PHILOSOPHY
AND
PSYCHOLOGY

VOLUME I

WIDENER LIBRARY SHELFLIST, 42

PHILOSOPHY
AND
PSYCHOLOGY

VOLUME I

CLASSIFICATION SCHEDULE
CLASSIFIED LISTING BY CALL NUMBER
CHRONOLOGICAL LISTING

Published by the Harvard University Library
Distributed by the Harvard University Press
Cambridge, Massachusetts
1973

SHELFLIST VOLUMES IN PRINT:

COPYRIGHT © 1973

BY THE PRESIDENT AND FELLOWS OF HARVARD COLLEGE

STANDARD BOOK NUMBER: 674–66486–8

LIBRARY OF CONGRESS CATALOGUE CARD NUMBER: 72–83389

PRINTED IN U.S.A.

Preface

As part of its effort to computerize certain of its operations, the Harvard University Library is converting to machine-readable form the shelflist and classification schedules of Widener Library, which houses Harvard's central research collection. After each class or group of related classes is converted, it is published in the *Widener Library Shelflist* series.

Volumes 42–43 of the series present the *Phil* classification, which contains nearly 59,000 books, periodicals, and pamphlets concerning metaphysics in general, cosmology, ontology, epistemology, logic, aesthetics, and psychology. Works on the philosophy of religion are included, but those on the philosophies of other disciplines are not. More detailed information on the scope and arrangement of this material can be found in the classification schedule and its introductory note.

This catalogue is arranged in four parts. The classification schedule is the first of these. It serves as an outline of the second part, which presents the entries in shelflist order; that is, in order by call number, as the books are arranged on the shelves. Together these two parts form a classified catalogue and browsing guide to the class. Part three lists the same items (excluding periodicals and other serials) in chronological order by date of publication. In addition to its obvious reference use, this list yields information on the quantity and rate of publication in the field. It can be helpful in determining patterns of collection development and in identifying existing strengths and weaknesses. Access to the collection by author and by title is provided by the alphabetical list which constitutes the fourth part of the catalogue. Computer-generated entries are included for titles of works listed elsewhere by author. (In these added entries the author's name follows the title and is enclosed in parentheses.) This section equips the reader with a subject-oriented subset of the card catalogue — a finding list which offers substantial advantages of conciseness and portability over the catalogue as a whole.

A note of caution is in order. A shelflist has traditionally served as an inventory record of the books in the library and as an indispensable tool for assigning call numbers to books as they are added to the collection. Designed and maintained to fulfill these two functions, the Widener shelflist was never intended to serve the purposes now envisaged for it. The bibliographical standards are not equal to those that prevail in the public card catalogues; shelflist entries are less complete than the public catalogue entries and may contain errors and inconsistencies which have not been eliminated during the conversion process. Cross references and name added entries are not included. Entries for serials rarely reflect changes in title, and serial holding statements give only the year or volume number of the first and last volumes in the library with no indication of gaps. If there is a plus sign after the beginning volume number or date, it can be inferred that the title is being currently received. For a complete record of the holdings of serial titles, the conventional serial records in the Widener Library should be consulted.

The list has other deficiencies. No classification system is perfect, and books are not always classified where the reader would expect to find them. Some books formerly in Widener and subsequently transferred to the Houghton Library or the New England Deposit Library are still to be found in the list; but others had been dropped from the original shelflist and could not be re-inserted.

Special notations indicate the locations of books which are in the shelflist but not in the Widener building. Books transferred to the Houghton Library (for rare books and special collections) are indicated by the letters *Htn*. Books that have been moved to special storage areas are designated by one of the following notations: *NEDL, X Cg*, or a *V* as the first letter of a call number prefix. These books should be requested, by their current numbers, through the Widener Circulation Desk. The letters *RRC* designate books in the Russian Research Center Library. The letter *A* following a call number in the alphabetical or chronological section indicates that the Library holds more than one copy of the book on this number. The classified list, however, includes all copies.

The shelflists of libraries not having classified catalogues have long been used by librarians and readers as implements for systematically surveying holdings in a particular subject. When perusing a shelflist one sees all the titles that have been classified in a given area, and not merely those which happen to be on the shelves and whose spine lettering is legible. In addition, one can take in at a glance the essential bibliographical description of a book — author, title, place and date of publication. However, the potential bibliographical usefulness of the shelflist has been difficult to exploit because it exists in only one copy, which is generally kept in a relatively inaccessible location. In Widener this problem is intensified because the handwritten sheaf shelflist is peculiarly awkward to read and difficult to interpret. Computer technology has made it possible to enlarge the concept of the shelflist and to expand its usefulness and accessibility while improving the techniques of maintaining it.

This shelflist catalogue will be of greatest utility to those using the libraries at Harvard, but in spite of its limitations, it can serve as a general bibliography of the subject and is therefore being made available to other interested libraries and individuals. The computer-based shelflist files are being maintained on a continuing basis so that updated editions of volumes in the series can be published as the need arises.

CHARLES W. HUSBANDS
Systems Librarian

Contents

Statistical Summaries of the *Phil* Class
September 1972

Analysis of Shelflist Entries by Language

Total Number of Entries   52,541

English	21,806	Rumanian	25	Bulgarian	61
French	7,313	Dutch	620	Hungarian	72
German	13,175	Swedish	645	Turkish	41
Russian	1,426	Danish	263	Finnish	17
Greek	40	Norwegian	69	Estonian	1
Latin	887	Icelandic	59	Latvian	4
Italian	3,241	Polish	325	Lithuanian	8
Spanish	1,152	Ukrainian	42	Other Languages	12
Portuguese	218	Czech & Slovak	168	Uncoded	745
Catalan	9	Yugoslav Languages	97		

Count of Titles

	Widener	Elsewhere	Total
Monographs	48,276	1,816	50,092
Serials	1,224	55	1,279
Pamphlets in Tract Volumes	6,342	619	6,961
Pamphlet Boxes	434	37	471
Total	56,276	2,527	58,803

Count of Volumes

	Widener	Elsewhere	Total
Monograph	54,322	2,082	56,404
Serial	9,899	962	10,861
Tract	592	107	699
Total	64,813	3,151	67,964

PHILOSOPHY
AND
PSYCHOLOGY

CLASSIFICATION SCHEDULE

NOTE ON THE CLASSIFICATION

The Phil class provides for nearly all works relating
to philosophy. In addition to speculative philosophy
(metaphysics in general, cosmology, ontology, and epistemology),
the class includes logic, psychology, esthetics, the philosophy
of religion, and ethics.

The accompanying Outline shows the major divisions of
the scheme. It was created by a person addicted to the
alphabetic arrangement of special topics. This is most
apparent in the sections for Special topics in Philosophy
(Phil 250-798), general Psychology (Phil 5300-5790), and
Ethics (Phil 9000-9579). It was also true, originally, in
the section for Abnormal Psychology, the special topics for
which were awkwardly scrambled together with those for
Parapsychology (Phil 6400-7249). At one time all the
books on Esthetics were transferred out of the Phil class to
the FA (Fine Arts) class. However, in 1963 when the
FA class was transferred to the Fine Arts Library, a new
section for Esthetics was inserted in Phil to provide for the
general works not limited to art. It should be noted that the
Philosophy of Religion is in the Phil class rather than in a
class for religion. But the philosophy of other disciplines
such as history and science goes in other classes. Likewise,
it should be noted that the section for Abnormal Psychology
also includes the medical aspects of Psychiatry.

A great many changes and additions have been made during
the revision of the scheme at this time. In the section for
Local Modern Philosophy (Phil 1798-4999), new numbers have
been inserted for many countries for which there was no
provision before. In the sections for Special topics in
Philosophy (Phil 250-798), Psychology (Phil 5300-5790), and
Ethics (Phil 9000-9579), numbers have been added for many
new topics and references have been inserted from alternate
terms. The section for Abnormal Psychology (Phil
6300-7249) has been almost completely reworked in order to
separate Abnormal Psychology and Parapsychology and to
provide a more detailed scheme; the arrangement of topics is
somewhat awkward because of the desire to retain as many of
the original numbers as possible. Many less notable
changes and additions have been made throughout. With the
available staff, it will be a long time before all the
books can be reclassified to fit properly into the revised
scheme.

Bartol Brinkler
Classification Specialist
August 1970

OUTLINE

10-70	Periodicals, Societies, Congresses
75-130	Reference works on philosophy
140-248	General treatises, etc. on philosophy
250-798	Special philosophical topics, systems, etc.
	History of philosophy
800-848	General history
	Ancient philosophy
850-898	General
900-1098	Oriental
1100-1298	Greek
1300-1398	Roman
	Medieval
1400-1498	Byzantine
1500-1598	Western
1600-1698	Renaissance
	Modern
1700-1790	General
1798-4999	Local
5000-5199	Logic
	Psychology
5200-5299	Generalia
5300-5790	Special aspects
5800-5839	Comparative psychology
5840-5844	Sex psychology
5845-5854	Applied psychology
5855-5859	Differential psychology
5860-5899	Genetic psychology
5900-6069	Phrenology; Physiognomy; Palmistry; Graphology
6100-6159	Mind and body; Psychopharmacology
6300-6999	Abnormal psychology (including Psychiatry)
7000-7249	Parapsychology
	Occultism. See Folklore class
8000-8449	Esthetics
8500-8799	Philosophy of religion
	Ethics
8800-8999	Generalia
9000-9579	Special topics
9585-9590	Miscellany

10-35   **Periodicals (A-Z)**
         [N.B. - Include here all philosophical
         periodicals; also periodicals dealing with Logic,
         Psychology, Philosophy of religion, and Ethics.
         See also Phil 40-65 and 70 for Societies and
         Congresses; see also Phil 8001-8026 for
         periodicals dealing with general esthetics.]

40-65   **Societies (A-Z)**
         [N.B. - Include here all philosophical and
         psychological societies. Class here a society's
         transactions and proceedings, annual reports,
         miscellaneous serial publications, histories, etc.;
         its general periodicals on philosophy or
         psychology go preferably in Phil 10-35.
         See also Phil 70 for Congresses. For
         societies devoted to the philosophy of religion,
         see Phil 8505.]

70   **Congresses, symposia, etc.**
         [N.B. - Include here all general philosophical
         and psychological congresses, symposia, etc.
         Congresses, etc. devoted to a specific subject
         go with the subject.]

         Reference works on philosophy
75   Bibliographies

         Dictionaries and encyclopedias
         [N.B. - See also Phil 130 and 150]
[80]   Folios [Discontinued]
85-110   Others (A-Z)

         Tables, outlines, syllabi, etc.
[125]   Folios [Discontinued]
126   Others
130   Biographical dictionaries
         [Include also general collections of
         biographies of philosophers]

         Pamphlet volumes on philosophy
140   General works
143   Münsterberg collection
         [N.B. - This number is used only for a large
         group of pamphlets on all aspects of philosophy
         assembled by Prof. Münsterberg and donated
         to the Library by him.]

150   **Terminology and nomenclature of philosophy**
         [N.B. - For dictionaries of philosophical
         terms, see Phil 85-110]

         Study and teaching of philosophy. See Educ

         General treatises on philosophy
         [N.B. - Include here primarily secondary
         works which discuss philosophy in a general way,
         e.g. essays, introductions, etc.; also works
         on the methods and scope of philosophy and
         its relations to other disciplines and subjects.
         At one time, general metaphysical works were
         classed here, especially if the writer was
         living; that practice has been discontinued, and
         such works are now classed with the writings of
         individual philosophers in Phil 1830-4999. For
         general histories of philosophy, see Phil 800-825.]
165   Collected authors
         [Include Festschriften and general anthologies
         of philosophical writings. For congresses, etc.,
         see Phil 70; for pamphlet volumes, see Phil
         140.]
[170]   Folios [Discontinued]
175-200 Individual authors (A-Z)
         [See note preceding Phil 165]

         Metaphysics, Speculative philosophy
         General treatises. See Phil 165-200; also with the
         writings of individual philosophers in
         Phil 1830-4999
210   General methodology
         [Include here very general works on methodology;
         also works on hermeneutics in general and the
         classification of knowledge in general.
         For works on historical Methodology, see H;
         for works on Biblical hermeneutics, see Bi;
         for works on the classification of books, see
         B; for works on the classification of science,
         see S.]

         Ontology. See Phil 540-566, etc.
         Cosmology. See Phil 280-306, etc.
         Epistemology. See Phil 330-356, etc.

         Special philosophical topics, systems, etc.
         [N.B. - The topics, systems, etc. are arranged
         alphabetically, rather than being grouped in a
         logical pattern.]

         Purely historical works. See Phil 830-848;
         also with special periods and countries in
         Phil 850-4999.

         Secondary treatises and discussions
         [N.B. - Original treatises by established
         philosophers should go with their writings
         in Phil 1830-4999.]
[250]   Folios [Discontinued]
252   Absolute
254   Abstraction
         [See also Phil 5360]

         Agnosticism. See Phil 8610
256   Alienation
         Analogy. See Phil 330-356
258   Analysis
         [See also Phil 5068]

         Animism. See R 211, etc.
         Anthroposophy. See Phil 970-978
260   Atomism
         Authority. See Gov and Soc
264   Banality
         Being. See Phil 540-566
266   Belief and certitude
         [See also Phil 5070 and 8622]

270   Causation
         [Include also works on cause and effect,
         chance, etc. See also Phil 384 and 440.
         For works on Final cause, see with
         Teleology in Phil 8735.]

         Chance. See Phil 270; also Phil 5145 and 9030.
272   Change
         [See also Phil 5350]

         Cognition. See Phil 330-356
274   Comparison and identity
         [See also Phil 5357]

         Comtism. See Phil 600
         Conceptualism. See Phil 630
276   Concrete
         Consciousness. See Phil 575; also Phil 5374
         Conservatism. See Gov

         Cosmology
         [Include here general works on cosmology -
         the theory of natural order, the processes of
         nature and the relation of its parts. Include
         also works on nature and natural philosophy,
         cosmic harmony, etc. See also
         special aspects of cosmology in Phil 270,
         378, 380, 450, 502, 505, 537, 590, 672,
         8655-8680, 8685, 8785, etc.]

Special philosophical topics, systems, etc. (cont.)
Secondary treatises and discussions (cont.)
Cosmology (cont.)
280   Pamphlet volumes
281-306   Monographs [A-Z]

Critical realism. See Phil 630
308   Criticism, Critical philosophy
[See also Existentialism, Phenomenalism
and Phenomenology, etc.]

Determinism. See Phil 384, 504, and 9215
310   Dialectic and Dialectical materialism
[See also with Logic]

Difference. See Phil 274 and 408
312   Dogmatism
Doubt and denial. See Phil 266 and 645
315   Dualism
[See also Pluralism in Phil 510]
320   Eclecticism
325   Empiricism
Energy. See Phil 378

Epistemology
[Include here general works on the theory of
knowledge; also works on the origin and
sources of knowledge, the limits of knowledge,
analogy, authority, the unknowable, etc.
See also special aspects of epistemology in
Phil 254, 258, 266, 274, 420, 573, 720, 735,
8622, 8630, etc.]
330   Pamphlet volumes
331-356   Monographs [A-Z]

Essence. See Phil 368
365   Evolutionism
[See also Phil 9150]
368   Existence and essence
370   Existentialism

Faith. See Phil 266; also Phil 8622
Fatalism. See Phil 384 and 535
Final cause. See Phil 8735
Finite. See Phil 410
378   Force and energy
380   Form
384   Freedom of the will
[Include also works on Determinism.
See also Phil 5750-5775.]

General semantics. See Phil 5520
Good and evil. See Phil 8620 and 9240
Hermeneutics. See Phil 210
Hope. See Phil 5421 and 8630
396   Humanism
[See also Pragmatism, Utilitarianism]
400   Idealism
[See also Individualism, Personalism,
Transcendentalism]

Identity. See Phil 274
402   Ideology
Immaterialism. See Phil 475-500
Immortality. See Phil 665; also Phil 8624-8650
Incarnation and reincarnation. See Phil 665,
970-978, and 8624-8650

Indeterminism. See Phil 384
406   Individualism
[See also Gov and Soc]
408   Individuation
[See also Phil 5855-5859, etc.]
410   Infinite and finite
[See also Phil 252 and 533]

Intellectualism. See Phil 623
418   Intention
420   Intuition
[See also Phil 5490]

Special philosophical topics, systems, etc. (cont.)
Secondary treatises and discussions (cont.)
Liberalism. See Gov
440   Liberty
[See also Phil 384; also Gov]
450   Life
Logical positivism. See Phil 5068
Man. See Phil 585

Materialism
[See also Naturalism, etc. For Historical
materialism, see Phil 310.]
474   Pamphlet volumes
475-500   Monographs (A-Z)
502   Matter
[See also Phil 378 and 380]
504   Mechanism
Meliorism. See Phil 579
Methodology. See Phil 210

505   Microcosm and macrocosm
Mind. See Phil 575, 5374, etc.
Monadology. See Phil 510
510   Monism and pluralism
514   Motion

Mysticism
[N.B. - Collections of mystical writings
should go in Phil 800-4999.]
525   General works
530   Local (By Special Local Table)
531   Naturalism
[See also Atomism, Dialectical materialism,
Materialism, Positivism, etc.]

Nature, Natural philosophy. See Phil 280-306
533   Necessity
Neorealism. See Phil 630
Neoscholasticism. See Phil 640
535   Nihilism
[Include here works on the general philosophy
of nihilism. Works on 19th century Russian
nihilism go in Slav.]

Nominalism. See Phil 630
537   Number and quantity
Objectivity. See Phil 720
538   Occasionalism

Ontology
[Include here general works on the nature
and relations of being. See also special
aspects of Ontology in Phil 252, 272, 276,
368, 410, 450, 533, 582, 585, 632, 643, 665,
684, 728, 760, etc.]
540   Pamphlet volumes
541-566   Monographs (A-Z)

Optimism. See Phil 579 and 9410
568   Order
570   Panpsychism
571   Pansophy
Pantheism. See Phil 8685
573   Perception
[See also Phil 5585, etc.]
574   Personalism

575   Personality
[N.B. - Include here only philosophical
works on personality; see Phil 5590, etc. for
psychological works. Include also works on
Self and Consciousness. See also Phil
665, 682, etc.]
577   Perspective
579   Pessimism and optimism
[See also Phil 9410 and 9430]
582   Phenomenalism
583   Phenomenology
585   Philosophical anthropology
[Include here general works on the philosophy
of man. See also Phil 575, 665, 682, etc.
See also Soc, etc.]

Special philosophical topics, systems, etc. (cont.)
    Secondary treatises and discussions (cont.)

        Pluralism. See Phil 510
        Plurality. See Phil 728

590   Plurality of worlds
            [Include philosophical speculation
            about life on other planets. See also
            Astr 8556-8560.]

596   Polarity
600   Positivism
            [For Logical positivism, see Phil 5068.]
610   Practice
615   Pragmatism
        Purpose. See Phil 8735
        Quantity. See Phil 537

623   Rationalism
            [Include also works on Intellectualism. See
            also Agnosticism, Skepticism, etc.]
627   Reaction
630   Realism and Neorealism
            [Include also works on Critical realism,
            Nominalism, and Conceptualism]
632   Reality
        Reincarnation. See Phil 665; also
            Phil 970-978 and 8624-8650
635   Relationism
         Scepticism. See Phil 645
640   Scholasticism and Neoscholasticism
            [See also Phil 1500-1540]

        Self. See Phil 575
        Semantics [Philosophy]. See Phil 5520
        Sensationalism. See Phil 402
643   Situation
645   Skepticism
665   Soul
            [Include also works on immortality, the
            spirit, etc.]
672   Space and time
            [Include also works on the philosophy of space
            alone or time alone and on the relationship
            of space and matter, time and motion, etc.]

        Spirit. See Phil 665
        Spiritualism. See Phil 7069
676   Spirituality
            [See also Phil 8740 and C.]
680   Structuralism
682   Subconsciousness
            [N.B. - Include here only philosophical
            works on the subconscious and the unconscious.
            For psychological works, see Phil 5722,
            6310-6335, 7080-7088, etc.]
683   Subject and object
         Subjectivity. See Phil 720
684   Substance
688   Syncretism
        Teleology. See Phil 8735
        Theism. See Phil 8655-8680
        Theosophy. See Phil 970-978
        Time. See Phil 672
703   Traditionalism
705   Transcendentalism
720   Truth
            [Include also works on objectivity and
            subjectivity]

        Unconsciousness. See Phil 682 and 5722
728   Unity and plurality
730   Universals
        Unknowable. See Phil 330-356
733   Utilitarianism
            [See also Phil 9550]

735   Value theory
            [N.B. - Include here only works on the
            philosophical theory of value or worth.
            See Econ for works on the economic theory
            of value. See also Phil 5785 and 8875-8900.]

Special philosophical topics, systems, etc. (cont.)
    Secondary treatises and discussions (cont.)
745   Vitalism
760   Whole and parts
        Worth. See Phil 735; also Phil 5785 and
            8875-8900.

History of philosophy

    General history
        [Include here works dealing with both western
        and oriental philosophy together through all
        periods; also works on western or European
        philosophy in general, ancient and medieval
        philosophy together or medieval and modern
        philosophy together. For works on oriental
        philosophy in general, see Phil 900.]
800-825   General works (A-Z)
    Metaphysics in general. See Phil 800-825

    Cosmology
830   General works
833   Special topics

    Epistemology
835   General works
838   Special topics

    Ontology
840   General works
843   Special topics
845   Humanism
848   Other special systems, etc.
            [Include Dualism, Empiricism,
            Idealism, Naturalism, etc.]

    General anthologies of philosophical writings.
        See Phil 165

    Ancient philosophy in general
        [N.B. - Include here works dealing with both
        western and oriental philosophy together; also
        works on the philosophy of the whole ancient
        Mediterranean world. For works on ancient
        Greek and Roman philosophy, see Phil 1100-1350.]

    History
850   General works
860   Special topics
870   Anthologies of philosophical writings

    Ancient and medieval oriental philosophy
        [This section is to be used for the history of
        non-European philosophy up to ca.1700.
        Eary oriental philosophy is so interwoven
        with religion that the texts are classed with
        the various religions or with the appropriate
        literature.]

    Oriental in general
        [For modern period, see Phil 4850, etc.]

    History
900   General works
910   Special topics

    Anthologies of philosophical writings. See OL

    China
        [For modern period, see Phil 4891-4893.]
930   History
        Anthologies of philosophical writings. See Ch
        Individual philosophers. See Ch

    Japan
        [For modern period, see Phil 4897-4899.]
935   History
        Anthologies of philosophical writings. See Jap
        Individual philosophers. See Jap

History of philosophy (cont.)
Ancient and medieval oriental philosophy (cont.)

Korea
[For modern period, see Phil 4894-4896.]
940   History
Anthologies of philosophical writings. See Jap
Individual philosophers. See Jap

India
[For modern period, see Phil 4870-4879.]
960   History
Anthologies of philosophical writings. See IndL
Individual philosophers. See IndL

Theosophy and Anthroposophy
[This system was placed here because its
doctrines are based on Buddhistic and
Brahmanistic theories.]
970   Pamphlet volumes
History
971   General works
972   Special topics
974   Biographies of theosophists
[Include criticism of their writings]
976   Anthologies of theosophical writings
978   Writings of individual theosophists

Persia
[For modern period, see Phil 4862-4864]
980   History
Anthologies of philosophical writings. See OL
Individual philosophers. See OL

Assyro-Babylonia. See AH and OL

Arabia
[Include also Arabic philosophy in general,
Medieval Islamic philosophy. For
modern period of Arabia alone, see
Phil 4859; for modern Islamic philosophy,
see Phil 4851.]

History
1020   General works
1030   Special topics

Anthologies of philosophical writings.
See OL and Asia

Individual philosophers. See OL
[1050] Jewish [Discontinued. See Jud and Heb]

Armenia
[For modern period, see Phil 4793-4794.]
1075   History
Anthologies of philosophical writings. See OL
Individual philosophers. See OL

Egypt, See Eg and OL; also Phil 1020
and 1150

Other countries of Asia and Africa. See with
the modern period in Phil 4850-4929

Ancient Greek philosophy
[Include here works on Greek philosophy from
the beginnings through the Hellenistic period
to the Alexandrian period, i.e. to about the
6th century A.D. Include also works covering
both ancient Greek and Roman philosophy.
For works on ancient Roman philosophy alone,
see Phil 1300-1350. For works on Greek
philosophy of the Byzantine period, see
Phil 1400-1430; for works on modern Greek
philosophy, see Phil 4843-4845.]
1100   Pamphlet volumes

History of philosophy (cont.)
Ancient Greek philosophy (cont.)

History
1105-1130   General works (A-Z)
1133   Special periods
[Include Pre-Socratic period in general,
Hellenistic or Graeco-Roman period in
general, etc.]
1135   Special topics
[Include relationship of Greek philosophy
to Christianity, cosmology and theories of
creation, theories of god and religion,
philosophy of nature, logic, etc.]
1140   Psychology
1145   Ethics

Special systems and schools
1150   Alexandrian School
1153   Cynics
1155   Eleatics
1158   Epicureans
[Include also Greek atomism]
1170   Neo-Platonists
[N.B. - Class here only works about
Greek and Graeco-Roman Neo-Platonism.
Works on the Platonism and Neo-Platonism
of the medieval and modern periods go with
those periods.]
1180   Pyrrhonism
1182   Pythagoreans
1190   Skeptics
1195   Sophists
1200   Stoics
1210   Other special
[Include Peripatetics, School of
Megarus, etc. See also Phil 1135-1145.]

Anthologies of philosophical writings. See G
Individual philosophers. See Ga-Gz

Ancient Roman philosophy
History
1300   General works
1350   Special topics
[Include Roman ethics, stoicism, etc.]

Anthologies of philosophical writings. See L
Individual philosophers. See La-Lz

Medieval philosophy in general. See Phil 1500-1530
Medieval oriental philosophy. See Phil 900-1099

Byzantine philosophy
[Include here works about medieval Greek
philosophy and the medieval philosophy of
eastern Europe.]

History
1400   General works
1430   Special topics
Local history. See Phil 4700-4849
[For Gnosticism, Manicheism, etc.,
see C]

Anthologies of philosophical writings. See C
or the appropriate literature class

Individual philosophers. See C or the
appropriate liteature class

Medieval western philosophy
[Include here works on the Christian and
scholastic philosophy of western Europe during
the Middle Ages; also works dealing with
oriental and occidental medieval philosophy in
general.]
[1500] Folios [Discontinued]
1501   Pamphlet volumes

History of philosophy (cont.)
Medieval western philosophy (cont.)

    History
      General works
1504   Collected authors
          [Include monograph series, congresses, etc.]
1505-1530   Individual authors (A-Z)
1535   Manuals, outlines, etc.
1540   Special topics
          [Include also special periods]

        Local history. See Phil 1800-4999
1560   Anthologies of philosophical writings
          [N.B. - See also C for anthologies of
          Patristic authors and later theologians;
          also with the appropriate literature class.]

        Individual philosophers. See C or the
          appropriate literature class.

    Renaissance philosophy
      [Include here primarily works dealing with
      western European philosophy during the 15th and
      16th centuries]

      History
        General works
1600   Collected authors
          [Include monograph series, congresses, etc.]
1601-1626   Individual authors (A-Z)
1630   Special topics
        Local history. See Phil 1800-4849
1660   Anthologies of philosophical writings
          [See also C,ML, etc.]

      Individual philosophers. See Phil 1800-4849 or
        the appropriate literature or subject class

    Modern philosophy in general
      [Include here works dealing with worldwide
      modern philosophy; also works about modern
      European philosophy in general - especially
      western European philosophy in general. For
      works on eastern European philosophy in general,
      see Phil 4700-4702.]

      History
        General works
          [Include here works covering the period
          since ca.1450 or since ca.1600]
1695   Collected authors
          [Include monograph series, congresses, etc.]
1700-1725   Individual authors (A-Z)

        Special periods
          15th-16th centuries. See Phil 1600-1630
1730   17th-18th centuries
            [Include the Enlightenment, Aufklärung]
1735   19th century
1740   20th century
1750   Special topics
          [Include Phenomenology (.115), Humanism
          (.116-.166), Existentialism (.167-.550),
          etc. Note that these topics are also
          included with Local history.]

        Local history. See Phil 1800-4999
1760   Anthologies of philosophical writings
          [See also with the special areas and
          countries in Phil 1800-4999]

      Individual philosophers. See Phil 1845-4999
    Local Modern philosophy
      Great Britain and United States
       ·[Include also Scotland and North America
       in general]
1798   Pamphlet volumes

History of philosophy (cont.)
Local Modern philosophy (cont.)
Great Britain and United States (cont.)

    History
      General works
1799   Collected authors
1800-1825   Individual authors (A-Z)
1828   Special topics
1830   Anthologies of philosophical writings

    Individual philosophers
1845   A
1850   Bacon, Francis
1855   Bain, Alexander
1857   Barfield, Owen
1860   Beattie, James
1865   Bentham, Jeremy
1870   Berkeley, George
1880   Bowen, Francis
1885   Bradley, Francis
1890   Brown, Thomas
1900   Butler, Joseph
1905   Other B
1915   Clarke, Samuel
1920   Craik, Kenneth J.W.
1925   Cudworth, Ralph
1928   Cumberland, Richard
1930   Other C
1955   D
1980   E
1990   Ferrier, James F.
2005   Other F
2020   Green, Thomas H
2030   Other G
2035   Hamilton, Sir William
2038   Hartley, David
2040   Herbert, Edward
2042   Hicks, George D.
2045   Hobbes, Thomas
2050   Hume, David
2053   Hutcheson, Francis
2055   Other H
2065   I
2070   James, William
2075   Other J
2100   K
2115   Locke, John
2120   Other L
2125   McCosh, James
2128   Mandeville, Bernard
2130   Mansel, Henry L.
2138   Mill, John Stuart
2145   More, Henry
2150   Other M
2175   N
2190   Occam, William
2193   Oswald, James
2200   Other O
2205   Paley, William
2215   Price, Richard
2218   Priestley, Joseph
2225   Other P
2230   Quimby, Phineas P.
2235   Other Q
2240   Reid, Thomas
2250   Royce, Josiah
2255   Other R
2262   Shaftesbury, Anthony Ashley Cooper, Earl of
2266   Smith, Adam
2268   Other Smiths
2270   Spencer, Herbert
2275   Stewart, Dugald
2280   Other S
        [See also Phil 2268]
2295   Toland, John
2300   Tucker, Abraham
2305   Other T
2310   U
2320   V

History of philosophy (cont.)
Local Modern philosophy (cont.)
Great Britain and United States (cont.)
Individual philosophers (cont.)

2340	W
2350	X
2360	Y
2370	Z

United States. See Phil 1798-2370

Canada
History
2380	General works
2383	Special topics
2385	Anthologies of philosophical writings

Individual philosophers. See Phil 1845-2370

Other English-speaking countries
British West Indies. See Phil 4958
Australia, etc. See Phil 4910-4919
British Africa. See Phil 4920-4929
India, etc. See Phil 4870-4879

Latin America. See Phil 4957-4987
France
2398	Pamphlet volumes

History
General works
2399	Collected authors
2400-2425	Individual authors (A-Z)
2428	Special topics
2430	Anthologies of philosophical writings

Individual philosophers
[Include here also Belgian and Swiss philosophers who wrote in French.]
[2435]	Alembert, Jean d' [Discontinued. See with French literature, etc.]
2438	Arnauld, Antoine
2445	Other A
2450	Bayle, Pierre [N.B. - Bayle's writings are classed with French literature. Criticism of his philosophical works and ideas may go here.]
2465	Bonnet, Charles
[2470]	Bossuet [Discontinued. See with French literature]
2475.1	Bergson, Henri
2477	Other B
2480	Cabanis, Pierre
2490	Comte, Auguste
2493	Condillac, Etienne [See also with French literature]
2494	Condorcet, Marie Jean [See also with French literature]
2496	Cousin, Victor
2515	Other C
2520	Descartes, René
2523	Destutt de Tracy, Antoine
2530	Diderot, Denis [See also with French literature]
2555	Other D
2580	E
2605	F
2610	Gassendi, Pierre
2630	Other G
2636	Helvetius, Claude
2648	Holbach, Paul
2651	Huet, Pierre
2655	Other H
2665	I
2668	Janet, Paul
2672	Jouffroy, Théodore
2675	Other J
2700	K
2705	La Mettrie, Julien
2725	Other L
2730	Maine de Biran, Pierre

History of philosophy (cont.)
Local Modern philosophy (cont.)
France (cont.)
Individual philosophers (cont.)

2733	Malebranche, Nicolas
2750	Other M
2775	N
2800	O
2805	Pascal, Blaise
2825	Other P
2830	Q
2835	Ramus (i.e. La Ramée, Pierre de)
[2838]	Renan, Ernest [Discontinued. See with French literature, etc.]
2840	Renouvier, Charles
2855	Other R
2880	S
2885	Taine, Hippolyte
2905	Other T
2910	U
2915	Voltaire, François [N.B. - See also with French literature, etc.]
2920	Other V
2940	W
2945	X
2950	Y
2955	Z

Belgium
History
2960	General works
2963	Special topics
2965	Anthologies of philosophical writings

Individual philosophers. See Phil 2435-2955

Netherlands, Holland. See Phil 3960-3965

Switzerland
History
2980	General works
2983	Special topics
2985	Anthologies of philosophical writings

Individual philosophers. See with French, German, or Italian philosophers (in Phil 2435-2955, 3085-3940, or 4060-4285) according to the person's customary language.

Germany
2998	Pamphlet volumes

History
General works
2999	Collected authors
3000-3025	Individual authors (A-Z)
3030	Special topics
3050	Anthologies of philosophical writings

Individual philosophers
[Include here also Austrian and Swiss philosophers who wrote in German; also philosophers from the Low Countries who wrote in Dutch or Flemish.]
3085	A
3090	Baader, Franz von
3092	Bachofen, J.J.
3095	Baumgarten, Alexander G.
3100	Beneke, Friedrich E.
3110	Böhme, Jakob
3120	Other B
3140	Clauberg, Johann
3160	Other C
3195	D
3200	E
3210	Fechner, Gustav T.
3235	Feuerbach, Ludwig
3245	Fichte, Immanuel H.
3246	Fichte, Johann G.
3255	Franck, Sebastian
3260	Fries, Jakob F.

History of philosophy (cont.)
Local Modern philosophy (cont.)
Germany (cont.)
Individual philosophers (cont.)
3270 Other F
3280 Geulincx, Arnold
3310 Other G
3415 Hartmann, Eduard von
3425 Hegel, Georg W.F.
3428 Herbart, Johann F.
[N.B. - His pedagogical writings and
works about them go in Educ]
3450 Other H
3455 I
3460 Jacobi, Friedrich H.
3475 Other J
Kant, Immanuel
3480 Writings
Biography and criticism
3481 Pamphlet volumes; Periodicals
3482-3507 Monographs (A-Z)
3508 Anonymous works
3525 Krause, Karl C.F.
3528 Krug, Wilhelm T.
3549 Other K
3552 Leibniz, Gottfried W.
3565 Lotze, Hermann
3585 Other L
3625 M (except Möbius)
3635 Möbius, Paul J.
3640 Nietzsche, Friedrich
3665 Other N
3705 O
3745 P
3750 Q
3778 Reinhold, Karl L.
3780 Rosenkranz, Karl
3790 Other R (except Riehl)
3791 Riehl, Alois
Schelling, Friedrich W.J. von
3800.1-.19 Bibliographies
3800.30-.49 Complete works
3800.50-.99 Selections
3800.100-.390 Individual works (By Special List)
3800.700-.799 Autobiography and letters
Biography and criticism
3801.1-.99 Pamphlet volumes; Periodicals
3801.100-.899 Monographs (800 scheme, A-Z)
3801.900-.999 Anonymous works
3805 Schleiermacher, Friedrich
3808 Schopenhauer, Arthur
Spinoza, Benedictus de
3819 Writings
Biography and criticism
3820-3845 Monographs (A-Z)
3846 Periodicals
3850 Other S
3890 T
3895 Ulrici, Hermann
3900 Other U
3903 V
3905 Weininger, Otto
3910 Wolff, Christian
3915 Wundt, Wilhelm
3925 Other W
3930 X
3935 Y
3940 Z

Austria. See Phil 2998-3940

Switzerland
History and anthologies. See Phil 2980-2985
Individual philosophers. See Phil 2435-2955,
3085-3940, or 4060-4285 according to the
person's customary language.

Netherlands, Holland
[Include here also works dealing with
the Low Countries in general.]

History of philosophy (cont.)
Local Modern philosophy (cont.)
Netherlands, Holland (cont.)

History
3960 General works
3963 Special topics
3965 Anthologies of philosophical writings
Individual philosophers. See Phil 3085-3940

Italy
3998 Pamphlet volumes

History
General works
3999 Collected authors
4000-4025 Individual authors (A-Z)
4030 Special topics
4050 Anthologies of philosophical writings

Individual philosophers
4060 A
4065 Bruno, Giordano
4070 Other B
4073 Campanella, Tommaso
4075 Cardano, Girolamo
4080 Other C
4090 D
4100 E
4110 F
4112 Galluppi, Pasquale
4114 Genovesi, Antonio
4115 Gioberti, Vincenzo
4120 Other G
4130 H
4135 I
4140 J
4150 K
4160 L
4170 M
4180 N
4190 O
4195 Pico della Mirandola, Giovanni
4196 Pico della Mirandola, Giovanni Francesco
4200 Other P
4205 Q
4210 Rosmini-Serbati, Antonio
4215 Other R
4225 S
4235 T
4250 U
4260 Vico, Giovanni B.
4265 Other V
4270 W
4275 X
4280 Y
4285 Z

Spain
[N.B. - For works relating to Spanish
American philosophy, see Phil 4957-4987.]
4298 Pamphlet volumes

History
General works
4300 Collected authors
4301-4326 Individual authors (A-Z)
4330 Special topics
4340 Anthologies of philosophical writings
4351-4376 Individual philosophers (A-Z)

Portugal
[N.B. - For works relating to Brazilian
philosophy, see Phil 4960.400-.599
and 4962-4987.]
4400 Pamphlet volumes

History
General works
4410 Collected authors

History of philosophy (cont.)
  Local Modern philosophy (cont.)
    Portugal (cont.)
      History (cont.)
        General works (cont.)

4411-4436	Individual authors (A-Z)
4440	Special topics
4450	Anthologies of philosophical writings
4461-4486	Individual philosophers (A-Z)

    Scandinavia
      History

4500	Scandinavia in general
4502	Denmark
4504	Iceland
4506	Norway
4508	Sweden
45.0	Anthologies of philosophical writings

      Individual philosophers

4513	A
4514	Borelius, Johann J.
4515	Boström, Christopher J.
4520	Other B
4525	C
4530	D
4535	E
4540	F
4570	G
4575	Höijer, Benjamin
4580	Höffding, Harold
4582	Other H
4585	I
4590	J
	Kierkegaard, Søren. See Scan 6664
4595	Other K
4600	L
4605	M
4610	N
4615	O
4620	P
4625	Q
4630	R
4635	S
4640	T
4645	U
4650	V
4655	W
4660	X-Z

    Finland

4665	History
4667	Anthologies of philosophical writings
4668	Individual philosophers (363 scheme)

    Baltic States in general

| 4670 | History |
| 4672 | Anthologies of philosophical writings |

    Estonia

4675	History
4677	Anthologies of philosophical writings
4678	Individual philosophers (363 scheme)

    Latvia

4680	History
4682	Anthologies of philosophical writings
4683	Individual philosophers (363 scheme)

    Lithuania

4685	History
4687	Anthologies of philosophical writings
4688	Individual philosophers (363 scheme)

    Eastern Europe in general

| 4700 | History |
| 4702 | Anthologies of philosophical writings |

History of philosophy (cont.)
  Local Modern philosophy (cont.)

    Russia
      History
        [N.B. - Class here works dealing with the whole of Russia and the Soviet Union or with European Russia. See also Phil 4670-4688, 4780-4799, and 4880-4889.]

4710	General works
4720	Special topics
4740	Anthologies of philosophical writings
4751-4776	Individual philosophers (A-Z)
	[N.B. - Include here only those writing in Russian. See also Phil 4670-4688, 4780-4799, and 4880-4889.]
[4777]	Poland [Discontinued. See Phil 4800-4803]

    White Russia

4780	History
4781	Anthologies of philosophical writings
4782	Individual philosophers (363 scheme)

    Ukraine

4783	History
4784	Anthologies of philosophical writings
4785	Individual philosophers (363 scheme)

    Moldavia

4786	History
4787	Anthologies of philosophical writings
4788	Individual philosophers (363 scheme)

    Caucasus in general

| 4790.1-.799 | History |
| 4790.800-.999 | Anthologies of philosophical writings |

    Georgia (Transcaucasia)
      [N.B. - All texts in Georgian go in OL]

4791.1-.799	History
4791.800-.999	Anthologies of philosophical writings
4792	Individual philosophers (363 scheme)

    Armenia
      [N.B. - All text in Armenian go in OL]

4793.1-.799	History
4793.800-.999	Anthologies of philosophical writings
4794	Individual philosophers (363 scheme)

    Azerbaijan
      [N.B. - All texts in Azerbaijani go in OL]

4795.1-.799	History
4795.800-.999	Anthologies of philosophical writings
4796	Individual philosophers (363 scheme)

    Dagestan
      [N.B. All texts in Dagestani go in OL]

4797.1-.799	History
4797.800-.999	Anthologies of philosophical writings
4798	Individual philosophers (363 scheme)

    Russian Asia. See Phil 4880-4889

    Poland

4800	History
4802	Anthologies of philosophical writings
4803	Individual philosophers (800 scheme)

    Czechoslovakia in general

| 4805 | History |
| 4806 | Anthologies of philosophical writings |

    Bohemia and Moravia
      [Include here works dealing with Czech philosophy]

4807	History
4808	Anthologies of philosophical writings
4809	Individual philosophers (800 scheme)

History of philosophy (cont.)
Local Modern philosophy (cont.)

Slovakia
4810	History
4811	Anthologies of philosophical writings
4812	Individual philosophers (800 scheme)

Hungary
4813	History
4814	Anthologies of philosophical writings
4815	Individual philosophers (800 scheme)

Rumania
4816	History
4817	Anthologies of philosophical writings
4818	Individual philosophers (800 scheme)

Balkan States in general
| 4820 | History |
| 4821 | Anthologies of philosophical writings |

Bulgaria
4822	History
4823	Anthologies of philosophical writings
4824	Individual philosophers (800 scheme)

Yugoslavia
[Include works dealing with the philosophy of Yugoslavia as a whole or its component states individually.]
4825	History
4826	Anthologies of philosophical writings
4829	Individual philosophers (800 scheme)

Albania
4840	History
4841	Anthologies of philosophical writings
4842	Individual philosophers (363 scheme)

Greece (Modern)
[N.B. - For Ancient Greece, see Phil 1100-1210; for Medieval Greece, see Phil 1400-1430.]
4843	History
4844	Anthologies of philosophical writings
4845	Individual philosophers (363 scheme)

Turkey. See Phil 4852-4854
| 4849 | Other European countries |

Asia in general
[Include also works dealing with oriental or non-European philosophy in general. See also Phil 4851, 4865, 4880, 4890, 4901, 4910, and 4920.]
| 4850.1-.799 | History |
| 4850.800-.999 | Anthologies of philosophical writings |

Southwest Asia in general, Near East in general
[Include also modern Islamic in general]
| 4851.1-.799 | History |
| 4851.800-.999 | Anthologies of philosophical writings |

Turkey
[N.B. - All texts in Ottoman Turkish go in OL, but texts in modern Turkish may be classed here.]
4852	History
4853	Anthologies of philosophical writings
4854	Individual philosophers (800 scheme)

Caucasus. See Phil 4790-4799

Syria
4855.1-.399	History
4855.400-.599	Anthologies of philosophical writings
4855.601-.963	Individual philosophers (363 scheme)

History of philosophy (cont.)
Local Modern philosophy (cont.)

Lebanon
4856.1-.399	History
4856.400-.599	Anthologies of philosophical writings
4856.601-.963	Individual philosophers (363 scheme)

Palestine, Israel
[Prefer Jud for Jewish philosophy]
4857.1-.399	History
4857.400-.599	Anthologies of philosophical writings
4857.601-.963	Individual philosophers (363 scheme)

Jordan
4858.1-.399	History
4858.400-.599	Anthologies of philosophical writings
4858.601-.963	Individual philosophers (363 scheme)

Arabia
[N.B. - All texts in Arabic go in OL.]
4859.1-.399	History
4859.400-.599	Anthologies of philosophical writings
4859.601-.963	Individual philosophers (363 scheme)

Minor states in southern Arabian Peninsula
4860.1-.399	History
4860.400-.599	Anthologies of philosophical writings
4860.601-.963	Individual philosophers (363 scheme)

Mesopotamia, Iraq
4861.1-.399	History
4861.400-.599	Anthologies of philosophical writings
4861.601-.963	Individual philosophers (363 scheme)

Persia, Iran
[N.B. - All texts in Persian go in OL]
4862	History
4863	Anthologies of philosophical writings
4864	Individual philosophers (363 scheme)

Southern Asia in general
| 4865.1-.799 | History |
| 4865.800-.999 | Anthologies of philosophical writings |

Afghanistan
[N.B. - All texts in Pushto go in OL.]
4866.1-.399	History
4866.400-.599	Anthologies of philosophical writings
4866.601-.963	Individual philosophers (363 scheme)

Tibet
[N.B. - All texts in Tibetan go in OL.]
4867.1-.399	History
4867.400-.599	Anthologies of philosophical writings
4867.601-.963	Individual philosophers (363 scheme)

Nepal
[N.B. - All texts in Nepali go in IndL.]
4868.1-.399	History
4868.400-.599	Anthologies of philosophical writings
4868.601-.963	Individual philosophers (363 scheme)

Sikkim and Bhutan
4869.1-.399	History
4869.400-.599	Anthologies of philosophical writings
4869.601-.963	Individual philosophers (363 scheme)

India
[N.B. - All texts in Indic languages go in IndL]
4870	History
4871	Anthologies of philosophical writings
4872	Individual philosophers (363 scheme)

Pakistan
[N.B. - All texts in Indic languages go in IndL.]
| 4873 | History |
| 4874 | Anthologies of philosophical writings |

History of philosophy (cont.)
  Local Modern philosophy (cont.)
    Pakistan (cont.)
4875   Individual philosophers (363 scheme)

    Ceylon
      [N.B. - All texts in Indic languages go
        in IndL.]
4876   History
4877   Anthologies of philosophical writings
4878   Individual philosophers (363 scheme)

    Russian Asia in general
4880.1-.799   History
4880.800-.999 Anthologies of philosophical writings

    Russian Central Asia in general
4881.1-.799   History
4881.800-.999 Anthologies of philosophical writings

    Turkmenistan
      [N.B. - All texts in Ural-Altaic
        languages go in OL.]
4882.1-.399   History
4882.400-.599 Anthologies of philosophical writings
4882.601-.963 Individual philosophers (363 scheme)

    Kazakhstan
      [N.B. - All texts in Ural-Altaic languages
        go in OL.]
4883.1-.399   History
4883.400-.599 Anthologies of philosophical writings
4883.601-.963 Individual philosophers (363 scheme)

    Uzbekistan
      [N.B. - All texts in Ural-Altaic languages
        go in OL.]
4884.1-.399   History
4884.400-.599 Anthologies of philosophical writings
4884.601-.963 Individual philosophers (363 scheme)

    Kirghizistan
      [N.B. - All texts in Ural-Altaic languages
        go in OL.]
4885.1-.399   History
4885.400-.599 Anthologies of philosophical writings
4885.601-.963 Individual philosophers (363 scheme)

    Tajikstan
      [N.B. - All texts in Ural-Altaic languages
        go in OL.]
4886.1-.399   History
4886.400-.599 Anthologies of philosophical writings
4886.601-.963 Individual philosophers (363 scheme)

    Siberia
      [N.B. - All texts in Ural-Altaic languages
        go in OL.]
4887.1-.399   History
4887.400-.599 Anthologies of philosophical writings
4887.601-.963 Individual philosophers (363 scheme)

    Outer Mongolia
      [N.B. - All texts in Ural-Altaic languages
        go in OL.]
4889.1-.399   History
4889.400-.599 Anthologies of philosophical writings
4889.601-.963 Individual philosophers (363 scheme)

    Russian Caucasus. See Phil 4790-4799

    Eastern Asia in general, Far East in general
4890.1-.799   History
4890.800-.999 Anthologies of philosophical writings

    China
      [N.B. - All texts in Chinese are in the
        Harvard Yenching Library. For Tibetan
        philosophy, see Phil 4867; for Mongol
        philosophy, see Phil 4889]

History of philosophy (cont.)
  Local Modern philosophy (cont.)
    China (cont.)
4891   History
4892   Anthologies of philosophical writings
4893   Individual philosophers (363 scheme)

    Korea
      [N.B. - All texts in Korean are in the
        Harvard Yenching Library.]
4894   History
4895   Anthologies of philosophical writings
4896   Individual philosophers (363 scheme)

    Japan
      [N.B. - All texts in Japanese are in the
        Harvard Yenching Library]
4897   History
4898   Anthologies of philosophical writings
4899   Individual philosophers (363 scheme)

    Southeast Asia in general
4901.1-.799   History
4901.800-.999 Anthologies of philosophical writings

    Indochina in general
4902.1-.799   History
4902.800-.999 Anthologies of philosophical writings

    Vietnam
      [N.B. - All texts in the native languages
        go in OL.]
4903.1-.399   History
4903.400-.599 Anthologies of philosophical writings
4903.601-.963 Individual philosophers (363 scheme)

    Laos
      [N.B. - All texts in the native languages
        go in OL.]
4904.1-.399   History
4904.400-.599 Anthologies of philosophical writings
4904.601-.963 Individual philosophers (363 scheme)

    Cambodia
      [N.B. - All texts in the native languages
        go in OL.]
4905.1-.399   History
4905.400-.599 Anthologies of philosophical writings
4905.601-.963 Individual philosophers (363 scheme)

    Burma
      [N.B. - All texts in the native languages
        go in OL.]
4906.1-.399   History
4906.400-.599 Anthologies of philosophical writings
4906.601-.963 Individual philosophers (363 scheme)

    Siam, Thailand
      [N.B. - All texts in the native languages
        go in OL.]
4907.1-.399   History
4907.400-.599 Anthologies of philosophical writings
4907.601-.963 Individual philosophers (363 scheme)

    Malaya
      [N.B. - All texts in the native languages
        go in OL.]
4908.1-.399   History
4908.400-.599 Anthologies of philosophical writings
4908.601-.963 Individual philosophers (363 scheme)

    Indonesia. See Phil 4916
    Philippines. See Phil 4917

    Oceania in general, Pacific Islands in general
4910.1-.799   History
4910.800-.999 Anthologies of philosophical writings

	History of philosophy (cont.)
	Local Modern philosophy (cont.)
	Australia
4911	History
4912	Anthologies of philosophical writings
4913	Individual philosophers (363 scheme)
	New Zealand
4914.1-.799	History
4914.800-.999	Anthologies of philosophical writings
4915	Individual philosophers (363 scheme)
	Indonesia
	[N.B. - All texts in the Malayan languages go in OL.]
4916.1-.399	History
4916.400-.599	Anthologies of philosophical writings
4916.601-.963	Individual philosophers (363 scheme)
	Philippines
	[N.B. - All texts in the Filipino languages go in OL.]
4917.1-.399	History
4917.400-.599	Anthologies of philosophical writings
4917.601-.963	Individual philosophers (363 scheme)
	Other islands of the Pacific Ocean
	[N.B. - All texts in the Malayo-Polynesian languages go in OL.]
4919.1-.599	History and anthologies
4919.601-.963	Individual philosophers (363 scheme)
	Africa in general
4920.1-.799	History
4920.800-.999	Anthologies of philosophical writings
	Egypt
	[N.B. - All texts in Arabic and Coptic go in OL]
4921.1-.799	History
4921.800-.999	Anthologies of philosophical writings
4922	Individual philosophers (363 scheme)
	Ethiopia
	[N.B. - All texts in the native languages of Ethiopia go in OL]
4923.1-.799	History
4923.800-.999	Anthologies of philosophical writings
4924	Individual philosophers (363 scheme)
	South Africa (Republic)
	[N.B. - All texts in native African languages go in Afr.]
4925.1-.799	History
4925.800-.999	Anthologies of philosophical writings
4926	Individual philosophers (363 scheme)
	Other countries of Africa
	[N.B. - All texts in the Afro-Asiatic languages go in OL or Afr.]
4929.1-.98	History and anthologies (By Special Table for Africa, omitting .15, .17, and .50-.54)
4929.101-.463	Individual philosophers (363 scheme)
[4931-4956]	Miscellany [Discontinued]
	Latin America in general
4957.1-.799	History
4957.800-.999	Anthologies of philosophical writings
	West Indies
	History and anthologies
4958.1-.199	General
4958.200-.299	Cuba
4958.300-.399	Puerto Rico
4958.400-.499	Haiti
4958.500-.599	Dominican Republic
4958.600-.699	Jamaica
4958.700-.999	Other islands (299 scheme, A-Z, by place)

	History of philosophy (cont.)
	Local Modern philosophy (cont.)
	West Indies (cont.)
	Individual philosophers. See Phil 4962-4987
	Central America
	History and anthologies
4959.1-.199	General
4959.200-.299	Mexico
4959.300-.399	British Honduras
4959.400-.499	Costa Rica
4959.500-.599	Guatemala
4959.600-.699	Honduras
4959.700-.799	Nicaragua
4959.800-.899	Panama
4959.900-.999	Salvador
	Individual philosophers. See Phil 4962-4987
	South America
	History and anthologies
4960.1-.199	General
4960.200-.399	Argentina
4960.400-.599	Bolivia
4960.600-.799	Brazil
4960.800-.999	Chile
4961.1-.199	Colombia
4961.200-.299	Ecuador
	Guianas
4961.300-.349	General
4961.350-.399	British Guiana, Guyana
4961.400-.449	Dutch Guiana, Surinam
4961.450-.499	French Guiana
4961.500-.599	Paraguay
4961.600-.799	Peru
4961.800-.899	Uruguay
4961.900-.999	Venezuela
4962-4987	Individual philosophers (A-Z)

	Logic
[5000]	Folios [Discontinued]
	Periodicals. See Phil 10-35
	Societies. See Phil 40-65
	General congresses. See Phil 70
	Reference works
5003	Bibliographies
5004	Dictionaries and encyclopedias
5005	Pamphlet volumes
	History
	General works
5009	Collected authors
5010-5035	Individual authors (A-Z)
5036	Special topics
	Special periods
	Ancient
	Oriental. See Phil 900-1099
	Greek. See Phil 1135
	Roman. See Phil 1350
	Medieval. See Phil 1430 and 1540
	Modern. See Phil 5009-5037
5037	Local (Geographic Table A)
	Biographies. See with history of philosophy or with their writings in Phil 5040-5065, etc.
	General works, treatises
	[Include here general introductions to logic and general works on deductive and inductive logic.]
5039	Collected authors
	[Include general anthologies of logic]
5040-5065	Individual authors (A-Z)
	Special kinds of logic
	Deductive logic. See Phil 5039-5065
	Inductive and empirical logic. See Phil 5039-5065; also Phil 5125 for works on induction as a special method.

Logic (cont.)

Special kinds of logic (cont.)

5066   Symbolic and mathematical logic
       [Include also modal logic, many-valued
       logic, etc.]

5067   Transcendental logic

5068   Logical positivism
       [Include also Analysis]

5069   Other special
       [Include Genetic and evolutionary logic,
       etc. See also Phil 5195.]

Special topics

5070   Belief
       [See also Phil 266 and 8622]

5075   Categories

5080   Concepts
       [See also Phil 5360]

5090   Evidence
       [Include also Proof]

5100   Fallacies
       [Include errors. See also Phil 5110]

5110   Hoaxes

5115   Hypothesis

5125   Induction
       [N.B. - Prefer Phil 5039-5065 for general
       works on Inductive logic.]

5130   Judgment
       [See also Phil 5500]

5135   Opinion

5145   Probability
       [Include also Logic of chance. See also
       Phil 270; also Math.]

5150   Relativity

5160   Sufficient reason

5170   Syllogism

5190   Other special
       [Include Argument and Persuasion,
       Axioms, Definition, Paradox, Contradiction,
       Possibility, Dilemma, Commands, etc.]

5195   Logic machines, mechanical logical methods

Psychology

[5200]   Folios [Discontinued]

Periodicals. See Phil 10-35

Societies. See Phil 40-65

Congresses, symposia, etc. See Phil 70; also
     with special subject below.

Reference works

5203   Bibliographies

5204   Dictionaries and encyclopedias

5205   Pamphlet volumes

[5207]   Dictionaries [Discontinued. See Phil 5204]

History

General works

5208   Collected authors

5210-5235   Individual authors (A-Z)

5236   Special topics

Special periods

Ancient

Oriental. See Phil 900-1099

Greek. See Phil 1140

Roman. See Phil 1350

Medieval. See Phil 1430 and 1540

Modern. See Phil 5208-5235

5237   Local (Geographical Table A)

Biographies of psychologists. See with
     history of philosophy or with their
     writings in Phil 5240-5265, etc.
     (e.g. Freud in Phil 6315.2)

General treatises

5238   Collected authors
       [Include Festschriften, monograph series, etc.
       For general congresses, symposia, see Phil 70]

5240-5265   Individual authors (A-Z)

Psychology (cont.)

General special treatises

Theory, scope, methods, relations

5270   General works
       [Include also general works on psychological
       research]

5272   Statistical methods
       [Include psychometrics]

5274   Other special research methods
       [Include factor analysis, etc.]

5275   Relations of psychology to other disciplines

5279   Other special

Special systems, schools, etc.

5280   Phenomenological psychology

5282   Existential psychology

5284   Behaviorism
       [See also Phil 5548]

5286   Gestalt psychology
       [See also Phil 5592-5599. For Gestalt
       therapy see Phil 6998.]

5289   Other special
       [See also Phil 5800-5899, etc.]

Physiological and experimental psychology

General works. See Phil 5238-5265, 5270-5274

Special topics. See Phil 5300-5790 passim

Mind and body. See Phil 6100-6159

Treatises on special topics

[Include here special topics of physiological
and experimental psychology; also general and
special aspects of consciousness and conscious
processes. Note that many of the same topics
may be classed with Genetic psychology. Note
also that the topics are arranged here in
alphabetic order except for groupings under
Emotions and Senses.]

[5300]   Folios [Discontinued]

Abnormal psychology. See Phil 6300-6999

Abstraction. See Phil 5360

Accommodation. See Phil 5435

Adolescence. See Phil 5876-5878

Affections. See Phil 5400

Aggressiveness. See Phil 5421

Anger. See Phil 5412

Animal psychology. See Phil 5800-5838

Anxiety. See Phil 5421

Applied psychology. See Phil 5845-5854

Apperception. See Phil 5374 and 5585

Apperception tests. See Phil 5592-5599

5325   Association of ideas
     [See also Phil 5545]

5330   Attention
     [See also Phil 5385]

5335   Attitude

Automatism. See Phil 7076-7079

Bashfulness. See Phil 5419

Belief. See Phil 5627; also Phil 266, 5070,
     and 8622

Boredom. See 5407

Brainwashing. See Phil 5780

5350   Change
     [Include here works on the psychology of
     change and the perception of change. See
     also Phil 272, 5867, etc.; also Soc 551-559.]

Character. See Phil 5590 and 9035

Child psychology. See Phil 5870-5875; also Educ

5352   Choice
     [See also Phil 5750-5780]

Cognition. See Phil 5520; also Phil 330-356

Color sense. See Phil 5645

Comparative psychology. See Phil 5800-5838

5357   Comparison
     [See also Phil 5500 and 5620; also Phil 274]

Psychology (cont.)
  Treatises on special topics (cont.)

5358	Compensation
	Comprehension. See Phil 5725
5360	Concept and concept building
	Conditioned reflex. See Phil 5625; also Phil 5398
	Confession (Crime). See Soc
	Confession (Religion). See Phil 5627; also C.
5365	Conflict
5374	Consciousness
	[See also Phil 5325, 5330, 5435, 5465, 5477, 5500, 5520, 5545, 5585, 5722, etc.]
	Courage. See Phil 5401
	Creative processes. See Phil 5465
[5380]	Crowds [Discontinued. See Soc 654.]
5385	Curiosity
	Cutaneous senses. See Phil 5648
5390	Degeneration (Mental)
	[Include here works on mental inefficiency, ignorance, stupidity. For works on feeblemindedness and mental retardation, see Phil 6730-6769. See also Soc 4285.]
	Deprivation. See Phil 5406 and 5640
	Desire. See Phil 5404
	Development. See Phil 5860-5899
	Difference. See Phil 5855-5859; also Phil 5590
	Elation. See Phil 5403
5398	Electronic behavior control
	Emotions
5400	General works
	[Include here general works dealing with all the emotions; also works on sensibility and feelings in general, the expression of emotion, etc. See also with Ethics]
	Special emotions, etc.
5401	Fear
	[Include also Courage. For works on fear in battle, see War 205. See also Phil 5421.10; also Phil 6610-6614.]
5402	Pleasure and pain
5403	Joy and elation
5404	Desire
5405	Enthusiasm
5406	Deprivation
	[Include general works on the psychology of deprivation. For works on sensory deprivation in general, see Phil 5640.]
5407	Ennui and boredom
5408	Surprise
5409	Expectation
5410	Gratitude and ingratitude
5411	Hatred
5412	Anger
5413	Envy and jealousy
5414	Shame and guilt
5415	Sympathy
	[See also Phil 5421.15]
5416	Prejudice
	[See also Phil 9455; also Soc 670]
5417	Frustration
	[Include also Failure]
5418	Loneliness
	[See also Phil 5406]
5419	Bashfulness
5420	Self-consciousness
5421	Others
	[The following dot numbers have been used:

	.5	Nostalgia
	.6	Security
	.10	Anxiety
	.15	Empathy

in next column

Psychology (cont.)
  Treatises on special topics (cont.)
    Emotions (cont.)
      Special emotions, etc. (cont.)
        Others (cont.)

	.20	Aggressiveness
	.25	Love
	.30	Stress
	.35	Hope
		Set up others as needed.]

	Empathy. See Phil 5421.15
	Ennui. See Phil 5407
	Enthusiasm. See Phil 5405
5423	Environment
	Envy. See Phil 5413
	Equilibrium. See Phil 5652
	Esthesiology. See Phil 5635 and 5640
	Evidence. See Phil 5090
	Example. See Phil 5475
	Expectation. See Phil 5409
	Expression of emotion. See Phil 5400
	Factor analysis. See Phil 5274
	Failure. See Phil 5417
	Faith. See Phil 5627; also Phil 8622
	Fanaticism. See Phil 9200
	Fatigue. See Phil 6110-6135
	Fear. See Phil 5401 and 6610-6614
	Feeling and feelings. See Phil 5400
	Fighting. See Phil 5421.20
	First impressions. See Phil 5585
	Fixed ideas. See Phil 6632
	Forgetting. See Phil 5545
	Frustration. See Phil 5417
	General semantics. See Phil 5520
	Genetic psychology. See Phil 5860-5899
5425	Genius
	[See also Phil 5390, 5465, etc.]
	Gestalt. See Phil 5286
	Gratitude. See Phil 5410
	Guilt. See Phil 5414
5435	Habit
	[See also Phil 5477]
	Hatred. See Phil 5411
	Hearing. See Phil 5650
5440	Heredity
	Hope. See Phil 5421.35
	Humor. See Phil 5525
	Ideas. See Phil 5480; also Phil 330-356
	Ignorance. See Phil 5390
5460	Illusions
	[Include here works on normal illusions. For works on optical illusions, see Phil 5643. For works on neurotic hallucinations, see Phil 6620-6624. For works on false illusions and hallucinations, see Phil 7202-7209.]
5465	Imagination
	[Include also works on the creative processes in general; also works on imagery.]
5467	Imitation
5470	Impulse
	[See also Phil 5838]
	Individuality. See Phil 5855-5859; also Phil 575, 5590, and 9035.
	Infancy. See Phil 5870-5875; also Educ
	Inferiority complex. See Phil 6816
5475	Influence
	[Include also works on the psychology of example and pattern. See also Soc 690.]
	Ingratitude. See Phil 5410
5477	Inhibition
[5478]	Inhibition - Special [Discontinued. See Phil 5417]
5480	Innate ideas

Psychology (cont.)
Treatises on special topics (cont.)
Inspiration. See Phil 5465; also Phil 8432
Instinct. See Phil 5838; also Phil 5590 and 6310-6335; also S 7980, etc.

5485   Intelligence
[See also Phil 5390]

Intelligence tests. See Phil 5592-5599; also Educ

Interest. See Phil 5330
Interference. See Phil 5435 and 5477
Interruption. See Phil 5545

5490   Intuition
[See also Phil 5374, 5520, and 5585; also Phil 420 and 5838]

Invention. See Phil 5465
Jealousy. See Phil 5413
Joy. See Phil 5403

5500   Judgment
[See also Phil 5357 and 5620; also Phil 5130.]

5520   Language and thought
[Include here general works on the psychology of thought and thinking, the psychology of language and speech, the psychology of meaning, and General semantics. See also Phil 5360, 5490, 5722, etc.]

5525   Laughter
[Include works on the psychology of the ludicrous, the psychology of wit and humor]

5528   Laziness
5535   Learning
[See also Phil 5545; also Educ]

Loneliness. See Phil 5418
Love. See Phil 5421.25; also Soc

5542   The Marvelous
Maturation. See Phil 5867

5545   Memory
[Include also works on memory training. See also Phil 5325. For works on disorders of the memory, including amnesia, see Phil 6440-6449.]

Mental ability and efficiency. See Phil 5485
Mental deficiency. See Phil 6730-6769
Mental imagery. See Phil 5465
Mental inefficiency. See Phil 5390
Mental tests. See Phil 5592-5599; also Educ
Military psychology. See War
Mimicry. See Phil 5467
Mnemonics. See Phil 5545

5548   Motivation
[See also Phil 5284, 5365, etc.]

Motor phenomena. See Phil 5649
Movement. See Phil 5649
Muscular sense. See Phil 5649
Nervous system. See Phil 6110-6135; also Phil 5625; also Med

Nostalgia. See Phil 5421.5
Observation. See Phil 5585
Opinion. See Phil 5135
Orientation. See Phil 5651
Originality. See Phil 5465
Parapsychology. See Phil 7000-7249
Pattern. See Phil 5475

5585   Perception
[Include works on perception in general; also works on the perception of space and time. See also Phil 5350, 5385, and 5695; also Phil 672. For works on sensory perception, see Phil 5640.]

Psychology (cont.)
Treatises on special topics (cont.)
Perseveration. See Phil 5545

5590   Personality
[Include general works on personality, personality change and adjustment, character, etc. For personality testing and evaluation, see Phil 5592. For differential psychology, see Phil 5855-5859. For disorders of personality, see Phil 6800-6859. For philosophical treatises on personality and the self, see Phil 575. See also Phil 5710.]

Personality tests and testing
[N.B. - Include here primarily tests and testing to evaluate personality. Most works on tests and testing to measure mental ability and intelligence are in Educ.]

5592   General works

Special tests
5593   Rorschach (By date, e.g. .60 for 1960)
5594   Q methodology (By date, e.g. .165 for 1965)
5599   Other special (99 scheme, A-Z, by name of test)
[See also Educ]

Persuasion. See Phil 5190
Pessimism. See Phil 9430
Pleasure and pain. See Phil 5402

5600   Posture
Pre-existence. See Phil 7180
Prejudice. See Phil 5416
Psychedelic experience. See Phil 6150-6159
Psychic research. See Phil 7000-7249
Psychopharmacology. See Phil 6150-6159
Psycho-physics. See Phil 5640 and 6110-6135

5610   Public speaking
[See also Phil 5685]
Reactions and reaction time. See Phil 5625 and 5649

5620   Reason and reasoning
[See also Phil 5500]

5625   Reflex action
[Include also works on conditioned response, reaction time, etc.]

Reinforcement. See Phil 5535, 5545, and 5625.

Religion
5627   General works (By date, e.g. .265 for 1965)
[Include works on the psychology of belief, faith, religious conversion, etc. Use .134 for works on the Oxford Group Movement and Buchmanism. For works on Moral Re-Armament, see Int 6879. For works on the philosophy of religion, see Phil 8500-8799.]
5628   Special topics
[Include religious ecstasy, stigmatization, glossolalia, etc. For mysticism, see Phil 525-530.]

Repression. See Phil 5477
Reproduction of ideas. See Phil 5325 and 5545
5630   Rumor
[See also Soc]
Security. See Phil 5421.6
Self-consciousness. See Phil 5420
Semantics (Philosophy). See Phil 5520
5635   Sensation
[See also Phil 5640-5655 and 5400-5421]

Sensibility. See Phil 5400, 5635, and 5640

Senses
5640   General works
[Include also works on sensory perception in general and sensory deprivation in general]

Psychology (cont.)
  Treatises on special topics (cont.)
    Senses (cont.)

5642   Synaesthesia

           Special senses
5643   Sight, Vision
             [Include also works on optical illusion
               and motion perception]
5645   Color sense
             [Include also color blindness]
5647   Temperature sense
5648   Touch
             [Include cutaneous sense in general]
5649   Muscular sense
             [Include works on motor phenomena,
               the psychology of movement, etc. See
               also Phil 5625.]
5650   Hearing
5651   Orientation
5652   Static sense, Equilibrium
5653   Taste
5655   Smell

         Sensory deprivation. See Phil 5640
         Sex psychology. See Phil 5840-5844
         Shame. See Phil 5414
         Sight. See Phil 5643
         Smell. See Phil 5655
         Social psychology. See Soc
         Space perception. See Phil 5585
5685   Stage fright
         Static sense. See Phil 5652
5690   Stereotype
         Stress. See Phil 5421.30
         Stupidity. See Phil 5390
         Subconscionsness. See Phil 5722
5695   Subliminal perception
            [See also Phil 5722]

         Superstition. See Phil 5627
         Surprise. See Phil 5408
5700   Symbolism
            [See also Phil 5520, 5627, and 8440;
              also R.]

         Sympathy. See Phil 5415
         Synaesthesia. See Phil 5642
         Taste. See Phil 5653
5710   Temperament
            [See also Phil 5590]

         Temperature sense. See Phil 5647
         Thought and thinking. See Phil 5520
         Time perception. See Phil 5585
         Touch. See Phil 5648
5715   Typology
            [See also Phil 5590, 5690, 6110-6135,
              6310-6335, etc.]
5722   Unconscious cerebration
            [Include general works on unconsciousness
              and the subconscious. See also Phil
              5695. For works on sleep phenomena,
              daydreaming, extrasensory perception, and
              other activities of the subconscious, see
              Phil 7000-7249.]
5725   Understanding
         Value. See Phil 5785
         Vigilance. See Phil 5330
         Vision. See Phil 5643

         Volition
5750-5775   General works (A-Z)
5780   Special topics
            [Include training and management
              of the will, brainwashing, etc.
              See also Phil 5352. For works
              on freedom of the will, see Phil
              5750-5775; also Phil 384.]
         Will. See Phil 5750-5780

Psychology (cont.)
  Treatises on special topics (cont.)
    Wit. See Phil 5525
    Work. See Phil 6110-6135
    Worry. See Phil 6110-6135
5785   Worth
       [N.B. - Prefer Phil 735 or 8875-8900]
5790   Miscellaneous minor topics
       [Include reaction to disaster, risks, etc.]

  Comparative psychology
     [Include here works comparing human and
      animal psychology; also works on the psychology
      of animals in general]
[5800]   Folios [Discontinued]
5803   Bibliographies
5808.00-5809.99   Pamphlet volumes

    General works
5809.100-.999   Collected authors
5810-5835   Individual authors (A-Z)

    Special topics
5838   Instinct (By date, e.g. .260 for 1960)
5839   Others
         [Include migratory impulse, motivation,
          sublimation, etc.]

  Sex psychology
     [Include here purely psychological works on sex.
      For works on sex relations, see Soc]
5840   Bibliographies
5841   General works

    Special topics
5843   Psychology of man
       Psychology of woman. See Soc
       Sexual perversions. See Phil 6830-6849

  Applied psychology
     [Include here works on Applied psychology
      in general. Works on applications to a
      special field go with the subject in the
      appropriate class, e.g. Industrial psychology
      in Econ.]
5845   Bibliographies
5848   Pamphlet volumes
5850   General works (299 scheme, A-Z)
       [Include also Interpersonal relations in
        general]
5853   Special topics
       [Include Counseling, Interviewing,
        Leadership, Negotiation, Peace of mind,
        Reconciliation, Success, etc.]

  Differential psychology
     [Include here works on the psychology of
      individual differences]
5855   Bibliographies
5856   General works

    Special topics
       Personality. See Phil 5590
       Personality tests. See Phil 5592-5599
5858   Other special

  Genetic psychology
     [Include here works on the psychology of mental
      development or evolution in the individual or
      race]
5863   Bibliographies
5865   General works
       [See also Phil 365 and 9150]
5867   General special
       [Include Maturation, Psychology of play,
        etc. See also Heredity in Phil 5440.]

    Child psychology
       [See also Child study and Educational
        psychology in Educ 2050-2098; also
        Soc 6000-6040.]

Psychology (cont.)
  Genetic psychology (cont.)
    Child psychology (cont.)
5870   General works
5871   General special
       [Include works relating to the child as
       an individual in relation to a family,
       e.g. only child, twins, foster child, etc.
       See also Soc 5775.]
5873   Emotions
5875   Other special topics
       [N.B. - For works on psychopathology in
       children, see Phil 6360.]

    Adolescence, Youth
      [See also Educ 2095, Soc 6000-6040, etc.]
5876   General works
5878   Special topics
5880   Adulthood
5883   Middle age
5886   Old age
      [See also Soc, Med, etc.]
5890   Class psychology in general
5893   Race and ethnic psychology in general
      [Include culture conflict in general.
      See also History of civilization in H.]
5896   Psychology of nations in general
      [See also H]

    Social psychology. See Soc
    Quasi-psychological systems
      Ethology, Character. See Phil 5590 and 9035
      Temperament. See Phil 5710

    Phrenology
[5900]   Folios [Discontinued]
5903   Bibliographies
5905   Dictionaries
5910   Pamphlet volumes
5912   History

     Biographies of phrenologists
5917.1-.99   Collected
5917.101-.399   Individual (A-Z, 299 scheme, by person)
5918.00-5919.99 Pamphlet file

     General treatises
5919.100-.899   Collected authors (800 scheme, A-Z)
5920-5945   Individual authors (A-Z)
5948   Special topics

    Physiognomy
[6000]   Folios [Discontinued]
6003   Bibliographies
6004   Dictionaries
6005   Pamphlet volumes
6007   History

     General treatises
6009   Collected authors
6010-6035   Individual authors (A-Z)
6038   Special topics

    Palmistry, Chiromancy
6040   Pamphlet volumes
6042   Bibliographies
6045-6050   General works (By date)
[6051]   Miscellany [Discontinued]
6053   Special topics

    Graphology
6055   Bibliographies
6060   General works
6063   Special topics

  Mind and body
    [Include here general works on the relationship
    between mind and body; also works on the
    physiology and functions of the brain and
    nervous system; also works on "New Thought"
    or menticulture and general works on mental
    health and hygiene. Do not include works on
    abnormal psychology.]

Psychology (cont.)
  Mind and body (cont.)
[6100]   Folios [Discontinued]
6102   Bibliographies
6103   Pamphlet volumes

    World Federation for Mental Health
6105.1-.99   Periodicals (A-Z, 99 scheme, by title)
6105.101-.399 Monographs (A-Z, 299 scheme, by title)

    General works
6109   Collected authors
6110-6135   Individual authors (A-Z)

    Special topics
     Psychoanalysis. See Phil 6300-6335
     Psychiatry. See Phil 6900-6998
     Psychosomatic medicine. See Med 1240
6140   Community mental health programs and services

  Psychopharmacology
    [Include here general works on the psychedelic
    experience; also studies on the effects of
    hallucinogenic drugs on perception and
    behavior. For works on drug addiction,
    see Soc. For chemotherapy, see Phil 6983.]
6152   Bibliographies
6153   Pamphlet volumes
6155   General works

    Special drugs
6158   LSD
6159   Others
      [Include mescaline, etc.]

  Abnormal psychology
    [Include here works on the behavior patterns of
    psychotic, psychoneurotic, and mentally
    deficient individuals; also works on Clinical
    psychology. Because of the fact that the
    Harvard Medical School is at a considerable
    distance, the decision was made many years ago
    that works on the medical aspects of psychoses
    and neuroses, their diagnosis and treatment,
    would be included here rather than in
    Widener's Med class.]
[6300]   Folios [Discontinued]
     Periodicals. See Phil 10-35
     Societies. See Phil 40-65
6302   Congresses

    Reference works
6303   Bibliographies
6304   Dictionaries and encyclopedias
6305   Pamphlet volumes

    History
     [See also Phil 6906-6907]
6306   General works
6307   Local (Geographic Table A)
     Biographies. See with their writings
      in Phil 6310-6335, etc.

    General treatises
     [Include here works dealing collectively with
     abnormal or pathological psychology,
     clinical psychology, and psychoanalysis.]
6309   Collected authors
      [See also Phil 6302]
6310-6335   Individual authors (A-Z)

    General special treatises
6340   Clinical psychology in general
     Psychiatry in general. See Phil 6950-6975
6350   Psychodiagnosis in general
     Psychotherapy. See Phil 6980-6999
     Psychosomatic medicine. See Med
6360   Psychopathology in children
      [See also Phil 6981]

	Psychology (cont.)
	Abnormal psychology (cont.)
	General special treatises (cont.)
	Psychoses
6380	General works
	Organic. See Phil 6500-6549
	Functional. See Phil 6950-6978
	Neuroses
6390	General works
	Special. See Phil 6400-6459, 6600-6659, and 6800-6859
	Conditions of a mixed nature
	Speech and language disorders
6400	General works
	[Include aphasia in general]
6405	Agraphia, disorders of writing
6410	Agnosia
6415	Apraxia
6420	Stammering and stuttering
	Memory disorders
6440	General works
6442	Amnesia
6449	Other special
	Sleep disturbances
6450	General works
6452	Insomnia
6459	Other special
[6480]	Dreaming [Discontinued. See Phil 7081-7084.]
	Organic psychoses
	[Include here works on conditions resulting from diseases of the nervous system.]
6503	Bibliographies
6510	General works
6515	Chorea
[6520]	Ecstasy [Discontinued. See Phil 7076 and 5628.]
	Epilepsy
6535	Reports
6536	Monographs
6540	Paresis
6548	Other special
	Functional psychoses. See Phil 6950-6978
	Psychoneurotic disorders
	General works. See Phil 6390
	Anxiety neuroses
6605	General
6606	Hypochondria
6609	Other special
	Phobias, Fear
6610	General works
6614	Special topics
	Hysteria
6615	General works
6619	Special topics
	Hallucinations
	[N.B. - Include here only works about hallucinatory states due to neurosis. See also Phil 7202-7209 for false illusions.]
6620	General works
6624	Special topics
	Psychogenic depression
	[N.B. - For manic-depressive psychoses, see Phil 6978.]
6625	General works
6626	Neurasthenia
6627	Nervous exhaustion

	Psychology (cont.)
	Abnormal psychology (cont.)
	Psychoneurotic disorders (cont.)
	Psychogenic depression (cont.)
6629	Other special
	Obsessive-compulsive states
6630	General works
6631	Tic
6632	Fixed ideas
6634	Other special
	[See also Phil 6850-6859]
	War neuroses
6635	General works
6636	Combat fatigue
6639	Other special
	Occupational neuroses
6640	General works
6644	Special topics
	Speech disorders. See Phil 6400-6439
	Memory disorders. See Phil 6440-6449
	Sleep disturbances. See Phil 6450-6459
	Personality disorders. See Phil 6800-6859
6659	Other psychoneuroses
[6660-6695]	Hypnotism [Discontinued. See Phil 7100-7149]
[6720]	Hysteria [Discontinued. See Phil 6615-6619]
	Mental deficiency
	[Include here works on feeblemindedness and mental retardation. For works on ignorance, stupidity, etc., see Phil 5390.]
6733	Bibliographies
6740	General works
	Idiocy, Imbecility
6745	Reports
6750	Monographs (By date, e.g. .260 for 1960)
	States due to injury
6760	Mongolism
6762	Cretinism
6769	Others
	Mental tests. See Phil 5592-5599; also Educ
	Education and training. See Educ
	Insanity. See Phil 6900-6978
	Personality disorders
	[Include disorders of character, behavior, etc.]
6803	Bibliographies
6805	General works
	Multiple personality. See Phil 7042
	Immature personality
6810	General works
6811	Emotional instability
6814	Other special
	Adult maladjustment
6815	General works
6816	Inferiority complex
6819	Other special
	Psychoneurotic addictions
6820	General works
	Alcoholism. See Soc
	Drug addiction. See Soc
	Tobacco habit. See Soc
6824	Others
	Psychopathic personality
	[Include here works on the antisocial or asocial personality]
6825	General works
6829	Special topics
	[See also Phil 6830-6859]

Psychology (cont.)
  Abnormal psychology (cont.)
    Personality disorders (cont.)

      Sexual deviations
        [N.B. - Include here works on the
        psychological aspects of sexual manias and
        perversions. Works on sexual crimes and
        delinquency go in Soc. Most of such
        material should be considered for XR.]

6830   General works
6832   Nymphomania
6834   Homosexuality
6836   Lesbianism
6840   Masochism
6842   Sadism
6844   Transvestism
6849   Other special

      Special compulsions
6850   Kleptomania
6852   Pyromania
6854   Homicidal and suicidal compulsion
        [See Soc for homicide and sucide as
        crimes]
6856   Compulsive lying and defrauding
6859   Others

      Mental deficiency. See Phil 6730-6769

     Mental disease
      [Include here works on functional psychoses,
      "insanity"; also works on the care and
      treatment of abnormal mental states,
      i.e. psychiatry.]

      Periodicals. See Phil 10-35
      Societies. See Phil 40-65
      Congresses. See Phil 6949

      Reference works
6903   Bibliographies
        Dictionaries and encyclopedias. See Phil 6304

      History of psychiatry
6906   General works
6907   Local (Geographic Table A)
        Biographies. See with their writings
        in Phil 6310-6335, etc.

      General treatises. See Phil 6950-6975
      Community mental health services. See Phil
      6140
[6930]   Melancholia [Discontinued. See
      Phil 6625-6629 or 6978]
6940   Law and legislation
      Insanity and crime. See Soc
6942   Psychiatric nursing

      Hospitals
6945   General works
        [Include treatment in general]
        Local (By special scheme)
        [N.B. - Offer to Medical School]
6946   United States and Canada
6947   Other countries
6948   Pamphlet volumes

      General treatises
      [Include also works on psychiatry in general]
6949   Collected authors (By date, e.g. .360 for 1960)
      [Include congresses, etc.]
6950-6975 Individual authors (A-Z)

      Special diseases and states
6976   Schizophrenia
6977   Paranoia and paranoid states
6978   Other special
        [Include Involutional melancholia,
        manic-depressive psychosis, Senile
        dementia, alcoholic psychoses, etc.]

Psychology (cont.)
  Abnormal psychology (cont.)
    Mental disease (cont.)

      Psychotherapy
6980.1-.799   General works (800 scheme, A-Z)
6981   Child psychotherapy
        [See also Phil 6360]
6983   Chemotherapy
6984   Shock therapy
6985   Group therapy
        [Include Psychodrama]
6988   Physical therapy
6990   Miraculous cures
        [Include faith healing, Lourdes, etc.]
6992   Suggestion therapy
        [Include use of hypnosis, etc.]
        Psychoanalysis. See Phil 6310-6335
6996   Surgery
6998   Other special
        [Include occupational therapy,
        recreational therapy, art therapy,
        music therapy, etc.]

     Social psychiatry. See Soc
    Parapsychology
     [Include in this section works on psychic
     research (spiritualism, automatism,
     telekinesis, etc.) and on the psychology
     of the unconscious (sleep phenomena,
     hallucinations, hypnotism, etc.). For
     New Thought, etc., see Phil 6100-6135.]

      Periodicals. See Phil 10-35
      Societies. See Phil 40-65
7002   Congresses, symposia, etc.

      Reference works
7003   Bibliographies
7004   Dictionaries
7005   Pamphlet volumes

      History
7006   General works
7008   Local (Geographic Table A)

        Biographies of researchers, etc.
        [N.B. - See also Phil 7055, 7109,
        and 7159.]
7009.1-.99   Collected
7009.101-.399 Individual (A-Z, 299 scheme, by person)

      General treatises
      [Include general discussions and controversial
      works. For works limited to Spiritualism,
      see Phil 7064-7069]
7010   Collected authors
7011-7036 Individual authors (A-Z)

      Reports of commissions, investigations, etc.
      [See also Phil 7138-7139 and 7163-7164]
7038   General works
7039   Special cases

      General special
[7040]   Disorders of personality [Discontinued.
      See Phil 6300-6978]
7042   Multiple consciousness, Dissociation of
      personality

      Unconscious mind, Subconsciousness in general.
      See Phil 5722
7048   Other special
      [Include animals and psychic research, etc.]

     Spiritualism
      [Include here works dealing with all forms
      of communication with discarnate spirits.]
[7050]   Folios [Discontinued]
      Bibliographies. See Phil 7061

	History
7052	General works
7053	Local (Geographic Table A)
[7054]	Miscellany [Discontinued]
	Biographies of mediums
	[See also Phil 7159]
7055.1-.99	Collected
7055.101-.399	Individual (299 scheme, A-Z, by person)
[7057]	Spirit writing [Discontinued. See Phil 7077]
[7059.1-.99]	Miscellany [Discontinued]
7059.500-.999	Pamphlet volumes
[7060]	General works [Discontinued. See Phil 7063-7069]
7061	Bibliographies
	General treatises
7063	Collected authors
	[See also Congresses in Phil 7002; also Phil 7059]
7064-7070	Individual authors (By date)
	General special
	Reports of commissions, investigations, etc. See Phil 7038-7039
	Exposure of mediums. See Phil 7038-7069
	Relation to religion, insanity, etc. See Phil 7063-7069
	Physical phenomena of spiritualism
7071	General works
	[Include telekineses in general]
7072	Special topics
	[Include Astral body, levitation, materialization and spirit photography, dematerialization and fourth dimension, raps, table moving, etc.]
	Mediumship, Psychometry
	General works. See Phil 7055-7069
	Spirit messages
7073	General works
7074	Special topics
	[Include alphabet and symbols, special persons, etc. See also Phil 7077.]
[7075]	Sexual perversion [Discontinued. See Phil 6830-6849.]
	Trance states
	[Include sensory and motor automatism]
7076	General works
	[Include ecstasy in general. For religious ecstasy, see Phil 5628. For extrasensory perception, see Phil 7152-7188.]
7077	Automatic communication
	[Include automatic writing, Ouija board messages, etc.]
7078	Automatic drawing
7079	Other special
	[Include trance utterances, etc. See also Phil 7151-7189 and 7222-7229.]
	Sleep phenomena
7080	General works
	Dreaming
	[See also Phil 7222-7229]
7081	Bibliographies
7082	General works
7084	Special topics
	Somnambulism
7085	General works
7088	Special topics

	Sleep disturbances. See Phil 6450-6459
	Hypnotism
	[Include also animal magnetism, Mesmerism, etc.]
	Periodicals. See Phil 10-35
	Societies. See Phil 40-65
7102	Congresses
7103	Bibliographies
7105	Pamphlet volumes
	History
7106	General works
7108	Local (Geographic Table A)
	Biographies of hypnotists
7109.1-.99	Collected
7109.101-.399	Individual (A-Z, 299 scheme, by person)
	General treatises
7110	Collected authors
	[See also Phil 7102 and 7105]
7111-7136	Individual authors (A-Z)
	Reports of commissions, investigations, etc.
7138	General works
7139	Special cases
	Special topics
7140	Suggestion and autosuggestion
	[See also Phil 6992]
7142	Catalepsy
7143	Stage hypnotism
7145	Personal magnetism
7147	Odylic force
7149	Other special
[7150]	Suicide [Discontinued. See Phil 6854]
	Extrasensory perception
	Periodicals. See Phil 10-35
	Societies. See Phil 40-65
7152	Congresses
7153	Bibliographies
7155	Pamphlet volumes
	History
7156	General works
7158	Local (Geographic Table A)
	Biographies
7159.1-.99	Collected
7159.101-.399	Individual (A-Z, 299 scheme, by person)
	General treatises
7160	Collected authors
7162	Individual authors (By date, e.g. .265 for 1965)
	Reports of commissions, investigations, etc.
7163	General works
7164	Special cases
	Special types
	Telepathy
	[Include mind reading, thought transference]
7165	General works
7169	Special topics
	Clairvoyance
	[Include second sight]
7170	General works
7172	Crystal gazing
7174	Other special topics
	Clairaudience
7175	General works
7179	Special topics
7180	Precognition

Psychology (cont.)
   Parapsychology (cont.)

      Hallucinations
         [N.B. - Include here works on false illusions.
         For works on normal illusions, see Phil 5460.]

7202	Bibliographies
7205	General works
7209	Special topics
	[Include deathbed hallucinations, mirage, etc. For neurotic hallucinations, see Phil 6620-6624.]

      Visions, apparitions

7212	Bibliographies
7215	General works
7219	Special topics

      Daydreams

7222	Bibliographies
7225	General works
7229	Special topics
[7230]	Trance [Discontinued. See Phil 7076-7079]

    Occult sciences. See the Folklore class

Esthetics
    [N.B. - This section is to be used for works on
    esthetics in general, especially those dealing
    with esthetics from the philosophical point of
    view. Books on the esthetics of music
    alone or of the fine arts alone will usually
    go to the Music Library or the Fine Arts
    Library; but if those libraries don't want the
    books, they may be classed here. Books on the
    esthetics of literature go in Lit 49, etc.
    General works on art and society or art and
    civilization being kept in Widener should go in
    H 5260-5269. Treatises on esthetics by well
    established philosophers or literary authors
    should go with their other writings.]

8001-8026	Periodicals (A-Z)
8028	Societies
	Congresses. See Phil 8400

    Reference works

8030	Bibliographies
8040	Dictionaries and encyclopedias
8045	Pamphlet volumes

    History of esthetic theory

| 8050 | General works |
| 8055 | Special topics |

      Special periods
        Ancient

8060	General
8062	Greek
8064	Roman
8066	Other

        Medieval

| 8070 | General |
| 8078 | Special |

        Modern

8080	General
8082	Renaissance
8084	16th century
8086	17th century
8088	18th century
8090	19th century
8092	20th century

      Local history
        Europe in general. See Phil 8050-8099

| 8110-8350 | Other countries, etc. (Geographic Table B, starting at 10) |

Esthetics (cont.)
   History of esthetic theory (cont.)

      Biographies. See Phil 8401-8426, etc.

    Treatises on esthetics
      [N.B. - See notes at the beginning of this
      section]

      General works

8400	Collected authors
	[Include congresses, Festschriften, monograph series, etc.]
8401-8426	Individual authors (A-Z)

      Special topics

8430	Relations of esthetics to other disciplines, etc.
	[Include esthetics and music, esthetics and religion, esthetics and information theory, etc. For general works on art and civilization, see H 5260-5269.]
8432	Inspiration
8434	Landscape, nature, etc.
8436	Grotesque, ugliness, etc.
8438	Harmony, symmetry, etc.
8440	Symbolism
8442	The Sublime, the Heroic, etc.
8444	The Comic, the Tragic, etc.
8446	Irony
8448	Other special

Philosophy of religion
    [This section is for purely philosophical works
    about religion. Note that some of the topics are
    also included in the R class, but from the
    point of view of comparative religion.]

[8500]	Folios [Discontinued]
	Periodicals. See Phil 10-35
8505	Societies
	[See also Phil 8615]

| | Congresses. See Phil 8575 |
| 8510 | Pamphlet volumes |

    Reference works

| 8515 | Bibliographies |
| 8518 | Dictionaries and encyclopedias |

    History

| 8520 | General works |
| 8525 | Special topics |

      Special periods
        Ancient
          Oriental. See Phil 900-1099
          Greek. See Phil 1135
          Roman. See Phil 1350

        Medieval. See Phil 1430 and 1540
        Modern. See Phil 8520-8525

| 8550 | Local (Geographical Table A) |
| | Biographies. See Phil 8580-8605, etc. |

    General treatises
      [Include Natural theology in general]

8575	Collected authors
	[Include congresses, Festschriften, etc. See also Phil 8510.]
8580-8605	Individual authors (A-Z)

    Treatises on special topics
      [See also R, etc. Note that the topics are
      arranged here in alphabetic order.]

8610	Agnosticism (By date, e.g. .960 for 1960)
	Anthropomorphism. See Phil 8654-8680; also R
	Atheism. See Phil 8654-8680
	Creation. See Phil 8689-8715; also Phil 280-306
8612	Death
	[See also Phil 8624-8650]

Philosophy of religion (cont.)
   Treatises on special topics (cont.)

      End of the world. See Phil 8689-8715
      Eschatology. See Phil 8624-8650; also R
8615   Ethical Culture Movement
8620   Evil
        [See also Phil 9240]
8622   Faith
      Freedom of the will. See Phil 5750-5775;
        also Phil 384

      Future life
        [See also Phil 8612; also R 265. For
        Spiritualism, etc. see Phil 7000-7099.]
8624   Pamphlet volumes; Collected authors
8625-8650   Individual authors (A-Z)

      God
        [Include here works on the nature and
        attributes of Deity.]
8654   Pamphlet volumes; Collected authors
8655-8680   Individual authors (A-Z)

      Immortality. See Phil 8624-8650; also R 265
      Monotheism. See Phil 8654-8680; also R 205
8685   Pantheism
      Polytheism. See Phil 8654-8680; also R 207
      Providence of God. See Phil 8654-8680 and 8735
      Psychology of religion. See Phil 5627
      Reincarnation. See Phil 8624-8650; also R 265

      Religion and science
8689   Pamphlet volumes; Collected authors
8690-8715   Individual authors (A-Z)

      Resurrection. See Phil 8624-8650; also R 265
8725   Secularism
      Soul. See Phil 8624-8650; also Phil 665
8735   Teleology
        [See also Phil 8654-8680 and 8685; also
        Phil 270, 280-306, 365, 570, etc.]

      Transmigration. See Phil 8624-8650; also
        Phil 665
8740   Worship
        [Include here only very general and
        philosophical works on worship. See also
        Phil 9320; also R.]

Ethics
   [Include in this section works on moral philosophy.
   Treatises by established philosophers should go
   with their writings in Phil 1830-4999.]
[8800]   Folios [Discontinued]
      Periodicals. See Phil 10-35
      Societies. See Phil 40-65
      Congresses. See Phil 8820 and 8870
8805   Pamphlet volumes
[8807]   Dictionaries [Discontinued. See Phil 8815]

   Reference works
8810   Bibliographies
8815   Dictionaries and encyclopedias

   History
     General works
8820   Collected authors
        [See also Phil 8805]
8825-8850   Individual authors (A-Z)
8855   Special topics

     Special periods
      Ancient
        Oriental. See Phil 900-1099
        Greek. See Phil 1145
        Roman. See Phil 1350

Ethics (cont.)
   History (cont.)
     Special periods (cont.)

      Medieval. See Phil 1430 and 1540
      Modern. See Phil 8820-8855
8865   Local (Geographical Table A)
      Biographies. See Phil 8875-8900, etc.

   General treatises
8870   Collected authors
       [Include selected readings of ethical writings,
       congresses, Festschriften, etc. See also
       Phil 8805]
8875-8900   Individual authors (A-Z)

   General special treatises
8905   Relations of ethics to other disciplines
       [Include works on relations to religion,
       law, science, etc. See also Phil 9450, etc.]
8910   Comparative ethics
8915   Evolutionary and genetic ethics
       [See also Phil 9150 and 365]
8920   Humanist ethics
8925   Positivist ethics
      Situation ethics. See Phil 8950-8975
      Ethical Culture Movement. See Phil 8615

     Religious ethics
8940   General works
       Buddhist. See Phil 910; also R
       Hindu. See Phil 960; also Ind
       Jaina. See Phil 960; also Ind
       Islamic. See Phil 1030; also Asia
       Jewish. See Jud
8950-8975   Christian (A-Z)

     Ethics of political and social systems
8980   Communist (800 scheme, A-Z)
8982   Socialist
8984   Totalitarian
8988   Other

   Treatises on special topics
     [Include special systems and topics relating
     to individual ethics, practical and applied
     ethics, etc. Note that the topics are
     arranged in alphabetical order except for
     grouping of vices and virtues.]

     Affections. See Phil 9420
     Aged. See Phil 9400
9003   Altruism
       [Include also Egoism, Self-interest, etc.]
9005   Ambition
9010   Amusements
       [Include works on moral aspects of the
       theater, dancing, billiards, etc. See
       also Phil 9230]

     Anger. See Phil 9558; also Phil 5412
9015   Asceticism
       [See also Phil 9435 and 9515; also
       Phil 5627.]
9020   Authority
       [See also Gov, Soc, etc.]

     Avarice. See Phil 9558
     Bachelors. See Phil 9339-9365
     Boys. See Phil 9160-9185
     Brotherliness. See Phil 9560
     Calumny. See Phil 9510
9027   Casuistry
9030   Chance
       [See also Phil 9230; also Phil 270]
9035   Character
       [Include here general works on ethics of the
       individual. See also Phil 9558 and 9560,
       etc.; also Phil 5590]

Ethics (cont.)
Treatises on special topics (cont.)

	Charity. See Phil 9560
	Chastity. See Phil 9495
	Cheerfulness. See Phil 9560
	Children. See Phil 9160-9185
9045	Citizens and citizenship
	[See also Gov]
9050	City life and country life
9055	Compassion
	[See also Phil 5415]
9060	Compensation
9065	Compromise
	[See also Phil 9540]
9070	Conduct of life
	[Include here general works on practical or applied ethics. See also Phil 9160-9185, 9530, etc.]
	Confidence. See Phil 9560
9075	Conscience
	Country life. See Phil 9050
	Courage. See Phil 9560; also Phil 5401
	Courtesy. See Phil 9145
	Courtiers. See Phil 9525
	Cruelty. See Phil 9558
	Determinism. See Phil 9215; also Phil 384
	Dishonesty. See Phil 9558
	Domestic duties. See Phil 9160-9185
9120	Duty
	[See also Phil 9470]
	Egoism. See Phil 9003
	Envy. See Phil 9558; also Phil 5413
	Ethical Culture Movement. See Phil 8615
9145	Etiquette
	[Include also works on the ethics of fashion and dress, the "evils of the age", Prefer H 5070-5079]
	Evil. See Phil 9240
9150	Evolution
	[See also Phil 365]
	Fairness. See Phil 9560
	Falsehood. See Phil 9558
	Family
	[Include here general works on the ethics of the family as a group, domestic duties, etc.; also works on the ethics of individual members of a family, e.g. parents, husbands, wives, children, etc. See also Phil 9400 for works on the ethics of the aged; also Phil 9339-9365.]
9159	Pamphlet volumes; Collected authors
9160-9185	Individual authors (A-Z)
9200	Fanaticism
	Fashion. See Phil 9145
	Fathers. See Phil 9160-9185
	Folly. See Phil 9558
9215	Freedom of the will
	[Prefer Phil 384 or Phil 5750-5775.]
9220	Friendship
9230	Gaming
	[Include works on the ethics of betting, gambling, etc.]
	Gentlemen. See Phil 9339-9365
9240	Good and evil
	[Include works on the origin of evil, the depravity of human nature, etc. See also Phil 8620; also Phil 9558 and 9560]
	Gratitude. See Phil 9560
	Grief. See Phil 9520
	Guilt. See Phil 9075; also Phil 5414
9245	Happiness
	[See also Phil 5402 and 5403]

Ethics (cont.)
Treatises on special topics (cont.)

	Hedonism. See Phil 9245
	Honesty. See Phil 9560
	Honor. See Phil 9560
	Husbands. See Phil 9160-9185
	Hypocrisy. See Phil 9558
	Ingratitude. See Phil 9558
9255	Irony
	Jealousy. See Phil 9558; also Phil 5413
	Joy. See Phil 9245; also Phil 5403
	Justice. See Phil 9450; also Gov
	Kindness. See Phil 9560
9290	Labor
	[Include here works on the ethics of work, leisure, etc.; also works on the ethics of the laboring class.]
	Ladies. See Phil 9339-9365
	Leisure. See Phil 9290; also Soc
	Loyalty. See Phil 9560
	Luxury. See Phil 9575
	Lying. See Phil 9558
	Magnanimity. See Phil 9560
	Manliness. See Phil 9560
9320	Meditative life
	[Include here general works on the active versus the contemplative life; also works on the spiritual life in general. See also Phil 9515.]
9330	Melancholy
	[See also Phil 9520]
	Men and women
	[Include here works on the ethics for men and women as groups; also works on Gentlemen, Ladies, Young persons, etc. See also Phil 9045, 9160-9185, 9375, 9400, 9490, 9513, 9525, and 9528.]
9339	Pamphlet volumes; Collected authors
9340-9365	Individual authors (A-Z)
9375	Merchants
	[Prefer Econ]
	Modesty. See Phil 9560
9380	Morale
	Mothers. See Phil 9160-9185
9390	Oaths and swearing
	Obedience. See Phil 9020
	Obligation. See Phil 9470
9400	Old age
	[Include here works on the ethics of the aged and elderly. See also Soc.]
9410	Optimism
	[See also Phil 9430]
9415	Pain and suffering
	[See also Phil 9500; also Phil 5402]
	Parents. See Phil 9160-9185
9420	Passions
	Patience. See Phil 9560
	Patriotism. See Phil 9045 and 9450
9425	Peace
9430	Pessimism
	[See also Phil 9410]
	Political ethics. See Phil 9450
9435	Poverty
	Pride. See Phil 9558
9440	Professional ethics
	[N.B. - Include here only very general works. Works on the ethics for a particular profession class with that profession, e.g. business in Econ, medicine in Med, etc. See also Phil 9290 and 9490]
	Prudence. See Phil 9560
9450	Public morals
	[Include political ethics, etc. See also Phil 9045; also Gov.]

Ethics (cont.)
Treatises on special topics (cont.)
9455   Public opinion
        [See also Soc]
9470   Responsibility
        [See also Phil 9120]

Rest. See Phil 9290
9480   Ridicule
Right and wrong. See Phil 9075 or 9240
Saving and thrift. See Econ
9490   Scholars
        [See also Phil 9528]

Self-interest. See Phil 9003
Self-respect. See Phil 9560
9495   Sexual ethics. (By date, e.g. .160 for 1960)
        [See also Phil 9159-9185, 9339-9365, etc.]
9500   Sickness
Silence. See Phil 9560
Sincerity. See Phil 9560
9510   Slander
Snobbishness. See Phil 9558
9513   Society, Social ethics
        [For Ethical Culture Societies, see
          Phil 8615]
9515   Solitude
9520   Sorrow
        [See also Phil 9330]
9525   Sovereigns and courtiers
Spiritual life. See Phil 9320
9528   Students
        [See also Phil 9490]
9530   Success
Suffering. See Phil 9415
Sympathy. See Phil 9055 or 9560; also
        Phil 5415

Swearing. See Phil 9390
9540   Toleration
        [See also Phil 9065]

Truthfulness. See Phil 9560
9550   Utilitarianism
        [See also Phil 733]
9558   Vice and vices
        [Include general works and works on
          particular vices. See also Phil 9390, 9480,
          9510, and 9575.]
9560   Virtue and virtues
        [Include general works and works on
          particular virtues. See also Phil 9005,
          9055, 9220, etc.]
9575   Wealth
Wives. See Phil 9160-9185
Women. See Phil 9339-9365
Work. See Phil 9290
Young people. See Phil 9339-9365

9590   **Miscellany**
        [N.B. - Use this number only for eccentric
        writings with a pseudo-philosophical and/or
        pseudo-religious basis which can not easily
        be classed elsewhere. See also Parapsychology
        in Phil 7000-7249.]

PHILOSOPHY

AND

PSYCHOLOGY

CLASSIFIED LISTING BY CALL NUMBER

Phil 10 - 35   Periodicals (A-Z)

	Phil 10.1	American journal of psychology. Baltimore. 1,1888+ 90v.
	Phil 10.1.5	American journal of psychology. Index. N.Y. 1-50,1926-1937 2v.
NEDL	Phil 10.2	Annales medico-psychologiques. Paris. 1843-1929 94v.
	Phil 10.2	Annales medico-psychologiques. Paris. 1930+ 73v.
NEDL	Phil 10.2.5	Annales medico-psychologiques. Table 1-2. Paris. 1-2,1843-1878
NEDL	Phil 10.3	Annales de philosophie chrétienne. Paris. 1830-1913 160v.
NEDL	Phil 10.3.5	Annales de philosophie chrétienne. Paris. 1884-1902
	Phil 10.4	L'année philosophique. Paris. 1-24,1890-1913 24v.
	Phil 10.4.5	L'année philosophique, études critiques. Paris. 1-2,1867-1868 2v.
	Phil 10.5	Martin, L.A. Annuaire philisophique. Paris. 1-5,1864-1868 5v.
	Phil 10.6	Archiv für Geschichte der Philosophie. Berlin. 1,1887+ 43v.
	Phil 10.6.5	Archiv für Geschichte der Philosophie. Register. Berlin. 1-20 2v.
NEDL	Phil 10.7	Archiv für Psychiatrie. Berlin. 1868-1929 27v.
	Phil 10.7	Archiv für Psychiatrie. Berlin. 1929-1942 12v.
	Phil 10.7.5	Archiv für Psychiatrie und Nervenkrankheiten vereinigt mit Zeitschrift für die gesamte Neurologie und Psychiatrie. Berlin. 179,1947+ 31v.
NEDL	Phil 10.7.15	Archiv für Psychiatrie und Nervenkrankheiten. General Register. Berlin. 1-45,1898-1909 2v.
	Phil 10.8	Archiv für systematische Philosophie. Berlin. 1-34,1895-1931 27v.
	Phil 10.8.5	Archiv für systematische Philosophie. Register. Berlin. 1-15
NEDL	Phil 10.9	Archives de neurologie. Paris. 1880-1929 11v.
	Phil 10.9	Archives de neurologie. Paris. 1930-1946 11v.
NEDL	Phil 10.10	American journal of insanity. Utica. 1-16,1844-1860 9v.
NEDL	Phil 10.11	Annals of phrenology. Boston. 1-2,1835-1836 2v.
NEDL	Phil 10.12	American phrenological journal. Philadelphia. 1838-1905 11v.
NEDL	Phil 10.12.5	American phrenological journal. Philadelphia.
	Phil 10.13	Archiv für die gesamte Psychologie. Leipzig. 1,1903+ 107v.
	Phil 10.13.5	Archiv für die gesamte Psychologie. Register. Leipzig. 1-75,1925-1931 2v.
	Phil 10.13.12	Archiv für die gesamte Psychologie. Erganzungsband. Leipzig. 1-4,1929-1937 5v.
	Phil 10.14	Archives de psychologie. Genève. 1,1902+ 38v.
	Phil 10.15	Journal of religious psychology. Worcester. 1-7,1904-1915 7v.
	Phil 10.16	Archivo de historia de la filosofía. Madrid. 1-2,1905-1907 2v.
	Phil 10.17	Archivos de psiquiatría y criminología. Buenos Aires. 6-12,1907-1913
	Phil 10.18	L'année psychologique. Paris. 1894+ 13v.
	Phil 10.19	Columbia University. Archives of psychology. N.Y. 1907-1945 37v.
	Phil 10.19.5	Columbia University. Archives of psychology.
	Phil 10.20	Anales de psicologia. Buenos Aires. 1911
	Phil 10.21	Archives du magnétisme animal. Paris. 1-4 2v.
	Phil 10.22	Abhandlungen zur Philosophie und ihrer Geschichte. Halle. 1-52 7v.
	Phil 10.22.8	Abhandlungen zur Philosophie und ihrer Geschichte. Leipzig. 1-25,1907-1916 3v.
	Phil 10.23	Archivos italiano di psicologia. Torino. 1-19,1920-1941 8v.
	Phil 10.24	Archiv für Religionspsychologie. Tübingen. 1914+ 4v.
	Phil 10.26	Abhandlungen zur Physiologie der Gesichtsempfindungen. Leipzig. 1-5 3v.
	Phil 10.27	Annalen der Philosophie. Leipzig. 1-8,1919-1929 8v.
	Phil 10.27.3	Erkenntnis; zugleich Annalen de Philosophie. Leipzig. 1-10 8v.
	Phil 10.27.8	Erkenntnis; zugleich Annalen de Philosophie. Leipzig. 1-9,1925-1929 7v.
	Phil 10.28	Australasian journal of psychology and philosophy. Sydney. 1,1923+ 29v.
	Phil 10.29	Arkiv för psykologi och pedagogik. Stockholm. 1-8,1922-1929 2v.
	Phil 10.30	Archives de philosophie. Paris. 1,1923+ 47v.
	Phil 10.30.3	Archives de philosophie. Tables generales. 1937
	Phil 10.31	Annali dello spiritismo in Italia; rivista psicologica. Torino. 1-35,1864-1898 21v.
	Phil 10.32	Annales des sciences psychiques. Paris. 1-7,1891-1897 7v.
	Phil 10.33	The American journal of neurology and psychiatry. N.Y. 1-4,1882-1883 2v.
	Phil 10.34	Archives of neurology and psycho-pathology. Utica, N.Y. 1-3 6v.
	Phil 10.36	Athenaeum; kiadja a filozofiai társaság. Budapest. 12-28,1926-1942 5v.
	Phil 10.37	Altenaeum; philosophische Zeitschrift. München. 1-3,1862-1864 3v.
	Phil 10.38	Annales du magnétisme animal. Paris. 1814-1817 4v.
	Phil 10.38.5	Bibliotheque du magnetisme animal. Paris. 1-8,1817-1819 4v.
	Phil 10.39	Acta psychologica Keijo. Keijo, Japan.
	Phil 10.40	Archivio di filosofia. Roma. 1-11,1931-1941 17v.
	Phil 10.41	Annalen der critische Philosophie. Assen. 1-29,1931-1959 21v.
	Phil 10.41.10	Algemeen Nederlands tijdschrift voor wijstegeerte en psychologie. Assen. 15,1921+ 19v.
	Phil 10.41.11	Algemeen Nederlands tijdschrift voor wijstegeerte en psychologie. Systemtisch en alfabetisch register. 1-50,1907-1958
	Phil 10.42	Aryan path. Bombay. 1,1930+ 45v.
	Phil 10.43	Archivio di storia della filosofia. Roma. 1-8,1932-1939 5v.
	Phil 10.45	Adyar pamphlets. Adyar. 13,1912
	Phil 10.47	The American journal of orthopsychiatry. Menasha, Wis. 1,1930+ 43v.
	Phil 10.47.3	The American journal of orthopsychiatry. Index. Menasha, Wis., 1941-1952. 2v.
	Phil 10.49	Acta philosophica Fennica edidit Societas Philosophica. Helsinki. 1,1935 9v.
	Phil 10.49.5	Acta psychologica Fennica. Helsingissä. 1,1951+
	Phil 10.50	Die Akademie. Erlangen. 2-3,1924-1925 2v.
	Phil 10.51	Analysis. Oxford, Eng. 1,1933+ 10v.
	Phil 10.52	The American image. Boston. 1,1939+ 23v.
	Phil 10.53	Archiv für den thierischen Magnetismus. Altenberg. 1-12,1817-1824 6v.

Phil 10 - 35   Periodicals (A-Z) - cont.

	Phil 10.54	Arya; a philosophical review. Pondicherry, India. 6-7,1920-1921
	Phil 10.55	Applied psychology monographs of American association for applied psychology. Stanford, Cal. 1-17,1943-1948 5v.
	Phil 10.57	The attendant. Philadelphia. 1-3,1944-1946
	Phil 10.58	Archiv für spiritualistische Philosophie und ihre Geschichte. Amsterdam.
	Phil 10.59	Australian journal of psychology. Victoria. 1,1949+ 11v.
	Phil 10.59.5	Australian journal of psychology. Cumulative index, 1-10,1949-1958. Melbourne, n.d.
	Phil 10.60	Arquivos brasileiros de psicotéchica. 1,1949+ 19v.
	Phil 10.61	Archiv für Philosophie. Stuttgart. 4,1950+ 8v.
	Phil 10.61.5	Archiv für mathematische Logik und Grundlagenforschung. Stuttgart. 5-7
	Phil 10.62	American Association for Applied Psychology. Directory of applied psychologists. Bloomington, Ind.
	Phil 10.63	Arkhé; revista de metafísica. Cordoba. 1-3,1952-1954 2v.
	Phil 10.65	Archiv für Begriffsgeschichte; Bausteine zu einem historischen Wörterbuch der Philosophie. Bonn. 1,1955+ 11v.
	Phil 10.68	The American nationalist. St. Louis. 1,1956+ 9v.
	Phil 10.70	Archiwum historii filozofii i myśli społecznej. Warszawa. 1-13 6v.
	Phil 10.72	Abhandlungen zur Philosophie und Psychologie. Dornach. 1,1951+ 2v.
	Phil 10.74	Archivio de psicologia, neurologia e psichiotrea. Milano. 5,1944+ 19v.
	Phil 10.76	Aquinas; rivista di filosofia. Roma. 1,1958+ 9v.
	Phil 10.78	Acta psychologica Taiwanica; science reports of the National Jaiwan University. Taipei. 1,1958+ 3v.
	Phil 10.80	Annual review of psychology. Palo Alto, California. 1+ 34v.
	Phil 10.82	American psychologist. Lancaster. 1,1946+ 29v.
	Phil 10.84	American philosophical quarterly. Pittsburgh. 1,1964+ 6v.
	Phil 10.86F	Aabo, Finland. Yliopisto. Institute of Psychology. Reports. Turku.
	Phil 10.88	The American journal of psychoanalysis. N.Y. 23,1963+ 8v.
	Phil 10.88.5	The American journal of psychoanalysis. Cumulative index. v.1-17,1941-1957. n.p., n.d.
	Phil 10.90	American journal of psychotherapy. Lancaster, Pa. 19,1965+ 5v.
	Phil 10.92	Adolescence. N.Y. 1,1966+ 3v.
	Phil 10.93	Adolescent psychiatry. N.Y. 1,1971+
	Phil 10.94	Acta psychologica Gothoburgensia. Stockholm. 1-7 2v.
	Phil 10.95	Australian psychologist. Queensland, Australia. 1,1956+
	Phil 10.96	Anuario filosofico. Pamplona. 1,1968+ 2v.
	Phil 10.97	Advances in the study of behavior. N.Y. 1,1965+ 2v.
	Phil 10.98	Anthropos. Ljubljana. 1969+
	Phil 10.99	Annali di psicologia. Milan. 1,1968+
	Phil 10.100	Annalen der Philosophie und der philosophischen Geistes von einer Gesellschaft gelehrter Männer. Reprinted 1970. Halle. 1-3,1795-1797// 2v.
	Phil 10.101	Acta paedopsychiatrica. Basel. 38,1971+
	Phil 10.102	Acta symbolica. Akron, Ohio. 1,1970+
	Phil 11.1	Philosophische Gesellschaft zu Berlin. Verhandlungen. v.1-21. Leipzig, 1875-82. 2v.
X Cg	Phil 11.2	The British journal of psychology. Cambridge. 1,1904
	Phil 11.2	The British journal of psychology. Cambridge. 2,1905+ 49v.
	Phil 11.2.5	The British journal of psychology. Monograph supplement. Cambridge. 1,1911 11v.
	Phil 11.2.8	The British journal of psychology. Medical section. Cambridge. 1,1920+ 26v.
	Phil 11.2.10	The British journal of psychology. Statistical section. London. 1,1947+ 9v.
	Phil 11.2.11	British journal of statistical psychology. Cumulative index, 1-14. n.p., n.d.
	Phil 11.3	Beiträge zur Philosophie. Heidelberg. 1-32,1912-1938+ 32v.
	Phil 11.4	Bibliothek für Philosophie. Berlin. 1-21+ 4v.
	Phil 11.5	Banner of light. Cambridge. 1907
	Phil 11.6	Psychopathic Hospital, Boston, Mass. Contributions. 1-63,1913-1914+
	Phil 11.7	Blätter für freies religiöses Leben. Philadelphia. 1-19,1857-1875+ 9v.
	Phil 11.8	Beiträge zur Psychologie der Aussage. Leipzig. 1903-1906 2v.
NEDL	Phil 11.9	Beiträge zur Philosophie des deutschen Idealismus. Erfurt. 1918-1927
	Phil 11.9.5	Folge der Beihefte. Erfurt. 3-13,1920-1924+ 4v.
	Phil 11.10	Buchanan's journal of man. Cincinnati. 1,1849 3v.
	Phil 11.10.2	Buchanan's journal of man. Cincinnati. 1849-1850
	Phil 11.12	British journal of psychical research. London. 1-2,1926-1929
	Phil 11.13	El buen deseo. Matanzas. 1-2,1884-1886
NEDL	Phil 11.14	Brain. N.Y. 1-52,1878-1929 82v.
	Phil 11.14	Brain. N.Y. 53,1930+ 83v.
	Phil 11.15	Blätter für deutsche Philosophie. Berlin. 1-16,1927-1943 16v.
	Phil 11.16	Beiträge und Psychologie. Stuttgart. 1-11,1928-1932 11v.
	Phil 11.17	Bollettino filosofico. Roma. 1-4,1935-1938 2v.
	Phil 11.18	Buenos Aires. University Nacional. Facultad de Filosofía y Letras. Publicaciones de filosofia contemporanea. Buenos Aires. 1-4,1938-1945
	Phil 11.18.5	Buenos Aires. University Nacional. Facultad de Filosofía y Letras. Publicaciones de filosofía argentina. Buenos Aires. 1-5 5v.
	Phil 11.18.10	Buenos Aires. University Nacional. Instituto de Psicología. Anales. Buenos Aires. 1-3,1935-1941 2v.
	Phil 11.19	Biosphical series. N.Y.
	Phil 11.20	Beiträge zur christlichen Philosophie. Mainz. 1-6,1947-1950
	Phil 11.25	Biblioteca de filosofía mexicana. Mexico. 1-10,1942-1943 2v.
	Phil 11.26	Breviarum litterarum. Berlin. 1-5 5v.
	Phil 11.27	Befreiung; Zeitschrift für kritisches Denken. Aaran. 1-3,1953-1955 3v.
	Phil 11.30	Bulletin de psychologie édité par le Groupe d'études de psychologie de l'Université de Paris. Paris. 7,1953+ 19v.
	Phil 11.33	Behavioral science. Ann Arbor. 1,1956+ 15v.
	Phil 11.35	Bibliothèque d'anthropotechnie. Paris. 1+ 2v.

Phil 10 - 35   Periodicals (A-Z) - cont.

Phil 11.37   Bulgarska Akademiiana naukite, Sofiia. Institut po
              Filosofiia. Izvestiia. Sofia. 1+ 14v.
Phil 11.39   British Psychological Society. Bulletin. London.
              11,1951+ 8v.
Phil 11.42   The British journal of social and clinical psychology.
              London. 1,1962+ 8v.
Phil 11.44   Bucharest Universitătea. Analele: seria acta logica.
              1,1958+ 3v.
Phil 11.46   Behavior research and therapy. Oxford. 4,1966+ 4v.
Phil 11.48   Bölcseleti közlemények. Budapest. 1-4,1935-1938
Phil 11.50   Bruenn. Universita. Knihovna. Přehled nové časopisecké
              literatury z oblasti. filosofie, estetiky, sociologie.
              Brno. 1965+
Phil 11.52   Bijdragen tot de psychologie. Assen. 2,1968+ 9v.
Phil 11.53   Bydgoskie Towarzystwo naukowe. Wydział nauk
              Humanistycznych. Komisja Filozofii i Pedagogiki. Prace.
              Bydgoszcz. 1,1969+
NEDL Phil 12.1   La critique philosophique, politique, scientifique,
              littéraire. Paris. 1872-1889 36v.
NEDL Phil 12.1.5   La critique philosophique. Supplemente. La critique
              religieuse. Paris. 1878-1885 7v.
Phil 12.2   Questions du temps present. Paris. 1911+ 2v.
Phil 12.4   La cultura filosofica. Firenze. 1-11,1907-1917 11v.
Phil 12.5   Comparative psychology monographs. Baltimore.
              1-21,1922-1951 10v.
Phil 12.6   Crisis; revista española de filosofia. Madrid. 1,1954+
              15v.
Phil 12.7   Contemporary psychology. Washington. 1,1956+ 11v.
Phil 12.8   Česká mysl; časopis filosofický. Praha. 1900-1947
              31v.
Phil 12.9   Complex; the magazine of psychoanalysis. N.Y.
              2-8,1950-1952
Phil 12.10   Characterologische Jahrbücher. Berlin.
Phil 12.12   Civiltá e idee. Torina. 1-20 2v.
Phil 12.15   Character and personality. Durham, N.C. 1,1932+ 38v.
Phil 12.17   Chinese journal of psychology. Peiping.
Phil 12.19   Contributions to psychological theory. Durham, N.C. 1
Phil 12.21   La caractérologie. Paris. 1,1960+ 2v.
Phil 12.23   The cultural world. Los Angeles. 2-3,1931-1932
Phil 12.25   Columbia studies in philosophy. N.Y. 1-10,1941-1948
              8v.
Phil 12.30   Charakter; eine Vierteljahresschrift für
              psychodiagnostische Studien und verwandte Gebiete. London.
              1-2,1932-1933
Phil 12.35   Convivium; estudios filosoficos. Barcelona. 1-2,1956-1957
Phil 12.40   Canadian journal of psychology. Toronto. 1,1947+ 14v.
Phil 12.45   Çulegere de studü de psihologie. Bucuresti. 4 2v.
Phil 12.50   Československá psychologie; časopis pro psychologickou
              teorii i praxi. Praha. 1,1957+ 13v.
Phil 12.55   Club Voltaire. München. 1,1963+ 4v.
Phil 12.60   Cahiers internationaux de symbolisme. Genève. 1-6+
              3v.
Phil 12.65   Cuadernos uruguayos de filosofia. Montevideo. 3,1964+
              3v.
Phil 12.70   Contemporary psychoanalysis. N.Y. 1,1964+ 3v.
Phil 12.75   Community mental health journal. Lexington, Mass. 1,1965+
              5v.
Phil 12.80   Cuyo. Mendoza. 1,1965+
Phil 12.90   Critica; revista hispano-americana de filosofia. Mexico.
              1,1967+
Phil 12.95   Contemporary thought in guidance and counseling.
              Washington. 1,1967+
Phil 12.100   The Ceylon rationalist ambassador. Colombo. 1,1968+
              4v.
Phil 12.105   Canadian journal of behavioral science. Toronto. 1,1969+
Phil 12.110   Cahiers pour l'analyse. Paris. 1,1966+ 2v.
Phil 12.115   The counseling psychologist. St. Louis. 1,1969+
Phil 12.120   Chinese studies in philosophy. White Plains, N.Y. 1,1969+
Phil 12.125   Concurrence; a review for the encounter of commitments.
              Basle. 1,1969+
Phil 12.130   Cognitive psychology. N.Y. 1,1970+
Phil 12.135   Les cahiers rationalistes. Paris. 108,1950+
Phil 12.140   Le courrier rationaliste. Paris. 12,1965+
Phil 12.145   Cognitive studies. N.Y. 1,1970+ 2v.
Phil 12.150   Canadian journal of philosophy. Edmonton. 1,1971+
Phil 13.1   Deutsche Psychologie. Langensolza. 1-7,1918-1932+ 5v.
Phil 13.1.5   Duesseldorfer philosophische Bausteine. Düsseldorf.
              1,1968+
Phil 13.2   Dialectica. Neuchâtel. 1,1947+ 10v.
Phil 13.5   Deucalion; cahiers de philosophie. Paris. 1-6 3v.
Phil 13.7   Deutsche Beiträge zur Philosophie der Zeit. München.
              1,1948
Phil 13.9   Deutsche Zeitschrift für Philosophie. Berlin. 1,1953+
              30v.
Phil 13.9.2   Deutsche Zeitschrift für Philosophie. Beiheft. Berlin.
              1,1953+
Phil 13.12   Doubleday papers in psychology. Garden City, N.Y. 1-17
              4v.
Phil 13.14   Dianoia; anuario de filosofia. Mexico. 1955+ 15v.
Phil 13.15   Diagnostica. Göttingen. 1,1955+ 8v.
Phil 13.16   Discorsi e prolusioni. Torino.
Phil 13.17   Dissertations philosophiques. Paris.
Phil 13.18   Dialoog; tydschrift voor wijsbegeerte. Antwerpen. 1,1960+
              9v.
Phil 13.19   Dialogue. Kingston, Ont. 1,1962+ 8v.
Phil 13.20   Danish yearbook of philosophy. Copenhagen. 1,1964+
Phil 13.22   De homine. Roma. 2,1962+ 12v.
Phil 13.23   Developmental psychology. Washington. 1,1969+
Phil 13.25   Dawes Hicks lecture on philosophy. London. 1970+
Phil 14.1   L'encéphale. Paris. 1-9 8v.
NEDL Phil 14.1.8   L'encéphale. Paris. 1906-1929
Phil 14.2   Ethical record. Philadelphia. 1-3 2v.
Phil 14.3   Ethical record. N.Y.
NEDL Phil 14.4   The esoteric. Boston. 1-13 12v.
Phil 14.5   Experimental studies in psychology and pedagogy. Boston.
              1-7,1902-1917 6v.
Phil 14.6   Les études philosophiques. Marseille. 1,1926+ 25v.
Phil 14.7   The ethological journal. London.
Phil 14.8   Erfahung und Denker, Schriften zur Forderung der
              Beziehungen zwischen Philosophie und Einzelwissenschaften.
              Berlin. 1-32 13v.
Phil 14.9   Experimental metaphysics. London. 1-2,1945-1947+
Phil 14.10   Enquiry. London. 1-3,1948-1950 2v.
Phil 14.11   Eranus. Kaunas. 2,1931
Phil 14.12   Episteme. Buenos Aires. 1947-1951
Phil 14.13   Eranos Jahrbuck. Zürich. 1,1933+ 33v.
Phil 14.13.5   Eranos Jahrbuck. Index. Zürich. 1,1933+ 2v.

Phil 10 - 35   Periodicals (A-Z) - cont.

Phil 14.14   Études d'epistemologie genetique. Paris. 1,1957+ 15v.
Phil 14.15   Episteme; anuario de filosofia. Caracas. 1,1957+ 4v.
Phil 14.15.3   Episteme. Biblioteca filosofica. Caracas. 1
Phil 14.16   Ensayos y estudios. Bonn. 1-17 8v.
Phil 14.17   Eidos. Cordoba. 1,1969+
Phil 14.18   Entretiens psychiatriques. Paris. 1,1952+ 13v.
Phil 14.19   The Edinburgh psychological review. Edinburgh.
Phil 14.20   Der erkenntnistheoretische Subjektivismus. München.
              1,1962+ 2v.
Phil 14.21   Experimental Psychology Society. Monograph. Cambridge.
              1,1961+ 3v.
Phil 14.22   Existential psychiatry. Chicago. 1,1966+
Phil 14.23   Révolution psychiatrique. Paris. 1948+ 33v.
Phil 14.23.2   Révolution psychiatrique. Tables des matieres. Paris.
              1925+
Phil 14.24   Etyka. Warzawa. 1,1966+ 3v.
Phil 14.25F   Ethical impact. N.Y. 1966-1967//
Phil 14.27   Etyka i estetyka. Kyïv. 1,1965+ 3v.
Phil 14.28   Etudes philosophiques et littéraires. Rabat.
              1-4,1967-1969//?
Phil 14.31   Energy and character; the journal of bio-energetic
              research. Abbotsbury, Eng. 1,1971+
Phil 15.1   Folia neuro-biologica. Leipzig. 1-12 11v.
Phil 15.2   Free thought magazine. Chicago. 1899-1919 3v.
Phil 15.3   Fortschritte der Psychologie und ihrer Anwendungen. 1-4
              4v.
Phil 15.4   La filosofia della scuoli italiane, revista bimestrale.
              Firenze. 1-16,1870-1885 16v.
NEDL Phil 15.5F   Freethinker. London. 10-48,1890-1928
Phil 15.5.10   Freethinker of America. Bulletin. N.Y. 1,1937+ 5v.
Phil 15.6   Forschungen zur Philosophie und ihrer Geschichte. Halle.
              1-16 9v.
Phil 15.7   Forum philosophicum. 1930-1931
Phil 15.8A   Filosofiskie zapiski. Moskva. 1-6,1946-1953 6v.
RRC Phil 15.8B   Filosofiskie zapiski. Moskva. 1,1946
Phil 15.9   Filosofia, per joy d'amor. Torino. 1-2,1945-1947
Phil 15.11   France. Centre d'Etudes et Recherches Psycho-Techniques.
              Bulletin. Paris. 5,1956+ 9v.
Phil 15.12   Filosofia, revista trimestrale. Torino. 1,1950+ 24v.
Phil 15.13   Felsefe arkivi. Istanbul. 1+ 3v.
Phil 15.14   Filosofska misül. Sofiiá. 1,1945+ 26v.
Phil 15.16   Filosófický časopis. Praha. 4,1956+ 20v.
Phil 15.17   Filosofia; revista do Centro de Estudos Escolásticos.
              Lisboa. 3,1956+ 8v.
Phil 15.18   Filozófiai évkönyv. Budapest. 1,1952
Phil 15.20   Filosofskie voprosy estestvoznaniia. Moskva. 1-3 3v.
Phil 15.25   Filosofski pregled. Sofiia. 1-4,1929-1942 18v.
Phil 15.30   Filozofija. Beograd. 1,1957+ 9v.
Phil 15.35   Filosofia e vita. Rome. 3,1962+ 7v.
Phil 15.35.2   Filosofia e vita. Indici generali. Roma. 1960+
Phil 15.40   Fortschritte der Psychoanalyse. Göttingen. 1-3 2v.
Phil 15.45   Frederic W.H. Mayers memorial lecture. London. 16,1966+
Phil 15.50   Filosofs'ka dumka. Kyïv. 1970+
Phil 15.55   Filosofskie voprosy logicheskogo analiza nauchnogo znaniia.
              Erevan. 1,1969+ 2v.
Phil 15.60   Forschungen zur Logik und zur Grundlegen der exakten
              Wissenschaften. Reprinted 1970. Leipzig. N.F.
              1-8,1937-1943//
Phil 15.65   Fédération française de la libre pensée. Bulletin mensuel
              de correspondance des groupes et adhérents fédérés. Paris.
              1890-1893
Phil 16.1   Giornale critico della filosofia italiana. Messina. 1920+
              43v.
Phil 16.2   Grenzfragen der Nerven und Seelenlebens. Wiesbaden. 1-130
              20v.
Phil 16.3   Genetic psychology monographs. Worcester. 1,1920+ 56v.
Phil 16.4   Der Gedanke. Berlin. 1-8,1860-1873 2v.
Phil 16.6   General semantics monographs. Chicago.
Phil 16.7   Giornale di metafisica; revista bimestrale di filosofica.
              1,1946+ 25v.
Phil 16.8   La gaceta filosófica de los Neokantianos de Mexico.
Phil 16.9   Geistige Überlieferung. Berlin. 1-2,1940-1942 2v.
Phil 16.10   Gawein; tydschrift van de psychologische kring aan de
              Vijneegen Universiteit. Vijneegen. 2,1953+ 10v.
Phil 16.11   Group Psychotherapy of Southern California. Annual report.
              Los Angeles. 1-2,1953-1955
Phil 16.12   Giornale italiano per la ricerca psichica. Milano.
              1,1963+
Phil 16.13   Georgia psychologist; official publication of Georgia
              Psychological Association. Atlanta. 20,1967+
Phil 16.14   Gruppenpsychotherapie und Gruppendynamik. Göttingen.
              1,1968+ 3v.
Phil 16.15   Granada, Spain (City). Universidad. Cátedra Francisco
              Suárez. Anales. Granada. 9,1969+
Phil 17.1   The Hibbert journal. London. 1,1902+ 73v.
X Cg Phil 17.1   The Hibbert journal. London. 8
Phil 17.1.5   The Hibbert journal. Index. v.1-10. Boston, 1902-1911.
Phil 17.2   Revue de l'hypnotisme. Paris. 1-13 13v.
Phil 17.2.5   Hoja de psicologia. Montevideo. 1-12,1947-1953
NEDL Phil 17.3   Human nature. London. 1-11,1807-1877 11v.
Phil 17.4   Heidelberger Abhandlungen zur Philosophie und ihrer
              Geschichte. Tübingen. 1-32,1924-1945 31v.
NEDL Phil 17.5   The hypnotic magazine. Chicago.
Phil 17.6   Handbuch der Philosophie. München. 1-4 4v.
Phil 17.7   Handbuch der biologischen Arbeitsmethoden. Abteilung VI.
              Berlin. 1920-1935+ 8v.
Phil 17.8   Harvard psychological studies. Lancaster, Pa.
              1-5,1903-1922 5v.
Phil 17.9   L'Hermes. Paris. 1-4,1826-1829 2v.
Phil 17.10   The hierophant. N.Y. 1-12,1842-1843
Phil 17.11   Journal of clinical and experimental hypnosis. N.Y.
              1,1953+ 15v.
Phil 17.12   Heinz Werner lecture series. Worcester, Mass. 1,1966
Phil 17.13   The Hampstead clinic psychoanalytic library. N.Y. 1,1969+
              3v.
Phil 18.1   International journal of ethics. Philadelphia. 1 69v.
Phil 18.1.5   International journal of ethics. Seventy-five year index.
              Chicago, 1890. 1v.
Phil 18.2   Illuminator. Boston. 1,1835
Phil 18.2.5   International journal for philosophy of religion.
              Tallahasse, Fla. 1,1970+
Phil 18.3   The Irish theosophist. Dublin. 1-5,1892-1897 5v.
Phil 18.3.10   The internationalist. Dublin. 1897-1898
Phil 18.3.10   The international theosophist. Dublin. 1,1898
Phil 18.4   Imago. Leipzig. 1-23 13v.
Phil 18.5   The Indian philosophical review. Bombay. 2-4 2v.
Phil 18.5.10   Individual psychology bulletin. Chicago. 4,1944+ 10v.

Phil 10 - 35   Periodicals (A-Z) - cont.

Phil 18.6	Ideen und Leben. Paderborn. 1-13 13v.
Phil 18.7	The international journal of psycho-analysis. London. 1,1920+ 44v.
Phil 18.7.5	International journal of psycho-analysis. Index. v.1-10. London, n.d.
Phil 18.7.10	International journal of Psycho-analysis. Supplement. Glossary for the use of translators of psycho-analytical works. London.
Phil 18.7.11	Richman, John. Development...psycho-analytical theory of psychosis, 1893-1926. London, 1928.
Phil 18.8	Zeitschrift für individual Psychologie. Continued as internationale Zeitschrift für individual Psychologie. Leipzig. 1-20,1914-1951 14v.
Phil 18.8.3	Internationale Zeitschrift für individual Psychologie. Leipzig. 1-2 2v.
Phil 18.8.5	Internationaler Psychoanalytischer Verlag. Almanach. Vienna. 1926-1936 11v.
Phil 18.9	Illinois. University. Psychological laboratory. Studies from the psychological laboratory of University of Illinois. Lancaster, Pa. 1,1909
Phil 18.10	Industrial psychology. Hamilton. 2,1927
Phil 18.11	Pamphlet box. Individualist pamphlets. London.
Phil 18.12	Indian journal of psychology. Calcutta. 1-33 9v.
Phil 18.13	International Tagung für angewandte Psychopathologie. Referate und Vorträge. Berlin. 1931
Phil 18.14	Idealismus. Zürich. 1,1934
Phil 18.15	International Philosophical Library. Periodical publication. Prague. 1-4,1935-1940 4v.
Phil 18.16	International journal of individual psychology. Chicago. 1935-1937 9v.
Phil 18.17	Index; revista ibero-americana. Buenos Aires. 3-4,1941-1945 5v.
Phil 18.18	International journal of professional ethics. Zürich.
Phil 18.19	International journal of group psychotherapy. N.Y. 1,1951+ 18v.
Phil 18.20	International journal of social psychiatry. London. 1,1955+ 10v.
Phil 18.21	De idee; orgaan van het Bolliano. Genootschap voor zuivore Rede. Utrecht. 1-19,1923-1941 18v.
Phil 18.22	Inquire. Oslo. 1,1958+ 10v.
Phil 18.23	International journal of parapsychology. N.Y. 1959+ 5v.
Phil 18.24	Indianejournal of philosophy. 1-4,1959-1964// 3v.
Phil 18.25	International philosophical quarterly. N.Y. 1,1961+ 10v.
Phil 18.26	Institute of Applied Psychology. Review. N.Y. 1,1961+ 3v.
Phil 18.27	International journal of psychiatry. N.Y. 1,1965+ 5v.
Phil 18.28	International journal of psychology. Paris. 1,1966+ 3v.
Phil 18.29	Interpretation. Montréal. 1,1967+ 2v.
Phil 18.30	International journal of symbology. Atlanta. 1,1969+
Phil 18.31	International logic review. Bologna. 1,1970+
Phil 18.32	Interpersonal development; international journal for humanistic approaches to group psychotherapy, sensitivity training, and organizational development. Basel. 1,1970+
Phil 18.33	Insikt och handling. Lund. 1,1955+
Phil 18.34	The Irish journal of psychology. Dublin. 1,1971+
NEDL Phil 19.1	Journal of mental science. London. 2-75,1856-1929 45v.
Phil 19.1	Journal of mental science. London. 76,1930+ 43v.
NEDL Phil 19.1.5	Journal of mental science. Index. London, n.d.
Phil 19.1.5	Journal of mental science. Index. London, 1879-1928.
NEDL Phil 19.2	Journal of nervous and mental disease. Chicago. 1-70,1874-1829 70v.
Phil 19.2	Journal of nervous and mental disease. Chicago. 71-105,1930-1947 35v.
NEDL Phil 19.2.6	Journal of nervous and mental disease. Index. N.Y., 1914-1925.
Phil 19.3	Journal of practical metaphysics. Boston. 1-3
Phil 19.4	Journal of speculative philosophy. St. Louis. 1-22,1867-1893 21v.
NEDL Phil 19.5	Jahrsbericht...Neurologie und Psychiatrie. Berlin. 1-23 23v.
Phil 19.6	Journal of philosophy, psychology and scientific methods. N.Y. 1,1904+ 95v.
X Cg Phil 19.6	Journal of philosophy, psychology and scientific methods. N.Y. 9
Phil 19.6.5	Journal of philosophy, psychology and scientifc methods. N.Y. 1-12,1904-1915 12v.
Phil 19.6.10	Journal of philosophy, psychology and scientific methods. Fifty year index, 1904-53; and ten year supplement, 1954-63. N.Y., 1962-64. 2v.
Phil 19.7	Journal de psychologie. Paris. 1+ 51v.
Phil 19.9	Husserl, E. Jahrbuch für Philosophie und phänomenologische Forschung. Halle, 1913. 13v.
Phil 19.10	Köhler, M.F. Jahrbücher der Philosophie. Berlin, 1913. 3v.
Phil 19.11	Journal of psycho-asthetics. Fairbault. 1+ 49v.
Phil 19.11.5	Journal of psycho-asthetics. Supplements. Fairbault, 1911.
Phil 19.12	Journal of applied psychology. Worcester. 1,1917+ 54v.
Phil 19.13	The journal of abnormal psychology. Boston. 1,1906+ 65v.
Phil 19.14	Jahrbuch für psychoanalytische Forschungen. Leipzig. 6,1914+ 6v.
Phil 19.15	The journal of neurology and psychopathology. Bristol. 1+ 34v.
Phil 19.16	Journal of experimental psychology. Princeton. 1,1916+ 76v.
Phil 19.17	Jahrbuch für Philosophie und spekulative Theologie. Paderborn, 1887. 25v.
Phil 19.17.5	Divus Thomas; Jahrbuch für Philosophie und spekulative Theologie. Wien. 1914-1953 23v.
Phil 19.17.8	Freiburger Zeitschrift für Philosophie und Theologie. Freiburg. 1,1954+ 13v.
Phil 19.17.9	Frejburger Zeitschrift für Philosophie und Theologie. Ökumenische Beihefte. Freiburg. 1,1968+
Phil 19.17.10	Divus Thomas; commentarium de philosophie. Piacenza. 41,1938+ 13v.
Phil 19.18	Journal du magnétisme. Paris. 1-20,1845-1861 20v.
Phil 19.20	Jahrbuch der Charakterologie. Berlin. 1-6,1924-1929 5v.
Phil 19.21	Journal of philosophical studies. London. 1,1926+ 38v.
Phil 19.22	Journal für Psychologie und Neurologie. 1-49 47v.
Phil 19.23	Journal of general psychology. Worcester. 1,1928+ 51v.
Phil 19.23.15	The journal of psychology. Worcester, Mass. 1,1935+ 48v.

Phil 10 - 35   Periodicals (A-Z) - cont.

Phil 19.24	The journal of social psychology. Worcester. 1,1930+ 56v.
Phil 19.25	Jahrbücher für speculative Philosophie und die philosophische Bearbeitung der empirischen Wissenschaften. Darmstadt. 1846-1847 4v.
Phil 19.26	Journal of thought and philosophy in general. Ocean Park, Calif. 1-4
Phil 19.27	The journal of Christian philosophy. N.Y.
Phil 19.28	The journal of symbolic logic. Menasha, Wis. 1,1936+ 24v.
Phil 19.29	Journal of consulting psychology. Lancaster, Pa. 1,1937+ 25v.
Phil 19.30	Journal of parapsychology. Durham, N.C. 1,1937+ 31v.
Phil 19.31	Psychiatry digest. Woodbourne. 1,1939+ 23v.
Phil 19.32	Jahrbuch für Psychologie und Psychotherapie. Würzburg. 1,1952+ 18v.
Phil 19.33	Journal of social therapy. N.Y. 1,1957+ 11v.
Phil 19.34	Journal of psychological researches. Madras. 1,1957+ 3v.
Phil 19.35	Journal of analytical psychology. London. 1,1955+ 7v.
Phil 19.36	Jahrbuch der Psychoanalyse; Beiträge zur Theorie und Praxis. Köhn. 1,1960+ 6v.
Phil 19.37	Journal of existential psychiatry. N.Y. 1-8,1960-1968// 8v.
Phil 19.38	Journal of the dynamic sciences. Hollywood. 1,1961+
Phil 19.39	Journal of humanistic psychology. Palo Alto. 1,1961+ 5v.
Phil 19.40	Journal of verbal learning and verbal behavior. N.Y. 1,1962+ 6v.
Phil 19.41	The Japanese psychological research. Tokyo. 1,1954+ 5v.
Phil 19.42	Journal of mathematical psychology. N.Y. 1,1964+ 5v.
Phil 19.43	Journal of the history of philosophy. Berkeley. 2,1964+ 6v.
Phil 19.44	Journal of personality and social psychology. Ann Arbor, Mich. 1,1965+ 10v.
Phil 19.45	Journal of experimental research in personality. N.Y. 1,1965+ 2v.
Phil 19.46	Journal for anthroposophy. N.Y. 1,1965+
Phil 19.47	Journal of modern subjectivism. Mercer Island, Washington. 59-71
Phil 19.48	Journal for philosophic understanding. Mercer Island, Washington. 1-2
Phil 19.49	Journal of psychophysical research. Oxford. 1,1967+
Phil 19.50	Journal of value enquiry. The Hague. 1,1967+
Phil 19.51	Journal at creative behavior. Buffalo. 1,1967+
Phil 19.53	Journal of applied behavior analysis. Lawrence, Kan. 1,1968+
Phil 19.55	The journal for the study of consciousness. Philadelphia. 1,1968+
Phil 19.57	Journal of transpersonal psychology. Stanford, California. 1,1969+
Phil 19.59	Journal of cross-cultural psychology; international and interdisciplinary. Bellingham, Washington. 1,1970+
Phil 19.60	J.B.S.P.; journal of the British society for phenomenology. Manchester, England. 1,1970+
Phil 19.62	Journal of Indian philosophy. Dordrecht. 1,1970+
Phil 19.63	Journal of philosophical logic. Dordrecht. 1,1972+
Phil 19.64	Journal of child development. Tokyo. 1,1965+
Phil 19.66	Journal of autism and childhood schizophrenia; devoted to all psychoses and severe disorders of behavior in childhood. Washington. 1,1971+
Phil 19.68	Journal of phenomenological psychology. Pittsburgh. 2,1971+
Phil 20.1	Krisis der Psychoanalyse. Leipzig. 1,1928
NEDL Phil 20.2	The Kalpaka; India's only psychic review. Tinnevelly.
Phil 20.3	Kwartalnik psychologiczny. Poznán. 1-6,1930-1935 6v.
Phil 20.5	Kwartalnik filozaficzny. Kraków. 1-18,1923-1949 11v.
Phil 20.6	Kulturphilosophische und philosophiegeschichtliche Studien. Würzburg. 1-3,1937-1938 3v.
Phil 20.8	Kiev. Universitet. Visnyk. Seriia filosofii. Kiev. 1,1967+
Phil 20.9	Katowice, Poland (city). Wyzsza Szkota Pedagogiczna. Sekcja Pedagogiczna. Prace psychologiczne. 1,1967+
Phil 20.10	Kinesis. Carbondale, Ill. 1,1968+
Phil 21.1	Logos. Tübingen. 1910-1943 23v.
Phil 21.2	Light and life. Glasgow. 1885-1887+ 2v.
Phil 21.3	Logos: rivista internazionale di filosofia. Napoli. 1914-1943 18v.
Phil 21.4	Logos; mezhdumarodnyi ezhegodnik. Praga. 1-2,1912-1913
Phil 21.5	Il libro pensiero. Milano. 1-11,1866-1876 8v.
Phil 21.6	Hubbard, Elbert. Little journeys to the homes of great philosophers. East Aurora, n.d.
Phil 21.7	Leiftur. Reykjavik. 1,1915
Phil 21.8	Lucifer. Point Loma, Calif. 68,1948 2v.
Phil 21.9	Light. London. 64,1944+
NEDL Phil 21.9	Light. London. 1881-1931
Phil 21.10	Studia logica. Warszawa. 1,1934
Phil 21.11	Logos. Kaunas.
Phil 21.12	Logos; revista de la mesa redonda. Mexico.
Phil 21.15	Leuchter; Weltanschauung von Lebensgestaltung. Darmstadt. 1919-1926 7v.
Phil 21.16	London. University. University College Psychological Laboratory. Collected papers. London. 1-10 5v.
Phil 21.17	Learning and motivation. N.Y. 1,1970+
Phil 21.18	Lublin, Poland. Uniwersytitu Marii Curie. Annales. Skodowskiej. 3,1948+ 5v.
Phil 21.19	Logique et analyse. Louvain. 1,1958+ 7v.
Phil 21.20	Leben und Weltenschauung; Beiträge zu geistiger Lebensgestaltung und Weltschau von Denkern aller Zeiten. Monatsschrift. Godesberg. 1-10,1926-1935 10v.
Phil 21.21	Lietuvos TSR aukštuju mokyklu mokslo darbai filosofija. Vilnius. 1-3 2v.
Phil 21.22	Der Leuchter. Darmstadt. 1930-1931//
Phil 22.1	Magazin zur Erfahrungsseelenkunde. Berlin. 1-10,1783-1793 10v.
Phil 22.2	Medical critic and psychological journal. London. 2-3,1862-1863 2v.
NEDL Phil 22.3	Metaphysical magazine. N.Y. 1-20,1895-1907 6v.
Phil 22.3.5	Intelligence. N.Y.
Phil 22.4	Mind. London. 1,1876+ 80v.
X Cgʳ Phil 22.4	Mind. London. 5-16
Phil 22.4.3	Mind. Index to new series. v. 1-12. London, 1904.
Htn Phil 22.4.6*	Mind. London. 1876-1910 35v.
Htn Phil 22.4.8*	Mind; a unique review of ancient philosophy (a parody). London, 1901.
Phil 22.5	Modern Thinker. 1-2,1870-1872

Phil 10 - 35   Periodicals (A-Z) - cont.

Phil 22.6   The monist. Chicago. 1890-1891+ 51v.
Phil 22.6.3   The monist. Complete index. v.1-17. Chicago, 1908.
Phil 22.6.5   Carus, P. Monism: its scope and review of The Monist. Chicago, 1890-1891.
Phil 22.6.15   Der Monismus. Berlin. 1-7,1906-1912 5v.
Phil 22.6.20   Das monistische Jahrhundert. Leipzig. 1-4,1912-1915 6v.
NEDL Phil 22.7   Mind. N.Y. 1-17,1897-1906 16v.
Phil 22.9   The magnet. N.Y.
Phil 22.10   Monatsschrift für Kriminalpsychologie und Strafrecht. Heidelberg. 3-11,1906-1915 9v.
Phil 22.11   Le magnétiseur spiritualiste. Paris. 1-2,1849-1851
Phil 22.12   Mental Hygiene. Concord. 1-30,1917-1946 31v.
Phil 22.13   Mysl' i slovo filosofskii ezhegodnik. Moskva, 1918-21.
Phil 22.14   Mental health. Baltimore. 1,1923
Phil 22.15   Münchener Studien zur Psychologie und Philosophie. Stuttgart. 1-5,1914-1920 5v.
Phil 22.16   The anti-mesmerist. London. 1-10
Phil 22.17   Mind power plus. St. Louis, Mo. 1-11
Phil 22.18   Mental health bulletin. Danville. 5-16,1928-1939
Phil 22.19   Monographien zur Grundlegung der philosophischen Anthropologie und Wirklichkeitsphilosophie. Berlin. 1-4,1929-1930 4v.
Phil 22.21   Morgunn; tímarit um andleg mál. Reykjavík. 1-9,1920-1928 2v.
Phil 22.22   Mind in nature. Chicago.
Phil 22.23   Mental hygiene news. New Haven.
Phil 22.24   The modern schoolman. St. Louis, Mo. 20,1942+ 18v.
Phil 22.24F   The modern schoolman. St. Louis, Mo. 11-19,1933-1942 6v.
Phil 22.25   The moralist. London. 1,1823
Phil 22.26   Mental health sentinal. Boston. 1940-1942
Phil 22.27   Mendoza, Argentine Republic (City). Universidad Nacional de Cuyo. Institute de Psicologia Experimental. Publicaciones. Mendoza. 1943-1945
Phil 22.30   México (city). Colegio de México a la Historia del Pensamiento Hispano-Americano. Contribuciones. Mexico. 2-3 2v.
NEDL Phil 22.35   México (city). Universidad Nacional. Facultad de Filosofía y Estudios Superiores. Centro de Estudios Filosoficos. Boletin bibliografico. Mexico.
Phil 22.37   Minerva. Buenos Aires. 1-2,1944-1945
Phil 22.38   Monographien zur philosophischen Forschung. Reutlingen. 1,1947+ 48v.
Phil 22.40   Methodos; Revista trimestrale di methodologi e di logica simbolica. Milano. 2,1950+ 11v.
Phil 22.42   Myśl filozoficzna. Warsaw. 1952-1957 9v.
Phil 22.42.5   Mekarski, S. Myśl filozoficzna Romunristow w Polsce. Londyn, 1953.
Phil 22.44   Magyar filozofiai szemle. Budapest. 1+ 14v.
Phil 22.46   Magjar pszichologiai szemle. Budapest. 9,1936+ 13v.
Phil 22.48   Mens en kosmos. Deventer. 17,1961+ 5v.
Phil 22.50   Monographien und Studien zur Konflikt-Psychologie. Konflikt-Anahyse. München. 1-6+ 6v.
Phil 22.52   Materialy prakseologiczne. Warszawa. 20,1965+ 3v.
Phil 22.53   Materialy do historii filozofii średniowiecznej w Polsce. Wrocław. 1,1970+
Phil 22.54   Man and world. State College, Pa. 1,1968+ 3v.
Phil 22.56   Milan. Università Cattolica del Sacro Cuore. Institutadi filosofia. Contributi. Milano. 1,1969+
Phil 22.58   Multivariate behavioral research. Fort Worth, Tex. 1,1966+
Phil 22.59   Multivariate behavioral research. Monographs. Fort Worth, Tex. 1966+
Phil 22.60   Merrill-Palmer quarterly of behavior and development. Detroit. 4,1957+ 12v.
Phil 22.61   Metaphilosophy. Oxford, England. 1,1970+
Phil 22.62   Mexico (City). Universidad Nacional. Facultad de Filosofia y Letras. Anuario psicologia. Mexico. 1-3,1962-1964//
NEDL Phil 23.2   The new world. Boston. 1-9 9v.
NEDL Phil 23.4   Mendel, E. Neurologisches Centralblatt. Leipzig, 1884-93. 10v.
NEDL Phil 23.5   The new century. N.Y. 1-14,1897-1910 11v.
Phil 23.6   Nervous and mental diseases. Chicago. 1907-1917 10v.
Phil 23.6.5   The nervous child. N.Y. 1-11,1941-1956 10v.
Phil 23.7   La nuova scienza. Todi. 1-6 2v.
Phil 23.8   National committee for mental hygiene, inc. 1,1924
Phil 23.9   Neudrucke zur Psychologie. 1-3,1917-1918
NEDL Phil 23.10   Neue metaphysische Rundschau. Berlin. 1897-1913 20v.
Phil 23.11   The new scholasticism. Washington, D.C. 1,1927+ 38v.
Phil 23.11.5   The new scholasticism. Index. v.1-40. Washington, 1968.
Phil 23.12   The new ideal. Boston. 3,1890
Phil 23.12F   The new ideal. Boston.
NEDL Phil 23.13   Neurobiologia. Pernambuco. 1-18 17v.
Phil 23.14   National laboratory of psychical research. Bulletin. London. 1-6,1931-1933
Phil 23.15   The new liberator. N.Y. 1-3 2v.
Phil 23.15F   The new liberator. N.Y. 3
Phil 23.16   Neve Deutsche Forschungen. Abteilung Philosophie. Berlin. 3-37 18v.
Phil 23.16.5   Neve Deutsche Forschungen. Abteilung Charakterologie, psychologische und philosophische Anthropologie. Berlin. 1-17 4v.
Phil 23.17   Nederlandsch tijdschrift voor de psychologie en hoor grensgevieden. Amsterdam. 1,1946+ 22v.
Phil 23.18   Nordisk psykologi. København. 1,1949+ 9v.
Phil 23.18.5   Nordisk Psykologi. Register, 1949-1960. København, n.d.
Phil 23.19   The New Zealand bulletin of psychology. Auckland. 1954-1955
Phil 23.20   Notas y estudios de filosofia. San Miguel de Tucuman. 3-5,1953-1954 3v.
Phil 23.21   Nekotorye voprosy filosofie. Nishinev. 2-4 2v.
Phil 23.22   Notre Dame journal of formal logic. Notre Dame, Ind. 1,1960+ 7v.
Phil 23.23   National Advisory Council on Radio in Education. Psychology series lecture. Chicago. 11-30
Phil 23.24   National Advisory Council on Radio in Education. Listener's notebook. Chicago. 1931-1932
Phil 23.25   Netherlands. Rijko Psychologische Dienst. Publikaties. 's Gravenhage. 1-2 2v.
Phil 23.26   New York. Psychoanalytic Institute. Ernst Kris Study Group. Monograph. 1,1965+
Phil 23.27   New race. Hyderabad. 1,1965+
Phil 23.28   Novye issledovaniia v psikhologii i vozrastnoi fiziologii. Moskva. 1,1970+
Phil 23.29   Noûs; nihil philosophici a nobis alienum putamus. Detroit. 1,1967+ 5v.

Phil 10 - 35   Periodicals (A-Z) - cont.

Phil 23.30   Nouvelle revue de psychanalyse. Paris. 1,1970+
Phil 23.32   Nekotorye voprosy marksistsko-leninskoi filosofii. Cheliabinsk. 2,1969+
Phil 24.1   The open court. Chicago. 1-50 31v.
Phil 24.1.5   Twenty Years of The Open Court. An index, 1887-1906. Chicago, 1907.
Phil 24.3   Ohio. State University. Department of Psychology. Contributions in psychology. Columbus. 8-12,1927-1934
Phil 24.4   Oregon. University. Studies in psychology. Eugene. 1-3,1943-1959 3v.
Phil 24.5   Oregon. University. Studies in psychology. Eugene. 2,1955
Phil 24.6   Organizational behavior and human performance. N.Y. 1,1966+ 3v.
Phil 24.7   Novosibirsk Universitet. Nauchnye trudy. Filosofskaia seriia. 2,1968+
Phil 24.8   The Ontario psychologist. Toronto. 1,1969+ 2v.
Phil 24.9   Omega; an international journal for the psychological study of dying, death, bereavement, suicide and other lethal behaviors. Westport, Conn. 1,1970+
Phil 25.1   The philosophical review. Boston. 1+ 80v.
Phil 25.1.5   The philosophical review. Index, 1892-1926. N.Y., n.d.
NEDL Phil 25.2   La philosophie positive. Paris. 1-15,1867-1875
Phil 25.2   La philosophie positive. Paris. 16-29,1876-1882 7v.
Phil 25.3   Philosophisches Journal. Neu-Strelite. 1-10,1795-1800 10v.
Phil 25.4   Philosophische Monatschafte. Berlin. 1-30,1868-1894 30v.
Phil 25.5   Philosophische Studien. Leipzig. 1-20,1881-1903 20v.
Phil 25.5.5   Philosophische Studien. Index, 1-20. Leipzig, n.d.
Phil 25.6   The plantonist. St. Louis. 1-4 3v.
Phil 25.6.5   Bibliotheca platonica. Osceola.
Phil 25.7   O positivismo. Porto. 1-4,1878-1882 4v.
Phil 25.7.5   El positivismo. Buenos Aires.
NEDL Phil 25.8   Prenological journal. London. 1823-1847 20v.
Phil 25.9   Psychological review. Lancaster, N.Y. 1,1894+ 73v.
Phil 25.9.5   Psychological monographs. Lancaster, N.Y. 8,1907+ 70v.
Phil 25.9.6   Psychological review. Philosophical monographs. Lancaster, N.Y. 1908-1916
Phil 25.9.9   Psychological review. Psychological index, 1894-1935. Lancaster, N.Y., n.d. 24v.
Phil 25.9.12   Psychological index. Abstract references of volumes 1-35,1894-1928. Colombia, n.d. 2v.
Phil 25.9.15   Psychological bulletin (literary section of Psychological Review). N.Y. 1,1904+ 73v.
Phil 25.10   Psychical review. Boston. 1-8
Phil 25.12   Die Philosophie der Gegenwart. Heidelberg. 1-5,1908-1912 5v.
Phil 25.12.10   Die Philosophie der Gegenwart in Selbstdarstellungen. Leipzig. 1-7 7v.
Phil 25.13   The positivist review. London. 1-31,1893-1923 15v.
Phil 25.14   Philosophisches Jahrbuch. Fulda. 1+ 69v.
Phil 25.14.5   Register zum philosophischen Jahrbuch. Fulda, 1912.
NEDL Phil 25.15   Theosophy. N.Y. 11-17,1896-1903 7v.
Phil 25.15.5   Psychoanalysis. N.Y. 1953-1958 5v.
Phil 25.16   Psychoanalytic review. N.Y. 1,1913+ 49v.
Phil 25.16.3   Psychoanalytic review. Subject author index, v.1-18,1913-1931. Washington, n.d.
Phil 25.17   Psychologische Studien. Leipzig. 1-10,1906-1918 10v.
Phil 25.17.3   Psychologische Studien. Leipzig. 1-7 6v.
Phil 25.17.4   Psychologische Studien. Leipzig.
Phil 25.17.5   The phrenological almanac and physiological guide. N.Y. 1845-1854
Phil 25.18   Philosophische Wochenschrift und Literatur-Zeitung. v.1-7. Leipzig, 1906-07. 7v.
Phil 25.19   Psiche, rivista di studi psicologici. v.1-4. Firenze, 1912. 4v.
Phil 25.20   The phreno-magnet and mirror of nature. London, 1843.
Phil 25.21   The illustrated annual of phrenology, 1882. N.Y., 1875.
Phil 25.22   The psychological review. London. 1-5 5v.
Phil 25.23   Psychobiology. Baltimore. 1-2,1917-1920 2v.
Phil 25.24   The psychic research quarterly. London. 1-17,1920-1937 17v.
Phil 25.25   Philosophische Arbeiten. Gieszen. 1-21+ 18v.
Phil 25.26   Psyche; popular-wissenschaftliche Zeitschrift. Leipzig, 1858-63. 3v.
Phil 25.27   Psychologische Forschung. Berlin. 1,1921+ 20v.
Phil 25.28   Psyke; tidskrift får psykologisk Farskuing. Stockholm. 1906-1920 4v.
Phil 25.29   Philosophie und Geschichte. Tübingen. 1-67,1922-1940 70v.
NEDL Phil 25.30   Psychische Studien. Leipzig. 1-26,1874-1899 26v.
Phil 25.31   Philosophische und psychologische Arbeiten. Langensalza. 1-15,1921-1932 15v.
Phil 25.32   Praktische Psychologie. 1-4,1919-1923 4v.
Phil 25.33   Psychologies of 1925. Worcester, 1926.
Phil 25.33.2   Psychologies of 1925. 2d ed. Worcester, 1827.
Phil 25.33.3   Psychologies of 1925. 3d ed. Worcester, 1928.
Phil 25.33.5A   Psychologies of 1930. Worcester, 1930.
Phil 25.33.5B   Psychologies of 1930. Worcester, 1930.
Phil 25.34   Philosophische Hefte. Berlin. 1-5,1928-1936 2v.
Phil 25.35   Psychological abstracts. Lancaster, Pennsylvania. 1,1927+ 41v.
Phil 25.36   Abhandlungen aus dem Gebeite der Psychotherapie. Stuttgart. 1-15,1925-1931 15v.
Phil 25.37F   Philosophischer Weltanzeiger. Berlin, n.d.
Phil 25.38   Philosophischer Anzeiger. Bonn. 1-4,1925-1930 4v.
Phil 25.39   Philosophie und Leben. Leipzig. 1-9,1925-1933
Phil 25.40   The philosophical quarterly. Calcutta. 1,1925+ 31v.
Phil 25.41   Il pensiero nuovo. Roma. 1-3,1898-1899
Phil 25.43   Philosophische forschungsberichte. Berlin. 1-36,1930-1955 18v.
Phil 25.44   Psychologische Rundschan. Basel. 1-4,1929-1933 2v.
Phil 25.45   Psikhotekhnika i psikhofiziologiia. Moskva. 1-7,1928-1934 4v.
Phil 25.45.5   Psikhotekhnika i psikhofiziologiia. Moskva. 1-7,1928-1934
Phil 25.46   Psikhologiia. Moskva. 1-5 4v.
Phil 25.49   Proteus; Blätter einer Welt. Kettwig. 1,1925
Phil 25.50   Psychological studies. Mysore. 1,1925
Phil 25.50.5   Psychological studies. Mysore. 1,1956+ 6v.
Phil 25.52   Practical ideals. Boston.
Phil 25.53   The philosopher. London.
Phil 25.54   Philosophische Abhandlungen. Frankfurt. 1,1935+ 29v.
Phil 25.55   Philosophia reformata. Amsterdam. 1,1936+ 14v.
Phil 25.55.3   Philosophia reformata. Register, v.1-20,1936-1955. n.p., n.d.

Classified Listing

Phil 10 - 35   Periodicals (A-Z) - cont.

Phil 25.56   Philosophia; philosophorum nostri temporis vox universa. Belgradi. 1-3,1936-1938 3v.
Phil 25.57   Psychological studies. Budapest.
Phil 25.59   The phrenological magazine. London.
Phil 25.60   Psyche and Eros. N.Y. 1-2,1920-1921 2v.
Phil 25.61   Papyaus. Le Caire.
Phil 25.62   Philosophiskt archiv og repertorium. Kjöbenhavn, n.d.
Phil 25.63.5   Psychosomatis medicine. Monograph. Washington, D.C. 1-3 2v.
Phil 25.65   Psychic science. London. 18-24,1939-1945 3v.
Phil 25.66   Philosophic abstracts. N.Y. 2+
Phil 25.66F   Philosophic abstracts. N.Y. 1-54,1940-1954 4v.
Phil 25.66.2   Philosophic abstracts. Index, 1-2,1939-1950. N.Y., n.d.
Phil 25.67   Psychoanalytic quarterly. Albany, N.Y. 2,1968+ 47v.
Phil 25.67.2   Psychoanalytic quarterly. Cumulative index, 1-35,1932-1966. n.p., n.d.
Phil 25.68   Psicotécnica. Madrid. 1-5,1939-1955 3v.
Phil 25.69   La pensée. Paris. 1,1944+ 5v.
Phil 25.70   Philosophy and phenomenological research. Buffalo. 1,1940+ 22v.
Phil 25.71   Psychometrika. Colorado Springs. 1,1936+ 32v.
Phil 25.71.5   Psychometrika. Topical and author indexes, 1936-1945. n.p., n.d.
Phil 25.71.6   Psychometrika. Monograph supplements. Toronto. 1,1938+
Phil 25.72   Psychological clinic. Philadelphia. 1-23,1907-1935 18v.
Phil 25.73A   Psychologische Arbeiten. Leipzig. 1-9,1895-1928 9v.
Phil 25.73B   Psychologische Arbeiten. Leipzig. 1-3 3v.
Phil 25.75   Praktisk psykologi. Stockholm. 1-4
Phil 25.76   Positivisme français; histoire et sciences sociales. Boulogne. 1945
Phil 25.77   Pensamiento, revista de investigacion e informacion filosofica. Madrid. 4,1948+ 22v.
Phil 25.77.5   Pensamiento, revista de investigacion filosofica. Indices generales, 1945-60. Madrid, n.d. 2v.
Phil 25.78   Psychoanalysis and the social sciences. London. 1-5,1947-1958 4v.
Phil 25.78.10   The psychoanalytic study of society. N.Y. 1,1960+ 3v.
Phil 25.79   Psychologische Hefte der Siemens-Studien Gesellschaft für praktische Psychologie. Hannover. 1949-1952 2v.
Phil 25.80   Psychologische Nachrichten für die Mitglieder der Siemens-Studien-Gesellschaft für praktische Psychologie. Hannover.
Phil 25.81   The plain view. London. 5,1930+ 9v.
Phil 25.82   Psychologische Rundschau. Göttingen. 1,1949+ 10v.
Phil 25.83   Philosophia. Mendoza. 2-9 9v.
Phil 25.84   Philosophische Studien. Berlin. 1-2,1949-1951 2v.
Phil 25.85   The philosophical quarterly. 1,1950+ 18v.
Phil 25.86   Philosophischen Literaturanzeiger. 1,1949+ 19v.
Phil 25.87   Psychological book preview. Princeton. 1-2,1951-1952 2v.
Phil 25.88   Philosophica slovaca. Bratislava. 1,1946+ 19v.
Phil 25.89   Philosophy East and West; a journal of Oriental and comparative thought. Honolulu. 1,1951+ 9v.
Phil 25.90   Parapsychology bulletin. Durham, N.C. 1,1946+ 3v.
Phil 25.91   Psychologische Schriftenreihe zur Zeitschrift der Psychologe. Schwarzenberg. 1-7,1952-1962//
Phil 25.92   Psychologische Beiträge. Vierteljahresschrift für alle Gekiete der Psychologie. Meisenheim. 1,1953+ 11v.
Phil 25.93   Philosophische Rundschau, eine Vierteljahresschrift für philosophische Kritik. Tübingen. 1,1953+ 14v.
Phil 25.93.3   Philosophische Rundschau;...Beiträge. Tübingen. 1-5 2v.
Phil 25.95   Psychologia. Jahrbuck. Zürich. 1955
Phil 25.97   Polska Akademia Nauk, Warsaw. Komitet filozoficzny. Studia logica. 1-24 10v.
Phil 25.99   Parapsicologia; rivista internazionale di studi, di ricerche ed orientamenti del pensiero relativo. Roma. 1,1955
Phil 25.100   Psychologica belgica; annales de la Société belge de psychologie. Louvain. 1,1946+ 6v.
Phil 25.103   Phronesis; a journal for ancient philosophy. Assen. 1,1961+ 5v.
Phil 25.105   La psychanalyse; recherche et enseignement freudiens de la Société française de psychanalyse. Paris. 1-7 6v.
Phil 25.108   Psychologie française; bulletin trimestriel de la Société française de psychologie. Paris. 3,1958+ 10v.
Phil 25.110   Psychologie und Praxis; Zeitschrift für die Anwendurgsgebiete der Psychologie. München. 1,1956+ 5v.
Phil 25.115   Il pensiero. Milano. 1,1956+ 10v.
Phil 25.120   Die psychoanalytische Bewegung. Wien. 1,1929+ 4v.
Phil 25.122   Praktische Arbeits- und Bildungs-Psychologie. Münster.
Phil 25.125   The Pakistan philosophical journal. Lahore. 1,1957+ 3v.
Phil 25.128   Psyche. Stuttgart. 1,1947+ 32v.
Phil 25.129   Thessalonike-Panepistémion. Philosophike-Schole Episticoniki epetires. 1,1927+ 10v.
Phil 25.130   Psychological issues. N.Y. 1,1959+ 10v.
Phil 25.131   Philosophical Association; Amravate. Journal. Nagpur. 2v.
Phil 25.132   Philosophical studies. Maynoach, Ire. 2,1954+ 12v.
Phil 25.133   Progress in clinical psychology. N.Y. 1,1952+ 9v.
Phil 25.134   Il pensiero critico; problemi del nostro tempo. Milano. 1,1959+ 4v.
Phil 25.135   Parapsychological monographs. N.Y. 1-6 3v.
Phil 25.136   Pacific philosophy forum. Stockton, Califorina. 1,1962+ 5v.
Phil 25.137   Philadelphia Associates for Psychoanalysis. Bulletin. Philadelphia. 15,1965+ 7v.
Phil 25.138   Philosophische Lesehefte. Wien. 1,1957+ 8v.
Phil 25.139   Psychotherapy; theory, research and practice. Menasha, Wis. 1,1963+ 2v.
Phil 25.140   Psychology. Savannah, Georgia.
Phil 25.141F   Psychological research bulletin. Lund. 4,1964+ 2v.
Phil 25.142   Psychonomic science. Goleta, Califorina. 1,1964+ 17v.
Phil 25.143   Praxis. Zagreb. 1,1965+ 6v.
Phil 25.143.5   Praxis. Jugoslovensko izdanje. Zagreb. 4,1967+ 8v.
Phil 25.144   Polska Akademia Nauk. Zakład historii filozofii starożytnej i srednoiwiecznej materiały i studia. Wrocław. 3-11,1964-1969//
Phil 25.145   Psikhologiia i tekhnika. Moskva. 1,1965+
Phil 25.146   The psychoanalytic forum. Beverly Hills, Calif. 1,1966+ 2v.
Phil 25.147   Pytannia ateizmu. Kyïv. 1,1965+
Phil 25.148   Problemy filosofii. Kyïv. 1,1966+ 4v.
Phil 25.149F   Philosophia Arhusiensis. Aarhus. 3,1965+
Phil 25.150   Psychologie vekonomické praci. Praha. 1,1966+ 2v.

Phil 25.151   Perception and psychophysics. Goleta, California. 1,1966+ 6v.
Phil 25.152   The psychology of learning and motivation. N.Y. 1,1967+ 5v.
Phil 25.153   Psychology today. Del Mar, California. 1,1967+ 3v.
Phil 25.155   Psychopathologie africaine. Dakar. 1,1965+ 3v.
Phil 25.157   Papers in psychology. Belfast. 1,1967+
Phil 25.159   La psychiatrie de l'enfant. Paris. 1,1958+ 6v.
Phil 25.160   Psikhologicheskie issledovaniia. Moskva. 1,1969+
Phil 25.162   Problemy differentsial'noi psikhofiziologii. Moskva. 1,1956+ 5v.
Phil 25.164   Philosophische Perspektiven; ein Jahrbuch. Frankfurt. 1,1969+ 2v.
Phil 25.166   Progress in experimental personality research. N.Y. 1,1964+ 5v.
Phil 25.170   Parapsychology review. N.Y. 1,1970+
Phil 25.172   Psychic; a bimonthly magazine devoted to every aspect of psychic phenomena and related topics. San Francisco. 1,1969+
Phil 25.173   Psychological perspectives; an interpretive review. Los Angeles. 1,1970+
Phil 25.175   Journal of psychedelic drugs. San Francisco. 1,1967+
Phil 25.177   Polish psychological bulletin. Warszawa. 1,1970+
Phil 25.179   Philosophy today. N.Y. 1,1968+
Phil 25.181   Problemy filosofii i nauchnogo kommunizma. Krasnoiarsk. 3,1970+
Phil 25.183   Psychologie du langage. Bruxelles. 1,1969+ 3v.
Phil 25.185   Problemy filosofii i sotsiologii. Moskva. 1,1969+
Phil 25.187   Philosophy and public affairs. Princeton. 1,1971+
Phil 25.191   Philosophia; phylosophical quarterly of Israel. Jerusalem. 1,1971+
Phil 25.195   Philosophic research and analysis; a bimonthly information and news journal. Boulder, Colo. 4,1971+
Phil 25.197   Process studies. Claremont, Calif. 1,1971+
Phil 26.1   The quest. London. 1-5,1909-1930 23v.
Phil 26.1.8   Pamphlet box. Quest society.
Phil 26.2   The quarterly journal of psychological medicine. N.Y.
Phil 26.3   The quarterly journal of experimental psychology. Cambridge, England. 1,1948+ 15v.
Phil 26.5   Question. London. 1,1968+ 4v.
Phil 26.7   Quality and quantity; European journal of methodology. Bologna. 1,1967+
Phil 26.8   Psychiatric opinion. Framingham, Mass. 8,1971+
Phil 27.1   Revue philosophique. Paris. 1+ 139v.
Htn   Phil 27.1.5*   Revue philosophique. Tables 1876-1912. Paris, 1888- 4v.
NEDL   Phil 27.1.10   Revue philosophique de la France et de l'étranger. Paris. 1-67,1876-1909 67v.
NEDL   Phil 27.2   Rivista di filosofia scientifica. Milano, 1881-1891. 10v.
Phil 27.3   Revue de metaphysique et de morale. Paris. 1+ 68v.
Phil 27.3.10   Revue de metaphysique et de morale. Table générale, 1893-1923. Paris, 1924.
Phil 27.4   Revue philosophique de Louvain. Louvain. 1,1894+ 70v.
Phil 27.4.2   Revue philosophique de Louvain. Table, 1894-1913. Louvain, 1914.
Phil 27.4.5   Répertoire bibliographique de la philosophie. Louvain. 1,1949+ 21v.
Phil 27.5   Revista filosofica. Pavia. 8
Phil 27.6   Revue des sciences psychologiques. Paris, n.d.
Phil 27.7   Revista de filosofia, cultura, ciencias, educacion. Buenos Aires. 1-30,1915-1929 24v.
Phil 27.8   Revue spiritualiste. Paris. 1-6 6v.
Phil 27.9   La ragione; foglio ebdomadario di filosofia. Torino. 1-8,1854-1857 7v.
Phil 27.10   Renaissance und Philosophie. Bonn, 1908. 13v.
Phil 27.11   Rivista di psicologia. Bologna. 1,1905+ 46v.
Phil 27.11.5   Rivista di psicologia. Indice generale, 1905-1936. Bologna, n.d. 2v.
Phil 27.12   Rivista di filosofia neo-scolastica. Firenze. 1,1909+ 57v.
Phil 27.13   Rivista italiana di filosofia. Roma. 1,1886+ 13v.
Phil 27.14   Rivista trimestrale di studi filosofici. Perugia. 1-4,1920-1923 3v.
Phil 27.15   La revue occidentale-philosophique. Versailles. 1878-1914 42v.
Phil 27.15.5   La revue occidentale. Tables des matières, 1878-1889. Paris, 1888.
Phil 27.17   Reichl's philosophischer Almanach. Darmstadt. 1923-1927 4v.
NEDL   Phil 27.18F   The religio-philosophical journal. Chicago. 1-3,1890-1893 3v.
Phil 27.19   Rivista di studi psichici. Padova. 1-4,1895-1898 3v.
Phil 27.20   Revue des études psychiques. Paris. 1-2
Phil 27.21   Rivista di filosofia e scienze affini. Padova. 1899-1908 10v.
Phil 27.22   Revue d'histoire de la philosophie. Paris. 1,1927+ 32v.
Phil 27.23   Religionspsychologie. Wien. 1-12,1926-1952 2v.
Phil 27.24   Ruch filosofický. Praze. 1-12,1920-1939 4v.
Phil 27.25   Revue théosophique. Paris. 1-2,1889-1890
Phil 27.26   La rationaliste. Genève. 1-9,1861-1870 9v.
Phil 27.27   Revue cosmique. Paris. 1-5,1901-1906 5v.
Phil 27.28   Revue de psychologie concrete. Paris. 1-2 2v.
Phil 27.29   Review of philosophy and religion. Poona. 1-9,1930-1940 3v.
Phil 27.30   Revue spirite. Paris. 1-9,1858-1866 9v.
Phil 27.31   Revista de psicologia i pedagogia. Barcelona. 3-5 3v.
Phil 27.32   The R.P.A. annual and ethical review. London. 1892+ 36v.
Phil 27.33   Recherches philosophiques. Paris. 1-6,1931-1937 6v.
Phil 27.34   Ricerche filosofiche. Messina. 1-9,1931-1939 4v.
Phil 27.34.5   Ricerche filosofiche. Index to 1-10 (1931-1940). Messina, n.d.
Phil 27.35   Rivista rosminiana. Torino. 1,1906+ 46v.
Phil 27.36   Revista de psicologia. Cluj. 3-4,1940-1941 4v.
Phil 27.37   Revue internationale de philosophie. Bruxelles. 2,1939+ 22v.
Phil 27.38   La revue psychologique. Bruxelles. 1-7,1908-1914 3v.
Phil 27.39   Revista de neurología e psiquiátria de São Paulo. São Paulo. 5-9,1939-1943 9v.
Phil 27.40   Revista de neuro-psiquiatría. Lima. 1-13,1938-1950 13v.
Phil 27.41   Revue de psychologie. Montreal. 1946-1952
Phil 27.42   Revista de psicologia. Madrid. 6,1947+ 18v.
Phil 27.43   Revista de psicologia; general y aplicada. Madrid. 1,1946+ 19v.
Phil 27.44   Rivista di storia della filosofia. Milano. 1,1946+ 23v.
Phil 27.45   The review of metaphysics. New Haven. 1,1947+ 27v.

Phil 27.45.3   The review of metaphysics. Index, 1947-1967. New Haven, n.d.
Phil 27.46   Revista cubana de filosofia. La Habana. 12,1959+
Phil 27.47   Rassegna di scienze filosofiche. Roma. 1,1948+ 12v.
Phil 27.48   Rassegna di filosofia. Roma. 1-7,1952-1958 7v.
Phil 27.50   Revista filosofica. Coimbra. 1-7,1951-1957 3v.
Phil 27.52   La raison; cahiers de psychopathologie scientifique. Villejuif. 4-22,1952-1958 5v.
Phil 27.54   Revista brasileira de filosofia orgão oficial do Instituto Brasileiro de Filosofia. São Paulo. 1,1951+ 17v.
Phil 27.56   Revista portuguesa de filosofia. Braga. 1,1945+ 25v.
Phil 27.56.5   Revista portuguêsa de filosofia. Suplemento bibliográfico. Braga. 1,1950+ 4v.
Phil 27.58   Revista de filosofia. La Plata. 1,1950+ 5v.
Phil 27.60   Rorschachiana Sonderhefte der schweizerischen Zeithschrift für Psychologie. Bern. 2-5
Phil 27.62   Rivista di psicologia della scrittura. Milano. 1,1955+ 7v.
Phil 27.64   Revista dominicana de filosofia. Ciudad Trujillo. 1956-1957 2v.
Phil 27.66   Revista pernambucana de filosofia. Recife.
Phil 27.68   Ratio. Oxford. 1,1957+ 3v.
Phil 27.70   Revista de filosofia de la Universidad de Costa Rica. San José. 1,1957+ 6v.
Phil 27.72   Revista de filosofia. Santiago. 3,1955+ 4v.
Phil 27.74   Revista de psihologie. Bucureşti. 4,1958+ 13v.
Phil 27.76   Ruch filozoficzny. Toruń. 18,1958+ 8v.
Phil 27.77   Rocznik woknej myśli. Warszawa. 1961+ 2v.
Phil 27.78   Rivista di filosofia. Torino. 3,1910+ 47v.
Phil 27.80   Revista de psicologia. Bogota. 1,1956+ 5v.
Phil 27.82   Review of existential psychology and psychiatry. Pittsburgh. 1,1961+ 6v.
Phil 27.84   Revista mexicana de psicologia. Guadalajara. 1963-1965+
Phil 27.86   Revue universitaire de science morale. Havre-lez-Mons. 1,1965+ 2v.
Phil 27.88   Revue du monde invisible. Paris. 1-10,1898-1908 10v.
Phil 27.90   Rational living. N.Y. 1,1966+
Phil 27.92   Royal Institute of Philosophy. Lectures. London. 1,1966+ 3v.
Phil 27.94   Revista de psicoanalisis, psiquiatria y psicologia. Mexico. 2,1968+
Phil 27.96   Revista latinoamericana de psicología. 1,1969+
Phil 28.1   The Saint Louis magnet. v.1-2. St. Louis, 1845.
Phil 28.2   Preyer, W. Sammlung physiologischer Abhandlungen. Jena, 1877. 2v.
Phil 28.3   Le spiritualiste de la Nouvelle Orleans. Nouvelle Orleans, 1857.
NEDL Phil 28.4   Spiritualist newspaper. London. 1869-1882 12v.
Phil 28.5   Schriften zur Psychologie der Berufseignung. Leipzig. 1918-1933 36v.
Phil 28.6   Scandinavian scientific review. Kristiania. 1-3,1922-1924 2v.
Phil 28.7   Facts; a monthly magazine devoted to mental and spiritual phenomena. Boston. 1-6,1882-1887 4v.
Phil 28.8   The standard. N.Y. 2,1915+ 26v.
Phil 28.10   Symposion; philosophische Zeitschrift für Forschung und Aussprache. Erlangen. 1-3
Phil 28.11   Studies in mental inefficiency. London. 1-12 3v.
Phil 28.11.20   Studia psychologica et paedagogica. Lund. 7-9,1955-1958 3v.
Phil 28.12   Schriften aus dem Euckenkreis. Langensalza. 1-31,1909-1929 2v.
Phil 28.13   Schriften zur Philosophie der Neuzeit. Augsburg. 1-2,1928-1931 2v.
Phil 28.13.20   Specchio umano. Napoli.
Phil 28.14   Studien und Bibliographien zur Gegenwartsphilosophie. Leipzig. 1-26,1932-1939 26v.
Phil 28.15   Sophia. Palermo. 15,1947+ 32v.
Phil 28.16   Studia philosophica; commentarii societates philosophiae polonorum. Leopoli. 3-4,1949-1950 2v.
Phil 28.17   Studia Anselmiana philosophica theologica edita a professoribus Instituti Pontificii S. Anselmi de Urbs. Roma. 1,1933+ 32v.
Phil 28.18   Sesamums. N.Y. 1937-1946 7v.
Phil 28.20   São Paulo (City). Universidade. Faculdade de Filosofia, Ciencias e Letras. Filosofia. São Paulo. 5
Phil 28.21   Symposion. Freiburg. 1-4,1948-1955 4v.
Phil 28.22   School case work manuels. Stanford.
Phil 28.23   Schweizerische philosophische Gesellschaft. Jahrbuch. Basel. 1,1941+ 28v.
Phil 28.23.10   Schweizerische philosophische Gesellschaft. Jahrbuch. Beihefte. Basel. 1,1943+ 11v.
Phil 28.25   Sociatry; journal of group and intergroup theory. Beacon, N.Y. 2,1948+ 15v.
Phil 28.27   Studi e recerche ed istoria della filosofia. Torino. 1-49 8v.
Phil 28.28   Studien zur diagnostischen Psychologie. Biel. 1-4+
Phil 28.30   Situation; contributions to phenomenological psychology and psychopathology. Utrecht. 1
Phil 28.32   Studiengesellschaft für praktische Psychologie. Jahrbuch. Lüneburg. 1953-1955 3v.
Phil 28.35   Stanford University. Department of Psychology. Technical report. 1-9,1953-1955 3v.
Phil 28.37   Southern philosopher. Chapel Hill. 5-6,1956-1957
Phil 28.39   Schweizerische Zeitschrift für Psychologie und ihre Anwendungen. Bern. 1,1942+ 17v.
Phil 28.41   The socratic; contemporary philosophy and christian faith. Oxford. 5
Phil 28.43   Szondiana. Bern. 6-7 2v.
Phil 28.45   Science of thought. Tokyo.
Phil 28.47   Sguardi su la filosofia contemporanea. Torino. 1-20 7v.
Phil 28.49   Stockholm studies in philosophy. Stockholm. 2 2v.
Phil 28.50   Sapientia; revista tomista de filosofía. La Plata. 1,1946+ 22v.
Phil 28.52   Salzburger Jahrbuch für Philosophie und Psychologie. Salzburg. 1,1957+ 8v.
Phil 28.55   Studia filosoficzne. Warszawa. 1957-1964 20v.
Phil 28.56   Studia filozoficzne. Izbrannye stat'i. Warszawa. 1,1962+
Phil 28.58   Studia parapsychologica. Roma.
Phil 28.60   The Scandinavian journal of psychology. Stockholm. 1,1960+ 10v.
Phil 28.62   Science and psycholoanalysis. N.Y. 1,1958+ 13v.
Phil 28.64   Soviet studies in philosophy. N.Y. 3,1964+ 4v.
Phil 28.66   Soviet psychology and psychiatry. N.Y. 1-4,1962-1966// 4v.
Phil 28.67   Soviet psychology. White Plains, N.Y. 5,1966+ 3v.

Phil 28.68   The southern journal of philosophy. Memphis, Tenn. 3,1965+ 4v.
Phil 28.70   Studia philosophica Gandensia. Gent. 1,1963+
Phil 28.72   Sapienza. Napoli. 18,1965+ 6v.
Phil 28.74   Studies in philosophy and the history of philosophy. Washington. 1,1961+ 4v.
Phil 28.76   Studia metodologiczne. Poznań. 1,1965+ 3v.
Phil 28.78   South African journal of philosophy. Rondebosch. 1,1964+ 2v.
Phil 28.80   Soviet neurology and psychiatry. White Plains, N.Y. 1,1968+ 2v.
Phil 28.82   Studien zur Wissenschaftstheorie. Meisenheim. 1,1968+ 2v.
Phil 28.83   The schizophrenic syndrome. N.Y. 1,1971+
Phil 28.84   Studia psychologiczne. Wrocław. 4,1963+
Phil 28.86   Southwestern journal of philosophy. Norman. 1,1970+
Phil 28.88   Savremene filozofske teme. Beograd. 1966-1969// 2v.
Phil 28.90   Studi internazionali di filosofia. Torino. 1,1969+
Phil 28.92   South African journal of psychology. Johannesburg. 1,1970+
Phil 29.1   The temple of reason. N.Y., 1800.
NEDL Phil 29.2   Theosophical quarterly. N.Y. 1-35,1906-1938 27v.
NEDL Phil 29.3   Theosophical path. Point Loma, Calif. 1-36,1911-1929 30v.
NEDL Phil 29.4   Theosophy. San Francisco. 1-15,1920-1927 15v.
NEDL Phil 29.5   The theosophist. Madras. 1-30 8v.
Phil 29.5.10   The theosophical movement. Bombay. 9-16,1938-1945 7v.
NEDL Phil 29.6   The truth promotor. v.1-3. London, 1849-55.
Phil 29.7   The theosophical forum. N.Y. 1-10,1889-1905 16v.
Phil 29.7.5   The theosophical forum. Point Loma, Calif.
Phil 29.8   Theosophical siftings. London. 1-7,1888-1895 7v.
Phil 29.9   The theosophical messenger. Los Angeles. 6-15,1918-1928 3v.
Phil 29.11   Die Tatwelt. Berlin. 7-17,1931-1941 5v.
Phil 29.13   Textes et études d'histoire de la philosophie. Paris.
Phil 29.17   Sendai, Japan. University. Tohoku psychologica folia. Sendai. 4,1936+ 10v.
Phil 29.20   Tulane studies in philosophy. New Orleans. 1,1952+ 6v.
Phil 29.25   Truth-seeker, or Present eye. London. 1849
Phil 29.26   Svokodna misel; glasilo Slovenske sekcye Svobodne misli. Praja. 1,1907+ 2v.
Phil 29.27   Theoria. Göteborg. 1,1935+ 19v.
Phil 29.27.2   Library of theoria. Lund. 1-11 4v.
Phil 29.28   Tydschrift voor philosophie. Leuven. 1939+ 57v.
Phil 29.30   Tu sei me; filosofia dell'unicita. Milano. 1,1956+ 13v.
Phil 29.35   Triades; revue trimestrielle de culture humaine. Paris. 1,1953+ 17v.
Phil 29.35.2   Triades; revue trimestrielle de culture humaine. Sommaires des numéros parus, 1953-1972. Paris, 1972.
Phil 29.40   La Tour Saint Jacques. Paris. 1-16,1955-1958 4v.
Phil 29.40.3   La Tour Saint Jacques. Cahiers. Paris. 1,1960+ 3v.
Phil 29.41   Tasmania. University. Hobart. Department of Psychology. Publication.
Phil 29.43   Theosofia. Amsterdam. 63,1962+ 9v.
Phil 29.45   Transcultural psychiatric research. Montreal. 1963+ 2v.
Phil 29.47   Terra nova. München. 3-4 2v.
Phil 29.49   Telos. Amherst, N.Y. 1,1968+ 2v.
Phil 30.1.5   United Lodge of Theosophists. U.L.T. pamphlet. Bombay.
Phil 30.2F   The univercoelum and spiritual philosopher. N.Y. 2,1848
Phil 30.5   Untersuchungen zur Psychologie, Philosophie und Pädagogik. Göttingen.
Phil 30.7   University of Southern California. Psychological Laboratory. Report. Los Angeles. 1,1952+
Phil 30.9   Universidad Nacional del Litoral. Santa Fe, Argentina. Instituto de Filosofia. Cuadernos filosóficos. Rosario.
Phil 30.12   Univers. Paris. 1,1964+
Phil 31.1   Vierteljahrsschrift für Wissen Philosophie. Leipzig. 1-40 38v.
Phil 31.1.5   Vierteljahrsschrift für Wissen Philosophie. Generalregister zu Jahrgang, I-XXX. Leipzig, 1908.
Phil 31.2   Vierteljahrschrift für Psychiatrie. Neuwied. 1-2,1867-1869 2v.
Phil 31.3   Voprosy filosofii i psikhologiia. Moskva. 1-28,1890-1917 29v.
Phil 31.4   Volná myslenka. Praha. 1-7 4v.
Phil 31.5   Voprosy filosofii. Moskva. 1947+ 15v.
Phil 31.5.5   Goerdt, Wilhelm. Fragen der Philosophie ein Materialbeitrag...im Spiegel der Zeitschrift "Voprosy Filosofii", 1947-1956. Köln, 1960.
Phil 31.6   Voprosy psikhologii. Moskva. 1955+ 27v.
Phil 31.6.10   Problems of psychology. N.Y. 1960+
Phil 31.7   Vita humana. Basel. 1,1958+ 6v.
Phil 31.7.4   Vita humana. Bibliotheca. 3,1965+
Phil 31.10   Vivarium. 1,1963+ 2v.
Phil 31.12   Voprosy filosofii i psikhologii. Leningrad. 1,1965+
Phil 31.14   Voprosy filosofii i sotsiologii. Leningrad. 1,1969+
Phil 31.15   Voprosy psikhologii vnimaniia. Saratov. 1,1969+
Phil 31.16   Voprosy gnoseologii, logiki i metodologii nauchnogo issledovaniia. Leningrad. 1,1969+
Phil 31.17   Voprosy dialektiki i logiki. Leningrad. 1,1964+
NEDL Phil 32.1   The word. N.Y. 9-25,1909-1917 17v.
Phil 32.2   The microcosm. N.Y.
Phil 32.3   Wissenschaft und Zeitgeist. Leipzig. 1-10,1935-1938
Phil 32.4   Wiener Zeitschrift für Philosophie, Psychologie, Pädagogik. Wien. 1,1947+ 5v.
Phil 32.4.5   Wiener Zeitschrift für Philosophie, Psychologie, Pädagogik. Beiheft. Wien. 1+
Phil 32.5   Wronskiana. Warszawa. 1939
Phil 32.6   Wiener Archiv für Psychologie, Psychiatrie und Neurologie. Wien. 1-6,1951-1956 4v.
Phil 32.7   Wijsgerig perspectief op maatschappij en wetenschap. Amsterdam. 2,1961+ 8v.
Phil 32.8   Wiener Jahrbuch für Philosophie. Wien. 1,1968+ 3v.
Phil 32.9   The Western psychologist. Alberta. 1,1969+
Phil 32.9.5   The Western psychologist. Monograph series. Alberta. 1,1969+
Phil 34.3   Year book of neurology, psychiatry and endocrinology. Chicago, 1943.
Phil 35.1   Zeitschrift für Philosophie. Bonn. 1-165 77v.
Phil 35.1.2   Zeitschrift für Philosophie und philosophische Kritik. Engänzungsheft. Leipzig. 1-2,1909-1910 2v.
Phil 35.1.5   Zeitschrift für Philosophie und philosophische Kritik. Register. Leipzig. 1914
Phil 35.1.15   Zeitschrift für Philosophie und philosophische Kritik. Verzeichnis der Abhundlungen. Leipzig. 1892
Phil 35.2   The zoist. London, 1848. 2v.
Phil 35.3   Zeitschrift für Religionspsychologie. Halle. 1-6 6v.

Phil 10 - 35   Periodicals (A-Z) - cont.

Phil 35.4	Zeitschrift für Timmanante Philosophie. Berlin, 1896-99. 4v.
Phil 35.5	Zeitschrift für positivistische Philosophie. Berlin. 1-2,1913-1914 2v.
Phil 35.6	Zeitschrift für Psychologie und Philosophie der Sinnesorgane. Leipzig. 1-40 40v.
Phil 35.6.2	Zeitschrift für Psychologie. Leipzig. 40-175 86v.
Phil 35.6.2.5	Zeitschrift für Psychologie. Register, 51-150. Leipzig, 1918-1943. 4v.
Phil 35.6.3	Zeitschrift für Sinnesphysiologie. Leipzig. 41-70 20v.
Phil 35.6.5	Zeitschrift für Psychologie. Leipzig. 1-24 13v.
Phil 35.7	Zeitschrift für angewandte Psychologie. Leipzig. 1-66,1908-1944 54v.
Phil 35.7.5	Zeitschrift für angewandte Psychologie. Beihefte. Leipzig. 1-93,1911-1948 24v.
Phil 35.8	Zeitschrift für Patho-Psychology. Leipzig. 1-2,1912-1914 2v.
Phil 35.9	Zeitschrift für die gesamte Neurologie und Psychiatrie. Berlin, 1910.
Phil 35.9.5	Zeitschrift für die gesamte Neurologie und Psychiatrie. Berlin, 1910.
Phil 35.10	Zentralblatt für Psychologie und...Pädagogik. Würzberg. 1914-1915
Phil 35.11	Zentralblatt für Psychoanalyse. Wiesbaden. 1-4,1910-1914 4v.
Phil 35.12	Zeitschrift für Philosophie und Pädogogik. Langensalza. 1895-1914 21v.
Phil 35.13	Zeitschrift für exacte Philosophie. Leipzig. 1-20,1861-1896 15v.
Phil 35.15	Zeitschrift für Menschenkunde. Heidelberg. 3-14,1927-1939 8v.
Phil 35.16	Zeitschrift für Psychotherapie. Stuttgart. 1-8,1909-1924 8v.
Phil 35.17	Zeitschrift für Hypnotismus, Psychotherapie. Leipzig. 1-10,1892-1902 10v.
Phil 35.18	Zalmoxis. Paris.
Phil 35.19	Zeitschrift für philosophische Forschung. Reutlingen. 1,1946+ 23v.
Phil 35.19.2	Zeitschrift für philosophische Forschung. Sach-, Namen und Autoren Register. 1,1946+ 2v.
Phil 35.19.3	Zeitschrift für philosophische Forschung. Beihefte. Meisenheim. 1,1951+ 15v.
Phil 35.19.5	Zeitschrift für philosophische Forschung. Sonderheft. Wurzach.
Phil 35.20	Zeitschrift für Psychoanalyse. Berlin. 1949-1950
Phil 35.25	Zeitschrift für experimentelle und angewandte Psychologie. Göttingen. 1,1853+ 14v.
Phil 35.30	Zeitschrift für diagnostische Psychologie und Persönlichkeitsforschung. Bern. 2-6,1954-1958 5v.
Phil 35.30.2	Zeitschrift für diagnostische Psychologie und Persönlichkeitsforschung. Beiheft. n.p., n.d.
Phil 35.35	Zeitschrift für Parapsychologie und Grenzgebiete der Psychologie. Bern. 1,1957+ 7v.
Phil 35.40	Zygon. Chicago. 1,1966+ 4v.
Phil 35.40.2	Zygon. Authors and titles, v. 1-5 (1966-1970). Chicago, 1971.
Phil 35.50	Zagreb. Univerzitet. Psihologijski Institut. Acta Instituti psychologici Universitatis Zagra iensis. 1,1964+

Phil 40 - 65   Societies (A-Z)

Phil 40.1	Aristotelian Society. Proceedings. London. 1,1887+ 70v.
Phil 40.1.3	Aristotelian Society. Synoptic index, 1900-49. Oxford, 1949. 2v.
Phil 40.1.5	Aristotelian Society. Supplementary volume. London. 1,1918+ 43v.
Phil 40.2	American Medico-Psychological Association. Proceedings. St. Louis. 60,1904
Phil 40.3	MacCracken, H.M. A propaganda of philosophy; a history of the American Institute of Christian Philosophy, 1881-1914. N.Y., 1914.
Phil 40.4	Pamphlet box. American psychological association.
Phil 40.4.3	American Psychological Association. Proceedings of the annual convention. Washington. 74,1966+ 5v.
Phil 40.4.5	American Psychological Association. Proceedings of annual meeting. Lancaster, Pa. 26-48,1917-1940 4v.
Phil 40.5	Australasian Association of Psychology and Philosophy. Monograph series. Sidney.
Phil 40.6	American Philosophical Association. Proceedings. 1-25,1902-1925 4v.
Phil 40.6.3	American Philosophical Association. Proceedings and addresses. 1,1927+ 9v.
Phil 40.7	Pamphlet box. Accademia di filosofia italica, Genoa.
Phil 40.8	American Catholic Philosophical Association. Proceedings. Washington, D.C. 1,1926+ 15v.
Phil 40.9	American Institute for Psychoanalysis. Curriculum. N.Y.
Phil 40.10	American Psychoanalytic Association. Journal. N.Y. 1,1953+ 21v.
Phil 40.10.5	American Psychoanalytic Association. Journal. Monograph series. N.Y. 1,1958+ 4v.
Phil 40.11	Academia Republici Populare Romine, Bucurest. Institutut de Filozofie. Arcetári filozofice. 4,1957+ 18v.
Phil 40.12	Associazione Filosofica Ligure. Relazione e discussione. Milano. 1951-1952
Phil 40.12.5	Associazione Filosofica Ligure. Atti. Milano. 2,1955+
Phil 40.13	American Psychoanalytic Association. Bulletin. N.Y. 1-8,1937-1952 4v.
Phil 40.15	Association for Research and Enlightenment. The A.R.E. journal. Virginia Beach. 1,1966+
Phil 40.20	Association Psychanalytique de France. Bulletin. Neully-sur-Seine. 4,1968+
Phil 41.1	Pamphlet box. British institute of philosophical studies.
Phil 41.2	Pamphlet box. Bureau for Scientific Investigation Demonstration of Psychic Phenomena.
Phil 41.3	Buenos Aires. Universidad Nacional. Instituto de Filosofía. Publicaciónes de clasicos de la filosofia. Buenos Aires. 3v.
Phil 41.4	Buenos Aires. Universidad Nacional. Facultad de Filosofia y Letras. Archivos del laboratorio de facultad de filosofia y letras psicologicas. Buenos Aires, 1931.
Phil 41.5	Buenos Aires. Universidad Nacional. Instituto de Filosofía. Publicaciónes de ensayos filosoficos. Buenos Aires. 1-4,1942-1945 2v.
Phil 41.6	Buenos Aires. Universidad Nacional. Instituto de filosofia. Cuadernos de filosofia. Buenos Aires. 1,1948+ 4v.

Phil 40 - 65   Societies (A-Z) - cont.

Phil 41.7	The philosophical forum; an annual published by the Boston University of Philosophical Club. Boston. 1-16,1943-1959 3v.
Phil 41.8	Buenos Aires. Universidad. Instituto de Filosofia. Sección de Psicologiá. Monógrafias psicologicas.
Phil 41.10	Bologna. Universita. Instituto di Filosofia. Sgione Teoretica. Ricerche filosofiche. 1,1959+ 5v.
Phil 41.12	British Psychological Society. The British Psychological Society, 1901-1961. London, 1901-1961.
Phil 42.1	Columbia College. Contributions to philosophy. N.Y. 1-12,1894-1903 12v.
Phil 42.1.5	Columbia College. Studies in the history of ideas. N.Y. 1-3,1918-1935 3v.
Phil 42.2	Cornell University. Studies in philosophy. N.Y. 1-17,1900-1925 3v.
Phil 42.3	California. University. Publications. Philosophy. Berkeley. 1-30,1904-1957 15v.
Phil 42.3.5	California. University. Publications. Psychology. Berkeley. 1-6,1910-1950 4v.
Phil 42.3.10	California. University. Institute of Human Development. Annual report. Berkeley. 1940+
Phil 42.4	Chicago. University. Contributions to philosophy. Chicago. 1,1904+ 3v.
Phil 42.4.5	Chicago. University. Philosophic studies. Chicago. 1-10 2v.
NEDL Phil 42.5	Córdoba, Argentina (City). Universidad Nacional. Centro de Estudios de Filosofía y Humanidades. Estudios de filosofía. Córdoba.
Phil 42.6	Connecticut. Society for Mental Hygiene. Publications.
Phil 42.6.3	Connecticut. Society for Mental Hygiene. Annual report. New Haven. 1912-1930
Phil 42.6.5	Pamphlet box. Connecticut society for mental hygiene.
Phil 42.7	College of the Pacific, Stockton, California. Publications in philosophy. Stockton. 1-3,1932-1934
Phil 42.7.5	College of the Pacific. Pacific Philosophy Institute. Publication. 1,1951+ 2v.
Phil 42.8	Catholic University of America. Studies in psychology and psychiatry. Washington. 1,1927+ 9v.
Phil 42.10	Circolo Giovanile Romano di Filosofia. Quaderni. 1-4,1953-1955
Phil 42.11	Colorado. University. University of Colorado studies. Series in philosophy. Boulder.
Phil 42.12	Canterbury. University College, Christchurch, New Zealand. Department of Psychology. Psychological report.
Phil 42.13	Chile. Universidad, Santiago. Instituto Central de Psicología. Archivos. Santiago. 2,1963+
Phil 43.1	Deutscher Monistenbund. Flugschriften. Brackwede. 3-30,1906-1914 16v.
Phil 43.2	Duke University psychological monographs. Durham, N.C. 1-3,1931-1934
Phil 44.2	Miller, W. The "philosophical". A short history of the Edinburgh Philosophical Institution. Edinburgh, 1949.
Phil 45.1	Laboratorio di Psicologia Sperimentale, Florence. Istituto di Studi Superiori. Ricerche psicologia. Firenze. 1-2,1905-1907
Phil 45.5	Ajatus; filosofisen yhdistyksen vuosikiya. Helsinki. 1-27 10v.
Phil 45.10	Foundation for Research on the Nature of Man. FRNM bulletin. Durham, N.C. 1,1965+
Phil 46.1	Schriften der Gesellschaft für psychologischer Forschung. Leipzig. 1
Phil 46.1.2	Schriften der Gesellschaft für psychologischer Forschung. Leipzig. 2
Phil 46.1.3	Schriften der Gesellschaft für psychologischer Forschung. Leipzig. 3-4
Phil 46.1.5	Schriften der Gesellschaft für psychologischer Forschung. Leipzig. 5
Phil 46.1.6	Schriften der Gesellschaft für psychologischer Forschung. Leipzig. 6
Phil 46.1.7	Schriften der Gesellschaft für psychologischer Forschung. Leipzig. 7-8
Phil 46.1.9	Schriften der Gesellschaft für psychologischer Forschung. Leipzig. 9-10
Phil 46.1.11	Schriften der Gesellschaft für psychologischer Forschung. Leipzig. 11
Phil 46.1.12	Schriften der Gesellschaft für psychologischer Forschung. Leipzig. 12
Phil 46.1.13	Schriften der Gesellschaft für psychologischer Forschung. Leipzig. 13-14
Phil 46.1.15	Schriften der Gesellschaft für psychologischer Forschung. Leipzig. 15
Phil 46.1.16	Schriften der Gesellschaft für psychologischer Forschung. Leipzig. 16
Phil 46.1.17	Schriften der Gesellschaft für psychologischer Forschung. Leipzig. 17
Phil 46.1.18	Schriften der Gesellschaft für psychologischer Forschung. Leipzig. 18-20
Phil 47.1.9	Harvard Medical School. Department of Neurology. Contributions from Massachusetts General Hospital. Boston. 1,1906
Phil 48.1	Iowa. University. Studies in psychology. Iowa City. 1-7,1897-1918 2v.
Phil 48.1.10	Iowa. University. Studies in character. Iowa City. 1-4,1927-1931 2v.
NEDL Phil 48.5	Institut Général Psychologique. Mémoires. Paris. 1-5+ 5v.
Phil 48.5.10	Institut Général Psychologique. Notes et documents concernant l'oeuvre, 1900-1921. Paris, 1921.
Phil 48.6F	Pamphlet box. Institute of general semantics.
Phil 48.7	International Institute for Psychical Research, Ltd. Bulletin. London.
Phil 48.8	Instituto di Studi Filosofici, Rome. Testi e documenti. Firenze. 1,1949
Phil 48.9	International Metaphysical League. Convention proceedings. Boston.
Phil 48.10	Institut Général Psychologique, Paris. Bulletin. Paris. 1-33,1900-1933 22v.
Phil 48.12	International Association of Applied Psychology. Bulletin. Paris. 1,1952+ 3v.
Phil 48.14	Indian Academy of Philosophy. Journal. Calcutta. 1,1961+
Phil 48.16	Institute of Psychophysical Research. Proceedings. Oxford. 1,1968+ 2v.
Phil 49.2	James Millikin University. Studies in linguistic psychology. Decatur, Ill.
Phil 49.4	Jung-Institut, Zürich. Studien. Zürich. 1,1949+ 18v.
Phil 49.6	Jowett papers, 1968-1969. Oxford, 1970.

Phil 50.1   Kantgesellschaft. Philosophische Vorträge. Berlin.
1-31,1912-1928 3v.

Phil 50.5   Keyserluig-Gesellschaft für freie Philosophie. Jahrbuch.
Düsseldorf. 2v.

Phil 50.7   Der neue Weg; Mittelungen der Keyserling Gesellschaft für
Freie Philosophie. Wiesbaden. 1-17,1950-1958

Phil 50.30   Ukrainskii. Psikhonevrologicheskii Institut, Kharkov.
Trudy. Kharkov.

Phil 50.35   Kaunas. Universitetas. Teologijos-Filosofijos Fakultetas.
Leidiniai. Kaunas. 8-18 2v.

Phil 51.1   Louvain. Université. Institute Supériéuse de Philosophe.
Annales. Louvain. 1-5,1912-1924 5v.

Phil 51.1.5   Louvain. Université. Laboratoire de Psychologie
Experimentale. Travaux. Louvain.

Phil 51.2   Coover, J.E. Experiments in psychical research at Stanford
Junior University. Stanford, 1917.

Phil 51.3   Lehigh University. Studies psychology series. Bethlehem,
Pa.

Phil 51.5   London. University. Council for Psychical Research.
Bulletin. London.

Phil 52.1   Michigan. University. Philosophical papers. Ann Arbor.
1-4

Phil 52.2   Minnesota. University. Department of Philosophy. Papers.
Minneapolis, 1893-

Phil 52.3   McGill University. Department of philosophy. Papers, 1-4.
Montreal, 1896-99.

Phil 52.4   Montana. University. Psychological series.
Missoula, 1908.

Phil 52.5   Missouri. University. Studies. Philosophie and education
series. Columbia, 1911.

Phil 52.6   Münchener philosophische Abhandlungen. Leipzig, 1911.

Phil 52.7   Massachusetts. Society for Social Hygiene. Bulletin.
Boston. 1918-1920

Phil 52.7.5   Massachusetts. Society for Social Hygiene. Bulletin.
Boston. 1-15,1931-1945

Phil 52.7.12   Massachusetts. Society for Mental Hygiene. Monthly
bulletin. Boston. 1-19,1922-1940 2v.

Phil 52.7.15   Massachusetts. Society for Mental Hygiene. Report of the
Boston Mental Hygiene Survey. Boston.

Phil 52.7.25   Massachusetts. Society for Mental Hygiene. Publication.
1-45 2v.

Phil 52.8   Metaphysical Club, Boston. Calendar. Boston, n.d.

Phil 52.9A   Brown, A.W. The metaphysical society. N.Y., 1947.

Phil 52.9B   Brown, A.W. The metaphysical society. N.Y., 1947.

Phil 52.10   Menninger Clinic. Bulletin. Topeka, Kan. 15,1951+
19v.

Phil 52.11   Milan. Università. Instituto di Storia della Filosofia.
Pubblicazioni. Milan. 1,1951+ 11v.

Phil 52.12   Mexico (City). Universidad Nacional. Facultad de Filosofía
y Letras. Anuario de filosofía.

Phil 53.2   National Association for Study of Epilepsy and Care and
Treatment of Epileptics. Transactions, 1901.
Buffalo, 1901.

Phil 53.3F   National Committee for Mental Hygiene. Eight annual
meeting (typed announcements). n.p., 1916.

Phil 53.3.5   National Committee for Mental Hygiene. Publication. N.Y.
1-12 2v.

Phil 53.3.9   National Committee for Mental Hygiene. Publication. N.Y.
2-196 2v.

Phil 53.4   New Mexico. University. Bulletin. Philosophical series.
Albuquerque. 1

Phil 53.5   Wangh, Martin. Fruition of an eden...in honor of the
fiftieth anniversary of the New York Psychoanalytics
Society. N.Y., 1962.

Phil 54.2   Oregon. University. Publications. Psychology series.
Eugene. 1929-1935

Phil 54.3   Oriental Esoteric Society, Washington, D.C. Bulletin.
Washington. 11-16,1915-1920 4v.

Phil 54.5   Obshchestvo Psikhologov, Moscow, 1. S"ezd, 1959. Tezisy
dokladov, 29 iiunia -4 iiulia 1959 g. v.1-3. Moskva, 1959.

Phil 55.1   Pennsylvania. University. Public series in philosophy.
Philadelphia. 1-4 2v.

Phil 55.1.10   Pennsylvina. University. Laboratory of Neuropathology.
Contributions. Philadelphia, 1905.

Phil 55.2   Princeton contributions to psychology. Princeton.
1-4,1895-1909 2v.

Phil 55.2.5   Princeton contributions to philosophy. Princeton.
1898-1905+

Phil 55.3   Pamphlet box. Psychic investigation association.

Phil 55.4.5   Philadelphia Neurological Society. Proceedings of the 30th
anniversary, November 27-28, 1914. Philadelphi? 1915.

Phil 55.5   Polska Akademja Umiejetności. Komisya do badania historji
filozofzi w Polsce archivum. Krakowie. 1-6,1915-1935
5v.

Phil 55.6   Thasmatological Society. Selections from the papers of the
society. Oxford 1,1882

Phil 55.7   Psychologists League, New York. Journal. N.Y.
1-4,1937-1940 2v.

Phil 55.8   Psychological Society of Great Britain. Papers. London.
1875-1876

Phil 55.9   Parapsychology Foundation. Newsletter. N.Y. 1,1953+
5v.

Phil 55.10   Parapsychology Foundation. Report on five years of
activities. N.Y., 1959.

Phil 55.11   Parapsychological Association. Proceedings. Bruges.
1957-1964+ 5v.

Phil 57.1   Rome. Universita. Scuola di Filosofia. Pabblicazioni.
Roma. 1-17 14v.

Phil 57.2   Rome. Pontificia Universitas Gregoriana. Textus et
documenta. Series philosophica. Romae. 1-14,1932-1938
13v.

Phil 57.3   Rome. Rome Universitas. Istituto di Psicologia
Sperimentale. Contributi psicologia dell' Instituto.
Roma. 1-6,1910-1933 6v.

Phil 57.5   Rostock. Universitat. Gesammelte Dissertationen. Rostock.

Phil 57.10   Rio de Janeiro. Universidade do Brasil. Instituto de
Psicologia. Annuario.

Phil 57.12   Rio de Janeiro. Universidade do Brasil. Instituto de
Psicologia. Boletim; revista de estudos psicológicos.
7,1957+ 2v.

Phil 57.14   Rhodes University, Grahamstown, South Africa. Department of
Philosophy. Philosophical papers. Grahamstown, 3,1967+

Phil 57.14F   Rhodes University, Grahamstown, South Africa. Department of
Philosophy. Occasional papers. Grahamstown. 1,1965+

Phil 58.1   Society for Psychical Research, London. Journal. London.
1,1884+ 36v.

Phil 58.2   Society for Psychical Research, London. Proceedings.
London. 1-49,1882-1952 43v.

Phil 58.2.3   Society for Psychical Research, London. Proceedings. v.1,
pt.2-3. London, 1883.

Phil 58.2.5   Society for Psychical Research, London. Presidential
addresses, 1882-1911. Glasgow, 1912.

Phil 58.2.25   Bradley, Herbert Dennis. An indictment of the present
administration of the Society for Psychical Research.
London, 1931.

Phil 58.3   American Society for Psychical Research. Proceedings.
Boston. 1885-1889

Phil 58.3.5   American Society for Psychical Research. Proceedings.
Boston. 1906-1927 22v.

Phil 58.3.9   American Society for Psychical Research. Journal. N.Y.
1,1907+ 52v.

Phil 58.4   Society for Psychical Research, London. Combined index.
London, 1904. 3v.

Phil 58.5   Pamphlet box. Society for psychical research.

Phil 58.6   Société Française de Philosophie. Bulletin, 1901-1914.
Paris. 1,1901+ 33v.

Phil 58.9   St. Andrews University. Publications of the departments of
philosophy and divinity. Glasgow, 1911.

Phil 58.10.3   Societá per gliStudi Filosofici, Palermo. Bibliotheca
Filosofica. Annuario. Palermo, 1912-

Phil 58.12   Smith College. William Allen Neilson Research Laboratory.
Studies in psychology. Northampton.

Phil 58.15   Société Belge de Philosophie. Archives. Bruxelles.
1-5,1928-1933

Phil 58.16   Sociedade Brasileira de Filosofía. Anais. Rio de Janeiro.
1-8,1939-1945+

NEDL Phil 58.17   San Miguel, Buenos Aires. Facultades de Filosofía y
Teología. Biblioteca. San Miguel.

Phil 58.18   South African Psychologial Association. Proceedings.
1,1950+

Phil 58.19   São Paulo Brazil (City). Universidade. Faculdade de
Filosofia, Ciencias e Letras. Psicologia. 4-7 2v.

Phil 58.20   Société Internationale pour l'Étude de la Philosophie
Mediévale. Bulletin. Louvain. 1,1959+ 4v.

Phil 58.21   Studies in Soviet thought. Dordrecht. 1,1961+ 8v.

Phil 59.1   Toronto. University. Studies. Psychological series.
Toronto. 1-5 3v.

Phil 59.1.5   Toronto. University. Studies. Philosophy. Toronto.
1,1914

Phil 59.2   Thirteen Club, New York. Annual report of the officers.
N.Y. 4-11,1884-1893+ 2v.

Phil 59.3   Theosophical Society in America. Annual convention. N.Y.
5-7,1891-1893

Phil 59.3.6   Theosophical Society in America. Oriental Department.
Pamphlet. N.Y. 1891-1897 2v.

Phil 59.4   Texas. Society of Mental Hygiene. Yearbook. Austin.

Phil 59.5   Tucumán. Universidad Nacional. Facultad de Filosofía y
Letras. Cuadernos de filosofía. Tucumán. 1,1942+
7v.

Phil 59.8   Tavistock Institute of Human Relations, London. Report.
1963+

Phil 59.8.5   Tavistock pamphlet. London. 1,1957+ 4v.

Phil 60.2   Utrecht. Rijksuniversiteit. Psychologisch Laboratorium.
Mededeelingen. Utrecht. 1-7,1924-1933 3v.

Phil 61.1   Vienna. Universität. Philosophische Gesellschaft.
WissenschaftlicheBeilage. Leipzig, 1902-1915. 2v.

Phil 61.1.5   Vienna. Universität. Philosophische Gesellschaft.
Veröffentlichungen. Leipzig, 1893- 3v.

Phil 61.5   Victoria College, Wellington, New Zealand. Department of
Psychology. Publications in psychology. 5+ 5v.

Phil 62.1   Society for Philosophical Inquiry, Washington, D.C.
Memoirs. Lancaster, Pa. 1-4,1893-1927+

Phil 62.2   Wyoming. University. Department of Psychology. Bulletin.
2. ed. no.1-3. Laramie, Wyoming, 1919-

Phil 62.3   Western Philosophical Association. Proceedings.
1-2,1901-1902

Htn Phil 62.4*   Wiener psychoanalytisches Verein. Wiesbaden.

Phil 62.5   Wiener, P.V. Minutes of the Vienna Psychoanalytic Society.
N.Y., 1962- 2v.

Phil 62.7   Western Behavioral Sciences Institute, La Jolla,
California. Report. La Jolla, California. 3-22

Phil 64.1   Yale Psychological Studies. The psychological review and
studies from Yale psychological laboratory. v.1., no.1-2
and supplement. New Haven, n.d. 3v.

Phil 65.1   Zeitschrift für sexual Wissenschaft. Bonn. 1-9 3v.

Phil 65.2   Hartmann, E.V. Phänomenologie des sittlechen Bewusstens. 3
Aufl. Berlin, 1924.

Phil 70   Congresses, symposia, etc.

Phil 70.1   International Congress of Philosophy, 1st, Paris, 1900.
Bibliothèque. Paris. 1900-1903

Phil 70.1.2   International Congress of Philosophy, 2nd, Geneva, 1904.
Rapports. Genève. 1905

Phil 70.1.3   International Congress of Philosophy, 3rd, Heidelberg,
1908. Bericht über den III International Kongress.
Heidelberg. 1909

Phil 70.1.3.2   International Congress of Philosophy, 3rd, Heidelberg,
1908. Kurzer Gesamt-Bericht die Tätigkeit in der Sektionen
und allgemeinen Sitzungen. Heidelberg. 1908

Phil 70.1.4   International Congress of Philosophy, 4th, Bologna, 1911.
Revue de metaphysique et de morale. Paris. 1911

Phil 70.1.5   International Congress of Philosophy, 5th, Naples, 1924.
Atti del v. congresso internazionale. Napoli. 1925

Phil 70.1.6   International Congress of Philosophy, 6th, Cambridge,
Mass., 1926. Proceedings. N.Y. 1927

Phil 70.1.7   International Congress of Philosophy, 7th, Oxford, 1930.
Proceedings. London. 1931

Phil 70.1.8   International Congress of Philosophy, 8th, Prague, 1934.
Actes du huitième congrés international de philosophie à
Prague. Prague. 1936

Phil 70.1.10   International Congress of Philosophy, 10th, Amsterdam,
1948. Proceedings. Amsterdam. 1949 2v.

Phil 70.1.11   International Congress of Philosophy, 11th, Brussels, 1953.
Proceedings. Amsterdam. 1953 4v.

Phil 70.1.12   International Congress of Philosophy, 12th, Venice, 1958.
Atti. Actes. Firenze. 1958-1961 12v.

Phil 70.1.12.5   International Congress of Philosophy, 12th, Venice, 1958.
Doklady i vystuplemia. Moskva. 1958

Phil 70.1.12.10   Prudian, Georg. Ital'ianskaia vstrecha filosov; o XII
Mezhdunarodnom filosofskom Kongresse. Erevan, 1959.

Phil 70.1.14   International Congress of Philosophy. Akten des XIV.
Wien. 1968 6v.

Phil 70   Congresses, symposia, etc. - cont.

Phil 70.2   Mental Hygiene Conference and Exhibit. Proceedings, 1911. N.Y., 1912.

Phil 70.2.15   International Congress on Mental Hygiene. Program.

Phil 70.3   International Congress of Psychology. Congrès international de psychologie physiologique. Paris. 1890

Phil 70.3.1   Internatonal Congress of Psychology, 1st, Paris, 1889. Congress international de psychologie physiologique. Paris. 1889

Phil 70.3.2   International Congress of Psychology, 2nd, London, 1892. Proceedings at the 2d session. London. 1892

Phil 70.3.3   International Congress of Psychology, 3rd, Munich, 1896. Dritter internationaler Congress für Psychologie in München. München. 1897

Phil 70.3.4   International Congress of Psychology, 4th, Paris, 1900. Compte rendu des séances et texte des mémoires. Paris. 1901

Phil 70.3.6   Pamphlet box. International congress of psychology, 4th, 1900.

Phil 70.3.10   International Congress of Psychology, 5th, Rome, 1905. Atti del V Congresso internazionale di psicologia. Roma. 1905

Phil 70.3.15   International Congress of Psychology, 6th, Geneva, 1909. Rapports et comptes rendus. Genève. 1910

Phil 70.3.25   International Congress of Psychology, 8th, Groningen, 1926. Proceedings and papers. Groningen. 1827

Phil 70.3.30   International Congress of Psychology, 9th, New Haven, 1929. Proceedings and papers. Princeton, N.J. 1930

Phil 70.3.35   International Congress of Psychology, 10th, Copenhagen, 1932. Papers read to the Xth International Congress of Psychology at Copenhagen, 1932. The Hague. 1935

Phil 70.3.40   International Congress of Psychology, 11th, Paris, 1937. Rapports et comptes rendus. Paris. 1938

Phil 70.3.45   International Congress of Psychology, 12th, Edinburgh, 1948. Proceedings and papers. Edinburgh. 1950

Phil 70.3.50   International Congress of Psychology, 13th, Stockholm, 1951. Proceedings and papers. Stockholm. 1952

Phil 70.3.52   International Congress of Psychology, 14th, Montreal, 1954. Proceedings. Actes. Amsterdam. 1955

Phil 70.3.55   International Congress of Psychology, 15th, Brussels, 1957. Actes. Proceedings. Amsterdam. 1959

Phil 70.3.60   International Congress of Psychology, 14th, Montreal, 1954. Proceedings. Amsterdam. 1955

Phil 70.3.63   International Congress of Psychology, 14th, Montreal, 1954. Doklady. Communications. Moskva. 1954

Phil 70.3.65   International Congress of Psychology, 17th, Washington, 1963. Proceedings. Comptes rendus. Amsterdam. 1963

Phil 70.3.70   International Congress of Psychology, 18th, Moscow, 1966. Tezisy soobshchenii. Abstracts of communications. Moskva. 1966 3v.

Phil 70.3.71   International Congress of Psychology, 18th, Moscow, 1966. Symposium. Moskva. 1966 19v.

Phil 70.3.75   Kussmann, Thomas. Achtzehne Internationale Kongress für Psychologie in Moskau, 1966. Göttingen, 1967.

Phil 70.3.90   International Congress of Psychology, 19th, London, 1969. Deviatnadtsatyi mezhdnnarodnyi psikhologicheskii kongress, 27 iialia - 2 avgusta 1969 g., London, Angliia. Moskva, 1970.

Phil 70.4   International Congress for Analytical Psychology, 1st, Zurich, 1958. Current trends in analytical psychology. London, 1961.

Phil 70.5   International Congress of Arts and Sciences, St. Louis, 1904. Proceedings. Philosophy and mathematics. Washington, 1906.

Phil 70.6   Human action: conceptual and empirical issues. N.Y., 1969.

Phil 70.7   Congrès des Sociétés Philosophiques, 1921. Congrès des société philosophique américaine, anglaises, belge, italienne. Paris, 1926.

Phil 70.8   Indian philosophical congress, 1st, Calcutta, 1925. Proceedings. Calcutta. 36,1927+ 4v.

Phil 70.8.5F   Indian Philosophical Congress. Silver jubilee commemoration volume. Madras, 1950. 2v.

Phil 70.9   Kongress für Experimentelle Psychologie. Bericht. Jena. 10,1927

Phil 70.9.25   Deutsche Gesellschaft für Psychologie. Bericht über den Kongress. Jena. 14,1934

Phil 70.10   Congresso Nazionale de Filosofia. Atti. Milano. 16-18 8v.

Phil 70.10.8   Milan. Universita Cattolica del Sacro Cuore. Faculta di Filosofia. Relazione e cumunicazioni presentate al Congresso Nazionale di Filosofia. Milano, 1935. 2v.

Phil 70.11   Congrés Polonais de Philosophie. Rapports et comptes rendus. Varsovie.

Phil 70.12   Conference on Individual Psychological Differences. Proceedings, Washington, D.C., May 9-10, 1930. Washington, D.C., 1930.

Phil 70.13   Congrès International de Philosophie Scientifique, 1st, Paris, 1935. Actes du Congrès International. Paris, 1936. 8v.

Phil 70.13.10   Congrès International de Philosophie des Science, Paris, 1949. Actes. Paris, 1951. 9v.

Phil 70.14   Conference of Psychologists, Hanover, New Hanpshire, 1925. Conference of psychologists called by Laura Spelman Rockefellar Memorial. n.p., 1925. 2v.

Phil 70.14.3   Conference of Psychologists, Hanover, New Hanpshire. Another, slightly variant report of the Thursday morning session. n.p., 1925.

Phil 70.15   Kongress für Synthetische Lebensforschung. Verhandlungsbericht. Prag, 1937.

Phil 70.16   Inter-American Congress of Philosophy, 1st, Port-au-Prince, 1944. Travaux du congrès international de philosophie. Port-au-Prince, 1947.

Phil 70.16.5   Interamerican Congress of Psychology. Actas. 1,1953 2 pam.

Phil 70.17   International Institute of Philosophy. Nature des problemes in philosophie. Paris, 1949.

Phil 70.18   Congrès des Sociétés de Philosophie de Langue Française, 4th, Neuchâtel, 1949. La liberté; actes. Neuchâtel. 1949

Phil 70.18.10   Congrès des Sociétés de Philosophie de Langue Française, 5th, Bordeaux, 1950. Les sciences et la sagesse. Paris. 1950

Phil 70.18.15   Congrès des Sociétés de Philosophie de Langue Française, 7th, Grenoblé, 1954. La vie, la pensée. Paris. 1954

Phil 70.19   Congreso Internacional de Filosofia, Barcelona. Actas. Madrid, 1949. 3v.

Phil 70.20   Congresso Nacional de Filosofia, Brazil. Anais. São Paulo. 1-4 4v.

Phil 70   Congresses, symposia, etc. - cont.

Phil 70.21   Congreso Nacional de Filosofia. Actas. Buenos Aires. 1-3 4v.

Phil 70.22   Centro di Studi Filosofici di Gallarate. Atti del convegno. Brescia. 1,1945+ 21v.

Phil 70.22.5   Centro di Studi Filosofici Cristiani, Gallarate. Il movimento di Gallarate. Padova. 1955

Phil 70.22.10   Centro di Studi Filosofici di Gallarate. Senso e valore del discorso metafisico. Padova, 1966.

Phil 70.23   Zur Psychoanalyse der Kriegsneurosen. Leipzig, 1919.

Phil 70.24   International Council for Philosophy and Humanistic Studies. International council for philosophy and humanistic studies. Paris, 1949.

Phil 70.25   Centre International de Synthèse, Paris. Valeur philosophique de la psychologie. Paris, 1951.

Phil 70.26   Deutscher Kongress für Philosophie, 3rd, Brenen, 1950. Symphilosophein. München. 1952

Phil 70.26.6   Deutscher Kongress für Philosophie, 6th, München, 1960. Das Problem der Ordnung. Meisenheim. 1962

Phil 70.26.7   Deutscher Kongress für Philosophie, 7th, Münster, 1962. Die Philosophie und die Frage nach dem Fortschritt. München. 1964

Phil 70.26.8   Deutscher Kongress für Philosophie, 8th, Heidelberg, 1966. Das Problem der Sprache. München. 1967

Phil 70.30   Science, language and human rights. Philadelphia, 1952.

Phil 70.32   Convegno degli Psicolozi Italiani. Atti. Firenze. 9-11,1951-1956 3v.

Phil 70.34   Vsesoiuznoe Soveshchanie po Voprosam Psikhologii, 2nd, Moskva, 1953. Doklady na soveshchanii po voprosam psikhologii 3-8 iiulia 1953 g. Moskva, 1954.

Phil 70.36   Nortisk Psykologmøte. Förhandlingar. 1947-1956 4v.

Phil 70.38   Congresso di Studi Metodologici, Turin, 1952. Atti del congresso di studi metodologici promosso del centro di studi metodologici. Torino, 1954.

Phil 70.40   Hook, Sidney. Determinism and freedom in the age of modern science. N.Y., 1958.

Phil 70.45   Congresso Internacional de Filosofia. Congresso Internacional de Filosofia. São Paulo, 1956.

Phil 70.45.5   International Institute of Philosophy. Entretiens philosophiques de Varsovie. Wrocław, 1958.

Phil 70.50   Semana Española de Filosofía, 4th, Madrid, 1957. La forma. Madrid, 1959.

Phil 70.50.5   Semana Española de Filosofía. Ponencias y conferencias. Madrid. 1-9 4v.

Phil 70.55   Association pour l'Etude Scientifique du Symbolisme. Congrès. Paris. 6,1957+ 3v.

Phil 70.60   Istituto di Studi Filosofici Serione di Torino. La ricerca filodofica. Roma, 1941.

Phil 70.63   Instituto di Studi Filosofici. Pubblicazione. Milano. 1940-1952 9v.

Phil 70.65   Group for the Advancement of Psychiatry. Symposium. N.Y. 1-7 2v.

Phil 70.67   Recent advances in biological psychiatry. N.Y. 4,1961+ 6v.

Phil 70.70   Caribbean Conference for Mental Health. Proceedings. San Juan. 2-3 2v.

Phil 70.72   Societá Filosofica Italiana. Veritá e libertá di Guzzo. Palumbo, 1960.

Phil 70.75.1   Congrès International de Philosophie Médiévale, 1st, Louvain and Brussels, 1958. L'homme et son destin, d'après les penseurs du moyen âge. Louvain. 1960

Phil 70.75.2A   Congrès International de Philosophie Médiévale, 2d, Cologne, 1961. Die Metaphysik im Mittelalter, ihr Ursprung und ihre Bedeutung. Berlin. 1963

Phil 70.75.2B   Congrès International de Philosophie Médiévale, 2d, Cologne, 1961. Die Metaphysik im Mittelalter, ihr Ursprung und ihre Bedeutung. Berlin. 1963

Phil 70.75.3   Congrès International de Philosophie Médiévale, 3rd, Passo della Mendola (Trento), 1964. La filosofia della natura nel medioevo. Milano. 1966

Phil 70.75.4   Congrès International de Philosophie Médiévale, 4th, Montreal, 1967. Arts liberaux et philosophie au moyen âge. Montreal. 1969

Phil 70.77   Conference on Psychological Scaling, Princeton, New Jersey. Psychological scaling: theory and applications. N.Y., 1960.

Phil 70.80   Winn, R.B. Psychotherapy in the Soviet Union. N.Y., 1961.

Phil 70.81   Reunion de Aproximacion Filosofica Cuntifica. La materia. v.2. Zaragoza, 1961.

Phil 70.82   Logic, methodology and philosophy of science. Amsterdam. 1,1962+ 3v.

Phil 70.83   International Congress of Applied Psychology, 14th, Copenhagen, 1961. Proceedings. Copenhagen, 1962. 5v.

Phil 70.83.16   International Congress of Applied Psychology, 16th, Amsterdam, 1968. Proceedings of the XVIth International Congress of Applied Psychology. Amsterdam, 1969.

Phil 70.84   Symposium Iberoamericano de Filosofia. Trabajos. Guatemala.

Phil 70.85   Symposium Iberoamericano de Filosofía. Primer Symposium Iberoamericano de Filosofía. Guatemala, 1961.

Phil 70.86   International Institute of Philosophy. Traditional cultural values. Mysore, 1959.

Phil 70.86.10   International Institute of Philosophy. Démonstration, vérification, justification. Liège, 1968.

Phil 70.88   East-West Philosopher Conference. Philosophy and culture. 1. ed. Honolulu, 1962.

Phil 70.89   Hayden Colloquium on Scientific Concept and Method, M.I.T. Parts and wholes. N.Y., 1963.

Phil 70.90   Gonseth, Ferdinand. La metaphysique et l'ouverture. Paris, 1961.

Phil 70.91   La philosophie analytique. Paris, 1962.

Phil 70.92   Conference on Science, Philosophy and Religion. Symbols and values; an initial study. N.Y., 1954.

Phil 70.93   Darmtaedter, Gespräch. Die Herausforderung. München, 1963.

Phil 70.94   Oberlin Colloguium in Philosophy, 3d, Oberlin College, 1962. Knowledge and experience. Pittsburgh, Pa. 1962

Phil 70.94.5   Oberlin Colloquium in Philosophy, 5th, Oberlin College, 1964. Metaphysics and explanation. Pittsburgh, Pa. 1966

Phil 70.94.6   Oberlin Colloquium in Philosophy, 6th, Oberlin College, 1965. Art, mind, and religion; proceedings. Pittsburgh. 1967

Phil 70.94.8   Oberlin Colloquium in Philosophy, 8th, Oberlin College, 1967. Perception and personal identity. Cleveland. 1969

Phil 70.94.10   Oberlin Colloquium in Philosophy. Society, revolution and reform; proceedings. Cleveland, 1971.

Classified Listing

Phil 70.95   Pakistan Philosophical Congress. Proceedings. 1,1954+
6v.
Phil 70.96   Archivio di Filosofia. Tecnica e casistica. Padova, 1964.
Phil 70.97   New York. Institute of Philosophy. Law and philosophy.
N.Y., 1964.
Phil 70.98   Kongres Psihologa Jugoslavije, 2d, Zagerb, 1964.
Materijali. Zagreb, 1964.
Phil 70.99   Gandillac, Maurice Patronnier de. Entretiens sur les
notions de genése et de structure. Paris, 1965.
Phil 70.100   International Congress of Philosophy, 13th, México, 1963.
Symposia. 1. ed. México. 1963
Phil 70.100.5   International Congress of Philosophy, 13th, México, 1963.
Memorias del XIII congreso internacional de filosofía,
México. México. 1-10 10v.
Phil 70.100.10   Problemy teorii poznaniia i logiki. Moskva, 1968.
Phil 70.100.15   Filosofiia i sovnemennost'. Moskva, 1971.
Phil 70.102   Wayne State University. Symposium in the Philosophy of
Mind, 1962. Intentionality, minds, and perecption.
Detroit, 1967.
Phil 70.103   Iubileinaia Nauchnaia Sessiia Vuzov Ural'skoi zony,
Sverdlovsk. Materialy. Sverdlovsk, 1967?
Phil 70.104   Interamerican Congress of Philosophy, 7th, Laval
University, 1967. Proceedings of the congress.
Quebec, 1967-68. 2v.
Phil 70.105   University of Western Ontario. Philosophy Colloquium. Fact
and existence; proceedings of the University of Western
Ontario philosophy colloquium, 1966. Oxford, 1969.
Phil 70.105.5   University of Western Ontario. Philosophy Colloquium. Fact
and existence; proceedings of the University of Western
Ontario philosophy colloquium, 1966. Toronto, 1969. 2v.
Phil 70.110   Madrid. Universidad. Seminario de Metafísica. Anales del
Seminario de Metafísica. Madrid, 1967.
Phil 70.112   The nature of philosophical inquiry. Notre Dame, 1970.
Phil 70.114   Banff Conference on Theoretical Psychology, 1st, 1965.
Toward unification in psychology. Toronto, 1970.
Phil 70.116   Contemporary philosophic thought. Albany, 1970. 4v.
Phil 70.118   Zonal'naia Konferentsiia Psikhologov Pribaltiki, 5th,
Tartu, Kääriku, 1968. Materialy V Zonal'noi Konferentsii
Psikhologov Pribaltiki. Tartu, 1968.
Phil 70.120   International Congress of Philosophy. Beiträge der
bulgarischen Teilnehmer an dem XIV. Wien, 1968.

Phil 75   Reference works on philosophy - Bibliographies

Phil 75.1   Averra, Adolfo. Bibliografia delle Scienze Filosofiche.
Torino, 1891.
Phil 75.2   Büchring, Adolph. Biliotheca philosophica.
Nordhausen, 1867.
Phil 75.3   Freude, C.G.A. Wegweiser. Ebersbach, 1858. 2v.
Phil 75.4   Geissler, C.A. Bibliographisches Handbuch der
philosophischer Literatur. Leipzig, 1850.
Phil 75.5   Gumposh, V.P. Die philosophische Literatur der Deutschen.
Regensburg, 1851.
Phil 75.6   Hiszmann, M. Anleitung der Literatur der Philosophie.
Göttingen, 1778.
Phil 75.7   Jonsius, Johannes. De scriptoribus historiae
philosophicae. Jena, 1716.
Phil 75.8   Schaller, Karl A. Handbuch der klassischen philosophischen
Literatur. Halle, 1816.
Phil 75.9   Struve, B.G. Bibliothecae philosphicae. Göttingen, 1740.
Phil 75.10   Pamphlet vol. Bibliography of philosophy.
Phil 75.11   Louvain. Université Catholique. Institut Supérieur de
Philosophie. Sommaire idéologique. Bruxelles.
1-20,1895-1914 4v.
Phil 75.12   Cosentini, F. Bibliotheca philosophica. Sassari, 1895.
Phil 75.13.5   Rand, Benjamin. Philosophical library for the American
continent. Cambridge, 1904.
Phil 75.13.9   Rand, Benjamin. Selected works on history of philosophy in
English language. Boston, 1906.
Phil 75.14   Valverde Téllez, E. Bibliografía. México, 1907.
Phil 75.15   Carus, P. Philosophy as a science. Chicago, 1909.
Phil 75.16   Levi, Alessandro. Bibliografia filosofica italiana,
1914-15. Roma, 1917.
Phil 75.17   Moog, Willy. Philosophie. Gotha, 1921.
NEDL Phil 75.18   Bibliographie der Philosophie und Psychologie. Leipzig.
1920
Phil 75.19   Herbertz, R. Die philosophische Literatur.
Stuttgart, 1912.
Phil 75.20   Literarische Berichte aus dem Gebiete der Philosophie.
Sonder Druck von Heft 9/10. Erfurt, 1926.
Phil 75.21   Deutsche Philosphische Gesellschaft. Literarische
Berichte. Erfurt. 8-26 19v.
Phil 75.22   Cohen, F. Philosphie. Antiquarists-Katalog 159/160.
Bonn, 1927.
Phil 75.23   Hoffmans, Jean. La philosophie et les philosophes.
Bruxelles, 1920.
Phil 75.24   Vaunérus, Allen. Svensk filosofi. Stockholm, 1930.
Phil 75.25   Index philosphique. Paris. 1-2,1902-1903 2v.
Phil 75.26   Alcan, Felix. La philosophie française contemporaine.
Paris, 1926.
Phil 75.27   National Research Council. Research Information Service.
Union list of foreign serials cited in Psychological
index, 1922. Washington, 1925.
Phil 75.28   Meiner, Felix. Philosophischer Handkatalog. 1er Nachtrag
über die Jahre 1927/28. Leipzig, 1928.
Phil 75.29   Renoir, Edmund. Bibliography of recent French philosophy,
1920. n.p. n.d.
Phil 75.30   Florence. Biblioteca Filosofica. Catalogo della Biblioteca
filosofica. Text and supplement. Firenze, 1910.
Phil 75.31   Fock, G. Philosophie. Leipzig, 1936.
Phil 75.32   New York. Public Library. List of books in the New York
Public Library relating to philosophy. N.Y., 1908.
Phil 75.33   Riedl, J.O. A catalogue of Renaissance philosophers.
Milwaukee, 1940.
Phil 75.34   Buenos Aires. Colegio Máximo. Nuestra bibliográfica de la
filosofía católica. Buenos Aires, 1939.
Phil 75.35   Hope, R. A guide to readings in philosophy. Ann
Arbor, 1939.
Phil 75.36   Argentine Republic. Comisión Nacional de Cooperación
Intelectual. Bibliografía argentina de publicaciones
filosóficas, años 1937 a 1943. Buenos Aires, 1943.
Phil 75.38   Brugger, Ilse. Filosofía alemana traducida al español.
Buenos Aires, 1942.
Phil 75.38.5   Brugger, Ilse. Filosofía alemana traducida al español.
Supplement. Pt.1. Buenos Aires, 1942.
Phil 75.39   Bibliographische Einführungen in das Studium der
Philosophie. Bern. 1948

Phil 75.40   Costa, M.G. Ineditos de filosofia em Portgal.
Porto, 1949.
Phil 75.41   Bibliografia filosofica italiana. Milano. 1949+ 17v.
Phil 75.42   Instituto di Studi Filosofci. Bibliografia filosofica
italiana dal 1900 al 1950. Roma, 1950. 4v.
Phil 75.42.5   Istituto di Studi Filosofici. Bibliografia ragionata delle
riviste filosofiche italiane dal 1900 al 1955. Roma, 1963.
Phil 75.43   Bril, G.A. de. Bibliographia philosophica. Rhenum, 1950.
2v.
Phil 75.44   Chan, Wing-Tsit. An outline and a bibliography of Chinese
philosophy. Hanover, N.H., 1953.
Phil 75.45   Pelzer, A. Répertoires d'incipit pour la littérature
latine philosophique. Roma, 1951.
Phil 75.46   Polska Akademia Nauk. Komitet Filozoficzny. Bibliografia
filozofii polskiej [1750-1830]. v.1,3. Warszawa, 1955.
2v.
Phil 75.47   Joó, Tibor. Magyar nyelvű filozófiai kézúratók a Széchenyi
Könyitárban. Budapest, 1940.
Phil 75.50   Bulgarska Akademiia na Naukite, Sofia. Biblioteka.
Abstracts of Bulgarian scientific literature. Philosophy
and pedagogics. Sofia. 1958+ 4v.
Phil 75.52   Totok, Wilhelm. Bibliographischer Wegweiser der
philosophischen Literatur. Frankfurt, 1959.
Phil 75.54   Emunds, Heinz. Zugange zur Philosophie. Köln, 1959.
Phil 75.55   Kwee, Swan Liat. Bibliography of humanism. Utrecht, 1957.
Phil 75.56   Philosophical books. Leicester. 1,1960+ 4v.
Phil 75.58   Inter-American Congress of Philosophy. Exposición del
libro americano. Buenos Aires, 1959?
Phil 75.59   Bibliographie der sowjetischen Philosophie. Freiburg. 1-4
2v.
Phil 75.60   Madrid. Universidad. Facultad de Filosofía y Letras.
Sumarios y extractos de las tesis doctorales en las
secciones de filosofía y pedagogía. 1940-1950
Phil 75.62   Martínez Gómez, Luis. Bibliografia filosófica.
Barcelona, 1961.
Phil 75.64   Bibliografia argentina de filosofía y ciencias de la
educación. La Plata.
Phil 75.64.5   Bibliografia argentina de filosofía. La Plata.
Phil 75.65   Totok, Wilhelm. Handbuch der Geschichte der Philosophie.
v.2, pt.1. Frankfurt, 1964. 2v.
Phil 75.66   Akademiia Nauk SSSR. Fundamental'naia Biblioteka
Obshchestvennykh Nauk. Istoriia zarubezhnoi domarksistskoi
filosofii, za 1917-1962 gody. Moskva, 1963.
Phil 75.67   Novaia sovetskaia literatura po filosofii. Moskva. 1965+
7v.
Phil 75.68   Berg, Jan. Selektiv bibliografi i teoretisk filosofi.
Stockholm, 1960.
Phil 75.69   Matica Slovenská, Turčiansky sv. Martin. Bibliografický
Odbor. Bibliografia filoszofíckéj Knižnej tvorby na
Slovensku. Martin, 1965.
Phil 75.70   Higgins, Charles L. The bibliography of philosophy. Ann
Arbor, 1965.
Phil 75.72   Verbinc, Franc. Filozofski tokovi na Slovenskem.
Ljubljana, 1966.
Phil 75.72.5   Verbinc, Franc. Filozofski tokovi na Slovenskem.
Ljubljana, 1970.
Phil 75.74   McLean, George F. An annotated bibliography of philosophy
in Catholic thought, 1900-1964. N.Y., 1967.
Phil 75.74.5   McLean, George F. A bibliography of Christian philosophy
and contemporary issue. N.Y., 1967.
Phil 75.75   Akademiia Nauk SSSR. Fundamental'naia Biblioteka
Obshchestvennykh Nauk. Kritika burzhuaznoi i reformistskoi
filosofii i sotsiologii epokhi imperializma. Moskva, 1967.
Phil 75.76   Bibliography of philosophy. Paris, 1966? 2 pam.
Phil 75.77   Dawe, Harold G.A. Philosophy in South Africa, 1950-1962.
Cape Town, 1964.
Phil 75.78   Bibliographie Philosophie. Berlin. 2,1968 4v.
Phil 75.78.2   Bibliographie Philosophie. Beiheft. 1,1967+
Phil 75.79   Ortloff, Johann Andreas. Handbuch der Literatur der
Geschichte der Philosophie. Düsseldorf, 1967.
Phil 75.82   Menchaca, José. Diccionario bio-bibliográfico de
filósofos. Bilbao, 1965.
Phil 75.84   Bendfeldt Rojas, Lourdes. Bibliografía filosófica de
publicaciones de las Universidades de Costa Rica y San
Carlos de Guatemala y de autores guatemaltecos que exhibió
la Biblioteca Nacional. Guatemala, 1964.
Phil 75.86   Richter, Richard. Humdert Jahre philosophische Bibliothek
1868-1968. Hamburg, 1968.
Phil 75.87   Philosphie; chronique annuelle. Paris. 1,1939+ 8v.
Phil 75.88   Adorno, Francesco. Il pensiero greco. Orientamenti
bibliografici a cura di Francesco Adorno. Bari, 1969.
Phil 75.88.5   Adorno, Francesco. Il pensiero greco-romano e il
cristianesimo. 1. ed. Bari, 1970.
Phil 75.89   Bibliografía filosófica mexicana. México. 1,1968+
Phil 75.90   Plott, John C. Sarva-darsana-sangraha; a bibliographical
guide to the global history of philosophy. Leiden, 1969.
Phil 75.92   Library of Congress. General Reference and Bibliography
Division. Philosophical periodicals. Washington, 1952.
Phil 75.94   Rassegna bibliografia di storia della filosofia; recavata
della riviste. Padova. 3,1968+ 2v.

Phil 80   Reference works on philosophy - Dictionaries and encyclopedias - Folios [Discontinued]

Phil 80.1   Chauvin, E. Lexicon rationale. Rotterdam, 1692.

Phil 85 - 110   Reference works on philosophy - Dictionaries and encyclopedias - Others (A-Z)

Phil 85.1   Arnaiz y Alcalde, N. Diccionario manual de filosofía.
Madrid, 1927.
Phil 85.5   Apel, Max. Philosophisches Wörterbuch. 4. Aufl.
Berlin, 1953.
Phil 85.10   Austeda, F. Kleines Worterbuch der Philosophie.
Frankfurt, 1954.
Phil 85.15   Abbagnano, Nicola. Dizionario di filosofia. Torino, 1961.
Phil 86.1   Bertrand, A. Lexique de philosophie. Paris, 1892.
NEDL Phil 86.3A   Baldwin, J.M. Dictionary of philosophy. v.1.
London, 1901-05.
Phil 86.3B   Baldwin, J.M. Dictionary of philosophy. London, 1901-05.
3v.
Phil 86.3.5   Baldwin, J.M. Dictionary of philosophy. v.1,3.
N.Y., 1911. 3v.
Phil 86.3.10   Baldwin, J.M. Dictionary of philosophy. v.2. N.Y., 1940.
Phil 86.4   Brothier, L. Ebauche d'un glossaire du langage
philosophique. Paris, 1863.
Phil 86.5   Boccalaro, M.A. Dizionario filosofico. Bologna, 1951.
Phil 86.6   Brugger, Walter. Philosophisches Wörterbuch. 5. Aufl.
Freiburg 1953.

il 85 - 110   Reference works on philosophy - Dictionaries and encyclopedias - Others (A-Z) - cont.

Phil 86.7   Blanc, Elie. Dictionnaire de philosophie ancienne. Paris, 1906.

Phil 87.1   Clauberg, K.N. Systematisches Wörterbuch der Philosophie. Leipzig, 1923.

Phil 87.3   Candou, José M. Diccionario manual de filosofía. Madrid, 1946.

Phil 87.4   Cantoro, Umberto. Vocabulario filosófico. Bologna, 1955.

Phil 87.12   Cuvillier, Armand. Petit vocabulaire de la langue philosophique. Paris, 1925.

Phil 87.12.5   Cuvillier, Armand. Kücük felsefesözlügü. Ankara, 1944.

Phil 87.13   Cuvillier, Armand. Nouveau vocabulaire philosophique. 2. éd. Paris, 1957.

Phil 87.14   Carrión, Joaquin. Diccionario de sinónimos ó sea la propiedad del lenguage filosófico. Madrid, 1873.

Phil 87.15   Chauvin, Etienne. Lexicon philosophicum. 2. Aufl. Dusseldorf, 1967.

Phil 88.1   Dorner, A. Encyklopädie der Philosophie. Leipzig, 1910.

Phil 88.5   Dizionario di filosofia. Milano, 1957.

Phil 88.10   Diemer, Alwin. Philosophie. Frankfurt, 1958.

Phil 89.1   Eisler, R. Wörterbuch der Philosophie Begriffe und aus Drücke. Berlin, 1899.

Phil 89.1.4   Eisler, R. Wörterbuch der Philosophie Begriffe und aus Drücke. 4. Aufl. Berlin, 1927-29. 3v.

Phil 89.1.5   Eisler, R. Handwörterbuch der Philosophie. Berlin, 1913.

Phil 89.1.7   Eisler, R. Handwörterbuch der Philosophie. 2. Aufl. Berlin, 1922.

Phil 89.1.8   Eisler, Rudolf. Wörterbuch der philosophischen Begriffe. 4. Aufl. Berlin, 1927-30. 3v.

Phil 89.1.15   Eisler, R. Philosophen - Lexikon. Berlin, 1912.

Phil 89.2   Eucken, R. Geschichte der philosophischen Terminologie. Leipzig, 1879.

Phil 89.3.10   English, Horace B. A student's dictionary of psychological terms. 3rd ed. Yellow Springs, Ohio, 1929.

Phil 89.4   Encyclopaedisch handboek van het moderne denken. Arnhem, 1931. 2v.

Phil 89.5.3   Elseviers filosofische en psychologische encyclopedie. 3. Druk. Amsterdam, 1966.

Phil 89.6   Enciclopedia filosofica. Venezia, 1957-58. 4v.

Phil 90.1   Fleming, William. Vocabulary of philosophy. London, 1858.

Phil 90.1.3   Fleming, William. Vocabulary of philosophy. London, 1857.

Phil 90.1.4   Fleming, William. Vocabulary of philosophy. 4th ed. N.Y., 1887.

Phil 90.2   Franck, Adolphe. Dictionnaire des sciences philosophiques. Paris, 1844. 6v.

Phil 90.2.2   Franck, Adolphe. Dictionnaire des sciences philosophiques. 2. éd. Paris, 1875.

Phil 90.2.3   Franck, Adolphe. Diccionaire des sciences philosophiques. 2e éd. Paris, 1875.

Phil 90.3   Furtmair, M. Philosophisches Real-Lexikon. Augsburg, 1853.

Phil 90.4   Ferrater Mora, José. Diccionario de filosofía. México, 1941.

Phil 90.4.10   Ferrater Mora, José. Diccionario de filosofía. 2. ed. México, 1944.

Phil 90.4.15   Ferrater Mora, José. Diccionario de filosofía. 3. ed. Buenos Aires, 1951.

Phil 90.4.16   Ferrater Mora, José. Diccionario de filosofía. 4. ed. Buenos Aires, 1958.

Phil 90.4.17   Ferrater Mora, José. Diccionario de filosofía. 5. ed. Buenos Aires, 1965.

Phil 90.5   Fachwörterbuch der Philosophie. Zürich, 1945.

Phil 90.6   Filosofskaia entsiklopediia. Moskva, 1960-70. 5v.

Phil 90.8   Foulquié, Paul. Dictionnaire de la langue philosophique. Paris, 1962.

Phil 91.3   Goblot, E. Le vocabulaire philosophique. Paris, 1901.

Phil 91.4   Giese, Fritz. Psychologisches Wörterbuch. Leipzig, 1921.

Phil 91.5   Grooten, J. Filosofisch lexicon. Antwerpen, 1958.

Phil 92.1   Hugon, Paul D. Our minds and our motives. N.Y., 1928.

Phil 92.2   Hamilton, James A. Englisch-Deutsch für Psychologen. Frankfurt, 1931.

Phil 92.3   Hauer, E. Philosophen Lexikon. Lief. 1-6. Berlin, 1937.

Phil 92.4   Hoffmeister, J. Wörterbuch der philosophischen Begriffe. Hamburg, 1955.

Phil 94.2   Jolivet, Régis. Vocabulaire de la philosophie. 4. ed. Lyon, 1957.

Phil 95.1   Kirchner, Friedrich. Wörterbuch der philosophischen Grundbegriffe. Heidelberg, 1890.

Phil 95.1.3   Kirchner, Friedrich. Wörterbuch der philosophischen Grundbegriffe. Heidelberg, 1886.

Phil 95.1.5   Kirchner, Friedrich. Wörterbuch der philosophischen Begriffe. Leipzig, 1944.

Phil 95.2   Krug, Wilhelm Traugott. Allgemeines Handwörterbuch der philosophischen Wissenschaften. Leipzig, 1827. 5v.

Phil 95.2.2A   Krug, Wilhelm Traugott. Allgemeines Handwörterbuch der philosophischen Wissenschaften. 2e Aufl. Leipzig, 1832-38. 5v.

Phil 95.2.2B   Krug, Wilhelm Traugott. Allgemeines Handworterbuch der philosophischen Wissenschaften. 2e Aufl. Leipzig, 1832-38. 6v.

Phil 95.3   Krauth, C.P. Vocabulary of the philosophical sciences. N.Y., 1878.

VPhil 95.4   Kratki slovar' po filosofii. Moskva, 1966.

Phil 95.4.2   Kratki slovar' po filosofii. Izd.2. Moskva, 1970.

Phil 95.5   Kratkii anglo-russkii filosofskii slovar'. Moskva, 1969.

Phil 96.1   Lossius, J.C. Neues Philosophie Real-Lexikon. Erfurt, 1803-06. 4v.

Phil 96.3   Lalande, A. Vocabulaire technique et critique de la philosophie. Paris, 1926. 2v.

Phil 96.4   Lalande, A. Vocabulaire technique et critique de la philosophie. 4. ed. Paris, 1932. 3v.

Phil 96.4.8   Lalande, A. Vocabulaire technique et critique de la philosophie. Paris, 1960.

Phil 96.5   Lamanna, E.P. Dizionario di termini filosofia. Firenze, 1951.

Phil 96.6   Lopes de Mattos, Carlos. Vocabulario filosófico. Sao Paulo, 1957.

Phil 97.1   Maimon, S. Philosophisches Wörterbuch. Berlin, 1791.

Phil 97.2   Mellin, G.S.A. Encyclopädisches Wörterbuch der Philosophie. Leipzig, 1797. 6v.

Phil 97.2.5   Mellin, G.S.A. Kunstsprache der kritischen Philosophie. Jena, 1798.

Phil 97.3   Mauthner, F. Wörterbuch der Philosphie. München, 1910. 2v.

Phil 97.4   Mayer, M.B. A primary glossary of psychological and philosophical terms. N.Y., 1932.

Phil 85 - 110   Reference works on philosophy - Dictionaries and encyclopedias - Others (A-Z) - cont.

Phil 97.5   Melzer, J.H. Guide to philosophical terminology. Ashland, Ohio, 1938.

Phil 97.6   Means, B.W. Selected glossary of philosophical terms. Hartford, Connecticut, 1943.

Phil 97.7   Miano, V. Dizionario filosofico. Torino, 1963.

Phil 97.10   Micraelius, Johann. Lexicon philosophicum terminorum philosophis usitatorum. Düsseldorf, 1966.

Phil 97.12   Metzke, Erwin. Handlexikon der Philosophie. Heidelberg, 1948.

Phil 98.1   Noack, L. Philosophie-Geschichtliches Lexikon. Leipzig, 1879.

Phil 98.2   Neuhaeusler, Anton Otto. Grundbegriffe der philosophischen Sprache. München, 1963.

Phil 98.3.2   Neff, Vladimir. Filosofiký sbornik pro sannonsy neboli autigorgias. 2. vyd. Praha, 1970.

Phil 99.1   Odebrecht, Rudolf. Kleines philosophisches Wörterbuch. Berlin, 1908.

Phil 99.2   Odebrecht, Rudolf. Kleines philosophiches Wörterbuch. Berlin, 1909.

Phil 100.2   Piquet, Jean Claude. Vocabulaire de philosophie. Paris, 1960.

Phil 100.5   Pallares, Eduardo. Diccionario de filosofía. 1. ed. México, 1964.

Phil 100.10.4   Philosophisches Wörterbuch. 4. Aufl. Leipzig, 1966.

Phil 100.10.7   Philosophisches Wörterbuch. 7. Aufl. Berlin, 1970. 2v.

Phil 100.15   La philosophie. Paris, 1969.

Phil 102.3   Ranzoli, C. Dizionario di scienze filosofiche. Milano, 1905.

Phil 102.3.2   Ranzoli, C. Dizionario di scienze filosofiche. 2a ed. Milano, 1916.

Phil 102.3.3   Ranzoli, C. Dizionario di scienze filosofiche. 3a ed. Milano, 1926.

Phil 102.3.4   Ranzoli, C. Dizionario di scienze filosofiche. 4. ed. Milano, 1943.

Phil 102.3.5   Ranzoli, C. Dizionario de scienze filosofiche. Milano, 1952.

Phil 102.3.6   Ranzoli, C. Dizionario de scienze filosofiche. 6. ed. Milano, 1963.

Phil 102.4   Ruckmick, C.A. German-English dictionary of psychological terms. Iowa City, 1928.

Phil 102.5   Rozental, Mark Moiseevich. Kratkii filosofskii slovar'. Moskva, 1939.

Phil 102.5.1   Rozental, Mark Moiseevich. Handbook of philosophy. N.Y., 1949.

Phil 102.5.2   Rozental', Mark Moiseevich. Kratkii filosofskii slovar'. Moskva, 1940.

Phil 102.5.3   Rozental', Mark Moiseevich. Kratkii filosofskii slovar'. Izd. 3. Moskva, 1951.

Phil 102.5.5   Rozental', Mark Moiseevich. Kratkii filosofskii slovar'. Izd. 4. Leningrad, 1954.

Phil 102.5.7   Rozental, Mark Moiseevich. Filosofskii slovar'. Moskva, 1963.

Phil 102.5.8   Rozental, Mark Moiseevich. Filosofskii slovar'. Izd. 2. Moskva, 1963.

Phil 102.5.10   Rozental, Mark Moiseevich. Filozoficky slovnik. Bratislava, 1965.

Phil 102.5.12   Rozental, Mark Moiseevich. Petit dictionnaire philosophique. Moscow, 1955.

Phil 102.5.14   Rozental, Mark Moiseevich. A dictionary of philosophy. Moscow, 1967.

Phil 102.6A   Runes, D.D. The dictionary of philosophy. N.Y., 1942.

Phil 102.6B   Runes, D.D. The dictionary of philosophy. N.Y., 1942.

Phil 102.6.5   Runes, D.D. Dictionary of thought. N.Y., 1959.

Phil 102.8   Radlov, Ernest L. Filosofskii slovar'. Sankt Peterburg, 1904.

Phil 102.8.2   Radlov, Ernest L. Filosofskii slovar'. Izd. 2. Moskva, 1913.

Phil 103.1   Signorrello, N. Lexicon peripateticum philosophico theologicum. Neapoli, 1872.

Phil 103.3   Schmidt, Heinrich. Philosophisches Wörterbuch. Leipzig, 1912.

Phil 103.3.20   Schmidt, Heinrich. Philosophisches Wörterbuch. 9. Aufl. Leipzig, 1934.

Phil 103.3.25   Schmidt, Heinrich. Philosophisches Wörterbuch. Stuttgart, 1943.

Phil 103.3.30   Schmidt, Heinrich. Philosophisches Wörterbuch. N.Y., 1945.

Phil 103.3.30.5 Schmidt, Heinrich. Philosophisches Wörterbuch. 11. Aufl. Stuttgart, 1951.

Phil 103.3.30.10 Schmidt, Heinrich. Philosophisches Wörterbuch. 13. Aufl. Stuttgart, 1955.

Phil 103.3.31   Schmidt, Heinrich. Philosophisches Wörterbuch. 14. Aufl. Stuttgart, 1957.

Phil 103.4   Semprini, G. Piccolo dizionario di coltura filosofica e scientifica. Milano, 1931.

Phil 103.4.5   Semprini, G. Nuovo dizionario di coltura filosofica e scientifica. Torino, 1952.

Phil 103.5   Sandström, C.I. Psykologisk ordbak. 2. uppl. Stockholm, 1951.

Phil 103.6   Sury, Kurt F. von. Wörterbuch der Psychologie und ihrer Grenzgebiete. Basel, 1951.

Phil 103.6.2   Sury, Kurt F. von. Wörterbuch der Psychologie und ihrer Grenzgebiete. 2. Aufl. Basel, 1958.

Phil 103.7   Stockhammer, Morris. Philosophisches Wörterbuch. Köln, 1967.

Phil 104.1   Taylor, I. Elements of thought. London, 1843.

Phil 104.1.5   Taylor, I. Elements of thought. London, 1863.

Phil 104.1.9   Taylor, I. Elements of thought. 2nd American ed. N.Y., 1851.

Phil 104.2.2   Thornmeyer, P. Philosophisches Wörterbuch. 2. Aufl. Leipzig, 1920.

Phil 104.2.3   Thornmeyer, P. Philosophisches Wörterbuch. 3e Aufl. Leipzig, 1924.

Phil 104.3   Thomson, J.R. A dictionary of philosophy in the words of philosophers. 2nd ed. London, 1892.

Phil 105.5   Urmson, J.O. The concise encyclopaedia of Western philosophy and philosophers. London, 1960.

Htn   Phil 106.1*   Voltaire, Francois Marie Arouet de. Dictionnaire philosophique. n.p., 1765.

Htn   Phil 106.1.2* Voltaire, Francois Marie Arouet de. Dictionnaire philosophique. Londres, 1765.

Htn   Phil 106.1.3* Voltaire, Francois Marie Arouet de. Dictionnaire philosophique. London, 1765.

Phil 106.1.4   Voltaire, Francois Marie Arouet de. Dictionnaire philosophique. Paris, 1816. 14v.

40

Classified Listing

Phil 85 - 110 Reference works on philosophy - Dictionaries and encyclopedias - Others (A-Z) - cont.

Phil 106.1.5 Voltaire, Francois Marie Arouet de. Dictionnaire philosophique. Paris, 1935-36. 2v.
Phil 106.1.6 Voltaire, Francois Marie Arouet de. The philosophical dictionary. v.1-2. London, 1819.
Phil 106.1.7 Voltaire, Francois Marie Arouet de. A philosophical dictionary. London, 1824. 6v.
Phil 106.1.10 Voltaire, Francois Marie Arouet de. Dictionnaire philosophique. Paris, 1954.
Phil 106.1.12 Voltaire, Francois Marie Arouet de. Dictionnaire philosophique. 6. ed. Londres, 1767. 2v.
Phil 106.1.13 Volataire, Francois Marie Arouet de. Dictionnaire philosophique. Paris, 1961.
Phil 106.1.15 Voltaire, Francois Marie Arouet de. Voltaire's philosophical dictionary. N.Y., 193-.
Phil 106.1.20 Voltaire, Francois Marie Arouet de. Philosophical dictionary. N.Y., 1969. 2v.
Phil 106.1.25 Voltaire, Francois Marie Arouet de. Aus dem philosophischen Wörterbuch. Frankfurt, 1967.
Phil 106.1.30 Voltaire, Francois Marie Arouet de. Dictionnaire philosophique. Paris, 1967.
Phil 107.1 Wynaendts Francken, C.J. Kort woordenboek van wijsgeerige kunstlermen. Haarlem 1925.
Phil 107.5 Winn, R.B. A concise dictionary of existentialism. N.Y., 1960.
Phil 110.5 Zaragueta Bengoechea, Juan. Vocabulario filosófico. Madrid, 1955.

Phil 125 Reference works on philosophy - Tables, outlines, syllabi, etc. - Folios [Discontinued]

Phil 125.1 Chicchitti-Suriani. Nozioni elementari di logica. Torino, 1887.
Phil 125.2 Rand, Benjamin. Tables of philosophy. Cambridge, 1882.
Phil 125.3 Schultze, F. Stammbaum der Philosophie. Jena, 1890.
Phil 125.4 Reiner, Julius. Philosophisches Wörterbuch. Leipzig, 1912.

Phil 126 Reference works on philosophy - Tables, outlines, syllabi, etc. - Others

Phil 126.1 Bouscaillou, R.P. Precis de philosophie. Paris, 1873.
Phil 126.2 Stier, J. Praecepta doctrinae logicae. London, 1671.
Phil 126.3 Stumpf, C. Tafeln zur Geschichte der Philosophie. Berlin, 1896.
Phil 126.3.2 Stumpf, C. Tafeln zur Geschichte der Philosophie. Berlin, 1900.
Phil 126.3.3 Stumpf, C. Tafeln zur Geschichte der Philosophie. Berlin, 1910.
Phil 126.3.4 Stumpf, C. Tafeln zur Geschichte der Philosophie. 4. Aufl. Berlin, 1928.
Phil 126.5 Quiles, Ismael. Gráficos de historia de la filosofía. Buenos Aires, 1940.
Phil 128.86 Southwestern journal of philosophy. Norman, Okla. 1,1970+

Phil 130 Reference works on philosophy - Biographical dictionaries

Htn Phil 130.1*A Martin, Benjamin. Biographia philosophica. London, 1764.
Htn Phil 130.1*B Martin, Benjamin. Biographia philosophica. London, 1764.
Phil 130.2 Lenoël, L. Les philosophes de l'antiquité. Paris, 1864.
Phil 130.3 Brasch, M. Die Klassiker der Philosophie. Leipzig, 1884-85. 3v.
Phil 130.4 Barni, Jules. Les martyrs de la libre pensée. 2. éd. Paris, 1880.
Phil 130.5 Tomlin, E.W.F. The great philosophers. London, 1949?
Phil 130.6 Hubscher, Arthur. Philosophen der Gegenwart. München, 1949.
Phil 130.6.5 Hubscher, Arthur. Denker unserer Zeit. München, 1956-57. 2v.
Phil 130.7 Decurtins, C. Kleines Philosophenlexikon. Affoltern, 1952.
Phil 130.8 Thieme, Karl. Philosophenbilden. Basel, 1952.
Phil 130.9 Neill, T.P. Makers of the modern mind. 2nd ed. Milwaukee, 1958.
Phil 130.10 De Selincourt, Audrey. Six great thinkers. London, 1958.
Phil 130.11F Słownik filozofów. Warszawa, 1966.
Phil 130.12 Directory of American philosophers. Albuquerque. 2,1967+ 4v.
Phil 130.13 Thomsen, Henrik. Hvem taenkfe hvad; filosofiens hvem-hvad-hvor. København, 1961.
Phil 130.14 Geldsetzer, L. Philosophengalerie. Düsseldorf, 1967.
Phil 130.15 American Psychological Association. Biographical directory. Washington. 1968+
Phil 130.16 International directory of philosophy and philosophers. Bowling Green, Ohio. 1,1965+

Phil 140 Pamphlet volumes on philosophy - General works

Phil 140 Pamphlet box. Philosophy. Collected biography and tracts.
Htn Phil 140.1* Pamphlet vol. Schelling, Fichte and Garnier. 4 pam.
Htn Phil 140.2* Pamphlet vol. Philosophical pamphlets. 8 pam.
Htn Phil 140.3* Pamphlet vol. Philosophical pamphlets. 9 pam.
Htn Phil 140.4* Pamphlet vol. Philosophical pamphlets. 6 pam.
Phil 140.5 Pamphlet vol. Philosophical pamphlets. 7 pam.
Phil 140.6 Pamphlet vol. Philosophical pamphlets. 10 pam.
Phil 140.7 Pamphlet vol. Philosophical pamphlets. 6 pam.
Phil 140.8 Pamphlet vol. Philosophical pamphlets. 6 pam.
Phil 140.9 Pamphlet vol. Philosophical pamphlets. 16 pam.
Phil 140.10 Pamphlet vol. Philosophical pamphlets. 8 pam.
Phil 140.11 Pamphlet vol. Philosophical pamphlets.
Phil 140.12 Pamphlet vol. Philosophical pamphlets. 16 pam.
Phil 140.12.2 Pamphlet vol. Philosophical pamphlets. 16 pam.
Phil 140.12.3 Pamphlet vol. Philosophical pamphlets. 11 pam.
Phil 140.12.4 Pamphlet vol. Philosophical pamphlets. 11 pam.
Phil 140.13 Pamphlet vol. Philosophy. German dissertations. 15 pam.
Phil 140.14 Pamphlet vol. Cosmology. Epistemology. Psychology. 9 pam.
Phil 140.15 Pamphlet vol. Philosophy. 9 pam.
Phil 140.16 Pamphlet vol. Miscellanee filosofiche. 10 pam.
Phil 140.17 Pamphlet vol. Tesi di filosofia e lettere. 8 pam.
Phil 140.18 Pamphlet vol. Metaphysics, 1893-1910. 6 pam.
Htn Phil 140.19* Pamphlet vol. Philosophy, 1877-1916. 9 pam.
Phil 140.20 Pamphlet vol. Philosophy, 1880-1909. 6 pam.
Phil 140.21F Pamphlet vol. Pragmatism.
Phil 140.22 Pamphlet box. Pragmatism.
Phil 140.23 Pamphlet box. Pragmatism. German dissertations.
Htn Phil 140.25PF* Pamphlet vol. Philosophy broadsides.
Phil 140.26 Pamphlet vol. Philosophy, 1880-1909. 6 pam.
Phil 140.30 Pamphlet vol. Philosophy, 1847-1926. 24 pam.
Phil 140.31F Pamphlet box. Philosophy, 1847-1926.
Phil 140.32 Pamphlet box. Philosophy. Miscellaneous pamphlets.
Phil 140.32.5 Pamphlet vol. Philosophy. 7 pam.

Phil 140 Pamphlet volumes on philosophy - General works - cont.

Phil 140.35 Pamphlet box. Philosophy. German dissertations.
Phil 140.40 Pamphlet box. Philosophy. Miscellaneous pamphlets.
Phil 140.45 Pamphlet vol. Philosophy. Miscellaneous pamphlets. 6 pam.
Phil 140.50 Baan, P.A.H. Psychiatrie in de maatschappij. Groningen, 1957. 8 pam.
Phil 140.51 Pamphlet vol. Philosophy. 5 pam.
Phil 140.52 Pamphlet vol. Philosophy. 7 pam.
Phil 140.55 Pamphlet vol. Wijsbegeerte. 4 pam.
Phil 140.56 Pamphlet vol. Philosophy. Russian. 4 pam.
Phil 140.57 Pamphlet vol. Philosophy. Russian. 7 pam.
Phil 140.58 Pamphlet vol. Dutch addresses on psychology. 3 pam.
Phil 140.59 Pamphlet vol. Philosophy (Russian). 4 pam.
Phil 140.60 Pamphlet vol. Philosophy. 4 pam.
Phil 140.63 Pamphlet vol. Philosophy (Russian). 5 pam.
Phil 140.64 Pamphlet vol. Philosophy (Russian). 4 pam.
Phil 140.65 Pamphlet vol. Essays on philosophy (Russian). 4 pam.
Phil 140.66 Pamphlet vol. Philosophy. Modern. 20th Century (Russian). 8 pam.
Phil 140.67 Pamphlet vol. Philosophy (Russian). 7 pam.
Phil 140.68 Pamphlet vol. Philosophy. 5 pam.
Phil 140.69 Pamphlet vol. Philosophy (Russian). 8 pam.

Phil 143 Pamphlet volumes on philosophy - Münsterberg collection

Phil 143.1 Pamphlet vol. Philosophy. A - Alr. 34 pam.
Phil 143.2 Pamphlet vol. Philosophy. Als - Arp. 38 pam.
Phil 143.3 Pamphlet vol. Philosophy. Arr - Bai. 19 pam.
Phil 143.4 Pamphlet vol. Philosophy. Bak - Bat. 24 pam.
Phil 143.5 Pamphlet vol. Philosophy. Bau - Ben. 23 pam.
Phil 143.6 Pamphlet vol. Philosophy. Ben - Bla. 30 pam.
Phil 143.7 Pamphlet vol. Philosophy. Bla - Bol. 22 pam.
Phil 143.8 Pamphlet vol. Philosophy. Bol - Bra. 30 pam.
Phil 143.9 Pamphlet vol. Philosophy. Bra - Bro. 20 pam.
Phil 143.10 Pamphlet vol. Philosophy. Bru - By. 33 pam.
Phil 143.11 Pamphlet vol. Philosophy. C - Car. 23 pam.
Phil 143.12 Pamphlet vol. Philosophy. Cas - Ch. 25 pam.
Phil 143.13 Pamphlet vol. Philosophy. Cl - Cla. 18 pam.
Phil 143.14 Pamphlet vol. Philosophy. Cle - Cou. 32 pam.
Phil 143.15 Pamphlet vol. Philosophy. Cow - Day. 25 pam.
Phil 143.16 Pamphlet vol. Philosophy. Dea - Dex. 26 pam.
Phil 143.17 Pamphlet vol. Philosophy. Die - Dre. 30 pam.
Phil 143.18 Pamphlet vol. Philosophy. Dru - Em. 29 pam.
Phil 143.19 Pamphlet vol. Philosophy. En - Fal. 29 pam.
Phil 143.20 Pamphlet vol. Philosophy. Fal - Fis. 31 pam.
Phil 143.21 Pamphlet vol. Philosophy. Fis - Fol. 32 pam.
Phil 143.22 Pamphlet vol. Philosophy. For - Fri. 30 pam.
Phil 143.23 Pamphlet vol. Philosophy. Fro - Gat. 31 pam.
Phil 143.24 Pamphlet vol. Philosophy. Gat - Glo. 28 pam.
Phil 143.25 Pamphlet vol. Philosophy. Go - Gom. 24 pam.
Phil 143.26 Pamphlet vol. Philosophy. Goo -Gro. 18 pam.
Phil 143.27 Pamphlet vol. Philosophy. Gro - Gu. 28 pam.
Phil 143.28 Pamphlet vol. Philosophy. H - Ham. 37 pam.
Phil 143.29 Pamphlet vol. Philosophy. Han - Has. 27 pam.
Phil 143.30 Pamphlet vol. Philosophy. Hat - Hel. 29 pam.
Phil 143.31 Pamphlet vol. Philosophy. Hel - Heu. 27 pam.
Phil 143.32 Pamphlet vol. Philosophy. Hey - Hir. 23 pam.
Phil 143.33 Pamphlet vol. Philosophy. Hir - Hol. 28 pam.
Phil 143.34 Pamphlet vol. Philosophy. Hol - How. 24 pam.
Phil 143.35 Pamphlet vol. Philosophy. Hoz - Jac. 32 pam.
Phil 143.36 Pamphlet vol. Philosophy. Jac - Jer. 24 pam.
Phil 143.37 Pamphlet vol. Philosophy. Jes - Kae. 24 pam.
Phil 143.38 Pamphlet vol. Philosophy. Kae - Kel. 30 pam.
Phil 143.39 Pamphlet vol. Philosophy. Kel - Kin. 28 pam.
Phil 143.40 Pamphlet vol. Philosophy. Kir - Kn. 29 pam.
Phil 143.41 Pamphlet vol. Philosophy. Ko - Kra. 28 pam.
Phil 143.42 Pamphlet vol. Philosophy. Kra - Ky. 32 pam.
Phil 143.43 Pamphlet vol. Philosophy. L - Lan. 19 pam.
Phil 143.44 Pamphlet vol. Philosophy. Lan - Las. 25 pam.
Phil 143.45 Pamphlet vol. Philosophy. Lay - Lei. 29 pam.
Phil 143.46 Pamphlet vol. Philosophy. Lei - Lic. 24 pam.
Phil 143.47 Pamphlet vol. Philosophy. Lie - Ll. 27 pam.
Phil 143.48 Pamphlet vol. Philosophy. Lo - Ly. 26 pam.
Phil 143.49 Pamphlet vol. Philosophy. M - McG. 16 pam.
Phil 143.50 Pamphlet vol. Philosophy. Mach - Mar. 31 pam.
Phil 143.51 Pamphlet vol. Philosophy. Mas - Mel. 32 pam.
Phil 143.52 Pamphlet vol. Philosophy. Mer - Min. 31 pam.
Phil 143.53 Pamphlet vol. Philosophy. Min - Mol. 23 pam.
Phil 143.54 Pamphlet vol. Philosophy. Mol - Moo. 20 pam.
Phil 143.55 Pamphlet vol. Philosophy. Mor - Mui. 30 pam.
Phil 143.56 Pamphlet vol. Philosophy. Mun - Nat. 34 pam.
Phil 143.57 Pamphlet vol. Philosophy. Nat - Nu. 27 pam.
Phil 143.58 Pamphlet vol. Philosophy. O - Op. 28 pam.
Phil 143.59 Pamphlet vol. Philosophy. Or - Pau. 29 pam.
Phil 143.60 Pamphlet vol. Philosophy. Pau - Pet. 24 pam.
Phil 143.61 Pamphlet vol. Philosophy. Pet - Pfe. 13 pam.
Phil 143.62 Pamphlet vol. Philosophy. Pfl - Pil. 34 pam.
Phil 143.63 Pamphlet vol. Philosophy. Pio - Pur. 23 pam.
Phil 143.64 Pamphlet vol. Philosophy. Put - Ran. 25 pam.
Phil 143.65 Pamphlet vol. Philosophy. Rap - Rei. 15 pam.
Phil 143.66 Pamphlet vol. Philosophy. Rei - Rit. 27 pam.
Phil 143.67 Pamphlet vol. Philosophy. Rob -Roy. 35 pam.
Phil 143.68 Pamphlet vol. Philosophy. Ru - Scha. 25 pam.
Phil 143.69 Pamphlet vol. Philosophy. Scha - Schl. 17 pam.
Phil 143.70 Pamphlet vol. Philosophy. Schm - Schr. 30 pam.
Phil 143.71 Pamphlet vol. Philosophy. Schr - Schu. 13 pam.
Phil 143.72 Pamphlet vol. Philosophy. Schu - Sel. 25 pam.
Phil 143.73 Pamphlet vol. Philosophy. Set - Sie. 25 pam.
Phil 143.74 Pamphlet vol. Philosophy. Sie - Sm. 33 pam.
Phil 143.75 Pamphlet vol. Philosophy. So - Spe. 27 pam.
Phil 143.76 Pamphlet vol. Philosophy. Spi - Ste. 18 pam.
Phil 143.77 Pamphlet vol. Philosophy. Ste - Sto. 25 pam.
Phil 143.78 Pamphlet vol. Philosophy. Str - Stu. 27 pam.
Phil 143.79 Pamphlet vol. Philosophy. Swi - Tho. 29 pam.
Phil 143.80 Pamphlet vol. Philosophy. Thu - Tr. 29 pam.
Phil 143.81 Pamphlet vol. Philosophy. Ts - Up. 21 pam.
Phil 143.82 Pamphlet vol. Philosophy. Ur - Vil. 15 pam.
Phil 143.83 Pamphlet vol. Philosophy. Vil - Wan. 28 pam.
Phil 143.84 Pamphlet vol. Philosophy. Wat - Wei. 20 pam.
Phil 143.85 Pamphlet vol. Philosophy. Wei - Wey. 16 pam.
Phil 143.86 Pamphlet vol. Philosophy. Wh - Wil. 23 pam.
Phil 143.87 Pamphlet vol. Philosophy. Wil - Wir. 27 pam.
Phil 143.88 Pamphlet vol. Philosophy. Wit - Woo. 20 pam.
Phil 143.89 Pamphlet vol. Philosophy. Woo - Wy. 22 pam.
Phil 143.90 Pamphlet vol. Philosophy. Y - Z. 20 pam.
Phil 143.91 Pamphlet vol. Philosophy. A - D. 37 pam.
Phil 143.92 Pamphlet vol. Philosophy. E - G. 21 pam.
Phil 143.93 Pamphlet vol. Philosophy. H - Hue. 34 pam.

Phil 143   **Pamphlet volumes on philosophy - Münsterberg collection - cont.**
Phil 143.94   Pamphlet vol. Philosophy. Hum - Kr. 30 pam.
Phil 143.95   Pamphlet vol. Philosophy. Ku - Me. 39 pam.
Phil 143.96   Pamphlet vol. Philosophy. Mi - Par. 20 pam.
Phil 143.97   Pamphlet vol. Philosophy. Par - Pot. 23 pam.
Phil 143.98   Pamphlet vol. Philosophy. Pr - Sha. 39 pam.
Phil 143.99   Pamphlet vol. Philosophy. She - St. 26 pam.
Phil 143.100   Pamphlet vol. Philosophy. T - Z. 26 pam.
Phil 143.101F   Pamphlet vol. Philosophy. 48 pam.
Phil 143.102F   Pamphlet vol. Philosophy. 12 pam.

Phil 150   **Terminology and nomenclature of philosophy**
Phil 150.01   Pamphlet box. Philosophical nomenclature.
Phil 150.1   Tönnies, F. Philosophische Terminologie. Leipzig, 1906.
Phil 150.5   Lalande, André. Sur la critique et la fixation du langage philosophique. Paris, 19- . 2 pam.
Phil 150.10   Mateucci, Arturo. Vocabularietto di termini filosofici. Milano, 1925.
Phil 150.15   Ranzoli, C. Il linguaggio dei filosofi. Padova, 1911.
Phil 150.20   Report of the committee on definitions of the American Philosophical Association. N.Y., 1911.
Phil 150.25   Belaval, Y. Les philosophes et leur langage. Paris, 1952.
Phil 150.26   Afnan, Soheil. Philosophical terminology in Arabic and Persian. Leiden, 1964.

Phil 165   **General treatises on philosophy - Collected authors**
Phil 165.1   Smith, T.V. From Descartes to Kant. Chicago, 1940.
Phil 165.2A   Muelder, Walter G. The development of American philosophy. Boston, 1940.
Phil 165.2B   Muelder, Walter G. The development of American philosophy. Boston, 1940.
Phil 165.2.5   Muelder, Walter G. The development of American philosophy. 2. ed. Boston, 1960.
Phil 165.3   Avey, A.E. Readings in philosophy. N.Y., 1936.
Phil 165.4   Clark, G.H. Selections from Hellenistic philosophy. N.Y., 1940.
Phil 165.5   Schmid, Bastian. Philosophisches Lesebuch zum Gebrauch an höheren Schulen und zum Selbststudium. Leipzig, 1906.
Phil 165.6   Bronstein, D.J. Basic problems of philosophy. N.Y., 1947.
Phil 165.7   Baldwin, R.C. An introduction to philosophy through literature. N.Y., 1950.
Phil 165.8   Ballauff, T. Das gnoseologische Problem. Göttingen, 1949.
Phil 165.9   Les quarante années scientifique de Theophile Boreas. Athénes, 1940. 2v.
Phil 165.10   Donum lustrale. Noviomagi, 1949.
Phil 165.11   Philosophie der Wirklichkeitsmäke. Wien, 1949.
Phil 165.12   Heinrich, Walter. Die Ganzheit in Philosophie und Wissenschaft. Wien, 1950.
Phil 165.13   Black, M. Philosophical analysis. Ithaca, 1950.
Phil 165.13.5A   Black, Max. Problems of analysis. Ithaca, 1954.
Phil 165.13.5B   Black, Max. Problems of analysis. Ithaca, 1954.
Phil 165.14   Glockner, H. Philosophisches lesebuch. Stuttgart, 1949-50. 2v.
Phil 165.15   Falkenhahn, W. Veritati. München, 1949.
Phil 165.16   Anteile. Frankfurt am Main, 1950.
Phil 165.17   Moore, C.A. Essays in East-West philosophy. Honolulu, 1951.
Phil 165.18   Essays in psychology. Uppsala, 1951.
Phil 165.19   Archivio di Filosofia. Il compito della Metafisica. Milano, 1952.
Phil 165.20   Radhakrishnan. London, 1951.
Phil 165.21   Ryan, J.K. Philosophical studies in honor of the very Reverend Ignatius Smith. Westminster, Maryland, 1952.
Phil 165.22   Piper, K. Olfener Horizont. München, 1953.
Phil 165.23   L'homme, le monde. Grenoble, 1948.
Phil 165.24   Hanslmeier, J. Natur, Geist, Geschichte. München, 1950.
Phil 165.25   Ordre, désordre, lumière. Paris, 1952.
Phil 165.26   Runes, D.D. Treasury of philosophy. N.Y., 1955.
Phil 165.27   Edman, Irwin. Landmarks for beginners in philosophy. N.Y., 1948?
Phil 165.28   Padovani, U.A. Grande antologia filosofica. Milano, 1954. 16v.
Phil 165.30   Analysis. Oxford, England. Philosophy and analysis. N.Y., 1954.
Phil 165.35   Wagner, Johannes. Was ist der Mensch? 2. Aufl. Braunschweig, 1954.
Phil 165.35.5   Wagner, Johannes. Vom Ursprung und Sinn des philosophischen Fragens. Braunschweig, 1954.
Phil 165.40   Gropp, R.O. Festschrift. Berlin, 1955.
Phil 165.40.5   Bloch, Ernest. Wissen und Hoffen. Berlin, 1955.
Phil 165.45   Palmeró, J. La philosophie par les textes. Paris, 1955.
Phil 165.50   Rader, M.M. The enduring questions. N.Y., 1956.
Phil 165.55   Organ, F.W. The examined life. Boston, 1956.
Phil 165.60   A.R. Wadia. Bangalore, 1954.
Phil 165.65   Archivio di Filosofia. Filosofia e simbolismo. Roma, 1956.
Phil 165.66   Archivio di Filosofia. La diaristica filosofica. Padova, 1959.
Phil 165.67   Archivio di Filosofia. Metafisica ed esperienza religiosa. Roma, 1956.
Phil 165.70   Burnett, Whit. This is my philosophy. 1st ed. N.Y., 1957.
Phil 165.75   Ohio State University, Columbus. Department of Philosophy. Perspectives in philosophy. Columbus, 1953.
Phil 165.80   Bari (City). Università. Istituto di Storia della Filosofia. Contributi di A. Corsana. Trani, 1955.
Phil 165.85   Mandelbaum, Maurice H. Philosophic problems. N.Y., 1957.
Phil 165.86   Mandelbaum, Maurice H. Philosophic problems. N.Y., 1961.
Phil 165.86.2   Mandelbaum, Maurice H. Philosophic problems. N.Y., 1966.
Phil 165.90   Levi, A.W. Varieties of experience. N.Y., 1957.
Phil 165.95   Mélanges de philosophie grecque. Paris, 1956.
Phil 165.100   Hommage á Gaston Bachelard. Paris, 1957.
Phil 165.105   Edwards, Paul. A modern introduction to philosophy. Glencoe, Illinois, 1957.
Phil 165.105.2   Edwards, Paul. A modern introduction to philosophy. N.Y., 1965.
Phil 165.110   Satin, J.H. Ideas in context. Boston, 1958.
Phil 165.115   Estudios de historia de la filosofía. Tucumán, 1957. 2v.
Phil 165.120   Ziegler, Klaus. Wesen und Wirklichkeit des Menschen. Göttingen, 1957.
Phil 165.125   Grateloup, Léon. Expérience - connaissance. Paris, 1957.
Phil 165.130   Derathé, Robert. La justice et la violence. Paris, 1958.
Phil 165.135   Sociedad Cubana de Filosofía. Conversaciones filosóficas interamericanas. Habana, 1955.
Phil 165.140   Im Dienste der Wahrheit. Bern, 1958.
Phil 165.145   O'Neil, Charles J. An Etienne Gilson tribute presented by his North American students. Milwaukee, 1959.

Phil 165   **General treatises on philosophy - Collected authors - cont.**
Phil 165.145.5   Mélanges offerts à Étienne Gilson de l'Académie Française. Toronto, 1959.
Phil 165.150   Koch, Adrienne. Philosophy for a time of crisis. N.Y., 1959.
Phil 165.155   Logica. Neuchâtel, 1959.
Phil 165.160   Philosophie der Toleranz. Graz, 1959.
Phil 165.165   Edel, Reiner F. Ein Weiser lebt unter uns. Marburg, 1958.
Phil 165.169   Ksiega pamiątkowa ku uczczeniu piętnastolecia pracy nauczycielskiej w Uniwersytecie Warszawskim profesora Tadeusza Kotarbińskiego. Warszawa, 1934.
Phil 165.170   Ksiega pamiątkowa ku uczczeniu czterdziestolecia pracy nauczycielskiej. Warszawa, 1959.
Phil 165.171   Fragmenty filozoficzne, seria trzecia. Warszawa, 1967.
Phil 165.173   For Roman Ingarden. 's Gravenhage, 1959.
Phil 165.175   Henrich, Dieter. Die Gegenwart der Griechen im neueren Denken. Tübingen, 1960.
Phil 165.175.5   Henrich, Dieter. Subjektivität und Metaphysik. Frankfurt, 1966.
Phil 165.180   Aristotelian Society for the Systematic Study of Philosophy. Concepts of continuity. v.4. London, 1924.
Phil 165.185   Huber, Gerhard. Philosophie und deristliche Existenz. Basel, 1960.
Phil 165.190   Le symbole. Paris, 1959.
Phil 165.195   Classics in philosophy and ethics. N.Y., 1960.
Phil 165.200   Collins, James. Readings in ancient and medieval philosophy. Westminster, 1960.
Phil 165.205   Clark, John A. The student seeks an answer. Waterville, Me., 1960.
Phil 165.210   Höfling, Helmut. Beiträge zer Philosphie und Wissenschaft. München, 1960.
Phil 165.215   Wisser, Richard. Sinn und Sein. Tubingen, 1960.
Phil 165.220   La philosophie et ses problèmes. Lyon, 1960.
Phil 165.225   Derbolav, Josef. Erkenntnis und Verantwortung. Düsseldorf, 1960.
Phil 165.230   Brinton, Crane. The fate of man. N.Y., 1961.
Phil 165.235   Comoth, R. Philosophes du dix neuvième siècle. Bruxelles, 1960.
Phil 165.240   Bergman, S. Studies in philosophy. Jerusalem, 1960.
Phil 165.245   Ramsey, J.T. Prospect for metaphysics. London, 1961.
Phil 165.250   Marcus, Aage. Livsanskuelse gennem tiderne. København, 1955-58. 10v.
Phil 165.255   Myers, G.E. Self, religion and metaphysics. N.Y., 1961.
Phil 165.265   Brunhold, C. De Montaigne à Luis de Broglie. 8. ed. Paris, 1958?
Phil 165.270   Magill, F.N. Masterpieces of world philosophy in summary form. 1st ed. N.Y., 1961.
Phil 165.275   Experiencia de la vida. Madrid, 1960.
Phil 165.280   Lieb, Irwin C. Experience, existence and good. Carbondale, 1961.
Phil 165.285   Charisteria; rozprawy filozoficzne, złozone w darze Władysłáawowi Tatarkiewiczowi. Warszawa, 1960.
Phil 165.290   Anscombe, G.E.M. Three philosophers. Ithaca, N.Y., 1961.
Phil 165.295   Bulgarska Akademiia na Naukite, Sofia. Vuprosi na dialekticheskiia materializum i na chastnite kauki. Sofiia, 1961.
Phil 165.300   Emge, Carl August. Kreise um Schopenhauer. Wiesbaden, 1962.
Phil 165.305   Logic and language. Holland, 1962.
Phil 165.310   Lucas, Eric. What is a man. London, 1962.
Phil 165.315   Perspectief; feestbundel. Kampen, 1961.
Phil 165.320   Temi e problemi di filosofia classica. Milano, 1960.
Phil 165.322   Studi di filosofia e di storia della filosofia in onore di Francesco Olgiati. Milano, 1962.
Phil 165.324   Drennen, D. A modern introduction to metaphysics. N.Y., 1962.
Phil 165.326   Joaquim de Carvalho no Brazil. Coimbra, 1958.
Phil 165.328   Hartmann, Klaus. Lebendiger Realismus. Bonn, 1962.
Phil 165.330   Essays in philosophy presented to Dr. T.M.P. Mahadevan. Madras, 1962.
Phil 165.332   Butler, R.J. Analytical philosophy. Oxford, 1962.
Phil 165.332.2   Butler, R.J. Analytical philosophy. 2nd series. Oxford, 1965.
Phil 165.334   Festschrift für Karl Joël zum 70. Geburtstage (27 März 1934). Basel, 1934.
Phil 165.336   Frank, J. Horizons of a philosopher. Leiden, 1963.
Phil 165.337   McMullin, Ethan. The concept of matter. Notre Dame, Indiana, 1963.
Phil 165.337.5   McMullin, Ethan. The concept of matter in Greek and medieval philosophy. Notre Dame, 1965.
Phil 165.338   Congrès des Sociétés de Philosophie de Langue Française, 11th, Montpelier, 1961. Existence et nature. Paris, 1962.
Phil 165.339   Oehler, K. Einsichten. Frankfurt a.M., 1962.
Phil 165.340A   Besch, L. Menschenbild und Lebensführung. München, 1963.
Phil 165.340B   Besch, L. Menschenbild und Lebensführung. München, 1963.
Phil 165.341   Cuvillier, A. Textes choisis des auteurs philosophiques. v.2. Paris, 1961.
Phil 165.342   Szkice filozoficzne; Romanowi Ingardinowi w darze. Warszawa, 1964.
Phil 165.343   Bunge, M. The critical approach to sciences and philosophy. N.Y., 1964.
Phil 165.344   Essays in ontology. Iowa City, 1963.
Phil 165.345   Davies, H.S. The English mind. Cambridge, Eng., 1964.
Phil 165.346   Rasheed, A. The notion of existence. Lahore, 1959.
Phil 165.347   Gerner-Beuerle, M. Schäpferisches Leben. München, 1964.
Phil 165.348   Reese, William L. Process and divinity. LaSalle, Illinois, 1964.
Phil 165.349   Rozprawy logiczne. Warszawa, 1964.
Phil 165.350   Ensayos filosóficos. Buenos Aires, 1963.
Phil 165.351   Tymieniecka, Anna Teresa. Contributions to logic and methodology in honor of J.M. Bochenski. Amsterdam, 1965.
Phil 165.352   Collegium Philosophicum; Studien Joachim Ritter zum 60. Geburtstage. Basel, 1965.
Phil 165.353   Institutiones philosophiae. Torino, 1961-63. 7v.
Phil 165.354   Philosophy and Christianity. Kampen, 1965.
Phil 165.355   American Academy for Jewish Research. Harry Austryn Wolfson. Jerusalem, 1965.
Phil 165.360   Delius, Harald. Argumentationen. Göttingen, 1964.
Phil 165.361   Ksiega pamiątkowa ku czci prof. W. Heinricha. Kraków, 1927.
Phil 165.362   Spirito, Ugo. Storia antologica dei problemi filosofici. Firenze, 1965. 7v.
Phil 165.364   Kennick, William E. Metaphysics; readings and reappraisals. Englewood Cliffs, N.J., 1966.
Phil 165.365   Koktanek, Anton Mirko. Philosophischer Eros im Wandel der Zeit. München, 1965.
Phil 165.366   Tamás, György. Selected studies. Budapest, 1965.

Phil 165   General treatises on philosophy - Collected authors - cont.

Phil 165.367   Daues, Vincent F. Wisdom in depth. Milwaukee, 1966.
Phil 165.368   Vaira. Budapest, 1960.
Phil 165.369   Science, folklore, and philosophy. N.Y., 1966.
Phil 165.370   Landgrebe, Ludwig. Beispiela. Den Haag, 1965.
Phil 165.372   Mann, Jesse Aloysius. Perspectives on reality; readings in metaphysics. N.Y., 1966.
Phil 165.373   Rouner, Leroy S. Philosophy, religion, and the coming world civilization. The Hague, 1966.
Phil 165.374   Dr. S. Radhakrishnan souvenir volume. Moradabad, 1964.
Phil 165.375   Friedman, Maurice Stanley. The worlds of existentialism. N.Y., 1964.
Phil 165.376   Feyerabend, Paul. Mind, matter, and method. Minneapolis, 1966.
Phil 165.378   Dommeyer, Frederick C. Current philosophical issues; essays in honor of Curt John Ducasse. Springfield, Illinois, 1966.
Phil 165.380   Ritzel, Wolfgang. Rationalität, Phänomenalität, Individualität. Bonn, 1966.
Phil 165.382   Kaulbach, Friedrich. Kritik und Metaphysik; Studien. Berlin, 1966.
Phil 165.384   Browning, Douglas. Philosophers of process. N.Y., 1965.
Phil 165.386   Findlay, John N. Studies in philosophy: British Academy lectures. London, 1966.
Phil 165.388   Iadir, C.A. The world of philosophy. Lahore, 1965.
Phil 165.390   Braun, Cornelis Gerardus Franciscus. Filia. Wijsgerige opstellen in vriendschap aangeboden aan Prof. Dr. J.H. Robbers. Nijmegen, 1966.
Phil 165.392   Adelmann, Frederick. The quest for the absolute. Chestnut Hill, 1966.
Phil 165.393   Schoenman, Ralph. Bertrand Russell, philosopher of the century. London, 1967.
Phil 165.395   L'histoire de la philosophie; ses problèmes, ses méthodes. Paris, 1964.
Phil 165.400   Philosophical essays, dedicated to Gunnar Aspelin on the occasion of his sixty-fifth birthday, the 23rd of September 1963. Lund, 1963.
Phil 165.402   Feigl, Herbert. Readings in philosophical analysis. N.Y., 1949.
Phil 165.405   Die Philosophie und die Wissenschaften. Simon Moser zum 65. Geburtstag. Meisenheim am Glan, 1967.
Phil 165.408   Festschrift für Joseph Klien zum 70. Geburtstag. Göttingen, 1967.
VPhil 165.409   Łowne zagadnienia filozofii. v.3. Warszawa, 1966.
Phil 165.410   Natur und Geschichte. Stuttgart, 1967.
Phil 165.412   Sidney Hook and contemporary world; essay on the pragmatie intelligence. N.Y., 1968.
Phil 165.415   World perspectives in philosophy, religion and culture. Patna, 1968.
Phil 165.418   Tradition und Kritik. Stuttgart 1967.
Phil 165.420   Strawson, Peter Frederick. Studies in the philosophy of thought and action. London, 1968.
Phil 165.422   L'endurance de la pensée; pour saluer Jean Beaufret. Paris, 1968.
Phil 165.424   Le réel et l'irréel. Paris, 1968.
Phil 165.426   Anton, John Peter. Naturalism and historical understanding. Albany, 1967.
Phil 165.427   Filosofskie nauki. Stavropol', 1967.
Phil 165.430   Gestalt und Wirklichkeit. Berlin, 1967.
Phil 165.432   Rescher, Nicholas. Essays in philosophical analysis. Pittsburg, 1969.
Phil 165.434A   Mélanges à la mémoire de Charles de Koninck. Québec, 1968.
Phil 165.434B   Mélanges à la mémoire de Charles de Koninck. Québec, 1968.
Phil 165.436   Probleme der Wissenschaftstheorie; Festschrift für Victor Kroft. Wien, 1960.
Phil 165.438   MacIntosh, John James. The business of reason. London, 1969.
Phil 165.440   Gadamer, Hans Georg. Philosophisches Lesebuch. Frankfurt a.M., 1965- 3v.
Phil 165.442   Essays in honor of Carl G. Hempel. Dordrecht, 1970.
Phil 165.444   Studenty - Oktiabriu. Moskva, 1968.
Phil 165.446   Wahrheit, Wert und Sein; Festgabe für Dietrich von Hildebrand zum 80. Geburtstag. Regensburg, 1970.
Phil 165.448   Einführung in die Psychologie. Frankfurt, 1969.
Phil 165.450   Phenomenology and social reality. The Hague, 1970.
Phil 165.452   Phaenomenologie, Rechtsphilosophie, Jurisprudenz. Frankfurt, 1969.
Phil 165.454   Giacon, Carlo. Saggi e ricerche su Alessandro di Afrodisia, Avicenna, Miceli, Brentano, Jaspers, Ingarden, Carr. Padova, 1970.
Phil 165.456   Wolff, Robert Paul. Philosophy. Englewood Cliffs, 1971.
Phil 165.458   Essays in metaphysics, by members of the philosophy department, the Pennsylvania State University. University Park, 1970.
Phil 165.460   Studi in onore di Antonio Corsano. Manduria, 1970.
Phil 165.462   Hommage à Jean Hyppolite. 1. ed. Paris, 1971.
Phil 165.464   Studi in memoria di Carlo Ascheri. Urbino, 1970.
Phil 165.466   Logic and art. Indianapolis, 1972.

Phil 170   General treatises on philosophy - Folios [Discontinued]

Phil 170.1   Chase, P.E. Intellectual symbolism. Philadelphia, 1863.
Htn   Phil 170.2*   Fludd, Robert. Mosaicall philosophy. London, 1659.
Htn   Phil 170.2.5F*   Fludd, Robert. Philosophia moysaica. Goudae, 1638.
Phil 170.3   Hutton, James. Investigation of the principles of knowledge. Edinburgh, 1794. 3v.
Phil 170.5   Holland, F.M. Facts about Hegel and other essays. Boston, 1880-81.

Phil 175 - 200   General treatises on philosophy - Individual authors (A-Z)

Phil 175.1   Abicht, J.H. System der Elementarphilosophie. Erlangen, 1795.
Phil 175.2   Alaux, J.E. L'analyse métaphysique. Paris, 1872.
Phil 175.2.5   Alaux, J.E. La raison. Paris, 1860.
Phil 175.2.8   Alaux, J.E. Métaphysique considérée comme science. Paris, 1879.
Phil 175.3   Alexander, A. Some problems of philosophy. N.Y., 1886.
Phil 175.4   Allibaco, W.A. Philosophic and scientific ultimatum. N.Y., 1864.
Phil 175.5   Amersin, F. Gemeinverständliche Weisheitslehre. Triest, 1881.
Phil 175.5.5   Amersin, F. Populäre Philosophie oder leichtfassliche Einfuhrung in die Weisheitslehre. Graz, 1872.
Phil 175.6   Ancillon, F. Essais de philosophie. Paris, 1832. 4v.
Phil 175.6.2   Ancillon, F. Essais de philosophie. Paris, 1832. 4v.
Phil 175.6.6   Ancillon, F. Essai sur la science. Paris, 1829.
Phil 175.6.9   Ancillon, F. Uber Glauben und Wissen in der Philosophie. Berlin, 1824.

Phil 175 - 200   General treatises on philosophy - Individual authors (A-Z) - cont.

Phil 175.6.15   Ancillon, F. Pensées sur l'homme, ses rapports. Berlin, 1829. 2v.
Phil 175.6.20   Ancillon, F. Mélanges de littérature et de philosophie. Paris, 1809. 2v.
Phil 175.8   Abhandlungen der Fries'schen Schule. Leipzig. 1847-1918 5v.
Phil 175.9   Argens, J.B. La philosophie du Bon-Sens. La Haye, 1765. 2v.
Phil 175.9.2   Argens, J.B. La philosophie du Bon-Sens. La Haye, 1755. 3v.
Phil 175.9.5   Argens, J.B. The impartial philosopher. London, 1749. 2v.
Phil 175.9.8   Argens, J.B. Philosophical dissertations. London, 1753. 2v.
Phil 175.10   Asmus, P. Das Ich. Halle, 1873.
Phil 175.11   Aulard, A. Éléments de philosophie. Paris, 1869.
Phil 175.12   Avenarius, R. Der menschliche Weltbegriff. Leipzig, 1891.
Phil 175.12.9   Ewald, Oskar. Richard Avenarius. Berlin, 1905.
Phil 175.13   Ampère, A.M. Philosophie. Paris, 1870.
Phil 175.13.9   Lorenz, B. Die Philosophie A.M. Ampères. Berlin, 1908.
Phil 175.14   Alexander, H.B. The problem of mataphysics and the meaning of metaphysical explenation. Diss. N.Y., 1902.
Phil 175.14.2   Alexander, H.B. The problem of mataphysics and the meaning of metaphysical explenation. N.Y., 1902.
Phil 175.14.5   Alexander, H.B. Nature and human nature. Chicago, 1923.
Phil 175.15   Armstrong, A.C. Transitional eras in thought. N.Y., 1904.
Phil 175.16   Arnold, R.B. Scientific fact and metaphysical reality. London, 1904.
Phil 175.17   Abbott, F.E. The syllogistic philosophy. Boston, 1906. 2v.
Phil 175.18   Arndt, Julius. Des Bewusstwerden der Menschheit. Halle, 1850.
Phil 175.19   Abauzit, Frank. L'absolutisme intellectuel. Saint-Blaise, 1909.
Phil 175.20   Appleton, J.H. Doctor Charles E.C.B. Appleton: his life and literary relics. London, 1881.
Phil 175.21   Andrews, S.P. Basic outlines of universology. N.Y., 1872.
Phil 175.22   Aars, K.B.R. Zur psychologischen Analyse der Welt. Leipzig, 1900.
Phil 175.24   Auerbach, Mathias. Einfälle und Betrachtungen. Dresden, 1904.
Phil 175.25   Ambrosi, Luigi. Il primo passo alla filosofia. v.3. 5a ed. Milano, 1915.
Phil 175.26   Aliotta, Antonio. La guerra eterna e il dramma dell'esistenza. Napoli, 1917.
Phil 175.26.2   Aliotta, Antonio. La guerra eterna e il dramma dell'esistenza. 2a ed. Napoli, 1920.
Phil 175.26.5   Aliotta, Antonio. La teoria di Einstein. Palmero, 1922.
Phil 175.26.9   Aliotta, Antonio. L'esperimento nella scienza. Napoli, 1936.
Phil 175.27   Anhuth, R.O. Das wahnsinnige Bewusstsein. Halle, 1877.
Phil 175.28.2   Avey, A.E. Readings in philosophy. N.Y., 1924.
Phil 175.29   Abbagnano, N. Le sorgenti irrazionali del pensiero. Genova, 1923.
Phil 175.30   Azais, H. Cours de philosophie générale. Paris, 1824. 8v.
Phil 175.31   Aquisto, B. d'. Elementi di filosofia fondamentale. Palermo, 1857.
Phil 175.33   Arch, Robert. Whence, whither, and why? London, 1926.
Phil 175.34   Ahlberg, Alf. De filosofiska grundproblemen. Stockholm, 1922.
Phil 175.35   Atterbom, P.D.A. Inledning till philosphiens system. Upsala, 1835.
Phil 175.36   Alstrin, Eric. Dissertationis academicae. pt.1-2. Upsaliae, 1728.
Phil 175.37   Adolph, Heinrich. Personalistische Philosophie. Leipzig, 1931.
Phil 175.38.4   Ayer, Alfred J. Language, truth and logic. London, 1938.
Phil 175.38.15A   Ayer, Alfred J. Language, truth and logic. N.Y., 1952.
Phil 175.38.15B   Ayer, Alfred J. Language, truth and logic. N.Y., 1952.
Phil 175.39   Accambray, Leon. Un testament philosophique. Paris, 1937.
Phil 175.40   Anderson, L.F. God and the cosmic order. N.Y., 1939.
Phil 175.40.5   Anderson, L.F. Logic and the cosmic order. N.Y., 1939.
Phil 175.41   Alessio, Roberto de. Ensayos de filosofía prática. Montevideo, 19- .
Phil 175.43   Alquié, Ferdinand. Le désir d'éternité. 1. ed. Paris, 1943.
Phil 175.43.4   Alquié, Ferdinand. Le désir d'éternité. 4th ed. Paris, 1963.
Phil 175.43.10   Alquié, Ferdinand. La nostalgie de l'être. Paris, 1950.
Phil 175.43.11   Alquié, Ferdinand. La nostalgie de l'être. Thèse. Paris, 1950.
Phil 175.44   Adams, George P. Man and metaphysics. N.Y., 1948.
Phil 175.45   Archivio di Filosofia. Il compito della fenomenologia. Padova, 1957.
Phil 175.50   Adamczyk, S. Matafzika ogólna czyli ontologia. Lublin, 1960.
Phil 175.52   Austin, John L. Philosophical papers. Oxford, 1961.
Phil 175.52.2   Austin, John L. Philosophical papers. 2d ed. Oxford, 1970.
Phil 175.52.5   Austin, John L. How to do things with words. Cambridge, 1962.
Phil 175.54   Abraches, Cassiano. Metafísica. Braga, 1956.
Phil 175.56   Armour, Leslie. The rational and the real. The Hague, 1962.
Phil 175.58   Ando, Takatuna. Metaphysics. Hague, 1963.
Phil 175.59   Amado Levy-Valensi, E. Les niveaux de l'être la connaissance et le mal. Paris, 1962.
Phil 175.60   Akademiia Nauk URSR, Kiev. Institut Filosofii. Liudyna i svitohliad. Kyiv, 1963.
Phil 175.61   Akademiia Nauk SSSR. Nauchnyi Sovet po Filosofskim Voprosam Estestvoznaniia. O sushchnosti zhizni. Moskva, 1964.
Phil 175.62   Adler, Mortimer Jerome. The conditions of philosophy. 1st ed. N.Y., 1965.
Phil 175.63   Arvasi, S. Ahmet. Insan ve insanötesi. Istanbul, 1970.
Phil 175.65   Almeida, Fernando Pinho de. A essência da matéria e o sentido da vida. Coimbra, 1967.
VPhil 175.66   Atanasijević, Ksenija. Smisao i vrednost eqzistencije. Beograd, 1968.
Phil 175.68   Abbagnano, Nicola. Per o contro l'uomo. Milano, 1968.
Phil 176.1   Bärenbach, F. Grundlegung der kritischen Philosophie. Leipzig, 1879.
Phil 176.2   Bäggesen, Jens. Philosophischer Nachlasz. Zürich, 1858. 2v.
Phil 176.2.10   Bäggesen, Jen. Aus J. Bäggesen's Briefwechsel mit K.L. Reinhold. Leipzig, 1931. 2v.

Classified Listing

Phil 175 - 200   General treatises on philosophy - Individual authors (A-Z) - cont.

Phil 176.3   Bahnsen, J. Beitrage zur Charakterologie. Leipzig, 1867. 2v.

Phil 176.3.3   Bahnsen, J. Zum Verhältniss Zwischen Wille und Motiv. Lauenburg, 1870.

Phil 176.3.5   Bahnsen, J. Wie ich Wurde was ich Ward. München, 1905.

Phil 176.3.7   Bahnsen, J. Wie ich Wurde was ich Ward. Leipzig, 1931.

Phil 176.3.9   Bahnsen, J. Das tragische als Weltgesetz und der Humor. Lauenburg, 1877.

Phil 176.3.10   Bahnsen, J. Das tragische als Weltgesetz und der Humor. Leipzig, 1931.

Phil 176.4A   Bailey, S. Essays on the pursuit of truth. London, 1829.

Phil 176.4B   Bailey, S. Essays on the pursuit of truth. London, 1829.

Phil 176.4.3   Bailey, S. Essays on the pursuit of truth. London, 1831.

Phil 176.5   Balfour, A.J. Defence of philosophic doubt. London, 1879.

Phil 176.5.5   Balfour, A.J. Foundations of belief. N.Y., 1895.

Phil 176.5.8   Balfour, A.J. Foundations of belief. London, 1901.

Phil 176.5.13   Balfour, A.J. Familiar belief and transcendent reason. London, n.d.

Phil 176.5.51   Rey, J. La philosophie de M. Balfour. Paris, 1897.

Phil 176.7   Barsalou-Fromenty, Gustave. La philosophie terrestre. Geneva, 1876.

Phil 176.9   Bascom, V. Science, philosophy and religion. N.Y., 1871.

Phil 176.10   Baumann, Julius J. Philosophie. Leipzig, 1872.

Phil 176.10.5   Baumann, Julius J. Elemente der Philosophie. Leipzig, 1891.

Phil 176.10.10   Baumann, Julius J. Welt- und Lebensansichte in Ihren. Gotha, 1906.

Phil 176.10.11   Baumann, Julius J. Die grundlegenden Thatsachen. 2e Aufl. Stuttgart, 1902.

Phil 176.11   Baumeister, F.C. Elementa philosophiae. Leipzig, 1755.

Phil 176.11.3   Baumeister, F.C. Institutiones metaphysicae. Wittenbergae, 1749.

Phil 176.11.5   Baumeister, F.C. Institutiones metaphysicae. Wittebergae, 1775.

Phil 176.11.10   Baumeister, F.C. Philosophia recens controversa complexa definitiones theoremata. Vratislaviae, 1766.

Phil 176.12   Baumgärtner, H. Die Weltzellen. Leipzig, 1875.

Phil 176.13   Baskin, M.P. Krizis burzhuaznogo soznaniia. Moskva, 1962.

Phil 176.14   Bax, E.B. Problem of reality. London, 1892.

Phil 176.14.5   Bax, E.B. The roots of reality. London, 1907.

Phil 176.14.10   Bax, E.B. The real, the rational and the alogical. London, 1920.

Phil 176.16   Belsham, T. Elements of the philosophy of the mind. London, 1801.

Phil 176.17   Bénard, Charles. Précis de philosophie. Paris, 1845.

Phil 176.17.2   Bénard, Charles. Précis de philosophie. Paris, 1857.

Phil 176.17.5   Bénard, Charles. Questions de philosophie. Paris, 1869.

Phil 176.19   Berger, J.E. Grundzuge zur Wissenschaft. Altona, 1817. 4v.

Phil 176.19.5   Berger, J.E. Philosophische Darstellung der Harmonien des Weltalls. Altona, 1808.

Phil 176.20   Bergmann, J. Sein und Erkennen. Berlin, 1880.

Phil 176.20.5   Bergmann, J. Vorlesungen über Metaphysik. Berlin, 1886.

Phil 176.21   Bersot, P.E. Libre philosophie. Paris, 1868.

Phil 176.21.5   Bersot, P.E. Essais de philosophie et de morale. Paris, 1864. 2v.

Phil 176.22   Biederman, G. Wissenschaft des Geistes. Leipzig, 1858.

Phil 176.23   Blein, A. Essais philosophiques. Paris, 1843.

Phil 176.24   Blignières, C. Exposition de la philosophie. Paris, 1857.

Phil 176.25   Bordas-Demoulin, Jean B. Mélanges philosophiques. Paris, 1846.

Phil 176.25.10   Borland, Hal Glen. Countyman: a summary of belief. 1st ed. Philadelphia, 1965.

Phil 176.26   Bouillier, F. Theorie de la raison impersonnelle. Paris, 1844.

Phil 176.26.10   Bouterwek, Friedrich. Die Epochen der Vernunft nach der Idee einer Apoditik. Bruxelles, 1968.

Phil 176.26.15   Bouterwek, Friedrich. Angangsgründe der speculaterien Philosophie. Bruxelles, 1968.

Phil 176.27   Bowne, B.P. Metaphysics. N.Y., 1882.

Phil 176.27.2   Bowne, B.P. Metaphysics. N.Y., 1898.

Phil 176.27.5   Bowne, B.P. Metaphysics. N.Y., 1882.

Phil 176.27.8   Flewelling, R.T. Personalism and the problems of philosophy. N.Y., 1915.

Phil 176.27.12   Bowne, B.P. Personalism. Boston, 1908.

Phil 176.30   Brisor de Warville, Jean Pierre. De la vérité. Neuchatel, 1782.

tn   Phil 176.31*   Browne, R. Liber...vetaribus rarum principia. London, 1678.

Phil 176.32   Buchez, P.T.B. Traité de philosophie. Paris, 1838. 3v.

Phil 176.33   Büchner, L. Aus Natur und Wissenschaft. Leipzig, 1874.

Phil 176.33.5   Büchner, L. Science et nature. v.1-2. Paris, 1866.

Phil 176.33.10   Büchner, L. Fremdes und Eignes. Leipzig, 1890.

Phil 176.33.15   Büchner, L. Im Dienste der Wahrheit. Giessen, 1900.

Phil 176.34   Buffier, Claude. Oeuvres philosophiques. Paris, 1843.

Phil 176.34.5   Buffier, Claude. First truths. London, 1780.

Phil 176.34.9F   Buffier, Claude. Cours de science. Paris, 1732.

Phil 176.35   Bunot, Albert Louis. Eléments de philosophie chretienne. Paris, 1869.

Phil 176.36   Burdach, K.F. Blicke ins Leben. v.1-4. Leipzig, 1842. 2v.

Cg   Phil 176.37   Burgersdijck, F.P. Collegium physicum disputationibus XXXII absolutum. Lugdunum Batavorum, 1642.

Cg   Phil 176.37.5   Burgersdijck, F.P. Institutionum metaphyricarum libri II. Hagae Comitis, 1657.

Phil 176.37.6   Burgersdijck, F.P. Institutionum metaphyricarum libri II. Lugdunum Batavorum, 1642.

Phil 176.37.10   Burgersdijck, F.P. Instituionum metaphysicarum libri II. n.p., 1647.

Phil 176.38   Burnouf, E.L. La vie et la pensée. Paris, 1886.

Phil 176.40   Batz, P. Philosophie der Erlösung. Berlin, 1876-86. 2v.

Phil 176.40.5   Batz, P. Die Philosophie der Erlösung. 2e Aufl. Berlin, 1879.

Phil 176.41   Monboddo, James Barnet. Ancient metaphysics. v.1-6. Edinburgh, 1779-99. 7v.

Phil 176.41.5   Knight, William. Lord Monboddo. London, 1900.

Phil 176.42.15   Boutroux, E. The beyond that is within. London, 1912.

Phil 176.43   Burdon, W. Materials for thinking. London, 1820. 2v.

Phil 176.44   Blackwell, A.B. The philosophy of individuality. N.Y., 1893.

Phil 176.44.5   Blackwell, A.B. Studies in general science. N.Y., 1869.

Phil 176.45   Baldwin, J.M. Fragments in philosophy and science. N.Y., 1902.

Phil 176.45.5   Baldwin, J.M. Imitation. n.p., 1894-1904. 8 pam.

Phil 176.46   Benvenuti, F. Saggi filosofici. Firenze, 1863.

Phil 175 - 200   General treatises on philosophy - Individual authors (A-Z) - cont.

Phil 176.47A   Blewett, G.J. Study of nature...with other essays. Toronto, 1907.

Phil 176.47B   Blewett, G.J. Study of nature...with other essays. Toronto, 1907.

Phil 176.48   Butler, N.M. Philosophy. N.Y., 1908.

Phil 176.48.3   Butler, N.M. Philosophy. N.Y., 1938.

Phil 176.49   Bourdeau, J. Pragmatisme et modernisme. Paris, 1909.

Phil 176.50   Bernès, M. Cours élémentaire de philosophie. Paris, n.d.

NEDL Phil 176.51.20   Bergson, H. Intuition og rerdensanskueke oversat af Knud Terlov. Kobenhavn, 1914.

NEDL Phil 176.51.25   Bergson, H. Den skabende udvikling. Kobenhavn, 1914.

Phil 176.51.29   Bergson, H. La filosofia dell'intuizione. Lanciano, 1922.

Phil 176.52   Bjorkman, E. Is there anything new under the sun? N.Y., 1911.

Phil 176.53   Bouterwek, F. Kleine schriften philosophischen. Bd.1. Göttingen, 1818.

Phil 176.53.2   Bouterwek, F. Lehrbuch der philosophischen Wissenschaften. Göttingen, 1820. 2v.

Phil 176.53.7   Bouterwek, F. Lehrbuch der philosophischen Vorkenntnisse. Göttingen, 1820.

Phil 176.53.15   Bouterwek, F. Idee einer Spoditik. Halle, 1799. 2v.

Phil 176.54A   Brochard, V. Etudes de philosophie ancienne et de philosophie moderne. Paris, 1912.

Phil 176.54B   Brochard, V. Etudes de philosophie ancienne et de philosophie moderne. Paris, 1912.

Phil 176.55   Berthelot, René. Un romantisme utilitaire. Paris, 1911. 3v.

Phil 176.56.2A   Bosanquet, B. Essays and addresses. London, 1891.

Phil 176.56.2B   Bosanquet, B. Essays and addresses. London, 1891.

Phil 176.56.7   Bosanquet, B. Science and philosophy and other essays. London, 1927.

Phil 176.57.2   Barzellotti, G. Santi, solitari e filosofi. 2nd ed. Bologna, 1886.

Phil 176.58   Bourdeau, J. La philosophie affective. Paris, 1912.

Phil 176.59   Blair, D. The master-key. Wimbledon, 1914.

Phil 176.60   Bruner, J.J. La experiencia y la especulación. Santiago de Chile, 1886.

Phil 176.61   Bierbower, A. Principles of a system of philosophy. N.Y., 1870.

Phil 176.63   Bertz, Eduard. Weltharmonie monistische Betrachtungen. Dresden, 1908.

Phil 176.64   Bourdeau, L. Problème de la vie, essai de sociologie générale. Paris, 1901.

Phil 176.65   Brass, T. Chapter from story of Pauline Parsons. Ashland, 1916.

Phil 176.66   Burton, Asa. Essays. Portland, 1824.

Phil 176.67   Pamphlet box. Billia, L.M. Miscellaneous pamphlets.

Phil 176.68   Boirac, Émile. L'idée du Phénomène. Thèse. Paris, 1894.

Phil 176.69   Bloch, Ernst. Geist der Utopie. München, 1918.

Phil 176.69.5   Bloch, Ernst. Tübinger Einleitung in die Philosophie. Berlin, 1923.

Phil 176.69.10   Bloch, Ernst. Spuren. Berlin, 1930.

Phil 176.69.12   Bloch, Ernst. Spuren. Berlin, 1960.

Phil 176.69.12.5   Bloch, Ernst. Spuren. 5. Aufl. Frankfurt, 1967.

Phil 176.69.15   Bloch, Ernst. Philosophische Grundfragen. Frankfurt, 1961.

Phil 176.69.80   Konferenz über Fragen der Blochschen Philosophie. Ernst Blochs Revision des Marxismus. Berlin, 1957.

Phil 176.69.80.5   Leipzig. Universität. Ernst Blochs Revision des Marxismus. Berlin, 1957.

Phil 176.70   Blood, B.P. Pluriverse. Boston, 1920.

Phil 176.71   Bonaventura, E. Le qualità del mondo fisico. Firenze, 1916.

Phil 176.72   Braun, Edmond. La logique de l'absolu. Paris, 1887.

Phil 176.73   Brunner, Constantin. Die Lehre von den Geistigen und vom Volke. Berlin, 1908. 2v.

Phil 176.73.2   Brunner, Constantin. Die Lehre von den Geistigen und vom Volk. 2. Aufl. Potsdam, 1927. 2v.

Phil 176.73.3   Brunner, Constantin. Die Lehre von den Geistigen und vom Volk. 3. Aufl. Stuttgart, 1962. 2v.

Phil 176.74   Pamphlet box. Bonatelli, Francesco. Miscellaneous pamphlets.

Phil 176.74.2F   Pamphlet box. Bonatelli, Francesco. Miscellaneous pamphlets.

Phil 176.74.5   Bonatelli, F. La coscienza e il meccanesimo interiore. Padova, 1872.

Phil 176.75   Barach, Carl S. Kleine philosophische Schriften. Wien, 1878.

Phil 176.76   Bilharz, Alfons. Metaphysik als Lehre vom Vorbewussten. Bd.I. Wiesbaden, 1897.

Phil 176.76.5   Bilharz, Alfons. Philosophie als Universalwissenschaft. Wiesbaden, 1912.

Phil 176.77   Brod, Max. Anschauung und Begriff. Leipzig, 1913.

Phil 176.78   Baillie, J.B. Studies in human nature. London, 1921.

Phil 176.79   Badoureau, A. Causeries philosophiques. Paris, 1920.

Phil 176.80   Burckhardt, Georg E. Was ist Individualismus? Leipzig, 1913.

Phil 176.80.5   Burckhardt, Georg E. Individuum und Welt als Werk. München, 1920.

Phil 176.80.10   Burckhardt, Georg E. Weltanschauungskrisis. v.1-2. Leipzig, 1925-26.

Phil 176.81   Bender, Hedwig. Zur Lösung des metaphysischen Problems. Berlin, 1886.

Phil 176.82   Baker, Arthur. Outlines of logic, psychology and ethics. London, 1891.

Phil 176.82.5   Bender, Hedwig. Philosophie, Metaphysik und Einzelforschung. Leipzig, 1897.

Phil 176.83   Boll, Marcel. Attardés et précurseurs. Paris, 1921.

Phil 176.84   Bonlnois, Helen. The law of being. London, 1921.

NEDL Phil 176.85.3   Brunschvicg, L. Introduction à la vie de l'esprit. 3e éd. Paris, 1920.

Phil 176.85.10   Brunschvicg, L. Nature et liberté. Paris, 1921.

Phil 176.85.13   Brunschvicg, L. L'idéalisme contemporain. Paris, 1905.

Phil 176.85.15   Brunschvicg, L. L'idéalisme contemporain. 2e éd. Paris, 1921.

Phil 176.85.20   Brunschvicg, L. La philosophie de l'esprit. 1. éd. Paris, 1949.

Phil 176.86   Bertrand, A. Principes de philosophie. Paris, 1893.

Phil 176.87   Benn, Alfred W. Revaluations. London, 1909.

Phil 176.88   Burne, C.D. The contact between minds. London, 1923.

Phil 176.88.10   Burne, C.D. The horizon of experience. N.Y., 1934.

Phil 176.89   Blundell, A. Idealism, possible and impossible. London, 1911.

Phil 176.90   Brausewetter, A. Die Weltanschauung als Erlebnis. Heft 3-4. Leipzig, 1920. 2v.

Phil 176.91   Bardonnet, L. L'univers-organisme. Paris, 1923. 4v.

Phil 175 - 200   General treatises on philosophy - Individual authors (A-Z) - cont.

Phil 176.93   Bexell, Carl E. Samvetet i forhallaude till natur. Jönköping, 1840.

Phil 176.94   Brightman, E.S. An introduction to philosophy. N.Y., 1925.

Phil 176.94.5   Brigtman, E.S. Person and reality. N.Y., 1958.

Phil 176.95   Bauch, Bruno. Anfangsgründe der Philosophie. Gotha, 1920.

Phil 176.96   Biunde, F.X. Fundamental-Philosophie. Trier, 1838.

Phil 176.97   Biese, Franz. Philosophie Propädeutik für Gymnasien und höhere Bildingssanstalten. Berlin, 1845.

Phil 176.98   Bouillier, D.R. Discours philosophiques. Amsterdam, 1759.

Phil 176.99   Bayrhoffer, K.T. Die Grundprobleme der Metaphysik. Marburg, 1835.

Phil 176.100   Braniss, C.J. System der Metaphysik. Breslau, 1834.

Phil 176.101   Backer, S. de. Disputationes metaphysicae. Fasc.1-3. Paris, 1920-1923.

Phil 176.102   Bellomia Barone, F. Il problema fondamentale dell'essere. Ortona a Mare, 1909.

Phil 176.103   Buddeus, J.F. Elementa philosophiae instrumentalis. Halae Saxonum, 1724-25.

Phil 176.103.3   Buddeus, J.F. Elementa philosophiae instrumentalis. v.1-2. Halae-Saxonum, 1719-20.

Phil 176.103.5   Buddeus, J.F. Elementa philosophiae instrumentalis. v.1-2. Halae Saxonum, 1724-25.

Phil 176.103.10   Buddeus, J.F. Elementa philosophiae practicae. Halaeo Magdeburgical, 1724.

Phil 176.104   Beck, Maximillian. Wesen und Wert. Berlin, 1925. 2v.

Phil 176.106   Buchanan, S.M. Possibility. London, 1927.

Phil 176.106.2   Buchanan, S.M. Possibility. N.Y., 1927.

Phil 176.106.10   Buchanan, S.M. Poetry and mathematics. N.Y., 1929.

Phil 176.107   Becher, Erich. Einführung in die Philosophie. München, 1926.

Phil 176.107.5   Becher, Erich. Einführung in die Philosophie. 2. Aufl. Berlin, 1949.

Phil 176.108   Bradford, Gamaliel. Life and I. Boston, 1928.

Phil 176.109   Brouwer, L.E.J. Wiskunde, waarheid, werkkeijkheid. Gröningen, 1919.

Phil 176.110   Becker, Carl. Die moderne Weltanschauung. Berlin, 1911.

Phil 176.110.5   Becker, Carl. Vom geistigen Leben und Schaffen. Berlin, 1912.

Phil 176.111   Benda, Julien. Lettres à Mélisande. Paris, 1926.

Phil 176.111.25   Benda, Julien. Essai d'un discours cohérent sur les rapports de Dieu et du monde. Paris, 1931.

Phil 176.112   Baudin, E. Introduction générale à la philosophie. Paris, 1927.

Phil 176.113   Barrett, Thomas S. An introduction to the study of logic and metaphysics. London, 1875.

Phil 176.114   Bauer, G.F. Die Welt als Subjekt-Objekt. Berlin, 1923.

Phil 176.115.2   Bierens de Haan, J.D. De verborgen harmonie. 2e druk. Amsterdam, 1918.

Phil 176.115.8   Bierens de Haan, J.D. Wysgeerige studies. 's-Gravenhage, 1904.

Phil 176.115.9   Bierens de Haan, J.D. Idee - studies. 3e druk. Amsterdam, 1920.

Phil 176.115.15   Bierens de Haan, J.D. Vergezichten. Studies. Amsterdam, 1921.

Phil 176.115.35   Bierens de Haan, J.D. De weg tot het inzicht. Amsterdam, 1920.

Phil 176.115.45   Bierens de Haan, J.D. Wereldorde engeestesleven. 2e Aufl. Amsterdam, 1922.

Phil 176.115.50   Bierens de Haan, J.D. Menschengeest. Amsterdam, 1926.

Phil 176.116   Bulgakov, S.N. Die Tragödie der Philosophie. Darmstadt, 1927.

Phil 176.117   Bruhn, Wilhelm. Einführung in das philosophische Denken für Anfanger und Alleinlermende. Leipzig, 1923.

Phil 176.118   Balfour, James. Philosophical essays. Edinburgh, 1768.

Phil 176.119   Baron, K. Metaphysica generalis. Londini, 1657?

Phil 176.121   Barthel, Ernst. Die Welt als Spannung und Rhythmus. Leipzig, 1928.

Phil 176.122   Burke, J.B. The mystery of life. London, 1931.

Phil 176.122.10   Burke, J.B. The emergence of life. London, 1931.

Phil 176.123   Baldini, Bernardino. Dialogi duo in quorum altero agitur de multitudine rerum. Mediolani, 1558. 3 pam.

Htn   Phil 176.123.5*   Maffei, G.C. Scala naturale. Venice, 1573.

Phil 176.124   Burkamp, Wilhelm. Die Struktur der Ganzheiten. Berlin, 1929.

Phil 176.125   Bardili, C.G. Sophylus oder Sittlichkeit und Natur. Stuttgart, 1794.

Phil 176.126   Burnham, James. Introductioon to philosophical analysis. N.Y., 1932.

Phil 176.128   Bertini, G.M. Idea di una filosofia della vita. Firenze, 1933.

Phil 176.129   Blondel, Maurice. Le problème de la philosophie catholique. Paris, 1932.

Phil 176.129.5   Blondel, Maurice. L'être et les êtres. Paris, 1935.

Phil 176.129.6   Blondel, Maurice. L'être et les êtres. Paris, 1963.

Phil 176.129.10   Blondel, Maurice. Dialogues avec les philosophes, Descartes, Spinoza. Paris, 1966.

Phil 176.130   Buscalioni, C.M. Carolus Michael Buscalioni Monregalensis ut philosophiae rationalis professor crearetur. Turin? 1848.

Phil 176.131   Bonghi, Ruggiero. Delle relazioni della filosofia colla società; prolusione. Milano, 1859.

Phil 176.132   Branford, B. Eros and Psyche. London, 1934.

Phil 176.133   Basch, Victor. Essais d'esthétique, de philosophie et de littérature. Paris, 1934.

Phil 176.134   Blondeau, Cyrille. Propositions de philosophie. Paris, 1932.

Phil 176.135   Barrett, Clifford. Philosophy. N.Y., 1935.

Phil 176.136   Bawden, Henry H. The principles of pragmatism. Boston, 1910.

Phil 176.137A   Burke, Kenneth. Permanence and change. N.Y., 1935.

Phil 176.137B   Burke, Kenneth. Permanence and change. N.Y., 1935.

Phil 176.137.2   Burke, Kenneth. Permanence and change. 2nd ed. Los Altos, Calif., 1954.

Phil 176.138   Berdiaev, Nikolai A. Méditations sur l'existence. Paris, 1936.

Phil 176.138.5   Berdiaev, Nikolai A. Solitude and society. London, 1938.

Phil 176.138.8   Berdiaev, Nikolai A. Solitude and society. London, 1947.

Phil 176.138.15   Berdiaev, Nikolai A. Slavery and freedom. London, 1943.

Phil 176.138.16   Berdiaev, Nikolai A. Slavery and freedom. N.Y., 1944.

Phil 176.138.20   Berdiaev, Nikolai A. Essai de metaphysique eschatologique. Paris, 1946.

Phil 176.139   Byers, R.P. Superuniversity studies. Boston, 1936.

Phil 176.140.5   Baur, Ludwig. Metaphysik. 3. Aufl. München, 1935.

Phil 176.141   Bontadini, G. Saggio di una metafisica dell'esperienza. Milano, 1938.

Phil 176.142   Bolaffio, C. Colui che si chiama "Io sono". Modena, 1936.

Phil 175 - 200   General treatises on philosophy - Individual authors (A-Z) - cont.

Phil 176.143   Bräuer, Ernst Wasa. Metaphysik als beobachtende Wissenschaft. Berlin, 1934.

Phil 176.144   Pamphlet box. Bixler, J.S. Minor works.

Phil 176.145   Bentley, J.E. Visual outline of philosophy. N.Y., 1939.

Phil 176.146   Bastide, George. De la condition humaine. Thèse. Paris, 1939.

Phil 176.147   Bryan, W.L. Wars of families of minds. New Haven, 1940.

Phil 176.148   Brownell, B. The philosopher in chaos. N.Y., 1941.

Phil 176.149   Benjamin, Harold. Man, the problem-solver. Boston, 1930.

Phil 176.150   Benzecri, E. Essai sur la nature et la portee d l'attitude metaphysique. Alcan, 1939.

Phil 176.151   Barth, Hans. Wahrheit und Ideologie. Zürich, 1945.

Phil 176.151.2   Barth, Hans. Wahrheit und Ideologie. 2. Aufl. Erlenbach, 1961.

Phil 176.152   Biese, Alfred. Die Philosophie des Metaphorischen. Hamburg, 1893.

Phil 176.153   Burgmüller, H. Zur Klarüng der Begriffe. 1. Aufl. München, 1947.

Phil 176.154   Botelho, Pero de. Da filosofia. 1. ed. Candeia, 1949.

Phil 176.155   Bouchet, Henri. Introduction à la philosophie de l'individu. Paris, 1949.

Phil 176.156   Barnes, W. The philosophical predicament. London, 1950.

Phil 176.157   Butler, J. Four philosophies. N.Y., 1951.

Phil 176.158   Brunner, August. Der Stufenbau der Welt. 1. Aufl. München, 1950.

Phil 176.158.5   Brunner, August. Die Grundragen der Philosophie. 4. Aufl. Freiburg, 1956.

Phil 176.160   Bense, Max. Literaturmetaphysik. 1. Aufl. Stuttgart, 1950.

Phil 176.160.5   Bense, Max. Einleitung in die Philosophie. München, 1941.

Phil 176.162   Beerling, R.F. Onsocratische gesprekken. Amsterdam, 1949.

Phil 176.166   Bloskhurst, J.B. Body, mind and creativity. N.Y., 1954.

Phil 176.168   Beck, Lewis White. Philosophic inquiry. N.Y., 1953.

Phil 176.168.5   Beck, Lewis White. Philosophic inquiry. Englewood Cliffs, N.J., 1958.

Phil 176.170   Blanshard, B. On philosophical style. Bloomington, 1954.

Phil 176.172   Bedetti, A. Filosofia della vita. Cremons, 1952.

Phil 176.175   Bounet, G. Introduction à tous les cours de philosophie. Paris, 1953.

Phil 176.180   Bosco, Giovanni. Ricerche filosofiche. Napoli, 1953.

Phil 176.185   Barth, Heinrich. Das Sein der Dinge. Wien, 1956.

Phil 176.190   Brates, Georg. Du und die Philosophie. Berlin, 1955.

Phil 176.195   Banerjee, N.V. Concerning human understanding. London, 1958.

Phil 176.200   Bauernfeind, Otto. Die Suingebung des Daseins. Meisenheim, 1957.

Phil 176.205   Bhattacharya, H.M. The principles of philosophy. Calcutta, 1948.

Phil 176.207   Barraud, Jean. Philosophie de la qualité. Paris, 1956.

Phil 176.210   Boas, George. The limits of reason. London, 1961.

Phil 176.212   Bennett, J.G. The dramatic universe. London, 1956-61. 2v.

Phil 176.213   La Rochefoucauld, Edmée de Fels. La nature et l'esprit. Paris, 1965.

Phil 176.214   Bochénski, I.M. Philosophy; an introduction. Dordrecht, 1963.

Phil 176.215   Brent, Duncan. Of the seer and the vision. Amsterdam, 1967.

Phil 176.217   Buchler, J. The concept of method. N.Y., 1961.

Phil 176.218   Bunge, Mario. The myth of simplicity. Englewood Cliff, N.J., 1963.

Phil 176.219   Becker, O. Dasein und Dawesen. Pfullingen, 1963.

Phil 176.220   Brito, Antonio J. Estudos de filosofia. Lisboa, 1962.

Phil 176.221   Berlin. Freie Universität. Freiheit als Problem der Wissenschaft. Berlin, 1962.

Phil 176.222   Bouwsma, O.K. Philosophical essays. Lincoln, Nebraska, 1965.

Phil 176.223   Beardsley, Monroe Curtis. Philosophical thinking. N.Y., 1965.

Phil 176.224   Burth, Edwin Arthur. In search of philosophic understanding. N.Y., 1966.

Phil 176.225   Bueno, Miguel. Conferencias. 1. ed. México, 1959.

Phil 176.226   Bartolone, Filippo. Struttura e significato nella storia della filosofia. Bologna, 1964.

Phil 176.227   Balthasar, Nicolas J.J. Mon moi dans l'être. Louvain, 1946.

Phil 176.228   Balmes, Raymond. Leçons de philosophie. Paris, 1965-66. 2v.

Phil 176.230   Britton, Karl. Philosophy and the meaning of life. London, 1969.

Phil 176.232   Bogliolo, Luigi. Nuovo corso di filosofia a norma del Concilio Vaticano II. Roma, 1969- 2v.

Phil 176.234   Bacchin, Giovanni Romano. L'immediato e la sua negazione. Perugia, 1967.

Phil 176.236   Bueno Martinez, Gustavo. El papel de la filosofia en el conjunto del saber. Madrid, 1970.

Phil 176.238   Boehme, Guenther. Der pädagogische Beruf der Philosophie. München, 1968.

Phil 176.240   Betancur, Cayetano. Filosofos y filosofias. Bogota, 1969.

Phil 176.242   Bihari, Péter. A philosophiai tudamányok encyclopaediája. Budapest, 1875.

Phil 177.1   Caird, Edward. Essays on literature and philosophy. N.Y., 1892. 2v.

Phil 177.1.5   Caird, Edward. Essays on literature and philosophy. Glasgow, 1892. 2v.

Phil 177.2   Calker, F. Propädeutik der Philosophie. Bonn, 1821.

Phil 177.2.5   Calker, F. Urgesetzlehre der wahren Guten und Schöne. Berlin, 1820.

Phil 177.3   Calinich, E.A.E. Philosophische Propädeutik. Dresden, 1847.

Phil 177.4   Cantoni, C. Corso elementare di filosofia. Milan, 1870.

Phil 177.4.12   Cantoni, C. Corso elementare di filosofia. Milan, 1901.

Phil 177.5   Cardaillac, M. Etudes élémentaires de philosophie. Paris, 1830. 2v.

Phil 177.6   Carey, H.C. The unity of law. Philadelphia, 1872.

Phil 177.7   Carpenter, W.B. Nature and man. London, 1888.

Phil 177.8   Carus, Paul. Fundamental problems. Chicago, 1889.

Phil 177.8.3   Carus, Paul. Fundamental problems. 2nd ed. Chicago, 1891.

Phil 177.8.5   Carus, Paul. The surd of metaphysics. Chicago, 1903.

Phil 177.8.9   Carus, Paul. Ursache Grund und Zweck. Dresden, 1883.

Phil 177.8.12A   Carus, Paul. Primer of philosophy. Chicago, 1893.

Phil 177.8.12B   Carus, Paul. Primer of philosophy. Chicago, 1893.

Phil 177.8.15   Carus, Paul. Philosophie als Wissenschaft. Chicago, 1911.

Phil 177.8.25   Carus, Paul. The point of view: an anthology. Chicago, 1927.

Phil 177.9   Catara-Lettieri, Antonio. L'omu nun l'usu di la ragiuni. Messina, 1869.

Phil 175 - 200 General treatises on philosophy - Individual authors (A-Z) - cont.

Phil 177.9.5 — Catara-Lettieri, Antonio. Sull' uomo; pensieri. Messina, 1869.

Phil 177.10 — Chalybäur, H.M. Fundamental Philosophie. Kiel, 1861.

Phil 177.11 — Changeux, P.J. Traiti des extrêmes. Amsterdam, 1767. 2v.

Phil 177.12 — Charma, Antoine. Réponses aux questions de philosophie. Paris, 1841.

Phil 177.13 — Clemente, A. Le bon sens. Paris, 1878. 2v.

Phil 177.14A — Clifford, W.K. Lectures and essays. London, 1879. 2v.

Phil 177.14B — Clifford, W.K. Lectures and essays. London, 1879. 2v.

X Cg   Phil 177.14.2 — Clifford, W.K. Lectures and essays. 2nd ed. London, 1886.

Htn   Phil 177.15* — Casaubon, M. Letter...concerning natural experimental philosophy. Cambridge, 1669.

Htn   Phil 177.16* — CJ.A. Physicae. Amsterdaam, 1645.

Phil 177.16.9 — Comenius, J.A. Natural philosophie reformed by divine light. London, 1651.

Phil 177.17 — Concord lecturer on philosophy. Cambridge, 1883.

Phil 177.18 — Consciousness. Boston, 1864.

Phil 177.19 — Conti, Augusto. Evidenza, amore e fede. Florence, 1858. 2v.

Phil 177.19.5 — Conti, Augusto. Filosofia elementare. Firenze, 1913.

Phil 177.19.10 — Conti, Augusto. Il vero nell'ordine o Ondologia e logica. 2a ed. Firenze, 1891. 2v.

Phil 177.19.15 — Conti, Augusto. L'armonia delle cose. Firenze, 1888. 2v.

Phil 177.19.20 — Conti, Augusto. Ai figli del popolo; consigli. Firenze, 1901.

Phil 177.20 — Cornwallis, C.F. Philosophical theories. Philadelphia, 1846.

Phil 177.21 — Cory, Isaac P. Metaphysical inquiry. London, 1833-37.

Phil 177.22 — Cournot, A.A. Traité des idées fondamentales. Paris, 1861.

Phil 177.22.5A — Cournot, A.A. Essai sur les fondations de nos connaissances. Paris, 1851. 2v.

Phil 177.22.5B — Cournot, A.A. Essai sur les fondations de nos connaissances. Paris, 1851. 2v.

Phil 177.22.5C — Cournot, A.A. Essai sur les fondations de nos connaissances. v.1. Paris, 1851.

Phil 177.22.10 — Cournot, A.A. An essay on the foundations of our knowledge. N.Y., 1956.

Phil 177.22.15 — Cournot, A.A. Critique philosophique. 1. ed. Paris, 1958.

Phil 177.23 — Courtney, W.L. Studies in philosophy. London, 1882.

Phil 177.24 — Curtis, M.M. Philosophy and physical science. Cleveleand, 1892.

Phil 177.25 — Canz, Israel Gottlieb. Meditationes philosophicae. Tubingae, 1750.

Phil 177.25.10 — Canz, Israle Gottlieb. Philosophicae Leibnitianae. Francofurti, 1749.

Phil 177.25.30 — Canz, Israel Gottlieb. Theologia naturalis thetico-polemica. Dresdae, 1742.

Phil 177.26 — Choraux, C. La pensée et l'amour. Paris, 1869.

Phil 177.26.5 — Choraux, C. L'ombre de Socrate. Paris, 1878.

Phil 177.27 — Cochin, D. La monde extérieur. Paris, 1895.

Phil 177.28A — Cohen, Hermann. Logik der reinen Erkenntnis. Berlin, 1902. 3v.

Phil 177.28B — Cohen, Hermann. Logik der reinen Erkenntnis. Berlin, 1902.

Phil 177.28.2 — Görland, A. Index zu Hermann Cohens Logik...Erkenntnis. Berlin, 1906.

Phil 177.28.10 — Cohens, Hermann. Schriften zur Philosophie und Zeitgeschichte. Berlin, 1928. 2v.

Phil 177.29 — Cornelius, H. Einleitung in die Philosophie. Leipzig, 1903.

Phil 177.29.2 — Cornelius, H. Einleitung in die Philosophie. 2e Aufl. Leipzig, 1919.

Phil 177.30 — Caspari, Otto. Zusammenhang der Dinge. Breslau, 1881.

Phil 177.31 — Crane, A. The new philosophy. San Francisco, 1904.

EDL   Phil 177.32 — Zoltowski, A. Graf August Cieszkowski's "Philosophie der Tat". Posen, 1904.

Phil 177.33.3 — Calkins, Mary Whiton. The persistent problems of philosophy. 3d ed. N.Y., 1912.

Phil 177.33.7 — Calkins, Mary Whiton. The persistent problems of philosophy. N.Y., 1936.

Phil 177.33.10 — Pamphlet vol. Calkins, Mary Whiton. Statistics of dreams. 14 pam.

Phil 177.34 — Cooley, W.F. The individual. N.Y., 1909.

Phil 177.35 — Croce, Benedetto. Saggi filosofici. Bari, 1910-52. 14v.

Phil 177.35.5 — Croce, Benedetto. Philosophie de la pratique. Paris, 1911.

Phil 177.35.9 — Croce, Benedetto. Philosophy of the practical. London, 1913.

Phil 177.35.25 — Croce, Benedetto. The conduct of life. N.Y., 1924.

Phil 177.35.30 — Croce, Benedetto. Eternitá storicità della filosofia. Rieti, 1930.

Phil 177.35.40 — Croce, Benedetto. Ultimi saggi. 2. ed. Bari, 1948.

Phil 177.36 — Carus, F.A. Ideen zur Geschichte der Philosophie. Leipzig, 1809.

Phil 177.37 — Caso, Antonio. Problemas filosóficos. México, 1915.

Phil 177.37.5 — Caso, Antonio. La existencia como economía como desinterés y como caridad. México, 1919.

Phil 177.38 — Caldwell, W. Pragmatism and idealism. London, 1913.

Phil 177.39 — Creative intelligence: Essays in pragmatic attitude. N.Y., 1917.

Phil 177.40 — Sabine, George H. Philosophical essays in honor of J.E. Creighton. N.Y., 1917.

Phil 177.40.5 — Creighton, J.E. Studies in speculative philosophy. N.Y., 1925.

Phil 177.41 — Commer, E. System der Philosophie. v.1-4. Münster, 1883.

Phil 177.42 — Christiansen, H. MeineLösung der Welträtsel. Wiesbaden, 1914.

Phil 177.43 — Cohn, Jonas. DerSinn der gegenwärtigen Kultur. Leipzig, 1914.

Phil 177.44 — Cohn, Jonas. Führende Denker. Leipzig, 1907.

Phil 177.44.5 — Cohn, Jonas. Gefühlston und Sättigung der Farben. n.p., 1899-1915. 16 pam.

Phil 177.45 — Charles, Emile. Éléments de philosophie. Paris, 1884-85. 2v.

Phil 177.46 — Cesca, Giovanni. La filosofia dell'azione. Milano, 1907.

Phil 177.46.5 — Cesca, Giovanni. La filosofia della vita. Messina, 1903.

Phil 177.47 — Cellarier, Felix. La métaphysique et sa méthode. Paris, 1914.

Phil 177.49 — Cunningham, H.E. An introduction to philosophy. Boston, 1920.

Phil 177.50 — Chainey, George. Times garland of grace. San Diego, 1918.

Phil 175 - 200 General treatises on philosophy - Individual authors (A-Z) - cont.

Phil 177.51 — Carneri, Bartolomeo. Der Mensch als Selbstjweck. Wien, 1877.

Phil 177.52 — Candidus, L. Das Weltstreben. München, 1913.

Htn   Phil 177.53* — Carpenter, Nathaniel. Philosophia libera. Ed. 2a. Oxoniae, 1622.

Phil 177.54 — Corbeil, S. La normalienne en philosophie. Montreal, 1914.

Phil 177.55 — Crowell, Frank. Man - God's masterpiece. N.Y., 1916.

Phil 177.56 — Cunynghame, H. Short talks upon philosophy. London, 1923.

Phil 177.57 — Calderoni, M. Il pragmatismo a cura di Giovanni Papini. Lanciano, 1920.

Phil 177.58 — Costa, Alessandro. Filosofia e buddhismo. Torino, 1913.

Phil 177.60 — Conrad-Martius, Hedwig. Metaphysiche Gespräche. Halle, 1921.

Phil 177.60.5 — Conrad-Martius, Hedwig. Bios und Psyche. Hamburg, 1949.

NEDL   Phil 177.61 — Cursus philosophicus in usum scholarum auctoribus pluribus philosophiae professoribus in collegiis Valkenburgenci et Stonyhurstensi S.J. Friburgi Brisgoviae. 1-6,1915-1919 4v.

Phil 177.62 — Cicala, F.B. Introduzione alla teoria dell'essere le relazioni ontotetiche. Città di Castello, 1923.

Phil 177.62.5 — Cicala, F.B. Filosofia e diritto. v.1-4. Città di Castello, 1924.

Phil 177.63.5 — Cunningham, G.W. Problem of philosophy. N.Y., 1935.

Phil 177.64 — Conger, G.P. A course in philosophy. N.Y., 1924.

Phil 177.65 — Carr, H.W. The scientific approach to philosophy. London, 1924.

Phil 177.65.5 — Carr, H.W. The unique status of man. N.Y., 1928.

Phil 177.66 — Chiocchetti, Emilio. Il pragmatismo. Milano, 1926.

Phil 177.67 — Cleve, Z.J, De principio philosophiae. Helsingfors, 1848.

Phil 177.68 — Chartier, Émile. Quatre-vingt un et un chapitres sur l'esprit et les passions. Paris, 1921.

Phil 177.68.10 — Chartier, Émile. Idées; Platon, Descartes, Hegel. Paris, 1932.

Phil 177.68.15 — Chartier, Émile. Sentiments, pasiions et signes. 2e éd. Paris, 1935.

Phil 177.68.20 — Chartier, Émile. Éléments de philosophie. Paris, 1949.

Phil 177.68.25 — Chartier, Émile. Propos sur des philosophes. Paris, 1961.

Phil 177.69 — Coellen, L. Von der Selbstoffenbarung des göttlichen Lebens. Darmstadt, 1924.

Phil 177.70 — Cifarelli, Natale. Abbozzi di filosofia umana. Bari, 1913.

Phil 177.71 — Ceballos Dosamantes, J. El perfeccionismo absoluto. México, 1888.

Phil 177.72 — Cuvillier, Armand. Manuel de philosophie. Paris, 1927. 2v.

Phil 177.72.5 — Cuvillier, Armand. Partis pris sur l'art. Paris, 1956.

Phil 177.73 — Constable, F.C. I am. London, 1928.

Phil 177.73.5 — Constable, F.C. Myself and dreams. N.Y., 1918.

Phil 177.74 — Clemens, F. Das Manifest der Vernunft. 3e Aufl. Berlin, 1875.

Phil 177.75 — Choisnard, Paul. La loi de relation et l'erreur séparatiste en science et en philosophie. Paris, 1923.

Phil 177.76 — Calò, G. Maestri e problemi di filosofia. Torino, 1924. 2v.

Phil 177.77 — Chevalier, Jacques. Trois conférences d'Oxford. Paris, 1928.

Phil 177.77.5 — Chevalier, Jacques. Trois conférences d'Oxford. 2. ed. Paris, 1933.

Htn   Phil 177.78* — Cointha, Jean des Boulez. Paradoxo ou Sentença, philosophica contra opinão do vulgo. Lixboa, 1866.

Phil 177.79A — Clemenceau, G. In the evening of my thought. Boston, 1929. 2v.

Phil 177.79B — Clemenceau, G. In the evening of my thought. Boston, 1929. 2v.

Phil 177.80 — Cresson, André. Les septèmes philosophiques. Paris, 1929.

Phil 177.81 — Cesalpino, Andrea. Questions péripatéliciennes. Paris, 1929.

Phil 177.82 — Calvet, Adolphe. Le discontinu dans la philosophie et dans les sciences exactes. Paris, 1923.

Phil 177.83 — Coaley, C.H. Life and the student. N.Y., 1927.

Phil 177.84 — Clark, S.C. The melody of life. N.Y., 1902.

Phil 177.84.5 — Clark, S.C. Key-notes for daily harmonies. Boston, 1898.

Phil 177.85 — Collingwood, R.G. An essay on philosophical method. Oxford, 1933.

Phil 177.85.2 — Collingwood, R.G. An essay on metaphysics. Oxford, 1940.

Phil 177.85.5 — Collingwood, R.G. Speculum mentis. Oxford, 1924.

Phil 177.85.10 — Collingwood, R.G. The new leviathan or Man, society, civilization and barbarism. Oxford, 1942.

Phil 177.86 — Camera, Ugo. Saggio di una sistema di filosofia busato sulla suggestione. Aquila, 1920.

Phil 177.86.10 — Camera, Ugo. Problemi filosofici. Roma, 1931. 2 pam.

Phil 177.87 — Cavour, G.B. de. Fragments philosophiques. Turin, 1841.

Phil 177.87.5 — Cavour, G.B. di. Discorso. Torino, 1861.

Phil 177.88 — Castaner, C. Soul and matter. London, 1933.

Phil 177.90 — Chávez, E.A. Dios, el universo y la libertad. Barcelona, 1935.

Phil 177.91 — Coffey, Peter. Ontology; or The theory of being. London, 1914.

Phil 177.92 — Casey, Joseph T. The primacy of metaphysics. Diss. Washington, D.C., 1936.

Phil 177.93 — Carneades, D. Matter, spirit and living intellect. London, 1936.

Phil 177.94 — Carra, J.L. Système de la raison. 3e éd. Paris, 1791.

Phil 177.95 — Carrasquilla R., Humberto. El hombre. Medellin, 1934.

Phil 177.96 — Cardone, D.A. Il problema del sovraumano. Firenze, 1936.

Phil 177.97 — Caramella, S. Introduzione alla filosofia e dottrina della practica. Messina, 1936.

Phil 177.98 — Coates, Adrian. A basis of opinion. London, 1938.

Phil 177.99 — Compton, A.H. Human meaning of science. Chapel Hill, 1940.

Phil 177.100 — Coviello, A. Crítica bibliográfica y análisis cultural. Tucumán, 1914.

Phil 177.101 — Christiansen, Broder. Das Gesicht unserer Zeit. München, 1914.

Phil 177.102 — Cobb, Henry V.Z. Man's way, a first book in philosophy. 1st ed. London, 1942.

Phil 177.103 — Cazals de Fabel, Gabriel. Précis de philosophie à l'usage des candidats au baccalaureat. Toulouse, 1937.

Phil 177.104 — Cysarz, Herbert. Das Schöpferische. Halle, 1943.

Phil 177.105 — Calogero, G. Lezioni di filosofia. v.2-3. Roma, 1946. 2v.

Phil 177.105.2 — Calogero, G. Lezioni di filosofia. Torino, 1960. 3v.

Phil 177.105.10 — Calogero, G. Filosofia del dialogo. Milano, 1962.

Phil 177.105.30 — Spirito, Ugo. Ideale del dialogo o ideale della scienza? Roma, 1966.

Phil 175 - 200 General treatises on philosophy - Individual authors (A-Z) - cont.

Phil 177.106 Chatterjee, S. The problems of philosophy. Calcutta, 1949.
Phil 177.107 Costello, H.T. A philosophy of the real and the possible. N.Y., 1954.
Phil 177.110 Cuvillier, Armand. Précis de philosophie: classe de philosophie. Paris, 1954. 2v.
Phil 177.110.5 Cuvillier, Armand. La dissertation philosophique. Paris, 1958-62. 2v.
Phil 177.112 Chaix-Reys, Jules. Les dimensions de l'être et du temps. Paris, 1953.
Phil 177.115 Connally, F.G. Science versus philosophy. N.Y., 1957.
Phil 177.120 Carré, Jean Raoul. Le point d'appui pris sur le néant. 1. éd. Paris, 1955.
Phil 177.122 Collins, William B. Metaphysics and man. Dubuque, 1959.
Phil 177.124 Cappellani, G. Dalla materia allo spirito. Mazara, 1959.
Phil 177.126 Caso, Antonio. Antología filosófica. México, 1957.
Phil 177.128 Coreth, Emerich. Metaphysik. Innsbruck, 1961.
Phil 177.128.2 Coreth, Emerich. Metaphysics. N.Y., 1968.
Phil 177.129 Collins, J.D. The lure of wisdom. Milwaukee, 1962.
Phil 177.130 Craig, Hardin. New lamps for old. Oxford, 1960.
Phil 177.132 Cruz Malpique, M. Una filosofia da cultura. Porto, 1962.
Phil 177.133 Corradi, Gemma. Philosophy and co-existence. Leyden, 1966.
Phil 177.136 Cernuschi, Alberto. Teoría del autodeísmo. Buenos Aires, 1962.
Phil 177.138 Ceccato, Silvio. Un tecnico fra i filosofi. Padova, 1964- 2v.
Phil 177.140 Claeys, R.H. Inleiding tot de metafysica. Gent, 1968.
Phil 178.1 Damiron, P. Cours de philosophie. Bruxelles, 1834. 3v.
Phil 178.2 Daumer, G.F. Andeutung eines Systems speculativer Philosophie. Nürnberg, 1831.
Phil 178.3 Dejean de Fonroque, Numd. Croyances philosophiques. Paris, 1872.
Phil 178.4 Dennys, E.N. The alpha. London, 1855.
Phil 178.4.2 Dennys, E.N. The alpha. London, 1855.
Phil 178.4.100 The Alpha Union for freedom through truth. 4th ed. Hertfordshire, 1909.
Phil 178.5 Deussen, P. Elemente der Metaphysik. 2. Aufl. Leipzig, 1890.
Phil 178.5.2 Deussen, P. Die Elemente der Metaphysik. Aachen, 1877.
Phil 178.5.3 Deussen, P. Die Elemente der Metaphysik. 6e Aufl. Leipzig, 1919.
NEDL Phil 178.5.5 Deussen, P. Elements of metaphysics. London, 1894. (Changed to KD 25702)
Phil 178.6 Dollfus, C. De la nature humaine. Paris, 1868.
Phil 178.7 Drummond, W. Academical questions. London, 1805.
Phil 178.7.5 Drummond, W. Academical questions. London, 1805.
Phil 178.8 Durand Désormeaux, Fernand. Réflexions et pensées. Paris, 1884.
Phil 178.9 Dutens, Louis. Recherches. v.1-2. Paris, 1766.
Phil 178.9.2 Dutens, Louis. Recherches. 2. éd. Paris, 1776. 2v.
Phil 178.9.3 Dutens, Louis. Origine des découvertes. 3e éd. Louvain, 1796.
Phil 178.9.4 Dutens, Louis. Origine des découvertes. 4e éd. Paris, 1812.
Phil 178.10 Dressler, J.G. Grundlehren der Psychologie und Logik. Leipzig, 1872.
Phil 178.11 Drious, C.J. Cours de philosophie. Paris, 1883.
Phil 178.12.05 Pamphlet box. Minor writings.
Phil 178.12.2 Dresser, H.W. In search of a soul. Boston, 1897.
Phil 178.12.5 Dresser, H.W. The perfect whole. Boston, 1896.
Phil 178.12.7 Dresser, H.W. The perfect whole. 3rd ed. Boston, 1898.
Phil 178.12.8 Dresser, H.W. The power of silence. Boston, 1895.
Phil 178.12.9.5 Dresser, H.W. The power of silence. 7th ed. Boston, 1898.
Phil 178.12.11 Dresser, H.W. The power of silence. N.Y., 1901.
Phil 178.12.11.9 Dresser, H.W. The power of silence. 2nd ed. N.Y., 1909.
Phil 178.12.12 Dresser, H.W. Voices of hope. Boston, 1898.
Phil 178.12.14 Dresser, H.W. Voices of freedom. N.Y., 1899.
Phil 178.12.16 Dresser, H.W. Education and the philosophical ideal. N.Y., 1900.
Phil 178.12.17 Dresser, H.W. Living by the spirit. N.Y., 1901.
Phil 178.12.18 Dresser, H.W. A book of secrets. N.Y., 1902.
Phil 178.12.19 Dresser, H.W. Methods and problems of spiritual healing. N.Y., 1899.
Phil 178.12.25 Dresser, H.W. Man and the divine order. N.Y., 1903.
Phil 178.12.26 Dresser, H.W. Philosophy of the spirit. N.Y., 1908.
Phil 178.12.27A Dresser, H.W. Health and the inner life. N.Y., 1906.
Phil 178.12.27B Dresser, H.W. Health and the inner life. N.Y., 1906.
Phil 178.12.29 Dresser, H.W. Human efficiency. N.Y., 1912.
Phil 178.12.33 Dresser, H.W. A message to the well. N.Y., 1910.
Phil 178.12.35 Dresser, H.W. Handbook of the new thought. N.Y., 1917.
Phil 178.12.37 Dresser, H.W. The spirit of the new thought. N.Y., 1917.
Phil 178.12.39 Dresser, H.W. The victorious faith, moral ideals in war time. N.Y., 1917.
Phil 178.12.40 Dresser, H.W. A physician to the soul. N.Y., 1908.
Phil 178.12.42 Dresser, H.W. A history of the new thought movement. N.Y., 1919.
Phil 178.12.43 Dresser, H.W. The religion of the spirit in modern life. N.Y., 1914.
Phil 178.12.47 Dresser, H.W. The Christ ideal. N.Y., 1901.
Phil 178.12.49 Dresser, H.W. On the threshold of the spiritual world. N.Y., 1919.
Phil 178.12.55 Dresser, H.W. The immanent God. Boston, 1895.
Phil 178.12.60 Dresser, H.W. The greatest truth. N.Y., 1907.
Phil 178.13 Dupont, A.H.H. Ontologie. Louvain, 1875.
Phil 178.14 Dietrich, K. Protest Gegen die moderne Wissenschaft. Hamburg, 1887.
Phil 178.15 Duboc, K.J. Hundert jahre Zeitgeist in Deutschland. Leipzig, 1889.
Phil 178.15.5 Duboc, K.J. Jenseits vom Wirklichen. Dresden, 1896.
Phil 178.16 Dumesni, G. Du role des concepts. Paris, 1892.
Phil 178.16.5 Dumesni, G. La sophistique contemporaine. Paris, 1912.
Phil 178.17 Dessoir, Max. Philosophisches Lesebuch. Stuttgart, 1903.
Phil 178.17.3 Dessoir, Max. Philosophisches Lesebuch. Stuttgart, 1910.
Phil 178.17.10 Dessoir, Max. Bibliographie des modernen Hypnotismus. n.p., 1888-1913. 25 pam.
Phil 178.17.15 Dessoir, Max. Einleitung in die Philosophie. Stuttgart, 1936.
Phil 178.17.17 Dessoir, Max. Einleitung in die Philosophie. 2. Aufl. Stuttgart, 1946.
Phil 178.18 Drews, Arthur. Das Ich als Grundproblem der Metaphysik. Freiburg, 1897.
Phil 178.19 Dunan, Charles. Essais de philosophie générale. 5th ed. Paris, 1902.
Phil 178.19.5 Dunan, Charles. Les deux idéalismes. Paris, 1911.

Phil 175 - 200 General treatises on philosophy - Individual authors (A-Z) - cont.

Phil 178.20 Domecq, J.B. Études analytiques sur les auteurs philosophiques. Tours, n.d.
Phil 178.21 Dubray, C.A. Introductory philosophy. N.Y., 1912.
Phil 178.22 Driesch, H. Ordnungslehre. Jena, 1912.
Phil 178.22.2 Driesch, H. Ordnungslehre. Jena, 1923.
Phil 178.22.4 Driesch, H. Wirklichkeitslehre. Leipzig, 1922.
Phil 178.22.4.5 Driesch, H. Wirklichkeitslehre. 3e Aufl. Leipzig, 1930.
Phil 178.22.5 Driesch, H. Das Ganze und die Summe. Leipzig, 1921.
Phil 178.22.7 Driesch, H. Metaphysik. Breslau, 1924.
Phil 178.22.9 Driesch, H. The possibility of metaphysics. London, 1924.
Phil 178.22.20 Driesch, H. Der Mensch und die Welt. Leipzig, 1928.
Phil 178.22.25 Driesch, H. Man and the universe. London, 1929.
Phil 178.22.30 Driesch, H. Philosophische Forschungswege. Leipzig, 1930.
Phil 178.22.35 Driesch, H. Philosophische Gegenwartsfragen. Leipzig, 1933.
Phil 178.24 Daub, E. Studien. Frankfurt, 1805. 6v.
Phil 178.24.5 Daub, Carl. Philosophische und theologische Vorlesungen. v.1-7. Berlin, 1838-44. 8v.
Phil 178.25 Dana, A.H. Inductive inquiries in physiology, ethics, and ethnology. N.Y., 1873.
Phil 178.26 Dilthey, Wilhelm. Einleitung in die Geisteswissenschaften. Leipzig, 1803.
Phil 178.26.5 Dilthey, Wilhelm. Introduction à l'étude des sciences humaines (Einleitung in die Geisteswissenschaften). 1re éd. Paris, 1942.
Phil 178.27 Driscoll, John T. Pragmatism and the problem of the idea. N.Y., 1915.
Phil 178.28 Pamphlet box. Dearborn, G.V.M. Minor writings.
Phil 178.28.1 Pamphlet box. Dearborn, G.V.M. Minor writings.
Phil 178.29 Dean, Amos. Philosophy of human life. Boston, 1839.
Phil 178.30 Durant, William. Philosophy and social problem. N.Y., 1917.
Phil 178.30.5 Durant, William. The mansions of philosophy. N.Y., 1929.
Phil 178.30.7 Durant, William. The mansions of philosophy. Garden City, 1941.
Phil 178.30.10 Durant, William. On the meaning of life. N.Y., 1932.
Phil 178.31 Dewing, A.S. Life as reality. N.Y., 1910.
Phil 178.32 Delbos, Victor. Figures et doctrines des philosophes. 4e éd. Paris, 1918.
Htn Phil 178.33* Duncan, R. Prometheus (les grandes crucifiés). Paris, 1919.
Phil 178.34 Dreher, Eugen. Philosophische Abhandlungen. Berlin, 1903.
Phil 178.34.5 Dreher, Eugen. Beiträge zu einer exacten Psycho-Physiologie. n.p., 1880-91. 4 pam.
Phil 178.35 Drossbach, M. Über die Verschiedenengrade. Berlin, 1873.
Phil 178.36 Dilles, Ludwig. Wieg zur Metaphysik als exakten Wissenschaft. Stuttgart, 1903-06. 2v.
Phil 178.37 Dingler, Hugo. Die Grundlagen der Naturphilosophie. Leipzig, 1913.
Phil 178.37.5 Dingler, Hugo. Der Zusammenbruch der Wissenschaft und der Primat derPhilosophie. München, 1926.
Phil 178.37.7 Dingler, Hugo. Der Zusammenbruch der Wissenschaft und der Primat der Philosophie. 2e Aufl. München, 1931.
Phil 178.37.10 Dingler, Hugo. Metaphysik als Wissenschaft vom Letzten. München, 1929.
Phil 178.37.15 Dingler, Hugo. Das System. München, 1930.
Phil 178.38.4 Dewey, John. Reconstruction in philosophy. Boston, 1948.
Phil 178.38.5A Dewey, John. Experience and nature. Chicago, 1925.
Phil 178.38.5B Dewey, John. Experience and nature. Chicago, 1925.
Phil 178.38.7A Dewey, John. Experience and nature. Chicago, 1926.
Phil 178.38.7B Dewey, John. Experience and nature. Chicago, 1926.
Phil 178.38.10 Dewey, John. The philosophy of John Dewey. N.Y., 1928.
Phil 178.38.15A Dewey, John. The quest for certainty. N.Y., 1929.
Phil 178.38.15B Dewey, John. The quest for certainty. N.Y., 1929.
Phil 178.38.16 Dewey, John. The quest for certainty. N.Y., 1929.
Phil 178.38.35 Dewey, John. Construction and criticism. N.Y., 1930.
Phil 178.38.40 Dewey, John. Philosophy and civilization. N.Y., 1931.
Phil 178.39 Durand, J.P. Variétés philosophiques. 2e éd. Paris, 1900.
Phil 178.40 Dyroff, Adolf. Über den Existenzialbegriff. Freiburg im Breisgau, 1902.
Phil 178.40.5 Dyroff, Adolf. Einleitung in die Philosophie. Bonn, 1948.
Phil 178.41 Dupont, Paul. Les problèmes de la philosophie et leur enchainement scientifique. Paris, 1920.
Phil 178.42 Dittes, Friedrich. Gesammelte Schriften. Heft I. Leipzig, 1893.
Phil 178.43 Dreyer, Friedrich. Studien zu Methodenlehre und Erkenntnisskritik. Leipzig, 1895-1903.
Phil 178.44 Delff, Heinrich K.H. Philosophie des Gemüths. Husum, 1893.
Phil 178.44.5 Delff, Heinrich K.H. Über den Weg, zum Wissen und zur Gewissheit zu Gesangen. Leipzig, 1882.
Phil 178.44.10 Delff, Heinrich K.H. Die Hauptprobleme der Philosophie und Religion. Leipzig, 1886.
Phil 178.45 Durand, Eugène. Cours de philosophie. Paris, 1909-21. 2v.
Phil 178.46 Decoster, Paul. Le règne de la pensée. Bruxelles, 1922.
Phil 178.46.5 Decoster, Paul. La réforme de la conscience. Bruxelles, 1919.
Phil 178.46.10 Decoster, Paul. Acte et synthèse. Bruxelles, 1928.
Phil 178.46.15 Decoster, Paul. De l'unité métaphysique. Bruxelles, 1934.
Phil 178.46.80 Gerard, Jacques. La metaphysique de Paul Decoster. Paris, 1945.
Phil 178.47 Danmar, W. World cognition. N.Y., 1923.
Phil 178.48 Dam, Axel. Opdragelsens hovedopgaver. 3. udg. Kobenhavn, 1923.
Phil 178.49 Dressler, Max. Die Welt als Wille zum Selbst. Seidelberg, 1904.
Phil 178.50 Dieterich, K. Grundzüge der Metaphysik. Freiburg im Breisgau, 1885.
Phil 178.51 Dubuc, Paul. Essai sur la méthode en métaphysique. Paris, 1887.
Phil 178.52 Descoqs, Paul. Institutiones metaphysicae generalis; éléments d'ontologie. Paris, 1925.
Phil 178.53 Delius, Rudolf von. Urgesetze des Lebens. Darmstadt, 1922.
Phil 178.54 Dandolo, G. Appunti di filosofia. v.1-3. Messina, 1903-1909.
Phil 178.54.3 Dandolo, G. Appunti di filosofia. 3. ed. Padova, 1894.
Phil 178.54.5 Dandolo, G. L'obbietto della filosofia e la verità. Padova, 1894.
Phil 178.55 Donati, G. La metafisica. Savignano, 1921.
Phil 178.56 Durand-Doat, J. Le sens de la mêtaphysique. Paris, 1928.
Phil 178.56.2 Durand-Doat, J. Le sens de la métaphysique. Thèse. Paris, 1928.
Phil 178.57 Dixon, E.T. The guidance of conduct. London, 1928.
Phil 178.58 Dewe, Joseph A. Les deux ordres, psychique el material. Paris, 1929.

Classified Listing

Phil 175 - 200 General treatises on philosophy - Individual authors (A-Z) - cont.

Phil 178.58.5 Dewe, Joseph A. Les deux ordres, psychique et materiel. Thèse. Paris, 1929.
Phil 178.59 Dotterer, Ray H. Philosophy by ways of the sciences. N.Y., 1929.
Phil 178.59.5 Dotterer, Ray H. Postulates and implications. N.Y., 1955.
Phil 178.60 Dakin, John E. Rhythmic affinity, a philosophic hypothesis. N.Y., 1929.
Phil 178.61 Drake, Durant. Invitation to philosophy. Boston, 1933.
Phil 178.62 Drago, P.C. La genesi del problema fenomenologico. Milano, 1933.
Phil 178.63 Dallago, Carl. Der grosse Universende. Innsbruch, 1924.
Phil 178.64 Dixon, W.M. The human situation. N.Y., 1937.
Phil 178.64.4 Dixon, W.M. The human situation. London, 1938.
Phil 178.64.4.5 Dixon, W.M. The human situation. London, 1954.
Phil 178.64.4.7 Dixon, W.M. The human situation. Harmondsworth, 1958.
Phil 178.64.5 Dixon, W.M. Thoughts for the times. N.Y., 1941.
Phil 178.64.6 Dixon, W.M. Thoughts for the times. Glasgow, 1941.
Phil 178.65 Ducasse, C.J. Philosophy as a science. N.Y., 1941.
Phil 178.67 Donat, Josef. Ontologia. 9. ed. Oeniponte, 1940.
Phil 178.68 Dempf, Alois. Selbstkritik der Philosophie und vergleichende Philosophiegeschichte im Umriss. Wien, 1947.
Phil 178.69 Deschoux, M. Initiation à la philosophie. 1. éd. Paris, 1951.
Phil 178.69.5 Deschoux, M. Itinéraire philosophique. Paris, 1964-1971. 5v.
Phil 178.70 Drews, A. Einführung in die Philosophie. Berlin, 1921.
Phil 178.71 Durkheim, E. Pragmatisme et socilologie. Paris, 1955.
Phil 178.74 Daval, Simone. Classe de philosophie. Paris, 1962. 2v.
Phil 178.75 Doeblin, Alfred. Unser Dasein. Olten, 1964.
Phil 178.76 Dilley, Frank B. Metaphysics and religious language. N.Y., 1964.
Phil 178.77 Dufrenne, Mikel. Jalons. La Haye, 1966.
Phil 178.78 Delhomme, Yeanne. La pensée et le réel, antique de l'ontologie. Paris, 1967.
VPhil 178.79 Dambska, Izydora. O narzedziach i przedmiotach poznamia. Wyd. 1. Warszawa, 1967.
Phil 178.81 Delavigne, A. Manual de filosophíe. Buçuresti, 1846.
Phil 178.82 Diéguez, Manuel de. Science et nescience. Paris, 1970.
Phil 178.84 Derisi, Octavio Nicolas. Los fundamentos metafisicos del orden moral. 3. ed. Madrid, 1969.
Phil 179.03 Eucken, R. Prolegomena...Einheit des Geisteslebens. Leipzig, 1885.
Phil 179.1 Engel, G.E. System der metaphysischen Grundbegriffe. Berlin, 1852.
Phil 179.2 Erhardt, F. Metaphysik. Leipzig, 1894.
Phil 179.3 Eucken, R. Die Einheit des Geisteslebens. Leipzig, 1888.
Phil 179.3.2 Eucken, R. Die Einheit des Geisteslebens. 2. Aufl. Berlin, 1925.
Phil 179.3.5 Eucken, R. Geistige Strömungen derGegenwart. Leipzig, 1904.
Phil 179.3.6 Eucken, R. Geistige Strömungen der Gegenwart. 4e Aufl. Leipzig, 1909.
Phil 179.3.7.4 Eucken, R. Main currents of modern thought. London, 1912.
Phil 179.3.8 Eucken, R. Fundamental concepts of modern philosophical thought. N.Y., 1880.
Phil 179.3.13 Eucken, R. Gesammelte Aufsätze zur Philosophie. Leipzig, 1903.
Phil 179.3.15 Eucken, R. Colleted essays. London, 1914.
Phil 179.3.17 Eucken, R. Geistigen Lebensinhalt. Leipzig, 1896.
Phil 179.3.19 Eucken, R. Der Kampf um einen Geistigen Lebensinhalt. Leipzig, 1918.
Phil 179.3.20 Eucken, R. Rudolf Eucken; ein Geistesbild. Berlin, 1927?
Phil 179.3.21 Eucken, R. The life of the spirit. London, 1909.
Phil 179.3.25 Eucken, R. Der Sinn und Wert des Lebens. Leipzig, 1910.
Phil 179.3.27 Eucken, R. Sinn und Wert des Lebens. 3rd ed. Leipzig, 1913.
Phil 179.3.27.3 Eucken, R. Der Sinn und Wert des Lebens. 6. Aufl. Leipzig, 1918.
Phil 179.3.27.15 Eucken, R. The meaning and value of life. London, 1909.
Phil 179.3.28.2 Eucken, R. Geistesprobleme und Lebensfragen. 2e Aufl. Leipzig, n.d.
Phil 179.3.28.5 Eucken, R. Geistesprobleme und Lebensfragen. Leipzig, 1918.
Phil 179.3.29 Eucken, R. Life's basis and life's ideal. London, 1911.
Phil 179.3.31 Eucken, R. Die Grundbegriffe der Gegenwart. 2. Aufl. Leipzig, 1893.
Phil 179.3.32 Eucken, R. Erkennen und Leben. Leipzig, 1912.
Phil 179.3.32.5 Eucken, R. Erkennen und Leben. Berlin, 1923.
Phil 179.3.35 Eucken, R. Religion and life. N.Y., 1912.
Phil 179.3.41 Eucken, R. Knowledge and life. N.Y., 1914.
Phil 179.3.45 Eucken, R. Zur Sammlung der Geistert. Leipzig, 1914.
Phil 179.3.50 Eucken, R. Die geistigen Forderungen der Gegenwart. 3e Aufl. Berlin, 1918.
Phil 179.3.52 Eucken, R. Prologomena und Epilog zu einer Philosophie des Geistlebens. Berlin, 1922.
Phil 179.3.55 Eucken, R. Naturalism or idealism? Photoreproduction. Cambridge, 1912.
Phil 179.3.60 Eucken, R. Geschichte und Kritik der grund Begriffe der Gegenwart. v.1-2. Leipzig, 1878.
Phil 179.3.61 Eucken, R. The spiritual outlook of Europe today. London, 1922.
Phil 179.3.65 Eucken, R. Mensch und Welt. 3e Aufl. Leipzig, 1923.
Phil 179.3.67 Eucken, R. Der Kampf um die Religion in der Gegenwart. 1. und 2. Aufl. Langensalza, 1922.
Phil 179.3.70 Eucken, R. Moral und Lebensanschauung. 2. Aufl. Leipzig, 1917.
Phil 179.3.75 Eucken, R. Lebenserinnerungen. Leipzig, 1921.
Phil 179.3.75.25 Eucken, R. Lebenserinnerungen. Stockholm, 1921.
Phil 179.3.76 Eucken, R. Rudolf Eucken, his life, work and travels. London, 1921.
Phil 179.3.80 Pamphlet box. Eucken, Rudolf.
Phil 179.3.81 Kessler, K. Rudolf Euckens Werk. Bunzlau, 1911.
Phil 179.3.81.5 Siebert, Otto. Rudolf Euckens Welt- und Lebensanschauung. 2. Aufl. Langensalza, 1911.
Phil 179.3.81.7 Boutroux, Émile. Rudolf Euckens Kampf um einen neuen Idealismus. Leipzig, 1911.
Phil 179.3.82 Gibson, W.R.B. Rudolf Eucken's philosophy of life. London, 1907.
Phil 179.3.84 Kappstein, T. Rudolf Eucken. Berlin, 1909.
Phil 179.3.86 Kade, Richard. Rudolf Euckens noologische Methode. Leipzig, 1912.
Phil 179.3.90 Kesseler, K. Rudolf Euckens Bedeutung für das modern Christentum. Bunzlau, 1912.
Phil 179.3.91 Kesseler, K. Die Vertiefung der kantischen Religions-Philosophie. Bunzlau, 1908.

Phil 175 - 200 General treatises on philosophy - Individual authors (A-Z) - cont.

Phil 179.3.99 Booth, Meyrick. Rudolf Eucken; his philosophy. London, 1914.
Phil 179.3.105 Höhlmann, Hans. Rudolf Euckens Theologie. Berlin, 1903.
Phil 179.3.106 Heussner, A. Einführung in Rudolf Euckens Lebens- und Weltanschauung. Göttingen, 1921.
Phil 179.3.109 Braun, Otto. Rudolf Euckens Philosophie und das Bildungsproblem. Leipzig, 1909.
Phil 179.3.112 Die Tatwelt, Zeitschrift für Erneuerung des Geiteslebens. Berlin, 1927.
Phil 179.3.114 Jones, Abel John. Rudolf Eucken. London, 1913.
Phil 179.3.125 Oldendorff, Paul. Von deutscher Philosophie des Lebens. Langensalza, 1916.
Phil 179.5 Eichbaum-Lange, W. Was heisst Philosophie? Leipzig, 1902.
Phil 179.6 Engle, J.S. Analytic interest psychology. Baltimore, 1904.
Phil 179.7 Eisler, R. Kritische Einführung in die Philosophie. Berlin, 1905.
Phil 179.8 Ewald, O. Gründe und Abgründe. v.1-2. Berlin, 1909.
Phil 179.9 Eusebietti, Pietro. Corso elementare di filosofia. Milano, 1912. 3v.
Phil 179.10 Ettinger-Reichmann, Regina. Die Immanenzphilosophie. Göttingen, 1916.
Phil 179.11 Eitle, Johannes. Grundriss der Philosophie. Freiburg, 1892.
Phil 179.12 Eno, Henry Lane. Activism. Princeton, N.J., 1920.
Phil 179.13 Elsenhans, T. Die Aufgabe einer Psychologie der Deutung als Vorarbeit für die Geisteswissenschaften. Giessen, 1904.
Phil 179.14F Eck, Samuel. Gedanke und Persönlichkeit. Giessen, 1914.
Phil 179.15 Einhorn, David. Der Kampf um einen Gegenstand der Philosophie. Wien, 1916.
Phil 179.16 Erberg, K. Tsel tvorchestva. Moskva, 1913.
Phil 179.17 Ellis, Havelock. The dance of life. Boston, 1923.
Phil 179.17.4 Ellis, Havelock. The dance of life. N.Y., 1923.
Phil 179.17.5 Ellis, Havelock. The dance of life. Boston, 1926.
Phil 179.17.15 Ellis, Havelock. The dance of life. Boston 1929.
Phil 179.17.18 Ellis, Havelock. The dance of life. N.Y., 1929.
Phil 179.17.20 Ellis, Havelock. The dance of life. N.Y., 1929.
Phil 179.18 Ettlinger, Max. Philosophische Fragen der Gegenwart. Kempten, 1911.
Phil 179.19 Emmelin, Axel. Enhets- och mangfaldsproblemet inom metfysiken. Lund, 1905.
Phil 179.20 Endres, J.A. Einleitung in die Philosophie. Kempten, 1920.
Phil 179.21 Eriksen, Richard. Tidens kurs. Kristiania, 1912.
Phil 179.22 Erdmann, J.E. Vermischte Aufsätze. Leipzig, 1846.
Phil 179.22.5 Erdmann, J.E. Filosofiska miniaturer. Stockholm, 1873.
Phil 179.22.10 Erdmann, J.E. Wir leben Nicht auf der Erde. Berlin, 1852-71. 5 pam.
Phil 179.22.15 Erdmann, J.E. Ernste Spiele. 3. Aufl. Berlin, 1875.
Phil 179.23 Edfeldt, Hans. Hvilken verldsförklaring uppfyller fordringarna för möjlighrtin of menniskans praktiska lif? Uppsala, 1868.
Phil 179.24 Edman, Irwin. Richard Kane looks at life. Boston, 1926.
Phil 179.24.2 Edman, Irwin. Richard Kane looks at life. Boston, 1926.
Phil 179.24.5 Edman, Irwin. The contemporary and his soul. N.Y., 1931.
Phil 179.25 Ekelund, V. Attiskt. Stockholm, 1919.
Phil 179.26 Eleutheropulos, A. Philosophie: allgemeine Weltanschauung. Zürich, 1911.
Phil 179.27 Ewast, John-Bart. Disquisitio philosophica de contingentia rerum. Aboae, 1735.
Phil 179.29 Eschenmayer, C.H. von. Einleitung in Natur und Geschichte. Erlangen, 1806.
Phil 179.30 Esser, Gerard. Metaphysica generalis in usum scholarum. Techny, Ill., 1933.
Phil 179.31 Egaña, Juan. Tractatus de re logica. Santiago, 1827.
Phil 179.32 Elrick, C.F. Tertium quid; ratiocination. St. Louis, 1934.
Phil 179.33 Emmet, D.M. Philosophy and faith. London, 1936.
Phil 179.33.5 Emmet, D.M. The nature of metaphysical thinking. London, 1945.
Phil 179.34 Everett, C.C. Immortality. Boston, 1902.
Phil 179.35 Esser, Pieter H. Levensaspecten. Zutphen, 1946.
Phil 179.36 Ewing, A.C. The fundamental questions of philosophy. N.Y., 1951.
Phil 179.36.3 Ewing, Alfred Cyril. The fundamental questions of philosophy. N.Y., 1962.
Phil 179.38A Eranos-Jahrbuch. Spirit and nature. N.Y., 1954.
Phil 179.38B Eranos-Jahrbuch. Spirit and nature. N.Y., 1954.
Phil 179.40 Einführung in die Philosophie. Greifswald, 1964. 2v.
Phil 179.42 Engel, S. Morris. The problem of tragedy. Frederiction, N.B., 1960.
Phil 179.44 Elders, Fons. Filosofie als science-fiction. Amsterdam, 1968.
Phil 180.1 Fabre, J. Cours de philosophie. Paris, 1870.
Phil 180.2 Fawcett, E.D. The riddle of the universe. London, 1893.
Phil 180.2.5 Fawcett, E.D. World as imagination. Series 1-2. London, 1916-1921. 2v.
Phil 180.2.9 Fawcett, E.D. The individual and reality. London, 1909.
Phil 180.2.15 Fawcett, E.D. The Zermatt dialogues. London, 1931.
Phil 180.2.35 Farkas, S. Filozófiai értekezések. Aiud-Nagyenyed, 1938.
Phil 180.5 Field, G. Outlines of analogical philosophy. London, 1839. 2v.
Phil 180.6 Fischer, K.P. Grundzüge des Systems der Philosophie. Frankfurt, 1848-1855. 3v.
Phil 180.6.2 Fischer, K.P. Grundzüge des Systems der Philosophie. v.2,3. Erlangen, 1850-1855. 2v.
Phil 180.6.7 Fischer, K.P. Die Wissenschaft der Metaphysik im Grundrisse. Stuttgart, 1834.
Phil 180.7 Flournoy, T. Métaphysique et psychologie. Genève, 1890.
Phil 180.7.2 Flournoy, T. Métaphysique et psychologie. 2. éd. Genève, 1919.
Phil 180.8 Franck, A. Moralistes et philosophes. Paris, 1872.
Phil 180.8.3 Franck, A. Essais de critique philosophique. Paris, 1885.
Phil 180.8.5 Franck, A. Nouveaux essais de critique philosophique. Paris, 1890.
Phil 180.9 Fraser, A.C. Rational philosophy. Edinburgh, 1858.
Phil 180.10A Frothingham, Ephraim L. Philosophy as absolute science. Boston, 1864.
Phil 180.10B Frothingham, Ephraim L. Philosophy as absolute science. Boston, 1864.
Phil 180.11 Pamphlet box. Frankland's miscellaneous philosophical writings.
Phil 180.12 Frohschammer, J. Einleitung in die Philosophie. München, 1858.
Phil 180.12.5 Frohschammer, J. System der Philosophie im Umriss. München, 1892.

Phil 180.12.10	Frohschammer, J. Die Philosophie als Idealwissenschaft und System. München, 1884.
Phil 180.12.15	Frohschammer, J. Über das Mysterium magnum des Daseins. Leipzig, 1891.
Phil 180.13	Funck-Brentano, T. Les sciences humaines: la philosophie. Paris, 1868.
Phil 180.14	Flourens, P. Fontenelle. Paris, 1847-1851. 5 pam.
Phil 180.16	Fiske, J. The unseen world and other essays. Boston, 1876.
Phil 180.17.2	Fullerton, G.S. A system of metaphysics. N.Y., 1914.
Phil 180.17.5	Fullerton, G.S. An introduction to philosophy. N.Y., 1906.
Phil 180.17.12	Fullerton, G.S. An introduction to philosophy. N.Y., 1921.
Phil 180.18	Flügel, D. Die Probleme der Philosophie und ihre Losungen. Cöthen, 1906.
Phil 180.18.5	Flügel, D. Die Probleme der Philosophie und ihre Lösungen historisch-critisch Dargestellt. 2.Aufl. Cöthen, 1888.
Phil 180.19	Fouillée, Alfred. La pensée. 2e éd. Paris, 1911.
Phil 180.19.5	Fouillée, Alfred. L'avenir de la metaphysique fondée sur l'experience. Paris, 1889.
Phil 180.19.9	Fouillée, Alfred. Extraits des grands philosophes. 6e éd. Paris, 1917.
Phil 180.20	Flint, Robert. Philosophy as scientia scientarum. N.Y., 1904.
X Cg Phil 180.21	Fortlage, Karl. Sechs philosophische Vorträge. 2. Ausg. Jena, 1872.
Phil 180.22	Frischeisen-Köhler, M. Moderne Philosophie. Stuttgart, 1907.
Phil 180.23	Faguet, Emile. Initiation into philosophy. N.Y., 1914.
Phil 180.23.2	Faguet, Emile. Initiation philosophique. Paris, 1913.
Phil 180.24	Faug, Balthasar. Les vraies bases de la philosophie. 3e éd. Paris, 1887.
Phil 180.25F	Ferri, Luigi. Della idea del vero e...dell'essere. Roma, 1887.
Phil 180.26	François Adolphe. Les grands problèmes. Paris, 1895.
Phil 180.27	Fabbricotti, Carlo A. Appunti critici di filosofia contemporanea. Firenze, 1910.
Phil 180.28.5	Field, G.C. Studies in philosophy. Bristol, 1935.
Phil 180.29	Ferrari, Giuseppe M. Scritti varj. v.1-3. Roma, 1899-1927. 3v.
Phil 180.30	Fazio-Allmayer, W. Materia e sensazione. Milano, 1913.
Phil 180.31	Fischer, Engelbert Lorenz. Das Grundproblem der Metaphysik. Mainz, 1894.
Phil 180.32	Frost, Walter. Naturphilosophie. v.1. Leipzig, 1910.
Phil 180.33	Fischer, Ludwig. Grundriss des Systems der Philosophie als Bestimmungslehre. Wiesbaden, 1890.
Phil 180.33.5	Fischer, Ludwig. Wirklichkeit, Wahrheit und Wissen. Berlin, 1919.
Phil 180.33.10	Fischer, Ludwig. Das Vollwirkliche und das Als-ob. Berlin, 1921.
Phil 180.34	Friedlaender, S. Schöpferische Indifferenz. München, 1918.
Phil 180.35	Freytag, Willy. Über den Begriff der Philosophie. Halle, 1904.
Phil 180.36	Fetzer, K.A. Philosophische Leitbegriffe. Tübingen, 1884.
Phil 180.37	Feldmann, J. Schule der Philosophie. Paderborn, 1925.
Phil 180.38	Freyer, Hans. Theorie des objektiven Geistes. Leipzig, 1923.
Phil 180.38.5	Freyer, Hans. Theorie des objektiven Geistes. 3. Aufl. Leipzig, 1934.
Phil 180.38.10	Freyer, Hans. Prometheus: Ideen zur Philosophie der Kultur. Jena, 1923.
Phil 180.39	Flewelling, R. Creative personality. N.Y., 1926.
Phil 180.40	Finckh, T. Lehrbuch der philosophischen Propädeutik. Heidelberg, 1909.
Phil 180.41	Ferro, A.A. Concetto della filosofia. Savona, 1902.
Phil 180.41.10	Ferro, A.A. Scritti filosofici. Milano, 1932.
Phil 180.42	Falco, Francesco. L'uomo:saggio popolare. Piacenza, 1870.
Phil 180.43	Feldkeller, Paul. Verständigung als philosophisches Problem. Erfurt, 1928.
Phil 180.44A	Farber, M. Phenomenology as a method and as a philosophical discipline. n.p., 1928.
Phil 180.44B	Farber, M. Phenomenology as a method and as a philosophical discipline. n.p., 1928.
Phil 180.45	Fritzsche, A.R. Vorschule der Philosophie. Leipzig, 1906.
Phil 180.46	Fremling, Matthaus. Dissertatio philosophica de ratione praecepta philosophiae theoreticae tradendi. Pt.1-3. Lundae, 1783-1787.
Phil 180.47	Falkenfeld, H. Einfuhrung in die Philosophie. Berlin, 1926.
Phil 180.48	Freund, Ludwig. Am Ende der Philosophie. München, 1930.
Phil 180.48.10	Freund, Ludwig. Philosophie: ein unlösbares Problem. München, 1933.
Phil 180.49	Faust, August. Der Möglichkeitsgedanke. Heidelberg, 1931-1932. 2v.
Phil 180.50	Feder, J.G.H. Philosophische Bibliothek. v.1-4. Göttingen, 1788-1791. 2v.
Phil 180.51	Felkin, F.W. A wordbook of metaphysics. London, 1932.
Phil 180.52	Fialko, N.M. Passivity and rationalization. N.Y., 1935.
Phil 180.52.5	Fialko, N.M. Passivnost'. Paris, 1927.
Phil 180.53	Finley, John H. The mystery of the mind's desire. N.Y., 1936.
Phil 180.54	Fersen, Alessandro. L'universo come guioco. Modena, 1936.
Phil 180.55	Fiszer, E. Unité et intelligibilité. Paris, 1936.
Phil 180.55.5	Fiszer, E. Unité et intelligibilité. Thèse. Paris, 1936.
Phil 180.56	Fischer-Mampoteng, F.C. Menschsein als Aufgabe. Heidelberg, 1928.
Phil 180.57	Forest, Aimé. Du consentement à l'être. Paris, 1936.
Phil 180.58	Finlayson Elliot, Clarence. Intuicion del ser. Santiago, 1938.
Phil 180.60	Flechtner, H.J. Freiheit und Bindung. Berlin, 1935.
Phil 180.61	La fase attuale della filosofia. Messina, 1936.
Phil 180.62	Fischer, E. Zum Geisteskampf der Gegenwart. Basel, 1941.
Phil 180.63A	Ferm, V. First adventures in philosophy. N.Y., 1936.
Phil 180.63B	Ferm, V. First adventures in philosophy. N.Y., 1936.
Phil 180.64	Foss, Martin. Symbol and metaphor in human experience. Princeton, N.J., 1949.
Phil 180.66	Friederichs, K. Die Selbstgestaltung des Lebendigen. München, 1955.
Phil 180.68	Foulquié, Paul. Précis de philosophie. 2. ed. v.2-3. Paris, 1955.
Phil 180.68.5	Foulquié, Paul. Nouveau précis de philosophie a l'usage des candidats au baccalauréat. Paris, 1955. 3v.
Phil 180.68.10	Foulquié, Paul. Quelques conseils pour la dissertation. 3. ed. Paris, 1956.
Phil 180.68.15	Foulquié, Paul. Cours de philosophie. Paris, 1961.

Phil 180.70	Fink, Eugen. Zur ontologischen Frühgeschichte von Raum, Zeit, Bewegung. Den Haag, 1957.
Phil 180.70.5	Fink, Eugen. Oase des Glücks. Freiburg, 1957.
Phil 180.70.10	Fink, Eugen. Sein. Den Haag, 1958.
Phil 180.72	Flam, Leopold. Profielen. Antwerpen, 1957.
Phil 180.72.5	Flam, Leopold. Le crépuscule des dieux et l'avenir de l'homme. Paris, 1966.
Phil 180.75	Feibleman, James. Inside the great mirror. The Hague, 1958.
Phil 180.76	Feibleman, James. Ontology. Baltimore, 1951.
Phil 180.77	Feibleman, James. Foundations of empiricism. The Hague, 1962.
Phil 180.78	Forest, Aimé. Orientazioni metafisiche. Milano, 1960.
Phil 180.80	Fougeyrollas, Pierre. La philosophie en question. Paris, 1960.
Phil 180.82	Foxe, Arthur N. The common sense from Heraclitus to Pierce. N.Y., 1962.
Phil 180.84	Franchini, Raffaello. L'oggetto della filosofia. Napoli, 1962.
Phil 180.84.5	Franchini, Raffaello. La logica della filosofia. Napoli, 1967.
Phil 180.86	Findlay, J.N. Language, mind and value. London, 1963.
Phil 180.88	Faggiotto, Pietro. Saggio sulla struttura della metafisica. Padova, 1965.
Phil 180.88.5	Faggiotto, Pietro. Il problema della metafisica nel pensiero moderno. Padova, 1969-
Phil 180.89	Friedberg, Felix. Thoughts about life. N.Y., 1954.
Phil 180.92	Fasel, Georg K. Metaphysik. Duisburg, 1969.
Phil 181.1	Gabler, G.A. Lehrbuch der philosophischen Propädeutik. Erlangen, 1827.
Phil 181.1.2	Gabler, G.A. Lehrbuch der philosophischen Propädeutik. Erlangen, 1827.
Phil 181.1.15	Gabler, G.A. De verae philosophiae erga religionem Christianam pietate. Berolini, 1836.
Phil 181.2	Gatien-Arnoult, A. Programe d'un cours de philosophie. Paris, 1835.
Phil 181.2.5	Gatien-Arnoult, A. Éléments de philosophie. Toulouse, 1864.
Phil 181.3	Garcia Tuduri, Mercedes. Introducción a la filosofía. 4. ed. Habana, 1957.
Phil 181.4	Genlis, S.F. de. Les diners baron D'Holbach. Paris, 1822.
Phil 181.5	Gerber, G. Das Ich. Berlin, 1893.
Phil 181.6	Gerhart, E.V. An introduction to study of philosophy. Philadelphia, 1858.
Phil 181.7	Géruzez, E. Cours de philosophie. Paris, 1840.
Phil 181.8	Gibon, A.E. Cours de philosophie. Paris, 1842. 2v.
Phil 181.9	Giner, F. Estudios filosoficos y religiosos. Madrid, 1876.
Phil 181.9.5	Giner, H. Filosofia y arte. Madrid, 1878.
Phil 181.10	Gioja, M. E. Elementi di filosofia. Lugano, 1834.
Phil 181.10.5	Gioja, M. Elementi di filosofia. Milano, 1818. 2v.
Htn Phil 181.11*	Glanvill, J. Essays...philosophy and religion. London, 1676.
Phil 181.11.2	Glanvill, J. Essays...philosophy and religion. London, 1676.
Phil 181.12	Gockel, C.F. Encyklopädische Einleitung in die Philosophie. Karlsruhe, 1855.
Phil 181.13	Göring, C. System der kritischen Philosophie. Leipzig, 1874. 2v.
Phil 181.14	Goodrich, Samuel G. A glance at philosophy. Boston, 1845.
Phil 181.15	Grazia, V. de. Saggio...della scienza umana. Napoli, 1839.
Phil 181.16	Green, Joseph Henry. Spiritual philosophy. London, 1865.
Phil 181.17	Greppo, C. The exegesis of life. N.Y., 1889.
Phil 181.18	Griffith, J. Behind the veil. London, 1876.
Phil 181.19	Gruppe, O.F. Antäus. Berlin, 1831.
Phil 181.20	Grote, J. Exploratio philosophica. Cambridge, 1865.
Phil 181.21	Gruyer, L.A. Méditations critiques. Paris, 1847.
Phil 181.21.5	Gruyer, L.A. Opuscules philosophiques. Bruxelles, 1851.
Phil 181.21.10	Gruyer, L.A. Observations sur le dieu-monde de M. Vacherot et de M. Tiberghien. Paris, 1860.
Phil 181.23	Gualberto, G. Raccolta di opuscoli filosofici. Pisa, 1766. 3v.
Htn Phil 181.24*	Gifford, A. Lectures. Frankfurt, n.d.
Phil 181.25	Gonçalvez de Magalhães, J.G. Factos do espirito humano. Rio de Janeiro, 1865.
Phil 181.25.5	Gonçalvez de Magalhães, J.G. Commentarios e pensamentos. Rio de Janeiro, 1880.
Phil 181.26.3	Gottsched, J.C. Erste Gründe. 3. Aufl. v.1-2. Leipzig, 1739.
Phil 181.26.5	Gottsched, J.C. Erste Grunder der Weltweisheit. Leipzig, 1749. 2v.
Phil 181.26.7	Gottsched, J.C. Erste Grunde der Weltweisheit. 7. Aufl. Leipzig, 1762. 2v.
Phil 181.27	Gourd, J.J. Le phénomène; esquisse de philosophie génerale. Paris, 1888.
Phil 181.28	Godlover, H.B. Science of minds. n.p., n.d.
Phil 181.29	Gravesande, J.G. Introductio ad philosophiam. Leidae, 1736.
Phil 181.31	Graham, C. The true philosophy of mind. Louisville, 1869.
Htn Phil 181.32*	Gale, Theophilus. Philosophia generalis in duas partes disterminata. London, 1676.
Phil 181.33	Geyer, D.L. Pragmatic theory of truth as developed by Peirce, James and Dewey. n.p., 1914?
Phil 181.34	Gourmont, Rémy de. Promenades philosophiques. 3rd series. Paris, 1913. 3v.
Phil 181.35	Garfein-Garski, Stan. Ein neuer Versuch über das Wesen der Philosophie. Heidelberg, 1909.
Phil 181.36	Grassmann, R. Das Weltleben oder die Metaphysik. Stettin, 1881.
Phil 181.37.2	Geiger, Joseph R. Some religious implications of pragmatism. Chicago, 1919.
Phil 181.38	Güttler, Karl. Gesammelte Abhandlungen. München, 1918.
Phil 181.39	Geyser, Joseph. Allgemeine Philosophie...der Natur. Münster, 1915.
Phil 181.39.5	Geyser, Joseph. Einige Hauptprobleme der Metaphysik. Freiburg, 1923.
Phil 181.40	Gleichen-Russwurm, A. von. Der freie Mensch. Berlin, 1916.
Phil 181.40.5	Gleichen-Russwurm, A. von. Philosophische Profile. Stuttgart, 1922.
Phil 181.41	González Serrano, U. En pro y en contra. Madrid, 1894.
Phil 181.42	Gans, Max E. Zur Psychologie der Begriffsmetaphysik. Wien, 1914.
Phil 181.43	Geissler, Kurt. Das System der Seinsgebiete als Grundlage einer umfassenden Philosophie. Leipzig, 1919.

il 175 - 200   General treatises on philosophy - Individual authors (A-Z) - cont.

Phil 181.44   Gurnhill, James. Christian philosophy discussed under the topics of absolute values. London, 1921.
Phil 181.44.5   Gurnhill, James. Interpretation of the spiritual philosophy. London, 1920.
Phil 181.45   Gentile, Giovanni. Saggi critici. Ser. I. Napoli, 1921.
Phil 181.45.5   Gentile, Giovanni. The theory of mind as pure act. London, 1922.
Phil 181.45.9   Gentile, Giovanni. Teoria generale dello spirito come atto puro. 2a ed. Pisa, 1918.
Phil 181.45.11   Gentile, Giovanni. Teoria generale dello spirito come atto puro. 3a ed. Bari, 1920.
Phil 181.45.15   Gentile, Giovanni. Teoria generale dello spirito come atto puro. 6a ed. Firenze, 1944.
Phil 181.45.19   Gentile, Giovanni. L'esprit, acte pur. Paris, 1925.
Phil 181.45.30   Gentile, Giovanni. Scritti vari. Lanciano, 1920-1926. 5v.
Phil 181.45.80   Orsi, Domenico d'. Lo spirito come atto puro in Giovanni Gentile. Padova, 1957.
Phil 181.46   Gille, E. Cours de philosophie. Paris, 1876.
Phil 181.47   Guillou, Henri. Essai de philosophie générale élémentaire. Paris, 1921.
Phil 181.48   Giovanni, V. di. Prelezioni di filosofia. Palermo, 1877.
Phil 181.48.5   Giovanni, V. di. Principii di filosofia prima. Palermo, 1878. 3v.
Phil 181.49   Geijer, Reinhold. Filosofiens historiska hufvudformer. Uppsala, 1916.
Phil 181.50   Grisebach, E. Wahrheit und Wirklichkeiten. Halle, 1919.
Phil 181.50.5   Grisebach, E. Gegenwart. Halle, 1928.
Phil 181.50.10   Grisebach, E. Freiheit und Zucht. Zurich, 1936.
Phil 181.51   Galli, Ettore. Alle soglie della metafisica. Milano, 1922.
Phil 181.52   Groos, Karl. Der Aufbau der Systeme. Leipzig, 1924.
Phil 181.53   Guyon, René. Essai de métaphysique materialiste. Paris, 1924.
Phil 181.55   Greca, Carlo. L'esistere quale oggetto di scienza e di storia. Parte 1a. Girgenti, 1925.
Phil 181.56   Grünbaum, A.A.. Herrschen und Leiben als Grundmotive der philosophische Weltanschauungen. Bonn, 1925.
Phil 181.57   Galli, Gallo. Spirito e realta. Milano, 1927.
Phil 181.57.5   Galli, Gallo. Saggio sulla dialettica della realta spirituale. Milano, 1933.
Phil 181.57.10   Galli, Gallo. Lineamenti di filosofia. Bologna, 1935.
Phil 181.57.15   Galli, Gallo. Tri studi di filosofia. Torino, 1956.
Phil 181.58   Gastelum, B.J. Inteligencia y simbolo. Madrid, 1927.
Phil 181.59   Germer, Hugo. Schönheit, Güte, Zweck. 1. Teil: Kant und Schopenhauer. Berlin, 1908.
Phil 181.60   Gener, Pompeyo. Inducciones, ensayos de filosofia y de crítica. Barcelona, 1901.
Phil 181.61   Geddes, Patrick. The world without and the world within. Bournville, 1905.
Phil 181.62   Goldberg, Isaac. Fine art of living. Boston, 1930.
Phil 181.63   Goedewaagen, T. Summa contra metaphysicos. Utrecht, 1931.
Phil 181.63.5   Goedewaagen, T. Het spectrum der philosophie in de 20e eeuw. Leiden, 1933.
Phil 181.64   Gamertsfelder, Walter Sylvester. Fundamentals of philosophy. N.Y., 1930.
Phil 181.65   Granberry, John C. Students' prolegomena to philosophy. Ann Arbor, 1931.
Phil 181.66   Grünhut, Ladislaus. Das Wesen und der Wert des Seins. Leipzig, 1931.
Phil 181.66.5   Gruenhut, Ladislaus. Metafizikai világnézet. Baja? 1934.
Phil 181.67   Giuliani, G. Intorno al principio..della filosofia civile. Napoli, 1862.
Phil 181.68   Gatti, Stanislao. Scritti varii di filosofia e letteratura. Napoli, 1861. 2v.
Phil 181.69   Gorce, M.M. Premiers principes de philosophie. Paris, 1933.
Phil 181.69.5   Gorce, M.M. Traité de philosophie. Paris, 1938.
Phil 181.69.10   Gorce, M.M. L'escalade des siècles. Saint-Imier, 1967.
Phil 181.70   Govi, Mario. Preludi filosofici e politici. Milano, 1935.
Phil 181.71   Guénon, R. Les états multiples de l'etre. Paris, 1932.
Phil 181.71.5   Guénon, R. Autorité spirituelle et pouvoir temporel. Paris, 1929.
Phil 181.71.10   Guénon, R. La métaphysique orientale. 2. ed. Paris, 1945.
Phil 181.72   Gessen, S.I. Weltanschauung Ideologie. Praha, 1934.
Phil 181.73   Gilson, E. Christianisme et philosophie. Paris, 1936.
Phil 181.73.5   Gilson, E. Being and some philosophers. Toronto, 1949.
Phil 181.73.7   Gilson, E. Being and some philosophers. 2. ed. Toronto, 1952.
Phil 181.73.10   Gilson, E. Le philosophe et la théologie. Paris, 1960.
Phil 181.73.15   Gilson, E. The philosopher and theology. N.Y., 1962.
Phil 181.74   Gotshalk, D.W. Structure and reality. N.Y., 1937.
Phil 181.74.5   Gilson, E. Metaphysics in modern times. Chicago, 1940.
Phil 181.75   Geiger, M. Die Wirklichkeit der Wissenschaften und die Metaphysik. Bonn, 1930.
Phil 181.76   Guthrie, H. Introduction au problème de l'histoire de la philosophie. Thèse. Paris, 1937.
Phil 181.76.5   Guthrie, H. Introduction au problème de l'histoire de la philosophie. Paris, 1937.
Phil 181.77   Gehlen, A. Wirklicher und unwirklicher Geist. Leipzig, 1931.
Phil 181.78   Gattell, B.B. The light of the mind. Philadelphia, 1938.
Phil 181.79   Gutkind, Eric. The absolute collective. London, 1937.
Phil 181.79.5   Gutkind, Eric. The body of God. N.Y., 1969.
Phil 181.80   Garcia Morente, Manuel. Lecciones preliminares de filosofia. Tucuman, 1938.
Phil 181.80.5   Garcia Morente, Manuel. Ensayos. Madrid, 1945.
Phil 181.80.10   Garcia Morente, Manuel. Ejercicios espirituales. Madrid, 1961.
Phil 181.81   Gould, G.M. The infinite presence. N.Y., 1910.
Phil 181.82   Gooch, L.C. Instinct vs. reason; the problem of man. Yazoo City, Miss., 1938.
Phil 181.83   Guardini, R. Der Gegensatz. Mainz, 1925.
Phil 181.84   Guzzo, Augusto. Idealisti ed empiristi; saggi. Firenze, 1935.
Phil 181.85   Guglielmini, H. Temas existenciales. Buenos Aires, 1939.
Phil 181.87   Guitton, Jean. Justification du temps. Paris, 1941.
Phil 181.87.5   Guitton, Jean. Man in time. Notre Dame, Ind., 1966.
Phil 181.88   Guitton, Jean. L'existence temporelle. Paris, 1949.
Phil 181.89   Glockner, Hermann. Einführung in das Philosophieren. Berlin, 1944.
Phil 181.90.5   Gredt, Joseph. Elementa philosophiae Aristotelico-Thomisticae. 7. ed. v.2. Friburgi, 1937.
Phil 181.102   Geiger, G.R. Philosophy and the social order. Boston, 1947.
Phil 181.104   Gaos, José. Filosofia de la filosofia e historia de la filosofia. México, 1947.

il 175 - 200   General treatises on philosophy - Individual authors (A-Z) - cont.

Phil 181.106   Gilby, Thomas. Phoenix and turtle. London, 1950.
Phil 181.108   Grenier, H. Thomistic philosophy. Charlotte-town, Canada, 1950. 4v.
Phil 181.110   Gunther, H.R.G. Personlichkeit und Geschichte. Augsburg, 1947.
Phil 181.112   Gignoux, Victor. Cours de philosophie. v.3. Paris, 1950.
Phil 181.114   Gusdorf, G. Mythe et métaphysique. Paris, 1953.
Phil 181.114.5   Gusdorf, G. Traité de métaphysique. Paris, 1956.
Phil 181.118   Gruber, F.C. The emergence of the modern mind. Philadelphia, 1958.
Phil 181.120   Gaigneron, L. de. Le secret de l'être. Paris, 1955.
Phil 181.122   Gonzalo Cosar, M. Introducción a la filosofia. Madrid, 1960.
Phil 181.125   Garin, Eugenio. La filosofia come sapere storico. Bari, 1959.
Phil 181.128   Garcia Bacca, J.D. Elementos de filosofia. 2. ed. Caracas, 1961.
Phil 181.128.5   Garcia Bacca, J.D. Introduccion literaria a la filosofia. 2. ed. Caracas, 1964.
Phil 181.128.10   Garcia Bacca, J.D. Metafisica natural estabilizada y problematica. Mexico, 1963.
Phil 181.130   Giannini, Giorgio. I presupposti della trascendenza. Milano, 1959.
Phil 181.131   Grenier, J. Entretiens sur le bon usage de la liberté. Paris, 1948.
Phil 181.131.5   Grenier, J. Conversations on the good uses of freedom. 1. American ed. Cambridge, 1967.
Phil 181.132   Gaos, José. De la filosofia. Mexico, 1962.
Phil 181.133   Gellner, Ernest. Thought and change. Chicago, 1965.
Phil 181.134   Giacon, Carlo. Interiorita e metafisica. Bologna, 1964.
Phil 181.135   Garcia Calderon, Francisco. Ideologías. Paris, 1918.
Phil 181.136   Goldmann, Lucien. Sciences humaines et philosophie. Paris, 1966.
Phil 181.136.5   Goldmann, Lucien. The human sciences and philosophy. London, 1969.
Phil 181.140.2   Gorovitz, Samuel. Philosophical analysis. N.Y., 1967.
Phil 181.145   Garulli, Enrico. Esperienza e metafisica nella filosofia moderna. Urbino, 1963.
NEDL Phil 181.150   Gregg, Richard B. What's it all about and what am I? N.Y., 1968.
Phil 181.150.5   Gregg, Richard B. What's it all about and what am I? 1. Indian ed. Ahmedabad, 1967.
Phil 181.152   Grlić, Danko. Zašto. Zagreb, 1968.
Phil 181.154   Grundfragen der Wissenschaften und ihre Wurzeln in der Metaphysik. Salzburg, 1967.
Phil 181.156   Granger, Gilles Gaston. Essai d'une philosophie du style. Paris, 1968.
Phil 181.158   Giorda, Renato. Psicologia dell'avere. Roma, 1968.
Phil 181.160   Gans, Abraham. Pathologie en therapie der filosofie. Wassenaar, 1968.
Phil 181.162   Gley, Gérard. Essai sur les éléments de la philosophie. Paris, 1817.
Phil 181.164.2   Gentile, Marino. Come si pone il problema meta fisico. 2. ed. Padova, 1965.
Phil 182.1   Hagemann, G. Elemente der Philosophie. v.1-3. Münster, 1870.
Phil 182.1.8   Hagemann, G. Elemente der Philosophie. Freiburg, 1911-1922. 3v.
Phil 182.1.10   Hagemann, G. Logik und Nötik. 9e und 10e Aufl. Freiburg, 1915.
Phil 182.1.81   Halasy-Nagy, J. A filozófia kis tükre. 2. kiad. Budapest, 193-?
Phil 182.4   Harms, F. Prolegomena zur Philosophie. Braunschweig, 1852.
Phil 182.4.3   Harms, F. Abhandlungen zur systematischen Philosophie. Berlin, 1868.
Phil 182.4.10   Harms, F. Metaphilosophie. Leipzig, 1895.
Phil 182.5   Harris, W.T. Introduction to the study of philosophy. N.Y., 1889.
Phil 182.5.5   Harris, W.T. A collection of philosophical and psychological essays; extracts from periodicals. n.p., n.d.
Phil 182.5.9   Harris, W.T. Philosophy in outline. N.Y., 1883.
Phil 182.6   Hartsen, F.A. Principes de philosophie. Paris, 1877.
Phil 182.6.5   Hartsen, F.A. Grundiss der Philosophie. Abt. 1. Nordhausen, 1875.
Phil 182.6.10   Hartsen, F.A. Die Philosophie als Wissenschaft. Heidelberg, 1876.
Phil 182.7   Hassler, K.D. Paragraphen für den Unterricht in der Philosophie. Ulm, 1832.
Phil 182.7.2   Hassler, K.D. Paragraphen für den Unterricht in der Philosophie. 2. Aufl. Ulm, 1852.
Phil 182.8   Hedge, F.H. Atheism in philosophy. Berlin, 1884.
Phil 182.9   Heinroths, J. Pisteodicee. Leipzig, 1829.
Phil 182.10A   Heereboort, A. Meletemata philosophica. Amsterdam, 1680.
Phil 182.10B   Heereboort, A. Meletemata philosophica. Amsterdam, 1680.
Htn Phil 182.10.3*   Heereboort, A. Meletemata philosophica. Amsterdam, 1665.
Phil 182.11   Helfferich, A. Der Organismus der Wissenschaft. Leipzig, 1856.
Phil 182.11.10   Helfferich, A. Die Metaphysik als Grundwissenschaft. Hamburg, 1846.
Phil 182.12   Hellenbach, L.B. Eine Philosophie des gesunden Menschenverstandes. Wien, 1876.
Phil 182.12.6   Hellenbach, L.B. Die Vorurtheile des gemeinen Verstandes. Wien, 1880.
Htn Phil 182.13*   Helmont, F.M. van. Macrocosm and microcosm. London, 1685.
Phil 182.13.5   Helmont, F.M. van. Eenige gedagten. Amsterdam, 1690.
Phil 182.14   Hemsterhuis, F. Oeuvres philosophiques. Paris, 1792. 2v.
Phil 182.14.1   Hemsterhuis, F. Oeuvres philosophiques. Paris, 1809. 2v.
Phil 182.14.2   Hemsterhuis, F. Oeuvres philosophiques. v.3. Leuwarde, 1850.
Phil 182.14.5   Hemsterhuis, F. Vermischte philosophische Schriften. Leipzig, 1782. 3v.
Phil 182.14.10   Hemsterhuis, F. Philosophische Schriften. Karlsruhe, 1912. 2v.
Phil 182.15   Heusde, P.W. Die Socratic Schule. v.1-2. Erlangen, 1838.
Phil 182.16   Hill, D.J. Genetic philosophy. N.Y., 1893.
Phil 182.17   Hillebrand, J. Philosophie des Geistes. Heidelberg, 1835-1836. 2v.
Phil 182.17.10   Hillebrand, J. Der Organismus der philosophischen Idee. Dresden, 1842.
Phil 182.17.15   Hillebrand, J. Lehrbuch der theoretischen Philosophie. Mainz, 1826.
Phil 182.17.20   Hillebrand, J. Universal-philosophische Prolegomena. Mainz, 1830.

Phil 175 - 200   General treatises on philosophy - Individual authors (A-Z) - cont.

Phil 182.18	Hinton, J. Man and his dwelling place. N.Y., 1859.
Phil 182.18.5	Henton, J. The art of thinking. London, 1879.
Phil 182.18.8	Henton, J. Philosophy and religion. London, 1881.
Phil 182.19	Hodgson, S.H. Philosophy and experience. London, 1885.
Phil 182.19.5	Hodgson, S.H. Philosophy of reflection. London, 1878. 2v.
Phil 182.19.8	Hodgson, S.H. Time and space. A metaphysical essay. London, 1865.
Phil 182.19.11	Hodgson, S.H. Metaphysic of experience. London, 1898. 4v.
Phil 182.19.13	Hodgson, S.H. The relation of philosophy to science, physical and psychological. London, 1884.
Phil 182.20	Hoffmann, K. Philosophische Propädeutik. Passan, 1872.
Phil 182.21	Hofmann, A.W. Inaugural address. Boston, 1883.
Phil 182.22	Holland, G. Réflexions philosophiques. Neuchâtel, 1775.
Htn Phil 182.23*	Hope, T. Essay on origin of man. London, 1831. 3v.
Phil 182.24	Huber, M. World unmasked. London, 1736.
Phil 182.24.2	Huber, M. World unmasked. London, 1786.
Phil 182.25	Huet, F. La science de l'esprit. Paris, 1864. 2v.
Phil 182.26	Hutcheson, F. Synopsis metaphysicae. Glasguae, 1756.
Phil 182.27	Hvalgrens, E. Grunddragen. Göteborg, 1879.
Phil 182.28	Hibben, J.G. The problems of philosophy. N.Y., 1898.
Phil 182.28.2	Hibben, J.G. The problems of philosophy. N.Y., 1899.
Phil 182.28.3	Hibben, J.G. The problems of philosophy. N.Y., 1908.
Phil 182.28.5	Hibben, J.G. A defence of prejudice. N.Y., 1911.
Htn Phil 182.29*	Heidfeld, J. Octavum renata. Herbornae Nassoviorum, 1621.
Phil 182.29.10	Heidfeld, J. Sphinx philosophica. Herbornae Nassoviorum, 1600.
Htn Phil 182.29.15*	Heidfeld, J. Quintum renata. Herbornae Nassoviorum, 1608.
Phil 182.30	Harris, J. Philosophical arrangements. London, 1775.
Phil 182.32	Holland, Henry. Fragmentary papers on science. London, 1875.
Phil 182.33	Hinton, C.H. Scientific romances. Nos. 1-5,7-8. London, 1884-1888. 7v.
Phil 182.33.2	Hinton, C.H. Scientific romances. London, 1886.
Phil 182.34	Hayward, J.K. A rebuttal of spiritism. N.Y., 1903.
Phil 182.35.2	Haldane, Richard B. The pathway to reality. London, 1905.
Phil 182.35.3	Haldane, Richard B. The pathway to reality. London, 1926.
Phil 182.35.5	Haldane, Richard B. The doctrine of degrees in knowledge, truth, and reality. London, n.d.
Phil 182.35.9	Haldane, Richard B. Human experience; a study of its structure. N.Y., 1926.
Phil 182.35.10	Haldane, Richard B. Human experience; a study of its structure. London, 1929.
Phil 182.36	Höffding, H. Philosophische Probleme. Leipzig, 1903.
Phil 182.36.5	Höffding, H. The problems of philosophy. N.Y., 1905.
Phil 182.36.6	Höffding, H. The problems of philosophy. N.Y., 1905.
Phil 182.36.7	Höffding, H. The problems of philosophy. N.Y., 1906.
Phil 182.36.15	Höffding, H. Der menschliche Gedanke. Leipzig, 1911.
Phil 182.36.17	Höffding, H. Den menneskelige tanke. Kjobenhavn, 1910.
Phil 182.37	Heymans, G. Einführung in die Metaphysik. Leipzig, 1905.
Phil 182.37.2	Heymans, G. Einführung in die Metaphysik. 2. Aufl. Leipzig, 1911.
Phil 182.37.10	Heymans, G. Gesammelte kleinere Schriften. Den Haag, 1927. 3v.
Phil 182.38	Hyslop, J.H. Problems of philosophy. N.Y., 1905.
Phil 182.39	Harriman, F. Philosophy of common sense. N.Y., 1907.
Phil 182.39.5	Harrison, F. The philosophy of common sense. London, 1907.
Phil 182.40	Hébert, M. Le pragmatisme. Paris, 1908.
Phil 182.41	Hartenstein, G. Probleme und Grundlehren der allgemeinen Metaphysik. Leipzig, 1836.
Phil 182.41.5	Hartenstein, G. Historisch-philosophische Abhandlungen. Leipzig, 1870.
Phil 182.42	Huizinga, A.V.C.P. The American philosophic pragmatism. Boston, 1911.
Phil 182.43	Häberlin, Paul. Wissenschaft und Philosophie. Basel, 1910. 2v.
Phil 182.43.5	Häberlin, Paul. Anthropologie philosophique. Paris, 1943.
Phil 182.43.10	Häberlin, Paul. Naturphilosophische Betrachtungen. Zurich, 1939-1940. 2v.
Phil 182.43.15	Häberlin, Paul. Philosophin perennis. Berlin, 1952.
Phil 182.44	Hartmann, F. The life of Jehoshua, the prophet of Nazareth. London, 1909.
Phil 182.44.5	Hartmann, F. The life of Jehoshua, the prophet of Nazareth. Boston, 1889.
Phil 182.45.5	Hannequin, A. Études d'histoire des sciences. Paris, 1908. 2v.
Phil 182.46	Hermance, W.E. Unorthodox conception of being. N.Y., 1912.
Phil 182.47	Hatch, D.P. Scientific occultism. Los Angeles, 1905.
Phil 182.48	Pamphlet vol. Hazard, Rowland G. 7 pam.
Phil 182.49	Hoernlé, R.F.A. Studies in contemporary metaphysics. N.Y., 1920.
Phil 182.49.5	Hoernlé, R.F.A. Matter, life, mind and God. London, 1923.
Phil 182.49.10	Hoernlé, R.F.A. Studies in philosophy. London, 1952.
Phil 182.49.10.2	Hoernlé, R.F.A. Studies in philosophy. Cambridge, Mass., 1952.
Phil 182.50	Herbertz, Richard. Philosophie und Einzelwissenschaften. Bern, 1913.
Phil 182.50.5	Herbertz, Richard. Das philosophische Urerlebnis. Bern, 1921.
Phil 182.51	Horion, Charles. Testament philosophique...essai de synthése evolutioniste. Bruxelles, 1900.
Phil 182.52	Hoffmann, Franz. Philosophische Schriften. v.1-2,4. Erlangen, 1868-1877. 3v.
Phil 182.53	Hoffner, Paul. Grundlinien der Philosophie als Aufgabe. Mainz, 1881. 2v.
Phil 182.54	Hallier, Ernst. Die Weltanschauung des Naturforschers. Jena, 1875.
Phil 182.55	Hudson, Jay W. The truths we live by. N.Y., 1921.
Phil 182.56.2	Hooper, Charles. Common sense and the rudiments of philosophy. 2d ed. London, 1920.
Phil 182.57	Haacke, Wilhelm. Vom Strome des Seins. Leipzig, 1905.
Phil 182.58	Hebler, Carl. Philosophische Aufsätze. Leipzig, 1869.
Phil 182.59	Hugueny, Charles. Systéme de la nature. Nancy, 1890.
Phil 182.60	Hubbe-Schleiden, Wilhelm. Das Dasein als Lust, Leid, und Liebe. Braunschweig, 1891.
Phil 182.61	Herpe, Hans. Einleitung in die Kategorienlehre. Leipzig, 1921.
Phil 182.61.10	Herpe, Hans. Idee und Existenz. Hamburg, 1935.
Phil 182.62	Holmes, Edmond. What is philosophy? London, 1905.
Phil 182.62.10	Holmes, Edmond. Philosophy without metaphysics. London, 1930.
Phil 182.62.15	Holmes, Edmond. The headquarters of reality. London, 1933.

Phil 175 - 200   General treatises on philosophy - Individual authors (A-Z) - cont.

Phil 182.63	Hallett, T.G.P. That life is the origin and purpose of the universe. London, 1916.
Phil 182.65	Henkel, Fred. Creative psychics, the art of regeneration Los Angeles, 1917.
Phil 182.66	Hauptmann, C. Die Metaphysik in der modernen Physiologie. Jena, 1894.
Phil 182.67	Husserl, Edmund. Ideen zu einer reinen Phänomenologie und phänomenologischen Philosophie. Halle, 1913.
Phil 182.67.4	Husserl, Edmund. Ideas: general introduction to pure phenomenology. London, 1931.
Phil 182.67.4.2	Husserl, Edmund. Ideas: general introduction to pure phenomenology. London, 1952.
Phil 182.67.5	Husserl, Edmund. Méditations cartésiennes. Paris, 1931.
Phil 182.67.80	Pierola, Raul A. Apuntes dispersos sobre fenomenologia. Santa Fe, 1943.
Phil 182.68	Huidobro, E. Programma analitico razonado de metafisica. Lima, 1923.
Phil 182.69F	Hoëné Wronski, J.M. Prospectus de la philosophie absolue et son développement. Paris, 1878.
Phil 182.70	Heegaard, S. Om opdragelse. 4e Opl. v.1-2. Kjøbenhavn, 1893.
Phil 182.71	Hansen, O. Opdrageslsaere. Kjobenhavn, 1898.
Phil 182.72	Huber, J. Kleine Schriften. Leipzig, 1871.
Phil 182.73	Hermann, E. Grundriss der Philosophie. Lahr, 1906.
Phil 182.74	Hugonin, F. Ontologie. Paris, 1856-1857. 2v.
Phil 182.75	Hollenberg, W. Philosophische Propädeutik. 2. Aufl. Elberfeld, 1875.
Phil 182.76	Abhandlungen aus dem Gebiete der Philosophie und ihrer Geschichte. Freiburg, 1913.
Phil 182.77	Hanan, F. A layman to his sons. London, 1924.
Phil 182.78	Heiler, Josef. Das Absolute. München, 1921.
Phil 182.79A	Herzberg, Alex. Zur Psychologie der Philosophie und der Philosophen. Leipzig, 1926.
Phil 182.79.5	Herzberg, Alex. The psychology of philosophers. London, 1929.
Phil 182.80	Hart, Joseph K. Inside experience. N.Y., 1927.
Phil 182.81	Hart, Julius. Die neue Welterkenntnis. Leipzig, 1902.
Phil 182.82	Hook, Sidney. The metaphysics of pragmatism. Chicago, 1927.
Phil 182.83	Heidrich, E. Die Gegenwartslinie, Wesen und Grenzen des Determinismus. Görlitz, 1925.
Phil 182.84	Hellmund, H. Das Wesen der Welt. Zürich, 1927.
Phil 182.85	Hartmann, Alma. Zwischen Dichtung und Philosophie. Berlin, 1912.
Phil 182.87	Hammarsköld, L. Strödda afhandlingar öfver ämnen inom philosophiens gebiet. Mariefred, 1827.
Phil 182.88A	Hocking, W.E. Types of philosophy. N.Y., 1929.
Phil 182.88B	Hocking, W.E. Types of philosophy. N.Y., 1929.
Phil 182.88C	Hocking, W.E. Types of philosophy. N.Y., 1929.
Phil 182.88.3	Hocking, W.E. Types of philosophy. 3d ed. N.Y., 1959.
Phil 182.88.7A	Hocking, W.E. Types of philosophy. N.Y., 1939.
Phil 182.88.7B	Hocking, W.E. Types of philosophy. N.Y., 1939.
Phil 182.90	Herrigel, E. Die metaphysische Form. Tübingen, 1929.
Phil 182.91	Hofmann, P. Metaphysik oder verstehende Sinnwissenschaft? Berlin, 1929.
Phil 182.91.5	Hofmann, P. Sinn und Geschichte. München, 1937.
Phil 182.93.5	Heidegger, M. Was ist Metaphysik? Bonn, 1931.
Phil 182.93.8	Heidegger, M. Qu'est-ce que la métaphysique? Paris, 1937.
Phil 182.93.10	Heidegger, M. Einführung in die Metaphysik. Tübingen, 1953.
Phil 182.93.10.2	Heidegger, M. Einführung in die Metaphysik. Tübingen, 1958.
Phil 182.93.12	Heidegger, M. An introduction to metaphysics. New Haven, 1959.
Phil 182.93.13	Heidegger, M. Introduction à la métaphysique. Paris, 1958.
Phil 182.94	Hartmann, N. Zum Problem der Realitätsgegebenheit. Berlin, 1931.
Phil 182.94.10	Hartmann, N. Das Problem des Geistigen Seins. Berlin, 1933.
Phil 182.94.10.5	Hartmann, N. Das Problem des geistigen Seins. 2. Aufl. Berlin, 1949.
Phil 182.94.12	Hartmann, N. Teleologisches Denken. Berlin, 1951.
Phil 182.94.15	Hartmann, N. Zur Grundlegung der Ontologie. Berlin, 1935.
Phil 182.94.16	Hartmann, N. Möglichkeit und Wirklichkeit. Berlin, 1938.
Phil 182.94.17	Hartmann, N. Philosophie der Natur. Berlin, 1950.
Phil 182.94.18	Hartmann, N. Neue Wege der Ontologie. Stuttgart, 194-.
Phil 182.94.18.3	Hartmann, Nicolai. Neue Wege der Ontologie. 3.Aufl. Stuttgart, 1949.
Phil 182.94.19	Hartmann, N. Der Aufbau der realen Welt. 2. Aufl. Meisenheim, 1949.
Phil 182.94.20	Hartmann, N. Einführung in die Philosophie. 3. Aufl. Osnabrück, 1954.
Phil 182.94.80	Alarco, L.F. Nicolai Hartmann y la idea de la metafisica. Lima, 1949.
Phil 182.94.82	Guggenberger, Alois. Der Menschengeist und das Sein. Krailling vor München, 1942.
Phil 182.94.85	Brandenstein, Béla. Teleologisches Denken. Bonn, 1960.
Phil 182.95	Haserot, F.S. Essays on the logic of being. N.Y., 1932.
Phil 182.96	Heydenreich, K.H. Encyclopädische Einleitung in das Studium der Philosophie. Leipzig, 1703.
Phil 182.97	Herz, M. Betrachtungen aus der Spekulativen Weltweisheit. Königsberg, 1771.
Phil 182.98	Horn, E. Der Begriff des Begriffes. Inaug. Diss. München, 1931.
Phil 182.98.5	Horn, E. Der Begriff des Begriffes. München, 1932.
Phil 182.99	Höcksmann, F.X. Der Weg zum Sinn des Seins. Wien, 1933.
Phil 182.100	Howison, G.H. George Holmes Howison, philosopher and teacher. Berkeley, 1934.
Phil 182.101	Haldane, J.S. The sciences and philosophy. London, 1928.
Phil 182.101.5A	Haldane, J.S. The philosophy of a biologist. Oxford, 1935.
Phil 182.101.5B	Haldane, J.S. The philosophy of a biologist. Oxford, 1935.
Phil 182.101.7	Haldane, J.S. The philosophy of a biologist. Oxford, 1935.
Phil 182.101.10	Haldane, John Burdon Sanderson. Science and life. London, 1968.
Phil 182.101.20	Sampson, A.H. The philosophy of John Scott Haldane. Philadelphia, 1938.
Phil 182.102	Haesaert, J. Introduction a la philosophie expérimentale. Gand, 1920.
Phil 182.103.5	Heineccius, J.G. Elementa philosophiae rationalis et moralis. Amstelodami, 1733.
Phil 182.104	Hersch, J. L'illusion philosophique. Paris, 1936.
Phil 182.104.2	Hersch, J. L'illusion philosophique. Paris, 1964.
Phil 182.105	Hawkins, D.J.B. Approach to philosophy. London, 1938.

Phil 175 - 200   General treatises on philosophy - Individual authors (A-Z) - cont.

Phil 182.105.5   Hawkins, D.J.B. Being and becoming. N.Y.,1954.
Phil 182.106.5   Huch, Ricarda. Vom Wesen des Menschen; Natur und Geist. 3. Aufl. Prein, 1922.
Phil 182.107   Heinemann, F. Odysseus oder die Zukunft der Philosophie. Stockholm, 1939.
Phil 182.108   Howells, T.H. Hunger for wholiness. Denver, 1940.
Phil 182.109   Huxley, A. Unser Glaube. Stockholm, 1939.
Phil 182.110   Humphreys, H.S. The cylindriad. Evansville, 1942.
Phil 182.111   Haldane, J.S. Materialism. London, 1932.
Phil 182.112   Hardie, C.D. Background to modern thought. London, 1947.
Phil 182.113   Henle, R.J. Method in metaphysics. Milwaukee, 1951.
Phil 182.114   Hospers, John. An introduction to philosophical analysis. London, 1956.
Phil 182.114.7   Hospers, John. An introduction to philosophical analysis. Englewood Cliffs, 1967.
Phil 182.115   Hedenius, I. Fyra dygder. Stockholm, 1955.
Phil 182.116   Hirschfeld, G. An essay on mankind. N.Y., 1957.
Phil 182.117   Hall, E.W. Philosophical systems. Chicago, 1960.
Phil 182.118   Herk, Konrad. Das leuchten des dunckels. Antwerpen, 1960.
Phil 182.120   Heyde, Johannes. Wege zur Klarheit. Berlin, 1960.
Phil 182.122   Hammond, A.L. Proprieties and vagaries. Baltimore, 1961.
Phil 182.124   Hengstenberg, Hans Edward. Freiheit und Seinsordnung. Stuttgart, 1961.
Phil 182.126   Havemann, Hans. Der polare Mensch. Hannover, 1923.
Phil 182.128   Halle, L.J. Men and nations. Princeton, 1962.
Phil 182.129   Hildebrandt, K. Ein Weg zur Philosophie. Bonn, 1962.
Phil 182.130   Hva er metafysikk: Aristoteles, Bergson, Heidegger. Oslo, 1962.
Phil 182.131   Hartnack, J. Philosophical problems. Copenhagen, 1962.
Phil 182.132   Harris, Errol E. The foundations of metaphysics in science. London, 1965.
Phil 182.133   Hurtado, Manuel. The positive absolutes. Mexico, 1963.
Phil 182.134   Horn, Joachim Christian. Monade und Begriff. Der Weg von Leibniz zu Hegel. Wien, 1965.
VPhil 182.136   Hit és haladás; mult és jövö tarsadalmi kifejlés fokozatos hitnyilvánulasaként fogvaföl. Torda, 1908.
Phil 182.138   Hors'kyï, Vilen S. Sotsial'ne seredovishche ta istoriko-filosofs'kyi protses. Kyïv, 1969.
Phil 182.140   Hammacher, Klaus. Kritik und Leben. v.2. München, 1969.
Phil 182.142   Hrušovský, Igor. Probleme der Philosophie. Bratislava, 1970.
Phil 182.144   Hilz, Selahattin. 100 soruda felsefe el kilabi. Istanbul, 1970.
Phil 182.146   Hessen, Johannes. Von der Aufgabe der Philosophie und dem Wesen des Philosophen; zwei Vorlesungen. Heidelberg, 1947.
Phil 183.1   Isbyam, I.C. The ego and physical force. London, 1925.
Phil 183.1.5   Isbyam, I.C. The ego and the spiritual truth. London, 1926.
Phil 183.2   Ingraham, A. Swain school lectures. Chicago, 1903. 2v.
Phil 183.3   Ipsen, J.J. Filosofi og filosofer. København, 1923.
Phil 183.4   Isola, I.G. Il metodo secondo dialogo filosofico. Modena, 1871.
Phil 183.6   Iadov, V.A. Ideologiia kak forma dukhovnoi deiatel'nosti obshchestva. London, 1961.
Htn   Phil 183.8   Incardona, Nunzio. Radicalità e filosofia. Palermo, 1968.
Htn   Phil 184.1*   Jack, G. Primae philosophiae institutiones. Lugdunum Batavorum, 1628.
Htn   Phil 184.1.2*   Jack, G. Primae philosophiae institutiones. Cantabrigia, 1649.
Phil 184.2   Jacques, A. Manuel de philosophie. Paris, 1855.
Phil 184.2.2   Jacques, A. Manuel de philosophie. Paris, 1857.
Phil 184.2.9   Jacques, A. Manuel de philosophie. 9. ed. Paris, 1883.
Phil 184.3   James, W. The will to believe and other essays. N.Y., 1897.
Phil 184.3.3   James, W. The will to believe and other essays in popular philosophy. N.Y., 1899.
Phil 184.3.3.5A   James, W. The will to believe and other essays in popular philosophy. N.Y., 1898.
Phil 184.3.3.5B   James, W. The will to believe and other essays in popular philosophy. N.Y., 1898.
Phil 184.3.3.7   James, W. The will to believe and other essays in popular philosophy. N.Y., 1899.
Phil 184.3.3.10   James, W. The will to believe and other essays in popular philosophy. London, 1905.
Phil 184.3.3.15   James, W. The will to believe and other essays in popular philosophy. London, 1912.
Phil 184.3.4.5   James, W. The will to believe and other essays in popular philosophy. 1st ed. N.Y., 1923.
Phil 184.3.5   James, W. The will to believe and other essays in popular philosophy. N.Y., 1927.
Phil 184.3.6   James, W. The will to believe. London, 1937.
Phil 184.3.7.15   James, W. La volonté de croire. Paris, 1920.
Phil 184.3.7.25   James, W. Der Wille zum Glauben. Stuttgart, 1899.
Phil 184.3.7.30   James, W. Viljan till tro och andra essayer. Stockholm, 1908.
Phil 184.3.10A   James, W. Essays in radical empiricism. N.Y., 1912.
Phil 184.3.10B   James, W. Essays in radical empiricism. N.Y., 1912.
Phil 184.3.12   James, W. Essays in radical empiricism. N.Y., 1943.
Phil 184.3.15   James, W. Pragmatism, a new name. N.Y., 1907.
Phil 184.3.16   James, W. Pragmatism, a new name. N.Y., 1908.
NEDL   Phil 184.3.16.2   James, W. Pragmatism, a new name. London, 1909.
Phil 184.3.16.3   James, W. Pragmatism, a new name. N.Y., 1912.
Phil 184.3.16.5   James, W. Pragmatism, a new name. N.Y., 1922.
Phil 184.3.17   James, W. Pragmatism, a new name. N.Y., 1928.
Phil 184.3.17.5   James, W. Pragmatism. N.Y., 1943.
Phil 184.3.18   James, W. Le pragmatisme. Paris, 1911.
Phil 184.3.19   James, W. Le pragmatisme. Paris, 1918.
Phil 184.3.20   James, W. Pragmatism. Stockholm, 1916.
Phil 184.3.21   James, W. Der Pragmatismus. Leipzig, 1908.
Phil 184.3.22.5A   James, W. The meaning of truth. N.Y., 1914.
Phil 184.3.22.5B   James, W. The meaning of truth. N.Y., 1914.
Phil 184.3.23A   James, W. A pluralistic universe. London, 1909.
Phil 184.3.23B   James, W. A pluralistic universe. London, 1909.
Phil 184.3.24   James, W. A pluralistic universe. London, 1920.
Phil 184.3.27A   James, W. Some problems of philosophy. N.Y., 1911.
Phil 184.3.27B   James, W. Some problems of philosophy. N.Y., 1911.
Phil 184.3.27C   James, W. Some problems of philosophy. N.Y., 1911.
Phil 184.3.28   James, W. Some problems of philosophy. N.Y., 1911.
Phil 184.3.30   James, W. Memories and studies. London, 1911.
Phil 184.3.30.5A   James, W. Memories and studies. N.Y., 1912.
Phil 184.3.30.5B   James, W. Memories and studies. N.Y., 1912.
Phil 184.3.30.10   James, W. Memories and studies. N.Y., 1968.
Phil 184.3.34A   James, W. Selected papers on philosophy. London, 1927.
Phil 184.3.34B   James, W. Selected papers on philosophy. London, 1927.
Phil 184.3.34.5   James, W. Selected papers on philosophy. London, 1929.
Phil 184.3.35   James, W. Collected essays and reviews. N.Y., 1920.

Phil 175 - 200   General treatises on philosophy - Individual authors (A-Z) - cont.

Phil 184.3.41   James, W. On the vital reserves. N.Y., 1922.
Phil 184.3.45   James, W. Essays on faith and morals. N.Y., 1943.
Phil 184.4   Jamieson, G. The essentials of philosophy. Edinburgh, 1859.
Phil 184.6   Javary, L.A. La certitude. Paris, 1847.
Phil 184.7   Johnson, Edward. Nuces philosophicae, or The philosophy of things. London, 1842.
Htn   Phil 184.8*   Johnson, Samuel. Elementa philosophica. v.1-2. Philadelphia, 1752.
Htn   Phil 184.8.3*   Johnson, Samuel. Elementa philosophica. Philadelphia, 1752.
Phil 184.8.5   Johnson, Samuel. Introduction to the study of philosophy. 2. ed. London, 1743.
Phil 184.9   Joly, H. Nouveau cours de philosophie. Paris, n.d.
Phil 184.9.5   Joly, H. Cours de philosophie. 7. ed. Paris, 1882.
Phil 184.10   Jouin, R.P.L. Compendium logicae et metaphysicae. N.Y., 1884.
Phil 184.11   Jacoby, L. Die Idee der Entwicklung. Berlin, 1874. 2v.
Phil 184.11.2   Jacoby, L. Die Idee der Entwicklung. Zürich, 1886.
Phil 184.12   Jerusalem, W. Einleitung in die Philosophie. Wien, 1899.
Phil 184.12.2   Jerusalem, W. Einleitung in die Philosophie. Wien, 1903.
Phil 184.12.3   Jerusalem, W. Einleitung in die Philosophie. Wien, 1923.
Phil 184.12.5   Jerusalem, W. Introduction to philosophy. N.Y., 1910.
Phil 184.12.7   Jerusalem, W. Introduction to philosophy. N.Y., 1932.
Phil 184.12.8   Jerusalem, W. Gedanken und Denker. Wien, 1905.
Phil 184.12.10   Jerusalem, W. Gedanken und Denker. 2. Aufl. Wien, 1925.
Phil 184.13   Jacoby, Günther. Der Pragmatismus. Leipzig, 1909.
Phil 184.13.6   Pamphlet vol. Jacoby, Günther. Der Pragmatismus. 10 pam.
Phil 184.13.7   Jacoby, Günther. Allgemeine der Wirklichkeit. Halle, 1925.
Phil 184.14   Jourdain, Charles. Nociones de filosofia. Valparaiso, 1870.
Phil 184.15.3   Jochnick, W. Menniskan. Stockholm, 1881. 5 pam.
Phil 184.15.5   Jochnick, W. Några grundlinjer fill filosofien. Stockholm, 1895.
Phil 184.16   Jodl, F. Aus der Werkstatt der Philosophie. Wien, 1911.
NEDL   Phil 184.16.5   Jodl, F. Vom Lebenswege. Stuttgart, 1916-1917. 2v.
Phil 184.18   Joussain, A. Esquisse d'une philosophie. Paris, 1912.
Phil 184.19   Jaspers, K. Psychologie der Weltanschauung. Berlin, 1919.
Phil 184.19.5A   Jaspers, K. Psychologie der Weltanschauung. Berlin, 1925.
Phil 184.19.5B   Jaspers, K. Psychologie der Weltanschauung. Berlin, 1925.
Phil 184.19.10   Jaspers, K. Philosophie. Berlin, 1932. 3v.
Phil 184.19.11   Jaspers, K. Philosophy. v.1-. Translation. Chicago, 1969-71. 3v.
Phil 184.19.15   Jaspers, K. Vernunft und Existenz. Groningen, 1935.
Phil 184.19.18   Tonquédec, J. de. L'existence d'après Karl Jaspers. Paris, 1945.
Phil 184.19.20   Jaspers, K. Existenzphilosophie. Berlin, 1938.
Phil 184.19.25   Jaspers, K. Der philosophische Glaube. München, 1948.
Phil 184.19.30   Jaspers, K. Die grossen Philosophen. München, 1957.
Phil 184.19.35   Jaspers, K. The great philosophers. 1. American ed. N.Y., 1962. 2v.
Phil 184.20   Jacquinet, M. Essai de philosophie pour tous. Paris, 1888.
Phil 184.21.9   Jourdain, Charles. Notions de philosophie. Paris, 1865.
Phil 184.21.15   Jourdain, Charles. Notions de philosophie. 15e ed. Paris, 1875.
Phil 184.22   Jung, E. Le principe constitutif de la nature organique. Paris, 1923.
Phil 184.23   Jones, R.M. Fundamental ends of life. N.Y., 1924.
Phil 184.24   Jacobsson, M. Pragmatiska uppfostringsprinciper. Lund, 1912.
Phil 184.25   Jacob, T. Aus der Lehre vom Ganzen. Berlin, 1855.
Phil 184.26   Joad, C.E.M. After-dinner philosophy. London, 1926.
Phil 184.26.5A   Joad, C.E.M. Matter, life and value. London, 1929.
Phil 184.26.5B   Joad, C.E.M. Matter, life and value. London, 1929.
Phil 184.26.12   Joad, C.E.M. Return to philosophy. London, 1935.
Phil 184.26.15   Joad, C.E.M. Return to philosophy. N.Y., 1936.
Phil 184.26.18   Joad, C.E.M. Guide to philosophy. London, 1936.
Phil 184.26.20   Joad, C.E.M. Guide to philosophy. N.Y., 1956.
Phil 184.26.25   Joad, C.E.M. Philosophy for our time. London, 1940.
Phil 184.26.30   Joad, C.E.M. Philosophy. London, 1944.
Phil 184.27   Joad, C.E.M. A first encounter with philosophy. London, 1952.
Phil 184.28   Jacobsen, O.T. Gennem modsabninger. København, 1905.
Phil 184.28.5   Janssen, O. Vorstudien zur Metaphysik. Halle, 1921. 2v.
Phil 184.29   Janssen, O. Dasein und Wirklichkeit. München, 1938.
Phil 184.30   Jones, W.T. Nature, thought and personal experience. London, 1926.
Phil 184.30.5   Janet, P. Philosophie; questions complémentaires. Paris, 1925.
Phil 184.30.15   Janet, P. Philosophie; questions complémentaires. 5e éd. Paris, 1936.
Phil 184.31   Janet, P. Philosophie. 8e éd. Paris, 1929.
Phil 184.32   Jakowenko, B. Vom Wesen des Pluralismus. Bonn, 1928.
Phil 184.34   Joël, K. Philosophenwege. Berlin, 1901.
Phil 184.34.5   Jørgensen, J. Filosofiens og apdragelsene grundproblemer. København, 1928.
Phil 184.35   Jørgensen, J. Filosofiske forelassninger son indledning tilvidenskabelige studier. København, 1926.
Phil 184.35.5   Jolivet, Régis. La notion de substance. Paris, 1929.
Phil 184.36   Jolivet, Régis. La notion de substance. Paris, 1929.
Phil 184.37   Johnson, E.V. Universal tradition. v.6. Alexandria, Va., 1932.
Phil 184.38   Jaller, Arthur. Doppeldenken; Grundlagen einer neuen Weltanschauung. Berlin, 1926.
Phil 184.39   Joseph, H.W.B. Essays in ancient and modern philosophy. Oxford, 1935.
Phil 184.39.5   Jankélévitch, V. L'alternative. Paris, 1938.
Phil 184.40   Jankélévitch, V. Philosophie première. 1. ed. Paris, 1954.
Phil 184.41   Josipovici, J. Fragments de vie intérieure. Aix-en-Provence, 1937.
Phil 184.42   Jordan, David S. The higher foolishness. Indianapolis, 1927.
Phil 184.45   Johnson, R.C. The imprisoned splendour. London, 1953.
Phil 184.47   Jeandidier, A. Le panpsychisme vital. Paris, 1954.
Phil 184.49   Jolivet, Régis. L'homme métaphysique. Paris, 1958.
Phil 184.50   Johnstone, Henry Webb. Philosophy and argument. State College, Pa., 1959.
Phil 184.50   Jorn, A. Naturens orden; de divisione naturae. 2. Opl. København.
Phil 184.52   Janssen, O. Gesammelte Abhandlungen zur Frage des Seins. München, 1963.

Phil 184.53 Jancke, Rudolf. Ursprung und Arten des realen Seins. Bern, 1963.

Phil 185.1 Keratry, A.H. Inductions. Paris, 1818.

Phil 185.1.2 Keratry, A.H. Inductions. Paris, 1841.

Phil 185.2 Kessler, R. Praktische Philosophie. Leipzig, 1691.

Phil 185.3 Keyserlingh, H. von. Menschen-Kenntnis oder Anthropologie. Berlin, 1827.

Phil 185.3.5 Keyserlingh, H. von. Metaphysik. Heidelberg, 1818.

Phil 185.4 Kirchmann, J. Katechismus der Philosophie. Leipzig, 1881.

Phil 185.5 Kirkman, T.P. Philosophy without assumptions. London, 1876.

Phil 185.6 Kirwan, R. Metaphysical essays. London, 1809.

Phil 185.6.5 Kirwan, R. Metaphysical essays. London, 1809.

Phil 185.7 Knight, W. Essays in philosophy. Boston, 1890.

Phil 185.7.5 Knight, W. Studies in philosophy and literature. London, 1879.

Phil 185.7.9 Knight, W. Varia; studies on problems of philosophy and ethics. London, 1901.

Phil 185.8 Koenig, E. La science du vrai. Paris, 1844.

Phil 185.9 Krönig, Prof. Das Dasein Gottes. Berlin, 1874.

Phil 185.10 Krug, W.T. Handbuch der Philosophie. Leipzig, 1828.

Phil 185.10.2 Krug, Wilhelm Traugott. Handbuch der Philosophie und der philosophischen Literatur. v.1-2. Düsseldorf, 1969.

Phil 185.10.15 Krug, W.T. Handbuch i philosophien. Stockholm, 1831.

Phil 185.10.30 Krug, W.T. De humanitate in philosophando rite servanda. Vitebergae, 1800.

Phil 185.11 Kym, A.L. Die Weltanschauungen. Zürich, 1854.

Phil 185.11.5 Kym, A.L. Metaphysische Untersuchungen. München, 1875.

Phil 185.12 Külpe, O. Introduction to philosophy. London, 1897.

Phil 185.12.4 Külpe, O. Einleitung in die Philosophie. 4. Aufl. Leipzig, 1907.

Phil 185.12.5 Külpe, O. Einleitung in die Philosophie. 5. Aufl. Leipzig, 1910.

Phil 185.12.7 Külpe, O. Einleitung in die Philosophie. Leipzig, 1895.

Phil 185.12.8 Külpe, O. Einleitung in die Philosophie. 6. Aufl. Leipzig, 1913.

Phil 185.12.20 Pamphlet vol. Külpe, O. Über das Problem der Willensfreiheit. 10 pam.

Phil 185.13 Kaufmann, P. The temple of truth. Cincinnati, 1858.

Phil 185.15 Keckermann, B. Systema physicum. Hanoviae, 1623.

Phil 185.16.5 Kreibig, J.C. Die intellektuellen Funktionen. Wien, 1909.

Phil 185.17 Kern, Berthold P. Das Problem des Lebens in kritischer Bearbeitung. Berlin, 1909.

Phil 185.18 Kaftan, Julius. Drei akademische Reden. Tübingen, 1908.

Phil 185.18.50 Festgabe für Julius Kaftan zu seinem 70. Geburtstage, 30 Sept. 1918. Tübingen, 1920.

Phil 185.19 Knowlson, T.S. A thought book on Socratic method. London, 1920?

Phil 185.21.2 Kinkel, Walter. Vom Sein und von der Seele. 2. Aufl. Giessen, 1914.

Phil 185.22 Koch, J.L.A. Die Wirchlichkeit und ihre Erkenntnis. Göppingen, 1886.

Phil 185.22.6 Koch, J.L.A. Grundriss der Philosophie. 2e Aufl. Göppingen, 1885.

Phil 185.23 Kanovitch, A. The will to beauty. N.Y., 1922.

Phil 185.23.2 Kanovitch, A. The will to beauty. N.Y., 1923.

Phil 185.25 Kralik, R. Weltweisheit. v.1-3. Wien, 1896.

Phil 185.25.5 Kralik, R. Weltwissenschaft. Wien, 1896.

Phil 185.26 Koppelmann, W. Weltanschauungsfragen. 2e Aufl. Berlin, 1922.

Phil 185.27 Kaulish, W. System der Metaphysik. Prag, 1874.

Phil 185.29 Kühne, B. Die höchste Aufgabe der Philosophie. Einsiedeln, 1880.

Phil 185.30 Kann, A. Ein philosophischer Gedankengang. Wien, 19- .

Phil 185.32 Kolmark P. Utkast til en systematisk afhandling i theoretiska och practiska philosophien. Stockholm, 1799.

Phil 185.33 Kaeppelin, E.R. El universo, Dios y el hombre, ó Creador, creacion y criaturas. Paris, 1864.

Phil 185.34 Kerler, D.H. Weltwille und Wertwille. Leipzig, 1925.

Phil 185.35 Keyserling, H. Philosophie als Kunst. Darmstadt, 1920.

Phil 185.35.2 Keyserling, H. Philosophie als Kunst. 2. Aufl. Darmstadt, 1922.

Phil 185.35.10 Keyserling, H. The recovery of truth. N.Y., 1929.

Phil 185.36 Kaíres, Theophilos. Philosophiká. Athens, 1910.

Phil 185.37 Kreyenbühl, J. Die Bedeutung der Philosophie für die Erfahrungswissenschaften. Heidelberg, 1885.

Phil 185.39 Kynast, R. Ein Weg zur Metaphysik. Leipzig, 1927.

Phil 185.40 Kolbenheyer, E.G. Die Bauhütte. München, 1925.

Phil 185.40.5 Kolbenheyer, E.G. Die Philosophie der Bauhütte. Wien, 1952.

Phil 185.40.10 Schaumann, Otto. Die Triebrichtungen des Gewissens. Frankfurt, 1967.

Phil 185.41 Kroner, Richard. Die Selbstverwirklichung des Geistes. Tübingen, 1928.

Phil 185.41.5 Skinner, J.E. Self and world; the religious philosophy of Richard Kroner. Philadelphia, 1963.

Phil 185.42 Kortmulder, R.J. Metaphysica ne rede. Amsterdam, 1925.

Phil 185.43 Knox,H.V. The evolution of truth and other essays. London, 1930.

NEDL Phil 185.44 Klages, Ludwig. Der Geist als Widersacher der Seele. v.1-3. Leipzig, 1929-1932. 4v.

NEDL Phil 185.44.2 Klages, Ludwig. Der Geist als Widersacher der Seele. v.1-3. Gesamtverzeichnis. Leipzig, 1933. 4v.

Phil 185.44.5 Klages, L. Der Geist als Widersacher der Seele. 3. Aufl. München, 1954. 2v.

Phil 185.45 Korzybski, A. Time-binding; the general theory. N.Y., 1924. 2 pam.

Phil 185.46 Keyser, Cassius Jackson. Humanism and science. N.Y., 1931.

Phil 185.47 Kremer, Josef. Einleitung in die Philosophie. Graz, 1931.

Phil 185.48 Köppen, Friedrich. Darstellung des Wesens der Philosophie. Nürnberg, 1810.

Phil 185.48.25 Schafberger, F. Kritik der Schrift Darstellung des Wesens der Philosophie. Nürnberg, 1813.

Phil 185.49 Kotarbiński, Tadeusz. Elementy. Lwów, 1929.

Phil 185.49.2 Kotarbiński, Tadeusz. Elementy teorii poznania. Wyd. 2. Wrocław, 1961.

Phil 185.49.5 Kotarbiński, Tadeusz. Gnosiology; the scientific approach to the theory of knowledge. 1. English ed. Oxford, 1966.

Phil 185.50 Kirchner, F. Die Hauptpunkte der Metaphysik. Cöthen, 1880.

Phil 185.51 Krueger, F. Ganzheit und Form. Berlin, 1932.

Phil 185.52 King, Mrs. E.D. The lotus path. Los Angeles, 1917.

Phil 185.52.5 King, Mrs. E.D. The higher metaphysics. Los Angeles, 1918.

Phil 185.52.10 King, Mrs. E.D. The flashlights of truth. Los Angeles, 1918.

Phil 185.52.15 King, Mrs. E.D. Aum, the cosmic silence. Los Angeles, 1918. 2 pam.

Phil 185.53 Khristov, M. Filosofskitě printsipi na prirodata. Sofia, 1935.

Phil 185.54 Klatzkin, Jakob. Der Erkenntnistrieb als Lebens und Todesprinzip. Zürich, 1935.

Phil 185.54.5 Klatzkin, Jakob. In praise of wisdom. N.Y., 1943.

Phil 185.55 Kraft, Julius. Die Unmöglichkeit der Geisteswissenschaft. Leipzig, 1934.

Phil 185.55.2 Kraft, Julius. Die Unmöglichkeit der Geisteswissenschaft. Frankfurt, 1957.

Phil 185.56 Kniepf, Albert. Theorie der Geisteswerthe. Leipzig, 1892.

Phil 185.57A Klibansky, Raymond. Philosophy and history. Oxford, 1936.

Phil 185.57B Klibansky, Raymond. Philosophy and history. Oxford, 1936.

Phil 185.58 Kahl-Furthmann, G. Das Problem des Nicht. Berlin, 1934.

Phil 185.59 Knowledge and society. N.Y., 1938.

Phil 185.59.5 Selected writings in philosophy. N.Y., 1939.

Phil 185.60 Kraus, O. Wege und Abwege der Philosophie. Prag, 1934.

Phil 185.60.10 Kraus, O. Selbstdarstellung. Leipzig, 1929.

Phil 185.62 Konczewska, H. Le probléme de la substance. Paris, 1937.

Phil 185.63 König, J. Sein und Denken. Halle, 1937.

Phil 185.64 Künkel, H. Die Lebensalter. Jena, 1939.

Phil 185.65 Kraft, Viktor. Einführung in die Philosophie. Wien, 1950.

Phil 185.66 Krueger, H. Zwischen Dekadenz und Erneuerung. Frankfurt, 1953.

Phil 185.67 Klubertanz, G.P. The philosophy of human nature. N.Y., 1953.

Phil 185.67.5 Klubertanz, G.P. Introduction to the philosophy of being. N.Y., 1955.

Phil 185.68 Kattsoff, L.O. Elements of philosophy. N.Y., 1953.

Phil 185.68.5 Kattsoff, L.O. Logic and the nature of reality. The Hague, 1956.

Phil 185.69 Krings, H. Fragen und Aufgaben der Ontologie. Tübingen, 1954.

Phil 185.70 Krishna, Daya. The nature of philosophy. Calcutta, 1955.

Phil 185.71 Knox, Crawford. The idiom of contemporary thought. London, 1956.

Phil 185.72 Kaufmann, Walter Arnold. Critique of religion and philosophy. 1. ed. N.Y., 1958.

Phil 185.75 Kaelin, Bernard. Einführung in die Logik, Ontologie, Kosmologie, Psychologie. 5. Aufl. Sarnen, 1957.

Phil 185.80 Koelbel, Gerhard. Über die Einsamkeit. München, 1960.

Phil 185.85 Krąpiec, M.A. Teoria analogii bytu. Lublin, 1959.

Phil 185.90 Kemp, Peter. Person og tänkning. København, 1960.

Phil 185.95 Keilbach, Wilhelm. Einübung ins philosophische Denken. München, 1960.

Phil 185.96 Koyré, Alexandre. Etudes d'histoire de la pensée philosophique. Paris, 1961.

Phil 185.97 Kalsbeek, L. Geloof en wetenschap. Baarn, 1962.

Phil 185.98 Keleher, James Francis. Disputed questions in philosophy. N.Y., 1965.

VPhil 185.99 Kudriavtsev-Platonov, Viktor D. Vvedenie v filosofiiu. Izd. 7. Sergiev Posad, 1908.

Phil 185.100 Kuhn, Helmut. Traktat über die Methode der Philosophie. München, 1966.

Phil 185.102 Kreiser, Lothar. Untersuchungen zur Möglichkeit Habilitationsschrift. Leipzig?, 1967?

Phil 185.104 Koerner, Stephan. What is philosophy? London, 1969.

Phil 185.106 Kuspit, Donald Burton. The philosophical life of the senses. N.Y., 1969.

VPhil 185.108 Kamiński, Stanisław. Z teorii i metodologii metafizyki. Wyd. 1. Lublin, 1962.

Phil 186.1 Landon, E. Le spiritualisme. Paris, 1872.

Phil 186.3 Laws, S.S. Metaphysics. Columbia, Mo., 1879.

Phil 186.4 Lazarus, M. Ideale Fragen. Berlin, 1878.

Phil 186.5 LeClerc, J. Opera philosophica. v.1-4. Amsterdam, 1698. 3v.

Phil 186.5.2 LeClerc, J. Opera philosophica. Amsterdam, 1722. 4v.

Phil 186.5.5 LeClerc, J. Logica, sive Ars ratiocinandi. London, 1692. 3 pam.

Phil 186.5.6 LeClerc, J. Logica, ontologia, et pneumatologia. 4. ed. Cambridge, 1704.

Phil 186.6 Lemaire, C. Initiation à la philosophie. Paris, 1843. 2v.

Phil 186.7 Lemoine, J.J. Les trois voyageurs. Paris, 1819.

Htn Phil 186.8* Lequier, J. La recherche d'une première vérité. Saint-Cloud, 1865.

Phil 186.9 Lévêque, J.C. La science de l'invisible. Paris, 1865.

Phil 186.10 Liard, L. La science positive. Paris, 1879.

Phil 186.10.5 Liard, L. La science positive. 5. ed. Paris, 1905.

Phil 186.12 Liebmann, O. Zur Analysis der Wirklichkeit. Strassburg, 1876.

Phil 186.12.5 Liebmann, O. Gedanken und Thatsachen. Strassburg, 1882-1899. 2v.

Phil 186.12.8 Liebmann, O. Über philosophische Tradition. Strassburg, 1883.

Phil 186.12.11 Liebmann, O. Die Klimax der Theorieen. Strassburg, 1884.

Phil 186.13 Lindner, G.A. Einleitung in das Studium der Philosophie. Wien, 1866.

Phil 186.14 Lindemann, H.S. Die Lehre vom Menschen. Zürich, 1844.

Phil 186.15 Lyall, W. Intellect, the emotions and moral nature. Edinburgh, 1855.

Phil 186.16 Ladd, G.T. Introduction to philosophy. N.Y., 1890.

Phil 186.16.5 Ladd, G.T. Theory of reality. N.Y., 1899.

Phil 186.16.15 Ladd, G.T. Knowledge, life and reality. New Haven, 1918.

Phil 186.17 Le Conte, J. Man's place in nature. N.Y., 1878.

Phil 186.18.5 Laugel, Auguste. Les problèmes de la nature. Paris, 1864.

Phil 186.18.9 Laugel, Auguste. Los problemas de la naturaleza. Barcelona, 18- ?

Phil 186.19 Laurie, S.S. Synthetica. London, 1906. 2v.

Phil 186.20 Lee, G.S. The voice of the machines. Northampton, 1906.

Phil 186.21 Leclére, A. Pragmatisme, modernisme, protestantisme. Paris, 1909.

Phil 186.22 Lorensen, C. Essay on positive theology or a new system of philosophy. Waterbury, 1899.

Phil 186.23 Lindsay, J. The fundamental problems of metaphysics. Edinburgh 1910.

Phil 186.24 Lagos, C.D. La doctrina de los siglos. Santiago, 1910.

Phil 186.25 Laguna, T. de. Dogmatism and evolution. N.Y., 1910.

Phil 186.26 Liddy, Ray Balmer. Relation of science and philosophy. Thesis. Toronto, 1914?

Phil 186.28 Leighton, J.A. The field of philosophy. Columbus, Ohio, 1918.

Phil 186.28.5 Leighton, J.A. The field of philosophy. 4.ed. N.Y., 1930.

Phil 186.29 Louage, Augustin. A course of philosophy. 4. ed. N.Y., 1895.

Classified Listing

Htn   Phil 186.30*   Lowde, James. A discourse concerning the nature of man. London, 1694.

Phil 186.31   Lightfoot, John. Studies in philosophy. Edinburgh, 1888.

Htn   Phil 186.33*   Lau, Theodor L. Meditationes philosophicae de Deo, mundo, homine. Frankfurt, 1717.

Phil 186.34   Lyon, Otto. Das Pathos der Resonanz. Leipzig, 1900.

Phil 186.35.5   Liebert, Arthur. Wie ist kritische Philosophie überhaupt möglich? Leipzig, 1919.

Phil 186.35.7   Liebert, Arthur. Wie ist kritische Philosophie überhaupt möglich? Leipzig, 1923.

Phil 186.35.15   Liebert, Arthur. Geist und Welt der Dialektik. Berlin, 1929.

Phil 186.36.4   Lehmann, R. Lehrbuch der philosophischen Propädeutik. 4. Aufl. Berlin, 1917.

Phil 186.36.5   Lehmann, R. Lehrbuch der philosophischen Propädeutik. 5. Aufl. Leipzig, 1922.

Phil 186.37   Lipps, Theodor. Philosophie und Wirklichkeit. Heidelberg, 1908.

Phil 186.38   Lipps, Gottlob F. Mythenbildung und Erkenntnis. Leipzig, 1907.

Phil 186.39   Liard, Louis. Wissenschaft und Metaphysik. Leipzig, 1911.

Phil 186.40.5   Lichtenfels, Johann. Lehrbuch zur Einleitung in die Philosophie. 5e Aufl. Wien, 1863.

Phil 186.41   Lipsius, Friedrich R. Naturphilosophie und Weltanschauung. Leipzig, 1918.

Phil 186.42   Lasson, Adolf. Zeitliches und Zeitloses. Leipzig, 1890.

Phil 186.43   Lublinski, Samuel. Die Humanität als Mysterium. Jena, 1907.

Phil 186.44   Lambeck, G. Philosophische Propädeutik. Leipzig, 1919.

Phil 186.45   Lasker, E. Die Philosophie des Unvollendbar. Leipzig, 1919.

Phil 186.46   Lapshin', I. Filosofia izobreteniia. Praga, 1924. 2v.

Phil 186.48.2   Pamphlet box. Lighthall, W.D.

Phil 186.48.5   Lighthall, W.D. Superpersonalism, the outer consciousness. Montreal, 1926.

Phil 186.48.10   Lighthall, W.D. The person of evolution. Montreal, 1930.

Phil 186.48.11   Lighthall, W.D. The person of evolution. Toronto, 1933.

Phil 186.49   Lambek, C. Indledning til kulturens filosofi. København, 1908.

Phil 186.49.5   Lambek, C. Growth of the mind in relation to culture. Copenhagen, 1936.

Phil 186.50   Ludowici, A. Das genetische Prinzip. München, 1913.

Phil 186.50.2   Ludowici, A. Spiel und Widerspiel. 2. Ausg. München, 1917.

Phil 186.50.10   Ludowici, A. Denkfibel; die Lehre vom organischen Gegensatz. München, 1927.

Phil 186.50.20   Ludowici, A. Zugleich. München, 1933.

Phil 186.51   Lyng, G.W. Philosophische Studien. n.p., 1877.

Phil 186.52   Lessing, T. Philosophie als Tat. Göttingen, 1914.

Phil 186.53.5   Luthardt, C.E. De moderna verldsàsigterna. Lund, 1880.

Htn   Phil 186.54*   Landino, C. Disputationum Camaldulensium. Bk. 4. Argentoraci, 1508.

Phil 186.54.5   Landino, C. Camaldolensische Gespräche. Jena, 1927.

Phil 186.55.5   Liljekrantz, B. Verklighetsproblemet i den antika filosofien. Göteborg, 1915.

Phil 186.56   Le Senne, R. Introduction à la philosophie. Paris, 1925.

Phil 186.56.5   Le Senne, R. Introduction à la philosophie. Paris, 1939.

Phil 186.56.10   Le Senne, R. Obstacle et valeur. Paris, 1934.

Phil 186.57   Lindsay, Norman. Creative effort. 1. ed. London, 1924.

Phil 186.58   Lehmann, Gerhard. Über Einzigkeit und Individualität. Leipzig, 1926.

Phil 186.59   Lehmann, Gerhard. Vorschule der Metaphysik. Berlin, 1927.

Phil 186.60   Litt, Theodor. Erkenntnis und Leben. Leipzig, 1923.

Phil 186.60.10   Litt, Theodor. Wissenschaft, Bildung, Weltanschauung. Leipzig, 1928.

Phil 186.60.15   Litt, Theodor. Einleitung in die Philosophie. Leipzig, 1933.

Phil 186.60.20   Litt, Theodor. Mensch und Welt. München, 1948.

Phil 186.61   Lafora, G.R. Don Juan, Los milagros y otros ensayos. Madrid, 1927.

Phil 186.63   Le Fébure, L.F.H. Essai sur l'organisation du monde physique et moral. Commercy, 1806.

Phil 186.64   Losskii, N.O. The world as an organic whole. London, 1928.

Phil 186.64.10   Losskii, N.O. Intellectual intuition and ideal being. Praha, 1934.

Phil 186.65.30   Lavelle, Louis. Science, esthétique, métaphysique. Paris, 1967.

Phil 186.65.35   Lavelle, Louis. Panorama des doctrines philosophiques. Paris, 1967.

Phil 186.66   Laffitte, Pierre. Cours de philosophie premiére. Paris, 1889-1894. 2v.

Phil 186.67   Leisegang, H. Denkformen. Berlin, 1928.

Phil 186.67.3   Leisegang, H. Denkformen. 2. Aufl. Berlin, 1951.

Phil 186.67.5   Leisegang, H. Einführung in die Philosophie. Berlin, 1951.

Phil 186.67.8   Leisegang, H. Einführung in die Philosophie. 3. Aufl. Berlin, 1956.

Phil 186.68   Larrabee, Harold A. What philosophy is. N.Y., 1928.

Phil 186.69   Laird, John. Modern problems in philosophy. London, 1928.

Phil 186.70   LeRoy, Edouard. La pensée intuitive. Paris, 1929.

Phil 186.71   La Hautière, E. de. Philosophie. Paris, 1895.

Phil 186.72   Langer, Mrs. S.K. The practice of philosophy. N.Y., 1930.

Phil 186.73   Lutosławski, W. The knowledge of reality. Cambridge, 1930.

Phil 186.73.10   Lutosławski, W. Wykłady jagiellońskie. Kraków, 1901-1902. 2v.

DL   Phil 186.73.20   Lutosławski, W. Iskierki Warszawskie. Ser. 1. Warszawa, 1911.

Phil 186.74   Lunn, A.H.M. The flight from reason. N.Y., 1931.

Phil 186.75   Lumbreras, Pedro. Estudios filosóficos. Madrid, 1930.

Phil 186.76   Le Dantec, Félix. Contre la métaphysique; questions de méthode. Paris, 1912.

Phil 186.76.5   Le Dantec, Félix. Le déterminisme biologique et la personnalité consciente. Paris, 1897.

Phil 186.76.15   Le Dantec, Félix. Le conflit. 6e ed. Paris, 1913.

Phil 186.77.5   Ludovici, August. Denkfibel; der Gegensatz als Richtmass. 2e Aufl. München, 1929.

Phil 186.78   Luquet, G.H. Logique, morale, métaphysique. Paris, 1931.

Phil 186.79.5   Lacuria, P.F.G. Les harmonies de l'être exprimées par les nombres. v.1-2. Paris, 1899.

Phil 186.80   Lombardi, F. L'esperienza e l'uomo. Firenze, 1935.

Phil 186.81   Lupasco, Stéphane. Du devenir logique et de l'affectivité. v.1-2. Thèse. Paris, 1935.

Phil 186.81.5   Lupasco, Stéphane. Du devenir logique et de l'affectivité. v.1-2. Paris, 1935-1936. 2v.

Phil 186.81.10   Lupasco, Stéphane. Qu'est-ce qu'une structure? Paris, 1967.

Phil 186.82   Lambert, Henri. Hypothèse sur l'évolution physique et métaphysique de l'énergie. Bruxelles, 1935.

Phil 186.83   LaSalle, A. de. La balance naturelle, ou Essai sur une loi universelle appliquée aux sciences. Londres, 1788. 2v.

Phil 186.84   Lodge, R.C. The questioning mind. N.Y., 1937.

Phil 186.85   Ladet, F. Méditations sur l'omnitude. Paris, 1936.

Phil 186.86   Leendertz, W. Dogma en existentie. Amsterdam, 1933.

Phil 186.86.10   Leendertz, W. Ratio en existentie. Amsterdam, 1936.

Phil 186.87   Lindemann, H.A. Weltgeschehen und Welterkenntnis. Baden, 1931.

Phil 186.88   Lin, Yu-t'ang. The importance of living. N.Y., 1937.

Phil 186.89.5   Lolli, E. La conception inductive de la vie. Paris, 1937.

Phil 186.91   Lambek, C. Studies in the dynamic coherence. Copenhagen, 1938.

Phil 186.92   Lins, I.M.de B. Escolas filosoficas. Rio, 1939.

Phil 186.93   Liebert, A. Von der Pflicht der Philosophie in unserer Zeit. Zürich, 1938.

Phil 186.94A   Living philosophies. N.Y., 1931.

Phil 186.94B   Living philosophies. N.Y., 1931.

Phil 186.95   Fadiman, Clifton. I believe. N.Y., 1939.

Phil 186.95.5   Fadiman, Clifton. I believe. London, 1940.

Phil 186.96   Laird, J. The limits of speculative humanism. London, 1940.

Phil 186.97   Langer, Mrs. S.K. Philosophy in a new key. Cambridge, Mass., 1942.

Phil 186.97.2   Langer, Mrs. S.K. Philosophy in a new key. 2d ed. Cambridge, Mass., 1951.

Phil 186.97.5   Langer, Mrs. S.K. Philosophy in a new key. 3d ed. Cambridge, Mass., 1957.

Phil 186.98   Ludendorff, M.S. Ist das Leben sinnlose Schinderei? München, 1935.

Phil 186.99   Losskii, N.O. Tipy mirovozzrenii. Parizh, 1931.

Phil 186.101   Lasaga y Travieso, J.I. Manual de introducción a la filosofia de acuerdo. 2. ed. Facs. 1-8. La Habana, 1944-1946.

Phil 186.103   Luporini, C. Filosofi vecchi e nuovi. Firenze, 1947.

Phil 186.105   Lévy-Bruhe, L. Les carnets. 1. ed. Paris, 1949.

Phil 186.107   Loos, A. The nature of man, his world. N.Y., 1950.

Phil 186.109   Lamprecht, S.P. Nature and history. N.Y., 1950.

Phil 186.111   Lodge, R.C. Applied philosophy. London, 1951.

Phil 186.113   Levitskii, S.A. Osnovy organicheskogo mirovozzreniia. n.p., 1946.

Phil 186.115   Liat, W.S. Methods of comparative philosophy. Leiden, 1955.

Phil 186.120   Lazerowitz, M. The structure of metaphysics. London, 1955.

Phil 186.120.2   Lazerowitz, M. The structure of metaphysics. N.Y., 1955.

Phil 186.120.4   Lazerowitz, M. Philosophy and illusion. London, 1968.

Phil 186.120.5   Lazerowitz, M. Studies in metaphilosophy. London, 1964.

Phil 186.125   Lalande, André. Vocabulaire technique et critique de la philosophie. 6. ed. Paris, 1951.

Phil 186.135   Loehrich, R.R. Modus operandi. McHenry, Ill., 1956.

Phil 186.140   Lovejoy, A.O. The reason, the understanding and time. Baltimore, 1961.

Phil 186.142   Lynch, W.F. The integrating mind. N.Y., 1962.

Phil 186.143   Lechat, Jean. Analyse et synthèse. Paris, 1962.

Phil 186.145   Lea, Frank A. A defence of philosophy. London, 1962.

Phil 186.146   Librizzi, Carmelo. Morale e conoscenza; saggi critici. Padova, 1961.

Phil 186.147   Lamouche, André. Rythmologie universelle et metaphysique de l'harmonie. Paris, 1966. 2v.

Phil 186.152   Leist, Fritz. Über Leben, Lüge und Liebe. Freiburg, 1966.

Phil 186.154   Lugarini, Leo. Filosofia e metafisica. Urbino, 1964.

Phil 186.156   Losskii, N.O. Types of world views; an introduction to metaphysics. Typescript. n.p., n.d.

Phil 186.158   Lemos, Ramon M. Experience, mind, and value. Leiden, 1969.

Phil 186.160   Lange, John. The cognitivity paradox. Princeton, 1970.

Phil 187.1   M'Cormac, H. Philosophy of human nature. London, 1837.

Phil 187.2   MacMahon, J.H. Treatise on metaphysics. London, 1860.

Phil 187.3   Macvicar, J.G. Sketch of a philosophy. v.1-4. London, 1868-1874.

Phil 187.4   Maguire, T. Lectures on philosophy. London, 1885.

Htn   Phil 187.5*   Magirus, J. Physiologiae peripateticae. Francofurti, 1610.

Phil 187.6   Makowski, J. Metaphysica. n.p., n.d.

Phil 187.6.2   Makowski, J. Metaphysica. Amsterdam, 1651.

Phil 187.7   Mallet, C.A. Études philosophiques. Paris, 1844. 2v.

Phil 187.8   Mancino, S. Elementi di filosofia. Palermo, 1846. 2v.

Phil 187.8.5   Marcel, Gabriel. Homo viator. London, 1951.

Phil 187.8.7   Marcel, Gabriel. Homo viator. Paris, 1952.

Phil 187.9   Martin, F. La perception extérieure. Paris, 1894.

Phil 187.10   Martin, T.H. Les sciences et la philosophie. Paris, 1869.

Phil 187.11   Martineau, J. Essays. Boston, 1866-1868. 2v.

Phil 187.11.2   Martineau, J. Essays. Boston, 1866. 2v.

Phil 187.11.9   Martineau, J. Essays. N.Y., 1875. 2v.

Phil 187.12   Matthiae, A.H. Manuel de philosophie. Paris, 1837.

Phil 187.13   Meyer, J.B. Philosophische Zeitfragen. Bonn, 1874.

Phil 187.14   Michelet, K.L. Das System der Philosophie. Berlin, 1876-1881. 5v.

Phil 187.15   Migeot, A. Philosophiae elementa. Carolopoli, 1784. 2v.

Phil 187.16   Miller, J. Metaphysics. N.Y., 1877.

Phil 187.17   Mivart, St. G. Nature and thought. London, 1882.

Phil 187.17.5   Mivart, St. G. On truth. London, 1889.

Phil 187.17.9   Mivart, St. G. The helpful science. N.Y., 1895.

Phil 187.19   Moreau de St. Elier, L. Les songes physiques. Amsterdam, 1781.

Phil 187.20   Morell, J.O. Philosophical tendencies of the age. London, 1848.

Phil 187.20.5   Morell, J.D. Philosophical fragments. London, 1878.

Phil 187.21   Pamphlet box. Monrad, M.T. Philosophical pamphlets. 6 pam.

Phil 187.22   Mühry, A. Kritik und Kurze Darlegung der exacten Natur-Philosophie. Göttingen, 1882.

Phil 187.23   Mercier, E. De la certitude. Paris, 1844.

Phil 187.23.7   Frischkopf, B. Die Psychologie der neuen Löwener-Schule. Luzern, 1908.

Phil 187.24   Müller, J.G. Philosophische Aufsäze. Breslau, 1795.

Phil 187.25   Mercier, D. Cours de philosophie. 3e éd. v.1. Louvain, 1902.

Phil 187.25.2   Mercier, D. Cours de philosophie. 3e éd. v.2. Louvain, 1902.

Phil 175 - 200   General treatises on philosophy - Individual authors (A-Z) - cont.

Phil 187.25.3 Mercier, D. Cours de philosophie. 6e éd. v.3. Louvain, 1903.

Phil 187.25.4 Mercier, D. Cours de philosophie. 4e éd. v.4. Louvain, 1900.

Phil 187.25.5 Mercier, D. Curso de philosophia. v.1. Logica. v.3. Psychologia. Vizeu, 1904. 2v.

Phil 187.26 Marvin, W.T. Introduction to systematic philosophy. N.Y., 1903.

Phil 187.26.5 Marvin, W.T. A first book in metaphysics. N.Y., 1912.

Phil 187.27 Mackenzie, J.S. Outlines of metaphysics. London, 1902.

Phil 187.27.5 Mackenzie, J.S. Lectures on humanism. London, 1907.

Phil 187.27.9 Mackenzie, J.S. Elements of constructive philosophy. London, 1917.

Phil 187.27.13 Mackenzie, J.S. Cosmic problems. London, 1931.

Phil 187.28 Mechnikov, I.I. Études sur la nature humaine. 2. ed. Paris, 1903.

Phil 187.28.2 Mechnikov, I.I. Études sur la nature humaine. Paris, 1903.

Phil 187.28.3 Mechnikov, I.I. Études sur la nature humaine. 5. ed. Paris, 1917.

Phil 187.28.4 Mechnikov, I.I. Studien über die Natur des Menschen. Leipzig, 1904.

Phil 187.28.6.7 Mechnikov, I.I. Nature of man. N.Y., 1911.

Phil 187.28.7 Mechnikov, I.I. Nature of man. London, 1938.

Phil 187.28.8 Mechnikov, I.I. Studier öfver människans natur. Stockholm, 1906.

Phil 187.28.11 Mechnikov, I.I. Essais optimistes. Paris, 1907.

Phil 187.28.13 Mechnikov, I.I. Beiträge zur einer optimistischen Weltauffassung. München, 1908.

Phil 187.28.15 Mechnikov, I.I. Etiudy optimizma. Moskva, 1907.

Phil 187.28.22 Mechnikov, I.I. Etiudy o prirode cheloveka. Izd. 2. Moskva, 1905.

Phil 187.28.25 Mechnikov, I.I. Sorok let iskaniia ratsional'nago mirovozzreniia. Moskva, 1913.

Phil 187.29 Morgan, C.L. The interpretation of nature. Bristol, 1905.

Phil 187.29.3 Morgan, C.L. The interpretation of nature. N.Y., 1906.

Phil 187.29.5 Morgan, C.L. Mind at the crossways. N.Y., 1930.

Phil 187.29.15A Morgan, C.L. The emergence of novelty. London, 1933.

Phil 187.29.15B Morgan, C.L. The emergence of novelty. London, 1933.

Phil 187.31 Malapert, P. Leçons de philosophie. Paris, 1907-1908. 2v.

Phil 187.31.7 Malapert, P. Leçons de philosophie. v.1. 6. ed.; v.2. 7. ed. Paris, 1916-1918. 2v.

Phil 187.32 Montgomery, E. Philosophical problems. N.Y., 1907.

Phil 187.32.5 Montgomery, E. Vitality and organization of protoplasm. Austin, Texas, 1904.

Phil 187.32.80 Lane, Charles A. Montgomery's philosophy of vital organization. Chicago, 1909.

Phil 187.32.85 Keeton, Morris. The philosophy of Edmund Montgomery. Dallas, 1950.

Phil 187.32.90 Stephens, I.K. The hermit philosopher of Liendo. Dallas, 1951.

Phil 187.33.5 Montague, W.P. Introductory course in philosophy. Syllabus. N.Y., 1920.

Phil 187.33.10 Montague, W.P. The ways of things: a philosophy of knowledge, nature, and value. N.Y., 1940.

Phil 187.34 Marin, V. Elementos de la filosofia del espiritu humano. Santiago, 1834.

Phil 187.34.5 Marin, V. Elementos de la filosofia del espiritu humano. 3d ed. Santiago, 1872.

Phil 187.35 Murray, D.L. Pragmatism. London, 1912.

Phil 187.38 Muller, W.T. De kennisleer van het Anglo-Amerikanisch pragmatisme. 's-Gravenhage, 1913.

Phil 187.39A Moore, A.W. Pragmatism and its critics. Chicago, 1910.

Phil 187.39B Moore, A.W. Pragmatism and its critics. Chicago, 1910.

Phil 187.41 Malter, Mrs. M.P. The world process. Fresno, Cal., 1914.

Phil 187.42 Mondolfo, Rodolfo. Saggi per la storia della morale utilitaria. Verona, 1903. 2 pam.

Phil 187.43 McTaggart, William. Absolute relativism. London, 1887.

Phil 187.44 Mann, William E. Theories about the truth of things. Franklin, Mass., 1919.

Phil 187.44.5 Mann, William E. The truth of things. Boston, 1922.

Phil 187.44.7 Mann, William E. A new theory of evolution. Walpole, Mass., 1923.

Phil 187.44.9 Mann, William E. A new theory of evolution. Walpole, Mass., 1924.

Phil 187.45 Marchesini, G. Saggio sulla naturale unità del pensiero. Firenze, 1895.

Phil 187.46 Menzer, Paul. Weltanschauungsfragen. Stuttgart, 1918.

Phil 187.47 Merz, John T. A fragment on the human mind. Edinburgh, 1919.

Phil 187.48 Mirbt, Ernst. Was heisst Philosophiren und was 1st Philosophie? Jena, 1839.

X Cg Phil 187.49 Malkani, G.R. The problem of nothing. Amalner, 1918.

Phil 187.49.5 Malkani, G.R. Metaphysics of energy. Amalner, 1920.

Phil 187.50 Marbe, Karl. Die Gleichförmigkeit in der Welt. München, 1916-1919. 2v.

Phil 187.50.6 Pamphlet vol. Marbe, Karl. Die Schwankungen der Gesichtsempfindungen. 15 pam.

Phil 187.51 Maudsley, Henry. Life in mind and conduct. London, 1902.

Phil 187.52 Michelis, Friedrich. Die Philosophie des Bewusstseins. Bonn, 1877.

Phil 187.52.80 Kowalewski, A. Die Philosophie des Bewusstseins von Friedrich Michelis. Berlin, 1897.

Phil 187.53 Michaltschew, Dimitri. Philosophische Studien. Leipzig, 1909.

Phil 187.54 Motion, George. Fragments of philosophy: Democracy. Nelson, B.C., 1920.

Phil 187.54.5F Pamphlet box. Motion, George. Fragments of philosophy.

Htn Phil 187.54.9F* Motion, George. Diagram of the celestial city. n.p., n.d.

Phil 187.55.3 Muñiz, Narcisse. Problèmes de la vie. Paris, 1914.

Phil 187.56 McTaggart, J.M.E. The nature of existence. Cambridge, Eng., 1921-1927. 2v.

Phil 187.56.4 McTaggart, J.M.E. Dare to be wise. London, 1910.

Phil 187.56.5 McTaggart, J.M.E. Philosophical studies. London, 1934.

Phil 187.56.9 McTaggart, J.M.E. Introduction to the study of philosophy. Cambridge, Eng., 190-.

Phil 187.57 McCarty, R.J. An essay in practical philosophy: relations of wisdom and purpose. Kansas City, Mo., 1922.

Phil 187.59 Moore, G.E. Philosophical studies. London, 1922.

Phil 187.59.80 Schilpp, P.A. The philosophy of G.E. Moore. Evanston, 1942.

Phil 187.59.82 Schilpp, P.A. The philosophy of G.E. Moore. 2. ed. N.Y., 1952.

Phil 187.59.85 White, Alan R. G.E. Moore. Oxford, 1958.

Phil 187.60.7 Maritain, J. An introduction to philosophy. London, 1937.

Phil 187.61 Maack, F. Naturforschung und Philosophie. Kiel, 1896.

Phil 175 - 200   General treatises on philosophy - Individual authors (A-Z) - cont.

Phil 187.62 Mahnke, D. Der Wille zur Ewigkeit. Halle, 1917.

Phil 187.63 Muirhead, J.H. Contemporary British philosophy. 1st Ser. N.Y., 1924.

Phil 187.63.5 Muirhead, J.H. Contemporary British philosophy. 2nd ser. N.Y., 1925.

Phil 187.63.8A Muirhead, J.H. Contemporary British philosophy. 3rd ser. London, 1956.

Phil 187.63.8B Contemporary British philosophy. 3d. series. London, 1956.

Phil 187.63.12 Muirhead, J.H. The use of philosophy. Cambridge, 1929.

Phil 187.65 Merten, J. Die Hauptfragen der Metaphysik in Verbindung mit der Speculation. Trier, 1840.

Phil 187.65.5 Merten, J. Grundriss der Metaphysik. Trier, 1848.

Phil 187.66 Moog, Willy. Das Verhältnis der Philosophie zu den Einzel-Wissenschaften. Halle, 1919.

Phil 187.68 Marty, Anton. Gesammelte Schriften. Halle, 1916-1918. 2v.

Phil 187.69 Muller, Aloys. Einleitung in die Philosophie. Berlin, 1925.

Phil 187.70 Müller, Josef. System der Philosophie. Mainz, 1898.

Phil 187.71 Mason, J.W.T. Creative freedom. N.Y., 1926.

Phil 187.72 Masci, Filippo. Elementi di filosofia per le scuole secondarie. Napoli, 1899-1904. 2v.

Phil 187.72.5 Masci, Filippo. Intellettualismo e pragmatismo. Napoli, 1911.

Phil 187.73F Madiedo, M.M. Una gran revolucion, ó La razon del hombre juzgada por sí misma. Caracas, 1876.

Phil 187.74 Mignosi, Pietro. Critica dell'identita. Palermo, 1926.

Phil 187.75 Maier, Heinrich. Philsophie der Wirklichkeit. Tübingen, 1926-1935. 3v.

Phil 187.76 Musatti, C.L. Analisi del concetto di realtà empirica. Castello, 1926.

Phil 187.77 Monaco, Nicolao. Praelectiones metaphysicae specialis. Romae, 1917-1920. 3v.

Phil 187.78 Maugeri, P. Antonino. Corso di lezioni di filosofia razionale. Catania, 1865-1866. 2v.

Phil 187.79 MacLeod, A.H.D. Sur diverses questions se présentant dans l'étude du concept de réalité. Paris, 1927.

Phil 187.79.2 MacLeod, A.H.D. Sur diverses questions se présentant dans l'étude du concept de réalité. Paris, 1927.

Phil 187.80 Maggiore, G. L'unita del mondo nel sistema del pensiero. Palermo, 1913.

Phil 187.81 Mossig, T. Wirklichkeit. Leipzig, 1927.

Phil 187.82 Moore, J.S. Rifts in the universe. New Haven, 1927.

Phil 187.83 Marchesini, A. L'imaginazione creatrice nella filosofia. Torino, 1905.

Phil 187.84 Maar, Jean. Le fondement de la philosophie. Paris, 1925.

Phil 187.85 Mehring, G. Grundzüge der speculativen Kritik. Heilbronn, 1844.

Phil 187.86 Müller-Freienfels, R. Metaphysik des Irrationalen. Leipzig, 1927.

Phil 187.86.10 Müller-Freienfels, R. Geheimnisse der Seele. München, 1927.

Phil 187.86.15 Müller-Freienfels, R. Mysteries of the soul. London, 1929.

Phil 187.87 Montalto, F. L'intuizione e la verità di fatto saggio; psicologico-metafisico. Roma, 1924.

Phil 187.87.5 Montalto, F. L'intuizione e la verità di fatto saggio; psicologico-metafisico. 2. ed. Roma, 1930.

Phil 187.88 Meek, Charles. The will to function. Bisley, 1929.

Phil 187.89 Muzquiz, J.M. La verdadera legitimidad y el verdadero liberalismo. Habana, 1886.

Phil 187.90 Masnovo, Amato. Problemi di metafisica e di criteriologia. Milano, 1930.

Phil 187.91 Meiklejohn, A. Philosophy. Chicago, 1926.

Phil 187.92 Moreau, J. Perspectives sur les relativités humaines. 2. ed. Paris, 1929.

Phil 187.93 Marcel, Gabriel. Journal métaphysique. Paris, 1927.

Phil 187.93.3 Marcel, Gabriel. Metaphysical journal. London, 1952.

Phil 187.93.5 Marcel, Gabriel. Être et avoir. Paris, 1935.

Phil 187.93.10 Marcel, Gabriel. Being and having. Westminster, 1949.

Phil 187.93.15 Marcel, Gabriel. Position et approches concrètes du mystère ontologique. Louvain, 1949.

Phil 187.93.30 Vassallo, Angel. Cuatro lecciones sobre metafísica. Buenos Aires, 1938.

Phil 187.94 McKerrow, J.C. Novius organum. London, 1931.

Phil 187.95 Manley, R.M. Synthetic philosophy. Cleveland, Ohio, 1931.

Phil 187.96 McDonald, M.F. Brief readings in philosophy. Brooklyn, 1931.

Phil 187.97 McCrossan, J.D. Logic and other nonsense. London, 1895.

Phil 187.98 Markovics, J.M. Assertiones ex universa philosophia. Pestini, 1802? 2 pam.

Phil 187.99 Muller, Maurice. Individualité, causalité, indeterminisme. Paris, 1932.

Phil 187.99.5 Muller, Maurice. Idées et archetypes de Platon à Elie Cartan. Neuchâtel, 1959.

Phil 187.100 Mead, George H. The philosophy of the present. Chicago, 1932.

Phil 187.100.5 Mead, George H. The philosophy of the act. Chicago, 1938.

Phil 187.101 Marci von Kronland, J.M. Philosophia vetus restituta. Francofurti, 1676.

Phil 187.102 Mannarino, G. La ragion d'essere della filosofia. Catanzaro, 1931.

Phil 187.104 Maltese, F. Il problema morale. Vittoria, 1896.

Phil 187.105 Melillo, F. Manuale di filosofia. Napoli, 1873.

Phil 187.106 Masson, T.L. The city of perfection. N.Y., 1927.

Phil 187.107 MacEachran, John M. Pragmatismus; eine neue Richtung der Philosophie. Leipzig, 1910.

Phil 187.108 Müller, G.E. Philosophy of our uncertainties. Norman, 1936.

Phil 187.108.5 Müller, G.E. Der Mensch im Sein. Stuttgart, 1938.

Phil 187.110 Mitchell, William. The place of minds in the world. London, 1933.

Phil 187.110.5 Mitchell, William. The quality of life. London, 1935?

Phil 187.111 My philosophy, by an unprofessional thinker. Oxford, 1934.

Phil 187.112 Monteath, K.M. The philosophy of the past. York, 1936.

Phil 187.113 Meyerson, E. Essais. Paris, 1936.

Phil 187.114 Masaryk, T.G. Das Ideale der Humanität. Wien, 1902.

Phil 187.114.5 Masaryk, T.G. The ideals of humanity and How to work. London, 1938.

Phil 187.114.10 Masaryk, T.G. Ideály humanitní. Praha, 1901.

Phil 187.115 Milville, H.L. Vers une philosophie de l'esprit ou de la totalité. Lausanne, 1937.

Phil 187.116 Maugé, F. L'esprit et le réel dans les limites du nombre et de la grandeur. Paris, 1937.

Phil 187.116.4 Maugé, F. L'esprit et le réel perçu. Paris, 1937.

Classified Listing

Phil 187.117 Morando, G. Corso elementare di filosofia. Milano, 1898-1899. 3v.

Phil 187.118 Monsarrat, K.W. Human powers and their relations. Liverpool, 1938.

Phil 187.118.5 Monsarrat, K.W. Thoughts, deeds and human happiness. London, 1944.

Phil 187.118.10 Monsarrat, K.W. Human desires and their fulfilment. Liverpool, 1950.

Phil 187.119 Murray, G. Stoic, Christian and humanist. London, 1940.

Phil 187.120 Markakis, A. A new philosophy and the philosophical sciences. N.Y., 1940. 2v.

Phil 187.121 Moore, E.C. The essence of the matter. Berkeley, 1940.

Phil 187.122 MacTaggart, M. Man, mind and psychology. London, 1940.

Phil 187.123 Muller, H.J. Science and criticism. New Haven, 1943.

Phil 187.125 Märker, F. Sinn und Gesetze des Lebens. Berlin, 1938.

Phil 187.127 Moore, C.F. The challenge of life. N.Y., 1925.

Phil 187.129 Morrish, Furze. Outline of metaphysics. London, 194-.

Phil 187.131 Masson-Oursel, Paul. Le fait métaphysique. Paris, 1941.

Phil 187.133 Mead, Hunter. Types and problems of philosophy. N.Y., 1946.

Phil 187.135 Medicus, Fritz. Natur und Geist. Erlenbach-Zurich, 1946.

Phil 187.135.5 Medicus, Fritz. Vom überzeitlichen in der Zeit. Zürich, 1954.

Phil 187.137 Matchette, F.J. Outline of a metaphysics. N.Y., 1949.

Phil 187.139 Marias Aquilera, J. El tema del hombre. Madrid, 1943.

Phil 187.141A Mumford, L. Man as interpreter. 1st ed. N.Y., 1950.

Phil 187.141B Mumford, L. Man as interpreter. 1st ed. N.Y., 1950.

Phil 187.143 Mallik, B.K. Related multiplicity. Oxford, 1952.

Phil 187.143.5 Mallik, B.K. The real and the negative. London, 1940.

Phil 187.144 Mayor, R.J.G. Reason and common sense. London, 1951.

Phil 187.145 MacCallum, R. Initiation and design, and other essays. Toronto, 1953.

Phil 187.146 Meimberg, R. Über die Einseitigkeit. Berlin, 1951.

Phil 187.147 Maisels, Misha. Thought and truth. N.Y., 1956.

Phil 187.148 Martin, W.O. The order and integration of knowledge. Ann Arbor, 1957.

Phil 187.149 Mueller, G.E. The interplay of opposites. N.Y., 1956.

Phil 187.149.5 Mueller, G.E. Dialectic; a way into and within philosophy. N.Y., 1953.

Phil 187.150 Meinertz, Josef. Philosophie. München, 1958.

Phil 187.151 Miceli di Serradileo, Riccardo. Introduzione alla filosofia. Roma, 1957.

Phil 187.152 Moser, Simon. Metaphysik einst und jetzt. Berlin, 1958.

Phil 187.152.5 Moser, Simon. Philosophie und Gegenwart. Meisenheim am Glan, 1960.

Phil 187.154 Mucchielli, Roger. Logique et morale. Paris, 1955.

Phil 187.156 Martin, Gottfried. Einleitung in die allgemeine Metaphysik. Köln, 1957.

Phil 187.156.5 Martin, Gottfried. An introduction to general metaphysics. London, 1961.

Phil 187.158 Martin, William O. Metaphysics and ideology. Milwaukee, 1959.

Phil 187.160 Maitra, Sushil. The main problems of philosophy. Calcutta, 1957. 2v.

Phil 187.165 MacIver, R.M. Life; its dimensions. N.Y., 1960.

Phil 187.170 Mel'nykov, V.M. Do pytannia pro pryrodu filosofs'kykh katehorii. Kyïv, 1959.

Phil 187.175 Myers, Henry. Systematic pluralism. Ithaca, 1961.

Phil 187.176 Murphy, Arthur E. Reason and the common good. Englewood Cliffs, 1963.

Phil 187.177 Melsen, Andreas Gerardus Maria van. Evolution and philosophy. Pittsburgh, 1965.

Phil 187.178 McGlynn, James. A metaphysics of being and God. Englewood Cliffs, 1966.

Phil 187.180 Machado Bandeira de Mello, Lydio. Crítica cosmológica da física quântica. Belo Horizonte, 1969.

Phil 187.182 Moretti-Costanzi, Teodorico. L'ora della filosofia. Bologna, 1968.

Phil 187.184 Maziarski, Stanisław. Prolegomena do filozofii przyrody inspiracji arystotelesowsko-tomistycznej. Lublin, 1969.

Phil 187.186 Marx, Werner. Vernunft und Welt. The Hague, 1970.

Phil 188.2 Nicole, P. Oeuvres philosophiques et morales. Paris, 1845.

Phil 188.3 Noack, L. Propädeutik der Philosophie. Weimar, 1854.

Phil 188.4 Noire, L. Die Welt als Entwicklung des Geistes. Leipzig, 1874.

Phil 188.5.2 Norris, J. Essay towards the theory of the world. London, 1701-1704. 2v.

Phil 188.6 Nourrison, J.F. Histoire et philosophie. Paris, 1860.

Phil 188.7A Nettleship, R.L. Philosophical lectures and remains. London, 1897.

Phil 188.7B Nettleship, R.L. Philosophical lectures and remains. London, 1897. 2v.

Phil 188.8 Newcomb, C.B. Principles of psychic philosophy. Boston, 1908.

Phil 188.9 Nelson, L. Ist metaphysikfreie Naturwissenschaft möglich? Göttingen, 1908.

Phil 188.9.5 Nelson, L. Die neue Reformation. v.1-2,4. n.p., n.d. 3v.

Phil 188.9.10 Nelson, L. Socratic method and critical philosophy. New Haven, 1949.

Phil 188.10 Neilson, W.A. Lectures on the five-foot shelf of books. 4. Philosophy. N.Y., 1913.

Phil 188.11 Naville, Ernest. Les systèmes de philosophie. Paris, 1909.

Phil 188.11.5 Naville, Ernest. La définition de la philosophie. Genève, 1894.

Phil 188.11.10 Naville, Ernest. Les philosophies négatives. Paris, 1900.

Phil 188.12 Natorp, Paul. Philosophische Propädeutik. Marburg, 1903.

Phil 188.12.5 Natorp, Paul. Jemand und ich. Stuttgart, 1906.

Phil 188.12.9 Natorp, Paul. Vorlesungen über praktische Philosophie. Erlangen, 1925.

Phil 188.12.20 Natorp, Paul. Philosophie: ihr Problem und ihre Probleme. Göttingen, 1911.

Phil 188.12.80 Brelage, Manfred. Fundamentalanalyse und Regionalanalyse. Köln, 1957.

Phil 188.13 Nyman, A. Kämpande intelligens. Malmö, 1911.

Phil 188.14 Nordenholz, A. Welt als Individuation. Leipzig, 1927.

Phil 188.14.5 Nordenholz, A. Scientologie. München, 1934.

Phil 188.14.7 Nordenholz, A. Scientologie. München, 1937.

Phil 188.15 Nielsen, F.K. Sjaele-og taenkelaere i almenfattelig. 4e udg. Kjøbenhavn, 1882.

Phil 188.16 Nuñez Requeiro, M. Tratado de metalogica. Rosario, 1936.

Phil 188.16.10 Nuñez Requeiro, M. Metafisica y ciencia. Buenos Aires, 1941.

Phil 188.17 Nevin, J.W. Human freedom and a plea for philosophy. Mercersburg, 1850.

Phil 188.18 Nohl, H. Einführung in die Philosophie. Frankfurt, 1935.

Phil 188.18.5 Nohl, H. Einführung in die Philosophie. 5. Aufl. Frankfurt, 1953.

Phil 188.19 Nicholson, J.A. Introductory course in philosophy. N.Y., 1939.

Phil 188.20 Neal, H.H. The universe and you. Laguna Beach, Calif., 1954.

Phil 188.21 Natzmer, G. von. Weisheit der Welt. Berlin, 1954.

Phil 188.22 Nicolas, M.P. Regards sur l'humain. Paris, 1958.

Phil 188.23 Nedeljković, Duš. Pragmatizm i djalektika. Beograd, 1960.

Phil 188.24 Natanson, M. Literature, philosophy and the social sciences; essays in existentialism and phenomenology. The Hague, 1962.

Phil 188.25 Nédoncelle, Maurice. Conscience et logos. Paris, 1961.

Phil 188.26 Negri, Antimo. Spirito del tempo e costume speculativo. Firenze, 1962.

Phil 188.28 Newell, Robert. The concept of philosophy. London, 1967.

Phil 188.30 Nott, Kathleen. Philosophy and human nature. London, 1970.

Phil 189.1 O'Connell, J. Vestiges of civilization. N.Y., 1851.

Htn   Phil 189.2* Ogilvie, J. Philosophical essays. Philadelphia, 1816.

Phil 189.4 Oersted, H.C. Gesammelte Schriften. Leipzig, 1850-1851. 6v.

Phil 189.4.2 Oersted, H.C. Samlede og efterladte skrifter. v.1-3, 4-6, 7-9. Kjøbenhavn, 1851-1852. 3v.

Phil 189.4.10 Oersted, H.C. Der Geist in der Natur. München, 1850-1851. 2v.

Phil 189.4.12 Oersted, H.C. The soul in nature. London, 1852.

Phil 189.4.14F Oersted, H.C. Naturvidenskabelige skrifter. København, 1920. 3v.

Phil 189.6 Ormond, A.T. Basal concepts in philosophy. N.Y., 1894.

Phil 189.6.5 Ormond, A.T. Concepts of philosophy. N.Y., 1906.

Phil 189.7 O'Sullivan, J.M. Old criticism and new pragmatism. Dublin, 1909.

Phil 189.8 Olzelt-Newin, A. Kleinere philosophische Schriften. Leipzig, 1903.

Phil 189.9 Opitz, H.G. Die Philosophie der Zukunft. Leipzig, 1910.

Phil 189.9.5 Opitz, H.G. Grundriss einer Seinswissenschaft. v.1-2. Leipzig, 1897-1899.

Phil 189.10 Olivier, Aimé. De l'absolu. Paris, 1887.

Phil 189.11 Otto, M.C. Things and ideals. N.Y., 1924.

Phil 189.12 Oppenheimer, F.J. The new tyranny; mysticism, scepticism. N.Y., 1927.

Phil 189.13 Ouy, A. Cahier d'études philosophiques. v.1-2. Paris, 1924-1925.

Phil 189.14 Pamphlet vol. Oxford lectures on philosophy, 1910-1923. 8 pam.

Phil 189.15 Opzoomer, C.W. De wijsbegeerte, den mensch met zich zelven verzoenende. Leiden, 1846.

Phil 189.15.5 Opzoomer, C.W. De waarheid en hare kenbronnen. Amsterdam, 1859.

Phil 189.16 Orestano, F. Nuovi principi. Roma, 1925.

Phil 189.16.5 Orestano, F. Verità dimostrate. Napoli, 1934.

Phil 189.17 Où chercher le réel? Paris, 1927.

Phil 189.18 Ott, Auguste. De la raison. Paris, 1873.

Phil 189.19 Ottaviano, C. Metafisica del concreto. Roma, 1929.

Phil 189.20 Osmond, A. My philosophy of life. Salt Lake City, 1927.

Phil 189.21.3 Overstreet, H.A. The enduring quest. N.Y., 1931.

Phil 189.22.5 Ortega y Gasset, José. The modern theme. London, 1931.

Phil 189.23 Oakeshott, Michael. Experience and its modes. Cambridge,Eng., 1933.

Phil 189.24 Oribe, Emilio. Teoría del nous. Buenos Aires, 1934.

Phil 189.24.5 Oribe, Emilio. Teoría del nous. Buenos Aires, 1944.

Phil 189.25 Oldfield, C.H. The kingdoms of the spirit. London, 1924.

Phil 189.26 Oegger, G. Nouvelles questions philosophiques. Tubingue, 1835.

Phil 189.27 Oro, A.M. dell'. Protologia; preludio al sapere. Milano, 1939.

Phil 189.28 O'Connor, E.M. Potentiality and energy. Diss. Washington, 1939.

Phil 189.29A Onians, R.B. The origins of European thought about the body, the mind, the soul. Cambridge, Eng., 1951.

Phil 189.29B Onians, R.B. The origins of European thought about the body, the mind, the soul. Cambridge, Eng., 1951.

Phil 189.29.2 Onians, R.B. The origins of European thought about the body, the mind, the soul. 2. ed. Cambridge, Eng., 1954.

Phil 189.30 Oliver, W.D. Theory of order. Yellow Springs, Ohio, 1951.

Phil 189.31 Ortuzar Arriaga, M. El ser y la accion en la dimension humana. Madrid, 1961.

Phil 189.32 Owens, Joseph. An elementary Christian metaphysics. Milwaukee, 1963.

Phil 189.33 Østerberg, Dag. Forståelsesformer. Et filosofisk bidrag. Oslo, 1966.

Phil 189.34 Oizerman, Teodor I. Problemy istoriko-filosofskoi nauki. Moskva, 1969.

Phil 190.2 Parr, S. Metaphysical tracts by English philosophers of the 18th century. London, 1837.

Phil 190.3.2 Paulsen, F. Einleitung in die Philosophie. Berlin, 1892.

Phil 190.3.3 Paulsen, F. Einleitung in die Philosophie. 3e Aufl. Berlin, 1895.

Phil 190.3.7 Paulsen, F. Introduction to philosophy. 2. American ed. N.Y., 1928.

Phil 190.3.7.5 Paulsen, F. Introduction to philosophy. 2. American ed. N.Y., 1930.

Phil 190.3.8 Paulsen, F. Introduzione alla filosofia. Milano, 1911.

Phil 190.3.8.5 Paulsen, F. Inleiding tot de wijsbegeerte. Amsterdam, 1910.

Phil 190.3.9 Paulsen, F. Philosophia militans. 3e und 4e Aufl. Berlin, 1908.

Phil 190.3.12 Paulsen, F. De metaphysiska problemen. Stockholm, 1904.

Phil 190.5 Peck, J.S. The ultimate generalization. N.Y., 1876.

Phil 190.6 Pellissier, P.A. Précis d'un cours complet de philosophie élémentaire. Paris, 1873. 2v.

Htn   Phil 190.7* Pemble, W. De Formarum origine. Cantabrigia, 1631.

Phil 190.10 Peters, C. Willenswelt und Weltwille. Leipzig, 1883.

Phil 190.11 Pezzani, A. Une philosophie nouvelle. Paris, 1872.

Phil 190.12 Picton, J.A. The mystery of matter. London, 1873.

Phil 190.14 Ploucquet, G. Commentationes philosophicae selectiores. Trajecti ad Rhenum, 1781.

Phil 190.15 Porter, N. Sciences of nature vs. sciences of man. N.Y., 1871.

Phil 190.15.5 Porter, N. Science and sentiment. N.Y., 1882.

Phil 190.16.2 Pressensé, E. de. Study of origins. 2d ed. N.Y., 1885.

Phil 190.16.5 Pressensé, E. de. Les origines. 3e éd. Paris, 1883.

Phil 190.16.10 Pressensé, E. de. Variétés morales et politiques. Paris, 1885.

Phil 190.17 Powell, J.W. Truth and error. Chicago, 1898.

56

Classified Listing

Phil 175 - 200 General treatises on philosophy - Individual authors (A-Z) - cont.

Phil 190.18A Perry, R.B. The approach to philosophy. N.Y., 1905.
Phil 190.18B Perry, R.B. The approach to philosophy. N.Y., 1905.
Phil 190.18.5 Perry, R.B. Studies in theory of knowledge. n.p., 1900-1910.
Phil 190.18.9 Perry, R.B. Philosophy. n.p., 1915.
Phil 190.18.15A Perry, R.B. A defence of philosophy. Cambridge, 1931.
Phil 190.18.15B Perry, R.B. A defence of philosophy. Cambridge, 1931.
Phil 190.18.20 Pamphlet vol. Perry, R.B. Miscellaneous essays. 14 pam.
Phil 190.18.25A Perry, R.B. One world in the making. 1st ed. N.Y., 1945.
Phil 190.18.25B Perry, R.B. One world in the making. 1st ed. N.Y., 1945.
Phil 190.19 Prantl, Karl. Die gegenwärtige Aufgabe der Philosophie. München, 1852. 8 pam.
Phil 190.20.3 Papini, Giovanni. Sul pragmatismo. Milano, 1913.
Phil 190.20.4 Papini, Giovanni. Pragmatismo, 1903-1911. 2. ed. Firenze, 1920.
Phil 190.20.7 Papini, Giovanni. L'altra metà. 3a ed. Firenze, 1919.
Phil 190.20.8 Papini, Giovanni. L'altra metà. 4a ed. Firenze, 1922.
Phil 190.21 Pearson, N. Some problems of existence. London, 1907.
Phil 190.23 Pratt, J.B. What is pragmatism. N.Y., 1909.
Phil 190.24 Perreaux, L.-G. Lois de l'univers. Paris, 1877. 2v.
Phil 190.26 Parker, DeWitt H. Self and nature. Cambridge, 1917.
Phil 190.27 Prat, Louis. Contes pour les métaphysiciens. Paris, 1910.
Phil 190.27.5 Prat, Louis. L'harmonisme. Paris, 1927.
Phil 190.28 Piat, Clodius. Insuffisance des philosophies de l'intuition. Paris, 1908.
Phil 190.29 Politeo, Giorgio. Scritti filosofici et letterari. Bologna, 1919.
Phil 190.30 Petitot, H. Introduction à la philosophie. Paris, 1914.
Phil 190.31 Pollack, Walter. Perspektive und Symbol in Philosophie und Rechtswissenschaft. Berlin, 1912.
Phil 190.32 Pitt, St. George Lane-Fox. Free will and destiny. London, 1920.
Phil 190.33 Philosophische Gesellschaft zu Berlin. Philosophische Aufsätze. Berlin, 1904.
Phil 190.34 Petrone, Igino. I limiti del determinismo scientifico. Modena, 1900.
Phil 190.35 Perriollat, Charles. Essai de philosophie scientifique. Paris, 1883.
Phil 190.36 Prather, Charles E. Divine science. Denver, Col., 1915.
Phil 190.37 Pfordten, Otto. Vorfragen der Naturphilosophie. Heidelberg, 1907.
Phil 190.38 Prandtl, Antonin. Einführung in die Philosophie. Leipzig, 1922.
Phil 190.38.5 Prandtl, Antonin. Das Problem der Wirklichkeit. München, 1926.
Phil 190.39 Poirson, Charles. Le dynamisme absolu. Lyon, 1898.
Phil 190.40.2 Piccoli, V. Introduzione alla filosofia. 2a ed. Milano, 1924.
Phil 190.41 Pichard, P. Doctrine du réel. Paris, 1889.
Phil 190.42 Pelazza, A. La metafisica dell'esperienza. Bergamo, 1907.
Phil 190.43 Polakov, W.N. Man and his affairs from an engineering point of view. Baltimore, 1925.
Phil 190.44 Page, Harvey L. Section I. Auto-philosophy founded on the straight and the curve; the 4 and the 9 of Pythagoras. San Antonio, 1927.
Phil 190.45 Pagani, Silvio. Umanismo antivitale. Milano, 1925.
Phil 190.46 Peladan, J. Traité des antinomies. Paris, 1901.
Phil 190.47 Peiser, Fritz. Systematische Philosophie in leichtfasslicher Darstellung. Berlin, 1923.
Phil 190.48 Pauler, A. von. Grundlagen der Philosophie. Berlin, 1925.
Phil 190.50 Paret, Hans. Der dialektische Ursprung der Glückseligkeit. Berlin, 1925.
Phil 190.51 Paget, Violet. Vital lies. London, 1912. 2v.
Phil 190.52 Pratt, James B. Adventures in philosophy and religion. N.Y., 1931.
Phil 190.53 Planck, Max. Positivismus und reale Aussenwelt. Leipzig, 1931.
Phil 190.53.10 Planck, Max. Religion und Naturwissenschaft. Leipzig, 1938.
Phil 190.54 Przywara, Erich. Analogia entis. München, 1932.
Phil 190.54.10 Przywara, Erich. Ringen der Gegenwart. Augsburg, 1929. 2v.
Phil 190.55 Philippe, Oscar. L'inconditionnalité de la philosophie. Paris, 1932.
Phil 190.55.5 Philippe, Oscar. L'inconditionnalité de la philosophie. Thèse. Nancy, 1932.
Phil 190.56 Patrick, G.T.W. Introduction to philosophy. Boston, 1924.
Phil 190.56.5 Patrick, G.T.W. Introduction to philosophy. London, 1935.
Phil 190.57 Pamphlet vol. Pennisi-Mauro, A. Il principio della sapienza. 3 pam.
Phil 190.58 Pirenne, H.E. Sur l'angoisse métaphysique; essai de philosophie. Bruxelles, 1934.
Phil 190.59 Palumbo, A. The mirror of your soul. Boston, 1935.
Phil 190.60 Poortman, J.J. Tweeërlei subjectiviteit. Haarlem, 1929.
Phil 190.60.5 Poortman, J.J. De grandparadox. Assen, 1961.
Phil 190.61A Philosophical essays for A.N. Whitehead. London, 1936.
Phil 190.61B Philosophical essays for A.N. Whitehead. London, 1936.
Phil 190.62 Die Philosophie; ihre Geschichte und ihre Systematik. Abt. 1,5,7,9,10,12,14,15. Bonn, 1934-1935. 8v.
Phil 190.63 Parodi, D. En quête d'un philosophie. Paris, 1935.
Phil 190.63.7 Parodi, D. En quête d'une philosophie; la conduite humaine et les valeurs idéales. Paris, 1939.
Phil 190.64 Pohl, Joachim. Philosophie der tragischen Strukturen. Wien, 1935.
Phil 190.65 Pöll, Wilhelm. Wesen und Wesenserkenntnis. München, 1936.
Phil 190.66 Paullier, W. Ciencia, filosofia y laicismo. Buenos Aires, 1937. 2v.
Htn Phil 190.67* Parité de la vie et de la mort. n.p., n.d.
Phil 190.68 Parkes, Henry B. The pragmatic test; essays on the history of ideas. San Francisco, 1941.
Phil 190.69 Pepper, Stephen C. World hypotheses; a study of evidence. Berkeley, 1942.
Phil 190.75 Popper, J. Das Individuum und die Beertung menschlicher Existenzen. 2. Aufl. Photoreproduction. Dresden, 1920.
Phil 190.76 Pegis, Anton C. Essays in modern scholasticism in honor of John F. McCormick. Westminster, Md., 1944.
Phil 190.77 Preface to philosophy. N.Y., 1947.
Phil 190.78 Pap, Arthur. Elements of analytic philosophy. N.Y., 1949.
Phil 190.79 Pfänder, A. Philosophie der Lebensziele. Göttingen, 1948.
Phil 190.80 Pieper, Josef. Musse und Kult. München, 1949.
Phil 190.80.6 Pieper, Josef. Leisure, the basis of culture. N.Y., 1964.
Phil 190.80.10 Pieper, Josef. Was heisst akademisch? München, 1952.
Phil 190.80.15 Pieper, Josef. Was heisst philosophieren? 3. Aufl. München, 1956.
Phil 190.80.20 Pieper, Josef. Die Wirklichkeit und das Gute. 6. Aufl. München, 1956.

Phil 175 - 200 General treatises on philosophy - Individual authors (A-Z) - cont.

Phil 190.80.25 Pieper, Josef. Verteidigungsrede für die Philosophie. München, 1966.
Phil 190.81 Pontifex, Mark. The meaning of existence. London, 1953.
Phil 190.82A Plessner, H. Zwischen Philosophie und Gesellschaft. Bern, 1953.
Phil 190.82B Plessner, H. Zwischen Philosophie und Gesellschaft. Bern, 1953.
Phil 190.83 Parpert, F. Philosophie der Einsamkeit. München, 1955.
Phil 190.84 Pears, D.F. The nature of metaphysics. London, 1957.
Phil 190.85 Piguet, Jean C. L'oeuvre de philosophie. Neuchâtel, 1960.
Phil 190.90 Peters, Johannes Arnold Josef. Metaphysica. Utrecht, 1957.
Phil 190.90.5 Peters, Johannes Arnold Josef. Metaphysics; a systematic survey. Pittsburgh, 1963.
Phil 190.95 Passmore, John Arthur. Philosophical reasoning. London, 1961.
Phil 190.100 Oromi, Miguel. Métodos y principios filosóficos. Madrid, 1960.
Phil 190.102 Barraud, Jean. Le message d'Amédée Ponceau. Paris, 1962.
Phil 190.103 Palacios, L.E. Filosofia del saber. Madrid, 1962.
Phil 190.104 Padovani, U.A. Metafisica classica e pensiero moderno. Milano, 1961.
Phil 190.106 Piaget, Jean. Sagesse et illusions de la philosophie. Paris, 1965.
Phil 190.106.5 Piaget, Jean. Insights and illusions of philosophy. Translation. 1st American ed. N.Y., 1971.
Phil 190.107 Pantskhava, Il'ia D. Chelovek, ego zhizn' i bessmertie. Moskva, 1967.
Phil 190.110 Peursen, Cornetis A. van. Feiten, waarden, gebeurtenissen. Een deiktische ontologie. Hilversum, 1965[1966].
Phil 190.112 Pavese, Roberto. Metafisica e pensiero. Padova, 1967.
Phil 190.114 Pacini, Dante. Sinteses e hipóteses de ser-humano. Rio de Janeiro, 1967.
Phil 190.116 Pezzani, André. Exposé d'un nouveau système philosophique. Paris, 1847.
Phil 191.1 Quinet, Edgar. L'esprit nouveau. 4. éd. Paris, 1875.
Phil 191.1.5 Quinet, Edgar. L'esprit nouveau. Paris, 1875.
Phil 191.2 Quensel, H. Geht es aufwärts? Cöln, 1904.
Phil 191.3 Quarto Di Palo, A. Sintesi di un sistema filosofica. Roma, 1935.
Phil 191.4 Quisling, Jörgen. Philosophie, das anthropokosmische System. Berlin, 1936.
Phil 192.1 Rabier, E. Leçons de philosophie. Paris, 1886. 2v.
Phil 192.1.9 Rabier, E. Leçons de philosophie. 9e éd. Paris, 1912.
Phil 192.2 Rabus, L. Lehrbuch zur Einleitung in die Philosophie. Erlangen, 1887-1895. 2v.
Phil 192.2.5 Rabus, L. Logik und Metaphysik. Erlangen, 1868.
Phil 192.3 Rands, W.B. Henry Holbeach. London, 1865. 2v.
Phil 192.3.2 Rands, W.B. Henry Holbeach. London, 1866. 2v.
Phil 192.3.8 Rands, W.B. Lilliput lectures. London, 1871.
Phil 192.4 Rattier, M.S. Cours complet de philosophie. Paris, 1843-1844. 4v.
Phil 192.5 Redern, S.E. de. Considerations sur la nature de l'homme. Paris, 1835. 2v.
Htn Phil 192.6* Reflections upon ancient and modern philosophy. London, 1678.
Phil 192.7 Reinhold, C.E. Theorie des menschlichen Erkenntnissvermögens. Gotha, 1832-1835. 2v.
Phil 192.7.2 Reinhold, C.E. System der Metaphysik. Jena, 1854.
Phil 192.8 Remusat, C. de. Essais de philosophie. Paris, 1842. 2v.
Phil 192.9 Riambourg, J.B. Oeuvres philosophiques. Paris, 1846. 3v.
Phil 192.10A Ritchie, D.G. Darwin and Hegel. London, 1893.
Phil 192.10B Ritchie, D.G. Darwin and Hegel. London, 1893.
Phil 192.10.5 Ritchie, D.G. Philosophical studies. London, 1905.
Phil 192.12 Ritter, Heinrich. System der Logik und der Metaphysik. Göttingen, 1856. 2v.
Phil 192.12.5 Ritter, Heinrich. Kleine philosophische Schriften. v.1-3. Kiel, 1839-1840.
Phil 192.12.7 Ritter, Heinrich. Encyklopädie der philosophischen Wissenschaften. Göttingen, 1862-1864. 3v.
Phil 192.12.15 Ritter, Heinrich. Philosophische Paradoxa. Leipzig, 1867.
Phil 192.13 Robertson, G.C. Elements of general philosophy. London, 1896.
Phil 192.13.5 Robertson, G.C. Philosophical remains. London, 1894.
NEDL Phil 192.16A Royce, Josiah. Religious aspect of philosophy. Boston, 1885. (Changed to KD 55178)
Htn Phil 192.16.5* Royce, Josiah. Religious aspect of philosophy. Boston, 1885.
Phil 192.16.7A Royce, Josiah. Studies of good and evil. N.Y., 1898.
Phil 192.16.7B Royce, Josiah. Studies of good and evil. N.Y., 1898.
Phil 192.16.7C Royce, Josiah. Studies of good and evil. N.Y., 1898.
Phil 192.16.10A Royce, Josiah. The world and the individual. N.Y., 1900-1901. 2v.
Phil 192.16.10C Royce, Josiah. The world and the individual. Ser. 2. N.Y., 1901.
Phil 192.16.10D Royce, Josiah. The world and the individual. Ser. 1. N.Y., 1900.
Htn Phil 192.16.10*B Royce, Josiah. The world and the individual. N.Y., 1900-1901. 2v.
Phil 192.16.10.5A Royce, Josiah. The world and the individual. N.Y., 1923-1927. 2v.
Phil 192.16.10.5C Royce, Josiah. The world and the individual. Ser. 1. N.Y., 1927.
Phil 192.16.11A Royce, Josiah. The world and the individual. N.Y., 1901. 2v.
Phil 192.16.11B Royce, Josiah. The world and the individual. Ser.1. N.Y., 1901.
Phil 192.16.15A Royce, Josiah. The sources of religious insight. N.Y., 1912.
Phil 192.16.15B Royce, Josiah. The sources of religious insight. N.Y., 1912.
Phil 192.16.18A Royce, Josiah. William James and other essays on the philosophy of life. N.Y., 1911.
Phil 192.16.18B Royce, Josiah. William James and other essays on the philosophy of life. N.Y., 1911.
Phil 192.16.18C Royce, Josiah. William James and other essays on the philosophy of life. N.Y., 1911.
Phil 192.16.18E Royce, Josiah. William James and other essays on the philosophy of life. N.Y., 1911.
Phil 192.16.18G Royce, Josiah. William James and other essays on the philosophy of life. N.Y., 1911.
Phil 192.17 Rozaven, J.L. Examen d'un ouvrage intitulé. Avignon, 1831.
Phil 192.18 Ruge, Arnold. Anekdota. Zürich, 1843. 2v.

Classified Listing

Phil 192.20   Richards, L.S. New propositions in...philosophy. Plymouth, 1903.

Phil 192.21   Rickert, H. Der Gegenstand der Erkenntniss. Freiburg, 1892.

Phil 192.21.2   Rickert, H. Der Gegenstand der Erkenntniss. Tübingen, 1904.

Phil 192.21.3   Rickert, H. Der Gegenstand der Erkenntniss. 3. Aufl. Tübingen, 1915.

Phil 192.21.3.6   Rickert, H. Der Gegenstand der Erkenntniss. 6. Aufl. Tübingen, 1928.

Phil 192.21.5   Rickert, H. Philosophie: ihr Wesen, ihre Probleme. Leipzig, 1912.

Phil 192.21.10   Pamphlet vol. Rickert, H. Zur Lehre von der Definition. 15 pam.

Phil 192.21.15   Rickert, H. Allgemeine Grundlegung der Philosophie. Tübingen, 1921.

Phil 192.21.20   Rickert, H. Grundprobleme der Philosophie. Tübingen, 1934.

Phil 192.22   Read, C. The metaphysics of nature. London, 1905.

Phil 192.23   Rageot, G. Les savants et la philosophie. Paris, 1908.

Phil 192.24   Richard, A. Souvenirs...d'un penseur moderne. Genève, 1905.

Phil 192.25   Rey, A. Leçons élémentaire de psychologie et de philosophie. Paris, 1908.

Phil 192.25.5   Rey, A. Les sciences philosophiques. 2. ed. Paris, 1911.

Phil 192.25.9   Rey, A. Logique et morale. 4. ed. Paris, 1916.

Phil 192.26   Rausch, Alfred. Elemente der Philosophie. Halle, 1909.

Phil 192.26.3   Rausch, Alfred. Elemente der Philosophie. 3. Aufl. Halle, 1914.

Phil 192.27   Rashdall, H. Philosophy and religion. London, 1909.

Phil 192.28   Russell, B. The problems of philosophy. London, 1912.

Phil 192.28.2A   Russell, B. The problems of philosophy. N.Y., 1912.

Phil 192.28.2B   Russell, B. The problems of philosophy. N.Y., 1912.

Phil 192.28.3   Russell, B. Les problèmes de la philosophie. Paris, 1923.

Phil 192.28.4   Russell, B. Die Probleme der Philosophie. Erlangen, 1926.

Phil 192.28.5A   Russell, B. Philosophical essays. London, 1910.

Phil 192.28.5B   Russell, B. Philosophical essays. London, 1910.

Phil 192.28.5C   Russell, B. Philosophical essays. London, 1910.

Phil 192.28.6   Russell, B. Philosophical essays. N.Y., 1967.

Phil 192.28.8   Russell, B. Scientific method in philosophy. Oxford, 1913.

Phil 192.28.8.5   Russell, B. Méthode scientifique en philosophie. Paris, 1929.

Phil 192.28.9   Russell, B. Our knowledge of the external world. Chicago, 1914.

Phil 192.28.9.5B   Russell, B. Our knowledge of the external world. Chicago, 1915.

Phil 192.28.14   Russell, B. Unser Wissen von der Aussenwelt. Leipzig, 1926.

Phil 192.28.17   Russell, B. Mysticism and logic and other essays. London, 1919.

Phil 192.28.19   Russell, B. Mysticism and logic. N.Y., 1929.

Phil 192.28.20.2   Russell, B. An outline of philosophy. London, 1956.

Phil 192.28.21A   Russell, B. A free man's worship. 2d ed. Portland, 1927.

Phil 192.28.21B   Russell, B. A free man's worship. 2d ed. Portland, 1927.

Phil 192.28.28   Jourdain, P. The philosophy of Mr. B*rtr*nd R*ss*ll. London, 1918.

Phil 192.29A   Russell, J.E. A first course in philosophy. N.Y., 1913.

Phil 192.29B   Russell, J.E. A first course in philosophy. N.Y., 1913.

Phil 192.30   Rümelin, G. Reden und Aufsätze. Freiburg, 1881. 3v.

Phil 192.30.5   Rümelin, G. Reden und aufsätze. Freiburg, 1881. 2v.

Phil 192.31   Roberty, E. de. Recherche de l'unité. Paris, 1893.

Phil 192.32   Roustan, D. Leçons de philosophie. Paris, 1912.

Phil 192.33   Reinke, J. Die Welt als That. Berlin, 1899.

Phil 192.33.5   Reinke, J. Die Welt als Tat. 3e Aufl. Berlin, 1903.

Phil 192.34   Ryland, F. Questions on psychology, metaphysics, and ethics. London, 1887.

Phil 192.35   Reiff, J.F. Der Anfang der Philosophie. Stuttgart, 1840.

Phil 192.36   Richardson, C.A. Spiritual pluralism and recent philosophy. Cambridge, 1919.

Phil 192.36.5   Richardson, C.A. The supremacy of spirit. London, 1922.

Phil 192.36.10   Richardson, C.A. Spiritual pluralism and recent philosophy. Cambridge, 1919.

Phil 192.37   Richter, Raoul. Einführung in die Philosophie. 4e Aufl. Leipzig, 1919.

Phil 192.37.3   Richter, Raoul. Einführung in die Philosophie. 3e Aufl. Leipzig, 1913.

Phil 192.37.5   Richter, Raoul. Essays. Leipzig, 1913.

Phil 192.37.10   Richter, Raoul. Dialoge über Religionsphilosophie. Leipzig, 1911.

Phil 192.38   Runze, Georg. Metaphysik. Leipzig, 1905.

Phil 192.39   Rée, Paul. Philosophie. Berlin, 1903.

Phil 192.40   Randall, J.H. The spirit of the new philosophy. London, 1919.

Phil 192.40.10   Randall, J.H. How philosophy uses its past. N.Y., 1963.

Phil 192.41   Rawson, F.L. Life understood from a scientific and religious point of view. 4th ed. London, 1917.

Phil 192.42   Redgrove, H.S. Matter, spirit and the cosmos. London, 1916.

Phil 192.43   Ruge, Arnold. Einführung in die Philosophie. Leipzig, 1914.

Phil 192.44.2   Rappoport, A.S. A primer of philosophy. London, 1916.

Phil 192.45   Roure, L. Doctrines et problèmes. Paris, 1900.

Phil 192.46   Richard, R.P. Le probablilisme moral et la philosophie. Paris, 1922.

Phil 192.49   Richter, H. Anrede bey Eröffnung von Vorlesungen über Metaphysik. Leipzig, 1823.

Phil 192.50   Ryan, J.H. An introduction to philosophy. N.Y., 1924.

Phil 192.51   Rattray, R.F. Fundamentals. Leicester, 1925.

Phil 192.52   Rein, Doris. Hvad er kultur? Kristiania, 1916.

Phil 192.53   Rudin, W. Tillvarons problem. Stockholm, 1905.

Phil 192.54   Rohrbaugh, L.G. The energy concept. Iowa City?, 1922.

Phil 192.54.5   Rohrbaugh, L.G. A natural approach to philosophy. N.Y., 1934.

Phil 192.55   Robef, Euthyme. De l'analyse réflexive. Thèse. Paris, 1925.

Phil 192.56   Rossi, M.M. Per una concezione attivistica della filosofia. Bologna, 1927.

Phil 192.57   Renda, Antonio. Il criticismo: fondamenti etico-religiosi. Palermo, 1927.

Phil 192.57.5   Renda, Antonio. Valori spirituali e realtà. Messina, 1930.

Phil 192.58   Roretz, Karl. Die Metaphysik: eine fiktion. Wien, 1927.

Phil 192.59   Rabeau, Gaston. Réalité et relativité. Paris, 1927.

Phil 192.60.5   Richet, Charles. L'homme impuissant. Paris, 1927.

Phil 192.60.10   Richet, Charles. The impotence of man. Boston, 1929.

Phil 192.61   Pamphlet vol. Rignano, E. Das biologische Gedächtnis. 10 pam.

Phil 192.62   Roguin, Ernest. Sociologie; partie de philosophie. Lausanne, 1928-1929. 3v.

Phil 192.63   Reiser, Beat. System der Philosophie. v.1. Einsiedeln, 1920.

Phil 192.64   Revel, Camille. Esquisse d'un essai sur les facultés humaines. Lyons, 1927.

Phil 192.65   Roisel, Godefroy de. La substance; essai de philosophie rationnelle. Paris, 1881.

Phil 192.66   Rothschild, R. The destiny of modern thought. N.Y., 1930.

Phil 192.67   Rintelen, Fritz J. von. Philosophia perennis. Regensburg, 1930. 2v.

Phil 192.67.5   Rintelen, Fritz J. von. Philosophie der Endlichkeit. Meisenheim, 1951.

Phil 192.67.10   Rintelen, Fritz J. von. Der europäische Mensch. Wien, 1957.

Phil 192.67.15   Rintelen, Fritz J. von. Beyond existentialism. London, 1961.

Phil 192.67.22   Rintelen, Fritz J. von. Der Aufstieg im Geiste. 2. Aufl. Frankfurt, 1968.

Phil 192.68   Ranke, Karl E. Die Kategorien des Lebendigen. München, 1928.

Phil 192.69   Ruyer, R. Esquisse d'une philosophie de structure. Paris, 1930.

Phil 192.69.2   Ruyer, R. Esquisse d'une philosophie de structure. Thèse. Paris, 1930.

Phil 192.70   Reininger, Robert. Metaphysik der Wirklichkeit. Wien, 1931.

Phil 192.70.5   Reininger, Robert. Metaphysik der Wirklichkeit. 2. Aufl. Wien, 1947. 2v.

Phil 192.71   Reiner, Hans. Phänomenologie und menschliche Existenz. Halle, 1931.

Phil 192.72.5   Rothacker, E. Einleitung in die Geistwissenschaften. 2e Aufl. Tübingen, 1930.

Phil 192.73   Rossignoli, Giovanni. Primi passi nello studio della metafisica. 8a ed. Torino, 1932.

Phil 192.74   Robertson, A. Philosophers on holiday. London, 1933.

Phil 192.75.5   Radulescu-Motin, C. Puterea sufleteasca. Bucuresti, 1930.

Phil 192.76   Rosa, Gabriele. Le meraviglio del mondo. Milano, 1851.

Phil 192.77   Robertson, J.M. Explorations. London, 1923.

Phil 192.77.5   Robertson, J.M. Spoken essays. London, 1925.

Phil 192.78   Rivier, W. Le problème de la vie. Paris, 1937.

Phil 192.78.5   Rivier, W. Les deux chemins. Bruxelles, 1951.

Phil 192.79   Restrepo, D. Nociones de alta critica. Manziales, 1937.

Phil 192.80   Rabeau, G. Le jugement d'existence. Wetteren, 1937.

Phil 192.80.2   Rabeau, G. Le jugement d'existence. Paris, 1938.

Phil 192.81   Rolbiecki, J.J. Prospects of philosophy. N.Y., 1939.

Htn   Phil 192.82*   Roas, A. Den amsteldamsen diogenes. Utrecht, 1684.

Phil 192.83   Rice, Cale Y. A new approach to philosophy. Lebanon, Tennesse, 1943.

Phil 192.85   Raeymaeker, Louis de. Introduction to philosophy. N.Y., 1948.

Phil 192.85.3   Raeymaeker, Louis de. Introduction à la philosophie. 4. ed. Louvain, 1956.

Phil 192.85.5.2   Raeymaeker, Louis de. Philosophie de l'être. 2. ed. Louvain, 1947.

Phil 192.85.5.5   Raeymaeker, Louis de. The philosophy of being. St. Louis, 1961.

Phil 192.85.10   Raeymaeker, Louis de. Riflessioni su temi filosofici fondamentali. Milano, 1958.

Phil 192.90   Roche, Jean. Discussions metaphysiques. Paris, 1950.

Phil 192.92   Rogge, E. Axiomatik alles möglichen Philosophierens. Meisenheim, 1950.

Phil 192.94   Rideau, E. Paganisme ou christianisme. Tournai, 1953.

Phil 192.96   Rosenberg, Max. Introduction to philosophy. N.Y., 1955.

Phil 192.98   Revel, Jean Francois. Pourquoi des philosophes? Paris, 1957. 2v.

Phil 192.98.2   Revel, Jean Francois. Pourquoi des philosophes? Paris, 1964.

Phil 192.98.3   Revel, Jean Francois. Pourquoi des philosophes? Utrecht, 1965. 2v.

Phil 192.99   Ribeiro, Alvaro. Estudos gerais. Lisboa, 1961.

Phil 192.100   Rinerso, Emmanuele. Metafisica e scientismo. Napoli, 1957.

Phil 192.102   Rivier, William. Le pouvoir de l'esprit. Neuchâtel, 1957.

Phil 192.104   Roig Gironella, J. Estudios de metafisica. Barcelona, 1959.

Phil 192.106   Rougier, Louis. La metaphysique et le langage. Paris, 1960.

Phil 192.108   Rosset, Clément. La philosophie tragique. Paris, 1960.

Phil 192.110   Rubert Condan, José Marin. Fenomenologia de la accion del hombre. Madrid, 1961.

Phil 192.112   Reinhardt, Kent F. A realistic philosophy. 2d ed. N.Y., 1962.

Phil 192.114   Raju, P. Introduction to comparative philosophy. Lincoln, 1962.

Phil 192.115   Rombach, Heinrich. Die Gegenwart der Philosophie. Freiburg, 1962.

Phil 192.115.5   Rombach, Heinrich. Substanz, System, Struktur. Freiburg, 1965. 2v.

Phil 192.116   Rahman, F. Philosophy, science, and other essays. 1st. ed. Lahore, 1961.

Phil 192.118   Reuss, Materhus. Vorlesungen über die theoretische und praktische Philosophie. Bruxelles, 1968.

Phil 193.1   Saint-Hyacinth, T. Recherches philosophiques. Rotterdam, 1743.

Phil 193.3   Saisset, E.E. Critique...de la philosophie. Paris, 1865.

Phil 193.3.5   Saisset, E.E. Mélanges d'histoire, de morale. Paris, 1859.

Phil 193.4   Salter, W.M. First steps in philosophy. Chicago, 1892.

Phil 193.5   Sanctis, F. de. La scienza e la vita. Philadelphia, 1884.

Phil 193.5.3   Sanctis, F. de. La scienza e la vita. Napoli, 1872.

Phil 193.6   Sargent, J. Transnatural philosophy, or Metaphysicks. London, 1687.

Htn   Phil 193.7*   Scheiblero, C. Philosophia compendiosa. Oxoniae, 1639.

Htn   Phil 193.7.2*   Scheiblero, C. Philosophia compendiosa. Oxoniae, 1639.

Phil 193.8   Schildener, H. Progress der Weltgeschichte. Greifswald, 1854.

Phil 193.9.2   Schiller, F.C.S. Riddles of the Sphinx. London, 1894.

Phil 193.9.3   Schiller, F.C.S. Riddles of the Sphinx. London, 1910.

Phil 193.9.5A   Schiller, F.C.S. Humanism philosophical essays. London, 1903.

Phil 193.9.5B   Schiller, F.C.S. Humanism philosophical essays. London, 1903.

58

Classified Listing

Phil 175 - 200 General treatises on philosophy - Individual authors (A-Z) - cont.

Phil 193.9.6 Schiller, F.C.S. Humanism philosophical essays. 2. ed. London, 1912.
Phil 193.9.9 Schiller, F.C.S. Studies in humanism. London, 1907.
Phil 193.9.13 Schiller, F.C.S. Études sur l'humanisme. Paris, 1909.
Phil 193.9.15 Schiller, F.C.S. Humanismus...pragmatische Philosophie. Leipzig, 1911.
Phil 193.9.18 Pamphlet box. Schiller, F.C.S.
Phil 193.9.25 Schiller, F.C.S. Must philosophers disagree? London, 1934.
Htn Phil 193.10* Schlegel, Friedrich von. Philosophische Vorlesungen. Bonn, 1836-37. 2v.
Htn Phil 193.10.3* Schlegel, Friedrich von. Die drey ersten Vorlesungen über die Philosophie des Lebens. Wien, 1827.
Phil 193.10.6 Schlegel, Friedrich von. Philosophy of life. London, 1847.
Phil 193.10.7 Schlegel, Friedrich von. Philosophy of life. N.Y., 1848.
Phil 193.10.9 Schlegel, Friedrich von. Philosophie de la vie. Paris, 1838.
Htn Phil 193.10.10* Schlegel, Friedrich von. Philosophie des Lebens. Wien, 1828.
Phil 193.10.15 Schlegel, Friedrich von. Neve philosophische Schriften. Frankfurt, 1935.
Phil 193.11 Schmid, F.X. Entwurf eines Systems der Philosophie. v.1-3. Wien, 1863-1868. 2v.
Phil 193.12 Schmid, J.H. Vorlesungen...Wesen der Philosophie. Stuttgart, 1836.
Phil 193.13 Schmid, L. Grundzüge der Einleitung in die Philosophie. Giessen, 1860.
Phil 193.14 Schoebel, C. Philosophie de la raison pure. Paris, 1865.
Phil 193.15 Schubert, G. von. Ansichten von der Nachseite der Naturwissenschaft. Dresden, 1840.
Phil 193.15.3 Schubert, G. von. Vermischte Schriften. Erlangen, 1857-1860. 2v.
Phil 193.16 Schubert-Soldern, R. von. Über Transcendenz der Objects und Subjects. Leipzig, 1882.
Phil 193.17 Schultze, F. Philosophie der Naturwissenschaft. Leipzig, 1881.
Phil 193.19 Scott, J. McD. Theories and criticisms. Halifax, 1883.
Phil 193.20 Scottish metaphysics. Edinburgh, 1887.
Phil 193.21 Secrétan, C. La philosophie de la liberté. Paris, 1849. 2v.
Phil 193.21.2 Secrétan, C. La philosophie de la liberté. 2e ed. Paris, 1866.
Phil 193.21.5 Secrétan, C. Pré3is élémentaire de philosophie. Lausanne, 1868.
Phil 193.21.25 Abauzit, Frank. L'enigme du monde. Paris, 1922.
Phil 193.22 Sengler, J. Über das Wesen und speculativen Philosophie. Mainz, 1834.
Phil 193.23 Seth Pringle-Pattison, A. Essays in philosophical criticism. London, 1883.
Phil 193.23.5 Seth Pringle-Pattison, A. Man's place in the cosmos. N.Y., 1897.
Phil 193.23.7 Seth Pringle-Pattison, A. Man's place in the cosmos. 2d ed. Edinburgh, 1902.
Phil 193.23.9 Seth Pringle-Pattison, A. The philosophical radicals and other essays. Edinburgh, 1907.
Phil 193.24 Sewall, F. The new metaphysics. London, 1888.
Phil 193.25 Shields, C.W. Philosophia ultima. Philadelphia, 1861.
Phil 193.25.3 Shields, C.W. The final philosophy. N.Y., 1877.
Phil 193.25.4 Shields, C.W. Philosophia ultima. N.Y., 1888-1889. 3v.
Phil 193.26 Shute, R. A discourse on truth. London, 1877.
Phil 193.27 Sigwart, Christoph von. Kleine Schriften. Freiburg, 1881. 2v.
Phil 193.27.5 Sigwart, H.C.W. Vermischte philosophische Abhandlungen. Tübingen, 1831.
Phil 193.28 Sigwart, H.C.W. Handbuch der theoretischen Philosophie. Tübingen, 1820.
Phil 193.29 Smart, Benjamin Humphrey. Beginnings of a new school of metaphysics. London, 1839.
Phil 193.30 Solger, K.W.F. Philosophische Gespräche. Berlin, 1817.
Phil 193.30.80 Wildbalz, A. Der philosophische Dialog als literarisches Kunstwerk. Bern, 1952.
Phil 193.31 Spir, A. von. Denken und Wirklichkeit. v.1-4. Leipzig, 1884-1885. 3v.
Phil 193.31.2 Pamphlet box. Spir, A. von. Pamphlets.
Htn Phil 193.31.5* Spir, A. von. Denken und Wirklichkeit. Leipzig, 1877. 2v.
Phil 193.31.6 Spir, A. von. Denken und Wirklichkeit. v.1-2. Leipzig, 1873.
Phil 193.31.7 Spir, A. von. Denken und Wirklichkeit. 4e aufl. Leipzig, 1908.
Phil 193.31.8 Spir, A. von. Moralität und Religion. 4e aufl. Leipzig, 1909.
Phil 193.31.9 Spir, A. von. Forschung nach der Gewissheit. Leipzig, 1869.
Phil 193.31.13 Spir, A. von. Vorschlag an die Freunde einer vernünftigen Lebensführung. Leipzig, 1869.
Phil 193.31.15 Spir, A. von. Esquisses de philosophie critique. Paris, 1887.
Phil 193.31.16 Spir, A. von. Esquisses de philosophie critique. Paris, 1930.
Phil 193.31.17 Spir, A. von. Philosophische Essays. Stuttgart, 18- .
Htn Phil 193.32* Stahli, D. Axiomata philosophica. London, 1651.
Phil 193.32.3 Stahli, D. Metaphysicae. Bredae, 1650.
Phil 193.34 Steffens, H. Grundzüge der philosophischen Naturwissenschaft. Berlin, 1806.
Phil 193.34.3 Steffens, H. Anthropologie. Breslau, 1822. 2v.
Phil 193.34.5 Steffens, H. Henrik Steffens indledning til förelaesninger in Kobenhavn 1803. Kobenhavn, 1905.
NEDL Phil 193.35 Stephen, L. An agnostic's apology. London, 1893.
NEDL Phil 193.35.1 Stephen, L. An agnostic's apology. N.Y., 1893.
X Cg Phil 193.35.2 Stephen, L. An agnostic's apology. 2d ed. N.Y., 1903.
Phil 193.35.4 Stephen, L. An agnostic's apology and other essays. 2d. ed. London, 1903.
Phil 193.36 Steudel, A. Philosophie im Umriss. Stuttgart, 1871-1884. 6v.
Phil 193.36.5 Steudel, A. Das goldene ABC der Philosophie. Berlin, 1891.
Phil 193.37.2 Stevens, Samuel Eugene. Science and superstition. N.Y., 1913.
Phil 193.37.5 Stöckl, Albert. Grundzüge der philosophie. 2e Aufl. v.1-2. Mainz, 1910.
Phil 193.38 Storchenau, S. Metaphysicae. v.1-4. Venice, 1819-1820. 2v.
Phil 193.40 Strada, G.J. de. Essai d'un ultimum organum. Paris, 1865. 2v.

Phil 175 - 200 General treatises on philosophy - Individual authors (A-Z) - cont.

Phil 193.41 Strümpell, L. Die Einleitung in die Philosophie. Leipzig, 1886.
Phil 193.42 Stuckenberg, J.H.W. Introduction to the study of philosophy. N.Y., 1888.
Phil 193.43 Swedenborg, E. Ontology. Photoreproduction. Philadelphia, 1880.
Phil 193.43.5 Swedenborg, E. Ontology. Boston, 1901.
Phil 193.44 Shoup, F.A. Mechanism and personality. Boston, 1891.
Phil 193.45 Scheffler, H. Die Naturgesetze. v.1-4 and Supplement 1-3. Leipzig, 1876-1883. 7v.
Phil 193.46 Sanz del Rio, D.J. Analisis del pensamiento racional. Madrid, 1877.
Phil 193.47 Sidgwick, H. Philosophy, its scope and relations. Photoreproduction. London, 1902.
Phil 193.47.2 Sidgwick, Henry. Philosophy; its scope and relations. N.Y., 1968.
Phil 193.48 Sanchez, C.L. Estudios de la filosofia. Buenos Aires, 1894.
Phil 193.49A Santayana, G. Life of reason. N.Y., 1905. 5v.
Phil 193.49B Santayana, G. Life of reason. N.Y., 1905. 5v.
Phil 193.49C Santayana, G. Life of reason. N.Y., 1905. 5v.
Phil 193.49.1 Santayana, G. Life of reason. N.Y., 1906. 5v.
Phil 193.49.2 Santayana, G. The life of reason. v.2-3. N.Y., 1921. 2v.
Phil 193.49.3 Santayana, G. The life of reason. v.1,3-5. N.Y., 1924-1925. 4v.
Phil 193.49.4 Santayana, G. The life of reason. v.3. N.Y., n.d.
Phil 193.49.5 Santayana, G. Winds of doctrine. London, 1913.
Phil 193.49.5B Santayana, G. Winds of doctrine. Studies in contemporary opinion. London, 1913.
Phil 193.49.7 Santayana, G. Winds of doctrine. Studies in contemporary opinion. N.Y., 1926.
Phil 193.49.8 Santayana, G. Winds of doctrine. N.Y., 1957.
Phil 193.49.9 Santayana, G. Philosophical opinion in America. London, 1918. 2v.
Phil 193.49.12 Santayana, G. The birth of reason and other essays. N.Y., 1968.
Phil 193.49.15 Santayana, G. Character and opinion in the United States. N.Y., 1920.
Phil 193.49.16 Santayana, G. Character and opinion in the United States. N.Y., 1921.
Phil 193.49.18 Santayana, G. Character and opinion in the United States. N.Y., 1934.
Phil 193.49.18.5 Santayana, G. Character and opinion in the United States. Garden City, 1956.
Phil 193.49.19 Santayana, G. Il pensiero americano e altri saggi. Milano, 1939.
Phil 193.49.20 Santayana, G. Little essays drawn from writings of George Santayana. N.Y., 1920.
Phil 193.49.23 Santayana, G. Little essays drawn from writings of George Santayana. N.Y., 1924.
Phil 193.49.25 Santayana, G. Dialogues in limbo. N.Y., 1925.
Phil 193.49.25.5 Santayana, G. Diálogos en el limbo. Buenos Aires, 1941.
Phil 193.49.25.10A Santayana, G. Dialogues in limbo. N.Y., 1948.
Phil 193.49.25.10B Santayana, G. Dialogues in limbo. N.Y., 1948.
Phil 193.49.25.15 Santayana, G. Dialogues in limbo. N.Y., 1926.
Phil 193.49.30 Santayana, G. Platonism and the spiritual life. N.Y., 1927.
Phil 193.49.35 Santayana, G. The realm of essence: book first of Realms of being. London, 1928.
Phil 193.49.37 Santayana, G. The realm of matter. Book second of Realms of being. N.Y., 1930.
Phil 193.49.38 Santayana, G. The realm of truth. N.Y., 1938.
Phil 193.49.39.8A Santayana, G. The realm of spirit. N.Y., 1940.
Phil 193.49.39.8B Santayana, G. The realm of spirit. N.Y., 1940.
Phil 193.49.40A Santayana, G. The genteel tradition at bay. N.Y., 1931.
Phil 193.49.40B Santayana, G. The genteel tradition at bay. N.Y., 1931.
Phil 193.49.40C Santayana, G. The genteel tradition at bay. N.Y., 1931.
Phil 193.49.41 Santayana, G. The genteel tradition; nine essays. Cambridge, 1967.
Phil 193.49.45A Santayana, G. Obiter dicta. N.Y., 1936.
Phil 193.49.45B Santayana, G. Obiter dicta. N.Y., 1936.
Phil 193.49.50 Santayana, G. The philosophy of Santayana; selections. N.Y., 1936.
Phil 193.49.60 Santayana, G. Vagabond scholar. N.Y., 1962.
Phil 193.49.65 Santayana, G. The wisdom of George Santayana. 2d. ed. N.Y., 1964.
Phil 193.49.80 Farré, Luis. Vida y pensamiento de Jorge Santayana. Madrid, 1953.
Phil 193.50 Studies in philosophy and psychology. Boston, 1906.
Phil 193.51 Shaler, S.P. The masters of fate...the power of the will. N.Y., 1906.
Phil 193.52 Systematische Philosophie. Berlin, 1907.
Phil 193.53 Stern, L.W. Person und Sache. Leipzig, 1906- 2v.
Phil 193.53.2 Stern, L.W. Person und Sache. Leipzig, 1923-1924. 3v.
Phil 193.53.5 Stern, L.W. Vorgedanken zur Weltanschauung. Leipzig, 1915.
Phil 193.54 Sortais, G. Traité de philosophie. Paris, 1906-1907. 3v.
Phil 193.55 Stein, Ludwig. Le sens de l'existence. Paris, 1909.
Phil 193.55.3 Stein, Ludwig. Der Sinn des Daseins. Tübingen, 1904.
Phil 193.55.9 Stein, Ludwig. Die Willensfreiheit...bei den jüdischen philosophen des Mittelalters. n.p., 1882-1908. 9 pam.
Phil 193.56 Snowden, J.H. The world a spiritual system. N.Y., 1910.
Phil 193.57A Searle, A. Essays I-XXX. Cambridge, 1910.
Phil 193.57B Searle, A. Essays I-XXX. Cambridge, 1910.
Phil 193.59.2A Simmel, G. Hauptprobleme der Philosophie. Leipzig, 1911.
Phil 193.59.2B Simmel, G. Hauptprobleme der Philosophie. Leipzig, 1911.
Phil 193.59.2.3A Simmel, G. Hauptprobleme der Philosophie. Leipzig, 1910.
Phil 193.59.2.3B Simmel, G. Hauptprobleme der Philosophie. Leipzig, 1910.
Phil 193.59.3 Simmel, G. Hauptprobleme der Philosophie. 7. Aufl. Berlin, 1950.
Phil 193.59.5 Simmel, G. Philosophische Kultur. Leipzig, 1911.
Phil 193.59.15 Simmel, G. Lebensanschauung; vier...Kapitel. München, 1918.
Phil 193.59.20A Simmel, G. Der Konflikt der modernen Kultur. 2. Aufl. München, 1921.
Phil 193.59.20B Simmel, G. Der Konflikt der modernen Kultur. 2. Aufl. München, 1921.
Phil 193.59.25A Simmel, G. Fragmente und Aufsätze. München, 1923.
Phil 193.59.25B Simmel, G. Fragmente und Aufsätze. München, 1923.
Phil 193.59.30 Simmel, G. Die Probleme der Geschichtsphilosophie. n.p., 1892-1909. 9 pam.

Classified Listing

Phil 175 - 200 General treatises on philosophy - Individual authors (A-Z) - cont.

Phil 193.60 Stewart, H.L. Questions of the day in philosophy and psychology. London, 1912.
Phil 193.61 Sopote, M. Mind and brain with other studies. Oxford, n.d.
Phil 193.62 Schuyler, A. Critical history of philosophical theories. Boston, n.d.
Phil 193.63 Stebbing, L.S. Pragmatism and French voluntarism. Cambridge, 1914.
Phil 193.64 Shaw, C.G. The ego and its place in the world. N.Y., 1913.
Phil 193.64.5 Shaw, C.G. The value and dignity of human life. Boston, 1911.
Phil 193.64.9 Shaw, C.G. The ground and goal of human life. N.Y., 1919.
Phil 193.65 Spicker, Gideon. Die Ursachen des Verfalls der Philosophie in alter und neuer Zeit. Leipzig, 1892.
Phil 193.65.5 Spicker, Gideon. Der Kampf zweier Weltanschauungen. Stuttgart, 1898.
Phil 193.66 Sellars, Roy Wood. Essentials of philosophy. N.Y., 1917.
Phil 193.66.5 Sellars, Roy Wood. Evolutionary naturalism. Chicago, 1922.
Phil 193.66.9 Sellars, Roy Wood. The principles and problems of philosophy. N.Y., 1926.
Phil 193.67A Stern, Paul. Grundprobleme der Philosophie. Berlin, 1903.
Phil 193.67B Stern, Paul. Grundprobleme der Philosophie. Berlin, 1903.
Phil 193.68 Schwarz, H. Grundfragen der Weltanschauung. 2e Aufl. Leipzig, 1912.
Phil 193.69 Stumpf, K. Philosophische Reden und Vorträge. Leipzig, 1910.
Phil 193.69.8 Stumpf, K. Gustav Engel...Klangfarbe. n.p., 1888-1915. 23 pam.
Phil 193.70 Sheldon, W.H. Strife of systems and productive duality. Cambridge, 1918.
Phil 193.70.5 Sheldon, W.H. America's progressive philosophy. New Haven, 1942.
Phil 193.71 Sketch of a new theory of man. Vivey, 1819.
Phil 193.72 Slesser, Henry H. The nature of being...essay in ontology. London, 1919.
Phil 193.72.5 Slesser, Henry H. The judicial office and other matters. London, 1943.
Phil 193.73 Snider, Denton J. Cosmos and diacosmos...nature psychologically treated. St. Louis, 1909.
Phil 193.73.5 Snider, Denton J. The biocomos...life psychologically ordered. St. Louis, 1911.
Phil 193.74 Stapfer, Paul. Questions esthétiques et religeuses. Paris, 1906.
Phil 193.75 Sedgwick, W. Man and his future. Philadelphia, 1913.
Phil 193.76 Schneider, Albert. Wirklichkeiten. Strassburg, 1910.
Phil 193.77 Schmitt, Eugen H. Kritik der Philosophie. Leipzig, 1908.
Phil 193.78 Sternberg, Kurt. Einführung in die Philosophie vom Stand...Kritizismus. Leipzig, 1919.
Phil 193.78.5 Sternberg, Kurt. Der Kampf zwischen Pragmatismus und Idealismus in Philosophie und Weltkrieg. Berlin, 1917.
Phil 193.79 Schnyder, Otto. Philosophische Reden. Zürich, 1916.
Phil 193.80 Schinz, Albert. Anti-pragmatism. Boston, 1909.
Phil 193.81 Spitzer, Hugo. Ueber das Verhältnis der Philosophie. Leipzig, 1883.
Phil 193.82 Schmitz-Dumont, A. Natur Philosophie als exakte Wissenschaft. Leipzig, 1895.
Phil 193.83 Strong, C.A. The wisdom of the beasts. Boston, 1922.
Phil 193.83.5 Strong, C.A. A creed for sceptics. London, 1936.
Phil 193.85 Schütz, Ludwig. Einleitung in die Philosophie. Paderborn, 1879.
Phil 193.86 Shearon, William. The hypothesis of the universality of life. St. Louis, 1922.
Phil 193.87 Spirito, U. Il pragmatismo nella filosofia contemporanea. Firenze, 1921.
Phil 193.88 Spalding, K.J. Desire and reason. London, 1922.
Phil 193.88.5 Spalding, K.J. Talks on philosophy. Oxford, 1931.
Phil 193.89 Sinibaldi, T. Elementos de philosophia. 3a ed. Coimbra, 1906. 2v.
Phil 193.90 Stuart, (Mrs.). C. The threshold of the new. London, 1920.
Phil 193.91.2 Saitschick, R. Der Mensch und sein Ziel. 2. Aufl. München, 1922.
Phil 193.92 Seltmann, Otto. Das Urteil der Vernunft. Caliv, 1920.
Phil 193.93.2 Sorel, Georges. De l'utilité du pragmatisme. 2e ed. Paris, 1928.
Phil 193.93.10 Sorel, Georges. D'Aristote à Marx. Paris, 1935.
Phil 193.94 Schulte-Tigges, A. Philosophische Propadeutik. n.p., n.d. 3 pam.
Phil 193.95 Singer, Edgar A. Modern thinkers and present problems. N.Y., 1923.
Phil 193.96 Schneidkunz, H. Philosophische Propädeutik in neuster Literatur. Halle, 1917.
Phil 193.97 Sharpe, A.B. The spectrum of truth. London, 1908.
Phil 193.98 Segal, Hyman. The law of struggle. N.Y., 1918.
Phil 193.99 Schneider, H. Metaphysik als exakte Wissenschaft. Pt.1-3. Leipzig, 1919-1921.
Phil 193.101 Sadler, G.T. A new world by a new vision. London, 1925. 2 pam.
Phil 193.102 Schenach, G. Metaphysik. Innsbruck, 1856.
Phil 193.103 Salat, J. Ueber den Geist der Philosophie. München, 1803.
Phil 193.104 Sauer, W. Philosophie der Zukunft eine Grundlegung der Kultur. Stuttgart, 1923.
Phil 193.104.2 Sauer, W. Philosophie der Zukunft. 2e Aufl. Stuttgart, 1926.
Phil 193.105 Schultz, J. Die Philosophie am Scheidewege. Leipzig, 1922.
Phil 193.106 Stuart, H.W. The logic of self-realization. Berkeley, 1904.
Phil 193.107 The three conventions; metaphysical dialogues, principia metaphysica, and commentary. N.Y., 1926.
Phil 193.108 Smith, H.B. The collective mind. Columbus, 1924.
Phil 193.109 Schiattarella, R. Note e problemi di filosofia contemporanea. Palermo, 1891.
Phil 193.110 Siegel, Carl. Grundprobleme der Philosophie. Wien, 1925.
Phil 193.111 Schmieder, J. Einführung in System und Geschichte der Philosophie. Leipzig, 1921.
Phil 193.112 Seailles, G. La philosophie du travail. Paris, 1923.
Phil 193.113 Schweizer, Robert. Der charakterwolle und der begriffiche Gegenstand. Leipzig, 1927.
Phil 193.114 Schütz, C.G. Einleitung in die speculative Philosophie. Lemgo, 1776.
Phil 193.115 Stickers, J. Die Wiedergeburt der systematischen Philosophie. Berlin, 1927.
Phil 193.116 Stern, Erich. Zufall und Schicksal. Karlsruhe, 1926.

Phil 175 - 200 General treatises on philosophy - Individual authors (A-Z) - cont.

Phil 193.117 Snellman, J.W. Philosophisk elementar-curs. 1. Psychologi; 2. Logik; 3. Rättslära. Stockholm, 1837-1840. 3 pam.
Phil 193.118 Svoboda, A.V. Ideale Lebensziele. Leipzig, 1901. 2v.
Phil 193.119 Schnass, F. Einführung in die Philosophie. Osterwieck, 1928.
Phil 193.120 Schöpfung und Mensch. Hamburg, 1871.
Phil 193.121 Saitta, G. Filosofia italiana e umanesimo. Venezia, 1928.
Phil 193.122 Sarlo, F. de. Introduzione alla filosofia. Milano, 1928.
Phil 193.123 Smith, Thomas V. Essays in philosophy by 17 Ph.D.'s of University of Chicago. Chicago, 1929.
Phil 193.123.5 Smith, Thomas V. The philosophic way of life. Chicago, 1929.
Phil 193.123.8 Smith, Thomas V. The philosophic way of life in America. 2d. ed. N.Y., 1943.
Phil 193.124 Sagcret, Emile. Essais de philosophie synthetique. Paris, 1928.
Phil 193.125 Söhngen, G. Sein und Gegenstand. Münster, 1930.
Phil 193.125.5 Söhngen, G. Philosophische Einübung in die Theologie. Freiburg, 1955.
Phil 193.126 Stone, Charles G. The social contract of the universe. London, 1930.
Phil 193.127 Scheler, Max. Philosophische Weltanschauung. Bonn, 1929.
Phil 193.128 Stout, G.F. Mind and matter. N.Y., 1931.
Phil 193.128.10 Stout, G.F. God and nature. Cambridge, Eng., 1952.
Phil 193.128.85 Wisdom, John. Problems of mind and matter. Cambridge, Eng., 1934.
Phil 193.129.5 Sainsbury, Geoffrey. The theory of polarity. London, 1931.
Phil 193.130 Stocks, J.L. The limits of purpose and other essays. London, 1932.
Phil 193.130.5 Stocks, J.L. Time; cause and eternity. London, 1938.
Phil 193.130.10 Stocks, J.L. Reason and intuition and other essays. London, 1939.
Phil 193.130.15 Stocks, J.L. Morality and purpose. N.Y., 1969.
Phil 193.131 Sills, Milton. Values; a philosophy of human needs. Chicago, 1932.
Phil 193.132 Samuel, Herbert S. Philosophy and the ordinary man. London, 1932.
Phil 193.132.10 Samuel, Herbert S. Creative man. Oxford, 1947.
Phil 193.132.15 Samuel, Herbert S. In search of reality. Oxford, 1957.
Phil 193.133 Seshagiri Row, T.V. New light on fundamental problems. Mylapore, Madras, 1932.
Phil 193.134 Shestov, L. Na vesakh Iova. Parizh, 1929.
Phil 193.134.5 Shestov, L. In job's balances. London, 1932.
Phil 193.134.10 Shestov, L. Apotheoz pespohveiossiti. Sankt Peterburg, 1905.
Phil 193.134.15 Déchet, Ferruccio. L'itinerario filosofico di Leone Sestov. Milano, 1964.
Phil 193.135 Somogyi, Jozsef. As ideák problémája. Budapest, 1931.
Phil 193.136 Segall-Socolin, I. Zur Verjüngung der Philosophie. 1e Reihe. Berlin, 1893.
Phil 193.137 Shahani, R.G. The coming of Karuna. London, 1934.
Phil 193.138 Stern, M.R. von. Weltanschauung; Ergenbnisse freien Denkens. Linz, 1921.
Phil 193.138.5 Stern, M.R. von. Das Welt-Vakuum. Linz, 1923.
Phil 193.139 Signpost (pseud.). In tune with the universe. London, 1932.
Phil 193.140 Spirito, Ugo. Scienza e filosofia. Firenze, 1933.
Phil 193.141 Schleier, S.T. An analysis of man and his philosophy. St. Louis, 1938.
Phil 193.142.5 Straub, L.W. Aufsatzentürufe. 3e Aufl. Leipzig, 1897.
Phil 193.143 Shah, R.V. Pourings of a struggling soul. Ahmedabad, 1932.
Phil 193.144 Steeksma, J. Philosophical inquiry. London, 1935.
Phil 193.145 Singer, E.A. On the contented life. N.Y., 1936.
Phil 193.146 Schmidt, Karl. The creative I and the Divine. N.Y., 1937.
Phil 193.147 Silverman, H.L. Random thoughts; liberalism in life and philosophy. N.Y., 1936. 2v.
Phil 193.147.5 Silverman, H.L. Philosophy and its significance in contemporary civilization. Boston, 1946.
Phil 193.148 Selsam, H. What is philosophy? N.Y., 1938.
Phil 193.148.3 Selsam, H. What is philosophy? N.Y., 1962.
Phil 193.148.5 Selsam, H. Philosophy in revolution. N.Y., 1957.
Htn Phil 193.149* Salicino, A. In lode della filosofia. Fiorenza, 1569.
Phil 193.150 Spakovski, A. Das menschliche Ich und die Kultur; der psychische Dynamismus und seine Gestabtung der Welt. Novi Sad, 1939.
Phil 193.150.5 Spakovski, A. Chelo-vecheskoe "ia" i kul'tura. Novyi Sad, 1936.
Phil 193.150.10 Spakovski, A. Razreshenie sud'by chelovecheskoi. Novyi Sad, 1934.
Phil 193.151 Schjoth, Emil. Gegenstands und verhältenislehre. Oslo, 1938.
Phil 193.152 Spanzini, Carlo. Philosophie und Pädagogik. Bern, 1936.
Phil 193.152.5 Sganzini, Carlo. Ursprung und Wirklichkeit. Bern, 1951.
Phil 193.153 Schmick, J.H. Geist oder Stoff? Leipzig, 1889.
Phil 193.154 Stace, W.T. The nature of the world; an essay in phenomenalist metaphysics. Princeton, 1940.
Phil 193.155 Stefanesco, Marin. Le problème de la méthode. Paris, 1938.
Phil 193.156 Schubart, W. Geistige Wandlung. Luzern, 1940.
Phil 193.157 Stapledon, Olaf. Philosophy and living. v.1-2. Harmondsworth, Eng., 1939.
Phil 193.158 Sinclair, W.A. An introduction to philosophy. London, 1944.
Phil 193.159A Souriau, Etienne. Les différents modes d'éxistence. Paris, 1943.
Phil 193.159B Souriau, Etienne. Les différents modes d'éxistence. Paris, 1943.
Phil 193.160 Szilasi, Wilhelm. Macht und Ohnmacht des Geistes. Bern, 1946.
Phil 193.160.5 Szilasi, Wilhelm. Philosophie und Naturwissenschaft. Bern, 1961.
Phil 193.161 Siger de Brabant. Question sur la metaphysique. Louvain, 1948.
Phil 193.162 Steenberghen, F. Ontologie. Louvain, 1946.
Phil 193.163 Spann, O. Philosophenspiegel. 2. Aufl. Wien, 1950.
Phil 193.163.3 Spann, Othmar. Philosophenspiegel; die Hauptlehren der Philosophie begrifflich und geschichtlich dargestellt. 3. Aufl. Graz, 1970.
Phil 193.164 Sadoleto, J. Elogia della sapienza. Napoli, 1950.
Phil 193.165 Speiser, A. Elemente der Philosophie und der Mathematik. Basel, 1952.
Phil 193.166 Società Italiana di Metapsichica. Oltre i cinque sensi. Torino? 1952.

60

Classified Listing

Phil 175 - 200 General treatises on philosophy - Individual authors (A-Z) - cont.

Phil 193.167 Steinberg, W. Grundfragen des menschlichen Seins. München, 1953.
Phil 193.168 Scarlata, G.P. Lineamenti di metalogica. Padova, 1951.
Phil 193.169 Schilfgaarde, P. von. Over de wijsgeerige verwondering. Assen, 1948.
Phil 193.170 Samuel, Otto. Die Ontologie der Kultur. Berlin, 1956.
Phil 193.172 Smith, J.W. Theme for reason. Princeton, 1957.
Phil 193.175 Schmidt, Franz. Ordnungslehre. München, 1956.
Phil 193.177 Schulz, Walter. Der Gott der neuzeitlichen Metaphysik. Pfullingen, 1957.
Phil 193.179 Sinha, Jadunath. Introduction to philosophy. 2d. ed. Calcutta, 1957.
Phil 193.181 Riconda, Guiseppe. Ugo Spirito. Torino, 1956.
Phil 193.183 Stefanini, Luigi. Metafisica dell'arte e altri saggi. Padova, 1948.
Phil 193.185 Silva Tarouca, Amadeo. Totale Philosophie und Wirklichkeit. Freiburg, 1937.
Phil 193.185.5 Silva-Tarouca, Amadeo. Aufsätze zur Sozialphilosophie. Wien, 1970.
Phil 193.190 Schneider, Erich. Auch ein Weg zur Philosophie. Berlin, 1947.
Phil 193.195 Gemeinschaft des Gustes. Wien, 1957.
Phil 193.200 Strawson, P.F. Individuals. London, 1959.
Phil 193.205 Shul'gyn, O. L'histoire el la vie. Paris, 1957.
Phil 193.210 Spier, Johannes. Van Thales tot sartre. Kampen, 1959.
Phil 193.215 Schapp, Wilhelm. Philosophie der Geschichten. Leer, 1959.
Phil 193.220 Siewerth, Gustav. Ontologie du langage. Bruges, 1958.
Phil 193.225 Scholz, H. Mathesis Universalis. Stuttgart, 1961.
Phil 193.225.7 Scholz, H. Metaphysik als strenge Wissenschaft. 2. Aufl. Darmstadt, 1965.
Phil 193.230 Schroedinger, Erwin. Meine Weltansicht. Hamburg, 1961.
Phil 193.230.3 Schroedinger, Erwin. My view of the world. Cambridge, 1964.
Phil 193.231 Smart, J. Philosophy and scientific realism. London, 1963.
Phil 193.231.2 Smart, J. Philosophy and and scientific realism. N.Y., 1963.
Phil 193.232 Salvucci, P. Saggi. Urbino, 1963.
Phil 193.233 Schazmann, P.E. Siegende Geduld. Bern, 1963.
Phil 193.234 Sweeney, Leo. A metaphysics of authentic existentialism. Englewood Cliffs, N.J., 1965.
Phil 193.235 Seijas, Rodolfo. Carta a Sartre, y otros ensayos. Buenos Aires, 1962.
Phil 193.236 Schneider, Herbert Wallace. Ways of being. N.Y., 1962.
Phil 193.237 Satyananda, Swami. World philosophy. Calcutta, 1959-1963. 3v.
Phil 193.238 Salazar Bondy, Augusto. Iniciación filosofia. Lima, 1964.
Phil 193.240 Schaeffler, Richard. Wege zu einer Ersten Philosophie. Frankfurt, 1964.
Phil 193.241 Sauvage, Micheline. L'aventure philosophique. Paris, 1966.
Phil 193.242 Strolz, Walter. Widerspruch und Hoffnung des Daseins. Frankfurt, 1965.
Phil 193.243 Staal, J.F. Euclides en Panini. Amsterdam, 1963.
Phil 193.244 Schneider, Peter K. Die Begründung der Wissenschaften durch Philosophie und Kybernetik. Stuttgart, 1966.
Phil 193.245 Suner, Soffet. Düsuncenin Tarihteki evrimi. Istanbul, 1967.
Phil 193.246 Specht, Ernst K. Sprache und Sein. Berlin, 1967.
Phil 193.247 Schmitz, Hermann. System der Philosophie. v.1-3. Pt.1-2. Bonn, 1964. 5v.
Phil 193.248 Siegwalt, Gérard. Nature et histoire; leur réalité et leur vérité. Leiden, 1965.
Phil 193.250 De Santillana, Giorgio. Reflections on men and ideas. Cambridge, 1968.
Phil 193.252 Sellars, Wilfrid. Philosophical perspectives. Springfield, 1967.
Phil 193.254 Stuettgen, Albert. Offenheit und Perspektive. Warendorf, 1966.
Phil 193.256 Sontag, Frederick. The existentialist prolegomena. Chicago, 1969.
Phil 193.258 Salazar Bondy, Augusto. Irrealidad e idealidad. 1. ed. Lima, 1958.
Phil 193.260 Shibles, Warren. Philosophical pictures. Dubuque, 1969.
Phil 193.262 Szymański, Jesy. Technika i mowa jako narsedsia pornania ludskiego. Pornań, 1971.
Phil 194.1 Taylor, B.S. Helps to understanding of nature. Albion, 1889.
Htn Phil 194.2* Taylor, B.S. Contemplatio philosophica. London, 1793.
Phil 194.4 Thornton, W.T. Old-fashioned ethics. London, 1873.
Phil 194.5 Tiberghien, G. Introduction a la philosophie. Bruxelles, 1868.
Phil 194.6 Tissot, C.J. Cours élémentaire de philosophie. Dijon, 1840.
Phil 194.6.2 Tissot, C.J. Cours élémentaire de philosophie. Paris, 1847.
Phil 194.7 Tobias, W. Grenzen der Philosophie. Berlin, 1875.
Phil 194.8 Tommaseo, N. Studii filosofici. Venezia, 1840. 2v.
Phil 194.8.5 Tommaseo, N. Studii filosofici. Lanciano, 1920.
Htn Phil 194.11* Taylor, A.E. Elements of metaphysics. London, 1903.
Phil 194.11.25 Taylor, A.E. Philosophical studies. London, 1934.
Phil 194.12 True, H.B. How to obtain our own. N.Y., 1909.
Phil 194.13 Trojano, P.R. Le basi dell'umanismo. Torino, 1907.
Phil 194.13.25 Venturini, M. La filosofia dell'umanesimo di P.R. Trojano, 1863-1909. Torino, 1919.
Phil 194.14 Thwing, E.P. Windows of character. N.Y., 1889.
Phil 194.15 Tounissoux, M. L'Abbé. L'homme dan sa triple vie. Paris, n.d.
Phil 194.16 Thayer, H.D. Physio-Psychics. Philadelphia, 1914.
Phil 194.16.10 Thayer, H.D. The Herodian me. Atlantic City, 1930.
Phil 194.17 Taft, Oren B. Hypothesis for a ceptacle theory. Chicago, 1900.
Phil 194.17.5 Taft, Oren B. Evolution of idea; a thesis. Chicago, 1926.
Phil 194.18 Teichmüller, G. Die Wirkliche und die scheinbare Welt. Breslau, 1882.
Phil 194.18.5 Teichmüller, G. Neue Grundlegung der Psychologie und Logik. Breslau, 1889.
Phil 194.19 Tarozzi, Giuseppe. Lezioni di filosofia. v.1-3. Torino, 1896-1898.
Phil 194.19.25 Tarozzi, Giuseppe. La racerca filosofica. Napoli, 1936.
Phil 194.19.30 Tarozzi, Giuseppe. L'idea di esistenza e la pensabilità del reale trascendente. Bologna, 1927.
Phil 194.19.35 Tarozzi, Giuseppe. L'esistenza e l'anima. Bari, 1930.
Phil 194.20 Tongiorgi, Salvator. Institutiones philosophicae. Romae, 1861. 3v.
Phil 194.21.2 Troward, Thomas. The Edinburgh lectures on mental science. N.Y., 1915.

Phil 175 - 200 General treatises on philosophy - Individual authors (A-Z) - cont.

Phil 194.21.3 Troward, Thomas. The Edinburgh lectures on mental science. 3d. ed. London, 1908.
Phil 194.21.5 Troward, Thomas. The creative process in the individual. London, 1910.
Phil 194.21.7 Troward, Thomas. The law and the word. N.Y., 1919.
Phil 194.22 Thomas, William C. Cosmic ethics. London, 1896.
Phil 194.23 Thalheimer, A. The meaning of terms 'existence' and 'reality'. Princeton, 1920.
Phil 194.24 Thone, Johannes F. System der Metaphysik. Dresden, 1908.
Phil 194.25.5 Thomas, P.F. Cours de philosophie pour les classes de philosophie A et B. 5e éd. Paris, 1921.
Phil 194.26 Turró, R. Filosofia critica. 1a ed. Madrid, 1919.
Phil 194.27 Tarner, George E. Some remarks on the axioms and postulates of athetic philosophy. Cambridge, 1922.
Phil 194.28 Tassy, E. La philosophie constructive. Paris, 1921.
Phil 194.30 Tilgher, A. Teoria del pragmatismo trascendentale. Milano, 1915.
Phil 194.30.80 Scalero, L. Adriano Tilgher. Padova, 1962.
Phil 194.31A Troilo, Erminis. Filosofia, vita e modernita. Roma, 1906.
Phil 194.31B Troilo, Erminis. Filosofia, vita e modernita. Roma, 1906.
Phil 194.31.5 Troilo, Erminis. Lo spirito della filosofia. Citta di Castello, 1925.
Phil 194.32 Tittmann, F.W. Aphorismen zur Philosophie. Dresden, 1859.
Phil 194.33 Teste, Paulin. Le precurseur. Le Haye, 1912.
Phil 194.34 Troxler, I.P.V. Naturlehre dis menschlichen Erkennens. Aarau, 1828.
Phil 194.34.10 Troxler, I.P.V. Blicke in das Wesen des Menschen. Aarau, 1812.
Phil 194.34.15 Troxler, I.P.V. Vorlesungen über Philosophie. Bern, 1835.
Phil 194.35 Thomas, E.E. The ethical basis of reality. London, 1927.
Phil 194.36 Taylor, H.O. Human values and verities. N.Y., 1928.
Phil 194.36.2 Taylor, H.O. Human values and verities. London, 1928.
Phil 194.36.3 Taylor, H.O. Human values and verities. Pt.I. N.Y., 1929.
Htn Phil 194.36.4* Taylor, H.O. Human values and verities. Pt.I. N.Y., 1929.
Phil 194.36.10 Taylor, H.O. Fact: the romance of mind. N.Y., 1932.
Phil 194.37 Thomas, Elyston. What existence means. London, 1928.
Phil 194.37.5 Thomas, Elyston. A view of all existence. London, 1936.
Phil 194.38 Traina, T. Saggio dei principali sistemi. Palermo, 1880.
Phil 194.39 Tourville, Henri. Precis de philosophie fondamentale d'apres la methode d'observation. Paris, 1928.
Phil 194.40 Thyssen, Johannes. Die philosophische Methode. Halle, 1930.
Phil 194.41 Twardowski, Kazimierz. Rozprawy i artykuly filozoficzne. Livów, 1927.
Phil 194.42 Tilby, Aubry W. Right; a study in physical and moral order. London, 1933.
Phil 194.43 Tardé, G. L'opposition universelle. Paris, 1897.
Phil 194.45 Tomlin, E.W.F. The approach to metaphysics. London, 1947.
Phil 194.45.5 Tomlin, E.W.F. Living and knowing. London, 1955.
Phil 194.46 Thiel, M. Versuch einer Ontologie der Persönlichkeit. Berlin, 1950.
Phil 194.47 Thévenaz, P. L'homme et sa raison. Neuchâtel, 1956. 2v.
Phil 194.48 Topitsch, Ernst. Vom Ursprung und Ende der Metaphysik. Wien, 1958.
Phil 194.49 Taulmin, St. E. Metaphysical beliefs. London, 1957.
Phil 194.50 Thomas, H. Understanding the great philosophers. 1st ed. Garden City, N.Y., 1962.
Phil 194.51 Tucuman, Argentina. Tornadas de filosofia, 21 al 26 de mayo de 1961. Tucuman, 1961.
Phil 194.54 Tanasescu, Horia. Existencialismo; pensamiento oriental y psicoanalisis. México, 1967.
Phil 194.56 Thayer, Horace Standish. Meaning and action. Indianapolis, 1968.
Phil 194.58 Topitsch, Ernst. Mythos, Philosophie, Politik. Freiburg, 1969.
Phil 194.60 Taylor, Daniel Malcolm. Explanation and meaning. Cambridge, Eng., 1970.
Phil 194.62 Trias, Eugenio. Metodologia del pensamiento mágico. Bercelona, 1970.
Phil 195.2.5 Unamuno, M. de. Das tragische Lebensgefühl. München, 1925.
Phil 195.3 Urtin, Henri. Vers une science du réel. Paris, 1930.
Phil 195.4 Utitz, Emil. Die Sendung der Philosophie in unserer Zeit. Leiden, 1935.
Phil 195.5 Urmeneta, F. de. Nuevos ensayos de critica filosofica. Barcelona, 1953.
Phil 195.6 Gulmer, Karl. Von der Sache der Philosophie. Freiburg, 1959.
Phil 195.8 Utrecht. Rijks Universiteit. Utrechts Universiteits fonds. Leven en dood. Haarlem, 1961.
Phil 195.9 Ulrich, Ferdinand. Homo Abyssus. Johannes, 1961.
Phil 195.10 Uemov, A.I. Veshchi, svoistva i otnosheniia. Moskva, 1963.
Phil 195.12 Unurn, George. What I believe. London, 1966.
Phil 195.13 Ulken, Hilmi Zuja. Felsejeye gini. Ankara, 1957. 2 pam.
Phil 195.13.5 Ulken, Hilmi Zuja. Varlik ve olus. Ankara, 1968.
Phil 196.1 Vacherot, E. La métaphysique. Paris, 1858. 2v.
Phil 196.1.2 Vacherot, E. La métaphysique et de science. 2d ed. Paris, 1863.
Phil 196.1.5 Vacherot, E. Essais de philosophie critique. Paris, 1864.
Phil 196.1.8 Vacherot, E. Le nouveau spiritualisme. Paris, 1884.
Phil 196.2 Ventura de Raulica, G. La philosophie chrétienne. Paris, 1861. 3v.
Phil 196.2.5 Ventura de Raulica, G. La raison philosophique et la raison catholique. Paris, 1854-1864. 4v.
Phil 196.2.10 Ventura de Raulica, G. La tradizione e i semi-Pelagiani della filosofia. pt.1-2. Milano, 1857.
Phil 196.4 Verworn, M. Naturwissenschaft und Weltanschauung. 2e Aufl. Leipzig, 1904.
Phil 196.5 Van Nostrand, J.J. Prefatory lessons in a mechanical philosophy. Chicago, 1907.
Phil 196.5.3F Van Nostrand, J.J. Prefatory lessons in a mechanical philosophy. Chicago, 1907.
Phil 196.5.7 Wake, C.S. Explanation of Van Nostrand's theory of the mental constitution. Chicago, 1892.
Phil 196.6 Varas, J. Miguel y Marin. Elementos de ideolojia. Santiago de Chile, 1830.
Phil 196.8 Varisco, B. The great problems. London, 1914.
Phil 196.8.3 Varisco, B. La conoscenza. Pavia, 1904.
Phil 196.8.7 Varisco, B. Scienza e opinioni. Roma, 1901.
Phil 196.8.12 Varisco, B. Studi di filosofia naturale. Roma, 1903.
Phil 196.8.15 Varisco, B. Sommario di filosofia. Roma, 1928.
Phil 196.8.20 Varisco, B. Lines de filosofia critica. 2a ed. Roma, 1931.

61

Classified Listing

il 175 - 200 General treatises on philosophy - Individual authors (A-Z) - cont.

Phil 196.8.80 Drago, Pietro C. La filosofia di Bernardino Varisco. Firenze, 1944.
Phil 196.9 Venetianer, M. Der allgeist. Grundzüge des Panpsychismus. Berlin, 1874.
Phil 196.11 Varnbüler, Theodore. Acht Aufsätze zur Apologie der menschlichen Vernunft. Leipzig, 1878.
Phil 196.11.5 Varnbüler, Theodore. Der Organismus der Allvernunft und das Leben der Menschheit in Ihm. Prag, 1891.
Phil 196.11.9 Varnbüler, Theodore. Die Lehre vom Sein. Leipzig, 1883.
Phil 196.12 Veitch, John. Knowing and being. Edinburg, 1889.
Phil 196.12.5 Veitch, John. Dualism and monism. Edinburg, 1895.
Phil 196.13 Vaz, F.M. Estudos philosóphicos. Porto, 1897. 2v.
Phil 196.14 Vogel, August. Die höchsten FragenBeleuchtet von den grössten Denkern der Neuzeit. Berlin, 1896-
Phil 196.16 Verweyen, J.M. Philosophie des Möglichen. Leipzig, 1913.
Phil 196.18 Vold, J.M. Verdensbetragtning, Sokrates og fantasi. Kristiania, 1889.
Phil 196.19 Vivante, L. Della intelligenza nell'espressione. Roma, 1922.
Phil 196.19.5 Vivante, Leone. Intelligence in expression. London, 1925.
Phil 196.20 Valensin, A. A travers la métaphysique. Paris, 1925.
n Phil 196.21* Varvaro, Paolo. Introduzione alla filosofia. Palermo, 1925.
Phil 196.22 Vincenzi, Moises. Mi segunda dimension. San José, 1928.
Phil 196.23 Vowinckel, E. Metaphysik des Ich. Berlin, 1924.
Phil 196.24 Veale, César. Mas espiritu, meuos materia. Buenos Aires, 1931.
Phil 196.25 Veuthy, L. La pensée contemporaine. Paris, 1938.
Phil 196.26 Vialle, L. Defense de la vie. Paris, 1938.
Phil 196.26.5 Vialle, L. Introduction a la vie imparfaite. 1. ed. Paris, 1947.
Phil 196.27 Vasconcelos, J. Tratado de metafisica. Mexico, 1929.
Phil 196.27.5 Vasconcelos, J. Manual de filosofia. Mexico, 1940.
Phil 196.28 Varela, F. Lecciones de filosofia. Havana, 1940.
Phil 196.29 Vassallo, Angel. Nuevos prolegómenos a la metafisica. Buenos Aires, 1938.
Phil 196.29.3 Vassallo, Angel. Elogio de la vigilia. Buenos Aires, 1939.
Phil 196.29.5 Vincenzi, M. Rionas y byondas. San José, 1921.
Phil 196.30 Vialatoux, J. L'intention philosophique. 1. ed. Paris, 1932.
Phil 196.32 Vancourt, R. La philosophie et sa structure. v.1,3. Paris, 1953. 2v.
Phil 196.34 Vogel, Arthur A. Reality. London, 1959.
Phil 196.35 Villoro, Luis. Paginas filosofias. Mexico, 1962.
Phil 196.36 Vita, Luis Washington. Que é filosofia. São Paulo, 1965.
Phil 196.36.5 Vita, Luis Washington. Tríptico de idéias. São Paulo, 1967.
Phil 196.36.10 Vita, Luis Washington. Introdução à filosofia. São Paulo, 1964.
Phil 196.40 Van Nuys, Kevin. Is reality meaningful? Static contradictions and dynamic resolutions between facts and value. N.Y., 1966.
Phil 196.42 Vazquez, Juan Adolfo. Que es la ontologia. Buenos Aires, 1964.
Phil 196.44 Vries, Joseph de. Philosophie im Grundriss. Würzburg, 1969.
Phil 197.1 Wagner, J. Organon der menschlichen Erkenntniss. Ulm, 1851.
Phil 197.1.5 Wagner, J. Erläuterungen zur Organon der menschlichen Erkenntniss. Ulm, 1854.
Phil 197.1.7 Wagner, J. System der Idealphilosophie. Leipzig, 1804.
Phil 197.1.10 Wagner, J. Religion, Wissenschaft, Kunst und Staat in ihren Gegenseitigen Verhältnissen. Erlangen, 1819.
Phil 197.1.15 Wagner, J. Praktische Philosophie enthaltend Religionslehre. Ulm, 1857.
Phil 197.2 Watson, J. Comte, Mill, and Spencer, an outline of philosophy. Glasgow, 1895.
Phil 197.2.2 Watson, J. Outline of philosophy with notes. 2d ed. Glasgow, 1898.
tn Phil 197.3* Watts, T. Philosophical essays. London, 1733.
Phil 197.3.15 Piozzi, H.L.T. (Mrs.). Mrs. Piozzi and Isaac Watts. London, 1934.
Phil 197.5 Werner, K. Grundlinien de Philosophie. Regensburg, 1855.
Phil 197.6.5 Whewell, W. On the philosophy of discovery. London, 1860.
Phil 197.7 Wijnperse, D. Institutiones metaphysicae. Lugdunum Batavorum, 1770.
Phil 197.8 Wilson, W.D. Introduction to metaphysics. Ithaca, 1872.
Phil 197.8.5 Wilson, W.D. Five questions in psychology and metaphysics. N.Y., 1877.
Phil 197.9A Windelband, W. Präludien. Freiburg, 1884.
Phil 197.9B Windelband, W. Präludien. Freiburg, 1884.
Phil 197.9.3A Windelband, W. Präludien. 3. ed. Tübingen, 1907.
Phil 197.9.3B Windelband, W. Präludien. 3. ed. Tübingen, 1907.
Phil 197.9.4 Windelband, W. Präludier. Stockholm, 1915.
Phil 197.9.7 Windelband, W. Die Hypothese des Unbewussten. Heidelberg, 1914.
Phil 197.9.13A Windelband, W. Einleitung in der Philosophie. Tübingen, 1914.
Phil 197.9.13B Windelband, W. Einleitung in der Philosophie. Tübingen, 1914.
Phil 197.9.14A Windelband, W. Einleitung in der Philosophie. 2. Aufl. Tübingen, 1920.
Phil 197.9.14B Windelband, W. Einleitung in der Philosophie. 2. Aufl. Tübingen, 1920.
Phil 197.9.15 Windelband, W. Introduction to philosophy. London, 1921.
Phil 197.10 Winter, N. Pan-Gnosticism. N.Y., 1895.
Phil 197.11 Wolff, Hermann. Zusammenhang unserer Vorstellungen. Leipzig, n.d.
Phil 197.12A Wright, C. Philosophical discussions. N.Y., 1877.
Phil 197.12B Wright, C. Philosophical discussions. N.Y., 1877.
Phil 197.12.5A Wright, C. Letters. Cambridge, 1877.
Phil 197.13 Wood, H. The symphony of life. Boston, 1901.
Phil 197.13.3 Wood, H. Studies in the thought world. Boston, 1896.
Phil 197.13.8 Wood, H. Studies in the thought world. 8th ed. Boston, 1906.
Phil 197.13.15 Wood, H. The new thought simplified. Boston, 1903.
Phil 197.14.5 Wentscher, Max. Metaphysik. Berlin, 1928.
Phil 197.15 Weber, H.B. von. Kleine Philosophie und politisc ie Schriften. Stuttgart, 1839.
Phil 197.16 Wells, H.G. First and last things. N.Y., 1908.
Phil 197.16.4 Wells, H.G. First and last things. London, 1918.
Phil 197.17 Wheeler, C.K. Hundredth century philosophy. Boston, 1906.
Phil 197.18 Willmann, O. Die Wichtigsten philosophischen Fachausdrücke in historischer Anordnung. Kempten, 1909.
Phil 197.18.5 Willmann, O. Philosophische Propädeutik. Freiburg, 1912-1914. 3v.

Phil 175 - 200 General treatises on philosophy - Individual authors (A-Z) - cont.

Phil 197.18.10 Willmann, O. Aus der Werkstatt der philosophia perennis. Freiburg, 1912.
Phil 197.19 Whittaker, T. Essays and notices: philosophical and psychological. London, 1895.
Phil 197.19.10 Whittaker, T. Prolegomena to a new metaphysic. Cambridge, Eng., 1931.
Phil 197.20 Wright, A.L. Modernism according to the law of sensual impression. Albany, 1910.
Phil 197.21 Wendelino, M.F. Philosophia moralis. v.2. n.p., n.d.
Phil 197.23 Woodbridge, F.J.E. Metaphysics. N.Y., 1908.
Phil 197.23.5 Woodbridge, F.J.E. The realm of mind. N.Y., 1926.
Phil 197.23.10 Woodbridge, F.J.E. Nature and mind. N.Y., 1937.
Phil 197.23.15 Woodbridge, F.J.E. An essay on nature. N.Y., 1940.
Phil 197.24 Walter, Johnston E. Subject and object. West Newton, Pa., 1915.
Phil 197.25 Williams, C.L. Creative involution. N.Y., 1916.
Phil 197.25.5 Williams, C.L. As if; a philosophical phantasy. San Francisco, 1914.
Phil 197.25.7 Williams, C.L. The passing of evolution. Berkeley, 1912.
Phil 197.26 Wahle, R. Das Ganze der Philosophie und ihr Ende. Wien, 1896.
Phil 197.27 Wilson, John. Thoughts on science, theology, and ethics. London, 1885.
Phil 197.28 Willy, Rudolf. Die Gesamterfahrung vom Gesichtspunkt des Primörmonismus. Zürich, 1908.
Phil 197.29 Walthoffen, H. Walter von. Lebensphilosophie und Lebenskunst. Wien, 1907.
Phil 197.30 Weber, Theodor. Metaphysik. v.1-2. Gotha, 1888-1891.
Phil 197.31 Widemann, P.H. Erkennen und Sein, Losung des Problems. Karlsruhe, 1885.
Phil 197.32 Weidenbach, Oswald. Mensch und Wirklichkeit. Giessen, 1907.
Phil 197.32.5 Weidenbach, Oswald. Weltanschauung aus der Geiste der Kritizismus. München, 1923.
Phil 197.33 Waldeck, Oscar. Zur Analyse der aesthetischen Substanz. Dresden, 1900.
Phil 197.34 Wille, Bruno. Philosophie der Befreiung. Berlin, 1894.
Phil 197.34.10 Wille, Bruno. Materie nie ohne Geist. Berlin, 1901.
Phil 197.35 Webster, Florence. The nature of life. N.Y., 1922.
Phil 197.36.12A Wittgenstein, Ludwig. Tractatus logico-philosophicus. London, 1961.
Phil 197.36.12B Wittgenstein, Ludwig. Tractatus logico-philosophicus. London, 1961.
Phil 197.36.45B Maslow, Alexander. A study in Wittgenstein's Tractatus. Berkeley, 1961.
Phil 197.37 Wrench, G.T. The grammar of life. London, 1908.
Phil 197.38 Widgery, A.G. Outlines of a philosophy of life. London, 1923.
Phil 197.38.5 Widgery, A.G. A philosopher's pilgrimage. N.Y., 1961.
Phil 197.39 Whitby, C.J. The open secret. London, 1912.
Phil 197.40 Wordsworth, J.C. Short essays in constructive philosophy. London, 1911.
Phil 197.40.5 Wordsworth, J.C. Adventures in philosophy. N.Y., 1926.
Phil 197.41 Wallerius, N. Compendium metaphysicae. Stockholmiae, 1755.
Phil 197.41.5 Wallerius, N. Systema metaphysicum. v.1-4. Stockholmiae, 1750-1752. 2v.
Phil 197.42.3 Wilson, F.B. Man limitless. 3d. ed. N.Y., 1905.
Phil 197.43 Wehnert, B. Wissenschaft, Philosophie, Kunst und Religion. Dortmund, 1910.
Phil 197.44 Wilson, George A. The self and its world. N.Y., 1926.
Phil 197.44.5 Wilson, George A. Reckoning with life. New Haven, 1942.
Phil 197.45 Ward, James. Essays in philosophy. Cambridge, Eng., 1927.
Phil 197.46 Wirth, William. Zur Orientierung der Philosophie am Bewusstseinsbegriff. München, 1919.
Phil 197.47 Worms, René. Eléments de philosophie scientifique et...morale. Paris, 1891.
Phil 197.48 Weinhandl, F. Einführung in das moderne philosophische Denken. Gotha-Stuttgart, 1924.
Phil 197.48.10 Weinhandl, F. Über das aufschliessende Symbol. Berlin, 1929.
Phil 197.49 Wattjes, J.G. Practische wijsbegeerte. 2e druk. Delft, 1926.
Phil 197.50 Wielenga, B. In de school ijer wysbegeerte. Amsterdam, 1924.
Phil 197.51 Wienstein, M.B. Welt- und libenanschauungen Hevoorgegangen aus Religion, Philosophie und Naturerkenntnis. Leipzig, 1910.
Phil 197.52 Wynaendts Franchen, C.J. Inleiding tot de wijsbegeerte. Haarlem, 1905.
Phil 197.53 Wetterburg, Jacobue. Dissertatio philosophica. Lundae, 1789.
Phil 197.54 Weber, Maximilian. Kritik der Weltanschaungen. Langensalza, 1926.
Phil 197.55 Walfenden, J.F. The approach to philosophy. London, 1932.
Phil 197.56 Wagner, J.J. Ueber das Wesen der Philosophie. Bamberg, 1804.
Phil 197.57 Woods, Elizabeth R. Music and meaning. Cambridge, 1932.
Phil 197.58 Wolff, Gustav. Leben und Erkennen. München, 1933.
Phil 197.59 Wells, Gabriel. Riddle of being. N.Y., 1934.
Phil 197.60 Weir, Archibald. Shallows and deeps. Oxford, 1934.
Phil 197.61 Watkin, E.I. A philosophy of form. London, 1935.
Phil 197.61.10 Watkin, E.I. A philosophy of form. London, 1950.
Phil 197.61.15 Watkin, E.I. Men and tendencies. London, 1937.
Phil 197.62 Wade, Joseph M. A few texts. Wise to the wise. Boston, 1892.
Phil 197.63 Wenzl, Aloys. Wissenschaft und Weltanschaaung. Leipzig, 1936.
Phil 197.63.3 Wenzl, Aloys. Wissenschaft und Weltanschauung. 2. Aufl. Hamburg, 1949.
Phil 197.63.5 Wenzl, Aloys. Philosophie als Weg von den Grenzen der Wissenschaft au die Grenzen der Religion. Leipzig, 1939.
Phil 197.63.7 Wenzl, Aloys. Metaphysik als Weg von den Grenzen der Wissenschaft au die Grenzen der Religion. 2. Aufl. Graz, 1956.
Phil 197.65 Wust, Peter. Ungewissheit und Wagnis. Salzburg, 1937.
Phil 197.65.5 Wust, Peter. Die Dialelitik des Geistes. Augsburg, 1928.
Phil 197.65.10 Wust, Peter. Der Mensch und die Philosophie. 2. Aufl. Münster, 1947.
Phil 197.66 Woods, A. The great quest. n.p., n.d.
Phil 197.67 World Wide Revival Prayer Movement. Preparing the way. Atlantic City, 1941.
Phil 197.68 White, S.E. Anchors to windward. N.Y., 1943.
Phil 197.69 Winderlich, R. Das Ding. Karlsruhe, 1924.
Phil 197.70 Woltereck, Richard. Ontologie des Lebendigen. Stuttgart, 1940.
Phil 197.71 Weil, Eric. Logique de la philosophie. Paris, 1950.

Classified Listing

Phil 175 - 200   General treatises on philosophy - Individual authors (A-Z) - cont.

Phil 197.72   Wahl, J.A. Traité de métaphysique. Paris, 1953.
Phil 197.72.5   Wohl, J.A. Un renouvellement de la métaphysique. Est-il possible? Paris, 1957.
Phil 197.72.10   Wohl, J.A. Essence et phénomènes. Paris, 1958.
Phil 197.73   Wasmuth, E. Von der Wahrheit der Philosophie. Köln, 1952.
Phil 197.74   Wells, H.K. Pragmatism. N.Y., 1954.
Phil 197.75   Wheelwright, Philip. The way of philosophy. N.Y., 1960.
Phil 197.80   Wagner, Hans. Philosophie und Reflexion. München, 1959.
Phil 197.85   Wedberg, Anders. Filosofins historia. Stockholm, 1958. 3v.
Phil 197.90   Watts, A.W. Psychotherapy. N.Y., 1961.
Phil 197.92   Wainwright, Donald S. Existentialist essays. N.Y., 1965.
Phil 197.93   Wisdom, John. Philosophy and psychoanalysis. Oxford, 1964.
Phil 197.94   Walendy, Udo. Die Weltanschauung des Wissens. 1. Aufl. Vlotho, 1969. 2v.
Phil 197.95   Wal, Goossen Albertus van der. Wereldbeschouwelijk denken als filosofisch probleem. Den Haag, 1968.
Phil 197.98   Wheatley, Jon. Prolegomena to philosophy. Belmont, Calif., 1970.
Phil 199.1   Young, A. The fractional family. N.Y., 1864.
Phil 199.2   Younghusband, F. The sense of community. London, 1916.
Phil 199.3   Yerington, William. Emerson and beyond. Columbus, Ohio, 1929.
Phil 199.4   Young, E.L. A philosophy of reality. Manchester, 1930.
Phil 199.5   Yura, T. Geisteswissenschaft und Willensgesetz. Berlin, 1931.
Phil 200.2   Zeller, E. Philosophische Aufsätze. Leipzig, 1887.
Phil 200.2.5   Zeller, E. Vorträge und Abhandlungen geschichtlichen Inhalts. Leipzig, 1865.
Phil 200.2.6   Zeller, E. Vorträge und Abhandlungen Geschichtlichen Inhalts. 1. Aufl. Leipzig, 1875.
Phil 200.2.7   Zeller, E. Vorträge und Abhandlungen Geschichtlichen Inhalts. 2. Aufl. Leipzig, 1877.
Phil 200.2.8   Zeller, E. Vorträge und Abhandlungen Geschichtlichen Inhalts. 3. Aufl. Leipzig, 1884.
Phil 200.2.15   Zeller, E. E. Zellers kleine Schriften, unter Mitwirking. Berlin, 1910. 3v.
Phil 200.2.75   Strassburger Abhandlungen zur Philosophie E. Zeller zu 70n Geburtstage. Freiburg, 1884.
Phil 200.3   Zimmermann, R. Anthroposophie. Wien, 1882.
Phil 200.3.5   Zimmermann, R. Philosophische Propaedeutik. Wien, 1867.
Phil 200.3.7   Zimmermznn, R. Studien und Kritiken zur Philosophie und Aesthetik. v.1-2. Wien, 1870.
Phil 200.3.12   Zimmermann, R. Was Erwarten wir von der Philosophie? Prag, 1852.
Phil 200.4   Zenetti, Jacob. Einfluss der Philosophie auf das Leben. München, 1829.
Phil 200.5   Zucca, Antioco. L'uomo e l'infinito. Roma, 1906.
Phil 200.5.5   Zucca, Antioco. Le veritable role de l'homme dans l'universe. Paris, 19- ?
Phil 200.5.10   Zucca, Antioco. I rapporti fra l'individuo e l'universo. Padova, 1937.
Phil 200.6.3   Ziegler, L. Gestaltwandel der Götter. 3. Aufl. Darmstadt, 1922. 2v.
Phil 200.7   Zarcone, O. Il genio dell'uomo. 2a ed. Palermo, 1850.
Phil 200.8   Zimmermann, K. Die Gemeinschaft der Einsamen. Jena, 1919.
Phil 200.9   Zafiropulo, J. La philosophie effective. Paris, 1931.
Phil 200.11   Zehnder, M. Universe and reality. Toronto, 1929.
Phil 200.12   Zur Philosophie der Gegenwart. Prag, 1934.
Phil 200.13   Zocher, R. Die philosophische Grundlehre. Tübingen, 1939.
Phil 200.15.5   Zerle, Herbert. Die Kunst des Kritisieren. Berlin, 1957.
Phil 200.17   Zafiropulo, Jean. Vox Zenanias. Paris, 1958.
Phil 200.17.5   Zafiropulo, Jean. Appollon et Dionysos. Paris, 1961.
Phil 200.19   Zaragüela Bengoechea, J. Los veinte lemas que le cultivado en los cincuenta. Madrid, 1958.
Phil 200.20   Zanstra, H. The construction of reality; lectures on the philosophy on science. N.Y., 1962.

Phil 210   Metaphysics, Speculative philosophy - General methodology

Phil 210.5   Palmer, Richard E. Hermeneutics; interpretation theory in Schlelermacher, Dilthey, Heidegger, and Gadamer. Evanston, 1969.
Phil 210.10   Henrichs, Norbert. Bibliographie der Hermeneutik und ihrer Anwendungs Gereiche seit Schleiermacher. Düsseldorf, 1968.
Phil 210.15   Il problema della domanda. Padova, 1968.
Phil 210.20   Lipps, Hans. Untersuchungen zu einer Hermeneutischen Logik. 2. Aufl. Frankfurt, 1959.
Phil 210.25   Consultation on Hermeneutics. Interpretation: the poetry of meaning. 1st ed. N.Y., 1967.
Phil 210.30   Gadamer, Hans Georg. Le problème de la conscience historique. Louvain, 1963.
Phil 210.31   Gadamer, Hans Georg. Wahrheit und Methode. Tübingen, 1960.
Phil 210.40   Interpretation, theory and practice. Baltimore, 1969.
Phil 210.45   Umanesimo e ermeneutica. Padova, 1963.
Phil 210.50   Esbroeck, Michel van. Herméneutique. Paris, 1968.
Phil 210.55   Ricoeur, Paul. Le conflit des interprétations; essais d'herméneutique. Paris, 1969.
Phil 210.60   Hirsch, Wolfgang. Über die Grundlagen einer universalen Methode der Philosophie. Bad Homburg, 1969.
Phil 210.65   Kaulbach, Friedrich. Philosophie der Beschreibung. Köln, 1968.
Phil 210.68   Hermeneutik und Dialektik. Aufsätze. Hans-Georg Gadamer zum 70. Geburtstag. Tübingen, 1970. 2v.
Phil 210.70.1   Chladenius, Johann Martin. Einleitung zur richtigen Auslegung vernünftiger Reden und Schriften. Düsseldorf, 1969.
Phil 210.72   Coreth, Emerich. Grundfragen der Hermeneutik. Freiburg, 1969.
Phil 210.74   Schueling, Hermann. Die Geschichte der axiomatischen Methode im 16. und Beginnenden 17. Jahrhundert. Hildesheim, 1969.
Phil 210.76   Hare, Richard Mervyn. Essays on philosophical method. London, 1971.
Phil 210.78   Hermeneutik als Weg heutiger Wissenschaft. Salzburg, 1971.

Phil 250   Special philosophical topics, systems, etc. - Secondary treatises and discussions - Folios [Discontinued]

Phil 250.1   Nancel, N. de. Analogia microcosmi. Paris, 1611.
Htn   Phil 250.2*   Giorgio, F. De harmonia mundi totius. Venice, 1525.

Phil 252   Special philosophical topics, systems, etc. - Secondary treatises and discussions - Absolute

Phil 252.5   Findlay, John Niemayer. Ascent to the absolute: metaphysical papers and lectures. London, 1970.

Phil 254   Special philosophical topics, systems, etc. - Secondary treatises and discussions - Abstraction

Phil 254.2   Vuillemin, Jules. La logique et le monde sensible. Paris, 1971.

Phil 258   Special philosophical topics, systems, etc. - Secondary treatises and discussions - Analysis

Phil 258.5   Pieretti, Antonio. Analisi linguistica e metafisica. Milano, 1968.
Phil 258.10   Lorenz, Kuno. Elemente der Sprachkritik; eine Alternative zum Dogmatismus und Skeptizismus in der analytischen Philosophie. 1. Aufl. Frankfurt am Main, 1970.
Phil 258.15   Gross, Barry R. Analytic philosophy; an historical introduction. N.Y., 1970.

Phil 260   Special philosophical topics, systems, etc. - Secondary treatises and discussions - Atomism

Phil 260.1   Sasswitz, K. Geschichte de Atomistik. Hamburg, 1890. 2v.
Phil 260.1.5   Sasswitz, K. Atomistik und Kriticismus. Braunschweig, 1878.
Phil 260.2A   Mabilleau, S. Histoire de la philosophie atomistique. Paris, 1895.
Phil 260.2B   Mabilleau, S. Histoire de la philosophie atomistique. Paris, 1895.
Phil 260.3   Welling, J.C. Atomic philosophy. Washington, 1884.
Phil 260.5   Hannequin, A. Essai critique sur l'hypothèse des Atoms. Paris, 1895.
Phil 260.6   Pfeifer, X. Die Controverse und der Beharren der Elemente. Dellingen, 1879.
Phil 260.8   Dahlbäck, Carl J. Om atomismen. Stockholm, 1857.
Phil 260.9   Lafaist, M. Dissertation sur la philosophie atomistique. Paris, 1833.
Phil 260.11   Alfieri, Vittorio Enpo. Atomos idea. Firenzo, 1953.
Phil 260.12   Mau, Jergen. Zum Problem des Infinitesimalen bei den antiken Atomisten. Berlin, 1957.
Phil 260.13   Whyte, Laucelot Law. Essay on atomism. 1st ed. Middletown, Conn., 1961.
Phil 260.14   Okál, M. Grécki atomisti a epikuros. Bratislava, 1953.
Phil 260.15   Zubor, Vasilii P. Razvitie atomisticheskikh predstavlenii do nachala XIX veka. Moskva, 1965.
Phil 260.16   Kargon, Robert. Atomism in England from Hariot to Newton. Oxford, 1966.
Phil 260.17   Kedrov, Bonifatii M. Triaspekta atomistiki. Moskva, 1969. 3v.

Phil 266   Special philosophical topics, systems, etc. - Secondary treatises and discussions - Belief and certitude

Phil 266.2   Quine, Willard Van Orman. The web of belief. N.Y., 1970.

Phil 270   Special philosophical topics, systems, etc. - Secondary treatises and discussions - Causation

Phil 270.01   Pamphlet vol. Philosophy. Special. Causation. 2 pam.
Phil 270.1   Barrett, T.S. Examination of Gillespie's "First Cause". London, 1869.
Phil 270.2   Barrett, T.S. Philosophy of science...on cause and effect. London, 1872.
Phil 270.2.5   Barrett, T.S. A new view of causation. London, 1871.
Phil 270.3   Bertauld, P.A. Introduction à la recherche des causes premières. Paris, 1876.
Phil 270.5   Christinnecke, J. Causalität und Entwicklung. Jena, 1891.
Phil 270.6   Foster, F.H. The doctrine of the transcendent use of the principle of causality. Leipzig, 1882.
Phil 270.7   Hazard, R.G. Man a creative first cause. Boston, 1883.
Phil 270.7.2   Hazard, R.G. Man a creative first cause. Boston, 1883.
Htn   Phil 270.7.3*   Hazard, R.G. Man a creative first cause. Boston, 1883.
Phil 270.7.10   Hazard, R.G. Causation and freedom in willing. Boston, 1889.
Phil 270.8   Houten, S. van. Causalitäs-Gesetz in der Socialwissen. Harlem, 1888.
Phil 270.9   Jamieson, G. Causality. London, 1872.
Phil 270.10   Journeyman (pseud.). Beneficence design in problem of evil...causation. N.Y., 1849.
Phil 270.11   Schellwein, R. Das Gesets der Causalität in der Natur. Berlin, 1876.
Phil 270.12   Scott, R.E. Inquiry into limits...nature of causation. Edinburgh, 1810.
Phil 270.13   Shepherd, M. Essays...doctrine of causation. London, 1827.
Phil 270.14   Wentscher, M. Über Physische und Psychische Kausalität. Leipzig, 1896.
Phil 270.15   Koenig, E. Entwickelung des Casualproblems. Leipzig, 1888.
Phil 270.16   Petersen, J. Kausalität Determinismus. München, 1909.
Phil 270.17   Lang, Albert. Das Kausalproblem. Köln, 1904.
Phil 270.17.5   Lang, Albert. Aphoristische Betrachtungen über das Kausalproblem. Köln, 1909.
Phil 270.18   Fonsegrive, G.L. La causalité efficiente. Thèse. Paris, 1891.
Phil 270.19   Meyer-Pforzheim, C.W. Der Kausalitätsbegriff. Hamburg, 1914.
Phil 270.20   Noiré, Ludwig. Die Doppelnatur der Causalität. Leipzig, 1875.
Phil 270.21   Erdmann, Benno. Über Inhalt und Geltung des Kausalgesetzes. Halle, 1905.
Phil 270.22   Heim, Gustav. Ursache und Bedingung. Leipzig, 1913.
Phil 270.24   Pastore, Annibale. Il problema della causalità con particolare reguardo alla teoria del metodo sperimentale. Torino, 1921. 2v.
Phil 270.25   L'Ange Huet, J. Nievve oplossing van een oud vraagstuk. Leiden, 1872.
Phil 270.26   Ducasse, Curt J. Causation and the types of necessity. Seattle, 1924.
Phil 270.26.5   Ducasse, Curt J. Truth, knowledge and causation. London, 1968.
Phil 270.27   Heuer, W. Warum Fragen die menschen Warum? Heidelberg, 1921.
Phil 270.28   Verworn, Max. Kausale und konditionale Weltanschauung. 2. aufl. Jena, 1918.
Phil 270.29   Neef, Fritz. Kausalität und Originalität. Tübingen, 1918.
Phil 270.30   Baglioni, B. Il principio di causalità. Perugia, 1908.
Phil 270.31   Mokrzycki, G. Relativisierung des Kausalitätsbegriffes. Leipzig, 1922.

Classified Listing

Phil 270 Special philosophical topics, systems, etc. - Secondary treatises and discussions - Causation - cont.

Phil 270.32 Rauschenberger, W. Über Identität und Kausalität. Leipzig, 1922.
Phil 270.33 Meinong, A. Zum Erweise des allgischen Kausalgesetzes. Wien, 1918.
Phil 270.34 Hessen, S. Individuelle Kausalität. Berlin, 1909.
Phil 270.35 Alstrin, Eric Praeses. Dissertatio philosophica, de concursu caussaē primaē cum secundis. Upsaliae, 1732.
Phil 270.37 Bang, Niels H. Aarsagsforestillingen. København, 1925.
Phil 270.38 Faggiotto, A. La causa trinitaria unica sostanza del cosmo. Padova, 1929.
Phil 270.39 Frank, Philipp. Das Kausalgesetz und seine Grenzen. Wien, 1932.
Phil 270.39.5 Frank, P. Le principe de causalité et ses limites. Paris, 1937.
Phil 270.40 Geyser, Joseph. Das Gesetz der Ursache. München, 1933.
Phil 270.41 Wentscher, E.S. Geschichte des Kausalproblems in der neueren Philosophie. Leipzig, 1921.
Phil 270.42 Silberstein, L. Causality. London, 1933.
Phil 270.43 Mercier, Charles A. On causation, with a chapter on belief. London, 1916.
Phil 270.44 Taube, M. Causation, freedom, and determinism. London, 1936.
Phil 270.45 Hawkins, D.J.B. Causality and implication. London, 1937.
Phil 270.46 Skilvierwski, S.L. Kausalität. Paderborn, 1930.
Phil 270.47 Brahma, N.K. Causality and science. London, 1939.
Phil 270.49 Miró Quesada, Oscar. El problema de la libertad y la ciencia. Lima, 1945.
Phil 270.50 Laporte, Jean. L'idee de necessité. Paris, 1941.
Phil 270.51 Junkersfeld, M.J. The Aristotelian-Thomistic concept of chance. Indiana, 1945.
Phil 270.52 Sageret, Jules. Le lasard et la destinée. Paris, 1927.
Phil 270.53 Windelband, W. Die Lehren vom Zufall. Berlin, 1870.
Phil 270.54 Foissac, Pierre. La chance ou la destinée. Paris, 1876.
Phil 270.55 Segond, J.L.P. Hasard et contingence. Paris, 1938.
Phil 270.56 Segond, J.L.P. Logique du pari. Paris, 1938.
Phil 270.57 Revel, Camille. Le hasard sa loi et ses conséquences dans les sciences et en philosophie. Paris, 1905.
Phil 270.58 Scholz, W. von. Der Zufall. Stuttgart, 1924.
Phil 270.59 Joachim, J. Das Problem der Gesetzlicheit. Hamburg, 1949- 2v.
Phil 270.60 Coculeseo, P. Hasard et probabilités. Paris, 1949.
Phil 270.61A Landau, M.A. Ul'mskaia noch': filosofi slucnaia. N'iu Iork, 1953.
Phil 270.61B Landau, M.A. Ul'mskaia noch': filosofi slucnaia. N'iu Iork, 1953.
Phil 270.62A Michotte, A.E. La perception de la causalité. 2. ed. Louvain, 1954.
Phil 270.62B Michotte, A.E. La perception de la causalité. 2. ed. Louvain, 1954.
Phil 270.62.5 Michotte, A.E. La perception de la causalité. Louvain, 1946.
Phil 270.62.10 Michotte, A.E. The perception of causality. London, 1963.
Phil 270.63 Giacon, Carlo. La causalità nel razionalismo moderno. Milano, 1954.
Phil 270.70 Brill, John. The chance character of human existence. N.Y., 1956.
Phil 270.75 Cohen, John. Risk and gambling. London, 1956.
Phil 270.75.5 Cohen, John. Chance, skill, and luck. Baltimore, 1960.
Phil 270.85 Gennaro, Guiseppe de. Saggio sui rapporti fra ubertá e causalità. Padova, 1958.
Phil 270.90 Bunge, Mario. Causality. Cambridge, 1959.
Phil 270.95 Cordoba, Martín de. Compendio de la fortuna. Madrid, 1958.
Phil 270.100 Baumann, Evert D. De harmonie der dingen. Leiden, 1933.
Phil 270.105 Akademiia Nauk SSSR. Institute Filosofii. Problema prichinnosti v sovremennoi biologie. Moskva, 1961.
Phil 270.105.5 Akademiia Nauk SSSR. Institute Filosofii. Problema prichinnost v sovremeni fizike. Moskva, 1960.
Phil 270.107 Musabaeva, N.A. Problemy prichinnosti v filosofii i giologii. Alma-Ata, 1962.
Phil 270.108 Musabaeva, N.A. Kibernetika i kategoriia prichinnosti. Alma-Ata, 1965.
Phil 270.110 Jaworski, M. Arystolelesowska i tomistyczna teoria przyczyry sprawczej na tle pojęcia bytu. Lublin, 1958.
Phil 270.115 Mazierski, S. Determinizm i indet w aspekcie fizykalrym i filozoficznym. Lublin, 1961.
Phil 270.129 Pakistan. Philosophical Congress, 7th, Dacca, Pakistan, 1960. Symposia on basic human values and causality. Lahore, 1960?
Phil 270.130 Šešić, Bogdan. Nužnost i sloboda. Beograd, 1963.
Phil 270.131 Hayden Colloquium on Scientific Method and Concept. Massachusetts Institute of Technology. Cause and effect. N.Y., 1965.
Phil 270.132 Pilipenko, Nikolai V. Neobkhodimost' i sluchainost'. Moskva, 1965.
Phil 270.133 Popov, Stoiko. Prichinnostta v obshtestvoto. Sofiia, 1964.
Phil 270.137 Grabbé, Geneviéve. Les conditions d'une perception de la causalité. Paris, 1967.
Phil 270.140 Selvaggi, Filippo. Causalità e indeterminismo. Roma, 1964.
Phil 270.141 Dzhioev, Otar. Priroda istoricheskoi neobkhodimosti. Tbilisi, 1967.
Phil 270.144 Titze, Hans. Der Kausalbegriff in Philosophie und Physik. Meisenheima, 1964.
Phil 270.146 Zwart, P.J. Causaliteit. Assen, 1967[1968]
Phil 270.148 Wright Georg Henrik van. Explanation and understanding. Ithaca, N.Y., 1971.
Phil 270.150 Komarov, Viktor N. Zagadka budushchego. Moskva, 1971.

Phil 274 Special philosophical topics, systems, etc. - Secondary treatises and discussions - Comparison and identity

Phil 274.2 Wiggins, David. Identity and spatio-temporal continuity. Oxford, 1967.
Phil 274.4 Deleuze, Gilles. Différence et répétition. Thèse. Paris, 1968.
Phil 274.6 Identity and individuation. N.Y., 1971.

Phil 280 Special philosophical topics, systems, etc. - Secondary treatises and discussions - Cosmology - Pamphlet volumes

Phil 280.01 Pamphlet box. Philosophy. Special. Cosmology.
Phil 280.5 Pamphlet vol. Philosophy of nature 1905-1911. 5 pam.

Phil 281 - 306 Special philosophical topics, systems, etc. - Secondary treatises and discussions - Cosmology - Monographs [A-Z

Phil 281.1 Ambler, R.P. Birth of the universe. N.Y., 1853.
Phil 281.2 Atkinson, J. Universe powers of nature revealed. London, 1856.
Phil 281.3 Alexejeff, W.G. Mathematik als Grundlage der Weltanschauung. Jurjew, 1903.
Phil 281.4 Bamberger, L. Die Vorstellung von Weltebäude im Wandel du Zeit. Leipzig, 1908.
Phil 281.4.5A Arrhenius, S. World's in the making. London, 1908.
Phil 281.4.5B Arrhenius, S. World's in the making. London, 1908.
NEDL Phil 281.4.9 Auerbach, Felix. Werden der Welten. Leipzig, 1913.
Phil 281.5 Fourviéro, Savié de. La creacioun dou mounde. Avignoun, 1891. 2v.
Phil 281.6.5 Ayais, H. Explication universelle. Paris, 1826. 2v.
Phil 281.6.10 Ayais, H. Constitution de l'univers. Paris, 1840.
Phil 281.6.15 Ambacher, Michel. Le précurseur philosophique. Paris, 1844.
Phil 281.7 Auerbach, Felix. Ektropismen en ny teori om livets bevarande i varldsprocessen. Stockholm, 1913.
Phil 281.8 Adler, Arthur. Das heutige Weltbild. Brieg, 1922.
Phil 281.9 Almeida, Theodoro de. Recreação filosofica. Lisboa, 1786-1805. 10v.
Phil 281.9.10 Palimodia manifesta. Sevilla, 1792?
Phil 281.10 Alvarea de Queiroz, M. Historia da creação do mundo conforme as ideas de Moizes. Porto, 1762.
Phil 281.11 Alt, Theodor. Fundamentum Weltanschauung. Mannheim, 1920.
Phil 281.12 Antieke en moderne kosmologie. Arnhem, 1941.
Phil 281.13 Ambacher, Michel. Méthode de la philosophie de la nature. Paris, 1961.
Phil 281.14 Adamczyk, S. Filozofia przyrody. Lublin, 1963.
Phil 281.20 Adams, George. Von dem ätherischen Raume. Stuttgart, 1964.
Phil 282.1 Barratt, A. Physical metempiric. London, 1883.
Phil 282.2 Boase, H.S. Few words on evolution and creation. London, 1882.
Phil 282.4 Batteux, C. Histoire des causes premières. Paris, 1769.
Phil 282.4.5 Batteux, C. Geschichte der Meynungen...Grundursachen. Leipzig, 1773.
Phil 282.4.9 Schenker, M. C. Batteux von seine nachahmungs Theorie in Deutsch. Leipzig, 1909.
Phil 282.5 Baxter, A. Matho; sive, Cosmotheoria puerilis. London, 1746.
Phil 282.5.5 Baxter, A. Matho, or, The cosmotheoria puerilis. London, 1745. 2v.
Phil 282.6 Baratsch, W. Kosmologische Gedanken. Leipzig, 1911.
Phil 282.6.2 Baratsch, W. Kosmologische Gedanken. 2. ed. Leipzig, 1912.
Phil 282.7 Becher, Erich. Naturphilosophie. Leipzig, 1914.
Phil 282.7.11 Becher, Erich. Weltgebäude, Weltgesetze, Weltentwicklung. Berlin, 1915.
Phil 282.7.16 Becher, Erich. Metaphysik und Naturwissenschaften. München, 1926.
Phil 282.7.19 Becher, Erich. Grundlagen und Grenzen des Naturerkennens. München, 1928.
Phil 282.8 Berdiaev, N. Smysl tvorchestva. Moskva, 1916.
Phil 282.9 Bardonnet, L. L'universe-organisme. Paris, 1912. 2v.
Phil 282.10 Bixby, J.T. The open secret; a study of life's deeper forces. Boston, 1912.
Phil 282.11 Busco, Pierre. Les cosmogonies modernes. Paris, 1924.
Phil 282.11.5 Busco, Pierre. Les cosmogonies modernes. Thèse. Paris, 1924.
Phil 282.12 Boodin, J.E. Cosmic evolution. N.Y., 1925.
Phil 282.12.10 Boodin, J.E. God and creation. N.Y., 1934. 2v.
Phil 282.13 Boreas, Theophilos. Tis filosofias i ipothesis ke i epitonvion ropi. Athens, 1913.
Phil 282.14 Bommersheim, P. Beiträge zur Lehre von Ding und Gesetz. Leipzig, 1927.
Phil 282.15 Bontecou, Daniel J. A chart of nature. Chicago, 1928.
Phil 282.16 Bolland, G.J.P.J. Hat wereldraadsel. Leiden, 1896.
Phil 282.17 Bernoulli, C. Romantiske Naturphilosophie. Jena, 1926.
Phil 282.18 Bürgel, B.H. Die Weltanschauung des modernen Menschen. Berlin, 1932.
Phil 282.19 Boulding, K.E. The image. Ann Arbor, 1956.
Phil 282.20 Bertrand, René. Le mystère de vivre. Monaco, 1957.
Phil 282.21 Bondi, Hermann. Cosmology. 2. ed. Cambridge, Eng., 1960.
Phil 282.21.5 Bondi, Hermann. The universe at large. Garden City, 1960.
Phil 282.22 Bleksley, A.E. The problems of cosmology. Johannesburg, 1956.
Phil 282.23 Bianchi, Ugo. Teogonie e cosmogonie. Roma, 1960.
Phil 282.24 Berger, Herman. Op zoek naar identiteit. Nijmegen, 1968.
Phil 282.26 Barth, Aron. The creation in the light of modern science. Jerusalem, 1968.
Phil 282.28.2 Balaban, Grigorii Iu. Real'nyi mir v svete uni persal'noi seorii podoishnogo ravnovesiia. 2. izd. Hamilton, 1970.
Phil 283.1 Carpenter, S.H. Philosophy of evolution. Madison, 1874
Phil 283.2 Carus, C.G. Natur und Idee. Wien, 1861.
Phil 283.4 Cuyás, F.G. Unidad del universo. Habana, 1874.
Phil 283.5 Clay, J. Schets eener kritische geschiedenis van het begrip natuurwet. Leiden, 1915.
Htn Phil 283.6* Contarini, N. De perfectione rerum, libri sex. Venetiis, 1576.
Htn Phil 283.8* Camilla, G. Enthosiasmo, de'misterii e maravigliose cause della compositione del mondo. Vinegia, 1564.
Htn Phil 283.9* Cattani da Diacceto, F. L'essamerone. Florenza, 1563.
Phil 283.10 Calter, A.C. Cosmologia. Boston, 1931.
Phil 283.12 Colligan, J.J. Cosmology. N.Y., 1936.
Phil 283.13 Collier, K.B. Cosmogonies of our fathers. N.Y., 1934.
Phil 283.14.5 Collingwood, Robin George. The idea of nature. Oxford, 1964.
Phil 283.15 Collin, R. The theory of celestial influence. London, 1954.
Phil 283.18 Colmoyer, Ciro. Due contributi di filosofia scientifica. Roma, 1967.
Phil 283.20 Collingwood, Francis. Philosophy of nature. Englewood Cliffs, N.J., 1961.
Phil 284.1 Durfee, J. The Panidèa. Boston, 1846.
Phil 284.2 Drossbach, M. Über Kraft und Bewegung. Halle, 1879.
Phil 284.3 Dinger, H. Prinzip der Entwickelung. Jena, 1896.
Phil 284.4 Duhem, P. La theorie physique. Paris, 1906.
Phil 284.4.2 Duhem, P. La theorie physique, son objet, sa structure. 2. éd. Paris, 1914.
Phil 284.4.7 Duhem, P. Ziel und Struktur der physikalischen Theorien. Leipzig, 1908.
Phil 284.4.10 Duhem, P. The aim and structure of physical theory. Princeton, 1954.
Phil 284.4.12 Duhem, P. The aim and structure of physical theory. N.Y., 1962.

Classified Listing

Phil 281 - 306   Special philosophical topics, systems, etc. - Secondary treatises and discussions - Cosmology - Monographs [A-Z - cont.

Phil 284.5   Dippe, Alfred. Naturphilosophie. München, 1907.
Phil 284.6   Driesch, Hans. Naturbegriffe und natururteile. Leipzig, 1904.
Phil 284.6.5   Driesch, Hans. Zwei Vorträge zur Naturphilosophie. Leipzig, 1910.
Phil 284.6.10 Driesch, Hans. Metaphysik der Natur. München, 1926.
Phil 284.7   Dario, J.M. Praelectiones cosmologiae. Paris, 1923.
Phil 284.8   Descoqus, P. Essai critique sur l'hytemorphisme. Paris, 1924.
Phil 284.9   Dandolo, G. La causa e la legge. Padova, 1901.
Phil 284.10   Dandolo, G. Intorno al valore della scienza. Padova, 1908.
Phil 284.11   Dennert, E. Die Weltanschauung des modernen Naturforschers. Stuttgart, 1907.
Phil 284.12   Dole, George Henry. The philosophy of creation. N.Y., 1906.
Phil 284.13   D'Arcy, C.F. Providence and the world-order. London, 1932.
Phil 284.14   Dupont de Nemours, P.S. Philosophie de l'univers. Paris, 1792.
Phil 284.15   Dessauer, Friedrich. Naturwissenschaftliches Erkennen. Frankfurt, 1958.
Phil 285.1   Ehrenfils, C. Kosmogonie. Jena, 1916.
Phil 285.2   Erdmann, J.E. Natur oder Schöpfung? Leipzig, 1840.
Phil 285.3   Eleutheropulos, A. Die exakten Grundlagen der Naturphilosophie. Stuttgart, 1926.
Phil 285.4   Embry, J. The Namic philosophy. N.Y., 1951.
Phil 285.5   Ehrenfels, C.F. Cosmogony. N.Y., 1948.
Phil 285.6   Eliade, Mircea. The myth of the eternal return. N.Y., 1954.
Phil 285.6.1   Eliade, Mircea. Le mythe de l'eternel retour. Paris, 1969.
Phil 285.6.2   Eliade, Mircea. Cosmos and history. N.Y., 1970.
Phil 285.6.5   Eliade, Mircea. Kosmos und Geschichte. Hamburg, 1966[1953]
Phil 285.8   Ehrhardt, Arnold. The begining. N.Y., 1968.
Phil 286.1   Faye, H.A.E. L'origine du monde. Paris, 1884.
Htn Phil 286.2*A Fiske, J. Outlines of cosmic philosophy. Boston, 1875. 2v.
Htn Phil 286.2*B Fiske, J. Outlines of cosmic philosophy. Boston, 1875. 2v.
Phil 286.2.2   Fiske, J. Outlines of cosmic philosophy. London, 1874. 2v.
Phil 286.2.3   Fiske, J. Outlines of cosmic philosophy. Boston, 1874. 2v.
Phil 286.2.5   Fiske, J. Outlines of cosmic philosophy. 11. ed. Boston, 1890. 2v.
Phil 286.2.9   Fiske, J. Outlines of cosmic philosophy. Boston, 1902. 4v.
Phil 286.2.1! Fiske, J. Outlines of cosmic philosophy. Boston, 1916. 4v.
Phil 286.4   Fullerton, G.S. The world we live in. N.Y., 1912.
Phil 286.5   Fouillée, Alfred. Esquise d'une interprétation du monde. Paris, 1913.
Phil 286.6   Frohschammer, J. Über die Aufgabe der Naturphilosophie. München, 1861.
Phil 286.7   Faria Gersão Ventura, Augusta. A maquina do mundo. Porto, 1944.
Phil 286.8   Frank, S.L. Smysl zhizni. Paris, 1925.
Phil 287.1   Gunkel, H. Schöpfung und Chaos. Göttingen, 1895.
Phil 287.2   Giera, Jules. Les deux creations. Paris, 1872.
Phil 287.3   Gomperz, Heinrich. Weltanschauungslehre. Jena, 1905-08. 2v.
Phil 287.4   Grave, F. Das Chaos als objektive Weltregion. Berlin, 1924.
Phil 287.5   Grant Watson, E.L. Man and his universe. London, 1940.
Phil 287.6   Garcia Bacca, Juan D. Tipos historicos del filosofar fisico. Tucuman, 1941.
Phil 287.7   Geymonat, Ludovico. La nuova filosofia della natura in Germania. Torino, 1934.
Phil 287.10   Guitton, Jean. De la signification du cosmos. Paris, 1966.
Phil 287.12   Ghirardi, Olsen A. Cosmología y ciencia ficcion. Córdoba, Argentina, 1970.
Phil 288.1   Hickok, S.P. Rational cosmology. N.Y., 1958.
Phil 288.1.8   Hickok, S.P. Review of rational cosmology. n.p., 18- ?
Phil 288.1.25 Pamphlet box. Hickok, Laurens. Perseus. Rational cosmology.
Phil 288.2   Hutchins, S. Theory of the universe. N.Y., 1868.
Phil 288.3   Heermance, E.L. Chaos or cosmos? N.Y., 1922.
Phil 288.4   Hahn, Otto. Die Philosophie des Bewussten. Tubingen, 1887.
Phil 288.5   Hartung, G. Philosophie und Naturwissenschaft. n.p., n.d.
Phil 288.6   Hartmann, L. Sind Naturgesetze veränderlich? Halle, 1926.
Phil 288.7   Hartung, J.F. Die physikalische Energie und die Brücke. Obersalzbrunn, 1928.
Phil 288.8   Häberlin, Paul. Leben und Lebensform. Basel, 1957.
Phil 288.10   Haber, Francis. The age of the world. Baltimore, 1959.
Phil 288.12   Hennemann, Gerhard. Naturphilosophie in 19. Jahrhundert. Freiburg, 1959.
Phil 288.15   Hoenen, Peter. Cosmologia. 5. ed. Romae, 1956.
Phil 288.15.2 Hoenen, Peter. Quaestiones noeticae de extensione corporea. Romae, 1955.
Phil 288.15.5 Hoenen, Peter. The philosophical nature of physical bodies. West Baden Springs, Ind., 1955.
Phil 288.15.10 Hoenen, Peter. The philosophy of inorganic compounds. West Baden Springs, Ind., 1960.
Phil 288.17   Hoenigswald, Richard. Schriften aus dem Nachlass. Stuttgart, 1957- 8v.
Phil 288.20   Hawley, Don. The nature of things. N.Y., 1959.
Phil 288.21   Hoyle, Fred. Man in the universe. N.Y., 1966.
Phil 288.22   Heimendahl, Eckart. Dialog des Abendlandes. München, 1966.
Phil 288.24   Hoerz, Herbert. Naturphilosophie von der Spekulation zur Wissenschaft. Berlin, 1969.
Phil 289.1   Inge, W.R. God and the astronomers. London, 1933.
Phil 289.2   Idée de monde et philosophie de la nature. Paris, 1966.
Phil 290.1   Jacobsson, M. Naturens lag. Stockholm, 1914.
Phil 290.2.3   Jellinek, K. Das Weltgeheimnis. Stuttgart, 1922.
Phil 290.3   Joffe, Isaac L. Expository history of the cosmos. N.Y., 1927.
Phil 290.5   Jaffe, Haym. Natural law as controlled but not determined by experiment. Thesis. Philadelphia, 1934.
Phil 291.1   Keyserling, H. Das Gefüge der Welt. München, 1906.
Phil 291.2F   Klyce, Scudder. Universe. Winchester, Mass., 1921.
Phil 291.3   Kern, Berthold. Weltanschauungen und Welterkenntnis. Berlin, 1911.

Phil 281 - 306   Special philosophical topics, systems, etc. - Secondary treatises and discussions - Cosmology - Monographs [A-Z - cont.

Phil 291.4   Kassowitz, Max. Welt - Leben - Seele. Wien, 1908.
Phil 291.5   Kaiser, Wilhelm. Kosmos und Menschenwesen im Spiegel der platonischen Körper. Basel, 1930.
Phil 291.6   Künkel, H. Das Gesetz deines Lebens. Jena, 1933.
Phil 291.7   Koyré, Alexandre. From the closed world to the infinite universe. Baltimore, 1957.
Phil 291.8   Koren, Henry. Readings in the philosophy of nature. Westminster, Md., 1958.
Phil 291.8.5   Koren, Henry. An introduction to the philosophy of nature. Pittsburg, 1960.
Phil 291.9   Kemeny, John G. A philosopher looks at science. Princeton, N.J., 1959.
Phil 291.10   Kapp, Reginald O. Towards a unified cosmology. London, 1960.
Phil 291.11   Komarov, V.N. Kosmos, log i vechnost' mira. Moskva, 1963.
Phil 291.12   Khudushin, Fedor S. Chelovck i priroda. Moskva, 1966.
Phil 291.14   Kiss, Elek. A világ fejlödése az atom szemléletében. Kolozsvár, 1946.
Phil 291.15   Kafka, Gustav. Naturgesetz, Freiheit und Wunder. Paderborn, 1940.
Phil 291.16   Kremianskii, Viktor I. Strukturnze urovni zhivoi materii. Moskva, 1969.
Phil 291.18   Kroeber, Günter. Der Gesetzesbegriff in der Philosophie und den Einzelwissenschaften. Berlin, 1968.
Phil 292.1   Luc, J.A. de. Lettres physiques et morales sur l'histoire...terre. Paris, 1779. 6v.
Phil 292.2   Lukas, F. Die Grundbegriffe...Kösmogonien. Leipzig, 1893.
Phil 292.3   Lassivitz, Kurd. Seelen und Ziele. Beiträge zum Weltverständnis. Leipzig, 1908.
Phil 292.4   Logan, J.D. Three papers reprinted. n.p., 1897-99.
Phil 292.5   Lilburne, H.A. The psychology of the atom. London, 1924.
Phil 292.6   LeBel, J.A. Cosmologie rationnelle. Le Mans, 1925.
Phil 292.7   Langdon-Davies, John. Man and his universe. N.Y., 1930.
Phil 292.7.5   Langdon-Davies, John. Man comes of age. 1st ed. N.Y., 1932.
Phil 292.8A   Lovejoy, A.O. The great chain of being. Cambridge, Mass., 1936.
Phil 292.8B   Lovejoy, A.O. The great chain of being. Cambridge, Mass., 1936.
Phil 292.8C   Lovejoy, A.O. The great chain of being. Cambridge, Mass., 1936.
Phil 292.8.5   Lovejoy, A.O. The great chain of being. Cambridge, Mass., 1957.
Phil 292.8.6   Lovejoy, A.O. The great chain of being. Cambridge, Mass., 1961.
Phil 292.9   Laberenne, P. L'origine des mondes. Paris, 1936.
Phil 292.10   Lecouturier, H. La cosmosphie. Paris, 1850.
Phil 292.11   Lavrov, A.S. V poiskakh istiny. Paris, 1940.
Phil 292.20   Lugones, Leopoldo. El tamaño del espacio. Buenos Aires, 1921.
Phil 292.22   Landesmann, Heinrich. Der Naturgenuss. Berlin, 1876.
Phil 293.1   Madiis, H. de. Le plan de la creation. Paris, 1864.
Phil 293.2   Magy, F. De la science et de la nature. Paris, 1865.
Phil 293.3   Martin, T.H. Philosophie spiritualiste de la nature. Paris, 1849. 2v.
Htn Phil 293.4* Memma, G.M. Sostanza et forma del mondo. Venice, 1545. 4v.
Phil 293.6   Meyer, E.H. Die eddische Kosmogonie. Freiburg, 1891.
Phil 293.7   Montagu, A. Cours de philosophie scientifique. Paris, 1879.
Phil 293.7.2   Montagu, A. Cours de philosophie scientifiques et ses conséquences sociales. 2. ed. Paris, 1881.
Phil 293.8   Maillet, Benoît de. Telliamed. v.1-2. Amsterdam, 1748.
Phil 293.8.2   Maillet, Benoît de. Telliamed. La Haye, 1755. 2v.
Phil 293.8.4   Maillet, Benoît de. Telliamed. La Haye, 1755. 2v.
Phil 293.8.6   Maillet, Benoît de. Telliamed. London, 1750.
Phil 293.8.8   Maillet, Benoît de. Telliamed. Urbana, 1968.
Htn Phil 293.8.15* Maillet, Benoît de. Telliamed. The world explained. Baltimore, 1797.
Phil 293.8.75 Neubert, Fritz. Einleitung in eine kritische Ausgabe von B. de Maillets Telliamed. Berlin, 1920.
Phil 293.9   McEwen, J.W. An essay on creation. Philadelphia, 1900
Phil 293.10.2 Maillard, Louis. Quand la lumiére fut. Les cosmogonies anciennes...modernes. Paris, 1922-23. 2v.
Htn Phil 293.11* Marsh, E.G. An oration on the truth of the Mosaic history of the creation. Hartford, 1798.
Phil 293.12   Merezhkovskii, K.S. Fragments du "Schema d'une nouvelle philosophie de l'univers". Genève, 1920.
Phil 293.14   Moraes Carvalho, A.A. de. Le problème de l'univers. Lisbonne, 1920.
Phil 293.15   Mikos, J. Hypothesen über einige kosmologische und geologische Momente. Leipzig, 1895.
Phil 293.16   Mitchell, William. Nature and feeling. Adelaide, 1929.
Phil 293.17   Marin de Carranrais, E. de. Etudes sur les origines. Paris, 1876.
Phil 293.18   McKaye, James. Dynamic universe. N.Y., 1931.
Phil 293.19   Momo, Giovanni. Sulla proposizione il mondo va da se. Lucca, 1827.
Phil 293.21   Mason, F.B. (Mrs.). The great design. N.Y., 1935.
Phil 293.22   Mitterer, Albert. Das Rinzen der alten Stoff-Form-Metaphysik mit der heutigen Stoff-Physik. Innsbruck, 1935.
Phil 293.22.5 Mittere, Albert. Wesensartwandel und Artensystem der physikalischen Körperwelt. Bressanone, 1936. 3v.
Phil 293.23   Minkowski, E. Vers une cosmologie. Paris, 1936.
Phil 293.24   Mally, E. Erlebnis und Wirklichkeit. Leipzig, 1935.
Phil 293.25   Matisse, G. La philosophie de la nature. Paris, 1938. 3v.
Phil 293.25.5 Matisse, G. L'incohérence universelle. 1. éd. Paris, 1953.
Phil 293.26   Morelli, C. Lo sviluppo del mondo nelle principali teorie filosofiche. Avellino, 1892.
Phil 293.27   Melsen, A.G.M. van. The philosophy of nature. Pittsburg, 1953.
Phil 293.28   Morin, J.A. The serpent and the satellite. N.Y., 1953.
Phil 293.29   Mugler, Charles. Deux thèmes de la cosmologie grecque. Paris, 1953.
Phil 293.30   Maier, Anneliese. Zwischen Philosophie und Mechanik. Roma, 1958.
Phil 293.31   Munitz, Milton Karl. Space, time, and creation. Glencoe, 1957.
Phil 293.31.5 Munitz, Milton Karl. The mystery of existence. N.Y., 1965.
Phil 293.32   Morin, Gérard. Vie et cosmos. Paris, 1962.
Phil 293.33   Merleau-Ponty, Jacques. Cosmologie du XXe siècle. Paris, 1965.

Classified Listing

Phil 281 - 306   Special philosophical topics, systems, etc. - Secondary treatises and discussions - Cosmology - Monographs [A-Z] - cont.

	Phil 293.34	Mueller, Aloys. Die Stellung des Menschen im Kosmos. Bonn, 1948.
	Phil 294.1	Nason, L.H. History of the prehistoric ages. Chicago, 1880.
	Phil 294.2	Nourrisson, J.F. Philosophies de la nature. Paris, 1887.
	Phil 294.3	Nichols, H. Treatise on cosmology. Cambridge, 1904.
Htn	Phil 294.4F*	Newcastle, M.L.C. Philosophical and physical opinions. London, 1663.
Htn	Phil 294.4.2F*	Newcastle, M.L.C. Grounds of natural philosophy. 2. ed. London, 1668.
	Phil 294.5	Newlyn, Herbert N. The relationship...mystical and the sensible world. London, 1918.
	Phil 294.6	Neeff, F. Prolegomena zu einer Kosmologie. Tübingen, 1921.
	Phil 294.7	Nernst, Walther. Zum Gültigkeitsbereich der Naturgesetze. Berlin, 1921.
	Phil 294.8	Nickel, E.J. Zugang zur Wicklichkeit. Freiburg, 1963.
	Phil 295.09	Ostwald, W. Vorlesungen über Naturphilosophie. Leipzig, 1902.
	Phil 295.1	Ostwald, W. Vorlesungen über Naturphilosophie. 2. Aufl. Leipzig, 1902.
	Phil 295.1.6	Ostwald, W. Natural philosophy. N.Y., 1910.
	Phil 295.2	O'Neill, John. Cosmology; an introduction to the philosophy of matter. London, 1923.
	Phil 295.4	Oliveira, I. de. Introduction du sens cosmique en philosophie. Paris, 1962.
	Phil 295.6	Orban, A.P. Les dénominations du monde chez les premiers auteurs chrétiens. Nijmegen, 1970.
	Phil 296.1	Petöcz, M. Ansicht der Welt. Leipzig, 1838.
	Phil 296.3	Piványi, J.A. Entwicklungsgeschichte des Welt...Organismen. Plauen, 1877.
	Phil 296.4	Pluche, N.A. The history of the heavens. London, 1740. 2v.
	Phil 296.6	Poincaré, H. Leçons sur les hypotheses cosmogoniques. Paris, 1911.
	Phil 296.6.2	Poincaré, H. Leçons sur les hypotheses cosmogoniques. 2. ed. Paris, 1913.
	Phil 296.7.2	Petzoldt, J. Das Weltproblem vom Standpunkte. 2. Aufl. Leipzig, 1912.
	Phil 296.8.3	Pesch, Tilmann. Die grossen Welträtsel. Freiburg, 1907. 2v.
	Phil 296.9	Portig, Gustav. Die Grundzüge der monistischen und dualistischen Weltanschauung. Stuttgart, 1904.
Htn	Phil 296.10*	Piccolomini, A. Della filosofia naturale. Venetia, 1585. 2v.
	Phil 296.14	Panizza, O. Der Illusionismus und die Rettung. Leipzig, 1895.
	Phil 296.15	Pavese, Roberto. Fisica e metafisica. Padova, 1964[1965]
	Phil 298.1	Richard, C. Les lois de Dieu. Paris, 1862.
	Phil 298.2	Rosley, Carl. Das Körpergesetz. San Francisco, 19- .
	Phil 298.2.10	Rosley, Carl. Life's reality. Hayward, 1932.
	Phil 298.3	Rindell, E. Framställning af teorierna om det kosmiska före Sölger och Hegel. Helsingfors, 1885.
	Phil 298.4	Reinke, J. Die Natur und Wir. Berlin, 1907.
	Phil 298.5	Rey, Abel. Le retour éternel et la philosophie de la physique. Paris, 1927.
	Phil 298.6	Riddell, Newton N. Science of creation. Des Moines, Iowa, 192-.
	Phil 298.7	Reichenbach, Hans. Ziele und Wege der heutigen Naturphilosophie. Leipzig, 1931.
	Phil 298.8	Richter, G. Die Philosophie der Eimmaligkeit. Wien, 1928-32. 3v.
	Phil 298.9	Rawson, F. Life understood from a scientific and religious point of view. 7. ed. London, 1947.
	Phil 298.10	Reinl, Kurt. Grundriss des Seins. München, 1958.
	Phil 298.12	Rieder, Albert. Die Pole der Gesamtnatur. Pfaffenhofen an der Ilm, 1959.
	Phil 298.14	Roth, Samuel. The peep-hole of the present. N.Y., 1945.
	Phil 298.16	Reitzer, Alfons. Das Problem des Materiebegriffes. München, 1960.
	Phil 298.18	Remits, E. The law in nature and anxiety-superior. Ottawa, 1962.
	Phil 298.18.5	Remits, E. The law in nature and the dynamics of openness. Ottawa, 1965.
	Phil 298.20	Rademaker, Hans. Die Welt in der Sicht der wissenschaftlichen Vernunft. Bonn, 1965.
	Phil 298.22	Rice, Laban Lucy. The universe, its origin, nature and destiny. N.Y., 1951.
	Phil 298.23	Reiser, Oliver Leslie. Cosmic humanism. Cambridge, 1966.
	Phil 299.1	Schlesinger, J. Die Entstehung der physischen...Welt. Wien, 1882.
	Phil 299.2	Silberstein, S.J. Disclosures of the universal mysteries. N.Y., 1896.
	Phil 299.3	Siljeström, P.A. Tretten aftnar hos en spiritist. Stockholm, 1886.
NEDL	Phil 299.4.2	Stallo, J.B. Concepts and theories of modern physics. N.Y., 1882.
	Phil 299.5	Spitzer, H. Über Ursprung...des Hylozoismus. Graz, 1881.
	Phil 299.6	Stunz, F. Naturbetrachtung und Naturkenntnis. Leipzig, 1904.
	Phil 299.7.5	Snyder, C. The world machine...cosmic mechanism. N.Y., 1907.
	Phil 299.8	Soury, Jules. Philosophie naturelle. Paris, 1882.
	Phil 299.9	Schnehen, W. Energetische Weltanschauung? Leipzig, 1908.
	Phil 299.10	Sageret, Jules. Le système du monde des chaldéens à Newton. 2. éd. Paris, 1913.
	Phil 299.11	Scheffler, Hermann. Die Grundlagen des Weltsystems. Braunschweig, 1898.
	Phil 299.11.5	Scheffler, Hermann. Realität und Ideelität ferner Naturkraft und Schöpfungskraft. Braunschweig, 1897.
	Phil 299.12	Schoeler, H. von. Kritik der wissenschaftlichen Erkenntnis. Leipzig, 1898.
	Phil 299.13	Schneider, K.C. Die Welt wie sie Jetzt ist und wie sie sein Wird. Wien, 1917.
	Phil 299.14	Sapper, Karl. Das Element der Wirklichkeit und die Welt der Erfahrung. München, 1924.
	Phil 299.15	Sidis, W.G. The animate and the inanimate. Boston, 1925.
	Phil 299.16	Society of Universal Science. Belmont, Mass. The system of the universe. Belmont, 1924.
	Phil 299.17	Spiller, P. Die Urkraft des Weltalls. Berlin, 1876.
	Phil 299.18	Snell, Karl. Philosophische Betrachtungen der Natur. Dresden, 1839.
	Phil 299.19	Sidereal evolution, or A new cosmology. Boston, 1889.
	Phil 299.20	Schneidewin, M. Die Unendlichkeit der Welt. Berlin, 1900.
	Phil 299.21	Schilder, Paul. Gedanken zur Naturphilosophie. Wien, 1928.

Phil 281 - 306   Special philosophical topics, systems, etc. - Secondary treatises and discussions - Cosmology - Monographs [A-Z] - cont.

	Phil 299.22	Stallknecht, N.P. Studies in the philosophy of creation. Princeton, 1934.
	Phil 299.24	Strömberg, G. The soul of the universe. Philadelphia, 1940.
	Phil 299.24.2	Strömberg, G. The soul of the universe. 2. ed. Philadelphia, 1948.
	Phil 299.25	Samtonge, F. Sumina cosmologiae. Montreal, 1941.
	Phil 299.26	Schöndorfer, Ulrich A. Philosophie des Materie. 1. Aufl. Graz, 1954.
	Phil 299.27	Shapley, Harlow. Of stars and men. Boston, 1958.
	Phil 299.27.5	Shapley, Harlow. Of stars and men. Boston, 1964.
	Phil 299.28	Spoerri, Walter. Spathellenistische Berichte über Welt. Basel, 1959.
	Phil 299.30	Sachsse, Hans. Naturerkenntnis und Wirklichkeit. Braunschweig, 1967.
	Phil 299.32	Sterneder, Hans. Das kosmische Weltbild. Freiburg, 1969.
NEDL	Phil 300.1	Toulmin, G.H. Eternity of the universe. Philadelphia, 1830.
	Phil 300.2	Tunzelmann, G.W. de. Treatise on electrical theory and problem of universe. London, 1910.
	Phil 300.3	Tieftrunk, J.H. Das Weltall nach menschlicher Ansicht. Halle, 1821.
	Phil 300.4	Trubetskoi, E.N. Smysl' zhizni. Berlin, 1922.
	Phil 300.6	Tramer, Moritz. Philosophie des schöpferischen. Bern, 1957.
	Phil 300.10	Third Programme. Rival theories of cosmology. London, 1960.
	Phil 300.13	Tuzet, Hélène. Le cosmos et l'imagination. Paris, 1965.
	Phil 300.15	Tollenaere, M. de. Lichaam en wereld. Brugge, 1967.
	Phil 300.15.5	Tollenaere, M. de. Le corps et le monde. Bruges, 1967.
	Phil 301.5	Uexkuell, T. von. Der Mensch und die Natur. Bern, 1953.
	Phil 302.1	Vinogradoff, I. Theory of cosmic reason. n.p., n.d.
	Phil 302.2	Vial, L.C.E. L'amour dans l'univers. Paris, 1896.
	Phil 302.4	Valsardieu, Paul. La révolution totale, en tout. Paris, 1968- 2v.
	Phil 303.2	Werther, C.A. Die Kräfte der unorganischen Natur. Dessau, 1852.
	Phil 303.3	Wuttke, A. Abhandlung über die Cosmogonie. Haag, 1850.
	Phil 303.4	Winslow, C.F. Cosmography. Boston, 1853.
	Phil 303.5	White, T. De mundo dialogi tres quibus. Paris, 1642.
	Phil 303.6	Wolff, H. Kosmos die Weltentwickelung. Leipzig, 1890.
	Phil 303.7	Weltanschauung. Philosophie und Religion. Berlin, 1911.
	Phil 303.8	Warrain, F. La synthèse concrète. Paris, 1910.
	Phil 303.9.3	Wille, Bruno. Das Lebendige all; idealistische Weltanschauung. Hamburg, 1905.
	Phil 303.10	Wälte, Théodore. Philosophie d'un ignorant. Genève, 1914.
	Phil 303.11	Waddington, M.F. Saggio sulla natura. Firenze, 1866.
	Phil 303.12	Whitehead, Alfred N. Process and reality. Cambridge, Eng., 1929.
	Phil 303.12.3	Whitehead, Alfred N. Process and reality. N.Y., 1929.
	Phil 303.12.5	Whitehead, Alfred N. Process and reality. N.Y., 1930.
	Phil 303.12.6	Whitehead, Alfred N. Process and reality; an essay in cosmology. N.Y., 1941.
	Phil 303.12.25	Lintz, E.J. The unity of the universe. Fribourg, 1939.
	Phil 303.13	Warren, W.F. The earliest cosmologies. N.Y., 1909.
	Phil 303.14	Whittaker, E. Space and spirit. London, 1946.
	Phil 303.18	Wein, Hermann. Zugang zu philosophischen Kosmologie. München, 1954.
	Phil 303.20.1	Wagner, Johann Jacob. Von der Natur der Dinge. Mit einer physiognomischen Kupfertafel. Leipzig, 1803. Bruxelles, 1968.
	Phil 305.1	Younghusband, F.E. The living universe. N.Y., 1933.
	Phil 306.1	Ziegler, Johann H. Die Struktur der Materie und das Welträtsel. Bern, 1908.
	Phil 306.2.2	Zehnder, Ludwig. Das Leben im Weltall. Tübingen, 1910.
	Phil 306.3	Ziegler, Konrat. Weltentstehung in Sage und Wissenschaft. Leipzig, 1925.
	Phil 306.3.5	Ziegler, Konrat. Weltuntergang in Sage und Wissenschaft. Leipzig, 1921.
	Phil 306.4	Ziehen, T. Grundlagen der Naturphilosophie. Leipzig, 1922.
	Phil 306.5	Zirm, E.K. Die Welt als Fühlen. Leipzig, 1937.

Phil 308   Special philosophical topics, systems, etc. - Secondary treatises and discussions - Criticism, Critical philosophy

	Phil 308.2	Atbert, Hans. Traktat über kritische Vernunft. Tübingen, 1968.
	Phil 308.4	Scholes, Robert E. The philosopher critic. Tulsa, Okla., 1970.
	Phil 308.6	Migliorini, Ermanno. Critica, oggetto e logica. Firenze, 1968.

Phil 310   Special philosophical topics, systems, etc. - Secondary treatises and discussions - Dialectic and Dialectical materialism

	Phil 310.1	Pamphlet vol. Dialectical materialism. 4 pam.
	Phil 310.1.1	Pamphlet vol. Dialectical materialism. 6 pam.
	Phil 310.1.2	Pamphlet vol. Dialectical materialism. 5 pam.
	Phil 310.1.3	Pamphlet vol. Dialectical materialism. 5 pam.
	Phil 310.1.4	Pamphlet vol. Dialectical materialism. 5 pam.
	Phil 310.1.5	Rozanov, Iakov S. Filosofsko-sotsiologicheskaia literatura marksizma za 1917-1927. Moskva, 1928.
	Phil 310.1.5.5	Rozanov, Iakov S. Istoricheskii materializm. Kiev, 1925.
	Phil 310.1.6	Pamphlet vol. Dialectical materialism. 5 pam.
	Phil 310.1.7	Pamphlet vol. Dialectical materialism. 3 pam.
	Phil 310.1.8	Asmus, Valentin F. Ocherki istorii dialektiki v novoi filosofii. 2. izd. Moskva, 1929. 2 pam.
	Phil 310.1.9	Pamphlet vol. Dialectical materialism. 4 pam.
	Phil 310.1.10	Pamphlet vol. "Dialectical materialism". (Russian). 5 pam.
	Phil 310.2	Cornforth, M.C. Dialectical materialism. London, 1952. 3v.
	Phil 310.2.2	Cornforth, M.C. Dialectical materialism. London, 1955-56. 3v.
	Phil 310.2.3	Cornforth, M.C. Dialectical materialism. v.1-3. 3d ed. London, 1955.
	Phil 310.2.5	Cornforth, M.C. Historical materialism. N.Y., 1954.
	Phil 310.3	Akadamiia Nauk SSSR. Institut Filosofii. Dialekticheskii materializm. Moskva, 1953.
	Phil 310.3.5	Rozental', M.M. Kategorii materialisti cheskoi dialektiki. Moskva, 1956.
	Phil 310.3.8	Rozental', M.M. Kategorien der materialistischen Dialektik. Berlin, 1959.
	Phil 310.3.10	Rozhin, V.P. Marksistsko-leninskaia dialektika. Leningrad, 1957.
	Phil 310.3.12	Rozhin, V.P. Predmet i struktura marksistsko-leninskoi filosofii. Leningrad, 1958.

Classified Listing

Phil 310   Special philosophical topics, systems, etc. - Secondary treatises and discussions - Dialectic and Dialectical materialism - cont.

Phil 310.3.15 — Shakhparonov, M.I. Dialekticheskii materializm i nekotorye problemy fiziki i khimii. Moskva, 1958.

Phil 310.4 — Velikaia sila idei lenimizma; sbornik statei. Moskva, 1950.

Phil 310.4.3 — Kovalgin, V.M. Dialekticheskii materializm o zakonakh nauki. Minsk, 1958.

Phil 310.4.5 — Protasenko, Z.M. Printsipy periodizatsii istorii marksistsko-leninskoi filosofii. Leningrad, 1957.

Phil 310.4.10 — Deborin, A.M. Vvedemie v filosofii dialekticheskogo materializma. Moskva, 1922.

Phil 310.5 — Pavlov, T. Ravnosmetka na edna idealistko reaktsionii filosofiia. Sofiia, 1953.

Phil 310.5.3 — Vorob'ev, M.F. Zakon otritsaniia otritsaniia. Moskva, 1958.

Phil 310.5.5 — Dialekticheskii materializm i sovremennoe estestvoznanie. Moskva, 1957.

VPhil 310.5.10 — Oshakov, Zhivko. Istoricheskiiat materializum. Sofiia, 1958.

Phil 310.5.12 — Oshakov, Zhivko. Istoricheskiiat materializum i sotsiologiiatu. 2. izd. Sofiia, 1970.

Phil 310.5.15 — Oshakov, Zhivko. Niakoi aktualni problemina nauchnogo. komunizum. Sofiia, 1961.

Phil 310.6 — Institut Filosofii. Akadamiia Nauk SSSR. O dialekticheskii materializme; sbornik statei. Moskva, 1952.

Phil 310.6.5 — Akadamiia Nauk SSSR. Institut Filosofii. Osnovy marksistskoi filosofii. Moskva, 1958.

Phil 310.6.6 — Akadamiia Nauk SSSR. Institut Filosofii. Osnovy marksistskoi filosofii. Izd. 2. Moskva, 1964.

Phil 310.6.7 — Osnovy marksistsko-leninskoi filosofii. Moskva, 1971.

Phil 310.6.10 — Bodrenski, J.M. Die dogmatischen Grundlagen der sowjetischen Philosophie. Dordrecht, Holland, 1959.

Phil 310.6.12 — Bodrenski, J.M. The dogmatic principles of Soviet philosophy. Dordrecht, Holland, 1963.

Phil 310.6.15 — Akadamiia Nauk SSSR. Institut Filosofii. Grundlagen der marxistischen Philosophie. Berlin, 1960.

Phil 310.7 — Akadamiia Nauk SSSR. Institut Filosofii. Dialekticheskii materializm. Moskva, 1954.

Phil 310.7.5 — Vostrikov, A.V. Marksistskii filosofskii materializm. Moskva, 1954.

Phil 310.7.7 — Vostrikov, A.V. Teoriia poznaniia dialekticheskogo materializma. Moskva, 1965.

Phil 310.7.10 — Golovakha, I.P. Marksistskaia filosofiia v poznavalmosti mira. Kiev, 1955.

Phil 310.8 — Lewis, John. Marxism and the irrationalists. London, 1955.

Phil 310.9A — Konstantinov, F.V. Istoricheskii materializm. Izd. 2. Moskva, 1954.

Phil 310.9B — Konstantinov, F.V. Istoricheskii materializm. Izd. 2. Moskva, 1954.

Phil 310.10 — Fedoseev, P.N. Usloviia materialicheskoi zhizni obshchestva. Moskva, 1954.

Phil 310.11 — Bol'shukhin, A.A. Oroli narodnogo max i lichnosti v istorii. Gor'kii, 1955.

RRC   Phil 310.12 — Russia (1917-   ). Upravlenie Prepodavatel'skogo Obshchestvennogo Nauk. Programma kursa dialekticheskogo i istoricheskogo materializma dlia vyshego uchebrogo zaved. Moskva, 1954.

Phil 310.12.10 — Moscow. Kafedra. Akadamiia Obshchestvennogo Nauk. Programma kursa dialekticheskogo i istori cheskogo materializma. Moskva, 1956.

Phil 310.12.12 — Moscow. Akadamiia Obshchestvennogo Nauk. Programmy po istorii filosofii. Moskva, 1958.

Phil 310.12.15 — Russia (1917-   ). Upravlenie Prepodavatel'skogo Obshchestvennogo Nauk. Programma kursa dialekticheskogo i istoricheskogo materializma. Moskva, 1957.

Phil 310.12.20 — Voprosy metodiki prepodavaniia marksistsko-leninskoi filosofii v vazakh. Moskva. 2,1967+

Phil 310.13 — Danilenko, D.I. Marksistskii filosofskii materializm. Moskva, 1953.

Phil 310.14A — Schaff, Adam. Zu einigen Fragen der marxistischen Theorie der Wahrheit. 1. Aufl. Berlin, 1954.

Phil 310.14B — Schaff, Adam. Zu einigen Fragen der marxistischen Theorie der Wahrheit. 1. Aufl. Berlin, 1954.

Phil 310.15 — Landesverband Nordshein-West-Tälischer Geschichte. Historie Materialismus und europäisches Geschichtsdenken. 1. Aufl. Düsseldorf, 1954.

Phil 310.16.5 — Merlean-Ponty, Maurice. Les aventures de la dialectique. Paris, 1961.

Phil 310.17 — Baskin, M.P. Materializm i religiia. Moskva, 1955.

Phil 310.18 — Hommes, Jakob. Der technische Eros. Freiburg, 1955.

Phil 310.19 — Mesaventures de l'anti-Marxisme. Paris, 1956.

Phil 310.20 — Pavlov, Todor D. Osnovnoto v Michurinskoto uchenie v svetlinata na dialekticheskai materializm. Sofia, 1955.

Phil 310.20.5 — Pavlov, Todor D. Teoriiata na otrazhenieto i nashata suvremennost. Sofia, 1961.

Phil 310.21 — Ivanov, A.I. Vozniknoveniie marksizma, revoliutsionnyi perevorst v filosofii. Moskva, 1956.

Phil 310.23 — Tuzarinov, V.P. Sootnoshenii kategorii dialekticheskoi marksizma. Leningrad, 1956.

Phil 310.24 — Plekhanov, G.V. The development of the monist view of history. Moscow, 1956.

Phil 310.25 — Fogarasi, Bela. Filozófiai elöadasok es tanulmányok. Budapest, 1952.

Phil 310.30 — Andreas, Theodor. Zur Widerlegung des dialectische und historische Materialismus. 5. Aufl. n.p., 1954.

Phil 310.35 — Probleme des historische Materialismus und der marxistische Sozialismus. Berlin, 1958.

Phil 310.40 — Baumgarten, A. Bemerkungen zur Erkenntnistheorie des dialektischen und historischen Materialismus. Berlin, 1957.

Phil 310.45 — Genevès, F. L'imposture scientifique du matérialisme historique allemand. Bordeaux, 1957.

Phil 310.50 — Gropp, Rugard Otto. Der dialektische Materialismus. Leipzig, 1958.

Phil 310.50.5 — Gropp, Rugard Otto. Zu Fragen der Geschichte der Philosophie und des dialektischen Materialismus. Berlin, 1959.

Phil 310.55 — Kutasov, D.A. V chem sostoit osnovnoi vopros filosofii. Moskva, 1958.

Phil 310.60 — Fataliev, K.M. Dialekticheskii materializm i voprosy estestvoznaniia. Moskva, 1958.

Phil 310.60.5 — Fataliev, K.M. Marksistko-leninskaia filosofii i estestroznaniia. Moskva, 1960.

Phil 310.65 — Dudel, S.P. Zakony materialicheskoi dialektiki. Moskva, 1958.

Phil 310   Special philosophical topics, systems, etc. - Secondary treatises and discussions - Dialectic and Dialectical materialism - cont.

Phil 310.70 — Moscow. Gosudarstvennaia Biblioteka SSSR imeni V.I. Lenina. Chto chitat' po filosofii. Moskva, 1958.

Phil 310.75 — Pantskhava, I.D. Dialekticheskii materializm. Moskva, 1958.

Phil 310.80 — Vries, Joseph de. Die Erkenntnistheorie des dialektischen Materialismus. München, 1958.

Phil 310.85 — Tugarinov, V.P. Sootnoshenie kategorii istoricheskögo materializma. Leningrad, 1958.

Phil 310.90 — Konimunisticheskaia Partiia Sovetskogo Soiuza Vysshaia Partiinaia Shkola. Kajedra dialektiki i istoricheskogo materializme. Moskva. 1-3,1958-1963+ 3v.

Phil 310.95 — Ogiermann, H.A. Materialistische Dialektik. München, 1958.

Phil 310.100 — Mal'tsev, V.I. Problemy dialekticheskoi logikii. Moskva, 1959.

Phil 310.101 — Problemy dialekticheskoi logiki. Alma-Ata, 1968.

Phil 310.105 — Duncher, Hermann. Einführungen in den Marxismus. Berlin, 1959. 2v.

Phil 310.110 — Kelle, V.Z. Formy obshchestvennogo soznaniia. Moskva, 1959.

Phil 310.115 — Sviderskii, Vladimir Io. Protivorechivost' dvizheniia i ee proiavleniia. Leningrad, 1959.

Phil 310.117 — Sviderskii, Vladimir Io. O dialektike elementov i struktury v ob"ektivnom mire i v poznanii. Moskva, 1962.

Phil 310.118 — Sviderskii, Vladimir Io. O nekotorykh formakh protivorechivosti v ob'ektivnom mire. Leningrad, 1968.

Phil 310.120 — Ai, Ssu-ch'i. Lektsii po dialekticheskom materializme. Moskva, 1959.

Phil 310.125 — Siusiukalov, B.I. Osnovnye zotkony materialisticheskoi dialektiki. Moskva, 1958.

Phil 310.130 — Presniakov, P.V. Teoriia poznaniia dialekticheskogo materializma. Alma-Ata, 1959.

Phil 310.135 — Schaff, Adam. Z zagadnień marksistowskiej teorii prawdy. Warszawa, 1959.

Phil 310.140 — Kurella, Alfred. Der Mensch als Schöpfer seiner Selbst. Berlin, 1958.

Phil 310.145 — Nesterenko, G.I. Obshchestvennoe soznanie i ego formy. Moskva, 1959. 2 pam.

Phil 310.146 — Teriaev, G.V. Due fazy kommunisticheskogo obshchestva i zakonomernosti pererastatelnogo sotsializma v kommunizm. Moskva, 1962.

Phil 310.150 — Mal'tsev, V.I. Bor'ba v SSSR protiv mekhanitsizma. Moskva, 1959.

Phil 310.151 — Mal'tsev, V.I. Marksistskaia dialektika i sovremennyi mekhanitsizm. Moskva, 1962.

Phil 310.155 — Goldmann, Lucien. Recherches dialectiques. 2. éd. Paris, 1959.

Phil 310.155.1 — Goldmann, Lucien. Dialektische Untersuchungen. Neuwied, 1966.

Phil 310.160 — Vranicki, Predrag. Dijalektički i historijski materijalizam i oḑabrani tekstovi. Zagred, 1958.

VPhil 310.163 — Vranicki, Predrag. Čovjek i historija. Sarajevo, 1966.

Phil 310.163.5 — Vranicki, Predrag. L'uomo e la storia. Roma, 1968.

Phil 310.165 — Hager, Kurt. Der dialektische Materialismus die theoretische Grundlage der Politik der SED. 3. Aufl. Berlin, 1959.

Phil 310.170 — Karavaev, G.G. Istoricheskii materializm. Leningrad, 1959.

Phil 310.175 — Rutkevich, M.N. Dialekticheskii materializm. Moskva, 1959.

Phil 310.180 — Andreev, I.D. Osnovnye zakony i kategorii materialisticheskoi dialektiki. Moskva, 1959.

Phil 310.185 — Academia Republicci Populare Romîne. Bucuresti, 1960.

Phil 310.190 — Pfoh, Werner. Philosophie und Gesellschaft. Berlin, 1958.

Phil 310.195 — Akadamiia Nauk SSSR. Institut Filosofii. Voprosy dialekticheskogo materializma. Moskva, 1960.

Phil 310.198 — Akadamiia Nauk SSSR. Institut Filosofii. Problemy istorii filosofskoi i sotsiologicreskoi mysli XIX veka. Moskva, 1960.

Phil 310.200 — Meurers, Joseph. Wissenschaft im Kollektiv. München, 1959.

Phil 310.205 — Makarov, A.D. Dialekticheskii materializm. Moskva, 1960.

Phil 310.210 — Narskii, I.S. Marksistskoe ponimanie predmeta filosofii i pozitivizm. Moskva, 1959.

Phil 310.212 — Narskii, I.S. Problema protivoreckiia v dialekticheskoi logike. Moskva, 1969.

Phil 310.215 — Novikov, A.I. Bor'ba marksizma-leninizma protiv sovremennogo filosofskogo revizionizma. Leningrad, 1959.

Phil 310.225 — Glezerman, G.E. Ozakonakh obskchestvennogo razvitiia. Moskva, 1960.

Phil 310.225.5 — Glezerman, G.E. The laws of social development. Moscow, 196-?

Phil 310.230 — Alekseev, M.N. Dialekticheskaia logika. Moskva, 1960.

Phil 310.235 — Moroz, K.V. Dialekticheskii materializm, ideinoe oruzoiie bor'by za Kommunizm. Moskva, 1960.

Phil 310.240 — Georgiev, F.I. Kategorii materialisticheskoi dialektiki. Moskva, 1960.

Phil 310.245 — Afanas'ev, V.G. Osnovy marksistskoi filosofii. Moskva, 1960.

Phil 310.250 — Akhmedli, D. Svoboda i neobkhodimost'. Baku, 1960.

Phil 310.255 — Kosanović, I. Dijalektički materijalizam. 4. vyd. Sarajevo, 1959.

Phil 310.256 — Kosanović, I. Istoriski materijalizam. 3. izd. Sarajevo, 1960.

Phil 310.260 — Meliukhin, S.I. O dialektike razvitiia neorganicheskoi prirody. Moskva, 1960.

Phil 310.265 — Tulenov, Z. Zakon kak filosofskaia kategoriia. Alma-Ata, 1959.

Phil 310.270 — Ehlen, Peter. Der Acheismus im dialektischen Materialismus. München, 1961.

Phil 310.275 — Gak, G.M. Uchenie ob obshchestvennom soznanii v svete teorii poznaniia. Moskva, 1960.

Phil 310.280 — Schaff, Adam. Wstęp do teorii marksizmu. Warszawa, 1948.

Phil 310.285 — Dubská, Irena. K problematice stranickosti a vědeckosti marksistsko-leninskaia filosofii. Praha, 1961.

Phil 310.290 — Rozental', Mark M. Kniga dlia chteniia po marksistsko filosofii. Moskva, 1960.

Phil 310.295 — Orlov, V.V. Dialekticheskii materializm i psikhofiziologicheskaia problema. Perm, 1960.

Phil 310.300 — Frantsev, I.P. Istoricheskii materializm i sotsial'naia filosofiia sovremennoi burzhazii. Moskva, 1960.

Phil 310.305 — Andreev, I.D. Dialekticheskii materializm. Moskva, 1960.

Phil 310.310 — Mitin, M.B. Filosofiia i sovremennost'. Moskva, 1960.

Phil 310.315 — Khrestomatiia po marksistsko-leninskoi filosofii. Moskva, 1961. 3v.

Phil 310.320 — Deborin, A.M. Filosofiia i politika. Moskva, 1961.

Classified Listing

Phil 310   Special philosophical topics, systems, etc. - Secondary treatises and discussions - Dialectic and Dialectical materialism - cont.

Phil 310.325   Witt-Hansen, J. Historical materialism. Copenhagen, 1960.
Phil 310.330   Gak, G.M. Formy obshchestvennogo soznaniia. Moskva, 1960.
Phil 310.335   Kopnin, P.V. Dialektika kak logika. Kiev, 1961.
Phil 310.340   Grushin, B.H. Ocherki logiki istoricheskogo issledovaniia. Moskva, 1961.
Phil 310.345   Praktika, kriterii istiny v nauke. Moskva, 1960.
Phil 310.350   Shirokanov, D.I. Dialektika neobkhodimosti i sluchainosti. Minsk, 1960.
Phil 310.355   Zakharov, F.I. Dialekticheskii materializm i nekotorye voprosy darvinizma. Moskva, 1961.
Phil 310.360   Danilenko, D.I. Dialekticheskii materializm. Moskva, 1961.
Phil 310.365   Kalatskii, V.P. Dialekticheskogo materializm. Moskva, 1961.
Phil 310.370   Podosetnik, V.M. Chto takoe dialekticheskii i istoricheskii materializm. Moskva, 1961.
Phil 310.370.5   Podosetnik, V.M. A glance at historical materialism. Moscow, 1965.
Phil 310.375   Kechov, B.M. O povtoriaemosti v protsesse razoitiia. Moskva, n.d.
Phil 310.380   Akademiia Nauk SSSR. Kafedra Filosofii. Russkie uchenye v bor'be protiv idealizma i metafiziki vozzrenii v estestvoznanii. Moskva, 1961.
Phil 310.385   Ahlberg, René. Dialektische Philosophie und Gesellschaft in der Sowiet-Union. Berlin, 1960.
Phil 310.390   Makarov, Aleksei D. Istoriko-filosofskoe vvedenie k kursu dialektiki i istoricheskogo materializma. Moskva, 1961.
Phil 310.390.2   Makarov, Aleksei D. Istoriko-filosofskoe vvedenie k kursu marksistsko-leninskoi filosofii. 2. Izd. Moskva, 1967.
Phil 310.395   Lehév, Iwere. Iyöväenluohan maailmankatsomus. Helsinki, 1959.
Phil 310.400   Kovalgin, V.M. Marksistskaia filosofiia protiv idealizma i metafiziki. Minsk, 1961.
Phil 310.405   Gropp, R.O. Was ist der dialektische Materalismus? München, 1960.
Phil 310.410   Hrzal, L. Predmet a metoda historického materialismu. Praha, 1961.
Phil 310.415   Cvekl, Jiři. Lid a osobnost v dějrhách. Praha, 1961.
Phil 310.415.5   Cvekl, Jiři. O zákonech dějin. Praha, 1957.
Phil 310.420   Iz istorii marksistsko-leninskoi filosofii posle vtoroi mirovoi voeny. Moskva, 1961.
Phil 310.421   Iovchuk, Mikhail T. Problemy marksistsko-leninskoi filosofii. Moskva, 1965.
Phil 310.425   Vorob'ev, L.V. Osnovnye kategorii i zakony materialisticheskoi dialektiki. Moskva, 1962.
Phil 310.430   Cherkesov, V.I. Materialisticheskaia dialektika kak logika i teoria poznaniia. Moskva, 1962.
Phil 310.435   Suvorov, L.M. Bor'ba marksistsko-leninskoi filosofii v SSSR. Moskva, 1961.
Phil 310.440   Hrušovský, I. Z minulosti a sučasnosti filozofi. Bratislava, 1961.
Phil 310.445   Schaff, Adam. Marksizm i egzystencjalizm. Warszawa, 1961.
Phil 310.445.4   Schaff, Adam. A philosophy of man. London, 1963.
Phil 310.445.5   Schaff, Adam. Filozofiia człowiekas. 2. Wyd. Warszawa, 1962.
Phil 310.445.10   Schaff, Adam. Marx oder Sartre? Wien, 1964.
Phil 310.445.15   Schaff, Adam. Filozofia człowieka. 3. Wyd. Warszawa, 1965.
Phil 310.445.25   Jaroszewski, Tadeusz M. Alienacja? Warszawa, 1965.
Phil 310.447   Schaff, Adam. Marxisme et existentialisme. Paris, 1962.
Phil 310.450   Platonov, G.V. Dialekticheskii materializm i voprosy genetike. Moskva, 1961.
Phil 310.455   Titarenko, Aleksandr I. Protiv fal'sifikatsii filosofii marksizma progmatistami SShA. Moskva, 1961.
Phil 310.456   Titarenko, Aleksandr I. Pragmatistskii filemarksizm filosofiia antikommunizme. Moskva, 1964.
Phil 310.460   Oizerman, T.I. Formirovanie filosofii marksizma. Moskva, 1962.
Phil 310.465   Leningrad. Universitet. Filosofskii Fakultet. Voprosy marksistskoi sotsiologii. Leningrad, 1962.
Phil 310.470   Novinskii, I.I. Poniatie sviazi v marksistskoi filosofii. Moskva, 1961.
Phil 310.475   Leningrad. Universitet. Nekotorye voprosy dialekticheskii materializma. Leningrad, 1962.
Phil 310.480   Iurova, I.L. Dialekticheskii materializm i chastnye nauki. Moskva, 1962.
Phil 310.485   Leningrad. Universitet. Filosofskie voprosy sovremennogo ucheniia o dvizhenii v prirode. Leningrad, 1962.
Phil 310.490   Nichyk, V.M. Dialektychnyi materializm pro katenoriiu prychynnosti. Kyiv, 1960.
Phil 310.495   Kolianskii, N.N. Mir i dusha. Frankfurt am Main? 1953.
Phil 310.500   Bogdanov, I.A. Sushchnost' i iavlenie. Kiev, 1962.
Phil 310.505   Afanas'ev, Viktor G. Osnovy filosofskikh znanii. 2. izd. Moskva, 1962.
Phil 310.506   Afanas'ev, Viktor G. Osnovy filosofskikh znanii. 3. izd. Moskva, 1965.
Phil 310.507   Afanas'ev, Viktor G. Nauchnyi kommunizm. Moskva, 1966.
Phil 310.510   Akademiia Nauk SSSR. Institut Filosofi. Zakony myshleniia. Moskva, 1962.
Phil 310.511   Akademiia Nauk SSSR. Institut Filosofii. Formy myshleniia. Moskva, 1962.
Phil 310.515   Akademiia Nauk SSSR. Nauchnyi Sovet po Filosofskim Voprosam Estestvoznanie. Dialekticheskii materializm i sovremennoe estestvoznanie. Moskva, 1962.
Phil 310.517   Matetialisticheskaia dialektika i metody estestvennykh nauk. Moskva, 1968.
Phil 310.520   Voitko, V.I. Dialekticheskii i istoricheskii materializm. Kiev, 1962.
Phil 310.525   Kursanov, G.A. Dialekticheskii materializm o poniatii. Moskva, 1963.
Phil 310.527   Vasil'ev, Iu. Al. V.I. Lenin i nekotorye voprosy nauchnogo predvideniia v obshchestvennom zhizni. Minsk, 1962.
Phil 310.530   Filosofiia marksizma i neopozitivizma. Moskva, 1963.
Phil 310.535   Sarab'ianov, V.N. Dialekticheskii i istoricheskii materializm. Moskva, 1934.
Phil 310.536   Simard, É. Communisme et science. Québec, 1963.
Phil 310.540   Gabrielian, G.G. Marksistskaia logika kak dialektika i teoriia poznaniia. Erevan, 1963.
Phil 310.543   Kaprielian, Henri. Osnovy marksistskoi logiki. Erevan, 1968.
Phil 310.545   Moscow. Moskovskii Institut Inzhenerov Zheleznogo Transporta. Nekotorye voprosy teorii poznaniia dialekticheskogo materializma. Moskva, 1962.
Phil 310.550   Pamphlet vol. Dialectical materialism. 5 pam.
Phil 310.551   Tsaregorodtsev, Gennadi I. Dialekticheskii materializm i meditsina. Moskva, 1963.

Phil 310   Special philosophical topics, systems, etc. - Secondary treatises and discussions - Dialectic and Dialectical materialism - cont.

Phil 310.551.2   Tsaregorodtsev, Gennadi I. Dialekticheskii materializm i meditsina. 2. Izd. Moskva, 1966.
Phil 310.552   Kedrov, B.M. Edinstvo dialektiki, logiki i teorii poznaniia. Moskva, 1963.
Phil 310.554   Kelle, Vladislav Zh. Istoricheskii materializm; kurs lektsii. Moskva, 1962.
Phil 310.554.2   Kelle, Vladislav Zh. Kurs istoricheskogo materializma. 2. Izd. Moskva, 1969.
Phil 310.555   Chesnokov, Dimitrii I. Istoricheskii materializm. Moskva, 1964.
Phil 310.555.2   Chesnokov, Dimitrii I. Istoricheskii materializm. izd. 2. Moskva, 1965.
Phil 310.555.3   Chesnokov, Dimitrii I. Historical materialism. Moscow, 1969.
Phil 310.556   Fomina, V.A. Aktual'nye problemy istoricheskogo materializma. Moskva, 1963.
Phil 310.558   Fingert, B.A. Kratkii uchebnik istoricheskogo materializma. Leningrad, 1930.
Phil 310.560   Babosov, E.M. Dialektika analiza i sinteza v nauchnom poznanii. Minsk, 1963.
Phil 310.562   Molnár, Erik. Les antécédents idéologiques du matérialisme historique. Budapest, 1965.
Phil 310.565   Javůrek, Zdenck. Dialektika oleccného a zuláštního. Praha, 1962.
Phil 310.567   Troise, Emilio. Materialismo dialectico. Buenos Aires, 1938.
Phil 310.570   Sheputo, L.L. Voprosy dialekticheskogo materializma i meditsina. v.2. Moskva, 1963.
Phil 310.575   Spizkin, A.G. Kurs marksistskoi filosofii. Moskva, 1963.
Phil 310.580   Academia Republicii Populare Romine. Biblioteca. Materialismus dialectic si stiintele contemporane ale naturii. Bucuresti, 1963.
Phil 310.581   Academia Republicii Populare Romine. Institut de Filosofie. Dialectica materialista. Bucuresti, 1963.
Phil 310.582   Gurvich, S.S. Voprosy dialektich materializma; k lektsiiam. Kiev, 1964.
Phil 310.582.5   Dialektiko-materialisticheskii analiz osnovnykh poniatii biologii i meditsiny. Kiev, 1968.
Phil 310.583   Biriukov, B.V. Dialekticheskii materializm. Moskva, 1964.
Phil 310.584   Vserossiiskii Seminar pre Poda Vatelei po Voprosam Sovet Estestvozaniia. Dialekticheskii materializm i sovremennoe estestvoznanie. Moskva, 1964.
Phil 310.585   Kosichev, A.D. Bor'ba marksizma-leninizma s ideologiei anarkhizma i sovremennost'. Moskva, 1964.
Phil 310.586   Tlustý, V. Dialektické rozpory a jejich zakonitosti. Praha, 1962.
Phil 310.587   Marsistsko-leninskaia filosofiia; uchebnoe posobie. Moskva, 1964.
Phil 310.587.2   Marksistsko-leninskaia filosofiia. 2. Izd. Moskva, 1966.
Phil 310.587.3   Marksistsko-leninskaia filosofiia. 3. Izd. Moskva, 1968.
Phil 310.588   Hrušovský, I. Tri iniciatívy v dejinách filozofie. Bratislava, 1959.
Phil 310.589   Klofáč, Jaroslav. O rozporech ve společnosti. Praha, 1962.
Phil 310.589.8   Klofáč, Jaroslav. Materialistické pojetí dějin. Vyd. 3. Praha, 1962.
Phil 310.590   Uvarov, A.I. Leninskii printsip ob''ektivnosti v poznanii. Tomsk, 1963.
Phil 310.591   Moscow. Institut Povyshennoi Kvalifikatsii Prepodovatelei Obshchestvennykh Nauk. Kafedra Dialekticheskogo i Istoricheskogo Materializma. Voprosy istoricheskogo materializma i nauchnogo kommunizma. Moskva, 1964.
Phil 310.592   Omel'ianovskyi, M.E. Dialektika v naukakh o nezhivoi prirode. Moskva, 1964.
Phil 310.594   Sabetti, Alfredo. Sulla fondazione del materialismo storico. Firenze, 1962.
Phil 310.595   Leningrad. Universitet. Rasprostranenie idei marksistskoi filosofii v Evrope. Leningrad, 1964.
Phil 310.596   Adajnyk, Walter. Marxism and existentialism. 1. ed. Garden City, N.Y., 1965.
Phil 310.597   Polikarov, A. Materiia i poznanie. Sofiia, 1961.
Phil 310.598   Planty-Bonjour, Guy. Les categories du materialisme dialectique. Dordrecht, 1965.
Phil 310.598.2   Planty-Bonjour, Guy. The categories of dialectical materialism. Dordrecht, 1967.
Phil 310.599.2   Kosík, Karel. Dialektika konkrétního. 2. Vyd. Praha, 1965.
Phil 310.600   Bulgarska Akademiia na Naukite, Sofia. Institut po Filosofiia. Sektsiia po Dialekticheskii Materializm i Logika. Problemi na zakonite i kategoriite na dialektikata i logikata. Sofiia, 1964.
Phil 310.601   Akademiia Nauk SSSR. Institut Filosofii. Marksistsko-leninskaia filosofiia i sotsiologiia v SSSR i evropeiskikh sotsialisticheskikh stranakh. Moskva, 1965.
Phil 310.602   Černík, Václav. Dialektický vedecký zákon. Bratislava, 1964.
Phil 310.603   Silipo, Luigi. Il materialismo dialettico e storico. Padova, 1962.
Phil 310.604   Mužík, Josef. Subjekt a objekt. Praha, 1964.
Phil 310.605   Guntau, Martin. Naturforschung und Weltbild. Berlin, 1964.
Phil 310.606   Samek, Antonín. Filosofie a politika. Praha, 1963.
Phil 310.607   Akademiia Nauk SSSR. Institut Filosofii. Protiv sovremennykh burzhuaznykh fal'sifikatorov marksistsko-leninskoi filosofii. Moskva, 1964.
Phil 310.608   Kon.munisticheskaia Partiia. Sovetskogo Soiuza. Zaochnaia Vysshaia Partiinaia Shkola. Katedra Marksistsko-Leninskoi Filosofii. Marksistsko-leninskaia filosofiia. Moskva, 1965.
VPhil 310.608.5   Marksistsko-leninskaia filosofiia. Moskva, 1967. 2v.
Phil 310.608.7   Marksistsko-leninskaia filosofiia. Moskva, 1971. 2v.
Phil 310.609   Verbin, Andrei. Mesto istoricheskogo materializma v sisteme nauk. Moskva, 1965.
Phil 310.610   Horbach, U.I. O vidakh protivorechii. Minsk, 1964.
Phil 310.611   Gregor, A. James. A survey of Marxism. N.Y., 1965.
Phil 310.612   Goerlich, J. Zur Problematik der materialistische Dialektischen. Berlin, 1964.
Phil 310.613   Die Wissenschaft im Lichte des Marxismus. Zürich, 1937.
Phil 310.614   Volovik, L.A. Istina v marksistskoi i domarksovoi filosofii. Moskva, 1965.
Phil 310.615   Vislobokov, Aleksei Dmitrievich. O dialektike protsessa poznaniia prirody i kibernetika. Moskva, 1965.
Phil 310.616   Rostov on the Don, Russia. Universitet. Kafedra Dialektichnskogo i Estoricheskogo Materializma. Nekotorye voprosy istoricheskogo materializma. Rostov-na-Donn, 1962.

Classified Listing

Phil 310   Special philosophical topics, systems, etc. - Secondary treatises and discussions - Dialectic and Dialectical materialism - cont.

Phil 310.617   Sheptulin, Aleksandr P. Dialekticheskii materializm. Moskva, 1965.

Phil 310.617.5   Sheptulin, Aleksandr P. Osnovnye zakony dialektiki. Moskva, 1966.

Phil 310.617.10   Sheptulin, Aleksandr P. Sistema kategorii dialektiki. Moskva, 1967.

Phil 310.618   Fedoseev, Petr. Dialektika sovremennoi epokhi. Moskva, 1966.

Phil 310.620   Szabó, András. Man and law. Budapest, 1965.

Phil 310.621   Nový, Lubomír. Filosofie v neklidné době. Praha, 1965.

Phil 310.622   Stepanov, V.I. Dialekticheskii materializm kak metodologiia estestvennonauchnogo poznaniia. Minsk, 1965.

Phil 310.623   Soveshchanie po Sovremennym Problemam Materialisticheskoi Dialektiki. Materialy. Moskva, 1966. 4v.

Phil 310.624   Deborin, Abram M. Dialektika i estestvoznanie. Izd. 3. Moskva, 1929.

Phil 310.625   Deborin, Abram M. Filosofiia i marksizm. Moskva, 1926.

Phil 310.626   Marksizm-leninizm, teoreticheskaia osnova stroitel'stva kommunizma. Moskva, 1965.

Phil 310.627   Sviderskii, Vladimir I. Nekotorye voprosy dialektiki izmeneniia i razvitiia. Moskva, 1965.

Phil 310.628   Kommunisticheskaia Akademiia, Moscow. Institut Filosofii. Materialy nauchnoi sessii. Moskva, 1934.

Phil 310.629   Filová, Elena. Materializmus proti holizmu. Bratislava, 1963.

Phil 310.630   Sverdlin, Matvei A. Nekotorye voprosy istoricheskogo materializma i nauchnogo kommunizma. Volgograd, 1965.

Phil 310.631   González Duran, Guillermo. La dialéctica comunista a la luz de la ciencia. La Paz, 1965.

Phil 310.632   Soldatov, Vasyl' I. Problema vzaiemovidnoshennia svitohliadu i metodu v dialektychnomu materializmi. Kyiv, 1966.

Phil 310.633   Rostov on the Don, Russia. Gosudarstvennyi Pedagogicheskii. Institut Kafedra Filosofii. Voprosy dialekticheskogo i istoricheskogo materializma. Rostov-na-Donn, 1966.

Phil 310.634   Barion, Jakob. Ideologie, Wissenschatt, Philosophie. Bonn, 1966.

Phil 310.635   Kalandarishvili, Grigorii. Problema otrazheniia dvizheniia v logike poniatii. Tbilisi, 1966.

Phil 310.636   DeGeorge, Richard T. Patterns of Soviet thought. Ann Arbor, 1966.

Phil 310.637   Kuz'min, Vsevolod P. Kategoriia mery v marksistkoi dialektike. Moskva, 1966.

Phil 310.638   Andreev, Kosta. Doktor Petur Genov za marksistkata filosofiia i bolshevizma. Sofiia, 1964.

Phil 310.639   Kopnin, Pavel V. Vvedenie v marksistskuiu gnoseologiiu. Kiev, 1966.

Phil 310.640   Krasnoiarsk, Siberia (City). Gosudarstvennyi Pedagogicheskii Institut. Kafedra Filosofii. Voprosy teoreticheskogo nasledstva V.I. Lenina. Krasnoiarsk, 1966.

Phil 310.641   Historický materialismus. Praha, 1965.

Phil 310.642   Ziherl, Boris. Dijalektički i istoriski materijalizam. 2. Izd. Beograd, 1952.

Phil 310.643   Garaudy, Roger. Marxisme du XXe siècle. Paris, 1966.

Phil 310.643.1   Garaudy, Roger. Marxism in the twentieth century. London, 1970.

Phil 310.644   Bosenko, Valerii A. Dialektika kak teoriia razvitiia. Kiev, 1966.

Phil 310.645   Sichirollo, Livio. Dialejesta-Dialektik voy Homer bis Aristoteles. Hildesheim, 1966.

Phil 310.646   Braga, Joaquim. Crítica do materialismo dialéctico. Lisboa, 1966.

Phil 310.647   Rus, Vojan. Dialektika človcka, misli in sveta. Ljubljana, 1967.

VPhil 310.647.10   Rus, Vojan. Sodobna filosofija med dialektiko in metafiziko. Ljubljana, 1968.

VPhil 310.648   Šešić, Bogdan. Dijalektički materijalizam. 2. Izd. Beograd, 1967.

Phil 310.649   Problemy istoricheskogo materializma. Dushambe. 1,1967+ 2v.

Phil 310.650.3   Kubeš, Miloslav. Človek, svět a filosofie. Vyd. 3. Praha, 1968.

Phil 310.651   Nekotorye voprosy marksistsko-leninskoi filosofii. Khar'kov, 1964.

Phil 310.652A   Jordan, Zbigniew A. The evolution of dialectical materialism. London, 1967.

Phil 310.652B   Jordan, Zbigniew A. The evolution of dialectical materialism. London, 1967.

Phil 310.653   Sutlič, Vanja. Bit i suvremenost. Sarajevo, 1967.

Phil 310.654   Kompaneets, Aleksei I. Leninskaia filosofiia i progress fizicheskikh nauk. Moskva, 1967.

Phil 310.655   Zaječaranovič, Gligorije. Analiza i sinteza u okviru dijalektike Hegela i Marksa. Beograd, 1966.

Phil 310.655.5   Zaječaranovič, Gligorije. Dijalektika ljudskog sveta. Novi Sad, 1969.

VPhil 310.656   Dialekticheskii i istoricheskii materializm. Moskva, 1967.

Phil 310.656.2   Dialekticheskii i istoricheskii materializm. Izd. 4. Moskva, 1971.

Phil 310.657   Protiv fal'sifikatorov marksistsko-leninskoi filosofii (sbornik statei). Moskva, 1967.

Phil 310.658   Parniuk, Mikhail A. Determinizm dialekticheskogo materializma. Kiev, 1967.

VPhil 310.659   Marković, Mihajlo. Humanizam i dijalektika. Beograd, 1967.

Phil 310.659.7   Marković, Mihajlo. Dijalektička teorija značenja. 2. izd. Beograd, 1971.

VPhil 310.660   Problemi filozofije marksizma. Beograd, 1967.

Phil 310.661   Huber, Eduard. Um eine "dialektische Logik". München, 1966.

Phil 310.662   Dudel', Savva P. Zakon edinstva i bor'by protivopolozhnostei. Moskva, 1967.

Phil 310.663   Rogachev, Petr M. Natsii - narod - chelovechestvo. Moskva, 1967.

Phil 310.665.2   Stiehler, Gottfried. Der dialektische Widusprud. 2. Aufl. Berlin, 1967.

Phil 310.665.5   Stiehler, Gottfried. Dialektik und Praxis. Berlin, 1968.

Phil 310.666   Voprosy marksistsko-leninskoi istorii filosofii. Deroslavl', 1967.

Phil 310.668   Marxistische Philosophie. Berlin, 1967.

Phil 310.669   Nekotorye voprosy dialekticheskogo materializma i marksistskoi sotsiologii. Rostov-na-Donn, 1967.

Phil 310.670   Zelený, Jindřich. O historickém materialismu. Vyd. 1. V Praze, 1960.

Phil 310.671   Kim, Makvim P. Istoriia i kommunizm. Moskva, 1968.

Phil 310.672   Sedlák, Jaromír. Marxisticko-leninská teorie tříd a třídního boje. Vyd. 1. Praha, 1959.

Phil 310   Special philosophical topics, systems, etc. - Secondary treatises and discussions - Dialectic and Dialectical materialism - cont.

Phil 310.673   Rozhim, Vasilii P. Voprosy filosofii i sotsiologii v reskeniiekh XXIII s'ezda KPSS. Leningrad, 1968.

Phil 310.674.2   Metodicheskoe posobre po filosofii. Izd. 2. Moskva, 1968.

Phil 310.675   Shliakhtenko, Sergei G. Kategorii kachestva i kolichestva. Leningrad, 1968.

Phil 310.676   Nedeljković, Dušan. Humanizam Marksove dijalektike i dijalektike humanizma danas. Beograd, 1968.

Phil 310.677   Iakhot, Ovshii O. Ocherk marksistskoi filosofii. Moskva, 1968.

Phil 310.681   Trendafilov, Nikola. Za deistvieto na zakona za edinstvoto i borbata na protivopolozhnostite pri sotsializma. Sofiia, 1968.

Phil 310.682   Aktual'nye voprosy istorii marksistsko-leninskoi filosofii. Moskva, 1968.

Phil 310.683   Ocherki istorii marksistsko-leninskoi filosofii v Belorussii, 1919-1968. Minsk, 1968.

Phil 310.684   Voprosy na istoricheskiia materializum. Sofiia. 1,1969+

Phil 310.685   Arkhiptsev, Fedor T. V.I. Lenin o nauchnom poniatii materii. Moskva, 1957.

Phil 310.686   Rusev, Pancho. Teoriiata na otrazhenieto v domarksovata filosofiia. Sofiia, 1968.

Phil 310.686.5   Problemy otrazheniia. Moskva, 1969.

Phil 310.687   Chagin, Boris A. Sub"ektivnyi faktor. Moskva, 1968.

Phil 310.688   Problemy filosofii i sotsiologii. Leningrad, 1968.

Phil 310.689   Problemy filosofii. Alma-Ata, 1968.

Phil 310.690   Ukraintsev, Boris S. Otobrazhenie v nezhivoi prirode. Moskva, 1969.

Phil 310.692   Kirschenmann, Peter. Kybernetik, Information, Widerspiegelung. München, 1969.

Phil 310.692.5   Kirschenmann, Peter Paul. Information and reflection on some problems of cybernetics and how contemporary dialectical materialism copes with them. Dordrecht, 1970.

VPhil 310.694   Ochocki, Aleksander. Materializm historyzcny. Warszawa, 1969.

Phil 310.696.2   Historical materialism: basic problems. Moscow, 1968.

Phil 310.696.5   Problèmes fondamentaux du matérialisme historique. Moscou, 1968.

Phil 310.698   Tomášek, Ladislav. Marxisticka' dialektika a neotomizmus. Vyd. 1. Bratislava, 1967.

Phil 310.699   Petrović, Gajo. Mognénost čovjeka. Zagreb, 1969.

Phil 310.700   Lojacono, Giorgio. L'ideología marxista. Roma, 1968. 3v.

Phil 310.701   Flam, Léopold. Wording en ontbinding van de filosofie. Amsterdam, 1969.

Phil 310.702   Leninizm i filosofskie problemy sovremennosti. Moskva, 1970.

Phil 310.703   Gritsenko, Ivan I. Istoricheskoe i logicheskoe v marksistskoi filosofii. Rostov-na-Donn, 1969.

VPhil 310.704   Kusý, Miroslav. Marxistická filozofia. 2. Vyd. Bratislava, 1969.

Phil 310.705   Furman, Aleksei E. Materialisticheskaia dialektika. Moskva, 1969.

Phil 310.706   Voprosy istoricheskogo materializma i kritika nekototorykh kontseptsii burzhnaznoi sotsiologii. Moskva, 1969.

VPhil 310.708.2   Sándor, Pál. A történelmi materializmus története. 2. kiad. Budapest, 1945.

Phil 310.710   Leninskata teoriia na otrazhenieto i sovremennostta. Sofiia, 1969.

Phil 310.712   Dahm, Helmut. Meuterei auf den Knien. Olten, 1969.

Phil 310.714   Piroschkow, Vera. Freiheit und Notwendigkeit in der Geschichte; zur Kritik des historischen Materialismus. München, 1970.

Phil 310.716   Leninskii etap v razvitii marksistskoi filosofii; sbornik nauchnykh rabot kafedry filosofii. Dnepropetrovsk, 1969.

Phil 310.718   Bagirov, Z.N. V.I. Lenin i dialekticheskoe ponimanie otritsaniia. Baku, 1969.

Phil 310.720   Filosofiia i nauchnyi kommunizm. Moskva, 1968.

Phil 310.722   Nekotorye aktual'nye problemy marksistsko-leninskoi filosofii. Perm', 1968.

Phil 310.724   Voprosy filosofii. Novosibirsk, 1968.

Phil 310.725   Lutai, Vadlen Stepanovich. O metode postroeniia sistemy dialekticheskogo materializma. Kiev, 1970.

Phil 310.726   Khotiakova, Valentina Alekseevna. Chelovek i istoriia. Moskva, 1970

Phil 310.728   Congrès des Sociétés de Philosophie de Langue Française, 14th, 1969. La dialectique. 1. éd. Paris, 1969.

Phil 310.730   Hollitscher, Jakob J. Das historische Gesetz; zur Kritik der materialistischen Geschichtsauffassung von Jakob Hollitscher. Dresden, 1901.

Phil 310.732   Becker, Werner. Idealistische und materialistische Dialektik; das Verhältnis von Herrschaft und Knechtschaft bei Hegel und Marx. Stuttgart, 1970.

Phil 310.734   Goerlich, Johann Wolfgang. Semantik und dialektischer Materialismus; Darstellung und Analyse der modernen marxistisch-leninistischen Wissenschaftstheorie in der DDR. Berlin, 1969.

Phil 310.736   Rohrmoser, Günter. Das Elend der kritischen Theorie. Theodor W. Adorno, Herbert Marcuse, Jürgen Habermas. Freiburg, 1970.

Phil 310.738   Anders, Georg. Wider die Fälscher der Geschichte. München, 1958.

Phil 310.740   Pawelzig, Gerd. Dialektik der Entwicklung objektiver Systeme. 1. Aufl. Berlin, 1970.

Phil 310.742   Problema urovnei i sistem v nauchnom poznanii. Minsk, 1970.

Phil 310.744   Dialektika i sovremennol estestvoznanie. Moskva, 1970.

Phil 310.745   Georgiev, Filipp I. Problema protivorechiia. Moskva, 1969.

Phil 310.746   Fajkus, Brětislav. Existence, realita, masérie. Vyd. 1. Praha, 1969.

Phil 310.747   Teoreticheskol nasledie V.I. Lenina i meditsina. Moskva, 1970.

Phil 310.748   Kategorii dialektiki i metodologiia sovremennoi nauki. Voronezh, 1970.

Phil 310.749   Nekotorye voprosy istoricheskogo materializma i nauchnogo kommunizma. Fergana, 1969.

Phil 310.750   Iurova, Inna L. Ob otnoshenii marksistski-leninskoi filosofii k estestrosnamiu. Moskva, 1970.

Phil 310.751   Spirkin, Aleksandr G. Teoriia, preobrasui ushchaia mir. Moskva, 1968.

Phil 310.751.6   Spirkin, Aleksandr G. The basic principles of dialectical and historical materialism. Moscow, 1971.

Phil 310.752   Simpozium po Dialekticheskoi Logike, Alma-Ata, 1968. Aktual'nye problemy dialekticheskoi logiki. Alma-Ata, 1971.

Phil 310.753   Problemy istoricheskogo materializma. Moskva, 1969.

Classified Listing

Phil 310 Special philosophical topics, systems, etc. - Secondary treatises and discussions - Dialectic and Dialectical materialism - cont.

Phil 310.754 Svidenskii, Vladimir I. Novye filosofskie aspekty elementno-strukturnykh otnoshenii. Leningrad, 1970.
Phil 310.755 Filozofia marksisłowska. Wyd. 1. Warszawa, 1970.
Phil 310.756 Conz, Gianni. Introduzione a una dialettica dei complementari. Padova, 1970.
Phil 310.758 Cassa, Mario. Ragione dialettica prassi marxista e profezia cristiana. Milano, 1966.
Phil 310.759 Zel'kina, Ol'ga S. Sistemno-strukturnyi analiz osnovnykh kategorii dialektilu. Saratov, 1970.
Phil 310.760 Tierno Galvan, Enrique. Razon mecanica y razon dialectica. Madrid, 1969.
Phil 310.762 Furman, Aleksei E. Istoricheskii materializon. Moskva, 1970.
Phil 310.764 Barulin, Vladimir S. Otnoshenie material'nogo i ideal'nogo v obshchestve kak problema istoricheskogo materializma. Barnaul, 1970.
Phil 310.766.2 Steininger, Herbert. Dialektik, Wissenschaft und Waffe. 2. Aufl. Berlin, 1967.
Phil 310.768.2 Enerstvedt, Regi Th. Dialektikk og samfunnsvitenskap. 2. oppl. Oslo, 1970.
Phil 310.770 Dialekticheskii materializm i voprosy estestvosnaniia. Perm', 1969.
Phil 310.772 Iovchuk, Mikhail T. Leninism, filosofskie traditsii i sovremennost'. Moskva, 1970.
Phil 310.774 Andrade, Almir de. Ensaio critico sôbre os fundamentos da filosofia dialética. Rio de Janeiro, 1971.
Phil 310.776 Iribadzhakov, Nikolai. Leninizum, filosofiia, ideologicheska borba. Sofiia, 1970.
Phil 310.777 V.I. Lenin i metodologicheskie voprosy sovremennoi nauki. Kiev, 1971.
Phil 310.778 Simpozium po Teme Ob"ektivnye Zakony Istorii i Nauchnoe Rukovodstov Obshchestvom, Moscow, 1967. Ob"ektirnye zako istorii i nauchnoe rukovodstov obshchestvom. Moskva, 1970.
Phil 310.779 Kissel', Mikhail A. Uchenie o dialektike v burzhnarnoi filosofii XX veka. Leningrad, 1970.
Phil 310.780 Das dialektische Gesetz. 1. vyd. Bratislava, 1964.
Phil 310.782 Shchekina, Liubov' I. Poniatiia "dvizhenie" i razvitie i ikhvol' v izuchsnii fizicheskikh protsessov. Moskva, 1970.
Phil 310.784 Fleischer, Helmut. Marxismus und Geschichte. Frankfurt, 1969.
Phil 310.786 Kategoriia dialektilei kak stupeni poznaniia. Moskva, 1971.
Phil 310.788 Rodin, Davor. Dijalektika gradjanskog drustva. Beograd, 1971.
Phil 310.790 Marc, Alexandre. De la méthodologie à la dialectique. Paris, 1970.
Phil 310.792 Leninskaia kontseptsiia razvitiia. Gor'kii, 1970.
Phil 310.794 Lenin i niakoi problemi na marksistkata filosofiia. Sofiia, 1970.
Phil 310.796.2 Cvekl, Jiři. Filosofie a soucăsnost. 2. vyd. Praha, 1969.
Phil 310.798 Mitin, Mark B. V.I. Lenin i aktual'nye problemy filosofii. Moskva, 1971.
Phil 310.800 Bŭnkov, Angel I. Dialekticheskaia logika. Sofiia, 1971.
Phil 310.803 MacIntyre, Alasdair C. Marxism and Christianity. N.Y., 1968.
Phil 310.805 Negt, Oskar. Abram Deborin/Nikolai Bucharin: Kontroversen über dialektischen und mechanistischen Materialismus. Frankfurt, 1969.
Phil 310.808 Fiorani, Eleonora. Friedrich Engels e il materialismo dialettico. Milano, 1971.

hil 315 Special philosophical topics, systems, etc. - Secondary treatises and discussions - Dualism

Phil 315.1 Laurie, S.S. Metaphysica nova et vetusta. London, 1884.
Phil 315.2 Stein, L. Dualismus oder Monismus. Berlin, 1909.
Phil 315.3 Stefanescu, M. Le dualisme logique. Paris, 1915.
Phil 315.4 Brandes, Georg. Dualismen i vor nyeste philosophie. Kjobenhavn, 1866.
Phil 315.5 Vierkandt, A. Der Dualismus mi modernen Weltbild. 2. Aufl. Berlin, 1923.
Phil 315.6A Lovejoy, A.O. The revolt against dualism. Chicago, 1930.
Phil 315.6B Lovejoy, A.O. The revolt against dualism. Chicago, 1930.
Phil 315.6.3 Lovejoy, A.O. The revolt against dualism. La Salle, Ill., 1955.
Phil 315.7 Nahile, Emilia. Il dualismo nella filosofia. Napoli, 1931.
Phil 315.8 Buckham, J.W. Dualism or duality? n.p., 1913.
Phil 315.10 Pétrement, Simone. Le dualisme chez Platon. Paris, 1947.
Phil 315.12 Singer, Kent. The idea of conflict. Melbourne, 1949.
Phil 315.16 Lavergne, Bernard. Individualisme contre autoritarisme. Paris, 1959.
Phil 315.17 Waterston, G.C. Order and counter-order. N.Y., 1966.
Phil 315.19 Vries, Joseph de. Materie und Geist. München, 1970.

il 325 Special philosophical topics, systems, etc. - Secondary treatises and discussions - Empiricism

Phil 325.1 Hoppe, R. Zulänglichkeit des Empirismus...Philosophie. Berlin, 1852.
Phil 325.2 Prat, Louis. Caractére empirique et la personne. Paris, 1906.
Phil 325.3 Sacheli, C.A. Fenomenismo. Genova, 1925.
Phil 325.4 Bertrand-Barraud, D. Des bases critique d'un empirisme psychologique. Paris, 1926.
Phil 325.5 Meurer, W. Gegen den Empirismus. Leipzig, 1925.
Phil 325.6 Morris, C.W. Logical positivism, pragmatism and scientific empiricism. Paris, 1937.
Phil 325.7 Hartnack, J. Analysis of the problem of perception in British empiricism. Thesis. Copenhagen, 1950.
Phil 325.8 Maravall, Jose Antonio. Las origenes del empirismo en el pensamiento político español del siglo XVII. Granada, 1947.
Phil 325.10 Hayden Colloquium on Scientific Concept and Method, M.I.T. Evidence and inference. Chicago, 1960.
Phil 325.12 Williams, Donald Cary. Principles of empirical realism. Springfield, Ill., 1966.
Phil 325.14 Evans, John Llewelyn. The foundations of empiricism. Cardiff, 1965.
Phil 325.16 Cowley, Fraser. A critique of British empiricism. London, 1968.
Phil 325.18 Aune, Bruce. Rationalism, empiricism, and pragmatism: an introduction. N.Y., 1970.
Phil 325.20 Formigari, Lia. Linguistica ed empirismo nel Seicento inglese. Bari, 1970.
Phil 325.22 Armstrong, Robert L. Metaphysics and British empiricism. Lincoln, 1970.

Phil 330 Special philosophical topics, systems, etc. - Secondary treatises and discussions - Epistemology - Pamphlet volumes

Phil 330.1 Pamphlet vol. Epistemology and logic. 16 pam.
Phil 330.2 Pamphlet vol. Epistemology. 6 pam.
Phil 330.3 Pamphlet vol. Monographs on epistemology. 4 pam.
Phil 330.4 Pamphlet vol. Epistemology. 5 pam.
Phil 330.5 Pamphlet vol. Epistemology. German diss. 1901-1931. 14 pam.
Phil 330.6 Pamphlet vol. Epistemology. German diss. 5 pam.
Phil 330.18 Mourelos, G. L'épistémologie positive et la critique. Paris, 1962.
Phil 330.18.2 Mourelos, G. L'épistémologie positive et la critique meyersonienne. Thése. Paris, 1962.

Phil 331 - 356 Special philosophical topics, systems, etc. - Secondary treatises and discussions - Epistemology - Monographs

Phil 331.1 Abbot, F.E. Scientific philosophy. London, 1882.
Phil 331.2 Avenarius, R. Kritik der Reinen Erfahrung. Leipzig, 1888.
Phil 331.2.5 Avenarius, R. Kritik der Reinen Erfahrung. Leipzig, 1907.
Phil 331.2.8 Carstanjen, F. Richard Avenarius' Biomechanische Grundlegung. München, 1894.
Phil 331.2.9 Raab, F. Philosophie von Avenarius' Biomechanische. Leipzig, 1912.
Phil 331.2.10 Avenarius, R. Zur Terminalfunktion. Berlin, 1913.
Phil 331.2.12 Avenarius, R. Philosophie als Denken der Welt Gemäss dem Prinzip des kleinsten Kraftmasses. Leipzig, 1876.
Phil 331.2.13 Avenarius, R. Philosophie als Denken der Welt Gemäss dem Prinzip des kleinsten Kraftmasses. 3. Aufl. Berlin, 1917.
Phil 331.2.21 Avenarius, R. L'empiriocriticismo. Roma, 1909.
Phil 331.2.25 Suter, Jules. Die Philosophie von Richard Avenarius. Zurich, 1910.
Phil 331.2.30 Bush, W.T. Avenarius and the stand point of pure experience. N.Y., 1905.
Phil 331.3 Avey, Albert E. An analysis of process of conceptual cognition. Cincinnati, 1915.
Phil 331.4 Aars, Kristian B. Die idee zum ursprung des gedankens. Kristiania, 1911.
Phil 331.5 Aster, Ernst von. Prinzipien der Erkenntnislehre. Leipzig, 1913.
Phil 331.5.10 Aster, Ernst von. Geschichte der neueren Erkenntnistheorie. Berlin, 1921.
Phil 331.6 Apel, Paul. Geist und Materie. Berlin, 1905. 2v.
Phil 331.7 Aaron, R.I. The nature of knowing. London, 1930.
Phil 331.8 Abicht, J.H. Philosophie der Erkenntnisse. Pt.1-2. Bayreuth, 1791.
Phil 331.9 Anderson, J.F. The bond of being. St. Louis, 1949.
Phil 331.9.5 Anderson, J.F. Reflections on the analogy of being. The Hague, 1967.
Phil 331.10 Anglès D'Auriac. Essai de philosophie génèrale. 1. ed. Paris, 1954. 2v.
Phil 331.11 Ayer, A.J. The problem of knowledge. London, 1956.
Phil 331.12 Alquié, Ferdinand. L'expérience. Paris, 1957.
Phil 331.15 Apostel, Léo. Logique apprentissage et probabilité. Paris, 1959.
Phil 331.20 Andreev, Ivan D. Osnovy teorii poznaniia. Moskva, 1959.
Phil 331.20.5 Andreev, Ivan D. Puti i trudnosti poznaniia. Moskva, 1968.
Phil 331.21 Akadamiia Nauk SSSR. Kafedra Filosofii. Voprosy teorii poznaniia i logiki. Moskva, 1960.
Phil 331.25 Albrecht, E. Beiträge zur Erkenntnistheorie und das Verhältnis von Sprache und Denken. Halle, 1959.
Phil 331.27 Alejandro, J.M. Estudios gnoseológicos. Barcelona, 1961.
Phil 331.29 Austin, J.L. Sense and sensibilia. Oxford, 1962.
Phil 331.30 Alexander, Peter. Sensationalism and scientific explanation. London, 1963.
Phil 331.31 Adamczyk, S. Krytyka ludzkiego poznania. Wyd.1. Lublin, 1962.
Phil 331.32 Asmus, V.F. Problema intuitsii v filosofii i matematike. Moskva, 1963.
Phil 331.33 Akademiia Nauk SSSR. Institut Filosofii. Dialektika teoriia poznaniia. Moskva, 1964- 3v.
Phil 331.33.10 Akademiia Nauk SSSR. Institut Filosofii. Erkenntnistheoretische und methodologische Probleme der Wissenschaft. Berlin, 1966.
Phil 331.34 Ackermann, Robert John. Theories of knowledge. N.Y., 1965.
Phil 331.35 Abrahamian, Lev. Gnoseologicheskie problemy teorii znakov. Erevan, 1965.
Phil 331.40 Aune, Bruce. Knowledge, mind and nature. N.Y., 1967.
Phil 331.41 Abdil'din, Zhabaikhan M. Problema nachala v teoreticheskom poznanii. Alma-Ata, 1967.
Phil 332.1 Bergmann, J. Grundlinien einer Theorie des Bewusstseins. Berlin, 1870.
Phil 332.2 Bowne, B.P. Theory of thought and knowledge. N.Y., 1897.
Phil 332.3 Brodbick, A. Das Wesen des Wissens. Stuttgart, 1884.
Phil 332.4 Bon, F. Die Dogmen der Erkenntnistheorie. Leipzig, 1902.
Htn Phil 332.4.9* Bon, F. Die Grundlagen der Logik und Mathematik. n.p., 193-. 2v.
Phil 332.5 Boodin, J.E. Truth and reality. N.Y., 1911.
Phil 332.5.5 Boodin, J.E. A realistic universe. N.Y., 1916.
Phil 332.5.10 Boodin, J.E. A realistic universe. N.Y., 1931.
Phil 332.6 Baumann, J. Der Wissensbegriff. Heidelberg, 1908.
Phil 332.7 Baillie, T.B. An outline of the idealistic construction of experience. London, 1906.
Phil 332.8 Bastian, Adolf. Die Lehre von Denken zur Ergänzung. v.1-3. Berlin, 1902-05.
Phil 332.9 Betz, H.J. Ervaringswijsbegeerte. 's-Gravenhage, 1881.
Phil 332.10 Brucker, Jacob. Historia philosophica doctrinae de ideis. Augustae Vindelicorum, 1723.
Phil 332.11 Bauch, Bruno. Die Idee. Leipzig, 1926.
Phil 332.12 Baumgarten, Arthur. Erkenntnis, Wissenschaft, Philosophie. Tübingen, 1927.
Phil 332.13 Beysens, J.T. Criteriologie of de leer over waarheid en zekerheid. 2. druk. Leiden, 1911.
Phil 332.14 Brentano, Franz. Versuch über die Erkenntnis. Leipzig, 1925.
Phil 332.14.2 Brentano, Franz. Versuch über die Erkenntnis. 2. Aufl. Hamburg, 1970.
Phil 332.14.10 Brentano, Franz. Wahrheit und Evidenz. Leipzig, 1930.
Phil 332.14.11 Brentano, Franz. Wahrheit und Evidenz. Hamburg, 1962.
Phil 332.14.12 Brentano, Franz. The true and the evident. London, 1966.
Phil 332.15 Barron, J.T. Elements of epistemology. N.Y., 1931.
Phil 332.16 Bendavid, L. Über den Ursprung unserer Erkenntniss. Berlin, 1802.
Phil 332.17 Bénézé, G. Critique de la mesure. Paris, 1937.
Phil 332.18 Boldt, Karl. Die Einheit des Erkenntnisproblems. Leipzig, 1937.
Phil 332.18.5 Boldt, Karl. Die Erkenntnisbeziehung. Tübingen, 1937.

Phil 331 - 356 Special philosophical topics, systems, etc. - Secondary treatises and discussions - Epistemology - Monographs - cont.

Phil 332.19   Bachelard, Gaston. La formation de l'esprit scientifique. Photoreproduction. Paris, 1938.

Phil 332.20A   Bon, F. Von den Begriffen, den Urteilen und der Wahrheit. Leipzig, 1913.

Phil 332.20B   Bon, F. Von den Begriffen, den Urteilen und der Wahrheit. Leipzig, 1913.

Phil 332.21   Burgh, W.G. Knowledge of the individual. London, 1939.

Phil 332.22   Bowers, David F. Atomism, empiricism, and scepticism. Abstract of thesis. Princeton, 1941.

Phil 332.23   Berger, Gaston. Recherches sur les conditions de la connaissance. Paris, 1941.

Phil 332.24   Barlow, K.E. The state of public knowledge. London, 1946.

Phil 332.25   Barth, Heinrich. Philosophie Erscheinung. Basel, 1947. 2v.

Phil 332.25.2 Barth, Heinrich. Philosophie der Erscheinung. 2. Aufl. Basel, 1966-

Phil 332.26   Bollnou, Atto. Das Verstechen. Mainz, 1949.

Phil 332.27   Bechert, R. Eine Semiphilosophie im Grundriss Dargestellt. München, 1941.

Phil 332.28   Bayer, R. Epistémalogie et logique depuis Kant jusqu'a nos jours. 1. éd. Paris, 1954.

Phil 332.29   Bologna, Italo. Il pensiero filosofico ed il suo fondamento. Milano, 1957.

Phil 332.30   Brain, W.R. The nature of experience. London, 1959.

Phil 332.35   Bonilla, Abelardo. Conocimiento, verdad y belleza. San Salvador, 1958.

Phil 332.36   Bruner, J.S. On knowing. Cambridge, 1962.

Phil 332.37   Battro, Antonio M. Dictionnaire d'epistémologie génétique. Dordrecht, 1966.

Phil 332.38   Begiashvili, Archie F. Problema nachala poznaniia v B. Rassela i E. Gusserlia. Tbilisi, 1969.

Phil 332.40   Born, Friedrich Gottlab. Versuch über die ursprünglichen Grundlagen des menschlichen Denkens und die davon Abhängigen Schranken unserer Erkenntniss. Bruxelles, 1969.

Phil 332.42   Bychko, Ihor Valentynovych. Poznanie i svoboda. Moskva, 1969.

Phil 332.44   Bollnow, Otto Friedrich. Philosophie der Erkenntnis; das Vorverständnis und die Erfahrung des Neuen. Stuttgart, 1970.

Phil 333.1   Carus, C.G. Organon der Erkenntniss. Leipzig, 1856.

Phil 333.2   Caspari, O. Grundprobleme der Erkenntnis. Berlin, 1876-79. 2v.

Phil 333.3   Cohen, H. Das Princip der Infinitesimal-Methode und seine Geschichte. Berlin, 1883.

Phil 333.4   Czolbe, H. Grundzüge einer extensionalen Erkenntnisstheorie. Plauen, 1875.

Phil 333.4.5   Czolbe, H. Die Grenzen und der Ursprung der menschlichen Erkenntniss. Jena, 1865.

Phil 333.5   Cassirer, Ernst. Das Erkenntnisproblem in der Philosophie. Berlin, 1906-57. 4v.

Phil 333.5.3   Cassirer, Ernst. Das Erkenntnisproblem in der Philosophie. 2. Aufl. Berlin, 1911. 2v.

Phil 333.5.5   Cassirer, Ernst. Substansbegriff und Funktionsbegriff. Berlin, 1910.

Phil 333.5.8A Cassirer, Ernst. Substance and function and Einstein's theory of relativity. N.Y., 1953.

Phil 333.5.8B Cassirer, Ernst. Substance and function and Einstein's theory of relativity. N.Y., 1953.

Phil 333.5.9   Cassirer, Ernst. Philosophie der symbolischen Formen. Berlin, 1923-29. 3v.

Phil 333.5.10 Cassirer, Ernst. Philosophie der symbolischen Formen. Index. Berlin, 1931.

Phil 333.5.12A Cassirer, Ernst. The philosophy of symbolic forms. New Haven, 1953- 3v.

Phil 333.5.12B Cassirer, Ernst. The philosophy of symbolic forms. v.1,3. New Haven, 1953- 2v.

Phil 333.5.15 Cassirer, Ernst. An essay on man. New Haven, 1944.

Phil 333.5.17 Cassirer, Ernst. An essay on man. New Haven, 1948.

Phil 333.5.18 Cassirer, Ernst. An essay on man. New Haven, 1962.

Phil 333.5.20 Cassirer, Ernst. The problem of knowledge. New Haven, 1950.

Phil 333.6   Coursault, J.H. The learning process. Theory of knowledge. N.Y., 1907.

Phil 333.7.2   Coffey, Peter. Epistemology. Gloucester, Mass., 1958. 2v.

Phil 333.8   Cohn, Jonas. Voraussetzungen und Ziele des Erkennens. Leipzig, 1908.

Phil 333.9   Cosalini, Alessandro. Studi filosofici sulla cognizione. Roma, 1914.

Phil 333.10   Cornelius, Hans. Transcendentale Systematik. Teil 1-2. München, 1916.

Phil 333.11   Calderoni, M. La previsione nella teoria della conoscenza. Milano, 1907.

Phil 333.12   Carnap, Rudolf. Der logische Aufbau der Welt. Berlin, 1928.

Phil 333.12.2 Carnap, Rudolf. The logical structure of the world. Berkeley, 1967.

Phil 333.12.5A Carnap, Rudolf. Scheinprobleme in der Philosophie. Berlin, 1928.

Phil 333.12.5B Carnap, Rudolf. Scheinprobleme in der Philosophie. Berlin, 1928.

Phil 333.13   Conger, George P. The horizons of thought. Princeton, 1933.

Phil 333.14PF Custard, Harry L. The unity of knowledge and the organization of thought. Washington, D.C., 1940.

Phil 333.15   Coninces, A. L'unité de la connaissance humaine. Bruges, 1943.

Phil 333.16   Childe, Vere G. Society and knowledge. 1st ed. N.Y., 1956.

Phil 333.17.1 Colorado. University. Psychology Department. Contemporary approaches to cognition. Cambridge, 1968.

Phil 333.19   Cortesi, Luigi. Le vie del sapere. Milano, 1959.

Phil 333.20   Chappell, Vere C. The philosophy of mind. Englewood Cliffs, 1962.

Phil 333.21   Canfield, J.V. Readings in the theory of knowledge. N.Y., 1964.

Phil 333.22   Chuvstvennoe poznanie. Moskva, ℾ965.

Phil 333.24   Connolly, William. Political science and ideology. st ed. N.Y., 1967.

Phil 333.26   Cornforth, Maurice Campbell. The theory of knowledge. N.Y., 1955.

Phil 333.28   Chomsky, Noam. Problems of knowledge and freedom: the Russell lectures. 1st ed. N.Y., 1971.

Phil 334.1   Dippe, A. Untersuchungen über die Bedeutung der Denkform. Jena, 1893.

Phil 331 - 356 Special philosophical topics, systems, etc. - Secondary treatises and discussions - Epistemology - Monographs - cont.

Phil 334.2   Du Bois-Reymond, P. Über die Grundlagen der Erkenntnis in der exacten Wissenschaften. Tübingen, 1890.

Phil 334.3   Della certitude des connaissance humaines. Londres, 1741.

Phil 334.4   Dürr, Ernst. Erkenntnis-Theorie. Leipzig, 1910.

Phil 334.5   Dorner, August. Das menschliche Erkennen. Berlin, 1887.

Phil 334.6   Dürr, Karl. Wesen und Geschichte der Erkenntnistheorie. Zürich, 1924.

Phil 334.7   Dietzgen, J. The positive outcome of philosophy. Chicago, 1906.

Phil 334.8.5   Donat, J. Critica. 9. ed. Monachü, 1945.

Phil 334.9   Decker, H.C. Das Denken in Begriffen als Kriterium (der Menschwerdung). Oosterhout, 1963.

Phil 334.10   Dobriianov, Velichko S. Metodologicheskie problemy teoreticheskogo i istoricheskogo poznaniia. Moskva, 1968.

Phil 334.12   Dretske, Fred I. Seeing and knowing. London, 1969.

Phil 334.14   Dooyeweerd, Herman. A new critique of theoretical thought. Amsterdam, 1953-58. 4v.

Phil 334.14.10 Bruemmer, Vincent. Transcendental criticism and Christian philosophy. Franeker, 1961.

Phil 334.16   Duchenko, Mykola V. Problema ob'iekta v marksysto'ko-lenins'kvi Seorii piznanoria. Kyiv, 1970.

Phil 335.1.2A Eisler, Rudolf. Einführung in die Erkenntnis-Theorie. 2. Aufl. Leipzig, 1925.

Phil 335.1.2B Eisler, Rudolf. Einführung in die Erkenntnis-Theorie. 2. Aufl. Leipzig, 1925.

Phil 335.1.5   Eisler, Rudolf. Das Bewusstsein der Aussenwelt. Leipzig, 1901.

Phil 335.2   Eaton, R.M. Symbolism and truth. Cambridge, 1925.

Phil 335.3   Ehrlich, Walter. Das unpersonale Erlebnis. Halle, 1927.

Phil 335.3.10 Ehrlich, Walter. Das Verstehen. Zürich, 1939.

Phil 335.4   Ehrat, P. Die Bedeutung der Logik. Zittau, 1896.

Phil 335.5   Elbert, J.W. Étude sur la phénoménologie. Thèse. Nancy, 1930.

Phil 335.6   Elie, H. Le complexe significabile. Paris, 1936.

Phil 335.6.2   Elie, H. Le complexe significabile. Thèse. Paris, 1936.

Phil 335.7A   Ewing, A.C. Reason and intuition. London, 1941.

Phil 335.7B   Ewing, A.C. Reason and intuition. London, 1941.

Phil 335.8   Earle, William A. Objectivity. N.Y., 1955.

Phil 335.9   Etcheverry, Auguste. L'homme dans le monde. Paris, 1963.

Phil 335.10   Danto, Arthur Coleman. Analytic philosophy of knowledge. Cambridge, Eng., 1968.

Phil 335.11   Essler, Wilhelm Karl. Wissenschaftstheorie. v.2. Freiburg, 1971.

Phil 336.1   Fouillée, A. L'évolutionnisme des idées-forces. Paris, 1890.

Phil 336.1.4   Fouillée, A. L'évolutionnisme des idées-forces. Paris, 1906.

Phil 336.1.5   Fouillée, A. La psychologie des idées-forces. Paris, 1893. 2v.

Phil 336.1.6   Fouillée, A. Morale des idées-forces. Paris, 1908.

Phil 336.1.7   Fouillée, A. Morale des idées-forces. 2. ed. Paris, 1908.

Phil 336.1.15 Pawlicki, S. A. Fouillée's Neue Theorie der Ideenlorëfts. Wien, 1893.

Phil 336.2   Furry, W.D. The aesthetic experience. Its nature in epistemology. Baltimore, 1908.

Phil 336.3   Frischeisen-Köhler, Max. Wissenschaft und Wirklichkeit. Leipzig, 1912.

Phil 336.4   Fischer, Englebert Lorenz. Die Grundfragen der Erkenntnistheorie. Mainz, 1887.

Phil 336.5   Fonsegrive, G. Essais sur la connaissance. 2. ed. n.p., n.d. 2v.

Phil 336.6   Franceschi, A. Ensayo sobre la teoría del conocimiento. La Plata, 1925.

Phil 336.7.5   Fischer, L. The structure of thought. London, 1930.

Phil 336.8   Fondard, L. De la forme a l'idée. Marseille, 1937.

Phil 336.10   Fireman, Peter. Sound thinking. N.Y., 1947.

Phil 336.11   Froschels, Emil. The human race. N.Y., 1947.

Phil 336.11.5 Froschels, Emil. The human race, a study in the nature of knowledge. N.Y., 1947.

Phil 336.12   Fischer, Anton. Die philosophischen Grundlagen der wissenschaftlichen Erkenntnis. Wien, 1947.

Phil 336.12.2 Fischer, Anton. Die philosophischen Grundlagen der wissenschaftlichen Erkenntnis. 2. Aufl. Wien, 1967.

Phil 336.14   Fireman, Peter. Perceptualistic theory of knowledge. N.Y., 1954.

Phil 336.16   Fink, Eugen. Alles und Nichts. Den Haag, 1959.

Phil 336.17   Flach, W. Zur Prinzipienlehre der Auschauung. Hamburg, 1963.

Phil 337.1   Grimm, E. Zur Geschichte der Erkenntnis Problems. Leipzig, n.d.

Phil 337.2   Gross, Felix. Form und Materie des Erkennens. Leipzig, 1910.

Phil 337.3   Gaillard, Gaston. De l'étude des phénomènes du point de vue leur probleme particular. Paris, 1903.

Htn   Phil 337.4*   Glanvill, Joseph. The vanity of dogmatizing. London, 1661. 2 pam.

Phil 337.4.5   Glanvill, Joseph. The vanity of dogmatizing. N.Y., 1931.

Phil 337.4.6   Glanvill, Joseph. The vanity of dogmatizing. Facsimile reprints of the London editions of 1661, 1665 and 1676. Brighton, 1970.

Phil 337.5   Grung, Frants. Das Problem der Gewissheit. Heidelberg, 1886.

Phil 337.5.5   Grung, Frants. Aandslaenker. Kjøbenhavn, 1886.

Phil 337.6   Gardair, M.J. Philosophie de Saint Thomas. La connaissance. Paris, 1895.

Phil 337.7   Glondys, Viktor. Einführung in die Erkenntnistheorie. Wien, 1923.

Phil 337.8   Gurland-Eljaschoff, E. Erkenntnistheoretische Studien auf antipsychologistischer Grundlage. Bern, 1910.

Phil 337.9   Günther, E. Die ontologischen Grundlagen der neueren Erkenntnislehre. Halle, 1933.

Phil 337.10   Goldschmidt, W. Der Linguismus und die Erkenntnistheorie der Verweisungen. Zürich, 1936.

Phil 337.11   Grisebach, E. Erkenntnis und Glaube. Halle an der Saale, 1923.

Phil 337.11.5 Grisebach, E. Probleme der wirklichen Bildung. München, 1923.

Phil 337.12   Gätschenberger, R. Zeichen, die Fundamente des Wissens. Stuttgart, 1932.

Phil 337.13   Gondin, W.R. Prefaces to inquiry; a study in the origins and relevance of modern theories of knowledge. N.Y., 1941.

Phil 337.14   Guia, Michele. Storia delle science ed epistemologia. Torino, 1945.

Phil 337.15   Grassi, E. Die Einheit unseres Wirklichkeitsbildes und die Grenzen der Einzelwissenschaftes. Bern, 1951.

Phil 331 - 356   Special philosophical topics, systems, etc. - Secondary treatises and discussions - Epistemology - Monographs - cont.

Phil 337.16   Garaudy, R. La théorie matérialiste de la connaissance. 1. ed. Paris, 1953.

Phil 337.16.5   Garaudy, Roger. Die materialistische Erkenntnistheorie. Berlin, 1960.

Phil 337.17   Greeve, T.M. Moral aesthetic and religious insight. New Brunswick, N.J., 1957.

Phil 337.18   Gregoire, F. La nature du psychique. 1. ed. Paris, 1957.

Phil 337.22   Granger, Gilles Gaston. Pensée formelle et sciences de l'homme. Paris, 1960.

Phil 337.23   Goidukov, I.G. Rot' praktiki v protsesse poznaniia. Moskva, 1964.

Phil 337.24   Gallagher, K.T. The philosophy of knowledge. N.Y., 1964.

Phil 337.25   Grossmann, Reinhardt Siegbert. The structure of mind. Madison, 1965.

Phil 337.26   Giovanni, Biagio de. L'esperienza come oggettivazione. Napoli, 1962.

Phil 337.27   Grene, Marjorie. The knower and the known. N.Y., 1966.

Phil 337.28   Guilhot, Jean. Introduction à la psychiatrie de la connaissance. Paris, 1966.

VPhil 337.29   Gabryl, Franciszek. Noetyka. Vyd. 2. Lublin, 1931.

Phil 337.35   Griffiths, A. Phillips. Knowledge and belief. London, 1967.

Phil 337.37   Gnoseologicheskie problemy formalizatsii. Minsk, 1969.

Phil 337.38   Golovanov, Viacheslaw N. Zakony i sisteme naukhnogo znaniia. Moskva, 1970.

Phil 338.1   Hobhouse, L.T. Theory of knowledge. London, 1896.

Phil 338.2   Hartmann, E. von. Das Grundproblem der Erkenntnissth. Leipzig, 1889.

Phil 338.3   Hodder, A. The adversaries of the sceptic. London, 1901.

Phil 338.4   Heim, Karl. Psychologismus oder Antipsychologismus. Berlin, 1902.

Phil 338.4.5   Heim, Karl. Das Weltbild der Zukunst. Berlin, 1904.

Phil 338.5   Hamelin, O. Essai sur les elements principaux de la représentation. Paris, 1907.

Phil 338.5.2   Hamelin, O. Essai sur les elements principaux de la représentation. 2. ed. Paris, 1925.

Phil 338.6   Heymans, G. Gesetze und Elemente des wissenschaftlichen Denkens. Leipzig, 1905.

Phil 338.6.2   Heymans, G. Gesetze und Elemente des wissenschaftlichen Denkens. Leipzig, 1894.

Phil 338.6.3   Heymans, G. Die Gesetze und Elemente des wissenschaftlichen Denkens. v.1-2. Leiden, 1890-94.

Phil 338.7   Hodgson, S.H. Some cardinal points in knowledge. London, n.d.

Phil 338.8   Hocking, William E. Papers on logic and epistemology. v.1-6. N.Y., 1905.

Phil 338.10   Haldane, R.B. The reign of relativity. New Haven, 1921.

Phil 338.10.2   Haldane, R.B. The reign of relativity. 2. ed. London, 1921.

Phil 338.10.4   Haldane, R.B. Le regne de la relativité. Paris, 1922.

Phil 338.10.5   Haldane, R.B. The philosophy of humanism. New Haven, 1922.

Phil 338.11   Hartmann, N. Grundzüge einer Metaphysik der Erkenntnis. Berlin, 1921.

Phil 338.12   Helmholtz, H. Schriften zur Erkenntnistheorie. Berlin, 1921.

Phil 338.13   Höfler, Alois. Erkenntnis Probleme und Erkenntnistheorie. Leipzig, n.d.

Phil 338.14   Hoppe, J.I. Die persönliche Denkthätigkeit. Würzburg, 1880.

Phil 338.15   Heyder, Carl. Die Lehre von den Ideen. Frankfurt am Main, 1874.

Phil 338.16   Haig, J. Philosophy, or The science of truth. London, 1861.

Phil 338.17   Höffding, H. Der Relationsbegriff. Leipzig, 1922.

Phil 338.17.5   Höffding, H. Erkenntnistheorie und Lebensauffassung. Leipzig, 1926.

Phil 338.17.9   Höffding, H. Les conceptions de la vie. Paris, 1928.

Phil 338.18   Hubert, René. Le sens du réel. Paris, 1925.

Phil 338.19   Honecker, M. Das Denken. Berlin, 1925.

Phil 338.20   Hönigswald, R. Geschichte der Erkenntnistheorie. Berlin, 1933.

Phil 338.21   Hahn, Hans. Logik, Mathematik und Naturerkennen. Wien, 1933.

Phil 338.22   Hausdorff, Felix. Das Chaos im kosmischer Auslese. Leipzig, 1898.

Phil 338.23   Hermann, M. Die Bedeutung der modernen Physik für die Theorie der Erkenntnis. Leipzig, 1937.

Phil 338.24   Hawkins, D.J.B. The criticism of experience. London, 1945.

Phil 338.25   Heynig, J.G. Plato und Aristoteles. Amberg, 1804.

Phil 338.26   Harris, E.E. Nature, mind of modern science. London, 1954.

Phil 338.27   Hartland-Swann, John. An analysis of knowing. London, 1958.

Phil 338.28   Hirst, R.J. The problems of perception. London, 1959.

Phil 338.32   Husser, Friedrich F. Zu einem Prinzip der Messung. Meisenhem am Glan, 1960.

Phil 338.34   Hill, T.E. Contemporary theories of knowledge. N.Y., 1961.

Phil 338.36   Hampshire, S. Feeling and expression. London, 1961.

Phil 338.38   Halt, Everett W. Our knowledge of fact and value. Chapel Hill, 1961.

Phil 338.39   Harris, E.E. Objectivity and reason. Johannesburg, 1955.

Phil 338.40   Hintikka, K.J.J. Knowledge and belief. Ithaca, 1962.

Phil 338.41   Hutten, Ernest. The origins of science. London, 1962.

Phil 338.42   Holzkamp, Klaus. Wissenschaft als Handlung. Berlin, 1968.

Phil 338.43   Hubenko, Volodymer I. Znannia i peretvorennia diistnosti. Kyiv, 1968.

Phil 338.44   Habermas, Jürgen. Erkenntnis und Interesse. Frankfurt am Main, 1968.

Phil 338.44.1   Habermas, Jürgen. Knowledge and interests. Boston, 1971.

Phil 338.45   Haering, Theodor Lorenz. Philosophie des Verstehens. Tübingen, 1963.

Phil 338.47   Hoffman, Robert. Language, minds, and knowledge. N.Y., 1970.

Phil 338.48   Hoeres, Walter. Kritik der transzendentalphilosophischen Erkenntnistheorie. Stuttgart, 1969.

Phil 339.1   Ingarden, Roman. Über die Stellung der Erkenntnistheorie im System der Philosophie. Halle an der Saale, 1926.

Phil 339.5   Iakushevskii, I.T. Praktika i ee rol' v protsese poznaniia. Moskva, 1961.

Phil 339.10   Iliadi, A.N. Prakticheskaia priroda chelovecheskogo poznaniia. Moskva, 1962.

Phil 340.1   Jaures, J. De la réalité du monde sensible. Paris, 1902.

Phil 340.1.2   Jaures, J. De la réalité du monde sensible. Paris, 1891.

Phil 331 - 356   Special philosophical topics, systems, etc. - Secondary treatises and discussions - Epistemology - Monographs - cont.

Phil 340.2   Jaja, Donato. L'intuito nella conoscenza. Napoli, 1894.

Phil 340.3   Jacob, T. Allgemeiner Theil der Erkenntnislehre. Berlin, 1853.

Phil 340.4   Jacobson, J. Über die Beziehungen zwischen Kategorien und Urtheilsfarmen. Inaug. Diss. Königsberg, 1877.

Phil 340.5   Jacoby, P.J. "Common sense" in ePistemology. Thesis. NOtre Dame, 1942.

Phil 340.6   Jordon, Bruno. Die Ideenlehre. Leipzig, 1928.

Phil 340.7   Jacques, E. Introduction au problème de la connaissance. Louvain, 1953.

Phil 340.8   Jonckheere, A. La lecture de l'expérience. Paris, 1958.

Phil 340.9   Jones, P. Chopin. The nature of knowledge. N.Y., 1964.

Phil 341.1   Kerry, B. System einer Theorie der Grenzbegriffe. Leipzig, 1890.

Phil 341.2   Koch, Emil. Das Bewusstsein der Transcendenz. Halle an der Saale, 1895.

Phil 341.3   Kleinseter, H. Erkenntnistheorie der Naturforschung. Leipzig, 1905.

Phil 341.4   Krug, W.T. Versuch einer systematischen Enzyklopädie. Whittenberg, 1796.

Phil 341.5   Külpe, O. Erkenntnistheorie und Naturwissenschaft. Leipzig, 1910.

Phil 341.6   Kleinpeter, Hans. Der Phänomenalismus. Leipzig, 1913.

Phil 341.7   Köhler, Watther. Geist und Freiheit. Tübingen, 1914.

Phil 341.8   Kehr, Theodor. Das Bewusstseinsproblem. Tübingen, 1916.

Phil 341.9   Kern, Berthold. Das Erkenntnisproblem...kritische Lösung. Berlin, 1911.

Phil 341.10   Kastenholz, Joseph. Der Begriff des Dinges in der Philosophie der Gegenwart. Inaug. Diss. Bonn, 1916.

Phil 341.11   Kauffmann, Max. Fundamente der Erkenntnistheorie und urssenschaftslehre. Leipzig, 1890.

Phil 341.13   Kynast, R. Das Problem der Phänomenologie. Breslau, 1917.

Phil 341.14   Keyserling, H. Graf von. Schöpferische Erkenntnis. Darmstadt, 1922.

Phil 341.14.5   Keyserling, H. Graf von. Creative understanding. N.Y., 1929.

Phil 341.15   Koch, Julius L. Erkenntnistheoretische Untersuchaungen. Göppingen, 1883.

Phil 341.16   Kruse, F.V. The foundation of human thought. London, 1949.

Phil 341.16.5   Kruse, F.V. Erkendelseslaeren og naturvidenskabens grundbegreber. København, 1960.

Phil 341.16.10   Kruse, F.V. Erkenntnis und Wertung; das Grundproblem. Berlin, 1960.

Phil 341.18   Kurth, R. Vonden Grenzen des Wissens. München, 1953.

Phil 341.20   Krapice, M.A. Realizm ludzkiego poznania. Poznań, 1959.

Phil 341.22   Kaufman, G.D. Relativism, knowledge and faith. Chicago, 1960.

Phil 341.25   Krausser, Peter. Untersuchuugen über den grundsatzlichen Auspruch der Wahrnehmung. Meisenheim am Glan, 1959.

Phil 341.30   Kalinowski, J. Teoria poznania praktycznego. Lublin, 1960.

Phil 341.32   Kraft, Victor. Erkenntnislehre. Wien, 1960.

Phil 341.34   Kurazhkovskaia, E.A. Dialektika protsessa poznaniia. Moskva, 1960.

Phil 341.35   Knowledge of other minds. Lahore, 1959.

Phil 341.36   Khaskhachikh, Fedor I. Voprosy teorii poznaniia dialekticheskogo materializma. Moskva, 1967.

Phil 341.37   Klein, Martin. Der zerstückelte Gott. München, 1967.

Phil 341.38   Kevorkian, Hamlet. Veroiatnoe i dostovernoe znanie. Erevan, 1965.

Phil 341.39   Kuemmel, Friedrich. Platon und Hegel zur ontologischen Begründung des Zirkels in der Erkenntnis. Tübingen, 1968.

Phil 341.42   Kraus, Hermann. Der Geist als Materie in Gehirnphysiologie und Kausalitätstheorie. Nurnberg, 1963.

Phil 341.44   Kanak, Fedvi M. Sub'ieks, ob'iekt i fizychne piznannia. Kyïv, 1970.

Phil 342.1   Ladd, G.T. Philosophie of knowledge. N.Y., 1897.

Phil 342.2   Leder, H. Untersuchungen über Augustins Erkenntnistheorie. Warburg, 1901.

Phil 342.3   Losskii, N. Die Grundlegung des Intuitivismus. Halle, 1908.

Phil 342.3.5   Losskii, N. The intuitive basis of knowledge. London, 1919.

Phil 342.3.10   Losskii, N. L'intuition, la matière et la vie. Paris, 1928.

Phil 342.4   Levy, Heinrich. Über die apriorischen Elemente. Leipzig, 1914.

Phil 342.5   Linke, Paul F. Die phänomenale Sphäre und das Bewusstsein. Halle an der Saale, 1912.

Phil 342.6   Lemaire, J. Notes complementiares sur une thèorie de la connaissance sensible. Bruges, 1923.

Phil 342.7   Leser, Hermann. Einfuhrung in die Grundprobleme der Erkenntnistheorie. Leipzig, 1911.

Phil 342.8   Lagerborg, R. Vetenskapliga vanföreställningars. Helsingfors, 1920.

Phil 342.9   Liljeckrantz, B. Ur världoförklaringarnas och kunskapsteoriernas urkunder. Stockholm, 1921.

Phil 342.10   Leclère, Albert. Essai critique sur le droit d'affirmer. Paris, 1901.

Phil 342.11   Lambek, C. Track af vor erkendelses psykologi. København, 1925.

Phil 342.11.5   Lambek, C. Essay on the foundation of cognition. Copenhagen, 1935.

Phil 342.12   Lipps, Hans. Untersuchungen zur Phänomenologie der Erkenntnis. v.1-2. Bonn, 1927-28.

Phil 342.13A   Lewis, Clarence I. Mind and the world-order. N.Y., 1929.

Phil 342.13B   Lewis, Clarence I. Mind and the world-order. N.Y., 1929.

Phil 342.13.5A   Lewis, Clarence I. An analysis of knowledge and value. La Salle, Ill., 1946.

Phil 342.13.5B   Lewis, Clarence I. An analysis of knowledge and value. La Salle, Ill., 1946.

Phil 342.13.10A   Lewis, Clarence I. Mind and the world-order. N.Y., 1956.

Phil 342.13.10B   Lewis, Clarence I. Mind and the world-order. N.Y., 1956.

Phil 342.14   Laird, John. Knowledge, belief and opinion. N.Y., 1930.

Phil 342.15   Lion, Alene. Anaknisses and the a priori. Oxford, 1935.

Phil 342.16   Lubboch, J.W. Remarks on the classification of the different branches of human knowledge. London, 1838.

Phil 342.17   Litt, Theodor. Denken und Sein. Stuttgart, 1948.

Phil 342.18.2   Lonergan, Bernard J.F. Insight. N.Y., 1964.

Phil 342.19   Lowenberg, Jacob. Reason and the nature of things. La Salle, Ill., 1959.

Phil 342.20   Leary, Lewis. The unity of knowledge. Garden City, N.Y., 1955.

Phil 342.26   Landesman, Charles. The foundations of knowledge. Englewood Cliffs, 1970.

Phil 342.28	Levin, Grigorii Aronovich. V.I. Lenin i sovremennye problemy teorii poznaniia. Minsk, 1970. 9v.
Phil 342.30	Ławniczak, Włodzimierz. O uzasadniającej roli analogii na przykładzie wnioskowań z zakresu historii sztaki. Poznań, 1971.
Phil 343.1	Mayer, A. Die Lehre von der Erkenntniss. Leipzig, 1875.
Phil 343.2	Mivart, G. The groundwork of science. N.Y., 1898.
Phil 343.3	Montgomery, G.R. The place of values. Bridgeport, 1903.
Phil 343.4	Mach, E. Erkenntnis und Irrtum. Leipzig, 1905.
Phil 343.4.3	Mach, E. Erkenntnis und Irrtum. 2. Aufl. Leipzig, 1906.
Phil 343.4.5	Mach, E. La connaissance et l'erreur. Paris, 1908.
Phil 343.4.6	Mach, E. Die Leitgedanken meiner naturwissenschaftlichen Erkenntnislehre und ire Aufnahme durch die Zeitenossen. Leipzig, 1919.
Phil 343.4.9	Schultz, R. Die Machsche Erkenntnistheorie. Berlin, n.d.
Phil 343.5	Meinong, A. Über Annahmen. Leipzig, 1902.
Phil 343.5.2	Meinong, A. Über Annahmen. 2. Aufl. Leipzig, 1910.
Phil 343.5.9	Meinong, A. Über die Stellung der Gegenstand Theorie im System der Wissenschaften. Leipzig, 1907.
Phil 343.5.15	Meinong, A. Über die Erfahrungsgrundlagen unseres Wissens. Berlin, 1906.
Phil 343.5.19	Meinong, A. Gesammelte Abhandlungen. Leipzig, 1913. 2v.
Phil 343.5.25	Meinong, A. Über Möglichkeit und Wahrscheinlichkeit. Leipzig, 1915.
Phil 343.5.50	Kerler, D.H. Über Annahmen; eine Streitschrift. Ulm, 1910.
Phil 343.6	Macintosh, D.C. Problem of knowledge. N.Y., 1915.
Phil 343.7	Messer, August. Einführung in die Erkenntnistheorie. Leipzig, 1912.
Phil 343.8	Maréchal, J. Le point de départ de la métaphysique. v.1-5. Bruges, 1922-47. 3v.
Phil 343.9	Merton, Adolf. Gedanken über Grundprobleme der Erkenntnistheorie. München, 1916.
Phil 343.10	Metzger, Arnold. Untersiechungen zur Frage die Differenz der Phänomenologie und des Kantianismus. Jena, 1915.
Phil 343.10.5	Metzger, Arnold. Phänomenologie und Metaphysik. Halle an der Saale, 1933.
Phil 343.11	Müller-Freienfels, R. Irrationalismus. Leipzig, 1922.
Phil 343.12	Mayer, J.V. Der welthistorische Prozess als die unzige Grundlage der Philosophie. Freiburg, 1857.
Phil 343.13A	Montague, William P. The ways of knowing. London, 1925.
Phil 343.13B	Montague, William P. The ways of knowing. London, 1925.
Phil 343.14	Meurer, W. Ist Wissenschaft überhaupt Möglich? Leipzig, 1920.
Phil 343.14.10	Meurer, W. Selbsterkenntnis. Berlin, 1931.
Phil 343.15	Mochi, Alberto. La connaissance scientifique. Paris, 1927.
Phil 343.15.5	Mochi, Alberto. De la connaissance à l'action. Paris, 1928.
NEDL Phil 343.16	Meyerson, Émile. Identité et réalité. Paris, 1908.
Phil 343.16.5	Meyerson, Émile. Identité et réalité. 2. éd. Paris, 1912.
Phil 343.16.10	Meyerson, Émile. Identity and reality. London, 1930.
Phil 343.16.11	Meyerson, Émile. Identité et réalité. 4. éd. Paris, 1932.
Phil 343.16.12	Meyerson, Émile. Identité et réalité. 5. éd. Paris, 1951.
Phil 343.16.15	Meyerson, Émile. Identität und Wirklichkeit. Leipzig, 1930.
Phil 343.16.16	Meyerson, Émile. Identity and reality. N.Y., 1962.
Phil 343.16.25	Meyerson, Émile. Du cheminement de la pensée. Paris, 1931. 3v.
Phil 343.17	Marcel, Victor. De l'activité purement immanente. Thèse. Nancy, 1932.
Phil 343.18	Mukerji, A.C. Self, thought and reality. Allahabad, 1933.
Phil 343.18.5	Mukerji, A.C. Thought and reality. Allahabad, 1930.
Phil 343.18.9	Mukerji, A.C. The nature of self. Allahabad, 1938.
Phil 343.19	Meisner, E. Erkenntniskritische Weltanschauung. Leipzig, 1936.
Phil 343.20	Miller, H. History and science. Berkeley, 1939.
Phil 343.21A	Moore, George E. Proof of an external world. London, 1939.
Phil 343.21B	Moore, George E. Proof of an external world. London, 1939.
Phil 343.22	Murphy, A.E. The uses of reason. N.Y., 1943.
Phil 343.23	Mack, R.D. The appeal to immediate experience. N.Y., 1945.
Phil 343.24	Morot, E. La pensée negative. Thèse. Paris, 1947.
Phil 343.25	Mouloud, N. Formes structurées et modes productifs. Paris, 195-?
Phil 343.26	Mayz Vallenilla, E. Ontologia del conocimiento. Caracas, 1960.
Phil 343.28	Martel, K. Podstawowe zagadnienia marksistowskiej teorii poznania. Warszawa, 1961.
Phil 343.30	Malcolm, N. Knowledge and certainty. Englewood Cliffs, 1963.
Phil 343.31	Millán Puellas, A. La función social de los saberes liberales. Madrid, 1961.
Phil 343.32	Martin Scheerer Memorial Meetings on Cognitive Psychology. University of Kansas, 1962. Cognition: theory, research, promise. N.Y., 1964.
Phil 343.33	Mandelbaum, M.H. Philosophy, science, and sense perception. Baltimore, 1964.
Phil 343.34	Mesthene, Emmanuel G. How language makes us know. The Hague, 1964.
Phil 343.35	Murphy, Arthur Edward. The theory of practical reason. La Salle, Ill., 1964[1965]
Phil 343.37F	MacLeod, Andries Hugo Donald. De psykiska företeelsernas förhallande till rum och tid. Stockholm, 1964.
Phil 343.38	Miani, Vincenzo. Problemi di gnoseologia e metafisica. Zürich, 1966.
Phil 343.40	Martins, Diamantino. Teoria do conhecimento. Braga, 1957.
Phil 343.45.5	Morandini, Francesco. Critica. 5. ed. Romae, 1963.
Phil 343.50	Mathieu, Vittorio. Il problema dell'esperienza. Trieste, 1963.
Phil 343.55	McInerny, Ralph M. Studies in analogy. The Hague, 1969.
Phil 343.56	Mamardashvili, M.K. Formy i soderzhanie mephleniia. Moskva, 1968.
Phil 343.60	Mercier, André. Erkenntnis und Wirklichkeit. Bern, 1968.
Phil 343.65	Moscato, Alberto. Ricerche sulla struttura della conoscenza formale. Milano, 1962.
Phil 344.1	Nelson, L. Über das sogenannte Erkenntnisproblem. Göttigen, 1908.
Phil 344.3	Nink, Caspar. Grundlegung der Erkenntnistheorie. Frankfurt am Main, 1930.
Phil 344.4	Negley, Glenn. The organization of knowledge...philosophical analysis. N.Y., 1942.
Phil 344.5	Nagel, Ernest. Meaning and knowledge. N.Y., 1965.

Phil 344.6	Nikitin, Evgenii P. Ob"iasnenie - funktsiia nauki. Moskva, 1970.
Phil 344.7	Nauchnoe otknjtie i ego vospriiatie. Moskva, 1971.
Phil 345.1	Ormond, A.T. Foundations of knowledge. London, 1900.
Phil 345.2	Ostwald, N. Die Wissenschaft. Leipzig, 1911.
Phil 345.3	Overhuber, H.E. Die Geltungsgrundlagen metaphysicher Urteile. München, 1928.
Phil 345.4	Ostler, H. Die Realität der Aussenwelt. Paderborn, 1912.
Phil 345.5	O'Neill, Reginald. Theories of knowledge. Englewood Cliffs, N.J., 1960.
Phil 345.6	Orlov, V.V. Osobennosti chuvstvennogo poznaniia. Perm, 1962.
Phil 346.1	Proelss, K.R. Vom Ursprung der Menschlichen Erkenntnis. Leipzig, 1879.
Phil 346.2	Petzoldt, J. Einführung in die Philosophie der reinen Erfahrung. v.1-2. Leipzig, 1900.
Phil 346.3	Philip, A. The dynamic foundation of knowledge. London, 1913.
Phil 346.3.5	Philip, A. Essays towards a theory of knowledge. London, 1915.
Phil 346.4	Pichler, H. Möglichkeit und Widerspruschlosigkeit. Leipzig, 1912.
Phil 346.4.5	Pichler, H. Über die Erkennbarkeit. Wien, 1909.
Phil 346.5	Piat, Clodius. L'intelligence et la vie. Paris, 1915.
Phil 346.6	Paoli, Giulio C. Considerazioni filosofiche sulla dottrina della conoscenza. Milano, 1911.
Phil 346.7	Petronievics, B. Prinzipien der Erkenntnislehre. Berlin, 1900.
Phil 346.8	Porten, Max von der. Entstehen von Empfindung und bewisstsein. Leipzig, 1910.
Phil 346.9	Portius, K.N. Ueber den Ursprung der Begriffe. Leipzig, 1848.
Phil 346.10	Piper, H. Prinzipielle Grundlagen. Göttingen, 1916.
Phil 346.11	Polak, L. Kennisleer contra materié-realisme. Amsterdam, 1912.
Phil 346.12	Phalén, Adolf. Beitrage zur Klärung des Begriffs. Uppsala, 1913.
Phil 346.13	Pos, Hendrik J. Filosofie der Wetenschappen. Arnhem, 1940.
Phil 346.14	Price, Henry H. Thinking and representation. London, 1946.
Phil 346.15	Pétrin, Jean. Connaissance spéculative et connaissance pratique. Ottawa, 1948.
Phil 346.16	Prichard, H.A. Knowledge and perception. Oxford, 1950.
Phil 346.17	Piaget, Jean. Introduction à l'épistémologie génétique. 1. éd. Paris, 1950. 3v.
Phil 346.17.5	Piaget, Jean. Biologie et connaissance, essai sur les relations entre les régulations organiques et les processus cognitifs. Paris, 1967.
Phil 346.18	Pardo, R. Del origen a la escencia del conocimiento. Buenos Aires, 1954.
Phil 346.19	Pap, Arthur. Analytische Erkenntnistheorie. Wien, 1955.
Phil 346.19.5	Pap, Athur. Semantics and necessary truth. New Haven, 1958.
Phil 346.20	Polanyi, Michael. Personal knowledge. London, 1958.
Phil 346.20.3	Polanyi, Michael. Personal knowledge. Chicago, 1960.
Phil 346.20.4	Polanyi, Michael. Personal knowledge towards a post-critical philosophy. Chicago, 1968[1958]
Phil 346.20.5A	Polanyi, Michael. The study of man. London, 1959.
Phil 346.20.5B	Polanyi, Michael. The study of man. London, 1959.
Phil 346.20.10	Polanyi, Michael. The tacet dimension. 1. ed. Garden City, N.Y., 1966.
Phil 346.20.15	Polanyi, Michael. Knowing and being. London, 1969.
Phil 346.22	Pasck, Alan. Experience and the analytic. Chicago, 1958.
Phil 346.26	París, Carlos. Ciencia. Santiago, 1957.
Phil 346.27	Popper, Karl Raimund. On the sources of knowledge and of ignorance. London, 1960.
Phil 346.27.5	Popper, Karl Raimund. Conjectures and refutations. N.Y., 1962.
Phil 346.27.8	Popper, Karl Raimund. Conjectures and refutations: the grouth of scientific knowledge. 3. ed. London, 1969.
Phil 346.28	Pasquinelli, Alberto. Nuevi principi di epistemología. Milano, 1964.
Phil 346.29	Powell, Betty. Knowledge of actions. London, 1967[1966]
Phil 346.30	Pape, Ingetrud. Tradition und Transformation der Modalitat Habilitationschrift. Hamburg, 1966-
Phil 346.31	Ponomarev, Iakov A. Psikhika i intuitsiia. Moskva, 1967.
Phil 346.32	Pondey, Rajendra Prasad. The problem of fact. Santiniketan, 1965.
Phil 346.33	Problemy poznaniia sotsial'nykh iavlenii. Moskva, 1968.
Phil 346.34	Podhorytov, Gennadii A. Istorizm kak metod nauchnogo poznaniia. Leningrad, 1967.
Phil 346.36	Puntel, L. Analogie und Geschichtlichkeit. Freiburg, 1969.
Phil 346.38	Pears, David Francis. What is knowledge? N.Y., 1971.
Phil 348.1	Ramsay, G. Instinct and reason. London, 1862.
Phil 348.2	Reinhold, C.E. Grundzüge...Erkenntnisslehre. Schleswig, 1822.
Phil 348.3	Ribot, T. L'évolution des idées générales. Paris, 1897.
Phil 348.3.4	Ribot, T. L'évolution des idées générales. 4. éd. Paris, 1915.
Phil 348.3.5	Ribot, T. Evolution of general ideas. Chicago, 1899.
Phil 348.4	Rehmke, J. Philosophie als Grundwissenschaft. Leipzig, 1910.
Phil 348.4.2	Rehmke, J. Philosophie als Grundwissenschaft. 2. Aufl. Leipzig, 1929.
Phil 348.4.3	Rehmke, J. Anmerkungen zur Grundwissenschaft. 2. Aufl. Leipzig, 1925.
Phil 348.4.5	Rehmke, J. Die Welt als Wahrnehmung und Begriff. Berlin, 1880.
Phil 348.4.80	Palmoe, E. Indledning til filosofi som grundvidenskab efter Johs. København, 1954.
Phil 348.5	Reininger, R. Philosophie des Erkennens. Leipzig, 1911.
Phil 348.5.5	Reininger, R. Das psycho-physische Problem. Wien, 1916.
Phil 348.6	Ratzenhofer, Gustav. Die Kritik des Intellects. Leipzig, 1902.
Phil 348.7.3	Rougier, Louis. Les paralogismes du rationalisme. Thèse. Paris, 1920.
Phil 348.7.5	Rougier, Louis A.P. Traité de la connaissance. Paris, 1955.
Phil 348.8	Rogers, A.K. What is truth? New Haven, 1923.
Phil 348.9	Rickert, H. Der Gegenstand der Erkenntnistheorie. 4. und 5. Aufl. Tübingen, 1921.
Phil 348.10	Reisner, E. Das Selbstopfer der Erkenntnis. München, 1927.

Phil 348.12   Roux, Antoine. Le problème de la connaissance. Paris, 1930.

Phil 348.13   Reichenbach, Hans. Experience and prediction. Chicago, 1938.

Phil 348.14   Raretz, Karl von. Au den Quellen unseres Denkens. Wien, 1937.

Phil 348.15   Riveline, M. Essai sur le problème le plus général, action et logique. Thèse. Paris, 1939.

Phil 348.16   Roque Pascual, R. Logical analysis of fictionalism with respect to the theory of truth. Chicago, Ill., 1940.

Phil 348.17   Riet, G. van. L'épistémologie thomiste. Louvain, 1946.
Phil 348.17.5 Riet, G. van. Problèmes d'épistémologie. Louvain, 1960.
Phil 348.18   Regnéll, Hans. Symbolization and fictional reference. Lund, 1949.

Phil 348.19   Rizzi, Erminio. L'esperienza e la sua possibilita. Padova, 1958.

Phil 348.19.10 Rizzi, Erminio. Il progresso delle conoscenze umane. Padova, 1967.

Phil 348.20   Reid, L.A. Ways of knowledge and experience. London, 1961.

Phil 348.22   Rozental, M.M. Qué es la teoria Marxista del conocimiento. Santiago, 1962.

Phil 348.24   Riet, G. van. Thomistic epistemology. St. Louis, 1963. 2v.

Phil 348.25   Ross, Jacob Joshua. The appeal to the given. London, 1970.

Phil 348.26   Reinisch, Leonhard. Grenzen der Erkenntnis. Freiburg, 1969.

Phil 349.1   Schubert-Soldern, R. von. Grundlagen einer Erkenntnisstheorie. Leipzig, 1884.

Phil 349.2   Sengler, J. Erkenntnisslehre. Heidelberg, 1858.
Phil 349.3   Spicker, G. Kant, Hume und Berkeley. Berlin, 1875.
Phil 349.4   Steiner, R. Die Grundfrage der Erkenntnisstheorie. n.p., 1891.

Phil 349.5   Schmitz-Dumont, O. Die mathematischen Elemente der Erkenntnisstheorie. Berlin, 1878.

Phil 349.6   Skrochowski, F. Human knowledge. Cnacow, 1893.
Phil 349.7   Störring, G. Einführung in die Erkenntnistheorie. Leipzig, 1909.

Phil 349.8   Prudhomme, Sully. Que Sais-je? Paris, 1896.
Phil 349.9   Schlick, Moritz. Allgemeine Erkenntnislehre. Berlin, 1918.

Phil 349.9.10 Schlick, Moritz. Sur le fondement de la connaissance. Paris, 1935.

Phil 349.10   Schuppe, W. Grundriss der Erkenntnistheorie und Logik. 2. Aufl. Berlin, 1910.

Phil 349.10.5A Schuppe, W. Grundriss der Erkenntnistheorie und Logik. Berlin, 1894.

Phil 349.10.5B Schuppe, W. Grundriss der Erkenntnistheorie und Logik. Berlin, 1894.

Phil 349.11   Smith, Walter. Methods of knowledge. N.Y., 1899.
Phil 349.12   Schwartzkopff, P. Das Wesen der Erkenntnis. Heidelberg, 1909.

Phil 349.12.5 Schwartzkopff, P. Was ist Denken? Wernigerode, 1906.
Phil 349.13   Stadler, A. Grundbegriffe der Erkenntnis. Leipzig, 1918.
Phil 349.13.2 Stadler, A. Die Grundbegriffe der Erkenntnis. Leipzig, 1913.

Phil 349.14   Schultz, J. Die drei Welten der Erkenntnistheorie. Göttingen, 1907.

Phil 349.15   Siegel, Carl. Zur Psychologie und Theorie der Erkenntnis. Leipzig, 1903.

Phil 349.16   Stein, Heinrich. Ueber Wahrnehmung. Berlin, 1877.
Phil 349.17   Shann, George. The evolution of knowledge. London, 1922.
Phil 349.18   Schaaf, Juluis Jakob. Über Wissen und Selbstbewisstsein. Stuttgart, 1947.

Phil 349.19   Sauerbeck, E. Vom Wesen der Wissenschaft. Leipzig, 1914.
Phil 349.20   Schultz, Julius. Die Maschinen-Theorie des Lebens. Göttingen, 1909.

Phil 349.20.5 Schultz, Julius. Die Maschinen-Theorie des Lebens. 2. Aufl. Leipzig, 1929.

Phil 349.20.25 Ditz, Erwin. Der Begriff der Maschine bei Julius Schultz. Inaug. Diss. Leipzig, 1935.

Phil 349.21   Strong, C.A. A theory of knowledge. N.Y., 1923.
Phil 349.22   Czernovitz. Gymnasium. Xenia Czernowiciensia. Czernowitz, 1900.

Phil 349.23   Switalski, B.N. Probleme der Erkenntnis. v.1-2. Münster in Westfalen, 1923.

Phil 349.24   Scheler, Max. Die Formen des Wissens und die Bildung. Bonn, 1925.

Phil 349.24.5 Scheler, Max. Die Wissensformen und die Gesellschaft. Leipzig, 1926.

Phil 349.25   Silfverberg, K.W. Der Wirklichkeitsdualismus. Helsingfors, 1912.

Phil 349.26   Suabedissen, D.T.A. Resultate des philosophischen Forschungen über...Erkenntnis. Marburg, 1805.

Phil 349.27   Schunck, Karl. Verstehen und Einsehen. Halle an der Saale, 1926.

Phil 349.28A   Smith, Norman K. Prolegomena to idealist theory of knowledge. London, 1924.

Phil 349.28B   Smith, Norman K. Prolegomena to idealist theory of knowledge. London, 1924.

Phil 349.29   Stern, Günther. Über das Haben. Bonn, 1928.
Phil 349.30   Salomaa, J.E. The category of relation. Helsinki, 1929.
Phil 349.31   Stürmann, J.F. Untersuchungen über das Wesen der philosophischen Erkenntnis. Inaug. Diss. Münster in Westfalen, 1931.

Phil 349.32   Stace, W.T. Theory of knowledge and existence. Oxford, 1932.

Phil 349.33   Sanford, H.W. Concerning knowledge. N.Y., 1935. 2v.
Phil 349.34   Swabey, William C. Being and being known. N.Y., 1937.
Phil 349.35   Schmidt, Franz. Kleine Logik der Geisteswissenschaften. München, 1938.

Phil 349.36   Stumpf, Karl. Erkenntnislehre. Bd. I-II. Leipzig, 1939-1940.

Phil 349.37   Schwarz, Baldwin. Der Irrtum in der Philosophie. Münster, 1934.

Phil 349.38   Smith, A.H. A treatise on knowledge. Oxford, 1943.
Phil 349.39.4 Steenberghen, Fernand van. Épistémologie. 4e éd. Paris, 1965.

Phil 349.39.5 Steenberghen, Fernand van. Épistémologie. 2e éd. Louvain, 1947.

Phil 349.39.6 Steenberghen, Fernand van. Épistémologie. 3e éd. Louvain, 1956.

Phil 349.40   Sinclair, W.A. The conditions of knowing. London, 1951.
Phil 349.41   Stark, Werner. The sociology of knowledge. London, 1958.
Phil 349.41.2 Stark, Werner. The sociology of knowledge. Glencoe, 1958.

Phil 349.41.3 Stark, Werner. The sociology of knowledge. London, 1960.
Phil 349.42   Schneider, Friedrich. Die haupt Probleme der Erkenntnistheorie. München, 1959.

Phil 349.42.5 Schneider, Friedrich. Kennen und Erkennen. 2. Aufl. Bonn, 1967.

Phil 349.43   Stempkovskaia, V.I. O roli abstraktsnii v poznanii. Moskva, 1959.

Phil 349.44   Sellars, W. Science, perception, and reality. London, 1963.

Phil 349.45   Shtoff, V.A. Rol' modelei v poznanii. Leningrad, 1963.
Phil 349.46   Stachowiak, Herbert. Denken und Erkennen im kybernetischen Modell. Wien, 1965.

Phil 349.47   Swartz, Robert Jason. Perceiving, sensing, and knowing. 1. ed. Garden City, N.Y., 1965.

Phil 349.48   Sikora, Joseph John. The Christian intellect and the mystery of being. The Hague, 1966.

Phil 349.52   Selvaggi, Filippo. Scienza e methologia; saggi de epistemologia. Roma, 1962.

Phil 349.54   Semerari, Giuseppe. La lotta per la scienza. 1. ed. Milano, 1965.

Phil 349.58   Study Group on the Unity of Knowledge. The anatomy of knowledge. Amherst, 1969.

Phil 349.61   Sukhotin, Anatoli K. Gnoselogicheskii analiz em kosti znaniia. Tomsk, 1968.

Phil 349.65   Schrag, Calvin Orville. Experience and being. Evanston, Ill., 1969.

Phil 349.70   Sarti, Sergio. Io cogitante ed io problematico. Brescia, 1969.

Phil 349.75   Stillwater Conference on the Nature of Concepts, their Structure and Social Inter-relation, Oklahoma Agricultural and Mechanical College, 1950. The nature of concepts, their inter-relation and role in social structure. Stillwater, Oklahoma, 1950.

Phil 349.80   Stroll, Avrum. Epistemology; new essays in the theory of knowledge. N.Y., 1967.

Phil 349.85   Studies in the theory of knowledge. Oxford, 1970.
Phil 349.90   Sadovskii, Grigorii I. Leninskaia kontseptsiia poniatiia i evoliutsiia poniatiia "vid". Minsk, 1970.

Phil 349.92   Sovremennye problemy seorii poznaniia dialecticheskogo materializma. Moskva, 1970. 2v.

Phil 349.94   Stegmueller, Wolfgang. Aufsätze zur Wissenschaftstheorie. Darmstadt, 1970.

Phil 350.1   Twardowski, K. Zur Lehre von Inhalt und Gegenstand. Wien, 1894.

Phil 350.2   Turner, F.S. Knowledge, belief and certitude. London, 1900.

Phil 350.3   Tauschinski, Hippolyt. Der Begriff. Wien, 1865.
Phil 350.4   Turró, R. La base trofica de la intelegencia. Madrid, 1918.

Phil 350.5   Tomov, Kiril. Poznanie i praktika. Sofiia, 1960.
Phil 350.6   Teoriia poznaniia i sovremennaia nauka. Moskva, 1967.
Phil 350.8.2   Thyssen, Johannes. Der philosophische Relativismus. 2. Aufl. Bonn, 1947.

Phil 351.1   Uphues, G.K. Psychologie des Erkennens I. Leipzig, 1893.
Phil 351.1.5   Uphues, G.K. Geschichte der Philosophie als Erkenntniskritik. Halle, 1909.

Phil 351.2   Ulrich, Georg. Grundlegung des Systems aller möglichen Erfahrung. Berlin, 1896.

Phil 351.3   Uexküll, T. von. Wirklichkeit als Geheimmis und Auftrag. Bern, 1945.

Phil 351.5   L'unificazione del sopere. Firenze, 1965.
Phil 351.7   Ülken, Hilmi Ziya. Bilgi ve değer. Ankara, 1965.
Phil 352.1   Volkelt, J. Erfahrung und Denken. Hamburg, 1886.
Phil 352.1.2   Volkelt, J. Erfahrung und Denken. Aufl. 2. Leipzig, 1924.
Phil 352.1.5   Volkelt, J. Die quellen der menschlichen Gewissheit. München, 1906.

Phil 352.1.15 Volkelt, J. Gewissheit und Wahrheit. München, 1918.
Phil 352.2   Vorlaender, F. Wissenschaft der Erkenntniss. Leipzig, 1847.

Phil 352.3   Volkmann, P. Erkenntnistheoretische Grundzüge der Naturwissenschaften. Leipzig, 1896.

Phil 352.3.5   Volkmann, P. Erkenntnistheoretische Grundzüge der Naturwissenschaften. Leipzig, 1910.

Phil 352.4   Voit, Carl von. Ueber die Entwicklung der Erkenntniss. München, 1878.

Phil 352.5.2   Verworm, Max. Die Frage nach den Grenzen der Erkenntnis. 2. Aufl. Jena, 1917.

Phil 352.6   Vialatoux, J. Le discours et l'intuition. Paris, 1930.
Phil 352.7   Vincent, Maxime. La vision interne. Paris, 1933.
Phil 352.8   Vries, Joseph de. Denken und Sein. Freiburg, 1937.
Phil 352.8.5.3 Vries, Joseph de. Critica. 3. ed. recognita et aucto. Barcinone, 1964.

Phil 352.9   Varga, A. von. Einführung in die Erkenntnislehre. München, 1919.

Phil 352.10   Voprosy teorii poznaniia. Perm, 1961.
Phil 352.11   Vardapetian, N. O nekotorykh osnovnykh voprosakh marks - leninskoi gnoseologii. Erevan, 1963.

Phil 352.12   Vakhtomin, Nikolai K. Zakony dialektiki, zakony poznaniia. Moskva, 1966.

Phil 352.13   Voprosy teorii poznaniia. Moskva, 1969.
Phil 353.1   Walter, J.E. The Principles of knowledge. West Newton, Pa., 1901. 2v.

Phil 353.2   Wodehouse, H. The presentation of reality. Cambridge, 1910.

Phil 353.3   Wyneken, Ernst. Das Ding an Sich und das Naturgesetz der Seele. Heidelberg, 1901.

Phil 353.4   Weinhandl, F. Die Methode der Gestaltanalyse. Leipzig, 1923.

Phil 353.5   Wijck, B.H.C.K. van der. De oorsprong en de grenzen der kennis. 2e Druk. Groningen, 1863.

Phil 353.6   Weisengrün, P. Das Problem. Leipzig, 1892.
Phil 353.7   Witte, J.H. Zur Erkenntnistheorie und Ethik. Berlin, 1877.

Phil 353.8   Windelband, W. Ueber die Gewissheit der Erkenntniss. Berlin, 1873.

Phil 353.9A   Whitehead, A.N. Symbolism: its meaning and effect. N.Y., 1927.

Phil 353.9B   Whitehead, A.N. Symbolism: its meaning and effect. N.Y., 1927.

Phil 353.9.2   Whitehead, A.N. Symbolism: its meaning and effect. Cambridge, Eng., 1928.

Phil 353.10   Weinmann, R. Philosophie, Welt und Wirklichkeit. München, 1922.

Phil 353.11   Wilkens, Claudius. Erkjendelsens problem. København, 1875.

Phil 353.12   Weinberg, Siegfried. Erkenntnistheorie. Berlin, 1930.

Classified Listing

Phil 331 - 356   Special philosophical topics, systems, etc. - Secondary treatises and discussions - Epistemology - Monographs - cont.

Phil 353.13   Wendel, Georg. Kritik des Erkennens. Bonn, 1914.
Phil 353.14   Weidauer, F. Objektivität, voraussetzungslose Wissenschaft und wissenschaftliche Wahrheit. Leipzig, 1935.
Phil 353.15   Weyl, H. Mind and nature. Philadelphia, 1934.
Phil 353.16   Weinschenk, C. Das Wirklichkeitsproblem der Erkenntnistheorie. Leipzig, 1936.
Phil 353.17   Wood, L. The analysis of knowledge. London, 1940.
Phil 353.18.5   Walsh, William Henry. Reason and experience. Oxford, 1947.
Phil 353.19   Woozley, A. Theory of knowledge. London, 1949.
Phil 353.20   Wein, Hermann. Das Problem des Relativismus. Berlin, 1950.
Phil 353.21   Wisdom, John. Other minds. Oxford, 1952
Phil 353.21.5   Wisdom, John. Other minds. Berkeley, 1968.
Phil 353.23   Wemme, G. Das Geheimnis der Gegensätze. Krailling, 1960.
Phil 353.25   Willam, Franz. Aristotelische Erkenntnislehre bei Whately und Newman. Freiburg, 1960.
Phil 353.27   Weigel, Gustave. Knowledge. Englewood Cliffs, N.J., 1961.
Phil 353.29   Wallraff, C.F. Philosophical theory and psychological fact. Tucson, 1961.
Phil 353.30   Wagner, J. Was Kann ich Wissen? 2. Aufl. Braunschweig, 1962.
Phil 353.31   Wisdom, John. Paradox and discovery. N.Y., 1965.
Phil 353.32   Vakhtomin, N.K. O roli kategorii sushchnost' i iavlenie v poznanii. Moskov, 1963.
Phil 353.33   Wiedmann, Franz. Das Problem der Gewissheit. Eine erkenntnismetaphsische Studie. München, 1966.
Phil 353.34   Weissman, David J. Dispositional properties. Carbondale, 1965.
Phil 356.1   Ziehen, T. Psychophysiologische Erkenntnistheorie. Jena, 1898.
Phil 356.1.5   Ziehen, T. Erkenntnistheorie...Grundlage. Jena, 1913.
Phil 356.1.10   Ziehen, T. Zum gegenwärtigen·Stand der Erkenntnistheorie. Wiesbaden, 1914.
Phil 356.2   Zilsel, Edgar. Das Anwendungsproblem. Leipzig, 1916.
Phil 356.3   Zocher, Rudolf. Die objektive Geltung Slogik und der Immanenzge Danke. Tübingen, 1925.
Phil 356.5   Zinkernagel, Peter. Omverdens problemet. København, 1957.
Phil 356.5.3   Zinkernagel, Peter. Conditions for description. London, 1962.

Phil 365   Special philosophical topics, systems, etc. - Secondary treatises and discussions - Evolutionism

Phil 365.01   Pamphlet box. Evolution.
Phil 365.02   Pamphlet vol. Evolution. 2 pam.
Phil 365.1   Carrau, V.M.J.L. Études sur la théorie de l'evolution. Paris, 1879.
Phil 365.3   Mivart, St. G. A limit to evolution. London? 1884.
Phil 365.4   Fiske, J. Excursions of an evolutionist. Boston, 1884.
Phil 365.5   Pearson, K. Chances of death...studies in evolution. London, 1897. 2v.
Phil 365.6   Baldwin, J.M. Development and evolution. N.Y., 1902.
Phil 365.7   Richard, G. L'idée d'evolution. Paris, 1903.
Phil 365.8   Thompson, H.C. New reading of evolution. Chicago, 1907.
Phil 365.9   Auvard, Alfred. L'evoluisme. Paris, 1914.
Phil 365.10   Cazalles, Emile. Outline of the evolution-philosophy. N.Y., 1875.
Phil 365.11   Preyer, W. Aus Natur- und Menschenleben. Berlin, 1885.
Phil 365.12   Morgan, Conwy L. Emergent evolution. London, 1923.
Phil 365.12.7   Morgan, Conwy L. Life, mind and spirit. N.Y., 1925.
Phil 365.13   Calderoni, G. L'evoluzione e i suoi limiti. Roma, 1907.
Phil 365.14   Lambek, C. Udkast til en sjaelelig bevaegelseslaere. København, 1901-1906.
Phil 365.15   Petronievics, B. L'évolution universelle. Paris, 1921.
Phil 365.16   Petavel-Oliiff, E. Le plan de Dieu dans l'évolution. Lausanne, 1902.
Phil 365.17   Valle, G. La psicogenesi della coscienza. Milano, 1905.
Phil 365.18.5   Cavling, Viggo. The collective spirit; an idealistic theory of evolution. N.Y., 1926.
Phil 365.19A   Smuts, J.C. Holism and evolution. N.Y., 1926.
Phil 365.19B   Smuts, J.C. Holism and evolution. N.Y., 1926.
Phil 365.19.60   Kolbe, F.C. A Catholic view of holism. N.Y., 1928.
Phil 365.20A   Noble, Edmund. Purposive evolution. N.Y., 1926.
Phil 365.20B   Noble, Edmund. Purposive evolution. N.Y., 1926.
Phil 365.22   Marichal, H. Essai de philosophie évolutive. Bruxelles, 1891.
Phil 365.24   Dominicis, S.F. de. La dottrina dell'evoluzione: I. Torino, 1878.
Phil 365.25   Hobhouse, L.T. Development and purpose. London, 1913.
Phil 365.25.2   Hobhouse, L.T. Development and purpose. London, 1927.
Phil 365.26   Bertinaria, F. La dottrina dell'evoluzione e la fil. Genova, 1876.
Phil 365.27   LeRoy, Edouard. L'exigence idéaliste et le fait de l'évolution. Paris, 1927.
Phil 365.27.5   LeRoy, Edouard. Les origines humaines et l'évolution de l'intelligence. Paris, 1928.
Phil 365.28   Wilson, J.C. On an evolutionist theory of axioms. Oxford, 1912.
Phil 365.29   Gizycki, G. von. Philosophische Consequenzen der Lamarck-Darwin. Leipzig, 1876.
Phil 365.30   Derr, Ezra Z. Evolution versus involution. N.Y., 1885.
Phil 365.31.5   Lalande, André. La dissolution opposée a l'évolution dans les sciences physiques et morales. Paris, 1899.
Phil 365.31.15   Lalande, André. Les illusions évolutionnistes. Paris, 1930.
Phil 365.32   Messenger, E.C. Evolution and theology. N.Y., 1932.
Phil 365.33   O'Brien, J.A. Evolution and religion. N.Y., 1932.
Phil 365.34.5   Ghose, Aurobinclo. Evolution. 2. ed. Calcutta, 1923.
Phil 365.35   Newsholme, H.P. Evolution and redemption. London, 1933.
Phil 365.36   Monsarrat, K.W. Desire and creation. Liverpool, 1932.
Phil 365.37   Tyler, J.M. The place of the church in evolution. Boston, 1914.
Phil 365.38   Bill, Annie C.B. Questions and answers on conscious evolution. N.Y., 1933.
Phil 365.38.5   Bill, Annie C.B. The conquest of death; an imminent step in evolution. Boston, 1935.
Phil 365.39   Collin, C. Brorskabets religion. Kristiania, 1912.
Phil 365.40   Joad, C.E.N. The meaning of life. London, 1928.
Phil 365.41   Mary Frederick, Sister. Religion and evolution since 1859. Diss. Notre Dame, 1934.
Phil 365.42   Jevons, Frank B. Evolution. London, 1900.
Phil 365.43   Kausika, N. The new evolution, being a general solution of all modern life problems, based on truth. Nemmara, 1936.
Phil 365.44   Kingson, B. The moving tent. Wellington, 1936.
Phil 365.45   Salis Goulart, J. O sentido da evolução. Porto Allegre, 1937.

Phil 365   Special philosophical topics, systems, etc. - Secondary treatises and discussions - Evolutionism - cont.

Phil 365.46   Heard, G. Pain, sex and time. N.Y., 1939.
Phil 365.47.10   Lecomte du Noüy, Pierre. L'avenir de l'esprit. Gallimard, 1941.
Phil 365.47.15   Lecomte du Noüy, Pierre. L'avenir de l'esprit. N.Y., 1943.
Phil 365.47.17   Lecomte du Noüy, Pierre. La dignité humaine. N.Y., 1944.
Phil 365.47.18   Lecomte du Noüy, Pierre. La dignité humaine. N.Y., 1947.
Phil 365.48   Bulford, S. Man's unknown journey. London, 1941.
Phil 365.49   Przyluski, Jean. L'évolution humaine. Paris, 1942.
Phil 365.50A   Wiener, P.P. Evolution and the founders of pragmatism. Cambridge, 1949.
Phil 365.50B   Wiener, P.P. Evolution and the founders of pragmatism. Cambridge, 1949.
Phil 365.51   Porter, C. Creative personality. N.Y., 1950.
Phil 365.52   Ewing, Upton Clary. Thresholds of existence. N.Y., 1956.
Phil 365.53   Rolle, Friedrich. Der Mensch, seine Abstammung und Gesittung. Frankfurt, 1866.
Phil 365.55   Gondge, Thomas A. The ascent of life. Toronto, 1961.
Phil 365.56   Bogomolov, A.S. Ideia razvitiia v burzhuaznoifilas, XIX i XV vekov. Moskva, 1962.
Phil 365.57   Gatewood, Willard B. Preachers, pedagogues, and politicians. Chapel Hill, 1966.
Phil 365.58   Benz, Ernst. Schöpfungsglaube und Endzeiterwartung. München, 1965.
Phil 365.60   George, Nicolas. D'Einstein à Teilhard. Paris, 1964.
Phil 365.62   Grillo, Ugo. Ultimo umanesimo. Bari, 1966.
Phil 365.64   Daniels, George H. Darwinism comes to America. Waltham, Mass., 1968.
Phil 365.66   Stuttgarter Gemeinschaft "Arzt und Seelsorger." Evolution; Fortschrittsglaube und Heilserwartung. Ein Tagungsbericht. Stuttgart, 1970.
Phil 365.68   Gebser, Hans. Der unsichtbare Ursprung. Evolution als Nachvollzug. Olten, 1970.

Phil 370   Special philosophical topics, systems, etc. - Secondary treatises and discussions - Existentialism

Phil 370.2   Musu, Aldo M. Educazione ed esistenza. Padova, 1967.

Phil 380   Special philosophical topics, systems, etc. - Secondary treatises and discussions - Form

Phil 380.2.5A   Whyte, Lancelot L. Accent on form. N.Y., 1954.
Phil 380.2.5B   Whyte, Lancelot L. Accent on form. N.Y., 1954.
Phil 380.2.10   Whyte, Lancelot L. Aspects of form. London, 1951.
Phil 380.4   Porter, Gene L. The nature of form in process. N.Y., 1969.
Phil 380.6   Shumilin, A.T. Problemy struktuny i soderzhaniia protsessa poznaniia. Moskva, 1969.

Phil 384   Special philosophical topics, systems, etc. - Secondary treatises and discussions - Freedom of the will

Phil 384.5   Spakovski, Anatol. Freedom, determinism, indeterminism. The Hague, 1963.
Phil 384.10   Dworkin, Gerald. Determinism, free will, and moral responsibility. Englewood Cliffs, 1970.
Phil 384.15   Welte, Bernhard. Determination und Freiheit. 1. Aufl. Frankfurt, 1969.
Phil 384.20   Fellowship of Religious Humanists. Freedom of choice. Yellow Springs, Ohio, 1970.
Phil 384.25   Lucas, John Randolph. The freedom of the will. Oxford, 1970.
Phil 384.30   Ofstad, Harald. Two new studies in moral philosophy. Stockholm, 1967.

Phil 396   Special philosophical topics, systems, etc. - Secondary treatises and discussions - Humanism

Phil 396.3   Reiser, Oliver Leslie. Planetary democracy. N.Y., 1944.
Phil 396.5   Ayer, Alfred Jules. The humanist outlook. London, 1968.
Phil 396.8   De ag ligt nog voor ons essays van humanisten. 's-Gravenhage, 1969.
Phil 396.10   Trinkaus, Charles Edward. In our image and likeness; humanity and divinity in Italian humanist thought. London, 1970. 2v.
Phil 396.12.2   Kurella, Alfred. Das Eigene und das Fremde. Neue Beiträge zum sozialist. Humanismus. 2. Aufl. Berlin, 1970.
Phil 396.14   Miro Quesada, Francisco. Humanismo y revolución. Lima, 1969.
Phil 396.16   Rodi, Frithjof. Provokation, Affirmation. Das Dilemma des kritischen Humanismus. Stuttgart, 1970.
Phil 396.18   Oppermann, Hans. Humanismus. Darmstadt, 1970.
Phil 396.20   Salzburger Humanismusgespräch. Die erschreckende Zivilisation. Wien, 1970.
Phil 396.22   Kofler, Leo. Perspektiven des revolutionären Humanismus. Reinbek, 1968.

Phil 400   Special philosophical topics, systems, etc. - Secondary treatises and discussions - Idealism

Phil 400.01   Pamphlet box. Philosophy. Special. Idealism.
Phil 400.1   Fischer, Friedrich. Über den Begriff der Philosophie. Tübingen, 1830.
Phil 400.2   Graham, W. Idealism. London, 1872.
Phil 400.3   Holmes, N. Realistic idealism in philosophy itself. Boston, 1888. 2v.
Phil 400.4   Laas, E. Idealistische und Positivistische. Berlin, 1879-1884. 3v.
Phil 400.4.15   Salamonowicz, L. Die Ethik des Positivismus nach Ernst Laas. Inaug. Diss. Dortmund, 1935.
Phil 400.5   Lyon, G. L'idéalisme en Angleterre. Paris, 1888.
Phil 400.5.5   Turner, J.P. Idealistic beginnings in England. n.p., 1910.
Phil 400.6   Webb, J.E. The veil of Isis...essays on idealism. Dublin, 1885.
Phil 400.7   Watson, J. Christianity and idealism. N.Y., 1897.
Phil 400.7.2   Watson, J. Christianity and idealism. N.Y., 1897.
Phil 400.10   Lloyd, A.H. Dynamic idealism. Chicago, 1898.
Phil 400.11   Willmann, O. Geschichte des Idealismus. Braunschweig, 1894-1897. 3v.
Phil 400.12   Howison, G.H. Limits of evolution. N.Y., 1901.
Phil 400.12.3   Howison, G.H. Limits of evolution. 2nd ed. N.Y., 1905.
Phil 400.13   Sturt, H. Personal idealism; philosophical essays of members of Oxford University. London, 1902.
Phil 400.13.5   Sturt, H. Idola theatri; a criticism of Oxford thought and thinkers. London, 1906.
Phil 400.14   Kretschmer, E. Die Ideale und die Seele. Leipzig, 1900.
Phil 400.16   Kassner, R. Die indische Idealismus. München, 1903.
Phil 400.17   Bergmann, J. System des objectiven Idealismus. Marburg, 1903.

Phil 400   Special philosophical topics, systems, etc. - Secondary treatises and discussions - Idealism - cont.

Phil 400.18   Muff, Christian. Idealismus. 3e Aufl. Halle, 1902.
Phil 400.18.5   Muff, Christian. Idealismus. 5e Aufl. Halle, 1911.
Phil 400.19   Münsterberg, H. Science and idealism. Boston, 1906.
Phil 400.20   Jerusalem, W. Der kritische Idealismus und die reine
                   Logik. Wien, 1905.
Phil 400.20.5   Villa, Guido. L'idealismo moderno. Torino, 1905. 2v.
Phil 400.21   Hinman, E.L. The physics of idealism. Lincoln, 1906.
Phil 400.21.5   Willems, C. Die Erkenntnislehre des modernen Idealismus.
                   Trier, 1906.
Phil 400.22   Schmidt, F.J. Zur Wiedergeburt des Idealismus.
                   Leipzig, 1908.
Phil 400.23   Kronenberg, M. Geschichte der deutschen Idealismus.
                   München, 1909. 2v.
Phil 400.24   Upward, A. The new world. N.Y., 1910.
Phil 400.24.5   Chiappelli, Alessandro. Dalla critica al nuovo idealismo.
                   Milano, 1910.
Phil 400.25.2   Jones, H. Idealism as a practical creed. 2nd ed.
                   Glasgow, 1910.
Phil 400.26   Caird, E. Idealism and theory of knowledge. London, 1903.
Phil 400.27   Ebbinghaus, J. Relativer und absoluter Idealismus.
                   Leipzig, 1910.
Phil 400.27.9   Morselli, Emilio. Il fondamento dell' idealismo etico.
                   Livorno, 1911.
Phil 400.27.15   Kinkel, Walter. Idealismus und Realismus.
                   Göttingen, 1911.
Phil 400.28   Fouilleé, A. Le mouvement idéaliste et la réaction contre
                   la science positive. 3. ed. Paris, 1913.
Phil 400.28.5   Marischini, G. La dottrina positiva delle idealità.
                   Roma, 1913.
Phil 400.29   Aliotta, A. La reazione idealistica contro la scienza.
                   Palermo, 1912.
Phil 400.29.5   Aliotta, A. The idealistic reaction against science.
                   London, 1914.
Phil 400.29.9   Aliotta, A. Relativismo e idealismo. Napoli, 1922.
Phil 400.30.5   Hyde, W. De W. Practical idealism. N.Y., 1899.
Phil 400.31   Howaleivsky, M. Über die Antinomienlehre als Begründung
                   des transzendentalen idealismus. Inaug. Diss.
                   Göttingen, 1914.
Phil 400.31.10   Sydow, Eckhart von. Der Gedanke des Ideal-Reichs in der
                   idealistischen Philosophie von Kant bis Hegel.
                   Leipzig, 1914.
Phil 400.32   Dide, Maurice. Les idealistes passionnés. Paris, 1913.
Phil 400.33   Sinclair, May. A defence of idealism. N.Y., 1917.
Phil 400.33.5   Sinclair, May. The new idealism. N.Y., 1922.
Phil 400.34   Eucken, Rudolf. Die Träger des deutschen Idealismus.
                   Berlin, 1915.
Phil 400.35   Mouw, J.A. der. Het absoluut idealisme. Leiden, 1905.
Phil 400.36   Lefèvre, Georges. Obligation morale et idéalisme. Thèse.
                   Paris, 1894.
Phil 400.37   Ricardon, A. De l'idéal. Étude philosophique.
                   Paris, 1890.
Phil 400.38   Adams, George P. Idealism and the modern age. New
                   Haven, 1919.
Phil 400.39   Coste, Adolphe. Dieu et l'âme. Paris, 1880.
Phil 400.40   Rauschenberger, W. Der kritische Idealismus.
                   Leipzig, 1918.
Phil 400.41   Carr, Herbert Wildon. The new idealist movement in
                   philosophy. London, 1918.
Phil 400.42   Schmidt, F.J. Der philosophische Sinn. Göttingen, 1912.
Phil 400.43   Ott, Auguste. Critique de l'idéalisme et du criticisme.
                   Paris, 1883.
Phil 400.44   Walker, W. Idealism. London, 1919.
Phil 400.45   Mukerji, N.C. The ethical and religious philosophy of
                   idealism. Allahabad, 1922.
Phil 400.46   Kingsland, William. Scientific idealism. London, 1909.
Phil 400.47   Seidenberger, J.B. Grundlinien idealer Weltanschauung.
                   Braunschweig, 1902.
Phil 400.48   Weber, Louis. Vers le positivisme absolu par l'idéalisme.
                   Paris, 1903.
Phil 400.49   Kröger, Otto. Die Philosophie des reinen Idealismus.
                   Bonn, 1921.
Phil 400.49.10   Kröger, Otto. Die Weltanschauung des absoluten Idealismus.
                   Harz, 1909.
Phil 400.50   Ovink, B.J.H. Het kritisch idealisme. Utrecht, 1913.
Phil 400.51   Jünemann, F. Der philosophische Idealismus und das
                   Grundproblem der Erkenntnistheorie. Neisse, 1913. 4v.
Phil 400.52   Hoernlé, R.F.A. Idealism as a philosophical doctrine.
                   London, 1924.
Phil 400.52.5   Hoernlé, R.F.A. Idealism as a philosophy. N.Y., 1927.
Phil 400.53   Ranzoli, C. L'idealismo e la filosofia. n.p., n.d.
Phil 400.55   Gaultier, J. de. Les raisons de l'idéalisme. 2e éd.
                   Paris, 1906.
Phil 400.56   Lugaro, E. Idealismo filosofico e realismo politico.
                   Bologna, 1920.
Phil 400.57   Giuliano, B. Il valore degl'ideali. Torino, 1916.
Phil 400.58   Cicala, F.B. Punto di partenza e punti di arrivo dell'
                   "idealismo attuale". Firenze, 1924.
Phil 400.59   Sternberg, K. Idealismus und Kultur. Berlin, 1923.
Phil 400.60   Heyde, Johannes E. Realismus oder Idealismus.
                   Leipzig, 1924.
Phil 400.61   Friedmann, H. Die Welt der Formen. Berlin, 1925.
Phil 400.61.5   Friedmann, H. Die Welt der Formen. 2e Aufl.
                   München, 1930.
Phil 400.62   Faye, Eugène de. Idéalisme et réalisme. Paris, 1920.
Phil 400.63   Chiapelli, A. Dottrina della realtà del mondo esterno.
                   Parte prima. Firenze, 1886.
Phil 400.64   Beggerow, H. Die Erkenntnis der Wirklichkeiten.
                   Halle, 1927.
Phil 400.65   Groos, H. Der deutsche Idealismus und das Christentum.
                   München, 1927.
Phil 400.66   Lippa, L. von. Der Aufstieg von Kant zu Goethe.
                   Berlin, 1929.
Phil 400.67   Guzzo, Augusto. Verità e realtà: apologia dell'idealismo.
                   Torino, 1925.
Phil 400.68   Pavese, R. L'idea e il mondo. Torino, 1925.
Phil 400.69   Redanò, Ugo. La crisi dell'idealismo attuale. Roma, 1924.
Phil 400.70   Mignosi, Pietro. L'idealismo. Milano, 1927.
Phil 400.71   Brightman, E.S. A philosophy of ideals. N.Y., 1928.
Phil 400.72   Corti, Settimio. La rivincita dell'idealismo.
                   Rieti, 1920.
Phil 400.73   Dwelshauvers, G. Les méthodes de l'idéalisme scientifique.
                   Paris, 1892. 2 pam.
Phil 400.74   Abbagnano, N. Il nuovo idealismo inglese ed americano.
                   Napoli, 1927.
Phil 400.75   Hartmann, Alma von. Zurück zum Idealismus. Berlin, 1902.

Phil 400   Special philosophical topics, systems, etc. - Secondary treatises and discussions - Idealism - cont.

Phil 400.76   Spann, Othmar. Der Schöpfungsgang des Geistes. Theil I.
                   Jena, 1928.
Phil 400.76.2   Spann, Othmar. Der Schöpfungsgang des Geistes. 2. Aufl.
                   Graz, 1969.
Phil 400.77   Spirito, Ugo. L'idealismo italiano e i suoi critici.
                   Firenze, 1930.
Phil 400.78   Muirhead, J.H. The Platonic traditions in Anglo-Saxon
                   philosophy. London, 1931.
Phil 400.79   Leese, Kurt. Philosophie und Theologie im Spätidealismus.
                   Berlin, 1929.
Phil 400.80   Keller, Erich. Das Problem des Irrationalen im
                   wertphilosophischen Idealismus der Gegenwart.
                   Berlin, 1931.
Phil 400.82   Mussmann, J.G. De idealismo, seu philosophia ideali. Diss.
                   Berolini, 1826.
Phil 400.83   Stefunini, L. Idealismo cristiano. Padova, 1931?
Phil 400.84   Barrett, Clifford. Contemporary idealism in America.
                   N.Y., 1932.
Phil 400.85.5   Papafava, N. L'attualismo considerazioni. Milano, 1932.
Phil 400.86   Cunningham, G.W. The idealistic argument in recent British
                   and American philosophy. N.Y., 1933.
Phil 400.87   Dasgupta, S.N. Indian idealism. Cambridge, Eng., 1933.
Phil 400.88   Ewing, Alfred C. Idealism. London, 1934.
Phil 400.88.3   Ewing, Alfred C. Idealism. 3. ed. London, 1961.
Phil 400.88.5   Ewing, Alfred C. The idealist tradition. Glencoe,
                   Illinois, 1957.
Phil 400.89   Etcheverry, A. L'idéalisme français contemporain.
                   Paris, 1934.
Phil 400.89.9   Etcheverry, A. Vers l'immanence intégrale. Thèse.
                   Paris, 1934.
Phil 400.90   Gardeil, H.D. Les étapes de la philosophie idéaliste.
                   Paris, 1935.
Phil 400.91   Wagner, G.F. Transcendental-Idealismus. Ulm, 1934.
Phil 400.91.25   Thanner, Ignaz. Der Transcendental-Idealismus.
                   München, 1805.
Phil 400.92   Astrada, Carlos. Idealismo fenomenológico y metafísica
                   existencial. Buenos Aires, 1936.
Phil 400.93   Liebert, Arthur. Die Krise des Idealismus. Zürich, 1936.
Phil 400.94   Ottaviano, C. Critica dell'idealismo. Napoli, 1936.
Phil 400.94.3   Ottaviano, C. Critica dell'idealismo. 3. ed.
                   Padova, 1960.
Phil 400.94.15   Parente, A. La morte dell'idealismo. Napoli, 1937.
Phil 400.95   Raju, P.T. Thought and reality; Hegelianism and Advaita.
                   London, 1937.
Phil 400.96   Gehlen, A. Idealismus und Existentialphilosophie.
                   Leipzig, 1933.
Phil 400.97   Kellner, Eva. Mann und Frau im deutschen Idealismus.
                   Inaug. Diss. Berlin, 1937.
Phil 400.98   Tallon, H.J. Concept of self in British and American
                   idealism. Washington, 1939.
Phil 400.99   Kränzlin, Gerhard. Die Philosophie vom unendlichen
                   Menschen. Leipzig, 1936.
Phil 400.99.5   Kränzlin, Gerhard. Das System des Panhumanismus.
                   Zürich, 1949.
Phil 400.100   Bartolomeis, F. de. Idealismo ed esistenzialismo.
                   Napoli, 1946.
Phil 400.102   Bianca, Giovanni. Essenza ed esistenza, idealità e realtà.
                   Catania, 1946.
Phil 400.104   La Via, Vincenzo. Idealismo e filosofia. Messina, 1942.
Phil 400.106   Blanchi, R. Les attitudes idéalistes. Paris, 1949.
Phil 400.108   Janssen, O. Seinsordnung und Gehalt der Idealitäten.
                   Meisenheim/Glan, 1950.
Phil 400.110   Cherkashin, P.P. O reaktsionnoi sushchnosti idealizma.
                   Moskva, 1953.
Phil 400.115   Archivio di Filosofia. Il solipsismo. Padova, 1950.
Phil 400.116   Todd, William. Analytical solipsism. The Hague, 1968.
Phil 400.117   Pareyson, L. L'estetica dell'idealismo tedesco.
                   Torino, 1950.
Phil 400.120   Baskin, M.P. Sovremennyi sub"ektivnyi idealizm.
                   Moskva, 1957.
Phil 400.121   Kursanov, Georgii A. Sovremennyi ob"ektivnyi idealizm.
                   Moskva, 1960.
Phil 400.121.5   Kursanov, Georgii A. Sovremennia idealisticheskaia
                   gnoseologiia. Moskva, 1968.
Phil 400.122   Novgorodtsev, P.I. Problemy idealizma. Moskva, 1903.
Phil 400.123   Cherkasin, P.P. Gnoseologicheskie korni idealizma.
                   Moskva, 1961.
Phil 400.124   Meynier, Philippe. Essai sur l'idéalisme moderne.
                   Paris, 1965.
Phil 400.128   Spisani, Franco. Natura e spirito nell'idealismo attuale.
                   Milano, 1968?
Phil 400.130   Zschimmer, Eberhard. Technik und Idealismus. Jena, 1920.
Phil 400.132   Stiehler, Gottfried. Der Idealismus von Kant bis Hegel.
                   Berlin, 1970.
Phil 400.134   Fichera, Giuseppe. La tematico religiosa nell idealismo
                   attuale. Catania, 1969.
Phil 400.136   Ciardo, Manlio. Un fallito tentativo di riforma dello
                   hegelismo. Bari, 1948.

Phil 402   Special philosophical topics, systems, etc. - Secondary treatises and discussions - Ideology

Phil 402.2   Corbett, Patrick. Ideologies. N.Y., 1966.
Phil 402.4   Lund, Erik. De europäiske ideers historie. 2. opl.
                   Gyldendal, 1963.
Phil 402.6   Aspelin, Gunnar. Världsbilder och livsidal. Lund, 1968.
Phil 402.8   Mongardini, Carlo. Storia del concetto di ideologia.
                   Roma, 1968.
Phil 402.10   Volpe, Galvano della. Critica dell'ideologia
                   contemporanea. Roma, 1967.
Phil 402.12   Cofrancesco, Dino. Appunti sull'ideologia. Milano, 1968.
Phil 402.14   Hoelzle, Erwin. Idee und Ideologie. Bern, 1969.
Phil 402.16B   Nauchna Sesiia, Posvetena na Borbata Sreshtu Burzhoaznata
                   Ideologiia v Naukata. Varna, 1969. Politika, ideologiia i
                   ideologicheska diversiia. Sofiia, 1970.
Phil 402.18   Leonardi, Franco. Sociologia dell'ideologia.
                   Catania, 1966.
Phil 402.20   Ratković, Radoslav. Ideoligija i politika. Beograd, 1971.
Phil 402.22   MacIntyre, Alasdair Chalmers. Against the self-images of
                   the age: essays on ideology and philosophy. London, 1971.

Classified Listing

Phil 408   Special philosophical topics, systems, etc. - Secondary treatises and discussions - Individuation

Phil 408.2   Simonond, Gilbert. L'individuation à la lumière des notions de forme et d'information. Thèse. Paris, 1964.
Phil 408.4   Meiland, Jack W. Talking about particulars. London, 1970.
Phil 408.6   Lefebvre, Henri. Le manifeste différentialiste. Paris, 1970.

Phil 410   Special philosophical topics, systems, etc. - Secondary treatises and discussions - Infinite and finite

Phil 410.01   Pamphlet box. Philosophy. Special. Infinite.
Phil 410.1   Calderwood, H. The philosophy of the infinite. Edinburgh, 1854.
Phil 410.1.2   Calderwood, H. The philosophy of the infinite. Cambridge, 1861.
Phil 410.2   Cantor, Georg. Grundlagen einer allgemeinen Monnichfaltigkeitslehre. Leipzig, 1883.
Phil 410.3   Evellin, F. Infini et quantité. Paris, 1880.
Phil 410.4.5   Swedenborg, E. The philosophy of the infinite. Boston, 1848.
Phil 410.5   Fullerton, G.S. Conception of the infinite. Philadelphia, 1887.
Phil 410.6   Příhonsky, F. F. B. Bolzano's Paradoxien des Unendlichen. Berlin, 1889.
Phil 410.6.5   Bolzano, B. Paradoxien des Unendlichen. Leipzig, 1920.
Phil 410.6.10   Bolzano, B. Paradoxes of the infinite. New Haven, 1950.
Phil 410.6.10.2   Bolzano, B. Paradoxes of the infinite. London, 1950.
Phil 410.7   Geissler, Kurt. Die Grundsätze und das Wesen des Unendlichen in der Mathematik und Philosophie. Leipzig, 1902.
Phil 410.8   Jourdain, E.F. On the theory of the infinite in modern thought. London, 1911.
Phil 410.9   Kuhns, Levi O. The sense of the infinite. N.Y., 1908.
Phil 410.10   Cohn, Jonas. Geschichte des Unendlichkeitsproblems im abendländischen Denken bis Kant. Leipzig, 1896.
Phil 410.11   Borel, Émile. Les paradoxes de l'infini. Paris, 1946.
Phil 410.75   Isenkrahe, Caspar. Das Endliche und das Unendliche. Münster, 1915.
Phil 410.75.5   Isenkrahe, Caspar. Untersuchungen über das Endliche und das Unendliche. Bonn, 1920. 3v.
Phil 410.77   Mozkowski, A. Der Abbau des "Unendlich". Berlin, 1925.
Phil 410.78   Garofalo, Lydia. Il problema dell'infinito dal rinascimento a Kant. Napoli 1931.
Phil 410.79   Latzin, H. Analysis des Unendlichen im Psychischen und Physischen. Wien, 1931.
Phil 410.80   Major, John. Le traité "De l'infini" de Jean Muir. Paris, 1938.
Phil 410.81   Benardete, José A. Infinity. Oxford, 1964.
Phil 410.82   Viderskii, Vladimir I. Konechnoe i beskonechnoe. Moskva, 1966.
Phil 410.84   Welte, Bernhard. Im Spielfeld von Endlichkeit und Unendlichkeit. Frankfurt, 1967.
Phil 410.85   Petron, Iurii A. Logicheskie problemy abstraktsii beskonechnosti i osushchestvimosti. Moskva, 1967.
Phil 410.90   Chany, Robert de. Sur les confins du fini, métaphysique, physique, mathématiques et religion. Paris, 1968.

Phil 418   Special philosophical topics, systems, etc. - Secondary treatises and discussions - Intention

Phil 418.5   Meiland, Jack W. The nature of intention. London, 1970.
Phil 418.10   Anscombe, Gertrude Elizabeth Margaret. Intention. Oxford, 1957.
Phil 418.16   Mohanty, Jitendra Nath. The concept of intentionality. St. Louis, 1971.

Phil 420   Special philosophical topics, systems, etc. - Secondary treatises and discussions - Intuition

Phil 420.2   Bahm, Archie J. Types of intuition. Albuquerque, 1960[1961].
Phil 420.4   Rothacker, Erich. Intuition und Begriff. Bonn, 1963.

Phil 440   Special philosophical topics, systems, etc. - Secondary treatises and discussions - Liberty

Phil 440.2   Adler, Mortimer J. The idea of freedom. Garden City, N.Y., 1958-61. 2v.
Phil 440.4   Fischer, Ernst. Freiheit und Persönlichkeit. Wien, 1947.
Phil 440.6   Centro di Studi Filosofici di Gallarate. Libertà e responsabilità. Padova, 1967.
Phil 440.8   Edwards, Rem Blanchard. Freedom, responsibiblity and obligation. The Hague, 1969.
Phil 440.10   Pavidovich, Vsevolod E. Grani svobody. Moskva, 1969.
Phil 440.12   Schuette, Hermann Günther. Freiheit ist anders. München, 1970.
Phil 440.14   Nauta, Lolle Wibe. Vrijheid, Horizon der Geschiedenis. Nijkerk, 1966.

Phil 450   Special philosophical topics, systems, etc. - Secondary treatises and discussions - Life

Phil 450.2   Clements, Tad S. Science and man; the philosophy of scientific humanism. Springfield, Illinois, 1968.
Phil 450.4   Mansuy, Michel. Etudes sur l'imagination de la vie. Paris, 1970.
Phil 450.6   Gradman, Hans. Menschsein ohne Illusionen. München, 1970.
VPhil 450.8   Retschlag, Max. Von der Urmaterie zum Urkraft-Elixier. Leipzig, 1906.
Phil 450.10   Steiner, Hans Friedrich. Marxiaten-Lennisten über den Sinn des Lebens. Essen, 1970.
Phil 450.12   Braun-Urban, Heiner. Wandlung der Welt durch Wandlung des Bewusstseins. München, 1969.

Phil 474   Special philosophical topics, systems, etc. - Secondary treatises and discussions - Materialism - Pamphlet volumes

Phil 474.1   Pamphlet box. Philosophy. Special. Materialism.

Phil 475 - 500   Special philosophical topics, systems, etc. - Secondary treatises and discussions - Materialism - Monographs (A-Z)

Phil 475.1   Abendroth, Robert. Das Problem der Materie. v.1. Leipzig, 1889.
Phil 475.2   Apel, Paul. Die Überwindung des Materialismus. 3e Aufl. Berlin, 1921.
Phil 475.3   Aksel'rod, L. I. Protiv idealizma. Moskva, 1933.
Phil 476.1   Bergier, N.S. Examen du matérialisme. Paris, 1771. 2v.
Phil 476.2   Böhner, A.N. Naturforschung und Kulturleben. Hannover, 1859.
Phil 476.2.5   Böhner, A.N. Du matérialisme. Genève, 1861.
Phil 476.3   Büchner, L. Kraft und Stoff. Frankfurt, 1859.
Phil 476.3.1   Büchner, L. Kraft und Stoff. Frankfurt, 1855.

Phil 475 - 500   Special philosophical topics, systems, etc. - Secondary treatises and discussions - Materialism - Monographs (A-Z) - cont.

Phil 476.3.2   Büchner, L. Kraft und Stoff. Leipzig, 1867.
Phil 476.3.2.4   Büchner, L. Kraft und Stoff. Frankfurt, 1898.
Phil 476.3.2.5   Büchner, L. Kraft und Stoff. Frankfurt, 1858.
Phil 476.3.2.10   Büchner, L. Der Humor in Kraft und Stoff. Darmstadt, 1856.
Phil 476.3.3   Büchner, L. Force et matière. Paris, 1863.
Phil 476.3.4.10   Büchner, L. Kraft och materia. Stockholm, 1869.
Phil 476.3.5   Büchner, L. Der Mensch. Leipzig, 1872.
Phil 476.3.6   Büchner, L. L'homme selon la science. Paris, 1870.
Phil 476.3.7   Büchner, L. Man in the past, present and future. London, 1872.
Phil 476.3.9   Büchner, L. Man in the past, present and future. N.Y., 1894.
Phil 476.3.11   Büchner, L. El hombre segum la ciencia. Barcelona, 1869.
Phil 476.3.15   Büchner, L. Natur und Geist. 2e Aufl. Hamm, 1865.
Phil 476.3.20   Büchner, L. Natur und Geist. Frankfurt, 1857.
Phil 476.3.50   Frauenstadt, J. Der Materialismus. Leipzig, 1856.
Phil 476.3.53   Strohecker, J.R. Die freie Naturbetrachtung. Augsburg, 1869.
Phil 476.5   Bliven, Eliza M. Materialism. n.p., n.d.
Phil 476.6   Bertini, G.M. Schiarimenti sulla controversia fra spiritualismo e materialismo. Torino, 1870.
Phil 476.8   Banfi, A. Storia del materialismo nei secoli XVI e XVII. v.1-2. Milano, 1951-53.
Phil 477.1   Cahagnet, A. Études sur le matérialisme. Argenteuil, 1869.
Phil 477.2   Caro, E.M. Le matérialisme et la science. Paris, 1867.
Phil 477.2.5   Caro, E.M. Le matérialisme et la science. 2e éd. Paris, 1868.
Phil 477.3   Castillon, J. de. Observations sur le livre "Système de la nature". Berlin, 1771.
Htn   Phil 477.4*   Coward, W. Grand essay. London, 1704.
Phil 477.5   Czolbe, H. Neue Darstellung des Sensualismus. Leipzig, 1855.
Phil 477.6   Cournot, A.A. Matérialisme, vitalisme, rationalisme. Paris, 1875.
Phil 477.6.5   Cournot, A.A. Matérialisme, vitalisme, rationalisme. Paris, 1923.
Phil 477.7   Cros, Antoine. Les nouvelles formules du matérialisme. Paris, 1897.
Phil 477.8   Cía y Alvarez, J.M. La función espiritual. Madrid, 1924.
Phil 477.9   Cohen, Chapman. Materialism: has it been exploded?...debate. London, 1928.
Phil 477.9.5   Cohen, Chapman. Materialism re-stated. London, 1927.
Phil 477.11   Coudenhove-Kalergi, R.N. Los von Materialismus! Wien, 1931.
Phil 477.14   Connell, Richard J. Matter and becoming. Chicago, 1966.
Phil 478.1   Duncan, W.S. Conscious matter. London, 1881.
Phil 478.2   Dauriac, L. Des notions de matière et de force. Paris, 1878.
Phil 478.3   Dreher, Eugen. Der Materialismus. Berlin, 1892.
Phil 478.4   Driesch, Hans. Die Überwindung des Materialismus. Zürich, 1935.
Phil 480.1   Ferraris, C.F. Il materialismo storico. Palermo, 1897.
Phil 480.2   Flentje, L. Das Leben und die todte Natur. Cassel, 1866.
Phil 480.3   Forichon, L. Le matérialisme et la phrénologie. Paris, 1840.
Phil 480.4   Fischer, K.P. Die Unwahrheit des Sensualismus und Materialismus. Erlangen, 1853.
Phil 480.5   Fabié, Antonio M. Exámen del materialismo moderno. Madrid, 1875.
Phil 480.6   Fernandez de Santanna, M. O materialismo em face da sciencia. Lisboa, 1899. 2v.
Phil 480.7   Franck, Otto. Der Weg zur Wirklichkeit. Leipzig, 1928.
Phil 480.10   Feibleman, James. The new materialism. The Hague, 1970.
Phil 481.1   Galitzine, E. De l'analyse de la force. v.1-3. Paris, 1845. 2v.
Phil 481.2   Glagolev, B. Materializm v svete sovremennoi nauki. Frankfurt, 1946.
Phil 481.4   Gurst, Guenter. Grosse Materialisten. Leipzig, 1965.
Phil 482.1   Heinroth, J.C. Über die Hypothese der Materie. Leipzig, 1828.
Phil 482.3   Hessen, Robert. Die Philosophie der Kraft. Stuttgart, 1913.
Phil 482.4   Haering, T.L. Die Materialisierung des Geistes. Tübingen, 1919.
Phil 482.5   Huré, Jules. Les origines judéo-chrétiennes du matérialisme contemporain. Paris, 1928.
Phil 482.6   Hoyle, Fred. Man and materialism. 1st ed. N.Y., 1956.
Phil 484.2   Jones, H.B. Croonian lectures on matter and force. London, 1868.
Phil 484.4   Juul, Jensen. Uffe sjoel og legeme. København, 1970.
Phil 485.1.5   Körner, F. Thierseele und Menschengeist. Leipzig, 1872.
Phil 486.1   Lange, F.A. Geschichte des Materialismus. Iserlohn, 1873-75. 2v.
Phil 486.1.5   Lange, F.A. History of materialism. London, 1877. 3v.
NEDL Phil 486.1.5.3   Lange, F.A. History of materialism. Boston, 1879-81. 3v.
Phil 486.1.5.7A   Lange, F.A. History of materialism and criticism of its importance. v.1-3. 3rd ed. London, 1925.
Phil 486.1.5.7B   Lange, F.A. History of materialism and criticism of its importance. v.1-3. 3rd ed. London, 1925.
NEDL Phil 486.1.5.8   Lange, F.A. The history of materialism and criticism of its present importance. v.1-3. 3rd ed. N.Y., 1925.
Phil 486.1.5.9   Lange, F.A. History of materialism and criticism of its present importance. Photoreproduction. Boston, 1880-81. 3v.
Phil 486.1.6A   Lange, F.A. Geschichte des Materialismus. 3e Aufl. Iserlohn, 1876-77. 2v.
Phil 486.1.6B   Lange, F.A. Geschichte des Materialismus. v.1-2. 3e Aufl. Iserlohn, 1876-77.
Phil 486.2   Leblais, A. Matérialisme et spiritualisme. Paris, 1865.
Phil 486.3   Lecomte, F.D. L'âme. Paris, 1869.
Phil 486.4   Lewins, R. Life and mind. Lewes, 1877.
Phil 486.5   Lucas, F. Le procès du matérialisme. Paris, 1867.
Phil 486.6   L, B.L. Matter and energy. London, 1874.
Phil 486.7   Löwenthal, E. System und Geschichte des Naturalismus. Leipzig, 1863.
Phil 486.8   Lovecchio, Antonino. Filosofia della prassi e filosofia dello spirito. Palmi, 1928.
Phil 486.9   Luce, A.A. Sense without matter, or Direct perception. Edinburgh, 1954.
Phil 486.10   Ley, Hermann. Studie zur Geschichte des Materialismus im Mittelalter. Berlin, 1957.
Phil 486.15   Lodetti, Milka. La matière imaginaire. Paris, 1959.

**Phil 475 - 500   Special philosophical topics, systems, etc. - Secondary
treatises and discussions - Materialism - Monographs (A-Z) - cont.**

Phil 486.25	Linssen, Robert. Spiritualité de la matière. Paris, 1966.
Phil 487.1	Moleschott, J. De Kreislauf des Lebens. Mainz, 1857.
Phil 487.1.3	Moleschott, J. Der Kreislauf des Lebens. Mainz, 1855.
Phil 487.1.4	Moleschott, J. Der Kreislauf des Lebens. Giessen, 1875-87. 2v.
Phil 487.1.5	Moleschott, J. Licht und Leben. Frankfurt, 1856.
Phil 487.1.10	Moleschott, J. La circulation de la vie. Paris, 1866.
Phil 487.2	Martineau, J. Modern materialism. London, 1876.
Phil 487.2.2	Martineau, J. Modern materialism. Boston, 1876.
Phil 487.2.5	Martineau, J. Religion affected by modern materialism. London, 1876-78. 2 pam.
Phil 487.2.6	Martineau, J. Religion affected by modern materialism. N.Y., 1875.
Phil 487.3	Mayer, Adolf. Los vom Materialismus! Heidelberg, 1906.
Phil 487.4	Maccall, William. The newest materialism. London, 1873.
Phil 487.5	Mayer, Charles L. L'homme, esprit ou matière?. Paris, 1949.
Phil 487.5.10	Mayer, Charles L. Man: mind or matter? Boston, 1951.
Phil 487.6.3	McDougall, William. Modern materialism and emergent evolution. N.Y., 1929.
Phil 487.6.5	McDougall, William. Modern materialism and emergent evolution. 2. ed. London, 1934.
Phil 487.7	Mann, Walter. Modern materialism. London, 1921.
Phil 487.8	Mins, H.F. Materialism; the scientific basis. N.Y., 1934.
Phil 487.9	Materialy dlia razoblacheniia materialisticheskago nigilizma. Photoreproduction. Sankt Peterburg, 1864.
Phil 488.1	Nizan, Paul. Les matérialistes de l'antiquité. Paris, 1936.
Phil 488.1.5	Nizan, Paul. Les matérialistes de l'antiquité. Paris, 1965.
Phil 488.2	Novack, George Edward. The origins of materialism. 1st ed. N.Y., 1965.
Phil 489.1A	Ostwald, W. Überwindung des wissenschaftlichen Materialismus. Leipzig, 1895.
Phil 489.1B	Ostwald, W. Überwindung des wissenschaftlichen Materialismus. Leipzig, 1895.
Phil 489.3	Eisenberg, Rafael. The East-West conflict. N.Y., 1967.
Phil 490.1	Discourse on the soul and instinct. N.Y., 1849.
Phil 490.1.5	Physiology of the soul and instinct. N.Y., 1872.
Phil 490.1.6	Physiology of the soul and instinct. N.Y., 1872.
Phil 490.2	Perty, M. Über die Bedeutung der Anthropologie. Bern, 1853.
Phil 490.3	Pictet, Raoul. Étude critique du matérialisme et du spiritualisme. Genève, 1897.
Cg Phil 490.4.3	Plekhanov, G.V. Beiträge zur Geschichte des Materialismus. 3. Aufl. Stuttgart, 1921.
Phil 490.4.7	Plekhanov, G.V. Essays in the history of materialism. London, 1934.
Phil 490.4.10	Plekhanov, G.V. Le matérialisme militant (materialismus militans). Paris, 1930.
Phil 490.4.10.12	Plekhanov, G.V. Materialismus militans (voinstvuiushchii materializm). Izd. 2. Moskva, 1931.
Phil 490.5	Pfaff, A.B.I.F. Die Entwicklung der Welt auf atomischer Grundlage. Heidelberg, 1883.
Phil 490.6	Pikler, G. Das Grundgesetz alles neuro-psychologischen Lebens. Leipzig, 1900.
Phil 490.7	Ploucquet, G. Dissertatio de materialismo. Tubingae, 1751.
Phil 490.8	Poortman, J.J. Achêma. v.1-2,6. Assen, 1954. 5v.
Phil 490.9	Pantin, Igor' K. Materialisticheskoe mirovozrenie i teoriia poznaniia russkikh revoliutsionnikh demokratov. Moskva, 1961.
Phil 491.2	Quarto di Palo, A. Materia (appunti di critica). Roma, 1928.
Phil 492.1	Renaud, H. Le matérialisme et la nature. Paris, 1870.
Phil 492.5	Roy, M.N. Materialism. 2nd ed. Calcutta, 1951.
Phil 492.10	Rossi, M.M. Alle fonti del deismo e del materialismo moderno. Firenze, 1942.
Phil 493.1	Simonin, A.H. Le matérialisme de masque. Paris, 1878.
Phil 493.2	Stevens, S.E. Philosophy of the great unconscious. Boston, 1908.
Phil 493.3	Svenson, S.G. Betraktelseröfver den materialistiska och idealistiska verldsäsigten. Stockholm, 1871.
Phil 493.4	Schilling, G. Beiträge zur Geschichte und Kritik des Materialismus. Leipzig, 1867.
Phil 493.5	Sellars, R.W. Philosophy for the future. N.Y., 1949.
Phil 493.6	Seely, Charles Sherlock. Philosophy and the ideological conflict. N.Y., 1953.
Phil 493.6.5	Seely, Charles Sherlock. Modern materialism. N.Y., 1960.
Phil 493.6.10	Seely, Charles Sherlock. The philosophy of science. N.Y., 1964.
Phil 493.6.15	Seely, Charles Sherlock. The essentials of modern materialism. N.Y., 1969.
Phil 493.7	Russo, F. Science et matérialisme. Paris, 1962.
Phil 493.10	Stiehler, G. Beiträge zur Geschichte des vormarxistischen Materialismus. 1. Aufl. Berlin, 1961.
Phil 493.12	Schmidt, Karl. Zur Überwindung des wissenschaftlichen Materialismus. Basel, 1968.
Phil 494.1	Townsend, H.G. Studies in philosophical naturalism. Eugene, 1931.
Phil 494.3	Tromp, Salco U. The religion of the modern scientist. Leiden, 1947.
Phil 494.4	Trakhtenberg, I.V. Razvetie materializma i ego bor'ba protiv idealizma. Moskva, 1956.
Phil 494.6	Timpanaro, Sebastiano. Sul materialismo. Pisa, 1970.
Phil 496.1	Volkmann, P. Die materialistische Epoche des neunzehnten Jahrhunderts. Leipzig, 1909.
Phil 497.1	Wagner, J.A. Naturwissenschaft und Bibel. Stuttgart, 1855.
Phil 497.2	Wagner, R. Menschenschöpfung und Seelensubstanz. Göttingen, 1854.
Phil 497.2.5	Wagner, R. Über Wissen und Glauben. Göttingen, 1854.
ɔL Phil 497.2.9	Vogt, C. Köhlerglaube und Wissenschaft...Wagner. Giessen, 1856.
Phil 497.3	Weis, L. Anti-Materialismus. v.1-2, 3. Berlin, 1871-73. 2v.
Phil 497.4	Weber, A. Die neueste Vergötterung des Stoffs. Giessen, 1858.
Phil 497.5	Wilder, S.H. Unscientific materialism. N.Y., 1881.
Phil 497.6	Wilson, A.S. The unity of matter. London, 1855.
ɔL Phil 497.7	Woltmann, L. Der historische Materialismus. Düsseldorf, 1900.
Phil 497.8	Wartenberg, Mzcislaw. Das idealistische Argument in der Kritik des Materialismus. Leipzig, 1904.
Phil 497.9.2	Wollny, F. Der Materialismus im Verhältnis zu Religion und Moral. 2e Aufl. Leipzig, 1902.

**Phil 475 - 500   Special philosophical topics, systems, etc. - Secondary
treatises and discussions - Materialism - Monographs (A-Z) - cont.**

Phil 497.10.5	Worrall, R. L. The outlook of science. 2nd ed. N.Y., 1946.

**Phil 504   Special philosophical topics, systems, etc. - Secondary treatises and
discussions - Mechanism**

Phil 504.2	Février, Paulette. Déterminisme et indéterminisme. 1. éd. Paris, 1955.
Phil 504.4	Sansgruber, Kurt. Einflüsse der Naturwissenschaften auf unser Weltbild. Brigenz, 1962.

**Phil 505   Special philosophical topics, systems, etc. - Secondary treatises and
discussions - Microcosm and macrocosm**

Phil 505.5.1	Conger, George Perrigo. Theories of macrocosms and microcosms in the history of philosophy. N.Y., 1967.
Phil 505.6	Andreev, Edvard P. Prostranstvo mikromira. Moskva, 1969.

**Phil 510   Special philosophical topics, systems, etc. - Secondary treatises and
discussions - Monism and pluralism**

Phil 510.01	Papers from the Monist. n.p., n.d.
Phil 510.1.1	Haeckel, Ernst. Der Monismus als Band zwischen Religion und Wissenschaft. 6e Aufl. Bonn, 1893.
Phil 510.1.1.5	Haeckel, Ernst. Monism. London, 1894.
Phil 510.1.1.7	Haeckel, Ernst. Monism. London, 1895.
Phil 510.1.2	Haeckel, Ernst. Die Welträthsel. 7e Aufl. Bonn, 1901.
Phil 510.1.2.4	Haeckel, Ernst. Die Welträthsel. 6e Aufl. Bonn, 1901.
Phil 510.1.2.5	Haeckel, Ernst. Die Welträthsel. Stuttgart, 1899.
Phil 510.1.2.6	Haeckel, Ernst. Die Welträtsel; gemeinverständliche Studien über monistische Philosophie. Berlin, 1961.
Phil 510.1.3	Haeckel, Ernst. Die Welträthsel. Bonn, 1903.
Phil 510.1.3.5	Haeckel, Ernst. Die Welträthsel. Stuttgart, 1903.
Phil 510.1.4	Haeckel, Ernst. Världsgåtorna. Stockholm, 1905.
Phil 510.1.6A	Haeckel, Ernst. The riddle of the universe. N.Y., 1900.
Phil 510.1.6B	Haeckel, Ernst. The riddle of the universe. N.Y., 1900.
Phil 510.1.7.5	Haeckel, Ernst. The riddle of the universe. London, 1925.
Phil 510.1.7.10	Haeckel, Ernst. The substance of the riddle of the universe. N.Y., 1927.
Phil 510.1.8	Haeckel, Ernst. Die wereldraadselen. Baarn, 1913.
Phil 510.1.9	Scarrett, W.R. The riddle of the universe; a review. n.p., 1902.
Phil 510.1.10	Haeckel, Ernst. Les énigmes de l'univers. Paris, 1903.
Phil 510.1.12	Lodge, Oliver. Life and matter. A criticism of Prof. Haeckel's riddle. N.Y., 1906.
Phil 510.1.13.5	Lodge, Oliver. Life and matter. 2nd ed. London, 1912.
Phil 510.1.14	Baumann, J. Häckels Welträthsel nach ihren starken und ihren schwachen Seiten. Leipzig, 1900.
Phil 510.1.15	Haeckel, Ernst. The wonders of life. N.Y., 1905.
Phil 510.1.16	Haeckel, Ernst. Haeckel und Allmers. Bremen, 1941.
Phil 510.1.17	McCabe, Joseph. Haeckel's critics answered. London, 1903.
Phil 510.1.18	McCabe, Joseph. Haeckel's critics answered. London, 1910.
Phil 510.1.19	Chwolson, O.D. Hegel, Haeckel, Kossuth und das zwölfte Gebot. Braunschweig, 1906.
Phil 510.1.20	Ballard, Frank. Haeckel's monism false. London, 1905.
Phil 510.1.21	Menzi, Theodor. Ernst Haeckels Welträtsel oder der Neomaterialismus. Zürich, 1901.
Phil 510.1.22	Wagner, Richard. Aether und Wille. Leipzig, 1901.
Phil 510.1.23	Haeckel, Ernst. Ewigkeit. Berlin, 1915.
Phil 510.1.24	Hansen, Adolf. Grenzen der Religion und Naturwissenschaft. Giessen, 1908.
Phil 510.1.25	Wobbermin, Georg. Ernst Haeckel im Kampf gegen die christliche Weltanschauung. Leipzig, 1906.
Phil 510.1.27	Loofs, F. Anti-Haeckel. 3rd ed. London, 1904.
Phil 510.1.29	Marcus, S.P. Monism? London, 1907.
Phil 510.1.31	Müller, D.A. Scheinchristentum und Haeckels Welträtsel. Inaug. Diss. Gotha, 1901.
Phil 510.1.33	Dennert, D.D. Die Wahrheit über Ernst Haeckel und seine "Welträtsel". Halle, 1920.
Phil 510.1.35	Steiner, R. Two essays on Haeckel. London, 19- .
Phil 510.1.37	Franz, Victor. Ernst Haeckel. v.1-2. Jena, 1944.
Phil 510.1.39	Schmidt, Heinrich. Was wir Ernst Haeckel Verdanken. Leipzig, 1914. 2v.
Phil 510.1.45	Shiltov., A. Ernst Gekkel' pered sudom logiki. Khar'kov, 1907.
Phil 510.1.50	Gasman, Daniel. The scientific origins of National Socialism: Social Darwinism in Ernst Haeckel and the German Monist League. London, 1971.
Phil 510.2	Romanes, G.J. Mind and motion and monism. N.Y., 1895.
Phil 510.3	Sack, J. Monistische Gottes und Weltanschauung. Leipzig, 1899.
Phil 510.4	Reichenau, W. Monistische Philosophie von Spinoza bis auf unserer Tage. Köln, 1884.
Phil 510.5	Ruckhaber, Erich. Des Daseins und Denkens Mechanik und Metamechanik. Hirschberg, 1910.
Phil 510.5.15	Ruckhaber, Erich. Der Mechanismus des menschlichen Denkens. Brackwede, 1911.
Phil 510.6A	Carus, P. Monism and meliorism. N.Y., 1885.
Phil 510.6B	Carus, P. Monism and meliorism. N.Y., 1885.
Phil 510.7	Wakeman, T.B. Addresses...at and in reference to the 1st Monist congress. Cos Cob, 1913.
Phil 510.8	Ostwald, W. Monism as the goal of civilization. Hamburg, 1913.
Phil 510.8.5	Ostwald, W. Monistische Sonntagspredigten. Series 1-3,4. Leipzig, 1911-13. 2v.
Phil 510.9	Noiré, Ludwig. Der monistische Gedanke. Leipzig, 1875.
Phil 510.9.6	Noiré, Ludwig. Aphorismen zur monistischen Philosophie. 2. ed. Mainz, 1884.
Phil 510.9.10	Noiré, Ludwig. Einleitung und Begründung einer monistischen Erkenntnis-Theorie. Mainz, 1877.
Phil 510.9.11	Noiré, Ludwig. Einleitung und Begründung einer monistischen Erkenntnis-Theorie. 2e Ausg. Mainz, 1884.
Phil 510.10	Saulze, J.B. Le monisme matérialiste. Paris, 1911.
Phil 510.11	Olivier, J. von. Monistische Weltanschauung, Leipzig, 1906.
Phil 510.13	Lipsius, Friedrich R. Die Religion des Monismus. Berlin, 1907.
Phil 510.13.5	Lipsius, Friedrich R. Einheit der Erkenntnis und Einheit des Seins. Leipzig, 1913.
Phil 510.14	Milliet, J. Paul. Remarques sur la monadologie. Paris, 1907.
Phil 510.15	Ziegler, J.H. Die wahre Einheit von Religion und Wissenschaft. Zürich, 1904.
Phil 510.16	Unold, Johannes. Der Monismus und seine Ideale. Leipzig, 1908.
Phil 510.17	Carneri, Bartolomäus von. Empfindung und Bewusstsein. Bonn, 1893.
Phil 510.17.5	Carneri, Bartolomäus von. Empfindung und Bewusstsein. 2e Aufl. Stuttgart, 1906.

Phil 510 Special philosophical topics, systems, etc. - Secondary treatises and discussions - Monism and pluralism - cont.

Phil 510.18 Schoeler, Heinrich von. Probleme. Leipzig, 1900.
Phil 510.19.2 Weiss, Bruno. Monismus, Monistenbund, Radikalismus und Christentum. 2e Aufl. Breme, 1908.
Phil 510.20 Volkmann, Paul. Fähigkeiten der Naturwissenschaften und Monismus der Gegenwart. Leipzig, 1909.
Phil 510.20.5 Volkmann, Paul. Die Eigenart der Natur und der Eigensinn des Monismus. Leipzig, 1910.
Phil 510.21 Marcus, Hugo. Die Philosophie des Monopluralismus. Berlin, 1907.
Phil 510.22 Frohschammer, J. Monaden und Weltphantasie. München, 1879.
Phil 510.23 Gutberlet, C. Der mechanische Monismus. Paderborn, 1893.
Phil 510.24 Wobbermin, Georg. Monismus und Monotheismus. Tübingen, 1911.
Phil 510.25 Heyde, Erich. Grundlegung der Wertlehre. Leipzig, 1916.
Phil 510.26 Stern, M.L. Philosophischer und naturwissenschaftlicher Monismus. Leipzig, 1885.
Phil 510.27 Loewenthal, Eduard. Der Bankrott der Darwin-Haeckel'schen Entwicklungstheories und die Krönung des monistischen Gebäudes. Berlin, 1900.
Phil 510.28 Rosny, J.H. Le pluralisme. Paris, 1909.
Phil 510.124 Erdmann, Benno. Über den modernen Monismus. Berlin, 1914.
Phil 510.125.4 Flügel, D. Monismus und Theologie. 4e Aufl. Gotha, 1914.
Phil 510.126 Wahl, Jean. Les philosophies pluralistes. Paris, 1920.
Phil 510.126.3 Wahl, Jean. Les philosophies pluralistes. Thèse. Paris, 1920.
Phil 510.126.9 Wahl, Jean. The pluralist philosophies of England and America. London, 1925.
Phil 510.127 Carr, H. Wildon. A theory of monads. London, 1922.
Phil 510.127.10 Carr, H. Wildon. Cogitans cogitata. Los Angeles, 1930.
Phil 510.128 Frutiger, P. Volonté er conscience. Genève, 1920.
Phil 510.129 Ashcroft, E.A. The world's desires. London, 1905.
Phil 510.130 Worsley, A. Concepts of monism. London, 1907.
Phil 510.131 Brooks, H.J. The riddle of the universe scientifically interpreted. n.p., 1924.
Phil 510.132 Rosenthal, L.A. Die monistische Philosophie. Berlin, 1880.
Phil 510.133 Jordan, H. Die Lebenserscheinungen. Leipzig, 1911.
Phil 510.134 Dieterich, K. Philosophie und Naturwissenschaft. Tübingen, 1875.
Phil 510.135 Mayer, A. Die monistische Erkenntnislehre. Leipzig, 1882.
Phil 510.137 Aliotta, A. Il problema di Dio e il nuovo pluralismo. Città di Castello, 1924.
Phil 510.137.5 Aliotta, A. L'éternité des esprits. Paris, 1924.
Phil 510.138 Wirth, R. Über Monismus (Pantheismus). Plauen, 1874.
Phil 510.139 Der Monismus dargestellt in Beiträgen seiner Vertreter. v.1-2. Jena, 1908.
Phil 510.140 Cassaigneau, M. Monisme vitaliste. Paris, 1925.
Phil 510.141 Wasmann, Erich. Entwicklungstheorie und Monismus. Innsbruck, 1910.
Phil 510.142 Eisler, Rudolf. Geschichte des Monismus. Leipzig, 1910.
Phil 510.143 Herzberg, L. Die philosophischen Hauptströmungen im Monistenbund. Inaug. Diss. Leipzig, 1928.
Phil 510.144 Wendland, J. Monismus in alter und neuer Zeit. Basel, 1908.
Phil 510.145 Penzler, Martin. Die Monadenlehre und ihre Beziehung zur griechischen Philosophie. Minden, 1878.
Phil 510.146 Friedrich, Gustav. Die Farce des Jahrhunderts oder Des monisten Glück und Ende. Leipzig, 1913.
Phil 510.147 Russell, C.W. Mind: creative and dynamic. N.Y., 1932.
Phil 510.148 Wightman, W.P.D. Science and monism. London, 1934.
Phil 510.149 Chang, T.S. Epistemological pluralism. Shanghai? 1932?
Phil 510.150 Bräuer, E.W. Überwindung der Materie. Leipzig, 1925.
Phil 510.152 Schmitz, Oscar A.H. Die Weltanschauung des Halbgebildeten. München, 1914.
Phil 510.153 Cramer, Wolfgang. Die Monade. Stuttgart, 1954.
Phil 510.154 Eyken, A. Reality and monads. Apeldoorn, 1950.
Phil 510.155 Malenovskii, A.A. Empiriomonizm. v.1-3. S'ankt Peterburg, 1905-06.
Phil 510.156 Carvalho, Rubens di Souza. Filosofia universitária. Rio de Janeiro, 1964.
Phil 510.157 Naumenko, Lev K. Monizm kak printsip dialekticheskoi logiki. Alma-Ata, 1968.
Phil 510.158 Waton, Harry. A true monistic philosophy. N.Y., 1947-1955. 2v.

Phil 525 Special philosophical topics, systems, etc. - Secondary treatises and discussions - Mysticism - General works

Phil 525.01 Pamphlet box. Philosophy. Special. Mysticism. General.
Phil 525.1 Du Prel, C.F. Die Philosophie der Mystik. Leipzig, 1885.
Phil 525.1.2 Du Prel, Karl. Die Philosophie der Mystik. 2e Aufl. Leipzig, 1910.
Phil 525.2 Du Prel, Karl. Philosophy of mysticism. London, 1889. 2v.
Phil 525.4 Story, T. (pseud.). Substantialism, or Philosophy of knowledge. Boston, 1879.
Phil 525.5.5 Récéjac, Edonard. Essays on the bases of mystic knowledge. London, 1899.
Phil 525.5.15 Troilo, E. Il misticismo moderno. Torino, 1899.
Phil 525.6 Gutiérrez, Marcelino. El misticismo ortodoxo en sus relaciones con la filosofia. Valladolid, 1886.
Phil 525.7.1 Underhill, Evelyn. Mysticism. 3rd ed. N.Y., 1911.
Phil 525.7.2 Underhill, Evelyn. Mysticism. 4th ed. N.Y., 1912.
NEDL Phil 525.7.3 Underhill, Evelyn. Mysticism. 8th ed. N.Y., 1919.
Phil 525.7.5 Underhill, Evelyn. Practical mysticism. London, 1914.
Phil 525.7.5.3 Underhill, Evelyn. Practical mysticism; a little book for normal people. N.Y., 1915.
Phil 525.7.7 Underhill, Evelyn. The essentials of mysticism and other essays. London, 1920.
Phil 525.7.10 Underhill, Evelyn. The mystic way. London, 1913.
Phil 525.7.15 Underhill, Evelyn. Collected papers of Evelyn Underhill. London, 1946.
Phil 525.7.20 Underhill, Evelyn. Concerning the inner life, with The house of the soul. London, 1947.
Phil 525.8 Seillière, E. Les mystiques du néo-romantisme. Paris, 1911.
Phil 525.8.5 Seillière, E. Mysticisme et domination. Paris, 1913.
Phil 525.8.9 Seillière, E. Le péril mystique dans l'inspiration des démocraties contemporaines. Paris, 1918.
Phil 525.9 Vaughan, R.A. Hours with the mystics. London, 1856. 2v.
Phil 525.9.2 Vaughan, R.A. Hours with the mystics. 2nd ed. London, 1860. 2v.
Htn Phil 525.10* Phelipeaux, J. Relation de l'origine, du progrès...du quiétisme. Ste. Ménehould, 1732.

Phil 525 Special philosophical topics, systems, etc. - Secondary treatises and discussions - Mysticism - General works - cont.

Phil 525.12 Heinroth, J.C.A. Geschichte und Kritik des Mysticismus. Leipzig, 1830.
Phil 525.12.7 Noack, Ludwig. Die christliche Mystik. Königsberg, 1853.
Phil 525.13 Reischle, Max. Ein Wort...über die Mystik in der Theologie. Freiburg, 1886.
Phil 525.14 Schmidt, C. Les libertins spirituels. Bale, 1876.
Phil 525.15 Seisdedos Sanz, J. Principios fundamentales de la mistica. v.1-2,3. Madrid, 1913. 2v.
Phil 525.15.5 Curtis, Adela M. The new mysticism. 3d ed. London, 1913.
Phil 525.15.15 Hasse, Karl P. Das Wesen der Persönlichkeit. Meerane, 1913.
Phil 525.16.5 Gem, S. Harvey. The mysticism of William Law. London, 1914.
Phil 525.16.9 Walton, C. Notes and materials for an adequate biography of...William Law. London, 1854.
Phil 525.16.13 Hobhouse, S.H. Fides et ratio; the book which introduced Jacob Boehme to William Law. n.p., 1936.
Phil 525.17 Paulhan, F. Le nouveau mysticisme. Paris, 1891.
Phil 525.18 Dawkins, M.B. Mysticism, an epistemological problem. New Haven, 1915.
Phil 525.19 Waite, A.E. Studies in mysticism and certain aspects of the secret tradition. London, 1906.
Phil 525.20 Hamilton, C.H. A psychological interpretation of mysticism. Diss. Chicago, 1916.
Phil 525.20.5 Salomon, Gotfried. Beitrag zur Problematik von Mystik und Glaube. Strassburg, 1916.
Phil 525.21 Perty, M. Die mystischen Erscheinungen der menschlichen Natur. With supplement. Leipzig, 1861.
Phil 525.21.2 Perty, M. Die mystischen Erscheinungen der menschlichen Natur. Bd.1-2. 2e Aufl. Leipzig, 1872.
Phil 525.22 Qu'est-ce que la mystique? Paris, 1925.
Phil 525.22.2 Lehmann, Edvard. Mystik in Heidentum und Christentum. 2e Aufl. Leipzig, 1918.
Phil 525.23 Pedrick, Katharine F. How to make perfection appear. Boston, 1919.
Phil 525.23.5 Pedrick, Katharinn F. Du moyen de manifester la perfection. Paris, 1921.
Phil 525.24 Zielinski, C. Der Begriff der Mystik. Jena, 1913.
Phil 525.25 Shirley, Ralph. Occultists and mystics of all ages. London, 1920.
Phil 525.26 Watkin, Edward Ingram. The philosophy of mysticism. London, 1920.
Phil 525.27 Sageret, Jules. La vague mystique. Paris, 1920.
Phil 525.28 Bain, James L.M. The Christ of the Holy Grail. London, 1909.
Phil 525.29 Brenier de Montmorand, Antoine F.J.H.L.M. Psychologie des mystiques catholiques orthodoxes. Paris, 1920.
Phil 525.30.2 Herman, E. The meaning and value of mysticism. 2nd ed. London, 1916.
Phil 525.31 The silent voice. 2d ser. London, 1916.
Phil 525.32 Montague, M.P. Twenty minutes of reality. N.Y., 1917.
Phil 525.33 Cobb, Stanwood. The essential mysticism. Boston, 1918.
Phil 525.34 Addison, C.M. What is mysticism. N.Y., 1923.
Phil 525.35 Butler, Cuthbert. Western mysticism. London, 1922.
Phil 525.35.5 Butler, Cuthbert. Western mysticism. 2d ed. London, 1927.
Phil 525.35.8 Butler, Cuthbert. Western mysticism: the teaching of Augustine, Gregory and Bernard. 3rd ed. London, 1967.
Phil 525.37 Maréchal, J. Dalla percezione sensible all'intuizione mistica. Firenze, 1913.
Phil 525.37.5 Maréchal, J. Études sur la psychologie des mystiques. v.1-2. Bruges, 1924-37.
Phil 525.38.2 Louismet, S. Miracle et mystique. 2e ed. Paris, 1923.
Phil 525.39 Joël, Karl. Der Ursprung der Naturphilosophie aus dem Geiste der Mystik. Jena, 1906.
Phil 525.40 Latteo, Ernesto. Il misticismo. Torino, 1908.
Phil 525.41 Helfferich, A. Die christliche Mystik. Gotha, 1842. 2v.
Phil 525.42 Gorres, J. Die christliche Mystik. Bd.1-2,3,4[1],4[2]. Regensburg, 1836-42.
Phil 525.43 Costa Guimaraes, Francisco da. Contribution à la pathologie des mystiques. Paris, 1908.
Phil 525.44 Specht, G. Die Mystik im Irrsinn. Wiesbaden, 1891.
Phil 525.45 Delacroix, H. Études d'histoire et de psychologie du mysticisme. Paris, 1908.
Phil 525.45.5 Delacroix, H. Essai sur le mysticisme spéculatif. Paris, 1900.
Phil 525.46 Elkinton, J. The light of mysticism. Philadelphia, 1907.
Phil 525.47 Latta, R. The old mysticism and the new pluralism. Glasgow, 1902.
Phil 525.48 Leclère, A. Le mysticisme catholique et l'âme de Dante. Paris, 1906.
Phil 525.49 Lejeune, Paul. Introduction à la vie mystique. Paris, 1899.
Phil 525.49.5 Lejeune, Paul. An introduction to the mystical life. London, 1915.
Phil 525.50.5 Poulain, A. Des graces d'oraison. 5e éd. Paris, 1906.
Phil 525.51.2 Sharpe, A.B. Mysticism: its true nature and value. London, 1910?
Phil 525.52 Oulmont, Charles. Le verger, le temple et la cellule. Paris, 1912.
Phil 525.53 Buckham, J.N. Mysticism and modern life. N.Y., 1915.
Phil 525.54 Bernhart, J. Die philosophische Mystik des Mittelalters. München, 1922.
Phil 525.54.5 Bernhart, J. Bernhardische und Eckhartische Mystik. Kempten, 1912.
Phil 525.55 Jones, Rufus M. Studies in mystical religion. London, 1919.
Phil 525.55.10 Jones, Rufus M. Some exponents of mystical religion. N.Y., 1930.
Phil 525.56.5 Steiner, R. Mystics of the Renaissance. N.Y., 1911.
Phil 525.57 Maw, M.B. Buddhist mysticism. Thèse. Bordeaux, 1924.
Phil 525.58 Janentzky, C. Mystik und Rationalismus. München, 1922.
Phil 525.59 Clemen, Carl. Die Mystik nach Wesen, Entwicklung und Bedeutung. Bonn, 1923.
Phil 525.60 Parke, Jean. The immaculate perception. N.Y., 1927.
Phil 525.61.5 Louismet, S. La contemplation chrétienne. Paris, 1923.
Phil 525.62 Levasti, A. I mistici. Firenze, 1925. 2v.
Phil 525.63 Bennett, C.A. A philosophical study of mysticism. New Haven, 1923.
Phil 525.63.5 Bennett, C.A. A philosophical study of mysticism. New Haven, 1931.
Phil 525.64 Mattiesen, Emil. Der jenseitige Mensch. Berlin, 1925.
Phil 525.65 Ihringer, Bernhard. Der Schuldbegriff bei den Mystikern der Reformationszeit. Bern, 1912.
Phil 525.66 Schwarz, Hermann. Auf Wegen der Mystik. Erfurt, 1924.
Phil 525.67 Buonaiuti, E. Il misticismo medioevale. Pinerolo, 1928.

Phil 525 Special philosophical topics, systems, etc. - Secondary treatises and
discussions - Mysticism - General works - cont.

Phil 525.68 Manacarda, A. Verso una nuova mistica. Bologna, 1922.
Phil 525.69 Riley, I.W. The meaning of mysticism. N.Y., 1930.
Phil 525.70 Bastide, Roger. Les problèmes de la vie mystique. Paris, 1931.
Phil 525.71 Gentilini, B. De la mística. Santiago de Chile, 1926.
Phil 525.72 Smith, Margaret. Studies in early mysticism in the Near and Middle East. London, 1931.
Phil 525.73 Thulié, H. La mystique divine. Paris, 1912.
Phil 525.74.5 Otto, Rudolf. Mysticism East and West. N.Y., 1932.
Phil 525.75 Anker-Larsen, Johannes. With the door open, my experience. N.Y., 1931.
Phil 525.76 Heppe, Heinrich. Geschichte der quietistischen Mystik in der katholischen Kirche. Berlin, 1875.
Phil 525.77 Cordelier, John. The path of the eternal wisdom. 2d ed. London, 1912.
Phil 525.78 Mehlis, G. Die Mystik. München, 1927.
Phil 525.79 Vellani, Giovanni E. La mistica dell'avenire. Modena, 1936.
Phil 525.81 Farges, Albert. Les phénomènes mystiques distingués de leurs contrefaçons humaines et diaboliques. Paris, 1920.
Phil 525.82 Mahnke, D. Unendliche Sphäre und Allmittelpunkt. Halle, 1937.
Phil 525.83 Mukerjee, R. Theory and art of mysticism. London, 1937.
Phil 525.84 Bailey, A.A. From intellect to intuition. N.Y., 1932.
Phil 525.85 Wieser, Max. Der sentimentale Mensch. Gotha, 1924.
Phil 525.85.2 Wieser, Max. Der sentimentale Mensch gesehen aus der Welt. Gotha, 1924.
Phil 525.86 Cailliet E. Mysticisme. Cahors, 1937.
Phil 525.87.5 Younghusband, F.E. Modern mystics. 1st ed. N.Y., 1935.
Phil 525.88 Concerning mysticism. Guilford, 1938.
Phil 525.89 Brockington, A.A. Mysticism and poetry. London, 1934.
Phil 525.90 Collins, J.B. Christian mysticism. Baltimore, 1940.
Phil 525.91 Récéjac, Edonard. Essai sur les fondements de la connaissance mystique. Paris, 1897.
Phil 525.92 Brenes Mesen, R. El misticismo como instrumento de investigación de la verdad. San José de Costa Rica, 1921.
Phil 525.93 Reinhold, Hans. The soul afire. N.Y., 1944.
Phil 525.93.5 Reinhold, Hans. The soul afire. N.Y., 1960.
Phil 525.95 Cheney, Sheldon. Men who have walked with God. N.Y., 1945.
Phil 525.97.5 Arsen'ev, N.S. Ostkirche und Mystik. 2. Aufl. München, 1943.
Phil 525.99 Serrano Plaja, A. Los místicos. Buenos Aires, 1943.
Phil 525.101 Allen, Warner. The timeless moment. London, 1946.
Phil 525.101.10 Allen, Warner. The happy issue. London, 1948.
Phil 525.103 Schnur, H.C. Mystic rebels. N.Y., 1949.
Phil 525.105 Marquette, Jacques de. Introduction to comparative mysticism. N.Y., 1949.
Phil 525.105.5 Marquette, Jacques de. Confessions d'un mystique contemporain. Paris, 1965.
Phil 525.107 Morot-Sir, E. Philosophie et mystique. Thèse. Paris, 1948.
Phil 525.109 Eustace, C.J. An infinity of questions. London, 1946.
Phil 525.111 Schreyer, L. Die Vallendeten. Heidelberg, 1949.
Phil 525.113 Bertin, G. I mistice medievali. Milano, 1944.
Phil 525.115 Summers, M. The physical phenomena of mysticism. N.Y., 1950.
Phil 525.117 Aegerter, E. Le mysticisme. Paris, 1952.
Phil 525.119 Thurston, H. The physical phenomena of mysticism. Chicago, 1952.
Phil 525.121 Albrecht, C. Psychologie des mystischen Bewusstseins. Bremen, 1951.
Phil 525.123.2 Walther, G. Phänomenologie der Mystik. 2. Aufl. Olten, 1955.
Phil 525.125 Mager, Alois. Mystik als seelische Wirklichkeit. Graz, 1947.
Phil 525.130 Froebe-Kapteyn, Olga. Mensch und Wandlung. Zürich, 1955.
Phil 525.131 Eranos-Jahorbuch. Man and transformation. N.Y., 1964.
Phil 525.135 Lemaître, S. Textes mystiques d'Orient et d'Occident. Paris, 1955.
Phil 525.140 Suzuki, D.T. Mysticism. N.Y., 1957.
Phil 525.145 Merkel, Rudolph Franz. Die Mystik im Kulturleben der Völker. Hamburg, 1940.
Phil 525.155 Schloetermann, Heinz. Mystik in den Religionen der Völker. München, 1958.
Phil 525.160 Graef, Hilda Charlotte. Der siebenfarbige Bogen auf den Spuren der grossen Mystiker. Frankfurt, 1959.
Phil 525.165 Gardet, Louis. Thèmes et textes mystiques. Paris, 1958.
Phil 525.170 Bordet, Louis. Religion et mysticisme. Paris, 1959.
Phil 525.175 Felice, Philippe de. Foules en délire. Paris, 1947.
Phil 525.180 Weyergans, Franz. Mystiques parmi nous. Paris, 1959.
Phil 525.185 Cognet, Louis. Post-Reformation spirituality. London, 1959.
Phil 525.190 Grandjean, Louis E. Alt anden gang. København, 1960.
Phil 525.200 Watts, Alan W. This is it. N.Y., 1960.
Phil 525.205 Stace, Walter T. Mysticism and philosophy. 1st ed. Philadelphia, 1960.
Phil 525.210 Zaehner, R.C. Hindu and Muslim mysticism. London, 1960.
Phil 525.215 Andrae, Tor. Islamische Mystiker. Stuttgart, 1960.
Phil 525.220 Baloković, J.B. Towards the center. N.Y., 1956.
Phil 525.225 Bennett, John G. Witness. London, 1962.
Phil 525.230 Happold, F.C. Mysticism. Baltimore, 1967.
Phil 525.231 Merlan, P. Monopsychism, mysticism. The Hague, 1963.
Phil 525.232 Colloque de Strasbourg, 1961. La mystique rhénane, Colloque de Strasbourg, 16-19 mai, 1961. Paris, 1963.
Phil 525.233 Mediaeval mystique tradition and S. John of the Cross. London, 1954.
Phil 525.234 Lodyzhenskii, M.V. Svet nezrimyi. Izd. 2. Petrograd, 1915.
Phil 525.235 Johnson, R.C. The light and the gate. London, 1964.
Phil 525.236 Gobry, Ivan. L'expérience mystique. Paris, 1964.
Phil 525.237 O'Brien, E. Varieties of mystic experience, an anthology and interpretation. 1st ed. N.Y., 1964.
Phil 525.238 Schnapper, Edith B. The inward Odyssey. London, 1965.
Phil 525.239 Bendiscioli, Mario. Der Quietismus zwischen Häresie und Orthodoxie. Wiesbaden, 1964.
Phil 525.240 Graef, Hilda Charlotte. The story of mysticism. 1st ed. Garden City, N.Y., 1965.
Phil 525.241 Bataille, Georges. L'expérience intérieure. 4. éd. Paris, 1954.
Phil 525.242 Shakhnovich, Mikhail. Sovremennaia mistika v svete nauki. Leningrad, 1965.
Phil 525.243 Ravier, André. La mystique et les mystiques. Bruges, 1965.
Phil 525.245 Choisy, Maryse. L'être et le silence. Genève, 1965.
Phil 525.246 Fausset, Hugh I'Anson. The lost dimension. London, 1966.

Phil 525 Special philosophical topics, systems, etc. - Secondary treatises and
discussions - Mysticism - General works - cont.

Phil 525.247 Knowles, David. What is mysticism? London, 1967.
Phil 525.249 Fremantle, Anne Jackson. The Protestant mystics. 1st ed. Boston, 1964.
Phil 525.250 Sunar, Cavit. Mistisizmin ana hatlari. Ankara, 1966.
Phil 525.252 L'homme et la connaissance. Paris, 1965.
Phil 525.254 Ghose, Sisirkumar. Mystics and society; a point of view. N.Y., 1968.
Phil 525.256.2 González Arintero, Juan. La evolución mística en el desenvolvimiento y vitalidad de la Iglesia. 2. ed. Madrid, 1968.
Phil 525.258 Bodmershof, Wilhelm. Geistige Versenkung. Zürich, 1965.
Phil 525.260 Vinkenoog, Simon. Weergaloos. Hilversum, 1968.
Phil 525.262 Katsaros, Thomas. The Western mystical tradition. New Haven, 1969-
Phil 525.264.1 Laski, Marghanita. Ecstasy; a study of some secular and religious experiences. N.Y., 1968.
Phil 525.266 Xirau, Ramón. Palabra y silencio. 1. ed. México, 1968.
Phil 525.268 Bieri, Edgard L. Un concetto dell'aldilà. Roma, 1970.
Phil 525.270 Congrès international de psychologie religieuse, 7th, Avon, 1950. Mystique et continence. Bruges, 1952.

Phil 530 Special philosophical topics, systems, etc. - Secondary treatises and
discussions - Mysticism - Local (By Special Local Table)

Phil 530.10 Hutin, Serge. Les disciples anglais de Jacob Boehme. Paris, 1960.
Phil 530.11.5 Inge, William R. Studies of English mystics. London, 1907.
Phil 530.11.6 Bullett, G.W. The English mystics. London, 1950.
Phil 530.11.7 Cloud of unknowing. A book of contemplation. London, 1912.
Phil 530.11.9 Cloud of unknowing. A book of contemplation. 4. ed. London, 1946.
Phil 530.11.10 The cloud of unknowing. London, 1924.
Phil 530.11.12 Cloud of Unknowing. The cloud of unknowing. London, 1959.
Phil 530.11.15 Knowles, David. The English mystics. London, 1927.
Phil 530.11.15.5 Knowles, David. The English mystical tradition. London, 1961.
Htn Phil 530.11.16* Philadelphian Society, London. Propositions. London, 1697.
Phil 530.11.18 Thune, Nils. The Behmenists and the Philadelphians. Inaug.-Diss. Uppsala, 1948.
Phil 530.11.20 Pepler, Conrad. The English religious heritage. Saint Louis, 1958.
Phil 530.11.22 Colledge, Eric. The mediaeval mystics of England. N.Y., 1961.
Phil 530.15.3 Matter, Jacques. Le mysticisme en France au temps de Fénelon. 2e éd. Paris, 1866.
Phil 530.15.5 Le Jonvello, H. Une mystique bretonne aux XVIIe siècle. Paris, 1913.
Phil 530.15.9 Sourian, M. Le mysticisme en Normandie au XVIIe siècle. Paris, 1923.
Phil 530.15.15 Jacob, A.A. La France mystique. v.1-2. 3e ed. Amsterdam, 1860.
Phil 530.15.20 The mirror of simple souls. London, 1927.
Phil 530.15.25 Jovy, Ernest. Une mystique en pays Perthois au XVIIe siècle Marie Darizy de Verget. Vitry-Le-François, 1913.
Phil 530.15.28 Daniel-Rops, Henry. Mystiques de France. Paris, 1941.
Phil 530.15.30 Buche, Joseph. L'école mystique de Lyon, 1776-1847. Paris, 1935.
Phil 530.15.37 Matter, Jacques. Le mysticisme en France au temps de Fénelon. 2e éd. Paris, 1865.
Phil 530.15.40 Paillard, Etienne. Lumière éternelle. Paris, 1944.
Phil 530.15.45 Cognet, Louis. Crépuscule des mystiques. Tournai, 1958.
Phil 530.20.5 Pfeiffer, Franz. Deutsche Mystiker des vierzehnten Jahrhunderts. Leipzig, 1845. 2v.
Phil 530.20.7 Pfeiffer, Franz. Deutsche Mystiker des vierzehnten Jahrhunderts. 2e Aufl. Göttingen, 1907. 2v.
Phil 530.20.9 Pfeiffer, Franz. Deutsche Mystiker des vierzehnten Jahrhunderts. v.2. Göttingen, 1914.
Phil 530.20.10 Böhringer, F. Die deutschen Mystiker. Zürich, 1855.
Phil 530.20.15 Greith, Carl. Die deutsche Mystik. Freiburg, 1861.
Phil 530.20.20 Hegler, A. Beiträge zur Geschichte der Mystik in der Reformationszeit. Berlin, 1906.
Phil 530.20.25 Preger, Wilhelm. Geschichte der deutschen Mystik im Mittelalter. Leipzig, 1874-1893. 3v.
Phil 530.20.30 Jundt, Auguste. Les amis de Dieu au quatorzième siècle. Paris, 1879.
Phil 530.20.32A Jones, R.M. The flowering of mysticism. N.Y., 1939.
Phil 530.20.32B Jones, R.M. The flowering of mysticism. N.Y., 1939.
Phil 530.20.35 Spamer, Adolf. Über die Zersetzung und Vererbung in den deutschen Mystikertexten. Diss. Giessen, 1910.
Phil 530.20.40 Vansteenberghe, E. Autour de la docte ignorance. Munster en Westphalie, 1914?
Phil 530.20.45 Schellenberg, E.L. Die deutsche Mystik. Berlin, 1919.
Phil 530.20.50 Denifle, H. Das geistliche Leben. 7. Aufl. Graz, 1920.
Phil 530.20.51 Denifle, H. Die deutschen Mystiker der 14. Jahrhunderts. Freiburg in der Schweiz, 1951.
Phil 530.20.53 Hornstein, X. de. Les grands mystiques allemands du XIVe siècle. Lucerne, 1922.
Phil 530.20.55 Grabmann, M. Die Kulturwerte der deutschen Mystik des Mittelalters. Augsburg, 1923.
Phil 530.20.65 Scholz, W. von. Deutsche Mystiker. Berlin, 1927.
Phil 530.20.67 Kunisch, H. Das Wort "Grund" in der Sprache der deutschen Mystik des 14. und 15. Jahrhunderts. Inaug.-Diss. Osnabrück, 1929.
Phil 530.20.75 Seesholtz, A.G. Friends of God. N.Y., 1934.
Phil 530.20.77 Zippel, W. Die Mystiker und die deutsche Gesellschaft des 13. und 14. Jahrhunderts. Inaug.-Diss. Düren, 1935.
Phil 530.20.80 Seitz, Jasy. Der Traktat des "unbekannten deutschen Mystikers" bei Greith. Leipzig, 1936.
Phil 530.20.85 Neuwinger, R. Die deutsche Mystik unter besonderer Berücksichtigung des "cherubinischen Wandersmannes" Johann Schefflers. Bleicherode am Harz, 1937.
Phil 530.20.86 Oehl, W. Deutsche Mystikerbriefe. München, 1931.
Phil 530.20.87 Quint, J. Deutsche Mystikertexte des Mittelalters. Bonn, 1929.
Phil 530.20.90 Clark, J.M. The great German mystics. Oxford, 1949.
Phil 530.20.93 Wentzlaff-Eggebert, F.W. Deutsche Mystik zwischen Mittelalter und Neuzeit. 2. Aufl. Tübingen, 1947.
Phil 530.20.93.3 Wentzlaff-Eggebert, F.W. Deutsche Mystik zwischen Mittelalter und Neuzeit. 3. Aufl. Berlin, 1969.
Phil 530.20.95 Quint, Josef. Textbuch zur Mystik des deutschen Mittelalters. Halle, 1952.
Phil 530.20.100 Gieraths, Gundolf Maria. Reichtum des Lebens. Düsseldorf, 1956.
Phil 530.20.105 Chuzeville, Jean. Les mystiques allemands du XVII au XIX siècle. Paris, 1935.

Phil 530   Special philosophical topics, systems, etc. - Secondary treatises and discussions - Mysticism - Local (By Special Local Table) - cont.

Phil 530.20.110	Marienwerder, Johannes. Vita Dorotheae Montoviensis. Graz, 1964.
Phil 530.20.115	Ruh, Kurt. Altdeutsche und altniederländische Mystik. Darmstadt, 1964.
Phil 530.20.120	Seyppel, Joachim Hans. Texte deutscher Mystik des 16. Jahrhunderts. Göttingen, 1963.
Phil 530.20.125	Firtel, Hilde. Dorothea von Montau. Freiburg in der Schweiz, 1968.
Phil 530.30.5	Muschg, Walter. Die Mystik in der Schweiz, 1200-1500. Frauenfeld, 1935.
Phil 530.30.10A	Muschg, Walter. Mystische Texte aus dem Mittelalter. Basel, 1943.
Phil 530.30.10B	Muschg, Walter. Mystische Texte aus dem Mittelalter. Basel, 1943.
Phil 530.35F	Misciattelli, Piero. Misticismo senese. Firenze, 1966.
Phil 530.35.5	Misciattelli, Piero. The mystics of Siena. Cambridge, Eng., 1929.
Phil 530.35.7	Misciattelli, Piero. L'Italia mistica. Firenze, 1932.
Phil 530.35.10	Jórgensenn, J. I det Höje. Kristiania, 1908.
Phil 530.35.15	Levasti, A. Mistici del duecento e del trecento. Milano, 1935.
Phil 530.35.20	Chuzeville, Jean. Les mystiques italiens. Paris, 1942.
Phil 530.35.25	Petrocchi, Giorgio. Ascesi e mistica trecentesca. Firenze, 1957.
Phil 530.35.30	Adriani, Maurilio. Italia mistica. Roma, 1968.
Phil 530.40.5	Rousselot, P. Les mystiques espagnols. Paris, 1869.
Phil 530.40.15	Rousselot, P. Los misticos españoles. Barcelona, 1907. 2v.
Phil 530.40.25	Peers, E.A. Spanish mysticism. London, 1924.
Phil 530.40.27	Peers, E.A. Studies of the Spanish mystics. London, 1927-30. 2v.
Phil 530.40.27.5	Peers, E.A. Studies of the Spanish mystics. 2nd ed. London, 1951-60. 3v.
Phil 530.40.40	Brouwer, Johan. Psychologie der Spaansche mystiek. Amsterdam, 1931.
Phil 530.40.42	Brouwer, Johan. De achtergrond der Spaansche mystiek. Zutphen, 1935.
Phil 530.40.45	Santullano, Luis. Místicos españoles. Madrid, 1934.
Phil 530.40.47	Peers, E.A. The mystics of Spain. London, 1951.
Phil 530.40.50	Behn, Irene. Spanische Mystik. Düsseldorf, 1957.
Phil 530.40.55	Sainz Rodriguez, P. Espiritualidad española. Madrid, 1961.
Phil 530.40.60	Gallegos Rocafull, J.M. La experiencia de Dios en los misticos españoles. México, 1945.
Phil 530.50.5	Groult, Pierre. Les mystiques des Pays-Bas. Louvain, 1927.
Phil 530.50.10	Arters, Stephanus. La spiritualité des Pays-Bas. Louvain, 1948.
Phil 530.55.7	Emilie, Sister. Une âme mystique au temps présent. v.1-2. Louvain, 1926-27.
Phil 530.70.5	Walter, R. von. Russische Mystik. Düsseldorf, 1957.
Phil 530.70.12	Espiritualidad rusa por San Serafin de Sarov. Madrid, 1965.
Phil 530.105	Dasgupta, S.N. Hindu mysticism. Chicago, 1927.
Phil 530.105.5	Govindacárya, Alkondavilli. A metaphysique of mysticism. Mysore, 1923.
Phil 530.155	Bridges, Leonard Hal. American mysticism, from William James to Zen. 1. ed. N.Y., 1970.

Phil 531   Special philosophical topics, systems, etc. - Secondary treatises and discussions - Naturalism

Phil 531.2	Pratt, James B. Naturalism. New Haven, 1939.
Phil 531.4	Cogny, Pierre. Le naturalisme. Paris, 1953.
Phil 531.6	Dennes, William R. Some dilemmas of naturalism. N.Y., 1960.
Phil 531.8	Skjeroheim, Hans. Objectivism and the study of man. Oslo, 1959.

Phil 535   Special philosophical topics, systems, etc. - Secondary treatises and discussions - Nihilism

Phil 535.5	Levin-Goldschmidt, Hermann. Der Nihilismus im Licht einer kritischen Philosophie. Thayngen, 1941.
Phil 535.10	Pannwitz, R. Der Nihilismus und die Welt. Nürnberg, 1951.
Phil 535.15	Thielicke, H. Der Nihilismus. Tübingen, 1950.
Phil 535.16	Thielicke, H. Nihilism, its origin and nature, with a Christian answer. 1st ed. N.Y., 1961.
Phil 535.20	Graaff, Frank de. Het Europese nihilisme. Amsterdam, 1956.
Phil 535.25	Mayer, Ernst. Kritik des Nihilismus. München, 1958.
Phil 535.30	Arendt, Dieter. Nihilismus. Köln, 1970.
Phil 535.35	Leon, Philip. Beyond belief and unbelief. London, 1965.
Phil 535.40	Goudsblom, Johan. Nihilisme en cultuur. Amsterdam, 1960.
Phil 535.45	Rosen, Stanley. Nihilism: a philosophical essay. New Haven, 1969.

Phil 541   -   566   Special philosophical topics, systems, etc. - Secondary treatises and discussions - Ontology - Monographs (A-Z)

Phil 551.1	Kichanova, Inga M. Desiat' ispovedi. Moskva, 1971.
Phil 552.3	Lanza del Vasto, Joseph Jean. Les quatre fléaux. Paris, 1971.
Phil 553.2	Misrahi, Robert. Lumière, commencement, liberté. Thèse. Paris, 1969.
Phil 559.2	Schmida-Wöllersderfer, Susanna. Perspektiven des Seins. München, 1968. 2v.
Phil 559.4	Seidel, George Joseph. Being nothing and God; a philosophy of appearance. Assen, 1970.

Phil 568   Special philosophical topics, systems, etc. - Secondary treatises and discussions - Order

Phil 568.2	The concept of order. Seattle, 1968.

Phil 573   Special philosophical topics, systems, etc. - Secondary treatises and discussions - Perception

Phil 573.2	Armstrong, David M. Perception and the physical world. London, 1961.
Phil 573.4	Chambers, Frank P. Perception, understanding and society. London, 1961.
Phil 573.6	Locke, Don. Perception and our knowledge of the external world. London, 1967.

Phil 574   Special philosophical topics, systems, etc. - Secondary treatises and discussions - Personalism

Phil 574.2	Janssens, Louis. Personalisme en democratisering. Brussel, 1957.
Phil 574.4	Stefanini, Luigi. Personalismo filosofico. Brescia, 1962.
Phil 574.6	Haering, Bernhard. The Christian existentialist. N.Y., 1968.
Phil 574.6.5	Haering, Bernhard. Personalismus in Philosophie und Theologie. München, 1968.
Phil 574.8	Escobar, Edmundo. Francisco Larroyo y su personalismo crítico. 1. ed. México, 1970.

Phil 575   Special philosophical topics, systems, etc. - Secondary treatises and discussions - Personality

Phil 575.01	Pamphlet box. Philosophy. Special. Personality.
Phil 575.1	Chantepie, E. Le presonnage humain. Paris, 1874.
Phil 575.2	Momerie, A.W. Personality. Edinburgh, 1879.
Phil 575.2.2	Momerie, A.W. Personality. 3rd ed. Edinburgh, 1886.
Phil 575.2.3	Momerie, A.W. Personality. 4th ed. Edinburgh, 1889.
Phil 575.2.5	Momerie, A.W. Personality. Edinburgh, 189-?
Phil 575.3	Oginski, T. Die Idee der Person. Breslau, 1853.
Phil 575.4	Olssen, W.W. Personality. N.Y., 1882.
Phil 575.5	Ritchie, E. The problem of personality. Ithaca, N.Y., 1889.
Phil 575.6	Thompson, H.M. The world and the wrestlers. N.Y., 1895.
Phil 575.7	Richmond, W. Essay on personality as a philosophical principle. London, 1900.
Phil 575.8	Lutosławski, W. Uber die Grundvoraussetzungen und Consequenzen der individualistischen Weltanschauung. Helsingfors, 1898.
Phil 575.9	Paulham, F. Les caractères. Paris, 1902.
Phil 575.10	Hyde, W. De W. From Epicurus to Christ...study in...personality. N.Y., 1904.
Phil 575.10.10	Hyde, W. De W. The five great philosophies of life. N.Y., 1932.
Phil 575.11	Jones, W.T. Idee der Persönlichkeit bei den englischen Denken. Jena, 1906.
Phil 575.12	Bruce, H.A. Riddle of personality. N.Y., 1908.
Phil 575.12.2	Bruce, H.A. Riddle of personality. N.Y., 1915.
Phil 575.12.5	Brockdorff, Cay. Die wissenschaftliche Selbsterkenntnis. Stuttgart, 1908.
Phil 575.13	Piat, C. La personne humaine. Paris, 1897.
Phil 575.13.2	Piat, C. La personne humaine. 2e éd. Paris, 1913.
Phil 575.14	Oesterreich, K. Die Phänomenologie des Ich in ihren Grundproblem. Leipzig, 1910.
Phil 575.16	Mouchet, E. Examen del concepto de identidad. Buenos Aires, 1910.
Phil 575.17	Carus, P. Personality. Chicago, 1911.
Phil 575.18A	Bosanquet, B. The principle of individuality and value. London, 1912.
Phil 575.18B	Bosanquet, B. The principle of individuality and value. London, 1912.
Phil 575.18.5	Bosanquet, B. Value and destiny of the individual. London, 1913.
Phil 575.19	Jevons, F.B. Personality. N.Y., 1913.
Phil 575.20	Frew, D.I. Cosmic inquiry pertaining to origin and development of individuality. Salt Lake City, 1907.
Phil 575.21	Merrington, E.N. The problem of personality. London, 1916.
Phil 575.22	Buckham, John W. Personality and the Christian ideal. Boston, 1909.
Phil 575.22.5	Buckham, John W. Christianity and personality. N.Y., 1936.
Phil 575.23	Ladd, George T. Secret of personality. N.Y., 1918.
Phil 575.24	Laird, John. Problems of the self. London, 1917.
Phil 575.25	Jeanmaire, Charles. L'idée de la personnalité. Thèse. Toulouse, 1882.
Phil 575.26	Moroney, Timothy. The idea of personality. Diss. Washington, 1919.
Phil 575.27	Schlaf, Johannes. Das absolute Individuum. Berlin, 1910.
Phil 575.28	Schulz, Bernhard. Das Bewusstseinsproblem. Wiesbaden, 1915.
Phil 575.29	König, Karl. Rhythmus, Religion, Persönlichkeit. Jena, 1908.
Phil 575.30	Platzhoff-Lejeune, E. Werk und Persönlichkeit. Minden, 1903.
Phil 575.31	Renouvier, Charles. Le personnalisme suivi d'une étude sur la perception extrême. Paris, 1903.
Phil 575.32	Dreyer, Hans. Personalismus und Realismus. Berlin, 1905.
Phil 575.33	Randall, J.H. The culture of personality. N.Y., 1912.
Phil 575.34	Müller-Freienfels, Richard. Persönlichkeit und Weltanschauung. Berlin, 1919.
Phil 575.34.2	Müller-Freienfels, Richard. Persönlichkeit und Weltanschauung. 2e Aufl. Berlin, 1923.
Phil 575.34.5.2	Müller-Freienfels, Richard. Philosophie der Individualität. 2e Aufl. Leipzig, 1923.
Phil 575.45	Heath, Arthur G. The moral and social significance of the conception of personality. Oxford, 1921.
Phil 575.47	Myerson, Abraham. The foundations of personality. Boston, 1921.
Phil 575.51	Klages, Ludwig. Prinzipien der Charakterologie. 3e Aufl. Leipzig, 1921.
Phil 575.51.4	Klages, Ludwig. Die Grundlagen der Charakterkunde. 4e Aufl. Leipzig, 1926.
Phil 575.51.8	Klages, Ludwig. Die Grundlagen der Charakterkunde. 7e und 8e Aufl. Leipzig, 1936.
Phil 575.51.9	Klages, Ludwig. Die Grundlagen der Charakterkunde. 5e Aufl. Jena, 1937.
Phil 575.51.12	Klages, Ludwig. Die Grundlagen der Charakterkunde. 11e Aufl. Bonn, 1951.
Phil 575.51.15	Klages, Ludwig. The science of character. London, 1929.
Phil 575.51.20	Klages, Ludwig. Les principes de la caractérologie. Paris, 1930.
Phil 575.51.30	Klages, Ludwig. Vorschule der Charakterkunde. 2e Aufl. Leipzig, 1937.
Phil 575.51.40	Hermann, Oskar. Dr. Klages, Entwurf einer Charakterkunde. Leipzig, 1920.
Phil 575.51.42	Breukers, Eugenio Marie Josephine. Levensvormen. Roermond, 1947.
Phil 575.52	Webb, C.C.J. God and personality. Aberdeen, 1919.
Phil 575.52.7	Webb, C.C.J. Divine personality and human life. London, 1920.
Phil 575.52.15	Webb, C.C.J. Our knowledge of one another. London, 1930
Phil 575.54	Wolf, H. De persoonlijkheidsidee bij meisterl Ekhart, Leibniz en Goethe. Amsterdam, 1920.
Phil 575.56	Zilsel, Edgar. Die Geniereligion. Wien, 1918.
Phil 575.57	Roback, A.A. Character and inhibition. n.p., 1925.

Classified Listing

Phil 575.57.10	Roback, A.A. Personality, the crux of social intercourse. Cambridge, Mass., 1931.
Phil 575.57.11	Roback, A.A. Personality. London, 1931.
Phil 575.58	Gordon, R.G. Personality. London, 1926.
Phil 575.58.3	Gordon, R.G. Personality. N.Y., 1928.
Phil 575.59	McBride, Peter. The riddle of personality: mechanism or mystery? London, 1926.
Phil 575.60	Braham, Ernest G. Personality and immortality in post Kantian thought. London, 1926.
Phil 575.60.5	Braham, Ernest G. Ourselves and reality. London, 1929.
Phil 575.61	Haering, T.L. Über Individualität in Natur- und Geistesewelt. Leipzig, 1926.
Phil 575.62	Valentine, P.F. The psychology of personality. N.Y., 1927.
Phil 575.64	Knudson, A.C. The philosophy of personalism. N.Y., 1927.
Phil 575.65	Rohracher, H. Persönlichkeit und Schicksal. Wien, 1926.
Phil 575.66	Fernandez, R. De la personne. Paris, 1928.
Phil 575.67	Volkelt, Johannes. Das Problem der Individualität. München, 1928.
Phil 575.68	Oakeley, Hilda D. A study in the philosophy of personality. London, 1928.
Phil 575.69	Lehmann, G. Über Einzigkeit und Individualität. Leipzig, 1926.
Phil 575.70	Prinzhorn, H. Um die Persönlichkeit. Bd.1. Heidelberg, 1927.
Phil 575.71	Daudet, Léon A. L'hérédo; essai sur le drame intérieur. Paris, 1916.
Phil 575.72	Bazaillas, Albert. La vie personnelle. Paris, 1904.
Phil 575.73	Vaughan, Richard M. The significance of personality. N.Y., 1930.
Phil 575.74	Denison, J.H. The enlargement of personality. N.Y., 1930.
Phil 575.75	Plant, Paul. Die Psychologie der produktiven Persönlichkeit. Stuttgart, 1929.
Phil 575.76	Ehrlich, Walter. Stufen der Personalität. Halle, 1930.
Phil 575.77	Stern, W. Studien zur Personwissenschaft. I. Leipzig, 1930.
Phil 575.78	Crutcher, Roberta. Personality and reason. London, 1931.
Phil 575.79	Hamilton, O.P. Dreamers and doers. London, 1931.
Phil 575.80	Thompson, Dow. A mind that was different. Wellston, 1932.
Phil 575.81	Dittrich, O. Individualismus, Universalismus, Personalismus. Berlin, 1917.
Phil 575.82	Lutosławski, W. El personalismo. Madrid, 1887.
Phil 575.83	Janet, Pierre. L'évolution psychologique de la personnalité. Paris, 1929.
Phil 575.84	Donahue, G.H. Parenthood and civilization. Boston, 1931.
Phil 575.85	Rădulescu-Motru, C. Personalismul energetic. Bucuresti, 1927.
Phil 575.86	Campbell, C.M. Human personality and the environment. N.Y., 1934.
Phil 575.87	Morgan, B.S. Individuality in a collective world. N.Y., 1935.
Phil 575.88	Langan, Hubert E. The philosophy of personalism and its educational applications. Diss. Washington, D.C., 1935.
Phil 575.89	Lemarié, O. Essai sur la personne. Paris, 1936.
Phil 575.90	Lochman, M. Inner life of humanity. Pt.1. n.p., 1936.
Phil 575.91A	Allport, G.W. Personality; a psychological interpretation. N.Y., 1937.
Phil 575.91B	Allport, G.W. Personality; a psychological interpretation. N.Y., 1937.
Phil 575.91.5	Allport, G.W. The field of personality. n.p., n.d.
Phil 575.92	Krout, M.H. Major aspects of personality. Chicago, 1933.
Phil 575.93	Rothacker, E. Die Schichten der Persönlichkeit. Leipzig, 1938.
Phil 575.93.15	Rothacker, E. Die Schichten der Persönlichkeit. 4e Aufl. Bonn, 1948.
Phil 575.95	Harvard University. Harvard Psychological Clinic. Explorations in personality. N.Y., 1938.
Phil 575.96	Thorpe, L.P. Psychological foundations of personality. N.Y., 1938.
Phil 575.97	Stuart, C. Achievement of personality. N.Y., 1938.
Phil 575.98	Stagner, R. Psychology of personality. N.Y., 1937.
Phil 575.99	Kamiat, A.H. Social forces in personality stunting. Cambridge, 1933.
Phil 575.100	McMorrow, G.J. A metaphysical study on the individual and the person. Diss. Notre Dame, 1940.
Phil 575.101	Hertel, François. Pour un ordre personnaliste. Montréal, 1942.
Phil 575.105	Larroyo, Francisco. Exposición y crítica del personalismo espiritualista de nuestro tiempo. México, 1941.
Phil 575.110	Lucka, E. Grenzen der Seele. Berlin, 1916.
Phil 575.115	Wolff, W. The expression of personality. N.Y., 1943.
Phil 575.120	Newcomb, Theodore Mead. Personality and social change. N.Y., 1943.
Phil 575.120.2.2	Newcomb, Theodore Mead. Personality and social change. N.Y., 1957.
Phil 575.127	Verweyen, J.M. Der Edelmensch und seine Werte. 2e Aufl. München, 1922.
Phil 575.130	Tietzen, Hermann. Die menschliche Persönlichkeit in Anlehnung an Zinzendorfsche Gedanken. Stuttgart, 1922.
Phil 575.135	Bañuelos García, M. Personalidad y caracter. Madrid, 1935.
Phil 575.136	Romero, F.A. Filosofía de la persona y otros ensayos de filosofía. Buenos Aires, 1944.
Phil 575.137	Mutius, Gerhard von. Jenseits von Person und Sache. München, 1925.
Phil 575.138	Stiefel, Kurt. Persönlichkeit und Form. Zürich, 1943.
Phil 575.139	Baudouin, Charles. Découverte de la personne, esquisse d'un personnalisme analytique. Paris, 1940.
Phil 575.140	Nédoncelle, Maurice. La réciprocité des consciences; essai sur la nature de la personne. Thèse. Paris, 1942.
Phil 575.140.5	Nédoncelle, Maurice. Vers une philosophie de l'amour et de la personne. Aubier, 1957.
Phil 575.141	Giordani, Roberto. Dalla dialettica alla apodittica. Roma, 1946.
Phil 575.142	Berdiaev, N.A. O rabstve i svobode cheloveka. Paris, 194-.
Phil 575.142.10	Berdiaev, N.A. Ia i mir ob"ektov. Paris, 193-?
Phil 575.145	Kern, Hans. Die Masken der Siecle. Leipzig, 194-.
Phil 575.146	Mounier, E. Le personnalisme. Paris, 1950.
Phil 575.146.5	Mounier, E. Personalism. London, 1952.
Phil 575.146.10	Mounier, E. The character of man. London, 1956.
Phil 575.147	Mounier, E. Be not afraid. London, 1952.
Phil 575.147.80	Zaza, N. Étude critique de la notion d'engagement chez E. Mounier. Genève, 1955.
Phil 575.148	Gent, Werner. Person und Psychotherapie. Göttingen, 1951.

Phil 575.149	Mel'vil', Iu.K. Amerikanskii personalizm-filosofiia imperialisticheskoi reaktsii. Moskva, 1954.
Phil 575.150	Massa, Eugenio. I fondamenti metafisici "dignitas hominis". Torino, 1954.
Phil 575.151A	Frondizi, R. The nature of the self. New Haven, 1953.
Phil 575.151B	Frondizi, R. The nature of the self. New Haven, 1953.
Phil 575.155	Stauenhagen, K. Person und Persönlichkeit. Göttingen, 1957.
Phil 575.160	Terlecki, Tymon. Krytyka personalistyczna. Londyn, 1957.
Phil 575.165	Macmurray, John. The self as agent. London, 1957. 2v.
Phil 575.170	Morley, Felix. Essays on individuality. Philadelphia, 1958.
Phil 575.180	La présence d'autrui. Paris, 1957.
Phil 575.185	Broad, Charlie P. Personal identity and survival. London, 1958.
Phil 575.190	Huibregtse, Kornelis. Anthropologisch-historische benadering van het moderne subjectgevoel. Haarlem, 1950.
Phil 575.200	Roem, H.A.C. Structuurphenomenologische systematisering van het menszijn door centraalstelling van de vrijheidsbeleving. 's-Gravenhage, 1952.
Phil 575.205	Wilde, Arie de. De persoon. Assen, 1951.
Phil 575.210	Michel, Ernst. Der Prozess "Gesellschaft contra Person". Stuttgart, 1959.
Phil 575.215A	Allport, G.W. Personality and social encounter. Boston, 1960.
Phil 575.215B	Allport, G.W. Personality and social encounter. Boston, 1960.
Phil 575.220	Chevalier, Charles. La confidence et la personne humaine. Paris, 1960.
Phil 575.225	Minkus, P.A. Philosophy of the person. Oxford, 1960.
Phil 575.230	Kaplan, Bert. Studying personality crossculturally. Evanston, Illinois, 1961.
Phil 575.235	Miller, Reinhold. Persönlichkeit und Gemeinschaft zur Kritik der neothomistischen Persönlichkeitsauffassung. Berlin, 1916.
Phil 575.240	Bui-Kim-Duong, J.B. L'épanouissement de la personnalité humaine par la conformité au Christ. Fribourg/Suisse, 1960.
Phil 575.245	Shoemaker, S. Self-knowledge and self-identity. Ithaca, 1963.
Phil 575.246	Parsons, Talcott. Social structure and personality. N.Y., 1964.
Phil 575.247	Nédoncelle, Maurice. Personne humaine et nature. Paris, 1963.
Phil 575.248	Kovály, Pavel. Americký personalismus; příspěvek k rozboru krize současného buržoazního myšlení. Praha, 1962.
Phil 575.250	Sanford, Nevitt. Self and society. 1st ed. n.p., 1966.
Phil 575.251	Lahbabi, Mohamed Aziz. De l'être à la personne. 1. éd. Paris, 1954.
Phil 575.253	Platonov, Konstantin K. Lichnost' i trud. Moskva, 1965.
Phil 575.253.5	Kalinin, Ananii I. Rol' truda v razvitii lichnosti v usloviiakh stroitelstva kommunizma. Cheboksary, 1969.
Phil 575.254	Jaroszewski, Tadeusz M. Osobowość i własność. Warszawa, 1965.
VPhil 575.255	Pešić-Golubović, Zagorka. Problemi savremene teorije ličnosti. Beograd, 1966.
Phil 575.256	Winckelmans de Cléty, Charles. The world of persons. Thesis. London, 1967.
Phil 575.258	To be or not to be...existential psychological perspectives on the self. Gainesville, 1967.
Phil 575.260	Merchant, Francis. A search for identity. Salem, 1967.
Phil 575.261	Koy, Igor' S. Sotsiologiia lichnosti. Moskva, 1967.
Phil 575.266	Ponzio, Augusto. La relazione interpersonale. Bari, 1967.
Phil 575.268	Morgan, George W. The human predicament and dissolution and wholeness. Providence, 1968.
Phil 575.270	Werff, Jacobus Johannes van der. Zelbeelden zelfideaal. Assen, 1965.
Phil 575.272	Conference on Comparative Philosophy and Culture. East-West studies on the problem of the self. The Hague, 1968.
Phil 575.274	Fair, Charles M. The dying self. 1st ed. Middletown, Conn., 1969.
Phil 575.276	Maaloee, Erik. Egenskab og faellesskab. København, 1969.
Phil 575.278	Watts, Alan Wilson. The book; on the taboo against knowing who you are. N.Y., 1966.
Phil 575.280	Evans, Cedric Oliver. The subject of consciousness. London, 1970.
Phil 575.282	Natanson, Maurice Alexander. The journeying self; a study in philosophy and social role. Reading, Mass., 1970.
Phil 575.284	Johnstone, Henry Webb. The problem of the self. University Park, 1970.
Phil 575.286	Frings, Manfred S. Person und Dasein. Zur Frage der Ontologie des Wertseins. Den Haag, 1969.
Phil 575.288	Gergen, Kenneth J. The concept of self. N.Y., 1971.
Phil 575.290	Ban'ka, Józef. Współczesne problemy filosofii aechniki. Poznań, 1971.
Phil 575.292	Slobodianuz, Sergei S. Lichnost' ilaaz asennost! Moskva, 1971.
Phil 575.294	Petander, Karl. Västerlandet inför personlighetstanken. Uppsala, 1969.
Phil 575.296	Karquel, André. La tragédie cosmique de la conscience. Paris, 1970.

Phil 577.2	Boehm, Gottfried. Studien zur Perspektivität. Thesis. Heidelberg, 1969.

Phil 582.2	Stegmueller, Wolfgang. Der Phänomenalismus und seine Schwierigkeiten. Darmstadt, 1969.
Phil 582.4	Moreau, Joseph. La conscience et l'être. Paris, 1958.
Phil 582.6	Chatterjee, Margaret. Our knowledge of other selves. Bombay, 1963.

Phil 583.2	Reyer, Wilhelm. Einführung in der Phänomenologie. Leipzig, 1926.
Phil 583.4	Strasser, Stephan. The idea of dialogal phenomenology. Pittsburgh, 1969.
Phil 583.6	Erickson, Stephen A. Language and being: an analytic phenomenology. New Haven, 1970.
Phil 583.8	Kockelmans, Joseph John. Phenomenology and physical science. Pittsburgh, 1966.

Phil 583   Special philosophical topics, systems, etc. - Secondary treatises and discussions - Phenomenology - cont.

Phil 583.8.5   Kockelmans, Joseph John. Phenomenology and the natural sciences: essays and translations. Evanston, 1970.

Phil 583.10   Colombo, Arrigo. Sulla fenomenologie e la rivelazione delle cose. Bologna, 1968.

Phil 583.12   Mohanty, Jitendra Nath. Phenomenology and ontology. Den Haag, 1970.

Phil 583.14   Mathur, Dinesh Chandra. Naturalistic philosophies of experience. St. Louis, 1971.

Phil 583.16   Zaner, Richard M. The way of phenomenology. N.Y., 1970.

Phil 583.18   Mokrejš, Antonín. Fenomenologie a problém intersubjektivity. 1. Vyd. Praha, 1969.

Phil 585   Special philosophical topics, systems, etc. - Secondary treatises and discussions - Philosophical anthropology

Phil 585.5   Siegmund, Georg. Der Mensch in seinem Dasein. Freiburg, 1953.

Phil 585.10   Burnett, Whit. The spirit of man. 1st ed. N.Y., 1958.

Phil 585.15   Emmet, D.M. Function. London, 1958.

Phil 585.20   Frank, W.D. The rediscovery of man. N.Y., 1958.

Phil 585.25   Jeffreys, M.V.C. Mystery of man. London, 1957.

Phil 585.30   Ehrlich, Walter. Philosophische Anthropologie. Tübingen, 1957.

Phil 585.35   Cardone, Domenico Antonio. Il divenire e l'uomo. v.1-3. 2. ed. Palmi, 1956-57.

Phil 585.45   Buytendijk, F.J.J. Das Menschliche. Stuttgart, 1958.

Phil 585.50   Biot, René. Poussière vivante. Paris, 1957.

Phil 585.55   Winkler, Franz E. Man: the bridge. N.Y., 1960.

Phil 585.60   Sabuco de Nantes Barrera, O. Nueva filosofía de la naturaleza del hombre. Madrid, 1728.

Phil 585.65   Kwant, Remy C. Encounter. Pittsburgh, 1960.

Phil 585.66   Kwant, Remy C. Wijsbegeerte van de ontmoeting. Utrecht, 1959.

Phil 585.70   Cantoni, Remo. Umano e disumano. 1. ed. Milano, 1958.

Phil 585.70.5   Cantoni, Remo. Il problema antropologico nella Filosofia Contemporanea. Milano, 1963.

Phil 585.70.10   Cantoni, Remo. Scienze umane e antropologia filosofica. Milano, 1966.

Phil 585.70.15   Cantoni, Remo. Storicismo e scienze dell'uomo. Milano, 1967.

Phil 585.75   Bruning, Walther. Philosophische Anthropologie. Stuttgart, 1960.

Phil 585.80   Radhakrishnan, Sarvepalli. The concept of man. London, 1960.

Phil 585.80.2   Radhakrishnan, Sarvepalli. The concept of man. London, 1960.

Phil 585.85F   Grünsteidl, Edmund. Der Mensch zwischen Atom und Universum. Wien, 1958?

Phil 585.90   Schoeps, H.J. Was ist der Mensch? Göttingen, 1960.

Phil 585.95   Langdon-Davies, J. On the nature of man. N.Y., 1961.

Phil 585.100   Nef, John U. Religion and the study of man. Houston, 1961.

Phil 585.105   Virasoro, M.A. Filosofía de la existencia y antropología filosófica. 1. ed. Bahía Blanca, 1960.

Phil 585.110   Gal'perin, S.I. Kritika teorii biologizatsii cheloveka. Leningrad, 1960.

Phil 585.115   Mercier, R. La réhabilitation de la nature humaine. Villemomble, 1960.

Phil 585.120   Landmann, Michael. De homine. Freiburg, 1962.

Phil 585.120.10   Wein, Hermann. Kentaurische Philosophie; Vorträge und Abhandlungen. München, 1968.

Phil 585.125   Aolliet, Joseph. L'homme social. Paris, 1942.

Phil 585.130   Desan, Wilfrid. The planetary man. Washington, 1961.

Phil 585.135   Plattel, Martinus Gulielmus. Sociale wijsbegeerte. v.1-2. Utrecht, 1960-64.

Phil 585.135.2   Plattel, Martinus Gulielmus. Social philosophy. Pittsburgh, 1965.

Phil 585.140   Becker, Ernest. The birth and death of meaning. N.Y., 1962.

Phil 585.140.2   Becker, Ernest. The birth and death of meaning. 2. ed. N.Y., 1971.

Phil 585.140.5   Becker, Ernest. The structure of evil. N.Y., 1968.

Phil 585.141   Dubos, René Jules. The torch of life. N.Y., 1962.

Phil 585.142   Wölcker, Joannes. Amussis vitae humanae. Olomucii, 1698.

Phil 585.143   Burr, Harold S. The nature of man and the meaning of existence. Springfield, 1962.

Phil 585.145   Martins, D. Mistério do homen. Braga, 1961.

Phil 585.147   Tsanoff, Radoslav. Worlds to know. N.Y., 1962.

Phil 585.148   Tsanoff, Radoslav. Science and human perspectives. London, 1963.

Phil 585.150   Ahlman, Erik. Ihmisen probleemi. Helsinki, 1953.

Phil 585.151   Marcel, Gabriel. Man against mass society. Chicago, 1962.

Phil 585.152   Muñoz Espinalt, Carlos. Saber-se entendre. Barcelona, 1961.

Phil 585.153   Leclerq, J. La révolution de l'homme au XXe siècle. Tournai, 1963.

Phil 585.154   Goltz, B. Hinter den Feigenblättern. Berlin, 1862-64.

Phil 585.155   Sullivan, L.H. Democracy: a man-search. Detroit, 1961.

Phil 585.156   Collingwood, F.J. Man's physical and spiritual nature. N.Y., 1963.

Phil 585.157   Chauchard, P. L'homme normal. Paris, 1963.

Phil 585.158   Plessner, H. Conditio humana. Pfullingen, 1964.

Phil 585.159   Virasoro, M.A. Para una nueva idea del hombre y de la antropología filosófica. Tucuman, 1963.

Phil 585.160   Rothacker, Erich. Philosophische Anthropologie. Bonn, 1964.

Phil 585.160.5   Rothacker, Erich. Zur Genealogie des menschlichen Bewusstseins. Bonn, 1966.

Phil 585.161   Browning, Douglas. Act and agent. Coral Gables, Fla., 1964.

Phil 585.162   Román, Julián. El hombre como síntesis del universo. 1. ed. Rosario, 1965.

Phil 585.163   Phenix, Philip H. Man and his becoming. New Brunswick, N.J., 1964.

Phil 585.164   Castell, Alburey. The self in philosophy. N.Y., 1965.

Phil 585.165   Patka, Frederick. Value and existence. N.Y., 1964.

Phil 585.166   International Congress of Philosophy, 13th, Mexico, 1963. Delegation from the USSR. Chelovek i epokha. Moskva, 1964.

VPhil 585.167   International Congress of Philosophy, 13th, Mexico, 1963. Clovek, kto si? Bratislava, 1965.

VPhil 585.167.5   Filipec, Jindřich. Člověk a moderní doba. Praha, 1966.

Phil 585.168   Taylor, Thomas. A vindication of the rights of brutes (1792). Gainesville, Fla., 1966.

Phil 585.169   Morra, Gianfranco. La riscoperta del sacro. Bologna, 1964.

Phil 585   Special philosophical topics, systems, etc. - Secondary treatises and discussions - Philosophical anthropology - cont.

Phil 585.170   Wein, Hermann. Philosophie als Erfahrungswissenschaft. Den Haag, 1965.

Phil 585.171   Endres, Josef. Man, as the ontological mean. N.Y., 1965.

Phil 585.172   Rieff, Philip. The triumph of the therapeutic. 1st ed. N.Y., 1966.

Phil 585.173   Mukerjee, Radhakamal. The dimensions of human evolution. London, 1963.

Phil 585.174   Cantoni, Remo. Società e cultura. Milano, 1964.

Phil 585.175   Silva Mello, Antonio da. A superioridade do homen tropical. Rio de Janeiro, 1965.

Phil 585.176   Jeuscher, Ernest. L'homme et son destin. Paris, 1961.

Phil 585.177   Taylor, Richard. Action and purpose. Englewood Cliffs, N.J., 1966.

Phil 585.177.5   Brown, Donald George. Action. Toronto, 1968.

Phil 585.178   Aaberg, Thorsten. Livsåskådningar. Stockholm, 1965.

Phil 585.179   Hidalgo, Alberto. El universo está cerca. Buenos Aires, 1945.

Phil 585.180   Platt, John Rader. New views of the nature of man. Chicago, 1965.

Phil 585.181   Hartung, Henri. Unité de l'homme. Paris, 1963.

Phil 585.182   Heschel, Abraham Joshua. Who is man? Stanford, Calif., 1965.

Phil 585.183   La filosofia dell'uomo di M.T. Antonelli. Roma, 1963.

Phil 585.184   Mukerjee, Radhakamal. The community of communities. Bombay, 1966.

Phil 585.185   Rombach, Heinrich. Die Frage nach dem Menschen. Freiburg, 1966.

Phil 585.186   Rendel, David. Earthling and Hellene; a psychological mechanism of evolution and its effect on the human race. Wimbledon, 1963.

Phil 585.187   Friedman, Maurice Stanley. To deny our nothingness. N.Y., 1967.

Phil 585.188   Chambliss, Rollin. Meaning for man. N.Y., 1966.

Phil 585.188.2   Auger, Pierre. L'homme microscopique. 2e éd. Paris, 1966.

Phil 585.190   Burkhardt, Hans. Dimensionen menschlicher Wirklichkeit. Schweinfurt, 1965.

VPhil 585.191   Suchodolski, Bogdan. Narodziny nowożytnej filozofii człowieka. Warszawa, 1963.

Phil 585.191.5   Suchodolski, Bogdan. Rozwój nowożytnej filozofii człowieka. Warszawa, 1967.

VPhil 585.191.5   Suchodolski, Bogdan. Rozwój nowożytnej filozofii człowieka. Warszawa, 1967.

VPhil 585.192   Šindelář, Jan. Co řeší filosofická antropologie. Vyd. 1. Praha, 1966.

Phil 585.195   Průcha, Milan. La recontre du cogito et du marxisme. Nancy, 1965.

Phil 585.196   Mynarek, Hubertus. Der Mensch: Sinnziel der Weltentwicklung. Inaug. Diss. München, 1967.

Phil 585.198   Melo, Roneu de. O homem contemporâneo. Lisboa, 1965.

Phil 585.205   Gabriel, Mesmin. Le mal de la culture. Port-au-Prince, 1962.

Phil 585.208   Adler, Mortimer Jerome. The difference of man and the difference it makes. N.Y., 1968.

Phil 585.210   Toesca, Maurice. Voyage autour de l'homme et au-delà. Paris, 1967.

Phil 585.212.2   Jones, Arthur. Menschsein als Auftrag. 2. Aufl. Bern, 1967.

Phil 585.213   Boehler, Walther. Der mensch zwischen Übernatur und Unternatur. Nürnberg, 1966.

Phil 585.214   Maaz, Wilhelm. Selbstschöpfung oder Selbstintegration des Menschen. Münster, 1967.

Phil 585.216   Plantiko, Otto. Rousseaus, Herders und Kants Theorie vom Zukunftsideal der Menschheitsgeschichte. Inaug. Diss. Greifswald, 1895.

Phil 585.220   Jolif, Jean Y. Comprendre l'homme. Paris, 1967-

Phil 585.222   Farré, Luis. Antropología filosófica. Madrid, 1968.

Phil 585.224   Silva, Antonio da. Filosofia social. Évora, 1966.

Phil 585.226   Silvestre, Georges. L'harmonie vitale; à temps nouveau, philosophie nouvelle. Paris, 1964.

Phil 585.228   Deho, Ambrogio. Alla scoperta della persona umana. Padova, 1967.

Phil 585.230   Strasser, Stephan. Bouwstenen voor een filosofische anthropologie. Hilversum, 1965.

Phil 585.235   Loewith, Karl. Gott, Mensch und Welt in der Metaphysik von Descartes bis zu Nietzsche. Göttingen, 1967.

Phil 585.240   Gattgno, Caleb. Conscience de le conscience. Neuchâtel, 1967.

Phil 585.245   Andriessen, J.H. Naar omega. Conceptie van nieuw denken. Den Haag, 1967.

Phil 585.250   Wirklichkeit der Mitte. Beiträge zu einer Strukturanthropologie. Freiburg, 1968.

Phil 585.255   Schwarz, Richard. Menschliche Existenz und moderne Welt. Ein internationales Symposion zum Selbstverständnis des heutigen Menschen. Berlin, 1967. 2v.

Phil 585.260   Pannenberg, Wolfhart. Was ist der Mensch? Die Anthropologie der Gegenwart im Lichte der Theologie. Göttingen, 1962.

Phil 585.260.3   Pannenberg, Wolfhart. Was ist der Mensch? Die Anthropologie der Gegenwart in Lichte der Theologie. 3e Aufl. Göttingen, 1968.

VPhil 585.261   Trstenjak, Anton. Hoja za človekom. Celje, 1968.

Phil 585.265   Masullo, Aldo. Il senso del fondamento. Napoli, 1967.

Phil 585.266   Il'enkov, Eval'd V. Ob idolakh i idealakh. Moskva, 1968.

Phil 585.270   Sonnemann, Ulrich. Negative Anthropologie. Reinbeck bei Hamburg, 1969.

Phil 585.275   Changing perspectives on man. Chicago, 1968.

Phil 585.280   Nobel Conference, 4th, Gustavus Adolphus College. The uniqueness of man. Amsterdam, 1969.

Phil 585.285   Metzger, Arnold. Existentialismus und Sozialismus. Pfullingen, 1968.

Phil 585.290   Werner, Karl. Speculative Anthropologie. Frankfurt, 1967.

Phil 585.295   Care, Norman S. Readings in the theory of action. Bloomington, 1968.

Phil 585.300   Tsatsos, Konstantinos. Aphorismoí kaí dialogismoí. v.1-2. Athens, 1965-68.

Phil 585.305   Anan'ev, Boris G. Chelovek kak predmet poznaniia. Leningrad, 1968.

Phil 585.310   Nabhani, Koribaa. Essai d'une détermination esthétique de l'humain. Thèse. Alger, 1964.

Phil 585.315   Riedweg, Franz. Konservative Evolution. München, 1968.

Phil 585.320   Lersch, Philipp. Der Mensch als Schnittpunkt. München, 1969.

Phil 585.325   Spicker, Stuart F. The philosophy of the body. Chicago, 1970.

Phil 585.330   Problema cheloveka v sovremennoi filosofii. Moskva, 1969.

Classified Listing

Phil 585   Special philosophical topics, systems, etc. - Secondary treatises and discussions - Philosophical anthropology - cont.

Phil 585.335   Podol'nyi, Roman Grigor'evich. Sviaz' vremen. Moskva, 1969.

Phil 585.340   Shaffer, Jerome A. Philosophy of mind. Englewood Cliffs, N.J., 1968.

Phil 585.345   Haeberlin, Paul. Der Mensch, eine philosophische Anthropologie. Zürich, 1969.

Phil 585.350   Hartmann, Otto Julius. Der Kampf um den Menschen in Natur, Mythos und Geschichte. Freiburg, 1969.

Phil 585.355   Bosio, Franco. Antropologia filosfica e occultamento ideologico. Urbino, 1968.

Phil 585.360   Williams, Gershom Antonio. The measure of a man. 1st ed. Toronto, 1970.

Phil 585.365   Passmore, John Arthur. The perfectibility of man. London, 1970.

Phil 585.370   Sviták, Ivan. Man and his world; a Marxian view. N.Y., 1970.

Phil 585.375   Antonovich, Ivan I. Sovremennaia "Anlosofskaia antropoligiia". Minsk, 1970.

Phil 585.380   Philibert, Michel André Jean. Les échelles d'âge dans la philosophie. Thèse. Paris, 1968.

Phil 585.385   Berger, Herman. De progressieve en de conservatieve mens in hermeneutisch perspectief. Nijmegen, 1969.

Phil 585.386   Berger, Herman. Progressive and conservative man. Pittsburgh, Pa., 1971.

Phil 585.390   Barbotin, Edmond. Humanité de l'homme. Paris, 1970.

Phil 585.392   Peterson, Forrest H. A philosophy of man and society. N.Y., 1970.

Phil 585.394   Larson, Victor E. Man: who-whence; a layman's attempt at a logical synthesis. N.Y., 1967.

Phil 585.396   Kakabadze, Zurab M. Chelovek kak filosofskaia problema. Tbilisi, 1970.

Phil 585.397   Váross, Marian. Esteticno, umenie a clovek. Bratislava, 1969.

Phil 585.400   Marías Aguilera, Julián. Antropología metafisica. Madrid, 1970.

Phil 585.402   Ferrater Mora, Jose. Els mots i els homes. 1. ed. Barcelona, 1970.

Phil 585.404   Légaut, Marcel. L'homme à la recherche de son humanité. Paris, 1971.

Phil 585.406.2   Claessens, Dieter. Instinkt, Psyche, Geltung. 2. Aufl. Köln, 1970.

Phil 585.408   Hermach, Yiří. Uskutecnění soucasného doveka. 1. vyd. Praha, 1969.

Phil 585.410   Nornengast, Urda. Der androgyne Mensch. Bellnhausen, 1970.

Phil 585.412   Borsodi, Ralph. Seventeen problems of man and society. 1. ed. Anand, 1968.

Phil 585.414   Morichon, René. Entretiens sur la destinée humaine. Limoges, 1970.

Phil 585.416   Schleissheimer, Bernhard. Der Mensch als Wissender und Glaubender. Inaug. Diss. Wien, 1970.

Phil 585.418   Riedel, Maximilian. Der Mensch und das Ganze. München, 1969.

Phil 585.420   Congressus Thomisticus Internationalis. v.1- Romae, 1970.

Phil 585.421   Groethuysen, Bernhard. Philosophische Anthprologie. München, 1931.

Phil 585.422   Groethuysen, Bernhard. Antropoligia filosofica. Napoli, 1969.

il 596   Special philosophical topics, systems, etc. - Secondary treatises and discussions - Polarity

Phil 596.2   Morris, Louis W. Polarity; a philosophy of tensions among values. Chicago, 1956.

il 600   Special philosophical topics, systems, etc. - Secondary treatises and discussions - Positivism

Phil 600   Pamphlet box. Philosophy. Special. Positivism.

Phil 600.01   Pamphlet vol. Philosophy. Special. Positivism. 10 pam.

Phil 600.1   Adam, W. Inquiry into theories of history. v.1-10. London, 1862.

Phil 600.2   Anguili, A. La filosofia e la ricerca positiva. Napoli, 1869.

Phil 600.3   Balfour, A.T. Religion of humanity. Edinburgh, 1888.

Phil 600.3.2   Balfour, A.T. Religion of humanity. London, 1888.

Phil 600.4   Broglie, A.T.P. La réaction contre le positivisme. Paris, 1894.

Phil 600.4.5   Broglie, Paul. Le postivisme et la science expérimentale. Paris, 1880-81. 2v.

Phil 600.5   Brütt, M. Der Positivismus. Hamburg, 1889.

Phil 600.6   Croly, D.G. A positivist primer. N.Y., 1871.

Phil 600.7   Littré, Émile. De la philosophie positive. v.1-2. Paris, 1845.

Phil 600.7.1   Littré, Émile. Paroles de philosophie positive. Paris, 1859.

Phil 600.7.2   Littré, Émile. Paroles de philosophie positive. Paris, 1863.

Phil 600.7.3   Littré, Émile. La science au point de vue philosophique. Paris, 1873.

Phil 600.7.5   Littré, Émile. Fragments de philosophie positive et de sociologie. Paris, 1876.

Phil 600.7.79   Pellarin, Charles. Essai critique sur la philosophie positive. Paris, 1864.

Phil 600.7.86   Poëy, Andrés. M. Littré et Auguste Comte. 2e éd. Paris, 1880.

Phil 600.7.95   Caro, Elme. M. Littré et le positivisme. Paris, 1883.

Phil 600.7.100   Aquarone, Stanislas. The life and works of Émile Littré. Leyden, 1958.

Phil 600.7.105   Six, J.F. Littré devant Dieu. Paris, 1962.

Phil 600.8   Peabody, A.P. The positive philosophy. Boston, 1867.

Phil 600.9   Ward, W. The clothes of religion. London, n.d.

Phil 600.11   Harrison, F. The creed of a layman. London, 1907.

Phil 600.11.2   Harrison, F. The creed of a layman. N.Y. 1907.

Phil 600.12   Cottin, P. Positivisme et anarchie. Paris, 1908.

Phil 600.13   Lagarrigue, J. Lettres sur le positivisme. Vincennes, 1886.

Phil 600.14   Jodl, F. L'etica del positivismo. Messina, 1909.

Phil 600.15   Maurras, C. L'avenir d'intelligence. Paris, 1909.

Phil 600.16   Petzoldt, Joseph. Das Weltproblem vom positivistischen Standpunkte aus. Leipzig, 1906.

Phil 600.17   Dubuisson, A. Positivisme intégral. Paris, 1910.

Phil 600.18   Brunetière, F. Sur les chemins de la croyance. Paris, 1905.

Phil 600.19   Rodrigues, Gustave. L'idée de relation. Paris, 1904.

Phil 600.20   Pacheu, Jules. Du positivisme au mysticisme. 2e éd. Paris, 1906.

Phil 600.21   Cantecor, Georges. Le positivisme. Paris, 1904.

Phil 600   Special philosophical topics, systems, etc. - Secondary treatises and discussions - Positivism - cont.

Phil 600.22   Estasén y Cortada, P. El positivismo. Barcelona, 1877.

Phil 600.23   Barzellotti, G. The ethics of positivism. N.Y., 1878.

Phil 600.24   Calderoni, Giuseppe. Il positivismo. Roma, 1900.

Phil 600.25   Greef, Guillaume. Problémes de philosophie positive. Paris, 1900.

Phil 600.26   Gamboa, Ignacio. El positivismo filosófico. Mérida, 1899.

Phil 600.27   Schinz, Max. Die Anfänge des französischen Positivismus. Teil I. Strassburg, 1914.

Phil 600.28   Marchesini, G. La crisi del positivismo...filosofico. Torino, 1898.

Phil 600.29   Bombard, Émile. La marche de l'humanité et les grands hommes d'après la doctrine positive. Paris, 1900.

Phil 600.30   Clavel, Adolphe. La morale positive. Paris, 1873.

Phil 600.31.5   Bridges, J.H. Illustrations of positivism. Chicago, 1915.

Phil 600.31.9   Bridges, J.H. Essays and addresses. London, 1907.

Phil 600.32   Deherme, G. Le positivisme dans l'action. Paris, 1923.

Phil 600.33   Boll, Marcel. La science et l'esprit positif chez les penseurs contemporains. Paris, 1921.

Phil 600.34   Senna Freitas, J.J. de. A doutrina positivista. Póvoa de Varzim, n.d.

Phil 600.35   Troilo, E. Il positivismo e i diritti dello spirito. Torino, 1912.

Phil 600.36   Robinet, E. Den positiva filosofien i sammandrag. Stockholm, 1889.

Phil 600.37   Nyström, Anton. Den gamla tiden inför den nya. Stockholm, 1875.

Phil 600.37.5   Nyström, Anton. Positivismen och Herbert Spencer. Stockholm, 1887.

Phil 600.38   Guthlin, A. Les doctrines positivistes en France. Paris, 1873.

Phil 600.39   Troeltsch, E. Die Dynamik der Geschichte nach der Geschichtsphilosophie des Positivismus. Berlin, 1919. 101v.

Phil 600.40   Mathis, René. La loi des trois états. Thèse. Nancy, 1924.

Phil 600.41   Laffitte, P. Les grandes types de l'humanité. Paris, 1875-76. 2v.

Phil 600.42   Grunicke, Lucia. Der Begriff der Tatsache in der positivistischen Philosophie des 19. Jahrhunderts. Halle, 1930.

Phil 600.43   McGee, John Edwin. A crusade for humanity. London, 1931.

Phil 600.44   Geymonat, L. Il problema della conoscenza nel positivismo. Torino, 1931.

Phil 600.45   Halleux, Jean. Les principes du positivisme contemporain. Paris, 19- ?

Phil 600.47   Weinberg, J.R. An examination of logical positivism. London, 1936.

Phil 600.48   Caso, A. Positivismo, neopositivismo y fenomenologia. México, 1941.

Phil 600.49   Kainer, J. Seven lectures on the doctrine of positivism...May, June and July, 1879. London, 1880.

Phil 600.50   Ducassé, Pierre. La méthode positive et l'intuition comtienne. Paris, 1939.

Phil 600.51   Cornforth, M. Science and idealism. N.Y., 1947.

Phil 600.52   Wojénski, T. Publicystyka okvesu pozytywizmu. Wrocław, 1953.

Phil 600.53   Broecker, Walter. Dialektik, Positivismus, Mythologie. Frankfurt, 1958.

Phil 600.54   Heyde, Johannes Erich. Entwertung der Kausalität. Zürich, 1957.

Phil 600.55   Charlton, D.G. Positivist thought in France. Oxford, 1959.

Phil 600.56   Poey, Andrés. El positivismo. Habana, 1960.

Phil 600.57   Narskii, Igor Sergeevich. Ocherki po istorii pozitivizma. Moskva, 1960.

Phil 600.57.10   Narskii, Igor Sergeevich. Positivismus in Vergangenheit und Gegenwart. Berlin, 1967.

Phil 600.58   Lins, Ivan Monteiro de Barros. História do positivismo no Brasil. São Paulo, 1964.

Phil 600.59   Kołakowski, Leszek. Filozofia pozytywistyczna. Warszawa, 1966.

Phil 600.59.5   Kołakowski, Leszek. The alienation of reason; a history of positivist thought. Garden City, N.Y., 1968.

Phil 600.60   Soler, Ricaurte. El positivismo argentino. Panamá, 1959.

Phil 600.61   Chicherin, Boris A. Polozhitel'naia filosofiia i edinstvo nauki. Moskva, 1892.

Phil 600.62   Lesevich, Vladimir V. Opyt kriticheskago izsledovaniia osnovonachal pozitivnoi filosofii. Sanktpeterburg, 1877. 2 pam.

Phil 600.64   Schnaedelbach, Herbert. Erfahrung, Begründing und Reflexion. 1. Aufl. Frankfurt, 1971.

Phil 600.65   Pozzo, Gianni M. Il problema della storia nel positivismo Pozzo. Padova, 1967.

Phil 610   Special philosophical topics, systems, etc. - Secondary treatises and discussions - Practice

Phil 610.2   Engelhardt, Paulus. Zur Theorie der Praxis. Mainz, 1970.

Phil 615   Special philosophical topics, systems, etc. - Secondary treatises and discussions - Pragmatism

Phil 615.1   Buozyńska, Hanna. Wartość i fakt. Wyd. 1. Warszawa, 1970.

Phil 623   Special philosophical topics, systems, etc. - Secondary treatises and discussions - Rationalism

Phil 623.01   Pamphlet box. Philosophy. Special. Rationalism.

Phil 623.1A   Lecky, W.E.H. History of the rise and influence of the spirit of rationalism in Europe. N.Y., 1866. 2v.

Phil 623.1B   Lecky, W.E.H. History of the rise and influence of the spirit of rationalism in Europe. N.Y., 1866. 2v.

Phil 623.1.5   Lecky, W.E.H. History of the rise and influence of the spirit of rationalism in Europe. London, 1865. 2v.

Phil 623.1.7   Lecky, W.E.H. History of the rise and influence of the spirit of rationalism in Europe. N.Y., 1968. 2v.

Phil 623.1.20   Lecky, W.E.H. History of the rise and influence of the spirit of rationalism in Europe. v.1-2. London, 1910.

Phil 623.2   Franchi, A. Il razionalismo del Popolo. Torino, 1861.

Phil 623.2.15   Bonarino, Cristoforo. Le rationalisme. Bruxelles, 1855.

Phil 623.3   Delvolvé, J. Rationalisme et tradition. Paris, 1910.

Phil 623.4   Robertson, J.M. Rationalism. London, 1912.

Phil 623.6   Bretschneider, K.G. Sendschreiben an einen Staatsmann über die Frage...Rationalismus. Leipzig, 1830.

Phil 623.7   Saintes, A. Histoire critique du rationalisme en Allemagne. Paris, 1841.

Phil 623.7.5   Saintes, A. Critical history of rationalism in Germany. 2nd ed. London, 1849.

Phil 623.8.3   Hurst, J.J. History of rationalism. N.Y., 1865.

Phil 623.8.5   Hurst, J.J. History of rationalism. London, 1867.

Classified Listing

Phil 623   Special philosophical topics, systems, etc. - Secondary treatises and discussions - Rationalism - cont.

Phil 623.9   Benn, A.W. The history of English rationalism in the nineteenth century. London, 1906. 2v.

Phil 623.9.5   Benn, A.W. The history of English rationalism in the nineteenth century. N.Y., 1962. 2v.

Phil 623.10.5   Hagenbach, K.R. German rationalism. Edinburgh, 1865.

Phil 623.11   Pusey, E.B. An historical enquiry into the probable causes of the rationalist character lately predominant in the theology of Germany. London, 1828.

Phil 623.12   Staudlin, C.F. Geschichte des Naturalismus. Göttingen, 1826.

Phil 623.14   Roulleaux Dugage, G. Théorie des principes de l'absolu. Paris, 1909.

Phil 623.15   Ziegler, Leopold. Der abendländische Rationalismus. Jena, 1905.

Phil 623.16   McCabe, Joseph. A biographical dictionary of modern rationalists. London, 1920.

Phil 623.16.5   McCabe, Joseph. A rationalist encyclopaedia. London, 1948.

Phil 623.17   Courtney, J.E. Freethinkers of the nineteenth century. London, 1920.

Phil 623.18   Scheele, K.H.G. von. Rationalismens förberedelser. Upsala, 1868.

Phil 623.19   Enriques, F. Scienza e razionalismo. Bologna, n.d.

Phil 623.20   Wolf, Hermann. Spekulation und Philosophie. v.1-2. Berlin, 1878.

Phil 623.21   Aliotta, A. Le origini dello irrazionalismo contemporaneo. Napoli, 1928.

Phil 623.22   Strich, Walter. Der irrationale Mensch. Berlin, 1928.

Phil 623.23   Busson, Henri. Les sources et le développement du rationalisme dans la littérature française de la Renaissance. Thèse. Paris, 1922.

Phil 623.23.5   Busson, Henri. Les sources et le développement du rationalisme dans la littérature française de la Renaissance. Paris, 1922.

Phil 623.23.10A   Busson, Henri. De Petrarque á Descartes. Paris, 1957.

Phil 623.23.10B   Busson, Henri. De Petrarque á Descartes. Paris, 1957.

Phil 623.24A   Busson, Henri. La pensée religieuse française de Charron à Pascal. Paris, 1933.

Phil 623.24B   Busson, Henri. La pensée religieuse française de Charron à Pascal. Paris, 1933.

Phil 623.25   Bachelard, G. Le rationalisme appliqué. Paris, 1949.

Phil 623.26   Benda, J. La crise du rationalisme. Paris, 1949.

Phil 623.28   Robertson, A. Rationalism in theory and practice. London, 1954.

Phil 623.30   Paranjpye, Raghunath Purushottam. Rationalism in practice. Calcutta, 1935.

Phil 623.35   Het rationalisme. Den Haag, 1960.

Phil 623.37   Brophy, B. Black ship to hell. 1. American ed. N.Y., 1962.

Phil 623.40   Bartley, William W. The retreat to commitment. 1st ed. N.Y., 1962.

Phil 623.42   Blanshard, Brand. Reason and analysis. La Salle, Ill., 1962.

Phil 623.43   Gol'dberg, N.M. Svobodomyslie i ateizm v SShA, XVII-XIX vv. Leningrad, 1965.

Phil 623.44   Hobson, John Atkinson. Rationalism and humanism. London, 1933.

Phil 623.45   Dictionnaire rationaliste. Paris, 1964.

Phil 623.46   Galifret, Yves. Le crépuscule des magiciens. 2. éd. Paris, 1965.

Phil 623.48   Gambra Ciudad, Rafael. El silencio de Dios. Madrid, 1968.

Phil 623.50   Vasa, Andrea. Ricerche sul razionalismo della prassi. Firenze, 1957.

Phil 630   Special philosophical topics, systems, etc. - Secondary treatises and discussions - Realism and Neorealism

Phil 630.01   Pamphlet box. Philosophy. Special. Realism.

Phil 630.02   Pamphlet box. Philosophy. Special. Realism.

Phil 630.1   Thouverez, E. Le réalisme métaphysique. Paris, 1894.

Phil 630.2   Herbert, T.M. Realistic assumptions of modern science. London, 1879.

Phil 630.3   Hodge, W.H. Intuitive perception, presented by a new philosophy of natural realism. Lancaster, 1903.

Phil 630.5.5A   Holt, E.B. The new realism. N.Y., 1912.

Phil 630.5.5B   Holt, E.B. The new realism. N.Y., 1912.

Phil 630.5.7   Holt, E.B. The new realism. N.Y., 1922.

Phil 630.5.10   Holt, E.B. The new realism. N.Y., 1925.

Phil 630.6   Bosanquet, B. Distinction between mind and its objects. Manchester, 1913.

Phil 630.6.5   Müller, Aloys. Wahrheit und Wirklichkeit: Untersuchungen zum realistischen Wahrheitsproblem. Bonn, 1913.

Phil 630.7A   Külpe, O. Die Realisierung. Leipzig, 1912. 3v.

Phil 630.7B   Külpe, O. Die Realisierung. v.1. Leipzig, 1912.

Phil 630.8   Dauriac, L. Croyance et réalité. Paris, 1889.

Phil 630.9   Sellars, R.W. Critical realism. N.Y., 1916.

Phil 630.9.10   Sellars, R.W. The philosophy of physical realism. N.Y., 1932.

Phil 630.10   Vance, John G. Reality and truth. London, 1917.

Phil 630.11   Lindsay, James. A philosophical system of theistic idealism. Edinburgh, 1917.

Phil 630.12A   Broad, Charles D. Perception, physics and reality. Cambridge, 1914.

Phil 630.12B   Broad, Charles D. Perception, physics and reality. Cambridge, 1914.

Phil 630.13   Sorley, W.R. Moral values and the idea of God. Cambridge, 1918.

Phil 630.13.7   Sorely, W. R. Moral values and the idea of God. 2nd ed. N.Y., 1921.

Phil 630.14   Cesca, Giovanni. Il nuovo realismo contemporaneo. Verona, 1883.

Phil 630.14.501   Case, Thomas. Physical realism. London, 1888.

Phil 630.15   Parkhurst, Helen. Recent logical realism. Thesis. Bryn Mawr, 1917.

Phil 630.16   Schwarz, Hermann. Was will der kritische Realismus? Leipzig, 1894.

Phil 630.18   McDowall, A.S. Realism, a study in art and thought. London, 1918.

Phil 630.19.2   Joad, Cyril Edwin. Essays in common sense philosophy. N.Y., 1920.

Phil 630.19.7   Joad, Cyril Edwin. Common sense theology. London, 1922.

Phil 630.20   Dürr, Ernst. Grundzüge einer realistischen Weltanschauung. Leipzig, 1907.

Phil 630.21A   Drake, Durant. Essays in critical realism. London, 1920.

Phil 630.21B   Drake, Durant. Essays in critical realism. London, 1920.

Phil 630.22   Laird, John. A study in realism. Cambridge, 1920.

Phil 630.23   Kremer, René. Le néo-réalisme américain. Louvain, 1920.

Phil 630   Special philosophical topics, systems, etc. - Secondary treatises and discussions - Realism and Neorealism - cont.

Phil 630.23.10   Kremer, René. La théorie de la connaissance chez les néo-réalistes anglais. Louvain, 1928.

Phil 630.25   Hawes, R.P. The logic of contemporary English realism. Thesis. N.Y., 1923.

Phil 630.26   Grün, Karl. Die Philosophie in der Gegenwart. Leipzig, 1876.

Phil 630.27   Roberts, George L. Objective reality. London, 1925.

Phil 630.28   Verda, Mary. New realism in the light of scholasticism. N.Y., 1926.

Phil 630.29.5   Turner, J.E. A theory of direct realism and the relation of realism to idealism. N.Y., 1925.

Phil 630.30   Evans, Daniel L. The status of values in new realism. Columbus, 1923.

Phil 630.30.5   Evans, Daniel L. New realism and old reality. Princeton, 1928.

Phil 630.31   Padovani, U.A. Il neorealismo anglo-americano. Firenze, 1916.

Phil 630.32   Boas, George. The datum as essence in contemporary philosophy. Niort, 1927.

Phil 630.33   Messer, August. Der kritische Realismus. Karlsruhe, 1923.

Phil 630.34   Hasan, S.Z. Realism: an attempt to trace its origin. Cambridge, 1928.

Phil 630.35   Keferstein, H. Die Realität der Aussenwelt in der Philosophie. Käthen, 1883.

Phil 630.36   Jaensch, Erich. Vorfragen der Wirklichkeitsphilosophie. Leipzig, 1931.

Phil 630.37   Harlow, V.E. Bibliography and genetic study of American realism. Oklahoma City, 1931.

Phil 630.38   Ranzoli, Cesare. Il realismo puro. Milano, 1932.

Phil 630.39   Heacock, Roger. Der monistische Realismus im amerikanischen Denken. Inaug. Diss. Berlin? 1933.

Phil 630.40   Chevalier, Jacques. L'idée et le réel. Grenoble, 1932.

Phil 630.41   Seth Pringle Pattison, Andrew. The Balfour lectures on realism. Edinburgh, 1933.

Phil 630.42   Spaulding, E.G. The new rationalism. N.Y., 1918.

Phil 630.42.15   Spaulding, E.G. A world of chance. N.Y., 1936.

Phil 630.43   Gilson, Étienne. Le réalisme méthodique. Paris, 1936?

Phil 630.43.7   Gilson, Étienne. Réalisme thomiste. Paris, 1939.

Phil 630.44   Pratt, James B. Personal realism. N.Y., 1937.

Phil 630.45   Olgiati, F. Il realismo. Milano, 1936.

Phil 630.46   Hicks, G.D. Critical realism. London, 1938.

Phil 630.47   Noël, L. Le réalisme immédiat. Louvain, 1938.

Phil 630.48   Carre, Meyrick H. Realists and nominalists. London, 1946.

Phil 630.49   Wild, John. Introduction to realistic philosophy. N.Y., 1948.

Phil 630.49.10   Wild, John. The return to reason. Chicago, 1955.

Phil 630.50   Urban, W.M. Beyond realism and idealism. London, 1949.

Phil 630.51   Pra, Mario dal. Il realismo e il trascendente. Padova, 1937.

Phil 630.53   Veatch, Henry B. Realism and nominalism revisited. Milwaukee, 1954.

Phil 630.54   Zykmund, V. Co je realismus? Praha, 1957.

Phil 630.55   Chisholm, R.M. Realism and the background of phenomenology. Glencoe, 1961.

Phil 630.56   Bakoš, Mik. O socialistickom realizme. Bratislava, 1952.

Phil 630.57   Schneider, H.W. Sources of contemporary philosophical realism in America. Indianapolis, 1964.

Phil 630.58   Hartnach, Justice. Den ydre verdens eksistens. København, 1964.

Phil 630.60   Ruvo, Vincenzo de. Introduzione al realismo critico. Padova, 1964.

Phil 630.62   Sosa López, Emilio. Fronteras de lo real. Córdoba, Argentina, 1965.

Phil 630.64   Eberle, Rolf A. Nominalistic systems. Dordrecht, 1970.

Phil 632   Special philosophical topics, systems, etc. - Secondary treatises and discussions - Reality

Phil 632.5   Europaeisches Forum, Alpach, Austria, 1948. Gesetz und Wirklichkeit. Innsbruck, 1949.

Phil 632.8   Streatfeild, D. Persephone: a study of two worlds. London, 1959.

Phil 632.10   Stommel, Joannes Antonius. L'unification du réel. Utrecht, 1964?

Phil 632.15   Das Wirklichkeitsverständnis der Gegenwart. Salzburg, 1970.

Phil 635   Special philosophical topics, systems, etc. - Secondary treatises and discussions - Relationism

Phil 635.2   Leisegang, Dieter. Die drei Potenzen der Relation. Inaug. Diss. Frankfurt, 1969.

Phil 640   Special philosophical topics, systems, etc. - Secondary treatises and discussions - Scholasticism and Neoscholasticism

Phil 640.2   Wichmann, Ottomar. Die Scholastiker. München, 1921.

Phil 640.4   Watzlaurk, Joseph. Leo XIII and the new scholasticism. Cebu City, 1966.

Phil 645   Special philosophical topics, systems, etc. - Secondary treatises and discussions - Skepticism

Phil 645.01   Pamphlet box. Philosophy. Special. Skepticism.

Phil 645.2.5   Glanvill, J. Scepsis scientifica: or, Confest ignorance, the way to science. London, 1885.

Phil 645.3   Owen, J. Evenings with skeptics. N.Y., 1881. 2v.

Phil 645.4   Robert, Louis. De la certitude et des formes recontes du scepticisme. Paris, 1880.

Phil 645.5   Saisset, E. Le scepticisme. Paris, 1865.

Phil 645.6   Stäudlin, C.F. Geschichte und Geist des Skepticismus. Leipzig, 1794.

Phil 645.8   Lloyd, A.H. The will to doubt. London, 1907.

Phil 645.9   Richter, Raoul. Der Skeptizismus in der Philosophie. Leipzig, 1904-08.

Phil 645.10   Rossi, G. Agrippa di Nettesheym e la direzione scettica. Torino, 1906.

Phil 645.15   Berthelot, M. Science et libre pensée. 2e éd. Paris, 1905.

Phil 645.16   Kreibig, J.K. Geschichte und Kritik des ethischen Skepticismus. Wien, 1896.

Phil 645.19   Calo, Giovanni. Il problema della libertà nel pensiero contemporaneo. Milano, 1906.

Phil 645.22   Rensi, Giuseppe. Lineamenti di filosofia scetica. Bologna, 1919.

Phil 645.22.2   Rensi, Giuseppe. Lineamenti di filosofia scetica. Bologna, 1921.

Phil 645.22.7   Rensi, Giuseppe. Lo scetticismo. Milano, 1926.

Phil 645.22.12   Rensi, Giuseppe. Apologia dello scetticismo. Roma, 1926.

Classified Listing

Phil 645 Special philosophical topics, systems, etc. - Secondary treatises and discussions - Skepticism - cont.

Phil 645.23 Hönigswald, Richard. Die Skepsis in Philosophie und Wissenschaft. Göttingen, 1914.
Phil 645.25A Santayana, G. Scepticism and animal faith. N.Y., 1923.
Phil 645.25B Santayana, G. Scepticism and animal faith. N.Y., 1923.
Phil 645.25.2 Santayana, G. Scepticism and animal faith. London, 1923.
Phil 645.27 Starcke, C.N. Skepticismen. Kjøbenhavn, 1890.
Phil 645.28 Levi, Adolfo. Sceptica. Torino, 1921.
Phil 645.29 Roberty, E. de. Agnosticisme. 2e éd. Paris, 1893.
Phil 645.30 Russell, B.A.W. Sceptical essays. N.Y., 1928.
Phil 645.31.5A Campbell, Charles A. Scepticism and construction. London, 1931.
Phil 645.31.5B Campbell, Charles A. Scepticism and construction. London, 1931.
Phil 645.32 Tafel, J.F.I. Geschichte und Kritik des Skepticismus und Irrationalismus. Tübingen, 1834.
Phil 645.33 Smith, T.V. Creative sceptics. Chicago, 1934.
Phil 645.35 Sánchez, Francisco. Que nada se sabe. Buenos Aires, 1944.
Phil 645.35.5 Sánchez, Francisco. Que nada se sabe. Madrid, 1926.
Phil 645.37 Preyre, A.E. The freedom of doubt. London, 1953.
Phil 645.39 Frenkian, Aram M. Scepticismul grec şi filosofia indianǎ. Bucuresti, 1957.
Phil 645.45 Baumer, Franklin. Religion and the rise of scepticism. 1st ed. N.Y., 1960.
Phil 645.50 Popkin, Richard H. The history of scepticism from Erasmus to Descartes. Assen, 1960.
Phil 645.50.5 Popkin, Richard H. The history of scepticism. Assen, 1964.
Phil 645.50.7 Popkin, Richard H. The history of scepticism from Erasmus to Descartes. N.Y., 1964.
Phil 645.55 Naess, Arne. Scepticism. London, 1968[1969]
Phil 645.60 Slote, Michael A. Reason and scepticism. London, 1970.
Phil 645.65 Cariddi, Walter. Filosofi della scepsi. Lecce, 1968.

Phil 665 Special philosophical topics, systems, etc. - Secondary treatises and discussions - Soul

Htn Phil 665.1.2* Baxter, A. An enquiry into nature of human soul. London, 1745. 2v.
Htn Phil 665.1.5* Baxter, A. Appendix to 1st pt. An enquiry into nature of human soul. v.3. London, 1750.
Phil 665.2 Colliber, S. Free thoughts concerning souls. London, 1734.
Htn Phil 665.3* Coward, William. Second thoughts concerning human souls. London, 1704.
Htn Phil 665.3.3* Coward, William. Just scrutiny...modern notions of the soul. London, 1705?
Htn Phil 665.4* Ramesey, W. Man's dignity. London, 1661.
Htn Phil 665.5* Warren, E. No praeexistence. London, 1667.
Htn Phil 665.6* Woolnor, H. The extraction of man's soul. London, 1655.
Phil 665.7 Lutosławski, W. Seelenmacht; Abriss einer zeitgemässen Weltanschauung. Leipzig, 1899.
Phil 665.7.5 Lutosławski, W. Nieśmiertelność duszy i wolność woli. Warszawa, 1909.
Phil 665.7.7 Lutosławski, W. Pre-existence and reincarnation. London, 1928.
Phil 665.7.15 Messer, Max. Die moderne Seele. 3e Aufl. Leipzig, 1903.
Phil 665.8A DuPrel, C. Die Entdeckung der Seele durch die Geheimwissenschaften. v.1-2. Leipzig, 1894-95.
Phil 665.8B DuPrel, C. Die Entdeckung der Seele durch die Geheimwissenschaften. Leipzig, 1894-95.
Phil 665.8.2 DuPrel, C. Die Entdeckung der Seele durch die Geheimwissenschaften. 2e Aufl. Leipzig, 1910. 2v.
Phil 665.10 Bradford, A.H. The ascent of the soul. N.Y., 1902.
Htn Phil 665.11* Reynolds, E. Treatise of the passions and faculties of the soule of men. London, 1640.
Htn Phil 665.12* Glanvill, Joseph. Lux orientalis. London, 1662.
Htn Phil 665.12.2* Glanvill, Joseph. Two choice and useful treatises: Lux orientalis and A discourse of truth, by Dr. Rust. London, 1682.
Phil 665.13 Glanvill, Joseph. A letter on praeexistence to Richard Baxter. Osceola, 1890.
Phil 665.14 ipper, P. Geistesleben and Descendenzlehre. Naumburg, 1885.
Phil 665.15 Carpenter, A. Pseuchographia anthropomagica. London, 1652.
Phil 665.17 Svoboda, A.V. Kritische Geschichte der Ideale. Leipzig, 1886.
Phil 665.18 Kostyleff, Nicolas. Les substituts de l'âme. Paris, 1906.
Phil 665.19 Corey, J.W. The soul; its organ and development. Los Angeles, 1913.
Phil 665.20 Kirk, Edward N. The greatness of the human soul. Boston, 1844.
Phil 665.21 Hygiene del alma. n.p., n.d.
Phil 665.22 Scheibler, Christoph. Liber de anima. Francofurti, 1665.
Phil 665.23 Révésy, Béla. Geschichte des Seelenbegriffes. Stuttgart, 1917.
Phil 665.24 Schmidt, Wilhelm. Der Kampf um die Seele. Gütersloh, 1909.
Phil 665.25 Christiansen, Broder. Vom Selbstbewusstsein. Berlin, 1912.
Phil 665.26 Melegari, Dora. Il destarsi delle anime. Milano, 1915.
Phil 665.27 Hirt, Walter. Ein neuer Weg zur Erforschung der Seele. München, 1917.
Phil 665.27.5 Hirt, Walter. Die Entschleierung der Seele: eine neue Theorie. Berlin, 1923.
Phil 665.28 Hein, Joseph. Aktualität oder Substantialität der Seele? Inaug. Diss. Paderborn, 1916.
Phil 665.29 Baraduc, H. L'âme humaine. Paris, 1896.
Phil 665.30 Joël, Karl. Seele und Welt. Jena, 1912.
Phil 665.32 Stone, M.M. A practical study of the soul. N.Y., 1901.
Phil 665.33 Gibbons, J. Theories of the transmigration of souls. London, 1907.
Phil 665.34 Larkin, E.L. The matchless altar of the soul. Los Angeles, 1916.
Phil 665.36 Falke, R. Gibt es eine Seelenwanderung? Halle, 1904.
Phil 665.37 Reich, E. Die Geschichte der Seele. Minden, 1884.
Phil 665.38 Coconnier, M.J. L'âme humaine. Paris, 1890.
Phil 665.39 Pietropaolo, F. L'anima nel mondo greco e romano nel medio evo e nella filosofia moderna. Roma, 1898.
Phil 665.40 Mackenzie, J.N. Landseer. The universal medium; a new interpretation of the soul. London, 1922.
Phil 665.41 Lutosławski, W. The world of souls. London, 1924.
Phil 665.42 Feilberg, Ludvig. Om ligeløb og Kredsning i Sjaelelivet. Kjøbenhavn, 1896.
Phil 665.42.5 Feilberg, Ludvig. Nutids själavård; om största utbytet av själens gåvor. Stockholm, 1917.

Phil 665 Special philosophical topics, systems, etc. - Secondary treatises and discussions - Soul - cont.

Phil 665.43 Beskow, B. von. Om själens helsa. 4e uppl. Stockholm, 1880.
Phil 665.43.2 Beskow, B. von. Om själens helsa. 2e uppl. Stockholm, 1867.
Phil 665.44 Aber, Mary R.A. Souls. Chicago, 1893.
Phil 665.45 Soul shapes. London, 1890.
Phil 665.46 Smith, O.J. A short view of great questions. N.Y., 1899.
Phil 665.48.5 Stosch, George. Själen och hennes historia. Stockholm, 1908.
Phil 665.49 Scofield, A. Insights and heresies. Boston, 1913.
Htn Phil 665.50* E., T. Vindiciae mentis. London, 1702.
Phil 665.51A Müller, Walter. Das Problem der Seelenschönheit im Mittelalter. Bern, 1923.
Phil 665.51B Müller, Walter. Das Problem der Seelenschönheit im Mittelalter. Bern, 1923.
Phil 665.52 Gardeil, A. La structure de l'âme et l'expérience mystique. Paris, 1927. 2v.
Phil 665.53 Coffin, Joseph H. The soul comes back. N.Y., 1929.
Phil 665.54 Bastian, Adolf. Die Seele indischer und hellenischer Philosophie in den Gespenstern moderner Geisterseherei. Berlin, 1886.
Phil 665.55 Fringe, J.W. Life everlasting and psychic evolution. London, 1919.
Phil 665.56 Flügel, O. Die Seelenfrage. Cöthen, 1878.
Phil 665.57 Sarlo, Francesco de. Il concetto dell'anima nella psicologia contemporanea. Firenze, 1900.
Phil 665.58.5 Knutzen, Martin. Philosophische Abhandlung von der immateriellen Natur der Seele. Königsberg, 1744.
Phil 665.59.5 Weidenbach, H. Die Mechanik der Seele. 3e Aufl. Mannheim, 1931.
Phil 665.60 Rank, Otto. Seelenglaube und Psychologie. Leipzig, 1930.
Phil 665.61 Rüsche, Franz. Das Seelenpneuma. Paderborn, 1933.
Phil 665.62 Laborier-Tradens, A. Le bonheur est en nous-mêmes. Paris, 1931.
Phil 665.63 Clymer, R.S. The science of the soul. Quakertown, 1922.
Phil 665.64 St. Cyr, E. The essay: let us think it over. 12th ed. Chicago, 1936.
Phil 665.65 Neuburger, E. Das Verständnis der Seele im Christentum und in der psychologischen Literatur der Gegenwart. Inaug. Diss. Tübingen, 1937.
Phil 665.66 Eckhardt, K.E. Irdische Unsterblichkeit. Weimar, 1937.
Phil 665.67 Ellis, W. The idea of the soul. London, 1940.
Phil 665.68 Sadler, W.S. The evolution of the soul. Chicago? 1941.
Phil 665.69 Schleich, C.L. Von der Seele. Berlin, 1921.
Phil 665.69.5 Schleich, C.L. Die Wunder der Seele. Berlin, 1940.
Phil 665.70 Crawshaw, William H. The indispensable soul. N.Y., 1931.
Phil 665.71 Syme, David. The soul. London, 1903.
Phil 665.72 Berdiaev, N.A. Dukh i real'nost'. Paris, 1941-.
Phil 665.73 Bury, R.G. The devil's puzzle. Dublin, 1949.
Phil 665.75A Frankel, Charles. The case for modern man. 1st ed. N.Y., 1956.
Phil 665.75B Frankel, Charles. The case for modern man. N.Y., 1956.
Phil 665.77 Gindl, I. Seele und Geist. Wien, 1955.
Phil 665.80 Strasser, Stephan. Seele und Beseeltes. Wien, 1955.
Phil 665.80.5 Strasser, Stephan. The soul in metaphysical and empirical psychology. Pittsburgh, 1957.
Phil 665.80.10 Strasser, Stephan. Het zielsbegrip in de metaphysische en in de empirische psychologie. Leuven, 1950.
Phil 665.82 Sausgruber, Kurt. Atom und Seele. Freiburg, 1958.
Phil 665.84 Morreale de Castro, Margherita. Versiones españolas de animus y anima. Granada? 1957.
Phil 665.86 Quarelli, Elena. Socrates and the animals. London, 1960.
Phil 665.88 Conrad-Martius, H. Die Geistseele des Menschen. München, 1960.
Phil 665.90 Pastuszka, J. Dusza ludzka, jej istnienie i natura. Lublin, 1947.
Phil 665.92 LaNoë, François de. L'appel de l'esprit. Paris, 1960.
Phil 665.93 Maeztu, Ramiro de. Defensa del espíritu. Madrid, 1958.
Phil 665.94 Bruch, Johann Friedrich. Die Lehre von der Präexistenz der Menschlichen Seelen. Strassburg, 1859.
Phil 665.95 Flew, Antony. Body, mind and death. N.Y., 1964.
Phil 665.96 Langre, Michel de. Ame humaine et science moderne. Paris, 1963.
Phil 665.98 Seele, Entwicklung, Leben. Bern, 1966.
Phil 665.100 Timeless documents of the soul. Evanston, 1968.
Phil 665.102 Zolla, Elémire. Le potenze dell'anima. Milano, 1968.
Phil 665.104 Heimann, Hans. Die Seele-Grenzbegriff der Naturwissenschaft und Theologie. Bern, 1966.
Phil 665.106 Cavarnos, Constantine. Modern Greek philosophers on the human soul. Belmont, 1967.
Phil 665.108 Krueger, Walter. Metaphysische Praxis als Schlüssel zur geistigen Welt. Freiburg, 1968.
Phil 665.110 Queis, Karl. Wege der Seele. Wien, 1968.

Phil 672 Special philosophical topics, systems, etc. - Secondary treatises and discussions - Space and time

Phil 672.01 Pamphlet box. Philosophy. Special. Space and time.
Phil 672.1 Baumann, J.J. Die Lehren von Raun, Zeit, und Mathematik. v.1-2. Berlin, 1868-69.
Phil 672.2 Bellermann, G. Beweis aus der neueren Raumtheorie. Berlin, 1889.
Phil 672.3 Dunan, C. Théorie psychologique de l'espace. Paris, 1895.
Phil 672.3.5 Dunan, C. Essai sur les formes a priori. Paris, 1884.
Phil 672.4A Funcke, D. Grundlagen der Raumwissenschaft. Hannover, 1875.
Phil 672.4B Funcke, D. Grundlagen der Raumwissenschaft. Hannover, 1875.
Phil 672.6 Lange, C.C.L. Die geschichtliche Entwickelung des Bewegungsbegriffes. Leipzig, 1886.
Phil 672.7 Place, C. That space is necesary being. London, 1728.
Phil 672.8 Rosanes, J. Über die neuesten Untersuchungen in Betreff unserer Anschauung vom Raume. Breslau, 1871.
Phil 672.9 Walter, J.E. Perception of space and matter. Boston, 1879.
Phil 672.9.5 Walter, J.E. Nature and cognition of space and time. W. Newton, Pa., 1914.
Phil 672.11 Nichols, H. Our notions of number and space. Boston, 1894.
Phil 672.12 Krause, A. Die Gesetze der menschlichen Herzens. Lahr, 1876.
Phil 672.13 Stumpf, C. Über den psychologischen Ursprung der Raumvorstellung. Leipzig, 1873.
Phil 672.14 The stars and the earth. 4th ed. London, 1850.
Phil 672.14.5 The star and the earth. 7th ed. London, 1861.
Phil 672.14.7 The stars and the earth. Boston, 1849.
Phil 672.14.9 The stars and the earth. 5th American ed. Boston, 1882.

Phil 672   Special philosophical topics, systems, etc. - Secondary treatises and
discussions - Space and time - cont.

Phil 672.15   Hinton, Charles H. A new era of thought. London, 1888.
Phil 672.15.5   Hinton, Charles H. The fourth dimension. London, 1904.
Phil 672.15.7   Hinton, Charles H. The recognition of the fourth
                   dimension. Washington, 1902.
Phil 672.15.10   Hinton, Charles H. A language of space. London, 1906.
Phil 672.16   Russell, B. Is position in time or space absolute or
                   relative? London, 1901.
Phil 672.17   Mach, E. Space and geometry. Chicago, 1906.
Phil 672.18   Lechalas, G. Etude sur l'espace et le temps. Paris, 1910.
Phil 672.20   Allan, A. Space and personality. Edinburgh, 1913.
Phil 672.21   Study, E. Die realistische Weltansicht und die Lehre vom
                   Raume. Braunschweig, 1914.
Phil 672.22   Eyfferth, Max. Der Begriff der Zeit. Berlin, 1870.
Phil 672.22.5   Eyfferth, Max. Über die Zeit; philosophische Untersuchung.
                   Berlin, 1871.
Phil 672.23   VanRiper, B.W. Some views of the time problem. Diss.
                   Menasha, 1916.
Phil 672.24   Guyau, M.J. La genèse de l'idée de temps. 2e éd.
                   Paris, 1902.
Phil 672.25   Stevens, E.M. Psychology of space perception. New
                   Orleans, 1915.
Phil 672.26   Luguet, Henry. Étude sur la notion d'espace d'après
                   Descartes. Thèse. Paris, 1875.
Phil 672.27   Ulrich, Georg. Der Begriff des Raumes. Berlin, 1907.
Phil 672.28   Gutberlet, Constantin. Die neue Raumtheorie. Mainz, 1882.
Phil 672.29.3   Browne, Robert T. The mystery of space. N.Y., 1919.
Phil 672.30   Schneid, Mathias. Die philosophische Lehre von Zeit und
                   Raum. Mainz, 1886.
Phil 672.32   Fallen angels. London, 1894.
Phil 672.33   Phalén, Adolf K. Über die Relativität der Raum- und
                   Zeitbestimmungen. Uppsala, 1922.
Phil 672.120   Alexander, S. Space, time and deity. London, 1920.
                   2v.
Phil 672.120.50   Liddell, Anna F. Alexander's space, time and deity.
                   Chapel Hill, 1925?
Phil 672.121   Smith, W.W. A theory of the mechanism of survival; the
                   fourth dimension. London, 1920.
Phil 672.122   Uspenskii, P.D. Tertium organum. 2nd American ed.
                   N.Y., 1922.
Phil 672.122.3   Uspenskii, P.D. Tertium organum. 2nd American ed.
                   N.Y., 1923.
Phil 672.122.5   Uspenskii, P.D. Tertium organum. 2nd American ed.
                   N.Y., 1930.
Phil 672.122.7   Uspenskii, P.D. Tertium organum. Rochester, 1920.
Phil 672.122.9   Uspenskii, P.D. Tertium organum. Berlin, 1931.
Phil 672.123   Nys, Désiré. La notion d'espace. Bruxelles, 1922.
Phil 672.123.10   Nys, Désiré. La notion de temps. 2e éd. Louvain, 1923.
Phil 672.124   Marty, Anton. Raum und Zeit. Halle, 1916.
Phil 672.125   Eriksen, R. Consciousness, life and the fourth dimension.
                   London, 1923.
Phil 672.126   Levi, Adolfo. Il concetto del tempo. Milano, 1919.
Phil 672.127.2   Rawitz, B. Raum, Zeit und Gott. Leipzig, 1923.
Phil 672.128   Eddington, A.S. Raum, Zeit und Schwere.
                   Braunschweig, 1923.
Phil 672.129   Weitzenböck, R. Over de vierde dimensie. Groningen, 1923.
Phil 672.130   Herbertz, R. Die Philosophie des Raumes. Stuttgart, 1912.
Phil 672.131   Zini, Zino. La doppa maschera dell'universo.
                   Milano, 1914.
Phil 672.132   Poppovich, N.M. Die Lehre vom diskreten Raum in der
                   neueren Philosophie. Wien, 1922.
Phil 672.133   Sturt, Mary. The psychology of time. London, 1925.
Phil 672.134.5   Benedicks, Carl. Space and time. London, 1924.
Phil 672.135   Volkelt, Johannes. Phänomenologie und Metaphysik der Zeit.
                   München, 1925.
Phil 672.136A   Dunne, John W. An experiment with time. N.Y., 1927.
Phil 672.136B   Dunne, John W. An experiment with time. N.Y., 1927.
Phil 672.136.5   Dunne, John W. An experiment with time. 3rd ed.
                   N.Y., 1949.
Phil 672.136.7   Dunne, John W. An experiment with time. London, 1952.
Phil 672.136.10   Dunne, John W. An experiment with time. 4th ed.
                   N.Y., 1938.
Phil 672.136.15   Dunne, John W. The serial universe. N.Y., 1938.
Phil 672.136.17   Dunne, John W. The new immortality. London, 1938.
Phil 672.136.25   Dunne, John W. Nothing dies. London, 1940.
Phil 672.136.30   Dunne, John W. Intrusions? London, 1955.
Phil 672.137   Ranzoli, C. Prime linee di una teoria realistica dello
                   spazio e del tempo. Messina, 1921.
Phil 672.138   Schultze, A. Ist die Welt vierdimensional? Leipzig, 1922.
Phil 672.139   Goldsbrough, G.F. Recent discussions on "Time".
                   London, 1927.
Phil 672.140   Lewis, Wyndham. Time and Western man. N.Y., 1928.
Phil 672.141   Jakubisiak, Augustin. Essai sur les limites de l'espace et
                   du temps. Paris, 1927.
Phil 672.142   Nordmann, Charles. Notre mâitre le temps. Paris, 1924.
Phil 672.142.5   Nordmann, Charles. The tyranny of time. London, 1925.
Phil 672.143   Alvarez de Toledo, A. Le problème de l'espace.
                   Paris, 1920.
Phil 672.144   Reichenbach, H. Philosophie der Raum-Zeit-Lehre.
                   Berlin, 1928.
Phil 672.144.3   Reichenbach, H. The philosophy of space and time.
                   N.Y., 1958.
Phil 672.145   Gunn, J.A. The problem of time. London, 1929.
Phil 672.146   Kaschmieder, E. Zeitbezug und Sprache. Berlin, 1929.
Phil 672.147   Sevin, Emile. Le temps absolu et l'espace à quatre
                   dimensions. Paris, 1928.
Phil 672.148   Durand-Doat, J. Essai sur l'étendue. Thèse. Paris, 1928.
Phil 672.148.5   Durand-Doat, J. Essai sur l'étendue. Paris, 1928.
Phil 672.149   Bonaventura, Enzo. Il problema psicologico del tempo.
                   Milano, 1929.
Phil 672.150   Hallett, H.F. Alternitas; a Spinozistic study.
                   Oxford, 1930.
Phil 672.151   Gent, Werner. Die Philosophie des Raumes und der Zeit.
                   Bonn, 1926.
Phil 672.151.2   Gent, Werner. Die Philosophie des Raumes und der Zeit. 2.
                   Aufl. v.1-2. Hildesheim, 1962.
Phil 672.151.10   Gent, Werner. Das Problem der Zeit. Hildesheim, 1965.
Phil 672.152   Jaffé, George. Zwei Dialoge über Raum und Zeit.
                   Leipzig, 1931.
Phil 672.152.5   Jaffé, George. Über Raum. Berlin, 1954.
Phil 672.153   Sander, Franz. Die Entwicklung der Raumtheorien in der 2.
                   Hälfte des 17. Jahrhunderts. Inaug.-Diss. Halle, 1931.
Phil 672.154   Poirier, René. Essai sur quelques caractères des notions
                   d'espace et de temps. Thèse. Paris, 1931.
Phil 672.155   Bachelard, Gaston. L'intuition de l'instant. Paris, 1932.
Phil 672.155.10   Bachelard, Gaston. La dialectique de la durée.
                   Paris, 1936.

Phil 672   Special philosophical topics, systems, etc. - Secondary treatises and
discussions - Space and time - cont.

Phil 672.156   Baker, John Tull. An historical and critical examination
                   of English space and time theories. Thesis. Bronxville,
                   N.Y., 1930.
Phil 672.157   Ramige, E.A. Contemporary concepts of time and the idea of
                   God. Boston, 1935.
Phil 672.158   Heath, L.R. The concept of time. Photoreproduction.
                   Chicago, 1936.
Phil 672.159   Ponsonby, A.P. Life here and now; conclusions derived from
                   an examination of the sense of duration. London, 1936.
Phil 672.160   Zawirski, Zygmunt. L'évolution de la notion du temps.
                   Cracovie, 1936.
Phil 672.161   Wiessner, Alexander. Die wesenhafte oder absolute Realität
                   des Raumes. Leipzig, 1877.
Phil 672.162   Souriau, Michel. Le temps. Paris, 1937.
Phil 672.163   Sivadjian, J. Le temps. Paris, 1938.
Phil 672.163.5   Sivadjian, J. Le temps. Paris, 1938. 6v.
Phil 672.164   Pemartin, J. Introducción a una filosofía de lo temporal.
                   Sevilla, 1937.
Phil 672.165   Burgelin, Pierre. L'homme et le temps. Photoreproduction.
                   Paris, 1945.
Phil 672.166   Allen, Chalinder. The tyranny of time. N.Y., 1947.
Phil 672.168   Coomaraswamy, A. Time and eternity. Ascona, 1947.
Phil 672.170   Plumbe, C.C. Release from time. London, 1950.
Phil 672.172   Bragdon, C.F. A primer of higher space. Rochester, 1913.
Phil 672.172.5   Bragdon, C.F. A primer of higher space. 2nd ed.
                   N.Y., 1923.
Phil 672.174   Goeje, C.H. de. Space, time and life; and, What is time?
                   v.1-2. Leiden, 1949.
Phil 672.176   Venturini, Saul. Chiacchierata sul concetto di spazio.
                   Milano, 1951.
Phil 672.178   Conrad-Martius, H. Die Zeit. 1. Aufl. München, 1954.
Phil 672.180   Aspecten van de tijd. Assen, 1950.
Phil 672.182   Reichenbach, Hans. The direction of time. Berkeley, 1956.
Phil 672.185   Pereira, I.R. The nature of space. 1st ed. N.Y., 1956.
Phil 672.190   Eranos-Jahrbuch. Man and time. N.Y., 1957.
Phil 672.195   Sviderskii, V.I. Filosofskoe znachenie
                   prostranstvenno-vremennykh predstavlenii v fizike.
                   Leningrad, 1956.
Phil 672.197   Archivio di Filosofia. Il tempo. Padova, 1958.
Phil 672.198   Archivio di Filosofia. Tempo e eternità. Padova, 1959.
Phil 672.199   Archivio di Filosofia. Tempo e intenzionalità.
                   Padova, 1960.
Phil 672.202   Samuells, Roberto. La dialéctica del espacio.
                   Madrid, 1952.
Phil 672.208   Fernández Suárez, Alvaro. El tiempo y el "hay".
                   Madrid, 1955.
Phil 672.210   Restrepo, F. Entre el tiempo y la eternidad.
                   Bogotá, 1960.
Phil 672.212   Whitrow, G.J. The natural philosophy of time.
                   London, 1961.
Phil 672.214   Matoré, Georges. L'espace humain. Paris, 1962.
Phil 672.215   MacIver, Robert Morrison. The challenge of the passing
                   years. N.Y., 1u962.
Phil 672.216   Kuemmel, F. Über den Begriff der Zeit. Tübingen, 1962.
Phil 672.218   Schlegel, R. Time and the physical world. East
                   Lansing? 1961.
Phil 672.219   Gruenbaum, A. Philosophical problems of space and time.
                   1st ed. N.Y., 1963.
Phil 672.220   Gonseth, F. Le problème du temps. Neuchâtel, 1964.
Phil 672.221   Priestley, J.B. Man and time. London, 1964.
Phil 672.222   Parsons, E. Time devoured. London, 1964.
Phil 672.223   Costa de Beauregard, Olivier. Le second principe de la
                   science du temps. Paris, 1963.
Phil 672.224   Tlustý, Vojtěch. Prostor a čas. 2. vyd. Praha, 1963.
Phil 672.225   Szumilewicz, Irena. O kierunku upływu czasu.
                   Warszawa, 1964.
Phil 672.226   Brandon, Samuel George Frederick. History, time and deity.
                   Manchester, 1965.
Phil 672.227   Nebel, Gerhard. Zeit und Zeiten. Stuttgart, 1965.
Phil 672.228   Reyner, John Hereward. God beyond time. London, 1965.
Phil 672.229   Smart, John Jamieson Carswell. Problems of space and time.
                   N.Y., 1964.
Phil 672.230   Guillaumaud, Jacques. Du temps physique au temps
                   romanesque. Paris, 1965.
Phil 672.231   Fraser, Julius Thomas. The voices of time. N.Y., 1966.
Phil 672.232   Costa de Beauregard, Olivier. La théorie physique et la
                   notion de temps. Bordeaux, 1963.
Phil 672.233   Needham, Joseph. Time and Eastern man. London, 1965.
Phil 672.234   Hatano, Seiichi. Time and eternity. Tokyo? 1963.
Phil 672.235   Hoelling, Joachim. Ontologische Beiträge zum
                   Raum-Zeit-Problem. Freiburg? 1965.
Phil 672.236   Durandeaux, Jacques. L'éternité dans la vie quotidienne.
                   Paris, 1964.
Phil 672.237   Askin, Iakov F. Problema vremeni. Moskva, 1966.
Phil 672.238   Pavlov, Vasilii T. Logicheskie funktsii kategorii
                   prostranstva i vremeni. Kiev, 1966.
Phil 672.239   Bachelard, Gaston. L'intuition de l'instant. Paris, 1966.
Phil 672.240   Wallis, Robert. Le temps, quatrième dimension de l'esprit.
                   Paris, 1966.
Phil 672.240.2   Wallis, Robert. Time, fourth dimension of the mind. 1st
                   ed. N.Y., 1968.
Phil 672.242   Gale, Richard. The language of time. London, 1968.
Phil 672.244   Cheek, John M. The perception of time. Charlotte,
                   N.C.? 1891.
Phil 672.246   Gold, Thomas. The nature of time. Ithaca, 1967.
Phil 672.250   Jacob, André. Temps et langage. Paris, 1967.
Phil 672.252   Swinburne, Richard. Space and time. London, 1968.
Phil 672.254   Popma, Klaas Johan. Nadenken over de tijd.
                   Amsterdam, 1965.
Phil 672.256   Entretiens sur le temps, sous la direction de Jeanne Hersch
                   et René Poirier. Paris, 1967.
Phil 672.258   Toulmin, Stephen Edelston. The discovery of time.
                   N.Y., 1965.
Phil 672.258.1   Toulmin, Stephen Edelston. The discovery of time.
                   London, 1965.
Phil 672.260   Tollenaere, M. de. Een philosophie van de tijd.
                   Leuven, 1962.
Phil 672.262   Versfeld, Marthinus. Wat is kontemporêr?
                   Johannesburg, 1966.
Phil 672.264   Jacobelli Isoldi, Angela Maria. Tempo e significato.
                   Roma, 1964.
Phil 672.266   Mostepanenko, Aleksandr M. Problema universal'nosti
                   osnovnykh svoistv prostranstva i vremeni. Leningrad, 1969.
Phil 672.268   Goelz, Walter. Dasein und Raum. Habilitationsschrift.
                   Tübingen, 1970.

Classified Listing

672 Special philosophical topics, systems, etc. - Secondary treatises and scussions - Space and time - cont.

Phil 672.270 Maneev, Aleksei K. Preemstvennost' v razoitii kategorii prostranstva, vremeni i dvizheniia. Minsk, 1971.

676 Special philosophical topics, systems, etc. - Secondary treatises and scussions - Spirituality

Phil 676.2 Rohrbach, Marc Adrien. L'éveil spirituel, accomplissement personnel par la pensée créatrice. Paris, 1969.

680 Special philosophical topics, systems, etc. - Secondary treatises and scussions - Structuralism

Phil 680.5 Jaeggi, Urs. Ordnung und Chaos. Frankfurt, 1968.
Phil 680.10 Caruso, Paolo. Conversazioni con Claude Lévi-Straws, Michel Foucault, Jacques Lacan. Milano, 1969.
Phil 680.15 Macksey, Richard. The language of criticism and the science of man. Baltimore, 1970.
Phil 680.20 Corvez, Maurice. Les structuralistes: les linguistes, Michel Foucault, Claude Lévi-Strauss, Jacques Lacan, Louis Althusser, les critiques littéraires. Paris, 1969.
Phil 680.25 Lane, Michael. Introduction to structuralism. N.Y., 1970.
Phil 680.26 Lane, Michael. Structuralism: a reader. London, 1970.
Phil 680.30 Millet, Louis. Le structuralisme. Paris, 1970.
Phil 680.35 Popovič, Anton. Štrukturalizmus v slovenskej vede. Martin, 1970.
Phil 680.40 Centro di studi filosofici di gallarate. Strutturalismo filosofico. Padova, 1970.
Phil 680.45 Chvotík, Květoslav. Strukturalismus a avantgarda. 1. vyd. Praha, 1970.
Phil 680.50 Lefebvre, Henri. Au-delà du structuralisme. Paris, 1971.
Phil 680.55 Francovich, Guillermo. Ensayos sobre el estructuralismo. La Paz, Bolivia, 1970.

683 Special philosophical topics, systems, etc. - Secondary treatises and scussions - Subject and object

Phil 683.2 Rosenthal, Klaus. Die Überwindung des Subjekt-Objekt-Denkens als philosophisches und theologisches Problem. Göttingen, 1970.

703 Special philosophical topics, systems, etc. - Secondary treatises and scussions - Traditionalism

Phil 703.3 Ehbinghaus, Julius. Traditionsfeindschaft und Traditionsgehundenheit. Frankfurt, 1969.

705 Special philosophical topics, systems, etc. - Secondary treatises and scussions - Transcendentalism

Phil 705.01 Pamphlet box. Philosophy. Special. Transcendentalism.
Phil 705.1 Essay on transcendentalism. Boston, 1842.
Phil 705.2 Johnson, S. Transcendentalism. n.p., n.d.
L Phil 705.3 Frothingham, Octavius Brooks. Transcendentalism in New England. N.Y., 1876.
Phil 705.3.5 Frothingham, Octavius Brooks. Transcendentalism in New England. Boston, 1903.
Phil 705.3.7A Frothingham, Octavius Brooks. Transcendentalism in New England, a history. Gloucester, Mass., 1965.
Phil 705.3.7B Frothingham, Octavius Brooks. Transcendentalism in New England, a history. Gloucester, Mass., 1965.
Phil 705.4 Dall, C.H. Transcendentalism in New England. Boston, 1897.
Phil 705.5 Goddard, H.C. Studies in New England transcendentalism. Thesis. N.Y., 1908.
Phil 705.5.5A Goddard, H.C. Studies in New England transcendentalism. N.Y., 1908.
Phil 705.5.5B Goddard, H.C. Studies in New England transcendentalism. N.Y., 1908.
Phil 705.6 Barthel, E. Elemente der transzendentalen Logik. Strassburg, 1913.
Phil 705.8 Tarrida del Mármol, F. Problemas trascendentales. Paris, 1908.
Phil 705.9 Bradford, Alden. Human learning favorable to true religion. Boston, 1841.
Phil 705.10 Rensi, Giuseppe. La trascendenza; studio sul problema morale. Torino, 1914.
Phil 705.11 Knittermeyer, Hinrich. Der Terminus transszendental in seiner historischen Entwickelung bis zu Kant. Inaug. Diss. Marburg, 1920.
Phil 705.11.5 Knittermeyer, Hinrich. Der Mensch der Erkenntnis. Hamburg, 1962.
Phil 705.12 Phalén, Adolf K. Kritik af subjektivismen. Uppsala, 1910.
Phil 705.13 Landström, Gustaf. Locke och Kant. Uppsala, 1900.
Phil 705.14 Plessner, H. Krisis der transzendentalen Wahrheit im anfang. Heidelberg, 1918.
Phil 705.16 Landmann, E. Die Transcendenz des erkennens. Berlin, 1923.
Phil 705.17 Byers, R.P. Transcendental values. Boston, 1925.
Phil 705.18 Girard, William. Du transcendentalisme considéré essentiellement dans sa définition et ses origines françaises. Berkeley, 1916.
Phil 705.19 Banfi, Antonio. Immanenza e trascendenza. Alessandria, 1924.
Phil 705.20 Leider, Kurt. Das Transzendentale. Diss. Königsberg, 1925.
Phil 705.21 Barkman, H. Bidrag till denTransscendentala kategorilären. Uppsala, 1901.
Phil 705.22 Pannwitz, R. Kosmos Atheos. München, 1926.
Phil 705.23 Christy, Arthur. The Orient in American transcendentalism. N.Y., 1932.
Phil 705.23.2 Christy, Arthur. The Orient in American transcendentalism. N.Y., 1963.
Phil 705.24 Schultzer, Bent. Transcendence and the logical difficulties of transcendence; a logical analysis. Copenhagen, 1935.
Phil 705.25 Bénézé, Georges. Allure du transcendental. Paris, 1936.
Phil 705.25.5 Bénézé, Georges. Allure du transcendental. Thèse. Paris, 1936.
Phil 705.26* Greene, William B. Transcendentalism. West Brookfield, 1849.
Phil 705.27 Selling, M. Studien zur Geschichte der Transzendantalphilosophie. Inaug. Diss. Lund, 1938.
Phil 705.28 Troilo, E. La ragioni della trascendenza o del realismo assoluto. Venezia, 1936.
Phil 705.29 Wells, R.V. Three Christian transcendentalists. N.Y., 1943.
Phil 705.30 Rogers, W.C. Transcendentalism truly remarkable. Boston, 1947.
Phil 705.31 Ezilasi, Wilhelm. Wissenschaft als Philosophie. Zürich, 1945.

Phil 705 Special philosophical topics, systems, etc. - Secondary treatises and discussions - Transcendentalism - cont.

Phil 705.33 Wahl, J. Existence humaine et transcendance. Neuchâtel, 1944.
Phil 705.35 Whicher, G.F. The transcendentalist revolt against materialism. Boston, 1949.
Phil 705.37 Hengstenberg, H.E. Autonomismus und Transzendenzphilosophie. Heidelberg, 1950.
Phil 705.39 Vuillemin, Jules. L'héritage Kantien et la révolution copernicienne. Paris, 1954.
Phil 705.40 Belzer, G. Das Problem der Transzendenz in der Geschichte der neueren Philosophie. Amsterdam, 1952.
Phil 705.42 Ellis, Charles Mayo. An essay on transcendentalism, 1842. Gainesville, 1954.
Phil 705.46 Fieschi, Andrea. Saggio sul trascendente e sul trascendentale. Padova, 1958.
Phil 705.48 Leighton, Walter Leatherbee. French philosophers and New England transcendentalism. Charlottesville, 1908.
Phil 705.49 Metzger, Arnold. Dämonie und Transzendenz. Pfullingen, 1964.
Phil 705.49.5 Metzger, Arnold. De Einzelne und der Einsame. Pfullingen, 1967.
Phil 705.50 Krings, Hermann. Transzendentale Logik. München, 1964.
Phil 705.51 Saur, Karl. Transzendenz als Wirklichkeit. Hamburg, 1965.
Phil 705.52 Giannini, Giorgio. La tematica della trascendenza. Roma, 1964.
Phil 705.54 Lauth, Reinhard. Zur Idee der Transzendentalphilosophie. München, 1965.
Phil 705.54.5 Lauth, Reinhard. Begriff. München, 1967.
Phil 705.55 Simon, Myron. Transcendentalism and its legacy. Ann Arbor, 1966.
Phil 705.57 Brelage, Manfred. Studien zur Transzendentalphilosophie. Berlin, 1965.
Phil 705.62 Schneider, Peter K. Die Wissenschaftsbegrundende Funktion der Transzendent alphilosophie. Freiburg, 1965.
Phil 705.64 Holz, Harald. Transzendentalphilosophie und Metaphysik. Mainz, 1966.
Phil 705.66 Dürckheim-Montmartin, Karlfried. Überweltliches Leben in der Welt. Weilheim, 1968.
Phil 705.68 The minor and later transcendentalists; a symposium. Hartford, 1969.
Phil 705.70 Schaumann, Johann Christian Gottlieb. Über die transcendentale Ästhetik. Bruxelles, 1968.
Phil 705.72 Struve, Wolfgang. Philosophie und Transzendenz. Freiburg, 1969.
Phil 705.74 Piclin, Michel. La notion de transcendance; son sens, son évolution. Paris, 1969.

Phil 720 Special philosophical topics, systems, etc. - Secondary treatises and discussions - Truth

Phil 720.01 Pamphlet box. Philosophy. Special. Truth and error.
Phil 720.1 Campbell, G.D. What is truth? Edinburgh, 1889.
Phil 720.1.2 Argyll, G.D.C. What is truth? N.Y., 1889.
Phil 720.2 Stokes, G.J. Objectivity of truth. London, 1884.
Phil 720.3 Tabor, J.A. The supreme law. Colchester, 1879.
Phil 720.5 Rhodes, D.P. Philosophy of change. N.Y., 1909.
Phil 720.6 Carus, P. Truth on trial. Chicago, 1910.
Phil 720.7 Strümpell, L. Die Unterschiede der Wahrneiten und der Irrthümer. Leipzig, 1897.
Phil 720.8 Carr, H.W. The problem of truth. London, n.d.
Phil 720.9 Ladd, G.T. What can I know? N.Y., 1914.
Phil 720.10 Stoner, J.R. Logic and imagination in the perception of truth. N.Y., 1910.
Htn Phil 720.11* Brooke, R.G. Nature of truth. London, 1640.
Phil 720.12 Bonucci, A. Verità e realtà. Modena, 1911.
Phil 720.13 Tonquédec, J. de. La notion de vérité dans la "philosophie nouvelle". Paris, 1908.
Phil 720.14.2 Brochard, V. De l'erreur. 2e éd. Paris, 1897.
Phil 720.15 Ramousse, Gatien. Essai d'une théorie scientifique du concept de vérité. Thèse. Saint-Amand, 1909.
Phil 720.16 Lelesz, H. La conception de la vérité. Thèse. Paris, 1921.
Phil 720.18 Reid, Louis A. Knowledge and truth. London, 1923.
Phil 720.21 Bauch, Bruno. Wahrheit, Wert und Wirklichkeit. Leipzig, 1923.
Phil 720.22 Arnauld, A. Des vrayes et des fausses idées. Cologne, 1683.
Phil 720.23 Aveling, Francis. The psychological approach to reality. London, 1929.
Phil 720.24 Borowne, S.S.S. A pragmatist theory of truth and reality. Thesis. Princeton, 1930.
Phil 720.25 Stern, Alfred. Die philosophischen Grundlagen von Wahrheit, Wirklichkeit, Wert. München, 1932.
Phil 720.26 Kearney, C.M. Two neglected aspects of the truth situation. Thesis. Chicago, 1933.
Phil 720.27 Lemaitre, C. L'amour du vrai. Louvain, 1929.
Phil 720.29 Price, H.H. Truth and corrigibility. Oxford, 1936.
Phil 720.30 Cleugh, M.F. Time and its importance to modern thought. London, 1937.
Phil 720.31 Belgodere, F.J.A. La verdad, la ciencia y la filosofía. México, 1939.
Phil 720.32 Ruja, H. A critique of the postulational theory of the a priori. Diss. Princeton, 1940.
Phil 720.33 Stefansson, V. The standardization of error. N.Y., 1927.
Phil 720.33.5 Stefansson, V. The standardization of error. London, 1928.
Phil 720.35 Grisebach, Eberhard. Was ist Wahrheit in Wirklichkeit? Bern, 1941.
Phil 720.37 Balthaser, Hans. Wahrheit. Einsiedeln, 1947.
Phil 720.39 Tarski, Alfred. De Wahrheitsbegriff in der...Sprachen. Photostat. Leopoli, 1935.
Phil 720.40 Medicus, F. Menschlichkeit. Zürich, 1951.
Phil 720.41 Erismann, T. Denken und Sein. v.1. Wien, 1950.
Phil 720.42 Kohn, David. More than truth. N.Y., 1956.
Phil 720.43 Aaron, Richard Ithamar. The true and the valid. London, 1955.
Phil 720.44 Casellato, Sante. Di alcune considerazioni intorno alla verità e all'errore. Padova, 1958.
Phil 720.45 Smith, Gerard. The truth that frees. Milwaukee, 1956.
Phil 720.46 Raab, Elmar F.X. Die Wahrheit als metaphysisches Problem. Dillingen, 1959.
Phil 720.50 King, Peter D. The principle of truth. N.Y., 1960.
Phil 720.55 Kamlah, Wilhelm. Wissenschaft, Wahrheit, Existenz. Stuttgart, 1960.
Phil 720.59 Khachaturian, Haig. The coherence theory of truth. Beirut, 1961.
Phil 720.60 Manzana Martinez de Marañon, José. Objektivität und Wahrheit. Vitoria, 1961.

Classified Listing

Phil 720.61	Jenny, Guido. Auf der Suche nach Wahrheit. Zürich, 1961.
Phil 720.62	Rivetti Barbo, Francesca. L'antinomia del mentitore nel pensiero contemporaneo da Peirce a Tarski. Milano, 1961.
Phil 720.63	Manzana Martinez de Marañón, José. Objektivität und Wahrheit. Vitoria, 1961.
Phil 720.64	Borne, Étienne. Passion de la vérité. Paris, 1962.
Phil 720.65	García López, Jesús. El valor de la verdad y otros estudios. Madrid, 1965.
Phil 720.67	Haensel, Carl. Über den Irrtum. Heidelberg, 1965.
Phil 720.68	Kittinger, Kenneth C. A cranium shake-up and a new philosophy to alter the war spirit in man. Los Angeles, 1967.
Phil 720.70	Lauth, Reinhard. Die absolute Ungeschichtlichkeit der Warhrheit. Stuttgart, 1966.
Phil 720.72	Congrès des Sociétés de Philosophie de Langue Française, 12th, Brussels et Louvain, 1964. La vérité. Louvain, 1964-65. 2v.
Phil 720.74	Joachim, Harold Henry. The nature of truth. Ann Arbor, 1969.
Phil 720.76	Pitcher, George Willard. Truth. Englewood Cliffs, N.J., 1964.
Phil 720.78	Semaine des Intellectuels Catholiques, 1969. Chercher la vérité, 5-12 mars 1969. Paris, 1969.
Phil 720.80	Armour, Leslie. The concept of truth. Assen, 1969.
Phil 720.82	Kalinowski, Jerzy. Le probléme de la vérité en morale et en droit. Thése. Lyon, 1967.
Phil 720.84	Scheffler, Israel. Science and subjectivity. Indianapolis, 1967.
Phil 720.86	Ulmer, Karl. Die Wissenschaften und die Wahrheit. Stuttgart, 1966.
Phil 720.88	Lane, Gilles. Être et langage; essai sur la recherche de l'objectivité. Paris, 1970.
Phil 720.90	Lanteri-Laura, Georges. Structures subjectives du champ transcendantal. Thèse. Paris, 1968.
Phil 720.92	Schär, Hans. Was ist Wahrheit? Eine theologisch-psychologische Untersuchung. Zürich, 1970.
Phil 720.94	Hennemann, Gerhard. Zum Problem der Voraussetzungslosigkeit und Objektivität in der Wissenschaft. Photoreproduction. Bonn, 1947.
Phil 720.96	Soggettività e intersoggettività. Padova, 1969.
Phil 720.98	Ruvo, Vincenzo de. Il problema della verità da Spinoza a Hume. Padova, 1970.
Phil 720.101	Rauche, Gerhard Albin. Contemporary philosophical alternatives and the crisis of truth; a critical study of positivism, existentialism and Marxism. The Hague, 1970.

Phil 728.5	Singevin, Charles. Essai sur l'un. Thèse. Paris, 1969.

Phil 730.5	Aaron, Richard Ithamar. The theory of universals. Oxford, 1952.
Phil 730.5.2	Aaron, Richard Ithamar. The Theory of universals. 2nd ed. London, 1967.
Phil 730.10A	Bocheński, Innocentius M. The problem of universals. Notre Dame, 1956.
Phil 730.10B	Bocheński, Innocentius M. The problem of universals. Notre Dame, 1956.
Phil 730.15	Schobinger, J.P. Vom Sein der Universalien. Winterthur, 1958.
Phil 730.20	Dalos, Patrick M. The critical value of concepts and universal ideas. 2. ed. Rome, 1960.
Phil 730.25	Afanas'ev, V.C. Problema tselostnosti v filosofii i biologii. Moskva, 1964.
Phil 730.26	Dar, B.A. Studies in the nature of universals. Lahore, 1958.
Phil 730.27	Iugai, Geragim A. Dialektika chasti i tselogo. Alma-Ata, 1965.
Phil 730.28	Zabeeh, Farhang. Universals; a new look at an old problem. The Hague, 1966.
Phil 730.30	Butchvarov, Panayot. Resemblance and identity. Bloomington, 1966.
VPhil 730.31	Admec, Josef. Holismus. Praha, 1966.
Phil 730.34	Pichler, Hans. Ganzheit und Gemeinschaft. Wiesbaden, 1967.
Phil 730.35	Korotkova, Galina P. Printsipy tselostnosti. Leningrad, 1968.
Phil 730.36	Wolterstorff, Nicholas Paul. On universals. Chicago, 1970.

Phil 735.01	Pamphlet box. Philosophy. Special. Values.
Phil 735.1	Berguer, G. La notion de valeur. Genève, 1908.
Phil 735.2A	Eisler, R. Studien zur Werttheorie. Leipzig, 1902.
Phil 735.2B	Eisler, R. Studien zur Werttheorie. Leipzig, 1902.
Phil 735.3	Nicholson, Anne M. The concept standard. N.Y., 1910.
Phil 735.4	Strich, Walter. Das Wertproblem in der Philosophie der Gegenwart. Berlin, 1909.
Phil 735.5	Dashiell, J.F. Philosophical status of values. N.Y., 1913.
Phil 735.6	Ostwald, W. Die Philosophie der Werte. Leipizig, 1913.
Phil 735.7	Hocking, William E. Papers on the theory of value. Lancaster, Pa., 1908. 2 pam.
Phil 735.8	Lüdemann, H. Das Erkennen und die Werturteile. Leipzig, 1910.
Phil 735.9	Vos, H. von de. Werte und Bewertungen in der Denkevolution. Berlin, 1909.
Phil 735.10	Urban, W.M. Valuation: its nature and laws. London, 1909.
Phil 735.10.5	Urban, W.M. The intelligible world. London, 1929.
Phil 735.11	Valli, Luigi. Il valore supremo. Genova, 1913.
Phil 735.12	Blechman, Nathan. The philosophic function of value. Boston, 1918.
Phil 735.13	Stuart, H.W. Valuation as a logical process. Thesis. Chicago, 1918.
Phil 735.14	Lessing, Theodor. Studien zur Wertaxiomatik. 2e Ausg. Leipzig, 1914.
Phil 735.15	Ritschel, Otto. Über Wethurteile. Freiburg, 1895.
Phil 735.16	Bougle, Celestin C. Leçons de sociologie sur l'évolution des valeurs. Paris, 1922.
Phil 735.17	Liebert, A. Das Problem der Geltung. 2e Aufl. Leipzig, 1920.
Phil 735.18.2	Scheler, Max. Vom Umsturz der Werte. 2e Aufl. Leipzig, 1919. 2v.

Phil 735.18.5	Scheler, Max. L'homme du ressentiment. Paris, 1933.
Phil 735.19	Mutius, Gerhard von. Gedanke und Erlebnis; Umriss einer Philosophie des Wertes. Darmstadt, 1922.
Phil 735.20.5A	Perry, Ralph Barton. General theory of value. N.Y., 1926.
Phil 735.20.5B	Perry, Ralph Barton. General theory of value. N.Y., 1926.
Phil 735.20.12	Perry, Ralph Barton. General theory of value. Cambridge, Mass., 1954.
Phil 735.75	Walker, Cyril T.H. The construction of the world. Oxford, 1919.
Phil 735.77	Picard, Maurice. Values immediate and contributory and their interrelation. N.Y., 1920.
Phil 735.78	Mackenzie, J.S. Ultimate values in the light of contemporary thought. London, 1924.
Phil 735.79	Vaucher, G. Le langage affectif et les jugements de valeur. Thèse. Paris, 1925.
Phil 735.79.1	Vaucher, G. Le langage affectif et les jugements de valeur. Paris, 1925.
Phil 735.80	Wiederhold, K. Wert Begriff und Wertphilosophie. Berlin, 1920.
Phil 735.81	Messer, August. Deutsche Wertphilosophie der Gegenwart. Leipzig, 1926.
Phil 735.82	Kühn, Lenore. Die Autonomie der Werte. Berlin, 1926-31. 2v.
NEDL Phil 735.83	Goldstein, M. Der Wert des Zwecklosen. Dresden, 1920.
Phil 735.84	Heyde, Johannes E. Wert. Erfurt, 1926.
Phil 735.85	Wilken, F. Grundzüge einer personalistischen Werttheorie. Jena, 1924.
Phil 735.86	Goblot, E. La logique des jugements de valeur. Paris, 1927.
Phil 735.87	Vetter, A. Kritik des Gefühls. Prien, 1923.
Phil 735.88	Bamberger, F. Untersuchungen zur Entstehung des Wertproblems in der Philosophie des 19. Jahrhunderts. Halle, 1924.
Phil 735.89A	Kreibig, J.C. Psychologische Grundlegung eines Systems der Wert-Theorie. Wien, 1902.
Phil 735.89B	Kreibig, J.C. Psychologische Grundlegung eines Systems der Wert-Theorie. Wien, 1902.
Phil 735.90	Münsterberg, H. Philosophie der Werte. Leipzig, 1908.
Phil 735.90.5	Münsterberg, H. The eternal values. Boston, 1909.
Phil 735.91.5	Ward, Leo Richard. Philosophy of value. Diss. N.Y., 1930.
Phil 735.91.10	Ward, Leo Richard. Values and reality. N.Y., 1935.
Phil 735.92	Laird, John. The idea of value. Cambridge, Eng., 1929.
Phil 735.93	Clarke, Mary E. A study in the logic of value. London, 1929.
Phil 735.94	Eaton, Howard O. The Austrian theory of value. Norman, 1930.
Phil 735.95	Pell, Orlie A.H. Value theory andCriticism. Thesis. N.Y., 1930.
Phil 735.96	Salomaa, J.E. Studien zur Wertphilosophie. Helsinki, 1930.
Phil 735.97	Parker, DeWitt H. Human values. N.Y., 1931.
Phil 735.98	Bommersheim, Paul. Wertrecht und Wertmacht. Berlin, 1931.
Phil 735.99	Ennismore, R.G. The values of life. London, 1931.
Phil 735.100	Rintelen, F.J. von. Der Wertgedanke in der europäischen Geistesentwicklung. Halle, 1932.
Phil 735.101	Cohn, Jonas. Wertwissenschaft. Stuttgart, 1932.
Phil 735.102	Osborne, Harold. Foundations of the philosophy of value. Cambridge, 1933.
Phil 735.103	Müller, Max. Über Grundbegriffe philosophischer Wertlehre. Inaug. Diss. Freiburg, 1932.
Phil 735.104	Groos, Karl. Zur Psychologie und Metaphysik des Wert-Erlebens. Berlin, 1932.
Phil 735.105	Rothschild, R. Reality and illusion. N.Y., 1934.
Phil 735.106	Cohn, Aron. Hauptprobleme der Wertphilosophie. Wien, 1934.
Phil 735.107	Losskii, Nikolai O. Value and existence. London, 1935.
Phil 735.108	Störring, G. Die moderne ethische Wertphilosophie. Leipzig, 1935.
Phil 735.109	Bénèzè, Georges. Valeur. Paris, 1936.
Phil 735.109.5	Bénèzè, Georges. Valeur. Thèse. Paris, 1936.
Phil 735.110	Jury, G.S. Value and ethical objectivity. London, 1937.
Phil 735.111	Garnett, Arthur C. Reality and value. New Haven, 1937.
Phil 735.112	Spiegelberg, H. Antirelativismus. Zürich, 1935.
Phil 735.113	Rodhe, S.E. Über die Möglichkeit einer Werteinteilung. Lund, 1937.
Phil 735.114	Kraft, V. Die Grundlagen einer wissenschaftlichen Wertlehre. Wien, 1937.
Phil 735.114.5	Kraft, V. Die Grundlagen einer wissenschaftlichen Wertlehre. 2. Aufl. Wien, 1951.
Phil 735.115	Katkov, Georg. Untersuchungen zur Werttheorie und Theodizee. Brünn, 1937.
Phil 735.116	Kraus, O. Die Werttheorien; Geschichte und Kritik. Brünn, 1937.
Phil 735.117	Reid, John R. A theory of value. N.Y., 1938.
Phil 735.118.2	Köhler, Wolfgang. The place of value in a world of facts. N.Y., 1959.
Phil 735.119	Larroyo, F. La filosofía de los valores. México, 1936.
Phil 735.120	Fiedler, K. Die Stufen der Erkenntnis. München, 1929.
Phil 735.121	Grenier, Jean. Le choix. Paris, 1941.
Phil 735.122	Sreenivasa Iyengar, K.R. The metaphysics of value. Mysore, 1942.
Phil 735.123	Polin, Raymond. Essai sur la compréhension des valeurs. Thèse. Paris, 1945.
Phil 735.124A	Lepley, Ray. Value; a cooperative inquiry. N.Y., 1949-50.
Phil 735.124B	Lepley, Ray. Value; a cooperative inquiry. N.Y., 1949-50.
Phil 735.124.5	Lepley, Ray. The language of value. N.Y., 1957.
Phil 735.125	Hilliard, A.L. The forms of value. N.Y., 1950.
Phil 735.126	Mukerjee, Radhakamal. The social structure of values. London, 1950.
Phil 735.126.2	Mukerjee, Radhakamal. The social structure of values. 2nd ed. New Delhi, 1965.
Phil 735.128	McCracken, D.J. Thinking and valuing. London, 1950.
Phil 735.130A	Hall, Everett W. What is value? London, 1952.
Phil 735.130B	Hall, Everett W. What is value? London, 1952.
Phil 735.132	Ruyer, R. Philosophie de la valeur. Paris, 1952.
Phil 735.134	Kurtz, Paul W. The problems of value theory. Thesis. N.Y., 1952.
Phil 735.136	Archivio di Filosofia. La crisi dei valori. Roma, 1945.
Phil 735.140	Lamont, W.D. The value judgement. Edinburgh, 1955.
Phil 735.145	Müller, A. Die Grundkategorien des Lebendigen. Meisenheim, 1954.
Phil 735.150	Glansdorff, Maxime. Théorie générale de la valeur et ses applications en esthétique et en économie. Bruxelles, 1954.

Classified Listing

Phil 735   **Special philosophical topics, systems, etc. - Secondary treatises and discussions - Value theory - cont.**

Phil 735.150.2 — Glansdorff, Maxime. Les déterminants de la théorie générale de la valeur et ses applications en esthétique, en religion, en morale, en économie et en politique. 2e éd. Bruxelles, 1966.
Phil 735.160 — Morris, C.W. Varieties of human value. Chicago, 1956.
Phil 735.165 — Halldén, Sören. Emotive propositions. Stockholm, 1954.
Phil 735.170 — Parker, D.H. The philosophy of value. Ann Arbor, 1957.
Phil 735.175 — Meimberg, Rudolf. Alternativen der Ordnung. Berlin, 1956.
Phil 735.180 — Pepper, Stephen C. The sources of value. Berkeley, 1958.
Phil 735.185 — Césari, Paul. La valeur. 1. ed. Paris, 1957.
Phil 735.190 — Pucelle, Jean. La source des valeurs. Lyon, 1957. 3v.
Phil 735.195 — Scientific Conference on New Knowledge...1st. New knowledge in human values. N.Y., 1959.
Phil 735.200 — Gruber, Frederick C. Aspects of value. Philadelphia, 1959.
Phil 735.205 — Coleburt, Russell. The search for values. London, 1960.
Phil 735.210 — Ehrlich, Walter. Hauptprobleme der Wertphilosophie. Tübingen, 1959.
Phil 735.220 — Dujoune, L. Teoría de los valores y filosofía de la historia. Buenos Aires, 1959.
Phil 735.225 — Pole, David. Conditions of rational inquiry. London, 1961.
Phil 735.230 — Mezing, Otto O. A grammar of human values. Pittsburgh, 1961.
Phil 735.235 — Graham, Angus C. The problem of value. London, 1961.
Phil 735.240 — Taylor, Paul. Normative discourse. Englewood, 1961.
Phil 735.242 — Frondizi, R. What is value? La Salle, 1963.
Phil 735.243 — Wittmann, M. Die moderne Wertethik. Münster, 1940.
Phil 735.244 — Langweg, R. Das Phänomen der Wertblindheit. Lingen-Ems, 1961?
Phil 735.245 — Mukerjee, Radhakamal. The dimensions of values. London, 1964.
Phil 735.250 — Makiguchi, Tsunesaburo. Philosophy of value. Tokyo, 1964.
Phil 735.252 — Loring, L.M. Two kinds of values. London, 1966.
Phil 735.254 — Kempff Mercado, Manfredo. Cuando valen los valores? Maracaibo, 1965.
Phil 735.256 — Hatcher, Harlan Henthorne. The persistent quest for values: what are we seeking? Columbia, 1966.
Phil 735.257 — Akademiia Nauk SSSR. Kafedra Filosofii, Leningrad. Problema tsennosti v filosofii. Leningrad, 1966.
Phil 735.260 — Bruederlin, Kurt. Zur Phänomenologie des Werterlebens. Winterthur, 1962.
Phil 735.261 — Antonovich, Ivan I. Amerikanskaia burzhuaznaia aksiologiia na sluzh e imperializma. Minsk, 1967.
Phil 735.262 — Hartman, Robert S. The structure of value; foundations of scientific axiology. Carbondale, 1967.
Phil 735.263 — Werkmeister, William H. Man and his values. Lincoln, 1967.
Phil 735.264 — Drobnitskii, Oleg G. Mir ozhivshikh predmetov. Moskva, 1967.
Phil 735.265 — Krohn, Sven. Totuus, arvo ja ihminen. Porvoo, 1967.
Phil 735.266 — Handy, Rollo. Value theory and the behavioral sciences. Springfield, Ill., 1969.
Phil 735.268 — Rescher, Nicholas. Introduction to value theory. Englewood Cliffs, N.J., 1969.
Phil 735.270 — Solimini, Maria. Genealogia e scienza dei valori. Manduria, 1968.
Phil 735.272 — Moritz, Manfred. Inledning i värdeteori. 2. uppl. Lund, 1968.
Phil 735.274 — Životić, Miladin. Čovek i vrednost. Beograd, 1969.
Phil 735.276 — Europaeisches Forum, Alpbach, Austria, 1946. Erkenntnis und Wert. Salzburg, 1946.
Phil 735.278 — Die Rolle der Werte im Leben. Festschrift für Johannes Hessen zu seinen 80. Geburtstag. Köln, 1969.
Phil 735.280 — Findlay, Niemeyer. Axiological ethics. London, 1970.
Phil 735.282 — Preti, Giulio. Fenomenologia del valore. Milano, 1942.
Phil 735.284 — Anisimov, Sergei F. Tseunoi real'nye i mnimye. Moskva, 1970.
Phil 735.286 — Ivin, Aleksandr A. Osnovaniia logiki otsenok. Moskva, 1970.

Phil 745   **Special philosophical topics, systems, etc. - Secondary treatises and discussions - Vitalism**

Phil 745.01 — Pamphlet box. Philosophy. Special. Vitalism.
Phil 745.3 — Bunge, Gustav von. Vitalismus und Mechanismus. Leipzig, 1886.
Phil 745.5 — Noll, Alfred. Die "Lebenskraft" in der Schriften der Vitalisten und ihrer Gegner. Leipzig, 1914.
Phil 745.6A — Driesch, H. The history and theory of vitalism. London, 1914.
Phil 745.6B — Driesch, H. The history and theory of vitalism. London, 1914.
Phil 745.6.7 — Driesch, H. Il vitalismo. Milano, 1911. 2v.
Phil 745.7 — Driesch, H. Geschichte des Vitalismus. 2e Aufl. Leipzig, 1922.
Phil 745.7.9A — Driesch, H. The problem of individuality. London, 1914.
Phil 745.7.9B — Driesch, H. The problem of individuality. London, 1914.
Phil 745.7.9C — Driesch, H. The problem of individuality. London, 1914.
Phil 745.7.15 — Driesch, H. Über der grundsätzliche Unmöglichkeit einer "Vereinigung" von universeller Teleologie und Mechanismus. Heidelberg, 1914.
Phil 745.8 — Rudy, Hirsch. Die Entwicklung der vitalistischen Naturphilosophie im 20. Jahrhundert. Inaug. Diss. Charlottenburg, 1927.
Phil 745.9 — Neal, Herbert V. Vitalism and mechanism. Lancaster, Pa., 1934.
Phil 745.10 — Losskii, Nikolai O. Materiia i zhizn'. Berlin, 1923.
Phil 745.12 — Bollnow, Otto F. Die Lebensphilosophie. Berlin, 1958.

Phil 760   **Special philosophical topics, systems, etc. - Secondary treatises and discussions - Whole and parts**

Phil 760.2 — González Asenjo, Florencio. El todo y las partes; estudios de ontología formal. Madrid, 1962.

Phil 800 - 825   **History of philosophy - General history - General works**
(A-Z)

Phil 800.1 — Allgemeine Geschichte der Philosophie. Berlin, 1909.
Phil 800.1.5 — Allgemeine Geschichte der Philosophie. 2. Aufl. Leipzig, 1913.
Phil 800.2 — Alexander, A.B.D. A short history of philosophy. Glasgow, 1907.
Phil 800.2.3 — Alexander, A.B.D. A short history of philosophy. 3. ed. Glasgow, 1922.
Phil 800.3 — Adams, C. Études sur les principaux philosophes. Paris, 1903.

Phil 800 - 825   **History of philosophy - General history - General works**
(A-Z)

Phil 800.4 — Albrich, K. Im Kampf um unsere Stellung zu Welt und Leben. Leipzig, 1924.
Phil 800.5 — Aall, Anothon. Filosofiens historie. Oslo, 1929.
Phil 800.6 — Amato, F. d'. Studi di storia della filosofia. Geneva, 1931.
Phil 800.7 — Alpern, Henry. The march of philosophy. N.Y., 1933.
Phil 800.8 — Aquilanti, F. Linei fondamentali di storia della filosofia. v.1-3. Milano, 1938-40. 2v.
Phil 800.10 — Akademiia Nauk SSSR. Institut Filosofii. Istoriia filosofii. Moskva, 1940-1941. 2v.
Phil 800.10.5 — Akademiia Nauk SSSR. Institut Filosofii. Istoriia filosofii. Moskva, 1957. 7v.
Phil 800.10.10 — Akademiia Nauk SSSR. Geschichte der Philosophie. Berlin, 1959- 6v.
Phil 800.12 — Aleksandrov, G.F. Istoriia zapnoevroplskoi filosofii. Izd. 2. Moskva, 1946.
Phil 800.12.10 — Zhdanov, A.A. Vystuplenie na diskussii po knige G.F. Aleksandrova. "Istoriia zapnoevropeiskoi filosofii". Moskva, 1947.
Phil 800.13.2 — Aleksandrov, G.F. A history of western European philosophy. 2d ed. New Haven, 1949.
Phil 800.14.14 — Aster, Ernst von. Geschichte der Philosophie. 14. Aufl. Stuttgart, 1963.
Phil 800.15 — Axelos, Kostas. Vers la pensée planétaire. Paris, 1964.
Phil 800.16 — Abbagnano, N. Storia della filosofia. 2. ed. Torino, 1963. 3v.
Phil 800.18 — Alfieri, Vittorio Enzo. Filosofia e filologia. Napoli, 1967.
Phil 800.20 — Ahlberg, A. Fran antikens och medeltidens tankevärd. Stockholm, 1966.
Phil 801.1 — Bauer, W. Geschichte der Philosophie. Halle, 1863.
Phil 801.2 — Box, E.B. Handbook...history of philosophy. London, 1886.
Phil 801.2.5 — Box, E.B. Handbook...history of philosophy. London, 1908.
NEDL   Phil 801.3 — Blakey, R. History of the philosophy of the mind. London, 1848. 4v.
Phil 801.3.2 — Blakey, R. History of the philosophy of the mind. London, 1850. 4v.
Phil 801.4 — Bouillier, F. Manuel de l'histoire de la philosophie. Paris, 1845.
Phil 801.4.5 — Bouillier, F. Analyses des ouvrages de philosophie. 3. ed. Paris, 1870.
Phil 801.5 — Brucker, J. Historia critica philosophiae. Lipsiae, 1742-67. 6v.
Phil 801.5.2 — Brucker, J. Historia critica philosophiae. Lipsiae, 1867. 6v.
Phil 801.5.3 — Brucker, J. Historia critica philosophiae. Lipsiae, 1867. 6v.
Phil 801.5.7 — Brucker, J. Institutiones historiae philosophicae. Lipsiae, 1747.
Phil 801.5.15 — Brucker, J. Kurtze Fragen aus der philosophischen Historie. Ulm, 1731-36. 7v.
Phil 801.5.20 — Brucker, J. Miscellanea historiae philosophicae literariae criticae. Augustae Vindelicorum, 1748.
Phil 801.6 — Budeus, J.F. Analecta historiae philosophicae. Halle, 1706.
Phil 801.6.2 — Budeus, J.F. Analecta historiae philosophicae. 2. ed. Halle, 1724.
Phil 801.7 — Buschings, A.F. Grundriss einer Geschichte de Philosophie. Berlin, 1772-4. 2v.
Phil 801.8 — Buhle, T.G. Lehrbuch der Geschichte der Philosophie. Göttingen, 1796-1804. 8v.
Phil 801.9 — Blainville, H. de. Historie des sciences de l'organisation. Paris, 1845. 3v.
Phil 801.10 — Boutroux, E. Etudes d'histoire de la philosophie. Paris, 1908.
Phil 801.10.5 — Boutroux, E. Historical studies in philosophy. London, 1912.
Phil 801.11 — Bascom, John. An historical interpretation of philosophy. N.Y., 1893.
Phil 801.12 — Bevan, J.O. Handbook of history and development of philosophy. London, 1916.
Phil 801.13 — Brockdorff, C. von. Die Geschichte der Philosophie. Hildesheim, 1906.
Phil 801.13.2 — Brockdorff, C. von. Die Geschichte der Philosophie. Osterwieck, 1908.
Phil 801.14 — Brothier, Léon. Histoire populaire de la philosophie. Paris, 1861.
Phil 801.14.3 — Brothier, Léon. Histoire populaire de la philosophie. 3. ed. Paris, 1907.
Phil 801.15 — Bergmann, J. Geschichte der Philosophie. Berlin, 1892-93. 2v.
Phil 801.16 — Baumann, J. Gesamtgeschichte der Philosophie. 2. Aufl. Gotha, 1903.
Phil 801.16.5 — Baumann, J. Geschichte der Philosophie nach Ideengehalt und Beweisen. Gotha, 1890.
Phil 801.17 — Bodrero, E. I limiti della storia della filosofia. Roma, 1919.
Phil 801.18 — Brøchner, Hans. Bidrag til opfattelsen of philosophiens historisk Udvikling. Kjøbenhavn, 1869.
Phil 801.18.3 — Brøchner, Hans. Philosophiens historie i Grundrids. Kjøbenhavn, 1873-74.
Phil 801.19 — Barr, Knut. Världsförklaringar och lifsåskådningar. Stockholm, 1910.
Phil 801.20 — Baker, A.E. How to understand philosophy. N.Y., 1926.
Phil 801.21 — Bréhier, É. Histoire de la philosophie. Paris, 1926. 9v.
Phil 801.21.5A — Bréhier, É. The history of philosophy. v.1-3,5-7. Chicago, 1963. 7v.
Phil 801.21.5B — Bréhier, É. The history of philosophy. Chicago, 1963.
Phil 801.21.6 — Bréhier, É. Histoire de la philosophie. Paris, 1963. 3v.
Phil 801.21.6.1 — Bréhier, É. Histoire de la philosophie. Paris, 1969.
Phil 801.22 — Bensow, Oscar. Grunddragen af filosofiens historia. Stockholm, 1916. 2v.
Phil 801.23 — Brunschvicg, L. Le progrès de la conscience dans la philosophie. Paris, 1927. 2v.
Phil 801.23.9 — Brunschvicg, L. Les âges de l'intelligence. Paris, 1934.
Phil 801.23.11 — Brunschvicg, L. Les âges de l'intelligence. 3. ed. Paris, 1934.
Phil 801.23.15 — Brunschvicg, L. La physique du vingtième siècle et la philosophie. Paris, 1936.
Phil 801.24 — Berthre de Bowinisseaux, P.V.J. La charlatanisme philosophique de tous les âges dévoilé. Paris, 1807.
Phil 801.25 — Bergmann, E. Weltanschauung. Breslau, 1926. 2v.
Phil 801.26 — Beccari, Arturo. Storia della filosofia e della scienza. Torino, 1928.

Phil 801.27	Bjarnason, A. Austurlönd. Reykjavik, 1908.
Phil 801.27.5	Bjarnason, A. Hellas. Reykjavik, 1910.
Phil 801.27.15	Bjarnason, A. Vesturlönd. Reykjavik, 1815.
Phil 801.27.20	Bjarnason, A. Nítjánda äldin. Reykjavik, 1906.
Phil 801.28	Boas, George. The adventures of human thought. N.Y., 1929.
Phil 801.28.5	Boas, George. The major traditions of European philosophy. N.Y., 1929.
Phil 801.29.5	Behn, Siegfried. The eternal magnet, a history of philosophy. N.Y., 1929.
Phil 801.30	Bayrhoffer, K.T. Die Idee und Geschichte der Philosophie. Marburg, 1838.
Phil 801.31	Bardili, C.G. Epochen der Vorzüglichsten philosophischen Begriffe. Halle, 1788. 2 pam.
Phil 801.32	Baumgarten, A. Die Geschichte der abendländischen Philosophie eine Geschichte des geistigen Fortschritts der Menscheit. Genève, 1945.
Phil 801.33	Bréhier, E. La philosophie et son passé. Paris, 1940.
Phil 801.33.5	Bréhier, E. La filosofia e il suo passato. Napoli, 1965.
Phil 801.34	Baillot, A.F. La notion d'existence. Paris, 1954.
Phil 801.35	Bueno, Miguel. Las grandes direcciones de la filosofia. México, 1957.
Phil 801.35.5	Bueno, Miguel. Prolegómenos filosóficos. México, 1963.
Phil 801.35.10	Bueno, Miguel. Ensayos liminares. México, 1962.
Phil 801.37	Baskin, M.P. Filosofiia i zhizn'. Moskva, 1961.
Phil 802.1	Cicchitti-Suriani, F. Sinossi della storia di filosofia. Torino, 1886.
Phil 802.2.1	Cousin, V. Cours d'histoire de la philosophie. Paris, 1828?
Phil 802.2.2	Cousin, V. Cours de philosophie. Paris, 1828.
Phil 802.2.3	Cousin, V. Cours de l'histoire de la philosophie. Paris, 1841.
Phil 802.2.5	Cousin, V. Histoire générale de la philosophie. 8e éd. Paris, 1867.
Phil 802.2.5.11	Cousin, V. Histoire générale de la philosophie. 11e éd. Paris, 1884.
Phil 802.2.8	Cousin, V. Introduction to the history of philosophy. Boston, 1832.
Phil 802.3	Crozier, F.B. History of intellectual development. v.1,3. London, 1897. 2v.
Phil 802.4A	Cushman, H.E. A beginner's history of philosophy. Boston, 1910-11. 2v.
Phil 802.4B	Cushman, H.E. A beginner's history of philosophy. Boston, 1910-11. 2v.
Phil 802.4.2A	Cushman, H.E. A beginner's history of philosophy. Boston, 1918-20. 2v.
Phil 802.4.2B	Cushman, H.E. A beginner's history of philosophy. Boston, 1918-20.
Phil 802.4.3	Cushman, H.E. A beginner's history of philosophy. Boston, 1918-19.
Phil 802.5	Cesca, Giovanni. I fattori della evoluzione filosofica. Padova, 1892.
Phil 802.6	Conti, Augusto. Storia della filosofia; lezioni. 6a ed. Roma, 1908-09. 2v.
Phil 802.6.5	Conti, Augusto. Histoire de la philosophie. Paris, n.d. 2v.
Phil 802.7	Cunz, T. Geschichte der Philosophie in gemeinverständlicher Darstellung. Marburg, 1911.
Phil 802.8.2	Carbonel, Pierre. Histoire de la philosophie depuis les temps les plus reculés jusqu'à nos jours. 2e éd. Avignon, 1882.
Phil 802.8.10	Carbonel, Pierre. Essai de philosophie classique. Paris, 1876.
Phil 802.9	Claeson, Gustaf. Filosofiens historia i sammandrag. n.p., n.d.
Phil 802.10	Cosentini, F. I grandi filosofi e i grandi sistemi filosofici. Torino, 1925.
Phil 802.11	Capone Braga, G. Il mondo delle idee. pt. 1a, 2a. Città di Cástello, 1928-33. 2v.
Phil 802.12	Calcagni, Gaetano. Compendio di storia della filosofia. Arce, 1931. 2v.
Phil 802.13	Caramella, S. Disegno storico della filosofia. Messina, 1931.
Phil 802.14	Challaye, F. Petite histoire des grandes philosophies. Paris, 1942.
Phil 802.15	Copleston, F. A history of philosophy. v.1,4-8. London, 1946-50. 6v.
Phil 802.15.5	Copleston, F. A history of philosophy. Westminster, 1960. 8v.
Phil 802.16	Chartier, Emile. Abreges pour les aveugles. Paris, 1943.
Phil 802.17	Casserley, J.V.L. The Christian in philosophy. London, 1949.
Phil 802.18	Casey, F. Thinking. London, 1922.
Phil 802.19	Ciardo, M. Filosofia dell'arte e filosofia come totalità. Bari, 1953.
Phil 802.20	La filosofia della storia della filosofia. Milano, 1954.
Phil 802.21	Clark, Gordon Haddon. Thales to Dewey. Boston, 1957.
Phil 802.22	Chevalier, Jacques. Histoire de la pensée. v.1-3. Paris, 1955- 2v.
Phil 802.23	Coleburt, Russell. An introduction to Western philosophy. N.Y., 1957.
Phil 802.25	Carlini, Armando. Breve storia della filosofia. Firenze, 1957.
Phil 803.1	Deslandes, A.F.B. Histoire critique de la philosophie. London, 1742. 3v.
Phil 803.1.5	Deslandes, A.F.B. Historie critique de la philosophie. Amsterdam, 1756. 4v.
Phil 803.2	Dühring, E. Kritische Geschichte der Philosophie. 2d Aufl. Berlin, 1873.
Phil 803.2.3	Dühring, E. Kritische Geschichte der Philosophie. 3e Aufl. Leipzig, 1878.
Phil 803.2.4	Duehring, Eugen. His Gesammtcursus der Philosophie. Leipzig, 1894-95. 2v.
Phil 803.3	Deussen, P. Allgemeine Geschichte der Philosophie. v.1, pts.1-3. v.2, pts.1-3. Leipzig, 1894-1917. 7v.
Phil 803.3.1A	Deussen, P. Allgemeine Geschichte der Philosophie. v.1-2. Leipzig, 1894-1920. 7v.
Phil 803.3.1B	Deussen, P. Allgemeine Geschichte der Philosophie. v.1, pt.1-3, v.2, pt.1. Leipzig, 1894-1920. 4v.
Phil 803.3.2	Deussen, P. Allgemeine Geschichte der Philosophie. Leipzig, 1907-020. 3v.
Phil 803.4.15	Deussen, P. Discours de la méthode pour bien étudier l'histoire de la philosophie. Paris, n.d.
Phil 803.5	Deter, C.J. Abriss der Geschichte der Philosophie. Berlin, 1913.
Phil 803.6.5A	Durant, W. The story of philosophy. N.Y., 1926.

	Phil 803.6.5B	Durant, W. The story of philosophy. N.Y., 1926.
	Phil 803.6.18	Durant, W. The story of philosophy. N.Y., 1933.
	Phil 803.6.19	Durant, W. The story of philosophy. N.Y., 1954.
	Phil 803.6.25	Durant, W. The story of philosophy. Cambridge, 1927.
	Phil 803.7	Dresser, H.W. A history of ancient and medieval philosophy. N.Y., 1926.
	Phil 803.8	Dressoir, M. Lehrbuch der Philosophie. Berlin, 1925. 2v.
	Phil 803.9	Duvall, T.G. Great thinkers; the quest of life for its meaning. N.Y., 1937.
	Phil 803.10	Devaux, P. De Thales à Bergson. Liége, 1955.
	Phil 803.12	Dempf, Alois. Kritik der historischen Vernunft. Wien, 1957.
	Phil 803.14	Delfgaauw, B.M.O. Beknopte geschiedenis der wijshegeerte. Baarn, 1954. 2v.
	Phil 803.16	Dolci, Alfredo. Da talete all'esistenzialismo. Milano, 1958.
	Phil 803.17	Dunham, B. Heroes and heretics. 1st ed. N.Y., 1964.
	Phil 804.1	Elmendorf, J.J. Outlines of lectures on history of philosophy. N.Y., 1876.
	Phil 804.2	Enfield, W. History of philosophy. London, 1791. 2v.
	Phil 804.2.2	Enfield, W. History of philosophy. Dublin, 1792. 2v.
	Phil 804.2.3	Enfield, W. History of philosophy. London, 1819. 2v.
	Phil 804.2.4	Enfield, W. History of philosophy. London, n.d. 2v.
	Phil 804.2.5	Enfield, W. History of philosophy. London, 1837.
	Phil 804.3	Erdmann, J.E. Grundriss der Geschichte der Philosophie. Berlin, 1869-70. 2v.
	Phil 804.3.3A	Erdmann, J.E. Grundriss der Geschichte der Philosophie. 3e Aufl. Berlin, 1878. 2v.
	Phil 804.3.3B	Erdmann, J.E. Grundriss der Geschichte der Philosophie. 3e Aufl. Berlin, 1878.
	Phil 804.3.4	Erdmann, J.E. Grundriss der Geschichte der Philosophie. 4. Aufl. Berlin, 1896. 2v.
	Phil 804.3.5	Erdmann, J.E. History of philosophy. London, 1890. 3v.
	Phil 804.3.6	Erdmann, J.E. History of philosophy. v.1, 2d ed.; v.2-3, 3d ed. London, 1891-92. 3v.
	Phil 804.3.7	Erdmann, J.E. History of philosophy. v.1, 2d ed.; v.2, 3d ed. London, 1890-92. 2v.
X Cg	Phil 804.3.7	Erdmann, J.E. History of philosophy. 2d ed. v.3. London, 1891.
	Phil 804.3.25	Pamphlet box. Erdmann, Benno. History of philosophy.
	Phil 804.6	Einhorn, D. Begründung der Geschichte der Philosophie als Wissenschaft. Wien, 1919.
	Phil 804.7	Ettlinger, M. Philosophisches Lesebuch. München, 1925.
	Phil 804.8	Ertsei, D. Philosophia historiaja. Debreczen, 1825.
	Phil 804.10	Ehrhardt, Walter E. Philosophiegeschichte und geschichtlicher Septizismus. Bern, 1967.
	Phil 804.15	Ehrlich, Walter. Philosophie der Geschichte der Philosophie. Bad Ragaz, 1965.
Htn	Phil 805.1*	Formey, J.H.S. History of philosophy. London, 1766.
Htn	Phil 805.1.3*	Formey, J.H.S. A concise history of philosophy. London, 1766.
	Phil 805.1.5	Formey, J.H.S. A concise history of philosophy and philosophers. Glasgow, 1767.
	Phil 805.1.9	Formey, J.H.S. Histoire abrégée de la philosophie. Amsterdam, 1760.
	Phil 805.2	Fries, J.F. Geschichte der Philosophie. Halle, 1837-40. 2v.
	Phil 805.2.5	Fries, J.F. Beträge zur Geschichte der Philosophie. Heidelberg, 1819.
	Phil 805.3	Fletcher, O.O. Introduction to philosophy. N.Y., 1913.
	Phil 805.4	Faguet, E. Initiation philosophique. Paris, 1912.
	Phil 805.4	Fouillée, Alfred. Histoire de la philosophie. 14e éd. Paris, 1919.
	Phil 805.6.2	Fiorentino, F. Manuele di storia della filosofia. Torino, 1921. 2v.
	Phil 805.6.3	Fiorentino, F. Compendio di storia della filosofia. vol. 1-2, pt.1. Firenze, 1921-22. 2v.
	Phil 805.7	Freudenberg, G. Die philosophiegeschichtliche Wahrheit. Inaug. Diss. Berlin, 1921.
	Phil 805.8	Fuller, B.A.G. A history of philosophy. N.Y., 1938.
	Phil 805.9	Foss, Martin. The idea of perfection in the western world. Princeton, 1946.
	Phil 805.10	Ferm, V. A history of philosophical systems. N.Y., 1950.
	Phil 805.11	Fischl, Johann. Geschichte der Philosophie. Graz, 1948-53. 5v.
	Phil 805.13	Ferrater Mora, José. Man at the crossroads. Boston, 1957.
	Phil 805.13.5.2	Ferrater, Mora José. El hombre en la encrucijada. 2. ed. Buenos Aires, 1965.
	Phil 805.14	Flam, Leopold. Verleden en toehomst van de filosofie. Amsterdam, 1962.
	Phil 805.15	Flam, Leopold. L'homme et la conscience tragique. Bruxelles, 1964.
	Phil 805.20	Franca, Leonel. Noções de história da filosofia. Rio de Janeiro, 1967.
	Phil 805.25	Fuelleborn, Georg Gustav. Beträge zur Geschichte der Philosophie. pt.1-12. Bruxelles, 1968. 5v.
	Phil 806.1	Gerando, J.M. de. Histoire comparée des systèmes de philosophie. Paris, 1822-23. 4v.
	Phil 806.2	Guillon, M.N.S. Histoire générale de la philosophie. Paris, 1835. 4v.
	Phil 806.3	Grosse Denker. Leipzig, n.d. 2v.
	Phil 806.4	Gonzalez, Z. Histoire de la philosophie. Paris, 1890-91. 4v.
	Phil 806.4.2	Gonzalez y Diaz Turion, Ceferinto. Historia de la filosofia. Madrid, 1886. 4v.
	Phil 806.5	Grätz, H. von. Geschichte der Philosophie. Langensalza, 1861.
	Phil 806.7	Gleich, S. von. Von Thales bis Steiner. Stuttgart, 1920.
	Phil 806.8	Gasc-Desfosses, E. Études sur les auteurs philosophiques: réponses aux questions. 3e éd. Paris, 1909.
	Phil 806.9	Geschichte der Philosophie. Leipzig, 1925.
	Phil 806.10	Grulle, Samuel. Dissertatio stationes successivas philosophiae progredientis abumbrans. Upsaliae, 1809.
	Phil 806.12	Gasiorowski, W. Historja filozofji. Sandomierz, 1928.
	Phil 806.13.1	Gilson, Etienne. The unity of philosophical experience. N.Y., 1937.
	Phil 806.13.2	Gilson, Etienne. The unity of philosophical experience. N.Y., 1946.
	Phil 806.14	Greca, Carlo. Storia della filosofia. Palermo, 1951.
	Phil 806.14.2	Greca, Carlo. Storia della filosofia. 2. ed. Firenze, 1956.
	Phil 806.15	Gabriel, Leo. Vom Brahma zur Existenz. 2. Aufl. Wien, 1954.

Phil 806.16   Geschichte der Philosophie. 2. Aufl. v.1-4,6,8-11.
Berlin, 1954. 6v.

Phil 806.17   Glockuer, H. Die europäische Philosophie.
Stuttgart, 1958.

Phil 806.18   Geymonat, Ludoviro. Storia del pensiero filosofico.
Milano, 1955-56.

Phil 806.20   Gladisch, August. Einleiteug in das Verständriss der
Weltgeschichte. Posen, 1844.

Phil 806.25   Galli, Dario. Sensei e soluzzi della filosofia europea.
Bologna, 1959.

Phil 806.30   Gambra Ciudad, R. Historia sencilla de la filosofia.
Madrid, 1961.

Phil 806.35   Guiliano, Balbino. Il cammino del pensiero.
Firenze, 1962.

Phil 806.36   Gonzalez Cominero, N. Historia philosophiae. v.1.
Romae, 1960. 2v.

Phil 806.37   García Bacca, Juan David. Siete modelos de filosofar.
Venezuela, 1963.

Phil 806.38   Gonzalez Alvarez, Angel. Manual de historia de la
filosofia. 3. ed. Madrid, 1964.

Phil 806.39   Gay, Peter. The enlightenment, an interpretation. 1st ed.
N.Y., 1966-69. 2v.

Phil 806.39.5   Gay, Peter. The bridge of criticism. 1st ed. N.Y., 1970.
Phil 807.1   Haven, J. A history of philosophy. N.Y., 1876.
Phil 807.2   Hegel, G.W.F. Lectures on history of philosophy.
London, 1892-96. 3v.

Phil 807.2.20   Hegel, G.W.F. Vorlesungen über die Geschichte der
Philosophie. Leiden, 1908.

Phil 807.2.25   Hegel, G.W.F. Hegels Geschichte der Philosophie.
München, 1923.

Phil 807.2.27   Hegel, G.W.F. Vorlesungen über die Geschichte der
Philosophie. Leipzig, 1938.

Phil 807.3   Hornius, G. Historiae philosophicae. Lugdunum
Batavorum, 1755.

Phil 807.4   Harms, F. Die Philosophie in ihrer Geschichte.
Berlin, 1878-81. 2v.

Phil 807.5   Hoffding, H. Filosofiske problemer. København, 1902.
Phil 807.6   Henry, C.S. An epitome of the history of philosophy.
N.Y., 1856. 2v.

Phil 807.8   Hunter, T. History of philosophy. N.Y., 1900.
Phil 807.9   Hasse, Karl P. Von Plotin zu Goethe. Leipzig, 1909.
Phil 807.9.2   Hasse, Karl P. Von Plotin zu Goethe. Jena, 1912.
Phil 807.10   Hamma, Mattheas. Geschichte der Philosophie. 2. Aufl.
Münster, 1908.

Phil 807.11   Hodgson, Shadworth H. Philosophy in relation to its
history. London, 1880.

Phil 807.12   Helms, Poul F. Fra Plato til Bergson. København, 1919.
Phil 807.13   Hamma, M. Geschichte und Grundfragen der Metaphysik.
Freiburg, 1876.

Phil 807.14   Hermann, C. Geschichte der Philosophie. Leipzig, 1867.
Phil 807.15   Habert, O. Le primat de l'intelligence dans l'histoire de
la pensée. Paris, 1926.

Phil 807.16   Heinemann, Fritz. Die Lehre von der Zweckbestimmung der
Menschen. Breslau, 1926.

Phil 807.16.5   Heinemann, Fritz. Die Philosophie im XX Jahrhundert.
Stuttgart, 1959.

Phil 807.17   Heinrich, W. Zarys historji filozofji. Warszawa, 1925-30.
Phil 807.17.2   Heinrich, W. Zarys historii filozofii średniowiecznej.
Warszawa, 1963.

Phil 807.18   Hirschberger, Johannes. Geschichte der Philosophie.
Freiburg, 1949-51. 2v.

Phil 807.18.5   Hirschberger, Johannes. Geschichte der Philosophie. 5.
Aufl. Freiburg, 1961-60. 2v.

Phil 807.19   Humbert, Pierre. Philosophes et savantes. Paris, 1953.
Phil 807.20   A history of philosophy. N.Y., 1962. 4v.
Phil 807.24   Hartnack, Justus. Filosofisns historie. København, 1969.
Phil 807.24.7   Hartnack, Justus. Filosofiske problemer og filosofiske
argumentationer. 2. Opl. København, 1970.

Phil 807.26   Hançerlióglu, Orhan. Düşünce tarihi. Istanbul, 1970.
Phil 808.1   Ingegnieros, José. Proposiciones relativas al porvenir de
la filosofia. v.1-2. Buenos Aires, 1918.

Phil 808.2   Istituto di Studi Filosofici, Rome. La philosophie de
l'histoire de la philosophie. Roma, 1956.

Phil 808.3   Inciarte, Fernando. Die Reflexionsbestimmungen un
dialektischen Denken. Köln, 1957.

Phil 808.4   Iovchuk, Mikhail T. Kratkii ocherk istorii filosofii. 2e
Izd. Moskva, 1969.

Phil 809.1   Joel, M. Beiträge zur Geschichte der Philosophie. Bd.1-2.
Breslau, 1876.

Phil 809.1.2   Joel, M. Beiträge zur Geschichte der Philosophie.
Breslau, 1885.

Phil 809.2   Janet, P. History of the problems of philosophy.
London, 1902. 2v.

Phil 809.2.10   Janet, P. Histoire de la philosophie. Paris, 1921.
Phil 809.2.15   Janet, P. Histoire de la philosophie. Supplement.
Paris, 1929.

Phil 809.3   Jansen, W. Geschiedenis der wijsbegeerte.
Zutphen, 1919-21. 2v.

Phil 809.4   Joad, C.E.M. Great philosophies of the world. N.Y., 1933.
Phil 809.5   Jones, W.T. A history of Western philosophy. N.Y., 1952.
Phil 809.5.2   Jones, W.T. A history of Western philosophy. 2d ed.
N.Y., 1969. 4v.

Phil 809.6   Jasinowski, Bogumil. Saber y dialectia. Santiago, 1957.
Phil 809.10   Jaspers, Karl. Aneignung und Polemik. München, 1968.
Phil 810.1   Kirchner, F. Katechismus der Geschichte der Philosophie.
Leipzig, 1877.

Phil 810.1.9   Kirchner, F. Geschichte der Philosophie. Leipzig, 1911.
Phil 810.2   Kinkel, W. Geschichte der Philosophie. v.1-2.
Giessen, 1906.

Phil 810.2.5   Kinkel, W. Allgemeine Geschichte der Philosophie.
Osterwieck, 1920-27. 4v.

Phil 810.3   Knauer, Vincenz. Die haupt Probleme der Philosophie.
Wien, 1892.

Phil 810.4   Karppe, S. Essais de critique et d'histoire de
philosophie. Paris, 1902.

Phil 810.5   Kaunitz, M.M. Philosophy for plain people. N.Y., 1926.
Phil 810.6   Kafka, G. Geschichtsphilosophie der Philosophiegeschichte.
Berlin, 1933.

Phil 810.7   Kratochvii, J. Rukovet filosofie. Brno, 1939.
Phil 810.8   Krakowski, Edouard. La philosophie gardienne de la cité de
Plotin à Bergson. Paris, 1946.

Phil 810.9   Kropp, Gerhard. Von Lao-Tse zu Sartre. Berlin, 1953.
Phil 810.10   Krueger, Gerhard. Grundfragen der Philosophie.
Frankfurt, 1958.

Phil 810.11   Kroner, Richard. Speculation and revelation in the history
of philosophy. London, 1952.

Phil 810.12   Kasm, Badi. L'ideé de preuve en imétaphysique.
Paris, 1959.

Phil 810.14   Ketoren, Oliva. Eurooppalaisen ihmisen maailmansatsomus.
Helsingissa, 1961.

Phil 810.15   Kopper, J. Reflexion und Raisonnement im ontologischen
Gottesbeweis. Köln, 1962.

Phil 810.16   Kempski, Jürgen von. Brechungen. Reinbek, 1964.
Phil 810.17   Keyserling, Arnold. Geschichte der Denkstile. Wien, 1968.
Phil 811.1   Laurent, P.M. Résumé de l'histoire de la philosophie.
Paris, 1826.

Phil 811.1.3   Landtman, G. Inledning till det filosofiska tänkandet.
Helsingfors, 1920.

Phil 811.2   Lefèvre, A. Philosophy. London, 1879.
Phil 811.2.5   Lefèvre, A. La Philosophie. 2e ed. Paris, 1884.
Phil 811.3   Lewes, G.H. A biographical history of philosophy. v.1-4.
London, 1845-46. 2v.

Phil 811.3.2   Lewes, G.H. A biographical history of philosophy.
London, 1857.

Phil 811.3.3   Lewes, G.H. History of philosophy. 3d ed. London, 1867.
2v.

Phil 811.3.5   Lewes, G.H. The biographical history of philosophy.
London, 1875.

Phil 811.3.6   Lewes, G.H. The biographical history of philosophy.
N.Y., 1859.

Phil 811.4   Savérien, A. Histoire des progrès de l'esprit humain dans
les sciences et dans les arts que en dépendent.
Paris, 1777.

Phil 811.5   Loewenthal, E. Geschichte der Philosophie im Umriss.
Berlin, 1896.

Phil 811.6   Lamanna, E. Paolo. Manuale di storia della filosofia ad
uso delle scuole. Firenze, 1928. 2v.

Phil 811.7   Losacco, Michele. Lineamenti di storia della filosofia.
Napoli, 1931.

Phil 811.8   Leon, M. The comedy of human philosophy. Boston, 1932.
Phil 811.9   Lewis, John. Introduction to philosophy. London, 1937.
Phil 811.10   Lindsay, James. Studies in European philosophy.
Edinburgh, 1909.

Phil 811.11A   Lovejoy, Arthur O. Essays in the history of ideas.
Baltimore, 1948.

Phil 811.11B   Lovejoy, Arthur O. Essays in the history of ideas.
Baltimore, 1948.

Phil 811.12   Ludat-Deniselle, A. Von Thales bis Heidegger.
Ratingen, 1952.

Phil 811.15   Lamprecht, S.P. Our philosophical traditions. N.Y., 1955.
Phil 811.16   Lamanna, E. Paolo. Storia della filosofia. Firenze, 1961.
6v.

Phil 811.17   Legowicz, J. Zarys historii filozofii. Warszawa, 1964.
Phil 811.20   Levin-Goldschmidt, Hermann. Dialogik; Philosophie auf dem
Boden der Neuzeit. Frankfurt, 1964.

Phil 811.22   Lindner, Herbert. Der Entwicklungsgang des philosophischen
Denkens. Berlin, 1966.

Phil 811.24   Ley, Hermann. Geschichte der Aufklärung und des Atheismus.
Berlin, 1966- 3v.

Phil 811.26   Louisgrand, Jean. De Lucrèce à Camus, littérature et
philosophie comme réflexion sur l'homme. Paris, 1970.

Phil 812.1   Maret, H.S.C. Philosophie et religion. Paris, 1856.
Phil 812.2   Matter, J. Histoire de la philosophie. Paris, 1854.
Phil 812.3   Maurice, J.F.D. Moral and metaphysical philosophy.
London, 1850.

Phil 812.3.2   Maurice, J.F.D. Moral and metaphysical philosophy. 2d ed.
London, 1854.

Phil 812.3.3   Maurice, J.F.D. Mediaeval philosophy. 2d ed.
London, 1859.

Phil 812.3.3.5   Maurice, J.F.D. Mediaeval philosophy. London, 1870.
Phil 812.3.4   Maurice, J.F.D. Modern philosophy. London, 1862.
Phil 812.3.9   Maurice, J.F.D. Moral and metaphysical philosophy.
London, 1873. 2v.

Phil 812.4   Marvin, W.T. The history of European philosophy.
N.Y., 1917.

Phil 812.5   Mannheimer, A. Geschichte der Philosophie in
übersichthcher Darstellung. v.1-3. Frankfurt, 1903-08.

Phil 812.6   Messer, August. Geschichte der Philosophie in Atlertum und
Mittelalter. Leipzig, 1919.

Phil 812.7   Michelis, F. Geschichte der Philosophie von Thales.
Braumsberg, 1865.

Phil 812.8   Mener, J.B. Geschichte der Philosophie zum Gebrauche.
Bonn, 1868.

Phil 812.9   Masson-Oursel, Paul. La philosophie comparée.
Paris, 1923.

Phil 812.9.2   Masson-Oursel, Paul. La philosophie comparée. Thèse.
Paris, 1923.

Phil 812.9.5   Masson-Oursel, Paul. Comparative philosophy. N.Y., 1926.
Phil 812.9.9   La sophistique étude de philosophie comparée. n.p., 1916.
Phil 812.10   Misch, Georg. Der Weg in die Philosophie. Leipzig, 1926.
Phil 812.10.5   Misch, Georg. Der Weg in die Philosophie. 2. Aufl.
München, 1950.

Phil 812.11   Macedo, Newton de. A luta pela liberdade no pensamento
europeu. Coimbra, 1930.

Phil 812.12   Myślicki, Ignacy. Historja filozofji. Warszawa, 1930.
Phil 812.13   Moog, W. Das Leben der Philosophen. Berlin, 1932.
Phil 812.14   Marbach, G.O. Lehrbuch des Geschichte der Philosophie.
v.1-2. Leipzig, 1838-41.

Phil 812.15   Melilli, F. Preliminari alla storia della filosofia.
Napoli, 1858.

Phil 812.16   Mehring, Franz. Zur Geschichte der Philosophie.
Berlin, 1931?

Phil 812.17   Moreira da Sá, A. Os precursores de Desartes.
Lisboa, 1944.

Phil 812.18   Miller, Hugh. An historical introduction to modern
philosophy. N.Y., 1947.

Phil 812.19   Marias Aguilera, J. San Anselmo y el insensato.
Madrid, 1944.

Phil 812.20   Mayer, F. A history of ancient and medieval philosophy.
N.Y., 1950.

Phil 812.21   Mantague, W. Great visions of philosophy. La Salle,
Ill., 1950.

Phil 812.22   Martin, S.G. A history of philosophy. N.Y., 1947.
Phil 812.23   Moore, Charles A. Philosophy - East and West.
Princeton, 1944.

Phil 812.25   Mondolfo, R. Problemi e metodi di ricerca nella storia
della filosofia. Firenze, 1952.

Phil 812.30   Mascia, Carmin. A history of philosophy. Paterson,
N.J., 1957.

Phil 812.35   Merleau-Ponty, Maurice. Les philosophes éelébres.
Paris, 1956.

Phil 812.40   Metzke, Erwin. Coincidentia oppositorum. Witten, 1961.

Classified Listing

Phil 812.41.2	Mondolfo, Rodolfo. En los origenes de la filosofia. 2. ed. Buenos Aires, 1960.
Phil 812.42	Mazzantini, Carlo. Filosofia e storia della filosofia, 1933-1959. Torino, 1960.
Phil 812.43	Mayr, Franz Karl. Geschichte der Philosophie. Kevelaer, 1966.
Phil 813.1	Nourrisson, J.F. Tableau des progrès de la pensée humaine. Paris, 1858.
Phil 813.1.2	Nourrisson, J.F. Tableau des progrès de la pensée humaine. Paris, 1867.
Phil 813.1.7	Nourrisson, J.F. Tableau des progrès de la pensée humaine. 7e éd. Paris, 1886.
Phil 813.2.3	Noire, L. A sketch...development of philosophical thought. London, 1908.
Phil 813.2.5	Noire, L. Die Entwickelung der abendländischen Philosophie Critik der reinen Vernunft. Mainz, 1883.
Phil 813.3	Noack, L. Geschichte der Philosophie. Weimar, 1853.
Phil 813.4	Nicolas, Michel. Introduction à l'étude de l'histoire de la philosophie. Paris, 1849-50. 2v.
Phil 813.5	Natzner, Gert von. Das Weltbild des Menschen. Berlin, 1962.
Phil 813.6	Negulescu, P.P. Scrieri inedite. Bucuresti, 1969.
Phil 814.1	Oldham, A. An introduction to the study of philosophy. Dublin, 1909.
Phil 814.2.5	Ondes Reggio, V. Sulla necessità della instaurazione. 2a ed. Palermo, 1861.
Phil 814.3	Oyen, Hendrik van. Philosophia. v.1-2. Utrecht, 1947-49. 2v.
Phil 814.4	Oizerman, T.I. Osnovnye etapy razvitiia domarksistskoi filosofii. Moskva, 1957.
Phil 814.5	Orientamenti filosofici e pedagogico. Milano, 1962. 4v.
Phil 814.6	O'Connor, Daniel J. A critical history of Western philosophy. N.Y., 1964.
Phil 815.1	Poetter, F.C. Die Geschichte der Philosophie. Elberfeld, 1874.
Phil 815.2	Pompa, R.P. Sommario della storia di filosofia. Napoli, 1865.
Phil 815.3	Perrin, R. St. J. The evolution of knowledge. N.Y., 1905.
Phil 815.4	Pfordten, Otto. Konformismus eine Philosophie der normatwen Werte. Heidelberg, 1910-13.
Phil 815.5	Perry, Rufus L. Sketch of philosophical systems. n.p., n.d.
Phil 815.6A	Pim, Herbert M. Short history of Celtic philosophy. Dundalk, 1920.
Phil 815.6B	Pim, Herbert M. Short history of Celtic philosophy. Dundalk, 1920.
Phil 815.7	Penjon, A. Précis d'histoire de la philosophie. Paris, 1896.
Phil 815.9	Palhariés, F. Vies et doctrines des grands philosophes à travers les âges. Paris, 1928. 3v.
Phil 815.15	Fabro, C. Storia della filosofia. Roma, 1954.
Phil 815.20	Rodovani, Umberto Antonio. Sommario di storia della filosofia, con particolare riguardo ai problemi morali e religiosi. Roma, 1966. 3v.
Phil 815.25	Perelman, C. An historical introduction to philosophical thinking. N.Y., 1965.
Phil 815.30	The Pelican history of European thought. v.1,4. Harmondsworth, Middlesex, 1968. 2v.
Phil 815.32	Paris. Institut Catholique. Faculte de Philosophie. Histoire de la philosophie et metaphysique. Paris, 1955.
Phil 815.33	Papalexandrou, K. Synoptike historia tes philosophias. 3. ed. Athens, 1969.
Phil 815.34	Pacini, Dante. Crise filosófica do século atual. Rio de Janeiro, 1969.
Phil 815.36	Petruzzellis, Nicola. Maestri di ieri. Napoli, 1970.
Phil 817.1	Reinhold, C.E.G. Geschichte der Philosophie. Jena, 1845. 2v.
Phil 817.2	Ritter, A.H. Geschichte der Philosophie. Hamburg, 1829-45. 12v.
Phil 817.2.1	Ritter, A.H. Geschichte der Philosophie. v.1-4. Hamburg, 1929-53.
Phil 817.2.2	Ritter, A.H. Zusätze und Verbesserungen. Hamburg, 1838.
Phil 817.2.4	Ritter, A.H. Geschichte der Philosophie. 2e Aufl. Hamburg, 1836-53. 12v.
Phil 817.4	Rogers, A.K. A student's history of philosophy. N.Y., 1901.
Phil 817.4.15	Rogers, A.K. A student's history of philosophy. N.Y., 1923.
Phil 817.4.20A	Rogers, A.K. A student's history of philosophy. 3d ed. N.Y., 1932.
Phil 817.4.20B	Rogers, A.K. A student's history of philosophy. 3d ed. N.Y., 1932.
Phil 817.5	Robert, A.A. Histoire de la philosophie. Québec, 1912.
Phil 817.6	Reyes Ruiz, Jesús Maria. Historia de la filosofia y terminología filosofica. 2. ed. Granada, 1910.
Phil 817.7	Rehmke, J. Grundriss der Geschichte der Philosophie. Berlin, 1896.
Phil 817.7.5	Rehmke, J. Grundriss der Geschichte der Philosophie. Bonn, 1959.
Phil 817.7.7	Rehmke, J. Grundriss der Geschichte der Philosophie. 5. Aufl. Frankfurt, 1965.
Phil 817.8	Ruggiero, Guido de. Storia della filosofia. v.1-2,4 (pt. 1.) Bari, 1918- 2v.
Phil 817.8.5	Ruggiero, Guido de. Storia della filosofia. pt. 1 (v.1-2), pt. 2 (v.1-3), pt. 3 (v.1-2), pt. 4 (v.1-5). Bari, 1934-48. 12v.
Phil 817.8.9	Ruggiero, Guido de. Sommario di storia della filosofia. Bari, 1927.
Phil 817.8.15	Ruggiero, Guido de. Breve storia della filosofia ad uso delle scuole. Bari, 1955. 3v.
Phil 817.8.20	Guggiero, Guido de. Storia della filosofia. v.1 (pt. 1-2), v.2 (pt. 1-3), v.3-10. Bari, 1958. 13v.
Phil 817.10	Roberty, E. de. L'ancienne et la nouvelle philosophie. Paris, 1887.
Phil 817.11	Rauschenberger, W. Das philosophische Genie und seine Rasseabstammung. Frankfurt, 1922.
Phil 817.12	Ribbing, Sigurd. Grundlinier till philosophiens historia. Upsala, 1864.
Phil 817.13	Ragnisco, P. Storia critica delle categorie dai primordj della filosofia Greca sino ad Hagel. v.1-2. Firenze, 1871.
Phil 817.14.5	Reinach, S. Lettres à Zoé sur l'histoire des philosophies. Paris, 1926. 3v.
Phil 817.15	Reichlin-Meldegg, K. Der Parallelismus der Alten und neuen Philosophie. Leipzig, 1866.
Phil 817.16	Rothenbücher, A. Geschichte der Philosophie. Berlin, 1904.

Phil 817.17	Reitmeister, L.A. The gist of philosophy. N.Y., 1936.
Phil 817.18	Rintelen, F.J. von. Philosophia perennis. Regensburg, 1930. 2v.
Phil 817.19A	Russell, B.R. A history of Western philosophy. N.Y., 1945.
Phil 817.19B	Russell, B.R. A history of Western philosophy. N.Y., 1945.
Phil 817.19C	Russell, B.R. A history of Western philosophy. N.Y., 1945.
Phil 817.19.4	Russell, B.R. Wisdom of the West. Garden City, 1959.
Phil 817.19.5	Russell, B.R. History of Western philosophy. London, 1947.
Phil 817.20	Ryan, Arthur H. Perennial philosophers. Dublin, 1946.
Phil 817.21	Rivaud, Albert. Histoire de la philosophie. Paris, 1948- 3v.
Phil 817.21.2	Rivaud, Albert. Histoire de la philosophie. 2. ed. Paris, 1960.
Phil 817.22	Radhakrishnan, S. History of philosophy. London, 1952. 2v.
Phil 817.23	Riel, Hans. Urwissen. 2. Aufl. Wien, 1956.
Phil 817.24	Rochedieu, Edmond. La pensée occidentale face à la sagesse de l'orient. Paris, 1963.
Phil 817.25	Rudmanški, S. Z dziejów filozofii. Warzawa, 1959.
Phil 817.26	Riverso, E. Il pensiero occidentale. v.1-3. Napoli, 1964.
Phil 817.27	Roncuzzi, Alfredo. Origini del pensiero europeo. Milano, 1964.
Phil 817.27.5	Roncuzzi, Alfredo. Umane certezze; il libro della verità ragionata. Roma, 1966.
Phil 817.28F	Runes, Dagobert. Pictorial history of philosophy. N.Y., 1965.
Phil 817.30	Revel, Jean François. Histoire de la philosophie occidentale. Paris, 1968-
Phil 818.1	Schwegler, F.C.A. Geschichte der Philosophie. Stuttgart, 1870.
Phil 818.1.3	Schwegler, F.C.A. Geschichte der Philosophie. 8e Aufl. Stuttgart, 1873.
Phil 818.1.3.3	Schwegler, F.C.A. Geschichte der Philosophie. Stuttgart, 1882.
Phil 818.1.4	Schwegler, F.C.A. Geschichte der Philosophie. 13. Aufl. Stuttgart, 1885.
Phil 818.1.4.5	Schwegler, F.C.A. Geschichte der Philosophie. 14. Aufl. Stuttgart, 1887.
Phil 818.1.5	Schwegler, F.C.A. History of philosophy in epitome. N.Y., 1856.
Phil 818.1.6.5	Schwegler, F.C.A. History of philosophy in epitome. N.Y., 1864.
NEDL Phil 818.1.7	Schwegler, F.C.A. Handbook of the history of philosophy. Edinburgh, 1867.
Phil 818.1.8	Schwegler, F.C.A. Handbook of the history of philosophy. 2d ed. Edinburgh, 1868.
Phil 818.1.12	Schwegler, F.C.A. Handbook of the history of philosophy. 5th ed. N.Y., 1873.
Phil 818.1.16	Schwegler, F.C.A. Handbook of the history of philosophy. 9th ed. Edinburgh, 1884.
Phil 818.2	Smyth, C.B. Christian metaphysics. London, 1851.
Phil 818.2.5	Starcke, C.N. Types af den filosofiske bankings historie. København, 1918.
Phil 818.3	Straszewski, M. Dzieje filozofü w zarysie. Krakowie, 1894.
Phil 818.5A	Stöckl, A. Handbook of the history of philosophy. N.Y., 1911.
Phil 818.5B	Stöckl, A. Handbook of the history of philosophy. N.Y., 1911.
Phil 818.7.3	Siebert, Otto. Was jeder Gebildete aus der Geschichte. 3e Aufl. Langensalza, 1912.
Phil 818.8	Sigwart, H.C.W. Geschichte der Philosophie. v.1-3. Stuttgart, 1844.
Phil 818.8.5	Sigwart, H.C.W. Die Propädeutik der Geschichte. Tübingen, 1840.
Phil 818.9	Sawicki, Franz. Lebensanschauungen Alter und neuer Denker. Paderborn, 1923. 3v.
Phil 818.10	Scholten, J.H. Kortfattet fremstilling ad filosofiens historie. 3. Opl. Kjøbenhavn, 1886.
Phil 818.10.5	Scholten, J.H. Manuel d'histoire comparée de la philosophie et de la religion. Paris, 1861.
Phil 818.12	Schmidt, Edward. Umrisse zur Geschichte der Philosophie. Berlin, 1890.
Phil 818.14	Sortais, G. Histoire de la philosophie ancienne. Paris, 1912.
Phil 818.15	Schwegler, A. Grunddragen of filosofiens historia. Örebro, 1856.
Phil 818.16	Snell, P.L. Kurzer Abriss der Geschichte der Philosophie. Giessen, 1819. 2v.
Phil 818.17	Schlunk, M. Die Weltanschauung von den Griechen bis zu Hegel. Hamburg, 1921.
Phil 818.18	Storia della filosofia. Milano. 1-3,1929-1930 2v.
Phil 818.18.5	Storia della filosofia. Milano. 1961 3v.
Phil 818.19	Sternberg, Kurt. Was Heisst und zu welchem Ende studiert man Philosophiegeschichte. Berlin, 1926.
Phil 818.20.5	Steiner, R. Gli enigmi della filosofia. Milano, 1935.
Phil 818.21	Sciacca, M.F. Studi sulla filosofia medioevale e moderna. Napoli, 1935.
Phil 818.22	Serra Hunter, J. Figures i perspectives de la história del pensamiento. Barcelona, 1935.
Phil 818.23	Serrano, J. História de filosofia; ou Pensamento filosófico atravês dos séculos. Rio de Janeiro, 1944.
Phil 818.24A	Schilling, Kurt. Geschichte der Philosophie. München, 1943-44. 2v.
Phil 818.24B	Schilling, Kurt. Geschichte der Philosophie. v.2. München, 1943-44.
Phil 818.24.5	Schilling, Kurt. Geschichte der Philosophie. München, 1951. 2v.
Phil 818.24.10	Schilling, Kurt. Einfurhrung in die Geschichte der Philosophie. Heidelberg, 1949.
Phil 818.25	Stallknecht, N.P. The spirit of Western philosophy. 1st ed. N.Y., 1950.
Phil 818.27	Schnittkind, H.T. Living biographies of great philosophers. Garden City, 1941.
Phil 818.28	Staerig, H.J. Kleine Weltgeschichte der Philosophie. 3. Aufl. Stuttgart, 1953.
Phil 818.29	Sheldon, W.H. God and polarity; a synthesis of philosophies. New Haven, 1954.
Phil 818.30	Strobach, W. Liebe zum Wissen. Wien, 1957.
Phil 818.32	Siewerth, G. Das Schicksal der Metaphysik von Thomas zu Heidegger. Einsiedeln, 1959.

Phil 818.32.5   Sierwerth, G. Grunfragen der Philosophie in Horizont der Seinsdiffereng. Düsseldorf, 1963.
Phil 818.34   Smart, Hawed. Philosophy and its history. La Salle, 1962.
Phil 818.35   Soares, L.R. Quatro meditacões sobre o filósofo. Porto, 1963.
Phil 818.36   Steenberghen, Ferdinand van. Histoire de la philosophie. Louvain, 1964.
Phil 818.37   Schilling, Kurt. Weltgeschichte der Philosophie. Berlin, 1964.
Phil 818.38   Swieżawski, Stefan. Zagadnienie historii filozofii. Warszawa, 1966.
Phil 818.39   Smuts, Johannes Petrus. Kruispaaie van die filosofie. Kaapstad, 1968.
Phil 818.40   Selbmann, Fritz. Wahrheit und Wirklichkeit. Dresden, 1947.
Phil 818.41.3   Sikora, Adam. Spotkania z filozofia. 3. Wyd. Warszawa, 1970.
Phil 819.1   Tennemann, W.G. Geschichte der Philosophie. v.1-11. Leipzig, 1798-1819. 12v.
Phil 819.1.3   Tennemann, W.G. Grundriss der Geschichte der Philosophie. Leipzig, 1820.
Phil 819.1.5   Tennemann, W.G. Grundriss der Geschichte der Philosophie. 5. Aufl. Leipzig, 1829.
Phil 819.1.7   Tennemann, W.G. Manuel de l'histoire de la philosophie. Paris, 1829. 2v.
Phil 819.1.8   Tennemann, W.G. Manuel de l'historie de la philosophie. Paris, 1839. 2v.
Phil 819.1.12   Tennemann, W.G. Manual of the history of philosophy. Oxford, 1832.
Phil 819.1.13A   Tennemann, W.G. Manual of the history of philosophy. London, 1852.
Phil 819.1.13B   Tennemann, W.G. Manual of the history of philosophy. London, 1852.
Phil 819.2   Tiberghien, G. Essai théorique et historique. Bruxelles, 1844.
Phil 819.3   Tiedemann, D. Geschichte der spekulativen Philosophie. Marburg, 1791-97. 6v.
Phil 819.4   Tissot, C.J. Histoire de la philosophie. Paris, 1840.
Phil 819.5.2   Turner, W. History of philosophy. Boston, 1903.
Phil 819.5.7   Turner, W. History of philosophy. Boston, 1929.
Phil 819.6   Tyler, S. The progress of philosophy. Philadelphia, 1888.
Phil 819.7.2A   Thilly, F. A history of philosophy. N.Y., 1914.
Phil 819.7.2B   Thilly, F. A history of philosophy. N.Y., 1914.
Phil 819.7.5   Thilly, F. A history of philosophy. N.Y., 1955.
Phil 819.7.7   Thilly, F. A history of philosophy. 3. ed. N.Y., 1957.
Phil 819.8   Troilo, E. Figure e studii de storia della filosofia. Roma, 1918.
Phil 819.8.5   Troilo, E. Sommario di storia della filosofia. Milano, 1929.
Phil 819.9   Tatarkiewiaz, W. Historja filozafji. Lwów, 1931. 2v.
Phil 819.10   Truc, Gonzague. Histoire de la philosophie. Paris, 1950.
Phil 819.11   Thonnard, F.J. A short history of philosophy. Paris, 1955.
Phil 820.01   Ueberweg, F. Grundriss der Geschichte der Philosophie. v.1-3. Berlin, 1863.
Phil 820.01.3   Ueberweg, F. Grundriss der Geschichte der Philosophie. 3rd ed. Berlin, 1867.
Phil 820.1   Ueberweg, F. Grundriss der Geschichte der Philosophie. v.1-3. Berlin, 1868-71. 2v.
Phil 820.1.1   Ueberweg, F. Grundriss der Geschichte der Philosophie. Berlin, 1894. 3v.
Phil 820.1.2   Ueberweg, F. Grundriss der Geschichte der Philosophie. v.1-2,3. 7. Aufl. Berlin, 1886-88. 2v.
Phil 820.1.2.5   Ueberweg, F. Grundriss der Geschichte der Philosophie. 5. Aufl. Berlin, 1880.
Phil 820.1.3   Ueberweg, F. Grundriss der Geschichte der Philosophie. Berlin, 1894-97. 5v.
Phil 820.1.4   Ueberweg, F. Grundriss der Geschichte der Philosophie. v.1-2,4. 9. Aufl. Berlin, 1902. 3v.
Phil 820.1.5   Ueberweg, F. Grundriss der Geschichte der Philosophie. 10. ed. Berlin, 1906. 4v.
Phil 820.1.6   Ueberweg, F. Grundriss der Geschichte der Philosophie. v.1-2. 6. ed. Berlin, 1880-1914.
Phil 820.1.6.5   Ueberweg, F. Grundriss der Geschichte der Philosophie. v.2. 10. ed. Berlin, 1915.
Phil 820.1.7   Ueberweg, F. Grundriss der Geschichte der Philosophie. v.2-4. 11. Aufl. Berlin, 1914-28. 3v.
Phil 820.1.7.5A   Ueberweg, F. Grundriss der Geschichte der Philosophie. 12. Aufl. Berlin, 1926-51. 5v.
Phil 820.1.7.5B   Ueberweg, F. Grundriss der Geschichte der Philosophie. v.3-5. 12. Aufl. Berlin, 1926-51. 3v.
Phil 820.1.7.7   Ueberweg, F. Grundriss der Geschichte der Philosophie. Basel, 1960.
Phil 820.1.8A   Ueberweg, F. History of philosophy. N.Y., 1872-4. 2v.
Phil 820.1.8B   Ueberweg, F. History of philosophy. N.Y., 1872-4. 2v.
Phil 820.1.10   Ueberweg, F. History of philosophy. N.Y., 1874. 2v.
Phil 820.1.14   Ueberweg, F. History of philosophy. London, 1874-75. 2v.
Phil 820.2   Ussher, Arland. Sages and schoolmen. Dublin, 1967.
Phil 821.1   Vorländer, K. Geschichte der Philosophie. v.1-2. Leipzig, 1903.
Phil 821.1.3   Vorländer, K. Geschichte der Philosophie. Leipzig, 1911. 2v.
Phil 821.1.6   Vorländer, K. Geschichte der Philosophie. 6. Aufl. Leipzig, 1921.
Phil 821.1.7   Vorländer, K. Geschichte der Philosophie. 7. Aufl. Leipzig, 1927. 2v.
Phil 821.1.9   Vorländer, K. Geschichte der Philosophie. 9. Aufl. Hamburg, 1949-55. 2v.
Phil 821.1.10   Vorländer, K. Volkstümliche Geschichte der Philosophie. 3. Aufl. Berlin, 1923.
Phil 821.1.15   Vorländer, K. Geschichte der Philosophie. Leipzig, 1964. 4v.
Phil 821.1.20   Vycinas, Vincent. Greatness and philosophy. The Hague, 1966.
Phil 821.2   Vogel, August. Überblick über der Geschichte der Philosophie. Leipzig, 1904-05. 2v.
Phil 821.3   Vallet, P. Histoire de la philosophie. 3e éd. Paris, 1886.
Phil 821.4   Visser, S. Zoekers naar wijsheid. Goes, 1938.
Phil 821.5   Varsencelos, Jóse. Historia del pensamiento filosofico. Mexico, 1937.

Phil 821.6   Vita, Luis Washington. Monólogos e diálogos. São Paulo, 1964.
Phil 821.7   Vollrath, Ernst. Die These der Metaphysik. Wuppertal, 1969.
Phil 822.1   Weber, A. Histoire de la philosophie européenne. Paris, 1872.
Phil 822.1.2   Weber, A. Histoire de la philosophie européenne. Paris, 1886.
Phil 822.1.3   Weber, A. Histoire de la philosophie européenne. 9e éd. Paris, 1925.
Phil 822.1.4   Weber, A. Histoire de la philosophie européenne. Paris, 1957. 3v.
Phil 822.1.5   Weber, A. History of philosophy. N.Y., 1896.
Phil 822.1.12   Weber, A. History of philosophy. N.Y., 1909.
Phil 822.1.14   Weber, A. History of philosophy. N.Y., 1912.
Phil 822.1.15A   Weber, A. History of philosophy. N.Y., 1925.
Phil 822.1.15B   Weber, A. History of philosophy. N.Y., 1925.
Phil 822.1.30   West, H.F. Rebel thought. Boston, 1953.
Phil 822.2A   Windelband, W. Geschichte der Philosophie. Freiburg, 1892.
Phil 822.2B   Windelband, W. Geschichte der Philosophie. Freiburg, 1892.
Phil 822.2.3   Windelband, W. Lehrbuch der Geschichte der Philosophie. 3. Aufl. Tübingen, 1903.
Phil 822.2.4   Windelband, W. Lehrbuch der Geschichte der Philosophie. Tübingen, 1935.
Phil 822.2.4.5   Windelband, W. Lehrbuch der Geschichte der Philosophie. Genf, 1945?
Phil 822.2.4.7   Windelband, W. Lehrbuch der Geschichte der Philosophie. Tübingen, 1957.
Phil 822.2.11   Windelband, W. History of philosophy. 2. ed. N.Y., 1901.
Phil 822.3   Wägner, S. Filosofiens historia i sammandrag. Lund, 1914.
Phil 822.5   Wolff, M. Bidrag till filosofiens historia. Stockholm, 1882.
Phil 822.6.2   Wahle, R. Die Tragikomödie der Weisheit die Ergebnisse und der Geschichte des Philosophierens. Wien, 1925.
Phil 822.6.5   Wahle, R. Geschichtlicher Überblick über die Entwicklung der Philosophie bis zu ihrer letzten Phase. Wien, 1895.
Phil 822.7   Wikner, Pontus. Filosofiens historia efter Pontus Wikner's kollegium. Rock Island, Ill., 1896.
Phil 822.8A   Whitehead, A.N. Adventures of ideas. N.Y., 1933.
Phil 822.8B   Whitehead, A.N. Adventures of ideas. N.Y., 1933.
Phil 822.9   Wundt, Max. Geschichte der Metaphysik. Berlin, 1931.
Phil 822.10   Walshe, Thomas J. The quest of reality. London, 1933.
Phil 822.11   Westaway, F.W. Obsessions and convictions of the human intellect. London, 1938.
Phil 822.12   Webb, Clement C.J. A history of philosophy. N.Y., 1915.
Phil 822.13   Wahl, Jean A. The philosopher's way. N.Y., 1948.
Phil 822.18.9   Wulf, M. Précis d'histoire de la philosophie. 9. ed. Louvain, 1950.
Phil 822.20   Weishedel, Wilhelm. Die philosophische Hintertreppe. München, 1966.
Phil 822.22   Weier, Winfried. Sinn und Teilhabe. Salzburg, 1970.
Phil 825.5   Zea, Leopoldo. Ensayos sobre filosofía en la historia. Mexico, 1948.
Phil 825.10   Zucchi, Hernan. Estudios de filosofía antiqua y moderna. Tucumán, 1956[1957]

Phil 830   History of philosophy - General history - Cosmology - General works
Phil 830.5   James, Edwin Oliver. Creation and cosmology. Leiden, 1969.

Phil 835   History of philosophy - General history - Epistemology - General works
Phil 835.2   Lauer, Hans Erhard. Die Wiedergeburt der Erkenntnis in der Entwicklungsgeschichte. Freiburg, 1946.
Phil 835.4   Thomas, Viktor. Das Erkenntnisproblem; ein historischkritischer Versuch. Stuttgart, 1921.
Phil 835.6   Kuntze, Friedrich. Erkenntnistheorie. München, 1927.

Phil 840   History of philosophy - General history - Ontology - General works
Phil 840.2   Brun, Jean. Les conquêtes de l'homme et la séparation ontologique. Thèse. Paris, 1961.

Phil 843   History of philosophy - General history - Ontology - Special topics
Phil 843.5.5   Boeckenhoff, J. Die Begegnungsphilosophie. Freiburg, 1970.

Phil 845   History of philosophy - General history - Humanism
Phil 845.2   Weinstock, Heinrich. Die Trajödie des Humanismus. Heidelberg, 1953.
Phil 845.2.5   Weinstock, Heinrich. Realer Humanismus. Heidelberg, 1955.
Phil 845.4   Schiavone, Michel. Problemi ed aspetti dell'Umanesimo. Milano, 1969.
Phil 845.6   Pozzo, Gianni M. Umanesimo moderno o tramonto dell'Umanesimo? Padova, 1970.

Phil 848   History of philosophy - General history - Other special systems, etc.
Phil 848.2   Carbonare, Cleto. La filosofia dell' espirenza e la fondazione dell' umanesims. 2. restampa. Napoli, 1961.
Phil 848.2.3   Carbonare, Cleto. La filosofia dell'espirenza e la fondazione dell Umanesimo. 3. ed. Napoli, 1969.
Phil 848.4   Franchini, Raffaello. Le origini della dialettica. Napoli, 1961.
Phil 848.4.2   Franchini, Raffaello. Le origini della dialettica. 2. ed. Napoli, 1965.
Phil 848.6   Fertig, Hermann. Die Auflösung der klassischen Substanzkonzeption und ein Versuch Rehabilitierung. Inaug. Diss. München, 1965.
Phil 848.8   Pamphlet vol. Haffner, Paul. Der Materialismus. 2 pam.
Phil 848.10   DeGrood, David H. Philosophies of essence; an examination of the category of essence. Groningen, 1970.

Phil 850   History of philosophy - Ancient philosophy in general - History - General works
Phil 850.1   Levesque de Bruiquy, J. Histoire de la philosophie payenne. La Haye, 1724.
Phil 850.2   Burnett, T. Archaeologiae philosophicae. v.1-2. London, 1728-33.
Phil 850.2.5   Burnett, T. Doctrina antigua. London, 1736. 3 pam.
Phil 850.3   Röth, E. Geschichte unserer abendländischen Philosophie. Mannheim, 1862. 2v.
Phil 850.4   Stöcke, A. Die speculative Lehre vom Menschen. Würzburg, 1858-59. 2v.
Phil 850.8   Eberhard, J.A. Der Geist des Urchristenthums. Halle, 1807-08. 3v.

Classified Listing

Phil 850   History of philosophy - Ancient philosophy in general - History - General works - cont.

Phil 850.10   Cocker, B.F. Christianity and Greek philosophy. N.Y., 1870.

Phil 850.11   Fabre, Joseph. La pensée antique (de Moise à Marcaurèle). Paris, 1902.

Phil 850.12   Tilgher, A. Filosofi antichi. Todi, 1921.

Phil 850.13   Faure, J.A. L'Egypte et les présocratiques. Paris, 1923.

Phil 850.14   Klippel, M. Philosophie et poésie: Les origines. Paris, 1925.

Phil 850.15   Hanus, G.J. Geschichte der Philosophie von ihren Uranfängen. Olmütz, 1850.

Phil 850.17   Georgov, Ivan. Istoriia na filosofiiata. Sofiia, 1926.

Phil 850.18   Ritter, Heinrich. Uber die Unanationslehre im Ubergange aus der Alterlhümlichen in die christlicheDenkeweise. Göttingen, 1847.

Phil 850.19   Verbeke, G. L'évolution de la doctriné du pneuma. Paris, 1945.

Phil 850.21A   Armstrong, A.H. An introduction to ancient philosophy. London, 1947.

Phil 850.21B   Armstrong, A.H. An introduction to ancient philosophy. London, 1947.

Phil 850.21.5 Armstrong, A.H. An introduction to ancient philosophy. 2d ed. London, 1949.

Phil 850.21.10 Armstrong, A.H. An introduction to ancient philosophy. 3d ed. London, 1957.

Phil 850.21.11 Armstrong, A.H. An introduction to ancient philosophy. 3d ed. Westminster, Md., 1959.

Phil 850.22   LaVia, V. Il problema della fondazione della filosofia e l'oggettivismo antico. 2. ed. Roma, 1946.

Phil 850.23   Misch, G. The dawn of philosophy. London, 1950.

Phil 850.23.2 Misch, G. The dawn of philosophy. Cambridge, 1951.

Phil 850.26   Marcer, S.A.B. Earliest intellectual man's idea of the cosmos. London, 1957.

Phil 850.29   Bogliolo, Luigi. La filosofia antica. Torino, 1955.

Phil 850.31   Legowiiz, J. Filozofia okresu sosarstwa rzymekiego. Warszawa, 1962.

Phil 850.32   Brady, Ignatius. A history of ancient philosophy. Milwaukee, 1959.

Phil 850.34   Cilento, Vincenzo. Primessa storica al pensiero antico. Bari, 1963.

Phil 850.40   Birand, Kámiran. Ilk cağ felsefesi torihi. Ankara, 1958.

Phil 850.45   Koje've, Alexandre. Essai d'une histoire raisonnée de la philosophie païenne. Paris, 1968.

Phil 850.48   Vogel, Cornelia Johanna de. Studies in Greek philosophy. Assen, 1970.

Phil 850.50   Komarova, Vera Ia. K tekstologicheskomu analizn antichnoi filosofi. Leningrad, 1969.

Phil 860   History of philosophy - Ancient philosophy in general - History - Special topics

Phil 860.2.2   Staudacher, Willibald. Die Trennung von Himmel und Erde; ein vorgriechischer Schöpfungsmythus bei Hesiod und den Orphikern. 2. Aufl. Darmstadt, 1968.

Phil 860.4   Adkins, Arthur William Hope. From the many to the one: a study of personality and views of human nature in the context of ancient Greek society, values and beliefs. London, 1970.

Phil 860.6   Ushida, Noriko. Étude comparative de la psychologie d'Aristote, d'Avicenne et de St.Thomas d'Aquin. Tokyo, 1968.

Phil 860.8   Dreyer, Oskar. Untersuchungen zum Begriff des Gottgeziemenden in der Antike. Hildesheim, 1970.

Phil 860.10   Stokes, Michael C. One and many in Presocratic philosophy. Washington, 1971.

Phil 900   History of philosophy - Ancient and medieval oriental philosophy - Oriental in general - History - General works

Phil 900.1   Windischmann, C.J.H. von. Die Philosophie im Fortgang. v.1-4. Bonn, 1827-34. 3v.

Phil 900.2   Fluegel, M. Philosophy, qabbala and vedánta. Baltimore, 1902.

Phil 900.3   Roth, E. Geschichte und abendländischen Philosophie. Mannheim, 1846.

Phil 900.4   Heurnius, O. Barbaricae philosophiae. Lugdunum Batavorum, 1600.

Phil 900.5   Horn, J. Über die biblische Gnosis. Hannover, 1805.

Phil 900.6   Grousset, René. Histoire de la philosophie orientale; Inde, Chine, Japan. Paris, 1923.

Phil 900.7   Pizzi, Italo. Pessimjsmo orientale. Bari, 1902.

Phil 900.8   Franck, Adolphe. Études orientales. Paris, 1861.

Phil 900.9   Motora, Y. An essay on Eastern philosophy. Leipzig, 1905.

Phil 900.10   Beck, Lily M.A. The story of Oriental philosophy. N.Y., 1928.

Phil 900.11   Grant, Francis. Oriental philosophy. N.Y., 1936.

Phil 900.13   Eaton, Gai. The richest vein. London, 1949.

Phil 900.14   Negelein, J. Deltanschauung des indogermanischen Asiens. Erlangen, 1924.

Phil 900.15   Le Renard, A. L'Orient et sa tradition. Paris, 1952.

Phil 900.25   Rádl, Emanuel. Západ a východ; filosofia úvahy z cest. Praze, 1925.

Phil 900.27   Krikorian, Sergei. Sovremennaia filosofskaia i sotsiologicheskaia mysl' stran vostoka. Moskva, 1965.

Phil 910   History of philosophy - Ancient and medieval oriental philosophy - Oriental in general - History - Special topics

Phil 910.2   Saddhatissa, Hammalaiva. Buddhist ethics: essence of Buddhism. London, 1970.

Phil 930   History of philosophy - Ancient and medieval oriental philosophy - China - History

Phil 930.01   Pamphlet box. Chinese philosophy pamphlets.

Phil 930.1   Carus, P. Chinese philosophy. Chicago, 1898.

Phil 930.1.2   Carus, P. Chinese thought. Chicago, 1907.

Phil 930.1.5   Carus, P. Chinese philosophy. 2d ed. Chicago, 1902.

Phil 930.5   Tucci, G. Storia della filosofia cinese antica. Bologna, 1912.

Phil 930.7   Forke, A. The world conception of the Chinese. London, 1925.

Phil 930.7.5   Forke, A. Geschichte der alten chinesischen Philosophie. Hamburg, 1927.

Phil 930.7.8   Forke, A. Geschichte der mittelalterlichen chinesischen Philosophie. Hamburg, 1934.

Phil 930.7.10 Forke, A. Geschichte der neueren chinesischen Philosophie. Hamburg, 1938.

Phil 930.7.50 Zach, E. von. Weitere Verbesserungen zu Forke's Geschichte der chinesischen Philosophie. Batavia, 1938.

Phil 930   History of philosophy - Ancient and medieval oriental philosophy - China - History - cont.

Phil 930.7.55 Zach, E. von. Einige Verbesserungen zu Forke's Geschichte der chinesischen Philosophie. Batavia, 1939.

Phil 930.9.5   Hoang, Tsen-Yue. Étude comparative sur les philosophies de Lao Tseu, Khong Tseu, Mo Tseu. Thèse. Lyon, 1925.

Phil 930.25   Rudd, H.F. Chinese moral sentiments before Confucius. Diss. Chicago? 1915?

Phil 930.25.2 Rudd, H.F. Chinese social organs. Chicago, 1928.

Phil 930.26   Lanessan, J.M. La morale des philosophies chinois. Paris, 1896.

Phil 930.27   Zenker, E.V. Geschichte der chinesischen Philosophie. Reichenberg, 1926-27. 2v.

Phil 930.28A   Hu, Suh. Development of logical method in China. Shanghai, 1922.

Phil 930.28B   Hu, Suh. Development of logical method in China. Shanghai, 1922.

Phil 930.29.5 Fung, Yu-lan. A history of Chinese philosophy. Peiping, 1937.

Phil 930.29.8 Fung, Yu-lan. A history of Chinese philosophy. Princeton, 1953. 2v.

Phil 930.29.10 Fung, Yu-lan. The spirit of Chinese philosophy. London, 1941.

Phil 930.30   Hackmann, H. Chinesische Philosophie. München, 1927.

Phil 930.30.10 Hackmann, H. Chinesche wijsgeeren. Amsterdam, 1930. 2v.

Phil 930.33   Suzuki, Daisetz T. A brief history of early Chinese philosophy. 2. ed. London, 1914.

Phil 930.34   Borel, Henri. De chinesche filosofi. 3. druk. Amsterdam, 1896-97. 2v.

Phil 930.35   Wilhelm, R. Chinesische Philosophie. Breslau, 1929.

Phil 930.36F   Eberhard, Wolfram. Beiträge zur Kosmologischen Spekulation der Chinesen der Han - Zert. Inaug. Diss. Berlin, 1933.

Phil 930.36.5 Eberhard, Wolfram. Guilt and sin in traditional China. Berkeley, 1967.

Phil 930.37   Northern Pacific Railroad Company. The story of the Monad. St. Paul, Minn., 1933.

Phil 930.38   Waley, Arthur. Three ways of thought in ancient China. London, 1939.

Phil 930.38.5 Waley, Arthur. Three ways of thought in ancient China. London, 1953.

Phil 930.39   Lin, Mou-Sheng. Men and ideas; an informal history of Chinese political thought. N.Y., 1942.

Phil 930.39.5 Scherbatskii, F.I. Teoriia poznaniia i logika po ucheniu pozdreishikh buddistov. Sankt Peterburg, 1903-09. 2v.

Phil 930.40   Wong, Gung-Hsing. The Chinese mind. N.Y., 1946.

Phil 930.41   Chen, Li-Fu. Philosophy of life. N.Y., 1948.

Phil 930.42   Creel, H.G. Chinese thought from Confucius to Mao Tse-tung. Chicago, 1953.

Phil 930.44   Chan, Wing-tsit. An outline and a bibliography of Chinese philosophy. Hanover, 1955.

Phil 930.44.2 Chan, Wing-tsit. An outline and annotated bibliography of Chinese philosophy. New Haven, 1961.

Phil 930.46   Antica filosofia cinese. v.1-2. Milano, 1956.

Phil 930.50   Chang, Carsun. China and Gandhian India. Calcutta, 1956.

Phil 930.52   Yang, Jung-kuo. Istoriia drevnekitaiskoi ideologii. Moskva, 1957.

Phil 930.54   Hou, Wai-lu. A short history of Chinese philosophy. Peking, 1959.

Phil 930.56   Kuo, Mo-jo. Bronzovij vek. Moskva, 1959.

Phil 930.58   Liou, Kia-hway. L'ésprit synthétique de la Chine. Paris, 1961.

Phil 930.60   Chow, Yih-ching. La philosophie chinoise. 2. ed. Paris, 1961.

Phil 930.62   Kuo, Mo-jo. Filosofy drevnego kitaia. Moskva, 1961.

Phil 930.64   Day, A.B. The philosophers of China. N.Y., 1962.

Phil 930.66   Akademiia Nauk SSSR. Institut Filosofii. Izbrannye proizuedeniia progeniia kitaiskikh myslitelei novogo vremeni, 1840-1898. Moskva, 1961.

Phil 930.67   Bykov, Fedor S. Zarozhdenie obshchestvenno-politicheskoi i filosofskoi mysli v kitae. Moskva, 1966.

Phil 930.68   Zempliner, Artur. Cínská filosofie v novověké evropské filosofii. Praha, 1966.

Phil 930.70   East-West Philosophers Conference. The Chinese mind. Honolulu, 1967.

Phil 930.72   Munro, Donald J. The concept of man in early China. Stanford, 1969.

Phil 930.74   Basic writings of Mo Tzu, Hsün Tzu and Han Fei Tzu. N.Y., 1967.

Phil 930.76   Rubin, Vitalii A. Ideologiia i kul'tura Drevnego Kitaia. Moskva, 1970.

Phil 935   History of philosophy - Ancient and medieval oriental philosophy - Japan - History

Phil 935.5   Kishinami, T. The development of philosophy in Japan. Princeton, 1915.

Phil 935.11   Lüth, Paul. Die japanische Philosophie. Tübingen, 1944.

Phil 935.12   Philosophical studies of Japan. Tokyo. 1,1959+ 3v.

Phil 935.13   East-West Philosophers' Conference. The Japanese mind. Honolulu, 1967.

Phil 940   History of philosophy - Ancient and medieval oriental philosophy - Korea - History

Phil 940.5   Chŏng, Chin-sŏk. Istoriia koreiskoi filosofii. Moskva, 1966.

Phil 960   History of philosophy - Ancient and medieval oriental philosophy - India - History

Phil 960.1   Brockie, W. Indian thought. Sunderland, 1876.

NEDL Phil 960.2   Colebrooke, H.T. Essais sur la philosophie des Hindous. Paris, 1833.

Phil 960.2.5   Colebrooke, H.T. Essays on the religion and philosophy of the Hindus. London, 1858.

Phil 960.3   Deussen, P. System des Vedânta. Leipzig, 1883.

Phil 960.3.2   Deussen, P. On the philosophy of the Vedânta in its relations to occidental metaphysics. Bombay, 1893.

Phil 960.3.3   Deussen, P. System of the Vedânta. Chicago, 1912.

Phil 960.3.4A Deussen, P. Outline of the Vedânta system of philosophy. 2d ed. N.Y., 1906.

Phil 960.3.4B Deussen, P. Outline of the Vedânta system of philosophy. 2. ed. N.Y., 1906.

Phil 960.3.4.5 Deussen, P. Outline of the Vedânta system of philosophy. Cambridge, 1906.

Phil 960.3.7   Deussen, P. The philosophy of the Upanishads. Edinburgh, 1906.

Phil 960.3.8   Deussen, P. The philosophy of the Upanishads. Edinburgh, 1908.

Phil 960.3.8.5 Deussen, P. The philosophy of the Upanishads. N.Y., 1966.

Classified Listing

Phil 960.3.9	Deussen, P. Outlines of Indian philosophy. Berlin, 1907.
Phil 960.3.15	Deussen, P. Vedânta, Platon und Kant. 2. Aufl. Wien, 1917.
Phil 960.3.19	Deussen, P. Vedânta und Platonismus im Lichte der kantischen Philosophie. Berlin, 1922.
Phil 960.4	Garbe, R. Die Samkhya - Philosophie. Leipzig, 1894.
Phil 960.4.5	Garbe, Richard. The philosophy of ancient India. Chicago, 1897.
Phil 960.6	Mullens, J. Religious aspects of Hindu philosophy. London, 1860.
Phil 960.7	Muller, F.M. The six systems of Indian philosophy. N.Y., 1899.
Phil 960.7.5	Muller, F.M. Three lectures on the Vedânta philosophy. London, 1894.
Phil 960.8	Valentin, O. Shaddarcaneshu en religionsstudie. Stockholm, 1899.
Phil 960.9.5	Sugivra, Sadajiro. Hindu logic as preserved in China and Japan. Philadelphia, 1900.
Phil 960.10.5	Schrader, F.O. Über den Stand der indischen Philosophie zur Zeit Mahávíras und Buddhas. Inaug. Diss. Strassburg, 1902.
Phil 960.11	Vidyabhusana, Satis Chandra. History...mediaeval school of Indian logic. Calcutta, 1909.
Phil 960.11.5	Vidyabhusana, Satis Chandra. A history of Indian logic. Calcutta, 1921.
Phil 960.12	Barnett, L.D. Brahma-knowledge, outline of philosophy of the Vedânta. London, 1907.
Phil 960.13	Oltramare, P. La formule bouddhique des douze causes. Geneve, 1909.
Phil 960.14.5	Gandhi, V.R. Speeches and writings of the Karma philosophy. Bombay, 1913.
Phil 960.15A	Rámanáthan, P. The spirit of the East contracted with spirit of the West. N.Y., 1906.
Phil 960.15B	Rámanáthan, P. The spirit of the East contracted with spirit of the West. N.Y., 1906.
Phil 960.16	Ánanda Achárya. Brahmadarsanam...introduction to the study of Hindu philosophy. London, 1917.
Phil 960.17	Noble, M.E. Religion and dharma. London, 1915.
Phil 960.17.5	Noble, M.E. Kali the mother. London, 1900.
Phil 960.17.40	Altekar, A.S. Sources of Hindu dharma in its socio-religious aspects. Shalapur, 1952?
Phil 960.18	Kitch, Ethel May. The origin of subjectivity in Hindu thought. Chicago, 1917.
Phil 960.18.5	Altekar, A.S. Sources of Hindu dharma in its socio-religious aspects. Chicago, 1917.
Phil 960.25	Shastri, Prabhu D. The conception of freedom in Hegel, Berigson and Indian philosophy. Calcutta, 1914.
Phil 960.26	Chamberlain, Houston. Arische Weltanschauung. 3. Aufl. München, 1916.
Phil 960.27	Suali, Luigi. Introduzione allo studio della filosofia indiania. Pavia, 1913.
Phil 960.28	Daqupta, S. A history of Indian philosophy. v. 2-5. Cambridge, Eng., 1922-49. 4v.
Phil 960.28.2	Dasgupta, Surendra Nath. A history of Indian philosophy. Cambridge, 1963.
Phil 960.28.5	Daqupta, S. Philosophical essays. Calcutta, 1941.
Phil 960.29	McGovern, W.M. A manual of Buddhist philosophy. London, 1923.
Phil 960.30	Belloni-Filippi, F. I maggiori sistemi filosofici indiani. Milano, 1914.
Phil 960.31	Masson-Oursel, Paul. Esquisse d'une histoire de la philosophie indienne. Thèse. Paris, 1923.
Phil 960.31.2	Masson-Oursel, Paul. Esquisse d'une histoire de la philosophie indienne. Thèse. Paris, 1923.
Phil 960.33	Atkinson, W.W. A series of lessons on the inner teachings of the philosophies and religions of India. Chicago, 1908.
Phil 960.35A	Ranade, R.D. A constructive survey of Upanishadic philosophy. Poona, 1926.
Phil 960.35B	Ranade, R.D. A constructive survey of Upanishadic philosophy. Poona, 1926.
Phil 960.36	Arunáchalam, P. Light from the East. London, 1927.
Phil 960.37	Strauss, Otto. Indische Philosophie. München, 1925.
Phil 960.38	Yevtić, Paul. Karma and reincarnation in Hindu. Thesis. London, 1927.
Phil 960.39	Shcherbatskii, F.I. Erkenntnistheorie und Logik. München, 1924.
Phil 960.39.5	Shcherbatskii, F.I. La théorie de la connaissance. Paris, 1926.
Phil 960.39.10	Shcherbatskii, F.I. Teoriia poznaniia i logika po ucheniiu pozdneishikh buddistov. Sankt Peterburg, 1903-09. 2v.
Phil 960.40	Barua, B.M. Prolegomena to a history of Buddhist philosophy. Calcutta, 1918.
Phil 960.40.4	Barua, B.M. A history of pre-Buddhistic Indian philosophy. Calcutta, 1921.
Phil 960.40.5	Barua, B.M. A history of pre-Buddhistic Indian philosophy. Delhi, 1970.
Phil 960.41	Shastri, P.D. The essentials of Eastern philosophy. N.Y., 1928.
Phil 960.42	Krishnachandra, B. Studies in Vedantism. Calcutta, 1909.
Phil 960.43	Belvalkar, S.K. History of Indian philosophy. v.2,7. Poona, 1927-33. 2v.
Phil 960.43.2	Belvalkar, S.K. An outline scheme for a history of Indian philosophy. Poona, 1919. 2v.
Phil 960.44	Gomperz, Heinrich. Die indische Theosophie. Jena, 1925.
Phil 960.118	Stephen, D.J. Studies in early Indian thought. Cambridge, 1918.
Phil 960.119	Dass, Satya. Self-expression and the Indian social problem. Lahore, 1937.
Phil 960.120	Oldenberg, Hermann. Vorwissenschaftliche Wissenschaft die Weltanschauung der Brahamana. Göttingen, 1919.
Phil 960.121	Dandoy, G. An essay on the doctrine of the unreality of the world in the Advaita. Calcutta, 1919.
Phil 960.124	Woodroffe, J.G. The world as power reality. Madras, 1921.
Phil 960.125	Woodroffe, J.G. The world as power, power as life. Madras, 1922.
Phil 960.127	Woodroffe, J.G. The world as power; power as mind. Madras, 1922.
Phil 960.128	Radhakrishnan, S. Indian philosophy. London, 1923. 2v.
Phil 960.128.10	Radhakrishnan, S. The Vedânta according to Samkara and Rámanuja. London, 1928.
Phil 960.129	Mitra, K.N. Pessimism and life's ideal: the Hindu outlook. Madras, 1926.
Phil 960.130	Desia, Shantaram Anant. A study of Indian philosophy. Bombay, 1906.

Phil 960.131	Jha, Ganganatha. The philosophical discipline. Calcutta, 1928.
Phil 960.132	Prasad, Jwala. Introduction to Indian philosophy. Allahabad, 1928.
Phil 960.134	Tombleson, J.B. As above, so below. London, 1928.
Phil 960.135	Grousset, René. Les philosophies indiennes, les systèmes. v.1-2. Paris, 1931.
Phil 960.136	Heimann, B. Studien zur Eigenart indischen Denkens. Tübingen, 1930.
Phil 960.136.5	Heimann, B. Indian and Western philosophy. London, 1937.
Phil 960.137	Hiriyanna, M. Outlines of Indian philosophy. London, 1932.
Phil 960.137.5	Hiriyanna, M. The quest after perfection. Madras, 1941.
Phil 960.137.8	Hiriyanna, M. The quest after perfection. Mysore, 1952.
Phil 960.137.10	Hiriyanna, M. The essentials of Indian philosophy. London, 1949.
Phil 960.137.15	Hiriyanna, M. Popular essays in Indian philosophy. Mysore, 1952.
Phil 960.137.20	Hiriyanna, M. Indian philosophical studies. Mysore, 1957.
Phil 960.137.25	Hiriyanna, M. The mission of philosophy. Mysore, 1960.
Phil 960.138	Modi, P.M. Aksara, a forgotten chapter in the history of Indian philosophy. Inaug. Diss. Baroda, 1932.
Phil 960.139	Syed, M.H. L'optimisme dans la pensée indienne. Thèse. n.p., 1932.
Phil 960.140	Oltramare, Paul. L'histoire des idées theosophiques dans l'Inde. Paris, 1906-23. 2v.
Phil 960.141	Mookerjee, S. The Buddhist philosophy of universal flux. Calcutta, 1935.
Phil 960.142	Griswold, Hervey De Witt. Brahman: a study in the history of Indian philosophy. N.Y., 1900.
Phil 960.144	Väth, Alfons. Im Kampfe mit der Zauberwelt des Hinduismus. Berlin, 1928.
Phil 960.145	Techoueyres, E. A la recherche de l'unité. Reims, 1934.
Phil 960.146	Astreya, B.L. The elements of Indian logic. 2d ed. Benares, 1934.
Phil 960.147	Malkani, G.R. Ajñana. London, 1933.
Phil 960.148	Sinha, Judunath. Indian realism. London, 1938.
Phil 960.149.5	Paul, N.C. A treatise on the Yoga philosophy. 3d ed. Bombay, 1888.
Phil 960.150	Jast, Louis S. Reincarnation and karma. N.Y., 1944.
Phil 960.152	Sommerfeld, S. Indienschau und Indiendeutung romantischer Philosophen. Zürich, 1943.
Phil 960.155	Abegg, Emil. Indische Psychologie. Zürich, 1945.
Phil 960.157	Bernard, Theos. Philosophical foundations of India. London, 1945.
Phil 960.161	Glasenapp, H. von. Die philosophie der Inder. Stuttgart, 1949.
Phil 960.163	Devanandan, P.D. The concept of Maya. London, 1950.
Phil 960.163.5	Ray Chaudhuri, A.K. The doctrine of Maya. 2nd ed. Calcutta, 1950.
Phil 960.163.10	Ray Chaudhuri, A.K. Self and falsity in Advaita Vedanta. 1st ed. Calcutta, 1955.
Phil 960.164	Zimmer, H.R. Philosophies of India. N.Y., 1951.
Phil 960.164.5	Zimmer, H.R. Philosophie und Religion Indiens. Zürich, 1961.
Phil 960.165	Chatterjee, S. An introduction to Indian philosophy. 4th ed. Calcutta, 1950.
Phil 960.165.5	Chatterjee, S. The fundamentals of Hinduism. Calcutta, 1950.
Phil 960.166	Masui, J. Approaches de l'Inde. Tours? 1949.
Phil 960.167	Chakravarti, A. Humanism and Indian thought. Madras, 1937.
Phil 960.168	Raju, P.T. Idealistic thought of India. London, 1953.
Phil 960.168.2A	Raju, P.T. Idealistic thought of India. Cambridge, Mass., 1953.
Phil 960.168.2B	Raju, P.T. Idealistic thought of India. Cambridge, Mass., 1953.
Phil 960.169	Frauwallner, E. Geschichte der indischen Philosophie. Salzburg, 1953. 2v.
Phil 960.170	Ruben, Walter. Geschichte der indischen Philosophie. Berlin, 1954.
Phil 960.172	Pal, B.C. An introduction to the study of Hinduism. 2. ed. Calcutta, 1951.
Phil 960.175	Sharma, C. Indian philosophy. Banaras, 1952.
Phil 960.175.5	Sharma, C. A critical survey of Indian philosophy. London, 1960.
Phil 960.180	Silburn, Lilian. Instant et cause. Paris, 1955.
Phil 960.190A	Umesha, Mishra. History of Indian philosophy. Allahabad, 1957.
Phil 960.190B	Umesha, Mishra. History of Indian philosophy. Allahabad, 1957.
Phil 960.195	Prabhavananda, Swami. Vedic religion and philosophy. Madras, 1950.
Phil 960.200	Challaye, Felicien. Les philosophes de l'Inde. 1. ed. Paris, 1956.
Phil 960.205	Tucci, Giuseppe. Storia della filosofia Indiana. Bari, 1957.
Phil 960.210	Fausset, H.I. Anson. The flame and the light. London, 1958.
Phil 960.212	Fausset, H.I. Anson. The flame and the light. N.Y., 1958[1959]
Phil 960.215	Prasad, Jwala. History of Indian epistemology. 2d ed. Delhi, 1958.
Phil 960.220	Rajadhyaksha, N.D. The six systems of Indian philosophy. Bombay, 1959.
Phil 960.225	Chennahesavan, Sarasvate. The concept of mind in Indian philosophy. London, 1960.
Phil 960.230	Wei-uri-wei (pseud.). Why Lazarus laughed. London, 1960.
Phil 960.235	Basanta Kumar Mallik. London, 1961.
Phil 960.240	Piatigorskii, A.M. Materialy po istorii indiiskoi filosofii. Moskva, 1962.
Phil 960.244	Litman, Aleksei D. Filosofskaia mysl' nezavisimoi Indii. Moskva, 1966.
Phil 960.245	Akademiia Nauk SSSR. Institut Narodov Azii. Obshchestvenno-politicheskaia i filosofskaia mysl' Indii. Moskva, 1962.
Phil 960.246	Organ, T.W. The self in Indian philosophy. London, 1964.
Phil 960.248.2	Dasgupta, Surama. Development of moral philosophy in India. N.Y., 1965.
Phil 960.249	Smart, Ninian. Doctrine and argument in Indian philosophy. London, 1964.
Phil 960.250	Pandeya, R.C. The problem of meaning in Indian philosophy. 1. ed. Delhi, 1963.
Phil 960.252	Anikeev, Nikolai P. O materialisticheskikh traditsiiakh v indiiskoi filosofii. Moskva, 1965.

Phil 960   History of philosophy - Ancient and medieval oriental philosophy -
India - History - cont.

Phil 960.253   Komarov, N. Ideologicheskie techeniia sovremennoi Indii.
Moskva, 1965.

Phil 960.255   Roy, Ellen (Gottschalk). In man's own image. 1. ed.
Calcutta, 1948.

Phil 960.256   Sircar, Mahendranath. Eastern lights; a brief account of
some phases of life, thought and mysticism in India.
Calcutta, 1935.

Phil 960.257   Damodaran, K. Indian thought; a critical survey.
Bombay, 1967.

Phil 960.258   Brodov, Vasilii V. Indiiskaia filosofiia novogo vremeni.
Moskva, 1967.

Phil 960.260   Gopinatha, Kaviraja. Aspects of Indian thought.
Burdwan, 1966.

Phil 960.265   East-west philosophers' conference. The Indian mind;
essentials of Indian philosophy and culture.
Honolulu, 1967.

Phil 960.270   Seneviratne, M.J. On the nature of man and society, and
other essays. 1st ed. Colombo, 1967.

Phil 960.272   Chethimattam, John B. Consciousness and reality.
Bangalore, 1967.

Phil 960.272.5   Chethimattam, John B. Patterns of Indian thought.
Maryknoll, N.Y., 1971.

Phil 960.274   Sharma, Dhirendra. The differentiation theory of meaning
in Indian logic. The Hague, 1969.

Phil 960.276   Bhagavad Datta. The story of creation as seen by the
seers. Delhi, 1968.

Phil 960.278   Ramaswami Aiyas C.P. Research Endowment Committee. A
bibliography of Indian philosophy. 1. ed. Madras, 1963-
2v.

Phil 960.280   The encyclopedia of Indian philosophies. 1st ed.
Delhi, 1970.

Phil 960.282   Riepe, Dale Maurice. The philosophy of India and its
impact on American thought. Springfield, 1970.

Phil 960.284   Filliozat, Jean. Les philosophies de l'Inde. Paris, 1970.

Phil 970   History of philosophy - Ancient and medieval oriental philosophy -
India - Theosophy and Anthroposophy - Pamphlet volumes

Phil 970.2   Pamphlet box. Oriental theosophy.
Phil 970.3   Pamphlet box. Oriental theosophy.
Phil 970.4   Pamphlet box. Oriental theosophy.
Phil 970.5   Pamphlet box. The path series.
Phil 970.6   Pamphlet box. Oriental theosophy.
Phil 970.15F   Pamphlet box. Oriental theosophy.
Phil 970.16   Pamphlet vol. Rudolf Steiner. 2 pam.

Phil 971   History of philosophy - Ancient and medieval oriental philosophy -
India - Theosophy and Anthroposophy - History - General works

Phil 971.5.5   Guénon, R. Le théosophie; histoire d'une pseudo-religion.
2. ed. Paris, 1929.

Phil 971.6   Negner, Helena. Beiträge zur Geschichte der
Weisheitsreligion. Pforzheim, 1960.

Phil 971.8   Lantier, Jacques. La théosophie. Paris, 1970.

Phil 971.10   Leiste, Heinrich. Ein Beitrag zur anthroposophischen
Hochschulfrage. Dornach, 1970.

Phil 972   History of philosophy - Ancient and medieval oriental philosophy -
India - Theosophy and Anthroposophy - History - Special topics

Phil 972.5   Olcott, H.S. Old diary leaves; story of theosophy.
N.Y., 1895.

Phil 972.9   Lazenby, C. The work of the masters. London, 1917.
Phil 972.12   Brander-Pracht, K. Der neue Mensch. Berlin, 1920.

Phil 972.15   Greenwalt, E.A. The Point Loma community in California,
1897-1942. Berkeley, 1955.

Phil 972.16   Schwarz, W. Hoffnung in Wichts. München, 1961.

Phil 972.17   Eek, Sven. Damodar and the pioneers of the theosophical
movement. Adyar, 1965.

Phil 972.18   Maendl, Hans. Vom Geist des Nordens. Stuttgart, 1966.
Phil 972.20   Panet, Edmond. La mort de Canopus. Paris, 1970.

Phil 972.22   Wehr, Gerhard. Der Urmensch und der Mensch der Zukunft.
Freiburg, 1964.

Phil 974   History of philosophy - Ancient and medieval oriental philosophy -
India - Theosophy and Anthroposophy - Biographies of theosophists

Phil 974.1   Pamphlet box. H.P. Blavatsky.

Phil 974.2   Coulomb, E. Some account of my intercourse with Mme.
Blavatsky. London, 1885.

Phil 974.2.5   Cleather, A.L. (Mrs.). H.P. Blavatsky, her life and work
for humanity. Calcutta, 1922.

Phil 974.2.7   Cleather, A.L. (Mrs.). H.P. Blavatsky, a great betrayal.
Calcutta, 1922.

Phil 974.2.9   Cleather, A.L. (Mrs.). H.P. Blavatsky as I knew her.
Calcutta, 1923.

Phil 974.2.10   Cleather, A.L. (Mrs.). H.P. Blavatsky as I knew her.
N.Y., 1923. 3 pam.

Phil 974.2.15   Tingley, K.A. (Mrs.). Helena Petrovna Blavatsky. Point
Loma, Calif., 1921.

Phil 974.2.20   Kingsland, W. Was she a charlatan? London, 1927.

Phil 974.2.25   Besant, A. The theosophical society and H.P.B. Three
articles. London, 1891?

Phil 974.2.30   Robert, C.E.B. The mysterious Madame Helena P. Blavatsky.
N.Y., 1931.

Phil 974.2.35   H.P.B. in memory of Helena Petrovna Blavatsky.
London, 1931.

Phil 974.2.40   Hare, H.E. Who wrote the Mahatma letters? London, 1936.

Phil 974.2.42   Cox, H.R.W. Who wrote the March-hare attack on the Mahatma
letters? Victoria, 1936.

Phil 974.2.44   Hudson, Irene B. Who wrote the Mahatma letters? Answered.
Victoria, 1936.

Phil 974.2.50   Hastings, B. (Mrs.). Defence of Madame Blavatsky.
Worthing, 1937. 2v.

Phil 974.2.55A   Williams, G.M. Priestess of the occult, Madame Blavatsky.
N.Y., 1946.

Phil 974.2.55B   Williams, G.M. Priestess of the occult, Madame Blavatsky.
N.Y., 1946.

Phil 974.2.60   Symonds, John. Madame Blavatsky. London, 1959.

Phil 974.2.65   Borborka, Geoffrey A. H.P. Blavatsky, Tibet and Tulka.
Madras, 1966.

Phil 974.2.70   Harris, Iverson L. Mme. Blatavsky defended. San
Diego, 1971.

Phil 974.3   Steiner, Rudolf. Mein Lebensgang. Geotheanum, 1925.

Phil 974.3.2   Steiner, Rudolf. Die Wirklichkeit der höheren Welten.
Dornach, 1962.

Phil 974.3.3   Steiner, Rudolf. Das Künstlerische in seiner Weltmission.
Dornach, 1961.

Phil 974.3.5   Steiner, Rudolf. The story of my life. London, 192-.

Phil 974.3.6   Steiner, Rudolf. Mein Legebensgang. Dornach, 1962.

Phil 974   History of philosophy - Ancient and medieval oriental philosophy -
India - Theosophy and Anthroposophy - Biographies of theosophists - cont.

Phil 974.3.7   Steiner, Rudolf. The story of my life. London, 1928.

Phil 974.3.8   Steiner, Rudolf. Die okkulten Grundlagen der Bhagavad
Gita. 3. Aufl. Dornach, 1962.

Phil 974.3.9   Pamphlet box. Pamphlets on Steiner.

Phil 974.3.10   Picht, C.S. Das literarische Lebenswerk Rudolf Steiners.
Dornach, 1926.

Phil 974.3.11   Boldt, Ernst. Von Luther bis Steiner. München, 1921.

Phil 974.3.15   Steiner, Rudolf. From Luther to Steiner. London, 1923.

Phil 974.3.16   Steiner, Rudolf. Die Weihnachtstagung zur Begründung. 3.
Aufl. Dornach, 1963.

Phil 974.3.20   Boldt, Ernst. Rudolf Steiner: ein kämpfer Gegen seine
Zeit. München, 1923.

Phil 974.3.25   Boldt, Ernst. Rudolf Steiner und das Epigonenturm.
München, 1923.

Phil 974.3.50   Rittelmeyer, F. Von der Theosophie Rudolf Steiners.
Nürnberg, 1919.

Phil 974.3.51   Rittelmeyer, F. Rudolf Steiner enters my life.
London, 1929.

Phil 974.3.55   Schmidt, J.W. Recht und Unrecht der Anthroposophie.
Göttingen, 1922.

Phil 974.3.60   Geyer, C.K.L. Rudolf Steiner und die Religion.
München, n.d.

Phil 974.3.65   Lévy, Eugène. Rudolf Steiners Weltanschauung und ihre
Gegner. 3. Aufl. Berlin, 1926?

Phil 974.3.70   Hovels, Karl. Beiträge zur Kritik der anthroposophischen
Welt- und Lebensanschauung. Inaug. Diss. Rheinland, 1926.

Phil 974.3.75   Schomerus, H.W. Die Anthroposophie Steiners und Indien.
Leipzig, 1922.

Phil 974.3.80   Steffen, Albert. Begegnungen mit Rudolf Steiner.
Zürich, 1926.

Phil 974.3.83   Steffen, Albert. Auf Geisteswegen. Dornach, 1942.

Phil 974.3.85   Tröger, Walter. Grundriss der Anthroposophie in engem
Anschluss an die Schriften Dr. Rudolf Steiners.
Breslau, 1921.

Phil 974.3.90   Lauer, Hans E. Rudolf Steiner's Lebenswerk. Basel, 1926.

Phil 974.3.91   Lauer, Hans E. Rudolf Steiners Anthroposophie in
Weltanschauungskampfe der Gegenwart. 8. Aufsätze.
Basel, 1927.

Phil 974.3.95   Hauer, J.W. Werden und Wesen der Anthroposophie.
Stuttgart, 1923.

Phil 974.3.105   Hoffmann, K. Die Anthroposophie Rudolf Steiners und die
moderne Geisleswissenschaft. Diss. Giessen, 1928.

Phil 974.3.108   Harwood, A.C. The faithful thinker. London, 1961.

Phil 974.3.109   Jellinek, Karl. Das Mysterium des Menschen. Zürich, 1960.
2v.

Phil 974.3.110   Apel, Max. Geheimwissenschaft. Charlettenburg, 1922.

Phil 974.3.112   Poepping, Fred. Rudolf Steiner, der grosse Unbekannte.
Wien, 1960.

Phil 974.3.115   Wachsmuth, G. Die Geburt der Geisteswissenschaft.
Dornach, 1941.

Phil 974.3.116   Wachsmuth, G. Bibliographie der Werke Rudolf Steiners in
die Geburt. Dornach, 1942.

Phil 974.3.117   Wachsmuth, G. Goethe in unserer Zeit. Dornach, 1949.

Phil 974.3.118   Kaufmann, G. Fruits of anthroposophy. London, 1922.

Phil 974.3.119   Steiner, M. Erinnerungen. v.1-2. Dornach, 1949.

Phil 974.3.119.5   Wiesberger, Halla. Aus dem Leben von Marie Steiner von
Silvers. Dornach, 1956.

Phil 974.3.120   Strakosch, A. Lebenswege mit Rudolf Steiner.
Strasbourg, 1947.

Phil 974.3.121   Stieglitz, K. von. Die Christosophie Rudolf Steiners.
Witten, 1955.

Phil 974.3.122.2   Krueck, M.J. Wir Erlebten Rudolf Steiner. 2. Aufl.
Stuttgart, 1957.

Phil 974.3.123   Muecke, Johanna. Erinnerungen an Rudolf Steiner.
Basel, 1955.

Phil 974.3.124   Zeylmans von Emmichoven, F.W. Rudolf Steiner.
Zeist, 1960.

Phil 974.3.126   Bock, Emil. Rudolf Steiner. Stuttgart, 1961.

Phil 974.3.128   Baltz, Karl von. Rudolf Steiners musikalische Inpulse.
Dornach, 1961.

Phil 974.3.130   Hahn, Herbert. Rudolf Steiner wie ich ihn Sah und Erlebte.
Stuttgart, 1961.

Phil 974.3.132   Kallert, Bernhard. Die Erkenntnistheorie Rudolf Steiners.
Stuttgart, 1960.

Phil 974.3.135   Rudolf Steiner-Nachlassverwaltung. Rudolf Steiner, das
literarische und künstlerische Werk. Dornach, 1961.

Phil 974.3.140   Sunden, Hjalmar. Rudolf Steiner. Stockholm, 1962.

Phil 974.3.145   Hartmann, Georg. Erziehung aus Menschenerkenntnis.
Dornach, 1961.

Phil 974.3.147   Hartmann, Georg. Erziehung aus Menschenerkenntnis: von
pädagogischen Impuls der Anthroposophie Rudolf Steiners. 2.
Aufl. Dornach, 1969.

Phil 974.3.150   Hiebel, Friedrich. Rudolf Steiner im Geistesgang des
Abendlandes. Bern, 1965.

Phil 974.3.155   Bugaev, Boris N. Rudolf Steiner i gete v mirovozzrenii
sovremennosti. Moskva, 1917.

Phil 974.3.160   Savitch, Marie. Marie Steiner von Sivers, Mitarbeiterin
von Rudolf Steiner. Dornach, 1965.

Phil 974.3.165   Walther, Kurt. Uber die neu Mysteriendramen Rudolf
Steiners. Freiburg, 1966-67. 3v.

Phil 974.3.170   Abendroth, Walter. Rudolf Steiner und die heutige Welt.
München, 1969.

Phil 974.3.175   Petersen, Klaus. Rudolf Steiner. Berlin, 1968.

Phil 974.4   New India, Madras. Annie Besant, servant of humanity.
Madras, 1924.

Phil 974.4.10   West, G. Mrs. Annie Besant. London, 1927.

Phil 974.4.13   Williams, Gertrude M. The passionate pilgrim. N.Y., 1931.

Phil 974.4.15   Williams, Gertrude M. The passionate pilgrim.
London, 1932.

Phil 974.4.20   Jinarajadasa, C. A short biography of Annie Besant.
Adyar, Madras, 1932.

Phil 974.4.25   Besterman, T. Mrs. Annie Besant. London, 1934.

Phil 974.4.30   Bhagavan Das. Annie Besant...and the changing world.
Adyar, 1934.

Phil 974.4.35   Gay, S.E. The life works of Mrs. Besant. London, 1913?

Phil 974.5   Zimmer, Heinrich. Der Weg zum Selbst. Zürich, 1944.

Phil 974.5.6   Zimmer, Heinrich. Der Weg zum Selbst. Zürich, 1954.

Phil 974.5.10   Osborne, Arthur. Ramana Maharshi and the path of
sell-knowledge. London, 1970.

Phil 974.6   Pamphlet box. Jiddu Krishnamurti.

Phil 974.7   Bolt, Ernst. Die Philosophie der Liebe. v.1-2.
Berlin, 1927.

Phil 974.8   Faivre, Antoine. Eckartshausen et la théosophie
chrétienne. Thèse. Paris, 1969.

Phil 976 History of philosophy - Ancient and medieval oriental philosophy - India - Theosophy and Anthroposophy - Anthologies of theosophical writings

	Phil 976.5	Lotusblueten. Leipzig. 4-99,1893-1900// 16v.

Phil 978 History of philosophy - Ancient and medieval oriental philosophy - India - Theosophy and Anthroposophy - Writings of individual theosophists

	Phil 978.5.1	Blavatsky, H.P. Collected writings. 1st American ed. v.5-8. Los Angeles, 1950. 4v.
	Phil 978.5.5	Blavatsky, H.P. Isis unveiled. v.1-2. Point Loma, California, 1919. 4v.
	Phil 978.5.6	Blavatsky, H.P. The secret doctrine. v.3. London, 1888-97.
	Phil 978.5.7	Blavatsky, H.P. Personal memoirs of H.P. Blavatsky. London, 1937.
	Phil 978.5.9	Blavatsky, H.P. The secret doctrine. v.1-2. Point Loma, Calif., 1925. 4v.
	Phil 978.5.9.25	Hyat, T.P. A check list of some books and authors. Stanford, 1940.
	Phil 978.5.11	Blavatsky, H.P. An abridgement by K. Hilliard of The secret doctrine. N.Y., 1907.
	Phil 978.5.12	Blavatsky, H.P. The voice of the silence. N.Y., 1889.
	Phil 978.5.13	Blavatsky, H.P. The voice of the silence. N.Y., 1889.
	Phil 978.5.15	Blavatsky, H.P. The voice of the silence. 5th ed. London, 1896.
	Phil 978.5.18	Blavatsky, H.P. The voice of the silence. 6th ed. London, 1903.
	Phil 978.5.20	Blavatsky, H.P. The voice of the silence. 4th ed. Point Loma, 1920.
	Phil 978.5.22	Blavatsky, H.P. The voice of the silence. Peking, 1927.
	Phil 978.5.24	Blavatsky, H.P. The key to theosophy. London, 1889.
	Phil 978.5.25	Blavatsky, H.P. The key to theosophy. 2nd American ed. N.Y., 1896.
	Phil 978.5.26	Blavatsky, H.P. The key to theosophy. Los Angeles, 1920.
	Phil 978.5.27	Blavatsky, H.P. The key to theosophy. 4th ed. Point Loma, Calif., 1923.
	Phil 978.5.28A	Blavatsky, H.P. The theosophical glossary. London, 1892.
	Phil 978.5.28B	Blavatsky, H.P. The theosophical glossary. London, 1892.
	Phil 978.5.30	Blavatsky, H.P. Studies in occultism. 2nd ed. Boston, 1897.
	Phil 978.5.85	Blavatsky, H.P. Some unpublished letters. London, 1929.
	Phil 978.5.90	Bleyi lotos. Burbank, Calif. 1958-1959 3v.
EDL	Phil 978.5.800	Sinnett, A.P. Incidents in the life of Madame Blavatsky. London, 1886.
	Phil 978.5.810	Ryan, C.J. H.P. Blavatsky and the theosophical movement. Point Loma, Calif., 1937.
	Phil 978.6	Pamphlet box. Besant, A. Minor writings.
	Phil 978.6.3	Besant, Annie. On the nature and the existence of God. London, 1875.
	Phil 978.6.4	Besant, Annie. Why I became a theosophist. N.Y., 1890.
	Phil 978.6.5	Besant, Annie. Why I became a theosophist. N.Y., 1891.
	Phil 978.6.9	Besant, Annie. The building of the kosmos. London, 1894.
	Phil 978.6.13	Besant, Annie. Essays and addresses. v.2-4. London, 1912-13. 3v.
	Phil 978.6.15	Besant, Annie. The ancient wisdom. London, 1897.
	Phil 978.6.20	Besant, Annie. Evolution of life and form. 2nd ed. London, 1900.
	Phil 978.6.25	Besant, Annie. Esoteric christianity. N.Y., 1902.
	Phil 978.6.30	Besant, Annie. Birth and evolution of the soul. 2nd ed. London, 1903.
	Phil 978.6.35	Besant, Annie. Some problems of life. 2nd ed. London, 1904.
	Phil 978.6.40	Besant, Annie. Theosophy and new psychology. London, 1904.
	Phil 978.6.43	Besant, Annie. Thought power; its control and culture. London, 1906.
	Phil 978.6.44A	Besant, Annie. Thought power; its control and culture. London, 1901.
	Phil 978.6.44B	Besant, Annie. Thought power; its control and culture. London, 1901.
	Phil 978.6.45	Besant, Annie. Study in consciousness. London, 1904.
	Phil 978.6.50	Besant, Annie. The changing world. Chicago, 1910.
	Phil 978.6.60	Besant, Annie. The seven principles of man. London, 1892.
	Phil 978.6.61	Besant, Annie. The seven principles of man. London, 1892.
	Phil 978.6.61.5	Besant, Annie. The seven principles of man. 15th ed. London, 189-?
	Phil 978.6.62	Besant, Annie. Reincarnation (Theosophical manual II). London, 1897.
	Phil 978.6.63	Besant, Annie. Death - and after? London, 1898.
	Phil 978.6.63.5	Besant, Annie. Death - and after? London, 1893.
	Phil 978.6.64	Besant, Annie. Karma. (Theosophical manual IV). London, 1897.
	Phil 978.6.70	Besant, Annie. The sphinx of theosophy. London, 189-?
	Phil 978.6.72	Besant, Annie. Thought-forms. Wheaton, Ill., 1969.
	Phil 978.6.85	Besant, Annie. Autobiographical sketches. Photoreproduction. London, 1885.
:g	Phil 978.6.86	Besant, Annie. Annie Besant: an autobiography. London, 1908.
	Phil 978.6.88	Besant, Annie. Theosophy and the theosophical society. Adyar, 1913.
	Phil 978.6.90	Nethercot, A.H. The first five lives of Annie Besant. Chicago, 1960.
	Phil 978.6.91	Nethercot, A.H. The last four lives of Annie Besant. London, 1963.
	Phil 978.6.97	Prakasa, Sri. Annie Besant. 2d ed. Bombay, 1954.
	Phil 978.7.2	Judge, W.Z. The ocean of theosophy. 2nd ed. N.Y., 1893.
	Phil 978.7.3	Judge, W.Z. The ocean of theosophy. Point Loma, Calif., 1926[1923]
	Phil 978.7.5	Judge, W.Z. Letters that have helped me. N.Y., 1891.
	Phil 978.7.9	Judge, W.Z. Letters that have helped me. 4th ed. N.Y., 1891.
	Phil 978.7.15	Judge, W.Z. Echoes from the Orient. 3rd ed. Point Loma, Calif., 1921.
	Phil 978.8.2	Leadbeater, C.W. The christian creed. 2nd ed. London, 1904.
	Phil 978.8.9	Leadbeater, C.W. Outline of theosophy. London, 1902.
	Phil 978.8.10	Leadbeater, C.W. Outline of theosophy. 2d ed. Chicago, 1903.
	Phil 978.8.11	Leadbeater, C.W. Outline of theosophy. London, 1915.
	Phil 978.8.15	Leadbeater, C.W. Man visible and invisible. N.Y., 1903.
	Phil 978.8.19	Leadbeater, C.W. Textbook of theosophy. Chicago, 1925.
	Phil 978.8.25	Leadbeater, C.W. Dreams; what they are and how they are caused. 4th ed. London, 1908.
	Phil 978.8.30	Leadbeater, C.W. Invisible helpers. London, 1899.
	Phil 978.8.35	Leadbeater, C.W. Reincarnation; a lecture. Harrogate, 1903.
	Phil 978.9.3	Sinnett, A.P. Esoteric Buddhism. 3rd ed. London, 1884.

Phil 978 History of philosophy - Ancient and medieval oriental philosophy - India - Theosophy and Anthroposophy - Writings of individual theosophists - cont.

	Phil 978.9.7	Sinnett, A.P. Esoteric Buddhism. 5th ed. London, 1885.
	Phil 978.9.8	Sinnett, A.P. Esoteric Buddhism. Boston, 1885.
	Phil 978.9.8.5	Sinnett, A.P. Esoteric Buddhism. 3d ed. Boston, 1886.
	Phil 978.9.9	Sinnett, A.P. Esoteric Buddhism. 6th ed. Boston, 1896.
	Phil 978.9.10	Sinnett, A.P. The occult world. Boston, 1882.
	Phil 978.9.18	Sinnett, A.P. The growth of the soul. 2nd ed. London, 1905.
	Phil 978.9.25	Sinnett, A.P. Collected fruits of occult teaching. London, 1919.
	Phil 978.10	Five years of theosophy. London, 1885.
	Phil 978.11	Olcott, H.S. Collection of lectures on theosophy and archaic religions. Madras, 1883.
	Phil 978.12	Fullerton, Alex. The Wilkesbarre letters on theosophy. N.Y., n.d.
	Phil 978.13	Tukarama Tatya. A guide to theosophy. Bombay, 1887.
	Phil 978.14	Solovef, V.S. Nodern priestess of Isis. London, 1895.
	Phil 978.15	Cook, M.C. Light on the path. Point Loma, California, 1897.
	Phil 978.15.2	Cook, M.C. Light on the path. Chicago, Ill., n.d.
	Phil 978.15.3	Cook, M.C. Light on the path. N.Y., 1886?
	Phil 978.15.4	Cook, M.C. Light on the path. Boston, 1889.
	Phil 978.15.4.5	Cook, M.C. Light on the path. N.Y., 18- .
	Phil 978.15.5	Cook, M.C. Through the gates of gold. Boston, 1901.
	Phil 978.16	Tingley, K.A. (Mrs.). The mysteries of the heart doctrine. Point Loma, Calif., 1902.
	Phil 978.16.5	Tingley, K.A. (Mrs.). Theosophy; the path ofthe mystic. 2d ed. Point Loma, Calif., 1922.
	Phil 978.16.13	Tingley, K.A. (Mrs.). The gods await. Point Loma, California, 1926.
	Phil 978.17	Man's place in the universe. London, 1902.
	Phil 978.18.3	Goffield, E.C. The past revealed. Boston, 1905.
	Phil 978.19	Iyer, S.S. Theosophical miscellanies. v.1-2. Calcutta, 1883.
	Phil 978.20	Hints on esoteric theosophy. no. 1-2. Calcutta, 1882.
	Phil 978.21	Fragments of occult truth. no. 1-8. n.p., 1881.
	Phil 978.22	Corbett, S. Extracts from the Vâhan. London, 1904.
	Phil 978.23.3	Edger, L. The elements of theosophy. London, 1907.
	Phil 978.24	Bruhn, Wilhelm. Theosophie und Theologie. Glückstadt, 1907.
	Phil 978.24.5	Bruhn, Wilhelm. Theosophie und Anthroposophie. Leipzig, 1921.
	Phil 978.25	Morrison, D. The open door of the soul. Boston, 1908.
	Phil 978.26	Theosophy Society in America. A primer of theosophy. Chicago, 1909.
	Phil 978.27	Bragdon, C. The beautiful necessity. Rochester, N.Y., 1910.
	Phil 978.28	Curtiss, H.A. The voice of Isis. Los Angeles, 1912.
	Phil 978.29	Farnsworth, E.C. Special teachings from the arcane science. Portland, Maine, 1913.
	Phil 978.29.5	Farnsworth, E.C. The heart of things. Portland, Maine, 1914.
	Phil 978.29.10	Farnsworth, E.C. The deeper mysteries. Portland, Maine, 1921.
	Phil 978.29.15	Farnsworth, E.C. Glimpses of inner truth. Portland, 1923.
	Phil 978.30	Speyer, J.S. Die indische Theosophie. Leipzig, 1914.
	Phil 978.30.5	Speyer, J.S. De indische theosophie en hare beteekenis voor ons. Leiden, 1910.
	Phil 978.31	Theosophy Publishing Company. The pitt and marrow of some sacred writings. N.Y., 1899.
	Phil 978.32.5	Street, J.C. The hidden way across the threshold. Boston, 1887.
	Phil 978.33	Brailsford-Bright, J. Theosophy and modern socialism. London, 1889.
	Phil 978.36.5	Constant, L. Unpublished writings. Calcutta, 1883.
	Phil 978.37	Kneisel, R. Die Lehre von der Seelenwanderung. Leipzig, 1889.
	Phil 978.38	Walker, E.D. Reincarnation. Boston, 1888.
	Phil 978.38.5	Walker, E.D. Reincarnation. Point Loma, Calif., 1923.
	Phil 978.39	Hume, A.C. No revelation infallible. Calcutta, 1883.
	Phil 978.40	Curtiss, F.H. Letters from the teacher. Denver, 1909?
	Phil 978.41	Mason, E.L. The discovery of discoveries. n.p., n.d.
	Phil 978.42	Theosophical manuals. v.1-18. Point Loma, 1910. 4v.
	Phil 978.43	Ver-Planck, J.C. (Mrs.). The wonder-light, true philosophy for children. N.Y., 1890.
X Cg	Phil 978.44	Kingsford, Anna. The perfect way, or The finding of Christ. London, 1909.
	Phil 978.45	Encausse, G. La réincarnation. Paris, 1912.
	Phil 978.46	Buck, J.D. The nature and aim of theosophy. Cincinnati, 1889.
	Phil 978.47	Darlès, Jean. Glossaire raisonné de la théosophie du qnosticisme et de l'ésotérisme. Paris, 1910.
	Phil 978.48	Theosophy and the higher life. London, 1880.
	Phil 978.49	Steiner, R. Theosophie. Stuttgart, 1922.
	Phil 978.49.7	Steiner, R. Theosophy. 18th ed. N.Y., 1910.
	Phil 978.49.16	Steiner, R. Knowledge of the higher worlds and its attainment. N.Y., 193-?
	Phil 978.49.17	Steiner, R. Knowledge of the higher worlds. 3d English ed. London, 1937.
	Phil 978.49.19	Steiner, R. An outline of occult science. Chicago, Ill., 1922.
	Phil 978.49.25	Steiner, R. The gates of knowledge. Chicago, Ill., 1922.
	Phil 978.49.30	Steiner, R. Die geistige Führung des Menschen und der Menschheit. Dornach, 1925.
	Phil 978.49.35	Steiner, R. The way of initiation. 1st American ed. N.Y., 1910.
	Phil 978.49.36	Steiner, R. Initiation and its results. N.Y., 1909.
	Phil 978.49.40	Steiner, R. Die Aufgabe der Geisteswissenschaft und deren Bau in Dornach. Berlin, 1921.
	Phil 978.49.45	Steiner, R. Die Schwelle der geistigen Welt. 10. Aufl. Berlin, 1921.
	Phil 978.49.50	Steiner, R. Der Hüter der Schwelle, Seelenvorgänge in scenischen Bildern. Berlin, 1922.
	Phil 978.49.55	Steiner, R. Der Seelen Erwachen. Berlin, 1922.
	Phil 978.49.60	Steiner, R. Die Mystik im Aufgange des neuzeitlichen Geisteslebens und ihr Verhältnis zur modernen Weltanschauung. 2. Aufl. Stuttgart, 1924.
	Phil 978.49.62	Steiner, R. Die Mystik im Aufgange des neuzeitlichen Geisteslebens und ihr Verhältnis zur modernen Weltanschauung. 3. Aufl. Stuttgart, 1924.
	Phil 978.49.65	Steiner, R. Die Pforte der Einweihung (Initiation). Dornach, 1925.
	Phil 978.49.70	Steiner, R. Wahrheit und Wissenschaft. Dornach, 1925.
	Phil 978.49.75	Steiner, R. Das Initiaten-Bewusstsein. Dornach, 1927.
	Phil 978.49.76	Steiner, R. Das Initiaten-Bewusstsein. Freiburg, 1955.

Classified Listing

Phil 978.49.77   Steiner, R. Das Initiaten-Bewusstsein: die Wahren und die falschen Wege der geistigen Forschung. Dornach, 1969.

Phil 978.49.80   Steiner, R. Praktische Ausbildung des Denkens. Stuttgart, 1927.

Phil 978.49.85   Steiner, R. Wendepunkte des Geisteslebens. Dornach, 1927.

Phil 978.49.86   Steiner, R. Wendepunkte des Geisteslebens. 3. Aufl. Freiburg, 1954.

Phil 978.49.90   Steiner, R. Von Seelenrätseln. Berlin, 1921.

Phil 978.49.95   Steiner, R. Esquisse d'une cosmogonie psychologique, d'après des conférences faites à Paris en 1906. Paris, 1928.

Phil 978.49.100   Steiner, R. The East in the light of the West. London, 1922.

Phil 978.49.110   Steiner, R. Philosophy and anthroposophy. London, 1928.

Phil 978.49.115   Steiner, R. Eurhythmy as visible song. London, 1923.

Phil 978.49.117   Steiner, R. Eurythmie als sichtbarer Gesang. 1. Aufl. Dornach, 1956.

Phil 978.49.120   Steiner, R. Eurhythmy as visible speech. London, 1931.

Phil 978.49.125   Steiner, R. Art in the light of mystery wisdom. N.Y., 1935.

Phil 978.49.130   Steiner, R. Anthroposophy. n.p., n.d. 5 pam.

Phil 978.49.135   Steiner, R. The problems of our time. London, 1934.

Phil 978.49.140   Spring, H.P. Essays on human science. Winter Park, 1943.

Phil 978.49.143   Steiner, R. Die Kunst der Rezitation und Deklamation. 2. Aufl. Dornach, 1967.

Phil 978.49.145   Steiner, R. Sprachgestaltung und dramatische Kunst. Dornach, 1926.

Phil 978.49.145.3   Steiner, R. Sprachgestaltung und dramatische Kunst. 3. Aufl. Dornach, 1969.

Phil 978.49.145.5   Steiner, R. Methodik und Wesen der Sprachgestaltung. Dornach, 1955.

Phil 978.49.150   Steiner, R. Veröffentlichungen aus dem literarischen Frühwerk. Dornach, 1939-41. 4v.

Phil 978.49.152   Steiner, R. Gesammelte Aufsätze zur Kultur- und Zeitgeschichte, 1887-1901. Dornach, 1966.

Phil 978.49.155   Steiner, R. Kosmische und menschliche Geschichte. Dornach, 1933-34. 5v.

Phil 978.49.157   Steiner, R. Kosmische und menschliche Geschichte. Dornach, 1964. 4v.

Phil 978.49.160   Steiner, R. Geschichtliche Notwendigkeit und Freiheit. Dornach, 1939.

Phil 978.49.162   Steiner, R. Geschichtliche Notwendigkeit und Freiheit. 2. Aufl. Dornach, 1966.

Phil 978.49.165   Steiner, R. Alte Mythen und ihre Bedeutung. Dornach, 1937.

Phil 978.49.170   Steiner, R. Bedeutsames aus dem äusseren Geistesleben um die Mitte des XIX Jahrhunderts. Dornach, 1939.

Phil 978.49.173   Steiner, R. Die okkulte Bewegung im Neunzehnten Jahrhundert und ihre Beiziehung zur Weltkultur. 3. Aufl. Dornach, 1969.

Phil 978.49.175   Steiner, R. Mysterienstätten des Mittelalters. Dornach, 1932.

Phil 978.49.180   Steiner, R. Charakteristisches zur Kennzeichnung der gegenwart Wirklichkeits-Entfremdung. Dornach, 1939.

Phil 978.49.185   Steiner, R. Die not Nach dem Christus. Dornach, 1942.

Phil 978.49.190   Steiner, R. Das Weltbild des deutschen Idealismus. Dornach, 1930.

Phil 978.49.195   Steiner, R. Goethes Geistesart in unseren Schicksalsschweren tagen und die deutsche Kultur. Dornach, 1930.

Phil 978.49.198   Steiner, R. Der Goetheanismus ein Umwandlungsimpuls und Auferstehungsgedanke: Menschenwissenschaft und Sozialwissenschaft. Dornach, 1967.

Phil 978.49.200   Freeman, Arnold. Who was Rudolf Steiner? Sheffield, 1944.

Phil 978.49.205   Steiner, R. Das volk Schillers und Fichtes. Dornach, 1930.

Phil 978.49.210   Steiner, R. Geschichte des Hypnotismus und des Somnambulismus. Basel, 1941.

Phil 978.49.215   Steiner, R. Die Geschichte des Spiritismus. Basel, 1941.

Phil 978.49.220   Steiner, R. Rudolf Steiner über Schauspielkunst (eine Fragenbeantwortung). Dornach, 1939.

Phil 978.49.225   Steiner, R. Welche Gesichtspunkte liegeni Errichtung der Waldorfschule zu Grunde? Dornach, 1942.

Phil 978.49.230   Steiner, R. Geisteswissenschaft und die Lebensforderungen der Gegenwart. pt.1-8. Dornach, 1950. 2v.

Phil 978.49.235   Pamphlet vol. Steiner, R. 6 pam.

Phil 978.49.240   Steiner, R. Drama und Dichtung im Bewusstseins-Umschwung der Neuzeit. Dornach, 1936.

Phil 978.49.245   Steiner, R. Der materialistische Erkenntnisimpuls und seine Bedeutung für die ganze Menscheitsentwicklung. Basel, 1953.

Phil 978.49.250   Steiner, R. Welt, Erde und Mensch. 2. Aufl. Freiburg, 1956.

Phil 978.49.255   Steiner, R. Die materialistische Weltanschauung des neunzehnten Jahrhunderts. Basel, 1955.

Phil 978.49.260   Steiner, R. Die Bedeutung der Anthroposophie im Geistesleben der Gegenwart. Dornach, 1957.

Phil 978.49.265   Steiner, R. Vier Mysteriendramen. 2. Aufl. Dornach, 1956.

Phil 978.49.270   Steiner, R. Rudolf Steiner in der Waldorfschule. 1. Aufl. Stuttgart, 1958.

Phil 978.49.275   Steiner, R. Das Johannes-Evangelium. 7. Aufl. Dornach, 1955.

Phil 978.49.278   Steiner, R. Menschheitsentwicklung und Christus-Erkenntnis. Dornach, 1967.

Phil 978.49.280   Steiner, R. Von der Initiation. 3. Aufl. Dornach, 1959.

Phil 978.49.285   Steiner, R. Die Erneuerung der pädagogisch-didaktischen Kunst. Dornach, 1958.

Phil 978.49.290   Pamphlet vol. Steiner, R. Lectures. 5 pam.

Phil 978.49.295   Steiner, R. Major writings. 1. ed. Englewood, 1959-6v.

Phil 978.49.300   Steiner, R. Aus Schicksals fragender Zeit. Dornach, 1959.

Phil 978.49.305   Steiner, R. Geisteswissenschaft als Lebensgut. Dornach, 1959.

Phil 978.49.310   Steiner, R. Luzifer-Gnosis, 1903-1908. Dornach, 1960.

Phil 978.49.315   Steiner, R. Menschenschichsale und Völkerschicksale. Dornach, 1960.

Phil 978.49.320   Steiner, R. Christus und die menschliche Seele. Dornach, 1960.

Phil 978.49.325   Steiner, R. Das Markus-Evangelium. Dornach, 1960.

Phil 978.49.330   Steiner, R. Ergebnisse der Geistesforschung. Dornach, 1960.

Phil 978.49.335   Steiner, R. Der goetheanumgedanke Insnitten der Kulturkreis der Gegenwart. Dornach, 1961.

Phil 978.49.340   Steiner, R. Kunst und Kunsterkunntniss. Dornach, 1961.

Phil 978.49.350   Steiner, R. Makrokosmos uund Mikrokosmos. Dornach, 1962.

Phil 978.49.360   Steiner, R. Methodische Grundlagen der Anthroposophie. Dornach, 1961.

Phil 978.49.370   Steiner, R. Geist und Stoff, Leben und Tod. Dornach, 1961.

Phil 978.49.375   Steiner, R. Alte und neue Einweihungsmethoden. Dornach, 1967.

Phil 978.49.383   Steiner, R. Exkurse in das Gebiet des Markus-Evangeliums. Dornach, 1963.

Phil 978.49.385   Steiner, R. Die Wissenschaft vom Werden des Menschen. Dornach, 1967.

Phil 978.49.390   Steiner, R. Menschengeschichte im Lichte der Geistesforschung. Berlin, 1962.

Phil 978.49.400   Steiner, R. Das Ewige in der Menschenseele. Dornach, 1962.

Phil 978.49.408   Steiner, R. Menschenwesen, Menschenschicksal und Weltentwicklunz. 3. Aufl. Dornach, 1966.

Phil 978.49.410   Steiner, R. Aus dem mitteleuropäschen Geisteleben. Dornach, 1962.

Phil 978.49.415   Steiner, R. Die soziale Grundforderung unserer Zeit in gländerter Zeitlage. Dornach, 1963.

Phil 978.49.420   Steiner, R. Geistige Wirkenskräfte. Dornach, 1964.

Phil 978.49.425   Steiner, R. Der Zusammenhang des Menschen mit der elementarischen Welt. Dornach, 1968.

Phil 978.49.430   Steiner, R. Neugestaltung, des sozialen Organismus. Dornach, 1963.

Phil 978.49.440   Steiner, R. Gesteswissenschaftliche Behandlung. Dornach, 1926.

Phil 978.49.445   Steiner, R. Initiationswissenschaft und Sternenerkenntnis. Dornach, 1964.

Phil 978.49.450   Steiner, R. Menschliche und menschheitliche Entwicklungswahrheiten. Dornach, 1964.

Phil 978.49.455   Steiner, R. Vorstufen zum Mysterium von Golgatha. Dornach, 1964.

Phil 978.49.460   Steiner, R. Die Erkenntnis der Seele und des Geistes. Dornach, 1965.

Phil 978.49.465   Steiner, R. Anthroposophie, Psychosophie, Pneumatosophie. Dornach, 1965.

Phil 978.49.470   Steiner, R. Das Ereignis der Christuserscheinung in der ätherischen Welt. Dornach, 1965.

Phil 978.49.483   Steiner, R. Heileurythmie; acht Vorträge. 3. Aufl. Dornach, 1966.

Phil 978.49.490   Steiner, R. Des Prinzip der spirituellen Ökonomie im Zusammenhang mit Wiederverkörperungsfragen; 22 Vorträge. Dornach, 1965.

Phil 978.49.502   Steiner, R. Die Impulsierung des weltgeschichtlichen Gescheheus durch geistige Mächte; sieben Vorträge. 2. Aufl. Dornach, 1966.

Phil 978.49.510   Steiner, R. Gegensätze in der Menschheitsentwickelung; 11 Vorträge. Dornach, 1967.

Phil 978.49.515   Steiner, R. Die tieferen Geheimnisse des Menschheitswerdens im Lichte der Evangelien. Dornach, 1966.

Phil 978.49.523   Steiner, R. Das Verhältnis der Sternenwelt zum Menschen und des Menschen zur Steinenwelt. 3. Aufl. Dornach, 1966.

Phil 978.49.525   Steiner, R. Das christliche Mysterium. Dornach, 1968.

Phil 978.49.530   Steiner, R. Geisteswissenschaft als Erkenntuis der Grundimpulse sozialer Gestaltung. Dornach, 1967.

Phil 978.49.535   Steiner, R. Die geistige Vereinigung der Menschheit durch den Christus-Impuls. 1. Aufl. Dornach, 1968.

Phil 978.49.540   Steiner, R. Das Geheimnis des Todes; Wesen und Bedeutung Mitteleuropas und die europäischen Volksgeister. Dornach, 1967.

Phil 978.49.545   Steiner, R. Meditative Betrachtungen und Anleitungen zur Vertiefung der Heilkunst. Dornach, 1967.

Phil 978.49.552   Steiner, R. Natur und Menschin geisteswissenschaftlicher Betrachtung. 2. Aufl. Dornach, 1967.

Phil 978.49.560   Steiner, R. Physiologisch-therapeutisches auf Grundlage der Geisteswissenschaft und zur Therapie und Hygiene. Dornach, 1965.

Phil 978.49.572   Steiner, R. Erdensterben und Weltenleben und anthroposophisdie Lebensgaben. 2. Aufl. Dornach, 1967.

Phil 978.49.578   Steiner, R. Heilpädagogischer Kursus. 3. Aufl. Dornach, 1965.

Phil 978.49.580   Steiner, R. Individuelle Geistwesen und ihr Wirken in der Seele des Menschen. Dornach, 1966.

Phil 978.49.585   Steiner, R. Okkultes Lesen und okkultes Hören. 4. Aufl. Dornach, 1967.

Phil 978.49.590   Steiner, R. Der Jahres kreislauf als Atmungsvorgang der Erde und die vier grossen Festeszeiten. Dornach, 1966.

Phil 978.49.595   Steiner, R. Der Tod als Lebenswandlung. 1. Aufl. Dornach, 1969.

Phil 978.49.600   Steiner, R. Die menschliche Seele in ihrem Zusammenhang mit göttlich-geistigen Individualitäten. Dornach, 1966.

Phil 978.49.605   Steiner, R. Der Mensch in seinem Zusammenhange mit dem Kosmos. v.5-6,9. Dornach, 1967- 3v.

Phil 978.49.610   Steiner, R. Kunst im Lichte der Mysterienweisheit. Dornach, 1966.

Phil 978.49.615   Steiner, R. Die Konstitution der Allgemeinen anthroposophischen Gesellschaft und der freien Hochschule. Dornach, 1966.

Phil 978.49.620   Steiner, R. Die spirituellen Hintergründe der äusseren Welt. Dornach, 1966.

Phil 978.49.625   Steiner, R. Geisteswissenschaftliche Grundlage zum Gedeihen der Landwirtschaft; landwirtschaftlicher Kursus. 4. Aufl. Dornach, 1963.

Phil 978.49.630   Steiner, R. Die Welträtsel und die Anthroposophie. 1. Aufl. Dornach, 1966.

Phil 978.49.635   Steiner, R. Mysterienwahrheiten und Weihnachtsimpulse. Dornach, 1966.

Phil 978.49.640   Steiner, R. Lebendiges Naturerkennen. Dornach, 1966.

Phil 978.49.645   Steiner, R. Briefwechel und Dokumente, 1901-1925. 1. Aufl. Dornach, 1967.

Phil 978.49.650   Steiner, R. Anthroposophische Gemeinschaftsbildung. Dornach, 1965.

Phil 978.49.655   Steiner, R. Geistige und soziale Wandlungen in der Menschheitsentwickelung; achtzehn Vorträge. Dornach, 196

Phil 978.49.660   Steiner, R. Nationalökonomischer Kurs. 4. Aufl. Dornach, 1965.

Phil 978.49.665   Steiner, R. Die Grundimpulse des weltgeschichtlichen Werdens der Menschheit. 2. Aufl. Dornach, 1965.

Phil 978.49.670   Steiner, R. Erdenwissen und Himmelserkenntnis. Dornach, 1966.

Phil 978.49.679   Steiner, R. Erziehungskunst; Methodisch-Didaktisches. 4. Aufl. Dornach, 1966. 2v.

Classified Listing

978 History of philosophy - Ancient and medieval oriental philosophy - India - Theosophy and Anthroposophy - Writings of individual theosophists - cont.

Phil 978.49.680 Steiner, R. Die Philosophie des Thomas von Aquino. 3. Aufl. Dornach, 1967.
Phil 978.49.685 Steiner, R. Menschenfragen und Weltenantworten. 1. Aufl. Dornach, 1969.
Phil 978.49.688 Steiner, R. Das Wesen des Musikaleschen und das Tonerlebnis im Menschen. 1. Aufl. Dornach, 1969.
Phil 978.49.690 Steiner, R. Biographien und biographische Skizzen, 1894-1905. 1. Aufl. Dornach, 1967.
Phil 978.49.692.4 Steiner, R. Aus der Akasha-Chronik. 4. Aufl. Dornach, 1969.
Phil 978.49.694 Steiner, R. Aus der Akasha-Forschung: Das Fünfte Evangelium. Dornach, 1963.
Phil 978.49.695 Steiner, R. Das Lukas-Evangelium. Ein Zyklus von zehn Vorträgen. 6. Aufl. Dornach, 1968.
Phil 978.49.696 Steiner, R. Die Verbindung zwischen Lebenden und Toten; acht Vorträge genalten im verschiedenen Stadten zwischen dem 16. Februar und 3. Dezember, 1916. 1. Aufl. Dornach, 1968.
Phil 978.49.697 Steiner, R. Anthoposophie. 3. Aufl. Dornach, 1968.
Phil 978.49.699.2 Steiner, R. Wie Kann die Menschheit den Christus Wiedertinden? 2. Aufl. Dornach, 1968.
Phil 978.49.700 Steiner, R. Christ and the spiritual world. London, 1963.
Phil 978.49.705 Steiner, R. Die Geschichte der Menschheit und die Weltanschauungen der Kulturvölker. Dornach, 1968.
Phil 978.49.710 Steiner, R. Der innere Aspekt des sozialen Rätsels. Dornach, 1968.
Phil 978.49.715 Steiner, R. Durch den Geist zur Wirklichkeits-Erkenntnis der Menschenrätsel. Dornach, 1965- 6v.
Phil 978.49.720 Steiner, R. Anweisungen für eine esoterische Schulung: aus den Inhalten der Esoterischen Schule. Dornach, 1968.
Phil 978.49.727 Steiner, R. Wahrspruchworte: anthroposophischer Selenkalender. 2. Aufl. Dornach, 1969.
Phil 978.49.729 Steiner, R. Die Beantwortung von Welt- und Lebensfragen durch Anthroposophie. Dornach, 1970.
Phil 978.49.730 Steiner, R. Die Naturwissenschaft und die welgeschichtliche Entwicklung der Menschheit seit dem Altertum. Dornach, 1969.
Phil 978.49.735 Steiner, R. Entwürfe, Fragmente und Paralipomenn zu den vier Mysteriendramen: Die Pforte der Einwiehung. Dornach, 1969.
Phil 978.49.740 Steiner, R. Das Geheimnis der Trinität. Dornach, 1970.
Phil 978.49.745 Steiner, R. Die Schöpfung der Welt und des Menschen. Dornach, 1969.
Phil 978.49.750.8 Steiner, R. Die Rätsel der Philosophie. 8. Aufl. Dornach, 1968.
Phil 978.49.759 Steiner, R. Grenzen der Naturerkenntnis. 4. Aufl. Dornach, 1969.
Phil 978.49.760 Steiner, R. Heilfaktoren für den sozialen Organismus. 1. Aufl. Dornach, 1969.
Phil 978.49.767 Steiner, R. Anthroposophie. 2. Aufl. Dornach, 1970.
Phil 978.49.770 Steiner, R. Die Polarität von Dauer und Entwickelung im Menschlenleben. Dornach, 1968.
Phil 978.49.778 Steiner, R. Die gesunde Entwickelung des Leiblich-Physischen als Grundlage der freien Entfaltung des Seelison-Geistigen. 3. Aufl. Dornach, 1969.
Phil 978.49.782 Steiner, R. Die neue Geistigkeit und das Christus-Erlebnis des zwanzigsten Jahrhunderts. 2. Aufl. Dornach, 1970.
Phil 978.49.785.3 Steiner, R. Die Grundsteinlegung der Allgemeinen Anthroposophischen Gesellschaft. 3. Aufl. Dornach, 1969.
Phil 978.49.800 Dornach. Goetheanum. Goetheanum. Dornach, 193-?
Phil 978.49.805 Lauer, H.E. Klassik. Basel, 1950.
Phil 978.49.805.5 Lauer, H.E. Die zwölf Sumie des Menschen. Basel, 1953.
Phil 978.49.810 Rihonët-Coroze, S. Rudolf Steiner. Paris, 1951.
Phil 978.49.815 Boos-Hamburger, H. Aus Gesprächen mit Rudolf Steiner. Basel, 1954.
Phil 978.49.820 Steffen, A. Begegnungen mit Rudolf Steiner. Dornach, 1955.
Phil 978.49.825 Allen, P.M. The writings and lectures of Rudolf Steiner. N.Y., 1956.
Phil 978.49.830 Peoppig, Fred. Schicksalswege zu Rudolf Steiner. 2. Aufl. Stuttgart, 1955.
Phil 978.49.835 Muellner, L. Rudolf Steiner und Brunn am Gebirge bei Wien. Wien, 1960.
Phil 978.49.840 Poppelbaum, H. Entwicklung, Vererbung und Abstammungs. Dornach, 1961.
Phil 978.49.845 Dornach, Switzerland. Goetheanum. Goetheanum. Dornach, 1961.
Phil 978.49.850 Haeusler, Friedrich. Weltenville und Menschenziele in der Geschichte. Dornach, 1961.
Phil 978.49.855 Fels, Alice. Studien zur Einführung in die Mysteriendramen Rudolf Steiners. 2. Aufl. Dornach, 1961.
Phil 978.49.860 Edmunds, L.F. Rudolf Steiner education. London, 1962.
Phil 978.49.870 Buehler, W. Meditation als Erkenntnisweg. Stuttgart, 1962.
Phil 978.49.875 Rudolf Steiner-Nachlassverwaltung. Nachrichten mit Veröffentlichungen aus dem Archiv. Dornach. 5-11
Phil 978.49.880 Steffen, Albert. Gegenwartsaufgaben der Menschheit. Schweiz, 1966.
Phil 978.49.885 Ballmer, Karl. Ernst Haeckel und Rudolf Steiner. Besazio, 1965.
Phil 978.49.890 Vallmer, Georg. Die Begegnung Max Heindel mit Rudolf Steiner. Darmstadt, 1965.
Phil 978.49.895 Steiner, Marie von Sivers. Gesammelte Schriften. Dornach, 1967.
Phil 978.49.900 Gabert, Erich. Die Weltgeschichte und das Menschen-Ish. Stuttgart, 1967.
Phil 978.49.905 Grosse, Rudolf. Erlebte Pädagogik. Dornach, 1968.
Phil 978.49.910 Lindenberg, Christoph. Individualismus und offenbare Religion. Stuttgart, 1970.
Phil 978.49.915 Ericsson-Skopnik, Brigitte. Nachweis der Zitate zu Rudolf Steiner Die Rätsel der Philosophie im ihrer Geschichte als Umriss Dargestellt. Dornach, 1969.
Phil 978.49.920 Schrey, Helmut. Waldorfpädagogik. Bad Godesberg, 1968.
Phil 978.50 Ferrier, John T. Life's mysteries unveiled. London, 1923.
Phil 978.51 Rogers, L.W. Elementary theosophy. 2d ed. Chicago, 1923.
Phil 978.51.3 Rogers, L.W. Elementary theosophy. 3rd ed. Chicago, 1929.
Phil 978.51.5 Rogers, L.W. Reincarnation, and other lectures. Chicago, 1925.
Phil 978.52 Willis, F.M. Theosophy in outline. Girard, 1923.
Phil 978.53 Murdoch, J. Theosophy unveiled. Madras, 1885.
Phil 978.55 Rees, J.R. The threefold path to peace. N.Y., 1904.
Phil 978.56 Clark, S.C. Short lessons in theosophy. Boston, 1892.
Phil 978.57 Stuart, C. A dialogue. n.p., 1901.
Phil 978.58 Frohnmeyer, L.J. Die theosophische Bewegung. Stuttgart, 1920.

Phil 978 History of philosophy - Ancient and medieval oriental philosophy - India - Theosophy and Anthroposophy - Writings of individual theosophists - cont.

Phil 978.59.2 Krishnamurti, J. The kingdom of happiness. N.Y., 1930.
Phil 978.59.5 Krishnamurti, J. At the feet of the master. Chicago, 1927?
Phil 978.59.7 Krishnamurti, J. Authentic notes of discussions and talks given by Kris at Ojai and Sarabia. Hollywood, 1940.
Phil 978.59.8 Krishnamurti, J. The song of life. Ommen, 1931.
Phil 978.59.10 Krishnamurti, J. The pool of wisdom; Who brings the truth; By what authority and three poems. Eerde, 1928.
Phil 978.59.14 Krishnamurti, J. The search. N.Y., 1927.
Phil 978.59.15 Krishnamurti, J. The search. N.Y., 1927[1928]
Phil 978.59.20 Krishnamurti, J. Life in freedom. N.Y., 1928.
Phil 978.59.22 Krishnamurti, J. Discussions with Krishnamurti in Europe, 1965. London, 1966.
Phil 978.59.25 Star bulletin. Ommen. 1929-1933 4v.
Phil 978.59.30 Krishnamurti, J. Talks, Ojai, California. Ojai, California, 1950.
Phil 978.59.35 Krishnamurti, J. The first and last freedom. London, 1954.
Phil 978.59.40 Krishnamurti, J. Commentaries on living. London, 1959.
Phil 978.59.41 Krishnamurti, J. Commentaries on living. N.Y., 1956.
Phil 978.59.42 Krishnamurti, J. Commentaries on living. London, 1957.
Phil 978.59.44 Krishnamurti, J. Commentaries on living. 1st ed. N.Y., 1960.
Phil 978.59.45 Krishnamurti, J. Life ahead. London, 1963.
Phil 978.59.50 Krishnamurti, J. Freedom from the known. 1st ed. N.Y., 1969.
Phil 978.59.55 Krishnamurti, J. Education and the significance of life. N.Y., 1953.
Phil 978.59.60 Krishnamurti, J. The only revolution. London, 1970.
Phil 978.59.65 Krishnamurti, J. Talks in Europe, 1968. Wassenaar, 1920.
Phil 978.59.70 Krishnamurti, J. Talks and dialogues, Saanen 1968. Wassenaar, 1970.
Phil 978.59.72 Krishnamurti, J. Talks and discussions at Brockwood Park, 1969. Wassenaar, 1970.
Phil 978.59.74 Krishnamurti, J. Talks with American students, 1968. Wassenaar, 1970.
Phil 978.59.90 Franceschi, G.J. El Señor Krishnamurti. Buenos Aires, 1935.
Phil 978.59.95 Heber, Lilly. Krishnamurti and the world crisis. London, 1935.
Phil 978.59.97 Suares, Carlo. Krishnamurti. Paris, 1933.
Phil 978.59.100 Fouéré, René. Krishnamurti. 2d ed. Bombay, 1954.
Phil 978.59.105 Matwani, Kewal. Krishnamurti. Madras, 1957.
Phil 978.59.110 Methorst-Kuiper, A. Krishnamurti. Amsterdam, 1961.
Phil 978.59.115 Dhopeshwarkar, A.D. Krishnamurti and the experience. Bombay, 1956.
Phil 978.59.120 Dhopeshwarkar, A.D. J. Kishnamurti and awareness in action. Bombay, 1967.
Phil 978.59.125 Bercou, Lydia. Krishnamurti, sa vie, sa parole. n.p., 1969.
Phil 978.60.2 Cooper, Irving S. Reincarnation, the hope of the world. 2d ed. Chicago, 1927.
Phil 978.60.15 Cooper, I.S. Theosophy simplified. 3d ed. Hollywood, 1919.
Phil 978.61 Jinarājadāsa, C. How we remember our past lives. Chicago, 1923.
Phil 978.61.5 Dhopeshwarkar, A.D. The divine vision. London, 1928.
Phil 978.61.10 Dhopeshwarkar, A.D. First principles of theosophy. 3d ed. Adyar, Madras, 1923.
Phil 978.62 Juste, Michael. The white brother; an occult autobiography. London, 192-?
Phil 978.63 Powell, F.G.M. Studies in the lesser mysteries. London, 1913.
Phil 978.64 Wachsmuth, G. Die ätherischen Bildekräfte in Kosmos, Erde und Mensch. Dornach, 1926.
Phil 978.64.5 Wachsmuth, G. Werdegang der Menschlheit. Dornach, 1953.
Phil 978.65 Sinnett, Patience E. The purpose of theosophy. London, 1885.
Phil 978.66 Crump, Basil. Evolution as outlined in the Archaic Eastern records. Peking, 1930.
Phil 978.67 Kuhn, Alvin Boyd. Theosophy. N.Y., 1930.
Phil 978.68 Purucker, G. de. Fundamentals of the esoteric philosophy. Philadelphia, 1932.
Phil 978.68.5 Purucker, G. de. Occult glossary. London, 1933.
Phil 978.68.10 Purucker, G. de. Studies in occult philosophy. Covina, California, 1945.
Phil 978.69 Rudolph, Hermann. Theosophischer Kulturbücher. Leipzig, 1932-33.
Phil 978.70 Pinchin, Edith F. The bridge of the gods in Gaelic mythology. London, 1934.
Phil 978.71 Coulomb, E.J. Le secret de l'absolu. Paris, 1892.
Phil 978.72 Ljungström, O. Graded lessons in theosophy. Lund, 1935.
Phil 978.72.5 Ljungström, O. Theosophy. n.p., n.d. 6 pam.
Htn Phil 978.72.10* Ljungström, O. A philosophical overhaul. Lund, 1937.
Phil 978.73 The theosophical movement, 1875-1925. N.Y., 1925.
Phil 978.74.5 Bailey, A.A. (Mrs.). A treatise on cosmic fire. 2d ed. N.Y., 1930[1925]
Phil 978.74.10 Bailey, A.A. (Mrs.). A treatise on white magic. N.Y., 1934.
Phil 978.74.15 Bailey, A.A. (Mrs.). A treatise on the seven rays. N.Y., 1936-42. 4v.
Phil 978.74.20 Bailey, A.A. (Mrs.). Initiation, human and solar. 3d. ed. N.Y., 1926.
Phil 978.74.25 Bailey, A.A. (Mrs.). Letters on occult meditation. 2d ed. N.Y., 1926.
Phil 978.74.30 Bailey, A.A. (Mrs.). The consciousness of the atom. 2d ed. N.Y., 1922.
Phil 978.74.35 Bailey, A.A. (Mrs.). The destiny of the nations. N.Y., 1949.
Phil 978.74.40 Bailey, A.A. (Mrs.). Unfinished autobiography. N.Y., 1951.
Phil 978.74.45 Bailey, A.A. (Mrs.). Education in the new age. 1st ed. N.Y., 1954.
Phil 978.75 Kauga, D.D. Where theosophy and science meet. Adyar, 1938.
Phil 978.76 Cannon, Alex. The power of karma in relation to destiny. London, 193-.
Phil 978.77.1 King, G.R. Unveiled mysteries. 2d ed. Chicago, 1935.
Phil 978.77.2 King, G.R. The magic presence. Chicago, 1935.
Phil 978.77.3 King, G.R. The "I am" discourses. 2d ed. Chicago, 1940.
Phil 978.77.6 King, G.R. Ascended master discourses. Chicago, 1937.
Phil 978.77.7 King, G.R. Ascended master light. Chicago, 1938.
Phil 978.78 Plummer, L.G. From atom to kosmos. Point Loma, 1940.
Phil 978.78.5 Plummer, L.G. Star habits and orbits. Covina, Calif., 1944.

Classified Listing

Phil 978   History of philosophy - Ancient and medieval oriental philosophy -
India - Theosophy and Anthroposophy - Writings of individual
theosophists - cont.
Phil 978.79   Dominguez Acosta, F. La exondida senda. Caracas, 1941.
Phil 978.80   Bragdon, C.F. Old lamps for new. N.Y., 1925.
Phil 978.80.10   Bragdon, C.F. The new image. N.Y., 1928.
Phil 978.81   Lee, Pi-cheng. An outline of Karma. n.p., 1941?
Phil 978.82   Stein, W.J. Weltgeschichte im Lichte des heiligen Gral.
                   Stuttgart, 1928.
Phil 978.83   Humphreys, Christmas. Karma and rebirth. London, 1943.
Phil 978.84   Demarquette, Jacques. De la liète á l'auge. Paris, 1937.
Phil 978.85   Poppelbaum, H. Man's eternal biography; three essays on
                   life and death. N.Y., 1945.
Phil 978.86   Lehrs, Ernst. Man or matter. London, 1951.
Phil 978.86.2   Lehrs, Ernst. Man or matter. 2d. ed. London, 1958.
Phil 978.86.7   Lehrs, Ernst. Mensch und Materie. 2. Aufl.
                   Frankfurt, 1966.
Phil 978.88   Schmidt, A.N. Iz rukopisei Anny Nikolaevny Shmidt.
                   Moskva, 1916.
Phil 978.90   Gleich, Sigismund. Die Wahrheit als Gesamtanfang aller
                   Weltansichten. Stuttgart, 1957.
Phil 978.91   Husemann, F. Wege und Irrwege in die geistige Welt.
                   Stuttgart, 1962.
Phil 978.92   Hartmann, F. Ausgewählte theasophische Werke.
                   Calw-Wimberg, Württ, 1959.
Phil 978.93   Kuhn, Hans. Es Ist an der Zeit. Nürnberg, 1965.
Phil 978.94   Boernsen, Hans. Naturwissenschaft an der Schwelle.
                   Stuttgart, 1964.
Phil 978.95   Barfield, Owen. Romanticism comes of age. 1st American ed.
                   Middletown, Conn., 1967[1966]
Phil 978.96   Lauer, Hans Erhard. Die Anthroposophie und die Zukunft des
                   Christentums. Stuttgart, 1966.
Phil 978.96.5   Lauer, Hans Erhard. Der Mensch in den Entscheidungen
                   unseres Jahrhunderts. Freiburg, 1968.
Phil 978.97   Skerst, Herman von. Der unbekannte Gott. Stuttgart, 1967.
Phil 978.98   Grohmann, Gerbert. Die Pflanze als Lichtsinnesorgan der
                   Erde. Stuttgart, 1962.
Phil 978.100   Wulf, Berthold. Athen und Ephesus. Freiburg, 1965.
Phil 978.105   Bockemnehl, Jochen. Naturwissenschaftliche Grundfragen.
                   Dornach, 1964.
Phil 978.108   Ballmer, Karl. Der Macher bim Ich. Besazio, 1967.
Phil 978.110   Ballmer, Karl. Deutschtum und Christentum in der
                   Theosophie des Goetheanismus. Besazio, 1966.
Phil 978.112   Poortman, Johannes Jocobus. Philosophy, theosophy,
                   parapsychology, some essays. Leyaen, 1965[1964]
VPhil 978.114   Merchant, Francis. The golden hoard. Houston, 1959.
VPhil 978.116   Wilmar, F.H.J. Kinderkrankheinten im Lichte der
                   Anthroposphie. Zeist, 1966.
Phil 978.118   Heuser, Annie. Bewisstseinsfragen des Erziehers.
                   Dornach, 1966.
Phil 978.120   Leevwen, A.J.H. van. Ganesha. Amsterdam, 1969.
Phil 978.122   Hagmann, Diego. Antwort auf Lebensrätsel. Zürich, 1968.
Phil 978.124   Lorenzen, Iwer Thor. Evolution durch Inkarnation und
                   Metamorphose. Hamburg, 1969.

Phil 980   History of philosophy - Ancient and medieval oriental philosophy -
Persia - History
Phil 990.1.2   Igbal, S.M. The development of metaphysics in Persia.
                   London, 1908.
Phil 990.1.3   Igbal, S.M. The development of metaphysics in Persia.
                   Lahore, 19- .
Phil 990.20   Foroughir, A.H. Civilisation et synthèse. Paris, 1936.
Phil 990.23   Foroughi, A.H. Systeme de philosophie dynamo synthetique.
                   Paris, 1940. 2v.
Phil 990.25   Beroukhim, Moussa. La pensée iranienne à travers
                   l'histoire. Thèse. Paris, 1938.
Phil 990.26   Horten, Max. Die philosophischen Ansichten von Razi und
                   Tusi. Bonn, 1910.

Phil 1020   History of philosophy - Ancient and medieval oriental philosophy -
Arabia - History - General works
Phil 1020.1   Schmölders, A. Essai...Écoles philosophiques chez les
                   Arabes. Paris, 1882.
Phil 1020.2   Dieterici, F. Die Philosophie der Araber im X.
                   Jahrhunderts. v.1-2,4-6,9,12-13. Leipzig, 1876-1895.
                   10v.
Phil 1020.3.6   Boer, T.J. de. The history of philosophy in Islam.
                   London, 1961.
Htn   Phil 1020.4.1*   Averroës. Destructio destructionú. Lugduni, 1529.
Phil 1020.4.5   Renan, E. Averrose et l'Averroisme. Paris, 1852.
Phil 1020.4.7   Fakhry, Majid. Islamic occasionalism and its critique by
                   Averroës and Aquinas. Paris, 1861.
Phil 1020.4.8   Fakhry, Majid. Islamic occasionalism and its critique by
                   Averroës and Aquinas. Paris, 1869.
Phil 1020.4.15   Christ, Paul S. The psychology of the active intellect of
                   Averroes. Thesis. Philadelphia, 1926.
Phil 1020.4.20   Grabmann, M. Der lateinische Awerroismus des 13
                   Jahrhunderts. München, 1931.
Phil 1020.4.25   Werner, Karl. Der Averroismus in der
                   christlich-peripatetischen Psychologie des späteren
                   Mittelalters. Wien, 1881.
Phil 1020.4.30   Reyes, A. Averroes y Lulio. Caracas, 1940.
Phil 1020.4.31   Reyes, A. El racionalismo averroísta y el razonamiento
                   luliano. Madrid, 1935.
Phil 1020.4.35   Fakhry, Majid. Islamic occasionalism and its critique by
                   Averroës and Aquinas. London, 1958.
Phil 1020.4.36   Fakhry, Majid. A history of Islamic philosophy.
                   N.Y., 1970.
Phil 1020.4.40   Kuksewicz, Zdzislaw. Averroïsme bolonais au XIVe siècle.
                   Wroclaw, 1965.
Phil 1020.4.41   Kuksewicz, Zdzislaw. De siger de Bredant à Jacques de
                   Plaisance. Wroclaw, 1968.
Phil 1020.5   Kayser, C. Das Buch von der Erkenntniss der Wahrheit.
                   Leizig, 1889.
Phil 1020.5.5   Dayser, C. Das Buch von der Erkenntniss der Wahrheit.
                   Strassburg, 1893.
Phil 1020.6   Mehren, A.F. Correspondance philosophique d'Ibn Sab'in.
                   Florence, 1879.
Phil 1020.7   Asin Palacios, M. Algazel. Dogmática, moral, ascética. v.
                   1-3. Zaragola, 1901. 2v.
Phil 1020.7.2   Asin Palacios, M. Obras escogidas. Madrid, 1946.
Phil 1020.7.3   Asin Palacios, M. La espiritualidad de Algozel y su
                   sentido critiano. Madrid, 1935-41.
Phil 1020.7.5   Carra de Vaux, Le Bon. Gazali. Photoreproduction.
                   Paris, 1902.
Phil 1020.7.10   Smith, Margaret. Al-Ghazáli, the mystic. London, 1944.
Phil 1020.8   Carra de Vaux. Avicenne. Paris, 1900.
Phil 1020.8.5   Pamphlet box. Ibn Sina.

Phil 1020   History of philosophy - Ancient and medieval oriental philosophy -
Arabia - History - General works - cont.
Phil 1020.8.9   Ibn Sina. Die metaphysik Ayicennas. Halle, 1907-09.
Phil 1020.8.12   Ibn Sina. Metaphysices compendium...Latinum...N. Carame.
                   Roma, 1926.
Phil 1020.8.15   Saliba, D. Étude sur la métaphysique d'Avicenne.
                   Paris, 1926.
Phil 1020.8.16   Saliba, D. Étude sur la métaphysique d'Avicenne. Thèse.
                   Paris, 1926.
Phil 1020.8.19   Gilson, Etienne. Avicenne et le point de départ de Duns
                   Scot. Paris, 1927.
Phil 1020.8.20   Goichon, A.M. La distinction de l'essence...d'aprés Ibn
                   Sina. Paris, 1937.
Phil 1020.8.20.2   Goichon, A.M. La distinction de l'essence...d'aprés Ibn
                   Sina. Thèse. Paris, 1937.
Phil 1020.8.21   Goichon, A.M. Lexique de la langue...d'Ibn Sina.
                   Paris, 1938.
Phil 1020.8.23   Goichon, A.M. La philosophie d'Avicenne et son influence
                   in Europe médiévale. Paris, 1944.
Phil 1020.9   Gauthier, L. La philosophie Musulmane. Paris, 1900.
Phil 1020.9.3   Gauthier, L. Introduction à l'étude de la philosophie
                   musulmane. Paris, 1923.
Phil 1020.9.5   Asian Palacios, M. Abenmasarra y su escuela.
                   Madrid, 1914.
Phil 1020.11   Anderson, M.B. Arabian philosophy. n.p., n.d.
Phil 1020.12   Gauthier, L. La théorie d'Ibn Rochd. Paris, 1909.
Phil 1020.13   Bauer, H. Die Psychologie Alhazens. Münster, 1911.
Phil 1020.14A   O'Leary, DeLacy. Arabic thought and its place in history.
                   London, 1922.
Phil 1020.14B   O'Leary, DeLacy. Arabic thought and its place in history.
                   London, 1922.
Phil 1020.14.5   O'Leary, DeLacy. Arabic thought and its place in history.
                   London, 1939.
Phil 1020.15   Bouyges, P.M. Notes sur les philosophes arabes.
                   Beyrouth, 1924.
Phil 1020.16   Ritter, H. Uber unsere Kenntniss der arabischen
                   Philosophie. Göttingen, 1844.
Phil 1020.17   Boer, Tjitze de. De wijsbegeerte in den Islam.
                   Haarlem, 1921.
Phil 1020.17.5   Boer, Tjitze de. Die Widersprüche der Philosophie nach al
                   Gozzali und ihr Ausgleich durch Ibn Rosd.
                   Strassburg, 1894.
Phil 1020.18.5   Horten, M. Die Philosophie des Islam. München, 1923.
Phil 1020.18.10   Horten, M. Die spekulative und positive Theologie des
                   Islam. Hildesheim, 1967.
Phil 1020.19   Pines, Salomon. Beiträge zur islamischen Atomenlehre.
                   Inaug Diss. Berlin, 1936.
Phil 1020.19.5   Pines, Salomon. Beiträge zur islamischen Atomenlehre.
                   Berlin, 1936.
Phil 1020.20   Wolfson, H.A. The amphibolous terms in Aristotle.
                   Cambridge, Mass., 1938.
Phil 1020.21   Affifi, A.E. The mystical philosophy of Muhyid din-ibnul
                   'Arabi. Cambridge, 1939.
Phil 1020.22.5   Nadvi, Muzaffar Uddir. Muslim thought and its source.
                   Lahore, 1946.
Phil 1020.22.7   Nadvi, Muzaffar Uddir. Muslim thought and its source. 4th
                   ed. Lahore, 1960.
Phil 1020.23   Quadri, G. La philosophie arabe dans l'Europe mediévale.
                   Paris, 1947.
Phil 1020.23.5   Quadri, G. La filosofia degli arabi nel suo fiore. v.1-2.
                   Firenze, 1939.
Phil 1020.28   Gardet, Louis. La pensée religieus d'Avicenne.
                   Paris, 1951.
Phil 1020.30   Farrukh, O.A. The Arab genius in science and philosophy.
                   2d ed. Washington, 1954.
Phil 1020.32   Cruz Hernández, Miguel. Historia de la filosofia española.
                   Madrid, 1957. 2v.
Phil 1020.32.10   Cruz Hernández, Miguel. La filosofía arabe. Madrid, 1963.
Phil 1020.34   Akademiia Nauk Uzbekskoi SSR, Tashkend. Otdel Filosofii i
                   Prava. Materialy poistorii progressivnoi obshchestvennoi
                   filosofskoi mysl v Uzbekistane. Tashkent, 1957.
Phil 1020.36   Lane-Poole, Stanley. Essay on the brotherhood of purity.
                   Lahore, 1954.
Phil 1020.38   Muminov, I.M. Iz istorii razvitiia...musli v uzbekistane.
                   Tashkent, 1957.
Phil 1020.39   Krikorian, Sergei. Srednevekovaia filosofiia narodov
                   Blizhnego i Srednego Vostoka. Moskva, 1966.
Phil 1020.40   Grigorian, S.N. Iz istorii filosofii Srednei Azii i Irana
                   VII-XII vv. Moskva, 1960.
Phil 1020.41   Grigorian, S.N. Izbrannye proizredenii myshtelei stran
                   Blizhnego Srednego Vostoka. Moskva, 1961.
Phil 1020.44   Walzer, Richard. Greek into Arabic. Cambridge, 1962.
                   2v.
Phil 1020.44.2   Walzer, Richard. Greek into Arabic. Oxford, 1962.
Phil 1020.46   Sharif, M.M. A history of Muslim philosophy.
                   Wiesbaden, 1963. 2v.
Phil 1020.47   Naso, S.H. An introduction to Islamic cosmological
                   doctrines. Cambridge, 1964.
Phil 1020.48   Corbin, H. Histoire de la philosophie islamique.
                   Paris, 1964.
Phil 1020.49   Bogoutdinov, Alautin M. Ocherki po istorii tadzhikskoi
                   filosofii. Stalinabad, 1961.
Phil 1020.50   Sheikh, M. Saeed. Studies in Muslim philosophy. 1st ed.
                   Lahore, 1962.
Phil 1020.55   Kamali, Sabin Ahmad. Types of Islamic thought in criticism
                   and reconstruction. Aligarh, 1963.
Phil 1020.60   Ulken, H.Z. Islam felsefesi kouynoklou ve teni.
                   Ankara, 1967.
Phil 1020.60.5   Ulken, H.Z. Islam duzancesi ve tarihteki yeri.
                   Ankara, 1959.
Phil 1020.62   Rescher, Nicholas. Studies in Arabic philosophy.
                   Pittsburgh, 1967[1968]
Phil 1020.64.2   Rafi-ud-din, Muhammad. Ideology of the future. 2nd ed.
                   Karachi, 1956.
Phil 1020.65   Jad'an, Fahme. L'influence du stoicisme sur la pensée
                   musulmane. Beyrauth, 1968.
Phil 1020.70   Çubukçu, I.A. Islâm felsefesinde Allah'in varliğinin
                   delilleri. Ankara, 1967.
Phil 1020.75   Sunar, Cavit. Islam felsefesi der'sleri. Ankara, 1967.
Phil 1020.80   Hanafi, Hasan. Les méthodes d'exegese. Le Caire, 1965.
Phil 1020.85   Badawi, Abdurrahman. Le transmission de la philosophie
                   grecque au monde arabe. Paris, 1968.

Phil 1030   History of philosophy - Ancient and medieval oriental philosophy - Arabia - History - Special topics

Phil 1030.5A   Rosenthal, Franz. Knowledge triumphant; the concept of knowledge in medieval Islam. Leiden, 1970.

Phil 1030.5B   Rosenthal, Franz. Knowledge triumphant; the concept of knowledge in medieval Islam. Leiden, 1970.

Phil 1050   History of philosophy - Ancient and medieval oriental philosophy - Jewish [Discontinued]

Phil 1050.1   Buddeus, J.F. Introductio ad historia philosophiae ebraeorum. Halae, 1702.

Phil 1050.2   Munk, S. Philosophie und Schriftsteller der Juden. Leipzig, 1852.

Phil 1050.3   Spiegler, J.S. Geschichte der Philosophie des Judenthums. Leipzig, 1890.

Phil 1050.4   Guttmann, J. Die philosophie der Soloman ibn Gabirol. Göttingen, 1889.

Phil 1050.4.5   Dukes, L. Salomo ben Gabirol. Hannover, 1860.

Phil 1050.4.9   Seyerlen, R. Die gegenseitigen Bezeihungen. Jena, 1899.

Phil 1050.4.13   Dreyer, Kare. Die religiöse Gedankenwelt des Salomo ibn Gabirol. Inaug. Diss. Leipzig, 1928.

Phil 1050.4.17   Solomon Ibn-Gabirol. La fuente de la vída. Madrid, 1901.

Phil 1050.4.20   Bieler, Majer. Der göttliche Wille (Logosbegriff) bei Gabirol. Breslau, 1933.

Phil 1050.4.25   Millás y Vallicrosa, José María. Sêlomó Ibn Gabirol como poeta y filósofo. Madrid, 1945.

Phil 1050.5   Munk, S. Mélanges de philosophie Juive et Arabe. Paris, 1859.

Phil 1050.5.5   Munk, S. Mélanges de philosophie Juive et Arabe. Paris, 1927.

Phil 1050.6   Husik, Isaac. Judah Messer Leon's commentary on the Vitus logica. Leiden, 1906.

Phil 1050.7   Neumark, D. Geschichte der jüdischen Philosophie der Mittelalters. Berlin, 1907. 3v.

Phil 1050.7.9   Neumark, D. Essays in Jewish philosophy. Vienna, 1929.

Phil 1050.8   Cearus, F.A. Psychologie der Hebräer. Leipzig, 1809.

Phil 1050.9   Bois, Henri. Essai sur les origines se la philosophie. Paris, 1890.

Phil 1050.10   Husik, I. History of medieval Jewish philosophy. N.Y., 1916.

Phil 1050.10.10   Husik, I. Philosophical essays. Oxford, 1952.

Phil 1050.12   Wolfson, Harry A. Maimonides and Halevi. Philadelphia, 1912.

Phil 1050.12.3   Wolfson, Harry A. The amphibolous terms in Aristotle. Cambridge, Mass., 1938.

Phil 1050.12.5   Wolfson, Harry A. The classification of sciences on mediaeval Jewish philosophy. Chicago, 1925.

Phil 1050.13   Wolfson, Harry A. Solomon Pappenheim on time and space and his relation to Locke and Kant. Vienna, 1927.

Phil 1050.14   Wolfson, Harry A. Note on Crescas's definition of time. Philadelphia, 1919.

Phil 1050.14.2   Wolfson, Harry A. Crescas on problem of divine attributes. Philadelphia, 1916.

Phil 1050.14.3   Wolfson, Harry A. Studies in Crescas. N.Y., 1934.

Phil 1050.14.5   Waxman, Meyer. The philosophy of Don Hasdai Crescas. N.Y., 1920.

Phil 1050.15   Weil, Isidore. Philosophie religieuse de Léi-ben-Gerson. Paris, 1868.

Phil 1050.15.5   Alderblum, N.H.H. A study of Gersonedes in his proper perspective. N.Y., 1926.

Phil 1050.15.9   Karo, Jakob. Kritische Untersuchungen zu Levi hen Gersons (Ralbag) Widerlegung des Aristotelischen Zeitbegriffes. Inaug. Diss. Leipzig, 1935.

Phil 1050.16   Neumark, D. Jehuda Hallevi's philosophy in its principles. Cinncinati, 1908.

Phil 1050.16.5   Berger, Emil. Das Problem der Erkenntnis in der Religions-Philosophie Jehuda Hallevis. Inaug-Diss. Berlin, 1915.

Phil 1050.17   Pamphlet box. Die Psychologie bei den judischen Religions.

Phil 1050.18   Gortein, H. Der Optimismus und Pessimismus in der jüdischen Religionsphilosophie. Berlin, 1890.

Phil 1050.19   Schmiedl, A. Studien über jüdische, Insonders jüdisch-arabische Religionsphilosophie. Wien, 1869.

Phil 1050.20   Efros, Israel I. The problem of space in Jewish mediaeval philosophy. N.Y., 1917.

Phil 1050.21   Guttmann, J. Die Philosophie des Judentums. München, 1933.

Phil 1050.22   Wolfson, Harry A. Isaac Israeli on the internal senses. N.Y., 1935.

Phil 1050.23   Macdonald, D.B. The Hebrew philosophical genius. Princeton, 1936.

Phil 1050.24   Levine, I. Faithful rebels; a study in Jewish speculative thought. London, 1936.

Phil 1050.25   Goldman, S. The Jew and the universe. N.Y., 1936.

Phil 1050.26   Ehrich, J. Das Problem der Theodizes in der jüdischen Religionsphilosophie des Mittelalters. Inaug. Diss. Breslau, 1936.

Phil 1050.27   Lichtigfeld, A. Philosophy and revelation in the work of contemporary Jewish thinkers. London, 1937.

Phil 1050.27.5   Lichtigfeld, A. Twenty centuries of Jewish thought. London, 1937.

Phil 1075   History of philosophy - Ancient and medieval oriental philosophy - Armenia - History

Phil 1075.1   Neumann, C.F. Memoire sur la vie et les ouvrages de David. Paris, 1829.

Phil 1075.1.5   Rose, Valentin. Leben des Heiligen David von Thessanilke. Berlin, 1887.

Phil 1075.5   Chaloian, V.K. Istoriia armians boi filosofii. Erevan, 1959.

Phil 1075.6   Gabriel'ian, Genri. Ocherk istorii armianskoi mysli. Erevan, 1962.

Phil 1100   History of philosophy - Ancient and medieval oriental philosophy - Pamphlet volumes

Phil 1100.1   Pamphlet vol. Greek philosophy. German. 8 pam.

Phil 1100.2   Pamphlet vol. Greek philosophy. German dissertations. 16 pam.

Phil 1100.3   Pamphlet box. Greek philosophy. German dissertations. 7 pam.

Phil 1100.5   Pamphlet box. Philosophy. Greek and Roman.

Phil 1100.7   Baumhauer, Theodor C.M. Disputatia literaria. Trajuti ad Rhinum, 1844. 4 pam.

Phil 1105 - 1130   History of philosophy - Ancient and medieval oriental philosophy - History - General works (A-Z)

Phil 1105.1   Anderson, W. Philosophy of ancient Greece. Edinburgh, 1791.

Htn   Phil 1105.2*   Agricola, R. De inventione. Libri III. Coloniae, 1518.

Htn   Phil 1105.2.5*   Agricola, R. De inventione dialectica. pt.3. Parisiis, 1535.

Phil 1105.3   Aquilianiis, S. Placitis philosophorum. Lipsiae, 1756.

Phil 1105.4   Adamson, Robert. The development of Greek philosophy. Edinburgh, 1908.

Phil 1105.5   Apell, Otto. Beiträge zur Geschichte der griechischen Philosophie. Leipzig, 1891.

Phil 1105.6   Appleton, R.B. The elements of Greek philosophy from Thales to Aristotle. London, 1922.

Phil 1105.7   Aster, E. Geschichte der antiken Philosophie. Berlin, 1920.

Phil 1105.8   Alfieri, V.E. Studi di filosofia greca. Bari, 1950.

Phil 1105.10   Asmus, Valentin F. Istoriia antichnoi filosofii. Moskva, 1965.

Phil 1105.12   Adorno, Francesco. Studi sul pensiero greco. Firenze, 1966.

Phil 1105.14   Anton, John Peter. Essays in ancient Greek philosophy. Albany, 1971.

Phil 1106.1A   Bakewell, C.M. Source book in ancient philosophy. N.Y., 1907.

Phil 1106.1B   Bakewell, C.M. Source book in ancient philosophy. N.Y., 1907.

Phil 1106.1.5   Bakewell, C.M. Source book in ancient philosophy. N.Y., 1907.

Phil 1106.1.7   Bakewell, C.M. Source book in ancient philosphy. N.Y., 1940.

Phil 1106.2   Benard, Charles. La philosophie ancienne. Paris, 1885.

Phil 1106.3   Benn, A.W. The Greek philosophers. London, 1882. 2v.

Phil 1106.3.2A   Benn, A.W. The Greek philosophers. London, 1914.

Phil 1106.3.2B   Benn, A.W. The Greek philosophers. London, 1914.

Phil 1106.3.5   Benn, A.W. The philosophy of Greece. London, 1898.

Phil 1106.3.9   Benn, A.W. Early Greek philosophy. London, 1908.

Phil 1106.3.10   Benn, A.W. Early Greek philosophy. N.Y., n.d.

Phil 1106.3.11   Benn, A.W. Early Greek philosophy. N.Y., 1909?

Phil 1106.3.15   Benn, A.W. History of ancient philosophy. London, 1912.

Phil 1106.4   Brandes, C.A. Handbuch der Geschichte der griechisch-römischen Philosophie. Berlin, 1835-60. 5v.

Htn   Phil 1106.5*   Burley, W. Von dem Leben, sitten und freyen Sprüchen der alten Philosophie. Ausburg, 1519.

Htn   Phil 1106.5.5*   Burley, W. Liber de vita et moribus philosophorum. Tübingen, 1886.

Htn   Phil 1106.5.6*   Burley, W. Vita omnium philosophorum et poetarum. n.p., n.d.

Phil 1106.6   Burt, B.C. Brief history of Greek philosophy. Boston, 1889.

Phil 1106.7   Butler, W.A. Lectures on the history of ancient philosophy. Cambridge, 1856. 2v.

Phil 1106.7.5   Butler, W.A. Lectures on the history of ancient philosophy. Philadelphia, 1857. 2v.

Phil 1106.8   Burnet, J. Greek philosophy. pt. 1. London, 1914.

Phil 1106.8.4   Burnet, J. Greek philosophy. pt.1. London, 1928.

Phil 1106.9   Blass, F. Ideale und materielle Lebensauschauung. Kiel, 1889.

Phil 1106.10   Bertling, Oskar. Geschichte der alten Philosophie. Leipzig, 1907.

Phil 1106.11   Boswell, F.P. A primer of Greek thought. Geneva, 1923.

Phil 1106.12   Bolland, G.J.P.J. De oorsprong der griekse wijsbegeerte. 3e uitg. Leiden, 1921.

Phil 1106.13   Bender, W. Mythologie und Metaphysik. Die Entstehung der Weltanschauungen im griechisch Altertums. Stuttgart, 1899.

Phil 1106.14   Büsching, A.F. Vergleichung der griechischen Philosophie mit der Neuern. Berlin, 1785.

Phil 1106.15   Bakhuizen Van Den Brink, R.C. Varias lectiones ex historia philosophiae antiquae. Lugduni-Batavorum, 1842.

Phil 1106.16   Bréhier, Emile. Etudes de philosophie antique. Paris, 1955.

Phil 1106.17   Bartolone, Félippi. L'origine dell'intellettualismo. Palermo, 1959.

Phil 1106.18   Bertozzi, A. Saggi sul pensiero antico. Padova, 1960.

Phil 1106.19   Brumbaugh, Robert S. The philosophers of Greece. N.Y., 1964.

Phil 1107.1   Cousin, Victor. Fragments philosophiques. Paris, 1840.

Phil 1107.2   Caspari, Otto. Die Irrthümer der altclassischen Philosophie. Heidelberg, 1868.

Phil 1107.3   Capelle, Wilhelm. Die griechische Philosophie. Berlin, 1922-34. 3v.

Phil 1107.4   Cornford, F.M. Before and after Socrates. Cambridge, Eng., 1932.

Phil 1107.4.3   Cornford, F.M. Before and after Socrates. Cambridge, Eng., 1960.

Phil 1107.4.5   Cornford, F.M. Principium sapientiae. Cambridge, Eng., 1952.

Phil 1107.5   Covotti, Aurelio. I piesocratici; saggi. Napoli, 1934.

Phil 1107.6   Covotti, Aurelio. Da Aristotele ai Bizantini. Napoli, 1935.

Phil 1107.7   Carbonara, Cleto. La filosofia greca. Napoli, 1951. 2v.

Phil 1107.7.2   Carbonara, Cleto. La filosofia greca: Aristotele. 2. ed. Napoli, 1967.

Phil 1107.7.3   Carbonara, Cleto. La filosofia greca. Platone. 2. ed. Napoli, 1969.

Phil 1107.8   Cresson, André. La philosophie antique. 4e ed. Paris, 1957.

Phil 1108.1   Döring, A. Geschichte der griechischen Philosophie. Leipzig, 1903. 2v.

Phil 1108.2   Deussen, P. Philosophie der Griechen. Leipzig, 1911.

Phil 1108.4   Dynnik, M.A. Ocherk istorii filosofii klassicheskoi Gretsii. Moskva, 1936.

Phil 1108.6   Detienne, Marcel. Les maîtres de vérité dans le Grèce archaique. Paris, 1967.

Phil 1108.8   Diels, Hermann. Kleine Schriften zur Geschichte der antiken Philosophie. Hildesheim, 1969.

Phil 1109.1   Eleutheropulos, A. Philosophie und der Lebensauffassung der Griechtens. Berlin, 1900-01. 2v.

Phil 1109.1.5   Eleutheropulos, A. Die Philosophie und der sozialen Züstande (materielle und ideele Entwicklung) des Greichentums. 3e Aufl. Zürich, 1915.

Phil 1109.2   Eckstein, F. Abriss der griechischen Philosophie. Frankfurt, 1955.

Phil 1109.5   Edelstein, Ludwig. The idea of progress in classical antiquity. Baltimore, 1967.

Classified Listing

Phil 1110.1.5	Ferrier, J.F. Lectures on Greek philosophy. v.2. Edinburgh, 1866.
Phil 1110.1.6	Ferrier, J.F. Lectures on Greek philosophy. 2nd ed. Edinburgh, 1875.
Phil 1110.1.7	Ferrier, J.F. Philosophical works. v.2. Edinburgh, 1888.
Phil 1110.4	Finley, John Huston. Four stages of Greek thought. Stanford, 1966.
Phil 1111.1	Gomperz, T. Griechische Denker. Leipzig, 1893. 3v.
Phil 1111.1.5	Gomperz, T. Griechische Denker. Leipzig, 1903-09. 3v.
Phil 1111.1.7	Gomperz, T. Griechische Denker. 4. Aufl. Berlin, 1922-31. 3v.
Phil 1111.1.9	Gomperz, T. Greek thinkers and history of ancient philosophy. v.4. London, 1901.
Phil 1111.1.11	Gomperz, T. Greek thinkers; a history of ancient philosophy. London, 1905-13. 4v.
Phil 1111.2	Grenet, P.B. Histoire de la philosophie ancienne. Paris, 1960.
Phil 1111.5	Garcia Bacca, J.D. Sobre estetica griega. Mexico, 1943.
Phil 1111.6	Groningen, B.A. In the grip of the past. Leiden, 1953.
Phil 1111.7	Gaos, José. Antologia filosofica; la filosofia griega. México, 1940.
Phil 1111.9	Gigon, Olof. Der Ursprung der griechischen Philosophie von Hesiod bis Parmenides. Berlin, 1945.
Phil 1111.9.5	Gigon, Olof. Grundprobleme der antiken Philosophie. Bern, 1959.
Phil 1111.12	Guthrie, William. The Greek philosophers from Thales to Aristotle. N.Y., 1950.
Phil 1111.12.5	Guthrie, William. Greek philosophy. Cambridge, Eng., 1953.
Phil 1111.12.10	Guthrie, William. A history of Greek philosophy. Cambridge, 1962. 3v.
Phil 1111.13	Galli, Dario. Il pensiero greco. Padova, 1954.
Phil 1111.14	Galli, Gallo. Corso di storia della filosofia; I sofisti. Socrate, Alcuni dialoghi platonici. Torino, 1954.
Phil 1112.1	History of Greek and Roman philosophy. London, 1853.
Phil 1112.2	Hampden, R.D. The fathers of Greek philosophy. Edinburgh, 1862.
Phil 1112.3	Hönigwald, R. Die Philosophie des Altertums. München, 1917.
Phil 1112.4	Hammarsköld, L. Grunddragen af philosophiens historia. 1a afd. Stockholm, 1825.
Phil 1112.5	Howald, E. Die Anfänge der europäischen Philosophie. München, 1925.
Phil 1112.6	Helms, Poul. Den graeske naturfilosofi indtil sofisterne. København, 1926.
Phil 1112.7	Hoffmann, Ernst. Die griechische Philosophie von Thales bis Platon. Leipzig, 1921.
Phil 1112.7.5	Hoffmann, Ernst. Die griechische Philosophie von Thales bis Platon. Heidelberg, 1951.
Phil 1112.8	Huonder, Quirin. Gott und Seele bin Lichte der griechischen Philosophie. München, 1954.
Phil 1112.10	Hoelscher, Vvo. Anfanchisches Fragen; Studien zur Frühen griechischen Philosophie. Göttingen, 1968.
Phil 1112.12	Hildebrandt, Kurt. Frühe griechische Denker. Bonn, 1968.
Phil 1114.1	Joël, Karl. Geschichte der antiken Philosophie. Tübingen, 1921.
Phil 1114.5	Jaeger, Werner W. The theology of the early Greek philosophers. Oxford, 1947.
Phil 1114.5.2	Jaeger, Werner W. The theology of the early Greek philosophers. London, 1968.
Phil 1114.10	Jaeger, Werner W. Die Theologie der Frühen griechischen Denker. Stuttgart, 1953.
Phil 1115.1	Kühnemann, E. Grundlehren der Philosophie. Berlin, 1899.
Phil 1115.2	Krug, W.T. Geschichte der Philosophie alter Zeit. Leipzig, 1827.
Phil 1115.3	Kinkel, Walter. Geschichte der Philosophie von Sokrates bis Aristoteles. Berlin, 1922.
Phil 1116.1	Laforet, N.J. Histoire de la philosophie ancienne. Bruxelles, 1866. 2v.
Phil 1116.3	Larsson, Hans. Den grekiska filosofien. Stockholm, 1921.
Phil 1116.4	Leisegang, H. Griechische Philosophie von Thales bis Platon. Breslau, 1922.
Phil 1116.4.5	Leisegang, H. Hellenistische Philosophie von Aristoteles bis Plotin. Breslau, 1923.
Phil 1116.5	Lasacco, Michele. Introduzione alla storia della filosofia greca e appendice di testi tradotti. Bari, 1929.
Phil 1117.1.2	Marshall, John. Short history of Greek philosophy. London, 1891.
Phil 1117.1.3	Marshall, John. Short history of Greek philosophy. London, 1898.
Phil 1117.2A	Mayor, J.B. Sketch of ancient philosophy. Cambridge, 1881.
Phil 1117.2B	Mayor, J.B. Sketch of ancient philosophy. Cambridge, 1881.
Phil 1117.2.5	Mayor, J.B. Sketch of ancient philosophy. Cambridge, 1885.
Phil 1117.2.7	Mayor, J.B. A sketch of ancient philosophy. Cambridge, Eng., 1889.
Phil 1117.3	Meiners, C. Geschichte des Ursprungs. Lemzo, 1781-82.
Phil 1117.3.5	Meiners, C. Histoire de l'origine...der sciences dans la Grèce. Paris, 1799. 5v.
Phil 1117.3.10	Meiners, C. Vermischte philosophische Schriften. Leipzig, 1775. 3v.
Phil 1117.4	Mallet, Charles. Histoire de la philosophie ionienne. Paris, 1842.
Phil 1117.5	Melli, G. La filosofia greca. Firenze, 1922.
Phil 1117.6	Meyer, Hans. Geschichte der alten Philosophie. München, 1925.
Phil 1117.7	Mitchell, E.M. (Mrs.). A study of Greek philosophy. Chicago, 1891.
Phil 1117.8	Mondolfo, Rodolfo. Problemi del pensiero antico. Bologna, 1935.
Phil 1117.8.5	Mondolfo, Rodolfo. La camprensione del soggeho. 1. ed. Firenze, 1958.
Phil 1117.8.10	Mondolfo, Rodolfo. El pensamiento antiguo. Buenos Aires, 1942. 2v.
Phil 1117.8.18	Mondolfo, Rodolfo. Il pensiero antico. 3. ed. Firenze, 1961.
Phil 1117.10	Maddalena, Antonio. Sulla cosmologia ionica da talete a eraclita. Padova, 1940.
Phil 1117.12	Menzel, Adolf. Hellenika. Baden, 1938.
Phil 1117.14	Michaelides, Konstantinos. Mensch und Kosmos in ihrer Zusammengehörigkeit bei den frühen griechischen Denkern. München? 1961?

	Phil 1117.16	Mondolfo, Rodolfo. Momenti del pensiero greco e cristiano. Napoli, 1964.
	Phil 1118.2	Natorp, Paul. Forschungen zur Geschichte der Erkenntnissproblems im Alterthum. Berlin, 1884.
	Phil 1118.3	Nestle, W. Griechische Weltanschauung in ihrer Bedeutung für die Gegenwart. Stuttgart, 1946.
	Phil 1119.1	Otten, Alois. Einleitung in die Geschichte der Philosophie. Paderborn, 1895.
	Phil 1119.2.21	Ovink, B.J.H. Overzicht der grieksche wijsbegeerte. 2e druk. Zutphen, 1906.
	Phil 1119.5	Olgiati, F. I fondamenti della filosofia classica. 2. ed. Milano, 1953.
	Phil 1119.6	Owens, Joseph. A history of ancient Western philosophy. N.Y., 1959.
	Phil 1120.1	Plessing, F.V.L. Versuche zur Aufklärung der Philosophie des ältesten Alterthums. Leipzig, 1788-90. 3v.
	Phil 1120.2	Prantl, K. Ubersicht der griech-römischen Philosophie. Stuttgart, 1854.
	Phil 1120.4	Peters, Francis E. Greek philosophical terms; a historical lexicon. N.Y., 1967.
	Phil 1120.5	Pra, Mario dal. La storiografia filosofica antica. 1.ed. Milano, 1950.
	Phil 1122.1	Renouvier, C.B. Manuel de philosophie ancienne. Paris, 1844. 2v.
	Phil 1122.2	Ritter, Heinrich. Histoire de la philosophie ancienne. Paris, 1835-36. 4v.
	Phil 1122.2.5	Ritter, Heinrich. History of ancient philosophy. Oxford, 1838-46. 4v.
	Phil 1122.2.6	Ritter, Heinrich. History of ancient philosophy. Oxford, 1838-46. 4v.
	Phil 1122.2.10	Ritter, Heinrich. Geschichte der jonischen Philosophie. Berlin, 1821.
	Phil 1122.3	Ritter, Heinrich. Historia philosophiae graeco-romanae. Hamburg, 1838.
	Phil 1122.3.5	Ritter, Heinrich. Historia philosophiae graeco-romanae. Gotha, 1857.
	Phil 1122.3.9	Ritter, Heinrich. Historia philosophiae graecae et romanae. Gotha, 1864.
	Phil 1122.3.11	Ritter, Heinrich. Historia philosophiae graecae et romanae. 5. ed. Gotha, 1875.
	Phil 1122.3.12	Ritter, Heinrich. Historia philosophiae graecae et romanae. 6. ed. Gotha, 1878.
	Phil 1122.3.13	Ritter, Heinrich. Historia philosophiae graecae et romanae. 7.ed. Gotha, 1888.
	Phil 1122.3.17	Ritter, Heinrich. Historia philosophiae graecae. Gotha, 1898.
	Phil 1122.3.25	Ritter, Heinrich. Historia philosophiae graecae. 9th ed. Gotha, 1913.
	Phil 1122.3.27	Ritter, Heinrich. Historia philosophiae graecae. 10 ed. Gotha, 1934.
	Phil 1122.4	Payot, E. Les auteurs philosophiques, grecs. Paris, 1898.
	Phil 1122.5	Rodier, Georges. Etudes de philosophie grecque. Paris, 1926.
	Phil 1122.6.3	Robin, Léon. La pensée grecque et les origines de l'esprit scientifique. Paris, 1928.
	Phil 1122.6.4	Robin, Léon. La pensée grecque et les origines de l'esprit scientifique. Paris, 1948.
	Phil 1122.6.5	Robin, Léon. Greek thought. N.Y., 1928.
	Phil 1122.6.10	Robin, Léon. La pensee hellenique des origines a epicule questions de methode. 1.ed. Paris, 1942.
	Phil 1122.7	Rivaud, Albert. Le problème du devenir et la notion de la matière dans la philosophie grecque depuis les origines jusqu'à Theophraste. Paris, 1906.
	Phil 1122.8	Rivaud, Albert. Les grands couvants de la pensée antique. Paris, 1929.
	Phil 1122.9.5	Rüfner, Vinzenz. Grundbegriffe griechischer Wissenschaftslehre. 2. Aufl. Bamberg, 1947.
	Phil 1122.10	Redlow, Götz. Theoria. Theoretische und praktische Lebensauffassung im philosophischen Denken der Antike. Berlin, 1966.
	Phil 1122.15	Rauche, Gerhard Albin. A student's key to ancient Greek thought. Fort Hare, 1966.
	Phil 1122.20	Robinson, Richard. Essays in Greek philosophy. Oxford, 1969.
	Phil 1122.25	Ráde, Emanuel. Dějiny filosofie. Praha, 1932-33. 2v.
	Phil 1123.1	Schulze, E. Ubersicht über die griechische Philosophie. Leipzig, 1886.
	Phil 1123.2	Schwegler, A. Geschichte der griechischen Philosophie. Tübingen, 1859.
Htn	Phil 1123.3*	Stanley, T. History of philosophy. London, 1687.
	Phil 1123.3.1	Stanley, T. History of philosophy. v.1-3. London, 1656-60. 2v.
I....	Phil 1123.3.2*	Stanley, T. History of philosophy. v.1-3. London, 1656-60. 2v.
	Phil 1123.3.3	Stanley, T. History of philosophy. London, 1701.
	Phil 1123.3.4	Stanley, T. Historia philosophiae. Lipsiae, 1711.
	Phil 1123.3.5	Stanley, T. Historia philosophiae. Lipsiae, 1743.
	Phil 1123.4	Snider, D.J. Ancient European philosophy...Greek. St. Louis, Mo., 1903.
	Phil 1123.5	Stace, W.T. Critical history of Greek philosophy. London, 1920.
	Phil 1123.6	Strümpell, L. Die Geschichte der griechischen Philosophie zur Ubersicht. pts.1-2. Leipzig, 1854-61.
	Phil 1123.7	Stenzel, Julius. Metaphysik des Altertums. München, 1931.
	Phil 1123.7.5	Stenzel, Julius. Kleine Schriften zur griechischen Philosophie. 2. Aufl. Darmstadt, 1957.
	Phil 1123.8	Smith, T.V. Philosophers in Hades. Chicago, Ill., 1932.
	Phil 1123.9	Schuhl, Pierre Maxime. Essai sur la formation de la pensée grecque. Paris, 1934.
	Phil 1123.9.10	Schuhl, Pierre Maxime. Essai sur la formation de la pensée grecque. 2.ed. Paris, 1949.
	Phil 1123.10	Sciacca, Michele F. Studi sulla filosofia antica. Napoli, 1935.
	Phil 1123.11	Schmekel, A. Forschungen. Berlin, 1938.
	Phil 1123.12	Stefanini, L. Il preimoginisimo dei Greci. Padova, 1953.
	Phil 1123.13	Schaerer, René. Le heros, le sage et l'événement dans l'humanisme grec. Paris, 1964.
	Phil 1123.13.5	Schaerer, René. L'homme devant ses choix dans la tradition grecque. Louvain, 1965.
	Phil 1123.13.10	Schaerer, René. L'homme antique et la structure du monde interieur d'Homère à Socrate. Paris, 1958.
	Phil 1123.16	Strycker, Emile de. Beknopte geschiedenis de de antieke filosofie. Antwerpen, 1967.
	Phil 1124.1	Teichmüller, G. Studien zur Geschichte der Begriffe. Berlin, 1874.

Classified Listing

Phil 1105 - 1130 History of philosophy - Ancient and medieval oriental philosophy - History - General works (A-Z) - cont.

Phil 1124.1.5	Teichmüller, G. Neue Studien zur Geschichte der Begriffe. Gotha, 1876-1879. 2v.
Phil 1124.2	Tiedemann, D. Griechenlands erste Philosophen. Leipzig, 1780.
Phil 1124.3	Taylor, M.E.J. Greek philosophy. London, 1924.
Phil 1124.4	Taylor, Thomas. Miscellanies in prose and verse. London, 1805.
Phil 1124.5	Tsatsos, K. He koinonikē filosofia tōn arkhaion Hellēnon. Athenai, 1938.
Phil 1126.2	Vogel, C. Greek philosophy. Leiden, 1950. 3v.
Phil 1126.3	Vos, Harmen de. Inleiding tot de wijsbegeerte van de Grieken en de Romeinen. Nijkerk, 1963.
Phil 1127.1	Wendland, Paul. Beiträge zur Geschichte der griechischen Philosophie. Berlin, 1895.
Phil 1127.2	Windelband, W. History of ancient philosophy. N.Y., 1899.
Phil 1127.2.5	Windelband, W. History of ancient philosophy. N.Y., 1901.
Phil 1127.2.7	Windelband, W. History of ancient philosophy. N.Y., 1956.
Phil 1127.2.9	Windelband, W. Geschichte der alten Philosophie. Nördlingen, 1888.
Phil 1127.3	Wundt, Max. Griechische Weltanschauung. Leipzig, 1910.
Phil 1127.4	Waddington, Charles. La philosophie ancienne et la critique historique. Paris, 1904.
Phil 1127.5A	Warbeke, John M. The searching mind of Greece. N.Y., 1930.
Phil 1127.5B	Warbeke, John M. The searching mind of Greece. N.Y., 1930.
Phil 1127.5C	Warbeke, John M. The searching mind of Greece. N.Y., 1930.
Phil 1127.5.3	Werner, Charles. La philosophie grecque. Paris, 1938.
Phil 1127.6	Weil, S. La source grecque. Paris, 1953.
Phil 1130.1	Zeller, Eduard. Die Philosophie der Griechen. Tubingen, 1856-68. 5v.
Phil 1130.2	Zeller, Eduard. Die Philosophie der Griechen. Leipzig, 1869-79. 3v.
Phil 1130.2.5	Zeller, Eduard. Die Philosophie der Griechen. v. 1-2,4-5. Leipzig, 1876-81. 4v.
Phil 1130.2.6	Zeller, Eduard. Die Philosophie der Griechen. Register. Leipzig, 1882.
Phil 1130.2.9	Zeller, Eduard. Die Philosophie der Griechen. v.2. Leipzig, 1892.
Phil 1130.2.11	Zeller, Eduard. Die Philosophie der Griechen. v. 1,3-6. Leipzig, 1892. 5v.
Phil 1130.2.15	Zeller, Eduard. Die Philosophie der Griechen. 6e Aufl. Leipzig, 1919-23. 6v.
Phil 1130.2.17	Zeller, Eduard. La filosofia dei Greci nel suo sviluppo storico. Firenze, 193-. 2v.
Phil 1130.3	Zeller, Eduard. Grundriss der Geschichte der griechischen Philosophie. Leipzig, 1883.
Phil 1130.3.8	Zeller, Eduard. Grundriss der Geschichte der griechischen Philosophie. 8th ed. Leipzig, 1907.
Phil 1130.3.9	Zeller, Eduard. Grundriss der Geschichte der griechischen Philosophie. 9th ed. Leipzig, 1909.
Phil 1130.3.13	Zeller, Eduard. Grundriss der Geschichte der griechischen Philosophie. 13e Aufl. Leipzig, 1928.
Phil 1130.4A	Zeller, Eduard. History of Greek philosophy. London, 1881. 2v.
Phil 1130.4B	Zeller, Eduard. History of Greek philosophy. London, 1881. 2v.
Phil 1130.4C	Zeller, Eduard. History of Greek philosophy. London, 1881. 2v.
Phil 1130.5	Zeller, Eduard. Outlines of history of Greek philosophy. N.Y., 1886.
Phil 1130.5.2	Zeller, Eduard. Outlines of history of Greek philosophy. London, 1886.
Phil 1130.5.3	Zeller, Eduard. Outlines of history of Greek philosophy. N.Y., 1890.
Phil 1130.5.4	Zeller, Eduard. Outlines of history of Greek philosophy. N.Y., 1889.
Phil 1130.5.5	Zeller, Eduard. Outlines of history of Greek philosophy. London, 1895.
Phil 1130.5.9	Zeller, Eduard. Outlines of history of Greek philosophy. London, 1922.
Phil 1130.5.15	Zeller, Eduard. Outlines of history of Greek philosophy. 13th ed. London, 1931.
Phil 1130.5.17	Zeller, Eduard. Outlines of history of Greek philosophy. 13th ed. London, 1931.
Phil 1130.6	Zeller, Eduard. Socrates and the Socratic schools. London, 1868.
Phil 1130.6.5	Zeller, Eduard. Socrates and the Socratic schools. London, 1877.
Phil 1130.6.8	Zeller, Eduard. Socrates and the Socratic schools. 3rd ed. London, 1885.
Phil 1130.6.9	Zeller, Eduard. Grundriss der Geschichte der griechischen Philosophie. Leipzig, 1911.
Phil 1130.7	Zeller, Eduard. Plato and the older academy. Leipzig, 1876.
Phil 1130.7.5	Zeller, Eduard. Plato and the older academy. London, 1888.
Phil 1130.8A	Zeller, Eduard. The Stoics, Epicureans, and Sceptics. London, 1870.
Phil 1130.8B	Zeller, Eduard. The Stoics, Epicureans, and Sceptics. London, 1870.
Phil 1130.8.3	Zeller, Eduard. The Stoics, Epicureans, and Sceptics. London, 1880.
Phil 1130.8.5	Zeller, Eduard. The Stoics, Epicureans, and Sceptics. London, 1892.
Phil 1130.9	Zeller, Eduard. History of eclecticism in Greek philosophy. London, 1883.

1 1133 History of philosophy - Ancient and medieval oriental philosophy - History - Special periods

Phil 1133.1.2	Burnet, John. Early Greek philosophy. London, 1892.
Phil 1133.1.12A	Burnet, John. Early Greek philosophers. 4th ed. London, 1952.
Phil 1133.1.12B	Burnet, John. Early Greek philosophers. 4th ed. London, 1952.
Phil 1133.5	Reesema, W.S. Parmenidas, anaxagorae, protagore principia. Lugduni, 1840.
Phil 1133.9	Cornwallis, C.F. Brief view of Greek philosophy. London, 1844.
Phil 1133.9.3	Cornwallis, C.F. Brief view of Greek philosophy. Philadelphia, 1846.
Phil 1133.10	Meyer, Hans. Geschichte der Lehre von den Keimkräften von der Stoa bis zum Ausgang der Patristik. Bonn, 1914.
Phil 1133.11	Leclère, Albert. La philosophie grecque avant Socrate. Paris, 1908.

Phil 1133 History of philosophy - Ancient and medieval oriental philosophy - History - Special periods - cont.

Phil 1133.15	Byk, S.A. Die vorsokratische Philosophie der Griechen. Leipzig, 1876-77. 2v.
Phil 1133.16	Nestle, W. Die Vorsokratiker. Auschauungen, 1908.
Phil 1133.16.5	Nestle, W. Die Sokratiker. Jena, 1922.
Phil 1133.16.10	Nestle, W. Die Nachsokratiker. Jena, 1923. 2v.
Phil 1133.17	Diès, Auguste. Le cycle mystique. Paris, 1909.
Phil 1133.18	Goebel, Karl. Die vorsokratische Philosophie. Bonn, 1910.
Phil 1133.19A	Kafka, Gustav. Die Vorsokratiker. München, 1921.
Phil 1133.19B	Kafka, Gustav. Die vorsokratiker. München, 1921.
Phil 1133.19.10	Kafka, Gustav. Der Ausklang der antiken Philosophie und das Erwachen einer neuen Zeit. n.p., n.d.
Phil 1133.20A	Fuller, Benjamin A.G. History of Greek philosophy. N.Y., 1923. 3v.
Phil 1133.20B	Fuller, Benjamin A.G. History of Greek philosophy. N.Y., 1923.
Phil 1133.21	Moulard, A. Metpon; étude sur l'idée de mesure dans la philosophie antésocratique. Thèse. Angers, 1923.
Phil 1133.22	More, Paul E. Hellenistic philosophies (From the death of Socrates to A.D. 451). Princeton, 1923.
Phil 1133.23	Scoon, Robert. Greek philosophy before Plato. Princeton, 1928.
Phil 1133.24	Frenkian, A.M. Etudes de philosophie presocratique. Cernăuti, 1933. 2v.
Phil 1133.25	Nassauer, Kurt. Denker der hellenischen Frühzeit. Frankfurt, 1948.
Phil 1133.26	Freeman, Kathleen. The pre-Socratic philosophers. Cambridge, Mass., 1946[1947]
Phil 1133.26.2	Freeman, Kathleen. The pre-Socratic philosophers. Oxford, 1946.
Phil 1133.28	McClure, Matthew T. The early philosophers of Greece. N.Y., 1935.
Phil 1133.30	Cornford, F.M. From religion to philosophy. N.Y., 1957.
Phil 1133.32	Paci, Enzo. Storia del pensiero presocratico. Torino, 1957.
Phil 1133.35A	Kirk, G.S. The presocratic philosophers. Cambridge, Eng., 1957.
Phil 1133.35B	Kirk, G.S. The presocratic philosophers. Cambridge, Eng., 1957.
Phil 1133.35C	Kirk, G.S. The presocratic philosophers. Cambridge, Eng., 1957.
Phil 1133.35.4	Kirk, G.S. The presocratic philosophers. Cambridge, Eng., 1962.
Phil 1133.37	Breden, Heribert. Grund und Gegenwart als Frageziel der frühgriechischen Philosophie. Den Haag, 1962.
Phil 1133.39	Vlolmans, A. De voorsokratici. Den Haag, 1961.
Phil 1133.40	Cleve, Felix M. The giants of pre-sophistic Greek philosophy. The Hague, 1965.
Phil 1133.40.2	Cleve, Felix M. The giants of pre-sophistic Greek philosophy. 2nd ed. The Hague, 1969. 2v.
Phil 1133.41	Mikhailova, Engelina N. Ioniiskaia filosofiia. Moskva, 1966.
Phil 1133.43	Armstrong, Arthur Hilary. The Cambridge history of later Greek and early medieval philosophy. London, 1967.
Phil 1133.44	Regnéll, Hans. Före Sokrates. Stockholm, 1969.
Phil 1133.45	Nebel, Gerhard. Die Geburt der Philosophie. Stuttgart, 1967.
Phil 1133.46	Broecker, Walter. Die Geschichte der Philosophie vor Sokrates. Frankfurt, 1965.
Phil 1133.47	Gadamer, Hans G. Um die Begriffswelt der Vorsokratiker. Darmstadt, 1968.
Phil 1133.48	Lahaye, Robert. La philosophie ionienne, l'École de Mileti Thales, Anaxemandre, Anaximène, Héraclite d'Ep'hèse. Paris, 1966.
Phil 1133.49	Maddalena, Antonio. Ionici; testimonianze e frammenti. Introduzione. 1. ed. Firenze, 1963.
Phil 1133.50	Legrand, Gérard. La pensée des présocratiques. Paris, 1970.
Phil 1133.52	Furley, David J. Studies in presocratic philosophy. London, 1970-
Phil 1133.54	McLean, George F. Ancient Western philosophy: the Hellenic emergence. N.Y., 1971.
Phil 1133.55	Chanyshev, Arsenii N. Egeiskaia predfilosofiia. Moskva, 1970.

Phil 1135 History of philosophy - Ancient and medieval oriental philosophy - History - Special topics

	Phil 1135.5	Zeller, Eduard. A history of eclecticism in Greek philosophy. London, 1883.
	Phil 1135.13	Breton, G. Essai sur la poésie philosophique en Grèce. Paris, 1882.
	Phil 1135.14	Wa Saïd, Dibinga. Theosophies of Plato, Aristotle and Plotinus. N.Y., 1970.
	Phil 1135.15	Simon, J. Études sur la Théodicée de Platon. Paris, 1840.
	Phil 1135.16	Plessing, F.V.L. Osiris und Sokrates. Berlin, 1783.
	Phil 1135.17	Fortlage, C. Ueber die Denkweise der ältesten Philosophen. München, 1829.
	Phil 1135.18	Krische, A.B. Die theologischen Lehren der griechischen Denker. Göttingen, 1840.
	Phil 1135.20	Caird, Edward. Volution of theology in Greek philosophers. Glasgow, 1904. 2v.
	Phil 1135.20.5	Caird, Edward. The evolution of theology in the Greek philosophers. Glasgow, 1923.
	Phil 1135.21	Hoffmann, F. Über die Gottes Idee des Anagoras. Wurzbrug, 1860.
	Phil 1135.22	Cocker, B.F. Christianity and Greek philosophy. N.Y., 1875.
	Phil 1135.22.4	Cocker, B.F. Christianity and Greek philosophy. N.Y., 1879.
	Phil 1135.23	Friedländer, M. Griechische Philosophie im alten Testament. Berlin, 1904.
	Phil 1135.23.9	Heinisch, Paul. Griechische Philosophie und altes Testament. Münster, 1913-14. 2v.
	Phil 1135.23.15	Sellin, Ernst. Die Spuren griechischer Philosophie. 1e and 2e Aufl. Leipzig, 1905.
	Phil 1135.24	Louis, M. Doctrines religieuses. Paris, 1909.
	Phil 1135.25	Gilbert, O. Griechische Religionsphilosophie. Leipzig, 1911.
Htn	Phil 1135.26F*	Picodella Mirandola, G.F. Examen vanitatis doctrinae gentium et veritatis Christianae disciplinae. Mirandulae, 1520.
	Phil 1135.28	Gruppe, O.F. Die kosmischen Systeme der Griechen. Berlin, 1851.
	Phil 1135.28.15	Bandry, J. Le problème de l'origine et de l'eternité du monde. Thèse. Paris, 1931.
	Phil 1135.28.20	Sternberg, Kurt. Das Problem des Ursprungs in der Philosophie des Altertums. Breslau, 1935.

Classified Listing

Phil 1135   History of philosophy - Ancient and medieval oriental philosophy - History - Special topics - cont.

Phil 1135.29   Neustadt, E. Die religiös-philosophische Bewegung der Hellenismus. Leipzig, 1914.

Phil 1135.30   Liebeck, H. Untersuchungen zur Philosophie der Griechen. Halle, 1873.

Phil 1135.31   Liebeck, H. Untersuchungen zur Philosophie der Griechen. 2nd ed. Freiburg, 1888.

Phil 1135.32   Liebeck, H. Quaestiones Duae de Philosophia Graecorum. Halle, 1872.

Phil 1135.33   Stettner, E. Antike Humanität in moderner Beleuchtung. Bieletz, 1912.

Phil 1135.34   Caiazzo, D. L'idea di giustizia nel pensiero greco. Roma, 1958.

Phil 1135.40   Goring, C. Über den Begriff der Ursache im der griechischen Philosophie. Leipzig, 1874.

Phil 1135.41   Gundel, Wilhelm. Beiträge zur...Ananke und Heimarmene. Giessen, 1914.

Phil 1135.44   Milliaud, G. Les philosophes-geometres de la Gréce. Paris, 1900.

Phil 1135.47   Kalthoff, A. Die Philosophie der Griechen. Berlin, 1901.

Phil 1135.50   Weisz, C.O.M. Metaphysische Theorie der griechischen Philosophie. Rostock, 1873.

Phil 1135.52   Poestion, J.C. Griechische Philosophinnen. Bremen, 1882.

Phil 1135.53   Joannides, A. Pragmateia peri tes par Athenagorai filosofikes geoses. Jena, 1883.

Phil 1135.56   Lwellengrebel, J.G.H. Veterum de Elementis Placita. Rhenum, 1844.

Phil 1135.57   Bouché-Leclerq, A. Placita Graecorum. Paris, 1871.

Phil 1135.60   Huit, C. Philosophie de la nature chez les anciens. Paris, 1901.

Phil 1135.62   Joël, Kar. Der Ursprung der Naturphilosophie aus dem Geiste der Mystik. Basel, 1903.

Phil 1135.63   Burle, E. Notion de droit naturel. Trevoux, 1908.

Phil 1135.64   Theiler, W. Zur Geschichte der teleologischen Naturbetrachtung bis auf Aristoteles. Inaug. Diss. Zürich, 1924.

Phil 1135.64.5   Theiler, W. Zur Geschichte der teleologischen Naturbetrachtung bis auf Aristoteles. Zürich, 1925.

Phil 1135.68   Baeumker, C. Das Probleme der Materie in der griechischen Philosophie. Münster, 1890.

Phil 1135.69   Apelt, O. Ansichten der griechischen Philosophen. Eisen, 1901.

Phil 1135.70   Müller, E. Die Idee der Menschheit. Leipzig, 1877.

Phil 1135.75   Montagni, G.R. L'evoluzione presocratica. Castello, 1912.

Phil 1135.76   Sikes, E.E. The anthropology of the Greeks. London, 1914.

Phil 1135.77   Giannini, Giorgio. Il problema antropologico. Roma, 1965.

Phil 1135.80   Heinze, M. Die Lehre vom Logos. Oldenburg, 1872.

Phil 1135.81   Trubetskoi, S.N. Uchenie o Logose. Moskva, 1900.

Phil 1135.81.5   Trubetskoi, S.N. Uchenie o Logose. Moskva, 1906.

Phil 1135.82   Kelber, Wilhelm. Die Logoslehre von Heraklit bis Origenes. Stuttgart, 1958.

Phil 1135.83   Thomas Aquinas, Sister. The pre-Socratic use of [Psyche]. Washington, 1915.

Phil 1135.85   Freytag, W. Die Entwicklung der Grossen Erkenntnistheorie. Hale, 1905.

Phil 1135.85.15   Salzi, Pierre. La genèse de la sensation...chez Protagoras. Paris, 1934.

Phil 1135.85.16   Salzi, Pierre. La genèse de la sensation...chez Protagoras, Platon et Aristote. Thèse. Paris, 1934.

Phil 1135.90   Walter, J. Die Lehre von der praktischen Vernunft. Jena, 1874.

Phil 1135.93   Chevalier, Jacques. Notion du Necessaire chez Aristote. Paris, 1915.

Phil 1135.94   Doerfler, Josef. Vom mythos zum logos. Freistadt, 1914.

Phil 1135.97   Deichmann, C. Das Problem des Raumes in der griechischen Philosophie bis Aristoteles. Halle, 1893.

Phil 1135.100   Laudowicz, Felix. Wesen und Ursprung der Lehre von der Präexistenz der Seele und von der Seelenwanderung in der griechischen Philosophie. Berlin, 1898.

Phil 1135.101   Stettner, Walter. Die Seelenwanderung bei Griechen und Römern. Inaug. Diss. Stuttgart, 1930.

Phil 1135.102   Sunne, D.G. Some phases...Post-Aristotelian period. Chicago, 1911.

Phil 1135.104   Peter, C.L. von. Problem des Zufalls in der griechischen Philosophie. Berlin, 1909.

Phil 1135.105   Bauch, B. Das Substanzproblem in der griechischen Philosophie bis zur Blütezeit. Heidelberg, 1910.

Phil 1135.115   Herbertz, R. Das Wahreitsproblem in der griechischen Philosophie. Berlin, 1913.

Phil 1135.125   Trubetskoi, S. Metafizika v drevnei Gretsii. Moskva, 1890.

Phil 1135.130   Swain, Joseph W. The Hellenic origins of Christian asceticism. N.Y., 1916.

Phil 1135.131   Bois, Henri. Le dogme grec. Paris, 1893.

Phil 1135.135   Rechenberg, C.M. Entwickelung des Gottesbegriffes. Leipzig, 1872.

Phil 1135.136   Hack, R.K. God in Greek philosophy. Princeton, 1931.

Phil 1135.145   Casel, Otto. De philosophorum graecorum silentis mystics. Giessen, 1919.

Phil 1135.150   Hopgner, T. Orient und griechische Philosophie. Leipzig, 1925.

Phil 1135.152   Boreas, Theophilos. Hē archē tēs ōeri metempsykōseōs doxēs tōn Hellēnōn philosophōn. Athens, 1913.

Phil 1135.153   Garve, C. Legendorum philosophorum veterum praecepta nonnulla et exemplum. Leipzig, 1770.

Phil 1135.154   Mondolfo, R. L'infinito nel pensiero dei Greci. Firenze, 1934.

NEDL Phil 1135.154.5   Mondolfo, R. El infinitio en el pensamiento de la antiguedad clasica. Buenos Aires, 1952.

Phil 1135.154.10   Mondolfo, R. L'infinito nel pensiero dell'antichita classica. Firenze, 1956.

Phil 1135.155   Guérin, Pièrre. L'idée de justice dans la conception de l'univers les premiers philosophes grecs. Paris, 1934.

Phil 1135.155.5   Guérin, Pièrre. L'idée de justice dans la conception de l'univers les premiers philosophes grecs. Thèse. Strasbourg, 1934.

Phil 1135.156   Delatte, A. Les conceptions de l'enthousiasme chez les philosophes presocratiques. Paris, 1934.

Phil 1135.157   Cornford, F.M. The laws of motion in ancient thought. Cambridge, Eng., 1931.

Phil 1135.158   Gentile, M. La metafisica presofistica. Padova, 1939.

Phil 1135.159   Moreau, J. L'âme du monde de Platon aux Stoiciens. Thèse. Paris, 1939.

Phil 1135.160   Fritz, K. von. Philosophie und sprachlicher Ausdruck. N.Y., 1938.

Phil 1135.161   Callahan, John F. Four views of time in ancient philosophy. Cambridge, 1948.

Phil 1135   History of philosophy - Ancient and medieval oriental philosophy - History - Special topics - cont.

Phil 1135.162   Long, Herbert S. A study of the doctrine of metempsychocis in Greece. Thesis. Princeton, 1948.

Phil 1135.163   Reidemeister, Kurt. Das Exakte denken der Griechen. Hamburg, 1949.

Phil 1135.164   Bochenski, I.M. Ancient formal logic. Amsterdam, 1951.

Phil 1135.165   Guyot, Henri. L'infinite divine depuis Philon le Juif jusqu'à Platin. Paris, 1906.

Phil 1135.166   Schroedinger, E. Nature and the Greeks. Cambridge, Eng., 1954.

Phil 1135.167   Grilli, A. Il problema della vita contemplativa nel mondo greco-romano. 1. ed. Milano, 1953.

Phil 1135.168   Beckmann, F. Humanitas. Münster, 1952.

Phil 1135.170   Robbers, Joannes Henricus. Antieke wijsgerige opvattingen in het christelijk denkleven. Roermond, 1959.

Phil 1135.172   Lieberg, Godo. Geist und Lust. Tübingen, 1959.

Phil 1135.173   Boas, Georje. Rationalism in Greek philosophy. Baltimore, 1961.

Phil 1135.174   Kienle, W. Die Berichte über die Sukressionen der Philosophen. Berlin, 1961.

Phil 1135.175   Precope, J. Iatrophilosophers of the Hellenic states. London, 1961.

Phil 1135.176   Voelke, Andre J. Les rapports avec Autrui dans la philosophie grecque d'Aristole à Panetius. Paris, 1961.

Phil 1135.177   Napoli, G. La concezione dell'essere nella filosofia. Milano, 1953.

Phil 1135.178   Welskopf, E.C. Probleme der Musse im alten Hellas. Berlin, 1962.

Phil 1135.179   Des Places, E. Syngeneia. Paris, 1964.

Phil 1135.180   Padellaro De Angelis, Rosa. Il problema cosmologica e l'antivomia unomalteplice. Milano, 1962.

Phil 1135.181   Maw, Jürgen. Isonomia. Berlin, 1964.

Phil 1135.182   Baldry, Harold Capame. The unity of mankind in Greek thought. Cambridge, Eng., 1965.

Phil 1135.183   Cogniot, Georges. Le materialisme gréco-romain. Paris, 1964.

Phil 1135.184   Lloyd, Geoffrey Ernest Richard. Polarity and analogy. Cambridge, Eng., 1966.

Phil 1135.184.5   Calogero, Giudo. Storia della logica antica. Bari, 1967-

Phil 1135.185   Pesce, Domenico. Idea, numero e anima. Padova, 1961.

Phil 1135.188   Kroeber, Günter. Wissenschaft und Weltanschauung in der Antike. Berlin, 1966.

Phil 1135.190   Sinnige, Theo G. Matter and infinity in the Presocratic school and Plato. Assen, 1968.

VPhil 1135.191   Kornatowski, Wiktor. Zarys driejów mysli politycznej starożytnosii. Wyd. 1. Warsawa, 1968.

Phil 1135.193   Carbonara Naddei, Mirella. Note sul realismo nel pensiero dei Greci. Napoli, 1965.

Phil 1135.194   Landmann, Michael. Ursprongsbild und Schöpfertat. München, 1966.

Phil 1135.195   Chicoteau, Marcel. Les attributs de l'ephectisme grec et leur survivance dans une cosmologie racinienne. Cardiff, 1943?

Phil 1135.200   Skovgaard Jensen, Søren. Dualism and demonology. Thesis. København, 1966.

Phil 1135.205   Whittaker, John. God, time, being; studies in the transcendental tradition in Greek philosophy. Thesis. Bergen, 1970.

Phil 1135.210   Roloff, Dietrich. Gottähnlichkeit, Vergöttlichung und Erhöhung zu seligem Leben. Berlin, 1970.

Phil 1135.215   Isnardi Parente, Margherita. Techne. 1. ed. Firenze, 1966.

Phil 1135.220   Conti, Rosario. Cosmogonie oriëntali e filosofia presocratica. Roma, 1967.

Phil 1135.225   West, M.L. Early Greek philosophy and the Orient. Oxford, 1971.

Phil 1135.230   Kurz, Dietrich. Akpibeia. Göppingen, 1970.

Phil 1135.235   Hager, Fritz-Peter. Der Geist und das Eine. Inaug. Diss. Bern, 1970.

Phil 1135.240   Stachowiak, Herbert. Rationalismus im Ursprung. Wien, 1971.

Phil 1135.245   Lotz, Johannes Baptist. Die Stufen der Liebe; Eros, Phila, Agape. 1. Aufl. Frankfurt, 1971.

Phil 1140   History of philosophy - Ancient and medieval oriental philosophy - History - Psychology

Phil 1140.1   Chaignet, A.E. Histoire de la Psychologie des Grecs. Paris, 1887-93. 5v.

Phil 1140.5   Beare, J.G. Greek theorie of elementary cognition. Oxford, 1906.

Phil 1140.7   Philippson, L. Hylē anthropinē. Berolini, 1831.

Phil 1140.8   Firniani, S. Le idee psicologiche in Grecia nel periodo presofistico e l'esposizione critica di Aristotele. Napoli, 1904.

Phil 1140.10   Movia, Giancarlo. Anima e intelletto. Padova, 1968.

Phil 1145   History of philosophy - Ancient and medieval oriental philosophy - History - Ethics

Phil 1145.3   Collection des moralistes anciens. Paris, 1782-83. 12v.

Phil 1145.5   Denis, J. Histoire des theories...dans l'Antiquité. Paris, 1856. 2v.

Phil 1145.6   Denis, J. Histoire des theories...dans l'Antiquité. Paris, 1879. 2v.

Phil 1145.8   Garnier, A. De la morale dans l'Antiquité. Paris, 1865.

Phil 1145.10   Holstein, R. Bedeutung des 7 Jahrhunderts. Stettin, 1903.

Phil 1145.11   Ménard, L. De la morale avant les philosophes. Paris, 1860.

Phil 1145.12   Ménard, L. De la morale avant les philosophes. 2e éd. Paris, 1863.

Phil 1145.15   Oakeley, Frederick. Remarks upon Aristotelian and Platonic ethics. Oxford, 1837.

Phil 1145.18   Schmidt, L. Die Ethik der alten Griechen. Berlin, 1882.

Phil 1145.18.1   Schmidt, L. Hé ethiké tón archaión Hellénón. Athenas, 1901.

Phil 1145.22   Kühn, O. Sittlichen Ideen der Griechen. Leipzig, 1888.

Phil 1145.32   Gomperz, H. Die Lebensauffassung der griechischen Philosophen. Jena, 1904.

Phil 1145.35   Jones, W.H.S. Greek morality in relation to institutions. London, 1906.

Phil 1145.37   Dobbs, A.E. Philosophy and popular morals in ancient Greece. Dublin, 1907.

Phil 1145.40   Wendt, M. Der Intellektualismus in der griechischen Ethik. Leipzig, 1907.

Phil 1145.41   Wendt, M. Geschichte der griechischen Ethik. Leipzig, 1908. 2v.

Phil 1145.45   Levi, A. Delitto e pena nel pensiero dei Greci. Torino, 1903.

Phil 1145 History of philosophy - Ancient and medieval oriental philosophy - History - Ethics - cont.

Phil 1145.50 Curtius, E. Der Freundschafts begriff der Alten. Göttingen, 1863.
Phil 1145.51 Dugas, L. L'amité antique d'après les moeurs populaires. Thèse. Paris, 1894.
Phil 1145.52 Dirlmeier, Franz. Filos und Filia im vorhellenistischen Griechentum. Inaug. Diss. München, 1931.
Phil 1145.53 Eernstman, J.P.A. Oikeios, etairos, epitedeios, filos; bejdtrage tot de kennis van de terminologie. Groningen, 1932.
Htn Phil 1145.55* Symonds, John A. A problem in Greek ethics. London, 1901.
Phil 1145.66 Hirzel, R. Was die Wahrheit war für die Griechen. Jena, 1905.
Phil 1145.70 Programm der koniglichen Bismarck-Gym? Pyritz, 1908.
Phil 1145.74 Oakeley, Hilda D. Greek ethical thought. London, 1925.
Phil 1145.75 Lavell, C.F. Evolution of Greek moral education. Kingston, 1911.
Phil 1145.76 Ziegler, T. Die Ethik der Griechen und Römer. Bonn, 1886.
Phil 1145.77 Heinze, Max. Der Eudämonismus in der griechischen Philosophie. Leipzig, 1883.
Phil 1145.78 Märcker, F.A. Das Princip des Bösen nach den Begriffen den Griechen. Berlin, 1842.
Phil 1145.79 Wehrli, Fritz. Lade biosas. Studien zur ältesten Ethik bei den Griechen. Leipzig, 1931.
Phil 1145.80 Gerlach, Julius. Haner hagados. Inaug. Diss. Munchen, 1932.
Phil 1145.81 Wal, L.G. Het objectiviteitsbeginsel in de oudste Grieksche ethiek. Groningen, 1934.
Phil 1145.82 Robin, L. La morale antique. Paris, 1938.
Phil 1145.83 Mondolfo, Rodolfo. Moralistas griegos. Buenos Aires, 1941.
Phil 1145.85 Heinimann, Felix. Nomos und physis. Basel, 1945.
Phil 1145.87 Schwartz, E. Ethik der Griechen. Stuttgart, 1951.
Phil 1145.90 Adkins, Arthur. Merit and responsibility. Oxford, 1960.
Phil 1145.90.1 Adkins, Arthur. Merit and responsibility. Oxford, 1960[1970]
Phil 1145.92 Pearson, L.I.C. Popular ethics in ancient Greece. Stanford, Calif., 1962.
Phil 1145.94 Riondato, E. Ethos. Padova, 1961.
Phil 1145.95 Barr, S. The three worlds of man. Columbia, 1963.
Phil 1145.96 Wankel, H. Kalos Kai Agaltos. Frankfurt, 1961.
Phil 1145.97 Luthardt, C.E. Die antike Ethik in ihrer geschichtlichen Entwicklung als Einleitung in die Geschichte der christlichen Moral. Leipzig, 1887.
Phil 1145.100 Banchetti, Silvestro. La persona umana nella morale dei Greci. Milano, 1966.
Phil 1145.102 Reinicke, Hans. Das Verhängnis der Übel im Weltbild griechischer Denker. Berlin, 1969.

Phil 1150 History of philosophy - Ancient and medieval oriental philosophy - History - Special systems and schools - Alexandrian School

Phil 1150.1 Barthélemy, H.J. De l'ecole d'Alexandrie. Paris, 1845.
Phil 1150.2 Simon, J. Histoire de l'ecole d'Alexandrie. Paris, 1845. 2v.
Phil 1150.3 Vacherot, E. Histoire critique de l'ecole d'Alexandrie. Paris, 1846-51. 3v.
Phil 1150.4 Kingsley, C. Alexandria and her schools. Cambridge, 1854.
Phil 1150.5 Dähne, A.F. Geschichtliche Darstellung der jüdisch-alexandrinischen Religions-Philosophie. Halle, 1834. 2v.
Phil 1150.9 Wolf, S. Hypatia, die Philosophin von Alexandria. Vienna, 1879.
Phil 1150.10 Hubbard, E. Hypatia. N.Y., 1908.
Phil 1150.11A Meyer, W.A. Hypatia von Alexandria. Heidelberg, 1886.
Phil 1150.11B Meyer, W.A. Hypatia von Alexandria. Heidelberg, 1886.
Phil 1150.12 Tollington, R.B. Alexandrine teaching on the universe. London, 1932.

Phil 1153 History of philosophy - Ancient and medieval oriental philosophy - History - Special systems and schools - Cynics

Phil 1153.5 Caspari, A. De cynicis. Chemnitz, 1896.
Phil 1153.7 Dudley, D.R. A history of cynicism from Diogenes to the 6th century A.D. London, 1937.
Phil 1153.10 Höistad, R. Cynic hero and cynic king. Uppsala, 1948.
Phil 1153.15 Sayre, Farrand. The Greek cynics. Baltimore, 1948.
VPhil 1153.20 Sebestyén, Károly. A einikusok. Budapest, 1902.

Phil 1155 History of philosophy - Ancient and medieval oriental philosophy - History - Special systems and schools - Eleatics

Phil 1155.5 Ranulf, Svend. Der eleatische satz vom widerspruch. Kjøbenhavn, 1924.
Phil 1155.10 Albertelli, P. Gli eleati. Bari, 1939.

Phil 1158 History of philosophy - Ancient and medieval oriental philosophy - History - Special systems and schools - Epicureans

Phil 1158.5 Guyau, M. La morale d'Epicure. Paris, 1878.
Phil 1158.6 Wallace, W. Epicureanism. London, 1880.
Phil 1158.7 Ferri, Luigi. L'epicureismo e l'atomismo. Firenze, 1871.
Phil 1158.9 Combes, M. Les vies d'Epicure de Platon et de Pythagore. Amsterdam, 1752.
Phil 1158.15.2 Pater, Walter. Marius the Epicurean. 2. ed. London, 1885. 2v.
DL Phil 1158.15.3 Pater, Walter. Marius the Epicurean. London, 1891.
Phil 1158.15.5 Pater, Walter. Marius the Epicurean. London, 1893.
Phil 1158.15.7 Pater, Walter. Marius the Epicurean. London, 1895.
Phil 1158.15.10 Pater, Walter. Marius the Epicurean. London, 1897.
Phil 1158.15.12 Pater, Walter. Marius the Epicurean. 4th ed. London, 1904. 2v.
Phil 1158.15.13 Pater, Walter. Marius the Epicurean. 4th ed. London, 1907. 2v.
Phil 1158.15.14A Pater, Walter. Marius the Epicurean. London, 1910. 2v.
Phil 1158.15.14B Pater, Walter. Marius the Epicurean. London, 1910.
Phil 1158.15.15A Pater, Walter. Marius the Epicurean. N.Y., 1930.
Phil 1158.15.15B Pater, Walter. Marius the Epicurean. N.Y., 1930.
Phil 1158.25A Bailey, Cyril. The Greek atomists and Epicurus. Oxford, 1928.
Phil 1158.25B Bailey, Cyril. The Greek atomists and Epicurus. Oxford, 1928.
Phil 1158.25.2 Bailey, Cyril. The Greek atomists and Epicurus. N.Y., 1964.
Phil 1158.27 Sedgwick, H.D. Art of happiness. Indianapolis, 1933.
Phil 1158.30 Fallat, Jean. Le plaisir et la mort dans la philosophie d'Epicure. Paris, 1951.
Phil 1158.35 Giuffrida, Pasquale. L'epicureismo nella letteratura latina nel I secolo a.c. Torino, 1940. 2v.
Phil 1158.37 Brun, Jean. L'épicurisme. Paris, 1959.

Phil 1158 History of philosophy - Ancient and medieval oriental philosophy - History - Special systems and schools - Epicureans - cont.

Phil 1158.38 Furley, David J. Two studies in the Greek atomists. Princeton, N.J., 1967.
Phil 1158.40 Neck, Gisela. Das Problem der Zeit im Epikureismus. Inaug. Diss. Köln, 1964.

Phil 1170 History of philosophy - Ancient and medieval oriental philosophy - History - Special systems and schools - Neo-Platonists

NEDL Phil 1170.5 Whittaker, Thomas. Neo-Platonists::Study in history of Hellenism. Cambridge, 1901.
Phil 1170.5.3 Whittaker, Thomas. Neo-Platonists. Photoreproduction. 2nd ed. Cambridge, 1928.
Phil 1170.5.5 Whittaker, Thomas. The Neo-Platonists. 4th ed. Olm, 1961.
Phil 1170.6A Bigg, C. Neoplatonism. London, 1895.
Phil 1170.6B Bigg, C. Neoplatonism. London, 1895.
Phil 1170.7 Elsee, Charles. Neoplatonism in relation to Christianity; an essay. Cambridge, 1908.
Phil 1170.8 Corbière, C. Le christianisme et la fin de la philosophie antique. Paris, 1921.
Phil 1170.9 Hultkrantz, C.A. Historisk framställning och granskning utaf hufvudpunkterna i Plotini theoretiska philosophi. Thesis. Stockholm, 1851.
Phil 1170.10 Decoster, V. Des antécédents du Néoplatonisme. Bruxelles, 1872.
Phil 1170.11 Merlan, Philip. From Platonism to Neoplatonism. The Hague, 1953.
Phil 1170.11.2 Merlan, Philip. From Platonism to Neoplatonism. 2nd ed. The Hague, 1960.
Phil 1170.11.3 Merlan, Philip. From Platonism to Neoplatomism. 3rd ed. The Hague, 1969.
Phil 1170.15 Feibleman, James. Religious Platonism. London, 1959.
Phil 1170.17 Koytsogiannopoyloy, D.I. Hellēnikē philosophia kai christianikon dogma. Athens, 1960.
Phil 1170.18 Rist, John M. Eros and Psyche. Toronto, 1964.
Phil 1170.20 Kremer, Klaus. Die neuplatonische Seinsphilosophie und ihre Wirkung auf Thomas von Aquin. Leiden, 1966.
Phil 1170.22 Esser, Hans Peter. Untersuchungen zu Gebet und Gottesverehrung der Neuplatoniker. Köln, 1967.
Phil 1170.24 Theiler, Willy. Forschungen zum Neuplatonismus. Berlin, 1966.
Phil 1170.26 Descombes, Vincent. Le platonisme. Paris, 1971.

Phil 1180 History of philosophy - Ancient and medieval oriental philosophy - History - Special systems and schools - Pyrrhonism

Phil 1180.5F Crousaz, J.P. Examen du Pyrrhonisme. La Haye, 1733.

Phil 1182 History of philosophy - Ancient and medieval oriental philosophy - History - Special systems and schools - Pythagoreans

X Cg Phil 1182.5 Bauer, W. Der altere Pythagoreismus. Berlin, 1897.
Phil 1182.10 Brunschvicg, Léon. Le rôle du pythagorisme dans l'évolution des idées. Paris, 1937.
Phil 1182.15 Fritz, K. Pythagorean politics in southern Italy. N.Y., 1940.
Phil 1182.20 Minar, Edwin L. Early Pythagorean politics and theory. Baltimore, 1942.
Phil 1182.25 Raven, John E. Pythagoreans and Eleatics. Cambridge, 1948.
Phil 1182.30 Ghyks, M.C. Le nombre d'or. v.1-2. Paris, 1952.
Phil 1182.35 Kerenyi, K. Pythagoras und Orpheus. 3. Aufl. Zürich, 1950.
Phil 1182.40 Maddalena, A. I Pitagorici. Bari, 1954.
Phil 1182.45 Rongier, Louis. La religion astrale des pythagoriciens. Paris, 1959.
Phil 1182.50 Capparelli, Vincenzo. Il contributo pilagorico alla scienza. Padova, 1955.
Phil 1182.52 Burkert, Walter. Weisheit und Wissenschaft. Nürnberg, 1962.
Phil 1182.53 Detienne, M. La notion de daimôn dans le pythagorisme ancien. Paris, 1963.
Phil 1182.54 Lévy, Isidore. Recherches esséniennes et pythagoriciennes. Genève, 1965.

Phil 1190 History of philosophy - Ancient and medieval oriental philosophy - History - Special systems and schools - Skeptics

Phil 1190.4 Maccoll, N. Greek sceptics from Pyrrho to Sextus. London, 1869.
Phil 1190.5 Pappenheim, E. Die Tropen der griechischen Skeptiker. Berlin, 1885.
Phil 1190.5.5 Pappenheim, E. Der angebliche Heraklitismus des Skeptikers. Berlin, 1889.
Phil 1190.6 Brochard, Victor. Les skeptiques grecs. Paris, 1887.
Phil 1190.6.5 Brochard, Victor. Les sceptiques grecs. Paris, 1959.
Phil 1190.7 Goedeckmeyer, A. Die Geschichte des griechischen Skeptizismus. Leipzig, 1905.
Phil 1190.9 Patrick, Mary M. The Greek sceptics. N.Y., 1929.
Phil 1190.10 Haas, Leander. De philosophorum scepticorum successionibus. Inaug. Diss. Wurciburgi, 1875.
Phil 1190.15 Robin, Léon. Pyrrkon et le scepticisme grec. 1. éd. Paris, 1944.
Phil 1190.18 Geffers, A. De arcesilae successoribus disputatio. Göttingen, 1845.
Phil 1190.20 Amand de Merdito, Emmanuel. Fatalisme et liberté dans l'antique grecque. Louvain, 1945.
Phil 1190.22 Pra, Mario dal. Lo scetticismo greco. Milano, 1950.
Phil 1190.25 Dumont, Jean-Paul. Les sceptiques grecs. Paris, 1966.
Phil 1190.30 Stough, Charlotte L. Greek skepticism; a study in epistemology. Berkeley, 1969.

Phil 1195 History of philosophy - Ancient and medieval oriental philosophy - History - Special systems and schools - Sophists

Phil 1195.3 Baumhauer, T.C.M. Disputatio literaria. Rhenum, 1844.
Phil 1195.4 Wecklein, N. Die Sophisten und die Sophistik nach den angaben Plato's. Wurzburg, 1866.
Phil 1195.5 Gunning, C.P. Dissertatio inauguralis de sophistis Graeciae. Amstelodami, 1915.
Phil 1195.7 Liljeqvist, Efraim. Antik och modern sofistik. Göteborg, 1896.
Phil 1195.8 Rascher, Wilhelm. De historicae doctrinae apud sophistas maiores vesligus. Inaug. Diss. Gottingae, 1838.
Phil 1195.9 Saitta, G. L'illuminismo della sofistica greca. Milano, 1938.
Phil 1195.10 Seitz, K. Die Schule von Gaza. Heidelberg, 1892.
Phil 1195.11 Dupréel, E. Les sophistes. Neuchâtel, 1949.
Phil 1195.12 Antonelli, M. Figures di sofisti in Platon. Torino, 1948.
Phil 1195.13 Untersteiner, M. Sofisti. Firenze, 1949-62. 2v.
Phil 1195.13.3 Untersteiner, M. The sophists. Oxford, 1954.

Classified Listing

Phil 1195 **Phil 1195   History of philosophy - Ancient and medieval oriental philosophy -**
History - Special systems and schools - Sophists - cont.

Phil 1195.15   Periphanakes, K. Les sophistes et le droit.
Athènes, 1953.

Phil 1195.16   Zadro, Attilio. Ricerche sul linguaggio e sulla logica del
sofista. Padova, 1961.

Phil 1195.17   Grieder, H. Die Bedeutung der Sophistik. Basel, 1962.

Phil 1195.18   Osipova, Valentina. O prirode sofistiki. Erevan, 1964.

Phil 1195.19   Wiśniewski, Bohdan. L'influence des sophistes sur
Aristote, Épicur, stoiciens et sceptiques. Wrocław, 1966.

Phil 1195.20   Levi, Adolfo. Storia della sofistica. Napoli, 1966.

Phil 1195.21   Bowersock, Glen Warren. Greek sophists in the Roman
empire. Oxford, 1969.

Phil 1200   History of philosophy - Ancient and medieval oriental philosophy -
History - Special systems and schools - Stoics

Phil 1200.1   Lipsius, J. Manuductionis ad stoicam philosophiam.
Antverpriae, 1604.

Phil 1200.1.5   Lipsius, J. Manuductionis ad stoicam philosophiam.
Lugduni Batavorum, 1644.

Htn   Phil 1200.2*   Thomasius, J. Exercitatio de stoica mundi exustione.
Leipzig, 1676.

Phil 1200.3   Capes, W.W. Stoicism. London, 1880.

Phil 1200.4.3   Holland, F.M. The reign of the Stoics. N.Y., 1879.

Phil 1200.5   Haake, A. Die Gesellschaftslehre der Stoiker.
Berlin, 1887.

Phil 1200.6   Favre, Jules. La morale des stoiciens. Paris, 1888.

Phil 1200.7   Schmekel, A. Die Philosophie der mittleren Stoa.
Berlin, 1892.

Phil 1200.8   Chollet, A. La morale stoicienne. Paris, n.d.

Phil 1200.9   Werzstein, Otto Heinrich Robert. Die Wandlung der stoichen
Lehre. Newstrelitz, 1892.

Phil 1200.10   Barth, P. Die Stoa. Stuttgart, 1903.

Phil 1200.10.6   Barth, P. Die Stoa. 5. Aufl. Stuttgart, 1941.

Phil 1200.10.7   Barth, P. Die Stoa. 6. Aufl. Stuttgart, 1946.

Phil 1200.11   Stock, St. George. Stoicism. London, 1908.

Phil 1200.13   Tiedemann, D. System der stoischen Philosophie.
Leipzig, 1776. 3v.

Phil 1200.14   Bevan, E.R. Stoics and sceptics. Oxford, 1913.

Phil 1200.14.5   Bevan, E.R. Stoïciens et sceptiques. Paris, 1927.

Phil 1200.15.7   Murray, G. The stoic philosophy. London, 1918.

Phil 1200.16   Thompson, J.W. The last pagan. Chicago, 1917.

Phil 1200.17   Davidson, W.L. The stoic creed. Edinburgh, 1907.

X Cg   Phil 1200.17   Davidson, W.L. The stoic creed. Edinburgh, 1907.

Phil 1200.18   Bréhier, Émile. La théorie des incorporels dans l'ancien
stoïcisme. Thèse. Paris, 1908.

Phil 1200.18.5   Bréhier, Émile. La théorie des incorporels dans l'ancien
stoïcisme. 2e éd. Paris, 1928.

Phil 1200.19   Thamin, Raymond. Un problème moral dans l'antiquité.
Paris, 1884.

Phil 1200.20   Avenel, J. Le stoïcisme et les stoïciens. Paris, 1886.

Phil 1200.21   Dourif, J. Du stoïcisme et du christianisme considérés
dans leurs rapports. Thèse. Paris, 186-?

Phil 1200.22   Brochard, Victor. De assensione Stoici quid Senserint.
Thesis. Parisiis, 1879.

Phil 1200.23   Wenley, R.M. Stoicism and its influence. Boston, 1924.

Phil 1200.24   Lafon, R. Les stoïciens. Paris, n.d.

Phil 1200.25   Karg, F. Stoicos' Aeatheiae falso suspectos.
Lipsiae, 1716.

Phil 1200.26   Sibbern, G. Den stoiske og epikuraeiske moral.
Kjobenhavn, 1853.

Phil 1200.27.2   Jordan, T. The stoic moralists, and the Christians in the
first two centuries. 2d ed. Dublin, 1884.

Phil 1200.28   Boza Masvidal, A.A. El estoicismo. Tesis. Habana, 1922.

Phil 1200.29   Ogereau, F. Essai sur le système philosophique des
stoïciens. Paris, 1885.

Phil 1200.30   Courdaveaux, V. De l'immortalité de l'âme dans le
stoïcisme. Paris, 1857.

Phil 1200.31   Conz, C.P. Abhandlungen für die Geschichte und das
Eigenthümliche der späteren stoischen Philosophie.
Tübingen, 1794.

Phil 1200.32   Hartmann, H. Gewissheit und Wahrheit; der Streit zwischen
Stoa und akademischer Skepsis. Halle (Saale), 1927.

Phil 1200.33   Bonnell, Karl E. Programm. Berlin, 1864.

Phil 1200.34   Gidionsen, W. De es quad stoici naturae comienienter
vivendum esse, principium ponunt. Lipsiae, 1852.

Phil 1200.35   Wevers, Friedrich. Quid Paulus, quid stoici de virtute
docuerint. Meursae, 1876? 3 pam.

Phil 1200.36   Thereianos. Dianeamma Stoikes philosophks.
Tergeoiē, 1892.

Phil 1200.37   Dyroff, Adolf. Die Ethik der alten Stoa. Berlin, 1897.

Phil 1200.38   Reichard, Elias C. Animi perturbationes ex mente
potissimum. Magdeburgi, 1764.

Phil 1200.39   Tsirimbas, Antonios. Die Allgemeinen pädagogischen
Gedanken der alten Stoa. Inaug. Diss. München, 1936.

Phil 1200.40   Mann, W. Beitrag zur Kenntnis der Sozial- und
Staats-philosophischen Anschauungen der Hauptvertreter der
neueren Stoa. Inaug. Diss. Halle (Saale), 1936.

Phil 1200.41   Wiersma, W. Peri telous. Groningen, 1937.

Phil 1200.42   Jong, K.H.E. De stoa; een wereld-philosophie.
Amsterdam, 1937.

Phil 1200.43   Mancini, Guido. L'etica stoica da Zenone a Crisippo.
Padova, 1940.

Phil 1200.44.2   Pohlenz, Max. Die Stoa. 2. und 4. Aufl. Göttingen, 1970.
2v.

Phil 1200.44.5   Pohlenz, Max. Stoa und Staiker. Zürich, 1950.

Phil 1200.50   Agostino, V. Studi sul reostoicismo. Torino, 1950.

Phil 1200.52   Virieux, A. La logique et l'épistémalogie des stoïciens.
Lausanne, 1950.

Phil 1200.53   Martinozzoli, F. Parataxeis. 1st ed. Firenze, 1953.

Phil 1200.55   Goldschmidt, V.E. Le système stoïcien et l'idée de temps.
Paris, 1953.

Phil 1200.56   Simon, Heinrich. Die alte Stoa und ihr Naturbegriff.
Berlin, 1956.

Phil 1200.58   Pire, Georges. Stoïcisme et pedagogie. Liege, 1958.

Phil 1200.60   Brun, Jean. Le stoïcisme. Paris, 1958.

Phil 1200.61   Christensen, J. An essay of the unity of Stoic philosophy.
Copenhagen, 1962.

Phil 1200.62   Edelstein, Ludwig. The meaning of stoicism.
Cambridge, 1966.

Phil 1200.63   Watson, Gerard. The Stoic theory of knowledge.
Belfast, 1966.

Phil 1200.64   Bridoux, André. Le stoïcisme et son influence.
Paris, 1966.

Phil 1200.65   Bodson, Arthur. La Morale sociale des derniers stoïciens,
Sénèque, Epictète et Marc Aurèle. Paris, 1967.

Phil 1200.67   Mignueci, Mario. Il siguificato della logica stoica.
Bologna, 1965.

Phil 1200   History of philosophy - Ancient and medieval oriental philosophy -
History - Special systems and schools - Stoics - cont.

Phil 1200.67.2   Mignueci, Mario. Il significato della logica stoica. 2.
edizione riveduta. Bologna, 1967.

Phil 1200.70   Rist, John Michael. Stoic philosophy. London, 1969.

Phil 1200.72   Rodis-Lewis, Geneviève. La morale stoïcienne.
Paris, 1970.

Phil 1200.74   Problems in stoicism. London, 1971.

Phil 1200.76   Hicks, Robert Drew. Stoic and Epicurean. N.Y., 1962.

Phil 1210   History of philosophy - Ancient and medieval oriental philosophy -
History - Special systems and schools - Other special

Phil 1210.2   Riambourg, Jean B.C. L'école d'Athènes. Paris, 1829.

Phil 1210.5   Henne, Désiré. École de Mégare. Paris, 1843.

Phil 1210.6   Mallet, Charles. Histoire de l'école de Mégare et des
écoles d'Élis et d'Érétrie. Paris, 1845.

Phil 1210.10   Dyroff, A. Der Peripatos über das Greisenalter.
Paderborn, 1939.

Phil 1210.15   Cornaeus, Melchior. Curriculum philosophiae peripateticae.
v.1-2. Herbipoli, 1657.

Phil 1210.16F   Weis, Georg. Nexus philosophiae theorico-politécae
pecipatentica. Prague, 1670.

Phil 1300   History of philosophy - Ancient Roman philosophy - History - General
works

Phil 1300.5   Aubertin, C. De sapientiae doctoribusqui, a ciceronis
morte ad neronis principatum. Parisiis, 1857.

Phil 1300.10A   Clarke, M.L. The Roman mind. London, 1956.

Phil 1300.10B   Clarke, M.L. The Roman mind. London, 1956.

Phil 1300.15   Clarke, M.L. The Roman mind. Cambridge, Mass., 1956.

Phil 1300.20   Levi, Adolfo. Storia della filosofia romana.
Firenze, 1949.

Phil 1350   History of philosophy - Ancient Roman philosophy - History - Special
topics

Phil 1350.5   Martha, Constant. Les moralistes sous l'Empire romain.
Paris, 1866.

Phil 1350.5.4   Martha, Constant. Les moralistes sous l'Empire romain. 4e
éd. Paris, 1881.

Phil 1350.6   Martha, Constant. Etudes morales sur l'antiquité.
Paris, 1883.

Phil 1350.6.3   Martha, Constant. Etudes morales sur l'antiquité.
Paris, 1896.

Phil 1350.7   Gentile, G. Studi sullo stoicismo romano. Trani, 1904.

Phil 1350.8   Arnold, E.V. Roman stoicism. Cambridge, 1911.

Phil 1350.9   Farrar, F.W. Seekers after God. Philadelphia, 1868.

Phil 1350.9.2   Farrar, F.W. Seekers after God. London, 1868.

Phil 1350.9.5   Farrar, F.W. Seekers after God. London, 1891.

Phil 1350.10   Schmidt, W.A. Geschichte der Denk- und Glaubensfreiheit.
Berlin, 1847.

Phil 1350.11   Montée, P. Le stoïcisme à Rome. Paris, 1865.

Phil 1350.12   Nemanic, D. De stoicorum romanorum. Görz, 1880.

Phil 1350.13   Calderini, A. Virtù romana. Milano, 1934.

Phil 1350.13.5   Opporrmann, Hans. Römische Wertbegriffe. Darmstadt, 1967.

Phil 1350.14   Ferrero, L. Storia del pitagorismo nel mondo romano.
Torino, 1955.

Phil 1400   History of philosophy - Byzantine philosophy - History - Special
topics - General works

Phil 1400.5   Tatakēs, B.N. Themata christianikes kai buzantinēs
philosophias. Athens, 1952.

Phil 1400.10   Olhler, Klaus. Antike Philosophie und byzan tinisches
Mittelalter. München, 1969.

Phil 1500   History of philosophy - Medieval western philosophy - Folios
[Discontinued]

Phil 1500.1   Werner, K. Die Entwicklung der mittelalterlicher
Psychologie. Wien, 1876.

Phil 1500.2   Bobenstuber, L. Philosophia thomistica salisburgensis.
Augusta Vindelicorum, 1724.

Phil 1500.3   Vinas, M. de. Philosophia scholastica. Genuae, 1709.
3v.

Phil 1501   History of philosophy - Medieval western philosophy - Pamphlet volumes

Phil 1501   Pamphlet box. Philosophy. Scholastic and mystic.

Phil 1501.2   Pamphlet box. Philosophy. Scholastic and mystic.

Phil 1504   History of philosophy - Medieval western philosophy - Pamphlet volumes -
Special topics - Collected authors

Phil 1504.1-.19.4   Beiträge zur Geschichte der
Philosophie des Mittelalters

Phil 1504.1   Correns, Paul. Die dem Boethius. v.1, pt.1.
Münster, 1891.

Phil 1504.1.2   Baeumker, C. Avencebrolis fons vitae. v.1, pt.2-3.
Münster, 1892. 2v.

NEDL Phil 1504.1.2   Baeumker, C. Avencebrolis fons vitae. v.1, pt.4.
Münster, 1892.

Phil 1504.2   Baumgartner, M. Die Erkenntnislehre. v.2, pt.1.
Münster, 1893.

Phil 1504.2.2   Doctor, Max. Die Philosophie. v.2, pt.2. Münster, 1895.

Phil 1504.2.3   Bülow, G. Des dominicus gundissalinus. v.2, pt.3.
Münster, 1897.

Phil 1504.2.4   Baumgartner, M. Die Philosophie. v.2, pt.4.
Münster, 1896.

Phil 1504.2.5   Nagy, A. Die philosophischen Abhandlungen. v.2, pt.5.
Münster, 1897.

Phil 1504.2.6   Baeumker, C. Die Impossibilia. v.2. pt.6. Münster, 1898.

Phil 1504.3   Domański, B. Die Psychologie des Nemesius. v.3, pt.1.
Münster, 1900.

Phil 1504.3.2   Baeumker, C. Witelo. v.3, pt.2. Münster, 1908.

Phil 1504.3.3   Wittman, M. Die Stellung. v.3, pt.3. Münster, 1900.

Phil 1504.3.4   Worms, M. Die Lehre von der Anfangslosigkeit. v.3, pt.4.
Münster, 1900.

Phil 1504.3.5   Espenberger, J.N. Die Philosophie des Petrus Lombardus.
v.3, pt.5. Münster, 1901.

Phil 1504.3.6   Switalski, B.W. Des Chalcidius Kommentar zu Platos
Timaeus. v.3, pt.6. Münster, 1902.

Phil 1504.4   Willner, H. Die Adelard von Bath Traktat. v.4, pt.1.
Münster, 1903.

Phil 1504.4.2   Baur, L. Gundissalinus de divisione philosophiae. v.4,
pt.2-3. Münster, n.d. 2v.

Phil 1504.4.4   Engelkemper, W. Die religions-philosophische Lehre. v.4.,
pt.4. Münster, 1903.

Phil 1504.4.5A   Schneider, A. Die Psychologie Alberts des Grossen. v.4,
pt.5-6. v.1 rejected 1971. Münster, 1906.

Phil 1504.4.5B   Schneider, A. Die Psychologie Alberts des Grossen. v.4,
pt.5-6. v.2 rejected 1971. Münster, 1906.

Phil 1504   History of philosophy - Medieval western philosophy - Pamphlet volumes - Special topics - Collected authors - cont.

Phil 1504.5	Wittmann, M. Zur Stellung Avencebrolis. v.5, pt.1. Münster, 1906.
Phil 1504.5.2	Hahn S. Thomas Bradwardinus. v.5, pt.2. Münster, 1905.
Phil 1504.5.3	Horten, M. Buch der Ringsteine Alfârâbis. v.5, pt.3. Münster, 1906.
Phil 1504.5.4	Minges, Parthenius. Ist duns scotus indeterminist? v.5, pt.4. Münster, 1905.
Phil 1504.5.5	Krebs, E. Meister Dietrich. v.5, pt.5-6. Münster, 1906.
Phil 1504.6	Ostler, H. Die Psychologie. v.6, pt.1. Münster, 1906.
Phil 1504.6.2	Lappe, J. Nicolaus von Autrecourt. v.6, pt.2. Münster, n.d.
Phil 1504.6.3	Grunwald, G. Geschichte der Gottesbewise. v.6, pt.3. Münster, 1907.
Phil 1504.6.4	Lutz, E. Die Psychologie bonaventuras. v.6, pt.4-5. Münster, 1909.
Phil 1504.6.6	Rousselot, P. Pour l'histoire du problème. v.6. pt.6. Münster, 1908.
Phil 1504.7	Minges, P. Der angebliche Exzessive Realismus Dons Scotus. v.7, pt.1. Münster, 1908.
Phil 1504.7.2	Geyer, B. Sententiae divinitatis. Ein Sentanzenbuch der gilbertschen Schule. v.7, pt.2-3. Münster, 1909.
Phil 1504.7.4	Keicher, O. Raymundus Lullus. v.7, pt.4-5. Münster, 1909.
Phil 1504.7.6	Grünfeld, A. Die Lehre vom göttlichen Willen. v.7, pt.6. Münster, 1909.
Phil 1504.8	Daniels, A. Quellenbeitrage und Untersuchungen zur Geschichte. v.8, pt.1-2. Münster, 1909.
Phil 1504.8.3	Endres, J.A. Petrus Damiani. v.8, pt.3. Münster, 1910.
Phil 1504.8.4	Soto, P.B. Petri Compostellani. v.8, pt.4. Münster, 1912.
Phil 1504.8.5	Reiners, J. Der Nominalismus in der Frühscholastik. v.8, pt.5. Münster, n.d.
Phil 1504.8.6	Vansteenberghe, E. Le "de Ignota Litteratura." v.8, pt.6-7. Münster, 1910.
Phil 1504.9	Baur, L. Die philosophischen Werke des Robert Grosseteste. v.9. Münster, 1912.
Phil 1504.10	Renz, O. Die Synteresis nach dem hl. Thomas von Aquin. v.10, pt.1-2. Münster, 1911.
Phil 1504.10.3	Fischer, J. Die Erkenntnislehre Anselms von Canterbury. Münster, 1911.
Phil 1504.10.4	Guttmann, J. Die philosophischen Lehren. v.10, pt.4. Münster, 1911.
Phil 1504.10.5	Bauer, H. Die Psychologie Alhazens. v.10, pt.5. Münster, 1911.
Phil 1504.10.6	Baeumker, F. Die Lehre Anselms von Canterbury. v.10, pt.6. Münster, 1912.
Phil 1504.11	Steinbüchel, T. Der Zweckgedanke in der Philosophie. v.11, pt.1-2. Münster, 1912.
Phil 1504.11.3	Krebs, E. Theologie und Wissenschaft nach de Lehre. v.11, pt.3-4. Münster, 1912.
Phil 1504.11.5	Rohner, A. Das Schöpfungsproblem bei Moses Maimonides. v.11, pt.5. Münster, 1913.
Phil 1504.11.6	Dreiling, R. Der Konzeptualismus. v.11, pt.6. Münster, 1913.
Phil 1504.12	Gaul, L. Alberts des Grossen Verhältnis zu Palto. v.12, pt.1. Münster, n.d.
Phil 1504.12.2	Kroll, J. Die Lehren des Hermes Trismegistos. v.12, pt.2-4. Münster, 1914.
Phil 1504.12.5	Würschmidt, J. Theodoricus Teutonicus de Vriberg De iride et radialibus impressionibus. v.12, pt.5-6. Münster, 1914.
Phil 1504.13	Schedler, M. Die Philosophie des Macrobius. v.13, pt.1. Münster, 1916.
Phil 1504.13.2	Probst, J.H. La mystique de Ramon Lull et l'art de contemplació. v.13, pt.2-3. Münster, 1914.
Phil 1504.13.5	Schulemann, G. Das Kausalprinzip. v.13, pt.5. Münster, 1915.
Phil 1504.13.6	Baeumker, F. Das Inevitable des Honorius Augustodunensis. v.13, pt.6. Münster, 1914.
Phil 1504.14	Graf, G. Des Theodor Abû Kurra Traktat. v.14, pt.1. Münster, n.d.
Phil 1504.14.2	Vansteenberghe, E. Autour de la "Docte Ignorance." v.14, pt.2-4. Münster, 1915.
Phil 1504.14.5	Hertling, G. von. Albertus Magnus, Beiträge zu seiner Würdigung. 2. Aufl. v.14, pt.5-6. Münster, 1914.
Phil 1504.15	Stadler, H.J. Albertus Magnus. v.15,16. Münster, 1916. 2v.
Phil 1504.17	Beemelmans, F. Zeit und Ewigkeit nach Thomas von Aquino. v.17, pt.1. Münster, 1914.
Phil 1504.17.2	Endes, J.A. Forschungen zur Geschichte der frümittelalterlichen Philosophie. v.17, pt.2-3. Münster, 1915.
Phil 1504.17.4	Schneider, A. Die abendländische Spekulation. v.17, pt.4. Münster, 1915.
Phil 1504.17.5	Grabmann, M. Forschungen über die lateinischen Aristoteles. v.17, pt.5-6. Münster, 1916.
Phil 1504.18	Michel, K. Der "liber de consonanci a nature et gracie." v.18, pt.1. Münster, 1915.
Phil 1504.18.2	Bliemetzrieder, P. Anselms von Laon systematische Sentenzen. v.18, pt.2-3. Münster, n.d.
Phil 1504.18.4	Baur, L. Die Philosophie des Robert Grosseteste. v.18, pt.4-6. Münster, n.d.
Phil 1504.19	Müller, W. Der Staat in seinen Beziehungen zur sittlichen. v.19, pt.1. Münster, 1916.
Phil 1504.19.2	Hessen, J. Die Begründung der Erkenntnis. v.19, pt.2-3. Münster, 1916.
Phil 1504.19.4	Ebner, J. Die Erkenntnislehre Richards von St. Viktor. v.19, pt.4-6. Münster, 1917.
Phil 1504.20	Beiträge zur Geschichte der Philosophie des Mittelalters. Münster. 20+ 60v.
Phil 1504.25	Beiträge zur Geschichte. Supplement. Münster. 2-3,1923-1935 3v.
Phil 1504.27	Medieval philosophical texts in translation. Milwaukee. 6-19+ 8v.
Phil 1504.30	Studia scholastico-Scotistica. Romae. 1,1968+ 4v.
Phil 1504.32	Minio-Palvello, Lorenzo. Twelfth century logic. Roma, 1956- 2v.
Phil 1504.50F	Les philosophes belges. Louvain. 1-15,1902-1941 12v.

Phil 1505 - 1530   History of philosophy - Medieval western philosophy - Pamphlet volumes - Special topics - Individual authors (A-Z)

Phil 1505.1	Appel, H. Lehre der Scholastiker von der Synteresis. Rostock, 1891.
Phil 1505.3	Association Guiellaume Bodé. Quelques aspects de l'humanisme médiéval. Paris, 1943.
Phil 1505.4	Aspelin, Gunnar. Ur medeltidens tankevärld. Stockholm, 1959.
Phil 1505.5	Abbagmano, N. La filosofia medievale. Bari, 1963.

Phil 1505 - 1530   History of philosophy - Medieval western philosophy - Pamphlet volumes - Special topics - Individual authors (A-Z) - cont.

Phil 1505.7	Alessio, Franco Paolo. Studi e ricerche di filosofia medievale. Pavia, 1961.
Phil 1506.1	Barach, C.S. Zur Geschichte des Nominalis von Roscellin. Wien, 1866.
Phil 1506.2	Blanc, Elie. Manuale philosophiae scholasticae. Lugduni, 1901. 2v.
Phil 1506.2.5	Blanc, Elie. Traité de philosophie scolastique. Lyon, 1909. 3v.
Phil 1506.4	Baeumker, Clemens. Platonismus in Mittelalter. München, 1916.
Phil 1506.7	Brade, W.R.V. From Plotinus to St. Thomas Aquinas. London, 1916.
Phil 1506.8	Bruni, Gerardo. Riflessioni sulla scolastica. Roma, 1927.
Phil 1506.8.10	Bruni, Gerardo. Progressive scholasticism. Saint Louis, Mo., 1929.
Phil 1506.9	Barbedette, D. Manière d'enseigner la philosophie scolastique. Paris, 1936.
Phil 1506.10	Brehser, Emile. La philosophie du moyen âge. Paris, 1949.
Phil 1506.11	Bertala, E. Saggi e studi di filosofia medievale. Padova, 1951.
Phil 1506.12	Bonafede, Giulio. Saggi sulla filosofia medievale. Torino, 1951.
Phil 1506.12.5	Bonafede, Giulio. Storia della filosofia medievale. 2. ed. Roma, 1957.
Phil 1506.13	Bogliolo, Luigi. Il problema della filosofia cristiana. Brescia, 1959.
Phil 1506.14	Burch, G.B. Early medieval philosophy. N.Y., 1951.
Phil 1507.1	Cupély. Esprit de la philosophie scolastique. Paris, 1867.
Phil 1507.3	Currie, F.J. Universal scholastic philosophy publicly defended. n.p., 1928.
Phil 1507.4	Coulton, G.G. Studies in medieval thought. London, 1940.
Phil 1507.5	Curtis, S.J. A short history of western philosophy in middle ages. London, 1950.
Phil 1507.6	Congresso Internationale di Studi Umanistici, Rome. Umanesimo e scienza politica. Milano, 1951.
Phil 1507.7	Copleston, F.C. Medieval philosophy. London, 1952.
Phil 1507.7.2	Copleston, F.C. Medieval philosophy. N.Y., 1952.
Phil 1507.8	Congressus Scholasticus Internationalis, Rome. Scholastico ratione historico-critica instaurada. Romae, 1951.
Phil 1507.9	Cilento, Vicenzo. Medioevo monastico e scolastico. Milano, 1961.
Phil 1508.1.2	Deussen, Paul. Die Philosophie des Mittelalters. 2. Aufl. Leipzig, 1919.
Phil 1508.2	Dempf, Alois. Die Hauptform mittelalterlicher Weltanschanung. München, 1925.
Phil 1508.2.5	Dempf, Alois. Das Unendliche in der mittelalterlichen Metaphysik und in der Kantischendialektik. Münster, 1925.
Phil 1508.2.12	Dempf, Alois. Christliche Philosophie. 2. Aufl. Bonn, 1952.
Phil 1508.3	Delhaye, Philippe. La philosophie chrétienne au Moyen Âge. Paris, 1959.
Phil 1509.5	Endres, J.A. Geschichte der mittelalterlichen Philosophie. 2. Aufl. Kemplin, 1911.
Phil 1510.5	Fremantle, A.J. The age of belief. Boston, 1955.
Phil 1510.10	Fleckenskein, J.O. Scholastik, Barock exakte Wissenschaften. Einsiedeln, 1949.
Phil 1511.1A	Grabmann, M. Geschichte der scholastischen Methode. Freiburg, 1909. 2v.
Phil 1511.1B	Grabmann, M. Geschichte der scholastischen Methode. v.2. Freiburg, 1909.
Phil 1511.1.5	Grabmann, M. Der Gegenwartswert der geschichtlichen Erforschung der mittelalterlichen Philosophie. Wien, 1913.
Phil 1511.1.10	Grabmann, M. Die Philosophie des Mittelalters. Berlin, 1921.
Phil 1511.1.15	Grabmann, M. Mittelalterliches Geistesleben. München, 1926-36. 3v.
Phil 1511.3	Gilson, Étienne. Études de philosophie médiévale. Strasbourg, 1921.
Phil 1511.3.5	Gilson, Étienne. La philosophie au moyen âge. v.2. Paris, 1922.
Phil 1511.3.7	Gilson, Étienne. La philosophie au moyen âge. 2e éd. Paris, 1944.
Phil 1511.3.10	Gilson, Étienne. L'esprit de la philosophie médiévale. Paris, 1932. 2v.
Phil 1511.3.11	Gilson, Étienne. L'esprit de la philosophie. Paris, 1948.
Phil 1511.3.12	Gilson, Étienne. L'esprit de la philosophie médiévale. 2e éd. Paris, 1944.
Phil 1511.3.13.5A	Gilson, Étienne. The spirit of mediaeval philosophy. N.Y., 1940.
Phil 1511.3.13.5B	Gilson, Étienne. The spirit of mediaeval philosophy. N.Y., 1940.
Phil 1511.3.13.5C	Gilson, Étienne. The spirit of mediaeval philosophy. N.Y., 1940.
Phil 1511.3.13.10A	Gilson, Étienne. History of Christian philosophy in the Middle Ages. N.Y., 1955.
Phil 1511.3.13.10B	Gilson, Étienne. History of Christian philosophy in the Middle Ages. N.Y., 1955.
Phil 1511.3.13.15	Gilson, Étienne. History of Christian philosophy in the Middle Ages. London, 1955.
Phil 1511.3.13	Gunn, W.W. A modern social philosophy. Cutting, 1937.
Phil 1511.3.15	Gilson, Étienne. Les sources gréco-arabes de l'augustinisme avicennisant. Paris, 1930.
Phil 1511.3.17	Gilson, Étienne. Introduction à la philosophie chrétienne. Paris, 1960.
Phil 1511.3.19	Gilson, Étienne. Die Geschichte der christlichen Philosophie. Paderborn, 1937.
Phil 1511.3.20	Boehner, Philotheus. Christliche Philosophie von ihren Anfängen bis Nikol von Cues. 3e Aufl. Paderborn, 1954.
Phil 1511.3.22	Gilson, Étienne. Reason and revelation in the Middle Ages. N.Y., 1959.
Phil 1511.3.23	Gilson, Étienne. Medieval universalism and its present value. N.Y., 1937.
Phil 1511.4	Glossner, M. Das Objektivität-Prinzip der aristotelisch-scholastische Philosophie. Regensburg, 1880.
Phil 1511.5	Gorce, M.M. Science moderne et philosophie médiévale. Paris, 1938.
Phil 1511.6	Garin, E. Dal medioeno al rinascimento. Firenze, 1950.
Phil 1512.1	Haureau, B. De la philosophie scolastique. Paris, 1850. 2v.
Phil 1512.1.2	Haureau, B. Histoire de la philosophie scolastique. Paris, 1872-80. 3v.

Phil 1512.2	Harper, Thomas. Metaphysics of the school. London, 1879. 3v.
Phil 1512.7	Hessen, John. Patristische und scholastische Philosophie. Breslau, 1922.
Phil 1512.9	Hochsteller, E. Die subjektiven GrundlagenDer scholastischen Ethik. Halle, 1915.
Phil 1512.10	Hart, C.A. Aspects of the new scholastic philosophy. N.Y., 1932.
Phil 1512.11	Hugon, Edward. Cursus philosophiae thomistica. 3. éd. v.1-6. Paris, 1928. 3v.
Phil 1512.12	Hawkins, D.J.B. A sketch of mediaeval philosophy. London, 1946.
Phil 1512.14	Hyman, Arthur. Philosophy in the Middle Ages. N.Y., 1967.
Phil 1514.2	Jeanneau, E. La philosophie médiévale. Paris, 1963.
Phil 1515.1	Kaulich, W. Geschichte der scholastischen Philosophie. Prag, 1863.
Phil 1515.2	Kleutgen, R.P. La philosophie scolastique. Paris, 1868-70. 4v.
Phil 1515.2.5	Gilen, Leonhard. Kleutgen und die Theorie des Erkenntnisbildes. Meisenheim, 1956.
Phil 1515.3	Knowles, David. The evolution of medieval thought. Baltimore, 1962.
Phil 1516.1.2	Littlejohn, J.M. Political theory of the schoolmen. College Springs, 1894.
Phil 1516.2	Ligeard, H. La théologie scolastique. Paris, 1908.
Phil 1516.3	Lehmen, Alfonso. Lehrbuch der Philosophie. 4e Aufl. n.p., 1912-19. 4v.
Phil 1516.3.5	Lehmen, Alfonso. Lehrbuch der Philosophie. Freiburg, 1923.
Phil 1516.4	Leff, Gordon. Medieval thought. Harmondsworth, 1958.
Phil 1517.1	Mignon, A. Les origines de la scolastique. Paris, n.d. 2v.
Phil 1517.3	Mercier, Désiré. A manual of modern scholastic philosophy. 2nd ed. London, 1917. 2v.
Phil 1517.3.5	Mercier, Désiré. A manual of modern scholastic philosophy. 3rd ed. London, 1928. 2v.
Phil 1517.4	Martigné, P. de. La scolastique et les traditions franciscaines. Paris, 1888.
Phil 1517.5	Masnovo, Amato. Da Guglielmo d'Auvergne a San Tomaso d'Aquino. Milano, 1930. 2v.
Phil 1517.5.5	Masnovo, Amato. Da Guglielmo d'Auvergne. 2. ed. Milano, 1946. 3v.
Phil 1517.6	Macdonald, A.J. Authority and reason in the early middle ages. London, 1933.
Phil 1517.7	Maier, A. Metaphysische Hintergrunde der spatscholastischen Naturphilosophie. Roma, 1955.
Phil 1517.8	Maier, A. Ausgehedes Mittelalter. Roma, 1964. 2v.
Phil 1517.10	Michalski, Konstanty. La philosophie au XIVe siècle; six études. Frankfurt, 1969.
Phil 1518.2	Nardi, Bruno. Studi di filosofia medievale. Roma, 1960.
Phil 1518.5	Nitsche, August. Naturer Kenntnis und politisches Handeln im Mittelalter. Körpen, 1967.
Phil 1519.1	Overbeck, Franz. Vorgeschichte und Jugend der mittelalterlichen Scholastek. Basel, 1917.
Phil 1520.2	Picavet, F. Histoire...des philosophies médiévales. Paris, 1905.
Phil 1520.2.5	Picavet, F. Essais sur l'histoire générale et comparée des theologies et des philosophies médiévales. Paris, 1913.
Phil 1520.3	Perrier, J.L. Revival of scholastic philosophy, XIX century. N.Y., 1909.
Phil 1520.3.3	Perrier, J.L. Revival of scholastic philosophy, XIX century. N.Y., 1909.
Phil 1520.4	Patru, G.A. De la philosophie du moyen âge. Paris, 1848.
Phil 1520.5	Pieper, Josef. Wahrheit der Dinge. München, 1947.
Phil 1520.5.5	Pieper, Josef. Scholastik. München, 1960.
Phil 1520.5.10	Pieper, Josef. Scholasticism. N.Y., 1960.
Phil 1520.6	Pelzer, Auguste. Etudes d'histoire littéraire sur la scolastique médiévale. Louvain, 1964.
Phil 1522.1	Ritter, A.H. Die christliche Philosophie. Göttingen, 1858-9.
Phil 1522.1.5	Ritter, A.H. Histoire de la philosophie chretienne. Paris, 1843-4. 2v.
Phil 1522.2	Rousselot, X. Etudes sur la philosophie...moyen âge. Paris, 1840-42. 3v.
Phil 1522.3	Rickaby, Joseph. Scholasticism. London, 1908.
Phil 1522.3.3	Rickaby, Joseph. Scholasticism. N.Y., 1908.
Phil 1522.4	Richard, J. Introduction à l'étude et à l'enseignement de la scolastique. Paris, 1913.
Phil 1522.5	Rougier, Louis. La scolastique et le thomisme. Paris, 1925.
Phil 1522.5.5	Rougier, Louis. Histoire d'une faillite philosophique: la scolastique. Paris, 1966.
Phil 1522.5.15	Descoqs, P. Thomisme et scolastique à propos de M. Rougier. 2e éd. Paris, 1935.
Phil 1522.6	Ryan, J.K. Basic principles and problems of philosophy. Washington, 1939.
Phil 1523.1	Stöckl, A. Geschichte der Philosophie der Mittelalters. Mainz, 1864-6. 3v.
Phil 1523.6	Saitta, Giuseppe. La scolastica del secolo XVI e la politica dei Gesuiti. Torino, 1911.
Phil 1523.6.5	Saitta, Giuseppe. Le origine del neo-tomismo. Bari, 1912.
Phil 1523.7	Stadelmann, R. Vom Geist des ausgehenden Mittelalters. Halle, 1929.
Phil 1523.8	Schneider, Artur. Die Erkenntnislehre bei Beginn der Scholastik. Fulda, 1921.
Phil 1523.10	Simard, G. Les maîtres chrétiens de nos pensées et de nos vies. Ottawa, 1937.
Phil 1523.11	Slesser, Henry H. Order and disorder; a study of mediaeval principles. London, 1945.
Phil 1523.12	Steenberghen, F. Atistote en Occident. Louvain, 1946.
Phil 1523.12.5	Steenberghen, F. Philosophie des Mittelalters. Bern, 1950.
Phil 1523.12.10	Steenberghen, F. Aristotle in the West. Louvain, 1955.
Phil 1523.12.15	Steenberghen, F. Directives pour la confection d'une monographie. Louvain, 1961.
Phil 1523.14	Shapiro, Herman. Medieval philosophy. N.Y., 1964.
Phil 1523.16	Sprengard, Karl Anton. Systematisch-historische Untersuchungen zur Philosophie des XIV. Jahrhunderts. Bonn, 196-.
Phil 1523.20	Sassen, Ferdinand. Wijsgerig denken in de middeleeuwen. Haarlem, 1965.
Phil 1524.1	Townsend, W.J. The great schoolmen of the Middle Ages. London, 1881.
Phil 1524.2	Taylor, H.O. The mediaeval mind. London, 1911. 2v.
Phil 1524.2.15A	Taylor, H.O. The mediaeval mind. 4th ed. Cambridge, Mass., 1949. 2v.

Phil 1524.2.15B	Taylor, H.O. The mediaeval mind. 4th ed. Cambridge, Mass., 1949. 2v.
Phil 1524.3	Trikál, Josef. Benezető a közepkori kereztény hölcselet tortenelmehe. Budapest, 1913.
Phil 1524.4	Thomas, Elliott C. History of the schoolmen. London, 1941.
Phil 1524.5	Traktenberg, O.V. Ocherki po istorii zapadno-evropeiskoi Srednovekovoi filosofii. Moskva, 1957.
Phil 1526.1	Verweyen, Johannes M. Philosophie und Theologie im Mittelalter. Bonn, 1911.
Phil 1526.2	Verweyen, Johannes M. Die Philosophie der Mittelalters. 2e Aufl. Berlin, 1926.
Phil 1526.3	Vaintrob, M. Istoriia srednevekovoi filosofii. Riga, 1929.
Phil 1526.4	Vignaux, Paul. Le pensée au moyen âge. Paris, 1938.
Phil 1526.4.5	Vignaux, Paul. Philosophie au moyen-âge. Paris, 1958.
Phil 1526.4.10	Vignaux, Paul. Philosophy in the Middle Ages. N.Y., 1959.
Phil 1527.1	Wulf, M. de. Histoire de la philosophie médiévale. Louvain, 1900.
Phil 1527.1.5A	Wulf, M. de. History of medieval philosophy. 3. ed. London, 1909.
Phil 1527.1.5B	Wulf, M. de. History of medieval philosophy. 3. ed. London, 1909.
Phil 1527.1.5.9	Wulf, M. de. History of medieval philosophy. London, 1926. 2v.
Phil 1527.1.5.20	Wulf, M. de. History of mediaeval philosophy. N.Y., 1952.
Phil 1527.1.6	Wulf, M. de. Histoire de la philosophie médiévale. 4e éd. Louvain, 1912.
Phil 1527.1.6.5	Wulf, M. de. Histoire de la philosophie médiévale. 5e éd. Louvain, 1924-25. 2v.
Phil 1527.1.6.7A	Wulf, M. de. Histoire de la philosophie médiévale. 6e éd. Louvain, 1934-47. 3v.
Phil 1527.1.6.7B	Wulf, M. de. Histoire de la philosophie médiévale. 6e éd. Louvain, 1934-47. 2v.
Phil 1527.1.6.25	Rand, E.K. Histoire de la philosophie médiévale. v.1-2. Cambridge, Mass., 1934.
Phil 1527.1.8	Wulf, M. de. Geschichte der mittelalterlichen Philosophie. Tübingen, 1913.
Phil 1527.1.9	Wulf, M. de. Scholasticism old and new. Dublin, 1910.
Phil 1527.1.9.5	Wulf, M. de. Scholasticism old and new. N.Y., 1907.
Phil 1527.1.10	Wulf, M. de. An introduction to scholastic philosophy. N.Y., 1956.
Phil 1527.1.15	Wulf, M. de. Philosophy and civilization in the Middle Ages. Princeton, 1922.
Phil 1527.1.16	Wulf, M. de. Philosophy and civilization in the Middle Ages. Princeton, 1922-24.
Phil 1527.1.17	Wulf, M. de. Mediaeval philosophy illustrated from the system of Thomas Aquinas. Cambridge. 1922.
Phil 1527.1.50	Hommage à Monsieur le Professeur Maurice de Wulf. Louvain, 1934.
Phil 1527.2	Werner, Karl. Die Scholastik des späteren Mittelalters. Wien, 1881. 4v.
Phil 1527.3	Wyser, Paul. Der Thomismus. Bern, 1951.
Phil 1527.4	Weinberg, J.R. A short history of medieval philosophy. Princeton, 1964.
Phil 1527.5	Weber, Hans Emil. Der Einfluss der protestantischen Schulphilosophie auf die orthodox-lutherische Dogmatik. Darmstadt, 1969.
Phil 1530.10	Zaragüeta Bengoechea, Juan. Una introducción moderna a la filosofía escolástica. Granada, 1946.

Phil 1535.1	Balmès, Jaime. Philosophie fondamentale. Paris, 1852. 3v.
Phil 1535.1.5	Balmès, Jaime. Filosofía fundamental. Paris, 18- . 2v.
Phil 1535.1.10	Balmes, Giacomo. La filosofia fondamentale. v.1-2. Napoli, 1851.
Phil 1535.1.15	Balmes, Giacomo. Corso di filosofia elementare. v.1-4. Firenze, 1854.
Phil 1535.1.25	Balmes, Jaime. Lehrbuch der Elemente der Philosophie. v.1-4. Regensburg, 1861.
Phil 1535.1.35	Balmes, Jaime. El criterio. Madrid, 1929.
Phil 1535.1.40	Balmes, Jaime. Habla Balmes. Barcelona, 1958.
Phil 1535.2	Boylesve, M. de. Cursus philosophie. Paris, 1855.
Phil 1535.3	Buscarini, G. Discussioni di filosofia razionale. Milano, 1857.
Htn Phil 1535.4*	Eustachius a S. Paulo. Summa philosophiae quadripartita. Cantabrigiae, 1698.
Htn Phil 1535.4.4*	Eustachius a S. Paulo. Summa philosophiae quadripartita. Cantabrigiae, 1640.
Htn Phil 1535.4.5*	Eustachius a S. Paulo. Summa philosophiae quadripartita. Cantabrigiae, 1640.
Phil 1535.5	Liberatore, M. Elementi di filosofia. Livorno, 1852.
Phil 1535.5.10	Liberatore, M. Della conoscenza intellectuale. 2e ed. Roma, 1873-74. 2v.
Phil 1535.5.15	Liberatore, M. Institutiones philosophicae. v.1-3. 10th ed. Romae, 1857.
Phil 1535.6.14	Rickaby, Joseph. Moral philosophy. 4th ed. London, 1919.
Phil 1535.6.20	Maher, Michael. Psychology. 6th ed. v.5. London, 1909.
Phil 1535.8	P. Institutiones philosophiae. Parisiis, 1868. 2v.
Phil 1535.9	Pesch, T. Institutiones philosophiae naturalis. Friburgi, 1880.
Phil 1535.9.5	Pesch, T. Institutiones logicae et ontologicae quas secundum principia S. Thomae Aguinatis. Friburgi, 1914.
Phil 1535.10	Pestalozza, A. Elementi di filosofia. Milano, 1857. 2v.
Phil 1535.11	Stöckl, A. Lehrbuch der Philosophie. Mainz, 1876. 2v.
Phil 1535.11.8	Stöckl, A. Lehrbuch der Philosophie. Mainz, 1905-12. 2v.
Phil 1535.12	Zigliara, F.T.M. Summa philosophica in usum scholarum. Lyon, 1884. 3v.
Phil 1535.12.5	Zigliara, F.T.M. Summa philosophica in usum scholarum. 15. ed. v.3. Paris, 1912.
Htn Phil 1535.13*	Mendoza, P.H. de. Disputationes de universa philosophia. Lugduni, 1617.
Htn Phil 1535.14*	Zabarella, J. De rebus naturalibus. Coloniae, 1597.
Htn Phil 1535.15*	Bonaventura, St., Cardinal. Cursus philosophicus. n.p., 1742.
Phil 1535.15.5	Bonaventura, St., Cardinal. Summa totius philosophiae Aristotelicae. pt.1-2. Romae, 1635. 2v.
Phil 1535.16	Schneider, C.M. Das Wissen Gottes. v.1-4. Regensburg, 1884-86. 3v.

Classified Listing

109

Phil 1535   History of philosophy - Medieval western philosophy - History - Manuals, outlines, etc. - cont.

Phil 1535.17	Farges, A. Études philosophiques. Paris, 1893-1902. 8v.
Phil 1535.18	Gredt, Joseph. Elementa philosophiae Aristotelico-Thomisticae. Romae, 1899.
Phil 1535.18.3	Gredt, Joseph. Elementa philosophiae Aristotelico-Thomisticae. 12. ed. Barcinone, 1958.
Phil 1535.18.4	Gredt, Joseph. Elementa philosophia. Barcinone, 1961. 2v.
Phil 1535.18.5	Gredt, Joseph. Die aristotellisch-thomistische Philosophie. Freiburg, 1935. 2v.
Phil 1535.19	Instittutionum philosophicarum cursus. v.2-3. Besancon, 1821. 2v.
Phil 1535.21	Biedermann, G. Natur-Philosophie. Prag, 1887-89. 3v.
Phil 1535.21.2	Biedermann, G. Philosophie des Geistes. Prag, 1886.
Phil 1535.22	Guidi, P.L. Principia philosophica. v.1-2. Florentiae, 1913-14.
Phil 1535.23	Levesque, l'abbé. Précis de philosophie. Paris, 1912.
Phil 1535.24	Urráburu, J.J. Institutiones philosophicae. Vallistoleli, 1891-1908. 8v.
Phil 1535.25	Bensa, A.M. Manuel de logique. Paris, 1855.
Phil 1535.26	Brothers of the Christian Schools. Elementary course of Christian philosophy. N.Y., 1893.
Phil 1535.27.2	Huber, Sebastian. Grundzüge der Logik und Noëtik. Paderborn, 1906.
Phil 1535.29	Carrasquilla, R.M. Lecciones de metafísica y ética. 2. ed. Bogotá, 1918.
Phil 1535.30	Shallo, Michael. Lessons in scholastic philosophy. Philadelphia, 1916.
Phil 1535.31	Guerinois, J.C. Clypeus philosophiae Thomisticae. Venetiis, 1729. 7v.
Phil 1535.32	Cherubini, F. Cursus philosophicus. Romae, 1904. 2v.
Phil 1535.33	La Scala, Puis. Cursus philosophicus ad usum seminariorum. Parisiis, 1910. 2v.
Phil 1535.34	Schneid, Mathias. Spezielle Metaphysik im Geiste des Heil. Paderborn, 1890-92. 2v.
Phil 1535.35	Vallet, Pa. Praelectiones philosophicae. Parisiis, 1878-9. 2v.
Phil 1535.36.12	Reinstadler, S. Elementa philosophiae scholasticae. 11. and 12. ed. Friburgi, 1923. 2v.
Phil 1535.36.13	Reinstadler, S. Elementa philosophiae scholasticae. 13. ed. Friburgi , 1929. 2v.
Phil 1535.37	Marxuach, F. Compendium dialecticae, critical et ontologial. Barcinone, 1926.
Phil 1535.38	LeRohellec, J. Problèmes philosophiques. Paris, 1932.

Phil 1540   History of philosophy - Medieval western philosophy - History - Special topics

Phil 1540.1	Koehler, H.O. Realismus und Nominalismus. Gotha, 1858.
Phil 1540.7.2	Jundt, A. Les anis de Dieu au quatorzième siècle. Thèse. Strasbourg, 1879.
Phil 1540.8	Knappe, O.F. The scholastic theory of the species sensibilis. Washington, 1915.
Phil 1540.9	Werner, Karl. Die nominalisirende Psychologie der Scholastik des späteren Mittelalters. Wien, 1882.
Phil 1540.11	Verweyen, Johannes. Das Problem der Willensfreiheit. Heidelberg, 1909.
Phil 1540.13	Serras, Pereira, M. A tese escolastica do composto humano. Diss. Coimbra, 1923.
Phil 1540.14	Heuel, Meinolf. Die Lehre vom Human Naturale bei Thomas Aquin, Bonaventura und Duns Scotus. Inaug. Diss. Koblenz, 1927.
Phil 1540.15	Reiners, Josef. Der aristotelische Realismus in der Frühscholastik. Inaug.-Diss. Bonn, 1907.
Phil 1540.16	Landry, Bernard. L'idée de chrétienté chez les scolastiques du XIIIe siècle. Paris, 1929.
Phil 1540.17A	Winter, E.K. Die Sozialmetaphysik der Scholastik. Leipzig, 1929.
Phil 1540.17B	Winter, E.K. Die Sozialmetaphysik der Scholastik. Leipzig, 1929.
Phil 1540.18	Heitz, T. Essai historique sur les rapports entre la philosophie et la foi. Thèse. Paris, 1909.
Phil 1540.19	Gessner, Jakob. Die Abstraktionslehre·in der Scholastik bis Thomas von Aquin. Inaug.-Diss. Tulda, 1930.
Phil 1540.20	Buonamici, G. La dottrina della conoscenza secondo Aristotele e la scuola. pt.1. Pisa, 1930.
Phil 1540.21	Garin, Pierre. La théorie de l'idée suivant l'école thomiste. Thèse. Bruges, 1932.
Phil 1540.22	Orth, Albert. Untersuchungen zu Prinzipien Fragen der scholastischen Erkenntnistheorie. Bahenhausen, 1933.
Phil 1540.23	Bonfarri, G. Lo studio della natura nell'umanesimo. Mantova, 1937.
Phil 1540.24	DeMatteis, F. L'occasionalismo e il suo sviluppo nel pensiero di N. Malebranche. Napoli, 193-.
Phil 1540.25	Rüegg, Walter. Cicero und der Humanismus; formale Untersuchungen über Petrarca und Erasmus. Zürich, 1946.
Phil 1540.26	Association Guillaume Bude, Paris. Quelques aspects de l'humanisme médiéval. Paris, 1943.
Phil 1540.27	Mélanges Auguste Pelzer. Louvain, 1947.
Phil 1540.28	Maier, A. An der Grenze von Scholastik und Naturwissenschaft. 2. Aufl. Roma, 1952.
Phil 1540.29	Strauss, Leo. Persecution and the art of writing. Glencoe, Ill., 1952. 2v.
Phil 1540.30	Böhner, P. Medieval logic. Chicago, 1952.
Phil 1540.30.2	Böhner, P. Medieval logic. Manchester, 1952.
Phil 1540.32	Renucci, P. L'aventure de l'humanisme européen au moyen-âge. Clermont-Ferrand, 1953.
Phil 1540.34	Steinbueckel, T. Vom Menschenbild des christlichen Mittelalters. Basel, 1953.
Phil 1540.35.5	Steenberghen, Fernand van. La philosophie au XIIE siècle. Louvain, 1966.
Phil 1540.36	Fortin, E.L. Christianisme et culture phillosophique au cinquième siècle. Paris, 1959.
Phil 1540.38	Zilli, José B. Introducción a la psicología de los conimbricenses. Bonn, 1961.
Phil 1540.40	Dempf, Alois. Metaphysik des Mittelalters. München, 1930.
Phil 1540.41	Ritter, Gerhard. Via Antigue und via Moderna auf den deutschen Universitaeten des XV Jahrhunderts. Darmstadt, 1963.
Phil 1540.43	Dempf, Alois. Metafisica de la Edad Media. Madrid, 1957.
Phil 1540.45	Egentin, Richard. Gottesfreundschaft. Augsburg, 1928.
Phil 1540.47	Talamo, Salvatore. L'aristotelismo della scolastica nella storia. 3. ed. Siena, 1881.
Phil 1540.50A	Garin, Eugenio. Studi sul platonismo medievale. Firenze, 1958.
Phil 1540.50B	Garin, Eugenio. Studi sul platonismo medievale. Firenze, 1958.

Phil 1540   History of philosophy - Medieval western philosophy - History - Special topics - cont.

Phil 1540.55	Gregory, Tullio. Platonismo medievale. Roma, 1958.
Phil 1540.60	Axters, Stephanus. Scholastick Lexicon. Antwerpen, 1937.
Phil 1540.70	Vallese, Giulia. Da Dante ad Erasmo. Napoli, 1962.
Phil 1540.72	Cilento, V. La forma Aristotelica in una "Quaestio" medievale. Napoli, 1961.
Phil 1540.74	Lemny, Richard. Abu Ma'shar and Lah'n Aristoteliaram. Beirut, 1962.
Phil 1540.75	Auer, J. Die Entwicklung der Grandenlehre in der Hochscholastik. v.2. Freiburg, 1951.
Phil 1540.77	Armstrong, O.H. Christian faith and Greek philosophy. N.Y., 1964.
Phil 1540.78	Nothdurft, Kalus Dieter. Studien zum Einfluss Senecas auf die Philosophie und Theologie des 12. Jahrhunderts. Leiden, 1963.
Phil 1540.79	Grabmann, Martin. Interpretazioni medievale del voüsnointinós. Padova, 1965.
Phil 1540.82	Krings, Hermann. Ordo. Halle, 1941.
Phil 1540.84	Prezioso, Faustino Antonio. La species medievale e i prodromi del fenomenismo moderno. Padova, 1963.
Phil 1540.85	Bérubé, Camille. La connaissance de l'individuel au Moyen Age. Montréal, 1964.
Phil 1540.87	Zimmermann, Albert. Ontologie oder Metaphysik? Die Diskussion über den Gegenstand der Metaphysik im 13. und 14. Jahrhundert. Habilitationeschrift. Leiden, 1965[1966].
Phil 1540.90	Behler, Ernst. Die Ewigkeit der Welt. München, 1965.
Phil 1540.92	Koelner Mediaevistentagung. Universalismus und Partikularismus in Mittelalter. Berlin, 1968.
Phil 1540.94	Cognet, Louis. Introduction aux mystiques rhéno-flamands. Paris, 1968.
Phil 1540.96	Beierwaltes, Werner. Platonismus in der Philosophie des Mittelalters. Darmstadt, 1969.

Phil 1560   History of philosophy - Medieval western philosophy - Anthologies of philosophical writings

Phil 1560.10	McKeon, Richard P. Selections from medieval philosophers. N.Y., 1929-1930. 2v.
Phil 1560.12	O'Donnell, J. Reginald. Nine medieval thinkers. Toronto, 1955.
Phil 1560.15	Michelet, Marcel. Le Rhin Mystique de Maitre Eckert à Thomas à Kempis. Paris, 1960.
Phil 1560.18	Wippel, John F. Medieval philosophy: from St. Augustine to Nicolas of Cusa. N.Y., 1969.

Phil 1600   History of philosophy - Renaissance philosophy - History - General works - Collected authors

Phil 1600.15	Céntre d'Études Supérieure. Courants religieux et humanisme à la fin de XVième et au début du XVIième siècle. Paris, 1959.
Phil 1600.20	Centro di studi umanistici di Montepulciano. Il pensiero italiano del Rinascimento e il tempo Nostro. Firenze, 1970.

Phil 1601 - 1626   History of philosophy - Renaissance philosophy - History - General works - Individual authors (A-Z)

Phil 1602.2	Bonicatti, Maurizio. Studi sull'Umanesimo. Secoli XIV-XVI. Firenze, 1969.
Phil 1603.2	Cassier, E. The indivudual and the cosmos in Renaissance philosophy. N.Y., 1963.
Phil 1607.5A	Gilbert, Neal. Renaissance concepts of method. N.Y., 1960.
Phil 1607.5B	Gilbert, Neal. Renaissance concepts of method. N.Y., 1960.
Phil 1607.10	Gelder, Herman Arend Enno van. The two reformations in the 16th century. The Hague, 1961.
Phil 1614.5	Nardi, Bruno. La crisi del Rinascimento e il dubbio cortesiano. Roma, 1950-51.
Phil 1614.10	Napoli, Giovanni di. Dal rinascimento all'illuminismo. Roma, 1969.
Phil 1618.2	Riekel, August. Die Philosophie der Renaissance. München, 1925.
Phil 1618.5	Rice, Eugene Franklin. The Renaissance idea of wisdom. Cambridge, 1958.
Phil 1619.2	Schultze, Fritz. Geschichte der Philosophie der Renaissance. Jena, 1874.
Phil 1619.5	Seigel, Jerrold Edward. Rhetoric and philosophy in Renaissance humanism. Princeton, 1968.
Phil 1620.5	Joffanin, Giuseppe. L'uomo antico nel pensiero del Rinascimento. Bologna, 1957.
Phil 1622.5	Vasoli, Cesare. Studi sulla cultura del Rinascimento. Manduria, 1968.

Phil 1630   History of philosophy - Renaissance philosophy - History - Special topics

Phil 1630.2	Zanta, Léontine. La renaissance du stoicisme au XVIe siècle. Paris, 1914.
Phil 1630.5	Archivio di Filosofia. Testi umanistici su l'ermetismo. Roma, 1955.
Phil 1630.10	Archivio di Filosofia. Umanesimo e esoterismo. Padova, 1960.
Phil 1630.15	Kristeller, P.O. La tradizione aristotelica nel Rinascimento. Padova, 1962.
Phil 1630.21	Mondolfo, R. Figure e idee della filosofia del Rinascimento. Firenze, 1963.
Phil 1630.22	Simone, F. La reductio artium ad Sacram scripturam. Torino, 1959?
Phil 1630.23	Rossi, P. I filosofi e le macchine, 1400-1700. Milano, 1962.
Phil 1630.23.5	Rossi, Paolo. Philosophy, technology, and the arts in the early modern era. N.Y., 1970.
Phil 1630.24	Callot, Emile. Doctrines et figures humanistes. Paris, 1963.
Phil 1630.30	Poppi, Antonino. Causalità e infinità nella scuola padovana dal 1480 al 1513. Padova, 1906.
Phil 1630.35	Vasoli, Cesare. La dialettica e la retorica dell'Umanesimo. Milano, 1968.
Phil 1630.40	Buck, August. Die humanistische Tradition in der Romania. Hamburg, 1968.
Phil 1630.45	Struever, Nancy S. The language of history in the Renaissance. Princeton, N.J., 1970.

Classified Listing

Phil 1660   History of philosophy - Renaissance philosophy - Anthologies of philosophical writings

Phil 1660.5   De Santillana, Giorgio. The age of adventure; the Renaissance philosophers. N.Y., 1956.
Phil 1660.5.2   De Santillana, Giorgio. The age of adventure; the Renaissance philosophers. Boston, 1957.

Phil 1695   History of philosophy - Modern philosophy in general - History - General works - Collected authors

Phil 1695.10   La morte della filosofia dopo Hegel e le correnti del pensiero contemporaneo. Roma, 1958.
Phil 1695.15   Barrett, William. Philosophy in the twentieth century. N.Y., 1962. 4v.
Phil 1695.20   Akademiia Nauk SSR. Institut Filosofii. Sovremennye religioznye filosofskie techeniia kapitalisticheskikh stran. Moskva, 1962.
Phil 1695.22   Alston, W. Readings in twentieth century philosophy. N.Y., 1936.
Phil 1695.23   Gaboriau, F. Novelle initiation philosophique. Tournai, 1962. 6v.
Phil 1695.25   Servadio, E. La psicoanalisi. Torino, 1963. 3v.
Phil 1695.29   Fromm, Erich. Socialist humanism. 1st ed. Garden City, N.Y., 1965.
Phil 1695.30   Nauka i filozofija. Beograd. 1,1963+
Phil 1695.31   Edie, James M. An invitation to phenomenology. Chicago, 1965.
Phil 1695.33   Qüestions de filosofi, Camus, Sartre, Ortega. v.21. Barcelona, 1964.
Phil 1695.34   Bogomdov, Aleksei S. Iz istorii zarubezhno filosofii XIX-XX vehov. Moskva, 1967.
Phil 1695.35   Verstehen und Vertranen. Otto Friedrich Bollnow zum 65. Geburtstag. Stuttgart, 1968.
Phil 1695.45   Contemporary philosophy. A survey. Firenze, 1968- 4v.
Phil 1695.48   Cardiel Reyes, Raul. Los filósofos modernos en la independencia latino-americana. 1. ed. México, 1964.

Phil 1700 - 1725   History of philosophy - Modern philosophy in general - History - Special topics - Individual authors (A-Z)

Phil 1700.1   Adamson, R. The development of modern philosophy. Photoreproduction. Edinburgh, 1903 2v.
Phil 1700.2   Anthologie der neueren Philosophie. Berlin, 1919.
Phil 1700.3   Atkinson, William W. The crucible of modern thought. Chicago, 1910.
Phil 1700.4   Arréat, Lucien. Dix années de philosophie. Paris, 1901.
Phil 1700.5   Armani, T. Da G. Bruno e da A. Gentile allo Spencer e all' Ardigò. Camerino, 1904.
Phil 1700.6   Ardley, Gavin. Aquinas and Kant. London, 1950.
Phil 1700.7   Aiken, H.D. The age of ideology. Boston, 1957.
Phil 1700.8   Aseev, I.A. Osnovnye napravleniia burzhuaznoi filosofii i sotsiologii XX veka. Leningrad, 1961.
Phil 1700.9   Akademiia Nauk SSSR. Institut Filosofii. Sektor Sovremennoi Burzhuaznoi Filosofii i Sotsiologii Stran Zapada. Noveishie priemy zashchity starogo mira. Moskva, 1962.
Phil 1700.10   Akademiia Nauk SSSR. Institut Filosofii. Sovremennaia filosofiia i sotsiologiia v stranakh Zapadnoi Evropy i Ameriki. Moskva, 1964.
Phil 1700.12   Adam, Antoine. Le mouvement philosophique dan la première moitie du XVIIIe siècle. Paris, 1967.
Phil 1701.1   Bowen, F. Modern philosophy. N.Y., 1877.
Phil 1701.1.2   Bowen, F. Modern philosophy. N.Y., 1877.
Phil 1701.1.3   Bowen, F. Modern philosophy. 2nd ed. N.Y., 1877.
Phil 1701.2   Braniss, C.J. Übersecht des Entwicklungsganges der Philosophie. Breslau, 1842.
Phil 1701.3   Buhle, J.G. Geschichte der neueren Philosophie. Göttlieb, 1800-1804. 6v.
Phil 1701.3.5   Buhle, J.G. Histoire de la philosophie moderne. Paris, 1816. 6v.
Phil 1701.4   Burt, Bery C. History of modern philosophy. Chicago, 1892. 2v.
Phil 1701.5   Burns, C. Delisle. The growth of modern philosophy. London, 1909.
Phil 1701.6   Benn, A.W. History of modern philosophy. London, 1912.
Phil 1701.6.25   Benn, A.W. History of modern philosophy. London, 1930.
X Cg   Phil 1701.7   Berr, Henri. Avenir de la philosophie. Paris, 1899.
Phil 1701.7.5   Berr, Henri. La synthèse des connaissances et l'histoire. Thèse. Paris, 1898.
Phil 1701.8   Bauch, Bruno. Neuere Philosophie bis Kant. 3. Aufl. Berlin, 1919.
Phil 1701.9.5   Busse, Ludwig. Die Weltanschauungen der grossen Philosophie der Neuzeit. 6e Aufl. Leipzig, 1917.
Phil 1701.10   Baumann, Julius. Deutsche und ausserdeutsche Philosophie. Gotha, 1903.
Phil 1701.11   Bosanquet, Bernard. The meeting of extremes in contemporary philosophy. London, 1921.
Phil 1701.12   Bertini, G. Maria. Storia della filosofia moderna. pt.1. Torino, 1881.
Phil 1701.14   Brasch, Moritz. Die Philosophie der Gegenwart. Leipzig, 1888.
Phil 1701.15   Bierens de Haan, J. Hoofdfiguren der geschiedenis van het urjsgcerig denden. 2e druk. Haarlem, 1927.
Phil 1701.16   Baratono, Adelchi. Filosofia in margine. Milano, 1930.
Phil 1701.17   Boas, George. Our new ways of thinking. N.Y., 1930.
Phil 1701.17.5   Boas, George. Dominant themes of modern philosophy. N.Y., 1957.
Phil 1701.18   Bagdasar, N. Filosofia contemporana a istorici. Bucureşti, 1930.
Phil 1701.19   Borkenan, Franz. Der Übergang vom Feudalen zum bügerlichen Weltbild. Paris, 1934.
Phil 1701.20   Bochénski, J.M. Europäische Philosophie der Gegenwart. Bern, 1947.
Phil 1701.20.5   Bochénski, J.M. Europäische Philosophie der Gegenwart. 2. Aufl. München, 1951.
Phil 1701.20.7   Bochénski, J.M. La philosophie contemporaine en Europe. 2. éd. Paris, 1951.
Phil 1701.20.10   Bochénski, J.M. Contemporary European philosophy. 2d ed. Berkeley, 1956.
Phil 1701.21   Brunner, Auguste. La personne incarnée, étude sur la phénoménologie et la philosophie existentialiste. Paris, 1947.
Phil 1701.22   Benda, J. Trois idoles romantique. Genève, 1948.
Phil 1701.23   Bréhier, Émile. Les thèmes actuels de la philosophie. 1. éd. Paris, 1951.
Phil 1701.23.3   Bréhier, Émile. Les thèmes actuels de la philosophie. Paris, 1954.
Phil 1701.23.5   Bréhier, Émile. Études de philosophie moderne. Paris, 1965.
Phil 1701.24   Bense, Max. Die Philosophie. Frankfurt a.M., 1951.

Phil 1700 - 1725   History of philosophy - Modern philosophy in general - History - Special topics - Individual authors (A-Z) - cont.

Phil 1701.25   Bousquet, J. Les capitals; ou De Jean Duns Scot à Jean Paulhan. Paris, 1955.
Phil 1701.26   Birro, Cela. The ways of enjoyment. N.Y., 1957.
Phil 1701.30   Berlinger, Rudolph. Das Werk der Freiheit. Frankfurt, 1959.
Phil 1701.35   Baudry, Bernard. Point de vue sur l'Occident. Paris, 1958.
Phil 1701.40   Bronowski, Jacob. The Western intellectual tradition. N.Y., 1960.
Phil 1701.45   Bakradze, K.S. Ocherki po istorii noveishei i sovremennoi burzhuaznoi filosofii. Tbilisi, 1960.
Phil 1701.47   Brytninger i tidens tankelin. Oslo, 1960.
Phil 1701.48   Baumer, Franklin Le van. Intellectual movements in modern European history. N.Y., 1965.
Phil 1701.50   Borzaga, Reynold. Contemporary philosophy; phenomenological and existential currents. Milwaukee, 1966.
Phil 1701.52   Bobbio, Norberto. Da Hobbes a Marx; saggi di storia della filosofia. Napoli, 1965.
Phil 1701.54   Bausola, Adriano. Indagini di storia della filosofia. Milano, 1969.
Phil 1701.56   Podnár, Ján. Od realizmu k iracionalizmu; zo súčasnej západnej filozofie. 1. vyd. Bratislava, 1966.
Phil 1701.58   Bonafede, Giulio. Interpretazioni della filosofia moderna. Palermo, 1965.
Phil 1702.1.2   Cousin, Victor. Cours de l'histoire de la philosophie, XVIIIe siècle. Paris, 1841. 2v.
Phil 1702.1.3   Cousin, Victor. Cours de l'histoire de la philosophie moderne. Paris, 1841.
Phil 1702.1.8   Cousin, Victor. Course of the history of modern philosophy. N.Y., 1854. 2v.
Phil 1702.1.9   Cousin, Victor. Course of the history of modern philosophy. N.Y., 1853. 2v.
Phil 1702.2.5   Chiappelli, A. La crisi del pensiero moderno. Citta di Castello, 1920.
Phil 1702.3   Cresson, André. La position actuelle des problèmes philosophiques. Paris, 1924.
Phil 1702.4   Correnti di filosofia contemporanea, a cura di circolo filosofico di Genova. Genova, 1913.
Phil 1702.6   Carlini, A. Orientamenti della filosofia conteporanea. Roma, 1931.
Phil 1702.6.15   Olgiati, F. Neo-scolastica, idealismo e spiritualismo. Milano, 1933.
Phil 1702.7   Castell, Alburey. An introduction to modern philosophy. N.Y., 1943.
Phil 1702.8   Ciardo, Manlio. Le quattro epoche dello storicismo. Bari, 1947.
Phil 1702.9   Campo, M. Variazioni sulla storia della filosofia moderna. Brescia, 1946.
Phil 1702.10   Cannabrava, Euryalo. Ensaios filosóficos. Rio de Janeiro, 1957.
Phil 1702.11   Collins, James Daniel. A history of modern European philosophy. Milwaukee, 1961.
Phil 1702.12   Ciardo, Manlio. Il dramma della metafisica nell'età contemporanea. Bologna, 1967.
Phil 1702.13   Cruickshank, John. Aspects of the modern European mind. Harlow, 1969.
Phil 1703.1   Dewing, Arthur Stone. Introduction to History of modern philosophy. Philadelphia, 1903.
Phil 1703.2   Drews, Arthur. Die Philosophie im ersten Drittel des 19. Jahrhunderts. Leipzig, 1912.
Phil 1703.2.3   Drews, Arthur. Die Philosophie im ersten Drittel des 19. Jahrhunderts. Berlin, 1920.
Phil 1703.2.5   Drews, Arthur. Die Philosophie im zweiten Drittel des 19. Jahrhunderts. Berlin, 1913.
Phil 1703.2.6   Drews, Arthur. Die Philosophie im zweiten Drittel des 19. Jahrhunderts. Berlin, 1922.
Phil 1703.2.10   Drews, Arthur. Die Philosophie im lekten Drittel des 19. Jahrhunderts. Berlin, 1921.
Phil 1703.2.15   Drews, Arthur. Die deutsche Philosophie der Gegenwart. Berlin, 1922.
Phil 1703.3   Du Marchie van Voorlhnipen, H. Nagelaten Geschriften. Arheim, 1886. 2v.
Phil 1703.5   Dresser, H.W. A history of modern philosophy. N.Y., 1928.
Phil 1703.6   Dingler, Hugo. Geschichte der Naturphilosophie. Berlin, 1932.
Phil 1703.7   Dempf, Alois. Weltordnung und Heilsgeschichte. Einsiedeln, 1958.
Phil 1703.10   Denkers in onze fijd. 2. druk. Francker, 1954-55. 3v.
Phil 1703.12   Datta, D.M. The chief currents of contemporary philosophy. Calcutta, 1950.
Phil 1703.12.2   Datta, D.M. The chief currents of contemporary philosophy. 2nd ed. Calcutta, 1961.
Phil 1703.16   Duméry, Henry. Regards sur la philosophie contemporaine. Tournai, 1957.
Phil 1703.17   Dictionnaire des idées contemporaines. Paris, 1964.
Phil 1704.1   Erdmann, J.E. Versuch...Geschichte der neuern Philosophie. Riga, 1834-53. 6v.
Phil 1704.1.5   Erdmann, J.E. Versuch...Geschichte der neuern Philosophie. Faksimile. Stuttgart, 1932-33. 10v.
Phil 1704.1.10   Ermolenko, D.V. Kritika sovremennoi burzuaznoi filosofii. Moskva, 1959.
Phil 1704.2   Eleutheropulos, A. Einführung in eine wissenschaftliche Philosophie. Leipzig, 1906.
Phil 1704.2.5   Eleutheropulos, A. Die Philosophie und die Lebensauffassung der germanisch-romanischen Völker. Berlin, 1901.
Phil 1704.4   Estiú, Emilio. Del arte a la historia en la filosofia moderna. La Plata, 1962?
Phil 1705.1   Falckenberg, R. Geschichte der neueren Philosophie. Leipzig, 1886.
Phil 1705.1.2   Falckenberg, R. Geschichte der neueren Philosophie. 2e Aufl. Leipzig, 1892.
Phil 1705.1.3   Falckenberg, R. Geschichte der neueren Philosophie. 8e Aufl. Berlin, 1921.
Phil 1705.1.4   Falckenberg, R. Geschichte der neueren Philosophie. 9. Aufl. Berlin, 1927.
Phil 1705.1.5   Falckenberg, R. History of modern philosophy. N.Y., 1893.
Phil 1705.1.7   Falckenberg, R. History of modern philosophy. N.Y., 1897.
Phil 1705.2   Feuerbach. Geschichte der neueren Philosophie. Ansbach, 1833-37. 2v.
Phil 1705.3   Fichte, T.H. Beiträge zur Charakteristik der neueren Philosophie. Sulzbach, 1841.
Phil 1705.3.5   Fichte, T.H. Beiträge zur Charakteristik der neueren Philosophie. Sulzbach, 1829.

Phil 1700 - 1725 History of philosophy - Modern philosophy in general - History - Special topics - Individual authors (A-Z) - cont.

Phil 1705.4	Fischer, K. Geschichte der neueren Philosophie. v.1-6. Mannheim, 1854-77. 7v.
Phil 1705.4.2	Fischer, K. Geschichte der neueren Philosophie. v.1-9. München, 1875-93. 10v.
Phil 1705.4.3	Fischer, K. Geschichte der neueren Philosophie. v.2-10. Heidelberg, 1898-1904. 7v.
Phil 1705.4.4	Fischer, K. Geschichte der neueren Philosophie. v.1-8. Heidelberg, 1889-1901. 10v.
Phil 1705.4.6	Fischer, K. History of modern philosophy. N.Y., 1887.
Phil 1705.4.8	Fischer, K. Kort inledning till nyare filosofia historia. Stockholm, 1866.
Phil 1705.4.9	Fischer, K. Einleitung in die Geschichte der neueren Philosophie. Heidelberg, 1908.
Phil 1705.4.50	Fischer, K. Geschichte der neueren Philosophie im Urteil der Jahrzehnte 1852-1924. Heidelberg, 1924.
Phil 1705.5	Franck, A. Philosophes modernes. Paris, 1879.
Phil 1705.6	Fabre, Joseph. La pensée moderne. Paris, 1908.
Phil 1705.6.1	Fabre, Joseph. La pensée moderne [de Luther à Leibniz]. Genève, 1970.
Phil 1705.7	Freyer, Johannes. Geschichte der Geschichte der Philosophie. Leipzig, 1912.
Phil 1705.8	Franchi, Ausonio. Letture su la storia della filosofia moderna. Milano, 1863. 2v.
Phil 1705.10	Fondane, B. La conscience malheureuse. Paris, 1936.
Phil 1705.11	Freeman, David. Recent studies in philosophy and theology. Philadelphia, 1962.
Phil 1705.12	Farré, Luis. Unamuno, William James y Kirkegaard y otros ensayos. Buenos Aires, 1967.
VPhil 1705.13	Filipović, Vladimir. Novija filozofija Zapada i odabrani telestovi. Zagreb, 1968.
Phil 1706.1	Gaultier, Jules de. De Kant à Nietzsche. Paris, 1900.
Phil 1706.1.6	Gaultier, Jules de. De Kant à Nietzsche. 6e éd. Paris, 19- .
Phil 1706.1.10	Gaultier, Jules de. From Kant to Nietzsche. London, 1961.
Phil 1706.1.13	Gaultier, Jules de. La philosophie officielle et la philosophie. Paris, 1922.
Phil 1706.1.23	Gaultier, Jules de. Le Bovarysme. 3. éd. Photoreproduction. Paris, 1902.
Phil 1706.1.25	Gaultier, Jules de. Bovarysm. N.Y., 1970.
Phil 1706.1.32	Gaultier, Jules de. Entretiens avec ceux d'hier et d'aujourd'hui. 2e éd. Paris, 1912.
Phil 1706.1.35	Gaultier, Jules de. La vie mystique de la nature. Paris, 1924.
Phil 1706.1.43	Gaultier, Jules de. La sensibilité métaphysique. 3e éd. Paris, 1924.
Phil 1706.2	Gaultier, P. La pensée contemporaine. Paris, 1911.
Phil 1706.3	Goldstein, J. Wandlungen in der Philosophie der Gegenwerk. Leipzig, 1911.
Phil 1706.5	Guttler, C. Einführung in die Geschichte der neueren Philosophie des Auslandes. München, 1922.
Phil 1706.5.10	Güttler, C. Einführung in die Geschichte der Philosophie seit Hegel. München, 1921.
Phil 1706.8	Gause, Hermann. Über die Problematik der neueren Philosophie. Inaug. Diss. Basel, 1928.
Phil 1706.9	Grevillot, J.M. Les grands courants de la pensée contemporaine. Paris, 1948.
Phil 1706.10	Grose. Grote filosofieën en de huidige mens. Amsterdam, 1959.
Phil 1706.11	Flam, Leopold. La philosophie au tournant de notre temps. Bruxelles, 1961.
Phil 1706.12	Gaos, José. Filosofía contemporanea. Caracas, 1962.
Phil 1706.15	Grenier, Jean. Essai sur l'esprit d'orthodoxie. Paris, 1967.
Phil 1707.1A	Höffding, H. Geschichte der Philosophie. Leipzig, 1895. 2v.
Phil 1707.1B	Höffding, H. Geschichte der Philosophie. Leipzig, 1895. 2v.
Cg Phil 1707.1.5	Höffding, H. History of modern philosophy. London, 1900.
Phil 1707.1.6	Höffding, H. History of modern philosophy. v.2. London, 1908.
Phil 1707.1.6.5	Höffding, H. A history of modern philosophy. London, 1920. 2v.
Phil 1707.1.6.10	Höffding, H. A history of modern philosophy. v.2. London, 1924.
Phil 1707.1.8	Höffding, H. Storia della filosofia moderna. Torino, 1913. 2v.
Phil 1707.1.9	Höffding, H. Moderne Philosophen. Leipzig, 1905.
Phil 1707.1.11	Höffding, H. Philosophes contemporains. Paris, 1908.
Phil 1707.1.12	Höffding, H. Histoire de la philosophie moderne. 2e éd. Paris, 1908. 2v.
Phil 1707.1.13	Höffding, H. Modern philosophers. London, 1915.
Phil 1707.1.15	Höffding, H. Lehrbuch der Geschichte der neueren Philosophie. Leipzig, 1907.
Phil 1707.1.19A	Höffding, H. A brief history of modern philosophy. N.Y., 1912.
Phil 1707.1.19B	Höffding, H. A brief history of modern philosophy. N.Y., 1912.
Phil 1707.1.25	Höffding, H. Compendio di storia della filosofia moderna. Torino, 1923.
Phil 1707.2A	Hibben, J.G. Philosophy of the enlightenment. N.Y., 1910.
Phil 1707.2B	Hibben, J.G. Philosophy of the enlightenment. N.Y., 1910.
Phil 1707.3	Hadley, A.T. Some influences in modern philosophic thought. New Haven, 1913.
Phil 1707.4A	Hegel, E.W.F. Vorlesungen und der Geschichte der Philosophie. Berlin, 1840. 3v.
Phil 1707.4B	Hegel, E.W.F. Vorlesungen und der Geschichte der Philosophie. Berlin, 1840. 2v.
Phil 1707.5	Hönigswald, R. Die Philosophie von der Renaissance bis Kant. Berlin, 1923.
Phil 1707.6	Hessen, Johannes. Die philosophischen Stromungen der Gegenwart. München, 1923.
Phil 1707.6.5	Hessen, Johannes. Die Geistesstromungen der Gegenwart. Freiburg, 1937.
Phil 1707.7	Hertling, G.F. von. Historische Beiträge zur Philosophie. München, 1914.
Phil 1707.8	Heimsoeth, H. Die sechs grossen Themen der abendländischen Metaphysik. Berlin, 1922.
Phil 1707.8.3	Heimsoeth, H. Die sechs grossen Themen der abendländischen Metaphysik. 3e Aufl. Stuttgart, 1954?
Phil 1707.8.6	Heimsoeth, H. Metaphysik der Neuzeit. München, 1967.
Phil 1707.9	Hammond, A.L. Anti-intellectualism in present philosophy. Diss. Baltimore, 1926.
Phil 1707.10	Heinemann, Fritz. Neue Wege der Philosophie, Geist, Leben, Existenz. Leipzig, 1929.
Phil 1707.11	Hartmann, Hans. Denkendes Europa; ein Gang durch die Philosophie der Gegenwart. Berlin, 1936.

Phil 1700 - 1725 History of philosophy - Modern philosophy in general - History - Special topics - Individual authors (A-Z) - cont.

Phil 1707.12	Hevigel, H. Das neue Denken. Berlin, 1928.
Phil 1707.13	Heiss, R. Der Gang des Geistes. Bern, 1948.
Phil 1707.14	Hubben, William. Four prophets of our destiny. N.Y., 1952.
Phil 1707.15	Hollenbach, J.M. Sein und Gewissen. Baden-Baden, 1954.
Phil 1707.16	Hawkins, D.J.B. Crucial problems of modern philosophy. London, 1957.
Phil 1707.16.5	Hawkins, D.J.B. Crucial problems of modern philosophy. Notre Dame, 1962.
Phil 1707.17	Haensel, Ludwig. Begegnungen und Auseinandersetzungen mit Denkern und Dichtern der Neuzeit. Wien, 1957.
Phil 1707.18	Heer, Friedrich. Die dritte Kraft. Frankfurt, 1959.
Phil 1707.20	Hadas, Mases. Humanism: the Greek ideal. 1. ed. N.Y., 1960.
Phil 1707.22	Holm, Søren. O plysningstiden. Kjøbenhavn, 1959.
Phil 1707.24	Hoenderdaal, G.J. De mens in tweeotrijd. Arnhem, 1956.
Phil 1707.26	Herzberg, G. Der Zeitgeist. Meisenheim, 1960.
Phil 1707.28	Huebscher, Arthur. Van Hegel zu Heidegger. Stuttgart, 1961.
Phil 1707.29	Haag, Karl Heinz. Die Lehre vom Sein in der modernen Philosophie. Frankfurt, 1963.
Phil 1709.1	Joël, Karl. Die philosophische Krisis der Gegenwart. Leipzig, 1914.
Phil 1709.1.2	Joël, Karl. Die philosophische Krisis derGegenwart. 2e Aufl. Leipzig, 1919.
Phil 1709.2	Joad, C.E.M. Introduction to modern philosophy. London, 1924.
Phil 1709.3	Jørgensen, J. Brudshjkher ar filosofiens historii. København, 1950.
Phil 1710.1	Knauer, V. Geschichte der Philosophie mit besonderer Berücksichtung der Neuzeit. Wien, 1876.
Phil 1710.1.2	Knauer, V. Geschichte der Philosophie mit besonderer Berücksichtung der Neuzeit. 2e Aufl. Wien, 1882.
Phil 1710.2	Kerler, D.H. Die auferstandene Metaphysik. Ulm, 1921.
Phil 1710.3	Krejčí, F. O filosofii přítomnosti. V Praze, 1904.
Phil 1710.3.5	Krejčí, F. Filosofie posledních let před válkou. 2. vyd. Praha, 1930.
Phil 1710.4	Kröner, Franz. Die Anarchie der philosophischen Systeme. Leipzig, 1929.
Phil 1710.5.3	Krutch, Joseph W. The modern temper. N.Y., 1929.
Phil 1710.5.5	Krutch, Joseph W. The modern temper. N.Y., 1930.
Phil 1710.5.10	Krutch, Joseph W. The measure of man. 1. ed. Indianapolis, 1954.
Phil 1710.6	Knight, Everett. The objective society. London, 1959.
Phil 1710.6.2	Knight, Everett. The objective society. N.Y., 1959.
Phil 1710.7	Klibasky, Raymond. La philosophie au milieu du 20e siècle. Firenze, 1958. 4v.
Phil 1710.10	Kaegi, Werner. Humanismus der Gegenwart. Zürich, 1959.
Phil 1710.12	Kaplan, A. The new world of philosophy. N.Y., 1961.
Phil 1710.13	Kline, George. European philosophy today. Chicago, 1965.
Phil 1710.16	Korn, Alejandro. Estudios de filosofía contemporánea. 1st ed. Buenos Aires, 1963.
Phil 1711.1	Liebert, A. Die geistige Krisis der Gegenwart. Berlin, 1923.
Phil 1711.1.5	Liehert, A. Zur Kritik der Gegenwart. Langensalza, 1927.
Phil 1711.2	Lenoir, R. Les historiens de l'esprit humain. Paris, 1926.
Phil 1711.5	Luppal, I.K. Istoriko-filosofskie etiudy. Moskva, 1935.
Phil 1711.6	Landgrebe, Ludwig. Philosophie der Gegenwart. Bonn, 1952.
Phil 1711.6.5	Landgrebe, Ludwig. Major problems in contemporary European philosophy. N.Y., 1966.
Phil 1711.7	Levi, Albert. Philosophy and the modern world. Bloomington, 1959.
Phil 1711.8A	Lovejoy, A.D. Reflections on human nature. Baltimore, 1961.
Phil 1711.8B	Lovejoy, A.D. Reflections on human nature. Baltimore, 1961.
Phil 1711.9	Laín Entralgo, Pedro. Teoría y realidad del otro. Madrid, 1961. 2v.
Phil 1711.10	Lee, Otis. Existence and inquiry, a study of thought in the modern world. Chicago, 1949.
Phil 1711.15	Láscaris Comneno, Constantino. Estudios de filosofía moderna. 1. ed. San Salvador, 1966.
Phil 1712.1	Morell, J.D. Historical and critical...philosophy, XIX century. London, 1846. 2v.
Phil 1712.1.2	Morell, J.D. Historical and critical...philosophy, XIX century. N.Y., 1848.
Phil 1712.1.6	Morell, J.D. Historical and critical...philosophy, XIX century. N.Y., 1856.
Phil 1712.2	Merz, J.T. History of European thought, 19th century. Edinburgh, 1896-1914. 4v.
Phil 1712.2.3A	Merz, J.T. History of European thought, 19th century. v.1-3. Edinburgh, 1907-1912. 2v.
Phil 1712.2.3B	Merz, J.T. History of European thought, 19th century. v.1-3. Edinburgh, 1907-1912. 2v.
Phil 1712.2.4	Merz, J.T. History of European thought, 19th century. Edinburgh, 1904. 2v.
Phil 1712.2.5	Merz, J.T. A history of European thought in the nineteenth century. Edinburgh, 1912-27. 4v.
Phil 1712.2.6	Merz, J.T. A history of European thought in the nineteenth century. N.Y., 1965. 4v.
Phil 1712.3	Merten, O. L'état présent de la philosophie. Namur, 1907.
Phil 1712.5	Messer, A. Geschichte der Philosophie. Leipzig, 1913.
Phil 1712.5.2	Messer, A. Geschichte der Philosophie vom Beginn der Neuzeit zum Ende des 18. Jahrhunderts. Leipzig, 1912.
Phil 1712.5.4	Messer, A. Geschichte der Philosophie vom Beginn der Neuzeit zum Ende des 18. Jahrhunderts. Leipzig, 1920.
Phil 1712.5.4.10	Messer, A. Geschichte der Philosophie vom Beginn der Neuzeit zum Ende des 18. Jahrhunderts. 6e und 7e Aufl. Leipzig, 1923.
Phil 1712.5.5	Messer, A. Die Philosophie der Gegenwart. 3e Aufl. Leipzig, 1913.
Phil 1712.5.10	Messer, A. Die Philosophie der Gegenwart. Leipzig, 1927.
Phil 1712.9	Mondolfo, R. Il dubbio metodico e la storia della filosofia. Padova, 1905.
Phil 1712.11	Mellone, S.H. The dawn of modern thought. London, 1930.
Phil 1712.12	Malisoff, William M. A calendar of doubts and faiths. N.Y., 1930.
Phil 1712.13	Maréchal, Joseph. Précis d'histoire de la philosophie moderne. Louvain, 1933.
Phil 1712.13.2	Maréchal, Joseph. Précis d'histoire de la philosophie moderne. 2e éd. Bruxelles, 1951.
Phil 1712.14A	Mead, George H. Movements of thought in the nineteenth century. Chicago, 1936.
Phil 1712.14B	Mead, George H. Movements of thought in the nineteenth century. Chicago, 1936.

Phil 1700 - 1725 History of philosophy - Modern philosophy in general - History - Special topics - Individual authors (A-Z) - cont.

Phil 1712.15   Magnino, Bianca. Alle origini della crisi contemporanea. Roma, 1946.

Phil 1712.16   McElroy, H.C. Modern philosophers. N.Y., 1950.

Phil 1712.17A   Mayer, Frederick. A history of modern philosophy. N.Y., 1951.

Phil 1712.17B   Mayer, Frederick. A history of modern philosophy. N.Y., 1951.

Phil 1712.18   Mehl, Roger. Images de l'homme. Genève, 1953.

Phil 1712.18.2   Mehl, Roger. Images of man. Richmond, 1965.

Phil 1712.19   Myers, Francis M. The warfare of democratic ideals. Yellow Springs, Ohio, 1956.

Phil 1712.20   Muller, Philippe. Itineraire philosophique. Neuchâtel, 1956.

Phil 1712.21   Mshvenieradze, V.V. Osnovnye fecheniia sovremennoi burzhuaznoi filosofii. Kiev, 1961.

Phil 1712.22   Moscow. Universitet Filosoficheskii Fakul'tet. Protiv sovremennoi burzhuaznoi filosofii. Moskva, 1963.

Phil 1712.23   Mañero Mañero, Salvador. El humanismo. Madrid, 1963.

Phil 1712.24   Moniuszko, Antoni. Aczyístość i synteza. Warszawa, 1962.

Phil 1712.25   Mueller, Max. Das christliche Menschenbild und die Weltanschauungen der Neuzeit im Breiszau. Freiburg, 1945.

Phil 1712.26   Marnell, William Henry. Man-made morals. 1st ed. Garden City, N.Y., 1966.

Phil 1712.27   Maier, Anneliese. Zwei Untersuchungen zur nachscholastischen Philosophie. 2e Aufl. Roma, 1968.

Phil 1712.28   Motroshilova, Nelli V. Poznanie i obshchestvo. Moskva, 1969.

Phil 1713.2   Nicholl, Donald. Recent thought in focus. N.Y., 1953.

Phil 1713.3   Newman, J. A time for truth. Dublin, 1955.

Phil 1713.4   Naess, Arne. Moderne filosofer. Stockholm, 1965.

Phil 1713.4.2   Naess, Arne. Four modern philosophers. Chicago, 1968.

Phil 1713.5   Nikolajević, Sietamir B. Misao kas odraz vremens. Beograd, 1971.

Phil 1714.1   Oischinger, J.N.P. Speculative Entwicklung...neueren Philosophie. Schaffhausen, 1853-4. 2v.

Phil 1714.2   Ollé-Laprune, L. La philosophie et le temps présent. 5e éd. Paris, 1908

Phil 1714.3   Olgiati, F. L'anima dell'umanesimo e del rinascimento. Milano, 1924.

Phil 1714.4   Oggioni, Emilio. Filosofia e psicologia nel pensiero postromantico. Bologna, 1955.

Phil 1714.5   Orsi, Domenico d'. Saggi varii di filosofia moderna e contemporanea. Padova, 1962.

Phil 1714.5.5   Orsi, Domenico d'. Il tramonto della filosofia moderna. Padova, 1962.

Phil 1714.5.8   Orsi, Domenico d'. Il tramonto della filosofia moderna. 3. ed. Padova, 1970.

Phil 1714.6   Oizerman, Teodor I. Zur Geschichte der vormarxschen Philosophie. Berlin, 1960.

Phil 1715.1   Papillen, Fernand. Histoire de la philosophie moderne. Paris, 1876. 2v.

Phil 1715.2   Papini, Giovanni. Il crepuscolo dei filosofi. Milano, 1906.

Phil 1715.2.5   Papini, Giovanni. Le crepuscule des philosophes. Paris, 1922.

Phil 1715.2.10   Papini, Giovanni. Gli amanti de Sofia, 1902-1918. Firenze, 1942.

Phil 1715.3.2   Perry, R.B. Present philosophical tendencies. London, 1912.

Phil 1715.3.5A   Perry, R.B. The present conflict of ideals. N.Y., 1918.

Phil 1715.3.5B   Perry, R.B. The present conflict of ideals. N.Y., 1918.

Phil 1715.3.8A   Perry, R.B. The present conflict of ideals. N.Y., 1922.

Phil 1715.3.8B   Perry, R.B. The present conflict of ideals. N.Y., 1922.

Phil 1715.3.9A   Perry, R.B. Philosophy of the recent past. N.Y., 1926.

Phil 1715.3.9B   Perry, R.B. Philosophy of the recent past. N.Y., 1926.

Phil 1715.5   Istoria filosofiei moderne. Bucurestti, 1937.

Phil 1715.6.5   Passmore, John Arthur. A hundred years of philosophy. London, 1962.

Phil 1715.6.7   Passmore, John Arthur. A hundred years of philosophy. 2nd ed. London, 1966.

Phil 1715.7   Paci, Enzo. La filosofia contemporanea. 1. ed. Milano, 1957.

Phil 1715.10   Pinilla, Antonio. El filósofo en la sociedad actual. Lima, 1959.

Phil 1715.11   Prosch, H. The genesis of twentieth century philosophy. 1. ed. Garden City, N.Y., 1964.

Phil 1715.12   Pepi, Sergio. Umanismo logico. Roma, 1963.

Phil 1715.13   Petrović, Gajo. Od Lockea do Ayera. Beograd, 1964.

Phil 1715.14   Pfeiffer, Johannes. Gegen den Strom. Itzehoe, 1964.

Phil 1715.16   Piovani, Pietro. Conoscenza storica e coscienza morale. Napoli, 1966.

Phil 1715.18   Pejović, Danilo. Sistem i egzistencija. Zagreb, 1970.

Phil 1717.1   Renouvier, C.B. Manuel de philosophie moderne. Paris, 1842.

Phil 1717.2   Ritter, A.H. Histoire de la philosophie moderne. Paris, 1861. 3v.

Phil 1717.3A   Royce, J. Spirit of modern philosophy. Boston, 1892.

Phil 1717.3B   Royce, J. Spirit of modern philosophy. Boston, 1892.

Phil 1717.3.5A   Royce, J. Spirit of modern philosophy. Boston, 1893.

Phil 1717.3.5B   Royce, J. Spirit of modern philosophy. Boston, 1893.

Phil 1717.3.8   Royce, J. The spirit of modern philosophy. Boston, 1896.

Phil 1717.3.20   Royce, J. The spirit of modern philosophy. N.Y., 1955.

Phil 1717.4   Rogers, A.K. A brief introduction to modern philosophy. N.Y., 1899.

Phil 1717.5.2   Riehl, Alois. Philosophie der Gegenwart. 2e Aufl. Leipzig, 1904.

Phil 1717.5.4   Riehl, Alois. Zur Einführung in die Philosophie der Gegenwart. 4. Aufl. Leipzig, 1913.

Phil 1717.5.5   Riehl, Alois. Zur Einführung in die Philosophie der Gegenwart. 5e Aufl. Leipzig, 1919.

Phil 1717.5.9   Riehl, Alois. Inleiding tot de hedendaagsche wijsbegeerte. Zutphen, 1918.

Phil 1717.6   Rand, Benjamin. Modern classical philosophers. Boston, 1908.

Phil 1717.6.3A   Rand, Benjamin. Modern classical philosophers. Boston, 1908.

Phil 1717.6.3B   Rand, Benjamin. Modern classical philosophers. Boston, 1908.

Phil 1717.6.5A   Rand, Benjamin. Modern classical philosophers. 2nd ed. Boston, 1924.

Phil 1717.6.5B   Rand, Benjamin. Modern classical philosophers. 2nd ed. Boston, 1924.

Phil 1717.6.6A   Rand, Benjamin. Modern classical philosophers. Boston, 1936.

Phil 1717.6.6B   Rand, Benjamin. Modern classical philosophers. Boston, 1936.

Phil 1700 - 1725 History of philosophy - Modern philosophy in general - History - Special topics - Individual authors (A-Z) - cont.

Phil 1717.7   Rey, A. La philosophie moderne. Paris, 1908.

Phil 1717.8   Ruggiero, G. de. La filosofia contemporanea. Bari, 1912.

Phil 1717.8.2   Ruggiero, G. de. La filosofia contemporanea. 2a ed. Bari, 1920. 2v.

Phil 1717.8.3   Ruggiero, G. de. La filosofia contemporanea. 3a ed. Bari, 1929. 2v.

Phil 1717.8.5A   Ruggiero, G. de. Modern philosophy. London, 1921.

Phil 1717.8.5B   Ruggiero, G. de. Modern philosophy. London, 1921.

Phil 1717.8.10   Ruggiero, G. de. Philosophische Strömungen des zivanzigsten Jahrhunderts. Köln, 1949.

Phil 1717.8.15   Ruggiero, G. de. Filosofi del novecento. Bari, 1934.

Phil 1717.8.20   Ruggiero, G. de. Filosofi del novecento. 3e ed. Bari, 1946.

Phil 1717.9   Rösener, Karl. Moderne Propheten. München, 1907.

Phil 1717.11   Robinson, D.S. Anthology of recent philosophy. N.Y., 1929.

Phil 1717.11.5   Robinson, D.S. Anthology of recent philosophy. N.Y., 1931.

Phil 1717.11.15   Robinson, D.S. An introduction to living philosophy. N.Y., 1932.

Phil 1717.11.20   Robinson, D.S. Crucial issues in philosophy. Boston, 1955.

Phil 1717.12   Russell, Leonard. An introduction to philosophy. London, 1929.

Phil 1717.14   Roberts, Michael. The modern mind. London, 1937.

Phil 1717.16   Roig Gironella, J. Filosofía y razón. Madrid, 1948.

Phil 1717.17   Reichenbach, H. The rise of scientific philosophy. Berkeley, 1951.

Phil 1717.17.7   Reichenbach, Hans. Der Aufsteig der wissenschaftlichen Philosophie. Braunschweig, 1968.

Phil 1717.18   Rosmini Serbati, Antonio. Breve schizzo dei sistemi di filosofia moderna e del proprio sistema. Napoli, 1952.

Phil 1717.18.4   Rosmini Serbati, Antonio. Breve schizzo dei sistemi di filosofia moderna e del proprio sistema. 4e ed. Firenze, 1964.

Phil 1717.19A   The revolution in philosophy. London, 1956.

Phil 1717.19B   The revolution in philosophy. London, 1956.

Phil 1717.20   La ricerca filosofia nella coscienza delle nuove generazioni. Bologna, 1957.

Phil 1717.21   Randall, John. The career of philosophy. N.Y., 1962. 2v.

Phil 1717.22   Russia, 1917. Ministerstvo vysshego Obrazovaniia. Kritika sovremennoi burzhuaznoi ideologii. Petrozavodsk, 1963.

Phil 1717.24   Rouche, Gerhard Albin. The philosophy of actuality. Fort Hare, 1963.

Phil 1717.26   Rossi, Paolo. Aspetti della rivoluzione scientifica. Napoli, 1971.

Phil 1718.1   Stöckl, A. Geschichte der neueren Philosophie. Mainz, 1883. 2v.

Phil 1718.2   Schellwien, R. Der Geist der neueren Philosophie. Leipzig, 1895.

Phil 1718.3   Schaller, J. Geschichte der Naturphilosophie, Bacon. pt.1-2. Leipzig, 1841-6.

Phil 1718.4   Stumpf, K. Die Wiedergeburt der Philosophie. Leipzig, 1908.

Phil 1718.5   Snider, Denton J. Modern European philosophy. Saint Louis, 1904.

Phil 1718.6   Sarlo, Francesco de. Filosofi del tempo nostro. Firenze, 1916.

Phil 1718.7   Stein, Ludwig. Philosophische Strömungen der Gegenwart. Stuttgart, 1908.

Phil 1718.7.5   Stein, Ludwig. Philosophical currents of the present day. Calcutta, 1918-19. 2v.

Phil 1718.8   Seth, Pringle-Pattison Andrew. The present position of the phisophical sciences. Edinburgh, 1891.

Phil 1718.9   Schjelderup, Harald K. Hauptlinien der Entwicklung der Philosophie von mitte des 19. Jahrhunderts bis zur Gegenwart. n.p., n.d.

Phil 1718.9.5   Schjelderup, Harald K. Filosofiens historie. Oslo, 1925.

Phil 1718.9.10   Schjelderup, Harald K. Geschichte der philosophischen Ideen von der Renaissance bis zur Gegenwart. Berlin, 1929.

Phil 1718.10   Sortais, Gaston. La philosophie moderne. Paris, 1921-22.

Phil 1718.11   Steinilber, E. Essais critiques sur les idées philosophiques contemporaines. Paris, 1912.

Phil 1718.12   Sageret, Jules. La revolution philosophique et la science. Paris, 1924.

Phil 1718.14   Stolzle, R. Das Problem des Lebens in der heutigen Philosophie. Paderborn, 1922.

Phil 1718.15   Steiner, Rudolf. Welt- und Lebensanschauungen im neunzehnten Jahrhundert. v.1-2. Berlin, 1901.

Phil 1718.15.5   Steiner, Rudolf. Die Rätsel der Philosophie in ihrer Geschichte. Stuttgart, 1924-26. 2v.

Phil 1718.17   Schaarschmidt, C. Der Entwicklungsgang der neueren Speculation. Bonn, 1857.

Phil 1718.19   Serra, Hunter J. Sentit i valor de la nova filosofia. Barcelona, 1934.

Phil 1718.20   Sassen, F. Geschiedenis van de wijsgeerte der negentiende eeuw. Antwerpen, 1934.

Phil 1718.21   Séronya, Henri. Initiation à la philosophie contemporaine. Paris, 1933.

Phil 1718.22A   Sorokin, P. Social philosophies of an age of crisis. Boston, 1950.

Phil 1718.22B   Sorokin, P. Social philosophies of an age of crisis. Boston, 1950.

Phil 1718.23   Smith, V.E. Idea man of today. Milwaukee, 1950.

Phil 1718.24   Sawicki, F. Lebensanschauungen moderner Denker. Paderborn, 1949-1952. 2v.

Phil 1718.25   Stegmüller, W. Hauptströmungen der Gegenwartphilosophie. Wien, 1952.

Phil 1718.25.1   Stegmüller, W. Main currents in contemporary German, British, and American philosophy. Bloomington, 1970.

Phil 1718.25.2   Stegmüller, W. Hauptströmungen der Gegenwartphilosophie. 2. Aufl. Stuttgart, 1960.

Phil 1718.26   Sahm, August. Jaspers als Blickpunkt für neue Einsichten. Worms am Rhein, 1952.

Phil 1718.27   Schneider, P. Philosophie der Gegenwart. München, 1953.

Phil 1718.28   Spenlé, J.E. Les grands maîtres de l'humanisme européen. Paris, 1952.

Phil 1718.29   Sciacca, Michele Federico. Il pensiero moderno. Brescia, 1949.

Phil 1718.29.5   Sciacca, Michele Federico. Les grands courants de la pensée modiale contemporaine. v.1-3. Milan, 1958- 6v.

Phil 1718.29.10   Sciacca, Michele Federico. Philosophical trends in the contemporary world. Notre Dame, 1964.

Phil 1718.30   Silva-Tarouca, Amadeo. Philosophie im Mittelpunkt. Graz, 1957.

Phil 1700 - 1725 History of philosophy - Modern philosophy in general - History - Special topics - Individual authors (A-Z) - cont.

Phil 1718.35 Strolz, Walter. Der vergessene Ursprung. Freiburg, 1959.
Phil 1718.37 Semerarí, Giuseppe. Da Schelling a Merkau-Ponty. Bologna, 1962.
Phil 1718.38 Stromberg, Roland N. An intellectual history of modern Europe. N.Y., 1966.
Phil 1718.40 Sándor, Pál. A filozófia is közügy! Tanulmányok. Budapest, 1968.
Phil 1718.42 Saffet, Mehmet. Muasir Aurupa felsefesi. Ankara, 1933.
Phil 1718.44 Semerari, Giuseppe. Esperienze del pensiero moderno. Urbino, 1969.
Phil 1718.46 Šarčević, Abdulah. Iskon i smisao. Sarajevo, 1971.
Phil 1719.1 Thilo, C.A. Kurze pragmatische Geschichte der neueren Philosophie. Göthen, 1874.
Phil 1719.2 Tullock, J. Modern theories in philosophy and religion. Edinburgh, 1884.
Phil 1719.3 Tonelli, L. L'anima moderna, da Lessing a Nietzsche. Milano, 1925.
Phil 1719.5 Thyssen, Johannes. Realismus und moderne Philosophie. Bonn, 1959.
Phil 1719.6 Thyssen, Johannes. Grundlinien eines realistischen Systems der Philosophie. Bonn, 1966. 2v.
Phil 1720.5 Urmson, J.O. Philosophical analysis. Oxford, 1956.
Phil 1721.1 Volkett, J. Vorträge zur Einführung in der Philosophie der Gegenwart. Photoreproduction. München, 1892.
Phil 1721.2 Vignoli, Tito. L'era nuova del pensiero. Milano, 1885.
Phil 1721.3 Veloso, A. Nos encruzilhadas do pensamento. Porto, 1956.
Phil 1721.4 Veit, Otto. Soziologie der Freiheit. Frankfurt a.M., 1957.
Phil 1721.5 Vloemans, Antoon. Europa in de spiegel. Den Haag, 1957.
Phil 1721.6 Verneaux, Roger. Histoire de la philosophie moderne. Paris, 1958.
Phil 1721.7 Vélez Correa, Jaime. Historia de la filosofía moderna y contemporánea. Bogotá, 1959.
Phil 1721.7.5 Vélez Correa, Jaime. Filosofía moderna y contemporanea. Madrid, 1965.
Phil 1721.8 Dalori, Paolo. Il pensiero filosofico odierno. Roma, 1959.
Phil 1721.9 Vieteck, George S. The seven against man. Scotch Plains, N.J., 1941.
Phil 1722.1 Weigelt, G. Zur Geschichte der neueren Philosophie. Hamburg, 1855.
Phil 1722.2A Windelband, W. Die Geschichte der neueren Philosophie. Leipzig, 1878-80. 2v.
Phil 1722.2B Windelband, W. Die Geschichte der neueren Philosophie. Leipzig, 1878-80. 2v.
Phil 1722.2.5 Windelband, W. Die Philosophie im Beginn des Zwanzigsten. Heidelberg, 1904.
Phil 1722.2.7 Windelband, W. Die Philosophie im Beginn des Zwanzigsten. Jahrhunderts. 2e Aufl. Heidelberg, 1907.
Phil 1722.2.8 Windelband, W. Die Philosophie im Beginn des zwanzigsten Jahrhunderts. Heidelberg, 1907.
Phil 1722.3 Webb, C.C.J. A history of philosophy. London, 1915.
Phil 1722.4.5 Wardwell, R.J. Contemporary philosophy. London, 1913.
Phil 1722.5.2 Wenzig, Carl. Die Weltanschuungen der Gegenwart. 2e Aufl. Leipzig, 1919.
Phil 1722.6 Ward, Charles H. Builders of delusion. Indianapolis, 1931.
Phil 1722.7 Wahl, Jean. Vers le concret; études d'histoire de la philosophie contemporaine. Paris, 1932.
Phil 1722.8 Wright, W.K. A history of modern philosophy. N.Y., 1941.
Phil 1722.9 White, M.G. The age of analysis. Boston, 1955.
Phil 1722.9.5 White, M.G. Toward reunion in philosophy. Cambridge, 1956.
Phil 1722.10 Werner, Charles. La philosophie moderne. Paris, 1954.
Phil 1722.11 Weber, Alfred. Histoire de la philosophie européenne. Paris, 1957.
Phil 1722.12 Waelkens, Alphonse de. Existence et signification. Louvain, 1958.
Phil 1722.12.5 Waelkens, Alphonse de. La philosophie et les experiences naturelles. La Haye, 1961.
Phil 1722.13 Warsaw. Univerystet. Główne zagadnienia i kierunki filozofii. v.1-2. 2. Wyd. Warszawa, 1960.
Phil 1725.1 Zuccante, Giuseppe. Uomini e dottrine. Torino, 1926.
Phil 1725.2 Zema, Demetrius. The thoughtlessness of modern thought. N.Y., 1934.

Phil 1730 History of philosophy - Modern philosophy in general - History - Special topics - 17th-18th centuries

Phil 1730.2 Starck, Johann G. Der Triumph der Philosophie im Achtzehnten Jahrhunderts. Germantown, 1804. 2v.
Phil 1730.4 Gourju, Pierre. La philosophie du dix-huitième siècle dévoilée par elle-même. Paris, 1816. 2v.
Phil 1730.6 Erdmann, Karl. Die theologische und philosophische Aufklärung des achtzshuten und neunzehuten Jahrhunderts. Leipzig, 1849.
Phil 1730.8 Lanfrey, Pierre. L'église et les philosophes au dix-huitième siècle. Paris, 1855.
Phil 1730.8.3 Lanfrey, Pierre. L'église et les philosophes au dix-huitième siècle. Paris, 1879.
Phil 1730.10 Seredi, P. Lajos. Az ismeret eredetének kérdése a XVII és XVIII szazad filozófiai küzdelmeiben Kantig. Eperjes, 1889.
Phil 1730.12 Marck, Siegfried. Das Jahrhundert der Aufklärung. Leipzig, 1923.
Phil 1730.14 DeAngelis, Eurico. Il metodo geometrico nella filosofia del Seicento. Pisa, 1964.
Phil 1730.16 Lively, Jack. The enlightenment. London, 1966.
Phil 1730.18 Winter, Eduard. Frühaufklärung; der Kampf Gegen den Konfessionalismus in Mittel- und Osteuropa und die deutsch-slawische Begegnung. Berlin, 1966.
Phil 1730.20 Studi sull'illuminismo di G. Solinas. Firenze, 1966.
Phil 1730.22 Denker, Rolf. Grenzen liberaler Aufklärung bei Kant und Anderen. Stuttgart, 1968.
Phil 1730.24 Goldmann, Lucien. Der christliche Bürger und die Aufklärung. Neuwied, 1968.
Phil 1730.26 Merker, Nicolao. L'illuminismo tedesco. Bari, 1968.
Phil 1730.27.1 Berlin, Isaiah. The age of enlightenment. Freeport, 1970.
Phil 1730.28 Mortier, Roland. Clartés et ombres du siècle des lumières. Études sur le 18e siècle littéraire. Genève, 1969.
Phil 1730.30 Venturi, Franco. Utopia e riforma nell'iluminismo. Torino, 1970.
Phil 1730.31 Venturi, Franco. Utopia and reform in the enlightenment. Cambridge, Eng., 1971.
Phil 1730.32 Ponte Orvieto, Marina da. L'unità de sapere nell'illuminismo. Padova, 1968.

Phil 1730 History of philosophy - Modern philosophy in general - History - Special topics - 17th-18th centuries - cont.

Phil 1730.34 Garin, Eugenio. Dal rinascimento all'illuminismo. Studi e ricerche. Pisa, 1970.
Phil 1730.36 Leyden, Wolfgang von. Seventeenth-century metaphysics. N.Y., 1968.

Phil 1735 History of philosophy - Modern philosophy in general - History - Special topics - 19th century

Phil 1735.2 Gruppe, Otto F. Wendepunkt der Philosophie im neunzehnten Jahrhundert. Berlin, 1834.
Phil 1735.4 Guepin, Anec. Philosophie du XIXe siècle. Paris, 1854.
Phil 1735.6 Gómez Izquierdo, Alberto. Historia de la filosofía del siglo XIX. Zaragoza, 1903.
Phil 1735.8 Bergmann, Ernst. Der Geist des XIX. Jahrhunderts. Breslau, 1922.
Phil 1735.8.2 Bergmann, Ernst. Der Geist des XIX. Jahrhunderts. 2. Aufl. Breslau, 1927.
Phil 1735.10 Tilgher, Adriano. Filosofi e moralisti del novecento. Roma, 1932.
Phil 1735.12 Rava, Adolfo. La filosofia Europea nel secolo decimonono. Padova, 1932.
Phil 1735.14 Istoriko filosofskii sbornik. Moskva, 1969.
Phil 1735.16 Mandelbaum, Maurice H. History, man, and reason; a study in nineteenth-century thought. Baltimore, 1971.

Phil 1740 History of philosophy - Modern philosophy in general - History - Special periods - 20th century

Phil 1740.2 Müller-Freienfels, Richard. Die Philosophie des zwanzigsten Jahrhunderts in ihren Hauptströmungen. Berlin, 1923.
Phil 1740.4 Runes, Dagobert D. Twentieth century philosophy; living schools of thought. N.Y., 1943.
Phil 1740.6 Hessen, Johannes. Die Philosophie des 20. Jahrhunderts. Rottenburg, 1951.
Phil 1740.8 Delfgaauw, Bernardus M.I. De wijsbegeerts va di 20. eeuw. Baarn, 1957.
Phil 1740.10 Banfi, Antonio. La filosofia degli ultími cinquanti anni. Milano, 1957.
Phil 1740.12 Ferrater Mora, José. La filosofía actual. Madrid, 1969.
Phil 1740.14 Dondeyne, Albert. Contemporary European thought and Christian faith. Pittsburgh, 1958.
Phil 1740.16.4 Stegmüller, Wolfgang. Hauptströmungen der Gegenwartsphilosophie. 4. Aufl. Stuttgart, 1969.
Phil 1740.18 Edmaier, Alois. Die Philosophie der Gegenwart. Aschaffenburg, 1970.
Phil 1740.20 Beyer, Wilhelm Raimund. Vier Kritiken. Heidegger, Sartre, Adorno, Lukácz. Köln, 1970.
Phil 1740.22 Rossi, Pietro. Lo storicismo contemporaneo. Torino, 1968.
Phil 1740.24 Raschini, Maria A. Riflessioni su filosofia e cultura. Milano, 1968.
Phil 1740.26 Calabró, Gaetano. La società fuori tutela. Napoli, 1970.
Phil 1740.28 López Quintás, Alfonso. Pensadores cristianos contemporáneos. v.1- Madrid, 1968-

Phil 1750 History of philosophy - Modern philosophy in general - History - Special top+cs

Phil 1750.1 Leib, J.R. Lecture on nature and objects of modern philosophy. Philadelphia, 1830-39. 3 pam.
Phil 1750.2 Price, E.K. Some phases of modern philosophy. Philadelphia, 1872. 2 pam.
Phil 1750.4 Janet, P. Les maîtres de la pensée moderne. Paris, 1883.
Phil 1750.5 Roberty, E. de. La philosophie du siècle. Paris, 1891.
Phil 1750.6 Huet, F. La révolution philosophique. Paris, 1871.
Phil 1750.9 Barthoemiss, C. Histoire critique des doctrines religieuses et philosophiques. Paris, 1855. 2v.
Phil 1750.10 Hermann, C. Der Gegensatz...der neueren Philosophie. Leipzig, 1877.
Phil 1750.11 Schmidt, H.J. Geschichte der Romantik...philosophische Geschichte. Leipzig, 1850. 2v.
Phil 1750.11.15 Maitra, S.K. The neo-romantic movement in contemporary philosophy. Thesis. Calcutta, 1922.
Phil 1750.12 Cousin, V. Philosophie sensualiste au XVIIIe siècle. Paris, 1866.
Phil 1750.14 Gratry, A.J.A. Étude sur la sophistique contemporaine. Paris, 1851.
Phil 1750.14.10 Gratry, A.J.A. Les sophistes et la critique. Paris, 1864.
Phil 1750.15 Funck-Brentano, T. Les sophistes grecs...et contemporains. Paris, 1879.
Phil 1750.16 Leschbrand, A. Substanzbegriff in der neueren Philosophie. Rostock, 1895.
Phil 1750.17 Haas, A. Über der Einfluss der Epicureischen...Philosophie des 16 und 17 Jahrhunderts. Berlin, 1896.
Phil 1750.20 McClure, M.T. Study of realistic movement in contemporary philosophy. Staunton, 1912.
Phil 1750.21 Chide, A. Le mobilisme moderne. Paris, 1908.
Phil 1750.22A Taylor, Henry O. Thought and expression in the 16th century. N.Y., 1920. 2v.
Phil 1750.22B Taylor, Henry O. Thought and expression in the 16th century. N.Y., 1920. 2v.
Phil 1750.22.5 Taylor, Henry O. Thought and expression in the 16th century. 2. ed. N.Y., 1930. 2v.
Phil 1750.22.10 Taylor, Henry O. Thought and expression in the 16th century. 2. ed. N.Y., 1959. 2v.
Phil 1750.23 McCutcheon, Roger Philip. The present-day relevance of eighteenth-century thought. Washington, 1956.
Phil 1750.24 Derisi, Octavio N. Filosofía moderna y filosofía tomista. Buenos Aires, 1941.
Phil 1750.25 Heitzman, M. Mikolaj Hill. Studjum z histoiji filozofji atomistycznej. Krakow, 192-?
Phil 1750.26 Ussher, A. Journey through dread. N.Y., 1955.
Phil 1750.27 Nicolas, M. De l'eclectisme. Paris, 1840.
Phil 1750.29 Grassi, E. Von Ursprung und Grenzen der Geistewissenschaften und Naturwissenschaften. Bern, 1950.
Phil 1750.31 Hazard, P. Die Herrschaft der Vermunft. Hamburg, 1949.
Phil 1750.33 Stackelberg, J. von. Schuld ist Schicksal. München, 1948.
Phil 1750.35 Vancourt, R. La phénoménologie et la foi. Tournai, 1953.
Phil 1750.38 Lyotard, Jean François. La phénoménologie. 3e éd. Paris, 1959.
Phil 1750.38.6 Lyotard, Jean François. La phénoménologie. 6e éd. Paris, 1967.
Phil 1750.40 Haas, William S. The destiny of the mind. N.Y., 1956.
Phil 1750.41 Herzberg, Günther. Die grosse Kontroverse. Meisenheim, 1953.
NEDL Phil 1750.45 Lukács, G. Az ész troufasztása. Budapest, 1954.
Phil 1750.50 Berg, J.H. van der. The phenomenological approach to psychiatry. Springfield, Ill., 1955.
Phil 1750.55 Damur, Carl. Das Test der Seele. Bern, 1947.

114

Classified Listing

Phil 1750 History of philosophy - Modern philosophy in general - History - Special top+cs - cont.

Phil 1750.60 Przywara, Erich. In und Gegen. Nürnberg, 1955.
Phil 1750.65 Flam, Leopold. De krisis van de burgerlijke moraal. Antwerpen, 1956.
Phil 1750.70 Gurwitsch, Aron. Théorie du champ de la conscience. Paris, 1957.
Phil 1750.70.5 Gurwitsch, Aron. The field of consciousness. Pittsburgh, 1964.
Phil 1750.75 Brecht, Franz Josef. Bewusstsein und Existenz. Bremen, 1948.
Phil 1750.78 Kittaka, Rin'ichi. New method of philosophy: an introduction to radiciology. Tokyo, 1967.
Phil 1750.80 Civilization du travail? Paris, 1956.
Phil 1750.82 Mihalich, J.C. Existentialism and Thomism. N.Y., 1960.
Phil 1750.85 Siu, Ralph G.H. The Tao of science. Cambridge, Mass., 1957.
Phil 1750.90.2 Hughes, Henry Stuart. Consciousness and society. N.Y., 1961.
Phil 1750.95 Engelhardt, Wolf von. Der Mensch in der technischen Welt. Köln, 1957.
Phil 1750.95.10 Charlesworth, Maxwell John. Philosophy and linguistic analysis. Pittsburgh, 1959.
Phil 1750.96 Farber, Marvin. Naturalism and subjectivism. Springfield, Ill., 1959.
Phil 1750.96.5 Boller, Paul F. American thought in transition: the impact of evolutionary naturalism, 1865-1900. Chicago, 1969.
Phil 1750.97 Cotereau, Jean. Que l'homme soit! Paris, 1959.
Phil 1750.98 Haag, Karl Hanz. Kritik der neueren Ontologie. Stuttgart, 1960.
Phil 1750.99 Breton, Stanislas. Approches phénoménologiques de l'idée d'être. Paris, 1959.
Phil 1750.100 Haag, Karl Hanz. Kritik der neueren Ontololgie. Stuttgart, 1960.
Phil 1750.101 Tymieniecka, Anna Teresa. Phenomenology and science in contemporary European thought. N.Y., 1962.
Phil 1750.101.5 Tymieniecka, Anna Teresa. Why is there something rather than nothing? Assen, 1966.
Phil 1750.102 Zaner, R.M. The problem of embodiment. The Hague, 1964.
Phil 1750.103 Compagnion, Jean. La philosophie scolastique au XXe siècle. Critique néo-scotiste du Thomisme. Paris, 1916.
Phil 1750.104 Zybura, John. S. Present-day thinkers and the new scholasticism. Saint Louis, 1926.
Phil 1750.105 Meglio, Gaetano. Prospettive filosofiche. Padova, 1966.
Phil 1750.106 Phillips, Richard P. Modern Thomistic philosophy. London, 1934-40. 2v.
Phil 1750.107 Muck, Otto. Die transzendentale Methode in der scholastischen Philosophie der Gegenwart. Innsbruck, 1964.
Phil 1750.107.2 Muck, Otto. The transcendental method. N.Y., 1968.
Phil 1750.110 Hengslenberg, Hans Eduard. Philosophische Anthropologie. Stuttgart, 1957.
Phil 1750.113 Boutroux, E. De l'idée de la loi naturelle. Paris, 1913.
VPhil 1750.115 Faragó, László. A harmadik humanismus és a harmadik birodalom. Budapest, 1935.
Phil 1750.115.2 Goodman, Nelson. The structure of appearance. Indianapolis, 1966.
Phil 1750.115.3A Goodman, Nelson. The structure of appearance. Cambridge, 1951.
Phil 1750.115.3B Goodman, Nelson. The structure of appearance. Cambridge, 1951.
Phil 1750.115.20 Archivio di Filosofia. Fenomenologia e sociologia. Padova, 1951.
Phil 1750.115.25 Merleau-Ponty, Maurice. Phénoménologie de la perception. Paris, 1945.
Phil 1750.115.26 Merleau-Ponty, Maurice. Phénoménologie de la perception. Paris, 1945.
Phil 1750.115.28 Merleau-Ponty, Maurice. Phenomenology of perception. London, 1966.
Phil 1750.115.30A Jeanson, F. La phénoménologie. Paris, 1951.
Phil 1750.115.30B Jeanson, F. La phénoménologie. Paris, 1951.
Phil 1750.115.35 Trân-Dúc-Thao. Phénoménologie et materialisme dialectique. Paris, 1951.
Phil 1750.115.37 Abellio, Raymond. La structure absolue; essai de phénoménologie génétique. Paris, 1965.
Phil 1750.115.40 Breda, H.L. Problémes actuels de la phénoménologie. Paris, 1952.
Phil 1750.115.50 Spiegelberg, Herbert. The phenomenological movement. Hague, 1960. 2v.
Phil 1750.115.55 Luijpen, Wilhelmus Antonius Maria. De fenomenologie is een humorisme. Amsterdam, 1961.
Phil 1750.115.56 Luijpen, Wilhelmus Antonius Maria. Phenomenology and humanism. Pittsburg, 1966.
Phil 1750.115.60 Thevenaz, Pierre. What is phenomenology? Chicago, 1967.
Phil 1750.115.62 Thevenaz, Pierre. De Husserl à Merleau-Ponty. Neuchâtel, 1966.
Phil 1750.115.65 Chatteyee, Margaret. Our knowledge of other selves. Bombay, 1963.
Phil 1750.115.70 Fink, Eugen. Studien zur Phänomenologie, 1930-1939. Den Haag, 1966.
Phil 1750.115.75 Nikolov, Elit I. Fenomenologiia i estetika. Sofiia, 1965.
Phil 1750.115.80 Schutz, Alfred. The phenomenology of the social world. Evanston, Ill., 1967.
Phil 1750.115.85 Phenomenology and existentialism. Baltimore, 1967.
Phil 1750.115.87 Micallef, John. Philosophy of existence. N.Y., 1969.
Phil 1750.115.90 Phenomenology in America. Chicago, 1967.
Phil 1750.115.95 Lexington. Conference on Pure and Applied Phenomenology. Phenomenology of will and action. Chicago, 1967.
Phil 1750.115.100 Funke, Gerhard. Phänomenologie- Metaphysik oder Methode? Bonn, 1966.
Phil 1750.115.115 Rollin, France. La phénoménologie au départ, Husserl, Heidagger, Gaboriau. Paris, 1967.
Phil 1750.115.120 Bakker, Reinout. De geschiedenis van het fenomenologisch denken. Antwerp, 1964.
Phil 1750.115.125 Merleau-Ponty, Maurice. Les sciences de l'homme et la phénoménologie. Paris, 1965.
Phil 1750.115.130 Landgrebe, Ludwig. Phänomenologie und Geschichte. 1. Aufl. Gütersloh, 1968.
Phil 1750.115.135 Forni, Guglielmo. Il sogno finito. Bologna, 1967.
Phil 1750.115.140 Sini, Carlo. Introduzione alla fenomenologia come scienza. Milano, 1965.
Phil 1750.115.145 Sinha, Debabrata. Studies in phenomenology. The Hague, 1969.
Phil 1750.115.150 Conci, Domenico. La conclusione della filosofia categoriale. Roma, 1967.
Phil 1750.115.155 Hoeven, Johannes van der. Kritische ondervraging van de fenomenologische rede. Amsterdam, 1963.
Phil 1750.115.160 Schmitz, Hermann. Subjektivität; Beiträge zur Phänomenologie und Logik. Bonn, 1968.

Phil 1750 History of philosophy - Modern philosophy in general - History - Special top+cs - cont.

Phil 1750.115.165 Sini, Carlo. La fenomenologia. 1. ed. Milano, 1965.
Phil 1750.115.170 Neri, Guido Davide. Prassi e conoscenza. 1. ed. Milano, 1966.
Phil 1750.115.175 Kwant, Remigius Cornelis. Phenomonology of expression. Pittsburgh, 1969.
Phil 1750.115.180 New essays in phenomenology. Chicago, 1969.
Phil 1750.115.185 Ehel, Gerhard. Untersuchungen zu einer realistischen Grundlegung der phänomenologischen Wesensschau. München, 1965.
Phil 1750.115.190 Prohić, Kasim. Odvažnost izricanja; fenomenologije životnih formi. Zagreb, 1970.
Phil 1750.115.195 Mailov, Anatolii Il'ich. Opisanie i ob"iasnenie. Tashkent, 1969.
Phil 1750.115.200 Brand, Gerd. Die Lebenswelt. Berlin, 1971.
Phil 1750.115.205 Schutz, Alfred. On phenomenology and social relations. Chicago, 1970.
Phil 1750.116 Marxist-Non-Marxist Humanist Dialogue, 2d, Herceg-Novi, 1969. Tolerance and revolution. Beograd, 1970.
Phil 1750.118 Hönigswald, R. Philosophische Motive im neuzeitlichen Humanismus. Breslau, 1918.
Phil 1750.122.2 Rickert, H. Die Philosophie des Lebens. Tübingen, 1922.
Phil 1750.123 Groot, J.V. de. Denkers van onzen tijd. Uitgevers, 1918.
Phil 1750.123.5 Denkers over zeil en leven. Amsterdam, 1917.
Phil 1750.124 Wach, Joachim. Das Verstehen. Tübingen, 1926-33. 3v.
Phil 1750.125 Tilgher, A. Relativisti contemporanei. Roma, 1923.
Phil 1750.126.3 Benda, Julien. The great betrayal. London, 1928.
Phil 1750.126.6A Benda, Julien. The treason of the intellectuals. N.Y., 1928.
Phil 1750.126.6B Benda, Julien. The treason of the intellectuals. N.Y., 1928.
Phil 1750.126.8 Benda, Julien. La trahison des clercs. Paris, 1958.
Phil 1750.126.8.2 Benda, Julien. La trahison des clercs. Paris, 1965.
Phil 1750.126.10 Bourquin, Constant. Itinéraire de Sirius a Jérusalem. Paris, 1931.
Phil 1750.127 Boehm, Benno. Sokrates im achtzehnten Jahrhundert. Leipzig, 1929.
Phil 1750.127.2 Boehm, Benno. Sokrates im achtzehnten Jahrhundert. Leipzig, 1929.
Phil 1750.129 Belgion, Montgomery. Our present philosophy of life. London, 1929.
Phil 1750.129.5 Belgion, Montgomery. The human parrot and other essays. London, 1931.
Phil 1750.130 Grattan, Clinton H. The critique of humanism; a symposium. N.Y., 1930.
Phil 1750.130.5A Grattan, Clinton H. The critique of humanism. N.Y., 1930.
Phil 1750.130.5B Grattan, Clinton H. The critique of humanism. N.Y., 1930.
Phil 1750.131 King, William Peter. Humanism. Nashville, 1931.
Phil 1750.132A McMahon, Francis E. Humanism of Irving Babbitt. Diss. Washington, D.C., 1931.
Phil 1750.132B McMahon, Francis E. Humanism of Irving Babbitt. Diss. Washington, D.C., 1931.
Phil 1750.132.10 Grosselin, O. The intuitive voluntarism of Irving Babbitt. Latrohe, Pa., 1951.
Phil 1750.133A Mercier, L.J.A. Challenge of humanism. N.Y., 1933.
Phil 1750.133B Mercier, L.J.A. Challenge of humanism. N.Y., 1933.
Phil 1750.134 Killeen, M.V. Man in the new humanism. Thesis. Washington, D.C., 1934.
Phil 1750.135 MacCampbell, D. Irving Babbitt. n.p., 1935.
Phil 1750.136 Richard, Christian. Le mouvement humaniste en Amerique. Paris, 1934.
Phil 1750.136.5 Richard, Christian. Le mouvement humaniste en Amérique et les courants de pensée similaire en France. Thèse. Paris, 1934.
Phil 1750.140 Krzesinski, André. Une nouvelle philosophie de l'immanence. Paris, 1931.
Phil 1750.141A Cassirer, Ernst. Die Philosophie der Aufklärung. Tübingen, 1932.
Phil 1750.141B Cassirer, Ernst. Die Philosophie der Aufklärung. Tübingen, 1932.
Phil 1750.141.3A Cassirer, Ernst. The philosophy of the enlightenment. Princeton, N.J., 1951.
Phil 1750.141.3B Cassirer, Ernst. The philosophy of the enlightenment. Princeton, N.J., 1951.
Phil 1750.141.7A Cassirer, Ernst. Rousseau, Kant, Goethe; two essays. Princeton, 1947.
Phil 1750.141.7B Cassirer, Ernst. Rousseau, Kant, Goethe; two essays. Princeton, 1947.
Phil 1750.142 Santayana, George. Some turns of thought in modern philosophy. Cambridge, Eng., 1933.
Phil 1750.142.2 Santayana, George. Some turns of thought in modern philosophy. N.Y., 1933.
Phil 1750.143 Juganaru, P. L'apologie de la guerre dans la philosophie contemporaine. Thèse. Paris, 1933.
Phil 1750.144A Bréhier, Emile. La notion de renaissance dans l'histoire de la philosophie. Oxford, 1934.
Phil 1750.144B Bréhier, Emile. La notion de renaissance dans l'histoire de la philosophie. Oxford, 1934.
Phil 1750.145 Hartshore, Charles. Beyond humanism. Chicago, 1937.
Phil 1750.146 Leander, F. Humanism and naturalism. Göteborg, 1937.
Phil 1750.147 Brémond, Henri. Autour de l'humanisme d'Erasme à Pascal. Paris, 1937.
Phil 1750.148 Rudiger, H. Wesen und Wandlung des Humanismus. Hamburg, 1937.
Phil 1750.149 Philippard, L. Connais-toi toi-même. Paris, 1937.
Phil 1750.150 Jansen, B. Die Pflege der Philosophie. Fulda, 1938.
Phil 1750.151 Elliott, George R. Humanism and imagination. Chapel Hill, 1938.
Phil 1750.152.10 Becker, Carl Lotus. The heavenly city of the eighteenth-century philosophers. New Haven, 1968.
Phil 1750.153 Association Guillaume Budé. L'humanisme en Alsace. Paris, 1939.
Phil 1750.155 Mercati, G. Ultimi contributi alla storia degli umanisti. pt.1-2. Città del Vaticano, 1939.
Phil 1750.156 Walsh, Gerald G. Medieval humanism. N.Y., 1942.
Phil 1750.157 Simond, D. Antipolitique. Lausanne, 1941.
Phil 1750.158 Sheldon, W.H. Process and polarity. N.Y., 1944.
Phil 1750.159 Rossi, Edmundo. Retorno à vida (ensaios). São Paulo, 1941.
Phil 1750.160 Fondy, John T. The educational principles of American humanism. Diss. Washington, D.C., 1945.
Phil 1750.161 Fiolle, Jean. La crise de l'humanisme. Paris, 1937.
Phil 1750.162 Richards, P.S. Humanism. London, 1934.
Phil 1750.163 Drewinc, H. VierGestalten aus den Zeitalter des Humanismus. Saint Gallen, 1946.
Phil 1750.164 Munson, G.B. The dilemma of the liberated. N.Y., 1930.

Classified Listing

Phil 1750 History of philosophy - Modern philosophy in general - History - Special top+cs - cont.

Phil 1750.165 Truc, G. De J.P. Sartre à L. Lavelle. Paris, 1946.
Phil 1750.166 Les grands appels de l'homme contemporain. Paris, 1946.
Phil 1750.166.5 Mercier, Louis J.A. American humanism and the new age. Milwaukee, 1948.
Phil 1750.166.10 Boucher, Maurice. Goethescher Geist und zwanzigstes Jahrhundert. Mainz, 1947.
Phil 1750.166.15 Granell Muñiz, M. El humanismo como responsabilidad. Madrid, 1959.
Phil 1750.166.17 Bottai, Giuseppe. Verteidigung des Humanismus. 2. Aufl. Berlin, 1942.
Phil 1750.166.20 Lamont, Corliss. Humanism as a philosophy. N.Y., 1949.
Phil 1750.166.21 Lamont, Corliss. Humanism as a philosophy. 2nd ed. N.Y., 1949.
Phil 1750.166.23 Lamont, Corliss. The philosophy of humanism. 5th ed. N.Y., 1965.
Phil 1750.166.24 Lamont, Corliss. The philosophy of humanism. 4th ed. N.Y., 1957.
Phil 1750.166.25 Ulmann, Andre. L'humanisme du 20e siècle. Paris, 1946.
Phil 1750.166.30 Heidegger, Martin. Über den Humanismus. Frankfurt, 1949.
Phil 1750.166.30.5 Heidegger, Martin. Lettre sur l'humanisme. Paris, 1957.
Phil 1750.166.35 Blackham, H.J. Living as a humanist. London, 1957.
Phil 1750.166.35.5 Blackham, H.J. The human tradition. Boston, 1953.
Phil 1750.166.35.7 Blackham, H.J. The human tradition. Boston, 1954.
Phil 1750.166.45 Mennesket i tiden. København, 1950.
Phil 1750.166.50 France. Centre National de la Recherche Scientifique. Pensée humaniste et tradition chrêtienne aux XVe et XVIe siècle. Paris, 1950.
Phil 1750.166.55 Bohlin, T.B. Debatt med profanhumanisien. Stockholm, 1951.
Phil 1750.166.60 Rey, Gabriel. Humanisme et surhumanisme. Paris, 1951.
Phil 1750.166.65 Przymara, E. Humanitus. Nuinberg, 1952.
Phil 1750.166.70 Sodalitas Erasmiana. Il valore universale dell'umanesimo. Napoli, 1950.
Phil 1750.166.75 Umanesimo e machiavellismo. Padova, 1949.
Phil 1750.166.80 Krueger, Gerhard. Abendländische Humanität. Stuttgart, 1953.
Phil 1750.166.85 Laloup, Jean. Hommes et machines. Tournai, 1953.
Phil 1750.166.85.5 Laloup, Jean. Communauté des hommes. 4e éd. Tournai, 1957.
Phil 1750.166.90 Huxley, J.S. Evolutionary humanism. Melbourne, 1954.
Phil 1750.166.91 Huxley, J.S. The humanist frame. London, 1961.
Phil 1750.166.92 Huxley, J.S. The humanist frame. N.Y., 1962.
Phil 1750.166.95 Hulst, H.C von. Phänomenologie en natuurwetenschap. Utrecht, 1953.
Phil 1750.166.100 Etcheverry, A. Le conflit actuel des humanismes. Paris, 1955.
Phil 1750.166.101 Etcheverry, A. Le conflit actuel des humanismes. Roma, 1964.
Phil 1750.166.105 Roshwald, M. Humanism in practice. London, 1955.
Phil 1750.166.110 Relgis, Eugen. El humanitarismo. Buenos Aires, 1956.
Phil 1750.166.115 Mensch und Menschlichkeit. Stuttgart, 1950.
Phil 1750.166.117 Paparelli, Gioacchino. Tra umanesimo e reforma. Napoli, 1946.
Phil 1750.166.120 Renaudet, Augustin. Humanisme et Renaissance. Genève, 1958.
Phil 1750.166.125 Zuidema, S.U. Baanbrekers van het humanisme. Franeker, 1959.
Phil 1750.166.130 Cobban, Alfred. In search of humanity. London, 1960.
Phil 1750.166.132 Cobban, Alfred. In search of humanity. N.Y., 1960.
Phil 1750.166.135 Dijkhuis, P. Polariteitsbesef als een der fundamenten van het humanisme. Assen, 1960.
Phil 1750.166.140 Frerichs, J.G. Waarde van de mens en menselijke waardigheid. Zaandam, 1960.
Phil 1750.166.145 Blackham, H.J. Objections to humanism. London, 1963.
Phil 1750.166.150 Kiley, W. Human possibilities. N.Y., 1963.
Phil 1750.166.153 Spongano, Raffaele. Due saggi sull'umanesimo. Firenze, 1964.
Phil 1750.166.155 Petrosian, M.J. Gumanizm; opyt filosofskoetich i potsial issled problemy. Moskva, 1964.
Phil 1750.166.160 Gastão, Manuel M. Humanismos e suas diversas interpretações. Lisboa, 1963.
Phil 1750.166.165 Rede en religie in het humanisme. Amsterdam, 1962.
Phil 1750.166.170 Amoroso Lima, Alcew. Pelo humanismo ameaçado. Rio de Janeiro, 1965.
Phil 1750.166.175 Mollenauer, Robert. Introduction to modernity. Austin, 1965.
Phil 1750.166.180 Panikkar, Raimundo. Humanismo y cruz. Madrid, 1963.
Phil 1750.166.185 Niel, André. Les grands appels de l'humanisme contemporain, christianisme, marxisme. Paris, 1966.
Phil 1750.166.190 Orrego, Antenor. Hacia un humanismo americano. Lima, 1966.
Phil 1750.166.195 Spirito, Ugo. Nuovo umanesimo. Roma, 1964.
Phil 1750.166.200 Hadas, Moses. The living tradition. N.Y., 1967.
Phil 1750.166.205 Castanos, Stelios. Réponse à Heidegger sur l'humanisme. Paris, 1966.
Phil 1750.166.210 Corts Grau, José. Los humanismos y el hombre. Madrid, 1967.
Phil 1750.166.215 Toesca, Pietro M. Verità e rivoluzione. Roma, 1965.
Phil 1750.166.220 Beaujon, Edmond. Némésis; ou, La limite. Paris, 1965.
Phil 1750.166.225 Dresden, Samuel. Het humanistische denken. Italië-Frankrijk 1450-1600. Amsterdam, 1968.
Phil 1750.166.230 Vogel, Cornelia Johanna de. Het humanisme en zijn historische achtergrond. Assen, 1968.
Phil 1750.166.235 Mukerjee, Radhakamal. The way of humanism, East and West. Bombay, 1968.
Phil 1750.166.240 Levi, Albert William. Humanism and politics. Bloomington, 1969.
Phil 1750.166.255 Millas, Orlando. El humanismo científico de los comunistas. Santiago de Chile, 1968.
Phil 1750.166.260 Mueller-Schwefe, Hans Rudolf. Humanismus ohne Gott. Stuttgart, 1967.
Phil 1750.166.270 Horosz, William. The promise and peril of human purpose. Saint Louis, 1970.
Phil 1750.166.275 Azevedo, Fernando de. Na batalho do humanismo. 2. ed. São Paulo, 1967.
Phil 1750.166.280 Legitimo, Gianfranco. Nuovo umanesimo sociale. Torino, 1968.
Phil 1750.166.285 Echandia, Dario. Humanismo y tecnica. Bogota, 1969.
Phil 1750.166.290 Santinello, Giovanni. Studi sull'Umanesimo europeo. Padova, 1969.
Phil 1750.167 Barrett, William. What is existentialism? N.Y., 1947.
Phil 1750.167.2 Barrett, William. What is existentialism? N.Y., 1947.

Phil 1750 History of philosophy - Modern philosophy in general - History - Special top+cs - cont.

Phil 1750.167.3A Barrett, William. What is existentialism? N.Y., 1964.
Phil 1750.167.3B Barrett, William. What is existentialism? N.Y., 1964.
Phil 1750.167.5 Barrett, William. Irrational man. Garden City, 1958.
Phil 1750.169 Beerling, Reimer. Het existentialisme. 's Gravenhage, 1947.
Phil 1750.171 Grene, M. Dreadful freedom. Chicago, 1948.
Phil 1750.172 Schrader, George Alfred. Existential philosophers. N.Y., 1967.
Phil 1750.173 Pesch, Edgar. L'existentialisme. Paris, 1946.
Phil 1750.175 Pruche, B. Existentialisme et acte d'être. Paris, 1947.
Phil 1750.177 Hessen, J. Existenzphilosophie. Essen, 1947.
Phil 1750.177.1 Hessen, Johannes. Existenzphilosophie. Basel, 1948.
Phil 1750.179 Bollnow, O.F. Existenzphilosophie. 2e Aufl. Stuttgart, 1942?
Phil 1750.179.5A Bollnow, O.F. Existenzphilosophie. 3. Aufl. Stuttgart, 1949.
Phil 1750.179.5B Bollnow, O.F. Existenzphilosophie. 3. Aufl. Stuttgart, 1949.
Phil 1750.179.10 Bollnow, O.F. Deutsche Existenzphilosophie. Bern, 1953.
Phil 1750.179.15 Bollnow, O.F. Neue Geborgenheit. Stuttgart, 1955.
Phil 1750.179.20 Bollnow, O.F. Existenzphilosophie. 4e Aufl. Stuttgart, 1955.
Phil 1750.181 Lefebvre, Henri. L'existentialisme. Paris, 1946.
Phil 1750.183 Harper, Ralph. Existentialism. Cambridge, 1948.
Phil 1750.183.2 Harper, Ralph. Existentialism. Cambridge, 1949.
Phil 1750.185 Wahl, Jean André. Petite histoire de "l'existentialisme". Paris, 1947.
Phil 1750.187 Wahl, Jean André. A short history of existentialism. N.Y., 1949.
Phil 1750.188 Wahl, Jean André. Esquisse pour une histoire de l'existentialisme. Paris, 1949.
Phil 1750.189 Wahl, Jean André. Les philosophies de l'existence. Paris, 1954.
Phil 1750.189.5 Wahl, Jean André. Philosophies of existence: an introduction to the basic thought of Kierkegaard. London, 1969.
Phil 1750.190 L'existence. Paris, 1945.
Phil 1750.195 Delfgaauw, B.M.I. Wat is existentialisme? Amsterdam, 1948.
Phil 1750.200 L'existentialisme. Paris, 1948.
Phil 1750.205 Bobbio, Norberto. The philosophy of decadentism; a study in existentialism. Oxford, 1948.
Phil 1750.210 Jolivet, Régis. Les doctrines existentialistes de Kierkegaard à J.P. Sartre. Paris, 1948.
Phil 1750.215 Marcel, Gabriel. The philosophy of existence. London, 1948.
Phil 1750.220 Foulquié, Paul. Existentialism. London, 1948.
Phil 1750.220.5 Foulquié, Paul. L'existentialisme. 9e éd. Paris, 1955.
Phil 1750.220.12 Foulquié, Paul. L'existentialisme. 12e éd. Paris, 1963.
Phil 1750.220.13 Foulquié, Paul. L'existentialisme. 13e éd. Paris, 1964.
Phil 1750.225 Mounier, Emman. Introduction aux existentialismes. Paris, 1947.
Phil 1750.230 Mounier, Emman. Existentialist philosophies. London, 1948.
Phil 1750.235 Benda, J. Tradition de l'existentialisme. Paris, 1947.
Phil 1750.240 Beauvoir, S. de. L'existentialisme et la sagesse des nations. Paris, 1948.
Phil 1750.245 Berger, G. Existentialism and literature in action. Buffalo, 1948.
Phil 1750.250 Peursen, C.A. van. Riskante philosophie. Amsterdam, 1948.
Phil 1750.255 Le choix, le monde, l'existence. Grenoble, 1947.
Phil 1750.263 Troisfontaines, R. Existentialisme et pensée chrétienne. 2e éd. Louvain, 1948.
Phil 1750.263.5 Troisfontaines, R. Existentialism and Christian thought. London, 1950.
Phil 1750.265 Steinbüchel, T. Existenzialismus und christliche Ethos. Heidelberg, 1948.
Phil 1750.270 Abbagnano, Nicola. Esistenzialismo positivo; due saggi. 1. ed. Torino, 1948.
Phil 1750.270.5 Abbagnano, Nicola. Introduzione all'esistenzialismo. Torino, 1947.
Phil 1750.270.8 Abbagnano, Nicola. Introduzione all'esistenzialismo. 3. ed. Torino, 1948.
Phil 1750.270.10 Abbagnano, Nicola. Philosophie des menschlichen Konflikts. Hamburg, 1957.
Phil 1750.270.15 Abbagnano, Nicola. Critical existentialism. 1. ed. Garden City, N.Y., 1969.
Phil 1750.275 Kanapa, J. L'existentialisme n'est pas un humanisme. Paris, 1947.
Phil 1750.280 Lepp, Ignoce. Existence et existentialismes. Paris, 1947.
Phil 1750.285 Jaspers, Karl. L'esistenzialismo. Roma, 1946.
Phil 1750.290 Vedaldi, A. Essere gli altri. 1. ed. Torino, 1948.
Phil 1750.295 Bence, Max. Technische Existenz, Essays. Stuttgart, 1949.
Phil 1750.295.5 Bense, Max. Rationalismus und Sensibilität. Krefeld, 1956.
Phil 1750.300 Verneaux, R. Leçons sur l'existentialisme et ses formes principales. Paris, 1949.
Phil 1750.301 Verneaux, R. Leçons sur l'existentialisme. 4e éd. Paris, 1964.
Phil 1750.305 Hartwig, T. Der Existentialismus. Wien, 1948.
Phil 1750.310 Siebers, G. Die Krisis des Existentialismus. Hamburg, 1949.
Phil 1750.315 Deledalle, G. L'existentiel, philosophies et littératures de l'existence. Paris, 1949.
Phil 1750.325 Reding, M. Die Existenzphilosophie. 1e Aufl. Düsseldorf, 1949.
Phil 1750.330 Paci, Enzo. Il mella e il problema dell'uomo. 1st ed. Torino, 1950.
Phil 1750.330.5 Paci, Enzo. Ancora sull'esistenzialismo. Torino, 1956.
Phil 1750.330.10 Paci, Enzo. Dall'esistenzialismo al relazionismo. Messina, 1957.
Phil 1750.335 Alonso-Fueyo, S. Existencialismo y existencialistas. Valencia, 1949.
Phil 1750.340 Pareyson, Luigi. Studi sull'esistenzialismo. 2. ed. Firenze, 1950.
Phil 1750.340.8 Pareyson, Luigi. Esistenza e persona. 3. ed. Torino, 1966.
Phil 1750.345 Rencontres Internationales. Pour un nouvel humanisme. Neuchâtel, 1949.
Phil 1750.346 Rencontres Internationales. La connaissance de l'homme on XVe siècle. Neuchâtel, 1952.
Phil 1750.350 Kuhn, H. Encounter with nothingness. London, 1951.
Phil 1750.350.2 Kuhn, H. Begegnung mit dem Nichts. Tübingen, 1950.
Phil 1750.351 Gabriel, Leo. Existenzphilosophie von Kierkegaard bis Sartre. Wien, 1951.
Phil 1750.351.2 Gabriel, Leo. Existenzphilosophie. 2e Aufl. Wien, 1968.

Classified Listing

Phil 1750 **History of philosophy - Modern philosophy in general - History - Special top + cs - cont.**

Phil 1750.352 — Müller, Max. Existenzphilosophie im geistigen Leben der Gegenwart. Heidelberg, 1949.

Phil 1750.352.3 — Müller, Max. Existenzphilosophie im geistigen Leben der Gegenwart. 3e Aufl. Heidelberg, 1964.

Phil 1750.353 — Spier, J.M. Calvinisme en existentie-philosophie. Kampen, 1951.

Phil 1750.353.5 — Spier, J.M. Christianity and existentialism. Philadelphia, 1953.

Phil 1750.354 — Lenz, Joseph. Der moderne deutsche und französische Existentialismus. 2e Aufl. Trier, 1951.

Phil 1750.355A — Collins, J.D. The existentialists. Chicago, 1952.

Phil 1750.355B — Collins, J.D. The existentialists. Chicago, 1952.

Phil 1750.355C — Collins, J.D. The existentialists. Chicago, 1952.

Phil 1750.356 — Möller, J. Existenzialphilosophie und katholische Theologie. Baden-Baden, 1952.

Phil 1750.357 — Stefanini, L. Esistenzialismo ateo et esistenzialismo teistro. Padova, 1952.

Phil 1750.359 — Frankl, V.C. Logos und Existenz. Wien, 1951.

Phil 1750.360A — Reinhardt, Kurt Frank. The existentialist revolt. Milwaukee, 1952.

Phil 1750.360B — Reinhardt, Kurt Frank. The existentialist revolt. Milwaukee, 1952.

Phil 1750.360.2 — Reinhardt, Kurt Frank. The existentialist revolt. 2nd ed. N.Y., 1960.

Phil 1750.361 — Straelen, H. van. Man the lonely. Tokyo, 1952.

Phil 1750.362 — Blackham, H.J. Six existentialist thinkers. London, 1952.

Phil 1750.363 — Haefliger, O. Wider den Existentialismus. Bern, 1949.

Phil 1750.364 — Allen, E.L. Existentialism from within. London, 1953.

Phil 1750.365 — Heinemann, Fritz. Existentialism and the modern predicament. London, 1953.

Phil 1750.365.5 — Heinemann, Fritz. Existentialism and the modern predicament. 2nd ed. London, 1954.

Phil 1750.365.7 — Heinemann, Fritz. Existentialism and the modern predicament. N.Y., 1958.

Phil 1750.365.10 — Heinemann, Fritz. Jenseits des Existentialismus. Zürich, 1957.

Phil 1750.365.15 — Heinemann, Fritz. Existenzphilosophie Lebendig oder Tat? 2e Aufl. Stuttgart, 1954.

Phil 1750.366 — Rognoni, L. L'espressionismo. Torino, 1953.

Phil 1750.367 — Hommes, Jakob. Zwiespältiges Dosein. Freiburg, 1953.

Phil 1750.367.5 — Hommes, Jakob. Dialektik und Politik. 1e Aufl. Köln, 1968.

Phil 1750.368 — Prini, P. Esistenzialismo. Roma, 1952.

Phil 1750.369 — Huebner, F.M. Umgang mit Gätterbilden. Frankfurt, 1950.

Phil 1750.370 — Knittermeyer, H. Dit Philosophie der Existenz von der Renaissance bis zur Gegenwart. Wien, 1952.

Phil 1750.371 — Archivio di Filosofia. Esistenzialismo cristiano. Padova, 1949.

Phil 1750.372 — Castelli, Enrico. Existentialisme théologique. Paris, 1948.

Phil 1750.372.2 — Castelli, Enrico. Existentialisme théologique. 2e éd. Paris, 1966.

Phil 1750.372.5 — Castelli, Enrico. Esistenzialismo teologico. Roma, 1966.

Phil 1750.373 — Astrada, C. La revolución existencialista. n.p., 1952.

Phil 1750.375 — Lepp, Ignace. La philosophie Chrêtiennie de l'existance. Paris, 1953.

Phil 1750.378 — Galamini, L. Esistenza e coesistenza. Milano, 1953.

Phil 1750.380 — Spoerri, Theophil F. Die Herausforderung des Existenzialismus. Hamburg, 1954.

Phil 1750.382 — Mougin, Henri. La sainte famille existentialiste. Paris, 1947.

Phil 1750.385 — Staritz, Ekkehart. Vom Schein zum Sein. Bonn, 1953.

Phil 1750.390 — Gregoire, Franz. Questions concernant l'existentialisme. 2. ed. Louvain, 1955.

Phil 1750.395 — Reidemeister, Kurt. Die Unsachlichkeit der Existenzphilosophie. Berlin, 1954.

Phil 1750.395.2 — Reidemeister, Kurt. Die Unsachlichkeit der Existenzphilosophie. 2. Aufl. Berlin, 1970.

Phil 1750.400A — Wild, John. The challenge of existentialism. Bloomington, 1955.

Phil 1750.400B — Wild, John. The challenge of existentialism. Bloomington, 1955.

Phil 1750.405 — Lukacs, G.S. Existentialismus oder Marxismus? Berlin, 1951.

Phil 1750.405.5 — Lukacs, G.S. Existentialisme ou Marxisme. 2e éd. Paris, 1961.

Phil 1750.410 — Grimsley, Ronald. Existentialist thought. Cardiff, 1955.

Phil 1750.410.2 — Grimsley, Ronald. Existentialist thought. 2nd ed. Cardiff, 1960.

Phil 1750.415 — Borrello, Oreste. L'estetica dell'esistenzialismo. Messina, 1956.

Phil 1750.420 — Ell, Johannes. Der Existenzialismus in seinem Wesen und Werden. Bonn, 1955.

Phil 1750.425 — Bertrand, Jean. L'énergie spirituelle et la destinée humaine. Nice, 1956.

Phil 1750.430 — Michalson, Carl. Christianity and the existentialists. N.Y., 1956.

Phil 1750.435 — Sourian, E. L'ombre de Dieum. 1e éd. Paris, 1955.

Phil 1750.440 — Redeker, Hans. Existentialisme. 2. druk. Amsterdam 1956.

Phil 1750.445 — Prohaska, L. Existentialismus und Padagogik. Freiburg, 1955.

Phil 1750.450 — Giannini, G. L'esistenzialismo positivo di Nicola Abbagnano. Brescia, 1956.

Phil 1750.450.5 — Simona, Maria. La notion de liberte dans l'existentialisme positif de Nicola Abbagnano. Fribourg, 1962.

Phil 1750.455 — Kaufmann, W.A. Existentialism from Dostoevsky to Sartre. N.Y., 1956.

Phil 1750.455.10 — Kaufmann, W.A. The owl and the nightingale. London, 1959.

Phil 1750.455.11 — Kaufmann, W.A. From Shakespeare to existentialism. Garden City, 1960.

Phil 1750.455.12 — Kaufmann, W.A. From Shakespeare to existentialism. Freeport, N.Y., 1971.

Phil 1750.460 — Anders, Günther. Die Antiquiertheit des Menschen. München, 1956.

Phil 1750.465 — Mende, Georg. Studien über die Existenzphilosophie. Berlin, 1956.

Phil 1750.470 — Campbell, Robert. L'esistenzialismo. Napoli, 1955.

Phil 1750.475 — Roberts, D.C. Existentialism and religious belief. N.Y., 1959.

Phil 1750.480 — Paci, Enzo. Esistenzialismo e storicismo. 1. ed. Milano, 1950.

Phil 1750.485A — Knight, E.W. Literature considered as philosophy. London, 1957.

Phil 1750.485B — Knight, E.W. Literature considered as philosophy. London, 1957.

Phil 1750 **History of philosophy - Modern philosophy in general - History - Special top + cs - cont.**

Phil 1750.490 — Universidad Nacional del Litoral. Santa Fé, Argentina. Instituto de Filosofía. Symposium sobre existencialismo. pts.1-7. Rosario, 195-?

Phil 1750.494 — Virasoro, Rafael. Existencialismo y moral. Argentina, 1957.

Phil 1750.495 — Virasoro, Rafael. Introducción al estudio de la fenomenologia de Husserl. Rosario, 195-?

Phil 1750.500 — Funke, Gerhard. Zur transzendentalen Phänomenologie. Bonn, 1957.

Phil 1750.505 — Existentialism. London, 1953. 2 pam.

Phil 1750.510 — Dutt, K. Guru. Existentialism. Basavagundi, 1953.

Phil 1750.510.2 — Dutt, K. Guru. Existentialism. Basavagundi, 1954.

Phil 1750.512.3 — Amoroso Lima, Alceu. El existencialismo, filosofia de nuestro tiempo. 3. ed. Buenos Aires, 1951.

Phil 1750.515 — Ferrier, Jean Louis. L'homme dans le monde. Neuchâtel, 1957.

Phil 1750.518 — Kern, Edith G. Existential thought and fictional technique; Kierkegaard, Sartre, Beckett. New Haven, 1970.

Phil 1750.520 — Muehlethaler, Jakob. Existenz und Transzendenz in der gegenwärtegen Philosophie. Basel, 1958.

Phil 1750.525 — Fabro, Cornelio. Dall'essere all'esistente. Brescia, 1957.

Phil 1750.530 — Sérouya, Henri. Les philosophies de l'existence. Paris, 1957.

Phil 1750.535 — Oggioni, Emilio. L'esistenzialismo. Bologna, 1956.

Phil 1750.540 — Flam, Leopold. Ontbinding en protest. Antwerpen, 1959.

Phil 1750.545 — Moscow. Akademiia Obshchestvennykh Nauk. Kritika sovremennoi burzhuaznoi filosofii. Moskva, 1959.

Phil 1750.550 — Gurr, John E. The principle of sufficient reason in some scholastic systems. Milwaukee, 1959.

Phil 1750.552 — Blankart, Franz André. Zweiheit, Bezug und Vermittlung. Zürich, 1966.

Phil 1750.552.5 — Lakebrink, Bernhard. Klassische Metaphysik. Freiburg, 1967.

Phil 1750.552.10 — Hijmans, Benjamin Lodwijk. Classics and the philosophy of existence. Winnipeg, 1965.

Phil 1750.552.15 — Lotz, Johannes Baptist. Sein und Existenz. Freiburg, 1965.

Phil 1750.552.20 — Stenström, Thure. Existentialismen. Stockholm, 1966.

Phil 1750.552.25 — Warnock, Mary. Existentialism. London, 1970.

Phil 1750.555.6 — Barnes, Hazel Estella. Humanistic existentialism; the literature of possibility. Lincoln, 1967.

Phil 1750.560 — Chiodi, Pietro. L'esistenzialismo. Torino, 1957.

Phil 1750.560.5 — Chiodi, Pietro. Il pensiero esistenzialista. Milano, 1959.

Phil 1750.560.10 — Chiodi, Pietro. Esistenzialismo e fenomenologia. Milano, 1963.

Phil 1750.560.15 — Bollnow, Otto Friedrich. Franzoesischer Existentialismus. Stuttgart, 1965.

Phil 1750.560.20 — Mancini, Italo. Filosofi esistenzialisti. Urbino, 1964.

Phil 1750.560.25 — Habachi, René. Une philosophie pour notre temps. Beirut? 1961.

Phil 1750.560.30 — Oizerman, Teodor I. Sovremennyi ekzistensialism. Moskva, 1966.

Phil 1750.560.35 — Habachi, René. Vers une pensée méditerranéenne. v.1-4. Beyrouth, 1959- 2v.

Phil 1750.565 — Hollenbach, Johannes. Der Mensch der Zukunft. Frankfurt, 1959.

Phil 1750.570 — Benitez, Claros. Une philosophie pour notre temps. Beirut? 1961.

Phil 1750.575 — Alonso-Fueyo, Sabino. El drama del hombre actual. Valencia, 1958.

Phil 1750.580 — Douglas, Kenneth. A critical bibliography of existentialism (the Paris School). New Haven, 1950.

Phil 1750.585 — Piccardt, Karel. Wijsbegeerte in verval. Amsterdam, 1959.

Phil 1750.590 — Marchello, Giuseppe. La crisi del concetto filosofico. Milano, 1959.

Phil 1750.595 — Bos, Julius G. Existentiële zin en onzim. Den Haag, 1960.

Phil 1750.600 — Naville, Pierre. Les conditions de la liberté. Paris, 1947.

Phil 1750.605 — Pfleger, Karl. Kundschafter der Existenztiefe. Frankfurt, 1959.

Phil 1750.610 — Sonnemann, Ulrich. Existence and therapy. N.Y., 1954.

Phil 1750.615 — Marck, Siegfried. Die Aufhebung des Irrationalismus. Wilhelmshaven, 1958.

Phil 1750.625 — Garin, Eugenio. Bilancio della fenomenologia. Padova, 1960.

Phil 1750.630 — Leist, Fritz. Existenz im Nichts. München, 1961.

Phil 1750.635 — Oizerman, T.I. Neotmoizm - filosofiia sovremennoi reaktsionoi burzhuazii. Moskva, 1959.

Phil 1750.635.5 — Jaroszewski, T.M. Renesans scholastyki. Warszawa, 1961.

Phil 1750.640 — Begiashvili, A.F. Metod analiza v sovremennoi burzhuaznoi filosofii. Tbilisi, 1960.

Phil 1750.645 — Moscow. Akademiia Obshchestvennykh Nauk. Kritika sovremennoi burzhuaznoi filosofii i sotsiologii. Moskva, 1963.

Phil 1750.646 — Moscow. Akademiia Obshchestvennykh Nauk. Kritika sovremennoi burzhuaznoi filosofii i sotsiologii. Moskva, 1963.

Phil 1750.655 — Hanna, Thomas. The lyrical existentialists. 1. ed. N.Y., 1962.

Phil 1750.660 — Meyer, H.J. Die Technisierung der Welt. Tübingen, 1961.

Phil 1750.665 — Schrag, C.O. Existence and freedom. Evanston, Ill., 1961.

Phil 1750.670 — Valori, Paolo. Il metodo fenomenologico e la fondazione della filosofia. Roma, 1959.

Phil 1750.675 — Oromi, Miguel. Introducción a la filosofía esencialista. Madrid, 1961.

Phil 1750.680 — Čivera, Marin. El hombre. México, 1956.

Phil 1750.685 — Černý, Václav. Proní sešit o existencialismii. Phraha, 1948.

Phil 1750.690 — Strasser, S. Fenomenologie en emperische Menskunde. Arnhem, 1962.

Phil 1750.695 — Martins, Diamantino. Existencialismo. Braga, 1955.

Phil 1750.700 — Breisach, Ernst. Introduction to modern existentialism. N.Y., 1962.

Phil 1750.705 — Adams, Robert. Better part of valor; More, Erasmus, Colet and Vives, on humanism, war, and peace. Seattle, 1962.

Phil 1750.710 — Olson, Robert. An introduction to existentialism. N.Y., 1962.

Phil 1750.715 — Molina, Fernando. Existentialism as philosophy. N.Y., 1962.

Phil 1750.720 — Wilde, Jean T. The search for being. N.Y., 1962.

Phil 1750.725 — Humanismus heute. Berlin, 1961.

Phil 1750.726 — Gonzalez Casanova, Pablo. El misoneismo y la modernidad cristiana en el siglo XVIII. México, 1948.

Classified Listing

Phil 1750   History of philosophy - Modern philosophy in general - History - Special top+cs - cont.

Phil 1750.730   Chalin, M.L. Filosofiia otohaianiia i strakha. Moskva, 1962.

Phil 1750.732   Noack, Hermann. Die Philosophie Westeuropus. Basel, 1962.

Phil 1750.733   Patha, Frederick. Existentialist thinkers and thought. N.Y., 1962.

Phil 1750.734   Flam, L. De onverzoenlijken. St. Niklaas, 1959.

Phil 1750.736   Straser, S. Phenomenology and the human scientific ideal. Pittsburg, 1963.

Phil 1750.738   Wild, John. Existence and the world of freedom. Englewood, 1963.

Phil 1750.740   Heiss, R. Die grossen Dialektiker des 19. Jahrhunderts. Köln, 1963.

Phil 1750.742   Roesch, E.J. The totalitarian threat. N.Y., 1963.

Phil 1750.744   Christianity and existentialism; essays. Evanston, Ill., 1963.

Phil 1750.744.5   Bartolone, Filippo. Valenze esistenziali del cristianesimo. Messina, 1964.

Phil 1750.745   Pollak, Oscar. Der neue Humanismus. Wien, 1962.

Phil 1750.747   Zinzen, A. Die ontologische Betrachtungsweise. Meisenheim, 1963.

Phil 1750.748   Utitz, Emil. Die Überwindung des Expressionismus. Stuttgart, 1927.

Phil 1750.749   Astrada, C. Existencialismo y crisis de la filosofía. 2. ed. Buenos Aires, 1963.

Phil 1750.750   Mueller-Schwefe, Hans Rudolf. Existenzphilosophie. Zürich, 1961.

Phil 1750.750.2   Mueller-Schwefe, Hans Rudolf. Existenzphilosophie. 2. Aufl. Göttingen, 1969.

Phil 1750.751   Rotenstreich, N. Humanism in the contemporary era. The Hague, 1963.

Phil 1750.752   Paci, Enzo. I problemi dell'economic e la fenomenologia. Milano, 1963.

Phil 1750.753   Roubiczek, P. Existentialism; for and against. Cambridge, 1964.

Phil 1750.754   La crise de la raison dans la pensée contemporaine. Bruges, 1960.

Phil 1750.755   Lanteri-Laura, G. La psychiatrie phénoménologique. Paris, 1963.

Phil 1750.756   Brancatisano, F. Per un umanesimo scientifico. Firenze, 1963.

Phil 1750.757   Borowitz, Eugene B. A layman's introduction to religious existentialism. Philadelphia, 1965.

Phil 1750.758   Marcel, Gabriel. La dignité humaine et ses assises existentielles. Paris, 1964.

Phil 1750.759   Williams, John Rodman. Contemporary existentialism and Christian faith. Englewood Cliffs, N.J., 1965.

Phil 1750.760   Lacroix, Jean. Histoire et mystère. Tournai, 1962.

Phil 1750.765   Paci, Enzo. Funzione delle scienze e significato dell'uomo. Milano, 1963.

Phil 1750.766   Bošnjak, Branko. Humanizam i socijalizam. Zagreb, 1963.

Phil 1750.767   MacColl, Sylvia. Structure and development of phenomenal reality. N.Y., 1965.

Phil 1750.768   Oizerman, Teodor Il'ich. Die Entfremdung als historische Kategorie. Berlin, 1965.

Phil 1750.769   Darmstaedter Gespräch, 8th, Darmstadt. Angst und Hoffnung in unserer Zeit. Darmstadt, 1965.

Phil 1750.770   Philosophes d'aujourd'hui en présence du droit. Paris, 1965.

Phil 1750.772   Bustos, Ismael. El sentido existencial de la política. Santiago de Chile, 1956.

Phil 1750.773   Gurwitsch, Aron. Studies in phenomenology and psychology. Evanston, 1966.

Phil 1750.774   Zea, Leopoldo. La cultura y el hombre de nuestros días. México, 1959.

Phil 1750.775   Wilson, Colin. Introduction to the new existentialism. London, 1966.

Phil 1750.776   Gaos, José. Museo de filosófos. 1. ed. México, 1960.

Phil 1750.777   Novak, George Edward. Existentialism versus Marxism. N.Y., 1966.

Phil 1750.778   Nuño Montes, Juan Antonio. Sentido de la filosofia contemporánea. Caracas, 1965.

Phil 1750.780   Natanson, Maurice Alexander. Essays in phenomenology. The Hague, 1966.

Phil 1750.782   John, Helen James. The Thomist spectrum. N.Y., 1966.

Phil 1750.783   Piana, Giovanni. I problemi della fenomenologia. 1. ed. Milano, 1966.

Phil 1750.784   Solov'ev, Erikh I. Ekzistentsializm i naunchnoe poznanie. Moskva, 1966.

Phil 1750.785   Soveral, Eduardo S. O método fenomenológico; estudo para a determinação do seu valor filosófico. Porto, 1965.

Phil 1750.786   Olafson, Frederick. Principles and persons. Baltimore, 1967.

Phil 1750.787   Wintrebert, Paul Marie Joseph. L'existense délivrée de l'existentialisme. Paris, 1965.

Phil 1750.788   Burnier, Michel Antoine. Les existentialistes et la politique. Paris, 1966.

Phil 1750.788.2   Burnier, Michel Antoine. Choice of action; the French existentialists on the political front line. 1st American ed. N.Y., 1968.

Phil 1750.790   Barnes, Hazel Estella. An existentialist ethics. 1st ed. N.Y., 1967.

Phil 1750.795   Salvan, Jacques León. The scandalous ghost; Sartre's existentialism as related to vitalism, humanism, mysticism, Marxism. Detroit, 1967.

Phil 1750.796   Tierno Galván, Enrique. Humanismo y sociedad. 1. ed. Barcelona, 1964.

VPhil 1750.797   Životić, Miladin. Pragmatizam i savremena filozofija. Beograd, 1966.

Phil 1750.798   Boelen, Bernard Jacques Marie. Existential thinking. Pittsburgh, 1968.

Phil 1750.799   Kanz, Heinrich. Der Sinn heutigen Philosophierens. Ratingen, 1967.

Phil 1750.800   Domenach, Jean Marie. Le retour de tragique, essai. Paris, 1967.

Phil 1750.805   Ketcham, Charles Brown. The search for meaningful existence. N.Y., 1968.

Phil 1750.810   DeFeo, Nicola Massimo. Kierkegaard, Nietzsche, Heidegeger. Milano, 1964.

Phil 1750.815   Wisser, Richard. Verantwortung im Wondel der Zeit. Mainz, 1967.

VPhil 1750.816   Existencializmus a fenomenológia. Bratislava, 1967.

Phil 1750.820   Paci, Enzo. Tempo e relazione. Milano, 1965.

Phil 1750.825   Sanborn, Patricia F. Existentialism. N.Y., 1968.

Phil 1750.830   Qu'est-ce que le structuralisme? Paris, 1968.

Phil 1750.830.5   Strukturalizam. Zagreb, 1970.

Phil 1750.830.8   Piaget, Jean. Le structuralisme. 3e éd. Paris, 1968.

Phil 1750   History of philosophy - Modern philosophy in general - History - Special top+cs - cont.

Phil 1750.830.10   Parain-Vial, Jeanne. Analyses structurales et idéologies structuralistes. Toulouse, 1969.

Phil 1750.835   Penati, Giancarlo. Introduzione alla filosofia come metocultura. Milano, 1968.

Phil 1750.840   Riu, Federico. Ontología del siglo XX: Husserl. Caracas, 1966.

Phil 1750.842   Pucci, Raffaele. La filosofia e l'unità della cultura. Napoli, 1970.

Phil 1750.845   Kamlah, Wilhelm. Utopie, Eschatologie, Geschichtsteleologie. Mannheim, 1969.

Phil 1750.848   Buchdahl, G. Metaphysics and the philosophy of science. Oxford, 1969.

Phil 1750.850   Protasenko, Zoia M. Lenin kak istorik filosofii. Leningrad, 1969.

Phil 1750.852   Ideologiia sovrcmennogo reformizma. Moskva, 1970.

Phil 1750.854   Leminizm i sovremennze problemy istoriko-filosofskoi nauki. Moskva, 1970.

Phil 1750.856   Clavel, Maurice. Qui est aliéné? Critique et métaphysique sociale de l'Occident. Paris, 1970.

Phil 1750.858   Schröder, Erich Christian. Abschied von der Metaphysik? Beiträge zu einer Philosophie der Endlichkeit. Trier, 1969.

Phil 1750.860   Schmidt, Siegfried Josef. Sprache und Denken als sprachphilosophisches Problem von Locke bis Wittgenstein. Den Haag, 1968[1969].

Phil 1750.862   Radev, R. Kritika va neotomizma. Sofiia, 1970.

Phil 1750.864   Tormey, Alan. The concept of expression. Princeton, N.J., 1971.

Phil 1750.866   Bernstein, Richard Jacob. Praxis and action. Philadelphia, 1971.

Phil 1760   History of philosophy - Modern philosophy in general - Anthologies of philosophical writings

Phil 1760.10   Krikorien, Yervant H. Contemporary philosophic problems, selected readings. N.Y., 1959.

Phil 1760.15A   Funke, Gerhard. Die Aufklärung, in ausgewählten Texten Dargestellt. Stuttgart, 1963.

Phil 1760.15B   Funke, Gerhard. Die Aufklärung, in ausgewählten Texten Dargestellt. Stuttgart, 1963.

Phil 1760.20   Rome, Sydney C. Philosophical interrogations. 1. ed. N.Y., 1964.

Phil 1798   History of philosophy - Local Modern philosophy - Great Britain and United States - Pamphlet volumes

Phil 1798   Pamphlet box. Philosophy. English.

Phil 1798.1   Pamphlet box. Philosophy. English

Phil 1800 - 1825   History of philosophy - Local Modern philosophy - Great Britain and United States - History - General works - Individual authors (A-Z)

Phil 1800.1   Aster, E. Geschichte der englischen Philosophie. Bielefeld, 1927.

Phil 1800.2   Adams, George P. Contemporary American philosophy. N.Y., 1930. 2v.

Phil 1800.2.5   Adams, George P. Contemporary American philosophy. N.Y., 1962. 2v.

Phil 1800.2.10   Contemporary American philosophy: second series. London, 1970.

Phil 1800.3A   Anderson, P.P. Philosophy in America. N.Y., 1939.

Phil 1800.3B   Anderson, P.P. Philosophy in America. N.Y., 1939.

Phil 1800.3.5   Anderson, P.P. Platonism in the Midwest. Philadelphia, 1963.

Phil 1800.5   Ayer, A.J. British empirical philosophers. London, 1952.

Phil 1800.6   Ames, Van Meter. Zen and American thought. Honolulu, 1962.

Phil 1801.1   Brougham, H. Lives of philosophers of the time of George III. London, 1855.

Phil 1801.2   Van Becelaere, L. La philosophie en Amériqe depuis les origine jusqu'à nos jours, 1607-1900. N.Y., 1904.

Phil 1801.3   Brockdorff, C. Die englische aufklärungs Philosophie. München, 1924.

Phil 1801.4   Baumgarten, E. Die geistigen Grundlagen des amerikanischen Gemeinwesens. Frankfurt, 1936-8. 2v.

Phil 1801.5   Barron, J.T. The idea of the absolute in modern British philosophy. Thesis. Washington, D.C., 1929.

Phil 1801.6   Boorstin, D.J. The lost world of Thomas Jefferson. N.Y., 1948.

Phil 1801.7.2A   Bethell, S.L. The cultural revolution of the seventeenth century. N.Y., 1951.

Phil 1801.7.2B   Bethell, S.L. The cultural revolution of the seventeenth century. N.Y., 1951.

Phil 1801.8A   Baker, H.C. The wars of truth. Cambridge, 1952.

Phil 1801.8B   Baker, H.C. The wars of truth. Cambridge, 1952.

Phil 1801.9A   Boman, Lars. Criticism and construction in the philosophy of the America new realism. Stockholm, 1955.

Phil 1801.9B   Boman, Lars. Criticism and construction in the philosophy of the America new realism. Stockholm, 1955.

Phil 1801.10   Baskin, M.P. Filosofiia amerikanskogo prosveshcheniia. Moskva, 1955.

Phil 1801.11   Bogomolov, A.S. Angle-amerikanskaia burzhuaznaia filosofiia epokhi imperializmo. Moskva, 1964.

Phil 1802.1   Carrau, L. La philosophie religieuse en Angleterre. Paris, 1888.

Phil 1802.2   Cousin, V. Philosophie écossaise. 3e éd. Paris, 1857. 2 pam.

Phil 1802.3   Carlson, J.S. Om filosofien i Amerika. Upsala, 1895.

Phil 1802.4   Coates, A. Sceptical examination of contemporary British philosophy. London, 1929.

Phil 1802.5   Cadman, S.P. Charles Darwin and other English thinkers. Boston, 1911.

Phil 1802.6   Carré, M.H. Phrases of thought in English. Oxford, 1949.

Phil 1802.8   Cragg, G.R. Reason and authority in the 18th century. Cambridge, Eng., 1964.

Phil 1802.10   Cassirer, E. The platonic renaissance in England. Edinburgh, 1953.

Phil 1802.12   Cohen, M.R. American thought. Glencoe, Ill., 1954.

Phil 1802.14   Colie, Rosalie L. Light and enlightenment. Cambridge, 1957.

Phil 1803.10   Deledalle, G. Histoire de la philosophie américaine. 1e éd. Paris, 1954.

Phil 1803.15   Donnell, Franklin H. Aspects of contemporary American philosophy. Würzburg, 1965.

Phil 1804.5   Ermolenko, Dimitrii V. Sovremennaia burzhuaznaia filosofiia SShA. Moskva, 1965.

Phil 1805.5   Fisch, M.H. Classic American philosophers. N.Y., 1951.

Classified Listing

Phil 1806.2   Ginestier, Paul. La pensée anglo-saxonne depuis 1900. 1e éd. Paris, 1956.

Phil 1806.5   Grant, George. Philosophy in the mass age. N.Y., 1960.

Phil 1806.10   Grave, Selwyn A. The Scottish philosophy of common sense. Oxford, 1960.

Phil 1807.1   Höffding, H. Einleitung in die englische Philosophie. Leipzig, 1889.

Phil 1807.1.5   Höffding, H. Den engelke philosophie i vortid. Kjøbenhavn, 1874.

Phil 1807.2   Halévy, E. La formation du radicalisme philosophique. Paris, 1901-04. 3v.

Phil 1807.2.15   Halévy, E. The growth of philosophic radicalism. London, 1949.

Phil 1807.2.20   Halévy, E. The growth of philosophic radicalism. London, 1952.

Phil 1807.3   Haldar, H. Neo-Hegelianism. London, 1927.

Phil 1807.4   Hocking, William E. Lectures on recent trends in American philosophy. Claremont, 1941.

Phil 1807.5A   Holmes, E.C. Social philosophy and the social mind. Thesis. N.Y., 1942.

Phil 1807.5B   Holmes, E.C. Social philosophy and the social mind. Thesis. N.Y., 1942.

Phil 1807.6   Holmes, E.C. Social philosophy and the social mind. N.Y., 1942.

Phil 1807.7   Harris, Victor I. All coherence gone. Chicago, 1949.

Phil 1807.8   Hutin, Serge. La philosophie anglaise et américaine. Paris, 1958.

Phil 1809.4   Jesuit Philosophical Association of the Eastern States. Phases of American culture. Freeport, 1969.

Phil 1810.1   Kortholti, C. De tribus impostoribus magnis liber. Hamburgi, 1701.

Phil 1810.2   Kallen, H.M. American philosophy today and tomorrow. N.Y., 1935.

Phil 1810.3   Koitko, D. Iu. Ocherki sovremennoi anglo-amerikanskoi filosofii. Moskva, 1936.

Phil 1810.4   Kennedy, Gail. Pragmatism and American culture. Boston, 1950.

Phil 1810.5   Kursanov, G.A. Gnoseologiia sovremennaia pragmatizma. Moskva, 1958.

Phil 1810.6   Kopnin, Pavel V. Sovremennaia burzhuaznaia filosofiia SShA. Kiev, 1966.

Phil 1811.1   Laurie, H. Scottish philosophy. Glasgow, 1902.

Phil 1811.2   Leroux, E. Le pragmatisme américain et anglais. Paris, 1923.

Phil 1811.2.2   Leroux, E. Le pragmatisme américain et anglais. Thèse. Paris, 1922.

Phil 1811.2.5   Leroux, E. Bibliographie méthodique du pragmatisme américain. Thèse. n.p., 1922.

Phil 1811.2.10   Leroux, E. La philosophie anglaise classique. Paris, 1951.

Phil 1811.3.5   Liard, Louis. Les logiciens anglais contemporains.'57 1811.3.5 44's. Les logiciens anglais contemporains. 5e éd. Paris, 1907.

Phil 1811.5   Van Leeuwen, H.G. The problem of certainty in English thought. The Hague, 1963.

Phil 1812.1   McCosh, J. The Scottish philosophy. N.Y., 1875.

Phil 1812.2   Masson, D. Recent British philosophy. N.Y., 1866.

Phil 1812.2.2   Masson, D. Recent British philosophy. London, 1867.

Phil 1812.2.5   Masson, D. Recent British philosophy. London, 1865.

Phil 1812.3   Morris, G.S. British thought and thinkers. Chicago, 1880.

Phil 1812.4   MacCunn, J. Six radical thinkers. London, 1907.

Phil 1812.4.5   MacCunn, J. Six radical thinkers. London, 1910.

Phil 1812.4.10   MacCunn, J. Six radical thinkers. N.Y., 1964.

Phil 1812.5   Merwe, A.J. van der. Het zondebegrip in de engelsche evolutionislische wijsbegeerte. Utrecht, 1925.

Phil 1812.5.10   Mel'vil, Iu.K. Amerikanskii pragmatizm. Moskva, 1957.

Phil 1812.6A   Metz, Rudolf. Die philosophischen Strömungen der Gegenwart in Grossbritannien. Leipzig, 1935. 2v.

Phil 1812.6B   Metz, Rudolf. Die philosophischen Strömungen der Gegenwart in Grossbritannien. Leipzig, 1935. 2v.

Phil 1812.6.5   Metz, Rudolf. England und die deutsche Philosophie. Stuttgart, 1941.

Phil 1812.7A   Müller, Gustav E. Amerikanische Philosophie. Stuttgart, 1936.

Phil 1812.7B   Müller, Gustav E. Amerikanische Philosophie. Stuttgart, 1936.

Phil 1812.7.5   Müller, Gustav E. Amerikanische Philosophie. 2. Aufl. Stuttgart, 1950[1936]

Phil 1812.8   Matthews, K. British philosophers. London, 1943.

Phil 1812.9   Mahony, M.J. History of modern thought, the English, Irish and Scotch schools. N.Y., 1933.

Phil 1812.10   Mure, G.R.G. Retreat from truth. Oxford, 1958.

Phil 1812.11A   Marcuse, Ludwig. Amerikanisches Philosophieren. Hamburg, 1959.

Phil 1812.11B   Marcuse, Ludwig. Amerikanisches Philosophieren. Hamburg, 1959.

Phil 1812.12   Moore, E.C. American pragmatism. N.Y., 1961.

Phil 1812.14   Milne, A.J.M. The social philosophy of English idealism. London, 1962.

Phil 1812.15   Mehta, Ved P. Fly and the fly-bottle. 1. ed. Boston, 1962.

Phil 1812.16   Mills, Charles W. Sociology and pragmatism. N.Y., 1964.

Phil 1812.20   Madden, Edward Harry. Civil disobedience and moral law in nineteenth century American philosophy. Seattle, 1968.

Phil 1813.5   Noble, D.W. The paradox of progressive thought. Minneapolis, 1958.

Phil 1813.10   Norak, Michael. American philosophy and the future. N.Y., 1968.

Phil 1815.1   Perry, C.M. The Saint Louis movement in philosophy. Norman, 1930.

Phil 1815.2   Pochmann, Henry A. New England transcendentalism and Saint Louis Hegelianism. Philadelphia, 1948.

Phil 1815.3   Persons, S. Evolutionary thought in America. New Haven, 1950.

Phil 1815.3.5   Persons, S. American minds. N.Y., 1958.

Phil 1815.5   Paul, L.A. The English philosophers. London, 1953.

Phil 1815.8   Pucelle, Jean. L'idéalisme en Angleterre. Neuchâtel, 1955.

Phil 1815.9   Philosophy. Englewood Cliffs, N.J., 1964.

Phil 1817.1   Rémusat, C.F. Histoire de la philosophie en Angleterre. Paris, 1875. 2v.

Phil 1817.2   Rusk, Robert R. Pragmatische und humanistische Strömung. Jena, 1906.

Phil 1817.3A   Riley, I.W. American philosophy. N.Y., 1907.

Phil 1817.3B   Riley, I.W. American philosophy. N.Y., 1907.

Phil 1817.3.5   Riley, I.W. American thought. N.Y., 1915.

Phil 1817.3.5.5   Riley, I.W. Le génie américain. Paris, 1921.

Phil 1817.3.7   Riley, I.W. American thought. 2nd ed. N.Y., 1923.

Phil 1817.3.8   Riley, I.W. American thought. Gloucester, 1959.

Phil 1817.3.9   Riley, I.W. La philosophie française en Amérique. Paris, 1919.

Phil 1817.4   Robertson, J.M. Pioneer humanists. London, 1907.

Phil 1817.5.3   Rogers, A.K. English and American philosophy since 1800. N.Y., 1923.

Phil 1817.7   Raffel, J. Die voraussetzungen Welche den empiresmus Lockis. Inaug.-Diss. Berlin, 1887?

Phil 1817.8   Reiser, O.L. Humanism and new world ideals. Yellow Springs, Colorado, 1933.

Phil 1817.9   Riley, I.W. La philsophie française en Amérique. Paris, n.d.

Phil 1817.10   Ritchie, A.D. British philosophers. London, 1950.

Phil 1817.12   Romanell, Patrick. Toward a critical naturalism. N.Y., 1958.

Phil 1817.15   Rossi Landi, Ferruccio. Il pensiero americano contemporaneo. Milano, 1958. 2v.

Phil 1817.16   Reck, A.J. Recent American philosophy. N.Y., 1964.

Phil 1817.18   Reck, A.J. The new American philosophers. Baton Rouge, 1968.

Phil 1817.20   Roberts, James Deotis. From Puritanism to Platonism in seventeenth century England. The Hague, 1968.

Phil 1817.22   Rucker, Darnell. The Chicago pragmatists. Minneapolis, 1969.

Phil 1818.1   Seth, A. Scottish philosophy. Edinburgh, 1885.

Phil 1818.1.5   Seth, A. Scottish philosophy. 3e ed. Edinburgh, 1899.

Phil 1818.2   Stephen, Leslie. History of English thought in XVIIIth century. N.Y., 1876. 2v.

Phil 1818.2.3   Stephen, Leslie. History of English thought in XVIIIth century. 3rd ed. London, 1902.

Phil 1818.2.4   Stephen, Leslie. History of English thought in the eighteenth century. 3rd ed. N.Y., 1949. 2v.

Phil 1818.2.5   Stephen, Leslie. The English Utilitarians. v.2. London, 1900.

Phil 1818.2.6   Stephen, Leslie. The English Utilitarians. n.p., n.d.

Phil 1818.2.7.5   Stephen, Leslie. History of English thought in the eighteenth century. v.2. 3rd ed. N.Y., 1902.

Phil 1818.2.8   Stephen, Leslie. History of English thought in the eighteenth century. v.2. London, 1927.

Phil 1818.2.10A   Stephen, Leslie. The English Utilitarians. London, 1950. 3v.

Phil 1818.2.10B   Stephen, Leslie. The English Utilitarians. London, 1950. 3v.

Phil 1818.2.15   Stephen, Leslie. History of English thought in the 18th century. N.Y., 1962. 2v.

Phil 1818.3.5   Seth, J. English philosophers and schools of philosophy. London, 1925.

Phil 1818.4   Stock, Saint George. English thought for English thinkers. London, 1912.

Phil 1818.5   Sorley, William R. A history of English philosophy. Cambridge, Eng., 1920.

Phil 1818.5.5   Sorley, William R. A history of English philosophy. N.Y., 1921.

Phil 1818.6   Salomaa, J.E. Idealismus undRealismus in der englische Philosophie der Gegenwart. Helsinki, 1929.

Phil 1818.7   Santayana, George. The genteel tradition in American philosophy...public address...1911. Berkeley, 1911.

Phil 1818.8   Schneider, H.W. A history of American philosophy. N.Y., 1946.

Phil 1818.8.2   Schneider, H.W. A history of American philosophy. 2nd ed. N.Y., 1963.

Phil 1818.9   Sakmann, Paul. Die Denker und Kämpfer der englischen Aufklärung. Stuttgart, 1946.

Phil 1818.10   Segerstedt, T.T. The problem of knowledge in Scottish philosophy. Lund, 1935.

Phil 1818.11   Smith, J.E. The spirit of American philosophy. N.Y., 1963.

Phil 1818.12   Savelle, Max. The colonial origins of American thought. Princeton, 1964.

Phil 1819.1   Thormeyer, Paul. Die grossen englischen Philosophen, Locke, Berkeley, Hume. Leipzig, 1915.

Phil 1819.2   Townsend, H.G. Philosophical ideas in the United States. N.Y., 1934.

Phil 1819.5   Trakhtenberg, O.V. Ocherki po istorii filosofii i sotsiologii Anglii XIX v. Moskva, 1959.

Phil 1819.7   Tedeschi, Paul. Paradoxe de la pensée anglaise au XVIIe siècle. Paris, 1961.

Phil 1819.10   Trawick, Leonard Moses. Backgrounds of romanticism. Bloomington, 1967.

Phil 1821.5   Vogt, P.B. From John Stuart Mill to William James. Washington, 1914.

Phil 1821.10   Van Wesep, Hendrikus. Seven sages. 1st ed. N.Y., 1960.

Phil 1821.15   Vitoux, Pierre. Histoire des idées en Grande-Bretagne. Paris, 1969.

Phil 1822.1   Waddington, M. The development of British thought. Toronto, 1919.

Phil 1822.2   Wentscher, E. Englische Philosophie. Leipzig, 1924.

Phil 1822.3   Warren, Austin. The Concord school of philosophy. n.p., 1929.

Phil 1822.4A   Wickham, H. The unrealists. N.Y., 1930.

Phil 1822.4B   Wickham, H. The unrealists. N.Y., 1930.

Phil 1822.4C   Wickham, H. The unrealists. N.Y., 1930.

Phil 1822.5   Weber, Conrad G. Studies in the English outlook in the period between the world wars. Bern, 1945.

Phil 1822.6   Werkmeister, W.H. A history of philosophical ideas in America. N.Y., 1949.

Phil 1822.7   Warnock, G.J. English philosophy since 1900. London, 1958.

Phil 1822.8   Williams, Bernard. British analytical philosophy. London, 1966.

Phil 1825.1   Zulen, P.S. Del neohegelianismo al neorealismo. Lima, 1924.

Phil 1825.2   Zazzo, René. Psychologues et psychologies et psychologies d'Amérique. Paris, 1942.

Phil 1828.2   Brown, Florence W. Alcott and the Concord school of philosophy. n.p., 1926.

Phil 1828.2.5   Cameron, Kenneth Walter. Concord harvest:publications of the Concord school of philosophy and literature. Hartford, 1970.

Phil 1828   History of philosophy - Local Modern philosophy - Great Britain and United States - History - Special topics - cont.

Phil 1828.4   Dubois, Pierre. Le problème de la connaissance d'autrui dans la philosophie anglaise contemporaine. Paris, 1969.

Phil 1828.6   Delaney, Cornelius F. Mind and nature; a study of the naturalistic philosophies of Cohen. Notre Dame, Ind., 1969.

Phil 1828.6.20   Crescenzo, Giovanni de. Patrick Romanelli e l'odierno naturalismo statunitense. 1. ed. Firenze, 1966.

Phil 1828.8   Riverso, Emanuele. La filosofia analitica in Inghilterra. Roma, 1969.

Phil 1828.10   Guffey, George Robert. Traherne and the seventeenth-century English platonists, 1900-1966. London, 1969.

Phil 1828.12   Ehrle, Franz. Gesammelte Aufsätze zur englischen Scholastik. Roma, 1970.

Phil 1828.14   Petersen, Richard J. Scottish common sense in America, 1768-1850. Thesis. Ann Arbor, 1972.

Phil 1830   History of philosophy - Local Modern philosophy - Great Britain and United States - Anthologies of philosophical writings

Phil 1830.2   Johnston, George A. Selections from the Scottish philosophy of common sense. Chicago, 1915.

Phil 1830.5A   Blau, Joseph L. American philosophic addresses. N.Y., 1946.

Phil 1830.5B   Blau, Joseph L. American philosophic addresses. N.Y., 1946.

Phil 1830.10   Hook, Sidney. Freedom and experience. Ithaca, 1947.

Phil 1830.11   Hook, Sidney. American philosophers at work. N.Y., 1956.

Phil 1830.12   Ratner, Sidney. Vision and action. New Brunswick, N.J., 1953.

Phil 1830.15   Winn, R.B. American philosophy. N.Y., 1955.

Phil 1830.17   Laslett, Peter. Philosophy. Oxford, 1956. 2v.

Phil 1830.17.5   Laslett, Peter. Philosophy, politics, and society, third series. N.Y., 1967.

Phil 1830.20   Mace, Cecil Alec. British philosophy in the mid-century. London, 1957.

Phil 1830.20.2   Mace, Cecil Alec. British philosophy in the mid-century. 2nd ed. London, 1966.

Phil 1830.25   Winny, James. The frame of order. London, 1957.

Phil 1830.30   Frankel, Charles. The golden age of American philosophy. N.Y., 1960.

Phil 1830.35   Kanvitz, Milton R. The American pragmatists. N.Y., 1960.

Phil 1830.40   Rigobello, Armando. La filosofia americana contemporanea. Torino, 1960.

Phil 1830.45   Società Filosofica Romana. La filosofia contemporanea in U.S.A. Roma, 1958.

Phil 1830.50   Pennsylvania. State University. Philosophy Department. Essays in philosophy. University Park, Penn., 1962.

Phil 1830.51   Robinson, D.S. The story of Scottish philosophy. 1st ed. N.Y., 1961.

Phil 1830.52   Amend, V.E. Ten contemporary thinkers. N.Y., 1964.

Phil 1830.53   Black, Max. Philosophy in America. London, 1965.

Phil 1830.54   Kurtz, Paul W. American thought before 1900. 1st ed. N.Y., 1966.

VPhil 1830.55   Amerikanskie prosvetiteli. Moskva, 1968-69. 2v.

Phil 1845   History of philosophy - Local Modern philosophy - Great Britain and United States - Individual philosophers - A

Phil 1845.1.25*   Allestree, Richard. The gentleman's calling. London, 1660.

Phil 1845.1.30*   Allestree, Richard. The ladies calling. Oxford, 1673.

Phil 1845.1.35F*   Allestree, Richard. The whole duty of man. London, 1725.

Phil 1845.2.30*   Ascham, Roger. The scholemaster. London, 1571.

Phil 1845.3.79   Pamphlet box. Alexander, Samuel.

Phil 1845.3.90   Devaux, P. Le système d'Alexander. Paris, 1929.

Phil 1845.3.95   Alexander, Samuel. Philosophical and literary pieces. London, 1939.

Phil 1845.3.100   Konvitz, Milton R. On the nature of value; the philosophy of Samuel Alexander. N.Y., 1946.

Phil 1845.3.105   Brettschneider, B.D. The philosophy of Samuel Alexander. N.Y., 1964.

Phil 1845.3.110A   Stiernotte, A.P.N.F. God and space time. N.Y., 1954.

Phil 1845.3.110B   Stiernotte, A.P.N.F. God and space time. N.Y., 1954.

Phil 1845.4.90   Abbot, F.E. Testimonials to his character. Boston, 1879.

Phil 1845.5.79   Pamphlet box. Allport, Gordon W.

Phil 1845.10   Ayer, Alfred Jules. Philosophical essays. London, 1954.

Phil 1845.10.5   Ayer, Alfred Jules. Metaphysics and common sense. London, 1969.

Phil 1845.11   Ayer, Alfred Jules. Philosophy and language. Oxford, 1960.

Phil 1845.11.5   Ayer, Alfred Jules. The concept of a person. N.Y., 1963.

Phil 1845.11.10   Gozzelino, Giorgio M. La filosofia di Alfred Jules Ayer. Zürich, 1964.

Phil 1845.12   Armstrong, A.E. In the last analysis. N.Y., 1956.

Phil 1845.14.2   Anscombe, G.E.M. Intention. Oxford, 1958.

Phil 1845.15   Anderson, John. Studies in empirical philosophy. Sydney, 1962.

Phil 1845.16   Furberg, M. Locutionary and illocutionary acts. Göteborg, 1963.

Phil 1845.16.5   Fann, K.T. Symposium on J.L. Austin. London, 1969.

Phil 1845.17   Armstrong, David M. A materialist theory of the mind. London, 1968.

Phil 1850   History of philosophy - Local Modern philosophy - Great Britain and United States - Individual philosophers - Bacon, Francis

VPhil 1850.1F   Bacon, F. Opera omnia. Frankfort, 1664-68.

VPhil 1850.1.2F   Bacon, F. Opera omnia. Frankfort, 1665.

VPhil 1850.1.3F   Bacon, F. Opera omnia. London, 1730. 4v.

Phil 1850.1.4F   Bacon, F. Opera omnia. London, 1730. 2v.

VPhil 1850.1.7F   Bacon, F. Opera omnia. Hafniae, 1694.

VPhil 1850.1.8F   Bacon, F. Opera omnia. Lipsiae, 1694.

Phil 1850.1.10*   Bacon, F. Operum moralium et civilium tomus. London, 1638.

Phil 1850.1.11F*   Bacon, Francis. Francisci Baconi operum moralium. Londini, 1638. 2 pam.

VPhil 1850.1.15F   Bacon, Francis. Works. London, 1740. 4v.

VPhil 1850.2F   Bacon, Francis. Works. London, 1753. 3v.

VPhil 1850.2.1F   Bacon, Francis. Works. London, 1765. 5v.

Phil 1850.2.2F   Bacon, Francis. Works. London, 1778. 5v.

Phil 1850.2.5   Bacon, Francis. Works. London, 1803. 10v.

Phil 1850.3.2*   Bacon, Francis. Advancement and proficience of learning. Oxford, 1640.

Phil 1850.3.3*   Bacon, Francis. Advancement and proficience of learning. Oxford, 1640.

Phil 1850.5.2F*   Bacon, Francis. Resuscitatio. 2nd ed. London, 1661.

Phil 1850.5.5F*   Bacon, Francis. The second part of the Resuscitatio. London, 1670.

Phil 1850   History of philosophy - Local Modern philosophy - Great Britain and United States - Individual philosophers - Bacon, Francis - cont.

Phil 1850.10   Bacon, Francis. Philosophical works. London, 1737. 3v.

Phil 1850.11   Bacon, Francis. Works. London, 1802-7. 12v.

Phil 1850.12   Bacon, Francis. Works. v.2. London, 1815.

Phil 1850.12.5   Bacon, Francis. Works. London, 1818. 12v.

Phil 1850.12.20   Bacon, Francis. Works. London, 1824. 10v.

Phil 1850.13   Bacon, Francis. Works. v.1-16. London, 1825-34. 17v.

Phil 1850.14   Bacon, Francis. Works. v.1-7, 9-14. London, 1857-74. 13v.

Phil 1850.15A   Bacon, Francis. Works. v.1-8, 10-15. Boston, 1861-64. 14v.

Phil 1850.15B   Bacon, Francis. Works. v.9. Boston, 1861-64.

Phil 1850.15.2   Bacon, Francis. Works. v.1,3-15. Paris, 1860-65. 14v.

Phil 1850.15.3   Bacon, Francis. Works. Faksimile-Neudruck. Stuttgart, 1963. 14v.

Phil 1850.15.5   Bacon, Francis. Works. London, 1870-72. 7v.

Phil 1850.16.15   Bacon, Francis. Francis Bacon. The great instauration. Garden City, 1937.

Phil 1850.17   Spedding, James. The collection of books used by James Spedding as his working library in preparing his...works of Sir F. Bacon. London, 19- ?

Htn Phil 1850.18*   Bacon, Francis. Remaines, being essayes and severall letters. London, 1648.

Phil 1850.21   Bacon, Francis. The works of Lord Bacon. London, 1838. 2v.

Phil 1850.23   Bacon, Francis. Oeuvres. Dijon, 1800. 3v.

Phil 1850.25   Bacon, Francis. Oeuvres philosophiques. Paris, 1834. 3v.

Phil 1850.25.5   Bacon, Francis. François Bacon. Paris, 1926.

Phil 1850.26   Bacon, Francis. Oeuvres philosophiques et morales. Paris, 1797. 2v.

Phil 1850.26.5   Bacon, Francis. Oeuvres philosophiques, morales et politiques. Paris, 1811.

Htn Phil 1850.27*   Bacon, Francis. Les oeuvres morales et politiques. Paris, 1637.

Htn Phil 1850.27.3*   Bacon, Francis. Les oeuvres morales et politiques. Paris, 1637.

Htn Phil 1850.27.5*   Bacon, Francis. Les oeuvres morales et politiques. Paris, 1633. 2v.

Htn Phil 1850.27.10* Bacon, Francis. Essays politiques et moraux. Paris, 1621.

Phil 1850.28   Bacon, Francis. Grosskanzlers von England moralische, politische und ökonomische Versuche. Breslau, 1762.

Htn Phil 1850.29*   Bacon, Francis. Essays or counsels, civil and moral...where unto is added the wisdom of the ancients. London, 1673.

Htn Phil 1850.29.10* Bacon, Francis. Essays or counsels, civil and moral...and discourse of the wisdom of the ancients. London, 1701.

Phil 1850.30   Bacon, Francis. Scripta in naturali...philosophia. Amsterdam, 1653.

Htn Phil 1850.31*   Bacon, Francis. The two books of proficience and advancement of learning. London, 1605.

Htn Phil 1850.31.15* Bacon, Francis. De dignitate et augmentis scientiarum. Libri IX. Paris, 1624.

Htn Phil 1850.32*   Bacon, Francis. De augmentis scientiarum. Libri IX. Lugdunum, 1652.

Htn Phil 1850.32.5*   Bacon, Francis. De augmentis scientiarum. Libri IX. Amsterdam, 1662.

Phil 1850.32.8   Bacon, Francis. De dignitate et augmentis scientarum. Libri IX. Argentorari, 1654.

Htn Phil 1850.33.5*   Bacon, Francis. Of the advancement and proficiencie of learning. London, 1674.

Phil 1850.34.2   Bacon, Francis. The books of Lord Verulam. London, 1825.

Phil 1850.34.3   Bacon, Francis. Of the proficience and advancement of learning. London, 1828.

Phil 1850.34.5   Bacon, Francis. Of the proficience and advancement of learning. London, 1838.

Phil 1850.35A   Bacon, Francis. Of the proficience and advancement of learning. London, 1851.

Phil 1850.35B   Bacon, Francis. Of the proficience and advancement of learning. London, 1851.

Phil 1850.35.1   Bacon, Francis. Of the proficience and advancement of learning. London, 1861.

Phil 1850.35.2A   Bacon, Francis. The advancement of learning. Oxford, 1869.

Phil 1850.35.2B   Bacon, Francis. The advancement of learning. Oxford, 1869.

Phil 1850.35.2.3   Bacon, Francis. The advancement of learning. 3rd ed. Oxford, 1885.

Phil 1850.35.3   Bacon, Francis. The advancement of learning. v.2. London, 1893-95.

Phil 1850.35.4   Bacon, Francis. The advancement of learning. 4th ed. Oxford, 1891.

Phil 1850.35.5   Bacon, Francis. The advancement of learning. 5th ed. Oxford, 1900.

NEDL Phil 1850.35.6   Bacon, Francis. The advancement of learning. St. Louis, 1901.

Phil 1850.35.7A   Bacon, Francis. The advancement of learning. Boston, 1904.

Phil 1850.35.7B   Bacon, Francis. The advancement of learning. Boston, 1904.

Phil 1850.35.7C   Bacon, Francis. The advancement of learning. Boston, 1904.

Phil 1850.35.8   Bacon, Francis. The advancement of learning. 1st ed. London, 1901-05. 2v.

Phil 1850.35.12   Bacon, Francis. Of the advancement of learning. 5th ed. Oxford, 1920.

Phil 1850.35.20   Bacon, Francis. The advancement of learning. London, 1950.

Phil 1850.36   Bacon, Francis. The advancement of learning. London, 1900.

Htn Phil 1850.37*   Bacon, Francis. Les progrez et avancement aux sciences divines et humaines. Paris, 1624.

Htn Phil 1850.38*   Bacon, Francis. Neuf livres de la dignité et de l'accroissement des sciences. Paris, 1632.

Htn Phil 1850.39*   Bacon, Francis. The essayes or counsels. London, 1625.

Phil 1850.40   Bacon, Francis. Essays. 3rd ed. London, 1857.

Phil 1850.40.2   Bacon, Francis. Essays. 3rd ed. London, 1858.

Phil 1850.40.4   Bacon, Francis. Essays. 2nd ed. London, 1857.

Phil 1850.41   Bacon, Francis. De dignitate et augmentis scientiarum. Wirceburgi, 1779-80. 2v.

Phil 1850.41.7   Bacon, Francis. Über die Würde und den Fortgang der Wissenschaften. Darmstadt, 1966.

Phil 1850.50.2   Bacon, Francis. Novum organum. T. Fowler. Oxford, 1878.

Phil 1850.50.3   Bacon, Francis. Novum organum. T. Fowler. Oxford, 1878.

Phil 1850.50.4   Bacon, Francis. Novum organum. T. Fowler. 2nd ed. Oxford, 1889.

**Phil 1850   History of philosophy - Local Modern philosophy - Great Britain and
United States - Individual philosophers - Bacon, Francis - cont.**

	Phil 1850.50.5A	Bacon, Francis. Novum organum. Rev. A. Johnson. London, 1859.
	Phil 1850.50.5B	Bacon, Francis. Novum organum. Rev. A. Johnson. London, 1859.
Htn	Phil 1850.50.6*	Bacon, Francis. Novum organum. Lugdunum Batavorum, 1650. 2 pam.
Htn	Phil 1850.50.7*	Bacon, Francis. Novum organum. 2a ed. Amsterdam, 1660.
	Phil 1850.50.8	Bacon, Francis. Neues Organon. J.H. Kirchmann. Berlin, 1870.
	Phil 1850.50.9	Bacon, Francis. Novum organum. Wirceburgi, 1779.
	Phil 1850.50.10	Bacon, Francis. Novum organum. Glasguae, 1803.
	Phil 1850.50.11	Bacon, Francis. Novum organum. Oxonii, 1813.
	Phil 1850.50.12	Bacon, Francis. Novum organum. St. Louis, 1901.
	Phil 1850.50.13A	Bacon, Francis. Novum organum. London, 1905.
	Phil 1850.50.13B	Bacon, Francis. Novum organum. London, 1905.
	Phil 1850.50.23	Bacon, Francis. Nuovo organo delle scienze. Bassano, 1788.
	Phil 1850.50.25	Bacon, Francis. Novum organum. Lanciano, 1928.
	Phil 1850.50.26	Bacon, Francis. Nuovo organo. Firenze, 1938.
	Phil 1850.51	Bacon, Francis. The novum organon. Oxford, 1855.
Htn	Phil 1850.55*	Bacon, Francis. A collection of some principall rules and maximes of the common laws of England. London, 1630.
Htn	Phil 1850.56*	Bacon, Francis. De Verulamio summi angliae. London, 1620.
Htn	Phil 1850.57*	Bacon, Francis. The historie of the raigne of...Henry VII. London, 1622.
Htn	Phil 1850.59*	Bacon, Francis. The use of the law. London, 1629.
X Cg	Phil 1850.59.10	Bacon, Francis. Exemplum tractatus de justitia universali. Metz, 1806. (Changed to XM 1503)
	Phil 1850.59.50	Bacon, Francis. Sermones fideles, ethici, politici, o economici, sive interiora rerum. Lugdunum Batavorum, 1659.
Htn	Phil 1850.60*	Bacon, Francis. Sermones fidelis. Amsterdam, 1662.
Htn	Phil 1850.61*	Bacon, Francis. A wise and moderate discourse concerning church affaires. n.p., 1641.
Htn	Phil 1850.62*	Bacon, Francis. True peace; or A moderate discourse. London, 1663.
Htn	Phil 1850.63*	Bacon, Francis. Historia vitae et mortis. Lugdunum Batavorum, 1636.
Htn	Phil 1850.64*	Bacon, Francis. Historia vitae et mortis. Lugdunum Batavorum, 1637.
Htn	Phil 1850.64.5*	Bacon, Francis. Historie of life and death. London, 1638.
Htn	Phil 1850.64.7*	Bacon, Francis. History naturall and experimentall, of life and death. London, 1638.
Htn	Phil 1850.65*	Bacon, Francis. Historia vitae et mortis. Amstelodami, 1663.
	Phil 1850.66	Bacon, Francis. Analyse de la philosophie. Leyde, 1756.
Htn	Phil 1850.71*	Bacon, Francis. Sylva Sylvarum. London, 1627.
Htn	Phil 1850.72*	Bacon, Francis. The confession of faith. London, 1641.
Htn	Phil 1850.73*	Bacon, Francois. Historia naturalis. Londini, 1622.
Htn	Phil 1850.74*	Bacon, Francis. Historia naturalis et experimentalis de ventis. Lugdunum Batavorum, 1638.
Htn	Phil 1850.74.5*	Bacon, Francis. The naturall and experimentall history of winds. London, 1653.
Htn	Phil 1850.75*	Bacon, Francis. Historia naturalis et experimentalis de ventis. Amstelodami, 1662. 3 pam.
Htn	Phil 1850.75.5*	Bacon, Francis. Histoire naturelle. Paris, 1631.
Htn	Phil 1850.75.10*	Bacon, Francis. Resuscitatio, or Bringing into public light. London, 1657.
Htn	Phil 1850.76*	Bacon, Francis. Opuscula varia posthuma, philosophica, civilia, et theologica. Londini, 1658.
	Phil 1850.79	Pamphlet box. Bacon, Francis.
	Phil 1850.80A	Abbott, E.A. Francis Bacon. London, 1885.
	Phil 1850.80B	Abbott, E.A. Francis Bacon. London, 1885.
	Phil 1850.81	Church, R.W. Bacon. London, 1884.
	Phil 1850.81.3	Church, R.W. Bacon. London, 1896.
	Phil 1850.81.4	Church, R.W. Bacon. N.Y., 1884.
	Phil 1850.81.5	Church, R.W. Bacon. N.Y., 1901.
	Phil 1850.81.6	Church, R.W. Bacon. N.Y., 1899.
	Phil 1850.81.9	Church, R.W. Bacon. London, 1908.
	Phil 1850.82	Fischer, K. Frances Bacon of Verulam. London, 1857.
	Phil 1850.82.5	Fischer, K. Francis Bacon und seine Nachfolger. 2e Aufl. Leipzig, 1875.
	Phil 1850.82.10	Fischer, K, Franz Bacon von Verulam. Leipzig, 1856.
	Phil 1850.83A	Fowler, J. Bacon. N.Y., 1881.
	Phil 1850.83B	Fowler, J. Bacon. N.Y., 1881.
	Phil 1850.84.2	Lovejoy, B.G. Francis Bacon. London, 1888.
	Phil 1850.85	Luc, J.A. de. Précis de la philosophie de Bacon. Paris, 1802. 2v.
	Phil 1850.86	Maestre, J. de. Examen de la philosophie de Bacon. Paris, 1836. 2v.
	Phil 1850.87	Nichol, J. Bacon. Philadelphia, 1888-89. 2v.
	Phil 1850.88	Rémusat, Charles de. Bacon. Paris, 1858.
	Phil 1850.89	Tyler, S. Discourse of the Baconian philosophy. Frederick City, 1844.
	Phil 1850.89.2	Tyler, S. Discourse of the Baconian philosophy. Frederick City, 1846.
	Phil 1850.89.3	Tyler, S. Discourse of the Baconian philosophy. N.Y., 1850.
	Phil 1850.89.5	Tyler, S. Discourse of the Baconian philosophy. 3rd ed. Washington, 1877.
	Phil 1850.90	Jung, E. Causa finalis. Eine Bakostudie. Giessen, 1893.
	Phil 1850.91F	Liebig, J.F. von. Rede in der...(F. Bacon...Geschichte...Naturwissenschaften). München, 1863.
	Phil 1850.92	Janet, P. Bacon Verulamius. Angers, 1889.
	Phil 1850.93	Reichel, E. Wer Schrieb das "Norum Organon" von Francis Bacon. Stuttgart, 1886.
	Phil 1850.94	Biechy, A. Essai sur la méthode de Bacon. Toulon, 1855.
	Phil 1850.95	Jacquinet, P. Francisci Baconi de re litteraria judicia. Paris, 1863.
	Phil 1850.96	Hoppus, J. An account of Lord Bacon's Novum Organon Scientiarum. London, 1827-28.
	Phil 1850.96.2	Hoppus, J. An account of Lord Bacons Novum Organon Scientiarum. London, 1827. 3 pam.
	Phil 1850.96.3	Hoppus, J. An account of Lord Bacons Novum Organon Scientiarum. London, 1827. 3 pam.
	Phil 1850.97	Sortain, J. The life of Francis Lord Bacon. London, n.d.
	Phil 1850.98	Fonsegrive, G.L. François Bacon. Paris, 1893.
	Phil 1850.100A	Craik, G.L. Bacon; his writings and his philosophy. London, 1846.
	Phil 1850.100B	Craik, G.L. Bacon; his writings and his philosophy. London, 1846.
	Phil 1850.100.5	Craik, G.L. Bacon; his writings and his philosophy. v.1-3. London, 1860.
	Phil 1850.100.7	Craik, G.L. Bacon; his writings and his philosophy. London, 1862.
NEDL	Phil 1850.101	Steeves, G.W. Francis Bacon, a sketch of his life. London, 1910.

**Phil 1850   History of philosophy - Local Modern philosophy - Great Britain and
United States - Individual philosophers - Bacon, Francis - cont.**

	Phil 1850.102	Wolff, E. Francis Bacon und seine Quellen. Berlin, 1910. 2v.
	Phil 1850.103	Adam, Charles. Philosophie de François Bacon. Paris, 1890.
	Phil 1850.104	Natge, Hans. Über Francis Bacons Formenlehre. Leipzig, 1891.
NEDL	Phil 1850.105	Laing, F.H. Lord Bacon's philosophy examined. London, 1877.
	Phil 1850.106	Finch, A. Elley. On the inductive philosophy. London, 1872.
	Phil 1850.107	Lemaire, Paul. François Bacon. Paris, 1913.
	Phil 1850.108	Wigston, William F. The Columbus of literature. Chicago, 1892.
	Phil 1850.109	Welhelmy, Gerrit. De vita et philosophia F. Baconi. Groningae, 1843.
	Phil 1850.110	Deleyre, A. Analyse de la philosophie du chancelier François Bacon avec sa vie. Leyde, 1778. 2v.
	Phil 1850.111	Barthélemy-Sainte-Hilaire, Jules. Étude sur François Bacon. Paris, 1890.
	Phil 1850.112	Heussler, Hans. Francis Bacon. Breslau, 1889.
	Phil 1850.113.3	Macaulay, Thomas Babington. Essay on Bacon. Oxford, 19- .
	Phil 1850.114	Liljeqvist, E. Om Francis Bacon filosofi med särskild hänsyn till det etiska problemet. Uppsala, 1893.
	Phil 1850.115	Stapfer, P. Qualis sapientae antiquae laudator qualis interpres Franciscus Baconus exstiterit. Paris, 1870.
	Phil 1850.116	Carrau, L. De sermonibus fidelibus F. Baconi Verulamii. Argentorati, 1870.
	Phil 1850.117	Lalande, A. Quid de mathematica senserit Baconus. Thesis. Lutetiae, 1899.
	Phil 1850.117.5	Lalande, A. L'interpretation de la nature dans le Valerius terminus. Mâcon, 1901.
	Phil 1850.118	Broad, C.D. The philosophy of Francis Bacon. Cambridge, Eng., 1926.
	Phil 1850.119	Kraus, Oskar. Der Machtgedanke und der Friedensidee in des Philosophie der Engländer, Bacon und Bentham. Leipzig, 1926.
	Phil 1850.120	Taylor, Alfred. Francis Bacon. London, 1926?
	Phil 1850.121	Frost, Walter. Bacon und die Naturphilosophie. München, 1927.
	Phil 1850.122	Patru, G.A. Esprit et méthode de Bacon en philosophie. Paris, 1854.
	Phil 1850.123	Levi, Adolfo. Il pensiero di Francesco Bacone. Torino, 1925.
	Phil 1850.124	Fazio-Allmayer, V. Saggio su Francesco Bacone. Palermo, 1928.
	Phil 1850.125	Catalano, E. Il naturalismo e l'individualismo di F. Bacone. Napoli, 1931.
	Phil 1850.126	The life and writings of Francis Bacon. Edinburgh, 1837.
	Phil 1850.127	Sturt, Mary. Francis Bacon; a biography. London, 1932.
	Phil 1850.128	Minkowski, Helmut. Einordnung, Wesen und Aufgaben...des Francis Bacon. Leyde, 1933.
	Phil 1850.129	Ossi, M.M. Saggio su Francesco Bacon. Napoli, 1935.
	Phil 1850.130	Réfutation de l'ouvrage intitulé; ou Reponse à un ecclésiastique sur cet ouvrage. n.p., n.d.
	Phil 1850.131	Tinivella, G. Baconee Locke. Milano, 1939.
	Phil 1850.133	Skemp, A.R. Francis Bacon. London, 1912.
	Phil 1850.135	Gundry, W.G.C. Francis Bacon, a map of days. London, 1946.
	Phil 1850.137	Green, Adwin W. Sir Francis Bacon. Syracuse, N.Y., 1948.
	Phil 1850.137.5	Green, Adwin W. Sir Francis Bacon. N.Y., 1966.
	Phil 1850.139	Anderson, Fulton H. The philosophy of Francis Bacon. Chicago, 1948.
	Phil 1850.140	Anderson, Fulton H. Francis Bacon. Los Angeles, 1962.
	Phil 1850.141	Farrington, B. Francis Bacon. N.Y., 1949.
	Phil 1850.143	Schuhl, P. La pensée de Lord Bacon. Paris, 1949.
	Phil 1850.145A	Jameson, T.H. Francis Bacon. N.Y., 1954.
	Phil 1850.145B	Jameson, T.H. Francis Bacon. N.Y., 1954.
	Phil 1850.147	Rossi, Paolo. L'interpretazione baconiana delle janole antiche. Roma, 1953.
	Phil 1850.147.5	Rossi, Paolo. Francesco Bacone, dalla magia alla scienza. Bari, 1957.
	Phil 1850.147.10	Rossi, Paolo. Francis Baconi from magic to science. London, 1968.
	Phil 1850.149	Haukart, Robert. François Bacon. Paris, 1957.
	Phil 1850.151	Pamer, C. Bacon von Verulam und seine Stellung in der Geschichte der Philosophie. Triest, 1888.
	Phil 1850.153	Patrick, J.M. Francis Bacon. London, 1961.
	Phil 1850.155	Saint Albans, England. City Council. Catalogue of exhibition organized by the St. Albans City Council in the Council Chamber. St. Albans, 1961.
	Phil 1850.157	Whitaker, Virgil Keeble. Francis Bacon's intellectual milieu. Los Angeles, 1962.
	Phil 1850.158	Bowen, Catherine. Francis Bacon. 1st ed. Boston, 1963.
	Phil 1850.159	Eiseley, Loren Corey. Francis Bacon and the modern dilemma. Lincoln, 1962.
	Phil 1850.160	Bacon, F.V. The philosophy of Francis Bacon. Liverpool, 1964.
	Phil 1850.162	Wallace, Karl Richards. Francis Bacon on the nature of man. Urbana, 1967.

**Phil 1855   History of philosophy - Local Modern philosophy - Great Britain and
United States - Individual philosophers - Bain, Alexander**

	Phil 1855.30	Bain, Alexander. Dissertaions on leading philosophical topics. London, 1903.
	Phil 1855.60	Bain, Alexander. Practical essays. London, 1884.
NEDL	Phil 1855.80	Bain, Alexander. Autobiography. London, 1904.

**Phil 1857   History of philosophy - Local Modern philosophy - Great Britain and
United States - Individual philosophers - Barfield, Owen**

	Phil 1857.1	Barfield, Owen. Unancestral voice. London, 1965.
	Phil 1857.2	Barfield, Owen. Worlds apart; a dialogue of the 1960's. 1st American ed. Middletown, Conn., 1964.

**Phil 1860   History of philosophy - Local Modern philosophy - Great Britain and
United States - Individual philosophers - Beattie, James**

	Phil 1860.10	Beattie, James. Dissertations moral and critical. Works 1-3. Philadelphia, 1809. 3v.
	Phil 1860.10.2	Beattie, James. Essays. Works 4-6. Philadelphia, 1809. 3v.
	Phil 1860.10.3	Beattie, James. Elements of moral science. Works 7-9. Philadelphia, 1809. 3v.
	Phil 1860.10.4	Beattie, James. The minstrel. Works 10. Philadelphia, 1809.
Htn	Phil 1860.40*	Beattie, James. Dissertations moral and critical. Dublin, 1783. 2v.

Classified Listing

Phil 1860 History of philosophy - Local Modern philosophy - Great Britain and United States - Individual philosophers - Beattie, James - cont.

	Phil 1860.40.2	Beattie, James. Dissertations moral and critical. London, 1783.
	Phil 1860.45	Beattie, James. Neue philosophische Versuche. Leipzig, 1779-80. 2v.
Htn	Phil 1860.50*	Beattie, James. Essay on the nature and immutability of truth. Edinburgh, 1770.
	Phil 1860.50.2	Beattie, James. Essay on the nature and immutability of truth. Dublin, 1773.
	Phil 1860.50.3	Beattie, James. Essay on the nature and immutability of truth. London, 1773.
	Phil 1860.50.4	Beattie, James. Essay on the nature and immutability of truth. London, 1774.
	Phil 1860.50.5	Beattie, James. Essay on the nature and immutability of truth. Edinburgh, 1777.
	Phil 1860.50.6	Beattie, James. Essay on the nature and immutability of truth. Edinburgh, 1805.
	Phil 1860.50.7	Beattie, James. Essay on the nature and immutability of truth. Philadelphia, 1809.
	Phil 1860.50.13	Beattie, James. Essay on the nature and immutability of truth. London, 1823.
	Phil 1860.60	Beattie, James. Elements of moral science. Philadelphia, 1792-94. 2v.
	Phil 1860.60.5	Beattie, James. Elements of moral science. v.1-2. Baltimore, 1813.

Phil 1865 History of philosophy - Local Modern philosophy - Great Britain and United States - Individual philosophers - Bent+am, mje-emy

	Phil 1865.05	Pamphlet box. Bentham, Jeremy. Political pamphlets, 1821-1825.
	Phil 1865.10	Bentham, Jeremy. Works. Edinburgh, 1843. 11v.
	Phil 1865.12	Bentham, Jeremy. The works of Jeremy Bentham. N.Y., 1962. 11v.
	Phil 1865.18	Bentham, Jeremy. Principios de la ciencia social. Salamanca, 1821.
	Phil 1865.19	Bentham, Jeremy. Panopticon. London, 1812-17. 4 pam.
	Phil 1865.22	Bentham, Jeremy. The limits of jurisprudence defined. N.Y., 1945.
	Phil 1865.25A	Bentham, Jeremy. Benthamiana. Edinburgh, 1843.
	Phil 1865.25B	Bentham, Jeremy. Benthamiana. Edinburgh, 1843.
	Phil 1865.28	Bentham, Jeremy. Of laws in general. London, 1970.
Htn	Phil 1865.29*	Bentham, Jeremy. A fragment on government. London, 1776.
	Phil 1865.30	Bentham, Jeremy. Deontology. v.1-2. London, 1834.
Htn	Phil 1865.30.2*	Bentham, Jeremy. Deontology. London, 1834. 2v.
	Phil 1865.30.30	Bentham, Jeremy. Deontologia. Torino, 1925.
	Phil 1865.30.35	Bentham, Jeremy. Deontologia. Torino, 1930.
Htn	Phil 1865.35*	Bentham, Jeremy. Panopticon. Dublin, 1791.
Htn	Phil 1865.40.2*	Bentham, Jeremy. The book of fallacies. London, 1824.
	Phil 1865.42	Bentham, Jeremy. The rationale of reward. London, 1830.
	Phil 1865.43	Bentham, Jeremy. Theorie des peines et des récompenses. v.1-2. London, 1811.
Htn	Phil 1865.49*	Bentham, Jeremy. An introduction to the principles of morals and legislation. London, 1789.
	Phil 1865.50	Bentham, Jeremy. Introduction to the principles of morals and legislation. v.1-2. London, 1823.
Htn	Phil 1865.50.1*	Bentham, Jeremy. Introduction to the principles of morals and legislation. London, 1823. 2v.
Htn	Phil 1865.50.5*	Bentham, Jeremy. Principles of legislation. Boston, 1830.
	Phil 1865.51A	Bentham, Jeremy. An introduction to the principles of morals and legislation. N.Y., 1948.
	Phil 1865.51B	Bentham, Jeremy. An introduction to the principles of morals and legislation. N.Y. 1948.
	Phil 1865.51.10	Bentham, Jeremy. An introduction to the principles of morals and legislation. Oxford, 1907.
	Phil 1865.51.15	Bentham, Jeromy. An introduction to the principles of morals and legislation. London, 1970.
	Phil 1865.53	Bentham, Jeremy. Official aptitude maximized. London, 1830.
Htn	Phil 1865.55*	Bentham, Jeremy. A table of the springs of action. London, 1815.
	Phil 1865.60	Bentham, Jeremy. Not Paul, but Jesus. Camden, 1917.
Htn	Phil 1865.60.5*	Bentham, Jeremy. Not Paul, but Jesus. London, 1823.
Htn	Phil 1865.65*	Bentham, Jeremy. Auto-icon. London, 1842?
	Phil 1865.66	Bentham, Jeremy. La religion naturelle...d'apres les papiers de J. Bentham. Paris, 1875.
	Phil 1865.80	Burton, J.H. Introduction to study of Bentham's works. Edinburgh, 1843.
	Phil 1865.81	Greyvenstein, J.H.J.A. Het sociale utilisme van Bentham. Utrecht, 1911.
Cg	Phil 1865.82	Atkinson, Charles M. Jeremy Bentham. London, 1905.
	Phil 1865.151A	Kraus, Oskar. Zur Theorie des Wertes. Halle, 1901.
	Phil 1865.151B	Kraus, Oskar. Zur Theorie des Wertes. Halle, 1901.
	Phil 1865.170	Lundin, Hilda G. The influence of J. Bentham on English democratic development. Iowa City, 1920.
	Phil 1865.171	Sánchez-Rivera de la Lastra, Juan. El utilitarismo; estudio de las doctrinas de Jeremías Bentham. Madrid, 1922.
	Phil 1865.175	Everett, Charles W. The education of Jeremy Bentham. N.Y., 1931.
	Phil 1865.176	Bentham, Jeremy. Bentham's theory of fictions. London, 1932.
	Phil 1865.176.2	Bentham, Jeremy. Bentham's theory of fictions. N.Y., 1932.
	Phil 1865.176.5	Ogden, Charles K. Jeremy Bentham 1832-2032...Bentham centenary lecture...on June 6th, 1930. London, 1932.
	Phil 1865.177	Wells, D.B. Saint Paul vindicated, being Part I of a reply...not Paul, but Jesus. Cambridge, 1824.
	Phil 1865.178	Stocks, John L. Jeremy Bentham (1748-1832). Manchester, 1933.
	Phil 1865.179	Himes, N.E. Jeremy Bentham and the genesis of English Neo-Malthusianism. London, 1936.
	Phil 1865.180	Surra, G. Studio sulla morale di Geremia Bentham. Torino, 1893.
	Phil 1865.181	Kayser, E.L. The grand social enterprise; a study of Jeremy Bentham in his relation to liberal nationalism. N.Y., 1932.
	Phil 1865.182	Keeton, G.W. Jeremy Bentham and the law. London, 1948.
	Phil 1865.183	London. University. University College Library. Jeremy Bentham, bicentenary celebrations. London, 1948.
	Phil 1865.184	Baumgardt, David. Bentham and the ethics of today. Princeton, 1952.
	Phil 1865.184.2	Baumgardt, David. Bentham and the ethics of today. N.Y., 1966.
	Phil 1865.185	London. University. University College Library. Catalogue of the manuscripts of Jeremy Bentham in the Library of University College. 2nd ed. London, 1962.

Phil 1865 History of philosophy - Local Modern philosophy - Great Britain and United States - Individual philosophers - Bent+am, mje-emy - cont.

	Phil 1865.185.2	London. University. University College Library. Catalogue of the manuscripts of Jeremy Bentham in the Library of University College. London, 1937.
	Phil 1865.186	Mack, Mary P. Jeremy Bentham; an odyssey of ideas. London, 1962.
	Phil 1865.186.2	Mack, Mary P. Jeremy Bentham. N.Y., 1963.
	Phil 1865.188	Burns, J.H. Jeremy Bentham and University College. London, 1962.
	Phil 1865.190	Hart, H.L.A. Bentham. London, 1962?
	Phil 1865.190.7	Atkinson, Charles. Jeremy Bentham. N.Y., 1969.
	Phil 1865.191	Nuñez, T. Sistema de la ciencia social. Salamanca, 1820.
	Phil 1865.192	The Utilitarians. Garden City, 1961.
	Phil 1865.193	Maślinśka, Hallna. Bentham i jcgo system ctyczny. Warszawa, 1964.
	Phil 1865.194	Robbins, Lionel. Bentham in the twentieth century. London, 1965.
	Phil 1865.195	Bentham, Jeremy. The correspondence of Jeremy Bentham. London, 1968. 3v.
	Phil 1865.196	Manning, David John. The mind of Jeremy Bentham. London, 1968.
	Phil 1865.198	Everett, Charles Warren. Jeremy Bentham. London, 1966.
	Phil 1865.200	el Shakankiri, Mohamed Abd el-Hadi. La philosophie juridique de Jeremy Bentham. Paris, 1970.

Phil 1870 History of philosophy - Local Modern philosophy - Great Britain and United States - Individual philosophers - Berkeley, George

	Phil 1870.10	Berkeley, G. Works. London, 1820. 3v.
	Phil 1870.10.5	Berkeley, G. Works. London, 1908. 3v.
	Phil 1870.11.5	Berkeley, G. Works. London, 1853. 2v.
	Phil 1870.12A	Berkeley, G. Works. Oxford, 1871. 4v.
	Phil 1870.12B	Berkeley, G. Works. v.2-4. Oxford, 1871. 3v.
	Phil 1870.13A	Berkeley, G. Works. Oxford, 1901.
	Phil 1870.13B	Berkeley, G. Works. v.2-3. Oxford, 1901. 2v.
	Phil 1870.13C	Berkeley, G. Works. v.4. Oxford, 1901.
	Phil 1870.15	Berkeley, G. Philosophische Werke. Leipzig, 192-. 3v.
	Phil 1870.17	Berkeley, G. Works. London, 1948-53. 9v.
	Phil 1870.20A	Berkeley, G. Selections. Oxford, 1874.
	Phil 1870.20B	Berkeley, G. Selections. Oxford, 1874.
	Phil 1870.20.3	Berkeley, G. Selections (Fraser). 3rd ed. Oxford, 1884.
	Phil 1870.20.4	Berkeley, G. Selections annotated. 5th ed. Oxford, 1899.
	Phil 1870.22	Berkeley, G. Philosophical writings. Edinburgh, 1952.
Htn	Phil 1870.29*	Berkeley, G. Alciphron. Dublin, 1732.
Htn	Phil 1870.30*	Berkeley, G. Alciphron. London, 1732. 2v.
Htn	Phil 1870.30.1*	Berkeley, G. Alciphron. 2d ed. London, 1732. 2v.
Htn	Phil 1870.30.2*	Berkeley, G. Alciphron. New Haven, 1803.
	Phil 1870.30.15	Berkeley, G. Alciphron. Leipzig, 1915.
	Phil 1870.30.25	Berkeley, G. Alcifrone. Dialoghi. v.1-5. Torino, 1932.
	Phil 1870.30.30	Berkeley, G. Alciphron. Paris, 1952.
Htn	Phil 1870.40.1*	Berkeley, G. Treatise...principles of human knowledge. Dublin, 1710.
Htn	Phil 1870.40.2*	Berkeley, G. Treatise...principles of human knowledge. London, 1734.
	Phil 1870.40.3	Berkeley, G. Treatise...principles of human knowledge. London, 1776.
	Phil 1870.40.9	Berkeley, G. Treatise concerning the principles of human knowledge. Chicago, 1878.
	Phil 1870.40.12	Berkeley, G. A treatise concerning the principles of human knowledge. Philadelphia, 1881.
	Phil 1870.40.13	Berkeley, G. A treatise concerning the principles of human knowledge. Chicago, 1904.
	Phil 1870.40.22	Berkeley, G. The principles of human knowledge. London, 1942.
	Phil 1870.40.25	Berkeley, G. Les principes de la connaissance humaine. Paris, 1920.
	Phil 1870.40.35	Berkeley, G. Abhandlung über die Prinzipien der menschlichen Erkenntnis. London, 1920.
	Phil 1870.40.45	Berkeley, G. Tratto dei principii della cognoscenza umana e tre dialogui. Bari, 1923.
	Phil 1870.40.50	Berkeley, G. Principi della conoscenza umana. Bologna, 1925.
Htn	Phil 1870.45.1*	Berkeley, G. Three dialogues...Hylas and Philonous. London, 1713.
	Phil 1870.45.3	Berkeley, G. Three dialogues...Hylas and Philonous. Chicago, 1901.
	Phil 1870.45.6	Berkeley, G. The dialogues between Hylas and Philonous. N.Y., 1954.
	Phil 1870.45.10	Berkeley, G. Dialogues entre Hylas et Philonous. Paris, 1925.
	Phil 1870.45.20	Berkeley, G. Drei Dialoge zwischen Hylas und Philonous. Leipzig, 1926.
	Phil 1870.45.21	Berkeley, G. Drei Dialoge zwischen Hylas und Philonous. Berlin, 1955.
	Phil 1870.45.25	Berkeley, G. Dialoghi tra Hylas e Filonous. Bari, 1939.
Htn	Phil 1870.60*	Berkeley, G. Essay towards a new theory of vision. Dublin, 1709.
Htn	Phil 1870.60.1*	Berkeley, G. Essay towards a new theory of vision. 2d ed. Dublin, 1709.
	Phil 1870.60.1.2	Berkeley, G. Essay towards a new theory. Dublin, 1709.
	Phil 1870.60.2	Berkeley, G. The theory of vision vindicated. Cambridge, 1860.
	Phil 1870.60.3A	Berkeley, G. A new theory of vision. London, 1906.
	Phil 1870.60.3B	Berkeley, G. A new theory of vision. London, 1906.
	Phil 1870.60.15	Berkeley, G. Versuch einer neuen Theorie der Gesichtswahrnehmung. Leipzig, 1912.
Htn	Phil 1870.65*	Berkeley, G. Siris: a chain of...reflexions. Dublin, 1744.
	Phil 1870.65.5	Berkeley, G. Recherches sur les vertus de l'eau de goudron. Amsterdam, 1745.
	Phil 1870.65.8	Berkeley, G. Recherches sur les vertus de l'eau de goudron. Genève, 1748.
Htn	Phil 1870.65.9*	Berkeley, G. Extrait des recherches sur les vertus de l'eau de goudron. Amsterdam, 1749.
	Phil 1870.65.15	Berkeley, G. Siris. Leipzig, 1915.
	Phil 1870.66.5	Berkeley, G. La siris. Paris, 1920.
	Phil 1870.70	Berkeley, G. Miscellany containing several tracts on various subjects. London, 1752.
Htn	Phil 1870.72*	Berkeley, G. A discourse addressed to magistrates and men in authority. Dublin, 1738.
	Phil 1870.73	Berkeley, G. Commonplace book. London, 1930.
	Phil 1870.73.5	Berkeley, G. Le journal philosophique. Commonplace book. Paris, 1908.
	Phil 1870.73.7	Berkeley, G. Gli appunti (commonplace book). Bologna, 1924.
	Phil 1870.73.13	Berkeley, G. Philosophisches Tagebuch (commonplace book). Leipzig, 1926.

Classified Listing

	Phil 1870.73.18	Berkeley, G. Philosophical commentaries generally called the commonplace book. London, 1944.
	Phil 1870.75	Berkeley, G. Memoirs. 2nd ed. London, 1784.
	Phil 1870.78	Jessop, T.E. A bibliography of George Berkeley. London, 1934.
	Phil 1870.79	Pamphlet box. Berkeley, G. German dissertations.
	Phil 1870.79.5	Pamphlet box. Berkeley, G.
Htn	Phil 1870.81*	Mandeville, B. A letter to Dion Bp. Berkeley on Alciphron. London, 1732.
	Phil 1870.82A	Abbot, T.K. Sight and touch...Berkeleian theory. London, 1864.
	Phil 1870.82B	Abbot, T.K. Sight and touch...Berkeleian theory. London, 1864.
	Phil 1870.82.5	Abbot, T.K. Bishop Berkeley and Professor Fraser. Dublin, 1877.
	Phil 1870.83	Bailey, S. Review of Berkeley's theory of vision. London, 1842.
NEDL	Phil 1870.84	Fraser, Alexander Campbell. Berkeley. Philadelphia, 1881.
	Phil 1870.84.1	Fraser, Alexander Campbell. Berkeley. Edinburgh, 1881.
	Phil 1870.84.2.3	Fraser, Alexander Campbell. Berkeley. Philadelphia, 1899.
	Phil 1870.84.3	Fraser, Alexander Campbell. Life and letters of George Berkeley. Oxford, 1871.
	Phil 1870.85	Dick, S.M. The principle of synthetic unity in Berkeley and Kant. Lowell, 1898.
	Phil 1870.86	Porter, N. The two-hundredth birthday of Bishop George Berkeley. N.Y., 1885.
	Phil 1870.87	Tower, C.V. The relation of Berkeley's later to his early ideal. Ann Arbor, 1899.
	Phil 1870.88	Freedman, L.A. Substanz und Causalitat bei Berkeley. Strassburg, 1902.
	Phil 1870.89	Raffel, Friedrich. Ist Berkeley ein Freihändler? Kiel, 1904.
	Phil 1870.90	Malan, D.F. Het idealisme van Berkeley. Utrecht, 1905.
	Phil 1870.92	Penjon, A. Étude sur vie et les oeuvres philosophiques de G. Berkeley. Paris, 1878.
	Phil 1870.93	David, M. Berkeley. Paris, n.d.
	Phil 1870.94	Cassirer, E. Berkeleys System. Giessen, 1914.
	Phil 1870.95	Berkeley, G. Berkeley and Percival. Cambridge, 1914.
Htn	Phil 1870.95.2*	Berkeley, G. Berkeley and Percival. Cambridge, 1914.
Htn	Phil 1870.96*	Pamphlet vol. The tar water controversy. 15 pam.
	Phil 1870.97	Levi, Adolfo. La filosofia di Giorgio Berkeley. Torino, 1922.
	Phil 1870.98	Joussain, André. Exposé critique de la philosophie de Berkeley. Paris, 1921.
	Phil 1870.98.3	Joussain, André. Exposé critique de la philosophie de Berkeley. Thèse. Paris, 1920.
	Phil 1870.99	Didier, Jean. Berkeley. Paris, 1911.
	Phil 1870.100	Johnston, G.A. The development of Berkeley's philosophy. London, 1923.
	Phil 1870.101	Metz, Rudolf. George Berkeley Leben und Lehre. Stuttgart, 1925.
	Phil 1870.102	Ueberweg, F. Berkeley's Abhandlung über Principien der menschlichen Erkenntnis. Berlin, 1869.
	Phil 1870.103	Ikbal Kishen, Shargha. A critical essay on Berkeley's theory of perception. Allababad, n.d.
	Phil 1870.105	Papini, G. Giorgio Berkeley. Milano, 1908.
	Phil 1870.106	Gerard, J. De idealismi aprud Berkeleium. Sancti Clodoaldi, 1874.
	Phil 1870.107	Olgiati, F. L'idealismo di G. Berkeley. Milano, 1926.
	Phil 1870.108	Norton, John N. The life of Bishop Berkeley. N.Y., 1861.
	Phil 1870.109A	Joseph, H.W.B. A comparison of Kant's idealism with that of Berkeley. London, 1929.
	Phil 1870.109B	Joseph, H.W.B. A comparison of Kant's idealism with that of Berkeley. London, 1929.
	Phil 1870.110	Hone, J.M. Bishop Berkeley. London, 1931.
	Phil 1870.111	Rand, Benjamin. Berkeley's American sojourn. Cambridge, 1932.
	Phil 1870.112	Hicks, G.D. Berkeley. London, 1932.
	Phil 1870.113	Aaron, Richard I. Locke and Berkeley's commonplace book. Aberdeen, 1931. 2 pam.
	Phil 1870.114	Oertel, Hans. George Berkeley und die englische Literatur. Halle, 1934.
	Phil 1870.115	Luce, Arthur A. Berkeley and Malebranche. London, 1934.
	Phil 1870.115.10	Luce, Arthur A. Berkeley's immaterialism. London, 1945.
	Phil 1870.115.15	Luce, Arthur A. The dialectic of immaterialism. London, 1963.
	Phil 1870.116	Kaveeshwar, G.W. The metaphysics of Berkeley critically examined in the light of modern philosophy. Mandleshwar, 1933.
	Phil 1870.117A	Wild, John. George Berkeley. Cambridge, 1936.
	Phil 1870.117B	Wild, John. George Berkeley. Cambridge, 1936.
	Phil 1870.118	Hedenius, Ingemar. Sensationalism and theology in Berkeley's philosophy. Inaug. Diss. Uppsala, 1936.
	Phil 1870.119	Stock, J. An account of the life of George Berkeley. 2nd ed. Dublin, 1777.
	Phil 1870.120A	Broad, C.D. Berkeley's argument about material substance. London, 1942.
	Phil 1870.120B	Broad, C.D. Berkeley's argument about material substance. London, 1942.
	Phil 1870.121	Baladi, Naguit. La pensée religieuse de Berkeley. La Caire, 1945.
	Phil 1870.122	Brayton, Alice. George Berkeley in Apulia. Boston, 1946.
	Phil 1870.122.5	Brayton, Alice. George Berkeley in Newport. Newport, R.I., 1954.
	Phil 1870.123	Bender, Frans. George Berkeley's philosophy re-examined. Amsterdam, 1946.
	Phil 1870.123.5	Bender, Frans. George Berkeley. Baarn, 1966.
	Phil 1870.124	Luce, Arthur A. The life of George Berkeley. London, 1949.
	Phil 1870.125A	Wisdom, J.O. The unconscious origin of Berkeley's philosophy. London, 1953.
	Phil 1870.125B	Wisdom, J.O. The unconscious origin of Berkeley's philosophy. London, 1953.
	Phil 1870.126	Warnock, G.J. Berkeley. London, 1953.
	Phil 1870.128	Hermathena. Homage to George Berkeley. Dublin, 1953.
	Phil 1870.130	Guéroult, Martial. Berkeley. Paris, 1956.
	Phil 1870.132	Sillem, E.A. George Berkeley and the proofs for the existence of God. London, 1957.
	Phil 1870.134	Dublin. University. Trinity College. Library. Catalogue of manuscripts. Dublin, 1953.
	Phil 1870.136	Bracken, Harry M. The early reception of Berkeley's immaterialism. The Hague, 1959.
	Phil 1870.136.5	Bracken, Harry M. The early reception of Berkeley's immaterialism, 1710-1733. The Hague, 1965.
	Phil 1870.138	Leroy, André Louis. George Berkeley. Paris, 1959.
	Phil 1870.140	Jessop, T.E. George Berkeley. London, 1959.

	Phil 1870.142	Armstrong, D.M. Berkeley's theory of vision. Victoria, 1960.
	Phil 1870.145	Rauschenberger, J.P. Über das Problem der Einheit un des Sinnes von Erscheinung bei Berkeley. Gernsbach, 1959.
	Phil 1870.150	Bogomolov, A.S. Kritika subektivno-idealisticheskoi filosofii D. Berkli. Moskva, 1959.
	Phil 1870.155	Steinkraus, Warren Edward. New studies in Berkeley's philosophy. N.Y., 1966.
	Phil 1870.160	Ritchie, Arthur David. George Berkeley, a reappraisal. Manchester, 1967.
	Phil 1870.165	Testa, Aldo. Meditazioni su Berkeley. Bologna, 1965.
	Phil 1870.170	Ardley, Gavin W.R. Berkeley's renovation of philosophy. The Hague, 1968[1969]
	Phil 1870.175	Olscamp, Paul J. The moral philosophy of George Berkeley. The Hague, 1970.
	Phil 1870.180	Stack, George J. Berkeley's analysis of preception. The Hague, 1970.
	Phil 1870.182	Bykhovskii, Bernard E. Dzhordzh Berkli. Moskva, 1970.

	Phil 1880.23	Pamphlet vol. Bowen, F. On the origin of species...Darwin. 8 pam.
	Phil 1880.25	Bowen, F. Critical essays. Boston, 1842.
	Phil 1880.25.5	Bowen, F. Critical essays. 2nd ed. Boston, 1845.
	Phil 1880.28	Bowen, F. Berkeley and his philosophy. Cambridge, 1838-57. 5 pam.
	Phil 1880.30	Bowen, F. Gleanings from a literary life 1830-80. N.Y., 1880.
	Phil 1880.40	Bowen, F. Principles of metaphysical and ethical science. Boston, 1855.
	Phil 1880.43	Bowen, F. Lowell lectures...metaphysics...science. Boston, 1849.
	Phil 1880.43.2	Bowen, F. Lowell lectures...metaphysics...science. Boston, 1849.
	Phil 1880.46	Bowen, F. Treatise on logic. Cambridge, 1864.
	Phil 1880.46.4	Bowen, F. Treatise on logic. 4th ed. Cambridge, 1866.
	Phil 1880.46.8	Bowen, F. Treatise on logic. 8th ed. Boston, 1880.
	Phil 1880.50	Bowen, F. The idea of cause. N.Y., 1879.
	Phil 1880.50.2	Bowen, F. The idea of cause. N.Y., 1879.

	Phil 1885.15	Bradley, Francis H. Collected essays. Oxford, 1935. 2v.
Htn	Phil 1885.30*	Bradley, Francis H. Ethical studies. London, 1876.
	Phil 1885.35	Bradley, Francis H. Essays on truth and reality. Oxford, 1914.
	Phil 1885.37	Bradley, Francis H. Appearance and reality. London, 1893.
	Phil 1885.37.3	Bradley, Francis H. Appearance and reality. London, 1899.
	Phil 1885.37.5A	Bradley, Francis H. Appearance and reality. 2d ed. London, 1902.
	Phil 1885.37.5B	Bradley, Francis H. Appearance and reality. 2d ed. London, 1902.
	Phil 1885.37.7	Bradley, Francis H. Appearance and reality. 2d ed. London, 1908.
	Phil 1885.37.15	Bradley, Francis H. Appearance and reality. Oxford, 1930.
	Phil 1885.37.20	Bradley, Francis H. Appearance and reality. Oxford, 1968.
	Phil 1885.80	Rashdall, H. The metaphysic of Mr. F.H. Bradley. London, 1912.
	Phil 1885.81	Francis Herbert Bradley, 1846-1924. London, n.d.
	Phil 1885.82	Pounder, R.M. The one and the many...Bradley's "Appearance and reality". Diss. Cambridge, 1928.
	Phil 1885.83	Kagey, Rudolf. The growth of F.H. Bradley's logic. N.Y., 1931.
	Phil 1885.84	Chappuis, A. Der theoretische Weg Bradley's. Paris, 1933.
	Phil 1885.85	Segerstedt, T.K. Value and reality in Bradley's philosophy. Lund, 1934.
	Phil 1885.86A	Loomba, R.M. Bradley and Bergson. Lucknow, 1937.
	Phil 1885.86B	Loomba, R.M. Bradley and Bergson. Lucknow, 1937.
	Phil 1885.87	Gamertsfelder, W.S. Thought, existence and reality as viewed by F.H. Bradley and B. Bosanquet. Columbus, 1920.
	Phil 1885.88	Ross, R.G. Scepticism and dogma; a study in philosophy of F.H. Bradley. N.Y., 1940.
	Phil 1885.89	Church, Ralph Withington. Bradley's dialectic. London, 1942.
	Phil 1885.90	Lofthouse, W.F. F.H. Bradley. London, 1949. 2v.
	Phil 1885.92	Ahmed, M. The theory of judgment in the philosophies of F.H. Bradley and John Cook Wilson. Dacca, 1955.
	Phil 1885.93	Wollheim, Richard. F.H. Bradley. Harmondsworth, 1960[1959]
	Phil 1885.93.2	Wollheim, Richard. F.H. Bradley. 2d ed. Harmondsworth, 1969.
	Phil 1885.94	Eliot, T.S. Knowledge and experience in the philosophy of F.H. Bradley. N.Y., 1964.
	Phil 1885.94.2	Eliot, T.S. Knowledge and experience in the philosophy of F.H. Bradley. London, 1964.
	Phil 1885.95	Saxena, Sushil Kumar. Studies in the metaphysics of Bradley. N.Y., 1967.
	Phil 1885.97	Vander Veer, Garrett L. Bradley's metaphysics and the self. New Haven, 1970.

	Phil 1890.30	Brown, T. Lectures on philosophy of human mind. Edinburgh, 1820. 4v.
	Phil 1890.30.2	Brown, T. Lectures on philosophy of human mind. Andover, 1822. 3v.
	Phil 1890.30.3	Brown, T. Lectures on philosophy of human mind. Philadelphia, 1824. 3v.
	Phil 1890.30.3.5	Brown, T. Lectures on philosophy of human mind. Hallowell, 1831.
	Phil 1890.30.4	Brown, T. Lectures on philosophy of human mind. Edinbrugh, 1846. 4v.
	Phil 1890.30.5	Brown, T. Lectures on philosophy of human mind. London, 1860.
	Phil 1890.30.6	Brown, T. Treatise on the philosophy of human mind. Cambridge, 1827. 2v.
	Phil 1890.30.7	Brown, T. Sketch of a system of human mind. Edinburgh, 1820.
	Phil 1890.40.2	Brown, T. Inquiry into relation of cause and effect. Andover, 1822.
	Phil 1890.80	Woods, J.H. Thomas Browns Causationstheorie. Leipzig, 1897.
	Phil 1890.85	Réthoré, François. Critique de la philosophie de Thomas Brown. Paris, 1863.

Phil 1900   History of philosophy - Local Modern philosophy - Great Britain and United States - Individual philosophers - Butler, Joseph

Phil 1900.9	Butler, Joseph. Works. Edinburgh, 1804. 2v.
Phil 1900.9.2	Butler, Joseph. Works. v.1-2. Cambridge, 1827.
Phil 1900.9.5	Butler, Joseph. Works. Oxford, 1844. 2v.
Phil 1900.9.9	Butler, Joseph. Works. Oxford, 1849-50. 2v.
Phil 1900.10	Butler, Joseph. Works. Oxford, 1807. 2v.
Phil 1900.11	Butler, Joseph. Works. Oxford, 1896. 2v.
Phil 1900.15	Butler, Joseph. Whole works. London, 1847.
Phil 1900.19	Butler, Joseph. Whole works. London, 1900. 2v.
Phil 1900.25	Butler, Joseph. Analogy of religion and sermons. London, 1852.
Phil 1900.28	Butler, Joseph. Analogy of religion and ethical discourses. Boston, 1860.
Htn Phil 1900.30*	Butler, Joseph. Analogy of religion. London, 1736.
Htn Phil 1900.30.2*	Butler, Joseph. Analogy of religion. London, 1736.
Phil 1900.31	Butler, Joseph. Analogy of religion. London, 1740.
Phil 1900.32A	Butler, Joseph. Analogy of religion. Bishop of Gloucester. Boston, 1793.
Phil 1900.32B	Butler, Joseph. Analogy of religion. Bishop of Gloucester. Boston, 1793.
Htn Phil 1900.32.6*	Butler, Joseph. Analogy of religion. Bishop of Gloucester. Boston, 1793.
Phil 1900.33	Butler, Joseph. Analogy of religion. London, 1798.
Phil 1900.34	Butler, Joseph. Analogy of religion. Boston, 1809.
Phil 1900.35	Butler, Joseph. Analogy of religion. Cambridge, 1827.
Phil 1900.35.5	Butler, Joseph. Analogy of religion. 2d ed. Cambridge, 1830.
Phil 1900.36	Butler, Joseph. Analogy of religion. London, 1834.
Phil 1900.37	Butler, Joseph. Analogy of religion. N.Y., 1839.
Phil 1900.37.3	Butler, Joseph. Analogy of religion. N.Y., 1843.
Phil 1900.37.3.5A	Butler, Joseph. Analogy of religion. 20th ed. N.Y., 1848.
Phil 1900.37.3.5B	Butler, Joseph. Analogy of religion. 20th ed. N.Y., 1848.
Phil 1900.37.3.6	Butler, Joseph. Analogy of religion. Cincinnati, 1849.
Phil 1900.37.15	Butler, Joseph. Analogy of religion. London, 1857.
Phil 1900.38	Butler, Joseph. Analogy of religion. Philadelphia, 1857.
Phil 1900.39	Butler, Joseph. Analogy of religion. London, 1860.
Phil 1900.39.5	Butler, Joseph. Analogy of religion. 20th ed. N.Y., 1860.
Phil 1900.40	Butler, Joseph. Analogy of religion. London, 1884.
Phil 1900.40.2	Butler, Joseph. Analogy of religion. London, 1873.
Phil 1900.41	Butler, Joseph. The analogy of religion, natural and revealed, to the constitution and course of nature. London, 1878.
Phil 1900.43	Butler, Joseph. The analogy of religion, natural and revealed. 1st ed. London, 1906.
Phil 1900.45	Holland, H.S. The optimism of Butler's "analogy". Oxford, 1908.
Phil 1900.60	Butler, Joseph. Fifteen sermons preached at the Rolls Chapel. London, 1726.
Phil 1900.60.2.6	Butler, Joseph. Fifteen sermons and six sermons. 6th ed. London, 1792.
Phil 1900.60.4	Butler, Joseph. Fifteen sermons and six sermons. 4th ed. London, 1749.
Phil 1900.60.5	Butler, Joseph. Fifteen sermons and six sermons. 5th ed. London, n.d.
Phil 1900.60.15	Butler, Joseph. Sermons. Cambridge, 1827.
Phil 1900.62	Butler, Joseph. Five sermons preached at the Rolls Chapel. N.Y., 1950.
Phil 1900.69	Butler, Joseph. Fifteen sermons. London, 1836.
Phil 1900.70	Butler, Joseph. Ethical discourses. Philadelphia, 1855.
Phil 1900.75	Butler, Joseph. Six sermons on moral subjects. Cambridge, 1849.
Phil 1900.76	Butler, Joseph. Sermons I, II, III upon human nature. Edinburgh, 1888.
Phil 1900.80	Bartlett, T. Memoirs...Joseph Butler D.C.L. London, 1839.
Phil 1900.81	Collins, W.L. Butler. Philadelphia, 1881.
Phil 1900.81.3	Collins, W.L. Butler. Edinburgh, 1881.
Phil 1900.82	Eaton, J.R.T. Bishop Butler and his critics. Oxford, 1877.
Phil 1900.83	Pynchon, T.R. Bishop Butler. N.Y., 1889.
Phil 1900.84	Gladstone, W.E. Studies subsidiary to works of...Butler. Oxford, 1896.
Phil 1900.85	Weeda, W.H. Joseph Butler als zedekundige. Utrecht, 1899.
Phil 1900.86	Taylor, W.E. Ethical and religious theories of Bishop Butler. Toronto, 1903.
Phil 1900.87	Ayer, Joseph Cullen. Versuch einer Darstellung der Ethik Joseph Butlers. Inaug. Diss. Leipzig, 1893.
Phil 1900.88	Baker, A.E. Bishop Butler. London, 1923.
Phil 1900.89	Hennell, Sara S. Essay on the sceptical tendency of Butler's "analogy". London, 1859.
Phil 1900.90	Tomkins, S.S. Conscience, self love and benevolence in the system of Bishop Butler. Thesis. Philadelphia, 1934.
Phil 1900.91	Mossner, E.C. Bishop Butler and the age of reason. N.Y., 1936.
Phil 1900.92	Norton, William J. Bishop Butler, moralist and divine. New Brunswick, 1940.
Phil 1900.93	Harris, W.G. Teleology in the philosophy of Joseph Butler and Abraham Tucker. Thesis. Philadelphia, 1941.
Phil 1900.94	Spooner, W.A. Bishop Butler. London, 1901.
Phil 1900.95	Duncan-Jones, A. Butler's moral philosophy. Harmondsworth, 1952.
Phil 1900.96	Carlsson, P.A. Butler's ethics. The Hague, 1964.
Phil 1900.98	Jeffner, Anders. Butler and Hume on religion. Stockholm, 1966.
Phil 1900.100	Sharma, Sukhde. Ethics of Butler and the philosophy of action in Bhogavadgita according to Madhusudana Sarasvati. Varanasi, 1961.
Phil 1900.175	Hughes, Henry. A critical examination of Butler's analogy. London, 1898.

Phil 1905   History of philosophy - Local Modern philosophy - Great Britain and United States - Individual philosophers - Other B

Phil 1905.9.6	Burthogge, R. The philosophical writings. Chicago, 1921.
Phil 1905.9.9*	Burthogge, R. An essay upon reason. London, 1694. 3 pam.
Phil 1905.9.30	Burthogge, R. Of the soul of the world of particular souls. London, 1699.
Phil 1905.10.75	Bosanquet, B. Bernard Bosanquet and his friends. London, 1935.
Phil 1905.10.79	Pamphlet box. Bosanquet, Bernard.
Phil 1905.10.80	Huang, Chia-cheng. Le néo-hegelianisme en Angleterre. Paris, 1954.
Phil 1905.10.80.2	Huang, Chia-cheng. Le néo-hegelianisme en Angleterre. Paris, 1954.
Phil 1905.10.80.5	Huang, Chia-cheng. De l'humanisme à l'absolutisme. Paris, 1954.
Phil 1905.10.90	Pfannenstill, Bertil. Bernard Bosanquet's philosophy of the state. Inaug.-Diss. Lund, 1936.

Phil 1905   History of philosophy - Local Modern philosophy - Great Britain and United States - Individual philosophers - Other B - cont.

Phil 1905.10.95	LeChevalier, C. Ethique et idéalisme. Paris, 1963.
Phil 1905.11.78	Bascom, John. Things learned by living. N.Y., 1913.
Phil 1905.11.80	Robinson, Sanford. John Bascom, prophet. N.Y., 1922.
Phil 1905.12.90	McLarney, James J. The theism of Edgar S. Brightman. Diss. Washington, 1936.
Phil 1905.13	Bowman, A.A. A sacramental universe. Princeton, 1939.
Phil 1905.14.79	Pamphlet box. E.G. Boring.
Phil 1905.14.100	Boring, E.G. Psychologist at large. N.Y., 1961.
Phil 1905.15	Blanshard, B. The nature of thought. N.Y., 1940. 2v.
Phil 1905.20A	Baker, H.C. The dignity of man. Cambridge, 1947.
Phil 1905.20B	Baker, H.C. The dignity of man. Cambridge, 1947.
Phil 1905.21	Beer, Samuel. The city of reason. Cambridge, 1949. 2v.
Phil 1905.22A	Broad, C.D. Ethics and the history of philosophy. London, 1952.
Phil 1905.22B	Broad, C.D. Ethics and the history of philosophy. London, 1952.
Phil 1905.22.10	Broad, C.D. Religion, philosophy and physical research. N.Y., 1953.
Phil 1905.22.10.2A	Broad, C.D. Religion, philosophy and physical research. London, 1953.
Phil 1905.22.10.2B	Broad, C.D. Religion, philosophy and physical research. London, 1953.
Phil 1905.22.79	Schilpp, Paul. The philosophy of C.D. Broad. N.Y., 1959.
Phil 1905.22.80	Lean, Martin. Sense - perception and matter. London, 1953.
Phil 1905.23	Baillie, J.B. Reflections on life and religion. London, 1952.
Phil 1905.24	Barnhart, F.J.C. Principles of the infinite philosophy. N.Y., 1955.
Phil 1905.25	Ball, Frank N. Intellectual calculus. Ipswich, 1957.
Phil 1905.26	Boodin, J.E. Studies in philosophy. Los Angeles, 1957.
Phil 1905.27.30	Bugbee, H.G. The inward morning. State College, Pa., 1958.
Phil 1905.30.30	Berlin, Isaiah. Two concepts of liberty. Oxford, 1959.
Phil 1905.32.30	Black, Max. Models and metaphores. N.Y., 1962.
Phil 1905.33.30	Banerje, N.V. Language. London, 1963.
Phil 1905.34	Buchler, Justus. Metaphysics of natural complexes. N.Y., 1966.

Phil 1915   History of philosophy - Local Modern philosophy - Great Britain and United States - Individual philosophers - Clarke, Samuel

Htn Phil 1915*	Clarke, Samuel. Miscellaneous pamphlets on Dr. Clarke. London, 1686-1834. 4 pam.
VPhil 1915.10F	Clarke, Samuel. Works. London, 1738. 4v.
Htn Phil 1915.10.2F*	Clarke, Samuel. Works. London, 1738. 2v.
Phil 1915.12F	Clarke, Samuel. Works. London, 1742. 2v.
Phil 1915.14	Clarke, Samuel. Oeuvres philosophiques. Paris, 1843.
Phil 1915.20	Clarke, Samuel. Sermons on several subjects and occasions. 8th ed. London, 1756. 8v.
Phil 1915.25	Clarke, Samuel. XVIII sermons. 3rd ed. London, 1734.
Phil 1915.60	Clarke, Samuel. Discourse...attributes of God. London, 1719. 2 pam.
Phil 1915.60.2	Clarke, Samuel. Discourse...attributes of God. London, 1719.
Phil 1915.60.3	Clarke, Samuel. Discourse...attributes of God. London, 1728.
Phil 1915.60.4	Clarke, Samuel. Discourse...attributes of God. London, 1706. 2 pam.
Phil 1915.60.5	Clarke, Samuel. Discourse...attributes of God. London, 1711. 2 pam.
Phil 1915.60.7	Clarke, Samuel. Discourse...attributes of God. 6th ed. London, 1725. 2 pam.
Phil 1915.61	Clarke, Samuel. The scripture-doctrine of the Trinity. London, 1712.
Phil 1915.61.2	Clarke, Samuel. The scripture-doctrine of the Trinity. 2d ed. London, 1719.
Phil 1915.61.3	Clarke, Samuel. The scripture-doctrine of the Trinity. 3d ed. London, 1732.
Phil 1915.63.2	Clarke, Samuel. An exposition of the church catechism. 2d ed. London, 1730.
Phil 1915.63.6	Clarke, Samuel. An exposition of the church catechism. 6th ed. London, 1756.
Htn Phil 1915.70*	Clarke, Samuel. Letter to Dodwell. London, 1708-13. 9 pam.
Phil 1915.70.5	Clarke, Samuel. Letters to Mr. Dodwell. London, 1731.
Phil 1915.75	Pamphlet vol. Philosophy. Clarke, Samuel. 5 pam.
Phil 1915.76	Pamphlet vol. Philosophy. Clarke, Samuel. 4 pam.
Phil 1915.77	Clarke, J. Defence of Dr. Clarke's...attributes. v.1-3. London, 1732-33.
Phil 1915.78	Pamphlet box. Samuel Clarke.
Phil 1915.80	Whiston, W. Historical memoires of...Dr. S. Clarke. London, 1730.
Phil 1915.81	Le Rossignol, J.E. Ethical philosophy of Samuel Clarke. Leipzig, 1892.
Phil 1915.82.2	A full account of the late proceedings in convocation relating to Dr. Clarke's writings about the Trinity. London, 1714.
Phil 1915.83	Fránquiz Ventura, José Antonio. Borden Parker Browne's treatment of the problem of change and identity. Rio Piedras, 1942.

Phil 1920   History of philosophy - Local Modern philosophy - Great Britain and United States - Individual philosophers - Craik, Kenneth J.W.

Phil 1920.1.30	Craik, Kenneth James Williams. The nature of explanation. Cambridge, 1943.
Phil 1920.1.32	Craik, Kenneth James Williams. The nature of explanation. Cambridge, Eng., 1952.
Phil 1920.1.35	Craik, Kenneth James Williams. The nature of psychology. Cambridge, Eng., 1966.

Phil 1925   History of philosophy - Local Modern philosophy - Great Britain and United States - Individual philosophers - Cudworth, Ralph

Phil 1925.1	Cudworth, R. True intellectual system of the universe. London, 1678.
Htn Phil 1925.1.2*	Cudworth, R. True intellectual system of the universe. London, 1678.
Htn Phil 1925.1.3*	Cudworth, R. True intellectual system of the universe. London, 1678.
Htn Phil 1925.30.2*	Cudworth, R. The true intellectual system of the universe. 2d ed. London, 1743. 2v.
Phil 1925.31	Cudworth, R. The true intellectual system of the universe. Andover, 1837-38. 2v.

Classified Listing

Phil 1925   History of philosophy - Local Modern philosophy - Great Britain and United States - Individual philosophers - Cudworth, Ralph - cont.

Phil 1925.31.55   Cudworth, R. The true intellectual system of the universe. London, 1820. 4v.

Phil 1925.32   Cudworth, R. The true intellectual system of the universe. London, 1845. 3v.

VPhil 1925.49F   Cudworth, R. Systema intellectuale huius universi. Jenae, 1733.

Phil 1925.50   Cudworth, R. Systema intellectuale. Lugduni Batavorum, 1773. 2v.

Htn   Phil 1925.55*   Cudworth, R. Eternal and immutable morality. London, 1731.

Phil 1925.65   Cudworth, R. A sermon preached before the House of Commons, March 31, 1647. N.Y., 1930.

NEDL Phil 1925.80   Lowrey, C.E. Philosophy of Ralph Cudworth. N.Y., 1884.

NEDL Phil 1925.81   Scott, William Robert. Introduction to Cudworth's treatise...with life. London, 1891.

Phil 1925.82   Schmitz, Kurt J. Cudworth und der Platonismus. Diss. Bonn, 1919.

Phil 1925.83   Beyer, Joseph. Ralph Cudworth als Ethiker, Staats-Philosoph und Usthetiker auf Grund des gedruckten Schriften. Inaug. Diss. Bottrop, 1935.

Phil 1925.84   Passmore, J.A. Ralph Cudworth. Cambridge, Eng., 1951.

Phil 1925.85   Gysi, Lydia. Platonism and Cartesianism. Bern, 1962.

Phil 1928   History of philosophy - Local Modern philosophy - Great Britain and United States - Individual philosophers - Cumberland, Richard

Htn   Phil 1928.30*   Cumberland, R. De legibus naturae. Dublin, 1720.

Phil 1928.30.2   Cumberland, R. De legibus naturae. London, 1672.

Htn   Phil 1928.30.5*   Cumberland, R. De legibus naturae. 3d ed. Lubecae, 1694.

Phil 1928.31   Cumberland, R. Traité philosophique des loix naturelles. Amsterdam, 1744.

Phil 1928.31.2   Cumberland, R. Loix de la nature. Leiden, 1757.

Htn   Phil 1928.33*   Cumberland, R. A treatise of the laws of nature. London, 1727.

Phil 1928.35   Cumberland, R. A philosophical enquiry into the laws of nature. Dublin, 1750.

Phil 1928.80   Spaulding, F.E. Richard Cumberland...englischen Ethik. Leipzig, 1894.

Phil 1930   History of philosophy - Local Modern philosophy - Great Britain and United States - Individual philosophers - Other C

Htn   Phil 1930.1.30*   Carlyle, Thomas. Sartor Resartus. Boston, 1836.

Htn   Phil 1930.2.30*   Channing, William E. A discourse on religion. Boston, 1821.

Htn   Phil 1930.3.30*   Coleridge, S.T. Aids to reflection. London, 1825.

Htn   Phil 1930.4.30*   Collier, Arthur. Clavis universalis. London, 1713. 2 pam.

Htn   Phil 1930.4.31*   Collier, Arthur. Clavis universalis. Edinburgh, 1836.

Phil 1930.4.35   Collier, Arthur. Clavis universalis. Chicago, 1909.

Phil 1930.4.81   Kowalewski, Arnold. Kritische Analyse von Arthur Colliers Clavis Universalis. Inaug. Diss. Griefswald, 1897.

Phil 1930.5.25   Collins, Anthony. Essai sur la nature de l'âme humaine. Londres, 1769.

Htn   Phil 1930.5.29*   Collins, Anthony. A discourse of the grounds and reasons of the Christian religion. v.1-2. London, 1724.

Htn   Phil 1930.5.30*   Collins, Anthony. A discourse of the grounds and reasons of the Christian religion. London, 1724-37.

Phil 1930.5.35   Collins, Anthony. A discourse of the grounds and reasons of the Christian religion. London, 1737. 2 pam.

Htn   Phil 1930.5.37*   Collins, Anthony. A discourse of the grounds and reasons of the Christian religion. London, 1737. 2 pam.

Htn   Phil 1930.5.50*   Collins, Anthony. The scheme of literal prophecy considered. London, 1727.

Phil 1930.5.51   Collins, Anthony. The scheme of literal prophecy considered. London, 1727.

Phil 1930.5.80   O'higgins, James. Anthony Collins; the man and his works. The Hague, 1970.

Htn   Phil 1930.5.95*   Bullock, T. The reasoning of Christ and his Apostles...sermons...Nov. and Dec., 1724. London, 1725.

Phil 1930.6.80   Pamphlet box. Caird, Edward. Biography.

Phil 1930.6.125   Jones, Henry. The life and philosophy of Edward Caird. Glasgow, 1921.

Phil 1930.7.80   Chamberlin, R.V. Life and philosophy. Salt Lake City, 1925.

Phil 1930.8.87   Collingwood, Robin George. An autotbiography. London, 1951.

Phil 1930.8.88A   Collingwood, Robin George. An autobiography. London, 1964.

Phil 1930.8.88B   Collingwood, Robin George. An autobiography. London, 1964.

Phil 1930.8.90   McCallum, R.B. Robin George Collingwood, 1889-1943. London, 1943.

Phil 1930.8.95   Tomlin, E.W.F. Robin George Collingwood, 1889-1943. London, 1953.

Phil 1930.8.100   Suranyi-Unger, Nora. Die politische Philosophie von R.G. Collingwood. München, 1960.

Phil 1930.8.105   Donagan, Alan. The later philosophy of R.G. Collingwood. Oxford, 1962.

Phil 1930.8.110   Johnston, William Murray. The formative years of R.G. Collingwood. The Hague, 1967[1968]

Phil 1930.8.115   Shalom, Albert. R.G. Collingwood, philosophie et historien. Paris, 1967.

Phil 1930.8.120   Mink, Louis O. Mind, History, and dialectic: the philosophy of R.G. Collingwood. Bloomington, 1969.

Phil 1930.8.125   Rubinoff, Lionel. Collingwood and the reform of metaphysics; a study in the philosophy of mind. Toronto, 1970.

Phil 1930.9   Pamphlet box. Chroust, Anton Hermann.

Phil 1930.10.10   Cohen, M.R. A dreamer's journey. (Autobiography). Boston, 1949.

Phil 1930.10.30   Cohen Morris, R. The faith of a liberal. Selected essays. N.Y., 1946.

Phil 1930.10.35   Cohen, Morris R. Studies in philosophy and science. N.Y., 1949.

Phil 1930.10.80   Baron, S.W. Freedom and reason. Glencoe, Ill., 1951.

Phil 1930.10.82   Kuhn, M. Arno. Morris Raphael Cohen. N.Y., 1957.

Phil 1930.10.85   Rosenfield, Leonora. Portrait of a philosopher. N.Y., 1962.

Phil 1930.10.90   Deregibus, A. Il razionalismo di Morris R. Cohen. Torino, 1960.

Phil 1930.11.30   Cargill, S.T. The philosophy of analogy and symbolism. London, 1946?

Phil 1930.12.32   Cornforth, Maurice Campbell. Science versus idealism. N.Y., 1946.

Phil 1930.13.30   Cattell, James M. James McKeen Cattell. Lancaster, Pa., 1947.

Phil 1930   History of philosophy - Local Modern philosophy - Great Britain and United States - Individual philosophers - Other C - cont.

Phil 1930.14.30   Cornforth, Maurice Campbell. In defence of philosophy against positivism and pragmatism. London, 1950.

Phil 1930.14.31   Cornforth, Maurice Campbell. In defence of philosophy against positivism and pragmatism. N.Y., 1950.

Phil 1930.15.30   Creegon, R.F. The shocky existence. Cambridge, 1954.

Phil 1930.16.30   Canger, Georg P. Synoptic naturalism. Minneapolis, 1960.

Phil 1930.17.80   Irvine, E.F. A pioneer of the new psychology. Chatham, 1963.

Phil 1930.18.80   Schilpp, Paul. The philosophy of Rudolf Carnap. La Salle, 1887.

Phil 1930.18.85   Krauth, Lothar. Die Philosophie Carnaps. Wien, 1970.

Phil 1930.19.30   Carlo, William E. The ultimate reductibility of essence to existence in existential metaphysics. The Hague, 1966.

Phil 1930.20   Cavell, Stanley. Must we mean what we say? N.Y., 1969.

Phil 1955   History of philosophy - Local Modern philosophy - Great Britain and United States - Individual philosophers - D

Htn   Phil 1955.1.30*   Darwin, Charles. On the origin of species. London, 1859.

Htn   Phil 1955.2.30*   De Morgan, Augustus. Formal logic. London, 1847.

Phil 1955.2.80   Pamphlet box. De Morgan, Augustus.

Htn   Phil 1955.3.30*   Digby, Kenelm. Of bodies and of man's soul. London, 1669.

Phil 1955.4.87   Durant, Will. Transition. N.Y., 1927.

Phil 1955.6.01   Thomas, Milton H. A bibliography of John Dewey. N.Y., 1929.

Phil 1955.6.02   Pamphlet box. Dewey, John.

Phil 1955.6.05A   Thomas, Milton H. Bibliography of John Dewey. 2d ed. N.Y., 1939.

Phil 1955.6.05B   Thomas, Milton H. Bibliography of John Dewey. 2d ed. N.Y., 1939.

Phil 1955.6.2   Thomas, Milton H. John Dewey. Chicago, 1962.

Phil 1955.6.3   The Dewey newsletter. Carbondale, Ill. 1,1967+

Phil 1955.6.20   Dewey, John. Freedom and culture. N.Y., 1939.

Phil 1955.6.22   Dewey, John. Intelligence in the modern world. N.Y., 1939.

Phil 1955.6.24   Dewey, John. John Dewey. 1st ed. Indianapolis, 1955.

Phil 1955.6.25   Gillio-Tos, M.T. Il pensiero di Giovanni Dewey. Napoli, 1938.

Phil 1955.6.30   Dewey, John. Problems of men. N.Y., 1946.

Phil 1955.6.32A   Dewey, John. Knowing and the known. Boston, 1949.

Phil 1955.6.32B   Dewey, John. Knowing and the known. Boston, 1949.

Phil 1955.6.33   Dewey, John. Knowing and the known. Boston, 1960.

Phil 1955.6.35   Dewey, John. The influence of Darwin on philosophy. N.Y., 1951.

Phil 1955.6.40A   Dewey, John. The wit and wisdom of J. Dewey. Boston, 1949.

Phil 1955.6.40B   Dewey, John. The wit and wisdom of J. Dewey. Boston, 1949.

Phil 1955.6.45   Dewey, John. Essays in experimental logic. N.Y., 1953.

Phil 1955.6.50   Dewey, John. Philosophy, psychology and social practice. N.Y., 1963.

Phil 1955.6.55   Dewey, John. The early works, 1882-1898. v.2,4. Carbondale, 1967- 2v.

Htn   Phil 1955.6.90F*   Klyce, S. Dewey's suppressed psychology. Winchester, Mass., 1928.

Phil 1955.6.91   Essays in honor of John Dewey...seventeenth birthday. N.Y., 1929.

Phil 1955.6.92   John Dewey, the man and his philosophy. Cambridge, 1930.

Phil 1955.6.95   Feldman, W.T. The philosophy of John Dewey. Baltimore, 1934.

Phil 1955.6.96   Feldman, W.T. The philosophy of John Dewey. Baltimore, 1934.

Phil 1955.6.101   Schilpp, P.A. The philosophy of John Dewey. Evanston, 1939.

Phil 1955.6.102   Schilpp, P.A. The philosophy of John Dewey. 2d ed. N.Y., 1951.

Phil 1955.6.103A   Hook, Sidney. John Dewey. N.Y., 1939.

Phil 1955.6.103B   Hook, Sidney. John Dewey. N.Y., 1939.

Phil 1955.6.104   Hook, Sidney. John Dewey. N.Y., 1950.

Phil 1955.6.106   The philosopher of the common man; essays in honor of John Dewey to celebrate his 80th birthday. N.Y., 1940.

Phil 1955.6.107   Mendoza de Montero, A. Líneas fundamentales de la filosofía de John Dewey. Buenos Aires, 1940.

Phil 1955.6.109   White, Stephen, S. A comparison of the philosophies of F.C.S. Schiller and John Dewey. Thesis. Chicago, 1940.

Phil 1955.6.112   Okun, Sid. John Dewey; a Marxian critique. Chicago, 1942.

Phil 1955.6.115   Wolstein, B. Experience and valuation. Thesis. N.Y., 1949.

Phil 1955.6.117   Pan American Union. Division of Philosophy, Letters and Sciences. John Dewey en sus noventa años. Washington, 1949.

Phil 1955.6.119   Nathanson, J. John Dewey. N.Y., 1951.

Phil 1955.6.120   Thayer, H.S. The logic of pragmatism. N.Y., 1952.

Phil 1955.6.122   Pra, Mario dal. Il pensiero di John Dewey. Milano, 1952.

Phil 1955.6.125   Crosser, P.K. The nihilism of John Dewey. N.Y., 1955.

Phil 1955.6.128   Battle, J.J. The metaphysical presuppositions of the philosophy of John Dewey. Thesis. Fribourg, 1951.

Phil 1955.6.130   Gutzke, M.G. John Dewey's thought and its implications for Christian education. N.Y., 1956.

Phil 1955.6.133   Pesce, Domenico. Il concetto dell'arte in Dewey e in Berensoni. 1. ed. Firenze, 1956.

Phil 1955.6.135   Verra, Valerio. Naturalismo umanistico e sperimentale di John Dewey. Torino, 1950.

Phil 1955.6.140   Geiger, George R. John Dewey in perspective. N.Y., 1958.

Phil 1955.6.145   Lamont, Corliss. Dialogue on John Dewey. N.Y., 1959.

Phil 1955.6.150   Handlin, Oscar. John Dewey's challenge to education. N.Y., 1959.

Phil 1955.6.155   Hendel, Charles W. John Dewey and the experimental spirit in philosophy. N.Y., 1959.

Phil 1955.6.160   Blewett, John. John Dewey. N.Y., 1960.

Phil 1955.6.165   Clark, Gordon H. Dewey. Philadelphia, 1960.

Phil 1955.6.170   Bansola, Adriano. L'etica di John Dewey. Milano, 1960.

Phil 1955.6.180   Nassif, E.N. En el centenario de John Dewey. La Plata, 1961.

Phil 1955.6.190   Lawson, D.E. John Dewey and the world view. Carbondale, 1964.

Phil 1955.6.200   Dewey, John. John Dewey and Arthur F. Bentley. New Brunswick, 1964.

Phil 1955.6.205   Mañach, Jorge. Dewey y el pensamiento americano. Madrid, 1959.

Phil 1955.6.210   Bernstein, Richard. John Dewey. N.Y., 1966.

Phil 1955.6.215   Nissen, Lowell. John Dewey's theory of inquiry and truth. The Hague, 1966.

Phil 1955.6.220   Debdalle, Gérald. L'idée d'expérience dans la philosophie de John Dewey. Thèse. Paris, 1966.

Phil 1955 History of philosophy - Local Modern philosophy - Great Britain and United States - Individual philosophers - D - cont.

Phil 1955.6.225 Banerjee, Gour Moham. The theory of democratic education; a critical exposition of John Dewey's philosophy of education. Calcutta, 1961.
Phil 1955.6.230 Granese, Alberto. Il Giovane Dewey. 1. ed. Firenze, 1966.
Phil 1955.6.235 Filograsso, Nando. Meditazioni deweyane. Urbino, 1968.
Phil 1955.6.240 Somjee, Abdulkarim Husseinbhay. The political theory of John Dewey. N.Y., 1968.
Phil 1955.6.245 Boyston, JoAnn. John Dewey; a checklist of translations, 1900-1967. Carbondale, 1969.
Phil 1955.6.250 Guide to the works of John Dewey. Carbondale, 1970.
Phil 1955.7.90 Luce, A.A. Charles Frederick D'Arcy, 1859-1938. London, 1938.
Phil 1955.8.30 DeBurgh, William G. The life of reason. London, 1949.
Phil 1955.9.30 Dunham, B. Giant in chains. 1st ed. Boston, 1953.
Phil 1955.10.30 Davis, Charles G. The philosophy of live. 2nd ed. Chicago, 1906.

Phil 1980 History of philosophy - Local Modern philosophy - Great Britain and United States - Individual philosophers - E

Htn Phil 1980.1.30* Edwards, Jonathan. A careful...enquiry. Boston, 1754.
Htn Phil 1980.2.30* Emerson, R.W. Nature. Boston, 1836.
Htn Phil 1980.2.35* Emerson, R.W. Essays. London, 1841.
Htn Phil 1980.2.80* Cabot, J.E. Memoir of Ralph Wlado Emerson. Boston, 1887. 2v.
Phil 1980.3.79 Pamphlet box. Ellis, Havelock.
Phil 1980.3.90 Peterson, Houston. Havelock Ellis, philosopher of love. Boston, 1928.
Phil 1980.3.92 Havelock Ellis, in appreciation. Berkeley Heights, N.J., 1929.
Phil 1980.3.94 Delisle, Françoise Roussel. Friendship's odyssey. London, 1946.
Phil 1980.3.95A Ellis, H. My life; autobiography of Havelock Ellis. Boston, 1939.
Phil 1980.3.95B Ellis, H. My life; autobiography of Havelock Ellis. Boston, 1939.
Phil 1980.3.98 Goldberg, I. Havelock Ellis; a biographical and critical survey. N.Y., 1926.
Phil 1980.3.100 Calde-Marshall, A. Havelock Ellis. London, 1959.
Phil 1980.3.102 Freeman-Ishill, Rose. Havelock Ellis. Berkeley Heights, N.J., 1959.
Phil 1980.3.104 Delisle, Françoise Roussel. The return of Havelock Ellis, or Limbo or the dove? London, 1968.
Phil 1980.4A Edman, Irwin. Philosophers holiday. N.Y., 1938.
Phil 1980.4B Edman, Irwin. Philosophers holiday. N.Y., 1938.
Phil 1980.4.7 Edman, Irwin. Four ways of philosophy. N.Y., 1937.
Phil 1980.4.11 Edman, Irwin. Candle in the dark. N.Y., 1939.
Phil 1980.4.15 Edman, Irwin. Philosopher's quest. N.Y., 1947.
Phil 1980.4.20A Edman, Irwin. Under whatever sky. N.Y., 1951.
Phil 1980.4.20B Edman, Irwin. Under whatever sky. N.Y., 1951.
Phil 1980.4.25 Edman, Irwin. The uses of philosophy. N.Y., 1955.
Phil 1980.4.30 Schneider, R.E. Positivism in the United States. Rosario, 1946.
Phil 1980.5 Experimental philosophy asserted and defended against some late attempts to undermine it. London, 1740.
Phil 1980.6 Ewing, Alfred Cyril. Non-linguistic philosophy. London, 1968.

Phil 1990 History of philosophy - Local Modern philosophy - Great Britain and United States - Individual philosophers - Ferrier, James F.

Phil 1990.10A Ferrier, J.F. Philosophical works. Edinburgh, 1875. 3v.
Phil 1990.10B Ferrier, J.F. Philosophical works. v.2. Edinburgh, 1875.
Phil 1990.10.5 Ferrier, J.F. Philosophical works. v.2. Edinburgh, 1881.
Phil 1990.30 Ferrier, J.F. Institutes of metaphysic. Edinburgh, 1854.
Phil 1990.30.2 Ferrier, J.F. Institutes of metaphysic. 2nd ed. Edinburgh, 1856.
Phil 1990.79 Pamphlet box. Ferrier, James Frederick.
Phil 1990.80 Haldane, E.S. Ferrier James Frederick. London, n.d.

Phil 2005 History of philosophy - Local Modern philosophy - Great Britain and United States - Individual philosophers - Other F

Phil 2005.1.80 Pamphlet box. Fiske, J.
Phil 2005.2.80 Pamphlet box. Fraser, A.C.
Phil 2005.2.81 Fraser, A.C. Biographica philosophica. 2d ed. Edinburgh 1905.
Phil 2005.3.80 Beresford, J.D. W.E. Ford: a biography. London, 1917.
Phil 2005.3.81 Beresford, J.D. W.E. Ford: a biography. N.Y., 1917.
Phil 2005.4.30F* Felltham, Owen. Resolves: Divine, moral, political. London, 1677.
Phil 2005.5.30* Filmer, Robert. Patriarcha. London, 1680.
Phil 2005.6.31 Friswell, J.H. Hä och der i verlden. Stockholm, 1870.
Phil 2005.7.25* Pamphlet box. Frankland, F.W. Collection of pamphlets, formerly property of William James.
Phil 2005.8.79 Pamphlet box. Frank, Jerome D.
Phil 2005.9.20 Feibleman, James. The two story world. 1st ed. N.Y., 1966.
Phil 2005.9.30 Feibleman, James. The revival of realism. Chapel Hill, 1946.
Phil 2005.9.32 Feibleman, James. Philosophers lead sheltered lives. London, 1952.
Phil 2005.9.34 Feibleman, James. The way of a man. N.Y., 1969.
Phil 2005.10.80 Allan, Donald James. Guy Cromwell Field. London, 1956.
Phil 2005.11 Kettler, David. The social and political thought of Adam Ferguson. Columbus, 1965.
Phil 2005.12 Frankel, Charles. The love of anxiety, and other essays. 1st ed. N.Y., 1945.
Phil 2005.13 Findlay, John N. The discipline of the cave. London, 1966.
Phil 2005.14 Findlay, John N. The transcendence of the cave. London, 1967.

Phil 2020 History of philosophy - Local Modern philosophy - Great Britain and United States - Individual philosophers - Green, Thomas H.

Phil 2020.10 Green, T.H. Works. v.1,3. London, 1886-88. 2v.
Phil 2020.15A Green, T.H. Works of Thomas H. Green. London, 1906. 3v.
Phil 2020.15B Green, T.H. Works of Thomas H. Green. v.1,3. London, 1906. 2v.
Phil 2020.30A Green, T.H. Prolegomena to ethics. Oxford, 1883.
Phil 2020.30B Green, T.H. Prolegomena to ethics. Oxford, 1883.
Phil 2020.30.2A Green, T.H. Prolegomena to ethics. 2d ed. Oxford, 1884.
Phil 2020.30.2B Green, T.H. Prolegomena to ethics. 2d ed. Oxford, 1884.
Phil 2020.30.3A Green, T.H. Prolegomena to ethics. 3d ed. Oxford, 1890.
Phil 2020.30.3B Green, T.H. Prolegomena to ethics. 3d ed. Oxford, 1890.
Phil 2020.30.4 Green, T.H. Prolegomena to ethics. 4th ed. Oxford, 1899.
Phil 2020.30.5 Green, T.H. Prolegomena to ethics. 5th ed. Oxford, 1924.

Phil 2020 History of philosophy - Local Modern philosophy - Great Britain and United States - Individual philosophers - Green, Thomas H. - cont.

Phil 2020.30.15 Green, T.H. Prolegomena to ethics. 5th ed. Oxford, 1929.
Htn Phil 2020.32* Green, T.H. The witness of God and faith. London, 1886.
Phil 2020.80.2A Fairbrother, W.H. Philosophy of Thomas Hill Green. 2nd ed. London, 1900.
Phil 2020.80.2B Fairbrother, W.H. Philosophy of Thomas Hill Green. 2nd ed. London, 1900.
Phil 2020.81 James, G.F. Thomas Hill Green und der Utilitarismus. Halle, 1894.
Phil 2020.82 Leland, A.P. Educational theory...T.H. Green. N.Y., 1911.
Phil 2020.83 Townsend, H.G. Principle of individuality in the philosophy of T.H. Green. Lancaster, 1914.
Phil 2020.84 Montagné, Paul. Un radical religieux. v.1-2. Thèse. Toulouse, 1927.
Phil 2020.85 Selsam, Howard. T.H. Green. N.Y., 1930.
Phil 2020.86 Lamont, W.D. Introduction to Green's moral philosophy. London, 1934.
Phil 2020.87 McKirachan, John C. The temporal and eternal in the philosophy of Thomas H. Green. Thesis. Ann Arbor, 1941.
Phil 2020.88 Richter, M. The politics of conscience. Cambridge, 1964.
Phil 2020.89 Richter, M. The politics of conscience. London, 1964.
Phil 2020.90 Pucelle, Jean. La nature et l'esprit dans la philosophie de T.H. Green. Louvain, 1960-65. 2v.
Phil 2020.135 Günther, Oskar. Das Verhältnis der Ethik T.H. Greens zu Derjenigen Kants. Inaug. Diss. Dresden, 1915.
Phil 2020.140 Mukhopadhyay, Amal Kumar. The ethics of obedience; a study of the philosophy of T.H. Green. Calcutta, 1967.

Phil 2030 History of philosophy - Local Modern philosophy - Great Britain and United States - Individual philosophers - Other G

Htn Phil 2030.1.30* Glanvill, Joseph. Scepsis scientifica. London, 1665.
Phil 2030.1.80 Greenslet, F. Joseph Glanvill. N.Y., 1900.
Phil 2030.1.81 Redgrove, H. Stanley. Joseph Glanvill and physical research in the seventeenth century. London, 1921.
Phil 2030.1.85 Cope, Jackson I. Joseph Glanvill. St. Louis, 1956.
Htn Phil 2030.2.30* George, Henry. Progress and poverty. San Francisco, 1879.
Htn Phil 2030.3.30* Godwin, William. An enquiry concerning political justice. London, 1793. 2v.
Phil 2030.4 Grote, George. Analysis of the influence of natural religion on the temporal happiness of mankind. London, 1822.
Phil 2030.5A Guérard, A.L. Battle in the sea. Cambridge, 1954.
Phil 2030.5B Guérard, A.L. Battle in the sea. Cambridge, 1954.
Phil 2030.5.5 Guérard, A.L. Fossils and presences. Standord, Calif., 1957.
Phil 2030.6A Goodman, Nelson. Fact, fiction and forecast. Cambridge, 1955.
Phil 2030.6B Goodman, Nelson. Fact, fiction and forecast. Cambridge, 1955.
Phil 2030.6.2 Goodman, Nelson. Fact, fiction and forecast. 2d ed. Indianapolis, 1965.
Phil 2030.6.5A Goodman, Nelson. Languages of art. Indianapolis, 1968.
Phil 2030.6.5B Goodman, Nelson. Languages of art. Indianapolis, 1968.
Phil 2030.6.10 Goodman, Nelson. Problems and projects. Indianapolis, 1972.
Phil 2030.7 Gotshalk, Dilman Walter. The promise of modern life. Yellow Springs, Ohio, 1958.
Phil 2030.7.5 Gotshalk, Dilman Walter. Human aims in modern perspective. Yellow Springs, Ohio, 1966.
Phil 2030.8 MacDonald, Lauchlin D. John Grote. The Hague, 1966.

Phil 2035 History of philosophy - Local Modern philosophy - Great Britain and United States - Individual philosophers - Hamilton, Sir William

Phil 2035.20 Hamilton, William. Philosophy. N.Y., 1853.
Phil 2035.30 Hamilton, William. Discussions on philosophy and literature. London, 1852.
Phil 2035.30.1 Hamilton, William. Discussions on philosophy and literature. 2nd ed. London, 1853.
Phil 2035.30.2 Hamilton, William. Discussions on philosophy and literature. N.Y., 1853.
Phil 2035.30.3 Hamilton, William. Discussions on philosophy and literature. N.Y., 1855.
Phil 2035.30.7 Hamilton, William. Discussions on philosophy and literature, education. N.Y., 1858.
Phil 2035.40 Hamilton, William. Lectures on metaphysics and logic. Boston, 1859-60. 2v.
Phil 2035.40.3 Hamilton, William. Lectures on metaphysics and logic. Edinburgh, 1859. 4v.
Phil 2035.40.5 Hamilton, William. Lectures on metaphysics and logic. Boston, 1860.
Phil 2035.40.10 Hamilton, William. Lectures on metaphysics and logic. N.Y., 1880.
Phil 2035.51 Hamilton, William. Metaphysics. Cambridge, 1861.
Phil 2035.51.9 Hamilton, William. Metaphysics. Cambridge, 1864.
Phil 2035.51.15 Hamilton, William. The metaphysics of Sir William Hamilton. Boston, 1872.
Phil 2035.51.19 Hamilton, William. The metaphysics of Sir William Hamilton. Boston, 1877[1861]
Phil 2035.60 Hamilton, William. Fragments de philosophie. Paris, 1840.
Phil 2035.65 Hamilton, William. Philosophy. N.Y., 1855.
Phil 2035.79 Pamphlet box. Hamilton, William.
Phil 2035.80A Mill, J.S. Examination...Hamilton's philosophy. London, 1865.
Htn Phil 2035.80*B Mill, J.S. Examination...Hamilton's philosophy. London, 1865.
Phil 2035.80.2 Mill, J.S. Examination...Hamilton's philosophy. 3rd ed. London, 1867.
Phil 2035.80.2.5 Mill, J.S. Examination...Hamilton's philosophy. 3rd ed. London, 1867.
Phil 2035.80.2.10 Mill, J.S. Examination...Hamilton's philosophy. Boston, 1868. 2v.
Phil 2035.80.6 Mill, J.S. Examination...Hamilton's philosophy. Boston, 1865. 2v.
Phil 2035.80.8 Mill, J.S. Examination...Hamilton's philosophy. 6th ed. London, 1889.
Phil 2035.80.17 Alexander, P.P. Moral causation, or Notes on Mr. Mill's notes to the chapter on freedom in the 3rd edition of his examination of Sir W. Hamilton's philosophy. Edinburgh, 1868.
Phil 2035.80.18 Alexander, P.P. Moral causation. Notes on Mr. Mill's examination. 2nd ed. Edinburgh, 1875.
Phil 2035.80.20A Grote, George. Review of the work of Mr. John Stuart Mill. London, 1868.
Phil 2035.80.20B Grote, George. Review of the work of Mr. John Stuart Mill. London, 1868.
Phil 2035.80.40 Mill, J.S. Eine Prüfung der Philosophie Sir William Hamiltons. Halle, 1908.

126

Classified Listing

Phil 2035 History of philosophy - Local Modern philosophy - Great Britain and United States - Individual philosophers - Hamilton, Sir William - cont.

Phil 2035.81 Battle of the two philosophies. London, 1866.
Phil 2035.82A Jones, J.H. Know the truth. Hamilton's theory. N.Y., 1865.
Phil 2035.82B Jones, J.H. Know the truth. Hamilton's theory. N.Y., 1865.
Phil 2035.83 Leaves from my writing desk. London, 1872.
Phil 2035.84 Mansel, H.L. Philosophy of the conditioned. London, 1866.
Phil 2035.85 Monck, W.H.S. Sir William Hamilton. English philosopher. London, 1881.
Phil 2035.86 Murray, J.C. Outline of Sir William Hamilton's philosophy. Boston, 1870.
Phil 2035.86.30 Rasmussen, S.V. Studier over W. Hamiltons filosofi. København, 1921.
Phil 2035.86.35 Rasmussen, S.V. The philosophy of Sir William Hamilton. Copenhagen, 1925.
Phil 2035.87 Sterling, J.H. Sir W. Hamilton. London, 1865.
Phil 2035.88 Veitch, J. Hamilton. Philadelphia, 1882.
Phil 2035.88.3 Veitch, J. Sir William Hamilton: the man and his philosophy. London, 1883.
Phil 2035.88.5 Veitch, J. Memoir of William Hamilton. Edinburgh, 1869.
Phil 2035.89 Bolton, M.P.W. Examination of the principles of the Scoto-Oxonian philosophy. London, 1869.

Phil 2038 History of philosophy - Local Modern philosophy - Great Britain and United States - Individual philosophers - Hartley, David

Htn Phil 2038.30* Hartley, D. Observations on man. London, 1749. 2v.
Phil 2038.31 Hartley, D. Observations on man. London, 1791. 3v.
Phil 2038.32 Hartley, D. Observations on man. London, 1801. 3v.
Phil 2038.33 Hartley, D. Observations on man. London, 1834.
Phil 2038.34 Hartley, D. Observations on man. v.1-2. Gainesville, Fla., 1966.
Phil 2038.50 Hartley, D. Theory of the human mind. London, 1775.
Phil 2038.80 Bower, G.S. Hartley and James Mill. London, 1881.
Phil 2038.80.5 Bower, G.S. Hartley and James Mill. N.Y., 1881.
Phil 2038.81 Schoenlank, B. Hartley und Priestley. Photoreproduction. Halle, 1882.
Phil 2038.82 Heider, Maria. Studien über David Hartley. Inaug. Diss. Bergisch Gladbach, 1913.

Phil 2040 History of philosophy - Local Modern philosophy - Great Britain and United States - Individual philosophers - Herbert, Edward

Htn Phil 2040.30* Herbert, E. De veritate. Paris, 1624.
Htn Phil 2040.30.2* Herbert, E. De veritate. London, 1633.
Htn Phil 2040.30.3* Herbert, E. De veritate. London, 1633.
Phil 2040.30.15 Herbert, E. De veritate. Bristol, 1937.
Htn Phil 2040.31* Herbert, E. De causis errorum. London, 1645.
Phil 2040.35.2 Herbert, E. De religione gentilium. Amsterdam, 1700.
Phil 2040.80 Carlini, Armando. Herbert di Cherbury e la scuola di Cambridge. Roma, 1917.

Phil 2042 History of philosophy - Local Modern philosophy - Great Britain and United States - Individual philosophers - Hicks, George D.

Phil 2042.5 DeBurgh, William George. George Dawes Hicks. London, 1944.

Phil 2045 History of philosophy - Local Modern philosophy - Great Britain and United States - Individual philosophers - Hobbes, Thomas

Phil 2045.02 Hobbes, Thomas. A bibliography by H. MacDonald and M. Hargreaves. London, 1952.
Phil 2045.1 Hobbes, Thomas. Moral and political works. London, 1750.
Htn Phil 2045.3* Hobbes, Thomas. Opera philosophica. Amstelodami, 1668. 2v.
Htn Phil 2045.4* Hobbes, Thomas. Works in Latin. Amsterdam, 1668-70.
Phil 2045.10 Hobbes, Thomas. Opera philosophica. London, 1839-45. 5v.
Phil 2045.10.5 Hobbes, Thomas. Opera philosophica. Aalen, 1961. 5v.
NEDL Phil 2045.11 Hobbes, Thomas. English works. v.1-7,9-11. London, 1839-45. 10v.
Phil 2045.12 Hobbes, Thomas. Opera philosophica. London, 1839-45. 5v.
Phil 2045.14 Hobbes, Thomas. The English works of Thomas Hobbes of Malmesbury. Aalen, 1962. 11v.
Phil 2045.14.2 Hobbes, Thomas. The English works of Thomas Hobbes of Malmesburg. Aalen, 1966. 11v.
Phil 2045.15 Hobbes, Thomas. Oeuvres philosophiques et politiques. Neufchatel, 1787. 2v.
Phil 2045.20 Hobbes, Thomas. The ethics of Thomas Hobbes, by E.H. Sneath. Photoreproduction. Boston, 1898.
Phil 2045.25 Hobbes, Thomas. Philosophy of Hobbes in extracts and notes from his philosophy. Minneapolis, 1903.
Phil 2045.26 Hobbes, Thomas. Selections. N.Y., 1930.
Phil 2045.27A Hobbes, Thomas. The metaphysical system of Hobbes. Chicago, 1905.
Htn Phil 2045.30* Hobbes, Thomas. Vita. Carolopoli, 1680-8-? 4 pam.
Htn Phil 2045.30.2* Hobbes, Thomas. Vita. Carolopoli, 1681.
Htn Phil 2045.31* Hobbes, Thomas. Tracts. London, 1678-82. 2 pam.
Htn Phil 2045.31.5* Hobbes, Thomas. Tracts. London, 1681.
Htn Phil 2045.32* Hobbes, Thomas. Tracts. London, 1682-84. 2 pam.
Htn Phil 2045.47.5* Hobbes, Thomas. Leviathan, sive de materia civitatis. London, 1678.
Htn Phil 2045.48* Hobbes, Thomas. Leviathan. London, 1651.
Htn Phil 2045.48.5F* Hobbes, Thomas. Leviathan. London, 1651.
Phil 2045.49 Hobbes, Thomas. Leviathan. Amsterdam, 1667.
Phil 2045.49.5 Hobbes, Thomas. Leviathan. Amstelodami, 1670.
NEDL Phil 2045.50.2 Hobbes, Thomas. Leviathan. Oxford, 1881.
Phil 2045.50.9 Hobbes, Thomas. Leviathan. Oxford, 1909.
Phil 2045.51.3A Hobbes, Thomas. Leviathan. 3rd ed. London, 1887.
Phil 2045.51.3B Hobbes, Thomas. Leviathan. 3rd ed. London, 1887.
Phil 2045.51.9 Hobbes, Thomas. Leviathan. London, 1894.
Phil 2045.52.5 Hobbes, Thomas. Leviathan. Cambridge, 1935.
Phil 2045.52.15 Hobbes, Thomas. Leviathan. London, 1940.
Phil 2045.52.20 Hobbes, Thomas. Leviathan. Oxford, 1946.
Phil 2045.52.25 Hobbes, Thomas. Leviathan. London, 1947.
Phil 2045.52.27 Hobbes, Thomas. Leviathan. Oxford, 1957.
Phil 2045.52.28 Hobbes, Thomas. Leviathan. Oxford, 1967.
Phil 2045.53 Hobbes, Thomas. Leviatano. Bari, 1911-12. 2v.
Phil 2045.53.10 Hobbes, Thomas. Il leviatano. Messina, 1930.
Phil 2045.54 Hobbes, Thomas. Leviathan. Paris, 1921.
Phil 2045.54.5 Hobbes, Thomas. Leviathan. Part I. Chicago, 1949.
Phil 2045.55 Hobbes, Thomas. Metaphysical system. Chicago, 1910.
Phil 2045.58 Hobbes, Thomas. Quadratura circuli. n.p., 1669.
Htn Phil 2045.59* Hobbes, Thomas. Human nature. London, 1650.
Htn Phil 2045.60* Hobbes, Thomas. Philosophical rudiments concerning goverment and society. London, 1651.
Htn Phil 2045.60.25* Hobbes, Thomas. Elementa philosophica de cive. Amsterdam, 1647.

Phil 2045 History of philosophy - Local Modern philosophy - Great Britain and United States - Individual philosophers - Hobbes, Thomas - cont.

Htn Phil 2045.61* Hobbes, Thomas. Elementa philosophica de cive. Amsterdam, 1657.
Htn Phil 2045.61.5* Hobbes, Thomas. Elementa philosophica de cive. Amsterdam, 1669.
Phil 2045.61.9 Hobbes, Thomas. Elementa philosophica de cive. n.p., 16-
Phil 2045.61.10 Hobbes, Thomas. Elementa philosophica de cive. Amsterdam, 1742.
Phil 2045.61.30 Hobbes, Thomas. Elemens philosophiques du bon citoyen. Paris, 1651.
Phil 2045.61.35 Hobbes, Thomas. De cive; or, The citizen. N.Y., 1949.
Htn Phil 2045.62* Hobbes, Thomas. Elements of philosophy. London, 1656.
Htn Phil 2045.63* Hobbes, Thomas. Of libertie and necessity. London, 1654.
Htn Phil 2045.64* Hobbes, Thomas. Mr. Hobbes considered in his loyalty, religion, reputation and manners. London, 1662.
Phil 2045.65 Hobbes, Thomas. Grundzüge der Philosophie. v.1-3. Leipzig, 1915-18.
Phil 2045.67 Hobbes, Thomas. Naturrecht und allgemeines Staatsrecht in den Anfangsgründen. Berlin, 1926.
Htn Phil 2045.70* Hobbes, Thomas. Decameron physiologicum. London, 1678.
Htn Phil 2045.75* Hobbes, Thomas. Historia ecclesiastica. Augustae, 1688.
Htn Phil 2045.77F* Hobbes, Thomas. Last sayings. London, 1680.
Htn Phil 2045.78.5F* Hobbes, Thomas. Life. London, 1680.
Phil 2045.79 Pamphlet box. Philosophy. English. Hobbes. German dissertations.
Phil 2045.80 Lyon, G. La philosophie de Hobbes. Paris, 1893.
NEDL Phil 2045.81 Roberstson, G.C. Hobbes. Philadelphia, 1886.
Phil 2045.81.4 Robertson, George Croan. Hobbes. St. Clair Shores, Michigan, 1970.
Phil 2045.82 Wille, B. Der Phänomenalismus des T. Hobbes. Kiel, 1888.
Phil 2045.83 Brandt, G. Grundlinien der Philosophie von T. Hobbes. Kiel, 1895.
Htn Phil 2045.84* Clarendon, Edward Hyde. A brief view and survey of the...errors...in Mr. Hobbes's book, entitled Leviathan. Oxford, 1676.
Htn Phil 2045.84.2* Clarendon, Edward Hyde. A brief view and survey of the...errors...in Mr. Hobbes's book, entitled Leviathan. Oxford, 1676.
Phil 2045.85 Tönnies, F. Hobbes Leben und Lehre. Stuttgart, 1896.
Phil 2045.85.2 Tönnies, F. Thomas Hobbes. 2e Aufl. Osterwieck, 1912.
Phil 2045.85.3 Tönnies, F. Thomas Hobbes. 3e Aufl. Stuttgart, 1925.
Phil 2045.86 Stephen, Leslie. Hobbes. London, 1904.
Phil 2045.86.2 Stephen, Leslie. Hobbes. London, 1904.
Htn Phil 2045.87* Rosse, A. Leviathan drawn out with a hook. London, 1653.
Phil 2045.88 Jodl, F. Studien...über Ursprung des Sittlichen; Hobbes. München, n.d.
Phil 2045.89 Taylor, A.E. Thomas Hobbes. London, 1908.
Htn Phil 2045.90* Graham, C.M. Loose remarks on certain positions to be found in Mr. Hobbes's Philosophical rudiments of government and society. 2nd ed. London, 1769.
Phil 2045.91 Messer, W.A. Das Verhältnis von Sittengesetz...bei Hobbes. Mainz, 1893.
Phil 2045.92 Chevrillon, André. Qui fuerint saeculo XVII imprimis apud Hobbesium Anglicae solutae orationis progressus. Insulae, 1893.
Phil 2045.93 Mandolfo, R. Saggi per la storia della morale utilitaria. Verona, 1903-04.
Phil 2045.94 Balz, Albert G.A. Idea and essence in the philosophies of Hobbes and Spinoza. N.Y., 1918.
Htn Phil 2045.95* Blackburne, Richard. Thomae Hobbes angli malmesburiensis vita. Carolopoli, 1681.
Htn Phil 2045.95.2* Blackburne, Richard. Magni philosophi Thomae Hobbes malmesburiensis vita. London, 1682.
Phil 2045.96 Larsen, Eduard. Thomas Hobbes' filosofi. København, 1891.
Htn Phil 2045.97* Wallis, John. Hobbius Heauton-timorumenos. Oxford, 1662.
Htn Phil 2045.97.5* Wallis, John. Thomae Hobbes quadratura circuli. 2. ed. Oxoniae, 1669.
Phil 2045.98 Catlin, George E.G. Thomas Hobbes as philosopher, publicist and man of letters. Oxford, 1922.
Phil 2045.99 Hönigswald, R. Hobbes und die Staatsphilosophie. München, 1924.
Phil 2045.100 Brockdorff, Cay von. Hobbes im Lichte seiner didaktischen und pädagogischen Bedeutung. Kiel, 1919.
Phil 2045.101 Iodice, A. Le teorie di Hobbes e Spinoza. Napoli, 1901.
Phil 2045.102 Feuerbach, P.J.A. Anti-Hobbes. Erfurt, 1798.
Htn Phil 2045.103* Eachard, John. Some opinions of Mr. Hobbs. London, 1673.
Htn Phil 2045.104* Lawson, George. An examination of the political part of Mr. Hobbs his Leviathan. London, 1657.
Phil 2045.105 Bramhall, J. Castigations of Mr. Hobbes. London, 1658.
Phil 2045.106 Tarantino, G. Saggio sulle idee morali e politiche di T. Hobbes. Napoli, 1900.
Htn Phil 2045.107* Tenison, Thomas. The creed of Mr. Hobbes examined. London, 1670.
Phil 2045.108 Brandt, Frithiof. Den mekaniske naturopfattelse hos Thomas Hobbes. København, 1921.
Phil 2045.108.5 Brandt, Frithiof. Thomas Hobbes' mechanical conception of nature. Copenhagen, 1928.
Phil 2045.109 Lips, Julius. Die Stellung des Thomas Hobbes zu den politischen Parteien der grossen englischen Revolution. Leipzig, 1927.
Phil 2045.110 Battelli, G. Le dottrine politiche dell'Hobbes e dello Spinoza. Firenze, 1904.
Phil 2045.111 Moser, H. Thomas Hobbes: seine logische Problematik. Bern, 1923.
Phil 2045.112 Levi, Adolfo. La filosofia di Thommaso Hobbes. Milano, 1929.
Phil 2045.113 Alloggio, Sabino. Critica della concezione dello stato in Tommaso Hobbes. Napoli, 1930.
Phil 2045.114 Łubieński, Z. Die Grundlagen des ethisch-politischen Systems von Hobbes. München, 1932.
Phil 2045.115 Laird, John. Hobbes. London, 1934.
Phil 2045.116 Brockdorff, Cay von. Die Urform der "Computatio sive logica" des Hobbes. Kiel, 1934.
Phil 2045.116.5 Pamphlet box. Hobbes, Thomas.
Phil 2045.117 Strauss, Leo. The political philosophy of Hobbes. Oxford, 1936.
Phil 2045.118 Vialatoux, J. La cité de Hobbes. Paris, 1935.
Phil 2045.119A Gooch, G.P. Hobbes; annual lecture on a master mind. London, 1939.
Phil 2045.119B Gooch, G.P. Hobbes; annual lecture on a master mind. London, 1939.
Phil 2045.119C Gooch, G.P. Hobbes; annual lecture on a master mind. London, 1939.
Phil 2045.120 Thorpe, C.D. The aesthetic theory of Thomas Hobbes. Ann Arbor, 1940.

Classified Listing

Phil 2045.121	A dissertation...according to the principles of Mr. Hobbes. London, 1706.
Phil 2045.122	Polin, Raymond. Politique et philosophie chez Thomas Hobbes. 1. éd. Paris, 1953.
Phil 2045.124	Davy, G. Thomas Hobbes et Jean-Jacques Rousseau. Oxford, 1953.
Phil 2045.125	Jessop, T.E. Thomas Hobbes. London, 1960.
Phil 2045.126	Konijnenburg, Willem van. Thomas Hobbes' Leviathan. Proefschrift. Assen, 1945.
Phil 2045.128	Peters, Richard. Hobbes. Harmondsworth, 1956.
Phil 2045.130	Warrender, H. The political philosophy of Hobbes. Oxford, 1957.
Phil 2045.132A	Mintz, Samuel. The hunting of Leviathan. Cambridge, 1962.
Phil 2045.132B	Mintz, Samuel. The hunting of Leviathan. Cambridge, 1962.
Phil 2045.133	Schnur, R. Individualismus und Absolutismus. Berlin, 1963.
Phil 2045.134	Hood, F.C. The divine politics of Thomas Hobbes. Oxford, 1964.
Phil 2045.135	Watkins, J.W.N. Hobbes' system of ideas; a study in the political significance of philosophical theories. London, 1965.
Phil 2045.136	Brown, Keith C. Hobbes. Cambridge, 1965.
Phil 2045.137	Mayer-Tasch, Peter Cornelius. Thomas Hobbes und das Widerstandsrecht. Mainz? 1964.
Phil 2045.139	Goldsmith, M.M. Hobbes's science of politics. N.Y., 1966.
Phil 2045.140	Braun, Dietrich. Der sterbliche Gott oder Leviathan gegen Behemoth. Thesis. Zürich, 1963.
Phil 2045.142	McNeilly, F.S. The anatomy of Leviathan. London, 1968.
Phil 2045.144	Foester, Winfried. Thomas Hobbes und der Puritanismus. Berlin, 1969.
Phil 2045.146	Gauthier, David Peter. The logic of Leviathan; the moral and political theory of Thomas Hobbes. Oxford, 1969.
Phil 2045.148	Wolf, Friedrich Otto. Die neue Wissenschaft des Thomas Hobbes. Stuttgart, 1969.
Phil 2045.150	Willms, Bernard. Die Antwort des Leviathan; Thomas Hobbes' politische Theorie. Neuwied, 1970.
Phil 2045.155	Wudel, Witold. Filozofia strachu i nadziei. Wyd. 1. Warszawa, 1971.
Phil 2045.160	Mayer-Tasch, Peter Cornelius. Autonomie und Autorität; Rousseau in den Spuren von Hobbes? Neuwied, 1968.
Phil 2045.165	Kriele, Martin. Die Herausforderung des Verfassungsstaates; Hobbes und englische Juristen. Neuwied, 1970.

Phil 2050.01	Metz, Rudolf. Bibliographie der Hume-Literatur. Erfurt, 1928.
Phil 2050.02	Jessop, T.E. A bibliography of David Hume. London, 1938.
Phil 2050.1	Hume, David. Essays and treatises. London, 1758.
Phil 2050.2	Hume, David. Essays and treatises. London, 1768. 2v.
Phil 2050.3A	Hume, David. Private correspondence...1761-76. London, 1820.
Phil 2050.3B	Hume, David. Private correspondence...1761-76. London, 1820.
Phil 2050.10	Hume, David. Philosophical works. Edinburgh, 1826. 4v.
Phil 2050.11A	Hume, David. Philosophical works. Edinburgh, 1854. 4v.
Phil 2050.11B	Hume, David. Philosophical works. Edinburgh, 1854. 4v.
Phil 2050.11C	Hume, David. Philosophical works. Edinburgh, 1854. 4v.
Phil 2050.15*	Hume, David. Essays. v.3-4. London, 1748-53. 2v.
Phil 2050.18	Hume, David. Dissertations sur les passions. Amsterdam, 1759.
Phil 2050.19	Hume, David. Le génie de M. Hume. London, 1770.
Phil 2050.20	Hume, David. Oeuvres philosophiques choisies. Paris, 1912. 2v.
Phil 2050.20.5	Hume, David. Oeuvres philosophiques choisies. Paris, 1930.
Phil 2050.23	Hume, David. Selections. N.Y., 1927.
Phil 2050.23.2	Hume, David. Selections. N.Y., 1955.
Phil 2050.24	Hume, David. Essay on miracles. London, 1882. 5 pam.
Phil 2050.30*	Hume, David. Four dissertations. London, 1757.
Phil 2050.31*	Hume, David. Essays and treatises on several subjects. London, 1760. 4v.
Phil 2050.32	Hume, David. Essays and treatises. Edinburgh, 1793. 2v.
Phil 2050.33	Hume, David. Essays and treatises. v.1-2,3-4. Basel, 1793. 2v.
Phil 2050.34	Hume, David. Essays and treatises on several subjects. n.p., n.d.
Phil 2050.34.25*	Hume, David. Philosophical essays concerning human understanding. 2nd ed. London, 1750.
Phil 2050.34.27*	Hume, David. Philosophical essays concerning human understanding. 2nd ed. London, 1751.
Phil 2050.34.50*	Hume, David. Essays moral and political. Edinburgh, 1741.
Phil 2050.34.55*	Hume, David. Essays moral and political. 2nd ed. Edinburgh, 1742.
Phil 2050.34.60	Hume, David. Essays and treatises on several subjects. London, 1764. 2v.
Phil 2050.35	Hume, David. Essays and treatises. Edinburgh, 1804. 2v.
Phil 2050.35.85	Hume, David. Philosophical essays. 1st American ed. Philadelphia, 1817. 2v.
Phil 2050.36	Hume, David. Essays: literary, moral, and political. London, 1880.
Phil 2050.36.5	Hume, David. Essays: moral, political and literary. London, 1882. 2v.
Phil 2050.37	Hume, David. Essays: moral, political and literary. N.Y., 1898. 2v.
Phil 2050.37.5	Hume, David. Essays: moral, political and literary. London, 1903.
Phil 2050.37.10	Hume, David. Essays: moral, political and literary. London, 1963.
Phil 2050.37.20	Hume, David. Pensées philosophiques, morales, critiques, littéraires et politiques. Londres, 1767.
Phil 2050.37.25	Hume, David. Eine Untersuchung über die Principien der Moral. Wien, 1883.
Phil 2050.39.5	Hume, David. An inquiry concerning the principles of morals. N.Y., 1957.
Phil 2050.40	Hume, David. An enquiry...human understanding. Oxford, 1894.
Phil 2050.41	Hume, David. An enquiry...human understanding. Chicago, 1904.

	Phil 2050.41.5A	Hume, David. An enquiry...human understanding. Chicago, 1907.
	Phil 2050.41.11A	Hume, David. An inquiry concerning human understanding. N.Y., 1955.
	Phil 2050.41.11B	Hume, David. An inquiry concerning human understanding. N.Y., 1955.
	Phil 2050.41.25	Hume, David. Enquiries concerning the human understanding and concerning the principles of morals. 2nd ed. Oxford, 1927.
	Phil 2050.41.30	Hume, David. An enquiry concerning human understanding. Chicago, 1956.
	Phil 2050.42	Hume, David. Eine Untersuchung über den menschlichen Verstand. Leipzig, 1893.
	Phil 2050.42.8	Hume, David. Eine Untersuchung über den menschlichen Verstand. 8e Aufl. Leipzig, 1920.
Htn	Phil 2050.42.12*	Hume, David. Eine Untersuchung über den menschlichen Verstand. Jena, 1793.
Htn	Phil 2050.43*	Hume, David. Essais philosophiques sur l'entendement humain. Amsterdam, 1758. 2v.
	Phil 2050.45	Hume, David. Ricerche sull'intelletto umano e sui principii della morale. Bari, 1910.
	Phil 2050.45.5	Hume, David. Ricerche sull'intelletto umano e sui principii della morale. 2a ed. Bari, 1927.
	Phil 2050.51	Hume, David. Treatise on human nature. London, 1874. 2v.
	Phil 2050.52	Hume, David. Treatise on human nature. v.2. London, 1878.
	Phil 2050.53	Hume, David. Treatise on human nature. Oxford, 1888.
	Phil 2050.58	Hume, David. Treatise on human nature. Oxford, 1928.
	Phil 2050.59	Hume, David. An abstract of a treatise of human nature, 1740. Cambridge, Eng., 1938.
	Phil 2050.59.2	Hume, David. An abstract of a treatise of human nature, 1740. Hamden, Conn., 1965.
	Phil 2050.59.3	Hume, David. A treatise of human nature. Oxford, 1964.
	Phil 2050.59.4	Hume, David. A treatise of human nature. Harmondsworth, 1969.
	Phil 2050.59.25	Hume, David. Moral and political philosophy. N.Y., 1948.
	Phil 2050.59.30	Hume, David. Theory of knowledge. Edinburgh, 1951.
	Phil 2050.59.35	Hume, David. Theory of politics. Edinburgh, 1951.
	Phil 2050.59.40	Hume, David. Political essays. N.Y., 1953.
	Phil 2050.60	Hume, David. Traité de la nature humaine. Paris, 1878.
	Phil 2050.60.5	Hume, David. Trattato della natura humana. Torino, 1924.
	Phil 2050.60.25	Hume, David. Über die menschliche Natur. Bd.2. Halle, 1791.
	Phil 2050.60.28	Hume, David. Traktat über die menschliche Natur. Hamburg, 1895-1906. 2v.
	Phil 2050.60.30	Hume, David. Traktat über die menschliche Natur. v.1-2. Leipzig, 1923.
	Phil 2050.64	Hume, David. Essays on suicide. London, 1789.
	Phil 2050.66	Hume, David. Anfänge und Entwicklung der Religion. Leipzig, 1909.
	Phil 2050.67A	Hume, David. Dialogues concerning natural religion. 2nd ed. London, 1779.
	Phil 2050.67.5	Hume, David. The natural history of religion. Stanford, 1957.
	Phil 2050.67.10	Hume, David. Dialogues sur la religion naturelle. Paris, 1964.
	Phil 2050.68	Hume, David. Dialogues concerning natural religion. Edinburgh, 1907.
	Phil 2050.68.3	Hume, David. Dialogues concerning natural religion. N.Y., 1948.
	Phil 2050.68.7	Hume, David. Hume's dialogues concerning natural religion. London, 1947.
Htn	Phil 2050.68.10*	Hume, David. Gespräche über natürliche Religion. Leipzig, 1781.
	Phil 2050.68.15	Hume, David. Dialoge über natürliche Religion. 3e Aufl. Leipzig, 1905.
	Phil 2050.68.17	Hume, David. Die Naturgeschichte der Religion. Frankfurt, 1911.
	Phil 2050.68.25	Hume, David. Storia naturale della religione e saggio sul suicidio. Bari, 1928.
Htn	Phil 2050.69.2*	Hume, David. An enquiry concerning...morals. London, 1751.
	Phil 2050.69.30	Hume, David. Untersuchung über diePrinzipien der Moral. Leipzig, 1929.
	Phil 2050.70	Hume, David. Treatise of morals. Photoreproduction. Boston, 1893.
	Phil 2050.71A	Hume, David. Philosophy of Hume. N.Y., 1893.
	Phil 2050.71B	Hume, David. Philosophy of Hume. N.Y., 1893.
	Phil 2050.72	Hume, David. David Hume: philosophical historian. Indianapolis, 1965.
Htn	Phil 2050.73*	Hume, David. Political discourses. Edinburgh, 1752.
	Phil 2050.75	Hume, David. Letters. Oxford, 1888.
	Phil 2050.76	Hume, David. Letters. Edinburgh, 1841.
	Phil 2050.77A	Hume, David. Unveröffentlichte Briefe David Humes. Leipzig, 1929.
	Phil 2050.77B	Hume, David. Unveröffentlichte Briefe David Humes. Leipzig, 1929.
	Phil 2050.77.15	Hume, David. Letters. Oxford, 1932. 2v.
	Phil 2050.77.20	Hume, David. New letters. Oxford, 1954.
	Phil 2050.77.25	Hume, David. A letter from a gentleman to his friend in Edinburgh (1745). Facsimile. Edinburgh, 1967.
Htn	Phil 2050.78*	Hume, David. Concise and genuine account of dispute between Mr. Hume and Mr. Rousseau. London, 1766.
	Phil 2050.78.5	Hume, David. Writings on economics. Madison, 1955.
	Phil 2050.78.80	Basson, A.H. David Hume. Harmondsworth, 1958.
	Phil 2050.79	Pamphlet vol. Philosophy. English. Hume, David. German dissertations. 19 pam.
	Phil 2050.79.2	Pamphlet box. Philosophy. English. Hume, David.
	Phil 2050.80A	Burton, J.H. Life and correspondence of Hume. Edinburgh, 1846. 2v.
	Phil 2050.80B	Burton, J.H. Life and correspondence of Hume. Edinburgh, 1846. 2v.
	Phil 2050.80.9A	Burton, J.H. Letters of eminent persons to Hume. Edinburgh, 1849.
	Phil 2050.80.9B	Burton, J.H. Letters of eminent persons to Hume. Edinburgh, 1849.
	Phil 2050.81	Howison, G.H. Hume and Kant. San Francisco, 1884. 2 pam.
Htn	Phil 2050.82.2*	Hume, David. Life. London, 1777.
Htn	Phil 2050.82.3*	Hume, David. Life. London, 1777. 5 pam.
	Phil 2050.83	Jodl, F. Leben und Philosophie David Hume's. Halle, 1872.
	Phil 2050.84	Pfleiderer, E. Empirismus und Skepsis...Hume's. Berlin, 1874.
	Phil 2050.85	Petzholtz, E. Die Hauptpunkte der Humeschen Erkenntnislehre. Berlin, 1895.
	Phil 2050.86	Ritchie, T.E. Account of life...D. Hume. London, 1807.

128

Classified Listing

Phil 2050 History of philosophy - Local Modern philosophy - Great Britain and United States - Individual philosophers - Hume, David - cont.

Phil 2050.87 Huxley, Thomas H. Hume. London, 1879.
Phil 2050.87.3 Huxley, Thomas H. Hume. N.Y., 1879.
Phil 2050.87.4A Huxley, Thomas H. Hume. N.Y., 1879.
Phil 2050.87.4B Huxley, Thomas H. Hume. N.Y., 1879.
Phil 2050.87.5 Huxley, Thomas H. Hume. N.Y., 189-?
Phil 2050.87.5.7A Huxley, Thomas H. Hume. N.Y., 19- ?
Phil 2050.87.5.7B Huxley, Thomas H. Hume. N.Y., 19- ?
Phil 2050.87.8 Huxley, Thomas H. Hume. London, 1909.
Phil 2050.87.10 Huxley, Thomas H. Hume. N.Y., 1894.
Phil 2050.88 Knight, William. Hume. Philadelphia, 1886.
Phil 2050.88.15 Knight, William. Hume. Edinburgh, 1905.
Htn Phil 2050.89* Pratt, Samuel J. An apology for life and writings of D. Hume. London, 1777.
Htn Phil 2050.89.10* Pratt, Samuel J. Curious particulars and genuine anecdotes respecting the late Lord Chesterfield and David Hume. London, 1788.
Phil 2050.90 Brede, W. Der Unterschied der lehren Humes. Halle, 1896.
Phil 2050.91 Goebel, H. Das Philosophie in Humes Geschichte von England. Marburg, 1897.
Phil 2050.92A Calderwood, H. David Hume. Edinburgh, n.d.
Phil 2050.92B Calderwood, H. David Hume. Edinburgh, n.d.
Phil 2050.93 Lechartier, G. David Hume. Paris, 1900.
Phil 2050.94 Kühne, R. Über das Verhältniss der Hume'schen und Kantischen Erkenntnisstheorie. Berlin, 1878.
Phil 2050.95 Elkin, W.B. Hume. Ithaca, 1904.
Htn Phil 2050.96* Specimen of the Scots Review. n.p., 1774.
NEDL Phil 2050.97 Latimer, J.E. Immediate perception as held by Reid and Hamilton. Leipzig, 1880.
Phil 2050.98 Thomsen, A. David Hume: sein Leben und seine Philosophie. Berlin, 1912.
Phil 2050.99 Didier, J. Hume. Paris, 1913.
Phil 2050.100 Shearer, Edna Aston. Hume's place in ethics. Diss. Bryn Mawr, 1915.
Phil 2050.101 Orr, James. David Hume and his influence on philosophy and theology. N.Y., 1903.
Phil 2050.101.3A Orr, James. David Hume and his influence on philosophy and theology. Edinburgh, 1903.
Phil 2050.101.3B Orr, James. David Hume and his influence on philosophy and theology. Edinburgh, 1903.
Phil 2050.101.5 Daiches, Sally. Über das Verhältnis der Geschichtsschreibung David Hume's zu seiner praktischen Philosophie. Leipzig, 1903.
Phil 2050.103 Kahle, C.M. De Davidis Humii philosophia. Inaug. Diss. Berolini, 1832?
Phil 2050.104 Masaryk, T.G. David Hume's Skepsis. Wien, 1884.
Phil 2050.104.5 Masaryk, T.G. Počet pravděpodobnosti a Humova skepse. Praha, 1883.
Phil 2050.105 Paoli, Alessandro. Hume e il principio di causa. Napoli, 1882.
Phil 2050.106 Sopper, A.J. David Hume's kenleer en ethiek. Leiden, 1907.
Phil 2050.107 Grimthorpe, E.B. A review of Hume and Huxley on miracles. London, 1883.
Phil 2050.108 Lüers, Adolf. David Humes religionsphilosophische Anschauungen. Berlin, 1901.
Phil 2050.109 Compayré, Gabriel. La philosophie de David Hume. Paris, 1873.
Phil 2050.110 Münster, O. Det Hume'ske problem. København, 1912.
Phil 2050.111 Phalén, Adolf. I. Hume's psykologiska härledning av kausalitetsföreställningeII. Hypotesen om det omedvetna i empirisk psykologi. Uppsala, 1914.
Phil 2050.112 Keller, Anton. Das Causalitätsproblem bei Malebranche und Hume. Rastatt, 1899.
Phil 2050.113 Kydd, Rachel M. Reason and conduct in Hume's treatise. London, 1946.
Phil 2050.175 Hasse, Heinrich. Das Problem der Gültigkeit. Leipzig, 1919.
Phil 2050.176A Hendel, C.W. Studies in the philosophy of David Hume. Princeton, 1925.
Phil 2050.176B Hendel, C.W. Studies in the philosophy of David Hume. Princeton, 1925.
Phil 2050.176C Hendel, C.W. Studies in the philosophy of David Hume. Princeton, 1925.
Phil 2050.177 Henschen, W.A. Bidrag till kännedomen af David Humes filosofiska betydelse. Upsala, 1863.
Phil 2050.178 Casazza, G. Hume, Kant e lo scetticismo filosofico. Roma, 1913.
Phil 2050.179 Wijnaendts Francken, C.J. David Hume. Haarlem, 1907.
Phil 2050.180 Long, William J. Über Hume's Lehre von den Ideen. Inaug. Diss. Heidelberg, 1897.
Phil 2050.181 Goldstein, J. Die empiristische Geschichtsauffassung Humes. Leipzig, 1903.
Phil 2050.182 Zimmermann, R. Über Hume's empirische Begründung der Moral. Wien, 1884.
Phil 2050.183 Speckmann, A. Über Hume's metaphysische Skepsis. Bonn, 1877.
Phil 2050.184 Taylor, A.E. David Hume and the miraculous. Cambridge, Eng., 1927.
Phil 2050.185 Radakovic, K. Die letzten Fundamente der Hume'schen Erkenntnistheorie. Graz, 1925.
Phil 2050.186 Linke, Paul. David Humes Lehre vom Wissen. Diss. Leipzig, 1901.
Phil 2050.187 Tvrdý, Josef. Problém skutečnosti u Davida Huma. Brno, 1925.
Phil 2050.188 Metz, Rudolf. David Hume: Leben und Philosophie. Stuttgart, 1929.
Htn Phil 2050.189* Jacobi, F.H. David Hume über den Glauben. Breslau, 1787.
Phil 2050.190 Kuypers, M.S. Studies in the eighteenth-century background of Hume's empiricism. Minneapolis, 1930.
Phil 2050.191 Jahn, Franz. David Humes Kausalitätstheorie. Inaug. Diss. Leipzig, 1895.
Phil 2050.192 Meinardus, H. David Hume als Religionsphilosoph. Inaug. Diss. Coblenz, 1897.
Phil 2050.193 Leroy, André. La critique et la religion chez David Hume. Paris, 1931.
Phil 2050.193.5 Leroy, André. La critique et la religion chez David Hume. Thèse. Paris, 1929.
Phil 2050.194 Howitz, Franz G. Determinismen eller Hume imod Kant. Kjøbenhavn, 1824.
Phil 2050.195 Rödder, Paul. Über Hume's Erkenntnistheorie. Gollnow, 1909.
Phil 2050.196 Greig, John Y.T. David Hume. London, 1931.
Phil 2050.197 Tegen, Einar. Humes uppfattning av jagets identitet. Uppsala, 1932.
Phil 2050.198 Laird, John. Hume's philosophy of human nature. N.Y., 1932.

Phil 2050 History of philosophy - Local Modern philosophy - Great Britain and United States - Individual philosophers - Hume, David - cont.

Phil 2050.199 Wegrich, Arno. Die Geschichtsauffassung David Hume's im Rahmen seines philosophischen Systems. Inaug. Diss. Köln, 1926.
Phil 2050.200 Pelikán, Ferdinand. Fikcionalism novověké filosofie zvláště u Humea a Kanta. Praha, 1928.
Phil 2050.201 Volpe, Galvano della. La teoria delle passioni di Davide Hume. Bologna, 1931.
Phil 2050.202 Schultze, W.F. Hume und Kant über den Causalbegriff. Inaug. Diss. Rostock, 1870.
Phil 2050.203 Laing, B.M. David Hume. London, 1932.
Phil 2050.204 Adams, William. An essay on Mr. Hume's essay on miracles. London, 1752.
Phil 2050.205 Church, R.W. Hume's theory of the understanding. London, 1935.
Phil 2050.206 Maund, Costance. Hume's theory of knowledge. London, 1937.
Phil 2050.208 Kruse, F.V. Hume's philosophy in his principal work, a treatise of human nature, and in his essays. London, 1939.
Phil 2050.209 Price, H.H. Hume's theory of the external world. Oxford, 1940.
Phil 2050.210 Smith, N.K. The philosophy of David Hume. London, 1941.
Phil 2050.211 Giżycki, G. von. Die Ethik David Hume's in ihrer geschichtlichen Stellung. Breslau, 1878.
Phil 2050.212 Mossner, E.C. The forgotten Hume, le bon David. N.Y., 1943.
Phil 2050.212.5 Mossner, E.C. The life of David Hume. Austin, 1954.
Phil 2050.213 Ross, William W.G. Human nature and utility in Hume's social philosophy. Garden City, N.Y., 1942.
Phil 2050.213.5 Ross, William G. Human nature and utility in Hume's social philosophy. Thesis. Garden City, N.Y., 1942.
Phil 2050.214 Brede, Wilhelm. Der Unterschied der Lehren Humes im Treatise und im Inquiry. Halle, 1896.
Phil 2050.215 Salmon, C.V. The central problem of David Hume's philosophy. Halle , 1929.
Phil 2050.216 Volpe, Galvano della. Hume, o Il genio dell'empirismo. Firenze, 1939.
Phil 2050.217 Heinemann, Fritz. David Hume. Paris, 1940.
Phil 2050.219 Baratono, A. Hume e l'illuminismo inglese. 2a ed. Milano, 1944.
Phil 2050.221 Martin, John J. Shaftesbury's und Hutcheson's Verhältnis zu Hume. Inaug. Diss. Halle, 1905.
Phil 2050.223 MacNabb, Donald George Cecil. David Hume. London, 1951.
Phil 2050.223.2 MacNabb, Donald George Cecil. David Hume. 2nd ed. Oxford, 1966.
Phil 2050.225 Cresson, A. David Hume. 1. éd. Paris, 1952.
Phil 2050.227.1 Passmore, John A. Hume's intentions. N.Y., 1968.
Phil 2050.229 Leroy, A.L. David Hume. 1. éd. Paris, 1953.
Phil 2050.230 Carsi, M. Natura e societá in David Hume. 1. ed. Firenze, 1953.
Phil 2050.232 Vlachos, Georges. Essai sur la politique de Hume. Athènes, 1955.
Phil 2050.234 Wallenfels, Walter. Die Rechtsphilosophie David Humes. Göttingen, 1928.
Phil 2050.236 Uhl, Josef. Humes Stellung in der englischen Philosophie. v.1-2. Prag, 1890-91.
Phil 2050.238 Zabeeh, F. Hume, precursor of modern empiricism. The Hague, 1960.
Phil 2050.240 Schaefer, Alfred. Erkenntnis. Berlin, 1960?
Phil 2050.242 Flew, A. Hume's philosophy of belief. London, 1961.
Phil 2050.243 Grieve, C.M. The man of (almost) independent mind. Edinburgh, 1962.
Phil 2050.244 Giarrizzo, G. David Hume politico e storico. Torino, 1962.
Phil 2050.245 Broad, C. D. Hume's doctrine of space. London, 1961.
Phil 2050.250 Mikhalenko, Iu.P. Filosofiia D. Iuma. Moskva, 1962.
Phil 2050.251 Snethlage, J.L. David Hume. Den Haag, 1963.
Phil 2050.252 Stewart, J.B. The moral and political philosophy of David Hume. N.Y., 1963.
Phil 2050.253.5 Pears, D.F. David Hume. London, 1966.
Phil 2050.254 Mall, Rom Adhar. Humes Bild vom Menschen. Köln, 1963.
Phil 2050.255 Belgion, Montgomery. David Hume. London, 1965.
Phil 2050.256 Price, John Valdimir. The ironic Hume. Austin, 1965.
Phil 2050.256.5 Price, John Valdimir. David Hume. N.Y., 1969.
Phil 2050.257 Pra, Mario dal. Hume. Milano, 1949.
Phil 2050.258 Brunetto, Filippo. La questione della vera causa in David Hume. Bologna, 1965.
Phil 2050.259 Sesonske, Alexander. Human understanding: studies in the philosophy of David Hume. Belmont, Calif., 1965.
Phil 2050.260 Castignone, Silvana. Giustizia e bene comune in David Hume. Milano, 1964.
Phil 2050.261 Anderson, Robert Fendel. Hume's first principles. Lincoln, 1966.
Phil 2050.262 Broiles, R. David. The moral philosophy of David Hume. The Hague, 1964.
Phil 2050.263 Ardal, Páll S. Passion and value in Hume's Treatise. Edinburgh, 1966.
Phil 2050.264 Brunet, Oliver. Philosophie et esthétique chez David Hume. Paris, 1965.
Phil 2050.265 Collins, James Daniel. The emergence of philosophy of religion. New Haven, 1967.
Phil 2050.266 Chappell, Vere Claiborne. Hume. 1st ed. Garden City, N.Y., 1966.
Phil 2050.267 Molinari, Ernesto. L'utopia controllata. Milano, 1964.
Phil 2050.268 Narskii, Igor' S. Filosofiia Davida Iuma. Moskva, 1967.
Phil 2050.270 Wenzel, Leonhard. David Humes politische Philosophie in ihrem Zusammenhang mit seiner gesamten Lehre. Inaug. Di Koln? 1959.
Phil 2050.272 Sabetti, Alfredo. David Hume, filosofo della religione. Napoli, 1965.
Phil 2050.275 Hume and present day problems; the symposia read at the joint session of the Aristotelian Society, the Scots Philosophical Club and the Mind Association at Edinburgh, July 7th-10th, 1939. N.Y., 1968.
Phil 2050.278 Wilbanks, Jan. Hume's theory of imagination. The Hague, 1968.
Phil 2050.280 Mall, Rom Adhar. Hume's concept of man. Bombay, 1967.
Phil 2050.282 Santucci, Antonio. Sistema e ricerca in David Hume. Bari, 1969.

Phil 2053 History of philosophy - Local Modern philosophy - Great Britain and United States - Individual philosophers - Hutcheson, Francis

Phil 2053.30 Hutcheson, F. System of moral philosophy. Glasgow, 1755. 2v.
Htn Phil 2053.30.1* Hutcheson, F. System of moral philosophy. London, 1755. 2v.
Phil 2053.40 Hutcheson, F. Philosophiae moralis. v.1-3. Glasgow, 1742.

Phil 2053 History of philosophy - Local Modern philosophy - Great Britain and United States - Individual philosophers - Hutcheson, Francis - cont.

Htn Phil 2053.41* Hutcheson, F. A short introduction to moral philosophy. v.1-3. Glasgow, 1753.
X Cg Phil 2053.41.2 Hutcheson, F. A short introduction to moral philosophy. v.1,2-3. Glasgow, 1764. 2v.
Htn Phil 2053.50* Hutcheson, F. Inquiry into...beauty and virtue. London, 1725.
Phil 2053.50.2 Hutcheson, F. Inquiry into...beauty and virtue. London, 1726.
Htn Phil 2053.50.3* Hutcheson, F. Inquiry into...beauty and virtue. London, 1729.
Phil 2053.50.4 Hutcheson, F. Inquiry into...beauty and virtue. London, 1738.
Phil 2053.52 Hutcheson, F. Metaphysicae synopsis. n.p., 1742.
Phil 2053.60 Hutcheson, F. Essay on nature and conduct of passions. London, 1728.
Htn Phil 2053.60.2* Hutcheson, F. Essay on nature and conduct of passions. London, 1728. 2 pam.
Phil 2053.60.3A Hutcheson, F. Essay on nature and conduct of passions. Glasgow, 1769.
Phil 2053.60.3B Hutcheson, F. Essay on nature and conduct of passions. Glasgow, 1769.
Phil 2053.65 Hutcheson, F. Illustrations on the moral sense. Cambridge, 1971.
Htn Phil 2053.70* Hutcheson, F. Reflections upon laughter. Glasgow, 1750.
Phil 2053.80 Scott, William Robert. Francis Hutcheson, his life, teaching and position in the history of philosophy. Cambridge, 1900.
Phil 2053.80.2 Scott, William Robert. Francis Hutcheson, his life, teaching and position in the history of philosophy. N.Y., 1966.
Phil 2053.81 Boerma, N.W. De Leer van den Zedelijken zin bij Hutcheson. n.p., n.d.
Phil 2053.90 Vigone, L. L'etica del senso morale in Francis Hutcheson. Milano, 1954.
Phil 2053.92 Blackstone, William T. Francis Hutcheson and contemporary ethical theory. Athens, Ga., 1965.
Phil 2053.125 Rampendahl, R. Eine Würdigung der ethik Hutchesons. Inaug.-Diss. Leipzig, 1892.

Phil 2055 History of philosophy - Local Modern philosophy - Great Britain and United States - Individual philosophers - Other H

Htn Phil 2055.1.30* Home, Henry. Essays on the principles of morality. Edinburgh, 1751.
Phil 2055.1.35 Homes, Henry. Versuche über die ersten Gründe der Sittlichkeit. Braunschweig, 1768.
Phil 2055.1.80 Bühler, K. Studien über Henry Home. Bonn, 1905.
Phil 2055.1.81 Norden, Joseph. Die Ethik Henry Homes. Inaug. Diss. Halle, 1895.
Phil 2055.1.82 Joseph, M. Die Psychologie Henry Home's. Inaug.-Diss. Halle, 1911.
Phil 2055.2.20 Hinton, James. Selections from manuscripts. London, 1870. 4v.
NEDL Phil 2055.2.80 Hinton, James. Life and letters. London, 1885.
Phil 2055.2.81 Ellis, Edith M. James Hinton. London, 1918.
Htn Phil 2055.3.30* Huxley, Thomas H. The Romanes lecture 1893. London, 1893.
Htn Phil 2055.4.30F* Harrington, James. The oceana of James Harrington. Dublin, 1737.
Phil 2055.5.90 Hobson, John A. L.T. Hobhouse; his life and work. London, 1931.
Phil 2055.5.95 Hobhouse, Leonard Trelawney. Sociology and philosophy. Cambridge, 1966.
Phil 2055.6 Harris, G. A philosophical treatise. London, 1876. 2v.
Phil 2055.7.5 Hocking, William E. What man can make of man. N.Y., 1942.
Phil 2055.7.10 Hocking, William E. Varieties of educational experience. Madison, N.H., 1952. 2v.
Phil 2055.7.15A Hocking, William E. Experiment in education. Chicago, 1954.
Phil 2055.7.15B Hocking, William E. Experiment in education. Chicago, 1954.
Phil 2055.7.80A Gilman, R.C. The bibliography of William E. Hocking. Waterville, Me., 1951.
Phil 2055.7.80B Gilman, R.C. The bibliography of William E. Hocking. Waterville, Me., 1951.
Phil 2055.7.85 Rouner, Leroy S. Within human experience; the philosophy of William Ernest Hocking. Cambridge, 1969.
Phil 2055.7.90 Luther, A.R. Existence as dialectical tension. The Hague, 1968[1969]
Phil 2055.8.30 Hyde, Lawrence. Isis and Osiris. London, 1946.
Phil 2055.8.35 Hyde, Lawrence. An introduction to organic philosophy. Reigate, 1955.
Phil 2055.9.30 Hartshorne, Charles. Reality as social process. Glencoe, Ill., 1953.
Phil 2055.9.35 Hartshorne, Charles. The logic of perfection. LaSalle, Ill., 1962.
Phil 2055.9.40 Hartshorne, Charles. Creative synthesis and philosophic method. London, 1970.
Phil 2055.10.30 Hampshire, Stuart. Thought and action. London, 1959.
Phil 2055.12.30 Hoor, Marten ten. Education for privacy. n.p., 1960.
Phil 2055.13.30 Hook, Sidney. The quest for being. N.Y., 1961.
Phil 2055.13.35 Hook, Sidney. Religion in a free society. Lincoln, 1967.
Phil 2055.15.30 Hulme, Thomas E. Further speculations. Minnesota, 1955.
Phil 2055.15.34A Hulme, Thomas E. Speculations; essays on humanism and the philosophy of art. N.Y., 1924.
Phil 2055.15.34B Hulme, Thomas E. Speculations; essays on humanism and the philosophy of art. N.Y., 1924.
Phil 2055.15.35 Hulme, Thomas E. Speculations. 2nd ed. London, 1958.
Phil 2055.15.37 Hulme, Thomas E. Speculations; essays on humanism and the philosophy of art. London, 1965.
Phil 2055.16.30 Hall, E.W. Categorical analysis. Chapel Hill, 1964.

Phil 2070 History of philosophy - Local Modern philosophy - Great Britain and United States - Individual philosophers - James, William

Phil 2070.01A Perry, Ralph B. Annotated bibliography of writings of William James. N.Y., 1920.
Phil 2070.01B Perry, Ralph B. Annotated bibliography of writings of William James. N.Y., 1920.
Phil 2070.01C Perry, Ralph B. Annotated bibliography of writings of William James. N.Y., 1920.
Phil 2070.03 Pamphlet box. Philosophy. English. James, William.
Phil 2070.07 James, William. The sense of dizziness in deaf-mutes. n.p., 1882-1911. 11 pam.
Phil 2070.09 James, William. The sentiment of rationality. n.p., 1879-1907. 8 pam.
Phil 2070.20 James, William. William James on psychical research. N.Y., 1960.

Phil 2070 History of philosophy - Local Modern philosophy - Great Britain and United States - Individual philosophers - James, William - cont.

Phil 2070.23 James, William. The writings of William James; a comprehensive edition. N.Y., 1967.
Phil 2070.25.5 James, William. The philosophy of William James, selected from his chief works. N.Y., 194-.
Phil 2070.25.7 James, William. The philosophy of William James, selected from his chief works. N.Y., 1953.
Phil 2070.26 James, William. Pragmatism. N.Y., 1925.
Phil 2070.27A James, William. Essays in pragmatism. N.Y., 1948.
Phil 2070.27B James, William. Essays in pragmatism. N.Y., 1948.
Phil 2070.27.5 James, William. Pragmatism. Chicago, 1955.
Phil 2070.27.10 James, William. Pragmatism. N.Y., 1949.
Phil 2070.28 James, William. The meaning of truth. N.Y., 1914.
Htn Phil 2070.30* James, William. Is life worth living? Philadelphia, 1896.
Phil 2070.30.5A James, William. Is life worth living? Philadelphia, 1895.
Phil 2070.30.5B James, William. Is life worth living? Philadelphia, 1895.
Phil 2070.31 James, William. On some Hegelisms. London, 1882.
Phil 2070.33 James, William. Introduction à la philosophie. Paris, 1914.
Phil 2070.34 James, William. The moral philosophy of William James. N.Y., 1969.
Phil 2070.35 James, William. Philosophie de l'expérience. Paris, 1917.
Phil 2070.35.10 James, William. Religiøse erfaringer en undersøgelse af den menneskelige natur. 3e udg. Nørregade, 1919.
Phil 2070.35.15 Études Théologiques et Religieuses. Cinquantenaire de la psychologie religieuse de William James. Montpellier, 1953.
Phil 2070.40 James, William. Causeries pédagogiques. 4th ed. Lausanne, 1917.
Phil 2070.46.10 James, William. Principî di psicologia (estratti). Torino, 1928.
Phil 2070.46.20A James, William. Psychology. Cleveland, 1948.
Phil 2070.46.20B James, William. Psychology. Cleveland, 1948.
Phil 2070.49 James, William. La théorie de l'émotion. 5e éd. Paris, 1917.
Phil 2070.50 James, William. Máttur manna. Reykjavík, 1925.
Phil 2070.51 James, William. Sentiment of rationality. Aberdeen, 18- .
Phil 2070.51.5 James, William. Sentiment of rationality. N.Y., 1905.
Phil 2070.54 James, William. William James. Harmondsworth, 1950.
Phil 2070.55 James, William. Saggi pragmatisti. Lanciano, 1919.
Phil 2070.60 James, William. L'idée de vérité. Paris, 1913.
Phil 2070.65.4 James, William. Gli ideali della vita. 4a ed. Torino, 1916.
Phil 2070.65.5 James, William. Gli ideali della vita. 5a ed. Torino, 1921.
Phil 2070.75A James, William. Letters. Boston, 1920. 2v.
Phil 2070.75B James, William. Letters. Boston, 1920. 2v.
Phil 2070.75.3A James, William. The letters of William James. Boston, 1920. 2v.
Phil 2070.75.3B James, William. The letters of William James. Boston, 1920. 2v.
Phil 2070.75.3C James, William. The letters of William James. Boston, 1920. 2v.
Phil 2070.75.3D James, William. The letters of William James. Boston, 1920. 2v.
Phil 2070.75.3E James, William. The letters of William James. v.2. Boston, 1920.
Phil 2070.75.5 James, William. The letters of William James. v.1-2. Boston, 1926.
Phil 2070.75.10 James, William. Selected letters. N.Y., 1961.
Phil 2070.75.15 James, William. The letters of William James and Théodore Flournoy. Madison, 1966.
Phil 2070.76 James, William. William James: extraits de sa correspondance. Paris, 1924.
Phil 2070.76.5A James, William. As William James said: extracts from the published writings. N.Y., 1942.
Phil 2070.76.5B James, William. As William James said: extracts from the published writings. N.Y., 1942.
Phil 2070.76.11 James, William. A William James reader. Boston, 1972.
Phil 2070.79 Pamphlet vol. Philosophy. English. James, William. German dissertations. 6 pam.
Phil 2070.79.5 Pamphlet vol. Philosophy. English. James, William. 4 pam.
Phil 2070.79.6 Pamphlet box. Philosophy. English. James, William.
Phil 2070.80A Knox, H.V. The philosophy of William James. London, 1914.
Phil 2070.80B Knox, H.V. The philosophy of William James. London, 1914.
Phil 2070.81A Kallen, H.M. William James and Henri Bergson. Chicago, 1914.
Phil 2070.81B Kallen, H.M. William James and Henri Bergson. Chicago, 1914.
Phil 2070.81C Kallen, H.M. William James and Henri Bergson. Chicago, 1914.
Phil 2070.82 Reverdin, H. La notion d'expérience d'après William James. Genève, 1913.
Phil 2070.82.5 Bloch, Werner. Der Pragmatismus von James und Schiller. Leipzig, 1913.
Phil 2070.82.8 Brett, George Sidney. William James and American ideals. Toronto? 1937.
Phil 2070.83 Brugmans, H.J.F.W. Waarheidstheorie van William James. Groningen, 1913.
Phil 2070.84A Flournoy, T. Philosophy of William James. N.Y., 1917.
Phil 2070.84B Flournoy, T. Philosophy of William James. N.Y., 1917.
Phil 2070.84.5 Flournoy, T. Die Philosophie von William James. Tübingen, 1930.
Phil 2070.85 Ubbink, J.G. Het pragmatisme van William James. Arnhem, 1912.
Phil 2070.86 Paetz, W. Die erkenntnis-theoretischen Grundlagen von William James "The Varieties of Religious Experience." Eilenburg, 1907.
Phil 2070.87 Teisen, N. William James' laere om retten til at tro. København, 1911.
Phil 2070.89 Dijk, I. van. Het pragmatisme van William James. Groningen, 1911.
Phil 2070.91 Stettheimer, E. Die Urteilsfreiheit als Grundlage der Rechtfertigung des religiösen Glaubens. Inaug. Diss. Wittenburg, 1903.
Phil 2070.91.2 Stettheimer, E. Die Urteilsfreiheit als Grundlage der Rechtfertigung des religiösen Glaubens. Inaug. Diss. Wittenburg, 1903.
NEDL Phil 2070.91.5 Stettheimer, E. The will to believe as a basis for defense of religious faith. N.Y., 1907.
Phil 2070.92 Hansen, V. William James og hans breve. Stockholm, 1922.
Phil 2070.92.5 Hansen, V. William James og det religiøse. København, 1936.
Phil 2070.93 Kortsen, K.K. William James' filosofi. København, n.d.
Phil 2070.108A Essays philosophical and psychological in honor of William James. N.Y., 1908.

Phil 2070   History of philosophy - Local Modern philosophy - Great Britain and
United States - Individual philosophers - James, William - cont.

Phil 2070.108B	Essays philosophical and psychological in honor of William James. N.Y., 1908.
Phil 2070.111A	Boutroux, E. William James. Paris, 1911.
Phil 2070.111B	Boutroux, E. William James. Paris, 1911.
Phil 2070.111.5	Boutroux, E. William James. Leipzig, 1912.
Phil 2070.112	Tarozzi, G. Compendio dei principii di psicologia. Milano, 1911.
Phil 2070.113	Cugini, U. L'empirismo radicale di William James. Genova, 1925.
Phil 2070.114	Leuba, J.H. The immediate apprehension of God according to William James and W.E. Hocking. n.p., 1924?
Phil 2070.119	Turner, J.E. An examination of William James's philosophy. Oxford, 1919.
Phil 2070.120	Stumpf, Carl. William James nach seinen Briefen. Berlin, 1927.
Phil 2070.120.2A	Stumpf, Carl. William James nach seinen Briefen. Berlin, 1928.
Phil 2070.120.2B	Stumpf, Carl. William James nach seinen Briefen. Berlin, 1928.
Phil 2070.126	Bixler, Julius S. Religion in the philosophy of William James. Boston, 1926.
Phil 2070.127	Le Breton, M. La personnalité de William James. Paris, 1928.
Phil 2070.127.5	Le Breton, M. La personnalité de William James. Paris, 1929.
Phil 2070.128	Blau, Théodore. William James. Thèse. Paris, 1933.
Phil 2070.129	Perry, R.B. William James. Boston? 1910.
Phil 2070.129.5A	Perry, R.B. The thought and character of William James. Boston, 1935. 2v.
Phil 2070.129.5B	Perry, R.B. The thought and character of William James. Boston, 1935. 2v.
Phil 2070.129.5C	Perry, R.B. The thought and character of William James. Boston, 1935. 2v.
Phil 2070.129.5D	Perry, R.B. The thought and character of William James. Boston, 1935. 2v.
Phil 2070.129.7A	Perry, R.B. The thought and character of William James. Cambridge, 1948.
Phil 2070.129.7B	Perry, R.B. The thought and character of William James. Cambridge, 1948.
X Cg Phil 2070.129.10	Perry, R.B. In the spirit of William James. New Haven, 1938.
Phil 2070.130	Switalski, B.W. Der Wahrheitsbegriff des Pragmatismus nach William James. Braunsberg, 1910.
Phil 2070.131	Maire, Gilbert. William James et le pragmatisme religieux. Paris, 1933.
Phil 2070.132	Delattre, F. William James Bergsonien. Paris, 192-.
Phil 2070.133	McGilvary, Evander B. The fringe of William James's psychology, the basis of logic. n.p., 1911.
Phil 2070.134	Cornesse, Marie. Le rôle des images dans la pensée de William James. Thèse. Grenoble, 1933.
Phil 2070.134.5	Cornesse, Marie. L'idée de Dieu chez William James. Thèse. Grenoble, 1933.
Phil 2070.135	Lapan, A. The significance of James' essay. Thesis. N.Y., 1936.
Phil 2070.136	Biró, B. A tudatalatti világ: William James lélektanában. Szeged, 1929.
Phil 2070.137	Raback, A.A. William James. Cambridge, 1942.
Phil 2070.138A	In commemoration of William James, 1842-1942. N.Y., 1942.
Phil 2070.138B	In commemoration of William James, 1842-1942. N.Y., 1942.
Phil 2070.139	Wisconsin. University. William James, the man and the thinker. Madison, 1942.
Phil 2070.140	Piane, A.L. delle. William James. Montevideo, 1943.
Phil 2070.141	Morris, Lloyd R. William James; the message of a modern mind. N.Y., 1950.
Phil 2070.141.5	Morris, Lloyd R. William James; the message of a modern mind. N.Y., 1969.
Phil 2070.142	Compton, C.H. William James. N.Y., 1957.
Phil 2070.143	Schmidt, Hermann. Der Begriff der Erfahrungskontinuität bei William James. Heidelberg, 1959.
Phil 2070.144	Riconda, G. La filosofia di William James. Torino, 1962.
Phil 2070.145	Linschoten, Johannes. Op weg naar een fenomenologische psychologie. Utrecht, 1959.
Phil 2070.145.5	Linschoten, Johannes. On the way toward a phenomenological psychology; the psychology of William James. Pittsburgh, 1968.
Phil 2070.147	Boutroux, Emile. William James. 2d ed. N.Y., 1912.
Phil 2070.147.5	Boutroux, Emile. Décès de M. William James. Paris, 1910.
Phil 2070.150	Brennan, Bernard P. The ethics of William James. N.Y., 1961.
Phil 2070.150.5A	Brennan, Bernard P. William James. N.Y., 1968.
Phil 2070.150.5B	Brennan, Bernard P. William James. N.Y., 1968.
Phil 2070.151	Martland, T. The metaphysics of William James and John Dewey. N.Y., 1963.
Phil 2070.152	Moore, Edward Carter. William James. N.Y., 1966.
Phil 2070.155A	Allen, Gay Wilson. William James; a biography. N.Y., 1967.
Phil 2070.155B	Allen, Gay Wilson. William James; a biography. N.Y., 1967.
Phil 2070.155.1	Allen, Gay Wilson. William James. Minneapolis, 1970.
Phil 2070.156	Anderson, Luke. The concept of truth in the philosophy of William James. Rome, 1965.
Phil 2070.157	Reck, Andrew J. Introduction to William James. Bloomington, 1967.
Phil 2070.158	Wild, John. The radical empiricism of William James. 1st ed. Garden City, N.Y., 1969.
Phil 2070.159	William James: unfinished business. Washington, 1969.
Phil 2070.161	Eisendrath, Craig Ralph. The unifying moment; the psychological philosophy of William James and Alfred North Whitehead. Cambridge, 1971.
Phil 2070.162	Roggerone, Giuseppe Agostino. James e la crisi della coscienza contemporanea. 2. ed. Milano, 1967.
Phil 2070.164	Roth, John K. Freedom and the moral life. Philadelphia, 1969.

Phil 2075   History of philosophy - Local Modern philosophy - Great Britain and
United States - Individual philosophers - Other J

Phil 2075.1.79	Pamphlet box. Philosophy. English. Joachim, H.H.
Phil 2075.4.30	Jones, G.V. Democracy and civilization. London, 1946.
Phil 2075.5.30	Joad, Cyril E.W. Decadence. London, 1948.
Phil 2075.5.31	Joad, Cyril E.W. Decadence. N.Y., 1949.
Phil 2075.6.90A	Warren, Austin. The elder Henry James. N.Y., 1934.
Phil 2075.6.90B	Warren, Austin. The elder Henry James. N.Y., 1934.
Phil 2075.7.30	Jordan, Elijah. Essays in criticism. Chicago, 1952.
Phil 2075.7.35	Jordan, Elijah. Metaphysics. Evanston, Ill., 1956.
Phil 2075.7.80	Barnett, George. Corporate society and education. Ann Arbor, 1962.

Phil 2075   History of philosophy - Local Modern philosophy - Great Britain and
United States - Individual philosophers - Other J - cont.

Phil 2075.8	Jonas, Hans. The phenomenon of life. 1st ed. N.Y., 1966.
Phil 2075.10	Johann, Robert O. Building the human. N.Y., 1968.

Phil 2100   History of philosophy - Local Modern philosophy - Great Britain and
United States - Individual philosophers - K

Htn	Phil 2100.1.30*	King, William. An essay on the origin of evil. 1st ed. and additions. London, 1731. 2v.
Htn	Phil 2100.1.30.2*	King, William. An essay on the origin of evil. London, 1732. 2v.
	Phil 2100.3.30	Kemble, Duston. The higher realism. Cincinnati, 1903.
	Phil 2100.4.30	Koren, H.J. An introduction to the philosophy of animate nature. St. Louis, 1955.

Phil 2115   History of philosophy - Local Modern philosophy - Great Britain and
United States - Individual philosophers - Locke, John

Htn	Phil 2115*	Locke, J. Essay concerning human understanding. 2nd American ed. Brattleboro, Vt., 1806. 3v.
	Phil 2115.1	Locke, J. Works. 1st ed. v.1,3. London, 1714. 2v.
	VPhil 2115.1.1	Locke, J. Works. 2nd ed. London, 1722. 3v.
	VPhil 2115.1.2	Locke, J. Works. 3rd ed. London, 1727. 3v.
	Phil 2115.1.3	Locke, J. Works. 4th ed. v.2. London, 1740.
	VPhil 2115.1.3	Locke, J. Works. 4th ed. v.1,3. London, 1740. 2v.
	VPhil 2115.1.5F	Locke, J. Works. 6th ed. London, 1759. 3v.
	Phil 2115.1.6F	Locke, J. Works. London, 1659. 3v.
	Phil 2115.1.8F	Locke, J. Works. 8th ed. London, 1777. 4v.
Htn	Phil 2115.2*	Locke, J. An essay concerning humane understanding. London, 1690.
Htn	Phil 2115.2.1F*	Locke, J. An essay concerning humane understanding. London, 1690.
Htn	Phil 2115.2.2*A	Locke, J. An essay concerning humane understanding. 2nd ed. London, 1694.
Htn	Phil 2115.2.2*B	Locke, J. An essay concerning humane understanding. 2nd ed. London, 1694.
Htn	Phil 2115.2.3F*	Locke, J. An essay concerning humane understanding. 2nd ed. London, 1694.
Htn	Phil 2115.2.5F*	Locke, J. An essay concerning humane understanding. 3rd ed. London, 1695.
Htn	Phil 2115.2.7F*	Locke, J. An essay concerning humane understanding. 4th ed. London, 1700.
Htn	Phil 2115.2.9F*	Locke, J. An essay concerning humane understanding. 5th ed. London, 1706.
	Phil 2115.4F	Lee, Henry. Anti-scepticism: or notes upon...Mr. Lock's essay. London, 1702.
	Phil 2115.5	Hartenstein, G. Locke's Lehre. Leipzig, 1861.
	Phil 2115.6	Moore, A.W. Existence, meaning, and reality in Locke's essay. Chicago, 1903.
	Phil 2115.10	Locke, J. Works. London, 1801. 10v.
	Phil 2115.10.5A	Locke, J. Works. London, 1812. 10v.
	Phil 2115.10.5B	Locke, J. Works. London, 1812. 10v.
	Phil 2115.11	Locke, J. Works. London, 1823. 10v.
	Phil 2115.11.2	Locke, J. Works. London, 1893. 10v.
	Phil 2115.12	Locke, J. Works. London, 1854. 2v.
	Phil 2115.13	Locke, J. Works. London, 1876.
	Phil 2115.14	Locke, J. Philosophical works. London, 1877. 2v.
	Phil 2115.14.7	Locke, J. Philosophical works. London, 1892. 2v.
Htn	Phil 2115.15*	Locke, J. Posthumous works. London, 1706.
Htn	Phil 2115.15.5*	Locke, J. Posthumous works. London, 1706.
	Phil 2115.19	Locke, J. Oeuvres philosophiques de Locke. Paris, 1821-25. 7v.
Htn	Phil 2115.20*	Locke, J. Oeuvres diverses. Rotterdam, 1710.
	Phil 2115.21	Locke, J. Two tracts on government. Cambridge, Eng., 1967.
Htn	Phil 2115.25*	Locke, J. Collection of several pieces. London, 1720.
	Phil 2115.26	Locke, J. Selections. Chicago, 1928.
	Phil 2115.27	Locke, J. The beauties of Locke. London, n.d.
	Phil 2115.27.5	Locke, J. Philosophical beauties. N.Y., 1828.
	Phil 2115.29	Locke, J. La filosofia di G. Locke. Firenze, 1920-21. 2v.
	Phil 2115.29.125F	Locke, J. De intellectu humano. Ed. 4a. London, 1701.
	Phil 2115.30	Locke, J. Essay concerning human understanding. London, 1726. 2v.
	Phil 2115.30.2	Locke, J. Essay concerning human understanding. London, 1748. 2v.
	Phil 2115.30.3	Locke, J. Essay concerning human understanding. London, 1716. 2v.
	Phil 2115.30.4	Locke, J. Essay concerning human understanding. v.2. London, 1735.
	Phil 2115.31	Locke, J. Essay concerning human understanding. London, 1753. 2v.
	Phil 2115.31.5	Locke, J. Essay concerning human understanding. v.2. Edinburgh, 1765.
	Phil 2115.32	Locke, J. Essay concerning human understanding. London, 1791. 2v.
	Phil 2115.32.3A	Locke, J. Essay concerning human understanding. v.1-2,3. London, 1795. 2v.
	Phil 2115.32.3B	Locke, J. Essay concerning human understanding. London, 1795.
	Phil 2115.32.5	Locke, J. Essay concerning human understanding. Edinburgh, 1798. 3v.
	Phil 2115.33	Locke, J. Essay concerning human understanding. v.1-3. Edinburgh, 1801.
	Phil 2115.34	Locke, J. Essay concerning human understanding. 1st American ed. Boston, 1803. 3v.
	Phil 2115.34.2	Locke, J. Essay concerning human understanding. v.1,3: 1st American ed. Boston, 1803-06. 3v.
Htn	Phil 2115.34.3*	Locke, J. Essay concerning human understanding. 2nd American ed. Brattleboro, Vt., 1806. 3v.
NEDL	Phil 2115.34.5	Locke, J. Essay concerning human understanding. v.2. 2nd American ed. Boston, 1813.
	Phil 2115.34.9	Locke, J. Essay concerning human understanding. 24th ed. London, 1817.
	Phil 2115.34.15	Locke, J. Essay concerning human understanding. London, 1823. 3v.
	Phil 2115.35	Locke, J. Essay concerning human understanding. v.1-2. N.Y., 1824.
	Phil 2115.35.5	Locke, J. Essay concerning human understanding. 25th ed. London, 1825.
	Phil 2115.35.15	Locke, J. Essay concerning human understanding. Philadelphia, 1849.
	Phil 2115.35.17	Locke, J. Essay concerning human understanding. Philadelphia, 185-?
	Phil 2115.35.19A	Locke, J. Essay concerning human understanding. Philadelphia, 185-?
	Phil 2115.35.19B	Locke, J. Essay concerning human understanding. Philadelphia, 185-?

Classified Listing

Phil 2115 History of philosophy - Local Modern philosophy - Great Britain and United States - Individual philosophers - Locke, John - cont.

Phil 2115.35.25 Locke, J. Essay concerning human understanding. London, 1870.
Phil 2115.36 Locke, J. Essay concerning human understanding. Oxford, 1894. 3v.
Phil 2115.36.25A Locke, J. Essay concerning human understanding. Oxford, 1924.
Phil 2115.36.25B Locke, J. Essay concerning human understanding. Oxford, 1924.
Phil 2115.36.30 Locke, J. Essay concerning human understanding. Cambridge, 1931.
Htn Phil 2115.36.31* Locke, J. Essay concerning human understanding. Cambridge, 1931.
Phil 2115.36.31.10 Locke, J. Essay concerning human understanding. London, 1947.
Phil 2115.36.31.12 Locke, J. Essay concerning human understanding. Chicago, 1956.
Htn Phil 2115.36.32* Locke, J. Essay concerning human understanding. Photostat copy of Locke's original ms. n.p., n.d.
Htn Phil 2115.36.33* Essay concerning human understanding. Editor's ms. for edition of 1931. n.p., n.d.
Phil 2115.36.35 Locke, J. Essay concerning human understanding. An early draft. Oxford, 1936.
Htn Phil 2115.44* Locke, J. An abridgment of Mr. Locke's Essay concerning humane understanding. London, 1696.
Htn Phil 2115.45* Locke, J. An abridgment of Mr. Locke's Essay concerning human understanding. London, 1700.
Phil 2115.45.2 Locke, J. An abridgment of Mr. Locke's Essay concerning human understanding. Boston, 1794.
Phil 2115.45.5 Locke, J. An abridgment of Mr. Locke's Essay concerning human understanding. Glasgow, 1744.
Phil 2115.45.40 Locke, J. I principi dell'illuminismo eclettico, estratti dal "Saggio sull'intelligenza umano". Torino, 1927.
Phil 2115.46 Locke, J. Philosophy of Locke in extracts. N.Y., 1891.
Phil 2115.47.5 Locke, J. Essay concerning human understanding. Chicago, 1917.
Phil 2115.48.2 Locke, J. Essai philosophique concernant l'entendement humaine. Amsterdam, 1700.
Phil 2115.48.5 Locke, J. Essai philosophique concernant l'entendement humaine. La Haye, 1714.
Phil 2115.48.7 Locke, J. Essai philosophique concernant l'entendement humaine. Amsterdam, 1735.
Phil 2115.48.10 Locke, J. Essai philosophique concernant l'entendement humaine. Abrégé. Genève, 1741.
Phil 2115.48.11 Locke, J. Essai philosophique concernant l'entendement humaine. 4e éd. Amsterdam, 1742.
Phil 2115.48.12 Locke, J. Essai philosophique concernant l'entendement humaine. Amsterdam, 1755.
Phil 2115.48.14 Locke, J. Essai philosophique concernant l'entendement humaine. 5e éd. Paris, 1799? 4v.
Phil 2115.48.15 Locke, J. Essai philosophique concernant l'entendement humaine. Abrégé. Upsal, 1792.
Phil 2115.48.25 Locke, J. Oeuvres de Locke et Leibnitz. Paris, 1839.
Phil 2115.49 Locke, J. Versuch über den menschlichen Verstand. Leipzig, 1913. 2v.
tn Phil 2115.49.5* Locke, J. Versuch vom menschlichen Verstand. Altenburg, 1757.
Phil 2115.49.8 Locke, J. Vom menschlichen Verstande. Mannheim, 1791.
Phil 2115.49.10 Locke, J. Versuch über den menschlichen Verstand. Jena, 1795. 3v.
Phil 2115.49.13 Locke, J. Versuch über den menschlichen Verstand. Berlin, 1872-73. 2v.
Phil 2115.49.15 Locke, J. Über den menschlichen Verstand. Leipzig, 1897. 2v.
Phil 2115.49.20 Locke, J. Libri IV de intellectu humano. Lipsiae, 1709.
Phil 2115.49.25 Locke, J. Libri IV de intellectu humano. Lipsiae, 1741.
Phil 2115.49.30 Locke, J. Über den menschlichen Verstand. Berlin, 1962. 2v.
Phil 2115.50 Locke, J. The conduct of the understanding. Boston, 1825.
Phil 2115.50.2 Locke, J. The conduct of the understanding. v.1-2. Boston, 1828.
Phil 2115.50.3 Locke, J. The conduct of the understanding. v.1-2. Boston, 1831.
Phil 2115.50.10 Locke, J. The conduct of the understanding. Cambridge, 1781.
Phil 2115.51A Locke, J. The conduct of the understanding. Oxford, 1881.
Phil 2115.51B Locke, J. The conduct of the understanding. Oxford, 1881.
Phil 2115.51.6 Locke, J. The conduct of the understanding. 5th ed. Oxford, 1901.
Phil 2115.51.7 Locke, J. The conduct of the understanding. N.Y., 1966.
Phil 2115.51.10 Locke, J. Leitung des Verstandes. Heidelberg, 1883.
Phil 2115.51.20 Locke, J. Della guida dell'intelligenza nella ricerca della verità. Lanciano, 1927.
n Phil 2115.58* Locke, J. The reasonableness of Christianity. London, 1695.
Phil 2115.58.5* Locke, J. The reasonableness of Christianity. Boston, 1811.
Phil 2115.58.9 Locke, J. The reasonableness of Christianity. London, 1836.
Phil 2115.60* Locke, J. Essay for the understanding of St. Paul's epistles. Boston, 1820.
Phil 2115.60.2 Locke, J. Essay for the understanding of St. Paul's epistles. Boston, 1820.
Phil 2115.61 Locke, J. Scritti editi e inediti sulla tolleranza. Torino, 1961.
Phil 2115.62 Locke, J. A paraphrase and notes on epistle of St. Paul. London, 1823.
Phil 2115.62.2* Locke, J. A paraphrase and notes on epistle of St. Paul. London, 1707.
Phil 2115.62.10 Locke, J. A paraphrase and notes on epistle of St. Paul. Cambridge, 1832.
Phil 2115.64* Locke, J. A common-place book to the Holy Bible. London, 1697.
Phil 2115.64.20 Locke, J. A common-place book to the Holy Bible. 3d ed. London, 1725.
Phil 2115.64.25 Locke, J. A common-place book to the Holy Bible. 4th ed. London, 1738.
Phil 2115.65 Locke, J. A commonplace book to the Holy Bible. London, 1824.
Phil 2115.65.25 Locke, J. A commonplace book to the Holy Bible. 5th London ed. N.Y., 18- ?
Phil 2115.67 Locke, J. On politics and education. N.Y., 1947.
Phil 2115.68 Locke, J. Of civil government and toleration. London, 1950.
Phil 2115.69 Locke, J. Locke's travels in France. Cambridge, 1953.

Phil 2115 History of philosophy - Local Modern philosophy - Great Britain and United States - Individual philosophers - Locke, John - cont.

Htn Phil 2115.70* Locke, J. Letter concerning toleration. London, 1689.
Htn Phil 2115.70.2* Locke, J. A third letter for toleration. London, 1692.
Htn Phil 2115.70.5* Locke, J. Letters concerning toleration. London, 1765.
Phil 2115.70.7 Locke, J. Ein Brief über Toleranz. Hamburg, 1957.
Phil 2115.70.15 Locke, J. Epistola su la tolleranza. Lanciano, 1920. 2v.
Phil 2115.70.16 Locke, J. Lettera sulla tolleranza. Firenze, 1961.
Phil 2115.70.20 Locke, J. A letter concerning toleration. The Hague, 1963.
Phil 2115.70.25 Locke, J. Lettre sur la tolérance. 1. éd. Montréal, 1964.
Htn Phil 2115.71* Locke, J. Some thoughts concerning education. London, 1693.
Phil 2115.72 Locke, J. Essays on the law of nature. Oxford, 1954.
Htn Phil 2115.73* Locke, J. A letter to Edward, Lord Bishop of Worcester. London, 1697.
Htn Phil 2115.73.5* Locke, J. Reply to the Lord Bishop of Worcester's answer to his letter. London, 1697.
Htn Phil 2115.73.7* Locke, J. Reply to the Lord Bishop of Worcester's answer to his second letter. London, 1699.
Htn Phil 2115.74* Locke, J. Two treatises of government. London, 1690.
Phil 2115.74.10 Locke, J. Zwei Abhandlungen über Regierung. Halle, 1906.
Phil 2115.74.15 Locke, J. O forgripelize. Stockholm, 1726.
Phil 2115.74.50 Locke, J. Some familiar letters between Mr. Locke and his friends. London, 1708.
Phil 2115.75 Locke, J. Familiar letters. London, 1742.
Phil 2115.75.2 Locke, J. Familiar letters. London, 1742.
Phil 2115.75.3 Locke, J. Familiar letters. London, 1830.
Phil 2115.75.9 Locke, J. The correspondence of John Locke and Edward Clarke. Cambridge, 1927.
Phil 2115.75.10 Locke, J. The correspondence of John Locke and Edward Clarke. London, 1927.
Htn Phil 2115.75.11* Locke, J. Correspondence of John Locke and Edward Clarke. Editor's ms. for Cambridge edition. n.p., n.d.
Phil 2115.76 Locke, J. Lettres inédites. La Haye, 1912.
Htn Phil 2115.77F* Locke, J. Catalogus librorum. Ms. photostat. n.p., n.d.
Htn Phil 2115.77.5F* Locke, J. Catalogue of Locke's library. Ms. photostat. n.p., n.d.
Phil 2115.78A Locke, J. An account of Mr. Lock's religion. London, 1700.
Phil 2115.78B Locke, J. An account of Mr. Lock's religion. London, 1700.
Phil 2115.79 Pamphlet box. Philosophy. English. Locke, J. German dissertations.
Phil 2115.79.5 Pamphlet box. Philosophy. English. Locke, J.
Htn Phil 2115.80* Carroll, William. A dissertation upon the tenth chapter of the fourth book of Mr. Locke's Essay concerning human understanding. London, 1706.
Phil 2115.81 Morell, T. Notes and annotations on Locke. London, 1794.
Htn Phil 2115.82* LeClerc, J. The life and character of Mr. John Locke. London, 1706-13.
Htn Phil 2115.82.1* LeClerc, J. The life and character of Mr. John Locke. London, 1706.
Htn Phil 2115.83* Stillingfleet, E. Answer to Mr. Locke's letter. London, 1697.
Htn Phil 2115.83.3* Stillingfleet, E. Answer to Mr. Locke's second letter. London, 1698.
Htn Phil 2115.85* Sergeant, J. Solid philosophy asserted. London, 1697.
Phil 2115.86 Tagart, E. Locke's writings and philosophy. London, 1855.
Phil 2115.87 Webb, T.E. Intellectualism of Locke. London, 1857.
Phil 2115.88 Manly, G.W. Contradictions in Locke's theory of knowledge. Leipzig, 1885.
Phil 2115.89A Geil, Georg. Über die Abhängigkeit Locke's von Descartes. Strassburg, 188-.
Phil 2115.89B Geil, Georg. Über die Abhängigkeit Locke's von Descartes. Strassburg, 188-.
Phil 2115.90 Fowler, T. Locke. London, 1880.
Phil 2115.90.3 Fowler, T. Locke. N.Y., 1880?
Phil 2115.90.4 Fowler, T. Life of Locke. N.Y., n.d.
Phil 2115.90.7 Fowler, T. Locke. N.Y., 1899.
Phil 2115.91A Bourne, H.R.F. The life of John Locke. London, 1876. 2v.
Phil 2115.91B Bourne, H.R.F. The life of John Locke. London, 1876. 2v.
Phil 2115.91.2A Bourne, H.R.F. The life of John Locke. N.Y., 1876. 2v.
Phil 2115.91.2B Bourne, H.R.F. The life of John Locke. N.Y., 1876. 2v.
Phil 2115.92 Fraser, A.C. Locke. Edinburgh, 1890.
Phil 2115.92.2A Fraser, A.C. Locke. Philadelphia, 1890.
Phil 2115.92.2B Fraser, A.C. Locke. Philadelphia, 1890.
Phil 2115.92.90 King, Peter. Life of John Locke. London, 1829.
Phil 2115.93A King, Peter. Life of John Locke. London, 1830. 2v.
Phil 2115.93B King, Peter. Life of John Locke. London, 1830. 2v.
NEDL Phil 2115.93.10 King, Peter. The life and letters of John Locke. London, 1858.
Phil 2115.94 Hertling, G. von. John Locke und die Schule von Cambridge. Freiburg, 1892. 2v.
Phil 2115.95 Martinak, E. Die Logik John Lockes'. Halle, 1894.
Htn Phil 2115.96* Grenville. Oxford and Locke. London, 1829.
Phil 2115.97 Ollion, H. La philosophie générale de John Locke. Paris, 1909.
Phil 2115.99 Alexander, S. Locke. London, 1908.
Phil 2115.100 Worcester, E.E. The religious opinions of John Locke. Thesis. Geneva, N.Y., 1889.
Phil 2115.100.5 Worcester, E.E. The religious opinions of John Locke. Geneva, N.Y., 1889.
Phil 2115.101 Didier, J. John Locke. Paris, 1911.
Phil 2115.102.4 Cousin, V. Philosophie de Locke. 4e éd. Paris, 1861.
Phil 2115.103 Benoit, G. von. Darstellung der Locke'schen Erkenntnisstheorie. Bern, 1869.
Phil 2115.104 Curtis, M.M. An outline of Locke's ethical philosophy. Leipzig, 1890.
Phil 2115.105 Krakowski, E. Les sources médiévales de la philosophie de Locke. Paris, 1915.
Phil 2115.106 Krakowski, E. Les sources médiévales de la philosophie de Locke. Thèse. Paris, 1915.
Htn Phil 2115.107* Burthogge, Richard. An essay upon reason and the nature of spirits. London, 1694-1755. 3 pam.
Phil 2115.108 Martinak, E. Zur Logik Lockes. Graz, 1887.
Phil 2115.109 Quaebicker, R. Lockii et Liebnitii de cognitione humana. Inaug.-Diss. Halis Saxonium, 1868.
Phil 2115.111.15A Gibson, James. John Locke. London, 1933.
Phil 2115.111.15B Gibson, James. John Locke. London, 1933.
Phil 2115.112A Hefelbower, S.G. The relation of John Locke to English deism. Chicago, 1918.

132

Classified Listing

Phil 2115 History of philosophy - Local Modern philosophy - Great Britain and United States - Individual philosophers - Locke, John - cont.

Phil 2115.112B Hefelbower, S.G. The relation of John Locke to English deism. Chicago, 1918.
Phil 2115.112C Hefelbower, S.G. The relation of John Locke to English deism. Chicago, 1918.
Phil 2115.113 Gerdil, G.S. L'immatérialité de l'âme...contre Locke. Turin, 1747.
X Cg Phil 2115.114 Lamprecht, S.P. The moral and political philosophy of John Locke. N.Y., 1918.
Phil 2115.114.5 Lamprecht, S.P. The moral and political philosophy of John Locke. N.Y., 1962.
Phil 2115.115 Lodge, Rupert C. The meaning...of...philosophy of John Locke. Minneapolis, 1918.
Htn Phil 2115.116* Memoirs of the life...of Mr. John Locke. London, 1742.
Phil 2115.117 Getschmann, W. Die Pädagogik des John Locke. Köthen, 1881.
Phil 2115.118 Fechtner, Eduard. John Locke, ein Bild aus den geistigen Kämpfen Englands. Stuttgart, 1898.
Phil 2115.119 Winter, Hermann. Darlegung und Kritik der Lokeschen Lehre vom empirischen Ursprung der sittlichen Grundsätze. Inaug.-Diss. Bonn, 1883.
Phil 2115.121 Kirchmann, J.H. Erläuterungen zu John Locke's Versuch über den menschlichen Verstand. Abt II. Berlin, 1874.
Phil 2115.122 Ferrari, M. Locke e il sensismo francese. Modena, 1900.
Phil 2115.123 Corti, S. La teoria della conoscenza in Locke e Leibnitz. Siena, 1908.
Phil 2115.124 Gregory, Raymond. A study of Locke's theory of knowledge. Wilmington, Ohio, 1919.
Phil 2115.124.5 Gregory, Raymond. A study of Locke's theory of knowledge. Thesis. Wilmington, Ohio, 1919.
Phil 2115.125 Burger, D. Locke's bewijs voor het bestaan van God. Amersfoort, 1872.
Htn Phil 2115.126* Perronet, Vincent. A vindication of Mr. Locke. London, 1736.
Htn Phil 2115.127* Perronet, Vincent. A second vindication of Mr. Locke. London, 1738.
Phil 2115.128 Rosell, Anton. Betraktelse af Lockes. Upsala, 1857.
Htn Phil 2115.129* Burnet, Thomas. Remarks upon an essay concerning humane understanding. London, 1697. 3 pam.
Htn Phil 2115.130* Lowde, J. Moral essays; wherein some of Mr. Locks and Monsir. Malbranch's opinions are briefly examin'd. York, 1699.
Phil 2115.131 Tex, Jan den. Locke en Spinoza over de tolerantie. Amsterdam, 1926.
Phil 2115.132 Reininger, R. Locke, Berkeley, Hume. München, 1922.
Phil 2115.133 Milhac, F. Essai sur les idées religieuses de Locke. Thèse. Genève, 1886.
Phil 2115.134 Marion, Henri. J. Locke: sa vie et son oeuvre. 2e éd. Paris, 1893.
Phil 2115.134.5 Marion, Henri. J. Locke: sa vie et son oeuvre. Paris, 1878.
Phil 2115.135 Tarantino, G. Giovanni Locke. Milano, 1886.
Phil 2115.136 Sommer, R. Locke's Verhältnis zu Descartes. Diss. Berlin, 1887.
Phil 2115.137 Nardi, Pietro de. Caratteri della filosofia di Giovanni Locke. Firenze, 1889.
Phil 2115.137.5 Nardi, Pietro de. Del rinnovamento delle dottrine di Gall e...di Locke. Firenze, 1890.
Phil 2115.138 Tellkamp, A. Das Verhältnis John Locke's zur Scholastik. Münster, 1927.
Phil 2115.139 Mellring, J.G. Specimen academicum. Upsaliae, 1792.
Htn Phil 2115.140* Animadversions on a late book entituled The reasonableness of Christianity. Oxford, 1697.
Htn Phil 2115.141* Bold, S. A collection of tracts. London, 1706.
Phil 2115.143 Christophersen, H.O. John Locke, en filosofis forberedelse og grunnleggelse (1632-1689). Oslo, 1932.
Phil 2115.144 Smith, N.K. John Locke, 1632-1704. Manchester, 1933.
Phil 2115.145A Thompson, S.M. A study of Locke's theory of ideas. Monmouth, Ill., 1934.
Phil 2115.145B Thompson, S.M. A study of Locke's theory of ideas. Monmouth, Ill., 1934.
Phil 2115.146 Hofstadter, A. Locke and scepticism. N.Y., 1935.
Phil 2115.147 MacLean, K. John Locke and English literature of the eighteenth century. New Haven, 1936.
Phil 2115.147.2 MacLean, K. John Locke and English literature of the eighteenth century. N.Y., 1962.
Phil 2115.148 Curti, M. The great Mr. Locke, America's philosopher, 1783-1861. n.p., 19- .
Phil 2115.149A Aaron, Richard Ithamar. John Locke. London, 1937.
Phil 2115.149.3 Aaron, Richard Ithamar. John Locke. 3rd ed. Oxford, 1971.
Phil 2115.149.5 Aaron, R.I. John Locke. 2nd ed. Oxford, 1955.
Phil 2115.151 Massie, J. An essay on...Mr. Locke. London, 1750.
Phil 2115.152 Massie, J. Observations. London, 1760.
Htn Phil 2115.153* Barbon, N. A discourse...in answer to Mr. Lock. London, 1696.
Phil 2115.154 Czajkowski, C.J. The theory of private property in John Locke's political philosophy. Notre Dame, 1941.
Phil 2115.155 Schärer, E. John Locke. Leipzig, 1860.
Phil 2115.157 An essay on personal identity, in 2 parts. London, 1769.
Phil 2115.159 Gough, J.W. John Locke's political philosophy. Oxford, 1950.
Phil 2115.161 Crons, E. Die religions philosophischen lehren Lockes. Halle, 1910.
Phil 2115.163 Yolton, John W. John Locke and the way of ideas. London, 1956.
Phil 2115.164 Ricci Garotti, Loris. Locke e i suoi problemi. Urbino, 1961.
Phil 2115.165 Bianca, Giuseppe G. La credenza come fondamento. Padova, 1950.
Phil 2115.167 Maag, Urs. Die psychologischen Ansichten John Lockes. Aarau, 1960.
Phil 2115.168 Cranston, M.W. John Locke. London, 1957.
Phil 2115.168.5 Cranston, M.W. Locke. London, 1961.
Phil 2115.170 Giganti, Maria A. John Locke e i limiti della scienza. Padova, 1957.
Phil 2115.172 Cox, Richard H. Locke on war and peace. Oxford, 1960.
Phil 2115.175 Narshii, I.S. Fislosofiia Dzhona Lokka. Moskva, 1960.
Phil 2115.180 Tuveson, E.L. The imagination as a means of grace. Berkeley, 1960.
Phil 2115.185 Viano, Carlo A. John Locke. Torino, 1960.
Phil 2115.190 Polin, Raymond. La politique morale de John Locke. 1e éd. Paris, 1960.
Phil 2115.195 Viano, Carlo A. John Locke. Torino, 1960.
Phil 2115.196 Morris, C.R. Locke, Berkeley, Hume. London, 1963.
Phil 2115.197 Leroy, A.L. Locke, sa vie. Paris, 1964.
Phil 2115.198 Bartolomeis, Francesco de. John Locke. Il pensiero filosofico e pedagogico. Firenze, 1967.

Phil 2115 History of philosophy - Local Modern philosophy - Great Britain and United States - Individual philosophers - Locke, John - cont.

Phil 2115.200 Rosa, Pasquale. Il pensiero filosofico e pedagogico di G. Locke. Napoli, 1965.
Phil 2115.205 Seligen, Martin. The liberal politics of John Locke. London, 1968.
Phil 2115.210 Yolton, John W. John Locke: problems and perspectives. London, 1969.
Phil 2115.215 Martin, Charles Burton. Locke and Berkeley: a collection of ciritical essays. London, 1968.
Phil 2115.220 Euchner, Walter. Naturrecht und Politik bei John Locke. Frankfurt am Main, 1969.
Phil 2115.225 Yolton, John W. Locke and the compass of human understanding; a selective commentary on the Essay. Cambridge, Eng., 1970.
Phil 2115.230 The Locke newsletter. Heslington, York, Eng. 1,1970+
Phil 2115.235 Baldini, Artemio Enzo. Il pensiero giovanile di John Locke. Milano, 1969.

Phil 2120 History of philosophy - Local Modern philosophy - Great Britain and United States - Individual philosophers - Other L

Phil 2120.1.80 Remacle, G. La philosophie de S.S. Laurie. Bruxelles, 1909.
Htn Phil 2120.2.30* Law, William. A serious call to a devout and holy life. London, 1729.
Htn Phil 2120.3.30* Lyly, John. Euphues and his England. London, 1588.
Phil 2120.4.90 Devaux, P. Le pragmatisme conceptuel de Clarence Irwing Lewis. Paris, 1934.
Phil 2120.4.95 Schilpp, Paul A. The philosophy of C.I. Lewis. 1. ed. Facsimile. La Salle, 1968.
Phil 2120.5 Cooper, B.S. The philosophy of Sir Oliver Lodge. Thesis. Nashville, 1934.
Phil 2120.6.30 Lewis, John. Marxism and modern idealism. London, 1944.
Phil 2120.7.79 Pamphlet box. Philosophy. English. Laird, John. Works by and about.
Phil 2120.8.30 Lamont, Corliss. The independent mind. N.Y., 1951.
Phil 2120.8.35 Pamphlet vol. Philosophy. English. Lamont, Corliss. 7 pam.
Phil 2120.9.30 Laucks, I.F. A speculation in reality. N.Y., 1953.
Phil 2120.10.20 Lindsay, A.D.L. Selected addresses. Cumberland, 1957.
Phil 2120.11.30 Langer, Susanne Katherina (Knauth). Philosophical sketches. Baltimore, 1962.
Phil 2120.12.30 Lovejoy, A.O. The thirteen pragmatisms. Baltimore, 1963.
Phil 2120.13 Laszlo, Ervin. Beyond scepticism and realism. The Hague, 1966.
Phil 2120.13.5 Laszlo, Ervin. Essential society; an ontological reconstruction. The Hague, 1963.
Phil 2120.15 Loewenberg, Jacob. Thrice-born. N.Y., 1968.
Phil 2120.18 Lewis, Clarence Irving. Collected papers. Stanford, 1970.

Phil 2125 History of philosophy - Local Modern philosophy - Great Brita.n and United States - Individual philosophers - McCosh, James

Phil 2125.30 McCosh, James. First and fundamental truths. N.Y., 1889.
Phil 2125.35 McCosh, James. The tests of the various kinds of truth. N.Y., 1891.
Phil 2125.40 McCosh, James. Philosophical papers. N.Y., 1869.
Phil 2125.45.2 Pamphlet box. Philosophy. English. McCosh, James.
Phil 2125.45.7 McCosh, James. A criticism of the critical philosophy. N.Y., 1884.
Phil 2125.50 McCosh, James. Psychology: the cognitive powers. N.Y., 1886.
Phil 2125.50.2 McCosh, James. Psychology: the cognitive powers. N.Y., 1889.
Phil 2125.50.3 McCosh, James. Psychology: the motive powers. N.Y., 1888.
Phil 2125.50.5 McCosh, James. Psychology: the cognitive powers. N.Y., 1906.
Phil 2125.52 McCosh, James. Intuitions of the mind. London, 1860.
Phil 2125.52.5 McCosh, James. Intuitions of the mind. 3rd ed. N.Y., 1874.
Phil 2125.55 McCosh, James. The emotions. N.Y., 1880.
Phil 2125.57 McCosh, James. The laws of discursive thought. N.Y., 1876.
Phil 2125.60 McCosh, James. Typical forms and special ends in creation. Edinburgh, 1857.
Phil 2125.62 McCosh, James. Christianity and positivism. N.Y., 1874.
Phil 2125.62.5 McCosh, James. Christianity and positivism. N.Y., 1871.
Phil 2125.65 McCosh, James. Method of divine government. N.Y., 1851.
Phil 2125.65.4 McCosh, James. Method of divine government. N.Y., 1855.
Phil 2125.65.5 McCosh, James. Method of divine government. Edinburgh, 1852.
Phil 2125.65.7 McCosh, James. Method of divine government. 2nd ed. Edinburgh, 1850.
Phil 2125.66 McCosh, James. The supernatural in relation to the natural. Cambridge, Eng., 1862.
Phil 2125.73 McCosh, James. Our moral nature, being a brief system of ethics. N.Y., 1892.
Htn Phil 2125.75* McCosh, James. Philosophy of reality: should it be favored by America? N.Y., 1894.
Phil 2125.77 Dulles, J.H. McCosh bibliography. Princeton, 1895.
Phil 2125.81 Volbeda, S. De intuitieve philosophie van James McCosh. Grand Rapids, n.d.

Phil 2128 History of philosophy - Local Modern philosophy - Great Britain and United States - Individual philosophers - Mandeville, Bernard

Htn Phil 2128.27* Mandeville, B. Fable of the bees. London, 1714.
Htn Phil 2128.28* Mandeville, B. Fable of the bees. London, 1723.
Phil 2128.29 Mandeville, B. Fable of the bees. 3rd ed. London, 1724.
Phil 2128.30 Mandeville, B. Fable of the bees. London, 1725.
Phil 2128.31 Mandeville, B. Fable of the bees. London, 1728-29. 2v.
Phil 2128.32 Mandeville, B. Fable of the bees. London, 1729-32. 2v.
Phil 2128.33.5 Mandeville, B. Fable of the bees. Pt.II. London, 1730.
Htn Phil 2128.33.12* Mandeville, B. Fable of the bees. Edinburgh, 1755. 2v.
Phil 2128.40A Mandeville, B. Bernard de Mandeville's Bienenfabel. Diss. Halle, 1886. 2v.
Phil 2128.40B Mandeville, B. Bernard de Mandeville's Bienenfabel. Diss. Halle, 1886. 2v.
Phil 2128.41A Mandeville, B. Fable of the bees. Oxford, 1924. 2v.
Phil 2128.41B Mandeville, B. Fable of the bees. Oxford, 1924. 2v.
Phil 2128.43 Mandeville, B. Fable of the bees. London, 1934.
Phil 2128.45 Mandeville, B. Fable of the bees. N.Y., 1962.
Htn Phil 2128.50* Mandeville, B. La fable des abeilles. London, 1750. 2v.
Phil 2128.55 Mandeville, B. Il paradosso Mandeville. Firenze, 1958.
Phil 2128.60 Mandeville, B. Enquiry into the origin of honour. London, 1732.

Classified Listing

Phil 2128 History of philosophy - Local Modern philosophy - Great Britain and United States - Individual philosophers - Mandeville, Bernard - cont.

Htn	Phil 2128.60.2*	Mandeville, B. Enquiry into the origin of honour. v.1-2. London, 1725-32.
	Phil 2128.61	Mandeville, B. A letter to Dion. Liverpool, 1954.
Htn	Phil 2128.65*	Mandeville, B. Free thoughts on religion. London, 1720.
	Phil 2128.80	Law, William. Remarks on...the fable of the bees. Cambridge, 1844.
Htn	Phil 2128.80.2*	Law, William. Remarks on...the fable of the bees. Cambridge, 1844.
	Phil 2128.80.5	Law, William. Remarks on...the fable of the bees. London, 1724.
	Phil 2128.81	Bluet. An enquiry whether a general practice of virtue tends to the wealth or poverty...of a people. London, 1725.
Htn	Phil 2128.82*	Dennis, John. Vice and luxury publick mischiefs. London, 1724.
	Phil 2128.83	Sakmann, Paul. Bernard de Mandeville und die Bienenfabel. Freiburg, 1897.
	Phil 2128.84	Stammler, B. Mandevilles Bienenfabel. Berlin, 1918.
	Phil 2128.85	Grégoire, F. Bernard de Mandeville et la "Fable des Abeilles". Thèse. Nancy, 1947.

Phil 2130 History of philosophy - Local Modern philosophy - Great Britain and United States - Individual philosophers - Mansel, Henry L.

	Phil 2130.30	Mansel, H.L. Metaphysics. Edinburgh, 1860.
	Phil 2130.31	Mansel, H.L. Metaphysics. N.Y., 1871.
	Phil 2130.33	Mansel, H.L. Psychology; the test of moral and metaphysical philosophy. Oxford, 1855.
	Phil 2130.35	Mansel, H.L. Prolegomena logica. Oxford, 1851.
	Phil 2130.35.2A	Mansel, H.L. Prolegomena logica. 2nd ed. Oxford, 1860.
	Phil 2130.35.2B	Mansel, H.L. Prolegomena logica. 2nd ed. Oxford, 1860.
	Phil 2130.35.3	Mansel, H.L. Prolegomena logica. Boston, 1860.
	Phil 2130.40	Mansel, H.L. Letters, lectures and reviews. London, 1873.
	Phil 2130.45	Mansel, H.L. The limits of religious thought. 1st American ed. Boston, 1859.
	Phil 2130.45.5	Mansel, H.L. The limits of religious thought. 3rd ed. London, 1859.
	Phil 2130.45.10	Mansel, H.L. The limits of religious thought. 1st American ed. Boston, 1875.
	Phil 2130.50	Mansel, H.L. Man's conception of eternity. London, 1854.
	Phil 2130.60	Mansel, H.L. Philosophy of the conditioned. London, 1866.
	Phil 2130.80	Freeman, Kenneth D. The role of reason in religion: a study of Henry Mansel. The Hague, 1969.

Phil 2138 History of philosophy - Local Modern philosophy - Great Britain and United States - Individual philosophers - Mill, John Stuart

	Phil 2138.02A	Mill, John S. Bibliography of the published writings of J.S. Mill. Evanston, Ill., 1945.
	Phil 2138.02B	Mill, John S. Bibliography of the published writings of J.S. Mill. Evanston, Ill., 1945.
	Phil 2138.02C	Mill, John S. Bibliography of the published writings of J.S. Mill. Evanston, Ill., 1945.
	Phil 2138.2	Mill, John S. Gesammelte Werke. v.1-3, 4-6, 7-9, 10-12. Leipzig, 1869-80. 4v.
	Phil 2138.11	Mill, John S. Collected works. v.2,3, 4(2), 5(2), 10,12,13. Toronto, 1963. 9v.
	Phil 2138.20	Mill, John S. The philosophy of John Stuart Mill. N.Y., 1961.
	Phil 2138.23	Mill, John S. John Stuart Mill; a selection of his works. N.Y., 1966.
	Phil 2138.25	Mill, John S. The spirit of the age. Chicago, 1942.
	Phil 2138.30A	Mill, John S. An examination of Hamilton's philosophy. Boston, 1865. 2v.
	Phil 2138.30B	Mill, John S. An examination of Hamilton's philosophy. Boston, 1865. 2v.
tn	Phil 2138.30.2*	Mill, John S. An examination of Hamilton's philosophy. London, 1865.
tn	Phil 2138.35.1*	Mill, John S. A system of logic. London, 1843. 2v.
EDL	Phil 2138.35.2	Mill, John S. A system of logic. 3rd ed. London, 1851. 2v.
EDL	Phil 2138.35.3	Mill, John S. A system of logic. N.Y., 1869.
	Phil 2138.35.3.15A	Mill, John S. A system of logic. 8th ed. London, 1872. 2v.
	Phil 2138.35.3.15B	Mill, John S. A system of logic. 8th ed. v.2. London, 1872.
	Phil 2138.35.3.19	Mill, John S. A system of logic. 8th ed. N.Y., 1874.
	Phil 2138.35.3.23	Mill, John S. A system of logic. 8th ed. N.Y., 1881.
	Phil 2138.35.4	Mill, John S. A system of logic. London, 1886.
	Phil 2138.35.5	Mill, John S. A system of logic. London, 1896.
	Phil 2138.35.5.3	Mill, John S. A system of logic. London, 1898.
	Phil 2138.35.5.10	Mill, John S. A system of logic. London, 1911.
	Phil 2138.35.6	Mill, John S. System der deductiven und inductiven Logik. 4e Aufl. v.1-2. Braunschweig, 1877.
	Phil 2138.35.8	Mill, John S. System der deductiven und inductiven Logik. 2e Aufl. Braunschweig, 1862-63. 2v.
	Phil 2138.35.10	Mill, John S. System der deductiven und inductiven Logik. Leipzig, 1872. 3 pam.
	Phil 2138.35.12	Mill, John S. Die inductive Logik. Braunschweig, 1849.
	Phil 2138.35.20	Mill, John S. A system of logic. London, 1965.
Cg	Phil 2138.37	Mill, John S. The student's handbook...of Mill's...logic. London, 1870.
	Phil 2138.37.15	Mill, John S. The student's handbook...of Mill's logic. London, 1891.
	Phil 2138.38.5	Mill, John S. Dissertations and discussions. v.2-5. v.1 rejected 1972. N.Y., 1873-75. 4v.
	Phil 2138.40	Mill, John S. On liberty. London, 1859.
1	Phil 2138.40.1*	Mill, John S. On liberty. London, 1859.
	Phil 2138.40.2.2	Mill, John S. On liberty. 2nd ed. Boston, 1863.
	Phil 2138.40.2.5	Mill, John S. On liberty. London, 1871.
	Phil 2138.40.3	Mill, John S. On liberty. London, 1874.
	Phil 2138.40.3.2	Mill, John S. On liberty. London, 1875.
	Phil 2138.40.4	Mill, John S. On liberty. London, 1878.
	Phil 2138.40.6	Mill, John S. On liberty. N.Y., 1895.
	Phil 2138.40.7	Mill, John S. On liberty. London, 19- .
	Phil 2138.40.8	Mill, John S. On liberty. N.Y., 19- .
	Phil 2138.40.10	Mill, John S. On liberty. London, 1903.
	Phil 2138.40.13	Mill, John S. Über die Freiheit. Frankfurt, 1860. 4 pam.
	Phil 2138.40.14	Mill, John S. Die Freiheit. Leipzig, 1928.
	Phil 2138.40.15	Mill, John S. Om friheten. Upsala, 1881.
	Phil 2138.40.16	Mill, John S. Die Freiheit (On Liberty) Übers. 3. Aufl. Darmstadt, 1970.
	Phil 2138.40.25	Mill, John S. La libertà. Torino, 1925.
	Phil 2138.40.35	Mill, John S. On liberty. N.Y., 1947.

Phil 2138 History of philosophy - Local Modern philosophy - Great Britain and United States - Individual philosophers - Mill, John Stuart - cont.

	Phil 2138.40.42	Mill, John S. On liberty. Considerations on representative government. Oxford, 1946.
	Phil 2138.40.45	Mill, John S. Prefaces to liberty. Boston, 1959.
	Phil 2138.40.46	Mill, John S. On liberty. N.Y., 1956.
	Phil 2138.40.47	Mill, John S. On liberty. London, 190-?
	Phil 2138.41	Mill, John S. On social freedom. N.Y., 1941.
	Phil 2138.45A	Mill, John S. Nature, the utility of religion and theism. London, 1874.
	Phil 2138.45B	Mill, John S. Nature, the utility of religion and theism. London, 1874.
	Phil 2138.45.2	Mill, John S. Three essays on religion. N.Y., 1874.
X Cg	Phil 2138.45.5	Mill, John S. Three essays on religion. N.Y., 1884.
	Phil 2138.45.10	Mill, John S. Three essays on religion. London, 1925.
	Phil 2138.45.12	Mill, John S. Nature, the utility of religion and theism. London, 1874.
	Phil 2138.45.15	Mill, John S. Nature, the utility of religion and theism. Westmead, Eng., 1969.
	Phil 2138.45.20	Mill, John S. Tre religions-filosofiska afhandlingar. Stockholm, 1883.
	Phil 2138.46	Mill, John S. Über Religion. Berlin, 1875.
	Phil 2138.48	Mill, John S. Philosophy of scientific method. N.Y., 1950.
Htn	Phil 2138.50.4*	Mill, John S. Utilitarianism. London, 1863.
	Phil 2138.50.5	Mill, John S. Utilitarianism. 4th ed. London, 1871.
	Phil 2138.50.6	Mill, John S. Utilitarianism. 12th ed. London, 1895.
	Phil 2138.50.8	Mill, John S. Utilitarianism. Chicago, 1906.
	Phil 2138.50.17	Mill, John S. L'utilitarisme. Paris, 1883.
	Phil 2138.50.20	Mill, John S. Utilitarianism. N.Y., 1953.
	Phil 2138.50.21	Mill, John S. Utilitarianism. Belmont, Calif., 1969.
	Phil 2138.53	Mill, John S. Considerations on representative government. N.Y., 1958.
	Phil 2138.54	Mill, John S. Essays on politics and culture. Garden City, 1962.
	Phil 2138.55	Mill, John S. The ethics of John Stuart Mill. Edinburgh, 1897.
Htn	Phil 2138.60*	Mill, John S. The subjection of women. London, 1869.
Htn	Phil 2138.65*	Mill, John S. Inaugural address to...University of St. Andrews. London, 1867.
	Phil 2138.75	Mill, John S. Lettres inédites. Paris, 1899.
	Phil 2138.76A	Mill, John S. Letters of John Stuart Mill. London, 1910. 2v.
	Phil 2138.76B	Mill, John S. Letters of John Stuart Mill. London, 1910. 2v.
	Phil 2138.77.5	Mill, John S. On Bentham and Coleridge. N.Y., 1962.
	Phil 2138.77.6	Mill, John S. Mill on Bentham and Coleridge. London, 1967.
Htn	Phil 2138.79.4*	Mill, John S. Autobiography. London, 1873.
X Cg	Phil 2138.79.6	Mill, John S. Autobiography. N.Y., 1874.
	Phil 2138.79.8.4	Mill, John S. Autobiography. N.Y., 1944.
	Phil 2138.79.8.5	Mill, John S. Autobiography. N.Y., 1957.
	Phil 2138.79.8.6	Mill, John S. Autobiography. N.Y., 1969.
	Phil 2138.79.9	Mill, John S. Mes mémoires: histoire de ma vie et de mes idées. 2e éd. Paris, 1875.
	Phil 2138.79.10	Pamphlet box. Philosophy. English. Mill, John S.
	Phil 2138.79.10.3	Mill, John S. Autobiography. N.Y., 1887.
	Phil 2138.79.10.5	Mill, John S. Autobiography. Early draft. Urbana, 1961.
	Phil 2138.79.11F	Pamphlet box. Philosophy. English. Mill, John S.
	Phil 2138.79.12	Mill, John S. John Mill's boyhood visit to France. Toronto, 1960.
	Phil 2138.80	Alexander, P.P. Mill and Carlyle. Edinburgh, 1866.
	Phil 2138.81A	Bain, A. John Stuart Mill. London, 1882.
	Phil 2138.81B	Bain, A. John Stuart Mill. London, 1882.
	Phil 2138.81C	Bain, A. John Stuart Mill. London, 1882.
	Phil 2138.81D	Bain, A. John Stuart Mill. London, 1882.
	Phil 2138.81.5	Bain, A. John Stuart Mill. N.Y., 1882.
	Phil 2138.82	Courtney, W.S. Metaphysics of John Stuart Mill. London, 1879.
	Phil 2138.82.5	Courtney, W.S. Life of John Stuart Mill. London, 1889.
	Phil 2138.82.7A	Courtney, W.S. Life of John Stuart Mill. London, 1889.
	Phil 2138.82.7B	Courtney, W.S. Life of John Stuart Mill. London, 1889.
	Phil 2138.83	Douglas, C. John Stuart Mill. Edinburgh, 1895.
	Phil 2138.84	Kohn, Benno. Untersuchungen über das Causalproblem. Wien, 1881.
	Phil 2138.85	McCosh, James. An examination of Mr. J.S. Mill's philosophy. London, 1866.
NEDL	Phil 2138.85.2	McCosh, James. An examination of Mr. J.S. Mill's philosophy. N.Y., 1866.
	Phil 2138.86	Spencer, H. John Stuart Mill. Boston, 1873.
	Phil 2138.87	Taine, H.A. Positivisme anglais. Paris, 1864.
	Phil 2138.88	Stebbing, W. Analysis of Mr. Miil's system of logic. London, 1875.
	Phil 2138.89F	Zuccante, G. La morale utilitaria dello Stuart Mill. Milano, 1899.
	Phil 2138.89.5	Zuccante, G. Giovanni Stuart Mill e l'utilitarismo. Firenze, 1922.
	Phil 2138.90	Lewels, Max. John Stuart Mill. Münster, 1902.
	Phil 2138.91	Jordan, W. Program des königlichen Gymnasiums. Stuttgart, 1870.
	Phil 2138.92	Archambault, P. Stuart Mill. Paris, n.d.
	Phil 2138.93	Gomperz, T. John Stuart Mill. Wien, 1889.
	Phil 2138.94	Crawford, J.F. The relation of inference to fact in Mill's logic. Chicago, 1916.
X Cg	Phil 2138.95	Vasey, George. Individual liberty, legal, moral, and licentious. 2nd ed. London, 1877.
	Phil 2138.96	Lauret, Henri. Philosophie de Stuart Mill. Thèse. Neufchâteau, 1885.
	Phil 2138.100	Löchen, Arne. Om J. Stuart Mills logik. Kristiania, 1885.
	Phil 2138.101	Michel, Henry. De Stuarti Millii individualismo. Thesis. Parisiis, 1895.
	Phil 2138.102	Winslow, Christian. Stuart Mills etik. København, 1909.
	Phil 2138.105	Martinazzoli, A.L. La teorica dell'individualismo secondo J.S. Mill. Milano, 1905.
	Phil 2138.106	Störring, G.W. John Stuart Mill's Theorie über den psychologischen Ursprung des Vulgärglaubens an die Aussenwelt. Inaug. Diss. Berlin, 1889.
	Phil 2138.107	Millet, J. An Millius veram mathematicorum axiomatum originem invenerit. Paris, 1867.
	Phil 2138.108	Wentscher, Ela. Das Problem des Empirismus, dargestellt an John Stuart Mill. Bonn, 1922.
	Phil 2138.110	Fabbricotti, Carlo A. Positivismo? John Stuart Mill. Firenze, 1910.
	Phil 2138.111	Street, Charles L. Individualism and individuality in the philosophy of John Stuart Mill. Milwaukee, 1926.
	Phil 2138.112	Wisniewski, J. Étude historique et critique de la théorie de la perception extérieure chez John Stuart Mill. Thèse. Paris, 1925.

134
Classified Listing

Phil 2138 History of philosophy - Local Modern philosophy - Great Britain and United States - Individual philosophers - Mill, John Stuart - cont.

Phil 2138.113 The Examiner, London. John Stuart Mill. London, 1873.
Phil 2138.114 Kubitz, O.A. Development of John S. Mill's system of logic. Thesis. Urbana, 1932.
Phil 2138.114.2 Kubitz, O.A. Development of John S. Mill's system of logic. Urbana, 1932.
Phil 2138.115 Castell, A. Mill's logic of the moral sciences. Diss. Chicago, 1936.
Phil 2138.117 Jackson, Reginald. An examination of the deductive logic of John S.Mill. London, 1941.
Phil 2138.118 Tennant, C. Utilitarianism explained and exemplified in moral and political government. In answer to John Stuart Mill's utilitarianism. London, 1864.
Phil 2138.119 Crawford, John F. The relation of inference to fact in Mill's logic. Chicago, 1916.
Phil 2138.120 Towers, C.M.D. John Stuart Mill and the London and Westminster review. v.1-2. Boston, 1892.
Phil 2138.121 Hayek, Friedrich Augustus von. John Stuart Mill and Harriet Taylor; their friendship and subsequent marriage. London, 1951.
Phil 2138.121.1 Hayek, Friedrich Augustus von. John Stuart Mill and Harriet Taylor; their correspondence and subsequent marriage. London, 1951.
Phil 2138.122 Casellato, S. Giovanni Stuart Mill e l'utilitarismo inglese. Padova, 1951.
Phil 2138.123 Anschutz, R.P. The philosophy of J.S. Mill. Oxford, 1953.
Phil 2138.124 Packe, M. The life of John Stuart Mill. London, 1954.
Phil 2138.125 Mueller, I.W. John Stuart Mill and French thought. Urbana, 1956.
Phil 2138.126 Rees, John C. Mill and his early critcs. Leicester, 1956.
Phil 2138.127 Borchard, Ruth. John Stuart Mill. London, 1957.
Phil 2138.132 Cranston, M.W. John Stuart Mill. London, 1958.
Phil 2138.135 Pappe, H. O. John Stuart Mill and the Harriet Taylor myth. Melbourne, 1960.
Phil 2138.140 Woods, Thomas. Poetry and philosophy. London, 1961.
Phil 2138.145 Berlin, Isaiah. John Stuart Mill and the ends of life. London, 1960?
Phil 2138.146 Cowling, M. Mill and liberalism. Cambridge, Eng., 1963.
Phil 2138.147 Ludwig, M. Die Sozialethik des John Stuart Mill. Zürich, 1963.
Phil 2138.148 Ellery, J.B. John Stuart Mill. N.Y., 1964.
Phil 2138.149 Arata, Fidia. La logica di J. Stuart Mill e la problematica eticosociale. Milano, 1964.
Phil 2138.150 The Mill news letter. Toronto. 1,1965+
Phil 2138.151 Weinberg, Adelaide. Theodor Gomperz and John Stuart Mill. Genève, 1963.
Phil 2138.152 Findikoğlu, Z.F. Stuart Mill ve Türkiyedeki tesirleri. Istanbul, 1963.
Phil 2138.153 Sharpless, F. Parvin. The literary criticism of J.S. Mill. The Hague, 1967.
Phil 2138.155 Robson, John Mercel. The improvement of mankind; the social and political thought of John Stuart Mill. Toronto, 1968.
Phil 2138.155.1 Robson, John Mercel. The improvement of mankind; the social and political thought of John Stuart Mill. Toronto, 1968.
Phil 2138.160 Nyman, Alf. Leviathan och folkviljan. Stockholm, 1948.
Phil 2138.165 Ryan, Alan. John Stuart Mill. N.Y., 1970.
Phil 2138.170 Schneewind, Jerome B. Mill, a collection of critical essays. Notre Dame, 1969.
Phil 2138.175 Restaino, Franco. J.S. Mill e la cultura filosofica britannica. Firenze, 1968.
Phil 2138.180 McCloskey, Henry John. John Stuart Mill: a critical study. London, 1971.

Phil 2145 History of philosophy - Local Modern philosophy - Great Britain and United States - Individual philosophers - More, Henry

Htn Phil 2145.1* More, Henry. Collection...philosophical writings. London, 1662.
Phil 2145.2 More, Henry. Collection...philosophical writings. 4th ed. London, 1712.
Htn Phil 2145.2.2* More, Henry. Collection...philosophical writings. London, 1712.
Phil 2145.15 More, Henry. Philosophical writings. N.Y., 1925.
Htn Phil 2145.40* More, Henry. Enchiridion metaphysicum. London, 1671.
Htn Phil 2145.48.5* More, Henry. Enchiridion ethicum. Amstelodami, 1679.
Htn Phil 2145.49* More, Henry. Enchiridion ethicum. Amstelodami, 1695.
Htn Phil 2145.49.5* More, Henry. Enchiridion ethicum. Amstelodami, 1695.
Phil 2145.50 More, Henry. Enchiridion ethicum. London, 1711.
Phil 2145.55A More, Henry. Enchiridion ethicum. N.Y., 1930.
Phil 2145.55B More, Henry. Enchiridion ethicum. N.Y., 1930.
Htn Phil 2145.60* More, Henry. Divine dialogues. London, 1668. 2v.
Htn Phil 2145.61* More, Henry. Divine dialogues. London, 1713.
Htn Phil 2145.65* More, Henry. Antidote against atheisme. London, 1653.
Htn Phil 2145.70* More, Henry. The immortality of the soul. London, 1659.
Phil 2145.80 Hutin, Serge. Henry More. Essai sur les doctrines théosophiques chez les platoniciens de Cambridge. Hildesheim, 1966.

Phil 2150 History of philosophy - Local Modern philosophy - Great Britain and United States - Individual philosophers - Other M

Phil 2150.1.80 Wenley, R.M. Life and work of George Sylvester Morris. N.Y., 1917.
Phil 2150.1.85 Jones, Marc Edmund. George Sylvester Morris; his philosophical career and theistic idealism. Philadelphia, 1948.
Phil 2150.1.130 Mott, F.J. The crisis of opinion. Boston, 1944.
Htn Phil 2150.2.30* Martineau, James. Types of ethical theory. Oxford, 1885. 2v.
Htn Phil 2150.3.30* Miller, William. Evidence from Scripture...the second coming of Christ. Troy, 1838.
Htn Phil 2150.4.30* Milton, Joannis. Angli pro populo anglicano defensio. Londini, 1651.
Htn Phil 2150.5.10* More, Thomas. Workes. London, 1557.
Htn Phil 2150.5.30* More, Thomas. De optimo reipublicae statu, deque nova insula Utopia. Basileae, 1518.
Htn Phil 2150.5.31* More, Henry. The immortality of the soul. London, 1659.
Htn Phil 2150.5.80* More, Thomas. Life of Sir Thomas More, by his great-grandson. London, 1726.
Phil 2150.6.01 Münsterberg, H. The library of H. Münsterberg. n.p., n.d.
Phil 2150.6.06 Pamphlet vol. Philosophy. English. Münsterberg, H. 41 pam.
Phil 2150.6.07F Pamphlet vol. Philosophy. English. Münsterberg, H. 18 pam.
Phil 2150.6.08 Pamphlet vol. Philosophy. English. Münsterberg, H. 3 vols. 85 pam.

Phil 2150 History of philosophy - Local Modern philosophy - Great Britain and United States - Individual philosophers - Other M - cont.

Phil 2150.6.30 Münsterberg, H. American patriotism and other social studies. N.Y., 1913.
Phil 2150.6.80 Münsterberg, M. Hugo Münsterberg, his life and work. N.Y., 1922.
Phil 2150.6.82F Ritschl, Otto. Die Causalbetrachtung in den Geisteswissenschaften. Bonn, 1901.
Phil 2150.6.83 Aspelin, G. Utgångspunkterna för Münsterbergs värdelära. Lund, 1929.
Phil 2150.7.90 Broad, Charles D. John McTaggart Ellis McTaggart, 1866-1925. London, 1928.
Phil 2150.7.95 Dickinson, G.L. John McTaggart Ellis McTaggart. Cambridge, Eng., 1931.
Phil 2150.7.99 Broad, Charles D. Examination of McTaggart's philosophy. Cambridge, Eng., 1933. 3v.
Phil 2150.8.79 Mackenzie, J.S. John Stuart Mackenzie. London, 1936.
Phil 2150.8.80 Testimonials in favor of J.S. Mackenzie. Glasgow, 1888. 2 pam.
Phil 2150.8.90 Muirhead, J.H. John Stuart Mackenzie, 1860-1935. London, 1936?
Phil 2150.9 Ralston, H.J. Emergent evolution...the philosophy of C. Lloyd Morgan. Boston, 1933.
Phil 2150.10.79 Pamphlet box. Philosophy. English. Murray, Henry A.
Phil 2150.11 Melzer, J.H. An examination of critical monism. Ashland, 1937.
Phil 2150.12 Muirhead, J.H. Reflections by a journeyman in philosophy. London, 1942.
Phil 2150.12.80 Ross, W.D. John Henry Muirhead. London, 1940?
Phil 2150.13A McKeon, Richard P. The philosophic bases of art and criticism. Chicago? 1944.
Phil 2150.13B McKeon, Richard P. The philosophic bases of art and criticism. Chicago? 1944.
Phil 2150.13.6 McKeon, Richard P. Thought, action and passion. Chicago, 1968.
Phil 2150.14.30 McMahon, T.E. A Catholic looks at the world. N.Y., 1945.
Phil 2150.15.20 Mead, George Herbert. Selected writings. Indianapolis, 1964.
Phil 2150.15.30 Mead, George Herbert. George Herbert Mead. N.Y., 1968.
Phil 2150.15.80 Lee, G.C. George Herbert Mead. N.Y., 1945.
Phil 2150.15.86 Pfuetze, P.E. Self, society, existence. N.Y., 1961.
Phil 2150.15.90 Victoroff, David. G.H. Mead, sociologue et philosophe. 1. ed. Paris, 1953.
Phil 2150.15.95 Mead, G.H. The social psychology of George Herbert Meal. Chicago, 1956.
Phil 2150.15.96 Meltzer, Bernard. The social psychology of George Herbert Mead. Kalamazoo, Michigan, 1964.
Phil 2150.15.100 Natanson, M. The social dynamics of George H. Mead. Washington, 1956.
Phil 2150.15.105 Tremmel, William C. The social concepts of George Herbert Mead. Emporia, 1957.
Phil 2150.15.107 Tremmel, William C. The social concepts of George Herbert Mead. Emporia, 1927.
Phil 2150.16.30 Mayer, Frederick. Essentialism. London, 1950.
Phil 2150.16.35 Mayer, Frederick. Patterns of a new philosophy. Washington, 1955.
Phil 2150.16.40 Mayer, Frederick. Education and the good life. Washington, 1957.
Phil 2150.16.45 Mayer, Frederick. New perspectives for education. Washington, 1962.
Phil 2150.17.90 Rossi-Landi, Ferruccio. Charles Morris. 1st ed. Roma, 1953.
Phil 2150.17.94A Mayo, Elton. Excerpts from civilization - the perilous adventure. Cambridge, Mass. 19- .
Phil 2150.17.94B Mayo, Elton. Excerpts from civilization - the perilous adventure. Cambridge, Mass., 19- .
Phil 2150.17.95A Mayo, Elton. Notes on a lecture on equilibrium. Cambridge, 1946?
Phil 2150.17.95B Mayo, Elton. Notes on a lecture on equilibrium. Cambridge, 1946?
Phil 2150.18.30 Moore, George Edward. Some main problems of philosophy. London, 1953.
Phil 2150.18.35 Moore, George Edward. Philosophical papers. London, 1959.
Phil 2150.18.40 Moore, George Edward. Commonplace book, 1919-1953. London, 1962.
Phil 2150.18.45 Addis, Laird. Moore and Ryle: two ontologists. Iowa City, 1965.
Phil 2150.18.50 Moore, George Edward. Lectures on philosophy. London, 1966.
Phil 2150.18.80 Campanale, D. Filosofia ed etica scientifica. Bari, 1962.
Phil 2150.18.85 Brunius, Teddy. G.E. Moore's analyses of beauty. Uppsala, 1964[1965].
Phil 2150.18.90 Lewy, C. G.E. Moore on the naturalistic fallacy. London, 1964.
Phil 2150.18.95 Hund, William Byrne. The theory of goodness in the writings of George Edward Moore, 1873-1958. Notre Dame, Ind., 1964.
Phil 2150.18.100 Olthuis, James H. Facts, values and ethics. Assen, 1968.
Phil 2150.18.105 Klemke, E.D. Studies in the philosophy of G.E. Moore. Chicago, 1969.
Phil 2150.18.105.5 Klemke, E.D. The epistemology of G.E. Moore. Evanston, 1969.
Phil 2150.18.110 Ambrose, Alice. G.E. Moore; essays in retrospect. London, 1970.
Phil 2150.18.115 Granese, Alberto. G.E. Moore e la filosofia analitica inglese. Firenze, 1970.
Phil 2150.19.30 McGilvary, E.B. Toward a perspective realism. LaSalle, Ill., 1956.
Phil 2150.20.30 Murty, K. Satchidanda. Metaphysics, man and freedom. N.Y., 1963.
Phil 2150.21.80 Carver, Vida. C.A. Mace: a symposium. London, 1962.
Phil 2150.22.30 Marcuse, Herbert. Kultur und Gesellschaft. Frankfurt, 1965. 2v.
Phil 2150.22.35 Marcuse, Herbert. An essay on liberation. Boston, 1969.
Phil 2150.22.38 Marcuse, Herbert. Negations; essays in critical theory. Boston, 1968.
Phil 2150.22.40.2 Marcuse, Herbert. Ideen zu einer kritischen Theorie der Gesellschaft. 2e Aufl. Frankfurt, 1969.
Phil 2150.22.42 Marcuse, Herbert. Five lectures. Boston, 1970.
Phil 2150.22.80 Antworten auf Herbert Marcuse. Frankfurt, 1968.
Phil 2150.22.85 Holz, Hans Heinz. Utopie und Anarchismus; zur Kritik der kritischen Theorie H. Marcuses. Köln, 1968.
Phil 2150.22.90 Perlini, Tito. Che cosa ha veramente detto Marcuse. Roma, 1968.
Phil 2150.22.97 Proto, Mario. Introduzione a Marcuse. 2. ed. Manduria, 1968.

Phil 2150 History of philosophy - Local Modern philosophy - Great Britain and United States - Individual philosophers - Other M - cont.

Phil 2150.22.100 Doria, Francisco Antônio. Marcuse, vida e obra. Rio de Janeiro, 1969.
Phil 2150.22.105 Perroux, François. François Perroux interroge Herbert Marcuse qui repond. Paris, 1969.
Phil 2150.22.110 Palmier, Jean Michel. Présentation d'Herbert Marcuse. Paris, 1969.
Phil 2150.22.115 Steigerwald, Robert Reinhold. Herbert Marcuses dritter Weg. Köln, 1969.
Phil 2150.22.120 Nicolas, André. Herbert Marcuse ou la Quête d'un univers trans-prométhéen. Paris, 1969.
Phil 2150.22.125 Ambacher, Michel. Marcuse et la critique de la civilisation américaine. Paris, 1969.
Phil 2150.22.130 Delbo, Charlotte. La théorie et la pratique, dialogue imaginaire mais non tout à fait apocryphe entre Herbert Marcuse et Henri Lefebvre. Paris, 1969.
Phil 2150.22.135 MacIntyre, Alasdair C. Herbert Marcuse: and exposition and a polemic. N.Y., 1970.
Phil 2150.22.140 Masset, Pierre. La pensée de Herbert Marcuse. Toulouse, 1969.
Phil 2150.22.145 Ulle, Dieter. E'rivoluzionaria la dottrina di Marcuse? Torino, 1969.
Phil 2150.22.150 Szewczyk, Jan. Eros i rewolucja. Wyd. 1. Warszawa, 1971.
Phil 2150.23 Morgan, Arthur Ernest. Observations. Yellow Springs, 1968.
Phil 2150.24.30 Mika, Lumir Victor. Thinker's handbook. Columbia, Mo., 1947.

Phil 2175 History of philosophy - Local Modern philosophy - Great Britain and United States - Individual philosophers - N

Htn Phil 2175.1.30* Newman, John H. Apologia pro vita sua. pt.1-7. London, 1864. 3 pam.
Htn Phil 2175.2.30* Norris, John. The theory and regulation of love. Oxford, 1688.
Htn Phil 2175.2.35* Norris, John. The picture of love unveil'd. 4. ed. London, 1744.
Htn Phil 2175.2.40* Norris, John. An essay towards the theory of the world. London, 1701. 2v.
Htn Phil 2175.2.45* Norris, John. Reflections on the conduct of human life. 2nd ed. London, 1691-93. 2 pam.
Htn Phil 2175.2.49* Norris, John. Reflections on the conduct of human life. London, 1690.
Htn Phil 2175.2.50*B Norris, John. Reflections on the conduct of human life. 2. ed. London, 1691.
Htn Phil 2175.2.55* Norris, John. An essay towards the theory of the ideal or intelligible world. pt.1-2. London, 1701-04. 2v.
Phil 2175.3.30 Neilson, Francis. The roots of our learning. N.Y., 1947.
Phil 2175.4.30 Northrop, F.S.C. The logic of the sciences and the humanities. N.Y., 1947.
Phil 2175.4.35 Northrop, F.S.C. Man, nature and God. N.Y., 1962.
Phil 2175.5.30 Nicoll, Maurice. Living time and the integration of the life. London, 1953.
Phil 2175.5.80 Pogson, Beryl. Maurice Nicoll. London, 1961.

Phil 2190 History of philosophy - Local Modern philosophy - Great Britain and United States - Individual philosophers - Occam, William

Phil 2190.5 Lornay, Stephen Clark. Ockham. LaSalle, Ill., 1938.
Phil 2190.10 Martin, G. Wilhelm von Ockham. Berlin, 1949.
Phil 2190.15 Giacon, C. Guglielmo di Occam. Milano, 1941. 2v.
Phil 2190.20 Miethke, Jürgen. Ockhams Weg zur Sozialphilosophie. Berlin, 1969.

Phil 2193 History of philosophy - Local Modern philosophy - Great Britain and United States - Individual philosophers - Oswald, James

Phil 2193.30 Oswald, J. An appeal to common sense in behalf of religion. Edinburgh, 1766-72. 2v.
Phil 2193.30.2 Oswald, J. An appeal to common sense in behalf of religion. London, 1768-72. 2v.

Phil 2200 History of philosophy - Local Modern philosophy - Great Britain and United States - Individual philosophers - Other O

Phil 2200.1 Otto, Max Carl. The human enterprise. N.Y., 1940.
Phil 2200.5A Otto, Max Carl. Science and the moral life. N.Y., 1949.
Phil 2200.5B Otto, Max Carl. Science and the moral life. N.Y., 1949.
Phil 2200.5.80 Burkhardt, F. The cleavage in our culture. Boston, 1952.
Phil 2200.10 Osborn, Arthur W. The expansion of awareness. Reigate, 1955.

Phil 2205 History of philosophy - Local Modern philosophy - Great Britain and United States - Individual philosophers - Paley, William

Phil 2205.1 Paley, W. Principles of moral and political philosophy. London, 1785.
Phil 2205.10 Paley, W. Works. Boston, 1810-12. 5v.
Phil 2205.10.5 Paley, W. Works. v.1,3-5. Boston, 1812. 4v.
Phil 2205.11 Paley, W. Works. London, 1825. 5v.
Phil 2205.11.5 Paley, W. Works. Cambridge, 1830. 6v.
Phil 2205.12 Paley, W. Works. Edinburgh, 1833.
Phil 2205.13 Paley, W. Works. London, 1823. 5v.
Phil 2205.13.15 Paley, W. Works. London, 1838. 4v.
Phil 2205.14 Paley, W. Works. Philadelphia, 1850.
Phil 2205.15 Paley, W. Works. London, 1851.
Phil 2205.30 Paley, W. Natural theology. London, 1803.
Phil 2205.30.2 Paley, W. Natural theology. Philadelphia, 1814.
DL Phil 2205.30.3 Paley, W. Natural theology. Philadelphia, 1814.
Phil 2205.30.4 Paley, W. Natural theology. London, 1822.
Phil 2205.30.5 Paley, W. Natural theology. Boston, 1854.
Phil 2205.30.6 Paley, W. Natural theology. N.Y., n.d. 2 pam.
Phil 2205.30.7 Paley, W. Natural theology. London, 1836. 2v.
Phil 2205.30.7.5 Paley, W. Natural theology. London, 1836. 2v.
Phil 2205.30.8 Brougham and Vaux, Henry Brougham. Discourse of natural theology. London, 1835.
Phil 2205.30.9 Paley, W. Natural theology. Boston, 1829.
DL Phil 2205.30.10 Paley, W. Natural theology. 10th ed. London, 1805.
DL Phil 2205.30.11 Paley, W. Natural theology. Philadelphia, 1814.
Phil 2205.30.12 Paley, W. Natural theology. Albany, 1803.
Phil 2205.30.13 Paley, W. Natural theology. Boston, 1831.
Phil 2205.30.14 Paley, W. Natural theology. Trenton, N.J., 1824.
Phil 2205.30.15 Paley, W. Natural theology. Boston, 1857.
Phil 2205.30.17* Paley, W. Natural theology. Hallowell, 1819.
Phil 2205.30.18 Paley, W. Natural theology. Hallowell, 1819.
Phil 2205.31 Paley, W. Theologia naturale. Roma, 1808.
Phil 2205.32 Paxton, J. Illustrations of Paley's natural theology. Boston, 1827.
Phil 2205.39* Paley, W. Principles of moral and political philosophy. London, 1785.
Phil 2205.39.5 Paley, W. Principles of moral and political philosophy. London, 1786.

Phil 2205 History of philosophy - Local Modern philosophy - Great Britain and United States - Individual philosophers - Paley, William - cont.

Phil 2205.40 Paley, W. Principles of moral and political philosophy. Paris, 1788.
Phil 2205.40.2 Paley, W. Principles of moral and political philosophy. Boston, 1795.
Phil 2205.40.2.5 Paley, W. Principles of moral and political philosophy. Boston, 1801.
Phil 2205.40.3 Paley, W. Principles of moral and political philosophy. London, 1804. 2v.
Phil 2205.40.4 Paley, W. Principles of moral and political philosophy. Boston, 1810.
Phil 2205.40.5 Paley, W. Principles of moral and political philosophy. Boston, 1811.
Phil 2205.40.6 Paley, W. Principles of moral and political philosophy. Boston, 1815.
Phil 2205.40.7 Paley, W. Principles of moral and political philosophy. Boston, 1830. 2v.
Phil 2205.40.8 Paley, W. Principles of moral and political philosophy. N.Y., 1817.
Phil 2205.40.8.5 Paley, W. Principles of moral and political philosophy. 11th American ed. Boston, 1825.
Phil 2205.40.9 Paley, W. Principles of moral and political philosophy. v.1-2. Boston, 1828.
Phil 2205.40.10 Paley, W. Principles of moral and political philosophy. N.Y., 1824.
Phil 2205.40.11 Paley, W. Principles of moral and political philosophy. Boston, 1827.
Phil 2205.40.13 Paley, W. Paley's moral philosophy. N.Y., 1828.
Phil 2205.40.14 Paley, W. The principles of moral and political philosophy. Boston, 1831. 2v.
Phil 2205.40.15 Paley, W. Paley's moral philosophy. London, 1859.
Phil 2205.40.30 Paley, W. Grundsätze der Moral und Politik. Leipzig, 1787. 2v.
Phil 2205.80 Pearson, Edward. Annotations on the practical part of Dr. Paley's Principles of moral and political philosophy. Ipswich, 1801.
Phil 2205.80.5 Pearson, Edward. Remarks on the theory of morals in which is contained an examination of the theoretical part of Dr. Paley's Principles of moral and political philosophy. Ipswich, 1800.
Phil 2205.81 Wainewright, L. A vindication of Dr. Paley's theory of morals. London, 1830.
Phil 2205.82 Croft, G. A short commentary, with strictures on certain parts of the moral writings of Dr. Paley and Mr. Gisborne. Birmingham, 1797.
Phil 2205.83 Meadley, G.W. Memoirs of William Paley, D.D. Sunderland, 1809. 2 pam.
Phil 2205.84.5 Holyoake, G.J. Paley's natural theology refuted in his own words. London, 1851.

Phil 2215 History of philosophy - Local Modern philosophy - Great Britain and United States - Individual philosophers - Price, Richard

Htn Phil 2215.30* Price, Richard. A review of the principal questions and difficulties in morals. London, 1758.
Phil 2215.30.2 Price, Richard. A review of the principal questions and difficulties in morals. 2d ed. London, 1769.
Phil 2215.30.3 Price, Richard. A review of the principal questions in morals. 3d ed. London, 1787.
Phil 2215.80 Cua, Antonio S. Reason and virtue; a study in the ethics of Richard Price. Athens, 1966.
Phil 2215.85 Hudson, William Donald. Reason and right: a critical examination of Richard Price's philosophy. London, 1970.

Phil 2218 History of philosophy - Local Modern philosophy - Great Britain and United States - Individual philosophers - Priestley, Joseph

Phil 2218.01 Pamphlet box. Philosophy. English. Priestley, Joseph.
Phil 2218.29 Priestley, Joseph. Disquisitions relating to matter and spirit. 1st ed. London, 1777.
Phil 2218.30 Priestley, Joseph. Disquisitions relating to matter and spirit. Birmingham, 1778-82. 3v.
Phil 2218.35 Priestley, Joseph. Institutes of natural and revealed religion. 2nd ed. Birmingham, 1782. 2v.
Phil 2218.40 Priestley, Joseph. An examination of Dr. Reid's Inquiry. 2d. ed. London, 1775.
Htn Phil 2218.45* Priestley, Joseph. The doctrine of philosophical necessity. London, 1777.
Phil 2218.47 Priestley, Joseph. A scientific autobiography of Joseph Priestley, 1733-1804. Cambridge, 1966.
Phil 2218.50 Priestley, Joseph. A continuation of the letters to the philosophers and politicians of France. Salem, 1795.
Phil 2218.55 Priestley, Joseph. Selections from his writings. University Park, 1962.
Phil 2218.60 Priestley, Joseph. Writings on philosophy, science and politics. 1st ed. N.Y., 1965.
Phil 2218.80 Corry, J. The life of Joseph Priestley. Birmingham, 1804.
Phil 2218.81 Priestley, Joseph. Memoirs. London, 1805-07. 2v.
Phil 2218.81.2 Priestley, Joseph. Memoirs. London, 1806. 2v.
Phil 2218.82 Birmingham, England. Priestley memorial. Photoreproduction. London, 1875.
Phil 2218.83 Pures, J. Observations. Philadelphia, 1797.
Phil 2218.84 Palmer, J. Observations. v.1-2. London, 1779.
Phil 2218.85 Observations on the emigration of Joseph Priestley. London, 1794.
Phil 2218.85.5 Cobbett, William. Observations on the emigration of Joseph Priestley. Philadelphia, 1794.
Phil 2218.86A Thorpe, J.E. Joseph Priestley. London, 1906.
Phil 2218.86B Thorpe, J.E. Joseph Priestley. London, 1906.
Phil 2218.87 Sigsbee, Ray A. Das philosophische System Joseph Priestleys. Heidelberg, 1912.
Phil 2218.88 Park, Mary Cathryne. Joseph Priestley and the problem of pantiscocracy. Diss. Philadelphia, 1947.
Phil 2218.89 Park, Mary Cathryne. Joseph Priestley and the problem of pantiscocracy. Philadelphia, 1947.
Phil 2218.90 Crook, Ronald E. A bibliography of Joseph Priestley, 1733-1804. London, 1966.

Phil 2225 History of philosophy - Local Modern philosophy - Great Britain and United States - Individual philosophers - Other P

Phil 2225.1.80 Judd, W.B. Noah Porters Erkenntnislehre. Jena, 1897.
Phil 2225.2.30A Perry, R.B. Realms of value. Cambridge, Mass., 1954.
Phil 2225.2.30B Perry, R.B. Realms of value. Cambridge, Mass., 1954.
Phil 2225.2.35 Perry, R.B. The humanity of man. N.Y., 1956.
Phil 2225.2.79 Pamphlet box. Philosophy. English. Perry, R.B.
Phil 2225.2.80 Jacoby, Günther. Die "neue Wirklichkeitslehre". Berlin, 1914?
Phil 2225.2.85 Steinberg, Ira Sherman. Ralph Barton Perry on education for democracy. Columbus, 1970.

Phil 2225   History of philosophy - Local Modern philosophy - Great Britain and United States - Individual philosophers - Other P - cont.

Htn   Phil 2225.3.30*   Paine, Thomas. The age of reason. Paris, 1794.
Htn   Phil 2225.3.35*   Paine, Thomas. Examination of...passages in the New Testament. N.Y., n.d.
Htn   Phil 2225.3.80*   Williams, Thomas. The age of infidelity...answer to the second part of The age of reason. Philadelphia, 1796.
Htn   Phil 2225.4.30*   Peacham, Henry. The compleat gentleman. London, 1622.
         Phil 2225.5.06   Pamphlet vol. Philosophy. English. Peirce, C.S. 9 pam.
         Phil 2225.5.07F   Pamphlet vol. Philosophy. English. Peirce, C.S. 3 pam.
         Phil 2225.5.10A   Peirce, C.S. Collected papers. Cambridge, 1931. 8v.
         Phil 2225.5.10B   Peirce, C.S. Collected papers. Cambridge, 1931.
         Phil 2225.5.20   Peirce, C.S. Essays in the philosophy of science. N.Y., 1957.
         Phil 2225.5.25   Peirce, C.S. The philosophy of Peirce; selected writings. London, 1940.
         Phil 2225.5.27   Peirce, C.S. Letters to Lady Welby. Photoreproduction. New Haven, 1953.
         Phil 2225.5.30   Peirce, C.S. Chance, love, and logic. N.Y., 1923.
         Phil 2225.5.35   Peirce, C.S. Chance, love, and logic. N.Y., 1949.
         Phil 2225.5.40   Peirce, C.S. Values in a universe of chance. Stanford, 1958.
         Phil 2225.5.50A   Peirce, C.S. Collected papers. v.1-6. Cambridge, 1960. 3v.
         Phil 2225.5.50B   Peirce, C.S. Collected papers. v.1-6. Cambridge, 1960. 3v.
         Phil 2225.5.55.5   Peirce, C.S. Über die Klarheit unserer Gedanken. Frankfurt, 1968.
         Phil 2225.5.80   Buchler, J. Charles Peirce's empiricism. N.Y., 1939.
         Phil 2225.5.85   Wiener, P.P. Studies in the philosophy of Charles Sanders Peirce. Cambridge, Mass., 1952.
         Phil 2225.5.88   Boler, J.F. Charles Peirce and scholastic realism. Seattle, 1963.
         Phil 2225.5.90   Hartshorne, Charles. Continuity, the form of forms in Charles Peirce. n.p., 1929.
         Phil 2225.5.93   Gallie, W.B. Peirce and pragmatism. Harmondsworth, 1952.
         Phil 2225.5.95   Feuer, L.S. Review: Collected papers of Charles Sanders Peirce. v.6. Scientific metaphysics. Bruges, 1932.
         Phil 2225.5.97   Freeman, Eugene. The categories of Charles Peirce. Diss. Chicago, 193-.
         Phil 2225.5.98   Thompson, M.H. The pragmatic philosophy of C.S. Pierce. Part of thesis. Chicago, 1945.
         Phil 2225.5.98.5   Thompson, M.H. The pragmatic philosophy of C.S. Peirce. Chicago, 1953.
         Phil 2225.5.100   Feibleman, James. An introduction to Peirce's philosophy. 1st ed. N.Y., 1946.
         Phil 2225.5.102   Goudge, T.A. The thought of C.S. Peirce. Toronto, 1950.
         Phil 2225.5.104   Murphey, M.G. The development of Peirce's philosophy. Cambridge, 1961.
         Phil 2225.5.106   Mullin, Albert A. Philosophical comments on the philosophies of Charles S. Peirce and Ludwig Wittgenstein. Urbana, Ill., 1961.
         Phil 2225.5.110   Haas, W.P. The conception of law. Fribourg, 1964.
         Phil 2225.5.115   Knight, Thomas Stanley. Charles Peirce. N.Y., 1965.
         Phil 2225.5.120A   Moore, Edward C. Studies in the philosophy of Charles Sanders Peirce. 2nd series. Amherst, 1964.
         Phil 2225.5.120B   Moore, Edward C. Studies in the philosophy of Charles Sanders Peirce. 2nd series. Amherst, 1964.
         Phil 2225.5.125   Bernstein, Richard J. Perspectives on Peirce. New Haven, 1965.
         Phil 2225.5.130   Buczyńska, Hanna. Peirce. Warszawa, 1965.
         Phil 2225.5.135   Fitzgerald, John J. Peirce's theory of signs as foundation for pragmatism. The Hague, 1966.
         Phil 2225.5.140   Charles S. Pierce Society. Transactions. Amherst. 1,1965+ 2v.
VPhil 2225.5.145   Dobrosielski, Marian. Filozoficzny pragmatyzm C.S. Peirce'a. Warszawa, 1967.
         Phil 2225.5.150   Potter, Vincent G. Charles S. Peirce on norms and ideals. Amherst, 1967.
         Phil 2225.5.155   Ayer, Alfred Jules. The origins of pragmatism: studies in the philosophy of Charles Sanders Peirce and William James. London, 1968.
         Phil 2225.5.160   Mel'vil', Iurii K. Charlz Pirs i pragmatizm. Moskva, 1968.
         Phil 2225.5.165   Reilly, Francis E. Charles Peirce's theory of scientific method. N.Y., 1970.
         Phil 2225.5.170   Fann, K.T. Peirce's theory of abduction. The Hague, 1970.
         Phil 2225.5.175   Salanitro, Niccolò. Peirce e i problemi dell'interpretazione. Roma, 1969.
         Phil 2225.6.80   Spettmann, P.H. Die Psychologie des Johannes Pecham. Inaug. Diss. Münster, 1919.
Htn   Phil 2225.7.30*   Palmer, George H. The teacher. Boston, 1908.
Htn   Phil 2225.7.32*   Fitzgerald, John J. The new education; three papers. Boston, 1887.
         Phil 2225.7.85A   Ayer, Alfred Jules. The autobiography of a philosopher. Boston, 1930.
         Phil 2225.7.85B   Ayer, Alfred Jules. The autobiography of a philosopher. Boston, 1930.
         Phil 2225.7.87   Ayer, Alfred Jules. The autobiography of a philosopher. Boston, 1930.
         Phil 2225.7.90A   George Herbert Palmer, 1842-1933; memorial addressses. Cambridge, 1935.
         Phil 2225.7.90B   George Herbert Palmer, 1842-1933; memorial addressses. Cambridge, 1935.
         Phil 2225.8   Paterson, William R. The passions of life. London, 1938.
         Phil 2225.9   Perry, C.M. Toward a dimensional realism. Norman, Okla., 1939.
         Phil 2225.10   Parker, D.H. Experience and substance. Ann Arbor, 1941.
         Phil 2225.11   Pepper, Stephen Coburn. A digest of purposive values. Berkeley, 1947.
         Phil 2225.11.5   Pepper, Stephen Coburn. World hypotheses. Berkeley, 1957.
         Phil 2225.11.10   Pepper, Stephen Coburn. Concept and quality; a world hypothesis. La Salle, 1967.
         Phil 2225.12   Paton, H.J. In defence of reason. London, 1951.
         Phil 2225.14   Pearson, A.N. A search for knowledge. Melbourne, 1889.
         Phil 2225.15   Pols, E. The recognition of reason. Carbondale, 1963.
         Phil 2225.16.80   Wellmer, Albrecht. Methodologie als Erkenntnistheorie. Frankfurt, 1967.
         Phil 2225.18   Langford, Thomas A. Intellect and hope; essays in the thought of Michael Polanyi. Durham, 1968.

Phil 2230   History of philosophy - Local Modern philosophy - Great Britain and United States - Individual philosophers - Quimby, Phineas P.

         Phil 2230.5A   Dresser, A.G. The philosophy of P.P. Quimby. Boston, 1895.
         Phil 2230.5B   Dresser, A.G. The philosophy of P.P. Quimby. Boston, 1895.
Htn   Phil 2230.10*   Quimby, P.P. The Quimby manuscripts. 1st ed. N.Y., 1921.
X Cg   Phil 2230.10.5   Quimby, P.P. The Quimby manuscripts. N.Y., 1921.
         Phil 2230.95   Dresser, J.A. The true history of mental science. Boston, 1899.

Phil 2240   History of philosophy - Local Modern philosophy - Great Britain and United States - Individual philosophers - Reid, Thomas

         Phil 2240.10   Reid, Thomas. Works. Charlestown, 1813-15. 4v.
         Phil 2240.12   Reid, Thomas. Works. N.Y., 1822. 3v.
         Phil 2240.14   Reid, Thomas. Works. Edinburgh, 1853. 2v.
         Phil 2240.20   Reid, Thomas. Oeuvres complètes. Paris, 1828-36. 6v.
         Phil 2240.25   Reid, Thomas. Essays on the active powers of the human mind. London, 1843.
         Phil 2240.30A   Reid, Thomas. An inquiry into the human mind. Edinburgh, 1764.
Htn   Phil 2240.30*B   Reid, Thomas. An inquiry into the human mind. Edinburgh, 1764.
         Phil 2240.30.2A   Reid, Thomas. An inquiry into the human mind. 2nd ed. Edinburgh, 1765.
         Phil 2240.30.2B   Reid, Thomas. An inquiry into the human mind. 2nd ed. Edinburgh, 1765.
         Phil 2240.31   Reid, Thomas. An inquiry into the human mind. 4th ed. London, 1785.
         Phil 2240.32   Reid, Thomas. An inquiry into the human mind. N.Y., 1824.
Htn   Phil 2240.33*   Reid, Thomas. Essays on the active powers of man. Edinburgh, 1788.
         Phil 2240.35   Reid, Thomas. The philosophy of Reid...in the "Inquiry into the human mind". N.Y., 1892.
         Phil 2240.49   Reid, Thomas. Essays on the intellectual and active powers of man. v.3. Dublin, 1790.
         Phil 2240.50   Reid, Thomas. Essays on the powers of the human mind. Edinburgh, 1803. 3v.
Htn   Phil 2240.58*   Reid, Thomas. Essays on the intellectual powers of man. Edinburgh, 1785.
         Phil 2240.59   Reid, Thomas. Essays on the intellectual powers of man. Dublin, 1786. 2v.
         Phil 2240.60   Reid, Thomas. Essays on the intellectual powers of man. Cambridge, 1850.
         Phil 2240.60.3   Reid, Thomas. Essays on the intellectual powers of man. 3rd ed. Cambridge, 1852.
Htn   Phil 2240.60.4*   Reid, Thomas. Essays on the intellectual powers of man. 4th ed. Cambridge, 1853.
         Phil 2240.60.6A   Reid, Thomas. Essays on the intellectual powers of man. 6th ed. Boston, 1855.
         Phil 2240.60.6B   Reid, Thomas. Essays on the intellectual powers of man. 6th ed. Boston, 1855.
         Phil 2240.60.30   Reid, Thomas. Essays on the intellectual powers of man. London, 1941.
         Phil 2240.60.31   Reid, Thomas. Essays on the intellectual powers of man. Cambridge, 1969.
         Phil 2240.61   Reid, Thomas. Philosophical orations of Thomas Reid. Aberdeen, 1937.
         Phil 2240.80   Garnier, A. Critique de la philosophie de Thomas Reid. Paris, 1840.
         Phil 2240.81   Fraser, A.C. Thomas Reid. London, 1898.
         Phil 2240.82   Kappes, M. Der "common sense" als Princip der Gewissheit. München, 1890.
         Phil 2240.84   Jones, O.McK. Empiricism and intuitionism in Reid's common sense philosophy. Princeton, 1927.
         Phil 2240.85   Sciacca, M.F. La filosofia di Tomaso Reid. Napoli, 1935.
         Phil 2240.85.3   Sciacca, M.F. La filosofia di Tommaso Reid. 3a ed. Milano, 1963.
         Phil 2240.87   Dür, Seweryn. Reid a Kant. Opole, 1963.
         Phil 2240.88   Reid, Thomas. Essays on the active powers of the human mind. Cambridge, Mass., 1969.

Phil 2250   History of philosophy - Local Modern philosophy - Great Britain and United States - Individual philosophers - Royce, Josiah

         Phil 2250.10   Royce, Josiah. Logical essays. Dubuque, Iowa, 1951.
         Phil 2250.15   Royce, Josiah. The basic writings of Josiah Royce. Chicago, 1969. 2v.
         Phil 2250.25   Royce, Josiah. Letters. Chicago, 1970.
Htn   Phil 2250.30*   Royce, Josiah. The intention of the Prometheus Bound of Aeschylus. Thesis. Berkeley, 1875.
Htn   Phil 2250.35*   Royce, Josiah. Primer of logical analysis. San Francisco, 1881.
         Phil 2250.43.5   Royce, Josiah. Il mondo e l'individuo. Bari, 1913-14. 4v.
         Phil 2250.45A   Royce, Josiah. Lectures on modern idealism. New Haven, 1919.
         Phil 2250.45B   Royce, Josiah. Lectures on modern idealism. New Haven, 1919.
         Phil 2250.45.5   Royce, Josiah. Lectures on modern idealism. New Haven, 1923.
         Phil 2250.51   Royce, Josiah. La filosofia della fedeltá. Bari, 1911.
         Phil 2250.55   Royce, Josiah. Fugitive essays. Cambridge, 1920.
         Phil 2250.60   Royce, Josiah. The social philosophy of Josiah Royce. Syracuse, 1950.
         Phil 2250.60B   Royce, Josiah. The social philosophy of Josiah Royce. Syracuse, 1950.
         Phil 2250.62   Royce, Josiah. The religious philosophy of Josiah Royce. Syracuse, 1952.
         Phil 2250.65   Royce, Josiah. Studies of good and evil. Hamden, 1898.
         Phil 2250.70   Royce, Josiah. The philosophy of Josiah Royce. N.Y., 1971.
         Phil 2250.79   Pamphlet box. Philosophy. English. Royce, Josiah. Biography.
         Phil 2250.80   Papers in honor of Josiah Royce on his sixtieth birthday. Lancaster, Pa., 1916.
         Phil 2250.85   Galgano, Maria. Il pensiero filosofico e morale di Josiah Royce. Roma, 1921.
         Phil 2250.86   Raccuglia, Pietro. Il concetto sintetico del reale e la sua evoluzione nel pensiero di Josiah Royce. Palermo, 1920.
         Phil 2250.87   Aronson, M.J. La philosophie morale de Josiah Royce. Paris, 1927.
         Phil 2250.87.2   Aronson, M.J. La philosophie morale de Josiah Royce. Thèse. Paris, 1927.
         Phil 2250.88   Rothman, W. Josiah Royces Versuch einer Synthese von Pragmatismus und Objektivität. Inaug. Diss. Jena, 1926.

Classified Listing

Phil 2250 History of philosophy - Local Modern philosophy - Great Britain and United States - Individual philosophers - Royce, Josiah - cont.

Phil 2250.88.2 Rothman, W. Josiah Royces Versuch einer Synthese von Pragmatismus und Objektivität. Jena, 1926.
Phil 2250.89 Albeggiani, F. Il sistema filosofico di Josiah Royce. Palermo, 1930.
Phil 2250.90 Leidecker, K.F. Josiah Royce and Indian thought. N.Y., 1931.
Phil 2250.91 Norborg, Sven. Josiah Royce. Oslo, 1934.
Phil 2250.92 Dykhuizen, George. The conception of God in the philosophy of Josiah Royce. Chicago, 1936.
Phil 2250.94 Marcel, Gabriel. La métaphysique de Royce. Paris, 1945.
Phil 2250.94.5 Marcel, Gabriel. Royce's metaphysics. Chicago, 1956.
Phil 2250.96 Smith, J.E. Royce's social infinite. N.Y., 1950.
Phil 2250.100A Catton, J.B. Royce on the human self. Cambridge, 1954.
Phil 2250.100B Catton, J.B. Royce on the human self. Cambridge, 1954.
Phil 2250.105A Loewenberg, j. Royce's synoptic vision. n.p., 1955.
Phil 2250.105B Loewenberg, J. Royce's synoptic vision. n.p., 1955.
Phil 2250.106 Costello, Harry. Josiah Royce's seminar, 1913-1914. New Brunswick, 1963.
Phil 2250.110 Humbach, K.T. Das Verhältnis von Einzelperson und Gemeinschaft nach Josiah Royce. Heidelberg, 1962.
Phil 2250.112 Buranelli, V. Josiah Royce. N.Y., 1964.
Phil 2250.113 Fuss, Peter Lawrence. The moral philosophy of Josiah Royce. Cambridge, 1965.
Phil 2250.116 Robinson, Daniel Sommer. Royce and Hocking: American idealists. Boston, 1968.

Phil 2255 History of philosophy - Local Modern philosophy - Great Britain and United States - Individual philosophers - Other R

Phil 2255.1.10A Russell, Bertrand Russell. Selected papers. N.Y., 1927.
Phil 2255.1.10B Russell, Bertrand Russell. Selected papers. N.Y., 1927.
Phil 2255.1.10C Russell, Bertrand Russell. Selected papers. N.Y., 1927.
Phil 2255.1.10D Russell, Bertrand Russell. Selected papers. N.Y., 1927.
Phil 2255.1.15 Russell, Bertrand Russell. The autobiography of Bertrand Russell, 1872-1914. 1st American ed. Boston, 1967. 3v.
Phil 2255.1.20 Russell, Bertrand Russell. La filosofía en el siglo XX y otros ensayos. Montevideo, 1962.
Phil 2255.1.30A Russell, Bertrand Russell. Philosophy. N.Y., 1927.
Phil 2255.1.30B Russell, Bertrand Russell. Philosophy. N.Y., 1927.
Phil 2255.1.32 Russell, Bertrand Russell. My philosophical development. London, 1959.
Phil 2255.1.35 Dewey, John. The Bertrand Russell case. N.Y., 1941.
Phil 2255.1.36 Russell, Bertrand Russell. Let the people think. 2nd ed. London, 1961.
Phil 2255.1.38 Russell, Bertrand Russell. The art of philosophizing. N.Y., 1968.
Phil 2255.1.40 Russell, Bertrand Russell. Philosophy and politics. London, 1947.
Phil 2255.1.43 Russell, Bertrand Russell. Political ideals. N.Y., 1963.
Phil 2255.1.45 Russell, Bertrand Russell. Human knowledge; its scope and limits. London, 1948.
Phil 2255.1.48 Russell, Bertrand Russell. Essays in skepticism. N.Y., 1962.
Phil 2255.1.50 Russell, Bertrand Russell. Unpopular essays. London, 1950.
Phil 2255.1.51 Russell, Bertrand Russell. Unpopular essays. N.Y., 1950.
Phil 2255.1.52 Russell, Bertrand Russell. Basic writings, 1903-1959. N.Y., 1961.
Phil 2255.1.55 Russell, Bertrand Russell. The wit and wisdom. Boston, 1951.
Phil 2255.1.58A Russell, Bertrand Russell. Bertrand Russell speaks his mind. 1st ed. Cleveland, 1960.
Phil 2255.1.58B Russell, Bertrand Russell. Bertrand Russell speaks his mind. 1. ed. Cleveland, 1960.
Phil 2255.1.60 Russell, Bertrand Russell. New hopes for a changing world. London, 1951.
Phil 2255.1.61 Russell, Bertrand Russell. New hopes for a changing world. N.Y., 1951.
Phil 2255.1.63 Russell, Bertrand Russell. Common sense and nuclear warfare. London, 1959.
Phil 2255.1.64 Russell, Bertrand Russell. Dear Bertrand Russell: a selection of his correspondence with the general public, 1950-1968. London, 1969.
Phil 2255.1.65 Russell, Bertrand Russell. Dictionary of mind, matter and morals. N.Y., 1952.
Phil 2255.1.68 Russell, Bertrand Russell. Has man a future? London, 1961.
Phil 2255.1.72 Russell, Bertrand Russell. The will to doubt. N.Y., 1958.
Phil 2255.1.73 Russell, Bertrand Russell. Fact and fiction. London, 1961.
Phil 2255.1.74A Russell, Bertrand Russell. Power; a new social analysis. N.Y., 1969.
Phil 2255.1.74B Russell, Bertrand Russell. Power; a new social analysis. N.Y., 1969.
Phil 2255.1.75 Russell, Bertrand Russell. Logic and knowledge. London, 1956.
Phil 2255.1.76 Russell, Bertrand Russell. The good citizen's alphabet. London, 1953.
Phil 2255.1.77 Russell, Bertrand Russell. The future of science. N.Y., 1959.
Phil 2255.1.78 Russell, Bertrand Russell. Portraits from memory. London, 1956.
Phil 2255.1.79 Russell, Bertrand Russell. Understanding history. N.Y., 1957.
Phil 2255.1.80 Pamphlet box. Philosophy. English. Russell, Bertrand Russell.
Phil 2255.1.90 Benjamin, A.C. The logical atomism of Bertrand Russell. Diss. Champaign, Ill., 1927?
Phil 2255.1.95 Lewis, John. Bertrand Russell: philosopher and humanist. London, 1968.
Phil 2255.1.100 Schilpp, Paul A. The philosophy of Bertrand Russell. Evanston, Ill., 1944.
Phil 2255.1.102 Schilpp, Paul A. The philosophy of Bertrand Russell. Evanston, Ill., 1946.
Phil 2255.1.103 Schilpp, Paul A. The philosophy of Bertrand Russell. N.Y., 1951.
Phil 2255.1.110 Leggett, H.W. Bertrand Russell. London, 1949.
Phil 2255.1.111 Leggett, H.W. Bertrand Russell. N.Y., 1950.
Phil 2255.1.112 Dorward, Alan. Bertrand Russell. London, 1951.
Phil 2255.1.113 Götlind, E. Bertrand Russell's theories of causation. Inaug. Diss. Uppsala, 1952.
Phil 2255.1.114 Narskii, I.S. Filosfiia Bertrana Rassela. Moskva, 1962.
Phil 2255.1.115 Fritz, C.A. Bertrand Russell's construction of the external world. London, 1952.
Phil 2255.1.118 Wood, Alan. Bertrand Russell. London, 1957.
Phil 2255.1.120 Riverro, Emmanuele. Il pensiero di Bertrand Russell. Napoli, 1958.

Phil 2255 History of philosophy - Local Modern philosophy - Great Britain and United States - Individual philosophers - Other R - cont.

Phil 2255.1.125 Bonifacino, V. Ensayos beligerantes: Bertrand Russell, James Joyce. Montevideo, 1960.
Phil 2255.1.126 Aiken, L.W. Bertrand Russell's philosophy of morals. N.Y., 1963.
Phil 2255.1.127 Park, J. Bertrand Russell on education. Columbus, 1963.
Phil 2255.1.128 Gottschalk, Herbert. Bertrand Russell: a life. London, 1965.
Phil 2255.1.130A Pears, David Francis. Bertrand Russell and the British tradition in philosophy. London, 1967.
Phil 2255.1.131 Russell, Bertrand Russell. A detailed catalogue of the archives of Bertrand Russell. London, 1967.
Phil 2255.1.135 Chisholm, John Edward. The theory of knowledge of Bertrand Russell. Rome, 1967.
VPhil 2255.1.140 Knjazeva-Adamović, Svetlana. Filozofija Bertranda Russella: strasno traženje izvesnosti. Zagreb, 1966.
Phil 2255.1.145 Vuillemin, Jules. Leçons sur la première philosophie de Russell. Paris, 1968.
Phil 2255.1.150 Clark, Robert J. Bertrand Russell's philosophy of language. The Hague, 1969.
Phil 2255.1.155 Eames, Elizabeth Ramsden. Bertrand Russell's theory of knowledge. London, 1969.
Phil 2255.1.160 Watling, John. Bertrand Russell. Edinburgh, 1970.
Phil 2255.1.165 Klemke, E.D. Essays on Bertrand Russell. Urbana, Illinois, 1970.
Phil 2255.1.170 Ayer, Alfred Jules. Russell and Moore: the analytical heritage. Cambridge, 1971.
Phil 2255.1.175 Russell: the journal of the Bertrand Russell Archives. Hamilton, Ont. 1,1971+
Phil 2255.1.180 Rizzacasa, Aurelio. Il pacifismo nella dottrina politico-pedagogica di Bertrand Russell. Bologna, 1969.
Phil 2255.1.185 Crawshay-Williams, Rupert. Russell remembered. London, 1970.
Phil 2255.1.190 Bertrand Russell; a collection of critical essays. 1st ed. Garden City, 1972.
Phil 2255.2.80 Pamphlet box. Philosophy. English. Robertson, George Croom.
Phil 2255.3 Young, Robert F. A Bohemian philosopher at Oxford in the 17th century. London, 1925.
Phil 2255.4 Reiser, Oliver L. A new earth and a new humanity. N.Y., 1942.
Phil 2255.4.5 Reiser, Oliver L. World philosophy. Pittsburgh, 1948.
Phil 2255.5 Reid, James K. Whither humanity; the philosophy of a doctor. London, 1945.
Phil 2255.6 Ritchie, Arthur D. Essays in philosophy and other pieces. London, 1948.
Phil 2255.7 Runes, Dagobert D. Letters to my son. N.Y., 1949.
Phil 2255.7.3 Runes, Dagobert D. Letters to my teacher. N.Y., 1961.
Phil 2255.7.5 Runes, Dagobert D. Of God, the devil and the Jews. N.Y., 1952.
Phil 2255.7.10 Runes, Dagobert D. On the nature of man. N.Y., 1956.
Phil 2255.7.15 Runes, Dagobert D. A book of contemplation. N.Y., 1957.
Phil 2255.7.20 Runes, Dagobert D. Letters to my God. N.Y., 1958.
Phil 2255.9 Rotenstreich, N. Spirit and man. The Hague, 1963.
Phil 2255.10.30 Rand, Ayn. The virtue of selfishness; a new concept of egoism. N.Y., 1965.
Phil 2255.10.32 Rand, Ayn. Introduction to objectivist epistemology. N.Y., 1967.
Phil 2255.10.34 Rand, Ayn. For the new intellectual; the philosophy of Ayn Rand. N.Y., 1961.
Phil 2255.10.36 The Ayn Rand letter. N.Y. 1,1971+
Phil 2255.10.80 Ellis, Albert. Is objectivism a religion? N.Y., 1968.
Phil 2255.11 Rhees, Rush. Without answers. London, 1969.
Phil 2255.12 Ryle. London, 1971.

Phil 2262 History of philosophy - Local Modern philosophy - Great Britain and United States - Individual philosophers - Shaftesbury, Anthony Ashley Cooper, Earl of

Phil 2262.2 Shaftesbury, A.A.C. Les oeuvres. v.1-3. Genève, 1769.
Htn Phil 2262.29* Shaftesbury, A.A.C. Characteristicks. London, 1711. 3v.
Htn Phil 2262.29.5* Shaftesbury, A.A.C. Characteristicks. 2nd ed. London, 1714. 3v.
Phil 2262.30 Shaftesbury, A.A.C. Characteristicks. London, 1723. 3v.
Phil 2262.30.2 Shaftesbury, A.A.C. Characteristicks. v.3. London, 17- .
Phil 2262.30.3 Shaftesbury, A.A.C. Characteristicks. v.2,3. London, 1727. 2v.
Phil 2262.30.4 Shaftesbury, A.A.C. Characteristicks. 4th ed. n.p., 1727. 3v.
Htn Phil 2262.30.5* Shaftesbury, A.A.C. Characteristicks. 5th ed. Birmingham, 1773. 3v.
Phil 2262.30.7 Shaftesbury, A.A.C. Characteristicks. London, 1732. 3v.
Phil 2262.31.2 Shaftesbury, A.A.C. Characteristicks. 5th ed. London, 1732. 3v.
Phil 2262.32 Shaftesbury, A.A.C. Characteristicks. 6th ed. London, 1737. 3v.
Htn Phil 2262.32.5* Shaftesbury, A.A.C. Characteristicks. London, 1749. 3v.
Phil 2262.33 Shaftesbury, A.A.C. Characteristicks. Basel, 1790. 3v.
Phil 2262.34 Shaftesbury, A.A.C. Characteristicks. v.1. London, 1870.
Phil 2262.35.3A Shaftesbury, A.A.C. Characteristicks. N.Y., 1900. 2v.
Phil 2262.35.4 Shaftesbury, A.A.C. Characteristics of men, manners, opinions, times. Gloucester, Mass., 1963. 2v.
Phil 2262.35.5 Shaftesbury, A.A.C. Characteristics of men. v.1-2. Indianapolis, 1964.
Phil 2262.39A Shaftesbury, A.A.C. Second characters. Cambridge, 1914.
Phil 2262.39B Shaftesbury, A.A.C. Second characters. Cambridge, 1914.
Htn Phil 2262.45* Shaftesbury, A.A.C. Characteristicks. Leipzig, 1768.
Htn Phil 2262.49* Shaftesbury, A.A.C. The moralists. London, 1709.
Phil 2262.50 Shaftesbury, A.A.C. Die Moralisten, eine philosophische Rhapsodie. Jena, 1910.
Phil 2262.51 Shaftesbury, A.A.C. Moralisterna, en filosofisk rhapsodi. Stockholm, 1926.
Phil 2262.55 Shaftesbury, A.A.C. Lettres sur l'enthousiasme de milord Shaftesbury. London, 1761.
Phil 2262.57 Shaftesbury, A.A.C. Ein Brief über den Enthusiasmus. Die Moralisten, eine philosophische Rhapsodie. Leipzig, 1909.
Phil 2262.59A Shaftesbury, A.A.C. Letter concerning enthusiasm. Paris, 1930.
Phil 2262.59B Shaftesbury, A.A.C. Letter concerning enthusiasm. Paris, 1930.
Phil 2262.60 Shaftesbury, A.A.C. Untersuchung über die Tugend. Leipzig, 1905.
Phil 2262.60.2 Shaftesbury, A.A.C. Religion und Tugend. Leipzig, 1905.

Phil 2262 History of philosophy - Local Modern philosophy - Great Britain and United States - Individual philosophers - Shaftesbury, Anthony Ashley Cooper, Earl of - cont.

Htn	Phil 2262.62*	Shaftesbury, A.A.C. Sensus communis. London, 1709.
	Phil 2262.63	Shaftesbury, A.A.C. Soliloquy. London, 1710.
Htn	Phil 2262.63*	Shaftesbury, A.A.C. Soliloquy. Photoreproduction. London, 1710.
	Phil 2262.75	Shaftesbury, A.A.C. Letters. London, 1750.
Htn	Phil 2262.76*	Shaftesbury, A.A.C. Letter concerning enthusiasm. London, 1708-09. 4 pam.
	Phil 2262.77	Shaftesbury, A.A.C. Life. Unpublished letters. London, 1900.
	Phil 2262.78	Pamphlet box. Philosophy. English. Shaftesbury, A.A.C.
	Phil 2262.78.5	Bacharach, A. Shaftesburys Optimismus und sein Verhältnis zum Leibnizschen. Inaug. Diss. Thann, 1912.
	Phil 2262.79	Brown, J. Essays on the characteristics. 2d ed. London, 1751.
Htn	Phil 2262.79.1*	Brown, J. Essays on the characteristics. London, 1751.
	Phil 2262.79.2	Brown, J. Essays on the characteristics. London, 1752.
	Phil 2262.80	Bierens de Haan, J.D. De beteekenis van Shaftesbury in de Engelsche ethiek. Proefschrift. Utrecht, 1891.
	Phil 2262.81A	Fowler, T. Shaftesbury and Hutcheson. London, 1882.
	Phil 2262.81B	Fowler, T. Shaftesbury and Hutcheson. London, 1882.
	Phil 2262.81.5A	Fowler, T. Shaftesbury and Hutcheson. N.Y., 1883.
	Phil 2262.81.5B	Fowler, T. Shaftesbury and Hutcheson. N.Y., 1883.
	Phil 2262.82	Gizycki, G. von. Die Philosophie Shaftesbury's. Leipzig, 1876.
	Phil 2262.83	Spicker, G. Die Philosophie des Grafen von Shaftesbury. Freiburg, 1872.
	Phil 2262.84	Weiser, C.F. Shaftesbury und das deutsche Geistesleben. Leipzig, 1916.
	Phil 2262.85	Rehorn, F. Moral sense und Moral-Prinzip bei Shaftesbury. Inaug. Diss. Bonn, 1882.
	Phil 2262.86	Waern, L.M. Shaftesbury's dygdelära. Upsala, 1875.
	Phil 2262.87	Hatch, Irvin C. Der Einfluss Shaftesburys auf Herder. Diss. Berlin? 1901?
	Phil 2262.88	Schonfeld, V. Die Ethik Shaftesburys. Diss. Budapest, 1920.
	Phil 2262.89	Schlosser, J.G. Über Schaftsbury von der Tugend. Basel, 1785.
	Phil 2262.90	Bandini, L. Shaftesbury; etica e religione, la morale del sentimento. Bari, 1930.
	Phil 2262.91	Lyons, Alexander. Shaftesbury's ethical principle of adaptation to universal harmony. N.Y., 1909?
	Phil 2262.92	Almer, T. Studier i Shaftesburys filosofi. Lund, 1939.
	Phil 2262.94	Brett, R.L. The third earl of Shaftesbury. London, 1951.
	Phil 2262.95	Zani, Lucio. L'etica di Lord Shaftesbury. Milano, 1954.
	Phil 2262.97	Schlegel, D.B. Shaftesbury and the French deists. Chapel Hill, 1956.
	Phil 2262.99	Wolff, Erwin. Shaftesbury und seine Bedeutung für die englische Literatur des 18. Jhs. Tübingen, 1960.

Phil 2266 History of philosophy - Local Modern philosophy - Great Britain and United States - Individual philosophers - Smith, Adam

	Phil 2266.20	Smith, Adam. Moral and political philosophy. N.Y., 1948.
	Phil 2266.30	Smith, Adam. Essays. London, 1795.
	Phil 2266.30.5	Smith, Adam. Essay on philosophical subjects. Basil, 1799.
	Phil 2266.30.10	Smith, Adam. Essays; philosophical and literary. London, 1880?
	Phil 2266.30.50A	Smith, Adam. Essays on I. Moral sentiment; II. Astronomical inquiries. London, 1869.
	Phil 2266.30.50B	Smith, Adam. Essays on I. Moral sentiment; II. Astronomical inquiries. London, 1869.
	Phil 2266.35	Smith, Adam. A dissertation on the origin of languages. Tübingen, 1970.
Htn	Phil 2266.36*	Smith, Adam. The theory of moral sentiments. London, 1759.
	Phil 2266.37	Smith, Adam. The theory of moral sentiments. 2nd ed. London, 1761.
	Phil 2266.38	Smith, Adam. The theory of moral sentiments. 7th ed. London, 1792. 2v.
	Phil 2266.41	Smith, Adam. The theory of moral sentiments. v.1-2. Boston, 1817.
	Phil 2266.41.2	Smith, Adam. The theory of moral sentiments. Philadelphia, 1817.
	Phil 2266.41.5	Smith, Adam. The theory of moral sentiments. N.Y., 1966.
	Phil 2266.41.10	Smith, Adam. The theory of moral sentiments. New Rochelle, 1969.
	Phil 2266.42	Smith, Adam. Theorie der ethischen Gefühle. Leipzig, 1926. 2v.
	Phil 2266.42.5	Smith, Adam. Theorie der sittlichen Gefühle. Leipzig, 1791-95. 2v.
	Phil 2266.43	Smith, Adam. Théorie des sentiments moraux. Paris, 1830. 2v.
	Phil 2266.43.5	Smith, Adam. La métaphysique de l'âme. Paris, 1764. 2v.
	Phil 2266.50	Smith, Adam. The early writings of Adam Smith. N.Y., 1967.
Htn	Phil 2266.68*	Smith, Adam. An inquiry into the nature and causes of the wealth of nations. London, 1776. 2v.
	Phil 2266.70	Smith, Adam. An inquiry into the nature and causes of the wealth of nations. London, 1796. 3v.
	Phil 2266.80	Farrer, J.A. Adam Smith. N.Y., 1881.
	Phil 2266.80.3	Farrer, J.A. Adam Smith. London, 1881.
	Phil 2266.81	Schubert, Johannes. Adam Smith's Moralphilosophie. Leipzig, 1890.
	Phil 2266.82	Paszkowski, W. Adam Smith als Moralphilosoph. Halle, 1890.
	Phil 2266.83	Muir, Ethel. The ethical system of Adam Smith. Thesis. Halifax, N.S., 1898.
	Phil 2266.90	Campbell, Thomas Douglas. Adam Smith's science of morals. London, 1971.
	Phil 2266.114	Limentani, L. La morale della simpatia; saggio sopra l'etica di Adamo Smith. Genova, 1914.
	Phil 2266.157	Preti, Giulio. Alle origini dell'etica contemporanea Adamo Smith. Bari, 1957.
	Phil 2266.165A	Rae, John. Life of Adam Smith. N.Y., 1965.
	Phil 2266.165B	Rae, John. Life of Adam Smith. N.Y., 1965.

Phil 2268 History of philosophy - Local Modern philosophy - Great Britain and United States - Individual philosophers - Other Smiths

Htn	Phil 2268.1.30*	Smith, Joseph. The book of Mormon. Palmyra, 1830.
	Phil 2268.2.79	Pamphlet box. Philosophy. English. Smith, Carl Ellsworth.
	Phil 2268.3.100	Smith, Charles. Sensism, the philosophy of the West. N.Y., 1956. 2v.

Phil 2270 History of philosophy - Local Modern philosophy - Great Britain and United States - Individual philosophers - Spencer, Herbert

	Phil 2270	Pamphlet box. Philosophy. English. Spencer, Herbert.
	Phil 2270.20	Spencer, Herbert. Select works. N.Y., 1886.
	Phil 2270.30	Spencer, Herbert. First principles. London, 1870.
	Phil 2270.30.2	Spencer, Herbert. Principles of biology. London, 1864-67. 2v.
	Phil 2270.30.3	Spencer, Herbert. Principles of psychology. London, 1870-72. 2v.
	Phil 2270.30.5	Spencer, Herbert. Data of ethics. London, 1887.
	Phil 2270.31	Spencer, Herbert. System der Synthetischen Philosophie: Grundlagen. Stuttgart, 1875.
	Phil 2270.31.2	Spencer, Herbert. System der synthetischen Philosophie: Biologie. Stuttgart, 1876-77. 2v.
	Phil 2270.31.3	Spencer, Herbert. System der synthetischen Philosophie: Psychologie. Stuttgart, 1882-86. 2v.
	Phil 2270.31.4	Spencer, Herbert. System der synthetischen Philosophie: Sociologie. Stuttgart, 1877-97. 4v.
	Phil 2270.31.5	Spencer, Herbert. System der synthetischen Philosophie: Ethik. Stuttgart, 1879-95. 2v.
	Phil 2270.35	Spencer, Herbert. Epitome of the synthetic philosophy. N.Y., 1889.
	Phil 2270.35.2	Spencer, Herbert. Epitome of the synthetic philosophy. N.Y., 1895.
	Phil 2270.39	Spencer, Herbert. Essays. v.2,3. London, 1868. 2v.
X Cg	Phil 2270.39	Spencer, Herbert. Essays. v.1. N.Y., 1868.
	Phil 2270.40	Spencer, Herbert. Essays. London, 1858.
	Phil 2270.40.2	Spencer, Herbert. Essays. N.Y., 1865.
	Phil 2270.40.3	Spencer, Herbert. Essays. N.Y., 1871.
	Phil 2270.40.3.5	Spencer, Herbert. Essays. N.Y., 1868.
	Phil 2270.40.4	Spencer, Herbert. Essays. N.Y., 1874.
	Phil 2270.40.5	Spencer, Herbert. Essays. N.Y., 1891. 3v.
	Phil 2270.40.8	Spencer, Herbert. Essays. N.Y., 1896. 3v.
	Phil 2270.40.30	Spencer, Herbert. Essais de morale, de science et d'esthétique. 5e éd. Paris, 1904.
	Phil 2270.40.35A	Spencer, Herbert. Essays on education and kindred subjects. London, 1910.
	Phil 2270.40.35B	Spencer, Herbert. Essays on education and kindred subjects. London, 1910.
	Phil 2270.41	Spencer, Herbert. Facts and comments. N.Y., 1902.
	Phil 2270.41.5	Spencer, Herbert. Facts and comments. N.Y., 1902.
	Phil 2270.41.6	Spencer, Herbert. Facts and comments. N.Y., 1902.
	Phil 2270.41.9	Spencer, Herbert. Faits et commentaires. 2e éd. Paris, 1904.
	Phil 2270.43	Spencer, Herbert. Various fragments. N.Y., 1898.
	Phil 2270.45	Spencer, Herbert. First principles. London, 1862.
Htn	Phil 2270.45.1*	Spencer, Herbert. First principles. London, 1862.
	Phil 2270.45.2	Spencer, Herbert. First principles. London, 1862.
Htn	Phil 2270.45.2.5*	Spencer, Herbert. First principles. London, 1862.
	Phil 2270.45.3	Spencer, Herbert. First principles. N.Y., 1864.
	Phil 2270.45.3.10	Spencer, Herbert. First principles. N.Y., 1865.
	Phil 2270.45.3.15	Spencer, Herbert. First principles. N.Y., 1866.
	Phil 2270.45.4	Spencer, Herbert. First principles. N.Y., 1873.
	Phil 2270.45.4.7	Spencer, Herbert. First principles. N.Y., 188-?
	Phil 2270.45.4.10	Spencer, Herbert. First principles. N.Y., 188-?
	Phil 2270.45.5	Spencer, Herbert. First principles. N.Y., 1886.
	Phil 2270.45.7	Spencer, Herbert. First principles. N.Y., n.d.
	Phil 2270.45.9	Spencer, Herbert. First principles. N.Y., 1900.
	Phil 2270.45.14	Spencer, Herbert. First principles. 4th ed. N.Y., 1885.
	Phil 2270.45.15	Spencer, Herbert. First principles. N.Y., 1892.
	Phil 2270.45.17	Spencer, Herbert. First principles. N.Y., 188-.
	Phil 2270.45.25	Spencer, Herbert. First principles. N.Y., 1894.
	Phil 2270.45.27	Spencer, Herbert. First principles. N.Y., 1896.
	Phil 2270.45.30	Spencer, Herbert. First principles. N.Y., 1958.
	Phil 2270.45.50	Spencer, Herbert. Les premiers principes. Paris, 1871.
	Phil 2270.50	Spencer, Herbert. Recent discussions in science. N.Y., 1873.
	Phil 2270.50.2	Spencer, Herbert. Recent discussions in science. N.Y., 1871.
	Phil 2270.55	Spencer, Herbert. Social statics. London, 1851.
Htn	Phil 2270.55.1*	Spencer, Herbert. Social statics. London, 1851.
	Phil 2270.55.2	Spencer, Herbert. Social statics. London, 1851.
	Phil 2270.55.3	Spencer, Herbert. Social statics. London, 1851.
	Phil 2270.55.4	Spencer, Herbert. Social statics. N.Y., 1865.
	Phil 2270.55.7.5	Spencer, Herbert. Social statics. N.Y., 1872.
	Phil 2270.55.8	Spencer, Herbert. Social statics. N.Y., 1882.
	Phil 2270.55.9	Spencer, Herbert. Social statics. N.Y., 1886.
NEDL	Phil 2270.56.5	Spencer, Herbert. Social statics. N.Y., 1893.
	Phil 2270.56.6	Spencer, Herbert. Social statics. N.Y., 1897.
	Phil 2270.56.7	Spencer, Herbert. Social statics. N.Y., 1904.
	Phil 2270.56.10	Spencer, Herbert. Social statics. N.Y., 1954.
Htn	Phil 2270.60*	Spencer, Herbert. The classification of the sciences. London, 1864.
	Phil 2270.60.3	Spencer, Herbert. The classification of the sciences. N.Y., 1864.
	Phil 2270.60.10	Spencer, Herbert. Classification des sciences. Paris, 1888.
	Phil 2270.65	Spencer, Herbert. Illustrations of universal progress. N.Y., 1864.
	Phil 2270.67.5	Spencer, Herbert. What knowledge is of most worth. N.Y., 1884.
	Phil 2270.70	Spencer, Herbert. Principles of psychology. London, 1855.
	Phil 2270.70.2	Spencer, Herbert. Principles of psychology. London, 1855.
	Phil 2270.70.4.15	Spencer, Herbert. Principles of psychology. N.Y., 1878. 2v.
	Phil 2270.70.5	Spencer, Herbert. Principles of psychology. London, 1881. 2v.
	Phil 2270.70.10	Spencer, Herbert. Principles of psychology. N.Y., 1894. 2v.
	Phil 2270.70.12	Spencer, Herbert. Principles of psychology. N.Y., 1895. 2v.
	Phil 2270.70.14	Spencer, Herbert. Principles of psychology. N.Y., 1901. 2v.
	Phil 2270.70.15	Spencer, Herbert. Principles of psychology. N.Y., 1926.
	Phil 2270.71.10	Spencer, Herbert. Uppfostran i intellektuelt, moraliskt och fysiskt afseende. 2a uppl. Stockholm, 1890.
	Phil 2270.72	Spencer, Herbert. L'evoluzione del pensiero. Milano, 1909. 2v.
	Phil 2270.73	Spencer, Herbert. Principles of ethics. N.Y., 1892-93. 2v.
	Phil 2270.73.3	Spencer, Herbert. Principles of ethics. N.Y., 1895. 2v.
	Phil 2270.73.4	Spencer, Herbert. Principles of ethics. N.Y., 1895-96. 2v.
	Phil 2270.73.5	Spencer, Herbert. Principles of ethics. N.Y., 1899.
	Phil 2270.74	Spencer, Herbert. Data of ethics. N.Y., 1879.
	Phil 2270.74.1.5	Spencer, Herbert. Data of ethics. N.Y., 1879.
	Phil 2270.74.4	Spencer, Herbert. Data of ethics. N.Y., 1883.

Classified Listing

Phil 2270.74.5	Spencer, Herbert. Data of ethics. London, 1879.
Phil 2270.74.7	Spencer, Herbert. Data of ethics. 3rd ed. London, 1881.
Phil 2270.74.12	Spencer, Herbert. Data of ethics. NY., 189-?
Phil 2270.74.20	Spencer, Herbert. Les bases de la morale évolutionniste. 8e éd. Paris, 1905.
Phil 2270.74.25	Spencer, Herbert. Le rôle moral de la bienfaisance. Paris, 1895.
Phil 2270.74.30	Spencer, Herbert. Qu'est-ce que la morale? Paris, 1909.
Phil 2270.74.35	Spencer, Herbert. La morale des différents peuples et la morale personnelle. Paris, 1896.
Phil 2270.75	Spencer, Herbert. Resumen sintético de los principios de la moral. Paris, 1910.
Phil 2270.76	Spencer, Herbert. L'evoluzione morale. Milano, 1909.
Phil 2270.76.5	Spencer, Herbert. Le basi della morale. 3a ed. Piacenza, 1920.
Phil 2270.77	Spencer, Herbert. Data of ethics. Pt. IV. Justice. N.Y., 1891.
Phil 2270.77.10	Spencer, Herbert. The coming slavery and other essays. N.Y., 1888.
Phil 2270.77.20	Spencer, Herbert. A rejoinder to Professor Weismann. London, 1893?
Phil 2270.78	Pamphlet box. Philosophy. English. Spencer, Herbert.
Phil 2270.79A	Spencer, Herbert. An autobiography. N.Y., 1904. 2v.
Phil 2270.79B	Spencer, Herbert. An autobiography. N.Y., 1904. 2v.
Phil 2270.79.10	Spencer, Herbert. Eine Autobiographie. Stuttgart, 1905. 2v.
Phil 2270.80	Birks, T.R. Modern physical fatalism. London, 1876.
Phil 2270.81	Greene, W.B. Facts of consciousness and philosophy of Spencer. Boston, 1871.
Phil 2270.82	Ground, W.D. Examination of Herbert Spencer's theory of the will. London, 1883.
Phil 2270.84	Guthrie, M. On Mr. Spencer's formula of evolution. London, 1878.
Phil 2270.84.5A	Guthrie, M. On Mr. Spencer's data of ethics. London, 1884.
Phil 2270.84.5B	Guthrie, M. On Mr. Spencer's data of ethics. London, 1884.
Phil 2270.84.8	Guthrie, M. On Mr. Spencer's unification of knowledge. London, 1882.
Phil 2270.85	Harrison, F. Nature and reality of religion. A controversy. N.Y., 1885.
Phil 2270.85.2	Gaupp, Otto. Herbert Spencer. Stuttgart, 1900.
Phil 2270.85.5	Gaupp, Otto. Herbert Spencer. Stuttgart, 1897.
Phil 2270.86	Herbert Spencer on the Americans and the Americans on Spencer. N.Y., 1883.
Phil 2270.87	Beard, G.M. Herbert Spencer on American nervousness. N.Y., 1883.
Phil 2270.88	Fischer, E.L. Über den Gesetz der Entwicklung. Würzburg, 1875.
Phil 2270.89	Michelet, C.L. Herbert Spencer's System der Philosophie. Halle, 1882.
Phil 2270.90	Bowne, B.P. The philosophy of Herbert Spencer. N.Y., n.d.
Phil 2270.90.2	Bowne, B.P. The philosophy of Herbert Spencer. N.Y., 1881.
Phil 2270.90.5	Bowne, Borden Parker. The philosophy of Herbert Spencer; being an examination of the first principles of his system. New York, 1881. Photoreproduction. Ann Arbor, Michigan, 1970.
Phil 2270.91A	Macpherson, H. Spencer and Spencerism. N.Y., 1900.
Phil 2270.91B	Macpherson, H. Spencer and Spencerism. N.Y., 1900.
Phil 2270.92	Dubois, J. Spencer et le principe de la morale. Paris, 1899.
Phil 2270.92.90	Hudson, William Henry. An introduction to the philosophy of Herbert Spencer. N.Y., 1894.
Phil 2270.93	Hudson, William Henry. An introduction to the philosophy of Herbert Spencer. 2nd ed. N.Y., 1900.
Phil 2270.93.16A	Hudson, William Henry. Herbert Spencer. London, 1916.
Phil 2270.93.16B	Hudson, William Henry. Herbert Spencer. London, 1916.
Phil 2270.94A	Royce, Josiah. Herbert Spencer; an estimate and review. N.Y., 1904.
Phil 2270.94B	Royce, Josiah. Herbert Spencer; an estimate and review. N.Y., 1904.
Phil 2270.94C	Royce, Josiah. Herbert Spencer; an estimate and review. N.Y., 1904.
Phil 2270.95	Harrison, F. The Herbert Spencer lecture. Oxford, 1905.
Phil 2270.96	Duncan, D. Life and letters of Herbert Spencer. N.Y., 1908. 2v.
Phil 2270.97	Quesada, E. Herbert Spencer y sus doctrinas sociológicas. Buenos Aires, 1907.
Phil 2270.98	Häberlin, P. Herbert Spencer's Grundlagen der Philosophie. Leipzig, 1908.
Phil 2270.99	Pace, E. Das Relativitätsprincip bei Herbert Spencer. Leipzig, 1891.
Phil 2270.100	Parisot, E. Herbert Spencer. Paris, n.d.
Phil 2270.101	Traina, Tommaso. La morale di Herbert Spencer. Torino, 1881.
Phil 2270.102	Blanc, Elie. Les nouvelles bases de la morale d'après Herbert Spencer. Lyon, 1881.
Phil 2270.103	Halleux, Jean. L'évolutionnisme en morale. Paris, 1901.
Phil 2270.104	Salvadori, Guglielmo. L'etica evoluzionista...di Herbert Spencer. Torino, 1903.
Phil 2270.105	Spicker, Gideon. Spencer's Ansicht über das Verhältniss der Religion zur Wissenschaft. Münster, 1889.
Phil 2270.106	Boutroux, E. La religion selon Herbert Spencer. Paris, 1905.
Phil 2270.107	Absi, Marcelle. La théorie de la religion chez Spencer et ses sources. Thèse. Beyrouth, 1952.
Phil 2270.112	Geraskoff, Michael. Die sittliche Erziehung nach Herbert Spencer. Zürich, 1912.
Phil 2270.113	Nörregård, Jens. Studier over Spencer, Lotze og Grundtvig. København, 1890.
Phil 2270.114	Dallari, Gino. Il pensiero filosofico di Herbert Spencer. Torino, 1904.
Phil 2270.115	Thyren, Johan. Kritisk framställning af Herbert Spencer's "Principles of Psychology". Akademisk afhandling. Lund, 1883.
Phil 2270.116	Ranzoli, C. La fortuna di Herbert Spencer in Italia. Verona, 1904.
Phil 2270.118	Stadler, August. Herbert Spencer. Spencers Ethik. Leipzig, 1918.
Phil 2270.118.2	Stadler, August. Herbert Spencer. Spencers Ethik. Leipzig, 1913.
Phil 2270.118.10	Stadler, August. Herbert Spencer; Zürcher Rathaus-Vortrag gehalten am 6. dezember 1906. Zürich, 1907.
Phil 2270.120	Elliot, Hugh S.R. Herbert Spencer. London, 1917.

Phil 2270.123	Santayana, George. The unknowable; Herbert Spencer lecture. Oxford, 1923.
Phil 2270.125	Grosse, Ernst. Herbert Spencer's Lehre von dem Unerkennbaren. Leipzig, 1890.
Phil 2270.126	Ardigó, R. La dottrina Spenceriana dell'inconoscibile. Roma, 1899.
Phil 2270.127A	Thomson, J.A. Herbert Spencer. London, 1906.
Phil 2270.127B	Thomson, J.A. Herbert Spencer. London, 1906.
Phil 2270.128	Ethical review. No. 4, Dec. 1906. Herbert Spencer memorial number. London, 1906.
Phil 2270.130	Thouverez, Émile. Herbert Spencer. Paris, 1913.
Phil 2270.131	Nardi, P. de. L'assoluto inconoscibile di H. Spencer. Forlì, 1904.
Phil 2270.132	Sacerdote, S. La vita di H. Spencer, ed "I primi principii". Torino, 1907.
Phil 2270.133	Jaeger, Max. Herbert Spencer's Prinzipien der Ethik. Hamburg, 1922.
Phil 2270.134	Arfvidsson, H.D. Religion och vetenskap...Spencers. Diss. Lund, 1894.
Phil 2270.135	Bager-Sjögren, J. Herbert Spencer och utvecklingsfilosofien. Lund, 1893.
Phil 2270.136	Pagnone, A. Le intuizioni morali e l'eredità nello Spencer. Torino, 1897.
Phil 2270.137	Juvalta, Erminio. La dottrina delle due etiche di H. Spencer, e la morale come scienza. n.p., n.d.
Phil 2270.138	Weber, Reinhard H. Die Philosophie von Herbert Spencer. Darmstadt, 1892.
Phil 2270.139	Rumney, J. Herbert Spencer's sociology. London, 1934.
Phil 2270.140	Diaconide, Elias. Etude critique sur la sociologie de Herbert Spencer. Paris, 1938.
Phil 2270.141	Lacy, William M. Examination of the philosophy of the unknowable as expounded by Herbert Spencer. Philadelphia, 1912.
Phil 2270.141.5	Lacy, William M. An examination of the philosophy of the unknowable as expounded by Herbert Spencer. Philadelphia, 1883.
Phil 2270.150	Shepperson, J. A comparative study of St. Thomas Aquinas and Herbert Spencer. Diss. Pittsburgh, 1923.
Phil 2270.151	Tillet, A.W. Herbert Spencer betrayed. London, 1939.
Phil 2270.160	Two (pseud.). Home life with Herbert Spencer. Bristol, 1906.
Phil 2270.165	Wiese, Leopold von. Herbert Spencers Einführung in die Soziologie. Köln, 1960.
Phil 2270.175	Allievo, Giuseppe. La psicologia di Herbert Spencer. 2a ed. Torino, 1913.
Phil 2270.180	Gol'denveizer, A.S. Gerbert Spencer. Idei svoboda i prava. Sankt Peterburg, 1904.
Phil 2270.185	Di Nola, Mario. Il presupposto biologico e individualista della sociologia spenceriana. Colombo, 1965.
Phil 2270.190	Peel, John David Yeadon. Herbert Spencer; the evolution of a sociologist. London, 1971.

	Phil 2275.10	Stewart, D. Works. Cambridge, 1829. 7v.
	Phil 2275.11	Stewart, D. Collected works. v.1-4, 6-10, and supplement. Edinburgh, 1854-60. 10v.
X Cg	Phil 2275.11	Stewart, D. Collected works. v.5. Edinburgh, 1854-60.
	Phil 2275.12	Stewart, D. Collected works. 2nd ed. Edinburgh, 1877. 11v.
	Phil 2275.20	Stewart, D. Oeuvres. Bruxelles, 1829. 5v.
	Phil 2275.22	Stewart, D. Oeuvres. Paris, 1829. 2v.
	Phil 2275.30	Stewart, D. Elements of the philosophy of the human mind. London, 1792.
	Phil 2275.31	Stewart, D. Elements of the philosophy of the human mind. Philadelphia, 1793.
	Phil 2275.31.5	Stewart, D. Elements of the philosophy of the human mind. London, 1802.
	Phil 2275.32	Stewart, D. Elements of the philosophy of the human mind. v.2. Boston, 1814.
	Phil 2275.33	Stewart, D. Elements of the philosophy of the human mind. Brattleborough, 1808.
	Phil 2275.33.2	Stewart, D. Elements of the philosophy of the human mind. Brattleborough, 1813.
	Phil 2275.34	Stewart, D. Elements of the philosophy of the human mind. Boston, 1814-27. 3v.
	Phil 2275.34.5	Stewart, D. Elements of the philosophy of the human mind. N.Y., 1818. 2v.
Htn	Phil 2275.34.6*	Stewart, D. Elements of the philosophy of the human mind. N.Y., 1818. 2v.
	Phil 2275.34.11	Stewart, D. Elements of the philosophy of the human mind. v.1-2. Boston, 1821.
	Phil 2275.34.15	Stewart, D. Elements of the philosophy of the human mind. v.1-2. Albany, 1822.
	Phil 2275.35	Stewart, D. Elements of the philosophy of the human mind. Cambridge, 1829. 2v.
	Phil 2275.35.2	Stewart, D. Elements of the philosophy of the human mind. v.1-2. Cambridge, 1829.
	Phil 2275.36	Stewart, D. Elements of the philosophy of the human mind. London, 1843.
	Phil 2275.37	Stewart, D. Elements of the philosophy of the human mind. Boston, 1866.
Htn	Phil 2275.38*A	Stewart, D. Philosophy of the active and moral powers. Boston, 1828. 2v.
Htn	Phil 2275.38*B	Stewart, D. Philosophy of the active and moral powers. Boston, 1828. 2v.
	Phil 2275.38.2	Stewart, D. Philosophy of the active and moral powers. v.1-2. Boston, 1828.
	Phil 2275.39	Stewart, D. Philosophy of the active and moral poweers. Cambridge, 1849.
	Phil 2275.39.2	Stewart, D. Philosophy of the active and moral powers. Boston, 1858.
	Phil 2275.40	Stewart, D. Philosophie des facultés actives et morales de l'homme. v.1-2. Paris, n.d.
	Phil 2275.50	Stewart, D. Elements of the philosophy of the human mind. Boston, 1854.
	Phil 2275.50.2	Stewart, D. Elements of the philosophy of the human mind. Boston, 1855.
	Phil 2275.50.10	Stewart, D. Anfangsgründe der Philosophie über die menschliche Seele. Berlin, 1794. 2v.
Htn	Phil 2275.59*	Stewart, D. Philosophical essays. Edinburgh, 1810.
	Phil 2275.60	Stewart, D. Philosophical essays. Philadelphia, 1811.
	Phil 2275.60.10	Stewart, D. Essais philosophique sur les systèmes de Locke, Berkeley. Paris, 1828.
	Phil 2275.65	Stewart, D. A general view of the progress of...philosophy. Boston, 1822.

140

Classified Listing

Phil 2275 History of philosophy - Local Modern philosophy - Great Britain and United States - Individual philosophers - Stewart, Dugald - cont.

Phil 2275.70 Stewart, D. Outlines of moral philosophy. Edinburgh, 1893.
Phil 2275.80 Stewart, D. Élémens de la philosophie de l'esprit humain. Genève, 1808. 3v.

Phil 2280 History of philosophy - Local Modern philosophy - Great Britain and United States - Individual philosophers - Other S

Htn Phil 2280.1.30* Sidgwick, Henry. The methods of ethics. London, 1874.
Phil 2280.1.79 Pamphlet box. Philosophy. English. Sidgwick, Henry.
Phil 2280.1.80 Sidgwick, A. Henry Sidgwick. London, 1906.
Phil 2280.1.86 Sinclair, A.G. Der Utilitarismus bei Sidgwick...Spencer. Heidelberg, 1907.
Phil 2280.1.90 Bradley, F.H. Mr. Sidgwick's hedonism. London, 1877.
Phil 2280.1.93 Bernays, Paul. Das Moralprinzip bei Sidgwick und bei Kant. Göttingen, 1910.
Phil 2280.1.95 Havard, William C. Henry Sidgwick and later utilitarian political philosophy. Gainesville, 1959.
Phil 2280.2.75 Sully, James. My life and friends. London, 1918.
Htn Phil 2280.3.30* Stoddard, Solomon. An answer to some cases of conscience. Boston, 1722.
Htn Phil 2280.4.30F* Sidney, Algernon. Discourses concerning government. London, 1698.
Phil 2280.5.7 Santayana, George. The works of George Santayana. N.Y., 1936-40. 14v.
Phil 2280.5.25 Santayana, George. The philosophy of Santayana. N.Y., 1953.
Phil 2280.5.30 Santayana, George. Animal faith and spiritual life. N.Y., 1967.
Phil 2280.5.79 Munson, T.N. The essential wisdom of George Santayana. N.Y., 1962.
Phil 2280.5.79.5 Santayana, George. Selected critical writing. Cambridge, Eng., 1968. 2v.
Phil 2280.5.84 Santayana, George. The idler and his works. N.Y., 1957.
Phil 2280.5.85A Santayana, George. Persons and places. v.1,3. N.Y., 1944-53. 2v.
Phil 2280.5.85B Santayana, George. Persons and places. v.1,2. N.Y., 1944-45. 2v.
Phil 2280.5.85C Santayana, George. Persons and places. v.1,2. N.Y., 1944-45. 2v.
Phil 2280.5.85D Santayana, Goerge. Persons and places. v.2. N.Y., 1945.
Phil 2280.5.87 Santayana, George. Persons and places. London, 1944.
Phil 2280.5.88 Santayana, George. The life of reason. N.Y., 1954.
Phil 2280.5.90 Larrabec, H.A. George Santayana. pt.1-2. n.p., 1931.
Phil 2280.5.91 Santayana, George. Physical order and moral liberty. Nashville, 1969.
Phil 2280.5.95 Kallen, H.M. America and the life of reason. N.Y., 1921.
Phil 2280.5.97 Hoor, M. George Santayana's theory of knowledge. Diss. n.p., 1923.
Phil 2280.5.99 MacCampbell, D. Santayana's debt to New England. n.p., 1935.
Phil 2280.5.101 Clemens, C. George Santayana; an American philosopher in exile. Webster Groves, 1937.
Phil 2280.5.102 Howgate, G.W. George Santayana. Philadelphia, 1938.
Phil 2280.5.102.2 Howgate, G.W. George Santayana. Thesis. Philadelphia, 1938.
Phil 2280.5.105 Munitz, M.K. Moral philosophy of Santayana. N.Y., 1939.
Phil 2280.5.106 Schilpp, P.A. The philosophy of Santayana. Evanston, 1940.
Phil 2280.5.106.2 Schilpp, P.A. The philosophy of George Santayana. 2nd ed. N.Y., 1951.
Phil 2280.5.107 Lida, R. Belleza, arte y poesía en la estética de Santayana. Tucumán, 1943.
Phil 2280.5.108 Duron, J. La pensée de George Santayana. Paris, 1950.
Phil 2280.5.108.2 Duron, J. La pensée de George Santayana. Thèse. Paris, 1950.
Phil 2280.5.109 Arnett, W.E. Santayana and the sense of beauty. Bloomington, Ind., 1955.
Phil 2280.5.110A Butler, Richard. The mind of Santayana. Chicago, 1955.
Phil 2280.5.110B Butler, Richard. The mind of Santayana. Chicago, 1955.
Phil 2280.5.115 Lamont, Corliss. Dialogue on George Santayana. N.Y., 1959.
Phil 2280.5.125 Cory, D. Santayana: the later years. N.Y., 1963.
Phil 2280.5.130A Singer, Irving. Santayana's aesthetics; a critical introduction. Cambridge, 1957.
Phil 2280.5.130B Singer, Irving. Santayana's aesthetics; a critical introduction. Cambridge, 1957.
Phil 2280.5.140 Lamont, C. The enduring impact of G. Santayana. N.Y., 1964.
Phil 2280.5.145 Ashmore, Jerome. Santayana, art, and aesthetics. Cleveland, 1966.
VPhil 2280.5.150 Szmyd, Jan. Filozofia moralna Santayany. Wyd. 1. Warszawa, 1968.
Phil 2280.5.155 Endovitskii, V.D. Kritika filosofii amerikanskogo kriticheskogo realizma. Moskva, 1968.
Phil 2280.5.161 Singer, Beth J. The rational society; a critical study of Santayana's social thought. Cleveland, 1970.
Phil 2280.6.87 Potter, H.C. A sermon, memorial of the Rev. Charles W. Shields. Princeton, N.J., 1905.
Phil 2280.7.30 Schiller, F.C.S. Our human truths. N.Y., 1939.
Phil 2280.7.35 Schiller, F.C.S. Humanistic pragmatism. N.Y., 1966.
Phil 2280.7.79 Pamphlet box. Philosophy. English. Schiller, F.C.S.
Phil 2280.7.80 Abel, Reuben. The pragmatic humanism of F.C.S. Schiller. N.Y., 1955.
Phil 2280.7.85 Winetrout, Kenneth. F.C.S. Schiller and the dimensions of pragmatism. Columbus, 1967.
Phil 2280.8.90 Baillie, J.B. Andrew Seth Pringle-Pattison, 1856-1931. London, 1931.
Phil 2280.8.93 Rahder, J. Pringle-Pattison's Gifford lectures. v.1-2. Leipzig, 1920.
Phil 2280.8.95 Seth Pringle-Pattison, Andrew. Testimonials in favor of Andrew Seth. Photoreproduction. Edinburgh, 1891.
Phil 2280.9.79 Pamphlet box. Philosophy. English. Schroeder, Theodore.
Phil 2280.10.79 Pamphlet box. Philosophy. English. Sanford, Robert Nevitt.
Phil 2280.11.79 Pamphlet box. Philosophy. English. Shevach, B.J., and Kendig, Isabel.
Phil 2280.12.79 Pamphlet box. Philosophy. English. Stevens, Stanley Smith.
Phil 2280.13.30 Swenson, D. Kierkegaardian philosophy in the faith of a scholar. Philadelphia, 1949.
Phil 2280.13.79 Pamphlet box. Philosophy. English. Swenson, David F.
Phil 2280.14.80 Philosophical essays in honor of Edgar Arthur Singer, Jr. Philadelphia, 1942.
Phil 2280.15.80 Stirling, Amelia H. James Hutchinson Stirling, his life and work. London, 1912.
Phil 2280.16.80 Aristotelian Society for the Systematic Study of Philosophy, London. Philosophical studies; essays in memory of L. Susan Stebbing. London, 1948.

Phil 2280 History of philosophy - Local Modern philosophy - Great Britain and United States - Individual philosophers - Other S - cont.

Phil 2280.17.80 Singer, Edgar. Experience and reflection. Philadelphia, 1959.
Phil 2280.18.5 Sikora, Joseph John. Inquiry into being. Chicago, 1965.
Phil 2280.20.30 Sulzberger, Cyrus. My brother death. 1st ed. N.Y., 1961.
Phil 2280.21.5 Schutz, Alfred. Collected papers. The Hague, 1962. 3v.
Phil 2280.21.10 Schutz, Alfred. Reflections on the problem of relevance. New Haven, 1970.
Phil 2280.22.80 Melchert, Norman P. Realism, materialism, and the mind: the philosophy of Roy Wood Sellars. Springfield, Ill., 1968.
Phil 2280.23.30 Stern, Alfred. The search for meaning: philosophical vistas. Memphis, 1971.

Phil 2295 History of philosophy - Local Modern philosophy - Great Britain and United States - Individual philosophers - Toland, John

Phil 2295.10 Toland, John. Collection of several pieces. London, 1726. 2v.
Phil 2295.15 Toland, John. Miscellaneous works. London 1747. 2v.
Htn Phil 2295.24* Toland, John. Letters to Serena. London, 1704.
Htn Phil 2295.27* Toland, John. Historical account of life. London, 1718-22. 3 pam.
Htn Phil 2295.34* Toland, John. Christianity not mysterious. v.1-3. London, 1696.
Htn Phil 2295.35* Toland, John. Christianity not mysterious. 2nd ed. London, 1696.
Phil 2295.36 Toland, John. Christianity not mysterious. Stuttgart, 1964.
Htn Phil 2295.39* Toland, John. Pantheisticon, sive formula celebrandae sodalitatis Socraticae. Cosmopoli, 1720.
Phil 2295.40.5 Toland, John. Das Pantheistikon. Leipzig, 1897.
Htn Phil 2295.65* Toland, John. Lettres philosophiques. London, 1768.
Htn Phil 2295.75* Toland, John. Vindicius liberius. London, 1702.
Htn Phil 2295.75.2* Toland, John. Vindicius liberius. London, 1702.
X Cg Phil 2295.80 Berthold, G. John Toland und der Monismus der Gegenwart. Heidelberg, 1876.
Phil 2295.85 Lantoine, Albert. Un précurseur de la franc-maçonnerie, John Toland, 1670-1722. Paris, 1927.
Htn Phil 2295.86* Beverley, Thomas. Christianity the great mystery; answer to a late treatise. Dondon, 1696.
Phil 2295.87 Seeber, Anna. John Toland als politischer Schriftsteller. Inaug. Diss. Schramberg, 1933.
Phil 2295.90 Muff, Margrit. Leibnizenz kritik der Reliogionsphilosophie von John Toland. Abhandlung. Affoltern, 1940.

Phil 2300 History of philosophy - Local Modern philosophy - Great Britain and United States - Individual philosophers - Tucker, Abraham

Phil 2300.30 Tucker, Abraham. Light of nature pursued. London, 1768-77. 7v.
Phil 2300.30.2 Tucker, Abraham. Light of nature pursued. London, 1768. 5v.
Phil 2300.30.3 Tucker, Abraham. Light of nature pursued. London, 1805. 7v.
Phil 2300.30.5 Tucker, Abraham. Light of nature pursued. Cambridge, 1831. 4v.
Phil 2300.30.15 Tucker, Abraham. An abridgment of the Light of nature pursued. London, 1807.
Htn Phil 2300.40* Tucker, Abraham. Freewill, foreknowledge. v.1-2. London, 1763.

Phil 2305 History of philosophy - Local Modern philosophy - Great Britain and United States - Individual philosophers - Other T

Htn Phil 2305.1.30* Taylor, Thomas. The mystical initiations. London, 1787.
Htn Phil 2305.1.35* Taylor, Thomas. The fable of Cupid and Psyche. London, 1795.
Htn Phil 2305.2.30* Tyndall, John. Address before...British association at Belfast. London, 1874.
Phil 2305.3.79 Pamphlet box. Philosophy. English. Taylor, Alfred E., 1869-1945.
Phil 2305.5.30 Thalheimer, Alvin. Existential metaphysics. N.Y., 1960.
Phil 2305.6.30 Stark, Franz. Das Problem der moralischen Rechtfertinung bei S.E. Toulmin. München, 1964.

Phil 2310 History of philosophy - Local Modern philosophy - Great Britain and United States - Individual philosophers - U

Phil 2310.1.30 Ushenko, A.P. Power and events. Princeton, 1946.

Phil 2340 History of philosophy - Local Modern philosophy - Great Britain and United States - Individual philosophers - W

Phil 2340.1.79 Pamphlet box. Philosophy. English. Wiener, Norbert.
Phil 2340.1.80 Maron, M.E. Norbert Wiener. Santa Monica, Calif., 1965.
Htn Phil 2340.2.80* Walker, O. Proposed for the press. Boston, 1757.
Htn Phil 2340.3.30* Waring, Robert. Amoris effigies. 4th ed. London, 1671.
Htn Phil 2340.3.31* Waring, Robert. The picture of love. 4th ed .v.1-2. London, 1744.
Htn Phil 2340.4.30* Wilson, Thomas. The use of reason. n.p., 1553.
Htn Phil 2340.5.30* Wollaston, William. The religion of nature. London, 1725.
Phil 2340.5.80 Thompson, C.G. The ethics of William Wollaston. Diss. Boston, 1922.
Phil 2340.6.90 Sorley, W.R. James Ward, 1843-1925. London, 192-.
Phil 2340.6.95 Murray, A.H. The philosophy of James Ward. Cambridge, Eng., 1937.
Phil 2340.7.01 Pamphlet box. Philosophy. English. Wilson, William Dexter.
Phil 2340.8.80 Kingston, Ontario. Queen's University. Faculty of Arts. Philosophical essays presented to John Watson. Kingston, 1922.
Phil 2340.9.79 Pamphlet box. Philosophy. English. Whewell, William.
Phil 2340.9.90 Stoll, Marion R. Whewell's philosophy of induction. Diss. Lancaster, Pa., 1929.
Phil 2340.9.93 Blanché, Robert. Le rationalisme de Whewell. Thèse. Paris, 1935.
Phil 2340.9.94 Blanché, Robert. Le rationalisme de Whewell. Paris, 1935.
Phil 2340.10.25 Whitehead, Alfred North. Alfred North Whitehead; an anthology. N.Y., 1953.
Phil 2340.10.26 Whitehead, Alfred North. Alfred North Whitehead. N.Y., 1961.
Phil 2340.10.28 Whitehead, Alfred North. American essays in social philosophy. N.Y., 1959.
Phil 2340.10.30A Whitehead, Alfred North. Wit and wisdom. Boston, 1947.
Phil 2340.10.30B Whitehead, Alfred North. Wit and wisdom. Boston, 1947.
Phil 2340.10.35A Whitehead, Alfred North. Dialogues of Alfred North Whitehead. 1st ed. Boston, 1954.
Phil 2340.10.35B Whitehead, Alfred North. Dialogues of Alfred North Whitehead. 1st ed. Boston, 1954.
Phil 2340.10.40 Whitehead, Alfred North. Alfred North Whitehead. 1st ed. N.Y., 1961.

Phil 2340 History of philosophy - Local Modern philosophy - Great Britain and United States - Individual philosophers - W - cont.

Phil 2340.10.80 Pamphlet box. Philosophy. English. Whitehead, Alfred North.
Phil 2340.10.90A Emmet, Dorothy M. Whitehead's philosophy of organism. London, 1932.
Phil 2340.10.90B Emmet, Dorothy M. Whitehead's philosophy of organism. London, 1932.
Phil 2340.10.93A Symposium in honor of the 70th birthday of Alfred North Whitehead. Cambridge, 1932.
Phil 2340.10.93B Symposium in honor of the 70th birthday of Alfred North Whitehead. Cambridge, 1932.
Phil 2340.10.95 Thompson, E.J. An analysis of the thought of Alfred N. Whitehead and William E. Hocking concerning good and evil. Diss. Chicago, 1935.
Phil 2340.10.96A Whitehead, Alfred North. Essays in science and philosophy. N.Y., 1947.
Phil 2340.10.96B Whitehead, Alfred North. Essays in science and philosophy. N.Y., 1947.
Phil 2340.10.96.2 Whitehead, Alfred North. Essays in science and philosophy. N.Y., 1948.
Phil 2340.10.97A Das, Ras-Vihari. The philosophy of Whitehead. London, 1938.
Phil 2340.10.97B Das, Ras-Vihari. The philosophy of Whitehead. London, 1938.
Phil 2340.10.98A Whitehead, Alfred North. Modes of thought. N.Y., 1938.
Phil 2340.10.98B Whitehead, Alfred North. Modes of thought. N.Y., 1938.
Phil 2340.10.98.5 Whitehead, Alfred North. Modes of thought. N.Y., 1956.
Phil 2340.10.99 Miller, D.L. The philosophy of A.N. Whitehead. Minneapolis, 1938.
Phil 2340.10.100 Blyth, J.W. Whitehead's theory of knowledge. Providence, R.I., 1941.
Phil 2340.10.101A Schilpp, Paul A. The philosophy of Alfred North Whitehead. Evanston, 1941.
Phil 2340.10.101B Schilpp, Paul A. The philosophy of Alfred North Whitehead. Evanston, 1941.
Phil 2340.10.102 Ely, Stephen Lee. The religious availability of Whitehead's God. Madison, 1942.
Phil 2340.10.105 Bera, M.A. A.N. Whitehead; un philosophe de l'expérience. Paris, 1948.
Phil 2340.10.110 Wells, Harry K. Process and unreality. N.Y., 1950.
Phil 2340.10.115 Shahan, E.P. Whitehead's theory of experience. N.Y., 1950.
Phil 2340.10.120A Lowe, Victor A. Whitehead and the modern world. Boston, 1950.
Phil 2340.10.120B Lowe, Victor A. Whitehead and the modern world. Boston, 1950.
Phil 2340.10.125 Cesselin, Felix. La philosophie organique de Whitehead. 1e éd. Paris, 1950.
Phil 2340.10.126 Cesselin, Felix. La philosophie organique de Whitehead. Thèse. 1e éd. Paris, 1950.
Phil 2340.10.127 Schilpp, Paul A. The philosophy of Alfred North Whitehead. 2nd ed. N.Y., 1951.
Phil 2340.10.130 Johnson, A.H. Whitehead's theory of reality. Boston, 1952.
Phil 2340.10.130.5 Johnson, A.H. Whitehead's philosophy of civilization. Boston, 1958.
Phil 2340.10.135 Lawrence, N.M. Whitehead's philosophical development. Berkeley, 1956.
Phil 2340.10.140 Orsi, Concetta. La filosofia dell'organismo di A.N. Whitehead. Napoli, 1955.
Phil 2340.10.145 Leclerc, Ivor. Whitehead's metaphysics. London, 1958.
Phil 2340.10.148 Leclerc, Ivor. The relevance of Whitehead. London, 1961.
Phil 2340.10.150 Christian, William A. An interpretation of Whitehead's metaphysics. New Haven, 1959.
Phil 2340.10.155 Mays, Wolfe. The philosophy of Whitehead. London, 1959.
Phil 2340.10.160 Sherburne, Donald W. A Whiteheadian aesthetic. New Haven, 1961.
Phil 2340.10.165 Palter, Robert M. Whitehead's philosophy of science. Chicago, 1960.
Phil 2340.10.170 Lowe, Victor A. Understanding Whitehead. Baltimore, 1962.
Phil 2340.10.175 Kline, George Louis. Alfred North Whitehead. Englewood Cliffs, 1963.
Phil 2340.10.180 Burgers, Johannes Martinus. Experience and conceptual activity. Cambridge, Mass., 1965.
Phil 2340.10.185 Sherburne, Donald W. A key to Whitehead's Process and realty. N.Y., 1966.
Phil 2340.10.190 Dunkel, Harold Baker. Whitehead on education. Columbus, 1965.
Phil 2340.10.200 Schmidt, Paul Frederic. Perception and cosmology in Whitehead's philosophy. New Brunswick, 1967.
Phil 2340.10.205 Pols, Edward. Whitehead's metaphysics. Carbondale, 1967.
Phil 2340.10.210 Adhin, Herman S. Whitehead en de wereld. Proefschrift. Delft, 1963.
Phil 2340.10.215 Paci, Enzo. La filosofia di Whitehead e i problemi del tempo e della struttura. Milano, 1965.
Phil 2340.10.220 Sini, Carlo. Whitehead e la funzione della filosofia. Vicenza, 1965.
Phil 2340.10.225 Parmentier, Alix. La philosophie de Whitehead. Paris, 1968.
Phil 2340.10.230 Jordan, Martin. New shapes of reality: aspects of A.N. Whitehead's philosophy. London, 1968.
Phil 2340.10.235 Weisenbeck, Jude D. Alfred North Whitehead's philosophy of values. Thesis. Waukesha, Wisconsin, 1969.
Phil 2340.10.240 Laszlo, Ervin. La métaphysique de Whitehead: recherche des prolongements anthropologiques. La Hague, 1970.
Phil 2340.11 Weiss, Paul. Reality. Princeton, 1938.
Phil 2340.11.30 Weiss, Paul. Nature and man. N.Y., 1947.
Phil 2340.11.40 Weiss, Paul. Man's freedom. New Haven, 1950.
Phil 2340.11.50 Weiss, Paul. Modes of being. New Haven, 1956. 2v.
Phil 2340.11.55 Weiss, Paul. Religion and art. Milwaukee, 1963.
Phil 2340.11.60 Weiss, Paul. Philosophy in process. Carbondale, 1963-64. 5v.
Phil 2340.13.30 Wylie, Philip. An essay on morals. N.Y., 1947.
Phil 2340.14.30 Wauchope, Oswald S. Deviation into sense. London, 1948.
Phil 2340.15.30 Watmough, J.R. Cambridge conversations. Cambridge, 1949.
Phil 2340.16.30 Weems, B.F. Challenge eternal. N.Y., 1955.
Phil 2340.17.30 White, Morton Gabriel. Religion, politics, and the higher learning. Cambridge, 1959.
Phil 2340.18.30 Wright, Chauncey. Philosophical writings. N.Y., 1958.
Phil 2340.18.80 Madden, E. Chauncey Wright and the foundations of pragmatism. Seattle, 1963.
Phil 2340.19.30 Wisdom, John. The metamorphosis of metaphysics. London, 1961?
Phil 2340.20.30 Wolff, Charlotte. On the way to myself: communications to a friend. London, 1969.
Phil 2340.21.5 Alan Watts journal. 1,1969+
Phil 2340.22.30 Wank, Martin. The real world. N.Y., 1970.

Phil 2398 History of philosophy - Local Modern philosophy - France - Pamphlet volumes

Phil 2398 Pamphlet box. Philosophy. French.

Phil 2399 History of philosophy - Local Modern philosophy - France - History - General works - Collected authors

Phil 2399.1 Vek Prosveshcheniia. Moskva, 1970.

Phil 2400 - 2425 History of philosophy - Local Modern philosophy - France - History - General works - Individual authors (A-Z)

Phil 2400.1 André, Y.M. Documents...l'histoire...philosophie. Caen, 1844-56. 2v.
Phil 2400.2 Adam, C. La philosophie en France. Paris, 1894.
Phil 2400.3 Avezac-Lavigne, C. Saint-Simonisme-Positivisme. Paris, 1905.
Phil 2400.4.5 Anthologie des philosophes français contemporains. 2e éd. Paris, 1931.
Phil 2401.1 Belin, J.P. Le mouvement philosophique, 1748-1789. Paris, 1913.
Phil 2401.2 Boas, George. French philosophies of the romantic period. Baltimore, 1925.
Phil 2401.2.10 Boas, George. The happy beast in French thought of the 17th century. Baltimore, 1933.
Phil 2401.3.5 Benrubi, Isaac. Contemporary thought of France. London, 1926.
Phil 2401.3.12 Benrubi, Isaac. Philosophische Strömungen der Gegenwart in Frankreich. Leipzig, 1928.
Phil 2401.3.15A Benrubi, Isaac. Les sources et les courants de la philosophie contemporaine en France. Paris, 1933. 2v.
Phil 2401.3.15B Benrubi, Isaac. Les sources et les courants de la philosophie contemporaine en France. Paris, 1933. 2v.
Phil 2401.4 Bondi, P. Études littéraires: essais sur les philosophes. Florence, 1918.
Phil 2401.5 Boutroux, E. Nouvelles études d'histoire de la philosophie. Paris, 1927.
X Cg Phil 2401.6 Bergson, H. La philosophie. Paris, 1915.
Phil 2401.7 Bonnard, A. Le mouvement antipositiviste contemporain en France. Thèse. Paris, 1936.
Phil 2401.8 Baruzi, Jean. Philosophes et savants français du XXe siècle. Paris, 1926. 3v.
Phil 2401.9 Benda, J. De quelques constantes de l'esprit humain. Paris, 1950.
Phil 2401.10 Bréhier, E. Transformation de la philosophie française. Paris, 1950.
Phil 2401.15 Barber, W.H. Leibniz in France. Oxford, 1955.
Phil 2401.16 Boguslavskii, Veniamin M. U istokov frantsuzskogo ateizma i materializma. Moskva, 1964.
NEDL Phil 2402.1 Caraman, V.A.C. Histoire des révolutions de la philosophie. Paris, 1845-48. 3v.
Phil 2402.2 Caro, E.M. Philosophie et philosophes. Paris, 1888.
Phil 2402.3 Carove, F.M. Philosophie in Frankreich. Göttingen, 1827. 2v.
Phil 2402.4 Cresson, A. Les courants de la pensée philosophie française. Paris, 1927. 2v.
Phil 2402.5 Capone Braga, G. La filosofia francese e italiana del settecenta. 3a ed. v.1-2. Padova, 1947.
Phil 2402.6 Caso, A. Filósofos y moralistas franceses. México, 1943.
Phil 2402.7 Crocker, Lester G. An age of crisis. Baltimore, 1959.
Phil 2402.8 Charlton, D.G. Secular religions in France, 1815-1870. London, 1963.
Phil 2402.9 Callot, E. Six philosophes français du XVIIIe siècle. Annecy, 1963.
Phil 2402.9.5 Callot, E. La philosophie de la vie au XVIIIe siècle. Paris, 1965.
Phil 2403.1 Damiron, J.P. Essai sur l'histoire...philosophie en France. Paris, 1846. 2v.
Phil 2403.1.5 Damiron, J.P. Memoires pour servir á l'histoire...philosophie au XVIIIe siècle. Paris, 1858. 2v.
Phil 2403.1.10 Damiron, J.P. Essai sur l'histoire...philosophie en France au dix-neuvième siècle. Paris, 1828. 2v.
Phil 2403.1.11 Damiron, J.P. Essai sur l'histoire...philosophie en France au XIXe siècle. Paris, 1834. 2v.
Phil 2403.1.50 Massias, N. Lettre à M.P. Damiron sur un article de son essai sur l'histoire de la philosophie en France au dix-neuvième siècle. Paris, 1828.
Phil 2403.3 DeLuc, J.F. Observations sur les Savans incredules. Genève, 1762.
Phil 2403.4 Duclaux, A.M.F.R. The French ideal. N.Y., 1911.
Phil 2403.7 Dauriac, L. Contingence et nationalisme. Paris, 1924.
Phil 2403.8 Daval, Roger. Histoire des idées en France. 2e éd. Paris, 1956.
Phil 2403.9 Diaz, F. Filosofia e politica nel Settecento francese. Torino, 1962.
Phil 2403.10 Deledalle, Gérard. Les philosophes français d'aujourd'hui par eux-mêmes. Paris, 1964?
Htn Phil 2404.1* Eloges de trois philosophes. London, 1753.
Phil 2404.2 Ewald, Oskar. Die französische Aufklärungsphilosophie. München, 1924.
Phil 2404.3 Ehrard, J. L'idée de nature en France. Paris, 1963. 2v.
Phil 2404.4 Emery, Leon. De Montaigne à Teilhard de Chardin via Pascal et Rousseau. Lyon, 1965.
Phil 2405.1 Ferraz, Marin. Étude sur la philosophie en France au XIXe siècle. Paris, 1877.
Phil 2405.2.2 Ferraz, Marin. Traditionalisme et ultramontanisme. 2e éd. Paris, 1880.
Phil 2405.2.3 Ferraz, Marin. Spiritualisme et libéralisme. 2e éd. Paris, 1887.
Phil 2405.2.5 Ferraz, Marin. Histoire de la philosophie pendant la révolution (1789-1804). Paris, 1889.
Phil 2405.3 Fonsegrive, G. De Taine à Régny. L'évolution des idées. Paris, 1917.
Phil 2405.4 Frankel, Charles. The faith of reason. N.Y., 1948.
Phil 2405.5.2 Farber, Marvin. Philosophic thought in France and the United States. 2. ed. Albany, 1968.
Phil 2405.5.5 Farber, Marvin. L'activité philosophique contemporaine en France. 1. éd. Paris, 1950. 2v.
Phil 2405.10 Foucher, Louis. La philosophie catholique en France au XIX siècle avant la renaissance Thomiste et dans son rapporrt avecelle. Paris, 1955.
Phil 2406.1 Gorham, Charles. Ethics of the great French rationalists. London, 1900.
Phil 2406.2 Gunn, J.A. Modern French philosophy. London, 1922.
Phil 2406.2.2 Gunn, J.A. Modern French philosophy. N.Y., 1922.
Phil 2406.3 Garaudy, Roger. Perspectives de l'homme. 2e éd. Paris, 1960.
Phil 2406.4A Gay, P. The party of humanity. 1st ed. N.Y., 1963.

Phil 2400 - 2425 History of philosophy - Local Modern philosophy - France - History - General works - Individual authors (A-Z) - cont.

Phil 2406.4B	Gay, P. The party of humanity. 1st ed. N.Y., 1963.
Phil 2406.6	Guittoy, Jean. Regards sur la pensée française, 1870-1940. Paris, 1968.
Phil 2407.5	Hansen, V. Gennembrudsmaend i nyere fransk filosofi. København, 1952.
Phil 2409.1	Janet, P. La crise philosophique. Paris, 1865.
Phil 2409.1.5	Janet, P. La philosophie française contemporaine. Paris, 1879.
Phil 2409.2	Joyau, Emmanuel. La philosophie en France pendant la révolution. Paris, 1893.
Phil 2410.1	Kuznetsov, Vitalii N. Frantsuzskaia burzhuaznaia filosofiia dvadtsatogo veka. Moskva, 1970.
Phil 2411.1	Lerminier, E. De l'influence de la philosophie du XVIIIe siècle. Paris, 1833.
Phil 2411.2	Levy-Bruhl, L. History of modern philosophy in France. London, 1899.
Phil 2411.4	Levi, Adolfo. L'indeterminismo nella filosofia francese contemporanea. Firenze, 1904.
Phil 2411.7	León, Ferdinand. Lebensquellen französischer Metaphysik. Hamburg, 1949.
Phil 2411.8	LeFlamanc, Auguste. Les utopies prérévolutionnaires et la philosophie du XVIIIe siècle. Brest, 1933.
Phil 2411.9	Lacroix, Jean. Panorama de la philosophie française contemporaine. Paris, 1966.
Phil 2412.1	Margerie, M.A. Philosophie contemporaine. Paris, 1870.
Phil 2412.2	Moreau, Jacob N. Nouveau mémoire pour servir à l'histoire des Cacouacs. Amsterdam, 1757. 2 pam.
Phil 2412.3	Maumus, Vincent. Les philosophes contemporains. Paris, 1891.
Phil 2412.4.7	Maritain, Jacques. Trois réformateurs; Luther, Descartes, Rousseau. Paris, 1939.
Phil 2412.5	Müller, Max. Die französische Philosophie der Gegenwart. Karlsruhe, 1926.
Phil 2412.6	Muller, Maurice. De Descartes à Marcel Proust. Neuchâtel, 1943.
Phil 2412.10.2	Mauzi, Robert. L'idée du bonheur dans la littérature et la pensée françaises. 2e éd. Paris, 1965.
Phil 2412.12A	Manuel, F.E. The prophets of Paris. Cambridge, 1962.
Phil 2412.12B	Manuel, F.E. The prophets of Paris. Cambridge, 1962.
NEDL Phil 2414.1	Owen, J. The skeptics of the French renaissance. London, 1893.
Phil 2415.2	Poitou, E.L. Les philosophes franĉais contemporains. Paris, 1864.
Phil 2415.3	Portalis, J.E.M. De l'usage et de l'abus de l'esprit philosophique durant le XVIIE siècle. Paris, 1834. 2v.
Phil 2415.3.25	Frégier, J.C. Portalis, philosophes-chrétien. Paris, 1861.
Phil 2415.4	Picavet, F. Les idealogues. Paris, 1891.
Phil 2415.5	Parodi, Dominique. La philosophie contemporaine en France. Paris, 1919.
Phil 2415.5.2	Parodi, Dominique. La philosophie contemporaine en France. Paris, 1920.
Phil 2415.5.10	Parodi, Dominique. Du positivisme à l'idéalisme. Paris, 1930. 2v.
Phil 2415.6	Philosophes et savants français du XXe siècle. Paris. 1-5,1926-1930 5v.
Phil 2415.7	Pickman, Edward M. Collapse of the scholastic hierarchy in 17th century France. Boston, 1931.
Phil 2415.8	Palmer, R.R. Catholics and unbelievers in eighteenth century France. Princeton, 1939.
Phil 2415.10	Pervicax (pseud.). Les infiltrations germaniques dans la pensée française. Paris, 1945.
Phil 2415.12A	Pintard, René. La libertinage érudit dans la première mortié du XVII siècle. v.1-2. Paris, 1943.
Phil 2415.12B	Pintard, René. La libertinage érudit dans la première mortié du XVII siècle. v.1-2. Paris, 1943.
Phil 2415.14	Popovych, M.V. Pokhid proty rozumu. Kyiv, 1960.
Phil 2417.1	Ravaisson, J.G.F. La philosophie en France au XIXe siècle. Paris, 1868.
Phil 2417.2A	Ripley, G. Philosophical miscellanies...Cousin, Jouffray. Boston, 1838. 2v.
Phil 2417.2B	Ripley, G. Philosophical miscellanies...Cousin, Jouffray. Boston, 1838. 2v.
Phil 2417.4A	Rosenfield, Leonora D.C. From beast-machine to man-machine. N.Y., 1941.
Phil 2417.4B	Rosenfield, Leonora D.C. From beast-machine to man-machine. N.Y., 1941.
Phil 2417.4.5	Rosenfield, Leonora D.C. From beast-machine to man-machine. N.Y., 1968.
Phil 2417.5	Rossi, Pietro. Gli illuministi francesi. Torino, 1962.
Phil 2418.1	Simon, Paul M. Der Pragmatisme in der modernen französischen Philosophie. Paderborn, 1920.
Phil 2418.2	Schelle, Meta. Studien zum französischen Pyrrhomismus. Inaug. Diss. Göttingen, 1930.
Phil 2418.3	Segond, J. Art et science dans la philosophie française contemporaine. Paris, 1936.
Phil 2418.4	Sève, L. La philosophie françise contemporaine et sa genèse de 1789 à nos jours. Paris, 1962.
Phil 2418.5	Stein, Jay W. The mind and the sword. N.Y., 1961.
Phil 2418.6	Smith, C. Contemporary French philosophy. N.Y., 1964.
Phil 2418.7	Spink, John Stephenson. French free-thought from Gassendi to Voltaire. London, 1960.
Phil 2419.1	Taine, Hippolyte Adolphe. Les philosophes français du XIXe siècle. Paris, 1857.
Phil 2419.1.2	Taine, Hippolyte Adolphe. Les philosophes français du XIXe siècle. Paris, 1860.
Phil 2419.1.2.5	Taine, Hippolyte Adolphe. Les philosophes français du XIXe siècle. Paris, 1966.
Phil 2419.1.3	Taine, Hippolyte Adolphe. Les philosophes clasiques du XIXe siècle. Paris, 1868.
Phil 2419.2	Tornezy, Albert. La légende des "philosophes". Paris, 1911.
Phil 2419.3	Théard. Tableau des trois époques, ou Les philosophes. Paris, 1829.
Phil 2419.4	La tradition philosophique et la pensée française. Paris, 1922.
Phil 2419.5	Tsebenko, M.D. Der Atheismus der französischen Materialisten des 18. Jarhunderts. 1. Aufl. Berlin, 1956.
Phil 2420.1	Urwin, Kenneth. A century for freedom; a survey of the French philosophers. London, 1946.
Phil 2421.1	Vorländer, Karl. Französische Philosophie. Breslau, 1923.
Phil 2421.2	Vyverberg, H.S. Historical pessimism in the French enlightenment. Cambridge, 1958.
Phil 2421.5	Volgin, V.P. Razvitie obshchestvennoi mysli vo Frantsii v XVIII veke. Moskva, 1958.

Phil 2400 - 2425 History of philosophy - Local Modern philosophy - France - History - General works - Individual authors (A-Z) - cont.

Phil 2421.7	Valentini, Francesco. La filosofia francese contemporanea. 1a ed. Milano, 1958.
Phil 2421.10	Vereker, Charles. Eighteenth-century optimism. Liverpool, 1967.
Phil 2422.1	Wulf, M. de. Histoire de la philosophie en Belgique. Bruxelles, 1910.
Phil 2422.2	Wijnaendts Francken, C.J. Fransche moralisten. Haarlem, 1904.
Phil 2422.3	Wade, Ira O. The Clandestine organization and diffusion of philosophic ideas in France from 1700 to 1750. Princeton, 1938.
Phil 2422.5	Wahl, Jean A. Tableau de la philosophie française. Paris, 1946.
Phil 2422.5.2	Wahl, Jean A. Tableau de la philosophie française. Paris, 1948.
Phil 2422.5.5	Wahl, Jean A. Französische Philosophie. 1e Aufl. Säkingen, 1948.
Phil 2422.6	Willard, Nedd. Le génie et la folie au dix-huitième siècle. Paris, 1963.
Phil 2422.8	White, Reginald James. The anti-philosophers; a study of philosophers in eighteenth century France. London, 1970.

Phil 2428 History of philosophy - Local Modern philosophy - France - History - Special topics

Phil 2428.5	Kingston, Frederick Temple. French existentialism; a Christian critique. Toronto, 1961.
Phil 2428.12	Trotignon, Pierre. Les philosophes français d'aujourd'hui. 2. éd. Paris, 1970.
Phil 2428.15	Denis, Jacques. Sceptiques ou libertins de la première moitié du XVIIe siècle. Genève, 1970.
Phil 2428.20	Schiwy, Günther. Der französische Strukturalismus. Reinbek, 1970.

Phil 2430 History of philosophy - Local Modern philosophy - France - Anthologies of philosophical writings

Phil 2430.2	Cuvillier, Armand. Anthologie des philosophes français. Paris, 1962.
Phil 2430.3	Torrey, Norman L. Les philosophes. N.Y., 1960.
Phil 2430.6	Desné, Roland. Les materialistes français de 1750 à 1800. Paris, 1965.

Phil 2438 History of philosophy - Local Modern philosophy - France - Individual philosophers - Arnauld, Antoine

Phil 2438.15	Arnauld, Antoine. Oeuvres philosophiques. Paris, 1843.
Phil 2438.16	Arnauld, Antoine. Oeuvres philosophiques. Paris, 1843.
Phil 2438.17	Arnauld, Antoine. Oeuvres de Messire Antoine Arnauld. v.1-43. Paris, 1964. 38v.

Phil 2445 History of philosophy - Local Modern philosophy - France - Individual philosophers - Other A

Phil 2445.1.30	Azaïs, Pierre H. Manuel du philosophe. Paris, 1816.
Phil 2445.1.79	Pamphlet box. Azaïs, Pierre H.
Phil 2445.2.6	Barthélemy-Saint-Hilaire, J. Philosophie des deux Ampère. Paris, 1866.
Phil 2445.3.1	André, Yves. Oeuvres. Paris, 1766-67. 4v.
Phil 2445.3.3	André, Yves. Oeuvres philosophiques. Paris, 1843.
Phil 2445.4.20	Alexandre, M. En souvenir de Michel Alexandre. Paris, 1956.
Phil 2445.5.30	Alguié, Ferdinand. Solitude de la raison. Paris, 1966.
Phil 2445.5.35	Alquié, Ferdinand. Signification de la philosophie. Paris, 1971.
Phil 2445.6.30	Axelos, Kôstas. Le jeu du monde. Paris, 1969.

Phil 2450 History of philosophy - Local Modern philosophy - France - Individual philosophers - Bayle, Pierre

Phil 2450.80	Denis, J. Bayle et Jurien. Caen, 1886.
Phil 2450.81	Feuerback, L.A. Pierre Bayle. Ansbach, 1838.
Phil 2450.81.2	Feuerback, L.A. Pierre Bayle. 2. Aufl. Leipzig, 1848.
Phil 2450.81.5A	Dibon, Paul. Pierre Bayle. Amsterdam, 1959.
Phil 2450.81.5B	Dibon, Paul. Pierre Bayle. Amsterdam, 1959.
Phil 2450.82	Rex, Walter. Essays on Pierre Bayle and religious controversy. The Hague, 1965.

Phil 2465 History of philosophy - Local Modern philosophy - France - Individual philosophers - Bonnet, Charles

Phil 2465.30	Bonnet, Charles. Essai analytique sur les facultés de l'âme. Copenhagen, 1760.
Phil 2465.30.5	Bonnet, Charles. Essai analytique sur les facultés de l'âme. v.1-2. 3e éd. Copenhagen, 1775.
Phil 2465.31	Claparède, E. La psychologie animale de Charles Bonnet. Genève, 1909.
Phil 2465.33	Bonnet, Charles. Psychologischer Versuch. Lemgo, 1773.
Phil 2465.79	Pamphlet box. Bonnet, Charles.
Phil 2465.80	Caraman, V.A.C.R. Charles Bonnet. Paris, 1859.
Phil 2465.81	Lemoine, Albert. Charles Bonnet de Genève. Thèse. Paris, 1850.
Phil 2465.82	Bonnet, Georges. Charles Bonnet (1720-1793). Thèse. Paris, 1929.
Phil 2465.85	Bonnet, Charles. Mèmoires autobiographiques de Charles Bonnet de Genève. Thèse. Paris, 1948.
Phil 2465.90	Savioz, R. La philosophie de Charles Bonnet de Genève. Thèse. 1e éd. Paris, 1948. 4v.

Phil 2475.1 History of philosophy - Local Modern philosophy - France - Individual philosophers - Bergson, Henri

Phil 2475.1.5	Bergson, Henri. Oeuvres. 1e éd. Paris, 1959.
Phil 2475.1.8	Bergson, Henri. Oeuvres. 3. éd. Paris, 1970.
Phil 2475.1.30	Bergson, Henri. The creative mind. N.Y., 1946.
Phil 2475.1.35	Bergson, Henri. Discours sur la politesse. Paris, 1945.
Phil 2475.1.37	Bergson, Henri. Le bon sens et études classiques. Clermont, 1947.
Phil 2475.1.38	Bergson, Henri. Les deux sources de la morale et de la religion. 14 éd. Paris, 1933.
Phil 2475.1.38.2	Bergson, Henri. Les deux sources de la morale et de la religion. Genève, 1945.
Phil 2475.1.38.4	Bergson, Henri. Les deux sources. Paris, 1932.
Phil 2475.1.38.6	Bergson, Henri. The two sources of morality and religion. N.Y., 1935.
Phil 2475.1.39	Bergson, Henri. Durée et simultanéité. 2e éd. Paris, 1923.
Phil 2475.1.39.5	Bergson, Henri. Durée et sumultanéité à propos de la théorie d'Einstein. Paris, 1923.
Phil 2475.1.39.10	Bergson, Henri. Duration and simultaneity. Indianapolis, 1965.
Phil 2475.1.40	Bergson, Henri. Essai sur les données immédiates de la conscience. Paris, 1889.

Phil 2475.1 History of philosophy - Local Modern philosophy - France - Individual philosophers - Bergson, Henri - cont.

Phil 2475.1.40.2	Bergson, Henri. Essai sur les données immédiates de la consciènce. 9. éd. Paris, 1911.
Phil 2475.1.40.4	Bergson, Henri. Essai sur les données immédiates de la conscience. 43. éd. Paris, 1944.
Phil 2475.1.40.6	Bergson, Henri. Essai sur les données immédiates de la conscience. Genève, 1945.
Phil 2475.1.40.10	Bergson, Henri. Essai sur les données immédiates de la conscience. Paris, 1961.
Phil 2475.1.41	Bergson, Henri. Time and free will; an essay on the immediate data of consciousness. N.Y., 1960.
Phil 2475.1.42	Bergson, Henri. Time and free will; an essay on the immediate data of consciousness. London, 1959.
Phil 2475.1.45	Bergson, Henri. L'énergie spirituelle. 5. éd. Paris, 1920.
Phil 2475.1.46	Bergson, Henri. Mind energy. London, 1920.
Phil 2475.1.50	Bergson, Henri. L'évolution créatrice. 4. éd. Paris, 1908.
Phil 2475.1.50.2A	Bergson, Henri. L'évolution créatrice. 5. éd. Paris, 1909.
Phil 2475.1.50.2B	Bergson, Henri. L'évolution créatrice. 5. éd. Paris, 1909.
Phil 2475.1.50.4	Bergson, Henri. L'évolution créatrice. 9. éd. Paris, 1912.
Phil 2475.1.50.6	Bergson, Henri. L'évolution créatrice. 10. éd. Paris, 1912.
Phil 2475.1.50.8	Bergson, Henri. L'évolution créatrice. 52. éd. Paris, 1940.
Phil 2475.1.50.10	Bergson, Henri. L'évolution créatrice. Genève, 1945.
Phil 2475.1.51	Bergson, Henri. Creative evolution. N.Y., 1944.
Phil 2475.1.51.2	Bergson, Henri. Creative evolution. N.Y., 1911.
Phil 2475.1.51.4	Bergson, Henri. Creative evolution. London, 1954.
Phil 2475.1.51.6	Bergson, Henri. Creative evolution. N.Y., 1911.
Phil 2475.1.51.8	Bergson, Henri. Creative evolution. N.Y., 1911.
Phil 2475.1.56	Bergson, Henri. An introduction to metaphysics. N.Y., 1912.
Phil 2475.1.56.2	Bergson, Henri. An introduction to metaphysics. London, 1913.
Phil 2475.1.57	Bergson, Henri. Einführung in die Metaphysik. Jena, 1909.
Phil 2475.1.60	Bergson, Henri. Matière et mémoire. 7. éd. Paris, 1911.
Phil 2475.1.60.2	Bergson, Henri. Matière et mémoire. 8. éd. Paris, 1912.
Phil 2475.1.60.4	Bergson, Henri. Matière et mémoire. 36. éd. Paris, 1941.
Phil 2475.1.60.6	Bergson, Henri. Matière et mémoire. Genève, 1946.
Phil 2475.1.61	Bergson, Henri. Matter and memory. N.Y., 1911.
Phil 2475.1.61.2	Bergson, Henri. Matter and memory. N.Y., 1912.
Phil 2475.1.61.4A	Bergson, Henri. Matter and memory. London, 1919.
Phil 2475.1.61.4B	Bergson, Henri. Matter and memory. London, 1919.
Phil 2475.1.63	Bergson, Henri. The meaning of the war. London, 1915.
Phil 2475.1.65	Bergson, Henri. La pensée et le mouvant. 5. éd. Paris, 1934.
Phil 2475.1.65.2	Bergson, Henri. La pensée et le mouvant. 12. éd. Paris, 1941.
Phil 2475.1.65.4	Bergson, Henri. La pensée et le mouvant. Genève, 1946.
Phil 2475.1.66	Bergson, Henri. The world of dreams. N.Y., 1958.
Phil 2475.1.66.5	Bergson, Henri. Dreams. N.Y., 1914.
Phil 2475.1.67	Bergson, Henri. La perception du changement. Oxford, 1911.
Phil 2475.1.69	Bergson, Henri. Le rire. 57. éd. Paris, 1941.
Phil 2475.1.69.5	Bergson, Henri. Le rire. Paris, 1928.
Phil 2475.1.69.6	Bergson, Henri. Laughter. London, 1911.
Phil 2475.1.69.7	Bergson, Henri. Le rire. Genève, 1945.
Phil 2475.1.71	Bergson, Henri. Discours de réception. Paris, 1918.
Phil 2475.1.73	Bergson, Henri. Schöpferische Entwicklung. Jena, 1921.
Phil 2475.1.75	Bergson, Henri. Zeit und Freiheit. Jena, 1920.
Phil 2475.1.76	Bergson, Henri. Memoire et vie. 1e éd. Paris, 1957.
Phil 2475.1.77	Columbia University. Library. A contribution to a bibliography of Henri Bergson. N.Y., 1913.
EDL Phil 2475.1.77	Columbia University. Library. A contribution to a bibliography of Henri Bergson. N.Y., 1913.
Phil 2475.1.78	Bergson, Henri. Écrits et paroles. Paris, 1957. 3v.
Phil 2475.1.79	Pamphlet box. Bergson, Henri.
Phil 2475.1.81	Solomon, J. Bergson. London, 1911.
Phil 2475.1.82	Stewart, J.W.K. A critical exposition of Bergson's philosophy. London, 1911.
Phil 2475.1.83	Lindsay, A.D. The philosophy of Bergson. London, 1911.
Phil 2475.1.85	Kitchin, D.B. Bergson for beginners. London, 1913.
Phil 2475.1.89	Segoud, J. L'intuition Bergsonienne. Paris, 1913.
Phil 2475.1.90	Carr, H.W. Henri Bergson; the philosophy of change. London, 1911.
Phil 2475.1.95	Coignet, C. De Kant à Bergson. Paris, 1911.
Phil 2475.1.99	Gillouin, R. Henri Bergson. Paris, 1910.
Phil 2475.1.103	Bergson, Henri. Choix de texte avec étude du...R. Gillouin. Paris, 1918.
Phil 2475.1.105	Gillouin, R. La philosophie de M. Henri Bergson. Paris, 1911.
Phil 2475.1.106	Gillouin, R. La philosophie de M. Henri Bergson. Paris, 1911.
Phil 2475.1.109A	Balsillie, D. An examination of Professor Bergson's philosophy. London, 1912.
Phil 2475.1.109B	Balsillie, D. An examination of Professor Bergson's philosophy. London, 1912.
Phil 2475.1.111	Desaymard, J. La pensée de Henri Bergson. Paris, 1912.
Phil 2475.1.113	LeRoy, E. Une philosophie nouvelle Henri Bergson. Paris, 1912.
Phil 2475.1.115	LeRoy, E. The new philosophy of Henri Berguson. N.Y., 1913.
Phil 2475.1.119	Dodson, G.R. Bergson and the modern spirit. Boston, 1913.
Phil 2475.1.125	Maritain, Jacques. La philosophie Bergsonienne. Paris, 1914.
Phil 2475.1.126	Maritain, Jacques. La philosophie Bergsonienne. 2. éd. Paris, 1930.
Phil 2475.1.128	Maritain, Jacques. Bergsonian philosophy and Thomism. N.Y., 1955.
Phil 2475.1.129	Russell, B. The philosophy of Bergson. Cambridge, 1914.
Phil 2475.1.132	Ruhe, A. Henri Bergson, an account of his life. London, 1914.
Phil 2475.1.133	Ruhe, A. Henri Bergson. Stockholm, 1914.
Phil 2475.1.135	Lovejoy, A.O. Bergson and romantic evolutionism. Berkeley, 1913.
Phil 2475.1.139	Sait, Una B. Ethical implications of Bergson's philosophy. N.Y., 1914.
Phil 2475.1.139.5	Florian, M. Der Begriff der Zeit bei Henri Bergson. Greifswald, 1914.
Phil 2475.1.145	Farges, Albert. Philosophie de M. Bergson. 2e ed. Paris, 1914.
Phil 2475.1.149	Olgiati, Francesco. La filosofia di Enrico Bergson. Torino, 1914.

Phil 2475.1 History of philosophy - Local Modern philosophy - France - Individual philosophers - Bergson, Henri - cont.

Phil 2475.1.152	Keller, Adolf. Eine Philosophie des Lebens. (H. Bergson). Jena, 1914.
Phil 2475.1.157	Cunningham, G.W. A study in the philosophy of Bergson. N.Y., 1916.
Phil 2475.1.158	Brockdorff, Cary. Die Wahrheit über Bergson. Berlin, 1916.
Phil 2475.1.165	Miller, L.H. Bergson and religion. N.Y., 1916.
Phil 2475.1.169	Höffding, Harald. Philosophie de Bergson. Paris, 1916.
Phil 2475.1.175	Grandjian, Frank. Une révolution dans la philosophie. 2e ed. Genève, 1916.
Phil 2475.1.179	Seillière, E. L'avenir de la philosophie Bergsonienne. Paris, 1917.
Phil 2475.1.185	Carr, Herbert W. The Philosophy of change. London, 1914.
Phil 2475.1.185.5	Carr, Herbert W. Henri Bergson; the philosophy of change. London, 1919.
Phil 2475.1.191	Benda, Julien. Sur le succès du Bergsonisme. Paris, 1914.
Phil 2475.1.192	Benda, Julien. Une philosophie pathétique. Paris, 1913.
Phil 2475.1.192.5	Benda, Julien. Une philosophie pathétique. Paris, 1914.
Phil 2475.1.194	Penido, M.T.L. La méthode intuitive de M. Bergson. Genève, 1918.
Phil 2475.1.195	Peckham, George W. Logic of Bergson's philosophy. N.Y., 1917.
Phil 2475.1.196	Kerler, Dietrich H. Henri Bergson und das Problem des Verhältnisses zwischen Leib und Seele. Ulm, 1917.
Phil 2475.1.197	Benda, Julien. Le bergsonisme. 5e éd. Paris, 1917.
Phil 2475.1.198	Meckauer, Walter. Der Intuitionismus und seine Elemente bei Henri Bergson. Leipzig, 1917.
Phil 2475.1.200	Zulen, P.S. La filosofía de lo inexpresable. Lima, 1920.
Phil 2475.1.201	Flewelling, Ralph. Bergson and personal realism. N.Y., 1920.
Phil 2475.1.202	Gunn, John Alex. Bergson and his philosophy. London, 1920.
Phil 2475.1.203	Mercanti, Pietro. Il pensiero filosofico cotemporaneo e la psicologia del Bergson. Roma, 1919?
Phil 2475.1.204	Hamilton, George R. Bergson and future philosophy. London, 1921.
Phil 2475.1.205	Stephen, Karin. The misuse of the mind. London, 1922.
Phil 2475.1.206	Luce, A.A. Bergson's doctrine of intuition. London, 1922.
Phil 2475.1.207	Pentimalli, G.H. Bergson. Torino, 1920.
Phil 2475.1.208	Nicolardot, F. Un pseudonyme Bergsonien? Paris, 1923.
Phil 2475.1.208.5	Nicolardot, F. Flore de G'nose, Laggrond, Pellis et Bergson. Paris, 1924.
Phil 2475.1.208.9	Nicolardot, F. A propos de Bergson. Paris, 1924.
Phil 2475.1.209	Rodrigues, G. Bergsonisme et moralité. Paris, 1921.
Phil 2475.1.210	Van Paassen, C.R. De antithesen in de philosophie van Henri Bergson. Haarlem, 1923.
Phil 2475.1.211	Hoogveld, J.E.H.J. "De nieuwe wijsbegeerte." Een studie over Henri Bergson. Utrecht, 1915.
Phil 2475.1.212	Jorgensen, J. Henri Bergson's filosofi i omrids. København, 1917.
Phil 2475.1.213	Schrecker, P. Henri Bergsons Philosophie der Persönlichkeit. München, 1912.
Phil 2475.1.214	Serini, P. Bergson e lo spiritualismo. Genova, 1923.
Phil 2475.1.216	Jacobbson, M. Henri Bergsons intuitionsfilosofi. Lund, 1911.
Phil 2475.1.219	Caramella, S. Bergson. Milano, 1925.
Phil 2475.1.222	Chevalier, Jacques. Bergson. Paris, 1926.
Phil 2475.1.222.5A	Chevalier, Jacques. Henri Bergson. N.Y., 1928.
Phil 2475.1.222.5B	Chevalier, Jacques. Henri Bergson. N.Y., 1928.
Phil 2475.1.222.10	Chevalier, Jacques. Henri Bergson. Paris, 1928.
Phil 2475.1.222.15	Chevalier, Jacques. Entretiens avec Bergson. Paris, 1959.
Phil 2475.1.223	Oxenstierna, G. Tids- och intuitionsproblemen i Bergson's filosofi. Thesis. Uppsala, 1926.
Phil 2475.1.224	Perego, Luigi. La dinamica dello spirito nella conoscenza: saggio...Bergson. Bologna, 1925.
Phil 2475.1.225	Wilm, E.C. Henri Bergson. N.Y., 1914.
Phil 2475.1.226	MacWilliam, J. Criticism of the philosophy of Bergson. Edinburgh, 1928.
Phil 2475.1.227	Challaye, F. Bergson. Paris, 1929.
Phil 2475.1.228	Jurēvičs, Pauls. Le problème de la connaissance dans la philosophie de Bergson. Paris, 1930.
Phil 2475.1.230	Mitchell, A. Studies in Bergson's philosophy. Lawrence, 1914-
Phil 2475.1.231	Laurila, K.S. La théorie du comique de M.H. Bergson. Helsinki, 1929.
Phil 2475.1.233	Jolivet, Régis. Essai sur la bergsonisme. Lyon, 1931.
Phil 2475.1.235	Basu, P.S. Bergson et le Vedanta. Montpellier, 1930.
Phil 2475.1.236	Rideau, Émile. Le dieu de Bergson. Thèse. Paris, 1932.
Phil 2475.1.237	Rideau, Émile. Le dieu de Bergson. Paris, 1932.
Phil 2475.1.238	Rideau, Émile. Les rapports de la matière et de l'esprit dans le bergsonisme. Paris, 1932.
Phil 2475.1.238.5	Rideau, Émile. Les rapports de la matière et de l'esprit dans le bergsonisme. Thèse. Paris, 1932.
Phil 2475.1.238.15	Rideau, Émile. Descartes, Pascal, Bergson. Paris, 1937.
Phil 2475.1.239	Pallière, Aimé. Bergson et le Judaïsme. Paris, 1933.
Phil 2475.1.241	Dryssen, Carl. Bergson und die deutsche Romantik. Marburg, 1922.
Phil 2475.1.243	Stallknecht, N.P. Bergson's idea of creation. Princeton, N.J., 1934?
Phil 2475.1.245	Loisy, Alfred. Y a-t-il deux sources de la religion et de la morale? Paris, 1933.
Phil 2475.1.247	Kann, Albert. Henri Bergson und meine Ideen. Wien, 1935.
Phil 2475.1.249	Maire, Gilbert. Bergson, mon maître. 6e éd. Paris, 1935.
Phil 2475.1.251	Córdoba, Argentina. Universidad Nacional. Instituto de Filosofía. Homenaje a Bergson. Córdoba, 1936.
Phil 2475.1.253	Sommer, Erika. Bergson's Einfluss auf die französische Schriftsprache. Inaug. Diss. München, 1935.
Phil 2475.1.255	Péguy, Charles. Note sur M. Bergson et la philosophie bergsonienne. 6e éd. Paris, 1935.
Phil 2475.1.257	Fénart, Michel. Les assertions bergsoniennes. Paris, 1936.
Phil 2475.1.259A	Szathmary, A. The aesthetic theory of Bergson. Cambridge, 1937.
Phil 2475.1.259B	Szathmary, A. The aesthetic theory of Bergson. Cambridge, 1937.
Phil 2475.1.261	Rolland, E. Le finalité morale dans le Bergsonisme. Paris, 1937.
Phil 2475.1.262	Stephen, Karin. The misuse of mind. N.Y., 1922.
Phil 2475.1.263	Jankélévitch, V. Bergson. Paris, 1931.
Phil 2475.1.263.5	Jankélévitch, V. Henri Bergson. Paris, 1959.

Phil 2475.1   History of philosophy - Local Modern philosophy - France -
Individual philosophers - Bergson, Henri - cont.

Phil 2475.1.264   Tonquédec, J. Sur la philosophie Bergsonienne.
                   Paris, 1936.
Phil 2475.1.265   Molina, Enrique. Proyecciones de la intuición. Santiago
                   de Chile, 1935.
Phil 2475.1.266   Figueroa, E.L. Bergson, exposición de sus ideas
                   fundamentales. La Plata, 1930.
Phil 2475.1.267   García Morente, M. La filosofía de Henri Bergson.
                   Madrid, 1917.
Phil 2475.1.269   Béguin, Albert. Henri Bergson. Essais et témoignages
                   inédits recueilles. Neuchâtel, 1941.
Phil 2475.1.270   Mexico City. Universidad Nacional. Facultad de Filosofía y
                   Estudios Superiores. Centro de Estudios Filosóficos.
                   Homenaje a Bergson. México, 1941.
Phil 2475.1.272   Sertillanges, A.G. Henri Bergson et le catholicisme.
                   Paris, 1941.
Phil 2475.1.274   Scharfstein, B.A. Roots of Bergson's philosophy.
                   N.Y., 1943.
Phil 2475.1.277   Coviello, A. El proceso filosófico de Bergson y su
                   bibliografía. 2. ed. Tucumán, 1941.
Phil 2475.1.280   Benrubi, Isaak. Souvenirs sur Henri Bergson.
                   Neuchâtel, 1942.
Phil 2475.1.282   Études Bergsoniennes, hommage à Henri Bergson (1859-1941).
                   Paris, 1942.
Phil 2475.1.284   Lacombe, R.E. La psychologie bergsonienne; étude critique.
                   Paris, 1933.
Phil 2475.1.286A   Cresson, André. Bergson; sa vie, son oeuvre, avec un
                   exposé de sa philosophie. Paris, 1941.
Phil 2475.1.286B   Cresson, André. Bergson; sa vie, son oeuvre, avec un
                   exposé de sa philosophie. Paris, 1941.
Phil 2475.1.288   Meyer, François. La pensée de Bergson. Grenoble, 1944.
Phil 2475.1.290   Benrubi, Isaak. Bergson. Buenos Aires, 1942.
Phil 2475.1.292   Valery, Paul. Henri Bergson. Paris, 1945.
Phil 2475.1.294   Adolphe, Lydie. La philosophie religieuse de Bergson.
                   Paris, 1946.
Phil 2475.1.294.4 Adolphe, Lydie. La dialectique des images chez Bergson.
                   Thèse. Paris, 1951.
Phil 2475.1.294.5 Adolphe, Lydie. La dialectique des images chez Bergson. 1.
                   éd. Paris, 1951.
Phil 2475.1.294.6 Adolphe, Lydie. L'univers bergsonien. Paris, 1955.
Phil 2475.1.296   Husson, León A. L'intellectualisme de Bergson.
                   Paris, 1947.
Phil 2475.1.297   Husson, León A. L'intellectualisme de Bergson. Thèse.
                   Paris, 1947.
Phil 2475.1.298   Sundén, Hjalmar. La théorie bergsonienne de la religion.
                   Thèse. Uppsala, 1940.
Phil 2475.1.298.5 Sundén, Jalmar. La théorie bergsonienne de la religion.
                   Paris, 1947.
Phil 2475.1.299   Politzer, Georges. Le Bergsonisme. Paris, 1947.
Phil 2475.1.299.5 Politzer, Georges. La fin d'une parade philosophique, le
                   Bergsonisme. Paris, 1967.
Phil 2475.1.300   Iliev, Alhanasso. Le Bergsonisme. Sofia, 193-?
Phil 2475.1.301   Les études bergsoniennes. Paris. 1-8 7v.
Phil 2475.1.302.5 Challaye, F. Bergson. Paris, 1947.
Phil 2475.1.303   Cavarnos, C.P. A dialogue between Bergson.
                   Cambridge, 1949.
Phil 2475.1.304   Jurēvičs, Pauls. Henri Bergson. Freiburg, 1949.
Phil 2475.1.305   Marietti, A. Les formes du mouvement chez Bergson. Le
                   Puy, 1953.
Phil 2475.1.306   Cuisa, Niso. Inchiesta sul Bergsonismo. Sassari, 1953.
Phil 2475.1.307   Delhomme, J. Vie et conscience de la vie. Thèse.
                   Paris, 1954.
Phil 2475.1.310   Mossé-Bastide, R.M. Bergson. Paris, 1955.
Phil 2475.1.315   Kelley, J.J. Bergson's mysticism. Thesis. Fribourg, 1954.
Phil 2475.1.320   Arbour, Romeo. Henri Bergson et les lettres françaises.
                   Paris, 1955.
Phil 2475.1.325   Montiani, Oddino. Bergson e il suo umanismo integrale.
                   Padova, 1957.
Phil 2475.1.330   Copleston, F.C. Bergson on morality. London, 1956.
Phil 2475.1.335   Heidsieck, F. Henri Bergson et la notion d'espace.
                   Paris, 1957.
Phil 2475.1.340   Alexander, I.W. Bergson. London, 1957.
Phil 2475.1.345   Lahbabi, Mohamed Aziz. Liberté ou libération?
                   Aubier, 1956.
Phil 2475.1.350   Mathieu, Vittorio. Bergson. Torino, 1954.
Phil 2475.1.355   Pflug, Günther. Henri Bergson. Berlin, 1959.
Phil 2475.1.360   Mossé-Bastide, Rose Marie. Bergson et Plotin. 1. éd.
                   Paris, 1959.
Phil 2475.1.360.5 Mossé-Bastide, Rose Marie. Bergson et Plotin. 1. éd.
                   Thèse. Paris, 1959.
Phil 2475.1.365   Bibliothèque Nationale, Paris. Henri Bergson; exposition.
                   Paris, 1959.
Phil 2475.1.370   Quintanilla, Louis. Bergonismo y política. 1. ed.
                   México, 1953.
Phil 2475.1.375   Černý, V. Ideové kořeny současného umění. Praha, 1929.
Phil 2475.1.380   Guitton, Jean. La vocation de Bergson. Paris, 1960.
Phil 2475.1.385   Chanyshev, A.N. Filosfiia Anri Bergsona. Moskva, 1960.
Phil 2475.1.390   Ades, Albert. Ades chez Bergson. Paris, 1949.
Phil 2475.1.395   Hanna, T. The Bergsonian heritage. N.Y., 1962.
Phil 2475.1.400   Gouhier, Henri. Bergson et le Christ des évangiles.
                   Paris, 1961.
Phil 2475.1.405   Trevisan, A. Essai sur le problèmes. Fribourg, 1963.
Phil 2475.1.410   Cresson, André. Bergson: sa vie, son oeuvre, avec un
                   exposé de sa philosophie. Paris, 1964.
Phil 2475.1.415   Elliots, Hugh Samuel Roger. Modern science and the
                   illusions of Professor Bergson. London, 1912.
Phil 2475.1.420   Darkaoui, Assad Arabi. Essai sur l'idée de pureté chez
                   Bergson. Damas, 1963.
Phil 2475.1.425   Mourélos, Giorgos. Bergson et les niveaux de réalité.
                   Paris, 1964.
Phil 2475.1.430   Giusso, Lorenzo. Bergson. Milano, 1949.
Phil 2475.1.435   Barthélemy-Madaule, Madeleine. Bergson, adversaire de
                   Kant. Paris, 1966.
Phil 2475.1.437   Barthélemy-Madaule, Madeleine. Bergson. Paris, 1967.
Phil 2475.1.440   Barlow, Michel. Henri Bergson. Paris, 1966.
Phil 2475.1.445   Wahl, Jean André. Bergson. Paris, 1965.
Phil 2475.1.450   Cavagna, Giordano Bruno. La dottrina della conoscenza in
                   Enrico Bergson. Napoli, 1965.
Phil 2475.1.455   Fressin, Augustin. La perception chez Bergson et chez
                   Merleau-Ponty. Paris, 1967.
Phil 2475.1.460   Ribeiro, Alvaro. Escritores doutrinados. Lisboa, 1965.
Phil 2475.1.465   Colletti, Giovanni. I fondamenti logico-metafisici del
                   bergsonismo e altri scritti. Padova, 1963.
VPhil 2475.1.470   Romanowski, Henryk. Nowa filozofja. Lublin, 1929.
Phil 2475.1.475   Milhand, Jean. A Bergson, la patrie reconnaissante.
                   Paris, 1967.

Phil 2475.1   History of philosophy - Local Modern philosophy - France -
Individual philosophers - Bergson, Henri - cont.

Phil 2475.1.480   Lebacqz, Joseph. De l'identique au multiple.
                   Québec, 1968.
Phil 2475.1.485   Violette, René. La spiritualité de Bergson.
                   Toulouse, 1968.
Phil 2475.1.490   Ebacher, Roger. La philosophie dans la cité technique.
                   Québec, 1968.
Phil 2475.1.495   Trotignon, Pierre. L'idée de vie chez Bergson et la
                   critique de la métaphysique. Paris, 1968.
Phil 2475.1.500   Gunter, Pete Addison Y. Bergson and the evolution of
                   physics. 1st ed. Knoxville, 1969.
Phil 2475.1.505   Callagher, Idella J. Morality in evolution: the moral
                   philosophy of Henri Bergson. The Hague, 1970.
Phil 2475.1.510   Janicaud, Dominique. Une généalogie du spiritualisme
                   français. La Haye, 1969.
Phil 2475.1.515   Theau, Jean. La critique bergsonienne du concept. Thèse.
                   Toulouse, 1967.

Phil 2477   History of philosophy - Local Modern philosophy - France - Individual
philosophers - Other B

Phil 2477.1.06   Boutroux, Émile. Philosophical pamphlets, 1888-1909.
                   Paris, 1888-1909.
Phil 2477.1.07   Boutroux, Émile. Philosophical pamphlets. Paris, 1904-05.
                   2 pam.
Phil 2477.1.08   Pamphlet box. Boutroux, Émile. Minor writings.
Phil 2477.1.25   Boutroux, Émile. Choix de textes. Paris, 1910.
Phil 2477.1.30   Boutroux, Émile. De la contingence des lois de la nature.
                   Thèse. Paris, 1874.
Phil 2477.1.32   Boutroux, Émile. De la contingence des lois de la nature.
                   3. éd. Paris, 1898.
Phil 2477.1.34   Boutroux, Émile. The contingency of the laws of nature.
                   Chicago, 1916.
Phil 2477.1.40   Boutroux, Émile. De l'idée de loi naturelle dans la
                   science et la philosophie contemporaines. Paris, 1895.
Phil 2477.1.41   Boutroux, Émile. De l'idée de loi naturelle dans la
                   science et la philosophie contemporaines. Paris, 1949.
Phil 2477.1.44   Boutroux, Émile. Natural law in science and philosophy.
                   London, 1914.
Phil 2477.1.50   Boutroux, Émile. Questions de morale et d'éducation.
                   Paris, 1895?
Phil 2477.1.55   Boutroux, Émile. La nature et l'esprit. Paris, 1926.
Phil 2477.1.63   Boutroux, Émile. Philosophy and war. London, 1916.
Phil 2477.1.64   Boutroux, Émile. Philosophy and war. N.Y., 1916.
Phil 2477.1.66   Boutroux, Émile. Certitude et vérité. London, 1915.
Phil 2477.1.100   LaFontaine, A.P. La philosophie d'E. Boutroux.
                   Paris, 1920.
Phil 2477.1.130   Ingenieros, José. Emilio Boutroux y la filosofía
                   universitaria en Francia. Buenos Aires, 1923.
Phil 2477.1.135   Crawford, L.S. The philosophy of Emil Boutroux. Thesis.
                   Charlotteville, 1924.
Phil 2477.1.136   Liguori-Barbieri, E. La filosofia di Émile Boutroux.
                   Pisa, 1926.
Phil 2477.1.139   Schyns, M. La philosophie d'Émile Boutroux. Paris, 1924.
Phil 2477.1.140   Baillot, A. Émile Boutroux et la pensée religieuse.
                   Paris, 1957.
Phil 2477.2.25   Bordas-Demoulin, J.B. Oeuvre posthumes. Paris, 1861.
                   2v.
Phil 2477.2.80   Huet, François. Histoire de la vie et des ouvrages de
                   Bordas-Demoulin. Paris, 1861.
Phil 2477.3.31   Barruel, Augustine. Les Helviennes. 5. éd. Paris, 1812.
                   4v.
Phil 2477.3.33   Barruel, Augustine. Les Helviennes. 7e éd. Paris, 1830.
                   4v.
Phil 2477.4.30   Bonald, L.G.A. Recherches philosophiques sur les premiers
                   objets des connaissances morales. Paris, 1818. 2v.
Phil 2477.5.30   Boberil, Roger. Essais philosophiques. Rennes, 1910.
                   2 pam.
Phil 2477.6.20   Blondel, Maurice. Correspondance, 1899-1912. Paris, 1957.
                   3v.
Phil 2477.6.30   Blondel, Maurice. Les premiers écrits de Maurice Blondel.
                   1. éd. Paris, 1956.
Phil 2477.6.32   Blondel, Maurice. Carnets intimes, 1883-1894.
                   Paris, 1961.
Phil 2477.6.34   Blondel, Maurice. Correspondance philosophique.
                   Paris, 1961.
Phil 2477.6.40   Blondel, Maurice. Lettres philosophiques. Paris, 1961.
Phil 2477.6.45   Blondel, Maurice. Blondel et Teilhard de Chardin.
                   Paris, 1965.
Phil 2477.6.80   Tonquedec, J. de. Immanence: essai critique sur le
                   doctrine de M. Maurice Blondel. 2e éd. Paris, 1913.
Phil 2477.6.80.5   Tonquedec, J. de. Deux études sur "La pensée de M.
                   Blondel". Paris, 1936.
Phil 2477.6.81   Gilbert, K. Maurice Blondel's philosophy of action.
                   Chapel Hill, 1924.
Phil 2477.6.85   Archambault, P. Vers un realisme intégral...Blondel.
                   Paris, 1928.
Phil 2477.6.87   Lefévre, Frédéric. L'itinéraire philosophique de M.
                   Blondel. Paris, 1928.
Phil 2477.6.89   Castelli, Enrico. Lettres reçues à propos de la
                   communication de M. Blondel. Marseille, 1933.
Phil 2477.6.92   Taymans d'Eypernon, F. Le blondelisme. Louvain, 1933.
Phil 2477.6.95   Scivittaro, F. L'azione e il pensiero. Roma, 1936.
Phil 2477.6.99   Valensin, A. Maurice Blondel. 2e éd. Paris, 1934.
Phil 2477.6.103   Federici Ajeoldi, G. Interpretazione del problema
                   dell'essere in M. Blondel. Firenze, 1936.
Phil 2477.6.105   Hommage à Maurice Blondel. Paris, 1946.
Phil 2477.6.108   Hayen, A. Bibliographie blondelienne. Bruxelles, 1953.
Phil 2477.6.110   Salvo, Franco. La logica della vita morale in Maurice
                   Blondel. Palermo, 1942.
Phil 2477.6.115   Crippà, Romeo. Rassegna di bibliografia blondeliana.
                   Torino, 1953.
Phil 2477.6.118   Crippà, Romeo. Il realismo integrale di M. Blondel.
                   Milano, 1954.
Phil 2477.6.120   Bonicelli, B.M. La logica morale in Maurice Blondel.
                   Torino, 1950.
Phil 2477.6.122   Ritz, Maria. Le problème de l'être dans l'ontologie de
                   Maurice Blondel. Fribourg, 1958.
Phil 2477.6.125   École, J. La métaphysique de l'être dans la philosophie
                   de Maurice Blondel. Louvains, 1959.
Phil 2477.6.130   Cartier, Albert. Existence et vérité. Paris, 1955.
Phil 2477.6.135   Bouillard, Henri. Blondel et le christianisme.
                   Paris, 1961.
Phil 2477.6.140   Tresmontant, C. Introduction à la metaphysique de Maurice
                   Blondel. Paris, 1963.
Phil 2477.6.145   Sciacca, M.E. Dialogo con M. Blondel. Milano, 1962.
Phil 2477.6.150   Lacroix, Jean. Maurice Blondel. Paris, 1963.

Phil 2477   History of philosophy - Local Modern philosophy - France - Individual
philosophers - Other B - cont.

Phil 2477.6.155   Saint-Jean, Raymond. L'apologétique philosophique. Paris, 1966.
Phil 2477.6.160   McNeill, John J. The Blondelian synthesis; a study of the influence of German philosophical sources on the formation of Blondel's method and thought. Leiden, 1966.
Phil 2477.6.165   Saint-Jean, Raymond. Genèse de l'action; Blondel, 1882-1893. Bruges, 1965.
Phil 2477.6.170   Scannone, Juan Carlos. Sein und Inkarnation. Diss. Freiburg, 1968.
Phil 2477.6.175   Parys, Jean M. van. La vocation de la liberté. Paris, 1968.
Phil 2477.6.180   Blondel, Maurice. Correspondance de Maurice Blondel et Joannès Wehrlé; extraits. Paris, 1969. 2v.
Phil 2477.6.185   Jouhaud, Michel. Le problème de l'être et l'expérience morale chez Maurice Blondel. Paris, 1970.
Phil 2477.7.81   Dippel, Joseph. Versuch einer systematischen Darstellung der Philosophie des C. Bovillus. Würzburg, 1865.
Phil 2477.8.81   Martin, Robert. Alfred Binet. Thèse. Paris, 1924.
Phil 2477.8.83   Bertrand, F.L. Alfred Binet et son oeuvre. Paris, 1930.
Phil 2477.8.84   Bertrand, F.L. Alfred Binet et son oeuvre. Thèse. Paris, 1930.
Phil 2477.8.90   Avanzini, Guy. La contribution de Binet à l'élaboration d'une pédagogie scientifique. Paris, 1969.
Phil 2477.9.81   Horton, W.M. The philosophy of the Abbé Bantain. N.Y., 1926.
Phil 2477.9.84   Bernard, Claude. Philosophie, manuscrit inédit. Paris, 19- .
Phil 2477.9.84.2   Bernard, Claude. Philosophie. Paris, 1954.
Phil 2477.9.85   Sertillanges, A.G. La philosophie de Claude Bernard. Paris, 1944.
Phil 2477.10.90   Latreille, C. Francisque Bouillier. Paris, 1907.
Phil 2477.11.30   Brunschvicg, Léon. Écrits philosphiques. 1. éd. Paris, 1951- 3v.
Phil 2477.11.90   Carbonara, C. Léon Brunschvicg. Napoli, 1930.
Phil 2477.11.91   Messaut, J. La philosophie de Léon Brunschvicg. Paris, 1938.
Phil 2477.11.93   Deschoux, Marcel. La philosophie de Léon Brunschvicg. Paris, 1949.
Phil 2477.11.94   Deschoux, Marcel. Léon Brunschvicg ou l'idéalisme à hauteur d'homme. Paris, 1969.
Phil 2477.11.95   Cochet, M.A. Commentaire sur la conversion spirituelle dans la philosophie de L. Branschvicg. Bruxelles, 1937.
Phil 2477.11.98   Deschoux, Marcel. La philosophie de Léon Brunschvicg. Thèse. Paris, 1949.
Phil 2477.11.105   Boirel, R. Brunschvicg; sa vie, son oeuvre avec un exposé de la philosophie. Paris, 1964.
Phil 2477.12   Bespaloff, R. Cheninement et carrefours. Paris, 1938.
Phil 2477.13   Bréhier, Émile. Science et humanisme. Paris, 1947.
Phil 2477.15   Bachelard, Gaston. Le matérialisme rationnel. Paris, 1953.
Phil 2477.15.5   Bachelard, Gaston. La poétique de l'espace. 1. éd. Paris, 1957.
Phil 2477.15.5.2   Bachelard, Gaston. La poétique de l'espace. 2. éd. Paris, 1958.
Phil 2477.15.6   Bachelard, Gaston. The poetics of space. N.Y., 1964.
Phil 2477.15.8   Bachelard, Gaston. The poetics of reverie. N.Y., 1969.
Phil 2477.15.10   Bachelard, Gaston. La poétique de la rêverie. Paris, 1960.
Phil 2477.15.13   Bachelard, Gaston. La poétique de la rêverie. 3. éd. Paris, 1965.
Phil 2477.15.22   Bachelard, Gaston. On poetic imagination and reverie; selections from the works of Gaston Bachelard. Indianapolis, 1971.
Phil 2477.15.32   Bachelard, Gaston. Le droit de rêver. 2. éd. Paris, 1970.
Phil 2477.15.35   Bachelard, Gaston. Études. Paris, 1970.
Phil 2477.15.80   Quillet, Pierre. Bachelard. Paris, 1964.
Phil 2477.15.85   Dagognet, François. Gaston Bachelard. Paris, 1965.
Phil 2477.15.90   Caws, Mary Ann. Surrealism and the literary imagination; a study of Breton and Bachelard. The Hague, 1966.
Phil 2477.15.95   Mansuy, Michel. Gaston Bachelard et les éléments. Paris, 1967.
Phil 2477.15.100   Pire, François. De l'imagination poétique dans l'oeuvre de Gaston Bachelard. Paris, 1967.
Phil 2477.15.110   Voisin, Marcel. Bachelard. Bruxelles, 1967.
Phil 2477.15.115   Gagey, Jacques. Gaston Bachelard; ou, La conversion à l'imaginaire. Paris, 1969.
Phil 2477.15.120   Therrien, Vincent. La révolution de Gaston Bachelard en critique littéraire. Paris, 1970.
Phil 2477.16.30   Brunet, Christian. Prolégomenes a une esthétique intégrale. Paris, 1962.
Phil 2477.17.30   Breton, Stanislas. Essence et existence. Paris, 1962.
Phil 2477.19.30   Berger, G. Phénoménologie du temps et prospective. Paris, 1964.
Phil 2477.19.80   Gouhier, Henri. Notice sur la vie et les travaux de Gaston Berger, 1896-1960. Paris, 1962.
Phil 2477.19.82   Ginisty, Bernard. Conversion spirituelle et engagement prospectif, essai pour une lecture de Gaston Berger. Paris, 1966.
Phil 2477.20.80   Pradines, Marie Thérèse. Georges Bastide, philosophe de la valeur. Toulouse, 1970.
Phil 2477.89.30   Bruaire, Claude. L'affirmation de Dieu. Paris, 1964.

Phil 2480   History of philosophy - Local Modern philosophy - France - Individual
philosophers - Cabanis, Pierre

Phil 2480.10   Cabanis, P.J.G. Oeuvres. Paris, 1823. 5v.
Phil 2480.15   Cabanis, P.J.G. Oeuvres philosophiques. 1. éd. Paris, 1956. 2v.
Phil 2480.20A   Cabanis, P.J.G. Choix de textes. Paris, n.d.
Phil 2480.20B   Cabanis, P.J.G. Choix de textes. Paris, 1910?
Phil 2480.30   Cabanis, P.J.G. Rapports du physique et du moral de l'homme. Paris, 1802. 2v.
Phil 2480.30.2   Cabanis, P.J.G. Rapports du physique et du moral de l'homme. Paris, 1805.
Phil 2480.30.5   Cabanis, P.J.G. Rapports du physique et du moral de l'homme. Paris, 1824. 3v.
Phil 2480.31   Cabanis, P.J.G. Rapports du physique et du moral de l'homme. Paris, 1843.
Phil 2480.31.5   Cabanis, P.J.G. Rapports du physique et du moral de l'homme. 8e éd. Paris, 1844.
Phil 2480.80   Vermeil de Conchard, P.P. Trois études sur Cabanis. Brive, 1914.
Phil 2480.81   Tencer, Marie. La psychophysiologie de Cabanis. Thèse. Toulouse, 1931.
Phil 2480.82   Peisse, L. Notice historique et philosophique sur la vie. Paris, 1844.

Phil 2480   History of philosophy - Local Modern philosophy - France - Individual
philosophers - Cabanis, Pierre - cont.

Phil 2480.85   Brive, France. Mussée Ernest Rupin. Cabanis, médecin, philosophe et l'époque révolutionnaire. Brive, 1957.
Phil 2480.88   Bigoni, Angelo. Vero rapporto del fisico e del morale dell'uomo. Padova, 1813.

Phil 2490   History of philosophy - Local Modern philosophy - France - Individual
philosophers - Comte, Auguste

Phil 2490.06   Pamphlet box. Comte, Auguste. Minor writings.
Phil 2490.12   Comte, Auguste. Opuscules de philosophie sociale. Paris, 1883.
Phil 2490.25   Hubert, René. Les grands philosophes...choix de textes. Paris, 1927.
Phil 2490.27   Comte, Auguste. Le prolétariat dans la societe moderne. Paris, 1946.
Phil 2490.29   Comte, Auguste. Oeuvres choisis. Paris, 1943.
Htn   Phil 2490.30*   Comte, Auguste. Cours de philosophie positive. Paris, 1830-42. 6v.
Phil 2490.31   Comte, Auguste. Cours de philosophie positive. Paris, 1869. 6v.
Phil 2490.31.5   Comte, Auguste. Cours de philosophie positive. 8. éd. Paris, 1946.
Phil 2490.32   Comte, Auguste. L'islamisme au point de vue social. Paris, 1911.
Phil 2490.41.1   Comte, Auguste. The positive philosophy. N.Y., 1855.
Phil 2490.41.1.5   Comte, Auguste. The positive philosophy. N.Y., 1853. 2v.
Phil 2490.41.2.2   Mill, John Stuart. The positive philosophy of Auguste Comte. N.Y., 1873.
Phil 2490.41.2.4A   Comte, Auguste. The positive philosophy. 2. ed. London, 1875. 2v.
Phil 2490.41.2.4B   Comte, Auguste. The positive philosophy. 2. ed. London, 1875. 2v.
Phil 2490.41.3   Comte, Auguste. The postive philosophy. London, 1896. 3v.
Phil 2490.41.4   Comte, Auguste. Die positive Philosophie. v.1-2. Heidelberg, 1884.
Phil 2490.41.5   Comte, Auguste. La philosophie positive. Paris, 1880-81. 2v.
Phil 2490.41.9   Comte, Auguste. Principios de filosofía positiva. Santiago, 1875.
Phil 2490.41.12A   Comte, Auguste. Principes de philosophie positive. Paris, 1868.
Phil 2490.41.12B   Comte, Auguste. Principes de philosophie positive. Paris, 1868.
Htn   Phil 2490.51*   Comte, Auguste. Discours sur l'ensemble du positivisme. Paris, 1848.
X Cg   Phil 2490.51.7   Comte, Auguste. A general view of positivism. 2d ed. London, 1880.
Phil 2490.51.15   Comte, Auguste. A general view of positivism. N.Y., 1957.
Phil 2490.52   Comte, Auguste. La méthode positive en seize leçons. Paris, 1917.
Phil 2490.53A   Comte, Auguste. Discours sur l'esprit positif. Paris, 1844.
Phil 2490.53B   Comte, Auguste. Discours sur l'esprit positif. Paris, 1844.
Phil 2490.53.15   Comte, Auguste. Abhandlung über den Geist des Positivismus. Leipzig, 1915.
Phil 2490.53.20   Comte, Auguste. Rede über den Geist des Positivismus. Hamburg, 1956.
Phil 2490.54   Edger, Henry. The positivist calendar. Long Island, N.Y., 1856.
Phil 2490.54.15   Comte, Auguste. Allmän öfversikt af positivismen. Stockholm, 1896.
Phil 2490.54.20   Comte, Auguste. Framställning öfver den positive anden. Stockholm 1875.
Phil 2490.55   Comte, Auguste. Catèchisme positiviste. Paris, 1852.
Phil 2490.55.2   Comte, Auguste. Catèchisme positiviste. Paris, 1874.
X Cg   Phil 2490.56   Comte, Auguste. Catechism of positive religion. London, 1858.
Phil 2490.57   Comte, Auguste. Appel aux conservateurs. Paris, 1855.
Phil 2490.58   Comte, Auguste. La religión universal. Santiago de Chile, 1938.
Phil 2490.58.5   Comte, Auguste. Religión universal, el amor por principio. Santiago de Chije, 1944.
Phil 2490.59   Comte, Auguste. Écrits de jeunesse, 1816-1828. Suivis du Mémoire sur la cosmogonie de Laplace, 1835. Paris, 1970.
Phil 2490.60   Comte, Auguste. Synthèse subjective. Paris, 1856.
Phil 2490.63   Comte, Auguste. Pensées et préceptes. Paris, 1924.
Phil 2490.65   Comte, Auguste. Auguste Comte méconnu. Extraits de son oeuvre finale (1851-1857). Paris, 1898.
Phil 2490.70   Comte, Auguste. Nouvelles lettres inédites. Paris, 1939.
Phil 2490.71   Comte, Auguste. Correspondance inédite. Paris, 1903-04. 4v.
Phil 2490.72   Comte, Auguste. Lettres d'Auguste Comte à divers. v.1-2. Paris, 1902-05. 3v.
Phil 2490.73   Comte, Aguste. Lettres d'Auguste Comte à M. Valat. Paris, 1870.
Phil 2490.74   Comte, Auguste. Lettres d'Auguste Comte à J.S. Mill. Paris, 1877.
Phil 2490.76   Comte, Auguste. Six lettres inédites à Romeo Pouzin. Paris, 1914.
Phil 2490.76.15   Comte, Auguste. Lettres inédites à C. de Blignières. Paris, 1932.
Phil 2490.77   Comte, Auguste. Testament. Paris, 1884.
Phil 2490.77.2   Comte, Auguste. Testament d'Auguste Comte, avec les documents qui s'y rapportent. Paris, 1896.
Phil 2490.78   Comte, Auguste. Lettres à des positivistes anglais. London 1889. 2v.
Phil 2490.78.10   Comte, Auguste. Lettres à Richard Congreve. London, 1889.
Phil 2490.79   Pamphlet box. Auguste Comte.
Phil 2490.80   Bridges, J.H. The unity of Comte's life and doctrine. London, 1853.
Phil 2490.81   Lewes, G.H. Comte's philosophy of the sciences. London, 1853.
Phil 2490.81.5   Lewes, G.H. Comte's philosophy of the sciences. London, 1871.
Phil 2490.83.2   Littré, M.P.E. Auguste Comte et la philosophie positive. Paris, 1864.
Phil 2490.84B   Mill, John Stuart. The positive philosophy of Auguste Comte. Boston, 1866.
Phil 2490.84.4   Mill, John Stuart. The positive philosophy of Auguste Comte. N.Y., 1887.
Phil 2490.84.6   Mill, John Stuart. The positive philosophy of Auguste Comte. N.Y., 1873.
Phil 2490.84.10   Mill, John Stuart. Auguste Comte et le positivisme. 2. éd. Paris, 1879.

Phil 2490   History of philosophy - Local Modern philosophy - France - Individual philosophers - Comte, Auguste - cont.

Phil 2490.84.15   Mill, John Stuart. Auguste Comte and positivism. London, 1908?

Phil 2490.84.20   Mill, John Stuart. Auguste Comte and positivism. Ann Arbor, 1965.

Phil 2490.85   Robinet, J.F. Notice sur l'oeuvre et sur la vie d'Auguste Comte. Paris, 1860.

Phil 2490.86   Spencer, Herbert. The classification of the sciences...philosophy of M. Comte. London, 1871.

Phil 2490.87   Schoff, W.F. A neglected chapter in the life of Comte. Philadelphia, 1896.

Phil 2490.88   Lévy-Bruhl, L. La philosophie d'Auguste Comte. Paris, 1900.

Phil 2490.88.3   Lévy-Bruhl, L. La philosophie d'Auguste Comte. 3. éd. Paris, 1913.

NEDL Phil 2490.88.5   Lévy-Bruhl, L. The philosophy of Auguste Comte. N.Y., 1903.

Phil 2490.88.10   Lévy-Bruhl, L. Die Philosophie August Comte's. Leipzig, 1902.

Phil 2490.89   Georges, A. Le système psychologique d'Auguste Comte. Lyon, 1908.

Phil 2490.90   Whittaker, T. Comte and Mill. London, 1908.

Phil 2490.91   Dupuy, P. Le positivisme. Paris, 1911.

Phil 2490.92   Chiappini, T. Les idées politiques d'Auguste Comte. Paris, 1913.

Phil 2490.93   Ostwald, W. Auguste Comte. Leipzig, 1914.

Phil 2490.94   Rouvre, C. de. L'amoureuse histoire d'Auguste Comte et de C. de Vaux. Paris, 1917.

Phil 2490.94.10   Rouvre, C. de. Auguste Comte et le catholicisme. Paris, 1928.

Phil 2490.95.5   Ingram, John K. Practical morals. London, 1904.

Phil 2490.96   Maurras, Charles. L'avenir de l'intelligence. 2e éd. Paris, 1917.

Phil 2490.97   Milhaud, Gaston. Le positivisme et le progrès de l'esprit. Paris, 1902.

Phil 2490.98A   Caird, Edward. The social philosophy...of Comte. 2nd ed. Glasgow, 1893.

Phil 2490.98B   Caird, Edward. The social philosophy...of Comte. 2nd ed. Glasgow, 1893.

Phil 2490.98.1   Caird, Edward. The social philosophy and religion of Comte. Glasgow, 1885.

Phil 2490.98.7   Caird, Edward. Philosophie sociale et religion d'Auguste Comte. Paris, 1907.

Phil 2490.99   Grasset, Joseph. Un demifou de génie. Montpelier, 1911.

Phil 2490.100   Deroisin, Hippolyte P. Notes sur Auguste Comte. Paris, 1909.

Phil 2490.101   Nyström, A. Positivism. Stockholm, 1879.

Phil 2490.102   Boyer de Sainte-Suzanne, Raymond de. Essai sur la pensée religieuse d'Auguste Comte. Paris, 1923.

Phil 2490.103   DeGrange, McQuilkin. The science of individuality. Thesis. Lyon, 1923.

Phil 2490.104   Fornelli, N. L'opera di Augusto Comte, in occasione del primo centenario della sua nascita. Milano, 1898.

Phil 2490.105   Harris, M.S. The positive philosophy of Auguste Comte. Thesis. Hartford, 1923.

Phil 2490.106   L'Ange-Huet, J. De methode der positieve filosofie volgens Auguste Comte. Leiden, 1866.

Phil 2490.107   Spielfogel, R. Comte's moralphilosophische Methode. Zürich, 1909.

Phil 2490.108   Deherme, G. Aus jeunes gens un maitre: Auguste Comte; une direction: le positivisme. Paris, 1921.

Phil 2490.109   Cirra, Émile. Appréciation générale du positivisme. Paris, 1898.

Phil 2490.110   Dumas, G. Psychologie de deux messies positivistes Saint-Simon et Auguste Comte. Paris, 1905.

Phil 2490.111   Dumas, G. Quid Auguste Comte de suae altatis psychologis senserit. Lutetiae, 1900.

Phil 2490.112   Seillière, E. Auguste Comte. Paris, 1924.

Phil 2490.113   Dussauze, W. Essai sur la religion d'apres A. Comte. Thèse. Saint-Amand, 1901.

Phil 2490.114   Hillemand, C. La vie et l'oeuvre de A.C. et de Pierre Laffitte. Paris, 1908.

Phil 2490.115   Mourgue, R. La philosophie biologique d'A.C. Lyon, 1909.

Phil 2490.116   Borchert, H. Der Begriff des Kulturzeitalters bei Comte. Diss. Halle, 1927.

Phil 2490.117   Style, Jane M. Auguste Comte thinker and lover. London, 1928.

Phil 2490.118   Uta, Michel. La théorie du savoir dans la philosophie d'Auguste Comte. Paris, 1928.

Phil 2490.118.5   Uta, Michel. La théorie du savoir dans la philosophie d'Auguste Comte. Thèse. Bourg, 1928.

Phil 2490.118.10   Uta, Michel. La loi des trois etats dans la philosophie d'Auguste Comte. Bourg, 1928.

Phil 2490.119   Schaefer, Albert. Die Moralphilosophie Auguste Comte's Versuch einer Darstellung und Kritik. Basel, 1906.

Phil 2490.120   Varney, M.M. L'influence des femmes sur Auguste Comte. Thèse. Paris, 1931.

Phil 2490.121   Marcuse, A. Die Geschichtsphilosophie Auguste Comtes. Inaug.-Diss. Stuttgart, 1932.

Phil 2490.122   Delvolvé, Jean. Réflexions sur la pensée comtienne. Paris, 1932.

Phil 2490.123   Gouhier, Henri. La jeunesse d'Auguste Comte et la formation du positivisme. Paris, 1933-36. 3v.

Phil 2490.124   Kühnert, H. August Comtes Verhältnis zur Kunst. Leipzig, 1910.

Phil 2490.125   Cherfils, C. L'esthétique positiviste. Paris, 1909.

Phil 2490.126   Mehlis, G. Die Geschichtsphilosophie Auguste Comtes. Leipzig, 1909.

Phil 2490.127   Peter, J. Auguste Comtes Bild vom Menschen. Inaug.-Diss. Stuttgart, 1936.

Phil 2490.129   Marvin, F.S. Comte, the founder of sociology. London, 1936.

Phil 2490.130   Ducassé, P. Méthode et intuition chez Auguste Comte. Thèse. Paris, 1939.

Phil 2490.131   Ducassé, P. Essai sur les origines intuitives du positivisme. Thèse. Paris, 1939.

Phil 2490.132   Lagarrigue, L. Politique internationale. Paris, 1928.

Phil 2490.134   Lagarrigue, L. La paz del mundo y la alianza universal de las doctrinas. Santiago de Chile, 1940.

Phil 2490.136A   Cresson, André. Auguste Comte; sa vie, son oeuvre, avec un exposé de sa philosophie. Paris, 1941.

Phil 2490.136B   Cresson, André. Auguste Comte; sa vie, son oeuvre, avec un exposé de sa philosophie. Paris, 1941.

Phil 2490.138   Darp, Jan van. De ethiek van Auguste Comte. Utrecht, 1910.

Phil 2490.140   Lacroix, Jean. La sociologie d'Auguste Comte. Paris, 1956.

Phil 2490   History of philosophy - Local Modern philosophy - France - Individual philosophers - Comte, Auguste - cont.

Phil 2490.140.5   Lacroix, Jean. La sociologie d'Auguste Comte. 2. éd. Paris, 1961.

Phil 2490.142   Arbouss-Bastide, Paul. La doctrine de l'éducation universelle dans la philosophie d'Auguste Comte. v.1-2. Paris, 1957.

Phil 2490.142.2   Arbousse-Bastide, Paul. La doctrine de l'éducation universelle dans la philosophie d'Auguste Comte. Paris, 1957.

Phil 2490.145   Aron, Raymond. War and industrial society. London, 1958.

Phil 2490.150   Sterzel, Georg Friedrick. A. Comte als Pädagog. Leipzig, 1886.

Phil 2490.155   Comte, Auguste. Early essays on social philosophy. London, 1911.

Phil 2490.160   Gurvitch, Georges. Les fondateurs de la sociologie. Paris, 1957.

Phil 2490.165   Clavel, Marcel. Le centenaire d'Auguste Comte et la nouvelle constitution française. Fontenay-sous-Bois, 1958.

Phil 2490.170   Sokoloff, Boris. The "mad" philosopher. 1st ed. N.Y., 1961.

Phil 2490.171   Mendieta y Núñez, L. Homenaje: Augusto Comte. 1. ed. México, 1961.

Phil 2490.172   Riezu, J. Sozialmoral. München, 1961.

Phil 2490.173   Negt, Oskar. Strukturbeziehungen Zwischen den Gesellschafteslehren Comtes und Heges. Frankfurt a.M., 1964.

Phil 2490.174   Massing, Otwin. Fortschritt und Gegenrevolution. Die Gesellschaftslehre Comtes in ihrer sozialen Funktion. Stuttgart, 1966.

Phil 2490.175   Steinhauer, Margarete. Die politische Soziologie Auguste Comtes und ihre Differenz zur liberalen Gesellschaftstheorie Condorcets. Meisenheim, 1966.

VPhil 2490.176   Skarga, Barbara. Ortodoksja i rewizja w pozytywizmie francuskim. Warszawa, 1967.

Phil 2490.180   Fletcher, Ronald. Auguste Comte and the making of sociology: delivered on November 4, 1965 at the London School of Economics. London, 1966.

Phil 2490.182   Kellermann, Paul. Kritik liner Soziologie der Ordnung: Organismus und System bei Comte, Spencer und Parsons. 1. Aufl. Freiburg, 1967.

Phil 2490.184   Arnaud, Pierre. Sociologie de Comte. Paris, 1969.

Phil 2490.184.5   Arnaud, Pierre. La pensée d'Auguste Comte. Paris, 1969.

Phil 2493   History of philosophy - Local Modern philosophy - France - Individual philosophers - Condillac, Etienne

Phil 2493.10   Condillac, Étienne Bonnot. Oeuvres. Paris, 1798. 23v.

Phil 2493.21   Condillac, Étienne Bonnot. Oeuvres philosophiques. Paris, 1795. 2v.

Phil 2493.22   Condillac, Étienne Bonnot. Oeuvres philosophiques. Paris, 1947-51. 3v.

Phil 2493.30   Condillac, Étienne Bonnot. La lógica. Caracas, 1812.

Phil 2493.30.2   Condillac, Étienne Bonnot. Logique. Paris, 1821.

Phil 2493.30.3   Condillac, Étienne Bonnot. Segunda edición de la Lógica puesta. Madrid, 1800.

Phil 2493.30.6   Condillac, Étienne Bonnot. The logic of Condillac. Philadelphia, 1809.

Phil 2493.30.10   Condillac, Étienne Bonnot. La logique. Paris, 1789.

Phil 2493.30.15   Condillac, Étienne Bonnot. Logique de Condillac à l'usage des élèves des prytanées. v.1-2. Paris, 1802. 2v.

Phil 2493.30.20   Condillac, Étienne Bonnot. La lógica, o Los primeros elementos del arte de pensar. Caracas, 1959.

Phil 2493.35   Condillac, Étienne Bonnot. Traité des animaux. Amsterdam, 1755.

Phil 2493.35.2   Condillac, Étienne Bonnot. Traité des animaux. Amsterdam, 1766.

Phil 2493.40   Condillac, Étienne Bonnot. Essai sur l'origine des connaissances humaines. v.1-2. Amsterdam, 1788.

Phil 2493.40.3   Condillac, Étienne Bonnot. Essai sur l'origine des connaissances humnaines. Paris, 1924.

Htn Phil 2493.40.5*   Contillac, Étienne Bonnot. An essay on the origin of human knowledge. London, 1756.

Phil 2493.40.10   Condillac, Étienne Bonnot. Essai sur l'origine des connaissances humaines. Paris, 1798.

Htn Phil 2493.45*   Condillac, Étienne Bonnot. Traité des sensations. v.1-2. Londres, 1754.

Phil 2493.45.2   Condillac, Étienne Bonnot. Traité des sensations. v.1-2. Londres, 1788.

Phil 2493.45.3   Condillac, Étienne Bonnot. Traité des sensations. Première partie. Photoreproduction. Paris, 1886.

Phil 2493.45.4   Condillac, Étienne Bonnot. Abhandlung über die Empfindungen. Berlin, 1870.

Phil 2493.45.20   Condillac, Étienne Bonnot. Trattato delle sensazioni. Bologna, 1927.

Phil 2493.45.30   Condillac, Étienne Bonnot. Condillac's treatise on the sensations. Los Angeles, 1930.

Phil 2493.50   Condillac, Étienne Bonnot. Traité des sistèmes. La Haye, 1749.

Phil 2493.51   Condillac, Étienne Bonnot. Traité des sistêmes. Amsterdam, 1771.

Phil 2493.80   Burger, K. Ein Beitrag zur Beurteilung Condillacs. Altenburg, 1885.

Phil 2493.81   Dewaule, L. Condillac et la psychologie anglaise contemporaine. Paris, 1892.

Phil 2493.82   Mülhaust, P. Darstellung der Psychologie bei Condillac und Bonnet. Cassel, 1874.

Phil 2493.83   Baguenault de Puchesse, Gustave. Condillac; sa vie, sa philosophie, son influence. Paris, 1910.

Phil 2493.84   Réthoré, François. Condillac. Paris, 1864.

Phil 2493.85   Robert, Louis. Les théories logiques de Condillac. Thèse. Paris, 1869.

Phil 2493.86   Saltykow, W. Die Philosophie Condillacs. Inaug.-Diss. Bern, 1901.

Phil 2493.87.5   Laromiguiere, P. Paradoxes de Condillac. Paris, 1825.

Phil 2493.88   Schaupp, Zora. The naturalism of Condillac. Lincoln, 1926.

Phil 2493.88.2   Schaupp, Zora. The naturalism of Condillac. Diss. n.p., 1926.

Phil 2493.89   Lenoir, Raymond. Condillac. Paris, 1924.

Phil 2493.90   Mondolfo, Rodolfo. Un psicologo associazionista: E.B. de Condillac. Bologna, 1923.

Phil 2493.92   LeRoy, Georges. La psychologie de Condillac. Paris, 1937.

Phil 2493.92.5   LeRoy, Georges. La psychologie de Condillac. Thèse. Paris, 1937.

Phil 2493.94   Salvucci, Pasquale. Linguaggio e mondo umano in Condillac. Urbino, 1957.

147

Classified Listing

Phil 2493 History of philosophy - Local Modern philosophy - France - Individual philosophers - Condillac, Etienne - cont.

Phil 2493.96 Meoli, Umberto. Il pensiero economico del Condillac. Milano, 1761.
Phil 2493.100 Knight, Isabel F. The geometric spirit; the Abbe de Condillac and the French Enlightenment. New Haven, 1968.

Phil 2494 History of philosophy - Local Modern philosophy - France - Individual philosophers - Condorcet, Marie Jean

Phil 2494.30 Condorcet, M.J.A.N. Esquisse d'un tableau historique. Paris, 1798.
Phil 2494.31 Condorcet, M.J.A.N. Esquisse d'un tableau historique. n.p., 1795.
Htn Phil 2494.31.5* Condorcet, N.J.A.N. Esquisse d'un tableau historique. Paris, 1795.
Phil 2494.32 Condorcet, M.J.A.N. Esquisse d'un tableau historique. 2e éd. Paris, 1866.
Phil 2494.35 Condorcet, M.J.A.N. Esquisse d'un tableau historique des progrès de l'esprit humain. Paris, 1933.
Phil 2494.36 Condorcet, M.J.A.N. Entwurf einer historischen Darsteillung. Frankfurt a.M., 1963.
Phil 2494.37 Condorcet, M.J.A.N. Esquisse d'un tableau historique des progrès de l'esprit humain. Paris, 1966.
NEDL Phil 2494.41 Condorcet, M.J.A.N. Outlines...historical...progress...human mind. Philadelphia, 1796.
Phil 2494.42 Condorcet, M.J.A.N. Outlines...historical...progress...human mind. Baltimore, 1802.
Phil 2494.80 Niedlich, J.K. Condorcet's "Esquisse d'un tableau historique". Sorai, 1907.
Phil 2494.81 Gillet, M. L'Utopie de Condorcet. Paris, 1883.
Phil 2494.82A Séverac, J.B. Condorcet. Paris, n.d.
Phil 2494.82B Séverac, J.B. Condorcet. Paris, n.d.
Phil 2494.83 Krynska, S. Entwicklung und Fortschritt nach Condorcet und A. Comte. Diss. Bern, 1908.
Phil 2494.87 Granger, Gilles Gaston. La mathématique sociale du marquis de Condorcet. 1. éd. Paris, 1956.

Phil 2496 History of philosophy - Local Modern philosophy - France - Individual philosophers - Cousin, Victor

Phil 2496.5 Cousin, Victor. Oeuvres de Victor Cousin. Bruxelles, 1840-41. 3v.
Phil 2496.30 Cousin, Victor. Fragments philosophiques. Paris, 1838. 2v.
Phil 2496.31 Cousin, Victor. Nouveaux fragmens philosophiques. Paris, 1828.
Phil 2496.32 Cousin, Victor. Fragments de philosophie moderne. Paris, 1856.
Phil 2496.35 Cousin, Victor. Philosophie populaire. Paris, 1848.
Phil 2496.40 Cousin, Victor. Cours de philosophie...Du Vrai, Du Bean, Du Bien. Paris, 1836.
Phil 2496.40.5 Cousin, Victor. Lectures on the true, the beautiful and the good. N.Y., 1854.
Phil 2496.40.6 Cousin, Victor. Lectures on the true, the beautiful, and the good. N.Y., 1855.
Phil 2496.40.10 Cousin, Victor. Lectures on the true, the beautiful and the good. N.Y., 1854.
Phil 2496.40.15 Cousin, Victor. The philosophy of the beautiful. London, 1848.
Phil 2496.45.2 Cousin, Victor. Défense de l'université et de la philosophie. 2e éd. Paris, 1844.
Phil 2496.45.3 Cousin, Victor. Défense de l'université et de la philosophie. Paris, 1844.
Phil 2496.45.4 Cousin, Victor. Defense de l'université et de la philosophie. 4e éd. Paris, 1845.
Phil 2496.50 Cousin, Victor. Elements of psychology. N.Y., 1838.
Phil 2496.50.2 Cousin, Victor. Elements of psychology. 3e éd. N.Y., 1842.
Cg Phil 2496.50.3 Cousin, Victor. Elements of psychology. N.Y., 1856.
Phil 2496.50.4 Cousin, Victor. Elements of psychology. N.Y., 1855.
Phil 2496.50.5 Cousin, Victor. Elements of psychology. Hartford, 1834.
Phil 2496.55.3 Cousin, Victor. Premiers essais de philosophie. 3e éd. Paris, 1855.
Phil 2496.79 Pamphlet box. Cousin, Victor.
Phil 2496.79.10 Ody, Hermann. Victor Cousin. Saarbrücken, 1953.
Phil 2496.80 Alaux, J.E. La philosophie de M. Cousin. Paris, 1864.
Phil 2496.81 Leroux, P. Réfutation de l'eclectisme. Paris, 1841.
Phil 2496.81.2 Leroux, P. Réfutation de l'eclectisme. Paris, 1839.
Phil 2496.82 Wallon, J. Du livre de M. Cousin. Paris, 1854.
Phil 2496.83 Mignet,M. Notice historique sur la vie...de Victor Cousin. Paris, 1869.
Phil 2496.84 Janet, Paul. Victor Cousin et son oeuvre. Paris, 1885.
Phil 2496.85 Deschamps, A.F. Reflexions sur l'instruction synodale de Mgr. l'évêque de Poitiers. Paris, 1855.
Phil 2496.86 Fuchs, C.E. Die Philosophie Victor Cousins. Berlin, 1847.
Phil 2496.87 Cornelius, Alfred. Die Geschichtslehre Victor Cousins. Genève, 1958.
Phil 2496.88 Will, Frederic. Flumen historicum: Victor Cousin's aesthetic and its sources. Chapel Hill, 1965.

Phil 2515 History of philosophy - Local Modern philosophy - France - Individual philosophers - Other C

Phil 2515.1.80 Louis Couturat (1868-1914). Coulomniers, 191-?
Phil 2515.2.27* Charron, P. De la sagesse, trois livres. 3e éd. Paris, 1614.
Phil 2515.2.30* Charron, P. De la sagesse. Leide, 1646.
Phil 2515.2.31* Charron, P. De la sagesse. Leide, 1658?
Phil 2515.2.32* Charron, P. De la sagesse. Amsterdam, 1662.
Phil 2515.2.33* Charron, P. Of wisdome. London, 1630.
Phil 2515.2.34* Charron, P. Charron on wisdom. London? n.d.
Phil 2515.2.35* Charron, P. La sagesse de Charron. Paris, 1672.
Phil 2515.2.36 Charron, P. Charron on wisdom. London, 1729. 3v.
Phil 2515.2.39 Charron, P. Charron on wisdom. London, 1707. 2v.
Phil 2515.2.40* Charron, P. Of wisdom, three books. London, 1651.
Phil 2515.2.41* Charron, P. Of wisdome. London, 1670.
Phil 2515.2.42 Charron, P. A treatise on wisdom. N.Y., 1891.
Phil 2515.2.45* Charron, P. Les trois veritez. 2e éd. Bordeaux, 1595.
Phil 2515.2.47* Charron, P. De la sagesse. v.1-3. Paris, 1604.
Phil 2515.2.48* Charron, P. De la sagesse. Rouen, 1614.
Phil 2515.2.49* Charron, P. De la sagesse. Bordeaux, 1601.
Phil 2515.2.50 Charron, P. Die wahre Weisheit. v.2. München, 1779.
Phil 2515.2.53 Charron, P. De la sagesse. Paris, 1820-24. 3v.
Phil 2515.2.55 Charron, P. De la sagesse. Paris, 1827. 3v.
Phil 2515.2.80 Pamphlet box. Charron, P.
Phil 2515.2.81 Sabrié, J.B. De l'humanisme au rationalisme. Pierre Charron. Paris, 1913.

Phil 2515 History of philosophy - Local Modern philosophy - France - Individual philosophers - Other C - cont.

Phil 2515.2.90 Chanet, P. Considérations sur la Sagesse de Charron. Paris, 1643.
Phil 2515.2.95 Piohetta, J.B. Pierre Chanet; une psychologie de l'instinct. Thèse. Paris, 1937.
Phil 2515.2.125 Liebscher, H. Charron und sien Werk, "de la Sagesse". Leipzig, 1890.
Phil 2515.3.32 Cresson, A. L'invérifiable; les problèmes de la métaphysique. 2e éd. Paris, 1920.
Phil 2515.4.90 Segond, J. Cournot et la psychologie vitaliste. Thèse. Paris, 1910.
Phil 2515.4.92 Battanelli, E.P. Cournot métaphysicien de la connaissance. Thèse. Paris, 1913.
Phil 2515.4.94 Ruyer, R. L'humanité de l'avenir, d'après Cournot. Paris, 1930.
Phil 2515.4.95 Ruyer, R. L'humanité de l'avenir, d'après Cournot. Thèse secondaire. Paris, 1930.
Phil 2515.4.97 Mentré, F. Pour qu'on lise Cournot. Paris, 1927.
Phil 2515.4.99 Lévêque, R. L'élément historique dans...Cournot. Paris, 1938.
Phil 2515.4.100 Lévêque, R. L'élément historique dans la connaissance humaine d'après Cournot. Thèse. Strasbourg, 1938.
Phil 2515.4.101 Floss, S.W. An outline of the philosophy of Antoine-Augustin Cournot. Philadelphia, 1941.
Phil 2515.5.90 Hess, G. Alain (Émile Chartier) in der Reihe der französischen Moralisten. Inaug.-Diss. Berlin, 1931.
Phil 2515.5.91 Hess, G. Alain (Émile Chartier) in der Reihe der französischen Moralisten. Berlin, 1932.
Phil 2515.5.92 Alain professeur par X.X., élève de roi Henri IV. Paris, 1932.
Phil 2515.5.93 Pascal, Georges. La pensée d'Alain. Paris, 1946.
Phil 2515.5.95 Maurois, André. Alain. Paris, 1950.
Phil 2515.5.97 Chartier, Émile. Lettres sur la philosophie première. 1. éd. Paris, 1955.
Phil 2515.6 Noel, J. Un philosophie belge, Colins. Mons, 1909.
Phil 2515.6.5 Rons, Ivo. Introduction au socialisme rationnel de Colins. Neuchâtel, 1968.
Phil 2515.7 Cochet, M.A. Le congrès Descartes...reflexions. Bruges, 1938.
Phil 2515.8.80 Guy, Alain. Métaphysique et intuition; le message de Jacques Chevalier. Paris, 1940.
Phil 2515.9.30 Corte, Marcel de. Philosophis des moeurs contemporaines. Bruxelles, 1945.
Phil 2515.10 Cioran, Émile M. La tentation d'exister. 2. éd. Paris, 1956.
Phil 2515.10.5 Cioran, Émile M. The temptation to exist. Chicago, 1968.
Phil 2515.10.10 Cioran, Émile M. Le Mauvais démiurge. Paris, 1969.
Phil 2515.10.15 Cioran, Émile M. La chute dans le temps. Paris, 1964.
Phil 2515.10.16 Cioran, Émile M. The fall into time. Chicago, 1970.
Phil 2515.12 LeChevalier, Charles. La confidence et la personne humaine. Aubier, 1960.
Phil 2515.14 Cordonnier, V. Le sacre de la liberté. Paris, 1958.
Phil 2515.16 Krauss, W. Cartaud de la Villate. Berlin, 1960. 2v.
Phil 2515.17 Chevalier, J. Cadences. Paris, 1939- 2v.
Phil 2515.18 Caraco, Albert. Huit essais sur le mal. Neuchâtel, 1963.
Phil 2515.18.5 Caraco, Albert. La luxure et la mort. Lausanne, 1968.
Phil 2515.20 Cordemoy, Géraud de. Oeuvres philosophiques, avec une étude bio-bibliographique. Paris, 1968.
Phil 2515.22.20 LaHarpe, Jacqueline Ellen Violette de. Jean-Pierre de Crousaz et le conflit des idées au siècle des lumières. Genève, 1955.

Phil 2520 History of philosophy - Local Modern philosophy - France - Individual philosophers - Descartes, René

Phil 2520.01 Paris. Bibliothèque National. Département des Imprimés. Catalogue des ouvrages de Descartes. Paris, 1909.
Phil 2520.2 Sebba, G. Bibliographia cartesiana. The Hague, 1964.
Htn Phil 2520.10* Descartes, René. Principia philosophiae. Amsterdam, 1650.
Htn Phil 2520.10.5* Descartes, René. Principia philosophiae. Amsterdam, 1644. 2 pam.
Phil 2520.10.8 Descartes, René. Opera philosophica. 4a ed. Amsterdam, 1664.
Htn Phil 2520.10.9* Descartes, René. Opera philosophica. 4a ed. Amsterdam, 1664.
Phil 2520.10.10 Descartes, René. Opera philosophica. 4a ed. Amsterdam, 1664.
Htn Phil 2520.10.15* Descartes, René. Opera philosophica. 5a ed. Amsterdam, 1672.
Htn Phil 2520.10.16* Descartes, René. Opera philosophica. 5a ed. Amsterdam, 1672.
Phil 2520.10.20 Descartes, René. Opera philosophica. 5a ed. Amsterdam, 1677-78. 2v.
Phil 2520.10.25 Descartes, René. Opera philosophica. Francofurti, 1692.
X Cg Phil 2520.11 Descartes, René. Opera philosophica. Francofurti, 1656-58.
Phil 2520.11.5 Descartes, René. Les principes de la philosophie. 2e éd. Paris, 1660.
Phil 2520.11.10 Descartes, René. Les principes de la philosophie. 4e éd. Paris, 1681.
Phil 2520.11.13 Descartes, René. Les principes de la philosophie. Paris, 1723.
Phil 2520.11.24 Descartes, René. Die Prinzipien der Philosophie. 3. Aufl. Leipzig, 1908.
Phil 2520.11.25 Descartes, René. Die Prinzipien der Philosophie. 4e Aufl. Leipzig, 1922.
Phil 2520.13.11 Descartes, René. Principia philosophiae. Amsterdam, 1685. 3 pam.
Phil 2520.13.12 Descartes, René. Geometria. 3a ed. Amsterdam, 1683. 2v.
Phil 2520.13.14 Descartes, René. Meditationeo de prima philosophia. Amsterdam, 1685.
Phil 2520.13.15 Descartes, René. Tractatus de homine et de formatione foetus. Amsterdam, 1686.
Phil 2520.13.15.5 Descartes, René. Treatise of man. Cambridge, 1972.
Phil 2520.13.16 Descartes, René. Epistolae, Pars prima-tertia. Amsterdam, 1682-83. 3v.
Phil 2520.13.20 Descartes, René. Opera omnia, novem tomis comprehensa. Amstelodami, 1692. 9v.
Phil 2520.14 Descartes, René. Meditationes de prima philosophia. Amsterdam, 1685.
Phil 2520.14.2 Descartes, René. Meditationes de prima philosophia. 2e. Aufl. München, 1912.
Phil 2520.14.9 Descartes, René. Meditationes de prima philosophia. München, 1901.
Phil 2520.15 Descartes, René. Oeuvres philosophiques. Paris, 1835. 4v.
Phil 2520.16 Descartes, René. Oeuvres. Paris, 1824-26. 11v.

148

Classified Listing

Phil 2520 History of philosophy - Local Modern philosophy - France - Individual philosophers - Descartes, René - cont.

Phil 2520.17 Descartes, René. Oeuvres morales et philosophiques. Paris, n.d.
Phil 2520.17.5 Descartes, René. Oeuvres morales et philosophiques. Paris, 1879.
Phil 2520.18A Descartes, René. Oeuvres philosophiques publiées. Paris, 1852.
Phil 2520.18B Descartes, René. Oeuvres philosophiques publiées. Paris, 1852.
Phil 2520.19 Descartes, René. Oeuvres de Descartes. Paris, 1897. 12v.
Phil 2520.19.2 Descartes, René. Oeuvres de Descartes. Suppl. Index général. Paris, 1913.
Phil 2520.19.3 Descartes, René. Oeuvres. Paris, 1860.
Phil 2520.19.4 Descartes, René. Oeuvres. Paris, 1844.
Phil 2520.19.4.5 Descartes, René. Oeuvres. Paris, 1850.
Phil 2520.19.5 Descartes, René. Oeuvres. Paris, 1865.
Phil 2520.19.7 Descartes, René. Oeuvres. Paris, 1868.
Htn Phil 2520.19.9* Descartes, René. Oeuvres choisies. Paris, 1865.
Phil 2520.19.11 Descartes, René. Oeuvres choisies. Paris, 1865.
Phil 2520.21.5 Descartes, René. Hauptschriften zur Grundlegung seiner Philosophie. Heidelberg, 1930.
Phil 2520.22 Descartes, René. Philosophical works. N.Y., 1955. 2v.
Phil 2520.22.5 Descartes, René. The philosophical works of Descartes. London, 1967. 2v.
Phil 2520.23A Descartes, René. Philosophical writings. N.Y., 1958.
Phil 2520.23B Descartes, René. Philosophical writings. N.Y., 1958.
Phil 2520.26 Descartes, René. Oeuvres choisies. Paris, 1877.
Phil 2520.26.2 Descartes, René. Oeuvres choisies. Paris, 1876.
Phil 2520.27 Descartes, René. Pensées de Descartes sur la religion et la morale. Paris, 1811.
Phil 2520.27.5 Descartes, René. Pensées, choisies. Paris, 1944.
Phil 2520.28A Descartes, René. Philosophy in extracts from his writings. N.Y., 1892.
Phil 2520.28B Descartes, René. Philosophy in extracts from his writings. N.Y., 1892.
Phil 2520.29A Descartes, René. Selections. N.Y., 1927.
Phil 2520.29B Descartes, René. Selections. N.Y., 1927.
Phil 2520.30 Descartes, René. Opuscula posthuma. Amsterdam, 1701.
Phil 2520.31 Descartes, René. Oeuvres et lettres. Paris, 1937.
Phil 2520.32 Descartes, René. Philosophische Werke. v.1-2. n.p., n.d.
Phil 2520.32.10 Descartes, René. Oeuvres philosophiques. Paris, 1963- 2v.
Phil 2520.32.15 Descartes, René. Oeuvres. v.1,2,6,8 (pt.1-2), 9 (pt.1-2), 10-11. Paris, 1964. 11v.
Htn Phil 2520.34* Descartes, René. L'homme et un traitte de la formation du Foetus. Paris, 1664.
Htn Phil 2520.34.2* Descartes, René. De homine, figuris, et latinitate donatus. Lugduni Batavorum, 1662.
Htn Phil 2520.34.3* Descartes, René. De homine...Schuye a Florentio Schuye. Lugduni Batavorum, 1664.
Phil 2520.34.5 Descartes, René. Tractatus de homine et de formatione Foetus. Amsterdam, 1677.
Htn Phil 2520.34.10* Descartes, René. L'homme de René Descartes et la formation du Foetus. Paris, 1677.
Htn Phil 2520.35.1* Descartes, René. Discours de la méthode pour bien conduire sa raison et chercher la vérité dans les sciences. Leyde, 1637.
Phil 2520.35.2 Descartes, René. Specimina philosophiae. Amsterdam, 1656.
Phil 2520.35.3 Descartes, René. Discours de la méthode pour bien conduire sa raison et chercher la vérité dans les sciences. Paris, 1668.
Phil 2520.35.4 Descartes, René. Discours de la méthode pour bien conduire sa raison et chercher la vérité dans les sciences. Paris, 1894.
Phil 2520.35.6 Descartes, René. Discours de la méthode pour bien conduire sa raison et chercher la vérité dans les sciences. Paris, 1876.
Phil 2520.35.8 Descartes, René. Discours de la méthode pour bien conduire sa raison et chercher la vérité dans les sciences. Paris, 1886.
Phil 2520.35.9 Descartes, René. Discours de la méthode pour bien conduire sa raison et chercher la vérité dans les sciences. Strasbourg, n.d.
Htn Phil 2520.35.10* Descartes, René. A discours of a method. London, 1649.
Htn Phil 2520.35.12* Descartes, René. Discours de la méthode pour bien conduire sa raison et chercher la vérité dans les sciences. Paris, 1668.
Htn Phil 2520.35.13* Descartes, René. Discours de la méthode pour bien conduire sa raison et chercher la vérité dans les sciences. Paris, 1668.
Phil 2520.35.14 Descartes, René. Discours de la méthode. Londres, 1913.
Phil 2520.35.15 Descartes, René. Discours de la méthode. Cambridge, Eng., 1923.
Phil 2520.35.16 Descartes, René. Discours de la méthode. Paris, 1925.
Phil 2520.35.17 Descartes, René. Discours de la méthode. Paris, 1926.
Phil 2520.35.19 Descartes, René. Discours de la méthode. Paris, 1927.
Phil 2520.35.21 Descartes, René. Discours de la méthode. Evreux, 1927.
Phil 2520.35.25 Descartes, René. Discours de la méthode. Paris, 1932.
Phil 2520.35.26 Descartes, René. Discours de la méthode. Paris, 1932.
Phil 2520.35.37 Descartes, René. Discours de la méthode. (Ouvrages de l'esprit). Manchester, 1941.
Phil 2520.35.39 Descarter, René. Discours de la méthode. Paris, 1937.
Phil 2520.35.40 Descartes, René. Discours de la méthode. Paris, 1951.
Phil 2520.35.45 Descartes, René. Discours de la méthode. Paris, 1950.
Phil 2520.35.47 Descarter, René. Discours de la méthode. 2. ed. Manchester, 1961.
Phil 2520.35.48 Descartes, René. Discours de la méthode. Paris, 1961.
Phil 2520.35.50 Descartes, René. Choix commenté du Discours de la méthode. Geneve, 1952.
Phil 2520.35.52 Descartes, René. Discorso sul metodo. Firenze, 1962.
Phil 2520.36 Descartes, René. The method, meditation and selections. Edinburgh, 1897.
Phil 2520.37 Descartes, René. Discourse on method. Chicago, 1899.
Phil 2520.37.10 Descartes, René. Discourse on method. London, 1901.
Phil 2520.38 Descartes, René. Discourse on the method of rightly conducting the reason. Edinburgh, 1850.
Htn Phil 2520.39* Descartes, René. Les principes de la philosophie. Paris, 1651.
Phil 2520.39.3 Descartes, René. Les principes de la philosophie. Paris, 1668.
Phil 2520.39.5 Descartes, René. Les principes de la philosophie. Paris, 1724.
Phil 2520.39.6 Descartes, René. Les principes de la philosophie. Paris, 1724.

Phil 2520 History of philosophy - Local Modern philosophy - France - Individual philosophers - Descartes, René - cont.

Htn Phil 2520.39.8* Descartes, René. Les principes de la philosophie. Paris, 1647.
Phil 2520.39.9 Descartes, René. Les principes de la philosophie. Rouen, 1706.
Htn Phil 2520.39.10* Descartes, René. Les principes de la philosophie. Paris, 1659.
Phil 2520.39.12 Descartes, René. Les principes de la philosophie. Rouen, 1698.
Phil 2520.39.16 Descartes, René. Les principes de la philosophie. Paris, 1950.
Phil 2520.39.20 Descartes, René. I principii della filosofia. Bari, 1914.
Phil 2520.39.30 Descartes, René. Principii di filosofia. Napoli, 1937.
Phil 2520.43 Descartes, René. Abhandlung über die Methode. Leipzig, 1919-20. 2 pam.
Phil 2520.44 Descartes, René. Philosophical writings. Edinburgh, 1954.
Phil 2520.45 Descartes, René. Discorso sul metodo e meditazioni. Bari, 1912. 2v.
Phil 2520.45.5 Descartes, René. Il discorso del metodo. Milano, 19- .
Phil 2520.45.12 Descartes, René. Il discorso del metodo. Assisi, 1911.
Phil 2520.45.18 Descartes, René. Il discorso sul metodo. Torino, 1926.
Phil 2520.45.25 Descartes, René. Discorso sul metodo. Napoli, 1937.
Phil 2520.50.5 Descartes, René. The meditations, and selections from the Principles of René Descartes. n.p., 1968.
NEDL Phil 2520.51 Descartes, René. Life and meditations. London, 1878.
Htn Phil 2520.52.7* Descartes, René. Les méditations métaphysics. Paris, 1647.
Phil 2520.52.8 Descartes, René. Les méditationes métaphysiques. 2e éd. Paris, 1661.
Phil 2520.52.10 Descartes, René. Les méditationes métaphysiques. 3e éd. Paris, 1673.
Htn Phil 2520.52.15* Descartes, René. Six metaphysical meditations. London, 1680.
Htn Phil 2520.52.17* Descartes, René. Meditationes de prima philosophia. 2a ed. Amstelodami, 1642. 2 pam.
Phil 2520.52.20 Descartes, René. Meditationes de prima philosophia. Amstelodami, 1644.
Phil 2520.52.25 Descartes, René. Meditationes de prima philosophia. Amstelodami, 1650. 3 pam.
Phil 2520.52.26 Descartes, René. Meditationes de prima philosophia. Amstelodami, 1654.
Phil 2520.52.27 Descartes, René. Meditationes de prima philosophia. Amstelodami, 1678.
Phil 2520.52.28 Descartes, René. Meditationes de prima philosophia. Amstelodami, 1698. 3 pam.
Phil 2520.52.32 Descartes, René. Meditationes de prima philosophia. Paris, 1944.
Phil 2520.52.35 Descartes, René. Les méditations métaphysiques. Paris, 1724. 2v.
Phil 2520.52.50 Descartes, René. Meditazioni filosofiche. Torino, 1927.
Phil 2520.52.60 Descartes, René. Meditationes de prima philosophia. Amsterdam, 1657. 5 pam.
Phil 2520.52.70 Descartes, René. The living thoughts of Descartes. Philadelphia, 1947.
Phil 2520.52.75 Descartes, René. Méditations. 4. éd. Paris, 1952.
Phil 2520.52.80 Descartes, René. Meditationen über die erste Philosophie. Hamburg, 1956.
Phil 2520.53.2 Descartes, René. Untersuchungen über die Grundlagen der Philosophie. 2e Aufl. Heidelberg, 1882.
Phil 2520.53.4 Descartes, René. Meditationen über die Grundlagen der Philosophie. 4e Aufl. Leipzig, 1915.
Phil 2520.53.10 Descartes, René. Meditações metafísicas. Coimbra, 1930.
Phil 2520.54 Descartes, René. Entretien avec Burman. Paris, 1937.
Phil 2520.55 Descartes, René. Regulae ad directionem ingenii. Torino, 1943.
Phil 2520.55.10 Descartes, René. Règles pour la direction de l'esprit. Paris, 1945.
Phil 2520.55.12 Descartes, René. Regulae ad directionem ingenii. La Haye, 1966.
Htn Phil 2520.60* Descartes, René. Passiones animae. Amstelodami, 1650.
Htn Phil 2520.60.1* Descartes, René. Passiones animae. Amstelodami, 1650.
Htn Phil 2520.60.5* Descartes, René. Passiones animae. Amstelodami, 1664.
Phil 2520.61.5 Descartes, René. Tractat von den Leidenschafften der Seele. Franckfurth, 1723.
Phil 2520.61.7 Descartes, René. Über die Leidenschaften der Seele. 3e Aufl. Leipzig, 1911.
Htn Phil 2520.61.12* Descartes, René. Les passions de l'âme. Rouen, 1651.
Phil 2520.61.15 Descartes, René. Les passions de l'âme. Paris, 1726.
Phil 2520.61.16 Descartes, René. Les passions de l'âme. Paris, 1955.
Phil 2520.61.19 Descartes, René. Traité des passions. Paris, 1928.
Phil 2520.61.20 Descartes, René. Traité des passions suivi de la correspondance avec la princess Elisabeth. Paris, 1965.
Htn Phil 2520.62.5* Descartes, René. Le monde. Paris, 1664.
Phil 2520.64 Descartes, René. Descartes. Paris, 1969.
Htn Phil 2520.65* Descartes, R. Excellent compendium of musik. London, 1653.
Phil 2520.66 Descartes, René. De Verhandeling van den Mensch, en de Makinge van de Vrugt. Middeleburg, 1682.
Phil 2520.67 Descartes, René. Principia philosophiae. Amstelodami, 1692.
Phil 2520.68 Descartes, René. Regln zur des Geistes. Leipzig, 1906.
Phil 2520.69 Descartes, René. Descartes. Paris, 1947.
Phil 2520.70 Descartes, René. Descartes, 1596-1650. Genève, 1948.
Phil 2520.75 Descartes, René. Epistolae. Amstelodami, 1682-83.
Phil 2520.75.2 Descartes, René. Epistolae. Francofurti ad Moenum, 1692.
Htn Phil 2520.75.3* Descartes, René. Epistolae. v.1-2. Amstelodami, 1668.
Htn Phil 2520.75.5* Descartes, René. Epistolae. v.1-2. Londini, 1668.
Phil 2520.75.15 Descartes, René. Epistolae. v.1-2. Amstelodami, 1714.
Htn Phil 2520.76* Descartes, René. Lettres ou sont traitées les plusieurs belles questions touchant la morale. Paris, 1663. 2v.
Htn Phil 2520.76.3* Descartes, René. Lettres ou sont traitées les plusieurs belles questions de la morale. Paris, 1657.
Htn Phil 2520.76.5* Descartes, René. Lettres ou sont traitées les plusieurs belles questions touchant la morale. v.1-3. Paris, 1666-67.
Phil 2520.76.55 Descartes, René. Lettres de Descartes. Paris, 1724-25. 6v.
Phil 2520.76.65 Descartes, René. Lettres sur la morale. Paris, 1935.
Htn Phil 2520.77* Descartes, René. Epistola...ad celeberrimum virum D. Gisbertum Voetium. Amsterodami, 1643.
Phil 2520.78 Swarte, V. de. Descartes, directeur spirituel. Paris, 1904.
Phil 2520.78.5 Descartes. Paris, 1957.
Phil 2520.78.25F Descartes, René. Correspondence of Descartes and Constantyn Huygeno, 1635-1647. Oxford, 1926.

520 History of philosophy - Local Modern philosophy - France - Individual losophers - Descartes, René - cont.

Phil 2520.78.30 Descartes, René. Correspondance publiée avec une introduction et des notes par C. Adam et G. Milhaud. 1. éd. Paris, 1936-51. 8v.
Phil 2520.78.35 Descartes, René. Correspondance avec Armaud et Marus. Paris, 1953.
Phil 2520.78.40 Descartes, René. Descartes par lui-meme. Paris, 1956.
Phil 2520.78.45 Descartes, René. Philosophical letters. Oxford, 1970.
Phil 2520.79 Pamphlet vol. Philosophy. French and Belgian. Descartes. German dissertations, 1881-1912. 19 pam.
Phil 2520.79.5 Pamphlet box. Philosophy. French and Belgian. Descartes.
Phil 2520.79.10 Serrurier, C. Descartes. Paris, 1951.
Phil 2520.80 Andrea, T. Brevis replicatia...notis Cartesii. Amstelodami, 1653.
Phil 2520.81 Baillet, A. La vie de Monsieur Des-Cartes. Paris, 1691.
Phil 2520.81.2* Baillet, A. La vie de Monsieur Des-Cartes. Paris, 1691. 2v.
Phil 2520.81.5* Baillet, A. La vie de Monsieur Des-Cartes. Paris, 1692.
Phil 2520.81.6 Baillet, A. La vie de Monsieur Des-Cartes. Paris, 1706.
Phil 2520.81.15 Baillet, A. Vie de Monsieur Descartes. Paris, 1946.
Phil 2520.82 Bordas-Demoulin, J.B. Le Cartésianisme. Paris, 1843. 2v.
Phil 2520.83.5 Bouillier, F. Histoire de la philosophie Cartésienne. Paris, 1854. 2v.
Phil 2520.83.6 Bouillier, F. Histoire de la philosophie Cartésienne. Paris, 1868. 2v.
Phil 2520.84 Bark, F. Descartes' Lehre von den Leidenschaften. Rostock, 1892.
Phil 2520.84.5 Twardowski, K. Idee und Perception. Wien, 1892.
Phil 2520.85 Bierendempfel, G. Descartes als Gegner des Sensualismus und Materialismus. Wolfenbüttel, 1884.
Phil 2520.85.30 Callot, Émile. Problèms du Cartesianisme. Annecy, 1956.
Phil 2520.86 Cousin, V. Fragments de philosophie Cartésienne. Paris, 1845.
Phil 2520.86.3 Cartesio nel terzo centenario nel "Discorso del metodo." Milano, 1937.
Phil 2520.86.5 Roth, Leon. Descartes' discourse on method. Oxford, 1937.
Phil 2520.87 Cunningham, William. The influence of Descartes on metaphysical speculation in England. London, 1876.
Phil 2520.88 Daniel, Gabriel. Voyage du monde de Descartes...Suite du voyage du monde de Descartes. Amsterdam, 1713.
Phil 2520.88.2 Daniel, Gabriel. Voyage du monde de Descartes. Paris, 1702.
Phil 2520.88.5* Daniel, Gabriel. Voiage du monde de Descartes. Paris, 1690.
Phil 2520.88.7 Daniel, Gabriel. Voiage du monde de Descartes. Paris, 1691.
Phil 2520.88.9 Daniel, Gabriel. Voyage du monde de Descartes. Paris, 1703.
Phil 2520.88.10 Daniel, Gabriel. Voyage du monde de Descartes. v.1-2. Amsterdam, 1706.
Phil 2520.88.20* Daniel, Gabriel. Voyage to the world of Cartesius. London, 1694.
Phil 2520.88.25 Daniel, Gabriel. Iter per mundum Cartesii. Amesteledami, 1694.
Phil 2520.88.30 Daniel, Gabriel. Nouvelles difficultez proposees par un peripateticien. Paris, 1693.
Phil 2520.89 Fouillée, A. Descartes. Paris, 1893.
Phil 2520.90 Hock, C.F. Cartesius und seine Gegner. Wien, 1835.
Phil 2520.91* Huetii, P.D. Censura philosophiae Cartesianae. Paris, 1689.
Phil 2520.92 Krantz, É. Essai sur l'esthétique de Descartes. Paris, 1882.
Phil 2520.93 Mahaffy, J.P. Descartes. Edinburgh, 1880.
Phil 2520.93.2.5 Mahaffy, J.P. Descartes. Edinburgh, 1884.
Phil 2520.93.3 Mahaffy, J.P. Descartes. Philadelphia, 1887.
Phil 2520.94 Mazure, P.A. Études du Cartésianisme. Paris, 1828.
Phil 2520.95 Millet, J. Histoire de Descartes avant 1637. Paris, 1867.
Phil 2520.95.5 Millet, J. Descartes; son histoire depuis 1637. Paris, 1876.
Phil 2520.96 Netter, A. Notes sur le vie de Descartes. Nancy, 1896.
Phil 2520.97 Saisset, Émile. Précurseurs et disciples de Descartes. Paris, 1862.
Phil 2520.97.3 Saisset, Émile. Précurseurs et disciples de Descartes. Paris, 1862.
Phil 2520.98 Schwarz, H. Die Lehre von den Sinnesqualitäten...Descartes. Halle, 1894.
Phil 2520.99 Jammes. Le sens commun de M. Gerbet. Paris, 1827.
Phil 2520.100 Touchard, G. La morale de Descartes. Paris, 1898.
Phil 2520.101 Boutroux, P. L'imagination et les Math Selon Descartes. Paris, 1900.
Phil 2520.102 Foucher de Careil, A. Descartes, la princesse Elizabeth et la reine Christine. Paris, 1879.
Phil 2520.102.2 Foucher de Careil, A. Descartes, la princesse Elizabeth et la reine Christine. Paris, 1909.
Phil 2520.102.5 Foucher de Careil, A. Descartes et la princesse palatine. Paris, 1862.
Phil 2520.103* Boyle, Pierre. Recueil de quelques...philosophie de Descartes. Amsterdam, 1684.
Phil 2520.105A Iverach, James. Descartes, Spinoza...new philosophy. N.Y., 1904.
Phil 2520.105B Iverach, James. Descartes, Spinoza...new philosophy. N.Y., 1904.
Phil 2520.105.2 Iverach, James. Descartes, Spinoza and the new philosophy. Edinburgh, 1904.
Phil 2520.106 Christiansen, B. Das Urteil bei Descartes. Hanau, 1902.
Phil 2520.107 Natorp, P. Descartes' Erkenntnisstheorie. Marburg, 1882.
Phil 2520.108.5 Hoffmann, A. René Descartes. Stuttgart, 1905.
Phil 2520.108.6 Hoffmann, A. René Descartes. 2. Aufl. Stuttgart, 1923.
Phil 2520.109A Haldane, E.S. Descartes, his life and times. London, 1905.
Phil 2520.109B Haldane, E.S. Descartes, his life and times. London, 1905.
Phil 2520.110 Koch, Anton. Die Psychologie Descartes. München, 1881.
Phil 2520.111 Hamelin, O. Le système de Descartes. Paris, 1911.
Phil 2520.111.2 Hamelin, O. Le système de Descartes. 2e éd. Paris, 1921.
Phil 2520.112 Debricon, L. Descartes. Paris, n.d.
Phil 2520.113 Heimsoeth, H. Die Methode der Erkenntnis bei Descartes. Giessen, 1912.
Phil 2520.114 Cochin, D. Descartes. Paris, 1913.
Phil 2520.114.11 Barth, Heinrich. Descartes' Begründung der Erkenntnis. Bern, 1913.
Phil 2520.115 Schmidt aus Schwarzenberg, X. René Descartes und seine Reform der Philosophie. Nördlingen, 1859.
Phil 2520.116 Gilson, E. La doctrine cartésienne de la liberté et la théologie. Paris, 1913.

Phil 2520 History of philosophy - Local Modern philosophy - France - Individual philosophers - Descartes, René - cont.

Phil 2520.116.5 Gilson, E. La liberté chez Descartes et la théologie. Paris, 1913.
Phil 2520.116.10 Gilson, E. Descartes et la métaphysique scolastique. Bruxelles, 1924.
Phil 2520.116.15 Gilson, E. Études sur le rôle de la pensée médiévale dans la formation du système cartésien. Paris, 1930.
Phil 2520.116.15.5 Gilson, E. Études sur le rôle de la pensée médiévale dans la formation du système cartésien. Paris, 1951.
Phil 2520.117 Gilson, E. Index scolastico-cartésien. Paris, 1912.
Phil 2520.118 Gröber, G. Descartes; Methode des richtigen Vernunftgebrauches 1637. Strassburg, 1914.
NEDL Phil 2520.119A Smith, N.K. Studies in the Cartesian philosophy. N.Y., 1902.
Phil 2520.119B Smith, N.K. Studies in the Cartesian philosophy. N.Y., 1902.
Phil 2520.119.2 Smith, N.K. Studies in the Cartesian philosophy. N.Y., 1962.
Phil 2520.119.5 Smith, N.K. New studies in the philosophy of Descartes. London, 1952.
Phil 2520.119.15.5 Fischer, Kuno. Descartes' Leben, Werke und Lehre. 5e Aufl. Heidelberg, 1912.
Phil 2520.120 Martin, W.A.P. The Cartesian philosophy before Descartes. Peking, 1888.
Phil 2520.121 Dimier, Louis. Descartes. Paris, 1917.
Phil 2520.121.5 Dimier, Louis. La vie raisonnable de Descartes. Paris, 1926.
Phil 2520.122 Liard, Louis. Descartes. 3e éd. Paris, 1911.
Phil 2520.123 Prost, Joseph. Essai sur l'atomisme...la philosophie cartesienne. Paris, 1907.
Phil 2520.124 Kahn, Lina. Metaphysics of the supernatural as illustrated by Descartes. N.Y., 1918.
Phil 2520.125 Ventura da Raulica, G. Essai sur l'origine des idées...sur le carthésianisme. Paris, 1853.
Phil 2520.126 Charpentier, T.V. Essai sur la méthode de Descartes. Thèse. Paris, 1869.
Phil 2520.127 Vincentius, Joannes. Discussio perysatitica. Tolosae, 1677.
Phil 2520.128 Opzoomer, C.W. Cartesius. Amsterdam, 1861.
Phil 2520.129 Jungmann, Karl. René Descartes, eine Einführung. Leipzig, 1908.
Phil 2520.130 Belharz, Alfons. Descartes, Hume und Kant. Wiesbaden, 1910.
Htn Phil 2520.131* Howard, E. Remarks on...new philosophy of Descartes. London, 1701.
Phil 2520.132 Hunze, Max. Die Sittenlehre des Descartes. Leipzig, 1872.
Phil 2520.133 Oprescu, Georg. Descartes' Erkenntnisslehre. Inaug.-Diss. Göttingen, 1889.
Phil 2520.134 Boutroux, Émile. De veritatibus aeternis apud Cartesium. Thesis. Parisiis, 1874.
Phil 2520.134.5 Boutroux, Émile. Des vérités éternelles chez Descartes. Paris, 1927.
Phil 2520.135 Chevalier, J. Descartes. Paris, 1921.
Phil 2520.136 Landormy, Paul. Descartes. 5e éd. Paris, 1917?
Phil 2520.137 Wahl, Jean. Du rôle de l'idée de l'instant dans la philosophie de Descartes. Paris, 1920.
Phil 2520.138 Milhaud, G.S. Descartes savant. Paris, 1921.
Phil 2520.138.5 Milhaud, G.S. Num Cartesii methodus tantum valeat in suo opere illustrando quantum ipse senserit. Thesis. Montpellier, 1894.
Phil 2520.139 Blanchet, Léon. Les antécédents historique du "Je pense, donc je suis". Paris, 1920.
Phil 2520.140.3 Gouhier, Henri. Essais sur Descartes. Paris, 1937.
Phil 2520.140.5 Gouhier, Henri. Essais sur Descartes. 2. éd. Paris, 1949.
Phil 2520.140.8 Gouhier, Henri. Les premières pensées de Descartes. Paris, 1958.
Phil 2520.141 Nordlindh, Arvid. Descates' lära om känslan. Akademisk afhaudling. Upsala, 1897.
Phil 2520.142 Grimm, E. Descartes' Lehre von den angeborenen Ideen. Inaug.-Diss. Jena, 1873.
Phil 2520.143 Meier, M. Descartes und die Renaissance. München, n.d.
Phil 2520.144 Liedtke, V. De Beweise für das dasein Gottes. Heidelberg, 1893.
Phil 2520.145 Bordas-Demoulin. Les cartésianisme. Paris, 1874.
Htn Phil 2520.146* Regis, P.S. Response au livre qui a pour titre P. Danielis Huetii. Paris, 1691.
Phil 2520.147 Labordère, Marcel. Une profession de foi cartésienne. Paris, 1919.
Htn Phil 2520.148* Ganguli, S. Descartes. Bombay, 1900.
Phil 2520.150 Schoock, Martin. Admiranda methodus novae philosophiae Renati des Cartes. Waesberge, 1643.
Phil 2520.151 Savérien, Alexandre. Vita di Renato Cartesio. Venezia, 1774.
Phil 2520.153 Kastil, Alfred. Studien zur neueren Erkenntnistheorie. Halle, 1909.
Phil 2520.154 Espinas, Alfred. Études sur l'histoire de la philosophie de l'action. Paris, 1925. 2v.
Phil 2520.155 Fog, B.J. Cartesius. Kjøbenhavn, 1856.
Phil 2520.156 Starcke, C.N. René Descartes. Kjøbenhavn, 1919.
Phil 2520.157 Brockdorff, Cay von. Descartes und die Fortbildung der kartesianischen Lehre. München, 1923.
Phil 2520.158 Giunchi, O. L'individualismo nel Cartesio e nel Rousseau. Novara, 1918.
Phil 2520.159 Rodrigues, G. Quid de mundi externi existentia...Cartesius. Thesis. Lutetiae Parisiorum, 1903.
Phil 2520.160 Aster, E. von. Einführung in die Philosophie Descartes. München, 1921.
Phil 2520.161 Koyré, A. Descartes und die Scholastik. Bonn, 1923.
Phil 2520.161.5 Koyré, A. Essai sur l'idée de Dieu...chez Descartes. Paris, 1922.
Phil 2520.161.10 Koyré, A. Entretiens sur Descartes. N.Y., 1944.
Phil 2520.162 Schmid, Paul J. Die Prinzipien der menschischen Erkenntniss nach Descartes. Leipzig, 187-?
Phil 2520.163.5 Spinoza, B. de. Descartes' Prinzipien der Philosophie. Leipzig, 1922.
Htn Phil 2520.163.15* Spinoza, B. de. Renatus des Cartes beginzelen der wijsbegeerte. Amsterdam, 1664.
Htn Phil 2520.163.20* Spinoza, B. de. Renati des Cartes principiorum philosophiaJ pars I, et II. Amstelodami, 1663.
Phil 2520.164 Chartier, A. Étude sur Descartes. Paris, 1928.
Phil 2520.165 Launay, Louis de. Descartes. Paris, 1923.
Htn Phil 2520.166* Geulincx, A. Annotata majora in principia philosophiae R. Des Cartes. Dordraci, 1691.
Phil 2520.167 Sirven, J. Les années d'apprentissage de Descartes (1596-1628). Albi, 1928.

Classified Listing

Phil 2520.167.2   Sirven, J. Les années d'apprentissage de Descartes (1596-1628). v.1-2. Thèse. Albi, 1928.
Phil 2520.168   Parenty, Henri. Les tourbillons de Descartes et la science moderne. Paris, 1903.
Phil 2520.169   Adam, C.E. De methodo apud Cartesium, Spinozam et Leibnitium. Lutetiae, 1885.
Phil 2520.169.10   Adam, C.E. Descartes; sa vie et son oeuvre. Paris, 1937.
Phil 2520.169.15   Adam, C.E. Descartes; ses amitiés féminines. Paris, 1937.
Phil 2520.170   Bohatec, Josef. Die cartesianische Scholastik. Leipzig, 1912.
Phil 2520.171   Alstrin, Eric. Dissertationis academicae. Holmiae, 1727.
Htn   Phil 2520.172*   Thomas, A.L. Eloge de René Descartes. Paris, 1765. 2 pam.
Phil 2520.172.5   Thomas, A.L. Eulogy of Descartes. Cheltenham, 1826.
Phil 2520.173   Grubbe, S. De philosophia Cartesii observationes. Diss. Upsaliae, 1807.
Phil 2520.174   Leroy, Maxime. Descartes le philosophie au masque. Paris, 1929. 2v.
Phil 2520.174.5   Leroy, Maxime. Descartes social. Paris, 1931.
Phil 2520.175   Palau, J.Y. Descartes y el idealismo subjetivista moderno. Barcelona, 1927.
Phil 2520.176   Petit, Henri. Images; Descartes et Pascal. Paris, 1930.
Phil 2520.177   Serrurier, C. Descartes leer en leven. 's-Gravenhage, 1930.
Phil 2520.178   Baumann, Julius. Doctrina Cartesiana de vero et falso explicata atque examinata. Berolini, 1860?
Phil 2520.179   Gibson, A.B. The philosophy of Descartes. London, 1932.
Phil 2520.180   Mitrovitch, R. La théorie des sciences chez Descartes d'après sa géométrie. Thèse. Paris, 192-?
Phil 2520.181   Giuli, Guido de. Cartesio. Firenze, 1933.
Htn   Phil 2520.182*   Gassendi, Pierre. Disquisitio metaphysica. Amsterodami, 1644.
Phil 2520.183   Barthel, A. Descartes' Leben und Metaphysik. Inaug.-Diss. Erlangen, 1885.
Phil 2520.185   Segond, J. La sagesse cartésienne et la doctrine de la science. Paris, 1932.
Phil 2520.186   Olgiati, Francesco. Cartesio. Milano, 1934.
Phil 2520.186.10   Olgiati, Francesco. La filosofia di Descartes. Milano, 1937.
Phil 2520.187   Keeling, Stanley V. Descartes. London, 1934.
Phil 2520.187.2   Keeling, Stanley V. Descartes. 2d ed. London, 1968.
Phil 2520.188   Serrus, Charles. La méthode de Descartes et son application à la métaphysique. Paris, 1933.
Phil 2520.188.5   Serrus, Charles. La méthode de Descartes et son application à la métaphysique. Thèse. Paris, 1933.
Phil 2520.189   Garin, Pierre. Thèses cartésiennes et thèses thomistes. Thèse. Bruges, 193-.
Phil 2520.190   Marcel, Victor. Étendue et conscience. Thèse. Nancy, 1932.
Phil 2520.191   Merryleęs, W.A. Descartes. Melbourne, 1934.
Phil 2520.192   Picard, Émile. Une édition nouvelle du discours de la méthode de Descartes. Paris, 1934.
Phil 2520.193   Alquié, F. Notes sur la première partie des principes de la philosophie de Descartes. Paris, 1933.
Phil 2520.193.5   Alquié, F. l'homme et l'oeuvre. Paris, 1956.
Phil 2520.193.10   Alquié, F. Descartes. Stuttgart, 1962.
Phil 2520.194   Laberthonnière, L. Études sur Descartes. Paris, 1935. 2v.
Phil 2520.195   Molitor, Emil. Über die Realitätstheorie Descartes'. Inaug.-Diss. Mayen, 1935.
Phil 2520.196   Mesnard, Pierre. Essai sur la morale de Descartes. Paris, 1936.
Phil 2520.196.5   Mesnard, Pierre. Essai sur la morale de Descartes. Thèse. Paris, 1936.
Phil 2520.196.10   Mesnard, Pierre. Descartes, ou Le combat pour la vérité. Paris, 1966.
Phil 2520.197   Iriarte, J. Kartesischer oder sanchezischer Zweifel? Inaug.-Diss. Bothrop, 1935.
Phil 2520.198   Beněs, J. Descartesova metoda ve vědách a ve filosofii. V Praze, 1936.
Phil 2520.199   Études sur Descartes. Paris, 1937.
Phil 2520.200A   Brunschvicg, L. René Descartes. Paris, 1937.
Phil 2520.200B   Brunschvicg, L. René Descartes. Paris, 1937.
Phil 2520.201   Buenos Aires. Universidad. Instituto de Filosofía. Descartes. Buenos Aires, 1937. 3v.
Phil 2520.202   Jaspers, Karl. Descartes und die Philosophie. Berlin, 1937.
Phil 2520.202.5   Jaspers, Karl. Descartes und die Philosophie. 2. Aufl. Berlin, 1948.
Phil 2520.203   Dem Gedächtnis au René Descartes. Berlin, 1937.
Phil 2520.204   Rochon, Antoine. Lettre d'un philosophie à un cartesien de ses amis. Paris, 1672.
Phil 2520.205   Cercle Philosophique, Lorrain. Tricentenaire de la parution du discours de la méthode, 1637-1937. Metz, 1937.
Phil 2520.206   La Plata. Universidad Nacional. Escritos en honor de Descartes. La Plata, 1938.
Phil 2520.207   Causeries cartésiennes à porpos du troisième centenaire du discours de la méthode. Paris, 1938.
Phil 2520.208   Cassirer, E. Descartes. Stockholm, 1939.
Phil 2520.208.5   Cassirer, E. Descartes, Corheille, Christine de Suede. Paris, 1942.
Phil 2520.209   Versfeld, M. An essay on the metaphysics of Descartes. London, 1940.
Phil 2520.210   An outline of Descartes' philosophy. Cambridge, 1938.
Phil 2520.211   Landermy, P.C.R. Descartes y su vida, su obra, su pensamiento. México, 1940.
Phil 2520.212   Monteiro de Barros Lius, Ivan. Descartes. Rio de Janeiro, 1940.
Phil 2520.214   Sergio, Antonio. Cartesianismo ideal e cartesianismo real. Lisboa, 1937.
Phil 2520.215   Cannabrava, E. Descartes e Bergson. São Paulo, 1942?
Phil 2520.216   Mattei, André. L'homme de Descartes. Paris, 1940.
Phil 2520.217   Cresson, André. Descartes; sa vie, son oeuvre, avec un exposé de sa philosophie. le éd. Paris, 1942.
Phil 2520.218   Descartes, René. Les pages immortelles de Descartes. Paris, 1942.
Phil 2520.218.5   Descartes, René. Les pages immortelles de Descartes. Paris, 1961.
Phil 2520.219A   Descartes, René. Descartes, 1596-1650. Genève, 1946.
Phil 2520.219B   Descartes, René. Descartes, 1596-1650. Genève, 1946.
Phil 2520.220   Mateu y Llopis, Felipe. Barcelona, 1945.
Phil 2520.221   Galli, Gallo. Studi cartesiani. Torino, 1943.
Phil 2520.222   Néel, Marguerite. Descartes et la princesse Elisabeth. Paris, 1946.
Phil 2520.223   Jacob, S.M. Notes on Descartes' règles pour la direction de l'esprit. London, 1948.

Phil 2520.224   Carbonara, Cleto. Renato Cartesio e la tradizione ontologica. Torino, 1945.
Phil 2520.224.5   Carbonara, Cleto. Renato Cartesio. Napoli, 1965.
Phil 2520.225   Carlini, Armando. Il problema di Cartesio. Bari, 1948.
Phil 2520.226   Bruno, A. Cartesio e l'illuminismo. Bari, 1949.
Phil 2520.227   Paris. Bibliotheque Nationale. Descartes. Paris, 1937.
Phil 2520.228   Lefebvre, H. Descartes. Paris, 1947.
Phil 2520.229   Alquié, F. La découverte métaphysique de l'homme chez Descartes. 1. éd. Paris, 1950.
Phil 2520.229.2   Alquié, F. La découverte métaphysique de l'homme chez Descartes. Thèse. Paris, 1950.
Phil 2520.229.5   Alquié, F. Science et métaphysique chez Descartes. Paris, 1965.
Phil 2520.230   Lewis, G. L'individualité selon Descartes. Paris, 1950.
Phil 2520.230.2   Lewis, G. L'individualité selon Descartes. Thèse. Paris, 1950.
Phil 2520.230.10   Lewis, G. Le problème de l'inconscient et le cartesianisme. 1. éd. Paris, 1950.
Phil 2520.230.20   Lewis, G. René Descartes. Paris, 1953.
Phil 2520.231   Finance, J. de. Cogito cartésien et réflexion thomiste. Thèse. Paris, 1946[1945].
Phil 2520.232   Balz, A.G.A. Cartesian studies. N.Y., 1951.
Phil 2520.233   Scholz, H. Descartes. Münster, 1951.
Phil 2520.234A   Descartes et le cartésianisme hollandais. Paris, 1950[1951].
Phil 2520.234B   Descartes et le cartésianisme hollandais. Paris, 1950[1951].
Phil 2520.235   Balz, A.G.A. Descartes and the modern mind. New Haven, 1952.
Phil 2520.236   Sykes, L.C. A philosopher for the modern university. Leicester, 1951.
Phil 2520.237   Scott, J.F. The scientific work of René Descartes. London, 1952.
Phil 2520.238   Beck, L.J. The method of Descartes. Oxford, 1952.
Phil 2520.239   Vartanian, A. Diderot and Descartes. Princeton, 1953.
Phil 2520.240   Berlin. Freie Universität. Gedenkfeier anlässlich des drei hundertjährigen Todestagen des Philosophen René Descartes. Berlin, 1950.
Phil 2520.241   Nardi, Bruno. Le meditizioni di Cartesio. Roma, 1952.
Phil 2520.242   Gueroult, Martial. Descartes, selon l'ordre des raisons. Paris, 1953. 2v.
Phil 2520.242.5   Gueroult, Martial. Nouvelles réflexions sur la preuve ontologique de Descartes. Paris, 1955.
Phil 2520.245   Leisegang, G. Descartes Dioptrik. Meisenheim am Glan, 1954.
Phil 2520.250   Hagmann, Moritz. Descartes. Winterthur, 1955.
Phil 2520.250.2   Hagmann, Moritz. Descartes in der Auffassung durch die Historiker der Philosophie. Winterthur, 1955.
Phil 2520.255   Lefèvre, Roger. La vocation de Descartes. v.1-3. Paris, 1956-1957. 2v.
Phil 2520.255.5   Lefèvre, Roger. L'humanisme de Descartes. Paris, 1957.
Phil 2520.255.10   Lefèvre, Roger. Le criticisme de Descartes. 1. éd. Paris, 1958.
Phil 2520.255.15   Lefèvre, Roger. La métaphysique de Descartes. 1. éd. Paris, 1959.
Phil 2520.255.20   Lefèvre, Roger. La bataille du "cogito". 1. éd. Paris, 1960.
Phil 2520.260   Joachim, H.H. Descartes's Rules for the direction of the mind. London, 1957.
Phil 2520.265   Ritter, Heinrich. Welcher Einfluss hat die Philosophie des Cartesius auf die Ausbildung der des Spinoza Gehabt. Leipzig, 1817.
Phil 2520.270   Bievre, C. de. Descartes und Pascal. Brasschaet, 1956.
Phil 2520.275   Rodis-Lewis, Geneviève. La morale de Descartes. 1. ed. Paris, 1957.
Phil 2520.275.10   Rodis-Lewis, Geneviève. Descartes et le rationalisme. Paris, 1966.
Phil 2520.276   Rodis-Lewis, Geneviève. La morale de Descartes. 3e ed. Paris, 1970.
Phil 2520.280   Behn, Irene. Der Philosoph und die Königin. Freiburg, 1957.
Phil 2520.285   Richter, L. René Descartes. Hamburg, 1942.
Phil 2520.290   Russier, Jeanne. Sagesse cartésienne et religion. Paris, 1958.
Phil 2520.295   Wolzogen, J.L. Urvagi do medytacji metafizycznych René Descartes. Warszawa, 1959.
Phil 2520.300   Sebba, Gregor. Descartes and his philosophy. Athens, Ga., 1959.
Phil 2520.305   Frédérix, Pierre. Monsieur Réné Descartes en son temps. Paris, 1959.
Phil 2520.310   Vuillemin, Jules. Mathématiques et métaphysique chez Descartes. Paris, 1960.
Phil 2520.315   Llanos, Alfredo. El problema del voluntarismo en Descartes. Bahia Blanca, 1960.
Phil 2520.320   Oggione, Emilio. Cartesio. Bologna, 1959.
Phil 2520.325   Cómbès, J. Le dessein de la sagesse cartésienne. Lyon, 1960.
Phil 2520.330   Hoeven, Pieter van der. Metafysica en fysica bij Descartes. Gorinchem, 1961.
Phil 2520.335   Waltheunis, O. De mens Descartes. Brussel, 1960.
Phil 2520.340   Pousa, Narciso. Moral y libertad en Descartes. La Plata, 1960.
Phil 2520.342   Gonhier, Henri. La pensée métaphysique de Descartes. Paris, 1962.
Phil 2520.343   Sassen, F. Descartes. Den Haag, 1963.
Phil 2520.344   Laporte, Jean. Le rationalisme de Descartes. Paris, 1950.
Phil 2520.345   Marshall, D.J. Physik und Metaphysik bei Descartes. München? 1961.
Phil 2520.346   Allard, J.L. Le mathématisme de Descartes. Ottawa, 1963.
Phil 2520.347   Roed, Wolfgang. Descartes. München, 1964.
Phil 2520.348   Barjonet-Huraux, Marcelle. Descartes. Paris, 1963.
Phil 2520.349   Watson, Richard A. The downfall of Cartesianism, 1673-1712. The Hague, 1966.
Phil 2520.350   Beck, Leslie John. The metaphysics of Descartes. Oxford, 1965.
Phil 2520.351   Rozsnyai, Ervin. Études sur Descartes. Budapest, 1964.
Phil 2520.352   Noce, Augusto del. Riforma cattolica e filosofia moderna. Bologna, 1965.
Phil 2520.353   Lefèvre, Roger. La pensée existentielle de Descartes. Paris, 1965.
Phil 2520.354   Chauvois, Louis. Descartes, sa "Méthode" et ses erreurs en physiologie. Paris, 1966.
Phil 2520.355   Schmidt, Gerhart. Aufklärung und Metaphysik. Die Neubegründung des Wissens durch Descartes. Tübingen, 1
Phil 2520.358.4   Sesonske, Alexander. Meta-meditations; studies in Descartes. Belmont, Calif., 1967[1965].

520   History of philosophy - Local Modern philosophy - France - Individual losophers - Descartes, René - cont.
Phil 2520.360   Specht, Rainer. Commercium mentis et corporis. Stuttgart, 1966.
Phil 2520.365   Mahnke, Detlef. Des Aufbau des philosophischen Wissens nach René Descartes. München, 1967.
Phil 2520.370   Doney, Willis. Descartes; a collection of critical essays. 1st ed. Notre Dame, 1968.
Phil 2520.375   Kenny, Anthony. Descartes; a study of his philosophy. N.Y., 1968.
Phil 2520.380   Schiavo, Mario. Il problema etico in Cartesio. Rome, 1948?
Phil 2520.385   Wegelingh, William. Cartesiaanse uitzichten. Lochem, 1966.
VPhil 2520.390   Kalocsai, Dezso. Descartes etikája. Budapest, 1964.
Phil 2520.395   Vrooman, Jack Rochford. René Descartes; a biography. N.Y., 1970.
Phil 2520.400   Broadie, Frederick. An approach to Descartes' meditations. London, 1970.
Phil 2520.405   Magnus, Bernd. Cartesian essays; a collection of critical studies. The Hague, 1969.
Phil 2520.410   Frankfurt, Harry G. Demons, dreamers, and madmen. Indianapolis, 1970.
Phil 2520.415   Negri, Antonio. Descartes politico o della ragionevole ideologia. Milano, 1970.
Phil 2520.420   Guéroult, Marital. Etudes sur Descartes, Spinoza, Hildesheim. N.Y., 1970.
Phil 2520.425   Denissoff, Élie. Descartes, premier théoricien de la physique mathematique. Louvain, 1970.
Phil 2520.430   Gabaude, Jean Marc. Liberté et raison. v. 1- Toulouse, 1970-
Phil 2520.435   Petit, Léon. Descartes et la princesse Elisabeth. Paris, 1969.

523   History of philosophy - Local Modern philosophy - France - Individual losophers - Destutt de Tracy, Antoine
Phil 2523.30   Destutt de Tracy, A.L.C. Élémens d'idéologie. Paris, 1817-18. 4v.
Phil 2523.31   Destutt de Tracy, A.L.C. Elementi d'ideologia Milano, 1817-19. 10v.
Phil 2523.31.2   Compagnoni, G. Saggio di un trattato di morale. Milano, 1819.
Phil 2523.32   Destutt de Tracy, A.L.C. Élémens d'idéologie. Paris, 1825-27. 5v.
Phil 2523.45   Destutt de Tracy, A.L.C. Principes logiques. Paris, 1817. 2 pam.
Phil 2523.50   Destutt de Tracy, A.L.C. Principes logiques. Paris, 1817.
Phil 2523.80   Pamphlet box. Destutt de Tracy, A.L.C.
Phil 2523.85   Cruet, Jean. La philosophie morale et sociale de Destutt de Tracy, 1754-1836. Tours, 1909.
Phil 2523.90   Kohler, Oskar. Die Logik des Destutt de Tracy. Inaug.-Diss. Borna, 1931.

530   History of philosophy - Local Modern philosophy - France - Individual losophers - Diderot, Denis
Phil 2530.15   Diderot, Denis. Oeuvres philosophiques. Bruxelles, 1829. 6v.
Phil 2530.15.5   Diderot, Denis. Oeuvres philosophiques. Paris, 1956.
Phil 2530.19   Diderot, Denis. Dederot's early philosophical works. Chicago, 1916.
Phil 2530.20   Diderot, Denis. Selected philosophical writings. Cambridge, Eng., 1953.
Phil 2530.30*   Diderot, Denis. Pensées philosophiques. La Haye, 1746.
Phil 2530.35*   Diderot, Denis. Lettre sur les aveugles. Londres, 1749.
Phil 2530.40*   Diderot, Denis. Lettre sur les sourds et muets. n.p., 1751.
Phil 2530.80A   Dieckmann, Herbert. Cinq leçons sur Diderot. Genève, 1959.
Phil 2530.80B   Dieckmann, Herbert. Cinq leçons sur Diderot. Genève, 1959.
Phil 2530.80.5   Dieckmann, Herbert. Diderot: sur Terence. n.p., 1958?
Phil 2530.80.10   Dieckmann, Herbert. Diderot's conception of genius. n.p., 1941?
Phil 2530.82   Roretz, Karl. Diderots Weltanschauung. Wien, 1914.
Phil 2530.84   Leo, Werner. Diderot als Kunstphilosophie. Inaug.-Diss. Erlangen, 1918.
Phil 2530.88   Lerel, A.C. Diderots Naturphilosophie. Wien, 1950.
Phil 2530.88.2   Lerel, A.C. Diderots Naturphilosophie. Wien, 1950.
Phil 2530.90   Heitmann, K. Ethos des Künstlers und Ethos der Kunst. Münster, 1962.

555   History of philosophy - Local Modern philosophy - France - Individual losophers - Other D
Phil 2555.1.80   Beaussire, É. Antécédents de l'hégélianisme...Dom Deschamps. Paris, 1865.
Phil 2555.1.85   Deschamps, L.M. Le vrai système. Paris, 1939.
Phil 2555.1.86   Deschamps, L.M. Le vrai système. Genève, 1963.
Phil 2555.2.80   Büchner, A. Un philosophe amateur, essai biographique sur Léon Dumont. Paris, 1884.
Phil 2555.3.30*   DuRefuge, E. Aulicus inculpatus. Amsterdam, 1644.
Phil 2555.4.31   Derepas, Gustave. De necessitate legum naturalium. Thesis. Lutetiae, 1883.
Phil 2555.5.90   Brulez, L. Delboeufs Bedeutung für die Logik. Diss. Berlin, 1919.
Phil 2555.6.90   Weber, Georg. Die Philosophie Debrye's. Inaug.-Diss. Augsburg, 1926.
Phil 2555.7.90   Cochet, M.A. La métaphysique de Paul Decoster et la science. Bruges, 1937.
Phil 2555.7.93   Molle, Germaine van. La philosophie de Paul Decoster. Bruxelles, 1940.
Phil 2555.8.30   Darbon, André. Philosophie de la volonté. 1. éd. Paris, 1951.
Phil 2555.8.35   Darbon, André. Les categories de la modalité. 1. éd. Paris, 1956.
Phil 2555.9.30   Dufrenne, Mikel. La notion d'a priori. 1. éd. Paris, 1959.
Phil 2555.9.31A   Dufrenne, Mikel. The notion of the a priori. Evanston, Ill., 1966.
Phil 2555.9.31B   Dufrenne, Mikel. The notion of the a priori. Evanston, Ill., 1966.
Phil 2555.10.81   Geissler, Rolf. Boureau-Deslandes, ein Materialist der Frühaufklärung. 1. Aufl. Berlin, 1967.
Phil 2555.11.71   Dupréel, Eugène. Similitude et dépassement. Paris, 1968.
Phil 2555.12.30   Dartan, Jacques. Franchir le Rubicon. Paris, 1968.

2605   History of philosophy - Local Modern philosophy - France - Individual philosophers - F
Phil 2605.1.79   Pamphlet box. Fouillée, Alfred.
Phil 2605.1.80   Guyau, Augustin. La philosophie...d'Alfred Fouillée. Paris, 1913.
Phil 2605.1.81   Pasmanik, D. Alfred Fouillées psychischen Monismus. Bern, 1899.
Phil 2605.1.83   Gaune de Beaucourdey, E. La psychologie et la métaphysique des idéesforces chez Alfred Fouillée. Thèse. Paris, 1936.
Phil 2605.1.85   Costanzi, T.M. Il pensiero di Alfredo Fouillée. Napoli, 1936.
Htn   Phil 2605.2.30*   Fontenelle, B. Entretiens sur la pluralité des mondes. Paris, 1766.
Htn   Phil 2605.3.30*   Fourier, C. Le nouveau monde. Paris, 1829.
Phil 2605.3.40   Theodore Flournoy, 1854-1920. Genève, 1928.
Phil 2605.4.31   Fonsegrive, George L. Éléments de philosophie. Paris, 1891-1892. 2v.
Phil 2605.5.95   Rabbe, Felix P. L'abbé Simon Foucher. Paris, 1867.
Phil 2605.6.31   Foucou, L. Les preliminaries de la philosophie. Paris, 1879.
Phil 2605.7.31   Fauré-Fremiet, P. Esquisse d'une philosophie concrète. 1. ed. Paris, 1954.
Phil 2605.8.30   Fouéré, René. Du temporel à l'intemporel. Paris, 1960. 2v.
Phil 2605.9.80   Hugo, C.L. Refutation du système de Monsr. Faidy. Luxemburg, 1699.
Phil 2605.10.30   Fontan, Pierre. L'intention réaliste. Paris, 1965.
Phil 2605.12.30   Finance, Joseph de. Connaissance de l'être, traité d'ontologie. Paris, 1966.

2610   History of philosophy - Local Modern philosophy - France - Individual philosophers - Gassendi, Pierre
Phil 2610.1   Gassendi, P. Opera omnia. Florentiae, 1727. 6v.
Phil 2610.7   Gassendi, P. Abregé de la philosophie de Gassendi. 2e ed. v.1-7. Lyon, 1684. 6v.
Htn   Phil 2610.7.5*   Gassendi, P. Abregé de la philosophie de Mr. Gassendi. Paris, 1675.
NEDL   Phil 2610.15   Gassendi, P. Institutio logica, et Philosophiae Epicuri syntagma. London, 1668.
Htn   Phil 2610.35*   Gassendi, P. Three discourses of happiness, virtue and liberty. London, 1699.
Phil 2610.81   Thomas, P. Felix. Philosophie de Gassendi. Paris, 1889.
Phil 2610.83   Bougerel, J. Vie de Pierre Gassendi. Paris, 1737.
Phil 2610.84   Andrieux, L. Pierre Gassendi. Thèse. Paris, 1927.
Phil 2610.86   Rochot, Bernard. Les travaux de Gassendi sur Épicure. Paris, 1944.
Phil 2610.87   Rochot, Bernard. Les travaux de Gassendi sur Épicure et sur l'atomisme. Thèse. Paris, 1944.
Phil 2610.95   Aquirre, Francisco Solano de. El atomismo de Gassendi. Barcelona, 1956.
Phil 2610.100   Comité du Tricentenaire de Gassendi. Actes du Congrès du Tricentenaire de Pierre Gassendi. Paris, 1957.
Phil 2610.100.5   Bloch, Olivier René. La philosophie de Gassendi. La Haye, 1971.
Phil 2610.105   Berr, Henri. Du scepticisme de Gassendi. Paris, 1960.
Phil 2610.110   Gregory, Tullio. Scetticismo ed empirismo. Bari, 1961.
Phil 2610.115   Pfeiffer, Adalbert. Die Ethik des Peter Gassendi. Inaug.-Diss. Borna, 1908.

2630   History of philosophy - Local Modern philosophy - France - Individual philosophers - Other G
Phil 2630.1.20   Gratry, Auguste. Studien. Regensburg, 1858-1859. 3v.
Phil 2630.1.25   Gratry, Auguste. Gratry, a cura di Angelica Marrucchi. Milano, 1923.
Phil 2630.1.35   Gratry, Auguste. Méditations inédites. Paris, 1926.
Phil 2630.1.79   Gratry, Auguste. Souvenirs de ma jeunesse. 5e ed. Paris, 1897.
Phil 2630.1.81   Pointud-Guillemot, B. Essai sur la philosophie de Gratry. Thèse. Paris, 1917.
Phil 2630.1.82   Perraud, A. Le P. Gratry; sa vie et ses oeuvres. 7e ed. Paris, 1933.
Phil 2630.1.83   Pointud-Guillemot, B. La doctrine sociale de Gratry. Thèse. Paris, 1917.
Phil 2630.1.84   Braun, Ludwig L. Gratrys Theorie der religiosen Erkenntnis. Strassburg, 1914.
Phil 2630.1.85   Marias Aguilera, J. La filosofia del Padre Gratry. 2. ed. Buenos Aires, 1948.
Phil 2630.1.86   Chauvin, A. Le père Gratry, 1805-1872. Paris, 1911.
Phil 2630.2.10   Guyau, J.M. Philosophische Werke. Leipzig, 1912-1914. 6v.
Phil 2630.2.35   Guyau, J.M. Sittlichkeit ohne Pflicht. Leipzig, 1909.
Phil 2630.2.122   Bergmann, Ernst. Die Philosophie Guyaus. Leipzig, 1912.
Phil 2630.2.125   Łuczewski, Kazimierz. Das Problem der Religion in der Philosophie Guyaus. Posen, 1915.
Phil 2630.2.127   Schumm, Felix. Jean Marie Guyaus Religionsphilosophie. Tübingen, 1913.
Phil 2630.2.129   Nilsson, A. Guyaus estetik. Lund, 1909.
Phil 2630.2.131   Bjarnason, Águst. Jean-Marie Guyau. Kobenhavn, 1911.
Phil 2630.2.133   Molina, Enrique. Dos filosofos contemporaneos; Guyau-Bergson. Santiago de Chile, 1925.
Phil 2630.3.82   Trial, Louis. Jean-Jacques Gourd 1850-1909. Nimes, 1914.
Phil 2630.3.84   Reymond, M. La philosophie de Jean-Jacques Gourd. Chambéry, 1949.
Phil 2630.4.90   Palante, Georges. La philosophie du Bovarysme. Paris, 1912.
Phil 2630.5.90   Kergomard, Jean. Edmond Goblot, 1858-1935. Paris, 1937.
Phil 2630.6.80   Barrenechea, M. Un idealismo estético; la filosofia de Jules de Gaultier. Buenos Aires, 1921.
Phil 2630.6.85   Spring, Gerald M. Man's invincible surmise; a personal interpretation of Bovarysm. N.Y., 1968.
Phil 2630.7.30   Guénon, René. The reign of quantity and the signs of the times. London, 1953.
Phil 2630.7.32   Guénon, René. La règne de la quantité et les signes des temps. 4. ed. Paris, 1950.
Phil 2630.7.39   Guénon, René. Symboles fondament aux de la science sacrée. Paris, 1962.
Phil 2630.7.90   Marcireau, J. René Guenon et son oeuvre. Poitiers, 1946.
Phil 2630.7.95   Sérant, Paul. René Guenon. Paris, 1953.
Phil 2630.7.98   Chacornac, Paul. La vie simple de René Guenon. Paris, 1958.
Phil 2630.7.105   Meroz, Lucien. René Guénon, ou La sagesse initiatique. Paris, 1962.
Phil 2630.8.21   Gilson, Étienne. A Gilson reader. Garden City, 1957.
Phil 2630.8.30   Gilson, Étienne. L'être et l'essence. Paris, 1948.
Phil 2630.8.32   Gilson, Étienne. L'être et l'essence. Paris, 1962.
Phil 2630.8.35   Gilson, Étienne. Breakdown of morals and Christian education. n.p., 1952?

Phil 2630.8.38   Gilson, Étienne. Introduction aux arts du beau.
                  Paris, 1963.
Phil 2630.8.80   Étienne Gilson. Paris, 1949.
Phil 2630.9   Gex, Maurice. Variétés philosophiques. Lausanne, 1948.
Phil 2630.10   Gerard, Jacques. L'être et la pensée. Paris, 1954.
Phil 2630.11   Guitton, Jean. Invitation a la pensée et à la vie.
                  Paris, 1956.
Phil 2630.11.2   Guitton, Jean. La pensée moderne et le catholicisme.
                  v.6,7,9,10. Aix, 1936. 5v.
Phil 2630.11.5   Guitton, Jean. Apprendre à vivre et à penser.
                  Paris, 1957.
Phil 2630.11.8   Guitton, Jean. Make your mind work for you. N.Y., 1958.
Phil 2630.11.10   Guitton, Jean. Journal. Paris, 1959. 2v.
Phil 2630.11.12   Guitton, Jean. The Guitton journals, 1952-1955.
                  London, 1963.
Phil 2630.11.15   Guitton, Jean. Une mère dans sa vallée. Paris, 1961.
Phil 2630.11.20   Guitton, Jean. Dialogue avec les précurseurs.
                  Aubier, 1962.
Phil 2630.11.25   Guitton, Jean. Le clair et l'obscur. Paris, 1962.
Phil 2630.11.30   Guitton, Jean. Oeuvres complètes. v.1-2. Paris, 1966.
Phil 2630.11.35   Jean Guitton, vu par Jacques André. Troyes, 1963.
Phil 2630.11.40   Guitton, Jean. Histoire et destinée. Paris, 1970.
Phil 2630.12   Geiger, Louis Bertrand. Philosophie et spiritualité.
                  Paris, 1963. 2v.
Phil 2630.13.80   Crispini, Franco. Lo strutturalismo dialettico di Lucien
                  Goldmann. Napoli, 1970.

Phil 2636.10   Helvétius, C.A. Oeuvres complètes. London, 1777.
                  2v.
Htn   Phil 2636.10.7*   Helvétius, C.A. Oeuvres complètes. v.1-2. London, 1781.
Phil 2636.11   Helvétius, C.A. Oeuvres complètes. v.3-7.
                  Deuxponts, 1784. 5v.
Phil 2636.12   Helvétius, C.A. Oeuvres complètes. Paris, 1793.
                  5v.
Phil 2636.12.2   Helvétius, C.A. Oeuvres complètes. Paris, 1793-97.
                  10v.
Phil 2636.25.5   Helvétius, C.A. De l'esprit, de l'homme. 4e éd.
                  Paris, 1909.
Phil 2636.25.6   Helvétius, C.A. De l'esprit. Paris, 1959.
Phil 2636.31   Helvétius, C.A. A treatise on man. London, 1877.
                  2v.
Phil 2636.31.2   Helvétius, C.A. A treatise on man. London, 1810.
                  2v.
Htn   Phil 2636.32*   Helvétius, C.A. De l'homme. London, 1773. 2v.
Phil 2636.34   Helvétius, C.A. De l'homme. London, 1776.
Htn   Phil 2636.40*   Helvétius, C.A. De l'esprit. Amsterdam, 1758.
Htn   Phil 2636.40.1*   Helvétius, C.A. De l'esprit. Paris, 1759.
Phil 2636.40.2   Helvétius, C.A. De l'esprit. v.1-4. Paris, 1793.
                  2v.
Phil 2636.40.6   Helvétius, C.A. De l'esprit. Paris, 1843.
Phil 2636.41   Helvétius, C.A. De l'esprit, or Essays on the mind.
                  London, 1759.
Phil 2636.41.2   Helvétius, C.A. De l'esprit, or Essays on the mind. 2. ed.
                  London, 1810.
Phil 2636.44   Helvétius, C.A. Le vrai sens du système de la nature.
                  Londres, 1774.
Phil 2636.79   Pamphlet box. Helvétius, C.A.
Phil 2636.80   Keim, A. Helvétius sa vie et son oeuvre. Paris, 1907.
Phil 2636.81   Séverac, J.B. Helvétius. Paris, n.d.
Phil 2636.82   Grossman, Mordecai. Philosophy of Helvetius. Thesis.
                  N.Y., 1926.
Phil 2636.82.3   Grossman, Mordecai. The philosophy of Helvetius.
                  N.Y., 1926.
Phil 2636.83   Stanganelli, Irma. La teoria pedagogica di Helvetius.
                  Napoli, 1919.
Phil 2636.85   Horowitz, I.L. Claude Helvetius. N.Y., 1954.
Phil 2636.88   Momdzhian, Khashik. Helvitius, ein streitbarer Atheist das
                  18. Jahrhunderts. Berlin, 1959.
Phil 2636.88.5   Momdzhian, Khashik. La philosophie d'Helvétius.
                  Moscow, 1959.
Phil 2636.90   Cumming, Ian. Helvetius. London, 1955.
Phil 2636.91   Smith, David Warner. Helvetius; a study in persecution.
                  Oxford, 1965.

Phil 2648.20   Holbach, Paul Henri T. Textes choisis. Paris, 1957.
Phil 2648.25   Holbach, Paul Henri T. D'Holbach portatif. Paris, 1967.
Htn   Phil 2648.29*   Holbach, Paul Henri T. Système de la nature.
                  London, 1770. 2v.
Htn   Phil 2648.30*   Holbach, Paul Henri T. Système de la nature.
                  London, 1770. 2v.
Phil 2648.30.5   Holbach, Paul Henri T. Système social. Paris, 1795.
                  2v.
Phil 2648.30.7   Holbach, Paul Henri T. Système social. v.1-2.
                  London, 1773.
Phil 2648.30.8   Holbach, Paul Henri T. Système social. London, 1774.
Phil 2648.30.9   Holbach, Paul Henri T. Système social. London, 1773.
                  3v.
Phil 2648.30.10   Holbach, Paul Henri T. Système de la nature. Paris, 1820.
                  2v.
Phil 2648.30.12   Holbach, Paul Henri T. Système de la nature. Paris, 1821.
                  2v.
Phil 2648.30.14   Holbach, Paul Henri T. Système de la nature.
                  Londres, 1777.
Phil 2648.31   Holbach, Paul Henri T. System of nature. N.Y., 1835.
Phil 2648.31.15   Holbach, Paul Henri T. Sociales System oder Naturliche
                  Principien der Moral und der Politik. Leipzig, 1898.
Htn   Phil 2648.32.80* Holbach, Paul Henri T. De la cruauté religieuse.
                  Londres, 1769.
Phil 2648.33   Holbach, Paul Henri T. De la cruauté religieuse.
                  Paris, 1826.
Phil 2648.34   Holbach, Paul Henri T. Le bon sens du Curé Meslier.
                  Paris, 1802.
Phil 2648.34.2   Holbach, Paul Henri T. Le bon sens du Curé Meslier.
                  Paris, 1802.
Phil 2648.34.3   Holbach, Paul Henri T. Le bon sens du Curé Meslier.
                  Paris, 1802.
Phil 2648.34.5   Holbach, Paul Henri T. Le bons sens du Curé Jean Meslier.
                  Hildesheim, 1970.
Phil 2648.35   Holbach, Paul Henri T. Good sense; or natural ideas.
                  N.Y., 1831.
Phil 2648.35.9   Holbach, Paul Henri T. Der gesunde Menschenverstand. 2e
                  Aufl. Baltimore, 1856.

Phil 2648.35.11   Holbach, Paul Henri T. Der gesunde Menschenverstand. 2e
                  Aufl. Baltimore, 1860.
Phil 2648.39   Holbach, Paul Henri T. Le bon-sens. London, 1782.
Phil 2648.39.2   Holbach, Paul Henri T. Le bon-sens, ou idées naturelles.
                  Londres, 1774.
Htn   Phil 2648.39.3*   Holbach, Paul Henri T. Le bon-sens. Londres, 1772.
Phil 2648.39.4   Holbach, Paul Henri T. Le bon-sens. Londres, 1772.
                  2 pam.
Phil 2648.39.5   Holbach, Paul Henri T. Le bon-sens. Londres, 1789.
Phil 2648.39.6   Holbach, Paul Henri T. Le bon-sens. Rome, 1792.
Htn   Phil 2648.40*   Holbach, Paul Henri T. Essai sur les préjugés.
                  Amsterdam, 1770.
Phil 2648.41   Holbach, Paul Henri T. Essai sur les préjugés. v.1-2.
                  Paris, 1800.
Phil 2648.41.2   Holbach, Paul Henri T. Essai sur les préjugés.
                  Paris, 1795.
Phil 2648.43.10   Holbach, Paul Henri T. Letters to Eugenia. Boston, 1870.
Phil 2648.43.25   Holbach, Paul Henri T. Cartas á Eugenia. Paris, 1810.
Phil 2648.45   Holbach, Paul Henri T. La contagion sacrée. v.1-2.
                  Londres, 1768.
Phil 2648.45.2   Holbach, Paul Henri T. La contagion sacrée. v.1-2.
                  Paris, 1796-97.
Htn   Phil 2648.49*   Holbach, Paul Henri T. La morale universelle.
                  Amsterdam, 1776. 3v.
Phil 2648.50   Holbach, Paul Henri T. La morale universelle.
                  Tours, 1792. 3v.
Phil 2648.52   Holbach, Paul Henri T. Le christianisme dévoilé.
                  Londres, 1767.
Htn   Phil 2648.52.2*   Holbach, Paul Henri T. Le christianisme dévoilé.
                  Londres, 1767.
Phil 2648.52.3   Holbach, Paul Henri T. Le christianisme dévoilé.
                  Paris, 1767.
Phil 2648.52.5   Holbach, Paul Henri T. Le christianisme dévoilé.
                  Suisse, 1796.
Phil 2648.52.6   Holbach, Paul Henri T. Le christianisme dévoilé.
                  Herblay, 1961.
Phil 2648.54   Holbach, Paul Henri T. L'enfer detruit. Londres, 1769.
Htn   Phil 2648.56*   Holbach, Paul Henri T. Tableau des saints. Londres, 1770.
                  2v.
Phil 2648.58   Holbach, Paul Henri T. Éthocratie. Amsterdam, 1776.
Htn   Phil 2648.60*   Holbach, Paul Henri T. Examen impartial des principales
                  religions. n.p., n.d.
Phil 2648.62   Holbach, Paul Henri T. Ausgewählte Texte. Berlin, 1959.
Phil 2648.64   Holbach, Paul Henri T. Bicentenaire du Système de la
                  nature. Paris, 1970.
Phil 2648.80   Petifils, E. Socialiste-révolution au commencement du
                  XVIII siècle. Paris, 1908.
Phil 2648.90   Hubert, René. D'Holbach et ses amis. Paris, 1928.
Phil 2648.91   Cushing, M.P. Baron d'Holbach. N.Y., 1914.
Phil 2648.92   Wickwar, William H. Baron d'Holbach; a prelude to the
                  French Revolution. London, 1935.
Phil 2648.93   Topazio, V.W. D'Holbach's moral philosophy. Geneva, 1956.
Phil 2648.94   Naville, Pierre. Paul Thiry d'Holbach et la philosophie
                  scientifique au XVIIIe siècle. 2. éd. Paris, 1943.
Phil 2648.94.3   Naville, Pierre. Paul Thiry d'Holbach et la philosophie
                  scientifique au XVIIIe siècle. Paris, 1967.
Phil 2648.96   Besthern, Rudolf. Textkritische Studien zum Werk Holbachs.
                  Berlin, 1969.

Phil 2651.30   Huet, Pierre Daniel. Traité philosophique de la faiblesse.
                  London, 1741.
Phil 2651.40   Huet, Pierre Daniel. Philosophical treatise concerning the
                  weakness of human understanding. London, 1728.
Phil 2651.80   DeGournay, M.F.A. Huet. Caen, 1854.
Phil 2651.81   Flottes, J.B.M. Etude sur Pierre Daniel Huet.
                  Montpellier, 1857.
Phil 2651.82   Bartholmess, B.J.W. Huet, évêque d'Avranches.
                  Paris, 1850.
Phil 2651.83   Tolmer, L. Pierre-Daniel Huet, 1630-1721. Bayeux, 1949.
Phil 2651.85   Sciacca, Giuseppe Maria. Scetticismo cristiano.
                  Palermo, 1968.

Phil 2655.1.79   Pamphlet box. Philosophy. French and Belgian. Hemsterhuis,
                  François.
Phil 2655.1.80   Grucker, E. François Hemsterhuis. Paris, 1866.
Phil 2655.1.81   Meyer, E. Der Philosoph Franz Hemsterhuis. Breslau, 1893.
Phil 2655.1.82   Bulle, F. Franziskus Hemsterhuis und der deutsche
                  Irrationalismus. Jena, 1911.
Phil 2655.2.80   Mirabaud, R. Charles Henry et l'idéalisme scientifique.
                  Paris, 1926.
Phil 2655.2.85   Warrain, F. L'oeuvre psychobiophysique. Paris, 1931.
Phil 2655.2.86   Warrain, F. L'oeuvre psychobiophysique. 2 ed.
                  Paris, 1938.
Phil 2655.3   Paris. École Libre des Sciences Politiques. Élie Halévy.
                  Paris, 1937.
Phil 2655.3.90   Carbonara, C. L'idealismo di O. Hamelin. Napoli, 1927?
Phil 2655.3.93   Beck, Leslie J. La méthode synthétique d'Hamelin.
                  Paris, 1935.
Phil 2655.3.100   Sesmat, A. Dialectique. Paris, 1955.
Phil 2655.3.105   Deregibus, Arturo. La metafisica critica di Octave
                  Hamelin. Torino, 1968.
Phil 2655.5.30   Hello, E. L'homme. Paris, 1872.
Phil 2655.6.30   Hyppolite, J. Leçon inaugurale faite le jeudi 19 déc.
                  1963. Nougent-le-Rotrou, 1964.
Phil 2655.7.30   Henry, Michel. L'essence de la manifestation.
                  Paris, 1963. 2v.

Phil 2668.30   Janet, Paul A.R. Traité élémentaire de philosophie.
                  Paris, 1880.
Phil 2668.35   Janet, Paul A.R. Le matérialisme contemporain.
                  Paris, 1875.
NEDL   Phil 2668.35.5   Janet, Paul A.R. The materialism of the present day.
                  London, 1866.
Phil 2668.40   Janet, Paul A.R. Les problèmes du XIXe siècle. 2e éd.
                  Paris, 1873.
Phil 2668.45   Janet, Paul A.R. Le cerveau et la pensée. Paris, 1867.
Phil 2668.50   Janet, Paul A.R. Les causes finales. Paris, 1876.
Phil 2668.50.4   Janet, Paul A.R. Final causes. 2d ed. N.Y., 1883.
Phil 2668.50.5   Janet, Paul A.R. Final causes. 3d ed. N.Y., 1894.
Phil 2668.55   Janet, Paul A.R. Petits éléments de morale. Paris, 1870.

Phil 2668 History of philosophy - Local Modern philosophy - France - Individual philosophers - Janet, Paul - cont.

Phil 2668.55.5 Janet, Paul A.R. Theory of morals. N.Y., 1883.
Phil 2668.60 Janet, Paul A.R. Philosophie du bonheur. Paris, 1864.
Phil 2668.65 Janet, Paul A.R. Éléments de philosophie scientifique. Paris, 1890.
Phil 2668.70 Janet, Paul A.R. Principes de la métaphysique et de psychologie. Paris, 1897. 2v.

Phil 2672 History of philosophy - Local Modern philosophy - France - Individual philosophers - Jouffroy, Théodore

Phil 2672.29 Jouffroy, Théodore S. Mélanges philosophiques. Paris, 1833.
Phil 2672.30 Jouffroy, Théodore S. Mélanges philosophiques. Paris, 1838.
Phil 2672.30.2 Jouffroy, Théodore S. Nouveaux mélanges philosophiques. Paris, 1842.
Phil 2672.30.3 Jouffroy, Théodore S. Nouveaux mélanges philosophiques. 2e éd. Paris, 1861.
Phil 2672.30.5 Jouffroy, Théodore S. Mélanges philosophiques. 4e éd. v.1-2. Paris, 1866.
Phil 2672.31 Jouffroy, Théodore S. Cours de droit naturel. Paris, 1835. 3v.
Phil 2672.31.5 Jouffroy, Théodore S. Cours de droit naturel. 4. éd. v.2. Paris, 1866.
Phil 2672.35 Jouffroy, Théodore S. Introduction to ethics. Boston, 1840. 2v.
Phil 2672.35.1 Jouffroy, Théodore S. Introduction to ethics. Boston, 1841. 2v.
Phil 2672.35.2 Jouffroy, Théodore S. Introduction to ethics. Boston, 1845. 2v.
Phil 2672.35.3 Jouffroy, Théodore S. Introduction to ethics. v.1-2. Boston, 1858.
Phil 2672.35.10 Jouffroy, Théodore S. Introduction to ethics. Boston, 1873. 2v.
Phil 2672.36 Jouffroy, Théodore S. Moral philosophy. N.Y., 1862.
Phil 2672.40 Jouffroy, Théodore S. Le cahier vert; comment les dogmes finissent. Lettres inédites. Paris, 1924.
Phil 2672.75 Jouffroy, Théodore S. Correspondance. Paris, 1901.
Phil 2672.79 Pamphlet box. Philosophy. French and Belgian. Jouffroy, Théodore Simon.
Phil 2672.80 Ollé-Laprune, L. Théodore Jouffroy. Paris, 1899.
Phil 2672.81 Leroux, Pierre. De la mutilation d'un écrit posthume de Théodore Jouffroy. Paris, 1843.
Phil 2672.90 Tissot, J. Théodore Jouffroy: sa vie et ses écrits. Paris, 1876.
Phil 2672.91 Pommier, J.J.M. Deux études sur Jouffroy et son temps. Paris, 1930.

hil 2675 History of philosophy - Local Modern philosophy - France - Individual philosophers - Other J

Phil 2675.1.31 Jaffre, F.A. Cours de philosophie adapté au programme du baccalauréat ès lettres. Lyon, 1878.
Phil 2675.2.80 Mayo, Elton. Some notes on the psychology of Pierre Janet. Cambridge, 1948.
Phil 2675.3.30 Jeanson, Francis. La vraie vérité, alibi. Paris, 1954.
Phil 2675.4 Jankélévitch, Vladimir. Le je-ne-sais-quoi et le presque-Dieu. 1. éd. Paris, 1957.
Phil 2675.4.5 Jankélévitch, Vladimir. Le pur et l'impur. Paris, 1960.
Phil 2675.4.10 Jankélévitch, Vladimir. Vladimir Jankélévitch, ou De l'Effectivité. Paris, 1969.
Phil 2675.4.30 Jankélévitch, Vladimir. Le pardon. Paris, 1967.
Phil 2675.5 Jakob, L.H. von. Essais philosophiques sur l'homme. Saint-Pétersbourg, 1822.
Phil 2675.6.80 Schmugge, Ludwig. Johannes von Jandun. Stuttgart, 1966.

il 2705 History of philosophy - Local Modern philosophy - France - Individual philosophers - La Mettrie, Julien

n Phil 2705.15* La Mettrie, Julien Offray de. Oeuvres philosophiques. London, 1751.
Phil 2705.20 La Mettrie, Julien Offray de. Textes choisis. Paris, 1954.
n Phil 2705.30* La Mettrie, Julien Offray de. L'homme machin. v.1-2. Leyde, 1748.
Phil 2705.30.55 La Mettrie, Julien Offray de. Der Mensch eine Maschine. Leipzig, 1909.
Phil 2705.31 La Mettrie, Julien Offray de. Man a machine. v.1-2. London, 1752.
Phil 2705.35 La Mettrie, Julien Offray de. L'homme machine, suivi de l'Art de jouir. Paris, 1921.
Phil 2705.35.5A La Mettrie, Julien Offray de. L'homme machine. Princeton, 1960.
Phil 2705.35.5B La Mettrie, Julien Offray de. L'homme machine. Princeton, 1960. 2v.
Phil 2705.35.6 La Mettrie, Julien Offray de. L'homme machine. Paris, 1966.
Phil 2705.37 La Mettrie, Julien Offray de. Man a machine. Chicago, 1927.
Phil 2705.40* La Mettrie, Julien Offray de. Histoire naturelle de l'ame. La Haye, 1745.
Phil 2705.45 La Mettrie, Julien Offray de. Un pamphlet médical au XVIIIe siècle. Thèse. Paris, 1931.
Phil 2705.80 Paquet, H.R.R. Essai sur La Mettrie. Paris, 1873.
DL Phil 2705.81 Du Bois-Reymond, E. La Mettrie. Berlin, 1875.
Phil 2705.81.2 Du Bois-Reymond, E. La Mettrie. Berlin, 1875.
Phil 2705.82 Poritzky, J.E. Julien Offray de La Mettrie. Berlin, 1900.
Phil 2705.83 Bergmann, Ernst. Die Satiren des Herrn Maschine. Leipzig, 1913.
Phil 2705.84 Boissier, Raymond. La Mettrie. Paris, 1931.
Phil 2705.84.2 Boissier, Raymond. La Mettrie. Thèse. Paris, 1931.
Phil 2705.85* Luface, Elie. L'homme plus que machine. Londres, 1748.
Phil 2705.86 Lemée, Pierre. Offray de la Mettrie. Saint-Servan, 1925.

2725 History of philosophy - Local Modern philosophy - France - Individual ilosophers - Other L

Phil 2725.1.80 Seyfarth, H. Louis de la Forge. Jena, 1887.
Phil 2725.1.81 Wolff, E. De la Forges Psychologie. Jena, 1893.
Phil 2725.2.10 Laffitte, Pierre. Moral positiva, sua necessidade atual. Rio de Janeiro, 1938.
Phil 2725.2.15 Laffitte, Pierre. Cours philosophique sur l'histoire générale de l'humanité; discours d'ouverture, ordre et progrès. Paris, 1859.
Phil 2725.2.30 Lamennais, F.R. de. Esquisse d'une philosophie. Paris, 1840-1846. 4v.
Phil 2725.2.31 Lamennais, F.R. de. Grundriss einer Philosophie. v.1-3. Paris, 1841. 3v.
Phil 2725.2.33 Lamennais, F.R. de. De la famille et de la propriété. Paris, 1848.

Phil 2725 History of philosophy - Local Modern philosophy - France - Individual philosophers - Other L - cont.

Phil 2725.2.34 Lamennais, F.R. de. M. Lamennais réfuté par lui-même. Paris, 1841.
Phil 2725.2.35 Lamennais, F.R. de. Discussions critiques, et pensées diverses sur la religion et la philosophie. Paris, 1841.
Phil 2725.2.35.5 Le Guillou, Louis. Les discussions critiques. Paris, 1967.
Htn Phil 2725.2.36* Lamennais, F.R. de. Paroles d'un croyant. Paris, 1834.
Phil 2725.2.37 Lamenais, F.R. de. Paroles d'un croyant. 7. éd. Paris, 1834.
Phil 2725.2.39 Lamenais, F.R. de. Paroles d'un croyant. 9. éd. Paris, 1834.
Htn Phil 2725.2.40* Lamennais, F.R. de. Paroles d'un croyant. Bruxelles, 1834.
Phil 2725.2.41 Lamennais, F.R. de. Les Paroles d'un croyant. Thèse. Paris, 1949.
Phil 2725.2.41.5 Lamennais, F.R. de. Paroles d'un croyant. Paris, 1949.
Phil 2725.2.43 Lamennais, F.R. de. Worte eines Gläubigen. Hamburg, 1834.
Phil 2725.2.46 Lamennais, F.R. de. Palabras de un creyente. 8. ed. Paris, 1834.
Phil 2725.2.47 Lamenais, F.R. de. Parole d'un credente. Bruxelles, 1834. 3 pam.
Phil 2725.2.48 Lamenais, F.R. de. Parole d'un credente. Italia, 1834.
Phil 2725.2.49 Lamenais, F.R. de. The words of a believer. London, 1834.
Phil 2725.2.50 Pamphlet vol. Lamennais' Paroles d'un croyante. 7 pam.
Htn Phil 2725.2.52* Lamennais, F.R. de. Le livre du peuple. Paris, 1838.
Phil 2725.2.52.5 Lamennais, F.R. de. Das Volksbuch von Félicité de Lamennais. Leipzig, 1905.
Phil 2725.2.53 Lamennais, F.R. de. Il libro del popolo. v.1-2. Firenze, 1848.
Phil 2725.2.54 Lamennais, F.R. de. Il libro del popolo. n.p., n.d. 2 pam.
Phil 2725.2.55 Lamennais, F.R. de. The people's own book. Boston, 1839.
Phil 2725.2.57 Lamennais, F.R. de. Essai sur l'indifférence en matière de religion. Paris, 1819-20. 2v.
Phil 2725.2.59 Lamennais, F.R. de. Essai sur l'indifférence en matière de religion. Paris, 1828. 5v.
Phil 2725.2.61 Lamennais, F.R. de. Essai sur l'indifférence en matière de religion. Paris, 1843. 4v.
Phil 2725.2.65 Lamennais, F.R. de. Libro per il popolo. Milano, 1874.
Phil 2725.2.66 Lamennais, F.R. de. Défense de l'essai sur l'indifférence. Paris, 1828.
Phil 2725.2.67 Maréchal, C. La Mennais. Paris, 1925.
Phil 2725.2.68 Bouchitté, Louis Herve. Réfutation de la doctrine. Paris, 1821.
Phil 2725.2.69 Flottes, J.B.M. M. l'abbé F. de Lamennais réfuté. Paris, 1825.
Phil 2725.2.70 Lamennais, F.R. de. Questions politiques et philosophiques. v.1-2. Paris, 1840.
Phil 2725.2.73 Lamennais, F.R. de. Les erreurs. Bruxelles, n.d.
Phil 2725.2.75 Lamennais, F.R. de. Una voce di prigione. Genova, 1850.
Phil 2725.2.76 Lamennais, F.R. de. Une voix de prison. Paris, 1954.
Phil 2725.2.77 Lamennais, F.R. de. Essai d'un système de philosophie catholique. Rennes, 1954.
Phil 2725.2.81 Lacordaire, H. Considérations sur le système philosophique de M. de Lamennais. Paris, 1834.
Phil 2725.2.82 Lamennais, F.R. de. Catalogue de livres rares et precieux provenant de la bibliothèque de M.F. de la Mennais. Paris, 1836.
Phil 2725.2.83 Lamennais, F.R. de. Études et notice biographique. Paris, 1835.
Phil 2725.2.85 Janet, Paul A.R. La philosophie de Lamennais. Paris, 1890.
Phil 2725.2.87 Du Plessis de Grenédan, L. Examen des Paroles d'un croyant et du Livre du peuple. Rennes, 1840.
Phil 2725.2.89 Maréchal, C. La Mennais. Paris, 1925.
Phil 2725.2.91 Pamphlet vol. Pensieri di un credente. 2 pam.
Phil 2725.2.95 Gioberti, V. Lettera intorno alle dottrine filosofiche e politiche del sig. di Lamennais. Lucca, 1845. 2 pam.
Phil 2725.2.95.2 Gioberti, V. Lettera intorno alle dottrine filosofiche e religiose del sig. di Lamennais. Milano, 1971.
Phil 2725.2.97 Poisson, Jacques. Le romantisme social de Lamennais. Thèse. Paris, 1931.
Phil 2725.2.99 Giraud, Victor. La vie tragique de Lamennais. Paris, 1933.
Phil 2725.2.101 Treves, P. Lamennais. Milano, 1934.
Phil 2725.2.103 Meinvielle, Jules. De Lamennais à Maritain. Paris, 1956.
Phil 2725.2.105 Bovard, René. Drame de conscience. Paris, 1961.
Phil 2725.2.110 Derre, Jean R. Lamennais, ses amis et le mouvement des idées à l'époque romantique, 1824-1834. Paris, 1962.
Phil 2725.2.115 Roe, William. Lamennais and England. Oxford, 1966.
VPhil 2725.2.120 Litwin, Jakub. Esejè o dialogach wewnętrznych: Diderot, Lamennais. Warszawa, 1967.
Phil 2725.2.125 Zadei, Guido. Il pensiero socio-politico di Lamennais. Napoli, 1969.
Phil 2725.2.130 Schmid, Beat. L'espérance et l'itinéraire de la certitude chez Lamennais. Berne, 1970.
Htn Phil 2725.3* LeGrand, A. An entire body of philosophy. London, 1694.
Htn Phil 2725.3.30* LeGrand, A. Institutio philosophiae. London, 1680.
Htn Phil 2725.3.35* LeGrand, A. Institutio philosophiae. London, 1678.
Phil 2725.4.81 Thomas, P. F. Pierre Leroux. Paris, 1904.
Phil 2725.4.85 Evans, David O. Pierre Leroux and his philosophy in relation to literature. n.p., 1929.
Phil 2725.4.87 Raillard, Célestin. Pierre Leroux et ses oeuvres. Chateauroux, 1899.
Phil 2725.4.89 Evans, David O. Le socialisme romantique. Paris, 1948.
Htn Phil 2725.5.30* Lamarck, J.B. Philosophie zoologique. Paris, 1809. 2v.
Htn Phil 2725.6.30* An account of the life and writings of Mr. John LeClerc. London, 1712. 2 pam.
Htn Phil 2725.6.31* LeClerc, Jean. Five letters concerning the inspiration of the Holy Scriptures. London, 1690.
Htn Phil 2725.7.30* Lipsius, Justus. Manuductionis ad stoicam. Antverpiae, 1604.
Phil 2725.8.80 Pamphlet box. Philosophy. French and Beligian. Laromiguière, Pierre.
Phil 2725.8.82 Lame, D. Étude sur la philosophie de Laromiguiere. Guéret, 1864.
Phil 2725.8.85 Alfaric, Prosper. Laromiguière et son école. Paris, 1929.
Phil 2725.9.86 LeGoff, François. De la philosophie de l'abbé de Lignac. Paris, 1863.
Phil 2725.10.30 Lahr, Charles. Cours de philosophie. 23e éd. Paris, 1920. 2v.
Phil 2725.11.15 Lachelier, Jules. Oeuvres. Paris, 1933. 2v.
Phil 2725.11.20 Lachelier, Jules. La nature. 1e éd. Paris, 1955.
Phil 2725.11.30 Lachelier, Jules. Du fondement de l'induction. Paris, 1871.

Classified Listing

Phil 2725.11.31	Lachelier, Jules. Études sur le syllogisme. Paris, 1907.
Phil 2725.11.75	Lachelier, Jules. The philosophy of Jules Lachelier. The Hague, 1960.
Phil 2725.11.81A	Séailles, G. La philosophie de Jules Lachelier. Paris, 1920.
Phil 2725.11.83	Brunschvicg, L. Notice sur la vie et les travaux de Jules Lachelier. Paris, 1921.
Phil 2725.11.85	Agosti, Vittorio. La filosofia di Jules Lachelier. Torino, 1952.
Phil 2725.11.90	Jolivet, Régis. De Rosmini à Lachelier. Paris, 1953.
Phil 2725.11.95	Millet, Louis. Le symbolisme dans la philosophie. Paris, 1959.
Phil 2725.11.100	Manchaussat, Gaston. L'idéalisme de Lachelier. Paris, 1961.
Phil 2725.12.81	Stosz, Wilhelm. Le Sage als Vorkämpfer der Atomistik. Inaug. Diss. Halle, 1884.
Phil 2725.13.32	Lequier, Jules. La liberté. Thèse. Paris, 1936.
Phil 2725.13.32.1	Lequier, Jules. La liberté. Paris, 1936.
Phil 2725.13.34	Lequier, Jules. La recherche d'une première vérité. Paris, 1924.
Phil 2725.13.80	Petterlini, Arnaldo. Jules Lequier e il problema della liberta. Milano, 1969.
Phil 2725.13.85	Roggerone, Giuseppe Agostino. La via nuova di Lequier. Milano, 1968.
Phil 2725.13.90	Grenier, Jean. La philosophie de Jules Lequier. Paris, 1936.
Phil 2725.13.91	Grenier, Jean. La philosophie de Jules Lequier. Thèse. Paris, 1936.
Phil 2725.13.95	Callot, Emile. Propos sur Jules Lequier. Paris, 1962.
Phil 2725.13.98	Tilliette, Xavier. Jules Lequier. Paris, 1964.
Phil 2725.14.85	Union pour l'Action Morale, Paris. Jules Lagneau. Paris, n.d.
Phil 2725.14.90	Chartier, Émile. Souvenirs concernant Jules Lagneau. 2. éd. Paris, 1925.
Phil 2725.14.92	Canivez, André. Jules Lagneau. Paris, 1965. 2v.
Phil 2725.14.93	Chartier, Émile. Souvenirs concernant Jules Lagneau. 5e éd. Paris, 1925.
Phil 2725.14.95	Madinier, G. Vers une philosophie réflexive. Neuchâtel, 1960.
Phil 2725.14.100	Lagneau, Jules. Célèbres leçons et fragments. 2. éd. Paris, 1964.
Phil 2725.15.30	Lasbax, E. La dialectique et le rythme de l'univers. Paris, 1925.
Htn Phil 2725.16.30*	Legouis, Émile. Histoire de la littérature anglaise. Paris, 1924.
Phil 2725.17.90	Bonnet, Georges. La morale de Félix Le Dantec (1869-1917). Thèse. Poitiers, 1930.
Phil 2725.19.90	Jolivet, R. A la recherche de Dieu. Paris, 1931.
Phil 2725.19.95	Gagnebin, S. La philosophie de l'institutio. St.-Blaise, 1912.
Phil 2725.20	Lamy, G. De principiis rerum. Paris, 1669.
Phil 2725.21	Lachièze-Rey, P. Le moi, le monde et Dieu. Paris, 1938.
Phil 2725.22	Laberthounière, L. Oeuvres. Paris, 1937.
Phil 2725.23.90	Chang Chi Chang. La morale...de M. Lucien Levy-Bruhl. Lyon, 1937.
Phil 2725.24	Lacroix, Jean. Marxisme, existentialisme, personnalisme. Paris, 1950.
Phil 2725.25	Centineo, E. René LeSenne. Palermo, 1952.
Phil 2725.25.5	Pirlot, J. Destinée et valeur. Namur, 1950?
Phil 2725.25.20	LeSenne, René. LeSenne ou le Combat pour la spiritualisation. Paris, 1968.
Phil 2725.25.90	Paumen, Jean. Le spiritualisme existentiel de René LeSenne. Paris, 1949.
Phil 2725.25.95	Magnani, Giovanni S.I. Itinerario al valore in R. Le Senne. Roma, 1971.
Phil 2725.30	Daniel-Rops, Henry. Edouard LeRoy et son fauteuil. Paris, 1956.
Phil 2725.30.30	LeRoy, Edouard. Essai d'une philosophie première. Paris, 1956- 2v.
Phil 2725.30.80	Miranda, Maria do Carmo Tavares de. Théorie de la vérité chez Edouard LeRoy. Paris, 1957.
Phil 2725.30.90	Polato, Franco. Il pragmatismo epistemológico e religioso di Edouard LeRoy. 1. ed. Padova, 1959.
Phil 2725.35	Lavelle, Louis. De l'intimité spirituelle. Paris, 1955.
Phil 2725.35.5	Lavelle, Louis. Morale et religion. Paris, 1960.
Phil 2725.35.10	Lavelle, Louis. Psychologie et spiritualité. Paris, 1967.
Phil 2725.35.20	Lavelle, Louis. Du temps et de l'eternité. Paris, 1945.
Phil 2725.35.30	Lavelle, Louis. Le moi et son destin. Paris, 1936.
Phil 2725.35.40	Lavelle, Louis. La présence totale. Paris, 1934.
Phil 2725.35.50	Lavelle, Louis. De l'être. Paris, 1928.
Phil 2725.35.55	Lavelle, Louis. De l'acte. Paris, 1937.
Phil 2725.35.60	Lavelle, Louis. La conscience de soi. Paris, 1933.
Phil 2725.35.65	Lavelle, Louis. Introduction à l'ontologie. 1. éd. Paris, 1947.
Phil 2725.35.70	Lavelle, Louis. Manuel de méthodologie dialectique. Paris, 1962.
Phil 2725.35.80	Ecole, Jean. La metaphysique de l'être dans la philosophie de Louis Lavelle. Louvain, 1957.
Phil 2725.35.85	Sargi, Bechara. La participation à l'être. Paris, 1957.
Phil 2725.35.87	Beschin, Giuseppe. Il tempo e la libertà in L. Lavelle. Milano, 1964.
Phil 2725.35.90	Piersol, Wesley. La valeur dans la philosophie de Louis Lavelle. Paris, 1959.
Phil 2725.35.95	Rothkopf, Wolfgang. Der Einfluss Kants auf die Erkenntnismetaphysik. München, 1964.
Phil 2725.35.100	Levert, Paul. L'être et le réel selon Louis Lavelle. Paris, 1960.
Phil 2725.35.105	Ainval, Christiane d'. Une doctrine de la présence spirituelle; la philosophie de Louis Lavelle. Louvain, 1967.
Phil 2725.35.110	Hardy, Gilbert G. La vocation de la liberté chez Louis Lavelle. Paris, 1968.
Phil 2725.35.115	Quito, Émerita. La notion de la liberté participée dans la philosophie de Louis Lavelle. Fribourg, 1969.
Phil 2725.36.30	LaRochefoucauld, Edmée. Pluralité de l'être. Paris, 1957.
Phil 2725.37.30	Lefebvre, Henri. La somme et le reste. Paris, 1959. 2v.
Phil 2725.37.35A	Lefebvre, Henri. Critique de la vie quotidienne. 2e éd. Paris, 1958-68. 2v.
Phil 2725.37.35B	Lefebvre, Henri. Critique de la vie quotidienne. v.1. Paris, 1958.
Phil 2725.37.40	Lefebvre, Henri. Métaphilosophie; prolégomènes. Paris, 1965.
Phil 2725.38	Leyvraz, Jean Pierre. Le temple et le Dieu. Paris, 1960.
Phil 2725.38.5	Leyvraz, Jean Pierre. Phénoménologie de l'expérience. La Haye, 1970.

Phil 2725.40	Drochner, Karl Heinz. Darstellung einiger Grundzüge des literarischen Werks von Pierre de la Primaudaye. Berlin, 1960.
Phil 2725.42	Levinas, Emmanuel. Totalité et l'infini. La Haye, 1961.
Phil 2725.42.5	Levinas, Emmanuel. Totality and infinity. Pittsburgh, Pennsylvania, 1969.
Phil 2725.44	Levert, Paule. L'idée de commencement. Paris, 1961.
Phil 2725.45	Lévêque, R. Unité et diversité. Paris, 1963.
Phil 2725.46	Cazeneuve, J. Lucien Lévy-Bruhl, sa vie, son oeuvre. Paris, 1963.
Phil 2725.50	Bertoni, Italo. Il neoilluminismo etico di André Lalande. Milano, 1965.
Phil 2725.55	Cossu, Maria. Il pensiero estetico di Charles Lalo. Cagliari, 1965.
Phil 2725.60	Tedeschi, Paul. Saint-Aubin et son oeuvre. Paris, 1968.

Phil 2730   History of philosophy - Local Modern philosophy - France - Individual philosophers - Maine de Biran, Pierre

Phil 2730.10	Maine de Biran, Pierre. Oeuvres philosophiques. Paris, 1841. 4v.
Phil 2730.11	Maine de Biran, Pierre. Oeuvres inédites. Paris, 1859. 3v.
Phil 2730.15	Maine de Biran, Pierre. Oeuvres. Paris, 1920-1939. 12v.
Phil 2730.21	Maine de Biran, Pierre. De l'existence, textes inédits. Paris, 1966.
Phil 2730.30	Maine de Biran, Pierre. Science et psychologie. Paris, 1887.
Phil 2730.35	Maine de Biran, Pierre. Influence de l'habitude. Paris, 1803.
Phil 2730.35.3	Maine de Biran, Pierre. Influence de l'habitude sur la faculté de penser. 1e éd. Paris, 1954.
Phil 2730.35.5	Maine de Biran, Pierre. The influence of habit on the faculty of thinking. Baltimore, 1929.
Phil 2730.40	Maine de Biran, Pierre. Mémoire sur les perceptions obscures. Paris, 1920.
Phil 2730.45	Maine de Biran, Pierre. Essai de restitution de l'ecrit...L'apperception immédiate. Thèse. Paris, 1908.
Phil 2730.50	Maine de Biran, Pierre. Nouvelles considerations sur les rapports du physique et du moral de l'homme. Paris, 1834.
Phil 2730.55	Maine de Biran, Pierre. Mémoire sur la décomposition de la pensée. v.1-2. Paris, 1952.
Phil 2730.60	Maine de Biran, Pierre. Journal intime. 5e éd. Paris, 1927-1931. 2v.
Phil 2730.60.2	Maine de Biran, Pierre. Journal. Neuchâtel, 1954. 3v.
Phil 2730.80	Naville, E. Maine de Biran. Paris, 1857.
Phil 2730.80.5	Naville, E. Maine de Biran. 3e éd. Paris, 1877.
Phil 2730.81	Truman, N.E. Maine de Biran's philosophy of will. N.Y., 1904.
Phil 2730.82	Couailhac, M. Maine de Biran. Paris, 1905.
Phil 2730.83	Favre, Charles. Essai sur la métaphysique...de Maine de Biran. Antibes, 1889.
Phil 2730.84	LaValette, Monbrun A. de. Essai de biographie historique...Maine de Biran. Paris, 1914.
Phil 2730.85	Tisserand, Pierre. L'anthropologie de Maine de Biran. Paris, 1909.
Phil 2730.86	Amendola, G. Maine de Biran. Firenze, 1911.
Phil 2730.87	Baumgarten, Franz. Die Erkenntnislehre von Maine de Biran. Krakau, 1911.
Phil 2730.88	Lang, Albert. Maine de Biran und die neuere Philosophie. Köln, n.d.
Phil 2730.89	Kühtmann, A. Maine de Biran. Bremen, 1901.
Phil 2730.90	Paliard, Jacques. Le raisonnement selon Maine de Biran. Paris, 1925.
Phil 2730.90.5	Paliard, Jacques. Le raisonnement selon Maine de Biran. Thèse. Paris, 1925.
Phil 2730.91	Robef, E. Leibniz et Maine de Biran. Thèse. Paris, 1925.
Phil 2730.92	Gérard, J. La philosophie de Maine de Biran. Paris, 1876.
Phil 2730.93	Rostan, E. La religion de Maine de Biran. Thèse. Paris, 1890.
Phil 2730.94	Barbillion, G. De l'idée de dieu dans la philosophie de Maine de Biran. Thèse. Grenoble, 1927. 2 pam.
Phil 2730.95	Delbos, Victor. Maine de Biran. Paris, 1931.
Phil 2730.96	LeRoy, Georges. L'expérience de l'effort et de la grace chez Maine de Biran. Paris, 1937.
Phil 2730.96.5	LeRoy, Georges. L'expérience de l'effort et de la grace chez Maine de Biran. Thèse. Paris, 1937.
Phil 2730.97	Fessard, G. La méthode de réflexion chez Maine de Biran. Paris, 1938.
Phil 2730.99.5	Vancourt, Raymond. La théorie de la connaissance chez Maine de Biran. 2e éd. Paris, 1944.
Phil 2730.100	Gouhier, Henri. Les conversions de Maine de Biran. Paris, 1947.
Phil 2730.102	Thibaud, Marguerite. L'effort chez Maine de Biran et Bergson. Thèse. Grenoble, 1939.
Phil 2730.104	Funke, Gerhard. Maine der Biran. Bonn, 1947.
Phil 2730.108	Hallie, P.P. Maine de Biran, reformer. Cambridge, 1959.
Phil 2730.110	Lassaigne, Jean. Maine de Biran, homme politique. Paris, 1958.
Phil 2730.111	Buol, J. Die Anthropologie Maine de Birans. Winterthur, 1961.
Phil 2730.112	Voutsinas, Dimitri. La psychologie de Maine de Biran, 1766-1824. Paris, 1964.
Phil 2730.113	Henry, Michel. Philosophie et phénoménologie du corps. Paris, 1965.
Phil 2730.114	Moore, Francis Charles Timothy. The psychology of Maine de Biran. Oxford, 1970.
Phil 2730.116	Lacroze, René. Maine de Biran. 1. éd. Paris, 1970.
Phil 2730.118	Holda, Bernard. La pensée de Maine de Biran. Paris, 1970.

Phil 2733   History of philosophy - Local Modern philosophy - France - Individual philosophers - Malebranche, Nicolas

Phil 2733.3	Malebranche, Nicolas. Oeuvres. v.1-4. Paris, 1871. 2v.
Phil 2733.4	Malebranche, Nicolas. Oeuvres. Paris, 1842. 2v.
Phil 2733.4.5	Malebranche, Nicolas. Oeuvres. Paris, 1859. 2v.
Phil 2733.5	Malebranche, Nicolas. Oeuvres complètes. Paris, 1837. 2v.
Phil 2733.5.5	Malebranche, Nicolas. Oeuvres complètes. Paris, 1938.
Phil 2733.5.10	Malebranche, Nicolas. Oeuvres complètes. v.1-20. Paris, 1958-63. 21v.
Phil 2733.5.11	Malebranche, Nicolas. Oeuvres complètes. Paris, 1970.
Htn Phil 2733.6.1F*	Malebranche, Nicolas. Treatise...Search for truth. Oxford, 1694.

Phil 2733   History of philosophy - Local Modern philosophy - France - Individual
    philosophers - Malebranche, Nicolas - cont.

Phil 2733.6.2   Malebranche, Nicolas. Father Malebranche, his
                   treatise...Search after truth. 2d ed. London, 1700.
Phil 2733.29   Malebranche, Nicolas. De la recherche de la verité.
                   Paris, 1676-78. 3v.
Phil 2733.29.3   Malebranche, Nicolas. De la recherche de la verité. 7e éd.
                   v.1-2. Paris, 1721.
Phil 2733.29.10   Malebranche, Nicolas. De la recherche de la vérité. 4e éd.
                   v.1-2. Amsterdam, 1688.
Phil 2733.29.20   Malebranche, Nicolas. De la recherche de la vérité. 2e éd.
                   Paris, 1675. 2v.
Phil 2733.29.30   Malebranche, Nicolas. De la recherche de la vérité.
                   Paris, 1935. 2v.
Phil 2733.29.35   Malebranche, Nicolas. De la recherche de la vérité.
                   Paris, 1962. 2v.
Phil 2733.30   Malebranche, Nicolas. De la recherche de la vérité. v.2.
                   Paris, 1886.
EDL Phil 2733.30.2 Malebranche, Nicolas. De la recherche de la vérité. v.2.
                   Paris, 1886.
Phil 2733.30.4   Malebranche, Nicolas. De la recherche de la vérité.
                   Paris, 1945. 2v.
tn Phil 2733.30.6* Malebranche, Nicolas. De inquirenda veritate.
                   Genevae, 1685.
Phil 2733.30.20   Malebranche, Nicolas. Erforschung der Wahrheit.
                   München, 1914.
tn Phil 2733.31*   Malebranche, Nicolas. Search after truth.
                   London, 1694-95. 2v.
tn Phil 2733.32*   Foucher, Simon. Critique de la recherche de la verité.
                   Paris, 1675.
Phil 2733.36   Malebranche, Nicolas. Entretiens sur la métaphysique.
                   Paris, 1871.
Phil 2733.36.4   Malebranche, Nicolas. Entretiens sur la métaphysique.
                   Paris, 1721. 2v.
Phil 2733.36.5   Malebranche, Nicolas. Entretiens sur la métaphysique.
                   v.1-2. Paris, 1922.
Phil 2733.36.10   Malebranche, Nicolas. Dialogues on metaphysics and on
                   religion. London, 1923.
Phil 2733.38   Malebranche, Nicolas. Lumière et mouvement de l'esprit.
                   Paris, 1962.
n Phil 2733.39*   Malebranche, Nicolas. Meditations chrétiennes et
                   métaphysiques. Lyon, 1707.
Phil 2733.40   Malebranche, Nicolas. Méditations métaphysiques.
                   Paris, 1841.
Phil 2733.41   Malebranche, Nicolas. Méditations chrétiennes.
                   Paris, 1928.
Phil 2733.43   Malebranche, Nicolas. Méditations pour se disposer à
                   l'humilité et à la pénitence. Paris, 1944.
Phil 2733.45   Malebranche, Nicolas. Pensiere metafisici.
                   Lanciano, 1911.
Phil 2733.50*   Malebranche, Nicolas. Traité de morale. pt.1-2.
                   Rotterdam, 1684.
Phil 2733.50.3*   Malebranche, Nicolas. Traité de morale. Lyon, 1697.
                   2v.
Phil 2733.50.5*   Malebranche, Nicolas. A treatise of morality. pt.1-2.
                   London, 1699.
Phil 2733.55   Malebranche, Nicolas. A treatise of nature and grace.
                   London, 1695. 2 pam.
Phil 2733.55.5*   Malebranche, Nicolas. Traité de la nature et de la grace.
                   Amsterdam, 1680. 2 pam.
Phil 2733.55.10   Malebranche, Nicolas. Traité de la nature et de la grace.
                   Rotterdam, 1712. 2 pam.
Phil 2733.56*   Malebranche, Nicolas. Trois lettres...la defense de Mr.
                   Arnauld. Rotterdam, 1685.
Phil 2733.57*   Malebranche, Nicolas. Réponse du Père Malebranche à la
                   troisième lettre de Mr. Arnauld. Amsterdam, 1704.
Phil 2733.60   Malebranche, Nicolas. Entretien d'un philosophe chrétien.
                   Paris, 1708.
Phil 2733.60.5   Malebranche, Nicolas. Entretien d'un philosophe chrétien
                   et d'un philosophe chinois. Paris, 1936.
Phil 2733.60.7   Malebranche, Nicolas. Entretien d'un philosophe chrétien
                   et d'un philosophe chinois. Thèse. Marseille, 1936.
Phil 2733.61   Malebranche, Nicolas. Conversations chrétiennes.
                   Rotterdam, 1685.
Phil 2733.61.2   Malebranche, Nicolas. Conversations chrétiennes.
                   Paris, 1702.
Phil 2733.61.5   Malebranche, Nicolas. Conversations chrétiennes dans
                   lesquelles on justifie la vérité de la religion. Thèse.
                   Paris, 1929.
Phil 2733.61.7   Malebranche, Nicolas. Conversations chrétiennes.
                   Paris, 1929.
Phil 2733.64   Malebranche, Nicolas. Malebranche et Leibniz. Thèse.
                   Paris, 1955.
Phil 2733.65   Malebranche, Nicolas. Traité de l'amour de Dieu.
                   Paris, 1922.
Phil 2733.65.1*   Malebranche, Nicolas. Traité de l'amour de Dieu.
                   Lyon, 1707.
Phil 2733.66*   Malebranche, Nicolas. Reflections sur la primation
                   physique. Paris, 1715.
Phil 2733.67   Malebranche, Nicolas. Traité de la nature et de la grâce.
                   Paris, 1958. 2v.
Phil 2733.78   Vidgrain, Joseph. Fragments philosophiques inédits et
                   correspondance. Thèse. Caen, 1923.
Phil 2733.78.2   Vidgrain, Joseph. Malebranche. Paris, n.d.
Phil 2733.79   Pamphlet box. Malebranche.
Phil 2733.80   André, Y.M. La vie du R.P. Malebranche, Bibliothèque
                   Oratorienne. Paris, 1886.
Phil 2733.81   Blampignon, Emile Antoine. Étude sur Malebranche.
                   Paris, 1862.
Phil 2733.82   Cruse, P.J. Malebranche en Zijne Bestrijders.
                   Utrecht, 1891.
Phil 2733.83   Ollé-Laprune, L. La philosophie de Malebranche.
                   Paris, 1870. 2v.
Phil 2733.84   Blampignon, Emile Antoine. Bibliographie de Malebranche.
                   Montbéliard, n.d.
Phil 2733.85   Joly, H. Malebranche. Paris, 1901.
Phil 2733.86   Martin, J. Malebranche. Paris, 1912.
Phil 2733.87   Gaonach, J.M. La théorie des idées dans la philosophie de
                   Malebranche. Brest, 1908.
Phil 2733.88   Novaro, Mario. Die Philosophie des Nicolaus Malebranche.
                   Berlin, 1893.
Phil 2733.89   Spehner, Edmund. Malebranches Lehre von der Erkenntnis in
                   psychologischer Hinsicht. Inaug.-Diss. Borna, 1915.
Phil 2733.90   Vidgrain, Joseph. Le christianisme dans la philosophie de
                   Malebranche. Thèse. Paris, 1923.
Phil 2733.92   Vidgrain, J. Le Christianisme dans la philosophie de
                   Malebranche. Paris, n.d.
Phil 2733.93   Stieler, Georg. Nikolaus Malebranche. Stuttgart, 1925.

Phil 2733   History of philosophy - Local Modern philosophy - France - Individual
    philosophers - Malebranche - cont.

Phil 2733.94   Gouhier, Henri. La philosophie de Malebranche et son
                   expérience religieuse. Paris, 1926.
Phil 2733.94.5   Gouhier, Henri. La philosophie de Malebranche et son
                   expérience religieuse. Thèse. Paris, 1926. 2 pam.
Phil 2733.94.6   Gouhier, Henri. La philosophie de Malebranche.
                   Paris, 1948.
Phil 2733.94.7   Gouhier, Henri. La vocation de Malebranche. Paris, 1926.
Phil 2733.94.10   Gouhier, Henri. Malebranche. Paris, 1929.
Phil 2733.95   Gerdil, G.S. Défense du sentiment du P. Malebranche.
                   Turin, 1748.
Phil 2733.96   Turbiglio, S. Le antitesi...in ispecie nella dottrina...di
                   Malebranche. Roma, 1877.
Phil 2733.97   Glaser, J.C. Vergleichung der Philosophie des Malebranche
                   und Spinoza. Berlin, 1846.
Phil 2733.98   Bonavino, C. Malebranche. Milano, 1926.
Phil 2733.99   Bouillier, F. Mémoire sur la vision en Dieu de
                   Malebranche. Orleans, 1852?
Phil 2733.100   Mouy, P. Les lois du choc des corps d'après Malebranche.
                   Paris, 1927.
Phil 2733.100.2   Mouy, P. Les lois du choc des corps d'après Malebranche.
                   Thèse. Paris, 1927.
Phil 2733.101   Mennicken, Peter. Die Philosophie des Nicolas Malebranche.
                   Leipzig, 1927.
Phil 2733.102   Bridet, L. La théorie de la connaissance dans la
                   philosophie de Malebranche. Paris, 1929.
Phil 2733.102.5   Bridet, L. La théorie de la connaissance dans la
                   philosophie de Malebranche. Thèse. Paris, 1929.
Phil 2733.103   Church, Ralph W. A study in the philosophy of Malebranche.
                   London, 1931.
Phil 2733.104   Labbas, Lucien. La grace et la liberté dans Malebranche.
                   Paris, 1931.
Phil 2733.104.10   Labbas, Lucien. L'idée de science dans Malebranche et son
                   originalité. Paris, 1931.
Phil 2733.104.15   Labbas, Lucien. La grace et la liberté dans Malebranche.
                   Thèse. Paris, 1931. 2 pam.
Phil 2733.105   LeMoine, A. Des vérités éternelles selon Malebranche.
                   Paris, 1936.
Phil 2733.105.5   LeMoine, A. Des vérités éternelles selon Malebranche.
                   Thèse. Marseille, 1936.
Phil 2733.106   Guéroult, Martial. Etendue et psychologie chez
                   Malebranche. Paris, 1939.
Phil 2733.106.5   Guéroult, Martial. Malebranche. Paris, 1955. 3v.
Phil 2733.107   Ducassé, Pierre. Malebranche; sa vie, son oeuvre, avec un
                   exposé de sa philosophie. 1e éd. Paris, 1942.
Phil 2733.108   Malebranche nel terzo centenario della nascita.
                   Milano, 1938.
Phil 2733.109   Montcheuil, Y. de. Malebranche et la quiétisme.
                   Paris, 1946.
Phil 2733.110   Cuvillier, A. Essai sur la mystique de Malebranche.
                   Paris, 1954.
Phil 2733.112   Blanchard, Pierre. L'attention à Dieu selon Malebranche.
                   Paris, 1956.
Phil 2733.115   Drefus, Ginette. La volonté selon Malebranche.
                   Paris, 1958.
Phil 2733.116   Rome, B.K. The philosophy of Malebranche. Chicago, 1963.
Phil 2733.117   Rodis-Lewis, G. Nicolas Malebranche. Paris, 1963.
Phil 2733.118   Banchetti, A. Il pensiero e l'opera di Nicola Malebranche.
                   Milano, 1963.
Phil 2733.119   Nicolosi, Salvatore. Causalità divina e libertà umana nel
                   pensiero di Malebranche. Padova, 1963.
Phil 2733.120   Robinet, Andre. Système et existence dans l'oeuvre de
                   Malebranche. Paris, 1965.
Phil 2733.121   Verga, Leonardo. La filosofia morale di Malebranche.
                   Milano, 1964.
Phil 2733.125   Journées Malebranche, Paris, 1965. Malebranche l'homme et
                   l'oeuvre, 1638-1715. Paris, 1967.
Phil 2733.130   Gonnell, Desmond. The vision in God; Malebranche's
                   scholastic sources. Louvain, 1967.

Phil 2750   History of philosophy - Local Modern philosophy - France - Individual
    philosophers - Other M

Phil 2750.1.79   Gusgens, J. Die Naturphilosophie des Joannes...Magnenus.
                   Bonn, 1910.
Phil 2750.2.80   Van der Elst, Robert. Michelet, naturaliste. Paris, 1914.
Htn Phil 2750.3.30* Marat, Jean Paul. A philosophical essay on man. v.1-2.
                   London, 1773.
Htn Phil 2750.5.30* Montaigne, Michel de. Les essais. Lyon, 1595.
Htn Phil 2750.5.35* Montaigne, Michel de. Essayes or Morall, politike, and
                   militarie discourses. 3d ed. London, 1632.
Htn Phil 2750.6.30* Montesquieu, Charles Louis de Secondat. Considerations sur
                   les causes de la grandeur des Romains et de leur décadence.
                   Amsterdam, 1734.
Phil 2750.7.35   Massias, Nicolas. Traité de philosophie
                   psycho-physiologique. Paris, 1830.
Phil 2750.7.37   Massias, Nicolas. Principe de la philosophie
                   psycho-physiologique sur lequel repose la science de
                   l'homme. Paris, 1829.
Phil 2750.7.39   Pamphlet vol. Massias, Nicolas. Philosophical essays.
                   4 pam.
Phil 2750.8.35   Maupertuis, P.L.M. de. Essai de philosophie morale.
                   Berlin, 1749.
Phil 2750.8.37   Maupertuis, P.L.M. de. Essai de philosophie morale.
                   Londres, 1750.
Phil 2750.8.50   Maupertuis, P.L.M. de. Lettres de Mr. de Maupertuis.
                   Dresden, 1752.
Phil 2750.8.79   Pamphlet box. Maupertuis, P.L.M. de.
Phil 2750.8.85   De la Beaumelle, Laurent A. Vie de Maupertuis.
                   Paris, 1856.
Phil 2750.8.87   Brunet, Pierre. Maupertuis. Thèse. Paris, 1929.
                   2 pam.
Phil 2750.8.89   Brunet, Pierre. Maupertuis. Paris, 1929, 2v.
Phil 2750.8.91   Tressan, Louis Élisabeth de la Vergne. Éloge de M. Moreau
                   de Maupertuis. Nancy, 17- .
Phil 2750.9.30   Merten, O. Des limites de la philosophie. Paris, 1896.
Phil 2750.10.79   Pamphlet box. Meyerson, Emile.
Phil 2750.10.90   Baas, George. A critical analysis of the philosophy of
                   Emile Meyerson. Baltimore, 1930.
Phil 2750.10.95   Sée, Henri. Science et philosophie d'après la doctrine de
                   Emile Meyerson. Paris, 1937.
Phil 2750.10.99   Kelley, T.R. Explanation and reality in the philosophy of
                   Emile Meyerson. Princeton, 1937.
Phil 2750.10.105   Bonnard, A. La notion d'irrationnel chez Emile Meyerson.
                   Thèse. Paris, 1936.
Phil 2750.10.106   Caso, A. Myerson y la fisica moderna. México, 1939.
Phil 2750.10.110   Marcucci, Silvestro. Emile Meyerson. Torino, 1962.

Phil 2750   **History of philosophy - Local Modern philosophy - France - Individual philosophers - Other M - cont.**

Phil 2750.10.111   LaLumia, Joseph. The ways of reason; a critical study of the ideas of Emile Meyerson. N.Y., 1966.

Phil 2750.11.20   Maritain, Jacques. Challenges and renewals. Notre Dame, 1966.

Phil 2750.11.33   Maritain, Jacques. Ransoming the time. N.Y., 1941.

Phil 2750.11.35   Maritain, Jacques. Redeeming the time. London, 1943.

Phil 2750.11.37   Maritain, Jacques. De Bergson à Thomas d'Aquin. Paris, 1944.

Phil 2750.11.37.5   Maritain, Jacques. De Bergson à Thomas d'Aquin. N.Y., 1944.

Phil 2750.11.38   Maritain, Jacques. De l'Église du Christ; la personne de l'Eglise et son personnel. Paris, 1970.

Phil 2750.11.40   Maritain, Jacques. Existence and the existent. N.Y., 1948.

Phil 2750.11.41   Maritain, Jacques. De la grâce et de l'humanité de Jèsus. Bruges, 1967.

Phil 2750.11.41.1   Maritain, Jacques. On the grace and humanity of Jesus. N.Y., 1969.

Phil 2750.11.42A   Maritain, Jacques. Court traité de l'existence et de l'existent. Paris, 1947.

Phil 2750.11.42B   Maritain, Jacques. Court traité de l'existence et de l'existent. Paris, 1947.

Phil 2750.11.43   Maritain, Jacques. An essay on Christian philosophy. N.Y., 1955.

Phil 2750.11.43.5   Maritain, Jacques. De la philosophie chrétienne. Paris, 1933.

Phil 2750.11.44   Maritain, Jacques. Le paysan de la Garonne. Paris, 1966.

Phil 2750.11.44.2   Maritain, Jacques. The peasant of the Garonne. 1. éd. N.Y., 1968.

Phil 2750.11.45A   Maritain, Jacques. Le crépuscule de la civilisation. Montreal, 1941.

Phil 2750.11.45B   Maritain, Jacques. Le crépuscule de la civilisation. 2.ed. Montreal, 1941.

Phil 2750.11.45.5   Maritain, Jacques. The twilight of civilization. N.Y., 1943.

Phil 2750.11.47   Maritain, Jacques. La personne et le bien commun. Paris, 1947.

Phil 2750.11.47.5   Maritain, Jacques. The person and the common good. N.Y., 1947.

Phil 2750.11.48   Maritain, Jacques. Distinguish to unite. N.Y., 1959.

Phil 2750.11.48.5   Maritain, Jacques. Distinguish to unite. London, 1959.

Phil 2750.11.48.10   Maritain, Jacques. The degree of knowledge. N.Y., 1938.

Phil 2750.11.48.15   Maritain, Jacques. Distinguer pour unir. Paris, 1932.

Phil 2750.11.48.20   Maritain, Jacques. Distinguer pour unir. 4. éd. Paris, 1946.

Phil 2750.11.49A   Maritain, Jacques. Confession de foi. N.Y., 1941.

Phil 2750.11.49B   Maritain, Jacques. Confession de foi. N.Y., 1941.

Phil 2750.11.50   Maritain, Jacques. Raison et raisons. 10. éd. Paris, 1947.

Phil 2750.11.51   Maritain, Jacques. Some reflections on culture and literature. Chicago, 1933.

Phil 2750.11.52   Maritain, Jacques. An introduction to philosophy. London, 1930.

Phil 2750.11.53   Maritain, Jacques. A preface to metaphysics. N.Y., 1940.

Phil 2750.11.54   Maritain, Jacques. Humanisme intégral. Paris, 1936.

Phil 2750.11.54.5   Maritain, Jacques. Integral humanism. N.Y., 1968.

Phil 2750.11.55   Maritain, Jacques. Neuf leçons sur les notions premières de la philosophie morale. Paris, 1951.

Phil 2750.11.56   Maritain, Jacques. De la vie d'oraison. Paris, 1947.

Phil 2750.11.57   Maritain, Jacques. Science et sagesse. Paris, 1935.

Phil 2750.11.57.5   Maritain, Jacques. Science and wisdom. N.Y., 1940.

Phil 2750.11.58   Maritain, Jacques. Christianisme et démocratie. N.Y., 1943.

Phil 2750.11.58.5   Maritain, Jacques. Christianity and democracy. N.Y., 1944.

Phil 2750.11.59   Maritain, Jacques. Éléments de philosophie. Paris, 1921-23. 2v.

Phil 2750.11.60   Maritain, Jacques. Pour une philosophie de l'éducation. Paris, 1959.

Phil 2750.11.61   Maritain, Jacques. The education of man. Garden City, 1962.

Phil 2750.11.62   Maritain, Jacques. Carnet de notes. Paris, 1965.

Phil 2750.11.63   Maritain, Jacques. Questions de conscience. Paris, 1938.

Phil 2750.11.64   Maritain, Jacques. Dieu et la permission du mal. Paris, 1964.

Phil 2750.11.65   Maritain, Jacques. Quatre essais sur l'esprit dans sa condition charnelle. Paris, 1939.

Phil 2750.11.65.3   Maritain, Jacques. Quatre essais sur l'esprit dans sa condition charnelle. Paris, 1956.

Phil 2750.11.66   Maritain, Jacques. La philosophie de la nature. Paris, 1936.

Phil 2750.11.67   Maritain, Jacques. Freedom in the modern world. London, 1935.

Phil 2750.11.68   Maritain, Jacques. La signification de l'athéisme contemporain. Paris, 1949.

Phil 2750.11.69   Maritain, Jacques. Reflexions sur l'intelligence et sur sa vie propre. Paris, 1931?

Phil 2750.11.70   Maritain, Jacques. The range of reason. London, 1953.

Phil 2750.11.70.5   Maritain, Jacques. The range of reason. N.Y., 1961.

Phil 2750.11.71A   Maritain, Jacques. Trois réformateurs: Luther-Descartes-Rousseau. Paris, 1925.

Phil 2750.11.71B   Maritain, Jacques. Trois réformateurs: Luther-Descartes-Rousseau. Paris, 1925.

Phil 2750.11.71.5   Maritain, Jacques. Trois réformateurs: Luther-Descartes-Rousseau. Paris, 1925. 2v.

Phil 2750.11.71.10   Maritain, Jacques. Three reformers: Luther, Descartes, Rousseau. Paris, 1929?

Phil 2750.11.72   Maritain, Jacques. The dream of Descartes. N.Y., 1944.

Phil 2750.11.72.5   Maritain, Jacques. Le songe de Descartes. Paris, 1932.

Phil 2750.11.73   Maritain, Jacques. Théonas. 2. éd. Paris, 1925.

Phil 2750.11.74   Maritain, Jacques. Sept leçons sur l'être. Paris, 1934?

Phil 2750.11.75   Maritain, Jacques. Approaches to God. 1st ed. N.Y., 1954.

Phil 2750.11.76   Maritain, Jacques. Scholasticism and politics. N.Y., 1940.

Phil 2750.11.77   Maritain, Jacques. Truth and human fellowship. Princeton, 1957.

Phil 2750.11.78   Maritain, Jacques. The social and political philosophy of Jacques Maritain. N.Y., 1955.

Phil 2750.11.79   Maritain, Jacques. On the philosophy of history. N.Y., 1957.

Phil 2750.11.80A   Maritain, Jacques. Reflections on America. N.Y., 1958.

Phil 2750.11.80B   Maritain, Jacques. Reflections on America. N.Y., 1958.

Phil 2750   **History of philosophy - Local Modern philosophy - France - Individual philosophers - Other M - cont.**

Phil 2750.11.81   Maritain, Jacques. Le philosophe dans la cité. Paris, 1960.

Phil 2750.11.82   Maritain, Jacques. Reflexions sur l'Amérique. Paris, 1958.

Phil 2750.11.83   Maritain, Jacques. On the use of philosophy. Princeton, N.J., 1961.

Phil 2750.11.84   Maritain, Jacques. Antimoderne. Paris, 1922.

Phil 2750.11.85   Maritain, Jacques. Art et scolastique. 3. éd. Paris, 1935.

Phil 2750.11.85.4   Maritain, Jacques. Art et scolastique. 4. éd. Paris, 1965.

Phil 2750.11.86   Maritain, Jacques. The responsibility of the artist. N.Y., 1960.

Phil 2750.11.87   Maritain, Jacques. La responsibilité de l'artiste. Paris, 1961.

Phil 2750.11.88   Maritain, Jacques. Liturgie et contemplation. Bruges, 1959.

Phil 2750.11.89   Maritain, Jacques. Art and poetry. N.Y., 1943.

Phil 2750.11.90   Phelan, G.B. Jacques Maritain. N.Y., 1937.

Phil 2750.11.91   Maritain, Jacques. Le songe de Descartes. Paris, 1965.

Phil 2750.11.95   Allen, E. Christian humanism...Jacques Maritain. London, 1950.

Phil 2750.11.100A   Fecher, C.A. The philosophy of Jacques Maritain. Westminster, 1953.

Phil 2750.11.100B   Fecher, C.A. The philosophy of Jacques Maritain. Westminster, 1953.

Phil 2750.11.105   Podellaro, N. Maritain. Brescia, 1953.

Phil 2750.11.110   Croteau, Jacques. Les fondements thornistes du personnalisme de Maritain. Ottawa, 1955.

Phil 2750.11.115   Cassata, M.L. La pedagogia di Jacques Maritain. Palermo, 1953.

Phil 2750.11.120   Michener, N.W. Maritain on the nature of man in a Christian democracy. Hull, 1955.

Phil 2750.11.130   Simonson, V.L. L'esthétique de Jacques Maritain. Copenhagen, 1956.

Phil 2750.11.140   Maritain, Jacques. Son oeuvre philosophique. Paris, 1949?

Phil 2750.11.142   Jacques Maritain. Paris, 1957.

Phil 2750.11.145   Bars, Henry. Maritain en notre temps. Paris, 1959.

Phil 2750.11.146   Bars, Henry. La politique selon Jacques Maritain. Paris, 1961.

Phil 2750.11.147   Jung, Hava Yol. The foundation of Jacques Maritain's political philosophy. Gainesville, Florida, 1960.

Phil 2750.11.148   Maritain, Jacques. Moral philosophy. N.Y., 1964.

Phil 2750.11.149   Maritain, Jacques. La philosophie morale. Paris, 1960.

Phil 2750.11.150   Viotto, Piero. Jacques Maritain. Brescia, 1957.

Phil 2750.11.150.3   Viotto, Piero. Jacques Maritain. 3. ed. Brescia, 1965.

Phil 2750.11.152   Gallagher, Donald. The achievement of Jacques and Raïssa Maritain. 1st ed. N.Y., 1962.

Phil 2750.11.153   Evans, J.W. Jacques Maritain. N.Y., 1963.

Phil 2750.11.160   Sampaio, L.F.A. L'intuition dans la philosophie de Jacques Maritain. Paris, 1963.

Phil 2750.11.170   Sullivan, S.M. Maritain's theory of poetic intuition. Fribourg, 1964.

Phil 2750.11.175   Mrówczyński, Tadeusz. Personalizm Maritaina i współczesna myśl Katolicka. Warszawa, 1964.

Phil 2750.11.180   Rover, Thomas Dominic. The poetics of Maritain. Washington, 1965.

Phil 2750.11.185   Daly, Mary F. Natural knowledge of God in the philosophy of Jacques Maritain. Rome, 1966.

Phil 2750.11.190   Martinez Paz, Fernando. Maritain, politica e ideologia; revolución cristiana en la Argentina. Buenos Aires, 1966.

Phil 2750.11.195   Forni, Guglielmo. La filosofia della storia nel pensiero politico di Jacques Maritain. Bologna, 1965.

Phil 2750.11.200   Reiter, Josef. Intuition und Transzendenz. München, 1967.

Phil 2750.11.210   Barbiellini Amidei, Gaspare. Dopo Maritain. Torino, 1967.

Phil 2750.11.215   Riccio, Franco. Maritain umano e metafisico. Trapani, 1968.

Phil 2750.11.220   Garofalo, Gaetano. Jacques Maritain. Saggio critico. Bari, 1969.

Phil 2750.11.225   Pavan, Antonio. La formazione del pensiero di J. Maritain. Padova, 1967.

Phil 2750.11.230   Pico, Cesar E. Carta a Jacques Maritain sobre la colaboración de los católicos con los movimientos de tipo fascista. Buenos Aires, 1937.

Phil 2750.11.235   Bauer, Hans Ludwig. Schopferische Erkenntnis. München, 1968.

Phil 2750.12.90   Iwanicki, J. Morin et les démonstrations mathématiques de l'existence de Dieu. Paris, 1936.

Phil 2750.13   Corte, Marcel de. La philosophie de Gabriel Marcel. Paris, 1937.

Phil 2750.13.30   Marcel, Gabriel. Du refus à l'invocation. 11. éd. Paris, 1956.

Phil 2750.13.80   Tavares, M. de la Salette. Aproximaçõa do pensamento concerto de Gabriel Marcel. Lisboa, 1948.

Phil 2750.13.85   Ricoeur, Paul. Gabriel Marcel et Karl Jaspers. Paris, 1948.

Phil 2750.13.90   Bernard, M. La philosophie religieuse de Gabriel Marcel. Le Puy, 1952.

Phil 2750.13.95   Troisfontaines, R. De l'existence à l'être. Namur, 1953. 2v.

Phil 2750.13.100   Lê Thanh Tri. L'idée de la participation chez Gabriel Marcel. Fribourg? 1959.

Phil 2750.14   Madinier, Gabriel. Conscience et amour. Paris, 1938.

Phil 2750.15   Madinier, Gabriel. Conscience et mouvement. Paris, 1938.

Phil 2750.15.1   Madinier, Gabriel. Conscience et mouvement. Thesis. Paris, 1938.

Phil 2750.16.30   Molle, G. van. La connaissance dialectique et l'expérience existentielle. Liège, 1945.

Phil 2750.17.30   Mieville, Henri L. Condition de l'homme. Genève, 1959.

Phil 2750.17.90   Hommage à Henri Mieville. Lausanne, 1948.

Phil 2750.18.80   Louvain. Université Catholique. Jubilé Albert Michotte. Louvain, 1947.

Phil 2750.19   Marcel, Gabriel. The mystery of being. London, 1950. 2v.

Phil 2750.19.5   Marcel, Gabriel. The mystery of being. Chicago, 1950-51. 2v.

Phil 2750.19.10   Marcel, Gabriel. Le mystère de l'être. Paris, 1951. 2v.

Phil 2750.19.20   Marcel, Gabriel. Men against humanity. London, 1952.

Phil 2750.19.25   Marcel, Gabriel. Les hommes contre l'humain. Paris, 1951.

Phil 2750.19.26   Marcel, Gabriel. L'homme problématique. Paris, 1955.

Phil 2750.19.30   Marcel, Gabriel. Le declin de la sagesse. Paris, 1954.

Phil 2750.19.31   Marcel, Gabriel. The decline of wisdom. London, 1954.

Phil 2750.19.32   Marcel, Gabriel. Creative fidelity. N.Y., 1964.

Phil 2750.19.35   Marcel, Gabriel. El misterio ontologico. Tucumán, 1959.

Phil 2750 History of philosophy - Local Modern philosophy - France - Individual philosophers - Other M - cont.

Phil 2750.19.37 Marcel, Gabriel. The philosophy of existentialism. 2nd ed. N.Y., 1962.
Phil 2750.19.39 Marcel, Gabriel. The existential background of human dignity. Cambridge, 1963.
Phil 2750.19.42 Marcel, Gabriel. Fragments philosophiques 1909-1914. Louvain, 1962.
Phil 2750.19.42.5 Marcel, Gabriel. Philosophical fragments, 1904. Notre Dame, Ind., 1965.
Phil 2750.19.43 Marcel, Gabriel. Pour une sagesse tragique et son au-delà. Paris, 1968.
Phil 2750.19.80 Rebollo Peña, A. Critica de la objetividad en el existencialism de Gabriel Marcel. Burgos, 1954.
Phil 2750.19.85 Sonsbeeck, Dawiet van. Het zijn als mysterie in de ervaring en het denken van Gabriel Marcel. Bilthoven, 1966.
Phil 2750.19.90 Rainho, Antonio Angelo Leite. L'existencialisme de M. Gabriel Marcel. Lisbonne, 1955.
Phil 2750.19.95 Peccorini Letona, Francisco. Gabriel Marcel. Barcelona, 1959.
Phil 2750.19.100 Cain, Seymour. Gabriel Marcel. London, 1963.
Phil 2750.19.105 Tilliette, X. Philosophes contemporains. Paris, 1962.
Phil 2750.19.110 O'Malley, John B. The fellowship of being; an essay on the concept of person in the philosophy of Gabriel Marcel. The Hague, 1966.
Phil 2750.19.115 Ricoeur, Paul. Entretiens Paul Ricoeur, Gabriel Marcel. Paris, 1968.
Phil 2750.19.120 Matera, Rocco. Problematico e meta-problematico in Gabriel Marcel. Bari, 1969.
Phil 2750.19.125 Berg, Randi. Alternativ til det absurde. Oslo, 1969.
Phil 2750.19.130 Widmer, Charles. Gabriel Marcel et le théisme existentiel. Paris, 1971.
Phil 2750.20 Waelhens, A. de. Un philosophie de l'ambiguité. Louvain, 1951.
Phil 2750.20.5 Touron del Pie, Eliseo. El mundo. Madrid, 1961.
Phil 2750.20.10 Merleau-Ponty, Maurice. Eloge de la philosophie. Paris, 1953.
Phil 2750.20.11 Merleau-Ponty, Maurice. Eloge de la philosophie. Paris, 1962.
Phil 2750.20.15 Merleau-Ponty, Maurice. In praise of philosophy. Evanston, 1963.
Phil 2750.20.20 Merleau-Ponty, Maurice. Sens et non-sens. Paris, 1948.
Phil 2750.20.24 Merleau-Ponty, Maurice. Sense and non-sense. Evanston, 1964.
Phil 2750.20.30 Merleau-Ponty, Maurice. Signes. Paris, 1960.
Phil 2750.20.32 Merleau-Ponty, Maurice. Signs. Evanston, 1964.
Phil 2750.20.35 Merleau-Ponty, Maurice. The primacy of perception. Evanston, 1964.
Phil 2750.20.40A Merleau-Ponty, Maurice. Le visible et l'invisible. Paris, 1964.
Phil 2750.20.40B Merleau-Ponty, Maurice. Le visible et l'invisible. Paris, 1964.
Phil 2750.20.45 Merleau-Ponty, Maurice. The visible and the invisible. Evanston, 1968.
Phil 2750.20.50 Merleau-Ponty, Maurice. Résumés de cours, Collège de France, 1952-1960. Paris, 1968.
Phil 2750.20.50.5 Merleau-Ponty, Maurice. Themes from the lectures at the Collège de France, 1952-1960. Evanston, 1970.
Phil 2750.20.55 Merleau-Ponty, Maurice. L'union de l'âme et du corps chez Malebranche, Biran et Bergson. Paris, 1968.
Phil 2750.20.60 Merleau-Ponty, Maurice. La prose du monde. Paris, 1969.
Phil 2750.20.80 Kwant, Remigius Cornelius. De fenomenologie van Merleau-Ponty. Utrecht, 1962.
Phil 2750.20.82 Kwant, Remigius Cornelius. Mens en expressie, in het licht van de wijsbegeerte van Merleau-Ponty. Utrecht, 1968.
Phil 2750.20.85 Roosfen, S. De idee der zelfvervramding. Delft, 1963.
Phil 2750.20.90 Rofinet, A. Merleau-Ponty. Paris, 1963.
Phil 2750.20.95 Bakker, Reinout. Merleau-Ponty. Bearn, 1965.
Phil 2750.20.100 Barral, Mary Rose. Merleau-Ponty. Pittsburgh, 1965.
Phil 2750.20.105 Langan, Thomas. Merleau-Ponty's critique of reason. New Haven, 1966.
Phil 2750.20.110 Kwant, Remigius Cornelius. From phenomenology to metaphysics. Pittsburgh, 1966.
Phil 2750.20.115 Rabil, Albert. Merleau-Ponty, existentialist of the social world. N.Y., 1967.
Phil 2750.20.120 Derossi, Giorgio. Maurice Merleau-Ponty. Torino, 1965.
Phil 2750.20.125 Bonomi, Andrea. Esistenza e struttura. Milano, 1967.
Phil 2750.20.130 Brena, Gian Luigi. La struttura della percezione. Milano, 1969.
Phil 2750.20.135 Maier, Willi. Das Problem der Leiblichkeit bei Jean Paul Sartre und Maurice Merleau-Ponty. Tübingen, 1964.
Phil 2750.20.140 O'Neill, John. Perception, expression, and history. Evanston, 1970.
Phil 2750.20.145 Tilliette, Xavier. Merleau-Ponty. Paris, 1970.
Phil 2750.20.150 Geraets, Théodore F. Vers une nouvelle philosophie transcendantale. La Haye, 1971.
Phil 2750.21 Marc, André. Dialectique de l'affirmation. Paris, 1952.
Phil 2750.22 Mounier, E. Mounier et sa generation. Paris, 1956.
Phil 2750.22.5 Mounier, E. Ouevres. Paris, 1961. 5v.
Phil 2750.22.30 Mounier, E. La petite peur du XXe siècle. Neuchâtel, 1959.
Phil 2750.22.80 Moix, Candide. Emmanuel Mounier. Paris, 1960.
Phil 2750.22.85 Melchione, Vuceolio. Il metodo di Mounier altri saggi. Milano, 1960.
Phil 2750.22.90 Guissard, L. Emmanuel Mounier. Paris, 1962.
Phil 2750.22.95 Conilh, Jean. Emmanuel Mounier, sa vie, son oeuvre, avec un exposé de sa philosophie. Paris, 1966.
Phil 2750.22.100 Charpentreau, Jacques. L'esthétique personnaliste d'Emmanuel Mounier. Paris, 1966.
Phil 2750.22.105 Siena, Primo. Il profeta della chiesa proletaria. Torino, 1965.
VPhil 2750.22.110 Jędrzejczak, Klara. Problemy rewolucji i socjalizmu we współczesnej katolickiej myśli filozoficznej. Poznań, 1967.
Phil 2750.22.115 Campanini, Giorgio. La rivoluzione cristiana. Brescia, 1968.
Phil 2750.22.120 Diaz, Carlos. Personalismo oberero. Madrid, 1969.
Phil 2750.22.125 Vu Duy Tu. Individualisme, collectivisme, personnalisme dans l'oeuvre d'Emmanuel Mounier. Bonn, 1962.
Phil 2750.22.130 Barlow, Michel. Le socialisme d'Emmanuel Mounier. Toulouse, 1971.
Phil 2750.23 Maréchal, Joseph. Mélanges Joseph Maréchal. Bruxelles, 1950. 2v.
Phil 2750.23.30 Maréchal, Joseph. A Maréchal reader. N.Y., 1970.
Phil 2750.23.80 Casula, Mario. Maréchal e Kant. Roma, 1955.
Phil 2750.23.85 Dirven, Edouard. De la forme à l'acte...Joseph Maréchal. Paris, 1965.

Phil 2750 History of philosophy - Local Modern philosophy - France - Individual philosophers - Other M - cont.

Phil 2750.24.30 Menetrier, Jacques. L'homme quelconque. Paris, 1959.
Phil 2750.25 Marc, André. L'être et l'esprit. Paris, 1958.
Phil 2750.26.30 Mathieu, Guy. Science du bonheur. Paris, 1957.
Phil 2750.27.30 Hyppolite, J. Sens et existence dans la philosophie de Maurice Merleau-Ponty. Oxford, 1963.
Phil 2750.28.30 Maudoussat, G. La liberté spirituelle. Paris, 1959.
Phil 2750.29.30 Michaud, Humbert. Analyse de la révolution moderne. Paris, 1968?
Phil 2750.30.30 Marc, André. Raison et conversion chrétienne. Paris, 1961.
Phil 2750.32.30 Mayer, Charles Leopold. L'homme face à son destin. Paris, 1964.
Phil 2750.32.35 Mayer, Charles Leopold. Man faces his destiny. London, 1968.
Phil 2750.33.30 Monnerot, Jules. Les lois du tragique. Paris, 1969.

Phil 2775 History of philosophy - Local Modern philosophy - France - Individual philosophers - N

Phil 2775.1.80 Naville, E. Ernest Naville, sa vie et sa pensée. Genève, 1913-17. 2v.
Phil 2775.2.30 Nizan, Paul. Les chiens de garde. Paris, 1960.
Phil 2775.3.30 Naulin, Paul. L'itinéraire de la conscience. Paris, 1963.
Phil 2775.4.80 Curtis, D.E. Progress and eternal recurrence in the work of Gabriel Naudé, 1600-1650. Hull, 1967.
Phil 2775.5.80 Valenziano, Crispino. Introduzione alla filosofia dell' amore di Maurice Nédoncelle. Roma, 1965.
Phil 2775.6.80 Levert, Paule. Jean Nabert; ou, L'exigence absolue. Paris, 1971.

Phil 2800 History of philosophy - Local Modern philosophy - France - Individual philosophers - O

Phil 2800.1.80 Pamphlet box. Philosophy. French and Belgian. Ollé-Laprune.
Phil 2800.1.87 Fonsegrive, Georges. Léon Ollé-Laprune, l'homme et le penseur. Paris, 1912.
Phil 2800.1.88 Blondel, M. Léon Ollé-Laprune. Paris, 1923.

Phil 2805 History of philosophy - Local Modern philosophy - France - Individual philosophers - Pascal, Blaise

Phil 2805.10 Pascal, Blaise. Oeuvres. La Haye, 1779. 5v.
Phil 2805.12 Pascal, Blaise. Oeuvres complètes. Paris, 1858. 2v.
Phil 2805.13 Pascal, Blaise. Oeuvres complètes. Bruges, 1964-
Phil 2805.15 Pascal, Blaise. Oeuvres de Blaise Pascal. Paris, 1886-95. 2v.
NEDL Phil 2805.17 Pascal, Blaise. Oeuvres. Paris, 1914-23. 14v.
Phil 2805.19 Pascal, Blaise. Oeuvres complètes. Paris, 1926. 2v.
Phil 2805.21 Pascal, Blaise. Oeuvres. Paris, 1928-29. 6v.
Phil 2805.22 Pascal, Blaise. L'oeuvre de Pascal. Argenteuil, 1936.
Phil 2805.24 Pascal, Blaise. Fragments philosophiques. Paris, 1875.
Phil 2805.25 Pascal, Blaise. Fragments philosophiques. Paris, 1876.
Phil 2805.25.50A Pascal, Blaise. The living thoughts of Pascal. N.Y., 1940.
Phil 2805.25.50B Pascal, Blaise. The living thoughts of Pascal. N.Y., 1940.
Phil 2805.25.52 Pascal, Blaise. Les pages immortelles de Pascal, choisies et expliquées par F. Mauriac. N.Y., 1941.
Phil 2805.26 Pascal, Blaise. Pascal; ein brevier seiner Schriften. Stuttgart, 1908.
Phil 2805.26.7 Pascal, Blaise. Pascal de l'esprit géométrique. Paris, 1871.
Phil 2805.27 Pascal, Blaise. Textes inédits. Bruges, 1962.
Htn Phil 2805.28* Pascal, Blaise. Les provinciales. Cologne, 1657.
Phil 2805.29 Pascal, Blaise. Litterae provinciales. Helmaestadt, 1664.
Phil 2805.29.3 Pascal, Blaise. Ludovici Montaltii Litterae provinciales. 6. éd. Coloniae, 1700. 2v.
Htn Phil 2805.29.5* Pascal, Blaise. Les provinciales. Cologne, 1685.
Htn Phil 2805.29.6* Pascal, Blaise. Les provinciales. 6. éd. Cologne, 1666.
Phil 2805.30.2 Pascal, Blaise. Les provinciales. Paris, 1819. 2v.
Phil 2805.30.3 Pascal, Blaise. Texte primitif des Lettres provinciales. Paris, 1867.
Phil 2805.30.4 Pascal, Blaise. Les provinciales. Paris, 1885. 2v.
Phil 2805.30.5 Pascal, Blaise. Lettres écrites à un provincial. Paris, 1885-86. 2v.
Phil 2805.30.6 Pascal, Blaise. Lettres écrites à un provincial. Paris, 1842.
Phil 2805.30.7 Pascal, Blaise. Les provinciales. Paris, 1816. 2v.
Phil 2805.30.9 Pascal, Blaise. Les provinciales. Amsterdam, 1734. 3v.
Phil 2805.30.11 Pascal, Blaise. Les provinciales. Leiden? 1761. 4v.
NEDL Phil 2805.30.12 Pascal, Blaise. Les provinciales. Paris, 1816. 2v.
Phil 2805.30.13 Pascal, Blaise. Les provinciales. Paris, 1851. 2v.
Phil 2805.30.14 Pascal, Blaise. Les provinciales. Paris, 1819. 2v.
Phil 2805.30.15 Pascal, Blaise. Les provinciales. Paris, 1815. 2v.
Htn Phil 2805.30.16* Pascal, Blaise. Les provinciales. Cologne, 1657.
Htn Phil 2805.30.18* Pascal, Blaise. Les provinciales. 7. éd. Cologne, 1669.
Phil 2805.30.19 Pascal, Blaise. Les provinciales. Strasbourg, n.d.
Phil 2805.30.21 Pascal, Blaise. Les provinciales. Mexico, 1841.
Phil 2805.30.23 Pascal, Blaise. Les provinciales. Paris, 1867.
Phil 2805.30.25 Pascal, Blaise. Les provinciales. Paris, 1853.
Phil 2805.30.26 Pascal, Blaise. Provinciales. 9. éd. Paris, 1913.
Phil 2805.30.27 Pascal, Blaise. The life of Mr. Paschal with his letters relating to the Jesuits. London, 1765-66. 2v.
Phil 2805.30.29 Pascal, Blaise. Quatorzième lettre provinciale. Paris, 1883.
Phil 2805.30.30 Pascal, Blaise. Pascal et les provinciales. Paris, 1956.
Phil 2805.30.800 Mignone, C. Rensi, Leopardi e Pascal. Milano, 1954.
Phil 2805.31 Pascal, Blaise. Première, quatrième et treizième lettres provinciales. Paris, 1882.
Phil 2805.31.2 Pascal, Blaise. Première, quatrième et treizième lettres provinciales. Paris, 1885.
Phil 2805.31.5 Pascal, Blaise. Les première, quatrième et treizième lettres provinciales. 13. éd. Paris, 188-.
Phil 2805.32 Pascal, Blaise. Provincial letters. N.Y., 1859.
Phil 2805.32.2 Pascal, Blaise. The provincial letters. Cambridge, Eng., 1880.
Phil 2805.32.4 Pascal, Blaise. The provincial letters. N.Y., 1850.
Phil 2805.32.5 Pascal, Blaise. The provincial letters. N.Y., 1828.
Phil 2805.32.6 Pascal, Blaise. The provincial letters. N.Y., 1856.
Phil 2805.32.6.20 Pascal, Blaise. The provincial letters. London, 1889.
Phil 2805.32.7 Pascal, Blaise. The provincial letters. 1st Canadian ed. Toronto, 19- ?
Htn Phil 2805.32.11* Pascal, Blaise. Les provinciales. London, 1657.
Htn Phil 2805.32.12* Pascal, Blaise. Les provinciales. London, 1658.
Htn Phil 2805.32.15* Pascal, Blaise. The mystery of jesuitism. London, 1689[1679].
Phil 2805.32.25 Pascal, Blaise. Les lettres provinciales. Manchester, 1920.

158

Classified Listing

Phil 2805 History of philosophy - Local Modern philosophy - France - Individual philosophers - Pascal, Blaise - cont.

Phil 2805.32.26 Pascal, Blaise. Les provinciales écrits des curés de Paris. Paris, 1962. 2v.
Phil 2805.32.27 Pascal, Blaise. Les provinciales. Paris, 1965.
Phil 2805.32.28 Pascal, Blaise. Provinciales. Paris, 1964.
Phil 2805.32.30 Pascal, Blaise. Les lettres de Blaise Pascal. Paris, 1922.
Phil 2805.33 Pascal, Blaise. Les provinciales. Berlin, 1878.
Phil 2805.35 Pascal, Blaise. Las celebres cartas provinciales. Madrid, 1846.
Phil 2805.36 Pascal, Blaise. Cartas escritas a un provincial. Paris, 1849.
Htn Phil 2805.39* Pascal, Blaise. Pensées...sur la religion. Paris, 1670.
Htn Phil 2805.39.2* Pascal, Blaise. Pensées. Paris, 1670.
Htn Phil 2805.39.5* Pascal, Blaise. Pensées. Paris, 1670.
Phil 2805.40 Pascal, Blaise. Oeuvres; Les pensées. Paris, 1830.
Phil 2805.40.2A Pascal, Blaise. Pensées, fragments et lettres. Paris, 1844. 2v.
Phil 2805.40.2B Pascal, Blaise. Pensées, fragments et lettres. Paris, 1844. 2v.
Phil 2805.40.3 Pascal, Blaise. Pensées. Paris, 1854.
Phil 2805.40.4A Pascal, Blaise. Pensées. v.1-2. Paris, 1866.
Phil 2805.40.4B Pascal, Blaise. Pensées. v.1-2. Paris, 1866.
Phil 2805.40.4.3 Pascal, Blaise. Pensées. 2e éd. v.1-2. Paris, 1866. 2v.
Phil 2805.40.5 Pascal, Blaise. Pensées. Tours, 1873.
Phil 2805.40.6 Pascal, Blaise. Pensées. Tours, 1873.
Phil 2805.40.6.5 Pascal, Blaise. Pensées de Blaise Pascal. Paris, 1873.
Phil 2805.40.7 Pascal, Blaise. Les pensées. Paris, 1877-79. 2v.
Phil 2805.40.10 Pascal, Blaise. Pensées...sur la religion. Paris, 1725.
Phil 2805.40.11 Pascal, Blaise. Pensées...sur la religion. Paris, 1734.
Phil 2805.40.12 Pascal, Blaise. Pensées...sur la religion. Paris, 1748.
Phil 2805.40.13 Pascal, Blaise. Pensées de Blaise Pascal. Paris, 1817. 2v.
Phil 2805.40.13.5 Pascal, Blaise. Pensées de Blaise Pascal. Paris, 1829.
Phil 2805.40.13.10 Pascal, Blaise. Pensées de Blaise Pascal. Paris, 1839.
Phil 2805.40.13.15 Pascal, Blaise. Pensées. Paris, 1842.
NEDL Phil 2805.40.14 Pascal, Blaise. Pensées. Paris, 1874.
Phil 2805.40.15 Pascal, Blaise. Pensées. Paris, 1897.
Phil 2805.40.16 Pascal, Blaise. Pensées. v.1-2. Paris, 1812.
Phil 2805.40.17A Pascal, Blaise. Pensées. Paris, 1904. 3v.
Phil 2805.40.17B Pascal, Blaise. Pensées. Paris, 1904. 3v.
Phil 2805.40.18 Pascal, Blaise. Pensées. Fribourg, 1896.
Phil 2805.40.19 Pascal, Blaise. Pensées. Paris, 1907.
Phil 2805.40.20 Pascal, Blaise. Pensées sur la vérité de la religion chrétienne par J. Chevalier. 2. éd. Paris, 1925. 2v.
Phil 2805.40.21 Pascal, Blaise. Pensées choisies. 6e éd. Paris, 1876.
Phil 2805.40.22 Pascal, Blaise. Pensées choisies. 2. éd. Paris, 1882.
Phil 2805.40.23 Pascal, Blaise. Pensées. Paris, 1924.
Phil 2805.40.25 Pascal, Blaise. Thoughts on religion and philosophy. London, 1894.
Phil 2805.40.28 Pascal, Blaise. Les pensées et oeuvres choisies. Paris, 1937.
Phil 2805.40.29 Pascal, Blaise. Pensées. Paris, 186-.
Phil 2805.40.30 Pascal, Blaise. Pensées contenant les lettres et opuscules. Paris, 1861.
Phil 2805.40.31 Pascal, Blaise. Pensées sur la religion. Paris, 1951. 3v.
Phil 2805.40.32 Pascal, Blaise. Pensées de Pascal. Paris, 1866.
Phil 2805.40.33 Pascal, Blaise. Pensées, opuscules et lettres. Paris, 1873. 2v.
Phil 2805.40.34 Pascal, Blaise. Pensées. Paris, 1869.
Phil 2805.40.35 Pascal, Blaise. Pensées et opuscules. 11e éd. Paris, 1923.
Phil 2805.40.36 Pascal, Blaise. Pensées et opuscules. 6. éd. Paris, 1912.
Phil 2805.40.37 Pascal, Blaise. Pensées. Paris, 1852.
Phil 2805.40.38 Pascal, Blaise. Pensées. Paris, 1934.
Phil 2805.40.39 Pascal, Blaise. Pensées sur la religion. v.1-2. Paris, 1948[1947]
Phil 2805.40.40 Pascal, Blaise. Tankar i religiösa frägor. 2. uppl. Stockholm, 1911.
Phil 2805.40.45 Pascal, Blaise. Pascal's apology for religion. Cambridge, Eng., 1942.
Phil 2805.40.50 Pascal, Blaise. Pensées sur la religion et sur quelques autres sujets. Monaco, 1962.
Phil 2805.40.55 Pascal présent, 1662-1962. Clermont, 1962.
Htn Phil 2805.41* Pascal, Blaise. Thoughts, meditations, and prayers, touching matters moral and divine. London, 1688.
X Cg Phil 2805.41.15 Pascal, Blaise. Thoughts, letters, and opuscules. N.Y., 1861.
Phil 2805.42.2 Pascal, Blaise. The thoughts of Blaise Pascal. London, 1888.
Phil 2805.42.3 Pascal, Blaise. Thoughts on religion. London, 1836.
Htn Phil 2805.42.4* Pascal, Blaise. Thoughts on religion. London, 1704.
Phil 2805.42.5 Pascal, Blaise. Thoughts on religion and other curious subjects. London, 1749.
Phil 2805.42.6A Pascal, Blaise. Miscelleneous writings. London, 1849.
Phil 2805.42.6B Pascal, Blaise. Miscelleneous writings. London, 1849.
NEDL Phil 2805.42.7 Pascal, Blaise. Thoughts on religion. London, 1825.
Phil 2805.42.9 Pascal, Blaise. The thoughts of Blaise Pascal. London, 1904.
Phil 2805.42.11 Pascal, Blaise. The pensées. Harmondsworth, 1961.
Phil 2805.42.25 Pascal, Blaise. Pascal's Pensées. Mt. Vernon, 1946?
Phil 2805.42.27 Pascal, Blaise. Pensées. London, 1947.
Phil 2805.42.30 Pascal, Blaise. Pensées. London, 1950.
Phil 2805.42.35 Pascal, Blaise. Pensées. Paris, 1942.
Phil 2805.42.37 Pascal, Blaise. Pensées. London, 1943.
Phil 2805.42.40 Pascal, Blaise. Pensées. Paris, 1958. 2v.
Phil 2805.42.45 Pascal, Blaise. Pensées. Paris, 1960. 2v.
Phil 2805.42.50 Pascal, Blaise. Pensées. N.Y., 1962.
Phil 2805.42.55 Pascal, Blaise. Pensées. Paris, 1962.
Phil 2805.42.58 Pascal, Blaise. Pensées. Paris, 1966.
Phil 2805.43 Pascal, Blaise. Pensamientos. Zaragoza, 1790.
Phil 2805.44 Pascal, Blaise. Gedanken. Leipzig, 1881.
Phil 2805.45 Pascal, Blaise. Pascal. Paris, 1946.
Phil 2805.46 Pascal, Blaise. Pascal. Paris, 1947.
Phil 2805.50 Pascal, Blaise. L'homme et l'oeuvre. Paris, 1956.
Phil 2805.55 Pascal, Blaise. Discours sur les passions de l'amour. Paris, 1900.
Htn Phil 2805.60* Pascal, Blaise. Traitez de l'equilibre. Paris, 1663.
Phil 2805.65 Pascal, Blaise. Deux pièces imparfaites sur la grâce et le concile de trente. Paris, 1947.
Phil 2805.70 Pascal, Blaise. Opuscules philosophiques. Paris, 1864.
Phil 2805.72 Pascal, Blaise. Opuscules philosophiques. Paris, 1887.

Phil 2805 History of philosophy - Local Modern philosophy - France - Individual philosophers - Pascal, Blaise - cont.

Phil 2805.73 Pascal, Blaise. Opuscules et lettres. Paris, 1955.
Phil 2805.74 Pascal, Blaise. Entretien avec de Saci sur Épictète et Montaigne. Paris, 1875.
Phil 2805.74.10 Pascal, Blaise. Entretien avec M. de Saci. 2. éd. Aix, 1946.
Phil 2805.74.20 Pascal, Blaise. L'entretien de Pascal et Sacy. Paris, 1960.
Phil 2805.77 Maire, Albert. L'oeuvre scientifique de Blaise Pascal. Paris, 1912.
Phil 2805.78 Maire, Albert. Bibliographie générale des oeuvres de Blaise Pascal. Paris, 1925-27. 5v.
Phil 2805.79 Pamphlet box. Philosophy. Pascal, Blaise. German dissertations.
Phil 2805.80 Cousin, Victor. Des pensées de Pascal. Paris, 1843.
Phil 2805.80.2 Cousin, Victor. Des pensées de Pascal. Paris, 1844.
Phil 2805.80.7 Cousin, Victor. Études sur Pascal. Paris, 1876.
Phil 2805.81 Collet, F. Fait inédit de la vie de Pascal. Paris, 1848.
Phil 2805.82 Droz, E. Étude sur le scepticisme de Pascal. Paris, 1886.
Phil 2805.83 Lelut, L.F. L'amulette de Pascal. Paris, 1846.
Phil 2805.84 Maynard, M.U. Pascal, sa vie et son charactère. Paris, 1850. 2v.
Phil 2805.85 Nourrisson, J.F. Pascal physicien et philosophe. Paris, 1885.
Phil 2805.85.5 Nourrisson, J.F. Pascal physicien et philosophe. Défense de Pascal. Paris, 1888.
Phil 2805.86 Tulloch, J. Pascal. Edinburgh, 1878.
Phil 2805.86.5 Tulloch, J. Pascal. Edinburgh, 1878.
Phil 2805.87 Souriau, M. Pascal. Paris, 1898.
Phil 2805.88 Bertrand, J.L.F. Blaise Pascal. Paris, 1891.
Phil 2805.89 Dreydorff, J.G. Pascal sein Leben und seine Kämpfe. Leipzig, 1870.
Phil 2805.90 Giraud, V. Pascal l'homme, l'oeuvre, l'influence. Fribourg, 1898.
Phil 2805.90.3 Giraud, V. Pascal l'homme, l'oeuvre, l'influence. Paris, 1905.
Phil 2805.90.5 Giraud, V. Blaise Pascal études d'histoire morale. Paris, 1910.
Phil 2805.90.9 Giraud, V. La vie héroique de Blaise Pascal. 15. éd. Paris, 1923.
Phil 2805.90.15 Giraud, V. Soeurs de grands hommes: J. Pascal. Paris, 1926.
Phil 2805.91 Vinet, A. Études sur Blaise Pascal. Paris, 1856.
Phil 2805.91.1 Vinet, A. Études sur Blaise Pascal. Paris, 1848.
Phil 2805.91.2 Vinet, A. Études sur Blaise Pascal. Lausanne, 1936.
Phil 2805.91.3 Nazelle, R.J. Étude sur Alexandre Vinet critique de Pascal. Alençon, 1901.
Phil 2805.92 Boutroux, E. Pascal. Paris, 1900.
Phil 2805.92.3 Boutroux, E. Pascal. 3. éd. Paris, 1903.
Phil 2805.92.7 Boutroux, E. Pascal. Manchester, 1902.
Phil 2805.92.9 Boutroux, E. Pascal. 5. éd. Paris, 1912.
Phil 2805.93 Lefranc, A. Défense de Pascal...est-il un faussaire? Paris, 1906.
Phil 2805.94 Köster, Adolph. Die Ethik Pascal. Tübingen, 1907.
Phil 2805.94.3 Köster, Adolph. Die Ethik Pascal. Inaug.-Diss. Tübingen, 1908.
Phil 2805.95 Strowski, F. Pascal et son temps. Paris, 1907-22. 3v.
Phil 2805.95.10A Strowski, F. Les pensées de Pascal; étude et analyse. Paris, 1930.
Phil 2805.95.10B Strowski, F. Les pensées de Pascal; étude et analyse. Paris, 1930.
Phil 2805.98 St. Cyres, S.H.N. Pascal. London, 1909.
Phil 2805.98.10 St. Cyres, S.H.N. Pascal. N.Y., 1910.
Phil 2805.99 Jordan, H.R. Blaise Pascal. London, 1909.
Phil 2805.100 Prudhomme, S. La vraie religion selon Pascal. Paris, 1905.
Phil 2805.101 Daniel, Gabriel. Réponse aux lettres provinciales. Amsterdam, 1697.
Phil 2805.101.5 Daniel, Gabriel. Réponse aux lettres provinciales. Bruxelles, 1698.
Phil 2805.101.8 Daniel, Gabriel. Réponse aux lettres provinciales. La Haye, 1716.
Phil 2805.101.15 Daniel, Gabriel. Entretiens de Cléandre et d'Eudoxe sur les lettres au provincial. 10. éd. Pierre Marteau, 1697.
Phil 2805.101.25 Daniel, Gabriel. The discourses of Cleander and Eudoxe. London, 1704.
Phil 2805.102 Gazier, A. Les derniers jours de Blaise Pascal. Paris, 1911.
Phil 2805.103 Archambault, P. Pascal. Paris, n.d.
Phil 2805.104 Petitot, H. Pascal sa vie religieuse. Paris, 1911.
Phil 2805.106 Hatzfeld, A. Pascal. Paris, 1901.
Phil 2805.107 Griselle, E. Pascal et les Pascalins d'après des documents contemporains. Fribourg, 1908.
Phil 2805.108 Beerens, J.F. De casuïstiek en Pascal. Utrecht, 1909.
Phil 2805.109 Janssens, Edgard. La philosophie et l'apologétique de Pascal. Louvain, 1906.
Phil 2805.110 Barrès, Maurice. L'angoisse de Pascal. Paris, 1918.
Phil 2805.110.5 Barrès, Maurice. L'angoisse de Pascal, suivi d'une étude sur les deux maisons de Pascal à Clermont-Ferrand. Paris, 1923.
Phil 2805.111 Jovy, Ernest. D'où irent l' "Ad tuum, Domine Jesu, de Pascal? Paris, 1916. 2 pam.
Phil 2805.111.5 Jovy, Ernest. Pascal et Saint Ignace. Paris, 1923.
Phil 2805.111.10 Jovy, Ernest. Pascal n'a pa inventé le haquet, démonstration lexicographique. Paris, 1923.
Phil 2805.111.15 Jovy, Ernest. Études pascaliennes. Paris, 1927-36. 9v.
Phil 2805.112.5 Stewart, Hugh F. La sainteté de Pascal. Paris, 1919.
Phil 2805.112.7 Stewart, Hugh F. The secret of Pascal. Cambridge, Eng., 1941.
Phil 2805.112.10 Stewart, Hugh F. Blaise Pascal. London, 1942.
Phil 2805.112.15 Stewart, Hugh F. The heart of Pascal. Cambridge, 1945.
Phil 2805.113F Faugère, Armand P. Défense de Blaise Pascal. Paris, 1868.
Phil 2805.115 Warmuth, K. Das religiös-ethische Ideal Pascals. Leipzig, 1901.
Phil 2805.165 La Vallette-Monbrun, A. de. Maine de Biran, critique et disciple de Pascal. Paris, 1914.
Phil 2805.175 Roux, Marie. Pascal en Poitou et les Poitevins. Paris, 1919.
Phil 2805.176 Maire, Albert. Essai sur la psychologie de Blaise Pascal. Paris, 1922.
NEDL Phil 2805.177 Chevalier, J. Pascal. Paris, 1922.
Phil 2805.177.5A Chevalier, J. Pascal. N.Y., 1930.
Phil 2805.177.5B Chevalier, J. Pascal. N.Y., 1930.
Phil 2805.178 Laros, M. Das Glaubensproblem bei Pascal. Düsseldorf, 1918.

159

Classified Listing

Phil 2805 History of philosophy - Local Modern philosophy - France - Individual philosophers - Pascal, Blaise - cont.

Phil 2805.179 Clark, William. Pascal and the Port Royalists. Edinburgh, 1902.
Phil 2805.180 Études sur Pascal. Paris, 1923.
Phil 2805.182 Chamaillard, E. Pascal, mondain et amoureux. Paris, 1923.
Phil 2805.183 Filleau de la Chaise, J. Discours sur les pensées de M. Pascal. Paris, 1922.
Phil 2805.185 Langenskjold, Agnes. Blaise Pascal. Uppsala, 1922.
Phil 2805.186 Bohlin, J. Blaise Pascal. v.1-2. Stockholm, 1920-21.
Phil 2805.187 Neri, F. Un ritratto immaginario di Pascal. Torino, 1921.
Phil 2805.188 Bremond, H. En prière avec Pascal. Paris, 1923.
Phil 2805.189 Lahorque, P.M. Le réalisme de Pascal. Paris, 1923.
Phil 2805.190 Picard, Émile. Pascal mathématicien et physicien. Paris, 1923.
Phil 2805.191 Malvy, A. Pascal et le problème de la croyance. Paris, 1923.
Phil 2805.192 Brunschvicg, L. Le génie de Pascal. Paris, 1924.
Phil 2805.192.10A Brunschvicg, L. Pascal. Paris, 1932.
Phil 2805.192.10B Brunschvicg, L. Pascal. Paris, 1932.
Phil 2805.192.15 Brunschvicg, L. Blaise Pascal. Paris, 1953.
Phil 2805.193 Nedelkovitch, D. La pensées philosophique créatrice de Pascal. Paris, 1925.
Phil 2805.194 Arsovitch, R. Pascal et l'expérience du Puy-de-Dome. Thèse. Montpellier, 1925.
Phil 2805.195.5 Duclaux, A.M.F.R. Portrait of Pascal. London, 1927.
Phil 2805.196 Valensin, A. A la suite de Pascal. Saint-Felicien-en-Vivarais, 1926.
Phil 2805.196.5 Valensin, A. Balthazar. Paris, 1934.
Phil 2805.196.7 Valensin, A. Balthazar. Paris, 1954.
Phil 2805.197 Gentile, F. Pascal: saggio d'interpretazione storica. Bari, 1927.
Phil 2805.200 Reuchlin, H. Pascal's Leben und der Geist seiner Schriften. Stuttgart, 1840.
Phil 2805.201 Nolhac, P. de. Pascal en Auvergne. Saint-Felicien-en-Vivarais, 1925.
Phil 2805.202.1 Soltau, R.H. Pascal: the man and the message. Westport, 1970.
Phil 2805.203 Bornhausen, K. Pascal. Basel, 1920.
Phil 2805.204 Droulers, C. La cité de Pascal. Paris, 1928.
tn Phil 2805.205* Petit-Didier, M. Apologie des lettres provinciales de Louis de Montalte. Delft, 1697-98.
:n Phil 2805.205.5* Petit-Didier, M. Apologie des lettres provinciales de Louis de Montalte. Pt.1-4. Delft, 1697-98. 2v.
Phil 2805.207 Shestor, Lev. La nuit de Gethsémani. Paris, 1923.
Phil 2805.208 Leavenworth, I. The physics of Pascal. N.Y., 1930.
Phil 2805.209 Bayet, Albert. Les provinciales de Pascal. Paris, 1929.
Phil 2805.209.5 Bayet, Albert. Les provinciales de Pascal. Paris, 1946.
Phil 2805.210 Chaix-Ruy, Jules. Le jansénisme; Pascal et Port-Royal. Paris, 1930.
Phil 2805.211 Orliac, Jehanne d'. Le coeur humain, inhumain, surhumain de Blaise Pascal. Paris, 1931.
Phil 2805.212 Lhermet, J. Pascal et la Bible. Thèse. Paris, 1931?
Phil 2805.213 Antoniadis, S. Pascal traducteur de la Bible. Thèse. Leyde, 1930.
Phil 2805.214 Mauriac, F. Blaise Pascal et sa soeur Jacqueline. Paris, 1931.
Phil 2805.215 Demahis, E. La pensée politique de Pascal. Thèse. St. Amand, 1931.
Phil 2805.216 Réguron, Paule. Les origines du mouvement antijanseniste. Thèse. Grenoble, 1934.
Phil 2805.216.5 Réguron, Paule. De la théologie à la prière de Pascal. Thèse. Grenoble, 1934.
Phil 2805.217 Desgrippes, George. Études sur Pascal de l'automatisme a la foi. Paris, 19- .
Phil 2805.218A Eastwood, D.M. The revival of Pascal. Oxford, 1936.
Phil 2805.218B Eastwood, D.M. The revival of Pascal. Oxford, 1936.
Phil 2805.219 Bishop, M. Pascal. N.Y., 1930.
Phil 2805.220 Guardini, R. Christliches Bewusstsein...Pascal. Leipzig, 1935.
Phil 2805.221 Lohde, Richard. Die Anthropologie Pascals. Halle, 1936.
Phil 2805.222 Suarès, André. Puissances de Pascal. Paris, 1923.
Phil 2805.223 Falcucci, C. Le problème de la vérité chez Pascal. Thèse. Toulouse, 1939.
Phil 2805.224 Finch, D. La critique philosophique de Pascal au XVIIIe siècle. Diss. Philadelphia, 1940.
Phil 2805.225 Desbruyères, P. Face à l'épreuve avec Pascal. Lyon, 1941.
Phil 2805.226 Cailliet, E. The clue to Pascal. London, 1944.
Phil 2805.226.5 Cailliet, E. Pascal; genius in the light of scripture. Philadelphia, 1945.
Phil 2805.226.6 Cailliet, E. Pascal. N.Y., 1961.
Phil 2805.227 Deschanel, E.A.E.M. Pascal, La Rochefoucauld, Bossuet. Paris, 1885.
Phil 2805.228 Benzécri, E. L'esprit humain selon Pascal. Paris, 1939.
Phil 2805.229.5 Cresson, André. Pascal; sa vie, son oeuvre, avec un exposé de sa philosophie. 2e éd. Paris, 1942.
Phil 2805.229.8 Cresson, André. Pascal; sa vie, son oeuvre, avec un exposé de sa philosophie. 5. éd. Paris, 1962.
Phil 2805.230 Michaut, Gustave. Pascal, Molière, Musset; essais de critique et de psychologie. Paris, 1942.
Phil 2805.231.5 Valot, Stephen. Regardons vivre Blaise Pascal. 2. éd. Paris, 1945.
Phil 2805.233 Boulan, Émile. De Pascal à Victor Hugo. Groningue, 1946.
Phil 2805.237 Merezhkovskii, Dimitrii S. Pascal. Paris, 1941.
Phil 2805.239 Patrick, D.G.M. Pascal and Kierkegaard. London, 1947. 2v.
Phil 2805.241 Tourneur, Zacharie. Une vie avec Blaise Pascal. Paris, 1943.
Phil 2805.241.5 Tourneur, Zacharie. Beauté poétique. Muln, 1933.
Phil 2805.242 Buchholz, E. Blaise Pascal. 2. Aufl. Göttingen, 1942.
Phil 2805.243 Humbert, Pierre. Cet effrayant génie...l'oeuvre scientifique de Pascal. Paris, 1947.
Phil 2805.245 Andreas, Peter. Pascal. Strasbourg, 1946.
Phil 2805.247A Baudin, Émile. Études historiques et critiques sur la philosophie de Pascal. v.1-3. Neuchâtel, 1946-47. 4v.
Phil 2805.247B Baudin, Émile. Études historiques et critiques sur la philosophie de Pascal. v.1. Neuchâtel, 1946-47.
Phil 2805.249A Lafuma, Louis. Trois pensées inédites de Pascal. Paris, 1945.
Phil 2805.249B Lafuma, Louis. Trois pensées inédites de Pascal. Paris, 1945.
Phil 2805.249.5 Lafuma, Louis. Controverses pascaliennes. Paris, 1952.
Phil 2805.249.10 Lafuma, Louis. Histoire des Pensées de Pascal. Paris, 1954.
Phil 2805.251 Tytgat, J. Pascal. Gand, 1948.
Phil 2805.253 Peters, F.E. Blaise Pascal. Hamburg, 1946.
Phil 2805.255 Russier, Jeanne. La foi selon Pascal. v.1-2. Thèse. Paris, 1949.

Phil 2805 History of philosophy - Local Modern philosophy - France - Individual philosophers - Pascal, Blaise - cont.

Phil 2805.256 Journet, C. Vérité de Pascal. St. Maurice, 1951.
Phil 2805.257 Daniel-Rops, Henry. Pascal et notre coeur. 6. éd. Strasbourg, 1949.
Phil 2805.259 Lefebvre, H. Pascal. Paris, 1949. 2v.
Phil 2805.261 Jungo, Michel. Le vocabulaire de Pascal. Paris, 1950.
Phil 2805.263A Mesnard, Jean. Pascal, l'homme et l'oeuvre. Paris, 1951.
Phil 2805.263B Mesnard, Jean. Pascal, l'homme et l'oeuvre. Paris, 1951.
Phil 2805.263.2 Mesnard, Jean. Pascal. London, 1952.
Phil 2805.265 Jaccard, L.F. Blaise Pascal. Neuchâtel, 1951.
Phil 2805.267 Holden, P.G. Pascal. London, 1951.
Phil 2805.268 Hubert, M.L., Sister. Pascal's unfinished Apology. New Haven, 1952.
Phil 2805.270 Guitton, Jean. Pascal et Leibniz. Paris, 1951.
Phil 2805.272 Pascal, Blaise. Pascal par lui-même. Paris, 1952.
Phil 2805.274 Rennes, J. Pascal et le libertin. Paris, 1950.
Phil 2805.276 Nasmuth, E. Die Philosophie Pascals. Heidelberg, 1949.
Phil 2805.277 Nasmuth, E. Der unbekannte Pascal. Regensburg, 1962.
Phil 2805.278 Moussalli, U. Le vrai visage de Blaise Pascal. Paris, 1952.
Phil 2805.280 Fletcher, F.T.H. Pascal and the mystical tradition. Oxford, 1954.
Phil 2805.282 Ducas, A. Discours sur les passions de l'amour de Pascal. Alger, 1953.
Phil 2805.284 Steinmann, Jean. Pascal. Paris, 1954.
Phil 2805.284.2 Steinmann, Jean. Pascal. Paris, 1962.
Phil 2805.284.5 Steinmann, Jean. Pascal. London, 1965.
Phil 2805.286 Jansen, Paule. De Blaise Pascal à Henry Hammond. Paris, 1954.
Phil 2805.288 Ehrenberg, H. In der Schule Pascals. Heidelberg, 1954.
Phil 2805.290 Demorest, Jean. Dans Pascal. Paris, 1953.
Phil 2805.291 Demorest, Jean. Pascal écrivain. Paris, 1937.
Phil 2805.300 Spoerri, T. Der verborgene Pascal. Hamburg, 1955.
Phil 2805.305 Vansina, Dirk. Pascal. Bussum, 1954.
Phil 2805.310 Maggioni, Mary J. The pensées of Pascal. Washington, 1950.
Phil 2805.315 Julien Eymard d'Angers. Pascal et ses précurseurs. Paris, 1954.
Phil 2805.320 Jerphagnon, L. Pascal et la souffrance. Paris, 1956.
Phil 2805.321 Jerphagnon, L. Le caractère de Pascal. Paris, 1962.
Phil 2805.325 Paris. Musée National des Granges de Port-Royal. Pascal et les provinciales. Paris, 1956.
Phil 2805.330 LeRoy, Georges. Pascal. 1. éd. Paris, 1957.
Phil 2805.335 Lacombe, R.E. L'apologétique de Pascal. Paris, 1958.
Phil 2805.340 Simonetti, Maria. Studi Pascaliani. Roma, 1957?
Phil 2805.345 Mortimer, Ernest. Blaise Pascal. London, 1959.
Phil 2805.350 Perdomo, Garcia José. La teoría del conocimiento en Pascal. Madrid, 1956.
Phil 2805.355 Scholtens, M. Études médico-psychologiques sur Pascal. Haarlem, 1958.
Phil 2805.360 Perdomo, Garcia José. La teoría del conocimiento en Pascal. Madrid, 1956.
Phil 2805.365 Francis, Raymond. Les pensées de Pascal en France de 1842 à 1942. Paris, 1959.
Phil 2805.370 Brunet, Georges. Un prétendu traité de Pascal. Paris, 1959.
Phil 2805.370.5 Brunet, Georges. Le Pari de Pascal. Paris, 1956.
Phil 2805.375 Alfieri, Vittorio Enzo. Il problema Pascal. Milano, 1959.
Phil 2805.380 Écrits sur Pascal. Paris, 1959.
Phil 2805.385 Baudouin, Charles. Blaise Pascal. Paris, 1962.
Phil 2805.386F Pascal et Port Royal. Paris, 1962.
Phil 2805.390 Terzi, Carlo. Pascal. Bergamo, 1960.
Phil 2805.391 Vloemans, A. Pascal. Den Haag, 1962.
Phil 2805.393 Pascal e Nietzsche. Padova, 1962.
Phil 2805.395 Chaigne, Louis. Pascal. Paris, 1962.
Phil 2805.397 Bibliothèque Nationale, Paris. Blaise Pascal, 1623-1662. Paris, 1962
Phil 2805.399 Hay, Malcolm. The prejudices of Pascal. London, 1962.
Phil 2805.400 Sciacca, M.F. Pascal. 3. ed. Milan, 1962.
Phil 2805.402 Daniel, Gabriel. Lettre de Mr. l'abbé...à Eudoxe. Cologne, 1698-99.
Phil 2805.404 Guitton, J. Génie de Pascal. Paris, 1962.
Phil 2805.406 Steinmann, J. Les trois nuits de Pascal. Paris, 1963.
Phil 2805.407 Jacques, E. Le troisième centenaire de la mort de la Blaise Pascal. Bruxelles, 1963.
Phil 2805.408 Rennes, A. Procès de Pascal. Paris, 1962.
Phil 2805.409 Clermont-Ferrand. Musée du Ranquet. Pascal, sa ville et son temps. Clermont-Ferrand, 1962.
Phil 2805.410 Ronnet, G. Pascal et l'homme moderne. Paris, 1963.
Phil 2805.412 Pascal. Barcelona, 1964.
Phil 2805.413A Pascal; testes du tricentenaire. Paris, 1963.
Phil 2805.413B Pascal; testes du tricentenaire. Paris, 1963.
Phil 2805.414 Borne, Étienne. De Pascal à Teilhard de Chardin. Clermont-Ferrand, 1963.
Phil 2805.415 Massis, Henri. Troisième centenaire de la mort de Pascal. Paris, 1962.
Phil 2805.416 L'oeuvre scientifique de Pascal. Paris, 1964.
Phil 2805.417 Moscato, Alberto. Pascal. Milano, 1963.
Phil 2805.418 Mauriac, François. La rencontre avec Pascal. Paris, 1926.
Phil 2805.419 Brooms, Jack Howard. Pascal. N.Y., 1966.
Phil 2805.420 Massis, Henri. Le réalisme de Pascal. St.-Felicien-en-Vivarais, 1924.
Phil 2805.421 Mesnard, Jean. Pascal. Bruges, 1965.
Phil 2805.421.1 Mesnard, Jean. Pascal. University, 1969.
Phil 2805.422 Mesnard, Jean. Pascal et les Roannez. Bruges, 1965. 2v.
Phil 2805.425 Académie des sciences, belles lettres et arts de Clermont-Ferrand. Cinq études sur Blaise Pascal. Clermont-Ferrand, 1962.
Phil 2805.428 Topliss, Patricia. The rhetoric of Pascal. Leicester, 1966.
Phil 2805.430 Gouhier, Henri. Blaise Pascal. Paris, 1966.
Phil 2805.432 Chinard, Gilbert. En lisant Pascal. Lille, 1948.
Phil 2805.435 Hoven, Pieter van der. Blaise Pascal. Baarn, 1964.
Phil 2805.440 Sellier, Philippe. Pascal et la liturgie. Paris, 1966.
Phil 2805.445 Pareyson, Luigi. L'etica di Pascal; corso di filiosfia morale dell'anno accademico 1965-1966. Torino, 1966.
Phil 2805.450 Goldmann, Lucien. Weltflucht und Politik. Neuwied, 1967.
Phil 2805.455 Pontet, Maurice. Pascal et Teilhard, témoins de Jésus-Christ. Paris, 1968.
Phil 2805.460 Miel, Jan. Pascal and theology. Baltimore, 1969.
Phil 2805.465 Le Guern, Michel. L'image dans l'oeuvre de Pascal. Paris, 1969.
Phil 2805.470 Garrone, Gabriel Marie. Ce que croyait Pascal. Tours, 1969.
Phil 2805.475 Eydoux, Emmanuel. Dialogue avec Blaise Pascal. Théâtre. Basel, 1968.

Phil 2805　History of philosophy - Local Modern philosophy - France - Individual philosophers - Pascal, Blaise - cont.

Phil 2805.480　Sellier, Philippe. Pascal et Saint Augustin. Paris, 1970.
Phil 2805.485F　Tricentenaire du mémorial de Blaise Pascal, 23 Novembre 1654-1954. Paris, 1955.
Phil 2805.490　Sina, Mario. L'anti-Pascal di Voltaire. Milano, 1970.
Phil 2805.495　Larraillet, Paul. Pascal et le problème de la destinée. Paris, 1970.

Phil 2825　History of philosophy - Local Modern philosophy - France - Individual philosophers - Other P

Phil 2825.5　Grappe, André. La pensée de Maurice Pradines. Paris, 1938.
Phil 2825.10　Le philosophe. St. Louis, 1948.
Phil 2825.15　Paliard, J. Profondeur de l'âme. Paris, 1954.
Phil 2825.15.80　Masset, Pierre. La dialectique de la conscience chez Jacques Paliard. Paris, 1959.
Phil 2825.20　Pradines, M. L'aventure de l'esprit dans les espèces. Paris, 1955.
Phil 2825.25　Piguet, Jean Claude. De l'esthétique à la métaphysique. La Haye, 1959.
Phil 2825.30　Amédée Ponceau, études et témoignages. Bruges, 1966.
Phil 2825.35　Politzer, Georges. Écrits...textes réunis par Jacques Debouzy. Paris, 1969. 2v.

Phil 2835　History of philosophy - Local Modern philosophy - France - Individual philosophers - Ramus (i.e. La Ramée, Pierre de)

Htn　Phil 2835.30*　Ramus, P. Dialecticae libri duo. London, 1669.
Phil 2835.35　La Ramée, P. de. Dialectique (1555). Genève, 1964.
Phil 2835.80　Downame, G. Commentarii in P. Rami Dialecticam. Francofurti, 1610.
Phil 2835.81　Waddington, C. Ramue (Pierre de la Ramée). Paris, 1855.
Phil 2835.82　Graves, F.P. Peter Ramus and educational reforms of the 16th century. N.Y., 1912.
Phil 2835.84　Ong, Walter J. Ramus, method and the decay of dialogue. Cambridge, 1958. 2v.
Phil 2835.84.5　Ong, Walter J. Ramus and Talon inventory. Cambridge, 1958.
Htn　Phil 2835.84.5*A　Ong, Walter J. Ramus and Talon inventory. Cambridge, 1958.
Phil 2835.86　Hooykaas, Reijer. Humanisme, science et réforme. Leyde, 1958.
Phil 2835.87　Verdonk, Johannes Jacobus. Petrus Ramus en de wiskunde. Assen, 1966.
Phil 2835.89　Desmaze, Charles. P. Ramus, professeur au Collège de France. Sa vie. Genève, 1970.

Phil 2840　History of philosophy - Local Modern philosophy - France - Individual philosophers - Renouvier, Charles

Phil 2840.30　Renouvier, C.B. Esquisse d'une classification systématique. Paris, 1885-86. 2v.
Phil 2840.40　Renouvier, C.B. Essais de critique générale. Paris, 1854-64. 4v.
Phil 2840.40.2　Renouvier, C.B. Essais de critique générale. v.1. pt.1-3; v.2, pt.1-3. Paris, 1875. 6v.
Phil 2840.41　Renouvier, C.B. Essais de critique générale. Premier essai. Paris, 1912. 2v.
Phil 2840.42　Renouvier, C.B. Essais de critique générale. Paris, 1912. 2v.
Phil 2840.50　Renouvier, C.B. Science de la morale. Paris, 1869. 2v.
Phil 2840.50.5　Renouvier, C.B. Science de la morale. Paris, 1908. 2v.
Phil 2840.55　Renouvier, C.B. Les dilemmes de la métaphysique pure. Paris, 1901.
Phil 2840.60　Renouvier, C.B. Histoire et solution des problèmes métaphysiques. Paris, 1901.
Phil 2840.70　Renouvier, C.B. Les derniers entretiens, recueillis par Louis Prat. Paris, 1904.
Phil 2840.70.3　Renouvier, C.B. Les derniers entretiens, recueillis par Louis Prat. Paris, 1930.
Phil 2840.70.5　Renouvier, C.B. As ultimas conversações. Coimbra, 1930.
Phil 2840.75　Renouvier, C.B. Correspondance de Renouvier et Secrétan. Paris, 1910.
Phil 2840.80　Janssens, B. Le néo-criticisme de Charles Renouvier. Louvain, 1904.
Phil 2840.81　Séailles, G. Philosophie de Charles Renouvier. Paris, 1905.
Phil 2840.82　Arnal, A. La philosophie religieuse de C. Renouvier. Paris, 1907.
Phil 2840.83A　Archambault, P. Renouvier. Paris, 1911.
Phil 2840.83B　Archambault, P. Renouvier. Paris, 1911.
Phil 2840.84　Picard, Roger. La philosophie sociale de Renouvier. Paris, 1908.
Phil 2840.85　Bonnard, Edmond. Le criticisme de M. Renouvier. Thèse. Lausanne, 1890.
Phil 2840.86　Cornwell, I. Les principes du droit dans la philosophie de C. Renouvier. Thèse. Paris, 1922?
Phil 2840.87　Montpellier. Université. Inauguration d'un buste de C. Renouvier le 4 mai 1911. Montpellier, 1911.
Phil 2840.88　Foucher, Louis. La jeunesse de Renouvier et sa première philosophie. Paris, 1927.
Phil 2840.88.2　Foucher, Louis. La jeunesse de Renouvier et sa première philosophie. Thèse. Paris, 1927. 2 pam.
Phil 2840.89　Milhaud, G. La philosophie de Charles Renouvier. Paris, 1927.
Phil 2840.90　Mouy, P. L'idée de progrès dans la philosophie de Renouvier. Paris, 1927.
Phil 2840.90.2　Mouy, P. L'idée de progrès dans la philosophie de Renouvier. Thèse. Paris, 1927.
Phil 2840.91　Concato, E. Introduzione alla filosofia del Renouvier. Marostica Vicenza, 1921.
Phil 2840.93　Hansen, Valdemar. Charles Renouvier og frihedsproblemet. København, 1928.
Phil 2840.93.5　Hansen, Valdemar. Charles Renouvier; hans liv og hans tanker. København, 1962.
Phil 2840.94　Yang, Pao-San. La psychologie de l'intelligence chez Renouvier. Thèse. Paris, 1930.
Phil 2840.95　Galli, Gallo. Studi storico-critici sulla filosofia di C. Renouvier. v.1-2. Gubbio, 1933-35.
Phil 2840.96　Wang, Tsun-Sheng. Le phénoménisme de Charles Renouvier. Thèse. Lyon, 1935.
Phil 2840.97　Prat, Louis. Charles Renouvier. Ariège, 1937.
Phil 2840.98　Hamelin, Octave. Le système de Renouvier. Paris, 1927.
Phil 2840.99　Verneaux, Roger. Renouvier. Thèse. Paris, 1944.
Phil 2840.99.5　Verneaux, Roger. L'idealisme de Renouvier. Thèse. Paris, 1943.
Phil 2840.99.10　Verneaux, Roger. L'idealisme de Renouvier. Paris, 1945.

Phil 2840　History of philosophy - Local Modern philosophy - France - Individual philosophers - Renouvier, Charles - cont.

Phil 2840.99.15　Verneaux, Roger. Renouvier, disciple et critique de Kant. Paris, 1945.
Phil 2840.99.20　Verneaux, Roger. Esquisse d'une théorie de la connaissance. Paris, 1954.
Phil 2840.100　Méry, Marcel. La critique du christianisme chez Renouvier. Thèse. Paris, 1952. 2v.

Phil 2855　History of philosophy - Local Modern philosophy - France - Individual philosophers - Other R

Phil 2855.1.31　Royer-Tollard. Les fragments philosophiques. Paris, 1913.
Phil 2855.2.81　Ribot, Théodule. Théodule Ribot; choix de textes. Paris, 1913.
Phil 2855.2.82　Robot, Théodule. Théodule Ribot; choix de textes. Paris, 1917?
Phil 2855.2.95　Krauss, S. Théodule Ribots Psychologie. Jena, 1905.
Phil 2855.2.97　Dugas, L. Le philosophie Théodule Ribot. Paris, 1924.
Phil 2855.3.15　Ravaisson-Mollien, Félix. Testament philosophique et fragments. Paris, 1933.
Htn　Phil 2855.3.30*　Ravaisson-Mollien, Felix. Essai sur la métaphysique. Paris, 1846.
Phil 2855.3.81　Dopp, Joseph. Félix Ravaisson. Louvain, 1933.
Phil 2855.3.83　Cazeneuve, Jean. Ravaisson et les médecins animistes et vitalistes. Paris, 1957.
Htn　Phil 2855.4.30*　Rousseau, J.J. Principes du droit politique. Amsterdam, 1762.
Phil 2855.5.31　Richard, C. Esquisse d'une philosophie synthésiste. Paris, 1875.
Phil 2855.5.33　Richard, C. Réponse à Charles Renouvier au sujet de son appreciation de l'Esquisse d'une philosophie synthésiste. Paris, 1875.
Phil 2855.6.25　Reymond, A. Philosophie spiritualiste. Lausanne, 1942. 2v.
Phil 2855.6.80　Mélanges de théologie et de philosophie offerts à Arnold Reymond. Lausanne, 1940.
Phil 2855.6.82　Arnold Reymond. Torino, 1956.
Phil 2855.7.30　Robinet, Jean Baptiste René. De la nature. Amsterdam, 1761.
Phil 2855.7.32　Robinet, Jean Baptiste René. De la nature. v.1-2. Amsterdam, 1763.
Phil 2855.7.35　Sitkovskii, E. Filosofiia Zh. B. Robine, ocherk iz istorii frantsuzskogo materializma XVIII v. Moskva, 1936.
Phil 2855.8.80　Griffiths, David Albert. Jean Reynaud, encyclopéciste de l'époque romantique d'après sa correspondance inédite. Paris, 1965.
Phil 2855.9.30　Rosset, Clément. Le monde et ses remèdes. Paris, 1964.
Phil 2855.9.35　Rosset, Clément. Lettre sur les chimpanzés. Paris, 1966.
Phil 2855.10.30　Revertin, Henri. Les exigences de la vie de l'esprit. Neuchâtel, 1966.
Phil 2855.11.80　Philibert, Michel André Jean. Paul Ricoeur. Paris, 1971.

Phil 2880　History of philosophy - Local Modern philosophy - France - Individual philosophers - S

Phil 2880.1.25　Saint-Martin, L.C. NachgelasseneWerke. Münster, 1833.
Phil 2880.1.30　Saint-Martin, L.C. Des erreurs et de la vérité. Edimbourg, 1782.
Htn　Phil 2880.1.33*　Saint-Martin, L.C. Des erreurs et de la vérité. Edimbourg, 1775.
Phil 2880.1.35　Saint-Martin, L.C. Irrtümer und Wahrheit. Stuttgart, 1925. 2v.
Htn　Phil 2880.1.40*　Saint-Martin, L.C. L'homme de désir. Lyon, 1790.
Phil 2880.1.42　Saint-Martin, L.C. L'homme de désir. Londres, 1808.
Phil 2880.1.45　Saint-Martin, L.C. Tableau naturel des rapports qui existent entre Dieu, l'homme et l'univers. Paris, 1900.
Phil 2880.1.47　Saint-Martin, L.C. Tableau naturel des rapports qui existent entre Dieu, l'homme et l'univers. Rochefort-sur-Mer, 1946.
Htn　Phil 2880.1.50*　Saint-Martin, L.C. Vom Geist und Wesen der Dinge. v.1-2. Leipzig, 1812.
Phil 2880.1.55　Saint-Martin, L.C. Der Dienst desGeist-Menschen. Münster, 1858.
Phil 2880.1.60　Saint-Martin, L.C. Ecce homo. Lyon, 1959.
Phil 2880.1.65　Saint-Martin, L.C. Mon portrait historique et philosophique. Paris, 1961.
Phil 2880.1.79　Saint-Martin, L.C. La correspondance inédite de L.C. Saint-Martin dit le philosophe inconnu et Kirchberger. Amsterdam, 1862.
Phil 2880.1.80　Caro, E.M. Essai sur la vie et la doctrine de St. Martin. Paris, 1852.
Phil 2880.1.81　Franck, A. La philosophie mystique...Saint-Martin. Paris, 1866.
Phil 2880.1.82　Waite, Arthur E. The life of Louis C. de Saint-Martin. London, 1901.
Phil 2880.1.82.5　Waite, Arthur E. Saint-Martin; the French mystic. London, 1922.
Phil 2880.1.83　Claassen, J. Ludwig von Saint-Martin. Stuttgart, 1891.
Phil 2880.1.85　Amadou, R. Louis C. de Saint-Martin et le Martinisme. Paris, 1946.
Phil 2880.1.87　Matter, Jacques. Saint-Martin. 2. ed. Paris, 1862.
Phil 2880.1.88　Chateautien, G. Bibliographie du Martinisme. Lyon, 1939.
Phil 2880.1.90　Suite des erreurs et de la vérité. Salomonopolis, 1784.
Phil 2880.1.95　Amadou, R. De l'agent inconnu au philosophe inconnu. Paris, 1962.
Phil 2880.2.80　Secrétan, L. Charles Secrétan: sa vie et son oeuvre. Lausanne, 1911.
Phil 2880.2.82　Pillon, F. La philosophie de Charles Secrétan. Paris, 1898.
Phil 2880.2.85　Grin, Edmond. Les origines et l'évolution de la pensée de Charles Secrétan. Lausanne, 1930.
Phil 2880.2.90　Lehner, Felix. Freiheit in Wirtschaft, Staat und Religion: die Philosophie der Gesellschaft von Charles Secrétan. Zürich, 1967.
Phil 2880.2.92　Salmona, Bruno. Il pensiero di Charles Secrétan. Milano, 1968.
Phil 2880.4.80　Hérnon, Camille. La philosophie de M. Sully Prudhomme. Paris, 1907.
Phil 2880.5.90　Boudeau, J.M.L. Ernest Seillière. Paris, 1925.
Phil 2880.6　Sauvage-Jousse, P. Le métaverbe. Paris, 1928.
Phil 2880.7　Sourian, E. Avoir une âme. Paris, 1938.
Phil 2880.8.20A　Sartre, Jean Paul. The philosophy of Jean Paul Sartre. N.Y., 1965.
Phil 2880.8.20B　Sartre, Jean Paul. The philosophy of Jean Paul Sartre. N.Y., 1965.
Phil 2880.8.20C　Sartre, Jean Paul. The philosophy of Jean Paul Sartre. N.Y., 1965.
Phil 2880.8.30　Sartre, Jean Paul. The psychology of imagination. N.Y., 1948.

Phil 2880 History of philosophy - Local Modern philosophy - France - Individual philosophers - S - cont.

Phil 2880.8.33 Sartre, Jean Paul. The psychology of imagination. N.Y., 1961.
Phil 2880.8.35 Sartre, Jean Paul. Essays in aesthetics. N.Y., 1963.
Phil 2880.8.40A Sartre, Jean Paul. L'existentialisme est un humanisme. 5. ed. Paris, 1946.
Phil 2880.8.40B Sartre, Jean Paul. L'existentialisme est un humanisme. 5. ed. Paris, 1946.
Phil 2880.8.40C Sartre, Jean Paul. L'existentialisme est un humanisme. 5. ed. Paris, 1946.
Phil 2880.8.40D Sartre, Jean Paul. L'existentialisme est un humanisme. 5. ed. Paris, 1946.
Phil 2880.8.41.2 Sartre, Jean Paul. Existentialism and humanism. London, 1960.
Phil 2880.8.41.3 Sartre, Jean Paul. Existentialism and humanism. London, 1965.
Phil 2880.8.42A Sartre, Jean Paul. Existentialism. N.Y., 1947.
Phil 2880.8.42B Sartre, Jean Paul. Existentialism. N.Y., 1947.
Phil 2880.8.43 Sartre, Jean Paul. Ist der Existentialismus ein Humanismus? Zürich, 1947.
Phil 2880.8.44 Sartre, Jean Paul. Esquisse d'une théorie des émotions. Paris, 1939.
Phil 2880.8.45 Sartre, Jean Paul. Esquisse d'une théorie des émotions. Paris, 1963.
Phil 2880.8.46 Sartre, Jean Paul. The emotions, outline of a theory. N.Y., 1948.
Phil 2880.8.52 Sartre, Jean Paul. Search for a method. 1st American ed. N.Y., 1963.
Phil 2880.8.55 Sartre, Jean Paul. L'être et le néant. Paris, 1943[1946].
Phil 2880.8.56.2 Sartre, Jean Paul. Being and nothingness. N.Y., 1965.
Phil 2880.8.56.3A Sartre, Jean Paul. Being and nothingness. N.Y., 1956.
Phil 2880.8.56.3B Sartre, Jean Paul. Being and nothingness. N.Y., 1956.
Phil 2880.8.57A Sartre, Jean Paul. Critique de la raison dialectique. Paris, 1960.
Phil 2880.8.57B Sartre, Jean Paul. Critique de la raison dialectique. Paris, 1960.
Phil 2880.8.58 Sartre, Jean Paul. Marxismus und Existentialismus. Reinbeck, 1964.
Phil 2880.8.60 Sartre, Jean Paul. Existential psychoanalysis. N.Y., 1953.
Phil 2880.8.62 Sartre, Jean Paul. Das Sein und das Nichts. Hamburg, 1952.
Phil 2880.8.64A Sartre, Jean Paul. The transcendence of the ego. N.Y., 1957.
Phil 2880.8.64.5 Sartre, Jean Paul. La transcendance de l'égo. Paris, 1965.
Phil 2880.8.65 Sartre, Jean Paul. Existentialism and human emotions. N.Y., 1957.
Phil 2880.8.70 Sartre, Jean Paul. The communists and peace, with a reply to Claude Lefort. N.Y., 1968.
Phil 2880.8.80 Campbell, Robert. Jean Paul Sartre; ou une littérature philosophique. Paris, 1945.
Phil 2880.8.81 Campbell, Robert. Jean Paul Sartre. Paris, 1946.
Phil 2880.8.82 Troisfontaines, Roger. Le choix de Jean Paul Sartre. Paris, 1945.
Phil 2880.8.82.2 Troisfontaines, Roger. Le choix de Jean Paul Sartre. 2. éd. Paris, 1946.
Phil 2880.8.86 Lefevre, Luc J. L'existentialiste est-il un philosophe? Paris, 1946. 2v.
Phil 2880.8.88 Boutang, P. Sartre, est-il un possédé? Paris, 1947.
Phil 2880.8.88.5 Boutang, P. Sartre, est-il un possédé? Paris, 1950.
Phil 2880.8.90 Juin, Hubert. Jean-Paul Sartre. Photoreproduction. Bruxelles, 1946.
Phil 2880.8.92 Henri-Hoyen, E. Sartre contre l'homme. Genève, 1947.
Phil 2880.8.94 Dauphin, E.J. Ekecrate; dialogue sur l'existentialisme. Montpellier, 1947.
Phil 2880.8.96 Bligbeder, Marc. L'homme Sartre. Paris? 1947.
Phil 2880.8.98 Jeanson, Francis. Le problème moral et la pensée de Sartre. Paris, 1947.
Phil 2880.8.99 Jeanson, Francis. Le problème moral et la pensée de Sartre. Paris, 1965.
Phil 2880.8.100 Fatone, V. El existencialismo y la libertad readoro. 1. ed. Buenos Aires, 1948.
Phil 2880.8.100.2 Fatone, V. El existencialismo y la libertad readoro. 2. ed. Buenos Aires, 1949.
Phil 2880.8.101 Manser, Anthony Richards. Sartre: a philosophic study. London, 1966.
Phil 2880.8.102 Paissac, H. Le dieu de Sartre. Grenoble, 1950.
Phil 2880.8.104 Stefoni, M. La libertà esistenziale in Jean Paul Sartre. Milano, 1949.
Phil 2880.8.106 Prucke, B. L'homme de Sartre. Grenoble, 1949.
Phil 2880.8.110 Holz, H.H. Jean Paul Sartre. Meisenheim, 1951.
Phil 2880.8.112 Gentiloni Silverj, F. Jean Paul Sartre contro la speranza. Roma, 1952.
Phil 2880.8.114 Streller, Justus. Zur Freiheit verurteilt. Hamburg, 1952.
Phil 2880.8.115 Streller, Justus. Jean Paul Sartre. N.Y., 1960.
Phil 2880.8.116 Stern, Alfred. Sartre. N.Y., 1953.
Phil 2880.8.116.2 Stern, Alfred. Sartre, his philosophy and existential psychoanalysis. 2.ed. N.Y., 1967.
Phil 2880.8.118 Desan, Wilfred. The tragic finale. Cambridge, Mass., 1954.
Phil 2880.8.120 Palumbo, Giovanni. La filosofia esistenziale di Jean Paul Sartre. Palermo, 1953.
Phil 2880.8.122 Natanson, M. A critique of Jean Paul Sartre's ontology. Lincoln, 1951.
Phil 2880.8.124 Quiles, Ismael. Sartre y su existencialismo. 2. ed. Buenos Aires, 1952.
Phil 2880.8.126 Naville, Pierre. L'intellectual communiste. Paris, 1956.
Phil 2880.8.128 Champigny, Robert. Stages on Sartre's way. Bloomington, 1959.
Phil 2880.8.130 Moeller, Joseph. Absurdes sein? Stuttgart, 1959.
Phil 2880.8.132 Greene, Norman. Jean Paul Sartre. Ann Arbor, 1960.
Phil 2880.8.134 Otto, Maria. Rene und Freiheit. Freiburg, 1961.
Phil 2880.8.136 Salvan, Jacques L. To be and not to be. Detroit, 1962.
Phil 2880.8.138 Kaelin, Eugene. An existentialist aesthetic. Madison, 1962.
Phil 2880.8.140 Hartmann, Klaus. Grundzüge der Ontologie Sartres in ihrem Verhältnis zu Hegels Logik. Berlin, 1963.
Phil 2880.8.142 Garaudy, Roger. Questions à Jean Paul Sartre. Paris, 1960.
Phil 2880.8.143 Laing, R.D. Reason and violence. London, 1964.
Phil 2880.8.145 Houbart, Jacques. Un père déuaturé. Paris, 1964.
Phil 2880.8.150 Fell, Joseph P. Emotion in thought of Sartre. N.Y., 1965.
Phil 2880.8.154 Jolivet, Régis. Sartre: the theology of the absurd. Westminster, 1967.
Phil 2880.8.155 Jolivet, Régis. Sartre, ou La théologie de l'absurde. Paris, 1965.

Phil 2880 History of philosophy - Local Modern philosophy - France - Individual philosophers - S - cont.

Phil 2880.8.156 Hana, Ghanem Georges. Freiheit und Person. München, 1965.
Phil 2880.8.157 Kohut, Karl. Was ist Literatur? Marburg, 1965.
Phil 2880.8.160 Hartmann, Klaus. Sartres Sozialphilosophie. Berlin, 1966.
Phil 2880.8.162 Niel, André. Jean-Paul Sartre. Paris, 1966.
Phil 2880.8.165 Audry, Colette. Sartre et la réalité humaine. Paris, 1966.
Phil 2880.8.170 Sotelo, Ignacio. Das Problem der dialektischen Vernunft bei Jean Paul Sartre. Köln, 1965.
Phil 2880.8.175 Goldstein, Walter. Jean Paul Sartre und Martin Buber. Jerusalem, 1965.
Phil 2880.8.180 Patte, Daniel. L'athéisme d'un chrétien; ou Un chrétien à l'écoute de Sartre. Paris, 1965.
Phil 2880.8.185 Zehm, Günter Albrecht. Historische Vernunft und direkte Aktion. Stuttgart, 1964.
Phil 2880.8.190 Nauta, Lolle Wibe. Jean Paul Sartre. Door, 1966.
Phil 2880.8.195 Jeason, Francis. Textes de Jean Paul Sartre. Paris, 1966.
Phil 2880.8.200 Borrello, Oreste. Studi su Sartre. Bologna, 1964.
Phil 2880.8.205 Tordai, Záder. Existance et realité polémique avec certaines thèses fondamentales dé "L'être et le néant" de Sartre. Budapest, 1967.
Phil 2880.8.210 Chiodi, Pietro. Sartre il marxismo. 1. ed. Milano, 1965.
Phil 2880.8.215 Lafarge, René. La philosophie de Jean Paul Sartre. Toulouse, 1967.
Phil 2880.8.216 Lafarge, René. Jean-Paul Sartre: his philosophy. Notre Dame, 1970.
Phil 2880.8.220 Warnock, Mary. Existentialist ethics. London, 1967.
Phil 2880.8.225 Gallo, Blas Raúl. Jean Paul Sartre y el marxismo. Buenos Aires, 1966.
Phil 2880.8.230 Herra, Rafael Angel. Sartre y los prolegómenos a la antropología. Ciudad Universitaria, 1968.
Phil 2880.8.235 Gahamanyi, Célestin. La conception de la liberté chez Jean-Paul Sartre et chez Maurice Merleau-Ponty. Fribourg? 1967.
Phil 2880.8.240 Struyker Boudier, C.E.M. Jean Paul Sartre. Tielt, 1967.
Phil 2880.8.245 Sheridan, James Francis. Sartre; the radical conversion. Athens, Ohio, 1969.
Phil 2880.8.250 Bauer, George Howard. Sartre and the artist. Chicago, 1969.
Phil 2880.8.255 Kuznetsov, Vitalii N. Zhan-Pol Sartr i ekzistentsializm. Moskva, 1969.
Phil 2880.8.260 Papone, Annagrazia. Esistenza e corporeità in Sartre. Firenze, 1969.
Phil 2880.8.265 Rovatti, Pier Aldo. Che cosa ha veramente detto Sartre. Roma, 1969.
Phil 2880.8.270 Suhl, Benjamin. Jean-Paul Sartre: the philosopher as a literary critic. N.Y., 1970.
Phil 2880.8.275 Aron, Raymond. Marxism and the existentialists. N.Y., 1970.
Phil 2880.8.282 Richter, Liselotte. Jean-Paul Sartre. N.Y., 1970.
Phil 2880.8.287 McMahon, Joseph H. Humans being; the world of Jean-Paul Sartre. Chicago, 1971.
Phil 2880.8.290 Schwarz, Theodor. Jean-Paul Sartres "Kritik der dialektischen Vernunft". Berlin, 1967.
Phil 2880.8.295 Cavaciuti, Santino. L'ontologia di Jean Paul Sartre. Milano, 1969.
Phil 2880.8.300 Pagano, Giacoma Maria. Sartre e la dialettica. Napoli, 1970.
Phil 2880.8.305 Fé, Franco. Sartre e il comunismo. Firenze, 1970.
Phil 2880.13.100 Scheurer, Pierre. An interior metaphysics. Weston, Mass., 1966.

Phil 2885 History of philosophy - Local Modern philosophy - France - Individual philosophers - Taine, Hippolyte

NEDL Phil 2885.30 Taine, Hippolyte Adolphe. De l'intelligence. Paris, 1878. 2v.
Phil 2885.30.5 Taine, Hippolyte Adolphe. De l'intelligence. 2. éd. v.1-2. Paris, 1870. 2v.
Phil 2885.30.8 Taine, Hippolyte Adolphe. De l'intelligence. 13. éd. Paris, 1914. 2v.
Phil 2885.31 Taine, Hippolyte Adolphe. On intelligence. pt. 1-2. London, 1871.
NEDL Phil 2885.31.1 Taine, Hippolyte Adolphe. On Intelligence. N.Y., 1871.
Phil 2885.31.3 Taine, Hippolyte Adolphe. On intelligence. N.Y., 1875. 2v.
Phil 2885.31.6 Taine, Hippolyte Adolphe. On intelligence. N.Y., 1889. 2v.
Phil 2885.31.8 Taine, Hippolyte Adolphe. Der Verstand. v.1-2. Bonn, 1880.
Phil 2885.32 Taine, Hippolyte Adolphe. Lectures on art. 1st series. N.Y., 1875.
Phil 2885.32.5A Taine, Hippolyte Adolphe. Lectures on art. 2nd series. N.Y., 1889.
Phil 2885.32.5C Taine, Hippolyte Adolphe. Lectures on art. 2nd series. N.Y., 1889.
Phil 2885.33 Taine, Hippolyte Adolphe. De l'ideal dans l'art. Paris, 1867.
Phil 2885.34A Taine, Hippolyte Adolphe. Philosophie de l'art. Paris, 1881. 2v.
Phil 2885.34B Taine, Hippolyte Adolphe. Philosophie de l'art. v.1. Paris, 1881.
Phil 2885.34.5 Taine, Hippolyte Adolphe. Philosophie de l'art. Paris, 1865.
Phil 2885.34.8 Taine, Hippolyte Adolphe. Philosophie de l'art. 8. éd. Paris, 1895?
Phil 2885.34.10 Taine, Hippolyte Adolphe. The philosophy of art. Photoreproduction. 2. ed. N.Y., 1873.
Phil 2885.34.12 Taine, Hippolyte Adolphe. The philosophy of art. Photoreproduction. London, 1867.
Phil 2885.34.14 Taine, Hippolyte Adolphe. The ideal in art. N.Y., 1874.
Phil 2885.34.16A Taine, Hippolyte Adolphe. Lectures on art. 3d ed. 1st series. N.Y., 1875. 2v.
Phil 2885.34.16B Taine, Hippolyte Adolphe. Lectures on art. 3d ed. 2nd series. N.Y., 1875. 2v.
Phil 2885.80 Barzellotti, G. Hippolito Taine. Roma, 1895.
Phil 2885.80.5 Barzellotti, G. La philosophie de H. Taine. Paris, 1900.
Phil 2885.81 Nève, P. La philosophie de Taine. Paris, 1908.
Phil 2885.82 Dutoit, E. Die Theorie des Milieu. Bern, 1899.
Phil 2885.83 Margerie, Amédée de. H. Taine. Paris, 1894.
Phil 2885.84 Lacombe, Paul. Taine historien et sociologue. Paris, 1909.
Phil 2885.84.5 Lacombe, Paul. La psychologie des individus et des societés chez Taine. Paris, 1906.
Phil 2885.85 Empart, L. L'empirisme et le naturalisme contemporain. Paris, 1870.
Phil 2885.86 Engel, Otto. Der Einfluss Hegels auf die Bildung der Gedankenwelt Hippolyte Taines. Stuttgart, 1920.

Phil 2885   History of philosophy - Local Modern philosophy - France - Individual philosophers - Taine, Hippolyte - cont.

Phil 2885.88   Gibaudan, R. Les idées sociales de Taine. Paris, 1928.
Phil 2885.89   Chevrillon, A. Taine; formation de sa pensée. Paris, 1932.
Phil 2885.90   Schmidt, O.A. Hippolyte Taines Theorie. Halle, 1936.
Phil 2885.100   Salomon, Michel. H. Taine. Paris, 1908.
Phil 2885.105   Schlaf, Johannes. Kritik der Taineschen Kunsttheorie. Wien, 1906.
Phil 2885.110   Zeitler, Julius. Die Kunstphilosophie von H.A. Taine. Leipzig, 1901.
Phil 2885.111   Begouëm, Henry. Quelques souvenirs sur H. Taine. Toulouse, 1923.
Phil 2885.112   Krzemień-Ojak, Sław. Taine. Wyd. 1. Warszawa, 1966.
Phil 2885.114   Mongardini, Carlo. Storia e sociologia nell'opera di H. Taine. Milano, 1965.

Phil 2905   History of philosophy - Local Modern philosophy - France - Individual philosophers - Other T

Phil 2905.1.1   Jarque i Jutglar, Joan E. Bibliographie générale des oeuvres et articles sur Pierre Teilhard de Chardin parus jusqu'a fin décembre 1969. Fribourg, 1970.
Phil 2905.1.2   Almago, Romano S. A basic Teilhard-bibliography, 1955 - Apr. 1968. N.Y., 1968.
Phil 2905.1.5   Teilhard de Chardin, Pierre. Oeuvres. Paris, 1956- 10v.
Phil 2905.1.7   Teilhard de Chardin, Pierre. L'oeuvre scientifique. Olten, 1971.
Phil 2905.1.10   Teilhard de Chardin, Pierre. The phenomenon of man. N.Y., 1959.
Phil 2905.1.12   Teilhard de Chardin, Pierre. The phenomonon of man. N.Y., 1965.
Phil 2905.1.15   Teilhard de Chardin, Pierre. The divine milieu. 1st ed. N.Y., 1960.
Phil 2905.1.18   Teilhard de Chardin, Pierre. Human energy. London, 1969.
Phil 2905.1.20   Cahiers Pierre Teilhard de Chardin. Paris. 1-5+ 6v.
Phil 2905.1.25   Teilhard de Chardin, Pierre. Sur le bonheur. Paris, 1966.
Phil 2905.1.27   Teilhard de Chardin, Pierre. Writings in time of war. London, 1968.
Phil 2905.1.28   Teilhard de Chardin, Pierre. Letters to two friends, 1926-1952. N.Y., 1968.
Phil 2905.1.29   Teilhard de Chardin, Pierre. Lettres à Léontine Zanta. Bruges, 1965.
Phil 2905.1.29.5   Teilhard de Chardin, Pierre. Letters to Léontine Zanta. London, 1969.
Phil 2905.1.30   Teilhard de Chardin, Pierre. Letters from a traveler. London, 1962.
Phil 2905.1.33   Teilhard de Chardin, Pierre. Album. London, 1966.
Phil 2905.1.35   Teilhard de Chardin, Pierre. Genèse d'une pensée. Paris, 1961.
Phil 2905.1.36   Teilhard de Chardin, Pierre. The making of a mind. London, 1965.
Phil 2905.1.40   Teilhard de Chardin, Pierre. Hymne de l'universe. Paris, 1961.
Phil 2905.1.42   Teilhard de Chardin, Pierre. Hymn of the universe. London, 1965.
Phil 2905.1.45   Teilhard de Chardin, Pierre. La place de l'homme dans la nature. Paris, 1962.
Phil 2905.1.48   Teilhard de Chardin, Pierre. The future of man. 1st American ed. N.Y., 1964.
Phil 2905.1.50   Teilhard de Chardin, Pierre. The future of man. London, 1964.
Phil 2905.1.55   Teilhard de Chardin, Pierre. Lettres d'Egypte, 1905-1908. Aubier, 1963.
Phil 2905.1.60   Teilhard de Chardin, Pierre. Letters from Egypt. N.Y., 1965.
Phil 2905.1.63   Teilhard de Chardin, Pierre. Science and Christ. London, 1968.
Phil 2905.1.65   Teilhard de Chardin, Pierre. Building the earth. 1st American ed. Wilkes-Barre, Pa., 1965.
Phil 2905.1.67   Teilhard de Chardin, Pierre. Building the earth. London, 1965.
Phil 2905.1.69   Teilhard de Chardin, Pierre. Je m'explique. Paris, 1966.
Phil 2905.1.69.1   Teilhard de Chardin, Pierre. Let me explain. London, 1970.
Phil 2905.1.70   Teilhard de Chardin, Pierre. La messe sur le monde. Paris, 1965.
Phil 2905.1.73   Teilhard de Chardin, Pierre. Lettres d'Hastings et de Paris, 1908-1914. Paris, 1965.
Phil 2905.1.80   Cristiani, Léon. La vie et l'âme de Teilhard de Chardin. Paris, 1957.
Phil 2905.1.82   Cristiani, Léon. Pierre Teilhard de Chardin. London, 1960.
Phil 2905.1.85   Teldy-Naim, Robert. Faut-il brûler Teilhard de Chardin? Paris, 1959.
Phil 2905.1.90   Leroy, Pierre. Pierre Teilhard de Chardin tel que je l'ai connu. Paris, 1958.
Phil 2905.1.95   Chauchard, Paul. L'être humain selon Teilhard de Chardin. Paris, 1959.
Phil 2905.1.96   Chauchard, Paul. Teilhard de Chardin. Paris, 1964?
Phil 2905.1.97   Chauchard, Paul. La pensée scientifique de Teilhard. Paris, 1965.
Phil 2905.1.100   Talhonët, Jean de. Le lyrisme et la mystique dans les oeuvres du Pierre Teilhard de Chardin. Paris, 1959.
Phil 2905.1.105   Wildiers, N.M. Het wereldbeeld van Pierre Teilhard de Chardin. 2. druk. Antwerpen, 1960.
Phil 2905.1.108   Martin-Deslias, Noël. Un aventurier de l'esprit, Pierre Teilhard de Chardin. Paris, 1963.
Phil 2905.1.110   Kahane, E. Teilhard de Chardin. Paris, 1960.
Phil 2905.1.115   Delfgaauw, B.M.I. Teilhard de Chardin. Baarn, 1961.
Phil 2905.1.115.5   Delfgaauw, B.M.I. Evolution; the theory of Teilhard de Chardin. London, 1969.
Phil 2905.1.120   Rabut, Oliver A. Dialogue with Teilhard de Chardin. London, 1961.
Phil 2905.1.125   Rabut, Oliver A. Teilhard de Chardin. N.Y., 1961.
Phil 2905.1.130   Wildiers, N.M. Teilhard de Chardin. Paris, 1961.
Phil 2905.1.130.5   Wildiers, N.M. An introduction to Teilhard de Chardin. 1st American ed. N.Y., 1968.
Phil 2905.1.140   Kopp, Josef Vital. Entstehung und Zukunft des Menschen. Luzern, 1961.
Phil 2905.1.145   Thérines, Jacques de. Quodlibets. Paris, 1958.
Phil 2905.1.150   Bailly, Thomas de. Quodlibets. Paris, 1960.
Phil 2905.1.155   Magloire, George. Présence de Pierre Teilhard de Chardin. Paris, 1961.
Phil 2905.1.160   Blanchard, Julien P. Méthode et principes du père Teilhard de Chardin. Paris, 1961.
Phil 2905.1.165   Grenet, Paul. Teilhard de Chardin. Paris, 1961.
Phil 2905.1.170   Cuénot, Claude. Teilhard de Chardin. Paris, 1962.

Phil 2905   History of philosophy - Local Modern philosophy - France - Individual philosophers - Other T - cont.

Phil 2905.1.172   Cuénot, Claude. Teilhard de Chardin. London, 1965.
Phil 2905.1.173   Cuénot, Claude. Science and faith in Teilhard de Chardin. London, 1967.
Phil 2905.1.175   Crespy, Georges. La pensée théologique de Teilhard de Chardin. Paris, 1961.
Phil 2905.1.176   Crespy, Georges. De la science à la théologie. Neuchâtel, 1965.
Phil 2905.1.177   Crespy, Georges. From science to theology. Nashville, 1968.
Phil 2905.1.180   Lubac, Henri de. La pensée religieuse du père Teilhard de Chardin. Paris, 1962.
Phil 2905.1.180.5   Lubac, Henri de. La prière du père Teilhard de Chardin. Paris, 1964.
Phil 2905.1.180.5.2   Lubac, Henri de. La prière du père Teilhard de Chardin. Paris, 1968.
Phil 2905.1.180.6   Lubac, Henri de. The faith of Teilhard de Chardin. London, 1965.
Phil 2905.1.180.7   Lubac, Henri de. L'éternel féminin, étude sur un texte du père Teilhard de Chardin. Paris, 1968.
Phil 2905.1.185   Raven, Charles. Teilhard de Chardin. London, 1962.
Phil 2905.1.190   Carnets Teilhard. Paris. 1-18 13v.
Phil 2905.1.195   Cuénot, Claude. Lexique Teilhard de Chardin. Paris, 1963.
Phil 2905.1.195.5   Cuénot, Claude. Nouveau lexique Teilhard de Chardin. Paris, 1968.
Phil 2905.1.196   Cuénot, Claude. Teilhard de Chardin et la pensée catholique: colloque de Venise sous les auspices de Pax Romana. Paris, 1965.
Phil 2905.1.196.5   Cuénot, Claude. Teilhard de Chardin e il pensiero cattolico. Firenze, 1966.
Phil 2905.1.200   Barthélemy-Madaule, Madeleine. Bergson et Teilhard de Chardin. Paris, 1963.
Phil 2905.1.200.5   Barthélemy-Madaule, Madeleine. La personne et le drame humain chez Teilhard de Chardin. Paris, 1967.
Phil 2905.1.205   Francoeur, Robert. The world of Teilhard. Baltimore, 1961.
Phil 2905.1.210   Onimus, J. Pierre Teilhard de Chardin. Paris, 1963.
Phil 2905.1.215   Pour comprendre Teilhard. Paris, 1962.
Phil 2905.1.220   Russo, F. Essais sur Teilhard de Chardin. Paris, 1962.
Phil 2905.1.225   Revue Teilhard de Chardin. Bruxelles. 1,1960+ 3v.
Phil 2905.1.230   Face au prophétisme de Teilhard de Chardin. Bruxelles, 1963.
Phil 2905.1.235   Charbonneau, B. Teilhard de Chardin, prophète d'un âge totalitaire. Paris, 1963.
Phil 2905.1.240   Teilhard de Chardin. Paris, 1963?
Phil 2905.1.245   Duroux, P.E. La prévie, la réconciliation de la science et la foi. Lyon, 1961.
Phil 2905.1.250   Hengstenberg, H.E. Evolution und Schöffung. München, 1963.
Phil 2905.1.255   Viallet, François A. L'univers personnel de Teilhard. Paris, 1955-61. 2v.
Phil 2905.1.257   Viallet, François A. Teilhard de Chardin. Nurnberg, 1963. 2v.
Phil 2905.1.260   Tresmoutant, Claude. Introduction à la pensée de Teilhard de Chardin. Paris, 1962.
Phil 2905.1.263   Tresmoutant, Claude. Introduccion al pensamiento de Teilhard de Chardin. 2. ed. Madrid, 1960.
Phil 2905.1.265   Smulders, P.F. Het visioen van Teilhard de Chardin. Brugge, 1962.
Phil 2905.1.266   Smulders, P.F. La vision de Teilhard de Chardin. Paris, 1964.
Phil 2905.1.267   Smulders, P.F. Theologie und Evolution. Essen, 1963.
Phil 2905.1.270   Mueller, Armin. Das naturphilosophische Werk Teilhard de Chardins. Freiburg, 1964.
Phil 2905.1.275   Madaule, J. Initiation à Teilhard de Chardin. Paris, 1963.
Phil 2905.1.280   Vigorelli, G. Il gesuita proibito. Milano, 1963.
Phil 2905.1.285   Vernet, M. La grande illusion de Teilhard de Chardin. Paris, 1964.
Phil 2905.1.290   Braybrook, N. Teilhard de Chardin. N.Y., 1964.
Phil 2905.1.295   Terra, Helmut de. Memories of Teilhard de Chardin. London, 1964.
Phil 2905.1.296   Terra, Helmut de. Perspektiven Teilhard de Chardins. München, 1966.
Phil 2905.1.300   Carles, Jules. Teilhard de Chardin. Paris, 1964.
Phil 2905.1.305   Barjon, L. La carrière scientifique de Pierre Teilhard de Chardin. Monaco, 1964.
Phil 2905.1.310   Magloire, G. Teilhard de Chardin. Paris, 1964.
Phil 2905.1.315   Colomer, Eusebi. Pierre Teilhard de Chardin. Barcelona, 1961.
Phil 2905.1.320   Périgord, Monique. L'esthétique de Teilhard. Paris, 1965.
Phil 2905.1.325   Barbour, George Brown. In the field with Teilhard de Chardin. N.Y., 1965.
Phil 2905.1.330   Barral, Louis Marie. Éléments du bâti scientifique Teilhardien. Monaco, 1964.
Phil 2905.1.335   Ormea, Ferdinando. Pierre Teilhard de Chardin. 2. ed. Torino, 1964.
Phil 2905.1.340   Chauchard, Paul. Man and cosmos. N.Y., 1965.
Phil 2905.1.345   Philippe de la Trinité, Father. Rome et Teilhard de Chardin. Paris, 1964.
Phil 2905.1.350   Teilhard de Chardin, Pierre. Écrits du temps de la guerre, 1916-1919. Paris, 1965.
Phil 2905.1.355   Martinazzo, Eusebio. Teilhard de Chardin. Romae, 1965.
Phil 2905.1.360   Corvez, Maurice. De la science à la foi. Tours, 1964.
Phil 2905.1.365   Rideau, Émile. La pensée du Père Teilhard de Chardin. Paris, 1965.
Phil 2905.1.366   Rideau, Émile. Teilhard de Chardin; a guide to his thought. London, 1967.
Phil 2905.1.370   Polgár, Ladislaus. Internationale Teilhard-Bibliographie. Freiburg, 1965.
Phil 2905.1.375   Murray, Michael Hunt. The thought of Teilhard de Chardin. N.Y., 1966.
Phil 2905.1.377   Mooney, Christopher F. Teilhard de Chardin et le mystère du Christ. Paris, 1966.
Phil 2905.1.380   Mooney, Christopher F. Teilhard de Chardin and the mystery of Christ. London, 1966.
Phil 2905.1.385   Luyten, Norbert Alfons. Teilhard de Chardin. Fribourg, 1965.
Phil 2905.1.390   Truhlar, Karel Vladimir. Teilhard und Solowjew. Freiburg, 1966.
Phil 2905.1.395   Monestier, André. Teilhard ou Marx? Paris, 1965.
Phil 2905.1.400   Frenaud, Georges. Pensée philosophique et religieuse du père Teilhard de Chardin. Le Chesnay, 1965.
Phil 2905.1.405   Calvet, Jean. Réflexions sur le "Phénomène humain" de Pierre Teilhard de Chardin. Paris, 1966.

Classified Listing

Phil 2905 History of philosophy - Local Modern philosophy - France - Individual philosophers - Other T - cont.

Phil 2905.1.410   Lubac, Henri de. Teilhard, missionnaire et apologiste. Toulouse, 1966.

Phil 2905.1.415   Decoux, René. L'énergie dans la cosmogenèse de Pierre Teilhard de Chardin. Cran-Annecy, 1964?

Phil 2905.1.420   Hugedé, Norbert. Le cas Teilhard de Chardin. Paris, 1966.

Phil 2905.1.425   Vernet, Maurice. Vernet contre Teilhard de Chardin. Paris, 1965.

Phil 2905.1.430   Coffy, Robert. Teilhard de Chardin et le socialisme. Lyon, 1966.

Phil 2905.1.435   Briones Toledo, Hernán. Pierre Teilhard de Chardin y otros ensayos. Santiago de Chile, 1966.

Phil 2905.1.440   Scaltriti, Giacinto. Teilhard de Chardin tra il mito e l'eresia. Roma, 1964.

Phil 2905.1.445   Teilhard de Chardin et l'unité du genre humain. Lisboa, 1965.

Phil 2905.1.450   Mallemann, René de. Notice sur la vie et les travaux de Pierre Teilhard de Chardin. Paris, 1962.

Phil 2905.1.455   Speaight, Robert. Teilhard de Chardin: a biography. London, 1967.

Phil 2905.1.456   Speaight, Robert. Teilhard de Chardin: re-mythologization. Chicago, 1970.

Phil 2905.1.460   Guerini, Edmund W. Evolution in the afterlife. 1st ed. N.Y., 1967.

Phil 2905.1.465   Faricy, Robert L. Teilhard de Chardin's theology of the Christian in the world. N.Y., 1967.

Phil 2905.1.470   Soucy, Claude. Pensée logique et pensée politique chez Teilhard de Chardin. Paris, 1967.

Phil 2905.1.475   Teilhard study library. London. 2,1967+ 4v.

Phil 2905.1.480   Solages, Bruno de. Teilhard de Chardin, témoignage et étude sur le développement de la pensée. Toulouse, 1967.

Phil 2905.1.485   Dussault, Gabriel. Panthéisme, action, oméga chez Teilhard de Chardin. Bruges, 1967.

Phil 2905.1.490   The Teilhard review. London. 1,1966+

Phil 2905.1.495   Schmitz-Moormann, Karl. Das Weltbild Teilhard de Chardins. Köln, 1966.

Phil 2905.1.500   Rideau, Émile. Teilhard, oui ou non? Paris, 1967.

Phil 2905.1.510   Mermod, Denis. La morale chez Teilhard. Paris, 1967.

Phil 2905.1.515   Mortier, Jeanne M. Avec Teilhard de Chardin, vues ardentes. Paris, 1967.

Phil 2905.1.520   Tilloy, Alain. Teilhard de Chardin, père de l'Église ou pseudo-prophète? Saint Cénère, 1968.

Phil 2905.1.525   Dimensions of the future; the spirituality of Teilhard de Chardin. Washington, 1968.

Phil 2905.1.530   Rivière, Claude. En Chine avec Teilhard. Paris, 1968.

Phil 2905.1.535   Trinité, Phillipe de la. Teilhard de Chardin. Paris, 1968.

Phil 2905.1.540   Rizzo, Enrico. La problematica di Teilhard de Chardin. Bologna, 1965.

Phil 2905.1.545   Tanner, Henri. Le grain de sénevé. De la science à la religion avec Teilhard de Chardin. Saint-Maurice, 1967.

Phil 2905.1.550   Teilhard de Chardin e a convergência das civilizações e das ciências. Lisboa, 1964?

Phil 2905.1.555   Vidoni, Egidio. L'individuo e il collettivo nella durata secondo Pierre Teilhard de Chardin. Milano, 1966[1965].

Phil 2905.1.560   Kraft, Ralph Wayne. The relevance of Teilhard. Notre Dame, 1968.

Phil 2905.1.565   Gosztonyi, Alexander. Der Mensch und die Evolution; Teilhard de Chardins philosophische Anthropologie. München, 1968.

Phil 2905.1.570   Reinhard, Edmond. Teilhard de Chardin. Pähl, 1966.

Phil 2905.1.575   Hemkben, Johannes. Pierre Teilhard de Chardin in Selbstzeugnissen und Bilddokumenten. Reinbek, 1966.

Phil 2905.1.580   Klohr, Olof. Beiträge zur Deutung von Teilhard de Chardin. Berlin, 1966.

Phil 2905.1.585   Mathieu, Pierre Louis. La pensée politique et économique de Teilhard de Chardin. Paris, 1969.

Phil 2905.1.590   Combes, André. Teilhard de Chardin et la sainte évolution. Paris, 1969.

Phil 2905.1.595   Gray, Donald P. The one and the many. N.Y., 1969.

Phil 2905.1.600   Cargas, Harry J. The continuous flame. St. Louis, 1969?

Phil 2905.1.605   Teilhard reassessed: a symposium of critical studies in the thought of Père Teilhard de Chardin attempting an evaluation of his place in contemporary Christian thinking. London, 1970.

Phil 2905.1.610   Bravo, Francisco. Teilhard de Chardin, su concepción de la historia. 1. ed. Barcelona, 1970.

Phil 2905.1.615   Imbrighi, Gastone. La paleogeografia in Teilhard de Chardin. L'Aguila, 1967.

Phil 2905.1.620   Rétif, André. Teilhard et l'évangélisation des temps nouveaux. Paris, 1970.

Phil 2905.1.625   Revol, Enrique Luis. Símbolo y evolución humana. Cordoba, 1970.

Phil 2905.1.630   Jarque i Jutglar, Joan E. Foi en l'homme; l'apologétique de Teilhard de Chardin. Paris, 1969.

Phil 2905.1.635   Babosov, Evgenii M. Teiiardizm. Minsk, 1970.

Phil 2905.1.640   Straniero, Giorgio. L'ontologia fenomenologica di Teilhard de Chardin. Milano, 1969.

Phil 2905.1.645   Grupo Español de Trabajo Teilhard de Chardin. En torno a Teilhard. Madrid, 1969.

Phil 2905.1.650   Canteni, Agostino. Il problema Teilhard de Chardin. Milano, 1969.

Phil 2905.1.655   Lecourt, Jacques. Cari Gustav Jung et Pierre Teilhard de Chardin. Goële, 1970.

Phil 2905.1.660   Philippe de la Trinité, Father. Pour et contre Teilhard de Chardin, penseur religieux. Saint-Cénéré, 1970.

Phil 2905.1.665   Nogare, Pedro Dalle. Pessoa e amor segundo Teilhard de Chardin. São Paulo, 1970.

Phil 2905.1.670   Ouince, René d'. Un prophète en procès. Paris, 1970. 2v.

Phil 2905.1.675   Goerres, Ida F.C. Teilhard de Chardin als Christ und als Mensch. Wiesbaden, 1971.

Phil 2905.1.680   Deckers, Marie Christine. Le vocabulaire de Teilhard de Chardin. Gembloux, 1968.

Phil 2905.2.30   Tonguèdec, J. La philosophie de la nature. v. 1-2. Paris, 1956. 4v.

Phil 2905.3.80   Chabanis, Christian. Gustave Thibon, témoin de la lumière. Paris, 1967.

2915 History of philosophy - Local Modern philosophy - France - Individual hilosophers - Voltaire, François

Phil 2915.30*   Voltaire, F.M.A. de. Le philosophe ignorant. n.p., 1766.

Phil 2915.31   Voltaire, F.M.A. de. The ignorant philosopher. N.Y., 185-?

Phil 2915.33   Voltaire, F.M.A. de. The ignorant philosopher. Glasgow, 1767.

Phil 2915 History of philosophy - Local Modern philosophy - France - Individual philosophers - Voltaire, François - cont.

Phil 2915.35   Voltaire, F.M.A. de. The ignorant philosopher. London, 1779.

Phil 2915.40   Voltaire, F.M.A. de. La philosophie. Paris, 1848.

Htn   Phil 2915.42*   Voltaire, F.M.A. de. Recueil necessaire. Leipsik, 1765[1766].

Htn   Phil 2915.50*   Candide ou L'optimisme. n.p., 1759.

Phil 2915.51   Voltaire, F.M.A. de. Traité de métaphysique, 1734. Manchester, 1937.

Phil 2915.70   Voltaire, F.M.A. de. Philosophical dictionary of M. de Voltaire. N.Y., 1830.

Htn   Phil 2915.74*   Voltaire, F.M.A. de. Lettre philosophique. Berlin, 1774.

Phil 2915.75   Voltaire, F.M.A. de. Lettres philosophiques. Paris, 1909. 2v.

Phil 2915.75.2   Voltaire, F.M.A. de. Lettres philosophiques. Paris, 1918.

Phil 2915.80   Saisset, E.E. Renaissance du Voltairianisme. Paris, 1845.

Phil 2915.81   Strauss, D.F. Voltaire. 4e Aufl. Bonn, 1877.

Phil 2920 History of philosophy - Local Modern philosophy - France - Individual philosophers - Other V

Phil 2920.1.80   Ollé-Laprune, L. Étienne Vacherot. Paris, 1898.

Phil 2920.2.30   Vallin, Georges. Être et individualite. Paris, 1959.

Phil 2920.2.35   Vallin, Georges. La perspective métaphysique. Paris, 1958.

Phil 2920.3.30   Valensin, Auguste. Auguste Valensin. Paris, 1961.

Phil 2920.3.32   Valensin, Auguste. Regards. Paris, 1955-56. 3v.

Htn   Phil 2925.2.35*   Vattel, Emmerich. The law of nations. v.1-2. London, 1760[1759].

Phil 2940 History of philosophy - Local Modern philosophy - France - Individual philosophers - W

Phil 2940.1.90   Manifestation en l'honneur de Monsieur Maurice de Wulf, 7 mars 1934. Louvain, 1934.

Phil 2940.2.30   Wahl, Jean André. L'expérience métaphysique. Paris, 1965.

Phil 2940.3.20   Weil, Éric. Essais et conférences. Paris, 1970. 2v.

Phil 2963 History of philosophy - Local Modern philosophy - Belgium - History - Special topics

Phil 2963.5   L'Humanisme belge. État de la question, vecherches, perspectives. Anvers, 1966.

Phil 2980 History of philosophy - Local Modern philosophy - Switzerland - History - General works

Phil 2980.5   Tumarkin, Anna. Wesen und Werden der schweizerischen Philosophie. Frauenfeld, 1948.

Phil 2980.8   Muralt, André de. Philosophes en Suisse française. Neuchâtel, 1966.

Phil 2980.10   Philosophie in der Schweiz. Erlenbach, 1946.

Phil 2998 History of philosophy - Local Modern philosophy - Germany - Pamphlet volumes

Phil 2998.01   Pamphlet box. Philosophy. German and Dutch.

Phil 2998.1   Anthologie aus F.W.J. von Schelling's Werken. Berlin, 1844-57. 8 pam.

Phil 2998.3   Pamphlet vol. Philosophy. German dissertations. 11 pam.

Phil 2998.4   Pamphlet vol. German dissertations.

Phil 2998.14   Pamphlet vol. German philosophers. A-H. German dissertations. 10 pam.

Phil 2998.15   Pamphlet vol. German philosophers. L-W. German dissertations. 9 pam.

Phil 2999 History of philosophy - Local Modern philosophy - Germany - History - General works - Collected authors

Phil 2999.2   La philosophie allemande au XIXe siècle. Paris, 1912.

Phil 3000 - 3025 History of philosophy - Local Modern philosophy - Germany - History - General works - Individual authors (A-Z)

Phil 3000.1   Adam, M. Vitae germanorum superiori. Franefort, 1615.

Phil 3000.1.2   Adam, M. Vitae germanorum philosophorum. Franefort, 1663.

Phil 3000.2   Allihn, F.H.T. Die Umkehr der Wissenschaft in Preussen. Berlin, 1855.

Phil 3000.4   Aster, E. Von. Die Philosophie der Gegenwart. Leiden, 1935.

Phil 3000.5   Adorno, Theodor W. Jargon der Eigentlichkeit; zur deutschen Ideologie. Frankfurt, 1967.

Phil 3000.6   Arvon, Henri. La philosophie allemande. Paris, 1970.

Phil 3000.8   Albrecht, Herbert. Deutsche Philosophie heute. Bremen, 1969.

Phil 3001.1   Barchou, A.T.H. Histoire de la philosophie allemande. Paris, 1836. 2v.

Phil 3001.2   Biedermann, F.C. Die deutsche Philosophie. Leipzig, 1842. 2v.

Phil 3001.3   Brasch, M. Leipziger Philosophen. Leipzig, 1894.

Phil 3001.4   Bartholmiss, C.J.W. Histoire philosophique de l'academie de Prusse. Paris, 1850. 2v.

Phil 3001.5   Bréhier, Emile. Histoire de la philosophie allemande. Paris, 1921.

Phil 3001.5.3   Bréhier, Emile. Histoire de la philosophie allemande. 3. ed. Paris, 1954.

Phil 3001.6   Borelius, J.J. En blick pa den newarande filosofien i Tyshland. Stockholm, 1879.

Phil 3001.6.5   Borelius, J.J. Blicke auf den Gegenwärtigen Standpunkt der Philosophie in Deutschland und Frankreich. Berlin, n.d.

Phil 3001.7   Slotemaker de Bruine, N.A.C. Eschatologie en Historie. Wageningen, 1925.

Phil 3001.8   Bruleg, Lucien. Holländische Philosophie. Breslau, 1926.

Phil 3001.9   Brockdorff, C. Die deutsche Auflslärungsphilosophie. München, 1926.

Phil 3001.10   Bauch, Bruno. Jena und die Philosophie des deutschen Idealismus. Jena, 1922.

Phil 3001.11   Becher, Erich. Deutsche Philosophen. München, 1929.

Phil 3001.12   Brock, Werner. An introduction to contemporary German philosophy. Cambridge, 1935.

Phil 3001.13   Baeumler, A. Studien zur dutschen Geistesgeschichte. Berlin, 1937.

Phil 3001.14   Bohne, F. Anti-Cartesianismus; deutsche Philosophie im Widerstand. Leipzig, 1938.

Phil 3001.15   Bense, M. Vom Wesen deutscher Denker. München, 1938.

Phil 3001.16   Balthasar, H.U. Apokalypse der deutschen Seele. Salzburg, 1937-39. 3v.

Phil 3001.16.5   Balthasar, H.U. Prometheus. Heidelburg, 1947.

Phil 3001.19   Benz, Ernst. Las sources mystiques de la phlosophie romantique allemande. Paris, 1968.

Phil 3001.20   Bogomolov, A.S. Nemetskaia burzhuaznaia filosofiia posle 1865 goda. Moskva, 1969.

Classified Listing

Phil 3001.22   Beck, Lewis White. Early German philosophy: Kant and his predecessors. Cambridge, 1969.

Phil 3001.24   Buggenhagen, Erich Arnold von. Contribuições à historia da filosofia alemã. São José, 1965.

Phil 3002.1   Chalybäus, H. Historie entwickelischen der speculativen Philosophie. Leipzig, 1860.

Phil 3002.1.5   Chalybäus, H. Historical survey of speculative philosophy. London, 1854.

Phil 3002.1.6   Chalybäus, H. Historical development of speculative philosophy. Edinburgh, 1854.

Phil 3002.1.7   Chalybäus, H. Historical survey of speculative philosophy. Andover, 1854.

Phil 3002.1.9   Chalybäus, H. Phänomenologische Blätter. Kiel, 1840.

Phil 3002.2   Crile, G.W. The fallacy of the German state philosophy. Garden City, 1918.

Phil 3002.3   Cassirer, Ernst. Freitheit und Form. 2e Aufl. Berlin, 1918.

Phil 3002.4   Cohn, Jonas. Der deutsche Idealismus. Leipzig, 1923.

Phil 3002.5   Carabellese, Pantaleo. Il problema della filosofia da Kant a Fichte (1781-1801). Palermo, 1929.

Phil 3002.6   Cousin, Victor. Uber französische und deutsche Philosophie. Stuttgant, 1834.

Phil 3002.7   Casper, Bernhard. Das dialogische Denken. Freiburg, 1967.

Phil 3003.1   Drews, A. Die deutsche Spekulation seit Kant. Berlin, 1893. 2v.

Phil 3003.2   Deutschthümler, W. Ueber Schopenhauer zu Kant; ein Kleines Geschichtsbild. Wien, 1899.

Phil 3003.3A   Dewey, John. German philosophy and politics. N.Y., 1915.

Phil 3003.3B   Dewey, John. German philosophy and politics. N.Y., 1915.

Phil 3003.3.5   Dewey, John. German philosophy and politics. N.Y., 1942.

Phil 3003.4   Delbos, Victor. L'esprit philosophique de l'Allemagne et la pensée française. Paris, 1915.

Phil 3003.5   Drechsler, Adolf. Charakteristik der philosophischen Systeme seit Kant. Dresden, 1863.

Phil 3003.6   Deutschlands Denker seit Kant. Dessan, 1851.

Phil 3003.8   Akademiia Nauk SSSR. Institut Filosofii. Die deutsche Philosophie. Berlin, 1961.

Phil 3003.9   Dussort, H. L'ecole de Marboug. Paris, 1963.

Phil 3003.10   Akademiia Nauk SSSR. Institut Filosofii. Die deutsche Philosophie nach 1945. Berlin, 1961.

Phil 3004.1.2   Eucken, Rudolf. Beiträge zur Einführung im die Geschichte der Philosophie. 2. Aufl. Leipzig, 1906.

Phil 3004.1.10   Eucken, Rudolf. Die Träger des deutschen Idealismus. Berlin, 1916.

Phil 3004.2   Ettlinger, Max. Geschichte der Philosophie von der Romantik bis zur Gegenwart. München, 1924.

Phil 3004.3   Ehrenberg, Hans. Die Parteiung der Philosophie. Leipzig, 1911.

Phil 3004.4   Ehrenberg, Hans. Disputation: drei Bücher vom Deutschen. München, 1923-25. 3v.

Phil 3004.5   Erdmann, J.E. Preussen und die Philosophie. Halle, 1954.

Phil 3004.6   Esliu, Emilio. De la vida a la existencia en la filosofia contemporanea. La Plata, 1964.

Phil 3004.8   Ebbinghaus, J. Gesammelte Aufsätze, Verträge und Reden. Hildesheim, 1968.

Phil 3005.1   Fortlage, K. Genetische Geschichte der Philosophie seit Kant. Leipzig, 1852.

Phil 3005.2   Fichte, T.H. Fragen und Bedenken. Leipzig, 1876.

Phil 3005.3.3   Falckenberg, Richard. Hilfslrich zur Geschichte der Philosophie seit Kant. 3e Aufl. Leipzig, 1917.

Phil 3005.3.7   Falckenberg, Richard. Über die gegenwärtige Lage der deutschen Philosophie. Leipzig, 1890.

Phil 3005.3.10   Falckenberg, Richard. La filosofia alemana desde Kant. Madrid, 1906.

Phil 3005.5   Friedrichs, A. Klassische Philosophie und Wirtschaftswissenschaft. Gotha, 1913.

Phil 3005.7   Franz, Erich. Deutsche Klassik und Reformation. Halle, 1937.

Phil 3005.9   Finger, Otto. Von der Materialität des Seele. Berlin, 1961.

Phil 3005.10   Faber, W. Wijsgeren in Nederland. Nijkerk, 1954.

Phil 3005.12   Frischeisen-Köhler, M. Geistige Werte. Berlin, 1915.

Phil 3006.1   Gruppe, O.F. Gegenwart und Philosophie in Deutschland. Berlin, 1855.

Phil 3006.3.2   Gramzow, Otto. Geschichte der Philosophie seit Kant. 2. Aufl. Charlottenburg, 1919-28. 2v.

Phil 3006.4   Gronau, Gotthard. Die Philosophie der Gegenwart. Langensalza, 1920-22. 2v.

Phil 3006.5   Günther, A. Die Juste-Milieus in der deutschen Philosophie. Wien, 1838.

Phil 3006.6   Groethuysen, B. Introduction a la pensée philosophie allemande depuis Nietzsche. Paris, 1926.

Phil 3006.7   Gurvitch, G. Les tendances actuelles de la philosophie allemande. Photoreproduction. Paris, 1930.

Phil 3006.7.5   Gurvitch, G. Les tendances actuelles de la philosophie allemande. Paris, 1949.

Phil 3006.8   Gehl, W. Der germanische Schichsalsglaube. Berlin, 1939.

Phil 3006.9   Gulyga, A.V. Iz istorii nemetskogo materializma. Moskva, 1962.

Phil 3006.9.5   Gulyga, A.V. Der deutsche Materialismus am Ausgang des 18. Jahrhunderts. Berlin, 1966.

Phil 3006.10   Gropp, Rugard Otto. Von Cusanus bis Marx. Leipzig, 1965.

Phil 3007.1   Harms, F. Der Anthropologismus. Leipzig, 1845.

Phil 3007.1.5   Harms, F. Die Philosophie seit Kant. Berlin, 1876.

Phil 3007.1.7   Harms, F. Die Philosophie seit Kant. Berlin, 1879.

Phil 3007.2   Heine, H. Religion and philosophy in Germany. London, 1882.

Phil 3007.2.5   Heine, H. Religion and philosophy in Germany. Boston, 1959.

Phil 3007.3   Heussner, Alfred. Die philosophischen Weltanschauungen. 5. Aufl. Göttingen, 1919.

Phil 3007.5   Hall, G.S. Aspects of German culture. Boston, 1881.

Phil 3007.5.5   Hall, G.S. Founders of modern psychology. N.Y., 1912.

Phil 3007.5.10   Hall, G.S. Founders of modern psychology. N.Y., 1924.

Phil 3007.6   Høffding, H. Philosophien i Tydskland efter Hegel. Kjøbenhavn, 1872.

Phil 3007.7.2A   Hartmann, N. Die Philosophie des deutschen Idealismus. 2. Aufl. Berlin, 1960.

Phil 3007.7.2B   Hartmann, N. Die Philosophie des deutschen Idealismus. 2. Aufl. Berlin, 1960.

Phil 3007.8.5   Helbing, Lothar. Der dritte Humanismus. 3. Aufl. Berlin, 1935.

Phil 3007.9   Hessen, Johannes. Die Ewigkeitswerte der deutschen Philosophie. Hamburg, 1943.

Phil 3007.10   Haering, Theodor Lorenz. Die deutsche und die europäische Philosophie. Stuttgart, 1943.

Phil 3007.10.5   Haering, Theodor Lorenz. Das deutsche in der deutschen Philosophie. 2. Aufl. Stuttgart, 1942.

Phil 3007.12   Hommes, Jakob. Krise der Freiheit. Regensburg, 1958.

Phil 3007.14   Haan, A.A.M. de. Het wijsgerig onderwijs aan het gymnasium illustre. Harderwijk, 1960.

Phil 3007.16   Heise, Wolfgang. Aufbruch in die Illusion. 1. Aufl. Berlin, 1964.

Phil 3009.1   Janet, P. Le matérialisme contemporaine...Allem. Paris, 1864.

Phil 3009.2   Jones, W.T. Contemporary thought of Germany. N.Y., 1931. 2v.

Phil 3010.1   Kirchner, C.K. Die speculativen Systeme seit Kant. Leipzig, 1860.

Phil 3010.2   Külpe, O. Die Philosophie der Gegenwart in Deutschland. Leipzig, 1905.

Phil 3010.2.5   Külpe, O. Die Philosophie der Gegenwart in Deutschland. Leipzig, 1911.

Phil 3010.2.26   Külpe, O. The philosophy of the present in Germany. N.Y., 1913.

Phil 3010.3   Kroner, R. Von Kant bis Hegel. Tübingen, 1921-24. 2v.

Phil 3010.3.2   Kroner, R. Von Kant bis Hegel. v.1-2. Tübingen, 1961.

Phil 3010.4   Rannengiesser, P. Dogmatismus und Skepticismus. Elberfeld, 1877.

Phil 3010.5   Kraft, J. Von Husserl zu Heidegger. Leipzig, 1932.

Phil 3010.5.2   Kraft, J. Von Husserl zur Heidegger. 2. Aufl. Frankfurt, 1957.

Phil 3010.6   Kauffmann, H.L. Essai sur l'anti-progressisme et ses origines dans la philosophie allemande moderne. Thèse. Paris, 1936.

Phil 3010.7   Klugen, A. von. Die Absage an die Romantik in der Zeit nach den Weltkriege. Berlin, 1938.

Phil 3010.8   Koyré, Alexandre. Mystiques. Paris, 1955.

Phil 3010.9   Kvochow, Christian C. von. Die Entscheidung. Stuttgart, 1958.

Phil 3010.10   Knauer, Rudolf. Der Voluntarismus. Berlin, 1907.

Phil 3010.11   Kurucz, J. Die Opposition der Jugendbrücken. Saar, 1958.

Phil 3010.14   Kronenberg, Moritz. Moderne Philosophen; Porträts und Charakteristiken. München, 1899.

Phil 3010.15   Krueger, Gustav. Die Religion der Goethezeit. Tübingen, 1931.

Phil 3011.1   Lotze, R.H. Geschichte der deutschen Philosophie - Kant. Leipzig, 1882.

Phil 3011.3   Lehmann, G. Geschichte der nachkantischen Philosophie. Berlin, 1931.

Phil 3011.3.10   Lehmann, G. Die Ontologie der Gegenwart in ihren Grundgestalten. Halle, 1933.

Phil 3011.3.15   Lehmann, G. Die deutschen Philosophie der Gegenwart. Stuttgart, 1943.

Phil 3011.4   Levy, H. Die Hegel-Renaissance in der deutschen Philosophie. Charlottenburg, 1927.

Phil 3011.5   Lewalter, E. Spanisch-Jesuisitische und Deutsch-Lutherische Metaphysik des 17. Jahrhunderts. Hamburg, 1935.

Phil 3011.6   Lukács, G. Die Zerstörung der Vernunft. Berlin, 1954.

Phil 3011.6.5   Lukács, G. La destruction de la raison. Paris, 1958-59. 2v.

Phil 3011.7   Linke, Paul F. Niedergangserscheinungen in der Philosophie der Gegenwart. München, 1961.

Phil 3011.8A   Loewith, Karl. Von Hegel bis Nietzsche. Zürich, 1941.

Phil 3011.8B   Loewith, Karl. Von Hegel bis Nietzsche. Zürich, 1941.

Phil 3011.8.2   Loewith, Karl. From Hegel to Nietzsche: the revolution in nineteenth century thought. 1st ed. N.Y., 1964.

Phil 3011.10   Liedman, Sven Eric. Det organiska livet i tysk debatt, 1795-1845. Thesis. Land, 1966.

Phil 3012.1   Michelet, C.L. Geschichte...Philosophie in Deutschland. Berlin, 1837-38. 2v.

Phil 3012.1.5   Michelet, C.L. Entwickelungsgeschichte der neuesten deutschen Philosophie. Berlin, 1843.

Phil 3012.2   Muirhead, J.H. German philosophy in relation to the war. London, 1917.

Phil 3012.3   Moog, Willy. Die deutsche Philosophie des 20. Jahrhunderts. Stuttgart, 1922.

Phil 3012.4   Murdock, J. Sketches of modern philosophy. Hartford, 1842.

Phil 3012.5   Meleshchenko, Zoia N. Nemctskaia filosofiia XIX - nachala XX vv. Leningrad, 1965.

Phil 3013.2   Noack, H. Deutsche Geisteswelt. Darmstadt, 1955. 2v.

Phil 3014.1A   Oesterreich, K. Die deutsche Philosophie inder zweiten Halfte des neunzehten Jahrhund. Tübingen, 1910.

Phil 3014.1B   Oesterreich, K. Die deutsche Philosophie inder zweiten Halfte des neunzehten Jahrhund. Tübingen, 1910.

Phil 3015.1   Papillault, G. Science française, scolastique allemande. Paris, 1917.

Phil 3015.2   Przygodda, Paul. Deutsche Philosophie v.2. Berlin, 1916.

Phil 3015.3   Petersen, Peter. Geschichte der aristotelischen Philosophie in protestantischen Deutschland. Leipzig, 1921.

Phil 3015.4   Pensa, M. Il pensiero tedesco. Bologna, 1938.

Phil 3015.5   Prang, Helmut. Der Humanismus. Bamburg, 1947.

Phil 3015.6   Pupi, A. Alla soglia dell'età romantica. Milano, 1962.

Phil 3017.1   Rémusat, C. de. De la philosophie allemande. Paris, 1845.

Phil 3017.2   Ritter, A.H. Versuch zur neueste deutsche Philosophie...Kant. Braunschweig, 1853.

Phil 3017.3   Rosenkranz, K. Neue Studien: IV Geschichte deutschen Philosophie. v.1-2. Leipzig, 1878. 3v.

Phil 3017.4   Riecke, H. Der Rassegedanke und die neuere Philosophie. Leipzig, 1936.

Phil 3017.5   Royce, J. Lectures on modern idealism. New Haven, 1964.

Phil 3017.6   Rádl, E. Romantická véda. V Praze, 1918.

Phil 3017.7   Razzug, Aŝad. Die Ansätze zu einer Kulturantropologie in der Gegenwärtigen deutschen Philosophie. Tübingen, 1963.

Phil 3017.9   Reichmann, Eberhard. Die Herrschaft der Zahl. Stuttgart, 1968.

Phil 3017.10   Rintelen, Fritz-Joachim von. Contemporary German philosophy and its background. Bonn, 1970.

Phil 3018.1   Schwab, J.C. Preisschriften...Metaphysik séet Leibnitz. Berlin, 1796.

Phil 3018.2   Sengler, J. Ueber das Wesen...Philosophie und Theologie in der gegenwärtigen Zeit...Religionsphilosophie. Heidelberg, 1837.

Phil 3018.3   Steininger, F. Examen critique de la philosophie allemande. Trèves, 1841.

Phil 3018.4   Seth, A. Developmnt from Kant to Hegel. London, 1882.

Phil 3018.5   Seibert, C. Geschichte der neueren deutschen Philosophie. Göttingen, 1898.

Phil 3000 - 3025 History of philosophy - Local Modern philosophy - Germany - History - General works - Individual authors (A-Z) - cont.

Phil 3018.5.3 Seibert, C. Geschichte der neueren deutschen Philosophie. 2e Aufl. Gottingen, 1905.
Phil 3018.6 Siegel, C. Geschichte der deutschen Naturphilosophie. Leipzig, 1913.
Phil 3018.7A Santayana, G. Egotism in German philosophy. Photoreproduction. London, 1916?
Phil 3018.7B Santayana, G. Egotism in German philosophy. Photoreproduction. London, 1916?
Phil 3018.7.7 Santayana, G. Egotism in German philosophy. N.Y., 1940.
Phil 3018.7.9 Santayana, G. L'erreur de la philosophie allemande. Paris, 1917.
Phil 3018.8 Stockum, T.C. Spinoza, Jacobi, Lessing. Groningen, 1916.
Phil 3018.9 Stählin, Leonhard. Kant, Lotze, and Ritschl. Edinburgh, 1889.
Phil 3018.9.5 Stählin, Leonhard. Kant, Lotze, and Ritschl. Leipzig, 1888.
Phil 3018.10 Strümpell, Ludwig. Abhandlungen zur Geschichte de Metaphysik, Psychologie. Leipzig, 1896.
Phil 3018.11 Spitzer, Hugo. Nominalismus und Realismus in der neuesten deutschen Philosophie. Leipzig, 1876.
Phil 3018.12 Schaller, J. Die Philosophie unserer Zeit. Leipzig, 1837.
Phil 3018.13 Seillière, E. Morales et religions nouvelles en Allemagne. Paris, 1927.
Phil 3018.14 Steiner, R. Vom Menschenrätsel. Berlin, 1918.
Phil 3018.15 Schwarz, H. Deutsche systematische Philosophie nach ihren Gestaltern. Berlin, 1931-34. 2v.
Phil 3018.16 Schram, J. Beitrag zur Geschichte der Philosophie. Bonn, 1836.
Phil 3018.17 Sannwald, A. Der Begriff der Dialektik und die Anthropologie. München, 1931.
Phil 3018.18 Schod, J.B. Geschichte der Philosophie unserer Zeit. Jena, 1800.
Phil 3018.19 Spenlé, J.E. La pensée allemande de Luther à Nietzsche. Paris, 1934.
Phil 3018.21 Schroeter, R. Geschichte und Geschichtlichkeit in der deutschen Philosophie der Gegenwart. Inaug. Diss. Kölm am Rhein, 1937.
Phil 3018.22 Schneider, P. Deutschen Philosophen des 19. Jahrhunderts. Berlin, 1927.
Phil 3018.24 Schwarz, Hermann. Grundzüge einer Geschichte der artdeutschen Philosophie. Berlin, 1937.
Phil 3018.25 Siebecke, H. Ernte deutscher Humanitat. 2. Aufl. Bad Nauheim, 1952.
Phil 3018.30 Scifert, F. Schäpferische deutsche Philosophie. Köhn, 1944.
Phil 3018.35 Schoch, Otto D. Der Völherbundsgedanke zur Zeit. Zürich, 1960.
Phil 3018.36 Stuke, H. Philosophie der Tat. Stuttgart, 1963.
Phil 3018.38 Sauer, Ernst Friedrich. Deutsche Philosophen: von Eckhart his Heidegger. Göttingen, 1968.
Phil 3018.40 Szyszkowka, Maria. Neokantyzm - filozofia spoleczna wraz a filozofia prawa natury o zmilnnej treści. Wyd. 1. Warszawa, 1970.
Phil 3019.5 Thijssen-Schoute, Caroline Louise. Uit de Republiek der Letteren. 's-Gravenhage, 1967[1968]
Phil 3022.1 Weber, T. Die Geschichte der neueren deutschen Philosophie. v.1-3. Münster, 1873.
Phil 3022.2 Willm, J. Histoire de la philosophie allemande. Paris, 1846-49. 4v.
Phil 3022.3 Windlband, Wilhelm. Die Philosophie im deutschen Geistesleben des 19. Jahrhunderts. 2e Aufl. Tübingen, 1909.
Phil 3022.3.2 Windlband, Wilhelm. Die Philosophie im deutschen Geistesleben des 19. Jahrhunderts. Tübingen, 1909.
Phil 3022.3.3 Windlband, Wilhelm. Die Philosophie im deutschen Geistesleben des 19. Jahrhunderts. 3. Aufl. Tübingen, 1927.
Phil 3022.3.15 Windlband, Wilhelm. Die Blüthezeit der deutschen Philosophie. Leipzig, 1880.
Phil 3022.4 Wust, Peter. Die Auferstehung Metaphysik. Leipzig, 1920.
Phil 3022.4.5 Wust, Peter. Gesammelte Werke. Münster, 1963. 10v.
Phil 3022.5 Wimmershoff, H. Die Lehre von Sündenfall in der Philosophie Schellings. Inaug. Diss. Selingen, 1934.
Phil 3022.6 Wundt, Max. Die Wurzeln der deutschen Philosophie in Staam und Vasse. Berlin, 1944.
Phil 3024.5 Young, William. Toward a reformed philosophy. Grand Rapids, Mich., 1952.
Phil 3025.1 Zart, G. Einfluss der englischen Philosophen...deutschen Philosophen. Berlin, 1881.
Phil 3025.2 Zeller, Eduard. Geschichte der deutschen Philosophie. München, 1873.
Phil 3025.2.2 Zeller, Eduard. Geschichte der deutschen Philosophie seit Liebniz. 2. Aufl. München, 1875.

il 3030 History of philosophy - Local Modern philosophy - Germany - History - Special topics

Phil 3030.4 Buhr, Manfred. Der Anspruch der Vernunft. Berlin, 1968.
Phil 3030.6 Oelmueller, W. Die unbefriedigte Aufklärung. Frankfurt, 1969.
Phil 3030.8 Habermas, Jürgen. Philosophisch-politische Profile. 7. Aufl. Frankkurt, 1971.

l 3050 History of philosophy - Local Modern philosophy - Germany - Anthologies of philosophical writings

Phil 3050.2 Bauer, Edgar. Bibliothek der deutschen Aufklärer des achtzehnten Jahrhunderts. Darmstadt, 1963. 2v.
Phil 3050.4 Protiv sovremennoi burzhuaznoi ideologii. Moskva, 1960.
Phil 3050.6 Loewith, Karl. Die Hegelsche Linke; Texte aus den Werken. Stuttgart, 1962.
Phil 3050.8 Taylor, Ronald Jack. The romantic tradition in Germany. London, 1970.

l 3085 History of philosophy - Local Modern philosophy - Germany - Individual philosophers - A

Phil 3085.1.30* Agrippa von Nettesheim, H.C. De nobilitate. n.p., 1532.
Phil 3085.1.32* Agrippa von Nettesheim, H.C. De occulta philosophia. Lugduni, 1550.
Phil 3085.1.35* Agrippa von Nettesheim, H.C. Henrici Cornelii Agrippae. Coloniae, 1575.
Phil 3085.1.36* Agrippa von Nettesheim, H.C. Apologia aduersus calumnias proptes declamationem. n.p., 1533.
Phil 3085.2.85 Aders, Fritz. Jacob Friedrich Abel als Philosophie. Inaug. Diss. Berlin, 1893.
Phil 3085.3.31 Apelt, E.F. Metaphysik. Leipzig, 1857.
Phil 3085.4.31 Adorno, F.W. Minima Moralia. Berlin, 1951.
Phil 3085.5.31 Andre, H. Wunderbare Wirklichkeit. Salzburg, 1955.

Phil 3085 History of philosophy - Local Modern philosophy - Germany - Individual philosophers - A - cont.

Phil 3085.5.35 Andre, H. Annäherung durch Abstand. Salzburg, 1957.
Phil 3085.5.40 Andre, H. Natur und Mysterium. Einsiedeln, 1959.
Phil 3085.5.80 Sieverth, Gustav. Andre's Philosophie des Lebens. Salzburg, 1959.
Phil 3085.6.80 Traaf, B. Alardus Amstelredamus. Amsterdam, 1958.
Phil 3085.6.85 Koelker, A. Alardus Amstelredamus en Cornelius Crocus. Nijmegen, 1963.
Phil 3085.7.1 Adorno, Theodor W. Gesammelte Schriften. 1. Aufl. Frankfurt, 1971.
Phil 3085.7.30 Adorno, Theodor W. Eingriffe. Frankfurt, 1963.
Phil 3085.7.31 Adorno, Theodor W. Negative Dialektik. Frankfurt, 1966.
Phil 3085.7.35 Adorno, Theodor W. Stichworte. Kritische Modelle. Frankfurt, 1969.
Phil 3085.7.40 Adorno, Theodor W. Aufsätze zur Gesellschaftstheorie und Methodologie. 1. Aufl. Frankfurt, 1970.
Phil 3085.7.45 Adorno, Theodor W. Kritik: kleine Schriften zur Gesellschaft. 1. Aufl. Frankfurt, 1971.
Phil 3085.7.80 Adorno, Theodor W. Mit Beiträgen von Kurt Oppens. Frankfurt, 1968.
Phil 3085.9.30 Alff, Wilhelm. Überlegungen; Vierzehn Essays. Heidelberg, 1964.
Phil 3085.10.81 Graaf, Bob de. Petrus Apherdianus, ludimagister ca. 1510-1580. Nieuwkoop, 1968.

Phil 3090 History of philosophy - Local Modern philosophy - Germany - Individual philosophers - Baader, Franz von

Phil 3090.01 Jost, J. Bibliographie der Schriften Franz v. Baaders. Bonn, 1926.
Phil 3090.10 Baader, Franz von. Sämmtliche Werke. Leipzig, 1851-60. 16v.
Phil 3090.20 Baader, Franz von. Philosophische Schriften und Aufsätze. v.1-2. Münster, 1831-33.
Phil 3090.22 Baader, Franz von. Sätze ans der erotischen Philosophie und andere Schriften. Frankfurt, 1966.
Phil 3090.23 Baader, Franz von. Schriften. Leipzig, 1921.
Phil 3090.24 Baader, Franz von. Schriften zur Gesellschaftsphilosophie. Jena, 1925.
Phil 3090.24.5 Baader, Franz von. Gesellschaftslehre. München, 1957.
Phil 3090.24.10 Baader, Franz von. Vom Sinn der Gesellschaft. Köln, 1966.
Phil 3090.25 Baader, Franz von. Kleine Schriften. Würzburg, 1847.
Phil 3090.27 Baader, Franz von. Leben und theosophische Werke. v.1-2. Stuttgart, 1886-87.
Phil 3090.28 Baader, Franz von. Über Liebe. München, 1953.
Phil 3090.30 Baader, Franz von. Über den Begriff des Gut-Oderpositiv und der Richtgut-Oder-Negative-Gewordnen. Luzern, 1829.
Phil 3090.31 Baader, Franz von. Beiträge zur dinamischen Philosophie im Gegensaze der Mechanischen. Berlin, 1809.
Phil 3090.35 Baader, Franz von. Sur la notion du tems. Munic, 1818.
Phil 3090.37 Baader, Franz von. Vorlesungen...über religiöse Philosophie. München, 1827.
Phil 3090.38 Baader, Franz von. Über die Freiheit der Intelligenz. München, 1826.
Phil 3090.39 Baader, Franz von. Von Segen und Fluch der Creatur. Strassburg, 1826.
Phil 3090.40 Baader, Franz von. Über das Verhalten des Wissens zum Glauben. Münster, 1833.
Phil 3090.41 Baader, Franz von. Vorlesungen über speculative Dogmatik. pt. 1-5. Stuttgart, 1828-38.
Phil 3090.42 Baader, Franz von. Fermenta cognitionis. pt. 1-6. Berlin, 1822-25. 5v.
Phil 3090.61 Baader, Franz von. Lettres inédites de Franz von Baader. Thèse. Paris, 1942.
Phil 3090.62 Baader, Franz von. Lettres inédites. Paris, 1942-51. 4v.
Phil 3090.64 Baader, Franz von. Über die Nothwendigkeit einer Revision der Wissenschaft natürlicher. Erlanzen, 1841.
Phil 3090.65 Baader, Franz von. Seele und Welt. Berlin, 1928.
Phil 3090.79 Pamphlet box. Philosophy. German.
Phil 3090.80 Hoffmann, F. Biographie Franz von Baader's. Leipzig, 1857.
Phil 3090.80.5 Hoffmann, F. Franz von Baader in seinem Verhällnitz zu Hegel und Schelling. Leipzig, 1850.
Phil 3090.80.10 Hoffmann, F. Zur Würdigung des Vorurthelie über der Lehre Baaders. Leipzig, 1855.
Phil 3090.80.15 Hoffmann, F. Vorhalle zur speculativen Lehre F. Baader's. Aschaffenburg, 1836.
Phil 3090.81 Hamberger, Julius. Die Fundamentalbegriffe von Franz von Baader's Ethik. Stuttgart, 1858.
Phil 3090.81.5 Hamberger, Julius. Die Cardinalpunkte der F. Baader'schen Philosophie. Stuttgart, 1855.
Phil 3090.82 Fischer, K.P. Zur hundertjährigen Geburtsfeier Franz von Baaders. Erlangen, 1865.
Phil 3090.83 Baumgardt, D. Franz von Baader und die philosophische Romantik. Halle, 1927.
Phil 3090.84 Reber, M. Franz von Baader und die Möglichkeit unbedingter pädagogischer Zielsetzung. Nürnburg, 1925.
Phil 3090.85 Lieb, Fritz. Franz Baaders Jugendgeschichte...von Baaders. München, 1926.
Phil 3090.86 Sauter, J. Baader und Kant. Jena, 1928.
Phil 3090.87 Susini, Eugene. Franz von Baader et le romantisme mystique. Thesis. Paris, 1942. 2v.
Phil 3090.87.5 Susini, Eugene. Franz von Baader et le romantisme mystique. v.2-3. Paris, 1942. 2v.
Phil 3090.88 Klamroth, Erich. Die Weltanschauung Franz von Baaders in ihrem Gegensatz zu Kant. Berlin, 1965.
Phil 3090.89 Siegl, Josef. Franz von Baader. München, 1957.
Phil 3090.90 Hemmerle, Klaus. Franz von Baaders philosophischer Gedanke der Schöpfung. Freiburg, 1963.
Phil 3090.91 Helberger-Frobenius, Sebastian. Macht und Gewalt in der Philosophie Franz von Baaders. Bonn, 1969.

Phil 3092 History of philosophy - Local Modern philosophy - Germany - Individual philosophers - Bachofen, J.J.

Phil 3092.1 Bachofen, J.J. Selbstbiographie undAntrittsrede. Halle, 1927.
Phil 3092.1.5 Kerényi, Karoly. Bach ofen und die Zukunft des Humanismus. Zürich, 1945.

Phil 3095 History of philosophy - Local Modern philosophy - Germany - Individual philosophers - Baumgarten, Alexander G.

Phil 3095.30 Baumgarten, A.G. Philosophia generalis. Halae, 1770.
Phil 3095.35 Baumgarten, A.G. Metaphysica. Halae, 1757.
Phil 3095.35.5 Baumgarten, A.G. Metaphysica. Halae, 1739.
Phil 3095.40 Baumgarten, A.G. Metaphysica. 7th ed. Halae, 1779.
Phil 3095.45 Baumgarten, A.G. Metaphysik. Halle, 1766.
Phil 3095.50 Baumgarten, A.G. Acroasis logica. Halae, 1773.

166

Classified Listing

Phil 3095 History of philosophy - Local Modern philosophy - Germany - Individual philosophers - Baumgarten, Alexander G. - cont.

	Phil 3095.51	Baumgarten, A.G. Meditationes philosophicae de nonnullis ad poema pertinentibus. Halae, 1735.
	Phil 3095.51.10	Baumgarten, A.G. Reflections on poetry. Berkeley, 1954.
	Phil 3095.52	Baumgarten, A.G. Initia philosophiae practicae primae acroamatice. Halae, 1760.
	Phil 3095.81	Poppe, B. Alexander G. Baumgarten. Borna, 1907.
	Phil 3095.82	Ruman, Albert. Die Aesthetik Alex Gottlieb Baumgartens. Halle, 1928.
	Phil 3095.83	Abbt, Thomas. Alexander Gottlieb Baumgartens Leben und Charakter. Halle, 1765.

Phil 3100 History of philosophy - Local Modern philosophy - Germany - Individual philosophers - Beneke, Friedrich E.

	Phil 3100.30	Beneke, F.E. System der Metaphysik and Religionsphilosophie. Berlin, 1840.
	Phil 3100.40	Beneke, F.E. System der Logik. Berlin, 1842. 2v.
	Phil 3100.42	Beneke, F.E. Grundlegung zur Physik der Sitten. Berlin, 1822.
	Phil 3100.43	Beneke, F.E. Schutzschrift für meine Grundlegung zur Physik der Sitten. Leipzig, 1823.
	Phil 3100.45	Beneke, F.E. Pragmatische Psychologie. v.1-2. Berlin, 1850.
	Phil 3100.46	Beneke, F.E. Lehrbuch der pragmatischen Psychologie. Berlin, 1853.
	Phil 3100.50	Beneke, F.E. Lehrbuch der Psychologie. Berlin, 1861.
	Phil 3100.50.2	Beneke, F.E. Die neue Psychologie. 2. Aufl. Berlin, 1845.
	Phil 3100.50.4	Beneke, F.E. Die neue Psychologie. 4. Aufl. Berlin, 1877.
	Phil 3100.51	Beneke, F.E. Neue Seelenlehre. Bautzen, 1854.
	Phil 3100.52	Beneke, F.E. Erfahrungsseelenlehre als Grundlage alles Wissens in ihren Hauptzügen Dargestellt. Berlin, 1820.
	Phil 3100.53	Beneke, F.E. Das Verhältniss von Seele und Leib. Göttingen, 1826.
	Phil 3100.55	Beneke, F.E. The elements of psychology. London, 1871.
	Phil 3100.60	Beneke, F.E. Grundlinien des natürlichen System der praktischen Philosophie. Berlin, 1837-41. 2v.
	Phil 3100.65	Beneke, F.E. Psychologische Skizzen. Göttingen, 1825-27. 2v.
	Phil 3100.70	Beneke, F.E. Syllogismorum analyticorum origines et ordinem naturalem. Berolini, 1839.
	Phil 3100.79	Pamphlet box.
	Phil 3100.80	Granzow, O. Friedrich Edward Benekes Leben. Bern, 1899.
	Phil 3100.81	Kempen, Aloys. Benekes religions Philosophie im Zusammenhang seines Systems, seine Gottes- und Unsterblickkeitslehre. Münster, 1914.
	Phil 3100.82	Wandschneider, A. Die Metaphysik Benekes. Berlin, 1903.
	Phil 3100.83	Hauffe, G. Professor Dr. Eduard Beneckes Psychologie als Naturwissenschaft. Borna, n.d.
	Phil 3100.84	Freimuth, F.W. Die wichtigsten Grundlehren und Vorzüge der Psychologie Dr. Beneke's. Bautzen, 1845.
	Phil 3100.85	Weber, Adalbert. Kritik der Psychologie von Beneke. Inaug-Diss. Weimar, 1872.
	Phil 3100.125	Löwenberg, Adolf. Friedrich Edward Beneke. Berlin, 1901.
	Phil 3100.127	Friedrich, J. Friedrich Edward Beneke. Wiesbaden, 1898.

Phil 3110 History of philosophy - Local Modern philosophy - Germany - Individual philosophers - Böhme, Jakob

	Phil 3110.5	Buddecke, W. Die Jakob Böhme-Ausgaben. Göttingen, 1937. 2v.
	Phil 3110.6	Jacob Boehme Society. Quarterly. 1-3,1952-1956 2v.
Htn	Phil 3110.10.2*	Böhme, J. Works. London, 1764- 4v.
	Phil 3110.11	Böhme, J. Sämmtliche Werke. v.1-7. Leipzig, 1860. 6v.
	Phil 3110.11.2	Böhme, J. Sämmtliche Werke. v.1-7. Leipzig, 1922. 6v.
	Phil 3110.12	Böhme, J. Schriften. Leipzig, 1938.
	Phil 3110.13	Böhme, J. Sämtliche Schriften. Stuttgart, 1942. 10v.
Htn	Phil 3110.15*	Böhme, J. Remainder of books. London, 1662.
	Phil 3110.22	Böhme, J. Works. Glasgow, 1886.
Htn	Phil 3110.23*	Böhme, J. Epistles. London, 1649-50.
	Phil 3110.24	Böhme, J. Die Lehre des deutschen Philosophen J. Böhme. München, 1844.
Htn	Phil 3110.25*A	Taylor, Edward. Jakob Böhme's theosophick philosophy. London, 1691.
Htn	Phil 3110.25*B	Taylor, Edward. Jakob Böhme's theosophick philosophy. London, 1691.
	Phil 3110.26	Böhme, J. Sein Leben und seine theosophischen Werke. Stuttgart, 1885.
	Phil 3110.27	Böhme, J. Six theosophic points, and other writings. London, 1919.
	Phil 3110.27.10	Böhme, J. Sex puncta theosophica. Leipzig, 1921.
	Phil 3110.28	Böhme, J. Schriften Jakob Böhme. Leipzig, 1923.
	Phil 3110.28.2	Böhme, J. Schriften. Leipzig, 1920.
Htn	Phil 3110.30*	Böhme, J. Questions concerning the soul. London, 1647.
	Phil 3110.31	Böhme, J. De electione gratiae and quaestiones theosophicae. London, 1930.
	Phil 3110.32	Böhme, J. Bedrachtingh vande goddelycke openbaringh. n.p., 1642.
Htn	Phil 3110.35*	Böhme, J. Concerning the three principles of divine essence. London, 1648.
	Phil 3110.35.5	Böhme, J. Concerning the three principles of divine essence. London, 1910.
Htn	Phil 3110.36.2*	Böhme, J. High and deep searching out. London, 1656.
	Phil 3110.36.5	Böhme, J. High and deep searching out. London, 1909.
	Phil 3110.36.30	Böhme, J. Vom dreifachen Leben des Menschen. Hamburg, 1924.
	Phil 3110.37.4	Böhme, J. The signature of all things, with other writings. London, 1926.
	Phil 3110.37.5	Böhme, J. The signature of all things, with other writings. London, 1934.
	Phil 3110.38	Böhme, J. De la signature des choses. Paris, 1908.
Htn	Phil 3110.39*	Böhme, J. Musterium magnum. London, 1654.
	Phil 3110.39.5	Böhme, J. Mysterium magnum. Amsterdam, 1682.
Htn	Phil 3110.40*	Böhme, J. Concerning the election of grace. London, 1655.
	Phil 3110.41	Böhme, J. Von der Genaden-Wahl. Amsterdam, 1682.
	Phil 3110.42	Böhme, J. Vom Lebendigen Glauben. Gütersloh, 1960.
	Phil 3110.43	Böhme, J. Über die Umkehr und die Einsicht. Wien, 1953.
	Phil 3110.45	Böhme, J. The confessions of Jacob Böhme. London, 1920.
	Phil 3110.45.10	Böhme, J. Confessions. N.Y., 1954.
	Phil 3110.47	Böhme, J. Clef, ou Explication des divers points et termes principaux. Paris, 1826.
Htn	Phil 3110.50*	Böhme, J. L'aurore naissante. Paris, 1800. 2v.
	Phil 3110.50.10	Böhme, J. L'aurore naissante. Milan, 1927.
	Phil 3110.55	Böhme, J. Der weeg zu Christo. Amsterdam, 1682.
	Phil 3110.55.5	Böhme, J. The way to Christ. 1st ed. N.Y., 1947.
	Phil 3110.55.15	Böhme, J. The way to Christ discovered. Manchester, 1752.

Phil 3110 History of philosophy - Local Modern philosophy - Germany - Individual philosophers - Böhme, Jakob - cont.

X Cg	Phil 3110.55.20	Böhme, J. The way to Christ discovered. N.Y., 1850. (Changed to XM 710, 1971)
	Phil 3110.55.25	Böhme, J. Vom übersinylichen Leben. Hamburg, 1954.
	Phil 3110.55.30	Böhme, J. Glaube und Tat. Berlin, 1957.
	Phil 3110.55.35	Böhme, J. Die lochteure Pforte. Berlin, 1921.
	Phil 3110.60	Böhme, J. Blüthen aus Jakob Böhme's Mystik. Stuttgart, 1838.
	Phil 3110.78	Buddecke, W. Verzeichnis von Jakob Böhme-Handschreften. Göttingen, 1934.
	Phil 3110.79	Pamphlet box. Böhme, J.
Htn	Phil 3110.80*	Werdenhagen, I.G. Psychologia. Amsterdam, 1632.
	Phil 3110.81	Okely, F. Memoris...Jacob Behrnen. Northampton, 1780.
	Phil 3110.84	Peip, A. Jakob Böhme der deutsche Philosoph. Leipzig, 1860.
	Phil 3110.84.5	Peip, A. Jakob Böhme, der deutsche Philosoph. Hamburg, 1862.
	Phil 3110.85	Martensen, Hans L. Jacob Böhme. Photoreproduction. London, 1885.
	Phil 3110.85.5	Martensen, Hans L. Jacob Böhme. Leipzig, 1882.
	Phil 3110.85.10	Martensen, Hans L. Jacob Boehme. London, 1949.
	Phil 3110.85.50	Penny. A.J. An introduction to the study of Jacob Boehme's writings. N.Y., 1901.
	Phil 3110.86	Penny, A.J. Jacob Boehme. London, 1912.
Htn	Phil 3110.87*	The life of one Jacob Boehmen. London, 1644.
Htn	Phil 3110.88*	Lamotte-Fouqué, Friedrich. Jakob Böhme. Greiz, 1831.
	Phil 3110.89	Harless, G.C.A. von. Jakob Böhme und die Alchymisten. Berlin, 1870.
	Phil 3110.90	Wernicke, A. Meister Jacob Böhme. Braunschweig, 1898.
	Phil 3110.91	Bornkamm, H. Luther und Böhme. Bonn, 1925.
	Phil 3110.92	Koyré, Alexandre. La philosophie de Jacob Boehme. Thèse. Paris, 1929.
	Phil 3110.92.5	Koyré, Alexandre. La philosophie de Jakob Boehme. Paris, 1929.
	Phil 3110.95	Grunsky, H.A. Jakob Böhme als Schöpfer einer germanischen Philosophie des Willens. Hamburg, 1940.
	Phil 3110.151	Deussen, Paul. Jakob Böhme. Leipzig, 1911.
	Phil 3110.155	Kielholz, A. Jakob Boehme. Leipzig, 1919.
	Phil 3110.163	Barker, C.J. Pre-requisites for the study of Jakob Böhme. London, 1920.
	Phil 3110.165	Swainson, W.P. Jacob Boehme, the Teutonic philosopher. London, 1921.
Htn	Phil 3110.169*	Vetterling, H. The illuminate of Görlitz, or Jakob Böhme's (1575-1624) life and philosophy. Leipzig, 1923.
	Phil 3110.171	Hankamer, P. Jakob Böhme, Gestalt und Gestaltung. Bonn, 1924.
	Phil 3110.172	Ludwig, Else. Jakob Böhme, der Görlitzer Mystiker. 2. Aufl. Bad Smiedeberg, 1924.
	Phil 3110.173	Peuckert, W.E. Das Leben Jakob Böhmes. Jena, 1924.
	Phil 3110.174	Brinton, H. The mystic will. N.Y., 1930.
	Phil 3110.175	Alleman, G.M. A critique of some philosophical aspects of the mysticism of Jacob Boehme. Thesis. Philadelphia, 1932.
	Phil 3110.176	Popp, K.R. Jakob Böhme und Issac Newton. Inaug. Diss. Leipzig, 1935.
	Phil 3110.177	Benz, E. Der Vollkommene Mensch nach Böhme. Stuttgart, 1937.
	Phil 3110.178	Sillig, J.F. Jakob Böhme. Perna, 1801.
	Phil 3110.179	Jecht, Richard. Jakob Böhme und Gorlitz. Gorlitz, 1924.
	Phil 3110.180	Baden, Hans J. Das reliqiöse Problem der Gegenwart bei Jakob Böhme. Leipzig, 1939.
	Phil 3110.185	Grunsky, H.A. Jacob Böhme. Stuttgart, 1956.
	Phil 3110.190	Weiss, Victor. Die Gnosis Jakob Böhmes. Zürich, 1955.
	Phil 3110.192	Solms-Rödelheim, Günther. Die Grundvorstellungen Jacob Böhme. München, 1960.
	Phil 3110.195	Staurt, J.J. Sunrise to eternity. Philadelphia, 1957.

Phil 3120 History of philosophy - Local Modern philosophy - Germany - Individual philosophers - Other B

	Phil 3120.1.80	Maosherr, T. J.A.E. Biedermann. Jena, 1893.
	Phil 3120.1.125	Hennig, M. A.E. Biedermanns Theorie...religiöse Erkenntnis. Leipzig, 1902.
	Phil 3120.2.3	Bolzano, Bernard. Gesammelte Schriften. 2. Ausg. Wien, 1882.
	Phil 3120.2.20	Bolzano, Bernard. Bernard Bolzano - Gesamtausgabe. Stuttgart, 1969.
	Phil 3120.2.30	Bolzano, Bernard. O pokroku a dobročinnosti. Praha, 1951.
	Phil 3120.2.35	Bolzano, Bernard. O nejlepšim státě. Praha, 1952.
	Phil 3120.2.40	Bolzano, Bernard. Wissenschaft und Religion in Vormärz. Berlin, 1965.
	Phil 3120.2.45	Bolzano, Bernard. Was ist Philosophie? Amsterdam, 1969.
	Phil 3120.2.61	Bolzano, Bernard. Bolzano-Brevier. Wien, 1947.
	Phil 3120.2.79	Pamphlet box. Philosophy. German and Dutch. Bolzano, Bernard.
	Phil 3120.2.80	Bergmann, H. Das philosophische Werk Bernard Bolzanos. n.p., 1909.
	Phil 3120.2.82	Gotthardt, J. Das Wahrheits Problem. Inaug. Diss. Trier, 1918.
	Phil 3120.2.84	Gotthardt. J. Bolzano Lehre vom "Satz an Sich". Berlin, 1909.
	Phil 3120.2.87	Frank, Paul. Die philosophischen Problem in Dr. Bolzano's "Erbauungsreden". Inaug. Diss. Pritzwalk, 1926.
	Phil 3120.2.90	Wiegand, H. Der Wahrheitsbegriff in der Lehre. Inaug. Diss. Alfeld Leine, 1928.
	Phil 3120.2.95	Fels, Heinrich. Bernard Bolzano. Leipzig, 1929.
	Phil 3120.2.96	Winter, E. Leben und Geistige. Halle, 1949.
	Phil 3120.2.97	Winter, E. Religion und Offenbarung in der Religionsphilosophie Bernard Bolzanos. Breslau, 1932.
	Phil 3120.2.98	Winter, E. Bernard Bolzano und sein Kreis. Leipzig, 1933.
	Phil 3120.2.98.5	Winter, E. Der Bolzanoprozess. Brünn, 1944.
	Phil 3120.2.99	Waldschmitt, L. Bolzano's Begründung des objektivismus in der theoretischen und praktischen Philosophie. Giessen, 1937.
	Phil 3120.2.101	Franzis, Emerich. Bernard Bolzano. Münster, 1933.
	Phil 3120.2.105	Dr. Bolzano und seine Gegner. Sulzbach, 1839.
	Phil 3120.2.110	Kolman, E. Bernard Bol'tsano. Moskva, 1955.
	Phil 3120.2.112	Kolman, E. Bernard Bolzano. Berlin, 1963.
	Phil 3120.2.115	Zimmermann, J. Krug und Bolzano. Sulzbach, 1837.
	Phil 3120.2.120	Seidlerová, I. Politické a pociálné názory Bernard Bolzano. Praha, 1963.
	Phil 3120.2.125	Zeil, Wilhelm. Bolzano und die Sorben. Bautzen, 1967.
	Phil 3120.3.30	Barnick, Johannes. Vierfaltigkeit in Logik und Welt oder die vier Bücher vom Sinn des Ganzen. Berlin, 1969.
Htn	Phil 3120.3.30*	Burgeridicii, F. Institutionum logicarum. Cantabrigiae, 1647. 2 pam.
Htn	Phil 3120.3.31*	Burgeridicii, F. Institutionum logicarum. Libri duo. Cantabrigiae, 1660.
Htn	Phil 3120.3.35*	Burgeridicii, F. Idea philosophiae. Oxonii, 1667.

Phil 3120   History of philosophy - Local Modern philosophy - Germany - Individual philosophers - Other B - cont.

Phil 3120.4.31   Bilfinger, G.B. Dilucidationes philosophicae de Deo. 3. ed. Tubingae, 1746.
Phil 3120.4.80   Liebing, H. Zurschen Orthodoxie und Aufklärung. Tubingen, 1961.
Phil 3120.5.80   Pamphlet box. Philosophy. German. Bratuschick, Ernst.
Phil 3120.6.85   Struck, Gustav. Friedrich Bouterwek. Inaug. Diss. Rostock, 1919.
Phil 3120.7.81   Seiling, Max. Mäinlander, ein neuer Messias. München, 1888.
Phil 3120.8.20   Brentano, Franz. Die Abkehr von Nichtrealen. Bern, 1966.
Phil 3120.8.30   Brentano, Franz. Was für ein Philosoph manchmal Epoche macht. Wien, 1876.
Phil 3120.8.31   Brentano, Franz. Meine Letzten wünsche für Oesterreich. Stuttgart, 1895.
Phil 3120.8.32   Brentano, Franz. Die vier Phasen der Philosophie und ihr augenblicklichen Stand. Leipzig, 1926.
Phil 3120.8.35   Brentano, Franz. Religion und Philosophie. Bern, 1954.
Phil 3120.8.40   Brentano, Franz. Über die Zukunft der Philosophie. Leipzig, 1929.
Phil 3120.8.45   Brentano, Franz. Die Lehre vom Nrichtigen Urteil. Bern, 1956.
Phil 3120.8.50   Brentano, Franz. Grundzüge der Ästhetik. Bern, 1959.
Phil 3120.8.60F   Brentano, Franz. Index. Highland Park, Illinois, 1959.
Phil 3120.8.81   Kraus, Oskar. Franz Brentano. München, 1919.
Phil 3120.8.82   Kraus, Oskar. Franz Brentanos Stellung zur Phänomenologie und Gegenstandstheorie. Leipzig, 1924.
Phil 3120.8.85   Hoppenstedt, W. von. Franz Brentanos Kantkritik. Inaug. Diss. Kiel, 1933.
Phil 3120.8.87   Hauber, V. Wahrheit und Evidenz bei Franz Brentano. Inaug. Diss. Stuttgart, 1936.
Phil 3120.8.89   Skrbensky, L.H. Franz Brentano als Religionsphilosophie. Zürich, 1937.
Phil 3120.8.91   Naturwissenschaft und Metaphysik. Brünn, 1938.
Phil 3120.8.92   Hartlich, C. Die ethischen Theorien Franz Brentanos. Wurzburg, 1939.
Phil 3120.8.94   Schneider, Karl. Zur Kritik der Urteilslehre Franz Brentanos. Heidelberg, 1915.
Phil 3120.8.96   Margolius, Hans. Die Ethic Franz Brentanos. Leipzig, 1929.
Phil 3120.8.98   Kastil, A. Die Philosophie Franz Brentanos. München, 1951.
Phil 3120.8.100   Winter, E. Fanz Brentanos Ringen um eine neue Gottessicht. Brünn, 1941.
Phil 3120.8.110   Mueller, Richard. Franz Brentanos Lehre von den Gemütsbewegungen. Brünn, 1943.
Phil 3120.8.115   Gilson, Lucie. Méthode et métaphysique selon Franz Brentano. Paris, 1955.
Phil 3120.8.120   Gilson, Lucie. La psychologie descriptive selon Franz Brentano. Paris, 1955.
Phil 3120.8.126   Taljaard, J.A.L. Franz Brentano as wysgeer. Franeker, 1955.
Phil 3120.8.130   Windischer, Johannes. Franz Brentano und die Scholastik. Innsbruck, 1936.
Phil 3120.8.135   Satue, A.A. La doctrina de la intencionalidad en Franz Brentano. Barcelona, 1961.
Phil 3120.8.140   Zawischa, E. Das Rätsel und sein Meister Franz Brentano. n.p., 1961.
Phil 3120.8.145   Bergmann, Gustav. Realism; a critique of Brentano and Meinong. Madison, 1967.
Phil 3120.8.150   Srzednicki, Jan. Franz Brentano's analysis of truth. The Hague, 1965.
Phil 3120.8.155   Dix, Petrus Gerandus. De verhouting van de psycologie tot de wijsbegeerte in der leer van Brentano. n.p., 1966.
Phil 3120.8.160   Rancurello, Antos C. A study of Franz Brentano; his psychological standpoint and his significance in the history of psychology. N.Y., 1968.
Phil 3120.8.165   Bausola, Adriano. Conoscenza e moralità in Franz Brentano. Milano, 1968.
Phil 3120.10.80   Theile, Günther. Philosophische Streifzüge an deutschen Hochschulen. Berlin, 1904.
Phil 3120.10.81   Eckstein, Ernst. Der Begriff des Daseins bei Julius Bergmann. Inaug. Diss. Erlangen, 1902.
Phil 3120.11.80   Thodoroff, C. Julius Bahnsen und die Hauptprobleme seiner charakterologie. Erlangen, 1910.
Phil 3120.11.82   Fechter, Paul. Die Grundlagen der Realdialektik. Inaug. Diss. München, 1906.
Phil 3120.11.84   Leiste, Heinrich. Die Charakterologie von Julius Bahnsen. Diss. Köln, 1928.
Phil 3120.11.85   Heydorn, H.J. Julius Bahnsen. Göttingen, 1952.
DL Phil 3120.11.90   Bolland, G.J.P.J. Collegium logicum. 2. druk. Amsterdam, 1931. 2v.
Phil 3120.11.92   Bolland, G.J.P.J. Zuivere rede. Leiden, 1904.
Phil 3120.11.93   Bolland, G.J.P.J. Verslag van de rede. Leiden, 1906.
Phil 3120.11.94   Bolland, G.J.P.J. Het schoone en de kunst of de naaste en onmiddellijke zelfbevrediging van absolute geestelijkheid in het kort besproken. Amsterdam, 1906.
Phil 3120.11.95   Bolland, G.J.P.J. Open brief aan den heer K.J.A.M. Schaepman. Leiden, 1899.
Phil 3120.11.96   Bolland, G.J.P.J. Aanschomving en verstand. Leiden, 1897.
Phil 3120.11.97   Bolland, G.J.P.J. De natuur. Leiden, 1915.
Phil 3120.11.98   Bolland, G.J.P.J. Spreuken. 's Gravenhage, 1962.
Phil 3120.12.80   Kegel, Martin. Bruno Bauers Übergang von der hegelschen Rechten zum Radikalismus. Inaug. Diss. Leipzig, 1908.
Phil 3120.13.9   Bolland, G.J.P.J. Briefwechsel mit E. von Hartmann. 's Gravenhage, 1937.
Phil 3120.13.90   Wigersma, I.B. Bolland. Amsterdam, 1927.
Phil 3120.14.90   Grubbe, Samuel. Dissertatio de realismo rationali Bardilii. Upsaliae, 1806.
Phil 3120.15.30   Brunner, Constantin. Kunst, Philosophie, Mystik, Gesammelte Anfsätze. Zürich, 1940.
Phil 3120.15.31   Brunner, Constantin. Unser Charakter, oder Ich bin der Richtige! Zürich, 1939.
Phil 3120.15.33   Brunner, Constantin. Der entlarvte Mensch. Haag, 1951.
Phil 3120.15.35   Brunner, Constantin. Materialismus und Idealismus. Köln, 1959.
Phil 3120.15.40   Brunner, Constantin. Science, spirit, superstition; a new enquiry into human thought. Toronto, 1968.
Phil 3120.15.47   Brunner, Constantin. Aus meinem Tagebuch. 2. Aufl. Stuttgart, 1967.
Phil 3120.15.50   Brunner, Constantin. Vom Einsiedler Constantin Brunner. Potsdam, 1924.
Phil 3120.15.90   Moebius, A. Constantin Brunners Lehre, das Evangelium. Berlin, 1910.
Phil 3120.15.95   Von Constantin Brunner und seinem Werk. Berlin, 1927.
Phil 3120.15.97   Bickel, Lothar. Wirklichkeit und Wahrheit des Denkens. Zürich, 1953.

Phil 3120   History of philosophy - Local Modern philosophy - Germany - Individual philosophers - Other B - cont.

Phil 3120.15.97.5   Bickel, Lothar. Kultur. Zürich, 1956.
Phil 3120.15.97.10   Bickel, Lothar. Das Leben - eine Aufgabe. Zürich, 1959.
Phil 3120.15.97.15   Bickel, Lothar. Aussen und Innen. Zürich, 1960.
Phil 3120.16.30   Brastberger, G.U. Philosophische Briefe an meine Schwester. Halle, 1779.
Phil 3120.17.90   Thöne, Fritz. Erich Becher als Vertreter des Eudämonismus. Diss. Giessen, 1933.
Phil 3120.18.90   Reiser, Joseph. Zur Erkenntnislehre Jakob Sigismund Becko. München, 1934.
Phil 3120.19.90   Keller, E. Die Philosophie Bruno Bauchs, als Ausdruck germanischer Geisteshaltung. Stuttgart, 1935.
Phil 3120.19.95   Strasser, Johano. Die Bedeutung des hypothetischen Imperativs in der Ethik Bruno Bauchs. Bonn, 1967.
Phil 3120.20   Burkamp, Wilhelm. Wirklichkeit und Sinn. v.1-2. Berlin, 1938.
Phil 3120.21   Beerling, Reinier Franciscus. Antithesen. Haarlem, 1935.
Phil 3120.21.5   Beerling, Reinier Franciscus. Heden en verleden. Arnhem, 1962.
Phil 3120.21.10   Beerling, Reinier Franciscus. Ideeën en idolen. Arnhem, 1968.
Phil 3120.22   Blüher, Hans. Empedokles, oder das Sakrament des freien Todes. n.p., 1918.
Phil 3120.22.5   Blüher, Hans. Gesammelte Aufsätze. Jena, 1919.
Phil 3120.22.10   Blüher, Hans. Philosophie auf Posten, Schriften 1916-21. Heidelberg, 1928.
Phil 3120.22.15   Blüher, Hans. Die Achse der Natur. Hamburg, 1949.
Phil 3120.22.20   Blüher, Hans. Werke und Tage. München, 1953.
Phil 3120.22.25F   Blüher, Hans. In medias res. Jena, 1920.
Phil 3120.22.30   Pamphlet vol. Blüher, Hans. Prien, 1920. 4 pam.
Phil 3120.22.35   Blüher, Hans. Die Wiedergeburt der platonischen Akademie. Jena, 1920. 4 pam.
Phil 3120.22.40   Blüher, Hans. Traktat über die Heilkunde. Jena, 1928.
Phil 3120.22.80   Thies, Heinz. Die Rolle der Erotik in der männlichen Gesellschaft. Baum, 193-.
Phil 3120.23.81   Bogdanski, A.A. The significance of Clemens Baeumker in neo-scholastic philosophy. Milwaukee, 1942.
Phil 3120.24.80   Zee, Teartse van der. Eat oer it libben fan Prof. Dr. Tj. de Boer, 1866-1942. Ljouwert, 1965.
Phil 3120.25   Bohnenblust, Gottfried. Vom Adel des Geistes; gesammelte Reden. Zürich, 1943.
Phil 3120.26.30   Brod, Max. Diesseits und Jenseits. Winterthur, 1947. 2v.
Phil 3120.27.25   Binswanger, L. Ausgewählte Vorträge und Aufsätze. Bern, 1961. 2v.
Phil 3120.27.30   Binswanger, L. Ausgewählte Vorträge und Aufsätze. Bern, 1947. 2v.
Phil 3120.27.32   Binswanger, L. Grundformen und Erkenntnis menschlichen Daseins. 2. Aufl. Zürich, 1953.
Phil 3120.27.40   Binswanger, L. Being in the world. N.Y., 1963.
Phil 3120.28.25   Pamphlet vol. Beck, M. A collection of reprints. 5 pam.
Phil 3120.30.7   Buber, Martin. Writings. N.Y., 1958.
Phil 3120.30.15   Buber, Martin. Werke. München, 1962. 3v.
Phil 3120.30.20   Buber, Martin. The way of response. N.Y., 1966.
Phil 3120.30.22A   Buber, Martin. Volker, Staaten und Zion. Berlin, 1917.
Phil 3120.30.22B   Buber, Martin. Volker, Staaten und Zion. Berlin, 1917.
Phil 3120.30.30   Buber, Martin. Urdistanz und Beziehung. Heidelberg, 1951.
Phil 3120.30.32   Buber, Martin. On Judaism. N.Y., 1967.
Phil 3120.30.35   Buber, Martin. Gottesfinsterrns. Zürich, 1953.
Phil 3120.30.37   Buber, Martin. Der Mensch und sein Gebild. Heidelberg, 1955.
Phil 3120.30.38   Buber, Martin. On the Bible; eighteen studies. N.Y., 1968.
Phil 3120.30.39   Buber, Martin. Ereignisse und Begegnungen. Leipzig, 1925.
Phil 3120.30.39.5   Buber, Martin. Ereignisse und Begegnungen. Berlin, 193-?
Phil 3120.30.39.10   Buber, Martin. Begegnung. Stuttgart, 1960.
Phil 3120.30.41   Buber, Martin. Das Problem des Menschen. Heidelberg, 1948.
Phil 3120.30.42   Buber, Martin. Ich und Du. Heidelberg, 1958.
Phil 3120.30.43   Buber, Martin. Ich und Du. Leipzig, 1923.
Phil 3120.30.43.5   Buber, Martin. Ich und Du. Köln, 1966.
Phil 3120.30.44   Buber, Martin. I and thou. Edinburg, 1958.
Phil 3120.30.44.3   Buber, Martin. I and thou. N.Y., 1970.
Phil 3120.30.44.5   Buber, Martin. I and thou. 2. ed. N.Y., 1958.
Phil 3120.30.45   Buber, Martin. Bilder von Gut und Böse. Köln, 1952.
Phil 3120.30.47   Buber, Martin. Zwei Glaubensweisen. Zürich, 1950.
Phil 3120.30.49   Buber, Martin. Die Rede. Leipzig, 1920.
Phil 3120.30.51   Buber, Martin. Die Frage an den Einzelnen. Berlin, 1936.
Phil 3120.30.53   Buber, Martin. Reden über Erziehung. Heidelberg, 1953.
Phil 3120.30.55   Buber, Martin. Rede über das Erzieherische. Berlin, 1926.
Phil 3120.30.56   Buber, Martin. Nachlese. Heidelberg, 1965.
Phil 3120.30.56.40   Buber, Martin. A believing humanism: my testament 1902-1965. N.Y., 1967.
Phil 3120.30.57   Buber, Martin. Die Stunde und die Erkenntnis. Berlin, 1936.
Phil 3120.30.60   Buber, Martin. Die Schriften über das dialogische Prinzip. Heidelberg, 1954.
Phil 3120.30.62   Buber, Martin. Hin Weise. Zürich, 1953.
Phil 3120.30.63   Buber, Martin. Dialogisches Leben. Zürich, 1947.
Phil 3120.30.64   Buber, Martin. Schuld und Schuldgefühle. Heidelberg, 1958.
Phil 3120.30.68A   Buber, Martin. Two types of faith. London, 1951.
Phil 3120.30.68B   Buber, Martin. Two types of faith. London, 1951.
Phil 3120.30.70   Buber, Martin. Pointing the way. London, 1951.
Phil 3120.30.71   Buber, Martin. Martin Buber, philosophe de la relation. Paris, 1968.
Phil 3120.30.72   Buber, Martin. Between man and man. London, 1947.
Phil 3120.30.73   Buber, Martin. Eclipse of God. N.Y., 1957.
Phil 3120.30.74   Buber, Martin. Images of good and evil. London, 1952.
Phil 3120.30.75   Buber, Martin. Good and evil. N.Y., 1953.
Phil 3120.30.76   Buber, Martin. Logos. Heidelberg, 1962.
Phil 3120.30.77   Buber, Martin. Zwischen Gesellschaft und Staat. Heidelberg, 1952.
Phil 3120.30.78   Buber, Martin. Israel and the world. 2. ed. N.Y., 1963.
Phil 3120.30.79   Buber, Martin. The knowledge of man. N.Y., 1965.
Phil 3120.30.80   Friedman, M.S. Martin Buber. Chicago, 1955.
Phil 3120.30.82   Cohen, A.A. Martin Buber. London, 1957.
Phil 3120.30.82.1   Cohen, A.A. Martin Buber. N.Y., 1957.
Phil 3120.30.83   Diamand, Malcolm L. Martin Buber, Jewish existentialist. N.Y., 1960.
Phil 3120.30.85   Kohn, Hans. Martin Buber. Hellerau, 1930.
Phil 3120.30.85.2   Kohn, Hans. Martin Buber, sein Werk und seine Zeit. Köln, 1961.

Classified Listing

Phil 3120   History of philosophy - Local Modern philosophy - Germany - Individual philosophers - Other B - cont.

Phil 3120.30.87   Goldstein, Walter Benjamin. Die Botschaft Martin Bubers. Jerusalem, 1952-56. 3v.

Phil 3120.30.88   Goldstein, Walter Benjamin. Martin Buber. Jerusalem, 1967.

Phil 3120.30.89   Goldstein, Walter Benjamin. Der Glaube Martin Bubers. Jerusalem, 1969.

Phil 3120.30.90   Balthasar, Hans von. Einsame Zinsprache; Martin Buber und das Christentum. Köln, 1958.

Phil 3120.30.91   Balthasar, Hans von. Martin Buber and Christianity. London, 1961.

Phil 3120.30.92   Hammerstein, Franz von. Das Messiasproblem bei Martin Buber. Stuttgart, 1958.

Phil 3120.30.95   Beek, Martinus Adrianus. Martin Buber. Baarn, 1964.

Phil 3120.30.95.5   Beek, Martinus Adrianus. Martin Buber: personalist and prophet. Westminster, 1968.

Phil 3120.30.100   Lang, Bernhard. Martin Buber und das dialogische Leben. Bern, 1963.

Phil 3120.30.105   Berkovits, Eliezer. A Jewish critique of the philosophy. N.Y., 1962.

Phil 3120.30.110   Anzenbacher, Arno. Die Philosophie Martin Bubers. Wien, 1965.

Phil 3120.30.115   Levin-Goldschmidt, Hermann. Abschied von Martin Buber. Köln, 1966.

Phil 3120.30.120   Babolin, Albino. Essere e alterità in Martin Buber. Padova, 1965.

Phil 3120.30.125   Kraft, Werner. Gespräche mit Martin Buber. München, 1966.

Phil 3120.30.130   München ehrt Martin Buber. München, 1961.

Phil 3120.30.135   Schaeder, Grete. Martin Buber, nebräischer Humanismus. Gottingen, 1966.

Phil 3120.30.140   Grünfeld, Werner. Der begegnungscharakter der Wirklichkeit...Martin Bubers. Ratingen, 1965.

Phil 3120.30.145   Smith, Ronald Gregor. Martin Buber. Richmond, 1967.

Phil 3120.30.150   Schilpp, Paul Arthur. The philosophy of Martin Buber. 1st ed. La Salle, 1967.

Phil 3120.30.155   Ben-Chorin, Schalom. Zwiesprache mit Martin Buber. München, 1966.

Phil 3120.30.160   Oliver, Roy. The wanderer and the way. Ithaca, N.Y., 1968.

Phil 3120.30.165   Levinson, Nathan P. Martin Buber. Frankfurt, 1966. 2v.

Phil 3120.30.170   Pilosof, Nelson. Martin Buber, profeta del diálogo. Montevideo, 1965.

Phil 3120.30.175   Dujoune, León. Martin Buber. Buenos Aires, 1966[1965]

Phil 3120.30.180   Wood, Robert E. Martin Buber's ontology. Evanston, 1969.

Phil 3120.30.185   Marcel, Gabriel. Martin Buber. L'homme et le philosophe. Bruxelles, 1968.

Phil 3120.30.190   Wehr, Gerhard. Martin Buber in Selbstzeugnissen und Bilddokumenten. Reinbek, 1968.

Phil 3120.30.195   Rosenblueth, Pinchas Erich. Martin Buber: sein Denken und Wirken. Hannover, 1968.

Phil 3120.30.200   Hodes, Aubrey. Martin Buber; an intimate portrait. N.Y., 1971.

Phil 3120.30.205   Wachinger, Lorenz. Der Glaubensbegriff Martin Bubers. 1. Aufl. München, 1970.

Phil 3120.30.210   Edwards, Paul. Buber and Buberism. Lawrence, 1971.

Phil 3120.31.30   Boem, W. Über die Möglichkeit systematischer Kulturphilosophie. Saale, 1927.

Phil 3120.32.21   Beth, Evert Willem. Science a road to wisdom: collected philosophical studies. Dordrecht, 1968.

Phil 3120.32.30   Beth, Evert Willem. Door wetenschap tot wijsheid. Assen, 1964.

Phil 3120.35.30   Bolland, G.J.P.J. Natuurbegrip en leuen. Leiden, 1917. 2 pam.

Phil 3120.40.30   Bierens de Haan, J.D. Het tragische schuld noodlot en bevrijding. Leiden, 1933.

Phil 3120.40.35   Bierens de Haan, J.D. De zin van het komische. Leiden, 1930.

Phil 3120.40.40   Bierens de Haan, J.D. De strijd tusschen idealisme en naturalisme in de 19. eeuw. Haarlem, 1929.

Phil 3120.40.45   Bierens de Haan, J.D. Het rijk van den geest. Zeist, 1938.

Phil 3120.40.50   Bierens de Haan. J.D. De norm der waarheid is in ons-zelf. Utrecht, 1897.

Phil 3120.40.55   Bierens de Haan, J.D. Innerlijk perspectief. Assen, 1966.

Phil 3120.40.80   Brahell Brujs, W.R. van. Ter herdenling van Dr. J.D. Bierens de Haan. Naarden, 1944.

Phil 3120.40.82   Feestbundel aangeboden aan Dr. J.D. Bierens de Haan. Assen, 1936.

Phil 3120.45.30   Brandenstein, Béla. Vom Sinn der Philosophie und ihrer Geschichte. Bonn, 1957.

Phil 3120.45.35   Brandenstein, Béla. Wahrheit und Wirklichkeit. Meisenheim, 1965.

Phil 3120.45.40   Brandenstein, Béla. Das Bild des Menschen und die Idee des Humanismus. Bregenz, 1948.

Phil 3120.45.45   Brandenstein, Béla. Grundlegung der Philosophie. Halle, 1926[1970] 6v.

Phil 3120.45.50   Brandenstein, Béla. Der Aufbau des Seins; System der Philosophie. Tübingen, 1950.

Phil 3120.50.30   Hertz-Eichenrode, Dieter. Der jünghegelianer Bruno Bauer im Vormärz. Berlin, 1959.

Phil 3120.55.20   Bloch, Ernst. Gesamtausgabe. Frankfurt, 1961. 15v.

Phil 3120.55.25   Bloch, Ernst. Die Kunst, Schiller zu sprechen und andere literarische Aufsätze. Frankfurt, 1969. 14v.

Phil 3120.55.30   Bloch, Ernst. Das Morgen im Heute; eine Auswahl. Frankfurt, 1960.

Phil 3120.55.35   Bloch, Ernst. Verfremdungen. Frankfurt, 1962. 2v.

Phil 3120.55.40   Bloch, Ernst. Wegzeichen der Hoffnung. Frankfurt, 1967.

Phil 3120.55.45   Bloch, Ernst. Auswahl aus seinen Schriften. Frankfurt, 1967.

Phil 3120.55.50   Bloch, Ernst. A philosophy of the future. N.Y., 1970.

Phil 3120.55.55   Bloch, Ernst. Tübinger Einleitung in die Philosophie I. Frankfurt, 1963.

Phil 3120.55.60   Bloch, Ernst. Pädagogica. 1.Aufl. Frankfurt, 1971.

Phil 3120.55.80   Buetow, H.G. Philosophie und Gesellschaft im Denken Ernst Blochs. Berlin, 1963.

Phil 3120.55.82   Marsch, Wolf. Hoffen worauf? Hamburg, 1963.

Phil 3120.55.85   Unseld, Siegfried. Ernst Bloch zu ehren. Frankfurt, 1965.

Phil 3120.55.90   Roeder von Diersburg, Egenolf. Zur Ontologie und Logik offener Systeme. Hamburg, 1967.

Phil 3120.55.95   Über Ernst Bloch. Frankfurt, 1968.

Phil 3120.55.100   Jager, Alfred. Reich ohne Gott; zur Eschatologie Ernst Blochs. Zürich, 1969.

Phil 3120.55.105   Kraenzle, Karl. Utopie und Ideologie. Bern, 1970.

Phil 3120.60.30   Buchheim, Karl. Logik der Tatsachen. München, 1959.

Phil 3120.61.30   Bueschel, Johann Gabriel Bernhard. Über die Charlatanerie der Gelehrten seit Menken. Leipzig, 1971.

Phil 3120   History of philosophy - Local Modern philosophy - Germany - Individual philosophers - Other B - cont.

Phil 3120.62.30   Bollnow, Otto Fredrich. Mass und Vermesserheit des Menschen. Göttingen, 1962.

Phil 3120.64.30   Bense, Max. Die abendländische Leidenschaft. München, 1938.

Phil 3120.65.30   Hammond, Kenneth R. The psychology of Egon Brunswik. N.Y., 1966.

Phil 3120.66.30   Barth, Heinrich. Erkenntnis der Existenz. Basel, 1965.

Phil 3120.67.80   Neuwinger, Rudolf. Die Philosophie Ernst Bergmanns. Stuttgart, 1938.

Phil 3120.68.79   Buhr, Manfred. Wilhelm Raimund Beyer, eine Bibliographie. Wien, 1967.

Phil 3120.69.30   Berg, Jan Hendrik van den. Metabletica van de materie. Nijkerk, 1968-

Phil 3140   History of philosophy - Local Modern philosophy - Germany - Individual philosophers - Clauberg, Johann

Phil 3140.1   Clauberg, Johann. Opera omnia philosophica. Reprint. Hildesheim, 1968. 2v.

Phil 3140.80   Müller, H. Johannes Clauberg. Jena, 1891.

Phil 3140.81   Göpfert. Claubergstudien. Meiningen, 1898.

Phil 3140.82   Brosch, P. Die Ontologie des J. Clauberg. Greifswald, 1926.

Phil 3140.85   Weier, Winfred. Die Stellung des Johannes Clauberg in der Philosophie. Diss. Mainz, 1960.

Phil 3160   History of philosophy - Local Modern philosophy - Germany - Individual philosophers - Other C

Phil 3160.1.79   Pamphlet box. Philosophy. German and Dutch. Class, Gustav.

Phil 3160.2.75   Carneri, B. Bartholomäus von Carneri's Briefwechsel mit E. Häckel und F. Jodl. Leipzig, 1922.

Phil 3160.2.79   Pamphlet box. Philosophy. German and Dutch. Carneri, B.

Phil 3160.2.85   Harpf, Adolf. Darwin in der Ethik. Leoben, 1901.

Phil 3160.2.87   Steiner, R. Bartholomäus Carneri, der Ethiker des Darwinismus. Dresden, 1900.

Phil 3160.3.79   Pamphlet box. Philosophy. German and Dutch. Cohen, Herma

Phil 3160.3.80   Philosophische Abhandlungen H. Cohen zum 70sten Geburtsta dargebracht. Berlin, 1912.

Phil 3160.3.81   Fritzsche, R.A. Hermann Cohen. Berlin, 1922.

Phil 3160.3.82   Natorp, Paul. Hermann Cohen. Marburg, 1918.

Phil 3160.3.83   Kinkel, N. Hermann Cohen. Stuttgart, 1924.

Phil 3160.3.84   Rosenzweig, L. La restauration de l'a priori kantien par H. Cohen. Paris, 1927.

Phil 3160.3.87   Jospe, Alfred. Die Unterscheidung von Mythos und Religion hei Hermann Cohen. Inaug. Diss. Oppeln, 1932.

Phil 3160.3.89   Rosmarin, T.W. (Mrs.). Religion of reason. N.Y., 1936.

Phil 3160.3.91   Kaplan, Simon. Das Geschichtsproblem in der Philosophie Hermann Cohen. Berlin, 1930.

Phil 3160.3.92   Cohen, Hermann. Briefe. Berlin, 1939.

Phil 3160.3.95   Levin-Goldschmidt, Hermann. Hermann Cohen und Martin Buber. Genève, 1946.

Phil 3160.3.98   Melher, Jehuda. Hermann Cohen's philosophy of Judaism. N.Y., 1968.

Phil 3160.3.100   Goldstein, Walter. Hermann Cohen. Jerusalem, 1963.

Phil 3160.4.3   Carriere, M. Gesammelte Werke. v.1-14. Leipzig, 1886-94. 12v.

Phil 3160.5.81   Saal, Ernst. Hans Cornelius Erkenntnistheorie im Verhältnis zu der Kants. Diss. Giessen, 1919.

Phil 3160.6.30   Crusius, Christian August. Die philosophischen Hauptwerke. v.1-3. Hildesheim, 1964- 3v.

Phil 3160.6.81   Festner, Carl. Christian August Crusius als Metaphysiker. Halle, 1892.

Phil 3160.6.85   Heimsoeth, H. Metaphysik und Kritik bei Christian August Crusius. Berlin, 1926.

Phil 3160.7.85   Friedmann, P. Darstellung und Kritik der naturalistischen Weltanschauung H. Czolbes. Inaug. Diss. Berlin, 1905.

Phil 3160.9   Carus, Karl Gustav. Lebens Erinnerungen und Denkwürdigkeiten. Weimar, 1966. 2v.

Phil 3160.9.30   Carus, Karl Gustav. Karl Gustav Carus und Carl Fr. Ph. von Martins. Halle, 1939.

Phil 3160.9.80   Kern, Hans. Die Philosophie des Carl Gustav Carus. Berlin, 1926.

Phil 3160.9.83   Langewisch, Eva. Das teleologische Prinzip bei Carl Gustav Carus. Inaug. Diss. Würzburg, 1927.

Phil 3160.9.85   Klink, Siegfried. Das Prinzip des Unbewussten bei Carl Gustav Carus. Tübingen, 1933.

Phil 3160.9.87   Wäsche, E. Carl Gustav Carus und die romantische Weltanschauung. Dusseldorf, 1933.

Phil 3160.9.90   Bakker, Reinout. Het wijsgerig en psychologisch denken van Carl Gustav Carus in het licht van zijn Godsbeschouwing. Assen, 1954.

Phil 3160.9.95   Kloppe, Wolfgang. Erinnerungen an Carl Gustav Carus. Berlin, 1969.

Phil 3160.10.90   Burg, Josef. Konstitution und Gegenstand im logistischen Neupositivismus Rudolf Carnaps. Inaug. Diss. Leipzig, 1933.

Phil 3160.10.95   Butrick, Richard. Carnap on meaning and analyticity. The Hague, 1970.

Phil 3160.11.5   Cysarz, Herbert. Das Unsterbliche. Halle, 1940.

Phil 3160.11.10   Cysarz, Herbert. Das seiende Sein. Wien, 1948.

Phil 3160.12.7   Schilpp, Paul. The philosophy of Ernst Cassirer. N.Y., 1958.

Phil 3160.12.10   Hamburg, C.H. Symbol and reality. The Hague, 1956.

Phil 3160.12.30   Cassirer, Ernst. Wesen und Wirkung des Symbolbegriffs. Oxford, 1956.

Phil 3160.12.40   Cassirer, Ernst. The logic of the humanities. New Haven, 1961.

Phil 3160.12.42   Cassirer, Ernst. Zur Logik der Kulturwissenschaften. 2. Aufl. Darmstadt, 1961.

Phil 3160.12.80   Rein, Mercedes. Ernst Cassirer. Montevideo, 1959.

Phil 3160.12.85   Gaona, Francisco. Das Raumproblem in Cassirers Philosophie der Mythologie. Tübingen, 1965.

Phil 3160.13   Cohn, Jonas. Wirklichkeit als Aufgabe. Stuttgart, 1955.

Phil 3160.15   Conrad-Martius, Hedwig. Das Sein. München, 1957.

Phil 3160.15.5   Avé-Lallemant, E. Der kategoriale Ort des Seelischen in der Naturwirklichkeit. München, 1959.

Phil 3160.15.10   Conrad-Martius, Hedwig. Schriften zur Philosophie. München, 1963-64. 3v.

Phil 3160.20   Cramer, Wolfgang. Die absolute Reflexion. Frankfurt, 1966- 2v.

Phil 3195 History of philosophy - Local Modern philosophy - Germany - Individual philosophers - D

Phil 3195.1.80 Neubert-Drobisch, W. Moritz Wilhelm Drobisch. Leipzig, 1902.
Phil 3195.1.81 Flügel, Otto. Religionsphilosophie der Schule Herbarts, Drobisch und Hartenstein. Langensalza, 1905.
Phil 3195.2.78 Pamphlet box. Philosophy. German and Dutch. Deutinger, Martin.
Phil 3195.2.79 Sattel, G. Martin Deutingers Gotteslehre. Regensburg, 1905.
Phil 3195.2.80 Sattel, G. Martin Deutinger als Ethiker. Paderborn, 1908.
Phil 3195.2.85 Deutinger, Martin. Martin Deutinger. München, 1938.
Phil 3195.2.90 Henckmann, Wolfhart. Das Wesen der Kunst in der$Ästhetik Martin Deutingers. München, 1966.
Phil 3195.2.93 Neudecker, G. Der Philosoph Deutinger und ultramontane Sophistik. Würzburg, 1877.
Phil 3195.2.95 Kastner, Lorenz. Martin Deutinger's Leben und Schriften. München, 1875.
Phil 3195.2.120 Endres, Joseph A. Martin Deutinger. Mainz, 1906.
Phil 3195.2.125 Ettlinger, Max. Die Ästhetik Martin Deutingers. Kempten, 1914.
Phil 3195.3 Dietzgen, Joseph. Sämtliche Schriften. Wiesbaden, 1911. 3v.
Phil 3195.3.6 Dietzgen, Joseph. Josef Dietzgens kleinere Philosophie. Stuttgart, 1903.
Phil 3195.3.10 Dietzgen, Joseph. Ausgewählte Schriften. 1. Aufl. Berlin, 1954.
Phil 3195.3.31 Dietzgen, Joseph. Das Acquisit der Philosophie und Briefe. Stuttgart, 1903.
Phil 3195.3.33 Dietzgen, Joseph. Das Wesen der menschlichen Kopfarbeit. Berlin, 1955.
Phil 3195.3.35 Dietzgen, Joseph. Schriften. Berlin, 1962.
Phil 3195.3.80 Dietzgen, Joseph. Joseph Dietzgens Philosophie. München, 1910.
Phil 3195.3.82 Hepner, Adolf. Josef Dietzgens philosophische Lehren. Stuttgart, 1916.
Phil 3195.3.84 Volkova, V.V. Iosif Ditsgen. Moskva, 1961.
Phil 3195.4.81 Rosenkranz, Karl. Erinnerungen an Karl Daub. Berlin, 1837.
Phil 3195.5.81 Deubler, Konrad. Tagebücher...Bauernphilosophen. Leipzig, 1886. 2v.
Phil 3195.6.01 Herrmann, Ulrich. Bibliographie Wilhelm Dilthey. Berlin, 1969.
Phil 3195.6.30 Dilthey, Wilhelm. Gesammelte Schriften. v.1-9,11-12. Leipzig, 1923-36. 11v.
Phil 3195.6.30.5 Dilthey, Wilhelm. Gesammelte Schriften. Stuttgart, 1957- 12v.
Phil 3195.6.30.10 Dilthey, Wilhelm. Gesammelte Schriften. v.1-17. Stuttgart, 1962- 16v.
Phil 3195.6.31 Dilthey, Wilhelm. Von deutscher Dichtung und Musik. Leipzig, 1933.
Phil 3195.6.31.2 Dilthey, Wilhelm. Von deutscher Dichtung und Musik. 2. Aufl. Stuttgart, 1957.
Phil 3195.6.33 Dilthey, Wilhelm. Briefwechsel zwischen Wilhelm Dilthey und den Grafen Paul York von Watenburg. Halle, 1923.
Phil 3195.6.35 Dilthey, Wilhelm. Die Philosophie des Lebens. Frankfurt, 1946.
Phil 3195.6.38 Dilthey, Wilhelm. The essence of philosophy. Chapel Hill, 1954.
Phil 3195.6.40 Dilthey, Wilhelm. Grundriss der allgemeinen Geschichte der Philosophie. Frankfurt, 1949.
Phil 3195.6.45 Dilthey, Wilhelm. Philosophy of existence. N.Y., 1957.
Phil 3195.6.50 Dilthey, Wilhelm. Meanings in history. London, 1961.
Phil 3195.6.75 Dilthey, Wilhelm. Der junge Dilthey. Leipzig, 1933.
Phil 3195.6.76 Dilthey, Wilhelm. Der junge Dilthey. 2. Aufl. Stuttgart, 1960.
Phil 3195.6.79.6 Dilthey, Wilhelm. Biographisch-literarischer Grundriss der allgemeinen Geschichte der Philosophie. 6. Aufl. Trebnitz, 189-.
Phil 3195.6.80 Pamphlet box. Dilthey, Wilhelm. German dissertations.
Phil 3195.6.81 Stein, Arthur. Der Begriff des Geistes bei Dilthey. Bern, 1913.
Phil 3195.6.83A Spranger, Eduard. Wilhelm Dilthey. Berlin, 1912.
Phil 3195.6.83B Spranger, Eduard. Wilhelm Dilthey. Berlin, 1912.
Phil 3195.6.84 Stein, Arthur. Der Begriff des Verstehens bei Dilthey. 2. Aufl. Tübingen, 1926.
Phil 3195.6.85 Wach, Joachim. Die Typenlehre Trendelenburgs und ihr Einfluss auf Dilthey. Tübingen, 1926.
Phil 3195.6.86 Unger, Rudolf. Weltanschauung und Dichtung...Dilthey. Zürich, 1917.
Phil 3195.6.89 Degener, Alfons. Dilthey und das Problem der Metaphysik. Bonn, 1933.
Phil 3195.6.91 Cüppers, Clemens. Die erkenntnistheoretischen Grundgedanken Wilhelm Diltheys. Leipzig, 1933.
Phil 3195.6.92 Cüppers, Clemens. Die erkenntnistheoretischen Grundgedanken Wilhelm Diltheys. Inaug. Diss. Leipzig, 1933.
Phil 3195.6.94 Hodges, Herbert A. Wilhelm Dilthey. London, 1944.
Phil 3195.6.94.5 Hodges, Herbert A. The philosophy of Wilhelm Dilthey. London, 1952.
Phil 3195.6.95 Hennig, J. Lebensbegriff und Lebenskategorie. Inaug. Diss. Aachen, 1934.
Phil 3195.6.97 Nicolai, Heinz. Wilhelm Dilthey und das Problem der dichterischen Phantasie. Inaug. Diss. München, 1934.
Phil 3195.6.99 Katsube, Kenzo. Wilhelm Diltheys Methode der Lebensphilosophie. Hiroschima, 1931.
Phil 3195.6.101 Bollnow, O.F. Dilthey, eine Einführung in seine Philosophie. Leipzig, 1936.
Phil 3195.6.102 Bollnow, O.F. Dilthey. 2. Aufl. Stuttgart, 1955.
Phil 3195.6.103 Steuzel, J. Über Diltheys Verhaltnis zu Hegel. n.p., n.d.
Phil 3195.6.105 Pucciarelli, E. Introduccion a la filosofía de Dilthey. Buenos Aires, 1944.
Phil 3195.6.107 Bork, A. Diltheys Auffassung des griechischen Geistes. Berlin, 1944.
Phil 3195.6.109 Misch, Georg. Vom Lebens- und Gedankenkreis Wilhelm Diltheys. Frankfurt, 1947.
Phil 3195.6.111 Roura-Parella, J. El mundo histórico social. México, 1948.
Phil 3195.6.113 Kluback, William. Philosophy of history. N.Y., 1956.
Phil 3195.6.114 Mayz Vallenilla, Ernesto. La idea de estructura psiquica in Dilthey. Caracas, 1949.
Phil 3195.6.115 Hoefer, Josef. Vom Leben zur Wahrheit. Freiburg, 1936.
Phil 3195.6.120 Negri, Antonio. Saggi sullo storicismo tedesco. Milano, 1959.
Phil 3195.6.125 Richey, H.G. Die Überwindung der Subjektivität in der empirischen Philosophie Diltheys und Deweys. Göttingen, 1935.

Phil 3195 History of philosophy - Local Modern philosophy - Germany - Individual philosophers - D - cont.

Phil 3195.6.130 Diaz de Cerio Ruiz, Franco. W. Dilthey y el problema del mundo historico. Barcelona, 1959.
Phil 3195.6.135 Suter, Jean F. Philosophie et histoire chez W. Dilthey. Bale, 1960.
Phil 3195.6.140 Waesimann, A. Dilthey o la lírica del historicismo. Tucumán, 1959.
Phil 3195.6.145 Grzesik, Juergen. Die Geschichtlichkeit als Wesensverfassung des Menschen. Bonn, 1961.
Phil 3195.6.150 Stefanovies, T. Dilthey; una filosofía de la vida. Montevideo, 1961.
Phil 3195.6.155 Diwald, Hellmut. Wilhelm Dilthey. Göttingen, 1963.
Phil 3195.6.157 Birand, Kâmiran. Dilthey ve Rickert'te manevi ilimlerin temellendirilmesi. Ankara, 1954.
Phil 3195.6.160 Mueller-Vollmer, K. Towards a phenomenological theory of literature. The Hague, 1963.
Phil 3195.6.170 Foejo, W. Introducción a Dilthey. Xalapa, 1962.
VPhil 3195.6.175 Kuderowicz, Zbigniew. Światopogląd a zycie u Dilheya. Warszawa, 1966.
VPhil 3195.6.180 Kuderowicz, Zbigniew. Dilthey. Warszawa, 1967.
Phil 3195.6.185 Marini, Giuliano. Dilthey e la comprensione del mondo umano. Milano, 1965.
Phil 3195.6.190 Krausser, Peter. Kritik der endlichen Vernunft. Frankfurt, 1968.
Phil 3195.6.195 Calabrò, Gaetano. Dilthey e il diritto naturale. Napoli, 1968.
Phil 3195.6.200 Rodi, Frithjof. Morphologie und Hermeneutik. Stuttgart, 1969.
Phil 3195.6.205 Tuttle, Howard Nelson. Wilhelm Dilthey's philosophy of historical understanding. Leiden, 1969.
Phil 3195.6.210 Herrmann, Ulrich. Die Pädagogik Wilhelm Diltheys. Göttingen, 1971.
Phil 3195.7.80 Deussen, Paul. Mein Leben. Leipzig, 1922.
Phil 3195.8.80 Birkenbihl, M. Georg Friedrich Daumer. Inaug. Diss. Aschaffenburg, 1905.
Phil 3195.8.85 Kühne, A. Der Religionsphilosoph Georg F. Daumer. Inaug. Diss. Berlin, 1936.
Phil 3195.9.75 Dühring, E. Cursus der Philosophie als streng wissenschaftlicher Weltanschauung und Lebensgestaltung. Leipzig, 1875.
Phil 3195.9.77 Dühring, E. Sache, Leben, und Feinde. 2. Aufl. Leipzig, 1903.
Phil 3195.9.80 Posner, S. Abriss der Philosophie Eugen Dührings. Inaug. Diss. Breslau, 1906.
Phil 3195.9.81 Lau, Hamann. Eugen Dühring als Religionsphilosoph. Inaug. Diss. Lübeck, 1907.
Phil 3195.9.83 Druskowitz, H. Eugen Dühring. Heidelberg, 1889.
Phil 3195.10.30 Driesch, H. Lebenserinnerungen. Basel, 1951.
Phil 3195.10.90 Heinichen, Otto. Driesch's Philosophie. Leipzig, 1924.
Phil 3195.10.95 Gehlen, Arnold. Zur Theorie der Setzung und des setzungshaften Wissens bei Driesch. Inaug. Diss. Leipzig, 1927.
Phil 3195.10.99 Burchard, H. Der entelechiebegriff bei Aristoteles und Driesch. Inaug. Diss. Quakenbrück, 1928.
Phil 3195.10.100 Festschrift Hans Driesch zum 60. Geburtstag. v.1-2. Leipzig, 1927.
Phil 3195.10.105 Gehlen, Arnold. Zur Theorie der Setzung und des setzungshaften Wissens bei Driesch. Leipzig, 1927.
Phil 3195.10.110 Zilberis, B. Kant und die Philosophie Drieschs. Inaug. Diss. Vilkaviskis, 1932.
Phil 3195.10.113 Sacher, Heinz. Vergleich zwischen Rehmkes und Drieschs Philosophie. Inaug. Diss. Dresden, 1933.
Phil 3195.10.117 Coviello, A. El filósofo Hans Driesch. Tucumán, 1942.
Phil 3195.10.120 Wenzl, Aloys. Hans Driesch. Basel, 1951.
Phil 3195.10.130 Teufel, Herbert. Der Begriff des Werdens und der Entwicklung bei Driesch. München, 1960.
Phil 3195.11.35 Dessoir, Max. Buch der Erinnerung. 2. Aufl. Stuttgart, 1947.
Phil 3195.11.90 Hermann, C. Max Dessoir Mensch und Werk. Stuttgart, 1929.
Phil 3195.12.90 Scheele, Fritz. Hugo Dinglers philosophisches System. Inaug. Diss. Corbach, 1933.
Phil 3195.13.90 Hamm, Anton. Die Philosophie Hugo Delffs als Begründung eine theistischen Idealrealismus im Sinne christlicher Weltanschauung. Inaug. Diss. Bottrop, 1934.
Phil 3195.14.34 Dacqué, Edgar. Urwelt, Sage und Menschheit, eine naturhistori-metaphysische Studie. 4. Aufl. München, 1927.
Phil 3195.14.40 Dacqué, Edgar. Das verlorene Paradies. 4. Aufl. München, 1953.
Phil 3195.14.45 Dacqué, Edgar. Leben als Symbol. München, 1928.
Phil 3195.14.50 Dacqué, Edgar. Vom Sinn der Erkenntnis. München, 1932.
Phil 3195.15.30 Dingler, Hugo. Der Glaube an die Weltmaschine und seine Überwindung. Stuttgart, 1932.
Phil 3195.15.35 Dingler, Hugo. Die Ergreifung des Wirklichen. München, 1955.
Phil 3195.15.80 Krampf, W. Die Philosophie Hugo Dinglers. München, 1955.
Phil 3195.15.81 Krampf, W. Hugo Dingler. München, 1956.
Phil 3195.15.83 Gorn, Erhard. Die Philosophie Hugo Dinglers. Dusseldorf, 1960.
Phil 3195.16.80 Szylkarski, W. Jugendgeschichte Adolf Dyroffs. 2. Aufl. Bonn, 1948.
Phil 3195.17.30 Diez, Max. Sprechen. Berlin, 1934.
Phil 3195.18.30 Dessauer, Friedrich. Durch die Tore der neuen Zeit. Göttingen, 1961.
Phil 3195.19.30 Dooyeweerd, H. Verkenningen in de wijsbegeerte. Amsterdam, 1962.
Phil 3195.19.35 Dooyeweerd, H. Vernieuwing en bezinning. 2. druk. Zutphen, 1963.
Phil 3195.20.30 Duynstee, Willem Jacob A.J. Verspreide opstellen. Roermond, 1963.

Phil 3200 History of philosophy - Local Modern philosophy - Germany - Individual philosophers - E

Htn Phil 3200.1.30* Erasmus, D. Colloquia. Lugdunum Batavorum, 1636.
Htn Phil 3200.1.35* Erasmus, D. Stultitiae laus. Basiliae, 1676.
Phil 3200.2.80 Pamphlet box. Philosophy. German and Dutch. Ebbinghaus, Hermann.
Phil 3200.3.80 Pamphlet box. Philosophy. German and Dutch. Eberhard, Johann August.
Phil 3200.3.81 Nicolai, Friedrich. Gedächtnisschrift auf Johann August Eberhard. Berlin, 1810.
Phil 3200.4.80 Pamphlet box. Philosophy. German and Dutch. Erdmann, Benno.
Phil 3200.5.90 Glockner, H. Johann Eduard Erdmann. Stuttgart, 1932.
Phil 3200.6 Eschenmayer, C.A. Die Philosophie. Erlangen, 1803.
Phil 3200.7 Erdmann, J.E. Über der Naturalismus. Halle, 1854.
Phil 3200.8 Ehrlich, W. Metaphysik. Tübingen, 1955.
Phil 3200.8.5 Ehrlich, W. Kulturgeschichtliche Autobiographie. Tübingen, 1961.

Phil 3200   History of philosophy - Local Modern philosophy - Germany - Individual philosophers - E - cont.

Phil 3200.8.10	Ehrlich, W. System der Philosophie. Bad Ragaz, 1966.
Phil 3200.8.15	Ehrlich, W. Metaphysik im erkenntniskritischen Grundriss. Halle, 1924.
Phil 3200.8.20	Ehrlich, W. Ontologie des Bewusstseins. Zürich, 1940.
Phil 3200.10	Goldmund, M. Die Philosophie Franz Erhardts. Leipzig, 1937.
Phil 3200.12	Einsiedel, August von. Ideen. Berlin, 1957.
Phil 3200.13	Sandmann, P. Das Weltproblem bei Ferdinand Ebner. München, 1962.
Phil 3200.14	Ebner, Ferdinand. Notizen, Tagebücher, Lebenserinnerungen. v.1-2,3. München, 1963. 2v.
Phil 3200.14.5	Ebner, Ferdinand. Gesammelte Werke. 2. Aufl. Wien, 1952.
Phil 3200.14.80	Steinbuechel, Theodor. Der Umbruch des Denkens. Darmstadt, 1966.
Phil 3200.15	Eberz, Otfried. Sophia und Logos oder die Philosophie der Wiederherstellung. München, 1967.
Phil 3200.16.30	Ebner, Felix. Moe obrashchenie. 2. izd. Moskva, 1903.
Phil 3200.17	Edelmann, Johann Christian. Sämtliche Schriften in Einzelausgaben. Stuttgart, 1970. 5v.

Phil 3210   History of philosophy - Local Modern philosophy - Germany - Individual philosophers - Fechner, Gustav T.

Phil 3210.25	Fechner, G.T. Ausgewählte Schriften. Berlin, 1907.
Phil 3210.26	Fechner, G.T. Kleine Schriften von Dr. Mises (pseud.). Leipzig, 1875.
Phil 3210.26.5	Fechner, G.T. Kleine Schriften. 2. Aufl. Leipzig, 1913.
Phil 3210.27	Pamphlet vol. Philosophy. German and Dutch. Fechner, G.T. 5 pam.
Phil 3210.28	Lasswitz, K. Gustav Theodor Fechner. Stuttgart, 1902.
Phil 3210.30A	Fechner, G.T. Tagesansicht gegenüber der Nachtansicht. Leipzig, 1879.
Phil 3210.30B	Fechner, G.T. Tagesansicht gegenüber der Nachtansicht. Leipzig, 1879.
Phil 3210.30.5	Fechner, G.T. Tagesansicht gegenüber der Nachtansicht. 3. Aufl. Leipzig, 1919.
Phil 3210.34	Fechner, G.T. Über die physikalische und philosophische Atomenlehre. Leipzig, 1855.
Phil 3210.35	Fechner, G.T. Atomenlehre. Leipzig, 1864.
Phil 3210.40	Fechner, G.T. Zend-Avesta. Hamburg, 1906.
Phil 3210.42	Fechner, G.T. Über das höchste Gut. Leipzig, 1846.
Phil 3210.45	Fechner, G.T. Über die Seelenfrage. Leipzig, 1861.
Phil 3210.45.10	Fechner, G.T. Über die Seelenfrage. 2. Aufl. Hamburg, 1907.
Phil 3210.47	Fechner, G.T. Elemente der Psychophysik. v.1-2. Leipzig, 1860.
Phil 3210.49	Fechner, G.T. In Sachen der Psychophysik. Leipzig, 1877.
Phil 3210.51	Fechner, G.T. Revision der Hauptpunkte der Psychophysik. Leipzig, 1882.
Phil 3210.53	Fechner, G.T. Über die Frage des Weber'schen Gesetzes. Leipzig, 1884.
Phil 3210.58	Fechner, G.T. Der Mensch im Kosmos. Berlin, 1949.
Phil 3210.59	Fechner, G.T. Nanna. Hamburg, 1908.
Phil 3210.61	Fechner, G.T. Einige Ideen zur Schöpfungs- und Entwickelungsgeschichte der Organismen. Leipzig, 1873.
Phil 3210.63	Fechner, G.T. Vorschule der Aesthetik. v.1-2. Leipzig, 1876.
Phil 3210.65A	Fechner, G.T. Drei Motive und Gründe des Glaubens. Leipzig, 1863.
Phil 3210.65B	Fechner, G.T. Drei Motive und Gründe des Glaubens. Leipzig, 1863.
Phil 3210.66	Fechner, G.T. Erinnerungen an die letzten Tage der Odlehre und ihre Urhebers. Leipzig, 1876.
Phil 3210.67	Fechner, G.T. Das Büchlein vom Leben nach dem Tode. Dresden, 1836.
Phil 3210.67.2	Fechner, G.T. Das Büchlein vom Leben nach dem Tode. 3. Aufl. Hamburg, 1887.
Phil 3210.67.3	Fechner, G.T. Das Büchlein vom Leben nach dem Tode. 6. Aufl. Hamburg, 1906.
Phil 3210.67.4	Fechner, G.T. Das Büchlein vom Leben nach dem Tode. 8. Aufl. Leipzig, 1922.
Phil 3210.67.5	Fechner, G.T. Little book of life after death. Boston, 1912.
Phil 3210.67.9	Fechner, G.T. On life after death. Chicago, 1914.
Phil 3210.67.10	Fechner, G.T. On life after death. Chicago, 1945.
Phil 3210.67.12	Fechner, G.T. On life after death. N.Y., 1943.
Phil 3210.69	Fechner, G.T. Kollektivmasslehre. Leipzig, 1897.
Phil 3210.70	Fechner, G.T. Über die Methode der richtigen und falschen Fälle. Leipzig, 1884.
Phil 3210.75	Fechner, G.T. Wissenschaftliche Briefe. Hamburg, 1890.
Phil 3210.77	Fechner, G.T. Religion of a scientist. N.Y., 1946.
Phil 3210.80	Pamphlet box. Philosophy. German and Dutch. Fechner, G.T. German dissertations.
Phil 3210.81	Lasswitz, Kurd. Gustav Theodor Fechner. Stuttgart, 1910.
Phil 3210.81.2	Lasswitz, Kurd. Gustav Theodor Fechner. Stuttgart, 1896.
Phil 3210.82	Wundt, W. Gustav Theodor Fechner. Leipzig, 1901.
Phil 3210.83	Liebe, R. Fechner's Metaphysik. Greifswald, 1903.
Phil 3210.83.2	Liebe, R. Fechner's Metaphysik. Leipzig, 1903.
Phil 3210.84	Pastor, Willy. Im GeisteFechners. Leipzig, 1901.
Phil 3210.85	Adolph, H. Die Weltanschauung G.T. Fechners. Stuttgart, 1923.
Phil 3210.86	Hollander, K. von. Über die Bedeutung von Fechners "Nanna". Göttingen, 1908.
Phil 3210.87	Dennert, E. Fechner als Naturphilosoph und Christ. Gütersloh, 1902.
Phil 3210.88	Lülmann, C. Monismus und Christentum bei G.T. Fechner. Berlin, 1917.
Phil 3210.89	Rezazadeh-Schafagh, Sadeg. Mystische Motive in Fechners Philosophie. Inaug. Diss. Charlottenburg, 1928.

Phil 3235   History of philosophy - Local Modern philosophy - Germany - Individual philosophers - Feuerbach, Ludwig

Phil 3235.10	Feuerbach, Ludwig. Sämmtliche Werke. Leipzig, 1846-90. 10v.
Phil 3235.11	Feuerbach, Ludwig. Gesammelte Werke. v.2-4,6-9. Berlin, 1967- 8v.
Phil 3235.15	Feuerbach, Ludwig. Ludwig Feuerbachs sämmtliche Werke. Stuttgart, 1903-11. 10v.
Phil 3235.20	Feuerbach, Ludwig. Manifestes philosophiques; textes choisis. Paris, 1960.
Phil 3235.25	Feuerbach, Ludwig. Grundsätze der Philosophie der Zukunft. Zürich, 1843.
Phil 3235.25.5	Feuerbach, Ludwig. Grundsätze der Philosophie der Zukunft. Frankfurt, 1967.
Phil 3235.28	Feuerbach, Ludwig. Aussprüche aus seinen Werken. Leipzig, 1879.

Phil 3235   History of philosophy - Local Modern philosophy - Germany - Individual philosophers - Feuerbach, Ludwig - cont.

	Phil 3235.45	Feuerbach, Ludwig. Das Wesen des Christenthums. Stuttgart, 1903.
	Phil 3235.45.2	Feuerbach, Ludwig. Das Wesen des Christenthums. Leipzig, 1841.
	Phil 3235.45.6	Feuerbach, Ludwig. Das Wesen des Christenthums. Leipzig, 1909.
	Phil 3235.50	Feuerbach, Ludwig. Qu'est-ce que la religion. Paris, 1850.
	Phil 3235.52	Feuerbach, Ludwig. Über Philosophie und Christenthum. Mannheim, 1839.
	Phil 3235.55	Feuerbach, Ludwig. Vorlesungen über das Wesen der Religion nebst Zusätzen und Anmerkungen. Stuttgart, 1908.
	Phil 3235.55.5	Feuerbach, Ludwig. Das Wesen der Religion. Leipzig, 1908.
	Phil 3235.60	Feuerbach, Ludwig. Philosophie der Zukunft. Stuttgart, 1922.
	Phil 3235.72	Feuerbach, Ludwig. The essence of Christianity. N.Y., 1855.
X Cg	Phil 3235.72.5	Feuerbach, Ludwig. The essence of Christianity. 2nd ed. London, 1881.
	Phil 3235.72.7	Feuerbach, Ludwig. The essence of Christianity. N.Y., 1957.
	Phil 3235.73	Feuerbach, Ludwig. The essence of religion. N.Y., 1873.
	Phil 3235.74	Feuerbach, Ludwig. Sämmtliche Werke. v.1-13. Stuttgart, 1964. 12v.
	Phil 3235.75	Feuerbach, Ludwig. Philosophische Charakterentwicklung. v.1-2. Leipzig, 1874.
	Phil 3235.76	Feuerbach, Ludwig. Briefwechsel zwischen L. Feuerbach und C. Kapp, 1832-1848. Leipzig, 1876.
	Phil 3235.77	Feuerbach, Ludwig. Ausgewählte Briefe von und an L. Feuerbach. v.1-2. Leipzig, 1904.
	Phil 3235.78	Feuerbach, Ludwig. Kleine philosophische Schriften. Leipzig, 1950.
	Phil 3235.79	Pamphlet box. Philosophy. German and Dutch. Feuerbach, Ludwig. German dissertations.
	Phil 3235.79.5	Pamphlet box. Philosophy. German and Dutch. Feuerbach, Ludwig.
	Phil 3235.80	Meyer, M. Ludwig Feuerbach's Moralphilosophie. Berlin, 1899.
	Phil 3235.81.5	Engels, Friedrich. Ludwig Feuerbach. Chicago, 1903.
	Phil 3235.81.8	Engels, Friedrich. Ludwig Feuerbach und der Ausgang der klassischen deutschen Philosophie. 5. Aufl. Stuttgart, 1910.
	Phil 3235.81.9	Engels, Friedrich. Ludwig Feuerbach und der Ausgang der klassischen deutschen Philosophie. 6. Aufl. Stuttgart, 1919.
	Phil 3235.81.12	Engels, Friedrich. Ludwig Feuerbach. Wien, 1927.
	Phil 3235.81.15	Engels, Friedrich. Ludwig Feuerbach and the outcome of classical German philosophy. N.Y., 1935.
	Phil 3235.81.17	Engels, Friedrich. Ludwig Feuerbach and the outcome of classical German philosophy. N.Y., 1941.
	Phil 3235.81.20	Engels, Friedrich. Liudvig Feierbakh. 2. izd. Geneva, 1905.
	Phil 3235.81.24	Engels, Friedrich. Ludwig Feuerbach et la fin de la philosophie classique allemande. Paris, 1945.
	Phil 3235.81.25	Engels, Friedrich. Ludwig Feuerbach and the end of classical German philosophy. Moscow, 1949.
	Phil 3235.81.27	Engels, Friedrich. Ludwig Feuerbach and the end of classical German philosophy. Moscow, 1950.
	Phil 3235.81.29	Gabaraev, S.S. Materializm Feierbakha. Tbilisi, 1955.
	Phil 3235.81.30	Engels, Friedrich. Ludwig Feuerbach. 3. Aufl. Berlin, 1952.
	Phil 3235.81.35	Engels, Friedrich. Ludwig Feuerbach. Chicago, 1906.
	Phil 3235.82	Lévy, Albert. La philosophie de Feuerbach. Thèse. Paris, 1904.
	Phil 3235.83	Schat Petersen, L.W. Ludwig Feuerbach og kristendommen. København, 1883.
	Phil 3235.84	Bolin, Wilhelm. Ludwig Feuerbach. Stuttgart, 1891.
	Phil 3235.84.10	Bolin, Wilhelm. Über Ludwig Feuerbach's Briefwechsel und Nachlass. Helsingfors, 1877.
	Phil 3235.85	Wintzer, Wilhelm. Der natürliche Sittenlehre Ludwig Feuerbachs. Leipzig, 1898.
	Phil 3235.87	Turban, Theodor. Das Wesen des Christentumes von Ludwig Feuerbach. Inaug. Diss. Karlsruhe, 1894.
	Phil 3235.88	Starcke, Carl N. Ludwig Feuerbach. Stuttgart, 1885.
	Phil 3235.89	Ardab'ev, A.I. Ateizm Ludviga Feierbakha. Moskva, 1963.
	Phil 3235.109	Kohut, Adolph. Ludwig Feuerbach, sein Leben und seine Werke. Leipzig, 1909.
	Phil 3235.110	Jodl, F. Ludwig Feuerbach. 2. Aufl. Photoreproduction. Stuttgart, 1921.
	Phil 3235.111	Starcke, C.N. L. Feuerbach; en monografi. Kjøbenhavn, 1883.
	Phil 3235.112	Rawidowicz, Simon. Ludwig Feuerbachs Philosophie. Berlin, 1931.
	Phil 3235.112.2	Rawidowicz, Simon. Ludwig Feuerbachs Philosophie. 2. Aufl. Berlin, 1964.
	Phil 3235.113	Schaller, Julius. Darstellung und Kritik der Philosophie Ludwig Feuerbach's. Leipzig, 1847.
	Phil 3235.114	Weser, H.A. Sigmund Freuds und Ludwig Feuerbachs Religionskritik. Inaug. Diss. Bettrop, 1936.
	Phil 3235.115	Chamberlain, W.B. Heaven wasn't his destination; the philosophy of Ludwig Feuerbach. London, 1941.
	Phil 3235.116	Ran, Albrecht. Ludwig Feuerbach's Philosophie. Leipzig, 1882.
	Phil 3235.117	Schilling, Werner. Feuerbach und die Religion. München, 1957.
	Phil 3235.118	Arvon, Henri. Ludwig Feuerbach. 1. éd. Paris, 1957.
	Phil 3235.120	Baskin, M.P. Filosofiia Ludviga Feierbakha. Moskva, 1957.
	Phil 3235.122	Esin, Ivan M. Die materialistische Philosophie Ludwig Feuerbachs. 1. Aufl. Berlin, 1956.
	Phil 3235.124	Bochmuell, Klaus. Leiblichkeit und Gesellschaft. Göttingen, 1961.
	Phil 3235.126	Feuerbach, Ludwig. Sockrinemia. Moskva, 1923.
	Phil 3235.126.5	Feuerbach, Ludwig. Istoriia filosofii. Moskva, 1967. 3v.
	Phil 3235.127	Cesa, C. Il giovane Feuerbach. Bari, 1963.
	Phil 3235.128	Bykhovskii, Bernard E. Liudvig Feierbakh. Moskva, 1967.
	Phil 3235.130	Klimkeit, Hans-Joachim. Das Wunderverstaendnis Ludwig Feuerbaches in religionsphanomenologischer Sicht. Bonn, 1965.
	Phil 3235.132	Kamenka, Eugene. The philosophy of Ludwig Feuerbach. London, 1970.
	Phil 3235.134	Gagen, Michael von. Ludwig Feuerbach. München, 1970.
	Phil 3235.136	Xhauffaire, Marcel. Feuerbach et la théologie de la sécularisation. Paris, 1970.
	Phil 3235.138	Elez, Iovo. Problema bytiia i myshleniia v filosofii Liudirga Feienbakha. Moskva, 1971.

Classified Listing

Phil 3245   History of philosophy - Local Modern philosophy - Germany - Individual philosophers - Fichte, Immanuel H.

Phil 3245.20   Fichte, Immanuel Hermann. Vernuschte Schriften zur Philosophie, Theologie und Ethik. Leipzig, 1869. 2v.

Phil 3245.25   Fichte, Immanuel Hermann. Zeitschrift für Philosophie und speculative Theologie. Bonn, 1937-56. 8v.

Phil 3245.30   Fichte, Immanuel Hermann. Grundzüge zur System der Philosophie. Heidelberg, 1833-46. 4v.

Phil 3245.32   Fichte, Immanuel Hermann. Sätze zur Vorschule der Theologie. Stuttgart, 1826.

Phil 3245.33   Fichte, Immanuel Hermann. Zur Seelenfrage. Leipzig, 1859.

Phil 3245.35   Fichte, Immanuel Hermann. Anthropologie: von der menschlichen Seele. Leipzig, 1860.

Phil 3245.40   Fichte, Immanuel Hermann. Über Gegen satz Wendepunkt und Zeit. Heidelberg, 1832.

Phil 3245.43   Fichte, Immanuel Hermann. Die Seelenfortdauer und die Weltstellung des Menschen. Leipzig, 1867.

Phil 3245.45   Fichte, Immanuel Hermann. Die theistische Weltansicht. Leipzig, 1873.

Phil 3245.50   Fichte, Immanuel Hermann. Die Idee der Persönlichkeit. Leipzig, 1855.

Phil 3245.50.2   Fichte, Immanuel Hermann. Die Idee der Persönlichkeit. Elberfeld, 1834.

Phil 3245.55   Fichte, Immanuel Hermann. Religion und Philosophie. Heidelberg, 1834.

Phil 3245.60   Fichte, Immanuel Hermann. Die speculative Theologie der Allgemeine Religionslehre. Heidelberg, 1846.

Phil 3245.65   Fichte, Immanuel Hermann. System der Ethik. Leipzig, 1850-51. 2v.

Phil 3245.70   Fichte, Immanuel Hermann. Psychologie. Leipzig, 1864-73. 2v.

Phil 3245.70.5   Fichte, Immanuel Hermann. Contributions to mental philosophy. London, 1860.

Phil 3245.75   Fichte, Immanuel Hermann. Grundsätze für die Philosophie der Zukunft. Stuttgart, 1847.

Phil 3245.79   Pamphlet box. Fichte, Immanuel Hermann. Philosophy. German and Dutch.

Phil 3245.80   Zeller, E. Antwort an...Dr. Immanuel Hermann Fichte. Berlin, 1876.

Phil 3245.82   Ambrosius, J.M. Om Immanuel Hermann Fichte's teism och etik. Lund, 1882.

Phil 3245.83   Swahn, F.O.B. Kritiska anmärkningar vid I.H. Fichtes ethiska grundsatzer. Lund, 1856.

Phil 3245.84   Herrmann, H.A. Die Philosophie Immanuel Hermann Fichtes. Berlin, 1928.

Phil 3245.85   Beckedorf, H. Die Ethik Immanuel Hermann Fichtes. Inaug. Diss. Hannover, 1912.

Phil 3245.86   Najdanović, D. Die Geschichtsphilosophie Immanuel Hermann Fichtes. Berlin, 1940.

Phil 3245.86.2   Najdanović, D. Die Geschichtsphilosophie Immanuel Hermann Fichtes. Berlin, 1940.

Phil 3245.87   Rakate, Georg. Immanuel Hermann Fichte. Leipzig, 1915.

Phil 3245.88   Serwe, Arthur. Die Raum- und Zeitlehre Immanuel Hermann Fichtes. Saarbrücken, 1959.

Phil 3246   History of philosophy - Local Modern philosophy - Germany - Individual philosophers - Fichte, Johann G.

Phil 3246.10   Fichte, Johann Gottlieb. Sämmtliche Werke. Berlin, 1845-46. 8v.

Phil 3246.11   Fichte, Johann Gottlieb. Sämmtliche Werke. Berlin, 1845-46. 11v.

Phil 3246.15   Fichte, Johann Gottlieb. Nachgelassene Werke. Bonn, 1934-35. 3v.

Phil 3246.17   Fichte, Johann Gottlieb. Werke. Leipzig, 1911. 6v.

Phil 3246.17.5   Fichte, Johann Gottlieb. Erganzungsband. Leipzig, 1934.

Phil 3246.18   Fichte, Johann Gottlieb. Sämmtliche Werke. Leipzig, 1924. 8v.

Phil 3246.18.3   Fichte, Johann Gottlieb. Nachgelassene Werke. Leipzig, 1924. 3v.

Phil 3246.18.3.5   Fichte, Johann Gottlieb. Nachgelassene Werke. Bonn, 1962. 3v.

Phil 3246.18.4   Fichte, Johann Gottlieb. Gesamtausgabe der Bauerischen Akademie der Wissenschaften. Stuttgart, 1962. 9v.

Phil 3246.18.5   Fichte, Johann Gottlieb. Eine Teilsammlung mit der Einfuhrung. Stuttgart, 1935.

Phil 3246.19   Fichte, Johann Gottlieb. Nachgelassene Schriften. Bd.2. Berlin, 1937.

n   Phil 3246.20*   Fichte, Johann Gottlieb. Über der Begriff der Wissenschaftslehre. Jena, 1798-1822. 4 pam.

n   Phil 3246.21*   Fichte, Johann Gottlieb. Das Herausgeber die philosophischen Journals. Jena, 1799-1815. 4 pam.

Phil 3246.25.5   Fichte, Johann Gottlieb. Popular works. London, 1873.

Phil 3246.26   Fichte, Johann Gottlieb. Popular works. London, 1889. 2v.

Phil 3246.28   Fichte, Johann Gottlieb. Predigten. Leipzig, 1918.

n   Phil 3246.30*   Fichte, Johann Gottlieb. Versuch einer Critik aller Offenbarung. Königsberg, 1792.

n   Phil 3246.30.5*   Fichte, Johann Gottlieb. Versuch einer Critik aller Offenbarung. Königsberg, 1793.

n   Phil 3246.32*   Pamphlet vol. Philosophy. German and Dutch. Fichte, Johann Gottlieb. 5 pam.

Phil 3246.32.5   Fichte, Johann Gottlieb. Eimige Vorlesungen über die Bestimmung des Gelehrten. Jena, 1954.

n   Phil 3246.34*   Fichte, Johann Gottlieb. Die Bestimmung des Menschen. Berlin, 1800.

Phil 3246.34.2   Fichte, Johann Gottlieb. Die Bestimmung der Menschen. Frankfurt, 1800.

Phil 3246.35   Fichte, Johann Gottlieb. Die Bestimmung des Menschen. Berlin, 1825.

Phil 3246.35.3A   Fichte, Johann Gottlieb. Die Bestimmung des Menschen. Leipzig, 1879.

Phil 3246.35.3B   Fichte, Johann Gottlieb. Die Bestimmung des Menschen. Leipzig, 1879.

Phil 3246.35.5   Fichte, Johann Gottlieb. Destination of man. London, 1846.

Phil 3246.35.7   Fichte, Johann Gottlieb. Die Bestimmung des Menschen. 2. Aufl. Berlin, 1801.

Phil 3246.35.8   Fichte, Johann Gottlieb. Die Bestimmung des Menschen. Leipzig, 1944.

Phil 3246.35.8.5   Fichte, Johann Gottlieb. Die Bestimmung des Menschen. 2. Aufl. Leipzig, 1944.

Phil 3246.35.9   Fichte, Johann Gottlieb. Destination de l'homme. Paris, 1832.

Phil 3246.35.10   Fichte, Johann Gottlieb. Die Bestimmung des Menschen. Stuttgart, 1966.

Phil 3246.35.12   Fichte, Johann Gottlieb. Männeskans bestammelse. Stockholm, 1923.

Phil 3246   History of philosophy - Local Modern philosophy - Germany - Individual philosophers - Fichte, Johann G. - cont.

Phil 3246.36   Fichte, Johann Gottlieb. Ideen über Gott und Unsterblichkeit. Leipzig, 1914.

Htn   Phil 3246.38*   Fichte, Johann Gottlieb. Grundlage des Naturrechts nach Prinzipien der Wissenschaftslehre. Jena, 1796.

Phil 3246.40   Fichte, Johann Gottlieb. Doctrine de la science...de la connaissance. Paris, 1843.

Htn   Phil 3246.44*   Fichte, Johann Gottlieb. Über den Begriff der Wissenschaftslehre. Weimar, 1794.

Phil 3246.44.5   Fichte, Johann Gottlieb. Darstellung der Wissenschaftslehre aus dem Jahre 1801, 1804. v.1-2. Leipzig, 1922.

Phil 3246.44.10   Fichte, Johann Gottlieb. Wissenschaftslehre 1804. Frankfurt, 1966.

Phil 3246.44.10.5   Fichte, Johann Gottlieb. Erste Wissenschaftslehre ven 1804. Stuttgart, 1969.

Phil 3246.45   Fichte, Johann Gottlieb. Grundlage der gesammten Wissenschaftslehre. Tübingen, 1802.

Phil 3246.45.6   Fichte, Johann Gottlieb. Grundlage der gesammten Wissenschaftslehre. Hamburg, 1956.

Htn   Phil 3246.45.8*   Fichte, Johann Gottlieb. Grundriss des Eigenthümlichen der Wissenschaftslehre. Jena, 1795.

Phil 3246.45.20   Fichte, Johann Gottlieb. Grundriss des Eigenthümlichen der Wissenschaftslehre in Rücksicht. Leipzig, 194-.

Phil 3246.46   Fichte, Johann Gottlieb. La theorie de la science expose de 1804. Thèse. Paris, 1967.

Htn   Phil 3246.47*   Fichte, Johann Gottlieb. Die Grundzüge des gegenwartigen Zeitalters. Berlin, 1806.

Phil 3246.47.25   Fichte, Johann Gottlieb. Die Grundzüge des gegenwartigen Zeitalters. 2. Aufl. Leipzig, 1922.

Phil 3246.47.26   Fichte, Johann Gottlieb. Die Grundzüge des gegenwartigen Zeitalters. Hamburg, 1956.

Phil 3246.49A   Fichte, Johann Gottlieb. Die Anweisung zum seeligen Leben. Berlin, 1828.

Phil 3246.49B   Fichte, Johann Gottlieb. Die Anweisung zum seeligen Leben. Berlin, 1828.

Htn   Phil 3246.49.2*   Fichte, Johann Gottlieb. Die Anweisung zum seeligen Leben. Berlin, 1806.

Phil 3246.49.5   Fichte, Johann Gottlieb. Die Anweisung zum seeligen Leben. Hamburg, 1954.

Phil 3246.50   Fichte, Johann Gottlieb. Méthode...a la vie bienheureuse. Paris, 1845.

Phil 3246.50.5   Fichte, Johann Gottlieb. The way toward the blessed life. London, 1849.

Phil 3246.50.9   Fichte, Johann Gottlieb. Första inledningen till vetenshapslären. Stockholm, 1914.

Phil 3246.53   Fichte, Johann Gottlieb. Nature of the scholar. London, 1845.

Phil 3246.53.2   Fichte, Johann Gottlieb. Nature of the scholar. 2nd ed. London, 1848.

Phil 3246.53.5   Fichte, Johann Gottlieb. Über die Bestimmung des Gelehrten. Berlin, 1812.

Phil 3246.53.10   Fichte, Johann Gottlieb. Über den Gelehrten. Berlin, 1956.

Phil 3246.54   Fichte, Johann Gottlieb. Johann Gottlieb Fichte über den Begriff des wahrhaften Kraiges. Leipzig, 1914.

Phil 3246.55   Fichte, Johann Gottlieb. Reden an die deutsche Nation. Leipzig, 1824.

Htn   Phil 3246.55.2*   Fichte, Johann Gottlieb. Reden an die deutsche Nation. Berlin, 1808.

Phil 3246.55.3   Fichte, Johann Gottlieb. Reden an die deutsche Nation. Leipzig, 1872.

Phil 3246.55.5   Fichte, Johann Gottlieb. Reden an die deutsche Nation. Leipzig, n.d.

Phil 3246.55.6A   Fichte, Johann Gottlieb. Reden an die deutsche Nation. Leipzig, 1909.

Phil 3246.55.6B   Fichte, Johann Gottlieb. Reden an die deutsche Nation. Leipzig, 1909.

Phil 3246.55.7   Fichte, Johann Gottlieb. Reden an die deutsche Nation. Leipzig, 1944.

X Cg   Phil 3246.55.10   Fichte, Johann Gottlieb. Discours a la nation allemande. Paris, 1895.

Phil 3246.55.12   Fichte, Johann Gottlieb. Addresses in the German nation. Photoreproduction. Chicago, 1923.

Phil 3246.58   Fichte, Johann Gottlieb. New exposition of the science of knowledge. Saint Louis, 1869.

X Cg   Phil 3246.58.2   Fichte, Johann Gottlieb. Science of knowledge. Philadelphia, 1868.

Phil 3246.59   Fichte, Johann Gottlieb. Rechtslehre vorgetragen von Ostern bis Michaelis 1812. Leipzig, 1920.

X Cg   Phil 3246.60   Fichte, Johann Gottlieb. Science of rights. London, 1889.

Phil 3246.60.5   Fichte, Johann Gottlieb. Science of rights. Philadelphia, 1869.

X Cg   Phil 3246.60.5   Fichte, Johann Gottlieb. Science of rights. Philadelphia, 1869.

Htn   Phil 3246.65*   Fichte, Johann Gottlieb. Die Thatsachen des Bewusstseyns. Stuttgart, 1817.

Phil 3246.66   Fichte, Johann Gottlieb. Philosophie der Maurerei. Leipzig, 1923.

Phil 3246.66.5   Fichte, Johann Gottlieb. Philosophy of masonry. Seattle, 1945.

Phil 3246.68   Fichte, Johann Gottlieb. Vocation of man. London, 1848.

Phil 3246.68.3   Fichte, Johann Gottlieb. Vocation of man. Chicago, 1906.

Phil 3246.68.15   Fichte, Johann Gottlieb. The vocation of man. N.Y., 1956.

Phil 3246.71   Fichte, Johann Gottlieb. Die philosophischen Schriften zum Atheismusstreit. Leipzig, 1910.

Phil 3246.71.20A   Fichte, Johann Gottlieb. Appellation an das Publikum über...atheistischen. Jena, 1799.

Phil 3246.71.20B   Fichte, Johann Gottlieb. Appellation an das Publikum über...atheistischen. Jena, 1799.

Htn   Phil 3246.72*   Fichte, Johann Gottlieb. Das System der Sittenlehre. Jena, 1798.

Phil 3246.72.2   Fichte, Johann Gottlieb. Das System der Sittenlehre nach Prinzipien der Wissenschaftslehre. Neuausgabe, 1963.

Phil 3246.72.3   Fichte, Johann Gottlieb. Das System der Sittenlehre nach Prinzipien der Wissenschaftslehre, 1798. 2. Aufl. Hamburg, 1969.

Phil 3246.72.5   Fichte, Johann Gottlieb. Science of ethics...based on Science of knowledge. London, 1897.

Phil 3246.73   Fichte, Johann Gottlieb. Über den Unterschied des Geistes und des Buchstabens in der Philosophie. Leipzig, 1924.

Phil 3246.74   Fichte, Johann Gottlieb. Rufe an die deutsche Nation. Berlin, 1943.

Htn   Phil 3246.75*   Fichte, Johann Gottlieb. Der geschlosse Handelsstaat. Tübingen, 1800.

Phil 3246.76   Fichte, Johann Gottlieb. Neue Fichte-funde, aus der Heimat und Schweiz. Gotha, 1919.

Phil 3246   History of philosophy - Local Modern philosophy - Germany - Individual
    philosophers - Fichte, Johann G. - cont.

Htn   Phil 3246.77*   Fichte, Johann Gottlieb. Staatslehre. Berlin, 1820.
       Phil 3246.77.2   Fichte, Johann Gottlieb. Grundlage des Naturrechts nach
                          Prinzipien der Wissenschaftslehre. 2. Aufl. Hamburg, 1967.
       Phil 3246.78   Fichte, Johann Gottlieb. Briefe, Ausgewahlt und
                          Herausgegeben von E. Bergmann. Leipzig, 1919.
       Phil 3246.78.5   Fichte, Johann Gottlieb. Achtundvierzig Briefe.
                          Leipzig, 1862.
       Phil 3246.78.9A   Fichte, Johann Gottlieb. Briefwechsel. Leipzig, 1925.
                          2v.
       Phil 3246.78.9B   Fichte, Johann Gottlieb. Briefwechsel. Leipzig, 1925.
                          2v.
       Phil 3246.79   Pamphlet vol. Philosophy. German and Dutch. Fichte, Johann
                          Gottlieb. 13 pam.
       Phil 3246.79.2   Pamphlet vol. Philosophy. German and Dutch. Fichte, Johann
                          Gottlieb. German dissertations. 15 pam.
       Phil 3246.79.3   Pamphlet vol. Philosophy. German and Dutch. Fichte, Johann
                          Gottlieb. German dissertations. 14 pam.
       Phil 3246.79.4   Pamphlet box. Philosophy. German and Dutch. Fichte, Johann
                          Gottlieb. German dissertations.
       Phil 3246.79.5   Pamphlet box. Philosophy. German and Dutch. Fichte, Johann
                          Gottlieb.
       Phil 3246.79.10   Fichte, Johann Gottlieb. Über die Einzig mögliche Störung
                          der akademischen Freiheit. Heidelberg, 1905.
       Phil 3246.79.15A   Fichte, Johann Gottlieb. Fichtes Freiheitslehre. 1. Aufl.
                          Düsseldorf, 1956.
       Phil 3246.79.15B   Fichte, Johann Gottlieb. Fichtes Freiheitslehre. 1. Aufl.
                          Düsseldorf, 1956.
       Phil 3246.79.20   Fichte, Johann Gottlieb. Erste und zweite Einleitung in
                          die Wissenschaftslehre und Versuch einer neuen Darstellung
                          der Wissenschaftslehre. Hamburg, 1954.
       Phil 3246.79.25   Fichte, Johann Gottlieb. Tat und Freiheit, ein Fichtebuch.
                          3. Aufl. Hamburg, 1922.
       Phil 3246.79.50   Meyer, Friedrich. Eine Fichte-Sammlung. Leipzig, 1921.
       Phil 3246.79.60   Fichte, Johann Gottlieb. Fichte für Heute. Bremen, 1944?
       Phil 3246.79.65   Fichte, Johann Gottlieb. Fichte Schriften zur
                          Gesellschaftsphilosophie. v.1-2. Jena, 1928-29.
       Phil 3246.80   Adamson, R. Fichte. Philadelphia, 1881.
       Phil 3246.80.3   Adamson, R. Fichte. Philadelphia, 1892.
       Phil 3246.80.5   Melzer, Ernst. Die Unsterblichkeitstheorie. Neisse, 1881.
       Phil 3246.81   Everett, C.C. Fichte's Science of knowledge.
                          Chicago, 1884.
       Phil 3246.82   Fichte, Immanuel Hermann. Johann Gottlieb Fichte's Leben
                          und Ritter. Sulzbach, 1830-31. 2v.
       Phil 3246.82.2   Fichte, Immanuel Hermann. Johann Gottlieb Fichte's Leben
                          und Ritter. Leipzig, 1862. 2v.
       Phil 3246.83   Schwabe, G. Fichtes und Schopenhauer's Lehre von Willen.
                          Jena, 1887.
       Phil 3246.84   Smith, W. Memoir. Boston, 1846.
       Phil 3246.85.2   Thompson, A.B. Unity of Fichte's Doctrine of knowledge.
                          Boston, 1895.
       Phil 3246.86   Raich, Maria. Fichte, seine Ethik...Problem des
                          Individualismus. Thesis. Tübingen, 1905.
       Phil 3246.86.5   Raich, Maria. Fichte, seine Ethik...Problem des
                          Individualismus. Tübingen, 1905.
       Phil 3246.87   Talbot, E.B. Fundamental principle of Fichte's philosophy.
                          Diss. N.Y., 1906.
       Phil 3246.87.2   Talbot, E.B. Fundamental principle of Fichte's philosophy.
                          N.Y., 1906.
       Phil 3246.88   Ivanoff, C. Darstellung der Ethik Johann Gottlieb Fichtes.
                          Leipzig, 1899.
       Phil 3246.89   Zimmer, F. Johann Gottlieb Fichte's Religionsphilosophie.
                          Berlin, 1878.
       Phil 3246.90   Wotschke, Theodor. Fichte und Erigena. Halle, 1896.
       Phil 3246.91   Janson, F. Fichtes Reden an die deutsche Nation.
                          Berlin, 1911.
       Phil 3246.91.9   Perego, Luigi. L'idealismo etico di Fichte. Modena, 1911.
       Phil 3246.92   Léon, Xavier. La philosophie de Fichte, ses rapports avec
                          la consciènce contemporaine. Paris, 1902.
X Cg   Phil 3246.92.5   Léon, Xavier. Fichte et son temps. Paris, 1922-24.
                          2v.
       Phil 3246.93A   Medicus, Fritz. Johann Gottlieb Fichte; Dreizehn
                          Vorlesungen gehalten and der Universität Halle.
                          Berlin, 1905.
       Phil 3246.93.5   Medicus, Fritz. Fichtes Leben. Leipzig, 1914.
       Phil 3246.94   Kabitz, Willy. Studien zur Entwicklungsgeschichte der
                          Fichteschen Wissenschaftslehre. Berlin, 1902.
       Phil 3246.95   Harms, F. Johann Gottlieb Fichte. Kiel, 1862.
       Phil 3246.95.9   Loewe, Johann H. Die Philosophie Fichte's.
                          Stuttgart, 1862.
       Phil 3246.96   Schad, Johann B. Gemeinfassliche Darstellung des
                          Fichteschen Systems and der daraus. Erfurt, 1800-02.
                          3v.
       Phil 3246.96.5   Fries, Jakob F. Fichte's und Schelling's neueste Lehren
                          von Gott und die Welt. Heidelberg, 1807.
       Phil 3246.97   Bensow, Oscar. Zu Fichtes Lehre von Nicht- ich.
                          Bern, 1898.
       Phil 3246.98   Erdmann, Johann E. Fichte, der Mann der Wissenschaft und
                          des Katheders. Halle, 1862.
       Phil 3246.99   Lindau, Hans. Johann Gottlieb Fichte und der neuere
                          Socialismus. Berlin, 1900.
       Phil 3246.99.5   Lindau, Hans. Die Schriften zu Johann Gottlieb Fichte's
                          Atheismusstreit. München, 1912.
       Phil 3246.99.10   Lindau, Hans. Johann Gottlieb Fichtes Lehren von Staat und
                          Gesellschaft in ihrem Verhältnis zum neueren Sozialismus.
                          n.p., 1899.
       Phil 3246.160   Hielscher, H. Das Denksystem Fichtes. Berlin, 1913.
       Phil 3246.169   Hidvall, Karl Z.K. Fichtes filosofi i förhallande till
                          Kants kriticism. Uppsala, 1914.
       Phil 3246.170   Gogarten, F. Fichte als religiöser Denker. Jena, 1914.
       Phil 3246.171   Fuchs, Emil. Vom Werden dreier Denker. Tübingen, 1914.
       Phil 3246.172   Lask, Emil. Fichtes Idealismus und die Geschichte.
                          Tübingen, 1914.
       Phil 3246.173   Bergmann, Ernst. Fichte, der Erzieher zum Deutschtum.
                          Leipzig, 1915.
       Phil 3246.173.2   Bergmann, Ernst. Johann Gottlieb Fichte der Erzieher. 2.
                          Aufl. Leipzig, 1928.
       Phil 3246.173.5   Bergmann, Ernst. Fichte und der Nationalsozialismus.
                          Breslau, 1933.
       Phil 3246.173.10   Bergmann, Ernst. Fichte und Carl Christian Erhard Schmid.
                          Leipzig, 1926?
       Phil 3246.174   Hirsch, Emanuel. Fichtes Religionsphilosophie.
                          Göttingen, 1914.
       Phil 3246.175   Strecker, Reinhard. Die Anfänge von Fichtes
                          Staatsphilosophie. Leipzig, 1916.
       Phil 3246.175.2   Strecker, Reinhard. Die Anfänge von Fichtes
                          Staatsphilosophie. Leipzig, 1917.

Phil 3246   History of philosophy - Local Modern philosophy - Germany - Individual
    philosophers - Fichte, Johann G. - cont.

       Phil 3246.176   Schwarz, Hermann. Fichte und Wir. Osterwieck, 1917.
       Phil 3246.177   Kerler, Dietrich H. Die Philosophie des Absoluten in der
                          Fichteschen Wissenschaftslehre. Inaug. Diss.
                          Ansbach, 1917.
       Phil 3246.178   Moog, Willy. Fichte über den Krieg. Darmstadt, 1917.
       Phil 3246.179   Messer, August. Fichte. Leipzig, 1920.
       Phil 3246.180   Maggiore, G. Fichte. Castello, 1921.
       Phil 3246.185   Leibholz, G. Fichte und der demokratischen Gedanke.
                          Freiburg, 1921.
       Phil 3246.187   Burman, E.O. Die Transscendentalphilosophie Fichte's und
                          Schelling's. Upsala, 1891.
       Phil 3246.188   Widmark, Elof. Historisk öfversigt af Fichtes naturrält
                          och Babergs outik deraf. Upsala, 1854.
       Phil 3246.189   Sahlin, Enar. Johann Gottlieb Fichtes idealism.
                          Upsala, 1888.
       Phil 3246.190   Nindelband, N. Fichte's Idee des deutschen Staates.
                          Tübingen, 1921.
       Phil 3246.191.5   Fries, Jakob F. Reinhold, Fichte und Schelling.
                          Leipzig, 1803.
       Phil 3246.192   Eberhard, J.A. Über den Gott des Herrn Professor Fichte.
                          Halle, 1799.
       Phil 3246.193   Trendelenburg, A. Zur Erinnerung an Johann Gottlieb
                          Fichte. Berlin, 1862.
       Phil 3246.195   Fichte und deutschlande Not. Berlin, 1919.
       Phil 3246.196   Spir, A. Johann Gottlieb Fichte nach seinen Briefen.
                          Leipzig, 1879.
       Phil 3246.197   Hirsch, E. Christentum und Geschichte in Fichtes
                          Philosophie. Tübingen, 1920.
       Phil 3246.198   Cesca, G. L'idealismo soggetivo di I.G. Fichte.
                          Padova, 1895.
       Phil 3246.199   Fischer, Kuno. Johann Gottlieb Fichte. Stuttgart, 1862.
       Phil 3246.199.5   Fischer, Kuno. Geschichte der neuern Philosophie.
                          Heidelberg, 1869.
       Phil 3246.200   Lott, F.C. Festrede zur Saecularfeier Fichtes.
                          Wien, 1862.
       Phil 3246.201   Kerler, D.H. Die Fichte-Schelling'sche Wissenschaftslehre.
                          Ulm, 1917.
       Phil 3246.202   Gurwitsch, G. Die Einheit der Fichteschen Philosophie.
                          Berlin, 1922.
       Phil 3246.202.5   Gurwitsch, G. Fichtes System der konkreten Ethik.
                          Tübingen, 1924.
       Phil 3246.203   Noack, Ludwig. Johann Gottlieb Fichte nach seinen Leben,
                          Lehren und Wirken. Leipzig, 1862.
       Phil 3246.204.2   Bauch, Bruno. Fichte und unsere Zeit. 2. Aufl.
                          Erfurt, 1921.
       Phil 3246.205   Horneffer, Martha. Die Identitätslehre Fichtes in den
                          Jahren 1801-1806. Leipzig, 1925.
       Phil 3246.206   Belthusen, J.C. Einige Fragen, veranlasst Durch.
                          Helmstädt, 1799.
       Phil 3246.207   Schwarz, H. Einführung in Fichtes Reden an die deutsche
                          Nation. 2. Aufl. Langensalza, 1925.
       Phil 3246.208   Heimsoeth, H. Fichte. München, 1923.
       Phil 3246.209   Ferro, A.A. La filosofia di G.A. Fichte. Savona, 1906.
       Phil 3246.210   Bayer, Karl. Zu Fichte's Gedächtniss. Ansbach, 1835.
       Phil 3246.211   Stahr, Adolf. Fichte, der Held unter der deutschen
                          Denkern. Berlin, 1862.
       Phil 3246.212   Wundt, Max. Johann Gottlieb Fichte. Stuttgart, 1927.
       Phil 3246.212.5   Wundt, Max. Fichte-Forschungen. Stuttgart, 1929.
       Phil 3246.213   Gelpcke, E. Fichte und die Gedankenwelt der Sturm und
                          Drang. Leipzig, 1928.
       Phil 3246.214   Wallner, Nico. Fichte als politischen Denker.
                          Halle, 1926.
       Phil 3246.215   Mayer, Otto. Fichte über das Volk. Leipzig, 1913.
       Phil 3246.216   Bergbom, F. De ortu et indole idealismi Fichtii. Diss.
                          Aboae, 1822.
       Phil 3246.217   Guerault, Martèal. L'evolution et la structure de la
                          doctrine et la science chez Fichte. Paris, 1930. 2v.
       Phil 3246.217.2   Guerault, Martèal. L'evolution et la structure de la
                          doctrine et la science chez Fichte. Thèse.
                          Strasbourg, 1930. 2 pam.
       Phil 3246.218   Heusinger, J.H.G. Über das idealistisch-atheistische
                          System des Professor Fichte in Jena. Dresden, 1799.
       Phil 3246.219   Et was über Herrn Professor Fichte. Hamburg, 1799.
       Phil 3246.220   Grusber, J.G. Eine Stimme aus dem Publikum über Gottes
                          Sein und Wesen. Leipzig, 1799.
       Phil 3246.221   Keyserlingk, H.W.E. von. Vergleich zwischen Fichtens
                          System. Königsberg, 1817.
       Phil 3246.222   Schäffer, W.F. Über des Herrn Professor Fichte Appellation
                          an das Publikum. Gotha, 1799.
       Phil 3246.223   Schaumann, J.C.G. Erklärung über Fichte's Appellation.
                          Giessen, 1799.
       Phil 3246.224   Walz, G.A. Die Staatsidee des Rationalismus...und die
                          Staatsphilosophie Fichte's. Berlin, 1928.
       Phil 3246.225   Boettger, Fritz. Ruf zur Tat; Johann Gottlieb Fichte. 1.
                          Aufl. Berlin, 1956.
       Phil 3246.226   Jensen, F.C. Kann man Herrn Professor Fichte mit Recht
                          beschuldigen. Kiel, 1799.
       Phil 3246.227   Lasson, Adolf. Johann Gottlieb Fichte im Verhältniss zu
                          Kirche und Staat. Berlin, 1863.
       Phil 3246.228   Engelbrecht, H.C. Johann Gottlieb Fichte. N.Y., 1933.
       Phil 3246.229   Oestereich, H. Freiheitsides und Rechtsbegriff in der
                          Philosophie von Johann Gottlieb Fichte. Jena, 1915.
       Phil 3246.230   Faust, August. Johann Gottlieb Fichte. Breslau, 1938.
       Phil 3246.231   Steinbeck, W. Das Bild des Menschen in der Philosophie
                          Fichtes. München, 1939.
       Phil 3246.232   Weischedel, W. Der Aufbruch der Freiheit. Leipzig, 1939.
       Phil 3246.233   Döring, W.O. Der Mann der Tat; eine Fichtebiographie.
                          Lübeck, 1926.
       Phil 3246.233.5   Döring, W.O. Fichte, der Mann und sein Werke.
                          Lübeck, 1925.
       Phil 3246.234   Schmidt, Erich. Fichtes Reden an die deutsche Nation.
                          Berlin, 1908.
       Phil 3246.235   Hase, K. von. Jenaisches Fichte - Büchlein.
       Phil 3246.236   Vysheslavtsev, B. Etika Fikhte. Moskva, 1914.
       Phil 3246.237   Stine, R.W. The doctrine of God in the philosophy of
                          Fichte. Philadelphia, 1945.
       Phil 3246.239   Unruh, G.F. von. Johann Gottlieb Fichte. Stuttgart, 1942.
       Phil 3246.240   Gehlen, Arnold. Deutschtum und Christentum bei Fichte.
                          Berlin, 1935.
       Phil 3246.241   Vlachos, G. Fédéralisme et raison d'état dans la pensée
                          internationale de Fichte. Paris, 1948.
       Phil 3246.241.5   Vlachos, G. Fédéralisme et raison d'état dans la pensée
                          internationale de Fichte. Thèse. Paris, 1948.
       Phil 3246.242   Heekman, H. Fichte und das Christentum. Wurzburg, 1939.
       Phil 3246.243   Massalo, A. Fichte e la filosofia. Firenze, 1948.

Phil 3246 History of philosophy - Local Modern philosophy - Germany - Individual philosophers - Fichte, Johann G. - cont.

Phil 3246.245 Stiner, Rudolf. Fichtes Geist mitten unter uns. Dornach, 1933.
Phil 3246.247 Schmidt-Warneck, J. von. Die Sociologie Fichte's. Berlin, 1884.
Phil 3246.250 Drechsler, J. Fichtes Lehre vom Bild. Stuttgart, 1955.
Phil 3246.253 Froelich, Franz. Fichtes Reden an die deutsche Nation. Berlin, 1907.
Phil 3246.255 Pareyson, L. Fichte. Torino, 1950.
Phil 3246.258 Ritzel, W.W. Fichtes Religionsphilosophie. Stuttgart, 1956.
Phil 3246.260 Fischer, F. Wohin, gehen wir? Langensalza, 1931.
Phil 3246.263 Gruner, C.G. Ein paar Worte zur Belehrung. Jena, 1799.
Phil 3246.265 Bergner, Dieter. Neue Bemerkungen zu Johann Gottlieb Fichte. Berlin, 1957.
Phil 3246.270 Koestlin, Karl. Fichte; ein Lebensbild. Tübingen, 1862.
Phil 3246.275 Bauch, Bruno. Fichte und der deutsche Staatsgedanke. Beyer, 1925.
Phil 3246.288 Johann Gottlieb Fichte; ein Vortrag zu Fichtes hundertjährischen Geburtstag. Raiserslauterer, 1862.
Phil 3246.290 Funche, Eduard. Neues zu den politischen Anschauungen des Jungen Fichte. Hildesheim, 1915.
Phil 3246.292 Hammacher, Vlans. Die ethische Teleologie in Fichtes System als Grundlage seiner Geschichtsphilosophie. Hadien, 1958.
Phil 3246.294 Severino, Emanuele. Per un innovamento nella interpretazione della filosofia Fichtiana. Brescia, 1968.
Phil 3246.296 Widmann, J. Analyse der formalen Strukturen des transzendentalen Wissens in Johann Gottlieb Fichtes. München? 1961.
Phil 3246.298 Buhr, Manfred. Akademie...Berlin. Berlin, 1962.
Phil 3246.298.5 Buhr, Manfred. Revolution und Philosophie. Berlin, 1965.
Phil 3246.299 Berlin. Deutsche Staats Bibliothek. Johann Gottlieb Fichte, 1762-1962. Berlin, 1962.
Phil 3246.300 Schindler, I.M.T. Reflexion und Bildung in Fichte Wissenschaftslehre. Bonn, 1962.
Phil 3246.300.1 Schindler, I.M.T. Reflexion und Bildung in Fichtes Wissenschaftslehre von 1794. 1. Aufl. Düsseldorf, 1966.
Phil 3246.301 Schulz, W. Johann Gottlieb Fichte. Pfullingen, 1962.
Phil 3246.302 Schuffenhauer, H. Die Padagogik Johann Gottlieb Fichtes. Berlin, 1963.
Phil 3246.303 Brueggen, Michael. Der Gang des Denkens in der Philosophie Johann Gottlieb Fichtes. München, 1964.
Phil 3246.304 Masullo, Aldo. La comunitá come fondamento. Napoli, 1965.
Phil 3246.305 Girndt, Helmut. Die Differenz des Fichteschen und Hegelschen Systems in der Hegelschen Differenzschrift. Bonn, 1965.
Phil 3246.306 Philonenko, Alexis. La liberté humaine dans la philosophie de Fichte. Paris, 1966.
Phil 3246.310 Baumgartner, Hans Michael. Johann Gottlieb Fichte; Bibliographie. Stuttgart, 1968.
Phil 3246.315 Schuhmann, Karl. Die Grundlage der Wissenschaftslehre in ihrem Umrisse. Den Haag, 1968[1969]
Phil 3246.320 Boeckelmann, Frank. Die Schriften zu Johann Gottlieb Fichtes Atheismus-Streit. München, 1969.
Phil 3246.325 Preul, Reiner. Reflexion und Gefühl. Berlin, 1969.
Phil 3246.330 Mader, Johann Karl. Fichte, Feierbach, Marx. Wien, 1968.
Phil 3246.335 Lassahn, Rudolf. Studien zur Wirkungsgeschichte Fichtes als Pädagoge Habilitationsschrift. Heidelberg, 1970.
Phil 3246.340 Ludwig, Karl Friedrich Ernst. Freymüthige Gedanken über Fichte's Appellation gegen die Anklage des Atheismus und deren Veranlassung. Bruxelles, 1968.
Phil 3246.345 Willms, Bernhard. Die totale Freiheit. Köln, 1967.
Phil 3246.350 Janke, Wolfgang. Ficht; Sein und Reflexion. Berlin, 1970.

Phil 3255 History of philosophy - Local Modern philosophy - Germany - Individual philosophers - Franck, Sebastian

Phil 3255.80 Hegler, Alfred. Geist und Schrift bei Sebastian Franck. Freiburg, 1892.
Phil 3255.80.5 Hegler, Alfred. Sebastian Francks lateinische Paraphrase der deutschen Theologie und seine hollandische erhaltenen Traktate. Tübingen, 1901.
Phil 3255.81 Körner, Hermann. Studien zur geistesgeschichtlichen Stellung S. Francks. Breslau, 1935.
Phil 3255.82 Kolbenheyer, Christiane. Die Mystik des Sebastian Franck von Wörd. Inaug-Diss. Würzburg, 1935.
Phil 3255.83 Klemm, Karl. Das Paradoxen als Ausdrucksform der spekulativen Mystik Sebastian Francks. Inaug-Diss. Leipzig, 1937.
Phil 3255.85 Hase, Karl A. Sebastian Frank von Wörd der Schwarmgeist. Leipzig, 1869.
Phil 3255.87 Bischof, Hermann. Sebastian Franck von deutsche Geschichtsschreibung. Tübingen, 1857.
Phil 3255.89 Haggenmacher, O. Uber Sebastian Francks Erstlingsschrift. Zürich, 1892.
Phil 3255.90 Koyré, Alexandre. Sebastian Franck. Paris, 1932.
Phil 3255.92 Peuckert, W.C. Sebastian Franck. München, 1943.
Phil 3255.94 Raeber, Kuno. Studien zur Geschichtsbibel Sebastian Francks. Basel, 1952.
Phil 3255.95 Raeber, Kuno. Studien zur Geschichtsbibel Sebastian Francks. Inaug. Diss. Basel, 1952.

Phil 3260 History of philosophy - Local Modern philosophy - Germany - Individual philosophers - Fries, Jakob F.

Phil 3260.30 Fries, J.F. System der Metaphysik. Heidelberg, 1824.
Phil 3260.31 Fries, J.F. Uber die Philosophie als evidente Wissenschaft. Leipzig, 1804.
Phil 3260.32 Fries, J.F. Wissen, Glaube und Ahndung. Jena, 1805.
Phil 3260.33A Fries, J.F. Handbuch der praktischen Philosophie oder der philosophischen Zwecklehre. Heidelberg, 1818-32. 2v.
Phil 3260.33B Fries, J.F. Handbuch der praktischen Philosophie oder der philosophischen Zwecklehre. pt.2. Heidelberg, 1818-32.
Phil 3260.35.2 Fries, Jakob Friedrich. Neue oder anthropologische Kritik der Vernunft. 2. Aufl. Berlin, 1935. 3v.
Phil 3260.39 Fries, J.F. Die mathematische Naturphilosophie. Heidelberg, 1822.
Phil 3260.40 Fries, J.F. Lehren der Liebe des Glaubens. Heidelberg, 1823.
Phil 3260.49 Fries, J.F. System der Logik. Heidelberg, 1811.
Phil 3260.50 Fries, J.F. System der Logik. Heidelberg, 1837.
Phil 3260.50.5 Fries, J.F. System der Logik. 3e Aufl. Leipzig, 1914.
Phil 3260.60 Fries, J.F. Handbuch der psychischen Anthropologie. Jena, 1837.
Phil 3260.79 Pamphlet box. Philosophy. German and Dutch. Fries, J.F.
Phil 3260.80 Strasosky, H. Jacob Friedrich Fries. Hamburg, 1891.
Phil 3260.81 Grape, Johannes. Die Prinzipien der Ethik bei Fries. Dessau, 1903.

Phil 3260 History of philosophy - Local Modern philosophy - Germany - Individual philosophers - Fries, Jakob F. - cont.

Phil 3260.82 Bliedner, E. Philosophie der Mathematik. Jena, 1904.
Phil 3260.83 Elsenhans, Theodor. Fries und Kant. v.1-2. Giessen, 1906.
Phil 3260.85 Henke, E.L.T. Jakob Friedrich Fries. Leipzig, 1867.
Phil 3260.86 Mechler, W. Die Erkenntnislehre bei Fries. Inaug. Diss. Berlin, 1911.
Phil 3260.87 Dubislav, W. Die Fries'che Lehre von der Begründung. Dömitz, 1926.
Phil 3260.88 Kastil, Alfred. Jakob F. Fries' Lehre von der unmittelbaren Erkenntnis. Göttingen, 1912.
Phil 3260.152 Weiss, Georg. Fries' Lehre von Ahndung in Ästhetik. Göttingen, 1912.
Phil 3260.152.5 Fraenkel, Georg. Die kritische Rechtsphilosophie bei Fries. Göttingen, 1912.

Phil 3270 History of philosophy - Local Modern philosophy - Germany - Individual philosophers - Other F

Phil 3270.1.31 Fischer, Kuno. Die Apologie meiner Lehre. Mannheim, 1854.
Phil 3270.1.32 Fischer, Kuno. Das Interdict meiner Vorlesungen. Mannhein, 1854.
Phil 3270.1.80 Windelband, W. Kuno Fischer Gedächtnisrede. Heidelberg, 1907.
Phil 3270.1.81 Falken, H.N. Kuno Fischer und der litterarhistorische Methode. Berlin, 1892.
Phil 3270.1.82 Sosnoioski, M.E.V. Kuno Fischer. Breslau, n.d.
Phil 3270.1.83 Türck, Hermann. Meine Erfahrungen mit Kuno Fischer. Jena, 1895.
Phil 3270.1.84 Hoffmann, E. Kuno Fischer: Rede...seine 100. Geburstages. Heidelberg, 1924.
Phil 3270.2.31 Fick, Adolf. Die Welt als Vorstellung. Würzburg, 1870.
Phil 3270.3.83 Münz, Bernhard. Briefe von und über Jakob Frohschammer. Leipzig, 1897.
Phil 3270.3.85 Münz, Bernhard. Jakob Frohschammer. Breslau, 1894.
Phil 3270.3.88 Friedrich, J. Jakob Frohschammer. Fürth, 1896.
Phil 3270.3.90 Johann, F. Systematische und kritische Darstellung der Psychologie Jakob Frohschammers. Würzburg, 1899.
Phil 3270.3.93 Reich, Edward. Weltanschauung und Menschenleben...Jakob Frohschammer's. Grossenhain, 1884.
Phil 3270.3.95 Fried, Günther. Phantasie Wahrheit und Erkenntnis. Inaug. Diss. Tübingen, 1929.
Phil 3270.4.30 Feuerbach, P.J.A. Über Philosophie und Empirie in ihrem Verhältnisse zur positiven Rechtswissenschaft. Landshut, 1804.
Phil 3270.4.79 Feuerbach, P.J.A. Biographischer Nachlass. v.1-2. Leipzig, 1853.
Phil 3270.4.80 Fleischmann, M. Anselm von Feuerbach der Jurist, als Philosoph. Inaug. Diss. München, 1906.
Phil 3270.4.82 Gielhammer, L. Die politischen Grundlagen. Berlin, 1928.
Phil 3270.4.84 Hartmann, Richard. P.J.A. Feuerbachs politische. Berlin, 1961.
Phil 3270.4.86 Kipper, Eberhard. Johann Paul Anselm Feuerbach. Köln, 1969.
Phil 3270.5.79 Feder, J.G.H. G.J.H. Feder's Lebens Natur und Grundsätze. Leipzig, 1825.
Phil 3270.5.80 Pachaly, E. J.G.H. Feders Erkenntnistheorie und Metaphysik. Inaug. Diss. Leipzig, 1906.
Phil 3270.6.80 Kurz, August. Über Christian Gabriel Fischers vernünftige Gedanken von der Natur. Inaug. Diss. Halle, 1908.
Phil 3270.7.80 Römer, Alfred. Der Gottesbegriff Franks. Inaug. Diss. Halle, 1912.
Phil 3270.8.80 Stamm, E. Konstantin Frantz' Jugendjahre und erste Schriften. Heidelberg, 1907.
Phil 3270.9.80 Berger, Herman. Julius Frauenstädt, sein Leben, seine Schriften und seine Philosophie. Inaug. Diss. v.8. Rostock, 1911.
Phil 3270.10.31 Flake, Otto. Das neuantike Weltbild. Darmstadt, 1922.
Phil 3270.11 Friedmann, H. Wissenschaft und Symbol. München, 1949.
Phil 3270.11.31 Friedmann, H. Sinnvolle Odyssee. München, 1950.
Phil 3270.11.35 Friedmann, H. Epilegomena. München, 1954.
Phil 3270.12.33 Frege, Gottlob. Translations from the philosophical writings of Gottlob Frege. Oxford, 1952.
Phil 3270.12.35 Frege, Gottlob. Translations from the philosophical writings of Gottlob Frege. Oxford, 1960.
Phil 3270.12.37 Frege, Gottlob. Translations from the philosophical writings. 2nd ed. Oxford, 1966.
Phil 3270.12.40 Frege, Gottlob. Funktion, Begriff, Bedeutung. Göttingen, 1962.
Phil 3270.12.45 Frege, Gottlob. Logische Untersuchungen. Göttingen, 1966.
Phil 3270.12.50 Frege, Gottlob. Kleine Schriften. Hildesheim, 1967.
Phil 3270.12.80 Bartelett, J.M. Funktion und Gegenstand. München, 1961.
Phil 3270.12.85 Walker, J.P.B. A study of Frege. Oxford, 1965.
Phil 3270.12.90 Sternfeld, Robert. Frege's logical theory. Carbondale, 1966.
Phil 3270.12.95 Angelelli, Ignacio. Studies on Gottlob Frege and Traditional philosophy. Dordrecht, 1967.
Phil 3270.12.100 Trinchero, Mario. La filosofia dell'aritmetica di Gottlob Frege. Giappichelli, 1967.
Phil 3270.12.105 Klemke, E.D. Essays on Frege. Urbana, 1968.
Phil 3270.12.110 Grossmann, Reinhardt S. Reflections on Frege's philosophy. Evanston, 1969.
Phil 3270.12.115 Largeault, Jean. Logique et philosophie chez Frege. Paris, 1970.
Phil 3270.13.21 Frank, Erich. Knowledge. Chicago, 1955.
Phil 3270.14.30 Feuling, Daniel. Hauptfragen der Metaphysik. 2. Aufl. Heidelberg, 1949.
Phil 3270.15.31 Frackenheim, Emil L. Metaphysics and historicity. Milwaukee, 1961.
Phil 3270.16.31 Fechner, O. Das System der ontischen Kategorien. Hildesheim, 1961.
Phil 3270.17.30 Flam, Leopold. Denken en existeren. Amsterdam, 1964.
Phil 3270.17.35 Flam, Leopold. Proeven over het tragisch bewiestzijn en de geschiedenis. Antwerpen, 1963.
Phil 3270.17.40 Flam, Leopold. Gestalten van de Westerse subjectiriteit. Amsterdam, 1965.
Phil 3270.17.45 Flam, Leopold. Zelfvervreemding en zelfzijn. Amsterdam, 1966.
Phil 3270.17.50 Falm, Leopold. De bezinning. Amsterdam, 1968.
Phil 3270.18.1 Herrmann, Friedrich Wilhelm von. Bibliographie Eugen Fink. Den Haag, 1970.

Phil 3280 History of philosophy - Local Modern philosophy - Germany - Individual philosophers - Geulincx, Arnold

Phil 3280.10 Geulincx, A. Opera philosophica. Hagae, 1891. 3v.
Phil 3280.30 Geulincx, A. Van de Hooft-Deuchden. Antwerp, 1895.
Phil 3280.31 Geulincx, A. De virtute et primis ejuis proprietatilius. Pretoria, 1961.

Classified Listing

Phil 3280 History of philosophy - Local Modern philosophy - Germany - Individual philosophers - Geulincx, Arnold - cont.

Phil 3280.50   Geulincx, A. Gnôthi Seauton, sive ethica. Amsterdam, 1709.

Phil 3280.55   Geulincx, A. Ethik, oder über die Kardinaltugenden. Hamburg, 1948.

Phil 3280.60   Geulincx, A. Arnold Geulincs collegium oratorium i. e. nova methodus omnis generis orationes. Amsterdam, 1968.

Phil 3280.81   Pfleiderer, E. Verzeichniss der Doctoren. Tübingen, 1882.

Phil 3280.82   Göpfert, E. Geulincx' ethisches System. Breslau, 1883.

Phil 3280.83   Terraillon, E. La morale de Geulincx. Paris, 1912.

Phil 3280.84   Grimm, Edward. Arnold Geulincx' Erkenntnisstheorie und Occasionalismus. Jena, 1875.

Phil 3280.85   Land, J.P.N. Arnold Geulincx und seine Philosophie. Haag, 1895.

Phil 3280.86   Land, J.P.N. Arnold Geulincx te Leiden. Amsterdam, 1887.

Phil 3280.87   Nagel, Karl. Das Substanzproblem bei Arnold Geulincx. Inaug. Diss. Köln, 1930.

Phil 3280.88   Hausmann, P. Das Freiheitsproblem in der Metaphysik und Ethik bei Arnold Geulincx. Inaug. Diss. Würzburg, 1934.

Phil 3280.91   Lattre, Alain de. L'Occasionalisme d'Arnold Geulincx. Paris, 1967.

Phil 3310 History of philosophy - Local Modern philosophy - Germany - Individual philosophers - Other G

Phil 3310.1.3   Günther, Anton. Gesammelte Schriften. Bd.1-9. Wien, 1882. 9v.

Phil 3310.1.30   Günther, Anton. Janusköpfe zur Philosophie und Theologie. Wien, 1834.

Phil 3310.1.80   Pamphlet box. Philosophy. German and Dutch. Günther, Anton.

Phil 3310.1.85   Dischinger, J.N.P. Die Günther'sche Philosophie. Schaffhausen, 1852.

Phil 3310.1.125   Knoodt, Peter. Anton Günther. Wien, 1881. 2v.

Phil 3310.1.127   Knoodt, Peter. Günther und Blemens. Wien, 1853-54.

Phil 3310.1.130   Lauden, V.J.C. Peter Franz Knoodt als Philosoph. Elberfeld, 1920.

Phil 3310.1.135   Wenzel, Paul. Das wissenschaftliche Anliger des Güntherianismus. Essen, 1961.

Phil 3310.2.80   Ganewa, R. Die Erkenntnistheorie von Carl Göring. Inaug. Diss. Heidelberg, 1910.

Phil 3310.3.31   George, L. System der Metaphysik. Berlin, 1844.

Phil 3310.4.80   Semmelink, J.H. Professor Dr. J.H. Gunning. Zeist, 1926.

Phil 3310.5.30   Gutberlet, C. Die Theodicee. Münster, 1878.

Phil 3310.5.31   Gutberlet, C. Die Metaphysik. Münster, 1880.

Phil 3310.5.32   Gutberlet, C. Die Psychologie. Münster, 1881.

Phil 3310.5.33   Gutberlet, C. Logik und Erkenntnisstheorie. Münster, 1882.

Phil 3310.5.34   Gutberlet, C. Ethik und Naturrecht. Münster, 1883.

Phil 3310.5.35   Gutberlet, C. Naturphilosophie. Münster, 1885.

Phil 3310.6.80   Stolleis, Michael. Die Moral in der Politik bei Christian Grane. Inaug. Diss. München, 1967.

Phil 3310.6.90   Schelle, K.G. Briefe über Garve's Schriften und Philosophie. Leipzig, 1800.

Phil 3310.7.90   Franzelin, B. Die neueste Lehre Geysers über des Kausali-Tatspriuzip. Innsbruck, 1924.

Phil 3310.8   Glockner, Hermann. Das Abenteuer des Geistes. Stuttgart, 1938.

Phil 3310.8.21   Glockner, Hermann. Gesammelte Schriften. Berlin, 1963-66.

Phil 3310.8.30   Glockner, Hermann. Bilderbuch meiner Jugend; Erinnerungen. Bonn, 1970. 2v.

Phil 3310.10   Grebe, W. Geist und Sache. Frankfurt, 1934.

Phil 3310.12   Gulden, P.H. Albert Görlands systematische Philosophie. Assen, 1943.

Phil 3310.14   Gomperz, H. Philosophical studies. Boston, 1953.

Phil 3310.15   Gehlen, Arnold. Theorie der Willensfeiheit und frühe philosophische Schriften. Neuvied, 1965.

Phil 3310.15.20   Jonas, Friedrich. Die Institutionenlehre Arnold Gehlens. Tübingen, 1966.

Phil 3310.16.80   Rauche, G.A. The problem of truth and reality in Grisebach's thought. Pretoria, 1966.

Phil 3310.17.80   Faber, Heije. Het christelijk humanisme. Assen, 1963.

Phil 3310.18   Gadamer, H.G. Kleine Schriften. Tübingen, 1967. 3v.

Phil 3310.19.80   Wucherer-Huldenfeld, Karl. Die Gegensatzphilosophie Romano Guardinis in ihren Grundlagen und Folgerungen. Wien, 1968.

Phil 3310.20   Geyer, H.F. Philosophisches Tagebuch. Freiburg, 1969. 3v.

Phil 3415 History of philosophy - Local Modern philosophy - Germany - Individual philosophers - Hartmann, Eduard von

Phil 3415.15   Hartmann, Eduard von. Ausgewählte Werke. Leipzig, 1888. 12v.

Phil 3415.19   Hartmann, Eduard von. Lichtstrahlen aus Eduard von Hartmann's sämmtlichen Werken. Berlin, 1881.

Phil 3415.30   Hartmann, Eduard von. Philosophie des Unbewusstsen. 5. Aufl. Berlin, 1873.

Phil 3415.30.1   Hartmann, Eduard von. Philosophie des Unbewusstsen. Berlin, 1869.

Phil 3415.30.1.2   Hartmann, Eduard von. Philosophie des Unbewusstsen. 4. Aufl. Berlin, 1872.

Phil 3415.30.2   Hartmann, Eduard von. Philosophie des Unbewusstsen. 8. Aufl. Berlin, 1878. 2v.

Phil 3415.30.3   Hartmann, Eduard von. Philosophie des Unbewusstsen. 6. Aufl. Berlin, 1874.

Phil 3415.30.9   Hartmann, Eduard von. Philosophie des Unbewusstsen. 9. Aufl. Berlin, 1882.

Phil 3415.30.15   Hartmann, Eduard von. Philosophie des Unbewusstsen. 2. Aufl. Leipzig, 1923. 3v.

Phil 3415.31   Hartmann, Eduard von. Philosophie de L'inconscient. Paris, 1877. 2v.

Phil 3415.32   Hartmann, Eduard von. Philosophy of the unconscious. London, 1884. 3v.

Phil 3415.32.2   Hartmann, Eduard von. Philosophy of the unconscious. London, 1884. 3v.

Phil 3415.32.8   Hartmann, Eduard von. Philosophy of the unconcious. 2nd ed. London, 1893. 2v.

Phil 3415.32.15   Hartmann, Eduard von. Philosophy of the unconscious. N.Y., 1931.

Phil 3415.32.16   Hartmann, Eduard von. Philosophy of the unconscious. N.Y., 1931.

Phil 3415.35   Hartmann, Eduard von. Das Umbewusste...Physiologie. Berlin, 1872.

Phil 3415.35.2   Hartmann, Eduard von. Das Umbewusste...Physiologie. 2. Aufl. Berlin, 1877.

Phil 3415.36   Hartmann, Eduard von. Erläuterungen zur Metaphysik der Bewusstsen. Berlin, 1874.

Phil 3415.38   Hartmann, Eduard von. Gesammelte philosophische Abhandlungen Philosophie Unbewusstsen. Berlin, 1872.

Phil 3415 History of philosophy - Local Modern philosophy - Germany - Individual philosophers - Hartmann, Eduard von - cont.

Phil 3415.39   Hartmann, Eduard von. Verldsprocessens väsen eller det omedvetnas filosofi. Stockholm, 1877-78.

Phil 3415.40   Hartmann, Eduard von. Das Ding an sich. Berlin, 1871.

Phil 3415.42   Hartmann, Eduard von. Neukantianismus, Schopenhauerianismus. Berlin, 1877.

Phil 3415.43   Hartmann, Eduard von. Philosophische Fragen. Leipzig, 1885.

Phil 3415.45   Hartmann, Eduard von. The sexes compared and other essays. London, 1895.

Phil 3415.48   Hartmann, Eduard von. Gesammelte Studien und Aufsätze. Berlin, 1876.

Phil 3415.50   Hartmann, Eduard von. Le Darwinisme. Paris, 1877.

Phil 3415.55   Hartmann, Eduard von. Kritische Grundlegung der trancedentalen Realismus. Berlin, 1875.

Phil 3415.57.2   Hartmann, Eduard von. Kategorienlehre. 2. Aufl. v.1-3. Leipzig, 1923.

Phil 3415.60   Hartmann, Eduard von. Die Religion des Geistes. Berlin, 1882.

Phil 3415.61   Hartmann, Eduard von. Die Selbstzersetzung des Christenthums. 2. Aufl. Berlin, 1874.

Phil 3415.61.3   Hartmann, Eduard von. Die des Christenthums. 3. Aufl. Leipzig, 1888.

Phil 3415.62   Hartmann, Eduard von. La religion de L'Avenir. Paris, 1877.

Phil 3415.62.2   Hartmann, Eduard von. La religion de L'Avenir. Paris, 1876.

Phil 3415.63   Hartmann, Eduard von. The religion of the future. London, 1886.

Phil 3415.65   Hartmann, Eduard von. Phänomenologie des sittlichen Bewussten. Berlin, 1879.

Phil 3415.65.2   Hartmann, Eduard von. Phänomenologie des sittlichen Bewusstseins. 3. Aufl. Berlin, 1924.

Phil 3415.66   Hartmann, Eduard von. Zur Geschichte und Begründung des Pessimismus. Berlin, 1880.

Phil 3415.67   Hartmann, Eduard von. Religious metaphysics. N.Y., 1883.

Phil 3415.68   Hartmann, Eduard von. Die Geisterhypothese des Spiritismus und seine Phantome. Leipzig, n.d.

Phil 3415.69   Hartmann, Eduard von. Ethische Studien. Leipzig, 1898.

Phil 3415.70   Hartmann, Eduard von. System der Philosophie im Grundriss. Bad Sachsa, 1907-09. 8v.

Phil 3415.71   Hartmann, Eduard von. Moderne Probleme. Leipzig, 1886.

Phil 3415.71.2   Hartmann, Eduard von. Moderne Probleme. 2. Aufl. Leipzig, 1888.

Phil 3415.72   Hartmann, Eduard von. Kritische Wanderungen durch die Philosophie der Gegenwart. Leipzig, 1889.

Phil 3415.73.5   Hartmann, Eduard von. Philosophie des Schonen. 2. Aufl. Berlin, 1924.

Phil 3415.74   Hartmann, Eduard von. Das Problem des Lebens. 2. Aufl. Berlin, 1925.

Phil 3415.79   Pamphlet box. Hartmann, Eduard von. Philosophy. German and Dutch.

Phil 3415.80   Fischer, J.C. Hartmann's Philosophie des Unbewussten. Leipzig, 1872.

Phil 3415.81   Hernan, C.F. Edward von Hartmann's Religion der Zukunft. Leipzig, 1875.

Phil 3415.82   Kluge, A. Philosophische Fragmente...Hartmann's Philosophie. Breslau, 1875-77. 2v.

Phil 3415.83   Knauer, G. Das Facit aus Eduard von Hartmann's Philosophie des Unbewussten. Berlin, 1873.

Phil 3415.84   Plümacher, O. Der Kampf um's Unbewusste. Berlin, 1881.

Phil 3415.84.2   Plümacher, O. Der Kampf um's Unbewusste. Leipzig, 1890.

Phil 3415.85   Schmidt, O. Die naturwissenschaftlichen Grundlagen der Philosophie des Unbewussten. Leipzig, 1877.

Phil 3415.86   Schwarz, H. Das Ziel der religiösen und wissenschaftlichen Gährung nachgewiesen Hartmann's Pessimismus. Berlin, 1875

Phil 3415.87   Vaihinger, H. Hartmann, Dühring und Lange. Faerlohn, 1876.

Phil 3415.88   Volkelt, J. Das Unbewusste und der Pessimismus. Berlin, 1873.

Phil 3415.89   Drews, A. Eduard von Hartmanns philosophisches System. Heidelberg, 1902.

Phil 3415.89.2   Drews, A. Eduard von Hartmanns philosophische System. Heidelberg, 1906.

Phil 3415.89.5   Drews, A. Das Lebens Werk Eduard von Hartmanns. Leipzig, n.d.

Phil 3415.90   Paulus, H. Die Gottesbeweise Eduard von Hartmanns. Würzburg, 1907.

Phil 3415.90.5   Kappstein, Theodor. Eduard von Hartmann. Gotha, 1907.

Phil 3415.91   Weckesser, A. Der empirische Pessimismus. Bonn, 1885.

Phil 3415.91.5   Koeber, Raphael. Das philosophische System Eduard von Hartmann's. Breslau, 1884.

Phil 3415.92   Ziegler, Leopold. Das Weltbild Hartmanns. Leipzig, 1910.

Phil 3415.93   Braun, Otto. Eduard von Hartmann, von Otto Braun. Stuttgart, 1909.

Phil 3415.94   Krüger, Gustav. Der Vitalismus Eduard von Hartmanns und seine philosophischen Grundlagen. Inaug. Diss. Schwerin, 1911.

Phil 3415.95   Weber, Alfred. Wille zum Leben oder Wille zum Guten? Strassburg, 1882.

Phil 3415.96   Heymons, C. Eduard von Hartmann. Berlin, 1882.

Phil 3415.97   Kurt, N. Wahrheit und Dichtung in den Hauptlehren Eduard von Hartmann's. Leipzig, 1894.

Phil 3415.98   Marcus, A. Hartmann's inductive Philosophie im Chassidismus. Wien, 1888.

Phil 3415.99   Steffes, J.P. Eduard von Hartmanns Religionsphilosophie des Unbewussten. Mergentheim, 1921?

Phil 3415.100   Schüz, A. Philosophie und Christentum. Stuttgart, 1884.

Phil 3415.101   König, N. Die metaphysische Begründung der Ethik in Eduard von Hartmanns philosophischen System. Leipzig, 1910.

Phil 3415.102   Rintelen, F.J. von. Pessimistische Religionsphilosophie der Gegenwart. München, 1924.

Phil 3415.103   Ebrard, A. Eduard von Hartmann's Philosophie des Unbewussten. Gütersloh, 1876.

Phil 3415.104   Lasson, A. Die Entwickelung der religiösen...nach Eduard von Hartmann. Halle, 1883.

Phil 3415.105   Hessen, J. Die Kategorienlehre Eduard von Hartmanns. Leipzig, 1924.

Phil 3415.106.8   Haacke, Hermann. Neuere Stimmen der Kritik über Eduard von Hartmanns Werke. Leipzig 1898.

Phil 3415.106.9   Haacke, Hermann. Stimmen der Kritik über Eduard von Hartmanns Werke. Leipzig, 1904.

Phil 3415.107   Pohorilles, N.E. Entwicklung und Kritik der Erkenntnistheorie Eduard von Hartmanns. Wien, 1911.

Phil 3415.108   Ebbinghaus, Hermann. Über die hartmannsche Philosophie des Unbewussten. Düsseldorf, 1873.

Phil 3415.109   Schnehen, W. von. Eduard von Hartmann. Stuttgart, 1929.

Phil 3415 History of philosophy - Local Modern philosophy - Germany - Individual philosophers - Hartmann, Eduard von - cont.

Phil 3415.110   Huber, Max. Eduard von Hartmanns Metaphysik und Religionsphilosophie. Winterthur, 1954.

Phil 3415.115   Darnoi, D.N.K. The unconcious and Eduard von Hartmann; a historico-critical monograph. The Hague, 1968.

Phil 3425 History of philosophy - Local Modern philosophy - Germany - Individual philosophers - Hegel, Georg W.F.

Phil 3425.01   Hellersberg firm, booksellers. Berlin. Hegel und die Hegelianer; eine Bibliothek. Charlottenburg, 1927?

Phil 3425.06   Pamphlet box. Philosophy. German and Dutch. Hegel, Georg Wilhelm Friedrich. Minor writings.

Phil 3425.5   The owl of Minerva. Tallahassee. 1,1969+

X Cg   Phil 3425.8   Hegel, Georg Wilhelm Friedrich. Werke. Berlin, 1832-45. 14v.

Phil 3425.9   Hegel, Georg Wilhelm Friedrich. Werke. Berlin, 1835-45. 20v.

Phil 3425.10   Hegel, Georg Wilhelm Friedrich. Werke. Berlin, 1832-87. 19v.

Phil 3425.11   Hegel, Georg Wilhelm Friedrich. Werke. Leipzig, 1909.

Phil 3425.12   Hegel, Georg Wilhelm Friedrich. Sämtliche Werke. Stuttgart, 1927-40. 29v.

Phil 3425.12.3   Hegel, Georg Wilhelm Friedrich. Hamann. Stuttgart, 1930.

Phil 3425.12.5A   Hegel, Georg Wilhelm Friedrich. Dokumente zu Hegels Entwicklung. Stuttgart, 1936.

Phil 3425.12.5B   Hegel, Georg Wilhelm Friedrich. Dokumente zu Hegels Entwicklung. Stuttgart, 1936.

Phil 3425.13A   Hegel, Georg Wilhelm Friedrich. Gesammelte Werke. v.4,7. Hamburg, 1968. 2v.

Phil 3425.13B   Hegel, Georg Wilhelm Friedrich. Gesammelte Werke. v.7. Hamburg, 1968.

Phil 3425.13.5   Hegel, Georg Wilhelm Friedrich. Werke. v.1-2,4-20. Frankfurt, 1969- 21v.

Phil 3425.14   Hegel, Georg Wilhelm Friedrich. Briefe von und an Hegel. Hamburg, 1952-53. 4v.

Phil 3425.14.5   Nicolin, Günther. Hegel in Berichten seines Zeitgenossen companion von to Briefe von und an Hegel. Hamburg, 1970.

Phil 3425.15   Hegel, Georg Wilhelm Friedrich. Politische Schriften. Frankfurt am Main, 1966.

Phil 3425.19   Hegel, Georg Wilhelm Friedrich. Schriften zur Gesellschaftsphilosophie. Jena, 1927.

Phil 3425.20   Hegel, Georg Wilhelm Friedrich. The philosophy of Hegel. N.Y., 1953.

Phil 3425.20.5   Hegel, Georg Wilhelm Friedrich. Hegel; highlights, an annotated selection. N.Y., 1968.

Phil 3425.20.10   Heidegger, Martin. Hegel's concept of experience. 1st ed. N.Y., 1970.

Phil 3425.22   Hegel, Georg Wilhelm Friedrich. Philosophie in wörtlichen Auszügen. Berlin, 1843.

Phil 3425.23   Hegel, Georg Wilhelm Friedrich. Hegels Philosophie. Berlin, 1917.

Phil 3425.24   Hegel, Georg Wilhelm Friedrich. Erste Druckschriften. Leipzig, 1928.

Phil 3425.25   Hegel, Georg Wilhelm Friedrich. Populäre Gedanken aus seinen Werker. Berlin, 1873.

Phil 3425.27A   Hegel, Georg Wilhelm Friedrich. The wisdom of religion of a German philosopher. London, 1897.

Phil 3425.27B   Hegel, Georg Wilhelm Friedrich. The wisdom of religion of a German philosopher. London, 1897.

Phil 3425.28   Hegel, Georg Wilhelm Friedrich. Selections. N.Y., 1929.

Phil 3425.28.5   Hegel, Georg Wilhelm Friedrich. Berliner Schriften. Hamburg, 1956.

Phil 3425.28.10   Hegel, Georg Wilhelm Friedrich. Hegel. Frankfurt, 1957.

Phil 3425.28.12   Hegel, Georg Wilhelm Friedrich. Hegel. Stuttgart, 1955.

Phil 3425.29*   Hegel, Georg Wilhelm Friedrich. Wissenschaft der Logik. Nürnberg, 1912. 3v.

Phil 3425.29.10   Hegel, Georg Wilhelm Friedrich. Wissenschaft der Logik. Leipzig, 1948.

Phil 3425.29.12   Hegel, Georg Wilhelm Friedrich. Wissenschaft der Logik. Göttingen, 1966-

Phil 3425.29.20   Hegel, Georg Wilhelm Friedrich. Hegel's political writings. Oxford, 1964.

Phil 3425.30   Hegel, Georg Wilhelm Friedrich. Glauben und Wissen. Hamburg, 1962.

Phil 3425.31   Hegel, Georg Wilhelm Friedrich. Logique. v.1-2. Paris, 1859.

Phil 3425.32   Hegel, Georg Wilhelm Friedrich. Logic. Oxford, 1874.

Phil 3425.32.2   Hegel, Georg Wilhelm Friedrich. Logic. 2nd ed. Oxford, 1892.

Phil 3425.33   Hegel, Georg Wilhelm Friedrich. Jenenser Logik Metaphysik und Naturphilosophie. Leipzig, 1923.

Phil 3425.33.10   Hegel, Georg Wilhelm Friedrich. Jenenser Realphilosophie. Leipzig, 1931-32. 2v.

Phil 3425.34   Hegel, Georg Wilhelm Friedrich. Wissenschaft der Logik. Leipzig, 1923. 2v.

Phil 3425.34.28   Hegel, Georg Wilhelm Friedrich. Hegel's Science of logic. N.Y., 1969.

Phil 3425.34.29   Hegel, Georg Wilhelm Friedrich. Science of logic. London, 1961. 2v.

Phil 3425.34.30   Hegel, Georg Wilhelm Friedrich. Science of logic. N.Y., 1929.

Phil 3425.34.31A   Hegel, Georg Wilhelm Friedrich. Science of logic. London, 1951. 2v.

Phil 3425.34.31B   Hegel, Georg Wilhelm Friedrich. Science of logic. London, 1951. 2v.

Phil 3425.34.32   Tavadze, I.K.V.I. Lenin o nauke logiki Gegelia. Tbilisi, 1959.

Phil 3425.34.35   Hegel, Georg Wilhelm Friedrich. Essence. n.p., n.d.

Phil 3425.35   Hegel, Georg Wilhelm Friedrich. Logique subjective. Paris, 1854.

Phil 3425.36   Hegel, Georg Wilhelm Friedrich. The subjective logic of Hegel. London, 1855.

Phil 3425.37   Hegel, Georg Wilhelm Friedrich. Hegel's doctrine of reflection. N.Y., 1881.

Phil 3425.38   Hegel, Georg Wilhelm Friedrich. Hegel; Volk, Staat. Stuttgart, 1942.

Phil 3425.39   Macran, H.S. Hegel's doctrine of formal logic. Oxford, 1912.

Phil 3425.39.2   Hegel, Georg Wilhelm Friedrich. Hegel's logic of world and idea. Oxford, 1929.

Phil 3425.40.5.6   Hegel, Georg Wilhelm Friedrich. The philosophy of history. N.Y., 1900.

Phil 3425.40.5.9A   Hegel, Georg Wilhelm Friedrich. The philosophy of history. N.Y., 1944.

Phil 3425.40.5.9B   Hegel, Georg Wilhelm Friedrich. The philosophy of history. N.Y., 1944.

Phil 3425 History of philosophy - Local Modern philosophy - Germany - Individual philosophers - Hegel, Georg W.F. - cont.

Phil 3425.40.5.10A   Hegel, Georg Wilhelm Friedrich. The philosophy of history. N.Y., 1956.

Phil 3425.40.5.10B   Hegel, Georg Wilhelm Friedrich. The philosophy of history. N.Y., 1956.

Phil 3425.40.6   Hegel, Georg Wilhelm Friedrich. Vorlesungen über die Philosophie der Geschichte. 1907.

X Cg   Phil 3425.40.7   Hegel, Georg Wilhelm Friedrich. Vorlesungen über die Philosophie der Weltgeschichte. v.2-5. Leipzig, 1920. 4v.

Phil 3425.40.10   Hegel, Georg Wilhelm Friedrich. Die Vernunft in der Geschichte. Hamburg, 1955.

Phil 3425.40.11   Hegel, Georg Wilhelm Friedrich. Vorlesungen über die Philosophie der Weltgeschichte. Leipzig, 1944. 4v.

Phil 3425.40.25   Hegel, Georg Wilhelm Friedrich. Leçons sur la philosophie de l'histoire. Paris, 1937.

Phil 3425.40.30   Hegel, Georg Wilhelm Friedrich. Reason in history. N.Y., 1953.

Phil 3425.40.50   Hegel, Georg Wilhelm Friedrich. Premières publications. Thèse. Paris, 1952.

Phil 3425.40.55   Hegel, Georg Wilhelm Friedrich. Differenz des Fichte'schen und Schelling'schen Systems der Philosophie. Hamburg, 1962.

Phil 3425.41   Hegel, Georg Wilhelm Friedrich. Schriften zur Politik und Rechtsphilosophie. Leipzig, 1913.

Phil 3425.42   Hegel, Georg Wilhelm Friedrich. Nürnberger Schriften. Leipzig, 1938.

Htn   Phil 3425.43*   Hegel, Georg Wilhelm Friedrich. Encyclopädie der philosophischen Wissenschaften. Heidelberg, 1817.

Phil 3425.44   Hegel, Georg Wilhelm Friedrich. Encyclopädie der philosophischen Wissenschaften. Heidelberg, 1827.

Phil 3425.45   Hegel, Georg Wilhelm Friedrich. Encyclopädie der philosophischen Wissenschaften. Heidelberg, 1830.

Phil 3425.45.4   Hegel, Georg Wilhelm Friedrich. Encyclopädie der philosophischen Wissenschaften. 4. Aufl. Berlin, 1845.

Phil 3425.45.20   Hegel, Georg Wilhelm Friedrich. Encyclopädie der philosophischen Wissenschaften. Leiden, 1906.

Phil 3425.46   Hegel, Georg Wilhelm Friedrich. Encyclopädie der philosophischen Wissenschaften. 2. Aufl. Leipzig, 1920.

Phil 3425.46.6   Hegel, Georg Wilhelm Friedrich. Enzyklopädie der philosophischen Wissenschaften. 6. Aufl. Hamburg, 1959.

Phil 3425.46.10   Hegel, Georg Wilhelm Friedrich. Hegel's philosophy of nature. Oxford, 1970.

Phil 3425.46.12   Hegel, Georg Wilhelm Friedrich. Hegel's philosophy of nature. London, 1970.

Phil 3425.48.2   Hegel, Georg Wilhelm Friedrich. Enciclopedia delle scienze filosofiche. 2. ed. v.1-3. Bari, 1923. 2v.

Phil 3425.50   Hegel, Georg Wilhelm Friedrich. Hegel's philosophy of mind. Oxford, 1894.

Phil 3425.52   Hegel, Georg Wilhelm Friedrich. Studienausgabe. Ausgewählt. Frankfurt, 1968. 3v.

Phil 3425.55   Hegel, Georg Wilhelm Friedrich. Die Verfassung des deutschen Reichs. Stuttgart, 1935.

Phil 3425.56   Hegel, Georg Wilhelm Friedrich. Cours d'esthétique. Paris, 1840-43. 2v.

Phil 3425.56.5   Hegel, Georg Wilhelm Friedrich. The introduction to Hegel's Philosophy of fine art. London, 1905.

Phil 3425.56.10   Hegel, Georg Wilhelm Friedrich. Asthetik. Berlin, 1955.

Phil 3425.56.15   Hegel, Georg Wilhelm Friedrich. The philosophy of art. Edinburgh, 1886.

Phil 3425.56.20   Hegel, Georg Wilhelm Friedrich. The introduction to Hegel's Philosophy of fine art. London, 1886.

Phil 3425.56.25   Hegel, Georg Wilhelm Friedrich. The philosophy of art. N.Y., 1879.

Phil 3425.56.30   Hegel, Georg Wilhelm Friedrich. The philosophy of fine art. London, 1920. 4v.

Phil 3425.56.35   Bartsch, Heinrich. Register zu Hegel's Vorlesungen über die Asthetik. Mainz, 1844.

Phil 3425.56.36   Bartsch, Heinrich. Register zu Hegel's Vorlesungen über die Asthetik. Stuttgart, 1966.

Phil 3425.60   Hegel, Georg Wilhelm Friedrich. Philosophie de la religion. Paris, 1876-78. 2v.

Phil 3425.60.3   Hegel, Georg Wilhelm Friedrich. Leçons sur la philosophie de la religion. pt.1-5. Paris, 1954-59. 3v.

Phil 3425.60.5   Hegel, Georg Wilhelm Friedrich. Lectures on the philosophy of religion. London, 1895. 3v.

Phil 3425.60.6   Hegel, Georg Wilhelm Friedrich. Lectures on the philosophy of religion. N.Y., 1962. 3v.

Phil 3425.60.10   Hegel, Georg Wilhelm Friedrich. Vorlesungen über die Philosophie der Religion. Berlin, 1840. 2v.

Phil 3425.60.12   Hegel, Georg Wilhelm Friedrich. Vorlesungen über die Philosophie der Religion. Hamburg, 1966. 2v.

Phil 3425.60.15   Hegel, Georg Wilhelm Friedrich. Vorlesungen über die Philosophie der Religion. Leiden, 1901. 2v.

Phil 3425.60.16   Hegel, Georg Wilhelm Friedrich. Vorlesungen über die Philosophie der Religion. Leipzig, 1944-

Phil 3425.60.17   Hegel, Georg Wilhelm Friedrich. Die Naturreligion. Leipzig, 1927.

Phil 3425.60.19   Hegel, Georg Wilhelm Friedrich. Die Religionen der geistigen Individualität. Leipzig, 1927.

Phil 3425.60.20   Hegel, Georg Wilhelm Friedrich. Vorlesungen über die Beweise vom Dasein Gottes. Leipzig, 1930.

Phil 3425.60.55   Hegel, Georg Wilhelm Friedrich. Hegels Religionsphilosophie in gekürzter Form. Jena, 1905.

Phil 3425.61   Hegel, Georg Wilhelm Friedrich. Theologische Judendschriften. Tübingen, 1907.

Phil 3425.62   Hegel, Georg Wilhelm Friedrich. Die absolute Religion. Leipzig, 1929.

Phil 3425.63   Hegel, Georg Wilhelm Friedrich. Early theological writings. Chicago, 1948.

Phil 3425.64   Hegel, Georg Wilhelm Friedrich. Das junge Hegel in Stuttgart. Marbach, 1970?

Phil 3425.65A   Hegel, Georg Wilhelm Friedrich. The ethics of Hegel. Boston, 1893.

Phil 3425.65B   Hegel, Georg Wilhelm Friedrich. The ethics of Hegel. Boston, 1893.

Phil 3425.66   Hegel, Georg Wilhelm Friedrich. Der Geist des Christentums und sein Schicksal. Gütersloh, 1970.

Phil 3425.68.5   Hegel, Georg Wilhelm Friedrich. System der Sittlichkeit. Osterwiech, 1893.

Phil 3425.69   Hegel, Georg Wilhelm Friedrich. Einleitung in die Asthetik. München, 1967.

Htn   Phil 3425.70.1*   Hegel, Georg Wilhelm Friedrich. Grundlinien der Philosophie des Rechts. Berlin, 1821.

Phil 3425 History of philosophy - Local Modern philosophy - Germany - Individual philosophers - Hegel, Georg W.F. - cont.

Phil 3425.70.5   Hegel, Georg Wilhelm Friedrich. Grundlinien der Philosophie des Rechts. Leipzig, 1911.

Phil 3425.70.9   Hegel, Georg Wilhelm Friedrich. Grundlinien der Philosophie des Rechts. 2. Aufl. Leipzig, 1921.

Phil 3425.70.10   Hegel, Georg Wilhelm Friedrich. Grundlinien der Philosophie des Rechts. 3. Aufl. Leipzig, 1930.

Phil 3425.70.15   Hegel, Georg Wilhelm Friedrich. Grundlinien der Philosophie des Rechts. Leiden, 1902.

Phil 3425.70.18   Hegel, Georg Wilhelm Friedrich. Grundlinien der Philosophie des Rechts. 4. Aufl. Hamburg, 1955.

Phil 3425.70.19   Hegel, Georg Wilhelm Friedrich. Grundlinien der Philosophie des Rechts. 4. Aufl. Berlin, 1956.

Phil 3425.70.50   Hegel, Georg Wilhelm Friedrich. Eigenhändige Raudhemerkungen zu seiner Rechtsphilosophie. Leipzig, 1930.

Phil 3425.70.75A   Hegel, Georg Wilhelm Friedrich. Einleitung in die Geschichte der Philosophie. 3. Aufl. Hamburg, 1959.

Phil 3425.70.75B   Hegel, Georg Wilhelm Friedrich. Einleitung in die Geschichte der Philosophie. 3. Aufl. Hamburg, 1959.

Phil 3425.71   Hegel, Georg Wilhelm Friedrich. Philosophy of right. London, 1896.

Phil 3425.71.5   Hegel, Georg Wilhelm Friedrich. Theory of right, duties, and religion. Ann Arbor, 1892.

Phil 3425.71.11   Hegel, Georg Wilhelm Friedrich. Philosophy of right. Oxford, 1967.

Phil 3425.72   Hegel, Georg Wilhelm Friedrich. System der Wissenschaft. Bamberg, 1807.

Phil 3425.72.90   Hegel, Georg Wilhelm Friedrich. Phänomenologie des Geistes. Leipzig, 1907.

Phil 3425.73   Hegel, Georg Wilhelm Friedrich. Phänomenologie des Geistes. Leipzig, 1907.

Phil 3425.73.1   Hegel, Georg Wilhelm Friedrich. Phänomenologie des Geistes. 2. Aufl. Leipzig, 1921.

Phil 3425.73.2   Hegel, Georg Wilhelm Friedrich. Phänomenologie des Geistes. 2. Aufl. Berlin, 1841.

Phil 3425.73.2.5   Hegel, Georg Wilhelm Friedrich. Phänomenologie des Geistes. Leipzig, 1937. 2v.

Phil 3425.73.2.10   Hegel, Georg Wilhelm Friedrich. Phänomenologie des Geistes. 6. Aufl. Hamburg, 1952.

Phil 3425.73.4   Hegel, Georg Wilhelm Friedrich. Einleitung in die Phänomenologie des Geistes. Frankfurt, 1964.

Phil 3425.73.5   Hegel, Georg Wilhelm Friedrich. The phenomenology of mind. London, 1910.

Phil 3425.73.8A   Hegel, Georg Wilhelm Friedrich. The phenomenology of mind. 2nd ed. London, 1955.

Phil 3425.73.8B   Hegel, Georg Wilhelm Friedrich. The phenomenology of mind. 2nd ed. London, 1955.

Phil 3425.73.9   Hegel, Georg Wilhelm Friedrich. The phenomenology of mind. 2nd ed. London, 1961.

Phil 3425.73.10A   Hegel, Georg Wilhelm Friedrich. The phenomenology of mind. 2nd ed. London, 1966.

Phil 3425.73.10B   Hegel, Georg Wilhelm Friedrich. The phenomenology of mind. 2nd ed. London, 1966.

Phil 3425.73.20   Hegel, Georg Wilhelm Friedrich. La phénoménologie de l'esprit. Paris, 1939-41. 2v.

Phil 3425.73.20.10   Heidegger, Martin. Hegel's concept of experience. 1st ed. N.Y., 1970.

Phil 3425.74   Hegel, Georg Wilhelm Friedrich. Hegels philosophiska propädentik. Helsingfors, 1845.

Phil 3425.74.2   Hegel, Georg Wilhelm Friedrich. Propédiutique philosophique. Paris, 1963.

Phil 3425.74.5   Hegel, Georg Wilhelm Friedrich. Hegel's first principle. Saint Louis, 1869.

Phil 3425.75   Hegel, Georg Wilhelm Friedrich. Neue Briefe...und Verwandtes. Leipzig, 1912.

Phil 3425.75.5   Hegel, Georg Wilhelm Friedrich. Hegel Brevier. Zürich, 1951.

Phil 3425.76   Hegel, Georg Wilhelm Friedrich. Der Staat. Leipzig, 1924.

Phil 3425.76.50   Hegel, Georg Wilhelm Friedrich. Hegel on tragedy. 1st ed. Garden City, N.Y., 1962.

Phil 3425.77   Hegel, Georg Wilhelm Friedrich. Hegels erstes System. Heidelberg, 1915.

Phil 3425.77.2   Hegel, Georg Wilhelm Friedrich. Hegels erstes System. Heidelberg, 1918.

Phil 3425.78A   Lowenberg, Jacob. Hegel's Entwürfe zur Enzyklopädie und Propadentik. Leipzig, 1912.

Phil 3425.78B   Lowenberg, Jacob. Hegel's Entwürfe zur Enzyklopädie und Propadentik. Leipzig, 1912.

Phil 3425.78.10   Lowenberg, Jacob. Hegel's phenomenology. La Salle, Ill., 1965.

Phil 3425.79   Pamphlet vol. Philosophy. German and Dutch. Hegel, Georg Wilhelm Friedrich. German dissertations. 18 pam.

Phil 3425.79.2   Pamphlet vol. Philosophy. German and Dutch. Hegel, Georg Wilhelm Friedrich. German dissertations. 13 pam.

Phil 3425.79.3   Pamphlet box. Philosophy. German and Dutch. Hegel, Georg Wilhelm Friedrich. German dissertations.

Phil 3425.79.5   Pamphlet box. Philosophy. German and Dutch. Hegel, Georg Wilhelm Friedrich.

Phil 3425.79.50   Internationales Hegelbund. Veroeffentlichungen. Tübingen. 1,1931 2v.

X Cg   Phil 3425.80   Caird, Edward. Hegel. Philadelphia, 1883.

X Cg   Phil 3425.80.3A   Caird, Edward. Hegel. Edinburgh, 1883.

NEDL   Phil 3425.80.5   Caird, Edward. Hegel. Philadelphia, 1896.

Phil 3425.80.7   Caird, Edward. Hegel. Edinburgh, 1891.

Phil 3425.81   Chlebik, F. Kraft und Stoff...Hegel'schen Prämissen. Berlin, 1873.

Phil 3425.82   Erner, F. Die Psychologie der Hegelschen Schule. Leipzig, 1842-44. 2v.

Phil 3425.83   Foucher de Careil, L.A. Hegel et Schopenhauer. Paris, 1862.

Phil 3425.84   Gabler, G.A. Die hegelsche Philosophie. Berlin, 1843.

Phil 3425.84.10   Gabler, G.A. Kritik des Bewusstseins. Leiden, 1901.

Phil 3425.85   George, L. Princip und Methode der Philosophie. Berlin, 1842.

Phil 3425.86   Harris, W.T. Hegel's logic. Chicago, 1890.

Phil 3425.86.5   Harris, W.T. Hegel's logic. 2d ed. Chicago, 1895.

Phil 3425.87   Goeschel, K.F. Hegel und seine Zeit. Berlin, 1832.

Phil 3425.88A   Haym, Rudolf. Hegel und seine Zeit. Berlin, 1857.

Phil 3425.88B   Haym, Rudolf. Hegel und seine Zeit. Berlin, 1857.

X Cg   Phil 3425.88.2   Haym, Rudolf. Hegel und seine Zeit. 2. Aufl. Leipzig, 1927.

Phil 3425.89   Keil, Oswald T. Einige Bemerkungen über den Standpankt, Welchen die deutsche Philosophie durch Hegel erreicht hat. Leipzig, 1828.

Phil 3425.90   Ott, A. Hegel et la philosophie allemande. Paris, 1844.

Phil 3425 History of philosophy - Local Modern philosophy - Germany - Individual philosophers - Hegel, Georg W.F. - cont.

Phil 3425.91   Rosenkranz, K. Kritische Erläuterungen des Hegel's...Systems. Königsberg, 1840.

Phil 3425.91.5   Rosenkranz, K. Apologie Hegel's gegen Dr. R. Haym. Berlin, 1858.

Phil 3425.91.7   Rosenkranz, K. Aus Hegels Leben. Leipzig, 1845.

Phil 3425.91.10   Rosenkranz, K. Georg Wilhelm F. Hegel's Leben. Berlin, 1844.

Phil 3425.91.13A   Rosenkranz, K. Hegel als deutscher Nationalphilosoph. Leipzig, 1870.

Phil 3425.91.13B   Rosenkranz, K. Hegel als deutscher Nationalphilosoph. Leipzig, 1870.

Phil 3425.91.15   Rosenkranz, K. Hegel as national philosopher of Germany. St.Louis, 1874.

Phil 3425.91.19   Rosenkranz, K. Erläuterungen zu Hegel's Encyklopädie der philosophischen Wissenschaften. Leipzig, 1920.

Phil 3425.91.22   Rosenkranz, K. Hegel's Naturphilosophie. Berlin, 1868.

Phil 3425.91.28   Bachmann, C.F. Anti-Hegel. Jena, 1835.

Phil 3425.91.30   Bachmann, C.F. Uber Hegel's System und die Nothwendigkeit. Leipzig, 1833.

Phil 3425.91.35   Rosenkranz, K. Hegel; Sendschreiben an...Carl Friedrich Bachmann. Königsberg, 1843.

Phil 3425.91.40   Rosenkranz, K. Über Schelling und Hegel. Königsberg, 1843.

Phil 3425.92A   Seth, A. Hegelianism and personality. Edinburgh, 1887.

Phil 3425.92B   Seth, A. Hegelianism and personality. Edinburgh, 1887.

Phil 3425.92.2   Seth, A. Hegelianism and personality. 2d ed. Edinburgh, 1893.

Phil 3425.93   Staudenmaier, F. Darstellung und Kritik des Hegelschen Systems. Mainz, 1844.

Phil 3425.94   Stirling, J.H. The secret of Hegel. London, 1865. 2v.

Phil 3425.95   Véra, A. Introduction à la philosophie de Hegel. Paris, 1845-55. 3 pam.

Phil 3425.95.4   Véra, A. Philosophie de l'esprit. Paris, 1867-69. 2v.

Phil 3425.95.8   Véra, A. Essais de philosophie hégélienne. Paris, 1864.

Phil 3425.95.12   Véra, A. L'hégélianisme et la philosophie. Paris, 1861.

Phil 3425.95.15   Véra, A. Introduction à la philosophie de Hegel. 2. éd. Paris, 1864.

Phil 3425.96A   Wallace, W. Prolegomena to Hegel's philosophy. Oxford, 1894.

Phil 3425.96B   Wallace, W. Prolegomena to Hegel's philosophy. Oxford, 1894.

Phil 3425.97   Werner, J. Hegels Offenbarungsbegriff. Leipzig, 1887.

NEDL   Phil 3425.98   McGilvary, E. Principle and method of the Hegelian dialectic. Berkeley, 1897.

Phil 3425.99   Noël, G. La logique de Hegel. Paris, 1897.

Phil 3425.100.2   McTaggart, John McTaggart Ellis. Studies in the Hegelian dialectic. 2. ed. Cambridge, 1922.

Phil 3425.100.2.1   McTaggart, John McTaggart Ellis. Studies in the Hegelian dialectic. 2. ed. N.Y., 1964.

Phil 3425.100.5A   McTaggart, John McTaggart Ellis. Studies in Hegelian cosmology. Cambridge, 1901.

Phil 3425.100.5B   McTaggart, John McTaggart Ellis. Studies in Hegelian cosmology. Cambridge, 1901.

Phil 3425.100.9   McTaggart, John McTaggart Ellis. A commentary on Hegel's logic. Cambridge, 1910.

Phil 3425.101   Kredenburch, W.C.A. De staatsleer van Hegel. Utrecht, 1896.

Phil 3425.102A   Morris, G.S. Hegel's philosophy of the state. Chicago, 1887.

Phil 3425.102B   Morris, G.S. Hegel's philosophy of the state. Chicago, 1887.

Phil 3425.103   Baillie, J.B. The origin and significance of Hegel's logic. London, 1901.

Phil 3425.104A   Mackintosh, R. Hegel and Hegelianism. Edinburgh, 1903.

Phil 3425.104B   Mackintosh, R. Hegel and Hegelianism. Edinburgh, 1903.

Phil 3425.105A   Hibben, J.G. Hegel's logic. N.Y., 1902.

Phil 3425.105B   Hibben, J.G. Hegel's logic. N.Y., 1902.

Phil 3425.105.15   Hibben, J.G. La logica di Hegel. Torino, 1910.

Phil 3425.106   Lévy-Bruhl, L. La théorie de l'état dans Hegel. Paris, 1889.

Phil 3425.108   Hegel...Gedankenwelt in Auszügen aus seine Werken. Stuttgart, 1906.

Phil 3425.108A   Lasson, G. Hegel...Gedankenwelt in Auszügen aus seine Werken. Stuggart, 1906.

Phil 3425.108.5   Lasson, G. Hegel; handschriftliche Zusätze zu seiner Rechtsphilosophie. Leipzig, 1914. 3v.

Phil 3425.108.7   Lasson, G. Beiträge zur Hegelforschung. Berlin, 1919-21. 2v.

Phil 3425.108.10   Lasson, G. Einführung in Hegels Religionsphilosophie. Leipzig, 1930.

Phil 3425.109   Croce, B. Lebendiges und Totes in Hegels Philosophie. Heidelberg, 1909.

Phil 3425.109.4   Croce, B. Ciò che è vivo e ciò che è morto della filosofia di Hegel. Bari, 1907.

Phil 3425.109.5   Croce, B. Ce qui est vivant et ce qui est mort de la philosophie de Hegel. Paris, 1910.

Phil 3425.109.10   Croce, B. Saggio sullo Hegel. Bari, 1913.

Phil 3425.109.14A   Croce, B. What is living and what is dead of the philosophy of Hegel. London, 1915.

Phil 3425.109.14B   Croce, B. What is living and what is dead of the philosophy of Hegel. London, 1915.

Phil 3425.109.15   Croce, B. Una pagina sconosciuta degli ultimi mesi della vita di Hegel. Bari, 1950.

Phil 3425.110   Windelband, W. Die Erneuerung des Hegelianismus. Heidelberg, 1910.

Phil 3425.111   Reiff, F. Uber die Hegel'sche Dialektik. Tübingen, 1866.

Phil 3425.112   Archambault, P. Hegel. Paris, n.d.

Phil 3425.113   Barrès, M. De Hegel aux cantines du nord. Paris, n.d.

Phil 3425.114   Roques, P. Hegel; sa vie et ses oeuvres. Paris, 1912.

Phil 3425.115   Phalén, A. Das Erkenntnisproblem in Hegels Philosophie. Upsala, 1912.

Phil 3425.116   Mackenzie, Millicent Hughes. Hegel's educational theory and practice. Photoreproduction. London, 1909.

Phil 3425.116.5   Brie, S. Der Volksgeist bei Hegel. Berlin, 1909.

Phil 3425.117   Schmitt, E.H. Das Geheimniss der hegelschen Dialektik. Halle, 1888.

Phil 3425.118   Fischer, Kuno. Hegels Leben, Werke und Lehre. v.1-2. Heidelberg, 1901.

Phil 3425.119   Åberg, Lawrence H. Hegel och Boströms rättsfilosofiska grundtankar. Upsala, 1885.

Phil 3425.120   Levi, Giuseppe. La dottrina dello stato di G.F.G. Hegel. Pavia, 1880-84.

Phil 3425.121   Mayer-Moreau, K. Hegels Socialphilosophie. Tubingen, 1910.

Phil 3425 History of philosophy - Local Modern philosophy - Germany - Individual philosophers - Hegel, Georg W.F. - cont.

Phil 3425.122   Purpus, Wilhelm. Zur Dialektik des Bewusstseins nach Hegel. Berlin, 1908.

Phil 3425.123   Schmid, Aloys. Entwicklungsgeschichte der Hegel'schen Logik. Regensburg, 1858.

Phil 3425.124   Reyburn, Hugh A. The ethical theory of Hegel. Oxford, 1921.

Phil 3425.125   Fazio-Allmayer, C. La teoria della libertà nella filosofia di Hegel. Messina, 1920.

Phil 3425.126   Thomsen, A. Hegel. København, 1905.

Phil 3425.127   Zóltowski, A. Metoda Hegla i zasady filosofii spekulatywej. Krakow, 1910.

Phil 3425.128   Aschkenasy, H. Hegels Einfluss auf die Religionsphilosophie in Deutschland. Berlin, 1907.

Phil 3425.180   Richert, Hans. Hegels Religionsphilosophie. Bromberg, 1900.

Phil 3425.191   Hammacher, Emil. Die Bedeutung der Philosophie Hegels. Leipzig, 1911.

Phil 3425.192   Bruijn, J.C. Hegel's phaenomenologie I-II, proeve van tekstverklaring. Proefschrift. Amsterdam, 1923.

Phil 3425.195   Kelly, Michael. Hegel's charlatanism exposed. London, 1911.

Phil 3425.198   Sedlák, F. A holiday with a Hegelian. London, 1911.

Phil 3425.199A   Stace, N.J. The philosophy of Hegel. London, 1924.

Phil 3425.199B   Stace, N.J. The philosophy of Hegel. London, 1924.

Phil 3425.199C   Stace, N.J. The philosophy of Hegel. London, 1924.

Phil 3425.200   Borelius, J.J. Det hegelska systemet och den spekulativa ethiken. Lund, 1853.

Phil 3425.200.5   Borelius, J.J. I hvad afseende är Hegel Pantheist? Upsala, 1851.

Phil 3425.200.10   Borelius, J.J. Om filosofiens supremati enligt Hegelska systemet. Lund, 1852.

Phil 3425.201   Boer, J. de. De beteekenis van de Hegel-studie voor onzen tijd. Baarn, 1915.

Phil 3425.202   Pen, K.J. Over het onderscheid tusschen de wetenschap van Hegel en de wijsheid van Bolland. Leiden, 1915.

Phil 3425.203   Afzelius, F.G. Hegelska philosophien. Upsala, 1843.

Phil 3425.203.5   Mager, K.W.E. Popular framstallning af Hegelska philosofeska. Stockholm, 1843.

Phil 3425.204   Nyblaeus, Axel. Ar en practisk philosophi möjlig efter Hegels verldsásigt? Lund, 1855.

Phil 3425.205   Edman, Alfred. Hegels lära om konstformerna. Helsingfors, 1856.

Phil 3425.206   Geijer, R. Hegelianism och positivism. Lund, 1883.

Phil 3425.207   Jong, K.H.E. de. Hegel und Plotin. Leiden, 1916.

Phil 3425.208   Stuhrmann, J. Die Wurzeln der Hegelschen Logik bei Kant. Neustadt, 1887.

Phil 3425.209   Gentile, G. La riforma della dialettica Hegeliana. Messina, 1913.

Phil 3425.209.5   Gentile, G. La riforma della dialettica Hegeliana. 2a ed. Messina, 1923.

Phil 3425.210   Bülow, F. Die Entwicklung der Hegelschen Sozialphilosophie. Leipzig, 1920.

Phil 3425.212   Caird, Edward. Hegel. Milano, 191-

Phil 3425.213   Maturi, S. L'idea di Hegel. Napoli, 1891.

Phil 3425.214   Bolland, G.J.P.J. Alte Vernunft und neuer Verstand. Leiden, 1902.

Phil 3425.215   Genberg, P. Belysning och granskning af Hegelska philosophiens. Lund, 1846.

Phil 3425.216   Lagus, R.E. De Hegeliana philosophiam juris tractandi ratione. Helsingforsiae, 1852.

Phil 3425.217   Wennerberg, G. Num recte et vere de Spinozismo judicavit Hegelius? Upsaliae, 1848.

Phil 3425.218   Chang, W.S. Hegel's ethical teaching. Shanghai, 1925.

Phil 3425.218.5   Chang, W.S. The development, significance and some limitatioms of Hegel's ethical teaching. Shanghai, 1926.

Phil 3425.219   Ulrici, Hermann. Uber Princip und Methode der hegelschen Philosophie. Halle, 1841.

Phil 3425.220   Heller, Hermann. Hegel und der nationale Machtstaatsgedanke in Deutschland. Leipzig, 1921.

Phil 3425.220.5   Heller, Hermann. Hegel und der nationale Machtstaatsgedanke in Deutschland. Aalen, 1963.

Phil 3425.221   Reichlin-Meldegg, Karl A. Die Autolatrie oder Selbstanbetung. Pforzheim, 1943.

Phil 3425.222   Norelius, G. Grunddragen af Hegels filosofi och ästetik. Norrköping, 1893.

Phil 3425.223   Heimann, B. System und Methode in Hegels Philosophie. Leipzig, 1927.

Phil 3425.224   Schmidt-Japing, J.W. Die Bedeutung der person Jesu...Hegel. Göttingen, 1924.

Phil 3425.225   Collan, F. De notione necessitatis Hegeliana. Diss. Helsingforsiae, 1850.

Phil 3425.226   Giese, G. Hegels Staatsidee und der Begriff der Staatserziehung. Halle, 1926.

Phil 3425.227   Quist, C.J. De philosophia juris Hegeliana. Thesis. Helsingforsiae, 1853.

Phil 3425.228   Lucia, V. de. L'Hegel in Italia. Vasto, 1888.

Phil 3425.229   Michelet, C.L. Hegel und der Empirismus. Berlin, 1873.

Phil 3425.229.10   Michelet, C.L. Einleitung in Hegel's philosophische Abhandlungen. Berlin, 1832.

Phil 3425.229.15   Michelet, C.L. Hegel, der unwiderlegte Weltphilosoph. Leipzig, 1870.

Phil 3425.230   Sturge, M.C. Opposite things. Bristol, 1927.

Phil 3425.231   Leese, Kurt. Die Geschichtsphilosophie Hegels. Berlin, 1922.

Phil 3425.232   Barth, Paul. Die Geschichtsphilosophie Hegels und der Hegelianer bis auf Marx und Hartman. 2. Aufl. Photoreproduction. Leipzig, 1925.

Phil 3425.232.5   Barth, Paul. Die Geschichtsphilosophie Hegels und der Hegelianer bis auf Marx und Hartman. Darmstadt, 1967.

Phil 3425.235   Köstlin, K.R. Hegel. Tübingen, 1870.

Phil 3425.236   Bullinger, A. Hegels Lehre vom Widerspruch. Dillingen, 1884.

Phil 3425.237   Allievo, G. L'Hegelianismo, la scienza e la vita. Milano, 1868.

Phil 3425.237.5   Allievo, G. Esame dell'Hegelianismo. Torino, 1897.

Phil 3425.238   Il'in, Ivan A. Filosofiia Gegelia. Moskva, 1918.

Phil 3425.239   Basch, Victor. Les doctrines politiques des philosophes de l'Allemagne; Leibnitz, Kant, Fichte, Hegel. Paris, 1927.

Phil 3425.240   Lassalle, F. Die hegelsche und rosenkranzsche Logik. Leipzig, 1927.

Phil 3425.241   Rosenzweig, Franz. Hegel und der Staat. v.1-2. Aalen, 1962.

Phil 3425.243   Ephraim, F. Untersuchungen über den Freiheitsbegriff Hegels in seinen Jugendarbeiten. Berlin, 1928.

Phil 3425.244   Grupe, Walter. Mundts und Kühnes Verhältnis zu Hegel und seinen Gegnern. Halle, 1928.

Phil 3425 History of philosophy - Local Modern philosophy - Germany - Individual philosophers - Hegel, Georg W.F. - cont.

Phil 3425.245   Lowenstein, Julius. Hegels Staatsidee. Berlin, 1927.

Phil 3425.246   Salditt, Maria. Hegels Shakespeare-Interpretation. Berlin, 1927.

Phil 3425.247   Hartmann, E. v. Ueber die dialektische Methode. Berlin, 1868.

Phil 3425.247.5   Purpus, Wilhelm. Eduard von Hartmanns Kritik der dialektischen Methode Hegels. Ansbach, 1911.

Phil 3425.248   Emge, C.A. Hegels Logik und die Gegenwart. Karlsruhe, 1927.

Phil 3425.249   Fischer, Hugo. Hegels Methode in ihrer ideengeschichtlichen Notwendigkeit. Habilitationsschrift. München, 1928.

Phil 3425.250   Larenz, Karl. Hegels Zurechnungslehre und der Begriff der objektiven Zurechnung. Leipzig, 1927.

Phil 3425.251   Nyblaeus, Axel. Bidrag till granskning af den Hegelska dialektiken och dess princip "Motsägelsen". Upsala, 1851.

Phil 3425.252   Sahlin, C. Yngve. Har Hegel öfvervunnit dualismen? Upsala, 1851.

Phil 3425.253   Brunswig, Alfred. Hegel. München, 1922.

Phil 3425.254   Haering, Theodor L. Hegel, sein Wollen und sein Werke. Leipzig, 1929-1938. 2v.

Phil 3425.255   Volpe, Galvano di. Hegel romantico e mistico (1793-1800). Firenze, 1929.

Phil 3425.256   Frost, Walter. Hegels Ästhetik. München, 1928.

Phil 3425.257   Wahl, Jean A. Le malheur de la conscience dans la philosophie de Hegel. Paris, 1929.

Phil 3425.257.10   Wahl, Jean A. Commentaire de la logique de Hegel. Paris, 1959.

Phil 3425.258   Glockner, Hermann. Hegel. Stuttgart, 1929.

Phil 3425.258.10   Glockner, Hermann. Die ethisch-politische Persönlichkeit des Philosophen. Tübingen, 1922.

Phil 3425.259   Negri, Enrico de. La nascita della dialettica Hegeliana. Firenza, 1930.

Phil 3425.260   Schelling-Wollny, Kurt. Hegels Wissenschaft von der Wirklichkeit und ihre Quellen. München, 1929.

Phil 3425.261   Foster, Michael B. Die Geschichte als Schicksal des Geistes in der hegelschenPhilosophie. Tübingen, 1929.

Phil 3425.262   Moog, Willy. Hegel und die hegelsche Schule. München, 1930.

Phil 3425.263   Noack, Ludwig. Der Religions begriff Hegel's. Darmstadt, 1845.

Phil 3425.264   Busse, Martin. Phänomenologie des Geistes und der Staat. Berlin, 1931.

Phil 3425.265A   Nink, Caspar. Kommentar zu den grundlegenden Abschnitten von Hegels Phänomenologie des Geistes. Regensburg, 1931.

Phil 3425.265B   Nink, Caspar. Kommentar zu den grundlegenden Abschnitten von Hegels Phänomenologie des Geistes. Regensburg, 1931.

Phil 3425.266   Nadler, Käte. Der dialektische Widerspruch in Hegels Philosophie und das Paradoxon des Christentums. Leipzig, 1931.

Phil 3425.267   Zu Georg Wilhelm Friedrich Hegels 100. Todestag (am 14 november 1931). Berlin, 1931.

Phil 3425.268   Hermann, Conrad. Hegel und die logische Frage der Philosophie in der Gegenwart. Leipzig, 1878.

Phil 3425.269   Allihn, F.H.T. Der verderbliche Einfluss der Hegelschen Philosophie. Leipzig, 1852.

Phil 3425.270   Trendelenburg, A. Die logische Frage in Hegel's System. Leipzig, 1843.

Phil 3425.271   Wenke, Hans. Hegels Theorie des objektiven Geistes. Halle, 1927.

Phil 3425.272   Eschenmayer, C.A. Die Hegel'sche Religions-Philosophie. Tübingen, 1834.

Phil 3425.273   Marheineke, Philipp. Einleitung in die öffentlichen Vorlesungen über die Bedeutung der hegelschen Philosophie in der christlichen Theologie. Berlin, 1842.

Phil 3425.274   Ott, Emil. Die Religionsphilosophie Hegels. Berlin, 1904.

Phil 3425.275   Springer, Anton T.H. Die Hegel'sche Geschichtsanschauung. Tübingen, 1848.

Phil 3425.276   Steinhart, C. Hegel und sein Werk. Naumburg, 1841.

Phil 3425.277   Hirä-Lâl, H. Hegelianism and human personality. Calcutta, 1910.

Phil 3425.278   Harms, F. Zur Erinnerungen an Georg W.F. Hegel. Berlin, 1871.

Phil 3425.279   Rackwitz, Max. Hegels Ansicht über die Apriorität von Zeit und Raum und die kantischen Kategorien. Halle, 1891.

Phil 3425.280   Siegel, Carl. Georg Wilhelm Freidrich Hegel. Graz, 1931.

Phil 3425.281   Sfard, D. Du role de l'idée de contradiction chez Hegel. Thèse. Nancy, 1931.

Phil 3425.282F   Spaventa, B. Le prime categorie della logica di Hegel; memoria. Napoli, 1864.

Phil 3425.282.5F   Spaventa, B. Studii sull'etica hegeliana; memoria. Napoli, 1869.

Phil 3425.283   Wacker, Herbert. Das Verhältnis des jungen Hegel zu Kant. Berlin, 1932.

Phil 3425.284   Steinbüchel, T. Das Grundproblem der hegelschen Philosophie. Bonn, 1933.

Phil 3425.285   Weisse, C.H. Ueber den gegenwärtigen Standpunct der philosophischen Wissenschaft. Leipzig, 1829.

Phil 3425.286   Trott zu Solz, A. v. Hegels Staatsphilosophie. Göttingen, 1932.

Phil 3425.287   Iakovenko, B.-V. Ein Beitrag zur Geschichte des Hegelianismus in Russland. Prag, 1934.

Phil 3425.287.5   Iakovenko, B.-V. Ein Beitrag zur Geschichte des Hegelianismus in Russland. Prag, 1934.

Phil 3425.288   Hoffmeister, J. Dokumente zu Hegels Entwicklung. Stuttgart, 1936.

Phil 3425.289   Flechtheim, O.K. Hegels Strafrechtstheorie. Brünn, 1936.

Phil 3425.290   Cross, G.J. Prologue and epilogue to Hegel. Oxford, 1935.

Phil 3425.291   Günther, G. Grundzüge einer neuen Theorie des Denkens in Hegels Logik. Leipzig, 1933.

Phil 3425.292   Marcuse, H. Hegels Ontologie und die Grundlegung einer Theorie der Geschichtlichkeit. Frankfurt, 1932.

Phil 3425.292.5   Marcuse, H. Reason and revolution; Hegel and the use of social theory. London, 1941.

Phil 3425.292.10A   Marcuse, H. Reason and revolution; Hegel and the use of social theory. 2nd ed. N.Y., 1954.

Phil 3425.292.10B   Marcuse, H. Reason and revolution; Hegel and the use of social theory. 2nd ed. N.Y., 1954.

Phil 3425.292.10C   Marcuse, H. Reason and revolution; Hegel and the use of social theory. 2nd ed. N.Y., 1954.

Phil 3425.292.12   Marcuse, H. Reason and revolution; Hegel and the use of social theory. 2nd ed. Boston, 1960.

Phil 3425.293   Trahndorff, K.F.E. Wie kann der Supernaturalismus sein Recht gegen Hegel's Religionsphilosophie behaupten? Berlin, 1840.

178

Classified Listing

Phil 3425 History of philosophy - Local Modern philosophy - Germany - Individual philosophers - Hegel, Georg W.F. - cont.

Phil 3425.294 Hegels Lehre von der Religion und Kunst von dem Standpuncte des Glauhens ausbeurtheilt. Leipzig, 1842.
Phil 3425.295 Fahrenhorst, E. Geist und Freiheit im System Hegels. Leipzig, 1934.
Phil 3425.296 Schultz, Werner. Die Grundprinzipien der Religionsphilosophie Hegels und der Theologie Schleiermachers. Berlin, 1937.
Phil 3425.297 Pelloux, L. La logica di Hegel. Milan, 1938.
Phil 3425.298 Schwarz, Justus. Hegels philosophische Entwicklung. Frankfurt, 1938.
Phil 3425.299 Müller, G.R. Hegel über Offenbarung. München, 1939.
Phil 3425.300 Lenin, V.I. Cahiers sur la dialectique de Hegel. Paris, 1938.
Phil 3425.300.5 Lenin, V.I. Hefte zu Hegels Dialektik. München, 1969.
Phil 3425.301 Contri, S. Tetralogia Hegeliana. Bologna, 1938-39. 2v.
Phil 3425.302 Mure, G.R.G. Introduction to Hegel. Oxford, 1940.
Phil 3425.303 Chyzhevs'kyi, Dmytro. Gegel' v Rossii. Parizh, 1939.
Phil 3425.303.2 Chyzhevs'kyi, Dmytro. Hegel bei den Slaven 2. Aufl. Bad Homburg, 1961.
Phil 3425.303.5 Chyzhevs'kyi, Dmytro. Hegel bei den Slaven. 2. Aufl. Darmstadt, 1961.
Phil 3425.304 Revue de Métaphysique et de Morale. Études sur Hegel. Paris, 1931.
Phil 3425.305 Burman, E.O. Hegels rättsfilosofi. Uppsala, 1939.
Phil 3425.306 Axmann, Walter. Zur Frage nach dem Ursprung des dialektischen Denkens bei Hegel. Inaug. Diss. Würzburg, 1939.
Phil 3425.307A Gray, J.G. Hegel's Hellenic ideal. N.Y., 1941.
Phil 3425.307B Gray, J.G. Hegel's Hellenic ideal. N.Y., 1941.
Phil 3425.308 Sterrett, James M. Studies in Hegel's philosophy of religion. N.Y., 1890.
Phil 3425.309 Werder, K. Logik. Als Commentar und Ergänzung zu Hegels Wissenschaft der Logik. Berlin, 1841.
Phil 3425.310 Myers, Henry Alonzo. The Spinoza-Hegel paradox. Ithaca, 1944.
Phil 3425.311 Dilthey, Wilhelm. Die Jugendgeschichte Hegels. Berlin, 1905.
Phil 3425.312 Niel, Henri. De la médiation dans la philosophie de Hegel. Paris, 1945.
Phil 3425.315 Il'in, Ivan A. Die Philosophie Hegels als kontemplative Gotteslehre. Bern, 1946.
Phil 3425.316 Niel, Henri. De la médiation dans la philosophie de Hegel. Thèse. Madrid, 1945.
Phil 3425.317 Antoni, Carlo. Considerazioni su Hegel e Marx. Napoli, 1946.
Phil 3425.318 Schmidt, Werner. Hegel und die Idee der Volksordnung. Leipzig, 1944.
Phil 3425.319 Hyppolite, Jean. Genèse et structure de la phénoménologie de l'esprit de Hegel. Thèse. Paris, 1946.
Phil 3425.319.5A Hyppolite, Jean. Genèse et structure de la phénoménologie de l'esprit de Hegel. Paris, 1946.
Phil 3425.319.5B Hyppolite, Jean. Genèse et structure de la phénoménologie de l'esprit de Hegel. Paris, 1946.
Phil 3425.319.10 Hyppolite, Jean. Logique et existence. 1. ed. Paris, 1953.
Phil 3425.319.15 Hyppolite, Jean. Introduction à la philosophie de l'historie de Hegel. Paris, 1948.
Phil 3425.320 Knoop, Bernhard. Hegel und die Franzosen. Stuttgart, 1941.
Phil 3425.321 Kojève, Alexandre. Introduction à la lecture de Hegel. Paris, 1947.
Phil 3425.321.5 Kojève, Alexandre. Introduction to the reading of Hegel. N.Y., 1969.
Phil 3425.321.10 Kojève, Alexandre. Hegel; eine Vergegenwäitigung. Stuttgart, 1958.
Phil 3425.322 Lukács, G. Der junge Hegel. Zürich, 1948.
Phil 3425.324 Bense, Max. Hegel und Kierkegaard. Köln, 1948.
Phil 3425.326A Mure, G.R.G. A study of Hegel's logic. Oxford, 1950.
Phil 3425.326B Mure, G.R.G. A study of Hegel's logic. Oxford, 1950.
Phil 3425.328 Negri, Enrico de. Interpretazione di Hegel. Firenze, 1943.
Phil 3425.328.1 Negri, Enrico de. Interpretazione di Hegel. Firenze, 1969.
Phil 3425.330 Wundt, M. Hegels Logik. Köln, 1949.
Phil 3425.332 Dürr, Agnes. Zum Problem der hegelschen Dialectik. Berlin, 1938.
Phil 3425.334 Bloch, Ernst. Subjekt-Objekt; Erläuterungen zu Hegel. Berlin, 1951.
Phil 3425.336 Glockner, Hermann. Hegel und seine Philosophie. Heidelberg, 1931.
Phil 3425.338 Guccione Monroy, Nino. Hegel ed il problema della moralità. Trapani, 1951.
Phil 3425.340 Weil, Eric. Hegel et l'état. Thèse. Paris, 1950.
Phil 3425.340.1 Weil, Eric. Hegel et l'état. Paris, 1950.
Phil 3425.342 Möller, Joseph. Der Geist und das Absolute. Paderborn, 1951.
Phil 3425.344 Sehring, L. Hegel. Berlin, 1908.
Phil 3425.346 Litt, Theodor. Hegel. Heidelberg, 1953.
Phil 3425.348 Bryant, W. McK. Hegel's educational ideas. N.Y., 1896.
Phil 3425.350 Coreth, Emerich. Das dialektische Sein in Hegel's Logik. Wien, 1952.
Phil 3425.354 Puglisi, F. L'estetica di Hegel e i suoi presupposti teoretici. Padova, 1953.
Phil 3425.356 Asveld, Paul. La pensée, religieuse du jeune Hegel. Louvain, 1953.
Phil 3425.358 Milan. Universita Cattolica del Sacro Cuare. Hegel nel centenario. Milano, 1932.
Phil 3425.360 Schmidt, E. Hegels Lehre von Gott. Gütersloh, 1952.
Phil 3425.362 Flügge, J. Die sittlichen Grundlagen des Denkens. Hamburg, 1953.
Phil 3425.364 Fusch, Carl-Ludwig. Der Bildungsbegriff des Jungen Hegel. Weinheim, 1953.
Phil 3425.366 Schlawin, H. Die Dialektik im System Hegels. Inaug. Diss. Bern, 1953.
Phil 3425.370 Contri, Siro. Punti di trascendenza nell'immanentismo hegeliano alla luce della momentalita storiosofica. Milano, 1954.
Phil 3425.372 Marx, Karl. Critique of Hegel's 'Philosophy of right.' Cambridge, Eng., 1970.
Phil 3425.375 Lakebrink, Bernhard. Hegels dialektische Ontologie und die thomistische Analektik. Köln, 1955.
Phil 3425.380 Beyer, W.R. Zwischen Phänomenologie und Logik. Frankfurt, 1955.
Phil 3425.385 Nicolin, F. Gründlinien einer geisteswissenschaftlichen Pädagogik bei G.W.F. Hegel. Bonn, 1955.

Phil 3425 History of philosophy - Local Modern philosophy - Germany - Individual philosophers - Hegel, Georg W.F. - cont.

Phil 3425.385.2 Nicolin, F. Hegels Bildungstheorie. Bonn, 1955.
Phil 3425.390 Hyppolite, Jean. Études sur Marx et Hegel. Paris, 1955.
Phil 3425.390.2 Hyppolite, Jean. Études sur Marx et Hegel. 2. éd. Paris, 1965.
Phil 3425.390.5 Hyppolite, Jean. Studies on Marx and Hegel. N.Y., 1969.
Phil 3425.395 Tinivella, Giovanni. Critica dell'idea di progresso. Milano, 1955.
Phil 3425.400 Cresson, André. Hegel. Paris, 1955.
Phil 3425.405 Adorno, Theodor W. Aspekte der Hegelschen Philosophie. Berlin, 1957.
Phil 3425.410 Poeggeler, Otto. Hegels Kritik der Romantik. Bonn, 1956.
Phil 3425.415 Wein, Hermann. Realdialektik. München, 1957.
Phil 3425.420 Banfi, Antonio. La filosofia di G.G.F. Hegel. Milano, 1956.
Phil 3425.422 Banfi, Antonio. Inconfro con Hegel. Urbino, 1965.
Phil 3425.425 Teyssèdre, Bernard. L'asthétique de Hegel. Paris, 1958.
Phil 3425.430A Grégoire, Franz. Études Hegeliennes. Louvain, 1958.
Phil 3425.430B Grégoire, Franz. Études Hegeliennes. Louvain, 1958.
Phil 3425.435 Dulckeit, Gerhard. Die Idee Gottes im Geiste der Philosophie Hegels. München, 1947.
Phil 3425.440 Henrici, Peter. Hegel und Blondel. Pullach, 1958.
Phil 3425.442 Heintel, Erich. Hegel und die Analogia Entis. Bonn, 1958.
Phil 3425.445 Kremer-Garietti, Angèle. La pensée de Hegel. Paris, 1957.
Phil 3425.450 Piérola, R.A. Hegel y la estatica. Tucumán, 1956.
Phil 3425.455 Erdmann, Johann Eduard. Abhandlung über Leib und Seele. Leiden, 1902.
Phil 3425.460 Findlay, John Niemayer. Hegel. London, 1958.
Phil 3425.465 Vecchi, Giovanni. L'estetica di Hegel. Milano, 1956.
Phil 3425.470 Meulen, Jan van der. Hegel. Hamburg, 1958.
Phil 3425.475 Schmandt, Jürgen. Hegel Ethik aus dem Geist der Religion. Bonn, 1957.
Phil 3425.480 Schulin, Ernst. Die weltgeschichtliche Erfassung des Orients bei Hegel und Ranke. Göttingen, 1958.
Phil 3425.485 Lacorte, Carmelo. Il primo Hegel. Firenze, 1959.
Phil 3425.490 Albrecht, Wolfgang. Hegels Gottesbeweis. Berlin, 1958.
Phil 3425.495 Beerling, R.F. De list de rede in de geschiedenisfilosofie van Hegel. Arnhem, 1959.
Phil 3425.500 Ovsiannikov, M.F. Filosofiia Gegelia. Moskva, 1959.
Phil 3425.505 Bakradze, K.S. Sistema i metod filosofii Gegelia. Tbilisi, 1958.
Phil 3425.510 Massolo, Arturo. Prime ricerche di Hegel. Urbino, 1959.
Phil 3425.515 Kruithof, J. Het uitgangspunt van Hegel's ontologie. Brugge, 1959.
Phil 3425.520 Gulian, C.I. Metoda si sistem la Hegel. Bucuresti, 1957. 2v.
Phil 3425.525 Mueller, Gustav E. Hegel. Bern, 1959.
Phil 3425.530 Fazio Allmayer, Vito. Ricerche hegeliane. Firenze, 1959.
Phil 3425.535 Oiserman, Teodor. Die Philosophie Hegels. 1. Aufl. Berlin, 1959.
Phil 3425.540 Wolf, Kurt. Die Religionsphilosophie des Jüngen Hegel. München, 1960.
Phil 3425.545 Stiehler, Gottfried. Hegel und der Marxismus über den Widerspruch. Berlin, 1960.
Phil 3425.550 Peperzak, Adrien. La jeune Hegel et la vision morale du monde. La Haye, 1960.
Phil 3425.552 Hegel-Studien. Bonn. 1-5 4v.
Phil 3425.553 Hegel-Studien; Beiheft. Bonn. 3-6 3v.
Phil 3425.554 Piontkovskii, A.A. Hegels Lehre über Staat und Recht und seine Strafrechtstheorie. Berlin, 1960.
Phil 3425.554.5 Piontkovskii, A.A. Uchenie Gegelia o prave i gosudarstve i ego ugolovno-pravovaia teoriia. Moskva, 1963.
Phil 3425.560 Chiereghin, F. L'influenza dello Spinozismo nella formazione. Padova, 1961.
Phil 3425.562 Schmidt, G. Hegel in Nürnberg. Tübingen, 1960.
Phil 3425.564 Rahrmoser, Günter. Subjektivität und verden Glichung. Gütersloh, 1961.
Phil 3425.566 Kaminsky, Jack. Hegel on art. N.Y., 1969.
Phil 3425.568 Georgiav, F.I. Protivopolozhnost' Marksistskogo i Gegelevskogo ucheniia o sozhanii. Moskva, 1961.
Phil 3425.570 Seeberger, W. Hegel, oder die Entwicklung. Stuttgart, 1961.
Phil 3425.572 Garaudy, Roger. Dieu est mort; étude sur Hegel. Paris, 1962.
Phil 3425.574 Focht, I. Mogućnost, nužnost, slučajnost, stvarnost. Sarajevo, 1961.
Phil 3425.576 Braum, Hermann. Realität und Reflexion. Heidelberg, 1960.
Phil 3425.577 Kedney, J.S. Hegel's aesthetics; a critical exposition. 2nd ed. Chicago, 1892.
Phil 3425.577.2 Kedney, J.S. Hegel's aesthetics; a critical exposition. Chicago, 1885.
Phil 3425.578 Kuhn, Helmut. Die Kulturfunkion der Kunst. Berlin, 1931. 2v.
Phil 3425.580 Travis, Don Carlos. A Hegel symposium. Austin, 1962.
Phil 3425.582 Hegel Jahrbuch. München. 1961+ 3v.
Phil 3425.584 Reining, Richard. Das Problem des polytechnischen Orbeitserziehung. Marburg, 1962.
Phil 3425.584.5 Reining, Richard. Zur Grundlegung der polytechnischen Bildung durch Hegel und Marx. Braunschweig, 1967.
Phil 3425.586 Kuderowicz, Z. Doktryna moralna mlodego Hegla. Warszawa, 1962.
Phil 3425.587 Serreau, R. Hegel et l'hégélianisme. Paris, 1962.
Phil 3425.588 Lauener, H. Die Sprache in der Philosophie Hegels. Berlin, 1962.
Phil 3425.589 Adorno, T.W. Drei Studien zu Hegel. Frankfurt, 1963.
Phil 3425.590 Guzzoni, Ute. Werden zu Sich. Freiburg, 1963.
Phil 3425.595 Beyer, W.R. Hegel-Bilder. Berlin, 1964.
Phil 3425.595.2 Beyer, W.R. Hegel-Bilder; Kritik der Hegel-Deutungen. 2. Aufl. Berlin, 1967.
Phil 3425.595.7 Beyer, W.R. Georg Wilhelm Friedrich Hegel in Nürnberg 1808-1816. Nürnberg, 1966.
Phil 3425.596 Stiehler, G. Die Dialektik in Hegels Phänomenologie des Geistes. Berlin, 1964.
Phil 3425.597 Shinkaruk, V.I. Logika dialektika i teoriia poznaniia Gegelia. Kiev, 1964.
Phil 3425.598 Luebbe, Hermann. Die Hegelsche Rechte. Stuttgart, 1962.
Phil 3425.599 Rehm, Margarete. Hegels spekulative Deutung der Infinitesimalrechnung. Köln, 1963.
Phil 3425.600 Redlich, A. Die Hegelsche Logik als Selbsterfassung der Persönlichkeit. Brinkum, 1964.
Phil 3425.601 Schmidt, H. Verheissung und Schrecken der Freiheit. Stuttgart, 1964.
Phil 3425.602 Merker, Nicolas. Le origini della logica hegeliana. Milano, 1961.
Phil 3425.603 Chapelle, A. Hegel et la religion. Paris, 1964.
Phil 3425.603.1 Chapelle, A. Hegel et la religion. Paris, 1964. 2v.
Phil 3425.603.2 Chapelle, A. Hegel et la religion. Annexes. Nanur, 1967.

Phil 3425 History of philosophy - Local Modern philosophy - Germany - Individual philosophers - Hegel, Georg W.F. - cont.

Phil 3425.604 Sass, H.M. Untersuchungen zur Religionsphilosophie. Münster, 1963.

Phil 3425.605 Kudrna, J. Studie k Hegel om pojetí historie. Praha, 1964.

Phil 3425.606 Bruaire, Claude. Logique et religion chrétiene dans la philosophie de Hegel. Paris, 1964.

Phil 3425.607 Vancourt, Raymond. La pensée religieuse de Hegel. Paris, 1965.

Phil 3425.608 Kaufmann, W.A. Hegel. 1st ed. Garden City, N.Y., 1965.

Phil 3425.609 Dooren, Willem van. Het tolaliteitsbegrip bij Hegel en zijn voorgangers. Assen, 1965.

Phil 3425.610 Mure, G.R.G. The philosophy of Hegel. London, 1965.

Phil 3425.611 Hegel, G.W. Propédeutique philosophique. Génève, 1964.

Phil 3425.612 Garauly, Roger. Le problème Hégélien. Paris, 196-.

Phil 3425.613 Sobotka, Milan. Die idealistische Dialektik der Praxis bei Hegel. Praha, 1965.

Phil 3425.614 Kissel, M.A. Etika Gegelia i Krizis sovremennoi burzhuaznoi etiki. Leningrad, 1966.

Phil 3425.615 Krueger, H.J. Theologie und Aufklärung. Stuttgart, 1966.

Phil 3425.616 Polska Akademia Nauk. Zakład Historii Filozofii Nowożytnej i Myśli Społecznej. Polskie spory o Hegla, 1830-1860. Warszawa, 1966.

Phil 3425.617 Maurer, R.K. Hegel und das Ende der Geschichte. Stuttgart, 1965.

Phil 3425.618 Riedel, Manfred. Theorie und Praxis im Denken Hegels. Stuttgart, 1965.

Phil 3425.619 Flam, Leopold. De bewustwording; beschouwingen bij de fenomenologie van de geest van Hegel. Bruxelles, 1966.

VPhil 3425.620 Kroński, Tadeusz. Hegel. wyd. 2. Warszawa, 1966.

Phil 3425.621 Koch, Traugott. Differenz und Versöhnung; eine Interpretation der Theologie G.W.F. Hegels nach seiner "Wissenschaft der Logik." 1. Aufl. Gütersloh, 1967.

Phil 3425.622 Benner, Dietrich. Theorie und Praxis. System theoretische Betrachtungen zu Hegel und Marx. Wien, 1966.

Phil 3425.623 Splett, Jörg. Die Trinitätslehre G.W.F. Hegels. Freiburg, 1965.

Phil 3425.624 Erdei, László. Der Anfang der Erkenntnis. Kritische Analyse des ersten Kapitels der Hegelschen Logik. Budapest, 1964.

Phil 3425.625 Marsch, Wolf Dieter. Gegenwart Christi in der Gesellschaft; eine Studie zu Hegels Dialektik. München, 1965.

Phil 3425.626 Rondet, Henri. Hegelianisme et christianisme. Paris, 1965.

Phil 3425.628 Hondt, Jacques d'. Hegel; philosophe de l'histoire vivante. Thèse. Paris, 1966.

Phil 3425.630 Easton, Loyd David. Hegel's first American followers. Athens, 1966.

Phil 3425.635 Oldrini, Guido. Gli Hegeliani di Napoli. Milano, 1964.

Phil 3425.640 Chiereghin, Franco. Hegel e la metafisica classica. Padova, 1966.

Phil 3425.641 Chiereghin, Franco. L'unità del sapere in Hegel. Padova, 1963.

Phil 3425.645 Polsko-Czechosłowacka Sesja Naukowa, Poświęcona Recepcji Filozofii Hegle w Krajach Słowianskich, Warsaw. Der Streit um Hegel bei den Slawen; Symposium. Prag, 1967.

Phil 3425.647 Incardona, Nunzio. L'assunzione hegeliana. Palermo, 1965.

Phil 3425.650 Fackenheim, Emil L. The religious dimension in Hegel's thought. Bloomington, Ind., 1968[1967]

Phil 3425.652 Hondt, Jacques d'. Hegel secret, recherches sur les sources cachées de la pensée de Hegel. Paris, 1968.

Phil 3425.654 Haag, Karl Heinz. Philosophischer Idealismus. Frankfurt, 1967.

Phil 3425.656 Fleishmann, Eugène. La science universelle ou la logique de Hegel. Paris, 1968.

Phil 3425.658 Waldemar, George. Présence de l'esthetique de Hegel. Paris, 1967.

Phil 3425.660 Hondt, Jacques d'. Hegel en son temps, Berlin, 1818-1831. Paris, 1968.

Phil 3425.662 Chatelet, François. Hegel. Paris, 1968.

Phil 3425.664.2 Lim, Sok-Zin. Der Begriff der Arbeit bei Hegel. 2. Aufl. Bonn, 1966.

Phil 3425.666.2 Parinetto, Luciano. La nozione di alienazione in Hegel, Feuerbach e Marx. 2. ed. Milano, 1969.

Phil 3425.668 Massolo, Arturo. Logica hegeliana e filosofia contemporanea. Firenze, 1967.

Phil 3425.670 Zuefle, Manfred. Prosa der Welt: die Sprache Hegels. Einsiedeln, 1968.

Phil 3425.675 Labarriere, Pierre Jean. Structures et mouvement dialectique dans la phenoménologie de l'esprit de Hegel. Paris, 1968.

VPhil 3425.676 Panasiuk, R. Lewica Heglowska. wyd. 1. Warszawa, 1969.

Phil 3425.678 Oldrini, Guido. Il primo hegelismo Italiano. Firenze, 1969.

Phil 3425.680 Rollwage, Jürgen. Das Modalproblem und die historische Handlung. München, 1969.

Phil 3425.682 Guereñu, Ernesto de. Das Gottesbild des Jungen Hegel. Thesis. Freiburg, 1969.

Phil 3425.688 Bourgeois, Bernard. La pensée politique de Hegel. Paris, 1969.

Phil 3425.690 Topitsch, Ernst. Die Sozialphilosophie Hegels als Heilslehre und Herrschaftsideologie. Neuwied, 1967.

Phil 3425.692 Horn, András. Kunst und Freiheit. Den Haag, 1969.

Phil 3425.693 Nedeljković, Dušan. Hegelova estetika, Marksovi osnovi estetike i dnašnje estetičke perspektive. Beograd, 1971.

Phil 3425.694 Rademaker, Hans. Hegels "objektive Logik" eine Einführung. Bonn, 1969.

Phil 3425.696 Grujié, P.M. Hegel und Sowjetphilosophie der Gegenwart. Bern, 1969.

Phil 3425.698 Hahn, Manfred. Bürgerlicher Optimismus im Niedergang. München, 1969.

Phil 3425.700 Bodanmer, Theodor. Hegel Deutung der Sprache. Hamburg, 1969.

Phil 3425.702 Ritta, Joachim. Metaphysik und Politik. Frankfurt, 1969.

Phil 3425.704 Weiss, Frederick Gustav. Hegel's critique of Aristotle's philosophy of mind. The Hague, 1969.

Phil 3425.706 Hagen, Eduard von. Abstraktion und Konkretion bei Hegel und Kierkegaard. Bonn, 1969.

Phil 3425.708 Sabetti, Alfredo. Hegel e il problema della filosofia come storia. Napoli, 1967.

Phil 3425.710 Treher, Wolfgang. Hegels Geisteskrankheit. Emmendin, 1969.

Phil 3425.712 Lakebrink, Bernhard. Studien zur Metaphysik Hegels. Freiburg, 1969.

Phil 3425.714 Brissoni, Armando. Ricerche sull'estetica di Hegel. Padova, 1968.

Phil 3425 History of philosophy - Local Modern philosophy - Germany - Individual philosophers - Hegel, Georg W.F. - cont.

Phil 3425.716 Colletti, Lucio. Il marxismo e Hegel. Bari, 1969.

Phil 3425.718 Soll, Ivan. An introduction to Hegel's metaphysics. Chicago, 1969.

Phil 3425.720 Reidinger, Otto. Gottes Tod und Hegels Auferstehung. Berlin, 1969.

Phil 3425.722 Brazill, William J. The young Hegelians. New Haven, 1970.

Phil 3425.724 Heintel, Peter. Hegel. Göttingen, 1970.

Phil 3425.726 Duso, Giuseppe. Hegel interprete di Platone. Padova, 1969.

Phil 3425.728 Schrader-Klebert, Karin. Das Problem des Anfangs in Hegels Philosophie. Wien, 1969.

Phil 3425.730 Wolff, Kurt Heinrich. Hingebung und Begriff. Neuwied, 1968.

Phil 3425.732 Boey, C. L'aliénation dans la phénoménologie de l'esprit de G.W.F. Hegel. Paris, 1970.

Phil 3425.734 Grégoire, Franz. L'attitude Hégélienne devant l'existence. Louvain, 1953.

Phil 3425.736 Fetscher, Iring. Hegels Lehre von Menschen. Stuttgart, 1970.

Phil 3425.738 Becker, Werner. Hegels Begriff der Dialektik und das Prinzip des Idealismus. Stuttgart, 1969.

Phil 3425.740 Rossi, Mario. Da Hegel a Marx. Milano, 1970- 2v.

Phil 3425.742 Wofford Symposium on Hegel and the Philosophy of Religion, Wofford College, 1968. Hegel and the philosophy of religion; the Wofford Symposium. The Hague, 1970.

Phil 3425.744 Golosov, Viktor F. Ratsional'noe i misticheskoe v gegelevskoi teorii iavliaiushchegosia dukha. Krasnoiarsk, 1969.

Phil 3425.746 Man'kovski, Boris S. Uchenie Gegelia o gosudarstve i sovremennost. Moskva, 1970.

Phil 3425.748 Dell'Aquila, Michele. Critica e letteratura in tre hegeliani di Napoli. Bari, 1969.

Phil 3425.750 Mueller, Friedrich. Entfremdung. Berlin, 1970.

Phil 3425.752 Kaufmann, Walter Arnold. Hegel's political philosophy. 1st ed. N.Y., 1970.

Phil 3425.754 Brockard, Hans. Subjekt; Versuch zur Ontologie bei Hegel. München, 1970.

Phil 3425.756 Bloch, Ernst. Über Methode und System bei Hegel. Frankfurt am Main, 1970.

Phil 3425.758 Bourgeois, Bernard. Hegel à Francfort; ou Judaisme, christianisme, hégélianisme. Paris, 1970.

Phil 3425.760 Carbonara, Cleto. Hegel e Marx nella polemica del diritto pubblico. Napoli, 1967.

Phil 3425.762 Palma, Norman. Moment et processus. Paris, 1970-

Phil 3425.764 Rohrmoser, Günter. Theologie et aliénation dans la pensée du jeune Hegel. Paris, 1970.

Phil 3425.766 Kaltenbrunner, Gerd Klaus. Hegel und die Folgen. 1. Aufl. Freiburg, 1970.

Phil 3425.768 Siep, Ludwig. Hegels Fichtekritik und die Wissenschaftslehre von 1804. Freiburg, 1970.

Phil 3425.770 Hondt, Jacques d'. Hegel et la pensée moderne. 1. éd. Paris, 1970.

Phil 3425.772 Theunissen, Michael. Hegels Lehre vom absoluten Geist als theologisch-politischer Traktat. Berlin, 1970.

Phil 3425.774 Gulyga, Arsenii V. Gegel'. Moskva, 1970.

Phil 3425.776 Negt, Oskar. Aktualität und Folgen der Philosophie Hegels. Frankfurt am Main, 1970.

Phil 3425.778 Léonard, Andre. La foi chez Hegel. Paris, 1970.

Phil 3425.780 Rebstock, Hans Otto. Hegels Auffassung des Mythos in seinen Frühschriften. Freiburg, 1971.

Phil 3428 History of philosophy - Local Modern philosophy - Germany - Individual philosophers - Herbart, Johann F.

Phil 3428.10 Herbart, J.F. Sämmtliche Werke. Leipzig, 1850-52. 12v.

Phil 3428.11 Herbart, J.F. Sämmtliche Werke. v.1-19. Langensalza, 1887-1912. 14v.

Phil 3428.15 Herbart, J.F. Kleinere philosophische Schriften und Abhandlungen. Leipzig, 1842-43. 3v.

Phil 3428.30 Herbart, J.F. Lehrbuch zur Einleitung in die Philosophie. Königsberg, 1837.

Phil 3428.30.5 Herbart, J.F. Lehrbuch zur Einleitung in die Philosophie. 2. Aufl. Königsberg, 1821.

Phil 3428.30.55 Herbart, J.F. Lehrbuch zur Einleitung in die philosophie. 4. Aufl. Leipzig, 1912.

Phil 3428.31 Herbart, J.F. Introduzione alla filosofia. 2. ed. Bari, 1927.

Phil 3428.34 Herbart, J.F. Allgemeine Pädagogik. Göttingen, 1806.

Phil 3428.35 Herbart, J.F. Allgemeine Metaphysik. Königsberg, 1828-29. 2v.

Phil 3428.36 Herbart, J.F. Allgemeine practische Philosophie. Göttingen, 1808.

Phil 3428.36.5 Herbart, J.F. Allgemeine praktische Philosophie. 3. Ausg. Hamburg, 1891.

Phil 3428.37 Herbart, J.F. Kurze Encyklopädie der Philosophie. Halle, 1841.

Phil 3428.40 Herbart, J.F. De attentionis. Regiomonti, 1822.

Phil 3428.43 Herbart, J.F. Lehrbuch zur Psychologie. Königsberg, 1816.

Phil 3428.43.5 Herbart, J.F. Lehrbuch zur Psychologie. 3. Aufl. Leipzig, 1887.

Phil 3428.44 Herbart, J.F. Lehrbuch zur Psychologie. Hamburg, 1900.

Phil 3428.45 Herbart, J.F. Text-book in psychology. N.Y., 1891.

Phil 3428.47 Herbart, J.F. Psychologie als Wissenschaft. Königsberg, 1824. 2v.

Phil 3428.61 Herbart, J.F. Gespräche über das Böse. Königsberg, 1817.

Phil 3428.63 Herbart, J.F. Über philosophisches Studium. Leipzig, 1873.

Phil 3428.65 Herbart, J.F. Über meiner Streit met der Modephilosophie. Königsberg, 1814.

Phil 3428.66 Herbart, J.F. Der principio logico exclusi medii. Gottingae, 1833.

Phil 3428.67 Herbart, J.F. Psychologische Untersuchungen. Göttingen, 1839-40.

Phil 3428.79 Pamphlet box. Philosophy. German and Dutch. Herbart, J.F. German dissertations.

Phil 3428.80 Capesius, J. Die Metaphysik Herbarts. Leipzig, 1878.

Phil 3428.81 Lange, F.A. Die Grundlegung der mathematischen Psychologie. Duisburg, 1865.

Phil 3428.82 Thomas, K. Herbart, Spinoza, Kant. Langensalza, 1875.

Phil 3428.83 Turic, G. Der Entschluss im dem Herbarts Metaphysik. Langensalza, 1892.

Phil 3428.84 Ivanoff, T. Die abweichungen Steinthals von Herbart. Jena, 1893.

Phil 3428.85 Ballauff, F. Entstehung und Bedeutung; Herbarts. Aurich, 1898.

Phil 3428.86 Ziechner, A. Herbarts Ästhetik. n.p., n.d.

Phil 3428 History of philosophy - Local Modern philosophy - Germany - Individual philosophers - Herbart, Johann F. - cont.

Phil 3428.87 Moosherr, T. Herbarts Metaphysik. Basel, 1898.
Phil 3428.88 Davidson, John. New interpretation of Herbart's psychology. Edinburgh, 1906.
Phil 3428.89 Flügel, Otto. Die Bedeutung der Metaphysik Herbarts. Langensalza, 1902.
Phil 3428.89.5 Flügel, Otto. Der philosophie J.F. Herbart. Leipzig, 1905.
Phil 3428.90F Trendelenburg, A. Herbarts praktische Philosophie. Berlin, 1856.
Phil 3428.90.5 Trendelenburg, A. Über Herbart's Metaphysik. Berlin, 1854.
Phil 3428.91 Felsh. Erläuterungen zu Herbarts Ethik. Langensalza, 1899.
Phil 3428.92 Franke, Friedrich. J.F. Herbart; Grundzüge seiner Lehre. Leipzig, 1909.
Phil 3428.93 Langenbeck, H. Die theoretische Philosophie Herbarts und seiner Schule. Berlin, 1867.
Phil 3428.94 Raaf, H. de. Herbarts' metafyzica, psychologie in ethiek. Groningen, 1904.
Phil 3428.95.2 Ostermann, W. Die Hauptsächlichstein der Herbartschen Psychologie. 2. Aufl. Oldenburg, 1894.
Phil 3428.96.4 Gleichmann, A. Über Herbarts Lehre von der Stufen des Unterrichts. 4. Aufl. Langensalza, 1904.
Phil 3428.97 Strümpell. Die Hauptpuncte der Herbartschen Metaphysik. Braunschweig, 1840.
Phil 3428.153 Kinkel, Walter. J.F. Herbart, sein Leben und seine Philosophie. Giessen, 1903.
Phil 3428.155 Zimmerman, R. Über Trendelenburg's Einwürfe gegen Herbarts praktische Ideen. Wien, 1872.
Phil 3428.155.5 Zimmerman, R. Über den Einfluss der Tonlehre auf Herbart's Philosophie. Wien, 1873.
Phil 3428.155.10 Zimmerman, R. Perioden in Herbart's philosophischen Geistesgang. Wien, 1876.
Phil 3428.155.15 Zimmerman, R. Leibnitz und Herbart. Wien, 1849.
Phil 3428.156 Drobisch, M.W. Über die Fortbildung der Philosophie durch Herbart. Leipzig, 1876.
Phil 3428.158 Schoel, A. Johann Friedrich Herbart's philosophische Lehre von der Religion. Dresden, 1884.
Phil 3428.159 Borelius, J.J. Anmärkningar vid Herbarts filosofiska system. Kalmar, 1866.
Phil 3428.160 Hartenstein, G. Über die neuesten Darstellungen und Beurtheilungen der Herbart'schen Philosophie. Leipzig, 1838.
Phil 3428.161 Poggi, Alfredo. La filosofia de G.F. Herbart. Genova, 1932.
Phil 3428.162 Hintz, R. Herbarts Bedeutung für die Psychologie. Berlin, 1900.
Phil 3428.163 Regler, Walter. Herbarts Stellung zum Eudämonismus. Leipzig, 1900.
Phil 3428.164 Schmitz, Josef Nikolaus. Herbart Bibliographie, 1842-1963. Weinheim, 1964.

Phil 3450 History of philosophy - Local Modern philosophy - Germany - Individual philosophers - Other H

Phil 3450.2.79 Pamphlet box. Hemsterhuis, F.
Phil 3450.2.80 Boulan, Emile. François Hemsterhuis, le Socrate hollandais. Groningue, 1924.
Phil 3450.2.85 Brummel, L. Frans Hemsterhuis, een philosofenleven. Haarlem, 1925.
Phil 3450.2.87 Paritzky, J.E. Franz Hemsterhuis, seine Philosophie und ihr Einfluss auf dei deutschen Romantiker. Berlin, 1926.
Htn Phil 3450.3.30* Heereboord, Adriani. Meletemata philosophica. Amsterdam, 1680.
Phil 3450.3.90 Stearne, John. Adriani Heereboordi. Dublinii, 1660.
Phil 3450.4.80 Engestrom, Sigfrid. Studier till Wilhelm Hermanns etik. Uppsala, 1920.
Phil 3450.4.85 Redeker, Martin. Wilhelm Herrmann im kampf Gegen die positivistische Lebensanschauung. Gotha, 1928.
Phil 3450.4.90 Fischer-Appelt, Peter. Metaphysik im Horizent der Theologie Wilhelm Herrmanns. München, 1965.
Phil 3450.5.80 Zirngiebl, Eberhard. Johannes Huber. Gotha, 1881.
Phil 3450.6.80 Zimmer, Friedrich. Grundriss der Philosophie nach Friedrich Harms. Tübingen, 1902.
Phil 3450.7.80 Heinze, Max. Philosophische Abhandlungen. Berlin, 1906.
Phil 3450.7.81 Eleutheropulos, A. Max Heinze. Leipzig, 1909.
Phil 3450.8.80 Philosophische Abhandlungen dem Andenken Rudolf Haymns. Halle, 1902.
Phil 3450.9.30 Astrov, V. Rudolf Maria Holzapfel. Jena, 1928.
Phil 3450.9.79 Pamphlet vol. Cuttings and notes on R.M. Holzapfel.
Phil 3450.9.80 Zbinden, H. Ein Künder neuer Lebenswege...R.M. Holzapfel. Jena, 1923.
Phil 3450.9.85 Rudolf Maria Holzapfel. Basel, 1930.
Phil 3450.10.80 Groenewegen, H.J. Paulus van Hermert, als godgeleerde en als wijsgeer. Proefschrift. Amsterdam, 1889.
Phil 3450.11.30 Husserl, Edmund. Gesammelte Werke. Haag, 1950-52. 12v.
Phil 3450.11.35 Husserl, Edmund. The phenomenology of internal time-consciousness. Bloomington, 1964.
Phil 3450.11.40A Husserl, Edmund. Cartesian meditations. The Hague, 1960.
Phil 3450.11.40B Husserl, Edmund. Cartesian meditations. The Hague, 1960.
Phil 3450.11.45 Husserl, Edmund. La philosophie comme science rigoureuse. Thèse. Paris, 1954.
Phil 3450.11.48 Husserl, Edmund. Philosophie als strenge Wissenschaft. Frankfurt am Main, 1965.
Phil 3450.11.50 Husserl, Edmund. The idea of phenomenology. The Hague, 1964.
Phil 3450.11.55 Husserl, Edmund. Phenomenology and the crisis of philosophy. N.Y., 1965.
Phil 3450.11.60 Husserl, Edmund. Briefe an roman ingarden. Den Haag, 1968.
Phil 3450.11.62 Husserl, Edmund. The crisis of European sciences and transcendental phenomenology. Evanston, 1970.
Phil 3450.11.75 Husserl, Edmund. The Paris lectures. The Hague, 1964.
Phil 3450.11.79 Pamphlet box. Husserl, Edmund.
Phil 3450.11.79.5 Giulietti, Giovanni. La filosofia del profondo in Husserl e in Zamboni. Treviso, 1965.
Phil 3450.11.80 Schmidt Degener, H. Proeve eener ver gelijkende studie over Plato en Husserl. Groningen, 1924.
Phil 3450.11.85 Paci, Enzo. Omaggio a Husserl. Milano, 1960.
Phil 3450.11.86 Paci, Enzo. Il problema del tempo nella fenomenologia di Husserl. Milano, 1960.
Phil 3450.11.87 Paci, Enzo. La formazione del pensiero di Husserl e il problema della costituzione della natura materiale e della natura animale. Milano, 1967.
Phil 3450.11.90 Grunwaldt, H.H. Ueber die Phänomenologie Husserl. Berlin, 1927.

Phil 3450 History of philosophy - Local Modern philosophy - Germany - Individual philosophers - Other H - cont.

Phil 3450.11.95 Festschrift Edmund Husserl. Halle an der Saale, 1929.
Phil 3450.11.97 Levinas, Emmanuel. La théorie de l'institution dans la phénoménologie de Husserl. Paris, 1930.
Phil 3450.11.98 Levinas, Emmanuel. La théorie de l'institution dans la phénoménologie de Husserl. Thèse. Paris, 1930.
Phil 3450.11.98.5 Levinas, Emmanuel. En découvrant l'existence avec Husserl et Heidegger. Paris, 1949.
Phil 3450.11.98.6 Levinas, Emmanuel. En découvrant l'existence avec Husserl et Heidegger. Paris, 1967.
Phil 3450.11.99 Bannes, Joachim. Versuch einer Darstellung und Beurteilung der Grundlagen der Philosophie E. Husserls. Breslau, 1930.
Phil 3450.11.100 Bannes, Joachim. Versuch einer Darstellung und Beurteilung der Grundlagen der Philosophie E. Husserls. Inaug. Diss. Breslau, 1930.
Phil 3450.11.101 Welch, E.P. Edmund Husserl's phenomenology. Los Angeles, 1939.
Phil 3450.11.101.50 Pedroli, Guido. La fenomenologia di Husserl. Torino, 1958.
Phil 3450.11.102 Zocher, Rudolf. Husserls Phänomenologie und Schuppes Logik. München, 1932.
Phil 3450.11.105 Illemann, U. Die Vor- phänomenologische philosophie Edmund Husserls. Inaug. Diss. n.p., 1932.
Phil 3450.11.110 Temuralk, T. Über die Grenzen der Erkennbarkeit bei Husserl und Scheler. Berlin, 1937.
Phil 3450.11.112 Temuralk, T. Über die Grenzen der Erkennbarkeit. Inaug. Diss. Berlin, 1937.
Phil 3450.11.113 Xirau, J. La filosofía de Husserl. Buenos Aires, 1941.
Phil 3450.11.114 Husserl, Edmund. Erfahrung und Urteil. Prag, 1939.
Phil 3450.11.115A Farber, Marvin. Philosophical essays in memory of Edmund Husserl. Cambridge, 1940.
Phil 3450.11.115B Farber, Marvin. Philosophical essays in memory of Edmund Husserl. Cambridge, 1940.
Phil 3450.11.116 Welch, E.P. Philosophy of Edmund Husserl...development of his phenomenology. N.Y., 1941.
Phil 3450.11.117 Farber, Marvin. The aims of phenomenology; the motives, methods, and impact of Husserl's thought. 1st ed. N.Y., 1966.
Phil 3450.11.118A Farber, Marvin. The foundation of phenomenology; Edmund Husserl. Cambridge, 1943.
Phil 3450.11.118B Farber, Marvin. The foundation of phenomenology; Edmund Husserl. Cambridge, 1943.
Phil 3450.11.118.3 Farber, Marvin. The foundation of phenomenology. 3d ed. n.p., 1967[1943]
Phil 3450.11.119 Berger, Gaston. Le cogito dans la philosophie de Husserl. Paris, 1941.
Phil 3450.11.120 Miro Quesada, F. Sentido del movimiento. Lima, 1941.
Phil 3450.11.122 Landgrabe, Ludwig. Edmund Husserl zum Gednachtnis. Prag, 1938.
Phil 3450.11.124 Fisch, Isidor. Husserl's Internationalitäts und Urteilslehre. Inaug. Diss. Basel, 1942.
Phil 3450.11.125A Osborn, A. Edmund Husserl. 2d ed. Cambridge, 1949.
Phil 3450.11.125B Osborn, A. Edmund Husserl. 2d ed. Cambridge, 1949.
Phil 3450.11.128 Landgrabe, Ludwig. Phänomenologie und Metaphysik. Hamburg, 1949.
Phil 3450.11.129 Landgrabe, Ludwig. Der Weg der Phäramenologie. Gütersloh, 1963.
Phil 3450.11.130 Reinach, Adolf. Was ist Phanomenologie. 1. Aufl. München, 1951.
Phil 3450.11.135 Lauer, Quentin. La genèse de l'intentionalité dans la philosophie de Husserl. Paris, 1954.
Phil 3450.11.140 Lauer, Quentin. Phénoménologie, existence. Paris, 1955.
Phil 3450.11.142 Lauer, Quentin. Phénoménologie de Husserl. 1st ed. Paris, 1955.
Phil 3450.11.142.5A Lauer, Quentin. The triumph of subjectivity. N.Y., 1958.
Phil 3450.11.142.5B Lauer, Quentin. The triumph of subjectivity. N.Y., 1958.
Phil 3450.11.145 Waelhens, A. de. Phénoménologie et vérité. Paris, 1953.
Phil 3450.11.150 Brand, Gerd. Welt. Den Haag, 1955.
Phil 3450.11.155 Casaubon, Juan A. Germenes de idealismo en las investigaciones logicas de Husserl. Buenos Aires? 1956?
Phil 3450.11.160 Adorno, T.W. Zur Metakritik der Erkenntnistheorie. Stuttgart, 1956.
Phil 3450.11.170 Breton, Stanislas. Conscience et intentionalité. Paris, 1956.
Phil 3450.11.180 Mueller, W.H. Die Philosophie Edmund Husserl den Grandzügen ihrer Entstefung. Bonn, 1956.
Phil 3450.11.190 Bachelard, Suzanne. La logique de Husserl. Paris, 1957.
Phil 3450.11.191 Bachelard, Suzanne. A study of Husserl's formal and transcendental logic. Evanston, 1968.
Phil 3450.11.195 Muralt, André de. L'idée de la phénoménologie. Paris, 1958.
Phil 3450.11.200 Wahle, Jean A. Husserl. v.1-2. Paris, 1958.
Phil 3450.11.202 Wahle, Jean A. Husserl. Paris, 1961.
Phil 3450.11.205 Wahle, Jean A. L'ouvrage posthume de Husserl. Paris, 1957. 2v.
Phil 3450.11.210 Edmund Husserl, 1859-1959. La Haye, 1959.
Phil 3450.11.215 Colloque International de Phénoménologie. Husserl et la pensée moderne. La Haye, 1959.
Phil 3450.11.220 Szilasi, Wilhelm. Einführung in die Phänomenologie Edmund Husserls. Tübingen, 1959.
Phil 3450.11.225 Boer, Theodorus de. De ontwikkelingsgang in het denken van Husserl. Assem, 1966.
Phil 3450.11.230 Kutschera, Franz. Über das Problem des Angangs der Philosophie im Spätwerk Edmund Husserl. München, 1960.
Phil 3450.11.235 Husserl. Paris, 1959.
Phil 3450.11.240 Gaos, J. Introducción a la fenomenología. México, 1960.
Phil 3450.11.245 Scrimieri, G. Problemi di logica. Bari, 1959.
Phil 3450.11.250 Roth, Alois. Edmund Husserls ethische Untersuchungen. Den Haag, 1960.
Phil 3450.11.255 Melandri, Enzo. Logica e esperienza in Husserl. Bologna, 1960.
Phil 3450.11.260 Witschel, Guenter. Edmund Husserls Lehre von den sekundären Qualitäten. Bonn, 1961.
Phil 3450.11.265 Hohl, Hubert. Lebenswelt und Geschichte. Areiburg, 1962.
Phil 3450.11.270 Fragata, Júlio. Problemas da fenomenologia de Husserl. Braga, 1962.
Phil 3450.11.275 Eley, Lathan. Die Krise des a priori in der Transzendentalen. Den Haag, 1762.
Phil 3450.11.280 Fragata, Júlio. A fenomenologia de Husserl como fundamento. Braga, 1959.
Phil 3450.11.285 Toulemont, Renę. L'essence de la société selon Husserl. Paris, 1962.

Classified Listing

Phil 3450 History of philosophy - Local Modern philosophy - Germany - Individual philosophers - Other H - cont.

Phil 3450.11.290 Druce, H. Edmund Husserls System der phänomenologischen Psychologie. Berlin, 1963.
Phil 3450.11.295 Pazanin, A. Das Problem der Philosophie als strenger Wissenschaft. Köln, 1962.
Phil 3450.11.300 Seebohm, W.T. Die Bedingungen der Möglichkeit der Transzendentalphilosophie. Bonn, 1961.
Phil 3450.11.305 Broekman, J.M. Phänomenologie und Egologie. Den Haag, 1963.
Phil 3450.11.310 Held, Klaus. Lebendige Gegenwart. Köln, 1963.
Phil 3450.11.311 Held, Klaus. Lebendige Gegenwart. Thesis. Den Haag, 1966.
Phil 3450.11.315 Mohanty, J.N. Edmund Husserl's theory of meaning. The Hague, 1964.
Phil 3450.11.320 Claesges, Ulrich. Edmund Husserls Theorie. Köln, 1962.
Phil 3450.11.322 Claesges, Ulrich. Edmund Husserls Theorie der Raumkonstitution. Den Haag, 1964.
Phil 3450.11.330 Huelsmann, H. Zur Theorie der Sprache bei E. Husserl. München, 1964.
Phil 3450.11.335 Sancipriano, Mario. Il logos di Husserl. Torino, 1962.
Phil 3450.11.336 Sancipriano, Mario. L'ethos di Husserl. Torino, 1967.
Phil 3450.11.340 Robberechts, L. Husserl. Paris, 1964.
Phil 3450.11.345 Sokolowski, Robert. The formation of Husserl's concept of constitution. The Hague, 1964.
Phil 3450.11.350 Keekell, Lothar. Husserl, sa vie, son oeuvre. Paris, 1964.
Phil 3450.11.355 Piana, G. Esistenza e storia negli inediti di Husserl. Milano, 1965.
Phil 3450.11.360 Petersen, Uwe. Das Verhältnis von Theorie und Praxis...Husserls. Heidelburg, 1964.
Phil 3450.11.365 Kakabadze, Zurab. Problema ekzistentsial'nogo krizisa i transtsendental'naia fenomenologiia Edmunda Gusserlia. Tbilisi, 1966.
Phil 3450.11.370 Ricoeur, Paul. Husserl; an analysis of his phenomenology. Evanston, 1967.
Phil 3450.11.375 Voltaggio, Franco. Fondamenti della logica di Husserl. Milano, 1965.
Phil 3450.11.380 Kockelmans, Joseph John. Edmund Husserl's phenomenological psychology. Pittsburgh, 1967.
VPhil 3450.11.385 Martel, Karol. U podstaw fenomenologii Husserla. Warszawa, 1967.
Phil 3450.11.390 Schérer, René. La phénoménologie des "Recherches logiques" de Husserl. Paris, 1967.
Phil 3450.11.395 Kockelmans, Joseph John. A first introduction to Husserl's phenomenology. Pittsburgh, 1967.
Phil 3450.11.400 Derride, Jacques. La voix et le phénomène, introduction au problème du signe dans la phénomenologie de Husserl. Paris, 1967.
Phil 3450.11.405 Tugendhat, Ernst. Der Wahrheitsbegriff bei Husserl und Heidegger. Berlin, 1967.
Phil 3450.11.410 Orth, Ernst Wolfgang. Bedeutung, Sim, Gegenstand. Thesis. Bonn, 1967.
Phil 3450.11.415 Janssen, Paul. Geschichte und Lebenswelt. Inaug. Diss. Köln, 1964.
Phil 3450.11.416 Janssen, Paul. Geschichte und Lebenswelt. Den Haag, 1970.
Phil 3450.11.420 Biral, Alessandro. L'unità del sapere in Husserl. Padova, 1967.
Phil 3450.11.425 Christoff, Daniel. Husserl; ou, Le retour aux choses. Paris, 1966.
Phil 3450.11.430 Beerling, Reiner F. De transcendentale vreemdeling. Hilversum, 1965.
Phil 3450.11.435 Oggioni, Emilio. La fenomenologia di Husserl e il pensiero contemporaneo. Bologna, 1963.
Phil 3450.11.440 Bosio, Franco. Fondazione della logica in Husserl. Milano, 1966.
Phil 3450.11.445 Raggiunti, Renzo. Husserl, dalla logica alla fenomenologia. Firenze, 1967.
Phil 3450.11.450 Wewel, Meinolf. Die Konstitution des transzendenten Etevas im Vollzug des Sehens. Düsseldorf, 1968.
Phil 3450.11.455 Granel, Gérard. Le sens du temps et de la perception chez E. Husserl. Paris, 1968.
Phil 3450.11.460 Boehm, Rudolf. Vom Gesichtspunkt des Phänomenologie. Den Haag, 1968[1969]
Phil 3450.11.465 Levin, David Michael. Reason and evidence in Husserl's phenomenology. Evanston, 1970.
Phil 3450.11.470 Elveton, R.O. The phenomenology of Husserl. Chicago, 1970.
Phil 3450.11.475 Baratta, Giorgio. L'idealismo fenomenologico di Edmund Husserl. Urbino, 1969.
Phil 3450.11.480 Pivčević, Edo. Husserl and phenomenology. London, 1970.
Phil 3450.11.485 Analecta Husserliana; the yearbook of phenomenological research. Dordrecht. 1,1971+
VPhil 3450.11.490 Logar, Cene. Fenomenologija analiza in kritika filosofije Edmunda Husserla. Ljubljana, 1970.
Phil 3450.11.495 Saraiva, Maria Manuela. L'imagination selon Husserl. La Haye, 1970.
Phil 3450.11.500 Herrmann, Friedrich-Wilhelm von. Husserl und die Meditationen des Descartes. Frankfurt, 1971.
Phil 3450.11.505 Aguirre, Antonio. Genetische Phänomenologie und Reduktion. Den Haag, 1970.
Phil 3450.11.510 Waldenfels, Bernhard. Das Zwischenreich des Dialogs. Den Haag, 1971.
Phil 3450.11.515 Altamore, Giovanni. Della fènomenologia all'ontologia. Padova, 1969.
Phil 3450.12.100 Hemsterhuis, F. Lettre sur l'homme et ses rapports. New Haven, 1964.
Phil 3450.13.32 Heusde, P.W. De Socratische school of Wijsgeerte. Utrecht, 1834. 2v.
Phil 3450.13.90 Kist, N.C. Memoriam Heusdii. Lugduni Batavorum, 1839.
Phil 3450.14.80 Flitner, Willy. August Ludwig Hülsen und der Bund der freien Männer. Naumberg, 1913.
Phil 3450.15.80 Barach, C.S. Hieronymus Hirnhaim. Wien, 1864.
Phil 3450.15.85 Hirnhaim, H. De typho generis humani. Prague, 1676.
Phil 3450.15.90 Klitzner, Julius. Hieronymus Hiruhaim: zum deutschen Geist im Barock Böhmens. Prag, 1943.
Phil 3450.16.10 Heusel, Paul. Kleine Schriften und Vorhäge. Tübingen, 1930.
Phil 3450.16.15 Wahl, Jean A. Sein Leben in seiner Briefen. Frankfurt, 1938.
L Phil 3450.16.90 Festschrift für Paul Hensel Erlangen. Greiz, 1923.
Phil 3450.17.90 Weinzierl, H. Zur Entwicklungsgeschichte der neuern katholischen Philosophie...Hertlings. Inaug. Diss. Reimlingen, 1928.
Phil 3450.17.92 Urbanowski, J. Georg von Hertlings Gesellschaftlslehre. Inaug. Diss. Battrop, 1936.
Phil 3450.18.79 Pamphlet box. Hartmann, N.
Phil 3450.18.80 Hartmann, N. Kleinere Schriften. Berlin, 1955. 3v.

Phil 3450 History of philosophy - Local Modern philosophy - Germany - Individual philosophers - Other H - cont.

Phil 3450.18.90 Gornshtein, T.N. Filosofiia Nikolaia Gartmana. Leningrad, 1969.
Phil 3450.18.95 Hirning, H. Nicolai Hartmanns Lehre. Tübingen, 1937.
Phil 3450.18.100 Daehler, J. Zur Freiheitslehre von Nicolai Hartmann. Inaug. Diss. Freiburg, 1952.
Phil 3450.18.105 Heimsoeth, H. Nicolai Hartmann, der Denker und sein Werk. Göttingen, 1952.
Phil 3450.18.110 Samuel, O. A foundation of ontology. N.Y., 1953.
Phil 3450.18.115F Fleischer, Helmut. Nicolai Hartmanns Ontologie des idealen Seins. Thesis. Erlangen? 1954.
Phil 3450.18.120 Wahl, Jean André. La théorie des catégories fondamentales dans Nicolai Hartmann. Paris, 1954.
Phil 3450.18.123 Wahl, Jean André. La structure du monde réel d'apres Nicolai Hartmann. Paris, 1953.
Phil 3450.18.125 Mohanty, J.N. Nicolai Hartmann and Alfred North Whitehead. Calcutta, 1957.
Phil 3450.18.130 Feuerstein, R. Die Modallehre Nicolai Hartmanns. Köln? 1957.
Phil 3450.18.135 Hülsmann, Heinz. Die Methode in der Philosophie Nicolai Hartmanns. 1e Aufl. Düsseldorf, 1959.
Phil 3450.18.140 Baumgartner, Hans Michael. Die Unbedingtheit des Sittlichen. München, 1962.
Phil 3450.18.145 Hanthack, K. Nicolai Hartmann und das Ende der Ontologie. Berlin, 1962.
Phil 3450.18.150 Beck, Heinrich. Möglichheit und Notwendigkeit. Pullach, 1961.
Phil 3450.18.155 Breton, S. L'être spirituel recherches sur la philosophie de N. Hartmann. Lyon, 1962.
Phil 3450.18.160 Grabes, H. Der Begriff des a priori in Nicolai Hartmanns Erkenntismetaphysik und Ontologie. Köln, 1962.
Phil 3450.18.170 Barone, Francisco. Nicolai Hartmann nella filosofia del novecento. Torino, 1957.
Phil 3450.18.175 Moeslang, Alois. Finalität. Freiburg, 1964.
Phil 3450.18.180 Theisen, Hans. Determination und Freiheit bei Nicolai Hartmanns. Köln, 1962.
Phil 3450.18.185 Wirth, I. Realismus und Apriorismus in Nicolai Hartmanns Erkenntnistheorie. Berlin, 1965.
Phil 3450.18.190 Koerschgen, Hans. Über die Raumlehre Nicolai Hartmanns und ihre Bezlehungen zur modernen Mathematik und Physik. Köln, 1959?
Phil 3450.18.195 Sirchia, Francesco. Nicolai Hartmann dal neokantismo all ontologia. Milano, 1969.
Phil 3450.18.200 Klösters, Joseph. Die "Kritische Ontologie" Nicolai Hartmanns und ihre Bedeutung für das Erkenntnisproblem. Inaug. Diss. Fulda, 1927.
Phil 3450.19.1.2 Feick, Hildegard. Index zu Heideggers "Sein und Zeit". 2e Aufl. Tübingen, 1968.
Phil 3450.19.2 Heideggeriana. Milano. 1,1967+
Phil 3450.19.10 Heidegger, Martin. Was ist Metaphysik? 4e Aufl. Frankfort, 1943.
Phil 3450.19.10.2 Heidegger, Martin. Was ist Metaphysik? 7e Aufl. Frankfort, 1955.
Phil 3450.19.10.5 Gelven, Michael. A commentary on Heidegger's Being and time. N.Y., 1970.
Phil 3450.19.15.1 Heidegger, Martin. Existence and being. Chicago, 1970.
Phil 3450.19.20 Heidegger, Martin. Holzwege. Frankfurt, 1950.
Phil 3450.19.23A Heidegger, Martin. Holzwege. 3e Aufl. Frankfurt, 1957.
Phil 3450.19.23B Heidegger, Martin. Holzwege. 3e Aufl. Frankfurt, 1957.
Phil 3450.19.25 Heidegger, Martin. Was ist Metaphysik? Bonn, 1929.
Phil 3450.19.28 Heidegger, Martin. German existentialism. N.Y., 1965.
Phil 3450.19.30 Heidegger, Martin. Sein und Zeit. 7e Aufl. Tübingen, 1953.
Phil 3450.19.30.10 Heidegger, Martin. Sein und Zeit. 10e Aufl. Tübingen, 1963.
Phil 3450.19.32 Heidegger, Martin. Being and time. London, 1962.
Phil 3450.19.35A Heidegger, Martin. Was heisst Denken? Tübingen, 1954.
Phil 3450.19.35B Heidegger, Martin. Was heisst Denken? Tübingen, 1954.
Phil 3450.19.36 Heidegger, Martin. What is called thinking? N.Y., 1968.
Phil 3450.19.38 Heidegger, Martin. Martin Heidegger. Frankfurt, 1969.
Phil 3450.19.40A Heidegger, Martin. Aus der Erfahrung des Denkens. Pfullingen, 1954.
Phil 3450.19.40B Heidegger, Martin. Aus der Erfahrung des Denkens. Pfullingen, 1954.
Phil 3450.19.45 Heidegger, Martin. Zur Seinsfrage. Frankfurt, 1956.
Phil 3450.19.50 Heidegger, Martin. Der Feldweg. Frankfurt, 1953.
Phil 3450.19.54 Heidegger, Martin. The essence of reasons. Evanston, 1969.
Phil 3450.19.55A Heidegger, Martin. Vom Wesen des Grundes. 4e Aufl. Frankfurt, 1955.
Phil 3450.19.55B Heidegger, Martin. Vom Wesen des Grundes. 4e Aufl. Frankfurt, 1955.
Phil 3450.19.56 Weplinger, F. Wahrheit und Geschichtlichkeit. Freiburg, 1961.
Phil 3450.19.57 Heidegger, Martin. Unterwegs zur Sprache. Pfullingen, 1959.
Phil 3450.19.58 Heidegger, Martin. Zur Sache des Denkens. Tübingen, 1969.
Phil 3450.19.59.1 Heidegger, Martin. Vom Wesen der Wahrheit. Frankfurt, 1949.
Phil 3450.19.60 Heidegger, Martin. Vom Wesen der Wahrheit. 3e Aufl. Frankfurt, 1954.
Phil 3450.19.63 Heidegger, Martin. Der Ursprung des Kunstwerkes. Stuttgart, 1960.
Phil 3450.19.64 Heidegger, Martin. Poetry, language, thought. 1. ed. N.Y., 1971.
Phil 3450.19.65 Heidegger, Martin. Was ist das - die Philosophie? Pfullingen, 1956.
Phil 3450.19.65.2 Heidegger, Martin. What is philosophy? N.Y., 1958.
Phil 3450.19.67 Heidegger, Martin. Was ist das- die Philosophie? 2. Aufl. Pfullingen, 1960.
Phil 3450.19.70 Heidegger, Martin. Vorträge und Anpätze. Pfullingen, 1954.
Phil 3450.19.70.5 Heidegger, Martin. Essais et conférences. 2e éd. Paris, 1958.
Phil 3450.19.73 Heidegger, Martin. The question of being. N.Y., 1958.
Phil 3450.19.74 Heidegger, Martin. Wegmarken. Frankfurt, 1967.
Phil 3450.19.74.1 Vycinas, V. Earth and gods. The Hague, 1961.
Phil 3450.19.75 Heidegger, Martin. Der Satz vom Grund. Pfullingen, 1957.
Phil 3450.19.76 Heidegger, Martin. Phänomenologie und Theologie. Frankfurt, 1970.
Phil 3450.19.77 Heidegger, Martin. Identität und Differenz. 2e Aufl. Pfullingen, 1957.
Phil 3450.19.77.5 Heidegger, Martin. Identity and difference. 1st ed. N.Y., 1969.
Phil 3450.19.78 Heidegger, Martin. Essays in metaphysics. N.Y., 1960.
Phil 3450.19.79 Pamphlet box. Chandra, Subhash. Heidegger.

Classified Listing

Phil 3450   History of philosophy - Local Modern philosophy - Germany - Individual philosophers - Other H - cont.

Phil 3450.19.79.5   Chandra, Subhash. Das Phänomen des Todes im Denken Heideggers und in der Lehre Buddhas. Köln, 1965.

Phil 3450.19.82   Heidegger, Martin. Die Technik und die Kehre. Pfullingen, 1962.

Phil 3450.19.85.2   Heidegger, Martin. Gelassenheit. 2e Aufl. Pfullingen, 1960.

Phil 3450.19.85.5   Heidegger, Martin. Discourse on thinking. N.Y., 1966.

Phil 3450.19.90   Vogl, A. Das Problem des Selhstseins bei Heidegger und Kierkegaard. Diss. Giessen, 1936.

Phil 3450.19.91   Wagner de Peyna, A. de. La ontologia fundamental de Heidegger. Buenos Aires, 1939.

Phil 3450.19.94A   Brecht, F.J. Heidegger und Jaspers. Wuppertal, 1948.

Phil 3450.19.94B   Brecht, F.J. Heidegger und Jaspers. Wuppertal, 1948.

Phil 3450.19.95   Pfeiffer, Johannes S. Existenzphilosophie; eine Einführung in Heidegger und Jaspers. Leipzig, 1933.

Phil 3450.19.95.3   Pfeiffer, Johannes S. Existenzphilosophie. 3e Aufl. Hamburg, 1952.

Phil 3450.19.95.5   Pfeiffer, Johannes S. Existenz und Offenbarung. Berlin, 1966.

Phil 3450.19.96   Waelhens, A. de. La filosofía de Martin Heidegger. Madrid, 1945.

Phil 3450.19.96.10   Waelhens, A. de. La philosophie de Martin Heidegger. 3e éd. Louvain, 1948.

Phil 3450.19.96.12   Waelhens, A. de. Chemins et impusses de l'ontologie Heideggerienne. Louvain, 1953.

Phil 3450.19.97   Fischer, Alois. Die Existenzphilosophie Martin Heideggers. Leipzig, 1935.

Phil 3450.19.98   Delp, A. Trogische Existenz; zur Philosophie Martin Heideggers. Freiburg, 1935.

Phil 3450.19.99   Folwart, H. Kant, Husserl, Heidegger. Breslau, 1936.

Phil 3450.19.100   Erro, C.A. Dialogo existencial. Buenos Aires, 1937.

Phil 3450.19.101   Hoberg, C.A. Das Dasein des Menschen. Zeuleuroda, 1937.

Phil 3450.19.102   Hoberg, C.A. Das Dasein des Menschen. Inaug. Diss. Zeuleuroda, 1937.

Phil 3450.19.103   Ballmer, Karl. Aber Herr Heidegger. Basel, 1933.

Phil 3450.19.104   Wagner de Reyna, A. La ontologia fundamental de Heidegger. Buenos Aires, 1939.

Phil 3450.19.106   Vanni Rovighi, S. Heidegger. Brescia, 1945.

Phil 3450.19.107A   Biemel, W. Le concept de inonde chez Heidegger. Louvain, 1950.

Phil 3450.19.107B   Biemel, W. Le concept de inonde chez Heidegger. Louvain, 1950.

Phil 3450.19.108   Chiodi, Pietro. L'esistenzialismo di Heidegger. Torino, 1947.

Phil 3450.19.108.3   Chiodi, Pietro. L'esistenzialismo di Heidegger. 3e ed. Torino, 1965.

Phil 3450.19.109   Chiodi, Pietro. L'ultimo. 1e ed. Torino, 1952.

Phil 3450.19.109.2   Chiodi, Pietro. L'ultimo Heidegger. 2e ed. Torino, 1960.

Phil 3450.19.110   Heidegger, Martin. Martin Heideggers Einfluss auf die Wissenschaften aus Anlass seines Sechzig sun Geburtstages verfasst Carlos Astrada. Bern, 1949.

Phil 3450.19.112   Marcia, Renè. Martin Heidegger und die Existenzialphilosophie. Bad Ischl, 1949.

Phil 3450.19.114   Graaff, F. de. Het schuldprableem ein de existentiephilosophie van Martin Heidegger. 's Gravenhage, 1951.

Phil 3450.19.116   Fritz, E. Die Seinsfrage bei Martin Heidegger. Stuttgart, 1950.

Phil 3450.19.118A   Lowith, Carl. Heidegger. Frankfurt, 1953.

Phil 3450.19.118B   Lowith, Carl. Heidegger. Frankfurt, 1953.

Phil 3450.19.120   Buddeberg, Else R. Heidegger und die Dichtting. Stuttgart, 1953.

Phil 3450.19.121   Buddeberg, Else R. Denken und Dichten des Seins. Stuttgart, 1956.

Phil 3450.19.125   Meulen, J.A. van der. Heidegger und Hegel. Groningen, 1953.

Phil 3450.19.130   Logstrup, K.E.C. Kierkegaards und Heideggers Existenzanalyse und ihr Verhaltnis. 1-3. Aufl. Berlin, 1950.

Phil 3450.19.135   Oberti, Elisa. L'estetica nel pensiero di Heidegger. Milano, 1955.

Phil 3450.19.140   Sepich, Juan R. La filosofía de Ser y tiempo de M. Heidegger. Buenos Aires, 1954.

Phil 3450.19.145   Raessingh, Karel Hendrik. Martin Heidegger als godsdienstwijsgeer. Assen, 1956.

Phil 3450.19.150   Grene, Marjorie. Martin Heidegger. London, 1957.

Phil 3450.19.155   Wahl, Jean A. Vers la fin de l'ontologie. Paris, 1956.

Phil 3450.19.160   Lüble, Hermann. Bibliographie der Heidegger. Literatur, 1917-1955. Meisenheim am Glan, 1957.

Phil 3450.19.165   Hühnerfeld, Paul. In Sachen Heidegger. Hamburg, 1959.

Phil 3450.19.170   Soler Grimma, Francisco. El origen de la obra de arte y la verdad en Heidegger. Bogota, 1953.

Phil 3450.19.175   Langan, Thomas. The meaning of Heidegger. N.Y., 1959.

Phil 3450.19.180   Llambías de Azevedo, Juan. El antiguo y el nuevo Heidegger y un dialogo con el. Montevideo, 1958.

Phil 3450.19.190   Neshe, Günther. Martin Heidegger zum siebzigsten Geburtstag. Pfullingen, 1959.

Phil 3450.19.200   Huebener, Wolfgang. Untersuchungen zur Denhart Martin Heideggers. Berlin, 1960.

Phil 3450.19.205   Kauthack, Katherina. Das Denken des Martin Heideggers. Berlin, 1959.

Phil 3450.19.210   Sacristán Luzón, Manuel. Las ideas gnoseologicas de Heidegger. Barcelona, 1959.

Phil 3450.19.215   Garcia Bacca, Juan David. Comentarios a la esencia de la poesia de Heidegger. Caracas, 1956.

Phil 3450.19.220   Ott, Heinrich. Denken und Sein. Zollikon, 1959.

Phil 3450.19.225   Mueller-Lauter, W. Möglichkeit und Wirklichkeit bei M. Heidegger. Berlin, 1960.

Phil 3450.19.230   Marx, Werner. Heidegger und die Tradition. Stuttgart, 1961.

Phil 3450.19.235   Padellaro De Angelis, Rosa. Heidegger e il problema Kantiano. Torino, 1960.

Phil 3450.19.240   Noller, Gerhard. Sein und Existenz. München, 1962.

Phil 3450.19.242   Noller, Gerhard. Heidegger und die Theologie. München, 1967.

Phil 3450.19.245   Schneeberger, Guido. Nachlese zu Heidegger. Bern, 1962.

Phil 3450.19.250   Kockelmans, A. Martin Heidegger. Teilt, 1962.

Phil 3450.19.253   Kockelmans, Joseph John. Martin Heidegger. Pittsburgh, 1965.

Phil 3450.19.255   Feick, Hildegard. Index zu Heideggers Sein und Zeit. Tübingen, 1961.

Phil 3450   History of philosophy - Local Modern philosophy - Germany - Individual philosophers - Other H - cont.

Phil 3450.19.260   Corvez, Maurice. La philosophie de Heidegger. Paris, 1961.

Phil 3450.19.265   Chapelle, Albert. L'ontologie phénoménologique de Heidegger. Paris, 1962.

Phil 3450.19.270A   Robinson, J.M.C. The later Heidegger and theology. N.Y., 1963.

Phil 3450.19.270B   Robinson, J.M.C. The later Heidegger and theology. N.Y., 1963.

Phil 3450.19.275   Sadzik, J. Esthétique de Martin Heidegger. Paris, 1963.

Phil 3450.19.280   Richardson, W.J. Heidegger: through phenomenology. The Hague, 1963.

Phil 3450.19.285   King, M. Heidegger's philosophy. N.Y., 1964.

Phil 3450.19.290   Poeggeler, Otto. Der Denkweg Martin Heideggers. Pfullingen, 1963.

Phil 3450.19.295   Demske, James M. Sein, Mensch und Tod. Freiburg, 1963.

Phil 3450.19.296   Demske, James M. Being, man and death: a key to Heidegger. Lexington, 1970.

Phil 3450.19.300   Cerezo Galan, Pedro. Arte, verdad y ser en Heidegger. Madrid, 1963.

Phil 3450.19.305   Wahl, J.A. Mots, mythes et réalité dans la philosophie de Heidegger. Paris, 1961.

Phil 3450.19.310   Seidel, G.J. Martin Heidegger and the pre-Socratics. Lincoln, 1964.

Phil 3450.19.315   Echauri, Raúl. El ser en la filosofía de Heidegger. Rosario, 1964.

Phil 3450.19.320   Finazzo, Giancarlo. L'umo e il mondo nella filosofia di M. Heidegger. Roma, 1963.

Phil 3450.19.325   Versényi, Laszlo. Heidegger, being and truth. New Haven, 1965.

Phil 3450.19.330   Ijsseling, Samuel. Heidegger. Antwerpen, 1964.

Phil 3450.19.335   Fraga, Gustavo A. Sobre Heidegger. Coimbra, 1965.

Phil 3450.19.340   Martin Heidegger, 26 September 1959. Messkirch, 1959.

Phil 3450.19.345   Schwan, Alexander. Politische Philosophie im Denken Heideggers. Köln, 1965.

Phil 3450.19.350   Trotignon, Pierre. Heidegger. Paris, 1965.

Phil 3450.19.355   Meyer, Hans. Martin Heidegger und Thomas von Aquin. München, 1964.

Phil 3450.19.360   Guilead, Reuben. Être et liberté. Louvain, 1965.

Phil 3450.19.365   Colombo, Arrigo. Martin Heidegger. Bologna, 1964.

Phil 3450.19.370   Manno, Mario. Heidegger e la filosofia. Roma, 1962.

Phil 3450.19.375   Bock, Irmgard. Heideggers Sprachdenken. München, 1964.

Phil 3450.19.380   Pugliese, Orlando. Vermittlung und Kehre. Freiburg, 1965.

Phil 3450.19.385   Rifga, Fuad. Studien zur Asthetik Martin Heideggers und Oskar Beckers. Inaug. Diss. Tübingen, 1965.

Phil 3450.19.390   Skirbekk, Gunnar. Dei filosofiske vilkår for sanning. Oslo, 1966.

Phil 3450.19.395   Macomber, William B. The anatomy of disillusion; Martin Heideggers notion of truth. Evanston, 1967.

Phil 3450.19.400   Penzo, Giorgio. L'unità del pensiero in Martin Heidegger; una ontologia estetica. Padova, 1965.

Phil 3450.19.405   Koza, Ingeborg. Das Problem des Grundes in Heideggers Auseinandersetzung mit Kant. Ratingen, 1967.

Phil 3450.19.410   Battaglia, Felice. Heidegger e la filosofia di valori. Bologna, 1967.

Phil 3450.19.415   Duintjer, Otto D. De vraag naar her transcendentale. Leiden, 1966.

Phil 3450.19.420   Vottimo, Gianni. Arte e verità nel pensiero di Martin Heidegger. Torino, 1966.

Phil 3450.19.425   Huch, Kurt Jürgen. Philosophiegeschichtliche Voraussetzungen der Heideggerschen Ontologie. Frankfurt, 1967.

Phil 3450.19.430   Heidegger and the quest for truth. Chicago, 1968.

Phil 3450.19.435   Floestad, Guttorm. Heidegger. En innfóring i hans filosofi. Oslo, 1968.

Phil 3450.19.440   Manno, Ambrogio Giacomo. Esistenza de essere in Heidegger. Napoli, 1967.

Phil 3450.19.445   Schmitt, Richard. Martin Heidegger on being human. N.Y., 1969.

Phil 3450.19.450   Laffoucrière, Odette. Le destin de la pensée et la mort de Dieu selon Heidegger. La Haye, 1968.

Phil 3450.19.455   Sass, Hans-Martin. Heidegger-Bibliographie. Meisenheim am Glan, 1968.

Phil 3450.19.460   Poeggeler, Otto. Heidegger; Perspektiven zur Deutung seines Werks. Köln, 1970.

Phil 3450.19.465   Dantlo, René. A la rencontre de Martin Heidegger. Toulouse, 1969.

Phil 3450.19.470   Martin Heidegger im Gespräch. München, 1970.

Phil 3450.19.475   Mehta, Jarava Lal. The philosophy of Martin Heidegger. Varanasi, 1967.

Phil 3450.19.480   Durchblicke: Martin Heidegger zum 80. Geburtstag. Frankfurt, 1970.

Phil 3450.19.485   Mazzantini, Carlo. Il tempo e quattro saggi su Heidegger. Parma, 1969.

Phil 3450.19.490   Palmier, Jean Michel. Les écrits politiques de Heidegger. Paris, 1968.

Phil 3450.19.495   Romano, Bruno. Tecnica e giustizia nel pensiero di Martin Heidegger. Milano, 1969.

Phil 3450.19.500   Heidegger and the path of thinking. Pittsburgh, 1970.

Phil 3450.19.505   Garulli, Enrico. Problemi dell'Ur-Heidegger. Urbino, 1969.

Phil 3450.19.510   Guzzoni, Giorgio. Considerazioni intorno alla prima sezione de Sein und Zeit. Urbino, 1969.

Phil 3450.19.515   De Cecchi Duso, Gianna. L'interpretazione heideggeriana dei presocratici. Padova, 1970.

Phil 3450.19.520   Sherover, Charles M. Heidegger, Kant and time. Bloomington, 1971.

Phil 3450.19.525   MacDowell, João Augusto A. Amazonas. A gênese da ontolo fundamental de Martin Heidegger. São Paulo, 1970.

Phil 3450.19.530   Regina, Umberto. Heidegger. Milano, 1970-

Phil 3450.19.535   Cauturier, Fernand. Monde e être chez Heidegger. Montréal, 1971.

Phil 3450.19.540   Magnus, Bernd. Heidegger's metahistory of philosophy: amor fati, being and truth. The Hague, 1970.

Phil 3450.19.545   Rosales, Alberto. Transzendenz und Differenz. Den Haag, 1970.

Phil 3450.20.10   Schreiher, H.W. Joseph Hillebraud. Diss. Giessen, 1937.

Phil 3450.21   Hoche, A. Jahresringe. München, 1937.

Phil 3450.22   Gerritsen, T.J.C. La philosophie de Heymass. Paris, 1938.

Phil 3450.22.1   Gerritsen, T.J.C. La philosophie de Heymass. Thèse. Paris, 1938.

Phil 3450.23   Kamm, P. Philosophie und Pädagogik Paul Häberlins in ehrer Wandlungen. Diss. Zürich, 1938.

Phil 3450.24   Hessing, Jacob. Das Selbsthewusstwerden des Geistes. Stuttgart, 1936.

Phil 3450.24.10   Hessing, Jacob. Logica als leer van zuivere rede. Deel. 1. Bussum, 1941.

Phil 3450 History of philosophy - Local Modern philosophy - Germany - Individual philosophers - Other H - cont.

Phil 3450.25 Hiller, Kurt. Der Aufbruch zum Paradies; Sätze. München, 1922.
Phil 3450.25.10 Hiller, Kurt. Die Weisheit der Langenweile. Leipzig, 1913.
Phil 3450.26 Hellpach, Willy. Zwischen Wittenberg und Rom. Berlin, 1931.
Phil 3450.26.10 Hellpach, Willy. Universitas litterarum. Stuttgart, 1948.
Phil 3450.27.80 Smits, Everard J.F. Herders humaniteitsphilosophie. Assen, 1939.
Phil 3450.28 Horkheimer, Max. Eclipse of reason. N.Y., 1947.
Phil 3450.28.10 Horkheimer, Max. Dialektik der Aufklärung. Amsterdam, 1947.
Phil 3450.28.15 Horkheimer, Max. Kritische Theorie. Frankfurt, 1968. 2v.
Phil 3450.28.20 Horkheimer, Max. Die Sehnsucht nach dem ganz Anderen. Hamburg, 1970.
Phil 3450.29 Haecker, Theodor. Journal in the night. London, 1950.
Phil 3450.29.5 Haecker, Theodor. Was ist der Mensch? 2e Aufl. Leipzig, 1934.
Phil 3450.29.7 Haecker, Theodor. Was ist der Mensch? München, 1965.
Phil 3450.29.10 Haecker, Theodor. Essays. Munchen, 1958.
Phil 3450.29.20 Haecker, Theodor. Satire und Polemik. München, 1961.
Phil 3450.29.70 Haecker, Theodor. Tag- und Nachtbücher. München, 1947.
Phil 3450.29.73 Haecker, Theodor. Tag- und Nachtbücher, 1939-1945. 3e Aufl. München, 1959.
Phil 3450.29.75 Haecker, Theodor. Vergil. Schönheit Metaphysik des Fühlens. München, 1967.
Phil 3450.29.80 Blessing, Eugen. Theodor Haecker. Nürnberg, 1959.
Phil 3450.29.85 Schnarwiler, W. Theodor Haeckers christliches Menschenbild. Frankfurt, 1962.
Phil 3450.29.90 Eid, Volker. Die Kunst in christlicher Daseinsverantwortung nach Theodor Haecker. Thesis. Würzburg, 1968.
Phil 3450.30 Hessen, Johannes. Lehrbuch der Philosophie. München, 1947-50. 3v.
Phil 3450.30.5 Hessen, Johannes. Im Ringen um eine zeitnahe Philosophie. Nürnberg, 1959.
Phil 3450.30.10 Hessen, Johannes. Lehrbuch der Philosophie. 2e Aufl. v.3. München, 1950-
Phil 3450.32.80 Bártschi, Lina. Der Berner Philosoph Carl Hebler. Bern, 1944.
Phil 3450.33 Hildebrand, D. von. The new tower of Babel. N.Y., 1953.
Phil 3450.33.2 Hildebrand, Christa. Die Wertethik bei Dietrick von Hildebrand. Düsseldorf, 1959.
Phil 3450.33.5 Hildebrand, D. von. Die Menschkeit am Scheideweg. Regensburg, 1955.
Phil 3450.33.7 Hildebrand, D. von. Metaphysik der Gemeinscheaft. Regensburg, 1955.
Phil 3450.33.8 Schwarz, Baldwin. The human person and the world of values. N.Y., 1960.
Phil 3450.33.10 Hartmann, N. Philosophische Gespräche. Göttingen, 1954.
Phil 3450.33.12 Maliandi, Ricardo G. Wertobjektivität und Realitätserfahrung. Bonn, 1966.
Phil 3450.33.13 Caspar, Caspar Toni. Grundlagen der Ontologie Nicolai Hartmanns. Tübingen, 1955.
Phil 3450.33.15 Stroeker, E. Zahl und Raum. Bonn, 1953.
Phil 3450.33.20 Reuter, Otfried. Sittichkert und ethische Werterkenntnis nach D. von Hildebrand. Münster? 1966.
Phil 3450.34 Heske, Franz. Organik. Berlin, 1954.
Phil 3450.36 Hessen, Johannes. Gustige Kämpf der Zeit im Spiegel und Lebens. Nürnberg, 1959.
Phil 3450.38 Hoffmann, Gustov. Genius der Menscheit. Delmenhorst, 1959.
Phil 3450.39.30 Hirsch, Wolfgang. Die Normen des Seins. Amsterdam, 1959?
Phil 3450.40 Husserl, Edmund. Cartesian meditations. The Hague, 1960.
Phil 3450.41 Haekstra, Sytze. Oratio de summae veritatis cognoscendae ratione atque via. Amstelodami, 1857.
Phil 3450.42 Ball, Thomas. Paul Leopold Hoffner als Philosophie. Mainz? 194-?
Phil 3450.43F Freed, Louis Franklin. R.F.A. Hoernle. Johannesburg, 1965.
Phil 3450.44 Hochgesang, Michael. Mythos und Logik im 20. Jahrhundert. München, 1965.
Phil 3450.46 Heintel, Erich. Die beiden Labyrinthe der Philosophie. Wien, 1968.
Phil 3450.48.80 Bittner, Gerhard. Sachlichkeit und Bildung; kritische Studie...Hans-Eduard Hengstenberg. München? 1965?

Phil 3455 History of philosophy - Local Modern philosophy - Germany - Individual philosophers - I

Phil 3455.1.01 Miller, Wilhelm A. Isenkrahe-Bibliographie. 3e Aufl. Berlin, 1927.
Phil 3455.2 Isendoorn, Gisbert. Cursus logicus systematicus et agonisticus. Francofurti, 1666.
Phil 3455.3.80 Hof, Ulrich im. Isaak Iselin. Basel, 1947. 2v.
Phil 3455.3.85 Hof, Ulrich im. Isaak Iselin und die Spätaufklärung. Bern, 1967.

Phil 3460 History of philosophy - Local Modern philosophy - Germany - Individual philosophers - Jacobi, Friedrich H.

Phil 3460.10 Jacobi, F.H. Werke. Leipzig, 1812-25. 7v.
Phil 3460.20 Jacobi, F.H. Nachlass. Ungedruckte Briefe. Leipzig, 1869.
Phil 3460.21 Jacobi, F.H. Schriften. Berlin, 1926.
Phil 3460.30.2 Jacobi, F.H. Von den göttlichen Dingen und ihrer Offenbarung. Leipzig, 1822.
Phil 3460.70 Jacobi, F.H. Jacobis auserlesener Briefwechsel. Leipzig, 1825. 2v.
Phil 3460.72* Jacobi, F.H. Jacobi an Fichte. Hamburg, 1799.
Phil 3460.75 Jacobi, F.H. Briefe an Friedrich Bouterwek. Göttingen, 1868.
Phil 3460.79 Pamphlet box. Philosophy. German and Dutch. Jacobi, F.H.
Phil 3460.80 Zirngiebl, E. F.H. Jacobis Seben, Dichten und Denken. Wien, 1867.
Phil 3460.81 Deyks, F. F.H. Jacobi im Verhaltniss zu seinen Zeitgenossen. Frankfurt, 1848.
Phil 3460.82 Schaumburg, E. Jacobis Garten zu Pempelfort. Aachen, 1873.
Phil 3460.83 Delius, J.F. Darstellung und Hauptgedanken F.H. Jacobi. Halle, 1878.
Phil 3460.84 Kusch, E. C.G.J. Jacobi und Helmholtz auf dem Gymnasium. Potsdam, 1896.
Phil 3460.85 Crawford, A.W. The philosophy of F.H. Jacobi. N.Y., 1905.
Phil 3460.86A Schmid, F.A. Friedrich Heinrich Jacobi. Heidelberg, 1908.
Phil 3460.86B Schmid, F.A. Friedrich Heinrich Jacobi. Heidelberg, 1908.
Phil 3460.87 Schlichtegroll, A.H.F. Friedrich Heinrich Jacobi. München, 1819.

Phil 3460 History of philosophy - Local Modern philosophy - Germany - Individual philosophers - Jacobi, Friedrich H. - cont.

Phil 3460.88 Lévy-Bruhl, L. La philosophie de Jacobi. Paris, 1894.
Phil 3460.89 Wiegand, Wilhelm. Zur Erinnerung an den Denker F.H. Jacobi und seine Weltansicht. Worms, 1863?
Phil 3460.90 Vecchiotti, Icilio. Premessa a Jacobi. 1. ed. Roma, 1959.
Phil 3460.91 Hebeisen, A. Friedrich Heinrich Jacobi. Bern, 1960.
Phil 3460.92 Baum, Guenther. Vernunft und Erkenntnis. Bonn, 1969.
Phil 3460.94 Weischedel, Wilhelm. Streit um die göttlichen Dinge. Darmstadt, 1967.
Phil 3460.94.5 Weischedel, Wilhelm. Jacobi und Schelling. Darmstadt, 1969.
Phil 3460.96 Olivetti, Marco M. L'esito teologico della filosofia del linguaggio di Jacobi. Padova, 1970.
Phil 3460.98 Friedrich, Heinrich Jacobi. Philosoph und Literat der Goethezeit. Frankfurt, 1971.

Phil 3475 History of philosophy - Local Modern philosophy - Germany - Individual philosophers - Other J

Phil 3475.1.80 Börner, W. Friedrich Jodl - eine Studie. Stuttgart, 1911.
Phil 3475.1.81 Jodl, Margarete. Friedrich Jodl sein Leben und Wirken. Stuttgart, 1920.
Phil 3475.2.90 Eckstein, W. Wilhelm Jerusalem; sein Leben und Werken. Wien, 1935.
Phil 3475.3.20 Jaspers, Karl. Three essays. 1st ed. N.Y., 1964.
Phil 3475.3.23 Jaspers, Karl. Werk und Wirkung. München, 1963.
Phil 3475.3.25 Jaspers, Karl. Schicksal und Wille. München, 1967.
Phil 3475.3.35 Jaspers, Karl. Die Schuldfrage. 2. Aufl. Zürich, 1946.
Phil 3475.3.37 Jaspers, Karl. Wahrheit und Wissenschaft. München, 1960.
Phil 3475.3.40 Jaspers, Karl. Die ontwort on Sigrid Undset. Konstang, 1947.
Phil 3475.3.42 Jaspers, Karl. Philosophie und Welt. München, 1958.
Phil 3475.3.47A Jaspers, Karl. The perennial scope of philosophy. N.Y., 1949.
Phil 3475.3.47B Jaspers, Karl. The perennial scope of philosophy. N.Y., 1949.
Phil 3475.3.52 Jaspers, Karl. Einführung in die Philosophie. Zürich, 1958.
Phil 3475.3.55 Jaspers, Karl. Vernunft und Existenz. Bremen, 1949.
Phil 3475.3.55.5 Jaspers, Karl. Vernunft und Existenz. München, 1960.
Phil 3475.3.56.1 Jaspers, Karl. Reason and existenz; five lectures. London, 1956.
Phil 3475.3.57 Jaspers, Karl. Chiffren der Transzendenz. München, 1970.
Phil 3475.3.58 Jaspers, Karl. Philosophie und Wissenschaft. Zürich, 1949.
Phil 3475.3.60 Jaspers, Karl. Vernunft und Windervernunft. München, 1950.
Phil 3475.3.61 Jaspers, Karl. Reason and anti-reason in our time. 1st British ed. London, 1952.
Phil 3475.3.62 Jaspers, Karl. Reason and anti-reason in our time. New Haven, 1952.
Phil 3475.3.65 Jaspers, Karl. Way of wisdom. New Haven, 1951.
Phil 3475.3.66 Jaspers, Karl. Philosophie und Offenbarungsglaube. Hamburg, 1963.
Phil 3475.3.67 Jaspers, Karl. Lebensfragen der deutschen Politik. München, 1963.
Phil 3475.3.70 Jaspers, Karl. Existentialism and humanism. N.Y., 1952.
Phil 3475.3.71 Jaspers, Karl. Existenzphilosophie. 2. Aufl. Berlin, 1950.
Phil 3475.3.72 Jaspers, Karl. Wo stehen wir heute. Olten, 1961.
Phil 3475.3.73 Jaspers, Karl. La bombe atomique et l'avenir de l'homme. Paris, 1958.
Phil 3475.3.74 Jaspers, Karl. Wahrheit, Freiheit und Friede. München, 1958.
Phil 3475.3.75 Jaspers, Karl. Rechenschaft und Ausbuik. München, 1951.
Phil 3475.3.76 Jaspers, Karl. Die Atombombe und die Zükunft des Menschen. München, 1960.
Phil 3475.3.77 Jaspers, Karl. The future of mankind. Chicago, 1961.
Phil 3475.3.78 Jaspers, Karl. Der philosophische Glaube Angesichts der Offenbarung. München, 1962.
Phil 3475.3.80 Feith, R.C. Psychologismus und Transzendentalismus bei K. Jaspers. Bern, 1945.
Phil 3475.3.85 Ramming, G. Karl Jaspers und Heinrich Richert Existenzialismus und Wertphilosophie. Bern, 1948.
Phil 3475.3.95 Dufrenne, M. Karl Jaspers et la philosophie de l'existence. Paris, 1947.
Phil 3475.3.105 Allen, L. The self and its hazards...K. Jaspers. London, 1950.
Phil 3475.3.110 Springer, J.L. Existentiele metaphysica. Assen, 1951.
Phil 3475.3.115 Karl Jaspers zum siebzigsten Geburtslag. Bern, 1953.
Phil 3475.3.120 Grunert, P.L. Objektive Norm. Inaug. Diss. Bonn, 1953.
Phil 3475.3.125 Schmidhauser, N. Allgemeine Wahrheit und existentielle Wahrheit. Bonn, 1953.
Phil 3475.3.130 Räber, T. Das Glasein in der "Philosophie" von K. Jaspers. Bern, 1955.
Phil 3475.3.135 Räber, T. Das Dasein in der Philosophie von Karl Jaspers. Diss. Freiburg, 1954.
Phil 3475.3.140 Schilpp, P.A. Karl Jaspers. Stuttgart, 1957.
Phil 3475.3.140.5 Schilpp, P.A. The philosophy of Karl Jaspers. 1st ed. N.Y., 1957.
Phil 3475.3.145 Armbruster, Ludwig. Objekt und Transzendenz bei Jaspers. Innsbruck, 1957.
Phil 3475.3.150 Piper, R.C. Karl Jaspers. München, 1958.
Phil 3475.3.155 Paumen, Jean. Raison et existence chez Karl Jaspers. Bruxelles, 1958.
Phil 3475.3.160 Lohff, Wenzel. Glaube und Freiheit. Gütersloh, 1957.
Phil 3475.3.165 Welte, Bernard. La foi philosophique chez Jaspers et Saint Thomas d'Aquin. Bruges, 1958.
Phil 3475.3.170 Caracciolo, Alberto. Studi Jaspersiani. Milano, 1958.
Phil 3475.3.175 Tilliette, Xavier. Karl Jaspers. Paris, 1960.
Phil 3475.3.180 Tollhoetter, Bernhard. Erziehung und Selbstsein. Rätingen, 1966.
Phil 3475.3.185F Bentz, Hans Wille. Karl Jaspers in Übersetzungen. Frankfurt, 1961.
Phil 3475.3.190 Horn, H. Philosophischer und christlicher Glaube. Essen, 1961.
Phil 3475.3.195 Jaspers, Karl. Hoffnung und Sorge. München, 1965.
Phil 3475.3.200 Gottschalk, Herbert. Karl Jaspers. Berlin, 1966.
Phil 3475.3.205 Jaspers, Karl. Philosophical faith and revelation. N.Y., 1967.
Phil 3475.3.210 Schneiders, Werner. Karl Jaspers in der Kritik. Bonn, 1965.
Phil 3475.3.215 Long, Eugene Thomas. Jaspers and Bultmenn. Durham, 1968.
Phil 3475.3.220 Jaspers, Karl. Provokationen; Gespräche und Interviews. München, 1969.
Phil 3475.3.225 Jaspers, Karl. Philosophische Aufsätze. Frankfurt, 1967.
Phil 3475.3.230 Jaspers, Karl. Kleine Schule des philosophischen Denkens. München, 1967.

Phil 3475 History of philosophy - Local Modern philosophy - Germany - Individual philosophers - Other J - cont.

Phil 3475.3.235 Hommel, Claus Uwe. Chiffer und Dogma. Zürich, 1968.
Phil 3475.3.240 Mekkes, Johan Peter Albertus. Teken en motief der creatuur. Amsterdam, 1965.
Phil 3475.3.245 Schrag, Oswald O. Existence, existenz, and transcendence. Pittsburgh, 1971.
Phil 3475.3.250 Saner, Hans. Karl Jaspers in Selbstzeugnissen und Bilddokumenten. Reinbek, 1970.
Phil 3475.4 Jacobi, Maximilian. Naturleben und Geistesleben. Leipzig, 1851.

Phil 3480 History of philosophy - Local Modern philosophy - Germany - Individual philosophers - Kant, Immanuel - Writings

Phil 3480.10 Kant, Immanuel. Opera ad philosophiam criticam. Leipzig, 1796-98. 4v.
Phil 3480.11 Kant, Immanuel. Werke. Leipzig, 1838-39. 10v.
Phil 3480.12 Kant, Immanuel. Sämmtliche Werke. Leipzig, 1838-40. 12v.
Phil 3480.13A Kant, Immanuel. Sämmtliche Werke. Leipzig, 1867-68. 8v.
Phil 3480.13B Kant, Immanuel. Sämmtliche Werke. Leipzig, 1867-68. 8v.
Phil 3480.14 Kant, Immanuel. Gesammelte Schriften. v.1-24,28. Berlin, 1900-36. 27v.
Phil 3480.14.1 Kant, Immanuel. Gesammelte Schriften. Personenindex. v.1-23. Bonn, 1962-
Phil 3480.14.2 Kant, Immanuel. Gesammelte Schriften. Personenindex. v.A-L. Bonn, 1964- 6v.
Phil 3480.14.2.2 Kant, Immanuel. Gesammelte Schriften. Personenindex. Nachträge. Bonn, 1966.
Phil 3480.14.4 Kant, Immanuel. Gesammelte Schriften. Allgemeiner Kantindex. Bonn, 1966. 3v.
Phil 3480.14.5 Kant, Immanuel. Gesammelte Schriften. Bd.X-XII. Berlin, 1922. 3v.
Phil 3480.15 Kant, Immanuel. Werke. v.1-7,9,11. Berlin, 1912. 9v.
X Cg Phil 3480.15 Kant, Immanuel. Werke. v.8,10. Berlin, 1912. 2v.
Phil 3480.16 Kant, Immanuel. Sämtliche Werke. v.1-9 und Ergänzungsband. 10. Aufl. Leipzig, 1913. 10v.
Phil 3480.16.25 Kant, Immanuel. Werke in acht Büchern. v.1-4,5-8. Berlin, 1921. 2v.
Phil 3480.17 Kant, Immanuel. Die philosophischen Hauptvorlesungen. München, 1924.
Phil 3480.18 Kant, Immanuel. Vermischte Schriften. Halle, 1799-1807. 4v.
Phil 3480.18.5 Kant, Immanuel. Vermischte Schriften und Briefwechsel. Berlin, 1873.
Phil 3480.18.7 Kant, Immanuel. Vermischte Schriften. Leipzig, 1912.
Phil 3480.18.9 Kant, Immanuel. Vermischte Schriften. Leipzig, 1922.
Phil 3480.18.12 Kant, Immanuel. Kleinere philosophische Schriften. Leipzig, 1921.
Phil 3480.18.16 Kant, Immanuel. Trois opuscules scientifiques. Mistral, 1914.
Htn Phil 3480.19* Kant, Immanuel. Kleine Schriften. Neuwied, 1793.
Htn Phil 3480.19.5* Kant, Immanuel. Zerstreute Aufsätze. Frankfurt, 1793.
Htn Phil 3480.19.7* Kant, Immanuel. Anhang zu den Zerstreuten Aufsatzen. Frankfurt, 1794.
Phil 3480.19.10 Kant, Immanuel. Frühere nocht nicht Gesammelte Kleine Schriften. Lintz, 1795.
Htn Phil 3480.19.11* Kant, Immanuel. Neue Kleine Schriften. Berlin? 1795.
Phil 3480.19.12 Kant, Immanuel. Sämmtliche Kleine Schriften. Königsberg, 1797. 3v.
Phil 3480.19.13 Kant, Immanuel. Ausgewählte Kleine Schriften. Leipzig, 1919.
Htn Phil 3480.19.15* Kant, Immanuel. Vorzügliche Kleine Schriften und Aufsätze. Bd.1-2. Leipzig, 1833.
Phil 3480.19.16 Kant, Immanuel. Vorzügliche Kleine Schriften und Aufsätze. v.1-2. Quedlinburg, 1838.
Htn Phil 3480.19.20* Kant, Immanuel. Sammlung einiger bisher unbekannt gebliebener kleiner Schriften. Königsberg, 1800.
Phil 3480.19.25 Kant, Immanuel. Populäre Schriften. Berlin, 1911.
Phil 3480.19.30 Kant, Immanuel. Kantische Blumenlese. v.1-2. Zittau, 1813-
Phil 3480.20 Kant, Immanuel. Grundlegung zur Metaphysik. Riga, 1792-98. 3 pam.
Htn Phil 3480.21* Kant, Immanuel. Der einzig mögliche Beweisgrund. Königsberg, 1763. 4 pam.
Phil 3480.21.3 Kant, Immanuel. Der einzig mögliche Beweis vom Daseyn Gottes. Königsberg, 1770.
Phil 3480.21.5 Kant, Immanuel. Der einzig mögliche Beweisgrund zu einer Demonstration des Daseyns Gottes. Königsberg, 1794.
Phil 3480.21.22 Kant, Immanuel. Der einzig mögliche Beweisgrund zu einer Demonstration des Daseyns Gottes. 2. Aufl. Leipzig, 1902.
Phil 3480.21.23 Kant, Immanuel. Der einzig mögliche Beweisgrund zu einer Demonstration des Daseyns Gottes. 3. Aufl. Leipzig, 1911.
Phil 3480.22 Kant, Immanuel. Deines Lebens Sinn. Wien, 1951.
Phil 3480.22.2 Kant, Immanuel. Deines Lebens Sinn. 2. Aufl. Wien, 1953.
Phil 3480.22.5 Kant, Immanuel. Über die Form und die Prinzipien der Sinnen - und Geisteswelt. Hamburg, 1958.
Phil 3480.24 Kant, Immanuel. Zur Logik und Metaphysik. 2. Aufl. Leipzig, 1921. 4v.
Phil 3480.24.2 Kant, Immanuel. Kleinere Schriften zur Logik und Metaphysik. v.1-4. 2. Aufl. Leipzig, 1905.
Phil 3480.24.5 Kant, Immanuel. Kleinere Schriften zur Logik und Metaphysik. Berlin, 1870.
Phil 3480.25 Kant, Immanuel. Philosophy of Kant as contained in extracts. N.Y., 1888.
Phil 3480.25.2 Kant, Immanuel. Philosophy of Kant as contained in extracts. N.Y., 1891.
Phil 3480.25.5 Kant, Immanuel. The philosophy of Kant. 2d ed. Glasgow, 1923.
Phil 3480.25.10 Kant, Immanuel. The philosophy of Kant. Glasgow, 1927.
Htn Phil 3480.25.15* Kant, Immanuel. Essays and treatises on moral, political and various philosophical subjects. London, 1798-99. 2v.
Phil 3480.25.20A Kant, Immanuel. Selectiones. N.Y., 1929.
Phil 3480.25.30 Kant, Immanuel. Kant. Oxford, 1963.
Phil 3480.25.40 Kant, Immanuel. Il pensiero filosofico di E.K. v.1-2. Firenze, 1926-25.
Phil 3480.25.50A Kant, Immanuel. The philosophy of Kant. N.Y., 1949.
Phil 3480.25.50B Kant, Immanuel. The philosophy of Kant. N.Y., 1949.
Phil 3480.25.50C Kant, Immanuel. The philosophy of Kant. N.Y., 1949.
Phil 3480.25.55 Kant, Immanuel. The living thoughts of Kant. N.Y., 1940.
Phil 3480.26 Kant, Immanuel. Les grands philosophes. Paris, 1909.
Phil 3480.26.10 Kant, Immanuel. Theorie und praxis. Leipzig, 1913.
Phil 3480.27.5 Kant, Immanuel. Lose Blätter aus Kants Nachloss. Königsberg, 1889-98.
Phil 3480.28 Kant, Immanuel. Kleinere Schriften zur Geschichts-Philosophie Ethik und Politik. Leipzig, 1913.

Phil 3480 History of philosophy - Local Modern philosophy - Germany - Individual philosophers - Kant, Immanuel - Writings - cont.

Phil 3480.28.4 Kant, Immanuel. Kants Weltanschanung. Darmstadt, 1919.
Phil 3480.28.12 Kant, Immanuel. Kleinere Schriften zur Ethik und Religionsphilosophie. Berlin, 1870.
Phil 3480.28.15 Kant, Immanuel. Kleinere Schriften zur Natur- Philosophie. v.1-2. Berlin, 1872-73.
Phil 3480.28.17 Kant, Immanuel. Schriften zur Naturphilosophie. 3. Aufl. Leipzig, 1922. 3v.
Phil 3480.28.25 Kant, Immanuel. Scritti minori. Bari, 1923.
Phil 3480.28.30 Kant, Immanuel. Antologia Kantiana. Torino, 1925.
Phil 3480.28.35 Kant, Immanuel. Ausgewählt und Bearbeitet von L. Weis. Hamburg, 1906.
Phil 3480.28.38 Kant, Immanuel. Frühschriften. Berlin, 1961. 2v.
Phil 3480.28.40 Kant, Immanuel. Kant- Aussprüche. Leipzig, 1901.
Phil 3480.28.40.3 Kant, Immanuel. Kant- Aussprüche. Leipzig, 1909.
Phil 3480.28.100A Kant, Immanuel. Die drei Kritiken. Leipzig, 1933.
Phil 3480.28.100B Kant, Immanuel. Die drei Kritiken. Leipzig, 1933.
Htn Phil 3480.29* Kant, Immanuel. Critik der reinen Vernunft. Riga, 1781.
Htn Phil 3480.29.2* Kant, Immanuel. Critik der reinen Vernunft. 2. Aufl. Riga, 1787.
Phil 3480.29.4 Kant, Immanuel. Critik der reinen Vernunft. 2. Aufl. Riga, 1787.
Htn Phil 3480.30* Kant, Immanuel. Critik der reinen Vernunft. 3. Aufl. Riga, 1790.
Phil 3480.30.01 Kant, Immanuel. Critik der reinen Vernunft. 3. Aufl. Frankfurt, 1791.
Htn Phil 3480.30.02* Kant, Immanuel. Critik der reinen Vernunft. 4. Aufl. Riga, 1794.
Phil 3480.30.03 Kant, Immanuel. Critik der reinen Vernunft. Neueste Aufl. Frankfurt, 1794.
Phil 3480.30.05 Kant, Immanuel. Critik der reinen Vernunft. 4. Aufl. Riga, 1794.
Phil 3480.30.07 Kant, Immanuel. Critik der reinen Vernunft. v.1-2,3-4. Grätz, 1795. 2v.
Phil 3480.30.1 Kant, Immanuel. Critik der reinen Vernunft. 5. Aufl. Leipzig, 1799.
Phil 3480.30.2 Kant, Immanuel. Critik der reinen Vernunft. 7. Aufl. Leipzig, 1828.
Phil 3480.30.2.10 Kant, Immanuel. Critik der reinen Vernunft. 6. Aufl. Leipzig, 1818.
Phil 3480.30.3 Kant, Immanuel. Kritik der reinen Vernunft. 2. Verb. Aufl. Leipzig, 1877.
Phil 3480.30.3.2A Kant, Immanuel. Kritik der praktischen Vernunft. Leipzig, 1878?
Phil 3480.30.3.2B Kant, Immanuel. Kritik der praktischen Vernunft. Leipzig, 1878?
Phil 3480.30.4 Kant, Immanuel. Kritik der reinen Vernunft. Leipzig, 1878.
Phil 3480.30.5A Kant, Immanuel. Kritik der reinen Vernunft. Berlin, 1889.
Phil 3480.30.5B Kant, Immanuel. Kritik der reinen Vernunft. Berlin, 1889.
Phil 3480.30.5.5 Kant, Immanuel. Kritik der reinen Vernunft. Hamburg, 1889.
Phil 3480.30.6 Kant, Immanuel. Kritik der reinen Vernunft. 5. Aufl. Berlin, 1900.
Phil 3480.30.6.5 Erdmann, B. Beiträge zur Geschichte...Anhang zur. 5. Aufl. Berlin, 1900.
Phil 3480.30.7 Kant, Immanuel. Kritik der reinen Vernunft. Kiel, 1881.
Phil 3480.30.8 Kant, Immanuel. Kritik der reinen Vernunft. Leipzig, 1853.
Phil 3480.30.9 Kant, Immanuel. Kritik der reinen Vernunft. Leipzig, 1868.
Phil 3480.30.10 Kant, Immanuel. Kritik der reinen Vernunft. Berlin, 1868-69.
Phil 3480.30.15 Kant, Immanuel. Kritik der reinen Vernunft. Halle, 1899?
Phil 3480.30.17 Kant, Immanuel. Critik der reinen Vernunft, 1781. 1. Aufl. Riga, 1905.
Phil 3480.30.18 Kant, Immanuel. Kritik der reinen Vernunft. 10. Aufl. Leipzig, 1913.
Phil 3480.30.20 Kant, Immanuel. Kritik der reinen Vernunft. Leipzig, 1920.
Phil 3480.30.25 Kant, Immanuel. Kritik der reinen Vernunft. 12. Aufl. Leipzig, 1922.
Phil 3480.30.27 Kant, Immanuel. Kritik der reinen Vernunft. Leipzig, 1925.
Phil 3480.30.29 Kant, Immanuel. Kritik der reinen Vernunft. Leipzig, 1926.
Phil 3480.30.35 Kant, Immanuel. Kritik der reinen Vernunft. München, 1920.
Phil 3480.30.40 Kant, Immanuel. Kritik der reinen Vernunft. Lübeck, 1926.
Phil 3480.30.44 Kant, Immanuel. Kritik der reinen Vernunft. Stuttgart, 1904.
Phil 3480.30.45 Kant, Immanuel. Kritik der reinen Vernunft. Berlin, 1928.
Phil 3480.30.56 Kant, Immanuel. Kritik der reinen Vernunft. Heldeberg, 1884.
Phil 3480.31 Kant, Immanuel. Critique de la raison pure. 2. éd. Paris, 1845. 2v.
Phil 3480.31.1 Kant, Immanuel. Critique de la raison pure. 1. éd. Paris, 1835. 2v.
Phil 3480.31.2 Kant, Immanuel. Critique de la raison pure. Paris, 1869. 2v.
Phil 3480.31.5 Kant, Immanuel. Critique de la raison pure. 3. éd. Paris, 1864. 2v.
Phil 3480.31.8 Kant, Immanuel. Critica della raigon pura. v.1-2. Bari, 1910.
Phil 3480.31.9 Kant, Immanuel. Critica della raigon pura. 2. ed. Bari, 1919-21. 2v.
Phil 3480.31.20 Kant, Immanuel. Critique de la raison pure. Paris, 1927.
Phil 3480.32 Kant, Immanuel. Critick of pure reason. London, 1838.
Phil 3480.32.2 Kant, Immanuel. Critique of pure reason. London, 1855.
Htn Phil 3480.32.3* Kant, Immanuel. Critique of pure reason. London, 1855.
Phil 3480.32.5 Kant, Immanuel. Critique of pure reason. London, 1869.
Phil 3480.32.6 Kant, Immanuel. Critique of pure reason. London, 1878.
Phil 3480.32.7.5 Kant, Immanuel. Critique of pure reason. N.y., 1900.
Phil 3480.32.8A Kant, Immanuel. Critique of pure reason. London, 1881. 2v.
Htn Phil 3480.32.8.2* Kant, Immanuel. Critique of pure reason. London, 1881. 2v.
Phil 3480.32.8.9 Kant, Immanuel. Critique of pure reason. London, 1887.
Phil 3480.32.9 Kant, Immanuel. Critique of pure reason. Edinburgh, 1881.
Phil 3480.32.10 Kant, Immanuel. Critique of pure reason. N.Y., 1882.
Phil 3480.32.17 Kant, Immanuel. Critique of pure reason. 2. ed. N.Y., 1927.
Phil 3480.32.20 Kant, Immanuel. Critique of pure reason. London, 1929.
Phil 3480.32.21 Kant, Immanuel. Critique of pure reason. London, 1933.
Phil 3480.32.26A Kant, Immanuel. Critique of pure reason. N.Y., 1961.
Phil 3480.32.26B Kant, Immanuel. Critique of pure reason. N.Y., 1961.

Phil 3480   History of philosophy - Local Modern philosophy - Germany - Individual
philosophers - Kant, Immanuel - Writings - cont.

Phil 3480.65B   Kant, Immanuel. Grundlegung zur Metaphysik der Sitten.
                   Riga, 1797.
Phil 3480.65.5   Kant, Immanuel. Grundlegung zur Metaphysik der Sitten.
                   v.1-2. Königsberg, 1803.
Phil 3480.65.6   Kant, Immanuel. Grundlegung zur Metaphysik der Sitten. 5.
                   Aufl. Leipzig, 1920.
Phil 3480.65.7   Kant, Immanuel. Grundlegung zur Metaphysik der Sitten.
                   Leipzig, 1906.
Phil 3480.65.8   Kant, Immanuel. Grundlegung zur Metaphysik der Sitten.
                   Leipzig, 1904.
Phil 3480.65.10   Kant, Immanuel. Grundlegung zur Metaphysik der Sitten.
                   München, 1925.
Phil 3480.65.12   Kant, Immanuel. Grundlegung zur Metaphysik der Sitten.
                   Gotha, 1930.
Phil 3480.65.13   Kant, Immanuel. Grundlegung zur Metaphysik der Sitten.
                   Stuttgart, 1967.
Phil 3480.65.15   Kant, Immanuel. Fondements de la métaphysique des moeurs.
                   2. éd. Paris, 1907?
Phil 3480.65.20   Kant, Immanuel. Principes métaphysiques de la morale.
                   Paris, 1837.
Phil 3480.65.23   Kant, Immanuel. Principes métaphysiques de la morale. 3.
                   éd. Paris, 1854.
Phil 3480.65.40   Kant, Immanuel. Fundamental principles of the metaphysics
                   of ethics. London, 1907.
NEDL Phil 3480.66.3 Kant, Immanuel. The metaphysics of ethics. 3. ed.
                   Edinburgh, 1871.
Phil 3480.66.49   Kant, Immanuel. Fondazione della metafisica dei costumi.
                   Torino, 1923.
Phil 3480.66.50   Kant, Immanuel. Fondazione della metafisica dei costumi.
                   Torino, 1925?
Phil 3480.66.51   Kant, Immanuel. La metafisica dei costumi. v.1-2.
                   Torino, 1923-25.
Phil 3480.67.10   Kant, Immanuel. Che cosa significa orientarsi nel pensare.
                   Lanciano, 1930.
Phil 3480.67.20   Kant, Immanuel. Qu'est-ceque s'orienter dans la pensée.
                   Paris, 1959.
Htn Phil 3480.67.50*   Kant, Immanuel. Metaphysische Anfangsgrunde der
                   Rechtslehre. Königsberg, 1797.
Phil 3480.67.50.5 Kant, Immanuel. Metaphysische Anfangsgrunde der
                   Rechtslehre. Frankfurt, 1797.
Htn Phil 3480.67.51*   Kant, Immanuel. Metaphysische Anfangsgrunde der
                   Rechtslehre. 2. Aufl. Königsberg, 1798.
Phil 3480.67.55   Kant, Immanuel. Principes métaphysiques du droit.
                   Paris, 1837.
Phil 3480.67.60   Kant, Immanuel. Éléments métaphysique de la doctrine du
                   droit. Paris, 1853.
Phil 3480.67.65   Kant, Immanuel. Eleinenta metaphysica juris doctrinae.
                   Amstelaedami, 1799.
Htn Phil 3480.67.70*   Kant, Immanuel. The metaphysic of morals, divided into
                   metaphisical elements of law and of ethics. v.1-2.
                   London, 1799.
Phil 3480.67.75   Kant, Immanuel. Lectures on ethics. London, 1930.
Phil 3480.67.80A   Kant, Immanuel. The moral law, or Kant's Groundwork of the
                   metaphysic of morals. London, 1947?
Phil 3480.67.80B   Kant, Immanuel. The moral law, or Kant's Groundwork of the
                   metaphysic of morals. London, 1947?
Phil 3480.67.85   Kant, Immanuel. Foundations of the metaphysics of morals.
                   Chicago, 1950.
Phil 3480.67.90   Kant, Immanuel. The moral law. N.Y., 1950.
Phil 3480.67.95   Kant, Immanuel. An Immanuel Kant reader. N.Y., 1960.
Phil 3480.67.100   Kant, Immanuel. The moral law. London, 1961.
Phil 3480.67.105   Kant, Immanuel. The philosophy of law. Edinburgh, 1887.
Phil 3480.67.110   Kant, Immanuel. The metaphysical elements of justice.
                   Indianapolis, 1965.
Htn Phil 3480.68*   Kant, Immanuel. Über moralische und politische
                   Gegenstände. Frankfurt, 1795.
Phil 3480.68.5   Kant, Immanuel. Zwo Abhandlungen über moralische
                   Gegenstände. 2. Aufl. Königsberg, 1796.
Phil 3480.69   Kant, Immanuel. Allgemeine Naturgeschichte. Theorie des
                   Himmels. Leipzig, 1890.
Htn Phil 3480.69.1*   Kant, Immanuel. Allgemeine Naturgeschichte. Theorie des
                   Himmels. Königsberg, 1755.
Phil 3480.69.2   Kant, Immanuel. Allgemeine Naturgeschichte. Theorie des
                   Himmels. Frankfurt, 1799.
Phil 3480.69.3   Kant, Immanuel. Allgemeine Naturgeschichte. Theorie des
                   Himmels. Zeitz, 1798.
Phil 3480.69.4   Kant, Immanuel. Allgemeine Naturgeschichte. Theorie des
                   Himmels. 4. Aufl. Zeitz, 1808.
Phil 3480.69.5   Kant, Immanuel. Cosmogony. Glasgow, 1900.
Phil 3480.69.5.10 Kant, Immanuel. Kant's cosmogony, as in his essay on The
                   retardation of the rotation of the earth and his national
                   history and theory of the heavens. N.Y., 1968.
Phil 3480.69.6   Kant, Immanuel. Allgemeine Naturgeschichte und Theorie des
                   Himmels. Berlin, 1955.
Htn Phil 3480.70*   Kant, Immanuel. Logik. Königsberg, 1800.
Phil 3480.70.1   Kant, Immanuel. Logik. Königsberg, 1801.
Phil 3480.70.2   Kant, Immanuel. Logik. Reutlingen, 1801.
Phil 3480.70.3   Kant, Immanuel. Logik. 3. Aufl. Leipzig, 1920.
Phil 3480.70.5   Kant, Immanuel. Logique. Paris, 1840.
Phil 3480.70.6   Kant, Immanuel. Logique. 2. éd. Paris, 1862.
Phil 3480.70.10A   Kant, Immanuel. Introduction to logic. Photoreproduction.
                   London, 1885.
Phil 3480.70.10B   Kant, Immanuel. Introduction to logic. Photoreproduction.
                   London, 1885.
Phil 3480.70.20   Kant, Immanuel. Logik. 2. Aufl. Leipzig, 1876.
Phil 3480.70.21   Kant, Immanuel. Kant's introduction to logic and his essay
                   on the mistaken subtilty of the four figures. N.Y., 1963
Htn Phil 3480.70.75*   Kant, Immanuel. Die Religion innerhalb der Grenzen der
                   blossen Vernunft. Königsberg, 1793.
Htn Phil 3480.70.80*   Kant, Immanuel. Ueber das radikale Böse in der
                   menschlichen Natur. Pt. 1. n.p., 1792.
Phil 3480.71.2   Kant, Immanuel. Die Religion innerhalb der Grenzen der
                   blossen Vernunft. Königsberg, 1784.
Htn Phil 3480.71.2.5* Kant, Immanuel. Die Religion innerhalb der Grenzen der
                   blossen Vernunft. Frankfurt, 1793.
Htn Phil 3480.71.2.6* Kant, Immanuel. Die Religion innerhalb der Grenzen der
                   blossen Vernunft. Frankfurt, 1793.
Phil 3480.71.2.7   Kant, Immanuel. Die Religion innerhalb der Grenzen der
                   blossen Vernunft. Frankfurt, 1794.
Phil 3480.71.4   Kant, Immanuel. Die Religion innerhalb der Grenzen der
                   blossen Vernunft. 4. Aufl. Leipzig, 1819.
Phil 3480.71.5   Kant, Immanuel. Religion within the boundary of Pure
                   reason. Edinburgh, 1838.
Phil 3480.71.7   Kant, Immanuel. Religion within the limits of reason
                   alone. Chicago, 1934.

Phil 3480   History of philosophy - Local Modern philosophy - Germany - Individual
philosophers - Kant, Immanuel - Writings - cont.

Phil 3480.71.8   Kant, Immanuel. Religion within the limits of reason
                   alone. 2sd ed. La Salle, 1960.
Phil 3480.71.10   Kant, Immanuel. Die Religion innerhalb der Grenzen der
                   blossen Vernunft. 2. Aufl. Leipzig, 1875.
Phil 3480.71.12   Kant, Immanuel. Die Religion innerhalb der Grenzen der
                   blossen Vernunft. 5. Aufl. Leipzig, 1937.
Phil 3480.71.13   Kant, Immanuel. Die Religion innerhalb der Grenzen der
                   blossen Vernunft. Hamburg, 1966.
Phil 3480.71.15   Kant, Immanuel. La religion dans les limites de la raison.
                   Paris, 1913.
Phil 3480.71.21   Kant, Immanuel. Theorie de Kant sur la religion dans
                   limites. Paris, 1842.
Htn Phil 3480.72*   Kant, Immanuel. Theorie der Reinmoralischen Religion.
                   Riga, 1796.
Htn Phil 3480.72.5*   Kant, Immanuel. Theorie der Reinmoralischen Religion.
                   Elberfeld, 1798.
Phil 3480.73   Kant, Immanuel. Vorlesungen über der philosophische
                   Religionslehre. Leipzig, 1830.
Htn Phil 3480.73.5*   Kant, Immanuel. Vorlesungen über der philosophische
                   Religionslehre. Leipzig, 1794-1817. 2 pam.
Phil 3480.74   Kant, Immanuel. Über Pädagogik. 3. Aufl.
                   Langensalza, 1901.
Htn Phil 3480.74.5*   Kant, Immanuel. Über Pädagogik. Königsberg, 1803.
Htn Phil 3480.74.7*   Kant, Immanuel. Über Pädagogik. Königsberg, 1803.
Phil 3480.74.15   Kant, Immanuel. Über Pädagogik. Leipzig, 1924.
Htn Phil 3480.75*   Kant, Immanuel. Uber des Ausgesetzte Preisfrage.
                   Königsberg, 1803-04. 2 pam.
Htn Phil 3480.75.15*   Kant, Immanuel. Von der verschiedenen Racen der Menschen.
                   Königsberg, 1775.
Phil 3480.75.20   Kant, Immanuel. Über den Gemeinspruch: Das mag in Theorie
                   richtig sein taugt, aber nicht für die Praxis.
                   Frankfurt, 1946.
Htn Phil 3480.75.25*   Kant, Immanuel. Über den Gemeinspruch: Das mag in Theorie
                   richtig sein taugt, aber nicht für die Praxis.
                   Berlin, 1793. 2 pam.
Phil 3480.75.30   Kant, Immanuel. Über den Gemeinspruch: Das mag in der
                   Theorie richtig sein taugt. Frankfurt, 1968.
Phil 3480.76   Kant, Immanuel. Das nachgelassene Werk. Lahr, 1888.
Phil 3480.77   Kant, Immanuel. En Andeskadares drömmar i ljusetay
                   metafysikens drömmar. Lund, 1921. 10v.
Htn Phil 3480.78*   Kant, Immanuel. Politische Meinungen. n.p., 1796.
Htn Phil 3480.78.5*   Kant, Immanuel. Politische Meinungen. n.p., 1794.
Htn Phil 3480.79*   Kant, Immanuel. Zum ewigen Frieden. Königsberg, 1795.
Htn Phil 3480.79.3*   Kant, Immanuel. Zum ewigen Frieden. Königsberg, 1795.
                   2 pam.
Htn Phil 3480.79.4*   Kant, Immanuel. Zum ewigen Frieden. Königsberg, 1796.
Phil 3480.79.7   Kant, Immanuel. Zum ewigen Frieden. Leipzig, 1881?
Phil 3480.79.10   Kant, Immanuel. Zum ewigen Frieden. Berlin, 1917.
Phil 3480.79.12   Kant, Immanuel. Zum ewigen Frieden. 2. Aufl.
                   Leipzig, 1919.
Phil 3480.80.15   Kant, Immanuel. Perpetual peace. Los Angeles, 1932.
Phil 3480.80.50   Kant, Immanuel. Vens la paix perpetuelle. 1. éd.
                   Paris, 1958.
Phil 3480.80.75   Kant, Immanuel. Ecrits politiques. Paris, 1917.
Phil 3480.80.79   Kant, Immanuel. Den evigi fred. Fagershand, 1889.
Phil 3480.80.80   Kant, Immanuel. Avhandlingar om fred och rätt.
                   Stockholm, 1915.
Phil 3480.80.125   Kant, Immanuel. Az örök héke. Budapest, 1918.
Htn Phil 3480.81*   Kant, Immanuel. Metaphysische Anfangsgründe der
                   Jugendlehre. Königsberg, 1797.
Htn Phil 3480.81.2*   Kant, Immanuel. Metaphysische Anfangsgründe der
                   Jugendlehre. 2. Aufl. Kreuznach, 1800.
Phil 3480.81.3   Kant, Immanuel. Metaphysische Anfangsgründe der
                   Jugendlehre. 2. Aufl. Königsberg, 1803.
Phil 3480.81.4   Kant, Immanuel. Metaphysische Anfangsgründe der
                   Naturwesenschaft. Leipzig, 1914.
Phil 3480.81.4.1   Kant, Immanuel. Metaphysical foundations of natural
                   science. Indianapolis, 1970.
Phil 3480.81.5   Kant, Immanuel. Metaphysische Anfangsgründe der
                   Jugendlehre. 2. Aufl. Kreuznach, 1800.
Htn Phil 3480.82*   Kant, Immanuel. Beobachtungen über das Gefühl des Schönen
                   und Erhabenen. Riga, 1771.
Htn Phil 3480.82.1*   Kant, Immanuel. Beobachtungen über das Gefühl des Schönen
                   und Erhabenen. Königsberg, 1764.
Phil 3480.82.4   Kant, Immanuel. Beobachtungen über das Gefühl des Schönen
                   und Erhabenen. Grätz, 1797.
Phil 3480.82.6   Kant, Immanuel. Beobachtungen über das Gefühl des Schönen
                   und Erhabenen. Berlin, 1910.
Phil 3480.82.8   Kant, Immanuel. Observations on the feeling of the
                   beautifull and sublime. Berkeley, 1960.
Phil 3480.82.25   Kant, Immanuel. Opmerkingen over het gevoll van Schoone en
                   Vorheveve. Sneck, 1919.
Phil 3480.83   Kant, Immanuel. Worin besteht der Fortschritt zum bessern
                   im Menschengeschlecht? Wiesbaden, 1917.
Phil 3480.84   Kant, Immanuel. Versuch den Begriff der negativen Grössen
                   in die Weltweisheit einzuführen. Grätz, 1797.
Htn Phil 3480.84.3*   Kant, Immanuel. Versuch den Begriff der negativen Grössen
                   in die Weltweisheit einzuführen. Königsberg, 1763.
Phil 3480.85.3   Kant, Immanuel. De kracht van den wil in het beheerschen
                   van ziekelijke aandoeningen. 3. druk. Leeuwarden, 1885.
Htn Phil 3480.85.5*   Kant, Immanuel. Von der Macht des Gemüths durch den
                   blossen Vorsatz seiner krankhaften Gefühle Meister zu seyn.
                   Jena, 1798.
Htn Phil 3480.85.6*   Kant, Immanuel. Von der Macht des Gemüths durch den
                   blossen Vorsatz seiner krankhaften Gefühle Meister zu seyn.
                   Jena, 1798.
Phil 3480.85.6.10 Kant, Immanuel. Von der Macht des Gemüths durch den
                   blossen Vorsatz seiner krankhaften Gefühle Meister zu seyn.
                   Königsberg, 1798?
Phil 3480.85.6.15 Kant, Immanuel. Von der Macht des Gemüths durch den
                   blossen Vorsatz seiner krankhaften Gefühle Meister zu seyn.
                   Leipzig, 1824?
Phil 3480.85.7   Kant, Immanuel. Von der Macht des Gemüths durch den
                   blossen Vorsatz seiner krankhaften Gefühle Meister zu seyn.
                   Frankfurt, 1800.
Phil 3480.85.9   Kant, Immanuel. Von der Macht des Gemüths durch den
                   blossen Vorsatz seiner krankhaften Gefühle Meister zu seyn.
                   2. Aufl. Leipzig, 1824.
Phil 3480.85.10   Kant, Immanuel. Von der Macht des Gemüths durch den
                   blossen Vorsatz seiner krankhaften Gefühle Meister zu seyn.
                   3. Aufl. Leipzig, 1836.
Phil 3480.85.11   Kant, Immanuel. Von der Macht des Gemüths durch den
                   blossen Vorsatz seiner krankhaften Gefühle Meister zu seyn.
                   6. Aufl. Leipzig, 1852.

hil 3480   History of philosophy - Local Modern philosophy - Germany - Individual
philosophers - Kant, Immanuel - Writings - cont.

Phil 3480.85.20   Kant, Immanuel. Von der Macht des Gemüths durch den
blossen Vorsatz seiner krankhaften Gefühle Meister zu seyn.
Heidelberg, 1924.

tn   Phil 3480.86*   Kant, Immanuel. Der streit der Facultaeten.
Königsberg, 1798.

tn   Phil 3480.86.2*   Kant, Immanuel. Der streit der Facultaeten.
Königsberg, 1798.

Phil 3480.86.5   Kant, Immanuel. Der Streit der Fakultäten. Leipzig, 1922.
Phil 3480.86.10   Kant, Immanuel. Der Streit der Fakultäten. Hamburg, 1959.
Phil 3480.86.25   Kant, Immanuel. Le conflit des facultes en trois sections,
1798. Paris, 1935.

Phil 3480.87   Kant, Immanuel. Die falsche Spitzfindigkeit der vier
syllogistischen Figuren. Frankfurt, 1797.

Phil 3480.88   Kant, Immanuel. Von dem ersten Grunde des Unterschiedes
der Gegenden im Raume. Steglitz, 1768[1920]

tn   Phil 3480.89*   Kant, Immanuel. Über die Büchmacheren. Königsberg, 1798.
Phil 3480.90   Kant, Immanuel. Briefwechsel. Leipzig, 1922.
Phil 3480.91   Kant, Immanuel. Briefwechsel. München, 1912. 3v.
Phil 3480.92   Kant, Immanuel. Briefwechsel. Leipzig, 1924. 2v.
Phil 3480.92.5   Kant, Immanuel. Briefe. Göttingen, 1970.
Phil 3480.93   Kant, Immanuel. Kants Briefe ausgewählt. Leipzig, 1911.
Phil 3480.94   Kant, Immanuel. Filosofía de la historia. México, 1941.
Phil 3480.97   Kant, Immanuel. Von der Würde des Menschen.
Leipzig, 1944.

Phil 3480.100   Kant, Immanuel. Die letzten Gedanken. Hamburg, 1902.

n   Phil 3480.101*   Kant, Immanuel. Physische Geographie. v.1-2.
Königsberg, 1802.

Phil 3480.101.2   Kant, Immanuel. Physische Geographie. Leipzig, 1803-07.
2v.

Phil 3480.105   Kant, Immanuel. Wörte Kants. Minden, 1911.
Phil 3480.110   Kant, Immanuel. Zwei Schriften über die Grundlegenden der
Naturwissenschaften. Berlin, 1920.

Phil 3480.115   Kant, Immanuel. De mundi sensibilis at que intelligibilis
forma. Hamburg, 1958.

Phil 3480.120   Kant, Immanuel. Réponse á Eberhard. Paris, 1959.
Phil 3480.125   Kant, Immanuel. Sochineniia. Moskva, 1963. 6v.
Phil 3480.126   Kant, Immanuel. Ausgewählte Kleine Schriften.
Hamburg, 1965.

Phil 3480.127   Kant, Immanuel. Philosophical correspondence.
Chicago, 1967.

Phil 3480.130   Kant, Immanuel. Selected pre-critical writings and
correspondence. Manchester, 1968.

Phil 3480.131.3   Kant, Immanuel. Kant Laienbrevier. 3. Aufl.
München, 1916.

Phil 3480.132   Kant, Immanuel. Kant's political writings.
Cambridge, 1970.

3481   History of philosophy - Local Modern philosophy - Germany - Individual
philosophers - Kant, Immanuel - Biography and criticism - Pamphlet
volumes; Periodicals

Phil 3481.1   Pamphlet vol. German and Dutch philosophy - Kant -
Biography and criticism. 39 pam.
Phil 3481.2   Pamphlet vol. German and Dutch philosophy - Kant -
Biography and criticism. 17 pam.
Phil 3481.3   Pamphlet vol. German and Dutch philosophy - Kant -
Biography and criticism. 24 pam.
Phil 3481.4   Pamphlet vol. German and Dutch philosophy - Kant -
Biography and criticism. 11 pam.
Phil 3481.5   Pamphlet vol. German and Dutch philosophy - Kant -
Biography and criticism. 9 pam.
Phil 3481.6   Pamphlet vol. German and Dutch philosophy - Kant -
Biography and criticism. 17 pam.
Phil 3481.7   Pamphlet vol. German and Dutch philosophy - Kant -
Biography and criticism. 19 pam.
Phil 3481.8   Pamphlet vol. German and Dutch philosophy - Kant -
Biography and criticism. German dissertations. 16 pam.
Phil 3481.9   Pamphlet vol. German and Dutch philosophy - Kant -
Biography and criticism. 11 pam.
Phil 3481.10   Pamphlet vol. German and Dutch philosophy - Kant -
Biography and criticism. 5 pam.
Phil 3481.11   Pamphlet vol. German and Dutch philosophy - Kant -
Biography and criticism. German dissertations. 17 pam.
Phil 3481.12   Pamphlet vol. German and Dutch philosophy - Kant -
Biography and criticism. 22 pam.
Phil 3481.13   Pamphlet vol. German and Dutch philosophy - Kant -
Biography and criticism. German dissertations. 17 pam.
Phil 3481.14   Pamphlet vol. German and Dutch philosophy - Kant -
Biography and criticism. German dissertations. 19 pam.
Phil 3481.15   Pamphlet vol. German and Dutch philosophy - Kant -
Biography and criticism. 15 pam.
Phil 3481.16   Pamphlet vol. German and Dutch philosophy - Kant -
Biography and criticism. German dissertations. 15 pam.
Phil 3481.17   Pamphlet vol. German and Dutch philosophy - Kant -
Biography and criticism. 5 pam.
Phil 3481.18   Pamphlet vol. German and Dutch philosophy - Kant -
Biography and criticism. German dissertations. 14 pam.
Phil 3481.19   Pamphlet box. German and Dutch philosophy - Kant -
Biography and criticism. German dissertations.
Phil 3481.20   Pamphlet box. German and Dutch philosophy - Kant -
Biography and criticism.
Phil 3481.50   Kant Studien; philosophische Studien. Berlin.
1-60,1904-1969 +   55v.
Phil 3481.50.5   Kant Studien. Ergänzungshefte. Berlin. 1-97,1915-1968 +
26v.
Phil 3481.51F   Kantiana. Wiesbaden.

3482   -   3507   History of philosophy - Local Modern philosophy - Germany -
Individual philosophers - Kant, Immanuel - Biography and criticism -
Monographs (A-Z)

Phil 3482.1   Adamson, R. Philosophy of Kant. Edinburg, 1879.
Phil 3482.1.5   Adamson, R. Über Kant's Philosophie. Leipzig, 1880.
Phil 3482.2   Adickes, E. Kant - Studien. Kiel, 1895. 2v.
Phil 3482.2.5   Adickes, E. German Kantian bibliography. v.1-3.
Boston, 1896[1893]
Phil 3482.2.7   Adickes, E. Kant als Naturforscher. Berlin, 1924.
2v.
Phil 3482.2.12   Adickes, E. Kants Ansichten über Geschichte und Bau der
Erde. Tübingen, 1911.
Phil 3482.2.16   Adickes, E. Kant und das Ding an sich. Berlin, 1924.
Phil 3482.2.20   Adickes, E. Untersuchungen zu Kants Physischer Geographie.
Tübingen, 1911.
Phil 3482.2.21   Adickes, E. Ein neu aufgefundenes Kollegheft nach Kants
Vorlesung über Psysischegeographie. Tübingen, 1913.
Phil 3482.2.25   Adickes, E. Kant und die als-ob-Philosophie.
Stuttgart, 1927.

3482   -   3507   History of philosophy - Local Modern philosophy - Germany -
Individual philosophers - Kant, Immanuel - Biography and criticism -
Monographs (A-Z) - cont.

Phil 3482.2.30   Adickes, E. Kants Lehre von der doppelten Affektion
unseres ich als Schlüssel zu seiner Erkenntnis Theorie.
Tübingen, 1929.
Phil 3482.2.35   Adickes, E. Kants Systematik als Systembilden der Factor.
Berlin, 1887.
Phil 3482.2.100   Aebi, Magdalena. Kant's Begründung der "Deutschen
Philosophie". Basel, 1947.
Phil 3482.3   Arnoldt, Emil. Kritische excurse im Gebiete der
Kant-Forschung. Köningsburg, 1894.
Phil 3482.3.5   Arnoldt, Emil. Kant's transcendentale idealität des Raumes
und der zeit. Pt.1-5. Königsberg, 1870-72.
Phil 3482.5   Apel, Max. Immanuel Kant. Berlin, 1904.
Phil 3482.5.3   Apel, Max. Kommentar zu Kants "Prologomena".
Schöneberg, 1908.
Phil 3482.5.5   Apel, Max. Kommentar zu Kants Prologomena. Leipzig, 1923.
Phil 3482.5.7   Apel, Max. Kants Erkenntnistheorie und seine Stellung zur
Metaphysik. Berlin, 1895.
Phil 3482.6.2   Aster, Ernst. Immanuel Kant. 2. Aufl. Leipzig, 1918.
Phil 3482.7   Aars, Kristian Birch-Reichenwald. Die Autonomie der Moral
mit besonderer Berucksichtigung der Morallehre Immanuel
Kants. Hamburg, 1896.
Phil 3482.8   Albert, Georg. Kant's transcendentale Logik. Wien, 1895.
Phil 3482.9   Aguanno, G. d'. La filosofia etico-giuridica de Kant a
Spencer. Pt.I. Palermo, 1895.
Phil 3482.10   Asmus, V.F. Dialektika Kanta. Moskva, 1929.
Phil 3482.11   Anceschi, T. I presupposti storici e teorici. n.p., 1955.
Phil 3482.12   Antonopoulos, Georg. Der Menschen als Bürger zweier
Welten. Bonn, 1958.
Phil 3482.13   Asmus, V.F. Die Philosophie Kants. Berlin, 1960.
Phil 3482.14   Alexandre, Michel. Lecture de Kant. Paris, 1961.
Phil 3482.15   Alquié, Ferdinand. La morale de Kant. Paris, 1965.
Phil 3482.15.5   Alquié, Ferdinand. La critique kantienne de la
metaphysique. Paris, 1968.
Phil 3482.20   Acton, Harry Burrows. Kant's moral philosophy.
London, 1970.
Phil 3483.1   Beck, J.S. Erläuternder Auszug. Riga, 1793-96.
3v.
Phil 3483.1.10   Beck, J.S. The principles of critical philosophy.
London, 1797.
Phil 3483.1.15   Beck, J.S. Grundriss der critischen Philosophie.
Halle, 1796.
Phil 3483.2   Bessel-Hagen, F. Die Grabstätte Immanuel Kants.
Königsberg, 1880.
Phil 3483.4   Boström, G. Kritisk framställning of Kants frihetslära.
Lund, 1897.
Phil 3483.5   Bridel, P. La philosophie de la religion. Lausanne, 1876.
Phil 3483.6   Basch, V. Essai critique sur L'esthétique de Kant.
Paris, 1896.
Phil 3483.6.2   Basch, V. Essai critique sur L'esthétique de Kant. 2. éd.
Paris, 1927.
Phil 3483.7   Bolliger, A. Anti-Kant oder. Basel, 1882.
Phil 3483.8   Bauch, Bruno. Geschichte der Philosophie. v.5.
Leipzig, 1911.
Phil 3483.8.3   Bauch, Bruno. Immanuel Kant. 3. Aufl. Berlin, 1920.
Phil 3483.8.5   Bauch, Bruno. Luther und Kant. Berlin, 1904.
Phil 3483.8.8   Bauch, Bruno. Immanuel Kant. Berlin, 1917.
Phil 3483.8.9   Bauch, Bruno. Immanuel Kant. 2. Aufl. Berlin, 1921.
Phil 3483.9   Barni, J. Philosophie de Kant. Examen de la Critique du
jugement. Paris, 1850.
Phil 3483.9.10   Barni, J. Philosophie de Kant. Examen des fondements de la
métaphysique des moeurs. Paris, 1851.
Phil 3483.10A   Bowne, B.P. Kant and Spencer. Boston, 1912.
Phil 3483.10B   Bowne, B.P. Kant and Spencer. Boston, 1912.
Phil 3483.11   Brunswig, A. Das Grundproblem Kants. Leipzig, 1914.
Phil 3483.12   Baumann, J. Anti-Kant. Gotha, 1905.
Phil 3483.13   Burger, D. Kants wipbegeerte, kortelijk verklaard. 's
Gravenhage, 1881.
Phil 3483.14   Bilharz, Altons. Erläuterungen zu Kant's Kritik der reinen
Vernunft. Wiesbaden, 1884.
Phil 3483.15   Borowski, L.E. Immanuel Kant. 2. Aufl. Halle, 1907.
Phil 3483.15.5   Borowski, L.E. Darstellung des Lebens und Charakters
Immanuel Kants. Königsberg, 1804.
Phil 3483.16   Bund, Hugo. Kant als Philosophie des Katholizismus.
Berlin, 1913.
Phil 3483.18   Buchenau, A. Kants Lehre vom kategorischen Imperativ.
Leipzig, 1913.
Phil 3483.18.2   Buchenau, A. Kants Lehre vom kategorischen Imperativ. 2.
Aufl. Leipzig, 1923.
Phil 3483.18.5   Buchenau, A. Grundprobleme der Kritik der reinen Vernunft.
Leipzig, 1914.
Phil 3483.19   Brennekam, M. Ein Beitrag zur Kritik der Kantschen Ethik.
Inaug. Diss. Greefswald, 1895.
Phil 3483.20   Brahn, Max. Die Entwicklung des Seelenbegriffes bei Kant.
Inaug. Diss. Leipzig, 18- ?
Phil 3483.21   Baake, Wilhelm. Kants Ethik bei den englischen
Moralphilosophen des 19. Jahrhunderts. Leipzig, 1911.
Phil 3483.22   Buchner, E.F. A study of Kant's psychology. N.Y., 1893.
Phil 3483.23   Bensow, O. Till Kants lära om tinget i och för sig.
Lund, 1896.
Phil 3483.24   Bring, Gustaf. Immanuel Kants förhallande till den
filosofiska teologien. Lund, 1876.
Phil 3483.25   Barkman, H. Categorilära enligt Kantiska principer.
Akademisk afhandling. Upsala, 1901.
Phil 3483.26   Boldt, Georg. Protestantismens idé och Immanuel Kant.
Helsingfors, 1900.
NEDL Phil 3483.28   Baeumler, Alfred. Kant's Kritik der Urteilskraft.
Halle, 1923.
Phil 3483.28.5   Baeumler, Alfred. Das Irrationalitätsproblem in der
Ästhetik und Logik. 2. Aufl. Darmstadt, 1967.
Phil 3483.29   Böckel, C.G.A. Die Todtenfeyer Kant's. 1. Aufl.
Königsberg, 1804.
Phil 3483.30   Biese, Reinhold. Die Erkenntnisslehre des Aristoteles und
Kant's. Berlin, 1877.
Phil 3483.31   Bergk, J. Briefe über Immanuel Kant's metaphysische
Anfangsgründe der Rechtslehre. Leipzig, 1797.
Phil 3483.32   Brotherus, K.R. Immanuel Kants Philosophie der Geschichte.
Helsingfors, 1905.
Phil 3483.33   Bendavid, L. Vorlesungen über die Critik des
Urtheilskraft. Wien, 1796.
Phil 3483.33.5   Bendavid, L. Vorlesungen über die Critik der practischen
Vernunft. Wien, 1796.
Phil 3483.33.10   Bendavid, L. Vorlesungen über die Critik der reinen
Vernunft. Wien, 1795.
Phil 3483.34   Bendixson, A. Kritiska studier till Kants transcendentala
ästetik. Upsala, 1885.

Classified Listing

Phil 3482 - 3507 History of philosophy - Local Modern philosophy - Germany - Individual philosophers - Kant, Immanuel - Biography and criticism - Monographs (A-Z) - cont.

Phil 3483.35   Boutroux, Émile. La philosophie de Kant. Paris, 1926.

Phil 3483.36   Böhringer, A. Kant's erkenntnis-theoretischer Idealismus. Freiburg, 1888.

Phil 3483.37   Boette, Werner. Kants religion. Langensalza, 1920.

Phil 3483.38   Bolin, W. Undersökning af läran om viljans frihet - Kants behandling af problemet. Helsingfors, 1868.

Phil 3483.39   Brastberger, G.U. Untersuchungen über Kants Critik der practischen Vernunft. Tübingen, 1792.

Phil 3483.39.5   Brastberger, G.U. Untersuchungen über Kants Critik der reinen Vernunft. Halle, 1790.

Phil 3483.40   Brückmann, R. Immanuel Kant: sein Leben und sein Lehre. v.1-2. Königsberg, 1918-19.

Phil 3483.41   Bernhardi, A.B. Gemeinfassliche Darstellung der Kantischen Lehren über Sittlichkeit, Freyheit, Gottheit und Unsterblichkeit. v.1-2. Freyberg, 1796-97.

Phil 3483.42   Barth, Heinrich. Philosophie der praktischen Vernunft. Tübingen, 1927.

Phil 3483.43   Biéma, Emile van. L'espace et les temps chez Leibnizet chez Kant. Paris, 1908.

Phil 3483.44   Borries, Kurt. Kant als Politiker. Leipzig, 1928.

Phil 3483.45   Bouterwek, F. Immanuel Kant. Hamburg, 1805.

Phil 3483.45.5   Bouterwek, F. Aphorismen den Freunden der Vernunftkritik nach Kantischer Lehre. Gottingen, 1793.

Phil 3483.46   Beneke, F. Eduard. Kant und die philosophische Aufgabe unserer Zeit. Berlin, 1832.

Phil 3483.47   Becher, Erich. Immanuel Kant. München, 1924.

Phil 3483.48   Barié, G.E. Oltre la critica. Milano, 1929.

Phil 3483.49   Breysig, Kurt. Der Aufbau der Persönlichkeit von Kant. Stuttgart, 1931.

Phil 3483.50   Beiträge zur Erläuterung und Prüfung des Kantischen Sistems in sechs Abhandlungen. Gotha, 1794.

Phil 3483.51   Bartling, Dirk. De structuur van het aesthetisch a priori bij Kant Proef. Assen, 1931.

Phil 3483.52   Bárány, Gerö. Kant Immanuel; halálának századik évfordulójára. Kolozsvár, 1904.

Phil 3483.53   Bohatec, J. Die Religionsphilosophie Kants. Hamburg, 1938.

Phil 3483.54   Bodansky, Siegfried. Kants Dissertation vom Jahre 1770 und ihre Beziehung zur Kritik der Reinen Vernunft. Friedele, 1911-13.

Phil 3483.55   Benda, Julien. El pensamiento vivo de Kant. Buenos Aires, 1939.

Phil 3483.58   Beier, Franz. Kants Apriorismus. Pfullingen, 1933.

Phil 3483.60   Burckhardt, W. Kant's objectiver Idealismus. Naumburg, 1898.

Phil 3483.65   Ballauff, Theodor. Vernünftiger Wille und gläubige Liebe. Meisenheim, 1957.

Phil 3483.70   Bobbio, Norberto. Diritto e stato nel pensiero di Emanuele Kant. Torino, 1957.

Phil 3483.75   Beck, Lewis White. A commentary on Kant's Critique of practical reason. Chicago, 1960.

Phil 3483.80   Bird, G. Kant's theory of knowledge. London, 1962.

Phil 3483.82   Berni, M. Il criticismo kantiano. Verona, 1960.

Phil 3483.83   Boeversen, F. Die Idee der Freiheit in der Philosophie Kants. Heidelberg, 1962.

Phil 3483.84   Besse, Guy. La morale selon Kant et selon Marx. Paris, 196-.

Phil 3483.85   Beck, Lewis White. Studies in the philosophy of Kant. 1st ed. Indianapolis, 1965.

Phil 3483.85.5   Beck, Lewis White. Kant studies today. La Salle, 1969.

Phil 3483.86   Bennett, Jonathan Francis. Kant's analytic. Cambridge, 1966.

Phil 3483.87   Borodai, I.M. Voobrazhenie i teoriia poznaniia. Moskva, 1966.

Phil 3483.88   Blaha, Ottokar. Die Ontologie Kants. Ihr Grundriss in der Transzendentalphilosophie. Habilitationsschrift. Salzburg, 1967.

Phil 3483.90   Bergk, Johann Adam. Reflexionen über I. Kant's Metaphysische Anfangsgründe der Tugendlehre. Bruxelles, 1968.

Phil 3483.92   Banfi, Antonio. Esegesi e letture kantiane. Urbino, 1969. 2v.

Phil 3483.94   Broecker, Walter. Kant über Metaphysik und Erfahrung. Frankfurt, 1970.

Phil 3483.96   Bruch, Jean Louis. La philosophie religieuse de Kant. Thèse. Paris, 1968.

Phil 3484.1   Caird, E. A critical account of the philosophy of Kant. Glasgow, 1877.

Phil 3484.1.2   Caird, E. A critical account of the philosophy of Kant. London, 1877.

Phil 3484.1.3A   Caird, E. A critical account of the philosophy of Kant. Glasgow, 1889. 2v.

Phil 3484.1.3B   Caird, E. A critical account of the philosophy of Kant. Glasgow, 1889. 2v.

Phil 3484.1.5   Caird, E. A critical account of the philosophy of Kant. v.2. N.Y., 1889.

Phil 3484.2   Cohen, H. Kant's Theorie der Erfahrung. Berlin, 1871.

Phil 3484.2.2   Cohen, H. Kant's Theorie der Erfahrung. 2. Aufl. Berlin, 1885.

Phil 3484.2.3   Cohen, H. Kant's Theorie der Erfahrung. 3. Aufl. Berlin, 1918.

Phil 3484.2.5A   Cohen, H. Kant's Begrundung der Ethik. Berlin, 1877.

Phil 3484.2.5B   Cohen, H. Kant's Begrundung der Ethik. Berlin, 1877.

Phil 3484.2.8   Cohen, H. Kant's Einfluss auf die deutsche Kultur. Berlin, 1883.

Phil 3484.2.15   Cohen, H. Kommentar zu Immanuel Kant's Kritik. Leipzig, 1907.

Phil 3484.2.16A   Cohen, H. Kommentar zu Immanuel Kant's Kritik. 2. Aufl. Leipzig, 1917.

Phil 3484.2.16B   Cohen, H. Kommentar zu Immanuel Kant's Kritik. 2. Aufl. Leipzig, 1917.

Phil 3484.2.17   Cohen, H. Kommentar zu Immanuel Kant's Kritik. 3. Aufl. Leipzig, 1920.

Phil 3484.2.25   Cohen, H. Kant's Begrundung der Aesthetik. Berlin, 1889.

Phil 3484.2.30   Cohen, H. Die systematischen Begriffe. Berlin, 1873.

Phil 3484.3   Cousin, V. Philosophie de Kant. Paris, 1857.

Phil 3484.3.5   Cousin, V. Philosophy of Kant. London, n.d.

Phil 3484.5   Carus, Paul. Kant and Spencer. Chicago, 1899.

Phil 3484.6   Chamberlain, H.S. Immanuel Kant. Die Persönlichkeit...in das Werke. München, 1905.

Phil 3484.6.3   Chamberlain, H.S. Immanuel Kant. Die Persönlichkeit...in das Werke. 3. Aufl. München, 1916.

Phil 3484.6.4   Chamberlain, H.S. Immanuel Kant. Die Persönlichkeit...in das Werke. 4. Aufl. München, 1921.

Phil 3484.6.5   Chamberlain, H.S. Immanuel Kant. London, 1914. 2v.

Phil 3482 - 3507 History of philosophy - Local Modern philosophy - Germany - Individual philosophers - Kant, Immanuel - Biography and criticism - Monographs (A-Z) - cont.

Phil 3484.6.18   Curtiner, Egon B. Chamberlain gegen Schopenhauer. Düsseldorf, 1910.

Phil 3484.7   Cantecor, G. Kant. Paris, n.d.

Phil 3484.8   Classen, August. Über den Einfluss Kants auf die Theorie der Sinneswahrnehmung. Leipzig, 1886.

Phil 3484.9   Cresson, André. La morale de Kant. Paris, 1904.

Phil 3484.9.5   Cresson, André. Kant; sa vie, son oeuvre, avec un exposé de sa philosophie. Paris, 1941.

Phil 3484.9.10   Cresson, André. Kant; sa vie, son oeuvre, avec un exposé de sa philosophie. 5. éd. Paris, 1959.

Phil 3484.10   Cantoni, Carlo. Emanuele Kant. v.1,3. Milano, 1879-84. 2v.

Phil 3484.10.2   Cantoni, Carlo. Emanuele Kant. 2. ed. Milano, 1907.

Phil 3484.11   Cassirer, Ernst. Kants Leben und Lehre. Berlin, 1921.

Phil 3484.12   Clark, Norman. An introduction to Kant's philosophy. London, 1925.

Phil 3484.13   Cornelius, Hans. Kommentar zu Kant's Kritik der reinen Vernunft. Erlangen, 1926.

Phil 3484.14   Cesca, G. La "cosa in se". Torino, 1887.

Phil 3484.15   Cavicchi, G. de. Saggio Culle contraddizioni di Emanuele Kant. Catania, 1929.

Phil 3484.16   Christiansen, B. Kritik der Kantischen Erkenntnislehre. Hanau, 1911.

Phil 3484.17F   Clasen, Karl H. Kant-Bildnisse. Königsberg, 1924.

Phil 3484.18   Cassirer, H.W. A commentary on Kant's Critique of judgement. London, 1938.

Phil 3484.18.5   Cassirer, H.W. Kant's first critique. London, 1954.

Phil 3484.19   Chartier, Emile. Lettres à Sergio Solmi sur la philosophie de Kant. Paris, 1946.

Phil 3484.20   Caracciolo, A. Arti e pensiero nelle laro istanze metafisiche. Roma, 1953.

Phil 3484.21   Composto, R. La quarta critica kantiana. Palermo, 1954.

Phil 3484.22   Caramella, Santino. Commentarii alla ragion pura. Palermo, 1956-57.

Phil 3484.23   Casula, Mario. Studi kantiani sul trascendente. Milano, 1963.

Phil 3484.23.5   Casula, Mario. L'illuminismo critico. Milano, 1967.

Phil 3484.24   Campo, M. La genesi del criticismo kantiano. v.1-2. Varese, 1953-

Phil 3484.24.10   Campo, M. Schizzo storico della esegesi e critica kantiana. Varese, 1959.

Phil 3484.25   Cavagna, G.B. La soluzione kantiana. Bologna, 1962.

Phil 3484.26   Chiodi, Pietro. Il pensiero di Immanuel Kant. Torino, 1963.

Phil 3484.27   Coninck, Antoine De. L'analytique transcendentale de Kant. Louvain, 1955-

Phil 3485.1   Deussen, Paul. Der kategorische Imperativ. Kiel, 1891.

Phil 3485.1.5   Deussen, Paul. Der kategorische Imperativ. 2. Aufl. Kiel, 1903.

Phil 3485.2   Dieterich, K. Kant und Newton. Tübingen, 1876.

Phil 3485.2.5   Dieterich, K. Kant und Rousseau. Tübingen, 1878.

Phil 3485.3   Ducros, L. Quando et quomodo Kantium humius. Burgigalae, 1883.

Phil 3485.4   Drews, A.C.H. Kants Naturphilosophie als Grundlage seines Systems. Berlin, 1894.

Phil 3485.5   Döring, W.O. Das Lebenswerk Immanuel Kants. 4. Aufl. Lübeck, 1917.

Phil 3485.6   Desdouits, T. La philosophie de Kant. Paris, 1876.

Phil 3485.7   Delbos, Victor. La philosophie pratique de Kant. Paris, 1905.

Phil 3485.8   Drobisch, M.W. Kants Dinge an sich und sein Erfahrungsbegriff. Hamburg, 1885.

Phil 3485.9   Dentrice di Accadia, C. Il razionalismo religioso di E. Kant. Bari, 1920.

Phil 3485.11   Deneffe, A. Kant und die catholische Wahrheit. Freiburg, 1922.

Phil 3485.12   Drago, Pietro C. La mistica kantiana. Messina, 1929.

Phil 3485.13   Dünnhaupt, Rudolf. Sittlichkeit, Staat und Recht bei Kant. Berlin, 1927.

Phil 3485.14   Dunham, B. A study in Kant's aesthetics. Diss. Lancaster, Pa., 1934.

Phil 3485.15   Dahl, J. Ernstes und Heiteres über Kant. Cottbus, 1933.

Phil 3485.16   Durante, Gaetano. Gli epigoni di Kant. Firenze, 1943.

Phil 3485.17   Denckmann, G. Kants Philosophie des Asthetischen. Heidelberg, 1947.

Phil 3485.18   Das, Ras-Vihari. A handbook to Kant's Critique of pure reason. Bombay, 1949.

Phil 3485.19   Daval, Roger. La métaphysique de Kant. 1. éd. Paris, 1950.

Phil 3485.19.2   Daval, Roger. La métaphysique de Kant. Thèse. Paris, 1950.

Phil 3485.20   Drossbach, P. Kant und die Gegenwärtige Naturwissenschaft. Berlin, 1943.

Phil 3485.21   Duncan, A.R.C. Practical reason and morality. London, 1957.

Phil 3485.22   Doerpinghaus, Wilhelm. Der Begriff der Gesellschaft bei Kant. Köln? 1959?

Phil 3485.23   Delekat, Friedrich. Immanuel Kant. Heidelberg, 1963.

Phil 3485.23.2   Delekat, Friedrich. Immanuel Kant. 2. Aufl. Heidelberg, 1966.

Phil 3485.24   Daxer, Georg. Über die Anlage. Hamburg, 1897.

Phil 3485.26   Dryer, D.P. Kant's solution for verification in metaphysics. London, 1966.

Phil 3485.28   Wolff, Robert. Kant; a collection of critical essays. 1st ed. Notre Dame, 1967.

Phil 3485.30   Daub, Carl. Predigten nach Kantischen Grundsätzen. Bruxelles, 1968.

Phil 3485.32   Destutt de Tracy, Antoine Louis Claude. La métaphysique de Kant. Bruxelles, 1968.

Phil 3485.34   Declève, Henri. Heidegger et Kant. La Haye, 1970.

Phil 3486.1   Erdmann, B. Reflexionen Kants zur kritischen Philosophie. Leipzig, 1882-84. 2v.

Phil 3486.1.5   Erdmann, B. Kant's Kriticismus. Leipzig, 1878. 3 pam.

Phil 3486.1.10   Erdmann, B. Historische Untersuchungen über Kants Prolegomena. Halle, 1904.

Phil 3486.2   Erhardt, Franz. Kritik der Kantischen Antinomienlehre. Cöthen, 1888.

Phil 3486.2.7   Erhardt, Franz. Die Grundgedanken der Kritik der reinen Vernunft. Leipzig, 1924.

Phil 3486.2.9   Erhardt, Franz. Bleibendes und Vergängliches in der Philosophie Kants. Leipzig, 1926.

Phil 3486.3   Edmunds, J. Kant's ethics: the Clavis to an index. Louisville, n.d.

Phil 3482 - 3507   History of philosophy - Local Modern philosophy - Germany -
Individual philosophers - Kant, Immanuel - Biography and criticism -
Monographs (A-Z) - cont.

Phil 3486.4   Evellin, F. La raison pure...essai sur la philosophie
               Kantienne. Paris, 1907.
Phil 3486.5   Ewald, O. Kants kritischer Idealismus. Berlin, 1908.
Phil 3486.6   Elsmann, W. Begriff des höchsten Gutes bei Kant und
               Schleiermacher. Leipzig, 1887.
Phil 3486.7   Ernst, W. Der Zweckbegriff bei Kant. Halle, 1909.
Phil 3486.9   Ewing, Alfred Cyril. Kant's treatment of causality.
               London, 1924.
Phil 3486.9.6A Ewing, Alfred Cyril. A short commentary on Kant's Critique
               of pure reason. Chicago, 1970.
Phil 3486.9.6B Ewing, Alfred Cyril. A short commentary on Kant's critique
               of pure reason. Chicago, 1970.
Phil 3486.10   Ehrlich, W. Kant und Husserl. Halle, 1923.
Phil 3486.10.5 Ehrlich, W. Der Freiheitsbegriff bei Kant und
               Schopenhauer. Berlin, 1920.
Phil 3486.11   Elsenhans, Theodor. Kants Rassentheorie und ihre bleibende
               Bedeutung. Leipzig, 1904.
Phil 3486.12   Edfeldt, Hans. Kants lära un det moraliskt onda.
               Upsala, 1878.
Phil 3486.13   England, Frederick E. Kant's conception of God.
               London, 1929.
Phil 3486.14   Eisler, Rudolf. Kant-Lexikon. Berlin, 1930.
Phil 3486.14.10 Eisler, Rudolf. Die Weiterbildung der Kant'schen
               Apriorïtatslehre bis zur Gegenwart. Inaug. Diss.
               Leipzig, 1895.
Phil 3486.15   Ewald, J.L. Über die Kantische Philosophie. Berlin, 1790.
Phil 3486.16   Eck, Samuel. Aus den grossen Tagen der deutschen
               Philosophie. Tübingen, 1901.
Phil 3486.18.2 Eberhard, John. Philosophisches Archiv. Bruxelles, 1968.
               2v.
Phil 3487.1   Fischer, Kuno. Kritik der Kantischen Philosophie.
               München, 1883.
Phil 3487.1.2 Fischer, Kuno. Kritik der Kantischen Philosophie. 2. Aufl.
               Heidelberg, 1892.
Phil 3487.1.4 Fischer, Kuno. Geschichte der neuern Philosophie. 2. Aufl.
               Bd.3,4. Heidelberg, 1869. 2v.
Phil 3487.1.5 Fischer, Kuno. Commentary on Kant's Critick of pure
               reason. London, 1866.
Phil 3487.1.8 Fischer, Kuno. Kant's leben und die Grundlagen seiner
               Lehre. Heidelberg, 1906.
Phil 3487.1.10 Trendelenburg, A. Kuno Fischer und sein Kant.
               Leipzig, 1869.
Phil 3487.1.15 Fischer, Kuno. Die hundertjährige Gedächtnissfeier der
               Kantischen Kritik der reinen Vernunft. 2. Aufl.
               Heidelberg, 1892.
Phil 3487.2   Falckenberg, R. Gedächtnisrede auf Kant. Erlangen, 1904.
Phil 3487.3.2 Fouillée, Alfred. Le moralisme de Kant et l'amoralisme
               contemporain. 2. éd. Paris, 1905.
Phil 3487.3.3 Fouillée, Alfred. Le moralisme de Kant et l'amoralisme
               contemporain. Paris, 1921.
Phil 3487.4   Frohschammer, J. Ueber die Bedeutung der Einbildungskraft.
               München, 1879.
Phil 3487.5   Fromm, E. Das Kantbildnis der grafen Keyserling.
               n.p., n.d.
Phil 3487.6   Feder, J.G.H. Ueber Raum und Caussalitat.
               Göttingen, 1787.
Phil 3487.7   Feder, Ernst. Von G.E. Schulze zu A. Schopenhauer. Diss.
               Aarau, 1901.
Phil 3487.8   Freytag, Willy. Über den Kantischen Idealismus.
               Leipzig, 1924.
Phil 3487.9   Frederichs, F. Ueber Kant's Princip der Ethik.
               Berlin, 1875.
Phil 3487.10   Färber, Max. Die Kantische Freiheitslehre. Berlin, 1921.
Phil 3487.11   Fricker, K.V. Kants Rechtsphilosophie. Lipsiae, 1885.
Phil 3487.12   Frost, Walter. Der Begriff der Urteilskraft bei Kant.
               Halle, 1906.
Phil 3487.13   Falkenheim, H. Die Entstehung der Kantischen Ästhetik.
               Diss. Berlin, 1890.
Phil 3487.14   Flatt, Johann F. Briefe über den moralischen
               Erkenntnisgrund der Religion überhaupt. Tübingen, 1789.
Phil 3487.15   Fröhlich, G. Immanuel Kant. Langensalza, 1890.
Phil 3487.16   Frauenstädt, J. Immanuel Kant. Leipzig, 1872.
Phil 3487.17   Freudenthal, Jacob. Immanuel Kant. Breslau, 1904.
Phil 3487.18   Flügge, C.W. Versuch einer historisch-kritischen
               Darstellung. Hannover, 1796-98. 2v.
Phil 3487.20   Fuentes Mares, J. Kant y la evolución de la conciencia
               socio-política moderna. México, 1946.
Phil 3487.25   Frankfurt Universität. Kant und die Wissenschaften.
               Frankfurt, 1955.
Phil 3487.26   Fang, Joong. Das Antinomenproblem im Entstehungsgang der
               Transzendentalphilosophie. Münster, 1957.
Phil 3487.27   Fang, Joong. Kant - Interpretationen. Münster, 1967-
Phil 3487.28   Falaturi, Abdal-Jawad. Zur Interpretation der Kantischen
               Ethik im Lichte der Achtung. Inaug. Diss. Bonn, 1965.
Phil 3487.29   Fazio-Allmayer, Bruna. L'uomo nella storia in Kant.
               Bologna, 1968.
Phil 3487.30   Francke, Georg Samuel. Über die Eigenschaft der Analysis
               und der analytis 'hen Methode in der Philosophie.
               Bruxelles, 1968.
Phil 3487.32   Falkenfeld, Hellmuth. Was ist uns Kant? Weimar, 1924.
Phil 3488.3   Galli, Gallo. Kant e Rosmini. Citta di Castello, 1914.
Phil 3488.4   Goldschmidt, L. Zur Wiedererweckung Kantischer Lehre.
               Gotha, 1910.
Phil 3488.4.5 Goldschmidt, L. Kant und Helmholtz. Hamburg, 1898.
Phil 3488.4.10 Goldschmidt, L. Kant Kritik oder Kantstudium?
               Gotha, 1901.
Phil 3488.4.15 Goldschmidt, L. Kant über Freiheit. Gotha, 1904.
Phil 3488.4.20 Goldschmidt, L. Kant's "Privatmeinungen" über das
               Jenseits. Gotha, 1905.
Phil 3488.4.25 Goldschmidt, L. Kant und Haeckel. Gotha, 1906.
Phil 3488.4.30 Goldschmidt, L. Weder Kant noch Goethe. Gotha, 1920.
Phil 3488.5   Gross, Felix. Kant und Wir. Heidelberg, 1913.
Phil 3488.6   Goldfriedrich, J.A. Kants Ästhetik. Leipzig, 1895.
Phil 3488.7   Goujon, H. Kant et Kantistes. Lille, 1901.
Phil 3488.7.23 Gallovich, J. Kant criticismusa az Isten létéröl. Inaug.
               Diss. Eger, 1887.
Phil 3488.8   Gerland, G. Immanuel Kant, seine geographischen und
               anthropologischen Arbeiten. Berlin, 1906.
Phil 3488.9   Gizycki, G. von. Kant und Schopenhauer. Leipzig, 1888.
Phil 3488.10   Gisevius, H. Kant's Lehre von Raum und Zeit.
               Hannover, 1890.
Phil 3488.11   Gerhard, Carl. Kant's Lehre von der Freiheit.
               Heidelberg, 1885.
Phil 3488.12   Gneisse, Karl. Das sittliche Handeln nach Kants Ethik.
               Colmar, 1895.

Phil 3482 - 3507   History of philosophy - Local Modern philosophy - Germany -
Individual philosophers - Kant, Immanuel - Biography and criticism -
Monographs (A-Z) - cont.

Phil 3488.13   Goretti, Cesare. Il carattere formale della filosofia
               giuridica Kantiana. Milano, 1922.
Phil 3488.14   Görland, A. Aristoteles und Kant bezüglich der idee der
               theoretischen Erkenntnis. Giessen, 1909.
Phil 3488.15   Gemelli, A. Immanuel Kant, 1724-1924. Milano, 1924.
Phil 3488.16   Garbeis, F.W. Das Problem des Bewusstseins in der
               Philosophie Kants. Wien, 1924.
Phil 3488.17   Guzzo, Augusto. Kant precritico. Torino, 1924.
Phil 3488.18   Grapengiesser, C. Kants Lehre von Raum und Zeit, Kuno
               Fischer und Adolf Trendelenburg. Jena, 1870.
Phil 3488.18.5 Grapengiesser, C. Erklärung und Vertheidigung von Kant's
               Kritik der reinen Vernueft wider die "sogenannten"
               Erläuterungen des J.H.v. Kirchmann. Jena, 1871.
Phil 3488.19   Grabowsky, N. Kants Grundirrtümer in seiner Kritik der
               reinen Vernunft, und die Reformation des geistigen
               Innenlebens der Menschheit. Leipzig, 1907.
Phil 3488.20   Goess, G.F.D. Ueber die Critik der reinen Vernunft.
               Erlangen, 1793.
Phil 3488.20.5 Goess, G.F.D. Systematische Darstellung der Kantischen
               Vernunftkritik zum gebrauch akademischer Vorlesungen.
               Nürnberg, 1794.
Phil 3488.21   Gertanner, Christoph. Ueber das Kantische Prinzip für die
               Naturgeschichte. Göttingen, 1796.
Phil 3488.22   Gartelmann, Henri. Sturz der Metaphysik als Wissenschaft.
               Berlin, 1893.
Phil 3488.24   Gračanin, G. La personnalité morale d'après Kant. Thèse.
               Paris, 1929.
Phil 3488.26   Goldmann, L. Mensch, Gemeinschaft und Welt in der
               Philosophie Immanuel Kants. Zürich, 1945.
Phil 3488.26.1 Goldmann, L. Immanuel Kant. London, 1971.
Phil 3488.26.5 Goldmann, L. La communauté humaine et l'univers chez Kant.
               Paris, 1948.
Phil 3488.27   Groyeff, F. Deutung und Darstellung der theoretischen
               Philosophie Kants. Hamburg, 1951.
Phil 3488.28   Giorgiantonio, M. Kant e la critica del nostro tiempo.
               Napoli, 1953.
Phil 3488.30   González Vicén, J. La filosofía del estado en Kant.
               Laguna, 1952.
Phil 3488.32   Glasenapp, H. von. Kant und die Religionen des Ostens.
               Kitzmingen, 1954.
Phil 3488.34   Gablentz, Otto Heinrich von der. Kants politische
               Philosophie und die Weltpolitik unserer Tage.
               Berlin, 1956.
Phil 3488.36   Goessl, Max. Untersuchungen zum Verhältnis von Recht und
               Sittlichkeit. München, 1941.
Phil 3488.38   Grigor'ian, B.T. Neokantianstvo. Moskva, 1962.
Phil 3488.39   Gregor, Mary J. Laws of freedom. N.Y., 1963.
Phil 3488.40   Gaos, José. Las críticas de Kant. Caracas, 1962.
Phil 3488.41   Gerresheim, E. Die Bedeutung des Terminus transzendental
               in Immanuel Kants Kritik der reinen Vernunft. Inaug. Diss.
               Köln, 1962.
Phil 3488.42   Garnett, Christopher Broune. The Kantian philosophy of
               space. Port Washington, N.Y., 1965.
Phil 3488.43   Gersch, Walter. Der transzendentale Existenzbeweis in
               Kants Kritischer Metaphysik der ausserbewussten
               Wirklichkeit. Würzburg, 1938.
Phil 3488.44   Gram, Moltke S. Kant: disputed questions. Chicago, 1967.
Phil 3488.47   Gattulo, Mario. Categoria e oggetto in Kant. 1. ed.
               Firenze, 1966.
Phil 3488.48   Grohmann, Johann Christian August. Dem Andenken Kants.
               Berlin 1804. Bruxelles, 1969.
Phil 3488.50   Granel, Gérard. L'équivoque ontologique de la pensée
               Kantienne. Paris, 1970.
Phil 3489.1   Hausius, K.G. Materialen zur Geschichte der critischen
               Philosophie. Leipzig, 1793. 2v.
Phil 3489.3   Hegler, A. Die Psychologie in Kant's Ethik.
               Freiburg, 1891.
Phil 3489.4   Heydenreich, C.H. Originalität über die kritische
               Philosophie. Leipzig, 1793.
Phil 3489.5   Hölder, Alfred. Darstellung der Kantischen
               Erkenntnisstheorie. Tübingen, 1873.
Phil 3489.6   Hoffmann, A. Immanuel Kant. Halle, 1902.
Phil 3489.7   Hauck, P. Urteile und Kategorien; eine Studie zu Kants
               Logik. Strassburg, 1903.
Phil 3489.8   Harris, John, of Montreal. Review of Kant's Critique of
               pure reason. Supplement to Theology and science of
               goverment. Montreal, 1874.
Phil 3489.9   Herrmann, C.G. Kant und Hemsterhuis in Rüksicht ihrer
               definitionen der Schönheit. Erfurt, 1791.
Phil 3489.10   Heinze, Max. Vorlesungen Kants über Metaphysik aus drei
               Semestern. Leipzig, 1894.
Phil 3489.11   Hägerström, Axel. Kants Ethik...dargestellt.
               Upsala, 1902.
Phil 3489.12   Hansen, Oscar. Undersøgelser verdrørende grundlaget for
               Kants erkendelsesteori. København, 1892.
Phil 3489.13   Hofmann, Paul. Kant's Lehre vom Schlusse. Inaug. Diss.
               Berlin, 1901.
Phil 3489.14   Hoar, Robert. Der angebliche Mysticismus Kants.
               Brugg, 1895.
Phil 3489.15   Huch, Lilly. Der Begriff Wissenschaft im Kantischen Sinne.
               Berlin, 1917.
Phil 3489.16   Höffding, H. Kontinuiteten i Kants filosofiske
               udviklingsgang. Kjøbenhavn, 1893.
Phil 3489.17   Hicks, G.D. Die Begriffe Phänomenon und Noumenon.
               Leipzig, 1897.
Phil 3489.18   Hochdorf, Max. Das Kantbuch. Berlin, 1924.
Phil 3489.19   Heller, Josef. Kants Persönlichkeit und Leben.
               Berlin, 1924.
Phil 3489.21   Heyse, Hans. Der Begriff der Ganzheit und die Kantische
               Philosophie. München, 1927.
Phil 3489.22   Hocking, William E. Immanuel Kant and international
               policies. Washington, D.C., 1924.
Phil 3489.23   Herrmann, Karl. Einführung in die neukantische
               Philosophie. Halle, 1927.
Phil 3489.24   Hirsch, Richard. Kant-Bibliothek. Wien, 1929.
Phil 3489.25   Heussner, A. Hilfs-Büchlein für Kant-Leser. v.1-2.
               Göttingen, 1921-22.
Phil 3489.25.3 Heussner, A. Kleines Kant-Wörterbuch. Göttingen, 1925.
Phil 3489.26   Hasse, J.G. Lezte aeusserungen Kant's von einem seiner
               Tischgenossen. Königsberg, 1804.
Phil 3489.27   Heidegger, Martin. Kant und das Problem der Metaphysik.
               Bonn, 1929.
Phil 3489.27.2 Heidegger, Martin. Kant und das Problem der Metaphysik. 2.
               Aufl. Frankfurt, 1951.

Phil 3482 - 3507 History of philosophy - Local Modern philosophy - Germany - Individual philosophers - Kant, Immanuel - Biography and criticism - Monographs (A-Z) - cont.

Phil 3489.27.10 Heidegger, Martin. Kant and the problem of metaphysics. Bloomington, 1962.
Phil 3489.27.15 Heidegger, Martin. Die Frage nach dem Ding. Tübingen, 1962.
Phil 3489.27.20 Heidegger, Martin. What is a thing? Chicago, 1968.
Phil 3489.28 Hacks, Jakob. Über Kant's synthetische Urteile a priori. Pt.1-4. Kattowitz, 1895-99.
Phil 3489.29 Heynig, J.G. Herausfoderung an Professor Kant in Königsberg. Leipzig, 1798.
Phil 3489.29.10 Heynig, J.G. Berichtigung der Urtheile des Publikums über Kant und seine Philosophie. Cölln, 1797.
Phil 3489.30 Harnack, Adolf von. Immanuel Kant, 1724-1924. Berlin, 1924.
Phil 3489.31 Hoppe, V. Dva základní problémy Kantova kriticismu. Brno, 1932.
Phil 3489.32 Herbart, J.F. Immanuel Kants Gedächtnissfeyer zu Königsberg am 22stem April 1812. Königsberg, 1811.
Phil 3489.33 Herbart, J.F. Haupt-Momente der kritischen Philosophie. Münster, 1883.
Phil 3489.34 Havet, Jacques. Kant et le problème du temps. Paris, 1946.
Phil 3489.36 Hendel, C.W. The philosophy of Kant and our modern world. N.Y., 1957.
Phil 3489.38 Henrich, Adolf. Kant's Deduktion der reinen Verstandesbegriffe. Emmerich, 1885.
Phil 3489.40 Hermann, Horst. Das Problem der objektiven Realität bei Kant. Mainz, 1961.
Phil 3489.42 Hofman, Franz. Kants erst Antinomie in ihrer Stellung als Indirekter. Mainz? 1961.
Phil 3489.43 Heimsoeth, Heinz. Transzendentale Dialektik. Ein Kommentar zu Kants Kritik der reinen Vernunft. Berlin, 1966- 4v.
Phil 3489.44 Heinz, Rudolf. Französische Kantinterpreten im 20. Jahrhundert. Bonn, 1966.
Phil 3489.45 Hartnack, Justus. Kant's theory of knowledge. N.Y., 1967.
Phil 3489.47 Hinske, Norbert. Kants Begriff des Transzendentalen. Pt.1. Stuttgart, 1970.
Phil 3489.48 Hermann, István. Kant teleológiájà. Budapest, 1968.
Phil 3489.50 Holzhey, Helmut. Kants Erfahrungsbegriff. Basel, 1970.
Phil 3489.52 Holst, Johann Ludolf. Über das Fundament der gesammten Philosophie des Herrn Kant. Halle, 1791. Bruxelles, 1968.
Phil 3491.1 Jonquière, Georg. Die grundsätzliche Unanehmbarkeit. Bern, 1917.
Phil 3491.2 Johansson, J. Kants eticka asikt. Lund, 1902.
Phil 3491.3 Jonson, Erik. Det kategoriska imperativet. Akademisk avhandling. Uppsala, 1924.
Phil 3491.4 Jackmann, R.B. Immanuel Kant. Königsberg, 1804.
Phil 3491.5 Jansen, B. Der Kritizismus Kants. München, 1925.
Phil 3491.5.15 Jansen, B. La philosophie religieuse de Kant. Paris, 1934.
Phil 3491.6 Jenisch, D. Über Grundlugen und Werth der Entdeckungen des Herrn Professor Kant. Berlin, 1796.
Phil 3491.7 Jahn, Max. Der Einfluss der Kantischen Psychologie auf die Pädagogik als Wissenschaft. Leipzig, 1885.
Phil 3491.8 Jünemann, Franz. Kantiana. Leipzig, 1909.
Phil 3491.9 Jacobson, Julius. Ueber die Auffindung des Apriori. Berlin, 1876.
Phil 3491.10 Jones, W.T. Morality and freedom in...Kant. London, 1940.
Phil 3491.12 Julia, Didier. La question de l'homne et la fondement de la philosophie. Aubier, 1964.
Phil 3491.14 Jacobs, Wilhelm Gustav. Trieb als sittliches Phänomen. Bonn, 1967.
Phil 3491.16 Jansohn, Heinz. Kants Lehre von der Subjektivität. Bonn, 1969.
Phil 3491.18 Juchem, Hans Georg. Die Entwicklung des Begriffs des Schönen bei Kant, unter besonderer Berücksichtigung des Begriffs verworrenen Erkenntnis. Bonn, 1970.
Phil 3491.20 Jones, Hardy E. Kant's principle of personality. Madison, 1971.
Phil 3492.1 Kirchmann, J. Erläuterungen zu Kant's Kritik. Berlin, 1869-73. 7 pam.
Phil 3492.1.5 Kirchmann, J. Erläuterungen zu Kant's kleinern Schriften. Berlin, 1873.
Phil 3492.2A Krause, A. Kant und Helmholtz. Lahr, 1878.
Phil 3492.2B Krause, A. Kant und Helmholtz. Lahr, 1878.
Phil 3492.2.5 Krause, A. Immanuel Kant wider Kuno Fischer. Lahr, 1884.
Phil 3492.2.10 Krause, A. Die letzten Gendanken Immanuel Kants. Hamburg, 1902.
Phil 3492.2.15 Krause, A. Populäre Darstellung von Immanuel Kant's Kritik der reinen Vernunft. Lahr, 1881.
Phil 3492.2.17 Krause, A. Populäre Darstellung von Immanuel Kant's Kritik der reinen Vernunft. 2. Aufl. Hamburg, 1911.
Phil 3492.2.55 Vold, John M. Albrecht Krause's Darstellung der Kantischen Raumtheorie und der Kantischen Lehre. Cristiania, 1885.
Phil 3492.3 Küpffer, C. Der Schädel Immanuel Kant's. Braunschweig, 1881?
Phil 3492.4 Kroeger, A.E. Immanuel Kant. New Haven, 1872.
Phil 3492.5 Kaftan, J. Rede...Jubiläums...Königreichs Preussen 18 Januar 1901. Berlin, 1901.
Phil 3492.6 Kuberka, F. Kant's Lehre von der Sinnlichkeit. Halle, 1905.
Phil 3492.7 Külpe, O. Immanuel Kant. Leipzig, 1907.
Phil 3492.8 König, E. Kant und die Naturwissenschaft. Braunschweig, 1907.
Phil 3492.9 Koppelmann, W. Die Ethic Kants. Berlin, 1907.
Phil 3492.10 Kalich, Karl. Cantii, Schellingii, Fichtii de filio divino sententiam. Diss. Lipsiae, 1870.
Phil 3492.12A Kelly, Michael. Kants philosophy as rectified by Schopenhauer. London, 1909.
Phil 3492.12B Kelly, Michael. Kants philosophy as rectified by Schopenhauer. London, 1909.
Phil 3492.12.5 Kelly, Michael. Kant's ethics and Schopenhauer's criticism. London, 1910.
Phil 3492.13 Kronenberg, M. Kant; sein Leben und sein Lehre. 5. Aufl. München, 1918.
Phil 3492.13.2 Kronenberg, M. Kant. 2. Aufl. München, 1904.
Phil 3492.13.3 Kronenberg, M. Kant. München, 1897.
Phil 3492.13.5 Kronenberg, M. Kant. 4. Aufl. München, 1910.
Phil 3492.13.6 Kronenberg, M. Kant; sein Leben und sein Lehre. 6. Aufl. München, 1922.
Phil 3492.14 Kinker, Johannes. Le dualisme de la raison humaine; ou, Le criticisme de E. Kant. Amsterdam, 1850-52. 2v.
Phil 3492.15 Kesseler, Kurt. Kant und Schiller. Bunzlau, 1910.
Phil 3492.15.5 Kesseler, Kurt. Die lösung der widersprüche des Dasiens. Bunzlau, 1909.
Phil 3492.16 Katzer, Ernst. Luther und Kant. Giessan, 1910.

Phil 3482 - 3507 History of philosophy - Local Modern philosophy - Germany - Individual philosophers - Kant, Immanuel - Biography and criticism - Monographs (A-Z) - cont.

Phil 3492.17 Kératry, A.H. de. Examen philosophique des Considérations sur le sentiment du sublime et du beau. Paris, 1823.
Phil 3492.18 Kroner, Richard. Kants Weltanschauung. Tübingen, 1914.
Phil 3492.18.5 Kroner, Richard. Kant's Weltanschauung. Chicago, 1956.
Phil 3492.19 Kühnemann, E. Kant. München, 1923-24. 2v.
Phil 3492.20 Kellermann, B. Das Ideal im System der Kantischen Philosophie. Berlin, 1920.
Phil 3492.21 Königsberg. Universität. Immanuel Kant. Leipzig, 1924.
Phil 3492.22 Klinberg, A.G. Kants kritik af heibnizianismen. Upsala, 1869.
Phil 3492.23 Kessler, A. Kants ansicht von der Grundlage der Empfindung. Darmstadt, 1903.
Phil 3492.24 Köster, Adolph. Der Junge Kant. Berlin, 1914.
Phil 3492.25 Keeling, S.V. La nature de l'expérience chez Kant et chez Bradley. Thèse. Montpellier, 1925.
Phil 3492.26 Kries, J. von. Immanuel Kant und seine Bedeutung für die Naturforschung der Gegenwart. Berlin, 1924.
Phil 3492.27 Kremer, Josef. Vorwärts zu Kant! Erfurt, 1924.
Phil 3492.27.5 Kremer, Josef. Kritik der Vernunftkritik. Erfurt, 1925.
Phil 3492.28 Kutter, Hermann. Im Anfang war die Tat: Versuch einer Orientierung in der Philosophie Kants. Basel, 1924.
Phil 3492.29 Kinkel, Walter. Kant zum Gedächtnis. Osterwieck, 1924.
Phil 3492.30 Kolb, Victor. Immanuel Kant: der modernen Zeit. 2. Aufl. Wien, 1919.
Phil 3492.31 Kynast, R. Kant: sein System als Theorie des Kulturbewusstseins. München, 1928.
Phil 3492.32 Kügelgen, C.W. von. Die Bibel bei Kant. Leipzig, 1904.
Phil 3492.32.5 Kügelgen, C.W. von. Immanuel Kant Auffassung von der Bibel und seine Auslegung derselben. Leipzig, 1896.
Phil 3492.33 Kunhardt, H. I. Kants Grundlegung zur Metaphysik der Sitten. Lübeck, 1800.
Phil 3492.34 Kiesewetter, J.G.K.C. Versuch einer...Darstellung der wichtigsten Wahrheiten der neuern Philosophie. Berlin, 1795.
Phil 3492.34.2 Kiesewetter, J.G.K.C. Versuch einer...Darstellung der wichtigsten Wahrheiten der kritischen Philosophie. Berlin, 1803. 2v.
Phil 3492.34.4 Kiesewetter, J.G.K.C. Darstellung der wichtigsten Wahrheiten der kritischen Philosophie. Berlin, 1824.
Phil 3492.34.15 Kiesewetter, J.G.K.C. Gedrängter Auszug aus Kants Kritik der reinen Vernunft. Berlin, 1795.
Phil 3492.35 Kress, Rudolf. Die soziologischen Gedanken Kants in Zusammenhang seiner Philosophie. Berlin, 1929.
Phil 3492.36 Köhler, W. Kant. Berlin, 1913.
Phil 3492.37 Krüger, Gerhard. Philosophie und Moral in der Kantischen Kritik. Tübingen, 1931.
Phil 3492.38 Kleuker, Johann. De libertate morali ex ratione Kantiana. Osnabrugi, 1789.
Phil 3492.39.5 Kuhrke, Walter. Kants Wohnhaus. 2. Aufl. Königsberg, 1924.
Phil 3492.40.2 Knox, Israel. The aesthetic theories of Kant. N.Y., 1958.
Phil 3492.41 Königsberg Universität. Zur Erinnerung an Immanuel Kant. Halle, 1904.
Phil 3492.42.5 Klinke, Willibald. Kant for everyman. N.y., 1962.
Phil 3492.43 Koenig, Ernst. Arzt und Ärztliches bei Kant. Kitzingen, 1954.
Phil 3492.44 Körner, Stephan. Kant. Harmondsworth, 1955.
Phil 3492.44.5 Koerner, Stephan. Kant. Harmondsworth, 1960.
Phil 3492.45 Kayser, Rudolf. Kant. Wien, 1935.
Phil 3492.50 Küpenberg, Max. Ethische Grundfragen...Ethikvorselung Kants. Innsbruck, 1925.
Phil 3492.50.5 Küpenberg, Max. Der Begriff der Pflicht in Kants vorkritischen Schriften. Innsbruck, 1927.
Phil 3492.55 Karapetian, H.A. Kriticheskii analiz filosofii Kanta. Erevan, 1958.
Phil 3492.65 Kaczmaeck, S. Początki Kantyzmu. Poznań, 1961.
Phil 3492.70 Kühnemann, Eugen. Kants und Schillers Begründung der Ästhetik. München, 1895.
Phil 3492.70.2 Kühnemann, Eugen. Kants und Schillers Begründung der Ästhetik. Marburg, 1895.
Phil 3492.75 Kern, Iso. Husserl und Kant. Den Haag, 1964.
Phil 3492.76 Kuypers, Karel. Immanuel Kant. Baarn, 1966.
Phil 3493.1 Laas, E. Kants Analogien der Erfahrung. Berlin, 1876.
Phil 3493.1.5 Laas, E. Kants Stellung in der Geschichte des Conflicts zwischen Glauben und Wissen. Berlin, 1882.
Phil 3493.2 Lorquet, N.H.A. Discussion des Antinomies Kantiennes. Paris, 1841.
Phil 3493.3 Lefkovits, M. Die Staatslehre auf Kantischer Grundlage. Bern, 1899.
Phil 3493.4 Lasswitz, K. Die Lehre Kants von der Idealität. Berlin, 1883.
Phil 3493.5 Levy, Heinrich. Kants Lehre vom Schematismus der reinen Verstandesbegriffe. Teil I. Halle, 1907.
Phil 3493.6 Liebmann, Otto. Kant und die Epigonen. Berlin, 1912.
Phil 3493.7 Larsson, Hans. Kants deduktion av kategorierna. 2. uppl. Lund, 1914.
Phil 3493.7.5 Larsson, Hans. Kants transscendentala deduktion af kategorierna. Lund, 1914.
Phil 3493.8 Last, E. Mehr Licht! Berlin, 1879.
Phil 3493.8.5 Last, E. Die realistische und die idealistische Weltanschauung entwickelt an Kants Idealität von Zeit und Raum. Leipzig, 1884.
Phil 3493.9 Lind, Paul von. Eine unsterbliche Entdeckung Kants. Leipzig, 1898.
Phil 3493.9.5 Lind, Paul von. Immanuel Kant und Alexander von Humboldt. Inaug. Diss. Erlangen, 1897.
Phil 3493.10 Lagerwall, A. Transscendentalfilosofiens problem och metod hos Kant. Göteborg, 1904.
Phil 3493.11 Landtman. Immanuel Kant. Stockholm, 1922.
Phil 3493.12 Ludwich, A. Zur Kantfeier der Albertina. Regimontii, 1889.
Phil 3493.13 Lamanna, E.P. Kant. Milano, 1926. 2v.
Phil 3493.13.5 Lamanna, E.P. Il fondamento morale...secondo Kant. Firenze, 1916.
Phil 3493.14 Lomber, Wilhelm. Die Gratistätte Immanuel Kants auf Grund authentischer Quellen dargestellt. Königsberg, 1924.
Phil 3493.14.5 Lomber, Wilhelm. Immanuel Kants letzte Lebensjahre und Tod. Königsberg, 1923.
Phil 3493.15 Lubnichi, Naum. Critique des eléments fondamentaux de la doctrine Kantienne. Paris, 1929.
Phil 3493.16 Litt, Theodor. Kant und Herder als Deuter der Geistigen Welt. Leipzig, 1930.
Phil 3493.16.5 Litt, Theodor. Kant und Herder als Deuter der Geistigen Welt. 2. Aufl. Heidelberg, 1949.
Phil 3493.17 Liebert, Arthur. Kants Ethik. Berlin, 1931.

Phil 3482 - 3507 History of philosophy - Local Modern philosophy - Germany - Individual philosophers - Kant, Immanuel - Biography and criticism - Monographs (A-Z) - cont.

Phil 3493.18 Lewan, Axel. Kring Kants "Tugendlehre". Lund, 1930.
Phil 3493.19 Laupichler, Max. Die Grundzüge der materialen Ethik Kants. Berlin, 1931.
Phil 3493.20 Lachièze-Rey, P. L'idéalisme Kantien. Thèse. Paris, 1931.
Phil 3493.20.5 Lachièze-Rey, P. L'idéalisme Kantien. Thèse. 2. éd. Paris, 1950.
Phil 3493.21 Lindsay, A.D. Kant. London, 1934.
Phil 3493.22 Lehmann, Otto. Über Kant's Principien der Ethik und Schopenhauer's Beurteilung derselben. Greifswald, 1880.
Phil 3493.23 Lembke, B. Immanuel Kants Geld-Theorie. Danzig, 1933.
Phil 3493.24 Lazzarini, Renato. Dalla religione naturale prekantiani alla religione morale di Kant. Roma, 1942.
Phil 3493.25 Leni di Spadafora, F. Kant nel realismo. Paris, 1953.
Phil 3493.26 Letocart, M. La morale Kantienne. Bruxelles, 1954.
Phil 3493.27 Lotz, J.B. Kant und die Scholastik Heute. Pullach, 1955.
Phil 3493.29 Lumia, Giuseppe. La dottrina Kantiana del diritto e dello stato. Milano, 1960.
Phil 3493.30 Luperini, Cesuce. Spazio e materia in Kant. Firenze, 1961.
Phil 3493.32 Löwisch, Dieter-Jürgen. Immanuel Kant und David Hume's, dialogues concerning natural religion. Bonn, 1964.
Phil 3493.33 Loegstrup, Kocud Ejler Christian. Kants aestetik. København, 1965.
Phil 3493.35 Liedtke, Max. Der Begriff der reflektierenden Urteilskraft in Kants Kritik der reinen Vernunft. Hamburg, 1964.
Phil 3493.38 Lugarini, Leo. La logica trascendentale Kantiana. Milano, 1950.
Phil 3493.40 Lacorte, Carmelo. Kant. Ancora un episodio dell' allanza di religione e filosofia. Urbino, 1969.
Phil 3493.42 Lauener, Henri. Hume und Kant. Bern, 1969.
Phil 3493.44.3 Lacroix, Jean. Kant et le Kantisme. 3. éd. Paris, 1969.
Phil 3493.46 Lamacchio, Ada. La filosofia della religione in Kant. Mandeiria, 1969-
Phil 3493.48 Lauter, Josef. Untersuchungen zur Sprache von Kants Kritik der reinen Vernunft. Köln, 1966.
Phil 3493.50 Loegstrup, Knud Ejler Christian. Kants Kritik af erkendelsen og refleksionen. København, 1970.
Phil 3493.52 Lebrun, Gérard. Kant et la mort de la métaphysique. Paris, 1970.
Phil 3493.54 Lehmann, Gerhard. Beiträge zur Geschichte und Interpretation der Philosophie Kants. Berlin, 1969.
Phil 3494.1 Mahaffy, J.P. Kant's critical philosophy. v.1,3. London, 1872. 2v.
Phil 3494.2 Marquardt, A. Kant und Crusius. Kiel, 1885.
Phil 3494.3 Maurial, E. Le scepticisme...Scepticisme de Kant. Montpellier, 1856.
Phil 3494.3.2 Maurial, E. Le scepticisme...Scepticisme de Kant. Supplément. Paris, 1857.
Phil 3494.4 Michelis, F. Kant vor und nach dem Jahre 1770. Braunsberg, 1871.
Phil 3494.5 Mirbt, E.S. Kant und seine Nachfolger. Jena, 1841.
Phil 3494.5.5 Mirbt, E.S. Kant's Philosophie. Jena, 1851.
Phil 3494.6 Monck, W.H.S. Introduction to the critical philosophy. Dublin, 1874.
Phil 3494.7 Montgomery, E. Die Kant'sche Erkenntnisslehre. München, 1871.
Phil 3494.8 Morris, G.S. Kant's Critique of pure reason. Chicago, 1882.
Phil 3494.9 Merren, R. Über der Bedeutung v. Leibniz...für Kant. Leipzig, 1908.
Phil 3494.10 Macmillan, R.A.C. Crowning phase of critical philosophy...Kant. London, 1912.
Phil 3494.11.5 Miller, E.M. Moral action and natural law in Kant. Melbourne, 1911.
Phil 3494.11.10 Miller, E.M. The basis of freedom: a study of Kant's theory. Sydney, 1924.
Phil 3494.11.15A Miller, E.M. Moral law and the highest good; a study of Kant's doctrine. Melbourne, 1928.
Phil 3494.11.15B Miller, E.M. Moral law and the highest good; a study of Kant's doctrine. Melbourne, 1928.
Phil 3494.12 Monzel, Alois. Die historischen Voraussetzungen,...der Kantischen Lehre. Bonn, 1912.
Phil 3494.12.10 Monzel, Alois. Die Lehre vom inneren Sinn bei Kant. Bonn, 1913.
Phil 3494.13 Messer, A. Kant's Ethik. Leipzig, 1904.
Phil 3494.13.5 Messer, A. Immanuel Kants Leben und Philosophie. Stuttgart, 1924.
Phil 3494.13.15 Messer, A. Kommentar zu Kants Kritik der reinen Vernunft. Stuttgart, 1923.
Phil 3494.13.20 Messer, A. Kommentar zu Kants ethischen und religionsphilosophischen Hauptschriften. Leipzig, 1929.
Phil 3494.14 Major, David R. The principle of teology. Ithaca, N.Y., 1897.
Phil 3494.15* Mellin, G.S.A. Marginalien und Register zu Kants Kritik der Erkentnissvermögen. Züllichau, 1794.
Phil 3494.15.3 Mellin, G.S.A. Marginalien und Register zu Kants Kritik der Erkenntnisvermögen. Pt. 1-2. Gotha, 1900-02.
Phil 3494.15.10 Mellin, G.S.A. Marginalien und Register zu Kants metaphysichen Anfangsgründen der Sittenlehre. Pt.1-2. Jena, 1801[1800]
Phil 3494.16 Morente, M.G. La filosofía de Kant. Madrid, 1917.
Phil 3494.16.5 Morente, M.G. La estética de Kant. Thesis. Madrid, 1912.
Phil 3494.17 Marck, S. Kant und Hegel. Tübingen, 1917.
Phil 3494.18 Menzer, Paul. Kants Lehre von der Entwicklung in Natur und Geschichte. Berlin, 1911.
Phil 3494.19.2 Marcus, Ernst. Der kategorische Imperativ. München, 1921.
Phil 3494.19.5 Marcus, Ernst. Kants Weltgebäude. München, 1917.
Phil 3494.19.6 Marcus, Ernst. Kants Weltgebäude. 2. Aufl. München, 1920.
Phil 3494.19.10 Marcus, Ernst. Die Zeit- und Raumlehre Kants. München, 1927.
Phil 3494.19.15 Marcus, Ernst. Logik. 2. Aufl. Herford, 1911.
Phil 3494.19.25 Marcus, Ernst. Die exakte Aufdeckung des Fundaments der Sittlichkeit und Religion...Kant. Leipzig, 1899.
Phil 3494.19.30 Marcus, Ernst. Kants Revolutionsprinzip (Kopernikanisches Prinzip). Herford, 1902.
Phil 3494.19.35 Marcus, Ernst. Aus den Tiefen der Erkennens...Kants. München, 1925.
Phil 3494.19.40 Marcus, Ernst. Die Bewersführung in der Kritik der reinen Vernunft. Essen, 1914.
Phil 3494.20 Meyer, Jürgen B. Kant's Psychologie. Berlin, 1870.
Phil 3494.21 Menzel, A. Kants Kritik der reinen Vernunft. Berlin, 1922.
Phil 3494.22 Manns, Richard. Die Stellung des Substanzbegriffes. Inaug. Diss. Bonn, 1887.

Phil 3482 - 3507 History of philosophy - Local Modern philosophy - Germany - Individual philosophers - Kant, Immanuel - Biography and criticism - Monographs (A-Z) - cont.

Phil 3494.23 Moog, Willy. Kants Ansichten über Krieg und Frieden. Leipzig, n.d.
Phil 3494.24 Meydenbauer, A. Kant oder Laplace? Marburg, 1880.
Phil 3494.25 Markull, G. Ueber Glauben und Wissen. Progr. Danzig, 1884.
Phil 3494.26 Myrho, F. Kritizismus: Eine Sammlung...Neu-Kantianismus. Berlin, 1926.
Phil 3494.27 Mamiani, T. Della psicologia di Kant. Roma, 1877.
Phil 3494.28 Miotti. Uiber die Falschheit und Gottlosigkeit des Kantischen System. Augsburg, 1802.
Phil 3494.28.5 Miotti. Uiber die Falschheit und Gottlosigkeit des Kantischen System. Wien, 1801.
Phil 3494.29 Michalsky, O. Kant's Kritik der reinen Vernunft und Herder's Metakritik. Diss. Breslau, 1883.
Phil 3494.31 Meissinger, K.A. Kant und die deutsche Aufgabe. Frankfurt, 1924.
Phil 3494.32 Mutschelle, S. Versuch einer solchen fasslichen Darstellung der Kantischen Philosophie. München, 1803. 2v.
Phil 3494.33 Metz, Andreas. Kurze und deutliche Darstellung des Kantischen Systemes. Bamberg, 1795.
Phil 3494.33.5 Metz, Andreas. Darstellung der Hauptimomente der Elementarlehre der Kantischen Kritik der reinen Vernunft. Pt. 1-2. Bamberg, 1802.
Phil 3494.34 Michaelis, C.F. Über die settliche Natur und Bestimmung des Menschen. v.1-2. Leipzig, 1796-97.
Phil 3494.35 Massonius, M. Ueber Kant's Transscendentale Aesthetik. Diss. Leipzig, 1890.
Phil 3494.36 Marchi, Vittore. La filosofia morale di Emmanuel Kant. Roma, 1931.
Phil 3494.37 Metzger, Wilhelm. Untersuchungen zur Sitten - und Rechtslehre Kants und Fichtes. Heidelberg, 1912.
Phil 3494.38 Marc-Wogau, K. Untersuchungen zur Raumlehre Kants. Inaug. Diss. Lund, 1932.
Phil 3494.39 Mortzfeldt, J.C. Fragmente aus Kants Leben. Königsberg, 1802.
Phil 3494.40 Marheinecke, P. De potiori vi quam ad commutandam. Erlangae, 1805.
Phil 3494.41 Munteano, B. Episodes Kantiens en Suisse et en France sous le Directoire. Paris, 1935.
Phil 3494.42 Maier, J. On Hegel's critique of Kant. N.Y., 1939.
Phil 3494.43 Mattern, C.D. Personal freedom within the third antimony. Thesis. Philadelphia, 1941.
Phil 3494.44 Massolo, Arturo. Introduzione alla analitica Kantiaña. Serie 2. Firenze, 1946.
Phil 3494.45 Martin, Gottfried. Immanuel Kant. Köln, 1951.
Phil 3494.45.4 Martin, Gottfried. Immanuel Kant. 4. Aufl. Berlin, 1969.
Phil 3494.45.5A Martin, Gottfried. Kant's metaphysics and theory of science. Manchester, Eng., 1955.
Phil 3494.45.5B Martin, Gottfried. Kant's metaphysics and theory of science. Manchester, Eng., 1955.
Phil 3494.45.10 Martin, Gottfried. Sachindex zu Kants Kritik der reinen Vernunft. Berlin, 1967.
Phil 3494.46 Maritz, M. Studien zum pflichtbegriff in Kants Kritischer Ethhik. Lund, 1951.
Phil 3494.47 Metzger, J.D. Aeusserungen über Kant. Königsberg, 1804.
Phil 3494.48 Mollowilz, Gerhard. Kants Platosuffassung. Berlin, 1935.
Phil 3494.50 Mueller, Johannes. Kantisches Staatsdenken und der Preussische Staat. Kitzingen, 1954.
Phil 3494.53A Miller, Oscar W. The Kantian thing-in-itself. N.Y., 1956.
Phil 3494.53B Miller, Oscar W. The Kantian thing-in-itself. N.Y., 1956.
Phil 3494.55 Marguard, Odo. Skeptische Methode im Blick auf Kant. Freiburg, 1958.
Phil 3494.58 Muralt, André. La conscience transcendentale. Paris, 1958.
Phil 3494.60 Meleschenko, Z.N. Neokantianstvo kak filosofskaia osnova revizionizma. Leningrad, 1960.
Phil 3494.61 Mathieu, V. La filosofia trascendentale. Torino, 1958.
Phil 3494.62 Milmed, Bella Kussy. Kant and current philosophical issues. N.Y., 1961.
Phil 3494.64 Mayz Vallenilla, Ernesto. El problema de la nada en Kant. Madrid, 1965.
Phil 3494.66.2 Miotti, Peter. Über die Nichtigkeit der Kantische Grundsätze in der Philosophie...Logik von Professor Kreil. Facsimile. Bruxelles, 1968.
Phil 3494.68 Moreau, Joseph. Le Dieu des philosophes. Paris, 1969.
Phil 3494.70.2 Mörchen, Hermann. Die Einbildungskraft bei Kant. 2. Aufl. Tübingen, 1970.
Phil 3494.72 Murphy, Jeffrie G. Kant: the philosophy of right. London, 1970.
Phil 3494.74 McFarland, John D. Kant's concept of teleology. Edinburgh, 1970.
Phil 3494.76 May, Joseph Austin. Kant's concept of geography and its relation to recent geographical thought. Toronto, 1970.
Htn Phil 3495.1* Nicolai, C.F. Über...kritischen Philosophie...Kant. Berlin, 1799.
Phil 3495.2 Nicolai, G.W. Ist der Begriff des Schönen bei Kant. Kiel, 1889.
Phil 3495.4 Nolen, D. Critique de Kant. Paris, 1875.
Phil 3495.5 Noiré, L. Die Lehre Kants...Vermorst. Mainz, 1882.
Phil 3495.6 Nelson, Leonard. Untersuchungen...Kantischen Erkenntnistheorie. Göttingen, 1909.
Phil 3495.6.5 Nelson, Leonard. Die kritische Ethik bei Kant, Schilles und Fries. Göttingen, 1914.
Phil 3495.7 Neumark, David. Die Freiheitslehre bei Kant. Hamburg, 1896.
Phil 3495.8 Noack, L. I. Kant's Auferstehung aus dem Grabe. Leipzig, 1861.
Phil 3495.8.5 Norelius, G. Om Kants sedelära. Upsala, 1889.
Phil 3495.9 Northwestern University. Evanston, Illinois. Immanuel Kant. Chicago, 1925.
Phil 3495.10 Natorp, Paul. Kant über Krieg und Frieden. Erlangen, 1924.
Phil 3495.10.10 Natorp, Paul. Kant und die Marburger Schule. Berlin, 1912.
Phil 3495.11 Neide, P.S. Die Kantische Lehre vom Schematismus der reinen Verstandesbegriffe. Diss. Halle, 1878.
Phil 3495.12 Nink, Casper. Kommentar zu Kants Kritik der reinen Vernunft. Frankfurt, 1930.
Phil 3495.13 Nehr, J.G. Kritik über die metaphysischen Aufangsgründe der Rechtslehre des I. Kant. Nürnberg, 1798.
Phil 3495.14.5 Neeb, Johann. Über Kant's Verdienste um das Interesse der philosophiren den Vernunft. 2. Aufl. Frankfurt, 1795.
Phil 3495.15 Nakashima, R. Kant's doctrine of the "thing-in-itself". New Haven, 1889.

Phil 3482 - 3507   History of philosophy - Local Modern philosophy - Germany -
Individual philosophers - Kant, Immanuel - Biography and criticism -
Monographs (A-Z) - cont.

Phil 3495.16   Nierkaus, F. Das Problem des psychophysischen Kommersiums
                in der Entwicklung der Kantischen Philosophie. Köln, 1962.
Phil 3495.17   Novák, Mirko. Kanův kriticismus a problém hodnoty. V
                Bratislave, 1936.
Phil 3495.18   Nieschmidt, Gerd Peter. Praktische Vernunft und Ewiger
                Friede. München, 1965.
Phil 3495.20.2 Negri, Antimo. La comunità estetica in Kant. 2. ed.
                Bari, 1968.
Phil 3496.1   Otto, R. Kantisch-Fries'sche Religionsphilosophie.
                Tübingen, 1909.
Phil 3496.2   Ortner, F. Kant in Österreich und Vincenz.
                Klagenfurt, 1904.
Phil 3496.3   Orestano, F. Der Tugendbegriff bei Kant. Inaug. Diss.
                Palermo, 1901.
Phil 3496.4   Obereit, J.H. Beobachtungen über die Quelle der
                Metaphysik. Meiningen, 1791.
Phil 3496.5   Odebrecht, Rudolf. Form und Geist. Berlin, 1930.
Phil 3496.6   Olivier, Paul. Zum Willinsproblem bei Kant und Reinhold.
                Berlin, 1941.
Phil 3497.2   Porter, N. Kant's ethics. Chicago, 1886.
Phil 3497.3A   Paulsen, Friedrich. Immanuel Kant. Stuttgart, 1898.
Phil 3497.3B   Paulsen, Friedrich. Immanuel Kant. Stuttgart, 1898.
Phil 3497.3.4.5 Paulsen, Friedrich. Immanuel Kant; his life and doctrine.
                N.Y., 1963.
Phil 3497.3.5   Paulsen, Friedrich. Immanuel Kant. 4. Aufl.
                Stuttgart, 1904.
Phil 3497.3.6   Paulsen, Friedrich. Immanuel Kant. 6. Aufl.
                Stuttgart, 1920.
Phil 3497.3.7   Paulsen, Friedrich. Kant. Milano, 1914.
Phil 3497.3.9   Paulsen, Friedrich. Kant der Philosophie des
                Protestantismus. Berlin, 1899.
Phil 3497.3.15 Paulsen, Friedrich. Versuch...Kantischen
                Erkenntnisstheorie. Leipzig, 1875.
Phil 3497.3.19 Paulsen, Friedrich. Kants Verhaltnis zur Metaphysik.
                Berlin, 1900.
Phil 3497.3.23 Paulsen, Friedrich. Was uns Kant sein kann?
                Leipzig, 1881.
Phil 3497.5   Prichard, H. Kant's theory of knowledge. Oxford, 1909.
Phil 3497.6   Piat, C. L'idée ou Critique du Kantisme. Paris, n.d.
Phil 3497.8   Pekelharing, C. Kant's Teleologie. Gröningen, 1916.
Phil 3497.9   Porten, M. von der. Die Grundlagen der Kantschen
                Philosophie. Leipzig, 1914.
Phil 3497.10   Pünjer, G.C. Die Religionslehre Kants. Jena, 1874.
Phil 3497.11   Petras, Otto. Der Begriff des Bösen in Kants Kritizismus.
                Leipzig, 1913.
Phil 3497.12   Palágyi, Melchiar. Kant und Bolzano. Halle, 1902.
Phil 3497.13   Pesch, T. Kant et la science moderne. Paris, 1894.
Phil 3497.13.6 Pesch, T. Le kantisme et ses erreurs. Paris, 1897.
Phil 3497.14   Poppovich, N.M. Die Entwicklungsgeschichte der
                vorkritischen Raumphilosophie Kants. Wien, 1925.
Phil 3497.15   Promnitz, C.F. Antischrift zur Vertheidigung der Vernunft
                und Religion. Berlin, 1796.
Phil 3497.16   Paul, Ludwig. Kant's Lehre vom Idealen Christus.
                Kiel, 1869.
Phil 3497.17   Pfleiderer, Edmund. Kantischer Kritizismus und englische
                Philosophie. Halle, 1881.
Phil 3497.18   Przywara, Erich. Kant Heute. München, 1930.
Phil 3497.19   Paton, Herbert J. Kant's metaphysic of experience.
                London, 1936. 2v.
Phil 3497.19.5 Paton, Herbert J. The categorical imperative.
                London, 1946.
Phil 3497.19.10 Paton, Herbert J. Kant on friendship. London, 1956.
Phil 3497.20   Panaev, I. Ras''iskateli istinyi: I. Kant. Sankt
                Peterburg, 1878.
Phil 3497.21   Popov, Sergei I. Kant i Kantianstvo. Moskva, 1961.
Phil 3497.22   Pascol, Georges. La pensée de Kant. 2. éd. Paris, 1957.
Phil 3497.23   Plaass, Peter. Kants Theorie der Naturwissenschaft.
                Göttingen, 1965.
Phil 3497.24   Philonenko, Alexis. Théorie et praxis dans la pensée
                morale et politique de Kant et de Fichte en 1793.
                Paris, 1968.
Phil 3497.25   Philonenko, Alexis. L'oeuvre de Kant. Paris, 1969-
Phil 3497.26   Pantaleo, Pasquale. La direzione coscienza-intenzione
                nella filosofia di Kant e Husserl. Bari, 1967.
Phil 3497.28   Papi, Fulvio. Cosmologia e civiltà. Urbino, 1969.
Phil 3497.30   Prauss, Gerold. Erscheinung bei Kant.
                Habilitationsschrift. Berlin, 1971.
Phil 3499.1   Immanuel Kant. Königsberg, 1882-87. 3 pam.
Phil 3499.1.5   Kant, Immanuel. Lose blätter aus Kants nach lass,
                Mitgetheit von Rudolf Reicke. Königsberg, 1889-98.
Phil 3499.2   Reinhold, K.L. Briefe über die Kantische Philosophie.
                Leipzig, 1790-92. 2v.
Phil 3499.2.3   Reinhold, K.L. Briefe über die Kantische Philosophie.
                Leipzig, 1924.
Phil 3499.2.5   Reinhold, K.L. Auswahl der besten Aufsätze über die
                Kantische Philosophie. Frankfurt, 1790.
Phil 3499.2.10 Reinhold, K.L. Uber die bisherigen Schicksale der
                Kantischen Philosophie. Jena, 1789.
Phil 3499.3   Riedel, O.J. Die monadologischen...Bestimmungen...Kant's.
                Hamburg, 1884.
Phil 3499.4   Rowland, D. Essay...unsolved ethical questions in Kant's.
                London, 1871.
Phil 3499.5   Ruyssen, T. Kant. Paris, 1900.
Phil 3499.5.5   Ruyssen, T. Quid de natura...senserit Kantius.
                Nemausi, 1903.
Phil 3499.6   Romundt, H. Kants philosophische Religionslehre.
                Gotha, 1902.
Phil 3499.6.5   Romundt, H. Die drei Fragen Kants. Berlin, 1887.
Phil 3499.6.9   Romundt, H. Ein neuer Paulus. Berlin, 1886.
Phil 3499.6.13 Romundt, H. Kants Kritik der reinen Vernunft Abgekürzt auf
                Grund ihrer Entstehungsgeschichte. Gotha, 1905.
Phil 3499.6.15 Romundt, H. Der Professorenkant. Gotha, 1906.
Phil 3499.6.18 Romundt, H. Antäus. Leipzig, 1882.
Phil 3499.6.20 Romundt, H. Grundlegung zur Reform der Philosophie.
                Berlin, 1885.
Phil 3499.7   Richter, Otto. Kants Auffassung des Verhaltnisses von
                Glaüben und Wissen. Lauban, 1905.
Phil 3499.8   Renouvier, C. Critique de la doctrine de Kant.
                Paris, 1906.
Phil 3499.9   Ruisch, Arnold. Freiheit Unstirblichkeit und Gott.
                Leipzig, 1919.
Phil 3499.10   Reininger, Robert. Kants Lehre vom Unneren sinn und seine
                Theorie der Erfahrung. Wein, 1900.
Phil 3499.10.5 Reininger, Robert. Kant, seine Anhänger und seine Gegner.
                München, 1923.

Phil 3482 - 3507   History of philosophy - Local Modern philosophy - Germany -
Individual philosophers - Kant, Immanuel - Biography and criticism -
Monographs (A-Z) - cont.

Phil 3499.10.10 Reininger, Robert. Kants kritischer Idealismus.
                Leipzig, 1912.
Phil 3499.11   Ruge, Arnold. Das Problem der Freiheit in Kants
                Erkenntnistheorie. Leipzig, 1910.
Phil 3499.12   Runze, Max. Kant's Bedeutung auf Grund der
                Entwicklungsgeschichte Seiner Philosophie. Berlin, 1881.
Phil 3499.12.5 Runze, Max. Kant's Kritikan Humes Skepticismus.
                Berlin, 1880.
Phil 3499.13   Rätze, J.G. Herder Gegen Kant. Leipzig, 1800.
Phil 3499.14   Rickert, H. Kant als Philosoph der Modernen.
                Tübingen, 1924.
Phil 3499.15   Remer, G.L. Kant's Theorie der reinmoralischen Religion.
                Rega, 1796.
Phil 3499.16   Roretz, Karl. Zur Analyse von Kants Philosoph des
                organischen. Wien, 1922.
Phil 3499.17   Reiche, L.P.A. De Kanti antinomüs. Thesis.
                Gottinage, 1838.
Phil 3499.18   Rauschenberger, W. Die Antinomien Kants. Berlin, 1923.
Phil 3499.19   Reichardt, W. Kant's Lehre vom den synthetischen
                Urtheilen...Mathematik. Leipzig, 1888.
Phil 3499.20   Roeder, E. De voce "a priori" in philosophia Kantii. Diss.
                Bonnae, 1866.
Phil 3499.21   Röver, G. Zur Lehre vom Raum...Lehre Kants.
                Oldenburg, 1923.
Phil 3499.23   Ratke, Heinrich. Systematisches Handlexikon zu Kants
                Kritik der reinen Vernunft. Leipzig, 1929.
Phil 3499.24   Roos, Andreas Praeses. Dissertatio philosophica de summo
                bono secundum decreta philosophiae criticae. Lundae, 1799.
Phil 3499.25   Reinhard, Walter. Über das Verhältnis von Sittlichkeit und
                Religion bei Kant. Bern, 1927.
Phil 3499.26   Rink, Friedrich T. Ansichten aus Immanuel Kant's Leben.
                Königsberg, 1805.
Phil 3499.26.5 Rink, Friedrich T. Mancherley zur Geschichte der
                metacritischen Invasion. Bruxelles, 1969.
Phil 3499.27   Rosikat, K.A. Kants Kritik der reinen Vernunft.
                Königsberg, 1901.
Phil 3499.28   Rüther, R. Kant und Antikant. Paderborn, 1921.
Phil 3499.29   Rasker, A.J. De ethick en het probleem van het booze.
                Proef. Assen, 1935.
Phil 3499.30   Renda, A. Conoscenza e moralita in Kant. Palermo, 1944.
Phil 3499.31   Rigobello, A. I limiti del trascendentale in Kant.
                Milano, 1963.
Phil 3499.32   Ross, H.D. Kant's ethical theory. Oxford, 1954.
Phil 3499.33   Reinig, Richard. Zur Kritik des Sowjetismus am Kritizismus
                Kants. Ratingen, 1964.
Phil 3499.34   Rotenstreich, Nathan. Experience and its systematization;
                studies in Kant. The Hague, 1965.
Phil 3499.36   Rousset, Bernard. La doctrine Kantienne de l'objectivité,
                l'autonomie comme devoir et devenir. Paris, 1967.
Phil 3499.40   Romano, Vincenzo. Kant; il problema della conoscenza.
                Napoli, 1965.
Phil 3499.42   Ruvo, Vincenzo de. Il pensiero filosofico di Kant, ovvero
                problemi di critica Kantiana. Paris, 1969.
Phil 3500.1   Saintes, A. Histoire de la vie et de la philosophie de
                Kant. Paris, 1844.
Phil 3500.2   Schaller, J. Darstellung Kantscher Philosophie.
                Halle, 1846.
Phil 3500.3   Scherer, G. Kritik über Kant's Subjektivität und
                Apriorität des Raumes und der Zeit. Frankfurt, 1871.
Phil 3500.4   Schmid, K.C.E. Wörterbuch zum leichtern Gebrauch der
                Kantischen Schriften. Jena, 1788.
Phil 3500.4.3   Schmid, K.C.E. Wörterbuch zum leichtern Gebrauch der
                Kantischen Schriften. 3. Ausg. Jena, 1795.
Phil 3500.4.5   Schmid, K.C.E. Critik der reinen Vernunft. Jena, 1784.
Phil 3500.5   Schmidt-Phiseldek, C. Criticae ratien. Purae expositio
                systematica. Hafniae, 1796.
Phil 3500.5.30 Schmidt-Phiseldek, C. Briefe ästhelischen Inhalts.
                Altona, 1797.
Phil 3500.6   Schneider, O. Die psychologische Entwickelung des
                Apriori...Kants Kritik der reinen Vernunft. Bonn, 1883.
Phil 3500.7   Schön, L.F. Philosophie transcendantale...Kant.
                Paris, 1831.
Phil 3500.8   Schurman, J.G. Kantian ethics. London, 1881.
Phil 3500.9   Spicker, G. Über das Verhältniss...Kantischen.
                Berlin, 1874.
Phil 3500.10   Stadler, A. Kant's Teleologie. Berlin, 1874.
Phil 3500.10.5 Stadler, A. Kant akademische Vorlesungen. Leipzig, 1912.
Phil 3500.10.10 Stadler, A. Kants Theorie der Materie. Leipzig, 1883.
Phil 3500.10.15 Stadler, A. Die Grundsätze der reinen Erkenntnisstheorie
                in der Kantischen Philosophie. Leipzig, 1876.
Phil 3500.12A   Stuelsenberg, J. Life of Immanuel Kant. London, 1882.
Phil 3500.12B   Stuelsenberg, J. Life of Immanuel Kant. London, 1882.
Phil 3500.13   Storr, D.G.C. Bemerkungen über Kant's Philosophie
                Religion. Tübingen, 1794.
Phil 3500.14   Schulze, J. Erläuterungen...Kant Critik der reinen
                Vernunft. Frankfurt, 1791.
Phil 3500.14.2 Schulze, J. Erläuterungen...K t Critik der reinen
                Vernunft. Königsberg, 1784.
Phil 3500.15   Schlaff, O. Kant's Lehre vom Genie. Göttingen, 1901.
Phil 3500.16   Schmidt, Karl. Beiträge zur Entwicklung der Kant'schen
                Ethik. Inaug. Diss. Marburg, 1900.
Phil 3500.16.5 Schmidt, Karl. Beiträge zur Entwicklung der Kant'schen
                Ethik. Inaug. Diss. Marburg, 1900.
Htn   Phil 3500.17*   Schwab, J.C. Vergleichung des Kantischen Moralprinzips.
                Berlin, 1800.
Htn   Phil 3500.17.10* Schwab, J.C. Neun Gespräche zwischen Christian Wolff.
                Berlin, 1798.
Phil 3500.17.15 Schwab, J.C. Bemerkungen ueber den Kantischen
                Begriff...metaphysischen Rechtslehre. Bruxelles, 1968.
Phil 3500.17.20 Schwab, J.C. Uber die Wahrheit der Kantischen
                Philosophie...Ausehung dieser Philosophie. Berlin, 1803.
Phil 3500.18   Sahlin, C.Y. Kants, Schleiermacher's och Bostroms etiska.
                Upsala, 1877.
Phil 3500.19   Sidgwich, H. Lectures on the philosophy of Kant.
                London, 1905.
Phil 3500.20   Simmel, G. Kant: sechzehn Vorlesungen. Leipzig, 1905.
Phil 3500.20.2 Simmel, G. Kant: sechzehn Vorlesungen. Leipzig, 1904.
Phil 3500.20.3 Simmel, G. Kant: sechzehn Vorlesungen. 3. Aufl.
                München, 1913.
Phil 3500.20.4 Simmel, G. Kant: sechzehn Vorlesungen. 4. Aufl.
                München, 1918.
Phil 3500.20.5 Simmel, G. Kant und Goethe. Berlin, 1906.
Phil 3500.20.6 Simmel, G. Kant: sechzehn Vorlesungen. 5. Aufl.
                München, 1921.

Classified Listing

Phil 3500.20.15   Simmel, G. Das Wesen der Materie nach Kants physischer Monadologie. Inaug. Diss. Berlin, 1881.

Phil 3500.21   Sentroul, C. L'objet de la métaphysique selon Kant. Louvain, 1905.

Phil 3500.21.5   Sentroul, C. Kant und Aristoteles. n.p., 1911.

Phil 3500.21.15   Sentroul, C. Kant et Aristote. 2. éd. Louvain, 1913.

Phil 3500.22   Seydel, R. Der Schlüssel zum objektiven Erkennen. Halle, 1889.

Phil 3500.23   Stehr, H. Über Immanuel Kant. Leipzig, 1896.

Phil 3500.24   Stériad, A. L'interprétation de la doctrine de Kant. Paris, 1913.

Phil 3500.25   Stefanescu, M. Essai sur le rapport entre le dualisme. Paris, 1915.

Phil 3500.26   Sänger, E.A. Kants Lehre vom Glauben. Leipzig, 1903.

Phil 3500.27   Smith, N.K. Commentary to Kant's Critique of pure reason. London, 1918.

Phil 3500.28   Sartiaux, F. Morale Kantienne et morale humaine. Paris, 1917.

Phil 3500.29   Schultze, F. Kant und Darwin. Jena, 1875.

Phil 3500.30   Strecker, Reinhard. Kants Ethik. Giessen, 1909.

Phil 3500.31   Sternberg, Kurt. Versuch einer Entwicklungsgeschichte des Kantischen...des Kriticismus. Berlin, 1909.

Phil 3500.32   Sornmerlath, Ernst. Kants Lehre vom Intelligiblencharakter. Leipzig, 1917.

Phil 3500.33.4   Stange, Carl. Der Gedankengang der Kritik der reinen Vernunft. Leipzig, 1920.

Phil 3500.33.6A   Stange, Carl. Die Ethik Kants zur Einführung in die Kritik der praktischen Vernunft. Leipzig, 1920.

Phil 3500.33.6B   Stange, Carl. Die Ethik Kants zur Einführung in die Kritik der praktischen Vernunft. Leipzig, 1920.

Phil 3500.34   Schweitzer, Albert. Die Religionsphilosophie Kants. Freiburg, 1899.

Phil 3500.35   Snell, E.W.D. Darstellung und Erläuterung I. Kant Critik. v.1-2. Mannheim, 1791.

Phil 3500.35.5   Snell, F.W.D. Menon oder Versuch in Gesprächen. Mannheim, 1789.

Phil 3500.35.7   Snell, F.W.D. Menon oder Versuch in Gesprächen. 2. Aufl. Mannheim, 1796.

Phil 3500.36   Schmidt, H. Immanuel Kants Leben. Halle, 1858.

Phil 3500.37   Stern, Albert. Über die Beziehungen Garve's zu Kant. Inaug. Diss. n.p., n.d.

Phil 3500.38   Scott, John W. Kant on the moral life. London, 1924.

Phil 3500.39   Steckelmacher, M. Die formale Logik Kant's in ihren Beziehungen zur Transcendentalen. Breslau, 1879.

Phil 3500.40   Schöndörffer, O. Kants Leben und Lehre. Leipzig, 1924.

Phil 3500.41   Schmalenbach, H. Die Kantische Philosophie und die Religion. Göttingen, 1926.

Phil 3500.41.10   Schmalenbach, H. Kants Religion. Berlin, 1929.

Phil 3500.42   Sarchi, Charles. Examen de la doctrine de Kant. Paris, 1872.

Phil 3500.43   Souviau, M. Le jugement réfléchissant dans la philosophie critique de Kant. Paris, 1926.

Phil 3500.43.2   Souviau, M. Le jugement réfléchissant dans la philosophie critique de Kant. Thèse. Paris, 1926.

Phil 3500.44   Samsom, A. Kants kennis van grieksche Philosophie. Thesis. Alphen aan den Rijn, 1927.

Phil 3500.45   Salits, Peter. Darstellung und Kritik des Kantischen Lehre von der Willensfreiheit. Rostock, 1898.

Phil 3500.46   Schreiber, C. Kant und die Gottesbeweise. Dresden, 1922.

Phil 3500.48   Selz, Otto. Kants Stellung in der Geistesgeschichte. Mannheim, 1924.

Phil 3500.49   Sturm, A. Kant, Schopenhauer, Nietzsche und deren...Gemüt. Langensalza, 1921.

Phil 3500.51   Schultheis, P. Kant's Lehre vom radicalen Bösen. Diss. Leipzig, 1873.

Phil 3500.52   Schultz, John. Prüfung der Kantischen Critik der reinen Vernunft. v.1-2. Königsberg, 1789.

Phil 3500.52.5   Schultz, John. Ensayo de una clara exposición del contenido de la crítica de la razón pura. Cordoba, 1942.

Phil 3500.53   Siehr, Carl. Kant und das freie Wort und Gerechtigkeit und...bei Kant. Königsberg, 1927.

Phil 3500.54   Schwarz, W. Immanuel Kant als Pädagoge. Langensalza, 1915.

Phil 3500.55   Schultz, Martin. Kants Religion innerhalb der Grenzen der blossen Vernunft. Königsberg, 1927.

Phil 3500.56   Schulze, Gottlob E. Einige Bemerkungen über Kants philosophische Religionslehre. Kiel, 1795.

Phil 3500.57   Stattler, B. Kurzer Entwurf der unausstehlichen Ungereimtheiten der Kantischen Philosophie. n.p., 1791.

Phil 3500.57.5   Stattler, B. Wahres Verhaltniss der Kantischen Philosophie. München, 1794.

Phil 3500.57.10   Stattler, B. Anti-Kant. München, 1788. 2v.

Phil 3500.58   Schilling, Georg. Kants Lebenswerk als Gabe und Aufgabe. Detmold, 1924.

Phil 3500.59   Serrus, C. L'esthétique transcendantale et la science moderne. Paris, 1930.

Phil 3500.60.5A   Smith, Norman K. A commentary to Kant's "Critique of pure reason". 2d ed. London, 1923.

Phil 3500.60.5B   Smith, Norman K. A commentary to Kant's "Critique of pure reason". 2d ed. London, 1923.

Phil 3500.62   Schramm, G. Kant's kategorischen Imperativ nach seiner Genesis und Bedeutung für die Wissenschaft. Bamberg, 1873.

Phil 3500.63   Schilpp, P.A. Kant's pre-critical ethics. Evanston, 1938.

Phil 3500.63.2   Schilpp, P.A. Kant's pre-critical ethics. 2d ed. Evanstown, 1960.

Phil 3500.65A   Smith, A.H. Kantian studies. Oxford, 1947.

Phil 3500.65B   Smith, A.H. Kantian studies. Oxford, 1947.

Phil 3500.67   Sander, J. Die Begründung der Notwehr in der Philosophie von Kant und Hegel. Bleicherode, 1939.

Phil 3500.69   Stavenhagen, F. Kant und Königsberg. Gottingen, 1949.

Phil 3500.71   Schneiberger, Guido. Kants Konzeption der Modalbegriffe. Basel, 1952.

Phil 3500.73   Stemberger, R. Immanuel Kant als Philosoph und Soziologe. Wien, 1953.

Phil 3500.75   Salvucci, Pasquale. La dottrina Kantiana dello schematismo transcendentale. Urbino, 1957.

Phil 3500.77   Schoeler, Wilhelm. Die transzendentale Einheit der Apperzeption von Immanuel Kant. Bern, 1958.

Phil 3500.80   Salvucci, Pasquale. Grandi interpreti di Kant. Urbino, 1958.

Phil 3500.85   Shashkevich, P.D. Teoriia poznaniia I. Kanta. Moskva, 1960.

Phil 3500.88   Schmucker, Josef. Das Problem der Kontingenz der Welt. Freiburg, 1969.

Phil 3500.90   Stoikhammer, Morris. Kants Zurechnungsidee und Freiheitsantinomie. Köln, 1961.

Phil 3500.91   Snell, Christian. Lehrbuch der Kritik des Geschmack. Leipzig, 1795.

Phil 3500.92   Schulz, H. Innerer Sinn und Erkenntnis in der Kantischen Philosophie. Düsseldorf, 1962.

Phil 3500.93   Salmony, H.A. Kants Schrift. Zürich, 1962.

Phil 3500.94   Santeler, J. Die Grundlegung der Menschenwürde bei I. Kant. Innsbruck, 1962.

Phil 3500.95   Sciacca, Guiseppe M. L'idea della libertà. Palermo, 1963.

Phil 3500.96   Santinello, Giovanni. Metafisica e critica in Kant. Bologna, 1965.

Phil 3500.98   Strawson, Peter Frederick. The bounds of sense: an essay on Kant's 'Critique of pure reason'. London, 1966.

Phil 3500.100   Schäfer, Lothar. Kants Metaphysik der Natur. Berlin, 1966.

Phil 3500.102   Saher, Hans. Kants Weg vom Krieg zum Frieden. München, 1968-

Phil 3500.103   Shcherbina, A.M. Uchenie Kanta o veshchi vě sebe. n.p., n.d.

Phil 3500.105   Studien zu Kants philosophischer Entwicklung. Hildesheim, 1967.

Phil 3500.106   Schwartlaender, Johannes. Der Mensch ist Person. Stuttgart, 1968.

Phil 3500.108   Swing, Thomas K. Kant's transcendental logic. New Haven, 1969.

Phil 3500.110   Schwab, Johann Christoph. Sendschreiben an einen Recensenten in der Gothaischen gelehrten Zeitung über den gerichtlichen Eyd. v.1-2. Bruxelles, 1968.

Phil 3500.112   Sellars, Wilfrid. Science and metaphysics; variations on Kantian themes. London, 1968.

Phil 3500.114   Salem, Joseph. Immanuel Kants Lehre und ihre Auswirkungen. Gelsenkirchen-Buer, 1969.

Phil 3500.116   Schaeffer, Wilhelm Friedrich. Inconsequenzen, und auffallende Widersprüche in der Kantischen Philosophie, Dessau, 1792. Bruxelles, 1969.

Phil 3501.1   Thiele, G. Kant's intellektuelle Anschauung. Halle, 1876.

Phil 3501.1.5   Thiele, G. Die Philosophie Immanuel Kant. Halle, 1882.

Phil 3501.2   Thomas, K. Kant und Herbart. Berlin, 1840-69. 2 pam.

Phil 3501.3   Troitzsch, J.G. Etwas über den Werth der kritischen Philosophie. Leipzig, 1780-1800. 3 pam.

Phil 3501.4   Tsanoff, P.A. Schopenhauer's criticism of Kant's Theory of experience. N.Y., 1911.

Phil 3501.5   Tocco, Felice. Studi Kantiani. Milano, 1909.

Phil 3501.6   Tegen, Einar. Studier till uppkomsten av Kants. Uppsala, 1918.

Phil 3501.7   Trivero, Camillo. Nuova critica della morale Kantiana. Milano, 1914.

Phil 3501.8   Thon, O. Die Grundprinzipien der Kantischen Moralphilosophie. Berlin, 1895.

Phil 3501.9   Theodor, J. Der Unendlichkeitsbegriff bei Kant und Aristoteles. Breslau, 1877.

Phil 3501.10   Toll, C.H. Die erste Antinomie Kants und der Pantheismus. Berlin, 1910.

Phil 3501.11   Troeltsch, E. Das Historische in Kants Religionsphilosophie. Berlin, 1904.

Phil 3501.12   Tittel, Gottlof August. Kantischen den Reformen oder Kategorien. Frankfurt, 1787.

Phil 3501.13   Trubetskoi, E. Metafizika predpolozheniia poznaniia opyt preodolevaniia Kanta. Moskva, 1917.

Phil 3501.14   Troilo, E. Emmanuele Kant. Roma, 1924.

Phil 3501.15   Teale, A.E. Kantian ethics. London, 1951.

Phil 3501.18   Tilling, Christian Gottfried. Gedanken zur Prüfung von Kants...der Sitten, Leipzig, 1789. Bruxelles, 1968.

Phil 3501.20   Taminiaux, Jacques. La nostalgie de la Grèce à l'aube de l'idéalisme allemand. La Haye, 1967.

Phil 3501.22   Takeda, Sueo. Kant und das Problem der Analogie. Den Haag, 1969.

Phil 3501.24   Tuschling, Burkhard. Metaphysische und transzendentale Dynamik in Kants opus postumum. Berlin, 1971.

Phil 3502.1   Uphues, G.K. Kant und seine Vorgänger. Berlin, 1906.

Phil 3502.2   Ueberhorst, C. Kant's Lehre von dem Verhältnisse der Kategorien zu der Erfahrung. Göttingen, 1878.

Phil 3502.3   Unold, J. Die ethnologischen und anthropogeographischen...bei I. Kant und J.R. Forster. Leipzig, 1886.

Phil 3502.4   Ueberweg, F. De priore et posteriore forma Kantianae critices. Berolini, 1862.

Phil 3502.5   Ueber Kant's philosophische Religionslehre. Augsburg? 1793.

Phil 3502.6   Ueber Theorie und Praxis. Frankfurt, 1967.

Phil 3503.1   Vaihinger, H. Commentar zu Kants Kritik der reinen Vernunft. Stuttgart, 1881. 2v.

Phil 3503.1.2   Vaihinger, H. Kommentar zu Kants Kritik der reinen Vernunft. 2. Aufl. Stuttgart, 1922. 2v.

Phil 3503.1.5   Vaihinger, H. Zu Kants Gedächtnis. Berlin, 1904.

Phil 3503.2   Villers, C. Philosophie de Kant. v.1-2. Metz, 1801.

Phil 3503.3   Venturini, Karl. Geist der kritischen Philosophie. Altona, 1796-97. 2v.

Phil 3503.4   Vorländer, K. Immanuel Kants Leben. Leipzig, 1911.

Phil 3503.4.2   Vorländer, K. Immanuel Kants Leben. 2. Aufl. Leipzig, 1921.

Phil 3503.4.3   Vorländer, K. Die Kantische Begründung der Moralprinzips. Solingen, 1889.

Phil 3503.4.5   Vorländer, K. Kant, Schiller, Goethe. Leipzig, 1907.

Phil 3503.4.6   Vorländer, K. Kant-Schiller-Goethe. 2. Aufl. Leipzig, 1923.

Phil 3503.4.10   Vorländer, K. Kant als Deutscher. Darmstadt, 1919.

Phil 3503.4.15   Vorländer, K. Immanuel Kant. Leipzig, 1924. 2v.

Phil 3503.4.25   Vorländer, K. Immanuel Kant und sein Einfluss auf der deutsche Denken. 2. Aufl. Bielefeld, 1922.

Phil 3503.4.30   Vorländer, K. Kant und der Sozialismus unter besonderer Verücksichtigung der neuesten theoretischen Bewegung innerhalb des Marxismus. Berlin, 1900.

Phil 3503.5   Volkelt, Johannes. Immanuel Kant's Erkenntnisstheorie nach ihren Grundprincipien Analysiert. Leipzig, 1879.

Phil 3503.5.5   Volkelt, Johannes. Kant's kategorischer Imperativ. Wien, 1875.

Phil 3503.5.10   Volkelt, Johannes. Kant als Philosoph des Unbedingten. Erfurt, 1924.

Phil 3503.6   Vallois, M. La formation de l'influence Kantienne en France. Paris, 1925?

Phil 3503.6.5   Vallois, M. La formation de l'influence Kantienne en France. Thèse. Paris, 1924.

194

Classified Listing

Phil 3482 - 3507 History of philosophy - Local Modern philosophy - Germany - Individual philosophers - Kant, Immanuel - Biography and criticism - Monographs (A-Z) - cont.

Phil 3503.7 Vogt, Carl. Darstellung und Beurtheilung der Kant'schen und Hegel'schen Christologie. Marburg, 1878.
Phil 3503.8 Vosters, J. La doctrine du droit de Kant. Bruxelles, 1920.
Phil 3503.9 Vleeschauwer, H.J. La déduction transcendentale dans l'oeuvre de Kant. v.1-2,3. Antwerp, 1934-36. 2v.
Phil 3503.9.10 Vleeschauwer, H.J. Development of Kantian thought. London, 1962.
Phil 3503.10 Vanni Rovighi, Sofia. Introduzione allo studio di Kant. Como, 1945.
Phil 3503.11 Vuillemin, Jules. Physique et métaphysique Kantiennes. 1. éd. Paris, 1955.
Phil 3503.12 Vialatoux, J. La morale de Kant. 1. éd. Paris, 1956.
Phil 3503.13 Vitier, M. Kant. La Habana, 1958.
Phil 3503.14 Vlachos, G. La pensée politique de Kant. Paris, 1962.
Phil 3503.15 Verondini, Enrico. La filosofia morale di Emanuele Kant. Bologna, 1966.
Phil 3503.20 Varga, Alexander von. Macht und Ohnmacht der Vernunft. Zur Einführung in die Philosophie Kants. München, 1967.
Phil 3503.25 Vas, Harmen de. Kant als theoloog. Baarn, 1968.
Phil 3503.30 Veca, Salvatore. Fondazione e modalita in Kant. Milano, 1969.
Phil 3503.35.4 Valentiner, Theodor. Kant und seine Lehre. Eine Einführung in die kritische Philosophie. 4. Aufl. Stuttgart, 1969.
Phil 3504.1 Wallace, William. Kant. Edinburgh, 1882.
Phil 3504.1.3 Wallace, William. Kant. Philadelphia, 1882.
Phil 3504.1.10 Wallace, William. Kant. Edinburgh, 1902.
Phil 3504.1.15 Wallace, William. Kant. Edinburgh, 1911.
Phil 3504.1.20 Wallace, William. Kant. Edinburgh, 1886.
Phil 3504.2 Wangenheim, F. Vertheidigung Kants Gegen Fries. Berlin, 1876.
Phil 3504.3A Watson, J. Kant and his English critics. N.Y., 1881.
Phil 3504.3B Watson, J. Kant and his English critics. N.Y., 1881.
Phil 3504.3.5 Watson, J. The philosophy of Kant explained. Glasgow, 1908.
Phil 3504.4 Weishaupt, A. Über die Kantischen Anschauungen. Nürnberg, 1788.
Phil 3504.4.10 Weishaupt, A. Zweifel über die Kantischen Begriffe von Zeit und Raum. Nürnberg, 1788.
Phil 3504.5 Willich, A.F.M. Elements of the critical philosophy...Kant. London, 1798.
Phil 3504.6 Wirgman, T. Kants works and life. n.p., n.d.
Phil 3504.6.2 Wirgman, T. Principles Kantesian...philosophy. London, 1824.
Htn Phil 3504.6.3* Wirgman, T. Principles Kantesian...philosophy. 2d ed. London, 1832.
Phil 3504.7 Wenley, R.M. An outline introduction of Kant's Critique of pure reason. N.Y., 1897.
Phil 3504.7.5 Wenley, R.M. An outline introduction of Kant's Critique of pure reason. N.Y., 1907.
Phil 3504.7.15 Wenley, R.M. Kant and his philosophical revolution. Edinburgh, 1910.
Phil 3504.8 Witte, J.H. Beiträge zum Verständniss Kant's. Berlin, 1874.
Phil 3504.8.5 Witte, J.H. Kantischer Kriticismus Gegenüber unkritischen Dilettantismus. Bonn, 1885.
Phil 3504.10 Wolf, Johannes. Verhaltnis des Beiden ersten Auflagen der Kritik der reinen Vernunft Zueinander. Inaug. Diss. Halle, 1905.
Phil 3504.11 Wheeler, C.K. Critique of pure Kant. Boston, 1911.
Phil 3504.12 Wernieke, A. Kant und kein Ende? 2. Aufl. Braunschweig, 1907.
Phil 3504.12.5 Wernieke, A. Theorie des Gegenstandes...bei I. Kant. Braunschweig, 1904.
Phil 3504.12.10 Wernieke, A. Die Begründung des deutschen Idealismus durch I. Kant. Braunschweig, 1910.
Phil 3504.12.15 Wernieke, A. Kants kritischer Werdegang. Braunschweig, 1911.
Phil 3504.13 Witter, C.E. Pragmatic elements in Kant's philosophy. Chicago, 1913.
Phil 3504.14 Whitney, G.J. An introduction to Kant's critical philosophy. N.Y., 1914.
Phil 3504.15 Wesselsky, Anton. Forberg und Kant. Leipzig, 1913.
Phil 3504.16 Wolff, Hermann. Neue Kritik der reinen Vernunft. Leipzig, 1897.
Phil 3504.16.5 Wolff, Hermann. Die metaphysische Grundanschauung Kants. Leipzig, 1870.
Phil 3504.17 Wohlrabe, Wilhelm. Kant's Lehre vom Gewissen. Halle, 1888.
Phil 3504.18 Windelband, W. Immanuel Kant und seine Weltanschauung. Heidelberg, 1904.
Phil 3504.19 Weber, Heinrich. Hamann und Kant. München, 1904.
Phil 3504.20 Warda, Arthur. Die Druckschriften Immanuel Kants. Wiesbaden, 1919.
Phil 3504.20.5 Warda, Arthur. Immanuel Kants Bücher. Berlin, 1922.
Phil 3504.20.9 Warda, Arthur. Immanuel Kants Cetzte Ehrung. Königsberg, 1924.
Phil 3504.21F Werner, Karl. Kant in Italien. Wien, 1881.
Phil 3504.22A Ward, James. A study of Kant. Cambridge, Eng., 1922.
Phil 3504.22B Ward, James. A study of Kant. Cambridge, Eng., 1922.
Phil 3504.22.5 Ward, James. Immanuel Kant. London, 1923.
Phil 3504.23A Wilm, E.C. Immanuel Kant. New Haven, 1925.
Phil 3504.23B Wilm, E.C. Immanuel Kant. New Haven, 1925.
Phil 3504.24 Wieser, F. Kant-Festschrift zu Kants 200. Geburststag am 22 April 1924. Berlin, 1924.
Phil 3504.24.2 Wieser, F. Kant-Festschrift zu Kants 200. Geburststag am April 1924. 2. Aufl. Berlin, 1924.
Phil 3504.25 Willems, C. Kant's Sittenlehre. Trier, 1919.
Phil 3504.25.5 Willems, C. Kant's Erkenntnislehre. Trier, 1919.
Phil 3504.26 Wegner, Gustav. Kantlexikon. Berlin, 1893.
Phil 3504.27 Wichmann, G. Platon und Kant. Berlin, 1920.
Phil 3504.28 Weis, Ludwig. Kant: Naturgesetze, Natur- und Gotteserkennen. Berlin, 1903.
Phil 3504.29 Wallenberg, G. Kants Zeitlehre. Berlin, 1896.
Phil 3504.30 Webb, Clement C.J. Kant's philosophy of religion. Oxford, 1926.
Phil 3504.31 Wasianski, E.A.C. Immanuel Kant. Upsala, 1810.
Phil 3504.31.5 Wasianski, E.A.C. Immanuel Kant in seinen letzen Lebensjahren. Königsberg, 1804.
Phil 3504.31.10 Wasianski, E.A.C. Immanuel Kant in seinen letzen Lebensjahren. Zürich, 1945.
Phil 3504.32 Wundt, Max. Kant als Metaphysiker. Stuttgart, 1924.
Phil 3504.33 Wagner, Walther. Die Vereinigung von Kant und Marx. Langensalza, 1921.
Phil 3504.34 Will, G.A. Vorlesungen über der Kantische Philosophie. Altdorf, 1788.
Phil 3504.35 Weber, Joseph. Versuch, die harten Urtheile über der Kantische Philosophie zu Mildern. Wirzburg, 1793.
Phil 3504.36 Weir, Archibald. The critical philosophy of Kant. London, 1881.
Phil 3504.37 Wyneken, G.A. Hegels Kritik Kants. Greifswald, 1898.
Phil 3504.37.5 Wyneken, G.A. Hegels Kritik Kants. Inaug. Diss. Greifswald, 1898.
Phil 3504.38A Wellek, René. Immanuel Kant in England, 1793-1838. Princeton, 1931.
Phil 3504.38B Wellek, René. Immanuel Kant in England, 1793-1838. Princeton, 1931.
Phil 3504.39 Wilmans, C.A. Dissertatio philosophica de similitudine. Halis Saxonum, 1797.
Phil 3504.40 Weissfeld, M. Kants Gesellschaftslehre. Bern, 1907.
Phil 3504.41 Weiller, K. Über den nachsten Zweck der Erziehung nach Kantischen Grunsätzen. Regensburg, 1798.
Phil 3504.42 Wiegershausen, H. Aenesidem-Schulze, der Gegner Kants. Inaug. Diss. Münster, 1910.
Phil 3504.43 Whitney, G.T. The heritage of Kant. Princeton, 1939.
Phil 3504.44 Weldon, Thomas D. Introduction to Kant's Critique of pure reason. Oxford, 1945.
Phil 3504.44.5 Weldon, Thomas D. Critique of pure reason. 2nd ed. Oxford, 1958.
Phil 3504.45 Washington, W.M. The formal and material elements of Kant's ethics. N.Y., 1898.
Phil 3504.46 Wolff, E.M. Étude du role de l'imagination dans la conaissance chez Kant. Thèse. Carcassonne, 1943.
Phil 3504.47 Wendel, J.A. Grundzüge und Kritik der Philosophien Kant's. Coburg, 1810.
Phil 3504.48 Wickenhagen, Ernst. Die Logik bei Kant. Inaug. Diss. Jena, 1869.
Phil 3504.50 Weil, Eric. Problems kantiens. Paris, 1963.
Phil 3504.50.2 Weil, Eric. Problemes kantiens. 2. éd. Paris, 1970.
Phil 3504.52 Walsh, William Henry. Kant's moral theology. London, 1963.
Phil 3504.53 Wolff, Robert Paul. Kant's theory of mental activity. Cambridge, 1963. 2v.
Phil 3504.55 Williams, T.C. The concept of the categorical imperative. Oxford, 1968.
Phil 3504.58 Wood, Allen W. Kant's moral religion. Ithaca, 1970.
Phil 3504.60 Weisskopf, Traugott. Immanuel Kant und die Pädagogik. Zürich, 1970.
Phil 3507.2 Zango, F. Über das Fundament der Ethik. Leipzig, 1872.
Phil 3507.3 Zickendraht, K. Kants Gedanken über Krieg und Frieden. Tübingen, 1922.
Phil 3507.4 Zimmerman, R. Über Kant's Widerlegung des Idealismus von Berkeley. Wien, 1871.
Phil 3507.4.5 Zimmerman, R. Kant und die positive Philosophie. Wien, 1874.
Phil 3507.5 Zwanziger, J.C. Commentar über Kant's Kritik der reinen Vernunft. Leipzig, 1794.
Phil 3507.5.2 Zwanziger, J.C. Commentar über Kant's Kritik der reinen Vernunft. Leipzig, 1792.
Phil 3507.6 Ziegeler, E. Kants Sittenlehre in gemeinverständlischer Darstellung. Leipzig, 1919.
Phil 3507.7 Zallinger, J.A. Disquisitionum philosophiae Kantianae. v.1-2. Augustae Vindelicorum, 1799.
Phil 3507.8 Zimmermann, Heinz. Der Befreier; eine Begegnung mit Kant. München, 1930.
Phil 3507.9 Zwingmann, H. Kants Staatstheorie. München, 19- ?
Phil 3507.9.5 Zwingmann, H. Kant. Berlin, 1924.
Phil 3507.10 Zocher, Rudolf. Kants Grundlehre. Erlangen, 1959.
Phil 3507.12 Zwingelberg, Hans Willi. Kants Ethik und das Problem der Einheit von Freiheit und Gesetz. Thesis. Bonn, 1969.

Phil 3508 History of philosophy - Local Modern philosophy - Germany - Individual philosophers - Kant, Immanuel - Biography and criticism - Anonymous works

Phil 3508.2 Verzeichniss der Bücher des Verstorben Professor Johann Friedrich Gensichen. Königsberg, 1808.
Phil 3508.4 Über das Studium der Kantischen Philosophie und ihren Werth. Bruxelles, 1968.

Phil 3525 History of philosophy - Local Modern philosophy - Germany - Individual philosophers - Krause, Karl C.F.

Phil 3525.06 Pamphlet box. Philosophy. German and Dutch. Krause, K.C.F. Minor writings.
Phil 3525.20 Krause, K.C.F. Handschriftlicher Nachlass; Logik. Göttingen, 1836.
Phil 3525.20.2 Krause, K.C.F. Handschriftlicher Nachlass; Anthropologie. Göttingen, 1848.
Phil 3525.20.3 Krause, K.C.F. Handschriftlicher Nachlass; Religionsphilosophie. Dresden, 1834-43. 2v.
Phil 3525.20.4 Krause, K.C.F. Handschriftlicher Nachlass; Rechtsphilosophie. Leipzig, 1874.
Phil 3525.23 Tiberghien, G. De la doctrine de Krause. Bruxelles, 1855.
Phil 3525.30 Krause, K.C.F. Emporleitende Theil der Philosophie. Prag, 1869.
Phil 3525.35 Krause, K.C.F. Erneute Vernunftkritik. Prag, 1868.
Phil 3525.40 Krause, K.C.F. Vorlesungen über das System der Philosophie. Göttingen, 1828.
Phil 3525.45 Krause, K.C.F. Abriss des Systemes der Philosophie. Göttingen, 1825.
Phil 3525.50 Krause, K.C.F. Das Urbild der Menschheit. Göttingen, 1851.
Phil 3525.55 Krause, K.C.F. Ideal de la humanidad para la vida. 2. ed. Madrid, 1871.
Phil 3525.60 Krause, K.C.F. Grundriss der historischen Logik. Jena, 1803.
Phil 3525.61 Krause, K.C.F. Abriss des Systemes der Logik. Göttingen, 1828.
Phil 3525.65 Krause, K.C.F. Vorlesung über psychische Anthropologie. Leipzig, 1905.
Phil 3525.70 Krause, K.C.F. System der Sittenlehre. Bd.1. Leipzig, 1810.
Phil 3525.75 Krause, K.C.F. Lebenlehre. 2. Aufl. Leipzig, 1904.
Phil 3525.79 Pamphlet box. Philosophy. German and Dutch. Krause, K.C.F
Phil 3525.80 Atienza y Medrano, A. El Krausismo. Madrid, 1877.
Phil 3525.81 Lindemann, H.S. Uebersichtliche Darstellung des Lebens und der Wissenschaftlehre K.C.F. Krause's. München, 1839.
Phil 3525.82 Ranft, M. Der Philosoph K.C.F. Krause als Erzieher. Halle, 1907.

195
Classified Listing

Phil 3525 History of philosophy - Local Modern philosophy - Germany - Individual philosophers - Krause, Karl C.F. - cont.

Phil 3525.83 Leonhardi, Hermann. Karl C.F. Krause's Leben und Lehre. Leipzig, 1902.
Phil 3525.84 Leonhardi, Hermann. Karl Christian Friedrich Krause als philosophischer Denker Gewürdigt. Leipzig, 1905.
Phil 3525.85 Martin, B.R. Karl Christian Friedrich Krause's Leben, Lehre und Bedeutung. Leipzig, 1885.
Phil 3525.86 Krause, K.C.F. Pädagogischen Gedenken K.C.F. Krauses in ihrem Zusammenhange mit seiner Philosophie Dargestellt. Inaug. Diss. Leipzig, 1911.
Phil 3525.86.5 Krause, K.C.F. Dei Briefwechsel Karl Christian Friedrich Krauses. Leipzig, 1903.
Phil 3525.87 Eucken, Rudolf. Zur Erinnerung an K.C.F. Krause. Leipzig, 1881.
Phil 3525.88 Hohlfeld, P. Die Krause'sche Philosophie. Jena, 1879.
Phil 3525.89 Reiff, F. Über Krause's Philosophie. n.p., n.d.
Phil 3525.90 MacCauley, Clay. Karl Christian Friedrich Krause. Berkeley, Calif., 1925.
Phil 3525.91 Opzoomer, C.W. De leer van God bij Schelling, Hegel en Krause. Leiden, 1846.
Phil 3525.92 Proksch, A. Karl Christian Friedrich Krause. Leipzig, 1880.
Phil 3525.95 Fernandez Valbuena, Ramiro. Se opone El Krausismo a la fé católica? Badajoz, 1882[1883]

Phil 3528 History of philosophy - Local Modern philosophy - Germany - Individual philosophers - Krug, Wilhelm T.

Phil 3528.10 Krug, Wilhelm Traugott. Gesammelte Schriften. Braunschweig, 1830-45. 12v.
Phil 3528.30 Krug, Wilhelm Traugott. System der theoretischen Philosophie. Königsberg, 1823-33. 3v.
Phil 3528.30.2 Krug, Wilhelm Traugott. System der theoretischen Philosophie. Königsberg, 1806-18. 2v.
Phil 3528.35 Krug, Wilhelm Traugott. System der praktischen Philosophie. 2. Aufl. Königsberg, 1817-19. 3v.
Phil 3528.35.2 Krug, Wilhelm Traugott. System der praktischen Philosophie. Königsberg, 1830-38. 2v.
Phil 3528.35.5 Krug, Wilhelm Traugott. System der praktischen Philosophie. Wien, 1818.
Phil 3528.37 Krug, Wilhelm Traugott. Bruchstücke aus meiner Lebensphilosophie. v.1-2. Berlin, 1800-01.
Phil 3528.40 Krug, Wilhelm Traugott. Fundamentalphilosophie. Leipzig, 1827.
Phil 3528.40.5 Krug, Wilhelm Traugott. Fundamentalphilosophie. 2. Aufl. Züllichan, 1819.
Phil 3528.45 Krug, Wilhelm Traugott. Universalphilosophische Vorlesungen für Gebildete beiderlei Geschlechts. Neustadt, 1831.
Phil 3528.50 Krug, Wilhelm Traugott. Über altes und neues Christenthum. Leipzig, 1836.
Phil 3528.55.2 Krug, Wilhelm Traugott. Der Widerstreit der Vernunft mit sich Selbst in der Versöhnungslehre. Bruxelles, 1968.
Phil 3528.58 Krug, Wilhelm Traugott. Briefe über die Wissenschaftslehre. Bruxelles, 1968.
Phil 3528.60.1 Krug, Wilhelm Traugott. Entwurf eines neuen Organon's der Philosophie. Meissen, 1801. Bruxelles, 1969.
Phil 3528.80 Fiedler, A. Die staatswissenschaftlichen Anschauungen und die politische-publizistische Tätigkeit des Nachkantianers Wilhelm Traugott Krug. Inaug. Diss. Dresden, 1933.

Phil 3549 History of philosophy - Local Modern philosophy - Germany - Individual philosophers - Other K

Phil 3549.1.85 Hartmann, E. von. J.H. von Kirchmanns erkentnisstheoretischer Realismus. Berlin, 1875.
Phil 3549.2.20 Blätter der Schule der Weisheit; eine Chronik der Weiterentwicklung der Schule der Weisheit für die Mitglieder des Vereins der Freunde des Keyserling-Archivs. v.1-2. Innsbruck, 1948-49.
Phil 3549.2.25 Keyserling, Hermann. Der Weg zur Vollendung. Darmstadt. 1-20,1924-1932 2v.
Phil 3549.2.30 Keyserling, Hermann. Südamerikanische Meditationen. Stuttgart, 1932.
Phil 3549.2.30.2 Keyserling, Hermann. South American meditations. 1st ed. N.Y., 1932.
Phil 3549.2.35 Keyserling, Hermann. Mensch und Erde in Darstellungen. Darmstadt, 1927.
Phil 3549.2.40 Keyserling, Hermann. Das Buch vom Ursprung. Baden-Baden, 1947.
Phil 3549.2.45 Keyserling, Hermann. The art of life. London, 1937.
Phil 3549.2.47 Keyserling, Hermann. Das Buch vom persönlichen Leben. Stuttgart, 1936.
Phil 3549.2.50 Keyserling, Hermann. Menschen als Sinnbilder. Darmstadt, 1926.
Phil 3549.2.52 Keyserling, Hermann. Wiedergeburt. Darmstadt, 1927.
Phil 3549.2.60 Keyserling, Hermann. Betractungen der Stille und Besinnlichkeit. Jena, 1942.
Phil 3549.2.70 Keyserling, Hermann. Graf Hermann Kyserling. Innsbruck, 1948.
Phil 3549.2.75.5 Keyserling, Hermann. Das Reisetagebuch eines Philosophen. 7. Aufl. Darmstadt, 1923. 2v.
Phil 3549.2.75.7 Keyserling, Hermann. Das Reisetagebuch eines Philosophen. Darmstadt, 1956. 3v.
Phil 3549.2.78 Keyserling, Hermann. The travel diary of a philosopher. London, 1925. 2v.
Phil 3549.2.78.2 Keyserling, Hermann. The travel diary of a philosopher. N.Y., 1925. 2v.
Phil 3549.2.78.5 Keyserling, Hermann. The travel diary of a philosopher. N.Y., 1929.
Phil 3549.2.79 Keyserling, Hermann. The world in the making. N.Y., 1927.
Phil 3549.2.79.2 Keyserling, Hermann. The world in the making. London, 1927.
Phil 3549.2.79.5 Keyserling, Hermann. Die neuentstehende Welt. Darmstadt, 1926.
Phil 3549.2.79.10 Keyserling, Hermann. Reise durch die Zeit. Innsbruck, 1948.
Phil 3549.2.79.15 Keyserling, Hermann. Kritik des Denkens. Innsbruck, 1948.
Phil 3549.2.80 Feldkeller, P. Graf Keyserlings Erkenntnisweg zum Übersinnlichen. Darmstadt, 1922.
Phil 3549.2.87 Boucher, M. La philosophie de H. Keyserling. 6. éd. Paris, 1927.
Phil 3549.2.90 Adolph, H. Die Philosophie des Grafen Keyserling. Stuttgart, 1927.
Phil 3549.2.92 Vondran, Hugo. Kritik der Philosophie des Grafen H. Keyserling. Diss. Erlangen, 1927.
Phil 3549.2.94 Shilpnagel, U. Graf Edward von Keyserling und seinepisches Werk. Inaug. Diss. Rostock, 1926.
Phil 3549.2.96 Hupfeld, R. Graf Hermann Keyserling. Bonn, 1922.

Phil 3549 History of philosophy - Local Modern philosophy - Germany - Individual philosophers - Other K - cont.

Phil 3549.2.99 Franceschi, G.J. Keyserling. 2. ed. Buenos Aires, 1929.
Phil 3549.2.100 Ocampo, Victoria. El viajero y una de sus sombras; Keyserling en mis memorias. Buenos Aires, 1951.
Phil 3549.2.105 Dyserinck, Hugo. Graf Hermann Keyserling und Frankereich. Bonn, 1970.
Phil 3549.4.80 Pamphlet box. Philosophy. German and Dutch. Kulpa, Oswald. Miscellaneous pamphlets.
Phil 3549.5.90 Erdmann, B. Martin Knutzen und seine Zeit. Leipzig, 1876.
Phil 3549.6.80 Pamphlet box. Philosophy. German and Dutch. Knoodt, Franz Peter. Miscellaneous pamphlets.
Phil 3549.7.90 Port, Kurt. Das System der Werte. München, 1929.
Phil 3549.8.2 Klages, Ludwig. Sämtliche Werke. v.1,2,6-8. Bonn, 1964. 5v.
Phil 3549.8.5 Klages, Ludwig. Sämmtliche Werke. Supplement. Bonn, 1966.
Phil 3549.8.30 Klages, Ludwig. Rhyghmen und Runen aus dem Nachlass. Leipzig, 1944.
Phil 3549.8.35 Klages, Ludwig. Mensch und Erde. Stuttgart, 1956.
Phil 3549.8.40 Klages, Ludwig. Vom Sinn des Lebens. Jena, 1943.
Phil 3549.8.45 Hestia. Bonn. 1963+
Phil 3549.8.79 Pamphlet box. Philosophy. German and Dutch. Klages, Ludwig. Miscellaneous pamphlets.
Phil 3549.8.80 Börlin, E. Darstellung und Kritik der Charakterologie von Ludwig Klages. Giessen, 1929.
Phil 3549.8.85 Klages, Ludwig. Die Wissenschaft am Scheidewege von Leben und Geist. Leipzig, 1932.
Phil 3549.8.90 Klages, Ludwig. Persönlichkeit. Potsdam, 1927.
Phil 3549.8.92 Klages, Ludwig. Mensch und Erde. München, 1920.
Phil 3549.8.95 Klages, Ludwig. Erforscher und Künder des Lebens. Linz, 1947.
Phil 3549.8.100 Benduk, Hugo. Der Gegensatz vom Seele und Geist bei Ludwig Klages. Werli, 1935.
Phil 3549.8.105 Bartels, Enno. Ludwig Klages seine Lebenslehre und das Vitalismusproblem. Meisenheim, 1953.
Phil 3549.8.110 Wandrey, Conrad. Ludwig Klages und seine Lebensphilosophie. Leipzig, 1933.
Phil 3549.8.115 Ganzoni, Werner. Die neue Schau der Seele. Wien, 1957.
Phil 3549.8.120 Hager, Wilhelm. Ludwig Klages im Memoriam. München, 1957.
Phil 3549.8.125 Bruhers, E.M.J. De bijdrage von Ludwig Klages tot de algemene psychologie. Roermond, 1941.
Phil 3549.8.130 Lewin, James. Geist und Seele. Berlin, 1931.
Phil 3549.8.135 Chidani, Shichiro. Mein Weg zu Ludwig Klages. Hamburg, 1967.
Phil 3549.8.140 Kasdorff, Hans. Ludwig Klages Werk und Wirkung. Bonn, 1969.
Phil 3549.8.145 Mueller, Roland. Das verzwistete Ich-Ludwig Klages und sein philosophisches Hauptwerk Der Geist als Widersacher der Seele. Bern, 1971.
Phil 3549.9.90 Kühnemann, E. Mit unbefangener Stirn. Heilbronn, 1937.
Phil 3549.10 Kassner, Rudolf. Buch der Erinnerung. Leipzig, 1938.
Phil 3549.10.2 Kassner, Rudolf. Buch der Erinnerung. 2. Aufl. Erlenbach, 1954.
Phil 3549.10.5 Kassner, Rudolf. Motive; essays. Berlin, 1906.
Phil 3549.10.30 Kassner, Rudolf. Der Gottmensch. Leipzig, 1938.
Phil 3549.10.35 Kassner, Rudolf. Transfiguration. Erlenbach, 1946.
Phil 3549.10.40 Kassner, Rudolf. Wandlung. Zürich, 1946.
Phil 3549.10.45 Kassner, Rudolf. Das neunzehnte Jahrhundert; Ausdruck und Grösse. Erlenbach, 1947.
Phil 3549.10.50 Kassner, Rudolf. Umgang der Jahre. Erlenbach, 1949.
Phil 3549.10.55 Kassner, Rudolf. Zahl und Gesichte. Wiesbaden, 1956.
Phil 3549.10.60 Kassner, Rudolf. Wer indische Gedanke. 2. Aufl. Leipzig, 1921.
Phil 3549.10.80 Wieser, T. Die Einbildungskraft bei Rudolf Kassner. Zürich, 1949.
Phil 3549.11 Kroner, Richard. The religious function of imagination. New Haven, 1941.
Phil 3549.11.5 Kroner, Richard. Freiheit und Gnade. Tübingen, 1969.
Phil 3549.15.80 Adickes, Erich. Vier Schriften des Herrn Professor Kappes. Pt.1-2. Berlin, 1903.
Phil 3549.17 Kanthack, Katharina. Vom Sinn der Selbsterkenntnis. Berlin, 1958.
Phil 3549.18 Kraus, Annie. Vom Wesen und Ursprung der Dummheit. Köln, 1961.
Phil 3549.19 Kaiser, Josef. Summe der Filosofie. München, 1961.
Phil 3549.20 Kwant, R.C. Mens en kritiek. Utrecht, 1962.
Phil 3549.21 Kuhn, H. Das Sein und das Gute. München, 1962.
Phil 3549.22 Kwant, R.C. Critique; its nature and function. Pittsburgh, 1967.
Phil 3549.24 Kuypers, Karel. Verspreide Geschriften. Assen, 1968. 2v.
Phil 3549.26 Kulenkampff, Arend. Antinomie und Dialektik. Stuttgart, 1970.
Phil 3549.28.30 Kudszus, Hans. Zaworte, Neimworte, Aphorismen. 1. Aufl. Frankfurt, 1970.
Phil 3549.30 Kosegarten, Chritian. Memnens Bildsäule in Briefen au Ida von Kosegarten. Berlin, 1799.

Phil 3552 History of philosophy - Local Modern philosophy - Germany - Individual philosophers - Leibniz, Gottfried W.

Phil 3552.01 Ravier, E. Bibliographie de la philosophie de Leibniz. Thèse. Caen, 1927.
Phil 3552.02 Ravier, E. Bibliographie des oeuvres de Leibniz. Paris, 1937.
Phil 3552.5 Studia Leibnitiana. Wiesbaden. 1,1969+
Phil 3552.6 Studia Leibnitiana. Supplementa. Wiesbaden. 1,1968+ 8v.
Phil 3552.7 Internationaler Leibniz-Kongress. Der Internationale Leibniz-Kongress in Hannover. Hannover, 1968.
Phil 3552.9 Leibniz, Gottfried Wilhelm. Oeuvres choisies. Paris, 1939.
Phil 3552.10 Leibniz, Gottfried Wilhelm. Oeuvres philosophiques. Amsterdam, 1765.
Htn Phil 3552.10.2* Leibniz, Gottfried Wilhelm. Oeuvres philosophiques. Amsterdam, 1765.
Phil 3552.10.15 Leibniz, Gottfried Wilhelm. Philosophische Werke nach Rapspens Sammlung. Halle 1778-80. 2v.
Phil 3552.11 Leibniz, Gottfried Wilhelm. Opera omnia. Genevae, 1768. 6v.
Phil 3552.12 Leibniz, Gottfried Wilhelm. Sämtliche Schriften und Briefe. v.1, pt.1-8. Darmstadt, 1923-50. 8v.
Phil 3552.13 Leibniz, Gottfried Wilhelm. Die Werke von Leibniz gemäss seinem handschriftlichen Nachlasse in der Königlichen Bibliothek zu Hannover. Hannover, 1864-84. 11v.
Phil 3552.14 Leibniz, Gottfried Wilhelm. Die philosophischen Schriften. Berlin, 1875-90. 7v.
Phil 3552.15 Leibniz, Gottfried Wilhelm. Opera philosophica. v.1-2. Berolini, 1839-40.

196

Classified Listing

Phil 3552 History of philosophy - Local Modern philosophy - Germany - Individual philosophers - Leibniz, Gottfried W. - cont.

Phil 3552.16 Leibniz, Gottfried Wilhelm. Oeuvres. Paris, 1842-45. 2v.

Phil 3552.17 Leibniz, Gottfried Wilhelm. Oeuvres. Paris, 1859-75. 7v.

Phil 3552.18 Leibniz, Gottfried Wilhelm. Oeuvres philosophiques. v.2. Paris, 1866.

Phil 3552.18.5 Leibniz, Gottfried Wilhelm. Oeuvres philosophiques. 2e éd. Paris, 1900. 2v.

Phil 3552.18.10 Leibniz, Gottfried Wilhelm. Oeuvres, publiées pour la première fois d'après les manuscrits. v.2-7. N.Y., 1969. 7v.

Phil 3552.19 Leibniz, Gottfried Wilhelm. Opuscules et fragments inédits. Paris, 1903.

Phil 3552.19.5 Leibniz, Gottfried Wilhelm. Lettres et opuscules inédits. Paris, 1854.

Phil 3552.20 Leibniz, Gottfried Wilhelm. Opusculum adscititio titulo Systema theologicum inscriptum. Lutetiae Parisiorum, 1845.

Phil 3552.21 Leibniz, Gottfried Wilhelm. Kleinere philosophische Schriften. Jena, 1740.

Phil 3552.21.5 Leibniz, Gottfried Wilhelm. Kleine Schriften zur Metaphysik. Frankfurt, 1965.

Phil 3552.22 Leibniz, Gottfried Wilhelm. Kleinere philosophische Schriften. Leipzig, 1883.

Phil 3552.23 Leibniz, Gottfried Wilhelm. Deutsche Schriften. Leipzig, 1916. 2v.

Phil 3552.23.5 Leibniz, Gottfried Wilhelm. Deutsche Schriften. Berlin, 1838-40. 2v.

Phil 3552.23.10 Leibniz, Gottfried Wilhelm. Ermahnung anu die Deutschen. Darmstadt, 1967.

Phil 3552.24 Leibniz, Gottfried Wilhelm. Hauptschriften zur Grundelung der Philosophie. Leipzig, 1904-06. 2v.

Phil 3552.24.5.3 Leibniz, Gottfried Wilhelm. Hauptschriften zur Grundelung der Philosophie. 3. Aufl. Hamburg, 1966. 2v.

Phil 3552.24.20 Leibniz, Gottfried Wilhelm. Werke. Stuttgart, 1949.

Phil 3552.24.25 Leibniz, Gottfried Wilhelm. Opera philosophica. Aalen, 1959.

Phil 3552.25 Leibniz, Gottfried Wilhelm. Philosophical works. New Haven, 1890.

Phil 3552.25.2 Leibniz, Gottfried Wilhelm. Philosophical works. 2nd ed. New Haven, 1908.

Phil 3552.26 Leibniz, Gottfried Wilhelm. Opere varie. Bari, 1912.

Phil 3552.27 Leibniz, Gottfried Wilhelm. Schäpferische Vernunft. Marbrug, 1951.

Phil 3552.28 Leibniz, Gottfried Wilhelm. Geist des Herrn von Leibniz. Wittenburg, 1775. 2v.

Phil 3552.28.5 Leibniz, Gottfried Wilhelm. Leibniz als Denker. Leipzig, 1863.

Htn Phil 3552.29* Leibniz, Gottfried Wilhelm. Otium hanoueranum sive Miscellanea. Lipsiae, 1718.

Htn Phil 3552.29.2* Leibniz, Gottfried Wilhelm. Otium hanoueranum sive Miscellanea. Lipsiae, 1718.

Phil 3552.29.25 Leibniz, Gottfried Wilhelm. Opere filosofiche; estratti. Bologna, 1929.

Phil 3552.29.35 Leibniz, Gottfried Wilhelm. Leibniz et la racine de l'existence. Par+s, 1962.

Htn Phil 3552.30.5* Leibniz, Gottfried Wilhelm. Principia philosophica. Lipsiae, 1728.

Phil 3552.30.10 Leibniz, Gottfried Wilhelm. Opuscula philosophica selecta. Paris, 1939.

Phil 3552.30.15 Leibniz, Gottfried Wilhelm. Opuscules philosophiques choisis. Paris, 1954.

Phil 3552.31 Leibniz, Gottfried Wilhelm. Gottfried Wilhelm Leibniz; Gott, Geist, Güte. Gütersloh, 1947.

Phil 3552.32 Leibniz, Gottfried Wilhelm. Philosophical papers and letters. Chicago, 1956. 2v.

Phil 3552.32.2 Leibniz, Gottfried Wilhelm. Philosophical papers and letters. 2nd ed. Dordrecht, 1969.

Phil 3552.33 Leibniz, Gottfried. Politische Schriften. v.1-2. Wien, 1966-67.

Phil 3552.34 Leibniz, Gottfried Wilhelm. Philosophical writings. London, 1956.

Phil 3552.35 Leibniz, Gottfried Wilhelm. General investigations concerning the analysis of concepts and truths. Athens, 1968.

Phil 3552.36 Leibniz, Gottfried Wilhelm. Selections. N.Y., 1951.

Phil 3552.38 Leibniz, Gottfried Wilhelm. Welträtsel und Lebensharmonie. Wiesbaden, 1949.

Phil 3552.39 Leibniz, Gottfried Wilhelm. Neue Abhandlungen über den menschlichen verstand. 3e Aufl. Leipzig, 1915.

Phil 3552.39.5 Leibniz, Gottfried Wilhelm. Neue Abhandlungen über den menschlichen verstand. Frankfurt, 1961. 2v.

Phil 3552.40A Leibniz, Gottfried Wilhelm. New essays concerning human understanding. N.Y., 1896.

Phil 3552.40B Leibniz, Gottfried Wilhelm. New essays concerning human understanding. N.Y., 1896.

Phil 3552.40.5 Leibniz, Gottfried Wilhelm. New essays concerning human understanding. 3rd ed. La Salle, 1949.

Phil 3552.41 Leibniz, Gottfried Wilhelm. Nouveaux essais sur l'entendement humain. Paris, 1899.

Phil 3552.41.5 Leibniz, Gottfried Wilhelm. Nouveaux essais sur l'entendement humain. Paris, 1886.

Phil 3552.41.10 Leibniz, Gottfried Wilhelm. Nouveaux essais sur l'entendement humain. Paris, 1966.

Phil 3552.42 Leibniz, Gottfried Wilhelm. Nové úvahy o lidské soudnosti od auktora Systému předjednané harmonie. Praha, 1932.

Htn Phil 3552.45* Leibniz, Gottfried Wilhelm. Réfutation inédite de Spinoza. Paris, 1854.

Htn Phil 3552.50* Leibniz, Gottfried Wilhelm. Disputatio metaphysica. Lipsiae, 1663.

Phil 3552.51 Leibniz, Gottfried Wilhelm. Discourse on metaphysics. Chicago, 1927.

Phil 3552.51.7 Leibniz, Gottfried Wilhelm. Discourse on metaphysics. Manchester, 1953.

Phil 3552.51.8 Leibniz, Gottfried Wilhelm. Discourse on metaphysics. La Salle, 1962.

Phil 3552.51.10 Leibniz, Gottfried Wilhelm. Discours de métaphysique. Paris, 1929.

Phil 3552.51.12 Leibniz, Gottfried Wilhelm. Discours de métaphysique et Correspondance aves Arnauld. Paris, 1957.

Phil 3552.51.15 Leibniz, Gottfried Wilhelm. Discorso di metafisica "Hortus conclusus". Napoli, 1934.

Phil 3552.52 Leibniz, Gottfried Wilhelm. Confessio philosophi. Paris, 1961.

Phil 3552.53 Leibniz, Gottfried Wilhelm. Den förutbestämda harmonien. Stockholm, 1927.

Phil 3552 History of philosophy - Local Modern philosophy - Germany - Individual philosophers - Leibniz, Gottfried W. - cont.

Phil 3552.54 Leibniz, Gottfried Wilhelm. Lehr-Satze über die Monadologie. Franckfurt, 1720.

Htn Phil 3552.55* Leibniz, Gottfried Wilhelm. Ars Combinatoria. Francofurti, 1690.

Phil 3552.56 Leibniz, Gottfried Wilhelm. Abhandlung über die beste philosophische Ausdrucksweise. Berlin, 1916.

Phil 3552.57A Leibniz, Gottfried Wilhelm. Die Hauptwerke. 3. Aufl. Stuttgart, 1949.

Phil 3552.57B Leibniz, Gottfried Wilhelm. Die Hauptwerke. 3. Aufl. Stuttgart, 1949.

Htn Phil 3552.58* Leibniz, Gottfried Wilhelm. Summi polyhistoris Godefridi Guilielmi Leibntii Protogaea. Goettingae, 1749.

Phil 3552.59 Leibniz, Gottfried Wilhelm. Protegée; ou De la formation et des révolutions du globe. Paris, 1859.

Htn Phil 3552.60* Leibniz, Gottfried Wilhelm. Essai de Theodicée. Amsterdam, 1710. 3 pam.

Phil 3552.60.5 Leibniz, Gottfried Wilhelm. Essais de Theodicée sur la bonté de Dieu. Amsterdam, 1720.

Phil 3552.60.10 Leibniz, Gottfried Wilhelm. Essais de Theodicée. Paris, 1962.

Phil 3552.61 Leibniz, Gottfried Wilhelm. Essais de Theodicée. Paris, 1720.

Phil 3552.62 Leibniz, Gottfried Wilhelm. Theodicaea. Paris, 1726.

Phil 3552.62.10 Leibniz, Gottfried Wilhelm. Theodicée. Hannover, 1744.

Htn Phil 3552.63* Leibniz, Gottfried Wilhelm. Theodicee. Hannover, 1763.

Phil 3552.63.10 Leibniz, Gottfried Wilhelm. Theodicy. New Haven, 1952.

Phil 3552.63.15 Leibniz, Gottfried Wilhelm. Die Theodicee. Leipzig, 1883. 2v.

Phil 3552.63.20 Leibniz, Gottfried Wilhelm. Tentamina theodicaeae de bonitate Dei libertate hominis et origine mali. Francofurti, 1719.

Phil 3552.63.25 Leibniz, Gottfried Wilhelm. Tentamina theodicaeae de bonitate Dei libertate hominis et origine mali. Tubingae, 1771.

Phil 3552.63.30 Leibniz, Gottfried Wilhelm. La monadologie. Paris, 1952.

Phil 3552.63.40 Leibniz, Gottfried Wilhelm. Plädoyer fur Gottes Gottheit. 1. Aufl. Berlin, 1947.

Htn Phil 3552.64* Leibniz, Gottfried Wilhelm. De la tolérance des religions. Paris, 1692.

Phil 3552.65 Leibniz, Gottfried Wilhelm. The monadology. Oxford, 1898.

Phil 3552.65.10 Leibniz, Gottfried Wilhelm. The monadology of Leibniz. Los Angeles, 1930.

NEDL Phil 3552.66 Leibniz, Gottfried Wilhelm. La monadologie, avec étude et notes. Paris, 1900.

Phil 3552.66.11 Leibniz, Gottfried Wilhelm. La monadologia. Milano, 1926.

Phil 3552.66.13 Leibniz, Gottfried Wilhelm. Monadologie. 2. Ausg. Stuttgart, 1954.

Phil 3552.66.16 Leibniz, Gottfried Wilhelm. La monadologia. Torino, 1929.

Phil 3552.67 Leibniz, Gottfried Wilhelm. La monadologie. Paris, 1881.

Phil 3552.67.3 Leibniz, Gottfried Wilhelm. La monadologie. Paris, 1883.

Phil 3552.67.5 Leibniz, Gottfried Wilhelm. La monadologie. 5. éd. Paris, n.d.

Phil 3552.67.15 Leibniz, Gottfried Wilhelm. Monadologie. Wien, 1847.

Phil 3552.67.20 Leibniz, Gottfried Wilhelm. Vernunftprinzipien der Natur und der Gnade. Hamburg, 1956.

Phil 3552.67.30 Leibniz, Gottfried Wilhelm. Grundwahrheiten der Philosophie. Frankfurt, 1962.

Phil 3552.67.40 Leibniz, Gottfried Wilhelm. Monadology, and other philosophical essays. Indianapolis, 1965.

Phil 3552.68 Leibniz, Gottfried Wilhelm. Exposition sur la religion. Paris, 1819.

Phil 3552.69 Leibniz, Gottfried Wilhelm. A system of theology. London, 1850.

Phil 3552.69.20 Leibniz, Gottfried Wilhelm. Theologisches System. Tübingen, 1860.

Phil 3552.69.30 Leibniz, Gottfried Wilhelm. System der Theologie. Mainz, 1820.

Phil 3552.70 Leibniz, Gottfried Wilhelm. Recueil...Pieces...Leibniz. Lausanne, 1759. 2v.

Phil 3552.71 Leibniz, Gottfried Wilhelm. A collection of papers. London, 1717.

Htn Phil 3552.71.1* Leibniz, Gottfried Wilhelm. A collection of papers. London, 1717.

Phil 3552.72 Leibniz, Gottfried Wilhelm. Textes inédits d'après les manuscrits de la Bibliothèque provinciale. Paris, 1948. 2v.

Phil 3552.73 Leibniz, Gottfried Wilhelm. Leibnizens geschichtliche Aufsätze und Gedichte. Hannover, 1847.

Phil 3552.73.5 Leibniz, Gottfried Wilhelm. Logical papers. Oxford, 1966.

Htn Phil 3552.74* Leibniz, Gottfried Wilhelm. Epistolae ad diversos. Cum annotationibus suis primum divulgavit christian. Lipsiae, 1734-42. 4v.

Phil 3552.75 Leibnizens Briefwechsel...Bernstorff. Hannover, 1882.

Phil 3552.76 Leibniz, Gottfried Wilhelm. Nouvelles lettres. Paris, 1857.

Phil 3552.77 Leibniz, Gottfried Wilhelm. Der Briefwechsel. Hannover, 1889.

Phil 3552.77.20 Leibniz, Gottfried Wilhelm. Correspondance de Leibniz avec l'électrice Sophie de Brunswick-Lunebourg. Hanovre, 1874. 3v.

Phil 3552.78 Leibniz, Gottfried Wilhelm. Briefwechsel zwischen Leibniz, Arnould, und dem Landgrafen Earnst von Hessen-Rheinfels. Hannover, 1846.

Phil 3552.78.5 Leibniz, Gottfried Wilhelm. Leibniz und Landgraf E. von Hessen-Rheinfels...Briefwechsel. v.1-2. Frankfurt, 1847.

Phil 3552.78.10 Leibniz, Gottfried Wilhelm. Sechzehn ungedruckte Briefe. Zürich, 1844.

Phil 3552.78.15 Leibniz, Gottfried Wilhelm. Correspondance Leibnitz-Clarke présentée d'après les manuscrits originaux des bibliothèques de Hanovre et de Londres. 1. éd. Paris, 1957.

Phil 3552.78.25 Leibniz, Gottfried Wilhelm. Leibniz' bref till Sparfrenfelt. n.p., n.d.

Phil 3552.78.30 Leibniz, Gottfried Wilhelm. Lettres et fragments inédits sur les problèmes philosophiques. Paris, 1934.

Phil 3552.78.35 Leibniz, Gottfried Wilhelm. Principes de la nature et de la grace fondés en raison. Paris, 1954.

Phil 3552.78.40 Leibniz, Gottfried Wilhelm. Leibniz korrespondiert mit Paris. Hamburg, 1940.

Phil 3552.78.50 Leibniz, Gottfried Wilhelm. Lettres de Leibniz à Arnauld. 1. éd. Paris, 1952.

Phil 3552.78.80 Leibniz, Gottfried Wilhelm. The Leibniz-Arnauld correspondence. Manchester, 1967.

Phil 3552.79 Pamphlet vol. Leibniz. 14 pam.

NEDL Phil 3552.79.2 Pamphlet vol. Leibniz. German dissertations, 1909-1929. 15 pam.

Phil 3552 History of philosophy - Local Modern philosophy - Germany - Individual philosophers - Leibniz, Gottfried W. - cont.

Phil 3552.79.3   Pamphlet box. Leibniz. German dissertations.
Phil 3552.79.5   Pamphlet box. Leibniz.
Phil 3552.79.20   Leibniz zu seinem 300. Geburtstag. 1-7. Berlin, 1946-52.
Phil 3552.79.25   Leibniz, Gottfried Wilhelm. Metaphysische Abhandlung. Hamburg, 1958.
Phil 3552.79.30   Leibniz, Gottfried Wilhelm. Saggi filosofici e lettere. Bari, 1963.
Phil 3552.80   Barchudarian, J. Inwiefern ist Leibniz in der Psychologie ein Vorgänger Herbarts. Jena, 1889.
Phil 3552.81   Braeutigam, L. Leibniz und Herbart über die Freiheit des menschlichen Willens. Heidelberg, 1882.
Phil 3552.82   Bilfingeri, G.B. Harmonia...praestabilita...Leibnitii. Tubingae, 1741.
Phil 3552.83.5   Dewey, J. Leibniz's new essays concerning the human understanding. Chicago, 1902.
Phil 3552.84   Encke, J.F. Rede...G.W. Leibnitz. Berlin, 1842.
Phil 3552.86   Foucher de Careil, Alexandre. Leibniz la philosophie juive et la cabale. Paris, 1861.
Phil 3552.86.5   Foucher de Careil, Alexandre. Leibniz et les deux sophies. Paris, 1876.
Phil 3552.86.10   Foucher de Careil, Alexandre. Leibniz et Pierre-le-Grand. Paris, 1874.
Phil 3552.86.15   Foucher de Careil, Alexandre. Leibniz, Descartes et Spinoza. Paris, 1862.
Phil 3552.87   Guhrauer, G.E. Gottfried Willhelm Freiherr von Leibnitz. Breslau, 1842. 2v.
Phil 3552.88   Jellinek, G. Die Weltanschauungen Leibnitz' und Schopenhauer's, ihre Gründe und ihre Berechtigung. Wien, 1872.
Phil 3552.89   Koppehl, H. Die Verwandtschaft Leibizens mit Thomas von Aquino. Jena, 1892.
Phil 3552.90   Ludovici, C.G. Ausfuhrlicher...Historie der leibnitzischen Philosophie. Leipzig, 1737. 2v.
Phil 3552.91   Mackie, J.M. Life of Godfrey William von Leibnitz. Boston, 1845.
Phil 3552.92A   Merz, J.T. Leibniz. Philadelphia, 1884.
Phil 3552.92B   Merz, J.T. Leibniz. Philadelphia, 1884.
Phil 3552.92.5   Merz, J.T. Leibniz. Edinburgh, 1907.
Phil 3552.93   Schmidt, J. Leibnitz und Baumgarten. Halle, 1875.
Phil 3552.93.5   Glöckner, G. Der Gottesbegriff bei Leibniz. Langensalza, 1888.
Phil 3552.94   Schwarz, H. Die Leibniz'sche Philosophie. Jena, 1888.
Phil 3552.94.5   Kirchner, Friedrich. Leibniz's Psychologie. Cöthen, 1875.
Phil 3552.94.9   Kirchner, Friedrich. Gottfried Wilhelm Leibniz. Cöthen, 1876.
Phil 3552.95   Secretan, C. La philosophie de Leibnitz. Genève, 1840.
Phil 3552.96   Stein, L. Leibniz und Spinoza. Berlin, 1890.
Phil 3552.97   Wernick, G. Der Begriff der Materie bei Leibniz. Jena, 1893.
Phil 3552.98   Leroy, G.V. Die philosophische Probleme...Leibniz und Clarke. Mainz, 1893.
Phil 3552.99   Volz, L. Die Erkenntnisstheorien bei Leibniz und Kant. Rostock, 1895.
Phil 3552.100   Renouvier, Charles. La nouvelle monadologie. Paris, 1899.
Phil 3552.101   Hahn, R. Die Entwickelung der leibnizischen Metaphysik. Halle, 1899.
Phil 3552.102   Werckmeister, Walther. Der leibnizsche Substanzbegriff. Halle, 1899.
Phil 3552.103   Willareth, O. Die Lehre vom Uebel. Strassburg, 1898.
Phil 3552.104.2   Russell, Bertrand Russell. A critical exposition of the philosophy of Leibniz..2d ed. London, 1967.
Phil 3552.105   Rall, H.F. Der leibnizsche Substanzbegriff. Halle, 1899.
*L Phil 3552.106   Couturat, L. La logique de Leibniz. Paris, 1901.
Phil 3552.107   Dillmann, E. Eine neue Darstellung der leibnizischen Monadenlehre. Leipzig, 1891.
Phil 3552.108   Archambault, P. Leibniz. Paris, n.d.
Phil 3552.109   Ward, A.W. Leibniz as a politician. Manchester, 1911.
Phil 3552.110   Bodemann, E. Die Leibniz-Handschriften. Hannover, 1895.
Phil 3552.110.5   Bodemann, E. G.W. Leibniz. Hannover, 1876.
Phil 3552.111   Cassirer, E. Leibniz' System. Marburg, 1902.
Phil 3552.111.9   Grassi-Bertazzi, G. L'inconscio nella filosofia di Leibnifd. Catania, 1903.
Phil 3552.111.15   Rydberg, Viktor. Leibniz' Theodicee. Leipzig, 1903.
Phil 3552.112   Baruzi, Jean. La pensée chretienne...Leibniz. Paris, 1909.
Phil 3552.112.5   Baruzi, Jean. Leibniz et l'organisation religieuse. Paris, 1907.
Phil 3552.113   Nourrisson, M. La philosophie de Leibniz. Paris, 1860.
Phil 3552.114   Davillé, L. Leibniz historien. Paris, 1909.
Phil 3552.114.5A   Kabitz, Willy. Die Philosophie des Jungen Leibniz. Heidelberg, 1909.
Phil 3552.114.5B   Kabitz, Willy. Die Philosophie des Jungen Leibniz. Heidelberg, 1909.
Phil 3552.115   Beneke, H.F. Leibniz als Ethiker. Erlangen, 1891.
Phil 3552.116   Ritter, P.H. De monadenleer van Leibniz. Leiden, 1882.
Phil 3552.116.5   Vallier, Charles A. De possibilibus apud Leibnitium. Thesis. Burdigalae, 1882.
Phil 3552.117   Gesche, Paul. Die Ethik Leibnizens. Halle, 1891.
Phil 3552.118   Schmarsow, A. Justus-Georgius Schottelius i. Leibniz und Schottelius. Strassburg, 1877.
Phil 3552.119   Pichler, A. Die Theologie des Leibniz. München, 1869. 2v.
Phil 3552.119.5   Grote, Ludwig. Leibniz und seine Zeit. Hannover, 1869.
Phil 3552.120   Kirchner, Friedrich. Leibnitz's Stellung zur katholischen Kirche. Berlin, 1874.
Phil 3552.120.5   Class, Gustav. Die metaphysischen Voraussetzungen. Tübingen, 1874.
Phil 3552.120.10   Class, Gustav. Der Determinismus von Leibniz. Tübingen, 1874.
Phil 3552.121   Piat, C. Leibniz. Paris, 1915.
Phil 3552.122   Halbwachs, Maurice. Leibniz. Paris, 1907.
Phil 3552.122.5   Halbwachs, Maurice. Leibniz. Paris, 1929.
Phil 3552.123   Blondel, Maurice. De vinculo substantiali. Thesis. Paris, 1893.
Phil 3552.123.5   Blondel, Maurice. Une énigme historique, le "vinculum substantiali" d'après Leibniz. 1. éd. Paris, 1930.
Phil 3552.124   Penjon, Auguste. De infinito apud Leibnitium. Thesis. Paris, 1878.
Phil 3552.125   Ganz, Hans. Das Unbewusste bei Leibniz...Theorien. Zürich, 1917.
Phil 3552.125.5   Wundt, Wilhelm. Leibniz, zu seinen Zweihundertzahrigen. Leipzig, 1917.
Phil 3552.125.9   Wundt, Wilhelm. Gottfried Wilhelm Leibniz. Gestorben 1716. Stuttgart, 1916.
Phil 3552.126   Lieder, F.W.C. Friedrich Spie and the théodicée of Leibniz. Urbana, 1912.

Phil 3552 History of philosophy - Local Modern philosophy - Germany - Individual philosophers - Leibniz, Gottfried W. - cont.

Phil 3552.127   Kiefl, Franz X. Der europäische Freiheitskampf. Mainz, 1913.
Phil 3552.127.5   Kiefl, Franz X. Leibniz und die religiöse Wiedervereinigung Deutschlands. 2. Aufl. München, 1925.
Phil 3552.128   Engler, Otto. Darstellung und Kritik der leibnitzischen Optimismus. Inaug.-Diss. Jena, 1883.
Phil 3552.129   Pichler, Hans. Leibniz. Graz, 1919.
Phil 3552.130   Mahnke, D. Leibniz als Gegner der Gelehrteneinseitigkeit. Stade, 1912.
Phil 3552.130.5   Mahnke, D. Leibniz und Goethe. Erfurt, 1924.
Phil 3552.130.10   Mahnke, D. Leibnizens Synthese von Universalmathematik und Individualmethaphysik. Halle, 1925.
Phil 3552.131   Carlotti, G. Il sistema die Leibniz. Messina, 1923.
Phil 3552.132   Geijer, K.R. Huru förhåller sig Leibnitz' metafysik. Upsala, 1876.
Phil 3552.133   Bolin, Wilhelm. Leibnitz ett forëbud till Kant. Akademisk afhandling. Helsingfors, 1864.
Phil 3552.135   Svahn, Oscar. Monadlärans uppkomst. Lund, 1863.
Phil 3552.227   Thilly, Frank. Leibnizens Streit gegen Locke. Heidelberg, 1891.
Phil 3552.229   Kvĕt, F.B. Leibnitz und Comenius. Prag, 1857.
Phil 3552.229.5   Kvĕt, F.B. Leibnitz'ens Logik. Prag, 1857.
Phil 3552.231   Durdik, Josef. Leibnitz und Newton. Halle, 1869.
Phil 3552.233   Eberhard, J.A. Charakteristik des Leibnitz. Leipzig, n.d.
Phil 3552.236   Bugarski, G.M. Die Natur des Willens bei Leibniz. Leipzig, 1889.
Phil 3552.238   Silberstein, Adela. Leibniz' Apriorismus. Weimar, 1902.
Phil 3552.242   Neff, L. Abfassungszeit von Leibnizens Unvorgreiflichen Gedanken. Durlach, 1880.
Phil 3552.242.5   Neff, L. Gottfried Wilhelm Leibniz als Sprachforscher und Etynologie. v.1-2. Heidelburg, 1870-71.
Phil 3552.244   Dafert, F.W. Gottfried Wilhelm Leibniz als Deutscher. Wien, 1883.
Phil 3552.246   Urbach, B. Leibnizens Rechtfertigung des Uebels. Prag, 1901.
Phil 3552.247   Ivaldi, I.G. Il platonismo di Plotino, Sant'Agosinto, Cartesio, Leibniz. Napoli, n.d.
Phil 3552.248   Schulze, G.E. Uber die Entdeckung, dass Leibniz ein Katholik gewesen sey. Göttingen, 1827.
Phil 3552.249   Ernst, Charles. Die Tierseele in der leibnizschen Philosophie. Wiesbaden, 1918.
Phil 3552.250   Hartenstein, G. De materiae apud Leibnitium notione et ad monadas relatione. Lipsiae, 1846.
Phil 3552.251   Emery, J.A. Esprit de Leibnitz. Lyon, 1772. 2v.
Phil 3552.251.5   Emery, J.A. Pensées de Leibnitz sur la religion. Paris, 1803. 2v.
Phil 3552.252   Hannequin, A. Quae fuerit prior Leibnitii philosophia. Thesis. Paris, 1895.
Phil 3552.253   Cresson, André. De liberate apud Leibnitium. Thesis. Paris, 1903.
Phil 3552.253.5   Cresson, André. Leibniz, sa vie, son oeuvre. Paris, 1946.
Phil 3552.253.8   Cresson, André. Leibniz, sa vie, son oeuvre. 3. éd. Paris, 1958.
Phil 3552.254   Bertereau, A. Leibnitz considéré comme historien de la philosophie. Thèse. Paris, 1843.
Phil 3552.255   Boirac, Aemilius. De spatio apud Leibnitium. Thesis. Paris, 1894.
Phil 3552.256   Sigorgne, P. Institutions léibnitiennes. Lyon, 1768.
Phil 3552.257   Nathan, Bernhard. Über das Verhältnis der leibnizischen Ethik zu Metaphysik und Theologie. Diss. Jena, 1916.
Phil 3552.258   Jasinowski, B. Die analytische Urteilslehre Leibnizens. Diss. Wien, 1918.
Phil 3552.259   Kolls. Zur Chronologie der leibnizischen Abhandlung "De vera methodo philosphiae et theologiae". Schönberg, 1906.
Phil 3552.260   Schmalenbach, H. Leibniz. München, 1921.
Phil 3552.261   Ravier, E. Le système de Leibniz et le problème des rapports de la raison et de la foi. Thèse. Caen, 1927.
Phil 3552.262   Auerbach, S. Zur Entwickelungsgeschichte der leibnitzschen Monadenlehre. Diss. Dessau, 1884.
Phil 3552.263   Köhler, Paul. Der Begriff der Repräsentation bei Leibniz. Bern, 1913.
Phil 3552.264   Rosenfeld, J. Die doppelte Wahrheit...Leibniz und Hurne. Diss. Bern, 1912.
Phil 3552.265   Brunswig, A. Leibniz. Wien, 1925.
Phil 3552.266   Ohse, Jakob. Untersuchungen über den Substansbegriff bei Leibniz. Inaug.-Diss. Dorpat, 1888.
Phil 3552.267   Caspari, Otto. Leibniz' Philosophie. Leipzig, 1870.
Phil 3552.268   Reinhardt, Arthur. Sind es Vorzugsweise speculative oder naturwissenschaftliche Gründe. Jena, 1873.
Phil 3552.270   Frenzel, Bernhard. Der Associationsbegriff bei Leibniz. Leipzig, 1898.
Phil 3552.272   Jaenicke, Kurt. Das Verhaltnis des Korperlichen zum Geistigen und die Entwicklung des Geistigen bei Leibniz. Cöthen, 1913.
Phil 3552.273   Jasper, Joseph. Leibniz und die Scholastik. Inaug. Diss. Münster, 1898-99.
Phil 3552.274   Mabilleau, L. De perfectione apud Leibnitium. Thesim. Paris, 1861.
Phil 3552.275   Schmoger, F. Leibniz in seiner Stellung zur tellurischen Physik. München, 1901.
Phil 3552.276   Trepte, Adolf. Die metaphysische Unvollkommenheit...bei Augustin und Leibniz. Inaug. Diss. Halle, 1889.
Phil 3552.277   Leibniz: zum Gedächtnis seines. 200. Jahrigen Todestages. Hannover, 1916.
Phil 3552.278   Jacoby, Daniel. De Leibnitii studiis Aristotelicis. Berolini, 1867.
Phil 3552.279   Carr, H.W. Leibniz. London, 1929.
Phil 3552.280   Wendt, Emil. Die Entwickelung der leibnizschen Monadenlehre bis zum Jahre 1695. Inaug. Diss. Berlin, 1885.
Phil 3552.281   Nolen, Désiré. Quid Leibniz uis Aristoteli debuerit. Parisiis, 1875.
Phil 3552.282   Hohenemser, E. Die Lehre von den kleinen Vorstellungen bei Leibniz. Heidelberg, 1899.
Phil 3552.283   Nithack, Emil. Darstellung und Kritik der Lehre Leibniz' von der menschlichen Wahlfreiheit. Inaug. Diss. Halle, 1893.
Phil 3552.284   Sjöberg, Gustaf M. Historisk öfversigt af den på monadlären grundade metafysikens utveckling. Upsala, 1868.
Phil 3552.285   Alstrin, Eric. Meditationes philosophicas. Upsala, 1731.
Phil 3552.286   Wanke, Georg. Das Stetigkeitsgesetz bei Leibniz. Inaug.-Diss. Kiel, 1892.
Phil 3552.287   Boutroux, Emile. La philosophie allemande au XVII siècle. Paris, 1929.
Phil 3552.288   Olgiati, Francesco. Il significato storico di Leibniz. Milano, 1929.
Phil 3552.289   Stammler, G. Leibniz. München, 1930.

Phil 3552   History of philosophy - Local Modern philosophy - Germany - Individual philosophers - Leibniz, Gottfried W. - cont.

Phil 3552.290	Klopp, O. Zur Ehrenrettung von Leibniz. Berlin, 1878.
Phil 3552.291	Leibniz-Archiv. Darmstadt. 1-3 3v.
Phil 3552.292	Zimmermann, R. Das Rechtsprinzip bei Leibnitz. Wien, 1852.
Phil 3552.293	Strahm, Hans. Die "Petites Perceptions" im System von Leibniz. Bern, 1930.
Phil 3552.294	Lamprecht, J.F. Leben des Freyherrn Gottfried Wilhelm von Leibnitz au das licht Gestellet. Berlin, 1740.
Phil 3552.294.5	Lamprecht, J.F. Vita del Signore Barone Goffredo G. di Leibnitz. Roma, 1787.
Phil 3552.295	Bussenius, Karl. Über die Theodicee des Leibniz. Halle, 1876.
Phil 3552.296	Pfleiderer, Edmund. Gottfried Wilhelm Leibniz. Leipzig, 1870.
Phil 3552.296.10	Pfleiderer, Edmund. Leibniz als Verfasser von Zwölf Anonymen. Leipzig, 1870.
Phil 3552.296.15	Pfleiderer, Edmund. Leibniz und Geulinx mit besonderer Beziehung auf ihr beiderseitiges Uhrengleichniss. Tübingen, 1884.
Phil 3552.297	Capesius, J. Der Apperceptionsbegriff bei Leipzig und dessen Nachfolgern. Hermannstadt, 1894.
Phil 3552.298	Merkel, Franz R. G.W. Leigniz und die China Mission. Leipzig, 1920.
Phil 3552.299	Dieckhoff, A.W. Leibnitz Stellung zur Offenbarung. Rostock, 1888.
Phil 3552.300	Pflugbell, R. Der Begriff der ewigen Wahrheiten bei Leibniz. Inaug. Diss. Leipzig, 1902.
Phil 3552.301	Le Chevallier, L. La morale de Leibniz. Paris, 1933.
Phil 3552.302	Tirtsch, Gergely. Leibniz erkolcatana. Balassagyarmat, 1898.
Phil 3552.303	Barié, G.E. La spiritualità dell'essere e Leibniz. Padova, 1933.
Phil 3552.304	Gueroult, M. Dynamique et métaphysique Leibniziennes. Paris, 1934.
Phil 3552.305	Iwanicki, Joseph. Leibniz et les démonstrations mathématiques de l'existence de Dieu. Strasbourg, 1933.
Phil 3552.305.5	Iwanicki, Joseph. Leibniz et les démonstrations mathématiques de l'existence de Dieu. Thèse. Strasbourg, 1933.
Phil 3552.306	Rolland, E. Le déterminisme monadique. Paris, 1935.
Phil 3552.306.5	Rolland, E. Le déterminisme monadique. Thèse. Paris, 1935.
Phil 3552.307A	Schrecker, Paul. Leibniz; ses idées sur l'organisation des relations internationales. London, 1937.
Phil 3552.307B	Schrecker, Paul. Leibniz; ses idées sur l'organisation des relations internationales. London, 1937.
Phil 3552.308	Politella, Joseph. Platonism, Aristotoleanism and Cabelism in the philosophy of Leibniz. Philadelphia, 1938.
Phil 3552.309	Boehm, A. Le "vinculum substantiale" chez Leibniz. Paris, 1938.
Phil 3552.311	Mönnich, Conrad Willem. De natuurlijke kennis gods bij Leibniz. Rotterdam, 1942.
Phil 3552.312	Friedmann, G. Leibniz et Spinoza. Paris, 1946.
Phil 3552.312.2	Friedmann, G. Leibniz et Spinoza. Paris, 1962.
Phil 3552.313	Berse, Max. Über Leibniz: Leibniz und seine Ideology. Jena, 1946.
Phil 3552.314	Drago del Boca, S. Leibniz. Milano, 1946.
Phil 3552.315	Guggenberger, Alois. Leibniz. Stuttgart, 1947.
Phil 3552.316	Kanthack, K.H. Leibniz. Berlin, 1946.
Phil 3552.317	Litt, Theodore. Leibniz und die deutsche Gegenwart. Wiesbaden, 1946.
Phil 3552.318	Hamburger Akademische Rundschau. Gottfried Wilhelm Leibniz. Hamburg, 1946.
Phil 3552.319	Fleckenstein, Joachim O. Gottfried Wilhelm Leibniz. München, 1908.
Phil 3552.320	Joseph, H.W.B. Lectures on the philosophy of Leibniz. Oxford, 1949.
Phil 3552.322	Meyer, R.W. Leibniz und die europäische Ordnungskrise. Hamburg, 1948.
Phil 3552.322.5	Meyer, R.W. Leibnitz and the seventeenth century revolution. Cambridge, Eng., 1952.
Phil 3552.324	Pape, Ingetrud. Leibniz. Stuttgart, 1949.
Phil 3552.326	Matzat, H.L. Gesetz und Freiheit. Köln, 1948.
Phil 3552.328	Richter, L. Leibniz und sein Russland. Berlin, 1946.
Phil 3552.330	Stieler, Georg. Gottfried Wilhelm Leibniz. Paderborn, 1950.
Phil 3552.332	Huber, Kurt. Leibniz. München, 1951.
Phil 3552.334	Kanitz, H.J. Das übergegensätzliche Gezeigt am Kontinuitätsprinzip bei Leibniz. Hamburg, 1951.
Phil 3552.336	Belaval, Yvor. Pour connaître la pensée de Leibniz. Paris, 1952.
Phil 3552.336.5	Belaval, Yvor. Leibniz; initiation à sa philosophie. Paris, 1962.
Phil 3552.338	Hildebrandt, Kurt. Leibniz und das Reich der Gnade. Haag, 1953.
Phil 3552.340	Brunner, F. Études sur la signification historique de la philosophie de Leibniz. Thèse. Paris, 1950[1951]
Phil 3552.342	Ottaviano, C. Le basi fisico-metafische della filosofia di Leibniz. Padova, 1952.
Phil 3552.344	Corsano, A. G.W. Leibniz. Napoli, 1952.
Phil 3552.346.2	Grua, Gaston. Jurisprudence universelle et théodicée selon Leibniz. Thèse. Paris, 1953.
Phil 3552.346.5	Grua, Gaston. La justice humaine selon Leibniz. Thèse. Paris, 1956.
Phil 3552.348	Preti, G. Il cristianesimo universale di G.W. Leibniz. 1. ed. Roma, 1953.
Phil 3552.350	Archivio di Filosofia. Leibniz. Il congresso internazionale di filosofia, Roma, 1946. Roma, 1947.
Phil 3552.352	Saw, R.L. Leibniz. Harmondsworth, Eng., 1954.
Phil 3552.355	Merz, J.T. Leibniz. N.Y., 1948.
Phil 3552.358	Moreau, Joseph. L'univers leibnizien. Paris, 1956.
Phil 3552.360	Barone, F. Leibniz e la logica formale. Torino, 1955.
Phil 3552.362	Gruber, J.D. Commercii epistolici Leibnitiani. Hanoverae, 1745. 2v.
Phil 3552.365	Blumenthal, Erwin. Herders Auseinaudersetzung mit der Philosophie Leibnitzens. Diss. Hamburg, 1934.
Phil 3552.370	Krueger, G. Leibniz als Friedensstifter. Wiesbaden, 1947.
Phil 3552.375A	Clarke, Samuel. The Leibniz-Clarke correspondence. Manchester, 1956.
Phil 3552.375B	Clarke, Samuel. The Leibniz-Clarke correspondence. Manchester, 1956.
Phil 3552.380	Holz, Hans H. Leibniz. Stuttgart, 1958.
Phil 3552.385	Herrmann, Karl. Das Staatsdenken bei Leibniz. Bonn, 1958.
Phil 3552.390	Naert, Emilienne. Leibniz et la querelle du pur amour. Paris, 1959.
Phil 3552.395	Costabel, Pierre. Leibniz et la dynamique. Paris, 1960.

Phil 3552   History of philosophy - Local Modern philosophy - Germany - Individual philosophers - Leibniz, Gottfried W. - cont.

Phil 3552.400	Belaval, Yvon. Leibniz critique de Descartes. Paris, 1960.
Phil 3552.405	Leibniz, G.W. Polemika G. Leibnitsa i S. Klarka po voprosam filosofii i estesvoznaniia, 1715-1716 gg. Leningrad, 1960.
Phil 3552.405.5	Leibniz, G.W. Fragmente zur Logik. Berlin, 1960.
Phil 3552.410	Wildermuth, A. Wahrheit und Schöpfung. Winterthur, 1960.
Phil 3552.415	Guerrier, V.I. Leibnits i ego vek. Sankt Peterburg, 1868.
Phil 3552.420	Saame, Otto. Der Satz vom Gound bei Leibniz. Mainz, 1961.
Phil 3552.425	Lion, Ferdinand. Lebensquellen der deutschen Metaphysik. Frankfurt, 1960.
Phil 3552.430	Leibniz, G.W. Confessio philosophi. Paris, 1961.
Phil 3552.431	Leibniz, G.W. Confessio philosophi. Ein Dialog. Frankfurt, 1967.
Phil 3552.435	Naert, Emilienne. Mémoire et conscience de soi selon Leibniz. Paris, 1961.
Phil 3552.438	Wiedeburg, P.H. Der junge Leibniz das Keich und Europa. Wiesbaden, 1962. 3v.
Phil 3552.440	Burgelin, Pierre. Commentaire du Discourse de métaphysique de Leibniz. Paris, 1959.
Phil 3552.441	Meyer, H.G. Leibniz und Baumgarten als Begründer der deutschen Aesthetik. Halle, 1874.
Phil 3552.442	Schnelle, H. Zeichensysteme zur wissenschaftlichen Darstellung. Stuttgart, 1962.
Phil 3552.444	Panzer, Ursula. Die Phänomenalität der Res Extensa bei Leibniz. Köln, 1962.
Phil 3552.445	Leibniz, G.W. The preface to Leibniz' Novissima Sinica. Honolulu, 1957.
Phil 3552.446	Naert, Emilienne. La pensée politique de Leibniz. Paris, 1964.
Phil 3552.447	Tymieniecka, A.T. Leibniz' cosmological synthesis. Assen, 1964.
Phil 3552.448	Parkinson, George H.R. Logic and reality in Leibniz's metaphysics. Oxford, 1965.
Phil 3552.449	Cione, Edmondo. Leibniz. Napoli, 1964.
Phil 3552.450	Vitale, Ignazio. L'armonia prestabilita in Leibniz. Padova, 1959.
Phil 3552.451	Newman, L.M. Leibniz, 1646-1716. London, 1966.
Phil 3552.452	Totok, Wilhelm. Leibniz. Hannover, 1966.
Phil 3552.454	Rescher, Nicholas. The philosophy of Leibniz. Englewood Cliffs, N.J., 1967.
Phil 3552.460	Nedergaard-Hansen, Leif. Bayle's og Leibniz' drøftelse af theodicé-problemet; en idéhistorisk redegørelse. v.1-2. København, 1965.
Phil 3552.461	Robinet, André. Leibniz und Wir. Göttingen, 1967.
Phil 3552.462	Mueller, Kurt. Leibniz-Bibliographie; die Literatur über Leibniz. Frankfurt, 1967.
Phil 3552.462.5	Mueller, Kurt. Leben und Werk von Gottfried Wilhelm Leibniz. Frankfurt, 1969.
Phil 3552.464	Martin, Gottfried. Leibniz: logique et métaphysique. Paris, 1960.
Phil 3552.464.5.2	Martin, Gottfried. Leibniz. Logik und Metaphysik. 2. Aufl. Berlin, 1967.
Phil 3552.468	Jalabert, Jacques. Le Dieu de Leibniz. 1. éd. Paris, 1960.
Phil 3552.470	Morawietz, Kurt. Gottfried Wilhelm Leibniz. Hannover, 1962.
Phil 3552.471	Chuchmarev, Vladimir I. G.W. Leibnits i russkaia kul'tura. Moskva, 1968.
Phil 3552.472	Vennelusch, Joachim. Gottfried Wilhelm Leibniz; philosopher and politician in the service of a universal culture. Bad Godesberg, 1966.
Phil 3552.474	Schering, Ernst. Leibniz und die Versöhnung der Konfessionen. Stuttgart, 1966.
VPhil 3552.476	Simonovits, Istvánné. A dialektika Leibniz filozófiá. Budapest, 1965.
Phil 3552.476.5	Simonovits, Istvánné. Dialektisches Denken in der Philosophie von Gottfried Wilhelm Leibniz. Budapest, 1968
Phil 3552.478	Peursen, Cornelis Anthonie van. Leibniz. Baarn, 1966.
Phil 3552.478.1	Peursen, Cornelis Anthonie van. Leibniz. London, 1969.
Phil 3552.480	Journées, Leibniz. Leibniz, 1646-1716, aspects de l'homme et de l'oeuvre. Paris, 1968.
Phil 3552.482	Serres, Michel. Le système de Leibniz et ses modèles mathématiques. Paris, 1968.
Phil 3552.484	Halz, Hans Heinz. Herr und Knecht bei Leibniz und Hegel. Berlin, 1968.
Phil 3552.486	Krueger, Lorenz. Rationalismus und Entwurf einer universalen Logik bei Leibniz. Frankfurt, 1969.
Phil 3552.488	Cichowicz, Stanislaw. Filosof i istnienie. Wyd. 1. Warszawa, 1970.
Phil 3552.490	Pogrebyskii, Iosif B. Gotfrid Vil'gel'm Leibnits, 1646-1716. Moskva, 1971.

Phil 3565   History of philosophy - Local Modern philosophy - Germany - Individual philosophers - Lotze, Hermann

Phil 3565.10	Lotze, Hermann. Kleine Schriften. Leipzig, 1885-91. 4v.
Phil 3565.30	Lotze, Hermann. System der Philosophie. Leipzig, 1874-79. 2v.
Phil 3565.30.3A	Lotze, Hermann. System der Philosophie. 2e Aufl. Leipzig, 1880-84. 2v.
Phil 3565.30.3B	Lotze, Hermann. System der Philosophie. v.2. 2e Aufl. Leipzig, 1884.
Phil 3565.30.25	Lotze, Hermann. System der Philosophie. Leipzig, 1912. 2v.
Phil 3565.30.30	Lotze, Hermann. Logik, drei Bücher vom Denken. 2e Aufl. Leipzig, 1928.
Phil 3565.31	Lotze, Hermann. Logic. Oxford, 1884.
Phil 3565.31.2	Lotze, Hermann. Metaphysic. Oxford, 1884.
Phil 3565.31.4	Lotze, Hermann. Metaphysic. 2. ed. Oxford, 1887. 2v.
Phil 3565.31.15	Lotze, Hermann. Métaphysique. Paris, 1883.
Phil 3565.32	Lotze, Hermann. Outline of Metaphysic. Boston, 1886.
Phil 3565.32.1.3	Lotze, Hermann. Outline of Metaphysic. Boston, 1884.
Phil 3565.32.3	Lotze, Hermann. Outline of practical philosophy. Boston, 1885.
Phil 3565.32.4	Lotze, Hermann. Outline of psychology. Boston, 1886.
Phil 3565.32.5	Lotze, Hermann. Outline of aesthetics. Boston, 1886.
Phil 3565.32.5.5	Lotze, Hermann. Outlines of logic and of encyclopaedia of philosophy. Boston, 1887.
Phil 3565.32.6	Lotze, Hermann. Outlines of logic and of encyclopaedia of philosophy. Boston, 1892.
Phil 3565.35	Lotze, Hermann. Grundzüge der praktischen Philosophie. 3. Aufl. Leipzig, 1899.
Phil 3565.35.2	Lotze, Hermann. Grundzüge der praktischen Philosophie. Leipzig, 1882.
Phil 3565.45	Lotze, Hermann. Metaphysik. Leipzig, 1841.

Classified Listing

Phil 3565.45.5A   Lotze, Hermann. Grundzüge der Metaphysik. Leipzig, 1883.
Phil 3565.45.5B   Lotze, Hermann. Grundzüge der Metaphysik. Leipzig, 1883.
Phil 3565.45.10   Lotze, Hermann. Metaphysik. Leipzig, 1879.
Phil 3565.45.12   Lotze, Hermann. Grundzüge der Metaphysik. 2. Aufl. Leipzig, 1887.
Phil 3565.50   Lotze, Hermann. Mikrokosmus. Leipzig, 1869-72. 3v.
Phil 3565.50.5   Lotze, Hermann. Mikrokosmus. v.1-3. Leipzig, 1885-1896. 2v.
Phil 3565.50.6   Lotze, Hermann. Mikrokosmus. 6e Aufl. Leipzig, 1923. 3v.
Phil 3565.51   Lotze, Hermann. Microcosmus. N.Y., 1885. 2v.
Phil 3565.51.1   Lotze, Hermann. Microcosmus. v.1-2. N.Y., 1886.
Phil 3565.51.2   Lotze, Hermann. Microcosmus. v.1-2. 2. ed. N.Y., 1885.
Phil 3565.51.4   Lotze, Hermann. Microcosmus. v.1-2. N.Y., 1897.
Phil 3565.51.5   Lotze, Hermann. An outline of the Microcosmus. Oberlin, 1895.
Phil 3565.51.10   Lotze, Hermann. Microcosmo. Pavia, 1911-16. 2v.
Phil 3565.51.50   Lotze, Hermann. Das Dasein der Seele. Leipzig, 1929?
Phil 3565.55   Lotze, Hermann. Streitschriften. Leipzig, 1857.
Phil 3565.58   Lotze, Hermann. Grundtraek af religionsfilosofien. København, 1886.
Phil 3565.60   Lotze, Hermann. Grundzüge der Naturphilosophie. Leipzig, 1882.
Phil 3565.60.2   Lotze, Hermann. Grundzüge der Naturphilosophie. 2. Aufl. Leipzig, 1889.
Phil 3565.64   Lotze, Hermann. Logik. Leipzig, 1843.
Phil 3565.65   Lotze, Hermann. Grundzüge der Logik. Leipzig, 1883.
Phil 3565.65.5   Lotze, Hermann. Grundzüge der Logik und Encyklopädie der Philosophie. 3e Aufl. Leipzig, 1891.
Phil 3565.68   Lotze, Hermann. Medicinische Psychologie. Leipzig, 1852.
Htn   Phil 3565.68.1*   Lotze, Hermann. Medicinische Psychologie. Leipzig, 1852.
Phil 3565.68.5   Lotze, Hermann. Principes généraux de psychologie physiologique. Paris, 1876.
Phil 3565.69   Lotze, Hermann. Grundzüge der Psychologie. Leipzig, 1881.
Phil 3565.70   Lotze, Hermann. Outline of psychology. Minneapolis, 188-?
Phil 3565.72   Lotze, Hermann. Grundzüge der Religionsphilosophie. 2e Aufl. Leipzig, 1884.
Phil 3565.74   Lotze, Hermann. Der Zusammenhang der Dinge. Berlin, 191-?
Phil 3565.78   Pfleiderer, E. Lotze's philosophische Weltanschauungen nach ihren Grundzügen. Berlin, 1882. 5 pam.
Phil 3565.79   Pamphlet vol. Philosophy. German and Dutch. Lotze. German dissertations. 21 pam.
Phil 3565.79.2   Pamphlet vol. Philosophy. German and Dutch. Lotze. German dissertations. 17 pam.
Phil 3565.79.3   Pamphlet vol. Philosophy. German and Dutch. Lotze. German dissertations. 4 pam.
Phil 3565.79.4   Pamphlet box. Philosophy. German and Dutch. Lotze. German dissertations.
Phil 3565.79.5   Pamphlet box. Philosophy. German and Dutch. Lotze.
Phil 3565.80   Caspari, O. Hermann Lotze. Breslau, 1883.
Phil 3565.80.5   Caspari, O. Hermann Lotze. 2. Aufl. Breslau, 1895.
Phil 3565.81   Hartmann, K.R.E. Lotze's Philosophie. Leipzig, 1888.
Phil 3565.82   Jones, Henry. A critical account of the philosophy of Lotze. N.Y., 1895.
Phil 3565.82.5   Jones, Henry. A critical account of the philosophy of Lotze. Glasgow, 1895.
Phil 3565.83   Powers, J.H. Kritische Bemerkungen zu Lotze's Seelenbegriff. Göttingen, 1892.
Phil 3565.84   Matagrin, A. Essai sur l'esthétique de Lotze. Paris, 1901.
Phil 3565.85   Kalweit, P.F.M. Die praktische Begründung des Gottesbegriffs bei Lotze. Jena, 1900.
Phil 3565.86   Schoen, H. La métaphysique de Hermann Lotze. Paris, 1902.
Phil 3565.87   Bauer, C. Programm der Realschule zu Meerane. n.p., 1885.
Phil 3565.88   Ambrosi, L. Ermanno Lotze e la sua filosofia. Milano, 1912.
Phil 3565.89   Wentscher, M. Hermann Lotze. Heidelberg, 1913.
Phil 3565.89.5   Wentscher, M. Fechner und Lotze. München, 1925.
Phil 3565.106   Simon, Theodor. Leib und Seele bei Fechner und Lotze als vertretern Zweier massgebenden Weltanschauungen. Göttingen, 1894.
Phil 3565.108   Lange, Paul. Die Lehre vom Instinkte bei Lotze und Darwin. Berlin, 1896.
Phil 3565.108.5   Tienes, Alfred. Lotze's Gedanken zur den Principienfragen der Ethik. Heidelberg, 1896.
Phil 3565.109   Thomas, Evan E. Lotze's theory of reality. London, 1921.
Phil 3565.111   Geijer, Reinhold. Hermann Lotzes tankar om tid och timlighet i kritisk belysning. Lund, 1886.
Phil 3565.112   Elgström, Albin. Hermann Lotzes uppfattning af människans valfrihet. Lund, 1892.
Phil 3565.113   Falckenberg, R. Hermann Lotze. Stuttgart, 1901.
Phil 3565.114   Rosenquist, G.G. Lotzes religionsfilosofi. Helsingfors, 1889.
Phil 3565.115   Otto, Clemens. Hermann Lotze über das Unbewusste. Labes, 1900.
Phil 3565.116   Vorbrodt, G. Principien der Ethick und Religionsphilosophie Lotzes. Dessau, 1891.
Phil 3565.117   Pfleiderer, E. Lotze's philosophische Weltanschauung nach ihren Grundzügen. Berlin, 1882.
Phil 3565.118   Hahn, Gustav. Der Allbeseelungsgedanke bei Lotze. Stuttgart, 1925.
Phil 3565.120   Seibert, F. Lotze als Anthropologe. Wiesbaden, 1900.
Phil 3565.122   Thieme, K. Gott und Wissen bei Lotze. Leipzig, 1888.
Phil 3565.123   Wentscher, E. Das Kausalproblem in Lotzes Philosophie. Halle, 1903.
Phil 3565.124   Kögel, Fritz. Lotzes Aesthetik. Göttingen, 1886.
Phil 3565.125   Schröder, Arthur. Geschichtsphilosophie bei Lotze. Diss. Leipzig, 1896.
Phil 3565.126   Nath, Max. Die Psychologie Hermann Lotzes in ihrem Verhältnis zu Herbart. Halle, 1892.
Phil 3565.127   Baerwald, Leo. Die Entwicklung der Lotzeschen Psychologie. Berlin, 1905.
Phil 3565.128   Bartell, Fr., pastor. Lotze's religionsphilosophische Gedanken im Lichte der göttichen Offenbarung. Hannover, 1884.
Phil 3565.129   Tuch, Ernst. Lotzes Stellung zum Occasionalismus. Halle, 1897.
Phil 3565.130   An, Ho-Sang. Hermann Lotzes Bedeutung für das Problem der Beziehung. Bonn, 1967.
Phil 3565.131   Wartenberg, Mscislaw. Das problem des Wirkens und die monistische Weltanschauung. Leipzig, 1900.
Phil 3565.132   Santayana, George. Lotze's system of philosophy. Bloomington, 1971.

Phil 3585.1.30   Lambert, Johann Heinrich. Logische und philosophische Abhandlungen. Berlin, 1782-87. 2v.
Phil 3585.1.35   Lambert, Johann Heinrich. Philosophische Schriften. Reprografischer Nachdruck. v.1-4,6-7,9. Hildesheim, 1965-7v.
Phil 3585.1.40   Lambert, Johann Heinrich. Anlage zur Architectonic oder Theorie. Riga, 1771. 2v.
Phil 3585.1.45F   Steck, Max. Bibliographia Lambertiana. Berlin, 1943.
Htn   Phil 3585.1.50*   Strnadt, A. Gedanken über die schönen und soliden Wissenschaften. Dresden, 1794.
Phil 3585.1.80   Baensch, Otto. Johann Heinrich Lamberts Philosophie und seine Stellung zu Kant. Inaug. Diss. Magdeburg, 1902.
Phil 3585.1.85   Peters, Wilhelm S. Johann Heinrich Lamberts Konzeption einer Geometrie auf einer imaginaren Kugel. Bonn, 1961.
Phil 3585.1.90   Lepsius, J. Johann Heinrich Lambert; eine Darstellung seiner kosmologischen und philosophischen Leistungen. München, 1881.
Phil 3585.1.95   Sterkman, P. De plaats van J.H. Lambert...idealisme voor Kant. 's-Gravenhage, 1928.
Phil 3585.1.100F   Loewenhaupt, Friedrich. Johann Heinrich Lambert. Mülhausen, 1943?
Phil 3585.1.105   Eisenring, Max F.E. Johann Heinrich Lambert und die wissenschaftliche Philosophie der Gegenwart. Zürich, 1942.
Phil 3585.2.80   Zum 70. Geburtstag Otto Liebmanns festschrift Kantstudien. Berlin, 1910.
Htn   Phil 3585.3.30*   Lessing, G.E. Zur Geschichte und Literatur. Braunschweig, 1777.
Htn   Phil 3585.4.30*   Luther, Martin. Theologia Deütsch. n.p., 1519.
Htn   Phil 3585.4.31*   Luther, Martin. Ob man für dem Sterben fliehen muge. Wittenberg, 1527.
Htn   Phil 3585.4.32*   Luther, Martin. Vermanug an die Geistlichen. Wittemberg, 1531.
Htn   Phil 3585.4.33*   Luther, Martin. Etliche schöne Predigten. n.p., 1533.
Htn   Phil 3585.4.34*   Luther, Martin. Warnung. Nürnberg, 1556.
Phil 3585.5.80   Pamphlet box. Philosophy. German and Dutch. Leonhardi, Hermann Karl von.
Phil 3585.6.80   Pamphlet box. Philosophy. German and Dutch. Lott, Karl Franz.
Phil 3585.7.80   Pamphlet box. Philosophy. German and Dutch. Lazarus, Moritz.
Phil 3585.7.86   Münz, Bernhard. Moritz Lazarus. Berlin, 1900.
Phil 3585.7.90   Leicht, Alfred. Lazarus, der Begründer der Volkerpsychologie. Leipzig, 1904.
Phil 3585.7.92   Leicht, Alfred. Lazarusstudien. Meissen, 1912.
Phil 3585.8.83   Gjurits, D. Erkenntnistheorie des Ernst Laas. Inaug. Diss. Leipzig, 1902.
Phil 3585.8.85   Hanisch, Rudolf. Der Positivismus von Ernst Laas. Inaug. Diss. Halle, 1902.
Phil 3585.9.80   Ellissen, O.A. Friedrich Albert Lange. Leipzig, 1894.
Phil 3585.9.81   Ellissen, O.A. Friedrich Albert Lange. Leipzig, 1891.
Phil 3585.10.80   Gothot, Heinrich. Die Grundbestimmungen über die Psychologie des Gefühls bei Theodor Lipps. Mülheim-Ruhr, 1921.
Phil 3585.10.82   Ahrem, Maximilien. Das Problem des tragischen bei Theodor Lipps und Johannes Volkelt. Inaug. Diss. Nürnberg, 1908.
Phil 3585.10.91   Pikler, Julius. Über Theodor Lipps' Versuch einer Theorie des Willens. Leipzig, 1908.
Phil 3585.10.94   Anschütz, G. Theodor Lipps' neuere Urteilslehre. Leipzig, 1913.
Phil 3585.10.97   Ehlen, Nikolaus. Die Erkenntnis der Aussenwelt nach Theodor Lipps. Inaug. Diss. Münster, 1914.
Phil 3585.11   Liebert, Arthur. Der Liberalismus als Fordering. Zürich, 1938.
Phil 3585.11.30   Liebert, Arthur. Der universale Humanismus. Zürich, 1946.
Phil 3585.12   Litt, Theodor. Die Selbsterkenntnis des Menschen. Leipzig, 1938.
Phil 3585.12.5   Litt, Theodor. Die Selbsterkenntnis des Menschen. 2. Aufl. Hamburg, 1948.
Phil 3585.12.80   Vogel, Paul. Theodor Litt. Berlin, 1955.
Phil 3585.12.85   Schlemper, Hans Otto. Reflexion und Geseteltungswille. Ratingen, 1964.
Phil 3585.12.90   Lassahn, Rudolf. Das Selbsterständnis der Pädagogik Theodor Litts. Wuppertal, 1968.
Phil 3585.13.30   Ludendurff, Mathilde. Statt Heiligenschein oder Hexenzeichen mein Leben. v.2- München, 193- 5v.
Phil 3585.13.90   Kurth, Hans. Die Weltdeutung Mathilde Ludendorffs. München, 1932.
Phil 3585.14.5   Lessing, Theodor. Die verfluchte Kultur. München, 1921.
Phil 3585.14.10   Lessing, Theodor. Gesammelte Schriften in zehn Bäuden. Prag, 1935.
Phil 3585.14.20   Hieronimus, E. Theodor Lessing. Hannover, 1964.
Phil 3585.15   Leisegang, H. Meine Weltanschaunng. Berlin, 1951.
Phil 3585.17   Lipps, Hans. Die Wirklichkeit des Menschen. Frankfurt, 1954.
Phil 3585.19   Lugmayer, Karl. Philosophie der Person. Salzburg, 1956.
Phil 3585.20   Luijpen, Wilhelmus Antonius Maria. Existentiële fenomenologie. Utrecht, 1959.
Phil 3585.20.4   Luijpen, Wilhelmus Antonius Maria. Nieuwe inleiding tot de existentiële fenomenologie. Utrecht, 1969.
Phil 3585.20.5   Luijpen, Wilhelmus Antonius Maria. Existential phenomenology. Pittsburgh, 1960.
Phil 3585.20.6   Luijpen, Wilhelmus Antonius Maria. A first introduction to existential phenomenology. Pittsburgh, 1969.
Phil 3585.20.10   Luijpen, Wilhelmus Antonius Maria. Fenomenologie en atheisme. Utrecht, 1963.
Phil 3585.20.15   Luijpen, Wilhelmus Antonius Maria. Phenomenology and atheism. Pittsburgh, 1964.
Phil 3585.20.20   Luijpen, Wilhelmus Anonius Maria. Phenomenology and metaphysics. Pittsburgh, 1965.
Phil 3585.20.22   Luijpen, Wilhelmus Antonius Maria. Fenomenologie en metafysica. Utrecht, 1966.
Phil 3585.20.25   Luijpen, Wilhelmus Antonius Maria. Phenomenology of natural law. Pittsburgh, 1967.
Phil 3585.20.30   Luijpen, Wilhelmus Antonius Maria. Fenomenologie van het natuurrecht door W. Luijpen. Utrecht, 1969.
Phil 3585.25   Landmann, M. Der Mensch als Schöpfer und Geschäpf der Kultur. München, 1961.
Phil 3585.26   Asser-Kramer, G. Neue nege zu Frieden und Freiheit. Pähl/Oberbayern, 1962.
Phil 3585.28   Lotz, Johannes Baptist. Der Mensch im Sein. Freiburg, 1967.
Phil 3585.28.5   Lotz, Johannes Baptist. Ich, du, wir. 1. Aufl. Frankfurt, 1968.
Phil 3585.28.10   Lotz, Johannes Baptist. Das Urteil und das Sein. München, 1957.
Phil 3585.28.20   Lotz, Johannes Baptist. Ontologia. Barcinone, 1963.

Phil 3585   History of philosophy - Local Modern philosophy - Germany - Individual philosophers - Other L - cont.

Phil 3585.30   Lask, Emil. Gesammelte Schriften. Tübingen, 1923.
                    3v.
Phil 3585.30.5   Sommerhäuser, Hanspeter. Emil Lask in der
                    Auseinander-Setzung mit Heinrich Rickert. Berlin, 1965.
Phil 3585.30.10   Sampaio Ferraz, Torcio. Die Zweidimensionalität des Rechts
                    als Voraussetzung für den Methodendualismus von Emil Lask.
                    Meisenheim am Glan, 1970.
Phil 3585.32   Luyten, Norbert Alfons. Ordo rerum. Freiburg, 1969.

Phil 3625   History of philosophy - Local Modern philosophy - Germany - Individual philosophers - M (except Möbius)

Phil 3625.1.5   Mendelssohn, Moses. Sämmtliche Werke. Wien, 1838.
                    3v.
Phil 3625.1.7   Mendelssohn, Moses. Moses Mendelssohn's sämmtliche Werke.
                    Wien, 1838.
Phil 3625.1.10   Mendelssohn, Moses. Gesammelte Schriften.
                    Leipzig, 1843-45. 8v.
Phil 3625.1.15A   Mendelssohn, Moses. Gesammelte Schriften. v.1-3,7,11,16.
                    Berlin, 1929-32. 6v.
Phil 3625.1.15B   Mendelssohn, Moses. Gesammelte Schriften.
                    Berlin, 1929-32.
Phil 3625.1.20   Mendelssohn, Moses. Opere filosofiche. Parma, 1800.
                    2v.
Phil 3625.1.25   Mendelssohn, Moses. Schriften zur Philosophie.
                    Leipzig, 1880.
Phil 3625.1.26   Mendelssohn, Moses. Philosophische Schriften. Verb. Aufl.
                    Berlin, 1771.
Phil 3625.1.30   Mendelssohn, Moses. Philosophische Schriften.
                    Berlin, 1777. 2v.
Phil 3625.1.31A   Mendelssohn, Moses. Philosophische Schriften.
                    Carlsruhe, n.d.
Phil 3625.1.31B   Mendelssohn, Moses. Philosophische Schriften.
                    Carlsruhe, n.d. 2v.
Phil 3625.1.32   Mendelssohn, Moses. Philosophische Schriften. v.1-2.
                    Carlsruhe, 1780.
Htn   Phil 3625.1.35*   Mendelssohn, Moses. Kleine philosophische Schriften.
                    Berlin, 1789.
Htn   Phil 3625.1.38*   Mendelssohn, Moses. Phädon. Berlin, 1767.
       Phil 3625.1.39   Mendelssohn, Moses. Phädon. Berlin, 1768.
X Cg   Phil 3625.1.39.3   Mendelssohn, Moses. Phädon. 3. Aufl. Berlin, 1769.
       Phil 3625.1.39.4   Mendelssohn, Moses. Phédon. Amsterdam, 1773.
       Phil 3625.1.39.5A   Mendelssohn, Moses. Phédon. 4. Aufl. Amsterdam, 1776.
       Phil 3625.1.39.5B   Mendelssohn, Moses. Phédon. 4. Aufl. Amsterdam, 1776.
       Phil 3625.1.39.9   Mendelssohn, Moses. Phédon. Amsterdam, 1821.
       Phil 3625.1.39.11   Mendelssohn, Moses. Phédon. Leipzig, 1869.
       Phil 3625.1.39.15   Mendelssohn, Moses. Phädon. London, n.d. 2 pam.
Htn   Phil 3625.1.40*   Mendelssohn, Moses. Schreiben an den Herrn Diaconus
                    Lavater. Berlin, 1770-87. 3 pam.
       Phil 3625.1.42A   Mendelssohn, Moses. Brautbriefe. Berlin, 1936.
       Phil 3625.1.42B   Mendelssohn, Moses. Brautbriefe. Berlin, 1936.
       Phil 3625.1.43   Mendelssohn, Moses. Briefe. Berlin, 1892.
       Phil 3625.1.44   Samuels, M. Memoirs of Moses Mendelssohn. London, 1825.
       Phil 3625.1.45   Samuels, M. Memoirs of Moses Mendelssohn. 2. ed.
                    London, 1827.
Htn   Phil 3625.1.47*   Mendelssohn, Moses. An die Freunde Lessings.
                    Berlin, 1786.
       Phil 3625.1.48   Mendelssohn, Moses. Moses Mendelssohn. Leipzig, 1883.
       Phil 3625.1.49   Mendelssohn, Moses. Moses Mendelssohn. Berlin, 1929.
       Phil 3625.1.53   Mendelssohn, Moses. Moses Mendelssohn. Berlin, 1929.
Htn   Phil 3625.1.55*   Mendelssohn, Moses. An die Freunde Lessings.
                    Berlin, 1786.
       Phil 3625.1.56   Mendlessohn, Moses. Moses Mendelssohn; eine Auswahl aus
                    seinen Schriften und Briefen. Frankfurt, 1912.
       Phil 3625.1.58A   Mendelssohn, Moses. Jerusalem, and other Jewish writings.
                    N.Y., 1969.
       Phil 3625.1.58B   Mendelssohn, Moses. Jerusalem, and other Jewish writings.
                    N.Y., 1969.
       Phil 3625.1.80   Pamphlet box. Philosophy. German and Dutch. Mendelssohn,
                    Moses.
       Phil 3625.1.85   Biltz, Otto. Der Phädo Platos und Mendelssohns. Inaug.
                    Diss. Berlin, 1897.
       Phil 3625.1.87   Guttenstein, B. M. Mendelssohn's Verdienste und die
                    Bildung seines Volkes. Heidelberg, 1829.
Htn   Phil 3625.1.89*   Das forschen Nach licht und recht. Berlin, 1782.
       Phil 3625.1.90   Schütz, F.W. von. Leben und Meinungen M. Mendelssohn.
                    Hamburg, 1787.
       Phil 3625.1.93   Kanngiesser, G. Die Stellung M. Mendelssohn's in der
                    Geschichte der Asthitik. Frankfurt, 1868.
       Phil 3625.1.96   Zöllner, J.F. Über Moses Mendelssohn's Jerusalem.
                    Berlin, 1784.
Htn   Phil 3625.1.100*   Jakob, Ludwig H. Prüfung der Mendelssohnschen
                    Morgenstunden oder aller spekulativen Beweise für das
                    Daseyn. Leipzig, 1786.
       Phil 3625.1.103   Dessauer, M. Der deutsche Plato. Berlin, 1879.
       Phil 3625.1.105   Kahut, Adolf. Moses Mendelssohn und seine Familie.
                    Dresden, 1886.
       Phil 3625.1.107   Kayserling, M. Moses Mendelssohn. Leipzig, 1862.
       Phil 3625.1.109   Schwab, Moise. Mendelssohn, sa vie et ses oeuvres.
                    Paris, 1868.
       Phil 3625.1.111   Goldstein, L. Die Bedeuterung Moses Mendelssohn. Inaug.
                    Diss. Konigsberg, 1897.
       Phil 3625.1.113   Goldstein, L. Moses Mendelssohn. Konigsberg, 1904.
       Phil 3625.1.117   Rothman, W. Mendelssohn's character and philosophy of
                    religion. n.p., 1929.
       Phil 3625.1.121   Freudenthal, M. Zum zweihundertjährigen Geburtstag Moses
                    Mendelssohns; vier Abhandlungen. Berlin, 1929.
       Phil 3625.1.125   Scholz, Heinrich. Die Hauptschriften zum pantheismus
                    Streit. Berlin, 1916.
       Phil 3625.1.129   Walter, Hermann. Moses Mendelssohn, critic and
                    philosopher. N.Y., 1930.
       Phil 3625.1.133   Wizenmann, T. Die Resultate der Jacobischen und
                    Mendelssohnschen Philosophie. Leipzig, 1786.
       Phil 3625.1.135   Ritter, I.H. Mendelssohn und Lessing. 2e Aufl.
                    Berlin, 1886.
       Phil 3625.1.139   Kornfeld, H. Moses Mendelssohn und die Aufgabe der
                    Philosophie. Berlin, 1896.
       Phil 3625.1.145   Mirabeau, H.G.R. Sur Moses Mendelssohn. Leipzig, 1853.
       Phil 3625.1.147   Mirabeau, H.G.R. Sur la réforme politique des Juifs.
                    Bruxelles, 1788.
       Phil 3625.1.150   Zarek, O. Moses Mendelssohn. Amsterdam, 1936.
       Phil 3625.1.153   Encyclopaidia Judaica. Moses Mendelssohn zur 200 jahrigen
                    Wiederkehr seines Gehertstages. Berlin, 1929.
Htn   Phil 3625.1.160*   Lavater, J.C. Antwort an den herrn Moses Mendelssohn zu
                    Berlin. Berlin, 1770.

Phil 3625   History of philosophy - Local Modern philosophy - Germany - Individual philosophers - M (except Möbius) - cont.

Phil 3625.1.163   Verland der vereine für Jüdische Geschichte und Literatur
                    in Deutschland. Gedenkbuch für Moses Mendelssohn.
                    Berlin, 1929.
Phil 3625.1.165   Richter, Liselotte. Philosophie der Dicht Kunst.
                    Berlin, 1948.
Phil 3625.1.170   Isaacs, Abram Samuel. Step by step. Philadelphia, 1910.
Phil 3625.1.175   Holdheim, Samuel. Moses Mendelssohn und die Dink.
                    Berlin, 1859.
Phil 3625.1.180   Richter, Johann Andreas Lebrecht. Moses Mendelssohn als
                    Mensch. Dessau, 1829.
Phil 3625.1.185   Baeck, Leo. Mendelssohn Gedenkfeier der Jüdischen Gemeinde
                    zu Berlin am 8, Sept. 1929. Berlin, 1929.
Phil 3625.1.190   Stadler, Károly. Mendelssohn Mózes, a zsidó Sokrates.
                    Szekesféhérvárott, 1895.
Phil 3625.1.195   Kayserling, Meyer. Moses Mendelssohn's philosophische und
                    religiöse Grundsätze mit Hinblick auf Lessing.
                    Leipzig, 1856.
Phil 3625.2   Michelet, K.L. Wahrheit aus meinem Leben. Berlin, 1884.
Phil 3625.2.6   Michelet, K.L. Naturrecht oder Rechts-Philosophie als die
                    praktische Philosophie. Berlin, 1866. Bruxelles, 1968.
                    2v.
Htn   Phil 3625.3.78*   Pamphlet box. Philosophy. German and Dutch. Mach, Ernst.
       Phil 3625.3.80   Henning, Hans. Ernst als Philosoph, Physiker und
                    Psycholog, eine Monographie. Leipzig, 1915.
       Phil 3625.3.82   Reinhold, Ferdinand. Machs Erkenntnistheorie.
                    Leipzig, 1908.
       Phil 3625.3.83   Hönigswald, R. Zur Kritik der Machschen Philosophie.
                    Berlin, 1903.
       Phil 3625.3.84   Moschetti, L. Fenomenismo e relativismo nel pensiero di E.
                    Mach. Genova, 1923.
       Phil 3625.3.85   Bouvier, Robert. La pensée d'Ernst Mach. Paris, 1923.
       Phil 3625.3.87   Dingler, Hugo. Die Grundgedanken der Machschen
                    Philosophie. Leipzig, 1924.
       Phil 3625.3.88   Weinberg, Carlton Berenda. Mach's empirio-pragmatism in
                    physical science. N.Y., 1937.
       Phil 3625.3.89   Wlassak, R. Ernst Mach: Gedächtnisrede. Leipzig, 1917.
       Phil 3625.3.91   Beer, Theodor. Die Weltanschauung eines modernen
                    Naturforschers. Dresden, 1903.
       Phil 3625.3.94   Mises, R. Ernst Mach. 's-Gravenhage, 1938.
       Phil 3625.3.100   Heller, K. Ernst Mach. Wien, 1964.
       Phil 3625.3.105   Adler, Friedrich. Ernst Machs Überwindung des mechanischen
                    Materialismus. Wien, 1918.
       Phil 3625.4.30   Müller, J. Vom Gebeimnis des Lebens. Stuttgart, 1953.
                    3v.
       Phil 3625.4.35   Müller, J. Ja zur Wirklichkeit. Weilheim, 1963.
       Phil 3625.4.81   Post, Karl. Johannes Müllers philosophische Anschauungen.
                    Inaug. Diss. Halle, 1905.
       Phil 3625.5.2   Maimon, Salomon. Gesammelte Werke. Hildesheim, 1965.
                    6v.
       Phil 3625.5.30   Maimon, Salomon. Über die Progressen der Philosophie.
                    Bruxelles, 1969.
       Phil 3625.5.34   Maimon, Salomon. Versuch einer neuen Logik, oder Theorie.
                    Berlin, 1794.
       Phil 3625.5.35   Maimon, Salomon. Versuch einer neuen Logik, oder Theorie.
                    Berlin, 1912.
       Phil 3625.5.40   Atlas, S. Kritische Untersuchungen über den menschlichen
                    Geist. Leipzig, 1797.
       Phil 3625.5.45   Atlas, S. From critical to speculative idealism. The
                    Hague, 1964.
       Phil 3625.5.60   Atlas, S. Geschichte des eigenen Lebens. Berlin, 1935.
       Phil 3625.5.78   Atlas, S. Lebensgeschichte. München, 1911.
       Phil 3625.5.78.2   Atlas, S. Lebensgeschichte. Berlin, 1792-93. 2 pam.
       Phil 3625.5.78.10   Maimon, Salomon. Salomon Maimon. Boston, 1888.
       Phil 3625.5.79   Maimon, Salomon. Autobiography. London, 1954.
       Phil 3625.5.80   Pamphlet box. Philosophy. German and Dutch. Maimon,
                    Salomon.
       Phil 3625.5.86   Bitte, I.H. Salomon Maimon. Berlin, 1876.
       Phil 3625.5.87   Kuntze, Friedrich. Die Philosophie Salomon Maimons.
                    Heidelberg, 1912.
       Phil 3625.5.89   Zubersky, A. Salomon Maimon und der kritischen Idealismus.
                    Leipzig, 1925.
       Phil 3625.5.91   Moeltzner, A. Salomon Maimons erkenntnistheoretische
                    Verbesserungsveruche der Kantischen Philosophie. Inaug.
                    Diss. Greifswald, 1889.
       Phil 3625.5.93   Gueroult, M. La philosophie transcendantale de Salomon
                    Maimon. Paris, 1929.
       Phil 3625.5.94   Gueroult, M. La philosophie transcendantale de Salomon
                    Maimon. Thèse. Paris, 1929.
       Phil 3625.5.95   Bergmann, Hugo. The philosophy of Salomon Maimon.
                    Jerusalem, 1967.
       Phil 3625.7.90   Gaquoin, Karl. Die transcendentale Harmonie bei Ernst
                    Marcus. Wiesbaden, 1907.
       Phil 3625.8.25   Meier, Georg Friedrich. Georg Friedrich Meiers Metaphysik.
                    v.1-4. Halle, 1755-59. 3v.
       Phil 3625.8.30   Meier, Georg Friedrich. Gedanken von Scherzen.
                    Halle, 1754.
       Phil 3625.8.31   Meier, Georg Friedrich. Betrachtung über den Fehler der
                    menschlichen Tugenden. Halle, 1755.
       Phil 3625.8.35   Meier, Georg Friedrich. Versuch einer Erklärung des
                    Nachtwandelns. Halle, 1758.
       Phil 3625.8.38   Meier, Georg Friedrich. Gedancken von der Ehre.
                    Halle, 1746.
       Phil 3625.8.41   Meier, Georg Friedrich. Gedanken vom philosophischen
                    Predigen. Halle, 1762.
       Phil 3625.8.42   Meier, Georg Friedrich. Philosophische Sittenlehre.
                    Halle, 1762. 2v.
       Phil 3625.8.43   Meier, Georg Friedrich. Philosophische Sittenlehre. 2.
                    Aufl. Halle, 1762-66. 5v.
       Phil 3625.8.50   Meier, Georg Friedrich. Philosophische Betrachtungen über
                    die chrislichen Religion. v.1-7. Halle, 1761-66. 2v.
       Phil 3625.8.52   Meier, Georg Friedrich. Versuch einer Allegemeinen
                    Auslegungskunst. Dusseldorf, 1965.
       Phil 3625.8.55   Meier, Georg Friedrich. Beweis: dass keine Materie dencken
                    Könne. Halel, 1742.
       Phil 3625.8.57   Meier, Georg Friedrich. Beweis: dass' keine Materie
                    dencken Könne. 2e Aufl. Halle, 1751. 7 pam.
       Phil 3625.8.58   Meier, Georg Friedrich. Beweis dass die menschliche Seele
                    ewig Lebt. Halle, 1751.
       Phil 3625.8.60   Meier, Georg Friedrich. Vernenftlehre. 2e Aufl.
                    Halle, 1762.
       Phil 3625.8.62   Meier, Georg Friedrich. Auszug aus der Vernunftlehre.
                    Halle, 1752.
       Phil 3625.8.65   Meier, Georg Friedrich. Vertheidigung der christlichen
                    Religion. 2e Aufl. Halle, 1749.

Phil 3625   History of philosophy - Local Modern philosophy - Germany - Individual
philosophers - M (except Möbius) - cont.

Phil 3625.8.85	Spitzer, David. Darstellung und Kritik der Thierpsychologie Georg Friedrich Meier's. Inaug. Diss. Györ, 1903.
Phil 3625.8.92	Langen, S.G. Leben Georg Friedrich Meiers. Halle, 1778.
Phil 3625.8.95	Bergmann, E. Georg Friedrich Meier als mitbegründer der deutschen Äthetik unter Benutzung ungedruckter Quellen. Leipzig, 1910.
Phil 3625.9.80	Kraus, Oskar. Anton Marty; sein Leben und seine Werke. Halle, 1916.
Phil 3625.10.30*	Münsterberg, H. Verse; von Hugo Terberg. Grossenhain, 1897.
Phil 3625.10.35*	Münsterberg, H. Science and idealism. Boston, 1906.
Phil 3625.11	Meinong, Alexius. Gesamtausgabe. Herausgeber: Rudolf Haller und R. Kindinger. Graz, 1968- 3v.
Phil 3625.11.80	Martinak, E. Meinong als Mensch und als Lehrer. Graz, 1925.
Phil 3625.11.82	Liljequist, E. Meinongs allmänna värdeteori. Göteborg, 1904.
Phil 3625.11.85	Findlay, J.N. Meinong's theory of objects. London, 1933.
Phil 3625.11.86	Findlay, J.N. Meinong's theory of objects and values. 2. ed. Oxford, 1963.
Phil 3625.11.90	Benndorf, H. Persönliche Erinnerungen an Alexius Meinong. Graz, 1951.
Phil 3625.12.80	Krieg, Max. Fritz Mauthners Kritik der Sprache. München, 1914.
Phil 3625.13.19	Müller, Aloys. Schriften zur Philosophie. Bonn, 1967. 2v.
Phil 3625.13.34	Müller, Aloys. Welt und Mensch in ihrem irrealen Aufbau. 4. Aufl. Leiden, 1951.
Phil 3625.13.90	Kluge, Fritz. Die Philosophie der Mathematik und Naturwissenschaft bei Aloys Müller. Inaug. Diss. Leipzig, 1935.
Phil 3625.14.90	Turner, William D. Georg Elias Müller. Cambridge, 1928.
Phil 3625.15.87	Messer, A. Glauben und Wissen. 3. Aufl. München, 1924.
Phil 3625.16.90	Grohrock, R. Der Kampf der Wesenskultur gegen die Bewusstseinskultur bei Johannes Müller. Inaug. Diss. Speyer, 1937.
Phil 3625.17.30	Medicus, Fritz. Das mythologische in der Religion. Erlenbach, 1944.
Phil 3625.18.30	Maier, A. Zwei Grundprobleme der scholastischen Naturphilosophie. 2. Aufl. Roma, 1951.
Phil 3625.20.30	Meyer, Hans. Systematische Philosophie. Paderborn, 1955. 4v.
Phil 3625.21	Marcuse, L. Aus den Papieren eines bejahrten Philosophie-Studenten. München, 1964.
Phil 3625.22	Meinong, Alexius. Philosophenbriefe aus den wissenschaftlichen Korrespondez mit Franz Brentano. Graz, 1965.
Phil 3625.24	Müller, Adam H. Schriften. Neuwield, 1967. 2v.
Phil 3625.26	Müller, Max. Symbolos. München, 1967.
Phil 3625.28.31	Maass, Johann Gebhard Ehrenreich. Kritische Theorie der Offenbarung. Bruxelles, 1969.

Phil 3635   History of philosophy - Local Modern philosophy - Germany - Individual
philosophers - Möbius, Paul J.

Phil 3635.6	Möbius, Paul. Ausgewählte Werke. Leipzig, 1905-11. 8v.
Phil 3635.90	Lorenz, Heinrich. Dr P.J. Möbius als Philosoph. Inaug. Diss. Wiesbaden, 1899.

Phil 3640   History of philosophy - Local Modern philosophy - Germany - Individual
philosophers - Nietzsche, Friedrich

Phil 3640.10A	Nietzsche, Friedrich. Werke. Leipzig, 1896-1926. 20v.
Phil 3640.10C	Nietzsche, Friedrich. Werke. Leipzig, 1895-1926. 15v.
Phil 3640.10.2	Nietzsche, Friedrich. Werke. Leipzig, 1895-1926. 19v.
Phil 3640.10.5	Nietzsche, Friedrich. Werke. Kritische Gesamtausgabe. Berlin, 1967. 9v.
Phil 3640.10.15	Nietzsche, Friedrich. Gesammelte Werke. München, 1929-29. 23v.
Phil 3640.11.2	Nietzsche, Friedrich. Menschliches, allzumenschliche sein Buch für freie Geister. Leipzig, 1886.
Phil 3640.11.4	Nietzsche, Friedrich. Der Fall Wagner; und die Geburt der Trajödie. Leipzig, 1888.
Phil 3640.11.5	Nietzsche, Friedrich. Unzeitgemässe Betrachtungen. Leipzig, 189-?
Phil 3640.11.10A	Nietzsche, Friedrich. Werke. Leipzig, 1906-09. 11v.
Phil 3640.11.10B	Nietzsche, Friedrich. Werke. v.7. Leipzig, 1906-09.
Phil 3640.12.10	Nietzsche, Friedrich. Gedichts. Leipzig, 1923.
Phil 3640.13	Nietzsche, Friedrich. Werke und Briefe. München, 1933-49. 5v.
Phil 3640.14	Nietzsche, Friedrich. Werke und Briefe. München, 1938-42. 4v.
Phil 3640.14.10	Nietzsche, Friedrich. Werke. Salzburg, 1952. 2v.
Phil 3640.14.15A	Nietzsche, Friedrich. Werke. München, 1954-56. 3v.
Phil 3640.14.15B	Nietzsche, Friedrich. Werke. München, 1954-56. 3v.
Phil 3640.14.16	Nietzsche, Friedrich. Nietzsche. Index. München, 1965.
Phil 3640.15	Nietzsche, Friedrich. Complete works. v.1,3,7,9-10,13,18. Edinburgh, 1910-13. 7v.
Phil 3640.15	Nietzsche, Friedrich. Complete works. v.2,4-6,8,11,14-15,17. Edinburgh, 1910-13. 9v.
Phil 3640.15.2	Nietzsche, Friedrich. Complete works. v.11,16. London, 1913. 2v.
Phil 3640.15.3	Nietzsche, Friedrich. Complete works. 3. ed. v.11. N.Y., 1914.
Phil 3640.15.5	Nietzsche, Friedrich. Complete works. N.Y., 1964. 18v.
Phil 3640.16	Nietzsche, Friedrich. Fünf Vorreden in fünf ungeschriebenen Büchern. Berlin, 1943.
Phil 3640.17	Nietzsche, Friedrich. Werke. v.1-11. Leipzig, 1931-59. 12v.
Phil 3640.17.2	Nietzsche, Friedrich. Un zeitgemässe Betrachtungen. Stuttgart, 1955.
Phil 3640.17.3	Nietzsche, Friedrich. Menschliches, Allzumenschliches; ein Buch für freie Geister. Stuttgart, 1960.
Phil 3640.17.4	Nietzsche, Friedrich. Morgenröte. Stuttgart, 1952. 2v.
Phil 3640.17.5	Nietzsche, Friedrich. Die fröhliche Wissenschaft. Stuttgart, 1956.
Phil 3640.17.6	Nietzsche, Friedrich. Also Sprach Zarathustra. Stuttgart, 1956.
Phil 3640.17.7	Nietzsche, Friedrich. Jenseits von Gut und Böse. Stuttgart, 1959.
Phil 3640.17.8	Nietzsche, Friedrich. Götzendämmerung. Stuttgart, 1954.
Phil 3640.17.9	Nietzsche, Friedrich. Der Wille zur Macht. Stuttgart, 1959.

Phil 3640   History of philosophy - Local Modern philosophy - Germany - Individual
philosophers - Nietzsche, Friedrich

Phil 3640.17.10	Nietzsche, Friedrich. Die Unschuld des Werdens. v.1-2. Leipzig, 1931.
Phil 3640.17.11	Oehler, R. Nietzsche. Register. Stuttgart, 1943.
Phil 3640.17.12	Nietzsche, Friedrich. Sämtliche Werke. Stuttgart, 1964-65. 12v.
Phil 3640.19	Nietzsche, Friedrich. Volks-Nietzsche. Berlin, 1931. 4v.
Phil 3640.20	Nietzsche, Friedrich. Werke. Leipzig, 1930. 2v.
Phil 3640.21	Nietzsche, Friedrich. Jugendschriften. München, 1923.
Phil 3640.22	Nietzsche, Friedrich. Nietzsche's Werke. v.2-4. Leipzig, 1931. 3v.
Phil 3640.22.8	Nietzsche, Friedrich. Nietzsche's Philosophie in Selbstzeugnissen. Leipzig, 1931. 4v.
Phil 3640.22.15	Nietzsche, Friedrich. Philosophy of Nietzsche. N.Y., 195-?
Phil 3640.23	Nietzsche, Friedrich. Studienausgabe in 4 Bänden. Frankfurt, 1968. 4v.
Phil 3640.24	Nietzsche, Friedrich. Germans, Jews and France. Newark, 1935.
Phil 3640.25	Nietzsche, Friedrich. Gedichte und Sprüche. Leipzig, 1908.
Phil 3640.25.7	Nietzsche, Friedrich. Gedichte und Sprüche. Leipzig, 1916.
Phil 3640.25.10	Nietzsche, Friedrich. Gedichte und Sprüche. Leipzig, 1901.
Phil 3640.26	Nietzsche, Friedrich. Pages choisies. 5e éd. Paris, 1899.
Phil 3640.27	Nietzsche, Friedrich. Das Vermächtnis Friedrich Nietzsches. Salzburg, 1940.
Phil 3640.27.1	Nietzsche, Friedrich. Umwertung aller Werte. München, 1969. 2v.
Phil 3640.28	Nietzsche, Friedrich. Nietzsche as critic. N.Y., 1901.
Phil 3640.30.5	Nietzsche, Friedrich. Aurora. Valencia, 1910?
Phil 3640.30.9	Nietzsche, Friedrich. Aurore. 7e éd. Paris, 1912.
Phil 3640.31A	Nietzsche, Friedrich. Beyond good and evil. N.Y., 1907.
Phil 3640.31B	Nietzsche, Friedrich. Beyond good and evil. N.Y., 1907.
Phil 3640.31.2	Nietzsche, Friedrich. Jenseits von Gut und Böse. Leipzig, 1886.
Phil 3640.31.3	Nietzsche, Friedrich. Beyond good and evil. N.Y., 1917.
Phil 3640.31.4	Nietzsche, Friedrich. Beyond good and evil. N.Y., 1924.
Phil 3640.31.5A	Nietzsche, Friedrich. Beyond good and evil. Chicago, 1949.
Phil 3640.31.5B	Nietzsche, Friedrich. Beyond good and evil. Chicago, 1949.
Phil 3640.31.9	Nietzsche, Friedrich. Beyond good and evil. N.Y., 1917.
Phil 3640.31.15	Nietzsche, Friedrich. Par delà le bien et le mal. Paris, 1951.
Phil 3640.32	Nietzsche, Friedrich. Götzen-Dämmerung. Leipzig, 1889.
Phil 3640.33	Nietzsche, Friedrich. Die fröhliche Wissenschaft. Leipzig, 1887.
Phil 3640.33.5	Nietzsche, Friedrich. Die fröhliche Wissenschaft. München, 1959.
Phil 3640.34	Nietzsche, Friedrich. The genealogy of morals. N.Y., 1918.
Phil 3640.34.5	Nietzsche, Friedrich. Zur Genealogie der Moral. Leipzig, 193-.
Phil 3640.35.5	Nietzsche, Friedrich. Humain, trop humain. Paris, 1899.
Phil 3640.36	Nietzsche, Friedrich. Humano, demasiado humano. Valencia, 1909?
Phil 3640.37	Nietzsche, Friedrich. Der Wanderer und sein Schatten. Chemnitz, 1880.
Phil 3640.38	Nietzsche, Friedrich. Kritik und Zukunft der Kultur. Zürich, 1933.
Phil 3640.39	Nietzsche, Friedrich. Ainsi parlait Zarathustra. 29e éd. Paris, 1914.
Phil 3640.40.2	Nietzsche, Friedrich. Thus spake Zararhustra. N.Y., 1908.
Phil 3640.40.3	Nietzsche, Friedrich. Thus spake Zarathustra. 2d ed. N.Y., 1911.
Phil 3640.40.5	Nietzsche, Friedrich. Thus spake Zarathustra. N.Y., 1896.
Phil 3640.40.10	Nietzsche, Friedrich. Thus spake Zarathustra. London, 1958.
Phil 3640.40.12	Nietzsche, Friedrich. Thus spake Zarathustra. Chicago, 1957.
Phil 3640.40.30	Nietzsche, Friedrich. Thus spake Zarathustra. N.Y., 1936.
Htn Phil 3640.41*	Nietzsche, Friedrich. Also sprach Zarathustra. Leipzig, 19- .
Phil 3640.41.4	Nietzsche, Friedrich. Also sprach Zarathustra. Leipzig, 1905?
Phil 3640.41.8A	Nietzsche, Friedrich. Also sprach Zarathustra. Leipzig, 1909.
Phil 3640.41.8B	Nietzsche, Friedrich. Also sprach Zarathustra. Leipzig, 1909.
Phil 3640.41.8C	Nietzsche, Friedrich. Also sprach Zarathustra. Leipzig, 1909.
Phil 3640.41.15	Nietzsche, Friedrich. Also sprach Zarathustra. Stuttgart, 1943.
Phil 3640.42	Nietzsche, Friedrich. Asi hablaba Zarathustra. Valencia, 19- ?
Phil 3640.43	Nietzsche, Friedrich. La gaya ciencia. Valencia, 1910?
Phil 3640.45	Nietzsche, Friedrich. Schwert des Geistes. Stuttgart, 1941.
Phil 3640.46	Nietzsche, Friedrich. Basic writings of Nietzsche. N.Y., 1968.
Phil 3640.47	Nietzsche, Friedrich. Menschliches, Allzumenschliches; ein Buch für freie Geister. v.1-2. Stuttgart, 1954.
Phil 3640.50	Nietzsche, Friedrich. Von neuen Freiheiten des Geistes. 1. Aufl. München, 1943.
Phil 3640.51	Nietzsche, Friedrich. Der Wille zur Macht. Stuttgart, 1952.
Phil 3640.51.10	Nietzsche, Friedrich. The will to power. N.Y., 1967.
Phil 3640.51.11	Nietzsche, Friedrich. The will to power. N.Y., 1968.
Phil 3640.52	Nietzsche, Friedrich. Der Fall Wagner. Frankfurt, 1946.
Phil 3640.52.5	Nietzsche, Friedrich. Der Fall Wagner. Leipzig, 1931.
Phil 3640.53.5	Nietzsche, Friedrich. Der Antichrist. 2. Aufl. Berlin, 1940.
Phil 3640.54	Nietzsche, Friedrich. Jenseits von Gut und Böse. Leipzig, 193-.
Phil 3640.56	Nietzsche, Friedrich. L'antéchrist. Paris, 1967.
Phil 3640.57A	Nietzsche, Friedrich. L'antéchrist. Paris, 1931.
Phil 3640.57B	Nietzsche, Friedrich. L'antéchrist. Paris, 1931.
Phil 3640.57C	Nietzsche, Friedrich. L'antéchrist. Paris, 1931.
Phil 3640.57D	Nietzsche, Friedrich. L'antéchrist. Paris, 1931.
Phil 3640.57E	Nietzsche, Friedrich. L'antéchrist. Paris, 1931.
Phil 3640.58	Nietzsche, Friedrich. Vorstufen der Geburt der Tragödie aus dem Geiste der Musik. Leipzig, 1926-28. 3v.
Phil 3640.58.5	Nietzsche, Friedrich. Die Geburt der Tragödie aus dem Geiste der Musik. Leipzig, 1931.

202

Classified Listing

Phil 3640 History of philosophy - Local Modern philosophy - Germany - Individual philosophers - Nietzsche, Friedrich - cont.

	Phil 3640.58.7	Nietzsche, Friedrich. Socrates und die griechische Tragödie. München, 1933.
	Phil 3640.58.20	Nietzsche, Friedrich. The birth of tragedy. N.Y., 1967.
	Phil 3640.60	Nietzsche, Friedrich. Pöesies complètes. Paris, 1948.
	Phil 3640.61	Nietzsche, Friedrich. La lirica di Nietzsche. Messina, 1948.
	Phil 3640.62	Nietzsche, Friedrich. Federico Nietzsche. 3. ed. Milano, 1944.
	Phil 3640.63	Nietzsche, Friedrich. Die Philosophie im tragischen Zeitalter der Griechen. Leipzig, 1931.
	Phil 3640.63.5	Nietzsche, Friedrich. Die Philosophie im tragischen Zeitalter der Griechen. München, 1923.
	Phil 3640.63.10	Nietzsche, Friedrich. Vom Nietzen un Nachteil der Historie für das Leben. Leipzig, 1931.
	Phil 3640.64.5	Nietzsche, Friedrich. Unzeigemässe Betrachtungen. Leipzig, 189-?
	Phil 3640.65	Nietzsche, Friedrich. Zeitgemässes und Unzeitgemässes. Frankfurt, 1956.
	Phil 3640.70	Nietzsche, Friedrich. The case of Wagner. Photoreproduction. Nietzsche, 1896.
	Phil 3640.72	Nietzsche, Friedrich. Fragments sur l'énergie et la puissance. Paris, 1957.
	Phil 3640.73	Nietzsche, Friedrich. The living thoughts of Nietzsche. London, 1946.
	Phil 3640.76A	Nietzsche, Friedrich. Briefe. v.1-5. 3rd ed. Berlin, 1902. 6v.
	Phil 3640.76B	Nietzsche, Friedrich. Briefe. v.2. 3rd ed. Berlin, 1902.
	Phil 3640.76.5	Nietzscher, Friedrich. Friedrich Nietzsches Briefe an Mutter und Schwester. Leipzig, 1909. 2v.
	Phil 3640.76.9	Nietzsche, Friedrich. Nietzsches Briefe. Leipzig, 1917.
	Phil 3640.76.15	Nietsche, Friedrich. Briefe an Peter Gast. Leipzig, 1908.
	Phil 3640.76.16	Nietzsche, Friedrich. Lettres à Peter Gast. Monaco, 1958. 2v.
	Phil 3640.76.17	Nietzsche, Friedrich. Nietzsche; a self-portrait from his letters. Cambridge, 1971.
	Phil 3640.77A	Nietzsche, Friedrich. Briefwechsel mit Franz Overbeck. Leipzig, 1916.
	Phil 3640.77B	Nietzsche, Friedrich. Briefwechsel mit Franz Overbeck. Leipzig, 1916.
	Phil 3640.77.5	Nietzsche, Friedrich. Unpublished letters. N.Y., 1959.
	Phil 3640.77.7	Nietzsche, Friedrich. Der werdende Nietzsche. München, 1924.
	Phil 3640.77.10	Nietzsche, Friedrich. Brevier. 2. Aufl. Wien, 1951.
	Phil 3640.77.15	Nietzsche, Friedrich. Ecce homo. Leipzig, 1908.
	Phil 3640.77.15.5	Nietzsche, Friedrich. Ecce homo. Leipzig, 1931.
	Phil 3640.77.15.10	Nietzsche, Friedrich. My sister and I. N.Y., 1951.
	Phil 3640.77.15.12	Nietzsche, Friedrich. My sister and I. N.Y., 1953.
	Phil 3640.77.20	Nietzsche, Friedrich. La vie de Friedrich Nietzsche d'après sa correspondance. Paris, 1932.
	Phil 3640.77.25	Nietzsche, Friedrich. The joyful wisdom. London, n.d.
	Phil 3640.77.27	Nietzsche, Friedrich. Joyful wisdom. N.Y., 1960.
	Phil 3640.78	Nietzsche, Friedrich. Selected letters. London, 1921.
	Phil 3640.78.5	Nietzsche, Friedrich. Selected letters of Friedrich Nietzsche. Chicago, 1969.
	Phil 3640.79	Pamphlet vol. Philosophy. German and Dutch. Nietzsche, Friedrich. German dissertations. 1901-1915. 17 pam.
	Phil 3640.79.2	Pamphlet vol. Philosophy. German and Dutch. Nietzsche, Friedrich. German dissertations. 1913-1932. 12 pam.
	Phil 3640.79.3	Pamphlet box. Philosophy. German and Dutch. Nietzsche, Friedrich. German dissertations.
	Phil 3640.79.4	Pamphlet box. Philosophy. German and Dutch. Nietzsche, Friedrich.
	Phil 3640.79.5	Pamphlet vol. Philosophy. German and Dutch. Nietzsche, Friedrich.
	Phil 3640.79.10	Nietzsche, Friedrich. The birth of tragedy and The genealogy of morals. 1. ed. Garden City, N.Y., 1956.
	Phil 3640.79.15	Nietzsche, Friedrich. Erkenntnistheoretische Schriften. Frankfurt, 1968.
	Phil 3640.79.20	Nietzsche, Friedrich. Van vornehmen Menschen. Klosterberg, 1945.
	Phil 3640.79.50	Ariadne; Jahrbuch der Nietzsche-Gesellschaft. München. 1925
	Phil 3640.79.55	Pamphlet vol. Philosophy. German and Dutch. Nietzsche-Gesellschaft.
	Phil 3640.79.60	Reichert, Herbert William. International Nietzsche bibliography. Chapel Hill, N.C., 1960.
	Phil 3640.79.60.5	Reichert, Herbert William. International Nietzsche bibliography. Chapel Hill, 1968.
	Phil 3640.79.100	Oehler, Richard. Nietzscheregister. Leipzig, 1926.
	Phil 3640.79.105	Oehler, Richard. Nietzscheregister. Stuttgart, 1943.
	Phil 3640.79.107	Oehler, Richard. Nietzscheregister. Stuttgart, 1965.
	Phil 3640.80	Gallwitz, H. Friedrich Nietzsche. Dresden, 1898.
	Phil 3640.80.5	Gallwitz, H. Friedrich Nietzsche. Ein Lebensbild. Dresden, 1898.
	Phil 3640.81	Zeitler, Julius. Nietzsches Asthetik. Leipzig, 1900.
	Phil 3640.82	Faguet, E. En lesant Nietzsche. Paris, 1904.
	Phil 3640.82.15	Willy, Rudolf. Friedrich Nietzsche. Zürich, 1904.
	Phil 3640.83	Drews, Arthur. Nietzsches Philosophie. Heidelberg, 1904.
	Phil 3640.84	Ewald, Oscar. Nietzsches Lehre. Berlin, 1903.
	Phil 3640.85	Albert, H. Frederic Nietzsche. Paris, 1903.
	Phil 3640.85.5	Orestano, Francesco. Le idee fondamentali de F. Nietzsche. Palermo, 1903.
	Phil 3640.86	Levy, Albert. Stirner et Nietzsche. Paris, 1904.
	Phil 3640.87	Kalthoff, A. Friedrich Nietzsche. Berlin, 1900.
	Phil 3640.87.7	Kalthoff, A. Zarathustra-Predigten. Jena, 1908.
	Phil 3640.88	Förster-Nietzsche, E. Das Leben Friedrich Nietzsche's. Leipzig, 1895. 2v.
	Phil 3640.88.3	Förster-Nietzsche, E. Der junge Nietzsche. Leipzig, 1912.
	Phil 3640.88.5	Förster-Nietzsche, E. Life of Nietzsche. N.Y., 1912-15. 2v.
	Phil 3640.88.6	Förster-Nietzsche, E. The young Nietzsche. London, 1912.
	Phil 3640.88.7	Förster-Nietzsche, E. Der einsame Nietzsche. München, 1915.
	Phil 3640.88.9	Förster-Nietzsche, E. Wagner und Nietzsche zur zeit Freundschaft. München, 1915.
	Phil 3640.88.10	Förster-Nietzsche, E. The Nietzsche-Wagner correspondence. N.Y., 1921.
	Phil 3640.88.15	Förster-Nietzsche, E. Friedrich Nietzsche and die Frauen seiner Zeit. München, 1935.
	Phil 3640.89	Ziegler, Theobald. Friedrich Nietzsche. Berlin, 1900.
	Phil 3640.90	Mencken, Henry. Philosophy of Friedrich Nietzsche. Boston, 1908.
Htn	Phil 3640.90*	Mencken, Henry. Philosophy of Friedrich Nietzsche. Boston, 1908.

Phil 3640 History of philosophy - Local Modern philosophy - Germany - Individual philosophers - Nietzsche, Friedrich - cont.

X Cg	Phil 3640.90.3	Mencken, Henry. Philosophy of Friedrich Nietzsche. 3d ed. Boston, 1913.
	Phil 3640.90.5	Bernoulli, Carl A. Franz Overbeck und Friedrich Nietzsche. Jena, 1908. 2v.
	Phil 3640.90.7	Bernoulli, Carl A. Nietzsche und die Schweiz. Leipzig, 1922.
	Phil 3640.90.12A	Gutersohn, U. Friedrich Nietzsche und der moderne Mensch. 2. Aufl. St. Gallen, 1945.
	Phil 3640.90.12B	Gutersohn, U. Friedrich Nietzsche und der moderne Mensch. 2. Aufl. St. Gallen, 1945.
	Phil 3640.91	Weber, Ernst. Die pädogogischen Gedanken...jungen Nietzsche. Leipzig, 1907.
	Phil 3640.93.2	Richter, R. Friedrich Nietzsche. 3. Aufl. Leipzig, 1917.
	Phil 3640.94	Tosi, T. F. Nietzsche, R. Wagner e la tragedie Greca. Firenze, 1905.
	Phil 3640.94.5	Joël, Karl. Nietzsche und die Romantik. Jena, 1905.
	Phil 3640.94.6	Joël, Karl. Nietzsche und die Romantik. 2. Aufl. Jena, 1923.
	Phil 3640.94.9	Dernoscheck, G.A. Das problem des egoistischen Perfektionismus in der Ethik Spinozas und Nietzsches. Annaberg, 1905.
	Phil 3640.95	Broene, J. Philosophy of Friedrich Nietzsche. n.p., n.d.
	Phil 3640.96	Halévy, D. Life of Friedrich Nietzsche. N.Y., 1911.
	Phil 3640.96.5A	Halévy, D. Nietzsche. Paris, 1944.
	Phil 3640.96.5B	Halévy, D. Nietzsche. Paris, 1944.
	Phil 3640.97	Fischer, W. Nietzsches Bild. München, 1911.
	Phil 3640.98	Ludovici, Anthony M. Nietzsche, his life and works. London, 1910.
	Phil 3640.98.5	Ludovici, Anthony M. Nietzsche and art. London, 1911.
	Phil 3640.98.9	Ludovici, Anthony M. Who is to be master of the world? Edinburgh, 1914.
	Phil 3640.98.15	Eckertz, Erich. Nietzsche als Künstler. München, 1910.
	Phil 3640.98.20	Ludovici, Anthony M. Nietzsche, his life and works. London, 1916.
	Phil 3640.99	Türck, Hermann. Friedrich Nietzsche und seine philosophischen Irrewege. München, 1894.
	Phil 3640.100A	Orage, A.R. Friedrich Nietzsche. Chicago, 1911.
	Phil 3640.100B	Orage, A.R. Friedrich Nietzsche. Chicago, 1911.
	Phil 3640.101	Kennedy, J.M. The quintessence of Nietzsche. London, 1909.
	Phil 3640.101.5	Kennedy, J.M. Nietzsche. London, 1914.
	Phil 3640.102	Morr, P.M. Nietzsche. Boston, 1912.
	Phil 3640.103	Hamblen, E.S. Friedrich Nietzsche and his new gospel. Boston, 1911.
	Phil 3640.104	Chatterton-Hill, G. Philosophy of Nietzsche. London, 1912.
	Phil 3640.105	Lichtenberger, H. La philosophie de Nietzsche. 3e éd. Paris, 1912.
	Phil 3640.105.5	Lichtenberger, H. Die Philosophie Friedrich Nietzsches. Dresden, 1899.
	Phil 3640.106A	Lichtenberger, H. The gospel of superman. N.Y., 1912.
	Phil 3640.106B	Lichtenberger, H. The gospel of superman. N.Y., 1912.
	Phil 3640.106.2	Lichtenberger, H. The gospel of superman. N.Y., 1926.
	Phil 3640.106.4	Lichtenberger, H. Friedrich Nietzsche. Dresden, 1900.
	Phil 3640.106.5	Lichtenberger, H. Friedrich Nietzsche. 2e Aufl. Dresden, 1900.
	Phil 3640.107	Brandes, G. Friedrich Nietzsche. N.Y., 1909.
	Phil 3640.107.5	Brandes, G. Friedrich Nietzsche. London, 1914.
	Phil 3640.108	Wolf, A. The philosophy of Nietzsche. London, 1915.
	Phil 3640.109	Stewart, H.L. Nietzsche and the ideals of modern Germany. London, 1915.
	Phil 3640.110	Wright, Willard H. What Nietzsche taught. N.Y., 1915.
	Phil 3640.111	Dowerg, R. Friedrich Nietzsches "Geburt der Tragödie". Leipzig, 1902.
	Phil 3640.112	Friedlaender, S. Friedrich Nietzsche, intellektuale Biographie. Leipzig, 1911.
	Phil 3640.113	Keiper, Wilhelm. Nietzsche, poeta. Buenos Aires, 1911.
	Phil 3640.114	Thilly, F. Philosophy of Friedrich Nietzsche. Photoreproduction. N.Y., 1905.
	Phil 3640.115	Figgis, J.N. The will to freedom. N.Y., 1917.
	Phil 3640.116A	Salter, William M. Nietzsche the thinker; a study. N.Y., 1917.
	Phil 3640.116B	Salter, William M. Nietzsche the thinker; a study. N.Y., 1917.
	Phil 3640.116.2	Salter, William M. Nietzsche the thinker; a study. N.Y., 1968.
	Phil 3640.117	Fouillée, Alfred E. Nietzsche et l'immoralisme. 3e éd. Paris, 1913.
	Phil 3640.117.5	Fouillée, Alfred E. Nietzsche et l'immoralisme. Paris, 1902.
	Phil 3640.118A	Riehl, Alois. Friedrich Nietzsche der Künstler und der Denker. Stuttgart, 1897.
	Phil 3640.118B	Riehl, Alois. Friedrich Nietzsche der Künstler und der Denker. Stuttgart, 1897.
	Phil 3640.118.2	Riehl, Alois. Friedrich Nietzsche der Künstler und der Denker. 2e Aufl. Stuttgart, 1898.
	Phil 3640.118.6	Riehl, Alois. Friedrich Nietzsche. 6e Aufl. Stuttgart, 1920.
	Phil 3640.118.7	Riehl, Alois. Friedrich Nietzsche. 7e Aufl. Stuttgart, 1920.
	Phil 3640.119	Huan, Gabriel. La philosophie de Frédéric Nietzsche. Paris, 1917.
	Phil 3640.119.10	Filser, Benno. Die Ästhetik Nietzsches. Passau, 1917.
	Phil 3640.120A	Carus, Paul. Nietzsche. Chicago, 1914.
	Phil 3640.120B	Carus, Paul. Nietzsche. Chicago, 1914.
	Phil 3640.121.2	Bertram, Ernst. Nietzsche. Berlin, 1918.
	Phil 3640.121.3	Bertram, Ernst. Nietzsche; Versuch einer Mythologie. Berlin, 1929.
	Phil 3640.121.3.5	Bertram, Ernst. Nietzsche. Bonn, 1965.
	Phil 3640.121.4	Bertram, Ernst. Nietzsche; essai de mythologie. Paris, 1932.
	Phil 3640.121.5	Horneffer, Ernst. Nietzsche-Vorträge. Leipzig, 1920.
	Phil 3640.121.10	Horneffer, Ernst. Vorträge über Nietzsche. Berlin, 1906.
	Phil 3640.121.15	Horneffer, Ernst. Vorträge über Nietzsche. Berlin, 1903.
	Phil 3640.122	Sánchez Torres, E. Nietzsche, Emerson, Tolstoy. Barcelona, 1902.
	Phil 3640.122.5	Eisler, Rudolf. Nietzsche's Erkenntnistheorie und Metaphysik. Leipzig, 1902.
	Phil 3640.123	Zoccoli, Ettore G. Federico Nietzsche. Modena, 1898.
	Phil 3640.124	Horneffer, Auguet. Nietzsche als Moralist und Schriftsteller. Jena, 1906.
	Phil 3640.125	Hollitscher, Jakob. Friedrich Nietzsche. Wein, 1904.
	Phil 3640.126.4	Vaihinger, Hans. Nietzsche als Philosoph. 4e Aufl. Berlin, 1916.
	Phil 3640.127	Meyer, Richard M. Nietzsche. München, 1913.

203
Classified Listing

Phil 3640 History of philosophy - Local Modern philosophy - Germany - Individual philosophers - Nietzsche, Friedrich - cont.

Phil 3640.128.2 Brahn, Max. Friedrich Nietzsches Meinung über Staaten und Kriege. 2e Aufl. Leipzig, 1915.
Phil 3640.155 De Villers, Sireyx. La faillite du surhomme et la physologie de Nietzsche. Paris, 1920.
Phil 3640.156 Muckle, Friedrich. Friedrich Nietzsche und der Zusammenbruch der Kultur. München, 1921.
Phil 3640.157 Strecker, Karl. Nietzsche und Strindberg. München, 1921.
Phil 3640.158 Andler, Charles. Nietzsche, sa vie et sa pensée. Paris, 1920-31. 6v.
Phil 3640.158.3 Andler, Charles. Nietzsche, sa vie et sa pensée. 3. éd. Paris, 1922.
Phil 3640.158.4 Andler, Charles. Nietzsche, sa vie et sa pensée. Paris, 1958. 3v.
Phil 3640.158.5 Andler, Charles. Nietzsche und Jakob Burckhardt. Basel, 1926.
Phil 3640.159.5 Grützmacher, R.H. Nietzsche. Leipzig, 1921.
Phil 3640.159.15 Grützmacher, R.H. Nietzsche und wir Christen. Berlin, 1910.
Phil 3640.160 Schacht, W. Nietzsche. Bern, 1901.
Phil 3640.161 Kohler, F.P. Friedrich Nietzsche. Leipzig, 1921.
Phil 3640.162 Messer, August. Erläuterungen zu Nietzsches Zarathustra. Stuttgart, 1922.
Phil 3640.163.2 Weichelt, Hans. Zarathustrakommentar. 2. Aufl. Leipzig, 1922.
Phil 3640.163.7 Weichelt, Hans. Nietzsche der Philosoph des Heroismus. Leipzig, 1924.
Phil 3640.164 Richter, Claire. Nietzsche et les théories biologiques contemporaines. 2. éd. Paris, 1911.
Phil 3640.165 Hildebrandt, K. Nietzsches Weltkampf mit Sokrates und Plato. Dresden, 1922.
Phil 3640.166 Pallarès, V. de. Le crépuscule d'une idole, Nietzsche, nietzschéisme, nietzscheens. Paris, 1910.
Phil 3640.167.2 Gaultier, J. de. Nietzsche et la réforme philosophique. 2. éd. Paris, 1904.
Phil 3640.167.5 Gaultier, J. de. Nietzsche. Paris, 1926.
Phil 3640.168 Römer, H. Nietzsche. Leipzig, 1921. 2v.
Phil 3640.169 Deussen, Paul. Erinnerungen an Friedrich Nietzsche. Leipzig, 1901.
Phil 3640.170 Rodriguez Aniceto, N. Maquiarelo y Nietzsche. Madrid, 1919.
Phil 3640.171 Duverger, A. Friedrich Nietzsche een levensbeeld. Amsterdam, 1913.
Phil 3640.172 Proost, K.F. Friedrich, Nietzsche, zijn leven en zijn werk. Uitgave, 1920.
Phil 3640.173 Wÿck, B.H.C.K. Friedrich Nietzsche. Baarn, 1920.
Phil 3640.174 Düringer, Adelbert. Nietzsche's Philosophie. 2. Aufl. Leipzig, 1906.
Phil 3640.175 Weigand, Wilhelm. Friedrich Nietzsche. München, 1893.
Phil 3640.176 Hocks, Erich. Das Verhältnis der Erkenntnis zur Unendlichkeit der Welt bei Nietzsche. Leipzig, 1914.
Phil 3640.177 Hasse, Heinrich. Das Problem des Sokrates. Leipzig, 1918.
Phil 3640.178 Ritschl, Otto. Nietzsches Welt und Lebensanschauung. 2. Aufl. Leipzig, 1899.
Phil 3640.178.5 Ritschl, Otto. Nietzsches Welt und Lebensanschauung. Freiburg, 1897.
Phil 3640.179 Binder, Elsa. Malwida vom Meysenburg und Friedrich Nietzsche. Berlin, 1917.
Phil 3640.180 Spindler, Josef. Nietzsches Persönlichkeit und Lehre. Stuttgart, 1913.
Phil 3640.181 Petrone, Igino. F. Nietzsche e L. Tolstoi. Napoli, 1902.
Phil 3640.182 Kämpfer, Hartfried. Zum Nietzsche-Verständnis. Celle, 1919.
Phil 3640.183 Havenstein, M. Nietzsche als Erzieher. Berlin, 1922.
Phil 3640.184 Griesser, Luitpold. Nietzsche und Wagner. Wien, 1923.
Phil 3640.185 Reiner, Julius. F. Nietzsche. Stuttgart, 1916.
Phil 3640.185.10 Reiner, Julius. Friedrich Nietzsche. 8. Aufl. Berlin, 191-.
Phil 3640.186 Reininger, R. Nietzsches Kampf um den Sinn des Lebens. Wien, 1922.
Phil 3640.187 Kaatz, Hugo. Die Weltanschauung Friedrich Nietzsches. Dresden, 1892.
Phil 3640.188 Fischer, E.L. F. Nietzsche. Regensburg, 1906.
Phil 3640.190 Bélart, Hans. Friedrich Nietzsches Ethik. Leipzig, 1901.
Phil 3640.190.5 Bélart, Hans. Friedrich Nietzsche und Richard Wagner. Berlin, 1907.
Phil 3640.190.11 Bélart, Hans. Friedrich Nietzsches Leben. 2. Aufl. Berlin, 1910?
Phil 3640.190.20 Bélart, Hans. Friedrich Nietzsches Freundschafts-Tragödie mit Richard Wagner und Cosime Wagner-Liszt. Dresden, 1912.
Phil 3640.190.30 Bélart, Hans. Nietzsches Metaphysik. Berlin, 1904.
Phil 3640.191 Würzbach, F. Dionysos. 2e Aufl. München, 1922.
Phil 3640.192 Gundolf, E. E. Gundolf und Kurt Heldebrandt, Nietzsche als Richter unsrer Zeit. Breslau, 1923.
Phil 3640.193 Howard, E. Friedirch Nietzsche und die klassische Philologie. Photoreproduction. Gotha, 1920.
Phil 3640.194 Norström, Vitalis. Friedrich Nietzsche. Stockholm, 1901.
Phil 3640.195 Schlaf, Johannes. Der "Fall" Nietzsche. Leipzig, 1907.
Phil 3640.195.5 Schlaf, Johannes. Die Kritik und mein "Fall Nietzsche". Leipzig, 1907.
Phil 3640.196 Bjerre, Poul. Det geniala vansinnet. Göteborg, 1903.
Phil 3640.197 Ekman, Karl. Nietzsches estetik. Helsingfors, 1920.
Phil 3640.198 Klages, Ludwig. Die psychologischen Errungenschaften Nietzsches. Leipzig, 1926.
Phil 3640.198.5 Klages, Ludwig. Die psychologischen Errungenschaften Nietzsches. 2e Aufl. Leipzig, 1930.
Phil 3640.198.15 Ellermann, H. Nietzsche und Klages. Inaug. Diss. Hamburg, 1933.
Phil 3640.199 Vetter, A. Nietzsche. München, 1926.
Phil 3640.200 Oehler, Richard. Nietzsches philosophisches Werden. München, 1926.
Phil 3640.200.9 Oehler, Richard. Friedrich Nietzsche und die Vorsokratiker. Leipzig, 1904.
Phil 3640.200.15 Oehler, Richard. Friedrich Nietzsche und die deutsche Zukunft. Leipzig, 1935.
Phil 3640.200.25 Oehler, Richard. Nietzsche als Bildner der Persönlichkeit. Leipzig, 1911?
Phil 3640.201 Odenwald, T. Friedrich Nietzsche und der heutige Christentum. Giessen, 1926.
Phil 3640.202 Kräutlein, Jonathan. Friedrich Nietzsches Morallehre. Leipzig, 1926.
Phil 3640.203 Kappstein, T. Einführung in Friedrich Nietzsches Zarathustradichtung. Bielefeld, 1925.
Phil 3640.204 Kalina, P.E. Fundament und Einheit in Friedrich Nietzsches Philosophie. Leipzig, 1898.
Phil 3640.205 Bubnoff, N. von. Friedrich Nietzsches Kulturphilosophie und Umwertungslehre. Leipzig, 1924.

Phil 3640 History of philosophy - Local Modern philosophy - Germany - Individual philosophers - Nietzsche, Friedrich - cont.

Phil 3640.206 Tissi, Silvio. Nietzsche. Milano, 1926.
Phil 3640.207 Andreas-Salomé, L. Friedrich Nietzsche in seinen Werken. Dresden, 1924?
Phil 3640.208 Barbat, V.J. Nietzsche, tendances et problèmes. Zürich, 1911.
Phil 3640.209 Liebmann, W. Nietzsche für und gegen Vaihinger. München, 1923.
Phil 3640.210 Salis-Marschlins, M. von. Philosoph und Edelmensch. Leipzig, 1897.
Phil 3640.211 Henne am Rhyn, O. Anti-Zarathustra. Altenburg, 1899.
Phil 3640.211.5 Henne am Rhyn, O. Anti-Zarathustra. 2e Aufl. Altenburg, 1901?
Phil 3640.212 Grimm, Eduard. Das Problem Friedrich Nietzsches. Berlin, 1899.
Phil 3640.213 Heckel, K. Nietzsche: sein Leben und seine Lehre. Leipzig, 1922.
Phil 3640.213.5 Heckel, K. Nietzsche: sein Leben und seine Lehre. Leipzig, 1922.
Phil 3640.214 Steiner, Rudolf. Friedrich Nietzsche: ein Kämpfer gegen seiner Zeit. Weimar, 1895.
Phil 3640.214.2 Steiner, Rudolf. Friedrich Nietzsche: ein Kämpfer gegen seiner Zeit. 2e Aufl. Dornich, 1926.
Phil 3640.215A Castiglioni, M. Il poema eroico di F. Nietzsche. Torino, 1924.
Phil 3640.215B Castiglioni, M. Il poema eroico di F. Nietzsche. Torino, 1924.
Phil 3640.216 Lasserre, Pierre. Les idées de Nietzsche sur la musique. Paris, 1919?
Phil 3640.216.10 Lasserre, Pierre. Les morale de Nietzsche. Paris, 1902.
Phil 3640.217 Rosen, Hugo. Livsproblemet hos Nietzsche. Stockholm, 1923.
Phil 3640.218 Mügge, M.A. Friedrich Nietzsche. London, 1912.
Phil 3640.218.2 Mügge, M.A. Friedrich Nietzsche. London, 1908.
Phil 3640.218.4 Mügge, M.A. Friedrich Nietzsche. 4th ed. London, 1914.
Phil 3640.218.5 Mügge, M.A. Friedrich Nietzsche. N.Y., 1915?
Phil 3640.219 Spitteler, Carl. Meine Beziehungen zu Nietzsche. München, 1908.
Phil 3640.220 Lessing, Theodor. Nietzsche. Berlin, 1925.
Phil 3640.221 Oehler, Max. Den Manen Friedrich Nietzsches. München, 1921.
Phil 3640.222 Stroux, Johannes. Nietzsches Professur in Basel. Jena, 1925.
Phil 3640.223 Biedenkapp, Georg. Friedrich Nietzsche und Friedrich Naumann als Politiker. Göttingen, 1901.
Phil 3640.224 Schian, Martin. Friedrich Nietzsche und das Christentum drei Vorträge. Görlitz, 1902.
Phil 3640.225 Simon, Theodor. Richtlinien christlicher Apologetik wider Nietzsche. Berlin, 1917.
Phil 3640.227 Hirsch, Moriz. Friedrich Nietzsche. Stuttgart, 1924.
Phil 3640.228 Haiser, Franz. Im Anfang war der Streit. München, 1921.
Phil 3640.229 Prinzhorn, Hans. Nietzsche und das XX Jahrhundert. Heidelberg, 1928.
Phil 3640.230 Bianquis, G. Nietzsche en France; l'influence de Nietzsche sur la pensée française. Paris, 1929.
Phil 3640.231A Foster, George B. Friedrich Nietzsche. N.Y., 1931.
Phil 3640.231B Foster, George B. Friedrich Nietzsche. N.Y., 1931.
Phil 3640.231C Foster, George B. Friedrich Nietzsche. N.Y., 1931.
Phil 3640.232 Brock, Werner. Nietzsches Idee der Kultur. Bonn, 1930.
Phil 3640.233 Langer, Norbert. Das Problem der Romantik bei Nietzsche. Münster, 1929.
Phil 3640.234 Mess, Friedrich. Nietzsche der Gesetzgeber. Leipzig, 1930.
Phil 3640.235 Podach, Erich F. Nietzsches Zusammenbruch. Heidelberg, 1930.
Phil 3640.235.10 Podach, Erich F. L'effondrement de Nietzsche. 4e éd. Photoreproduction. Paris, 1931.
Phil 3640.235.15 Podach, Erich F. Gestalten um Nietzsche. Weimar, 1932.
Phil 3640.235.20 Podach, Erich F. Friedrich Nietzsche und Lou Salomé. Zürich, 1938.
Phil 3640.235.25 Podach, Erich F. Friedrich Nietzsches Werke des Zusammenbruchs. Heidelberg, 1961.
Phil 3640.235.30 Podach, Erich F. Ein Blick in Notizbücher Nietzsches. Heidelberg, 1963.
Phil 3640.236 Fischer, Hugo. Nietzsche apostata, oder die Philosophie des Argernisses. Erfurt, 1931.
Phil 3640.237 Hirschhorn, S. Vom Sinn des Tragischen bei Nietzsche. Freiburg, 1930.
Phil 3640.238 Brann, H.W. Nietzsche und die Frauen. Leipzig, 1931.
Phil 3640.239 Rauch, Karl. Nietzsches Wirkung und Erbe. Berlin, 1930.
Phil 3640.240A Baeumler, Alfred. Nietzsche der Philosoph und Politiker. Leipzig, 1931.
Phil 3640.240B Baeumler, Alfred. Nietzsche der Philosoph und Politiker. Leipzig, 1931.
Phil 3640.240.3 Baeumler, Alfred. Nietzsche der Philosoph und Politiker. 3e Aufl. Leipzig, 1937.
Phil 3640.240.5 Baeumler, Alfred. Bachofen und Nietzsche. Zürich, 1929.
Phil 3640.241 Hellenbrecht, H. Das Problem der freien Rhythmen mit Bezug auf Nietzsche. Berlin, 1931.
Phil 3640.242 Kretzer, Eugen. Friedrich Nietzsche. Leipzig, 1895.
Phil 3640.243 Kaftan, Julius. Das Christentum und Nietzsches Herremoral. Berlin, 1897.
Phil 3640.244 Vaihinger, Hans. Nietzsche als Philosoph. Berlin, 1902.
Phil 3640.245 Düringer, Adelbert. Nietzsches Philosophie und das neutige Christentum. Leipzig, 1907.
Phil 3640.246 Kerler, D.H. Nietzsche und die Vergeltungsidee. Ulm, 1910.
Phil 3640.247 Jesinghaus, W. Nietzsche und Christus. Berlin, 1913.
Phil 3640.247.5 Jesinghaus, W. Nietzsches Stellung zu Weib. 3e Aufl. Leipzig, 1907.
Phil 3640.248 Schrempf, Christof. Friedrich Nietzsche. Göttingen, 1922.
Phil 3640.249 Tönnies, Ferdinand. Der Nietzsche-Kultus; eine Kritik. Leipzig, 1897.
Phil 3640.250 Giorgianni, E. Nietzsche. Roma, 1931.
Phil 3640.251 Gerhard, H.F. Die künstlerischen Mittel der Darstellung in Nietzsches "Zarathustra". Berlin, 1896.
Phil 3640.252 Kramer, H.G. Nietzsche und Rousseau. Inaug. Diss. Borna, 1928.
Phil 3640.253 Beckenhaupt, D. Nietzsche und das gegenwärtige Geistesleben. Leipzig, 1931.
Phil 3640.254 O'Brien, Edward J. Son of the morning; a portrait of F. Nietzsche. N.Y., 1932.
Phil 3640.255 Pourtalès, Guy de. Nietzsche en stalie. 15. éd. Paris, 1929.
Phil 3640.255.5 Pourtalès, Guy de. Amor fati; Nietzsche in Italien. Freiburg, 1930.
Phil 3640.256 Vialle, Louis. Détresses de Nietzsche. Paris, 1932.

Phil 3640 History of philosophy - Local Modern philosophy - Germany - Individual philosophers - Nietzsche, Friedrich - cont.

Phil 3640.256.5 — Vialle, Louis. Détresses de Nietzsche. Thèse. Paris, 1932.
Phil 3640.257 — Abraham, G.E.H. Nietzsche. London, 1933.
Phil 3640.257.5 — Abraham, G.E.H. Nietzsche. N.Y., 1933.
Phil 3640.258 — Dippel, P.G. Nietzsche und Wagner. Bern, 1934.
Phil 3640.259 — Visser, H.L.A. Nietzsche de goede Europeaan. Zutphen, 1933.
Phil 3640.260 — Knight, A.H.J. Some aspects of the life and work of Nietzsche. Cambridge, 1933.
Phil 3640.261 — Löwith, Karl. Kierkegaard und Nietzsche. Frankfurt am Main, 1933.
Phil 3640.261.5A — Löwith, Karl. Nietzsches Philosophie der ewigen Wiederkunft des Gleichen. Berlin, 1935.
Phil 3640.261.5B — Löwith, Karl. Nietzsches Philosophie der ewigen Wiederkunft des Gleichen. Berlin, 1935.
Phil 3640.261.10 — Löwith, Karl. Nietzsches Philosophie der ewigen Wieder kehr des Gleichen. Stuttgart, 1956.
Phil 3640.262 — Rosengarth, W. Nietzsche und George. Leipzig, 1934.
Phil 3640.263 — Crookshank, F.G. Individual psychology and Nietzsche. London, 1933.
Phil 3640.264 — Wahle, Aloys. Der weltanschauliche Gehalt von Nietzsches Dichtungen. Inaug. Diss. Dillingen, 1933.
Phil 3640.265 — Hellenbrecht, H. Das Problem der freien Rhythmen mit Bezug auf Nietzsche. Inaug. Diss. Bern, 1931.
Phil 3640.266 — Klein, Johannes. Die Dichtung Nietzsches. München, 1936.
Phil 3640.267 — Jaspers, Karl. Nietzsche. Berlin, 1936.
Phil 3640.267.3 — Jaspers, Karl. Nietzsche. 2e Aufl. Berlin, 1947.
Phil 3640.267.4 — Jaspers, Karl. Nietzsche: an introduction to the understanding of his philosophical activity. Tucson, 1965.
Phil 3640.267.5 — Jaspers, Karl. Nietzsche und das Christentum. Hameln, 1946.
Phil 3640.270 — Nicolas, M.P. De Nietzsche à Hitler. Paris, 1936.
Phil 3640.270.90 — Ritteleyer, F. Friedrich Nietzsche und das Erkenntnisproblem. Leipzig, 1903.
Phil 3640.271 — Rittelmeyer, F. Friedrich Nietzsche und die Religion. Ulm, 1904.
Phil 3640.272 — Gil Salguero, L. Persona y destino. Buenos Aires, 1934.
Phil 3640.273 — Nietzsche, Frau Franziska O. Der kranke Nietzsche. Wien, 1937.
Phil 3640.274 — Siegel, Carl. Nietzsches Zarathustra; Gehalt und Gestalt. München, 1938.
Phil 3640.275 — Goedewaagen, T. Nietzsche. 's-Gravenhage, 1933.
Phil 3640.276 — Cohn, Paul. Um Nietzsches Untergang; Beiträge zum Verständnis des Genies. Hannover, 1931.
Phil 3640.277A — Nietzsche, Friedrich. The living thoughts of Nietzsche. N.Y., 1939.
Phil 3640.277B — Nietzsche, Friedrich. The living thoughts of Nietzsche. N.Y., 1939.
Phil 3640.278 — Scheuffler, G. Friedrich Nietzsche im Dritten Reich. Erfurt, 1933.
Phil 3640.279 — Lonsbach, R.M. Friedrich Nietzsche und die Juden. Stockholm, 1939.
Phil 3640.280 — Härtle, H. Nietzsche und der Nationalsozialismus. 2e Aufl. München, 1939.
Phil 3640.281 — Lefebvre, H. Nietzsche. Paris, 1939.
Phil 3640.281.5 — Lefebvre, H. Nietzsche. Mexico, 1940.
Phil 3640.282.1 — Brinton, Clarence Crane. Nietzsche. 1. ed. N.Y., 1965.
Phil 3640.283 — Goday, V. Bersanelli. Humanidad. Buenos Aires, 1940.
Phil 3640.284 — Heintel, E. Nietzsches "System" in seinen Grundbegriffen. Leipzig, 1939.
Phil 3640.285 — Kniggendorf, W. Friedrich Nietzsche - der Deutsche! Erfurt, 1938.
Phil 3640.286 — Kroekel, F. Europas Selbsbesinnung durch Nietzsche. München, 1929.
Phil 3640.287 — Michel, W. Nietzsche in unserern Jahrhundert. Berlin, 1939.
Phil 3640.289 — Sanz y Escartin, Eduardo. Federico Nietzsche y el anarquismo intelectual. Madrid, 1898.
Phil 3640.290 — Furstenthal, Achim. Maske und Scham bei Nietzsche. Diss. Basel, 1940.
Phil 3640.291.5 — Ackerknecht, E. Friedrich Nietzsche, der Prophet der schenkenden Tugend. 2e Aufl. Stettin, 1926.
Phil 3640.292 — Copleston, F. Friedrich Nietzsche. London, 1942.
Phil 3640.293 — Beonio-Brocchieri, V. Federico Nietzsche. Roma, 1926.
Phil 3640.294 — Endres, Hans. Rasse, Ehe, Zucht und Züchtung bei Nietzsche und Heute. Heidelberg, 1938.
Phil 3640.295 — Arevalo Martinez, R. Nietzsche el conquistador. Guatemala, 1943.
Phil 3640.296 — Garcia Barcena, R. Responso heroico. La Habana, 1943.
Phil 3640.297 — Daffner, H. Friedrich Nietzsches Randglassen zu Bizets Carmen. Regenburg, 1938.
Phil 3640.298 — Kassler, K. Nietzsche und das Recht. München, 1941.
Phil 3640.299 — Umland, Karl. Nietzsches Würdigung des Menschen. Würzburg, 1938.
Phil 3640.300 — Stein, Ludwig. Friedrich Nietzsches Weltanschauung und ihre Gefahren. Berlin, 1893.
Phil 3640.301 — Gawronsky, Dimitry. Friedrich Nietzsche und das Dritte Reich. Bern, 1935.
Phil 3640.302 — Naumann, Gustav. Zarathustra-Commentar. Leipzig, 1899-1901. 4v.
Phil 3640.303 — Zickendraht, Karl. Sieben Thesen wider den Nietzsche-Geist. Basel, 193-.
Phil 3640.304 — Blanco, Julio E. Homenaje a Friedrich Nietzsche en el primer centenario de su nacimiento. Baranquilla, 1944.
Phil 3640.305.10 — Martin, A.W.O. von. Nietzsche und Burckhardt; zwei geistige Welten im Dialog. 3e Aufl. Basel, 1945.
Phil 3640.306 — Cresson, André. Nietzsche; sa vie, son oeuvre, avec un exposé de sa philosophie. 1e éd. Paris, 1942.
Phil 3640.307 — Roos, Carl Nissen. Nietzsche und das Labyrinth. Copenhagen, 1940.
Phil 3640.308 — Nietzsche; conférences prononcées à Genève sous les auspices de la fondation Marie Gretler. Erlenbach, 1945.
Phil 3640.310 — Guisso, Lorenzo. Nietzsche. Milano, 1942.
Phil 3640.311 — Smelik, Evert Louis. Vergelden en wergeven. Thesis. 's-Gravenhage, 1943.
Phil 3640.312 — Molina, Enrique. Nietzsche, dionisíaco y asceta. Santiago, 1944.
Phil 3640.314 — Kronenberg, M. Friedrich Nietzsche und seine Herrenmoral. München, 1901.
Phil 3640.316 — Baranger, William. La pensée de Nietzsche. Paris, 1946.
Phil 3640.318 — Giese, Fritz. Nietzsche...die Erfüllung. Tübingen, 1934.
Phil 3640.320 — Bataille, Georges. Sur Nietzsche. Paris, 1945.
Phil 3640.325 — Hauff, R. von. Nietzsches Stellung zur christlichen Demut. Inaug. Diss. Tübingen, 1939.
Phil 3640.330 — Heinze, Kurt. Verbrechen und Strafe bei Friedrich Nietzsche. Berlin, 1939.

Phil 3640 History of philosophy - Local Modern philosophy - Germany - Individual philosophers - Nietzsche, Friedrich - cont.

Phil 3640.334 — Flake, Otto. Nietzsche. 2e Aufl. Baden-Baden, 1947.
Phil 3640.336 — Reyburn, Hugh A. Nietzsche. London, 1948.
Phil 3640.338A — Hofmiller, Josef. Friedrich Nietzsche. Hamburg, 1947.
Phil 3640.338B — Hofmiller, Josef. Friedrich Nietzsche. Hamburg, 1947.
Phil 3640.340 — Brin, Slata G.R. Kollektivistisches in der Philosophie Nietzsches. Basel, 1948.
Phil 3640.342 — Johnsson, Milker. Nietzsche och tredje riket. Stockholm, 1943.
Phil 3640.345 — Ackermann, O. Kant im Urteil Nietzsches. Tübingen, 1939.
Phil 3640.347 — Knight, George W. Christ and Nietzsche. London, 1948.
Phil 3640.349 — Lavrin, Janko. Nietzsche; an approach. London, 1948.
Phil 3640.351 — Thibon, G. Nietzsche; ou Le declin de l'espirit. 13e éd. Lyon, 1948.
Phil 3640.353 — Lange, Wilhelm. Nietzsche, Krankheit und Wirking. Hamburg, 1948.
Phil 3640.355 — Jungen, F. Nietzsche. Frankfurt, 1949.
Phil 3640.357 — Götz, K.A. Nietzsche als Ausnahme. Freiburg, 1949.
Phil 3640.359 — Giesz, Ludwig. Nietzsche. Stuttgart, 1950.
Phil 3640.361 — Études nietzschéennes. Aix-en-Provence.
Phil 3640.363 — Landry, H. Friedrich Nietzsche. Berlin, 1931.
Phil 3640.366 — Challaye, F. Nietzsche. Paris, 1950.
Phil 3640.368B — Kaufmann, Walter Arnold. Nietzsche: philosopher. Princeton, N.J., 1950.
Phil 3640.368C — Kaufmann, Walter Arnold. Nietzsche: philosopher. Princeton, N.J., 1950.
Phil 3640.368.3 — Kaufmann, Walter Arnold. Nietzsche: philosopher, psychologist, antichrist. Cleveland, 1964.
Phil 3640.368.4 — Kaufmann, Walter Arnold. Nietzsche: philosopher, psychologist, antichrist. 3. ed. Princeton, N.J., 1968.
Phil 3640.370 — Zahn, L. Friedrich Nietzsche. Düsseldorf, 1950.
Phil 3640.372 — Pfeie, H. Friedrich Nietzsche und die Religion. Regensburg, 1948.
Phil 3640.374 — Schoeck, H. Nietzsches Philosophie. Tübingen, 1948.
Phil 3640.376 — Farré, R. De l'influence de Nietzsche sur la pensée politique allemande. Thèse. Baden-Baden, 1947.
Phil 3640.378 — Thompson, R.M. Nietzsche and Christian ethics. London, 1951.
Phil 3640.380 — Brunngraber, Rudolf. Was zu Kommen hat. Wien, 1947.
Phil 3640.384 — Landmann, M. Geist und Leben. Bonn, 1951.
Phil 3640.384.5 — Landmann, M. Zum Stil des Zarathustra. n.p., 1944.
Phil 3640.386 — Diefke, Max. Was Muss man von Nietzsche Wissen? Berlin, 1903.
Phil 3640.388 — Würzbach, F. Nietzsche. Berlin, 1942.
Phil 3640.392 — Vitens, Siegfried. Die Sprachkunst Friedrich Nietzsches in Also sprach Zarathustra. Bremen, 1951.
Phil 3640.393 — Kesselring, M. Nietzsche und sein Zarathustra in psychiatrischer Beleuchtung. Aehren Verlag, 1954.
Phil 3640.394A — Société Française d'Études Nietzschéennes. Nietzsche. Paris, 1950.
Phil 3640.394B — Société Française d'Études Nietzschéennes. Nietzsche. Paris, 1950.
Phil 3640.396 — Williams, W.D. Nietzsche and the French. Oxford, 1952.
Phil 3640.398 — Pannwitz, Rudolf. Nietzsche und die Verwandlung des Menschen. Amsterdam, 1939.
Phil 3640.400 — Gerbes, Hans E. Zum 50. Todestag Friedrich Nietzsches. n.p., 195-.
Phil 3640.402 — Mittasch, A. Friedrich Nietzsche als Naturphilosoph. Stuttgart, 1952.
Phil 3640.404 — Blunck, R. Friedrich Nietzsche. München, 1953.
Phil 3640.406 — Wiser, Edwin. Nietzsche als Prophet und das Geheimnis des Übermenschen. Affaltern, 1953.
Phil 3640.408 — Schlechta, Karl. Nietzsches grosser Mittag. Frankfurt, 1954.
Phil 3640.409 — Schlechta, Karl. Der Fall Nietzsche. München, 1958.
Phil 3640.409.2 — Schlechta, Karl. Der Fall Nietzsche. München, 1959.
Phil 3640.410 — Lotz, J.B. Zwischen Seligkeit und Verdamnis. Frankfurt, 1953.
Phil 3640.412 — Zur Erinnerung an Friedrich Nietzsche. Leipzig, 190-?
Phil 3640.414A — Lannoy, Joris C. Nietzsche, ou L'histoire d'un égocentrisme athée. Paris, 1952.
Phil 3640.414B — Lannoy, Joris C. Nietzsche, ou L'histoire d'un égocentrisme athée. Paris, 1952.
Phil 3640.416 — Bindschedler, M.B. Nietzsche und die poetische Lüge. Basel, 1954.
Phil 3640.418 — Dournes, P. Nietzsche vivant. n.p., 1948.
Phil 3640.420 — Lauscher, A. Friedrich Nietzsche. Essen, 1909.
Phil 3640.422 — Noll, B. Zeitalter der Feste. Bonn, 1947.
Phil 3640.425 — Obenauer, K.J. Friedrich Nietzsche der erkstatische Nihilist. Jena, 1924.
Phil 3640.430 — Siegmund, G. Nietzsche der Atheist und Anti-christ. 4e Aufl. Paderborn, 1946.
Phil 3640.433 — Augustin, G. Nietzsches religiöse Entwicklung. Stuttgart, 1936.
Phil 3640.435 — Mette, H.J. Der handschriftliche Nachlass Friedrich Nietzsches. Leipzig, 1932.
Phil 3640.436 — Mette, H.J. Sachlicher Vorbericht zur Gesamtausgabe der Werke Friedrich Nietzsches. n.p., 193-?
Phil 3640.440 — Noll, Baldwin. Das Wesen von Friedrich Nietzsches Idealismus. Köln, 1940.
Phil 3640.442 — Weyland, M. Una nueva imagen del hombre a través de Nietzsche y Freud. Buenos Aires, 1953.
Phil 3640.445 — Olzien, Otto H. Nietzsche und das Problem der dichterischen Sprache. Berlin, 1941.
Phil 3640.450 — Flam, Leopold. Nietzsche. Bussum, 1955.
Phil 3640.452 — Flam, Leopold. Wie was Nietzsche? Antwerpen, 1960.
Phil 3640.455A — Wolff, H.M. Friedrich Nietzsche. Bern, 1956.
Phil 3640.455B — Wolff, H.M. Friedrich Nietzsche. Bern, 1956.
Phil 3640.460 — Sonns, Stefan. Das Gewissen in der Philosophie Nietzsches. Winterthur, 1955.
Phil 3640.465 — Hartmann, H. Nietzsche, critique d'art. Manosque, 1955.
Phil 3640.470 — Manthey-Zorn, Otto. Dionysus. Amherst, 1956.
Phil 3640.475 — Drain, Henri. Nietzsche et Gide. Paris, 1932.
Phil 3640.480 — Quinot, Armand. Nietzsche, philosophe de la valeur. Manosque, 1956.
Phil 3640.485 — Benz, Ernst. Nietzsches Ideen zur Geschichte des Christentum wider die Kirche. Leiden, 1956.
Phil 3640.490 — Lea, F.A. The tragic philosopher. London, 1957.
Phil 3640.495 — Liebmann, H. Nietzsche. München, 1943.
Phil 3640.500 — Diem, Gudrun. Das Wesen der Kunst im Denken Nietzsches. Schorndorf, 1953.
Phil 3640.505 — Pannwitz, Rudolf. Nietzsche und die Verwandlung des Menschen. Amsterdam, 1943.
Phil 3640.510 — Kremer-Marietti, Angèle. Thèmes et structures dans l'oeuvre de Nietzsche. Paris, 1957.
Phil 3640.515 — Mehring, Franz. Friedrich Nietzsche. Berlin, 1957.

Classified Listing

Phil 3640   History of philosophy - Local Modern philosophy - Germany - Individual philosophers - Nietzsche, Friedrich - cont.

Phil 3640.520	Klein, Werner. Nietzsches Kampf gegen den göttlichen Zwang. Stuttgart, 1940.
Phil 3640.525	Verweyen, J. Wagner und Nietzsche. Stuttgart, 1926.
Phil 3640.530	Grau, Gerd Günther. Christlicher Glaube und intellektuelle Redlichkeit. Frankfurt, 1958.
Phil 3640.535	Rohde, Erwin. Afterphilologie. Leipzig, 1872.
Phil 3640.540	Schulze, Friedrich. Der junge Nietzsche in den Jahren. Leipzig, 1941.
Phil 3640.545	Rogachev, B. Fr. Nitsshe. Parizh, 1909.
Phil 3640.550	Salin, Edgar. Vom deutschen Verhängnis. Hamburg, 1959.
Phil 3640.555	Bianquis, Genevieve. Nietzsche devant ses contemporains. Monaco, 1959.
Phil 3640.560	Welke, Bernhard. Nietzsches Atheismus und das Christentum. Darmstadt, 1958.
Phil 3640.570	Roeschl, Herbert. Nietzsche et la solitude. Manosque, 1958.
Phil 3640.570.5	Roeschl, Herbert. Nietzsche. Paris, 1960.
Phil 3640.575	Hotter, Karl. Das Bildungsproblem in der Philosophie Nietzsches. München, 1958.
Phil 3640.580	Binder, J. Nietzsches Raatsauffassung. Göttingen, 1925.
Phil 3640.585	Troenle, Ludwig. Elitebildung durch agonale Auslese. Wien, 1958.
Phil 3640.590	Hohn, Hans. Die metaphysischen und anthropologischen Voraussetzungen der Politik bei Friedrich Nietzsche. Bonn, 1959.
Phil 3640.595	Oduev, S.F. Reaktsionnaia sushchnost' nitssheanstva. Moskva, 1959.
Phil 3640.595.5	Oduev, S.F. Tropami Zaratustry. Moskva, 1971.
Phil 3640.600	Stambaugh, Joan. Untersuchungen zum Problem der Zeit bei Nietzsche. Den Haag, 1959.
Phil 3640.605	Nejedlý, Zděnek. Nietzscheova tragedie. Vinohrady, 1926.
Phil 3640.610	Wahl, J.A. La pensée philosophique de Nietzsche. Paris, 1959.
Phil 3640.611	Wahl, J.A. L'avant dernière pensée de Nietzsche. Paris, 1961.
Phil 3640.615	Morawa, Hans. Sprache und Stil von Nietzsches Zarathustra. München, 1958.
Phil 3640.620	Heidegger, M. Nietzsche. Pfullingen, 1961. 2v.
Phil 3640.625	Weiss, Tomasz. Fryderyk Nietzsche w piśmiennictwie polskim lat 1890-1914. Wrocław, 1961.
Phil 3640.630	Savounet, Marie. Nietzsche et DuBos. Paris, 1960.
Phil 3640.635	Melo, R. de. Considerações sobre Frederico Nietzsche. Coimbra, 1961.
Phil 3640.640	Slobodskoi, I. Fridrikh Nitsche. Sankt Peterburg, 1905.
Phil 3640.645	Brzozowski, S.L. Fryderyk Nietzsche. Stanisławów, 1907.
Phil 3640.650	Baroni, C. Nietzsche éducateur. Paris, 1961.
Phil 3640.655	Wien, Hermann. Positives antichristentum. Den Haag, 1962.
Phil 3640.670	Deleuze, Gilles. Nietzsche et la Philosophie. Paris, 1962.
Phil 3640.675	Steiner, Rudolf. Friedrich Nietzsche, ein Kampfer gegen seine Zeit. Dornach, 1963.
Phil 3640.680	Rukser, Udo. Nietzsche in der Hispania; ein Beitrag zur hispanischen Kultur- und Geistesgeschichte. Bern, 1962.
Phil 3640.681	Biser, Eugen. Gott ist tot. München, 1962.
Phil 3640.682	Heftrich, Eckhard. Nietzsches Philosophie. Frankfurt, 1962.
Phil 3640.684	Love, F.R. Young Nietzsche and the Wagnerian experience. Chapel Hill, 1963.
Phil 3640.686	Gaède, E. Nietzsche et Valéry. Paris, 1962.
Phil 3640.688	Puetz, Heinz Peter. Kunst und Künstlerexistenz bei Nietzsche und Thomas Mann. Bonn, 1963.
Phil 3640.690	Doisy, M. Nietzsche, homme et surhomme. Bruxelles, 1946.
Phil 3640.692	Martinez Estrada, E. Nietzsche. Buenos Aires, 1947.
Phil 3640.694	Wilhelm, J. Friedrich Nietzsche und der französische Geist. Hamburg, 1939.
Phil 3640.695	Hess, K. Von Nietzsche zu Pannwitz. Lagnau, 1963.
Phil 3640.696	Broecker, W. Das was kommt gesehen von Nietzsche und Hölderlin. Pfullingen, 1963.
Phil 3640.697	Sørensen, V. Friedrich Nietzsche. København, 1963.
Phil 3640.698	Société Française d'Etudes Nietzschéennes. Bulletin. Paris.
Phil 3640.699	Heller, E. Nietzsche. Frankfurt am Main, 1964.
Phil 3640.700A	Stavrou, C.N. Whitman and Nietzsche. Chapel Hill, 1964.
Phil 3640.700B	Stavrou, C.N. Whitman and Nietzsche. Chapel Hill, 1964.
Phil 3640.701	Leider, Kurt. Friedrich Nietzsche. Lübeck, 1963.
Phil 3640.702	Vincenzi, M. El caso Nietzsche. San Juan, 1963.
Phil 3640.703	Hollingsdale, Reginald J. Nietzsche: the man and his philosophy. London, 1965.
Phil 3640.704	Fink, Eugen. La philosophie de Nietzsche. Paris, 1965.
Phil 3640.705	Gillner, Helmut. Fryderyk Nietzsche. Warszawa, 1965.
Phil 3640.706	Danto, Arthur Coleman. Nietzsche as philosopher. N.Y., 1965.
Phil 3640.707	Bartuschat, Wolfgang. Nietzsche. Heidelberg? 1964.
Phil 3640.708	Deleuze, Gilles. Nietzsche; sa vie, son oeuvre. Paris, 1965.
Phil 3640.709	Schieder, Theodor. Nietzsche und Bismarck. Krefeld, 1963.
Phil 3640.710	Brassard, Werner à. Untersuchungen zum Problem des Übermenschen bei Friedrich Nietzsche. Freiburg, 1962.
Phil 3640.711	Solov'ev, Evgenii A. Nitsshe. Sankt Peterburg, 1902.
Phil 3640.712	Garnier, Paul-Louis. Réflexions sur Nietzsche. Paris, 1902.
Phil 3640.713	Siegmund, Georg. Nietzsches Kunde vom Tode Gottes. Berlin, 1964.
Phil 3640.714	Kuczyński, Janusz. Zmierzch mies zczaństwa. Warszawa, 1967.
Phil 3640.715	Granier, Jean. Le problème de la vérité dans la philosophie de Nietzsche. Paris, 1966.
Phil 3640.716	Sandvoss, E. Sokrates und Nietzsche. Leiden, 1966.
Phil 3640.717	Colloque Philosophique International de Royaumont, 7th, 1964. Nietzsche. Paris, 1967.
Phil 3640.720	Vogel, Martin. Apollinisch und Dionysisch; Geschichte eines genialen Irrtums. Regensburg, 1966.
Phil 3640.722	Jette, Celine. The philosophy of Nietzsche in the light of Thomistic principles. 1st ed. N.Y., 1967.
Phil 3640.723	DeFeo, Nicola M. Analitica e dialettica in Nietzsche. Bari, 1965.
Phil 3640.725	Stobbe, Erhard. Nietzsches Lehre vom Verbrecher. Inaug. Diss. Marburg, 1964.
Phil 3640.726	Vaglia, Anna Teresa. Nietzsche e la letteratura francese. Brescia, 1967.
Phil 3640.730	Sobejano, Gónzalo. Nietzsche en España. Madrid, 1967.
Phil 3640.735	Frenzel, Ivo. Friedrich Nietzsche; an illustrated biography. N.Y., 1967.
Phil 3640.736	Frenzel, Ivo. Friedrich Nietzsche in Selbstzeugnissen und Bilddokumenten. Reinbek, 1968.
Phil 3640.740	Mei, Flavio. Tramonto della ragione. Milano, 1967.

Phil 3640   History of philosophy - Local Modern philosophy - Germany - Individual philosophers - Nietzsche, Friedrich - cont.

Phil 3640.745	Puetz, Heinz Peter. Friedrich Nietzsche. Stuttgart, 1967.
Phil 3640.750	Vattimo, Gianni. Ipostesi su Nietzsche. Torino, 1967.
Phil 3640.755	Volkmann-Schluck, Karl Heinz. Leben und Denken. Frankfurt, 1968.
VPhil 3640.760	Borský, Lev. Bedřich Nietzsche. Praha, 1912.
Phil 3640.765	Lannoy, Joris C. Dionysos of God. Brugge, 1968.
VPhil 3640.766	Grlić, Danko. Ko je Niče. Beograd, 1969.
Phil 3640.770	Dickopp, Karl-Heinz. Nietzsches Kritik des Ich-denke. Bonn, 1965.
Phil 3640.775	Ries, Wiebrecht. Grundzüge des Nietzsche-Verständnisses in der Deutung seiner Philosophie. Maulburg, 1967?
Phil 3640.780	Klossowski, Pierre. Nietzsche et le cercle vicieux. Paris, 1969.
Phil 3640.785	Fink, Eugen. Nietzsches Philosophie. 2e Aufl. Köln, 1968.
Phil 3640.790	Bulhof-Rutgers, Ilse Nina. Apollos Wiederkehr; eine Untersuchung der Rolle des Kreises in Nietzsches Denken. 's-Gravenhage, 1969.
Phil 3640.795	Gruenter, Karlfried. Der Streit um Nietzsches "Geburt der Tragödie". Hildersheim, 1969.
Phil 3640.800	Goth, Joachim. Nietzsche und die Rhetorik. Tübingen, 1970.
Phil 3640.805	Boudot, Pierre. Nietzsche et l'au-delà de la liberté; Nietzsche et les écrivains français de 1930 à 1960. Paris, 1970.
Phil 3640.810	Thatcher, David S. Nietzsche in England, 1890-1914. Toronto, 1970.
Phil 3640.815	Steinbuechel, Theodor. Nietzsche; eine christliche Besinnung. Photoreproduction. Stuttgart, 1946.
Phil 3640.820	Engadine; organe de la Société Nietzsche. Paris. 1,1969+
Phil 3640.825	Simpozium na temu Niče i Marksizam, Belgrade, 1968. Niče i marksizam. Beograd, 1969.
Phil 3640.830	Massuh, Victor. Nietzsche y el fin de la religión. Buenos Aires, 1969.
Phil 3640.836	Mann, Thomas. Nietzsches Philosophie im Lichte unserer Erfahrung. Berlin, 1948.
Phil 3640.840A	Morel, Georges. Nietzsche; Introduction à une première lecture. Paris, 1970-71. 3v.
Phil 3640.840B	Morel, Georges. Nietzsche; Introduction à une première lecture. Paris, 1970-71. 3v.
Phil 3640.845	Boudot, Pierre. L'ontologie de Nietzsche. Paris, 1971.
Phil 3640.850	Rey, Jean Michel. L'enjeu des signes; lecture de Nietzsche. Paris, 1971.
Phil 3640.855	Schmidt, Otto Ernst. Nietzsche der falsche Prophet. Leipzig, 1914.

Phil 3665   History of philosophy - Local Modern philosophy - Germany - Individual philosophers - Other N

Phil 3665.1.30	Natorp, Paul. Philosophische Systematik. Hamburg, 1958.
Phil 3665.1.70	Pamphlet box. Philosophy. German and Dutch. Natorp, Paul.
Phil 3665.1.79	Gschwind, H. Die philosophischen Grundlagen von Natorps Sozialpadagogik. Leipzig, 1920.
Phil 3665.1.80	Festschrift für Paul Natorp zum siebzigsten Geburtstage. Berlin, 1924.
Phil 3665.1.85	Jørgensen, J.F. Paul Natorp som repraesentant for den kritiske idealisme. København, 1918.
Phil 3665.2.31	Naumann, M.E.A. Über die Grenzen zwischen Philosophie und Naturwissenschaft. Leipzig, 1823.
Phil 3665.2.35	Naumann, M.E.A. Die Naturwissenschaften und Materialismus. Bonn, 1869.
Phil 3665.3.31	Neeb, Johann. Vernunft gegen Vernunft. Frankfurt, 1797. Bruxelles, 1969.
Phil 3665.3.80	Jentgens, Gerhard. Der philosophische Entwicklungsgang des Johannes Neeb 1767-1843. Düsseldorf, 1922.
Phil 3665.4.30	Nieuwenlijt, B. Gronden van zekerheid of Die regte betooguyse der wiskundigen. Amsterdam, 1728.
Phil 3665.5.2	Nelson, Leonard. Gesammelte Schriften. v.1-8. Hamburg, 1970. 7v.
Phil 3665.5.30	Nelson, Leonard. Fortschritte und Rückschritte der Philosophie. Frankfurt, 1962.
Phil 3665.5.32	Nelson, Leonard. Progress and regress in philosophy, from Hume and Kant to Hegel and Fries. Oxford, 1970.
Phil 3665.5.90	Hauer, Eugen. Person und Handlung in der Ethik Leonard Nelsons. Inaug. Diss. Bonn, 1928.
Phil 3665.5.95	Specht, Minna. Leonard Nelson zum Gedächtnis. Frankfurt, 1953.
Phil 3665.6.30	Noll, Baldwin. Philosophie und Politik. Bonn, 1953.
Phil 3665.7.30	Nicolai, Friedrich. Philosophische Abhandlungen. Bruxelles, 1968. 2v.
Phil 3665.8.30	Neeb, Johann. System der kritischen Philosophie auf den Satz des Bewustseyns gegründet. Bruxelles, 1968. 2v.
Phil 3665.9.30	Neuhaeusler, Anton Otto. Fragmente keines Vorsokratikers. München, 1968.

Phil 3705   History of philosophy - Local Modern philosophy - Germany - Individual philosophers - O

Phil 3705.1.80	Zehme, Berthold. Jakob Hermann Abereit. Inaug. Diss. Lindau, 1920.
Phil 3705.2.80	Sandberg, A.J. Het stelsel der ervaring van Mr. C.W. Opzoomer. Zeist, 1865.
Phil 3705.2.85	Veer, Hendrik. Mr. C.W. Opzoomer als wijsgeer. Assen, 1961.
Phil 3705.2.86	Veer, Hendrik. Mr. C.W. Opzoomer als wijsgeer. Assen, 1961.
Phil 3705.3.90	Rolla, A. La filosofia energetica. Torino, 1907.
Phil 3705.3.95	Rodnyi, Naum I. Vil'gel'm Ostval'd. Moskva, 1969.
Phil 3705.4	Odebrecht, R. Welterlebnis. Berlin, 1938.
Phil 3705.5	Hauck, W.A. Das Geheimnis des Lebens. Heidelburg, 1947.
Phil 3705.6.20	Oesterreich, Trangott K. Trangott Konstanin Österreich. Stuttgart, 1954.
Phil 3705.7	Oberth, Hermann. Stoff und Leben. Remagen, 1959.

Phil 3745   History of philosophy - Local Modern philosophy - Germany - Individual philosophers - P

Phil 3745.1.30A	Platner, E. Philosophische Aphorismen. Leipzig, 1793-1800. 2v.
Phil 3745.1.30B	Platner, E. Philosophische Aphorismen. Leipzig, 1793-1800. 2v.
Phil 3745.1.31	Platner, E. Philosophische Aphorismen. Leipzig, 1776.
Phil 3745.1.40	Platner, E. Lehrbuch der Logik und Metaphysik. Leipzig, 1795.
Phil 3745.1.50	Platner, E. Anthropologie für Ärzte und Weltweise. Leipzig, 1772.
Phil 3745.1.80	Bergemann, P. Ernst Platner als Moralphilosophe. Halle, 1891.
Phil 3745.1.153	Bergmann, Ernst. Ernst Platner und die Kunstphilosophie. Leipzig, 1913.

Phil 3745 History of philosophy - Local Modern philosophy - Germany - Individual philosophers - P - cont.

Phil 3745.2.31 Ploucquet, Gottfried. Sammlung der Schriften welche den logischen calcul Herrn Prof. Ploucquets Betreffen, mit neuen Zusäben, Frankfurt und Leipzig, 1766. Stuttgart, 1970.
Phil 3745.2.80 Pamphlet box. Philosophy. German and Dutch. Ploucquet, G.
Phil 3745.3.06F Pamphlet box. Philosophy. German and Dutch. Prantl, Carl von.
Phil 3745.3.80 Pamphlet box. Philosophy. German and Dutch. Prantl, Carl von.
Phil 3745.5.79 Pamphlet box. Philosophy. German and Dutch. Paulsen, F.
Phil 3745.5.85 Paulsen, Friedrich. Aus meinen Leben. Jena, 1909.
Phil 3745.5.90 Speck, Johannes. Friedrich Paulsen, sein Leben und sein Werk. Langensalza, 1926.
Phil 3745.6.35 Planck, K.C. Testament eines Deutschen; Philosophie der Natur und Menschheit. 3e Ausg. Jena, 1925.
Phil 3745.6.90 Borne, G. von dem. Karl Christian Plancks Anthropologie auf der Grundlage seiner Logik des reinen Denkens. Inaug. Diss. Winnendens, 1930.
Phil 3745.6.95 Planck, M. Karl Christian Planck. Stuttgart, 1950.
Phil 3745.7 Plessner, Helmuth. Die Stufen des Organischen und des Marisch; Einleitung in die philosophische Anthropologie. Berlin, 1928.
Phil 3745.8 Pfannwitz, Rudolf. Lebenshilfe. Zürich, 1938.
Phil 3745.8.5 Pfannwitz, Rudolf. Logos eidos, bios. München, 1930.
Phil 3745.8.10 Jäckle, E. Rudolf Pannwitz. Hamburg, 1937.
Phil 3745.9 Poortman, J.J. De noodzaak. Assen, 1936.
Phil 3745.10.5 Spiegelberg, H. Alexander Pfänders phänomenologie. Den Haag, 1963.
Phil 3745.10.10 Pfaender, Alexendar. Phenomenology of willing and motivation and other phaenomenologica. Evanston, 1967.
Phil 3745.10.15 Pfaender, Alexander. Phänomenologie des Wollens; eine psychologische Analuse. 3. Aufl. München, 1963.
Phil 3745.12 Pfeil, Hans. Überwindung des Massenmenschen durch echte Philosophie. 1. Aufl. Graz, 1956.
Phil 3745.14 Pieper, Josef. Kleines Lesebuch von den Tugenden des menschlichen Herzens. 5. Aufl. München, 1957.
Phil 3745.14.5 Pieper, Josef. Glück und Kontemplation. 1. Aufl. München, 1957.
Phil 3745.14.15 Pieper, Josef. Belief and faith. N.Y., 1963.
Phil 3745.15 Przywara, Erich. Mensch. Nürnberg, 1959.
Phil 3745.16 Popma, Klaas. Wijsbegeerte en anthropologie. Amsterdam, 1963.
Phil 3745.18 Perls, Hugo. Die Komödie der Wahrheit. 10 essays. Bern, 1967.
Phil 3745.20 Peprzak, Adrien T.B. Gronden en Grenzen. Haarlem, 1966.
Phil 3745.21 Polak, Leo. Verzamelde werken. Amsterdam, 1947.

Phil 3778 History of philosophy - Local Modern philosophy - Germany - Individual philosophers - Reinhold, Karl L.

Phil 3778.6 Reinhold, K.L. Auswahl vermischter Schriften. Jena, 1796-97. 2v.
Phil 3778.30 Reinhold, K.L. Beyträge zur leichtern Übersicht des Zustandes der Philosophie. v.1-6. Hamburg, 1802. 2v.
Phil 3778.32 Reinhold, K.L. Beyträge zur Berichtigung bisheriger Missverständnisse der Philosophen. Jena, 1790. 2v.
Phil 3778.35 Reinhold, K.L. Über die Paradoxien der neuesten Philosophie. Hamburg, 1799.
Phil 3778.36 Reinhold, K.L. Sendschreiben an J.C. Lavater und J.G. Fichte über den Glauben an Gott. Hamburg, 1799. 3 pam.
Phil 3778.38 Reinhold, K.L. Anleitung zur Kenntniss und Beurtheilung der Philosophie in ihren sämmtlichen Lehrgebäuden. Wien, 1805.
Phil 3778.39 Reinhold, K.L. Verhandlungen über die Grundbegriffe und Grundsätze der Moralität. Lübeck, 1798.
Phil 3778.40 Reinhold, K.L. Über das fundament des philosophischen Wissens. Jena, 1791.
Phil 3778.41 Reinhold, K.L. Die alte Frage: was ist die Wahrheit? Altona, 1820.
Phil 3778.90 Reinhold, E. Karl Leonhard Reinholds Leben. Jena, 1825.
Phil 3778.91 Pfeifer, A. Die Philosophie der Kantperiode Karl Leonhard Reinholds. Inaug. Diss. W. Elberfeld, 1935.
Phil 3778.92 Klemmt, Alfred. Karl Leonard Reinholds Elementarphilosophie. Hamburg, 1958.
Phil 3778.94 Spickhoff, K. Die Vorstellung in der Polemik zwischen Reinhold. München, 1961.
Phil 3778.96 Pupi, Angelo. La formazione della filosofia di K.L. Reinhold, 1784-1794. Milano, 1966.

Phil 3780 History of philosophy - Local Modern philosophy - Germany - Individual philosophers - Rosenkranz, Karl

Phil 3780.30 Rosenkranz, Karl. Studien. v.1-5. Berlin, 1839-48. 4v.
Phil 3780.35 Rosenkranz, Karl. Wissenschaft der logischen Idee. v.1-2. Königsberg, 1858-59.
Phil 3780.35.2 Rosenkranz, Karl. Wissenschaft der logischen Idee. Königsberg, 1858-59. 2v.
Phil 3780.36 Rosenkranz, Karl. Epilegomena...Wissenschaft der logischen Idee. Königsberg, 1862.
Phil 3780.37 Rosenkranz, Karl. Psychologie oder die Wissenschaft vom subjectiven Geist. Königsberg, 1837.
Phil 3780.38 Rosenkranz, Karl. System der Wissenschaft. Königsberg, 1850.
Phil 3780.79 Rosenkranz, Karl. Meine Reform der hegelschen Philosophie. Königsberg, 1852.
Phil 3780.90 Metzke, Erwin. Karl Rosenkranz und Hegel. Leipzig, 1929.
Phil 3780.91 Japtok, E. Karl Rosenkranz als Literaturkritiker. Freiburg, 1964.

Phil 3790 History of philosophy - Local Modern philosophy - Germany - Individual philosophers - Other R (except Riehl)

Phil 3790.1.80 Pamphlet box. Reimarus, H.S.
Phil 3790.1.90 Scherer, C.C. Der biologisch-psychologische Gottesbeweis bei Herman S. Reimarus. Würzburg, 1899.
Phil 3790.1.93 Scherer, C.C. Das Tier in der Philosophie des H.S. Reimarus. Diss. Würzburg, 1898.
Phil 3790.1.95 Engert, Joseph. Herman S. Reimarus als Metaphysiker. Inaug. Diss. Paderborn, 1908.
Phil 3790.1.97 Büttner, Wilhelm. Hermann S. Reimarus als Metaphysiker. Inaug. Diss. Paderborn, 1909.
Phil 3790.1.100 Starauss, D.F. Herman S. Reimarus und seine Schitzschrift für die vernünftigen Verehrer Gottes. Leipzig, 1862.
Phil 3790.2.30.8 Rathenau, W. Zur Mechanik des Geistes. 8e und 9e Aufl. Berlin, 1918.
Phil 3790.3.80 Pamphlet box. Rümelin, Gustav von.
Phil 3790.4.79 Pamphlet box. Riekert, Heinrich.

Phil 3790 History of philosophy - Local Modern philosophy - Germany - Individual philosophers - Other R (except Riehl) - cont.

Phil 3790.4.81 Schlunke, Otto. Die Lehre vom Bewusstsein bei Heinrich Rickert. Inaug. Diss. Leipzig, 1911.
Phil 3790.4.82 Schneider, Max. Die erkenntnistheoretischen Grundlagen in Rickerts Lehre von der Transzendenz. Inaug. Diss. Dresden, 1918.
Phil 3790.4.83 Leenmans, H.A. De logica der geschiedeniswetenschap's van H. Rickert. 's Gravenhage, 1924.
Phil 3790.4.85 Beck, Friedrich. Heinrich Rickert und der philosophische transzendenta subjektivismus. Inaug. Diss. Erlangen, 1925.
Phil 3790.4.87 Bloch, Ernst. Kritische Erörterungen über Rickert. Diss. Ludwigshafen, 1909.
Phil 3790.4.88 Faust, August. Heinrich Rickert und seine Stellung innerhalb der eutschen Philosophie der Gegenwart. Tübingen, 1927.
Phil 3790.4.90 Miller-Rostoska, A. Das Individuelle als Gegenstand der Erkenntnis. Winterthur, 1955.
Phil 3790.4.95 Seidel, Hermann. Wert und Wirklichkeit in der Philosophie Heinrich Rickerts. Bonn, 1968.
Phil 3790.5.31 Rosenkrantz, Wilhelm. Die Wissenschaft des Wissens und Begründung der besonderer Wissenschaften durch die allgemeine Wissenschaft. v.1-2. München, 1866-68.
Phil 3790.6.31 Rauscher, J.O. Darstellung der Philosophie. Salugan, 1891.
Phil 3790.7.81 Hasse, Heinrich. Die Philosophie Raoul Richters. Leipzig, 1914.
Phil 3790.8.80 Keirstead, W.C. Metaphysical presuppositions of Ritschl. Chicago, 1905.
Phil 3790.8.82 Rosén, Hugo. Föhållandet mellan moral och religion...den Ritschelska skolan. Lund, 1919.
Phil 3790.8.85 Hack, Valentin. Die Auffassung vom Wesen der Religion bei A. Ritschl. Diss. Leipzig, 1911.
Phil 3790.9.20 Rehmke, J. Gesammelte philosophische Aufsätze. Erfurt, 1928.
Phil 3790.9.30 Rehmke, J. Die philosophische Erbsunde; Was in ich? Marburg, 1924.
Phil 3790.9.80 Rehmke, J. Johannes Rehmke. Leipzig, 1921.
Phil 3790.10.91 Bertele, H. Paul Rée's Lehre vom Gewissen. Thesis. München, 1927.
Phil 3790.11.85 Reimarus, J.A.H. Lebensbeschreibung, von ihm selbst. Hamburg, 1814.
Htn Phil 3790.11.87* Reimarus, J.A.H. De vita sua commentarius. Hamburgi, 1815.
Phil 3790.11.90 Ebeling, C.D. Memoriae J.A.H. Reimari. Hamburgi, 1815.
Phil 3790.12.81 Motsch, Karl E. Matern Reuss. Freiburg, 1932.
Phil 3790.13 Raab, F. Philosophische Gespräche. Berlin, 1937.
Phil 3790.14 Reinwald, J.G. Kultur und Barbarei. 2e Aufl. Mainz, 1828.
Phil 3790.15.30 Riezler, K. Man, mutable and immutable. Chicago, 1950.
Phil 3790.16.30 Reidemeister, Kurt. Geist und Wirklichkeit. Berlin, 1953.
Phil 3790.20 Rosenstock, Eugen. Zurück in das Wagnis der Sprache. Berlin, 1957.
Phil 3790.20.5 Rosenstock, Eugen. Die Sprache des Menschengeschlechts. Heidelberg, 1963-64. 2v.
Phil 3790.20.10 Rosenstock, Eugen. Ja und Nein. Heidelberg, 1968.
Phil 3790.22 Riessen, Hendrick van. Mens en werk. Amsterdam, 1962.
Phil 3790.22.5 Riessen, Hendrick van. Op wijsgerige wegen. Wageningen, 1963.
Phil 3790.24 Rothacker, E. Heitere Erinnerungen. Frankfurt, 1963.
Phil 3790.30 Richtscheid, Hans. Existenz in dieser Zeit. München, 1965.
Phil 3790.30.5 Richtscheid, Hans. Helle Nächte; drei Stücke Existenzphilosophie. München, 1968.
Phil 3790.32 Rothert, Helmut. Welt, All, Einheit. München, 1969.
Phil 3790.34 Ruemke, Henricus Cornelius. Levenstijdperken van de naan. Amsterdam, 1968.

Phil 3791 History of philosophy - Local Modern philosophy - Germany - Individual philosophers - Riehl, Alois

Phil 3791.06 Riehl, Alois. Moral und Dogma. n.p., 1871-92. 5 pam.
Phil 3791.30 Riehl, Alois. Über Begriff und Form der Philosophie. Berlin, 1872.
Phil 3791.31 Eiehl, Alois. Über wissenschaftliche und nichtwissenschaftliche Philosophie. Freiburg, 1883.
Phil 3791.35 Riehl, Alois. Der philosophischeKriticismus. v.1-2. Leipzig, 1876-1887.
Phil 3791.35.2A Riehl, Alois. Der philosophische Kritcismus. 2e Aufl. Leipzig, 1908.
Phil 3791.35.2B Riehl, Alois. Der philosophische Kritcismus. 2e Aufl. Leipzig, 1908.
Phil 3791.35.3 Riehl, Alois. Der philosophische Kritizismus. Leipzig, 1924-1926. 3v.
Phil 3791.36 Riehl, Alois. Introduction to theory of science and metaphysics. London, 1894.
Phil 3791.40 Riehl, Alois. Führende Denker und Forscher. Leipzig, n.d.
Phil 3791.45 Riehl, Alois. Realistische Grundzüge. Graz, 1870.
Phil 3791.50 Riehl, Alois. Zur Einführung in der Philosophie des Gegenwart. Leipzig, 1903.
Phil 3791.75 Riehl, Alois. Philosophische Studien aus 4 Jahrzehnten. Leipzig, 1925.
Phil 3791.124 Festschrift für Alois Riehl. Halle, 1914.
Phil 3791.125 Siegel, Carl. Alois Riehl. Graz, 1932.
Phil 3791.126 Ramlow, Lilli. Alois Riehl und H. Spencer. Inaug. Diss. Saalfeld, 1933.

Phil 3800.1 - .19 History of philosophy - Local Modern philosophy - Germany - Individual philosophers - Schelling, Friedrich W.J. von - Bibliographies

Htn Phil 3800.5* Pamphlet box. Schelling bibliography.
Phil 3800.10 Jost, J. F.W.J. von Schelling: Bibliographie. Bonn, 1927.
Phil 3800.12 Schneeberger, G. Friederich Wilhelm Joseph von Schelling. Bern, 1954.

Phil 3800.30 - .49 History of philosophy - Local Modern philosophy - Germany - Individual philosophers - Schelling, Friedrich W.J. von - Complete works

Phil 3800.30A Schelling, F.W.J. von. Sämtliche Werke. v.1. pt.1-10, v.2. pt.1-4. Stuttgart, 1856-61. 14v.
Phil 3800.30B Schelling, F.W.J. von. Sämtliche Werke. Stuttgart, 1856-61. 10v.
Htn Phil 3800.30.5* Schelling, F.W.J. von. Sämmtliche Werke. v.1. pt.1-10, v.2. pt.1-4. Stuttgart, 1856-61. 14v.
Phil 3800.32 Schelling, F.W.J. von. Schellings Werke. München, 1927-28. 5v.
Phil 3800.32.3 Schelling, F.W.J. von. Schellings Werke. München, 1943. 6v.
Phil 3800.33 Schelling, F.W.J. von. Écrits philosophiques. Paris, 1847.

Classified Listing
207

Phil 3800.30 - .49 History of philosophy - Local Modern philosophy - Germany - Individual philosophers - Schelling, Friedrich W.J. von - Complete works - cont.

Htn Phil 3800.33.2* Schelling, F.W.J. von. Écrits philosophiques. Paris, 1847.
Phil 3800.36 Schelling, F.W.J. von. Schelling als persönlichkeit Briefe, Reden, Aufsätze. Leipzig, 1908.

Phil 3800.50 - .99 History of philosophy - Local Modern philosophy - Germany - Individual philosophers - Schelling, Friedrich W.J. von - Selections

Htn Phil 3800.50*A Schelling, F.W.J. von. Philosophische Schriften. Landshut, 1809.
Htn Phil 3800.50*B Schelling, F.W.J. von. Philosophische Schriften. Landshut, 1809.
Htn Phil 3800.51* Schelling, F.W.J. von. Anthologie aus Schelling's Werken. Berlin, 1844.
Phil 3800.57 Schelling, F.W.J. von. Schöpferisches Handeln. Herausgegeben und Eingeleitet von Emil Fuchs. Jena, 1907.
Phil 3800.59 Schelling, F.W.J. von. Darlegung des wahren Verhältnisses der Naturphilosophie zu der verbesserten Fichte'schenLehre. n.p., n.d. 4 pam.
Phil 3800.61A Schelling, F.W.J. von. Gedichte und poetische Ubersetzungen. Leipzig, 1913.
Phil 3800.61B Schelling, F.W.J. von. Gedichte und poetische Ubersetzungen. Leipzig, 1913.
Phil 3800.63 Schelling, F.W.J. von. Shellings Schriften zur Gesellschaftsphilosophie. Jena, 1926.
Phil 3800.65 Schelling, F.W.J. von. Philosophie. Berlin, 1918?
Phil 3800.67 Schelling, F.W.J. von. Gedichte. Jena, 1917.

Phil 3800.100 - .390 History of philosophy - Local Modern philosophy - Germany - Individual philosophers - Schelling, Friedrich W.J. von - Individual works (By Special List)

Htn Phil 3800.100* Schelling, F.W.J. von. Antiquissimi de prima malorum humanorum origine. Tubingae, 1792.
Htn Phil 3800.105* Schelling, F.W.J. von. Über Mythen. Leipzig, 1793.
Htn Phil 3800.120* Schelling, F.W.J. von. Über die Möglichkeit einer Form der Philosophie überhaupt. Tübingen, 1795.
Htn Phil 3800.120.5* Schelling, F.W.J. von. Über die Moglichkeit einer Form der Philosophie überhaupt. Tubingen, 1795.
Htn Phil 3800.130* Schelling, F.W.J. von. Vom ich als Princip der Philosophie. Tübingen, 1795.
Phil 3800.135 Schelling, F.W.J. von. Briefe über Dogmatismus und Kritizismus. Leipzig, 1914.
Htn Phil 3800.140* Schelling, F.W.J. von. Ideen zu einer Philosophie der Natur. v.1-2. Leipzig, 1797.
Phil 3800.140.2 Schelling, F.W.J. von. Ideen zu einer Philosophie der Natur. v.1-2. Leipzig, 1797.
Htn Phil 3800.140.5*A Schelling, F.W.J. von. Ideen zu einer Philosophie der Natur. 2e Aufl. Landshut, 1803.
Htn Phil 3800.140.5*B Schelling, F.W.J. von. Ideen zu einer Philosophie der Natur. 2e Aufl. Landshut, 1803.
Htn Phil 3800.150* Schelling, F.W.J. von. Von der Weltseele. Hamburg, 1798.
Phil 3800.150.2 Schelling, F.W.J. von. Von der Weltseele. 3e Aufl. Hamburg, 1809.
Htn Phil 3800.150.3* Schelling, F.W.J. von. Von der Weltseele. 2e Aufl. Hamburg, 1806.
Htn Phil 3800.150.6*A Schelling, F.W.J. von. Von der Weltseele. 3e Aufl. Hamburg, 1809.
Htn Phil 3800.150.6*B Schelling, F.W.J. von. Von der Weltseele. 3e Aufl. Hamburg, 1809.
Htn Phil 3800.160*A Schelling, F.W.J. von. Erster Entwurf eines Systems der Naturphilosophie. Jena, 1799.
Htn Phil 3800.160*B Schelling, F.W.J. von. Erster Entwurf eines Systems der Naturphilosophie. Jena, 1799.
Htn Phil 3800.170* Schelling, F.W.J. von. Einleitung zu seinem Entwurf eines Systems der Naturphilosophie. Jena, 1799.
Htn Phil 3800.170.5* Schelling, F.W.J. von. Einleitung zu seinem Entwurf eines Systems der Naturphilosophie. Jena, 1799. 2 pam.
Phil 3800.170.10 Schelling, F.W.J. von. Einleitung zu seinem Entwurf eines Systems der Naturphilosophie. Leipzig, 1911.
Htn Phil 3800.180* Schelling, F.W.J. von. System des transscendentalen Idealismus. Tübingen, 1800.
Htn Phil 3800.180.5* Schelling, F.W.J. von. System des transscendentalen Idealismus. Tübingen, 1800.
Phil 3800.180.7 Schelling, F.W.J. von. System des transscendentalen Idealismus. Hamburg, 1957.
Phil 3800.180.10 Schelling, F.W.J. von. Système de l'idéalisme trancendental. Paris, 1812.
Phil 3800.180.15 Schelling, F.W.J. von. Sistema dell'idealismo trancendentale. Bari, 1908.
Htn Phil 3800.190* Schelling, F.W.J. von. Über die jenaische allgemeine Literaturzeitung. Jena, 1800.
Htn Phil 3800.190.2* Schelling, F.W.J. von. Über die jenaische allgemeine Literaturzeitung. Jena, 1800. 3 pam.
Phil 3800.195.5 Schelling, F.W.J. von. Esposizione del mio sistema filosofico. Bari, 1923.
Phil 3800.200* Schelling, F.W.J. von. Bruno. Berlin, 1802.
Phil 3800.200.5* Schelling, F.W.J. von. Bruno. Reutlingen, 1834.
Phil 3800.200.7 Schelling, F.W.J. von. Bruno. Hamburg, 1954.
Phil 3800.200.10* Schelling, F.W.J. von. Bruno. 2e Aufl. Berlin, 1842.
Phil 3800.200.11A Schelling, F.W.J. von. Bruno. 2. Aufl. Berlin, 1842.
Phil 3800.200.11B Schelling, F.W.J. von. Bruno. 2. Aufl. Berlin, 1842.
Phil 3800.200.17 Schelling, F.W.J. von. Bruno. Leipzig, 1928.
Phil 3800.200.20 Schelling, F.W.J. von. Bruno. Paris, 1845.
Phil 3800.200.30 Schelling, F.W.J. von. Bruno. Torino, 1906.
Phil 3800.210* Schelling, F.W.J. von. Vorlesungen über die Methode des academische Studium. Tübingen, 1803.
Phil 3800.210.5* Schelling, F.W.J. von. Vorlesungen über die Methode des academische Studium. 2e Ausg. Stuttgart, 1813.
Phil 3800.210.10* Schelling, F.W.J. von. Vorlesungen über die Methode des academische Studium. 3e Ausg. Stuttgart, 1830.
Phil 3800.210.15 Schelling, F.W.J. von. Studium generale. Stuttgart, 1954.
Phil 3800.220* Schelling, F.W.J. von. Philosophie und Religion. Tübingen, 1804.
Phil 3800.230*A Schelling, F.W.J. von. Darlegung der wahren Verhältnisses der Naturphilosophie. Tübingen, 1806.
Phil 3800.230*B Schelling, F.W.J. von. Darlegung der wahren Verhältnisses der Naturphilosophie. Tübingen, 1806.
Phil 3800.230*C Schelling, F.W.J. von. Darlegung der wahren Verhaltnisses der Naturphilosophie. Tübingen, 1806.
Phil 3800.240* Schelling, F.W.J. von. Über das Verhältniss der Realen und Idealen in der Natur. Hamburg, 1806.
Phil 3800.250* Schelling, F.W.J. von. Über das Verhältniss der bildenden Künste zu der Natur. München, 1807.
Phil 3800.250.5* Schelling, F.W.J. von. Rede über das Verhältniss der bildenden Künste zu der Natur. Upsala, 1818.

Phil 3800.100 - .390 History of philosophy - Local Modern philosophy - Germany - Individual philosophers - Schelling, Friedrich W.J. von - Individual works (By Special List) - cont.

Htn Phil 3800.250.10* Schelling, F.W.J. von. Über das Verhätniss der bildenden Künste zu der Natur. Wien, 1825.
Htn Phil 3800.250.15* Schelling, F.W.J. von. Über das Verhältniss der bildenden Künste zu der Natur. Berlin, 1843.
Phil 3800.250.20 Schelling, F.W.J. von. Über das Verhältniss der bildenden Künste zu der Natur. Marbach, 1954.
NEDL Phil 3800.250.50 Schelling, F.W.J. von. The philosophy of art. London, 1845.
Htn Phil 3800.260* Schelling, F.W.J. von. Denkmal der Schrift von den göttlichen Dingen des Herrn F.H. Jacobi. Tübingen, 1812.
Htn Phil 3800.270* Schelling, F.W.J. von. Über die Gottheiten von Samothrace. Stuttgart, 1815.
Htn Phil 3800.270.1* Schelling, F.W.J. von. Über die Gottheiten von Samothrace. Stuttgart, 1815.
Htn Phil 3800.270.5* Schelling, F.W.J. von. Über die Gottheiten von Samothrace. Stuttgart, 1815.
Phil 3800.280 Schelling, F.W.J. von. Philosophie der Mythologie. Darmstadt, 1957. 2v.
Htn Phil 3800.290* Schelling, F.W.J. von. Rede zum siebzigsten in öffentlicher Sitzung gefeyerten Jahrestag der K. Akademie der Wissenschaften. München, 1829.
Htn Phil 3800.300* Schelling, F.W.J. von. Zur öffentlichen Sitzung der k. Academie der Wissenschaften am Vorabend des Ludwigs-Tages 1829. München, 1829.
Htn Phil 3800.310* Schelling, F.W.J. von. Rede an die Studierenden der Ludwig-Maximilians-Universität...29 dec. 1830. München, 1831.
Htn Phil 3800.320* Schelling, F.W.J. von. Rede zum zwei und Siebzigsten...Jahrestag der k. Academie der Wissenschaften. München, 1831.
Htn Phil 3800.330* Schelling, F.W.J. von. Über Faradays neueste EntdIckung. München, 1832.
Htn Phil 3800.340* Schelling, F.W.J. von. Philosophische Untersuchungen über das Wesen der menschlichen Freiheit. Reutlingen, 1834.
Phil 3800.340.1 Schelling, F.W.J. von. Das Wesen der menschlichen Freiheit. 1. Aufl. Düsseldorf, 1950.
Phil 3800.340.5 Schelling, F.W.J. von. Über das Wesen der menschlichen Freiheit. Leipzig, 1911.
Phil 3800.340.20 Schelling, F.W.J. von. Ricerche filosofiche su...libertá umana. Lanciano, 1910.
Phil 3800.340.25 Schelling, F.W.J. von. Of human freedom. Chicago, 1936.
Htn Phil 3800.350* Schelling, F.W.J. von. Rede zum 75. Jahrestag der k. Academie der Wissenschaften. München, 1834.
Htn Phil 3800.380*A Schelling, F.W.J. von. Erste Vorlesung in Berlin, 15 nov. 1841. Stuttgart, 1841.
Htn Phil 3800.380*B Schelling, F.W.J. von. Erste Vorlesung in Berlin, 15 nov. 1841. Stuttgart, 1841.
Htn Phil 3800.385* Steffens, Henrik. Nachgelassene Schriften...Vorwort von Schelling. Berlin, 1846.
Htn Phil 3800.385.5* Schelling, F.W.J. von. Vorwort zu H. Steffens Nachgelassenen Schriften. Berlin, 1846.
Phil 3800.386.2 Schelling, F.W.J. von. Münchener Vorlesungen. Leipzig, 1902.
Phil 3800.386.5 Schelling, F.W.J. von. Zur Geschichte der neueren Philosophie; Münchener Vorlesungen. Stuttgart, 1955.
Phil 3800.387 Schelling, F.W.J. von. The ages of the world. N.Y., 1942.
Phil 3800.387.5 Schelling, F.W.J. von. The ages of the world. N.Y., 1942.
Phil 3800.387.10 Schelling, F.W.J. von. Die Weltalter; Fragmente. München, 1946.
Htn Phil 3800.390* Schelling, F.W.J. von. Clara. Stuttgart, 1862.
Htn Phil 3800.390.5* Schelling, F.W.J. von. Clara. 2e Aufl. Stuttgart, 1865.
Phil 3800.390.10 Schelling, F.W.J. von. Clara. München, 1948.

Phil 3800.700 - .799 History of philosophy - Local Modern philosophy - Germany - Individual philosophers - Schelling, Friedrich W.J. von - Autobiography and letters

Htn Phil 3800.715* Fichtes und Schellings philosophischer Briefwechsel. Stuttgart, 1856.
Phil 3800.720 Schelling, F.W.J. von. Aus Schellings Leben. In briefe. v.1, 2-3. Leipzig, 1869-70. 2v.
Phil 3800.722 Schelling, F.W.J. von. Briefwechsel mit Niethammer von seiner Berufung nach Jena. Leipzig, 1913.
Phil 3800.725 Horn, F. Schelling und Swedenborg. Zürich, 1954.
Phil 3800.730 Schelling, F.W.J. von. Briefe und Dokumente. Bonn, 1962.
Phil 3800.735 Schelling, F.W.J. von. Schelling und Cotta. Stuttgart, 1965.

Phil 3801.1 - .99 History of philosophy - Local Modern philosophy - Germany - Individual philosophers - Schelling, Friedrich W.J. von - Biography and criticism - Pamphlet volumes; Periodicals

Phil 3801.1 Pamphlet box. Philosophy. German and Dutch. Schelling. Biography and criticism.
Phil 3801.5 Pamphlet vol. Philosophy. German and Dutch. Schelling. Biography and criticism. Dissertations, 1908-1913. 10 pam.
Phil 3801.6 Pamphlet box. Philosophy. German and Dutch. Schelling. Biography and criticism. Dissertations.

Phil 3801.100 - .899 History of philosophy - Local Modern philosophy - Germany - Individual philosophers - Schelling, Friedrich W.J. von - Biography and criticism - Monographs (800 scheme, A-Z)

Phil 3801.125 Afzelius, F.G. Von Schelling's nya lära. Upsala, 1843.
Phil 3801.134 Allwohn, Adolf. Der Mythos bei Schelling. Charlottenburg, 1927.
Phil 3801.168 Assunto, Rosario. Estetica dell'identita. Urbino, 1962.
Htn Phil 3801.185* Schelling, der Philosoph in Christo. Berlin, 1842.
Phil 3801.194 Bausola, Adriano. Metafiscia e rivelazione nella filosofia positiva di Schelling. Milano, 1965.
Phil 3801.194.5 Bausola, Adriano. Lo svolgimento del pensiero di Schelling. Milano, 1969.
Htn Phil 3801.197* Beckers, Hubert. F.W.J. von Schelling. München, 1855.
Htn Phil 3801.197.10*A Beckers, Hubert. Über die Bedeutung des Schelling'schen Metaphysik. München, 1861.
Htn Phil 3801.197.10*B Beckers, Hubert. Über die Bedeutung des Schelling'schen Metaphysik. München, 1861.
Htn Phil 3801.197.16* Beckers, Hubert. Historisch-kritische Erläuterungen zu Schelling's Abhandlungen über die Quelle der ewigen Wahrheiten. München, 1858.
Phil 3801.197.20 Beckers, Hubert. Die Unsterblichkeitslehre Schelling's im ganzen Zusammenhange ihrer Entwicklung. München, 1865.
Htn Phil 3801.197.25* Beckers, Hubert. Über die Wahre und bleibende Bedeutung der Naturphilosophie Schelling's. München, 1864.

Phil 3801.100 - .899 History of philosophy - Local Modern philosophy - Germany - Individual philosophers - Schelling, Friedrich W.J. von - Biography and criticism - Monographs (800 scheme, A-Z) - cont.

Htn Phil 3801.197.30*A Beckers, Hubert. Schelling's Geistesentwicklung in Ihrem inneren Zusammenhang. München, 1875.

Htn Phil 3801.197.30*B Beckers, Hubert. Schelling's Geistesentwicklung in Ihrem inneren Zusammenhang. München, 1875.

Htn Phil 3801.198* Berg, Franz. Sextus oder über die absolute Erkenntniss von Schelling. Würzburg, 1804.

Phil 3801.203 Benz, Ernst. Schelling. Zürich, 1955.

Htn Phil 3801.210* Biedermann, K. Degenetica philosophandi ratione et methods praesertim Fichti, Schellingii, Hegelii. Lipsiae, 1835.

Phil 3801.222 Bolland, G.J.P.L. Schelling, Hegel, Fechner en de nieuwere theosophie. Leiden, 1910.

Phil 3801.232 Bréhier, Émile. Schelling. Paris, 1912.

Phil 3801.233 Braun, Otto. Hinauf zum Idealismus! Schelling-Studien. Leipzig, 1908.

Phil 3801.233.5 Braun, Otto. Schellings geistige Wandlungen in den Jahren 1800-1810. Inaug. Diss. Leipzig, 1906.

Phil 3801.233.8 Braun, Otto. Schellings geistige Wandlungen in den Jahren 1800-1810. Leipzig, 1906.

Htn Phil 3801.234* Brandis, Christian A. Gedächtnissrede auf Friedrich Wilhelm Joseph von Schelling. Berlin, 1856.

Phil 3801.272 Cesa, Claudio. La filosofia politica di Schelling. Bari, 1969.

Htn Phil 3801.293* Cousin, Victor. Über französische und deutsche Philosophie...Nebst einer Beurtheilen den Vorrede des...Schelling. Stuttgart, 1834.

Phil 3801.319 Dekker, Gerbrand J. Die Rückwendung zum Mythos. München, 1930.

Phil 3801.320 Delbos, Victor. De posteriore Schellingii philosophia. Thesim. Lutetiae, 1902.

Phil 3801.320.10 Dempf, Alois. Schelling; zwei Reden. München, 1955.

Phil 3801.367 Erdmann, Johann E. Über Schelling. Halle, 1857.

Htn Phil 3801.367.2* Erdmann, Johann E. Über Schelling. Halle, 1857.

Phil 3801.386 Ferri, Ettore de. La filosofia dell'identità di F. Schelling. Torino, 1925.

Htn Phil 3801.391* Fichte, I.H. Über die Bedingungen eines spekulativen Theismus. Elberfeld, 1835.

Htn Phil 3801.392* Fick, Georg Karl. Vergleichende Darstellung der philosophen Systeme von Kant, Fichte, Schelling. Heilbronn, 1825.

Htn Phil 3801.405* Frauenstädt, J. Schelling's Vorlesungen in Berlin. Berlin, 1842.

Phil 3801.405.5 Frauenstädt, J. Schelling's Vorlesungen in Berlin. Berlin, 1842.

Phil 3801.406 Frantz, Constantin. Schelling's positive Philosophie. Pt.1-3. Cöthen, 1879-80.

Phil 3801.406.20 Frigo, Gianfranco. Matematismo e spinozismo nel primo Schelling. Padova, 1969.

Htn Phil 3801.407* Fries, Jakob F. Reinhold, Fichte und Schelling. Leipzig, 1803.

Htn Phil 3801.407.5* Fries, Jakob F. Fichte's und Schelling's neueste Lehren von Gott und die Welt. Heidelberg, 1807.

Htn Phil 3801.407.10* Fries, Jakob F. Von deutscher Philosophie...ein Votum für F.H. Jacobi gegen...Schelling. Heidelberg, 1812.

Phil 3801.410 Fuhrmans, H. Schelling's Philosophie der Weltalter. Düsseldorf, 1954.

Htn Phil 3801.419* Gerlach, G.W. De differentia, quae inter Plotini et Schellingii doctrinam de numine summo intercedit. Thesis. Vitebergae, 1811.

Phil 3801.426 Gibelin, Jean. L'esthétique de Schelling d'après la philosophie de l'art. Thèse. Clermont-Ferrand, 1934.

Htn Phil 3801.428* Glaser, Johann K. Differenz der Schelling'schen und Hegel'schen Philosophie. Leipzig, 1842.

Htn Phil 3801.431* Goetz, Johann K. Anti-Sextus, oder über der absolute Erkenntniss von Schelling. Heidelberg, 1807.

Phil 3801.431.2 Goetz, Johann K. Anti-Sextus, oder über der absolute Erkenntniss von Schelling. Heidelberg, 1807.

Phil 3801.434A Gray-Smith, R. God in the philosophy of Schelling. Diss. Philadelphia, 1933.

Phil 3801.434B Gray-Smith, R. God in the philosophy of Schelling. Diss. Philadelphia, 1933.

Htn Phil 3801.435* Grohmann, J.C.A. De recentissimae philosophiae vanitate. Vitebergae, 1809.

Phil 3801.436 Grubbe, Samuel. Animadversiones in constructionem materiae Schellingianam. Pt.1-4. Upsaliae, 1818.

Phil 3801.437 Groos, Friedrich. Die Schellingische Gottes- und s freiheits - Lehre. Tübingen, 1819.

Phil 3801.445 Habluetzel, Rudolf. Dialektik und Einbildungskraft. Basel, 1954.

Phil 3801.445.50 Habermas, J. Das Absolute und die Geschichte. Bonn, 1954.

Htn Phil 3801.446* Hartmann, K.R.E. von. Schelling's positive Philosophie. Berlin, 1869.

Phil 3801.446.2 Hartmann, K.R.E. von. Schelling's positive Philosophie. Berlin, 1869.

Htn Phil 3801.447* Hast, Johann. Andeutungen über Glauben und Wissen. Münster, 1842.

Phil 3801.448 Heinrich, W. Schellings Lehre von den Letzten Dingen. Salzburg, 1955.

Phil 3801.448.5 Hayner, Paul Collins. Reason and existence; Schelling's philosophy of history. Leiden, 1967.

Htn Phil 3801.449* Hegel, Georg W.F. Differenz des Fichte'schen und Schelling'schen Systems der Philosophie. Jena, 1801.

Htn Phil 3801.450* Herbart, Johann F. Hauptpuncte der Metaphysik. Göttingen, 1808.

Phil 3801.450.5 Hemmerle, Klaus. Gott und das Denken nach Schellings Spätphilosophie. Freiburg, 1968.

Phil 3801.451 Heussler, Hans. Schellings Entwicklungslehre dargestellt. Frankfurt, 1882.

Phil 3801.464 Jäger, G. Schellings politische Anschauungen. Berlin, 1939.

Phil 3801.465 Jankélévitch, V. L'odyssée de la conscience dans la dernière philosophie de Schelling. Thèse. Paris, 1932.

Phil 3801.465.5 Jankélévitch, V. L'odyssée de la conscience dans la dernière philosophie de Schelling. Paris, 1933.

Phil 3801.465.10 Jaspers, Karl. Schelling. München, 1955.

Phil 3801.465.15 Jaehnig, Dieter. Schelling. v.2. Pfullingen, 1966.

Htn Phil 3801.469* Jung, Alexander. F.W.J. von Schelling. Leipzig, 1864.

Htn Phil 3801.470* Kapp, Christian. F.W.J. von Schelling. Leipzig, 1843.

Phil 3801.470.2 Kapp, Christian. F.W.J. von Schelling. Leipzig, 1843.

Htn Phil 3801.471* Kapp, Christian. Sendschreiben an den...von Schelling. n.p., 1830.

Htn Phil 3801.471.10* Kapp, Christian. Über den Ursprung der Menschen und Völker nach der mosaischen Genesis. Nürnberg, 1829.

Phil 3801.100 - .899 History of philosophy - Local Modern philosophy - Germany - Individual philosophers - Schelling, Friedrich W.J. von - Biography and criticism - Monographs (800 scheme, A-Z) - cont.

Phil 3801.472 Kahr-Wallerstein, C. Schellings Frauen: Caroline und Pauline. Bern, 1959.

Phil 3801.474 Kasper, Walter. Das Absolute in der Geschichte. Mainz, 1965.

Phil 3801.485 Kile, Frederick O. Die theologischen Grundlagen von Schellings Philosophie der Freiheit. Leiden, 1965.

Htn Phil 3801.488* Klein, Georg M. Betrachtungen über den gegenwartigen Zustand der Philosophie...Schellingsche Philosophie. Nürnberg, 1813.

Phil 3801.491 Knittermeyer, H. Schelling und die romantische Schule. München, 1929.

Phil 3801.493 Koktanek, A.M. Schellings erste münchner Vorlesung. Inaug. Diss. München, 1959.

Htn Phil 3801.494* Köppen, Friedrich. Schellingslehre. Hamburg, 1803.

Phil 3801.494.2 Köppen, Friedrich. Schellingslehre. Hamburg, 1803.

Phil 3801.495 Kotzias, Nikolaos. Skellighios iti oligha tina peri ton vion ke tis filosofias aftou. Athena, 1855.

Phil 3801.496 Koktanek, A.M. Schellings Seinslehre und Kierkegaard. München, 1962.

Phil 3801.496.5 Ko Ktanck, Anton Mirko. Schelling-Studien. München, 1965.

Htn Phil 3801.498* Krug, W.T. Schelling und Hegel. Leipzig, 1835.

Phil 3801.499 Kunz, Hans. Schellings Gedichte und dichtischer Pläne. Zürich, 1955.

Phil 3801.516 Lendi-Wolff, Christian. Friedrich Wilhelm Joseph von Schelling. Bad Ragaz, 1954.

Phil 3801.522 Lisco, Heinrich. Geschichtsphilosophie Schellings, 1792-1809. Inaug. Diss. Jena, 1884.

Phil 3801.529 Losacco, Michele. Schelling. Milano, 1914?

Htn Phil 3801.539* Lyng, Georg V. Studier over Schelling. Thesis. Christiania, 1866.

Htn Phil 3801.544* Matter, Jacques. Schelling, ou La philosophie de la nature. Paris, 1845.

Phil 3801.544.2 Matter, Jacques. Schelling, ou La philosophie de la nature. Paris, 1845.

Htn Phil 3801.545* Marheineke, P. Zur Kritik der Schellingschen Offenbarungsphilosophie. Berlin, 1843.

Htn Phil 3801.546* Marbach, G.O. Schelling, Hegel, Cousin und Krug. Leipzig, 1835.

Phil 3801.560 Massolo, Arturo. Il primo Schelling. Firenze, 1953.

Phil 3801.563 Meier, F. Die Idee der Transzendentalphilosophie. Winterthur, 1961.

Htn Phil 3801.564* Schelling und die Theologie. Berlin, 1845.

Phil 3801.564.2 Schelling und die Theologie. Berlin, 1845.

Phil 3801.565 Mehlis, Georg. Schellings Geschichtsphilosophie in den Jahren 1799-1804. Heidelberg, 1906.

Phil 3801.566 Metzger, Wilhelm. Die Epochen der Schellingschen Philosophie von 1795 bis 1802. Heidelberg, 1911.

Htn Phil 3801.570*A Michelet, Carl L. Schelling und Hegel. Berlin, 1839.

Htn Phil 3801.570*B Michelet, Carl L. Schelling und Hegel. Berlin, 1839.

Phil 3801.570.2 Michelet, Carl L. Schelling und Hegel. Berlin, 1839.

Htn Phil 3801.570.10* Michelet, Carl L. Entwickelungsgeschichte der neuesten deutschen Philosophie...Schelling. Berlin, 1843.

Htn Phil 3801.606* Nicolai, F. Leben und Meinungen Sempronius Gundibert's. Berlin, 1798.

Htn Phil 3801.612* Noack, Ludwig. Schelling und der Philosophie des Romantik. Berlin, 1859. 2v.

Phil 3801.612.2 Noack, Ludwig. Schelling und der Philosophie des Romantik. v.1-2. Berlin, 1859.

Phil 3801.637 Oeser, Erhard. Die antike Dialektik in der Spätphilosophie Schellings. Wein, 1965.

Htn Phil 3801.669* Paulus, H.E.G. Die endlich offenbar Gewordene positive Philosophie der Offenbarung. Darmstadt, 1843.

Phil 3801.669.2 Paulus, H.E.G. Die endlich offenbar Gewordene positive Philosophie der Offenbarung. Darmstadt, 1843.

Htn Phil 3801.669.10* Paulus, H.E.G. Vorläufige Appellation...Contra das Philosophie...Schelling. Darmstadt, 1843.

Phil 3801.674 Pereyson, Luigi. L'estetica di Schelling. Torino, 1964.

Htn Phil 3801.685*A Pfleiderer, Otto. Friedrich Wilhelm Joseph Schelling. Stuttgart, 1875.

Htn Phil 3801.685*B Pfleiderer, Otto. Friedrich Wilhelm Joseph Schelling. Stuttgart, 1875.

Htn Phil 3801.697* Planck, Adolf. Schellings nachgelassene Werke. Erlangen, 1858.

Htn Phil 3801.734* Reichlin-Meldegg, C.A. von. Bedenken eines süddeutschen Krebsfeindes über Schellings erste Vorlesung in Berlin. Stuttgart, 1842.

Htn Phil 3801.743* Schellings religiongeschichtliche Ansicht. Berlin, 1841.

Htn Phil 3801.749* Rosenkranz, J.K.F. Schelling Vorlesungen. Danzig, 1843.

Phil 3801.749.2 Rosenkranz, J.K.F. Schelling Vorlesungen. Danzig, 1843.

Htn Phil 3801.749.5* Rosenkranz, J.K.F. Über Schelling und Hegel. Königsberg, 1843.

Htn Phil 3801.749.6* Rosenkranz, J.K.F. Über Schelling und Hegel. Königsberg, 1843. 2 pam.

Htn Phil 3801.749.10* Paulus, H.E.G. Entdeckungen über des Entdeckungen unserer neuesten Philosophen. Bremen, 1835.

Htn Phil 3801.763* Salat, Jakob. Erläuterung einiger Hauptpunкt der Philosophie. Landshut, 1812.

Htn Phil 3801.763.5* Salat, Jakob. Schelling in München. pt.I. Freiburg, 1837.

Phil 3801.763.7 Salat, Jacob. Schelling in München. pt.1-2. Heidelberg, 1845.

Htn Phil 3801.763.10* Salat, Jacob. Schelling und Hegel. Heidelberg, 1842.

Htn Phil 3801.764* Saldanha, J.C. de S. de B.D. de. Concordancia das sciencas naturaes. Vienna, 1845.

Phil 3801.765 Sandberg, Sven. Nägra anteckningar om Schellings philosophi. Lund, 1856.

Phil 3801.768 Sandkuehler, Hans-Jörg. Freiheit und Wirklichkeit. Frankfurt, 1968.

Phil 3801.768.10 Sandkuehler, Hans-Jörg. Friedrich Wilhelm Joseph Schelling. Stuttgart, 1970.

Htn Phil 3801.772* Schleiden, M.J. Schelling's und Hegel's Verhältniss zur Naturwissenschaft. Leipzig, 1844.

Htn Phil 3801.773* Schwarz, J.L. Schelling's alte und neue Philosophie. Berlin, 1844.

Htn Phil 3801.774* Schmidt, A. Beleuchtung der neuen Schellingschen Lehre. Berlin, 1843.

Phil 3801.774.10 Schneiter, Rudolf. Schellings Gesetz der Polarität. Winterthur, 1968.

Phil 3801.775 Schilling, Kurt. Natur und Wahrheit; Untersuchungen über Entstehung...der Schellingschen Systems. München, 1934.

Phil 3801.775.10 Schlanger, Judith E. Schelling et la réalité finie. Paris, 1966.

Phil 3801.775.20 Schulz, Walter. Die Vollendung des deutschen Idealismus in der Spätphilosophie Schellings. Stuttgart, 1955.

Htn Phil 3801.776* Schaffroth, J.A.G. Blicke auf die Schellingsch-Jacobi'sche Streitsache. Stuttgart, 1812.

Phil 3801.100 - .899   History of philosophy - Local Modern philosophy -
Germany - Individual philosophers - Schelling, Friedrich W.J. von -
Biography and criticism - Monographs (800 scheme, A-Z) - cont.

	Phil 3801.777	Schirnhafer, R. von. Vergleich zwischen den Lehren Schelling's und Spinoza's. Zürich, 1889.
	Phil 3801.777.25	Schröder, C.M. Das Verhältnis von Heidentum und Christentum in Schellings Philosophie der Mythologie und Offenbarung. München, 1936.
Htn	Phil 3801.778*	Schütz, C.G. Vertheidigung gegen Herren Schellings...Erläuterungen. Jena, 1800. 4v.
Htn	Phil 3801.779*	Seuberg, J.A. Ob Schelling? ob Schmitt? Mainz, 1845.
	Phil 3801.780	Schneider, R. Schellings und Hegels schwäbische Geistesahnen. Würzburg, 1938.
	Phil 3801.781	Semerari, Giuseppe. Interpretazione di Schelling. Napoli, 1958.
Htn	Phil 3801.801*A	Schellings religionsgeschichtliche Ansicht. Berlin, 1841.
Htn	Phil 3801.801*B	Schellings religionsgeschichtliche Ansicht. Berlin, 1841.
	Phil 3801.806	Staiger, Emil. Der Geist der Liebe und das Schicksal. Frauenfeld, 1935.
	Phil 3801.807	Stefansky, Georg. Das hellenisch-deutsche Weltbild. Bonn, 1925.
Htn	Phil 3801.812*	Süskind, F.G. von. Prüfung der Schellingischen Lehren von Gott. Tübingen, 1812.
Htn	Phil 3801.831*	Thürmer, J. Versuch die Anhänger Hegel's und Schelling's. Berlin, 1843.
	Phil 3801.837	Tillich, Paul. Die religionsgeschichtliche Konstruktive in Schellings positiver Philosophie. Breslau, 1910.
	Phil 3801.837.15	Tilliette, Xavier. Schelling: une philosophie en devenir. Paris, 1970. 2v.
Htn	Phil 3801.846*	Trahndorff, Karl F.E. Schelling und Hegel. Berlin, 1842.
Htn	Phil 3801.872*	Vogel, Emil F. Schelling oder Hegel oder Keiner von Beyden? Leipzig, 1843.
	Phil 3801.872.25	Volkmann-Schluck, Karl Heinz. Mythos und Logos. Berlin, 1969.
Htn	Phil 3801.874*	Watson, John. Schelling's transcendental idealism. Chicago, 1882.
	Phil 3801.874.2A	Watson, John. Schelling's transcendental idealism. Chicago, 1882.
	Phil 3801.874.2B	Watson, John. Schelling's transcendental idealism. Chicago, 1882.
	Phil 3801.874.5	Watson, John. Schelling's transcendental idealism. 2nd ed. Chicago, 1892.
Htn	Phil 3801.875*	Weiller, K. von. Der Geist der allerneuesten Philosophie der Herren Schelling, Hegel. v.1-2. München, 1803-05.
Htn	Phil 3801.876*	Wendell, Johann A. Grundzüge und Kritik der Philosophien Kant's, Fichte's und Schelling's. 2. Aufl. Coburg, 1824.
	Phil 3801.876.30	Weber, Alfred. Examen critique de la philosophie religieuse se Schelling. Thèse. Strasbourg, 1860.
Htn	Phil 3801.876.40*	Wegscheider, J.A.L. Über die von der neusten Philosophie. Hamburg, 1804.
	Phil 3801.878	Wild, Christoph. Reflexion und Erfahrung. Freiburg, 1968.
	Phil 3801.879	Wieland, W. Schellings Lehre von der Zeit. Heidelberg, 1956.
	Phil 3801.895A	Zeltner, Hermann. Schelling. Stuttgart, 1954.
	Phil 3801.895B	Zeltner, Hermann. Schelling. Stuttgart, 1954.
Htn	Phil 3801.896*	Zimmermann, R. Schelling's Philosophie der Kunst. Wien, 1875.

Phil 3801.900 - .999   History of philosophy - Local Modern philosophy -
Germany - Individual philosophers - Schelling, Friedrich W.J. von -
Biography and criticism - Anonymous works

Htn	Phil 3801.923*	Die Enthullte Geheimlehre des Herren von Schelling. Schaffhausen, 1844.
Htn	Phil 3801.934*	Die Grundlehren der neu- Schelling'schen und der Hegel'schen Philosophie. Reutlingen, 1847.
	Phil 3801.934.2	Die Grundlehren der neu- Schelling'schen und der Hegel'schen Philosophie. Reutlingen, 1847.
tn	Phil 3801.959*	Schelling, F.W.J. von. Der neue Reineke Fuchs in acht philosophischen Fabeln. Stuttgart, 1844.
	Phil 3801.959.2	Schelling, F.W.J. von. Der neue Reineke Fuchs in acht philosophischen Fabeln. Stuttgart, 1844.
tn	Phil 3801.979*	Schellings Offenbarungsphilosophie. Drei Briefe. Berlin, 1843.
	Phil 3801.982	Schelling und die Offerbarung. Leipzig, 1842.
tn	Phil 3801.989*	Über den neuesten Idealismus der Herren Schelling und Hegel. München, 1803.

Phil 3805   History of philosophy - Local Modern philosophy - Germany - Individual
philosophers - Schleiermacher, Friedrich

	Phil 3805.10	Schleiermacher, Friedrich. Sämmtliche Werke. Berlin, 1826-64. 29v.
	Phil 3805.12	Schleiermacher, Friedrich. Sämmtliche Werke. 2. Aufl. Berlin, 1884.
	Phil 3805.15	Schleiermacher, Friedrich. Werke. Leipzig, 1910-11. 4v.
	Phil 3805.17	Schleiermacher, Friedrich. Werke. Berlin, 1924.
	Phil 3805.18	Schleiermacher, Friedrich. Kleine Schriften und Predigten. Berlin, 1969-70. 3v.
	Phil 3805.20	Schleiermacher, Friedrich. Friedrich Schleiermacher. Langensalza, 1912.
	Phil 3805.22	Schleiermacher, Friedrich. Dialektik. Berlin, 1903.
	Phil 3805.25	Schleiermacher, Friedrich. Ideen, Reflexionen und Betrachtungen aus Schleiermachers Werken. Berlin, 1854.
	Phil 3805.29	Schleiermacher, Friedrich. Ein poetischer Brief Schleiermachers. Halle, 1917.
	Phil 3805.30*	Schleiermacher, Friedrich. Über die Religion. Berlin, 1799.
	Phil 3805.30.2	Schleiermacher, Friedrich. Über die Religion. Berlin, 1806.
	Phil 3805.30.3	Schleiermacher, Friedrich. Über die Religion. Berlin, 1821.
	Phil 3805.30.4	Schleiermacher, Friedrich. Über die Religion. Berlin, 1831.
	Phil 3805.30.5	Schleiermacher, Friedrich. Über die Religion. Leipzig, 1868-69.
	Phil 3805.30.10	Schleiermacher, Friedrich. Über die Religion. Berlin, 191-.
	Phil 3805.30.12	Schleiermacher, Friedrich. Über die Religion. Hamburg, 1958.
	Phil 3805.30.12.6	Schleiermacher, Friedrich. Über die Religion. 6. Aufl. Göttingen, 1914.
	Phil 3805.30.15	Schleiermachers Glaubenslehre. Leipzig, 1910.
	Phil 3805.30.20	Thönes, Friedrich. Schleiermacher's handschriftlichen Anmerkungen zur I. Theil der Glaubenslehre. Berlin, 1873.
	Phil 3805.31.5	Schleiermacher, Friedrich. On religion. N.Y., 1958.
	Phil 3805.31.6	Schleiermacher, Friedrich. On religion. N.Y., 1955.
	Phil 3805.32	Schleiermacher, Friedrich. Der christliche Glaube. Bd.1-2. Reutlingen, 1828.

Phil 3805   History of philosophy - Local Modern philosophy - Germany - Individual
philosophers - Schleiermacher, Friedrich - cont.

	Phil 3805.32.5	Schleiermacher, Friedrich. Der christliche Glaube. 2. Aufl. Berlin, 1830-31. 2v.
	Phil 3805.32.10	Schleiermacher, Friedrich. Der christliche Glaube. 5. Aufl. Berlin, 1861. 2v.
	Phil 3805.32.15	Schleiermacher, Friedrich. Der christliche Glaube; nach den Grundsätzen. Berlin, 1960. 2v.
	Phil 3805.33	Schleiermacher Kurze Darstellung des theologischen Studiums. Leipzig, 1910.
	Phil 3805.33.10	Schleiermacher, Friedrich. Kurze Darstellung des theologischen Studiums. Berlin, 1811.
	Phil 3805.33.20	Schleiermacher, Friedrich. Brief outline of the study of theology. Edinburgh, 1850.
Htn	Phil 3805.34*	Schleiermacher, Friedrich. Über Offenbarung und Mythologie. Berlin, 1799.
	Phil 3805.34.10	Schleiermacher, Friedrich. Räthsel und Charaden. Berlin, 1874.
	Phil 3805.35	Schleiermacher, Friedrich. Grundlinien eines Kritik...Sittenlehre. Berlin, 1803.
	Phil 3805.36	Schleiermacher, Friedrich. Grundriss der philosophischen Ethik. Leipzig, 1911.
	Phil 3805.36.5	Schleiermacher, Friedrich. Grundriss der philosophischen Ethik. Berlin, 1841.
	Phil 3805.37	Schleiermacher, Friedrich. Entwurf eines Systems der Sittenlehre. Berlin, 1835.
	Phil 3805.40	Schleiermacher, Friedrich. Monologen. Berlin, 1800.
	Phil 3805.41	Schleiermacher, Friedrich. Monologen. Berlin, 1868.
	Phil 3805.45	Schleiermacher, Friedrich. Monologen nebst den Vorarbeiten. 2. Aufl. Leipzig, 1914.
	Phil 3805.49	Schleiermacher, Friedrich. Soliloquies. Chicago, 1926.
	Phil 3805.50	Schleiermacher, Friedrich. Die Weihnachtsfeier. Leipzig, 1908.
	Phil 3805.50.5	Schleiermacher, Friedrich. Die Weihnachtsfeier. Halle, 1806.
	Phil 3805.50.10	Schleiermacher, Friedrich. Die Weihnachtsfeier. 3. Ausg. Berlin, 1837.
	Phil 3805.50.15	Schleiermacher, Friedrich. Die Weihnachtsfeier. Basel, 1954.
	Phil 3805.55	Schleiermacher, Friedrich. Asthetik. Berlin, 1931.
	Phil 3805.75	Schleiermacher, Friedrich. Aus Schleiermacher's Leben. Berlin, 1860. 2v.
	Phil 3805.76	Schleiermacher, Friedrich. Briefe. Berlin, 1923.
	Phil 3805.76.5	Schleiermacher, Friedrich. Schleiermacher als Mensch...Briefe. Gotha, 1922. 2v.
	Phil 3805.76.9	Schleiermacher, Friedrich. Briefwechsel mit seiner Braut. 2. Aufl. Gotha, 1920.
	Phil 3805.78	Schleiermacher, Friedrich. Briefwechsel mit J.C. Gass. Berlin, 1852.
	Phil 3805.79	Pamphlet vol. Philosophy. German and Dutch. Schleiermacher, Friedrich. 12 pam.
	Phil 3805.79.2	Pamphlet vol. Philosophy. German and Dutch. Schleiermacher, Friedrich. German dissertations. 12 pam.
	Phil 3805.79.3	Pamphlet box. Philosophy. German and Dutch. Schleiermacher, Friedrich. German dissertations.
	Phil 3805.79.5	Pamphlet box. Philosophy. German and Dutch. Schleiermacher, Friedrich.
	Phil 3805.80	Aus F.D.E. Schleiermacher's Leben. Berlin, 1858-63. 4v.
	Phil 3805.81	The life of F.D.E. Schleiermacher. London, 1860. 2v.
	Phil 3805.82	Theil. Friedrich Daniel Ernst Schleiermacher. Berlin, 1835.
	Phil 3805.83	Bender, W. Schleiermachers Theologie. v.1-2. Nördlingen, 1876-78.
	Phil 3805.84	Esselborn, F.W. Die philosophischen Voraussetzingen von Schleiermachers Determinismus. Ludwigshafen, 1897.
	Phil 3805.85	Dilthey, Wilhelm. Leben Schleiermachers. Berlin, 1870.
	Phil 3805.85.2	Dilthey, Wilhelm. Leben Schleiermachers. 2. Aufl. Berlin, 1922.
	Phil 3805.86	Weissenborn, G. Vorlesungen über Schleiermacher's Dialektik und Dogmatik. v.1-2. Leipzig, 1847-49.
	Phil 3805.87	Fischer, M. Schleiermacher. Berlin, 1899.
	Phil 3805.88	Fuchs, Emil. Schleiermachers Religionsbegriff und religiöse Stellung zur Zeit der ersten Ausgabe der Reden, 1799-1806. Inaug. Diss. Giessen, 1900.
	Phil 3805.89	Wickert, R. Über Schleiermachers. Leipzig, 1907.
	Phil 3805.90	Bachmann, F. Entwickelung der Ethik Schleiermachers. Leipzig, 1892.
	Phil 3805.91	Iuäbicker, R. Über Schleiermachers erkenntnisstheoretische Grundausicht. Berlin, 1871.
	Phil 3805.92	Schürer, Emil. Schleiermacher's Religionsbegriff. Leipzig, 1868.
	Phil 3805.93	Schleiermacher, Friedrich. Philosophische Sittenlehre. Berlin, 1870.
	Phil 3805.94	Schweizer, A. Schleiermachers Wirksamkeit als Prediger. Halle, 1834.
	Phil 3805.95	Uhlhorn, Otto. Schleiermachers Entwurf einer Kritik der bisherigen Sittenlehre dargestellt. Oldenburg, 1894. 2v.
	Phil 3805.96	Wendland, J. Die Religiöse Entwicklung Schleiermachers. Tübingen, 1915.
	Phil 3805.97	Munro, R. Schleiermacher, personal and speculative. Paisley, 1903.
	Phil 3805.98	Cramaussel, E. La philosophie religieuse de Schleiermacher. Genève, 1909.
	Phil 3805.99	Goebel, Louis. Herder und Schleiermachers Reden. Gotha, 1904.
	Phil 3805.100	Vorlander, Franz. Schleiermachers Sittenlehre ausführlich. Marburg, 1851.
	Phil 3805.101	Vowinckel, Ernst. Religion und Religionen bei Schleiermacher und Hegel. Erlangen, 1896.
	Phil 3805.102	Eck, Samuel. Über die Herkunft des Individualitäts - Gedankens bei Schleiermacher. Giessen, 1908.
	Phil 3805.103	Thilo, C.A. Schleiermachers Religionsphilosophie. Langensalza, 1906.
	Phil 3805.104	Alin, Folke. Studier öfver Schleiermachers uppfattning af det evangeliska skapelsebegreppet. Lund, 1909.
	Phil 3805.153	Dentice di Accadia, Cecilia. Schleiermacher. Milano, 1918.
	Phil 3805.155	Selbie, W.B. Schleiermacher. London, 1913.
	Phil 3805.155.5	Siegmund-Schultze, F. Schleiermachers Psychologie. Tübingen, 1913.
	Phil 3805.155.7	Stammer, Martin O. Schleiermachers Asthetizismus in Theorie und Praxis wahrend der Jahre 1796 bis 1802. Leipzig, 1913.
	Phil 3805.156	Völter, Hans. Schleiermacher und die Gegenwart. Heilbronn, 1919.
	Phil 3805.157	Schaller, Julius. Vorlesungen über Schleiermacher. Halle, 1844.

Phil 3805   History of philosophy - Local Modern philosophy - Germany - Individual philosophers - Schleiermacher, Friedrich - cont.

Phil 3805.158   Braniss, C.J. Über Schleiermachers Glaubenslehre. Berlin, 1824.

Phil 3805.159   Ritschl, Otto. Schleiermacher's Stellung zum Christentum. Gotha, 1888.

Phil 3805.160   Lindroth, H. Schleiermachers religionsbegrepp. Thesis. Uppsala, 1926.

Phil 3805.161   Willich, E. von. Aus Schleiermacher's Hause: Jugender'en seiner Stiefsohnes. Berlin, 1909.

Phil 3805.162   Schmidt, P. Spinoza und Schleiermacher. Berlin, 1868.

Phil 3805.163   Strobel, Anton. Die Pädagogik und Philosophie Schleiermachers in ihren Bezienungen zu J.J. Tousseau. Inaug. Diss. n.p., 1927.

Phil 3805.164   Holstein, Günther. Die Staatsphilosophie Schleiermachers. Bonn, 1923.

Phil 3805.165   Geyer, Otto. Friedrich Schleiermachers Psychologie. Inaug. Diss. Leipzig, 1895.

Phil 3805.166   Diebow, Paul. Die Pädagogik Schleiermachers im Lichte seiner und unserer Zeit. Halle, 1894.

Phil 3805.167   Kügelgen, C. von. Schleiermachers Reden und Kants Predigten. Leipzig, 1901.

Phil 3805.168   Petrelli, C.M.J. In Schleiermacherianam christianae fidei expositionem. Diss. Upsaliae, 1840.

Phil 3805.169   Steinberg, Julius. Liebe und Ehe in Schleiermachers Kreis. Dresden, 1921.

Phil 3805.170   Frahne, A. Der Begriff der Eigentümlichkeit oder Individualität bei Schleiermacher. Halle, 1884.

Phil 3805.171   Müsebeck, Ernst. Schleiermacher in der Geschichte der Staatsides. Berlin, 1927.

Phil 3805.172   Wehrung, Georg. Schleiermacher in der Zeit seines Werdens. Gütersloh, 1927.

Phil 3805.173   Ungern-Sternberg, Arthur Freiherr von. Freiheit und Wirklichkeit. Gotha, 1931.

Phil 3805.173.5   Ungern-Sternberg, Arthur Freiherr von. Schleiermachers völkische Botschaft. Gotha, 1933.

Phil 3805.174   Hartenstein, G. De ethice a Schleiermachero propositae fundamento. Pt.1-2. Lipsiae, 1837.

Phil 3805.175   Rosenkranz, Karl. Kritik der Schleiermacherschen Glaubenslehre. Königsberg, 1836.

Phil 3805.176   Schenkel, D. Friedrich Schleiermacher, ein Lebens- und Charakterbild. Elberfeld, 1868.

Phil 3805.177   Osborn, A.R. Schleiermacher and religious education. London, 1934.

Phil 3805.178   Herz, Henriette de Lemos. Schleiermacher und seine Lieben. Magdeburg, 1910.

Phil 3805.179   Runze, G. Schleiermacher's Glaubenslehre in ihrer Abhängigkeit von seiner Philosophie. Berlin, 1877.

Phil 3805.180   Odebrecht, Rudolf. Schleiermachers System der Asthetik. Berlin, 1932.

Phil 3805.181   Graeber, Martin. Die Sakramentstheorie Schleiermachers und ihre Weiterbildung innerhalb der kritischen Theologie des 19. Jahrhunderts. Inaug. Diss. Wuppertal, 1937.

Phil 3805.182   Kroker, P. Die Tugendlehre Schleiermachers. Erlangen, 1889.

Phil 3805.183   Brandt, R.B. The philosophy of Schleiermacher. N.Y., 1941.

Phil 3805.184   Süskind, H. Der Einfluss Schellings auf die Entwicklung von Schleiermachers System. Tübingen, 1909.

Phil 3805.185   Ritschl, Alfrecht. Schleiermachers Reden über die Religion und ihre Nachwirkungen auf die evangelische Kirche Deutschlands. Bonn, 1874.

Phil 3805.186   Flückiger, Felix. Philosophie und Theologie bei Schleiermacher. Basel, 1947?

Phil 3805.187   Bredow, G. Wertanalysen zu Schleiermachers. Diss. Würzburg, 1941.

Phil 3805.188   Neumann, J. Schleiermacher. Berlin, 1936.

Phil 3805.190   Vogelsang, A.A. De preeken von Schleiermacher Praefschrift. Leiden, 1916.

Phil 3805.195   Schuffenhauer, Heinz. Der fortschrittliche Gehalt der Pädagogik Schleiermachers. Berlin, 1956.

Phil 3805.200   Meisner, Heinrich. Schleiermachers Lehrjahre. Berlin, 1934.

Phil 3805.205   Luetgert, Wilhelm. Schleiermacher. Berlin, 1934.

Phil 3805.210   Jorgensen, Paul. Die Ethik Schleiermachers. München, 1959.

Phil 3805.215   Beckmann, Klaus. Der Begriff der Häresie bei Schleiermacher. München, 1959.

Phil 3805.220   Ariebel, Horst. Die Bedeutung des Bösen für die Entwiklung. Ratingen, 1961.

Phil 3805.221   Birkner, Hans J. Schleiermachers christliche Sittenlehre, im Zusammenhang seines philosophisch-theologischen Systems. Berlin, 1964.

Phil 3805.222   Niebuhr, Richard R. Schleiermacher on Christ and religion. N.Y., 1964.

Phil 3805.223   Suenkel, Wolfgang. Friedrich Schleiermachers Begründung der Pädagogik als Wissenschaft. Düsseldorf, 1964.

Phil 3805.224   Dawson, Jerry F. Friedrich Schleiermacher: the evolution of a nationalist. Austin, 1966.

Phil 3805.226   Spiegel, Yorick. Theologie der bürgerlichen Gesellschaft. München, 1968.

Phil 3805.228   Redeker, Martin. Friedrich Schleiermacher. Berlin, 1968.

Phil 3805.230   Vattimo, Gianni. Schleiermacher filosofo dell'interpretazione. Milano, 1968.

Phil 3805.235   Hirsch, Emanuel. Schleiermachers Christusglaube drei Studien. 1. Aufl. Gütalsoh, 1968.

Phil 3805.240   Wintsch, Hans Ulrich. Religiosität und Bildung. Thesis. Zürich, 1967.

Phil 3805.245   Preuss, Eckhardt. Die Stellung und Bedeutung der Familie in der Pädagogik Schleiermachers. Münster? 1966?

Phil 3805.250   Groell, Johannes. Rezeptivität und Spontaneität. Inaug. Diss. Münster? 1966?

Phil 3805.252   Oranje, Leendert. God en wereld. Kampen, 1968.

Phil 3805.255   Stalder, Robert. Grundlinien der Theologie Schleiermachers. Wiesbaden, 1969.

Phil 3805.260   Fuchs, Emil. Von Schleiermacher zu Marx. Berlin, 1969.

Phil 3805.265   Daur, Martin. Die eine Kirche und das zweifache Recht. Thesis. München, 1970.

Phil 3805.270   Miller, Marlin E. Der Ubergang. 1. Aufl. Gütersloh, 1970.

Phil 3808   History of philosophy - Local Modern philosophy - Germany - Individual philosophers - Schopenhauer, Arthur

Phil 3808.10   Schopenhauer, Arthur. Sämmtliche Werke. Leipzig, 1873-77. 6v.

Phil 3808.11   Schopenhauer, Arthur. Werke. 2. Aufl. Leipzig, 1891. 2v.

Phil 3808.11.2   Schopenhauer, Arthur. Werke. Leipzig, 1891. 2v.

Phil 3808   History of philosophy - Local Modern philosophy - Germany - Individual philosophers - Schopenhauer, Arthur - cont.

Phil 3808.12   Schopenhauer, Arthur. Sämmtliche Werke. Leipzig, 1891. 6v.

Phil 3808.13   Schopenhauer, Arthur. Sämmtliche Werke. v.1-6,9-11,13-16. München, 1911-42. 13v.

Phil 3808.15   Schopenhauer, Arthur. Sämmtliche Werke. 2. Aufl. Leipzig, 1877. 6v.

Phil 3808.15.7   Schopenhauer, Arthur. Sämmtliche Werke. 2. Aufl. Leipzig, 1908. 6v.

Phil 3808.17   Schopenhauer, Arthur. Sämmtliche Werke in fünf Bänden. Leipzig, 1919. 5v.

Phil 3808.18   Schopenhauer, Arthur. Sämmtliche Werke. Leipzig, 1919. 2v.

Phil 3808.19   Schopenhauer, Arthur. Sämmtliche Werke. Leipzig, 1937-41. 7v.

Phil 3808.20   Schopenhauer, Arthur. Aus A. Schopenhauer's handschriftlichen Nachlass. Leipzig, 1864.

Phil 3808.20.10   Schopenhauer, Arthur. Philosophische Aphorismen. Leipzig, 1924.

Phil 3808.21   Schopenhauer, Arthur. Lichtstrahlen aus seinen Werken. Leipzig, 1867.

Phil 3808.22   Schopenhauer, Arthur. The works of Schopenhauer, abridged. N.Y., 1928.

Phil 3808.22.3   Schopenhauer, Arthur. The works of Schopenhauer, abridged. Garden City, 1928.

Phil 3808.22.15   Schopenhauer, Arthur. The wisdom of Schopenhauer. London, 1911.

Phil 3808.22.20   Schopenhauer, Arthur. Works. Abridged. N.Y., 1931.

Phil 3808.23   Schopenhauer, Arthur. Handschriftlicher Nachlass. Leipzig, 1895.

Phil 3808.23.5   Schopenhauer, Arthur. Der handschriftliche Nachlass. v.1-3,5. Frankfurt, 1966. 4v.

Phil 3808.24   Schopenhauer, Arthur. Über Urtheil, Kritik, Beifall, Ruhm, Warheit und Irrthum. Leipzig, 1891.

Phil 3808.24.14   Schopenhauer, Arthur. Arthur Schopenhauer. n.p., n.d.

Phil 3808.24.15   Schopenhauer, Arthur. Die Persönlichkeit und das Werk. Leipzig, 1925.

Phil 3808.24.17   Schopenhauer, Arthur. Das Bild des Menschen in Schopenhauers Philosophie. Berlin, 1932.

Phil 3808.24.20   Schopenhauer, Arthur. Über den Satz vom Grunde. Leipzig, 1891.

Phil 3808.25.5   Schopenhauer, Arthur. Aphorismen zur Lebensweisheit. Stuttgart, 1924.

Phil 3808.25.7   Schopenhauer, Arthur. Aphorismen zur Lebensweisheit. Leipzig, 1920.

Phil 3808.25.25   Schopenhauer, Arthur. The wisdom of life. London, 1963.

Phil 3808.25.30   Schopenhauer, Arthur. Counsels and maxims. London, 1890.

Phil 3808.26   Schopenhauer, Arthur. Counsels and maxims. London, 1891.

Phil 3808.26.50   Schopenhauer, Arthur. Schopenhauer und Schleiermacher über die Lebensalter. Leipzig, 1925?

Phil 3808.27   Schopenhauer, Arthur. Religion: a dialogue. London, 1890.

Phil 3808.28   Schopenhauer, Arthur. Art of literature. London, 1891.

Phil 3808.29.5   Schopenhauer, Arthur. Studies in pessimism. London, 1891.

Phil 3808.29.10   Schopenhauer, Arthur. Studies in pessimism. London, 1923.

Phil 3808.29.15   Schopenhauer, Arthur. Uren met Schopenhauer. Baarn, 1916.

Phil 3808.29.25   Schopenhauer, Arthur. La pensée de Schopenhauer. Paris, 1918.

Phil 3808.30   Schopenhauer, Arthur. Art of controversy. London, 1896.

Phil 3808.31.2   Schopenhauer, Arthur. On human nature. London, 1897.

Phil 3808.31.5   Schopenhauer, Arthur. On human nature; essays. London, 1957.

Htn   Phil 3808.33*   Schopenhauer, Arthur. Die Welt als Wille und Vorstellung. Leipzig, 1819.

Htn   Phil 3808.35*   Schopenhauer, Arthur. Die Welt als Wille und Vorstellung. Leipzig, 1859. 2v.

Phil 3808.35.2   Schopenhauer, Arthur. Die Welt als Wille und Vorstellung. Leipzig, 1873. 2v.

Phil 3808.35.2.3   Schopenhauer, Arthur. Die Welt als Wille und Vorstellung. Leipzig, 1873. 2 pam.

Phil 3808.35.3   Schopenhauer, Arthur. Die Welt als Wille und Vorstellung. Halle, 1891? 2v.

Phil 3808.35.4   Schopenhauer, Arthur. Die Welt als Wille und Vorstellung. 5. Aufl. Leipzig, 1879. 2v.

Phil 3808.35.5   Schopenhauer, Arthur. Die Welt als Wille und Vorstellung. München, 1912-13. 2v.

Phil 3808.35.6   Schopenhauer, Arthur. Die Welt als Wille und Vorstellung. Stuttgart, 19- ? 2v.

Phil 3808.35.10   Schopenhauer, Arthur. Die Welt als Wille und Vorstellung. Berlin, 1930.

Phil 3808.35.28   Schopenhauer, Arthur. Le monde comme volonté et comme représentation. 8. éd. v.3. Paris, 1943.

NEDL   Phil 3808.36.2   Schopenhauer, Arthur. The world as will and idea. Boston, 1883-86. 3v.

Phil 3808.36.5   Schopenhauer, Arthur. The world as will and idea. v.2. London, 1896.

Phil 3808.36.10   Schopenhauer, Arthur. The world as will and idea. London, 19- . 3v.

Phil 3808.36.10.3   Schopenhauer, Arthur. The world as will and idea. London, 1906-09. 3v.

Phil 3808.36.10.5   Schopenhauer, Arthur. The world as will and idea. 7th ed. London, 19- . 3v.

Phil 3808.36.10.10   Schopenhauer, Arthur. The world as will and representation. Indian Hills, Colo., 1958. 2v.

Phil 3808.37   Schopenhauer, Arthur. De vier hocksteenen der Wereld en harr Bouwmeester. v.1-2. 's-Gravenhage, 1893.

Phil 3808.38.5   Schopenhauer, Arthur. Il mondo come volontà e rappresentazione. 2. ed. Bari, 1920-21. 2v.

Phil 3808.43   Schopenhauer, Arthur. Complete essays. v.1-7. N.Y., 1942.

Phil 3808.44   Schopenhauer, Arthur. The essays of Arthur Schopenhauer. N.Y., n.d.

Phil 3808.45   Schopenhauer, Arthur. Selected essays. Milwaukee, 1881.

Phil 3808.45.15   Schopenhauer, Arthur. Selected essays. London, 1926.

Phil 3808.45.20   Schopenhauer, Arthur. Selections. N.Y., 1956.

Phil 3808.47   Schopenhauer, Arthur. Das Erwacher aus dem Leben- Fraum. Pfullingen, 1961.

Htn   Phil 3808.48*   Schopenhauer, Arthur. Über die vierfache Wurzel des Satzes vom zureichen Grunde. 2. Aufl. Frankfurt, 1847.

Phil 3808.49   Schopenhauer, Arthur. Über die vierfache Wurzel des Satzes vom zureichen Grunde. 3. Aufl. Leipzig, 1864.

Phil 3808.49.5   Schopenhauer, Arthur. Über die vierfache Wurzel des Satzes vom zureichen Grunde. 4. Aufl. Leipzig, 1875.

Phil 3808.49.10   Schopenhauer, Arthur. Über die vierfache Wurzel des Satzes vom zureichen Grunde. Hamburg, 1957.

Phil 3808.50   Schopenhauer, Arthur. De la quadruple racine du principe de la raison suffisante. Paris, 1882.

Phil 3808.51.5   Schopenhauer, Arthur. Two essays. London, 1889[1888]

Classified Listing

Phil 3808.51.6   Schopenhauer, Arthur. On the fourfold root of the principle of sufficient reason and on the will in nature; two essays. London, 1891.

Phil 3808.51.7   Schopenhauer, Arthur. On the fourfold root of the principle of sufficient reason. London, 1903.

Phil 3808.53   Schopenhauer, Arthur. Philosophische Meschenkunde. Stuttgart, 1957.

Phil 3808.55   Schopenhauer, Arthur. Pensées et fragments. 9. éd. Paris, 1889.

Phil 3808.55.11   Schopenhauer, Arthur. Pensées et fragments. 25. éd. Paris, 1911.

tn   Phil 3808.59*   Schopenhauer, Arthur. Kan menneskets frie villie bevises af dets selvebevidsthed. Trodhjem, 1840.

Phil 3808.60   Schopenhauer, Arthur. Parerga und Paralipomena. Berlin, 1862.

Phil 3808.60.2   Schopenhauer, Arthur. Parerga und Paralipomena. v.1-2. Berlin, 1851.

Phil 3808.60.8   Schopenhauer, Arthur. Parerga en Paralipomena. Amsterdam, 1908. 2v.

Phil 3808.60.10   Schopenhauer, Arthur. Philosophie et philosophes. 2. éd. Paris, 19- .

Phil 3808.60.30   Schopenhauer, Arthur. Parerga et Paralipomena: fragments sur l'histoire de la philosophie. Paris, 1912.

Phil 3808.60.40   Schopenhauer, Arthur. Frammenti di storia della filosofia. Milano, 1926?

Phil 3808.60.50   Schopenhauer, Arthur. The philosophy of Schopenhauer. N.Y., 1956.

Phil 3808.61   Schopenhauer, Arthur. Essays from the Parerga and Paralipomena. London, 1951?

Phil 3808.61.5   Schopenhauer, Arthur. Essays and aphorisms. Harmondsworth, Eng., 1970.

Phil 3808.62   Schopenhauer, Arthur. Morale e religione. Torino, 1921.

Phil 3808.62.5   Schopenhauer, Arthur. Aforismi sulla saggezza della vita. Torino, 1923.

n   Phil 3808.63*   Schopenhauer, Arthur. Über das Sehn und die Farben. Leipzig, 1816.

Phil 3808.63.10   Schopenhauer, Arthur. Über das Sehn und die Farben. 3. Aufl. Leipzig, 1870.

Phil 3808.63.20   Schopenhauer, Arthur. Parapsychologische Schriften. Basel, 1961.

Phil 3808.65*   Schopenhauer, Arthur. Über den Willen in der Natur. Frankfurt, 1836.

Phil 3808.65.2   Schopenhauer, Arthur. Über den Willen in der Natur. Leipzig, 1867.

Phil 3808.65.5*   Schopenhauer, Arthur. Über den Willen in der Natur. Frankfurt, 1854.

Phil 3808.65.30   Schopenhauer, Arthur. La volontà nella natura. Milano, 1927.

Phil 3808.68   Schopenhauer, Arthur. Essai sur le Libre Arbitre. Paris, 1877.

Phil 3808.68.5   Schopenhauer, Arthur. Essai sur le Libre Arbitre. 13. éd. Paris, 1925.

Phil 3808.69.3   Schopenhauer, Arthur. Le fondement de la morale. 3. éd. Paris, 1888.

Phil 3808.69.8   Schopenhauer, Arthur. Le fondement de la morale. 11. éd. Paris, 1925.

Phil 3808.70*   Schopenhauer, Arthur. Die beiden Grundprobleme der Ethik. Frankfurt, 1841.

Phil 3808.70.5   Schopenhauer, Arthur. Die beiden Grundprobleme der Ethik. 5. Aufl. Leipzig, 1908.

Phil 3808.70.10   Schopenhauer, Arthur. Die beiden Grundprobleme der Ethik. Leipzig, 1860.

Phil 3808.70.10*B   Schopenhauer, Arthur. Die beiden Grundprobleme der Ethik. Leipzig, 1860.

Phil 3808.70.12A   Schopenhauer, Arthur. Die beiden Grundprobleme der Ethik. Leipzig, 1881.

Phil 3808.70.12B   Schopenhauer, Arthur. Die beiden Grundprobleme der Ethik. Leipzig, 1881.

Phil 3808.71   Schopenhauer, Arthur. The basis of morality. London, 1903.

Phil 3808.71.2   Schopenhauer, Arthur. The basis of morality. 2nd ed. London, 1915.

Phil 3808.72   Schopenhauer, Arthur. Lebensweisheit. Berlin, 1943.

Phil 3808.73   Schopenhauer, Arthur. Die wahren Güter des Lebens. München, 194-?

Phil 3808.74   Schopenhauer, Arthur. Zur Ästhetik der Poesie, Musik und der bildend en Künste. Leipzig, n.d.

Phil 3808.75   Schopenhauer, Arthur. Über Schriftstellerei und Stil. Leipzig, 1913.

Phil 3808.75.5   Schopenhauer, Arthur. Écrivains et style. Paris, 1905.

Phil 3808.75.10   Schopenhauer, Arthur. Gedanken über Schriftstellerei und ahnliche Gegenslande. Dortmund, 1943.

Phil 3808.76   Schopenhauer, Arthur. Brieftasche, 1822-1823. Berlin, n.d.

Phil 3808.76.15   Schopenhauer, Arthur. Briefe. Leipzig, 1893.

Phil 3808.76.20   Schopenhauer, Arthur. Briefwechsel und andere Dokumente; Ausgewählt und Herausgegeben von Mar Brahn. Leipzig, 1911.

Phil 3808.76.30   Schopenhauer, Arthur. Schopenhauer und Brockhaus. Leipzig, 1926.

Phil 3808.76.40   Schopenhauer, Arthur. Schopenhauer-Brevier. Wiesbaden, 1955.

Phil 3808.76.50   Schopenhauer, Arthur. Arthur Schopenhauer; Mensch und Philosoph in seinen Briefen. Wiesbaden, 1960.

Phil 3808.77   Schopenhauer, Arthur. Schopenhauer et ses disciples. Paris, 1920.

Phil 3808.78   Schopenhauer, Arthur. Reisetagebücher aus den Jahren 1803-1804. Leipzig, 1923.

Phil 3808.79   Pamphlet vol. Philosophy. German and Dutch. Schopenhauer, Arthur. 18 pam.

Phil 3808.79.2   Pamphlet vol. Philosophy. German and Dutch. Schopenhauer, Arthur. German dissertations. 20 pam.

Phil 3808.79.3   Pamphlet vol. Philosophy. German and Dutch. Schopenhauer, Arthur. German dissertations. 15 pam.

Phil 3808.79.4   Pamphlet box. Philosophy. German and Dutch. Schopenhauer, Arthur. German dissertations.

Phil 3808.79.5   Pamphlet box. Philosophy. German and Dutch. Schopenhauer, Arthur.

Phil 3808.80   Asher, D. Arthur Schopenhauer. Berlin, 1871.

Phil 3808.80.2   Asher, D. Das Endergebniss der Arthur Schopenhauer Philosophie. Leipzig, 1885.

Phil 3808.81   Busch, O. Arthur Schopenhauer. Heidelberg, 1877.

Phil 3808.82   Frauenstädt, C.M.J. Briefe über des Schopenhauerische Philosophie. Leipzig, 1854.

Phil 3808.82.5   Frauenstädt, C.M.J. Neue Brief über Schopenhauerische Philosophie. Leipzig, 1876.

Phil 3808.83   Frauenstädt, C.M.J. Schopenhauer-Lexikon. Leipzig, 1871. 2v.

Htn   Phil 3808.83.1*   Frauenstädt, C.M.J. Schopenhauer-Lexikon. Leipzig, 1871. 2v.

Phil 3808.84   Frommann, H. Arthur Schopenhauer. Jena, 1872.

Phil 3808.85   Grisebach, E.R. Edita und Inedita Schopenhaueriana.

Phil 3808.85.15   Reich, Emil. Schopenhauer als Philosoph der Tragödie. Wien, 1888.

Phil 3808.86   Gwinner, W. Arthur Schopenhauer. Leipzig, 1862.

Phil 3808.86.3   Gwinner, W. Arthur Schopenhauer. Leipzig, 1922.

Phil 3808.86.5   Gwinner, W. Schopenhauer's Leben. Leipzig, 1878.

Phil 3808.86.7   Gwinner, W. Schopenhauer's Leben. Leipzig, 1910.

Phil 3808.86.10   Gwinner, W. Schopenhauer und seine Freunde. Leipzig, 1863.

Phil 3808.86.15   Gwinner, W. Denkrede auf Arthur Schopenhauer. Leipzig, 1888.

Phil 3808.87   Hecker, M.F. Schopenhauer. Köln, 1897.

Phil 3808.87.5   Hecker, M.F. Metaphysik und Asketik. Bonn, 1896.

Phil 3808.88   Hertslet, M.L. Schopenhauers-Register. Leipzig, 1890.

Phil 3808.89   Koeber, R. von. Schopenhauer's Erlösungslehre. Leipzig, 1881?

Phil 3808.89.5   Koeber, R. von. Die Philosophie Arthur Schopenhauers. Heidelberg, 1888.

Phil 3808.90.1   Laban, Ferdinand. Die Schopenhauer-Literatur. N.Y., 1970.

Phil 3808.91   Lehmann, E. Die verschiedenartigen Elemente der Schopenhauer'schen Willenslehre. Strassburg, 1889.

Phil 3808.92   Lehmann, R. Schopenhauer. Berlin, 1894.

Phil 3808.93   Lindner, E.O. Arthur Schopenhauer. Berlin, 1863.

Phil 3808.94   Ribot, T. La philosophie de Schopenhauer. Paris, 1874.

Phil 3808.94.10   Ribot, T. La philosophie de Schopenhauer. Paris, 1909.

Phil 3808.95   Sommerlad, F. Darstellung und Kritik. Offenbach, 1895.

Phil 3808.95.5   Crämer, Otto. Arthur Schopenhauer's Lehre von der Schuld in ethischer Beziehung. Inaug. Diss. Heidelberg, 1895.

Phil 3808.96   Thilo, C.A. Über Schopenhauer's ethischen Atheism. Leipzig, 1868.

Phil 3808.97   Venetianer, M. Schopenhauer als Scholastiker. Berlin, 1873.

Phil 3808.98   Zimmern, H. Arthur Schopenhauer. London, 1876.

Phil 3808.99   Meyer, J.B. Weltelend und Weltschmerz. Bonn, 1872.

Phil 3808.100A   Wallace, W. Life of Arthur Schopenhauer. London, 1890.

Phil 3808.100B   Wallace, W. Life of Arthur Schopenhauer. London, 1890.

Phil 3808.100.5   Wallace, W. Life of Arthur Schopenhauer. N.Y., 1890.

Phil 3808.101   Colvin, S.S. Schopenhauer's doctrine of the Thing-in-itself. Providence, 1897.

Phil 3808.102   Möbius, P.J. Über Schopenhauer. Leipzig, 1899.

Phil 3808.103   Volkelt, J. Arthur Schopenhauer. Stuttgart, 1901.

Phil 3808.104   Schlüter, R. Schopenhauers Philosophie. Leipzig, 1900.

Phil 3808.105   Caldwell, W. Schopenhauer's system...philosophical significance. Edinburgh, 1896.

Phil 3808.106   Hauff, W. Die Überwindung des Schopenhauerschen Pessimismus durch F. Nietzsche. Halle, 1904.

Phil 3808.107   Baer, J. Schopenhauer - Bibliothek. Frankfurt, 1905.

Phil 3808.107.5   Melli, Giuseppe. La filosofia di Schopenhauer. Firenze, 1905.

Phil 3808.107.10   Grisebach, Eduard. Schopenhauer. Berlin, 1905.

Phil 3808.108   Simmel, G. Schopenhauer und Nietzsche. Leipzig, 1907.

Phil 3808.108.3   Simmel, G. Schopenhauer und Nietzsche. 3. Aufl. München, 1923.

Phil 3808.108.5   Scheffer, Wessel. Arthur Schopenhauer; de philosophie. Leiden, 1870.

Phil 3808.109A   Kowaleski, A. Arthur Schopenhauer und seine Weltanschaung. Halle, 1908.

Phil 3808.109B   Kowaleski, A. Arthur Schopenhauer und seine Weltanschaung. Halle, 1908.

Phil 3808.110   Whittaker, T. Schopenhauer. London, 1909.

Phil 3808.111   Wagner, G.F. Encyclopädisches Register...Schopenhauer. Karlsruhe, 1909.

Phil 3808.112   Ruyssen, T. Les grands philosophes; Schopenhauer. Paris, 1911.

Phil 3808.112.9   Covotti, Aurelio. La vita e il pensiero di Arturo Schopenhauer. Milano, 1910.

Phil 3808.112.13   Covotti, Aurelio. La metafisica del bello e dei costumi di...Schopenhauer. Napoli, 1934.

Phil 3808.112.15   Kusten, Wallebald. Zürück zu Schopenhauer. Berlin, 1910.

Phil 3808.112.20   Mülethaler, J. Die Mystik bei Schopenhauer. Berlin, 1910.

Phil 3808.113   Seillière, E. Arthur Schopenhauer. Paris, 1911.

Phil 3808.113.5   Warschauer, Erich. Schopenhauers Rechts- und Staatslehre. Kattowitz, 1911.

Phil 3808.114.5   Fauconnet, A. L'esthetique de Schopenhauer. Paris, 1913.

Phil 3808.114.10   Hasse, Heinrich. Schopenhauer Erkenntnislehre. Leipzig, 1913.

Phil 3808.114.12   Hasse, Heinrich. Schopenhauers Religionsphilosophie und ihre Bedeutung für die Gegenwart. Frankfurt, 1924.

Phil 3808.114.15   Hasse, Heinrich. Schopenhauer. München, 1926.

Phil 3808.115   Anspach, F.W. Schopenhauer und Chamfort. Göttingen, 1914.

Phil 3808.116.3   Bossert, Adolphe. Schopenhauer. 3. éd. Paris, 1912.

Phil 3808.116.10   Bossert, Adolphe. Schopenhauer als Mensch und Philosoph. Dresden, 1905.

Phil 3808.117   Rzewuski, S. L'optimisme de Schopenhauer. Paris, 1908.

Phil 3808.118   Dueros, Louis. Schopenhauer. Thèse. Paris, 1883.

Phil 3808.119   Richert, Hans. Schopenhauer; seine Persönlichkeit. 3. Aufl. Leipzig, 1916.

Phil 3808.119.5   Pforrdten, T. von der. Staat und Recht bei Schopenhauer. München, 1916.

Phil 3808.120   Paoli, Alessandro. Lo Schopenhauer i il Rosmini. Roma, 1878.

Phil 3808.121   Tschofen, Johann. Die Philosophie Arthur Schopenhauers. München, 1879.

Phil 3808.121.5   Penzig, Rudolph. Arthur Schopenhauer und die menschliche Willensfreiheit. Halle, 1879.

Phil 3808.122   Lehman, Rudolf. Schopenhauer und die Entwickelung der monistischen Weltanschauung. Berlin, 1892.

Phil 3808.123   Damm, Oscar. Schopenhauers Ethik im Verhaltnis zu seiner Erkenntnislehre und Metaphysik. Annaberg, 1898.

Phil 3808.124   Schopenhauer - Gesellschaft. Jahrbuch der...Gesellschaft. Kiel. 1912-1969+ 48v.

Phil 3808.125   Sannders, T.B. Schopenhauer; a lecture. London, 1901.

Phil 3808.126.2   Medilch, P. La theorie de l'intelligence chez Schopenhauer. Paris, 1923.

Phil 3808.127   Irvine, David. Philosophy and Christianity; an introduction to the works of Schopenhauer. London, 1907.

Phil 3808.129   Millioud, Maurice. Etude critique système philosophique de Schopenhauer. Lausanne, 1893.

Phil 3808 History of philosophy - Local Modern philosophy - Germany - Individual philosophers - Schopenhauer, Arthur - cont.

Phil 3808.130 Kiehl, Daniel. Naturlÿke historie van den Filistijn. 's Gravenhage, 1895.
Phil 3808.131 Zini, Zino. Schopenhauer. Milano, 1923.
Phil 3808.132 Flink, Carl G. Schopenhauers Seelenwanderungslehre. Berlin, 1906.
Phil 3808.133 Kiy, Victor. Der Pessimismus und die Ethik Schopenhauers. Berlin, 1866.
Phil 3808.134 Plumacher, G. Zwei Individualisten der Schopenhauer'schen Schule. Wien, 1881.
Phil 3808.135 Frost, Walter. Schopenhauer als erbe Kants in der philosophischen Seelenanalyse. Bonn, 1918.
Phil 3808.136 Stern, I. Arthur Schopenhauer. Zürich, 1883.
Phil 3808.137 Keutel, Otto. Über die Zweck Mässigkeit in der Natur bei Schopenhauer. Leipzig, 1897.
Phil 3808.138 Calas, T. Schopenhauer; pessimisme-athéisme. Thèse. Montauban, 1909.
Phil 3808.139 Jellinck, G. Die Weltanschauungen Leibnitz und Schopenhauer's ihre Gründe und ihre Berechtigung. Wien, 1872.
Phil 3808.140 Rodhe, J. Schopenhauers filosofiska grundtankar i systematisk framställning och Kritisk belysning. Lund, 1888.
Phil 3808.141 Groener, M. Schopenhauer und die Juden. München, 1920.
Phil 3808.142 Hohenemser, Richard. Arthur Schopenhauer als Psychologie. Leipzig, 1924.
Phil 3808.143 Herrig, Hans. Gesammelte Aufsätze über Schopenhauer. Leipzig, 1894.
Phil 3808.144 Ahlberg, Alf. Arthur Schopenhauer. Stockholm, 1924.
Phil 3808.145 Damm, O.F. Arthur Schopenhauer. Leipzig, 1912.
Phil 3808.146 Eichler, Oskar. Die Wurzeln des Frauenhasses bei Arthur Schopenhauer. Bonn, 1926.
Phil 3808.147 Ebstein, W. Arthur Schopenhauer seine wirklichen und vermeintlichen Krankheiten. Stuttgart, 1907.
Phil 3808.148 Haym, R. Arthur Schopenhauer. Berlin, 1864.
Phil 3808.149 Allievo, G. Giobbe e Schopenhauer. Torino, 1912.
Phil 3808.150 Fahsel, H. Die Überwindung des Pessimismus. Freiburg, 1927.
Phil 3808.151.2 Baillot, A. Influence de la philosophie de Schopenhauer en France. Thèse. Paris, 1927. 2 pam.
Phil 3808.152 Francken, C.J. Wijnaendts. Arthur Schopenhauer, een levensbeeld. Haarlem, 1905.
Phil 3808.153 Beer, Margrieta. Schopenhauer. London, 1914.
Phil 3808.154 Hochfeld, Sophus. Das künstlerische in der Aprache Schopenhauers. Leipzig, 1912.
Phil 3808.155 Eymer, Karl. Arthur Schopenhauer. n.p., 1915.
Phil 3808.156 Gebhardt, Carl. Schopenhauer-Bilder, Grundlagen einer Ikonographie. Frankfurt, 1913.
Phil 3808.157 Kaplan, Leo. Schopenhauer und der Animismus. Leipzig, 1925.
Phil 3808.158 Zuccante, G. Osservazioni critiche alla filosofia di Arturo Schopenhauer. Milano, 1929.
Phil 3808.159 Friedlander, Salomo. Schopenhauer, seine Persönlichkeit in seinen Werken. Bd.II. Stuttgart, 1907.
Phil 3808.160 Cornill, Adolph. Arthur Schopenhauer. Heidelberg, 1856.
Phil 3808.161 McGill, Vivian J. Schopenhauer; pessimist and pagan. N.Y., 1931.
Phil 3808.162 Rappaport, S. Spinoza und Schopenhauer. Berlin, 1899.
Phil 3808.163 Richter, Raoul. Schopenhauer's Verhältnis zu Kant in seinen Grundzügen. Leipzig, 1893.
Phil 3808.164.5 Zimmern, Helen. Schopenhauer, his life and philosophy. London, 1932.
Phil 3808.165 Wyczolkowska, A. Schopenhauers Lehre von der menschlichen Freiheit in ihrer Beziehung zu Kant und Schelling. Inaug. Diss. Wien, 1893.
Phil 3808.166 Bamberger, Herz. Das Tier in der Philosophie Schopenhauer's. Inaug. Diss. Wirzburg, 1897.
Phil 3808.167 Siedel, K.G. Die Lehre von der Freiheit bei Kant und Schopenhauer. Inaug. Diss. Erlangen, 1888.
Phil 3808.168 Padovani, Umberto A. Arturo Schopenhauer. Milano, 1934.
Phil 3808.169 Hübscher, Arthur. Arthur Schopenhauer. Leipzig, 1938.
Phil 3808.169.5 Hübscher, Arthur. Schopenhauer. Stuttgart, 1952.
Phil 3808.169.10 Hübscher, Arthur. Leben mit Schopenhauer. Frankfurt, 1966.
Phil 3808.170 Costa, Alessandro. Il pensiero religioso di Arturo Schopenhauer. Roma, 1935.
Phil 3808.171 Michaelis, G. Arthur Schopenhauer. Leipzig, 1937.
Phil 3808.172 Bierens de Haan, J.D. Schopenhauer. 's Gravenhage, 1933.
Phil 3808.173 Schneider, W. Schopenhauer. Vienna, 1937.
Phil 3808.174A Mann, Thomas. Schopenhauer. Stockholm, 1938.
Phil 3808.174B Mann, Thomas. Schopenhauer. Stockholm, 1938.
Phil 3808.175 Mignosi, P. Schopenhauer. Brescia, 1934.
Phil 3808.176 Schopenhauer, Arthur. Living thoughts presented by Thomas Mann. N.Y., 1939.
Phil 3808.177 Adams, J.S. The aesthetics of pessimism. Philadelphia, 1940.
Phil 3808.178 Rasche, F. Der Pessimismus Schopenhauers und das Wert Problem. Crimmitschau, 1924.
Phil 3808.179 Lessing, Theodor. Schopenhauer, Wagner, Nietzsche. München, 1906.
Phil 3808.180 Doring, W.O. Schopenhauer. Zürich, 1919.
Phil 3808.181 Bonanno, S. La "Volanta" in Arturo Schopenhauer. Torino, 1903.
Phil 3808.182 Salomaa, J.E. Schopenhauer ja von Hartmann. Turku, 1918.
Phil 3808.184 Cresson, André. Schopenhauers a vie, son oeuvre. Paris, 1946.
Phil 3808.184.3 Cresson, André. Schopenhauer. Paris, 1957.
Phil 3808.186 Copleston, Frederick. Arthur Schopenhauer. London, 1946.
Phil 3808.188 Borch, Rudolf. Schopenhauer. Boston, 1941.
Phil 3808.190 Busch, Hugo. Das Testament Arthur Schopenhauer. Wiesbaden, 1950.
Phil 3808.192 Nietzsche, F.W. Schopenhauer als Erzieher. Leipzig, 1931.
Phil 3808.194 Kurth, K.O. Arthur Schopenhauer. Kitzingen, 1952.
Phil 3808.196 Keyserling, H. Schopenhauer als Verbilder. Leipzig, 1910.
Phil 3808.198 Stefano Escher di, Anna. La filosofia di Arturo Schopenhauer. Padova, 1958.
Phil 3808.200 Zint, Hans. Schopenhauer als Erlebnis. München, 1954.
Phil 3808.205 Terzi, Carlo. Schopenhauer. Romae, 1955.
Phil 3808.207 Guetzlaff, Victor. Schopenhauer ueber die Thiere und den Tierschutz. Berlin, 1879.
Phil 3808.210 Biscardo, R. Il pessimismo romantico nel mondo di Schopenhauer. 1. ed. Bolzano, 1955.
Phil 3808.212 Holn, Søren. Schopenhauer ethik. Kjøbenhavn, 1932.
Phil 3808.215 Arthur Schopenhauer. Berlin, 1955.
Phil 3808.220 Emge, Carl August. Gedachtnisschrift für Arthur Schopenhauer zur 150. Wiederkehr seines Geburtstages. Berlin, 1938.

Phil 3808 History of philosophy - Local Modern philosophy - Germany - Individual philosophers - Schopenhauer, Arthur - cont.

Phil 3808.225 Franz-Schneider, Lucia. Erinnerungen an das Schopenhauers Schöne Aussicht. Frankfurt, 1959.
Phil 3808.230 Wolff, H.M. Arthur Schopenhauer. Bern, 1960.
Phil 3808.231 Arnold, Otto. Schopenhauer padägogische. Leipzig, 1906.
Phil 3808.232 Klee, Hermann. Grundzüge einer Ästhetik nach Schopenhauer. Berlin, 1875.
Phil 3808.233 Garewicz, Jan. Rozdroza pesymizmu. Wyd. 1. Wroctaw, 1965.
Phil 3808.234 Frankfurt am Main. Stadt- und Universitätsbibliothek. Arthur Schopenhauer. Frankfurt, 1960.
Phil 3808.235 Mei, Flavio. Etica e politica nel pensiero di Schopenhauer. Milano, 1966.
Phil 3808.236 Hoyack, Louis. Schopenhauer, waarheid en dwaling. Deventer, 1968.
Phil 3808.237 Abendroth, Walter. Arthur Schopenhauer in Selbstzeugnissen und Bilddokumenten. Reinbek, 1967.
Phil 3808.238 Dauer, Dorothoa W. Schopenhauer as transmitter of buddhist ideas. Berne, 1967.
Phil 3808.240 Riconda, Giuseppe. Schopenhauer interprete dell'iccidente. Milano, 1969.
Phil 3808.242 Hübscher, Arthur. Schopenhauer-Bildnisse. Frankfurt, 1968.
Phil 3808.244 Sørensen, Villy. Schopenhauer. København, 1969.
Phil 3808.246 Rosset, Clément. L'esthetique de Schopenhauer. Paris, 1969.
Phil 3808.248 Bahr, Hans Dieter. Das gefesselte Engagement; zur Ideologie der Kontemplativen Ästhetik Schopenhauer. Bonn, 1970.
Phil 3808.250 Garewicz, Jan. Schopenhauer. Wyd. 1. Warszawa, 1970.
Phil 3808.252 Vecchiotti, Icilio. La dottrina di Schopenhauer. Roma, 1969.

Phil 3819 History of philosophy - Local Modern philosophy - Germany - Individual philosophers - Spinoza, Benedictus de - Writings

Phil 3819.5 Wetlesen, Jon. A Spinoza bibliography, particularly on the period 1940-1967. Oslo, 1968.
Phil 3819.10 Spinoza, Benedictus de. Opera quae supersunt omnia. Ienae, 1802. 2v.
Phil 3819.10.2 Spinoza, Benedictus de. Opera philosophische omnia. v.3. Stuttgardiae, 1830.
Phil 3819.10.3 Spinoza, Benedictus de. Opera quae supersunt omnia. Lipsiae, 1843-46. 3v.
Phil 3819.10.4 Spinoza, Benedictus de. Opera quae supersunt omnia supplementum. Amstelodami, 1862.
Phil 3819.10.8 Spinoza, Benedictus de. Opera quotquot reperta sunt. Hagae, 1882-83. 2v.
Phil 3819.10.9 Spinoza, Benedictus de. Opera quotquot reperta sunt. 2. ed. Hagae, 1895-96. 3v.
Phil 3819.10.9.3 Spinoza, Benedictus de. Opera quotquot reperta sunt. 3. ed. v.1-4. Hagae, 1913-14. 2v.
Phil 3819.10.10 Spinoza, Benedictus de. Opera, im Auftrag der Heidelberg Akademie der Wissenschaften Herausgegeben. Heidelberg, 1925. 4v.
Htn Phil 3819.10.11* Spinoza, Benedictus de. Opera posthuma. Pt.2. Amstelodami, 1677.
Phil 3819.10.14 Spinoza, Benedictus de. Benedictus de Spinoza's Sämmtliche Werke. Stuttgart, 1871. 2v.
Phil 3819.11 Spinoza, Benedictus de. Sämmtliche philosophische Werke. Berlin, 1869-71. 2v.
Phil 3819.11.2 Spinoza, Benedictus de. Sämmtliche Werke. Leipzig, 1914-22. 3v.
Phil 3819.12 Spinoza, Benedictus de. Oeuvres. Paris, 1842.
Phil 3819.12.2 Spinoza, Benedictus de. Oeuvres. Paris, 1861.
Phil 3819.12.3 Spinoza, Benedictus de. Oeuvres. Paris, 1872. 3v.
Phil 3819.12.4 Spinoza, Benedictus de. Oeuvres complètes. Paris, 1954.
Phil 3819.14.5 Spinoza, Benedictus de. Chief works. v.2. London, 1919.
Phil 3819.14.10 Spinoza, Benedictus de. Chief works. N.Y, 1955[1951] 2v.
Phil 3819.15 Spinoza, Benedictus de. Oeuvres de Spinoza. Paris, 1914. 2v.
NEDL Phil 3819.18 Spinoza, Benedictus de. Spisy filosofické. Prag, 1932.
Phil 3819.20 Spinoza, Benedictus de. Die Unvollendeten lateinischen Abhandlungen. Heidelberg, 1882.
Phil 3819.25 Spinoza, Benedictus de. Renati des Cartes et Benedicti de Spinoza praecipua opera. Lipsiae, 1843.
Phil 3819.27 Spinoza, Benedictus de. Uren met Spinoza. 2. druk. Baarn, 1917.
Phil 3819.28 Spinoza, Benedictus de. Von den festen und ewigen Dingen. Heidelberg, 1925.
Phil 3819.29A Spinoza, Benedictus de. The philosophy of Spinoza. N.Y., 1927.
Phil 3819.29B Spinoza, Benedictus de. The philosophy of Spinoza. N.Y., 1927.
Phil 3819.29.30 Spinoza, Benedictus de. The living thoughts of Spinoza. N.Y., 1939.
Phil 3819.29.40 Spinoza, Benedictus de. Spinoza dictionary. N.Y., 1951.
Phil 3819.30 Spinoza, Benedictus de. Die Ethik. Leipzig, 1875.
Phil 3819.30.5 Spinoza, Benedictus de. Ethik. Berlin, 1868. 2 pam.
Phil 3819.30.25 Spinoza, Benedictus de. Die Ethik. Leipzig, 1910.
Phil 3819.30.29 Spinoza, Benedictus de. Ethik nebst Briefen Welche sich auf die Gegenstände der Ethik. Bd.1. Berlin, 1812.
Phil 3819.30.30 Spinoza, Benedictus de. Ethik. 7. Aufl. Leipzig, 192-?
Phil 3819.30.35 Spinoza, Benedictus de. Ethik. 10. Aufl. Leipzig, 1922.
Phil 3819.30.50 Spinoza, Benedictus de. Sittenlehre. Frankfurt, 1744.
Phil 3819.30.55 Spinoza, Benedictus de. Die Ethik nach geometrischer Methode dargestellt. Hamburg, 1955.
Phil 3819.31 Spinoza, Benedictus de. Ethik demonstrated in geometrical order. London, 1883.
Phil 3819.31.6 Spinoza, Benedictus de. Ethic demonstrated in geometrical order. N.Y., 1894.
Phil 3819.31.9 Spinoza, Benedictus de. Ethic demonstrated in geometrical order. London, 1927.
Phil 3819.32 Spinoza, Benedictus de. Ethics, demonstrated after the methods of geometers. N.Y., 1888.
Phil 3819.33 Spinoza, Benedictus de. Éthique. Paris, 1907.
Phil 3819.33.3 Spinoza, Benedictus de. Éthique. Paris, 1908.
Phil 3819.33.5 Spinoza, Benedictus de. Éthique. Paris, 1908.
Phil 3819.33.10 Spinoza, Benedictus de. Éthica. Amsterdam, 19- .
Phil 3819.33.15 Spinoza, Benedictus de. Éthique démontrée suivant l'ordre géométrique et divisée en cinq parties. v.1-2. Paris, 1953.
Phil 3819.33.20 Spinoza, Benedictus de. Éthique. Paris, 1961.
Phil 3819.33.25 Spinoza, Benedictus de. L'étique. Paris, 1930. 2v.
Phil 3819.35 Spinoza, Benedictus de. Philosophy of Spinoza. N.Y., 1894.
Phil 3819.35.3 Spinoza, Benedictus de. Philosophy of Spinoza. N.Y., 1892.

Phil 3819 History of philosophy - Local Modern philosophy - Germany - Individual philosophers - Spinoza, Benedictus de - Writings - cont.

Phil 3819.35.25A Spinoza, Benedictus de. Ethics. N.Y., 1949.
Phil 3819.35.25B Spinoza, Benedictus de. Ethics. N.Y., 1949.
Phil 3819.35.26 Spinoza, Benedictus de. Ethics and De intellectus emendatione. London, 1922.
Phil 3819.35.30A Spinoza, Benedictus de. The road to inner freedom. N.Y., 1957.
Phil 3819.35.30B Spinoza, Benedictus de. The road to inner freedom. N.Y., 1957.
Phil 3819.36 Spinoza, Benedictus de. Ethica. 's Gravenhage, 1895.
Phil 3819.36.5 Spinoza, Benedictus de. Ethica op meelkundige wijze uiteengezet. 3. druk. Amsterdam, 1923.
Phil 3819.36.20 Spinoza, Benedictus de. L'etica. Milano, 1914.
Phil 3819.36.25 Spinoza, Benedictus de. Etica. Pt.1-2. Firenze, 1924.
Phil 3819.36.30 Spinoza, Benedictus de. L'etica. Milano, 1913.
Phil 3819.36.31 Spinoza, Benedictus de. Ethica ordine geometrico demonstrata. Hagae, 1905.
Phil 3819.36.33 Spinoza, Benedictus de. Ethica, ordine geometrico demonstrata. Hagae, 1914.
Phil 3819.36.35 Spinoza, Benedictus de. Etica...testo latino. Bari, 1915.
Phil 3819.36.40 Spinoza, Benedictus de. Etica. Milano, 1939.
Phil 3819.36.60 Spinoza, Benedictus de. Ethica. München, 1919.
Phil 3819.36.70 Spinoza, Benedictus de. Etica. Madrid, 1940.
Phil 3819.37 Spinoza, Benedictus de. Tractatus de Deo et homine eiusque felicitate lineamenta atque adnotationes ad tractatum theologico politicum. Halae, 1852.
Phil 3819.38 Spinoza, Benedictus de. God, man, and human welfare. Chicago, 1909.
Phil 3819.38.3 Spinoza, Benedictus de. Spinoza's short treatise on God, man and human welfare. Chicago, 1909.
Phil 3819.38.5 Spinoza, Benedictus de. Spinoza's short treatise on God, man and his well-being. London, 1910.
Phil 3819.38.6 Spinoza, Benedictus de. Short treatise on God, man and his well-being. N.Y., 1963.
Phil 3819.39 Spinoza, Benedictus de. Improvement of the understanding. Washington, 1901.
Phil 3819.39.5 Spinoza, Benedictus de. Improvement of the understanding. N.Y., 1901.
Phil 3819.39.7 Spinoza, Benedictus de. On the improvement of the understanding. N.Y., 1958.
Phil 3819.39.10 Spinoza, Benedictus de. How to improve your mind. N.Y., 1956.
Phil 3819.40 Spinoza, Benedictus de. Korte verhandeling van God. Amsterdam, 1869.
Phil 3819.41 Spinoza, Benedictus de. Kurzer Tractat von Gott. Freiburg, 1881.
Phil 3819.41.15 Spinoza, Benedictus de. Kurze Abhandlung von Gott dem Menschen und seinen Glück. Leipzig, 1922.
Phil 3819.43 Spinoza, Benedictus de. Das Endliche und Unendliche. Wiesbaden, 1947.
Phil 3819.45 Spinoza, Benedictus de. Tractus De intellectus emendatione. N.Y., 1895.
Phil 3819.45.7A Spinoza, Benedictus de. Ethics and "De intellectus emendatione". London, 1930.
Phil 3819.45.7B Spinoza, Benedictus de. Ethics and "De intellectus emendatione". London, 1930.
Phil 3819.45.9 Spinoza, Benedictus de. Abhandlung über die Verbesserung des Verstandes. 4. Aufl. Leipzig, 1922.
Phil 3819.45.15 Spinoza, Benedictus de. Traité de la réforme de l'ertendement. Paris, 1937.
Phil 3819.50 Spinoza, Benedictus de. A treatise partly theological, and partly political. London, 1689.
Phil 3819.57 Spinoza, Benedictus de. Spinoza; theologisch-politischer Traktat. 4. Aufl. Leipzig, 1922.
Phil 3819.57.5 Spinoza, Benedictus de. Der theologisch-politische Traktat. 2. Aufl. Leipzig, 1910.
Phil 3819.57.15A Spinoza, Benedictus de. The political works. Oxford, 1958.
Phil 3819.57.15B Spinoza, Benedictus de. The political works. Oxford, 1958.
Phil 3819.57.20 Spinoza, Benedictus de. Spinoza on freedom of thought. Montreal, 1962.
Phil 3819.57.25 Spinoza, Benedictus de. Bogoslovsko-politicheskii traktat. Moskva, 1935.
Phil 3819.58 Spinoza, Benedictus de. Adnotationes ad tractatum theologico politicum. Hagae, 1802.
Phil 3819.59 Spinoza, Benedictus de. Tractatus politicus. Lanciano, 1915.
Phil 3819.59.5 Spinoza, Benedictus de. Trattato politico. Torino, 1958.
Phil 3819.60 Spinoza, Benedictus de. Dio. Lanciano, 1911.
Phil 3819.61 Spinoza, Benedictus de. Stelkonstige reeckening van den regenboog. Leiden, 1884.
Phil 3819.63 Spinoza, Benedictus de. Letters to friend and foe. N.Y., 1966.
Phil 3819.70 Spinoza, Benedictus de. Briefwechsel; Einleitung. Leipzig, 1876.
Phil 3819.70.5 Spinoza, Benedictus de. Briefwechsel; Übertragen und mit Einleitung. Leipzig, 1914.
Phil 3819.71 Spinoza, Benedictus de. Lettres inédites en français. Paris, 1884.
Phil 3819.72 Spinoza, Benedictus de. Briefwechsel und andere Dokumente. Leipzig, 1916.
Phil 3819.72.5 Spinoza, Benedictus de. Briefwechsel und andere Dokumente. Leipzig, 1923.
Phil 3819.73 Spinoza, Benedictus de. Der Briefwechsel Spinozas. Halle, 1919. 2v.
Phil 3819.73.10F* Spinoza, Benedictus de. Nachbildung der im Jahre 1902 noch Erhaltenen...Briefe. Haag, 1903.
Phil 3819.74 Spinoza, Benedictus de. Brieven,,,vertoog over het zuivere denken. Amsterdam, 1897.
Phil 3819.75 Gebhardt, Carl. Spinoza, Lebensbeschreibung und Gespräche. Leipzig, 1914.
Phil 3819.76 Spinoza, Benedictus de. The correspondence of Spinoza. London, 1928.
Phil 3819.77 Spinoza, Benedictus de. Lettere. Lanciano, 1938. 2v.
Phil 3819.79 Pamphlet vol. Philosophy. German and Dutch. Spinoza, Benedictus de. 14 pam.
Phil 3819.79.2 Pamphlet vol. Philosophy. German and Dutch. Spinoza, Benedictus de. 15 pam.
Phil 3819.79.3 Pamphlet box. Philosophy. German and Dutch. Spinoza, Benedictus de.
Phil 3819.79.5 Pamphlet box. Philosophy. German and Dutch. Spinoza, Benedictus de. German dissertations.

Phil 3820 - 3845 History of philosophy - Local Modern philosophy - Germany - Individual philosophers - Spinoza, Benedictus de - Biography and criticism - Monographs (A-Z)

Phil 3820.1 Auerbach, B. Spinoza. Mannheim, 1854.
Phil 3820.1.8 Auerbach, B. Spinoza; ein Denkerleben. Berlin, 1911.
Phil 3820.2 Avenarius, R. Ueber die...Spinozischen Pantheismus. Leipzig, 1868.
Phil 3820.3 Altkircli, Ernst. Spinoza im Porträt. Jena, 1913.
Phil 3820.3.5 Altkircli, Ernst. Maledictus und Benedictus: Spinoza. Leipzig, 1924.
Phil 3820.4 Alexander, Samuel. Spinoza and time. London, 1921.
Phil 3820.4.5 Alexander, Samuel. Spinoza; an address...tercentenary...birth. Manchester, 1933.
Phil 3820.5 Alexander, B. Spinoza. München, 1923.
Phil 3820.6 Appuhn, C. Spinoza. Paris, 1927.
Phil 3820.7 Amzalak, M.B. Spinoza. Lisboa, 1927.
Phil 3820.8 Alquié, Ferdinand. Nature et vérité dans la philosophie de Spinoza. Paris, 1965.
Phil 3821.1 Baltzer, A. Spinoza's Entwicklungsgang. Kiel, 1888.
Phil 3821.3 Brunschvicg, L. Spinoza. 2. éd. Paris, 1894.
Phil 3821.3.3 Brunschvicg, L. Spinoza, et ses contemporaines. 3. éd. Paris, 1923.
Phil 3821.4 Busolt, Georg. Grundzuge der Erkenntnisztheorie Spinozas. Berlin, 1875.
Phil 3821.5 Berendt, M. Spinoza's Erkenntnisslehre. Berlin, 1881.
Phil 3821.6 Borrell, Philippe. Benôit Spinoza. Paris, 1911.
Phil 3821.7 Betz, H.J. Levenschets van Baruch de Spinoza. 's Gravenhage, 1876.
Phil 3821.7.5 Betz, H.J. Spinoza en Kant. 's Gravenhage, 1883.
Phil 3821.7.7 Betz, H.J. Spinoza en de vrijheid. 's Gravenhage, 1877.
Phil 3821.8 Bierens de Haan, J.D. Levensleer naar de beginselen van Spinoza. 's Gravenhage, 1900.
Phil 3821.10 Bohin, Vilhelm. Spinoza. Berlin, 1894.
Phil 3821.11 Brunner, Constantin. Spinoza Gegen Kant und die Sache der geistigen Wahrheit. Berlin, 1910.
Phil 3821.12 Bellangé, C. Spinoza et la philosophie moderne. Paris, 1912.
Phil 3821.13 Bolland, G.J.P.J. Spinoza. Leiden, 1899.
Phil 3821.14 Bäck, Leo. Spinozas Erste Einwirkungen auf Deutschland. Berlin, 1895.
Phil 3821.15 Brasch, Moritz. Spinoza's System der Philosophie. Berlin, 1870.
Phil 3821.16 Boumann, L. Explicatío spinozismi. Diss. Berlin, 1828.
Phil 3821.17 Brockdorff, C. Beiträge über die Verhältnis Schopenhauers zu Spinoza. Hildesheim, 1900.
Phil 3821.18 Bröchner, Hans. Benedict Spinoza. Kjøbenhavn, 1857.
Phil 3821.19 Browne, Lewis. Blessed Spinoza. N.Y., 1932.
Phil 3821.20 Brakell Buys, W.R. de V. van. Het Godsbegrip bij Spinoza. Utrecht, 193-?
Phil 3821.21 Bernard, Walter. The philosophy of Spinoza and Brunner. N.Y., 1934.
Phil 3821.23 Bidney, David. Psychology and ethics of Spinoza. New Haven, 1940.
Phil 3821.23.2 Bidney, David. The psychology and ethics of Spinoza. 2nd ed. N.Y., 1962.
Phil 3821.24 Brandt, C. Spinoza y el panteismo. Buenos Aires, 1941.
Phil 3821.25 Benincá, A. La libertà umana. Caravate, 1952.
Phil 3821.26 Belen'kii, M.S. Spinoza. Moskva, 1964.
Phil 3821.27 Baer, Joseph. Spinoza. Frankfurt, 191-?
Phil 3821.30 Bonfi, Antonio. Spinoza e il suo tempo. Firenze, 1969.
Phil 3821.32 Boschavini, Emilia Giancotti. Lexicon Spinozanum. La Haye, 1970.
Phil 3822.1 Caird, John. Spinoza. Philadelphia, 1888.
Phil 3822.1.10 Caird, John. Spinoza. Edinburgh, 1902.
Phil 3822.2 Camerer, T. Die Lehre Spinoza's. Stuttgart, 1877.
Phil 3822.2.5 Camerer, T. Spinoza und Schleiermacher. Stuttgart, 1903.
Phil 3822.2.10 Camerer, T. Die Lehre Spinozas. 2. Aufl. Stuttgart, 1914.
Phil 3822.3 Couchond, P.L. Benoit de Spinoza. Paris, 1902.
Phil 3822.4 Colerus, Johannes. La vie de Benoit de Spinoza. La Haye, 1706.
Htn Phil 3822.4.5* Colerus, Johannes. The life of Benedict de Spinoza. London, 1706.
Phil 3822.4.6A Colerus, Johannes. The life of Benedict de Spinoza. London, 1706.
Phil 3822.4.6B Colerus, Johannes. The life of Benedict de Spinoza. London, 1706.
Phil 3822.4.10 Colerus, Johannes. Korte, dog waaragtige levens-beschrijving van Benedictus de Spinoza. Amsterdam, 1705[1910]
Phil 3822.4.15 Colerus, Johannes. Das Leben des Benedict von Spinoza. Frankfurt, 1733.
Phil 3822.4.25 Colerus, Johannes. Das Leben des Benedict von Spinoza. Heidelberg, 1952.
Phil 3822.5 Colsenet, Edmond. De mentis essentia Spinoza quid senserit. Thesis. Parisiis, 1880.
Phil 3822.6.5 Chartier, Emile A. Spinoza. 5. éd. Paris, 19- .
Phil 3822.7A Chronicon Spinozanum. Hagae, 1921-27. 8v.
Phil 3822.7B Chronicon Spinozanum. v.1-4. Hagae, 1921-27.
Phil 3822.8 Cleve, Z.J. De cognitionis generibus Spinozae. Thesis. Helsingforsiae, 1850.
Phil 3822.10 Cresson, André. Spinoza. Paris, 1940.
Phil 3822.10.4 Cresson, André. Spinoza. 4. éd. Paris, 1959.
Phil 3822.12 Curley, E.M. Spinoza's metaphysics. Cambridge, 1969.
Phil 3823.1 Dessauer, M. Der Sokrates der Neuzeit...Spinoza's. Cöthen, 1877.
Phil 3823.1.5 Dessauer, M. Spinoza und Hobbes. Breslau, 1868.
Phil 3823.2 Dörffling, M. Die Ansichten Spinozas. Leipzig, 1873.
Phil 3823.3 Duff, R.A. Spinoza's political and ethical philosophy. Glasgow, 1903.
Phil 3823.5 Dunin-Borkowski, Stanislaus von. Der Junge de Spinoza. Münster, 1910.
Phil 3823.5.5 Dunin-Borkowski, Stanislaus von. Spinoza aus den Tagen Spinozas. Münster, 1933. 3v.
Phil 3823.6 Delblos, Victor. Le spinozisme. Paris, 1916.
Phil 3823.6.5 Delblos, Victor. Le problème moral dans la philosophie de Spinoza. Paris, 1893.
Phil 3823.7 Dumrath, O.H. Spinoza. Stockholm, 1908.
Phil 3823.8 De Casseres, B. Spinoza, liberator of God and man, 1632-1932. N.Y., 1932.
Phil 3823.9 Dunham, J.H. Freedom and purpose; an interpretation of the psychology of Spinoza. Princeton, N.J., 1916.
Phil 3823.10 Darbon, A.D. Etudes Spinozistes. Paris, 1946.
Phil 3823.11 Dujovne, Leon. Spinoza. Buenos Aires, 1941-45. 4v.
Phil 3823.12 Dunner, J. Baruch Spinoza and western democracy. N.Y., 1955.
Phil 3823.14 Deregilris, Arturo. La filosofía etico-politica di Spinoza. Torino, 1963.

Phil 3820 - 3845 History of philosophy - Local Modern philosophy - Germany - Individual philosophers - Spinoza, Benedictus de - Biography and criticism - Monographs (A-Z) - cont.

Phil 3823.16 Deugd, Cornelis de. The significance of Spinoza's first kind of knowledge. Assen, 1966.
Phil 3823.18 Deleuze, Gilles. L'idée de expression dans la philosophie de Spinoza. Thèse. Paris, 1968.
Phil 3823.18.1 Deleuze, Gilles. Spinoza et le problème de l'expression. Paris, 1968.
Phil 3824.1 Elbogen, Ismar. Der Tractatus de Intellectus emendatione. Breslau, 1898.
Phil 3824.1.5 Elbogen, Ismar. Der Tractatus de Intellectus emendatione. Diss. Breslau, 1898.
Phil 3824.2 Erhardt, Franz. Die Philosophie des Spinoza. Leipzig, 1908.
Phil 3824.2.5 Erhardt, Franz. Die Weltanschauung Spinozas. Stuttgart, 1928.
Htn Phil 3824.3* Earbery, Matthias. Deism examin'd and confuted in...Tractatus Theologico Politicus. London, 1697.
Phil 3824.4 Espinosa, G. Un pretendido interprete suramericano de Spinoza. Caracas, 1943.
Phil 3825.2 Fullerton, G.S. On Spinozistic immortality. Philadelphia, 1899.
Phil 3825.3 Ferriere, E. La doctrine de Spinoza. Paris, 1899.
Phil 3825.4 Freudenthal, J. Spinoza, sein Leben und seine Lehre. Stuttgart, 1904.
Phil 3825.4.2 Freudenthal, J. Spinoza: Leben und Lehre. 2. Aufl. v.1-2. Heidelberg, 1927.
Phil 3825.5 Forsberg, N.A. Jemförande betraktelse af Spinozas och Malebranches metafysiska principier. Upsala, 1864.
Phil 3825.6 Ferrari, G.M. L'etica di B. Spinoza. Napoli, 1902.
Phil 3825.7 Fischer, Kuno. Baruch Spinoza's Leben und Charakter. Mannheim, 1865.
Phil 3825.7.2A Fischer, Kuno. Baruch Spinoza's Leben und Charakter. Heidelberg, 1946.
Phil 3825.7.2B Fischer, Kuno. Baruch Spinoza's Leben und Charakter. Heidelberg, 1946.
Phil 3825.8 Francès, Madeleine. Spinoza dans les pays Néerlandais. Paris, 1937.
Phil 3825.8.5 Francès, Madeleine. Spinoza. Paris, 1937.
Phil 3825.9 Friedrichs, Max. Der Substanzbegriff Spinozas neu und gegen die herrschenden Ansichten zu Gunsten des Philosophen erläutert. Inaug. Diss. Greifswald, 1896.
Phil 3825.10 Feuer, L.S. Spinoza and The use of liberalism. Boston, 1958.
Phil 3826.1 Gaspary, A. Spinoza und Hobbes. Berlin, 1873.
Phil 3826.2 Godfernaux, A. De Spinoza. Paris, 1894.
Phil 3826.3 Gordon, A. Spinoza's Psychologie der Affekte mit Rücksicht auf Descartes. Breslau, 1874.
Phil 3826.4 Grunwald, Max. Spinoza in Deutschland. Gekrönte Preisschrift. Berlin, 1897.
Phil 3826.5 Gunning, J.H. Spinoza en de idee der personlijkleid. 2. druk. Baarn, 1919.
Phil 3826.6 Gans, M.E. Spinozismus. Wien, 1907.
Phil 3826.7 Gunn, J.A. Benedict Spinoza. Melbourne, 1925.
Phil 3826.8 Guzzo, Augusto. Il pensiero di B. Spinoza. Firenze, 1924.
Phil 3826.8.2 Guzzo, Augusto. Il pensiero di B. Spinoza. 2. ed. Torino, 1964.
Phil 3826.9 Grzymisch, S. Spinoza's Lehren von der Ewigkeit und Unsterblichkeit. Breslau, 1898.
Phil 3826.10 Bolin, Wilhelm. Spinoza. 2. Aufl. Darmstadt, 1927.
Phil 3826.11 Gebhardt, Carl. Spinoza; vier Reden. Heidelberg, 1927.
Phil 3826.12 Gelbraus, Samuel. Die Metaphysik der Ethik Spinozas im Quellenlichte der Kabbalah. Wien, 1917.
Phil 3826.14 Garulli, Enrico. Saggi su Spinoza. Urbino, 1958.
Phil 3826.15 Gallicet Calvetti, Carla. Spinoza. Milano, 1968.
Phil 3827.1 Hann, F.G. Die Ethik Spinozas und die Philosophie Descartes. Innsbruck, 1875.
Phil 3827.2 Hissbach, K. Ist ein Durch...Spinoza und Leibniz Vorchanden? Weimar, 1889.
Phil 3827.3 Høffding, H. Spinozas liv og laere. København, 1877.
Phil 3827.3.5 Høffding, H. Spinozas ethica, analyse og karakteristik. København, 1918.
Phil 3827.3.7 Høffding, H. Spinozas ethica, analyse og karakteristik. Heidelberg, 1924.
Phil 3827.4 Horn, J.F. Spinoza's Staatslehre. Dessau, 1851.
Phil 3827.5 Helfferich, A. Spinoza und Leibniz. Hamburg, 1846.
Phil 3827.6 Huan, G. Le Dieu de Spinoza. Arras, 1913.
Phil 3827.8 Hessing, Siegfried ed. Spinoza-Festschrift. Heidelberg, 1933.
Phil 3827.8.5 Hessing, Siegfried. Spinoza dreihundert Jahre Ewigkeit. Den Haag, 1962.
Phil 3827.9 Hamphire, S. Spinoza. Harmondsworth, 1951.
Phil 3827.9.3 Hamphire, S. Spinoza. London, 1956.
Phil 3827.10 Hebler, Carl. Spinoza's Lehre vom Verhältniss der Substanz zu ihren Bestimmtheiten Dargestellt. Bern, 1850.
Phil 3827.12 Hallett, H.F. Benedict de Spinoza. London, 1957.
Phil 3827.12.5 Hallett, H.F. Creation, emanation and salvation, a Spinozistic study. The Hague, 1962.
Phil 3827.14 Hampshire, Stuart. Spinoza and the idea of freedom. London, 1960.
Phil 3827.15 Hubbeling, H.G. Spinoza's methodology. Assen, 1964.
Phil 3827.15.5 Hubbeling, H.G. Spinoza. Baarn, 1966.
Phil 3827.16 Hoyack, Louis. Spinoza als uitgangspant. Deventer, 1965.
Phil 3829.1 Joachim, H.H. A study of the Ethics of Spinoza. Oxford, 1901.
Phil 3829.1.7 Joachim, H.H. Spinoza's Tractus. Oxford, 1940.
Phil 3829.1.10 Joachim, H.H. A study of the Ethics of Spinoza. N.Y., 1964.
Phil 3829.2 Joel, Manuel. Spinoza's theologisch-politischer Traktat. Breslau, 1870.
Phil 3829.3 Jacobi, F.E. Über die Lehre des Spinoza. Breslau, 1789.
Phil 3829.3.10 Jacobi, F.E. Sulla dottrina dello Spinoza. Bari, 1914.
Htn Phil 3829.3.20* Jacobi, F.E. Wider Mendelssohns Beschuldigungen Betreffend die Briefe über die Lehre des Spinoza. Leipzig, 1786.
Phil 3829.3.25 Jacobi, F.E. Jacobi's Spinoza Büchlein. München, 1912.
Phil 3830.1 Kirchmann, J.H. von. Erlauterungen zu Benedict von Spinoza's. Berlin, 1870-72. 5 pam.
Phil 3830.1.5 Kirchmann, J.H. von. Erläuterungen zu Benedict von Spinoza's Ethik. Berlin, 1869.
Phil 3830.2 Knight, E. Spinoza, essays by Land, Fischer, Vloten, and Renan. London, 1882.
Phil 3830.3 Kühnemann, E. Über die Grundlagen der Lehre des Spinoza. Halle, 1902.
Phil 3830.4 Kniat, Joseph. Spinoza's Ethik gegenüber der Erfahrung. Posen, 1888.
Phil 3830.5 Kratz, H. Spinoza's Ansicht über den Zweckbegriff. Newied, 1871.
Phil 3830.6 Kellermann, B. Die Ethik Spinozas über Gott und Geist. Berlin, 1922.
Phil 3830.7 Kołakowski, L. Jednostka i mieskończoność. Warszawa, 1958.
Phil 3830.8 Klaar, Alfred. Spinoza, sein Leben und seine Lehre. Berlin, 1926.
Phil 3830.9 Kettner, F. Spinoza, the biosopher. N.Y., 1932.
Phil 3830.10 Kayser, Rudolf. Spinoza; Bildnis eines geistigen Helden. Wien, 1932.
Phil 3830.10.5 Kayser, Rudolf. Spinoza. N.Y., 1946.
Phil 3830.11 Kaim, J.R. Die Philosophie Spinozas. München, 1921.
Phil 3830.12 Kline, G.L. Spinoza in Soviet philosophy. London, 1952.
Phil 3830.13 Kechek'ian, Stepan F. Eticheskoe mirosezaresanie Spinozy. Moskva, 1914.
Phil 3831.1 Ledinský, F. Die Philosophie Spinoza's. Budweis, 1871.
Phil 3831.2 Leibnitz, G.W. A refutation...Spinoza. Edinburgh, 1855.
Phil 3831.3 Linde, A. van der. Spinoza. Göttingen, 1862.
Phil 3831.4 Loewenhardt, S.E. Benedict von Spinoza. Berlin, 1872.
Phil 3831.5 Linde, A. van der. Benedictus Spinoza. Gravenhage, 1871.
Phil 3831.6 Lesbazeilles, P. De logica Spinozae. Paris, 1883.
Phil 3831.7 Léon, Albert. Les éléments cartésiens. Paris, 1907.
Phil 3831.8 Leopold, J.H. Ad Spinozae opera posthuma. Hagae, 1902.
Phil 3831.9.3 Lasbax, Émile. La hiérarchie dans l'univers chez Spinoza. Thèse. Paris, 1919.
Phil 3831.10 Lotsij, M.C.L. Spinoza's wijsbegeerte. Utrecht, 1888-?
Phil 3831.11 Lévêque, Raphail. Le problème de la vérité dans la philosophie de Spinoza. Strasbourg, 1923.
Phil 3831.13 Lehmans, J.B. Spinoza. Würzburg, 1864.
Phil 3831.14 Lénström, C.J. De principiis philosophiae practicae Spinozae. Gevaliae, 1843.
Phil 3831.15 Lachièze-Rey, P. Les origines cartésiennes du Dieu de Spinoza. Thèse. Paris, 1932.
Phil 3831.16 Lacharrière, R. Études sur la théorie démocratique. Paris, 1963.
Phil 3831.17 Levin, Dan. Spinoza, the young thinker who destroyed the past. N.Y., 1970.
Phil 3831.18 Lacroix, Jean. Spinoza et le problème du salut. Paris, 1970.
Phil 3832.1A Martineau, J. A study of Spinoza. London, 1882.
Phil 3832.1B Martineau, J. A study of Spinoza. London, 1882.
Phil 3832.2 Meyer, M. Die Tugendlehre Spinoza's. Fleusburg, 1885.
Phil 3832.3 Meinsma, K.O. Spinoza en zijn kring. 's Gravenhage, 1896.
Phil 3832.3.15 Meinsma, K.O. Spinoza und sein Kreis. Berlin, 1909.
Phil 3832.4 Matthes, Ewald. Die Unsterblichkeitslehre des Benedictus Spinoza. Inaug. Diss. Heidelberg, 1892.
Phil 3832.5 Mauthner, Fritz. Spinoza. Berlin, 1906.
Phil 3832.5.5 Mauthner, Fritz. Spinoza; eine Umriss seine Lebens und Wirkens. Dresden, 1921.
Phil 3832.5.7 Mauthner, Fritz. Spinoza. 16. Aufl. Dresden, 1922.
Phil 3832.6 Malapert, P. De Spinozae politica. Thesis. Paris, 1897.
Phil 3832.7 Müller, J. Der Begriff die sittlichen Unvollkommenheit bei Descartes und Spinoza. Leipzig, 1890.
Phil 3832.8 Mänoloff, P. Willensfreiheit und Erziehungsmöglichkeit Spinoza. Diss. Bern, 1904.
Phil 3832.9 Meozzi, A. Le dottrine politiche e religiose di B. Spinoza. Arezzo, 1915.
Phil 3832.10 Meijer, W. Spinozana 1897-1922. Heidelberg, 1922.
Phil 3832.10.15 Meijer, W. Spinoza, een levensbeeld. Amsterdam, 1915.
Phil 3832.11A McKeon, R. The philosophy of Spinoza. N.Y., 1928.
Phil 3832.11B McKeon, R. The philosophy of Spinoza. N.Y., 1928.
Phil 3832.12 Meurling, H. Fullkomlighetsbegreppet i Spinozas filosofi. Diss. Uppsala, 1928.
Phil 3832.13 Melames, S.M. Spinoza and Buddha. Chicago, Ill., 1933.
Phil 3832.14 Meli, Fausto. Spinoza e due antecedenti italiani dello Spinozismo. Firenze, 1934.
Phil 3832.15 Mansveld, R. Adversus anonymun theologs-politicum. Amstelaedami, 1674.
Phil 3832.16 Milan. Universita Cattolica del Sacro Cuore-Facolta di Filosofia. Spinoza nel terzo centenario della sua nascita. Milano, 1934.
Phil 3832.17 Millner, Simond. The face of Benedictus Spinoza. N.Y., 1946.
Phil 3832.18 Marbach, G.O. Gedächtnissrede auf Benedict von Spinoza. Halle, 1831.
Phil 3832.19 McShea, Robert J. The political philosophy of Spinoza. N.Y., 1968.
Phil 3832.20 Misrahi, Robert. Spinoza; présentation, choix et traduction des textes. 2. éd. Paris, 1966.
Phil 3832.22 Matheron, Alexandre. Individu et communauté chez Spinoza. Paris, 1969.
Phil 3832.24 Millet, Louis. La pensée de Spinoza. Paris, 1970.
Phil 3832.26 Moreau, Joseph. Spinoza et le spinozisme. 1. éd. Paris, 1971.
Phil 3833.1 Nourrisson, J.F. Spinoza et la naturalisme contemporain. Paris, 1866.
Phil 3833.2 Nossig, Alfred. Ueber die bestimmende Ursache des Philosophirens. Stuttgart, 1895.
Phil 3833.3 Nordwall, A.L. De Spinozismi initiis aphorismi. Upsaliae, 1852.
Phil 3833.5 Norinder, A.V. Försök till en framställning, af Spinozismens nufvidsatser. Upsala, 1851.
Phil 3833.6 Meniţescu, Joan. Die Affectenlehre Spinoza's. Leipzig, 1887.
Phil 3834.1 Orelli, J.C. von. Spinoza's Leben und Lehre. Aurau, 1843.
Phil 3834.2 An outline of the philosophy of Spinoza. Boston, 1939.
Phil 3834.3 Oko, Adolph S. The Spinoza bibliography. Boston, 1964.
Phil 3835.1.2 Pollock, F. Spinoza. 2nd ed. London, 1899.
Phil 3835.1.15 Pollock, F. Spinoza. London, 1935.
Phil 3835.1.16.2 Pollock, F. Spinoza; his life and philosophy. 2nd ed. N.Y., 1966.
Phil 3835.2 Picton, Allanson. Spinoza, handbook to the Ethics. London, 1907.
Phil 3835.3 Préposiet, Jean. Spinoza et la liberté des hommes. Paris, 1967.
Phil 3835.4.2 Powell, E.E. Spinoza and religion. Chicago, 1906.
Phil 3835.5 Philipson, M. Leben Benedikt's von Spinoza. Braunschweig, 1790.
Phil 3835.6 Pulcini, C. L'etica di Spinoza. Genova, 1914.
Phil 3835.7 Palmodo, Kurt. Der Freiheitsbegriff in der Lehre Spinozas. Weiden, 1920.
Phil 3835.8 Parkinson, G.H.R. Spinoza's theory of knowledge. Oxford, 1854.
Phil 3835.9 Pasig, Walter. Spinozas Rationalismus und Erkenntnislehre im Lichte. Leipzig, 1892.

Phil 3820 - 3845   History of philosophy - Local Modern philosophy - Germany -
Individual philosophers - Spinoza, Benedictus de - Biography and
criticism - Monographs (A-Z) - cont.

Phil 3837.1   Rehorn, K.W.A. G.E. Lessing's Stellung zur Philosophie des
                 Spinoza. Frankfurt, 1877.
Phil 3837.2   Roe, E.D. The probability; a critique of Spinoza's
                 demonstration. Andover, 1894.
Phil 3837.3   Rosenkranz, C. De Spinozae philosophia dissertatio.
                 Halae, 1828.
Phil 3837.4   Rovijen, A.J.L. van. Inventaire de livrés de B. Spinoza.
                 La Haye, 1888.
Phil 3837.6   Ricardou, A. De hrimauae mentis aeternitate apud Spinoza.
                 Lutet, 1890.
Phil 3837.7   Richter, G.T. Spinozas philosophische Terminologie.
                 Leipzig, 1913.
Phil 3837.8   Renan, Ernest. Spinoza; Rede...gehalten im Haag.
                 Leipzig, 1877.
Phil 3837.8.5   Renan, Ernest. Spinoza; conference tenue à La Haye.
                 Paris, 1877.
Phil 3837.9   Rivaud, Albert. Les notions d'essence...de Spinoza.
                 Paris, 1906.
Phil 3837.10   Rabenort, W.L. Spinoza as educator. N.Y., 1911.
Phil 3837.11   Robinson, L. Metafizika Spinozy. Sankt Peterburg, 1913.
Phil 3837.12A   Roth, Leon. Spinoza, Descartes and Maimonides.
                 Oxford, 1924.
Phil 3837.12B   Roth, Leon. Spinoza, Descartes and Maimonides.
                 Oxford, 1924.
Phil 3837.12.5   Roth, Leon. Spinoza. London, 1929.
Phil 3837.12.7   Roth, Leon. Spinoza, Descartes and Maimonides.
                 N.Y., 1963.
Phil 3837.13   Rauh, F. Quatenus doctrina quam Spinoza de fide. Thesis.
                 Tolosae, 1890.
Phil 3837.14   Ricco, Cesare. Le dottrine giuridiche...di Spinoza e
                 Hobbes. Giovinazzo, 1884.
Phil 3837.15   Robinson, Lewis. Kommentar zu Spinozas Ethik. v.1-2.
                 Leipzig, 1928.
Phil 3837.16   Rousset, Bernard. La perspective finale de l'éthique et le
                 problème de la coherence du Spinozisme. Paris, 1968.
Phil 3837.17   Richter, Raoul. Der Willensbegriff in der Lehre Spinoza's.
                 Leipzig, 1898.
Phil 3837.18   Rietz, J.E. De Spinozismi fonte orientali. Diss.
                 Lundae, 1839.
Phil 3837.19   Ratner, J. Spinoza on God. N.Y., 1930.
Phil 3837.20.5   Rensi, Giuseppe. Spinoza. 2. ed. Milano, 1944.
Phil 3837.25   Rackwitz, Max. Studien über Causalität und Identität als
                 Grundprincipien des Spinozismus. Halle, 1884.
Phil 3837.30   Rava, Adolfo. Studi su Spinoza e Fichte. Milano, 1958.
Phil 3837.35   Révah, J.S. Spinoza et le Dr. Juan de Prado. Paris, 1959.
Phil 3837.40   Roehrich, Welfried. Staat der Freiheit. Darmstadt, 1969.
Phil 3838.1   Saintes, A. Histoire...ouvrages de B. de Spinoza.
                 Paris, 1842.
Phil 3838.2   Sigwart, H.C.W. Der Spinozismus. Tübingen, 1839.
Phil 3838.3   Smith, H. Spinoza...environment. Cincinnatti, 1886.
Phil 3838.4   Santayana, G. The ethical doctrine of Spinoza.
                 Cambridge, 1886.
Phil 3838.5   Scheidemantel, H. Die Grundprobleme der Ethik Spinoza's.
                 Leipzig, 1898.
Phil 3838.6   Severijn, Johannes. Spinoza en de gereformeerde theologie
                 zijner dagen. Utrecht, 1919.
Phil 3838.7   Stockum, T.C. van. Spinoza's beoordeeling en invloed in
                 duitschland van 1677 tob 1750. Groningen, 1916.
Phil 3838.8   Stern, Jakob. Die Philosophie Spinoza's. 2. Aufl.
                 Stuttgart, 1894.
Phil 3838.8.5   Stern, Jakob. Die Philosophie Spinoza's. 3. Aufl.
                 Stuttgart, 1908.
Phil 3838.9   Starcke, C.N. Baruch de Spinoza. København, 1923.
Phil 3838.10   Saisset, Émile. Introduction critique aux oeuvres de
                 Spinoza. Paris, 1860.
Phil 3838.11   Sabatier, A. de Castres. Apologie de Spinoza et du s'isme.
                 Altona, 1805.
Phil 3838.12   Schlüter, C.B. Die Lehre des Spinoza. Münster, 1836.
Phil 3838.13   Stumpf, K. Spinozastudien. Berlin, 1919.
Phil 3838.14   Spinoza Redivivus: eine Fibel für Anfanger. Berlin, 1917.
Phil 3838.15   Siwek, Paul. L'ame et le corps d'après Spinoza.
                 Paris, 1930.
Phil 3838.15.5   Siwek, Paul. Spinoza et le panthéisme religieux.
                 Paris, 1937.
Phil 3838.15.7   Siwek, Paul. Spinoza et le panthéisme religieux.
                 Paris, 1950.
Phil 3838.15.10 Siwek, Paul. An coeur du Spinozisme. Paris, 1952.
Phil 3838.16   Sigwart, Christoph von. Spinoza's neuentdeckter Tractat
                 von Gott. Gotha, 1866.
Phil 3838.17   Schaub, E.L. Spinoza, the man and his thought.
                 Chicago, 1933.
Phil 3838.18   Segond, J. La vie de Benoit de Spinoza. Paris, 1933.
Phil 3838.19   Sérouya, Henri. Spinoza. Paris, 1933.
Phil 3838.20   Stern, Alfred. Über einen Bisher unbeachteten Brief
                 Spinozas. Göttingen, 1872?
Phil 3838.21   Shauki, Alexander. An introduction to Spinoza's Ethic.
                 London, 1938.
Phil 3838.22   Schmoldt, H. Der Spinozastreit. Inaug. Diss.
                 Würzburg, 1938.
Phil 3838.23   Societas Spinoza. Septimana Spinozana. Hagae, 1933.
Phil 3838.26   Sikkes, J.W.T.E. Spinoza. Den Haag, 1946.
Phil 3838.28   Semerari, G. Il problemi dello Spinozismo. Trani, 1952.
Phil 3838.29   Delouit, A. Lettre d'un ami du sens commun à un Hollandois.
                 Utrecht, 1938.
Phil 3838.30   Sokolov, V.V. Filosofiia Spinozy i sovremennost'.
                 Moskva, 1964.
Phil 3838.31   Stransno, Leo. Spinoza's critique of religion. N.Y., 1965.
Phil 3838.32   Shepo, Elias. The strange death of Barukh Spinoza.
                 Cambridge, 1952.
Phil 3838.34   Stybe, Svend Erik. Spinoza. København, 1969.
Phil 3839.1   Thomas, K. Spinoza als Metaphysiker. Königsberg, 1840.
Phil 3839.2   Thomas, J. Spinoza systema philosophicum adumbratum.
                 Borussorum, n.d.
Phil 3839.4   Turbiglio, S. Benedetto Spinoza. v.3. Roma, 1874.
Phil 3839.5   Tak, W.G. van der. Bento de Spinoza. 's Gravenhage, 1928.
Phil 3839.6.5   Traité des trois imposteurs. Amsterdam? 1768?
Phil 3839.6.10* Traité des trois imposteurs. Amsterdam, 1777.
Phil 3839.6.15   Traité des trois imposteurs. Luïsse, 1793.
Phil 3841.1.2   Vloten, J. van. Baruck d'Espinoza. Amsterdam, 1865.
Phil 3841.1.10   Vloten, J. van. Spinoza. 's Gravenhage, 1880.
Phil 3841.1.15   Vloten, J. van. Benedictus de Spinoza. 2. Aufl.
                 Schiedam, 1871.
Phil 3841.2   Vold, J.M. Spinozas erkjendelsestheori. Kristiania, 1888.
Phil 3841.4   Vloemans, Antoon. Spinoza, de mensch, het leven en het
                 werk. 's Gravenhage, 1931.

Phil 3820 - 3845   History of philosophy - Local Modern philosophy - Germany -
Individual philosophers - Spinoza, Benedictus de - Biography and
criticism - Monographs (A-Z) - cont.

Phil 3841.5   Vaz Dias, A.M. Spinoza, mercator en autodidactus. 's
                 Gravenhage, 1932.
Phil 3841.6   Vulliaud, P. Spinoza d'après les livres de la
                 bibliothèque. Paris, 1934.
Phil 3841.7   Vernière, P. Spinoza et la pensée française avant la
                 révolution. Paris, 1954. 2v.
Phil 3841.7.2   Vernière, P. Spinoza et la pensée française avant la
                 révolution. Thèse. Paris, 1954. 2v.
Phil 3841.8   Vries, Theun de. Baruch de Spinoza in Selbstzeugnissen und
                 Bilddokumenten. Reinbek, 1970.
Phil 3842.1   Weise, H. Über das Erste Buch der Ethik des Spinoza.
                 Salzwede, 187-?
Phil 3842.2   Willis, R. Benedict de Spinoza. London, 1870.
Phil 3842.3   Wahle, R. Kurze Erklarung Ethic von Spinoza. Wien, 1899.
Phil 3842.5   Wenzel, Alfred. Die Weltanschauung Spinozas. Bd.1.
                 Leipzig, 1907.
Phil 3842.6   Worms, René. La morale de Spinoza. Paris, 1892.
Phil 3842.7   Wrzecionko, R. Der Grundganke der Ethik des Spinoza.
                 Wien, 1894.
Phil 3842.8   Wolf, Abraham. The oldest biography of Spinoza.
                 London, 1927.
Phil 3842.8.5   Wolf, Abraham. Spinoza, 1632-1677. Amsterdam, 1950.
Phil 3842.9   Wetzel, Paul. Der Zweckbegriff bei Spinoza. Thesis.
                 Leipzig, 1873.
Phil 3842.10   Wijck, J. van. Spinoza. Groningen, 1877.
Phil 3842.11   Wolfson, Abraham. Spinoza; a life of reason. N.Y., 1932.
Phil 3842.11.2   Wolfson, Abraham. Spinoza; a life of reason. 2nd ed.
                 N.Y., 1969.
Phil 3842.12   Waton, Harry. The kabbalah and Spinoza's philosophy.
                 N.Y., 1931-32. 2v.
Phil 3842.13A   Wolfson, H.A. The philosophy of Spinoza. Cambridge, 1934.
                 2v.
Phil 3842.13B   Wolfson, H.A. The philosophy of Spinoza. Cambridge, 1934.
                 2v.
Phil 3842.13.2   Wolfson, H.A. The philosophy of Spinoza. v.1-2.
                 N.Y., 1958.
Phil 3842.13.5   Wolfson, H.A. Some guiding principles in determining
                 Spinoza's mediaeval sources. Philadelphia, 1937.
Phil 3842.13.10 Wolfson, H.A. Spinoza and religion. N.Y., 1950.
Phil 3842.13.12 Wolfson, H.A. Spinoza and religion. N.Y., 1950.
Phil 3842.13.15 Pamphlet vol. Philosophy. German and Dutch. Spinoza.
                 Biographie and criticism. Wolfson, H.A. 4 pam.
Phil 3842.14   Wolff, Hans M. Spinozas Ethik. München, 1958.
Phil 3845.1   Zulawski, J. Problem der Kausalitat bei Spinoza.
                 Bern, 1899.
Phil 3845.3   Zac, Sylvain. La morale de Spinoza. Paris, 1959.
Phil 3845.3.2   Zac, Sylvain. La morale de Spinoza. 2. éd. Paris, 1966.
Phil 3845.3.5   Zac, Sylvain. L'idée de vie dans la philosophie de
                 Spinoza. Paris, 1963.
Phil 3845.3.10   Zac, Sylvain. Spinoza et l'interpretation de l'écriture.
                 Paris, 1965.
Phil 3845.4   Zweig, Arnold. Baruch de Spinoza. Darmstadt, 1968.
Phil 3845.25   Zum Charakter Spinozas. 2. Aufl. Halle, 1919.

Phil 3846   History of philosophy - Local Modern philosophy - Germany - Individual
philosophers - Spinoza, Benedictus de - Biography and criticism -
Periodicals
Phil 3846.5   Spinozistisch Bulletin. Zeist. 1-2,1938-1940
Phil 3846.10   Rijnsburg, Netherlands. Spinozahuis. Mededeslingen.
                 Leiden. 1,1934+ 3v.

Phil 3850   History of philosophy - Local Modern philosophy - Germany - Individual
philosophers - Other S
Phil 3850.1.29   Strauss, D.F. Der alte und der neue Glaube.
                 Leipzig, 1872.
Phil 3850.1.30   Strauss, D.F. Der alte und der neue Glaube. Bonn, 1873.
                 2v.
Phil 3850.1.35   Strauss, D.F. Der alte und der neue Glaube. 2. Aufl.
                 Bonn, 1881.
Phil 3850.1.36   Strauss, D.F. The old faith and the new. London, 1873.
Phil 3850.1.37   Strauss, D.F. The old faith and the new. v.1-2.
                 N.Y., 1873.
Phil 3850.1.43   Strauss, D.F. The opinions of Professor D.F. Strauss.
                 London, 1844.
Phil 3850.1.45   Strauss, D.F. Essais d'histoire religieuse et mélanges
                 littéraires. Paris, 1872.
Phil 3850.1.75   Strauss, D.F. Der papier-Reisende. Weimar, 1907.
Phil 3850.1.79   Pamphlet box. Philosophy. German and Dutch. Strauss, D.F.
Phil 3850.1.80   Reuschle, C.G. Philosophie und Naturwiss...D.F. Strauss.
                 Bonn, 1874.
Phil 3850.1.83   Ulrici, H. Der Philosoph Strauss. Halle, 1873.
Phil 3850.1.84   Kuenkler, Heinrich. Zum Gedächtnis an David Friedrich
                 Strauss. Wiesbaden, 1898.
Phil 3850.1.86   Harraeus, K. David Friedrich Strauss. Leipzig, n.d.
Phil 3850.1.87   Ziegler, T. David Friedrich Strauss. Strassburg, 1908.
                 2v.
Phil 3850.1.91   Zeller, Eduard. David Friedrich Strauss. 2. Aufl.
                 Bonn, 1874.
Phil 3850.1.93   Zeller, Eduard. David Friedrich Strauss. London, 1874.
Phil 3850.1.94   Zeller, Eduard. Strauss and Renan. London, 1866.
Phil 3850.1.95   Fischer, Kuno. Über David Friedrich Strauss.
                 Heidelberg, 1908.
X Cg Phil 3850.1.96   Kohut, Adolph. David Friedrich Strauss als Denker und
                 Erzieher. Leipzig, 1908.
Phil 3850.1.98   Lévy, Albert. David Frédéric Strauss, la vie et l'oeuvre.
                 Paris, 1910.
Phil 3850.1.102 Plasman, L.C. de. Lettres à Gambetta...sur le dernier
                 ouvrage de Strauss. Paris, 1877.
Phil 3850.1.105 Müller, Gotthold. Identität und Immanenz; zur Genese der
                 Theologie von David Friedrich Strauss, eine theologie- und
                 philosophiegeschichtliche Studie. Zürich, 1968.
Phil 3850.2.80A Lemoine, A. Le vitalisme et l'animisme de Stahl.
                 Paris, 1864.
Phil 3850.2.80B Lemoine, A. Le vitalisme et l'animisme de Stahl.
                 Paris, 1864.
Phil 3850.3.80   Hildenbrand, R. Gotthilf Samuel Steinbart. Herne, n.d.
Phil 3850.3.81   Alberty, Gerhard. Gotthilf Samuel Steinbart, 1738-1809.
                 Inaug. Diss. Gotha, 1930.
Phil 3850.4.80   Pamphlet box. Philosophy. German and Dutch. Sailor, J.M.
                 2 pam.
Phil 3850.4.81   Wolf, L. John Michael Sailer's Lehre vom Menschen. Diss.
                 Giessen, 1937.
Phil 3850.5.8   Spir, Afrikan. Paroles d'un sage. Paris, 1938.
Phil 3850.5.9   Spir, Afrikan. Saggi di filosofia critica. Firenze, 1939.
Phil 3850.5.15   Spir, Afrikan. Right and wrong. Edinburgh, 1954.

Phil 3850 History of philosophy - Local Modern philosophy - Germany - Individual philosophers - Other S - cont.

Phil 3850.5.80 Pamphlet box. Philosophy. German and Dutch. Spir, African von.
Phil 3850.5.85 African Spir und die Bedeutung seiner Philosophie. Leipzig, 1881.
Phil 3850.5.90 Humanus. African Spir. Leipzig, 1892.
Phil 3850.5.93 Claparède-Spir, H. Un pprécurseur. Lausanne, 1920.
Phil 3850.5.94 Claparède-Spir, H. Evocation. Genève, 1944.
Phil 3850.5.95 Lessing, Theodor. African Spir's Erkenntnislehre. Inaug. Diss. Giessen, 1900.
Phil 3850.5.100 Spir, Afrikan. Lettres inédites au professeur. Neuchâtel, 1948.
Phil 3850.6.75 Schubert, G.H. Gotthilf Heinrich Schubert in seinen Briefen. Stuttgart, 1918.
Phil 3850.6.79 Schubert, G.H. Der Erwerb aus...Leben: eine Selbstbiographie. Erlangen, 1854-56. 3v.
Phil 3850.6.80 Pamphlet box. Philosophy. German and Dutch. Schubert, G.H.
Phil 3850.6.81 Merkel, Franz R. Der Naturphilosoph Gotthilf Heinrich Schubert und die deutsche Romantik. München, 1913.
Phil 3850.7.81 Pelazza, Aurelio. W. Schuppe and the immanent philosophy. London, 1915.
Phil 3850.8.81 Michelis, F. Staudenmaier's Wissenschaftliche Leistung. Freiburg, 1877.
Phil 3850.8.85 Weindel, Phil. Das Verhältnis von Glauben und Wissen in der Theologie Franr Anton Staudenmaiers. Düsseldorf, 1940.
Phil 3850.9.80 Pamphlet box. Philosophy. German and Dutch. Sigivart, Christoph.
Phil 3850.9.90 Philosophische Abhandlungen Christoph Sigwart zu seine 70. Geburtstage gewidmet. Tübingen, 1900.
Phil 3850.9.92 Pira, Karl. Framställning och kritik af J.S. Mills, Lotzes och Sigwarts...i logiken. Stockholm, 1897.
Htn Phil 3850.10.30* Schlegel, Friedrich von. Die drey ersten Vorlesungen über die Philosophie des Lebens. Wien, 1827.
Phil 3850.10.50 Schlegel, Friedrich von. Lifrets philosophie. Stockholm, 1834.
Phil 3850.10.80 Serch, Paul. Friedrich Schlegels Philosophie Anschauungen in ihrer Entwicklung und systematischen Ausgestaltung. Berlin, 1905.
Phil 3850.10.85 Oppenburg, Ursula. Quellenstudien zu Friedrich Schlegels Übersetzungen aus dem Sanskrit. Diss. Narburg, 1965.
Phil 3850.11.80 Pamphlet box. Philosophy. German and Dutch. Schegk, J.
Phil 3850.12.31 Stoy, Karl V. Philosophische Propädentik. Leipzig, 1869.
Phil 3850.12.85 Fröhlich, Gustaf. Dr. Karl Volkmar Stoys Leben. Dresden, 1885.
Phil 3850.13.25 Schulze, G.E. Grundriss der philosophischen Wissenschaften und Zerbst. Wittenberg, 1788-90. 2v.
Phil 3850.13.27 Schulze, G.E. Über den höchsten Zweck des Studiums der Philosophie. Leipzig, 1789.
Phil 3850.13.30 Schulze, G.E. Kritik der theoritischen Philosophie. Hamburg, 1801. 2v.
Phil 3850.13.31 Schulze, G.E. Encyklopaedie der philosophischen Wissenschaften. Göttingen, 1823.
Phil 3850.13.32 Schulze, G.E. Encyklopaedie der philosophischen Wissenschaften. Göttingen, 1824.
Phil 3850.13.33 Schulze, G.E. Aenesidemus öder über die Fundamenta. , Helmstadt, 1792.
Phil 3850.13.35 Schulze, G.E. Aenesidemus. Berlin, 1911.
Phil 3850.13.40 Schulze, G.E. Psychische Anthropologie. Göttingen, 1816.
Phil 3850.13.42 Schulze, G.E. Psychische Anthropologie. 2. Aufl. Göttingen, 1819.
Phil 3850.13.44 Schulze, G.E. Psychische Anthropologie. Göttingen, 1826.
Phil 3850.13.55 Schulze, G.E. Grundsätze der allgemeinen Logik. Göttingen, 1831.
Phil 3850.13.60 Schulze, G.E. Leitfaden der Entwickelung der philosophischen Prinzipien. Göttingen, 1813.
Phil 3850.13.70 Schulze, G.E. Ueber die Menschliche Erkenntnis. Göttingen, 1832.
Phil 3850.14.30 Hasenfuss, Josef. Herman Schell als existentieller Denker und Theologie. 1. Aufl. Würzburg, 1951.
Phil 3850.14.80 Pamphlet box. Philosophy. German and Dutch. Schell, Herman.
Phil 3850.14.85 Schneider, Theodor. Teleologie als theologische Kategorie bei Herman Schell. Essen, 1966.
Phil 3850.15.31 Staegmann, B.A. von. Die Theorie des Bewusstseyns im Wesen. Berlin, 1864.
Phil 3850.16.21 Simmel, Georg. Georg Simmel, 1858-1918. Columbus, 1959.
Phil 3850.16.31 Simmel, Georg. Brüche und Tür. Stuttgart, 1957.
Phil 3850.16.41 Simmel, Georg. The conflict in modern culture and other essays. N.Y., 1968.
Phil 3850.16.45 Simmel, Georg. Das individuelle Gesetz. Frankfurt, 1968.
Phil 3850.16.79 Pamphlet box. Philosophy. German and Dutch. Simmel, Georg. German dissertations.
Phil 3850.16.81 Adler, Max. Georg Simmels Bedeutung für die Geistesgeschichte. Wien, 1919.
Phil 3850.16.85 Knevels, Wilhelm. Simmels Religionstheorie. Leipzig, 1920.
Phil 3850.16.89 Fabian, W. Kritik der Lebensphilosophie Georg Simmels. Breslau, 1926.
Phil 3850.16.92 Mamelet, A. Le relativisme philosophique chez G. Simmel. Paris, 1914.
Phil 3850.16.95 Frischeisen-Köhler, Max. Georg Simmel. Berlin, 1919.
Phil 3850.16.96 Mueller, H. Lebensphilosophie und Religion bei Georg Simmel. Berlin, 1960.
Phil 3850.16.100 Luongo, M.R. Il relativismo di G. Simmel e de Pirandello. Napoli, 1955?
Phil 3850.16.105 Gassen, Kurt. Zuch des Dankes an G. Simmel. Berlin, 1958.
Phil 3850.16.110 Bauer, Isidora. Die Tragik in der Existenz des modernen Menschen bei Georg Simmel. München, 1961.
Phil 3850.16.112 Bauer, Isidora. Die Tragik in der Existenz des modernen Menschen bei Georg Simmel. Berlin, 1961.
Phil 3850.16.115 Weingartner, R.H. Experience and culture; the philosophy of G. Simmel. Middletown, 1962.
Phil 3850.16.118 Coser, Lewis A. Georg Simmel. Englewood, 1965.
Phil 3850.18.5 Scheler, Max. Mensch und Geschichte. Zürich, 1929.
Phil 3850.18.10 Scheler, Max. Bildung und Wissen. Frankfurt, 1947.
Phil 3850.18.15 Scheler, Max. Abhandlungen und Aufsätze. Leipzig, 1915. 2v.
Phil 3850.18.20A Scheler, Max. Philosophische Weltanschauung. Bern, 1954.
Phil 3850.18.20B Scheler, Max. Philosophische Weltanschauung. Bern, 1954.
Phil 3850.18.25 Scheler, Max. Vom Umsturz der Werte. 4. Aufl. v.2,3,5,6,8,10. Bern, 1955. 7v.
Phil 3850.18.30A Scheler, Max. Liebe und Erkenntnis. Bern, 1955.
Phil 3850.18.30B Scheler, Max. Liebe und Erkenntnis. Bern, 1955.
Phil 3850.18.35 Scheler, Max. Ressentiment. N.Y., 1961.
Phil 3850.18.40 Scheler, Max. Philosophical perspectives. Boston, 1958.
Phil 3850.18.45 Scheler, Max. On the eternal in man. N.Y., 1960.
Phil 3850.18.80 Wittmann, Michael. Max Scheler als Ethiker. Düsseldorf, 1923.

Phil 3850 History of philosophy - Local Modern philosophy - Germany - Individual philosophers - Other S - cont.

Phil 3850.18.81 Geyser, Joseph. Max Schelers Phänomenologie der Religion. Freiburg, 1924.
Phil 3850.18.82 Kerler, D.H. Max Scheler. Ulm, 1917.
Phil 3850.18.83 Kreppel, F. Die Religionsphilosophie Max Schelers. Inaug. Diss. München, 1926.
Phil 3850.18.84 Hügelmann, H. Max Schelers Persönlichkeitsidee. Diss. Leipzig, 1927.
Phil 3850.18.86 Lützeler, Heinrich. Der Philosoph Max Scheler. Bonn, 1947.
Phil 3850.18.87 Neive, Heinrich. Max Schelers Auffassung. Diss. Photoreproduction. Würzburg, 1928.
Phil 3850.18.88 Herrmann, J. Die Prinzipien der formalen Gesetzes Ethik Kants und der materialen Wertethik Schelers. Diss. Breslau, 1928.
Phil 3850.18.90 Kürth, Herbert. Das Verhältnis von Ethik und Ästhetik bei Max Scheler. Diss. Leipzig, 1929.
Phil 3850.18.92 Nota, J. Max Scheler. Utrecht, 1947.
Phil 3850.18.95 Herzfeld, Hans. Begriff und Theorie vom Geist bei Max Scheler. Diss. Leipzig, 1930.
Phil 3850.18.100 Hafkesbrink, H. Das Problem des religiösen Gegenstandes bei Max Scheler. Diss. Gütersloh, 1930.
Phil 3850.18.105 Eklund, H. Evangelisches und Katholisches in Max Schelers Ethik. Inaug. Diss. Uppsala, 1932.
Phil 3850.18.106 Eklund, H. Evangelisches und Katholisches in Max Schelers Ethik. Inaug. Diss. Uppsala, 1932.
Phil 3850.18.108 Frick, Paul. Der weltanschauliche Hintergrund der materialen Wertethik Max Schelers. Diss. Stuttgart, 1933.
Phil 3850.18.109 Przywara, Erich. Religionsbegründung: Max Scheler, J.H. Neuman. Freiburg, 1923.
Phil 3850.18.113 Bachus, A. Enzelmensch Familie und Staat in der Philosophie Max Schelers. Inaug. Diss. Düsseldorf, 1936.
Phil 3850.18.115 Alpheus, Karl. Kant und Scheler. Diss. Freiburg, 1936.
Phil 3850.18.120F Povina, Alfredo. La obra sociologica de Max Scheler. Cordoba, 1941.
Phil 3850.18.125 Gongora Perea, C. El espiritu y la vida en la filosofía de Max Scheler. Lima, 1943.
Phil 3850.18.130 Hessen, J. Max Scheler. Essen, 1948.
Phil 3850.18.135 Konthock, K. Max Scheler. Berlin, 1948.
Phil 3850.18.140 Hartmann, Wilfried. Die Philosophie Max Schelers in ihren Beziehungen zu Eduard von Hartmann. Düsseldorf, 1956.
Phil 3850.18.142 Hartmann, Wilfried. Max Scheler; Bibliographie. Stuttgart, 1963.
Phil 3850.18.145 Lorschield, Bernhard. Max Schelers Phänomenologie des Psychischen. Bonn, 1957.
Phil 3850.18.150 Dupuy, Maurice. La philosophie de la religion. Paris, 1959.
Phil 3850.18.151 Dupuy, Maurice. La philosophie de la religion chez Max Scheler. Paris, 1959.
Phil 3850.18.152 Dupuy, Maurice. La philosophie de Max Scheler. 1. éd. Paris, 1959. 2v.
Phil 3850.18.153 Dupuy, Maurice. La philosophie de Max Scheler. Paris, 1959. 2v.
Phil 3850.18.155 Doerry, Gerd. Der Begriff des Wertpersontypus bis Scheler und Spranger. Berlin, 1958.
Phil 3850.18.160 Lenk, Kurt. Von der Ohnmacht des Geistes. Tübingen, 1959.
Phil 3850.18.165 Wojtyta, K.B. Ocena mózliwósci zbudowania etybi chresc. Lublin, 1959.
Phil 3850.18.170 Heidemann, I. Untersuchungen zur Kantkritik Max Schelers. Köln? 1955.
Phil 3850.18.175 Lorscheid, B. Das Leibphänomen. Bonn, 1962.
Phil 3850.18.180 Filippone, Vincenzo. Societá e cultura nel pensiero di Max Scheler. Milano, 1964. 2v.
Phil 3850.18.185 Martin-Izquierdo, Honorio. Das religiöse Apriori bei Max Scheler. Bonn, 1964.
Phil 3850.18.190 Frings, Manfred S. Max Scheler. Pittsburgh, 1965.
Phil 3850.18.195 Ranly, Ernest W. Scheler's phenomenology of community. The Hague, 1966.
Phil 3850.18.200 Haskamp, Reinhold J. Spekulativer und Phänomenologischer. Freiburg, 1966.
Phil 3850.18.205 Staude, John Raphael. Max Scheler, 1874-1928; an intellectual portrait. N.Y., 1967.
Phil 3850.18.210 Uchiyam, Mivoru. Das Wertwidrige in der Ethik Max Schelers. Bonn, 1966.
Phil 3850.18.215 Mandrioni, Héctor Delfor. Max Scheler; un estudio sobre el concepto de espíritu en el formalismu de Max Scheler. Buenos Aires, 1965.
Phil 3850.18.220 Rutishauser, Bruno. Max Schelers Phänomenologie des Fühlens. Bern, 1969.
Phil 3850.19.30 Suabedissen, D.T.A. Die Grundzüge der Metaphysik. Marburg, 1836.
Phil 3850.19.40 Suabedissen, D.T.A. Zur Einleitung in die Philosophie. Marburg, 1827.
Phil 3850.19.50 Suabedissen, D.T.A. Die Grundzüge der philosophischen Tugend- und Rechtslehre. Marburg, 1839.
Phil 3850.20.80 Bruck, Reinhard. Heinrich Steffens. Diss. Borna, 1906.
Phil 3850.20.84 Smits, J.P. Filosofies opooedkundige sketse. Amsterdam, 1929.
Phil 3850.21.91 Schroeder, B. Leopold Schmid's Leben und Denken. Leipzig, 1871.
Phil 3850.22.90 Heller, Joseph E. Solgers Philosophie der ironischen Dialektik. Berlin, 1928.
Phil 3850.22.90.2 Heller, Joseph E. Solgers Philosophie der ironischen Dialektik. Diss. Berlin, 1928.
Phil 3850.22.93 Boucher, Maurice K.N.F. Solger; esthétique et philosophie de la présence. Thèse. Paris, 1934.
Phil 3850.22.95 Herzog, Reinhart. Die Bewahrung der Vernunft. Inaug. Diss. München, 1967.
Phil 3850.24.90 Beuschlein, K. Die Möglichkeit der Gotteserkenntnis in der Philosophie Gideon Spickers. Diss. Würzburg, 1914.
Phil 3850.25.80 Schmidt, Hugo. Die Lehre von der psychologischen Kausalität in der Philosophie Ludwig Strümpells. Inaug. Diss. Leipzig, 1907.
Phil 3850.26.90 Semewald, L. Carl Christian Ehrhard Schmid und sein Verhältnis zu Fichte. Inaug. Diss. Leipzig, 1929.
Phil 3850.27.16 Seaver, George. Albert Schweitzer; the man and his mind. 6th ed. London, 1969.
Phil 3850.27.21 Schweitzer, A. An anthology. N.Y., 1947.
Phil 3850.27.23 Schweitzer, A. Vom Lich in Uns. Stuttgart, 1947.
Phil 3850.27.30 Schweitzer, A. Waffen des Lichts. 1. Aufl. Heilbronn, 1940.
Phil 3850.27.35 Schweitzer, A. Memoirs of childhood and youth. 1st American ed. N.Y., 1949.
Phil 3850.27.40 Schweitzer, A. Albert Schweitzers Leben und Denken. N.Y., 1949.
Phil 3850.27.45 Schweitzer, A. Das Christentum und die Welterligionen. München, 1949.

217
Classified Listing

Phil 3850 History of philosophy - Local Modern philosophy - Germany - Individual philosophers - Other S - cont.

Phil 3850.27.50 Schweitzer, A. Denken und Fat. Hamburg, 1950.
Phil 3850.27.55 Schweitzer, A. The animal world of Albert Schweitzer. Boston, 1950.
Phil 3850.27.60 Ehrfurcht vor dens Leben. Bern, 1954?
Phil 3850.27.65 Schweitzer, A. Strassburger Predigten. München, 1966.
Phil 3850.27.65.5 Schweitzer, A. Reverence for life. N.Y., 1969.
Phil 3850.27.75 Schweitzer, A. Die Lehre von der Ehrfurcht von dem Leben. München, 1966.
Phil 3850.27.90 Regester, John D. Albert Schweitzer. N.Y., 1931.
Phil 3850.27.93 Robock, A.A. The Albert Schweitzer jubilee book. Cambridge, 1945.
Phil 3850.27.93.1 The Albert Schweitzer Jubilee Book. Westport, Conn., 1970.
Phil 3850.27.94 Robock, A.A. In Albert Schweitzer's realms. Cambridge, 1962.
Phil 3850.27.95 Kraus, Oskar. Albert Schweitzer. 2. Aufl. Berlin, 1929.
Phil 3850.27.97 Kraus, Oskar. Albert Schweitzer. London, 1943.
Phil 3850.27.98 Barthelemy, Guy. Chez le Docteur Schweitzer. Laussame, 1953.
Phil 3850.27.99 Raab, Karl. Albert Schweitzer, Persönalichkeit und Denken. Inaug. Diss. Düsseldorf, 1937.
Phil 3850.27.101 Buri, Fritz. Christentum und Kulture bei Albert Schweitzer. Beru, 1941.
Phil 3850.27.101.5 Buri, Fritz. Albert Schweitzer und Karl Jaspers. Zürich, 1950.
Phil 3850.27.102 Joy, C.R. Music in the life of Albert Schweitzer. 1st ed. N.Y., 1951.
Phil 3850.27.103 Russell, L.M. The path to reconstruction...Albert Schweitzer's philosophy of civilization. London, 1941.
Phil 3850.27.103.5 Russell, L.M. The path to reconstruction. London, 1943.
Phil 3850.27.105 Henrich, R. They thought he was mad; Albert Schweitzer. N.Y., 1940.
Phil 3850.27.106 Grabs, R. Albert Schweitzer. Berlin, 1949.
Phil 3850.27.106.10 Grabs, R. Sinngeburg des Lebens. Hamburg, 1950.
Phil 3850.27.108 Seaver, George. Albert Schweitzer: revolutionary christian. N.Y., 1944.
Phil 3850.27.109 Seaver, George. Albert Schweitzer. London, 1947.
Phil 3850.27.110 Seaver, George. Albert Schweitzer. 4th ed. London, 1951.
Phil 3850.27.110.2 Seaver, George. Albert Schweitzer. Boston, 1951.
Phil 3850.27.111 Hagedorn, Hermann. Prophet in the wilderness. N.Y., 1947.
Phil 3850.27.112 Lind, Emil. Die Universalmenschen Goethe und Schweitzer. Neustadt, 1964.
Phil 3850.27.113 Lind, Emil. Albert Schweitzer. Bern, 1948.
Phil 3850.27.113.5 Lind, Emil. Ein Meister der Menscheit Albert Schweitzer. Bühl, 1954.
Phil 3850.27.114 Amadou, Robert. Albert Schweitzer. Bruxelles, 1951.
Phil 3850.27.114.5 Amadou, Robert. Albert Schweitzer. Paris, 1952.
Phil 3850.27.116 Christolles, H. Albert Schweitzer. Stuttgart, 1953.
Phil 3850.27.117 Ratter, Magnus C. Albert Schweitzer, life and message. Boston, 1950.
Phil 3850.27.119 Grabs, R. Albert Schweitzer. Berlin, 1948.
Phil 3850.27.120 Lotar, Peter. Von Sinn des Lebens. Strasbourg, 1951.
Phil 3850.27.122 Feschotte, Jacques. Albert Schweitzer. Paris, 1952.
Phil 3850.27.122.4 Feschotte, Jacques. Albert Schweitzer. 4. éd. Paris, 1958.
Phil 3850.27.125 Babel, Henry. Que pensé Albert Schweitzer? Genève, 1953.
Phil 3850.27.127 Babel, Henry. Schweitzer tel qu'il fut. Boudry-Neuchâtel, 1966.
Phil 3850.27.128 Anderson, E. The world of Albert Schweitzer. N.Y., 1955.
Phil 3850.27.130 Hommage a Albert Schweitzer. Paris, 1955.
Phil 3850.27.132 Steinitz, Benno. Albert Schweitzer. Wien, 1955.
Phil 3850.27.135 Tau, Max. Albert Schweitzer und der Friede. Hamburg, 1955.
Phil 3850.27.140 Hygen, J.B. Albert Schweitzers Kulturkritik. Göttingen, 1955.
Phil 3850.27.141 Hygen, J.B. Albert Schweitzers tanker om kulturen. Oslo, 1954.
Phil 3850.27.145 Pierhal, Jean. Albert Schweitzer. N.Y., 1957.
Phil 3850.27.150 Payne, Robert. The three worlds of Albert Schweitzer. N.Y., 1957.
Phil 3850.27.155 Kirschner, Carol F. A selection of writings of and about Albert Schweitzer. Boston, 1958.
Phil 3850.27.160 Phillips, Herbert M. Safari of discovery. N.Y., 1958.
Phil 3850.27.165 Langfeldt, Gabriel. Albert Schweitzer. London, 1960.
Phil 3850.27.166 Langfeldt, Gabriel. Albert Schweitzer. N.Y., 1960.
Phil 3850.27.170 Cousins, Norman. Dr. Schweitzer of Lambaréné. N.Y., 1960.
Phil 3850.27.175 Mueller, Herbert. Albert Schweitzer. Duisburg, 1956.
Phil 3850.27.180 Rode, Ebbe. Møde med Albert Schweitzer. København, 1959.
Phil 3850.27.185 Albert Schweitzer, Mensch und Werk. Bern, 1959.
Phil 3850.27.190 Spinosa, Antonio. Dottor Schweitzer e dintorni. Roma, 1960.
Phil 3850.27.195 Picht, Werner. Albert Schweitzer. Hamburg, 1960.
Phil 3850.27.197 Picht, Werner. The life and thought of Albert Schweitzer. N.Y., 1964.
Phil 3850.27.200 Buri, Fritz. Albert Schweitzer und unsere Zeit. Zürich, 1947.
Phil 3850.27.205 Gittleman, D. Albert Schweitzer. n.p., 1959.
Phil 3850.27.210 Clark, Henry. The ethical mysticism of Albert Schweitzer. Boston, 1962.
Phil 3850.27.215 Baehr, Hans N. Albert Schweitzer, sein Denken und sein Weg. Tübingen, 1962.
Phil 3850.27.220 Loennebo, M. Albert Schweitzers etisk-religiösa iderl. Stockholm, 1964.
Phil 3850.27.225 Anderson, E. Albert Schweitzer's of friendship. 1st ed. N.Y., 1964.
Phil 3850.27.230 Marshall, George. An understanding of Albert Schweitzer. N.Y., 1966.
Phil 3850.27.230.5 Marshall, George N. Schweitzer; a biography. 1st ed. Garden City, 1971.
Phil 3850.27.235 Phillips, Herbert M. Albert Schweitzer, prophet of freedom. Evanston, Ill., 1957.
Phil 3850.27.240 Friends of Albert Schweitzer. A tribute on the ninetieth birthday of Albert Schweitzer. Boston, 1964.
Phil 3850.27.245 Corah, Hakki. Aborra oganga. Istanbul, 1967.
Phil 3850.27.250 Kantzenbach, Friedrich Wilhelm. Albert Schweitzer, Wirklichkeit und Legende. Göttingen, 1969.
Phil 3850.27.255 Götting, Gerald. Albert Schweitzer- Pionier der Menschlichkeit. Berlin, 1970.

Phil 3850 History of philosophy - Local Modern philosophy - Germany - Individual philosophers - Other S - cont.

Phil 3850.27.260 Al'bers Shveitser - velikii gumanist XX veka. Moskva, 1970.
Phil 3850.27.265 Nosik, Boris M. Shveitser. Moskva, 1971.
Phil 3850.28.80 Pamphlet box. Philosophy. German and Dutch. Siebeck, Hermann. Paris.
Phil 3850.29.20 Schlich, M. Gesemmelte Aufsätze, 1926-1936. Wien, 1938.
Phil 3850.29.30 Schlick, M. Gesetz, Kausalität und Wahrscheinlichkeit. Wien, 1948[1938]
Phil 3850.30.90 Fassbender, Johann. Erkenntnislehre und Metaphysik Jakob Seuglers, 1799-1878. Inaug. Diss. Bonn, 1937.
Phil 3850.31 Schmalenbach, H. Geist und Sein. Basel, 1939.
Phil 3850.32 Räber, H. Othmar Spanns Philosophie. Jena, 1937.
Phil 3850.32.10 Spann, Othmar. Erkenne dich Selbst. Jena, 1935.
Phil 3850.32.10.2 Spann, Othmar. Erkenne dich Selbst. 2. Aufl. Graz, 1968.
Phil 3850.32.20 Spann, Othmar. Naturphilosophie. Jena, 1937.
Phil 3850.32.22 Spann, Othmar. Naturphilosophie. 2. Aufl. Graz, 1963.
Phil 3850.32.24 Spann, Othmar. Gespräch über Unsterblichkeit; Betrachtungen zweier Krieger im Felde. Graz, 1965.
Phil 3850.32.80 Schneller, Martin. Zurischen Romantik und Faschismus. 1. Aufl. Stuttgart, 1970.
Phil 3850.32.85 Rieber, Arnulf. Vom Positivismus zum Universalismus. Berlin, 1971.
Phil 3850.33 Schramm, A. Philosophische Studien zum Begriff der Entscheidung. Inaug. Diss. Berlin, 1940.
Phil 3850.35 Stumpf, Karl. Zur Einteilung der Wissenschaften. Berlin, 1907.
Phil 3850.37 Spann, Othmar. Das philosophische Gesamtinerk im Auszug. Wien, 1950.
Phil 3850.40 Schnitzler, Otto. Von der Feststellung. Bonn, 1953.
Phil 3850.42 Speiser, Andreas. Die geistige Arbeit. Basel, 1955.
Phil 3850.44.3 Schrempf, Christof. Gesammelte Werke. Stuttgart, 1930-40.
Phil 3850.46 Neu, Theodor. Bibliographie Eduard Spranger. Tübingen, 1958.
Phil 3850.46.1 Spranger, Eduard. Gesammelte Schriften. v.1-3,8. Tübingen, 1969- 4v.
Phil 3850.47 Seifert, Hans. Heinrich Scholz. Münster, 1958.
Phil 3850.48 Sydow, W. Das Geheimnis des ewigen Lebens und des jüngsten Tages. Berlin, 1960?
Phil 3850.50 Huenermann, Peter. Trinitorische Anthropologie bei Franz Anton Staudenmaiet. Freiburg, 1962.
Phil 3850.51 Berning, V. Das Denken Herman Schells. Essen, 1964.
Phil 3850.52.30 Stallaert, L. Voor alleenstaanden. Rotterdam, 1958.
Phil 3850.52.35 Stallaert, L. Peilingen. Rotterdam, 1956. 3v.
Phil 3850.52.40 Stallaert, L. Onze nonger naar oprechtheid. Brugge, 1958.
Phil 3850.53 Spengler, Oswald. Urfragen. München, 1965.
Phil 3850.54 Steinheim, Salomon Ludwig. Salomon Ludwig Steinheim zum Gedenken. Leiden, 1966.
Phil 3850.54.80 Andorn, Hans. Salomon Ludwig Steinheims "Offenbarung nach dem Lehrbegriff der Synagoge". Berlin, 1930.
Phil 3850.55 Scherrer, Eduard. Wissenschaftslehre. Bern, 1968.
Phil 3850.56 Malan, Daniel Johannes. 'n Kritiese studie van die wysbegeerte van H.G. Stoker vanuit die standpunt van H. Dooye weerd. Amsterdam, 1968.
Phil 3850.60 Sander, Heinrich. Von der Güte und Weisheit Gottes in der Natur. Carlsruhe, 1780.
Phil 3850.62 Schaumann, Johann Christian Gottlieb. Versuch eines neuen Systems des natürlichen Rechts. Bruxelles, 1969.
Phil 3850.64 Stern-Mitcherlich, Axel Ludwig. The science of freedom; an essay in applied philosophy. London, 1969.
Phil 3850.66 Spann, Othmar. Kämpfende Wissenschaft. 2. Aufl. Graz, 1969.
Phil 3850.68 Struve, Wolfgang. Der andere Zug. Salzburg, 1969.
Phil 3850.70 Selle, Christian Gottlieb. Grundsätze der reinen Philosophie. Bruxelles, 1969.
Phil 3850.72.2 Stegmueller, Wolfgang. Metaphysik, Skepsis, Wissenschaft. 2. Aufl. Berlin, 1969.

Phil 3890 History of philosophy - Local Modern philosophy - Germany - Individual philosophers - T

Phil 3890.1.30 Trendelenburg, A. Historische Beiträge zur Philosophie. Berlin, 1846-67. 3v.
Phil 3890.1.41 Trendelenburg, A. Logische Untersuchungen. 2. Aufl. Leipzig, 1862. 3v.
Phil 3890.1.42 Trendelenburg, A. Logische Untersuchungen. Berlin, 1840. 2v.
Phil 3890.1.45A Trendelenburg, A. Logische Untersuchungen. 3. Aufl. Leipzig, 1870. 2v.
Phil 3890.1.45B Trendelenburg, A. Logische Untersuchungen. 3. Aufl. Leipzig, 1870. 2v.
Phil 3890.1.75 Trendelenburg, A. Contribution to history of the word person. Chicago, 1910. 2 pam.
Phil 3890.1.80 Veeck, O. Darstellung...Trendelenburgs. Gotha, 1888.
Phil 3890.1.81 Bonitz, Hermann. Zur Erinnerung an Friedrich Adolf Trendelenburg. Boston, 1872.
Phil 3890.1.83 Orphal, H. Die religionsphilosophischen Anschauungen Trendelenburg's. Eisleben, 1891.
Phil 3890.1.84 Weiss, Antonia R. Friedrich Adolf Trendelenburg. Kallmünz, 1960.
Phil 3890.1.85 Petersen, Peter. Die Philosophie Friedrich Adolf Trendelenburgs. Hamburg, 1913.
Phil 3890.1.105 Hoffmann, Edmund. Die Psychologie Friedrich Adolf Trendelenburgs. Inaug. Diss. Greifswald, 1892?
Phil 3890.1.110 Gál, Keleman. Trendelenburg Bölcseleti rendszere tekintettie. Kolozsvárt, 1895.
Phil 3890.1.115 Rosensbock, G.G. F.A. Trendelenburg. Carbondale, 1964.
Phil 3890.2.30 Tschirnhaus, E.W. von. Medicina mentis. Lipsiae, 1695.
Phil 3890.2.80 Verweyen, J. Ehrenfried Walther von Tschirnhaus. Bonn, 1905.
Phil 3890.2.85 Winter, Eduard. E.W. von Tschirnhaus. Berlin, 1960.
Htn Phil 3890.3.30F* Tauler, J. Des heilige Lerers Predigfast. Basel, 1621.
Phil 3890.4.80 Pamphlet vol. Philosophy. German and Dutch. Trahudorf, Karl Friedrich Eusebius.
Phil 3890.5.80 Pamphlet box. Philosophy. German and Dutch. Tennemann, Wilhelm G.
Phil 3890.6.80 Störring, Gustav. Die Erkenntnistheorie von Tetens. Leipzig, 1901.
Phil 3890.6.83 Schinz, Max. Die Moralphilosophie von Tetens. Leipzig, 1906.
Phil 3890.6.84 Uebele, Wilhelm. Johann Nicolaus Tetens. Inaug. Diss. Berlin, 1911.
Phil 3890.6.85 Schweig, Helmut. Die Psychologie des Enkennens bei Bonnet und Tetens. Trier, 1921.
Phil 3890.6.86 Seidel, A. Tetens Einfluss auf die kritische Philosophie Kants. Inaug. Diss. Würzburg, 1932.
Phil 3890.7.81 Jacobskötter, A. Die Psychologie Dieterich Liedemanns. Inaug. Diss. Erlangen, 1898.

Classified Listing

Phil 3890.8.6   Thomasius, Christian. Allerhand bissher Publicirte Kleine deutsche Schriften. Halle, 1701.

Phil 3890.8.30   Thomasius, Christian. Von der Kunst vernünftig und tugendhafft zu Lieben als dem eintzigen Mittel zu einen Glückselingen. Halle, 1692.

Phil 3890.8.30.1   Thomasius, Christian. Einleitung zur Sittenlehre. Hildesheim, 1968.

Phil 3890.8.35   Thomasius, Christian. Von der Artzeney widner die Unvernunfftige Lieben und die zuvorher Nöthigen Erkäntniss sein Sellst. Halle, 1696.

Phil 3890.8.40   Thomasius, Christian. Ausübung der Sittenlehre. Hildesheim, 1968.

Phil 3890.8.45.1   Thomasius, Christian. Ausübung der Vernunftlehre. Hildesheim, 1968.

Phil 3890.8.79   Pamphlet box. Philosophy. German and Dutch. Thomasius, Christian.

Phil 3890.8.85   Thomasiana; Arbeiten aus dem Institut für Staats und Rechtsgeschichte bei der Martin Luther. Universität Halle-Wittenberg. Weimar. 1-4

Phil 3890.8.95   Pufendoy, Samne. Briefe an Christian Thomasius. München, 1897.

Phil 3890.8.101   Kayser, R. Christian Thomasius und der Pietismus. Hamburg, 1900.

Phil 3890.8.105   Neisser, Liselotte. Christian Thomasius und seine Beziehungen zum Pietismus. Inaug. Diss. München, 1928.

Phil 3890.8.110   Bloch, E. Christian Thomasius. Berlin, 1953.

Phil 3890.8.115   Schneiders, Werner. Recht. Münster, 1961.

Phil 3890.8.120   Thomasius, Christian. Kleine deutsche Schriften. Halle, 1894.

Phil 3890.9.85   Troxler, I.P.V. Der Briefwechsel zwischen Ignoz Paul Vital Troxler. Aran, 1953.

Phil 3890.9.88   Troxler, I.P.V. Philosophische Enzyklopädie und Methodologie der Wissenschaften. Beromünster, 1956.

Phil 3890.9.90   Gamper, J. Paul Vital Ignoz Troxlers Leben und Philosophie. Diss. Bern, 1907.

Phil 3890.9.95   Spiess, Emil Jakob. Ignoz Paul Vital Troxler. Bern, 1967.

Phil 3890.10.90   Liehrich, H. Die historische Wahrheit bei Ernst Troeltsch. Diss. Giessen, 1937.

Phil 3890.10.100   Brachmann, W. Ernst Troeltschs historische Weltanschauung. Halle, 1940.

Phil 3890.10.110   Schaaf, J.J. Geschichte und Begriff. Tübingen, 1946.

Phil 3890.10.120   Waismann, A. Ernst Troeltsch o el drama del historicismo. Cordoba, 1955.

Phil 3890.10.130   Kasch, W.F. Die Sozialphilosophie von Ernst Troeltsch. Tübingen, 1963.

Phil 3890.11   Schabad, M. Die Wiederenteleskung des ich in der Metaphysik Teichmüllers. Basel, 1940.

Phil 3890.14   Treher, W. Das Oknosprinzip. München, 1962.

Phil 3890.16   Tiedemann, Dieterich. Idealistische Briefe Marburg. Bruxelles, 1969.

Phil 3895.30   Ulrici, H. Glauben und Wissen. Leipzig, 1858.

Phil 3895.35   Ulrici, H. Gott und der Mensch. Bd.1. Leipzig, 1873.

Phil 3895.35.2   Ulrici, H. Gott und der Mensch. 2. Aufl. Bd.1-2. Leipzig, 1874. 2v.

Phil 3895.40   Ulrici, H. Gott und die Natur. Leipzig, 1862.

Phil 3895.40.2   Ulrici, H. Gott und die Natur. Leipzig, 1875.

Phil 3895.40.5   Ulrici, H. Gott und die Natur. 2. Aufl. Leipzig, 1866.

Phil 3895.45   Ulrici, H. Das Grundprincip der Philosophie. Leipzig, 1845-46. 2v.

Phil 3895.49   Ulrici, H. Über die Logik. Leipzig, 1852.

Phil 3895.50   Ulrici, H. Compendium der Logik. Leipzig, 1860.

Phil 3895.53   Ulrici, H. Compendium der Logik. 2. Aufl. Leipzig, 1872.

Phil 3895.80   Pamphlet box. Philosophy. German and Dutch. Ulrici, H. 2 pam.

Phil 3900.1.80   Brasch, M. Welt- und Lebensanschauung Friedrich Ueberweg. Leipzig, 1889.

Phil 3900.1.81   Dilthey, W. Zum Andenken an Friedrich Ueberweg. n.p., n.d.

Phil 3900.1.82   Lange, F.A. Friedrich Ueberweg. Berlin, 1871.

Phil 3900.1.83   Hallmer, Lars. Om Friedrich Ueberwegs "System der logik". Lund, 1877.

Phil 3900.1.85   Berger, Herbert. Begründung des Realismus. Bonn, 1958.

Phil 3900.2   Unger, A. The imagination of reason. London, 1952.

Phil 3900.2.5   Unger, Erich. Das Lebendige und das Goettliche. Jerusalem, 1966.

Phil 3903.1.80   Pamphlet vol. Philosophy. German and Dutch. Volkelt, Johannes.

Phil 3903.1.81   Festschrift Johannes Volkelt zum 70. Geburtstag. München, 1918.

Phil 3903.1.86   Schuster, Willy. Zwischen Philosophie und Kunst, Johannes Volkelt zum 100 Lehrsemester. Leipzig, 1926.

Phil 3903.1.91   Ferro, A.A. La teoria della conoscenza in G. Volkelt. Aosta, 1903.

Phil 3903.1.95   Ponnér, Jarl W. Johannes Volkelts lära am det tragiska. Lund, 1956.

Phil 3903.2.125   Jung, Johannes. Karl Vogts Weltanschauung. Paderborn, 1915.

Phil 3903.2.126   Jung, Johannes. Karl Vogts Weltanschauung. Inaug. Diss. Paderborn, 1915.

Phil 3903.3.30   Vaihinger, Hans. Die Philosophie des Als Ob. Berlin, 1911.

Phil 3903.3.33   Vaihinger, Hans. Die Philosophie des Als Ob. 3. Aufl. Leipzig, 1918.

Phil 3903.3.34   Vaihinger, Hans. Die Philosophie des Als Ob. 2. Aufl. Leipzig, 1924.

Phil 3903.3.40   Vaihinger, Hans. The philosophy of "As if". London, 1924.

Phil 3903.3.43   Vaihinger, Hans. The philosophy of "As if"; a system of the theoretical, practical and religious fictions of mankind. 2. ed. London, 1968.

Phil 3903.3.50   Vaihinger, Hans. Der Atheismusstreit gegen die Philosophie des Als Ob. Berlin, 1916.

Phil 3903.3.80   Smit, H.W.V.D.V. Hans Vaihinger en de als-ob-philosophie. Baarn, 1925.

Phil 3903.3.90   Strauch, W. Die Philosophie des "Als-Ob" und...Rechtswissenschaft. München, 1923.

Phil 3903.3.92   Spickerbaum, P. Das Vaihingersche Als-Ob und die Methode der Formensprache in Religion und Theologie. München, 1922.

Phil 3903.3.95   Fliess, B. Einführung in die Philosophie des Als Ob. Bielefeld, 1922.

Phil 3903.3.97   Valeton, Matthée. De "Als ob" philosophie en het psychisch monisme. Amsterdam, 1923.

Phil 3903.3.99   Reininger, R. Über H. Vaihingers "Philosophie des Als Ob". Leipzig, 1912.

Phil 3903.3.102   Bausteine zu einer Philosophie des "Als-Ob". München. 1-14,1922-1927   13v.

Phil 3903.3.105   Leidel, A. Die Philosophie des Als Ob und das Leben Festschrift. Berlin, 1932.

Phil 3903.3.109   Willrodt, S. Semifiktionen und Vollfiktionen in der Philosophie des Als Ob von H. Vaihinger. Inaug. Diss. Gräfenhainichen, 1933.

Phil 3903.3.110   Vossius, G.J. Universalis philosophiae. Leiden, 1955.

Phil 3903.3.113   Richtscheid, H. Das Problem des philosophischen Skeptizismus. Diss. Düsseldorf, 1935.

Phil 3903.4.80   Zuidema, Sytse Uebe. Wetenschappelijke bijdragen door leerigen van D.H.M. Vollenhoveu. Franeker, 1951.

Phil 3903.5.30   Verhoeven, Cornelius W.M. Inleiding tot de verwondering. Utrecht, 1967.

Phil 3903.5.31   Verhoeven, Cornelius Wilhelmus Maria. The philosophy of wonder. N.Y., 1972.

Phil 3903.5.35   Verhoeven, Cornelius W.M. Het grote gebeuren. Utrecht, 1966.

Phil 3903.5.40   Verhoeven, Cornelius W.M. Rondom de leegte. Utrecht, 1967.

Phil 3903.5.45   Verhoeven, Cornelius W.M. Symboliek van de voet. Assen, 1956.

Phil 3905.30   Weininger, Otto. Geschlecht und Charakter. Wien, 1903.

Phil 3905.30.3   Weininger, Otto. Geschlecht und Charakter. 3. Aufl. Wien, 1904.

Phil 3905.30.10   Weininger, Otto. Geschlecht und Charakter. Berlin, 1932.

Phil 3905.30.15   Weininger, Otto. Sex and character. Photoreproduction. London, 1910.

Phil 3905.31   Weininger, Otto. Sex and character. London, 1906.

Phil 3905.35   Weininger, Otto. Über die letzen Dinge. Wien, 1904.

Phil 3905.80   Lucka, E. Otto Weininger: sein Werk und Persönlichkeit. Wien, 1905.

Phil 3905.82   Biró, Paul. Die Sittlichkeitsmetaphysik Otto Weiningers. Wien, 1927.

Phil 3905.82.2   Biró, Paul. Die Sittlichkeitsmetaphysik Otto Weiningers. Diss. Wien, 1927.

Phil 3905.84   Abrahamsen, David. The mind and death of a genius. N.Y., 1946.

Phil 3905.86   Swoboda, H. Otto Weiningers Tod. 2. Aufl. Wien, 1923.

Phil 3905.88   Dallago, Carl. Otto Weiningers und sein Werk. Innsbruck, 1912.

Phil 3905.90   Sturm, Bruno. Gegen Weininger. Wien, 1912.

Phil 3905.92   Klaren, Georg. Otto Weininger, der Mensch, sein Werk und sein Leben. Wien, 1924.

Phil 3910.1   Wolff, Christian von. Philosophia rationalis suie logica. Veronae, 1735.

Phil 3910.2   Wolff, Christian von. Philosophia rationalis suie logica. Helmstadia, 1746.

Phil 3910.10   Wolff, Christian von. Gesammlete kleine Philosophie Schrifften. Magdeburg, 1736-40. 6v.

Phil 3910.12   Wolff, Christian von. Gesammlete Werke. Hildesheim, 1962-22v.

Phil 3910.25   Wolff, Christian von. Wolffsche Begriffsbestimmungen. Leipzig, 1910.

Phil 3910.29   Wolff, Christian von. Philosophia prima. Francofurti, 1730.

Phil 3910.30   Wolff, Christian von. Philosophia prima suie ontologia. Francofurti, 1736.

Htn   Phil 3910.34*   Wolff, Christian von. Meinung von dem Wesen der Seele. Leipzig, 1727.

Phil 3910.35   Wolff, Christian von. Psychologia empirica. Francofurti, 1732.

Phil 3910.35.5F   Wolff, Christian von. Psychologia empirica. Veronae, 1736.

Htn   Phil 3910.40*   Wolff, Christian von. Psychologia rationalis. Francofurti, 1734.

Phil 3910.40.5   Wolff, Christian von. Psychologia rationalis. Veronae, 1737.

Phil 3910.45   Wolff, Christian von. Vernunfftige Gedancken. Halle, 1749-53.

Phil 3910.50   Wolff, Christian von. Theologia naturalis. Francofurti, 1736-41. 2v.

Phil 3910.50.5   Wolff, Christian von. Theologia naturalis. Veronae, 1738. 2v.

Phil 3910.54   Wolff, Christian von. Philosophia practica. Francofurti, 1738-39. 2v.

Phil 3910.54.5   Wolff, Christian von. Philosophia practica. Veronae, 1739-42. 2v.

Phil 3910.55   Wolff, Christian von. Philosophia moralis suie ethica. Halae, 1750-53. 5v.

Phil 3910.56   Wolff, Christian von. Der Vernunftigen Gedancken von Gott. 2. Aufl. Pt.2. Franckfurt, 1733.

Phil 3910.57   Wolff, Christian von. Vernunfftige Gedancken von Gott. 7. Aufl. Frankfurt, 1735.

Phil 3910.57.15   Wolff, Christian von. Vernunfftige Gedancken von Gott. Halle, 1752-40. 2v.

Phil 3910.58   Wolff, Christian von. Cosmologia generalis methodo scientifica. Francofurti, 1737.

Phil 3910.59.5   Wolff, Christian von. Vernunfftige Gedancken von der Menschen. 2. Aufl. Halle, 1723.

Phil 3910.59.15   Wolff, Christian von. Vernunfftige Gedancken von der Menschen. Magdeburgischen, 1752.

Phil 3910.60   Wolff, Christian von. Oeconomica. Halae, 1754.

Phil 3910.66   Wolff, Christian von. Logic. London, 1770.

Phil 3910.68.6   Wolff, Christian von. Vernunfftige Gedancken von dem gesellschafftlichen. 6. Aufl. Franckfurt, 1747.

Phil 3910.70.5   Wolff, Christian von. Vernunfftige Gedancken von dem Würckungen der Natur. 5. Aufl. Halle, 1746.

Phil 3910.72.15   Wolff, Christian von. Vernunfftige Gedancken von dem Absichten. Magdeburgischen, 1752.

Phil 3910 History of philosophy - Local Modern philosophy - Germany - Individual philosophers - Wolff, Christian - cont.

Phil 3910.73.15	Wolff, Christian von. Vernunfftige Gedancken von dem Gebrauche. Magdeburgischen, 1753.
Phil 3910.75	Wolff, Christian von. Briefe...aus 1719-1753. St. Petersburg, 1860.
Phil 3910.76	Wolff, Christian von. Eigene Lebensbeschreibung. Leipzig, 1841.
Phil 3910.77	Baumeister, F.C. Philosophia definitiva. Vitembergae, 1767.
Phil 3910.77.3	Baumeister, F.C. Institutiones philosophiae rationalis methodo Wolfii conscriptae. 5. ed. Vitembergae, 1741.
Phil 3910.77.10	Baumeister, F.C. Historiam doctrinae recentius controversiae de mundo optimo. Lipsiae, 1741.
Phil 3910.77.15	Baumeister, F.C. Institutiones philosophiae naturalis. Olomueii, 1774.
Phil 3910.78	Pamphlet box. Philosophy. German and Dutch. Wolff, Christian von.
Phil 3910.80	Breslau. Prussia Magdalinisch-Gymnas. Christian ven Wolf. Breslau, 1831.
Phil 3910.81	Richler, H. Über Christian Wolffs Ontologie. Leipzig, 1910.
Phil 3910.82	Des Champs, J. Cours abrégé de la philosophie Wolffienne. Amsterdam, 1743-47. 2v.
Phil 3910.83	Gottsched, J.C. Historische Lobschrift des Herrn C. von Wolf. Halle, 1755.
Phil 3910.84	Ludovici, Karl G. Sammlung Auszüge der sämmtlichen Wegen der Wolffischen Philosophie. Pt.1-2. Leipzig, 1737-38.
Phil 3910.84.5	Pamphlet vol. Philosophy. German and Dutch. Wolff, Christian von. 4 pam.
Phil 3910.125	Arnsperger, W. Christians Wolff's Verhältnis zu Lubniz. Weimar, 1897.
Phil 3910.126	Frauendienst, W. Christian Wolff als Staatsdenker. Berlin, 1927.
Phil 3910.128	Kohlmeyer, Ernst. Kosmos und Kosmonomie bei Christian Wolff. Göttingen, 1911.
Phil 3910.130	Burns, John V. Dynamism in the cosmology of Christian Wolf. 1st ed. N.Y., 1966.
Phil 3910.132	Bissinger, Anton. Die Stuktur der Gotteserkenntnis. Bonn, 1970.
Phil 3910.134.1	Meissner, Heinrich Adam. Philosophischer Lexicon aus Christian Wolffs sämtlichen deutschen Schriften. Düsseldorf, 1970.

Phil 3915 History of philosophy - Local Modern philosophy - Germany - Individual philosophers - Wundt, Wilhelm

Phil 3915.01	Wundt, E.W. Wolff's Werk: ein Verzeichnis seiner sämtlischen Schriften. München, 1927.
Phil 3915.06	Wundt, Wilhelm. Der Spiritismus. Leipzig, 1879-1913. 7 pam.
Phil 3915.3	Wundt, Wilhelm. Collected papers; articles. n.p., n.d.
Phil 3915.6	Wundt, Wilhelm. Zur Psychologie und Ethik. Leipzig, 1911.
Phil 3915.8	Wundt, Wilhelm. Kleine Schriften. Leipzig, 1910-11. 2v.
Phil 3915.30	Wundt, Wilhelm. System der Philosophie. Leipzig, 1889.
Phil 3915.30.2	Wundt, Wilhelm. System der Philosophie. 2. Aufl. Leipzig, 1897.
Phil 3915.30.5	Wundt, Wilhelm. System der Philosophie. 3. Aufl. v.1-2. Leipzig, 1907.
Phil 3915.35	Wundt, Wilhelm. Einleitung in die Philosophie. Leipzig, 1902.
Phil 3915.36	Wundt, Wilhelm. Über die Einfluss der Philosophie. Leipzig, 1876.
Phil 3915.38	Wundt, Wilhelm. Philosophie und Psychologie. Leipzig, 1902.
Phil 3915.40	Wundt, Wilhelm. Logik. Stuttgart, 1880-83. 2v.
Phil 3915.40.2	Wundt, Wilhelm. Logik. Stuttgart, 1893-95. 3v.
Phil 3915.40.2.2	Lindan, Hans. Namenverzeichniss und Sachregister zu Wundt's Logik. 2. Aufl. Stuttgart, 1902.
Phil 3915.40.3	Wundt, Wilhelm. Logik. 3. Aufl. Stuttgart, 1906-08. 3v.
Phil 3915.40.4	Wundt, Wilhelm. Logik. 4. Aufl. Stuttgart, 1919-21. 3v.
Phil 3915.43	Wundt, Wilhelm. Hypnotismus und Suggestion. Leipzig, 1892.
Phil 3915.44	Wundt, Wilhelm. Untersuchungen zur Mechanik der Nerven. v.1-2. Erlangen, 1871-76.
Phil 3915.45	Wundt, Wilhelm. Grundzüge der physiologischen Psychologie. Leipzig, 1874.
Phil 3915.45.2	Wundt, Wilhelm. Grundzüge der physiologischen Psychologie. v.1-2. Leipzig, 1880.
Phil 3915.45.3	Wundt, Wilhelm. Grundzüge der physiologischen Psychologie. Leipzig, 1887- 2v.
Phil 3915.45.4	Wundt, Wilhelm. Grundzüge der physiologischen Psychologie. 4. Aufl. Leipzig, 1893. 2v.
Phil 3915.45.5	Wundt, Wilhelm. Grundzüge der physiologischen Psychologie. 5. Aufl. Leipzig, 1902. 3v.
Phil 3915.45.6	Wundt, Wilhelm. Grundzüge der physiologischen Psychologie. 6. Aufl. Leipzig, 1910. 3v.
Phil 3915.46	Wundt, Wilhelm. Eléments de psychologie physiologique. Paris, 1886. 2v.
Phil 3915.46.6	Wundt, Wilhelm. Principles of physiological psychology. London, 1904.
Phil 3915.47	Wundt, Wilhelm. Outlines of psychology. Leipzig, 1897.
Phil 3915.47.2	Wundt, Wilhelm. Outlines of psychology. Leipzig, 1902.
Phil 3915.47.3	Wundt, Wilhelm. Outlines of psychology. 3rd ed. Leipzig, 1907.
Phil 3915.47.4	Wundt, Wilhelm. Grundriss des Psychologie. 2. Aufl. Leipzig, 1897.
Phil 3915.47.5	Wundt, Wilhelm. Grundriss des Psychologie. 7. Aufl. Leipzig, 1905.
Phil 3915.47.7	Wundt, Wilhelm. Grundriss des Psychologie. Leipzig, 1896.
Phil 3915.47.9	Wundt, Wilhelm. Grundriss des Psychologie. 9. Aufl. Leipzig, 1909.
Phil 3915.47.10	Wundt, Wilhelm. Grundriss des Psychologie. 4. Aufl. Leipzig, 1901.
Phil 3915.47.25	Wundt, Wilhelm. Leerboek der zielkunde. Amsterdam, 1898?
Phil 3915.48	Wundt, Wilhelm. Einführung in die Psychologie. Leipzig, 1911.
Phil 3915.49A	Wundt, Wilhelm. Introduction to psychology. London, 1912.
Phil 3915.49B	Wundt, Wilhelm. Introduction to psychology. London, 1912.
Phil 3915.50	Wundt, Wilhelm. Naturwissenschaft und Psychologie. Leipzig, 1903.
Phil 3915.52	Wundt, Wilhelm. Beiträge zur Theorie der Sinneswahrnehm. Leipzig, 1862.
Phil 3915.53	Wundt, Wilhelm. Die Lehre von der Muskelbewegung. Braunschweig, 1858.

Phil 3915 History of philosophy - Local Modern philosophy - Germany - Individual philosophers - Wundt, Wilhelm - cont.

Phil 3915.55	Wundt, Wilhelm. Vorlesungen über die Menschen- und Thierseele. Leipzig, 1863. 2v.
Phil 3915.55.5A	Wundt, Wilhelm. Lectures on human and animal psychology. London, 1894.
Phil 3915.55.5B	Wundt, Wilhelm. Lectures on human and animal psychology. London, 1894.
Phil 3915.55.7	Wundt, Wilhelm. Lectures on human and animal psychology. London, 1896.
Phil 3915.55.8	Wundt, Wilhelm. Vorlesungen über die Menschen- und Thierseele. 2. Aufl. Hamburg, 1892. 2v.
Phil 3915.55.12	Wundt, Wilhelm. Vorlesungen über die Menschen- und Thierseele. Hamburg, 1906. 2v.
Phil 3915.56.2	Wundt, Wilhelm. Reden und Aufsätze. 2. Aufl. Leipzig, 1914.
Phil 3915.59	Wundt, Wilhelm. Elements of folk psychology. London, 1916.
Phil 3915.59.3	Wundt, Wilhelm. Elemente der Völkerpsychologie. 2. Aufl. Leipzig, 1913.
Phil 3915.59.7	Wundt, Wilhelm. Probleme der Völkerpsychologie. 2. Aufl. Stuttgart, 1921.
Phil 3915.60	Wundt, Wilhelm. Die Psychologie im Kampf ums Dasein. Leipzig, 1913.
Phil 3915.65	Wundt, Wilhelm. Ethik. Stuttgart, 1886.
Phil 3915.65.5	Wundt, Wilhelm. Ethik. London, 1897-1901. 3v.
Phil 3915.65.10	Wundt, Wilhelm. Ethik. 4. Aufl. Stuttgart, 1912. 3v.
Phil 3915.66.2	Wundt, Wilhelm. Griechische Weltanschauung. 2. Aufl. Leipzig, 1917.
Phil 3915.67	Wundt, Wilhelm. Sinnliche und übersinnliche Welt. Leipzig, 1914.
Phil 3915.69	Wundt, Wilhelm. Die physikalischen Axiome und ihre Beziehung zum Causal Princip. Erlangen, 1866.
Phil 3915.69.5	Wundt, Wilhelm. Die Prinzipien der mechanischen Naturlehre. Stuttgart, 1910.
Phil 3915.70	Wundt, Wilhelm. Völkerpsychologie. Leipzig, 1900- 5v.
Phil 3915.70.2	Wundt, Wilhelm. Völkerpsychologie. 2nd ed. Leipzig, 1908-20. 12v.
Phil 3915.70.10	Wundt, Wilhelm. Die Zukunft der Kultur. Leipzig, 1920.
Phil 3915.71	Wundt, Wilhelm. Die Nationen und ihre Philosophie. Leipzig, 1916.
Phil 3915.71.2	Wundt, Wilhelm. Nationen und ihre Philosophie. Leipzig, 1915.
Phil 3915.75	Wundt, Wilhelm. Sprachgeschichte und Sprachpsychologie. Leipzig, 1901.
Phil 3915.76	Wundt, Wilhelm. Essays. Leipzig, 1906.
Phil 3915.76.3	Wundt, Wilhelm. Essays. Leipzig, 1885.
Phil 3915.77.50	Wundt, Wilhelm. Erlebtes und Erkanntes. Stuttgart, 1920.
Phil 3915.78	Wundt, Wilhelm. Erlebtes und Erkanntes. 2. Aufl. Stuttgart, 1921.
Phil 3915.79	Pamphlet vol. Philosophy. German and Dutch. Wundt, Wilhelm. German dissertations. 14 pam.
Phil 3915.79.2	Pamphlet box. Philosophy. German and Dutch. Wundt, Wilhelm. German dissertations.
Phil 3915.79.5	Pamphlet box. Philosophy. German and Dutch. Wundt, Wilhelm.
Phil 3915.80	Schumann, H. Wundts Lehre vom Willen. Leipzig, 1912.
Phil 3915.82	Sommer, Hugo. Individualismus oder Evolutionismus? Berlin, 1887.
Phil 3915.83	Cesca, Giovanni. L'animismo di Guglielmo Wundt. n.p., 1891.
Phil 3915.85	König, Edmund. Wilhelm Wundt. Stuttgart, 1901.
Phil 3915.85.5	König, Edmund. Wilhelm Wundt als Psycholog und als Philosoph. Stuttgart, 1902.
Phil 3915.105	Vannérus, Allen. Vid studiet af Wundts psykologi. Stockholm, 1896.
Phil 3915.105.5	Vannérus, Allen. Zur Kritik des Seelenbegriffs. n.p., n.d.
Phil 3915.145	Szczurat, Vassil. Wundt's Apperzeptionstheorie. Brody, 1903.
Phil 3915.148	Klenke, Friedrich. Der Mensch. Graz, 1908.
Phil 3915.150	Heinzelmann, G. Der Begriff der Seele und die Idei der Unsterblichkeit. Tübingen, 1910.
Phil 3915.152	Passkönig, Oswald. Die Psychologie Wilhelm Wundts. Leipzig, 1912.
Phil 3915.153	Nef, Willi. Die Philosophie Wilhelm Wundts. Leipzig, 1923.
Phil 3915.154	Bernstein, Xenja. Die Kunst nach Wilhelm Wundt. Nürnberg, 1914.
Phil 3915.156	Svensson, P.I.K. Wundts etik, framställning och granskning. Lund, 1913.
Phil 3915.158	Svensson, P.I.K. Kunskapsteoretiska studier med särskild hänsyn till Wundts åsikt. Lund, 1904.
Phil 3915.159	Prever, G. La filosofia di Guglielmo Wundt. Cuorgné, 1904.
Phil 3915.160	Heussner, A. Einführung in Wilhelm Wundt's Philosophie und Psychologie. Göttingen, 1920.
Phil 3915.161	Petersen, Peter. Wilhelm Wundt und seine Zeit. Stuttgart, 1925.
Phil 3915.162	Benzoni, R. Esposizione analitica del sistema di filosofia di Guglielmo Wundt. Palermo, 1890.

Phil 3925 History of philosophy - Local Modern philosophy - Germany - Individual philosophers - Other W

Phil 3925.1.79	Pamphlet box. Philosophy. German and Dutch. Wagner, J.J.
Phil 3925.2.80	Pamphlet box. Philosophy. German and Dutch. Wasmann, Erich
Phil 3925.2.90	Weishedel, Wilhelm. Wirklichkeit und Wirklichkeiten. Berlin, 1960.
Phil 3925.2.95	Weischedel, Wilhelm. Philosophische Grunzgänge. Stuttgart, 1967.
Phil 3925.3.31	Weisse, Christian Hermann. Grundzüge der Metaphysik. Hamburg, 1835.
Phil 3925.3.35	Weisse, Christian Hermann. Philosophische Dogmatik oder Philosophie des Christenthums. Leipzig, 1855-62. 3v.
Phil 3925.3.40	Weisse, Christian Hermann. Psychologie und Unsterblichkeitslehre. Leipzig, 1869.
Phil 3925.3.45	Weisse, Christian Hermann. Das philosophische Problem der Gegenwart. Leipzig, 1842.
Phil 3925.3.50	Weisse, Christian Hermann. Kleine Schriften zur Aesthetik und ästhetischen Kritik. Leipzig, 1867.
Phil 3925.3.52	Weisse, Christian Hermann. Kleine Schriften zur Ästhetik und ästhetischen Kritik. Hildesheim, 1966.
Phil 3925.3.80	Seydel, Rudolf. Christian Hermann Weisse. Leipzig, 1866.
Phil 3925.4.80	Funker, O. Über Wirblichkeit und Logik; eine kritische Darlegung der Lehre Richard Wahles. Cernauti, 1924.
Phil 3925.5.80	Goldstandt, H. Weissenborns Stellung zum Theismus. Inaug. Diss. Würzburg, 1917.

Phil 3925 History of philosophy - Local Modern philosophy - Germany - Individual philosophers - Other W - cont.

Phil 3925.6.06 Windelband, W. Ueber den Gegenwärtigen stand der Psychologie. n.p., 1876-1914. 12 pam.
Phil 3925.6.79 Pamphlet box. Philosophy. German and Dutch. Windelband, W.
Phil 3925.6.90 Rickert, H. Wilhelm Windelband. Tübingen, 1915.
Phil 3925.6.92 Ruge, Arnold. Wilhelm Windelband. Leipzig, 1917.
Phil 3925.7.85 Wirth, Wilhelm. Wie ich zur Philosophie und Psychologie Ram. Leipzig, 1931.
Phil 3925.8.81 Trefzger, Hermann. Der philosophische Entwicklungsgang von Joseph Weber. Freiburg, 1933.
Phil 3925.9.90 Becker, J. Die Religionsphilosophie Karl Werners. Inaug. Diss. Bonn, 1935.
Phil 3925.10 Wimmer, H.A. Neue Dialoge; zwischen Hylas und Philoneris. Heidelberg, 1938.
Phil 3925.11.20 Wust, Peter. Wege einer Freundschaft. Heidelberg, 1951.
Phil 3925.11.25 Wust, Peter. Briefe an Freunde. Münster, 1955.
Phil 3925.11.26 Wust, Peter. Briefe an Freunde. 2. Aufl. Münster, 1956.
Phil 3925.11.28 Wust, Peter. Brief und Aufsätze. Münster, 1958.
Phil 3925.11.30 Wust, Peter. Gestalten und Gedanken. 4. Aufl. München, 1950.
Phil 3925.11.40 Wust, Peter. Im Sinnkreis des Ewigen. 1. Aufl. Graz, 1954.
Phil 3925.11.50 Schmidt, R.H. Peter Wust. Saarbrüchen, 1954.
Phil 3925.11.60 Wust, Peter. Unterwegs zur Heimat. Münster, 1956.
Phil 3925.11.70 Leenhouwen, Albuinus. Ungesichertheit und Wagnis. Essen, 1964.
Phil 3925.11.80 Alcorta, José Ignacio. Peter Wust, filosofo espiritualista de nuestro tiempo. Bilbao, 1965.
Phil 3925.12 Weber, Alfred. Das Tragische und die Geschichte. Hamburg, 1943.
Phil 3925.15 Wendel, G. Vermischte Schriften. Berlin, 1912.
Phil 3925.16 Wittgenstein, Ludwig. Philosophical investigations. Oxford, 1953.
Phil 3925.16.2 Wittgenstein, Ludwig. Philosophical investigations. N.Y., 1953.
Phil 3925.16.3 Wittgenstein, Ludwig. Philosophical investigations. 3rd ed. N.Y., 1968[1958]
Phil 3925.16.3.1 Wittgenstein, Ludwig. Philosophical investigations. 3rd ed. Oxford, 1968.
Phil 3925.16.3.2 Wittgenstein, Ludwig. Philosophical investigations. 3rd ed. Oxford, 1968.
Phil 3925.16.4 Wittgenstein, Ludwig. Remarks on the foundations of mathematics. Oxford, 1956.
Phil 3925.16.5 Wittgenstein, Ludwig. Remarks on the foundations of mathematics. Oxford, 1964.
Phil 3925.16.10 Wittgenstein, Ludwig. Preliminary studies for the "Philosophical investigations" generally known as the Blue and Brown books. Oxford, 1958.
Phil 3925.16.12 Wittgenstein, Ludwig. Preliminary studies for the "Philosophical investigations" generally known as the Blue and Brown books. 2nd ed. Oxford, 1969.
Phil 3925.16.15A Wittgenstein, Ludwig. Notebooks. Oxford, 1961. 2v.
Phil 3925.16.15B Wittgenstein, Ludwig. Notebooks. Oxford, 1961. 2v.
Phil 3925.16.20 Wittgenstein, Ludwig. Philosophische Bemerkungen; aus dem Nachlass. Oxford, 1964.
Phil 3925.16.25 Wittgenstein, Ludwig. Lectures and conversations on asthetics. Berkeley, 1966.
Phil 3925.16.30 Wittgenstein, Ludwig. Zettel. Oxford, 1967.
Phil 3925.16.35A Wittgenstein, Ludwig. On certainty. Oxford, 1969.
Phil 3925.16.35B Wittgenstein, Ludwig. On certainty. Oxford, 1969.
Phil 3925.16.41 Wittgenstein, Ludwig. Tractatus logico-philosophicus. London, 1922.
Phil 3925.16.45 Wittgenstein, Ludwig. Tractatus logico-philosophicus. London, 1960.
Phil 3925.16.46 Wittgenstein, Ludwig. Tractatus logico-philosophicus. Paris, 1961.
Phil 3925.16.47A Wittgenstein, Ludwig. Tractatus logico-philosophicus. London, 1961.
Phil 3925.16.47B Wittgenstein, Ludwig. Tractatus logico-philosophicus. London, 1961.
Phil 3925.16.50A Wittgenstein, Ludwig. Schriften. Frankfurt, 1960-64. 2v.
Phil 3925.16.50B Wittgenstein, Ludwig. Schriften. Frankfurt, 1960-64.
Phil 3925.16.52 Wittgenstein, Ludwig. Schriften...Beiheft. Frankfurt, 1960.
Phil 3925.16.60 Wittgenstein, Ludwig. Tractatus logico-philosophicus. Milano, 1954.
Phil 3925.16.80 Barone, Francesco. Wittgenstein inedito. Torino, 1953.
Phil 3925.16.82 Campanale, Domenico. Studi su Wittgenstein. Bari, 1956.
Phil 3925.16.84 Malcolmi, Norman. Ludwig Wittgenstein. London, 1958.
Phil 3925.16.86 Pole, David. The later philosophy of Wittgenstein. London, 1958.
Phil 3925.16.88 Hawkins, Dennis John Bernard. Wittgenstein and the cult of language. London, 1957.
Phil 3925.16.90 Stenius, Erik. Wittgenstein's Tractatus. Ithaca, 1960.
Phil 3925.16.92 Hartnack, Justus. Wittgenstein und die Moderne Philosophie. Stuttgart, 1962.
Phil 3925.16.93 Hartnack, Justus. Wittgenstein and modern philosophy. Garden City, 1965.
Phil 3925.16.95 Pitcher, George Willard. The philosophy of Wittgenstein. Englewood Cliffs, 1964.
Phil 3925.16.96 Copi, Irving Marmer. Essays on Wittgenstein's Tractatus. London, 1966.
Phil 3925.16.98 Peursen, Cornelis Anthonie van. Ludwig Wittgenstein. Baarn, 1965.
Phil 3925.16.98.1 Peursen, Cornelis Anthonie van. Ludwig Wittgenstein: an introduction to his philosophy. London, 1969.
Phil 3925.16.100 Griffin, J.P. Wittgenstein's logical atomism. Oxford, 1964.
Phil 3925.16.105 Favrholdt, D. An interpretation and critique of Wittgenstein's Tractatus. Copenhagen, 1964.
Phil 3925.16.110 Black, Max. A companion to Wittgenstein's Tractatus. Ithaca, 1964.
Phil 3925.16.115 Burkhardt, Jörg R. Die Bildtheorie der Sprache. München, 1965.
Phil 3925.16.120 Pitcher, George Willard. Wittgenstein: the philosophical investigation. 1st ed. Garden City, N.Y., 1966.
Phil 3925.16.125 Hubbeling, Hubertus Gerinus. Inleiding tot het denken van Wittgenstein. Assen, 1965.
Phil 3925.16.130 Hallett, Garth. Wittgenstein's definition of meaning as use. N.Y., 1967.
Phil 3925.16.135 Engelmann, Paul. Letters from Ludwig Wittgenstein with a memoir. Oxford, 1967.
Phil 3925.16.140 Waismann, Friedrich. Wittgenstein und der Wiener Kreis. Oxford, 1967.
Phil 3925.16.145 High, Dallas. Language, persons, and belief studies in Wittgenstein's Philosophical investigations. N.Y., 1967.

Phil 3925 History of philosophy - Local Modern philosophy - Germany - Individual philosophers - Other W - cont.

Phil 3925.16.150 Morick, Harold. Wittgenstein and the problem of other minds. N.Y., 1967.
VPhil 3925.16.155 Wolniewicz, Bogustaw. Rzeczy i fakty. Warszawa, 1968.
Phil 3925.16.160 Morrison, James. Meaning and truth in Wittgenstein's Tractatus. The Hague, 1968.
Phil 3925.16.165 Schulz, Walter. Wittgenstein; die Negation der Philosophie. Pfullingen, 1967.
Phil 3925.16.170 Gargani, Aldo Giorgio. Linguaggio di esperienza in Ludwig Wittgenstein. Firenze, 1966.
Phil 3925.16.175.2 Hermans, Willem Frederich. Wittgenstein in de mode en karze mier niet. 2. druk. Amsterdam, 1967.
Phil 3925.16.180 Riverso, Emanuele. Il pensiero di Ludovico Wittgenstein. Napoli, 1965?
Phil 3925.16.185 Mueller, Anselm. Ontologie in Wittgensteins "Tractatus". Bonn, 1967.
Phil 3925.16.190 Ganguly, Sachindranath. Wittgenstein's Tractatus, a preliminary. Santiniketan, 1968.
Phil 3925.16.195 Specht, Ernst Konrad. The foundations of Wittgenstein's late philosophy. Manchester, 1969.
Phil 3925.16.200 Winch, Peter. Studies in the philosophy of Wittgenstein. N.Y., 1969.
Phil 3925.16.205 Über Ludwig Wittgestein. Frankfurt, 1968.
Phil 3925.16.210 Fann, K.T. Wittgenstein's conception of philosophy. Oxford, 1969.
Phil 3925.16.215 Borgis, Ilona. Index zu Ludwig Wittgensteins "Tractatus logico-philosophicus" und Wittgenstein - Bibliographie. Frieburg, 1968.
Phil 3925.16.220 Glebe Møller, Jens. Wittgenstein or religionen. København, 1969.
Phil 3925.16.225 Giegel, Hans Joachim. Die Logik der seelischen Ereignisse. Thesis. Frankfurt, 1969.
Phil 3925.16.230 Wuchteil, Kurt. Strukur und Sprachspiel bei Wittgenstein. Frankfurt, 1969.
Phil 3925.16.235 Rhees, Rush. Discussions of Wittgenstein. London, 1970.
Phil 3925.16.240 Rielkopf, Charles F. Strict finitism. The Hague, 1970.
Phil 3925.16.245 Antiseri, Dario. Dopo Wittgenstein. Roma, 1967.
Phil 3925.16.250 Cristaldi, Mariano. Wittgenstein; l'ontologia inibita. Bologna, 1970.
Phil 3925.16.255 Novielli, Valeria. Wittgenstein e la filosofia. Bari, 1969.
Phil 3925.16.260 Pear, David Francis. Ludwig Wittgenstein. N.Y., 1970.
Phil 3925.16.265 Anscombe, Gertrude Elizabeth Margaret. An introduction to Wittgenstein's Tractatus. London, 1959.
Phil 3925.16.270 Polochmann, George Kimball. Terms in their proportional contexts in Wittgenstein's Tractatus; an index. Carbondale, 1962.
Phil 3925.16.275 Maslow, Alexander. A study in Wittgenstein's Tractatus. Berkeley, 1961.
Phil 3925.16.280 Shibles, Warren. Wittgenstein; language and philosophy. Dubuque, Iowa, 1969.
Phil 3925.16.285 Leeds, England. University. Department of Philosophy. A Witttgenstein workbook. Berkeley, 1970.
Phil 3925.16.290 Finch, Henry Leroy. Wittgenstein - the early philosophy. N.Y., 1971.
Phil 3925.16.295 Engelmann, Paul. Ludwig Wittgenstein: Briefe und Begegnungen. Wien, 1970.
Phil 3925.16.300 Marconi, Diego. Il mito del linguaggio scientifico. Studi su Wittgenstein. Milano, 1971.
Phil 3925.16.305 Egidi, Rosaria. Studi di logica e filosofia della scienza. Roma, 1971.
Phil 3925.17.25 Wigeroma, Baltus. Wordende waarheid. 's Gravenhage, 1959.
Phil 3925.18.30 Waismann, Friedrich. How I see philosophy. N.Y., 1968.

Phil 3935 History of philosophy - Local Modern philosophy - Germany - Individual philosophers - Y

Phil 3935.1.30 Yorck von Wartenburg, Paul. Bewusstseinsstellung und Geschichte. Tübingen, 1956.
Phil 3935.1.80 Gruender, Karl Fried. Zur Philosophie des Grafen Paul Vorck von Wartenburg. Göttingen, 1970.

Phil 3940 History of philosophy - Local Modern philosophy - Germany - Individual philosophers - Z

Phil 3940.1.85 Zeller, Eduard. Erinnerungen eines Neunzigjährigen. Stuttgart, 1908.
Phil 3940.1.90 Diels, Hermann. Gedächtnisrede auf Eduard Zeller. Berlin, 1908.
Phil 3940.2.30 Ziegler, L. Spätlese eigener Hand. München, 1953.
Phil 3940.2.35 Ziegler, L. Das Lehrgespräch vom Allgemeinen Menschen in Lieben Abenden. Hamburg, 1956.
Phil 3940.2.40 Ziegler, L. Dienst an der Welt. Darmstadt, 1925.
Phil 3940.2.45 Ziegler, L. Briefe, 1901-1958. München, 1963.
Phil 3940.3.30 Saager, Q. Der Winterthurer Naturphilosoph J.H. Ziegler. Winterthur, 1930.
Phil 3940.4 Zwanziger, Johann Christian. Die Religion des Philosoph und sein Glaubenskenntniss. Bruxelles, 1968.

Phil 3960 History of philosophy - Local Modern philosophy - Netherlands, Holland - History - General works

Phil 3960.1 Repertorium der Nederlanden wijsbegeerte. Amsterdam, 1948- 3v.
Phil 3960.10 Antal, Geza von. Die holländische Philosophie im neunzehnten Jahrhundert. Utrecht, 1888.
Phil 3960.12 Land, Jan P.N. De wijsbegeerte in de Nederlanden. 's Gravenhage, 1899.
Phil 3960.14 Brulez, Lucien. Holländische Philosophie. Breslau, 1926.
Phil 3960.16 Sassen, Ferdinand. De wijsbegeerte der middeleeuvren in de Nederlanden. Lochen, 1944.
Phil 3960.16.5 Sassen, Ferdinand. Geschiedenis van de wijsbegeerte in Nederland tot het einde der negentiende eeuw. Amsterdam, 1959.
Phil 3960.16.13 Sassen, Ferdinand. Wijsgerig leven in Nederland in de twintigste eeuw. 3. druk. Amsterdam, 1960.
Phil 3960.18 Dibon, Paul. La philosophie néerlandaise au siècle d'ov. Paris, 1954.
Phil 3960.20 Faber, W. Wijsgerin in Nederland. Nijkork, 1954.

Phil 3963 History of philosophy - Local Modern philosophy - Netherlands, Holland - History - Special topics

Phil 3963.2 Stien, Hendrik. Das Leib-Seele-Problem in der Philosophie Hollands im 19. und 20. Jahrhundert. Lengerich, 1937.
Phil 3963.4 Constandse, Anton Levien. Geschiedenis van het humanisme in Nederland. Den Haag, 1967.

Phil 3998   History of philosophy - Local Modern philosophy - Italy - Pamphlet volumes

Phil 3998   Pamphlet box. Italian philosophy.
Phil 3998.1   Pamphlet box. Italian philosophy.
Phil 3998.2   Pamphlet vol. Philosophy. Miscellanee filosofiche. 15 pam.
Phil 3998.3   Pamphlet vol. Philosophy. Miscellanee filosofiche. 17 pam.
Phil 3998.4   Pamphlet vol. Philosophy. Italian philosophical pamphlets. 39 pam.
Phil 3998.5   Pamphlet vol. Philosophy. Italian philosophy. 7 pam.
Phil 3998.6   Pamphlet vol. Philosophy. Italian philosophers. Biographical pamphlets. 9 pam.

Phil 4000   - 4025   History of philosophy - Local Modern philosophy - Italy - History - General works - Individual authors (A-Z)

Phil 4000.10   Acri, Francesco. Critica di alcune critiche di spaventa. Bologna, 1875.
Phil 4000.15   Alberghi, Sante. Metafisica e spiritualisti italiani contemporanei. Milano, 1960.
Phil 4000.16   Alorpio, F. de. Storia e dialogo. Bologna, 1962.
Phil 4000.17   Alliney, G. I pensatori della seconda metà del secolo XIX. Milano, 1942.
Phil 4001.1   Berthé de Besaucèle, Louis. Les Cartériens d'Italie. Thèse. Paris, 1920.
Phil 4001.2   Bertinaria, F. Sull'indole e le vicende della filosofia italiana. Torino, 1846.
Phil 4001.3   Braschi, C. I filosofi italiani dal XVIII al XIX secolo. Milano, 1916.
Phil 4001.4   Bonavino, C. L'introduzione alla filosofia delle scuole italiane. Italia, 1852.
Phil 4001.4.5   Bonavino, C. La filosofia delle scuole italiane. Capolago, 1852.
Phil 4001.4.6   Bonavino, C. La filosofia delle scuole italiane. 2. ed. Firenze, 1863.
Phil 4001.4.9   Bonavino, C. Appendice alla filosofia delle scuole italiane. 2. ed. Milano, 1866.
Phil 4002.1   Charbonnel, J.R. La pensée italienne au XVIe siècle. Paris, 1919.
Phil 4002.2   Conti, Augusto. La philosophie italienne contemporaine. Paris, 1865.
Phil 4002.3   Crespi, Angelo. Contemporary thought of Italy. London, 1926.
Phil 4002.4   Colangelo, F. Storia dei filosofi e dei matematici napolitani. v.1-3. Napoli, 1833-34.
Phil 4002.5   Contri, Siro. La filosofia scolastica in Italia nell'ora presente. Bologna, 1931.
Phil 4002.6   La collaboration philosophique. Bologna, 1958.
Phil 4002.7   Corsano, A. Il pensiero religioso italiano dall'umanesimo al giurisdizionalismo. Bari, 1937.
Phil 4002.8   Carbonara, Cleto. Il secolo XV. Milano, 1943.
Phil 4002.9   Cassirer, Ernst. The Renaissance philosophy of man. Chicago, 1948.
Phil 4002.9.5   Cassirer, Ernst. The Renaissance philosophy of man. Chicago, 1956.
Phil 4003.1   Debrit, M. Histoire des doctrines philosophiques dans l'Italie. Paris, 1859.
Phil 4003.5   Dezza, Paolo. I neotomisti italiani del XIX secolo. Milano, 1942-44. 2v.
Phil 4003.6   Il dialogo prospettive filosofiche. Bologna, 1964.
Phil 4004.1   Espinas, Alfred. La philosophie expérimentale en Italie. Paris, 1880.
Phil 4004.2   Efirov, Svetozar A. Ital'ianskaia burzhuaznaia filosofiia XX veka. Moskva, 1968.
Phil 4005.1   Ferri, L. Essai sur l'histoire de la philosophie en Italie. Paris, 1869. 2v.
Phil 4005.2   Fiorentino, F. La filosofia contemporanea in Italia. Napoli, 1876.
Phil 4005.2.5   Fiorentino, F. Scritti varii di letteratura, filosofia e critica. Napoli, 1876.
Phil 4005.5   La filosofia contemporanea in Italia dal 1870 al 1920. Napoli, 1928.
Phil 4005.6   Fontana, B. La filosofia della storia nei pensatori italiani. Imola, 1873.
Phil 4005.10   La filosofia italiana fra Ottocento e Novecento. Torino, 1954.
Phil 4005.11   La filosofia contemporanea in Italia. 1. ed. Roma, 1958. 2v.
Phil 4005.12   Faggiotto, Pietro. Esperienza e metafisica. Padova, 1959.
Phil 4006.1   Gabotto, F. L'epicureismo italiano. Piemonte, 1889.
Phil 4006.2   Gentile, G. I problemi della scolastica e il pensiero italiano. Bari, 1913.
Phil 4006.2.2   Gentile, G. I problemi della scolastica e il pensiero italiano. 2a ed. Bari, 1923.
Phil 4006.2.5A   Gentile, G. Le origini della filosofia contemporanea in Italia. v. 1-3. Messina, 1917-21. 4v.
Phil 4006.2.5B   Gentile, G. Le origini della filosofia contemporanea in Italia. v. 1. Messina, 1917.
Phil 4006.2.7   Gentile, G. Dal Genovesi al Galuppi. Napoli, 1903.
Phil 4006.2.8   Gentile, G. Storia della filosofia italiani dal Genovesi al Galuppi. 2a ed. Milano, 1930. 2v.
Phil 4006.2.9   Gentile, G. Studi sul rinascimento. Firenze, 1923.
Phil 4006.2.10   Gentile, G. Studi sul rinascimento. 2a ed. Firenze, 1936.
Phil 4006.2.15   Gentile, G. Il pensiero italiano del secolo XIX. Milano, 1928.
Phil 4006.2.18   Gentile, G. Il pensiero italiano del rinascimento. 3. ed. Firenze, 1940.
Phil 4006.2.20   Gentile, G. Memorie italiane e problemi della filosofia e della vita. Firenze, 1936.
Phil 4006.2.30   Gentile, G. La filosofia italiana contemporanea. Firenze, 1941.
Phil 4006.3   Giovanni, V. Storia della filosofia in Sicilia. Palermo, 1873. 2v.
Phil 4006.3.10*   Giovanni, V. Sullo stato attuale...filosofici in Sicilia. Palermo, 1854.
Phil 4006.3.12   Giovanni, V. Sullo stato attuale...filosofici in Sicilia. Palermo, 1854.
Phil 4006.3.15   Giovanni, V. Della filosofia moderna in Sicilia libri due. Palermo, 1868.
Phil 4006.4   Gemelli, A. Il mio contributo alla filosofia neoscolastica. Milano, 1926.
Phil 4006.5.33   Garin, Eugenio. Filosofi italiani del quattro cento. Firenze, 1942.
Phil 4006.5.35   Garin, Eugenio. Der italienische Humanismus. Bern, 1947.
Phil 4006.5.37   Garin, Eugenio. L'umanesemio italiano. Bari, 1952.
Phil 4006.5.38   Garin, Eugenio. Italian humanism. Oxford, 1965.
Phil 4006.5.40   Garin, Eugenio. La filosofia. v.1-2. Milano, 1947.

Phil 4000   - 4025   History of philosophy - Local Modern philosophy - Italy - History - General works - Individual authors (A-Z) - cont.

Phil 4006.5.45   Garin, Eugenio. Cronache di filosofia italiana. Bari, 1955.
Phil 4006.5.50   Garin, Eugenio. Cronache di filosofia italiana. 2. ed. Bari, 1959.
Phil 4006.5.55   Garin, Eugenio. Cronache di filosofia italiana, 1900-1943. Bari, 1966.
Phil 4006.5.60   Garin, Eugenio. Storia della filosofia italiana. Torino, 1966. 3v.
Phil 4006.5.80   Bibliografia degli scritti di Eugenio Garin. Bari, 1969.
Phil 4006.6.30   Garilli, G. La crisi dell'immanentismo. Palermo, 1953.
Phil 4006.7.30A   Guzzo, A. Gli hegeliani d'Italia. Torino, 1953.
Phil 4006.7.30B   Guzzo, A. Gli hegeliani d'Italia. Torino, 1953.
Phil 4006.8.30   Giusso, Lorenzo. La tradizione ermetica nella filosofia italiana. Roma, 1955?
Phil 4006.9.30   Galli, Gallo. Filosofi italiani d'oggi e altri scritti. Torino, 1958.
Phil 4007.1   Hönigswald, R. Denker der italienischen Renaissance; Gestalten und Probleme. Basel, 1938.
Phil 4007.5   Guerra, Augusto. Il mondo della sicurezza; Ardigo, Labriola, Croce. Firenze, 1963.
Phil 4007.10   Hoellhuber, Ivo. Geschichte der italienischen Philosophie von den Anfängen des 19. Jahrhunderts biz zur Gegenwart. München, 1969.
Phil 4010.2   Kristeller, P.O. Eight philosophers of the Italian Renaissance. Stanford, 1964.
Phil 4011.1   Levi, A. Saggio di una bibliografia filosofia italiana. Bologna, 1908.
Phil 4011.2   Lenoir, E. Trois novateurs. Paris, 1939.
Phil 4011.3   Librizzi, C. Il risorgimento filosofica in Italia. Padova, 1952. 2v.
Phil 4011.3.5   Librizzi, C. Lo spiritualismo religioso nell'età del Risorgimento italiano. Catania, 1955.
Phil 4011.4   Lombardi, Franco. La filosofia italiana negli ultimi cento anni. Asti, 1958?
Phil 4012.1   Mamiani di Rovere, T. Del rinnovamento della filosofia antica italiana. Milano, 1836.
Phil 4012.1.3   Mamiani di Rovere, T. Del rinnovamento della filosofia antica italiana. Parigi, 1834.
Phil 4012.1.4   Mamiani di Rovere, T. Del rinnovamento della filosofia antica italiana. 3. ed. Firenze, 1836.
Phil 4012.1.5   Mamiani di Rovere, T. Sei lettere...intorno al libro filosofia antica italiana. Parigi, 1838.
Phil 4012.1.7   Mamiani di Rovere, T. Sei lettere...intorno al libro filosofia antica italiana. 2. ed. Firenze, 1842.
Phil 4012.2   Mario, A. I nostri filosofi contemporanei; rivista. Napoli, 1862.
Phil 4012.3   Mariano, R. La philosophie contemporaine. Paris, 1868.
Phil 4012.4   Miranda, L. Die Hegel a Croce e da Jellinek a Chiovenda. Bari, 1921.
Phil 4012.5   Masnovo, A. Il neo-tomismo in Italia (origini e prime vicende). Milano, 1923.
Phil 4012.6   Miceli di Serradileo, R. Filosofia. Verona, 1937.
Phil 4012.6.5   Miceli di Serradileo, R. La philosophie contemporaine en Italie. Paris, 1939.
Phil 4012.6.10   Miceli di Serradileo, R. La filosofia italiana actual. Buenos Aires, 1940.
Phil 4012.7   Mondolfo, Rodolfo. La filosofia politica de Italia en el siglo XIX. Buenos Aires, 1942.
Phil 4012.7.5   Mondolfo, Rodolfo. Da Ardigò a Gramsci. Milano, 1962.
Phil 4012.8   Mueller, F.L. La pensée contemporaine en Italie et l'influence de Hegel. Genève, 1941.
Phil 4012.9   Montanari, Fausto. Riserve su l'umanesimo. Milano, 1943.
Phil 4012.12   Marciano, Francesco. Storia della filosofia italiana. Roma, 1959.
VPhil 4012.13   Mikecin, Vjekoslav. Suvremena talijanska filozofija. Zagreb, 1966.
Phil 4013.2   Nardi, Bruno. Saggi sull'aristotelismo padovana dal secolo XIV al XVI. Firenze, 1958.
Phil 4013.5   Noventa, Giacomo. Nulla di nuova. 1. ed. Milano, 1960.
Phil 4013.7   Nowicki, Andrzej. Filozofia włoskiego odrodzenia. Warszawa, 1967.
Phil 4013.10   Namer, Émile. La philosophie italienne. Paris, 1970.
Phil 4014.1   Owen, J. Skeptics of the Italian Renaissance. Photoreproduction. London, 1893.
Phil 4015.1   Puglia, F. Il risorgimento filosofico in Italia. Napoli, 1891.
Phil 4015.2   Piccoli, V. Storia della filosofia italiano. Torino, 1924.
Phil 4015.3   Pennisi, S. Intorno allo stato e ai bisogni attuali della filosofia teoretica in Italia. Firenze, 1862. 3v.
Phil 4015.4   Pompa, Raffaele. L'Italia filosofica contemporanea. Salerno, 1875.
Phil 4015.6   Poppi, Antonino. Introduzione all'aristotelismo padovano. Padova, 1970.
Phil 4017.1   Rava, Adolfo. Descartes, Spinoza et la pensée italienne. Paris, 1927.
Phil 4017.5   Rossi, Mario. Sviluppi dello hegelismo in Italia. Torino, 1957.
Phil 4017.5.5   Rossi, Mario. Svilluppi dello hegelismo in Italia. Torino, 1962.
Phil 4018.1   Siciliani, P. Sul rinnovamento della filosofia positiva in Italia. Firenze, 1871.
Phil 4018.2   Spaventa, Bertrando. La filosofia italiana. Bari, 1908.
Phil 4018.2.5   Spaventa, Bertrando. La filosofia italiana. 3. ed. Bari, 1926.
Phil 4018.2.10   Spaventa, Bertrando. La Circolarità del pensiero europeo. Palermo, 1964.
Phil 4018.3   Spirito, Ugo. Il nuovo idealismo italiano. Roma, 1923.
Phil 4018.4   Simoni, M. Il nuovo spiritualismo in Italia. Napoli, 1936.
Phil 4018.5   Saitta, G. Il pensiero italiano nell'umanesimo e nel Rinascimento. Bologna, 1949. 3v.
Phil 4018.5.2   Saitta, G. Il pensiero italiano nell'umanesimo e nel Rinascimento. 2. ed. Firenze, 1961. 3v.
Phil 4018.6   Sciacca, M.F. Il secolo XX. Milano, 1947. 2v.
Phil 4018.6.5   Sciacca, M.F. Il pensiero italiano nell'età del Risorgimento. 2. ed. Milano, 1963.
Phil 4018.7   Sciacca, M.F. La philosophie italienne contemporaine. Lyon, 1953.
Phil 4018.8   Santucci, Antonio. Esistenzialismo e filosofia italiana. Bologna, 1959.
Phil 4018.8.5   Santucci, Antonio. Il pragmatismo in Italia. Bologna, 1963.
Phil 4019.1   Tilgher, A. Antologia dei filosofi italiani del dopoguerra. 2. ed. Modena, 1937.

Phil 4000 - 4025   History of philosophy - Local Modern philosophy - Italy -
History - General works - Individual authors (A-Z) - cont.

Phil 4019.10   Tozzi, Antonio. L'eredità del neo-idealismo italiana.
                    Firenze, 1953.
Phil 4021.1   Vailati, Giovanni. De quelques caractères du mouvement
                    philosophique contemporain en Italie. Paris, 1907.
Phil 4021.2   Vanni Ronighi, S. Il problema morale nella filosofia
                    italiana dell prima metà de secolo XIX. Milano, 1951.
Phil 4022.1   Werner, K. Die italienische Philosophie. v. 1-5.
                    Wien, 1884-86. 2v.
Phil 4022.1.5   Werner, K. Die cartesische-malebranche'sche Philosophie in
                    Italien. Pt.1-2. Wien, 1883.
Phil 4025.1   Zerella, F. L'eclettisma francese e la cultura filosofica
                    meridionale. 1. ed. Roma, 1953.
Phil 4025.5   Zeppi, Stelio. Il problema del dialogo nel pensiero
                    italiano contemporaneo. Firenze, 1960.

Phil 4030   History of philosophy - Local Modern philosophy - Italy - History -
Special topics

Phil 4030.5   Archivio di Filosofia. Testi umanistici inediti sul De
                    anima. Padova, 1951.

Phil 4060   History of philosophy - Local Modern philosophy - Italy - Individual
philosophers - A

Phil 4060.1.2   Ardigo, Roberto. Opere filosofiche. Padova, 1901-13.
                    11v.
Phil 4060.1.23   Ardigo, Roberto. Pagine scelte. Genova, 1913.
Phil 4060.1.25   Ardigo, Roberto. Scritti vari. Firenze, 1920.
Phil 4060.1.30   Ardigo, Roberto. An inconsistent preliminary objection
                    against positivism. Cambridge, 1910.
Phil 4060.1.35   Ardigo, Roberto. Natura naturans. Ostiglia, 1918.
Phil 4060.1.40   Ardigo, Roberto. L'idealismo e la scienza. Roma, 1919.
Phil 4060.1.80   Bluwstein, J. Die Weltauschauung Roberto Ardigo.
                    Leipzig, 1911.
Phil 4060.1.81   Marchesini, G. Roberto Ardigo, l'uomo e l'umanista.
                    Firenze, 1922.
Phil 4060.1.82   Marchesini, G. Lo spirito evangelico di Roberto Ardigo.
                    Bologna, 1919.
Phil 4060.1.83   Marchesini, G. La vita e il pensiero di Roberto Ardigo.
                    Milano, 1907.
Phil 4060.1.85   Carelle, Antonio. Naturalismo italiano. Padova, 1911.
Phil 4060.1.87   Zamboni, G. Il valore scientifico del positivismo di
                    Roberto Ardigò. Verona, 1921.
Phil 4060.1.88   Mondolfo, Rodolfo. Il pensiero di Roberto Ardigo.
                    Mantova, 1908.
Phil 4060.1.91   Troilo, Erminio. Ardigò. Milano, 1926.
Phil 4060.1.93   Tarozzi, Giuseppe. Roberto Ardigo. Roma, 1928.
Phil 4060.1.95   Ghisleri, Arcangelo. Nel LXX compleanno di Roberto Ardigò.
                    Cremona, 1898.
Phil 4060.1.97   Quadrelli, Ercole. Le problème des origines. Gerace
                    Marina, 1911.
Phil 4060.1.98   Groppali, A. Nel settantesimo anniversario di Roberto
                    Ardigò. Torino, 1898.
Phil 4060.1.100   Saloni, Alfredo. Il positivismo e Roberto Ardigò.
                    Roma, 1969.
Htn Phil 4060.2.33*   Leo Hebraeus. Dialoghi di amore. Vinegia, 1552.
Htn Phil 4060.2.35*   Leo Hebraeus. Los dialogos de amor. Venetia, 1568.
Htn Phil 4060.2.37*   Leo Hebraeus. Los dialogos de amor. Venetia, 1572.
Phil 4060.2.38   Leo Hebraeus. Diálogos de amor. 1. ed. Romano, 1953.
Phil 4060.2.40   Leo Hebraeus. Dialoghi d'amore. Bari, 1929.
Phil 4060.2.42   Leo Hebraeus. Dialoghi d'amore. Heidelberg, 1929.
Phil 4060.2.50   Leo Hebraeus. The philosophy of love. London, 1937.
Phil 4060.2.55   Leo Hebraeus. Dialogos de amor. Madrid, 1949. 2v.
Phil 4060.2.80   Carvalho, Joaqium de. Leão Hebreu, filósofo.
                    Coimbra, 1918.
Phil 4060.2.82   Zimmels, B. Leo Hebraeus, ein jüdischer Philosoph.
                    Breslau, 1886.
Phil 4060.2.83   Sonne, I. Intorno alla vita di Leone Ebreo.
                    Firenze, 1934.
Phil 4060.2.85   Fontanesi, Giuseppina. Il problema dell'amore nell'opera
                    di Leone Ebreo. Venezia, 1934.
Phil 4060.3.30   Allievo, G. Saggi filosofici. Milano, 1866.
Phil 4060.3.35   Allievo, G. G. Allievo...per essere aggregato...Universita
                    di Torino. Torino, 1858.
Phil 4060.4.2   Aliotta, Antonio. Opere complete. Roma, 1947. 7v.
Phil 4060.4.35   Aliotta, Antonio. Critica dell'esistenzialismo. 2. ed.
                    v.2,5. Roma, 1957. 2v.
Phil 4060.4.80   Gentiluomo, Domenico. Il relativismo sperimentale di
                    Antonio Aliotta nel suo svolgimento storico. Roma, 1955.
Phil 4060.4.85   Pallavicini, Gian Luigi. Il pensiero di Antonio Aliotta.
                    Napoli, 1968.
Phil 4060.5.30   Anguilli, A. La filosofia e la scuola. Napoli, 1888.
Phil 4060.5.80   Taura, Giacoma. La vita ed il pensiero di Andrea Anguilli.
                    Milano, 1914.
Phil 4060.5.85   Mandolfo, Santo. I positivisti italiani. Anuilli, 1966.
Phil 4060.5.90   Cordaro, Philip. Andrea Angiulli e l'eredità dell'800.
                    Castanissetta, 1969.
Phil 4060.6.90   Giovanni, V. di. D'acquisto e la filosofia della creazione
                    in Sicilia. Firenze, 1868.
Phil 4060.7   Acari, P. Un meccanismo umano. Milano, 1909.
Phil 4060.8.30   Calderaro, Francesco. Francesco Arri e il suo
                    spiritualismo. Roma, 1941.
Phil 4060.8.81   Cancarini, Itala. Acri. Brescia, 1945.
Phil 4060.8.83   Paggiaro, L. La filosofia di Francesco Acri.
                    Padova, 1953.
Phil 4060.9.30   Amendala, G. Etica e biografia. Milano, 1953.
Phil 4060.9.35   Amendola, Evakühn. Vita can Giovanni Amendola.
                    Firenze, 1960.
Phil 4060.9.40   Antoni, Giuseppe. Pensiero ed esistenza. Padova, 1965.
Phil 4060.10.30   Abbagnano, Nicola. Scritti scelti. Torino, 1967.
Phil 4060.10.80   Travaglia, Sandro. La nozione di possibilità nel pensiero
                    di Nicola Abbagnano. Padova, 1969.

Phil 4065   History of philosophy - Local Modern philosophy - Italy - Individual
philosophers - Bruno, Giordano

Htn Phil 4065.01*   Salvestrini, V. Bibliografia delle opere di Giordano
                    Bruno. Pisa, 1926.
Phil 4065.02   Salvestrini, V. Bibliografia di Giordano Bruno. 2. ed.
                    Firenze, 1958.
Phil 4065.10A   Bruno, Giordano. Opere. Lipsia, 1830. 2v.
Phil 4065.10B   Bruno, Giordano. Opere. v.1-2. Lipsia, 1830. 2v.
Phil 4065.11   Bruno, Giordano. Opere italiane. Bari, 1907. 2v.
Phil 4065.12A   Bruno, Giordano. Opera latine. v. 1-3. Neapoli, 1879-91.
                    6v.
Phil 4065.12B   Bruno, Giordano. Opera latine. Neapoli, 1879-91.
Phil 4065.13   Bruno, Giordano. Opere italiane. Bari, 1907. 2v.
Phil 4065.14A   Bruno, Giordano. Dialoghi italiani. Firenze, 1958.
Phil 4065.14B   Bruno, Giordano. Dialoghi italiani. Firenze, 1958.

Phil 4065   History of philosophy - Local Modern philosophy - Italy - Individual
philosophers - Bruno, Giordano - cont.

Phil 4065.15   Bruno, Giordano. Gesammelte Werke. Leipzig, 1904-09.
                    6v.
Phil 4065.25   Bruno, Giordano. Giordano-Bruno-Buch. Bad Oldesloe, 1927.
Phil 4065.27   Bruno, Giordano. Giordano Bruno. 2. ed. Milano, 1944.
Phil 4065.28   Bruno, Giordano. Opere di G. Bruno e di T. Campanella.
                    Milano, 1956.
Htn Phil 4065.30*   Bruno, Giordano. Philothei Jordani. Paris, 1582.
Phil 4065.31   Bruno, Giordano. Caudelaio. Strasburgo, n.d.
Phil 4065.32   Bruno, Giordano. De umbris idearum. Berolini, 1868.
Htn Phil 4065.32.5*   Bruno, Giordano. De umbris idearum. Paris, 1582.
Phil 4065.32.20   Bruno, Giordano. Le ombre delle idee. Catania, 1901.
Htn Phil 4065.35*   Bruno, Giordano. Camoeracensis acrotismus.
                    Vitebergae, 1588.
Phil 4065.40   Bruno, Giordano. Spaccio de la bestia trionfante.
                    Roma, 1888.
Phil 4065.41   Bruno, Giordano. Reformation des Himmels. Leipzig, 1889.
Phil 4065.43   Bruno, Giordano. L'éthique et le deuxième dialogue du
                    spaccio. Paris, 1919.
Phil 4065.45   Bruno, Giordano. Spaccio della bestia trionfante. v.1-2.
                    Lanciano, 1920.
Phil 4065.45.5   Bruno, Giordano. The expulsion of the triumphant beast.
                    New Brunswick, 1964.
Phil 4065.50.2   Bruno, Giordano. Von der Ursache, dem Princip und dem
                    Einen. 2. Ausg. Heidelberg, 1889.
Phil 4065.50.4   Bruno, Giordano. Giordano Bruno von der Ursache dem
                    Prinzip und dem Einen. 4e aufl. Leipzig, 1923.
Phil 4065.50.10   Bruno, Giordano. Cause, principe et unité. Paris, 1930.
Phil 4065.50.12   Bruno, Giordano. Cause, principle, and unity. N.Y., 1964.
Phil 4065.50.15   Boyanov, Slavi. Filosofiiata na Dzhordano Bruno.
                    Sofiia, 1969.
Phil 4065.52   Bruno, Giordano. De la causa. Padova, 1941.
Htn Phil 4065.55*   Bruno, Giordano. De monade, numero et figura.
                    Franco, 1591.
Htn Phil 4065.58*   Bruno, Giordano. De gl'heroici furori. Parigi, 1585.
Phil 4065.60   Bruno, Giordano. The heroic enthusiasts. pt.1-2.
                    London, 1887-1889. 2v.
Phil 4065.60.30   Bruno, Giordano. Eroici furori, Übersetzt von L.
                    Kuhlenbeck. Leipzig, 1898.
Phil 4065.61   Bruno, Giordano. De gl'heroici furori. Torino, 1928.
Phil 4065.62   Bruno, Giordano. Des fureurs héroiques. Paris, 1954.
Phil 4065.65   Bruno, Giordano. La cena de le cenerè. Torino, 1955.
Phil 4065.65.5   Bruno, Giordano. Das Aschermitt Wochsmahl.
                    Frankfurt, 1969.
Phil 4065.70   Bruno, Giordano. Due dialoghi sconosciuti e due dialoghi
                    noti. Roma, 1957.
Phil 4065.75   Bruno, Giordano. Heroische Leidenschaften und
                    individuelles Leben. Hamburg, 1957.
Phil 4065.79   Pamphlet box. Bruno, Giordano.
Phil 4065.80   Bartholmess, C. Jordano Bruno. Paris, 1846-47. 2v.
Phil 4065.80.5   Bartholmess, C. Jordano Bruno. Paris, 1846-47. 2v.
Phil 4065.81   Clemens, F.J. Giordano Bruno und Nicolaus von Cusa.
                    Bonn, 1847.
Phil 4065.82   Berti, D. Giordano Bruno da Nola. Torino, 1889.
Phil 4065.83   Morselli, E. Giordano Bruno. Torino, 1888.
Phil 4065.84   Stein, H. von. Giordano Bruno, Gedanken über seine Lehre.
                    Leipzig, 1900.
Phil 4065.85   Schiattarella, R. La dottrina di Giordano Bruno.
                    Palermo, 1888.
Phil 4065.86   Louis, G. Giordano Bruno. Berlin, 1900.
Phil 4065.87   McIntyre, J.S. Giordano Bruno. London, 1903.
Phil 4065.88   Giancola, Francesco. Giordano Bruno. Roma, 1885.
Phil 4065.88.12   Paris Zezin, Luis. Fray Giordano Bruno y su tiempo. 2a ed.
                    Madrid, 1886.
Phil 4065.89   Riehl, A. Giordano Bruno. Edinburgh, 1905.
Phil 4065.89.5   Riehl, A. Giordano Bruno. 2e, Aufl. Leipzig, 1900.
Phil 4065.89.20   Riehl, A. Giordano Bruno. Leipzig, 1889.
Phil 4065.90   Hartung, E.B. Grundlinien einer Ethik bei Giordano Bruno.
                    Leipzig, 1878.
Phil 4065.91   Troilo, Erminio. La filosofia di Giordano Bruno.
                    Torino, 1904.
Phil 4065.91.5   Troilo, Erminio. Giordano Bruno. Roma, 1918.
Phil 4065.92   Frith, I. Life of Giordano Bruno. London, 1887.
Phil 4065.92.3   Frith, I. Life of Giordano Bruno. Boston, 1887.
Phil 4065.93   Turnbull, C. Life and teachings of Giordano Bruno,
                    1548-1600. San Diego, 1913.
Phil 4065.94A   Brinton, D.G. Giordano Bruno. Philadelphia, 1890.
Phil 4065.94B   Brinton, D.G. Giordano Bruno. Philadelphia, 1890.
Phil 4065.95   Charbonnel, J.R. L'éthique de Giordano Bruno.
                    Paris, 1919.
Phil 4065.96   Tocco, Felice. Giordano Bruno. Firenze, 1886.
Phil 4065.97   Wilde, Georg. Giordano Bruno's Philosophie in den
                    Hauptbegriffen Materie und Form. Breslau, 1901.
Phil 4065.98   Spampanato, V. Vita di Giordano Bruno. v.1-2.
                    Messina, 1921.
Phil 4065.98.5   Spampanato, V. Documenti della vita di Giordano Bruno.
                    Firenze, 1933.
Phil 4065.99.2   Kuhlenbeck, L. Bruno. 2e Aufl. Leipzig, 1899.
Phil 4065.100   Levi, David. Giordano Bruno. Torino, 1887.
Phil 4065.101   Boulting, William. Giordano Bruno, his life, thought and
                    martyrdom. London, 1916.
Phil 4065.101.2   Boulting, William. Giordano Bruno. London, 1914.
Phil 4065.102   Gentile, G. Giordano Bruno i el pensiero de rinascimento.
                    Firenze, 1920.
Phil 4065.102.2   Gentile, G. Giordana Bruno i el pensiero del rinascimento.
                    2a ed. Firenze, 1925.
Phil 4065.102.8   Gentile, G. Giordano Bruno nella storia della cultura.
                    Milano, 1907.
Phil 4065.103   Labriola, Arturo. Giordano Bruno. Roma, 1924?
Phil 4065.103.5   Labriola, Arturo. Giovanni Bovio e Giordano Bruno.
                    Napoli, 1911.
Phil 4065.104   Wickström, V.H. Giordano Brunos metafysik. Lund, 1883.
Phil 4065.105   Brunnhofer, H. Giordano Bruno's Weltanschauung.
                    Leipzig, 1882.
Phil 4065.105.15   Brunnhofer, H. Giordano Bruno's Lehre vom Kleinsten als
                    die Quelle der prastabilierten Harmonie des Leibnitz. 2.
                    Aufl. Leipzig, 1899.
Phil 4065.106   Atanassievitch, K. Atanasijević, Ksenija, 1894.
                    Belgrade, 1923.
Phil 4065.107   Namer, Émile. Les aspects de Dieu dans la philosophie de
                    Giordano Bruno. Thèse. Paris, 1926.
Phil 4065.107.5   Namer, Émile. Les aspects de Dieu dans la philosophie de
                    Giordano Bruno. Paris, 1926.
Phil 4065.107.10   Namer, Émile. Giordano Bruno, ou L'univers infini comme
                    fondement de la philosophie moderne. Paris, 1966.
Phil 4065.108   Maturi, Sebastiano. Bruno e Hegel. Firenze, 1926.
Phil 4065.109   Mariano, R. Giordano Bruno: la vita e l'uomo. Roma, 1881.

Phil 4065 History of philosophy - Local Modern philosophy - Italy - Individual philosophers - Bruno, Giordano - cont.

Phil 4065.110 Olschki, L. Giordano Bruno. Bari, 1927.
Phil 4065.111 Acanfora-Venturelli, R. Il monismo teosofico di G.B. Palermo, 1893.
Phil 4065.112 Cotugno, R. Giordano Bruno e le sue opere. Trani, 1907.
Phil 4065.113 Reiner, Julius. Giordano Bruno und seine Weltanschauung. Berlin, 19- ?
Phil 4065.114 Ferrari, Sante. G. Bruno, F. Fiorentino, T. Mamiani. Mantova, 1887.
Phil 4065.115 Soliani, B. La filosofia di Giordano Bruno. Firenze, 1930.
Phil 4065.116 Battaglini, F. Giordano Bruno e il Vaticano. Roma, 1889.
Phil 4065.117 Sigwart, C. Die Lebensgeschichte Giordano Bruno's. Tübingen, 1880.
Phil 4065.118 Guzzo, Augusto. I dialoghi del Bruno. Torino, 1932.
Phil 4065.118.5 Guzzo, Augusto. Giordano Bruno. Torino, 1960.
Phil 4065.119 Fiorentino, F. Il panteismo di Giordano Bruno. Napoli, 1861.
Phil 4065.120 Brambilla, E. Studi letterari. Sugli eroici furori di G. Bruno. Milano, 1892.
Phil 4065.121 Comandini, A. Per Giordano Bruno dal 1876 al 1889. Roma, 1889.
Phil 4065.122 Saracista, M. La filosofia di Giordano Bruno nei suoi motivi plotiniani. Firenze, 1935.
Phil 4065.123 Schwartz, M. Giordano Bruno. Erfurt, 1939.
Phil 4065.124 Brandt, C. Giordano Bruno. Buenos Aires, 1940.
Phil 4065.125 Il sommario del processo di Giordano Bruno. Citta del Vaticano, 1942.
Phil 4065.126 Greenberg, S. The infinite in Giordano Bruno. N.Y., 1950.
Phil 4065.127 Singer, D. (Waley). Giordano Bruno. N.Y., 1950.
Phil 4065.128 Cicuttini, L. Giordano Bruno. Milano, 1950.
Phil 4065.129 Fraccari, G. G. Bruno. 1. ed. Milano, 1951.
Phil 4065.130A Horowitz, I.L. The Renaissance philosophy of Giordano Bruno. N.Y., 1952.
Phil 4065.130B Horowitz, I.L. The Renaissance philosophy of Giordano Bruno. N.Y., 1952.
Phil 4065.135 Baldi, E. Giordano Bruno. Firenze, 1955.
Phil 4065.140 Badaloni, Nicola. La filosofia di Giordano Bruno. Firenze, 1955.
Phil 4065.145 Firpo, Luigi. Il processo di Giordano Bruno. Napoli, 1949.
Phil 4065.150 Giusso, Lorenzo. Scienza e filosofia in Giordano Bruno. Napoli, 1955.
Phil 4065.155 Nelson, J.C. Renaissance theory of love. N.Y., 1958.
Phil 4065.160 Saraw, Julie. Der Einfluss Plotins auf Giordano Brunos Degli eroici furori. Borna-Leipzig, 1916.
Phil 4065.165 Ciardo, Manlio. Giordano Bruno tra l'umanesimo e lo stoicismo. Bologna, 1960.
Phil 4065.170 Michel, Paul. La caemologie de Giordano Bruno. Paris, 1962.
Phil 4065.172 Nowicki, A. Centralne Kategorie filozofii Giordana Bruna. Warszawa, 1962.
Phil 4065.173 Yates, F.A. Giordano Bruno. London, 1964.
Phil 4065.174 Gorfunkel', Aleksandr K. Dzhordano Bruno. Moskva, 1965.
Phil 4065.176 Previti, Luigi. Giordano Bruno e i suoi tempi. Prato, 1887.
Phil 4065.178 Szemere, Samu. Giordano Bruno. Budapest, 1917.
Phil 4065.180 Védrine, Hélène. La conception de la nature chez Giordano Bruno. Paris, 1967.
Phil 4065.182 Huber, Karl. Einheit und Vielheit in Denken und Sprache Giordano Brunos. Winterthur, 1965.
Phil 4065.184 Paterson, Antoinette Mann. The infinite worlds of Giordano Bruno. Springfield, 1970.
Phil 4065.186 Kuznetsov, Boris G. Dzhordano Bruno i genesis klassicheskoi nauki. Moskva, 1970.

4070 History of philosophy - Local Modern philosophy - Italy - Individual philosophers - Other B

Phil 4070.1.35 Bonavino, Cristoforo. Studi filosofici e religiosi; del sentimento. 1. ed. Torino, 1854.
Phil 4070.1.36 Bonavino, Cristoforo. Studi filosofici e religiosi; del sentimento. 2. ed. Torino, 1854.
Phil 4070.1.45 Bonavino, Cristoforo. Su la teoria del giudizio. Milano, 1871. 2v.
Phil 4070.1.50 Bonavino, Cristoforo. Saggi di critica e polemica per Ausonio Franchi (pseud.). Milano, 1871-72. 3v.
Phil 4070.1.60 Bonavino, Cristoforo. Ultima critica. Milano, 1889-93. 3v.
Phil 4070.1.65 Bonavino, Cristoforo. Il razionalismo del popolo dei Ausonio Franchi. 3a ed. corretta et aumentata. Milano, 1864.
Phil 4070.1.80 Angelini, A. Ausonio Franchi. Roma, 1897.
Phil 4070.1.85 Galletti, B. Critica dell'Ultima critica di Cristoforo Bonavino. Palermo, 1889.
Phil 4070.1.90 I nuovi auspizi all'Italia e le confessioni di Ausonio Franchi. Genova, 1852.
Phil 4070.1.93 Romano, P. Ausonio Franchi. Savona, 1896.
Phil 4070.1.96 Gotran, P. Due del 48 - Ernest Renan and Cristoforo Bonavino saggio critico filosofico. Firenze, 1891.
Phil 4070.2.80 Cheula, Pietro. Saggio su la filosofia di Francesco Bonatelli. Milano, 1934.
Phil 4070.3 Brunello, B. Lineamenti di filosofia dell'azione. Modena, 1938.
Phil 4070.4.30 Bertini, Giovanni M. Scritti filosofici. Milano, 1942.
Phil 4070.5.30 Boni, Guido. L'essere nella spontaneità creativa e nella riffessione razionale. Roma, 1953.
Phil 4070.6.80 Marchello, G. Felice Battaglia. Torino, 1953.
Phil 4070.7.5 Banfi, Antonio. Principi di una teoria della ragione. Milano, 1960.
Phil 4070.7.10 Banfi, Antonio. La filosofia e la vita spirituale. Roma, 1967.
Phil 4070.7.30 Banfi, Antonio. La ricerca della realta. Firenze, 1959. 2v.
Phil 4070.7.35 Banfi, Antonio. Filosofi contemporanei. v.1-2. Milano, 1961.
Phil 4070.7.40 Banfi, Antonio. Studi sulla filosofia del novecento. Roma, 1965.
Phil 4070.7.45 Banfi, Antonio. Filosofia dell'arte; scelta. Roma, 1962.
Phil 4070.7.50 Banfi, Antonio. I problemi di una estetica filosofica. Milano, 1961.
Phil 4070.7.55 Banfi, Antonio. La crisi. Milano, 1967.
Phil 4070.7.60 Banfi, Antonio. L'uomo copernicano. Milano, 1965.
Phil 4070.7.80 Papi, Fulveo. Il pensiero di Antonio Banfi. Firenze, 1961.
Phil 4070.7.85 Carbonare, Cleto. L'estetica filosofica di Antonio Banfi. Napoli, 1966.

Phil 4070 History of philosophy - Local Modern philosophy - Italy - Individual philosophers - Other B - cont.

Phil 4070.7.90 Convegno di Studi Banfiani, Reggio Emilia. Antonio Banfi e il pensiero contemporaneo. Firenze, 1969.
Phil 4070.8.80 Heuser, H. Ludwig Buzorinis. München, 1961.
Phil 4070.9.1 Bozzetti, Giuseppe. Opere complete: saggi, scritti inediti, opere minori, recensioni. Milano, 1966. 3v.
Phil 4070.10.30 Papuli, Giovanni. Girdamo Balduino. Manduzia, 1967.

Phil 4073 History of philosophy - Local Modern philosophy - Italy - Individual philosophers - Campanella, Tommaso

Phil 4073.20 Campanella, Tommaso. Tommaso Campanella, poeta. Salerno, 1957.
Phil 4073.30 Campanella, Tommaso. Del senso delle cose e delle magia. Bari, 1925.
Phil 4073.31 Campanella, Tommaso. Telogia. Milano, 1936.
Phil 4073.32A Campanella, Tommaso. Epilogo magno (fisiologia italiana). Roma, 1939.
Phil 4073.32B Campanella, Tommaso. Epilogo magno (fisiologia italiana). Roma, 1939.
Phil 4073.33 Campanella, Tommaso. De antichristo. Roma, 1965.
Phil 4073.34 Campanella, Tommaso. Legazioni ai Maomettani. Firenze, 1960.
Htn Phil 4073.35* Campanella, Tommaso. Ludovico iusto XIII; Atheismus Tsiumphatus. Parisiis, 1636.
Phil 4073.36 Campanella, Tommaso. Monarchia Messiae. Torino, 1960.
Phil 4073.37 Campanella, Tommaso. Artiveneti. Firenze, 1945.
Phil 4073.39 Campanella, Tommaso. Opuscali inediti. Firenze, 1951.
Phil 4073.39.5 Campanella, Tommaso. Magia e grazia. Roma, 1957.
Phil 4073.40 Campanella, Tommaso. De sancta mono triade. Roma, 1958.
Phil 4073.42 Campanella, Tommaso. Della necessita di una filosofia cristiana. Torino, 1953.
Phil 4073.43 Campanella, Tommaso. Il peccato originale. Roma, 1960.
Phil 4073.45 Campanella, Tommaso. La prima e la seconda resurrezione. Roma, 1955.
Phil 4073.50 Campanella, Tommaso. Cristologia. Roma, 1958. 2v.
Phil 4073.52 Campanella, Tommaso. Apologia di Galileo. Torino, 1968.
Phil 4073.55 Campanella, Tommaso. Della grazia gratificante. Roma, 1959.
Phil 4073.58 Campanella, Tommaso. De dictis Christi. Roma, 1969.
Phil 4073.60 Campanella, Tommaso. Dio e la predestinazione. Firenze, 1949-51. 2v.
Phil 4073.62F Campanella, Tommaso. Metaphysica. Torino, 1961.
Phil 4073.65 Campanella, Tommaso. De homine. Roma, 1960.
Phil 4073.65.2 Campanella, Tommaso. De homine. Roma, 1961.
Phil 4073.66 Campanella, Tommaso. I sacri segni, inediti. Roma, 1965. 6v.
Phil 4073.67 Campanella, Tommaso. Cosmologia, inediti; theologicorum liber III. Roma, 1964.
Phil 4073.68 Campanella, Tommaso. Vita Christi. Roma, 1962. 2v.
Phil 4073.70 Campanella, Tommaso. Escatologia. Roma, 1969.
Phil 4073.72 Campanella, Tommaso. Le creature sovrannaturali. Roma, 1970.
Phil 4073.75 Campanella, Tommaso. Lettere. Bari, 1927.
Phil 4073.79 Pamphlet box. Campanella, Tommaso.
Phil 4073.80 Cyprian, E. Vita T. Campanella. Amstelodami, 1722.
Htn Phil 4073.81* Berti, D. Nuovi documenti su T. Campanella. Roma, 1881.
Phil 4073.82 Amabile, L. Fra Tommaso Campanella: la sua congiura. Napoli, 1882-. 3v.
Phil 4073.84 Blanchet, Léon. Campanella. Paris, 1920.
Phil 4073.85 Dentice di Accadia, C. Tommaso Campanella. Firenze, 1921.
Phil 4073.86 Treves, Paulo. La filosofia politica di Tommaso Campanella. Bari, 1930.
Phil 4073.87 Sante Felici, G. Die religionsphilosophischen Grundanschauungen des Thomas Campanella. Inaug. Diss. Halle, 1887.
Phil 4073.88 Rossi, M.M. T. Campanella metafisico. Firenze, 1923.
Phil 4073.89 Mattei, R. de. La politica di Campanella. Roma, 1927.
Phil 4073.90 Mattei, R. de. Studi Campanelliani. Firenze, 1934.
Phil 4073.95 Gardner, E.G. Tommaso Campanella and his poetry. Oxford, 1923.
Phil 4073.97 Firpo, Luigi. Bibliografia degli scritti di Tommaso Campanella. Torino, 1940.
Phil 4073.97.5 Firpo, Luigi. Ricerche Campanelliane. Firenze, 1947.
Phil 4073.99 Orestano, F. Tommaso Campanella. Roma, 1940.
Phil 4073.100 Amerio, Romano. Campanella. Brescia, 1947.
Phil 4073.102 Jacabelli Isaldi, A.M. Tomaso Campanella. Milano, 1953.
Phil 4073.104 Grillo, F. Tommaso Campanella in America. N.Y., 1954.
Phil 4073.104.2 Grillo, F. A supplement to the critical bibliography. N.Y., 1957. 2v.
Phil 4073.104.10 Grillo, F. Questioni Campanelliane. Cosenza, 1961.
Phil 4073.112 Corpano, Antonio. Tommaso Campanella. Bari, 1961.
Phil 4073.113 Firpo, Luigi. L'iconografia di Tommaso Campanella. Firenze, 1964.
Phil 4073.115 Shtekli, Al'fred E. Kampanella. Izd. 3. Moskva, 1966.
Phil 4073.116 Testa, Aldo. Meditazioni su Campanella. Bologna, 1965.
Phil 4073.117 Badaloni, Nicola. Tommaso Campanella. 1. ed. Milano, 1965.
Phil 4073.120 Femiano, Salvatore Beniamino. Lo spiritualismo di Tommasco Campanella. Napoli, 1965. 2v.
Phil 4073.120.5 Femiano, Salvatore Beniamino. La metafisica di Tommaso Campanella. Milano, 1968.
Phil 4073.122 Squillace, Mario. La vita eroica di Tommaso Campanella. Roma, 1967.
Phil 4073.124 Bonansea, Bernardino M. Tommaso Campanella. Washington, 1969.
Phil 4073.126 Gonfunkel', Aleksandrkh. Tommaso Kampanella. Moskva, 1969.
Phil 4073.128 Ducros, Franc. Tommaso Campanella, poète. Paris, 1969.
Phil 4073.130 Thomas Campanella, 1568-1639. Milleciquecentoses santotto-millescicentotrentanove. Napoli, 1969.

Phil 4075 History of philosophy - Local Modern philosophy - Italy - Individual philosophers - Cardano, Girolamo

Phil 4075.1F Cardano, Girolamo. Opera. Lugduni, 1663. 10v.
Htn Phil 4075.31* Cardano, Girolamo. De consolatione. Venetijs, 1542.
Htn Phil 4075.40* Cardano, Girolamo. De libris propriis, eorumque ordinis et usu. Lugduni, 1557.
Phil 4075.45 Cardano, Girolamo. Arcana politica. Lugduni, 1635.
Phil 4075.45.15 Cardano, Girolamo. La science du monde. 4e ed. Paris, 1661.
Htn Phil 4075.51* Cardano, Girolamo. De utililate-ex adversis capienda libri. Amsterdam, 1672.
Phil 4075.55 Cardano, Girolamo. The book on games of chance. N.Y., 1961.
Phil 4075.78 Cardano, Girolamo. Hieronymi Cardani mediolanensis. Amstelaedami, 1654.
Htn Phil 4075.79* Cardano, Girolamo. De propria vita liber. Parisiis, 1643.

Classified Listing

Phil 4075   History of philosophy - Local Modern philosophy - Italy - Individual philosophers - Cardano, Girolamo - cont.

Phil 4075.79.10   Cardano, Girolamo. Vita di Girolamo Cardano. Milano, 1821.

Phil 4075.79.15   Cardano, Girolamo. Des Girolamo Cardano von Mailand (Buergers von Bologna) eigene Lebensbeschreibung. Jena, 1914.

Phil 4075.79.16   Cardano, Girolamo. Des Girolamo Cardano von Mailand eigene Lebensbeschreibung. München, 1969.

Phil 4075.79.20A   Cardano, Girolamo. The book of my life. N.Y., 1930.

Phil 4075.79.20B   Cardano, Girolamo. The book of my life. N.Y., 1930.

Phil 4075.79.25   Cardano, Girolamo. Ma vie. Paris, 1936.

Phil 4075.80   Morley, H. Jerome Cardan. v.2. London, 1854.

Phil 4075.81   Waters, W.G. Jerome Cardan. London, 1898.

Phil 4075.83   Cumston, Charles Greene. Notes on life and writings of Gironimo Cardano. Boston, 1902.

Phil 4075.84   Bellini, Angelo. Girolamo Cardano e il suo tempo. Milano, 1947.

Phil 4075.85   Ore, Oystein. Cardano, the gambling scholar. Princeton, 1953.

Phil 4075.86   Lucas Dubreton, D. Le monde enchanté de la Renaissance. Paris, 1954.

Phil 4080   History of philosophy - Local Modern philosophy - Italy - Individual philosophers - Other C

Phil 4080.1.80   Mabilleau, L. Étude historique...Cesare Cremonini. Paris, 1881.

Phil 4080.1.85   Del Torre, Maria A. Studi su Cesare Cremonini. Padova, 1968.

Phil 4080.2.79   Pamphlet box. Chiapelli, Alessandro.

Phil 4080.3.1   Pamphlet box. Croce, Benedetto. Works.

Phil 4080.3.10   Croce, Benedetto. Gesammelte philosophische Schriften in deutscher Übertragung. v.1 (no.1-4), v.2 (no. 1-3). Tübingen, 1927-1930. 7v.

Phil 4080.3.12   Pamphlet vol. Croce, Benedetto. 4 pam.

Phil 4080.3.15   Croce, Benedetto. Tre saggi filosofici. Palermo, 1932.

Phil 4080.3.20   Croce, Benedetto. Punti di orientamento della filosofia moderna. Bari, 1931.

Phil 4080.3.22   Croce, Benedetto. Saggi filosofici. v. 1,3-5,11. Bari, 1948-54. 5v.

Phil 4080.3.23   Croce, Benedetto. Epistolario. v.2. Napoli, 1967.

Phil 4080.3.25   Croce, Benedetto. Etica e politica. Bari, 1931.

Phil 4080.3.28   Croce, Benedetto. Etica e politica. 3. ed. Bari, 1945.

Phil 4080.3.30   Croce, Benedetto. Il presupposto filosofico della concezione liberale Nota. Napoli, 1927.

Phil 4080.3.31   Croce, Benedetto. Estetica come scienza dell'espressione e linguistica generale. Milano, 1902.

Phil 4080.3.31.3   Croce, Benedetto. Estetica come scienza dell'espressione e linguistica generale. 3a ed. Bari, 1908.

Phil 4080.3.31.4   Croce, Benedetto. Estetica come scienza dell'espressione e linguistica generale. 4a ed. Bari, 1912.

Phil 4080.3.31.10   Croce, Benedetto. Estetica come scienza dell'espressione e linguista generale. 10. ed. Bari, 1958.

Phil 4080.3.33   Croce, Benedetto. Problemi di estetica e contributi alla storia dell'estetica italiana. Bari, 1910.

NEDL   Phil 4080.3.34   Croce, Benedetto. Brevario di estetica. Laterza, 1913.

Phil 4080.3.34.5   Croce, Benedetto. Brevario de estetica. Lisboa, 1914.

Phil 4080.3.34.12   Croce, Benedetto. Breviario di estetica; quattro lezioni. 12. ed. Bari, 1954.

Phil 4080.3.35   Croce, Benedetto. La prima forma della estetica e della logica. Messina, 1900.

Phil 4080.3.36   Croce, Benedetto. The essence of aesthetic. London, 1921.

Phil 4080.3.37   Croce, Benedetto. Breviaire d'esthétique. Paris, 1923.

Htn   Phil 4080.3.38*   Croce, Benedetto. Aesthetica in nuce. Napoli, 1929.

Phil 4080.3.38.3   Croce, Benedetto. Aesthetica in nuce. 3. ed. Laterza, 1954.

Phil 4080.3.40   Croce, Benedetto. Perche non possiamo non derci cristiani. Bari, 1944.

Phil 4080.3.42   Croce, Benedetto. Aesthetic as science of expression and general linguistic. N.Y., 1953.

Phil 4080.3.42.10   Croce, Benedetto. Aesthetic as science of expression and general linguistic. N.Y., 1968.

Phil 4080.3.45   Croce, Benedetto. Pensieri vari (ristampa). Bari, 1944.

Phil 4080.3.47   Croce, Benedetto. Nuove pagini sparse. Napoli, 1948-49. 2v.

Phil 4080.3.47.2   Croce, Benedetto. Nuove pagini sparse. 2. ed. Bari, 1966. 2v.

Phil 4080.3.48.2   Croce, Benedetto. Nuovi saggi di estetica. 2. ed. Bari, 1926.

Phil 4080.3.50   Croce, Benedetto. Considerazioni sul problema morale del tempo nostro. Bari, 1945.

Phil 4080.3.54   Croce, Benedetto. Der Begriff des Barock. Zürich, 1925.

Phil 4080.3.55   Croce, Benedetto. Il concetto moderno della storia. Bari, 1947.

Phil 4080.3.58   Croce, Benedetto. Liberismo e liberalismo. Milano, 1957.

Phil 4080.3.60   Croce, Benedetto. My philosophy. London, 1949.

Phil 4080.3.65   Croce, Benedetto. Filosofia e storiografia. Bari, 1949.

Phil 4080.3.70   Croce, Benedetto. Intorno alla dialettica. v.1-2. Bari, 1952.

Phil 4080.3.75   Croce, Benedetto. La Borghesia. Bari, 1945.

Phil 4080.3.78   Croce, Benedetto. An autobiography. Oxford, 1927.

Phil 4080.3.79   Pamphlet box. Croce, Benedetto.

Phil 4080.3.80   Carr, Herbert Wildon. The philosophy of Benedetto Croce. London, 1917.

Phil 4080.3.81   Carr, Herbert Wildon. The philosophy of Benedetto Croce. N.Y., 1969.

Phil 4080.3.85   Masnovo, Omero. L'estetica di Benedetto Croce. Parma, 1914.

Phil 4080.3.90   Settimelli, Emilio. La critica di Benedetto Croce. Bologna, 1912.

Phil 4080.3.93   Romano Palazzo, F. Influssi del pensiero Kantiano vell Croce. Bari, 1938.

Phil 4080.3.120   Castellano, G. Introduzione allo studio...B. Croce. Bari, 1920.

Phil 4080.3.121   Castellano, G. Benedetto Croce. Napoli, 1924.

Phil 4080.3.121.5   Castellano, G. Benedetto Croce. 2a ed. Bari, 1936.

Phil 4080.3.121.20   Castellano, G. Ragazzate letterarie: appunti...Croce. Napoli, 1919.

Phil 4080.3.122   Chiocchetti, E. La filosofia di Benedetto Croce. 2a ed. Milano, 1920.

Phil 4080.3.123   Chiocchetti, E. La filosofia di Benedetto Croce. 3a ed. Milano, 1924.

Phil 4080.3.127   Zacchi, Angelo. Il nuovo idealismo italiano di Benedetto Croce. 2a ed. Roma, 1925.

Phil 4080.3.129   Zanacchi, G. L'intuizione di Benedetto Croce. Palermo, 1925.

Phil 4080.3.132   Flora, F. Croce. Milano, 1927.

Phil 4080   History of philosophy - Local Modern philosophy - Italy - Individual philosophers - Other C - cont.

Phil 4080.3.135   Spirito, Ugo. Benedetto Croce. Roma, 1929.

Phil 4080.3.137   Righi, Gaetano. Il Croce interprete del Vico. Bologna, 1931.

Phil 4080.3.139   Pardo, Ferruccio. La filosofia teoretica di Benedetto Croce. Napoli, 1928.

Phil 4080.3.141   Calogero, G. Studi crociani. Rieti, 1930.

Phil 4080.3.143   Colorni, E. L'estetica di Benedetto Croce. Milano, 1932.

Phil 4080.3.145   Molina, G. Saggio su Benedetto Croce. Genova, 1928.

Phil 4080.3.147   Lameere, Jean. L'esthétique de Benedetto Croce. Paris, 1936.

Phil 4080.3.150   Carnevale, Luigi. Il concetto puro della filosofia dello spirito e la storia del secolo XIX di B. Croce. Varese, 1934.

Phil 4080.3.155   Ascoli, M. Intorno alla concezione del diritto nel sistema di Benedetto Croce. Roma, 1925.

Phil 4080.3.160   Cione, Edmondo. L'opera filosofica...di Benedetto Croce. Bari, 1942.

Phil 4080.3.160.2   Cione, Edmondo. Benedetto Croce. 2. ed. Milano, 1953.

Phil 4080.3.160.5   Cione, Edmondo. Bibliografia crociana. 1. ed. Milano, 1956.

Phil 4080.3.165   Romarell, Patrick. Croce versus Gentile. N.Y., 1946.

Phil 4080.3.170   Nicolini, Fausto. Benedetto Croce. Napoli, 1944.

Phil 4080.3.172   Nicolini, Fausto. Benedetto Croce. Torino, 1962.

Phil 4080.3.175   Parente, Alfredo. Il pensiero politico di Benedetto Croce e u nuovo liberalismo. 2. ed. Napoli, 1944.

Phil 4080.3.180   Sgoi, Carmelo. Benedetto Croce. Messina, 1947.

Phil 4080.3.185   Fano, Giorgio. La filosofia del Croce. 1a ed. Milano, 1946.

Phil 4080.3.190   LaVia, Pietro. Mente e realtà; il pensiero di Benedetto Croce. Firenze, 1947. 2v.

Phil 4080.3.195   Lombardi, A. La filosofia di Benedetto Croce. Roma, 1946.

Phil 4080.3.200   Derisi, Octavio N. La filosofia de espíritu. Madrid, 1947.

Phil 4080.3.201   Merlotti, Eric. L'intention spéculative de Benedetto Croce. (Filosofia dello spirito). Neuchâtel, 1970.

Phil 4080.3.205   Gramsci, Antonio. Il materialismo storico e la filosofia di Benedetto Croce. 2. ed. Torino, 1949.

Phil 4080.3.210   Sprigge, Cecil Jackson Squire. Benedetto Croce. Cambridge, Eng., 1952.

Phil 4080.3.211   Sprigge, Cecil Jackson Squire. Benedetto Croce. New Haven, 1952.

Phil 4080.3.215   Corsi, Mario. Le origini del pensiero di Benedetto Croce. 1. ed. Firenze, 1951.

Phil 4080.3.220   Marra, Dara. Conversazioni con Benedetto Croce su alcuni libri della sua biblioteca. Milano, 1952.

Phil 4080.3.225   Vettori, V. Benedetto Croce e gli studi contemporanei d'estetica e storia. Firenze, 1952.

Phil 4080.3.230   Sainati, V. L'estetica di Benedetto Croce. Firenze, 1953.

Phil 4080.3.235   Franchini, R. Note biografiche di Benedetto Croce. Torino, 1953.

Phil 4080.3.240   Olgiati, F. Benedetto Croce e lo storicismo. Milano, 1953.

Phil 4080.3.245   Osterwalder, T. Die Philosophie Benedetto Croces als moderne Ideenlehre. Berne, 1954.

Phil 4080.3.250   Guzzo, A. Croce e Gentile. Lugano, 1953.

Phil 4080.3.255   Letterature Moderne. Benedetto Croce. Milano, 1953.

Phil 4080.3.260   Antoni, Carlo. Commento a Croce. 1. ed. Venezia, 1955.

Phil 4080.3.265   Attisani, A. Interpretazioni crociane. Messina, 1953.

Phil 4080.3.270   Raggiunti, R. La conoscenza storica. Firenze, 1955.

Phil 4080.3.275   Comoth, René. Introduction à la philosophie politique de Benedetto Croce. Liège, 1955.

Phil 4080.3.280   Abbate, Michele. La filosofia di Benedetto Croce e la crisi della società italiano. Torino, 1955.

Phil 4080.3.281   Abbate, Michele. La filosofia di Benedetto Croce e la crisi della società italiana. Torino, 1966.

Phil 4080.3.285   Montano, Rocco. Arte. 1. ed. Napoli, 1951.

Phil 4080.3.290   Buenos Aires. Universidad Nacional. Benedetto Croce. Buenos Aires, 1954.

Phil 4080.3.295   Sartori, G. Croce etico-politico e filosofo. Firenze, 1956.

Phil 4080.3.300   Galati, Vito Giuseppe. Colloqui con Benedetto Croce. Brescia, 1957.

Phil 4080.3.305   Cantoni, Carlo. In memoria di Carlo Cantoni. Pavia, 1908.

Phil 4080.3.315   Vinceguerra, Mario. Croce. Napoli, 1957.

Phil 4080.3.320   Iofrida, Vincenzo. La liberta come fondamento dello stato. Milano, 1959.

Phil 4080.3.325   Bruno, Antonino. Economia ed etica nello svolgimento. Siracusa, 1958.

Phil 4080.3.330   Omaggio a Benedetto Croce. Torino, 1953.

Phil 4080.3.335   Tanga, Igino. L'estetica di Benedetto Croce nella storia del pensiero e della letteratura. Roma, 1959.

Phil 4080.3.340   Giordano-Orsini, Gian Napoleon. Benedetto Croce. Carbondale, 1961.

Phil 4080.3.345   Bulletin of Croce studies in U.S. Madison, Wis. 1-5,1959-1964//

Phil 4080.3.350   Gandolfo, Antonio. Benedetto Croce, critico dei contemporanei. Padova, 1958.

Phil 4080.3.355   Viola, Italo. Problemi di critica crociana. Milano, 1960.

Phil 4080.3.360   DeGennaro, Angelo A. The philosophy of Benedetto Croce. 1st ed. N.Y., 1961.

Phil 4080.3.365   Albeggiani, Ferdinando. Inizio e svolgimento della filosofia dello spirito di Benedetto Croce. Palermo, 1960?

Phil 4080.3.370   Svenaeus, G. Methodologie et spéculation esthétique. Lund, 1961.

Phil 4080.3.375   Agazzi, E. Il Giovane Croce e il Marxismo. Torino, 1962.

Phil 4080.3.380   Onufrio, Salvatore. La politica nel pensiero di Benedetto Croce. Milano, 1962.

Phil 4080.3.385   Murray, G. Benedetto Croce. London, 1953.

Phil 4080.3.390   Garosci, A. Il pensiero politico di Benedetto Croce. Torino, 1962.

Phil 4080.3.395   Grandi, M. Benedetto Croce e il seicento. Milano, 1962.

Phil 4080.3.400   Nicolini, F. Il Croce minore. Milano, 1963.

Phil 4080.3.405   Puppo, Mario. Croce critico e prosatore. Torino, 1953.

Phil 4080.3.405.5   Puppo, Mario. Il metodo e la critica di Benedetto Croce. Milano, 1964.

Phil 4080.3.405.10   Puppo, Mario. Croce e d'annunzio, e altri saggi. Firenze, 1964.

Phil 4080.3.410   Nicolini, F. Benedetto Croce. Roma, 1954.

Phil 4080.3.415   Rivista di studi crociani. Napoli. 1,1964+

Phil 4080.3.420   Focher, Ferruccio. Profilo dell'opera di Benedetto Croce. Cremona, 1963.

Phil 4080.3.425   Marone, Gherardo. Ensayo sobre el pensamiento de Benedet Croce. Buenos Aires, 1946.

Phil 4080.3.430   Capriviis, Vittorio de. Benedetto Croce. Milano, 1963.

Phil 4080.3.435   Mager, Wolfgang. Benedetto Croces literarisches und politisches Interesse an der Geschichte. Koln, 1965.

225

Classified Listing

Phil 4080 History of philosophy - Local Modern philosophy - Italy - Individual philosophers - Other C - cont.

Phil 4080.3.440 Capanna, Francesco. La religione in Benedetto Croce. Bari, 1964.
Phil 4080.3.445 Borsari, Silvano. L'opera di Benedetto Croce. Napoli, 1964.
Phil 4080.3.450 Brown, Merle Elliott. Neo-idealistic aesthetics. Detroit, 1966.
Phil 4080.3.455 Bausola, Adriano. Filosofia e storia nel pensiero crociano. Milano, 1965.
Phil 4080.3.456 Bausola, Adriano. Etica e politica. Milano, 1966.
Phil 4080.3.458 Feo, Italo de. Benedetto Croce e il suo mondo. Torino, 1966.
Phil 4080.3.460 Franchini, Raffaello. Croce interprete di Hegel e altri saggi filosofici. Napoli, 1964.
Phil 4080.3.461 Franchini, Raffaello. La teoria della storia di Benedetto Croce. Napoli, 1966.
Phil 4080.3.465 Lönne, Karl-Egon. Benedetto Croce als Kritiker seiner Zeit. Tübingen, 1967.
Phil 4080.3.470 Convegno Crociano, Bari. Interpretazioni crociane di R. Assunto. Bari, 1965.
Phil 4080.3.472 Roggerone, Giuseppe A. Benedetto Croce e la fondazione del concetto di libertà. Milano, 1966.
Phil 4080.3.475 Pagliano Ungari, Graziella. Croce in Francia; ricerche sulla fortuna dell'opera crociana. Napoli, 1967.
Phil 4080.3.480 Lentini, Giacinto. Croce e Gramsci. Palermo, 1967.
Phil 4080.3.485 Ricci, Angelo. Benedetto Croce. Pôrto Alegre, 1966.
Phil 4080.3.490 Topuridze, Elena I. Estetika Benedetto Kroche. Tbilisi, 1967.
Phil 4080.3.495 Alfieri, Vittorio Enzo. Pedagogia crociana. Napoli, 1967.
Phil 4080.3.498 Trieste. Università Facoltà di Lettere e Filosofia. Lezioni crociane. Trieste, 1967.
Phil 4080.3.500 Mattioli, Raffaele. Fedeltà a Croce. Milano, 1966.
Phil 4080.3.505 Benedetti, Ulisse. Benedetto Croce e il fascismo. Roma, 1967.
Phil 4080.3.510 Contini, Bian Franco. L'influenza culturale di Benedetto Croce. Milano, 1967.
Phil 4080.3.515 Benedetto Croce. Napoli, 1967.
Phil 4080.3.520 Biscione, Michele. Interpreti do Croce. Napoli, 1968.
Phil 4080.3.525 Sartori, Giovanni. Stato e politica nel pensiero di Benedetto Croce. Napoli, 1966.
Phil 4080.3.530 Dujovne, León. El pensamiento histórico de Benedetto Croce. Buenos Aires, 1968.
Phil 4080.3.535 Roggerone, Giuseppe A. Prospettive crociane. Lecce, 1968.
Phil 4080.3.540 Colapietra, Raffaele. Benedetto Croce e la politica italiana. Bari, 1969.
Phil 4080.3.545 Cotroneo, Girolamo. Croce e l'illuminismo. Napoli, 1970.
Phil 4080.3.550 Vitiello, Vincenzo. Storiografia e storia nel pensiero di Benedetto Croce. Napoli, 1968.
Phil 4080.4.30* Castilio, Baldessa. The courtier. London, 1588.
Phil 4080.5.31 Corleo, Simone. Filosofia universale. Palermo, 1860-63. 2v.
Phil 4080.5.32 Corleo, Simone. Il sistema della filosofia universale. Roma, 1879.
Phil 4080.5.90 Carlo, E. di. Simone Corleo. Palermo, 1924.
Phil 4080.6.80 Varchi, B. Vita di Francesco Cattani da Diacceto. Ancona, 1843.
Phil 4080.7.31 Colecchi, O. Sopra alcune quistioni...della filosofeia. Napoli, 1843.
Phil 4080.7.80 Cristallini, Alessandro. Ottario Colecchi, un filosofo da riscoprire. Padova, 1968.
Phil 4080.8.31 Conti, Augusto. Il buono nel vero. Libri quattro. Firenze, 1873. 2v.
Phil 4080.8.35 Conti, Augusto. Nuovi discorsi del tempo o famiglia, patria e Dio. Firenze, 1896-97. 2v.
Phil 4080.8.40 Conti, Augusto. Dio e il male. Prato, 1866.
Phil 4080.8.79 Pamphlet vol. Conti, Augusto. 5 pam.
Phil 4080.8.80 Romano, Pietro. La filosofia di Augusto Conti. Genova, 1895.
Phil 4080.8.83 Alfani, Augusto. Della vita e delle opere. Firenze, 1906.
Phil 4080.8.85 Barzellotti, G. Due filosofi italiani. Roma, 1908.
Phil 4080.8.87 Lantrua, A. La filosofia di Augusto Conti. Padova, 1955.
Phil 4080.9.33 Carlini, Armando. Avviamento allo studio della filosofia. 3a ed. Firenze, 1921.
Phil 4080.9.35 Carlini, Armando. La vita dello spirito. Firenze, 1921.
Phil 4080.9.39 Carlini, Armando. Il mito del realismo. Firenze, 1936.
Phil 4080.9.40 Carlini, Armando. Alla ricerca di me stesso. Firenze, 1951.
Phil 4080.9.45 Carlini, Armando. Dalla vita dello spirito al mito del realismo. Firenze, 1959.
Phil 4080.10.35 Ceretti, Pietro. Saggio circa la ragione logica di tutte le cose (Pasaelogices specimen). v.1-5. Torino, 1888-1905. 7v.
Phil 4080.10.60 Ceretti, Pietro. Opere postume. Torino, 1890.
Phil 4080.10.80 Ercole, P. d'. Il saggio di panlogica ovvero l'enciclopedia filosofica. Torino, 1911.
Phil 4080.10.85 Ercole, P. d'. Notizia degli scritti e del pensiere filosofico di Pietro Ceretti. Torino, 1866.
Phil 4080.10.88 Alemanni, V. Pietro Ceretti. Milano, 1904.
Phil 4080.11.80F Ferrari, G.M. Giovanni Caroli e la sua dottrina filosofica. Modena, 1926.
Phil 4080.12.30 Castelli, Enrico. Filosofia della vita. Roma, 1924.
Phil 4080.12.35 Castelli, Enrico. Introduction à une phenomenologie de notre epoque. Paris, 1949.
Phil 4080.12.45 Castelli, Enrico. L'enquête quotidienne. Paris, 1959.
Phil 4080.12.50 Castelli, Enrico. Le temps Larcelant. Paris, 1952.
Phil 4080.12.62 Castelli, Enrico. Il tempo esaurito. 2. ed. Milano, 1954.
Phil 4080.12.65 Castelli, Enrico. I paradossi del senso comune. Padova, 1970.
Phil 4080.13.30 Caria, G.M. de. Identità o contraddizione? Palermo, 1925.
Phil 4080.14.2 Celesia, Paolo. Opere. v.1-7. Roma, 1923-30. 8v.
Phil 4080.15.81 Renauld, J.F. L'oeuvre inachevée de Mario Calderoni. n.p., n.d.
Phil 4080.16 Consentino, A. Temps, espace devenir, moi. Paris, 1938.
Phil 4080.17 Carabellese, P. L'idealismo italiano. Napoli, 1938.
Phil 4080.17.5 Nobile Ventura, O.M. Filosofia e religione in un metafisico laico. 1. ed. Milano, 1951.
Phil 4080.17.10 Tebaldeschi, I. Il problema della natura nel pensiero di Pantaleo Carabellese. Roma, 1955.
Phil 4080.17.15 Semerari, G. Storia e storicismo. Trani, 1953.
Phil 4080.17.20 Giornate di Studi Carabellesiani, Bologna, 1960. Giornate di studi carabellesiani. Genoa, 1964.
Phil 4080.18 Calogero, Guido. La conclusione della filosofia del conoscere. Firenze, 1938.
Phil 4080.18.5 Calogero, Guido. Scritti. Firenze, 1960. 2v.
Phil 4080.18.10 Calogero, Guido. Quaderno laico. Bari, 1967.
Phil 4080.18.80 Raggiunti, Renzo. Tre brevi studi: La conclusione della filosofia del conoscere di Guido Calogero. Firenze, 1946.
Phil 4080.18.85 Raggiunti, Renzo. Logica e linguistica nel pensiero di Guido Calogero. Firenze, 1963.
Phil 4080.19 Chiavacci, G. La ragione poetica. Firenze, 1947.
Phil 4080.20.30 Cairola, G. Scritti. Torino, 1954.
Phil 4080.21 Caracciolo, A. La persona e il tempo. 1. ed. pt. 1. Arona, 1955.
Phil 4080.22.31 Coresi, Vincenzo. Assoluto e relativo. 1. ed. Bergamo, 1959.
Phil 4080.23 Cicinato, Dante. Verso il trascendimento. Palmi, 1959.
Phil 4080.24 Corsini, Edoardo. Institutiones philosophicae. Venetius, 1743.
Phil 4080.25 Cini, Giovanni. Senso e natura. Firenze, 1959?
Phil 4080.26 Cantoni, Remo. Tragico e senso comune. Cremona, 1963.
Phil 4080.26.10 Cantoni, Remo. La vita quotidiana. Milano, 1966.
Phil 4080.27 Crescini, Angelo. Per una metafisica concreta. Padova, 1963.
Phil 4080.28 Ciardo, Manlio. Esteticità della dialettica nella vita dello spirito. Pisa, 1965.
Phil 4080.30 Cristaldi, Giuseppe. Filosofia e verità; saggi e note. Milano, 1965.
Phil 4080.32 Martano, Giuseppe. La filosofia dell'esperienza di Cleto Carbonara. Napoli, 1965.
Phil 4080.34 Carena, Giacinto. Essai d'un parallèle entre les forces physiques et les forces morales. Turin, 1817.
Phil 4080.36 Grocholl, Wolfgang. Der Mensch in seinem ursprünglichen Sein nach der Lehre Landulfs von Neapel. München, 1969.
Phil 4080.38 Campanale, Domenico. Fondamento e problemi della metafisica. Bari, 1968-
Phil 4080.40 Cardone, Domenico Antonio. L'ozio, la contemplazione, il giuoco, la tecnica. Roma, 1968.
Phil 4080.40.5 Cardone, Domenico Antonio. La filosofia nella storia civile del mondo. Roma, 1966.

Phil 4110 History of philosophy - Local Modern philosophy - Italy - Individual philosophers - F

Htn Phil 4110.1.30F* Ficino, Marsilio. Opera. Basileae, 1576. 2v.
Phil 4110.1.80 Saitta, Giuseppe. La filosofia di Marsilio Ficino. Messina, 1923.
Phil 4110.1.85 Hobert, Werner. Metaphysik des Marsilius Ficinus. Inaug. Diss. Koblenz, 1930.
Phil 4110.1.89 Kristeller, Paul Oskar. The philosophy of Marsilio Ficino. Gloucester, Mass., 1964.
Phil 4110.2.31 Florenzi Waddington, Marianna. Saggi di psicologia e di logica. Firenze, 1864.
Phil 4110.2.35 Florenzi Waddington, Marianna. Saggio sulla filosofia dello spirito. Firenze, 1867.
Phil 4110.2.81 In morte della M. sa Marianna Florenzi Waddington tributo di dolore. Perugia, 1870.
Phil 4110.2.85 Leonij, Lorenzo. Notizie della vita di Marianna Florenzi Waddington. Todi, 1865.
Phil 4110.3.80 Marino, L. Gli elementi di filosofia del professore Francesco Fiorentino. Napoli, 1878.
Phil 4110.3.83 Onoranze funebri a Francesco Fiorentino. Napoli, 1885.
Phil 4110.3.86 La Giovine Calabria. Giornale, Catanzaro. Per Francesco Fiorentino nella inaugurazione del monumento in Catanzaro. Catanzaro, 1889.
Phil 4110.3.89 Ferrari, G.M. Commemorazione di Francesco Fiorentino. Roma, 1891.
Phil 4110.3.92 Chimirri, Bruno. Inaugurazione del monumento a Francesco Fiorentino in Sambiase, 15 novembre 1908. Catanzaro, 1908.
Phil 4110.3.95F In memoria di Francesco Fiorentino. Catanzaro, 1889.
Phil 4110.4.79 Pamphlet box. Ferri, Luigi.
Phil 4110.4.90F Ferri commemorazione prof. Luigi. Roma, 1885.
Phil 4110.4.93 Cantoni, Carlo. Luigi Ferri. Roma, 1895.
Phil 4110.4.95 Dejob, Charles. Notice sur Luigi Ferri. Versailles, 1896.
Phil 4110.4.98 Barzellotti, G. Commemorazione dell'accademico Luigi Ferri. Roma, 1895.
Phil 4110.4.99 Barzellotti, G. Luigi Ferri. Roma, 1895.
Phil 4110.4.102 Tauro, G. Luigi Ferri. Roma, 1896.
Phil 4110.5.28 Ferrari, G. Filosofia della rivoluzione. v.1-2. Londra, 1851.
Phil 4110.5.30 Ferrari, G. Filosofia della rivoluzione. v.1-2. 2. ed. Milano, 1873.
Phil 4110.5.33 Ferrari, G. Filosofia della rivoluzione. 2. ed. Milano, 1923.
Phil 4110.5.80 Rota Ghibandi, Silvia. Giuseppe Ferrari. L'evoluzione del suo pensiero (1838-1860). Firenze, 1969.
Phil 4110.5.90 Cantoni, Carlo. Giuseppe Ferrari. Milano, 1878.
Phil 4110.5.95F Ferri, Luigi. Cenno su Giuseppe Ferrari e le sul dottrine. Roma, 1877.
Phil 4110.6.30 Filippi, Liutprando. Realtà e idealità. Napoli, 1937.
Phil 4110.8.30 Fedi, Remo. Il bene e la libertà. Milano, 1944.
Phil 4110.9.30 Fabro, Cornelio. Problemi dell'esistenzialismo. Roma, 1945.
Phil 4110.10.30 Fabi, Bruno. Il tutto e il nulla. 1. ed. Milano, 1952.
Phil 4110.11.30 Schiavone, Michelle. Problemi filosofia in Marsilio Ficino. Milano, 1951.
Phil 4110.11.35 Kuczyńska, Alicja. Filozofia i seoria piękna Marsilia Ficina. Wyd. 1. Warszawa, 1970.
Phil 4110.12.30 Fancelli, M. Discorso sulla speranza. Messina, 1960.
Phil 4110.13.30 Fortunato da Brescia. Philosophia sensuum mechanica methodice tractata atque ad usus academicos accommodata. Venetiis, 1756.
Phil 4110.14.30 Fichera, G. Crisi e valori, ed altri saggi. Padova, 1958.
Phil 4110.15.80 Fazio-Allmayer, Bruna. Esistenza e realtà nella fenomenologia di Vito Fazio-Allmayer. Bologna, 1968.

Phil 4112 History of philosophy - Local Modern philosophy - Italy - Individual philosophers - Galluppi, Pasquale

Phil 4112.30 Galluppi, Pasquale. Elementi di filosofia. v.1-2. Firenze, 1834.
Phil 4112.30.2 Galluppi, Pasquale. Elementi di filosofia. Bologna, 1837. 3v.
Phil 4112.30.5 Galluppi, Pasquale. Elementi di filosofia. v.1-6. 3. ed. Napoli, 1834-37. 3v.
Phil 4112.30.6 Galluppi, Pasquale. Elementi di filosofia. v.2. Roma, 1963-
Phil 4112.31 Galluppi, Pasquale. Introduzione allo studio della filosofia. Milano, 1832.
Phil 4112.35 Galluppi, Pasquale. Saggio filosofico. v.1-6. 1a ed. Milano, 1846-47. 3v.
Htn Phil 4112.39* Galluppi, Pasquale. Lettere filosofiche. Messina, 1827.
Phil 4112.39.5 Galluppi, Pasquale. Lettere filosofiche. Firenze, 1842.
Phil 4112.40 Galluppi, Pasquale. Lettere filosofiche. Firenze, 1833.
Phil 4112.40.2 Galluppi, Pasquale. Lettere filosofiche. Napoli, 1838.

Classified Listing

Phil 4112.40.6   Galluppi, Pasquale. Lettere filosofiche. 2a ed. Firenze, 1925.

Phil 4112.40.7   Galluppi, Pasquale. Lettere filosofiche e lezioni di logica e metafisica. Torino, 1925?

Phil 4112.41   Galluppi, Pasquale. Lettres philosophiques. Paris, 1844.

Phil 4112.45   Galluppi, Pasquale. Lezioni di logica e metafisica. v.1-4. Milano, 1845-46. 2v.

Phil 4112.50   Galluppi, Pasquale. Filosofia della volonta. Napoli, 1832-40. 4v.

Phil 4112.55.3   Galluppi, Pasquale. Considerazioni filosofiche sull'idealismo transcendentale. 3a ed. Torino, 1857.

Phil 4112.60   Galluppi, Pasquale. Sull'analisi e la sintesi. Firenze, 1935.

Phil 4112.75   Galluppi, Pasquale. Una memoria. Padova, 1957.

Phil 4112.79   Pamphlet vol. Galluppi, Pasquale. 4 pam.

Phil 4112.80   Lastrucci, V. Pasquale Galluppi; studio critico. Firenze, 1890.

Phil 4112.81   Palhoriès, F. La theorie idéologique de Galluppi. Paris, 1909.

Phil 4112.82   Pagano, V. Galluppi e la filosofia italiana. Napoli, 1897.

Htn   Phil 4112.83*   Arnone, N. Pasquale Galluppi giacobino. Napoli, 1912.

Phil 4112.84   Campari, A. Galluppi e Kant nella dottrina morale. Conegliano, 1907.

Phil 4112.85   Tranfo, C.T. Saggio sulla filosofia del Galluppi. Napoli, 1902.

Phil 4112.86   Cursi, C.M. Onori funebri che alla memoria di Pasquale Galluppi. Napoli, 1847.

Phil 4112.87   Giuli, G. de. La filosofia di Pasquale Galluppi. Palermo, 1935.

Phil 4112.88   Auria, Renata d'. Il Galluppi. Roma, 1942.

Phil 4112.89   Napoli, G. di. La filosofia di Pasquale Galluppi. Padova, 1947.

Phil 4112.90   Cardone, Elsa. La teologia razionale di P. Galluppi. Palmi, 1959.

Phil 4114 History of philosophy - Local Modern philosophy - Italy - Individual philosophers - Genovesi, Antonio

Phil 4114.20   Genovesi, Antonio. Autobiografia, lettere e altri scritti. Milano, 1962.

Phil 4114.23   Genovesi, Antonio. Elementorum artis logico criticae. n.p., 1766.

Phil 4114.23.10   Genovesi, Antonio. Elementorum artis logico criticae. Neapoli, 1778.

Phil 4114.25   Genovesi, Antonio. Elementa metaphysicae mathematicum in morem adornata. 2a ed. Neapoli, 1751-56. 4v.

Phil 4114.25.3   Genovesi, Antonio. Disciplinarum metaphysicarum elementa. Bassani, 1785. 5v.

Phil 4114.30   Genovesi, Antonio. Delle scienze metafisiche. Venezia, 1782.

Phil 4114.31   Genovesi, Antonio. Delle scienze metafisiche. Napoli, 1791.

Phil 4114.32   Genovesi, Antonio. Denoihnsion stoixeia, metafisikis. Vienna, 1806.

Phil 4114.40   Genovesi, Antonio. La logica. Napoli, 1790.

Phil 4114.45   Genovesi, Antonio. Della diceosina o sia della filosofia sul religione. Napoli, n.d. 3v.

Phil 4114.47   Genovesi, Antonio. Meditazioni filosofiche sulla religione e sulla morale. Bassano, 1783.

Phil 4114.50   Genovesi, Antonio. Lettere filosofiche. Napoli, 1785.

Phil 4114.71   Genovesi, Antonio. Opuscoli e lettere familiari. Venezia, 1827.

Phil 4114.75   Genovesi, Antonio. Lettere familiari. Venezia, 1844. 2v.

Phil 4114.80   Racioppi, G. Antonio Genovesi. Napoli, 1871.

Phil 4114.81   Pamphlet vol. Robba, R. Commemorazione di A. Genovesi. 2 pam.

Phil 4114.85   Demarco, Domenico. Quello che è vivo del pensiero economico di Antonio Genovesi. Napoli, 1957.

Phil 4114.90   Corpaci, Francesco. Antonio Genovesi. Milano, 1966.

Phil 4115 History of philosophy - Local Modern philosophy - Italy - Individual philosophers - Gioberti, Vincenzo

Phil 4115.12   Gioberti, V. Opere edite ed inedite. v. 1-7, 13. Brusselle, 1843-44. 6v.

Phil 4115.14   Gioberti, V. Opere. v. 1-16. Napoli, 1845- 7v.

Phil 4115.20   Gioberti, V. Scritti scelti. Torino, 1954.

Phil 4115.23   Gioberti, V. Pagine scelte, edite ed inedite. Torino, 1922.

Phil 4115.24   Gioberti, V. L'Italia, la chiesa e la civiltà universale. Torino, 1926.

Phil 4115.25   Gioberti, V. Nuova protologia brani scelti da tutte le sue opere. Bari, 1912. 2v.

Phil 4115.27   Gioberti, V. Pensieri. Torino, 1859-60. 2v.

Phil 4115.28   Gioberti, V. Studi filologici. Torino, 1867.

Phil 4115.30   Gioberti, V. Del buono, del bello. Firenze, 1850.

Phil 4115.30.2   Gioberti, V. Del buono, del bello. Firenze., 1853.

Phil 4115.30.5   Gioberti, V. Del buono. Napoli, 1848.

Phil 4115.31   Gioberti, V. Cours de philosophie, 1841-1842. Milano, 1947.

Phil 4115.33   Gioberti, V. Introduzione allo studio della filosofia. v.1-2. Brusselle, 1840. 3v.

Phil 4115.33.5   Gioberti, V. Introduzione allo studio della filosofia. 2a ed. v.1-4. Capolago, 1845-46. 2v.

Phil 4115.33.10   Gioberti, V. Introduzione allo studio della filosofia. v.1-4. Napoli, 1846-47.

Phil 4115.34   Gioberti, V. Introduzione allo studio della filosofia. Milano, 1850. 2v.

Phil 4115.34.6   Gioberti, V. Introduzione allo studio della filosofia. Firenze, 1926.

Phil 4115.35   Gioberti, V. Introduction à l'étude de la philosophie. Moulins, 1845-47. 4v.

Phil 4115.36   Pigliano, V. Introduction à l'étude de la philosophie. Paris, 1847. 3v.

Phil 4115.40   Gioberti, V. Della protologia. Torino, 1857-58. 2v.

Phil 4115.40.5   Gioberti, V. Protologia; estratti. Torino, 1924.

Phil 4115.42   Gioberti, V. La teorica delle mente umana. Milano, 1910.

Phil 4115.50   Gioberti, V. Teorica del sovranaturale. Capolago, 1850. 2v.

Phil 4115.50.5   Gioberti, V. Teorica del sovranaturale. Venezia, 1850.

Phil 4115.51   Gioberti, V. Della filosofia della rivelazione. Torino, 1856.

Phil 4115.53   Gioberti, V. Meditazioni filosofiche inedite. Firenze, 1909.

Phil 4115.55   Gioberti, V. Essay on the beautiful. London, 1871.

Phil 4115.60   Gioberti, V. Il pensiero civile. Torino, 1901.

Phil 4115.65   Gioberti, V. Grundzüge eines Systems der Ethik. Mainz, 1848.

Phil 4115.75   Gioberti, V. Epistolario. Firenze, 1927-37. 11v.

Phil 4115.76   Gioberti, V. Lettere inedite di V. Gioberti e P. Galluppi. Roma, 1920.

Phil 4115.79   Bruers, A. Gioberti. (Guide bibliografiche). Roma, 1924.

Phil 4115.80   Rosmini-Serbati, A. Vincenzo Gioberti. Lucca, 1853.

Phil 4115.80.5   Rosmini-Serbati, A. Vincenzo Gioberti e il panteismo. Milano, 1847.

Phil 4115.80.10   Rosmini-Serbati, A. Vincenzo Gioberti e il panteismo. Napoli, 1847.

Phil 4115.81   Gioberti, V. Primo centenario di V. Gioberti. Torino, 1901. 2 pam.

Phil 4115.82   Zarelli, T. Il sistema filosofico di V. Gioberti. Paris, 1848.

Phil 4115.82.5   Gioberti e Zarelli. Pisa, 1851.

Phil 4115.83   Morkos, D. Spiegazione analitica della formola ideale di V. Gioberti. Torino, 1865.

Phil 4115.84   Ern, V.F. Filosofiia dzhoberti. Moskva, 1916.

Phil 4115.85   Saitta, Giuseppe. Il pensiero di Vincenzo Gioberti. Messina, 1917.

Phil 4115.85.2   Saitta, Giuseppe. Il pensiero di Vincenzo Gioberti. 2a ed. Firenze, 1927.

Phil 4115.86   Piccoli, Valentino. Vincenzo Gioberti. Roma, 1923.

Phil 4115.86.5   Piccoli, Valentino. L'estetica di Vincenzo Gioberti. Milano, 1917.

Phil 4115.87   Sgroi, Carmelo. L'estetica e la critica letteraria in V. Gioberti. Firenze, 1921.

Phil 4115.87.10   Calcaterra, C. Polemica giobertiana. Torino, 1923.

Phil 4115.88   Caramella, S. La formazione della filosofia giobertiana. Genova, 1926.

Phil 4115.89   Palhories, F. Gioberti. Paris, 1929.

Phil 4115.90   Bonnetty, A. Examen critique de la philosophie de Gioberti. Paris, 1847-49. 2 pam.

Phil 4115.91   Spaventa, B. La filosofia di Gioberti. v.1. Napoli, 1863.

Phil 4115.91.2   Spaventa, B. La filosofia di Gioberti. Napoli, 1870.

Phil 4115.92   Luciani, P. Gioberti e la filosofia nuova italiana. Napoli, 1866-72. 3v.

Phil 4115.93   Balbino, G. Il primato d'un popolo; Fichte e Gioberti. Catania, 1916.

Phil 4115.94   Rinaldi, R. Gioberti e il problema religioso del risorgimento. Firenze, 1929.

Phil 4115.96   Gioberti, V. Réponse à un article. Bruxelles, 1844.

Phil 4115.98   Gioberti, V. Una lettera inedita a Taparelli d'Azeglio. Roma, 1923.

Phil 4115.99   Gentile, G. Rosmini e Gioberti. Pisa, 1898.

Phil 4115.100   Sordi, Serafino. I misteri di Demofilo. Milano, 1850. 3 pam.

Phil 4115.105   Fusco, Maria. Vincenzo Gioberti, critico letterario. Catania, 1940.

Phil 4115.106   Crescenzo, G. de. Pietro Luciani e il giobertismo. Napoli, 1960.

Phil 4115.107   Ercole, Pasquale d'. Commemorazione della personalità e del pensiero filosofico. Torino, 1901.

Phil 4115.110   Portale, Vincenzo. L'ontologismo di Vincenzo Gioberti; antologia sistematica. Cosenza, 1968.

Phil 4120 History of philosophy - Local Modern philosophy - Italy - Individual philosophers - Other G

Phil 4120.1.8   Gioja, Melchiorre. Opere principali. Lugano, 1838-40. 16v.

Phil 4120.1.10   Gioja, Melchiorre. Opere minori. Lugano, 1832-37. 17v.

Phil 4120.1.30   Gioja, Melchiorre. Elementi di filosofia ad uso de'Giovanetti. Milano, 1822. 2v.

Phil 4120.1.31   Gioja, Melchiorre. Elementi di filosofia ad uso de'Giovanetti. v.1-2. Milano, 1838.

Phil 4120.1.32F   Gioja, Melchiorre. Del merito e delle ricompense; trattato storico e filosofico. v. 1-2. 2. ed. Lugano, 1830.

Phil 4120.1.33   Gioja, Melchiorre. Del merito e delle ricompense. Lugano, 1839. 2v.

Phil 4120.1.35   Gioja, Melchiorre. Del merito e delle ricompenae. Torino, 1853. 2v.

Phil 4120.1.40   Gioja, Melchiorre. Ideologia. Milano, 1822-23. 2v.

Phil 4120.1.45   Gioja, Melchiorre. Esercizio logico sugli errori d'ideologia. Milano, 1824.

Phil 4120.1.50   Gioja, Melchiorre. La causa di Dio e degli uomini difesa dagl'insulti degli empj e dalle pretensioni dei fanatici. Lugano, 1834.

Phil 4120.1.80   Pamphlet vol. Gioja, Melchiorre. 4 pam.

Phil 4120.1.81   Semprini, G. Melchiorre Gioia e la sua dottrina politica. Genova, 1934.

Phil 4120.2.30   Guastella, Cosmo. Le ragioni del fenomenismo. v. 1-3. Palermo, 1921-23. 2v.

Phil 4120.2.90   Carlo, Eugenio di. Cosmo Guastella. Palermo, 1923.

Phil 4120.2.92   Albeggiani, F. Il sistema filosofico di Cosmo Guastella. Firenze, 1927.

Phil 4120.3.30   Giovanni, V. di. Principii di filosofia prima. Palermo, 1863. 2v.

Phil 4120.3.32   Giovanni, V. di. Sofismi e buon senso, serati campestri. 2. ed. Palermo, 1873.

Phil 4120.3.90   Titoli del professore Vincenzo di Giovanni. Palermo, 1870.

Phil 4120.4.11   Gentile, Giovanni. Opere. v. 1-28,30-38,42. Firenze, 1942. 36v.

Phil 4120.4.31   Gentile, Giovanni. Discorsi di religone. 3. ed. Firenze, 1934.

Phil 4120.4.35   Gentile, Giovanni. I fondamenti della filosofia del oiritto. 3. ed. Firenze, 1937.

Phil 4120.4.45   Gentile, Giovanni. Introduzione alla filosofia. Milano, 1933.

Phil 4120.4.47   Puglisi, F. La pedagogia di G. Gentile. v.1-2. Catania, 1953-54.

Phil 4120.4.50   Piglianu, A. Giovanni Gentile. Sassari, 1953.

Phil 4120.4.55   Gentile, Giovanni. Gentile. Roma, 1966.

Phil 4120.4.79   Pamphlet box. Miscellaneous pamphlets.

Phil 4120.4.80   Volpe, Galvano della. L'idealismo dell'atto e il problema delle categorie. Bologna, 1924.

Phil 4120.4.81   Chiocchetti, E. La filosofia di Giovanni Gentile. Milano, 1922.

Phil 4120.4.82   La Via, M. L'idealismo attuale di Giovanni Gentile. Trani, 1925.

Phil 4120.4.83   Sarlo, F. de. Gentile e Croce. Firenze, 1925.

Phil 4120.4.84   Aebischer, Max. Der Einzelne und der Staat nachtreibung Giovanni Gentile. Schweiz, 1954.

Phil 4120.4.85   Holmes, Roger W. The idealism of Giovanni Gentile. N.Y., 1937.

Classified Listing

Phil 4120 History of philosophy - Local Modern philosophy - Italy - Individual philosophers - Other G - cont.

Phil 4120.4.87 Romanelli, P. Gentile. N.Y., 1938.
Phil 4120.4.89 Harris, Henry S. The social philosophy of Giovanni Gentile. Urbana, 1960.
Phil 4120.4.90 Gentile, Giovanni. Introduzione alla filosofia. 2. ed. Firenze, 1952.
Phil 4120.4.95 Fondazione Giovanni Gentile per gli Studi Filosofici. Giovanni Gentile. Firenze, 1948-51. 13v.
Phil 4120.4.100 Andreola, A. Giovanni Gentile a la sua scuola. Milano, 1951.
Phil 4120.4.105 Vettori, V. Giovanni Gentile. Firenze, 1954.
Phil 4120.4.110 Spirito, Ugo. Note sur pensiero di Giovanni Gentile. Firenze, 1954.
Phil 4120.4.115 Puglisi, Filippo. La concezione estetico-filosofica di Giovanni Gentile. Catania, 1955.
Phil 4120.4.120 Liguori, Ersilia. La pedagogia come scienza filosofica di Giovanni Gentile. Padova, 1951.
Phil 4120.4.125 Gentile, Giovanni. Il concetlo moderno della scienza e il problema universitario. Roma, 1921.
Phil 4120.4.126 Gentile, Giovanni. La religione: il modernismo e i rapporti tra religione e filosofia. Firenze, 1965.
Phil 4120.4.130 Spirito, Ugo. Giovanni Gentile. Firenze, 1969.
Phil 4120.4.135 Signorini, Alberto. Il giovane Gentile e Marx. Milano, 1966.
Phil 4120.4.140 Smith, William Aloysius. Giovanni Gentile on the existence of God. Louvain, 1970.
Phil 4120.6.90 Fiorentino, F. Della vita e delle opere di Vincenzo de Grazia. Napoli, 1877.
Phil 4120.6.95 Varano, F.S. Vincenzo de Grazia. Napoli, 1931.
Htn Phil 4120.7.30* Galilei, Galileo. Dialogo. Fiorenza, 1632.
Phil 4120.8.30 Guzzo, Augusto. La scienza. Torino, 1955.
Phil 4120.8.35 Guzzo, Augusto. La moralitá. Torino, 1950.
Phil 4120.8.40 Guzzo, Augusto. Parerga. Torino, 1956.
Phil 4120.8.45 Guzzo, Augusto. Discorsi, 1938-50. Torino, 1951.
Phil 4120.9.30 Galli, Gallo. Linee fondamentali d'une filosofia dello spirito. Torino, 1961.
Phil 4120.9.35 Galli, Gallo. L'uomo nell'assoluto. Torino, 1965.
Phil 4120.9.82 Gallo Galli. 2. ed. Torino, 1968.

Phil 4135 History of philosophy - Local Modern philosophy - Italy - Individual philosophers - I

Phil 4135.1 Iaja, Donato. Saggi filosofici. Napoli, 1886.

Phil 4140 History of philosophy - Local Modern philosophy - Italy - Individual philosophers - J

Phil 4140.80 Cristallini, Alessandro. Il pensiero filosofico de Donato Jaja. Padova, 1970.

Phil 4160 History of philosophy - Local Modern philosophy - Italy - Individual philosophers - L

Phil 4160.1.33 Labanca, Baldassare. Della filosofia razionale. 2a ed. Firenze, 1868. 2v.
Phil 4160.1.40 Labanca, Baldassare. Il mio testamento. Agnone, 1913.
Phil 4160.1.85 Labanca, Baldassare. Ricordi autobiografici. Agnone, 1913.
Phil 4160.5.30 Lazzerini, Virgilio. Annotaziori per un nuovo criticismo. Milano, 1965.
Phil 4160.5.230 Lazzarini, Renato. Valore e religione nell'orizzonte esistenziale. Padova, 1965.
Phil 4160.5.280 Modenato, Francesca. Intenzionalità e storia in Renato Lazzarini. Bologna, 1967.
Phil 4160.41.30 Librizzi, Carmelo. Morale e religione. Padova, 1962.
Phil 4160.41.35 Librizzi, Carmelo. Letteratura, arte, filosofia. Padova, 1969.
Phil 4160.66.12 Lombardi, Franco. Scritti; saggi. v.10-13. Firenze, 1965- 4v.
Phil 4160.66.12.2 Lombardi, Franco. Scritti; saggi. v.11- 2. ed. Firenze, 1970-
Phil 4160.66.14 Lombardi, Franco. Scritti. Opere. Firenze, 1963- 6v.

Phil 4170 History of philosophy - Local Modern philosophy - Italy - Individual philosophers - M

Htn Phil 4170.1.30* Manuzio, Paolo. De gli elementi. Venetia, 1557.
Phil 4170.2.80 Pamphlet box. Moglia, Agostino.
Phil 4170.3.80 Vecchio-Veneziani, Augusta del. La vita e l'opere di A.C. de Meis. Bologna, 1921.
Phil 4170.3.82 Amante, B. Un santo nel secolo XIX: A.C. de Meis. Lanciano, 1920.
Phil 4170.3.84 Croce, B. Ricerche e documenti Desanctisiani. Dal carteggio inedito di A.C. de Meis. Napoli, 1915.
Phil 4170.3.86 Negrelli, Giorgio. Storicismo e moderatismo nel pensiero politico di Angelo Camillo de Meis. Milano, 1968.
Phil 4170.4.31 Masci, F. Pensiero e conoscenza. Torino, 1922.
Phil 4170.5.30 Maturi, S. Introduzione alla filosofia. Bari, 1913.
Phil 4170.5.80 Pra, Mario dal. Il pensiero di Sebastiano Maturi. Milano, 1943.
Phil 4170.6.30 Marchesini, G. La dottrina positiva delle idealità. Roma, 1913.
Phil 4170.6.35 Marchesini, G. Il simbolismo nella conoscenza. Torino, 1901.
Phil 4170.6.40 Marchesini, G. Le finzioni dell'anima. Bari, 1905.
Phil 4170.7 Richerche di psichiatria...dedicate al...E. Morselli. Milano, 1907.
Phil 4170.7.30 Mamiani della Rovere, Terenzio. Compendio e sintesi della propriafilosofia. Torino, 1876.
Phil 4170.7.33 Mamiani della Rovere, Terenzio. Confessioni di un metafisico. Firenze, 1865. 2v.
Phil 4170.7.35 Mamiani della Rovere, Terenzio. Dell'ontologia e del metodo. Parigi, 1841.
Phil 4170.7.36 Mamiani della Rovere, Terenzio. Dell'ontologia e del metodo. 2a ed. Firenze, 1843.
Phil 4170.7.37 Mamiani della Rovere, Terenzio. Dell'ontologia e del metodo. 2a ed. Firenze, 1848.
Phil 4170.7.40 Mamiani della Rovere, Terenzio. Della religione positiva e perpetua. Milano, 1880.
Phil 4170.7.43 Mamiani della Rovere, Terenzio. Critica delle rivelazioni. Roma, 1873.
Phil 4170.7.46 Mamiani della Rovere, Terenzio. Dialoghi di scienza prima. Parigi, 1846.
Phil 4170.7.48 Mamiani della Rovere, Terenzio. Lo Spedalieri. Roma, 1894.
Phil 4170.7.50 Mamiani della Rovere, Terenzio. Discorso proemiale letto li 10 nov. 1850. Genova, 1850.
Phil 4170.7.52 Mamiani della Rovere, Terenzio. Nuovo discorso proemiale. Genova, 1852.
Phil 4170.7.60 Mamiani della Rovere, Terenzio. Le meditazioni cartesiane rinnovate nel seccolo XIX. Firenze, 1869.

Phil 4170 History of philosophy - Local Modern philosophy - Italy - Individual philosophers - M - cont.

Phil 4170.7.90 Angelini, A. Di Terenzio Mamiani filosofo. Roma, 1885. 2v.
Phil 4170.7.93 Mamini, C. Diagnosi comparativa della filosofia di Rosmini e di Mamiani. Bologna, 1860.
Phil 4170.7.96 Pamphlet vol. The philosophy of Mamiani della Rovere, Terenzio. 3 pam.
Phil 4170.7.98 Tavianini, U. Una polemica filosofica dell'1800. Padova, 1955.
Phil 4170.8.90 Giovanni, V. di. Il Miceli ovvero dell'ente uno e reale. Palermo, 1864.
Phil 4170.9.30 Mancino, Salvatore. Lettere inedito di S. Mancino a V. Coasin. Palermo, 1936.
Phil 4170.9.90 Giovanni, V. di. Salvatore Mancino e l'ecletticismo in Sicilia. Palermo, 1867.
Phil 4170.10.30 Martinetti, P. Il compito della filosofia e altri saggi inediti ed editi. 1. ed. Torino, 1951.
Phil 4170.10.80 Sciacca, Michele F. Martinetti. Brescia, 1943.
Phil 4170.10.85 Pellegrino, U. Religione ed educazione nell'idealismo trascendente di Piero Martinetti. Brescia, 1956.
Phil 4170.10.90 Romano, F. Il pensiero filosofico di Piero Martinetti. Padova, 1959.
Phil 4170.11.80 Pietrangeli, Alfonso. Filippo Maxi e il suo neocriticismo. Padova, 1962.
Phil 4170.12 Mei, F. Storia e significato del superuomo. Milano, 1962.
Phil 4170.12.5 Mei, Flavio. La missione del filosofo. Milano, 1964.
Phil 4170.12.10 Mei, Flavio. Eroicità ed ereticalità della filosofia. Milano, 1968.
Phil 4170.13 Monti, G.F. Anima brutorum secundum sanioris. Neapoli, 1742.
Phil 4170.14 Mazzilli, Stefano. I sommi problemi. Padova, 1963. 2v.
Phil 4170.16 Pró Diego F. Rodolfo Mondolfo. v.1-2. Buenos Aires, 1967-68.
Phil 4170.16.5 Bassi, Enrico. Rodolfo Mondolfo nella vita e nel pensiero socialista. Bologna, 1968.
Phil 4170.16.10 Omaggio a Rodolfo Mondolfo. Urbino, 1963.
Phil 4170.18.30 Magnini, Carlomagno. Introduzione alla critica della scienza. Bologna, 1969.

Phil 4180 History of philosophy - Local Modern philosophy - Italy - Individual philosophers - N

Phil 4180.1 Nizzoli, Mario. De veris principiis et vera ratione philosophandi contra pseudophilosophos. Roma, 1956. 2v.
Phil 4180.2 Nobile-Ventura, Attilio. La maschera e il volto della nostra società. Milano, 1965.

Phil 4190 History of philosophy - Local Modern philosophy - Italy - Individual philosophers - O

Phil 4190.1.30 Orestano, Francesco. Nuovi princèpi. Milano, 1939.
Phil 4190.1.35 Orestano, Francesco. Idee econcetti. Milano, 1939.
Phil 4190.1.40 Orestano, Francesco. Il nuovo realismo. Milano, 1939.
Phil 4190.1.45 Orestano, Francesco. Nuove vedute logiche. Milano, 1939.
Phil 4190.1.80 Dollo, Corrado. Il pensiero filosofico di Francesco Orestano. Padova, 1967.
Phil 4190.1.90 Ottaviano, Carmelo. Il pensiero di Francesco Orestano. Palermo, 1933.
Phil 4190.2.30 Ottaviano, Carmelo. La tragicita del reale. Padova, 1964.
Phil 4190.2.80 Mazzarella, Pasquale. Ira finito e infinito; saggio sul pensiero di Carmelo Ottaviano. Padova, 1961.
Phil 4190.3.30 Ottonello, Pier Paolo. Dialogo e silenzio. Milano, 1967.

Phil 4195 History of philosophy - Local Modern philosophy - Italy - Individual philosophers - Pico della Mirandola, Giovanni

Phil 4195.3F Pico della Mirandola, Giovanni. Opera omnia. Reggio, 1506.
Htn Phil 4195.5* Pico della Mirandola, Giovanni. Opera omnia. Basileae, 1573. 2v.
Phil 4195.6F Pico della Mirandola, Giovanni. Opera quae extant omnia. Basileae, 1601.
Phil 4195.7F Pico della Mirandola, Giovanni. Joannes Pieus Mirandulanus Opera omnia. Torino, 1971.
Phil 4195.10 Pico della Mirandola, Giovanni. Ausgewählte Schriften. Jena, 1905.
Htn Phil 4195.30* Pico della Mirandola, Giovanni. Conclusiones nongentae. n.p., 1532.
Phil 4195.32 Pico della Mirandola, Giovanni. Le sette sposizioni. Pescia, 1555.
Phil 4195.34 Pico della Mirandola, Giovanni. Disputationes adversus astrolo;iam divinatricem. Firenze, 1946-52. 2v.
Phil 4195.36 Pico della Mirandola, Giovanni. Dignità dell'uomo. 3. ed. Firenze, 1945.
Phil 4195.36.2 Pico della Mirandola, Giovanni. Dignità dell'uomo. 2. ed. Firenze, 1943.
Phil 4195.36.5 Pico della Mirandola, Giovanni. La dignità dell'uomo. Matera, 1963.
Phil 4195.37 Pico della Mirandola, Giovanni. De dignitate hominis. Bad Homburg, 1968.
Phil 4195.38 Pico della Mirandola, Giovanni. Oration on the dignity of man. Chicago, 1956.
Phil 4195.39 Pico della Mirandola, Giovanni. On the dignity of man. Indianapolis, 1965.
Phil 4195.40 Rigg, J.M. Giovanni Pico della Mirandola: his life. London, 1890.
Phil 4195.40.5 Pico della Mirandola, Giovanni. Ioannis Pici Mirandulae...vita. Modena, 1963.
Phil 4195.80 Giovanni, V. di. Giovanni Pico. Palermo, 1894.
Phil 4195.81 Dreydorff, Georg. Das System des Johannes Pico. Warburg, 1858.
Phil 4195.82 Dorez, Léon. Pic de la Mirandole en France, 1485-1488. Paris, 1897.
Phil 4195.83 Massetani, D.G. La filosofia cabbalistica di Giovanni Pico. Empoli, 1897.
Phil 4195.84 Semprini, G. Giovanni Pico della Mirandola. Todi, 1921.
Phil 4195.85 Semprini, G. La filosofia di Pico della Mirandola. Milano, 1936.
Phil 4195.86 Garin, Eugenio. Giovanni Pico della Mirandola. Firenze, 1937.
Phil 4195.87 Dulles, A. Princeps concordiae: Pico della Mirandola. Cambridge, 1941.
Phil 4195.88 Garin, Eugenio. Giovanni Pico della Mirandola. Parma? 1963.
Phil 4195.89 Sloek, Johannes. Tradition og nybrud. København, 1957.
Phil 4195.90 Condier, Pierre Marie. Jean Pic de la Mirandole. Paris, 1957.
Phil 4195.95 Remé, Richard W. Darstellung des Inhalts der Disputationes in astrologiam. Hamburg, 1933.

Phil 4195 History of philosophy - Local Modern philosophy - Italy - Individual philosophers - Pico della Mirandola, Giovanni - cont.

Phil 4195.100   Monnerjahn, E. Giovanni Pico della Mirandola. Wiesbaden, 1960.

Phil 4195.105   Gautier-Vignal, L. Pic de la Mirandole, 1463-94. Paris, 1937.

Phil 4195.106A   Convegno Internazionale per il V Centenario della Nascita di Giovanni Pico della Mirandola, Mirandola, 1963. L'opera e il pensiero di Giovanni Pico della Mirandola nella storia dell'umanesimo. Firenze, 1965.

Phil 4195.106B   Convegno Internazionale per il V Centenario della Nascita di Giovanni Pico della Mirandola, Mirandola, 1963. L'opera e il pensiero di Giovanni Pico della Mirandola nella storia dell'umanesimo. Firenze, 1965.

Phil 4195.107   Napoli, Giovanni di. Giovanni Pico della Mirandola. Roma, 1965.

Phil 4195.110   Convegno di Studi Pichiani per il V Centenario della Nascita di Giovanni Pico della Mirandola. Studi pichiani; atti e memorie del Convegno di studi pichiani per il V centenario della nascita di Giovanni Pico della Mirandola, Mondena, Mirandola, 25-26 maggio, 1963. Modena, 1965.

Phil 4196 History of philosophy - Local Modern philosophy - Italy - Individual philosophers - Pico della Mirandola, Giovanni Francesco

Htn   Phil 4196.5*   Pico, G.F. Opera. n.p., 1508.

Phil 4196.30   Pico, G.F. Le epistole de imitatione di G. Pico. Firenze, 1954.

Phil 4196.80   Schmitt, Charles B. Gianfrancesco Pico della Mirandola, 1469-1533. The Hague, 1967.

Phil 4196.85   Raith, Werner. Die Macht des Bildes. München, 1967.

Phil 4200 History of philosophy - Local Modern philosophy - Italy - Individual philosophers - Other P

Phil 4200.1.5F   Ferri, L. La psicologia di Pietro Pomponazzi. Roma, 1876.

Phil 4200.1.6   Fiorentino, F. Luigi Ferri: la psicologia di Pietro Pomponazzi. Napoli, 1877.

Htn   Phil 4200.1.10*   Pomponazzi, Pietro. Opera. Basileae, 1567.

Phil 4200.1.15   Pomponazzi, Pietro. De fato. Lucani, 1957.

Phil 4200.1.30   Pomponazzi, Pietro. Les causes des merveilles de la nature, ou Les enchantements. Paris, 1930.

Phil 4200.1.32   Pomponazzi, Pietro. Corsi inediti dell'insegnamento padovano. Padova, 1966.

Phil 4200.1.34.1   Pomponazzi, Pietro. De naturalium effectuum causis, sive, De incantionibus. Hildesheim, 1970.

Phil 4200.1.80   Douglas, A.H. Philosophy and psychology of...Pomponazzi. Cambridge, 1910.

Phil 4200.1.81   Betzendörfer, Walter. Die Lehre von der zweifachen Wahrheit bei Petrus Pomponatius. Inaug. Diss. Tübingen, 1919.

Phil 4200.1.82   Fiorentino, F. Pietro Pomponazzi. Firenze, 1868.

Phil 4200.1.83   Ardigò, R. Pietro Pomponazzi. Mantova, 1869.

Phil 4200.1.84   Nardi, Bruno. Studi su Pietro Pomponazzi. Firenze, 1965.

Phil 4200.1.90   Poppi, Antonio. Saggi sul pensiero inedito di Pietri Pomponazzi. Padova, 1970.

Phil 4200.2.01   Premec, Vladimir. Franciskus Patricijus. Beograd, 1968.

Htn   Phil 4200.2.10*   Patrizzi, F. Nova de universis philosophia. Venetiis, 1593.

Phil 4200.2.15   Brickman, Benjamin. An introduction to Francesco Patrizi's Nova de universis philosophia. Thesis. N.Y., 1941.

Phil 4200.2.20   Lamprecht, F. Zur Theorie der humanistischen Geschichtschreibung. Zürich, 1950.

Phil 4200.2.30   Patrizzi, F. L'amorosa filosofia di F. Patrizzi. Firenze, 1963.

Phil 4200.2.79   Pamphlet box. Patrizzi, F.

Htn   Phil 4200.3.30*   Pasi, Bartholomeo. Tariffa. Vinetia, 1540.

Phil 4200.4.30   Pastore, A. Il pensiero puro. Milano, 1913.

Phil 4200.4.35   Pastore, A. Il solipsismo. Torino, 1924.

Phil 4200.5.30   Pusci, F. Lettere. Firenze, 1955. 2v.

Phil 4200.6.30   Petruzzellis, Nicola. Meditazione critiche. Napoli, 1960.

Phil 4200.6.32.2   Petruzzellis, Nicola. Problemi e aporie del pensiero contemporaneo. 2. ed. Napoli, 1970.

Phil 4200.6.80   Firrito, Giovanni. Ontologia e assiologia critica nel pensiero di Nicola Petruzzellis. Napoli, 1967.

Phil 4200.7.06   Pergulensis, Paulus. Logica and tractatus de sensu composito et diviso. St. Bonaventure, 1961.

Phil 4200.8.30   Paci, Enzo. Relazioni e significati. v.1-3. Milano, 1965. 3v.

Phil 4200.9.30   Pucci, Raffaele. La fenomenologia contemporanea e il problema dell'uomo. Napoli, 1963.

Phil 4200.9.35   Pucci, Raffaele. Linguaggio e interpretrazione. Napoli, 1966.

Phil 4210 History of philosophy - Local Modern philosophy - Italy - Individual philosophers - Rosmini-Serbati, Antonio

Phil 4210.2   Collana di studi filosofici Rosminiani. Milano. 1-12,1951-1956 4v.

Phil 4210.5   Rosmini-Serbati, Antonio. Per Antonio Rosmini nel 1o centenario dalla sua nascita. Milano, 1897. 2v.

Phil 4210.8   Rosmini-Serbati, Antonio. Opere edite e inedite. v.5, 11-14, 20, 27-30. Milano, 1837. 10v.

Phil 4210.10   Rosmini-Serbati, Antonio. Opere. v.1, 9-10, 11-12, 15. Napoli, 1842-47. 4v.

Phil 4210.11   Rosmini-Serbati, Antonio. Anthologie philosophique. Lyon, 1954.

Phil 4210.12   Rosmini-Serbati, Antonio. Opere edite e inedite. Roma, 1934-63. 42v.

Phil 4210.14   Rosmini-Serbati, Antonio. Antologia pedagogica. 1. ed. Brescia, 1955.

Phil 4210.15   Rosmini-Serbati, Antonio. Breve esposizione della filosofia di Melchiorre Gioja. Milano, 1840. 8 pam.

Phil 4210.20   Rosmini-Serbati, Antonio. Introduzione alla filosofia. Casalle, 1850.

Phil 4210.20.10   Rosmini-Serbati, Antonio. Introduzione alla filosofia. v.1-4. Torino, 1924-25. 2v.

Phil 4210.21   Rosmini-Serbati, Antonio. Filosofia del diritto. Napoli, 1856. 2v.

Phil 4210.22   Rosmini-Serbati, Antonio. Nouovo saggio sull'origine delle idee. Milano, 1836-37. 3v.

Phil 4210.22.5   Rosmini-Serbati, Antonio. Ideologia (Nuovo saggio sull'origine delle idee). Torino, 1851-52. 3v.

Phil 4210.22.10   Rosmini-Serbati, Antonio. Nuovo saggio sull'origine delle idee. 3. ed. Bari, 1948.

Phil 4210.23   Rosmini-Serbati, Antonio. Logica. Intra, 1867.

Phil 4210.23.2   Rosmini-Serbati, Antonio. Logica. Torino, 1853.

Phil 4210.24.5   Rosmini-Serbati, Antonio. Il rinnovamento della filosofia in Italia. Milano, 1836. 3 pam.

Phil 4210.25   Rosmini-Serbati, Antonio. Trattato della coscienza morale. Milano, 1844.

Phil 4210 History of philosophy - Local Modern philosophy - Italy - Individual philosophers - Rosmini-Serbati, Antonio - cont.

Phil 4210.25.20   Rosmini-Serbati, Antonio. Sul principio: Pa legge dubia non obliga. Milano, 1851.

Phil 4210.26   Rosmini-Serbati, Antonio. Antropologia. Novara, 1847.

Phil 4210.27   Rosmini-Serbati, Antonio. Psicologia. v.1-2. Napoli, 1858.

Phil 4210.28   Rosmini-Serbati, Antonio. Teosofia. Torino, 1859-74. 2v.

Phil 4210.29   Rosmini-Serbati, Antonio. Il principio della morale. Bari, 1924.

Phil 4210.30   Rosmini-Serbati, Antonio. Principi della scienza morale. Torino, 1928.

Phil 4210.32   Rosmini-Serbati, Antonio. Storia comparativa e critica dei sistemi intorno al principio della morale, a cura di C. Caviglione. Pt. 1. Torino, 1928.

Phil 4210.35   Rosmini-Serbati, Antonio. Compendio di etica e breve storia di essa. Roma, 1907.

Phil 4210.38   Rosmini-Serbati, Antonio. Esposizione del sistema morale dell'autore e compendio di etica. Mozara, 1952.

Phil 4210.40   Rosmini-Serbati, Antonio. Philosophisches System. Regensburg, 1879.

Phil 4210.41   Rosmini-Serbati, Antonio. The philosophical system. London, 1882.

Phil 4210.41.20   Rosmini-Serbati, Antonio. Sistema filosofico. Torino, 1924.

Phil 4210.41.30   Rosmini-Serbati, Antonio. Il sistema filosofico. Torino, 1951.

Phil 4210.42   Rosmini-Serbati, Antonio. Il razionalismo. Prato, 1882.

Phil 4210.45   Rosmini-Serbati, Antonio. Opuscali morali. Milano, 1841.

Phil 4210.50   Rosmini-Serbati, Antonio. The origin of ideas. London, 1883-84. 3v.

Phil 4210.55   Bollettino rosminiano. Rovereto. 1,1886

Phil 4210.57   Rosmini-Serbati, Antonio. Gnoseologia. Messina, 1953.

Phil 4210.60   Rosmini-Serbati, Antonio. Psychology. London, 1886-88. 3v.

Phil 4210.62   Rosmini-Serbati, Antonio. Letteratura e arti belle. pt.1-2. Intra, 1870-73.

Phil 4210.65   Rosmini-Werbati, Antonio. Quaranta proposizioni attribute ad A. Rosmini. Milano, 1889.

Phil 4210.67   Rosmini-Serbati, Antonio. La societa teocratico. Brescia, 1963.

Phil 4210.68   Rosmini-Serbati, Antonio. Il pensiero giuridico e politico di Antonio Rosmini. Firenze, 1962.

Phil 4210.69   Rosmini-Serbati, Antonio. Saggio sul comunismo e socialismo. Pescara, 1964.

Phil 4210.70   Rosmini-Serbati, Antonio. Saggio storico critico sulle categorie e la dialettica. v.1-2. Torino, 1885.

Phil 4210.72   Rosmini-Serbati, Antonio. Il giovane Rosmini. Urbino, 1963.

Phil 4210.73   Rosmini-Serbati, Antonio. Saggio sui divertimenti pubblici. Roma, 1964.

Phil 4210.74   Rosmini-Serbati, Antonio. Leitsätze für Christen von Antonio Rosmini. Einsiedeln, 1964.

Phil 4210.75   Rosmini-Serbati, Antonio. Epistolario. pt.1, v.1-2. Torino, 1857. 2v.

Phil 4210.76   Rosmini-Serbati, Antonio. Giovane età e primi studi di Antonio Rosmini-Serbati. Italia, 1860.

Phil 4210.77   Sulla difesa del...A. Rosmini-Serbai. Firenze, 1841.

Phil 4210.78   Caviglione, C. Bibliografia delle opere di A. Rosmini. Torino, 1925.

Phil 4210.79   Pamphlet vol. Rosmini-Serbati, Antonio. 37 pam.

Phil 4210.79.10   Bergamaschi, Cirillo. Bibliografia rosminiana. Milano, 1967. 2v.

Phil 4210.80   Calza, G. Esposizione ragionata della filosofia. Intra, 1878-79. 2v.

Phil 4210.81   Nardi, P. de. Antonio Rosmini ed i gesuiti. Torino, 1882.

Phil 4210.81.4   Nardi, P. de. La filosofia di Antonio R-S. Pt. 1. Bellinzona, 1881.

Phil 4210.81.8   Nardi, P. de. Rosmini e Kant. Forli, 1902.

Phil 4210.81.12F   Nardi, P. de. Di Antonio Rosmini-Serbati reformatore. Forli, 1894.

Phil 4210.81.15   Nardi, P. de. La compagnia di Gesu e la recente condanna di A. Rosmini. Intra, 1888. 5 pam.

Phil 4210.82   Paoli, F. Della vita di Antonio Rosmini-Serbati. Torino, 1880-84. 2v.

Phil 4210.83   Lockhart, W. Life of Antonio Rosmini-Serbati. 2. ed. London, 1886. 2v.

Phil 4210.83.2   Lockhart, W. An outline of the life of...Antonio Rosmini. London, 1856.

Phil 4210.83.3   Lockhart, W. Vie d'Antonio Rosmini-Serbati. Paris, 1889.

Phil 4210.83.5   MacWalter, G.S. Life of Antonio Rosmini-Serbati. London, 1883.

Phil 4210.84   Garelli, V. Antonio Rosmini. Torino, 1861.

Phil 4210.85   Vidari, G. Rosmini e Spencer. Milano, 1899.

Phil 4210.86   Ferre, Pietro Maria. Esposizione del principio filosofico di Rosmini. Verona, 1859.

Phil 4210.87   Avogadro della Motta, Emiliano. La filosofia dell'abate Antonio Rosmini esaminata. 4a ed. Napoli, 1877.

Phil 4210.87.5   Avogadro della Motta, Emiliano. Sul valore scientifico e sulle pratiche consequenze. Napoli, 1853.

Phil 4210.88.2   Stresa, Italy. Istituto della Carità. Cenni biografici di Antonio Rosmini. 2a ed. Milano, 1857.

Phil 4210.88.5   Stresa, Italy. Istituto della Carità. Cenni biografici di Antonio Rosmini. Firenze, 1924.

Phil 4210.89   Bruno, J.F. Rosmini's contribution to ethical philosophy. N.Y., 1916.

Phil 4210.90   Sarlo, Francesco de. Le basi della psicologia e della biologia secondo il Rosmini. Roma, 1893.

Phil 4210.91   Jarvis, Stephen E. Rosmini, a Christian philosopher. 2. ed. Market Weighton, 1888.

Phil 4210.92   Gioberti, Vincenzo. Degli errori filosofici di Antonio Rosmini. Napoli, 1845.

Phil 4210.92.2   Gioberti, Vincenzo. Degli errori filosofici di Antonio Rosmini. 2a ed. Capolago, 1846. 3v.

Phil 4210.92.15   Gioberti, Vincenzo. Risposta agli attachi di G. di Cavour. Torino, 1848.

Phil 4210.93   Lettere intorno al nuovo paggio sull'origine delle idea dell'ab. A. Rosmini-Serbati. Modena, 1843. 2 pam.

Phil 4210.93.10   Tommaseo, N. Esposizione sul sistema filosofico del nuovo saggio. Torino, 1840?

Phil 4210.93.15   Tommaseo, N. Antonio Rosmini. Domodossola, 1958.

Phil 4210.94   Pestalozza, A. La mente di Antonio Rosmini. Milano, 1855.

Phil 4210.106   Dyroff, Adolf. Rosmini. Mainz, 1906.

Phil 4210.107   Pagani, G.B. Vita di Antonio Rosmini scritta da un sacerdote dell'istituto della carità. Rovereto, 1959. 2v.

Phil 4210 History of philosophy - Local Modern philosophy - Italy - Individual philosophers - Rosmini-Serbati, Antonio - cont.

Phil 4210.107.5 Pagani, G.B. The life of Antonio Rosmini-Serbati. London, 1907.
Phil 4210.108 Palhoriès, F. La philosophie de Rosmini. Thèse. Paris, 1908.
Phil 4210.108.5 Palhoriès, F. Rosmini. Paris, 1908.
Phil 4210.112 Caviglione, C. Il Rosmini vero. Voghera, 1912.
Phil 4210.113 Carabellese, P. La teoria della percezione intellettiva. Bari, 1907.
Phil 4210.114 Schwaiger, Georg. Die Lehre vom sentimento fondamentale bei Rosmini nach ihrer Anlage. Inaug. Diss. Fulda, 1914.
Phil 4210.115 Ferré, Pietro M. Degli universali secondo la teoria rosminiana. Casale, 1880-86. 11v.
Phil 4210.116F Buroni, Giuseppe. Dell'essere e del conoscere. Torino, 1877.
Phil 4210.116.5 Buroni, Giuseppe. Nozioni di ontologia. 2a ed. Torino, 1878.
Phil 4210.116.10 Buroni, Giuseppe. Risposta 1a al padre Cornoldi in difesa delle nozioni di ontologia. Torino, 1878.
Phil 4210.116.20 Buroni, Giuseppe. Della nuova dichiarazione quasi ultima della S. Congregazione dell'Indice. Torino, 1882.
Phil 4210.117 Gentile, G. Rosmini e Gioberti. Pisa, 1898.
Phil 4210.117.2 Gentile, G. Rosmini e Gioberti. 2. ed. Firenze, 1955.
Phil 4210.118 Cornelio, A.M. Antonio Rosmini e il suo monumento in Milano. Torino, 1896.
Phil 4210.119 Cornoldi, G.M. Il rosminiamismo. Roma, 1881.
Phil 4210.120 Bianciardi, S. Antonio Rosmini o il filosofo cristiano. Firenze, 1858.
Phil 4210.121F Zucchi, N. Parole dette da N. Zucchi per l'inaugurazione del monumento ad Antonio Rosmini in Milano. n.p., 1896.
Phil 4210.122F Fogazzaro, A. La figura di Antonio Rosmini. Milano, 1897.
Phil 4210.123F Lilla, V. Le fonti del sistema filosofico di Antonio Rosmini. Milano, 1897.
Phil 4210.124 Morando, G. Esame critico delle XL proposizioni rosminiane condaunate dalla S.R.U. inquisizione. Milano, 1905.
Phil 4210.125 Werner, Karl. Die italien Philosophie. Wien, 1884.
Phil 4210.125.10F Werner, Karl. A. Rosmini's Stellung in der Geschichte der neueren Philosophie. Wien, 1884.
Phil 4210.126 Brogialdi, Adolfo. Elogio di Antonio Rosmini letto l'11 giugno 1863 all'Accademia degli Eutelet. Firenze, 1863.
Phil 4210.127 Galli, Gallo. Kant e Rosmini. Città de Castello, 1914.
Phil 4210.128 Paoli, A. Lo Schopenhauer e il Rosmini. Roma, 1878.
Phil 4210.129 Petri, Giuseppe. Lo dottrine di Antonio Rosmini...ed altri esaminate da Giuseppe Petri. Torino, 1878.
Phil 4210.129.5 Petri, Giuseppe. Risposta ad alcuni appunti...sul libro A. Rosmini ed i neoscolastici. Torino 1879.
Phil 4210.130 Moglia, A. I suareziani e l'abate Rosmini. Piacenza, 1882.
Phil 4210.131 Calzi, Carlo. L'antropologia soprannaturale di A. Rosmini. Firenze, 1885.
Phil 4210.132 Pederzolli, G. La filosofia di Antonio Rosmini. Rovereto, 1887.
Phil 4210.133 Bulgarini, G.B. La storia della questione rosminiana. Milano, 1888.
Phil 4210.134 Sernagiotto, L. Antonio Rosmini all'estero. Venezia, 1889.
Phil 4210.135 Rovereto. Comitato Centrale per la Commemorazione di A. Rosmini. Commemorazione del primo centenario dalla nascita di A. Rosmini. Milano, 1897.
Phil 4210.135.10 Bettanini, A. Anniversario della festa secolare per Antonio Rosmini. n.p., 1901.
Phil 4210.136 Stopppani, Pietro. Antonio Rosmini. Milano, 1905.
Phil 4210.137F Pedrotti, Pietro. Discorso...per Antonio Rosmini. Rovereto, 1908.
Phil 4210.138 Capone-Braga, G. Saggio su Rosmini il mondo delle idee. Milano, 1914.
Phil 4210.139 Ballarini. Principj della scuola Rosminiana. Milano, 1850. 2v.
Phil 4210.140 Bozzetti, Giuseppe. Rosmini nell'ultima critica di Ausonio Franchi. Firenze, 1917.
Phil 4210.140.5 Rosmini. Roma, 1943.
Phil 4210.141.5 Trullet, Angelo Parere intorno alle dottrine ed alle opere di Antonio Rosmini-Serbati. Modena, 1882.
Phil 4210.142.5 Pestalozza, A. Le postille di un anonimo. Milano, 1850.
Phil 4210.143 Cheula, Pietro. Rapporti fra Kant e Rosmini. Milano, 1934.
Phil 4210.144 Massolo, A. Il problema dell'individuo nella filosofia di A. Rosmini. Palermo, 1934.
Phil 4210.145 Ceriani, G. L'ideologia rosminiana nei rapporti con la gnoseologia agostiniano-tomistica. Milano, 1937.
Phil 4210.146 Anastasia, M. I principii della politica nella filosofia di Antonio Rosmini. Osimo, 1934.
Phil 4210.147 Bulferetti, Luigi. Antonio Rosmini nella restaurazione. Firenze, 1942.
Phil 4210.149 Morando, Dante. Rosmini. 2a ed. Brescia, 1945.
Phil 4210.149.3 Morando, Dante. Antonio Rosmini. Brescia, 1958.
Phil 4210.151 Brunello, Bruno. Antonio Rosmini. Milano, 1945.
Phil 4210.152 Callovini, C. Antonio Rosmini come uomo del risorgimento italiano. Roma, 1953.
Phil 4210.153 Donati, B. Rosmini e Gioia. Firenze, 1949.
Phil 4210.153.5 Donati, B. Antonio Rosmini. Modena, 1941.
Phil 4210.154 Rovea, G. Filosofia e religione in Antonio Rosmini. Domodossola, 1951.
Phil 4210.155 Esposito, G. Il sistema filosofico di Antonio Rosmini. 2a ed. Milano, 1933.
Phil 4210.157 Incontro Internazionale Rosminiano, Bolzana. La problematica politico-sociale nel pensiero di Antonio Rosmini. Roma, 1955.
Phil 4210.159 Garioni Bertolatti, G. Antonio Rosmini. Torino, 1957.
Phil 4210.160 Congresso Internazionale di Filosofia Antonio Rosmini, Stresa and Rovereto, 1955. Atti del congresso internazionale di filosofia Antonio Rosmini. Firenze, 1957. 2v.
Phil 4210.161 Gambaro, Angiolo. Antonio Rosmini nella cultura del sus tempo. Torino, 1955?
Phil 4210.165 Leetham, C.R. Rosmini. London, 1957.
Phil 4210.166 Riva, Clemente. Antonio Rosmini nel primo centenario della morte. Firenze, 1958.
Phil 4210.170 Pusineri, Giovanni. Antonio Rosmini, uomo di pensiero, di azione, di virtu. Milano, 1956.
Phil 4210.175 Piovani, Pietro. La teodicea sociale di Rosmini. Padova, 1957.
Phil 4210.180 Galli, Dario. Studi rosminiani. Padova, 1957.
Phil 4210.185 Emery, Cuthbert Joseph. Rosmini on human rights. London, 1957.
Phil 4210.185.5 Emery, Cuthbert Joseph. The Rosminians. London, 1960.

Phil 4210.190 Sciacca, M.F. La filosofia morale di Antonio Rosmini. 3a ed. Milano, 1958.
Phil 4210.190.5 Sciacca, M.F. Interpretarioni rosminiane. Milano, 1958.
Phil 4210.191 Giacon, Carlo. L'oggettivita in Antonio Rosmini. Milano, 1960.
Phil 4210.192 Raschini, Maria A. Il principio dialettico nella filosofia di Antonio Rosmini. Milano, 1961.
Phil 4210.193 Brunello, B. Rosmini. Bologna, 1963.
Phil 4210.194 Beschin, G. La comunicazione delle persone nella filosofia. Milano, 1964.
Phil 4210.197 Zolo, Danilo. Il personalismo rosminiano. Brescia, 1963.
Phil 4210.198 Solari, Gioele. Studi rosminiani. Milano, 1957.
Phil 4210.200 Colonna, Salvatore. L'educazione religiosa nella pedagogia di A. Rosmini. Lecce, 1963.
Phil 4210.202 Cuciuffo, Michele. Morale e politica in Rosmini. Milano, 1967.
Phil 4210.205 Cristaldi, Giuseppe. Prospettive rosminiane. Milano, 1965.
Phil 4210.210 Manganelli, Maria. Persona e personalità nell'antropologia di Antonio Rosmini. Milano, 1967.
Phil 4210.215 Radice, Gianfranco. Annali di Antonio Rosmini Serbati. Milano, 1967. 2v.
Phil 4210.220 Piemontese, Filippo. La dottrina del sentimento fondamentale nella filosofia di A. Rosmini. Milano, 1966.
Phil 4210.225 Ottonello, Pier Paolo. L'essere iniziale nell'ontologia di Rosmini. Milano, 1967.
Phil 4210.230 Verondini, Enrico. Leffere sulla spiritualitá rosminiana. Milano, 1966.
Phil 4210.235 Traniello, Francesco. Società religiosa e società civile in Rosmini. Bologna, 1966.
Phil 4210.240 Cristaldi, Mariano. Rosmini antiromantico. Catania, 1967.
Phil 4210.245 Brancaforte, Antonio. Discussioni rosminiane. Catania, 1968.
Phil 4210.250 Quacquarelli, Antonio. La lezione liturgica di Antonio Rosmini. Milano, 1970.
Phil 4210.255 Rosmini e il Rosminianesimo nel veneto. Padova, 1970.

Phil 4215 History of philosophy - Local Modern philosophy - Italy - Individual philosophers - Other R

Phil 4215.1.01 Cusani Confalonieri, L.G. G.D. Romagnosi. Carate Brianza, 1928.
Phil 4215.1.10 Opere di G.D. Romagnosi. Pt. 1-2. Milano, 1841. 16v.
Phil 4215.1.25 Romagnosi, G.D. Opuscoli filosofici. Lanciano, 1923.
Phil 4215.1.30 Romagnosi, G.D. Opere di Romagnosi. Milano, 1957.
Phil 4215.1.78 Pamphlet vol. Romagnosi, G.D. 8 pam.
Phil 4215.1.79 Pamphlet box. Romagnosi, G.D.
Phil 4215.1.80 Ferrari, Giuseppe. La mente di G.D. Romagnosi. Prato, 1839.
Phil 4215.1.80.5 Ferrari, Giuseppe. La mente di G.D. Romagnosi. Milano, 1913.
Phil 4215.1.81 Nova, Alessandro. Delle censure dell'abate A. Rosmini-Serbati contro la dottrina religiosa di G.D Romagnosi. Milano, 1842.
Phil 4215.1.82 Stiattesi, Andrea. Notizia storica di Gian Domenico Romagnosi. Firenze, 1878.
Phil 4215.1.83 Bartolomei, A. Del significato e del valore delle dottrine di Romagnosi per il criticismo contemporaneo. Roma, 1901.
Phil 4215.1.85 Caboara, L. La filosofia del diritto di G.D. Romagnosi. Citta, 1930.
Phil 4215.1.86 Caboara, L. La filosofia politica di Romagnosi. Roma, 1936.
Phil 4215.1.87 Norsa, Achille. Il pensiero filosofico di Giandomenico Romagnosi. Milano, 1930.
Phil 4215.1.89 Levi, G. Del carattere meglio determinante la filosofia di Romagnosi. Parma, 1885.
Phil 4215.1.91 Aguanno, Giuseppe d'. Gian Domenico Roamgnosi filosofo e giureconsulto. Pt.2. Parma, 1906.
Phil 4215.1.95 Cantù, Cesare. Notizia di G.D. Romagnosi. 2a ed. Prato, 1840.
Phil 4215.1.97 Giorgi, A. de. Biografia di G.D. Romagnosi e catalogo delle sue opere. Parma, 1874.
Phil 4215.1.100 Martino, R. de. Saggio su G.D. Romagnosi. Napoli, ,1887.
Phil 4215.1.103 Mistrali, Dario. G.D. Romagnosi. Borgo San Donnino, 1907.
Phil 4215.1.105 Credali, A. G.D. Romagnosi. Modena, 1935.
Phil 4215.1.110 Alecci, Romolo. La dottrina di G.D. Romognosi intorno alla civiltá. Padova, 1966.
Phil 4215.1.115 Dentone, Adriana. Il problema morale in Romagnosi e Cattaneo. Milano, 1968.
Phil 4215.2.81 Ventura, L. Tommaso Rossi e la sua filosofia. Genova, 1912.
Phil 4215.2.83 Ragnisco, P. Tommaso Rossi e Benedetto Spinoza, saggio storico-critico. Salerno, 1873.
Phil 4215.2.86 Giordano-Zocchi, V. Tommaso Rossi. Napoli, 1866.
Phil 4215.3.30 Rensi, Giuseppe. Le antinomie dello spirito. Piacenza, 1910.
Phil 4215.3.31 Rensi, Giuseppe. Formalismo e amoralismo giuridico. Verona, 1914.
Phil 4215.3.32 Rensi, Giuseppe. Polemiche antidogmatiche. Bologna, 1920.
Phil 4215.3.33 Rensi, Giuseppe. La filosofia dell'autorita. Palermo, 1920.
Phil 4215.3.35 Rensi, Giuseppe. L'irrazionale, il lavoro, l'amore. Milano, 1923.
Phil 4215.3.38 Rensi, Giuseppe. Il genio etico, ed altri saggi. Bari, 1912.
Phil 4215.3.40 Rensi, Giuseppe. Le ragioni dell'irrazionalismo. 2a ed. Napoli, 1933.
Phil 4215.3.45 Rensi, Giuseppe. La filosofia dell'assurdo. Milano, 1937.
Phil 4215.3.80 Buonaiui, E. Giuseppe Rensi. Roma, 1945.
Phil 4215.3.83 Nonis, Piero. La scepsi etica di Giuseppe Rensi. Roma, 1957.
Phil 4215.3.85 Morra, Gianfranco. Scetticismo e misticismo nel pensiero di Giuseppe Rensi. Siracuse, 1958.
Phil 4215.3.90 Giornata Rensiana, Genova. Giuseppe Rensi. Milano, 1967.
Phil 4215.4.80 Gentiluomo, D. L'ontognoseologia di Cesare Ranzoli. Padova, 1951.
Phil 4215.8.21 Ruggiero, Guido de. Scritti politici, 1912-26. Bologna, 1963.
Phil 4215.8.30 Ruggiero, Guido de. Existentialism. London, 1946.
Phil 4215.8.32 Ruggiero, Guido de. L'esistenzialismo. 1. ed. Bari, 1943.
Phil 4215.8.34 Ruggiero, Guido de. Existentialism: disintegration of man's soul. N.Y., 1948.
Phil 4215.8.35 Ruggiero, Guido de. Myths and ideals. London, 1946.
Phil 4215.9.80 Caracciolo, C. L'idealismo e i suoi limiti nel pensiero di Antonio Renda. Palermo, 1960.
Phil 4215.10.30 Raya, Gino. La fame. 2. ed. Roma, 1963.

Phil 4225 History of philosophy - Local Modern philosophy - Italy - Individual philosophers - S

Phil 4225.1	Spaventa, Bertrando. Scritti filosofici. Napoli, 1900.
Phil 4225.1.21	Spaventa, Bertrando. Scritti inediti e rari, 1840-1880. Padova, 1966.
Phil 4225.1.32	Spaventa, Bertrando. Logica e metafisica. Bari, 1911.
Phil 4225.1.40	Spaventa, Bertrando. Principii di etica. Napoli, 1904.
Phil 4225.1.52	Spaventa, Bertrando. Prolusione e introduzione alle lezioni di filosofia nella Università di Napoli. 2a ed. Napoli, 1886.
Phil 4225.1.85	Vacca, Giuseppe. Politica e filosofia in Bertrando Spaventa. Bari, 1967.
Phil 4225.1.90	Onoranze funebri a Bertrando Spaventa. Napoli, 1883.
Phil 4225.1.95	Gentile, Giovanni. Bertrando Spaventa. Firenze, 1920.
Phil 4225.1.100	Bortot, Renato. L'hegelismo di Bertrando Spaventa. Firenze, 1968.
Phil 4225.2.31	Sarlo, Francesco de. Saggi di filosofia. Torino, 1896-97. 2v.
Phil 4225.3.89	Sichirollo, G. La mia conversione dal Rosmini a S. Tommaso. Padova, 1887.
Phil 4225.4	Sacheli, C.A. Atto e valore. Firenze, 1938.
Phil 4225.5	Nel primo centenario della morte di Nicola Spedalieri. Roma, 1899.
Phil 4225.5.2	Spedalieri, Nicola. De diritti dell'uomo libri 6. Assisi, 1791.
Phil 4225.7	Severgnini, D. L'interiorità teologica dello storicismo. Roma, 1940. 3v.
Phil 4225.8.2	Sciacca, Michele Federico. Opere complete. Milano, 1952-56. 7v.
Phil 4225.8.30	Sciacca, Michele Federico. L'interiorità oggettiva. Milano, 1958.
Phil 4225.8.32	Sciacca, Michele Federico. La filosofia oggi. 3. ed. Milano, 1958. 2v.
Phil 4225.8.34	Sciacca, Michele Federico. Morte ed immortalità. Milano, 1959.
Phil 4225.8.34.2	Sciacca, Michele Federico. Morte e immortalità. 2. ed. Milano, 1962.
Phil 4225.8.36	Sciacca, Michele Federico. Atto ed essere. 2. ed. Milano, 1958.
Phil 4225.8.37	Sciacca, Michele Federico. Akt und Sein. 4. Aufl. Freiburg, 1964.
Phil 4225.8.38	Sciacca, Michele Federico. Come si vince a Waterloo. Milano, 1957.
Phil 4225.8.40	Sciacca, Michele Federico. L'uomo. 2. ed. Milano, 1958.
Phil 4225.8.42	Sciacca, Michele Federico. La clessidra. 3. ed. Milano, 1960.
Phil 4225.8.44	Sciacca, Michele Federico. In spirito e verità. 4. ed. Milano, 1960.
Phil 4225.8.46	Sciacca, Michele Federico. Filosofia e metafisica. v.1-2. 2. ed. Milano, 1962.
Phil 4225.8.48	Sciacca, Michele Federico. Gliarieti contro la verticale. Milano, 1969.
Phil 4225.8.50	Sciacca, Michele Federico. Dull'attualismo. Milano, 1961.
Phil 4225.8.52	Sciacca, Michele Federico. Cosi mi parlano le cose muti. Milano, 1962.
Phil 4225.8.55	Sciacca, Michele Federico. Studi sulla filosofia moderna. 3. ed. Milano, 1964.
Phil 4225.8.58	Sciacca, Michele Federico. Filosofia e antifilosofia. Milano, 1968.
Phil 4225.8.60	Sciacca, Michele Federico. Il problema di Dio e della religione nella filosofia attuale. 4. ed. Milano, 1964.
Phil 4225.8.62	Sciacca, Michele Federico. L'oscuramento dell'intelligenza. Milano, 1970.
Phil 4225.8.65	Sciacca, Michele Federico. La libertà e il tempo. Milano, 1965.
Phil 4225.8.67.2	Sciacca, Michele Federico. La chiesane la civiltà moderna. 2. ed. Milano, 1969.
Phil 4225.8.68	Sciacca, Michele Federico. Lettere dalla campagna, e scritti affini. 2. ed. Milano, 1966.
Phil 4225.8.70	Sciacca, Michele Federico. Dallo spiritualismo critico allo spiritualismo cristiano, 1939-1951. Milano, 1965. 2v.
Phil 4225.8.75	Michele F. Sciacca in occasione del trenta anno di cattedra universitaria, 1938-1968. Milano, 1968.
Phil 4225.8.79	Ottonello, Pier Paolo. Bibliografia di M.F. Sciacca. Milano, 1969.
Phil 4225.8.80	Nobile-Ventura, Attilio. Crisi dell uomo e conquista. Milano, 1958.
Phil 4225.8.85	Antonelli, M.T. Studi in onore di M.F. Sciacca. Milano, 1959.
Phil 4225.8.90	Pignoloni, Emilio. Genesi e sviluppo del rosminianesimo nel pensiero di Michele F. Sciacca. Milano, 1964. 2v.
Phil 4225.8.95	El pensamiento de Michele Federico Sciacca; homenaje, 1908-1958. Buenos Aires, 1959.
Phil 4225.8.102	Nobile-Ventura, Attilo. Colloquio con Michele Federico Sciacca. Milano, 1966.
Phil 4225.8.105	Dentone, Adriana. La problematica morale nella filosofia della integralita. 2. ed. Milano, 1966.
Phil 4225.8.110	Giannuzzi, Eugenio. L'uomo e il suo destino. Cosenza, 1968.
Phil 4225.9	Stefanini, Luigi. Metafisica della forma. Padova, 1949.
Phil 4225.15.30	Spirito, Ugo. La vita come arte. Firenze, 1941.
Phil 4225.15.40	Spirito, Ugo. Dal mito alla scienza. Firenze, 1966.
Phil 4225.15.80	Barrello, O. L'estetica di M. Spirito. Lugano, 1958.
Phil 4225.15.85	Conti, O. Polemica sull'immanenza in Ugo Spirito. Milano, 1963.
Phil 4225.15.90	Lizzio, Maria. Marxismo e metafisica. Catania, 1968.
Phil 4225.23.15	Stellini, J. Opera omnia. Patavii, 1778-79. 4v.
Phil 4225.23.30	Stellini, J. Scritti filosofica. Milano, 1942.
Phil 4225.66.80	Antonaci, Antonio. Francesco Storella. Galatina, 1966.
Phil 4225.77.30	Sarti, Sergio. L'azione creatice di Sergio Sarti. Brescia, 1959.
Phil 4225.90.30	Severino, Emanuele. Studi di filosofia della prassi. Milano, 1962.

Phil 4235 History of philosophy - Local Modern philosophy - Italy - Individual philosophers - T

Phil 4235.1.30	Telesius, B. Consentini de rerum. Neapoli, 1570.
Phil 4235.1.35	Telesius, B. De rerum natura. Modena, 1910. 3v.
Phil 4235.1.40	Telesius, B. Varii de naturalibus rebus libelli. Hildesheim, 1971.
Phil 4235.1.80	Bartholmes, C. De Bernardino Telesio. Paris, 1849.
Phil 4235.1.82	Fiorentino, Francesco. Bernardino Telesio ossia studi storici su l'idea della natura nel risorgimento italiano. Firenze, 1872-74. 2v.
Phil 4235.1.85	Gentile, G. Bernardino Telesio. Bari, 1911.
Phil 4235.1.90	Troilo, E. Bernardino Telesio. Modena, 1910.

Phil 4235 History of philosophy - Local Modern philosophy - Italy - Individual philosophers - T - cont.

Phil 4235.1.95	Zavattari, E. La visione della vita...Telesio. Torino, 1923.
Phil 4235.1.97	Abbagnano, Nicola. Bernardino Telesio. Milano, 1941.
Phil 4235.1.99	Van Deusen, Neil C. Telesio, the first of the moderns. N.Y., 1932.
Phil 4235.2.79	Pamphlet box. Turamini, Alessandro.
Phil 4235.3.31	Testa, Alfonso. Della filosofia della mente. Piacenza, 1836.
Phil 4235.3.90	Credaro, L. Alfonso Testa e i primordii del Kantismo in Italia. Catania, 1913.
Phil 4235.4.81	Catania. R. Scuola Normale Maschile Superiore. Per le solenni onoranze al filosofo Vincenzo Tedeschi Paterno Castello. Catania, 1892.
Phil 4235.5.30	Taddeo da Parma. Le quaestiones de anima de Taddeo da Parma. Milano, 1951.
Phil 4235.9.80	Fiorensoli, Dario. Il pensiero filosofico di Guiseppe Tarozzi. Padova, 1964.
Phil 4235.10.80	Silvestro da Valsanzibio. Vita e dottrina di Laetano di Thiene. 2. ed. Padova, 1949.
Phil 4235.11.30	Tradu, L. Saggi filosofici vari. Padova, 1960.

Phil 4260 History of philosophy - Local Modern philosophy - Italy - Individual philosophers - Vico, Giovanni B.

Phil 4260.05	Croce, Benedetto. Bibliografia vichiana. Napoli, 1904-10.
Phil 4260.05.5	Croce, Benedetto. Bibliografia vichiana. Quinto supplemento. Napoli, 1932.
Phil 4260.07	Croce, Benedetto. Biblografia vichiana. Napoli, 1947-48. 2v.
Phil 4260.08	Gianturco, Elio. A selective bibliography of Vico scholarship, 1948-68. Firenze, 1968.
Phil 4260.12	Vico, G.B. Opere. v.1-4. Napoli, 1840-41. 5v.
Phil 4260.15	Vico, G.B. Opere. v.1-6. Milano, 1854- 3v.
Phil 4260.16	Vico, G.B. Opere. Milano, 1953.
Phil 4260.17	Vico, G.B. Opere. Bari, 1914. 6v.
Phil 4260.17.5	Vico, G.B. Tutte le opere di Giambattista Vico. Milano, 1957.
Phil 4260.17.7	Vico, G.B. The autobiography of Giambattista Vico. Ithaca, 1944.
Phil 4260.17.10	Vico, G.B. Opere. Milano, 1959.
Phil 4260.17.15	Vico, G.B. Autobiografia e scienza nuova. Torino, 1932.
Phil 4260.17.16	Vico, G.B. Autobiografia. 1. ed. Torino, 1965.
Phil 4260.23	Vico, G.B. Scritti vari e pagine sparse. Bari, 1940.
Phil 4260.25	Vico, G.B. Oeuvres. Paris, 1835. 2v.
Phil 4260.25.5	Vico, G.B. Vico, d'après la traduction de Michelet. Paris, 1927.
Phil 4260.27	Vico, G.B. L'estetica di G.B. Vico allraverso la scienza nuova e gli scritti minari. Napoli, 1926.
Phil 4260.28	Vico, G.B. La scienza nuova e opere scelte di Giambattista Vico. Torino, 1952.
Phil 4260.30	Vico, G.B. La difesa dell'umanesimo. Firenze, 1958.
Phil 4260.31	Vico, G.B. Il pensiero di Giambattista Vico. Torino, 1959.
Htn Phil 4260.33*	Vico, G.B. Principi di scienza nuova. v.1-2. Napoli, 1744.
Phil 4260.34	Vico, G.B. The new science of Giambattista Vico. Ithaca, 1948.
Phil 4260.34.2A	Vico, G.B. The new science of Giambattista Vico. Ithaca, 1968.
Phil 4260.34.2B	Vico, G.B. The new science of Giambattista Vico. Ithaca, 1968.
Phil 4260.35	Vico, G.B. Principi di una scienza nuova. Napoli, 1826.
Phil 4260.35.5	Vico, G.B. La science nouvelle. Paris, 1844.
NEDL Phil 4260.35.9	Vico, G.B. La science nouvelle. Bari, 1911-16. 3v.
Phil 4260.35.20	Vico, G.B. Principi di una scienza nuova. Milano, 1903.
Phil 4260.35.32	Vico, G.B. Scienza nuova...a cura di G. Flores d'Arcais. 2. ed. Padova, 1939.
Phil 4260.35.33	Vico, G.B. Scienza nuova...a cura di G. Flores d'Arcais. 3. ed. Padova, 1943.
Phil 4260.36A	Vico, G.B. Principes de la philosophie de l'histoire. Paris, 1827.
Phil 4260.36B	Vico, G.B. Principes de la philosophie de l'histoire. Paris, 1827.
Phil 4260.36.5	Vico, G.B. Principes de la philosophie de l'histoire. Bruxelles, 1835.
Phil 4260.37	Vico, G.B. Die neue Wissenschaft über die gemeinschaftliche Natur der Völker. Munchen, 1924.
Phil 4260.37.1	Vico, G.B. Die neue Wissenschaft über die gemeinschaftliche Natur der Völker. Hamburg, 1966.
Phil 4260.38	Vico, G.B. Sabiduría primitiva de los italianos. Buenos Aires, 1939.
Phil 4260.39	Vico, G.B. Vom Wesen und Weg der geistigen Bildung. Godesberg, 1947.
Phil 4260.41	Vico, G.B. L'ideale educativo. Napoli, 1954.
Phil 4260.42	Omaggio a Vico di A. Corsano, Paolo Romi, A.M. Jacobelli Inoldi. Napoli, 1968.
Phil 4260.44	Vico, Giovanni Battista. De antiquissima Italorum sapientia. Roma, 1969.
Phil 4260.79	Pamphlet box. Vico, G.B.
Phil 4260.80	Cantoni, C. G.B. Vico. Torino, 1867.
Phil 4260.81	Ferrari, G. La mente di Giambattista Vico. Milano, 1837.
Phil 4260.81.5	Ferrari, G. Vico et l'Italie. Paris, 1839.
Phil 4260.81.10	Ferrari, G. Il genio di Vico. Lanciano, 1922.
Phil 4260.82	Flint, R. Vico. Philadelphia, 1884.
Phil 4260.83	Klemm, Otto. G.B. Vico als Geschichtsphilosoph. Inaug. Diss. Leipzig, 1906.
Phil 4260.83.2	Klemm, Otto. G.B. Vico als Geschichtsphilosoph. Leipzig, 1906.
Phil 4260.84	Arcari, P. Processi...di scienza nuova in G.B. Vico. Friburgo, 1911.
Phil 4260.85	Croce, B. The philosophy of Giambattista Vico. London, 1913.
Phil 4260.85.2	Croce, B. La filosofia di Giambattista Vico. 2a. ed. Bari, 1922.
Phil 4260.85.5	Croce, B. Le fonti della gnoseologia Vichiana. Napoli, 1912.
Phil 4260.85.8	Croce, B. The philosophy of Giambattista Vico. N.Y., 1964.
Phil 4260.85.25	Scrocca, A. Giambattista Vico nella critica di Benedetto Croce. Napoli, 1919.
Phil 4260.86	Apologia del genere umano. Venezia, 1768.
Phil 4260.87	Werner, K. Giambattista Vico als Philosophie und Gelehrterforscher. Wien, 1881.
Phil 4260.87.5	Werner, K. Emerico Amari in seinern Verhaltniss zu G.B. Vico. Wien, 1880.

Classified Listing

Phil 4260.88   Werner, K.   Über Giambattista Vico als Geschichtsphilosophen und begründer der neueren italienischen Philosophie. Wien, 1877.

Phil 4260.89   Vadalà-Papale, G.   Dati psicologici nella dottrina giuridica. Roma, 1889.

Phil 4260.90   Longo, Michele.   Giambattista Vico. Torino, 1921.

Phil 4260.91   Donati, Benvenuto.   Autografi e documenti vichiani inediti o dispersi. Bologna, 1921.

Phil 4260.91.5   Donati, Benvenuto.   Nuovi studi sulla filosofia civile di G.B. Vico. Firenze, 1936.

Phil 4260.92   Gemmingen, Otto.   Vico, Hamann und Herder. Inaug. Diss. Borna, 1918.

Phil 4260.93   Galasso, Antonio.   Del criterio della verita nella scienza e nella storia secondo G.B. Vico. Milano, 1877.

Phil 4260.94   Gentile, Giovanni.   Studi vichiani. Messina, 1915.

Phil 4260.94.5   Gentile, Giovanni.   Studi vichiani. Firenze, 1927.

Phil 4260.95   Cochery, M.   Les grandes lignes de la philosophie historique et juridique de Vico. Paris, 1923.

Phil 4260.97   Rivista internationale di filosofia del diritto. Per il secondo centenario della "Scienza nuova" di Vico. Roma, 1925.

Phil 4260.98   Sorrentino, A.   La retorica et la poetica di G.B. Vico. Torino, 1927.

Phil 4260.99   Ferrari, G.M.   Il Leibnitz gindicato da G.B. Vico. n.p., n.d.

Phil 4260.100   Gemelli, A.   G.B. Vico: volume commemorativo. Milano, 1926.

Phil 4260.101   Sarchi, Carlo.   Della dottrina di B. Spinoza e di G.B. Vico. Milano, 1877.

Phil 4260.102   Cotugno, R.   La sorte di G.B. Vico e le polemiche...della fine del XVII alla metà del XVIII secolo. Bari, 1914.

Phil 4260.102.10   Cotugno, R.   Giovambattista Vico. Il suo secolo e le sue opere. Pt.1. Trani, 1890.

Phil 4260.103   Peters, Richard.   Der Aufbau der Weltgeschichte bei Giambattista Vico. Stuttgart, 1929.

Phil 4260.104   Caramella, S.   Antologia vichiana. Messina, 1930.

Phil 4260.105   Tommaseo, Niccolo.   G.B. Vico. Torino, 1930.

Phil 4260.106   Löhde, Hermann.   Giambattista Vico und das Problem der Bildung. Inaug. Diss. Erlangen, 1932.

Phil 4260.107F   Ranieri, A.   Discorso recitato il di primo anniversario del plebiscito dell'Italia meridionale. Napoli, 1861.

Phil 4260.108   Chiocchetti, E.   La filosofia di Giambattista Vico. Milano, 1935.

Phil 4260.109   Adams, Henry P.   The life and writings of Giambattista Vico. London, 1935.

Phil 4260.110   Corsano, Antonio.   Umanesino e religione in G.B. Vico. Bari, 1935.

Phil 4260.110.5   Corsano, Antonio.   Giambattista Vico. Bari, 1956.

Phil 4260.111   Fornaca, Remo.   Il pensiero educativo di Giambattista Vico. Torino, 1957.

Phil 4260.112   Finetti, Giovanni F.   Difesa dell'autorità della sacra scrittura contro Giambattista Vico. Bari, 1936.

Phil 4260.113   Witzemann, Walter.   Politischer Aktivismus und sozialer Mythos. Berlin, 1935.

Phil 4260.116   Chaix-Ruy, Jules.   Vie de J.B. Vico. Gap, 1943.

Phil 4260.116.5   Chaix-Ruy, Jules.   J.B. Vico et l'illuminisme athée. Paris, 1968.

Phil 4260.117   Luginbühl, Johannes.   Die Axiomatik bei Giambattista Vico. Bern, 1946.

Phil 4260.118   Fubini, Mario.   Stile i umanità di Giambattista Vico. Bari, 1946.

Phil 4260.118.5.2   Fubini, Mario.   Stile e umanità di Giambattista Vico. 2. ed. Milano, 1965.

Phil 4260.119   Giusso, Lorenzo.   La filosofia di G.B. Vico e l'età barocca. Roma, 1943.

Phil 4260.120   Chaix-Ruy, Jules.   La formation de la pensée philosophique de G.B. Vico. Gap, 1943.

Phil 4260.121   Amerio, Franco.   Introduzione allo studio di G.B. Vico. Torino, 1947.

Phil 4260.122   Buenos Aires. Universidad Nacional.   Vico y Herder. Buenos Aires, 1948.

Phil 4260.123   Nicolini, F.   Commento storico alla seconda Scienza nuova. Roma, 1949- 2v.

Phil 4260.124   Nicolini, F.   La giovinezza di Giambattista Vico. 2. ed. Bari, 1932.

Phil 4260.124.5   Nicolini, F.   Saggi vichiani. Napoli, 1955.

Phil 4260.124.10   Nicolini, F.   La religiosità di Giambattista Vico. Bari, 1949.

Phil 4260.125   Berry, Thomas.   The historical theory of Giambattista Vico. Washington, 1949.

Phil 4260.126   Paci, Enzo.   Ingens sylva. 1. ed. Milano, 1949.

Phil 4260.128   Cantone, Carlo.   Il concetto filosofico di diritto in Giambattista Vico. Mazara, 1952.

Phil 4260.129   Caponigri, A.R.   Time and idea. London, 1953.

Phil 4260.130   Bellofiore, L.   La dottrina del diritto naturale in G.B. Vico. Milan, 1954.

Phil 4260.130.5   Bellofiore, L.   La dottrina providenza in G.B. Vico. Padova, 1962.

Phil 4260.131   Sabarini, Raniero.   Il tempo in G.B. Vico. Milano, 1954.

Phil 4260.132   Banchetti, Silvestro.   Il significato morale dell'estetica vichiana. Milano, 1957.

Phil 4260.133   Grimaldi, A.A.   The universal humanity of Giambattista Vico. N.Y., 1958.

Phil 4260.135   Columbu, Mario.   Giambattista Vico. Trani, 1957.

Phil 4260.137   Severgnini, Dante.   Studi vichiani. Milano, 1954-56. 2v.

Phil 4260.140   Badaloni, Nicola.   Introduzione a G.B. Vico. Milano, 1961.

Phil 4260.145   Jacobelli Isoldi, Angela Maria.   G.B. Vico. Bologna, 1960.

Phil 4260.146   Croce, B.   Giambattista Vico, primo scopritore della scienza estetica. Napoli, 1901.

Phil 4260.147   Lanza, Franco.   Saggi di poetica vichiana. Varese, 1961.

Phil 4260.148   Uscatescu, George.   Juan Batista Vico y el mundo histórico. 1. ed. Madrid, 1956.

Phil 4260.149   Marini, Cesare.   Grambattista Vico al cospetto del secolo XIX. Napoli, 1852.

Phil 4260.152   Varela Domínguez de Ghiolai, Delfina.   Filosofía argentina: Vico en los escritos de Sarmiento. Buenos Aires, 1950.

Phil 4260.153   Manno, Ambrogio G.   Lo storicismo di G.B. Vico. Napoli, 1965.

Phil 4260.155   Nicolini, F.   Vico storico. Napoli, 1967.

Phil 4260.157   Bianca, Giovanni A.   Il concetto di poesia in Giambattista Vico. Messina, 1967.

Phil 4260.160   Tagliacozzo, Giorgio.   Giambattista Vico. Baltimore, 1969.

Phil 4260.165   Manson, Richard.   The theory of knowledge of Giambattista Vico. Hamden, Conn., 1969.

Phil 4260.170   Studi vichiani. Napoli. 1,1969+

Phil 4260.175   Rossi, Paolo.   Le sterminate antichità. Studi vichiani. Pisa, 1969.

Phil 4260.180   Brancato, Francesco.   Vico nel risorgimento. Palermo, 1969.

Phil 4260.185   Falco, Enrico de.   La biografia di G.B. Vico. Roma, 1968.

Phil 4260.190   Candela, Silvestro.   L'unità e la religiosità del pensiero di Giambattista Vico. Napoli, 1969.

Phil 4260.195   Sciacca, Michele Federico.   Verità e storia in Vico. Roma, 1968.

Phil 4260.200   Giambattista Vico nel terzo centenario della nascita. Napoli, 1971.

Phil 4260.205   Daus, Hans-Jürgen.   Selbstverständnis und Menschenbild in den Selbstdarstellungen Giambattista Vicos und Pietro Giannones. Thesis. Genève, 1962.

Phil 4260.210   Donzelli, Maria.   Natura e humanitas nel Giovane Vico. Napoli, 1970.

Phil 4260.215   Iannizzotto, Matteo.   L'empirismo nella gnoseologia di Giambattista Vico. Padova, 1968.

Phil 4260.220   Candela, Mercurio.   Diritto e umanità in G.B. Vico. Empoli, 1968.

Phil 4265   History of philosophy - Local Modern philosophy - Italy - Individual philosophers - Other V

Phil 4265.1.15   Vanini, Lucilio, afterwards Giulio Cesare.   Oeuvres philosophiques. Paris, 1842.

Phil 4265.1.18   Vanini, Lucilio, afterwards Giulio Cesare.   Opere. Lecce, 1912. 2v.

Phil 4265.1.20   Vanini, Lucilio, afterwards Giulio Cesare.   Le opere di Giulio Cesare Vanini e le loro fonti. Milano, 1933-34. 2v.

Htn   Phil 4265.1.30*   Vanini, Lucilio, afterwards Giulio Cesare.   De admirandis naturae reginae deaeque mortalium arcanis. Lutetieae, 1616.

Phil 4265.1.35   Rutenburg, V.I.   Velikii ital'ianskii ateist Vanini. Moskva, 1959.

Phil 4265.1.40   Vivante, Leone.   Elementi di una filosofia della potenzialità. Firenze, 1953.

Phil 4265.1.41   Vivante, Leone.   A philosophy of potentiality. London, 1955.

Phil 4265.1.80   Palumbo, R.   Giulio Cesare Vanini e i suo tempi. Napoli, 1878.

Phil 4265.1.81   Baudouin, A.   Histoire critique de Jules César Vanini. Toulouse, n.d.

Phil 4265.1.83   Schramm, J.M.   De vita et scriptis...Julii Caesaris Vanini. 2. ed. Ciistrini, 1715.

Phil 4265.1.84   Vie et les sentimens de Lucilio Vanini. Rotterdam, 1717.

Phil 4265.1.85   Cattaneo, G.   Idee di G.C. Vanini sull...evoluzione. Milano, 1885.

Htn   Phil 4265.1.90*   Arpe, P.F.   Apologia J. Caesare Vanino neapolitano. Csmomopoli, 1712.

Phil 4265.1.95   Nowicki, Andrzej.   Centralne kategorie filosofii Vaniniego. Wyd. 1. Warszawa, 1970.

Phil 4265.2.10   Ventura da Raulica, G.   Opere. v.1-13. Napoli, 1856-64. 11v.

Phil 4265.2.30   Ventura da Raulica, G.   Della vera e della falsa filosofia. Napoli, 1854.

Phil 4265.2.31   Mariano, R.   Le bellezze della fede ne misteri. Milano, 1867. 3v.

Phil 4265.2.32   Ventura, J.   De methodo philosphandi. Romae, 1828.

Phil 4265.2.90   Cristofoli, A.   Il pensiero religioso di P.G. Ventura. Milano, 1927.

Phil 4265.2.91   Cultrera, Paolo.   Della vita e delle opere del Rev. P.D. Geovachino Ventura. Palermo, 1877.

Phil 4265.2.93   Rémusat, Charles.   Il padre Ventura e la filosofia. Milano, 1853.

Phil 4265.2.94   Rémusat, Charles.   Il padre Ventura e la filosofia. Milano, 1853.

Phil 4265.2.96   Rizzo, R.   Teocrazia e neo-cattaluisimo nel risorgimento. Palermo, 1938.

Phil 4265.3.30   Vera, A.   Introduction to speculative logic and philosophy. St. Louis, 1873.

Phil 4265.3.32   Vera, A.   In inquiry into speculative and experimental science. London, 1856.

Phil 4265.3.33   Vera, A.   Ricerche sulla scienza speculativa e esperimentale. Parigi, 1864.

Phil 4265.3.35   Vera, A.   Problema dell'assoluto. v.1-4. Napoli, 1872-82.

Phil 4265.3.37   Vera, A.   Mélanges philosophiques. Paris, 1862.

Phil 4265.3.39   Vera, A.   Saggi filosofici. Napoli, 1883.

Phil 4265.3.45   Vera, A.   Prolusioni alla storia della filosofia. Milano, 1861.

Phil 4265.3.80   Mariano, R.   Augusto Vera. Napoli, 1887.

Phil 4265.3.85   Longoni, G.   Il sistema filosofico di Hegel...sulla pena di morte di A. Vera. Milano, 1863.

Phil 4265.4.5F   Vailati, G.   Scritti (1863-1909). Leipzig, 1911.

Phil 4265.4.10   Vailati, G.   El metodo della filosofia. Bari, 1957.

Phil 4265.4.81   L'anima; saggi e guidizi. Maggio 1911. G. Vailati. Firenze, 1911.

Phil 4265.4.85   Ricci, Umberto.   Necrologio di Giovanni Vailati. Roma, 1909.

Phil 4265.5.30   Vanni, Icilio.   Saggi di filosofia sociale e giuridica. Bologna, 1906-11. 2v.

Phil 4265.6.80   Librizzi, C.   Il pensiero di B. Varisco. Padova, 1942.

Phil 4265.6.90   Librizzi, C.   La filosofia di B. Varisco. Catania, 1936.

Phil 4265.6.95   Calogero, G.   La filosofia di Bernardino Varisco. Messina, 1950.

Phil 4285   History of philosophy - Local Modern philosophy - Italy - Individual philosophers - Z

Phil 4285.1.90   Ragnisco, P.   Giacomo Zabarella il filosofo Pietro Pompanazzi. Roma, 1886-87.

Phil 4285.1.95   Labanca, B.   Sopra Giacomo Zabarella. Napoli, 1878.

Phil 4285.1.100   Aliotta, S.   Un precursore della neoscolastica. Noto, 1970.

Phil 4285.2.80   Studi sul pensiero di Giuseppe Zamboni. Milano, 1957.

Phil 4301 - 4326   History of philosophy - Local Modern philosophy - Spain - History - General works - Individual authors (A-Z)

Phil 4301.1   Avelino, Andres.   Prolegomenos a la unica metafisica posible. Ciudad Trujillo, 1941.

Phil 4301.1.5   Avelino, Andres.   Une lettre à Jacques Maritain. Ciudad Trujillo, 1944.

Phil 4301.2   Abellán, José Luis.   Filosofía española en America, 1936-1966. Madrid, 1967.

Phil 4302.4   Bonilla y San Martin, A.   Historia de la filosofía española. Madrid, 1908.

Classified Listing

Phil 4301 - 4326   History of philosophy - Local Modern philosophy - Spain - History - General works - Individual authors (A-Z) - cont.

Phil 4302.4.5   Bonilla y San Martin, A. Historia de la filosofía española. Madrid, 1911.

Phil 4302.5   Bullón y Fernández, E. Los precursores españoles de Bacon y Descartes. Salamanca, 1905.

Phil 4303.1   Carreras y Artau, T. Introduccio a la història del pensament filosofic a Catalunya. Barcelona, 1931.

Phil 4303.1.5   Carreras y Artau, T. Estudios sobre médicos-filosófos españoles del siglo XIX. Barcelona, 1952.

Phil 4303.5.5   Cruz Costa, João. Alguns aspétos da filosofia no Brazil. São Paulo, 1938?

Phil 4303.6   Carreras y Artau, J. Apports hispaniques à la philosophie chrétienne. Louvain, 1962.

Phil 4303.7   Carreras y Artau, J. Estudios filosóficos. v.1-2. Barcelona, 1966-1968.

Phil 4303.10   Cartezon Alvarez, Daniel. De la saudade y sus formas. Nueva York, 1960.

Phil 4307.1   Gaos, José. Pensamiento español. México, 1945.

Phil 4307.2   Guy, Alain. Les philosophes espagnols d'hier et d'aujourd'hui. Toulouse, 1956. 2v.

Phil 4307.4   Gil Cremades, Juan José. El reformismo español; Krausismo. Barcelona, 1969.

Phil 4308.1   Höllhuber, I. Geschichte der Philosophie im spanischen Kulturbereich. München, 1967.

Phil 4309.1   Ingenieros, José. La cultura filosófica en España. Madrid, 1916.

Phil 4309.5   Iriarte, Joaquin S.J. Menendez Pelayo y la filosofia española. Madrid, 1947.

Phil 4312.5A   Lopez Morillas, Juan. El krausismo español. 1. ed. México, 1956.

Phil 4312.5B   Lopez Morillas, Juan. El krausismo español. 1. ed. México, 1956.

Phil 4312.8   Lopez Quintas, Alfonso. Filosofía española contemporánea; temas y autores. Madrid, 1970.

Phil 4313.1   Menéndez y Pelayo, M. Discurso leído en la universidad central. Madrid, 1889.

Phil 4313.2   Mendez Bejarano, M. Historia de la filosofía en España hasta el siglo XX. Madrid, 192-.

Phil 4313.5   Marias Aguilera, Julian. La escuela de Madrid. Buenos Aires, 1959.

Phil 4313.5.5   Marias Aguilera, Julian. El oficio del pensamiento. Madrid, 1958.

Phil 4313.5.10   Marias Aguilera, Julian. Filosofía actual, y Existencialismo en España. Madrid, 1955.

Phil 4314.2   Nicol, Eduardo. El problema de la filosofía hispanica. Madrid, 1961.

Phil 4316.1   Parpal y Marques, C. Antecedentes de la escuela filosófica Catalana del siglo XIX. Barcelona, 1914.

Phil 4316.3   Puy Munõoz, Francisco. El pensamiento tradicional en la España del siglo XVIII, 1700-1760. Madrid, 1966.

Phil 4317.5   Quiroz-Martinez, Olga Victoria. La introducción de la filosofía moderna en España. 1. ed. Mexico, 1949.

Phil 4318.2   Rodriguez Aranda, Luis. El desarrollo de la razón en la cultura española. Madrid, 1962.

Phil 4318.4   Robledo, Maria N. El mundo clásico en el pensamiento español contemporáneo. Madrid, 1965.

Phil 4319.1   Solana, Marcial. Los grandes escolásticos espanoles de los siglos XVI y XVII. Madrid, 1928.

Phil 4319.1.5   Solana, Marcial. Historia de la filosofía española. Madrid, 1940-41. 3v.

Phil 4319.2   Segovia Canosa, R. Tres salvaciones del siglo XVIII español. Xalapa, 1960.

Phil 4319.3   Spain. Filosofía española y portuguesa de 1500 a 1650. Madrid, 1948.

Phil 4320.10A   Le temps et la mort dans la philosophie espagnole contemporaine. Toulouse, 1968.

Phil 4320.10B   Le temps et la mort dans la philosophie espagnole contemporaine. Toulouse, 1968.

Phil 4322.1   Vidart, Louis. La filosofía española. Madrid, 1866.

Phil 4325.2   Yamuni, Tabush. Concepts e imágenes en pensadores. México, 1951.

Phil 4326.1   Zambrano, M. Pensamiento y poesía en la vida española. México, 1939.

Phil 4330   History of philosophy - Local Modern philosophy - Spain - History - Special topics

Phil 4330.5   El mundo clasico en el pensamiento español contemporaneo. Madrid, 1960.

Phil 4330.10   Puy, Francisco. El pensamiento tradicional en la España del siglo XVIII, 1700-1760. Madrid, 1966.

Phil 4330.15   Clascar, Federico. Estudi sobre la filosofia a Catalunya en el siglo XVIII. Barcelona, 1918.

Phil 4340   History of philosophy - Local Modern philosophy - Spain - Anthologies of philosophical writings

Phil 4340.5   Castro y Rossi, Adolf de. Obras escogidas de filósofos. Madrid, 1953.

Phil 4340.10   Batlori, Miguel. Il pensiero delea rinascenza in Spagna e Portogallo. Milano, 1964.

Phil 4340.15   Academia...Madrid. Academia Española, Madrid. Discursos leídos en las recepciones públicas de la Real Academia Española. Ser. 2. Madrid, 1945- 6v.

Phil 4340.20   Caponigri, Aloysius Robert. Contemporary Spanish philosophy; an anthology. Notre Dame, 1967.

Phil 4351 - 4376   History of philosophy - Local Modern philosophy - Spain - Individual philosophers (A-Z)

Phil 4351.1.25   Amoroso Lima, A. Las edades del hombre. Buenos Aires, 1943.

Phil 4351.1.33   Arteaga, E. La belleza ideal. Madrid, 1943.

Phil 4351.2   Arias, Alejandro C. Sobre la cultura. Montevideo, 1943.

Phil 4351.2.5   Arias, Alejandro C. Estudios literarios y filosóficos. Montevideo, 1941.

Phil 4351.3   Morreale deCastro, M. Pedro Simon Abril. Madrid, 1949.

Phil 4351.4   Alvarado, Francisco. Obras escogidas del filosofo rancio. Madrid, 1912.

Phil 4351.4.5   Alvarado, Francisco. Las cartas inéditas del filosofo rancio. Madrid, 1916.

Phil 4351.4.10   Alvarado, Francisco. Cartas del filósofo rancio. Sevilla, 1811-14. 3v.

Phil 4351.4.15   Alvarado, Francisco. Cartas criticas. Madrid, 1824-25. 5v.

Phil 4351.4.20   Alvarado, Francisco. La maza de fraga sobre los filosofastros liberales del día. Madrid, 1812.

Phil 4351.4.80   Fernández Largo, Jacinto. Introduccion al estudio del filósofo rancio. Madrid, 1959.

Phil 4351.5   Astrada, Carlos. Ensayos filosoficos. Bahia Blanca, 1963.

Phil 4351 - 4376   History of philosophy - Local Modern philosophy - Spain - Individual philosophers (A-Z) - cont.

Phil 4351.5.80   Llanos, Alfredo. Carlos Astrada. Buenos Aires, 1962.

Phil 4351.6.80   Delgado Varela, José M. La gracia divina en el correlativismo. Madrid, 1961.

Phil 4351.6.85   Barreiro Gomez, José. Sistematización de lo personal y lo sobrenatural. Lugo, 1964.

Phil 4352.1.33   Balmes, Jaime. Art d'arriver au vrai. Paris, 1852.

Phil 4352.1.35   Balmes, Jaime. Curso de filosofia elemental. v.1-4. Barcelona, 1911.

Phil 4352.1.40   Balmes, Jaime. Filosofia fundamental. 2. ed. Barcelona, 1848. 4v.

Phil 4352.1.45   Balmes, Jaime. Filosofia elemental. Madrid, 1935.

Phil 4352.1.50   Balmes, Jaime. Elements of logic. N.Y., 1880.

Phil 4352.1.55   Balmes, Jaime. Obras completas. Madrid, 1948- 8v.

Phil 4352.1.60   Baucells Serra, Ramón. Balmes y el nacionalismo espanol. Vich, 1940.

Phil 4352.1.79   Dios Mendoza, J. de. Bibliografia balmesiana. Barcelona, 1961.

Phil 4352.1.80   Roure, Narciso. La vida y las obras de Balmes. Madrid, 1910.

Phil 4352.1.82   Roure, Narciso. Las ideas de Balmes. Madrid, 1910.

Phil 4352.1.85   Blanche-Raffin, A. de. Jacques Balmes, sa vie et ouvrages. Paris, 1849.

Phil 4352.1.89   Menendez y Pelayo, D.M. Das palabras sobre centenario de Balmes. Vich, 1910.

Phil 4352.1.95   Ruano y Corbo, J.M. Balmes apologista. Santiago, 1911.

Phil 4352.1.99   Hermkes, Maria. Die Fundamental-Philosophie des Jaime Balmes. Inaug. Diss. Krefeld, 1919.

Phil 4352.1.101   Briones Ortún, Juan. En torno a Balmes. Bilboa, 1933.

Phil 4352.1.103   Kruse, Paul. Die pädagogischen Elemente in der Philosophie des Jakob Balmes. Inaug. Diss. Neuherberg, 1935.

Phil 4352.1.105   Urmeneta, F. de. Principios de filosofia de la historia. Madrid, 1952.

Phil 4352.1.107   Sagarra y de Castellarnau, Fernando. Encrucijada. Barcelona, 1957.

Phil 4352.1.110   Prados y Lopez, M. Balmes, el buen amigo de la verdad. Madrid, 1954?

Phil 4352.1.112   Batelari, Miguel. Balmes i Casanovas. Barcelona, 1959.

Phil 4352.1.115   Instituto de España. Centenario de Jaime Balmes. Madrid, 1949.

Phil 4352.1.120   Garcia Los Santos, B. Vida de Balmes. Madrid, 1848.

Phil 4352.1.125   Barcelona. Biblioteca Central. Catálogo de la exposicion bibliográfica. Barcelona, 1948.

Phil 4352.1.130   Auhofer, H.J. La sociologia de Jaime Balmes. Madrid, 1959.

Phil 4352.1.135   Solaguren, Celestino. Metodalogía filosófica de Balmes. Madrid, 1961.

Phil 4352.1.140   Casanovas, J. Balmes. Barcelona, 1932. 3v.

Phil 4352.1.145   Sainz de Robles, Federico Carlos. Jaime Balmes; estudio y antologia. Madrid, 1964.

Phil 4352.1.150   Feliu Egidio, Vicente. Sistematizacion del pensamiento de Balmes en orden a la filosofia de la historia. Madrid, 1952.

Phil 4352.1.155   Corts Grau, José. Ideario político de Balmes. Madrid, 1934.

Phil 4352.1.160   Arboleya y Martinéz, Maximiliane. Balmes politico. Barcelona, 1911.

Phil 4352.1.165   Sáiz Barberá, Juan. Pensamiento histórico cristiano. 1. ed. Madrid, 1967.

Phil 4352.2   Rabello, Sylvio. Farias Brito. Rio de Janeiro, 1941.

Phil 4352.2.2   Rabello, Sylvio. Farias Brito. Rio de Janeiro, 1967.

Phil 4352.2.5   Cruz Costa, Joao. Farias Brito on uma adventura do esprito. Sao Paulo, 1942.

Phil 4353.5   Chavarri B., Misael. Diez y siete divagaciones. Santiago de Chile, 1940. 2v.

Phil 4353.10   Cencillo, J.L. Experiencia profunda del ser. Madrid, 1959.

Phil 4353.12   Gomez Izquierdo, A. Un filosofo catalan, Antonio Comellas y Cluet. Madrid, 1907.

Phil 4353.15   Caba, Pedro. Sintesis de su obra filosofica: antroposofica y metafisica de la presencia. Mexico, 1959.

Phil 4355.5   Echarri, Jaime. Philosophia entis sensibilis. Romae, 1959.

Phil 4356.1.80   Ronilla y San Martin, A. Fernando de Córdoba. Madrid, 1911.

Phil 4356.2.81   Lueben, Robert. Sebastian Fox Morzillo und seine erkenntnistheoretische Stellung zur Naturphilosophie. Inaug. Diss. Bonn, 1911.

Phil 4356.3   Ferrater Mora, José. Obras selectas. Madrid, 1967. 2v.

Phil 4356.3.5   Ferrater Mora, José. El ser y el sentido. Madrid, 1967.

Phil 4356.3.10   Ferrater Mora, José. Variaciones sobre el espíritu. Buenos Aires, 1945.

Phil 4357.1.81   Carvalho, Joaquim de. Antonio de Gouveia e o Aristotelismo la renascenca. Coimbra, 1916.

Phil 4357.2.3   Giner de los Rios, Francisco. Obras completas. v.1-19. Madrid, 1916-27. 15v.

Phil 4357.2.30   Giner de los Rios, Francisco. Ensayos y cartas. Mexico, 1965.

Phil 4357.2.31   Giner de los Rios, Francisco. El pensamiento vivo de Giner de los Rios. Buenos Aires, 1949.

Phil 4357.2.79   Pamphlet box. Gastelum, B.J.

Phil 4357.2.80   Navarro, Martin. Vida y obras de Don Francisco Giner de los Rios. 1. ed. Mexico, 1945.

Phil 4357.2.85   Villalopos, José. El pensamiento filsofico de Giner. Sevilla, 1969.

Phil 4357.3.32   Garcia Bacca, J.D. Inoitacion a filosofar. v.1-2. Mexico, 1940-42.

Phil 4357.5   Gastelum, B.J. En el reino de las sombras; Maria de la Luz. Mexico, 1937.

Phil 4357.6.80   Alonso, Manuel. Temas filosoficos medievales. Comillas, 1959.

Phil 4357.8   Caragorri, P. La paradoja del filósofo. Madrid, 1959.

Phil 4357.9   Rubert Candau, José Maria. El siglo XIV. Madrid, 1952.

Phil 4357.10   García Lahiguera, Fernando. La libertad. Valencia, 1961.

Phil 4357.12.2   García Hoz, Victor. El nacimiento de la intimidad, y otros estudios. 2. ed. Madrid, 1970.

Phil 4357.14.80   Rubert Candau, José Maria. El conocimiento de Dios en la filosofía de Guillermo Rubió. Madrid, 1952?

Phil 4359.1.81   Endara, Julio. José Ingenieros y el porvenir de la filosofía. 2a ed. Buenos Aires, 192-.

Phil 4359.1.83   Bermann, G. José Ingenieros. Buenos Aires, 1926.

Phil 4360.2   Joannes XXI. Obras filosoficas. 2. ed. Madrid, 1961.

Phil 4362.1.80   Gutierrez, P.F.M. Fr. Luis de León y la filosofia espanole. Madrid, 1885.

Phil 4362.2   Leret, Carlos. La Trinidad, principio fundamental del universo. Madrid, 1938.

Classified Listing

Phil 4362.5 Lloreus y Barba, F.J. Lecciones de filosofia.
Barcelona, 1920. 3v.

Phil 4362.10 Soler Puigoriol, Pedro. El hombre, ser indigente: el
pensamiento antropológico de Pedro Lain Entralgo.
Madrid, 1966.

Phil 4363.1.80 Rodriguez, J.I. Vida del Doctor José Manuel Mestre.
Habana, 1909.

Phil 4363.2.5 Molinos, M. de. Guia espiritual. Barcelona, 1906.

Htn Phil 4363.2.30* Molinos, M. de. The spiritual guide. Venice, 1688.

Phil 4363.2.35 Molinos, M. de. The spiritual guide of Michael de Molinos.
Philadelphia, 1897.

Phil 4363.2.36 Molinos, M. de. The spiritual guide of Michael de Molinos.
London, 191-?

Phil 4363.2.37 Molinos, M. de. Golden thoughts from the spiritual guide.
N.Y., 1883.

Phil 4363.2.40 Entrambasaguas y Pena, J. de. Miguel de Molinos, siglo
XVII. Madrid, 1935?

Phil 4363.2.80A Bigelow, John. Molinos the quietist. N.Y., 1882.
Phil 4363.2.80B Bigelow, John. Molinos the quietist. N.Y., 1882.

Htn Phil 4363.2.81* Bigelow, John. Moljnos the quietist. N.Y., 1882.

Phil 4363.2.82 Reynier, Frédéric. Étude sur la doctrine de Molinos.
Thèse. Strasbourg, 1856.

Phil 4363.2.84 Dudon, P. Le quiétiste espanol. Paris, 1921.

Phil 4363.2.85 Sanchez-Castañer, Francisco. Miguel de Molinos en Valencia
y Roma, nuevos datas biográficos. Valencia, 1965.

Phil 4363.3.35 Manara Vincentelo de Leca, M. de. Discurso de la verdad
dedicado á la Imperial Majestad de Dios. Madrid, 1878.

Phil 4363.3.38 Manara Vicentelo de Leca, M. de. Discurso de la verdad
dedicado á la Imperial Majestad de Dios. Zaragoza, 1967.

Phil 4363.3.80 Latour, A. de. Don Miguel de Manara. Paris, 1857.

Phil 4363.3.85 Lede, Luis Perez de Guzman y Sanjuan. Discurso de la
verdad. Bilboa, 1954.

Phil 4363.3.90 Cardenas, Juan. Breve relacion de la muerte.
Sevilla, 1732.

Phil 4363.3.95 Tassara y Sangian, Luz. Mañara. Sevilla, 1959.

Phil 4363.3.101 Homenaje al venerable siervo de dios, Don Miguel.
Sevilla, 1925.

Phil 4363.3.105 Granero, Jesus Maria. Don Miguel Mañara. Sevilla, 1963.

Phil 4363.3.110 Gestoso y Pérez, José. Valdes y Mañara. Sevilla, 1890.

Phil 4363.4.30 Menéndez y Pelayo, M. Ensayos de crítica filosófica.
Madrid, 1918.

Phil 4363.5.31 Macedo, J.A. de. Cartas filosoficas a Attico.
Lisboa, 1815.

Phil 4363.6 Molina, E. De lo espiritual. Concepcion, 1937.

Phil 4363.6.10 Molina, E. Confesión filosófica y llamado de superación a
la América Hispana. Santiago, 1942.

Phil 4363.7 Marias Aguilera, Julián. Reason and life. New
Haven, 1956.

Phil 4363.7.2 Marias Aguilera, Julián. Obras. Madrid, 1958-60.
8v.

Phil 4363.7.5 Marias Aguilera, Julián. Idea de la metafísica. Buenos
Aires, 1954.

Phil 4363.7.6 Marias Aguilera, Julián. Idée de la métaphysique.
Toulouse, 1969.

Phil 4363.7.10 Marias Aguilera, Julián. Ensayos de convivencia. Buenos
Aires, 1955.

Phil 4363.7.15 Marias Aguilera, Julián. El tiempo que ni vuelve ni
tropieza. Barcelona, 1964.

Phil 4363.7.20 Marias Aguilera, Julián. Nuevos ensayos de filosofía. 2.
ed. Madrid, 1968.

Phil 4363.7.25 Marías Aguilera, Julián. Historia de la filosofía. 19. ed.
Madrid, 1966.

Phil 4363.7.33 Marias Aguilera, Julián. Ensayos de teoria. 3. ed.
Madrid, 1966.

Phil 4363.8 Mirabeut Vilaplana, Francisco. Estudios estéticos.
Barcelona, 1957. 2v.

Phil 4363.9 Weber, Wilhelm. Wirtschaftethik am Vorabend des
Liberalismus. Münster, 1959.

Phil 4363.11 Martinez, Martin. Philosophia sceptica. Madrid, 1730.

Phil 4363.12 Madariaga, Salvador de. Portrait of a man standing.
London, 1968.

Phil 4363.14 Mestre, Antonio. Ilustración y reforma de la Iglesia.
Valencia, 1968.

Phil 4364.1.70 Núñez Regueiro, M. On the knowledge and progress of
oneself. Rosario, 1941.

Phil 4365.1.5 Ors y Rovira, E. d'. Aprendizaje y heroismo.
Madrid, 1915.

Phil 4365.1.10 Ors y Rovira, E. d'. Grandeza y servidumbre de la
intelegencia. Madrid, 1919.

Phil 4365.1.15 Aranguren, José. La filosofia de Eugenio d'Ors.
Milano, 1953.

Phil 4365.1.80 Rojo Perez, E. La ciencia de la cultura, teoría
histórиologica de Eugenio d'Ors. Barcelona, 1963.

Phil 4365.1.82 Capdevila, José Maria. Eugeni d'Ors. Barcino, 1965.

Phil 4365.2.33A Ortega y Gasset, José. Concord and liberty. 1st. ed.
N.Y., 1946.

Phil 4365.2.33B Ortega y Gasset, José. Concord and liberty. 1st. ed.
N.Y., 1946.

Phil 4365.2.35 Ortega y Gasset, José. Origen y epílogo de la filosofía.
Mexico, 1960.

Phil 4365.2.36 Ortega y Gasset, José. The origin of philosophy. 1st. ed.
N.Y., 1967.

Phil 4365.2.38 Ortega y Gasset, José. The modern theme. N.Y., 1933.

Phil 4365.2.40 Ortega y Gasset, José. Unas lecciones de metafisica.
Madrid, 1966.

Phil 4365.2.41 Ortega y Gasset, José. Some lessons in metaphysics. 1st
ed. N.Y., 1969.

Phil 4365.2.42 Ortega y Gasset, José. Ideas y creencias. Buenos
Aires, 1940.

Phil 4365.2.45 Cepeda Calzada, Pablo. La doctrina de la sociedad en
Ortega y Gasset. Valladolid, 1968.

Phil 4366.79.30 Pascual Ferrández, Antonio. Ensayos. Barcelona, 1961.
20v.

Phil 4368.1.79 Pamphlet box. Ruiz, D.

Phil 4368.1.80 Rigau, P. La obra del filósofo español Diego Ruiz.
Paris, 1913.

Phil 4368.2.33 Romero, Francisco. Filosofia contemporanea estudios y
notas. Buenos Aires, 1941.

Phil 4368.2.35 Romero, Francisco. Filosofia contemporanea estudios y
notas. 2. ed. Buenos Aires, 1944.

Phil 4368.2.40 Romero, Francisco. Ideas y figuras. 2. ed. Buenos
Aires, 1958.

Phil 4368.2.45 Romero, Francisco. Teoría del hombre. Buenos Aires, 1952.

Phil 4368.2.47 Romero, Francisco. Theory of man. Berkeley, 1964.

Phil 4368.2.50 Romero, Francisco. Ortega y Gasset y el problema de la
jefatura espiritual. Buenos Aires, 1960.

Phil 4368.2.55 Romero, Francisco. Relaciones de la filosofía: la
filosofía y el filósofo. Buenos Aires, 1958.

Phil 4368.2.60 Romero, Francisco. Filósofos y problemas. 2. ed. Buenos
Aires, 1957.

Phil 4368.2.80 Harris, Marjorie. Francisco Romero on problems of
philosophy. N.Y., 1960.

Phil 4368.2.85 Rodriguez Acala, Hugo. Mision y pensamiento de Francisco
Romero. 1. ed. Mexico, 1959.

Phil 4368.2.90 Rodríguez Acala, Hugo. Francisco Romero, 1891: vija y
obra. N.Y., 1954.

Phil 4368.3.5 Rouges, Alberto. Obras completas. Tucumán, 1960.

Phil 4368.4 Baliñas, Carlos A. El pensamiento de Amor Ruibal.
Madrid, 1968.

Htn Phil 4369.1.30* Sebon, Raymond. La theologie naturelle. 2. ed.
Paris, 1640.

Phil 4369.2 Marcos Coujáles, B. Miguel Sabuco. Madrid, 1923.

Phil 4369.2.80 Cazac, H.P. Le lieu d'origine, du philosophe Francisco
Sanchez. Bordeaux, 1903.

Phil 4369.2.82 Cruz Costa, João. Ensaio sobre a vida e a obra do filósofo
Francisco Sanchez. São Paulo, 1942.

Phil 4369.2.84 Giarratano, C. Il pensiero di Francesco Sanchez.
Napoli, 1903.

Phil 4369.2.86 Sanches, Francisco. Opera philosophica. Coimbra, 1955.

Phil 4369.2.90 Miccolis, Salvatore. Francesco Sanchez. Bari, 1965.

Phil 4369.3 Soto, Juan B. La tragedia del pensamiento. Rio
Piedras, 1937.

Phil 4369.5 Sondereguér, Pedro. El enigma de la realidad. Buenos
Aires, 1941.

Phil 4369.7 Sanz del Rio, Julián. Cartas ineditas. Madrid, 1873?

Phil 4369.7.3 Sanz del Rio, Julián. Sanz del Río, 1814-1869.
Madrid, 1969.

Phil 4369.7.5 Manrique, Gervasio. Sanz del Rio. Madrid, 1935.

Phil 4370.5 Tagle, L. La experiencia humana. Buenos Aires, 1938.

Phil 4370.7 Tierno, G. E. Tradicíon y modernismo. Madrid, 1962.

Phil 4370.10 Torner, F.M. Doña Oliva Sabuco de Nantes. Madrid, 1935.

Phil 4370.15 Tallet, Jorge. The absolute being. N.Y., 1958.

Phil 4371.5 Montseny y Carret, Juan. La evolución de la filosofía en
España. v.1-2. Barcelona, 1934.

Phil 4371.10 Montseny y Carret, Juan. La evolución de la filosofía en
España. Barcelona 1968.

Phil 4372.1.1A Vives, Juan Luis. Obras completas. Madrid, 1947-48.
2v.

Phil 4372.1.1B Vives, Juan Luis. Obras completas. Madrid, 1947-48.
2v.

Phil 4372.1.5 Vives, Juan Luis. Opera omnia. London, 1964. 8v.

Htn Phil 4372.1.31* Vives, Juan Luis. I.L. Vívis Valentini, de disciplinis
libri XII. Batavorum Lugduni, 1636.

NEDL Phil 4372.1.35 Vives, Juan Luis. Causas de la decadencia de las artes.
Buenos Aires, 1948.

Phil 4372.1.36 Vives, Juan Luis. Obras sociales y políticas.
Madrid, 1960.

Phil 4372.1.39 Vives, Juan Luis. Satellitium animi. Wien, 1883.

Phil 4372.1.40 Vives, Juan Luis. De anima et vita. Torino, 1959.

Phil 4372.1.45 Vives, Juan Luis. De veritate fidei christianae libri
quinque. Lupluni, 1551.

Phil 4372.1.79 Pamphlet box. Vives, Juan Luis.

Phil 4372.1.80 Hoppe, G. Psychologie des Juan Luis Vives. Berlin, 1901.

Phil 4372.1.82 Gomis, J.B. Criterio social de Luis Vives. Madrid, 1946.

Phil 4372.1.84 Rivari, Enrico. La sapienza psicologica e pedagogica di
Giovanni L. Vives. Bologna, 1922.

Phil 4372.1.85 Bonilla y San Martin, D.A. Luis Vives y la filosofía del
renacimiento. Madrid, 1903.

Phil 4372.1.87 Gutiérrez, Alberto. El pensamiento filosófico de Juan Luis
Vives. Buenos Aires, 1940.

Phil 4372.1.90 Mateu y Llopez, F. Catálogo de la exposición bibliográfica
celebrada con motivo del IV centenario de la muerte de Luis
Vives. Barcelona, 1940.

Phil 4372.1.93 Ríos Sarmiento, Juan. Juan Luis Vives. 1. ed.
Madrid, 1940.

Phil 4372.1.95 Paris. Bibliotheque Nationale. Vives. Paris, 1942.

Phil 4372.1.97 Marañon, G. Luis Vives. Madrid, 1942.

Phil 4372.1.100 Vivés. Paris, 1951.

Phil 4372.1.105 Manzoni, Bruno. Vives. Lugano, 1960.

Phil 4372.1.110 Sancipriano, M. Il pensiero ssicologico e morale di G.L.
Vives. Firenze, 1958.

Phil 4372.1.115 Watson, Foster. Les relacions de Juan Luis Vives amb els
Anglesos i amb l'Angleterra. Barcelona, 1918.

Phil 4372.1.120 Puigdollers Oliver, Mariano. La filosofía española de Luis
Vives. Barcelona, 1940.

Phil 4372.1.125 Sanz, Victor. Vigencia actual de Luis Vives.
Montevideo, 1967.

Phil 4372.1.130 Riba y García, Carlos. Luis Vives y el pacifismo.
Zaragoza, 1933.

Phil 4372.1.135 Noreña, Carlos G. Juan Luis Vives. The Hague, 1970.

Phil 4372.1.140 Montegú, Bernardo. Filosofía del humanismo de Juan Luis
Vives. Madrid, 1961.

Phil 4372.1.145 Gayano, Lluch Rafael. El folklore en las obras de Luis
Vives. Valencia, 1941.

Phil 4372.3.85 Ortega, Euselio. Francisco de Valles, el Divino.
Madrid, 1914.

Phil 4374.5.20 Xirau, Joaquín. Obras. 1. ed. Mexico, 1963.

Phil 4374.5.30 Xirau, Joaquín. Lo fugaz y lo eterno. Mexico, 1942.

Phil 4374.5.80 Larroya, Francisco. El romanticismo filosófico
observaciones a la weltanschauung de Joaquin Xirau.
Mexico, 1941.

Phil 4376.2 Zambrano, Maria. España, sueño y verdad. Barcelona, 1965.

**Phil 4400   History of philosophy - Local Modern philosophy - Portugal - Pamphlet
volumes**

Phil 4400.01 Pamphlet box. Philosophy. Portuguese.

**Phil 4440   History of philosophy - Local Modern philosophy - Portugal - History -
Special topics**

Phil 4440.2 Carmen Rovira, María del. Eclécticos portugueses del siglo
XVIII y algunas de sus. Mexico, 1958.

**Phil 4450   History of philosophy - Local Modern philosophy - Portugal - Anthologies
of philosophical writings**

Phil 4450.6 Andrade, A.A. de. Filósofos portugueses do séc. XVIII.
v.1-3. Lisboa, 1957-

Phil 4461 - 4486 History of philosophy - Local Modern philosophy -
Portugal - Individual philosophers (A-Z)

Phil 4462.1.30	Bevilaqua, Clovis. Esboços e fragmentos. Rio de Janeiro, 1899.
Phil 4462.3	Serrão, Joel. Sampaio Bruno. Lisboa, 1958.
Phil 4463.5	Moraes, Manuel. Cartesianismo em Portugal: Antonio Cordeiro. Braga, 1966.
Phil 4464.1.30	Diniz, Almachio. Questões actuaes de philosophia e direito. Rio de Janeiro, 1909.
Phil 4466.1.80	Louzada de Magalhaes, J.J. Silvestre Pinheiro Ferreira. Bonn, 1881.
Phil 4466.2.80	Uedelhofen, M. Die Logik Petrus Fonseca's mit Ausschluss des Sprachlogischen. Inaug. Diss. Bonn, 1914.
Phil 4466.4.30	Ferreira, A. Ensaios de filosofia para a história. Coimbra, 1962.
Phil 4466.5.30	Feijó, Diogo Antonio. Cadernos de filosofia. São Paulo, 1967.
Phil 4467.1.30	Guimarães, M. A grand concepcão de Deus. Rio, 1940.
Phil 4467.2.30	Govies, Pinharanda. Peregrinação do absoluto. Lisboa, 1965.
Phil 4472.1.30	Lapas de Gusmão. Virtudes e defeitas dos homens. Lisboa, 1957.
Phil 4472.89.30	Lourencao, Eduardo. Heterodoxia. Coimbra, 1967. 2v.
Phil 4473.1.30	Marinho, José. Teoria do ser e da verdade. Lisboa, 1961.
Phil 4473.78.30	Martins, Diamantino. Filosofia da plenitude. Braga, 1966.
Phil 4475.1.80	Moniz Barreto, G. Oliveira Martins: estudo de psychologia. Paris, 1892.
Phil 4476.1.30	Peceigueiro, Jose. Problemas da ciencia e da filosofia contemporanea. Coimbra, 1966.
Phil 4476.2.30	Cardoso Rangel de Souza Coelho, Maria Luiza. A filosofia de Silvestre Penheiro Ferreira. Braga, 1958.
Phil 4478.1.30	Rocha, Germano da Costa. Nova filosofia cristã. Lisboa, 1961?
Phil 4479.1.30	Sylvan, F. Filosofia e politica no destino de Portugal. Lisboa, 1963.
Phil 4479.2.30	Santos, Delfin. Meditação sobre a cultura. Lisboa, 1946.
Phil 4482.1.90	Andrade, Antonio Alberto de. Vernei a filosofia portuguesa. Braga, 1946.
Phil 4482.1.95	Cabral de Moncada, L. Um iluminista portugues do século XVIII; Luiz Antonio Verney. Coimbra, 1941.
Phil 4482.1.97	Vieira de Almeida, Francisco. Pontos de referência. Lisboa, 1961.
Phil 4482.1.100	Andrade, António Alberto de. Vernei e a cultura do seu tempo. Coimbra, 1966.
Phil 4482.2.80	Sant'Anna, Dionisio. Teólogo laico. Scara Nova, 1961.

Phil 4500 History of philosophy - Local Modern philosophy - Scandinavia -
History - Scandinavia in general

Phil 4500.2	Aall, Anathon. Filosofien i Norden. Kristiania, 1919.
Phil 4500.4	Holm, Søren. Filosofien i Norden før 1900. København, 1967.
Phil 4500.4.5	Holm, Søren. Filosofien i Norden efter 1900. København, 1967.

Phil 4502 History of philosophy - Local Modern philosophy - Scandinavia -
History - Denmark

Phil 4502.2	Hansen, Oscar. Filosofien i Danmark i dit 18. og 19. aarhundrede. København, 1897.

Phil 4508 History of philosophy - Local Modern philosophy - Scandinavia -
History - Sweden

Phil 4508.2	Hammarsköld, Lorenzo. Historiska antickningar rörande fortgängen och utvecklingen af det philosophiska studium i Sverige. Stockholm, 1821.
Phil 4508.4	Nyblaseus, Axel. Den filosofiska forskningen i Sverige. Lund, 1873-97. 3v.
Phil 4508.5	Höffding, Harald. Filosofien i Sverige. Stockholm, 1879.
Phil 4508.7	Adelborg, Gustaf Otto. Om det personligt andliga. Stockholm, 1907.
Phil 4508.10	Ryding, Erik. Den svenska filosofins historia. Stockholm, 1959.

Phil 4510 History of philosophy - Local Modern philosophy - Scandinavia -
Anthologies of philosophical writings

Phil 4510.10	Märre skrifter. Stockholm. 1-45,1908-1917 9v.
Phil 4510.35	Corpus philosophorum danicorum medii aevi. Hauniae, 1955-1963. 4v.

Phil 4513 History of philosophy - Local Modern philosophy - Scandinavia -
Individual philosophers - A

Phil 4513.1.31	Ahlberg, A. Filosfiska essayer. Stockholm, 1918.
Phil 4513.1.35	Ahlberg, A. Filosfi och vetenskap. Stockholm, 1919.
Phil 4513.1.38	Ahlberg, A. Filosofi och dikt. Stockholm, 1924.
Phil 4513.1.40	Ahlberg, A. Det ondas problem. Stockholm, 1923.
Phil 4513.1.42	Ahlberg, A. Tidoreflexer; filosofiska uppsatser. Stockholm, 1926.
Phil 4513.2.31	Aars, K.B.R. Tanker og syn En liden studie. Kristiania, 1894.
Phil 4513.2.35	Aars, K.B.R. Haben die naturgesetze Wirklichkeit? Christiania, 1907.
Phil 4513.3.33	Åberg, L.N. Fyra föreläsningar. Uppsala, 1891.
Phil 4513.4.31	Asp, Matthia. Disputatio gradualis de philosopho curioso. Upsaliae, 1730.
Phil 4513.4.33	Asp, Matthia. Dissertatio academica potiores antiquorum. Upsaliae, 1732.
Phil 4513.4.35	Asp, Matthia. Dissertatio gradualis de vera perfectionis idea. Upsaliae, 1732.
Phil 4513.4.37	Asp, Matthia. Exercitium academicum de philosophia parabolica. Upsaliae, 1733.
Phil 4513.4.39	Asp, Matthia. Stylus character animi. Upsaliae, 1732.
Phil 4513.4.41	Asp, Matthia. Dissertatio academica de caussis obscuritatis philosophorum. Upsaliae, 1733.
Phil 4513.4.43	Asp, Matthia. Mexethma philosophicum de subordinatione veritatum. Upsaliae, 1733.
Phil 4513.4.45	Asp, Matthia. Dissertatio gradualis de usu philosophiae in convertendis gentilibus. Upsaliae, 1737.
Phil 4513.4.47	Asp, Matthia. Dissertatio academica de syncretismo philosophico. Upsaliae, 1737.
Phil 4513.5.90	Festskrift til Anathon Aall på 70:årsdagen hans, 15 Aug. 1837. Oslo, 1937.
Phil 4513.6.31	Aall, H.H. Interessen som normativ idé. Kristiania, 1913.
Phil 4513.8.31	Aspelin, Gunnar. Lek och allvar. Lund, 1968.

Phil 4514 History of philosophy - Local Modern philosophy - Scandinavia -
Individual philosophers - Borelius, Johann J.

Phil 4514.1.35	Borelius, J.J. Den dogmatiska rationismens strid mot den spekulativa filosofien. Stockholm, 1857.
Phil 4514.1.40	Borelius, J.J. Menniskans naturlif i dess förhållande de till det andliga lifvet. Stockholm, 1855.
Phil 4514.1.80	Boström, C.J. Den specultiva philosophen Johann Jacob Borelius Calmar. Upsala, 1860.

Phil 4515 History of philosophy - Local Modern philosophy - Scandinavia -
Individual philosophers - Boström, Christopher J.

Phil 4515.10	Boström, C.J. Skrifter af C.J. Boström utgifna af H. Edfeldt. v.1-3. Upsala, 1883-1901. 2v.
Phil 4515.30.2	Boström, C.J. Satser om lag och lagstiftning med tillägg och anmärkningar å nyo utgifne. 2e uppl. Upsala, 1871.
Phil 4515.31	Boström, C.J. Grundlinier till philosophiska civil- och criminalrätten. Stockholm, 1903.
Phil 4515.31.3	Boström, C.J. Grundlinier till philosophiska civil- och criminalrätten. Upsala, 1883.
Phil 4515.32.2	Boström, C.J. Grundlinier till philosophiska statslärans propaedeutik. 2. uppl. Upsala, 1884.
Phil 4515.32.3	Boström, C.J. Grundlinier till philosophiska statslärans propaedeutik. 3. uppl. Stockholm, 1901.
Phil 4515.32.5	Boström, C.J. Grundlinier till philosophiska statslärans propaedeutik. Upsala? 1859?
Phil 4515.33	Boström, C.J. Anmärkningar om helveteslären. 2. uppl. Upsala, 1864.
Phil 4515.34	Boström, C.J. Grundlinien eines philosophischen Systems. Leipzig, 1923.
Phil 4515.35	Boström, C.J. Föreläsningar i religionsfilosofi. Stockholm, 1885.
Phil 4515.36	Boström, C.J. Philosophy of religion. New Haven, 1962.
Phil 4515.40	Boström, C.J. Föreläsningar i etiken. Upsala, 1897.
Phil 4515.45	Boström, C.J. Dissertatio de notionibus religionis. Upsala, 1841.
Phil 4515.48	Boström, C.J. De nexu rerum cum Deo ex ratione pantheismi positiones. Upsaliae, 1827.
Phil 4515.50	Boström, C.J. Om religion, vishet och dygd. Stockholm, 1943.
Phil 4515.81	Nybläeus, A. Tvänne uppsatser om den Boströmska filosofien. Lund, 1885.
Phil 4515.81.5	Nybläeus, A. Bidrag till en karakteristik af den Boströmska filosofien. Lund, 1892.
Phil 4515.82	Hellström, Carl. Om viljefrihetsläran i Boströms definitiva filosofi. Uppsala, 1919.
Phil 4515.83	Edfeldt, Hans. Om Boströms ideelära. Uppsala, 1884.
Phil 4515.83.10	Edfeldt, Hans. Granskning af kandidaten Waldemar. Upsala, 1875.
Phil 4515.84	Vannérus, Allen. Till Boströms teoretiska filosofi. Stockholm, 1897.
Phil 4515.85	Liljeqvist, Efraim. Om Boströms äldsta skrifter. Göteborg, 1897.
Phil 4515.85.5	Liljeqvist, Efraim. Boströms äldsta latinska dissertationer. Thesis. Lund, 1915.
Phil 4515.86	Leander, P.J.H. Boströms lära om guds ideer. Lund, 1886.
Phil 4515.87	Sahlin, K.Y. Om ministrarne i den konstitutionela monarkien enligt Boströms statslära. Upsala, 1877.
Phil 4515.87.2	Sahlin, K.Y. Om menistrarne i den konstitutionela monarkien enligt Boströms statslära. Upsala, 1877.
Phil 4515.88	Kalling, P. Om kunskapen; studier. Upsala, 1875.
Phil 4515.89	C.J. Boström och hans filosofi. Örebro, 1859.
Phil 4515.90	Theorell, Sven L. Betraktelser i samhällslären med granskning af Boströmska statsläräns grundinier. Stockholm, 1860.
Phil 4515.91	Åberg, L.H. Den Boströmska verldsåsigten i sina grunddrag framstäld. Stockholm, 1882.
Phil 4515.91.5	Åberg, L.H. Försök till en lärobok i allmän samhällslära. Upsala, 1879.
Phil 4515.92	Dons, Waldemar. Om Boströmianismen. Christiania, 1874.
Phil 4515.93	Ljunghoff, Johannes. Christopher Jacob Boström Sveriges Platon. Uppsala, 1916.
Phil 4515.94	Landström, Gustaf. Om tänkaren Kristofer Jakob Boström och hans filosofi. Stockholm, 1903.
Phil 4515.96	Borelius, J.J. Kritik öfver den Boströmska filosofien. v.1-2. Stockholm, 1859-60.
Phil 4515.97	Kalling, P. Framställning af Boströmska filosofien. Örebro, 1868.
Phil 4515.98	Wikner, P. Om den svenske tänkaren Boström. Göteborg, 1888.
Phil 4515.99	Åt minnet af C.J. Boström, 1797-1897. Festskrift. Stockholm, 1897.
Phil 4515.100	Larsson, Hans. Minnesteckning över Christopher Jacob Boström. Stockholm, 1931.
Phil 4515.101	Wedberg, A. Den logiska strukturen hos Boströms filosofi. Uppsala, 1937.

Phil 4520 History of philosophy - Local Modern philosophy - Scandinavia -
Individual philosophers - Other B

Phil 4520.1.31	Blomquist, G. Lyckovägar. Stockholm, 1916.
Phil 4520.2.3	Biberg, N.F. Samlade skrifter. Upsala, 1828-30. 3v.
Phil 4520.2.30	Biberg, N.F. In jus natuarae recentiorum stricturae. Diss. Upsaliae, 1818.
Phil 4520.2.32	Biberg, N.F. Notionum ethicarum quas formales dicunt, dialexis critica. Diss. Pt.1-2. Upsaliae, 1823-24.
Phil 4520.2.34	Biberg, N.F. Commentationum Stoicarum. Diss. Upsaliae, 1815-1821.
Phil 4520.3.31	Björkman, N.O. Om det absoluta förnuftet. Stockholm, 1888.
Phil 4520.4.31	Bastholm, Christopher. Philosophie för olarde. Lund, 1795.
Phil 4520.5.20	Kant, Immanuel. Grundlaggning till metaphysiken för seder. Upsala, 1797.
Phil 4520.5.25	Boethius, Daniel. Dissertatio philosophica, de angustis rationis humanae limitibus. Upsaliae, 1774.
Phil 4520.5.30	Boethius, Daniel. Dissertatio philosophica de origine atque indole nimiae divitiarum aestimationis. Upsaliae, 1788.
Phil 4520.5.32	Boethius, Daniel. Dissertatio philosophica de morali ordine in eventu rerum jure postulato. Upsaliae, 1790.
Phil 4520.5.34	Boethius, Daniel. De modo inculcandi veritates morales in concione publica. Diss. Upsaliae, 1800.
Phil 4520.6.2	Björklund, G. Skrifter. Upsala, 1924.
Phil 4520.8.30	Bjarnason, Ágúst. Austurlönd. Reykjavík, 1908.
Phil 4520.8.32	Bjarnason, Ágúst. Drauma-joi, sannar sagnir. Reykjavík, 1915.
Phil 4520.8.34	Bjarnason, Ágúst. Hellas. Reykjavík, 1910.
Phil 4520.8.36	Bjarnason, Ágúst. Níjtánda öldin. Reykjavík, 1906.
Phil 4520.8.38	Bjarnason, Ágúst. Vesturlönd. Reykjavík, 1915.

Classified Listing

Phil 4520   History of philosophy - Local Modern philosophy - Scandinavia -
Individual philosophers - Other B - cont.
Phil 4520.8.40	Bjarnason, Ágúst. Andatrúin. Reykjavík, 1905.
Phil 4520.8.42	Bjarnason, Ágúst. Almenn rökfraeð Reykjavík, 1913.
Phil 4520.8.44	Bjarnason, Ágúst. Siðraeð Reykjavík, 1924.
Phil 4520.8.46	Bjarnason, Ágúst. Upphaf kristninnar og...Jesús Kristur. Reykjavík, 1904.
Phil 4520.8.48	Bjarnason, Ágúst. "Andatrúin" krufin. Reykjavík, 1906.
Phil 4520.8.50	Mjarnason, Ágúst. Rannsókn dularfullra fyrirbrigð. Reykjavík, 1914.
Phil 4520.8.52	Bjarnason, Ágúst. Almenn sálarfraeð Reykjavík, 1916.
Phil 4520.9.90	Festskrift tillägnad E.O. Burman. Upsala, 1910.

Phil 4525   History of philosophy - Local Modern philosophy - Scandinavia -
Individual philosophers - C
Phil 4525.1.31	Christensen, S. Indad. København, 1918.
Phil 4525.2.5	Claeson, Krist. Skrifter. Stockholm, 1860. 2v.
Phil 4525.2.90	Myrberg, Otto F. Om förhållandet mellan teologi och filosofi. v.2. Upsala, 1861.
Phil 4525.3.30	Cavallin, P. Identiska och syntetiska satser. Lund, 1894.

Phil 4540   History of philosophy - Local Modern philosophy - Scandinavia -
Individual philosophers - F
Phil 4540.5	Feilberg, Ludvig. Samlede skrifter. 3. udg. København, 1949- 2v.
Phil 4540.10	Favrhold, David. Filosofi og samfund. København, 1968.

Phil 4570   History of philosophy - Local Modern philosophy - Scandinavia -
Individual philosophers - G
Phil 4570.1.5	Grubbe, Samuel. Filosofiska skrifter i Urval. v.1-5. Lund, 1876. 7v.
Phil 4570.1.20	Grubbe, Samuel. Bidrag till utredandet af samhällslärans grundbegrepp. 1. delen. Upsala, 1826.
Phil 4570.1.30	Grubbe, Samuel. Filosofisk rätts- och samhälls-lära. Upsala, 1839.
Phil 4570.1.60	Grubbe, Samuel. Dissertatio de harmonia religionis et moralitatis. Upsaliae, 1810.
Phil 4570.1.81	Schéele, Frans von. Samuel Grubbe's skönhetslära. Akademisk afhandling. Upsala, 1885.
Phil 4570.1.83	Meden, Carl. Om Grubbes deduktion af rättsbegreppet. Uppsala, 1869.
Phil 4570.1.85	Cuelberg, John. Samuel Grubbe; en studie i transcendental religionsfilosofi. Upsala, 1926.
Phil 4570.2.6	Genberg, P. Valda skrifter. v.1-2. Stockholm, 1878.
Phil 4570.3.31	Geijer, R. Samvetet. Stockholm, 1905.
Phil 4570.3.81	Geijer, R. Humanistiska sektionen contra den sakkunniga nämden. Lund, 1887.
Phil 4570.4.81	Spongberg, V.H. The philosophy of Erik Gustaf Geijer. Rock Island, 1945.

Phil 4575   History of philosophy - Local Modern philosophy - Scandinavia -
Individual philosophers - Höijer, Benjamin
Phil 4575.10	Höijer, B.C.H. Samlade skrifter. Stockholm, 1825-27. 5v.
Phil 4575.25	Höijer, B.C.H. Filosofiska föreläsningar, 1806-1812. Lund, 1931.
Phil 4575.93	Bygdén, Anders L. Benjamin Höijer. Akademisk afhandling. Upsala, 1872.
Phil 4575.94	Leufren, E.J. Kritisk exposition of Benjamin Höijers. Upsala, 1897.
Phil 4575.95	Liljekrantz, B. Benjamin Höijer. Lund, 1912.

Phil 4580   History of philosophy - Local Modern philosophy - Scandinavia -
Individual philosophers - Höffding, Harold
Phil 4580.15	Høffding, Harald. Mindre arbejder. Räkke 1-2. København, 1899-1905.
Phil 4580.20	Høffding, Harald. Correspondence entre H. Høffding et G. Meyerson. Copenhague, 1939.
Phil 4580.30	Høffding, Harald. Danske filosofer. København, 1909.
Phil 4580.31	Køffding, Harald. Formel logik. København, 1884.
Phil 4580.32	Høffding, Harald. Ved aarhundredeskiftet. København, 1901.
Phil 4580.33.5	Høffding, Harald. Personlighetsprincipen i filosofin. Stockholm, 1911.
Phil 4580.35.7	Høffding, Harald. Kort oversigt over den nyere filosofis historie. 7e ed. Kjøbenhavn, 1919
Phil 4580.35.9	Høffding, Harald. Kort oversigt over den nyere filosofis historie. 9e ed. Kjøbenhavn, 1925.
Phil 4580.36	Høffding, Harald. Den nyere filosofis historie. København, 1894-95. 2v.
Phil 4580.36.3	Høffding, Harald. Den nyere filosofis historie. v.1-10. Kjøbenhavn, 1921-22. 2v.
Phil 4580.37	Høffding, Harald. O plevelse og tydning religionsfilosofiske studier. Kjøbenhavn, 1918.
Phil 4580.37.5	Høffding, Harald. Erlebnis und Deutung; eine vergleichende Studie zur Religionspsychologie. Stuttgart, 1923.
Phil 4580.38.15	Høffding, Harald. Regionsphilosophie. Leipzig, 1901.
Phil 4580.38.20	Høffding, Harald. Religionsfilosofi. 3e ed. København, 1924.
Phil 4580.40	Høffding, Harald. Totalitet som kategori en erkendelsesteoretisk undersøgelse. København, 1917.
Phil 4580.50	Høffding, Harald. Der totalitätsbegriff. Leipzig, 1917.
Phil 4580.51	Høffding, Harald. La relativité philosophique. Paris, 1924.
Phil 4580.62	Høffding, Harald. Morale essai sur les principes théoriques. Paris, 1903.
Phil 4580.63	Høffding, Harald. Den store humor. Kjøbenhavn, 1916.
Phil 4580.64	Høffding, Harald. Om grundlaget for den humane ethik. Kjøbenhavn, 1876.
Phil 4580.65	Høffding, Harald. Etiske undersøgelser. København, 1891.
Phil 4580.66	Høffding, Harald. Der Begriff der Analogie. Leipzig, 1924.
Phil 4580.66.10	Høffding, Harald. Le concept d'analogie. Paris, 1931.
Phil 4580.67	Høffding, Harald. Religiøse tankotyper. København, 1927.
Phil 4580.79	Høffding, Harald. Erindringer. København, 1928.
Phil 4580.81	Rindom, E. Samtaler med Harald Høffding, 1909-1918. København, 1918.
Phil 4580.81.5	Rindom, E. Harald Høffding. Kjøbenhavn, 1918.
Phil 4580.82	Schiodte, C. Bemaerkninger om den Høffdingske filosofi. København, 1900.
Phil 4580.113	Schott, Georg. Harald Høffding, als Religionsphilosoph. München, 1913.
Phil 4580.113.3	Schott, Georg. Harald Høffding als Religionsphilosoph. Inaug. Diss. München, 1913.
Phil 4580.115	La Harpe, J. La réligion comme conservation de la valeur dans ses rapports avec...H. Høffding. Lausanne, 1920.
Phil 4580.116	Hansen, V. Harald Høffding som religionsfilosof. København, 1923.

Phil 4580   History of philosophy - Local Modern philosophy - Scandinavia -
Individual philosophers - Höffding, Harold - cont.
Phil 4580.117	Hürtgen, Robert. Das Gottesproblem bei Harald Høffding. Inaug. Diss. Bonn, 1928.
Phil 4580.118	Meis, Hans. Darstellung und Würdigung der Ethik Harald Høffdings. Inaug. Diss. Obersassel, 1928.
Phil 4580.119	Harald Høffding in memoriam. København, 1932.
Phil 4580.120	Horreüs de Hass, G. Harald Høffding en zijne beteekenis voor godsdienstwipbegeerte a zedeleer. Huister Heide, 1930.

Phil 4582   History of philosophy - Local Modern philosophy - Scandinavia -
Individual philosophers - Other H
Phil 4582.1.30	Herrlin, Axel. Filosofi och facksetenskap. Lund, 1905.
Phil 4582.1.81	Leljeqvist, E. Marginalanmärkningar till Docenten Herrlins skrift "Filosofi och fackvetenskap". Göteborg, 1905.
Phil 4582.1.83	Festskrift till ägnad Axel Herrlin den 30 mars 1935. Lund, 1935.
Phil 4582.2.31	Hofstedt, A. Arbetets ära kulturhistorisk undersökning. Stockholm, 1900.
Phil 4582.3.31	Hwasser, Israel. Om vår tids ungdom. Upsala, 1842.
Phil 4582.3.32	Hwasser, Israel. Mannens ynglingaålder. Upsala, 1856.
Phil 4582.4.31	Hägerström, Axel. Undersökning af den empiristiska etikens möjlighet. Upsala, 1895.
Phil 4582.4.33	Hägerström, Axel. Om moraliska föreställningars sanning. Stockholm, 1911.
Phil 4582.4.35	Hägerström, Axel. Om den moraliska känslan och driften sasom förnuftiga. Upsala, 1895.
Phil 4582.4.38	Hägerström, Axel. Stat och rätt. Upsala, 1904.
Phil 4582.4.40	Hägerström, Axel. De socialistiska idéernas historia. Stockholm, 1946.
Phil 4582.4.45	Hägerström, Axel. Inquiries into the nature of law and morals. Stockholm, 1953.
Phil 4582.4.46	Hägerström, Axel. Ratten och Viljan. Lund, 1961.
Phil 4582.4.49	Hägerström, Axel. Socialfilosofiska uppsatser. Stockholm, 1966.
Phil 4582.4.83	Leander, P.H.J. Svar på kritik af ett kompetensutlåtande. Lund, 1898.
Phil 4582.4.88	Festskrift tillägnad Axel Hägerström den 6 september 1928. Upsala, 1928.
Phil 4582.4.90	Vannérus, Allen. Hägerströmstudier. Stockholm, 1930.
Phil 4582.4.95	Klingberg, Wilhelm. Den intellektuella spärren; trous svårigheter i belysning av Axel Hägerströms filosofi. Stockholm, 1966.
Phil 4582.4.100	Marc-Wogan, Konrad. Studier till Axel Hägerströms filosofi. Stockholm, 1968.
Phil 4582.5.30	Halvorson, G. Grundtraek af metafysik. Kristiania, 1891.
Phil 4582.6.30	Hermansson, J. Quaestio philosophica an philosophus passit errare? Upsaliae, 1728.
Phil 4582.6.35	Hermansson, J. Speciminis academici. Upsaliae, 1733.
Phil 4582.6.40	Hermansson, J. Dissertatio philosophica. Upsaliae, 1736.
Phil 4582.7.90	Thomsen, O. F.G. Howitz, 1789-1826. København, 1924.

Phil 4585   History of philosophy - Local Modern philosophy - Scandinavia -
Individual philosophers - I
Phil 4585.1.31	Ibsen, Sigurd. Menneskelig kvintessens. Kristiania, 1911.
Phil 4585.9.81	Rubin, E. En ung dansk filosof. Kjøbenhavn, 1920.

Phil 4595   History of philosophy - Local Modern philosophy - Scandinavia -
Individual philosophers - Other K
Phil 4595.1.31	Krebs, C. Handling og iagttagelse. København, 1913.
Phil 4595.3.31	Karitz, Anders. Philosophie und Spezialforschung. Lund, 1932.
Phil 4595.4.30	Hansen, Valdemar. K. Kroman. København, 1955.

Phil 4600   History of philosophy - Local Modern philosophy - Scandinavia -
Individual philosophers - L
Phil 4600.1.31	Landquist, John. Filosofiska essayer. Stockholm, 1906.
Phil 4600.1.35	Landquist, John. Essayer. Stockholm, 1913.
Phil 4600.1.40	Landquist, John. Det levande forflutna. Stockholm, 1919.
Phil 4600.2.30	Larsson, Hans. Postscriptum. Stockholm, 1944.
Phil 4600.2.32	Larsson, Hans. Ideer om makter. 2. uppl. Lund, 1909.
Phil 4600.2.33	Larsson, Hans. Nagot om den fria viljan. n.p., n.d.
Phil 4600.2.34	Larsson, Hans. Viljans frihet. Lund, 1899.
Phil 4600.2.35	Larsson, Hans. Viljans frihet. Lund, 1910.
Phil 4600.2.36	Larsson, Hans. Studier och meditationer. 4e uppl. Lund, 1912.
Phil 4600.2.37	Larsson, Hans. Hemmabyarna världsbetraklelser i femton kapitel. Stockholm, 1916.
Phil 4600.2.38	Larsson, Hans. Under världskrisen. Stockholm, 1920.
Phil 4600.2.39	Larsson, Hans. Kunskapslivet. 3e uppl. Stockholm, 1920.
Phil 4600.2.40	Larsson, Hans. Psykologi paa Dansk red Stig Bredstrup. København, 1914.
Phil 4600.2.44	Larsson, Hans. Intuitionsproblemet. Stockholm, 1912.
Phil 4600.2.45	Larsson, Hans. Intuition. 3e uppl. Stockholm, 1910.
Phil 4600.2.46	Larsson, Hans. Intuition. 4e uppl. Stockholm, 1910.
Phil 4600.2.48	Larsson, Hans. Filosofien och politiken. Stockholm, 1915.
Phil 4600.2.50	Larsson, Hans. Gränsen mellan sensation och emotion. 2e uppl. Lund, 1911.
Phil 4600.2.52	Larsson, Hans. Den intellektuella askadningens filosofi. Stockholm, 1920.
Phil 4600.2.53	Larsson, Hans. Reflexioner för dagen. Lund, 1911.
Phil 4600.2.80	Nyman, Alf. Hans Larsson. Stockholm, 1945.
Phil 4600.2.90	Festskrift tillägnad Hans Larsson. Stockholm, 1927.
Phil 4600.3.31	Leander, P.J.H. Om substansbegreppet hos Cartesius, Spinoza och Liebnitz. Akademisk afhandling. Lund, 1862. 2 pam.
Phil 4600.4.30	Lidforss, Bengt. Dagsbilder. Malmö, 1917.
Phil 4600.4.32	Lidforss, Bengt. Fragment och miniatyrer. 2. uppl. Malmö, 1912.
Phil 4600.4.35	Lidforss, Bengt. Onda makter och goda. Malmö, 1909.
Phil 4600.4.36	Utkast och silhuetter. Malmö, 1909.
Phil 4600.4.38	Lidforss, Bengt. Modärna apologeter. Malmö, 1911.
Phil 4600.4.40	Lidforss, Bengt. Polemiska inlägg. Malmö, 1913.
Phil 4600.4.45	Lidforss, Bengt. Bengt Lidforss i urral. Stockholm, 1965.
Phil 4600.4.80	Geijerstam, G.L. af. Så minns Bengt Lidforss. Stockholm, 1908.
Phil 4600.4.85	Beyer, Nils. Bengt Lidforss. Stockholm, 1968.
Phil 4600.5.31	Ljunglund, L. Livets bejakande. Stockholm, 1914.
Phil 4600.6.21	Lagerwall, A. Skrifter. Göteborg, 1921.
Phil 4600.7.30	Lagerborg, Rolf. Invita Minerva. Stockholm, 1918.
Phil 4600.8	Asfelin, G. Studier Aillägnade Efraim Liljequish. Lund, 1930. 2v.

Phil 4605 History of philosophy - Local Modern philosophy - Scandinavia - Individual philosophers - M

Phil 4605.1.31 Monrad, M.J. Tro og viden. Kristiania, 1892.
Phil 4605.1.36 Monrad, M.J. Philosophisk propaedentik. 5. opl. Christiania, 1896.
Phil 4605.1.41 Monrad, M.J. Om det skjønne. Christiania, 1873.
Phil 4605.1.46 Monrad, M.J. Tankeretninger i den nyere tid. 2 opl. Christiania, 1884.
Phil 4605.1.49 Monrad, M.J. Denkrichtungen der neueren Zeit. Bonn, 1879.
Phil 4605.1.80 Christophersen, Halfdan. Marcus Jacob Monrad. Oslo, 1959.
Phil 4605.2.31 Menzinger, A. Fra før Kant. København, 1918.
Phil 4605.74.31 Marc-Wogan, Konrad. Filosofiska dis Kussioner. Stockholm, 1967.

Phil 4610 History of philosophy - Local Modern philosophy - Scandinavia - Individual philosophers - N

Phil 4610.6.2 Nyblaeus, Axel. Trenne religiousfilosfiska uppsatser. 2. uppl. Lund, 1874.
Phil 4610.6.3 Trenne filosofiska uppsatser. Lund, 1878.
Phil 4610.6.31 Nyblaeus, Axel. Om straffrätten. Lund, 1852.
Phil 4610.7.10 Norström, V. Tankelinier. Stockholm, 1905.
Phil 4610.7.13 Norström, V. Tankar och forskningar. Stockholm, 1915.
Phil 4610.7.15 Norström, V. Religion och tanke. Stockholm, 1912.
Phil 4610.7.18 Norström, V. Hvad är sanning. Göteborg, 1899.
Phil 4610.7.25 Norström, V. Religion und Gedanke. Lund, 1932.
Phil 4610.7.31 Norström, V. Om pligt, frihet och förnuft. Upsala, 1891.
Phil 4610.7.32 Norström, V. Om natursammanhang och frihet. Göteborg, 1895.
Phil 4610.7.33 Norström, V. Naturkunskapens självbesinning. Stockholm, 1907.
Phil 4610.7.35 Norström, V. Hvad vi behöfva. Stockholm, 1901.
Phil 4610.7.38 Norström, V. Masskultur. Stockholm, 1910.
Phil 4610.7.40 Norström, V. Om viljans frihet. Stockholm, 1917.
Phil 4610.7.45 Norström, V. Tal och tankar. Stockholm, 1919.
Phil 4610.7.50 Norström, V. Den nyaste människan. Stockholm, 1906.
Phil 4610.7.85 Norström, V. Brev, 1889-1916. Stockholm, 1923.
Phil 4610.7.87 Liljedal, E. Vitalis Norström. Stockholm, 1917-18. 2v.
Phil 4610.7.88 Akesson, Elof. Norströmiana. Stockholm, 1924.
Phil 4610.7.90 Festskrift tillägnad Vitalis Norström. Göteborg, 1916.
Phil 4610.9.31 Nielsen, R. Natur og aand. Kjøbenhavn, 1873. 2 pam.
Phil 4610.9.35 Nielsen, R. Om personlig sanning och sann personlighet. Upsala, 1856.
Phil 4610.9.80 Asmussen, E. Entwicklungsgang und grundprobleme der philosophie Rasmus Nielsens. Inaug. Diss. Flensburg, 1911.
Phil 4610.9.85 Steen, H. Problemet om tro og viden. Kjøbenhavn, 1813.
Phil 4610.10.30 Naess, Arne. Hva er filosofi? Oslo, 1965.
Phil 4610.12.80 Mustelin, Olof. Hjalmar Neiglick. Helsingfors, 1966.

Phil 4620 History of philosophy - Local Modern philosophy - Scandinavia - Individual philosophers - P

Phil 4620.1 Péturss, Helgi. Nýall Nokkur íslenzk drög til heimsfraeð og liffraeð Reykjavík, 1922.
Phil 4620.1.5 Péturss, Helgi. Erlendar Greiner. Reykjavík, 1955.
Phil 4620.2.90 Hedenius, I. Adolf Phalén in memoriam. Uppsala, 1937.
Phil 4620.3 Péturss, Helgi. Nýall. Reykjavík, 1919.
Phil 4620.3.5 Péturss, Helgi. Sannyall. Reykjavík, 1943.

Phil 4630 History of philosophy - Local Modern philosophy - Scandinavia - Individual philosophers - R

Phil 4630.1.31 Ribbing, Sigurd. Grundlinier till anthropololgien. 4. uppl. Upsala, 1870.
Phil 4630.1.35 Ribbing, Sigurd. Eristiska blad. Upsala, 1852.
Phil 4630.2.31 Rein, T. Uppsatser och tal. Helsingfors, 1903.
Phil 4630.2.36 Rein, T. Lärobok i den formella logiken. Helsingfors, 1886.
Phil 4630.2.38 Rein, T. Grunddragen af den filosofiska imputationsläran. Helsingfors, 1863.
Phil 4630.2.39 Rein, T. Om kunskapens möjlighet. Helsingfors, 1867.
Phil 4630.2.40 Rein, T. Om den filosofiska methoden. Helsingfors, 1868.
Phil 4630.2.43 Rein, T. Anteckningar i filosofi och historia. Helsingfors, 1889.
Phil 4630.2.45 Rein, T. Lefnadsminnen. Helsingfors, 1918.
Phil 4630.2.80 Juhlajulkaisu omistettu Th. Reinille hänen täyttäessään 80 vuotta. Helsingissä, 1918.
Phil 4630.3.31 Rydelius, Anders. Förnufts-öfningar. Linköping, 1737.
Phil 4630.3.35 Rydelius, Anders. Dissertatio philosophica mepi...seu de excessu subtilitatis in philosophicae. Lund, 1726.
Phil 4630.3.37 Rydelius, Anders. Dissertatio metaphysica de novis...axiomatibus...Leibnitus et Volfius. Lundini, 1725.
Phil 4630.3.39 Rydelius, Anders. Aphorismi philosophici de moderamine libertatis philosophicae. Diss. Lundini, 1726.
Phil 4630.3.42 Rydelius, Anders. Dissertatio philosophica, gradualis de tempore. Diss. Lundini, 1726.
Phil 4630.3.44 Rydelius, Anders. Dissertatio philosophica, fidelem praeceptorem...privatum adumbrans. Diss. Lundini, 1726.
Phil 4630.3.46 Rydelius, Anders. Dissertatio philosophica de vera rationis humanae definitione. Diss. Lund, 1727.
Phil 4630.3.80 Almguist, Karl Gustaf. Andreas Rydelius etiska åkådning. Lund, 1955.
Phil 4630.4.30 Ruin, Waldemar. Kunskap och ideal. Helsingfors, 1886.
Phil 4630.4.40 Ruin, Waldemar. Kulturen och tiden. Helsingfors, 1920.
Phil 4630.5.2 Rydberg, V. Filosofiska föreläsningar. Stockholm, 1900-01. 4v.
Phil 4630.6.30 Rubin, E. Af efterladte papirer. København, 1956.
Phil 4630.7.80 Aaberg, Bengt. Individualitet och universalitet hos Waldemar Rudin. Lund, 1968.

Phil 4635 History of philosophy - Local Modern philosophy - Scandinavia - Individual philosophers - S

Htn Phil 4635.1.30* Swedenborg, E. Prodromus philosophiae. Dresdae, 1734.
Phil 4635.2.31 Starcke, C.N. Samvittighedslivet. København, 1894-97.
Phil 4635.2.33 Starke, C.N. Etikens teoretiske grundlag. Kjøbenhavn, 1889.
Phil 4635.2.34F Starcke, C.N. Den menneskelige tänkning. Kopenhagen, 1916.
Phil 4635.2.90 Naesgaard, S. Starkes psykologi. Köbenhavn, 1916.
Phil 4635.2.92 Naesgaard, S. Starckes forsvar, metoder og resultater. Köbenhavn, 1917.
Phil 4635.3.31 Sylwan, O.C. Naturvetenskap eller metafysik? Stockholm, 1881.
Phil 4635.3.33 Sylwan, O.C. Vetenskapens evangelium. Stockholm, 1879.
Phil 4635.4.31 Schéele, Frans von. Filosofiens uppgift. Upsala, 1899.
Phil 4635.4.33 Schéele, Frans von. Filosofiska studier. Första samlingen. Stockholm, 1899.
Phil 4635.5.81.3 Rein, T. Juhana Vilhelm Snellman. Helsingissa, 1928.
Phil 4635.6.30 Sjöholm, L.A. Det historiska sammanhanget mellan Humes skepticism och Kants kriticism. Upsala, 1869.

Phil 4635 History of philosophy - Local Modern philosophy - Scandinavia - Individual philosophers - S - cont.

Phil 4635.7.9 Stjernhjelm, Georg. Filosofiska fragment. v.1-2. Stockholm, 1924.
Phil 4635.8.31 Sibbern, F.C. Om philosophiens begreb. Kjøbenhavn, 1843.
Phil 4635.8.33 Sibbern, F.C. Speculativ kosmologie med grundlag. Kjøbenhavn, 1846.
Phil 4635.9.30 Grieg, Harald V. Torgny Segershedt. Oslo, 1945.
Phil 4635.9.80 Ancker, E. Torgny Segerstedt, 1876-1945. Stockholm, 1962.
Phil 4635.10.30 Skjervheim, Hans. Vitskapen om mennesket ogden filosofiske refleksjon. Oslo, 1964.

Phil 4640 History of philosophy - Local Modern philosophy - Scandinavia - Individual philosophers - T

Phil 4640.1.30 Treschow, N. Om den menneskelige natur. København, 1812.
Phil 4640.2.30 Fórólfsson, S. Dulmaetti og dultrú. Reykjavík, 1922.

Phil 4650 History of philosophy - Local Modern philosophy - Scandinavia - Individual philosophers - V

Phil 4650.1.31 Vannérus, Allen. Till kritiken af den religiösa kunskapen. Stockholm, 1902.
Phil 4650.1.33 Vannérus, Allen. Ateism contra teism. Stockholm, 1903.
Phil 4650.1.35 Vannérus, Allen. Kulturidealism. Stockholm, 1903.
Phil 4650.1.37 Vannérus, Allen. Lära och lif. Stockholm, 1904.
Phil 4650.1.39 Vannérus, Allen. Kunskapslära. Stockholm, 1905.
Phil 4650.1.40 Vannérus, Allen. Vetenskapernas system. Stockholm, 1892.
Phil 4650.1.41 Vannérus, Allen. Vetenskapssystematik. Stockholm, 1907.
Phil 4650.1.43 Vannérus, Allen. Logik och vetenskapslära. Stockholm, 1918.
Phil 4650.1.45 Vannérus, Allen. Til det andliga lifvets filosofi. Stockholm, 1910.
Phil 4650.1.47 Vannérus, Allen. Om erfarenheten ett kunskapsteoretiskt studieförsök. Akademisk afhandling. Stockholm, 1890.
Phil 4650.1.48 Vannérus, Allen. Det yttersta tankegångar. Stockholm, 1924.
Phil 4650.1.51 Vannérus, Allen. Filosofiska konturer. Göteborg, 1902.
Phil 4650.1.53 Vannérus, Allen. Metafysik. Lund, 1914.
Phil 4650.1.56 Vannérus, Allen. Ursprungens filosofi. Stockholm, 1925.
Phil 4650.1.59 Vannérus, Allen. Materiens värld. Stockholm, 1925.
Phil 4650.1.69 Vannérus, Allen. Etiska tankegångar. Stockholm, 1922.
Phil 4650.1.70 Vannérus, Allen. Den empiriska naturuppfattningen. 2. ed. Stockholm, 1913.

Phil 4655 History of philosophy - Local Modern philosophy - Scandinavia - Individual philosophers - W

Phil 4655.1.2 Wikner, Pontus. Skrifter. Stockholm, 1920-27. 12v.
Phil 4655.1.18 Wikner, Pontus. Vittra skrifter. 3. uppl. Stockholm, 1894.
Phil 4655.1.25 Wikner, Pontus. Anteckningar till filosofiens historia efter P. Wikners kollegium af K.S. Upsala, 18- .
Phil 4655.1.30 Wikner, Pontus. Om egenskapen och närgränsande tankeföremål. Upsala, 1880.
Phil 4655.1.35 Wikner, Pontus. Kultur och filosofi i deras förhällande till hvarandra. Stockholm, 1869.
Phil 4655.1.38 Wikner, Pontus. Om auktoritet och sjelfständighet. Upsala, 1872.
Phil 4655.1.40 Wikner, Pontus. Öppet sändebref till teologisk tidskrift. Upsala, 1881.
Phil 4655.1.43 Wikner, Pontus. Undersökningar om enhet och mängfald. Upsala, 1863.
Phil 4655.1.45 Wikner, Pontus. Lärobok i anthropologien. Upsala, 1870.
Phil 4655.1.48 Wikner, Pontus. "Gud är kärleken." 2. uppl. Stockholm, 1895.
Phil 4655.1.50 Wikner, Pontus. Några drag af kulturens offerväsen. Upsala, 1880.
Phil 4655.1.52 Wikner, Pontus. Kan philosophien bringa någon välsignelse åt mensklighten? 2. uppl. Upsala, 1864.
Phil 4655.1.53 Wikner, Pontus. Hvad vi behöfva. Upsala, 1865.
Phil 4655.1.55 Wikner, Pontus. Narkissos-sagan och platonismen. Upsala, 1880.
Phil 4655.1.58 Wikner, Pontus. Tankar och frågor inför menniskones son. 4. uppl. Stockholm, 1893.
Phil 4655.1.62 Wikner, Pontus. Promotionspredikan. Upsala, 1872.
Phil 4655.1.64 Wikner, Pontus. Undersökningar angående den materialistiska verldsåskådningen. Stockholm, 1870.
Phil 4655.1.67 Wikner, Pontus. Naturens förbannelse. Upsala, 1866.
Phil 4655.1.70 Wikner, Pontus. Uppsatser i religiösa ämnen. Stockholm, 1871.
Phil 4655.1.72 Wikner, Pontus. I mensklighetens lifsfrågor. Stockholm, 1889. 2v.
Phil 4655.1.80 Åberg, L.H. Carl Pontus Wikner. Sockholm, 1889.
Phil 4655.1.80.2 Åberg, L.H. Granskning af P. Wikners kritik. Stockholm, 1882.
Phil 4655.1.81 Eklund, J.A. Pontus Wikner. Stockholm, 1903.
Phil 4655.1.82 Kjellberg, Elis. Carl Pontus Wikner. Upsala, 1888.
Phil 4655.1.82.2 Kjellberg, Elis. Carl Pontus Wikner. Stockholm, 1902.
Phil 4655.1.83 Kjellberg, Elis. Mer om och af Pontus Wikner. Upsala, 1913.
Phil 4655.1.84 Werin, A. Pontus Wikner. Lund, 1937.
Phil 4655.1.85 Lange, Dagmar M. Pontus Wikner som vitter författare. Nora, 1946.
Phil 4655.2.30 Wildhagen, A. Vor tids determinisme. Kristiania, 1887.
Phil 4655.3.30 Waerland, Are. Materie eller ande? 3. uppl. Uppsala, 1919.
Phil 4655.3.33 Waerland, Are. Idealism och materialism. Uppsala, 1924.
Phil 4655.4.30 Wedberg, Anders. Philosophical papers. Stockholm, 1968-

Phil 4668 History of philosophy - Local Modern philosophy - Finland - Individual philosophers (363 scheme)

Phil 4668.40.30 Castrén, Zacharias. Uskonnonfilosofian käsitteestä ja metoodista. Helsingissä, 1899.
Phil 4668.121.80 Harva, Uno. Die Philosophie von G.I. Hartman. Turku, 1935.
Phil 4668.123.30 Hintikka, Kaarlo Jaakko Juhani. Tieto on valtaa ja muita aatehistoriallisia esseitä. Porvoo, 1969.

Phil 4680 History of philosophy - Local Modern philosophy - Latvia - History

Phil 4680.312 Valeskalns, Peteris. Ocherk razvitiia progressivnoi filosofskoi iobshchestvenno-politicheskoi mysli v Latvii. Riga, 1967.

Phil 4683   History of philosophy - Local Modern philosophy - Latvia - Individual philosophers (363 scheme)

Phil 4683.37.30   Buduls, Hermanis. Cilvēks dzives spoguli. Stockholm, 1954.

Phil 4683.55.31   Dāle, Pauls. Vērojumi un pārdomas par cilvēku un gara kultūru. Chicago, 1952.

Phil 4683.161.30   Jurevičs, Pauls. Idejas un istenība; esejas. 2. izd. Stockholm, 1965.

Phil 4688   History of philosophy - Local Modern philosophy - Lithuania - Individual philosophers (363 scheme)

Phil 4688.110.30   Girnius, Juozas. Idealas ir laikas. Chicago, 1966.

Phil 4688.110.32   Girnius, Juozas. Laisve ir būtist. Brooklyn, 1953.

Phil 4688.110.34   Girnius, Juozas. Žmogus de Dievo. Chicago? 1964.

Phil 4688.110.36   Girnius, Juozas. Tauta ir tautine ištikimybė. Chicago, 1961.

Phil 4710   History of philosophy - Local Modern philosophy - Russia - History - General works

Phil 4710.01   Pamphlet vol. Philosophy. Russian. 6 pam.

Phil 4710.02   Pamphlet vol. Philosophy. Russian. 5 pam.

Phil 4710.03   Pamphlet vol. Philosophy. Russian. 5 pam.

Phil 4710.04   Pamphlet vol. Philosophy. Russian. 4 pam.

Phil 4710.1   Bezobrazova, M. Handschriftliche...Philosophie in Russland. Leipzig, 1892.

Phil 4710.2   Koyré, A. Études sur l'histoire de la pensée philosophique en Russie. Paris, 1950.

Phil 4710.3   Lobkowicz, Nikolaus. Das Widerspruchsprinzie in der neueren sowjetischen Philosophie. Reidel, 1959.

Phil 4710.4   Jakovenko, B. Filosofi Russi: saggio di storia della filosofia. Firenze, 1925.

Phil 4710.4.10   Jakovenko, B. Ocherki russkoi filosofii. Berlin, 1922.

Phil 4710.5   Lourié, Osip. La philosophie russe contemporaine. Paris, 1902.

Phil 4710.5.2A   Lourié, Osip. La philosophie russe contemporaine. 2. ed. Paris, 1905.

Phil 4710.5.2B   Lourié, Osip. La philosophie russe contemporaine. 2. ed. Paris, 1905.

Phil 4710.6   Schultze, B. Russische Denker. Wien, 1950.

Phil 4710.7   Moscow. Universitet. Filosofskii Fakul'tet. Iz istorii russkoi filosofii, sbornik. Leningrad, 1949.

Phil 4710.7.5   Moscow. Universitet. Filosofskii Fakul'tet. Iz istorii russkoi filosofii, sbornik. Moskva, 1951.

Phil 4710.7.5.2   Moscow. Universitet. Filosofskii Fakul'tet. Iz istorii russkoi filosofii, sbornik. Moskva, 1952.

Phil 4710.7.7   Moscow. Universitet. Filosofskii Fakul'tet. Iz istorii russkoi filosofii, XVIII-XIX vv. Moskva, 1952.

Phil 4710.7.10A   Moscow. Universitet. Filosofskii Fakul'tet. Izbrannye proizvedeniia russkikh myslitelei vtoroi poloviny XVIII v. Leningrad, 1952. 2v.

Phil 4710.7.10B   Moscow. Universitet. Filosofskii Fakul'tet. Izbrannye proizvedeniia russkikh myslitelei vtoroi poloviny XVIII v. Leningrad, 1952. 2v.

Phil 4710.7.15   Iz istorii russkoi filosofii XIX-go-nachala XX-go veka. Moskva, 1969.

Phil 4710.9   Wetter, G.A. Die Umkehrung Hegels. Köln, 1963.

X Cg   Phil 4710.10   Problemy russkago religioznogo soznaniia. Berlin, 1924.

Phil 4710.11   Khaskhachikh, F.I. Materiia i soznanie. Moskva, 1951.

Phil 4710.11.5   Khaskhachikh, F.I. Materie und Bewusstsein. 5. Aufl. Berlin, 1957.

Phil 4710.12   Losskii, N.O. Dialekticheskii materializm v SSSR. Paris, 193-?

Phil 4710.15   Billig, Joseph. Der russische Idealismus der 30er Jahre und seine Überwindung. Inaug. Diss. Berlin, 1930.

Phil 4710.16   Bobrov, E.A. Filosofiia v Rossii; materialy. Kazan, 1899.

Phil 4710.17A   Akademiia Nauk SSSR. Institut Filosofii. Ocherki po istorii filosoficheskoi i obshchestvenno-politicheskoi mysli narodov SSSR. Moskva, 1955. 2v.

Phil 4710.17B   Akademiia Nauk SSSR. Institut Filosofii. Ocherki po istorii filosoficheskoi i obshchestvenno-politicheskoi mysli narodov SSSR. Moskva, 1955. 2v.

Phil 4710.18   Vysheslavtsev, B.P. Vechnoe v russkoi filosofii. N.Y., 1955.

Phil 4710.19   Laszlo, Ervin. Philosophy in the Soviet Union. Dordrecht, 1967.

Phil 4710.20.5   Radloff, E. von. Russische Philosophie. Bredau, 1925.

Phil 4710.25   Pelikán, Ferdinand. Současná filosofie u Slovanů. Praha, 1932.

Phil 4710.25.5   Pelikán, Ferdinand. Aus der philosophischen Riffamationsliteratur. Prag, 1934.

Phil 4710.30   Kruzhkov, U.S. O russkoi klassicheskoi filosofii XIX v. Moskva, 1945.

Phil 4710.35A   Losskii, N.O. History of Russian philosophy. N.Y., 1951.

Phil 4710.35B   Losskii, N.O. History of Russian philosophy. N.Y., 1951.

Phil 4710.36   Zen'kovskii, V.V. O mnimom materializme russkoi nauki i filosofii. Miunkhen, 1956.

Phil 4710.37   Bubnov, Nikolai M. Russische Religionsphilosophen. Heidelberg, 1956.

Phil 4710.40   Kulchitskii, Aleksandr. Die marxistisch-sowjetische Konzeption des Menschen. München, 1956.

Phil 4710.50   Chizhevskii, O. Filosofiia na Ukraini. Vyd. 2. Praga, 1928.

Phil 4710.50.5   Akademiia Nauk URSR, Kiev. Instytut Filosofii. Z istorii filosofs'koi dumki na Ukraini. Kyïv, 1962.

Phil 4710.50.10   Akademiia Nauk URSR, Kiev. Instytut Filosofii. Borot'ba mizh materializmom ta idealizmom na Ukraini. Kyïv, 1964.

Phil 4710.50.15   Ievdokymenko, V.I. Z istorii filosofs'koi dumky na Ukraini. Kyïv, 1965.

Phil 4710.50.20   Akademiia Nauk URSR, Kiev. Instytut Filosofii. Narys istorii filosofii na Ukraini. Kyïv, 1966.

Phil 4710.50.25   Akademiia Nauk URSR, Kiev. Pobudova naukovoi teorii. Kyïv, 1965.

Phil 4710.50.30   Buchvarov, Mikhail D. Ukraïns'ko-bolgars'ki filosofs'ki zv'iazki. Kyïv, 1966.

Phil 4710.50.35   Respublikans'ka Naukova Konferentsiia za Aktual'nykh Pytan' Istorii Filosofii na Ukraini, Kiev, 1965. Z istorii filosofii na Ukraïni. Kyïv, 1967.

Phil 4710.50.45   Rozvytok filosofii v Ukrainskii RSR. Kyïv, 1968.

Phil 4710.50.50   Z istorii filosofii i sotsiolohii na Ukraini. Kyïv, 1968.

Phil 4710.50.55   Oleksiuk, Myroslav M. Borot'ba filosofs'kykh techii na zakhidnoukraïns'kykh zemliak u 20-30kh rokakh XX st. L'viv, 1970.

Phil 4710.55   Chizhevskii, D. Narysy z istorii filosofii na Ukraïni. Praga, 1931.

Phil 4710.60   Jakovenko, B.U. Geschichte des Hegelianismus in Russland. Prag, 1938.

Phil 4710.65   Jovchuk, M.T. Osnovnye cherty russkoi klassicheskoi filosofii XIX v. Moskva, 1945.

Phil 4710   History of philosophy - Local Modern philosophy - Russia - History - General works - cont.

Phil 4710.66   Berdiaev, N.A. Sofiia; problemy dukhovnoi kul'tury i religioznoi filosofii. Berlin, 1923-

Phil 4710.70   Zen'kovskii, V.V. Russkie mysliteli i Evropa. Paris, 1926.

Phil 4710.70.2   Zen'kovskii, V.V. Russkie mysliteli i Evropa. Izd. 2. Paris, 1955.

Phil 4710.70.10   Zen'kovskii, V.V. Pravoslavie i kul'tura. Berlin, 1923.

Phil 4710.70.15   Zen'kovskii, V.V. Russian thinkers and Europe. Ann Arbor, 1953.

Phil 4710.75   Mitin, M.B. Filosofskaia nauka v SSSR za 25 let. Moskva, 1943.

Phil 4710.78   Moskalenko, F.Ia. Uchenie ob induktivnykh vyrodakh v istorii russkoi logiki. Kiev, 1955.

Phil 4710.79   Moskalenko, F.Ia. Gnoseologicheskoe soderzhanie logicheskikh form i metodov. Kiev, 1960.

Phil 4710.80   Khaskhachikh, F.I. O poznavaemosti mira. Moskva, 1946.

Phil 4710.82   Vasetskii, G.S. Russkaia progressivnaia filosficheskaia mysl' XIX veka. Moskva, 1959.

Phil 4710.83   Budilova, E.A. Bor'ba materializma i idealizma v russkoi psikhologicheskoi nauke. Moskva, 1960.

Phil 4710.84   Shchipanov, I.Ia. Russkaia materialisticheskaia filosofiia XVIII-IX vekov i ee istoricheskoe znachenie. Moskva, 1953.

Phil 4710.85   Zen'kovskii, V.V. Istoriia russkoi filosofii. Paris, 1949. 2v.

Phil 4710.85.5   Zen'kovskii, V.V. A history of Russian philosophy. N.Y., 1953. 2v.

Phil 4710.90   Pokrovskii, S.A. Fal'sifkatsiia istorii russkoi politicheskoi mysli v sovremennoi reaktsionnoi burzhuaznoi literature. Moskva, 1957.

Phil 4710.96   Pamphlet vol. Russian philosophy. 7 pam.

Phil 4710.100   Shchipanov, I.Ia. Protiv sovremennykh fal'sifikatorov istorii russkoi filosofii. Moskva, 1960.

Phil 4710.110   Blakeley, Thomas J. Soviet scholasticism. Dordrecht, 1961.

Phil 4710.110.5   Blakeley, Thomas J. Soviet philosophy; a general introduction to contemporary Soviet thought. Dordrecht, 1964.

Phil 4710.110.10   Blakeley, Thomas J. Soviet theory of knowledge. Dordrecht, 1964.

Phil 4710.115   Chupakhin, I.Ia. Voprosy teorii poniatiia. Leningrad, 1961.

Phil 4710.125   Walicki, Andrzej. Filozofia i myśl społeczna rosyjska, 1825-1861. Warzawa, 1961.

Phil 4710.130   Galaktionov, A.A. Istoriia russkoi filosofii. Moskva, 1961.

Phil 4710.135   Bashilov, B. Pravye i levye, blizkie i dal'nie. Buenos Aires, 194-?

Phil 4710.140   Kogan, Iu.Ia. Ocherki po istorii russkoi ateisticheskoi mysli XVIII v. Moskva, 1962.

Phil 4710.141   Malinin, V.A. Osnovnye problemy kritiki idealisticheskoi istorii russkoi filosofii. Moskva, 1963.

Phil 4710.142   Ballestrem, Karl G. Russian philosophical terminology. Dordrecht, 1964.

Phil 4710.143   Frank, Semen L. Iz istorii russkoi filosofskoi mysli kontsa XIX i nachala XX v. Washington, 1965.

Phil 4710.144   Edie, James M. Russian philosophy. 1. ed. Chicago, 1965. 3v.

Phil 4710.145   Gershenzon, Mikhail O. Istoriia molodoi Rossii. Moskva, 1923.

Phil 4710.146   Shchipanov, I.Ia. Russkie prosvetiteli, ot Radishcheva do dekabristov. Moskva, 1966. 2v.

Phil 4710.147   Novikov, Avraam I. Leninizm i progressivnye traditsii russkoi obshchestvennoi mysli. Leningrad, 1965.

Phil 4710.148   Kogan, Leonid A. Krepostnye vol'nodumtsy, XIX vek. Moskva, 1966.

Phil 4710.149   Zonal'naia Nauchnaia Konferentsiia po Filosofskim Naukam, 2d, Perm', 1965. Materialy. Perm', 1965.

Phil 4710.150   Zimin, Petr P. Voprosy psikhologii myshleniia v trudakh klassikov russkoi filosofii XIX v. Tashkent, 1966.

Phil 4710.151   Aznaurov, Artem A. Ocherki po etike velikikh russkikh revoliutsionnykh demokratov. Baku, 1966.

Phil 4710.152   Goerdt, Wilhelm. Die Sowjetphilosophie. Basel, 1967.

Phil 4710.153   Istoriia filosofii v SSSR. v.1- Moskva, 1968- 4v.

Phil 4710.154   Leningrad. Universitet. Filosofskii Fakul'tet. Materialy k nauchnoi sessii, posviashchennoi 50-letiiu Velikoi Oktiabr'skoi sotsialisticheskoi revoliutsii. Leningrad, 1967.

Phil 4710.155   Ballestrem, Karl G. Die sowjetische Erkenntnismetaphysik und ihr Verhältnis zu Hegel. Dordrecht, 1968.

Phil 4710.156   Shein, Louis J. Readings in Russian philosophical thought. The Hague, 1968.

Phil 4710.158   Frank, Semen L. Die russiche Weltanschauung. 1. Aufl. Darmstadt, 1967.

Phil 4710.159   Levitskii, Sergei A. Ocherki po istorii russkoi filosofskoi i obshchestvennoi mysli. Frankfurt, 1968.

Phil 4710.160   Abdullaev, Magomed A. Iz istorii filosofskoi i obshchestvenno-politicheskoi mysli narodov Dagestana v XIX v. Moskva, 1968.

Phil 4710.168   Galaktionov, Anatolii A. Russkaia filosofiia XI-XIX vekov. Leningrad, 1970.

Phil 4710.170   Okulov, Aleksandr F. Sovetskaia filosofskaia nauka i ee problemy. Moskva, 1970.

Phil 4710.172.3   Bogatov, Vitalii V. Istoriia filosofii narodov SSSR. Izd. 3. Moskva, 1970.

Phil 4720   History of philosophy - Local Modern philosophy - Russia - History - Special topics

Phil 4720.2   Jeu, Bernard. La philosophie soviétique et l'Occident. Paris, 1969.

Phil 4720.5   Zuev, Ivan E. Ob"ektivnoe i sub"ektivnoe v poznanii i prakticheskoi deiatel'nosti. Moskva, 1969.

Phil 4720.6   Kamenskii, Zakhar A. Filosofskie idei russkogo prosveshcheniia. Moskva, 1971.

Phil 4720.7   V.I. Lenin i istoriia filosofii narodov SSSR. Moskva, 1970.

Phil 4720.9   Rapp, Friedrich. Gesetz und Determination in der Sowjetphilosophie. Dordrecht, 1968.

Phil 4751 - 4776   History of philosophy - Local Modern philosophy - Russia - Individual philosophers (A-Z)

Phil 4751.1.30   Arsen'ev, N.S. Zhazhda podlinnago Bytiia. Berlin, n.d.

Phil 4751.1.32   Arsen'ev, N.S. Pravoslavie, katolichestvo, protestantizm. Parizh, 1948.

Phil 4751.2.80   Peunova, M.N. Mirovozzrenie M.A. Antonovicha. Moskva, 1960.

Phil 4751.3.6   Aikhenval'd, Iu.I. Otdel'nyia stranitsy. Moskva, 1910.

Classified Listing

Phil 4751 - 4776   History of philosophy - Local Modern philosophy - Russia - Individual philosophers (A-Z) - cont.

	Phil 4751.4.25	Asmus, Valentin F. Izbrannye filosofskie trudy. v.1- Moskva, 1969- 2v.
	Phil 4752.1.30	Malinovskii, Aleksandr A. Allgemeine Organisationslehre Tektologie. Berlin, 1926-28. 2v.
	Phil 4752.1.32	Malinovskii, Aleksandr A. Filosofiia zhivogo opyta. Moskva, 1920.
	Phil 4752.1.35	Shcheglov, A.V. Bor'ba Lenina protiv Bogdanovskoi revizii marksizma. Moskva, 1937.
X Cg	Phil 4752.2.30	Berdiaev, Nikolai Aleksandrovich. Sub specie aeternitatis. Sankt Peterburg, 1907.
	Phil 4752.2.33A	Berdiaev, Nikolai Aleksandrovich. The beginning and the end. London, 1952.
	Phil 4752.2.33B	Berdiaev, Nikolai Aleksandrovich. The beginning and the end. London, 1952.
	Phil 4752.2.35	Berdiaev, Nikolai Aleksandrovich. Russkaia ideia. Parizh, 1946.
	Phil 4752.2.38	Berdiaev, Nikolai Aleksandrovich. Nicolas Berdiaeff ou la Révolte contre l'objectivation. Paris, 1967.
	Phil 4752.2.40	Berdiaev, Nikolai Aleksandrovich. Dialectique existentielle du divin et de l'humain. Paris, 1947.
	Phil 4752.2.43	Berdiaev, Nikolai Aleksandrovich. Ekzistentsial'naia dialektika bozhestvennogo i chelovecheskogo. Parizh, 1952.
	Phil 4752.2.45	Berdiaev, Nikolai Aleksandrovich. The divine and the human. London, 1949.
	Phil 4752.2.50	Berdiaev, Nikolai Aleksandrovich. Tsarstvo dukha i tsarstvo kesaria. Parizh, 1951.
	Phil 4752.2.55	Berdiaev, Nikolai Aleksandrovich. Dream and reality. London, 1950.
	Phil 4752.2.60	Berdiaev, Nikolai Aleksandrovich. Khristianstvo i antisimitizm. Parizh, 1946.
	Phil 4752.2.63	Berdiaev, Nikolai Aleksandrovich. Essai d'autobiographie spirituelle. Paris, 1958.
	Phil 4752.2.65	Berdiaev, Nikolai Aleksandrovich. Das Ich und die Welt der Objekte. Darmstadt, 195-?
	Phil 4752.2.68	Berdiaev, Nikolai Aleksandrovich. De l'esprit bourgeois. Neuchâtel, 1949.
	Phil 4752.2.70	Berdiaev, Nikolai Aleksandrovich. The realm of spirit and the realm of Caesar. London, 1952.
	Phil 4752.2.72	Berdiaev, Nikolai Aleksandrovich. The meaning of the creative act. N.Y., 1955.
	Phil 4752.2.73	Berdiaev, Nikolai Aleksandrovich. Le sens de la création. Paris, 1955.
	Phil 4752.2.75	Berdiaev, Nikolai Aleksandrovich. Royaume de l'esprit et royaume de César. Neuchâtel, 1951.
	Phil 4752.2.77A	Berdiaev, Nikolai Aleksandrovich. Truth and revelation. London, 1953.
	Phil 4752.2.77B	Berdiaev, Nikolai Aleksandrovich. Truth and revelation. London, 1953.
	Phil 4752.2.78	Berdiaev, Nikolai Aleksandrovich. Christianity and anti Semitism. Aldington, 1952.
	Phil 4752.2.78.2	Berdiaev, Nikolai Aleksandrovich. Christianity and anti-Semitism. N.Y., 1954.
	Phil 4752.2.79	Berdiaev, Nikolai Aleksandrovich. Christian existentialism. London, 1965.
	Phil 4752.2.80	Lampert, Evengu. Nicolas Berdyaev and the new middle ages. London, 194-.
	Phil 4752.2.85	Spinka, M. Nicholas Berdyaev. Philadelphia, 1950.
	Phil 4752.2.90	Clarke, O.G. Introduction to Berdyaev. London, 1950.
	Phil 4752.2.95	Seaver, George. Nicolas Berdyaev. London, 1950.
	Phil 4752.2.100	Porret, Eugene. La philosophie chrétienne en Russie. Neuchâtel, 1944.
	Phil 4752.2.105	Allen, E. Freedom in God...on Berdyaev. London, 1950. 4 pam.
	Phil 4752.2.110	Vallon, Michell A. An apostle of freedom. N.Y., 1960.
	Phil 4752.2.115	Porret, Eugene. Berdiaeff. Neuchâtel, 1951.
	Phil 4752.2.120	Osipov, N. Kleveta druzei. Miunkhen, 1958.
	Phil 4752.2.125	Caín, Lucienne. Berdiaev en Russie. Paris, 1962.
	Phil 4752.2.130	Segundo, J.L. Berdiaeff. Paris, 1963.
	Phil 4752.2.135	Klamroth, E. Der Gedanke der ewigen Schoepfung. Hamburg, 1963.
	Phil 4752.2.140	Davy, M.M. Nicolas Berdiaev, l'homme du huitième jour. Paris, 1964.
	Phil 4752.2.145	Calian, Carnegie Samuel. The significance of eschatology in the thoughts of Nicolas Berdiaev. Leiden, 1965.
	Phil 4752.2.150	Nucho, Fuad. Berdyaev's philosophy. London, 1967.
	Phil 4752.2.155	Poltoratskii, Nikolai P. Berdiaev i Rossia. N.Y., 1967.
	Phil 4752.2.160	Wernham, James C.S. Two Russian thinkers: essays in Berdyaev and Shestov. Toronto, 1968.
	Phil 4752.2.170	Meusel, Joachim. Geschichtlichkeit und Mystik im Denken Nikolaj Berdjaycws. Berlin? 1962?
	Phil 4752.2.180	Zoppo, Franco. La rivelazione della libertà. Firenze, 1966.
	Phil 4752.2.185	Richardson, David B. Berdyaev's philosophy of history. The Hague, 1968.
	Phil 4752.2.190	Gaith, Jérome. Nicolas Berdiaeff. Beyrouth, 1968.
	Phil 4752.2.195	Déchet, Ferruccio. L'ottavo giorno della creazione. Saggio su N. Berdijaev. Milano, 1969.
	Phil 4753.1.30	Chelpanov, G. Vvedenie v filosofiiu. Riga, 1923.
	Phil 4753.1.35	Chelpanov, G. Uchebnik logiki. Kharbin, 1921.
	Phil 4753.2.30	Chernyshevskii, N.G. Antropologicheskii printsip v filosofii. Moskva, 1943.
	Phil 4753.2.35	Chernyshevskii, N.G. Das anthropologische Prinzip. Berlin, 1956.
	Phil 4753.2.40	Chernyshevskii, N.G. Estetika. Moskva, 1958.
	Phil 4753.3	Chernov, Vladimir I. Analiz filosofskikh poniatii. Moskva, 1966.
	Phil 4753.4	Chernovolenko, Vilen F. Mirovozzronie i nauchnoe poznanie. Kiev, 1970.
	Phil 4754.1.30	Ahlberg, René. A.M. Deborin. Berlin, 1959.
	Phil 4755.1	Ern, Vladimir F. Bor'ba za Logos. Moskva, 1911.
	Phil 4756.1.29	Frank, Semen L. Filosofiia i zhizn', etiudy i nabroski po filosofii kul'tury. Sankt Peterburg, 1910.
	Phil 4756.1.30	Frank, Semen L. Vvedenie v filosofiiu. Berlin, 1923.
	Phil 4756.1.33	Frank, Semen L. Zhivoe znanie. Berlin, 1923.
	Phil 4756.1.35	Frank, Semen L. Krushenie kumirov. Berlin, 1924.
	Phil 4756.1.37	Frank, Semen L. Svet vo t'me; opyt khristianskoi etikhi i sotsial'noi filosofii. Parizh, 1949
	Phil 4756.1.40	Frank, Semen L. Dusha cheloveka. Moskva, 1917.
	Phil 4756.1.41	Frank, Semen L. Dusha cheloveka. Izd.2. Paris, 1964.
	Phil 4756.1.42	Frank, Semen L. Real'nost' i chelovek; metafizika chelovecheskogo bytiia. Parizh, 1956.
	Phil 4756.1.43	Frank, Semen L. Reality and man. London, 1965.
	Phil 4756.1.45	Frank, Semen L. La connaissance et l'être. Paris, 1935.
	Phil 4756.1.45.5	Frank, Semen L. God with us; three meditations. London, 1946.

Phil 4751 - 4776   History of philosophy - Local Modern philosophy - Russia - Individual philosophers (A-Z) - cont.

Phil 4756.1.46	Frank, Semen L. S nami Bog; tri razmyshleniia. Paris, 1964.
Phil 4756.1.47.1	Frank, Semen L. Nepostizhimoe. München, 1971.
Phil 4756.1.48	Frank, Semen L. Religiia i nauka. Posev, 1959.
Phil 4756.1.49	Zen'kovskii, V.V. Sbornik pamiati Semena L. Franka. Miunkhen, 1954.
Phil 4756.2.30	Fedorov, N.F. Filosofiia obshchago dela. Izd.2. Kharbin, 1928-
Phil 4756.2.30.5	Fedorov, N.F. Filosofiia obshchago dela. v.2. Vernyi, 1913-
Phil 4756.2.31	Setniskii, N.A. Kapitalisticheskii stroi v izobrazhenii N.F. Fedorova. Kharbin, 1926. 2 pam.
Phil 4756.2.35	Ostromirov, A. Nikolai Fedorovich Fedorov i sovremennost'. v.1-3. Kharbin, 1928.
Phil 4756.5.30	Giliarov-Platonov, N.P. Sbornik sochinenii. v.1-2. Moskva, 1899-1900.
Phil 4756.5.31	Giliarov-Platonov, N.P. Voprosy very i tserkvi. Moskva, 1905.
Phil 4756.6.50	Platonov, G.V. Kh.M. Fataliev. Makhachkala, 1964.
Phil 4757.1.30	Gershenzon, M.O. Kliuch very. Peterburg, 1922.
Phil 4757.1.35	Gershenzon, M.O. Troistvennyi obraz sovershenstva. Moskva, 1918.
Phil 4757.2.30A	Gurdjieff, Georges Ivanovitch. All and everything. v.1-2. 1st ed. N.Y., 1950. 2v.
Phil 4757.2.30B	Gurdjieff, Georges Ivanovitch. All and everything. v.1. 1st ed. N.Y., 1950.
Phil 4757.2.32	Gurdjieff, Georges Ivanovitch. The herald of coming good. Chicago, 1966.
Phil 4757.2.80	Pauwels, L. Monsieur Gurdjieff. Paris, 1954.
Phil 4757.2.90	Walker, K.M. Venture with ideas. London, 1951.
Phil 4757.2.95	Walker, K.M. A study of Gurdjieff's teaching. London, 1957.
Phil 4757.2.97	Walker, K.M. The making of man. London, 1963.
Phil 4757.2.100	Nicoll, Maurice. Psychological commentaries on the teaching of G.I. Gurdjieff and P.D. Ouspensky. London, 1955-57. 5v.
Phil 4757.2.105	Nott, C.S. Teachings of Gurdjieff. London, 1961.
Phil 4757.2.110	Peters, Arthur A. Boyhood with Gurdjieff. N.Y., 1964.
Phil 4757.2.115	Peters, Arthur A. Gurdjieff remembered. London, 1965.
Phil 4757.2.120	Ekkev, Martin H. Gurdjieff, de mens en zijn werk. Amsterdam, 1968.
Phil 4757.3.20	Vvedenskii, Aleksei I. Protoierei Feodor Aleksandrovich Golubinski. Sergiev, 1898.
Phil 4757.3.25	Golubinskii, F.A. Premudrost' i blagost' Bozhiia v sud'bakh mira i cheloveka; o konechnych prichinakh. 4. izd. Sankt Peterburg, 1894.
Phil 4757.4	Nikolai Iakovlevich Grot v ocherkakh, vospominaniiakh i pis'makh tovarishchei . Sankt Peterburg, 1911.
Phil 4757.5	Tsallaev, Khariton K. Filosofskie i obshchestvenno-politicheskie vozzreniia Afanasiia Gassieva. Ordzhonikidze, 1966.
Phil 4759.1.30	Il'in, I.A. Religioznyi smysl filosofii. Paris,, n.d.
Phil 4759.1.35	Il'in, I.A. O soprotivlenii zlu siloiu. Berlin, 1925.
Phil 4759.1.40	Il'in, I.A. Aksiomy religioznago opyta. Paris, 1953.
Phil 4759.1.45	Il'in, I.A. Poiushchee serdtse. Miunkhen, 1958.
Phil 4759.1.50	Il'in, I.A. Put' k ochevidnosti. Miunkhen, 1957.
Phil 4761.1.80	Askoldov, C. Aleksei Aleksandrovich Kozlov. Moskva, 1912.
Phil 4761.2.30	Karsavin, L.P. O comnenii, nauke i vere. Berlin, 1925.
Phil 4761.2.35	Karsavin, L.P. O nachalakh. Berlin, 1925.
Phil 4761.2.40	Karsavin, L.P. Tserkov', lichnost' i gosudarstvo. Parizh, 1927.
Phil 4761.3.30	Kratkoe poniatie o cheloveke. n.p., 18-?
Phil 4761.4.80	Kogan, Iu.Ia. Prosvetitel' XVIII veka Ia.P. Kozel'skii. Moskva, 1958.
Phil 4761.5.80	Rabinovich, Valerii I. Revoliutsionnyi prosvetitel' F.V. Karzhaviv. Moskva, 1966.
Phil 4762.1.30	Losskii, Nikolai Onufrievich. Vvedenie v filosofiiu. Petrograd, 1918.
Phil 4762.1.35	Losskii, Nikolai Onufrievich. Sbornik zadach po logike. Praga, 1924.
Phil 4762.1.36	Losskii, Nikolai Onufrievich. Vospominaniia. München, 1968.
Phil 4762.1.37	Losskii, Nikolai Onufrievich. Svoboda voli. Paris, n.d.
Phil 4762.1.38	Losskii, Nikolai Onufrievich. Obshchedostupnoe vvedenie v filosofiiu. Frankfurt, 1956.
Phil 4762.1.39	Kohanskii, A.S. Lossky's theory of knowledge. Nashville, 1936.
Phil 4762.1.42	Losskii, Nikolai Onufrievich. Philosophical essays. n.p., 1941.
Phil 4762.1.90	Polanowska, Fejga. Losskij's erkenntnistheoretischer Intuitionismus. Inaug. Diss. Berlin, 1931.
Phil 4762.1.95	Festschrift N.O. Losskij zum 60. Geburtstage. Bonn, 1934.
Phil 4762.2.30	Lopatin, Lev M. Filosofskiia kharakteristiki i rechi. Moskva, 1911.
Phil 4762.2.90	Ognev, A.I. Lev Mikhailovich Lopatin. Petrograd, 1922.
Phil 4762.3.80	Laroche, P.G. Ossip-Leurié (L'homme et l'oeuvre). Paris, 1934.
Phil 4762.4.30	Lapshin, I.I. La synergie spirituelle. Praha, 1935.
Phil 4763.1.30	Malinovskii, V.F. Izbrannye obshchestvenno-politicheskie sochineniia. Moskva, 1958.
Phil 4765.1	Bem, A.K. Zhizn' i smert'; sbornik pamiatniki N.E. Osipova. Praga, 1936.
Phil 4768.1	Rozental', M.M. Materialisticheskaia dialektika. Moskva, 1937.
Phil 4768.1.5	Rozental', M.M. Chto takoe marksistskaia teoriia poznaniia. Moskva, 1955.
Phil 4768.2.5	Rubinshtein, Sergei L. Bytie i soznanie o meste psikhologii. Moskva, 1957.
Phil 4768.2.6	Rubinshtein, Sergei L. Sein und Bewusstsein. 4. Aufl. Berlin, 1966.
Phil 4768.2.7	Rubinshtein, Sergei L. O myshlenii i putiakh ego issledovaniia. Moskva, 1958.
Phil 4768.2.9	Rubinshtein, Sergei L. Printsipy i puti razvitiia psikhologii. Moskva, 1959.
Phil 4768.5	Payne, T.R. S.L. Rubinstein and the philosophical foundations of Soviet psychology. Dordrecht, 1969.
Phil 4769.1.10	Solov'ev, V.S. Ausgewählte Werke. Jena, 1914-16. 2v.
Phil 4769.1.40	Solov'ev, V.S. Werke. v.2,3,6,7. Freiburg, 1953. 4v.
Phil 4769.1.45	Solov'ev, V.S. Kritika otvlechennykh nachal. Moskva, 1880.
Phil 4769.1.50	Solov'ev, V.S. Det onda. Tre samtal. Stockholm, 1918.
Phil 4769.1.60	Solov'ev, V.S. A Solovyov anthology. London, 1950.
Phil 4769.1.65	Chicherin, Boris N. Mistitsizm v nauke. Moskva, 1880.
Phil 4769.1.70	Solov'ev, V.S. The meaning of love. London, 1945.

Phil 4751 - 4776 History of philosophy - Local Modern philosophy - Russia - Individual philosophers (A-Z) - cont.

Phil 4769.1.75 Solov'ev, V.S. Crise de la philosophie occidentale. Paris, 1947.
Phil 4769.1.78 Solov'ev, V.S. Tri razgovora. N'iu-Iork, 1954.
Phil 4769.1.80 Pamphlet box. Solov'ev, V.S.
Phil 4769.1.81 Solov'ev, V.S. La grande controverse et la politique chrétienne. Paris, 1953.
Phil 4769.1.82A Severac, B. Vladimir Soloviev. Paris, n.d.
Phil 4769.1.82B Severac, B. Vladimir Soloviev. Paris, n.d.
Phil 4769.1.85 Solov'ev, V.S. Pis'ma. Sankt Peterburg, 1908-09.
Phil 4769.1.86 Usnadse, D. von. Wladimir Ssolowiow. Halle, 1909.
Phil 4769.1.89 Herbigny, Michel d'. Un Neuman Russe: Vladimir Soloviev (1853-1900). 2. ed. Paris, 1911.
Phil 4769.1.90 Kireev, A.A. Slavianofil'stvo i natsionalizm; otvet k Solov'evy. Petrograd, 1890.
Phil 4769.1.91 Vladimire Solov'eve. Moskva, 1911.
Phil 4769.1.92 Luk'ianov, S.M. O Vl. S. Solov'eve v ego molodye gody. Kniga 3. Vyp. I. Petrograd, 1921. 2v.
Phil 4769.1.94 Bayer, J.J.M. Solowiew. Den Haag, 1964.
Phil 4769.1.95 Sacke, G. W.S. Solowjews Geschichtsphilosophie. Berlin, 1929.
Phil 4769.1.96 Lange, E.M. Solowjew. Mainz, 1923.
Phil 4769.1.97 Ambrozaitis, K. Die Staatslehre W. Solowjews. Paderborn, 1927.
Phil 4769.1.99 Kaschewnikoff, A. Die Geschichtsphilosophie Wladimir Solowjews. Bonn, 1930.
Phil 4769.1.101 Skobtsov, E. Mirosozertsanie Vl. Solov'eva. Paris, 1929.
Phil 4769.1.102 Müller, Ludolf. Solovjev und der Protestantismus. Freiburg, 1951.
Phil 4769.1.102.5 Müller, Ludolf. Das religionsphilosophische System Vladimir Solowjews. Berlin, 1956.
Phil 4769.1.103 Mochul'skiĭ, K. Vladimir Solov'ev; zhizn' i uchenie. Paris, 1936.
Phil 4769.1.104 Mochul'skiĭ, K. Vladimir Solov'ev. 2. izd. Parizh, 1951.
Phil 4769.1.105 Truhetskoĭ, E.N. Mirosozertsanie Vl.C. Solov'eva. v.1-2. Moskva, 1913.
Phil 4769.1.107 Strémooukhoff, D. Vladimir Soloviev et son oeuvre messianique. Paris, 1935.
Phil 4769.1.107.5 Strémooukhoff, D. Vladimir Soloviev et son oeuvre messianique. Thèse. Strasbourg, 1935.
Phil 4769.1.108 Solove'ev, V.S. I fondamenti spirituali della vita. Bologna, 1922.
Phil 4769.1.110 Radlov, E.L. Vladimir Solov'ev; zhizn' i uchenie. Sankt Peterburg, 1913.
Phil 4769.1.112 Munzer, Egbert. Solovyev. London, 1956.
Phil 4769.1.115 Piaskovskii, N.Ia. Kak myslil Vladimir Solov'ev o voskresenie. Moskva, 1901.
Phil 4769.1.120 Solov'ev, V.S. Tri rechi v pamiat' Dostoevskogo. Berlin, 1925.
Phil 4769.1.122 Solov'ev, V.S. Russkaia ideia. Moskva, 1911.
Phil 4769.1.125 Klum, Edith. Natur, Kunst und Liebe in der Philosophie Vladimir Solov'evs. München, 1965.
Phil 4769.1.130 Solov'ev, V.S. O khristianskom edinstve. Briussell, 1967.
Phil 4769.1.135 Velichko, Vasilii L. Vladimir Solov'ev. Sankt Peterburg, 1902.
Phil 4769.1.140 Dahm, Helmut. Vladimir Solov'ev und Max Scheler. München, 1971.
Phil 4769.3 Spektorskii, E. Khristianstvo i kul'tura. Sankt Peterburg, 1925.
Phil 4769.4.5 Shpet, Gustav. Ocherk razvitiia russkoi filosofii. Petrograd, 1922.
Phil 4769.4.10 Shpet, Gustav. Esteticheskie fragmenti. Pts.1-3. Peterburg, 1923.
Phil 4769.4.15 Shpet, Gustav. Iavlenie i smysl. Moskva, 1914.
Phil 4769.5 Setnitskii, N.A. O konechnom ideale. Kharbin, 1932.
Phil 4769.6.81 Belov, P.T. Materializm I.M. Sechenova. Moskva, 1963.
Phil 4769.6.82 Kaganov, V. Mirovozzrenie I.M. Sechenova. Moskva, 1943.
Phil 4769.6.83 Budilova, E.A. Uchenie I.M. Sechenova ob oshchushchenii i myshlenii. Moskva, 1924.
Phil 4769.6.83.5 Rubinshtein, Sergei L. I.M. Sechenov. Moskva, 1957.
Phil 4769.6.84 Iaroshevskii, Mikhail G. Ivan Mikhailovich Sechenov 1825-1905. Leningrad, 1968.
Phil 4769.7.32 Shestov, Lev. Potestas clavium. München, 1926.
Phil 4769.7.33 Shestov, Lev. Potestas clavium. Athens, Ohio, 1968.
Phil 4769.8.20 Strakhov, N.N. Mir kak tseloe. 2. izd. Sankt Peterburg, 1892.
Phil 4769.8.21 Strakhov, N.N. Filosofskie ocherki. Sankt Peterbrug, 1895.
Phil 4769.9.21 Maday, J. Wladimir Sergejewitsch Solowjew. Düsseldorf, 1961.
Phil 4769.10 Skvortsov, Lev V. Obretaet li metafizika vtoroe dykhanie. Moskva, 1966.
Phil 4770.1 Trubetskoi, S.N. Sobranie sochinenii. v.1-2,5-6. Moskva, 1907. 4v.
Phil 4770.2 Praxl, Franz. Die Rechtfertigung Gottes nach Eugen H. Trubetskoj. Inaug. Diss. München, 1967.
Phil 4770.5 Avaliani, S.Sh. Filosofskie vzgliady I.R. Tarkhnishvili. Tbilisi, 1957.
Phil 4771.1A Uspenskii, P.D. In search of the miraculous. 1. ed. N.Y., 1949.
Phil 4771.1B Uspenskii, P.D. In search of the miraculous. 1. ed. N.Y., 1949.
Phil 4771.3A Uspenskii, P.D. The fourth way. 1st American ed. N.Y., 1957.
Phil 4771.3B Uspenskii, P.D. The fourth way. 1st American ed. N.Y., 1957.
Phil 4771.5.2 Uspenskii, P.D. A new model of the universe. 2d ed. N.Y., 1956.
Phil 4772.1 Veideman, A. Opravdanie zla. Riga, 1939.
Phil 4772.10 Vvedenskii, A.I. Logika, kak chast' teorii poznaniia. 2. izd. Sankt Peterburg, 1912.
Phil 4772.10.5 Vvedenskii, A.I. Filosofskie ocherki. Praga, 1924.
Phil 4773.5 Tutundzhian, Ovsep. Psikhologicheskaja kontseptsiia Anri Vallona. Erevan, 1966.

4777 History of philosophy - Local Modern philosophy - Poland [Discontinued]

Phil 4777.282.10 Roszkowski, Antonio. Poględy spoleczne i ekonomiczne Augusta Cieszkowskiego. Poznań, 1923.
Phil 4777.433 Harassek, S. Józef Goluchowski. Kraków, 1924.
Phil 4777.536.80 Pamphlet box. Lutoslawski, W.
Phil 4777.536.100 Lutoslawski, W. Postannictwo polskiego narodu. Warszawa, 1939. (Changed to XP 5137; 3/20/72)
Phil 4777.894 Z dziejów polskiej myśli filozoficznej i spolecznej. Warszawa, 1956- 3v.

Phil 4780 History of philosophy - Local Modern philosophy - White Russia - History

Phil 4780.2 Lushchytski, I.N. Narysy pa historyi hramadska-palitychnai i filosofskai dumki u Belarusi u drukoi palavine XIX veku. Minsk, 1958.
Phil 4780.4 Akademiia nauk BSSR, Minsk. Instytut filosofii. Iz istorii filosofskoi i obshchestvenno-politicheskoi mysli Belorussii. Minsk, 1962.

Phil 4783 History of philosophy - Local Modern philosophy - Ukraine - History

Phil 4783.1 Ostrianyn, Danylo Kh. Rozvytok materialistychnoi filosofii na Ukrainii. Kyiv, 1971.

Phil 4791.1 - .799 History of philosophy - Local Modern philosophy - Georgia (Transcaucasia) - History

Phil 4791.2 Nutsubidze, Shalva Isakovich. Istoriia gruzinskoi filosofii. Tbilisi, 1960.
Phil 4791.4 Beritashvili, Ivan Solomonovich. Uchenie o prirode cheloveka v drevnei Gruzii. Tbilisi, 1961.
Phil 4791.6 Khidasheli, Shalva Vasil'evich. Osnovnye mirovozzrencheskie napravleniia v feodal'noi Gruzii. Tbilisi, 1962.
Phil 4791.8 Sheroziia, Apollon Epifonovich. Filosofskaia mysl' v Gruzii v pervoi chetverti XX veka. Tbilisi, 1963.

Phil 4795.1 - .799 History of philosophy - Local Modern philosophy - Azerbaijan - History

Phil 4795.2.2 Guseinov, Geidar. Iz istorii obshechestvennoi i filosofskoi mysli v Azerbaidzhane. Izd. 2. Baku, 1958.
Phil 4795.4 Rzaev, Agababa. Peredovaia politicheskaia mysl' Rossii i Azerbaidzhana XIX vekai ikh vzaimosviazi. Baku, 1967.
Phil 4795.6 Kasumov, Mekhbaly Mamedovich. Ocherki po istorii peredovoi filosofskoi i obshchestvenno-politicheskoi mysli azerbaidzhanskogo naroda v XIX veke. Baku, 1959.
Phil 4795.8 Mamedov, Sheidabek Faradzhievich. Razvitie filosofskoi mysli v Azerbaidzhane. Moskva, 1965.
Phil 4795.10 Akademiia nauk Azerbaidzhanskoi SSR, Baku. Sektor filosofii. Ocherki po istorii Azerbaidzhanskoi filosofii. Baku, 1966.

Phil 4796 History of philosophy - Local Modern philosophy - Azerbaijan - Individual philosophers (363 scheme)

Phil 4796.96.20 Fath 'Ali-Akhund-zada. Izbrannye filosofskie proizvedeniia. Baku, 1953.
Phil 4796.96.21 Fath 'Ali-Akhund-zada. Izbrannye filosfskie proizvedeniia. Moskva, 1962.
Phil 4796.96.80 Kasumov, Mekhbaly Mamedovich. M.F. Akhundov i russkaia revoliutsionno-demokraticheskaia estetika. Baku, 1954.

Phil 4800 History of philosophy - Local Modern philosophy - Poland - History

Phil 4800.2.2 Struve, Henryk. Historya logiki jako teoryi pozuania w Polsce. Wyd. 2. Warszawa, 1911.
Phil 4800.4 Kozlowski, Wladyslaw M. Les ideés françaises dans la philosophie nationale et la poésie patriotique de la Bologne. Grenoble, 1923.
Phil 4800.6 Harassek, Stefan. Kant w Polsce przed rokiem 1830. Kraków, 1916.
Phil 4800.8 Tyszyński, Aleksander. Piérwsze zasady krytyki powszechnéj. v.1-2. Warszawa, 1870.
Phil 4800.10 Mediaevalia philosophica polonorum. Warszawa. 1,1958+
Phil 4800.12 Suchodolski, Bogdan. Studia z dziejów polskiej myśli filozoficznej i naukowej. Wyd. 1. Wroclaw, 1959.
Phil 4800.14 Narskii, Igor' Sergeevich. Pol'skie mysliteli epokhi Vozrozhdeniia. Moskva, 1960.
Phil 4800.16 Osipova, Elena Vladimirovna. Filosofiia pol'skogo Prosveshcheniia. Moskva, 1961.
Phil 4800.18 Wasik, Wiktor. Historia filozofii polskiej. Warszawa, 1958-66. 2v.
Phil 4800.20 Jordan, Zbigniew A. Philosophy and ideology. Dordrecht, 1963.
Phil 4800.22 Skarga, Barbara. Naroziny pozytywizmu polskiego, 1831-1864. Warszawa, 1964.
Phil 4800.22.10 Skarbek, Janusz. Koncepcja nauki w pozytywizmie polskim. Wroclaw, 1968.
Phil 4800.24 Kuksewicz, Zdzislaw. Z dziejów filosofii na Uniwersytecie Krakowskim w XV wieku. Wroclaw, 1965.
Phil 4800.26 Filozofia polska. Warszawa, 1967.
Phil 4800.28 Skolimowski, Henryk. Polish analytical philosophy. London, 1967.

Phil 4802 History of philosophy - Local Modern philosophy - Poland - Anthologies of philosophical writings

Phil 4802.1 Jakiej filozofii Polacy potrzebują. Wyd. 1. Warszawa, 1970.
Phil 4802.2 Straszewski, Maurycy. Polska filozofja narodowa, 15 wykladow. Krakow, 1921.
Phil 4802.4 Moscow. Universitet. Filosofskii fakultet. Izbrannye proizvedeniia progressivnykh pol'skikh myslitelei. Moskva, 1956-58. 3v.
Phil 4802.6 Hinz, Henryk. Polska mysl filosoficzna. Warszawa, 1964.

Phil 4803 History of philosophy - Local Modern philosophy - Poland - Individual philosophers (800 scheme)

Phil 4803.108.1 Abramowski, Edward. Pisma. Warszawa, 1924.
Phil 4803.108.25 Abramowski, Edward. Filozofia spoleczna. Warszawa, 1965.
Phil 4803.108.90 Krawczyk, Zbigniew. Socjologia Edwarda Abramowskiego. Warszawa, 1965.
Phil 4803.108.95 Jezierski, Romuald. Poglądy etyczne Edwarda Abramowskiego. Wyd. 1. Poznań, 1970.
Phil 4803.130.30 Ajdukiewicz, Kazimierz. Zagadnienia i Kierunki filozofii. W Krakowie, 1949.
Phil 4803.130.35 Ajdukiewicz, Kazimierz. Jezyk i poznanie. Wyd. 1. Warszawa, 1960-
Phil 4803.186.30 Baczko, Bronislaw. Czlowiek i światopoglady. Warszawa, 1965.
Phil 4803.241.30 Brzozowski, Stanislaw L. Idee. Lwów, 1910.
Phil 4803.241.90 Trzebuchowski, Pavel. Filozofia pracy Stanislawa Brzozowskiego. Wyd. 1. Warszawa, 1971.
Phil 4803.281.20 Chwistek, Leon. Pisma filozoficzne i logiczne. Warszawa, 1961-63. 2v.
Phil 4803.281.80 Pasenkiewicz, Kazimierz. Pierwsze systemy semantyki Leona Chwistka. Krakow, 1961.
Phil 4803.282.80 Kowalski, Kazimierz Józef. Filozofja Augusta Hr. Cieszkowskiego w świetle zasad filozofji. Poznań, 1929.
Phil 4803.313.20 Czezowski, Tadeusz. Filozofia na rozdrozu. Wyd. 1. Warszawa, 1965.
Phil 4803.313.30 Czezowski, Tadeusz. O uniwersytecie i studiach uniwersyteckick. Toruń, 1946.

Phil 4803.313.35   Czezowski, Tadeusz. O naukach humanistycznych. Toruń, 1946.

Phil 4803.320.30   Dembowski, Bronisław. Spór o metafizyke. Warszawa, 1969.

Phil 4803.334.80   Kaczmarek, Stefan. Anioł Dowgird, filozof nieznany. Poznań, 1963.

Phil 4803.334.81   Kaczmarek, Stefan. Anioł Dowgird, filozof nieznany. Warszawa, 1965.

Phil 4803.334.85   Doroshevich, Engel's Konstantinovich. Aniol Dovgird - myslitel' epokhi Prosveshcheniia. Minsk, 1967.

Phil 4803.360.20   Elzenberg, Henryk. Proby kontaktu; eseje i studia krytyczme. Kraków, 1966.

Phil 4803.360.30   Elzenberg, Henryk. Kłopot z istnieniem. Kraków, 1963.

Phil 4803.434.30   Gołuchowski, Józef. Dumania nad najwyzszemi zagadnieniami człowieka. Wilno, 1861. 2v.

Phil 4803.435.30   Grzegorczyk, Andrzej. Schemały i człowiek. Kraków, 1963.

Phil 4803.454.1   Hoene-Wroński, Józef Maria. Hoëné Wronski. Paris, 1970.

Phil 4803.454.5   Hoene-Wroński, Józef Maria. L'oeuvre philosophique de Hoené Wronski. Paris, 1933-36. 2v.

Phil 4803.454.20   Pamphlet vol. Hoene-Wroński, Józef Maria. Miscellaneous writings. 4 pam.

Phil 4803.454.21   Hoene-Wroński, Józef Maria. Sept manuscrits inédits, écrits de 1803 à 1806. Paris, 1879.

Phil 4803.454.22F   Pamphlet vol. Hoene-Wroński, Józef Maria. Miscellaneous writings. 9 pam.

Phil 4803.454.23   Pamphlet vol. Hoene-Wroński, Józef Maria. Miscellaneous writings. 3 pam.

Phil 4803.454.30   Hoene-Wroński, Józef Maria. Messianisme; ou Réforme absolue du savoir humain. Paris, 1847. 3v.

Phil 4803.454.32   Hoene-Wroński, Józef Maria. Lit do papiezy o maglacej potrzebie obechej spełnienia religli. Warszawa, 1928.

Phil 4803.454.35   Hoene-Wroński, Józef Maria. Messianisme; philosophie absolue. Paris, 1876.

Phil 4803.454.40   Hoene-Wroński, Józef Maria. Le destin de la France, de l'Allemagne, et de la Russie, comme prolégomènes du messianisme. Paris, 1842.

Phil 4803.454.41   Hoene-Wroński, Józef Maria. Prolegomena do mesjanizmu. Lwów, 1922-25. 3v.

Phil 4803.454.45   Hoene-Wroński, Józef Maria. Propédeutigue messianique. v.2. Paris, 1875.

Phil 4803.454.46   Hoene-Wroński, Józef Maria. Propedeutyka mesjaniczna. v.2. Warszawa, 1925.

Phil 4803.454.50   Hoene-Wroński, Józef Maria. Messianisme, union finale de la philosophie et de la religion. Paris, 1831.

Phil 4803.454.51   Hoene-Wroński, Józef Maria. Prodrom mesjanizmu albo filozofji absolutnej. Lwów, 1921.

Phil 4803.454.55   Hoene-Wroński, Józef Maria. Metapolityke. Warszawa, 1923.

Phil 4803.454.60   Hoene-Wroński, Józef Maria. Kodeks prawodawstwa społecznego absolutnego. Warszawa, 1923.

Phil 4803.454.61   Hoene-Wroński, Józef Maria. Reforma absolutna przeto ostateczna wiedzy ludzkiej. Paryz, 1891.

Phil 4803.454.65F   Hoene-Wroński, Józef Maria. Nomothétique messianique. Paris, 1881.

Phil 4803.454.66   Hoene-Wroński, Józef Maria. Adresse aux nations slaves sur les destinées du monde. Paris, 1847.

Phil 4803.454.70   Hoene-Wroński, Józef Maria. Caméralistique; économie politique et finances. Paris, 1884.

Phil 4803.454.72   Hoene-Wroński, Józef Maria. Epitre secrète à son altesse le Prince Louis-Napoléon sur les destinées de la France. Metz, 1851.

Phil 4803.454.74F   Hoene-Wroński, Józef Maria. Odezwa do narodóv slawianskich wzgledem przeznaczeń świata. Paryz, 1848.

Phil 4803.454.79   Dickstein, Samuel. Katalog dzieł i rekopisów Hoene-Wrońskiego. Kraków, 1896.

Phil 4803.454.79.5   Gawecki, Bolesław J. Wroński i o Wrońskim; katalog. Warszawa, 1958.

Phil 4803.454.80   Gennadii, abbot. Zakon tvoreniia. Buenos Aires, 1956.

Phil 4803.454.85   Zieleńczyk, Adam. Hoene-Wroński. Warszawa, 1930-?

Phil 4803.454.91   Warrain, Francis. Wiązanie metafizyczne sporządzone według prawa stworzenia Hoene-Wrońskiego. Warszawa, 1928.

Phil 4803.454.95   Ujejski, Józef. O cenę absolutu; rzecz o Hoene-Wrońskim. Warszawa, 1925.

Phil 4803.454.100   Bukaty, Antoni. Hoene-Wroński i jego udział w rozwinięciu ostatecznem wiedzy ludzkiej. Paryz, 1844.

Phil 4803.454.105   Brawn, Jérzy Bronislaw. Apercu de la philosophie de Wroński. Rome, 1969?

Phil 4803.462.1   Ingarden, Roman. Spór o istnienie świata. Kraków, 1947-48. 2v.

Phil 4803.462.2   Ingarden, Roman. Spór o istnienie świata. Wyd. 2. Warszawa, 1960-61. 2v.

Phil 4803.462.5   Ingarden, Roman. Studia z estetyki. Warszawa, 1957-70. 3v.

Phil 4803.462.10   Ingarden, Roman. U podsław sevrii poznania. Wyd. 1. Warszawa, 1971.

Phil 4803.462.20   Ingarden, Roman. Szkice z filozofii literatury. Łódź, 1947.

Phil 4803.462.21   Ingarden, Roman. O dziele literackim. Warszawa, 1960.
Phil 4803.462.30   Ingarden, Roman. Issledovaniia po estetike. Moskva, 1962.
Phil 4803.462.35   Ingarden, Roman. Der Streit um die Existenz der Welt. v.1-2. Tübingen, 1964-65. 3v.

Phil 4803.462.40   Ingarden, Roman. Przezijni, dzieło, wartość. Czyli, Kraków, 1966.

Phil 4803.462.45   Ingarden, Roman. Erlebnis, Kunstwerk und Wert. Tübingen, 1969.

Phil 4803.462.50   Ingarden, Roman. Psycho-fizjologiuzna teorja poznania i jejkrytyka. Lwów, 1930.

Phil 4803.462.55   Ingarden, Roman. Vom Erkennen des literarischen Kunstwerks. Tübingen, 1968.

Phil 4803.462.60   Ingarden, Roman. Z badań nad folozofią współczesną. Warszawa, 1963.

Phil 4803.462.80   Tymieniecka, Anna Teresa. Essence et existence. Paris, 1957.

Phil 4803.465.86   Bańka, Józef. Narodziny filozofii nauki o pracy w Polsce. Wyd. 1. Warszawa, 1970.

Phil 4803.468.80   Lipkowski, Otton. Józefa Joteyko. Wyd. 1. Warszawa, 1968.

Phil 4803.472.20   Kamieński, Henryk. Filozofia ekonomii materialnej ludzkiego społecznstwa. Warszawa, 1959.

Phil 4803.495.20   Kotarbiński, Leszek. Kultura i fetysze; zbiór rozpraw. Wyd. 1. Warszawa, 1967.

Phil 4803.495.21   Kotakowski, Leszek. Traktat über die Sterblichkeit der Vernunft. München, 1967.

Phil 4803.495.220   Kołłątaj, Hugo. Porządek fizyczno-moralny oraz Pomysty do dzieta Porządek fizyczno-moralny. Warszawa, 1955.

Phil 4803.496.30   Kossak, Jerzy. Bunt na kolanach. Warszawa, 1960.

Phil 4803.497.6   Kotarbiński, Tadeusz. Studia z zakresu filozofii, etyki i nauk społecznych. Wrocław, 1970.

Phil 4803.497.25   Kotarbiński, Tadeusz. Wybór pism. Warszawa, 1957-58. 2v.

Phil 4803.497.30   Kotarbiński, Tadeusz. Hasło dobrej roboty. Wyd. 1. Warszawa, 1968.

Phil 4803.497.35   Kotarbiński, Tabeusz. Sprawność i bład. Warszawa, 1956.

Phil 4803.497.40   Kotarbiński, Tadeusz. Wykłady z dziejów logiki. Łódź, 1957.

Phil 4803.497.45   Kotarbiński, Tadeusz. Medytacje o życiu godziwym. Warszawa, 1966.

Phil 4803.497.90   Jawonski, Manek. Tadeusz Kotarbiński. Wyd. 1. Warszawa, 1971.

Phil 4803.497.230   Kowalski, Kazimierz Józef. Podstawy filozofji. Guiezano, 1930.

Phil 4803.497.420   Kozłowski, Władysław M. Szkice filozoficzne. Warszawa, 1900.

Phil 4803.497.480   Gawecki, Bolesław J. Władysław Mieczysław Kozłowski, 1858-1935. Wrocław, 1961.

Phil 4803.498.20   Krajewski, Władysław. Szkice filozofcze. Wyd. 1. Warszawa, 1963.

Phil 4803.500.20   Kroński, Tadeusz. Rozwazania wokół Hegla. Warszawa, 1960.
Phil 4803.502.20   Kuczyński, Janusz. Zyć i filozofować. Wyd. 1. Warszawa, 1969.

Phil 4803.522.5   Libelt, Karol. Estetyka czyli umnictwo piękne. v.1-2. Petersburg, 1854. 3v.

Phil 4803.522.10   Libelt, Karol. Pisma promniejsze. Poznań, 1849-51. 6v.

Phil 4803.522.15   Libelt, Karol. Filozofia i krytyka. Wyd. 2. v.1-6. Poznań, 1874-75. 3v.

Phil 4803.522.20   Libelt, Karol. Feleton polityczno-literacki. Poznań, 1846.

Phil 4803.522.30   Libelt, Karol. Pisma o oświacie i wychowaniu. Wrocław, 1971.

Phil 4803.522.35   Libelt, Karol. Samowładztwo rozumu i objawy filozofii słowiańskiej. Warszawa, 1967.

Phil 4803.522.80   Kosmowska, J.W. Karol Libelt jako działacz polityczny i społeczny. ur. 1807 um. 1875. Poznań, 1918.

Phil 4803.536.20   Lukasiewicz, Jan. L zagadnień logiki i filozofii; pisma wybrane. Warszawa, 1961.

Phil 4803.537.30   Lutosławski, Wincenty. Iskierki warszawskie. Warszawa, 1911.

Phil 4803.537.37   Lutosławski, Wincenty. Pewniki polityki polskiej. Wyd. 2. W Szamotułach, 1926.

Phil 4803.537.40   Lutosławski, Wincenty. Eine Bekehrung. Kempten, 19- .
Phil 4803.537.45F   Lutosławski, Wincenty. Jeden łatwy zywot. Dzięgielów? 1932.

Phil 4803.537.80   Information about Professor Wincenty Lutosławski for those who wish to organize his lectures. Wilno, 1930.

Phil 4803.555.32   Mankowski, Mieczysław. Złoty dar człowieka. Wyd. 2. Kraków, 1912.

Phil 4803.558.20   Mahrburg, Adam. Pisma filozoficzne. Warszawa, 1914. 2v.

Phil 4803.570.80   Usovicz, Aleksandr. Ksiądz Konstanty Michalski, 1879-1947. Wyd. 1. Kraków, 1949.

Phil 4803.592.20   Mysłakowski, Zygmunt. Pisma wybrane. Wyd. 1. Warszawa, 1971.

Phil 4803.592.30   Mysłakowski, Zygmunt. Zatracone ścieżki, zagubione ślady. Warszawa, 1967.

Phil 4803.680.30   Pełka-Peliński, Stanisław. Na drogach współczesnej kultury. Łódz, 1946.

Phil 4803.727.80   Cáceres, Alfredo. La obra psicológica de Radecki, 1910-35. Montevideo, 1936.

Phil 4803.755.80   Kliauchenia, Aliaksandr S. Stefan Rudnianskii. Minsk, 1968.

Phil 4803.794.30   Skolimowski, Henryk. Polski Marksizm. Londyn, 1969.
Phil 4803.799.2   Śniadecki, Jan. Dziela. v.1-7. Warszawa, 1837-39. 3v.

Phil 4803.799.20   Śniadecki, Jan. Pisma rozmaite. Wilno, 1818-22. 4v.
Phil 4803.799.21   Śniadecki, Jan. Wybor pism naukowych. Warszawa, 1954.
Phil 4803.799.22   Śniadecki, Jan. Pisma pedagogiczne. Wrocław, 1961.
Phil 4803.799.23   Śniadecki, Jan. Pisma filozoficzne. Warszawa, 1958. 2v.

Phil 4803.799.25   Śniadecki, Jan. Korespondencja Jana Śniadeckiego; listy z Kraków. Krakow, 1932-54. 2v.

Phil 4803.799.80   Świezawski, Leon. Jan Śniadecki, jego zycie i działalność naukowa. Petersburg, 1898.

Phil 4803.799.85   Chrzanowski, Ignacy. Jan Śniadecki jako nauczyciel narodu. Kraków, 1930.

Phil 4803.799.90   Chamcówna, Mirosława. Jan Śniadecki. Kraków, 1963.
Phil 4803.799.95   Baliński, Michał. Pamiętniki o Janie Śniadeckim. Wilno, 1865. 2v.

Phil 4803.810.30   Straszewski, Maurycy. Dzieje filozoficznej myśli polskiej w okresie porozbiorowym. Kraków, 1912.

Phil 4803.822.30   Tatarkiewicz, Władysław. Droga do filozofii i inne rozprawy filozoficzne. Wyd. 1. v.1- Warszawa, 1971-

Phil 4803.846.30   Trentowski, Bronisław F. Grundlage der universellen Philosophie. Karlsruhe, 1837.

Phil 4803.846.35   Trentowski, Bronisław F. Wizerunki duszy narodowej s końca ostatniego szesnastolecia. Paryż, 1847.

Phil 4803.846.40   Trentowski, Bronisław F. Myślini czyli catokształt loiki narodowéj. Poznań, 1844. 2v.

Phil 4803.846.45   Trentowski, Bronisław F. Stosunek filozofii do cybernetyki czyli sztuki rządzenia narodem. Poznań, 1843.

Phil 4803.846.80   Horodyski, Władysław. Bronisław Trentowski (1808-1869). Kraków, 1913.

Phil 4803.854.20   Twardowski, Kazimierz. Wybrane pisma filozoficzne. Warszawa, 1965.

Phil 4803.879.06   Wiszniewski, Michał. Charaktery rozumów ludzkich. Warszawa, 1876. 2 pam.

Phil 4803.879.90   Bańku, Józef. Poglądy filozoficzno-społeczne Michała Wiszniewskiego. Wyd. 1. Warszawa, 1967.

Phil 4803.879.95   Dybiec, Julian. Michał wiszniewski. Wrocław, 1970.
Phil 4803.896.20   Znamierowski, Czesław Stanisław. Oceny i normy. Warszawa, 1957.

Phil 4803.896.230   Znaniecki, Florian. Studja nad filozofja wartosci. Warszawa, 1912.

Phil 4803.896.235   Znaniecki, Florian. Humanizm i poznanie. Warszawa, 1912.

Phil 4805   History of philosophy - Local Modern philosophy - Czechoslovakia in general - History

Phil 4805.5   Král, Josef. Československá filosofie. Praha, 1937.
Phil 4805.10   Iakovenko, Boris V. La philosophie tchécoslovaque contemporaine. Prague, 1935.

Phil 4805.15   Zich, Otakar. Lidová přísloví s logického hlediska. Praha, 1956.

Phil 4805.20   Popelová, Jiřina. Studie o současné české filosofii. Praha, 1946.

Phil 4805   History of philosophy - Local Modern philosophy - Czechoslovakia in general - History - cont.
Phil 4805.25   Strohs, Slavomil. Marxisticko-leninská filosofie v Československu mezi dvěma světovými válkami. Vyd. 1. Praha, 1962.

Phil 4806   History of philosophy - Local Modern philosophy - Czechoslovakia in general - Anthologies of philosophical writings
Phil 4806.2   Československá akademie věd. Antologie z dějin československé filosofie. Praha, 1963.

Phil 4807   History of philosophy - Local Modern philosophy - Bohemia and Moravia - History
Phil 4807.2   Bělka, František. Kapitaly z dějin českého revolučního myšlení. Vyd. 1. Havlíčkův Brod, 1960.
Phil 4807.4   Konference o dějinách české filosofie, Liblice, 1958. Filosofie v dějinách českého národa. Vyd. 1. Praha, 1958.
Phil 4807.6F   Česká akademie věd a umění. Památník na oslavu padesátiletého panovnického jubilea jeho veličenstva císaře a krále Františka Josefa I. Praha, 1898.

Phil 4809   History of philosophy - Local Modern philosophy - Bohemia and Moravia - Individual philosophers (800 scheme)
Phil 4809.393   Fischer, Josef L. Filosofické studie. Praha, 1968.
Phil 4809.393.330   Fišer, zbyněk. Útěcha z ontologie. Vyd. 1. Praha, 1967.
Phil 4809.447.90   Loužil, Jaromír. Ignác Jan Hanuš. Vyd. 1. Praha, 1971.
Phil 4809.465.30   Jahn, Jiljí. Pozmání a život. Praha, 1948.
Phil 4809.486.20   Kiselimchev, Asen. Izbrani proizvedeniia. Sofiia, 1964.
Phil 4809.489.2   Klíma, Ladislav. Dílo. v.2- Praha, 1948-
Phil 4809.497.30   Kozák, Jan Blahoslav. Věda a duch. Praha, 1938.
Phil 4809.498.30   Krejčí, František. Pozitivní etika jakožto mravanka na základě přirozeném. Praha, 1922.
Phil 4809.498.80   Šimsa, Jaroslav. Sboruiík ku poctě Frantiska Krejciho. Praha, 1929.
Phil 4809.524.80   Král, Josef. Studie o G.A. Lindnerovi. Bratislava, 1930.
Phil 4809.727.11   Pamphlet vol. Rádl, Emanuel. Co soudím o spiritismu. 3 pam.
Phil 4809.727.12   Pamphlet vol. Rádl, Emanuel. Essays. 6 pam.
Phil 4809.727.30   Rádl, Emanuel. Úvahy vědeché a filosofické. Praha, 1914.
Phil 4809.727.35   Rádl, Emanuel. Moderní věda. Praha, 1926.
Phil 4809.727.80   Hromádka, Josef Lukl. Don Quijote české filosofie, Emanuel Rádl, 1873-1942. V New Yorku, 1943.
Phil 4809.779.80   Shaw, Nellie. A Czech philosopher on the Cotswolds...Francis Sedlák. London, 1940.
Phil 4809.796.1   Smetana, Augustin. Sebrané spisy. Praha, 1960- 2v.
Phil 4809.796.30   Smetana, Augustin. Vznik a zánik ducha. Praha, 1923.
Phil 4809.796.36   Smetana, Augustin. Úvahy o budoncnosti lidstva. Praha, 1903.
Phil 4809.796.80   Michňáková, Irena. Augustin Smetana. Praha, 1963.
Phil 4809.814.30   Sviták, Ivan. Lidský smysl kultury. Vyd. 1. Praha, 1968.
Phil 4809.894.1   Zahradmk, Vincenc. Filosofické spisy. Praha, 1907-18. 3v.
Phil 4809.895.11   Pamphlet vol. Želivan, Pavel. Půvuod vesmíru; and Půvuod života. 2 pam.

Phil 4810   History of philosophy - Local Modern philosophy - Slovakia - History
Phil 4810.2   Muenz, Teodor. Filosofia slovenského osvietenstva. Vyd. 1. Bratislava, 1961.
Phil 4810.2.5   Muenz, Teodor. Náhľady filozofov malohontstkej spoločnosti. Bratislava, 1954.
Phil 4810.4   Uher, Ján. Filozofia v boji o dnešok. Vyd. 1. Bratislava, 1961.
Phil 4810.6   Várossová, Elena. Kapitoly z dějin slovenskej filozofie. Bratislava, 1957.
Phil 4810.6.5   Várossová, Elena. Prehľad dejín slovenskej filozofie. Bratislava, 1965.

Phil 4812   History of philosophy - Local Modern philosophy - Slovakia - Individual philosophers (800 scheme)
Phil 4812.196.80   Felber, Stanislav. Ján Bayer, slovenský baconista XVII storočia. Bratislava, 1953.
Phil 4812.457.20   Hrušovský, Igor. Kapitoly z téorie vedy. Bratislava, 1968.
Phil 4812.457.31   Hrušovský, Igor. Strukturation und Apperzeption des Konkreten. Bratislava, 1966.
Phil 4812.457.35   Hrušovský, Igor. Problémy, portréty, retrospektívy. Vyd. 1. Bratislava, 1965.

Phil 4813   History of philosophy - Local Modern philosophy - Hungary - History
Phil 4813.10   Szontagh, Gusztav. Propylaeumok a' magyar philosophiákoz. Budán, 1839.

Phil 4815   History of philosophy - Local Modern philosophy - Hungary - Individual philosophers (800 scheme)
Phil 4815.223.30   Bodnár, Zsigmond. Szellemi haladásunk törvénye. Budapest, 1892.
Phil 4815.223.35   Bodnár, Zsigmond. Az erkölcsi világ. Budapest, 1896.
Phil 4815.368.30   Erösdi, Mihály. Kritikus objectiv metaphysíka. Budapest, 1885.
Phil 4815.558.80   Fraknói, Vilmos. Martinovicsnak istentagadó elvelet hirdető, imént fölfedezett francia munkája. Budapest, 1920.
Phil 4815.558.85   Fraknói, Vilmos. Martinovics élete. Budapest, 1921.
Phil 4815.672.80   Wurmb, Albert. Darstellung und Kritik der logischen Grundbegriffe der Naturphilosophie Melchior Palagyis. Weisswasser, 1931.
Phil 4815.790.30   Simòn, Józsaf Sándor. A spekulativ termeszettudomány alapgondolatai mint az egységes érzet filozofia rendszere. Budapest, 1904.

4816   History of philosophy - Local Modern philosophy - Rumania - History
Phil 4816.6   Problemy filosofii. Moskva, 1960.
Phil 4816.8   Gulian, C.I. Peredovye rumynskie mysliteli XVIII-XIXVV. Moskva, 1961.
Phil 4816.10   Academia Republicii Socialiste România, Bucharest. Institutul de Filozofie. Istoria gîradirii sociale şi filozofice în Romînia. Bucureşti, 1964.

4817   History of philosophy - Local Modern philosophy - Rumania - Anthologies philosophical writings
Phil 4817.5   Academia Republicii Socialiste România, Bucharest. Philosophes roumains contemporains. Bucureşti, 1958.
Phil 4817.6   Academia Republicii Socialiste România, Bucharest. Institutu I de Filozofie. Antologiia iz istoriiata na rumunskata progresivna misul. Sofiia, 1965.

Phil 4818   History of philosophy - Local Modern philosophy - Rumania - Individual philosophers (800 scheme)
Phil 4818.298.15   Conta, Vasile. Opera filozofice. Bucureşti, 1967.
Phil 4818.298.80   Badareu, Dan. Un système matérialiste métaphysique au XIXe siècle: la philosophie de Basile Conta. Paris, 1924.
Phil 4818.410.80   Vance, Wilson. René Fülöp-Miller's search for reality. London, 1930.
Phil 4818.571.20   Michăilescce, Ştefan C. Pagini filozofice alese. Bucureşti, 1955.

Phil 4822   History of philosophy - Local Modern philosophy - Bulgaria - History
Phil 4822.1   Istoriia na filosofskata misul v Bulgariia. Sofiia, 1970-
Phil 4822.2   Grozev, Groziu. Istoriia na bŭlgarskata filosofiia. Sofiia, 1957- 2v.
Phil 4822.4   Bunkov, Angel Iliev. Prinos kum istoriiata na bulgarskata filosofska misul'. Sofiia, 1943.
Phil 4822.4.5   Bunkov, Angel Iliev. Razvitie na filosofskata misul v Bulgariia. Sofiia, 1966.
Phil 4822.6   Penev, Mikho. Za religiozno-idealisticheskata sŭshtnost na bŭlgarskata burzhoazno filosofiia. Sofiia, 1964.
Phil 4822.8   Andreev, Kosta. Kritikata na Dimitur Blagoev na neokantianstvoto v Bulgariia po vuprosite na filosofiiata. Sofiia, 1968.

Phil 4824   History of philosophy - Local Modern philosophy - Bulgaria - Individual philosophers (800 scheme)
Phil 4824.676.30   Pavlov, Todor Dimitrov. Izkustvoiživot. Sofiia, 1953.

Phil 4825   History of philosophy - Local Modern philosophy - Yugoslavia - History
Phil 4825.1   Vrtačiă, Ludvík. Einführung in den Jugoslawischen Marxismus-Leninismus; Organisation und Bibliographie. Dordrecht, 1963.
Phil 4825.10   Nedeljkovič, Dušan. Aperçu de la philosophie contemporaine en Yougoslavie. Beograd, 1934.
Phil 4825.11   Nedeljkovič, Dušan. Od Heraklita do njegoša i Svetozara. Beograd, 1971.
Phil 4825.12   Atanasijavič, Ksenija. Penseurs yougoslaves. Belgrade, 1937.
Phil 4825.14   Zeremski, Sava D. Essays aus der südslawischen Philosophie. Novisad, 1939.
Phil 4825.16   Stojković, Andrija B. Počeci filosofije Srba od Save do Dositeja na osnovama narodne mudrosti. Beograd, 1970.
Phil 4825.18   Urbančič, Juan. Poglavitne ideje slovenskih filozofov med sholastiko in neosholako. Ljubljana, 1971.

Phil 4826   History of philosophy - Local Modern philosophy - Yugoslavia - Anthologies of philosophical writings
Phil 4826.2   Filozofi. Novi Sad, 1966.

Phil 4829   History of philosophy - Local Modern philosophy - Yugoslavia - Individual philosophers (800 scheme)
Phil 4829.160.80   Despot, Branko. Filozofija Djue Arnolda. Zagreb, 1970.
Phil 4829.203.80   Brida, Marija. Benedikt Benković. Beograd, 1967.
Phil 4829.344.20   Dvorniković, Vladimir. Barba ideja. Beograd, 1937.
Phil 4829.491.80   Grubačić, Kosta. Božidar Knežević. Sarajevo, 1962.
Phil 4829.616.30   Novaković, Staniša. Problem metafizike u savremenoj analitickoj filozofiji. Beograd, 1967.
Phil 4829.680.30   Pejović, Danilo. Protiv struje. Zagreb, 1965.
Phil 4829.749.30   Rodin, Davor. Metafizika i čudoredje. Zagreb, 1971.
Phil 4829.803.20   Spakovski, Anatol. Kleinere philosophische Schriften. Velika Kikinda, 1938.
Phil 4829.860.2   Ušeničnik, Aleš. Izbrani spisi. Ljubljana, 1939-41. 10v.
Phil 4829.867.80   Zečević, Seraphinus. Francisci Veber theoria de persona; internum drama philosophi sloveni. Montréal, 1954.
Phil 4829.896.30   Zimmermann, Stjepan. Religija i život. Zagreb, 1938.

Phil 4843   History of philosophy - Local Modern philosophy - Greece (Modern) - History
Phil 4843.1   Boumblinopoulos, Georgios E. Bibliographie critique de la philosophie grecque...1453-1953. Athènes, 1966.
Phil 4843.2   Cavarnos, Constantine Peter. Modern Greek thought. Belmont, Mass., 1969.
Phil 4843.4   Henderson, George Patrick. The revival of Greek thought, 1620-1830. Albany, 1970.
Phil 4843.6   Apostolopoulos, Ntimes. Syntomè historia tès neoellenikès philosophias. Athena? 1949.
Phil 4843.8   Kissabou, Maria I. Hè philosophia en Helladi apo tès Anostaseòs tou ethnous. Athena, 1951.

Phil 4845   History of philosophy - Local Modern philosophy - Greece (Modern) - Individual philosophers (363 scheme)
Phil 4845.227.30   Papanoutsos, Euangelos. Ho logos kai ho anthrōpos. Athena, 1971.
Phil 4845.227.32   Papanoutsos, Euangelos. Ho kosmos toù pneumatos. 2. ed. Athena, 1953-56. 3v.
Phil 4845.227.32.2   Papanoutsos, Euangelos. Gnosiologia. 2. ed. Athena, 1962.
Phil 4845.227.32.3   Papanoutsos, Euangelos. The foundations of knowledge. Albany, 1968.
Phil 4845.227.34   Papanoutsos, Euangelos. Epikaira kai anepikaira. Athena, 1962.
Phil 4845.227.36   Papanoutsos, Euangelos. Philosophia kai paideia. Athena, 1958.
Phil 4845.227.38   Papanoutsos, Euangelos. Hè èthikè syneidèsè kai tä problèmata tes. Athena, 1962.
Phil 4845.227.40   Papanoutsos, Euangelos. Philosophika problemata. Athena, 1964.
Phil 4845.227.44   Papanoutsos, Euangelos. Neollènikè philosophia. 2. ed. v.1-2. Athena, 1956-59.

Phil 4851.1 - .799   History of philosophy - Local Modern philosophy - Southwest Asia in general, Near East in general - History
Phil 4851.10A   Amin, Osman. Lights on contemporary Moslem philosophy. Cairo, 1958.
Phil 4851.10B   Amin, Osman. Lights on contemporary Moslem philosophy. Cairo, 1958.

Phil 4870   History of philosophy - Local Modern philosophy - India - History
Phil 4870.10   Ray, Benoy Gopal. Contemporary Indian philosophers. Allahabad, 1947.
Phil 4870.12   Naravane, Vishwanath S. Modern Indian thought; a philosophical survey. Bombay, 1964.
Phil 4870.14   Srivastava, Rama Shanker. Contemporary Indian philosophy. Delhi, 1965.

Classified Listing

Phil 4870   History of philosophy - Local Modern philosophy - India - History - cont.
Phil 4870.16   Anikeev, Nikolai Petrovich. Modern ideological struggle for the ancient philosophical heritage of India. Calcutta, 1969.
Phil 4870.18   Gessler, Clara. Westlicher Wissensdrang-Indische Weisheit. Zürich, 1970.

Phil 4871   History of philosophy - Local Modern philosophy - India - Anthologies of philosophical writings
Phil 4871.5   Radhakrishnan, Sarvepalli. Contemporary Indian philosophy. London, 1936.
Phil 4871.5.2   Radhakrishnan, Sarvepalli. Contemporary Indian philosophy. 2nd ed. London, 1952.

Phil 4872   History of philosophy - Local Modern philosophy - India - Individual philosophers (363 scheme)
Phil 4872.55.20   D'Andrade, Joseph C.P. Philosophy and life and other papers. Bombay, 1952.
Phil 4872.55.220   Damle, Prabhakar R. Philosophical essays. Bombay, 1954.
Phil 4872.109.2   Ghose, Aurobindo. The life divine. N.Y., 1949.
Phil 4872.109.3   Ghose, Aurobindo. The life divine. 3rd ed. N.Y., 1965.
Phil 4872.109.80   Sailley, Robert. Crî Aurobindo, philosophe du yoga intégral. Paris, 1970.
Phil 4872.187.30   Mallik, Basanta Kumar. The towering wave. London, 1953.
Phil 4872.193.30   Mukerjea, Jyoti S. Humanism. Nagpur, 19- .
Phil 4872.242.20   Radhakrishnan, Sarvépalli. Radhakrishnan; an anthology. London, 1952.
Phil 4872.242.22   Radhakrishnan, Sarvépalli. Radhakrishnan reader; an anthology. 1st ed. Bombay, 1969.
Phil 4872.242.30   Radhakrishnan, Sarvépalli. My search for truth. 2nd ed. Agra, 1956.
Phil 4872.242.80   Schilpp, Paul A. The philosophy of Sarvepalli Radhakrishnan. N.Y., 1952.
Phil 4872.242.85   Arapura, John G. Radhakrishnan and integral experience. London, 1966.
Phil 4872.242.1030   Radhas Vamidayal. The Sär Bachan; an abstract of the teachings of Swamiji Maharaj. 4th ed. Beas, 195-?
Phil 4872.247.30   Roy, Manendra Nath. Reason, romanticism and revolution. Calcutta, 1952-55. 2v.

Phil 4873   History of philosophy - Local Modern philosophy - Pakistan - History
Phil 4873.5   Stepovniants, Marietta Tigranovna. Filosofiia i sotsiologiia v Pakistane. Moskva, 1967.
Phil 4873.10   Smet, Richard V. de. Philosophical activity in Pakistan. Lahore, 1961.

Phil 4882.1 - .399   History of philosophy - Local Modern philosophy - Turkmenistan - History
Phil 4882.1   Ocherki istorii filosofskoi i obshchestvenno-politicheskoi mysli v Turkmenistane. Ashkhabad, 1970.

Phil 4883.1 - .399   History of philosophy - Local Modern philosophy - Kazakhstan - History
Phil 4883.2   Beisembiev, Kasym Beisembievich. Ideino-politicheskie techeniia v Kazakhstane Kontsa XIX-nachala XX veka. Alma-Ata, 1961.
Phil 4883.2.5   Beisembiev, Kasym Beisembievich. Progressivno-demokraticheskaia i marksistskaia mysl' v Kazakhstane nachala XX veka. Alma-Ata, 1965.

Phil 4890.1 - .799   History of philosophy - Local Modern philosophy - Eastern Asia in general, Far East in general - History
Phil 4890.10   Tsuchida, Kyoson. Contemporary thought of Japan and China. London, 1927.
Phil 4890.10.2   Tsuchida, Kyoson. Contemporary thought of Japan and China. N.Y., 1927.

Phil 4891   History of philosophy - Local Modern philosophy - China - History
Phil 4891.1   Chan, Wing-tsit. Chinese philosophy, 1949-1963; an annotated bibliography of mainland China publications. Honolulu, 1966-67.
Phil 4891.10   Brière, O. Fifty years of Chinese philosophy, 1898-1950. London, 1956.
Phil 4891.10.2   Brière, O. Fifty years of Chinese philosophy, 1898-1848. N.Y., 1965.

Phil 4897   History of philosophy - Local Modern philosophy - Japan - History
Phil 4897.10   Piovesana, Gino K. Recent Japanese philosophical thought, 1862-1962. Tokyo, 1963.
Phil 4897.10.5   Piovesana, Gino K. Contemporary Japanese philosophical thought. N.Y., 1969.
Phil 4897.15   Nakamura, Hajime. A history of the development of Japanese thought from 592 to 1868. v.1-2. Tokyo, 1967.

Phil 4899   History of philosophy - Local Modern philosophy - Japan - Individual philosophers (363 scheme)
Phil 4899.162.30   Kaneko, Shōseki. Über das Wesen und den Ursprung des Menschen. Osaka, 1932.
Phil 4899.255.80   Radul'-Zatulovskii, Iakov B. Ando Sëëki, filosof, materialist XVIII veka. Moskva, 1961.

Phil 4912   History of philosophy - Local Modern philosophy - Australia - Anthologies of philosophical writings
Phil 4912.5   Brown, Robert. Contemporary philosophy in Australia. London, 1969.

Phil 4926   History of philosophy - Local Modern philosophy - South Africa (Republic) - Individual philosophers (363 scheme)
Phil 4926.160.30   Jordan, Rudolf. The new perspective, an essay. Chicago, 1951.

Phil 4931 - 4956   History of philosophy - Local Modern philosophy - Miscellany [Discontinued]
Htn   Phil 4931.1.30*   Augustinus, S. Of the citie of God. London, 1610.
Htn   Phil 4931.2.30F*   Alexander, A. In Aristotelis meteoricus libros commentaria. n.p., 1527.
Htn   Phil 4931.3.80*   Dénes, Lajos. Emlekkönyv Alexander Bernat hatvanadik születése napjára. Budapest, 1910.
Htn   Phil 4932.2.30F*   Bernard of Clairvaux, St. Opera. n.p., 1508.
Htn   Phil 4934.1.30*   Diogenes Laertius. De vita et moribus philosophorum. Basiliae, 1524.
Htn   Phil 4934.2.30*   Dionysius Areopagita. Theologia vivificans. Argetine, 1502.
Htn   Phil 4938.1.30*   Hermes Trismegistus. The divine Pymander. London, 1650.
Htn   Phil 4938.2.30*   Hus, J. Liber egregius de unitate ecclesiae. n.p., n.d.
Htn   Phil 4939.1.30*   Iamblichus. Iamblichus de mysteriis. Lugduni, 1570.

Phil 4931 - 4956   History of philosophy - Local Modern philosophy - Miscellany [Discontinued] - cont.
Phil 4941.9   Kriezes, T.A. To Ellinikon ethnos ke i sighxroni epoxi. Athena, 1958.
Htn   Phil 4946.1.30*   Philo Iudaeus. De vita Mosis. Paris, 1554.
Htn   Phil 4946.2.30F*   Philostratus. Quae supersunt omnia. Lipsiae, 1709.
Htn   Phil 4950.1.30F*   Thomas Aquinas, St. Summa theologica. Duaci, 1614.
X Cg   Phil 4952.1.5   Vvedenskii, A.I. Psikhologiia bez vsiakoi metafiziki. Petrograd, 1915.

Phil 4957.1 - .799   History of philosophy - Local Modern philosophy - Latin America in general - History
Phil 4957.5   Larroyo, Francisco. La filosofía americana, su razón y su sinrazón de ser. Mexico, 1958.
Phil 4957.10   Gaos, José. Pensamiento de lengua española. México, 1945.
Phil 4957.15   Montevideo. Universidad. Facultad de Humanidades y Ciencias. Aportes a una bibliografía anotada de historía de las ideas en América. Montevideo, 1964.
Phil 4957.20   Sánchez Reulet, Aníbal. La filosofía latinoamericana contemporanea. Washington, 1949.
Phil 4957.20.5   Sanchez Reulet, Aníbal. Contemporary Latin-American philosophy. New Mexico, 1954.
Phil 4957.25   Larrayo, Francisco. Histora de las doctrinas filosóficas en Latinoamérica. 1. ed. México, 1968.
Phil 4957.30   Caturla Brú, Victoria de. Cuáles son los grandes temas de la filosofía latinoamericana? México, 1959.
Phil 4957.35   Romero, Francisco. Sobre la filosofía en América. Buenos Aires, 1952.
Phil 4957.40   Carrillo Narváez, Alfredo. La tragectoria del pensamiento filosófico en Latinoamérica. Quito, 1959.
Phil 4957.45   Kempff Mercado, Manfredo. Historia de la filosofía en Latinoamérica. Santiago de Chile, 1958.
Phil 4957.50   Zea, Leopoldo. América como conciencia. México, 1953.
Phil 4957.55   Villegas, Abelardo. Panorama de la filosofía iberoamericana actual. Buenos Aires, 1963.
Phil 4957.60   The Ibero-American enlightenment. Urbana, 1971.
Phil 4957.65   Salazar, Bondy Augusto. Existe una filosofía de nuestra América? 1. ed. México, 1968[1969]

Phil 4957.800 - .999   History of philosophy - Local Modern philosophy - Latin America in general - Anthologies of philosophical writings
Phil 4957.805   Zea, Leopoldo. Antología de la filosofía americana contemporánea. México, 1968.
Phil 4957.810   Zea, Leopoldo. La filosofía americana como filosofia sin más. 1. ed. México, 1969.

Phil 4958.200 - .299   History of philosophy - Local Modern philosophy - West Indies - History and anthologies - Cuba
Phil 4958.205   Piñera Llera, Humberto. Panorama de la filosofía cubana. Washington, 1960.
Phil 4958.210   Mestre, José Manuel. De la filosofía en la Habana. Habana, 1862.

Phil 4958.500 - .599   History of philosophy - Local Modern philosophy - West Indies - History and anthologies - Dominican Republic
Phil 4958.505   Sánchez, Juan Francisco. El pensamiento filosófico en Santo Domingo. Ciudad Trujillo, 1956?
Phil 4958.510   Cordero, Armando. Panorama de la filosofía en Santo Domingo. Santo Domingo, 1962.

Phil 4959.1 - .199   History of philosophy - Local Modern philosophy - Central America - History and anthologies - General
Phil 4959.5   Lascaris Comneno, Constantino. Historia de las ideas en Centroamerica. 1. ed. San José de Costa Rica, 1970.

Phil 4959.200 - .299   History of philosophy - Local Modern philosophy - Central America - History and anthologies - Mexico
Phil 4959.205   Mayagoitia, David. Ambiente filosófico de la Nueva España. México, 1945.
Phil 4959.210   Navarro, Bernabé. La introducción de la filosofía moderna en México. México, 1948.
Phil 4959.210.5   Navarro, Bernabé. Cultura mexicana moderna en el siglo XVIII. 1. ed. México, 1964.
Phil 4959.215   Gaos, José. Filosofía mexicana de nuestros días. México, 1954.
Phil 4959.220   Gallegos Rocafull, José Manuel. El pensamiento mexicano en los siglos XVI y XVII. México, 1951.
Phil 4959.225   Romanell, Patrick. La formación de la mentalidad mexicana. 1. ed. México, 1954.
Phil 4959.230.2   Zea, Leopoldo. El positivismo en México. 2. ed. México, 1953.
Phil 4959.230.5   Zea, Leopoldo. La filosofía en México. v.1-2. Mexico, 1955.
Phil 4959.230.10   Zea, Leopoldo. La filosofía como compromiso, y otros ensayos. 1. ed. México, 1952.
Phil 4959.235   Villegas, Abelardo. La filosofía en la historía política de México. 1. ed. México, 1966.
Phil 4959.240   Robles, Oswaldo. Filósofos mexicanos del siglo XVI. Mexico, 1950.
Phil 4959.245   México (City). Universidad Nacional. Consejo Técnico de Humanidades. Estudios de historía de la filosofía en México. 1. ed. México, 1963.
Phil 4959.245.5   México (City). Universidad Nacional. Consejo Técnico de Humanidades. Major trends in Mexican philosophy. Notre Dame, 1966.

Phil 4959.400 - .499   History of philosophy - Local Modern philosophy - Central America - History and anthologies - Costa Rica
Phil 4959.405   Láscaris Comneno, Constantino. Desarrollo de las ideas filosóficas en Costa Rica. Costa Rica, 1964.

Phil 4960.200 - .399   History of philosophy - Local Modern philosophy - South America - History and anthologies - Argentina
Phil 4960.205   Copelli y Marroni, Francisco. Esencialismo. 1. ed. Buenos Aires, 1957.
Phil 4960.210.2   Lombardo Toledano, Vicente. Las corrientes filosóficas en la vida de México. 1. ed. México, 1963.
Phil 4960.215   Ingenieros, José. Las direcciones filosóficas de la cultura argentina. Buenos Aires, 1963.
Phil 4960.220   Alberini, Coriolano. Problemas de la historía de las ideas filosóficas en la Argentina. La Plata, 1966.
Phil 4960.220.5   Alberini, Coriolano. Die deutsche Philosophie in Argentinien. Berlin, 1930.
Phil 4960.225   Farré, Luis. Cincuenta años de filosofía en Argentina. Buenos Aires, 1958.
Phil 4960.230   Fúrlong Cárdiff, Guillermo. Nacimiento y desarollo de la filosofía en el Rio de la Plata, 1536-1810. Buenos Aires, 1952.

Classified Listing

Phil 4960.200 - .399   History of philosophy - Local Modern philosophy - South America - History and anthologies - Argentina - cont.

Phil 4960.235   Torchia Estrada, Juan Carlos. La filosofía en la Argentina. Washington, 1961.

Phil 4960.240   Vázquez, Juan Adolfo. Antología filosófica argentina del siglo XX. Buenos Aires, 1965.

Phil 4960.245   Caturelli, Alberto. La filosofía en Argentina actual. Córdoba, 1963.

Phil 4960.250   Korn, Alejandro. El pensamiento argentino. Buenos Aires, 1961.

Phil 4960.255   Lipp, Solomon. Three Argentine thinkers. N.Y., 1969.

Phil 4960.260   Varela Dominguez de Ghioldi, Delfina. Filosofía argentina; los ideólogos. Buenos Aires, 1938.

Phil 4960.265   Roig, Arturo Andres. Los krausistas argentinos. Puebla, Mexico, 1969.

Phil 4960.270   Influenza italiana nella filosofia rioplatense. Firenze, 1969.

Phil 4960.272   Vazela Dominiguez de Ghioldi, Delfina. Para la historia de las ideas argentinas. 1. ed. Buenos Aires, 1952.

Phil 4960.400 - .599   History of philosophy - Local Modern philosophy - South America - History and anthologies - Bolivia

Phil 4960.405   Francovich, Guillermo. La filosofía en Bolivía. Buenos Aires, 1945.

Phil 4960.600 - .799   History of philosophy - Local Modern philosophy - South America - History and anthologies - Brazil

Phil 4960.605   Cruz Costa, João. Contribuição à história das idéias no Brasil. Rio de Janeiro, 1956.

Phil 4960.605.2   Cruz Costa, João. Contribuição à história das idéias no Brasil. 2. ed. Rio de Janeiro, 1967.

Phil 4960.605.5   Cruz Costa, João. A history of ideas in Brazil. Berkeley, 1964.

Phil 4960.605.10   Cruz Costa, João. A filosofía no Brasil. Pôrto Alegre, 1945.

Phil 4960.605.15   Cruz Costa, João. O positivismo na república. São Paulo, 1956.

Phil 4960.605.20   Cruz Costa, João. Esbozo de una historía de las ideas en el Brasil. México, 1957.

Phil 4960.605.25   Cruz Costa, João. Panorama of the history of philosophy in Brazil. Washington, 1962.

Phil 4960.610   Torres, João Camillo de Oliveira. O positivismo no Brasil. Petropolis, 1943.

Phil 4960.610.2   Torres, João Camillo de Oliveira. O positivismo no Brasil. 2. ed. Rio de Janeiro, 1957.

Phil 4960.615   Textos brasileiros de filosofia. Rio de Janeiro. 1-5,1957-1960// 4v.

Phil 4960.620   Souza, Remy de. Vocação filosófica do Brasil. Salvador, 1960.

Phil 4960.625   Vita, Luís Washington. Tendências do pensamento estético contemporâneo no Brasil. Rio de Janeiro, 1967.

Phil 4960.625.5   Vita, Luís Washington. Antología do pensamento social e político no Brasil, seleção e notas. São Paulo, 1968.

Phil 4960.625.10   Vita, Luís Washington. Panorama da filosofía no Brasil. Pôrto Alegre, 1969.

Phil 4960.625.15   Vita, Luís Washington. A filosofía contemporânea em São Paulo nos seus textos. São Paulo, 1969.

Phil 4960.630   Acerboni, Lidia. La filosofia contemporanea in Brasile. Milano, 1968.

Phil 4960.635   Gómez Robledo, Antonio. La filosofía en el Brasil. México, 1946.

Phil 4960.640   Paim, Antônio. A filosofía da escola do Recife. Rio de Janeiro, 1966.

Phil 4960.640.5   Paim, Antônio. Història das idéias filosóficas no Brasil. São Paulo, 1967.

Phil 4960.645   Roméro, Sylvio. A philosophia no Brasil. Pôrto Alegre, 1878.

Phil 4960.650   Reale, Miguel. Filosofía em São Paulo. São Paulo, 1962.

Phil 4960.655   Francovich, Guillermo. Filósofos brasileños. Buenos Aires, 1943.

Phil 4960.660   Buggenhagen, Erich Arnold von. Pensamento filosófico brasileiro na atualidade. São Paulo, 1968.

Phil 4960.800 - .999   History of philosophy - Local Modern philosophy - South America - History and anthologies - Chile

Phil 4960.805   Hanisch Espíndola, Walter. En torno a la filosofía en Chile, 1594-1810. Santiago, 1963.

Phil 4961.1 - .199   History of philosophy - Local Modern philosophy - South America - History and anthologies - Colombia

Phil 4961.45.3   Romanell, P. La formación de la mentalidad mexicana. México, 1954.

Phil 4961.65   García Bacca, J.D. Antologia del pensamiento filosófico en Colombia. Bogotá, 1955.

Phil 4961.116   Jaramillo Uribe, Jaime. El pensamiento colombiano en el siglo XIX. Bogotá, 1964.

Phil 4961.126.5   Ibarguengoitía, Antonio. Filosofía mexicana. 1. ed. Mexico, 1967.

Phil 4961.140   Pan American Union. Fuentes de la filosofía latinoamericana. Washington, 1967.

Phil 4961.600 - .799   History of philosophy - Local Modern philosophy - South America - History and anthologies - Peru

Phil 4961.605   Salazar Bondy, Augusto. La filosofía en el Perú. Wáshington, 1955.

Phil 4961.605.5   Salazar Bondy, Augusto. Historía de las ideas en el Perú contemporáneo. Lima, 1965.

Phil 4961.615   Mejia Valera, Manuel. Fuentes para la história de la filosofía en el Perú. Lima, 1963.

Phil 4961.800 - .899   History of philosophy - Local Modern philosophy - South America - History and anthologies - Uruguay

Phil 4961.805   Ardao, Arturo. Filosofía pre-universitaria en el Uruguay. Montevideo, 1945.

Phil 4961.805.5   Ardao, Arturo. Espiritualismo y positivismo en el Uruguay. México, 1950.

Phil 4961.805.10   Ardao, Arturo. La filosofía en el Uruguay en el siglo XX. México, 1956.

Phil 4961.805.15   Ardao, Arturo. Racionalismo y liberalismo en el Uruguay. Montevideo, 1962.

Phil 4961.900 - .999   History of philosophy - Local Modern philosophy - South America - History and anthologies - Venezuela

Phil 4961.905   Beltrán Guerrero, Luis. Introducción al positivismo venezolano. Caracas, 1956?

Phil 4961.910   Granell Muñiz, Manuel. Del pensar venezolano. Caracas, 1967.

Phil 4961.900 - .999   History of philosophy - Local Modern philosophy - South America - History and anthologies - Venezuela - cont.

Phil 4961.915   García Bacca, Juan David. Antología del pensamiento filosófico venezolano. Caracas, 1954.

Phil 4961.918   Nuño, Alicia de. Ideas sociales del positivismo en Venezuela. Caracas, 1969.

Phil 4962 - 4987   History of philosophy - Local Modern philosophy - South America - Individual philosophers (A-Z)

Phil 4962.5   Abad Carretero, Luis. Niñez y filosofía. México, 1957.

Phil 4962.5.5   Abad Carretero, Luis. Vida y sentido. México, 1960.

Phil 4962.10   Alvarez, González. Introducción a una metafisica de la contingencia. Cuenca, 1959.

Phil 4962.20   Arroyave Calle, J.C. El ser del hombre. Medellín, 1952.

Phil 4963.1   Buzzi, E. De donde venimos. Lima, 1942.

Phil 4963.2   Cannabrava, Euryalo. A cultura brasileira e seus equivocos. Rio de Janeiro, 1955.

Phil 4963.2.5   Cannabrava, Euryalo. Estética da crítica. Rio de Janeiro, 1963.

Phil 4963.3   Ardao, Arturo. Battle y Ordoñez y el positivismo filosófico. Montevideo, 1951.

Phil 4963.4   Basave Fernandez del Valle, A. Ideario filosófico, 1953-1961. Monterrey, 1961.

Phil 4963.5   Barros, Roque Spencer Maciel de. A evolução do pensamento de Pereira Barreta. São Paulo, 1967.

Phil 4963.6   Barreto, Luís Pereira. Obras filosóficas. São Paulo, 1967.

Phil 4964.5   Agramonte y Pichardo, R. José Augustin Caballero y las origines de la conciencia cubana. La Habana, 1952.

Phil 4964.10   Chaves, Osvaldo. Historía y filosofía. Buenos Aires, 1958.

Phil 4964.67   Coviello, Alfredo. Una página de historía en la naciente filosofía argentina y otros ensayos criticos. Tucumán, 1942.

Phil 4965.2   Diaz de Gamarra y Dávalos, J.B. Elementos de filosofía moderna. México, 1963.

Phil 4965.4   Bibliografía de las obras del Dr. Dn. Alejandro O. Deustua. Lima, 1939.

Phil 4966.2   Estable, C. Psicología de la vocación. Montevideo, 1942.

Phil 4967.5   Francovich, Guillermo. Hijos de la roca. México, 1954.

Phil 4967.5.5   Francovich, Guillermo. El cinismo. Puebla, 1963.

Phil 4967.5.10   Francovich, Guillermo. Supay; diálogos. Sucre, 1939.

Phil 4967.5.80   Zelada C., Alberto. El pensamiento de Guillermo Francovich. Sucre, 1966.

Phil 4967.10   Elias de Tejada, Francisco. Las doctrinas políticas de Raimundo de Farias Brito. Sevilla, 1953.

Phil 4967.15   Asociación de Egresados de la Facultad de Derecho y Ciencias Sociales de la Universidad de Buenos Aires. La acusación de plagio contra el rector Frondizi. Buenos Aires? 1959.

Phil 4967.20   Farias Brito, Raymundo de. A base physica do espirito. Rio de Janeiro, 1912.

Phil 4967.20.5   Farias Brito, Raymundo de. O mundo interior. Rio de Janeiro, 1951.

Phil 4967.20.10   Farias Brito, Raymundo de. Finalidade do mundo. 2. ed. Rio de Janeiro, 1957. 3v.

Phil 4967.20.15   Farias Brito, Raymundo de. Ineditos e dispersos, notas e variaçoes sôbre assuntos diversos. São Paulo, 1966.

Phil 4967.20.20   Farias Brito, Raymundo de. Trechos escolhidos. Rio de Janeiro, 1967.

Phil 4967.20.80   Nogueira, A. Farias Brito e a filosofia do espirito. Rio de Janeiro, 1962.

Phil 4967.20.85   Lopes de Maltos, C. O pensamento de Farias Brito. São Paulo, 1962.

Phil 4967.32   Fontes, Gloria Marly Duarte. Alexandre Rodrigues Ferreira: aspectos de sua vida e obra. Manaus, 1966.

Phil 4967.35   Franceschi, Alfredo. Escritos filosóficos. La Plata, 1968.

Phil 4968.4.80   Cordiel Reyes, Raúl. Del modernismo al liberalismo. México, 1967.

Phil 4970.1.11   Ingenieros, José. Obras completas. Buenos Aires, 1962. 8v.

Phil 4970.1.20   Ingenieros, José. Antología; su pensamiento en sus mejores páginas. Buenos Aires, 1961.

Phil 4970.1.30   Ingenieros, José. La simulación en la lucha por la vida. Valencia, 191-?

Phil 4972.5.5   Korn, Alejandro. Obras completas. Buenos Aires, 1949.

Phil 4972.5.10   Korn, Alejandro. Ensayos críticos. Buenos Aires, 193-.

Phil 4972.5.15   Korn, Alejandro. Obras. La Plata, 1938-40. 3v.

Phil 4972.5.20   Korn, Alejandro. De San Agustín a Bergson. Buenos Aires, 1959.

Phil 4972.5.50   Malmurca Sánchez, Ernesto. Para una posición argentina. La Plata, 1940.

Phil 4972.5.53   Romero, Francisco. Alejandro Korn. La Plata, 1938.

Phil 4972.5.55   Romero, Francisco. Alejandro Korn. Buenos Aires, 1940.

Phil 4972.5.56   Romero, Francisco. Alejandro Korn. Buenos Aires, 1956.

Phil 4972.5.60   Universidad Nacional del Litoral. Alejandro Korn. Rosario, 1963.

Phil 4972.5.80   La Plata. Universidad Nacional. Estudios sobre Alejandro Korn. La Plata, 1963.

Phil 4972.6.30   Kelly, Celso. Valores do espirito; ensaios. Rio de Janeiro, 195-?

Phil 4972.22   Kehl, Renato. Bio-perspectivas. Rio de Janeiro, 1938.

Phil 4973.5.6   Lombardo Toledano, Vicente. Escritos filosóficos. México, 1937.

Phil 4973.7   Lins, Mario. Foundations of social determinism. Rio de Janeiro, 1959.

Phil 4973.41   Lizarte Martínez, Angel. Dios, espíritu y materia; esencia. 2. ed. Montevideo, 1944.

Phil 4974.5   Massera, José P. Estudios filosóficos. v.12. Montevideo, 1954.

Phil 4974.24   Menezes, O. Raízes pré-socráticas do pensamento atual. Ceará, 1958.

Phil 4974.27.20   Mestre, Jose Manuel. Obras. Habana, 1965.

Phil 4974.50.2   Molina, Enrique. Tragedia y realización del espíritu. 2. ed. Santiago, 1953.

Phil 4974.65   Bazán, Armando. Vida y obra del maestro Enrique Molina. Santiago, 1954.

Phil 4976.5.80   Flores Caballero, Luis. Humanismo y revolución en América Latina; bosquejo de interpretación del pensamiento materialista de Antenor Orrego. Lima, 1968.

Phil 4977.5   Pessoa, Fernando. Textos filosóficos. Lisboa, 1968. 2v.

Phil 4979.5.30   Ramos, Samuel. Hacia un nuevo humanismo. 1. ed. México, 1940.

Phil 4979.5.80   Hernández Luna, Juan. Samuel Ramos. México, 1956.

Phil 4979.5.85   Hernández Luna, Juan. Dos ideas sobre la filosofía en la Nueva España. México, 1959.

Phil 4962 - 4987   History of philosophy - Local Modern philosophy - South America - Individual philosophers (A-Z) - cont.

Phil 4979.10.30   Rodríguez Delgado, Rafael. Introducción a una filosofía de la era atómica. Habana, 1950.

Phil 4979.15.30   Romero, Francisco. La estructura de la historia de la filosofía y otros ensayos. Buenos Aires, 1967.

Phil 4979.41.30   Rio, Manuel. La liberté; choix, amour, création. Paris, 1961.

Phil 4979.65.30   Romero, Sylvio. Obra filosófica. Rio de Janeiro, 1969.

Phil 4980.1.30   Sabato, Ernesto R. Hombres y engranajes. Buenos Aires, 1951.

Phil 4980.3   Silva Mello, Antonio da. Man; his life, his education, his happiness. N.Y., 1956.

Phil 4980.41   Sánchez Reulet, Aníbal. Raíz y destino de la filosofía. Tucumán, 1942.

Phil 4980.52.30   Silva, Vicente Ferreira da. Obras completas. São Paulo, 1964. 2v.

Phil 4981.41.100   Tierno Galvan, Enrique. La realidad como resultado. Rio Piedras, 1966.

Phil 4983.1.5   Vaz Ferreira, Carlos. Obras. v.1-25. Montevideo, 1957. 20v.

Phil 4983.1.30   Vaz Ferreira, Carlos. Fermentario. Buenos Aires, 1940.

Phil 4983.1.32   Vaz Ferreira, Carlos. Fermentario. Montevideo, 1953.

Phil 4983.1.79   Montevideo. Universidad. Facultad de Humanidades y Ciencias. Bibliografía de Carlos Vaz Ferreira. Montevideo, 1962.

Phil 4983.1.80   Arias, Alejandro. Vaz Ferreira. 1. ed. México, 1948.

Phil 4983.1.85   Campo, Aníbal del. El problema de la creencia y el intelectualismo de Vaz Ferreira. Montevideo, 1959.

Phil 4983.1.90   Ardao, Arturo. Introducción a Vaz Ferreira. Montevideo, 1961.

Phil 4983.5.6   Varela, Félix. Miscelanea filosófica. Habana, 1944.

Phil 4983.5.20   Varela, Félix. Lecciones de filosofía. 5. ed. Habana, 1961. 2v.

Phil 4983.5.22   Varela, Félix. Cartas a Elpidio (Selección). Habana, 1960.

Phil 4983.5.85   Varela, Félix. Cartas a Elpidio sobre la impiedad. v.1-2. Habana, 1944.

Phil 4983.5.90   Rodriguez, José Ignacio. Vida del presbítero don Félix Varela. N.Y., 1878.

Phil 4983.5.95   McCadden, Joseph James. Father Varela. N.Y., 1969.

Phil 4983.8.6   Varona, Enrique. Conferencias filosóficas. Ser.1, 3. Habana, 1880. 2v.

Phil 4983.8.90   Cabrera, Francisco de A. Razón contra razón...de Enrique José de Varona. 3. ed. Habana, 1893.

Phil 4983.9.30   Vasconcelos, J. Todología. México, 1952.

Phil 4983.41   Villegas, Abelardo. La filosofía de lo mexicano. México, 1960.

Phil 4983.74.31   Virasoro, M.A. Desesperación y rebeldía en la conciencia contemporanea. Bahia Blanca, 1959.

Phil 4987.53.30   Zambrano, María. Hacia un saber sobre el alma. Buenos Aires, 1950.

Phil 4987.60.61   Zunino Dubois, J.C. Entre robles y tilos. La Plata, 1962.

Phil 4987.89.20   Zubiri, Xavier. Estudios filosóficos. Madrid, 1963.

Phil 4987.89.30   Zubiri, Xavier. Naturaleza, historia, Dios. Buenos Aires, 1948.

Phil 4987.89.80   Homenaje a Xavier Zubiri. Madrid, 1953.

Phil 4987.89.85   Marquinez Argote, Germán. En torno a Zubiri. Madrid, 1965.

Phil 4987.89.90   Homenaje a Xavier Zubiri. Madrid, 1970. 2v.

Phil 5000   Logic - Folios [Discontinued]

Htn   Phil 5000.1*   Burley, Walter. Expositio super artem veterem Porphyrii et Aristotelis. Pts.1,2. Manuscripts. n.p., 1442?

Phil 5000.2   Keckermanni, B. Systema systematum. Hanoviae, 1613.

Htn   Phil 5000.3*   Monti, Panfilo. Logica pamph. v.1-3. Venice, 1512.

Phil 5000.4F   Zabarella, Giacomo. Opera logica. 16a ed. Tarvisii, 1604.

Phil 5000.5   Pierce, C.S. Logic of relatives. Cambridge, 1870.

Phil 5003   Logic - Reference works - Bibliographies

Phil 5003.5   Cambridge. University. Library. Catalog of a collection of books on logic. Cambridge, 1889.

Phil 5003.6A   Weiss, Paul. A preliminary draft of a bibliography of contributions to modern logic. Supplement. n.p., n.d.

Phil 5003.6B   Weiss, Paul. A preliminary draft of a bibliography of contributions to modern logic. Supplement. n.p., n.d.

Phil 5003.10   Primakovskii, A.P. Bibliografiia po logike. Moskva, 1955.

Phil 5003.12   Risse, Wilhelm. Bibliographia logica. Hildesheim, 1965.

Phil 5004   Logic - Reference works - Dictionaries and encyclopedias

Phil 5004.1   Kondakov, Nikolai I. Logicheskii slovar'. Moskva, 1971.

Phil 5005   Logic - Pamphlet volumes

Phil 5005.1   Pamphlet vol. Logic, 1896-1910.

Phil 5005.3   Pamphlet vol. Logic, 1901-1908. 5 pam.

Phil 5005.4   Pamphlet vol. Logic. 35 pam.

Phil 5005.5   Pamphlet vol. Logic. German pamphlets and dissertations, 1910-1922. 11 pam.

Phil 5005.6   Pamphlet box. Logic.

Phil 5005.7   Pamphlet box. Logic. German dissertations.

Phil 5010 - 5035   Logic - History - General works - Individual authors (A-Z)

Phil 5010.1   Adamson, R. A short history of logic. Edinburgh, 1911.

Phil 5010.2   Ahlander, J.A. De prascipuis philosophorum recentioris aevi logicam tractandi rationibus. Diss. Lundae, 1849.

Phil 5011.1   Blakey, R. Historical sketch of logic. London, 1851.

Phil 5011.2   Brevis ad artem cogitandi. London, 1770.

Phil 5011.3   Binde, Robert. Begriff, Urteil und Schluss in ihrer gemeinsamen Wurze. pt.1-2. Glogan, 1886-87.

Phil 5011.4   Boll, Marcel. La logique. Paris, 1935.

Phil 5011.5   Barbu, Z. Le développement de la pensée dialectique. Paris, 1947.

Phil 5011.6   Bochénski, I.M. Formale Logik. Freiburg, 1956.

Phil 5011.6.5   Bochénski, I.M. Logisch-philosophische Studien. Freiburg, 1959.

Phil 5011.6.6   Bochénski, I.M. A history of formal logic. Notre Dame, Ind., 1961.

Phil 5011.6.10   Bochénski, I.M. Logico-philosophical studies. Dordrecht, 1962.

Phil 5011.7   Beth, Evert Willem. Geschiedenis der logica. Den Haag, 1948.

Phil 5011.8   Bowne, G.D. The philosophy of logic, 1880-1908. The Hague, 1966.

Phil 5012.2A   Clark, Joseph. Conventional logic and modern logic. Woodstock, 1952.

Phil 5012.2B   Clark, Joseph. Conventional logic and modern logic. Woodstock, 1952.

Phil 5010 - 5035   Logic - History - General works - Individual authors (A-Z) - cont.

Phil 5014.1   Enriques, Federigo. Per la storia della logica. Bologna, 1922.

Phil 5014.1.5   Enriques, Federigo. Zur Geschichte der Logik. Leipzig, 1927.

Phil 5014.1.20   Enriques, Federigo. L'évolution de la logique. Paris, 1926.

Phil 5014.1.30   Enriques, Federigo. The historic development of logic. N.Y., 1929.

Phil 5015.1   Franck, A. Esquisse d'une histoire de la logique. Paris, 1838.

Phil 5015.2   Filipor, R.P. Logic and dialecta in the Soviet Union. N.Y., 1952.

Phil 5015.3   Feys, Robert. De onturkkeling van het logisch denken. Antwerpen, 1949.

Phil 5015.4   Filkorn, V. Pre-dialectical logic. Bratislava, 1963.

VPhil 5015.5   Flam, Leopold. De geschiedenis van de dialektiek. St. Niklaas, 1964.

Phil 5016.1   Göldel, R.W. Die Lehre von der Identität in der deutschen Logik-Wissenschaft seit Lotze. Inaug. Diss. Leipzig, 1935.

Phil 5016.2   Gurvitch, Georges. Dialectique et sociologie. Paris, 1962.

Phil 5016.4   Geach, Peter Thomas. A history of the corruptions of logic: an inaugural lecture. Leeds, 1968.

Phil 5017.5   Howell, W.S. Logic and rhetoric in England. Princeton, 1956.

Phil 5017.6   Howell, W.S. Logic and rhetoric in England. N.Y., 1961.

Phil 5017.6.5   Howell, W.S. Eighteenth-century British logic and rhetoric. Princeton, 1971.

Phil 5019.5   Joja, A. Studii de logica. Bucuresti, 1960. 3v.

Phil 5020.5   Kneale, William Calvert. The development of logic. Oxford, 1962.

Phil 5020.5.10   Kneale, William Calvert. The development of logic. Oxford, 1968.

Phil 5020.10   Kotarbiński, Tadeusz. Leçons sur l'histoire de la logique. Warszawa, 1965.

Phil 5021.1   Liard, L. Les logiciens anglais contemporains. Paris, 1878.

Phil 5021.5   Lamouche, André. Logique de la simplicité. Paris, 1959.

Phil 5022.1   Marck, Siegfried. Die Dialektik in der Philosophie der Gegenwart. v.1-2. Tübingen, 1929-31.

Phil 5022.2   Meckies, H. Beiträge zur Geschichte des Induktionsproblems. Münster, 1933.

Phil 5022.4   Moscow. Universitet. Filosofskii Fakul'tet. Ocherki po istorii logiki v Rossii. Moskva, 1962.

Phil 5022.5   Makovel'skii, Aleksandr O. Istoriia logiki. Moskva, 1967.

Phil 5023.1   Nidditch, Peter. The development of mathematical logic. London, 1962.

Phil 5024.1   Öner, Nécoti. Fromsy sosydojiokuluna göre mokhyinmensei. Ankara, 1965.

Phil 5025.1   Prantl, Carl von. Geschichte der Logik. Leipzig, 1855-70. 3v.

X Cg   Phil 5025.1   Prantl, Carl von. Geschichte der Logik. v.4. Leipzig, 1855-70.

Phil 5025.1.1   Prantl, Carl von. Geschichte der Logik. v.2. 2e Aufl. Leipzig, 1855-1885.

Phil 5025.1.2   Prantl, Carl von. Geschichte der Logik. v.2. Leipzig, 1885.

Phil 5025.1.3   Prantl, Carl von. Geschichte der Logik im Abendlande. v.1-4. Graz, 1955. 3v.

Phil 5025.1.4   Prantl, Carl von. Geschichte der Logik im Abendlande. v.1-4. Berlin, 1957. 3v.

Phil 5025.2   Platzeck, E.W. Von der Analogie zum Syllogismus. Paderborn, 1954.

Phil 5025.3   Popov, P.S. Istoriia logiki novogo vremeni. Moskva, 1960.

Phil 5027.1   Rabus, L. Der neuesten Bestrebung...Logik. Erlangen, 1880.

Phil 5027.2   Rijh, Lambertus. Logica modernorum. Assen, 1962. 3v.

Phil 5027.3   Rescher, N. Studies in the history of Arabic logic. Pittsburgh, 1963.

Phil 5027.3.5   Rescher, N. The development of Arabic logic. Pittsburgh, 1964.

Phil 5027.4   Risse, Wilhelm. Die Logik der Neuzeit. Stuttgart, 1964-2v.

Phil 5028.1   Sanseverino, G. Philosophia Christiana cum antiqua et nova comparata. Neapoli, 1862-66. 3v.

Phil 5028.2   Scholz, Heinrich. Geschichte der Logik. Berlin, 1931.

Phil 5028.2.10   Scholz, Heinrch. Concise history of logic. N.Y., 1961.

Phil 5028.3   Sándor, Pál. Histoire de la dialectique. Paris, 1947.

Phil 5028.4   Stiazhkin, N.I. Kratkii ocheesk istorii obshchei i matemaficheskoi logiki v Rossii. Moskva, 1962.

Phil 5029.1   Tellbom, J.P. De progressibus disciplinae logicae. Diss. Upsaliae, 1830.

Phil 5031.1   Vollenhoven, D.H.T. De noodzakelijkheid eener christelijke logica. Amsterdam, 1932.

Phil 5032.1   Weinberg, Julius Rudolph. Abstraction, relation, and induction. Madison, 1965.

Phil 5032.5   Wilson, Curtis. William Heytesbury. Madison, 1956.

Phil 5039   Logic - General works, treatises - Collected authors

Phil 5039.2   Houde, Roland. Readings in logic. Dubuque, 1958.

Phil 5039.4   Runes, Dagobert D. Classics in logic. N.Y., 1962.

Phil 5039.6   Copi, Irving M. Readings on logic. N.Y., 1965.

Phil 5039.6.5   Copi, Irving M. Contemporary readings in logical theory. N.Y., 1967.

Phil 5039.8   Poloka Akademia Nauk. Instytut Filozofii i Socjologii. Teoria y doświadczenie. Warszawa, 1966.

Phil 5039.10   Problemi na logikata. Sofiia, 1967- 2v.

Phil 5039.12   Studies in logical theory. Oxford, 1968.

Phil 5039.14   Probleme de logică. Bucuresti, 1968. 3v.

Phil 5039.16   Sju filosofiska studier, tillägnade Anders Wedberg. Stockholm, 1963.

Phil 5039.18   Foster, Marguerite H. Probability, confirmation, and simplicity; readings in the philosophy of inductive logic. N.Y., 1966.

Phil 5039.20   Hintikka, Kaarlo Jaakko J. Aspects of inductive logic. Amsterdam, 1966.

Phil 5039.22   Philosophical problems in logic. Dordrecht, 1970.

Phil 5039.24   Lambert, Karel. The logical way of doing things. New Haven, 1969.

Phil 5039.26   Bober, Juraj. Problémy dialektiky. 1. vyd. Bratislava, 1968.

Phil 5039.28   Davis, J.W. Philosophical logic. Dordrecht, 1969.

Phil 5039.30   Centro di Studi Filosofici di Gallarate. Teoria della demostrazione. Padova, 1963.

Phil 5039.32   Sootnoshenie istorii i logiki nauki. Dnepopetrovsk, 1970.

Phil 5040 - 5065 Logic - General works, treatises - Individual authors (A-Z)

	Phil 5040.1	Aldrich, H. Artis logicae rudimenta. Oxford, 1852.
	Phil 5040.1.2	Aldrich, H. Artis logicae rudimenta. Oxford, 1856.
	Phil 5040.1.3	Aldrich, H. Artis logicae rudimenta. Oxford, 1862.
	Phil 5040.1.5	Aldrich, H. Artis logicae rudimenta. 5th ed. Oxford, 1835.
	Phil 5040.1.6	Aldrich, H. Artis logicae rudimenta. 6th ed. Oxford, 1850.
	Phil 5040.1.7	Aldrich, H. Artis logicae rudimenta. Oxonae, 1723.
	Phil 5040.1.8	Aldrich, H. Artis logicae compendium. Oxonii, 1844.
	Phil 5040.2	Allihn, F.H.T. Des antibarbarus logicus. Halle, 1853.
	Phil 5040.3.5	Arnauld, Antoine. Logique de Port Royal. Paris, 1854.
	Phil 5040.3.9	Arnauld, Antoine. Logique de Port Royal. Paris, 1861.
	Phil 5040.3.12	Arnauld, Antoine. Logique de Port Royal. Paris, 1869.
NEDL	Phil 5040.3.15	Arnauld, Antoine. Logique de Port Royal. Paris, 1878.
	Phil 5040.3.18	Arnauld, Antoine. Logique de Port-Royal. Facsimile. Lille, 1964.
	Phil 5040.3.20	Arnauld, Antoine. The art of thinking. Indianapolis, 1964.
	Phil 5040.3.25	Arnauld, Antoine. L'art de penser; la logique de Port Royal. v.1-3. Stuttgart, 1965- 2v.
	Phil 5040.4	Arnauld, Antoine. Logik, or The art of thinking. London, 1702.
	Phil 5040.4.2	Arnauld, Antoine. Logic, or The art of thinking. London, 1717.
	Phil 5040.4.3	Arnauld, Antoine. Logic, or The art of thinking. London, 1723.
	Phil 5040.4.4	Arnauld, Antoine. Logic, or The art of thinking. Edinburgh, 1850.
	Phil 5040.4.4.7	Arnauld, Antoine. La logique, ou L'art de penser. Paris, 1965.
	Phil 5040.4.5	Arnauld, Antoine. The Port Royal logic. Edinburgh, 1861.
	Phil 5040.6	Atwater, L.H. Manual of elementary logic. Philadelphia, 1867.
	Phil 5040.6.2	Atwater, L.H. Manual of elementary logic. Philadelphia, 1867.
	Phil 5040.7	Aikins, H.A. The principles of logic. N.Y., 1902.
	Phil 5040.7.1	Aikins, H.A. The principles of logic. 2nd ed. N.Y., 1904.
	Phil 5040.10	Alfonso, N.R. d'. Principii di logica reale. Torino, 1894.
	Phil 5040.11	Afzelius, F.G. Lärobok i logiken for elementar-undervisningen. Upsala, 1852.
	Phil 5040.12	Alstedius, J.H. Logicae systema harmonicum. Herbonae Nassoviorum, 1614.
	Phil 5040.13	Almquist, S. Vårt tankelif. Stockholm, 1906.
	Phil 5040.14	Avey, A.E. The function and forms of thought. N.Y., 1927.
	Phil 5040.15	Andreasi, A. Arte logica. Verona, 1882.
	Phil 5040.16	Anderson, Louis. Das logische; seine Gesetze und Kategorien. Leipzig, 1929.
	Phil 5040.17	Abicht, Johann H. Vom dem Nutzen und der Einrichtung eines zu logischen uebingen Bestimmten Collegimus. Leipzig, 1790.
	Phil 5040.17.5	Abicht, Johann H. Verbesserte Logik. Fürth, 1802.
	Phil 5040.19	Adjukiewicz, Kazimierz. Glówne zasady metodologji nauk i logiki. Warszawa, 1928.
	Phil 5040.19.5	Adjukiewicz, Kazimierz. Logika pragmatyczna. Warszawa, 1965.
	Phil 5040.20.5	Aragón, G.A. Lógica elemental. 4a ed. Habana, 1926.
	Phil 5040.21.5	Abbott, F.K. The elements of logic. London, 1947.
	Phil 5040.22	Asmus, V.F. Logika. Moskva, 1947.
	Phil 5040.22.5	Asmus, V.F. Uchenie logiki o dokazatel'stvi oprovrrzheniia. Moskva, 1954.
	Phil 5040.23	Akademiia Nauk SSSR. Institut Filosofii. Vaprosy logiki. Moskva, 1955.
	Phil 5040.24	Alekseev, M.N. Dialektika farm myshlemiia. Moskva, 1959.
	Phil 5040.25	Ambrose, A. Logic. N.Y., 1961.
	Phil 5040.26	Akademiia Nauk SSSR. Institut Filosofii. Filosofskie voprosy sovremennoi formal'noi logiki. Moskva, 1962.
	Phil 5040.27	Akademiia Nauk Kazakhskoi SSSR, Alma-Ata. Institut Literatury i Prava. Problemy logiki dialektiki poznaniia. Alma-Ata, 1963.
	Phil 5040.28	Astat'ev, Vsevdod K. Zakony myshleniia v formal'noi i dialketicheskoi logike. L'vov, 1968.
	Phil 5040.30	Alejandro, Jose Maria de. La lógica y el hombre. Madrid, 1970.
	Phil 5040.32	Albrecht, Erhard. Die Beziehungen von Erkenntnistheorie, Logik und Sprache. Halle, 1956.
	Phil 5041.1	Bachmann, C.F. System der Logik. Leipzig, 1828.
	Phil 5041.2	Bailey, Samuel. The theory of reasoning. London, 1852.
	Phil 5041.2.5	Bailey, Samuel. The theory of reasoning. London, 1851.
	Phil 5041.3	Bain, Alexander. Logic. London, 1870. 2v.
	Phil 5041.3.5	Bain, Alexander. Logic deductive and inductive. N.Y., 1887.
	Phil 5041.3.10	Bain, Alexander. Logique déductive et inductive. 3e éd. Paris, 1894. 2v.
	Phil 5041.4	Ballantine, W.G. Inductive logic. Boston, 1896.
	Phil 5041.5	Bardili, C.G. Grundriss der ersten Logik. Stuttgart, 1800.
	Phil 5041.6	Barnes, William. An outline of Rede-Craft (Logic). London, 1880.
L	Phil 5041.7	Baynes, T.S. Essay...new analytic. Logical forms. Edinburgh, 1850.
	Phil 5041.8	Barron, William. Elements of logic. N.Y., 1856.
	Phil 5041.9	Bergmann, J. Allgemeine Logik. Berlin, 1879.
	Phil 5041.11*	Beurhusius, F. In P. Rami. London, 1581.
	Phil 5041.12	Biedermann, Gustav. Zur logischen Frage. Prag, 1870.
	Phil 5041.13	Blakey, Robert. Essay towards...system of logic. London, 1834.
	Phil 5041.14	Bobrik, Eduard. Neues praktisches System der Logik. Zürich, 1838.
	Phil 5041.15	Boole, George. The laws of thought. London, 1854.
	Phil 5041.15.1*	Boole, George. The laws of thought. London, 1854.
	Phil 5041.15.2	Boole, George. The laws of thought. Chicago, 1916.
	Phil 5041.15.3	Boole, George. The laws of thought. Chicago, 1940.
	Phil 5041.15.4	Boole, George. Studies in logic and probability. London, 1952.
	Phil 5041.15.6	Boole, George. An investigation of the laws of thought. N.Y., 1951.
	Phil 5041.16	Bosanquet, B. Logic, or The morphology of knowledge. Oxford, 1888. 2v.
	Phil 5041.16.2A	Bosanquet, B. Logic, or The morphology of knowledge. Oxford, 1911. 2v.
	Phil 5041.16.2B	Bosanquet, B. Logic, or The morphology of knowledge. Oxford, 1911.
	Phil 5041.16.5	Bosanquet, B. The essentials of logic. London, 1895.
	Phil 5041.16.9	Bosanquet, B. The essentials of logic. London, 1914.
	Phil 5041.16.15	Bosanquet, B. Implication and linear inference. London, 1920.

Phil 5040 - 5065 Logic - General works, treatises - Individual authors (A-Z) - cont.

	Phil 5041.16.80	LeChevalier, Charles. La pensée morale de Bernard Bosanquet. Paris, 1963.
	Phil 5041.17	Bosanquet, S.R. A new system of logic. London, 1839.
	Phil 5041.18	Bouttier, M.Z. Essai de philosophie française. Paris, 1844.
	Phil 5041.20	Bradley, F.H. Principles of logic. London, 1883.
	Phil 5041.20.3	Bradley, F.H. Principles of logic. N.Y., 1912.
	Phil 5041.20.5A	Bradley, F.H. Principles of logic. 2nd ed. London, 1922. 2v.
	Phil 5041.20.5B	Bradley, F.H. Principles of logic. 2nd ed. London, 1922.
Htn	Phil 5041.20.5*B	Bradley, F.H. Principles of logic. 2nd ed. v.2. London, 1922.
Htn	Phil 5041.20.5*C	Bradley, F.H. Principles of logic. 2nd ed. London, 1922.
	Phil 5041.20.8	Bosanquet, B. Knowledge and reality. London, 1885.
	Phil 5041.21	Braniss, C.J. Die Logik...Verhaltniss zur philosophische Geschichte betrachter. Berlin, 1823.
	Phil 5041.21.10	Braniss, C.J. Grundriss der Logik. Breslau, 1830.
Htn	Phil 5041.23*	Brerewood, E. Tractatus guidam logici. Oxoniae, 1631. 3 pam.
	Phil 5041.24	Buhle, J.G. Einleitung in die allgemeine Logik und die Kritik der reinen Vernunft. Göttingen, 1795.
Htn	Phil 5041.25*	Burgersdijck, Franco. Institutionum logicarum. Lugdunum Batavorum, 1642-60. 2 pam.
Htn	Phil 5041.25.2*	Burgersdijck, Franco. Institutionum logicarum. Cantabrigiae, 1647-80. 3 pam.
Htn	Phil 5041.25.3*	Burgersdijck, Franco. Institutionum logicarum. Cantabrigiae, 1668-1670. 3 pam.
Htn	Phil 5041.25.4*	Burgersdijck, Franco. Institutionum logicarum libri duo. Cantabrigiae, 1680. 3 pam.
Htn	Phil 5041.26*	Burgersdijck, Franco. Monitio logica, or An abstract and translation of Burgersdicius his Logick. London, 1697.
	Phil 5041.27	Bahnsen, J. Der Widerspruch im Wessen und Wesen der Welt. Berlin, 1880-82. 2v.
	Phil 5041.28	Black, George A. Problem: science (function) analysis. N.Y., 1905.
	Phil 5041.28.3	Black, George A. Problem; science-analysis. N.Y., 1911.
	Phil 5041.29	Baldwin, J.M. Thought and things. London, 1906-11. 3v.
	Phil 5041.29.2	Baldwin, J.M. Genetic theory of reality. N.Y., 1915.
	Phil 5041.30	Bode, B.H. An outline of logic. N.Y., 1910.
Htn	Phil 5041.31*	Best, William. A concise system of logics. N.Y., 1796.
	Phil 5041.33	Buffier, Claude. Les principis du raisonment exposez en deux logiques nouvéles. Paris, 1714.
	Phil 5041.34	Barker, Johnson. A digest of deductive logic for the use of students. London, 1897.
	Phil 5041.35	Baumgartner, M. Logik und Erkentnistheorie. Facsimile. n.p., 1905-06.
	Phil 5041.36.5	Borelius, J.J. Lärobok i den formella logiken. 4. Uppl. Lund, 1882.
Htn	Phil 5041.37*	Bentham, G. Outline of a new system of logic. London, 1827.
	Phil 5041.38	Bertini, G.M. La logica. Roma, 1880.
	Phil 5041.39	Bogoslovsky, B.B. The technique of controversy. N.Y., 1928.
	Phil 5041.39.2	Bogoslovsky, B.B. The technique of controversy. London, 1928.
NEDL	Phil 5041.40	Burtt, Edwin Arthur. Principles and problems of right thinking. N.Y., 1928.
	Phil 5041.40.5	Burtt, Edwin Arthur. Principles and problems of right thinking. N.Y., 1931.
	Phil 5041.40.10	Burtt, Edwin Arthur. Principles and problems of right thinking. N.Y., 1938.
	Phil 5041.40.20	Burtt, Edwin Arthur. Right thinking. 3rd ed. N.Y., 1946.
	Phil 5041.41	Brandt, F. Formel logik. København, 1927.
	Phil 5041.41.5	Brandt, F. Formel logik til brug ved filosofikum. 3e udg. København, 1930.
	Phil 5041.42	Bachelard, G. Essai sur la connaissance approchée. Thèse. Paris, 1927.
	Phil 5041.43	Bolland, G.J.P.J. G.J.P.J. Bolland's colleges uitgegeven door Ester vas Hunes. Haarlem, 1923.
	Phil 5041.44	Beysens, J.T. Logica of Denkleer. 3e druk. Hilversum, 1923?
	Phil 5041.45	Behn, Siegfried. Romantische oder klassische Logik? Münster, 1925.
	Phil 5041.47.5	Balzano, Bernard. Wissenschaftslehre. Leipzig, 1929-31. 4v.
	Phil 5041.47.7	Balzano, Bernard. Grundlegung der Logik. Ausgewählte Paragraphen aus der Wissenschaftslehre. Hamburg, 1963.
	Phil 5041.48	Baudry, L. Petit traité de logique formelle. Paris, 1929.
	Phil 5041.49	Bonnot, Lucien. Logique positive; essai d'un théorie nouvelle de la connaissance. Dijon, 1930.
	Phil 5041.50	Burkamp, W. Logik. Berlin, 1932.
	Phil 5041.51	Binder, Frank. Dialectic, or The tactics of thinking. London, 1932.
Htn	Phil 5041.52.5*	Blundeville, Thomas. The arte of logicke. London, 1619.
	Phil 5041.52.6	Blundeville, Thomas. The art of logike. Facsimile. Menston, 1967.
	Phil 5041.53	Baudin, E. Précis de logique des sciences. Paris, 1938.
	Phil 5041.54	Biser, I. A general scheme for natural systems. Philadelphia, 1938.
	Phil 5041.55	Bennett, A.A. Formal logic. N.Y., 1939.
	Phil 5041.57	Baumgarten, Arthur. Logik als Erfahrungswissenschaft. Kaunas, 1939.
	Phil 5041.58	Beth, Evert Willem. Summulae logicales. Groningen, 1942.
	Phil 5041.58.7	Beth, Evert Willem. Moderne logica. 2. druk. Assen, 1967.
	Phil 5041.58.8	Beth, Evert Willem. Aspects of modern logic. Dordrecht, 1970.
	Phil 5041.59.2	Black, Max. Critical thinking. N.Y., 1947.
	Phil 5041.59.5	Black, Max. Critical thinking. 2nd ed. N.Y., 1954.
	Phil 5041.60	Beardsley, M.C. Pratical logic. N.Y., 1950.
	Phil 5041.61	Becker, O. Einführung in die Logistik. Meisenheim, 1951.
	Phil 5041.63	Bochenski, I. Mario. Die zeitgenossischen Denkmethoden. München, 1954.
	Phil 5041.65	Bilsky, Manuel. Logic and effective argument. N.Y., 1956.
	Phil 5041.70	Blyth, J.W. A modern introduction to logic. Boston, 1957.
	Phil 5041.72	Brunstaed, Friedrich. Logik. München, 1933.
	Phil 5041.75	Bachhuber, A.H. Introduction to logic. N.Y., 1957.
	Phil 5041.78	Blanché, Robert. Introduction à la logique contemporaine. Paris, 1957.
	Phil 5041.80	Brennan, Joseph Gerard. A handbook of logic. N.Y., 1957.
	Phil 5041.80.2	Brennan, Joseph Gerard. A handbook of logic. 2nd ed. N.Y., 1961.
	Phil 5041.85	Boll, Marcel. Les étapes de la logique. 4. éd. Paris, 1957.
	Phil 5041.87	Bocheński, Innocentius M. Die zeitgenossischen Denkmethoden. 2. Aufl. Bern, 1959.

Phil 5040 - 5065   Logic - General works, treatises - Individual authors (A-Z) - cont.

Phil 5041.89   Babaiants, M.S. Zakon iskheichennogo tret'ego. Moskva, 1962.

Phil 5041.90   Bierman, Arthur Kalmer. Logic: a dialogue. San Francisco, 1964.

Phil 5041.91   Barker, Stephen Francis. The elements of logic. N.Y., 1965.

Phil 5041.92   Bocheński, Innocentius M. The methods of contemporary thought. Dordrecht, 1965.

Phil 5041.93   Blanché, Robert. Structures intellectuelles. Paris, 1966.

Phil 5041.93.10   Blanché, Robert. Raison et discours, dépense de la logique réflexive. Paris, 1967.

Phil 5041.95   Bentham, Edward. An introduction to logick, 1773. Menston, 1967.

Phil 5041.96.3   Berg, Innocentius Jozefus Marie van den. Beginselen der logica. 3. druk. Bilthaven, 1963.

Phil 5041.97   Bakanialze, Mamiie I. Problema subordinatsii logicheskikh form. Alma-Ata, 1968.

Phil 5042.1   Calker, J.F.A. Denklehre oder Logik und Dialektik...Geschichte und Literatur. Bonn, 1822.

Phil 5042.2   Collard, John. The essentials of logic. London, 1796.

Phil 5042.2.5   Collard, John. A praxis of logic. London, 1799.

Phil 5042.4   Coppée, Henry. Elements of logic. Philadelphia, 1858.

Phil 5042.4.2   Coppée, Henry. Elements of logic. Philadelphia, 1860.

Phil 5042.5   Crousaz, J.P. de. New treatise...art of thinking. London, 1724. 2v.

Phil 5042.5.5   Crousaz, J.P. de. La logique. 2e éd. Amsterdam, 1720. 3v.

Phil 5042.6   Cuffelaer, A.J. Specimen artes ratiocinandi. v.1-3. Hamburgi, 1684.

Phil 5042.7   Creighton, J.E. An introductory logic. N.Y., 1898.

Phil 5042.7.2   Creighton, J.E. An introductory logic. N.Y., 1900.

Phil 5042.7.3   Creighton, J.E. An introductory logic. 3rd ed. N.Y., 1909.

Phil 5042.7.10   Creighton, J.E. An introductory logic. 4th ed. N.Y., 1927.

Phil 5042.8   Couturat, L. L'algèbre de la logique. 1st ed. Paris, 1905.

Phil 5042.8.2   Couturat, L. L'algèbre de la logique. 2e éd. Paris, 1905.

Phil 5042.8.5A   Couturat, L. The algebra of logic. Chicago, 1914.

Phil 5042.8.5B   Couturat, L. The algebra of logic. Chicago, 1914.

Phil 5042.9   Croke, J.L.O. Logic. London, 1906.

Phil 5042.10   Croce, B. Logica come scienza del concetto puro. Bari, 1909.

Phil 5042.10.3   Croce, B. Logica come scienza del concetto puro. 5a ed. Bari, 1928.

Phil 5042.10.4   Croce, B. Logica come scienza del concetto puro. 4a ed. Bari, 1920.

Phil 5042.10.5   Croce, B. Logic as the science of the pure concept. London, 1917.

Phil 5042.10.6   Croce, B. Logica come scienza del concetto puro. 7. ed. Bari, 1947.

Phil 5042.11   Coffey, P. The science of logic. London, 1912. 2v.

Phil 5042.12   Clauberg, Johann. Logica vetus et nova. 2a ed. Amsterdam, 1658.

Phil 5042.13   Cordier, Paul. Les problèmes de la logique. Paris, 1916.

Phil 5042.14   Commer, Ernst. Logik. Paderborn, 1897.

Phil 5042.15A   Columbia Association in Philosophy. An introduction to reflective thinking. Boston, 1923.

Phil 5042.15B   Columbia Association in Philosophy. An introduction to reflective thinking. Boston, 1923.

Phil 5042.16   Charma, A. Leçons de logique. Paris, 1840.

Htn   Phil 5042.17*   Crakanthorp, R. Logicae, libri quinque. London, 1622.

Phil 5042.17.3   Crakanthorp, R. Logicae libri quinque. 3a ed. Oxoniae, 1670.

Phil 5042.18   Cohn, Jonas. Theorie der Dialektik. Leipzig, 1923.

Phil 5042.19   Cunningham, H.E. Textbook of logic. N.Y., 1924.

Phil 5042.20   Crumley, T. Logic, deductive and inductive. N.Y., 1926.

Phil 5042.21A   Carnap, Rudolf. Abriss der Logistik. Wien, 1929.

Phil 5042.21B   Carnap, Rudolf. Abriss der Logistik. Wien, 1929.

Phil 5042.21.9A   Carnap, Rudolf. Logische Syntax der Sprache. Wien, 1934.

Phil 5042.21.9B   Carnap, Rudolf. Logische Syntax der Sprache. Wien, 1934.

Phil 5042.21.14   Carnap, Rudolf. The logical syntax of language. N.Y., 1937.

Phil 5042.21.14.5A   Carnap, Rudolf. The logical syntax of language. London, 1954.

Phil 5042.21.14.5B   Carnap, Rudolf. The logical syntax of language. London, 1954.

Phil 5042.21.14.10   Carnap, Rudolf. The logical syntax of language. London, 1967.

Phil 5042.21.15   Carnap, Rudolf. Philosophy and logical syntax. London, 1935.

Phil 5042.21.17   Carnap, Rudolf. Notes for symbolic logic. Chicago, 1937.

Phil 5042.21.20   Carnap, Rudolf. The continuum of inductive methods. Chicago, 1952.

Phil 5042.22A   Carmichael, R.D. The logic of discovery. Chicago, 1930.

Phil 5042.22B   Carmichael, R.D. The logic of discovery. Chicago, 1930.

Phil 5042.23.5   Cotter, Anthony C. Logic and epistemology. 2nd ed. Boston, 1931.

Phil 5042.23.8   Cotter, Anthony C. Logic and epistemology. Boston, 1940.

Phil 5042.24   Chapman, Frank M. The fundamentals of logic. N.Y., 1933.

Phil 5042.25   Cohen, Morris R. Introduction to logic and scientific method. N.Y., 1934.

Phil 5042.25.2   Cohen, Morris R. Introduction to logic and scientific method. N.Y., 1936.

Phil 5042.25.5A   Cohen, Morris R. A preface to logic. N.Y., 1944.

Phil 5042.25.5B   Cohen, Morris R. A preface to logic. N.Y., 1944.

Phil 5042.25.5C   Cohen, Morris R. A preface to logic. N.Y., 1944.

Phil 5042.26   Conze, E. Der Satz vom Widerspruch. Hamburg, 1931.

Phil 5042.27   Castell, Alburey. A college logic; an introduction to the study of argument and proof. N.Y., 1935.

Phil 5042.28.5   Cochet, J. La clef des sciences et des beaux arts, ou La logique. Paris, 1757.

Phil 5042.29   Creighton, J.E. An introductory logic. N.Y., 1938.

Phil 5042.29.5   Creighton, J.E. An introductory logic. 4th ed. N.Y., 1923.

Phil 5042.30   Churchman, C.W. Elements of logic. Phildelphia, 1940.

Phil 5042.35   Chwistek, Leon. The limits of science. London, 1948.

Phil 5042.40   Chase, Stuart. Guides to straight thinking. 1st ed. N.Y., 1956.

Phil 5042.45   Czech, Albert. Grundkurs der Logik. Bonn, 1970.

Phil 5042.50   Crawshay-Williams, Rupert. Methods and criteria of reasoning. London, 1957.

Phil 5042.55   Chauveneau, Jean. La logique moderne. 1. éd. Paris, 1957.

Phil 5040 - 5065   Logic - General works, treatises - Individual authors (A-Z) - cont.

Phil 5042.60   Carnap, Rudolf. Induktive Logik und Wahrscheinlichkeit. Wien, 1959.

Phil 5042.65   Clark, Romane. Introduction to logic. Princeton, N.J., 1962.

Phil 5042.70   Chesnokov, P.V. Logicheskaia fraza i predlozhenie. Rostov-na-Donu, 1961.

Phil 5042.75   Carbonard, Cleto. Psicologia, logica, dialettica. Napoli, 1963.

Phil 5042.80   Coke, Zachary. The art of logic, 1654. Menston, Eng., 1969.

Phil 5043.1   Damiron, M.J.P. Cours de philosophie. Paris, 1836.

Phil 5043.2   Davis, N.K. The theory of thought. N.Y., 1880.

Phil 5043.2.5   Davis, N.K. Elements of inductive logic. N.Y., 1895.

Phil 5043.3   Day, Henry N. Elements of logic. N.Y., 1867.

Phil 5043.3.10   Day, Henry N. Logical praxis. N.Y., 1876.

Phil 5043.4   Delboeuf, J. Essai de logique scientifique. Liége, 1865.

Phil 5043.5   DeMorgan, Augustus. Formal logic. London, 1847.

Phil 5043.5.3   DeMorgan, Augustus. Formal logic (1847). London, 1926.

Phil 5043.5.5A   DeMorgan, Augustus. Syllabus of a proposed system of logic. London, 1860.

Phil 5043.5.5B   DeMorgan, Augustus. Syllabus of a proposed system of logic. London, 1860.

Phil 5043.6   Devey, Joseph. Logic; or The science of inference. London, 1854.

Phil 5043.7   Dittes, Friedrich. Praktische Logik. Wien, 1873.

Phil 5043.8   Dodgson, C.L. The game of logic. London, 1886.

Phil 5043.8.7   Dodgson, C.L. Symbolic logic. pt.1. 4th ed. London, 1897.

Phil 5043.9   Dressler, J.G. Praktisch Denklehre. Bautzen, 1852.

Phil 5043.10   Drobisch, Moritz Wilhelm. Neue Darstellung der Logik. Leipzig, 1851.

Phil 5043.10.3   Drobisch, Moritz Wilhelm. Die moralische Statistik und die menschliche Willens Freiheit. Leipzig, 1867.

Phil 5043.10.4   Drobisch, Moritz Wilehlm. Neue Darstellung der Logik nach ihren einfaschsten Verhältnissen mit Rücksicht auf Mathematik und Naturwissenschaft. 4. Aufl. Leipzig, 1875.

Phil 5043.11   Dühring, E.K. Logik und Wissenschaftstheorie. Leipzig, 1878.

Phil 5043.11.5   Dühring, E.K. Natürliche Dialektik. Berlin, 1865.

Htn   Phil 5043.12*   DuMoulin, Pierre. Elementa logica. Breamae, 1622.

Phil 5043.13   Duncan, William. The elements of logick. London, 1764.

Phil 5043.13.2   Duncan, William. The elements of logick. Edinburgh, 1776.

Phil 5043.13.3   Duncan, William. The elements of logick. Philadelphia, 1792.

Phil 5043.13.4   Duncan, William. The elements of logick. N.Y., 1802.

Phil 5043.13.7   Duncan, William. The elements of logick. Albany, 1811.

Phil 5043.14   Duval-Jouve, J. Traité de logique. Paris, 1855.

Phil 5043.15   Duhamel, J.M.C. Des méthodes dans les sciences de raisonnement. v.1-5. Paris, 1865-73. 3v.

Phil 5043.15.2   Duhamel, J.M.C. Des méthodes dans les sciences de raisonnement. pt.1. Paris, 1865.

Phil 5043.16A   Dewey, J. Studies in logical theory. Chicago, 1903.

Phil 5043.16B   Dewey, J. Studies in logical theory. Chicago, 1903.

Phil 5043.16.3A   Dewey, J. Logic; the theory of inquiry. N.Y., 1938.

Phil 5043.16.3B   Dewey, J. Logic; the theory of inquiry. N.Y., 1938.

Phil 5043.16.5   Dewey, J. Essays in experimental logic. Chicago, 1916.

Phil 5043.17   Döring, A. Grundlinien der Logik. Leipzig, 1912.

Phil 5043.18A   Driesch, H. Die Logik als Aufgabe. Tübingen, 1913.

Phil 5043.18B   Driesch, H. Die Logik als Aufgabe. Tübingen, 1913.

Phil 5043.18.10   Driesch, H. Wessen und Denken. Leipzig, 1922.

Phil 5043.19   Davies, A.E. A text-book of logic. Columbus, 1915.

Phil 5043.20   Dinwiddie, William. Essentials of logic. N.Y., 1914.

Phil 5043.21   Davidson, William L. The logic of definition. London, 1885.

Phil 5043.22   Dotterer, Ray H. Beginners' logic. N.Y., 1924.

Phil 5043.22.5   Dotterer, Ray H. Beginners' logic. N.Y., 1938.

Phil 5043.23   Dam, Axel. Logik til brug under laereruddannelsen paa seminarierne. København, 1915.

Phil 5043.24   Dahlbäck, Carl J. Om logikens studium vid elementarläroverken. Umea, 1864.

Phil 5043.25   Drbal, M. Propadeutische Logik. Wien, 1885.

Phil 5043.26   Donati, G. La logica. Forli, 1920.

Phil 5043.27   Dubs, Homer. Rational induction. Chicago, 1930.

Phil 5043.29   Dingler, Hugo. Philosophie der Logik und Arithmetik. München, 1931.

Phil 5043.30   Dialectica. Neuchâtel. Pouvoir de l'esprit sur le réel. Neuchâtel, 1948.

Phil 5043.33   Dopp, Joseph. Leçons de logique formelle. v.1-3. Louvain, 1949-50. 2v.

Phil 5043.33.5   Dopp, Joseph. Formal logic. N.Y., 1960.

Phil 5043.33.10   Dopp, Joseph. Notions de logique formelle. Louvain, 1965.

Phil 5043.35   Drieschner, Rudolf. Untersuchungen zur dialogischen Deutung der Logik. Diss. Hambirg, 1966.

Phil 5043.38   DiBernardo, Giuliano. Logica, norme, azione. Trento, 1969.

Phil 5044.1A   Erdmann, B. Logik. Halle, 1892.

Phil 5044.1B   Erdmann, B. Logik. Halle, 1892.

Phil 5044.1.2   Erdmann, B. Logik. 2e Aufl. Halle, 1907.

Phil 5044.1.3   Erdmann, B. Logik. 3e Aufl. Berlin, 1923.

Phil 5044.1.6   Erdmann, B. Umrisse zur Psychologie des Denkens. 2e Aufl. Tübingen, 1908.

Phil 5044.2   Esser, Wilhelm. System der Logik. Münster, 1830.

Phil 5044.3.4   Everett, C.C. The science of thought. Boston, 1882.

Phil 5044.3.5   Everett, C.C. The science of thought. Rev. ed. Boston, 1890.

Phil 5044.4   Erhard, A. Handbuch der Logik. München, 1839.

Phil 5044.5.2   Erdmann, J.E. Grundriss der Logik und Metaphysik. 2e Aufl Halle, 1843.

Phil 5044.5.4   Erdmann, J.E. Grundriss der Logik und Metaphysik. Halle, 1864.

Phil 5044.5.10   Erdmann, J.E. Outlines of logic and metaphysics. 4th rev. ed. London, 1896.

Phil 5044.6   Eaton, Ralph M. General logic. N.Y., 1931.

Phil 5044.7   Ehrlich, W. Intentionalität und Sinn. Halle, 1934.

Phil 5044.8   Evans, D.L. Logic, theoretical and applied. Garden City, 1937.

Phil 5044.9   Emmet, Eric Revell. Thinking clearly. N.Y., 1962.

Phil 5044.10   Efiroo, S.A. Ot Gegelia k Dzhennago. Moskva, 1960.

Phil 5044.12   Essler, Wilhelm Karl. Induktive Logik. Habilitationsschrift. Freiburg, 1970.

Phil 5045.1   Fischer, Friedrich. Lehrbuch der Logik. Stuttgart, 1838.

Phil 5045.2   Fowler, Thomas. The elements of deductive logic. Oxford, 1867.

Phil 5045.2.5   Fowler, Thomas. Inductive logic. Oxofrd, 1876.

Phil 5045.2.6   Fowler, Thomas. Inductive logic. Oxford, 1883.

Phil 5045.2.15   Fowler, Thomas. Logic, deductive and inductive. Oxford, 1904-05.

Phil 5045.3   Freyer, Paul. Beispiele zur Logik. Berlin, 1889.

Phil 5040 - 5065   Logic - General works, treatises - Individual authors (A-Z) - cont.

Phil 5045.4   Ferrari, Ambrogio. Introduzione alla logica. Alessandria, 1895.
Phil 5045.5   Friedlaender, S. Logik, die Lehre von Denken. Berlin, 191-?
Phil 5045.6.2   Fischer, Kuno. System der Logik und Metaphysik oder Wissenschaftslehre. 2e Aufl. Heidelberg, 1865.
Phil 5045.6.3   Fischer, Kuno. Philosophische Schriften. System der Logik und Metaphysik. 3e Aufl. Heidelberg, 1909.
Phil 5045.7   Freytag, Willy. Der Realismus und Dastransscendenzproblem. Halle, 1902.
Phil 5045.7.3   Freytag, Bruno baron von. Logik. Stuttgart, 1955-67. 2v.
Phil 5045.7.5   Fretag, Bruno baron von. Irrational oder Rational? Berlin, 1935.
Phil 5045.8   Feder, J.G.H. Logik und Metaphysik. Göttingen, 1769.
Phil 5045.8.5   Feder, J.G.H. Logik und Metaphysik. Wien, 1779.
Phil 5045.8.14   Feder, J.G.H. Institutiones logical et metaphysicae. 4a ed. Gottingae, 1797.
Phil 5045.8.20   Feder, J.G.H. Erklaerung der Logik. Wien, 1793-94. 3v.
Phil 5045.9   Fischhaber, G.C.F. Lehrbuch der Logik. Stuttgart, 1818.
Phil 5045.10   Friedrich, E.F. Beiträge zur Förderung der Logik. Leipzig, 1864.
Phil 5045.11   Frey, T. Die Theorie der diskursiven Erkenntnis. Dorpat, 1929.
Phil 5045.12   Feys, R. Le raisonnement entermes de faite dans la logique russellienne. Louvain, 1928.
Phil 5045.13   Fechner, Oskar. Das Verhältnis der Kategorienlehre zur formalen Logik. Rostock, 1927.
Phil 5045.14A   Frye, A.M. Rational belief. N.Y., 1941.
Phil 5045.14B   Frye, A.M. Rational belief. N.Y., 1941.
Phil 5045.15   Fischl, J. Logik; ein Lehrbuch. 2. Aufl. Graz, 1952[1946].
Phil 5045.16   Fogarasi, Béla. Logik. Berlin, 1956.
Phil 5045.16.2   Fogarasi, Béla. Logika. 2. kiadás. Budapest, 1953.
Phil 5045.17   Flach, W. Negation und Andersheit. München, 1959.
Phil 5045.18   Fougeyrollas, Pierre. Contradiction et totalité. Paris, 1964.
Phil 5045.19.2   Fraunce, Abraham. The lawyer's logic, 1588. Menston, Eng., 1969.
Phil 5045.19.5   Fraunce, Abraham. The shepherd's logic. Menston, 1969.
Phil 5046.1   George, L. Die Logik als Wissenschaftslehre Dargestellt. Berlin, 1868.
Phil 5046.3   Gilbart, J.W. Logic for the million. London, 1860.
Phil 5046.3.5   Gilbart, J.W. Logic for the million. 5th ed. London, 1857.
Phil 5046.4   Gockel, C.F. Propädentische Logik und Hodegetik. Karlsruhe, 1839.
Phil 5046.5   Garden, F. An outline of logic or the use of teachers and students. 2nd ed. London, 1871.
Phil 5046.6   Gratry, A.J.A. Logique. Paris, 1868. 2v.
Phil 5046.6.1   Gatry, A.J.A. Logic. LaSalle, Ill., 1944.
Phil 5046.6.2   Gatry, A.J.A. Philosophie. Logique. Paris, 1855. 2v.
Phil 5046.7   Gneisse, K. Deduction und Induction. Strassburg, 1899.
Phil 5046.8   Gibson, W.R.B. The problem of logic. London, 1908.
Phil 5046.9   Gilmore, J.H. Outlines of logic. Rochester, 1876.
Phil 5046.9.5   Gilmore, J.H. Outlines of logic. N.Y., 1888.
Phil 5046.10   Gregory, D.S. Practical logic. Philadelphia, 1881.
Phil 5046.11   Gentile, G. Sistema di logica come teoria del conscere. Pisa, 1917.
Phil 5046.12.4   Goblot, Edmond. Traité de logique. Paris, 1922.
Phil 5046.13   Gruber, F.X. Philosophie des Denkens. Bern, 1842.
Phil 5046.14   Gustrin, E.F. Några anmarkningar angående den formella logiken. Lund, 1876.
Phil 5046.15   Gross, Peter. Vorschule der Logik. Berlin, 1890.
Phil 5046.16   Geyser, J. Grundlagen der Logik und Erkenntnislehre. Munster, 1909.
Phil 5046.16.5   Geyser, J. Auf dem Kampffelde der Logik. Freiburg, 1926.
Phil 5046.17   Gerlach, G.W. Grundriss der Logik. 2e Aufl. Halle, 1822.
Phil 5046.18   Goesch, H. Uber die kritische Logik. Berlin, 1904.
Phil 5046.19   Grassmann, R. Die Logik. Stettin, 1900.
Phil 5046.20   Grau, Kurt J. Grundriss der Logik. Leipzig, 1918.
Phil 5046.21   Govi, Mario. Fondazione della metodalogia. Torino, 1929.
Phil 5046.22   Grebe, Wilhelm. Die Form des Erkennens. München, 1929.
Phil 5046.22.10   Grebe, Wilhelm. Erkennen und Zeit. München, 1931.
Phil 5046.23   Grote, Albert. Uber die Funktion der Copula. Leipzig, 1935.
Phil 5046.24   Garciá, David. Introducció a la logística. Barcelona, 1934. 2v.
Phil 5046.25   Gabriel, Leo. Logik der Weltanschauung. 1. Aufl. Graz, 1949.
Phil 5046.25.5   Gabriel, Leo. Integrale Logik. Wien, 1965.
Phil 5046.26   Gesellschaft für Deutsch-Ravjetische Freundschaft. Über formale Logik und Dialektik. Berlin, 1954.
Phil 5046.27   Gorskii, D.D. Logika. Moskva, 1956.
Phil 5046.30   Guenther, Gotthard. Idee und Grundriss einer nicht-aristotalischen Logik. Hamburg, 1959.
Phil 5046.32   Garcia Tuduri, R. Lógica. 7. ed. Habana, 1959.
Phil 5046.34   Greenwood, David. The nature of science. N.Y., 1959.
Phil 5046.36   Geach, Peter. Reference and generality. Ithaca, N.Y., 1962.
Phil 5046.37   Grosser, S. Pharus intellectus, sive logica. Lipsiae, 1703.
Phil 5046.38   Gokieli, Levan P. Logika. v.1- Tbilisi, 1965. 2v.
Phil 5046.40   Good, Thomas. A brief English tract of logick, 1677. Facsimile. Leeds, 1967.
Phil 5046.42   Grize, Jean Blaise. Logique et connaissance. Genève, 1965.
Phil 5046.44   Georgius, Trapezuntius. De re dialectica libellus. Frankfurt, 1966.
Phil 5046.46   Goclenius, Rudolph. Problemata logica. v.1-5. Frankfurt, 1967.
Phil 5046.48.2   Gortari, Eli de. Introducción a la lógica dialéctica. 2. ed. México, 1959.
Phil 5046.50   Guttenplan, Samuel D. Logic: a comprehensive introduction. N.Y., 1971.
Phil 5047.1   Halle, H.F. Exact philosophy. London, 1848.
Phil 5047.2   Hartsen, F.A. Grundzüge der Logik. Berlin, 1873.
Phil 5047.2.5   Hartsen, F.A. Principes de logique exposés d'après une méthode nouvelle. Paris, 1872.
Phil 5047.3.2   Hedge, Levi. Elements of logick. Boston, 1818.
Phil 5047.3.5   Hedge, Levi. Elements of logick. Boston, 1823.
Phil 5047.3.7   Hedge, Levi. Elements of logick. Boston, 1835.
Phil 5047.3.12   Hedge, Levi. Elements of logick. N.Y., 1864.
Phil 5047.4   Heereboord, Adriano. Ermnheia logica...burgersdicianae. Cantabridgiae, 1663.

Phil 5040 - 5065   Logic - General works, treatises - Individual authors (A-Z) - cont.

Phil 5047.4.5   Heereboord, Adriano. Ermhneia logica...burgersdicianae. London, 1676.
Phil 5047.5   Hill, Walter H. Elements of philosophy comprising logic, ontology or general metaphysics. Baltimore, 1884.
Phil 5047.6   Hinds, Samuel. Introduction to logic. Oxford, 1827.
Phil 5047.7   Hoffbauer, J.C. Unfangsgrunde der Logik. Halle, 1810.
Phil 5047.8   Hibben, J.G. Inductive logic. N.Y., 1896.
Phil 5047.8.7L   Hibben, J.G. Logic, deductive and inductive. N.Y., 1905.
Phil 5047.8.8   Hibben, J.G. Logic, deductive and inductive. N.Y., 1910[1905].
Phil 5047.9   Hyslop, J.H. Elements of logic. N.Y., 1892.
Phil 5047.9.5   Hyslop, J.H. Logic and argument. N.Y., 1907.
Phil 5047.10   Hoffman, F.S. Sphere of science. N.Y., 1898.
Phil 5047.11   Husserl, Edmund. Logische Untersuchungen. Halle, 1900.
Phil 5047.11.2   Husserl, Edmund. Logische Untersuchungen. 2. Aufl. v. 1-2, pt. 1-2. Halle, 1913. 3v.
Phil 5047.11.3   Husserl, Edmund. Logische Untersuchungen. v. 1-2, pt. 1-2. Tübingen, 1968[1913]. 3v.
Phil 5047.11.4   Husserl, Edmund. Logical investigations. 2nd ed. N.Y., 1970. 2v.
Phil 5047.11.10   Husserl, Edmund. Formale und transzendentale Logik. Halle, 1929.
Phil 5047.11.15   Husserl, Edmund. Logique formelle et logique transcendantale. Paris, 1957.
Phil 5047.11.20   Husserl, Edmund. Recherches logiques. Paris, 1959. 3v.
Phil 5047.11.25   Husserl, Edmund. Formal and transcendental logic. The Hague, 1969.
Phil 5047.12   Hamilton, E.J. The modalist, or The laws of rational conviction. Boston, 1891.
Phil 5047.12.3   Hamilton, E.J. Perzeptionalismus und Modalismus. N.Y., 1911.
Phil 5047.12.9   Hamilton, E.J. Erkennen und Schlieszen. N.Y., 1912.
Phil 5047.13   Hooper, C.E. The anatomy of knowledge. London, 1906.
Phil 5047.14   Höfler, Alois. Grundlehren der Logik und Psychologie. Leipzig, 1906.
Phil 5047.14.5   Höfler, Alois. Philosophische Propädeutik. Prag, 1890.
Phil 5047.14.10   Höfler, Alois. Logik. 2e Aufl. Wien, 1922.
Phil 5047.15   Hourticq, R. Leçons de logique et de morale. Paris, 19- ?
Phil 5047.16   Hermant, Paul. Les principales théories de la logique contemporaine. Paris, 1909.
Phil 5047.17   Hoag, C.G. The logic of argument. Haverford, 1909.
Phil 5047.18   Holman, Henry. Questions on logic. 2nd ed. London, 1915.
Phil 5047.19   Harms, Friedrick. Logik. Leipzig, 1886.
Phil 5047.20   Herbertz, Richard. Prolegomena zu einer realistischen Logik. Halle, 1916.
Phil 5047.22   Hoppe, James. Die kleine Logik. Paderborn, 1869.
Phil 5047.23   Høffding, Harald. Formel logik, til brug ved forelaesninger. 6. udgave. København, 1913.
Phil 5047.23.5   Høffding, Harald. Det psykologiske grundlag for logiske domme. København, 1899.
Phil 5047.24   Hjelmérus, Alfred. Formella logiken baserad på identitetsprincipen. Lund, 1889.
Phil 5047.24.5   Hjelmérus, Alfred. Den aristoteliska logiken jämförd med modern logik. Umea, 1918.
Phil 5047.26   Hinrichs, H.F.W. Grundlinien der Philosophie der Logik. Halle, 1826. 2 pam.
Phil 5047.27   Holman, H. A key to Holman and Irvine's questions on logic. London, n.d.
Phil 5047.29   Hillebrand, J. Grundriss der Logik. Heidelberg, 1820.
Phil 5047.30   Hontheim, J. Der logische Algorithmus. Berlin, 1895.
Phil 5047.31   Heilner, R. System der Logik. Leipzig, 1897.
Phil 5047.32   Honecker, M. Logik: eine Systematik der logischen Probleme. Berlin, 1927.
Phil 5047.32.10   Honecker, M. Gegenstandslogik und Denklogik Vorschlag zu einer Neugestaltung der Logik. 2. Aufl. Berlin, 1928.
Phil 5047.33A   Hilbert, David. Grundzüge der theoretischen Logik. Berlin, 1928.
Phil 5047.33B   Hilbert, David. Grundzüge der theoretischen Logik. Berlin, 1928.
Phil 5047.33.5   Hilbert, David. Grundzüge der theoretischen Logik. 2e Aufl. Berlin, 1938.
Phil 5047.33.10   Hilbert, David. Principles of mathematical logic. N.Y., 1950.
Phil 5047.34   Hönigswald, R. Beiträge zur Erkenntnistheorie uhd Methodenlehre. Leipzig, 1906.
Phil 5047.35   Heiss, Robert. Logik des Widerspruchs. Berlin, 1932.
Phil 5047.35.5   Heiss, Robert. Wesen und Formen der Dialektik. Köln, 1952.
Phil 5047.36   Hlučka, F. Das Problem der Logik als Entwicklung des Prinzips der Heterothese. Leipzig, 1939.
Phil 5047.37   Hartman, S.J. A textbook of logic. N.Y., 1936.
Phil 5047.38   Holmes, R.W. The rhyme of reason; a guide to accurate and mature thinking. N.Y., 1939.
Phil 5047.39   Holmes, R.W. Exercises in reasoning, with an outline of logic. N.Y., 1940.
Phil 5047.40   Harvard University. Department of Philosophy. Logic cases for philosophy, 1919-1920. Cambridge, Mass., 1920.
Phil 5047.41   Hawley, Thomas de R. Infallible logic. Lansing, 1896.
Phil 5047.42   Hepp, M.H. Thinking things through. N.Y., 1956.
Phil 5047.43   Huppé, B.J. Logic and language. 1st ed. N.Y., 1956.
Phil 5047.44   Horn, Heinz. Widerspiegelung und Begriff. Berlin, 1958.
Phil 5047.46   Hartkopf, Werner. Die Strukturformen der Probleme. Berlin, 1958.
Phil 5047.47   Hughes, G.E. The elements of formal logic. N.Y., 1965.
Phil 5047.48   Hampel, Hans-Jürgen. Variabilität und Disziplinierung des Denkens. München, 1967.
Phil 5047.49   Hartnack, Justus. Logik. Klassik og moderne. København, 1968.
Phil 5048.1   Ingleby, C.M. Outlines of theoretical logic. Cambridge, 1856.
Phil 5048.2   Iversen, H. To essays om vor erkendelse. Kjøbenavn, 1918.
Htn   Phil 5049.1*   Jack, Gilbert. Grammatica rationis sive institutiones logicos. Oxonii, 1675.
Phil 5049.2   Jardine, George. Outlines. Philosophy. Education. Logic. Glasgow, 1818.
Phil 5049.3.4   Jevons, W.S. Logic (science primers). N.Y., 1880.
Phil 5049.3.6   Jevons, W.S. Logic (science primers). N.Y., 1884.
Phil 5049.4.2.5   Jevons, W.S. Elementary lessons in logic. London, 1888.
Phil 5049.4.4.5   Jevons, W.S. Elementary lessons in logic. London, 1870.
Phil 5049.4.4.7   Jevons, W.S. Elementary lessons in logic. London, 1871.
Phil 5049.5.2   Jevons, W.S. Studies in deductive logic. London, 1880.
Phil 5049.6   Jevons, W.S. The principles of science. London, 1874. 2v.
Phil 5049.6.2.5   Jevons, W.S. The principles of science. N.Y., 1874.

Phil 5040 - 5065 Logic - General works, treatises - Individual authors (A-Z) - cont.

Phil 5049.6.6   Jevons, W.S. The principles of science. London, 1887.
Phil 5049.6.18   Jevons, W.S. The principles of science. N.Y., 1958.
Phil 5049.7   Jevons, W.S. Pure logic. London, 1864.
Phil 5049.7.5   Jevons, W.S. The substitution of similars. London, 1869.
Phil 5049.8   Jevons, W.S. Pure logic and other minor works. London, 1890.
Phil 5049.9   Jevons, W.S. Logica. Milano, 1920.
Phil 5049.9.2.1   Joseph, Horace William Brindley. An introduction to logic. 2nd rev. ed. Oxford, 1967.
Phil 5049.9.5   Joseph, Horace William Brindley. An introduction to logic. 2nd rev. ed. Oxford, 1931.
Phil 5049.10   Joyce, G.A. Principles of logic. London, 1908.
Phil 5049.11.2   Jones, A.L. Logic inductive and deductive. N.Y., 1909.
Phil 5049.12   Jones, E.E.C. A new law of thought and its logical bearings. Cambridge, 1911.
Phil 5049.12.5   Jones, E.E.C. An introduction to general logic. London, 1892.
Phil 5049.12.9   Jones, E.E.C. Elements of logic as a science of propositions. Edinburgh, 1890.
Phil 5049.14   Johnstone, Lawrence. A short introduction to the study of logic. London, 1887.
Phil 5049.15   Joannes XXI, Pope. Summulae logicales. Venetiis, 1597.
Phil 5049.15.10   Alcala, P. de. Petri hispani summulae logicales. Venetiis, 1572.
Phil 5049.15.15   Joannes XXI, Pope. Petri hispani summulae logicales. Torino, 1947.
Phil 5049.16A   Johnson, William Ernest. Logic. pt.1. Cambridge, Eng., 1921-24. 3v.
Phil 5049.16C   Johnson, William Ernest. Logic. pt.1. Cambridge, Eng., 1921-24.
Phil 5049.16.1   Johnson, William Ernest. Logic. N.Y., 1964. 3v.
Phil 5049.17   Johanson, Johan. Apharismi e logica transcendali quas praeside Samuel Grubbs. Upsaliae, 1815.
Phil 5049.18   Jorgenson, J. A treatise of formal logic. Copenhagen, 1931. 3v.
Phil 5049.19   Joachim, Harold H. Logical studies. Oxford, 1948.
Phil 5049.20   Jaspers, Karl. Von der Wahrheit. München, 1947.
Phil 5049.20.3   Jaspers, Karl. Truth and symbol. N.Y., 1959.
Phil 5049.20.5   Jaspers, Karl. Philosophische Logik. München, 1958.
Phil 5049.20.10   Jaspers, Karl. Über das tragische. München, 1952.
Phil 5049.22   Jeffrey, Richard C. Formal logic: its scope and limits. N.Y., 1967.
Phil 5049.24   Jelenský, Šimon. Logika. Praha, 1926.
Phil 5049.25   Jepson, R.W. Clear thinking. 4th ed. London, 1948.
Phil 5049.26   Jacoby, G. Die Ansprüche der Logistiker. Stuttgart, 1962.
Phil 5049.28   Johnston, Frederick S. The logic of relationship. N.Y., 1968.
Htn   Phil 5050.2*   Keckermann, B. Systema logicae minus. Hanoviae, 1606.
Phil 5050.2.5   Keckermann, B. Systema logicae. Coloniae, 1611. 2 pam.
Phil 5050.3   Keynes, J.N. Studies and exercises in formal logic. London, 1884.
Phil 5050.3.2   Keynes, J.N. Studies and exercises in formal logic. 2nd ed. London, 1887.
Phil 5050.3.5   Keynes, J.N. Studies and exercises in formal logic. 4th ed. London, 1928.
Phil 5050.4   Kidd, R.B. A deliniation, primary principal reasoning. London, 1856.
Phil 5050.5   Kiesewetter, J.G.C.C. Grundriss einer allgemeinen Logik. Leipzig, 1824-25. 2v.
Phil 5050.5.2   Kiesewetter, J.G.C.C. Grundriss einer allgemeinen Logik. 2. Aufl. Berlin, 1795-96. 2v.
Phil 5050.5.3   Kiesewetter, J.G.C.C. Compendum einer allgemeinen Logik. Berlin, 1796.
Phil 5050.5.4   Kiesewetter, J.G.C.C. Grundriss einer allgemeinen Logik. Berlin, 1796-1802. 2v.
Phil 5050.5.5   Kiesewetter, J.G.C.C. Logik zum Gebrauch für Schulen. Leipzig, 1832.
Phil 5050.5.6   Kiesewetter, J.G.C.C. Grundriss einer reinen allgemeinen Logik nach kantischen Grundsaetzen. Berlin, 1791.
Phil 5050.5.15   Kiesewetter, J.G.C.C. Lärobok i logiken. Abo, 1806.
Phil 5050.7   Krause, K.H. Versuchplanmässiger und Naturgemässer unmittelbarer Denkübungen. Halle, 1844. 3v.
Phil 5050.8   Kells, S.C. Typical methods of thinking. N.Y., 1910.
Phil 5050.9   Koppelmann, W. Untersuchungen zur Logik Gegenwart. Berlin, 1913-18. 2v.
Phil 5050.10   Kries, Johannes von. Logik. Tübingen, 1916.
Phil 5050.11   König, Julius. Neue Grundlagen der Logik Arithmetic. Leipzig, 1914.
Phil 5050.12   Kulpe, Oswald. Vorlesungen über Logik. Leipzig, 1923.
Phil 5050.13   Kirchner, F. Katechismus der Logik. Leipzig, 1890.
Phil 5050.14   Keeling, S.V. Logic and reasoning. London, 1929.
Phil 5050.15   Knutzen, M. Elementa philosophiae rationalis seu logicae. Regiomonti, 1747.
Phil 5050.16   Knauss, G. Gegenstand und Umgreifendes. Basel, 1954.
Phil 5050.17   Kyle, William M. The elements of deductive logic. 4th ed. Brisbane, 1957.
Phil 5050.20F   Kauger, F. Handbok i logik. Stockholm, 1959.
Phil 5050.24   Kutschera, Franz von. Die Antinomien der Logik. Freiburg, 1964.
Phil 5050.25   Kutschera, Franz von. Elementare Logik. Wien, 1967.
Phil 5050.26   Kondakov, Nikolai I. Vvedenie v logiku. Moskva, 1967.
Phil 5051.1   Lambert, J.H. Neues organon Gedanken. Leipzig, 1764. 2v.
Phil 5051.2   Lange, F.A. Logische Studien. Iserlohn, 1877.
Phil 5051.3   Latham, R.G. Logic..application to language. London, 1856.
Phil 5051.4   Lindemann, H.S. Die Denkkunde oder die Logik. Solothurn, 1846.
Phil 5051.5   Lask, E. Die Logik der Philosophie und die Kategorienlehre. Tübingen, 1911.
Phil 5051.6   Luquet, G.H. Essai d'une logique systematique et simplifiée. Lille, 1913.
Phil 5051.6.5   Luquet, G.H. Eléments de logique formelle. Paris, 1909.
Phil 5051.6.13   Luquet, G.H. Logique formelle. Paris, 1925.
Phil 5051.7A   Lafleur, P.T. Illustrations of logic. Boston, 1899.
Phil 5051.7B   Lafleur, P.T. Illustrations of logic. Boston, 1899.
NEDL   Phil 5051.8   Logical compendium. Glasguae, 1756.
Phil 5051.9   Lecomte, A. La logique populaire. Paris, 1832.
Phil 5051.10.2   Lewis, Clarence I. A survey of symbolic logic. Berkeley, 1918.
Phil 5051.10.10   Lewis, Clarence I. Symbolic logic. N.Y., 1932.
Phil 5051.10.12   Lewis, Clarence I. Symbolic logic. 2nd ed. N.Y., 1959.
Phil 5051.10.14   Lewis, Clarence I. A survey of symbolic logic. N.Y., 1960.
Phil 5051.11   Lasson, Adolf. Der Satz vom Widerspruch. Halle, 1885.

Phil 5040 - 5065 Logic - General works, treatises - Individual authors (A-Z) - cont.

Phil 5051.12   Lodge, Rupert C. An introduction to modern logic. Minneapolis, 1920.
Phil 5051.13   Leechman, John. Logic. 4th ed. London, 1864.
Phil 5051.14   Lightfoot, John. Logic and education. London, 1899.
Phil 5051.15   Lyng, Georg V. Grundtankernes system. v.1-3. Christiania, 1882-1887.
Phil 5051.15.5   Lyng, Georg V. Laerebog i den objektive logik. Christiania, 1891.
Phil 5051.16.6   Lindner, Gustav A. Lehrbuch der allgemeinen Logik. 6e Aufl. Wien, 1914.
Phil 5051.17.9   Liard, Louis. Logique. 9e éd. Paris, 1917?
Phil 5051.18   Lambek, C. Om psychologische beviser. København, 1909.
Htn   Phil 5051.19*   Lever, Ralph. The arte of reason. London, 1573.
Phil 5051.20   Labanca, B. Della dialettica. v.1-2. Firenze, 1874.
Phil 5051.21   Loeive, J.H. Lehrbuch der Logik. Wien, 1881.
Phil 5051.22   Lutosławski, W. Logika ogolna czyli Teorja poznania i logika formalna. London, 1906.
Phil 5051.23.4   Losskiĭ, N.O. Logika. Berlin, 1923.
Phil 5051.23.7   Losskiĭ, N.O. Handbuch der Logik, Übersetzung von W. Sesemann. Leipzig, 1927.
Phil 5051.24A   Latta, Robert. The elements of logic. London, 1929.
Phil 5051.24B   Latta, Robert. The elements of logic. London, 1929.
Phil 5051.25   Lünemann, Arthur. Logik der Philosophie. Wien, 1929.
Phil 5051.26   LeLeu, Louis. La logique; l'art de penser. Paris, 1930.
Phil 5051.27A   Langer, S.K. (Mrs.). An introduction to symbolic logic. Boston, 1937.
Phil 5051.27B   Langer, S.K. (Mrs.). An introduction to symbolic logic. Boston, 1937.
Phil 5051.28   Lukasiewicz, Jan. Elementy logiki matematycznej. Warszawa, 1929.
Phil 5051.28.5   Lukasiewicz, Jan. Elements of mathematical logic. 2nd ed. Oxford, 1964.
Phil 5051.28.10   Lukasiewicz, Jan. Selected works. Amsterdam, 1970.
Phil 5051.28.15   Jermen, Frane. Med logiko in filozofijo. Ljubljana, 1971.
Phil 5051.29   Lieber, Lillian R. Mits, wits and logic. 1st ed. N.Y., 1947.
Phil 5051.29.3   Lieber, Lillian R. Mits, wits and logic. 3d ed. N.Y., 1960.
Phil 5051.30   Lipps, T. Grundzüge der Logik. Hamburg, 1893.
Phil 5051.31   LaHarpe, J. de. La logique de l'assertion pure. Paris, 1950.
Phil 5051.32   Leblanc, H. An introduction to deductive logic. N.Y., 1955.
Phil 5051.33   Little, W.W. Applied logic. Boston, 1955.
Phil 5051.37   Losev, Aleksei F. Muzyka kak predmet logiki. Moskva, 1927.
Phil 5051.40   Lossada, Luis de. Institutiones dialecticae, vulgo summulae, ad primam partem philosophici cursus pertinentes. Salmanticae, 1721.
Phil 5051.42   Lefebvre, Henri. Logique formelle, logique dialectique. 2e éd. Paris, 1969.
Phil 5051.44.4   Larroyo, Francisco. Lecciones de lógica y etica. 4. ed. México, 1970.
Phil 5051.46.4   Lorenzen, Paul. Formale Logik. 4. Aufl. Berlin, 1970.
Phil 5052.1   McGregor, P. A system of logic. N.Y., 1862.
Phil 5052.4   Mora, J.J. de. Cursos de lojica y etica segun la escuela de Edinburgo. Lima, 1832.
Phil 5052.6   Minto, William. Logic. N.Y., 1894.
Phil 5052.7   Moberly, Charles Edward. Lectures on logic. Photoreproduction. Oxford, 1848.
Phil 5052.8   Monck, W.H.S. An introduction to logic. Dublin, 1880.
Phil 5052.9.9   Mellone, S.H. An introductory text-book of logic. 9th ed. Edinburgh, 1917.
Phil 5052.10   Müller, E. Uber die Algebra der Logik. v. 1-2. Leipzig, 1900-01.
Phil 5052.11   Monrad, M.J. Udsigt over den høiere logik. Christiania, 1881.
Phil 5052.12   MacColl, H. Symbolic logic and its applications. London, 1906.
Phil 5052.13   Macleane, D. Reason, thought and language. London, 1906.
Phil 5052.14   Mercier, C. A new logic. London, 1912.
Phil 5052.16   Marchisini, G. Logica elementare. Firenze, 1917.
Phil 5052.18   Macfarlane, Alexander. Principles of the algebra of logic. Edinburgh, 1879.
Phil 5052.19   McLachlan, D.B. Reformed logic. London, 1892.
Phil 5052.20   Mendive, José. Elementos de lógica. 2a ed. Valladolid, 1887.
Phil 5052.21   Matičević, Stephan. Zur Grundlegung der Logik. Wien, 1909.
Phil 5052.22   McCosh, James. The laws of discursive thought. London, 1870.
Phil 5052.22.3   McCosh, James. The laws of discursive thought. N.Y., 1870.
Phil 5052.23   Mukerji, A.C. A text-book of inductive logic. Allahabad, 1919.
Phil 5052.24.6   Mitra, A.C. The principles of logic deductive and inductive. Calcutta, 1922. 2v.
Phil 5052.25   Moog, Willy. Logik, Psychologie und Psychologismus. Halle, 1919.
Phil 5052.26   Mackaye, James. The logic of conduct. N.Y., 1924.
Phil 5052.27   McClure, M.T. An introduction to the logic of reflection. N.Y., 1925.
Phil 5052.28   Maier, H. Logik und Erkenntnistheorie. 2. abd. Tübingen, 1918.
Phil 5052.29   Mosso, Pietro. Principii di logica del potenziamento. Torino, 1924.
Phil 5052.30   Morselli, E. Principios de lógica. Buenos Aires, 1928.
Htn   Phil 5052.31*   Melanchthon, Philipp. Erotemata dialectices. Lipsiae, 1559. 2 pam.
Phil 5052.32   Manheim, Ernst. Zur Logik des Konkreten Begriffs. München, 1930.
Phil 5052.34   Morris, C.R. Idealistic logic. London, 1933.
Phil 5052.35   Mahan, Asa. The science of logic. N.Y., 1857.
Phil 5052.36   Maritain, J. An introduction to logic. London, 1937.
Phil 5052.37   Miller, James N. The structure of Aristotelian logic. London, 1938.
Phil 5052.38   Mally, Ernst. Gegenstandstheoretische Grundlagen der Logik und Logistik. Leipzig, 1912.
Phil 5052.38.5   Mally, Ernst. Logische Schriften. Dordrecht, 1971.
Phil 5052.39   Mander, Alfred E. Logic for the millions. N.Y., 1947.
Phil 5052.40   Marriott, J.W.O.E.D. Some hints on arguing. London, 1948.
Phil 5052.41   Morell, J.D. Handbook of logic. London, 1866.
Phil 5052.42   Meyer, H. Le rôle médiateur de la logique. Assen, 1956.
Phil 5052.43   Maneev, A.K. Predmet formal'noi logiki i dialektika. Minsk, 1964.
Phil 5052.44.2   Marc-Wogau, Konrad. Logik för nybörjare. 2. uppl. Stockholm, 1967.

Phil 5040 - 5065 Logic - General works, treatises - Individual authors (A-Z) - cont.

Phil 5052.44.7   Marc-Wogau, Konrad. Logik, vetenskapsteori, argumentationsanalys. 2. tryckningen. Stockholm, 1969.

Phil 5052.45   Menne, Albert. Einführung in die Logik. Bern, 1966.

Phil 5052.46   Mała encyklopedia logiki. Wrocław, 1970.

Phil 5052.48.2   Miro, Quesada Cantuarias. Iniciación lógica. 2. ed. Lima, 1969.

Phil 5053.1   Neil, Samuel. The art of reasoning. London, 1853.

Phil 5053.2   Nieuwenhuis, Jacobi. Initia philosophiae logicae. Lugdunum Batavorum, 1831.

Phil 5053.3   Naville, A. Logique de l'identité...contradiction. Genève, 1909.

Phil 5053.4   Nagy, Albino. Fondamenti del calcolo logico. Napoli, 1890.

Phil 5053.5.2   Nitsche, Adolf. Lehrbuch der Logik. 2e Aufl. Innsbruck, 1890.

Phil 5053.6   Neudecker, G. Grundlegung der reinen Logik. Würzburg, 1882.

Phil 5053.7   Nielsen, R. Grundideernes logik. Kjøbenhavn, 1864-66. 2v.

Phil 5053.7.4   Nicoli, P. Elementi di logica. Milano, 1912.

Phil 5053.8   Newman, F.W. Lectures on logic. Oxford, 1838.

Phil 5053.10   Narbutt, Olgierd. O pierwszym polskim podręczniku logiki. Lódź, 1958.

Phil 5054.1   Oldfield, J. An essay towards the improvement of reason. London, 1707.

Phil 5054.2.2   Opzoomer, C.W. Het weyen der kennis. 2e druk. Amsterdam, 1867.

Phil 5054.3.5   Orti y Lara, J.M. Lógica. Madrid, 1885.

Phil 5055.1   Pierce, C.S. Logical papers. n.p., n.d.

Phil 5055.1.5A   Pierce, C.S. Studies in logic. Boston, 1883.

Phil 5055.1.5B   Pierce, C.S. Studies in logic. Boston, 1883.

Htn   Phil 5055.1.9*   Pierce, C.S. Three papers on logic. n.p., 1867?

Htn   Phil 5055.1.15*   Pierce, C.S. Papers on logic. n.p., 1867?

Phil 5055.2   Perrard, M.J.F. Logique classique. Paris, 1860.

Phil 5055.3   Planck, K.C. Logisches Kausalgesetz. Nördlingen, 1877.

Phil 5055.5A   Prantl, C. Die Bedeutung der Logik. München, 1849.

Phil 5055.5B   Prantl, C. Die Bedeutung der Logik. München, 1849.

Phil 5055.5.5   Prantl, C. Verstehen und Beurtheilen. München, 1877.

Phil 5055.6   Püllenberg, Johann. Kurze Darstellung des Hauptinhalts der Logik. Coblenz, 1854.

Phil 5055.7   Pokorny, T. Beiträge zur Logik der Urtheile und Schlüsse. Leipzig, 1901.

Phil 5055.8   Paulhan, F. La logique de la contradiction. Paris, 1911.

Phil 5055.9   Pesloüan, C.L. de. Les systèmes logiques et la logistique. Paris, 1909.

Phil 5055.10   Piola, Giuseppe. Elementi di logica guiridica. Roma, 1894.

Phil 5055.11   Palágyi, Melchior. Der streit der Psychologisten. Leipzig, 1902.

Phil 5055.11.5   Palágyi, Melchior. Die Logik auf dem Scheidewege. Berlin, 1903.

Phil 5055.12   Phalen, A.K. Om det kvantitativa betraktelsesättet i logiken. Uppsala, 1911.

Phil 5055.13.2   Poetter, F.C. Logik. 2. Aufl. Gütersloh, 1887.

Phil 5055.14.5   Pira, Karl. Om grundformerna i den reella logiken. Stockholm, 1907.

Phil 5055.15   Plenning, J. Logica, usui juniorum. Holmiae, 1746.

Phil 5055.16   Pfänder, A. Logik. Halle, 1921.

Phil 5055.16.5   Pfänder, A. Logik. 2. aufl. Halle, 1929.

Phil 5055.16.6   Pfänder, A. Logik. 3. Aufl. Tübingen, 1963.

Phil 5055.17   Patterson, Charles H. Problems in logic. N.Y., 1926.

Phil 5055.17.5   Patterson, Charles H. Principles of correct thinking. Minneapolis, 1936.

Phil 5055.18   Pichler, Hans. Zur Logik der Gemeinschaft. Tübingen, 1924.

Phil 5055.18.5   Pichler, Hans. Die Logik der Seele. Erfurt, 1927.

n   Phil 5055.19*   Piccolomini, A. L'instrumento de la filosofia. Roma, 1561.

Phil 5055.20   Pastore, Annibale. Logica formale...modelli meccanici. Torino, 1906.

Phil 5055.20.5   Pastore, Annibale. Logicalia. Padova, 1957.

Phil 5055.21.5   Pauler, Akás. Logik. Berlin, 1929.

Phil 5055.21.10   Madárászné Zsigmond Anna. A tiszta logika alapkérdesei. Budapest, 1965.

Phil 5055.22   Papineau, Arthur B. Philosophy II and III in Harvard College. Cambridge, 1889.

Phil 5055.23   Prot, Marcel. Language et logique. Paris, 1949.

Phil 5055.25A   Prior, Arthur N. Formal logic. Oxford, 1955.

Phil 5055.25B   Prior, Arthur N. Formal logic. Oxford, 1955.

Phil 5055.25.2   Prior, Arthur N. Formal logic. 2nd ed. Oxford, 1962.

Phil 5055.27   Pavese, Roberto. Compendio di logica sintetica. Padova, 1954.

Phil 5055.27.3   Pavese, Roberto. Commento alla logica sintetica. Padova, 1963.

Phil 5055.29   Perelman, Chaim. Traité de l'argumentation. v.1-2. Paris, 1958.

Phil 5055.29.5   Perelman, Chaim. The new rhetoric: a treatise on agrumentation. Notre Dame, Ind., 1969.

Phil 5055.29.10   Perelman, Chaim. Logique et argumentation. Bruxelles, 1968.

Phil 5055.29.15   Perelman, Chaim. Le champ de l'argumentation. Bruxelles, 1970.

Phil 5055.29.20   Perelman, Chaim. Éléments d'une théorie de l'argumentation. Bruxelles, 1968.

Phil 5055.30   Penev, Mikho. Kritika na logicheskite vuzgledi na burzhoaznite filosofi v Bulgariia. Sofiia, 1958.

Phil 5055.31   Puzikov, Petr D. Analiticheskaia sposobnost' myshleniia. Minsk, 1965.

Phil 5055.32   Problemy logiki i teorii poznaniia. Moskva, 1968.

Phil 5055.34   Papanoutsos, Euangelos. Logiké. Athéna, 1970.

Phil 5055.36   Paulus Venetus. Logica. Hildesheim, 1970.

Phil 5055.38   Patzig, Günther. Sprache und Logik. Göttingen, 1970.

Phil 5055.40   Poern, Ingmar. The logic of power. Oxford, 1970.

Phil 5055.42   Putnam, Hilary. Philosophy of logic. N.Y., 1971.

Phil 5056.1A   Quine, Willard Van Orman. A system of logistic. Cambridge, 1934.

Phil 5056.1B   Quine, Willard Van Orman. A system of logistic. Cambridge, 1934.

Phil 5056.1.01   Pamphlet box. Quine, Willard Van Orman. Collection of papers.

Phil 5056.1.5   Pamphlet vol. Quine, Willard Van Orman. Papers on symbolic logic. 1932-1936. 21 pam.

Phil 5056.1.10A   Quine, Willard Van Orman. A short course in logic. Cambridge, 1946.

Phil 5056.1.10B   Quine, Willard Van Orman. A short course in logic. Cambridge, 1946.

Phil 5056.1.15   Quine, Willard Van Orman. Methods of logic. N.Y., 1950.

Phil 5040 - 5065 Logic - General works, treatises - Individual authors (A-Z) - cont.

Phil 5056.1.20   Quine, Willard Van Orman. Methods of logic. N.Y., 1959.

Phil 5056.1.22   Quine, Willard Van Orman. Methods of logic. N.Y., 1953.

Phil 5056.1.23   Quine, Willard Van Orman. Methods of logic. N.Y., 1964.

Phil 5056.1.25   Quine, Willard Van Orman. Philosophy of logic. Englewood Cliffs, N.J., 1970.

Phil 5057.1   Reichlin-Meldegg, K.A.F. System der Logik. v.1-2. Wien, 1870.

Phil 5057.2   Reimarus, H.S. Die Vernunstlehre. Hamburg, 1790.

Phil 5057.3   Reinhold, Ernest. Versuch einer Begrundung und neuen Darstellung der logischen Formen. Leipzig, 1819.

Phil 5057.3.5   Reinhold, Ernest. Die Logik oder die allgemeine Denkformenlehre. Jena, 1827.

Phil 5057.5   Richter, Heinrich. Über den Gegenstand und den Umfang der Logik. Leipzig, 1825.

Phil 5057.6   Rion, J. Gemeinfassliche Darstellung der Denklehre. Reutlingen, 1844.

Phil 5057.7   Rösling, C.L. Die Lehren der reinen Logik. Ulm, 1826.

Phil 5057.8   Royce, J. Primer of logical analysis. San Francisco, 1881.

Phil 5057.9   Read, C. Logic; deductive and inductive. London, 1898.

Phil 5057.10   Regnaud, P. Précis de logique évolutionniste. Paris, 1897.

Phil 5057.11   Russell, J.E. An elementary logic. N.Y., 1906.

Phil 5057.12   Ritter, Heinrich. Abriss der philosophischen Logik. Berlin, 1824.

Phil 5057.12.4   Ritter, Heinrich. Abriss der philosophischen Logik. 2. Aufl. Berlin, 1829.

Phil 5057.13   Robinson, A.T. The applications of logic. N.Y., 1912.

Phil 5057.14   Russell, L.J. An introduction to logic. London, 1914.

Phil 5057.15   Restrepo-Hernandez, J. Lecciones de lógica dictadas en el Colegio. 2. ed. Bogota, 1914.

Phil 5057.16   Re, Alfonso del. Lezioni di algebra della logica. Napoli, 1907.

Phil 5057.17   Rehmke, Johannes. Logik, oder Philosophie als Wissenslehre. Leipzig, 1918.

Phil 5057.18   Ritschl, Otto. Program zur Feier des Gedächtnisses. Bonn, n.d.

Phil 5057.19   Rieber, Charles H. Footnotes to formal logic. Berkeley, 1918.

Phil 5057.20   Robinson, D.S. The principles of reasoning. N.Y., 1924.

Phil 5057.20.2   Robinson, D.S. The principles of reasoning. 2nd ed. N.Y., 1930.

Phil 5057.20.5   Robinson, D.S. The principles of reasoning. 3rd ed. N.Y., 1949.

Phil 5057.20.7   Robinson, D.S. Illustrations of the methods of reasoning. N.Y., 1927.

Phil 5057.21   Richter, A. Grundlegung der philosophischen Wissenschaften und Elemente der Logik. Halle, 1888.

Phil 5057.22   Robert, Arthur. Leçons de logique. Québec 1914.

Phil 5057.23   Reiser, Oliver L. Humanistic logic for the mind in action. N.Y., 1930.

Phil 5057.24   Rosenkranz, Karl. Die Modification en des Logik. Leipzig, 1846.

Phil 5057.25   Reymond, Arnold. Les principes de la logique et la critique contemporaine. Paris, 1932.

Phil 5057.25.2   Reymond, Arnold. Les principes de la logique et la critique contemporaine. Paris, 1957.

Phil 5057.26   Raphael, Max. Zur Erkenntnistheorie der konkreten Dialektik. Paris, 1934.

Phil 5057.26.2   Raphael, Max. La théorie marxiste de la connaissance. Paris, 1937.

Phil 5057.27   Romagnosi, G.D. Vedute fondamentali sull'arte logica. Roma, 1936.

Phil 5057.28   Reajifo, F.M. Elementos de logica. Bogota, 1930.

Phil 5057.30   Romero, Francisco Argentine. Lógica y nóciones de teoria del conocimiento. 2. ed. Buenos Aires, 1938.

Phil 5057.30.5   Romer, Francisco Argentine. Lógica y nóciones de teoria del conocimiento. 5. ed. Buenos Aires, 1942.

Phil 5057.32   Reichenbach, Hans. Nomological statements and admissible operations. Amsterdam, 1954.

Phil 5057.34   Roure, Marie Louise. Logique et métalogique. Paris, 1957.

Phil 5057.36   Ruby, Lionel. The art of making sense. London, 1956.

Phil 5057.38   Rozental', M.M. Prenlsipy dialekticheskoi logiki. Moskva, 1960.

Phil 5057.41   Rescher, N. Introduction to logic. N.Y., 1964.

Phil 5057.42   Regnier, André. Les infortunes de la raison. Paris, 1966.

VPhil 5057.43   Rodin, Davor. Aspekti odnosa izmedju Hegelove i Marxove dijalektike. Beograd, 1967.

Phil 5058.1   Sandersono, R. Logicae artis compend. Oxoniae, 1741.

Phil 5058.2.2   Sargent, J. The method to science. London, 1696.

Phil 5058.3   Schaden, E.A. System der Positiven Logik. Erlangen, 1841.

Phil 5058.4   Schlötel, W. Die Logik. Göttingen, 1854.

Phil 5058.5   Schröder, E. Der Operationskries der Logikkalkuls. Leipzig, 1877.

Phil 5058.5.5   Schröder, E. Vorlesungen über der Algebra der Logik. Leipzig, 1891-95. 4v.

Phil 5058.5.9A   Schröder, E. Abriss der Algebra der Logik. Leipzig, 1909. 2v.

Phil 5058.5.9B   Schröder, E. Abriss der Algebra der Logik. Leipzig, 1909. 2v.

Phil 5058.7   Schuppe, W. Erkenntnisstheoretische Logik. Bonn, 1878.

Phil 5058.7.5   Schuppe, W. Das menschliche Denken. Berlin, 1870.

Phil 5058.7.18   Pelazza, Amelio. Guglielmo Schuppe e la filosofia dell'immanerza. Milano, 1914.

Phil 5058.8   Schuyler, A. The principles of logic. Cincinnatti, n.d.

Phil 5058.9   Seydel, R. Logik. Leipzig, 1866.

Phil 5058.10   Shedden, T. The elements of logic. London, 1864.

Phil 5058.11   Sigwart, H.C.W. Handbuch zu Vorlesungen über Logik. Tübingen, 1835.

Phil 5058.12   Sigwart, H.C.W. Logik. Tübingen, 1873-78. 2v.

Phil 5058.12.2   Sigwart, H.C.W. Logik. Freiberg, 1889-1893. 2v.

Phil 5058.13   Sigwart, H.C.W. Logic. 2nd ed. London, 1895. 2v.

Phil 5058.13.5   Sigwart, H.C.W. Logik. 5e aufl. Tübingen, 1924. 2v.

Phil 5058.13.15   Sigwart, H.C.W. Die Impersonalien. Freiburg, 1888.

Phil 5058.14   Smith, J.C. Culmination of the science of logic. Brooklyn, 1888.

Htn   Phil 5058.15*   Smith, Samuel. Aditis at logicam. Oxoniae, 1656-1657.

Htn   Phil 5058.15.3*   Smith, Samuel. Aditus ad logicam. Oxoniae, 1634.

Phil 5058.16   Solly, T. A syllabus of logic. Cambridge, 1839.

Phil 5058.17   Spalding, W. An introduction to logical science. Edinburgh, 1857.

Phil 5058.18   Strümpell, L. Entwurf der Logik. Mitau, 1846.

Phil 5058.18.5   Strümpell, L. Grundriss der Logik. Leipzig, 1881.

Phil 5058.20   Swinburne, A.J. Picture logic. London, 1881.

Phil 5058.21   Smith, G.H. Logic. N.Y., 1901.

Phil 5058.22   Sidgwick, A. The use of words in reasoning. London, 1901.

Phil 5040 - 5065   **Logic - General works, treatises - Individual authors (A-Z) - cont.**

	Phil 5058.22.5	Sidgwick, A. Elementary logic. Cambridge, 1914.
	Phil 5058.22.9	Sidgwick, A. Distinction and the criticism of beliefs. London, 1892.
	Phil 5058.22.15	Sidgwick, A. The process of argument. London, 1893.
	Phil 5058.22.19	Sidgwick, A. The application of logic. London, 1910.
Htn	Phil 5058.23*	Strode, R. Consequentie. Venice, 1493.
	Phil 5058.24	Schiller, F.C.S. Formal logic. London, 1912.
	Phil 5058.24.10	Schiller, F.C.S. Logic for use. London, 1929.
	Phil 5058.25	Shearman, A.T. The scope of formal logic. London, 1911.
	Phil 5058.26	Stinson, J.H. Organon of science. Eureka, Calif., 1879.
	Phil 5058.27	Sellars, R.W. Essentials of logic. Boston, 1917.
	Phil 5058.27.5	Sellars, R.W. The essentials of logic. Boston, 1925.
	Phil 5058.27.7	Sellars, R.W. The essentials of logic. Boston, 1945.
	Phil 5058.28	Smith, Henry B. A primer of logic. Pulaski, 1917.
	Phil 5058.28.5	Smith, Henry B. A first book in logic. N.Y., 1922.
	Phil 5058.28.9	Smith, Henry B. Non-Aristotelian logic. Philadelphia, 1919.
	Phil 5058.28.15	Smith, Henry B. Letters on logic, to a young man. Philadelphia, 1920.
	Phil 5058.28.17	Smith, Henry B. Foundations of formal logic. Philadelphia, 1922.
	Phil 5058.28.18	Smith, Henry B. A system of formal logic. Ann Arbor, 1925.
	Phil 5058.28.19	Smith, Henry B. A system of formal logic. pt.1. Columbus, 1926.
	Phil 5058.28.21	Smith, Henry B. How the mind falls into error. N.Y., 1923.
	Phil 5058.28.28	Smith, Henry B. Symbolic logic: method and development. N.Y., 1927.
	Phil 5058.28.50	Pamphlet box. Logic. Smith, Henry B.
	Phil 5058.29	Stadler, A. Logik. Leipzig, 1912.
	Phil 5058.30	Störring, Gustav. Logik. Leipzig, 1916.
	Phil 5058.30.10	Störring, Gustav. Experimentelle Untersuchungen über Einfache schlussprozesse. Leipzig, 1908.
	Phil 5058.31	Stöhr, Adolf. Leitfaden der Logik in psychologisierender Darstellung. 2e Aufl. Leipzig, 1915.
	Phil 5058.31.5	Stöhr, Adolf. Lehrbuch der Logik in psychologisierender Darstellung. Leipzig, 1910.
	Phil 5058.32	Schultze, Fritz. Grundlinien der Logik in schematischer Darstellung. Leipzig, 1902.
	Phil 5058.33.4	Subrahmanyam, A. Logic, inductive and deductive. Madras, 1916.
	Phil 5058.34	Sjoberg, Gustaf. Lärobok i logik af Gustaf Sjöberg och Gustaf Klingberg. Stockholm, 1887.
	Phil 5058.36	Starcke, Carl N. Formel logik, grundlag for forelaesninger. 2. udg. Kjøbenhavn, 1922.
	Phil 5058.37	Sibbern, F.C. Taenkelaere eller logik i sammentraengt fremstilling. 3. udg. Kjøbenhavn, 1866.
	Phil 5058.37.5	Sibbern, F.C. Logik sem taenkelaere. 2. udg. Kjöbenhavn, 1835.
	Phil 5058.38	Switalski, B.W. Vom Denken und Erkennen. Kempten, n.d.
	Phil 5058.39	Smiglecki, Marcin. Logica Martini. Oxonii, 1658.
	Phil 5058.41	Smart, Harold R. The philosophical presuppositions of mathematical logic. Thesis. N.Y., 1925.
	Phil 5058.42	Snell, F.W.D. Erste Grundlinien der Logik oder Verstandeslehre. Gieosen, 1828.
	Phil 5058.43	Stammler, G. Begriff, Urteil, Schluss. Halle, 1928.
	Phil 5058.44	Storchenau, S. Institutiones logicae. Venetiis, 1819.
	Phil 5058.45	Swabey, Marie. Logic and nature. N.Y., 1930.
	Phil 5058.46	Stebbing, Lizzie S. A modern introduction to logic. London, 1930.
	Phil 5058.46.3	Stebbing, Lizzie S. A modern introduction to logic. 2. ed. N.Y., 1933.
	Phil 5058.46.7	Stebbing, Lizzie S. A modern introduction to logic. 7. ed. London, 1961.
	Phil 5058.46.10A	Stebbing, Lizzie S. Logical positivism and analysis. London, 1933.
	Phil 5058.46.10B	Stebbing, Lizzie S. Logical positivism and analysis. London, 1933.
	Phil 5058.46.15	Stebbing, Lizzie S. Logic in practice. London, 1934.
	Phil 5058.46.20	Stebbing, Lizzie S. Thinking to some purpose. Harmondsworth, 1939.
	Phil 5058.46.25	Stebbing, Lizzie S. A modern elementary logic. London, 1943.
	Phil 5058.46.30	Stebbing, Lizzie S. Logic in practice. 4. ed. London, 1954.
	Phil 5058.47	Schingnitz, Werner. Prolegomenon zu einer Logik als Lehre von der Vergegrifflichten Gegenständlichkeit. Leipzig, 1931.
	Phil 5058.47.5	Schingnitz, Werner. Mensch und Begriff. Leipzig, 1935.
	Phil 5058.48	Shaw, Charles G. Logic in theory and practice. N.Y., 1935.
	Phil 5058.50	Sinclair, W.A. The traditional formal logic. London, 1937.
	Phil 5058.51	Serrus, Charles. Essai sur la signification de la logique. Paris, 1939.
	Phil 5058.53A	Searles, Herbert L. Logic and scientific methods. N.Y., 1948.
	Phil 5058.53B	Searles, Herbert L. Logic and scientific methods. N.Y., 1948.
	Phil 5058.53.5	Searles, Herbert L. Logic and scientific methods. 2. ed. N.Y., 1956.
	Phil 5058.55	Strogovich, M.S. Logika. Moskva, 1949.
	Phil 5058.57	Sesmat, A. Logique. Paris, 1950.
	Phil 5058.60	Strawson, P.F. Introduction to logic theory. London, 1952.
	Phil 5058.65	Swabey, M. Logic and nature. 2nd ed. N.Y., 1955.
	Phil 5058.70.9	Suppes, Patrick. Introduction to logic. Princeton, N.J., 1966.
	Phil 5058.70.10	Suppes, Patrick. Introduction to logic. Princeton, N.J., 1968.
	Phil 5058.75	Schipper, Edith Watson. Principles of applied logic. Dubuque, 1956.
	Phil 5058.80	Spann, Othmar. Gangheitliche Logik. v.1-2. Salzburg, 1957.
	Phil 5058.82	Spann, Othmar. Ganzheitliche Logik. 2. Aufl. Graz, 1971.
	Phil 5058.85	Sichirollo, Livio. Logica e dialettica. Milano, 1957.
	Phil 5058.90	Saarnio, Uuno. Logikens Uppkomst och Väsen. Helsingfors, 1957.
	Phil 5058.92	Saarnio, Uuno. Ord och Mängd. Helsingfors, 1960.
	Phil 5058.94	Salmon, W. Logic. Englewood, 1963.
	Phil 5058.96	Shirwood, William. William of Sherwood's introduction to logic. Minneapolis, 1966.
	Phil 5058.96.5	Shirwood, William. William of Sherwood's treatise on syncategorematic words. Minneapolis, 1968.
	Phil 5058.98	Schock, Rolf. Logics without existence assumptions. Uppsala, 1968.

Phil 5040 - 5065   **Logic - General works, treatises - Individual authors (A-Z) - cont.**

	Phil 5058.100	Schulze, Ernst. Grundriss der Logik und Übersicht über die Griechische Philosophie für die prima der Gymnasien. Leipzig, 1886.
	Phil 5058.102	Skyrms, Brian. Choice and chance; an introduction to inductive logic. Belmont, Calif., 1968.
	Phil 5058.104	Skolem, Thoralf. Selected works in logic. Oslo, 1970.
	Phil 5058.106.1	Spencer, Thomas. The art of logic. 1628. Facsimile. Menston, Eng., 1970.
	Phil 5058.108	Strombach, Werner. Die Gesetze unseres Denkens. München, 1970.
	Phil 5058.110	Serebriannikov, Oleg F. Evristicheskie printsipy i logicheskie ischisleniia. Moskva, 1970.
	Phil 5059.1	Tagart, Edward. Remarks on mathematical or demonstrative reasoning. London, 1837.
	Phil 5059.2	Tappan, H.P. Elements of logic. N.Y., 1844.
	Phil 5059.4	Thomson, W. Outline of the necessary laws of thought. London, 1849.
	Phil 5059.4.2	Thomson, W. Outline of the necessary laws of thought. Cambridge, 1859.
	Phil 5059.4.3	Thomson, W. Outline of the necessary laws of thought. N.Y., 1879.
	Phil 5059.4.4	Thomson, W. Outline of the necessary laws of thought. 4th ed. London, 1857.
	Phil 5059.5	Tiberghein, G. Logique. Paris, 1865. 2v.
	Phil 5059.6	Tissot, C.J. Essai de logique objective. Paris, 1868.
	Phil 5059.8	Trieu, A.R.P.P.D. Manuductio ad logicam. Oxoniae, 1662.
	Phil 5059.9	Troxler, I.P.V. Logik. Stuttgart, 1829-30. 3v.
	Phil 5059.10	True, C.K. The elements of logic. Boston, 1840.
	Phil 5059.11	Turrell, H.J. A manual of logic. London, 1870.
	Phil 5059.12	Turner, W. Lessons in logic. Washington, 1911.
	Phil 5059.13	Tookey, J.J. An elementary handbook of logic. N.Y., 1918.
	Phil 5059.14	Taylor, William J. Elementary logic. N.Y., 1909.
	Phil 5059.16	Thiele, G. Grundriss der Logik und Metaphysik. Halle, 1878.
	Phil 5059.17	Templin, Olin. A guide to thinking; a beginner's book in logic. Garden City, N.Y., 1927.
	Phil 5059.18	Tricot, Jules. Traité de logique formelle. Paris, 1930.
	Phil 5059.19	Tieftrunk, J.H. Grundriss der Logik. Halle, 1801.
	Phil 5059.20.2	Thouless, R.H. Straight and crooked thinking. N.Y., 1932.
	Phil 5059.20.5	Thouless, R.H. How to think straight. N.Y., 1939.
	Phil 5059.20.10	Thouless, R.H. How to think straight. N.Y., 1941.
	Phil 5059.21	Tavanets, P.V. Suzhdenie i ego vidy. Moskva, 1953.
	Phil 5059.21.6A	Tavanets, P.V. Izbrannye trudy russkikh XIX v. Moskva, 1956.
	Phil 5059.21.6B	Tavanets, P.V. Izbrannye trudy russkikh XIX v. Moskva, 1956.
	Phil 5059.22	Toms, Eric. Being, negation, and logic. Oxford, 1962.
	Phil 5059.24.2	Thomasius, Christian. Einleitung zur Vernunftlehre. Hildesheim, 1968.
	Phil 5060.1	Ueberweg, F. System der Logik. Bonn, 1857.
	Phil 5060.1.5	Ueberweg, F. System of logic. London, 1871.
	Phil 5060.1.6	Ueberweg, F. System der Logik. 5e Aufl. Bonn, 1882.
	Phil 5060.2	Ufford, H.G. Elementary treatise on logic. N.Y., 1823.
	Phil 5060.3	Uphues, G. Zur Krisis in der Logik. Berlin, 1903.
	Phil 5060.3.5	Uphues, G. Erkenntniskritische Logik. Halle, 1909.
	Phil 5060.3.10	Uphues, Karl. Grundlagen der Logik. Breslau, 1883.
	Phil 5060.5	Ubahgs, G.C. Logicae seu philosophiae rationalis elementa. 6. ed. Lovanii, 1860.
	Phil 5060.6	Ushenko, A.P. The theory of logic. N.Y., 1936.
	Phil 5060.6.5	Ushenko, A.P. The problems of logic. London, 1941.
	Phil 5060.6.7	Ushenko, A.P. The problems. Princeton, 1941.
	Phil 5061.1	Venn, J. Principles of empirical or inductive logic. London, 1889.
	Phil 5061.1.2	Venn, J. Principles of empirical or inductive logic. London, 1907.
	Phil 5061.1.6	Venn, J. Symbolic logic. London, 1894.
	Phil 5061.1.8	Venn, J. The logic of chance. London, 1876.
	Phil 5061.1.9	Venn, J. The logic of chance. London, 1866.
	Phil 5061.1.11	Venn, J. The logic of chance. London, 1888.
X Cg	Phil 5061.1.11	Venn, J. The logic of chance. London, 1888.
	Phil 5061.2	Varona, E.J. Nociones de lógica. Habana, 1902.
	Phil 5061.3	Veitch, John. Institutes of logic. Edinburgh, 1885.
	Phil 5061.4.5	Vaz Ferreira, Carlos. Lógica viva. Montevideo, 1920.
	Phil 5061.4.15	Vaz Ferreira, Carlos. Lógica viva (adaptación prática y didáctica). Buenos Aires, 1945.
	Phil 5061.5	Volpe, G. della. Logica come scienza positiva. Messina, 1950.
	Phil 5061.5.2	Volpe, G. della. Logica come scienza positiva. 2. ed. Messina, 1956.
	Phil 5061.6	Voishvillo, Evgenii K. Predmet i znachenie logiki. Moskva, 1960.
	Phil 5061.6.5	Voishvillo, Evgenii K. Poniatie. Moskva, 1967.
	Phil 5061.8	Vries, Joseph de. Logica, cui praemittitur. Friburgi, 1952.
	Phil 5061.10	Veatch, Henry B. Two logics. Evanston, 1969.
	Phil 5062.1	Waddington, C. Essais de logique. Paris, 1857.
	Phil 5062.1.5	Waddington, C. De l'utilité des études logiques. Paris, 1851.
	Phil 5062.2	Waitz, F.H.W. Die Hauptlehren der Logic. Erfurt, 1840.
	Phil 5062.3	Wallis, J. Institutio logicae. Oxonii, 1715.
Htn	Phil 5062.4.2*	Watts, S. Logick. London, 1725.
NEDL	Phil 5062.4.3	Watts, S. Logick. 6th ed. London, 1736.
	Phil 5062.4.3.5	Watts, S. Logick. 8th ed. London, 1745.
NEDL	Phil 5062.4.4	Watts, S. Logick. 9th ed. London, 1751.
	Phil 5062.4.5	Watts, S. Logick. 10th ed. London, 1755.
	Phil 5062.4.5.2	Watts, S. Logick. 12th ed. London, 1763.
NEDL	Phil 5062.4.6	Watts, S. Logick. London, 1786.
Htn	Phil 5062.4.7*	Watts, S. Logick. 16th ed. Philadelphia, 1789.
Htn	Phil 5062.4.8*	Watts, S. Logick. 2nd American ed. Newburyport, 1796.
NEDL	Phil 5062.4.8.5	Watts, S. Logic. London, 1801.
NEDL	Phil 5062.4.9	Watts, S. Logic. London, 1802.
Htn	Phil 5062.4.10*	Watts, S. Logic. 3rd American ed. Exeter, 1806.
NEDL	Phil 5062.4.11	Watts, S. Logic. Edinburgh, 1807.
	Phil 5062.4.11.5	Watts, S. Logic. London, 1813.
Htn	Phil 5062.4.12*	Watts, S. Logic. 6th American ed. Boston, 1819.
	Phil 5062.4.25	Watts, S. Logic. London, 17- .
Htn	Phil 5062.5*	Wendelin, M.F. Logicae institutiones. Amstelrodami, 1654.
	Phil 5062.6	Whately, Richard. Elements of logic. London, 1829.
	Phil 5062.6.2	Whately, Richard. Elements of logic. N.Y., 1832.
	Phil 5062.6.3.5	Whately, Richard. Elements of logic. N.Y., 1836.
	Phil 5062.6.5	Whately, Richard. Elements of logic. London, 1840.
	Phil 5062.6.6	Whately, Richard. Elements of logic. London, 1844.
	Phil 5062.6.7.5	Whately, Richard. Elements of logic. Boston, 1852.
	Phil 5062.6.8	Whately, Richard. Elements of logic. 2nd ed. London, 1852.
	Phil 5062.6.8.5	Whately, Richard. Elements of logic. Boston, 1859.
	Phil 5062.6.55	Smart, B.H. A letter to Dr. Whately. London, 1852.
	Phil 5062.7	Smart, B.H. Easy lessons on reasoning. Boston, 1857.

Phil 5040 - 5065 **Logic - General works, treatises - Individual authors (A-Z) - cont.**

Phil 5062.8	Whewell, W. Novum organon renovatum. London, 1858.
Phil 5062.9	Wijnperse, D. van de. Institutiones logicae. Groningae, 1767.
Phil 5062.11	Wilson, W.D. Elementary treatise on logic. N.Y., 1856.
Phil 5062.11.5	Wilson, W.D. Logic. Ithaca, N.Y., 1872.
Phil 5062.14	Wyttenback, D. Praecepta philosophiae logicae. Hallae, 1820.
Phil 5062.16	Weinstein, B. Die philosophische Grundlagen der Wissenschaften. Leipzig, 1906.
Phil 5062.17	Welton, James. An intermediate logic. London, 1911.
Phil 5062.17.5	Welton, James. Intermediate logic. 4th ed. London, 1938.
Phil 5062.17.8	Welton, James. Groundwork of logic. London, 1921.
Phil 5062.18	Ruge, Arnold. Logic. London, 1913.
Phil 5062.18.3	Ruge, Arnold. Encyclopädie der philosophischen Wissenschaften in Verbindung mit W. Windelband. Pt.1. Logik. Photoreproduction. Tübingen, 1912.
Phil 5062.19	Williams, S. Principles of logic. London, n.d.
Phil 5062.20	Windelband, W. Die Prinzipien der Logik. Tübingen, 1913.
Phil 5062.20.10	Windelband, W. Theories in logic. N.Y., 1961.
Phil 5062.22	Wolf, Abraham. Exercises in logic and scientific method. London, 1919.
Phil 5062.22.5	Wolf, Abraham. The existential import of categorical predication. Cambridge, 1905.
Phil 5062.22.9	Wolf, Abraham. Essentials of logic. London, 1926.
Phil 5062.22.12	Wolf, Abraham. Textbook of logic. N.Y., 1930.
Phil 5062.22.16	Wolf, Abraham. Textbook of logic. 2nd ed. London, 1961.
Phil 5062.23	Wolff, Hermann. Logik und Sprachphilosophie. Berlin, 1880.
Phil 5062.23.5	Wolff, Hermann. Logik und Sprachphilosophie. Leipzig, 1883.
Phil 5062.24	Wesley, John. A compendium of logic. 2nd ed. London, 1756.
Phil 5062.25	Waller, A.D. A contribution to the psychology of logic. London, 1912.
Phil 5062.26	Waite, Dorothy J. First lessons in logic. London, 1923.
Phil 5062.27	Wadstein, E.A. "Moralens matematik". Stockholm, 1888.
Phil 5062.28	Weissborn, G. Logik und Metaphysik. Halle, 1850.
Phil 5062.29	Williams, Henry H. The evaluation of logic. Chapel Hill, 1925.
Phil 5062.29.5	Williams, Henry H. Logic for living. N.Y., 1951.
Phil 5062.30.1	Wilson, John Cook. Statement and inference. Oxford, 1969. 2v.
Phil 5062.30.15	Robinson, Richard. The province of logic; an interpretation of certain parts of Cook Wilson's "Statement and inference". London, 1931.
Phil 5062.31	Wrzecionko, R. Das Wesen des Denkens. Wien, 1896.
Phil 5062.32	Walcott, G.D. An elementary logic. N.Y., 1931.
Phil 5062.34	Willcox, J.M. Elementary philosophy. Philadelphia, 1875.
Phil 5062.35	Weil, R. The art of practical thinking. N.Y., 1940.
Phil 5062.36	Wallas, G. The art of thought. London, 1926.
Phil 5062.37	Wérkmeister, W.H. An introduction to critical thinking. Lincoln, 1948.
Phil 5062.38	Wright, G.H. von. Logical studies. London, 1957.
Phil 5062.39	Wheelwright, P.E. Valid thinking. 1st ed. N.Y., 1962.
Phil 5065.1A	Zuhen, Theodor. Lehrbuch der Logik. Bonn, 1920.
Phil 5065.1B	Zuhen, Theodor. Lehrbuch der Logik. Bonn, 1920.

Phil 5066 **Logic - Special kinds of logic - Symbolic and mathematical logic**

Phil 5066.1	Greenwood, T. Les fondements de la logique symbolique. v.1-2. Paris, 1938.
Phil 5066.5	Hermes, H. Semiotik; eine Theorie der Zeichengestalten als Grundlage für Untersuchungen von formalisierten Sprachen. Leipzig, 1938.
Phil 5066.7	Mathematics-deductive theory of rate learning. New Haven, 1940.
Phil 5066.8	Carnap, Rudolf. Introduction to semantics. Cambridge, 1942.
Phil 5066.8.2	Carnap, Rudolf. Introduction to semantics and formalization of logic. Cambridge, 1959.
Phil 5066.8.5	Carnap, Rudolf. Einführung in die symbolische Logik. Wien, 1954.
Phil 5066.8.6	Carnap, Rudolf. Einführung in die symbolische Logik mit besonderer Berucksichtigung. Wien, 1960.
Phil 5066.8.10	Carnap, Rudolf. Introduction to symbolic logic and its applications. N.Y., 1958.
Phil 5066.9	Cooley, J.C. An outline of formal logic. Pt.1. Cambridge, 1939.
Phil 5066.9.5A	Cooley, J.C. A primer of formal logic. N.Y., 1942.
Phil 5066.9.5B	Cooley, J.C. A primer of formal logic. N.Y., 1942.
Phil 5066.10	Bochénski, I.M. Noue lezioni di logica simbolica. Roma, 1938.
Phil 5066.10.5	Bochénski, I.M. Précis de logique mathématique. Bussum, 1948.
Phil 5066.10.7	Bochénski, I.M. A precis of mathematical logic. Dordrecht, 1959.
Phil 5066.11	Quine, Willard van Orman. Mathematical logic. N.Y., 1940.
Phil 5066.11.7	Quine, Willard van Orman. Mathematical logic. Cambridge, Mass., 1951.
Phil 5066.11.10A	Quine, Willard van Orman. Elementary logic. Boston, 1941.
Phil 5066.11.10B	Quine, Willard van Orman. Elementary logic. Boston, 1941.
Phil 5066.11.11	Quine, Willard van Orman. Elementary logic. N.Y., 1965.
Phil 5066.11.12	Quine, Willard van Orman. Elementary logic. Cambridge, 1966.
Phil 5066.11.20	Quine, Willard van Orman. From a logical point of view. Cambridge, Mass., 1953.
Phil 5066.11.21	Quine, Willard van Orman. From a logical point of view. 2nd ed. N.Y., 1963.
Phil 5066.11.25	Quine, Willard van Orman. On functions of relations. Santa Monica, 1949.
Phil 5066.11.30	Quine, Willard van Orman. Commutative Boolean functions. Santa Monica, 1949.
Phil 5066.11.35	Quine, Willard van Orman. A theorem on parametric Boolean functions. Santa Monica, 1949.
Phil 5066.11.40A	Quine, Willard van Orman. Word and object. Cambridge, 1960.
Phil 5066.11.40B	Quine, Willard van Orman. Word and object. Cambridge, 1960.
Phil 5066.11.45	Quine, Willard van Orman. The ways of paradox. N.Y., 1966.
Phil 5066.11.50	Quine, Willard van Orman. Ontological relativity, and other essays. N.Y., 1969.
Phil 5066.11.80	Words and objections. N.Y., 1969.
Phil 5066.12	Peano, G. Aritmetica generale e algebra elementare. Torino, 1902.
Phil 5066.12.5	Peano, G. Arithmétique. Turin, 1898.
Phil 5066.12.10	Peano, G. Notations de logique mathématique. Turin, 1894.

Phil 5066 **Logic - Special kinds of logic - Symbolic and mathematical logic - cont.**

Phil 5066.12.15	Peano, G. I principii di geometria logicamente esposti. Torino, 1889.
Phil 5066.13	Studies in semantics. Cambridge, Mass. 1-2,1942-1943 2v.
Phil 5066.14.5A	Church, Alonzo. Introduction to mathematical logic. Princeton, 1956.
Phil 5066.14.5B	Church, Alonzo. Introduction to mathematical logic. Princeton, 1956.
Phil 5066.14.10	Church, Alonzo. A bibliography of symbolic logic. Monasha, Wisconsin, 1936.
Phil 5066.16	Schröber, Karl. Ein allgemeiner Kalkülbegriff. Leipzig, 1941.
Phil 5066.17	Wernick, William. Complete sets of logical functions. Thesis. N.Y., 1942.
Phil 5066.18	Churchman, C.W. Towards a general logic of propositions. Thesis. Philadelphia, 1942.
Phil 5066.20	Jörgensen, J. Traek af deduktionsteoriens Udvikling i den nyere Tid. København, 1937.
Phil 5066.22	Daval, R. Le raisonnement mathématique. Paris, 1945.
Phil 5066.24	Feys, Robert. Logistiek geformaliseerde logica. Antwerpen, 1944.
Phil 5066.24.5	Feys, Robert. Modal logics. Louvain, 1965.
Phil 5066.24.10	Segerberg, Krister. Results in non-classical propositional logic. Lund, 1968.
Phil 5066.26	Reichenbach, H. Elements of symbolic logic. N.Y., 1947.
Phil 5066.26.5	Reichenbach, H. Nomalogical statements and admissable operations. Amsterdam, 1954.
Phil 5066.28	Ackermann, W. Ein System der typenfreien Logik. Pt.1. Leipzig, 1941-
Phil 5066.28.5	Ackermann, W. Soluable cases of the decision problem. Amsterdam, 1954.
Phil 5066.30	Kiss, Stephen A. Transformations on lattices and structures of logic. N.Y., 1947.
Phil 5066.32	Ambrose, Alice. Fundamentals of symbolic logic. N.Y., 1948.
Phil 5066.34	Boole, George. The mathematical analysis of logic. Oxford, 1948.
Phil 5066.36	Piaget, Jean. Traité de logique. Paris, 1949.
Phil 5066.36.10	Piaget, Jean. Essai sur les transformations des óperations logiques. 1. ed. Paris, 1952.
Phil 5066.36.15	Piaget, Jean. Logic and psychology. Manchester, Eng., 1953.
Phil 5066.36.20	Piaget, Jean. Classes, relations et nombres. Paris, 1942.
Phil 5066.38A	Henle, Paul. Structure, method, and meaning. N.Y., 1951.
Phil 5066.38B	Henle, Paul. Structure, method, and meaning. N.Y., 1951.
Phil 5066.40	Collection de logique mathématique. Serie A. Paris. 1-23 10v.
Phil 5066.42	Rosenbloom, P.C. The elements of mathematical logic. 1st ed. N.Y., 1950.
Phil 5066.44	Wright, G.H. van. An essay in modal logic. Amsterdam, 1951.
Phil 5066.46	Fitch, F.B. Symbolic logic. N.Y., 1952.
Phil 5066.48	Becker, O. Untersuchungen über den Modalkalkül. Meinsenheim/Glan, 1952.
Phil 5066.50	Rosser, J.B. Many-valued logics. Amsterdam, 1952.
Phil 5066.50.5	Rosser, J.B. Logic for mathematicians. N.Y., 1953.
Phil 5066.52.2	Langer, S.K.K. An introduction to symbolic logic. 2nd ed. N.Y., 1953.
Phil 5066.54.2	Copi, Irving M. Symbolic logic. 2nd ed. N.Y., 1965.
Phil 5066.56	Dürr, K. Lehrbuch der Logistik. Basel, 1954.
Phil 5066.58	Basson, A.H. Introduction to symbolic logic. London, 1953.
Phil 5066.58.2	Basson, A.H. Introduction to symbolic logic. 2nd ed. London, 1957.
Phil 5066.60	Juhos, B. van. Elemente der neuen Logik. Frankfurt, 1954.
Phil 5066.65	Menne, Albert. Logik und Existenz. Meisenheim/Glan, 1954.
Phil 5066.70	Hilbert, D. Grundzüge der theorelischen Logik. 2. Aufl. Berlin, 1949.
Phil 5066.75	Zeisler, E.B. Foundations of logic and math. 1. ed. Chicago, 1955- 3v.
Phil 5066.80	Berkeley, E.C. Symbolic logic. N.Y., 1955.
Phil 5066.85	Wiskundig Genootschap. Amsterdam. Mathematical interpretation of formal systems. Amsterdam, 1955.
Phil 5066.90	Robinson, A. Complete theories. Amsterdam, 1956.
Phil 5066.100	Prior, Arthur Norman. Time and modality. Oxford, 1957.
Phil 5066.102	Prior, Arthur Norman. Past, present and future. Oxford, 1967.
Phil 5066.103	Prior, Arthur Norman. Papers on time and tense. Oxford, 1968.
Phil 5066.105	Miller, J.W. Exercises in introductory symbolic logic. Montreal? 1955.
Phil 5066.110	Ferrater Mora, José. Lógica matemática. México, 1955.
Phil 5066.115	Halldén, Sören. On the logic of 'better'. Lund, 1957.
Phil 5066.120	Curry, Haskell Brooks. Combinatory logic. Amsterdam, 1958.
Phil 5066.122	Curry, Haskell Brooks. Foundations of mathematical logic. N.Y., 1963.
Phil 5066.125	Goodstein, R.L. Mathematical logic. Leicester, 1957.
Phil 5066.130	Crahay, Franz. Le formalisme logic-mathématique et le problème du non-sens. Paris, 1957.
Phil 5066.135	Akademiia Nauk SSSR. Institut Filosofii. Logicheskie issledovaniia. Moskva, 1959.
Phil 5066.140	Pasquinelli, Alberto. Introduzione alla logica simbolica. Torino, 1957.
Phil 5066.145	Martin, Richard M. The motion of analytic truth. Philadelphia, 1959.
Phil 5066.150	Popov, A.I. Vredenie v matematicheskuiu logiku. Leningrad, 1959.
Phil 5066.155	Stahl, Gerold. Introduccion a la logica simbolica. Santiago, Chile, 1956.
Phil 5066.160	Schmidt, H.A. Mathematische Gesetze der Logik. Berlin, 1960.
Phil 5066.165	Tavanets, P.V. Primenie logiki v nauke i tekhnika. Moskva, 1960.
Phil 5066.170	Zinov'ev, Aleksandr A. Filosofskie problemy mnogoznachnoi logiki. Moskva, 1960.
Phil 5066.171	Zinov'ev, Aleksandr A. Philosophical problems. Dordrecht, 1963.
Phil 5066.172	Zinov'ev, Aleksandr A. Kompleksnaia logika. Moskva, 1970.
Phil 5066.175	Iwanicki, J. Dedukcja naturalna i logistyczna. Warszawa, 1949.
Phil 5066.180	Day, John P. Inductive probability. N.Y., 1961.
Phil 5066.180.5	Day, John P. Inductive probability. London, 1961.
Phil 5066.185	Scholz, H. Grundrüge der mathematischen Logik. Berlin, 1961.
Phil 5066.190	Freudenthal, Hans. Exacte logica. Haarlem, 1961.
Phil 5066.190.2	Freudenthal, Hans. Exacte logica. 2. druk. Haarlem, 1967.

Phil 5066   Logic - Special kinds of logic - Symbolic and mathematical logic - cont.

Phil 5066.195   Beth, Evert W. Formal methods. Dordrecht, 1962.

Phil 5066.195.5   E.W. Beth Memorial Colloquium, Institut Henri Poincaré, 1964. Logic and foundations of science. Dordrecht, 1968.

Phil 5066.200   Lee, Harold Newton. Symbolic logic. N.Y., 1961.

Phil 5066.210   Zinov'ev, Aleksandr A. Logika vyskazyvanii i teoriia vyvoda. Moskva, 1962.

Phil 5066.211   Zinov'ev, Aleksandr A. Osnovy logicheskoi teorii nauchnykh znanii. Moskva, 1967.

Phil 5066.212   Zinov'ev, Aleksandr A. Logika nauki. Moskva, 1971.

Phil 5066.214   Wang, Hao. A survey of mathematical logic. Peking, 1962.

Phil 5066.215   Wang, Hao. A survey of mathematical logic. Peking, 1963.

Phil 5066.220   Nelson, Leonard. Beiträge zur Philosophie. Frankfurt, 1959.

Phil 5066.223   Stonert, H. Język i nauka. Warszawa, 1964.

Phil 5066.224   Akademiia Nauk SSSR. Institut Filosofii. Problemy logiki nauchnogo poznaniia. Moskva, 1964.

Phil 5066.224.5   Akademiia Nauk SSSR. Institut Filosofii. Problems of the logic of scientific knowledge. Dordrecht, 1970.

Phil 5066.225   Akademiia Nauk SSSR. Institut Filosofii. Problemy logiki. Moskva, 1963.

Phil 5066.225.5   Akademiia Nauk SSSR. Institut Filosofii. Formal'naia logika i metodologiia nauki. Moskva, 1964.

Phil 5066.226   Novikov, P.S. Elements of mathematical logic. Edinburgh, 1964.

Phil 5066.227   Dopp, J. Logiques construites par une methode de déduction naturelle. Louvain, 1962.

Phil 5066.228   Keene, G.B. First-order functional calculus. London, 1964.

Phil 5066.229   Karp, Carol R. Languages with expressions of infinite length. Amsterdam, 1964.

Phil 5066.230   Kharin, N.N. Matematicheskaia logika i teoriia mnozhestv. Moskva, 1963.

Phil 5066.231   Mates, Benson. Elementary logic. N.Y., 1965.

Phil 5066.232   Logic Colloquiam, 8th, Oxford, 1963. Formal systems and recursive functions. Amsterdam, 1965.

Phil 5066.232.20   Leicester, England. University. Summer School in Mathematical Logic. Sets, models and recursion theory. Amsterdam, 1967.

Phil 5066.233   Dickoff, James. Symbolic logic and language. N.Y., 1965.

Phil 5066.234   Kaluzhnin, Lev A. Chto takoe matematicheskala logika. Moskva, 1964.

Phil 5066.235   Hilton, Alice Mary. Logic, computing machines, and automation. Cleveland, 1964.

Phil 5066.240   Martin, Roger. Logique contemporaine et formalisation. Paris, 1964.

Phil 5066.241   Laserna, Mario. Klassenlogik und formale Einteilung der Wissenschaft. Berlin, 1963?

Phil 5066.242   Stiazhkin, Nikolai Ivanovich. Stanovlenie idei matematischeskoi logiki. Moskva, 1964.

Phil 5066.242.1   Stiazhkin, Nikolai Ivanovich. History of mathematical logic from Leibniz to Peano. Cambridge, Mass., 1969.

Phil 5066.242.5   Stiazhkin, Nikolai Ivanovich. Formirovanre matematicheskoi logiki. Moskva, 1967.

Phil 5066.243   Toernelohm, Håkan. Information and confirmation. Göteborg, 1964.

Phil 5066.245   Andrews, Peter Bruce. A transfinite type theory with type variables. Amsterdám, 1965.

Phil 5066.247   Hermes, Hans. Einführung in die Mathematische Logik: klassische Prädikatenlogik. Stuttgart, 1963.

Phil 5066.250   Daigneault, Aubert. Théorie des modèles en logique mathématique. Montréal, 1963.

Phil 5066.251   Leblanc, Hugues. Techniques of deductive inference. Englewood Cliffs, 1966.

Phil 5066.252   Tavanets, P.V. Logicheskaia struktura nauchnogo znaniia. Moskva, 1965.

Phil 5066.253   Freudenthal, Hans. The language of logic. Amsterdam, 1966.

Phil 5066.254   Mostowski, Andrzej. Thirty years of foundational studies. Oxford, 1966.

Phil 5066.255   Lyndon, Roger C. Notes on logic. Princeton, N.J., 1966.

Phil 5066.256   Tondl, Ladislav. Problémy sémantiky. Praha, 1966.

Phil 5066.257   Richter, Vladimir. Untersuchungen zur operativen Logik der Gegenwart. Freiburg, 1965.

Phil 5066.258   Hackstaff, L.H. Systems of formal logic. Dordrecht, 1966.

Phil 5066.259   Van Heijenoort, Jean. From Frege to Gödel; a source book in mathematical logic, 1879-1931. Cambridge, 1967.

Phil 5066.259.5   Van Heijenoort, Jean. Frege and Gödel; two fundamental texts in mathematical logic. Cambridge, 1970.

Phil 5066.260   Algebra i matematicheskaia logika. Kiev, 1966.

Phil 5066.261   Kleene, Stephen Cole. Mathematical logic. N.Y., 1967.

Phil 5066.261.5   Kleene, Stephen Cole. The foundations of intuitionistic mathematics. Amsterdam, 1965.

Phil 5066.262   Ciger, Juraj. Základy infinitezimálnej logiky a jej axiómy. Bratislava, 1949.

Phil 5066.263   Shoenfield, Joseph R. Mathematical logic. Reading, Mass., 1967.

Phil 5066.264   Biriukov, Boris Vl. Krushenie metafizicheskoi kontseptsii univeral'nosti predmetnoi oblasti v logike. Moskva, 1963.

Phil 5066.265   McCall, Storrs. Polish logic, 1920-1939 papers. Oxford, 1967.

Phil 5066.266   Jdel'son, A.V. Matematicheskaia teoriia logicheskogo vyvoda. Moskva, 1967.

Phil 5066.268   Kreisel, Georg. Elements of mathematical logic. Amsterdam, 1967.

Phil 5066.269   The logic of decision and action. Pittsburgh, 1966.

Phil 5066.270   Hausman, Alan. Carnap and Goodman: two formalists. Iowa City, 1967.

Phil 5066.273   Agazzi, Evandro. La logica simbolica. Brescia, 1964.

Phil 5066.276   Quine, Willard van Orman. Selected logic papers. N.Y., 1966.

Phil 5066.277   Kuzichev, Aleksandr S. Diagrammy Venna. Moskva, 1968.

Phil 5066.280   Logic Colloquium, 11th, Hannover, 1966. Contributions to mathematical logic; proceedings of the logic colloquium, Hannover, 1966. Amsterdam, 1968.

Phil 5066.282   Herbrand, Jacques. Ecrits logiques. Paris, 1968.

Phil 5066.284   Kac, Mark. Mathematics and logic. N.Y., 1968.

Phil 5066.286   Feys, Robert. Dictionary of symbols of mathematical logic. Amsterdam, 1969.

Phil 5066.288   Robison, Gerson B. An introduction to mathematical logic. Englewood Cliffs, 1969.

Phil 5066.300   Robbin, Joel W. Mathematical logic; a first course. N.Y., 1969.

Phil 5066.304   Spisani, Franco. Neutralizzacione dello spazio per sintesiproduttiva. 2. ed. Milano, 1968.

Phil 5066.306   Die Struktur realisierter Sprachen. Darmstadt, 1965.

Phil 5066.308   Penzov, Inrii E. Elementy matematicheskoi logiki i teorii mnozhestva. Saratov, 1968.

Phil 5066   Logic - Special kinds of logic - Symbolic and mathematical logic - cont.

Phil 5066.310   Crossley, John N. Constructive order types. London, 1969.

Phil 5066.312   Mostowski, Andrzej. Constructable sets with applications. Warszawa, 1969.

Phil 5066.314   Hintikka, Kaarlo Jaakko Johani. Models for modalities. Dordrecht, Holland, 1969.

Phil 5066.316   Rescher, Nicholas. Topics in philosophical logic. Dordrecht, Holland, 1968.

Phil 5066.316.5   Rescher, Nicholas. Temporal logic. Wien, 1971.

Phil 5066.318   Massey, Gerald J. Understanding symbolic logic. N.Y., 1970.

Phil 5066.320   Grünberg, Teo. Sembolik mantik. Istanbul, 1968.

Phil 5066.322   Neklassicheskniia logika. Moskva, 1970.

Phil 5066.324   Amato, Nicolò. Logica simbolica e diritto. Milano, 1969.

Phil 5066.326   Issledovanie logicheskikh sistem. Moskva, 1970.

Phil 5066.328   Problemy matematicheskoi logiki. Moskva, 1970.

Phil 5068   Logic - Special kinds of logic - Logical positivism

Phil 5068.5   Mises, R.E. von. Kleines Lehrbuch des Positivismus. The Hague, 1939.

Phil 5068.5.5A   Mises, R.E. von. Positivism. Cambridge, 1951.

Phil 5068.5.5B   Mises, R.E. von. Positivism. Cambridge, 1951.

Phil 5068.6   Ayer, A.J. Foundations of empirical knowledge. London, 1940.

Phil 5068.7.4   Russell, Bertrand Russell. An inquiry into meaning and truth. London, 1951.

Phil 5068.7.6   Russell, Bertrand Russell. An inquiry into meaning and truth. London, 1966.

Phil 5068.8   Frank, P. Between physics and philosophy. Cambridge, 1941.

Phil 5068.11   Zuurdeeg, Willem Frederik. A research for the consequences of the Vienna circle philosophy for ethics. Proefschrift. Utrecht, 1946.

Phil 5068.12   Joad, C.E.M. A critique of logical positivism. London, 1950.

Phil 5068.14   Albrecht, Erhard. Darstellung und Kritik der erkenntnistheoretischen Grundlagen der Kausalitätsauffassung und der Ethik des Neopositivismus. Rostock, 1949.

Phil 5068.16A   Kraft, Viktor. Der Wiener Kreis. Wien, 1950.

Phil 5068.16B   Kraft, Viktor. Der Wiener Kreis. Wien, 1950.

Phil 5068.16.2   Kraft, Viktor. Der Wiener Kreis. Der Ursprung des Neopositivismus. Ein Kapitel der jüngsten Philosophiegeschichte. 2. Aufl. Wien, 1968.

Phil 5068.18.2   Bergmann, Gustav. The metaphysics of logical positivism; papers. 2. ed. Madison, 1967.

Phil 5068.18.5   Bergmann, Gustav. Meaning and existence. Madison, 1960.

Phil 5068.18.10   Bergmann, Gustav. Logic and reality. Madison, 1964.

Phil 5068.20   Simàn, B. Der logische Positivismus und das Existenzproblem der höheren Ideen. Tel-Aviv, 1950.

Phil 5068.22   Copleston, F.C. Contemporary philosophy. London, 1956.

Phil 5068.24   Haeberli, Hans. Der Begriff der Wissenschaft im logischen Positivismus. Bern, 1955.

Phil 5068.26   Giorgianni, Virgilio. Neopositivismo e scienza de diritto. Roma, 1956.

Phil 5068.28   Korneeva, Anna I. Kritika neopoz, vzgliadov na prizodu poznaniia. Moskva, 1962.

Phil 5068.29   Korneeva, Anna I. Leninskaia kritika malchizma i bor'ba protiv sovremennogo idealizma. Moskva, 1971.

Phil 5068.30   Baknadze, K.S. Sub"ektivnyi idealizm. Tbilisi, 1955.

Phil 5068.32   Beckwith, B.P. Religion. N.Y., 1957.

Phil 5068.34   Martin, R.M. Truth and denotation. London, 1958.

Phil 5068.38   Miles, Thomas R. Religion and the scientific outlook. London, 1959.

Phil 5068.40   Naese, Arne. Wie fördert man heute die empirische Bewegung? Oslo, 1956.

Phil 5068.42   Gellner, Ernest. Words and things. London, 1959.

Phil 5068.44   Filiasi Carcano, Paolo. La metodologia nel rinnovarsi del pensiero. Napoli, 1957.

Phil 5068.46   Wilson, Max. Über das Kriterium der Verifizierbarkeit. Berlin, 1959.

Phil 5068.48   Narskii, I.S. Sovremennyi pozitivizm. Moskva, 1960.

Phil 5068.50   Mshvenieradze, V.V. Filosofiia reopozitivizma i semantiki. Moskva, 1961.

Phil 5068.52   Astrada, C. Dialéctica y positivismo lógico. Tucumán, 1961.

Phil 5068.53   Küng, Gaide. Ontologie und logistiche Analyse der Sprache. Wien, 1963.

Phil 5068.53.1   Küng, Gaide. Ontology and the logistic analysis of language. Dordrecht, 1967.

Phil 5068.54   Ruml, Vladimir. Základné otázky filosofie logického pozitivismu. Praha, 1962.

Phil 5068.54.5   Ruml, Vladimir. Der logische Positivismus. (Übersetzung aus den Techechischen). Berlin, 1965.

Phil 5068.55   Ponte Orvieto, Marina da. L'unità del sapere nel neopositivismo. Padova, 1965.

Phil 5068.56   Waismann, Friedrich. The principles of linguistic philosophy. London, 1965.

Phil 5068.56.5   Cornman, James W. Metaphysics, reference, and language. New Haven, 1966.

Phil 5068.56.10   Weingartner, Paul. Deskription, Analytizität und Existenz. Salzburg, 1966.

Phil 5068.56.15   Crescini, Angelo. Le origini del metodo analitico. Udine, 1965.

Phil 5068.56.20   Nuchelmans, Gabriël. Proeven van analytisch filosopesen. Hilversum, 1967.

Phil 5068.56.25   Nuchelmans, Gabriël. O verzicht van de analytische wijsbegeeste. Utrecht, 1969.

Phil 5068.57   Shvyrev, Vladimir S. Neopozitivizm i problemy empiricheskogo oboshovaniia nauki. Moskva, 1966.

Phil 5068.58   Logica e analisi. Scritti di P. Filiasi Carcano (et al.). Padova, 1966.

Phil 5068.60   Fogelin, Robert J. Evidence and meaning: studies in analytic philosophy. London, 1967.

Phil 5068.65   Kyserling, Arnold. Der Wiener Denkstil: Mach, Carnap. Graz, 1965.

Phil 5068.67   Ganguli, Hermanta Kumar. Philosophy of logical construction. 1st ed. Calcutta, 1963.

Phil 5068.68   Khachaturian, Haig. A critical study in method. The Hague, 1967.

Phil 5068.70   Maros dell'Oro, Angiolo. Il pensiero scientifico in Italia negli anni 1930-1960. Cremona, 1963.

Phil 5068.71   Pushkin, Veniamin N. Evristika-nauka o tvorcheskom myshlenii. Moskva, 1967.

Phil 5068.75   Frisch, Joseph C. Extension and comprehension in logic. N.Y., 1969.

Phil 5068.80   Przelecki, Marian. The logic of empirical theories. London, 1969.

Phil 5068   Logic - Special kinds of logic - Logical positivism - cont.
Phil 5068.82   Lorenzen, Paul. Normative logic and ethics. Mannheim, 1969.
Phil 5068.84   Statera, Gianni. Logica, linguaggio e sociologia. Torino, 1967.
Phil 5068.86   The legacy of logical positivism. Baltimore, 1969.
Phil 5068.88   Fano, Giorgio. Neopositivismo, analisi del linguaggio e cibernetica. Torino, 1968.
Phil 5068.90   Hoffbauer, Johann Christoph. Versuch über die sicherste und leichteste Anwendung der Analysis in den philosophischen Wissenschaften (Leipzig). Bruxelles, 1968.
Phil 5068.92   Petzäll, Ake. Logistischer Positivismus. Göteborg, 1931.
Phil 5068.94   Narskii, Igor S. Dialekticheskoe protivorechie i logika poznaniia. Moskva, 1969.
Phil 5068.96   Reintel'dt, Boris K. Zakon edinstva i bor'by protivopolzhnostei. Ioshkar-Ola, 1969.
Phil 5068.98   Vax, Louis. L'empirisme logique. Paris, 1970.
Phil 5068.100   Zaichenko, Georgii A. K voprosu o kritike sovremennogo angliiskogo pozitivizma. Khar'kov, 1971.
Phil 5068.102   Moscato, Alberto. Intenzionalità e dialettica. Firenze, 1969.

Phil 5069   Logic - Special kinds of logic - Other special
Phil 5069.2   Spisoni, Franco. Logica ed esperienz. Milano, 1967.
Phil 5069.4   Eley, Lothar. Metakritik der formalen Logik. Den Haag, 1969.
Phil 5069.6   Tammelo, Ilmar. Outlines of modern legal logic. Wiesbaden, 1969.
Phil 5069.8   Hilpinen, Risto. Deontic logic: introductory and systematic readings. Dordrecht, 1971.

Phil 5070   Logic - Special topics - Belief
Phil 5070.1   Lowndes, R. Introduction...philosophy of primary beliefs. London, 1865.
Phil 5070.1.2   Lowndes, R. Introduction...philosophy of primary beliefs. London, 1865.
Phil 5070.2   Venn, J. On some of the characteristics of belief; scientific and religious. London, 1870.
Phil 5070.3   Ward, Wilfred. The wish to believe. Photoreproduction. London, 1885.
Phil 5070.5   Payot, J. De la croyance. Paris, 1896.
Phil 5070.6   Inge, William R. Faith. London, 1909.
Phil 5070.6.5   Inge, William R. Faith and its psychology. N.Y., 1910.
Phil 5070.7   Lindsay, J. The psychology of belief. Edinburgh, 1910.
Phil 5070.8   Sollier, P. Le doute. Paris, 1909.
Phil 5070.9   Ladd, G.T. What should I believe? London, 1915.
Phil 5070.10   Forbes, Waldo. Cycles of personal belief. Boston, 1917.
Phil 5070.11   Coke, Henry J. The domain of belief. London, 1910.
Phil 5070.12   Lowrié, Ossip. Croyance religieuse et croyance intellectuelle. Paris, 1908.
Phil 5070.13   Bazaillas, A. La crise de la croyance. Paris, 1901.
Phil 5070.14   Le Bon, Gustave. La vie des vérités. Paris, 1917.
Phil 5070.15   Vorbrodt, Gustav. Psychologie des Glaubens. Göttingen, 1895.
Phil 5070.16   Schiller, F.C.S. Problems of belief. London, 1924.
Phil 5070.16.5   Schiller, F.C.S. Problems of belief. N.Y., 1924.
Phil 5070.17   Mertens, Paul. Zur Phänomenologie des Glaubens. Inaug. Diss. Fulda, 1927.
Phil 5070.19   Ahmet, Nureltin. Conformisme et révolte. Thèse. Paris, 1934.
Phil 5070.20   Wagner, Hans. Elements des Glaubens. Inaug. Diss. München, 193-.
Phil 5070.21   Lundholm, H. The psychology of belief. Durham, 1936.
Phil 5070.23   Lebacqz, Joseph. Certitude et volonté. Bruges, 1962.
Phil 5070.24   Lindner, Herbert. Der Zweifel und seine Grenzen. Berlin, 1966.
Phil 5070.26   Mynarek, Hubertus. Der Mensch, das Wesen der Zukunft. München, 1968.
Phil 5070.28   Price, Henry Habberley. Belief: the Gifford lectures delivered at the University of Aberdeen in 1960. London, 1969.
Phil 5070.30   Martin, Richard Milton. Belief, existence, and meaning. N.Y., 1969.
Phil 5070.32   Sprigge, Timothy Lauro Squire. Facts, words, and beliefs. N.Y., 1970.

Phil 5075   Logic - Special topics - Categories
Phil 5075.1   Stirling, J.H. The categories. Edinburgh, 1903.
Phil 5075.2   Dupréel, Eugène. Essai sur les catégories. Bruxelles, 1906.
Phil 5075.3   Spann, Othmar. Kategorienlehre. Jena, 1924.
Phil 5075.3.3   Spann, Othmar. Kategorienlehre. 3. Aufl. Graz, 1969.
Phil 5075.4   Brentano, F. Kategorienlehre. Leipzig, 1933.
Phil 5075.5   Moschetti, A.M. L'unità come categoria. Milano, 1952. 2v.
Phil 5075.6   Fuerstengerg, Hans. Dialectique du XX siècle. Paris, 1956.
Phil 5075.7   Shirokanov, Imitri I. Vzaimosviaz' kategorii dialektiki. Minsk, 1969.
Phil 5075.8   Koerner, Stephan. Categorial frameworks. Oxford, 1970.

5080   Logic - Special topics - Concepts
Phil 5080.01   Pamphlet box. Philosophy. Concepts.
Phil 5080.2   Dubs, Arthur. Das Wesen des Begriffs und des Begreifens. Halle, 1911.
Phil 5080.3   Burkamp, W. Begriff und Beziehung. Leipzig, 1927.
Phil 5080.4   Pauler, Akos. A fogalom problémája a teozta logikaban. Budapest, 1915.
Phil 5080.5   Aaron, Richard I. Our knowledge of universals. London, 1945.
Phil 5080.6   Koerner, S. Conceptual thinking. Cambridge, Eng., 1955.
Phil 5080.7   Flew, A. Essays in conceptual analysis. London, 1956.
Phil 5080.8   Combès, Michel. Le concept de concept formel. Toulouse, 1969.

5090   Logic - Special topics - Evidence
Phil 5090.01   Pamphlet box. Evidence.
Phil 5090.1   Finch, A.E. The pursuit of truth. London, 1873.
Phil 5090.2   Gambier, J.E. Introduction...moral evidence. v.1- . London, 1808-1818.
Phil 5090.3A   Newman, J.H. Grammar of assent. N.Y., 1870.
Phil 5090.3B   Newman, J.H. Grammar of assent. N.Y., 1870.
Phil 5090.3.2   Newman, J.H. An essay in aid of a Grammar of assent. London, 1901.
Phil 5090.3.80   Zeno, Father. John Henry Newman. Leiden, 1957.
Phil 5090.4   Gréard, Mlle. La certitude philosophique. Paris, 1883.
Phil 5090.5   Franck, A. De la certitude. Paris, 1847.

Phil 5090   Logic - Special topics - Evidence - cont.
Phil 5090.6   Smedley, E.A. Treatise on moral evidence. Cambridge, 1850.
Phil 5090.7   Milhaud, G. Essai sur les conditions et les limites. 3e éd. Paris, 1912.
Phil 5090.7.5   Milhaud, G. Le rationnel. Paris, 1898.
Phil 5090.8   Dellepiane, A. Les sciences et la méthode reconstructives. Paris, 1915.
Phil 5090.9   Meinhandl, F. Über Urteilswahrheit. Leipzig, 1923.
Phil 5090.11   Sengupta, Pradip Kumar. Demonstration and logical truth. 1st ed. Calcutta, 1968.
Phil 5090.12.2   Klotz, Hans. Der philosophische Beweis. 2. Aufl. Berlin, 1969.

Phil 5100   Logic - Special topics - Fallacies
Phil 5100.2A   Sidgwick, A. Fallacies. N.Y., 1884.
Phil 5100.2B   Sidgwick, A. Fallacies. N.Y., 1884.
Phil 5100.3   Kamiat, A.H. Critique of poor reason. N.Y., 1936.
Phil 5100.5   Moore, William H. Frequent fallacies. Boston, 1931.
Phil 5100.8   Hamblin, Charles Leonard. Fallacies. London, 1970.
Phil 5100.10   Carcaterra, Gaetano. Il problema della fallacia naturalistica. Milano, 1969.

Phil 5110   Logic - Special topics - Hoaxes
Phil 5110.1   MacDougall, C.D. Hoaxes. N.Y., 1940.
Phil 5110.5   Capaldi, Nicholas. The art of deception. N.Y., 1971.

Phil 5115   Logic - Special topics - Hypothesis
Phil 5115.01   Pamphlet box. Philosophy. Hypothesis.
Phil 5115.1   Naville, J.E. La logique de l'hypothèse. Paris, 1880.
Phil 5115.1.5   Varano, Francesco S. L'ipotesi nella filosofia di Ernesto Naville. Gubbio, 1931.
Phil 5115.2   Sigwart, C. Beigefügt sind Beiträge zur Lehre vom hypothetischen Urtheile. Tübingen, 1871.
Phil 5115.3   Joyau, E. De l'invention dans les arts. Paris, 1879.
Phil 5115.4   Poincaré, Henri. La science et l'hypothèse. Paris, 1903.
Phil 5115.4.5   Poincaré, Henri. Science and hypothesis. N.Y., 1905.
Phil 5115.4.6   Poincaré, Henri. Science and hypothesis. London, 1905.
Phil 5115.4.7   Poincaré, Henri. Science and hypothesis. London, 1914.
Phil 5115.5   Ashley, M.L. The nature of hypothesis. Chicago, 1903.
Phil 5115.6   Görland, Albert. Die Hypothese. Göttingen, 1911.
Phil 5115.7   Crane, Esther. The place of the hypothesis in logic. Chicago, 1924.
Phil 5115.8   Hillebrand, F. Zur Lehre von der Hypothesenbildung. Wien, 1896.
Phil 5115.10   Rescher, Nicholas. Hypothetical reasoning. Amsterdam, 1964.

Phil 5125   Logic - Special topics - Induction
Phil 5125.1   Apelt, E.F. Die Theorie der Induction. Leipzig, 1854.
Phil 5125.2   Biéchy, A. L'induction. Paris, 1869.
Phil 5125.4   Whewell, W. Of induction. London, 1849.
Phil 5125.5   Erhardt, F. Der Satz von Grunde als Prinzip der Schliessens. Halle, 1891.
Phil 5125.6   Naden, Constance C.W. Induction and deduction. London, 1890.
Phil 5125.7   Benzoni, Roberto. L'induzione. Pt.1-3. Genova, 1894.
Phil 5125.8   Hughes, Henry. The theory of inference. London, 1894.
Phil 5125.9   Nicod, Jean. Le problème logique de l'induction. Paris, 1924.
Phil 5125.10   Dorolle, M. Les problèmes de l'induction. Paris, 1926.
Phil 5125.11   Patterson, C.H. Problems in logic. N.Y., 1926.
Phil 5125.12   Störring, G. Das urteilende und schliessende Denken in kausaler Behandlung. Leipzig, 1926.
Phil 5125.13   Lalande, André. Les théories de l'induction et de l'expérimentation. Paris, 1929.
Phil 5125.14   Rougier, Louis. La structure des théories déductives. Paris, 1921.
Phil 5125.15   Planella Guille, J. El razonamiento inductivo. Barcelona, 1929?
Phil 5125.16   Poirier, René. Remarques sur la probabilité de inductions. Thèse. Paris, 1931.
Phil 5125.17   Ballantine, William G. The basis of belief, proof by inductive reasoning. N.Y., 1930.
Phil 5125.18   Reade, W.H.F. The problem of inference. Oxford, 1938.
Phil 5125.19.5A   Williams, Donald C. The ground of induction. N.Y., 1963.
Phil 5125.19.5B   Williams, Donald C. The ground of induction. N.Y., 1963.
Phil 5125.20   Kneale, William Calvert. Probability and induction. Oxford, 1949.
Phil 5125.20.1   Kneale, William Calvert. Probability and induction. Reprint. Oxford, 1966.
Phil 5125.21   Wright, G.H. von. A treatise on induction and probability. London, 1951.
Phil 5125.21.5   Wright, G.H. von. The logical problem of induction. 2nd ed. N.Y., 1957.
Phil 5125.21.7   Wright, G.H. von. The logical problem of induction. 2nd ed. Oxford, 1957.
Phil 5125.22   Bagchi, S. Inductive reasoning. Calcutta, 1953.
Phil 5125.23   Harrod, R.F. Foundations of inductive logic. London, 1956.
Phil 5125.24.6   Carnap, Rudolf. Logical foundations of probability. 2nd ed. Chicago, 1962.
Phil 5125.27A   Quine, Willard van Orman. Theory of deduction. Pts.1-4. Cambridge, 1948.
Phil 5125.27B   Quine, Willard van Orman. Theory of deduction. Pts.1-4. Cambridge, 1948.
Phil 5125.29   Katz, Jerrold J. The problem of induction and its solution. Chicago, 1962.
Phil 5125.30   Wesleyan Conference on Induction. Induction: some current issues. 1st ed. Middleton, 1963.
Phil 5125.32   Ackermann, Robert John. Nondeductive inference. London, 1966.
VPhil 5125.34   Arandjelović, Jovan T. Uloga indukcije u naučnom istraživanju. Beograd, 1967.
Phil 5125.38   Swain, Marshall. Induction, acceptance and rational belief. Dordrecht, 1970.
Phil 5125.40   Cohen, Laurence Jonathan. The implications of induction. London, 1970.

Phil 5130   Logic - Special topics - Judgment
Phil 5130.2   Lenk, Hans. Kritik der logischen Konstanten. Berlin, 1968.
Phil 5130.4   Antonov, Georgii V. Ot formal'noi logiki k dialektike. Moskva, 1968.
Phil 5130.6   Czayka, Lothar. Grundzüge der Aussagenlogik. München, 1971.

Classified Listing

Phil 5135   Logic - Special topics - Opinion
Phil 5135.1   Bailey, S. Essays...opinions. London, 1826.
Phil 5135.1.3   Bailey, S. Essays...opinions. London, 1831.
Phil 5135.1.4   Bailey, S. Essays on the formation and publication of
                 opinions. London, 1837.
Phil 5135.1.5   Bailey, S. Essays on opinions and truth. Boston, 1854.
Phil 5135.2   Lewis, G.C. An essay on the influence of authority
                 opinion. London, 1849.
Phil 5135.3   Le Bon, Gustave. Les opinions et les croyances.
                 Paris, 1911.
Phil 5135.4   Coleridge, J.D. Thinking for ourselves. v.1-2.
                 London, 1890.
Phil 5135.6   Stoetzel, Jean. Théorie des opinions. 1. éd. Paris, 1943.
Phil 5135.7   Bzhalava, Iosif T. Vospriiatie i ustanovka.
                 Tbilisi, 1965.
Phil 5135.7.5   Bzhalava, Iosif T. Psikhologiia ustanovki i kibernetika.
                 Moskva, 1966.

Phil 5145   Logic - Special topics - Probability
Phil 5145.2   Leblanc, Hugues. Statistical and inductive probabilities.
                 Englewood Cliffs, 1962.
Phil 5145.3   Kyburg, Henry E. Studies in subjective probability.
                 N.Y., 1964.
Phil 5145.4   Byrne, Edmund F. Probability and opinion. The
                 Hague, 1968.
Phil 5145.6   Boursin, Jean Louis. Autopsie du hasard. Paris, 1970.

Phil 5150   Logic - Special topics - Relativity
Phil 5150.1   Sheffer, H.M. General theory of notational relativity.
                 Cambridge, 1921.
Phil 5150.1.5   Sheffer, H.M. Notational relativity. n.p., 1926?

Phil 5160   Logic - Special topics - Sufficient reason
Phil 5160.1   Fitzgerald, Penelope F. A treatise...sufficient reason.
                 London, 1887.
Phil 5160.5.2   Granger, Giles. La raison. 2. éd. Paris, 1958.
Phil 5160.6   Espersen, Jon. Logik og argumenter. København, 1969.

Phil 5170   Logic - Special topics - Syllogism
Phil 5170.1   Poretsky, P. Sept lois fondamentales de la théorie des
                 égalités logiques. Kazan, 1899.
Phil 5170.3   Pastore, A. Sillogismo e proporzione. Milano, 1910.
Phil 5170.4   Rodier, G. De vi propria syllogismi. Thesis. v.1-2.
                 Parisiis, 1891.
Phil 5170.5   Billia, Lorenzo M. Quatres règles inexactes du syllogisme.
                 Heidelberg, 1908?
Phil 5170.6   Hillebrand, F. Die neuen theorien der Kategorischen
                 Schlüsse. Wien, 1891.
Phil 5170.7   Wilcox, Stanley. The destructive hypothetical syllogism in
                 Greek logic and in Attic oratory. n.p., 1938.
Phil 5170.8   Howard, D.T. Analytical syllogistics. Evanston, 1946.
Phil 5170.9   Wright, G.H. Form and content in logic. Cambridge, 1949.
Phil 5170.10   Lebzeltern, G. Der Syllogismus. Graz, 1948.
Phil 5170.11   Țuțugan, F. Silogistica judecaților de predicație.
                 Bucuresti, 1957.
Phil 5170.12   Schuhl, Pierre M. Le dominateur el les possibles. 1. éd.
                 Paris, 1960.
Phil 5170.13   Korcik, Antoni. Teoriia sylogizmu zdań asertorycznych u
                 azystotelesa. Lublin, 1948.
Phil 5170.14   Subbotin, Aleksandr L. Teoriia sillogistiki v sovremennoi
                 formal'noi logike. Moskva, 1965.
Phil 5170.14.5   Subbotin, Aleksandr L. Traditsionnaia i sovremennaia
                 formal'naia logika. Moskva, 1969.
Phil 5170.15   DeMorgan, Augustus. On the syllogism, and other logical
                 writings. London, 1966.
Phil 5170.18   Bradley, Raymond. Logic, physics and metaphysics.
                 Auckland, 1967.

Phil 5190   Logic - Special topics - Other special
Phil 5190.1   Oesterlen, F. Medical logic. London, 1855.
Phil 5190.2   Kramp, Leo. Das Verhältnis von Urteil und Satz.
                 Bonn, 1916.
Phil 5190.3   Schultz, Julias. Psychologie der Axiome. Göttingen, 1899.
Phil 5190.4   Rickert, H. Zur Lehre von der Definition. 2e Aufl.
                 Tübingen, 1915.
Phil 5190.4.2   Rickert, H. Zur Lehre von der Definition. 3. Aufl.
                 Tübingen, 1929.
Phil 5190.4.5   Rethwisch, E. Der Begriff der Definition. Berlin, 1880.
Phil 5190.4.10   Dubislav, W. Über die Definition. 2. Aufl. Berlin, 1927.
Phil 5190.4.10.3 Dubislav, W. Über die Definition. 3. Aufl. Leipzig, 1931.
Phil 5190.4.15F Piccolomineus, F. De rerum definitionibus liber unus.
                 Venetiis, 1600.
Phil 5190.4.20   Scholz, H. Die sogenannten Definitionen durch Abstraktion.
                 Leipzig, 1935.
Phil 5190.4.25   Robinson, R. Definition. Oxford, 1950.
Phil 5190.4.30   Tamás, György. Die wissenschaftliche Definition.
                 Budapest, 1964.
Phil 5190.5   Rondelet, A. Théorie logique des propositions modales.
                 Paris, 1861.
Phil 5190.10   MacPherson, William. The psychology of persuasion.
                 London, 1920.
Phil 5190.10.1   MacPherson, William. The psychology persuasion.
                 N.Y., 192-?
Phil 5190.10.10 Dolce, Danilo. Conversazioni contedine. Milano, 1966.
Phil 5190.10.15 Prezzalini, G. L'arte di persuadere. Firenze, 1907.
Phil 5190.10.20 Miller, Clyde R. The process of persuasion.
                 Firenze, 1907.
Phil 5190.10.26 Yale University. Institute of Human Relations. The order
                 of presentation in persuasion. New Haven, 1961.
Phil 5190.15   Joachim, Harold. Immediate experience and meditation.
                 Oxford, 1919.
Phil 5190.17   Aspects de la dialectique. Paris, 1956.
Phil 5190.20   Thiede, J. Über die Negation, den Widerspruch und den
                 Gegensatz. Inaug.-Diss. Berlin, 1883.
Phil 5190.21.5   Adler, M.J. Dialectic. N.Y., 1927.
Phil 5190.22   Hänssler, Ernst H. Zur Theorie der Analogie und des
                 sogenannten Analogschlusses. Diss. Basel, 1927.
Phil 5190.23   Alstrin, Eric. Dissertatio gradualis. Upsaliae, 1725.
Phil 5190.24   Schilder, Klaas. Zur Begriffsgeschichte des "Paradoxon".
                 Inaug. Diss. Kampen, 1933.
Phil 5190.24.5   Melhwish, George. The paradoxical universe. Bristol,
                 Eng., 1959.
Phil 5190.24.10 Slaatte, Howard Alexander. The pertinence of the paradox.
                 N.Y., 1968.
Phil 5190.24.15 Toensma, E. The paradoxes. Assen, 1969.
Phil 5190.25   Schultzer, B. Observation and protocolstatement.
                 Copenhagen, 1938.
Phil 5190.27   Tavanets, P.V. Voprosy teorii suzhdeniia. Moskva, 1955.

Phil 5190   Logic - Special topics - Other special - cont.
Phil 5190.28.2   Ryle, G. Dilemmas. Cambridge, Eng., 1962.
Phil 5190.30   Toulmin, S.E. The uses of argument. Cambridge,
                 Eng., 1958.
Phil 5190.35   Korchyns'ka, H. Try abo chotyry zakony diialektyky.
                 Miunkhen, 1956.
Phil 5190.36   Agazzi, Evandro. Introduzione ai problemi
                 dell'assiomatica. Milano, 1961.
Phil 5190.37   Faris, John A. Truth-functional logic. London, 1962.
Phil 5190.38   Brown, J.A.C. Techniques of persuasion. Baltimore, 1963.
Phil 5190.40   Akademiia Nauk SSSR. Kafedra Filosofii, Leningrad.
                 Problema vozmozhnosti i deistvitel'nosti.
                 Leningrad, 1964.
Phil 5190.41   Cackowski, Zdzisław. Problemy i pseudoproblemy.
                 Warszawa, 1964.
Phil 5190.42   Rescher, Nicholas. The logic of commands. London, 1966.
Phil 5190.43   Fotheringham, Wallace C. Perspectives on persuasion.
                 Boston, 1966.
Phil 5190.45   Rosnow, Ralph L. Experiments in persuasion. N.Y., 1967.
Phil 5190.50   Guha Mozumdar, Roby. Possibilism. Calcutta, 1966.
Phil 5190.60   Patel, Peter. Logische und methodologische Probleme der
                 wissenschaftlichen Erklärung. München, 1965.
Phil 5190.65   Finazzo, Giancarlo. Sulla dialettica dell'apriori.
                 Roma, 1966.
Phil 5190.70   Das, Adhar Chandra. Negative fact, negation and truth.
                 Calcutta, 1942.
Phil 5190.72   Martin, Robert L. The paradox of the liar. New
                 Haven, 1970.
Phil 5190.75   Barker, John A. A formal analysis of conditionals.
                 Carbondale, 1969.
Phil 5190.80   Morales Encina, Carlos. Técnica de la persuasión.
                 Santiago de Chile, 1969.
Phil 5190.85   Abelson, Herbert Irving. Persuasion; how opinions and
                 attitudes are changed. N.Y., 1959.
Phil 5190.85.2   Karlins, Marvin. Persuasion; how opinions and attitudes
                 are changed. 2nd ed. N.Y., 1970.
Phil 5190.88   Hare, Richard Mervyn. Practical inferences. London, 1971.
Phil 5190.90   Andersen, Kenneth E. Persuasion: theory and practice.
                 Boston, 1971.
Phil 5190.92   Wybramec-Skardowska, Urszula. Z badań nad seoria zdań
                 odrzuconyeh. Opole, 1969.
Phil 5190.94   Thilo, Ingmar. Vom Fragen. Inaug. Diss. München, 1969.

Phil 5195   Logic - Logic machines, mechanical logical methods
Phil 5195.2   Gardner, Martin. Logic machines and diagrams. N.Y., 1958.

Phil 5203   Psychology - Reference works - Bibliographies
Phil 5203.1   Bibliographie der Psycho-Physiologischen. Hamburg, 1890.
Phil 5203.2   Laehr, H. Die Literatur der Psychiatrie, Neurologie und
                 Psychologie. v.1-3. Berlin, 1900. 4v.
Phil 5203.3   Grässe, J.G.T. Bibliotheca psychologica. Leipzig, 1848.
Phil 5203.4   Psykologische tidsskrifter; liste over ikke-nordishe
                 tidsskrifter av psykologisk interesse på nordishe
                 biblioteker. Oslo.
Phil 5203.5   Psycho-pathological references, English and American.
Phil 5203.6   Gunn, John A. Psyche and Minerva. Melbourne, 1930.
Phil 5203.7   Spek, J. van der. Literatuurlijsten en atlas.
                 Groningen, 1927.
Phil 5203.8   Murchison, C.A. The psychological register. v.3.
                 Worcester, 1932.
Phil 5203.8A   Murchison, C.A. The psychological register. v.2-3.
                 Worcester, 1929.
Phil 5203.8B   Murchison, C.A. The psychological register. v.2.
                 Worcester, 1929.
Phil 5203.9   Estey, H.G. A bibliography on psychology. Gardner, 1926.
Phil 5203.10   Hawes, M. What to read on psychology. Chicago, 1942.
Phil 5203.11   Harvard University. Psychology Library. Selected reference
                 list. Cambridge, 1936.
Phil 5203.11.10 Harvard University. Department of Psychology. Books in
                 psychology. v.1-2. Cambridge, 1938.
Phil 5203.11.15 Harvard University. The Harvard list of books in
                 psychology. Cambridge, 1949.
Phil 5203.11.20 Harvard University. The Harvard list of books in
                 psychology. Cambridge, 1955.
Phil 5203.11.22A Harvard University. The Harvard list of books in
                 psychology. 3. ed. Cambridge, 1964.
Phil 5203.11.22B Harvard University. The Harvard list of books in
                 psychology. 3. ed. Cambridge, 1964.
Phil 5203.11.24 Harvard University. The Harvard list of books in
                 psychology. Compiled and annotated by the psychologists in
                 Harvard University. 4th ed. Cambridge, 1971.
Phil 5203.12   Carron, René. Guide de l'étudiant en psychologie.
                 Paris, 1953.
Phil 5203.14   Benedek, László. Magyar pszichológiai irodalom 1945-66.
                 Budapest, 1967.
Phil 5203.15   Moscow. Gosudarstvennaia Biblioteka SSSR. Imeni V.I.
                 Lenina. Kak nauka ob"iasniaet psikhologicheskoi
                 deiatel'nosti cheloveka. Moskva, 1954.
Phil 5203.16   United States. National Institute of Mental Health.
                 Reference guide. Bethesda, Md.
Phil 5203.18   Baatz, Walter. Geistes und naturwissenschaftliche
                 Abhandlungen der Mitglieder des Wiener Arbeitskreises.
                 Wien, 1957.
Phil 5203.20   Emanuilova, E. Suvremenna materialisticheska psikhologiia.
                 Sofiia, 1959.
Phil 5203.22   Quarterly check-list of psychology. Darien, Conn. 1,1961+
Phil 5203.24   Bibliographie der psychologischen Literatur der
                 sozialistischen Länder. Berlin. 3,1960+ 5v.
Phil 5203.25   Wellek, Albert. Gesamtverzeichnis der deutschsparchigen
                 psychologischen Literatur der Jahre 1942 bis 1960.
                 Göttingen, 1965.
VPhil 5203.26   Ostvold, Harald. Manual of reference sources in
                 psychology. St. Louis? 1949.
Phil 5203.27   Jugoslovenska psihološka bibliografija, period od 1952-1964
                 god. Beograd, 1964.
Phil 5203.30   Kullman, Siv-Aino. Tôrster Husén. Tryckataskrifter
                 1940-1965. Stockholm, 1966.
Phil 5203.31   Klingelhofer, Edward L. A bibliography of psychological
                 research and writings on Africa. Uppsala, 1967.
Phil 5203.34   Schueling, H. Bibliographie der psychologischen Literatur
                 des 16. Jahrhunderts. Hildesheim, 1967.
Phil 5203.35   Soviet psychology; a continuing bibliography. North
                 Hollywood, Calif. 1,1950+
Phil 5203.37   Loattit, Chauncey McKinley. Handbook of psychological
                 literature. Bloomington, Ind., 1932.

Classified Listing

04 Psychology - Reference works - Dictionaries and encyclopedias

Phil 5204.6.2 Giese, Fritz. Psychologische Wörterbuch. Tübingen, 1950.
Phil 5204.8.2 Essen, Jac van. Beschrijvend en verklarend woordenboek der psychologie. 2. Druk. Haarlem, 1953.
Phil 5204.10.2 Psykologisk-pedagogisk uppslagsbok. 2. uppl. Stockholm, 1956. 3v.
Phil 5204.10.2.1 Psykologisk-pedagogisk uppslagsbok. Supplement. Stockholm, 1956.
Phil 5204.12.2 Piéron, Henri. Vocabulaire de la psychologie. 2. éd. Paris, 1957.
Phil 5204.12.3 Piéron, Henri. Vocabulaire de la psychologie. 3. éd. Paris, 1963.
Phil 5204.14 The encyclopedia of mental health. N.Y., 1963. 6v.
Phil 5204.16 Telberg, Ina. Russian-English glossary of psychiatric terms. N.Y., 1964.
Phil 5204.18.3 Sury, Kurt F. von. Wörterbuch der Psychologie und ihrer Gunzgebiete. 3. Aufl. Basel, 1967.
Phil 5204.20 Hinsée, Leland Earl. Psychiatric dictionary, with encyclopedic treatment of modern terms. N.Y., 1940.
Phil 5204.22.2 Zeddies, Adolf. Worterbuch der Psychologie. 2. Aufl. Dortmund, 1948.
Phil 5204.24 Berka, M. Kleines psychologisches Lexicon. Wien, 1949.

05 Psychology - Pamphlet volumes

VPhil 5205.1 Pamphlet box. Psychological papers.
VPhil 5205.2 Pamphlet box. Psychological essays.
VPhil 5205.3 Pamphlet box. Psychology.
VPhil 5205.4 Pamphlet vol. Psychology. General experimental. 19 pam.
VPhil 5205.5 Pamphlet vol. Psychology. General. 11 pam.
VPhil 5205.6 Pamphlet box. Psychology. 1824-1909.
VPhil 5205.7 Pamphlet box. Psychology. 1829-1906.
VPhil 5205.8 Pamphlet box. Psychology. 1903-1908.
VPhil 5205.11 Pamphlet vol. Psychology.
VPhil 5205.11.1 Pamphlet vol. Psychology.
VPhil 5205.11.2 Pamphlet vol. Psychology.
VPhil 5205.11.3 Pamphlet vol. Psychology.
VPhil 5205.11.4 Pamphlet vol. Psychology.
VPhil 5205.11.5 Pamphlet vol. Psychology.
VPhil 5205.11.6 Pamphlet vol. Psychology.
VPhil 5205.11.7 Pamphlet vol. Psychology.
VPhil 5205.11.8 Pamphlet vol. Psychology.
VPhil 5205.12 Pamphlet box. Calkins on association.
VPhil 5205.13 Pamphlet box. Monographs in psychology and anthropology.
VPhil 5205.14 Pamphlet box. Psychology. Monographs on anomalies.
Phil 5205.15 Pamphlet vol. Psychology. 10 pam.
VPhil 5205.16 The American journal of psychology. Worcester, Mass., 1895-96.
VPhil 5205.18 Pamphlet vol. Psychology. 1845-1928. 27 pam.
VPhil 5205.20 Pamphlet vol. Psychology. German dissertations. 21 pam.
VPhil 5205.21 Pamphlet vol. Psychology. German dissertations. 22 pam.
VPhil 5205.22 Pamphlet vol. Psychology. German dissertations. 17 pam.
VPhil 5205.25 Pamphlet vol. Psychology. 22 pam.
VPhil 5205.26 Pamphlet vol. Psychology. 22 pam.
VPhil 5205.27 Pamphlet vol. Psychology. 20 pam.
Phil 5205.28 Pamphlet box. Psychology.
Phil 5205.30 Pamphlet box. Psychology. German dissertations.
Phil 5205.32 Behavior Research Fund, Chicago. A community's adventure. Chicago, 1931? 5 pam.
Phil 5205.34 Hildebrant, R. Zur Kritik der Psychologie. Marburg, 1946. 4 pam.
Phil 5205.35 Pamphlet vol. Psychology. (Russian). 3 pam.
VPhil 5205.36 Pamphlet vol. Psychology. Dissertations (A-E). 10 pam.
VPhil 5205.37 Pamphlet vol. Psychology. Dissertations. (F-K). 7 pam.
VPhil 5205.38 Pamphlet vol. Psychology. Dissertations. (L-R). 8 pam.
VPhil 5205.39 Pamphlet vol. Psychology. Dissertations. (S-Z). 8 pam.
VPhil 5205.40 Pamphlet vol. Psychology. German dissertations. 5 pam.
VPhil 5205.41 Pamphlet vol. Experimental psychology. Dissertations. (A-F). 7 pam.
VPhil 5205.42 Pamphlet vol. Experimental psychology. German dissertations. (G-J). 6 pam.
VPhil 5205.43 Pamphlet vol. Experimental psychology. German dissertations. (K). 8 pam.
VPhil 5205.44 Pamphlet vol. Experimental psychology. Dissertations. (L-Z). 8 pam.
VPhil 5205.45 Pamphlet box. Experimental psychology. Dissertations.

207 Psychology - Dictionaries [Discontinued]

Phil 5207.10 Warren, Howard Crosby. Dictionary of psychology. N.Y., 1934.

210 - 5235 Psychology - History - General works - Individual authors Z)

Phil 5210.1 Aall, A. Psykologiens historie i Norge. Kristiania, 1911.
Phil 5210.2 Arnold, V.H. La psychologie de réaction en Amérique. Thèse. Paris, 1926.
Phil 5210.3 Adams, Grace K. Psychology. N.Y., 1931.
Phil 5210.5 Anan'ev, B.G. Ocherki po istorii russkoi psikhologii XVII i XIX v. Moskva, 1947.
Phil 5210.8 Akademiia Pedagogicheskikh Nauk RSFSR, Moscow. Institut Psikhologii. Psikhologicheskaia nauk a v SSSR. Moskva, 1959. 2v.
Phil 5210.8.5 Akademiia Pedagogicheskikh Nauk RSFSR, Moscow. Institut Psikhologii. Ergebnisse der sowjetischen Psychologie. Berlin, 1967.
Phil 5210.10 Akademiia Nauk SSSR. Institut Filosofii. Sovremennaia psikhologiia v kapitalisticheskikh stranakh. Moskva, 1963.
Phil 5210.11 Anzieu, Didier. Esquisse de la psychologie française. Paris, 1962?
Phil 5210.15 Appley, Mortimertt. Psychology in Canada. Ottawa, 1967.
Phil 5210.20 Alarcón, Reynaldo. Panorama de la psicología en el Perú. Lima, 1968.
Phil 5211.1 Brett, G.S. History of psychology. London, 1912-21. 3v.
Phil 5211.1.5 Brett, G.S. History of psychology. London, 1953.
Phil 5211.2A Baldwin, J.M. History of psychology. N.Y., 1913. 2v.
Phil 5211.2B Baldwin, J.M. History of psychology. N.Y., 1913. 2v.
Phil 5211.2.5 Baldwin, J.M. Sketch of the history of psychology. Lancaster, 1905.
Phil 5211.3.2 Bühler, Karl. Die Kirse der Psychologie. 2. Aufl. Jena, 1929.
Phil 5211.4A Boring, E.G. A history of experimental psychology. N.Y., 1929.
Phil 5211.4B Boring, E.G. A history of experimental psychology. N.Y., 1929.
Phil 5211.4C Boring, E.G. A history of experimental psychology. N.Y., 1929.

Phil 5210 - 5235 Psychology - History - General works - Individual authors (A-Z) - cont.

Phil 5211.4.5 Boring, E.G. A history of experimental psychology. 2. ed. N.Y., 1950.
Phil 5211.4.7A Boring, Edwin Garrigues. A history of experimental psychology. 2. ed. N.Y., 1957.
Phil 5211.4.7B Boring, Edwin Garrigues. A history of experimental psychology. 2. ed. N.Y., 1957.
Phil 5211.4.20 Boring, E.G. Sensation and perception in the history of experimental psychology. N.Y., 1942.
Phil 5211.5 Bierviet, J.J. van. La psychologie d'aujourd'hui. Paris, 1927.
Phil 5211.6 Brennan, R.E. History of psychology. N.Y., 1945.
Phil 5211.7 Bamborough, J.B. The little world of man. London, 1952.
Phil 5211.10 Bochorishvili, A.t. Prints'pial'nye voprosy psikhologii. Tbilisi, 1957- 2v.
Phil 5212.1 Carus, F.A. Geschichte der Psychologie. Leipzig, 1808.
Phil 5212.2 Cattell, J.M. The progress of psychology. N.Y., 1893?
Phil 5212.5 Chin, Robert. Psychology in America. N.Y., 1929.
Phil 5212.10 Clark, Kenneth. America's psychologists. Washington, 1957.
Phil 5212.15 Chin, Robert. Psychological research in Communist China, 1949-1966. Cambridge, Mass., 1969.
Phil 5212.20.2 Chaplin, James Patrik. Systems and theories of psychology. 2. ed. N.Y., 1968.
Phil 5213.1 Dessoir, M. Geschichte der neueren deutschen Psychologie. Berlin, 1897.
Phil 5213.1.5 Dessoir, M. Abriss einer Geschichte der Psychologie. Heidelberg, 1911.
Phil 5213.1.9A Dessoir, M. Outline...history of psychology. N.Y., 1912.
Phil 5213.1.9B Dessoir, M. Outline...history of psychology. N.Y., 1912.
Phil 5213.2 Dwelshauvers, Georges. La psychologie française contemporaine. Paris, 1920.
Phil 5213.3 Diehl, Frank. An historical and critical study of radical behaviorism. Baltimore, 1934.
Phil 5214.2 Esper, E.A. A history of psychology. Philadelphia, 1964.
Phil 5214.4 Ebert, Manfred. Die Bedeutung der Philosophie für die Entwicklung der Psychologie zur Einzelwissenschaft. Inaug. Diss. München, 1966.
Phil 5215.1 Friedländer, A.A. Die neuzeitliche psychologische Strömungen. Lubeck, 1926.
Phil 5215.2.5 Flügel, J.C. A hundred years of psychology, 1833-1933. 2nd ed. London, 1951.
Phil 5215.2.10 Flügel, J.C. A hundred years of psychology, 1833-1933. London, 1964.
Phil 5215.2.12 Flügel, J.C. A hundred years of psychology, 1833-1933. N.Y., 1964.
Phil 5215.3 Fay, J.W. American psychology. New Brunswick, N.J., 1939.
Phil 5215.4 Farbstein, Wolf. Romantische Einflüsse in der Geschichte der Psychologie. Zürich, 1953.
Phil 5215.5 Foulquié, Paul. La psychologie contemporaine. Paris, 1951.
Phil 5216.1 Gilardin, Alphonse. Considérations sur les divers systèmes de psychologie. Paris, 1883.
Phil 5216.2 Garrett, Henry E. Great experiments in psychology. N.Y., 1930.
Phil 5216.2.5 Garrett, Henry E. Great experiments in psychology. N.Y., 1941.
Phil 5216.5 Gučas, Alfonsas. Psichologijos raidci Lietuvoje. Vilnius, 1968.
Phil 5217.1 Hart, Charles A. The Thomistic concept of mental faculty. Diss. Washington, 1930.
Phil 5217.5 Heidbreder, Edna. Seven psychologies. N.Y., 1961.
Phil 5217.6 Hoyos, C.G. Denkschrift zur Lage der Psychologie. Wiesbaden, 1964.
Phil 5217.7 Hearnshaw, L.S. A short history of British psychology, 1840-1940. London, 1964.
Phil 5217.8.2 Hehlmann, Wilhelm. Geschichte der Psychologie. 2. Aufl. Stuttgart, 1967.
Phil 5218.5 Iaroshevskii, Mikhail G. Istoriia psikhologii. Moskva, 1966.
Phil 5218.5.5 Iaroshevskii, Mikhail G. Psikhologiia v XX stoletii. Moskva, 1971.
Phil 5220.1 Klemm, O. Geschichte der Psychologie. Leipzig, 1911.
Phil 5220.1.5 Klemm, O. A history of psychology. N.Y., 1914.
Phil 5220.3 Knauer, V. Grundlinien zur Aristotelisch-Thomistischen Psychologie. Wien, 1885.
Phil 5220.4 Keller, F.S. The definition of psychology. N.Y., 1937.
Phil 5220.5 Kantor, J.R. The scientific evolution of psychology. Chicago, 1963. 2v.
Phil 5220.6 Kvasov, Dmitrii G. Fiziologicheskaia shkola I.P. Pavlova. Leningrad, 1967.
Phil 5220.7 Klein, David Ballin. A history of scientific psychology. N.Y., 1970.
Phil 5221.1 Levine, A.J. Current psychologies. Cambridge, 1940.
Phil 5221.5 Lottin, Odon. Psychologie et morale aux XIIe et XIIIe siècles. v.1-6. Louvain, 1942. 8v.
Phil 5221.8 Leigh, D. The historical development of British psychiatry. Oxford, 1961.
Phil 5222.1 Mercier, D. Les origines de la psychologie contemporaine. Paris, 1897.
Phil 5222.1.5 Mercier, D. The origins of contemporary psychology. N.Y., 1918.
Phil 5222.2 Mantorani, Giuseppe. Psicologia fisiologica. 2. ed. Milano, 1905.
Phil 5222.3 Murphy, Gardner. Historical introduction to modern psychology. N.Y., 1929.
Phil 5222.3.5A Murphy, Gardner. Historical introduction to modern psychology. N.Y., 1949.
Phil 5222.3.5B Murphy, Gardner. Historical introduction to modern psychology. N.Y., 1949.
Phil 5222.3.5.2 Murphy, Gardner. An historical introduction to modern psychology. 2. ed. N.Y., 1930.
Phil 5222.3.10 Murphy, Gardner. Approaches to personality. N.Y., 1932.
Phil 5222.4 Müller-Freienfelds, R. Die Hauptrichtungen der gegenwärtigen Psychologie. Leipzig, 1929.
Phil 5222.4.5 Müller-Freienfelds, R. The evolution of modern psychology. New Haven, 1935.
Phil 5222.5A Murchinson, C.A. A history of psychology in autobiography. Worcester, 1930-36. 4v.
Phil 5222.5B Murchinson, C.A. A history of psychology in autobiography. v.1-2,4. Worcester, 1930-36. 3v.
Phil 5222.6 Manoll, A. La psychologie expérimentale en Italie. Paris, 1938.
Phil 5222.7 Mace, C.A. Current trends in British psychology. London, 1953.
Phil 5222.8 Müller, T.L. Histoire de la psychologie. Paris, 1960.

Classified Listing

Phil 5210 - 5235   **Psychology - History - General works - Individual authors**
(A-Z) - cont.

Phil 5222.9   Muller, Philippe. La psychologie dans le monde moderne. Bruxelles, 1964.

Phil 5222.9.5   Muller, Philippe. Psychology in the modern world. N.Y., 1969.

Phil 5222.10   Manswrov, N.S. Sovremennaia curzhuazhaia psikhologiia. Moskva, 1962.

Phil 5222.11   Meyer, Donald Burton. The positive thinkers. 1. ed. Garden City, N.Y., 1965.

Phil 5222.12   Massucco Costa, Angiola. Psicologia sovietica. Torino, 1963.

Phil 5222.13   Misiak, Henryk. Catholics in psychology. N.Y., 1954.

Phil 5222.16   Murphy, Gardner. Asian psychology. N.Y., 1968.

Phil 5222.20   McPherson, Marion White. Problems and procedures in oral histories of the Archives of the History of American Psychology. Akron, 1967.

Phil 5222.22   Madsen, K.B. Moderne psykologiske teorier. 2. oplag. København, 1969.

Phil 5222.22.5   Madsen, K.B. Psykologiens udvikling. København, 1970.

Phil 5223.1   Nuttin, Jozef. Tendences nouvelles dans la psychologie contemporaine. Louvain, 1951.

Phil 5223.5   Nuttin, Jozef. Tôche relussité et échec. Bruxelles, 1953.

Phil 5223.10   Nuttin, Jozef. Psychology in Belgium. Louvain, 1961.

Phil 5224.1   Orth, Johannes. Der psychologische Begriff des Unbewuzten in der Schelling'schen Schule. Heidelberg, 1914.

Phil 5225.1A   Pillsbury, W.B. The history of psychology. N.Y., 1929.

Phil 5225.1B   Pillsbury, W.B. The history of psychology. N.Y., 1929.

Phil 5225.2   Petermann, Bruno. Die Wertheimer-Koffka-Köhlersche Gestalttheorie und das Gestaltproblem systematische und kritisch Dargestellt. Leipzig, 1928.

Phil 5225.3   Prinzhorn, H. Leib-Seele-Linheit. Potsdam, 1927.

Phil 5225.4.1   Postman, Leo Joseph. Psychology in the making; histories of selected research problems. N.Y., 1968.

Phil 5225.5   Petrovskii, Artur V. Istoriia sovetskoi psikhologii. Moskva, 1967.

Phil 5225.10   Pongratz, Ludwig Jakob. Problemgeschichte der Psychologie. Bern, 1967.

VPhil 5225.11   Pasluszha, Yózet. Historia psychologii. Lublin, 1971.

Phil 5227.1   Ribot, T. La psychologie anglaise contemporaine. Paris, 1870.

Phil 5227.1.5   Ribot, T. English psychology. London, 1892.

Phil 5227.1.10   Ribot, T. English psychology. London, 1873.

Phil 5227.2   Ribot, T. La psychologie allemande contemporaine. Paris, 1879.

Phil 5227.2.3   Ribot, T. La psychologie allemande contemporaine. 2. éd. Paris, 1885.

Phil 5227.2.5   Ribot, T. German psychology of to-day. N.Y., 1886.

Phil 5227.2.6   Ribot, T. German psychology of to-day. N.Y., 1899.

Phil 5227.3A   Rand, B. The classical psychologists. Boston, 1912.

Phil 5227.3B   Rand, B. The classical psychologists. Boston, 1912.

Phil 5227.4   Ruin, Hans. Erlebnis und Wissen. Helsingfors, 1921.

Phil 5227.5   Recent experiments in psychology. 1st ed. N.Y., 1938.

Phil 5227.6   Roback, A.A. History of American psychology. N.Y., 1951.

Phil 5227.6.2   Roback, A.A. History of American psychology. N.Y., 1964.

Phil 5227.6.10   Roback, A.A. History of psychology and psychiatry. N.Y., 1961.

Phil 5227.7   Reinle, Rico. Das Problems der Entwicklung in der neueren Psychologie. Basel, 1952.

Phil 5227.8   Reeves, Joan Wynn. Body and mind in Western thought. Harmondsworth, 1958.

Phil 5227.8.10   Reeves, Joan Wynn. Thinking about thinking. London, 1965.

Phil 5227.10   Reith, Herman. An introduction to philosophical psychology. Englewood Cliffs, N.J., 1956.

Phil 5228.1   Siebeck, H. Geschichte der Psychologie. Gotha, 1880-84.

Phil 5228.1.2   Siebeck, H. Geschichte der psychologie. v.1-2. Amsterdam, 1961.

Phil 5228.1.5   Siebeck, H. Beiträge...Psychologie. Giessen, 1891.

Phil 5228.2   Sommer, R. Grundzüge einer Geschichte der deutschen Psychologie. Würzburg, 1892.

Phil 5228.3   Sganzini, Carlo. Die Fortschritte der Völkerpsychologie. Bern, 1913.

Phil 5228.4   Sanseverino, G. Philosophia christianacum antigua et nova comparata. Neapoli, 1862-66. 3v.

Phil 5228.5   Seifert, Friedrich. Die Wissenschaft von Menschen in der Gegenwart. Leipzig, 1930.

Phil 5228.6   Sinha, Jadunath. Indian psychology; perception. London, 1934.

Phil 5228.6.5   Sinha, Jadunath. Indian psychology. Calcutta, 1958.

Phil 5228.7   Streeter, B.H. The church and modern psychology. Evanston, Ill., 1934.

Phil 5228.8   Spearman, C. Psychology down the ages. London, 1937. 2v.

Phil 5228.12   Schiller, P. von. Aufgabe der Psychologie. Wien, 1948.

Phil 5228.14   Skard, Ase Gruda. Psykologi og psykologar i Norge. Oslo, 1959.

Phil 5228.16   Suarez Soto, Vicente. Psicología abismal del mexicano. 2. ed. Puebla de Zaragoza, 1967.

Phil 5228.18   Schultz, Duane P. A history of modern psychology. N.Y., 1969.

Phil 5229.2   Thomson, Robert. The Pelican history of psychology. Harmondsworth, 1968.

Phil 5230.1   Ullersperger, J.B. Die Geschichte der Psychologie und der Psychiatrik in Spanien. Würzburg, 1871.

Phil 5231.5   Voutsinas, Dimitri. Documentation sur la psychologie française. v.1-6. Paris, 1958- 5v.

Phil 5232.1   Windelband, W. Über den...psychologische Forschung. Leipzig, 1876.

Phil 5232.2   Wollny, F. Historisch-psychologischer Tractat. Leipzig, 1892.

Phil 5232.3   Wray, W.J. The new psychology and the gospel. London, 1926.

Phil 5232.4   Wickham, H. The misbehaviorists. N.Y., 1928.

Phil 5232.5A   Woodworth, R.S. Contemporary schools of psychology. N.Y., 1931.

Phil 5232.5B   Woodworth, R.S. Contemporary schools of psychology. N.Y., 1931.

Phil 5232.5.10   Woodworth, R.S. Contemporary schools of psychology. N.Y., 1936.

Phil 5232.5.15A   Woodworth, R.S. Contemporary schools of psychology. N.Y., 1948.

Phil 5232.5.15B   Woodworth, R.S. Contemporary schools of psychology. N.Y., 1948.

Phil 5232.5.17   Woodworth, R.S. Contemporary schools of psychology. 3. ed. N.Y., 1967.

Phil 5232.6   Wolfson, H.A. The internal senses in Latin, Arabic, and Hebrew philosophic texts. Cambridge, 1935.

Phil 5210 - 5235   **Psychology - History - General works - Individual authors**
(A-Z) - cont.

Phil 5232.8   Westerhof, A.C. Representative psychologists. Union Bridge, Md., 1938.

Phil 5232.9   Wells, H.K. Pavlov and Freud. N.Y., 1956. 2v.

Phil 5232.10   Watson, Robert Irving. The great psychologists. Philadelphia, 1963.

Phil 5232.10.2   Watson, Robert Irving. The great psychologists from Aristotle to Freud. 2. ed. Philadelphia, 1968.

Phil 5232.11   Wickert, F.R. Readings in African psychology. East Lansing, 1967.

Phil 5232.12   Wolman, Benjamin B. Historical roots of contemporary psychology. N.Y., 1968.

Phil 5234.2   Young, Robert Maxwell. Mind, brain and adaptation in the nineteenth century. Oxford, 1970.

Phil 5235.1   Ziehen, T. Über die Beziehungen zwischen Gehirn und Seelenleben. Leipzig, 1902.

Phil 5235.2   Zharikbaev, Kubigul B. Razvitie psikhologicheskoi mysli v Kazakhstane (so vtoroi poloviny XIXlveka i do nashikh dnei . Alma-Ata, 1968.

Phil 5237   **Psychology - History - Local (Geographical Table A)**

Phil 5237.512   Slobin, Dan Isaac. Handbook of Soviet psychology. White Plains, N.Y., 1966.

Phil 5237.516   Ocherki po istorii russkoi psikhologii. Moskva, 1957.

Phil 5237.516.5   Sokolov, Mikhail V. Ocherki istorii psikhologicheskikh vozznenii v Rossii v XI-XVIII vekakh. Moskva, 1963.

Phil 5237.516.10   Sokolov, Mikhail V. Iz istorii russkoi psikhologii. Moskva, 1961.

Phil 5238   **Psychology - General treatises - Collected authors**

Phil 5238.1   Angell, J.R. Chapters from modern psychology, 1911. London, 1912.

Phil 5238.2   Martius, Götz. Beiträge zur Psychologie und Philosophie. Leipzig, 1905.

Phil 5238.3   Colorado. College. Publication. Education and psychology. Colorado Springs. 1,1919

Phil 5238.4   Milan. Università Cattolica del Sacro Cuore. Laboratorio di Psicologia di Biologia. Contributi. Milano. 1-29 26v.

Phil 5238.5   Collection de psychologie experimentale et de métapsychie. Paris. 1-22,1908-1912 18v.

Phil 5238.6   Scritti di psicologia raccolti in onore di Federico Kiesow. Torino, 1933.

Phil 5238.7   Centenaire de T. Ribot, jubilé de la psychologie scientifique française, 1839-1939. Ägen, 1939.

Phil 5238.8   Psychologischer Club, Zürich. Die kulturelle Bedeutung der komplexen Psychologie. Berlin, 1935.

Phil 5238.10A   Current trends in psychology. Pittsburgh, 1947.

Phil 5238.10B   Current trends in psychology. Pittsburgh, 1947.

Phil 5238.10.2   Current trends in psychological theory. Pittsburgh, 1961.

Phil 5238.12   Louvain. Université Catholique. Institute Supérieur de Philosophie. Miscellanea psychologica Albert Michotte. Louvain, 1947.

Phil 5238.14A   Problems of personality: studies presented to Dr. Morton Prince. N.Y., 1925.

Phil 5238.14B   Problems of personality: studies presented to Dr. Morton Prince. N.Y., 1925.

Phil 5238.16   Baumgarten, F. Progress de la psycotechnique. Bern, 1949-

Phil 5238.18   Stevens, S.S. Handbook of experimental psychology. N.Y., 1951.

Phil 5238.20   Rapaport, D. Organization and pathology of thought. N.Y., 1951.

Phil 5238.22   Wilbur, G.B. Psychoanalysis and culture. N.Y., 1951.

Phil 5238.24   Beiträge aus der Sowjetpsychologie. Berlin, 1952.

Phil 5238.24.5   Soviet psychology. N.Y., 1961.

Phil 5238.26   Current trends. Pittsburgh, 1952.

Phil 5238.28   Austen Riggs Center, Stockbridge, Massachusetts. Psychoanalytic psychiatry and psychology. N.Y. 1,1954

Phil 5238.30   Annual survey of psychoanalysis; a comprehensive survey of current psychoanalytic theory and practice. N.Y. 1-9,1950-1958 8v.

Phil 5238.32   Behavior theory and social science. New Haven, 1955.

Phil 5238.35   Farrell, B.A. Experimental psychology. N.Y., 1955.

Phil 5238.38A   Grinker, R.R. Toward a unified theory of human behavior. 1. ed. N.Y., 1956.

Phil 5238.38B   Grinker, R.R. Toward a unified theory of human behavior. 1. ed. N.Y., 1956.

Phil 5238.40   Simon, Brian. Psychology in the Soviet Union. Stanford, Calif., 1957.

Phil 5238.45   Moderne Entwicklungsologie. Berlin, 1956.

Phil 5238.60   Johnston, D.K. Religion und wissenschaftliches Heilverfahren. Bahn, 1925. 7 pam.

Phil 5238.65   Beiträge zur genetischen Charakterologie. Bern. 1-3

Phil 5238.67   Association de Psychologie Scientifique de Langue Française. Les problèmes de la mesure en psychologie. Paris, 1962.

Phil 5238.70   Dunlap and Associates, Stanford, Conn. Mathematical models of human behavior. Stanford, 1962.

Phil 5238.75   Rencontre. Utrecht, 1957.

Phil 5238.80   Current trends in the description and analysis of behavior. Pittsburgh, 1958.

Phil 5238.85   May, Rollo. Existence. N.Y., 1958.

Phil 5238.88.2   May, Rollo. Existential psychology. 2d ed. N.Y., 1969.

Phil 5238.90   Roe, Anne. Behavior and evolution. New Haven, 1958.

Phil 5238.95   Däumling, Adolf. Seelenleben und Menschenbild. München, 1958.

Phil 5238.100   Koch, Sigmund. Psychology. v.2-6. v.1 lost. N.Y., 1959. 5v.

Phil 5238.105   Halmos, Paul. Readings in general psychology. London, 1959.

Phil 5238.110   Ciba Foundation. Ciba Foundation symposium on the neurological basis of behaviour. Boston, 1958.

Phil 5238.115   Cantril, Hadley. Reflections on the human venture. N.Y., 1960.

Phil 5238.120   Kaplan, Bernard. Perspectives in psychological theory. N.Y., 1960.

Phil 5238.125   Harris, Dale B. The concept of development. Minneapolis, 1957.

Phil 5238.130   Peatman, J.G. Festschrift for Gardner Murphy. N.Y., 1960.

Phil 5238.135   Decision, values and groups; report from the Interdisciplinary Conference in the Behavioral Science Division. N.Y. 1,1960+ 2v.

Phil 5238.140   Kuhlen, Raymond. Psychological studies of human development. N.Y., 1952.

Phil 5238.142   Rasey, Marie I. The nature of being human. Detroit, 1959.

Phil 5238   Psychology - General treatises - Collected authors - cont.

Phil 5238.145   Weinhandl, Ferdinand. Gestalthaftes Sehen...zum hundertjährigen Geburtstag von Christian von Ehrenfels. Darmstadt, 1960.
Phil 5238.150   Ehrhardt, H. Psychiatrie und Gesellschaft. Bern, 1958.
Phil 5238.155   Shipley, T. Classics in psychology. N.Y., 1961.
Phil 5238.160   O'Connor, N. Recent Soviet psychology. N.Y., 1961.
Phil 5238.165   Archivio di Filosofia. Filosofia della alienazione e analisi esistenziale. Padova, 1961.
Phil 5238.170   Marx, Melvin Herman. Psychological theory. N.Y., 1961.
Phil 5238.175   Nelson, Harry. Theoretical foundations of psychology. Princeton, 1959.
Phil 5238.176   New directions in psychology. N.Y., 1962.
Phil 5238.177   Bauer, Raymond A. Some views on Soviet psychology. Washington, 1962.
Phil 5238.178   Novosibirsk. Gosudartvennyi Pedagogicheskii Institut. Voprosy psikhologii. Omsk, 1965.
Phil 5238.180   Katholieke Centrale Vereniging voor Geestelijke Volksgezondheid. Serie geestelijke volksgezondheid. 20-42 6v.
Phil 5238.182   Hommage à Georges Henyer. Paris, 1961.
Phil 5238.184   Psychological studies. The Hague. 1,1961+ 6v.
Phil 5238.185   Psychological studies. Minor series. The Hague. 1,1967+
Phil 5238.186   White, R.W. The study of lives; essays on personality in honour of Henry A. Murray. N.Y., 1963.
Phil 5238.188   Association de Psychologie Scientifique de la Langue Française. Les attitudes; symposium, Bordeaux. Paris, 1961.
Phil 5238.188.10   Association de Psychologie Scientifique de Langue Française. Le comportement, symposium de l'association de psychologie...(Rome, 1967). Paris, 1968.
Phil 5238.189   Hiltmann, H. Dialektik und Dynamik der Person. Köln, 1963.
Phil 5238.190   Herlrich, E. Der Mens als Persönlichkeit und Problem. München, 1963.
Phil 5238.191   Farberow, N.L. Taboo topics. N.Y., 1963.
Phil 5238.192   Henle, Mary. Documents of Gestalt psychology. Berkeley, 1961.
Phil 5238.194   King, R.A. Readings for an introduction to psychology. N.Y., 1961.
Phil 5238.195   Gaskill, H.S. Counterpoint. N.Y., 1963.
Phil 5238.196   Fraisse, Paul. Traite de psychologie expérimentale. Paris, 1963. 9v.
Phil 5238.196.1   Fraisse, Paul. Experimental psychology. N.Y., 1968.
Phil 5238.197   Atkinson, R.C. Studies in mathematical psychology. Stanford, 1964.
Phil 5238.198   Wann, T.W. Behaviorism and phenomenology. Chicago, 1964.
Phil 5238.199   Margarete Eberhardt, zum 18. August, 1961. Hamburg, 1961.
Phil 5238.200   Cohen, J. Readings in psychology. London, 1964.
Phil 5238.201   Abrams, A. Unfinished tasks in the behavioral sciences. Baltimore, 1964.
Phil 5238.202   Mandler, J.M. Thinking. N.Y., 1964.
Phil 5238.203   Harper, Robert J.C. The cognitive processes. Englewood Cliffs, N.J., 1964.
Phil 5238.204   Hernnstein, Richard J. A source book in history of psychology. Cambridge, 1965.
Phil 5238.205   Wolman, Benjamin B. Scientific psychology: principles and approaches. N.Y., 1965.
Phil 5238.206   Frey-Wehrlin, Caspar J. Spectrum Psychologiae, ein Freundesgabe. Zürich, 1965.
Phil 5238.207   Psychológia a nicktoré otázky súčasnosti. Bratislava, 1962.
Phil 5238.208   Banks, Charlotte. Stephanos. London, 1965.
Phil 5238.210   Interamerican Congress of Psychology. 3rd, Austin, Texas, 1955. Psychological approaches to intergroup and international understanding. Austin, 1956.
Phil 5238.210.6   Interamerican Congress of Psychology. 6th, Rio de Janeiro, 1959. Promovido pela Sociedade Interamericana de Psicologia com a cooperação de Associação Brasileira de Psicologia Aplicada. Rio de Janeiro, 1966.
Phil 5238.211   Psychological research in the U.S.S.R. Moscow, 1966.
Phil 5238.211.5   Psikhologicheskie issledovaniia. Tbilisi, 1966.
Phil 5238.212   Transzendenz als Erfahrung: Beitrag und Widerhall. Weilheim, 1966.
Phil 5238.213   Vdruženje Psihologa Jugoslavije. Stanje i perspektive jugoslovenske psihologije. Beograd, 1965.
Phil 5238.215   Matson, Floyd W. Being, becoming and behavior; the psychological sciences. N.Y., 1967.
Phil 5238.220   The reach of mind. N.Y., 1968.
Phil 5238.221   Nauchnaia Sessiia Posviashchennaia 50-Letiui Velikoi Oktiabr'skoi Sotsialisticheskoi Revoliutsii, Sverdlovsk, 1967. Voprosy psikhologii. Sverdlovsk, 1967.
Phil 5238.222   Dialog über den Menschen. Stuttgart, 1968.
Phil 5238.224   Sahakian, William S. History of psychology. Itasca, Ill., 1968.
Phil 5238.226   Cole, Michael. Handbook of contemporary Soviet psychology. N.Y., 1969.
Phil 5238.228   Person als Prozess. Bern, 1968.
Phil 5238.230   Breger, Louis. Clinical-cognitive psychology. Englewood Cliffs, N.J., 1969.
Phil 5238.232   Behavioral and Social Sciences Survey Committe. Psychology. Englewood Cliffs, N.J., 1970.
Phil 5238.234   Pribram, Karl H. Brain and behaviour. Harmondsworth, Middlesex, Eng., 1969. 4v.
Phil 5238.236   Schools of psychology. N.Y., 1969.
Phil 5238.238   El'kin, David G. Konspekt lektsii po psikhologii. v.3. Odessa, 1966.
Phil 5238.240   Festschrift for B.F. Skinner. N.Y., 1970.
Phil 5238.242   Struktur und Dynamik des menschlichen Verhaltens; zum Stand der modernen Psychologie. Stuttgart, 1970.
Phil 5238.244   Hardesty, Francis P. Forderungen an die Psychologie. Bern, 1965.
Phil 5238.246   Psühholoogia ja kaasaeg. Tallinn, 1968.
Phil 5238.248   Husén, Torsten. Psykologisk bredvielläsning. v. 1-2. Stockholm, 1967.

5240 - 5265   Psychology - General treatises - Individual authors (A-Z)

Phil 5240.1   Abercrombie, J. Inquiries...intellectual powers. Edinburgh, 1831.
Phil 5240.1.2   Abercrombie, J. Inquiries...intellectual powers. N.Y., 1832.
Phil 5240.1.3   Abercrombie, J. Inquiries...intellectual powers. Boston, 1835.
Phil 5240.1.4   Abercrombie, J. Inquiries...intellectual powers. N.Y., 1838.
Phil 5240.1.12   Abercrombie, J. The culture and discipline of the mind. 6th ed. Edinburgh, 1837.

Phil 5240 - 5265   Psychology - General treatises - Individual authors (A-Z) - cont.

Phil 5240.2   Ahrens, Heinrich. Cours de psychologie. v.1-2. Paris, 1836-38.
Phil 5240.2.5   Ahrens, Heinrich. Curso de psicología. Madrid, 1873. 2v.
Phil 5240.3   Atkinson H.G. Letters...laws of man's nature. London, 1851.
Phil 5240.3.2   Atkinson, H.G. Letters...laws of man's nature. Boston, 1851.
Phil 5240.4   Arnold, G.F. Psychology applied to legal evidence. Calcutta, 1906.
Phil 5240.5   Abelson, R. Mental fatigue - 1908. Leipzig, 1908.
Phil 5240.5.30   Angell, J.R. Psychology. 2. ed. N.Y., 1905.
Phil 5240.6.2   Angell, J.R. Psychology. 4. ed. N.Y., 1908.
Phil 5240.6.9   Angell, J.R. An introduction to psychology. N.Y., 1918.
Phil 5240.6.15   Angell, J.R. The relations of structural and functional psychology to philosophy. Chicago, 1903.
Phil 5240.7   Anschütz, Georg. Die Intelligenz, eine Einführung in die Hauptatdachenfet. Harz, 1913.
Phil 5240.7.5   Anschütz, Georg. Über die Erforschung der Denkvorgänge. Osterwieck, 1913.
Phil 5240.7.10   Anschütz, Georg. Psychologie. Hamburg, 1953.
Phil 5240.8   Aveling, Francis. On the consciousness of the universal. Thesis. London, 1912.
Phil 5240.9   Pamphlet box. Philosophy. Psychology.
Phil 5240.10   Pamphlet box. Philosophy. Psychology.
Phil 5240.16   Alfonso, N.R. I limiti dell'esperimento in psicologia. Roma, 1905.
Phil 5240.17.2   Aster, Ernst von. Einführung in die Psychologie. 2. Aufl. Leipzig, 1919.
Phil 5240.19   The alternative. London, 1882.
Phil 5240.21   Adumkiewicz, A. Die Eigenkraft der Materie. Wien, 1906.
Phil 5240.22   Atkinson, William W. Your mind and how to use it. Holyoke, Mass., 1911.
Phil 5240.23   Adams, H.F. The ways of the mind. N.Y., 1925.
Phil 5240.24   Aars, K.B.R. Inledning til psychologien. Kristiania, 1898.
Phil 5240.25   Abel, Jacob Friedrich von. Einleitung in die Seelenlehre. Stuttgart, 1786. 2 pam.
Phil 5240.25.5   Abel, Jacob Friedrich von. Erläuterungen wichtiger Gegenstände aus der philosophischen und christlichen Moral. Tübingen, 1790.
Phil 5240.25.10   Abel, Jacob Friedrich von. Versuch über die Seelenstärke. Tübingen, 1804.
Phil 5240.25.15   Abel, Jakob Friedrich von. Rede über das Genie. Marbach, 1955.
Phil 5240.25.20   Abel, Jacob Friedrich von. Versuch über die Natur der speculativen Vernunft zur Prüfung des Kantischen Systems. Frankfurt, 1787.
Phil 5240.26   Apfelbach, Hans. Das Denkgefühe, eine Untersuchung über den emotionalen Charakter der Denkprozesse. Wien, 1922.
Phil 5240.27   Anthony, R. Réflexions d'un biologiste sur l'objet...de la psychologie. Paris, 1925.
Phil 5240.28   Ahlenstiehl, H. Über die Stellung der Psychologie im Stammbaum der Wissenschaften. Berlin, 1923.
Phil 5240.29   Aliotta, A. La misura in psicologia sperimentale. Firenze, 1905.
Phil 5240.30.2   Mairet, Philippe. A.B.C. of Adler's psychology. N.Y., 1929.
Phil 5240.31   Alrutz, S.G.L.R. Om själslifvets studium på fysiologisk grundval. Stockholm, 1899.
Phil 5240.32   Armstrong-Jones, K. The growth of the mind. Edinburgh, 1929?
Phil 5240.33   Alexander, S. Foundations and sketch plan of a conational psychology. Cambridge, Eng., 1911.
Phil 5240.34   Allen, A.H.B. The self in psychology. London, 1935.
Phil 5240.35   Anastasi, Anne. Differential psychology. N.Y., 1937.
Phil 5240.35.2   Anastasi, Anne. Differential psychology. N.Y., 1949.
Phil 5240.35.3   Anastasi, Anne. Differential psychology. N.Y., 1956.
Phil 5240.36.5   Adler, M.J. What man has made of man. N.Y., 1938.
Phil 5240.37   Anderson, L.F. Psychology and the cosmic order. n.p., 1939.
Phil 5240.39   Agramonte y Richardo, R. Compendio de psicología. Habana, 1939.
Phil 5240.39.15   Agramonte y Richardo, R. Tratado de psicología general. v.1-2, pt.1. 4a ed. Habana, 1940.
Phil 5240.40   Anile, Antonio. La salute del pensiero "I libro d'oro". Bari, 1922.
Phil 5240.41   Adams, John. Everyman's psychology. 1. ed. Garden City, 1929.
Phil 5240.42.5   Ananiew, B.G. Hamptaufgaben der sowjetischen psychologischen Wissenschaft. Berlin, 1952.
Phil 5240.43   Andrews, T.G. Methods of psychology. N.Y., 1948.
Phil 5240.44   Aeppli, E. Psychologie des Bewussten und Unbewussten. Zürich, 1947.
Phil 5240.45   Adcock, C.J. Factorial analysis for non-mathematicians. Carlton, 1954.
Phil 5240.46A   Allport, Gordon Willard. Becoming. New Haven, 1955.
Phil 5240.46B   Allport, Gordon Willard. Becoming. New Haven, 1955.
Phil 5240.46.2   Allport, Gordon Willard. Becoming. New Haven, 1964.
Phil 5240.46.5.2   Allport, Gordon Willard. Becoming. New Haven, 1967.
Phil 5240.47   Aktuelle Probleme der Gestalttheorie. Bern, 1954.
Phil 5240.49   Adrian, E.D.A. Factors in mental evolution. Oxford, 1960.
Phil 5240.51   Abella Gibert, D. El nostre caracter. Barcelona, 1961.
Phil 5240.52   American Psychological Association. Project on Scientific Information. Exchange in Psychology. Reports. Washington, 1963- 3v.
Phil 5240.53   Anrich, Ernst. Moderne Physik und Tiefenpsychologie. Stuttgart, 1963.
Phil 5240.54   Akademiia Nauk SSSR. Institut Filosofii. Osnovnye napravleniia issledovanii psikhologii myshleniia v kapitalisticheskikh stranakh. Moskva, 1966.
Phil 5240.55   Ariete, Silvano. The intrapsycic self. N.Y., 1967.
Phil 5240.58.2   Andreas, Burton G. Experimental psychology. 2. ed. N.Y., 1972.
Phil 5240.60   Analysis of behavioral change. N.Y., 1968.
Phil 5240.65   Alvarez Villar, Alfonso. Psicología de los pueblos primitivos. Madrid, 1969.
Phil 5240.70   Evans, Richard Isadore. Gordon Allport. 1. ed. N.Y., 1970[1971]
Phil 5241.1   Bailey, S. Letters...philosophy...human mind. London, 1855.
Phil 5241.1.2   Bailey, S. Letters...philosophy...human mind. London, 1858.
Phil 5241.2   Bain, A. Mental science. N.Y., 1868.
Phil 5241.2.2   Bain, A. Mental science. N.Y., 1873.
Phil 5241.2.5   Bain, A. Mental science. N.Y., 1880.
Phil 5241.2.10   Bain, A. The emotions and the will. London, 1865.

Classified Listing

Phil 5240 - 5265   Psychology - General treatises - Individual authors (A-Z) - cont.

Phil 5241.2.10.15	Bain, A. The emotions and the will. 3. ed. N.Y., 1875.
Phil 5241.2.13	Bain, A. The emotions and the will. N.Y., 1886.
Phil 5241.2.15	Bain, A. Le émotions et la volonté. 3e éd. Paris, 1885.
Phil 5241.2.20	Bain, A. The senses and the intellect. London, 1855.
Phil 5241.2.21	Bain, S. The senses and the intellect. 2. ed. London, 1864.
Phil 5241.2.21.5	Bain, A. The senses and the intellect. 3. ed. N.Y., 1872.
Phil 5241.2.22	Bain, A. The senses and the intellect. N.Y., 1879.
Phil 5241.2.27	Bain, A. The senses and the intellect. 4th ed. N.Y., 1894.
Phil 5241.3	Baldwin, J.M. Hand book of psychology. Senses and intellect. 1. ed. N.Y., 1889.
Phil 5241.3.2	Baldwin, J.M. Handbook of psychology...feeling and will. N.Y., 1891.
Phil 5241.3.3	Baldwin, J.M. Handbook of psychology. Senses and intellect. N.Y., 1890.
Phil 5241.3.5A	Baldwin, J.M. Social and ethical interpretations. Mental development. N.Y., 1897.
Phil 5241.3.5B	Baldwin, J.M. Social and ethical interpretations. Mental development. N.Y., 1897.
Phil 5241.3.6	Baldwin, J.M. Social and ethical interpretations. Mental development. N.Y., 1902.
Phil 5241.3.6.10	Baldwin, J.M. Social and ethical interpretations. Mental development. 5. ed. N.Y., 1913.
Phil 5241.3.8	Baldwin, J.M. Mental development. 2. ed. N.Y., 1897.
Phil 5241.3.9	Baldwin, J.M. Interpretation sociale et morale des principes du développement mental. Paris, 1899.
Phil 5241.3.15	Baldwin, J.M. Elements of psychology. N.Y., 1893.
Phil 5241.3.24	Baldwin, J.M. The story of the mind. N.Y., 1901.
Phil 5241.3.28	Baldwin, J.M. The story of the mind. N.Y., 1898.
Phil 5241.3.30A	Baldwin, J.M. The individual and society. Boston, 1911.
Phil 5241.3.30B	Baldwin, J.M. The individual and society. Boston, 1911.
Phil 5241.4	Ballantyne, J. An examination of the human mind. Edinburgh, 1828.
Phil 5241.5	Ballauff, L. Die Elemente der Psychologie. Cöthen, 1877.
Phil 5241.5.3	Ballauf, L. Die Grundlehren der Psychologie und ihre Anwendung auf die Lehre. Cöthen, 1890.
Phil 5241.6	Barlow, J. Connection. Physiology. Intellectual philosophy. 2. ed. Philadelphia, 1846.
Phil 5241.7	Bascom, J. The principles of psychology. N.Y., 1869.
Phil 5241.7.2	Bascom, J. The science of mind. N.Y., 1881.
Phil 5241.9	Bautain, L.E.M. Psychologie experimentale. Strasbourg, 1839. 2v.
Phil 5241.9.5	Bautain, L.E.M. L'esprit humain et ses facultés. Paris, 1859. 2v.
Phil 5241.10	Beasley, F. A search of truth. Philadelphia, 1822.
Phil 5241.12	Bishop, D. An introduction...study...mind. London, 1849.
Phil 5241.12.5	Bishop, D. An introduction...study...mind. London, 1857.
Phil 5241.14	Bonstetten, C.V. de. Etudes de l'homme. Genève, 1821. 2v.
Phil 5241.15	Bowne, B.P. Introduction to psychological theory. N.Y., 1887.
Phil 5241.16	Brodie, B.C. Psychological inquiries. London, 1854.
Phil 5241.16.2	Brodie, B.C. Psychological inquiries. London, 1856.
Phil 5241.16.4	Brodie, B.C. Psychological inquiries. London, 1862.
Phil 5241.17.5	Brentano, Franz. Psychologie vom empirischen Standpunkt. Leipzig, 1924-25. 2v.
Phil 5241.17.13A	Brentano, Franz. Von der Klassifikation der psychischen Phänomene. Leipzig, 1911.
Phil 5241.17.13B	Brentano, Franz. Von der Klassifikation der psychischen Phänomene. Leipzig, 1911.
Phil 5241.17.17	Brentano, Franz. La classificazione delle attivitapsichiche. Lanciano, 1913.
Phil 5241.17.20	Brentano, Franz. Vom sinnlichen und noetischen Bewusstsein. Leipzig, 1928.
Phil 5241.17.23	Brentano, Franz. Psychologie du point de vue empirique. Paris, 1944.
Phil 5241.17.25A	Brentano, Franz. Psychologie vom empirischen Standpunkt. Hamburg, 1955.
Phil 5241.17.25B	Brentano, Franz. Psychologie vom empirischen Standpunkt. Hamburg, 1955.
Phil 5241.19	Buccola, G. La legge del tempo. Milano, 1883.
Phil 5241.20	Buchanan, Joseph. The philosophy of human nature. Richmond, 1812.
Phil 5241.20.2	Buchanan, Joseph. The philosophy of human nature. Weston, Mass., 1970.
Phil 5241.21	Bouillier, F.C. Études familières de psychologie et de morale. Paris, 1884.
Phil 5241.21.5	Bouillier, F.C. Nouvelles études familières de psychologie et de morale. Paris, 1887.
Phil 5241.22	Brooks, H.J. The elements of mind. London, 1902.
Phil 5241.23	Bawden, H.H. A syllabus of psychology. Poughkeepsie, N.Y., 1902.
Phil 5241.24.2A	Bosanquet, B. Psychology of the moral self. London, 1904.
Phil 5241.24.2B	Bosanquet, B. Psychology of the moral self. London, 1904.
Phil 5241.24.5A	Bosanquet, B. Three chapters on the nature of the mind. London, 1923.
Phil 5241.24.5B	Bosanquet, B. Three chapters on the nature of the mind. London, 1923.
Phil 5241.25	Brackenbury, L. Primer of psychology. London, 1907.
Phil 5241.26	Boucher, J. Psychologie. Paris, 1908.
Phil 5241.27	Berger, H. Über die körperlichen Ausserungen psychologischen Zuständen. Jena, 1904. 2v.
Phil 5241.28	Brown, W. Essentials of mental measurement. Cambridge, 1911.
Phil 5241.28.2A	Brown, W. Essentials of mental measurement. 2. ed. Cambridge, Eng., 1921.
Phil 5241.28.2B	Brown, W. Essentials of mental measurement. 2. ed. Cambridge, Eng., 1921.
Phil 5241.28.3	Brown, W. Essentials of mental measurement. 3. ed. Cambridge, Eng., 1925.
Phil 5241.28.4	Brown, W. Essentials of mental measurement. 4. ed. Cambridge, Eng., 1940.
Phil 5241.28.7	Brown, W. Psychology and the sciences. London, 1924.
Phil 5241.28.10	Brown, W. Psychology and psychotherapy. London, 1922.
Phil 5241.28.13	Brown, W. Mind and personality. London, 1926.
Phil 5241.28.17	Brown, W. Science and personality. New Haven, 1929.
Phil 5241.28.20	Brown, W. Personality and religion. London, 1946.
Phil 5241.28.25	Brown, W. College psychology. N.Y., 1950.
Phil 5241.30	Bekhterev, V. La psychologie objective. Paris, 1913.
Phil 5241.30.15	Bekhterev, V. General principles of human reflexology. London, 1933.
Phil 5241.31	Bramshausen, N. Einführung in die experimentelle Psychologie. Leipzig, 1915.
Phil 5241.32	Ballard, J.H. Some phases of the psychology of puzzle learning. N.Y., 1915.
Phil 5241.33	Buck, J.D. Constructive psychology. Chicago, 1908.

Phil 5240 - 5265   Psychology - General treatises - Individual authors (A-Z) - cont.

Phil 5241.34	Bilharz, A. Neue Denklehre. Wiesbaden, 1908.
Phil 5241.35.2	Breese, B.B. Psychology. N.Y., 1921.
Phil 5241.37	Benedikt, M. Die Seelenkunde des Menschen als eine Erfahrungswissenschaft. Leipzig, 1895.
Phil 5241.38	Buell, C.S. Essentials of psychology. Boston, 1898.
Phil 5241.39	Bierens de Haan, P. Hoofdlijnen eener psychologie met metafysischen grondslag. Amsterdam, 1898.
Phil 5241.40	Bocci, Balduino. I primi teoremi di psicologia. Siena, 1915.
Phil 5241.41	Batson, W.H. Acquisition of skill. Princeton, 1916.
Phil 5241.42.5	Baudin, E. Cours de psychologie. 5e éd. Paris, 1927.
Phil 5241.43	Benigni, Edvige. Elementi di psicologia sperimentale positiva. Torino, 1900.
Phil 5241.44	Bunge, Carlos O. Estudios filosóficos. Buenos Aires, 1919.
Phil 5241.44.5	Bunge, Carlos O. Principes de psychologie. Paris, 1903.
Phil 5241.45	Baratono, Adelchi. I fatti psichici elementari. Torino, 1900.
Phil 5241.45.5	Baratono, Adelchi. Fondamenti di psicologia sperimentale. Torino, 1906.
Phil 5241.46	Billia, Lorenzo M. Has the psychological laboratory proved helpful. Chicago, 1909.
Phil 5241.47	Betz, W. Psychologie des Denkens. Leipzig, 1918.
Phil 5241.48	Biervliet, Jules Jean van. Eléments de psychologie humaine. Gand, 1895.
Phil 5241.48.5	Biervliet, Jules Jean van. La psychologie quantitative. Gand, 1907.
Phil 5241.49	Bleibtreu, K. Zur Psychologie der Zukunft. Leipzig, 1890.
Phil 5241.50	Briffault, Robert. Psyche's lamp. London, 1921.
Phil 5241.51	Bumke, Oswald. Psychologische Vorlesungen für Hörer aller Fakultälen. Wiesbaden, 1919.
Phil 5241.51.2	Bumke, Oswald. Psychologische Vorlesungen für Hörer aller Fakultälen. 2. Aufl. München, 1923.
Phil 5241.52	Brierley, S.S. (Mrs.). An introduction to psychology. London, 1921.
Phil 5241.53	Brunswig, A. Einführung in die Psychologie. München, 1921.
Phil 5241.54	Binet, Alfred. L'étude expérimentale de l'intelligence. Photoreproduction. Paris, 1922.
Phil 5241.54.5	Binet, Alfred. The experimental psychology of Alfred Binet; selected papers. N.Y., 1969.
Phil 5241.55.10	Beck, Joseph. Grundriss der empirischen Psychologie und Logik. 7. Aufl. Stuttgart, 1887.
Phil 5241.55.21	Fürst, Joseph. Grundriss der empirischen Psychologie und Logik. 21e Aufl. Stuttgart, 1928.
Phil 5241.57	Baudouin, C. The power within us. N.Y., 1923.
Phil 5241.57.10	Baudouin, C. Makten i vår själ. Stockholm, 1925.
Phil 5241.58	Bennett, H.E. Psychology and self-development. Boston, 1923.
Phil 5241.59	Bentley, I.M. The field of psychology. N.Y., 1924.
Phil 5241.59.5	Bentley, I.M. The psychology of mental arrangement. Worcester, 1902.
Phil 5241.59.15	Bentley, I.M. The new field of psychology. N.Y., 1934.
Phil 5241.60	Bjerre, Poul. Studier i själstäkekonst. Stockholm 1914.
Phil 5241.61	Baumgartner, M. Grundriss der Psychologie. Dillingen, 1906.
Phil 5241.63	Brough, J. The study of mental science. London, 1903.
Phil 5241.64	Binswanger, L. Einführung in die Probleme der allgemeinen Psychologie. Berlin, 1922.
Phil 5241.65	Bertrand-Barraud, D. Les valeurs affectives et l'exercice discursif de la pensée. Paris, 1924.
Phil 5241.65.5	Bertrand-Barraud, D. Les valeurs affectives et l'exercice discursif de la pensée. Thèse. Paris, 1924.
Phil 5241.65.10	Bertrand-Barraud, D. De la nature affective de la conscience. Paris, 1927.
Phil 5241.66	Broad, C.D. The mind and its place in nature. London, 1925.
Phil 5241.66.5	Broad, C.D. The mind and its place. N.Y., 1927.
Phil 5241.67	Badareu, D. Essai sur la pensée. Thèse. Paris, 1924.
Phil 5241.68	Bourdon, B. L'intelligence. Paris, 1926.
Phil 5241.69	Bonsfield, Paul. The mind and its mechanism. London, 1927.
Phil 5241.70	Bühler, Karl. Handbuch der Psychologie. Jena, 1922.
Phil 5241.70.5	Bühler, Karl. Das Gestaltprinzip im Leben des Menschen und der Tiere. Bern, 1960.
Phil 5241.71	Britz, Carl August. Eine theoretische und experimentelle Untersuchung über den psychologischen der Klarheit. Diss. Saarlouis, 1913.
Phil 5241.72	Berman, Louis. The religion called behaviorism. N.Y., 1927.
Phil 5241.73	Brugmans, H.J. Psychologische methoden en begrippen. Haarlem, 1922.
Phil 5241.74	Brockdorff, Cay L.G.C. Die philosophischen Anfangsgründe der Psychologie. Heldesheim, 1905.
Phil 5241.75	Burloud, Albert. La pensée d'après les recherches experimentales de H.J. Watt, de Messer et de Bühler. Paris, 1927.
Phil 5241.75.2	Burloud, Albert. La pensée d'après les recherches experimentales de H.J. Watt, de Messer et de Bühler. Thèse. Paris, 1927.
Phil 5241.75.12	Burloud, Albert. La pensée conceptuelle. Thèse. Paris, 1927.
Phil 5241.75.15	Burloud, Albert. Principles d'une psychologie des tendances. Paris, 1938.
Phil 5241.75.80	La Garanderie, Antoine de. Le dynamisme des structures inconscientes dans la psychologie d'Albert Burloud. Louvain, 1969.
Phil 5241.76	Baar, Jacob. Psychology. N.Y., 1928.
Phil 5241.77	Baade, Walter. Allgermeine Einfuhrung in das Gesamtgebiet der Psychologie. Leipzig, 1928.
Phil 5241.78	Breitwieser, Joseph V. Psychological experiments. Colorado Springs, 1914.
Phil 5241.79	Bridges, J.W. Psychology, normal and abnormal. N.Y., 1930.
Phil 5241.79.10	Bridges, J.W. Personality, many in one. Boston, 1932.
Phil 5241.80	Bernhard, E.A. Philosophische und naturwissenschaftliche Grundlagen der Psychologie. Berlin, 1930.
Phil 5241.81	Bailey, A.A. (Mrs.). The soul and its mechanism (the problem of psychology). N.Y., 1930.
Phil 5241.82	Badley, John H. The will to live. London, 1931.
Phil 5241.83	Barthel, Ernst. Vorstellung und Denken. München, 1931.
Phil 5241.84	Bleuler, Eugen. Naturgeschichte der Seele und ihres Bewusst-Werdens. Berlin, 1921.
Phil 5241.85	Barbado, M. Introducción a la psicologia experimental. Madrid, 1928.
Phil 5241.86.5	Barrett, J.F. Elements of psychology. 2. ed. Milwaukee, 1931.

Phil 5240 - 5265 Psychology - General treatises - Individual authors (A-Z) - cont.

Phil 5241.87   Bingham, Walter V. Psychology today. Chicago, 1932.
Phil 5241.88   Bühler, Charlotte M. Der menschliche Lebenslauf als psychologisches Problem. Leipzig, 1933.
Phil 5241.88.3   Bühler, Charlotte M. Psychologie im Leben unserer Zeit. München, 1962.
Phil 5241.88.3.5   Bühler, Charlotte M. Psychology for contemporary living. 1st American ed. N.Y., 1969.
Phil 5241.88.5   Bühler, Charlotte M. Der menschliche Lebenslauf als psychologisches Problem. 2. Aufl. Göttingen, 1959.
Phil 5241.88.10   Bühler, Charlotte M. Psychologische Probleme unserer Zeit. Stuttgart, 1968.
Phil 5241.89   Butler, J.R. Human nature. N.Y., 1933.
Phil 5241.89.10   Butler, J.R. Human psychology. N.Y., 1936.
Phil 5241.90   Blondel, M. La pensée. Paris, 1934. 2v.
Phil 5241.90.5   Blondel, M. La pensée. 4. éd. Paris, 1948.
Phil 5241.91   Burridge, William. A new physiological psychology. London, 1933.
Phil 5241.92A   Boring, E.G. Psychology; a factual textbook. N.Y., 1935.
Phil 5241.92B   Boring, E.G. Psychology; a factual textbook. N.Y., 1935.
Phil 5241.92.10   Boring, E.G. The relation of the attributes of sensation to the dimensions of the stimulus. Baltimore, 1935. 3 pam.
Phil 5241.92.15   Wedell, C.H. Handbook in psychology, to accompany Boring's Psychology. N.Y., 1936.
Phil 5241.92.20   Boring, E.G. History, psychology and science. N.Y., 1963.
Phil 5241.93   Bentley, A.F. Behavior, knowledge, fact. Bloomington, 1935.
Phil 5241.94   Blanché, Robert. La notion de fait psychique. Thèse. Paris, 1934.
Phil 5241.95   Bone, H. Une étude du préjugé au moyen des tests. Thèse. Paris, 1934.
Phil 5241.96   Bergström, J.A. An experimental study of some of the conditions of mental activity. Worcester, 1894.
Phil 5241.97   Burrow, Trigant. Altering frames of reference in the sphere of human behavior. N.Y., 1937.
Phil 5241.97.5   Burrow, Trigant. Science and man's behavior. N.Y., 1953.
Phil 5241.97.10   Burrow, Trigant. The neurosis of man. London, 1949.
Phil 5241.97.15   Burrow, Trigant. A search for man's sanity. N.Y., 1958.
Phil 5241.98   Boynton, P.L. Intelligence, its manifestations and measurement. N.Y., 1933.
Phil 5241.99   Brennan, R.E. General psychology. N.Y., 1932.
Phil 5241.100   Billings, E.G. Handbook of elementary psychology. N.Y., 1939.
Phil 5241.101   Baker, H.J. The art of understanding. Boston, 1940.
Phil 5241.102   Beck, M. Psychologie. Leiden, 1938.
Phil 5241.103   Bills, A.G. General experimental psychology. N.Y., 1934.
Phil 5241.104   Brandt, F. Psykoligi. v.1-2. København, 1934-40.
Phil 5241.105   Boris, J.S. Anselme. Le bonheur s'apprend. 2. éd. Montreal, 1941.
Phil 5241.106   Bernal del Riesgo, A. Iniciación a la psicologia. v.1-2. La Habana, 1936.
Phil 5241.107   Barboza, Enrique. Psicologia. Lima, 1940.
Phil 5241.108   Bittle, Alestine N.C. The whole man. Milwaukee, 1945.
Phil 5241.109   Blackburn, J.M. Psychology and the social pattern. London, 1945.
Phil 5241.110   Barnard, Chester Irving. Mind in everyday affairs. Princeton, 1936.
Phil 5241.111   Burt, Cyril. Intelligence and fertility. London, 1947.
Phil 5241.112   Boring, E.G. Foundations of psychology. N.Y., 1948.
Phil 5241.113   Benda, Julien. Du style d'idées. Paris, 1948.
Phil 5241.114   Bauer, R.A. The new man in Soviet psychology. Cambridge, Mass., 1952.
Phil 5241.115   Barakin, E.W. Quantitative theory on human behavior. Santa Monica, 1952.
Phil 5241.116   Barrell, Joseph. A philosophical study of the human mind. N.Y., 1954.
Phil 5241.117   Brill, Albert. Fundamental fundamentals. N.Y., 1955.
Phil 5241.117.5   Brill, Albert. Ascendant psychology. Guilford, Conn., 1959.
Phil 5241.118   Bruner, J.S. A study of thinking. N.Y., 1956.
Phil 5241.119   Balint, Michael. Problems of human pleasure and behavior. London, 1957.
Phil 5241.120   Brecht, F.J. Vom menschlichen Denken. Heidelberg, 1955.
Phil 5241.122   Brrermann, Ernst. Allgemeine Psychologie. Paderborn, 1958.
Phil 5241.126   Banterwek, Heinrich. Charakter als Naturgesetz. Ulm, 1959.
Phil 5241.128   Baker, Lawrence. General experimental psychology. N.Y., 1960.
Phil 5241.130   Boehme, Edwin. Das Gedankenleben und seine Beherrschung. Cöln, 1959.
Phil 5241.135   Bulyne, D.E. Conflict. N.Y., 1960.
Phil 5241.140   Birnbaum, W. Organisches Denken. Tübingen, 1960.
Phil 5241.145   Berg, Jan Hendrik van den. The changing nature of man. 1. ed. N.Y., 1961.
Phil 5241.145.5.2   Berg, Jan Hendrik van den. De dingen. 2. druk. Nijkerk, 1966.
Phil 5241.150   Broadlunt, Donald Eric. Behaviour. 1. ed. N.Y., 1961.
Phil 5241.155   Berg, Charles. Mankind. London, 1962.
Phil 5241.160   Buytendijk, F.J.J. Academische redeväringen. Utrecht, 1961.
Phil 5241.165   Bachrach, Arthur. Experimental foundations of clinical psychology. N.Y., 1962.
Phil 5241.166   Bijkerk, R.J. Psycho-logica. Amsterdam, 1962.
Phil 5241.167   Brain, Walter. Science and man. London, 1966.
Phil 5241.170   Bertalanffy, Ludwig von. Robots, men, and minds; psychology in the modern world. N.Y., 1967.
Phil 5241.172   Bowlby, John. Attachment and loss. London, 1969.
Phil 5241.174   Becker, Ernest. Angel in armor; a post Freudian perspective on the nature of man. N.Y., 1969.
Phil 5241.178   Baeumker, Clemens. Anschauung und Denken. Paderborn, 1913.
Phil 5241.180   Berdelle, Philipp. Kleine Theorie des praktischen Denkens. Mainz, 1969.
Phil 5241.182   Berg, Jan Hendrik van den. De zuilen van het Panthéon en andere studies. Nijkerk, 1969.
Phil 5241.184.80   Dummer, Ethel Sturges. Mary Everest Boole; a pioneer student of the unconscious. n.p., 19- ?
Phil 5241.186   Biasutti, Bruno. Critica della società competitiva. Roma, 1968.
Phil 5241.188   Biran, Sigmund. Die ausserpsychologischen Voraussetzungen der Tiefenpsychologie. München, 1966.
Phil 5242.1   Carus, C.G. Vorlesungen über Psychologie. Leipzig, 1831.
Phil 5242.1.5   Carus, C.G. Psychologie zur Entwicklungsgeschichte der Seele. Pforzheim, 1846.
Phil 5242.2   Cesca, G. Le teorie nativistiche e genetiche della localizzazione spaziale. Verona, 1883.

Phil 5240 - 5265 Psychology - General treatises - Individual authors (A-Z) - cont.

Phil 5242.2.5   Cesca, G. L'attività psichica. Messina, 1904.
Phil 5242.3   Chardel, C. Essai de psychologie. Paris, 1838.
Phil 5242.4   Champlin, J.T. Text-book in intellectual philosophy. Boston, 1860.
Phil 5242.5   Collineau, J.C. Analyse physiologique. Paris, 1843-44. 2 pam.
Phil 5242.6   Collins, T.W. Humanics. N.Y., 1860.
Phil 5242.7   Colsenet, E. La vie inconsciente. Paris, 1880.
Phil 5242.8   Cornelius, H. Psychologie. Leipzig, 1897.
Phil 5242.9   Claparède, E. Rapport sur la terminologie psychologique. Genève, 1909.
Phil 5242.10   Costa, P. Del modo di comporre l'idee. Firenze, 1837. 2 pam.
Phil 5242.11   Cox, E.W. The mechanism of man. London, 1876. 2v.
Phil 5242.12   Cyples, W. An inquiry into the process of human experience. London, 1880.
Phil 5242.13   Calkins, M.W. An introduction to psychology. N.Y., 1901.
Phil 5242.13.5   Calkins, M.W. Der doppelte Standpunkt...Psychologie. Leipzig, 1905.
Phil 5242.13.9   Calkins, M.W. A first book in psychology. N.Y., 1910.
Phil 5242.13.10   Calkins, M.W. A first book in psychology. 2. ed. N.Y., 1911.
Phil 5242.13.12   Calkins, M.W. A first book in psychology. 4. ed. N.Y., 1914.
Phil 5242.14.12   Crane, A.M. Right and wrong thinking. Boston, 1914.
Phil 5242.15   Clark University, Worcester, Mass. Lectures and addresses before departments of psychology and pedagogy...20 anniversary. Worcester, 1910.
Phil 5242.16   Campbell, P.A. The game of mind. N.Y., 1913.
Phil 5242.17   Clark, William. The formation of opinion. Cambridge, 1888?
Htn   Phil 5242.18.2*   Charleton, Walter. Two discourses. 2. ed. London, 1675.
Phil 5242.19   Cohn, Max. Uber das Denken. Berlin, 1910.
Phil 5242.20   Cardols, Joseph. Éléments de psychologie. Namur, 1890.
Phil 5242.21   Campion, George G. Elements in thought and emotion. London, 1923.
Phil 5242.22   Cuvillier, Armand. ABC de psychologie. Paris, 1923.
Phil 5242.23   Pamphlet box. Psychology. Cason, Hulsey.
Phil 5242.24   Crüger, J. Grundritz der Psychologie. 2. Aufl. Leipzig, 1902.
Phil 5242.25   Cartault, A. L'intellectuel. Paris, 1914.
Phil 5242.26   Cros, A. Les fonctions supérieures du système nerveux. Paris, 1874.
Phil 5242.27   Choisnard, P. L'éducation psychologique à propos de la grande guerre. Paris, 1920.
Phil 5242.28   Cutten, George. Mind; its origin and goal. New Haven, 1925.
Phil 5242.29   Cunningham, G.W. Five lectures on the problem of mind. Austin, 1925.
Phil 5242.30   Collins, Mary. Experimental psychology. London, 1926.
Phil 5242.30.5   Collins, Mary. A first laboratory guide in psychology. London, 1926.
Phil 5242.30.7   Collins, Mary. A first laboratory guide in psychology. London, 1926.
Phil 5242.31   Challaye, F. Psychologie et métaphysique. Paris, 1925.
Phil 5242.32   Carlill, H.F. Socrates, or The emancipation of mankind. London, 1927.
Phil 5242.33   Coleman, L.R. Psychology; a simplification. N.Y., 1927.
Phil 5242.34   Cramaussel, E. Psychologie expérimentale. Paris, 1925.
Phil 5242.35   Carpenter, Edward. L'arte della creazione. Roma, 1909.
Phil 5242.35.10   Carpenter, Edward. The art of creation. London, 1904.
Phil 5242.36   Chavigny, P. L'esprit de contradiction. Paris, 1927.
Phil 5242.37   Claremont, C.A. Intelligence, and mental growth. N.Y., 1928.
Phil 5242.38   Cresson, André. Les réactions intellectuelles élémentaires. Paris, 1922.
Phil 5242.39   Cole, Lawrence W. Factors of human psychology. Boulder, 1926.
Phil 5242.39.4   Cole, Lawrence W. Factors of human psychology. Boulder, 1930[1935]
Phil 5242.40   Crawley, Sumner Lee. Syllabus for the first course in experimental psychology. N.Y., 1930.
Phil 5242.41   Calabresi, R. La determinazione del presente psichico. Firenze, 1930.
Phil 5242.42   Chircoulesco, D. Essai sur les principes d'une psychologie évolutive. Bucarest, 1929.
Phil 5242.43   Clergué, G. Essai de psychologie critique sur la nature première. Thèse. Paris, 1930.
Phil 5242.44   Claparède, Édouard. Causeries psychologiques. Genève, 1933.
Phil 5242.44.5   Claparède, Édouard. Causeries psychologiques. Ser. 2. Genève, 1935.
Phil 5242.45   Chiavacci, G. Saggio sulla natura dell'uomo. Firenze, 1936.
Phil 5242.46   Cattell, R.B. General psychology. Cambridge, Mass., 1941.
Phil 5242.46.5   Cattell, R.B. Personality and social psychology. San Diego, 1964.
Phil 5242.47   Clarke, Edwin L. The art of straight thinking. N.Y., 1932.
Phil 5242.48   Clarke, Edwin L. The art of straight thinking. N.Y., 1929.
Phil 5242.50   Carlsson, N.G. Dimensions of behaviour. Lund, 1949.
Phil 5242.51   Clawson, J. Psychology in action. N.Y., 1946.
Phil 5242.52   Cantrie, H. The "why" of man's experience. N.Y., 1950.
Phil 5242.53   Carus, K.G. Vorlesungen über Psychologie. Erlerbach, 193-?
Phil 5242.53.2   Carus, K.G. Vorlesungen über Psychologie. Darmstadt, 1958.
Phil 5242.54   Château, J. Psychologie et métaphysique. Paris, 1949.
Phil 5242.55   Carmichael, L. The making of modern mind. Houston, 1956.
Phil 5242.55.5   Carmichael, L. Basic psychology. N.Y., 1957.
Phil 5242.56   Cohen, John. Humanistic psychology. London, 1958.
Phil 5242.56.5   Cohen, John. Homs psychologicus. London, 1970.
Phil 5242.58   Coleman, J.C. Personality dynamics and effective behavior. Chicago, 1960.
Phil 5242.60   Candland, D.K. Exploring behavior. 1. ed. N.Y., 1961.
Phil 5242.62   Conklin, Edmund Smith. Introductory psychology for students of education. N.Y., 1939.
Phil 5242.64   Cooley, William. Multivariate procedures for the behavioral sciences. N.Y., 1962.
Phil 5242.65   Construction of a simulation process for initial psychiatric interviewing. Santa Monica, 1964.
Phil 5242.66   Charakchiev, Asen. Deistvenostta na misleneto. Sofiia, 1961.
Phil 5242.67   Cruchon, Georges E. Dynamic psychology. N.Y., 1965.
Phil 5242.70   Curi, Umberto. Il problema dell'unità del sapere nel comportamentismo. Padova, 1967.

Phil 5240 - 5265   Psychology - General treatises - Individual authors (A-Z) - cont.

Phil 5243.1   Damiron, J.P. Cours de philosophie. Paris, 1837. 2v.
Phil 5243.2   Davies, J. An estimate of the human mind. London, 1828. 2v.
Phil 5243.3   Day, H.N. Elements of psychology. N.Y., 1876.
Phil 5243.4   Delaperche, H. Essai de philosophie analytique. Paris, 1872.
Phil 5243.5   Delboeuf, J.R.L. Examen critique de la loi psychophysique. Paris, 1883.
Phil 5243.5.5   Delboeuf, J.R.L. La psychologie. Paris, 1876.
Phil 5243.5.10   Delboeuf, J.R.L. Étude psychophysique. Belgium, 1873.
Phil 5243.5.50   Delgrado, Honario. El tiempo y la vida animica normal. Lima, 1944.
Phil 5243.6   Despine, P. Psychologie naturelle. Paris, 1868. 3v.
Phil 5243.7   Dewey, John. Psychology. N.Y., 1887.
Phil 5243.7.2   Dewey, John. Psychology. N.Y., 1889.
NEDL Phil 5243.7.3   Dewey, John. Psychology. 3d ed. N.Y., 1896.
Phil 5243.7.16   Dewey, John. Psychology and social practice. Chicago, 1909.
Phil 5243.8   Dittes, F. Lehrbuch der Psychology. Wien, 1873.
Phil 5243.9   Irbal, M. Lehrbuch der empirischen Psychologie. Wien, 1885.
Phil 5243.10   Drobisch, M.W. Empirische Psychologie. Leipzig, 1842.
Phil 5243.10.1   Drobisch, M.W. Empirische Psychologie. 2e Aufl. Hamburg, 1898.
Phil 5243.10.2   Drobisch, M.W. Erste Grundlehren der mathematischen Psychologie. Leipzig, 1850.
Phil 5243.12   Durand, M.J.P. Essais de physiologie philosophique. Paris, 1866.
Phil 5243.13   Dubray, C.A. The theory of psychical dispositions. Washington, 1905.
Phil 5243.14   Dwelshauvers, George. La synthèse mentale. Paris, 1908.
Phil 5243.14.9   Dwelshauvers, George. L'étude de la pensée. Paris, 1934.
Phil 5243.15   Dunlap, K. A system of psychology. N.Y., 1912.
Phil 5243.15.5   Dunlap, K. The elements of scientific psychology. St. Louis, 1922.
Phil 5243.15.7   Dunlap, K. Elements of psychology. St. Louis, 1936.
Phil 5243.15.9   Dunlap, K. Old and new viewpoints in psychology. St. Louis, 1925.
Phil 5243.15.20   Dunlap, K. Concerning fluctuating and inaudible sounds. n.p., 1908-1916. 15 pam.
Phil 5243.16   Dromard, Gabriel. Les mensonges de la vie intérieure. 2e éd. Paris, 1914.
Phil 5243.17   Dubot, T. Psychologie. Paris, 1897.
Phil 5243.18.4   Dyroff, Adolf. Einführung in die Psychologie. 4e Aufl. Leipzig, 1919.
Phil 5243.19   Damm, Hermann. Korrelative Beziehungen zwischen Elementarenvergleichsleistungen. Inaug. Diss. Leipzig, 1914.
Phil 5243.20   Doll, Edgar Arnold. The growth of intelligence. Diss. Princeton, 1920.
Phil 5243.22   Dressler, Max. Vorlesungen über Psychologie. Heidelberg, 1900.
Phil 5243.23.5   Dumville, B. The fundamentals of psychology. London, 1921.
Phil 5243.23.7   Dumville, B. The fundamentals of psychology. 2d ed. London, 1924.
Phil 5243.24.5   Dresser, H. Psychology in theory and application. N.Y., 1924.
Phil 5243.25   Dessoir, Max. Vom Diesseits der Seele. Leipzig, 1923.
Phil 5243.25.5   Dessoir, Max. Psychologische Briefe. Berlin, 1948.
Phil 5243.26   Dam, Axel. Om muligheden af formel opdragelse af de intellektuelle evner. København, 1912.
Phil 5243.27   Davis, N.K. Elements of psychology. N.Y., 1892.
Phil 5243.28   Driesch, Hans. The crisis in psychology. Princeton, 1925.
Phil 5243.28.5   Driesch, Hans. Grundprobleme der Psychologie. Leipzig, 1926.
Phil 5243.28.8   Driesch, Hans. Alltagsrätsel des Seelenlebens. Stuttgart, 1938.
Phil 5243.29   Dumas, George. Traité de psychologie. Paris, 1923. 2v.
Phil 5243.29.10   Dumas, George. Nouveau traité de psychologie. v.1-8. Paris, 1930-36. 7v.
Phil 5243.30   Drake, Durant. Mind and its place in nature. N.Y., 1925.
Phil 5243.31   Dide, Maurice. Introduction à l'étude de la psychogénèse. Paris, 1926.
Phil 5243.31.5   Dide, Maurice. Introduction à l'étude de la psychogénèse. Thèse. Paris, 1925. 2 pam.
Phil 5243.32   Dattino, Giovanni. La psicologia dei testimoni. Napoli, 1909.
Phil 5243.33.3   Dearden, H. Understanding ourselves. N.Y., 1926.
Phil 5243.34.3   Dimnet, E. The art of thinking. N.Y., 1929.
Phil 5243.34.5A   Dimnet, E. The art of thinking. N.Y., 1929.
Phil 5243.34.5C   Dimnet, E. The art of thinking. N.Y., 1929.
Phil 5243.34.9A   Dimnet, E. The art of thinking. N.Y., 1929.
Phil 5243.34.9B   Dimnet, E. The art of thinking. N.Y., 1929.
Phil 5243.34.10   Dimnet, E. The art of thinking. London, 1929.
Phil 5243.34.15   Dimnet, E. L'art de penser. Paris, 1930.
Phil 5243.36   Dashiell, J.F. Fundamentals of objective psychology. Boston, 1928.
Phil 5243.36.10   Dashiell, J.F. Fundamentals of general psychology. Boston, 1937.
Phil 5243.36.12   Dashiell, J.F. An experimental manual in psychology. Boston, 1931.
Phil 5243.36.15   Dashiell, J.F. Manual to accompany Fundamentals of general psychology. Boston, 1931.
Phil 5243.37   Dodge, Raymond. Conditions and consequences of human variability. New Haven, 1931.
Phil 5243.37.10   Dodge, Raymond. The craving for superiority. New Haven, 1931.
Phil 5243.38   Dockeray, F.C. General psychology. N.Y., 1932.
Phil 5243.39   Delgadio, H.F. Psicología. Lima, 1933.
Phil 5243.40   Dorsey, J.M. The foundations of human nature. N.Y., 1935.
Phil 5243.41.2   Dreikurs, Rudolf. Grundbegriffe der Individualpsychologie. Stuttgart, 1969.
Phil 5243.41.5   Dreikurs, Rudolf. An introduction to individual psychology. London, 1935.
Phil 5243.42   Delacroix, Henri. Les grandes formes de la vie mentale. Paris, 1934.
Phil 5243.43   Duflo, J. Esquisse d'une énergétique mentale. Paris, 1936.
Phil 5243.44   Deut, John Y. Reactions of the human machine. London, 1936.
Phil 5243.44.5   Deut, John Y. The human machine. N.Y., 1937.
Phil 5243.45   Dexter, E.S. Introduction to the fields of psychology. N.Y., 1938.
Phil 5243.46   Dearborn, W.F. Predicting the child's development. Cambridge, Mass., 1941.

Phil 5240 - 5265   Psychology - General treatises - Individual authors (A-Z) - cont.

Phil 5243.46.2   Dearborn, W.F. Predicting the child's development. 2d rev. ed. Cambridge, Mass., 1963.
Phil 5243.47   Pamphlet box. Philosophy. Psychology. General. Diven, Kenneth.
Phil 5243.48   Delay, Jean P.L. Les ondes cérébrales et la psychologie. Paris, 1942.
Phil 5243.49   Devoto, Andrea. Saggio sulla psicologia contemporanea. Firenze, 1959.
Phil 5243.50   Dobbelstein, Herman. Der normale Mensch im Urteil der Psychiatrie. Einsiedeln, 1955.
Phil 5243.52   Daval, Simone. Psychologie. Paris, 1956. 2v.
Phil 5243.55   Deutsch, Jaroslav A. The structural basis of behavior. Chicago, 1960.
Phil 5243.60   Donceel, Joseph. Philosophical psychology. 2d ed. N.Y., 1961.
Phil 5243.65   Dirks, Heinz. Psychologie. Gütersloh, 1960.
Phil 5243.66   Daujat, J. Psychologie contemporaine et pensée chrétienne. Tournai, 1962.
Phil 5243.68.2   Duncker, Karl. Zur Psychologie des Produktiven Denkens. 2e Neudruck. Berlin, 1966.
Phil 5243.70   Dubouchet-Buffet, Jeanne. Essai de formalisation de la psychologie fondé sur l'analogie des phénomènes psychiques et des phénomènes physiques. Thèse. Paris, 1965.
Phil 5243.72   Dembicki, Leo. Psychologie: Modell und Wirklichkeit. Bodman/Bodensee, 1969.
Phil 5243.74   D'Amato, Michael Richard. Experimental psychology. N.Y., 1970.
Phil 5244.1   Eberhard, J.A. Allgemeine Theorie des Denkens und Empfindens. Berlin, 1776.
Phil 5244.2   Erdmann, J.E. Psychologische Briefe. Leipzig, 1856.
Phil 5244.2.8   Erdmann, J.E. Grundriss der Psychologie. 4. Aufl. Leipzig, 1862.
Phil 5244.2.9   Erdmann, J.E. Grundriss der Psychologie. 5e Aufl. Leipzig, 1873.
Phil 5244.2.10   Erdmann, J.E. Psychologische Briefe. 3e Aufl. Leipzig, 1863.
Phil 5244.2.12   Erdmann, J.E. Psychologische Briefe. 5e Aufl. Leipzig, 1875.
Phil 5244.3   Eschenmayer, C.A.A. Psychologie. Stuttgart, 1817.
Phil 5244.4   Esser, W. Psychologie. Münster, 1854.
Phil 5244.5   Exner, S. Entwurf zu einer physiologischen Erklärung der psychischen Erscheinungen. Leipzig, 1894.
Phil 5244.6   Elsenhans, T. Psychologie und Logik. Leipzig, 1898.
Phil 5244.7   Ebbinghaus, H. Abriss der Psychologie. Leipzig, 1908.
Phil 5244.7.4   Ebbinghaus, H. Abriss der Psychologie. 6e Aufl. Leipzig, 1919.
Phil 5244.7.5   Ebbinghaus, H. Psychology, an elementary text-book. Boston, 1908.
Phil 5244.7.9   Ebbinghaus, H. Précis de psychologie. Paris, 1910.
Phil 5244.7.15   Ebbinghaus, H. Grundzüge der Psychologie. Leipzig, 1911. 2v.
Phil 5244.8   Eisenmeier, J. Die Psychologie und ihre Zentralestellung in der Philosophie. Halle, 1914.
Phil 5244.9.5   Erismann, T. Psychologie. Berlin, 1920.
Phil 5244.9.15   Erismann, T. Die Eigenart des Geistigen. Leipzig, n.d.
Phil 5244.9.23   Erismann, Theodor. Allgemeine Psychologie. 3. Aufl. Berlin, 1962-1965. 4v.
Phil 5244.10   Elsenhans, Theodor. Psychologie und Logik. 5e Aufl. Berlin, 1920.
Phil 5244.10.6   Elsenhans, Theodor. Lehrbuch der Psychologie. Tübingen, 1920.
Phil 5244.10.9   Elsenhans, Theodor. Lehrbuch der Psychologie. 3e Aufl. Tübingen, 1937-1938.
Phil 5244.10.10   Elsenhans, Theodor. Selbstbeobachtung und Experiment in der Psychologie. Freiburg, 1897.
Phil 5244.11   Eichberg, T. Psychologische Probleme. Stuttgart, 1907.
Phil 5244.12.3   Eisler, Rudolf. Psychologie im Umriss. 3e Aufl. Leipzig, 1903.
Phil 5244.13   Ehrenberg, Hans. Kritik der Psychologie als Wissenschaft. Tübingen, 1910.
Phil 5244.14   Elsas, Adolf. Über die Psychophysik. Marburg, 1886.
Phil 5244.15   Erdmann, B. Grundzüge der Reproduktions Psychologie. Berlin, 1920.
Phil 5244.17   Eriksen, R. Taenkningens psychologiske utviklingsbetingelser. Kristiania, 1915.
Phil 5244.18   Ellefsen, Olaf. Om moralens oprindelse. Kristiania, 1893.
Phil 5244.19   Edgell, B. Mental life. London, 1926.
Phil 5244.20   Elder, William. Studies in psychology. London, 1927.
Phil 5244.21   Evans, John E. The effect of distraction on reaction time. N.Y., 1916.
Phil 5244.22   Ellis, Willis D. Gestalt psychology and meaning. Berkeley, 1930.
Phil 5244.22.5   Ellis, Willis D. A source book of Gestalt. London, 1950.
Phil 5244.23   English, V.P. Human mind and its physical machine...human body. San Diego, 1937.
Phil 5244.24   Ehrenstein, Walter. Einführung in die Ganzheitspsychologie. Leipzig, 1934.
Phil 5244.24.5   Ehrenstein, Walter. Probleme des höheren Seelenlebens. München, 1965.
Phil 5244.25   Edwards, Allen L. Statistical analysis for students in psychology and education. N.Y., 1946.
Phil 5244.25.2   Edwards, Allen L. Statistical analysis. N.Y., 1958.
Phil 5244.25.5   Edwards, Allen L. Statistical methods for the behavioral sciences. N.Y., 1964.
Phil 5244.30   Eysenck, H.J. Sense and nonsense in psychology. Harmondsworth, Middlesex, 1957.
Phil 5244.34   Coles, Robert. Erik H. Erikson; the growth of his work. 1st ed. Boston, 1970.
Phil 5244.36   Egidius, Henry. Första människor. Lund, 1971.
Phil 5245.1   Fabre d'Envieu, J. Cours de philosophie. Paris, 1863-1866. 2v.
Phil 5245.2   Fearn, J. First lines of the human mind. London, 1820.
Phil 5245.2.2   Fearn, J. A manual of the physiology of mind. London, 1829.
Phil 5245.4   Feuchtersleben, E. von. Principles of medical psychology. London, 1847.
Phil 5245.6   Filachou, J.E. Éléments de psychologie mathématique. Montpelier, 1877.
Htn Phil 5245.7*   Fiske, J. The composition of mind. N.Y., 1872. 3 pam.
Phil 5245.8   Flögel, C.F. Geschichte des menschlichen Verstandes. Breslau, 1776.
Phil 5245.9   Fortlage, A.R.K. Acht psychologische Vorträge. Jena, 1869.
Phil 5245.9.5   Fortlage, A.R.K. System der Psychologie. Leipzig, 1855. 2v.
Phil 5245.9.10   Fortlage, A.R.K. Beiträge zur Psychologie. Leipzig, 1875.

Phil 5240 - 5265   Psychology - General treatises - Individual authors (A-Z) - cont.

Phil 5245.9.15	Fortlage, A.R.K. Vier psychologische Vorträge. Jena, 1874.
Phil 5245.10	Fournié, É. Essai de psychologie. Paris, 1877.
Phil 5245.12	Frohschammer, J. Die Phantasie als Grundprincip des Weltprocesses. München, 1877.
Phil 5245.13	Faggi, A. Principi di psicologia moderna. Palermo, 1895.
Phil 5245.14	François, A. Leçons élémentaires de psychologie. Paris, 1897.
Phil 5245.15	Foucault, Marcel. La psychophysique. Paris, 1901.
Phil 5245.15.5	Foucault, Marcel. Cours de psychologie. Paris, 1926.
Phil 5245.15.10	Foucault, Marcel. Premières leçons de psychologie expérimentale a l'usage des candidats au baccalauréat. Paris, 1930.
Phil 5245.16.3	Friedreich, J.B. System der gerichtlichen Psychologie. 3e Aufl. Regensburg, 1852.
Phil 5245.17	Falinski, E. Cahiers de psychologie rationnelle. v.1-4. Paris, 1926.
Phil 5245.18	Ford, Corydon. The synthesis of mind. n.p., 1883-1893.
Phil 5245.19	Feldegg, F. Das Gefühl als Fundament der Weltordnung. Wien, 1890.
Phil 5245.19.5	Feldegg, F. Beiträge zur Philosophie des Gefühls. Leipzig, 1900.
Phil 5245.20	Fischer, E.L. Theorie der Gesichtswahrnehnung. Mainz, 1891.
Phil 5245.21	Fröbes, Joseph. Lehrbuch der experimentellen Psychologie. Freiburg, 1917. 2v.
Phil 5245.21.2A	Fröbes, Joseph. Lehrbuch der experimentellen Psychologie. 2. und 3. Aufl. Freiburg, 1922-1923. 2v.
Phil 5245.21.2B	Fröbes, Joseph. Lehrbuch der experimentellen Psychologie. 2. und 3. Aufl. Freiburg, 1922-1923. 2v.
Phil 5245.21.7	Fröbes, Joseph. Cursus brevior psychologiae speculativae in usum scholarum. Parisiis, 1933.
Phil 5245.22	Ferrari, G.C. Psychological papers. Reggio, 1896-1900.
Phil 5245.23	Flourens, Pierre. De la raison du genié et...folie. Paris, 1861.
Phil 5245.23.5	Flourens, Pierre. De la vie et de l'intelligence. 2. éd. Paris, 1858.
Phil 5245.25	Farnsworth, B.B. Practical psychology for men and women. N.Y., 1923.
Phil 5245.26	Finnbogason, G. L'intelligence sympathetique. Paris, 1913.
Phil 5245.27	Foster, William S. Experiments in psychology. N.Y., 1923.
Phil 5245.27.5	Foster, William S. Experiments in psychology. N.Y., 1923.
Phil 5245.28F	Farpon y Tuñón, José. Discurso leido...2 de julio de 1898. Manila, 1898.
Phil 5245.29	Felsch. Die Hauptpunkte der Psychologie. Cöthen, 1904.
Phil 5245.30	Foltz, Otto. Grundriss der Psychologie für Lehrer- und Lehrerinnen-Bildungs-Anstalten. Österwiech-Harz, 1910.
Phil 5245.31	Flower, J.C. Psychology simplified. London, 1928.
Phil 5245.32.5	Ford, Adelbert. Group experiments in elementary psychology. N.Y., 1932.
Phil 5245.33	Fox, Charles. Mind and its body. London, 1931.
Phil 5245.34	Field, G.C. Prejudice and impartiality. London, 1932.
Phil 5245.35	Franz, S.I. Psychology. 1. ed. N.Y., 1933.
Phil 5245.37	Fauré-Fremiet, P. Pensée et re-création. Paris, 1934.
Phil 5245.38	Fuller, B. The tyranny of the mind. London, 1935.
Phil 5245.39	Finner, P.F. An introduction to experimental psychology. N.Y., 1935.
Phil 5245.40	Focht, Mildred. What is Gestalt-theory. Diss. N.Y., 1935.
Phil 5245.41	Fryer, D. An outline of general psychology. N.Y., 1936.
Phil 5245.42	Fernberger, Samuel W. Elementary general psychology. N.Y., 1937.
Phil 5245.43	Freeman, E. Principles of general psychology. N.Y., 1939.
Phil 5245.44	Fisher, R.A. The psychology of desire. Saskatoon, 1930.
Phil 5245.45.2	Flügel, John Carl. Man, morals and society. London, 1945.
Phil 5245.45.5	Flügel, John Carl. Man, morals and society. N.Y., 1955.
Phil 5245.45.6	Flügel, John Carl. Man, morals and society. Harmondsworth, 1962.
Phil 5245.46	Fales, Walter. Wisdom and responsibility. Princeton, 1946.
Phil 5245.47	French, T.M. The integration of behavior. Chicago, 1952-58. 3v.
Phil 5245.48	Falorni, M.L. Studio psicologica dell'intelligenza e della matricità. Firenze, 1952.
Phil 5245.49	Feldkeller, P. Das unpersönliche Denken. Berlin, 1949.
Phil 5245.50	Fraisse, Paul. Manuel pratique de psychologie experimentale. 1. éd. Paris, 1956.
Phil 5245.55	Fraser, John Munro. Psychology. N.Y., 1956.
Phil 5245.60	Furtado, Diogo. Vultos e problemas. Coimbra, 1957.
Phil 5245.65	Finkelstein, Ben A. Psychologische skizzen. Amsterdam, 1957.
Phil 5245.70	From, Franz. Menneske kundskab. København, 1959. 2v.
Phil 5245.75	Ferrière, A. L'orthogenèse lumaine. Neuchâtel, 1959.
Phil 5245.80	Fischel, Werner. Struktur und Dynamik. Bern, 1962.
Phil 5245.81	Fingerman, G. Estudios de psicologia y de estetica. Buenos Aires, 1926.
Phil 5245.82	Friedman, Neil. The social nature of psychological research. N.Y., 1967.
Phil 5245.84	Fromme, Allan. Our troubled selves. N.Y., 1967.
Phil 5245.86	Fodor, Jerry A. Psychological explanation. N.Y., 1968.
Phil 5246.1.2A	Galton, F. Inquiries into the human faculty. N.Y., 1883.
Phil 5246.1.2B	Galton, F. Inquiries into the human faculty. N.Y., 1883.
Phil 5246.1.5B	Galton, F. Inquiries into the human faculty. London, 1919.
Phil 5246.1.9	Galton, F. Inquiries into the human faculty. London, 1928.
Phil 5246.1.10	Galton, F. Inquiries into human faculty and its development. London, 1907.
Phil 5246.2	Garnier, A. La psychologie et la phrénologie comparées. Paris, 1839.
Phil 5246.2.10	Garnier, A. Traite des facultés de l'âme. Paris, 1865. 3v.
Phil 5246.3	Garreau, P. Essai sur les bases ontologiques...l'homme. Paris, 1846.
Phil 5246.4	George, J. Lehrbuch der Psychologie. Berlin, 1854.
Phil 5246.5	Gerando, J.M. de. Des signes et de l'art de penser. Paris, 1800. 4v.
Phil 5246.6	Giner de los Rios, Francisco. Lecciones sumarias de psicología. Midrid, 1877.
Phil 5246.7	Godfernaux, A. Le sentiment et la pensée. Paris, 1894.
Phil 5246.7.3	Godfernaux, A. Le sentiment et la pensée. 3. éd. Paris, 1907.
Phil 5246.8	Granger, F.S. Psychology. London, 1891.
Phil 5246.9	Gratry, A.J.A. De la connaissance de l'âme. Paris, 1857. 2v.

Phil 5240 - 5265   Psychology - General treatises - Individual authors (A-Z) - cont.

Phil 5246.9.8A	Boole, M.E. The mathematical psychology of Gratry and Boole. London, 1897.
Phil 5246.9.8B	Boole, M.E. The mathematical psychology of Gratry and Boole. London, 1897.
Phil 5246.10	Gruyer. L.A. Les causes...phénomènes de l'âme. Paris, 1844.
Phil 5246.12.12	Gordy, J.P. New psychology. N.Y., 1902.
Phil 5246.14	Geyser, J. Grundlegung der empirischen Psychologie. Bonn, 1902.
Phil 5246.14.5	Geyser, J. Lehrbuch der allegemeinen Psychologie. 2. Aufl. Munster, 1912.
Phil 5246.14.10	Geyser, J. Die Seele, ihr Verhältnis zum Bewusstsein. Leipzig, 1914.
Phil 5246.15	Gerard-Varet, G. L'ignorance et l'irréflexion. Paris, 1899.
Htn	Phil 5246.16*	Gurley, R.R. Skeleton project of a science of psychology. n.p., n.d.
Htn	Phil 5246.16.2*	Gurley, R.R. Skeleton project of a science of psychology. n.p., n.d.
Phil 5246.17	Givler, Robert C. The conscious cross-section. Seattle, 1915.
Phil 5246.17.7	Givler, Robert C. Psychology; the science of human behavior. N.Y., 1922.
Phil 5246.18	Glover, William. Know your own mind...book of practical psychology. Cambridge, 1915.
Phil 5246.19	Gutberlet, C. Die Psychologie. 2. Aufl. Münster, 1890.
Phil 5246.19.10	Gutberlet, C. Psychophysik. Mainz, 1905.
Phil 5246.20	Goddard, H.H. Psychology of the normal and subnormal. N.Y., 1919.
Phil 5246.20.5	Goddard, H.H. Human efficiency and levels of intelligence. Princeton, 1920.
Phil 5246.21	Gabius, P. Denkökonomie und Energieprinzip. Berlin, 1913.
Phil 5246.22	Gonzalez Serrano, U. Estudios psicológicos. Madrid, 1892.
Phil 5246.23	Giese, Fritz. Psychologische Beiträge. Langensalza, 1916-
Phil 5246.23.9	Giese, Fritz. Psychotechnisches Praktikum. Halle, 1923.
Phil 5246.24	Guérin, Jules. Les différentes manifestations. Paris, 1899.
Phil 5246.25.3	Gemelli, Agostino. Psicologia e biologia. 3. ed. Firenze, 1913.
Phil 5246.25.5	Gemelli, Agostino. Nuovo orizzonti della psicologia sperimentale. 2. ed. Milano, 1923.
Phil 5246.25.10	Gemelli, Agostino. Introducione alla psicologia. Milano, 1947.
Phil 5246.25.80	Spaltro, Enzo. Agostino Gemelli e la psicologia del lavoro in Italia. Milano, 1966.
Phil 5246.26B	Gruender, Hubert. An introductory course in experimental psychology. Chicago, 1920.
Phil 5246.27	Glogau, Gustav. Grundriss der Psychologie. Breslau, 1884.
Phil 5246.27.5	Glogau, Gustav. Die Form und die Bewegungsgesetze des Geistes. Breslau, 1880. 2 pam.
Phil 5246.28	Gale, Harlow. Psychological studies. Minneapolis, 1900.
Phil 5246.29	Garrett, Henry E. A study of the relation of accuracy to speed. N.Y., 1922.
Phil 5246.29.5	Garrett, Henry E. Psychology. N.Y., 1950.
Phil 5246.29.6	Garrett, Henry E. General psychology. 2. ed. N.Y., 1961.
Phil 5246.30	Gates, G.S. Individual differences as affected by practice. N.Y., 1922.
Phil 5246.31.2	Griffith, C.R. General introduction to psychology. N.Y., 1928.
Phil 5246.31.5	Griffith, C.R. General introduction to psychology. N.Y., 1924.
Phil 5246.31.10	Griffith, C.R. Principles of systematic psychology. Urbana, 1943.
Phil 5246.32.5	Green, G.H. The mind in action. London, 1923.
Phil 5246.33	Galli, Ettore. Nel mondo dello spirito. Milano, 1920.
Phil 5246.33.5	Galli, Ettore. Nel mondo dello spirito. Milano, 1919.
Phil 5246.34	Güttler, C. Psychologie und Philosophie. München, 1896.
Phil 5246.35	Giran, Paul. Les origines de la pensée. Paris, 1923.
Phil 5246.36	Gates, Arthur I. Elementary psychology. N.Y., 1925.
Phil 5246.37	Gault, Robert H. Outline of general psychology. N.Y., 1925.
Phil 5246.38	Geiger, Moritz. Methodologische und experimentelle Beiträge zur Quantitätslehre. Leipzig, 1907.
Phil 5246.39	Griffith, Percy. A synthetic psychology. London, 1927.
Phil 5246.40	Gomperz, H. Über Sinn und Sinngebilde. Tübingen, 1929.
Phil 5246.41	Gilliland, A.R. General psychology for professional students. Boston, 1930.
Phil 5246.41.4	Gilliland, A.R. Psychology of individual differences. N.Y., 1939.
Phil 5246.42	Garnett, Arthur C. The mind in action. London, 1931.
Phil 5246.42.5	Garnett, Arthur C. The mind in action. N.Y., 1932.
Phil 5246.43	Guillaume, Paul. Psychologie. Paris, 1931.
Phil 5246.43.5	Guillaume, Paul. La psychologie de la forme. Paris, 1937.
Phil 5246.43.10	Guillaume, Paul. Manuel de psychologie. Paris, 1944.
Phil 5246.44	Garvey, M.A. A manual of human culture. London, 1866.
Phil 5246.45	Galt, William. Phyloanalysis. London, 1933.
Phil 5246.46	Goodenough, Florence L. Developmental psychology. N.Y., 1934.
Phil 5246.46.5	Goodenough, Florence L. Developmental psychology. 2. ed. N.Y., 1945.
Phil 5246.47	Guilford, Joy Paul. Laboratory studies in psychology. N.Y., 1934.
Phil 5246.47.5A	Guilford, Joy Paul. Psychometric methods. 1. ed. N.Y., 1936.
Phil 5246.47.5B	Guilford, Joy Paul. Psychometric methods. 1. ed. N.Y., 1936.
Phil 5246.47.5C	Guilford, Joy Paul. Psychometric methods. 1. ed. N.Y., 1936.
Phil 5246.47.6	Guilford, Joy Paul. Psychometric methods. N.Y., 1954.
Phil 5246.47.8	Guilford, Joy Paul. Fields of psychology. N.Y., 1940.
Phil 5246.47.10A	Guilford, Joy Paul. Fundamental statistics in psychology and education. N.Y., 1942.
Phil 5246.47.10B	Guilford, Joy Paul. Fundamental statistics in psychology and education. N.Y., 1942.
Phil 5246.47.12	Guilford, Joy Paul. Fundamental statistics in psychology and education. 4. ed. N.Y., 1965.
Phil 5246.47.15	Guilford, Joy Paul. The nature of human intelligence. N.Y., 1967.
Phil 5246.48	Groves, Ernest R. Understanding yourself, the mental hygiene of personality. N.Y., 1935.
Phil 5246.49	Gaskell, John. New elements from old subjects presented as the basis for a science of mind. Philadelphia, 1874.
Phil 5246.50	Grassi-Bertazzi, G.B. I fenomeni psichici. Catania, 1898.
Phil 5246.51	Gregg, F.M. Psychology of a growing personality. Lincoln, 1938.
Phil 5246.52A	Goldstein, K. Human nature. Cambridge, 1940.
Phil 5246.52B	Goldstein, K. Human nature. Cambridge, 1940.

262

Classified Listing

Phil 5240 - 5265 Psychology - General treatises - Individual authors (A-Z) - cont.

Phil 5246.53 Goldstein, K. Human nature in the light of psychopathology. Cambridge, Mass., 1947.
Phil 5246.54 Guerrero, L.J. Psicología. 4. ed. Buenos Aires, 1943.
Phil 5246.56 Glaser, E.M. An experiment in the development of critical thinking. Thesis. N.Y., 1941.
Phil 5246.58 Gibson, A.B. Thinkers at work. London, 1946.
Phil 5246.60 Gruhle, H.W. Verstehen und Einfühlen. Berlin, 1953.
Phil 5246.60.5 Gruhle, H.W. Verstehende Psychologie. 2. Aufl. Stuttgart, 1956.
Phil 5246.62 Geyer, Horst. Über die Dummheit. Göttingen, 1954.
Phil 5246.65 Graber, Gustav Hans. Psychologie des Mannes. Bern, 1957.
Phil 5246.68 Guirdham, Arthur. Man: divine or social. London, 1960.
Phil 5246.70 Gibb, Andrew. In search of sanity. N.Y., 1942.
Phil 5246.72 Geldard, F.A. Fundamentals of psychology. N.Y., 1962.
Phil 5246.74 Gendlin, Eugene. Experiencing and the creation of meaning. N.Y., 1962.
Phil 5246.75 Gómez Ibars, J. En el món del invidents. Barcelona, 1963.
Phil 5246.76A Garner, W.R. Uncertainty and structure as psychological concepts. N.Y., 1962.
Phil 5246.76B Garner, W.R. Uncertainty and structure as psychological concepts. N.Y., 1962.
Phil 5246.77 Garan, D.G. The paradox of pleasure and relativity. N.Y., 1963.
Phil 5246.77.5 Garan, D.G. Relativity for psychology. N.Y., 1968.
Phil 5246.78 Gernhammer, Vilhelm. And og sjael; symboler og symbolik. v.1-2. Silkeborg, 1968.
Phil 5246.80 Gilmer, Beverly von Haller. Psychology. N.Y., 1970.
Phil 5246.82 Gagey, Jacques. Analyse spectacle de la psychologie. Paris, 1970.
Phil 5246.84 Goldman, Alvin I. A theory of human action. Englewood Cliffs, N.J., 1970.
Phil 5246.86 Gelinas, Robert P. The teenager and psychology. 1. ed. N.Y., 1971.
Phil 5246.88 Gosselin, Albert. L'homme en ce monde et le sens de la vie. Paris, 1970.
Phil 5247.1.2 Halleck, R.P. Psychology and psychic culture. N.Y., 1895.
Phil 5247.2 Hamilton, D.H. Autology...mental science. Boston, 1873.
Phil 5247.3 Hamilton, E.J. The human mund. N.Y., 1883.
Phil 5247.3.7 Hamilton, E.J. The perceptionalist. N.Y., 1912.
Phil 5247.3.9 Hamilton, E.J. The perceptionalist. N.Y., 1891.
Phil 5247.3.300 Hartmann, George W. A collection of miscellaneous papers. n.p., n.d.
Phil 5247.4 Hartsen, F.A. Grundzüge der Psychologie. Berlin, 1874.
Phil 5247.4.5 Hartsen, F.A. Princepes de psychologie. Paris, 1872.
Phil 5247.4.10 Hartsen, F.A. Untersuchungen über Psychologie. Leipzig, 1869.
Phil 5247.5 Haslam, J. Sound mind. London, 1819.
Phil 5247.6.1 Haven, J. Mental philosophy. Boston, 1872.
Phil 5247.7 Henle, F.G.J. Anthropologische Vorträge. Braunschweig, 1876-80.
Phil 5247.9 Hickok, L.P. Rational psychology. Auburn, 1849.
Phil 5247.9.4 Hickok, L.P. Empirical psychology. Boston, 1882.
Phil 5247.9.5 Hickok, L.P. Rational psychology. N.Y., 1876.
Phil 5247.9.7 Hickok, L.P. Empirical psychology. 2. ed. N.Y., 1854.
Phil 5247.10.3 Höffding, H. Psykologi i omrids paa grundlag af erfarung. 3. ed. København, 1892.
Phil 5247.10.4 Höffding, H. Psykologi i omrids paa grundlag af erfarung. 9. ed. København, 1920.
Phil 5247.10.6 Höffding, H. Outlines of psychology. London, 1892.
Phil 5247.10.8 Höffding, H. Outlines of psychology. London, 1904.
Phil 5247.10.13 Höffding, H. Psychologie in Umrissen auf Grundläge der Erfahrung. Leipzig, 1887.
Phil 5247.10.14 Höffding, H. Psychologie in Umrissen auf Grundläge der Erfahrung. Leipzig, 1893.
Phil 5247.10.15 Höffding, H. Pensée humaine. Paris, 1911.
Phil 5247.10.19 Höffding, H. Psykologiske undersogeler. Kjøbenhavn, 1889.
Phil 5247.11.3 Hopkins, M. An outline study of man. N.Y., 1883.
Phil 5247.11.7 Hopkins, M. An outline of man; or, The body and mind in one system. N.Y., 1889.
Phil 5247.12 Horwicz, A. Psychologische Analysen. v.1-2. Halle, 1872-78. 3v.
Htn Phil 5247.13* Huarte de San Juan, J. Examen de ingenios para las sciencias. Antwerp? 1603.
Phil 5247.13.3 Huarte de San Juan, J. Examen de ingenios para las sciencias. Barcelona, 1917.
Phil 5247.13.4 Huarte de San Juan, J. Examen de ingenios para las sciencias. Madrid, 1930. 2v.
Htn Phil 5247.13.5* Huarte de San Juan, J. The examination of men's wits. London, 1596.
Htn Phil 5247.13.7* Huarte de San Juan, J. Examen de ingenios. London, 1594.
Htn Phil 5247.13.9* Huarte de San Juan, J. Examen de ingenios. London, 1604.
Phil 5247.13.13 Huarte de San Juan, J. Examen des esprits et naiz aux sciences. Rouen, 1607.
Phil 5247.13.15 Huarte de San Juan, J. L'examen des esprits pour les sciences. Paris, 1661.
Phil 5247.13.17 Huarte de San Juan, J. Examen de ingenios. London, 1698.
Phil 5247.13.18 Huarte de San Juan, J. Examen de ingenios. Gainesville, 1959.
Phil 5247.13.19 Huarte de San Juan, J. Essai sur l'ouvrage. Paris, 1855.
Phil 5247.13.21 Huarte de San Juan, J. Prüfung der Köpfe zu den Wissenschaften. Zerbst, 1752.
Htn Phil 5247.13.22* Huarte de San Juan, J. Anacrise, ou Parfait jugement et examen. Lyon, 1580.
Phil 5247.13.25 Klein, Anton. Juan Huarte und der Psychognosis der Renaissance. Inaug. Diss. Bonn, 1913.
Phil 5247.13.26 Guibelet, J. Examen de l'examen des esprits. Paris, 1631.
Phil 5247.13.27 Iriarte, Mauricio de. Dr. Juan Huarte de San Juan. Münster, 1938.
Phil 5247.13.28 Iriarte, Mauricio de. El Doctor Huarte de San Juan y su examen de ingenios. Madrid, 1940.
Phil 5247.13.29 Herrero Pouas, Antolin. Juan Huarte de San Juan. Madrid, 1941.
Phil 5247.13.32 Ramis Alonso, M. A propósito de examen de ingenios del Dr. Huarte. Palma de Mallorca, 1943.
Phil 5247.13.33 Franzbach, Martin. Lessings Huarte-Übersetzung, 1752. Hamburg, 1965.
Phil 5247.13.80 Dantin Gallego, J. La filosofia natural de Huarte de San Juan. Madrid, 1952.
Phil 5247.14 Histoire philosophique de l'homme. Londres, 1766.
Phil 5247.15 Hebberd, S.S. An introduction...science of thought. Madison, 1892.
Phil 5247.16 Hollingworth, H.L. Outlines for experimental psychology. N.Y., 1914.
Phil 5247.16.5 Hollingworth, H.L. Outlines for applied and abnormal psychology. N.Y., 1914.
Phil 5247.16.15 Hollingworth, H.L. The psychology of thought approached through studies of sleeping and dreaming. N.Y., 1926.

Phil 5240 - 5265 Psychology - General treatises - Individual authors (A-Z) - cont.

Phil 5247.16.16 Hollingworth, H.L. The psychology of thought approached through studies of sleeping and dreaming. N.Y., 1927.
Phil 5247.16.22 Hollingworth, H.L. Mental growth and decline. N.Y., 1928.
Phil 5247.16.25 Hollingworth, H.L. Psychology: its facts and principles. N.Y., 1928.
Phil 5247.17 Hartmann, E. Die moderne Psychologie. Leipzig, 1901.
Phil 5247.18 Harvey, N.A. Elementary psychology. Chicago, 1914.
Phil 5247.19.2 Hunter, W.S. General psychology. Chicago, 1919.
Phil 5247.19.7 Hunter, W.S. General psychology. Chicago, 1927.
Phil 5247.19.25 Hunter, W.S. Human behavior. Chicago, 1928.
Phil 5247.20 Hamelinck, M. Étude préparatoire à la détermination experimentale de diverses individuel intellects. Gand, 1915.
Phil 5247.21 Hanspaul, F. Die Seelentheorie und die Gesetze. 2. Aufl. Berlin, 1901.
Phil 5247.22 Heymans, G. Das Künftige Jahrhundert der Psychologie. Leipzig, 1911.
Phil 5247.22.5 Heymans, G. Quantitative Untersuchungen über der öptische Paradoxon. n.p., 1896-1913. 13 pam.
Phil 5247.22.20 Heymans, G. Einführung in die spezielle Psychologie. Leipzig, 1932.
Phil 5247.23.4 Höfler, Alois. Grundlehren der Psychologie. 4. Aufl. Wien, 1908.
Phil 5247.23.7 Höfler, Alois. Grundlehren der Psychologie. 7. Aufl. Wien, 1919.
Phil 5247.23.8 Höfler, Alois. Physiologische oder experimentelle Psychologie am Gymnasium? Wien, 1898.
Phil 5247.23.15 Höfler, Alois. Hundert psychologische Schulversuche. 4. Aufl. Leipzig, 1918.
Phil 5247.23.20 Höfler, Alois. Psychologie. 2e Aufl. Wien, 1930.
Phil 5247.23.25 Höfler, Alois. Zur Propädeutik-Frage. Wien, 1884.
Phil 5247.25 Harms, F. Psychologie. Leipzig, 1897.
Phil 5247.26 Hering, Ewald. Die Deutungen des psychophysischen Gesetzes. Tübingen, 1909.
Phil 5247.27 Hill, Owen Aloysuis. Psychology and natural theology. N.Y., 1921.
Phil 5247.28 Haas, Wilhelm. Die psychische Dingwelt. Bonn, 1921.
Phil 5247.29 Humphrey, G. The story of man's mind. Boston, 1923.
Phil 5247.29.5 Humphrey, G. The story of man's mind. N.Y., 1932.
Phil 5247.29.15 Humphrey, G. The nature of learning in its relation to the living system. London, 1933.
Phil 5247.29.20 Humphrey, G. Directed thinking. N.Y., 1948.
Phil 5247.30 Häberlin, Paul. Der Gegenstand der Psychologie. Berlin, 1921.
Phil 5247.30.5 Häberlin, Paul. Der Geist und die Triebe: eine Elementarpsychologie. Basel, 1924.
Phil 5247.31.5 Hayward, C.W. What is psychology? N.Y., 1923.
Phil 5247.32 Harford, C.F. Mind as a force. London, 1924.
Phil 5247.33 Hautefeuille, F. d'. Le privilege de l'intelligence. Paris, 1923.
Phil 5247.33.2 Hecke, Gustav. Psychologie. 2. Aufl. Braunschweig, 1919.
Phil 5247.35.5 Bertinaria, F. La psicologia fisica ed iperfisica di Hoenato Wronski. Torino, 1877.
Phil 5247.36 Hannahs, E.H. Lessons in psychology. Albany, 1908.
Phil 5247.37.2 Hönigswald, R. Die Grundlagen der Denkpsychologie. 2. Aufl. Leipzig, 1925.
Phil 5247.37.10 Hönigswald, R. Vom Problem des Rhythmus. Leipzig, 1926.
Phil 5247.38 Helson, Harry. The psychology of Gestalt. Urbana, 1926.
Phil 5247.39 Heinroth, J.C.A. Die Psychologie als Selbsterkenntnisslehre. Leipzig, 1827.
Phil 5247.40 Heilmann, K. Psychologie und Logik. 15. Aufl. Berlin, 1913.
Phil 5247.41 Hertz, Paul. Über das Denken...Auschauung. Berlin, 1923.
Phil 5247.42A Hocking, W.E. The self: its body and freedom. New Haven, 1928.
Phil 5247.42B Hocking, W.E. The self: its body and freedom. New Haven, 1928.
Phil 5247.43 Heath, Archie E. How we behave. London, 1927.
Phil 5247.44 Henning, Hans. Psychologie der Gegenwart. Berlin, 1925.
Phil 5247.45.2 Herrick, C.J. The thinking machine. 2. ed. Chicago, 1929.
Phil 5247.46 Hamilton, Hughbert C. The effect of incentives on accuracy of discrimination measured on the Galton bar. Thesis. N.Y., 1929.
Phil 5247.47A Holt, Edwin B. Animal drive and the learning process. N.Y., 1931.
Phil 5247.47B Holt, Edwin B. Animal drive and the learning process. N.Y., 1931.
Phil 5247.48.2 Higginson, G. Fields of psychology. N.Y., 1932.
Phil 5247.48.5 Higginson, G. Psychology. N.Y., 1936.
Phil 5247.49 Hungerford, H. Bunkless psychology. Washington, 1933.
Phil 5247.50 Harmon, F.L. The effects of noise upon certain psychological and physical processes. Thesis. N.Y., 1933.
Phil 5247.51 Hadfield, J.A. Psychology and modern problems. London, 1935.
Phil 5247.52 Hempel, Carl G. Der Typus Begriff im Lichte der neuen Logik. Leiden, 1936.
Phil 5247.53 Hartmann, G.W. Gestalt psychology. N.Y., 1936.
Phil 5247.54 Harrower, M.R. The psychologist at work. London, 1937.
Phil 5247.55 Hoggland, H. Pacemakers. N.Y., 1935.
Phil 5247.56 Hull, C.L. Mind, mechanism and adaptive behavior. Lancaster, 1937.
Phil 5247.56.5 Hull, C.L. Principles of behavior. N.Y., 1943.
Phil 5247.57 Hill, D.J. Elements of psychology. N.Y., 1888.
Phil 5247.58 Hughes, P. Introduction to psychology. Bethlehem Pa., 1928.
Phil 5247.59 Hook, A. The human mind. London, 1940.
Phil 5247.60.01 Pamphlet box. Philosophy. Psychology. Holway, Alfred H.
Phil 5247.61 Harriman, P.L. Twentieth century psychology. N.Y., 1946.
Phil 5247.62 Heinrich, W. Zur Prinzipienfrage der Psychologie. Zürich, 1899.
Phil 5247.63 Hayek, F.A. von. Individualism: true and false. Dublin, 1946.
Phil 5247.64 Huber, Kurt. Grundbegriffe der Seelenkunde. Ettal, 1955.
Phil 5247.65 Herrick, C.J. The evolution of human nature. Austin, 1956.
Phil 5247.66.3 Hilgard, Ernest R. Introduction to psychology. 3. ed. N.Y., 1962.
Phil 5247.67 Hartley, Eugene Leonard. Outside readings in psychology. N.Y., 1950.
Phil 5247.68 Hadley, John M. Clinical and counseling psychology. 1. ed. N.Y., 1958.
Phil 5247.69 Holzner, Burket. Amerikanische und deutsche Psychologie. Würzburg, 1958?
Phil 5247.70 Hoejgaard, Mogens. Mennesker og andre dyr. København, 1959.
Phil 5247.72 Henryson, Sten. Applicability of factor analysis in the behavioral science. Stockholm, 1957.

Phil 5240 - 5265	Psychology - General treatises - Individual authors (A-Z) - cont.
Phil 5247.73	Holland, James G. The analysis of behavior. N.Y., 1961.
Phil 5247.74	Hunt, J. Intelligence and experience. N.Y., 1961.
Phil 5247.75	Hellpach, W. Das Wellengesetz unseres Lebens. Hamburg, 1941.
Phil 5247.76	Hays, W. Statistics for psychologists. N.Y., 1963.
Phil 5247.77	Harris, Chester. Problems in measuring change. Madison, 1963.
Phil 5247.78	Heard, G. The five ages of man. N.Y., 1964[1963]
Phil 5247.79	Hyman, R. The nature of psychological inquiry. Englewood Cliffs, N.J., 1964.
Phil 5247.80	Holzkamp, Klaus. Theorie und Experiment in der Psychologie. Berlin, 1964.
Phil 5247.81	Hunt, Morton M. The thinking animal. Boston, 1964.
Phil 5247.84.4	Husén, Torsten. Psykologi. 4. uppl. Stockholm, 1966.
Phil 5247.86	Hector, Heinz. Gedankengänge in Psychologie. Paderborn, 1965.
Phil 5248.1	Ideler, K.W. Grundriss der Seelenheilkunde. Berlin, 1835-38. 2v.
Phil 5248.2	Ingenieros, J. Principios de psicología biológica. Madrid, 1913.
Phil 5248.2.5	Ingenieros, J. Prinzipien der biologischen Psychologie. Leipzig, 1922.
Phil 5248.2.25	Gonzalez Velez, J. Resumen sintético y brevísemo del sistema de psicología. Habana, 192-.
Phil 5248.3	Isaacson, Robert Lee. Psychology, the science of behavior. N.Y., 1965.
Phil 5249.1	Jahn, M. Psychologie als Grundwissenschaft der Pädagogik. Leipzig, 1883.
Phil 5249.1.2	Jahn, M. Psychologie als Grundwissenschaft der Pädagogik. Leipzig, 1897.
Phil 5249.2A	James, William. Principles of psychology. N.Y., 1890. 2v.
Phil 5249.2B	James, William. Principles of psychology. N.Y., 1890. 2v.
Phil 5249.2*	James, William. Principles of psychology. N.Y., 1890. 2v.
Phil 5249.2.01A	James, William. Principles of psychology. N.Y., 1890. 2v.
Phil 5249.2.01B	James, William. Principles of psychology. N.Y., 1890. 2v.
EDL Phil 5249.2.01	James, William. Principles of psychology. v.2. N.Y., 1890.
Phil 5249.2.02	James, William. The principles of psychology. London, 1891. 2v.
Phil 5249.2.1	James, William. Principles of psychology. N.Y., 1896. 2v.
Phil 5249.2.2	James, William. Principles of psychology. v.2. N.Y., 1899.
Phil 5249.2.3	James, William. Principles of psychology. N.Y., 1927.
Phil 5249.2.4A	James, William. Psychology. N.Y., 1892.
Phil 5249.2.4B	James, William. Psychology. N.Y., 1892.
Phil 5249.2.5.3	James, William. Psychology. N.Y., 1891.
Phil 5249.2.5.5	James, William. Psychology. N.Y., 1923.
Phil 5249.2.5.10	James, William. Psychology. N.Y., 1961.
Phil 5249.2.6	James, William. Psychology. N.Y., 1900.
Phil 5249.2.6.10	James, William. Psychology. N.Y., 1907.
Phil 5249.2.11	James, William. Psychology. N.Y., 1893.
Phil 5249.2.13	James, William. Psychologie. Leipzig, 1909.
Phil 5249.2.13.5	James, William. Psychologie. N.Y., 1909.
Phil 5249.2.16	James, William. Psykologi. Uppsala, 1925.
Phil 5249.2.20	James, William. Sjalslifrets. Uppsala, 1898.
Phil 5249.2.21	James, William. Principios de psicología. Madrid, 1909. 2v.
Phil 5249.2.24	James, William. Principii di psicología. Milano, 1901.
Phil 5249.2.28A	Flournoy, T. La philosophie de William James. St. Blaise, 1911.
Phil 5249.2.28B	Flournoy, T. La philosophie de William James. St. Blaise, 1911.
Phil 5249.2.35	James, William. Précis de psychologie. 3. éd. Paris, 1912.
Phil 5249.2.38	James, William. On some of life's ideals. N.Y., 1900.
Phil 5249.2.39B	James, William. On some of life's ideals. N.Y., 1912.
Phil 5249.2.39D	James, William. On some of life's ideals. N.Y., 1912.
Phil 5249.2.40	James, William. Några livsideal samt de store männen och deres omgiming. Stockholm, 1917.
Phil 5249.2.45	James, William. Energies of men. N.Y., 1917.
Phil 5249.2.48	James, William. Energies of men. N.Y., 1926.
Phil 5249.2.80	Pamphlet box. Philosophy. Psychology. James, William.
Phil 5249.2.81	Ménard, A. Analyse et critique des princepes de la psychologie de W. James. Paris, 1911.
Phil 5249.2.81.5	Wilshire, Bruce. William James and phenomenology. Bloomington, 1968.
Phil 5249.2.85	Shargha, I.K. Examination of Prof. W. James' psychology. London, 1909.
Phil 5249.2.89	Jastrow, J. Notes in psychology. Madison, 1912.
Phil 5249.2.95	Ménard, A. Analyse et critique des princepes de la psychologie. Paris, 1911.
Phil 5249.2.99	Myers, F.W.H. The principles of psychology. London, 1891.
Phil 5249.3	Janes, Elijah. Human psychology. Oakland, 1885.
Phil 5249.3.2	Janes, Elijah. Human psychology. N.Y., 1886.
Phil 5249.3.5	Janes, Elijah. Human psychology. Oakland, 1884.
Phil 5249.4	Jardine, R. Elements of the psychology of cognition. London, 1874.
Phil 5249.5	Jodl, Friedrich. Lehrbuch der Psychologie. Stuttgart, 1896.
Phil 5249.5.5	Jodl, Friedrich. Lehrbuch der Psychologie. 2. Aufl. v.1-2. Stuttgart, 1903.
DL Phil 5249.6	Jastrow, J. Fact and fable in psychology. Boston, 1901.
Phil 5249.6.5	Jastrow, J. The psychology of conviction. Boston, 1918.
Phil 5249.6.10	Jastrow, J. The time-relations of mental phenomena. n.p. 1890-1912. 10 pam.
Phil 5249.6.15	Jastrow, J. Effective thinking. N.Y., 1931.
Phil 5249.6.20	Jastrow, J. Wish and wisdom. N.Y., 1935.
Phil 5249.6.25	Jastrow, J. The betrayal of intelligence. N.Y., 1938.
Phil 5249.7	Judd, C.H. Psychology. General introduction. N.Y., 1907.
Phil 5249.7.2	Judd, C.H. Psychology. General introduction. Boston, 1917.
Phil 5249.7.5.2	Judd, C.H. Laboratory manual of psychology. N.Y., 1907.
Phil 5249.7.5.3	Judd, C.H. Laboratory equipment for psychological experiments. N.Y., 1907.
Phil 5249.8	Jerusalem, W. Lehrbuch der Psychologie. Wien, 1902.
Phil 5249.8.10	Jerusalem, W. Lehrbuch der Psychologie. 4. Aufl. Wien, 1907.
Phil 5249.10	Jessen, Peter. Physiologie des menschlichen Denkens. Hannover, 1872.
Phil 5249.10.5	Jessen, Peter. Versuch einer wissenschaftlichen Begründung der Psychologie. Berlin, 1855.

Phil 5240 - 5265	Psychology - General treatises - Individual authors (A-Z) - cont.
Phil 5249.11	Jander, E. Leitfaden der Psychologie. Berlin, 1908.
Phil 5249.12	Jäger, Hermann. Die gemeinsame Wurzel der Kunst, Moral und Wissenschaft. Berlin, 1909.
Phil 5249.13	Jung, Carl G. Psychological types. London, 1923.
Phil 5249.13.5	Jung, Carl G. Psychological types. n.p., 192-.
Phil 5249.13.7	Jung, Carl G. Psychologische Typen. Zürich, 1925.
Phil 5249.13.8	Jung, Carl G. Psychologische Typen. Zürich, 1921.
Phil 5249.13.9	Jung, Carl G. Psychologische Typen. Zürich, 1930.
Phil 5249.13.10	Jung, Carl G. Psychologische Typen. Zürich, 1946.
Phil 5249.13.15	Jung, Carl G. Psychological factors determining human behavior. Cambridge, 1937.
Phil 5249.13.20	Jung, Carl G. Contributions to analytical psychology. London, 1928.
Phil 5249.13.25	Jung, Carl G. Psychologische Betrachtungen; eine Auslese aus den Schriften. Zürich, 1945.
Phil 5249.13.27	Jung, Carl G. Psychological reflections. N.Y., 1953.
Phil 5249.13.28	Jung, Carl G. C.G. Jung: psychological reflections. Princeton, 1970.
Phil 5249.13.30	Jung, Carl G. Bericht über das Berliner Seminar. Berlin, 1933.
Phil 5249.13.95	Corrie, Joan. C.G. Jung's Psychologie im Abriss. Zürich, 1929.
Phil 5249.13.99	Kellner, Kurt. C.G. Jung's Philosophie auf der Grundlage seiner Tiefenpsychologie. Inaug. Diss. Düren, 1937.
Phil 5249.14	Johanson, A.M. Influence of incentive and punishment upon reaction-time. N.Y., 1922.
Phil 5249.15	Jochnick, W. Mensklighetens vitigaste frågor. v.1-2. Stockholm, 1880-81.
Phil 5249.16	Jascalevich, A.A. Three conceptions of mind. N.Y., 1926.
Phil 5249.17	Jordan, G.J. The story of psychology. London, 1926.
Phil 5249.19	Jaensch, Erich. Über Gestaltpsychologie und Gestalttheorie. Langensalza, 1929.
Phil 5249.20	Joussain, A. Les sentiments et l'intelligence. Paris, 1930.
Phil 5249.21	Janet, Pierre. Les débuts de l'intelligence. Paris, 1935.
Phil 5249.21.3	Janet, Pierre. L'intelligence avant le langage. Paris, 1936.
Phil 5249.21.5	Janet, Pierre. La pensée interieure et ses troubles. pts.1-6. Paris, 1927.
Phil 5249.22	Jones, Llewellyn W. An introduction to theory and practice of psychology. London, 1934.
Phil 5249.23.5	Joly, Henri. Psychologie des grands hommes. 2. éd. Paris, 1891.
Phil 5249.24	Jaeger, Marc A. Relativitätstheorie des Menschengeistes. Zürich, 1958.
Phil 5249.25	Joereskog, K.G. Statistical estimation in factor analysis. Stockholm, 1963.
Phil 5249.26	Jeffrey, Melville. Beyond sense perception. 1. ed. Los Angeles, 1953.
Phil 5249.27	Jones, Harold Ellis. Studies in human development. N.Y., 1966.
Phil 5249.29	Jaeger, Adolf Otto. Dimensionen der Intelligenz. Göttingen, 1967.
Phil 5249.30	Jourard, Sidney Marshall. Disclosing man to himself. Princeton, 1968.
Phil 5249.31	Jordan, Nehemiah. Themes in speculative psychology. London, 1968.
Phil 5249.32	Jaeger, Marc A. Geist und Seele im technischen Zeitalter. Zürich, 1968.
Phil 5250.1	Kirchmann, J.H. von. Die Lehre vom Wissen. Berlin, 1871.
Phil 5250.2	Külpe, Oswald. Outlines of psychology. London, 1895.
Phil 5250.2.3A	Külpe, Oswald. Outlines of psychology. London, 1921.
Phil 5250.2.3B	Külpe, Oswald. Outlines of psychology. London, 1921.
Phil 5250.2.5	Külpe, Oswald. Grundriss der Psychologie. Leipzig, 1893.
Phil 5250.2.8	Külpe, Oswald. Vorlesungen über Psychologie. Leipzig, 1920.
Phil 5250.2.9	Külpe, Oswald. Vorlesungen über Psychologie. 2. Aufl. Leipzig, 1922.
Phil 5250.3	Kirkpatrick, E.A. Inductive psychology. N.Y., 1895.
Phil 5250.3.6	Kirkpatrick, E.A. Genetic psychology. N.Y., 1925.
Phil 5250.4	Kroell, H. Die Seele im Lichte des Monismus. Strassburg, 1902.
Phil 5250.4.5	Kroell, H. Die Aufbau der menschlichen Seele. Leipzig, 1900.
Phil 5250.5	Kellogg, A.M. Elementary psychology. N.Y., 1894.
Phil 5250.6	Kostyleff, N. La crise de la psychologie expérimentale. Paris, 1911.
Phil 5250.7	Koffka, K. Zur Analyse der Vorstellungen und ihre Gesetze. Leipzig, 1912.
Phil 5250.7.10	Koffka, K. Beiträge zur Psychologie der Gestalt. Leipzig, 1919.
Phil 5250.7.15	Koffka, K. Principles of Gestalt psychology. N.Y., 1935.
Phil 5250.7.19	Koffka, K. Principles of Gestalt psychology. N.Y., 1935.
Phil 5250.9	Körner, F. Die Seele und ihre Thätigkeiten. 2. Aufl. Leipzig, 1890.
Phil 5250.10	Kirchner, F. A student's manual of psychology. London, 1888.
Phil 5250.10.5	Kirchner, F. Katechismus der Psychologie. Leipzig, 1883.
Phil 5250.11	Kaploun, Albert. Psychologie générale. Lausanne, 1919.
Phil 5250.12	Kroman, Kristian. Korfattet taenke-og sjaelelaere. 5. udg. København, 1914.
Phil 5250.12.3	Kroman, Kristian. Korfattet taenke-og sjaelelaere. 3. udg. København, 1899.
Phil 5250.12.15	Kroman, Kristian. Grundtraek af sjaelelaeren. 6. udg. København, 1920.
Phil 5250.12.17	Kroman, Kristian. Grundtraek af sjaelelaeren. 7. udg. København, 1928.
Phil 5250.13	Krueger, Felix. Über Entwicklungspsychologie. Leipzig, 1915.
Phil 5250.13.5	Krueger, Felix. Ist Philosophie ohne Psychologie möglich? Eine Erwiderung. München, 1896.
Phil 5250.13.9	Krueger, Felix. Neue psychologische Studien. München. 1926-1939 23v.
Phil 5250.13.20	Krueger, Felix. Beobachtungen über zweiklänge. Leipzig, 1900-08. 10 pam.
Phil 5250.13.25	Krueger, Felix. Zur Philosophie und Psychologie der Ganzheit. Berlin, 1953.
Phil 5250.13.80	Odebrecht, Rudolf. Gefühl und Ganzheit. Berlin, 1929.
Phil 5250.13.85	Wellek, Albert. Die Wiederherstellung der Seelenwissenschaft im Lebenswerk Felix Kruegers. Hamburg, 1950.
Phil 5250.13.87	Wellek, Albert. Das Problem des seelischen Seins. 2. Aufl. Meisenheim, 1953.
Phil 5250.14	Königbauer, J. Grundzüge der Psychologie und Logik. 2. Aufl. Regensburg, 1893.
Phil 5250.15.11	Köhler, Wolfgang. Gestalt psychology. N.Y., 1929.

Classified Listing

Phil 5250.15.15   Köhler, Wolfgang. Gestalt psychology. N.Y., 1929.
Phil 5250.15.15.5   Köhler, Wolfgang. Gestalt psychology. N.Y., 1947.
Phil 5250.15.15.10   Köhler, Wolfgang. Gestalt psychology. N.Y., 1947.
Phil 5250.15.16   Köhler, Wolfgang. Dynamics in psychology. N.Y., 1940.
Phil 5250.15.17   Köhler, Wolfgang. Dynamische Zusammenhänge in der Psychologie. Bern, 1958.
Phil 5250.15.18   Köhler, Wolfgang. The task of Gestalt psychology. Princeton, 1969.
Phil 5250.15.80   Franquiz Ventura, José A. La filosofía de las ciencias de Wolfgang Köhler. México, 1941.
Phil 5250.16   Kramar, W. Neue Grundlagen zur Psychologie des Denkens. Brünn, 1914.
Phil 5250.17   Kantor, J.R. Principles of psychology. N.Y., 1924-26. 2v.
Phil 5250.17.2A   Kantor, J.R. Problems of physiological psychology. Bloomington, 1947.
Phil 5250.17.2B   Kantor, J.R. Problems of physiological psychology. Bloomington, 1947.
Phil 5250.17.5   Kantor, J.R. A survey of the science of psychology. Bloomington, 1933.
Phil 5250.17.10   Kantor, J.R. Psychology and logic. Bloomington, 1945. 2v.
Phil 5250.18   Kraepelin, Emil. Om sjalsarbete. Stockholm, 1894.
Phil 5250.18.10   Kraepelin, Emil. Über die Beeinflussung einfacher psychischer Vorgänge durch einige Arzneimittel. Jena, 1892.
Phil 5250.19   Key, Ellen. Krinns-psykologi och krinnlig logik. Stockholm, 1896.
Phil 5250.20   Kaulich, W. Handbuch der Psychologie. Graz, 1870. 3 pam.
Phil 5250.21   König, Josef. Der Begriff der Intuition. Halle, 1926.
Phil 5250.22   Keyser, C.J. Thinking about thinking. N.Y., 1926.
Phil 5250.23   Kaim, J.R. Psychologische Probleme in der Philosophie. München, 1921.
Phil 5250.24   Kiesewetter, J.G.C. Fassliche Darstellung der Erfahrungsseelenlehre. Wien, 1817.
Phil 5250.25   Krejči, F.V. Základy vědeckého systému psychologie. Praha, 1929.
Phil 5250.26   King, W.P. Behaviourism; a symposium by Josiah Morse. London, 1930.
Phil 5250.28   Kleinpeter, H. Vorträge zur Einführung in die Psychologie. Leipzig, 1914.
Phil 5250.29   Kozlowski, W.M. Thought considered as action and the logical axioms. N.Y., 1927.
Phil 5250.30   Krauss, S. Der seelische Konflikt; Psychologie und existenziale Bedeutung. Stuttgart, 1933.
Phil 5250.31   Kastein, G.W. Eine Kritik der Ganzheitstheorien. Leiden, 1937.
Phil 5250.32.5   Kaila, Eino. Personlighetens psykologi. Helsingfors, 1935.
Phil 5250.33   Konczewski, C. La pensée préconsciente. Paris, 1939.
Phil 5250.34.5   Katona, George. Organizing and memorizing. N.Y., 1949.
Phil 5250.35   Kornilov, K.N. Psikhologiia. Moskva, 1941.
Phil 5250.35.2   Kornilov, K.N. Psikhologiia. Moskva, 1946.
Phil 5250.35.3   Kornilov, K.N. Psikhologiia. Izd. 8. Moskva, 1948.
Phil 5250.36A   Kardiner, Abram. The psychological frontiers of society. N.Y., 1945.
Phil 5250.36B   Kardiner, Abram. The psychological frontiers of society. N.Y., 1945.
Phil 5250.36C   Kardiner, Abram. The psychological frontiers of society. N.Y., 1945.
Phil 5250.37.5   Katz, David. Psychologischer Atlas. Basel, 1945.
Phil 5250.37.6   Katz, David. Psychological atlas. N.Y., 1948.
Phil 5250.37.10   Katz, David. Handbuch der Psychologie. Basel, 1951.
Phil 5250.37.11   Katz, David. Handbuch der Psychologie. Basel, 1960.
Phil 5250.37.20   Katz, David. Studien zur experimentellen Psychologie. Basel, 1953.
Phil 5250.38   Kahn, T.C. The Kahn test of symbol arrangement. n.p., 1949.
Phil 5250.39   Künkel, Fritz. In search of maturity. N.Y., 1944.
Phil 5250.40   Karn, H.W. An introduction to psychology. N.Y., 1955.
Phil 5250.42   Knight, Rex. A modern introduction to psychology. 5. ed. London, 1957.
Phil 5250.45.2   Krech, David. Elements of psychology. N.Y., 1965.
Phil 5250.50   Kunz, Hans. Über den Sinn und die Grenzen des psychologischen Erkennens. Stuttgart, 1957.
Phil 5250.55   Keller, F. Principles of psychology. N.Y., 1950.
Phil 5250.60   Kremers, Johan. Scientific psychology and naive psychology. Nijmegen, 1960.
Phil 5250.65   Kelly, William L. Die neuscholastische und die empirische Psychologie. Meisenheim, 1961.
Phil 5250.70   Kotarbiński, Tadeusz. Osnova primena prakseologije. Beograd, 1961.
Phil 5250.72   Kagan, J. Birth to maturity. N.Y., 1962.
Phil 5250.75   Kopnin, P.V. Problemy myshleniia v sovremennoi nauke. Moskva, 1964.
Phil 5250.76   Kahn, Jack Harold. Human growth and the development of personality. 1. ed. N.Y., 1965.
Phil 5250.78   Kotarbiński, Tadeusz. Praxiology; an introduction to the sciences of efficient action. 1. English ed. Oxford, 1965.
Phil 5250.79.4   Kotarbiński, Tadeusz. Traktat o dobrej robocie. Wyd. 4. Wrocław, 1969.
Phil 5250.80   Koestler, Arthur. The ghost in the machine. London, 1967.
VPhil 5250.81   Kozielecki, Józef. Zagadnienia psychologii myślenia. Wyd. 1. Warszawa, 1966.
Phil 5250.84   Knapp, Franz. Das geistige Leben der Person in den persönlichkeitspsychologischen Schichttheorien. Inaug. Diss. Heidelberg? 1967?
Phil 5250.86   Keiter, Friedrich. Verhaltensforschung im Rahmen der Wissenschaften vom Menschen. Göttingen, 1969.
Phil 5251.1.2   Ladd, G.T. Primer of psychology. N.Y., 1894.
Phil 5251.1.5   Ladd, G.T. Philosophy of mind. N.Y., 1895.
Phil 5251.1.10   Ladd, G.T. Psychology descriptive and explanatory. N.Y., 1895.
Phil 5251.1.15   Ladd, G.T. Elements of physiological psychology. N.Y., 1887.
Phil 5251.1.15.3   Ladd, G.T. Elements of physiological psychology. London, 1889.
NEDL Phil 5251.1.15.8   Ladd, G.T. Elements of physiological psychology. N.Y., 1896.
Phil 5251.1.16   Ladd, G.T. Outlines of physiological psychology. N.Y., 1896.
Phil 5251.1.18   Ladd, G.T. Elements of physiological psychology. N.Y., 1911.
Phil 5251.1.20   Ladd, G.T. Descriptive psychology, N.Y., 1898.

Phil 5251.1.22   Ladd, G.T. Elements of physiology, psychology. N.Y., 1911.
Phil 5251.1.30   Mills, Eugene S. George Trumbull Ladd: pioneer American psychologist. Cleveland, 1969.
Phil 5251.2   Lallebasque. Introduzione alla filosofia naturale di pensiero. Lugano, 1824.
Phil 5251.3   Langer, P. Die Grundlagen der Psychophysik. Jena, 1876.
Phil 5251.3.5   Langer, P. Psychophysische Streitfragen. Ohrdruf, 1893.
Phil 5251.3.50.01   Pamphlet box. Psychology. Langer, Walter C.
Phil 5251.4   Langel, A. Les problèmes. Paris, 1873.
Phil 5251.4.5   Langel, A. Les problèmes de la vie. Paris, 1867.
Phil 5251.6.2.6   Lewes, G.H. Problems of life and mind. 1st series. London, 1874-75. 2v.
Phil 5251.6.3   Lewes, G.H. Problems of life and mind. 1st-3rd series. London, 1874. 5v.
Phil 5251.6.4   Lewes, G.H. The study of psychology. London, 1879.
Phil 5251.6.4.5   Lewes, G.H. Problems of life and mind. 3rd series. Boston, 1879-80. 2v.
Phil 5251.6.5   Lewes, G.H. The physical basis of mind. London, 1893.
Phil 5251.6.5.2   Lewes, G.H. The physical basis of mind. Boston, 1891.
Phil 5251.7   Lindner, G.A. Lehrbuch der empiriochen Psychologie. Wien, 1872.
Phil 5251.7.3   Lindner, G.A. Lehrbuch der empiriochen Psychologie. 9. Aufl. Wien, 1889.
Phil 5251.7.5   Lindner, G.A. Manual of empirical psychology. Boston, 1889.
Phil 5251.7.7   Lindner, G.A. Leerbaek der empirische zielkunde. Zutphen, 18- .
Phil 5251.8   Lipps, T. Seelenlebens. Bonn, 1883.
Phil 5251.8.5   Lipps, T. Leitfaden der Psychologie. Leipzig, 1903.
Phil 5251.8.7   Lipps, T. Psychologische Studien. Heidelberg, 1885.
Phil 5251.8.8   Lipps, T. Psychologische Studien. Leipzig, 1905.
Phil 5251.8.15   Lipps, T. Psychological studies. 2d ed. Baltimore, 1926.
Phil 5251.8.25   Lipps, T. Psychologie der Komik. n.p., 1888-1906. 23 pam.
Phil 5251.9   Lichthorn, C. Die Erforschung der physiologische Naturgesetze. Breslau, 1875.
Phil 5251.10   Lazarus, M. Das Leben der Seele. Berlin, 1876. 3v.
Phil 5251.10.9   Lazarus, M. Über Tact, Kunst, Freundschaft und Sitten. 3e Aufl. Berlin, 1896.
Phil 5251.11   Liguet, G.H. Idée générales de psychologie. Paris, 1906.
Phil 5251.12   Lipmann, O. Grundriss der Psychologie für Juristen. Leipzig, 1908.
Phil 5251.13   Lloyd, W.E. Psychology, normal and abnormal. Los Angeles, 1908.
Phil 5251.13.2   Lloyd, W.E. Psychology, normal and abnormal. N.Y., 1910.
Phil 5251.16   Louden, D.M. van. Onderzoek naar den duur der eenvoudige psychische processen v.n. bij de Psychosen. Amsterdam, 1905.
Phil 5251.17   Lanfeld, H.S. Elementry laboratory course in psychology. Boston, 1916.
Phil 5251.18   Lynch, Arthur. Psychology; a new system. London, 1912. 2v.
Phil 5251.18.5   Lynch, Arthur. Principles of psychology. London, 1923.
Phil 5251.19   Lubac, Émile. Esquisse d'un système de psychologie rationnelle. Paris, 1903.
Phil 5251.20   Lehmann, Alfred. Grundzüge der Psychophysiologie. Leipzig, 1912.
Phil 5251.20.5   Lehmann, Alfred. Lehrbuch der psychologischen Methodik. Leipzig, 1906.
Phil 5251.20.9   Lehmann, Alfred. Die körperlichen Äusserungen psychischer Zustände. Leipzig, 1899-1905. 4v.
Phil 5251.20.15   Lehmann, Alfred. Den individuelle sjaelelige udrikling. København, 1920.
Phil 5251.20.20   Lehmann, Alfred. Uppfostran till arbete. Stockholm, 1920.
Phil 5251.21   Langwieser, Karl. Der Bewusstseinsmechanismus. Leipzig, 1897.
Phil 5251.22   Leuchtenberger, G. Houptbegriffe der Psychologie. Berlin, 1899.
Phil 5251.23   Losskii, N.O. Die Grundlehren der Psychologie. Leipzig, 1904.
Phil 5251.23.5   Losskii, N.O. Chuvstvennaia, intellektual'naia i misticheskaia intuitsiia. Paris, 1938.
Phil 5251.24   Liqueno, Jose M. Compendio de psicologia contemporanea. Córdoba, 1919.
Phil 5251.25   Larguier des Bancels, Jean. Introduction à la psychologie. Paris, 1921.
Phil 5251.27   Lothian, A.J.D. An outline of psychology for education. London, 1923.
Phil 5251.28   Lambek, C. Psychologiske studier. Supplementhefte til tidsschrift for aandskultur. København, 1904.
Phil 5251.28.7   Lambek, C. The structure of our apprehension of reality. Copenhagen, 1933.
Phil 5251.29   Lloyd, R.E. Life and word. London, 1924.
Phil 5251.30   Laromiguière, P. Leçons de philosophie, ou Essai sur les facultés de l'ame. Paris, 1815-18. 2v.
Phil 5251.30.5   Laromiguière, P. Leçons de philosophie:sur les principes de l'intelligence. 5. ed. Paris, 1833. 2v.
Phil 5251.31   Lungwitz, H. Die Entdeckung der Seele. Leipzig, 1925.
Phil 5251.32   La Vaissière, J. de. Elements of experimental pseyhology. St. Louis, 1926.
Phil 5251.33   Love, Mary C. Human conduct and the law. Menasha, 1925.
Phil 5251.34.3   Lindworsky, J. Theoretische Psychologie im Umriss. 3. Aufl. Leipzig, 1926.
Phil 5251.34.10   Lindworsky, J. Theoretical psychology. St. Louis, 1932.
Phil 5251.34.15   Lindworsky, J. Experimental psychology. London, 1931.
Phil 5251.35   Lund, F.H. Psychology: the science of mental activity. N.Y., 1927.
Phil 5251.35.9   Lund, F.H. Psychology: an empirical study of behavior. N.Y., 1933.
Phil 5251.36   Leary, Daniel Bell. Modern psychology, normal and abnormal. Philadelphia, 1928.
Phil 5251.38   Loomans, Charles. De la connaissance de soi-même. Bruxelles, 1880.
Phil 5251.39   Landquist, J. Människokunskap. Stockholm, 1920.
Phil 5251.40.5A   Luria, A.R. The nature of human conflicts. N.Y., 1932.
Phil 5251.40.5B   Luria, A.R. The nature of human conflicts. N.Y., 1932.
Phil 5251.41A   Lewin, Kurt. A dynamic theory of personality. N.Y., 1935.
Phil 5251.41B   Lewin, Kurt. A dynamic theory of personality. N.Y., 1935.
Phil 5251.41.9   Lewin, Kurt. Principles of topological psychology. 1st ed. N.Y., 1936.
Phil 5251.41.15A   Lewin, Kurt. Resolving social conflicts. 1st ed. N.Y., 1948.
Phil 5251.41.15B   Lewin, Kurt. Resolving social conflicts. 1st ed. N.Y., 1948.
Phil 5251.41.25   Lewin, Kurt. Field theory in social science. 1st ed. N.Y., 1951.

Classified Listing

Phil 5240 - 5265 Psychology - General treatises - Individual authors (A-Z) - cont.

Phil 5251.41.80   Ossicuri, Adriano. L'opera di Kurt Lewin nella psicologia contemporanea. Messina, 1960.

Phil 5251.41.85   Schwermer, Josef. Die experimentelle Willenspsychologie Kurt Lewin. Meisenheim, 1966.

Phil 5251.41.90   Kaufmann, Pierre. Kurt Lewin, une théorie du change dans les sciences de l'homme. Paris, 1968.

Phil 5251.41.95   Marrow, Alfred Jay. The practical theorist; the life and work of Kurt Lewin. N.Y., 1969.

Phil 5251.42   Levy, Hyman. Thinking. London, 1936.

Phil 5251.43   Lévy, Albert. Le sens intime en psychologie. Bruxelles, 1896.

Phil 5251.44.7   Link, Henry C. The rediscovery of man. N.Y., 1939.

Phil 5251.46   Loux, Samuel. Man and his fellowmen. London, 1945.

Phil 5251.50   Lawrence, Merle. Studies in human behavior. Princeton, 1949.

Phil 5251.51   Lundholm, H. God's failure or man's folly? Cambridge, 1949.

Phil 5251.52   Leithauser, J.C. Das unbekannte Ich. Berlin, 1955.

Phil 5251.53   Lückert, Heinz Rolf. Konflikt-Psychologie. München, 1957.

Phil 5251.54   Lafitte, Paul. The person in psychology. N.Y., 1957.

Phil 5251.56   Lewis, Don. Quantitative methods in psychology. N.Y., 1960.

Phil 5251.57   Leyden. Universiteit. De toekomst der psychologie. Leiden, 1960.

Phil 5251.58A   Lashley, K.S. The neuropsychology of Lashley. N.Y., 1960.

Phil 5251.58B   Lashley, K.S. The neuropsychology of Lashley. N.Y., 1960.

Phil 5251.60   Luce, Robert D. Development in mathematical psychology. Glencoe, 1960.

Phil 5251.60.10   Luce, Robert D. Handbook of mathematical psychology. N.Y., 1963. 2v.

Phil 5251.62   Lamouche, André. Psychologie. Paris, 1957.

Phil 5251.64   Leonhard, Karl. Biologische Psychologie. Leipzig, 1962.

Phil 5251.65   Levitov, N.D. O psikhicheskikh sostoianiiakh cheloveka. Moskva, 1964.

Phil 5251.66   Linschoten, Johannes. Idolen van de psycholoog. Utrecht, 1964.

Phil 5251.67   Lorenz, Konrad Zacharias. Evolution and modification of behavior. Chicago, 1965.

Phil 5251.68   Leont'ev, Aleksei N. Problemy razvitiia psikhiki. Moskva, 1959.

Phil 5251.70   Lacroze, René. Eléments d'anthropologie. Paris, 1966.

Phil 5251.72   Leite, Dante M. Psicologia diferencial. São Paulo, 1966.

Phil 5251.74   Losskii, N.O. Principles of voluntaristic psychology. n.p., 1935. 2v.

Phil 5251.76   Lauer, Hans Erhard. Die Rätsel der Seele: Tiefenpsychologie und Anthroposophie. 2. Aufl. Freiburg, 1964.

Phil 5252.2   Mahan, A. System of intellectual philosophy. N.Y., 1847.

Phil 5252.2.5   Mahan, A. System of mental philosophy. 4th ed. Chicago, 1886.

Phil 5252.5   Martin, T. Zetemata dianoetika. Liverpool, 1821.

Phil 5252.6   Mehring, G. Philosophische-Kritische Grundsätze der Selbsterkenntniss. Stuttgart, 1857.

Phil 5252.7A   Mill, J. Analysis of the phenomena of human mind. London, 1829. 2v.

Phil 5252.7B   Mill, J. Analysis of the phenomena of human mind. v.1. London, 1829.

Phil 5252.7.2   Mill, J. On the mind. London, 1869. 2v.

Phil 5252.8   Moore, G. Power of the soul. London, 1845.

Phil 5252.9   Morell, J.D. Elements of psychology. pt. 1. Photoreproduction. London, 1853.

Phil 5252.9.5   Morell, J.D. Introduction to mental philosophy. London, 1862.

Phil 5252.10   Müller, F.A. Das Axiom der Psychophysik. Marburg, 1882.

Phil 5252.11   Munsell, O.S. Psychology. N.Y., 1880.

Phil 5252.12   Münsterberg, H. Beiträge zur experimentische Psychologie. Freiberg, 1888-92.

Phil 5252.12.9A   Münsterberg, H. Grundzüge der Psychologie. Leipzig, 1900.

Phil 5252.12.9B   Münsterberg, H. Grundzüge der Psychologie. Leipzig, 1900.

Phil 5252.12.10   Münsterberg, H. Grundzüge der Psychologie. 2. Aufl. Leipzig, 1918.

Phil 5252.12.13.2   Münsterberg, H. On the witness stand. N.Y., 1909.

Phil 5252.12.17   Münsterberg, H. American problems. N.Y., 1910.

Phil 5252.12.18   Münsterberg, H. On the witness stand. N.Y., 1933.

Phil 5252.12.29   Münsterberg, H. Social studies of today. London, 1913.

Phil 5252.12.35   Münsterberg, H. Psychology and social sanity. Garden City, 1914.

Phil 5252.12.45   Münsterberg, H. Psychology general and applied. N.Y., 1914.

Phil 5252.13   Murphy, J.J. Habit and intelligence. London, 1869. 2v.

Phil 5252.13.2   Murphy, J.J. Habit and intelligence. 2d. ed. London, 1879.

Phil 5252.14   Murray, J.C. Handbook of psychology. Boston, 1888.

Phil 5252.14.5   Murray, J.C. An introduction to psychology. Boston, 1904.

Phil 5252.15   Mercier, C.A. Psychology normal and morbid. London, 1901.

Phil 5252.16   Mitchell, W. Structure and growth of the mind. London, 1907.

Phil 5252.17   Mellone, Sydney Herbert. Elements of psychology. Edinburgh, 1907.

Phil 5252.18.3   McDougall, William. An introduction to social psychology. 15th ed. Boston, 1923.

Phil 5252.18.5.4   McDougall, William. An introduction to social psychology. 3d ed. London, 1910.

Phil 5252.18.6   McDougall, William. An introduction to social psychology. Boston, 1926.

Phil 5252.18.8   McDougall, William. The group mind. Cambridge, 1920.

Phil 5252.18.8.2   McDougall, William. The group mind. 2d ed. N.Y., 1920.

Phil 5252.18.8.3   McDougall, William. The group mind. N.Y., 1920.

Phil 5252.18.11A   McDougall, William. Psychology, the study of behavior. N.Y., 1912.

Phil 5252.18.11B   McDougall, William. Psychology, the study of behavior. N.Y., 1912.

Phil 5252.18.12   McDougall, William. Psychology, the study of behavior. London, 1912.

Phil 5252.18.12.10   McDougall, William. Psychology. 2d ed. London, 1952.

Phil 5252.18.13   McDougall, William. Psychologi. København, 1926.

Phil 5252.18.15   McDougall, William. Outline of psychology. N.Y., 1923.

Phil 5252.18.16   McDougall, William. Outline of psychology. N.Y., 1926.

Phil 5252.18.25   McDougall, William. The energies of men. N.Y., 1933.

Phil 5252.18.30   McDougall, William. A contribution towards an improvement in psychological method. n.p., 1898-1914. 8 pam.

Phil 5252.18.35   McDougall, William. Religion and the sciences of life. London, 1934.

Phil 5252.18.37   McDougall, William. The frontiers of psychology. N.Y., 1934.

Phil 5240 - 5265 Psychology - General treatises - Individual authors (A-Z) - cont.

Phil 5252.18.38   McDougall, William. The riddle of life. London, 1938.

Phil 5252.18.50   Hollander, B. McDougall's social psychology anticipated by 100 years. n.p., 1924.

Phil 5252.18.54   Fochtman, V.A. Das Lieb-Seele-Problem bei George Trumbull Ladd und William McDougall. Inaug. Diss. München, 1928.

Phil 5252.18.60   Becker, F. Die Instinkt-Psychologie William McDougalls. Reichenberg, 1933.

Phil 5252.18.65   Robinson, A.L. William McDougall, M.B., D.S.C., F.R.S.: a bibliography. Durham, 1943.

Phil 5252.19   Myers, C.S. Text-book of experimental psychology. N.Y., 1909.

Phil 5252.19.2.5   Myers, C.S. A text book of experimental psychology with laboratory exercises. 2nd ed. pt.1. Cambridge, 1911.

Phil 5252.19.3   Myers, C.S. Text-book of experimental psychology. 3d ed. Cambridge, 1925.

Phil 5252.19.8   Myers, C.S. An introduction to experimental psychology. Cambridge, 1911.

Phil 5252.19.20   Myers, C.S. A psychologist's point of view. London, 1933.

Phil 5252.20   March, J.L. A theory of mind. N.Y., 1908.

Phil 5252.21   Milliet, J.P. La dynamis et les trois ames. Paris, 1908.

Phil 5252.22   Miller, T.E. The psychology of thinking. N.Y., 1909.

Phil 5252.23   Pamphlet box. MacDougall, R. Minor writings.

Phil 5252.23.5   MacDougall, R. The general problems of psychology. N.Y., 1922.

Phil 5252.23.20   MacDougall, R. The physical characteristics of attention. n.p., 1896-1904. 15 pam.

Phil 5252.25   Etudes de psychologie. Louvain, 1912.

Phil 5252.26   Meyer, Semi. Probleme der Entwicklung des Geistes. Leipzig, 1913.

Phil 5252.26.10   Meyer, Semi. Die geistige Wirklichkeit. Stuttgart, 1925.

Phil 5252.27   Meynert, T. Sammlung von populär- wissenschaftlichen Vorträgen über den bau und die leistungen des gehirns. Wien, 1892.

Phil 5252.28   Messer, A. Psychologie. Stuttgart, 1914.

Phil 5252.28.2   Messer, A. Psychologie. 2. Aufl. Stuttgart, 1920.

Phil 5252.28.5   Messer, A. Empfindung und Denken. Leipzig, 1908.

Phil 5252.30   Müller, G.E. Zur Grundlegung der Psychophysik. 2. Ausg. Berlin, 1879.

Phil 5252.30.5   Müller, G.E. Die Gesichtspunkte und der Tatsachen der psychophysischen Methodik. Wiesbaden, 1904.

Phil 5252.30.9   Müller, G.E. Abriss der Psychologie. Göttingen, 1924.

Phil 5252.31   Morando, G. Psicologia. 2a. ed. Voghera, 1915.

Phil 5252.32   Marchesini, Giovanni. Psicologia elementare, ad uso dei licei. pt.1-3. Firenze, 1916. 2v.

Phil 5252.33.5   Monrad, Marcus. Psychologie; grundrids til brug. Christiania, 1892.

Phil 5252.34   Marbe, K. Grundzüge der forensichen Psychologie. München, 1913.

Phil 5252.36.2   Meerkatz. Einführung in die Psychologie. 2. Aufl. Halle, 1919.

Phil 5252.37   Marett, R.R. Psychology and folk-lore. N.Y., 1920.

Phil 5252.38   Müller-Freienfels, R. Das Denken und die Phantasie. Leipzig, 1916.

Phil 5252.38.5   Müller-Freienfels, R. Grundzüge einer Lebenspsychologie. Leipzig, 1924-25. 2v.

Phil 5252.38.10   Müller-Freienfels, R. Tagebuch eines Psychologen. Leipzig, 1931.

Phil 5252.38.15   Müller-Freienfels, R. Die Seele des Alltags. 2. Aufl. Berlin, 1925.

Phil 5252.38.20   Müller-Freienfels, R. Menschenkenntnis und Menschenbehandlung. Berlin, 1951.

Phil 5252.39.2   Mobius, P. Die Hoffnungslosigkeit allen Psychologie. Halle, 1907.

Phil 5252.40   Martin, Otto. Zur Psychologie des Verstehens wissenschaftlicher Texte. Inaug. Diss. Freiburg, 1914.

Phil 5252.41   McKim, William D. A study for the times. N.Y., 1920.

Phil 5252.42   Meyer, M.F. Psychology of the other one. Columbia, 1921.

Phil 5252.42.15   Meyer, M.F. Über Tonverschmelzung. n.p., 1898-1913. 20 pam.

Phil 5252.43   Moore, J.S. The foundations of psychology. Princeton, 1921.

Phil 5252.43.5   Moore, J.S. The foundations of psychology. 2d ed. Princeton, 1924.

Phil 5252.44   Pamphlet box. Psychology. MacDonald, Arthur.

Phil 5252.44.2F   Pamphlet box. Psychology. MacDonald, Arthur.

Phil 5252.45   Masci, Filippo. El materialismo psicofisico. Napoli, 1901.

Phil 5252.45.5   Masci, Filippo. Introduzione generale alla psicologia. Milano, 1926.

Phil 5252.46   Mentré, F. Espèces et variétés d'intelligences. Thèse. Paris, 1920.

Phil 5252.46.5   Mentré, F. Espèces et variétés d'intelligences. Thèse. Paris, 1920.

Phil 5252.47   McKerrow, J.C. The appearance of mind. London, 1923.

Phil 5252.48   Montet, C. de. Les problemes fondamentaux de la psychologie medical. Berne, 1922.

Phil 5252.49   Montet, C. de. Psychologie et development de l'enfance à la vieillesse. Berne, 1922.

Phil 5252.49.5   Montet, C. de. Le relativisme psychologique et la recherche médicale. Paris, 1926.

Phil 5252.50   Moore, T.V. Dynamic psychology. Philadelphia, 1924.

Phil 5252.50.2   Moore, T.V. Dynamic psychology. 2d ed. Philadelphia, 1926.

Phil 5252.50.10   Moore, T.V. Cognitive psychology. Chicago, 1939.

Phil 5252.51   Mortensen, M. Grundrids af psykologi og paedogogik. 2. utg. København, 1901.

Phil 5252.52   Meyer, Hans. Zur Psychologie der Gegenwart. Köln, 1909.

Phil 5252.53   Mischer. Psychologische Fragen. Stendal, 1884.

Phil 5252.54   Michelet, C.L. Anthropologie und Psychologie. Berlin, 1840.

Phil 5252.55   Meier, M. Der Seelenbegriff in der modernen Psychologie. München, n.d.

Phil 5252.56   Mayer, A. Zur Seelenfrage. 1866.

Phil 5252.58   Martin, E.D. Psychology. pt.1-20. N.Y., 1924.

Phil 5252.58.2   Martin, E.D. Psychology. N.Y., 1924.

Phil 5252.60   McDowall, R.J.S. The mind. N.Y., 1927.

Phil 5252.60.12   McDowall, R.J.S. Sane psychology. 2d ed. London, 1944.

Phil 5252.61   MacCurdy, J.T. Common principles in psychology and physiology. N.Y., 1928.

Phil 5252.61.2   MacCurdy, J.T. Common principles in psychology and physiology. Cambridge, 1928.

Phil 5252.62   Martin, L.J. Zur Analyse der Unterschiedsempfindlichkeit. Leipzig, 1899.

Htn   Phil 5252.62.5*   Martin, L.J. Psychology of aesthetics. n.p., 1905-1907. 4 pam.

Phil 5252.63A   Murchison, C.A. The foundations of experimental psychology. Worcester, 1929.

Classified Listing

Phil 5240 - 5265 **Psychology - General treatises - Individual authors (A-Z) - cont.**

Phil 5252.63B   Murchison, C.A. The foundations of experimental psychology. Worcester, 1929.

Phil 5252.63.10   Murchison, C.A. Handbook of general experimental psychology. Worcester, 1934.

Phil 5252.64   Marston, W.M. Integrative psychology. London, 1931.

Phil 5252.65   Mathaei, Rupprecht. Das Gestaltproblem. München, 1929.

Phil 5252.66   Musmann, J.G. Lehrbuch der Seelenwissenschaft. Berlin, 1827.

Phil 5252.67   Morgan, John J.B. An introduction to psychology. N.Y., 1927.

Phil 5252.68.5   Morris, Charles W. Six theories of mind. Chicago, 1959.

Phil 5252.69A   Murphy, Gardner. General psychology. N.Y., 1933.

Phil 5252.69B   Murphy, Gardner. General psychology. N.Y., 1933.

Phil 5252.69.10   Murphy, Gardner. A briefer general psychology. N.Y., 1935.

Phil 5252.69.15   Murphy, Gardner. An introduction to psychology. N.Y., 1951.

Phil 5252.69.20   Murphy, Gardner. Encounter with reality. Boston, 1968.

Phil 5252.69.25   Murphy, Gardner. Psychological thought from Pythagoras to Freud. 1st. ed. N.Y., 1968.

Phil 5252.70   Marconi, A. Oggetto ed uficio della psicologia. Milano, 1875.

Phil 5252.71   Mead, George H. The definition of the psychical. Chicago, 1903.

Phil 5252.72   Munn, Norman L. A laboratory manual in general experimental psychology. Pittsburgh, 1934.

Phil 5252.73   Mantell, U. Aktualgenetische Untersuchungen an Situationsdarstellungen. Inaug. Diss. München, 1936.

Phil 5252.74   Malgand, W. De l'action à la pensée. Paris, 1935.

Phil 5252.74.5   Malgand, W. Devant la réalité. 1. éd. Paris, 1953.

Phil 5252.75   Mander, A.E. Psychology for everyman. London, 1939.

Phil 5252.76   Munzinger, K.F. Psychology. Denver, 1939.

Phil 5252.76.5   Munzinger, K.F. Psychology. N.Y., 1942.

Phil 5252.77   Mackenzie, M. The human mind. Philadelphia, 1941.

Phil 5252.78A   Miller, N.E. Social learning and imitation. New Haven, 1941.

Phil 5252.78B   Miller, N.E. Social learning and imitation. New Haven, 1941.

Phil 5252.78.5   Miller, N.E. Social learning and imitation. New Haven, 1953.

NEDL Phil 5252.79   Mouchet, E. Percepción instinto y razon. Buenos Aires, 1941.

Phil 5252.80   Mira y Lopez E. Problemas psicologicos actuales. Buenos Aires, 1940.

Phil 5252.81A   Masserman, J.H. Behavior and neurosis. Chicago, 1943.

Phil 5252.81.2   Masserman, J.H. Behavior and neurosis. N.Y., 1964.

Phil 5252.82.2A   Morgan, Clifford Thomas. Physiological psychology. 2. ed. N.Y., 1950.

Phil 5252.82.3   Morgan, Clifford Thomas. Physiological psychology. 3. ed. N.Y., 1965.

Phil 5252.82.13   Morgan, Clifford Thomas. Introduction to psychology. 3d ed. N.Y., 1966.

Phil 5252.83   Marf, Gustav. Grundriss der Psychologie. Bern, 1943.

Phil 5252.84   Murphy, L.B. Emotional factors in learning. N.Y., 1945.

Phil 5252.84.2   Murphy, L.B. Emotional factors in learning. N.Y., 1946.

Phil 5252.85   Merleau-Ponty, M. La structure du comportement. 1. ed. Paris, 1942.

Phil 5252.85.5   Merleau-Ponty, M. La structure du comportement. 3. ed. Paris, 1955.

Phil 5252.85.10A   Merleau-Ponty, M. The structure of behavior. Boston, 1963.

Phil 5252.85.10B   Merleau-Ponty, M. The structure of behavior. Boston, 1963.

Phil 5252.85.10C   Merleau-Ponty, M. The structure of behavior. Boston, 1963.

Phil 5252.86   Major, David R. The elements of psychology. Columbus, 1913.

Phil 5252.87   Miller, Edmond M. Brain capacity and intelligence. Sydney, 1926.

Phil 5252.88   Mourad, Youssef. L'eveil de l'intelligence. Paris, 1939.

Phil 5252.89   Munn, Norman Leslie. Psychology. Boston, 1946.

Phil 5252.89.2   Munn, Norman Leslie. Psychology. 2. ed. Boston, 1951.

Phil 5252.89.4A   Munn, Norman Leslie. Psychology. 2. ed. Boston, 1961.

Phil 5252.89.4B   Munn, Norman Leslie. Psychology. 2. ed. Boston, 1961.

Phil 5252.89.5   Munn, Norman Leslie. Psychology. 5. ed. Boston, 1966.

Phil 5252.91   MacKinnon, D.W. Experimental studies in psychodynamics. Cambridge, 1948. 2v.

Phil 5252.93   Meinertz, Josef. Moderne Seinsprobleme in ihrer Bedeutung für die Psychologie. Heidelberg, 1948.

Phil 5252.95A   May, Rollo. Man's search for himself. N.Y., 1953.

Phil 5252.95B   May, Rollo. Man's search for himself. N.Y., 1953.

Phil 5252.96   May, Rollo. Psychology and the human dilemma. Princeton, 1967.

Phil 5252.97   Morgan, J.J.B. Psychology. N.Y., 1947.

Phil 5252.100   Metzger, W. Psychologie. 2. Aufl. Darmstadt, 1954.

Phil 5252.102   Matte Blanco, Ignacio. La psiquica y la naturaleza humana. Santiago, 1954.

Phil 5252.105   Mertsalov, V.S. K issledovaniiu problem psikhologicheskoi voiny; sbornik statei. Miunkhen, 1955.

Phil 5252.110   Monsarrat, K.W. On human thinking. London, 1955.

Phil 5252.115   Maslow, Paul. Intuition versus intellect. N.Y., 1957.

Phil 5252.120   Messer, August. Einführung in die Psychologie und die psychologischen Richtungen der Gegenwart. 2. Aufl. Leipzig, 1931.

Phil 5252.125A   Miller, George. Plans and the structure of behavior. N.Y., 1960.

Phil 5252.125B   Miller, George. Plans and the structure of behavior. N.Y., 1960.

Phil 5252.130   Murphy, James G. The human mind. Belfast, 1873.

Phil 5252.135   Misiak, H. The philosophical roots of scientific psychology. N.Y., 1961.

Phil 5252.140   Menert, Evžen. Fysiologický základ logického myšlení. Praha, 1960.

Phil 5252.141A   Miller, George A. Psychology, the science of mental life. N.Y., 1962.

Phil 5252.141B   Miller, George A. Psychology, the science of mental life. N.Y., 1962.

Phil 5252.150   Mauchart, I.D. Neues allgemeines Repertorium. Leipzig, 1802-03.

Phil 5252.151   Mann, J.H. Frontiers of psychology. N.Y., 1963.

Phil 5252.152   Marx, M.H. Systems and theories in psychology. N.Y., 1963.

Phil 5252.153   Michotte, A.E. Les compléments amodaux des structures perceptives. Louvain, 1964.

Phil 5252.154   Merlin, Vol'f S. Tipologicheskie issledovaniia po psikhologii lichnosti i po psikhologii truda. Perm', 1964.

Phil 5240 - 5265 **Psychology - General treatises - Individual authors (A-Z) - cont.**

Phil 5252.155   Marx, Melvin Herman. Theories in contemporary psychology. N.Y., 1965.

Phil 5252.156   Morávek, Milan. Otázky vzniku a povahy psychiky. Praha, 1965.

Phil 5252.157A   Morris, Desmond. The naked ape; a zoologist's study of the human animal. 1. ed. N.Y., 1967.

Phil 5252.157B   Morris, Desmond. The naked ape; a zoologist's study of the human animal. 1. ed. N.Y., 1967.

Phil 5252.158   Madden, Edward Harry. Philosophical problems of psychology. N.Y., 1922.

Phil 5252.159   Meza, César. Mimo, dependencia, depresión, alcoholismo. 1. ed. Guatemala, 1967.

Phil 5252.160   Murphy, Gardner. Western psychology. N.Y., 1969.

Phil 5252.162   Mucchielli, Roger. Introduction à la psychologie structurale. 2. ed. Bruxelles, 1968.

Phil 5252.164   Boersenverein des deutschen Buchhandels, Frankfurt am Main. Alexander Mitscherlich: Ansprachen anlässlich der Verleihung des Friedenspreises. Frankfurt, 1969.

Phil 5252.166   Meyerson, Ignace. Les fonctions psychologiques et les oeuvres. Thèse. Paris, 1948.

Phil 5252.168   Malcolm, Norman. Problems of mind. N.Y., 1971.

Phil 5252.170   Morris, Desmond. Intimate behaviour. London, 1971.

Phil 5252.175   Madsen, K.B. Almen psykologi. 3. opl. v.1-2. København, 1968.

Phil 5253.1   Natorp, P. Einleitung in die Psychologie. Freiburg, 1888.

Phil 5253.1.5   Natorp, P. Allgemeine Psychologie. Tübingen, 1912.

Phil 5253.1.9   Natorp, P. Allgemeine Psychologie. 2. Aufl. Marburg, 1910.

Phil 5253.2   Noel, R.R. Physical basis of mental life. London, 1873.

Phil 5253.3   Nourrisson, J.F. La nature humaine. Paris, 1865.

Phil 5253.4   Netter, S. De l'intuition. Strasbourg, 1879.

Phil 5253.5   Nicati, W.M. La psychologie naturelle. Paris, 1898.

Phil 5253.6   Naccarati, S. The morphologic aspect of intelligence. N.Y., 1921.

Phil 5253.7   Naesgaard, S. Kortfattet sjaelelaere. København, 1919.

Phil 5253.7.2   Naesgaard, S. Kortfattet sjaelelaere. København, 1928.

Phil 5253.7.5   Naesgaard, S. Begrebet som psykologisk element. København, 1924.

Phil 5253.8   Nelson, Leonard. Die kritische Methode und das Verhaltnis der Psychologie zur Philosophie. Göttingen, 1904.

Phil 5253.8.50   Naess, Arne. Notes on the foundation of psychology as a science. Oslo, 1960.

Phil 5253.9   Noltenius, F. Die Gefühlswerte. Leipzig, 1927.

Phil 5253.10   Neurath, Otto. Einheitswissenschaft und Psychologie. Wien, 1933.

Phil 5253.11   Mason, Phillips. The X of psychology. Cambridge, 1940.

Phil 5253.12   Nicol, Eduardo. Psicología de las situaciones vitales. Mexico, 1941.

Phil 5253.13   Nahoum, Charles. L'entretien psychologique. Paris, 1958.

Phil 5253.14   Nassefat, Mortega. Étude quantitative sur l'évolution des opérations inteslectuelles. Neuchâtel, 1963.

Phil 5253.15   Neimark, Edith. Stimulus sampling theory. San Francisco, 1967.

Phil 5253.20   Nicoletti, Ivan. Analisi quantitativa e programmi di ricerca in psicologia epsichiatria. Torino, 1968.

Phil 5253.21   Novik, Il'ia B. Filosofskie voprosy modelirovaniia psikhiki. Moskva, 1969.

Phil 5254.1   Ogden, R.M. An introduction to general psychology. N.Y., 1914.

Phil 5254.2   Ogden, C.K. The meaning of psychology. N.Y., 1926.

Phil 5254.2.15   Ogden, C.K. The ABC of psychology. Harmondsworth, 1944.

Phil 5254.3   Overstreet, H. Allen. About ourselves. N.Y., 1927.

Phil 5254.3.5   Overstreet, H. Allen. The great enterprise. 1st. ed. N.Y., 1952.

Phil 5254.3.7   Overstreet, H. Allen. The mind goes forth. 1st. ed. N.Y., 1956.

Phil 5254.4   Oreg, J. Gondslkodastan az eggetemesitö (inductiv) s lehoźo (deductiv) módazer alapján. Nagy Köros, 1877.

Phil 5254.5   Osborn, John K. A comparison of reactions to personality and achievement test items. Diss. Ann Arbor, 1936.

Phil 5254.6   Orr, T.V. Applied mental efficiency. Chicago, 1913.

Phil 5254.7A   Osgood, C.E. Method and theory in experimental psychology. N.Y., 1956.

Phil 5254.7B   Osgood, C.E. Method and theory in experimental psychology. N.Y., 1956.

Phil 5254.8   O'Neil, William Matthew. An introduction to method in psychology. 2d. ed. Parkville, 1962.

Phil 5254.9   Oraison, Mark. Illusion and anxiety. N.Y., 1963.

Phil 5255.1   Paine, A.W. The new philosophy. Bangor, 1884.

Phil 5255.2   Paulhan, F. L'activité mentale. Paris, 1889.

Phil 5255.2.2   Paulhan, F. L'activité mentale. 2. éd. Paris, 1913.

Phil 5255.2.6   Paulhan, F. Esprits logiques et esprits faux. Paris, 1914.

Phil 5255.2.12   Paulhan, F. Analystes et esprits synthétiques. Paris, 1902.

Phil 5255.3   Petvin, J. Letters concerning mind. London, 1750.

Phil 5255.3.5   Pauli, Richard. Psychologisches Praktikum. 6. Aufl. Stuttgart, 1957.

Phil 5255.4   Planck, K.C. Anthropologie und Psychologie. Leipzig, 1874.

Phil 5255.4.5   Plank, K.C. Seele und Geist. Leipzig, 1871.

Phil 5255.5.6   Porter, Noah. The human intellect. 4th ed. N.Y., 1887.

Phil 5255.5.9   Porter, Noah. The elements of intellectual science. N.Y., 1872.

Phil 5255.6   Psychological Laboratory. Bedford College for Women. University of London. Psychological studies. London, 1914.

Phil 5255.7   Pillsbury, W.B. Fundamentals of psychology. N.Y., 1916.

Phil 5255.7.5   Pillsbury, W.B. The essentials of psychology. N.Y., 1915.

Phil 5255.7.8   Pillsbury, W.B. The essentials of psychology. N.Y., 1925.

Phil 5255.7.15   Pillsbury, W.B. Handbook of general psychology. N.Y., 1942.

Phil 5255.8   Pfänder, A. Einführung in die Psychologie. Leipzig, 1904.

Phil 5255.8.2   Pfänder, A. Einführung in die Psychologie. 2. Aufl. Leipzig, 1920.

Phil 5255.8.15   Pfänder, A. Die Seele des Menschen. Halle, 1933.

Phil 5255.9   Putnam, Daniel. A text book of psychology. N.Y., 1901.

Phil 5255.11   Pikler, Gyula. The psychology of belief in objective existence. pt.1. London, 1890.

Phil 5255.11.5   Pikler, Gyula. Zwei Vorträge über dynamische Psychologie. Leipzig, 1908.

Phil 5255.11.9   Pikler, Gyula. Das Beharren und die Gegensätzlichkeit des Erlebens. Stuttgart, 1908.

VPhil 5255.11.10   Pikler, Gyula. A lelektan alapelvei. Budapest, 1909.

Phil 5255.12   Petrescu, Nicolaus. Die Denkfunktion der Verneinung. Leipzig, 1914.

Phil 5240 - 5265   Psychology - General treatises - Individual authors (A-Z) - cont.

Phil 5255.13   Panizza, Mario. Nuova teorica fisiologica della conoscenza. Roma, 1899.

Phil 5255.13.5   Panizza, Mario. I nuovi elemente della psicofisiologia. Roma, 1898.

Phil 5255.14   Piat, Clodius. L'intellect actif. Thèse. Paris, 1890.

Phil 5255.16B   Platt, Charles. The psychology of thought and feeling. N.Y., 1921.

Phil 5255.17   Le procès de l'intelligence. Paris, 1922.

Phil 5255.18.5   Piéron, Henri. Psychologie experimentale. Paris, 1927.

Phil 5255.18.10   Piéron, Henri. Principles of experimental psychology. London, 1929.

Phil 5255.18.15   Piéron, Henri. Le développment mental et l'intelligence. Paris, 1929.

Phil 5255.18.20   Piéron, Henri. Les problémes fondamentaux de la psychophysique dans la science actuelle. Paris, 1951.

Phil 5255.19   Pfister, O. Zur Psychologie des philosophischen Denkens. Bern, 1923.

Phil 5255.20   Petrini, Edvard. Om känslolagar. Upsala, 1900.

Phil 5255.22   Pioger, J. La vie et la pensée. Paris, 1893.

Phil 5255.23   Palágyi, M. Naturphilosophische Vorlesungen über die Grundprobleme des Bewusstseins und des Lebens. Charlottenburg, 1907.

Phil 5255.23.2   Palágyi, M. Naturphilosophische Vorlesungen über die Grundprobleme des Bewusstseins und des Lebens. Leipzig, 1924.

Phil 5255.24   Paget, Violet. Proteus or The future of intelligence. London, 1925.

Phil 5255.25.5   Paliard, Jacques. Intuition et réflexion. Thèse. Paris, 1925.

Phil 5255.26   Perrin, Fleming. Psychology. N.Y., 1926.

Phil 5255.27   Pyne, John K. The mind. N.Y., 1926.

Phil 5255.28   Poffenberger, A.T. Experimental psychology; loose leaf laboratory manual. Chicago, 1926.

Phil 5255.28.2   Poffenberger, A.T. Experimental psychology; loose leaf laboratory manual. N.Y., 1925?

Phil 5255.29   Preyer, W. Über die Grenzen der Tonwahrnehmung. n.p., 1876-89. 9 pam.

Phil 5255.30   Phillips, D.E. An elementary psychology. Boston, 1927.

Phil 5255.31   Pauli, R. Psychologisches Praktikum. Jena, 1920.

Phil 5255.31.10   Pauli, R. Über psychische Gesetzmässigkeit. Jena, 1920.

Phil 5255.32.5   Putnam, J.J. Human motives. Boston, 1921.

Phil 5255.33   Petermann, B. Die Wertheimer-Koffka-Köhlersche Gestalttheorie und das Gestaltproblem. Leipzig, 1929.

Phil 5255.33.10   Petermann, B. The gestalt theory and the problem of configuration. London, 1932.

Phil 5255.34   Prengowski, P. Le concept, le jugement et l'attention. Paris, 1930.

Phil 5255.36   Psychologische Studien. Festschrift gewidmet Paul Ranschburg. Budapest, 1929.

Phil 5255.37   Politzer, Georges. Critique des fondements de la psychologie. Paris, 1928.

Phil 5255.38   Paterson, D.G. Physique and intellect. N.Y., 1930.

Phil 5255.40   Palmés, F.M. Psicología. Barcelona, 1928.

Phil 5255.41   Patrick, G.T.W. What is the mind? N.Y., 1929.

Phil 5255.42   Potts, John. Know thyself; a study in mental qualities. Philadelphia, 1935.

Phil 5255.43A   Pratt, Carroll C. The logic of modern psychology. N.Y., 1939.

Phil 5255.43B   Pratt, Carroll C. The logic of modern psychology. N.Y., 1939.

Phil 5255.44   Prinzhorn, H. Persönlichkeitspsychologie. Leipzig, 1932.

Phil 5255.44.2   Prinzhorn, H. Persönlichkeits-Psychologie. 2. Aufl. Heidelberg, 1958.

Phil 5255.45   Pennsylvania. University. Bicentennial Conference. Modern psychology. Philadelphia, 1941.

Phil 5255.46   Paton, S. Human behavior. N.Y., 1921.

Phil 5255.47A   Pressey, Sidney Leavitt. Life; a psychological survey. 1st ed. N.Y., 1939.

Phil 5255.47B   Pressey, Sidney Leavitt. Life; a psychological survey. 1st ed. N.Y., 1939.

Phil 5255.48   Pulver, Max. Selbsterfahrung. Zürich, 1941.

Phil 5255.49   Pradines, Maurice. Traité de psychologie générale. 1st éd. v.1-2, pt.1-2. Paris, 1943-46. 3v.

Phil 5255.50   Pyle, William H. The science of human nature. Boston, 1917.

Phil 5255.51   Piaget, Jean. The psychology of intelligence. N.Y., 1950.

Phil 5255.51.8   Piaget, J. La psychologie de l'intelligence. 3. ed. Paris, 1952.

Phil 5255.53   Psychologie moderne et réflexion chrétienne. Paris, 1953.

Phil 5255.54   Pronko, N.H. Empirical foundations of psychology. N.Y., 1952.

Phil 5255.56   Progoff, Ira. Depth psychology and modern man. N.Y., 1959.

Phil 5255.58   Pastuszka, J. Charakter cztowieka. Lublin, 1959.

Phil 5255.58.5   Pastuszka, J. Charakter cztowieka. Lublin, 1962.

Phil 5255.60   Piela, Franz. Die Psychologie. Köln, 1959.

Phil 5255.62   Ponomarev, Ia.A. Psikhologiia tvorcheskogo myshleniia. Moskva, 1960.

Phil 5255.64   Pikunas, J. Psychology of human development. N.Y., 1961.

Phil 5255.66   Palmade, G. L'unité des science humaines. Paris, 1961.

Phil 5255.68   Perlenghini, A. Psicologia degli animali e filosofia del sentimento. Genova, 1961.

Phil 5255.70   Platonov, Konstantin Konstantinovich. Psychology as you may like it. Moscow, 1965.

Phil 5255.72   Paulus, Jean. Les fondements théoriques et méthodologiques de la psychologie. Bruxelles, 1965.

Phil 5255.75   Piret, Roger. Psychologie différentielle des sexes. Paris, 1965.

Phil 5255.76   Prangishvili, Aleksandr S. Issledovaniia po psikhologii ustanovki. Tbilisi, 1967.

Phil 5255.78   Psychologische Testtheorie. Bern, 1968.

Phil 5255.80   Porteus, Stanley David. A psychologist of sorts. Palo Alto, 1969.

Phil 5255.82   Papanoutsos, Euangelos. Psychologia. Athēnai, 1970.

Phil 5256.5   Quastler, H. Information theory in psychology. Glencoe, 1955.

Phil 5257.1   Rauch, F.A. Psychology. N.Y., 1840.

Phil 5257.1.2   Rauch, F.A. Psychology. N.Y., 1841.

Phil 5257.2   Reed, S. Observations on the growth of the mind. Boston, 1838.

Phil 5257.2.2   Reed, S. Observations on the growth of the mind. Boston, 1829.

Phil 5257.2.5   Reed, S. Observations on the growth of the mind. 5th ed. Boston, 1859.

Phil 5257.3   Rehmke. J. Lehrbuch der allgemeinen Psychologie. Hamburg, 1894.

Phil 5257.3.5   Rehmke, J. Die Seele des Menschen. Leipzig, 1902.

Phil 5240 - 5265   Psychology - General treatises - Individual authors (A-Z) - cont.

Phil 5257.3.10   Rehmke, J. Der Mensch. Leipzig, 1928.

Phil 5257.3.25   Baumann. Rehmke, Joh: Lehrbuch der allgemeinen Psychologie. Göttingen, 1894.

Phil 5257.4   Reinhold, E.C. Lehrbuch der philosophisch propädeutischen Psychologie und der formalen Logik. 2. Aufl. Jena, 1839.

Phil 5257.5   Reinhold, K.L. Versuch einer neuen Theorie des menschlichen Vorstellungs-Vermögens. Prag, 1789.

Phil 5257.6   Richet, Charles. L'homme et l'intelligence. Paris, 1884.

Phil 5257.6.5   Richet, Charles. Essai de psychologie général. 10. éd. Paris, 1919.

Phil 5257.6.10   Richet, Charles. L'intelligence et l'homme. Paris, 1927.

Phil 5257.7   Robertson, G.C. Elements of psychology. London, 1896.

NEDL Phil 5257.8   Röse, F. Die Psychologie. Göttingen, 1856.

Phil 5257.9   Raue, C.G. Psychology as a natural science. Philadelphia, 1889.

Phil 5257.10   Rubinstein, Susanna. Psychologisch-ästhetische Essays. Heidelberg, 1877-88. 2v.

Phil 5257.11A   Royce, Josiah. Outlines of psychology. N.Y., 1903.

Phil 5257.11B   Royce, Josiah. Outlines of psychology. N.Y., 1903.

Phil 5257.11.3   Royce, Josiah. Outlines of psychology. N.Y., 1908.

Phil 5257.11.5   Royce, Josiah. Outlines of psychology. N.Y., 1906.

Phil 5257.11.15   Royce, Josiah. Lineamenti di psicologia. Bari, 1928.

Phil 5257.13   Ruger, Henry A. Psychology of efficiency. N.Y., 1910.

Phil 5257.15   Rey, A. Leçons de psychologie et de philosophie. 3. éd. Paris, 1911.

Phil 5257.16   Rith, L. L'intelligence. Thèse. Paris, 1912.

Phil 5257.17   Reichwein, G. Die neueren Untersuchungen über Psychologie des Denkens. Halle, 1910.

Phil 5257.18   Rehwoldt, F. Über respiratorische Affektsymptome. Leipzig, 1911.

Phil 5257.19   Robert, Arthur. Leçons de psychologie. Québec, 1915.

Phil 5257.19.3   Robert, Arthur. Leçons de psychologie. 3. éd. Québec, 1921.

Phil 5257.20   Rémond, A. Recherches expérimentales sur la durée des actes psychiques les plus simples et sur la vitesse des courants. Paris, 1888.

Phil 5257.21   Dessoir, Max. Psychologische Skizzen, von Edmund W. Rells. Leipzig, 1893.

Phil 5257.22.3   Ryland, F. Psychology. 7. ed. London, 1897.

Phil 5257.22.5   Ryland, F. The story of thought and feeling. London, 1900.

Phil 5257.23   Riche, A. Essai de psychologie; sur le cerveau. Paris, 1881.

Phil 5257.24   Raaf, H. de. Die Elemente der Psychologie. 3. Aufl. Langensalza, 1908.

Phil 5257.25   Russell, Bertrand Russell. The analysis of mind. London, 1921.

Phil 5257.25.2   Russell, Bertrand Russell. The analysis of mind. London, 1924.

Phil 5257.25.5   Russell, Bertrand Russell. Analyse de l'esprit. Paris, 1926.

Phil 5257.26.2   Rüegg, H.R. Grundriss der Seelenlehre. 2. Aufl. Bern, 1864.

Phil 5257.26.8   Rüegg, H.R. Lehrbuch der Psychologie. 3. Aufl. Bern, 1876.

Phil 5257.27   Robinson, E.S. Readings in general psychology. Chicago, 1923.

Phil 5257.27.3   Robinson, E.S. Readings in general psychology. Chicago, 1929.

Phil 5257.27.6   Robinson, E.S. Practical psychology; human nature in everyday life. N.Y., 1927.

Phil 5257.27.10   Robinson, E.S. Man as psychology sees him. N.Y., 1934.

Phil 5257.28   Roback, A.A. Behaviorism and psychology. Cambridge, 1935.

Phil 5257.28.5   Roback, A.A. Psychology. Rahway, 1923.

Phil 5257.28.8   Roback, A.A. Popular psychology. Cambridge, 1928.

Phil 5257.28.10   Roback, A.A. The psychology of common sense. Cambridge, 1939.

Phil 5257.28.15   Roback, A.A. Psychorama; a mental outlook and analysis. Cambridge, 1942.

Phil 5257.28.25   Pamphlet box. Roback, A.A.

Phil 5257.28.30   Roback, A.A. Behaviorism at twenty-five. Cambridge, Mass., 1937.

Phil 5257.28.35   Roback, A.A. Present day psychology. N.Y., 1955.

Phil 5257.29   Rhodes, G. The mind at work. London, 1914.

Phil 5257.30   Radziwillowicz, P. Zagadnienia psychologii. Kraków, 1911?

Phil 5257.31   Radha-Krishnan, S. Essentials of psychology. London, 1912.

Phil 5257.32   Rogers, M.C. Adenoids and diseased tonsils; their effect on general intelligence. N.Y., 1922.

Phil 5257.33   Ruttmann, W.J. Die Hauptergebnisse der modernen Psychologie. Leipzig, 1914.

Phil 5257.34   Ruckmick, C.A. The brevity book on psychology. Chicago, 1920.

Phil 5257.34.5   Ruckmick, C.A. The mental life. N.Y., 1928.

Phil 5257.35   Ruddell, G.A.R. Some things that matter. London, 1922.

Phil 5257.36   Rignano, E. Come funziona la nostra intelligenza. Bologna, 1922.

Phil 5257.37   Reiff, Paul. Der moderne psychophysische Parallelismus. Inaug. Diss. Heilbronn, 1901.

Phil 5257.38   Reyburn, H.A. An introduction to psychology. Cape Town, 1924.

Phil 5257.39.2   Raup, R.B. Complacency; the foundation of human behavior. N.Y., 1925.

Phil 5257.40   Richter, Conrad. Human vibrations. Harrisburg, 1925.

Phil 5257.40.5   Richter, Conrad. Principles in bio-physics. Harrisburg, 1927.

Phil 5257.41   Roffenstein, G. Das Problem des psychologischen Verstehens. Stuttgart, 1926.

Phil 5257.42   Rostohar, M. Studie z vyvojové psychologie. Brno, 1928.

Phil 5257.43   Rupp, Hans. Probleme und Apparate zur experimentellen Pädagogik und Jugendpsychologie. Leipzig, 1919.

Phil 5257.44   Rexroad, Carl N. General psychology for college students. N.Y., 1929.

Phil 5257.45   Rattray, Robert F. An outline of genetic psychology according to the theory of inherited mind. London, 1931.

Phil 5257.46   Radecki, Wacław. Tratado de psicología. Buenos Aires, 1933.

Phil 5257.47   Russell, J.T. Applicability of the probable error formulae to psychological data. Diss. Chicago, 1934.

Phil 5257.48   Ritchie, Arthur D. The natural history of mind. London, 1936.

Phil 5257.49   Richmond, W.V. Personality: its development and hygiene. N.Y., 1937.

Phil 5257.50   Rosling, B. Some aspects of psychology. London, 1936.

Phil 5257.51   Rosett, Joshua. The mechanism of thought. N.Y., 1939.

Phil 5257.52   Reinhardt, J.M. Social psychology. Chicago, 1938.

Phil 5257.53   Ruch, F.L. Psychology and life. Chicago, 1937.

Phil 5240 - 5265   Psychology - General treatises - Individual authors (A-Z) - cont.

Phil 5257.54   Ryland, F. A student's handbook of psychology and ethics. London, 1885.

Phil 5257.55   Rexroad, Carl N. Psychology and personality development. Boston, 1940.

Phil 5257.56   Ranschburg, Pál. Az emberi elme. Budapest, 1923. 2v.

Phil 5257.57   Révész, Géza. Die Bedeutung der Psychologie für die Wissenschaft. Bern, 1947.

Phil 5257.58.5   Rohracher, Hubert. Einführung in die Psychologie. 2. Aufl. Wien, 1947.

Phil 5257.58.6   Rohracher, Hubert. Einführung in die Psychologie. 6. Aufl. Wien, 1958.

Phil 5257.59   Ram, T. Psycho-astrologische Encyclopedie. Lochem, 1950-51. 2v.

Phil 5257.60   Roubiczek, Paul. Thinking in opposites. London, 1952.

Phil 5257.62   Ramus, Carl. Behind the scenes with ourselves. N.Y., 1931.

Phil 5257.64   Reuchlin, Maurice. Histoire de la psychologie. Paris, 1957.

Phil 5257.64.5   Reuchlin, Maurice. Les méthodes quantitatives en psychologie. Paris, 1962.

Phil 5257.66   Rohrbach, M.A. La pensée vivante; réales et techniques de la pensée créatrice. Paris, 1959.

Phil 5257.68   Rubinshtein, Sergei L. Grundlagen der allgemeinen Psychologie. Berlin, 1958.

Phil 5257.69   Akademiia Nauk SSSR. Institut Filosofii, Sektor Psikologii. Protsess myshleniia i zakonomernosti analiza, Sinteza i obobshcheniia. Moskva, 1960.

Phil 5257.70   Ryle, Gilbert. A puzzling element in the notion of thinking. London, 1958.

Phil 5257.70.5   Ryle, Gilbert. A rational animal. London, 1962.

Phil 5257.71   Rudolph, Rigmor. Er jeg nig? Traek of Jeg'ets psykologi. Kjøbenhavn, 1960.

Phil 5257.72   Rein, Thiodolf. Sielutieteen oppikirja. Helsingissa, 1884.

Phil 5257.75   Reitman, Walter Ralph. Cognition and thought. N.Y., 1965.

VPhil 5257.76   Rostohar, Mihajlo. Psihologija. Ljubljana, 1966.

Phil 5257.78   Reese, Ellen P. The analysis of human operant behavior. Dubuque, Iowa, 1966.

Phil 5257.80   Roskam, Edwarda Elias Charles Iben. Metric analysis of ordinal data in psychology. Proefschrift. Voorschoten, 1968.

Phil 5257.82   Ringness, Thomas A. Psychology in theory and practice. Boston, 1959.

Phil 5258.1   Sagra, R. de la. L'âme. Paris, 1868.

Phil 5258.2   Sailer, J.D.M. Vernunftlehre für Menschen, wie sie sind. München, 1785.

Phil 5258.3   Saisset, E.E. L'âme et la vie. Paris, 1864.

Phil 5258.4   Sanford, E.C. Course in experimental psychology. Boston, 1895.

Phil 5258.4.3   Sanford, E.C. Course in experimental psychology. Boston, 1894.

Phil 5258.4.4   Sanford, E.C. Course in experimental psychology. Boston, 1901.

Phil 5258.5   Schaller, J. Das Seelenleben des Menschen. Weimar, 1860.

Phil 5258.6   Schmucker, S.S. Psychology. N.Y., 1842.

Phil 5258.7   Schubert, G.H. von. Altes und Neues aus dem Gebiet der innren Seelenkunde. Leipzig, 1825-44. 5v.

Phil 5258.7.3   Schubert, G.H. von. Altes und Neues aus dem Gebiet der innren Seelenkunde. Leipzig, 1817.

Phil 5258.7.5   Schubert, G.H. von. Die Geschichte der Seele. Stuttgart, 1833.

Phil 5258.7.6   Schubert, G.H. von. Die Geschichte der Seele. Stuttgart, 1850. 2v.

Phil 5258.7.10   Schubert, G.H. von. Lehrbuch der Menschen- und Seelenkunde. Erlangen, 1838.

Phil 5258.7.80   Elschenbroich, Adalbert. Romantische Sehnsucht und Kosmogonie. Tübingen, 1971.

Phil 5258.8   Schubert-Soldern, R. von. Reproduction, Gefühl und Wille. Leipzig, 1887.

Phil 5258.10   Schultz-Schultzenstein, K.H. Die Bildung der menschlichen Geistes. Berlin, 1855.

Phil 5258.10.25   Schultz-Schultzenstein, K.H. Naturstudium und Kultur. Berlin, 1866.

Phil 5258.12   Scott, R.E. Elements of intellectual philosophy. Edinburgh 1805.

Phil 5258.13   Scripture, E.W. Problem of psychology. London, 1891.

Phil 5258.13.5   Scripture, E.W. Thinking, feeling, doing. Meadville, 1895.

Phil 5258.13.6   Scripture, E.W. Thinking, feeling, doing. N.Y., 1907. 2v.

Phil 5258.13.10   Scripture, E.W. The new psychology. London, 1897.

Phil 5258.13.15   Scripture, E.W. The new psychology. London, 1901.

Phil 5258.15   Setchénov, J. Études psychologiques. Paris, 1884.

Phil 5258.16   Siciliani, P. Prolégomènes a la psychogénie moderne. Paris, 1880.

Phil 5258.17   Simonin, A. Traité de psychologie. Paris, 1876.

Phil 5258.19   Snider, D.J. Psychology and the psychosis. St.Louis, 1896.

Phil 5258.19.5   Snider, D.J. Feeling psychologically treated. St.Louis, 1905.

Phil 5258.20   Steele, G.M. Rudimentary psychology. Boston, 1890.

Phil 5258.21   Schweden, P. Über elementarische psychische Prozesse. Berlin, 1894.

Phil 5258.22   Strümpell, L. Grundriss der Psychologie. Leipzig, 1884.

Phil 5258.22.5   Unger, Rudolf. Die kinderpsychologischen Bestrebungen L. Strümpells. Strassburg, 1912.

Phil 5258.23   Stricker, S. Studien über die Bewegungsvorstellungen. Wien, 1882.

Phil 5258.24   Struve, H. von. Zur Entstehung der Seele. Tübingen, 1862.

Phil 5258.25.2   Sully, J. Outlines of psychology. N.Y., 1885.

Phil 5258.25.3   Sully, J. Outlines of psychology. 6th ed. London, 1889.

Phil 5258.25.3.5   Sully, J. Outlines of psychology. N.Y., 1900.

Phil 5258.25.4   Sully, J. Outlines of psychology. London, 1920.

Phil 5258.25.5   Sully, J. Teacher's handbook of psychology. London, 1886.

Phil 5258.25.5.3   Sully, J. Teacher's handbook of psychology. N.Y., 1888.

Phil 5258.25.5.5   Sully, J. Teacher's handbook of psychology. 3d ed. N.Y., 1892.

Phil 5258.25.6   Sully, J. Teacher's handbook of psychology. N.Y., 1897.

Phil 5258.25.11   Sully, J. Human mind. N.Y., 1892. 2v.

Phil 5258.25.16   Sully, J. Sensation and intuition. 2d ed. London, 1880.

Phil 5258.26   Sunderland, La Ray. Pathetism. Boston, 1847.

Phil 5258.27   Stout, G.F. A manual of psychology. v.1-2. London, 1898-99.

Phil 5258.27.1   Stout, G.F. A manual of psychology. 2d ed. London, 1901.

Phil 5258.27.2   Stout, G.F. A manual of psychology. N.Y., 1899.

Phil 5258.27.5   Stout, G.F. Groundwork of psychology. N.Y., 1903.

Phil 5240 - 5265   Psychology - General treatises - Individual authors (A-Z) - cont.

Phil 5258.27.6   Stout, G.F. Groundwork of psychology. 2d ed. London, 1927.

Phil 5258.27.9   Stout, G.F. A manual of psychology. 3. ed. London, 1913.

Phil 5258.27.10   Stout, G.F. A manual of psychology. 4th ed. London, 1929.

Phil 5258.27.12   Stout, G.F. Analytic psychology. N.Y., 1896. 2v.

Phil 5258.27.15   Stout, G.F. Analytic psychology. London, 1902. 2v.

Phil 5258.27.25   Stout, G.F. Studies in philosophy and psychology. London, 1930.

Phil 5258.28   Schultze, F. Psychologie der Naturvölker. Leipzig, 1900.

Phil 5258.29.5   Stratton, G.M. Experimental psychology. N.Y., 1914.

Phil 5258.30.3   Spiller, G. The mind of man. "Ethical series." London, 1902.

Phil 5258.33   Swoboda, H. Studien zur Grundlegung der Psychologie. Leipzig, 1905.

Phil 5258.34.4   Seashore, C.E. Elementary experiments in psychology. N.Y., 1909.

Phil 5258.34.10   Seashore, C.E. Psychology in daily life. N.Y., 1928.

Phil 5258.34.13   Seashore, C.E. Introduction to psychology. N.Y., 1923.

Phil 5258.35   Stern, W. Die differentielle Psychologie. Leipzig. 1911.

Phil 5258.35.3   Stern, W. Die differentielle Psychologie. Leipzig, 1921.

Phil 5258.35.5   Stern, W. Die Psychologie und der Personalismus. Leipzig, 1917.

Phil 5258.35.12   Stern, W. Über Psychologie der individuellen Differenzen. Leipzig, 1900.

Phil 5258.35.15   Stern, W. Allgemeine Psychologie auf personalistischer Grundlage. Haag, 1935.

Phil 5258.35.20   Stern, W. General psychology from the personalistic standpoint. N.Y., 1938.

Phil 5258.37   Stern, N. Das Denken und sein Gegenstand. München, 1909.

Phil 5258.38   Schmied-Kowarzik, W. Umrisz einer neuen analytischen Psychologie. Leipzig, 1912.

Phil 5258.38.5   Schmied-Kowarzik, W. Umriss einer analytischen Psychologie. 2. Aufl. Teil I. Leipzig, 1928.

Phil 5258.39   Sturt, Henry. Principles of understanding. Cambridge, 1915.

Phil 5258.40   Sullivan, H. Mediation; the function of thought. Andover, 1871.

Phil 5258.41   Sterrett, John D. The power of thought. N.Y., 1896.

Phil 5258.42   Schulz, B. Psychologische Wanderungen auf Seitenwegen. Jena, 1913.

Phil 5258.43   Schmidt, E. Zum Begriff und Sitz der Seele. Freiburg, 1897.

Phil 5258.44   Sarlo, Francesco de. Psicologia e filosofia. Firenze, 1918. 2v.

Phil 5258.44.5   Sarlo, Francesco de. Idati della esperienza psichica. Firenze, 1903.

Phil 5258.45   Spitta, Heinrich. Einleitung in die Psychologie als Wissenschaft. Freiburg, 1886.

Phil 5258.45.5   Spitta, Heinrich. Die psychologische Forschung und ihre Aufgabe in der Gegenwart. Freiburg, 1889.

Phil 5258.46   Spamer, K. Physiologie der Seele. Stuttgart, 1877.

Phil 5258.47   Stirling, James H. What is thought? Edinburgh, 1900.

Phil 5258.49   Sallwürk, Ernst von. Die Seele des Menschen. Karlsruhe, 1918.

Phil 5258.50   Schuchter, Josef. Kurzgefaszte empirische Psychologie. Wien, 1902.

Phil 5258.50.5   Schuchter, Josef. Empirische Psychologie. Brixen, 1897.

Phil 5258.58   Stadler, August. Einleitung in die Psychologie. Leipzig, 1918.

Phil 5258.59   Selz, Otto. Über die Gesetze des geordneten Denkverlaufs. Stuttgart, 1913. 2v.

Phil 5258.59.7   Selz, Otto. Über die Persönlichkeitstypen. Jena, 1924.

Phil 5258.60   Schultz, Paul. Gehirn und Seele. Leipzig, 1906.

Phil 5258.61.3   Schilling, Gustav, of Giessen. Lehrbuch der Psychologie. Langensalza, 1913.

Phil 5258.62   Staak, Hermann. Aufbau der höheren geistigen Entwicklung. Rostock, 1921.

Phil 5258.62.15   Pamphlet box. Staak, Hermann.

Phil 5258.63   Stöhr, Adolf. Psychologie. Wien, 1917.

Phil 5258.64   Segond, J. Intuition et anitié. Paris, 1919.

Phil 5258.65   Schindler, Ferdinand. Lehrbuch der Psychologie. Troppau, 1913.

Phil 5258.66.2   Smith, Stevenson. General psychology. N.Y., 1927.

Phil 5258.66.3   Smith, Stevenson. Chapters in general psychology. Seattle, 1921.

Phil 5258.68   Spearman, C. The nature of "intelligence" and the principles of cognition. London, 1923.

Phil 5258.68.2   Spearman, C. The nature of "intelligence" and the principles of cognition. London, 1927.

Phil 5258.68.5A   Spearman, C. The abilities of man; their nature and measurement. N.Y., 1927.

Phil 5258.68.5B   Spearman, C. The abilities of man; their nature and measurement. N.Y., 1927.

Phil 5258.68.10   Spearman, C. Human ability. London, 1950.

Phil 5258.68.30   Garcia de Onrubia, Luis Felipe. Ensayo sobre la teoria. Buenos Aires, 1949.

Phil 5258.69   Sullivan, E.T. Mood in relation to performance. N.Y., 1922.

Phil 5258.70   Sergi, G. La psychologie physiologique. Paris, 1888.

Phil 5258.70.5   Sergi, G. L'origine dei fenomeni psichici e il loro significato biologico. 2. ed. Torino, 1904.

Phil 5258.71   Snow, Adolph J. Problems in psychology. N.Y., 1923.

Phil 5258.72   Scheele, Frans von. Det mänskliga själslifvet. Stockholm, 1896.

Phil 5258.72.5   Scheele, Frans von. Lärobok i psykologi. Stockholm, 1899.

Phil 5258.74.4   Spranger, Eduard. Lebensformen; geisteswissenschaftliche Psychologie und Ethik der Personlichkeit. 4. Aufl. Halle, 1924.

Phil 5258.74.5   Spranger, Eduard. Gedanken zur Daseinsgestaltung. München, 1954.

Phil 5258.74.9A   Spranger, Eduard. Types of men. Halle, 1928.

Phil 5258.74.9B   Spranger, Eduard. Types of men. Halle, 1928.

Phil 5258.76.3   Starcke, C.N. Psychologi. 3. udg. Kjøbenhavn, 1923.

Phil 5258.76.10   Starcke, C.N. Kritiken af min psychologi svar til mine kritikere. Kjøbenhavn, 1916.

Phil 5258.77   Sibbern, F.C. Psychologie, indledet ved almindelig biologie, i sammentroengt fremstilling. Kjøbenhavn, 1856.

Phil 5258.77.5   Sibbern, F.C. Loeren om de menneskelige Folelser. Kjøbenhavn, 1885.

Phil 5258.78   Schultz, J. Briefe über genetische Psychologie. Berlin, 1906.

Phil 5258.80   Suabedissen, D.T.A. Von dem Begriffe der Psychologie. Marburg, 1819.

Phil 5258.81   Syrkin, N. Was muss man von der Psychologie wissen? Berlin, n.d.

Phil 5258.82   Schmid, C.C.E. Empirische Psychologie. Jena, 1791.

Phil 5258.83   Sièrebois, R.P. Psychologie réaliste. Paris, 1876.

Phil 5240	-	5265	Psychology - General treatises - Individual authors (A-Z) - cont.

Phil 5258.84 Strasser, Vera. Psychologie der Zusammenhänge und Beziehungen. Berlin, 1921.

Phil 5258.85 Schleich, Carl Ludwig. Das ich und die Dämonien. Berlin, 1924.

Phil 5258.85.5 Schleich, Carl Ludwig. Jaget och demonierna. Stockholm, 1925.

Phil 5258.85.15 Schleich, Carl Ludwig. Von Schaltwerk der Gedanken. 47. bis 49. Aufl. Berlin, 1926.

Phil 5258.86 Schweizer, Walter. Erklären und Verstehen in der Psychologie. Bern, 1924.

Phil 5258.87 Saxby, I.B. The psychology of the thinker. London, 1926.

Phil 5258.88 Souriau, Etienne. Pensée vivante et perfection formelle. Thèse., Paris, 1925.

Phil 5258.88.5 Souriau, Étienne. Pensée vivante et perfection formelle. 2. éd. Paris, 1952.

Phil 5258.89 Schjelderup, H. Referat av H. Schjelderups forelaesninger over psykologi. Oslo, 192-.

Phil 5258.89.5 Schjelderup, H. Psychologie. Berlin, 1928.

Phil 5258.90 Saint-Paul, G. Thèmes psychologiques. Paris, 1926.

Phil 5258.91 Singer, Edgar A. Mind as behavior and studies in empirical idealism. Columbus, Ohio, 1924.

Phil 5258.92.2 Spaier, A. La pensée concrète. Thèse. Paris, 1927.

Phil 5258.94 Sahai, Mahajot. A new primer of psychology. London, 1928.

Phil 5258.95 Shastri, Prabhu D. Elementary psychology. Calcutta, 1928.

Phil 5258.96.5 Schulze, Rudolf. Die moderne Seelenlehre; Begabungsforschung und Berufsberatung. 3. Aufl. Leipzig, 1921.

Phil 5258.97.5 Stephen, Henry. Elements of analytical psychology. 5th. ed. Calcutta, 1922.

Phil 5258.98 Surbled, Georges. Éléments de psychologie. Paris, 1894.

Phil 5258.98.2 Surbled, Georges. Éléments de psychologie. 2e éd. Paris, 1894.

Phil 5258.99 Stanley, H.M. An outline sketch. Chicago, 1899.

Phil 5258.100 Spencer, Willard Wylie. Our knowledge of other minds. New Haven, 1930.

Phil 5258.101 Scheidemann, Norma Valentine. Experiments in general psychology. Chicago, 1929.

Phil 5258.102A Schoen, M. Human nature; a first book in psychology. N.Y., 1930.

Phil 5258.102B Schoen, M. Human nature; a first book in psychology. N.Y., 1930.

Phil 5258.103 Szymanski, J.S. Psychologie vom Standpunkt der Abhängigkeit des Erkennens von den Lebensbedürfnissen. Leipzig, 1930.

Phil 5258.104 Strecker, Edward A. Discovering ourselves. N.Y., 1931.

Phil 5258.104.5 Strecker, Edward A. Discovering ourselves. 2d ed. N.Y., 1943.

Phil 5258.105 Swift, Edgar J. The jungle of the mind. N.Y., 1931.

Phil 5258.106 Sollier, Paul. La répression mentale. Paris, 1930.

Phil 5258.107 Segond, Joseph. Traité de psychologie. Paris, 1930.

Phil 5258.108 Scheerer, M. Die Lehre von der Gestalt. Berlin, 1931.

Phil 5258.109 Schein, Josef. Zentralistische Organisation und Seelenleben. München, 1931. 2v.

Phil 5258.110 Schröder, Paul. Stimmungen und Verstimmungen. Leipzig, 1930.

Phil 5258.112 Stoelting, C.H., Co., Chicago. Psychology and physiology apparatus and supplies. Chicago, 1923.

Phil 5258.113.5 Skaggs, E.B. A textbook of experimental and theoretical psychology. Boston, 1935.

Phil 5258.114 Straus, Erwin. Vom Sinn der Sinne. Berlin, 1935.

Phil 5258.114.5 Straus, Erwin. The primary world of senses. N.Y., 1963.

Phil 5258.114.10 Straus, Erwin. Phenomenological psychology. N.Y., 1966.

Phil 5258.115 Starch, Daniel. Controlling human behavior. N.Y., 1936.

Phil 5258.116 Sprott, W.J.H. General psychology. London, 1937.

Phil 5258.116.5 Sprott, W.J.H. Psychology for everyone. London, 1937.

Phil 5258.117 Schering, W.M. Zuschauen oder Handeln? Leipzig, 1937.

Phil 5258.118 Society of Applied Psychology. Psychology and achievement. San Francisco, 1914.

Phil 5258.120 Skinner, Burrhus F. Behavior of organisms. N.Y., 1938.

Phil 5258.120.8 Skinner, Burrhus F. Science and human behavior. Cambridge, Mass.? 1951.

Phil 5258.120.10 Skinner, Burrhus F. Science and human behavior. N.Y., 1953.

Phil 5258.120.12 Skinner, Burrhus F. Science and human behavior. N.Y., 1958.

Phil 5258.120.13 Skinner, Burrhus F. Science and human behavior. N.Y., 1964.

Phil 5258.120.15 Skinner, Burrhus F. Verbal behavior. N.Y., 1957.

Phil 5258.120.20A Skinner, Burrhus F. Beyond freedom and dignity. 1st ed. N.Y., 1971.

Phil 5258.120.20B Skinner, Burrhus F. Beyond freedom and dignity. 1st ed. N.Y., 1971.

Phil 5258.121A Sheldon, W.H. Psychology and the promethean will. N.Y., 1936.

Phil 5258.121B Sheldon, W.H. Psychology and the promethean will. N.Y., 1936.

Phil 5258.122 Scheidemann, N.V. Lecture demonstrations for general psychology. Chicago, 1939.

Phil 5258.123 Sherman, M. Basic problems of behavior. N.Y., 1941.

Phil 5258.124 Schilder, Paul. Mind: perception and thought in their constructive aspects. N.Y., 1942.

Phil 5258.124.5 Schilder, Paul. Medical psychology. N.Y., 1953.

Phil 5258.125.5 Soria, T.D. Psicología. 4. ed. México, 1940.

Phil 5258.132 Simon, M. Tratado de psicología. Lima, 1944. 2v.

Phil 5258.134 Sherman, Mandel. Intelligence and its deviations. N.Y., 1945.

Phil 5258.136A Symonds, P.M. The dynamics of human adjustment. N.Y., 1946.

Phil 5258.136B Symonds, P.M. The dynamics of human adjustment. N.Y., 1946.

Phil 5258.136.5A Symonds, P.M. The ego and the self. N.Y., 1951.

Phil 5258.136.5B Symonds, P.M. The ego and the self. N.Y., 1951.

Phil 5258.140 Sanctis, Sante de. Psicologia sperimental. Roma, 1929-30. 2v.

Phil 5258.140.5 Appecciafuoco, Romolo. La psicologia sperimentale di Sante de Panctis. Roma, 1946.

Phil 5258.142 Streletski, C. Clavier psychologigue. Paris, 1942.

Phil 5258.143 Seashore, R.H. Fields of psychology. N.Y., 1942.

Phil 5258.144 Störring, G. Psychologie. Leipzig, 1923.

Phil 5258.145 Stagner, Ross. Psychology. 1st ed. N.Y., 1952.

Phil 5258.145.2 Stager, Ross. Psychology. Instructor's manual. 1st ed. N.Y., 1952.

Phil 5258.146 Seliger, Josef. Das sociale Verhalten. Bern, 1903.

Phil 5258.149 Suter, Jules. Psychologie; Grundlagen und Aufbau. Frauenfeld, 1942.

Phil 5258.152 Salber, Wilhelm. Der psychische Gegenstand. Bonn, 1959.

Phil 5240	-	5265	Psychology - General treatises - Individual authors (A-Z) - cont.

Phil 5258.152.10 Salber, Wilhelm. Morphologie des seelischen Geschehens. Ratingen, 1965.

Phil 5258.155A Skinner, Burrhus F. Cumulative record. N.Y., 1959.

Phil 5258.155B Skinner, Burrhus F. Cumulative record. N.Y., 1959.

Phil 5258.155.5A Skinner, Burrhus F. Cumulative record. N.Y., 1961.

Phil 5258.155.5B Skinner, Burrhus F. Cumulative record. N.Y., 1961.

Phil 5258.160 Sjöbring, Henrik. Struktur och utveckling. Lund, 1958.

Phil 5258.165 Sechenov, Ivan M. Oeuvres philosophiques et psychologiques choisies. Moscou, 1957.

Phil 5258.165.10 Sechenov, Ivan M. Selected works. Moscow, 1935.

Phil 5258.170 Shands, Harley. Thinking and psychotherapy. Cambridge, 1960.

Phil 5258.175 Sarbin, Theodore. Clinical inference and cognitive theory. N.Y., 1960.

Phil 5258.180 Sykes, G. The hidden remnant. 1. ed. N.Y., 1962.

Phil 5258.180.5 Sykes, G. The hidden remnant. London, 1962.

Phil 5258.185 Smith, Frederick Viggers. The explanation of human behavior. London, 1951.

Phil 5258.187 Scott, William. Introduction to psychological research. N.Y., 1962.

Phil 5258.190 Simões, M.B. Pora uma psicologia na premeira pessoa. Lisboa, 1961.

Phil 5258.192 Sander, F. Ganzheitspsychologie::Grundlagen. München, 1962.

Phil 5258.193 Szasz, Thomas Stephen. Law, liberty and psychiatry. N.Y., 1963.

Phil 5258.194 Staats, A.W. Complex human behavior. N.Y., 1964.

Phil 5258.195 Spence, Kenneth Wartenbee. Behavior theory and learning; selected papers. Englewood Cliffs, 1960.

Phil 5258.196 Schmitt, Friedrich. ABC des Helfens. Stuttgart, 1965.

Phil 5258.197 Serebriakoff, Victor. I.Q.: a Mensa analysis and history. London, 1965.

Phil 5258.198 Shorokhova, Ekaterina V. Issledovaniia myshleniia v sovetskoi psikhologii. Moskva, 1966.

Phil 5258.199 Schroeder, Theodore. An evolutionary psychologist. Berkeley Heights, N.J., 1965.

Phil 5258.200 Schultz, Hans Jürgen. Was weiss man von der Seele? Stuttgart, 1967.

Phil 5258.202 Nobel Conference, 3d, Gustavus Adolphus College, 1967. The human mind. Amsterdam, 1967.

Phil 5258.203 Slavskaia, Kseniie A. Mysl' v deistvii. Moskva, 1968.

Phil 5258.204 Sokolov, Aleksandr N. Vnutrenniaia rech' i myshlenie. Moskva, 1968.

Phil 5258.205 Szondi, Lipot. Freiheit und Zwang im Schicksal des Einzelnen. Bern, 1968.

Phil 5258.206 Schleiden, Matthias Jacob. Zur Theorie des Erkennens durch den Gesichtssinn. Leipzig, 1861.

Phil 5258.208 Salvat, Henri. L'intelligence; mythes et réalités. Paris, 1969.

Phil 5258.210 Sighele, Scipio. Mentre il secolo muore. Milano, 1899.

Phil 5259.2 Taylor, T. World of mind. N.Y., 1858.

Phil 5259.3 Thompson, D.G. System of psychology. London, 1884. 2v.

Phil 5259.4 Tissot, C.J. Anthropologie. Paris, 1843. 2v.

Phil 5259.5A Titchener, E.B. A primer of psychology. N.Y., 1898.

Phil 5259.5B Titchener, E.B. A primer of psychology. N.Y., 1898.

Phil 5259.5.5 Titchener, E.B. An outline of psychology. N.Y., 1897.

Phil 5259.5.9 Titchener, E.B. Experimental psychology. v.1-2; v.2, pt.1. n.p., 1901-27. 5v.

Phil 5259.5.9.5 Titchener, E.B. Experimental psychology. v.1-2. N.Y., 1927. 4v.

NEDL Phil 5259.5.10A Titchener, E.B. Lectures on the experimental psychology of the thought-processes. N.Y., 1909.

NEDL Phil 5259.5.10B Titchener, E.B. Lectures on the experimental psychology of the thought-processes. N.Y., 1909.

Phil 5259.5.10.5 Titchener, E.B. Lectures on the experimental psychology of the thought-processes. N.Y., 1926.

Phil 5259.5.16 Titchener, E.B. Manuel de psychologie. Paris, 1922.

Phil 5259.5.18 Titchener, E.B. A beginner's psychology. N.Y., 1916.

Phil 5259.5.19 Titchener, E.B. A beginner's psychology. N.Y., 1924.

Phil 5259.5.25 Titchener, E.B. Elementos de psicologia. Paris, 1913.

Phil 5259.5.28 Studies in psychology. Worcester, 1917.

Phil 5259.5.35 Titchener, E.B. A text-book of psychology. N.Y., 1924.

Phil 5259.5.37 Titchener, E.B. A text-book of psychology. N.Y., 1926.

Phil 5259.5.38 Titchener, E.B. A text-book of psychology. N.Y., 1928.

Phil 5259.5.50 Titchener, E.B. Systematic psychology; prolegomena. N.Y., 1929.

Phil 5259.6 Tetens, J.N. Philosophische Versuche über die menschliche Natur. Leipzig, 1777. 2v.

Phil 5259.6.8 Tetens, J.N. Über die allgemeine speculativische Philosophie. Berlin, 1913.

Phil 5259.6.15 Pamphlet box Tetens, J.N.

Phil 5259.7 Thorndike, E.L. The human nature club. N.Y., 1901.

Phil 5259.7.3 Thorndike, E.L. The human nature club. N.Y., 1900.

Phil 5259.7.5 Thorndike, E.L. The elements of psychology. N.Y., 1905.

Phil 5259.7.6 Thorndike, E.L. The elements of psychology. 2d ed. N.Y., 1905.

Phil 5259.7.15 Thorndike, E.L. The psychology of wants, interests and attitudes. N.Y., 1935.

Phil 5259.7.20 Thorndike, E.L. Human nature and the social order. N.Y., 1940.

Phil 5259.7.22 Thorndike, E.L. Human nature and the social order. Cambridge, 1969.

Phil 5259.7.30 Thorndike, E.L. Man and his works. Cambridge, 1943.

Phil 5259.7.76 Pamphlet vol. Thorndike, E.L. Papers. 1900-1910. 17 pam.

Phil 5259.7.77 Pamphlet vol. Thorndike, E.L. Papers. 1911-1921. 17 pam.

Phil 5259.7.78 Pamphlet vol. Thorndike, E.L. Papers. 1899-1908. 9 pam.

Phil 5259.9 Thompson, H.B. The mental traits of sex. Chicago, 1903.

Phil 5259.10 Toulouse. Technique de psychologie experiment. Paris, 1911. 2v.

Phil 5259.11.5 Trabue, M.R. Measure your mind. Garden City, 1921.

Phil 5259.13.2 Tansley, A.G. The new psychology. London, 1920.

Phil 5259.13.10 Tansley, A.G. The new psychology. N.Y., 1924.

Phil 5259.13.15 Tansley, A.G. Mind and life. London, 1952.

Phil 5259.14 Theone, Alois S. Die Mechanik des Seelenlebens. Bonn, 1911.

Phil 5259.15 Tumarkin, Anna. Prolegomena zu einer wissenschaftliche Psychologie. Leipzig, 1923.

Phil 5259.15.10 Tumarkin, Anna. Die Methoden der psychologischen Forschung. Leipzig, 1929.

Phil 5259.16.2 Thoden van Velzen, H. De wetenschap van ons geestelijk wezen. 2. druk. Amsterdam, 1894.

Phil 5259.17 Thurstone, L.L. The nature of intelligence. London, 1924.

Phil 5240 - 5265 Psychology - General treatises - Individual authors (A-Z) - cont.

Phil 5259.18 Tapy, George H. Outline of psychology. Crawfordsville, 19- ?
Phil 5259.19 Troland, L.T. The mystery of mind. N.Y., 1926.
Phil 5259.19.9 Troland, L.T. The fundamentals of human motivation. N.Y., 1928.
Phil 5259.19.15A Troland, L.T. The principles of psychology. N.Y., 1929. 3v.
Phil 5259.19.15B Troland, L.T. The principles of psychology. v.3. N.Y., 1929.
Phil 5259.19.50 Pamphlet box. Psychology. General works.
Phil 5259.20 Tassy, Edme. L'activité psychique. Paris, 1925.
Phil 5259.21 Thomson, M.K. The springs of human action. N.Y., 1927.
Phil 5259.22 Tarozzi, G. Nozioni di psicologia. Bologna, 1925.
Phil 5259.23 Ten Seldam, W.H. Psychologische hoofdstukken. Amsterdam, 1926.
Phil 5259.24.2 Tickell, Sydney. Psychology really simplified in terms of machinery. Cirencester, 1927.
Phil 5259.25 Trejos, J. Resumen de psicología. San José, 1929.
Phil 5259.25.5 Trejos, J. Cuestiones de psicologiá racional. 2. ed. San José de Costa Rica, 1935.
Phil 5259.26 Tripp, Erich. Untersuchungen zur Rechtspsychologie des Individuums. Leipzig, 1931.
Phil 5259.27 Thomas, Frank C. Ability and knowledge: the London school. London, 1935.
Phil 5259.28 Torrey, D.C. The normal person. Jaffrey, New Hampshire, 1927.
Phil 5259.29 Taylor, J.G. Popular psychological fallacies. London, 1938.
Phil 5259.30 Tiffin, J. The psychology of normal people. Boston, 1940.
Phil 5259.31 Thomae, Hans. Das Wesen der menschlichen Antriebsstruktur. Leipzig, 1944.
Phil 5259.32 Tilquin, A. Le behaviorisme. Thèse. Paris, 1942-45.
Phil 5259.34 Tyler, Leona E. The psychology of human differences. N.Y., 1947.
NEDL Phil 5259.36 Teplov, B.M. Psikhologiia. Moskva, 1948.
Phil 5259.38 Thirring, H. Homo sapiens. 2. Aufl. Wien, 1948.
Phil 5259.40A Tolman, Edward C. Collected papers in psychology. Berkeley, 1951.
Phil 5259.40B Tolman, Edward C. Collected papers in psychology. Berkeley, 1951.
Phil 5259.40.5 Tolman, Edward C. Behavior and psychological man. Berkeley, 1958.
Phil 5259.42 Tyrrell, G.N.M. Homo faber. London, 1952.
Phil 5259.45 Thurner, Franz K. Kurzzeitige nacheffekte unserer Wahrnehmungen. Berlin, 1961.
Phil 5259.50 Teplov, B.M. Problemy individual'nykh razlichii. Moskva, 1961.
Phil 5259.55 Toman, Walter. Family constellation. N.Y., 1961.
Phil 5259.55.2 Toman, Walter. Family constellation. 2d ed. N.Y., 1969.
Phil 5259.56 Taylor, Charles. The explanation of behavior. London, 1964.
Phil 5259.58 Turner, Merle. Philosophy and the science of behavior. N.Y., 1967.
Phil 5259.60 Thines, Georges. La problématique de la psychologie. La Haye, 1968.
Phil 5260.1 Upham, T.C. Elements of intellectual philosophy. Portland, 1827.
Phil 5260.1.2 Upham, T.C. Elements of mental philosophy. Portland, 1831. 2v.
Phil 5260.1.3 Upham, T.C. Mental philosophy. N.Y., 1869. 2v.
Phil 5260.1.4 Upham, T.C. Elements of mental philosophy. 3. ed. Portland, 1839. 2v.
Phil 5260.1.5 Upham, T.C. Elements of mental philosophy. N.Y., 1841.
Phil 5260.1.8 Upham, T.C. Elements of mental philosophy. N.Y., 1857.
Phil 5260.1.9 Upham, T.C. Elements of mental philosophy. N.Y., 1859.
Phil 5260.1.15 Upham, T.C. Mental philosophy. v.2. N.Y., 1875.
Htn Phil 5260.4* Pamphlet vol. Urban, F.M. L'analyse des sphygmogrammes. 1906-1913. 14 pam.
Phil 5260.5 Uphues, G. Erkenntniskritische Psychologie. Halle, 1909.
Phil 5260.6 Ude, Johnson. Einführung in die Psychologie. Graz, 1916.
Phil 5260.8.5 Ufer, Christian. Systematische Psychologie für Oberlyzeen und Seminare. Leipzig, 1912.
Phil 5260.9 United States. Department of Agriculture. Graduate School. The adjustment of personality. Washington, 1939.
Phil 5260.9.5 United States. Department of Agriculture. Graduate School. Understanding ourselves. Washington, 1938.
Phil 5260.10 Uznadze, Dmitrii N. Eksperimental'nye osnovy psikhologii ustanovki. Tbilisi, 1961.
Phil 5260.10.5 Uznadze, Dmitrii N. Psikhologicheskie issledovaniia. Moskva, 1966.
Phil 5261.1 Volkmann, W. Lehrbuch der Psychologie. Göthen, 1875-76. 2v.
Phil 5261.1.2 Volkmann, W. Lehrbuch der Psychologie. v.1-2. Göthen, 1884-85.
Phil 5261.1.3 Volkmann, W. Lehrbuch der Psychologie. Göthen, 1884-8. 2v.
Phil 5261.2 Vignoli, T. Myth and science. N.Y., 1882.
Phil 5261.2.5 Vignoli, T. Peregrinazioni psicologiche. Milano, 1895.
Phil 5261.3 Villa, G. La psicologia contemporanea. Torino, 1899
Phil 5261.3.5 Villa, G. Contemporary psychology. London, 1903.
Phil 5261.3.9 Villa, G. La psicologia contemporanea. Milano, 1911.
Phil 5261.3.12 Villa, G. Enleitung in die Psychologie der Gegenwart. Leipzig, 1902.
Phil 5261.4 Vaz Ferreira, C. Ideas y observaciones. Montevideo, 1905.
Phil 5261.5 Varona, Enrique José. Conferencias filosoficas. Havana, 1888.
Phil 5261.5.5 Varona, Enrique José. Curso de psicologia. Fascimile 2. Havana, 1906.
Phil 5261.6 Van Norden, Charles. The psychic factor; outline of psychology. N.Y., 1894.
Phil 5261.7 Valdarnini, Angelo. Elementi scientifici di psicologia ē logica. 3-4. ed. pt.1-2. Torino, 1915.
Phil 5261.8 Varendonck, J. La psychologie du témoinage. Gand, 1914.
Phil 5261.8.5 Varendonck, J. L'évolution des facultés conscientes. Thèse. Gand, 1921.
Phil 5261.8.8 Varendonck, J. The evolution of the concious faculties. N.Y., 1923.
Phil 5261.9 Vogt, P. Studenbilder der philosophischen Propadeutik. Freiburg, 1909. 2v.
Phil 5261.10.2 Verluys, J. Beginselen der Zielkunde. 2e. Druk. Amsterdam, 1899.
Phil 5261.11 Vannérus, A. Om psykisk energi. Stockholm, 1896.
Phil 5261.12 Vannérus, A. De psykologiska vetenskapernas system. Stockholm, 1907.
Phil 5261.13 Vorländer, F. Grundlinien einer organischen Wissenschafte der menschlichen Seele. Berlin, 1841.

Phil 5240 - 5265 Psychology - General treatises - Individual authors (A-Z) - cont.

Phil 5261.14 Visser, H.L.A. Collectief-psychologische omtrekken. Haarlem, 1920.
Phil 5261.15 Vaughan, W.F. The lure of superiority. N.Y., 1928.
Phil 5261.15.10 Vaughan, W.F. General psychology. Garden City, 1936.
Phil 5261.15.25 Vaughan, W.F. General psychology. 1st ed. N.Y., 1939.
Phil 5261.16 Varvaro, P. L'intelligenza. Palermo, 1927.
Phil 5261.17 Valentine, Willard Lee. Readings in experimental psychology. 1. ed. N.Y., 1931.
Phil 5261.17.10 Valentine, Willard Lee. Psychology laboratory manual. N.Y., 1932.
Phil 5261.17.12 Valentine, Willard Lee. Psychology laboratory manual. N.Y., 1933.
Phil 5261.17.19 Valentine, Willard Lee. Student's guide for beginning the study of psychology. N.Y., 1935.
Phil 5261.17.25 Valentine, Willard Lee. Experimental foundations of general psychology. N.Y., 1938.
Phil 5261.17.26 Valentine, Willard Lee. Experimental foundations of general psychology. N.Y., 1946.
Phil 5261.18 Vogel, C.L. Psychology and the Franciscan school. N.Y., 1932.
Phil 5261.19 Vialle, L. Le désir du néant. Paris, 1933.
Phil 5261.19.5 Vialle, L. Le désir du néant. Thèse. Paris, 1932.
Phil 5261.20 Vaughn, J. Positive versus negative instruction. N.Y., 1928.
Phil 5261.21 Varnuar, W.C. Psychology in everyday life. N.Y., 1938.
Phil 5261.22 Vetter, A. Wirklichkeit des Menschlichen. Freiburg, 1960.
Phil 5261.23 Valdefievre, P. La psychologie du poéte. Paris, 1933.
Phil 5262.1 Wagner, M. Beyträge zur philosophischen Anthropologie. Wien, 1794-96. 2v.
Phil 5262.2 Waitz, T. Grundlegung der Psychologie. Hamburg, 1846.
Phil 5262.2.5 Waitz, T. Lehrbuch der Psychologie. Braunschweig, 1849.
Phil 5262.3 Warden, R.B. Familiar forensic view of man and law. Columbus, 1860.
Phil 5262.4 Wayland, F. Elements of intellectual philosophy. Boston, 1854.
Phil 5262.4.9 Wayland, F. Elements of intellectual philosophy. N.Y., 1865.
Phil 5262.4.50 Wellek, Albert. Der Kückfall in die Methodenkrise der Psychologie. Göttingen, 1959.
Phil 5262.5 Whately, R. Introductory lessons on mind. Boston, 1859.
Phil 5262.5.2 Whately, R. Introductory lessons on mind. London, 1859.
Phil 5262.6 Winslow, H. Elements of intellectual philosophy. Boston, 1850.
Phil 5262.6.3 Winslow, H. Elements of intellectual philosophy. Boston, 1856.
Phil 5262.6.10 Winslow, H. Intellectual philosophy. 8th ed. Boston, 1863.
Phil 5262.8 Watt, H.J. Experimentelle...Theorie des Denkens. Leipzig, 1904.
Phil 5262.8.5 Watt, H.J. Psychology. A lecture. London, 1913.
Phil 5262.9 Woodworth, R.S. Psychology. N.Y., 1908.
Phil 5262.9.10 Woodworth, R.S. Psychology. N.Y., 1924.
Phil 5262.9.15 Woodworth, R.S. Psychology. N.Y., 1929.
Phil 5262.9.20 Woodworth, R.S. Psychology. 3d ed. N.Y., 1935.
Phil 5262.9.25 Woodworth, R.S. Psychology. 4th ed. N.Y., 1940.
Phil 5262.9.30 Woodworth, R.S. Adjustment and mastery. Baltimore, 1933.
Phil 5262.9.35 Woodworth, R.S. Experimental psychology. N.Y., 1938.
Phil 5262.9.40 Woodworth, R.S. Experimental psychology. N.Y., 1950.
Phil 5262.9.42 Woodworth, R.S. Experimental psychology. N.Y., 1954.
Phil 5262.9.43 Woodworth, R.S. Experimental psychology. N.Y., 1965.
Phil 5262.10 Welch, A.S. The teacher's psychology. N.Y., 1889.
Phil 5262.11 Witasek, S. Grundlinien der Psychologie. Leipzig, 1908.
Phil 5262.12 Wenzlaff, G.G. The mental man. N.Y., 1909.
Phil 5262.13 Whipple, G.M. Manual of mental and physical tests. Baltimore, 1910.
Phil 5262.13.2 Whipple, G.M. Manual of mental and physical tests. Pt. 1-2. Baltimore, 1914-15. 2v.
Phil 5262.14 Wirth, W. Psychophysik. Leipzig, 1912.
Htn Phil 5262.16* Willis, T. De anima Brutorum. Oxonii, 1672.
Phil 5262.17.2 Witmer, L. Analytical psychology. Boston, 1902.
Phil 5262.18 Witte, J.H. Das Wesen der Seele und die Natur der geistigen Vorgänge im Lichte. Halle-Saale, 1888.
Phil 5262.19 Ward, James. Psychological principles. Cambridge, 1918.
Phil 5262.19.3A Ward, James. Psychological principles. 2d ed. Cambridge, Eng., 1920.
Phil 5262.19.3B Ward, James. Psychological principles. 2d ed. Cambridge, Eng., 1920.
Phil 5262.19.5 Ward, J. Naturalism and agnosticism. 4th ed. London, 1915.
Phil 5262.20 Warren, H.C. Human psychology. Boston, 1919.
Phil 5262.20.5 Warren, H.C. Elements of human psychology. Boston, 1922.
Phil 5262.20.7 Warren, H.C. Elements of human psychology. Boston, 1930.
Phil 5262.20.9 Warren, H.C. Précis de psychologie. Paris, 1923.
Phil 5262.21B Watson, John B. Psychology from the standpoint of a behaviorist. Philadelphia, 1919. 2v.
Phil 5262.21.2 Watson, John B. Psychology from the standpoint of a behaviorist. 2d ed. Philadelphia, 1924.
Phil 5262.21.3 Watson, John B. Psychology from the standpoint of a behaviorist. 3d ed. Philadelphia, 1929.
Phil 5262.21.5 Watson, John B. Behaviorism. N.Y., 1925.
Phil 5262.21.6 Watson, John B. Behaviorism. N.Y., 1925.
Phil 5262.21.7 Watson, John B. Behaviorism. N.Y., 1930.
Phil 5262.21.10A Watson, John B. The ways of behaviorism. 1st ed. N.Y., 1928.
Phil 5262.21.10B Watson, John B. The ways of behaviorism. 1st ed. N.Y., 1928.
Phil 5262.21.15 Watson, John B. The battle of behaviorism. London, 1928.
Phil 5262.22 Waddington, Charles. L'âme humaine. 2. série. Paris, 1862.
Phil 5262.22.2 Waddington, Charles. De l'âme humaine. 2. série. Paris, 1862.
Phil 5262.23 Walsemann, Hermann. Methodisches Lehrbuch der Psychologie. Potsdam, 1905.
Phil 5262.24 Wollny, F. Grundriss der Psychologie. Leipzig, 1887.
Phil 5262.25 Wahle, Richard. Über den Mechanismus des geistigen Lebens. Wien, 1906.
Phil 5262.26 Wada, Tomi. An experimental study of hunger in its relation to activity. N.Y., 1922.
Phil 5262.28 Wentzke, J.A. Compendium der Psychologie und Logik. Leipzig, 1868.
Phil 5262.29 Ward, Henshaw. Thobbing; a seat at the circus of the intellect. Indianapolis, 1926.
Phil 5262.30 Weiss, Albert P. A theoretical basis of human behavior. Columbus, 1925.
Phil 5262.30.5 Weiss, Albert P. A theoretical basis of human behavior. 2d ed. Columbus, 1929.

5240 - 5265   Psychology - General treatises - Individual authors (A-Z) - cont.

Phil 5262.31   Wertheimer, M. Drei Abhandlungen zur Gestalttheorie.
                 Erlangen, 1925.
Phil 5262.31.5   Pamphlet vol. Wertheimer, M. Psychologische
                 Tatbestandsdiagnostik. 1904-1912. 4 pam.
Phil 5262.31.9   Wertheimer, M. Uber Gestalttheorie. Erlangen, 1925.
Phil 5262.31.15 Wertheimer, M. Gestalt theory. N.Y., 1944.
Phil 5262.31.25A Wertheimer, M. Productive thinking. N.Y., 1959. 2v.
Phil 5262.31.25B Wertheimer, M. Productive thinking. N.Y., 1959.
Phil 5262.31.26 Wertheimer, M. Productive thinking. London, 1961.
Phil 5262.32   Werner, Heinz. Einführung in die Entwicklungspsychologie.
                 Leipzig, 1926.
Phil 5262.32.5   Werner, Heinz. Einführung in die Entwicklungspsychologie.
                 3. Aufl. München, 1953.
Phil 5262.32.6   Werner, Heinz. Einführung in die Entwicklungspsychologie.
                 4. Aufl. München, 1959.
Phil 5262.33   Pamphlet vol. Wells, F.L. A statistical study of literary
                 merit. 1907-16. 37 pam.
Phil 5262.34   Weld, Harry P. Psychology as science, its problems and
                 points of view. London, 1928.
Phil 5262.34.2   Weld, Harry P. Psychology as science, its problems and
                 points of view. N.Y., 1928.
Phil 5262.35   Wexberg, Erwin. Individual psychology. N.Y., 1929.
Phil 5262.35.5   Wexberg, Erwin. Individualpsychologie. 2. Aufl.
                 Leipzig, 1931.
Phil 5262.36   Wheeler, R.H. The science of psychology. N.Y., 1929.
Phil 5262.36.2   Wheeler, R.H. The science of psychology. N.Y., 1940.
Phil 5262.36.5   Wheeler, R.H. Readings in psychology. N.Y., 1930.
Phil 5262.36.10 Wheeler, R.H. Laws of human nature. N.Y., 1932.
Phil 5262.37   Wyatt, Horace G. Psychology of intelligence and will.
                 London, 1930.
Phil 5262.38   Witwicki, W. Psychologja. v.1-2. Lwów, 1930.
Phil 5262.39A   Wild, K.W. Intuition. Cambridge, Eng., 1938.
Phil 5262.39B   Wild, K.W. Intuition. Cambridge, Eng., 1938.
Phil 5262.40   Weinhandl, F. Die Gestaltanalyse. Erfurt, 1927.
Phil 5262.41   Wait, W.T. Science of human behavior. N.Y., 1938.
Phil 5262.42   Wiggam, Albert E. Exploring your mind with the
                 psychologists. Indianapolis, 1928.
Phil 5262.43   Walker, Kenneth M. Diagnosis of man. London, 1942.
Phil 5262.43.5   Walker, Kenneth M. The circle of life. London, 1942.
Phil 5262.44   Weiser-Aall, Lily. Volkskunde und Psychologie; eine
                 Einführung. Berlin, 1937.
Phil 5262.45.10 Weatherhead, L.D. Psychology and life. N.Y., 1940.
Phil 5262.46.01 Pamphlet box. White, Robert W.
Phil 5262.47   Wolff, W. What is psychology? N.Y., 1947.
Phil 5262.48.5   Weizäcker, Viktor. Der Gestaltkreis. 3. Aufl.
                 Stuttgart, 1947.
Phil 5262.48.20 Weizäcker, Viktor. Gestalt und Zeit. 2. Aufl.
                 Göttingen, 1960.
Phil 5262.49   Wellek, A. Ganzheitspsychologie und Strukturtheorie.
                 Bern, 1955.
Phil 5262.50   Wolfenstein, M. Disaster, a psychological essay. Glencoe,
                 Ill., 1957.
Phil 5262.51   Wenzl, Aloys. Theorie der Begabung. 2. Aufl.
                 Heidelberg, 1957.
Phil 5262.53   Wolman, Benjamin B. Contemporary theories and systems in
                 psychology. N.Y., 1960.
Phil 5262.54   Webb, W.B. The profession of psychology. N.Y., 1962.
Phil 5262.55   Within, Herman A. Psychological differentiation.
                 N.Y., 1962.
Phil 5262.56   Waffenschmidt, Walter. Denkformen und Denktechnik.
                 Meisenheim, 1961.
Phil 5262.57   Williamson, George Scott. Science, synthesis and sanity.
                 London, 1965.
Phil 5262.57.5   Williamson, George Scott. Science, synthesis and sanity.
                 Chicago, 1965.
Phil 5262.60   Willwoll, Alexander. Psychologia metaphysica, in Usum
                 scholarum. Friburgi, 1952.
Phil 5262.62   Whitla, Dean. Handbook of measurement and assessment in
                 behavioral sciences. Reading, 1968.
Phil 5262.65   Westcott, Malcolm Robert. Toward a contemporary psychology
                 of intuition. N.Y., 1968.
Phil 5262.66   Witvrouw, Marcel. Le comportement humain.
                 Bruxelles, 1966.
Phil 5262.68   Wulf, Berthold. Idee und Denken. Stuttgart, 1964.
Phil 5262.70   Wiseman, Stephen. Intelligence and ability.
                 Baltimore, 1967.
Phil 5264.1   Young, J. Lectures on intellectual philosophy.
                 Glasgow, 1835.
Phil 5264.2.2   Yerkes, R.M. Introduction to psychology. N.Y., 1911.
Phil 5264.3   Young, P.T. Motivation of behavior. N.Y., 1936.
Phil 5264.3.5   Young, P.T. Motivation of behavior. N.Y., 1950.
Phil 5264.4   Yolton, J.W. Thinking and perceiving. Lasalle,
                 Ill., 1962.
Phil 5265.1   Ziehen, Theodor. Leitfaden der physiologischen
                 Psychologie. Jena, 1891.
Phil 5265.1.2   Ziehen, Theodor. Leitfaden der physiologischen
                 Psychologie. 3. Aufl. Jena, 1896.
Phil 5265.1.3   Ziehen, Theodor. Leitfaden der physiologischen
                 Psychologie. Jena, 1908.
Phil 5265.1.4   Ziehen, Theodor. Leitfaden der physiologischen
                 Psychologie. 5. Aufl. Jena, 1900.
Phil 5265.1.4.2 Ziehen, Theodor. Leitfaden der physiologischen
                 Psychologie. 7. Aufl. Jena, 1906.
Phil 5265.1.4.3 Ziehen, Theodor. Leitfaden der physiologischen
                 Psychologie. 10. Aufl. Jena, 1914.
Phil 5265.1.4.5 Ziehen, Theodor. Leitfaden der physiologischen
                 Psychologie. 12. Aufl. Jena, 1924.
Phil 5265.1.5   Ziehen, Theodor. Introduction to physiological psychology.
                 n.p., 1892.
Phil 5265.1.6   Ziehen, Theodor. Introduction to physiological psychology.
                 London, 1895.
Phil 5265.1.9   Ziehen, Theodor. Die Grundlagen der Psychologie. v.1-2.
                 Leipzig, 1915.
Phil 5265.1.15   Ziehen, Theodor. Allgemeine Psychologie. Berlin, 1923.
Phil 5265.2   Zwanenburg, S. Inleiding tot de psychologie.
                 Utrecht, 1926.
Phil 5265.3F   Zapan, Georg. Übbarkeit verschiedener Aufgaben.
                 München, 1932.
Phil 5265.4   Zürcher, W. Über die Intelligenz und ihren Ort im Gefüge
                 des Verhalttens. Bern, 1941.
Phil 5265.5   Zippert, Erwin. Vom Gleichgewicht der Seele. Ulm, 1958.
Phil 5265.6   Zimny, George. Method in experimental psychology.
                 N.Y., 1961.
Phil 5265.7   Zhdanov, D.A. Vozniknovenie abstraktnogo myshleniia.
                 Khar'kov, 1969.

Phil 5270   Psychology - General special treatises - Theory, scope, methods,
relations.- General works

Phil 5270.1   Kerlinger, Frederick, N. Foundations of behavioral
                 research. N.Y., 1965.
Phil 5270.2   Kurtz, Kenneth Hassett. Foundations of psychological
                 research. Boston, 1965.
Phil 5270.3   Shwayder, David S. The stratification of behaviour.
                 N.Y., 1965.
Phil 5270.3.1   Shwayder, David S. The stratification of behaviour.
                 London, 1965.
Phil 5270.4   Sidowski, Joseph B. Experimental methods and
                 instrumentation in psychology. N.Y., 1966.
Phil 5270.6   Bakan, David. On method: toward a reconstruction of
                 psychological investigation. 1st ed. San Francisco, 1967.
Phil 5270.8   Traxel, Werner. Uber Gegenstand und Methode der
                 Psychologie. Bern, 1968.
Phil 5270.10   Devereux, George. From anxiety to method in the behavioral
                 sciences. The Hague, 1968.
Phil 5270.12   Gobar, Ash. Philosophic foundations of genetic psychology
                 and Gestalt psychology. The Hague, 1969.
Phil 5270.14   Naturalistic viewpoints in psychological research.
                 N.Y., 1969.
Phil 5270.16   Metodologicheskie i teoreticheskie problemy psikhologii.
                 Moskva, 1969.
Phil 5270.18   Rosenthal, Robert. Artifact in behavioral research.
                 N.Y., 1969.
Phil 5270.20   Schneewind, Klaus Alfred. Methodisches Denken in der
                 Psychologie. Bern, 1969.
Phil 5270.22   Brown, Clarence William. Scientific method in psychology.
                 N.Y., 1955.
Phil 5270.24   Lagache, Daniel. L'unité de la psychologie. 2. éd.
                 Paris, 1969.
Phil 5270.26   Borger, Robert. Explanation in the behavioral sciences.
                 Cambridge, Eng., 1970.
Phil 5270.28   Eckensberger, Lutz H. Methodenprobleme der
                 kulturvergleichenden Psychologie. Saarbrücken, 1970.
Phil 5270.30   Miller, Arthur G. The social psychology of psychological
                 research. N.Y., 1971.
Phil 5270.32   Jung, John. The experimenter's dilemma. N.Y., 1971.
Phil 5270.36   Anderson, Barry F. The psychology experiment. 2d ed.
                 Belmont, Calif., 1971.

Phil 5272   Psychology - General special treatises - Theory, scope, methods,
relations - Statistical methods

Phil 5272.2   Du Bois, Philip Hunter. An introduction to psychological
                 statistics. N.Y., 1965.
Phil 5272.3   Luce, Robert D. Readings in mathematical psychology.
                 N.Y., 1963-65. 2v.
Phil 5272.4   Coombs, Clyde. A theory of data. N.Y., 1967.
Phil 5272.5   Lord, Frederick M. Estimating true-score distributions in
                 psychological testing. Princeton, 1967.
Phil 5272.6   Nunnally, Jum Clarence. Psychometric theory. N.Y., 1967.
Phil 5272.6.5   Delbeke, L. Construction of preference spaces.
                 Louvain, 1968.
Phil 5272.7   Wike, Edward L. Data analysis. Chicago, 1971.
Phil 5272.8   Gulliksen, Harold. Mathematical solutions for
                 psychological problems. n.p., 1958.
Phil 5272.10   Restle, Frank. Introduction to mathematical psychology.
                 Reading, Mass., 1970.
Phil 5272.10.3   Hofstaetter, Peter Robert. Quantitative Methoden der
                 Psychologie. 3. Aufl. München, 1967.
Phil 5272.11   Sixtl, Friedrich. Messmethoden der Psychologie.
                 Weinheim, 1967.
Phil 5272.12   Bock, R. Darrell. The measurement and prediction of
                 judgment and choice. San Francisco, 1968.
Phil 5272.14   Rydberg, Sven. Bias in prediction; on correction methods.
                 Uppsala, 1963.
Phil 5272.16   Rey, André. Techniques inédites pour l'examen
                 psychologique. Neuchâtel, 1967.
Phil 5272.18   Pfanzogl, Johann. Theory of measurement. Würzburg, 1968.
Phil 5272.20   Edwards, Allen Louis. Experimental design in psychological
                 research. N.Y., 1951.
Phil 5272.20.3   Edwards, Allen Louis. Experimental design in psychological
                 research. 3d ed. N.Y., 1968.
Phil 5272.22   Kristof, Walter. Untersuchungen zur Theorie
                 psychologischen Messens. Meisenheim, 1969.
Phil 5272.24   Courts, Frederick A. Psychological statistics. Homewood,
                 Ill., 1966.
Phil 5272.26.2   Tyler, Leona Elizabeth. Tests and measurements. 2d ed.
                 Englewood Cliffs, 1971.

Phil 5274   Psychology - General special treatises - Theory, scope, methods,
relations - Other special research methods

Phil 5274.2   Colloque International sur les Modèles et la Formalisation
                 du Comportement, Paris, 1965. Les modèles et la
                 formalisation du comportement. Paris, 1967.
Phil 5274.3   Bobneva, Margarita I. Tekhnicheskaia psikhologiia.
                 Moskva, 1966.
Phil 5274.4   Kochergin, A.N. Problemy modelirovaniia psikhicheskoi
                 deiatel'nosti. v.2. Photoreproduction. Moskva, 1969. 2v.
Phil 5274.5   Modelirovanie psikhicheskoi deiatel'nosti. Moskva, 1969.
Phil 5274.6   Apter, Michael John. The computer simulation of behavior.
                 London, 1970.
Phil 5274.8   Burt, Cyril. The factors of the mind. London, 1940.
Phil 5274.10   Butler, John M. Quantitative naturalistic research.
                 Englewood Cliffs, 1963.
Phil 5274.12   Harmon, Harry Horace. Some observations on factor
                 analysis. Santa Monica, 1955.
Phil 5274.14   Symposium on Psychological Factor Analysis, Uppsala
                 University, 1953. Uppsala symposium on psychological
                 factor analysis, 17-19 March 1953. Copenhagen, 1953.
Phil 5274.16   Pawlik, Kurt. Dimensionen des Verhaltens. Bern, 1968.
Phil 5274.18   Oléron, Pierre. Les composantes de l'intelligence d'après
                 les recherches factorielles. Paris, 1957.
Phil 5274.20   Johnson, Homer H. An introduction to experimental design
                 in psychology. N.Y., 1971.
Phil 5274.23   Mulaik, Stanley A. The foundations of factor analysis.
                 N.Y., 1971.

Phil 5275   Psychology - General special treatises - Theory, scope, methods,
relations - Relations of psychology to other disciplines

Phil 5275.5   Střizenec, Michal. Psychológia a kybernetika.
                 Bratislava, 1966.
Phil 5275.7   Domin, Georg. Psychologie, philosophie, Menschenbild.
                 Halle, 1964.
Phil 5275.10   Pelikán, Pavel. Homo informationicus, réflexions sur
                 l'homme et l'informatique. Nancy, 1967.

Phil 5275   Psychology - General special treatises - Theory, scope, methods, relations - Relations of psychology to other disciplines - cont.

Phil 5275.15   Simon, Herbert Alexander. The sciences of the artificial. Cambridge, 1969.

Phil 5275.20   Psychologie et sous-développement. Paris, 1963.

Phil 5279   Psychology - General special treatises - Theory, scope, methods, relations - Other special

Phil 5279.5   Malewski, Andrzej. Verhalten und Interaktion. Tübingen, 1967.

Phil 5279.10   Rosenthal, Robert. Experimenter effects in behavioral research. N.Y., 1966.

Phil 5279.25.2   Geer, Johannes Petrus van de. De mening van de psycholoog. 2. druk. Haarlem, 1968.

Phil 5279.25.5   Kelly, Everett Lowell. The prediction of performance in clinical psychology. N.Y., 1969.

Phil 5280   Psychology - General special treatises - Special systems, schools, etc. - Phenomenological psychology

Phil 5280.5   Owens, Thomas J. Phenomenology and intersubjectivity. The Hague, 1971.

Phil 5282   Psychology - General special treatises - Special systems, schools, etc. - Existential psychology

Phil 5282.5   Existential humanistic psychology. Belmont, Calif., 1971.

Phil 5284   Psychology - General special treatises - Special systems, schools, etc. - Behaviorism

Phil 5284.2   Kaminski, Gerhard. Verhaltenstheorie und Verhaltensmodifikation. Stuttgart, 1970.

Phil 5284.4   The psychology of private events; perspectives on covert response systems. N.Y., 1971.

Phil 5286   Psychology - General special treatises - Special systems, schools, etc. - Gestalt psychology

Phil 5286.7   Wellek, Albert. Ganzheitspsychologie und Strukturtheorie. 2. Aufl. Berlin, 1969. 4v.

Phil 5286.10   Katz, David. Gestaltpsychologie. Basel, 1944.

Phil 5286.10.2   Katz, David. Gestaltpsychologie. 2. Aufl. Basel, 1948.

Phil 5286.10.4   Katz, David. Gestaltpsychologie. 4. Aufl. Basel, 1969.

Phil 5286.15   Petermann, Bruno. Das Gestaltproblem in der Psychologie im Lichte analytischer Besimmung. Leipzig, 1931.

Phil 5300   Psychology - Treatises on special topics - Folios [Discontinued]

NEDL Phil 5300.1   Mantegazza, P. Atlante della espressione del dolore. Firenze, 1876.

Phil 5300.2A   James, W. The feeling of effort. Boston, 1880.

Phil 5300.2B   James, W. The feeling of effort. Boston, 1880.

Phil 5300.2C   James, W. The feeling of effort. Boston, 1880.

Phil 5300.3   Cyon, E. de. Recherches éxperimentales sur les fonctions des canaux semi-circulaires. Thèse. Paris, 1878.

Phil 5300.4   Angell, J.R. A preliminary study...partial tones...of sound. Chicago, 1902.

Phil 5311.2.5   Bjerre, P. Von der Psychoanalyse zur Psychosynthese. Halle, 1925.

Phil 5325   Psychology - Treatises on special topics - Association of ideas

Phil 5325.1   Pamphlet vol. Association of ideas. 1900-12. 11 pam.

Phil 5325.1.2   Pamphlet box. Association of ideas.

Phil 5325.2   Ferri, L. La psychologie de l'association. Paris, 1883.

Phil 5325.2.5   Ferri, L. La psicologia dell'associazione dall'Hobbes. Roma, 1894.

Phil 5325.2.10   Stricker, Salomon. Studien über die Association der Vorstellungen. Wien, 1883.

Phil 5325.3   Hissmann, M. Geschichte der Lehre...Association der Ideen. Göttingen, 1777.

Phil 5325.5   Arnold, Felix. The psychology of association. N.Y., 1906.

Phil 5325.5.2   Arnold, Felix. The psychology of association. N.Y., 1906.

Phil 5325.7   Sollier, Paul. Essai sur l'association. Paris, 1907.

Phil 5325.8   Culler, A.J. Interference and adaptability. N.Y., 1912.

Phil 5325.9   Scripture, E.W. Über der associativen Verlauf der Vorstellungen. Leipzig, 1891.

Phil 5325.9.5   Scripture, E.W. Vorstellung und Gefühl. Leipzig, 1891.

Phil 5325.10   Sutherland, A.H. Critique of word association reactions; an experimental study. Menasha, Wisc., 1913.

Phil 5325.10.2   Sutherland, A.H. Critique of word association reactions. n.p., 191-.

Phil 5325.10.5   Popp, Walter. Kritische Bemerkungen zur Associationstheorie. Teil 1. Leipzig, 1913.

Phil 5325.11   Stern, L.W. Analogie in volkstümlichen Denken. Berlin, 1893.

Phil 5325.13   Mervoyer, P.M. Étude sur l'association des idées. Paris, 1864.

Phil 5325.14   Sganzini, Carlo. Neuere Einsichten...Ideenassoziationen. Bern, 1918.

Phil 5325.15   Jung, Carl G. Über das Verhalten der Reaktionszeit. Leipzig, 1915.

Phil 5325.15.7   Jung, Carl G. Die psychologische Diagnose des Tatbestandes. Zurich, 1941.

Phil 5325.16   Burchhardt, F. Die Vorstellungsreihe. Meissen, 1888.

Phil 5325.17   Warren, Howard C. A history of the association psychology. N.Y., 1921.

Phil 5325.17.2   Warren, Howard C. A history of the association psychology. Diss. Baltimore, 1921.

Phil 5325.18   Hintermann, H. Experimentelle Untersuchung der Bewusstseinsvorgänge. Zürich, 1916.

Phil 5325.19   Pétrovitch, D. L'association des idées obéitelles à des lois? Thèse. Caen, 1920.

Phil 5325.20   Renda, A. La dissociazione psicologica. Torino, 1905.

Phil 5325.21   Paulhan, Fr. Le mensonge du monde. Paris, 1921.

Phil 5325.22   Lehmann, A. Om gedenkelse. Kjøbenhavn, 1888.

Phil 5325.23   Claparède, Edouard. L'association des idées. Paris, 1903.

Phil 5325.24   Kern, B. Assoziationspsychologie und Erkenntnis. Berlin, 1913.

Phil 5325.25   Bardili, C.G. Über die Geseze der Ideenassoziation. Tübingen, 1796.

Phil 5325.26   Robinson, E.S. Association theory today. N.Y., 1932.

Phil 5325.27   Lévêque, R. L'éclosion des pensées. Paris, 1938.

Phil 5325.28   Herrick, C.J. Awareness. Philadelphia, 1939.

Phil 5325.30A   Festinger, Leon. A theory of cognitive dissonance. Evanston, Ill., 1957.

Phil 5325.30B   Festinger, Leon. A theory of cognitive dissonance. Evanston, Ill., 1957.

Phil 5325.35   Brehm, Jack W. Explorations in cognitive dissonance. N.Y., 1962.

Phil 5325.37   Jaspars, Joseph Maria Franciscus. De vrienden van mijn vrienden. Leiden, 1967.

Phil 5325   Psychology - Treatises on special topics - Association of ideas - cont.

Phil 5325.40F   Jordan, Nehemiah. The theory of cognitive dissonance. Washington, 1964.

Phil 5325.42   Deese, James. The structure of association in language and thought. Baltimore, 1966.

Phil 5325.44   Cramer, Phede. Word association. N.Y., 1968.

Phil 5325.46   Håseth, Kjell Johan. Norske ord-assosiasjonsnormer. Oslo, 1968.

Phil 5325.48   Zimbardo, Philip G. The cognitive control of motivation: the consequences of choice and dissonance. Glenville, Ill., 1969.

Phil 5325.50   Kallich, Martin. The association of ideas and critical theory in eighteenth-century England. The Hague, 1970.

Phil 5325.155   Loring, Mildred W. Methods of studying controlled word associations. Baltimore, 1919.

Phil 5325.156   Lévêque, R. L'éclosion des pensées. Thèse. Strasbourg, 1938.

Phil 5330   Psychology - Treatises on special topics - Attention

Phil 5330.01   Pamphlet box. Attention.

Phil 5330.05   Pamphlet vol. Attention. German dissertations. 6 pam.

Phil 5330.1   Aiken, C. Methods for mind training. N.Y., 1889.

Phil 5330.1.3   Aiken, C. Methods for mind training. N.Y., 1897.

Phil 5330.1.15   Pilzecker, A. Die Lehre von der sinnlichen Aufmerksamkeit. Inaug. Diss. München, 1889.

Phil 5330.2   Kohn, H.E. Zur Theorie der Aufmerksamkeit. Halle, 1894.

Phil 5330.3   Müller, G.E. Zur Theorie der sinnlichen Aufmerksamkeit. Leipzig, 1874?

Phil 5330.4.5   Ribot, T. Psychology of attention. N.Y., 1889.

Phil 5330.4.6   Ribot, T. Psychologie de l'attention. Paris, 1889.

Phil 5330.4.7   Ribot, T. The psychology of attention. Chicago, 1890.

Phil 5330.4.10   Ribot, T. Uppmärksamhetens psykologi. Stockholm, 1891.

Phil 5330.4.15   Ribot, T. Die Psychologie der Aufmerksamkeit. 9 Aufl. Leipzig, 1908.

Phil 5330.5   Uhl, L.L. Attention. Baltimore, 1890.

Phil 5330.6   Heinrich, W. Die moderne psysiologische Psychologie...Aufmerksamkeit. Zürich, 1899.

Phil 5330.6.2   Heinrich, W. Die moderne psysiologische Psychologie...Aufmerksamkeit. Leipzig, 1895.

Phil 5330.6.5   Braunschweiger, D. Die Lehre von der Aufmerksamkeit. Leipzig, 1899.

Phil 5330.7.7   Pillsbury, W.B. Attention. London, 1921.

Phil 5330.8   Nayrac, J.P. Physiologie et psychologie de l'attention. Paris, 1906.

Phil 5330.9   Roehrich, E. L'attention spontanée et volontaire. Paris, 1907.

Phil 5330.10   Dürr, E. Die Lehre von der Aufmerksamkeit. Leipzig, 1907.

Phil 5330.11   Arnold, F. Attention and interest...study in psychology. N.Y., 1910.

Phil 5330.12   Geissler, L.R. The measurement of attention. n.p., 1909.

Phil 5330.14   Stevens, H.C. Plethysmographic study of attention. n.p., 1905.

Phil 5330.16   Mitchell, David. Influence of distractions on the formation of judgments in lifted weight experiments. Princeton, 1914.

Phil 5330.17   Morgan, H.H.B. The overcoming of distraction and other resistances. N.Y., 1916.

Phil 5330.18   Ostermann, W. Das Interesse. 3e Aufl. Oldenburg, 1912.

Phil 5330.19   Dohrn, H. Das Problem der Aufmerksamkeit. Schleswig, 1876.

Phil 5330.20   Hylan, J.P. The fluctuation of attention. N.Y., 1898.

Phil 5330.21   Patrizi, M.L. Il tempo di reazione semplice. Reggio-Emilia, 1897.

Phil 5330.21.5   Patrizi, M.L. La graphique psychométrique de l'attention. Turin, 1895.

Phil 5330.22   Henning, H. Die Aufmerksamkeit. Berlin, 1925.

Phil 5330.23   Suter, Jules. Zur Theorie der Aufmerksamkeit. Zürich, 1914.

Phil 5330.24   Woodrow, H. The measurement of attention. Princeton, 1914.

Phil 5330.25   Yeh, Ling. La psychologie de l'intérêt. Thèse. Lyon, 1929.

Phil 5330.26   Reynax. L'attention. Paris, 1930.

Phil 5330.27   Strong, E.K. Change of interest with age. Palo Alto, 1931.

Phil 5330.28   Knowlson, T.S. The secret of concentration. 1st. ed. N.Y., 1931.

Phil 5330.29   Kreibig, Josef C. Die Aufmerksamkeit. Wien, 1897.

Phil 5330.31   Buckner, D. Vigilance. Los Angeles, 1963.

Phil 5330.32   Käellen, Elov. Uppmärksamhetsförloppens psykologi. Akademisk avhandling. Göttesburg, 1949.

Phil 5330.34   Rutten, Josephus W.H.M. Attentiviteit als psychodiagnosticum. Proefschrift. Maastricht, 1964.

Phil 5330.36   Leplat, Jacques. Attention et incertitude dans les travaux de surveillance et d'inspection. Paris, 1968.

Phil 5330.38   Moray, Neville. Listening and attention. Baltimore, 1969.

Phil 5330.40   Meldman, Monte Jay. Diseases of attention and perception. 1st ed. Oxford, 1970.

Phil 5330.42   Mackworth, Jane F. Vigilance and habituation: a new psychological approach. Harmondsworth, 1969.

Phil 5330.42.5   Mackworth, Jane F. Vigilance and attention; a signal detection approach. Harmondsworth, 1970.

Phil 5335   Psychology - Treatises on special topics - Attitude

Phil 5335.2   Bem, Daryl J. Beliefs, attitudes and human affairs. Belmont, Calif., 1970.

Phil 5335.4   Elms, Alan C. Role playing, reward, and attitude change. N.Y., 1969.

Phil 5335.6   Rokeach, Milton. The open and closed mind. N.Y., 1960.

Phil 5335.8   Freyhold, Michaela von. Autoritarismus und politische Apathie. Frankfurt, 1971.

Phil 5335.10   Triandis, Harry C. Attitude and attitude change. N.Y., 1971.

Phil 5350   Psychology - Treatises on special topics - Change

Phil 5350.1   Stern, L.W. Psychologie der Veränderungsauffassung. Breslau, 1898.

Phil 5350.2.8A   Carr, H.W. Henry Bergson: philosophy of change. London, 1911.

Phil 5350.2.8B   Carr, H.W. Henry Bergson: philosophy of change. London, 1911.

Phil 5350.2.8C   Carr, H.W. Henry Bergson: philosophy of change. London, 1911.

Phil 5350.3   Dobler, J. Die Lebenswende als Reifungskrisis. München, 1961.

Phil 5350.5A   Birren, James E. The psychology of aging. Englewood Cliffs, N.J., 1964.

Phil 5350   Psychology - Treatises on special topics - Change - cont.

Phil 5350.5B   Birren, James E. The psychology of aging. Englewood Cliffs, N.J., 1964.
Phil 5350.5.5   Geist, Harold. The psychological aspects of the aging process with sociological implications. St. Louis, 1968.
Phil 5350.5.10   Riley, Matilda White. Aging and society. N.Y., 1968. 2v.
Phil 5350.6   Coleman, James Samuel. Models of change and response uncertainty. Englewood Cliffs, N.J., 1964.
Phil 5350.7   Munn, Norman Leslie. The evolution and growth of human behavior. 2d ed. Boston, 1965.
Phil 5350.8   Mann, John Harvey. Changing human behavior. N.Y., 1965.
Phil 5350.10   Persistence and change: Bennington College and its students after twenty-five years. N.Y., 1967.

Phil 5352   Psychology - Treatises on special topics - Choice

Phil 5352.5   Luce, Robert. Individual choice behavior. N.Y., 1959. 2v.
Phil 5352.10   Thomae, Hans. Der Mensch in der Entscheidung. München, 1960.
Phil 5352.15   Restle, Frank. Psychology of judgment and choice. N.Y., 1961.
Phil 5352.16   Downs, A. The value of unchosen alternatives. Santa Monica, 1964.
Phil 5352.18   Siegel, Sidney. Choice, strategy and utility. N.Y., 1964.
Phil 5352.20   Broadbent, Donald Eric. Decision and stress. London, 1971.

Phil 5357   Psychology - Treatises on special topics - Comparison

Phil 5357.1   Brunswig, A. Vergleichen und die Relationserkenntnis. Leipzig, 1910.
Phil 5357.2   Jaensch, E.R. Einige allgemeinere Fragen der Psychologie und Biologie des Denkens. Leipzig, 1920.
Phil 5357.3   Gulliksen, Harold. Reliability for the law of comparative judgment. n.p., 1957. 2 pam.

Phil 5358   Psychology - Treatises on special topics - Compensation

Phil 5358.2   Seifert, Karl Heinz. Grundformen und theoretische Perspektiven psychologischer Kompensation. Meisenheim, 1969.

Phil 5360   Psychology - Treatises on special topics - Concept and concept building

Phil 5360.01   Pamphlet box. Psychology. Conception.
Phil 5360.1   Maennel, B. Über abstraktion. Gütersloh, 1890.
Phil 5360.2   Heinrich, E. Untersuchungen zur Lehre vom Begriff. Inaug. Diss. Göttingen, 1910.
Phil 5360.3   Stöhr, Adolf. Die Vieldeutigkeit des Urtheiles. Leipzig, 1895.
Phil 5360.4   Queyrat, F. L'abstraction et son rôle dans l'éducation intellectuelle. 2e éd. Paris, 1907.
Phil 5360.5   Willwoll, A. Begriffsbildung: eine psychologische Untersuchung. Leipzig, 1926.
Phil 5360.6   Paulhan, F. Les puissances de l'abstraction. Paris, 1928.
Phil 5360.7   Peillaude, E. Théorie des concepts. Paris, n.d.
Phil 5360.8   Fisher, S.C. The process of generalizing abstraction. Thesis. Princeton, N.J., 1916.
Phil 5360.9   Pellet, R. Des premières perceptions du concret à la conception de l'abstrait. Thèse. Lyon, 1938.
Phil 5360.10   Laporte, J.M.F. Le problème de l'abstraction. Paris, 1940.
Phil 5360.12   Bouisson, R. Essai sur l'abstraction. Gap, 1942.
Phil 5360.13   Geach, P.T. Mental acts. N.Y., 1957.
Phil 5360.14   Gorskii, D.P. Vopsosy abstraktsii i obrazovanie poniatiia. Moskva, 1961.
Phil 5360.15   Pavlov, V.T. Otnosheniia mezhdu poniatiiami. Kiev, 1961.
Phil 5360.16.1   Hunt, Earl Busby. Concept learning. N.Y., 1966.
Phil 5360.17   Wilson, J. Thinking with concepts. Cambridge, 1963.
Phil 5360.18   Pikas, Anatol. Abstraction and concept formation. Cambridge, 1944.
Phil 5360.19   Rozov, Mikhail A. Nauchnaia abstraktsiia i ee vidy. Novosibirsk, 1965.
Phil 5360.20   Schroder, Harold M. Human information processing. N.Y., 1967.
Phil 5360.22   Symposium on Cognition, 2d, Pittsburgh, 1966. Concepts and the structure of memory. N.Y., 1967.
Phil 5360.24   Schon, Donald A. Displacement of concepts. London, 1963.
Phil 5360.25   Alexander, Hubert Griggs. Language and thinking; a philosophical introduction. Princeton, N.J., 1966.
Phil 5360.26   Reenpää, Yrjö. Wahrnehmen, Beobachten, Konstituieren. Frankfurt, 1967.
Phil 5360.27   Borisov, Vadim N. Urovni logicheskogo protsessa i osnovnye napravleniia ikh issledovaniia. Novosibirsk, 1967.
Phil 5360.30   Klerk, Lein Friedrich Wolfgang de. Probabilistic concept learning. Proefschrift. Leiden? 1968.
Phil 5360.32   Reumann, Kurt. Das antithetische Kamptbild. Inaug. Diss. Berlin, 1966.
Phil 5360.34   Tenzer, Oliver. Abstrakcia. 1. vyd. Bratislava, 1966.
Phil 5360.36   Weinberg, Julius Rudolph. Ideas and concepts. Milwaukee, 1970.

Phil 5365   Psychology - Treatises on special topics - Conflict

Phil 5365.2   Nesswetha, Wilhelm. Formen der Reaktion auf Konflikte. Diss. Bonn, 1964.
Phil 5365.4   Fisch, Rudolf. Konfliktmtivation und Examen. Meisenheim am Glan, 1970.

Phil 5374   Psychology - Treatises on special topics - Consciousness

Phil 5374.1   Pamphlet vol. Consciousness. 1866,1902-15. 10 pam.
Phil 5374.1.2   Pamphlet box. Consciousness.
Phil 5374.2   Morrill, J.S. Self-consciousness of noted persons. Boston, 1887.
Phil 5374.3   Drossbach, M. Genesis des Bewusstseins. Leipzig, 1860.
Phil 5374.4   Fitzgerald, P.F. Essay on the philosophy of self-consciousness. London, 1882.
Phil 5374.5   Stricker, S. Studien über das Bewusstsein. Wien, 1879.
Phil 5374.6   Bertrand, A. L'aperception du corps humain. Paris, 1880.
Phil 5374.7   Lange, K.M. Über Apperception. Plauen, 1879.
Phil 5374.7.5   Lange, K.M. Apperception. Boston, 1893.
Phil 5374.7.6   Lange, K.M. Apperception. Boston, 1893.
Phil 5374.8   Bergson, H. Essai sur les données immédiates de la conscience. 2. éd. Paris, 1898.
L Phil 5374.8.5   Bergson, H. Essai sur les données immédiates de la conscience. 2. èd. Paris, 1898.
Phil 5374.9   Hall, L. The evolution of consciousness. London, 1901.
Phil 5374.9.9   Kries, Johannes. Über die materiellen Grundlagen der Bewusstseins-Erscheinungen. Tübingen, 1901.
Phil 5374.10   Lipps, Theodor. Einheiten und Relationen. Leipzig, 1902.
Phil 5374.11.3   Wolff, J. Das Bewusstsein und sein Object. Berlin, 1889.

Phil 5374   Psychology - Treatises on special topics - Consciousness - cont.

Phil 5374.12   Perry, R.B. Conceptions and misconceptions of conciousness. N.Y., 1904.
Phil 5374.14   Mittenzwey, K. Über abstrahierende Apperception. Leipzig, 1907.
Phil 5374.14.9   Hoffmann, Alfred. Vom Bewusstsein. Leipzig, 1907.
Phil 5374.15   Wheeler, C.K. The autobiography of the I or ego. Boston, 1903.
Phil 5374.16   Herbertz, R. Bewusstsein und Unbewusstes. Köln, n.d.
Phil 5374.17   Rehmke, J. Das Bewusstsein. Heidelberg, 1910.
Phil 5374.17.5   Pikler, Gyula. Die Stelle des Bewusstseins in der Natur. Leipzig, 1910.
Phil 5374.18   Halt, E.B. The concepts of consciousness. London, 1914.
Phil 5374.20   Turró, R. Origines de la connaissance. Paris, 1914.
Phil 5374.21   Strong, Charles A. The origin of consciousness. London, 1918.
Phil 5374.22   Montague, W.P. Consciousness a form of energy. N.Y., 19-? 2 pam.
Phil 5374.23   Hofmann, Paul. Die antithetische Struktur des Bewusstseins. Berlin, 1914.
Phil 5374.24.5   Legahn, August F. Entricklungsgeschichte des Bewusstseins. Leipzig, 1926.
Phil 5374.25   Schlegel, Emil. Das Bewusstsein. Stuttgart, 1891.
Phil 5374.26   Fischer, J.C. Das Bewusstsein. Leipzig, 1874.
Phil 5374.27   Koch, Julius L.A. Vom Bewusstsein in Zustanden sogennanten Bewusstlosigkeit. Stuttgart, 1877.
Phil 5374.28   Richter, Rudolf. Herbart'sch und Bergmann'sche Problem des Bewusstseins. Inaug. Diss. Greifswald, 1883?
Phil 5374.29   Uphues, Goswin. Vom Bewusstsein. Osterwieck, 1904.
Phil 5374.30   Tilby, A Wyatt. The evolution of consciousness. London, 1922.
Phil 5374.31   Nasgaard, S. Die Form der Bewusstheit. München, 1923.
Phil 5374.31.5   Nasgaard, S. Bevidsthedens form. Kóbenhavn, 1922.
Phil 5374.32   Ambrosi, L. I principii della conoscenza. Roma, 1898.
Phil 5374.33   Kodis, J. Zur Analyse des Apperceptions begriffes. Berlin, 1893.
Phil 5374.34   Czolbe, Heinrich. Entstehung des Selbstbewusstseins. Leipzig, 1856.
Phil 5374.35   Mager, Alois. Die Enge des Bewusstseins. Stuttgart, 1920.
Phil 5374.36   Pavese, R. Il meccanismo della coscienza. Milano, 1922.
Phil 5374.37   Galli, Ettore. Nel domonio dell' "io". Milano, 1919.
Phil 5374.38   Heisler, N. Ein Ausflug in das Gebiet des Bewusstseins. Basel, 1892.
Phil 5374.39   Müller, R. Das normale Bewusstsein. Leipzig, 1898.
Phil 5374.41   Hesnard, A. La relativité de la conscience de soi. Paris, 1924.
Phil 5374.42   Giése, Fritz. Das ausserpersönliche Unbewusste. Braunschweig, 1924.
Phil 5374.43   Marshall, H.R. Consciousness. London, 1909.
Phil 5374.44.2   Klages, Ludwig. Vom Wesen des Bewusstseins. 2e Aufl. Leipzig, 1926.
Phil 5374.44.5   Klages, Ludwig. Vom Wesen des Bewusstseins. 4. Aufl. München, 1955.
Phil 5374.45.2   Burrow, Trigant. The social basis of consciousness. N.Y., 1927.
Phil 5374.46   Saint Prix, J. de. La conscience comme principe spirituel. Paris, 1927.
Phil 5374.47   Dwelshauvers, G. Psychologie de l'apperception. Bruxelles, 1890.
Phil 5374.48   Fite, Warner. The living mind. N.Y., 1930.
Phil 5374.49   Ishyam, J.C. Infinity and ego. London, 1930.
Phil 5374.50.15   Saunders, H.S. The higher consciousness. Toronto, 1924.
Phil 5374.51   Bostock, John. The neural energy constant. London, 1930.
Phil 5374.52   Jaesche, E. Werden, Sein und Erscheinungsweise des Bewusstseins. Heidelberg, 1887.
Phil 5374.53   King, C. Daly. The psychology of consciousness. London, 1932.
Phil 5374.54   Weir, A. Light, a philosophy of consciousness. Oxford, 1932.
Phil 5374.55   Brunschvicg, Léon. De la connaissance de soi. Paris, 1931.
Phil 5374.56   Minot, C.S. The problem of consciousness in its biological aspects. N.Y., 1902.
Phil 5374.57   Boring, E.G. The physical dimensions of consciousness. N.Y., 1933.
Phil 5374.58   Campbell, P.A. Consciousness, brain-child. East Cleveland, 1933.
Phil 5374.60   Ruyer, Raymond. La conscience et le corps. Paris, 1937.
Phil 5374.61   Campbell, Percy A. Body and self, one and inseparable. San Francisco, 1942.
Phil 5374.63   Gusdorf, G. La découverte de soi. Thèse. 1. éd. Paris, 1948.
Phil 5374.65   Latour, M. Autour des fondements de l'être et du connaître selon l'analyse psychologique. Paris, 1949. 2v.
Phil 5374.67   Lang, Ernst Hildegard. Das wahre Wesen und Wirken des Bewusstseins in seiner normalen und anormalen Erscheinungen. München, 1960.
Phil 5374.69   Arnold, Magda. Story sequence analysis. N.Y., 1962.
Phil 5374.148   Geley, Gustave. L'être subconscient. 4e éd. Paris, 1919.
Phil 5374.148.2   Geley, Gustave. L'être subconscient. Paris, 1899.
Phil 5374.149   Geley, Gustave. De l'inconscient au conscient. Paris, 1919.
Phil 5374.150   Geley, Gustave. From the unconscious to the conscious. Glasgow, 1920.
Phil 5374.151   Geney, Gustave. From the unconcious to the conscious. N.Y., 1921.
Phil 5374.153   Reed, Charles J. The law of vital transfusion and the phenomenon of consciousness. San Francisco, 1921.
Phil 5374.154   Peucesco, M.G. Le mécanisme du courant de la conscience. Paris, 1922.
Phil 5374.154.2   Peucesco, M.G. Le mécanisme du courant de la conscience. Thèse. Paris, 1921.
Phil 5374.154.9   Peucesco, M.G. Mouvement et pensée. Paris, 1927.
Phil 5374.156   Seidel, A. Bewusstsein als Verhangnis. Bonn, 1927.
Phil 5374.158   Nogué, J. Essai sur l'activité primitive du moi. Paris, 1936.
Phil 5374.158.5   Nogué, J. Essai sur l'activité primitive du moi. Thèse. Paris, 1936.
Phil 5374.159   Ganne de Beaucoudrey, E. Perception et courant de conscience. Thèse. Paris, 1936.
Phil 5374.161   Paliard, J. Théorème de la connaissance. Paris, 1938.
Phil 5374.162   Wirth, Wilhelm. Die experimentelle analyse der Bewusstseinsphänomenma. Brauschweig, 1908.
Phil 5374.163   Neumann, E. Ursprungsgeschichte des Bewusstseins. 1. Aufl. Zürich, 1949.
Phil 5374.163.7   Neumann, E. The origins and history of consciousness. N.Y., 1964.

Phil 5374 Psychology - Treatises on special topics - Consciousness - cont.

Phil 5374.165 — Nevratil, Michel. Introduction critique à une découverte de la pensée. Paris, 1954.
Phil 5374.170 — Vincent, M. L'image dynamique. Paris, 1955.
Phil 5374.180 — Brach, Jacques. Conscience et connaissance. Paris, 1957.
Phil 5374.185 — Port, Kurt. Die Enge des Bewusstseins. Esslingen, 1955.
Phil 5374.190 — Joussain, André. Les systèmes de la vie. Paris, 1958.
Phil 5374.195 — Sodan, Guenter. Über den Gebrauch des Ausdrücke "Intention". Berlin, 1958.
Phil 5374.200 — Chauchard, P. Physiologie de la conscience. 4. éd. Paris, 1959.
Phil 5374.205 — Spirkin, A.G. Proiskhozhdenie soznaniia. Moskva, 1960.
Phil 5374.210 — Protasenia, P.F. Proiskhozhdenie soznaniia i ego osobennosti. Minsk, 1959.
Phil 5374.215 — Shorokhova, E.V. Problema soznaniia v filosofii i estestvoznanii. Moskva, 1961.
Phil 5374.220 — Greidanus, J.H. Fundamental physical theory and the concept of consciousness. Oxford, 1961.
Phil 5374.225 — Eriksen, Charles. Behavior and awareness. Durham, 1962.
Phil 5374.232 — Wildangel, G. Beiträge zur Grundlegung der Elementaranalytik des Bewusstseins. Köln, 1962.
Phil 5374.234.30 — Leary, Timothy Francis. High priest. N.Y., 1968.
Phil 5374.235.5 — Castaneda, Carlos. The teachings of Don Juan; a yaqui way of knowledge. Berkeley, 1968.
Phil 5374.235.10 — Castaneda, Carlos. A separate reality; further conversations with Don Juan. N.Y., 1971.
Phil 5374.236 — Psychedelic Review. The psychedelic reader. New Hyde Park, N.Y., 1965.
Phil 5374.239 — Leont'ev, Aleksei N. Problemy razvitiia psikhiki. 2. izd. Moskva, 1965.
Phil 5374.243 — Accademia...Vatican City. Pontificia Accademia delle Scienze, Vatican City. Brain and conscious experience. Study Week, September 28 to October 4, 1964. N.Y., 1966.
Phil 5374.244 — Young, Warren R. L.S.D. on campus. N.Y., 1966.
Phil 5374.245.2 — Schueling, Hermann. Denkstil. Beschreibung und Deutung der Denkformen. 2. Aufl. Düsseldorf, 1967.
Phil 5374.245.10 — Gorsen, Peter. Zur Phänomenologie des Bewusstseinsstroms. Bonn, 1966.
Phil 5374.252 — Neisser, Ulric. Cognitive psychology. N.Y., 1967.
Phil 5374.255 — Petrilowitsch, Nikolaus. Das Gewissen als Problem. Darmstadt, 1966.
Phil 5374.260 — Otto, Herbert Arthur. Ways of growth. N.Y., 1968.
Phil 5374.265 — Kalmar, Jacques M. Frontières de l'homme. Neuchâtel, 1968.
Phil 5374.270 — Structuur en sanctie van het bewustzijn. Wassenaar, 1967.
Phil 5374.275 — Moutada, Leo. Über die Funktion der Mobilität in der geistigen Entwicklung. Stuttgart, 1968.
Phil 5374.276 — Soznanie i obshchenie. Frunze, 1968.
Phil 5374.278 — Tart, Charles T. Altered states of consciousness. N.Y., 1969.
Phil 5374.280 — Smith, Kendon Rasey. Behavior and conscious experience. Athens, 1969.
Phil 5374.282 — Tugarinov, Vasilii P. Filosifiia soznaniia. Moskva, 1971.
Phil 5374.284 — Stevens, John O. Awareness: exploring, experimenting, experiencing. Lafayette, Calif., 1971.
Phil 5374.286 — Drury, Michael. The inward sea. 1st ed. Garden City, 1972.

Phil 5380 Psychology - Treatises on special topics - Crowds [Discontinued]

Phil 5380.01 — Pamphlet box. Psychology. Crowds.
Phil 5380.3.3 — Tarde, G. L'opinion et la foule. 3rd éd. Paris, 1910.
Phil 5380.5.15 — Trotter, Wilfred. Instincts of the herd in peace and war. 3. ed. N.Y., 1941.
Htn — Phil 5380.77* — Freud, Sigmund. Massenpsychologie und Ich-Analyse. Leipzig, 1921.
Phil 5380.90.5 — Cantril, H. The invasion from Mars. Princeton, 1947.

Phil 5385 Psychology - Treatises on special topics - Curiosity

Phil 5385.5 — Nemberg, Herman. Curiosity. N.Y., 1961.
Phil 5385.6 — Fowler, Harry. Curiosity and exploratory behavior. N.Y., 1965.

Phil 5390 Psychology - Treatises on special topics - Degeneration (Mental)

Phil 5390.2.2 — Erdmann, Johann Eduard. Über Dummheit. Berlin, 1866.
Phil 5390.4 — Loewenfeld, Leopold. Über die Dummheit. Wiesbaden, 1909.
Phil 5390.6 — Richet, Charles. L'homme stupide. Paris, 1919.
Phil 5390.8 — Pitkin, Walter B. A short introduction to the history of human stupidity. N.Y., 1932.
Phil 5390.10 — Tabori, Paul. The natural science of stupidity. 1. ed. Philadelphia, 1959.
Phil 5390.12 — Musil, Robert. Über die Dummheit. Wien, 1937.

Phil 5398 Psychology - Treatises on special topics - Electronic behavior control

Phil 5398.5 — Delgado, José M.R. Physical control of the mind. N.Y., 1969.

Phil 5400 Psychology - Treatises on special topics - Emotions - General works

Phil 5400.01 — Pamphlet box. Psychology. Emotions.
Phil 5400.02 — Pamphlet box. Psychology. Emotions.
Phil 5400.05 — Pamphlet box. Psychology. Emotions. German dissertations.
Phil 5400.1 — Burgess, S.W. Historical illustrations of the origin and progress of the passions. London, 1825. 2v.
Htn — Phil 5400.2* — Charleton, W. Natural history of the passions. London, 1674.
Phil 5400.3 — Vernier, I. Caractère des passions. Paris, 1807. 2v.
Phil 5400.4 — Stael-Holstein, Anne Louise G. Treatise on the influence of the passions. London, 1798.
Htn — Phil 5400.4.2* — Stael-Holstein, Anne Louise G. De l'influence des passions. Lausanne, 1796.
NEDL — Phil 5400.5 — Watts, I. The doctrine of the passions. London, 175?.
Htn — Phil 5400.5.6* — Watts, I. The doctrine of the passions. Trenton, n.d.
Phil 5400.6.2 — Letourneau, C. Physiologie des passions. 2. éd. Paris, 1878.
Phil 5400.6.3 — Letourneau, C. Physiologie des passions. Paris, 1868.
Phil 5400.7 — Frédault, F. Les passions. Paris, n.d.
Phil 5400.8 — Maillet, E. De l'essence des passions. Paris, 1877.
Phil 5400.9 — Bottschew, N. Die Gefühlslehre... von Kant bis auf unsere Zeit. Leipzig, 1888.
Htn — Phil 5400.10* — Wright, Thomas. The passions of the minde in generall. London, 1604.
Htn — Phil 5400.10.2* — Wright, Thomas. The passions of the minde in generall. London, 1604.
Htn — Phil 5400.10.5* — Wright, Thomas. The passions of the minde in generall. London, 1630.
Phil 5400.11 — Stanley, Hiram Miner. Studies in the evolutionary psychology of feeling. London, 1895.

Phil 5400 Psychology - Treatises on special topics - Emotions - General works - cont.

Phil 5400.12 — Waldstein, C. Balance of emotion and intellect. London, 1878.
Phil 5400.13 — Nahlowsky, J.W. Das Gefühlsleben. Leipzig, 1884.
Phil 5400.15 — Lehmann, A. Die Hauptgesetze des menschlichen Gefühlslebens. Leipzig, 1892.
Phil 5400.15.2 — Lehmann, A. Die Hauptgesetze des menschlichen Gefühlslebens. 2. Aufl. Leipzig, 1914.
Phil 5400.16 — Kröner, E. Das körperliche Gefühl. Breslau, 1887.
Phil 5400.17 — Steinitzer, M. Die menschlichen und tierischen Gemütsbewegungen. München, 1889.
Phil 5400.18 — Ribot, T. The psychology of the emotions. London, 1897.
Phil 5400.18.4 — Ribot, T. La psychologie des sentiments. Paris, 1896.
Phil 5400.18.5 — Ribot, T. La psychologie des sentiments. 16. éd. Paris, 1939.
Phil 5400.18.6 — Ribot, T. Psychologie der Gefühle. Altenburg, 1903.
Phil 5400.18.9 — Ribot, T. La logique des sentiments. 2. éd. Paris, 1907.
Phil 5400.18.12 — Ribot, T. La logique des sentiments. 5. éd. Paris, 1920.
Phil 5400.18.15 — Ribot, T. Essai sur les passions. Paris, 1907.
Phil 5400.18.19 — Ribot, T. Essai sur les passions. 4. éd. Paris, 1917.
Phil 5400.18.25 — Ribot, T. Problèmes de psychologie affective. Paris, 1910.
X Cg — Phil 5400.18.50 — Darwin, Charles. The expression of the emotions in man and animals. London, 1872.
Phil 5400.19 — Darwin, Charles. The expression of the emotions in man and animals. N.Y., 1873.
Phil 5400.19.2 — Darwin, Charles. Der Ausdruck der Gemüthsbewegungen bei dem Menschen und den Thieren. 4. Aufl. Stuttgart, 1884.
Phil 5400.19.3.5 — Darwin, Charles. The expression of the emotions in man and animals. N.Y., 1894.
Phil 5400.19.3.10 — Darwin, Charles. The expression of the emotions in man and animals. N.Y., 1896.
Phil 5400.19.4 — Darwin, Charles. The expression of the emotions in man and animals. N.Y., 1899.
Phil 5400.19.7 — Darwin, Charles. The expression of the emotions in man and animals. N.Y., 1897.
Phil 5400.20 — Rauh, F. De la méthode dans la psychologie des sentiments. Paris, 1899.
Phil 5400.21 — Schutz, L.H. Die Lehre von den Leidenschaften. Hagen, 1901.
Phil 5400.22 — Gent, W. Volumpulscurven bei Gefühlen und Affecten. Leipzig, 1903.
Phil 5400.23 — Sollier, P. Le mécanisme des émotions. Paris, 1905.
Phil 5400.24 — Hayes, Samuel P. Study of the affective qualities. n.p., 1906.
Phil 5400.25 — Titchener, E.B. Lectures on the elementary psychology of feeling and attention. N.Y., 1908.
Phil 5400.25.5 — Titchener, E.B. Lectures on the elementary psychology of feeling and attention. N.Y., 1924.
Phil 5400.26 — Revault d'Allonnes, G. Les inclinations; leur role dans la psychologie des sentiments. Paris, 1907.
Phil 5400.27 — Chabrier. Les émotions et les états organiques. Paris, 1911.
Phil 5400.28 — Dussauze, H. Les règles esthétiques et les lois du sentiment. Montauban, 1911.
Phil 5400.29 — Latour, Marius. Premiers principes d'une théorie générale des émotions. Paris, 1912.
Phil 5400.29.5 — Latour, Marius. Premiers principes d'une théorie générale des émotions. Paris, 1935.
Phil 5400.29.15 — Latour, Marius. Premiers principes d'une théorie générale des émotions. Observations complémentaires. 3me série. Bayonne, 1937.
Phil 5400.29.20 — Latour, Marius. Premiers principes d'une théorie générale des émotions. Observations complémentaires. 4me série. Bayonne, 1937.
Phil 5400.29.25 — Latour, Marius. Premiers principes d'une théorie générale des émotions. Observations complémentaires. 5me série. Bayonne, 1937.
Phil 5400.30 — Harvey, N.A. The feelings of man. Baltimore, 1914.
Phil 5400.31.9 — Cannon, W.B. Bodily changes in pain, hunger, fear and rage. 2d ed. N.Y., 1929.
Phil 5400.32 — Crile, George W. The origin and nature of the emotions. Philadelphia, 1915.
Phil 5400.33 — Klencke, P.F.H. Diätetik der Seele. 2e Aufl. Leipzig, 1873.
Phil 5400.36 — Alibert, J.L. Physiologie des passions. 2e éd. Paris, 1827. 2v.
Phil 5400.37 — Maier, H. Psychologie des emotionalen Denkens. Tübingen, 1908.
Phil 5400.38 — Luys, Jules. Les émotions chez les sujets en état d'hypnotisme. Paris, 1887.
Phil 5400.39 — Bhagavan, Das. The science of the emotions. London, 1900.
Phil 5400.39.3 — Bhagavan, Das. La science des émotions. Bruxelles, 1921.
Phil 5400.39.9 — Bhagavan, Das. The science of the emotions. 3rd ed. Adyar, 1924.
Phil 5400.40 — Vives, Juan L. Tratado del alma. Madrid, 1916.
Phil 5400.41 — Störring, Gustav. Psychologie des menschlichen Gefühlslebens. Bonn, 1916.
Phil 5400.42 — Andrews, Cyril B. Life, emotion, and intellect. London, 1913.
Phil 5400.42.5 — Koch, Bernhard. Experimentelle Untersuchungen. Leipzig, 1913.
Phil 5400.43 — Frey, Max von. Die Gefühle und ihr Verhältnis zu den Empfindungen. Leipzig, 1894.
Phil 5400.44 — Gurewitsch, Aron. Zur Geschichte des Achtungsbegriffes und zur Theorie der sittlichen Gefühle. Inaug. Diss. Würzburg, 1897.
Phil 5400.45 — Paulhan, Frédéric. Les transformations sociales des sentiments. Paris, 1920.
Phil 5400.45.9 — Paulhan, Frédéric. Les phénomènes affectifs et les lois de leur apparition. 3d éd. Paris, 1912.
Phil 5400.45.15 — Paulhan, Frédéric. Laws of feeling. London, 1930.
Phil 5400.46 — Oelzelt-Newin, A. Über sittliche Dispositionen. Graz, 1892.
Phil 5400.49 — Sergio, Antonio. Da natureza da affecção. Rio de Janeiro, 1913.
Phil 5400.50 — Lange, C.G. Om sindsbevaegelser. Kjobenhavn, 1885.
Phil 5400.50.5 — Lange, C.G. Über Gemüthsbewegungen. Leipzig, 1887.
Phil 5400.50.6 — Lange, C.G. Die Gemüthsbewegungen. 2e Aufl. Würzburg, 1910.
Phil 5400.50.20A — Lange, C.G. The emotions. Baltimore, 1922.
Phil 5400.50.20B — Lange, C.G. The emotions. Baltimore, 1922.
Phil 5400.51 — Festa, Alfonso. Introduzione alla filosofia dell'affetto. Piacenza, 1911.
NEDL — Phil 5400.52 — Feleky, A. Feelings and emotions. N.Y., 1922.
Phil 5400.53 — Cartault, A. Les sentiments généraux. Paris, 1912.
Phil 5400.55 — Rikimaru, J. Emotion and endocrine activities. n.p., 1924.

Phil 5400   Psychology - Treatises on special topics - Emotions - General works - cont.

Phil 5400.56   Thomas, Félix. L'éducation des sentiments. Paris, 1899.
Phil 5400.57   Phelan, G.B. Feeling experience and its modalities. London, 1925.
Phil 5400.59   Sourian, E. L'abstraction sentimentale. Thèse. Paris, 1925.
Phil 5400.59.2   Sourian, E. L'abstraction sentimentale. Paris, 1925.
Phil 5400.59.5   Sourian, E. L'abstraction sentimentale. 2. ed. Paris, 1951.
Phil 5400.60   Szymanski, J.S. Gefühl und Erkennen. Berlin, 1926.
Phil 5400.61   Savescu, Michael. Die Gefühlslehre in der neuesten französischen Psychologie. Leipzig, 1900.
Phil 5400.62   Ferrari, G.C. Le emozioni e la vita del subcosciente. Bologna, 1911.
Phil 5400.63   Picard, Ernest. Problème de la vie affective. Paris, 1926.
Phil 5400.64   Wechsler, David. The measurement of emotional reactions. N.Y., 1925.
Phil 5400.65A   Regmert, Martin L. Feelings and emotions. Worcester, Mass., 1928.
Phil 5400.65B   Regmert, Martin L. Feelings and emotions. Worcester, Mass., 1928.
Phil 5400.66   Marston, W.M. Emotions of normal people. London, 1928.
Phil 5400.68   Ambrosi, L. La dottrina del sentimento nella storia della filosofia. Roma, 1894.
Phil 5400.69   Loosmore, W.C. Ourselves and our emotions. London, 1928.
Phil 5400.71   Joussain, A. Les passions humaines. Paris, 1928.
Phil 5400.72   Brunswick, D. The effects of emotional stimuli on the gastro-intestinal tone. Baltimore, 1924.
Phil 5400.73   Jungmann, J. Das Gemüth. 2e Aufl. Freiburg, 1885.
Phil 5400.74   Lagerborg, R. Das Gefühlsproblem. Leipzig, 1905.
Phil 5400.75   Ziegler, T. Das Gefühl. Stuttgart, 1893.
Phil 5400.75.5   Ziegler, T. Das Gefühl. 5e Aufl. Berlin, 1912.
Phil 5400.76   Kratz, H. Ästhetik. Gütersloh, 1891.
Phil 5400.77   Begtrup, Julius. Some prominent characteristics of human nature and a new conception of God. London, 1929.
Phil 5400.78   Volkelt, J. Versuch über Fühlen und Wollen. München, 1930.
Phil 5400.79   Lund, Frederick H. Emotions of men. N.Y., 1930.
Phil 5400.79.5   Lund, Frederick H. Emotions of men. N.Y., 1939.
Phil 5400.80   Wreschner, Arthur. Das Gefühl. Leipzig, 1931.
Phil 5400.81   Petrażycki, L. Wstęp do nauki prawa i moralności. Warszawa, 1930.
Phil 5400.82   Wang, Ging Hsi. Galvanic skin reflex and the measurement of emotions. Canton, China, 1930?
Phil 5400.83   Britan, H.H. The affective consciousness. N.Y., 1931.
Phil 5400.84   Lashley, K.S. Studies in the dynamics of behavior. Chicago, 1932.
Phil 5400.84.6   Lashley, K.S. The thalamus and emotion. Lancaster, 1938.
Phil 5400.85   Dyett, E.G. Une étude des émotions au moyen des tests. Thèse. Paris, 1932.
Phil 5400.86.5   Fourier, C. The passions of the human soul. London, 1851. 2v.
Phil 5400.87   Maas, J.G.E. Versuch über die Leidenschaften. Halle, 1805-07. 2v.
Phil 5400.88   Wyatt, H.G. The art of feeling. Boston, 1932.
Phil 5400.89   Marucci, A. Le passioni nella filosofia e nell'arte. Torino, 1932.
Phil 5400.90   Ruckmick, C.A. The psychology of feeling and emotion. 1st ed. N.Y., 1936.
Phil 5400.91   Janet, Pierre. L'amour et la haine. Paris, 1932.
Phil 5400.92   Landis, Carney. Studies of emotional reactions. n.p., 1924.
Phil 5400.93.1   Gardiner, Harry Norman. Feeling and emotion. Westport, 1970.
Phil 5400.94   Lacroze, R. L'angoisse et l'émotion. Paris, 1938.
Phil 5400.94.5   Lacroze, R. L'angoisse et l'émotion. Paris, 1938.
Phil 5400.95   Dunbar, H.F. Emotions and bodily changes. N.Y., 1938.
Phil 5400.95.5   Dunbar, H.F. Psychosomatic diagnosis. N.Y., 1943.
Phil 5400.96   Phillips, M. The education of the emotions. London, 1937.
Phil 5400.97   Vleugel, E.S. De samenhang tussen psycho-galvanische reflex en grondeigenschappen van het temperament. Proefschrift. Groningen, 1939.
Phil 5400.99   Foster, George S. Our hunches; the effect of emotions on our lives and habits. N.Y., 1942.
Phil 5400.100   Rapaport, David. Emotions and memory. Baltimore, 1942.
Phil 5400.101   Young, Paul T. Emotion in man and animal. N.Y., 1943.
Phil 5400.103   Bisch, L.E. Your nerves. N.Y., 1945.
Phil 5400.105   Hinsie, L.E. The person in the body. N.Y., 1945.
Phil 5400.107   Zazzo, Revné. Le devenir de l'intelligence. Paris, 1946.
Phil 5400.109   Dumas, G. La vie affective. 1. éd. Paris, 1948.
Phil 5400.110   Bull, Nina. The attitude theory of emotion. N.Y., 1951.
Phil 5400.112   Haecker, T. Metaphysik des Fühlens. 4. Aufl. München, 1950.
Phil 5400.114   Forti, E. L'émotion. 1. éd. Paris, 1952.
Phil 5400.116   McGill, V.J. Emotions and reason. Springfield, 1954.
Phil 5400.118   Burloud, A. Psychologie de la sensibilité. Paris, 1954.
Phil 5400.120   Flugel, J.C. Studies in feeling and desire. London, 1955.
Phil 5400.122   Strasser, S. Das Gemüt. Antwerpen, 1956.
Phil 5400.126   Lakobson,P.M. Psikhologiia chuvstv. Moskva, 1956.
Phil 5400.128   Bollnow, O.F. Das Wesen der Stimmungen. 3. Aufl. Frankfurt, 1956.
Phil 5400.130   Frijda, N.H. De betekenis van de gelaatsexpressie. Amsterdam, 1956.
Phil 5400.130.5   Frijda, N.H. Gelaat en karakter. Haarlem, 1958.
Phil 5400.132   Michaud, H. La sensibilité. Lyon, 1954?
Phil 5400.134   Ginneken, J. van. Gelaat, gebaar en klankexpressie. Leiden, 1919.
Phil 5400.136   Maisonneuve, Jean. Les sentiments. 4. ed. Paris, 1957.
Phil 5400.136.5   Maisonneuve, Jean. Les sentiments. 5. ed. Paris, 1960.
Phil 5400.138   Bellingroth, Friedhelm. Triebwirkung des Films auf Jugendliche. Bern, 1958.
Phil 5400.140   Holzkamp, Klaus. Ausdrucksverstehen im Erlebnisaspekt. Inaug. Diss. Berlin, 1956.
Phil 5400.145   Arnold, Magda B. Emotion and personality. N.Y., 1960. 2v.
Phil 5400.150   Muszynski, Franz. Unsere Leidenschaften. 2. Aufl. Paderborn, 1926.
Phil 5400.155   Hillman, J. Emotion. London, 1960.
Phil 5400.157   Grossart, Friedrich. Gefühl und Strebung. München, 1961.
Phil 5400.159   Kenny, A. Action, emotion and will. London, 1963.
Phil 5400.160   Gellhorn, Ernest. Emotions and emotional disorders. N.Y., 1963.
Phil 5400.162   Simonov, P.V. Metod K.S. Stanislavskogo i fiziologiia emotsii. Moskva, 1962.
Phil 5400.164   Schneiders, A.A. The anarchy of feeling. N.Y., 1963.
Phil 5400.165   Symposium on Expression. Expression of the emotions in man. N.Y., 1963.

Phil 5400   Psychology - Treatises on special topics - Emotions - General works - cont.

Phil 5400.166   Callwood, J. Love, hate, fear, anger and the other lively emotions. Garden City, 1964.
Phil 5400.167   Canolland, D.K. Emotion::bodily change, an enduring problem in psychology. Princeton, 1962.
Phil 5400.168   Tomkins, Silvan Solomon. Affect, cognition, and personality. N.Y., 1965.
Phil 5400.169   Vieira, Manuel. Emoções e felicidade. Lisboa, 1964.
Phil 5400.170   Davitz, Joel Robert. The communication of emotional meaning. N.Y., 1964.
Phil 5400.172   Rochlin, Gregory. Griefs and discontents. 1. ed. Boston, 1965.
Phil 5400.174   Riese, Walther. La théorie des passions à la lumière de la pensée médicale du XVIIe siècle. N.Y., 1965.
Phil 5400.175   Jacobson, Edmund. Biology of emotions::new understanding derived from biological multidisciplinary investigation. Springfield, 1967.
Phil 5400.180   Carstens, Erik. HAD. Kóbenhavn, 1967.
Phil 5400.185   Monakow, Constantin. The emotions, morality and the brain. Washington, 1925.
Phil 5400.190   Kaufmann, Pierre. L'expérience émotionnelle de l'espace. Thèse. Paris, 1967.
Phil 5400.192   Franke, Joachim. Ausdruck und Konvention. Habilitationsschrift. Göttingen, 1967.
Phil 5400.196   Senault, Jean Francois. De l'usage des passions. Paris, 1964.
Phil 5400.198   Davitz, Joel Robert. The language of emotion. N.Y., 1969.
Phil 5400.200   Krueger, Felix. Über das Gefühl. Darmstadt, 1967.
Phil 5400.202   Sartre, Jean-Paul. Sketch for a theory of the emotions. London, 1962.
Phil 5400.204   Dermon, Emiir. Sinirlenmeden yaşayeniz. Izmir, 1970.
Phil 5400.206   Physiological correlates of emotion. N.Y., 1970.
Phil 5400.208   Izard, Carroll E. The face of emotion. N.Y., 1971.

Phil 5401   Psychology - Treatises on special topics - Emotions - Special emotions, etc. - Fear

Phil 5401.01   Pamphlet box. Fear.
Phil 5401.1   Mosso, A. La paura. Milano, 1884.
Phil 5401.1.5   Mosso, A. La peur. Paris, 1886.
X Cg Phil 5401.1.10   Mosso, A. Fear. London, 1896.
Phil 5401.1.12   Mosso, A. Die Furcht. Leipzig, 1889.
Phil 5401.2   Hall, G.S. Study of fears. Worcester, 1897.
Phil 5401.3   Dugas, L. La timidité. Paris, 1910.
Phil 5401.3.5   Dugas, L. Les timides dans la littérature et l'art. Paris, 1925.
Phil 5401.4   Morse, P. The psychology and neurology of fear. Worcester, 1907.
Phil 5401.5   Lord, H.G. The psychology of courage. Boston, 1918.
Phil 5401.6   Marks, J. Courage today and tomorrow. N.Y., 1919.
Phil 5401.7   Walsh, W.S. The mastery of fear. N.Y., 1924.
Phil 5401.8   Williams, E.H. Our fear complexes. London, 1924.
Phil 5401.9   Marrel, P. Les phobies. Paris, 1895.
Phil 5401.10   Gratia, L.E. Le "trac" et la timidité. 2e éd. Paris, 1926.
Phil 5401.11   Mones, L. Why be afraid? Boston, 1931.
Phil 5401.12   Liebeck, O. Das Unbekannte und die Angst. Leipzig, 1928.
Phil 5401.13.10   Oliver, John R. Fear. N.Y., 1931.
Phil 5401.14   Lunn, H.K. Courage; an anthology. London, 1939.
Phil 5401.15   Fletcher, P. Life without fear. N.Y., 1939.
Phil 5401.16   Watkins, D.E. Stage fright and what to do about it. Boston, 1940.
Phil 5401.16.5   Dollard, John. Victory over fear. N.Y., 1942.
Phil 5401.18   Litwinski, Léon de. La timidité constitutionnelle et ses formes passive et active. Lisbonne, 1944.
Phil 5401.20F   Vassos, John. Phobia. N.Y., 1931.
Phil 5401.22   Wandruszka von Wanstetten, M.W. Angst und Mut. Stuttgart, 1950.
Phil 5401.24   Schwartz, C. Neurotic anxiety. N.Y., 1954.
Phil 5401.26A   May, Rollo. The meaning of anxiety. N.Y., 1950.
Phil 5401.26B   May, Rollo. The meaning of anxiety. N.Y., 1950.
Phil 5401.28   Leroy, Paul. Angst und Lachen. Wien, 1954.
Phil 5401.30   Bitter, Wilhelm. Die Angstneurose. Bern, 1948.
Phil 5401.32   Lyon, Josette. L'angoisse. Paris, 1957.
Phil 5401.34   Palou, Jean. La peur dans l'histoire. Paris, 1958.
Phil 5401.36   Woodworth, H.M. Sanity. 1st ed. Victoria, B.C., 1958.
Phil 5401.38   Stein, Maurice R. Identity and anxiety. Glencoe, 1960.
Phil 5401.38.2   Stein, Maurice R. Identity and anxiety. Glencoe, 1962.
Phil 5401.40   March, Hans. Verfolgung und Angst in ihren leib-seelischen Auswirkungen. Stuttgart, 1960.
Phil 5401.44   Odier, Charles. Anxiety and magic thinking. N.Y., 1956.
Phil 5401.46   Hiltner, S. Constructive aspects of anxiety. N.Y., 1950.
Phil 5401.47   Riemann, Fritz. Grundformen der Angst und die Antinomien des Lebens. München, 1961.
Phil 5401.48   Réal, Pierre. Triomphez de l'angoisse. Verviers, 1963.
Phil 5401.49   Mexico (City). Universidad Nacional. Facultad de Filosofia y Letras. La esencia del valor. México, 1964.
Phil 5401.50   Panse, Friedrich. Angst und Schreck in klinisch psychologischer und sozialmedizinischer Sicht. Stuttgart, 1952.
VPhil 5401.51   Alvarez, Martins d'. O medo no seculo XX. Rio de Janeiro, 1964.
Phil 5401.52   Barker, John Charles. Scared to death; an examination of fear. London, 1968.
Phil 5401.53.2   Diel, Paul. La peur et l'angoisse, phénomène central de la vie et de son évolution. 2e éd. Paris, 1968.
Phil 5401.54   Vestdijk, Simon. Het wezen van de angst. Amsterdam, 1968.
Phil 5401.56   Angst; psychische und somatische Aspekte. Bern, 1967.
Phil 5401.58   Starnberger Gespräche. Aspekte der Angst. Stuttgart, 1965.
Phil 5401.60   Marks, Issac M. Fears and phobias. N.Y., 1969.

Phil 5402   Psychology - Treatises on special topics - Emotions - Special emotions, etc. - Pleasure and pain

Phil 5402.1   Dumont, L. Théorie scientifique de la sensibilité. Paris, 1875.
Phil 5402.1.3   Dumont, L. Vergnügen und Schmerz. Leipzig, 1876.
Phil 5402.2   Gilman, B.T. Syllabus of...lectures on the psychology of pain. Worcester, Mass., 1893.
Phil 5402.3   Mantegazza, P. Le estase umane. Milano, 1887. 2v.
Phil 5402.3.5   Mantegazza, P. Fisiologia del dolore. Firenze, 1880.
Phil 5402.3.10   Mantegazza, P. Physiologie du plaisir. Paris, 1886.
Phil 5402.3.15   Mantegazza, P. L'anima delle cose. Torino, 1921.
Phil 5402.4   Levesque de Pouilly, L.J. Theorie des sentiments agreables. Paris, 1748.
Phil 5402.4.2   Levesque de Pouilly, L.J. Theorie des sentiments agreables. Paris, 1774.
Phil 5402.4.5   Levesque de Pouilly, L.J. Theory of agreeable sensations. Boston, 1812.

Classified Listing

Phil 5402   Psychology - Treatises on special topics - Emotions - Special emotions,
etc. - Pleasure and pain - cont.

Phil 5402.6	Ioteyko, I. Psycho-physiologie de la douleur. Paris, 1909.
Phil 5402.7	Fulliquet, G. Le problème de la souffrance. Genève, 1909.
Phil 5402.8	Bouillier, F. Du plaisir et de la douleur. Paris, 1865.
Phil 5402.8.3	Bouillier, F. Du plaisir et de la douleur. 3e ed. Paris, 1885.
Phil 5402.9	Harbin, R.M. Paradoxical pain. Boston, 1916.
Phil 5402.10	Zimmermann, O. Die Wonne des Leids. 2e Aufl. Leipzig, 1885.
Phil 5402.11	Marshall, H.R. Pain, pleasure, and aesthetics. N.Y., 1894.
Phil 5402.12	Wells, Frederic L. Pleasure and behavior. N.Y., 1924.
Phil 5402.13	Castez, G. La douleur physique. Paris, 1905.
Phil 5402.14	Schwarz, Balduin. Untersuchungen zur Psychologie des Weinens. Inaug. Diss. München, 1928.
Phil 5402.15	Nádejde, D.C. Die biologische Theorie der Lust und Unlust. Leipzig, 1908.
Phil 5402.16	Bousfield, P. Pleasure and pain. London, 1926.
Phil 5402.17	Burlton Allen, A.H. Pleasure and instinct. London, 1930.
Phil 5402.18	Bendavid, L. Versuch über das Vergnügen. Wien, 1794.
Phil 5402.19	Beebe-Center, J.G. The psychology of pleasantness and unpleasantness. N.Y., 1932.
Phil 5402.20	Spitz, C. Zur Psychologie des Weinens. Inaug. Diss. Zeulenroda, 1935.
Phil 5402.21.10	Lewis, Clive Staples. The problem of pain. London, 1943.
Phil 5402.22.15	Jones, Eli Stanley. Christ and human suffering. N.Y., 1933.
Phil 5402.23	Szasz, T.S. Pain and pleasure. N.Y., 1957.
Phil 5402.24	Heidsieck, François. Plaisir et tempérance. Paris, 1962.
Phil 5402.25	McKenna, A.G. Les réactions psycho-physiologiques à la douleur. Louvain, 1963.
Phil 5402.26.2	Sauerbruch, F. Wesen und Bedeutung des Schmerzes. 2. Aufl. Frankfurt, 1961.
Phil 5402.27	Heath, R.G. The role of pleasure in behavior. N.Y., 1964.
Phil 5402.28	Sarano, Jacques. La douleur. Paris, 1965.
Phil 5402.29	Prescott, Frederick. The control of pain. N.Y., 1965.
Phil 5402.35	Petrie, Asenath. Individuality in pain and suffering. Chicago, 1967.
Phil 5402.36	Bakan, David. Disease, pain and suffering. Chicago, 1968.
Phil 5402.37	Cowan, Joseph Lloyd. Pleasure and pain: a study in philosophical psychology. London, 1968.
Phil 5402.39	Sternbach, Richard A. Pain; a psychophysiological analysis. N.Y., 1968.
Phil 5402.40	Metz, Willem. Het verschijnsel pijn. Proefschrift. Haarlem, 1964.
Phil 5402.42	Trigg, Roger. Pain and emotion. Oxford, 1970.
Phil 5402.44	Lowen, Alexander. Pleasure: a creative approach to life. N.Y., 1970.

Phil 5403   Psychology - Treatises on special topics - Emotions - Special emotions,
etc. - Joy and elation

Phil 5403.1.3	Dearborn, Gran N. The emotion of joy. N.Y., 1899.
Phil 5403.2	Piderit, Theodor. Die Theorie des Glücks. Leipzig, 1867.
Phil 5403.3	Mignard, M. La joie passive. Paris, 1909.
Phil 5403.4	Lindner, Gustav. Das Problem des Glücks. Wien, 1864.
Phil 5403.4.5	Lindner, Gustav. Lyckans problem. Stockholm, 1869.
Phil 5403.4.10	Lindner, Gustav. Zahada štěstí. Praha, 1931.
Phil 5403.5	Lange, C.G. Bidrag til nydelsernes fysiologi som grundlag for en rationel aestetik. Kjobenhavn, 1899.
Phil 5403.6	Dumas, G. La tristesse et la joie. Paris, 1900.
Phil 5403.9	Cazeneuve, Jean. Psychologie de la joie. Paris, 1952.
Phil 5403.10	Rochlin, Gregory. Griefs and discontents. London, 1965.
Phil 5403.11	Cazeneuve, Jean. Bonheur et civilisation. Paris, 1966.
Phil 5403.12	Schutz, William Carl. Joy; expanding human awareness. N.Y., 1968.
Phil 5403.14	Durand, Leo. The psychology of happiness. Blackstone, 1968.
Phil 5403.16	Monedero Gil, Carmelo. La alegría. Madrid, 1970.

Phil 5404   Psychology - Treatises on special topics - Emotions - Special emotions,
etc. - Desire

Phil 5404.1	Urban, J. L'epithymologie. Paris, 1939.
Phil 5404.4	Martinon, Jean Pierre. Les métamorphoses du désir et l'oeuvre. Paris, 1970.

Phil 5405   Psychology - Treatises on special topics - Emotions - Special emotions,
etc. - Enthusiasm

Phil 5405.5.2	Taylor, I. Natural history of enthusiasm. Boston, 1830.
Phil 5405.5.3	Taylor, I. Natural history of enthusiasm. London, 1830.
Phil 5405.5.5	Taylor, I. Natural history of enthusiasm. London, 1830.
Phil 5405.5.10	Taylor, I. Natural history of enthusiasm. 10th ed. London, 1845.
Htn Phil 5405.6*	Casaubon, M. A treatise concerning enthusiasme. 2. ed. London, 1656.
Phil 5405.6.2	Casaubon, M. A treatise conserning enthusiasme (1655). 2. ed. Gainsville, 1970.

Phil 5406   Psychology - Treatises on special topics - Emotions - Special emotions,
etc. - Deprivation

Phil 5406.2	United States. National Institute of Child Health and Human Development. Perspectives on human deprivation: biological, psychological, and sociological. Washington, 1968.

Phil 5407   Psychology - Treatises on special topics - Emotions - Special emotions,
etc. - Ennui and boredom

Phil 5407.5.2	Tardieu, E. L'ennui; étude psychologique. Paris, 1903.
Phil 5407.6	Cruz Malpique, Manuel da. Psicologia do tédio. Porto, 1963.
Phil 5407.7	Jankélévitch, Vladimir. L'aventure, l'ennui, le sérieux. Paris, 1963.

Phil 5409   Psychology - Treatises on special topics - Emotions - Special emotions,
etc. - Expectation

Phil 5409.5	Hitchcock, C.M. The psychology of expectation. N.Y., 1903.
Phil 5409.6	Pyle, W.H. Experimental study of expectation. n.p., 1909.
Phil 5409.7	Sack, Max. Die Verzweiflung: eine Untersuchung ihres Wesens und ihrer Entstehung. Inaug. Diss. Kallmünz, 1930.
Phil 5409.8	Union des Religieuses Enseignantes. L'éducation de l'espérance. Paris, 1959?

Phil 5410   Psychology - Treatises on special topics - Emotions - Special emotions,
etc. - Gratitude and ingratitude

Phil 5410.5	Litwinski, Léon. La psychologie de l'ingratitude. Bruxelles, 1927.

Phil 5411   Psychology - Treatises on special topics - Emotions - Special emotions,
etc. - Hatred

Phil 5411.5.4	Mantegazza, P. Fisiologia dell'odio. 4a ed. Milano, 1889.
Phil 5411.5.10	Mantegazza, P. Die Physiologie des Hasses. Jena, 1889.
Phil 5411.6	Pfister, Oskar. Analytische Untersuchungen über die Psychologie des Hasses und der Versöhnung. Leipzig, 1910.
Phil 5411.7	Mathis, René. La haine. Thèse. Nancy, 1927.
Phil 5411.8	Gonçalves Viana, Mário. Psicologia do ódio. Porto, 196-.
Phil 5411.10	Haesler, Alfred A. Leben mit dem Hass. Reinbeck, 1969.
Phil 5411.12	Salgado, Enrique. Radiografía del odio. Madrid, 1969.

Phil 5412   Psychology - Treatises on special topics - Emotions - Special emotions,
etc. - Anger

Htn Phil 5412.3*	Wier, Johann. Ioannis VVieri De ira morbo. Basileae, 1577.
Phil 5412.5	Stratton, G.M. Anger; its religious and moral significance. N.Y., 1923.
Phil 5412.7	Dembo, Tamara. Der Arger als dynamisches Problem. Inaug. Diss. Berlin, 1931.
Phil 5412.10	Saul, Leon Joseph. The hostile mind. N.Y., 1956.
Phil 5412.15	Borra, Edoardo. Quando gli uomini perdono le staffe. Roma, 1959.
Phil 5412.20	Madow, Leo. Anger. N.Y., 1972.

Phil 5413   Psychology - Treatises on special topics - Emotions - Special emotions,
etc. - Envy and jealousy

Phil 5413.5	Friedmann, Max. Über die Psychologie der Eifersucht. Wiesbaden, 1911.
Phil 5413.10	Raiga, Eugène. L'envie. Paris, 1932.
Phil 5413.13	Gesell, Arnold L. Jealousy. Diss. Worcester, 1906.
Phil 5413.14	Ankles, T.M. A study of jealousy as differentiated from envy. Boston, 1939.
Phil 5413.15	Delpierre, Guy. De la jalousie. Paris, 1954.
Phil 5413.16	Schoeck, Helmut. Der Neid. Freiburg, 1966.
Phil 5413.16.5	Schoeck, Helmut. Envy; a theory of social behaviour. London, 1969.
Phil 5413.20	Klein, Melanie. Envy and gratitude. London, 1957.

Phil 5414   Psychology - Treatises on special topics - Emotions - Special emotions,
etc. - Shame and guilt

Phil 5414.15A	Piers, Gerhart. Shame and guilt. Springfield, Ill., 1953.
Phil 5414.15B	Piers, Gerhart. Shame and guilt. Springfield, Ill., 1953.
Phil 5414.20.2	Lynd, Helen Merrell. On shame and the search for identity. N.Y., 1958.
Phil 5414.25	Airas, Erkki. Syyllisyydentunoton vaikuttavista tekijöistä. Helsinki, 1956.
Phil 5414.30	Tournier, Paul. Guilt and grace. London, 1962.
Phil 5414.35	McKenzie, John. Guilt. London, 1962.
Phil 5414.40	Schlederer, Franz. Schuld, Reue und Krankheit. München, 1970.
Phil 5414.45	Benda, Clemens Ernst. Gewissen und Schuld. Stuttgart, 1970.
Phil 5414.50	Fornari, Franco. Psicanalisi della situazione atomica. Milano, 1970.

Phil 5415   Psychology - Treatises on special topics - Emotions - Special emotions,
etc. - Sympathy

Phil 5415.01	Pamphlet box. Sympathy.
Phil 5415.3	Petrini, E. Om sympatiska känslor. Upsala, 1900.
Phil 5415.5	Jones, J.W.L. Sociality and sympathy. N.Y., 1903.
Phil 5415.7	Scheler, Max. Wesen und Formen der Sympathie. Bonn, 1923
Phil 5415.7.5	Scheler, Max. Zur Phänomenologie und Theorie der Sympathiegefühle. Halle, 1913.
Phil 5415.7.9	Scheler, Max. The nature of sympathy. Hamden, 1970.
Phil 5415.8	Fremling, Matthaus. Dissertatio philosophica, de sympathia. Lundae, 1789.
Phil 5415.9	Prandtl, A. Die Einfühlung. Leipzig, 1910.
Phil 5415.10	Ochanine, D. La sympathie. Paris, 1938.
Phil 5415.11	Maucorps, P.H. Empathies et connaissance d'autrui. Paris, 1960.

Phil 5416   Psychology - Treatises on special topics - Emotions - Special emotions,
etc. - Prejudice

Phil 5416.2	Loeb, Robert H. The sins of bias. N.Y., 1970.

Phil 5418   Psychology - Treatises on special topics - Emotions - Special emotions,
etc. - Loneliness

Phil 5418.2	Stuttgarter Gemeinschaft "Arzt und Seelsorger". Einsamkeit in medizinisch-psychologischer, theologischer und soziologischer Sicht. Stuttgart, 1967.
Phil 5418.4	Mannin, Ethel Edith. Loneliness; a study of the human condition. London, 1966.
Phil 5418.6	Dreitzel, Hans Peter. Die Einsamkeit als soziologisches Problem. Zurich, 1970.

Phil 5420   Psychology - Treatises on special topics - Emotions - Special emotions,
etc. - Self-consciousness

Phil 5420.5	Roback, A.A. Self-consciousness and its treatment. Cambridge, 1933.
Phil 5420.5.5	Roback, A.A. Getting rid of self-consciousness. n.p., 1934.
Phil 5420.5.10	Roback, A.A. Self-consciousness self-treated. Cambridge, 1936.
Phil 5420.5.11	Roback, A.A. Varför hämmar jag mig själo? Stockholm, 1939.
Phil 5420.15	Schouten, Jan. De verlegenheid. Proefschrift. Groningen, 1935.
Phil 5420.16	Milsen, G. Studies in self-confrontation. Copenhagen, 1962.
Phil 5420.20	Vom menschlichen Selbst. Stuttgart, 1965.

Phil 5421   Psychology - Treatises on special topics - Emotions - Special emotions,
etc. - Others

Phil 5421.5	Ernst, F. Vom Heimweh. Zürich, 1949.
Phil 5421.5.5	Ramming-Thoen, Fortunata. Das Heimweh. Thesis. Zürich, 1958.
Phil 5421.6	Faulkner, Edwin Jerome. Man's quest for security; a symposium. Lincoln, 1966.
Phil 5421.10	Remits, Ernest L. The feeling of superiority and anxiety-superior. Ottawa, 1955.
Phil 5421.10.3	Friedlaender, Julius. Der Pessimismus im Lichte einer höheren Weltauffassung. Berlin, 1893.

Classified Listing
277

Phil 5421 Psychology - Treatises on special topics - Emotions - Special emotions, etc. - Others - cont.

Phil 5421.10.5	Eysenck, H.J. The dynamics of anxiety and hysteria. London, 1957.
Phil 5421.10.10	Silva-Tarouca, Amadeo. Die Logik der Angst. Innsbrucke, 1953.
Phil 5421.10.15	Lain Entraglo, Pedro. La espera y la esperanza. Madrid, 1957.
Phil 5421.10.16	Lain Entraglo, Pedro. La espera y la esperanza. 2. ed. Madrid, 1958.
Phil 5421.10.20	Levitt, Eugene Elmer. The psychology of anxiety. Indianapolis, 1967.
Phil 5421.10.25	Marchisa, Ernestina. Ansietà e carenze affettive. Napoli, 1968.
Phil 5421.10.30	Özcan, Mehmed Tevfik. Angoisse (sikinti). Ankara, 1966.
Phil 5421.10.35	Barraud, Jean. L'homme et son angoisse. Paris, 1969.
Phil 5421.10.40	Hellner, Hans. Über die Angst. Stuttgart, 1969.
Phil 5421.10.45	Fischer, William Frank. Theories of anxiety. N.Y., 1970.
Phil 5421.15	Stewart, David A. Preface to empathy. N.Y., 1956.
Phil 5421.15.5	Katz, R.L. Empathy, its nature and uses. N.Y., 1963.
Phil 5421.15.12	Stein, Edith. On the problem of empathy. 2d ed. The Hague, 1970.
Phil 5421.15.20	Stewart, David A. Money, power, and sex. N.Y., 1965.
Phil 5421.15.25	Smith, Henry Clay. Sensitivity to people. N.Y., 1966.
Phil 5421.15.30	Bezembinder, Thomas G.G. Een experimentele methode om de juistheid van interpersonale perceptie zuiver te bepalen. Proefschrift. Groningen, 1961.
Phil 5421.15.35	Trost, Jan. Om bildandet av dyader. Uppsala, 1966.
Phil 5421.20	Scott, John Paul. Aggression. Chicago, 1958.
Phil 5421.20.5	Folkard, M.S. A sociological contribution to the understanding of aggression and its treatment. Coulsdon, 1961.
Phil 5421.20.10	Berkourt, L. Aggression; a social psychological analysis. N.Y., 1962.
Phil 5421.20.15	Bovet, Pierre. L'instinct combatif; problèmes de psychologie et d'éducation. 3. éd. Neuchâtel, 1961.
Phil 5421.20.20	Lorenz, Konrad Zacharias. Das sogenannte Böse. 2. Aufl. Wien, 1964.
Phil 5421.20.21	Lorenz, Konrad Zacharias. On aggression. N.Y., 1966.
Phil 5421.20.25	Carthy, John D. The natural history of aggression. London, 1964.
Phil 5421.20.30	Rof Carballo, Juan. Violincía y ternura. Madrid, 1967.
Phil 5421.20.35	Denker, Rolf. Aufklärung über Aggression: Kant, Darwin, Freud, Lorenz. Stuttgart, 1966.
Phil 5421.20.37	Denker, Rolf. Aufklärung über Aggression: Kant, Darwin, Freud, Lorenz. 2. Aufl. Stuttgart, 1968.
Phil 5421.20.40	Storr, Anthony. Human aggression. 1. American ed. N.Y., 1968.
Phil 5421.20.45	Montagn, Ashley. Man and aggression. London, 1968.
Phil 5421.20.50	Czapiewski, Winfried. Der Aggression trieb und das Böse. Essen, 1967.
Phil 5421.20.55	Russell, Claire. Violence, monkeys, and man. London, 1968.
Phil 5421.20.60	Selg, Herbert. Diagnostik der Aggressivität. Habilitationsschrift. Göttingen, 1968.
Phil 5421.20.65	Carp, Eugène Antoine. Agressie en agressiviteit. Utrecht, 1968.
Phil 5421.20.70	Toch, Hans. Violent men; an inquiry into the psychology of violence. Chicago, 1969.
Phil 5421.20.75	Berkowitz, Leonard. Roots of aggression. 1. ed. N.Y., 1969.
Phil 5421.20.80	Mitscherlich, Alexander. Bis hierher und nicht weiter. München, 1969.
Phil 5421.20.85	Mitscherlich, Alexander. Die Idee des Friedens und die menschliche Aggressivität. Frankfurt, 1969.
Phil 5421.20.90	Gamm, Hans-Jochen. Aggression und Friedensfähigkeit in Deutschland. München, 1968.
Phil 5421.20.95	Buss, Arnold H. The psychology of aggression. N.Y., 1961.
Phil 5421.20.100	Megargee, Edwin I. The dynamics of aggression. N.Y., 1970.
Phil 5421.20.105	Eibl-Eibesfeld, Irenäus. Liebe und Hass. München, 1970.
Phil 5421.20.110	Rattner, Josef. Aggression und menschliche Natur. Olten, 1970.
Phil 5421.20.115	Schindler, Sepp. Aggressionshandlungen Jugendlicher. Wien, 1969.
Phil 5421.20.120	Kneutgen, Johannes. Der Mensch, ein kriegerisches Tier. Stuttgart, 1970.
Phil 5421.20.125	Feshbach, Seymour. Television and aggression. 1. ed. San Francisco, 1971.
Phil 5421.20.130	Hollitscher, Walter. Aggression im Menschenbild. Wien, 1970.
Phil 5421.20.135	Keil, Siegfried. Aggression und Mitmenschlichkeit. Stuttgart, 1970.
Phil 5421.20.140	Lepenies, Wolf. Kritik der Anthropologie. München, 1971.
Phil 5421.20.145	Stokes, Allen W. Aggressive man and aggressive beast. Logan, 1968?
Phil 5421.25	Nesbitt, Michael. Friendship, love, and values. Princeton, 1959.
Phil 5421.25.5	Benda, Clemen Ernst. The image of love. N.Y., 1961.
Phil 5421.25.10	Helwig, Paul. Liebe und Feindschaft. München, 1964.
Phil 5421.25.15	Hazo, Robert G. The idea of love. N.Y., 1967.
Phil 5421.25.20	Sadler, William Alan. Existence and love. N.Y., 1969.
Phil 5421.25.25	Blais, Gerard. L'amour humain. Sherbrooke, 1968.
Phil 5421.25.30	Hodge, Marshall B. Your fear of love. Garden City, 1967.
Phil 5421.25.35	Philipp, Wolfgang. Die Dreigestalt der Liebe. 1. Aufl. Konstanz, 1967.
Phil 5421.25.40	Zweig, Paul. The heresy of self-love. N.Y., 1968.
Phil 5421.25.45	Evory, John J. The man and the woman; psychology of human love. N.Y., 1968.
Phil 5421.25.50	Lemaire, Ton. De tederheid. Gedachten over de liefde. Utrecht, 1968.
Phil 5421.25.55	Mannin, Ethel Edith. Practitioners of love: some aspects of the human phenomenon. London, 1969.
Phil 5421.25.60	May, Rollo. Love and will. 1. ed. N.Y., 1969.
Phil 5421.25.65	Rosenberg, Stuart E. More loves than one. N.Y., 1963.
Phil 5421.25.70	Worms, Jeannine. D'une malédiction. Paris, 1963.
Phil 5421.25.76	Suttie, Ian Dishart. The origins of love. N.Y., 1966.
Phil 5421.30	Mechanu, David. Students under stress. N.Y., 1962.
Phil 5421.30.5	Rourke, Byron P. Explorations in the psychology of stress and anxiety. Don Mills, Ontario, 1969.
Phil 5421.35.5	Lynch, William F. Images of hope. Baltimore, 1965.
Phil 5421.35.10	Edmaier, Alois. Horizonte der Hoffnung. Regensburg, 1968.
Phil 5421.35.15	Stotland, Ezra. The psychology of hope. 1. ed. San Francisco, 1969.

Phil 5425 Psychology - Treatises on special topics - Genius

	Phil 5425.01	Pamphlet Box. Psychology. Special. Genius.
Htn	Phil 5425.1*	Duff, W. Essay on original genius. London, 1767.
	Phil 5425.1.3	Duff, W. An essay on original genius. Gainesville, Fla., 1964.
Htn	Phil 5425.1.5*	Duff, W. Critical observations. London, 1770.
	Phil 5425.2A	Galton, F. Hereditary genius. London, 1869.
	Phil 5425.2B	Galton, F. Hereditary genius. London, 1869.
	Phil 5425.2.2	Galton, F. Hereditary genius. 2. ed. London, 1892.
	Phil 5425.2.5	Galton, F. Hereditary genius. N.Y., 1891.
	Phil 5425.2.6	Galton, F. Hereditary genius. London, 1925.
	Phil 5425.2.7	Constable, F.C. Poverty and hereditary genius (criticism of Galton's theory). London, 1905.
	Phil 5425.2.8	Galton, F. English men of science. London, 1874.
	Phil 5425.2.9	Galton, F. English men of science. N.Y., 1875.
	Phil 5425.2.13	Galton, F. Noteworthy families (Modern science). London, 1906.
	Phil 5425.2.18	Galton, F. Memories of my life. London, 1908.
	Phil 5425.2.20	Galton, F. Memories of my life. N.Y., 1909.
	Phil 5425.3	Nisbet, J.F. Insanity of genius. London, 1891.
	Phil 5425.4	Lombroso, C. L'uomo di genio. Torino, 1894.
	Phil 5425.4.5	Lombroso, C. L'homme de génie. Paris, 1889.
NEDL	Phil 5425.4.9	Lombroso, C. The man of genius. London, 1891.
	Phil 5425.4.15	Lombroso, C. Entartung und Genie. Leipzig, 1894.
	Phil 5425.5	Hirsch, William. Genius and degeneration. N.Y., 1896.
	Phil 5425.5.6	Hirsch, William. Genie und Entartung. 2. Aufl. Berlin, 1894.
	Phil 5425.6	Macdonald, A. Genius and insanity. Lewes, 1892.
	Phil 5425.7.3	Nordau, M. Entartung. 2. Aufl. Berlin, 1893. 2v.
	Phil 5425.7.5	Nordau, M. Dégénérescence. Paris, 1894. 2v.
	Phil 5425.7.10	Nordau, M. Degeneration. 2. ed. N.Y., 1895.
	Phil 5425.7.12	Nordau, M. Degeneration. 4. ed. N.Y., 1895.
	Phil 5425.7.12.5	Nordau, M. Degeneration. 5. ed. London, 1895.
NEDL	Phil 5425.7.13	Nordau, M. Degeneration. 6. ed. London, 1895.
	Phil 5425.8	Regeneration. A reply to Max Nordau. N.Y., 1896.
	Phil 5425.9	Radestock, P. Genie und Wahnsinn. Breslau, 1884.
	Phil 5425.10	Cooley, C.H. Genius, fame and the comparison of races. Philadelphia, 1897.
	Phil 5425.11	Scripture, E.W. Arithmetical prodigies. Worcester, 1891.
	Phil 5425.13	Candolle, A. de. Histoire des sciences et des savants. Genève, 1885.
	Phil 5425.13.15	Candolle, A. de. Zur Geschichte der Wissenschaften und der Gelehrten. Leipzig, 1911.
	Phil 5425.14	Carus, Karl G. Über ungleiche Befähigung der verschiedenen Menschheitstämme. Leipzig, 1849.
	Phil 5425.15	Türck, H. Der geniale Mensch. Berlin, 1899.
	Phil 5425.15.10	Türck, H. Der geniale Mensch. 8. Aufl. Berlin, 1917.
	Phil 5425.15.15	Türck, H. Der geniale Mensch. 10. Aufl. Berlin, 1920?
	Phil 5425.15.27	Türck, H. The man of genius. London, 1923.
	Phil 5425.16	Bovio, G. Il genio. Milano, 1900.
	Phil 5425.17	Gerard, Alexander. An essay on genius. London, 1774.
X Cg	Phil 5425.17	Gerard, Alexander. An essay on genius. London, 1774.
	Phil 5425.17.5	Gerard, Alexander. An essay on genius, 1774. München, 1966.
	Phil 5425.18	Ellis, H. Study of British genius. London, 1904.
	Phil 5425.18.5A	Ellis, H. A study of British genius. Boston, 1926.
	Phil 5425.18.5B	Ellis, H. A study of British genius. Boston, 1926.
	Phil 5425.20	Ramos Mejia, J.M. Los simuladores del talento. Barcelona, n.d.
	Phil 5425.21	Roscoe, T.G. Mental and physical decadence. London, 1914.
	Phil 5425.23	Hancock, Thomas. Essay on capacity and genius. London, 1817.
	Phil 5425.24	Ostwald, W. Grosse Männer. Leipzig, 1909.
	Phil 5425.26	Knowlson, Thomas S. Originality, a popular study of creative mind. Philadelphia, 1918.
	Phil 5425.28	Reibmayr, Albert. Die Entwicklungsgeschichte des Talentes und Genies. München, 1908. 2v.
	Phil 5425.29.3	Gerhardi, Karl A. Das Wesen des Genies. Jauer, 1908.
	Phil 5425.30	Wendel, Georg. Über das Genie. Strassburg, 1909.
	Phil 5425.31	Herrlin, Axel. Snille och sjalssjukdom. Lund, 1903.
	Phil 5425.32	Rauschenberger, W. Das Talent und das Genie. Frankfurt, 1922.
	Phil 5425.33	Pacheco, Albino Augusto. Degenerescencia. Diss. inaug. Coimbra, 1901.
	Phil 5425.34.3	Padovan, A. Il genio. 3. ed. Milano, 1923.
	Phil 5425.35A	Brentano, F. Das Genie. Leipzig, 1892.
	Phil 5425.35B	Brentano, F. Das Genie. Leipzig, 1892.
	Phil 5425.36	Bleibtreu, K. Letzte Wahrheiten. Leipzig, 1894.
NEDL	Phil 5425.37	Legrain, M. Les dégénérés. Paris, 1895.
	Phil 5425.38	Sanborn, K.A. The vanity and insanity of genius. N.Y., 1886.
	Phil 5425.39	Zilsel, Edgar. Die Entstehung des Geniebegriffes. Tübingen, 1926.
	Phil 5425.40	Palcos, Alberto. El genio; ensayo sobre su génesis. Buenos Aires, 1920.
	Phil 5425.41	Hankin, Ernest H. Common sense and its cultivation. London, 1926.
	Phil 5425.42	Duche, Émile. De la precocité intellectuelle. Paris, 1901.
	Phil 5425.43	Marks, Jeannette. Genius and disaster. London, 1928.
	Phil 5425.44	Lange, Wilhelm. Genie-Irrsinn und Ruhm. München, 1928.
	Phil 5425.44.3	Lange, Wilhelm. Genie, Irrsinn und Ruhm. 3. Aufl. München, 1942.
	Phil 5425.44.4	Lange, Wilhelm. Genie, Irrsinn und Ruhm. München, 1967.
	Phil 5425.44.5	Lange, Wilhelm. Das Genie-Problem; eine Einführung. München, 1931.
	Phil 5425.44.10	Lange, Wilhelm. Das Genie-Problem. 3. Aufl. München, 1941.
	Phil 5425.44.15	Lange, Wilhelm. The problem of genius. London, 1931.
	Phil 5425.44.23	Lange, Wilhelm. Genies als Problem. 2. Aufl. München, 1941.
	Phil 5425.44.25	Lange, Wilhelm. Genie, Irrsinn und Ruhm. 4. Aufl. München, 1956.
	Phil 5425.45	Hock, Alfred. Die methodische Entwicklung der Talente und des Genies. Leipzig, 1920.
	Phil 5425.46	Jacobson, A.C. Genius: some revaluations. N.Y., 1926.
	Phil 5425.47.3	Kretschmer, Ernst. Geniale Menschen. 5. Aufl. Berlin, 1958.
	Phil 5425.47.5	Kretschmer, Ernst. The psychology of men of genius. London, 1931.
	Phil 5425.48	Segoud, Joseph. Le problème du génie. Paris, 1930.
	Phil 5425.49	Cabanès, Auguste. Grands Névropathes. Paris, 1930-31. 3v.
	Phil 5425.50	Durant, William. Adventures in genius. N.Y., 1931.
	Phil 5425.51	Hirsch, N.D.M. Genius and creative intelligence. Cambridge, 1931.
	Phil 5425.54	Nicolle, Charles. Biologie de l'invention. Paris, 1932.

Classified Listing

Phil 5425   Psychology - Treatises on special topics - Genius - cont.

Phil 5425.54.5   Guerster, Eugen. Macht und Geheimnis der Dummheit. Zürich, 1967.

Phil 5425.57   Hayward, F.H. Professionalism and originality. Chicago, 1917.

Phil 5425.58   Somogyi, J. Begabung im Lichte der Eugenik. Leipzig, 1936.

Phil 5425.59   Hamann, Otto. Biologie deutscher Dichter und Denker. Zürich, 1923.

Phil 5425.60   Holste, Maria. Das Erlebnis und die Leistung. Inaug. Diss. Düsseldorf, 1936.

Phil 5425.61   Palmer, William J. Genius. Los Angeles, 1937.

Phil 5425.62   Koller, A.H. The Abbé Du Bos - his advocacy of the theory of climate. Champaign, 1937.

Phil 5425.63   Voronoff, Serge. Du crétin au génie. N.Y., 1941.

Phil 5425.65   Royse, Noble K. A study of genius. Chicago, 1890.

Phil 5425.67   Austin, Mary Hunter. Everyman's genius. Indianapolis, 1925.

Phil 5425.70   Veiga Azvedo, A.V. O problema do génio; ensaio para uma tesse de redução. Lisboa, 1944.

Phil 5425.72   Müller, Willy. Genie und Talent. München, 1940.

Phil 5425.74   Bowerman, Walter. Studies in genius. N.Y., 1947.

Phil 5425.76A   Dovski, Lee van. Genie und Eros. Olten-Bern, 1949. 3v.

Phil 5425.76B   Dovski, Lee van. Genie und Eros. v.3. Olten-Bern, 1949.

Phil 5425.78   Scheffler, K. Lebensbild des Talents. Berlin, 1948.

Phil 5425.80   Kenmare, D. Stolen fire. London, 1951.

Phil 5425.82   Belt, W.R. The infirmities of genius. London, 1952.

Phil 5425.84   Révész, Géza. Talent und Genie. Bern, 1952.

Phil 5425.86   Gun, W.T.J. Studies in hereditary ability. London, 1928.

Phil 5425.88   Roe, Anne. The making of a scientist. N.Y., 1953.

Phil 5425.90   Carroll, H.A. Genius in the making. N.Y., 1940.

Phil 5425.92   Bryant, J.E. Genius and epilepsy. Concord, Mass., 1953.

Phil 5425.94   Lenk, Emil. Das Liebesleben des Genies. 2. Aufl. Badeburg, 1926.

Phil 5425.96   Talent and society. Princeton, 1958.

Phil 5425.100   Kotsovsky, D. Tragödie des Genius. München, 1959.

Phil 5425.102   Gemant, Andrew. The nature of the genius. Springfield, Ill., 1961.

Phil 5425.104   Princeton Meeting on the Recognition of Excellence, Princeton, 1959. The recognition of excellence. Washington, 1959.

Phil 5425.106   Konferentsiia po Problemam Sposobnostei, Leningrad, 1960. Problemy sposobnostei. Moskva, 1962.

Phil 5425.107   Venzmer, Gerhard. Genius und Wahn. Stuttgart, 1964.

Phil 5425.108   Grant, Vernon W. Great abnormals; the pathological genius of Kafka, Van Gogh, Strindenberg and Poe. N.Y., 1968.

Phil 5425.110   Wolfle, Dael Lee. The discovery of talent. Cambridge, 1969.

Phil 5425.112   Kuhn-Foelix, August. Vom Wesen des genialen Menschen. Zürich, 1968.

Phil 5425.114.1   Barlow, F. Mental prodigies. N.Y., 1969.

Phil 5435   Psychology - Treatises on special topics - Habit

Phil 5435.01   Pamphlet box. Psychology. Special. Habit.

Phil 5435.1   Creighton, C. Illustrations of unconscious memory in disease. London, 1886.

Phil 5435.4   Ravaisson-Mollien, Felix. De l'habitude. Paris, 1938.

Phil 5435.4.2   Ravaisson-Mollien, Felix. De l'habitude. 2. éd. Paris, 1957.

Phil 5435.4.5   Ravaisson-Mollien, Felix. De l'habitude. Paris, 1927.

Phil 5435.5   Nicolardot, F. Habitude ou train? Paris, 1922.

Phil 5435.6   Erdmann, J.E. Uber Gewohnheiten und Angewohnheiten. Berlin, 1858.

Phil 5435.7   Brown, Warner. Habit interference in sorting cards. Berkeley, 1914.

Phil 5435.8A   James, William. Habit. N.Y., 1890.

Phil 5435.8B   James, William. Habit. N.Y., 1890.

Phil 5435.8.3A   James, William. Habit. N.Y., 1914.

Phil 5435.8.3B   James, William. Habit. N.Y., 1914.

Phil 5435.9   Chevalier, J. L'habitude, essai de métaphysique scientifique. Paris, 1929.

Phil 5435.10.5   Dunlap, Knight. Habits, their making and unmaking. N.Y., 1945.

Phil 5435.11   Gurney, Joseph J. Thoughts on habit and discipline. Philadelphia, 1877.

Phil 5435.12   Veldt, Jacobus van der. L'apprentissage du mouvement et l'automatisme. Louvain, 1928.

Phil 5435.13   Khodzhava, Z.I. Problema navyka v psikhologii. Tbilisi, 1960.

Phil 5435.14   Guillaume, Paul. La formation des habitudes. Paris, 1968.

Phil 5435.16   Association de Psychologie Scientifique de Langue Française. Les processus d'adaptation; Xe symposium, Marseille, 1965. 1. éd. Paris, 1967.

Phil 5440   Psychology - Treatises on special topics - Heredity

Phil 5440.01   Pamphlet Box. Psychology. Special. Heredity.

Phil 5440.1   Bradford, A.H. Heredity and Christian problems. N.Y., 1895.

Phil 5440.2   Nisbet, J.F. Marriage and heredity. London, 1889.

Phil 5440.3   Galton, F. Record of family faculties. London, 1884.

Phil 5440.4.2   Ribot, T. Heredity. N.Y., 1891.

Phil 5440.4.3   Ribot, T. Die Erblichkeit. v.1-4. Leipzig, 1876.

Phil 5440.4.5   Ribot, T. Die Erblichkeit. Paris, 1897.

Phil 5440.4.9   Ribot, T. L'hérédité psychologique. 2. éd. Paris, 1882.

Phil 5440.5   Sanson, A. L'hérédité. Paris, 1893.

Phil 5440.6   Thompson, E. Rowell. Heredity. Boston, 1882.

Phil 5440.7   Féré, C. La famille névropathique. Paris, 1898.

Phil 5440.8   Proctor, R.A. Hereditary traits. N.Y., 1882.

Phil 5440.9   Woods, F.A. Mental and moral heredity in royalty. N.Y., 1906.

Phil 5440.9.5   Spillman, W.J. "Mental and moral heredity in royalty" · Woods. Lancaster, 1909.

Phil 5440.9.25   Pamphlet box. Woods, F.A. Heredity, minor publications.

Phil 5440.10   Kendall, H. The kinship of men. Boston, 1888.

Phil 5440.11   Walker, Alexander. Intermarriage. N.Y., 1839.

Htn   Phil 5440.11.2*   Walker, Alexander. Intermarriage. N.Y., 1839.

Phil 5440.12   Galippe, V. L'hérédité des stigmates de dégénérescence. Paris, 1905.

Phil 5440.14   Withington, C.F. Consanguineous marriages; their effect upon offspring. Boston, 1885.

Phil 5440.15   Strahan, S.A.K. Marriage and disease. London, 1892.

Phil 5440.16   Harris, George. Christ's teaching concerning heredity. n.p., 1887.

Phil 5440.17   Fernald, W.M. View at the foundatiuons...of character. Boston, 1865.

Phil 5440.18   Josefovici, U. Die psychische Vererbung. Leipzig, 1912.

Phil 5440   Psychology - Treatises on special topics - Heredity - cont.

Phil 5440.19   Sériot, Pauline. Effets nocifs du croisement des races sur la formation du caractère. Thèse. Paris, 1918.

Phil 5440.20   Sommer, Georg. Geistige Veranlagung und Vererbung. Leipzig, 1916.

Phil 5440.23   Retzius, Gustaf. Om förvärfvade egenskapers ärftlighet. Stockholm, 1895.

Phil 5440.25   Poyer, Georges. Les problèmes généraux de l'hérédité psychologique. Paris, 1921.

Phil 5440.25.3   Poyer, Georges. Les problèmes généraux de l'hérédité psychologique. Thèse. Paris, 1921. 2 pam.

Phil 5440.26   Kellogg, V.L. Mind and heredity. Princeton, 1923.

Phil 5440.27   Gjellerup, Karl. Arvelighed og moral. Kjøbenhavn, 1881.

Phil 5440.28   Peters, Wilhelm. Die Vererbung geistiger Eigenschaften und die psychische Constitution. Jena, 1925.

Phil 5440.28.5   Peters, Wilhelm. Über Vererbung psychischer Fähigkeiten. Leipzig, 1915.

Phil 5440.29   Outhit, M.C. A study of the resemblance of parents and children in general intelligence. Thesis. N.Y., 1933.

Phil 5440.30   Revda, A. Il destino delle dinastie. Torino, 1904.

Phil 5440.31   Bumke, O. Kultur und Ertartung. Berlin, 1922.

Phil 5440.32.5   Schwesinger, G. Heredity and environment. N.Y., 1933.

Phil 5440.33   Sen Gupta, N. Heredity in mental traits. 1. ed. London, 1941.

Phil 5440.34   Barker, Roger Garlock. Ecological psychology. Stanford, Calif., 1968.

Phil 5440.35   Geurts, P.M.M. De erfelijkheid in de oudere Grieksche wetenschap. Nijmegen, 1941.

Phil 5440.38   Behavioral genetics; method and research. N.Y., 1969.

Phil 5440.40   Mottram, Vernon Henry. The physical basis of personality. Harmondsworth, 1944.

Phil 5460   Psychology - Treatises on special topics - Illusions

Phil 5460.1.2   Sully, J. Illusions: a psychological study. pt.1-2. N.Y., 1884.

Phil 5460.1.3   Sully, J. Illusions: a psychological study. N.Y., 1884.

Phil 5460.1.5   Sully, J. Die Illusionen. Leipzig, 1884.

Phil 5460.2   Leyendecker, Herbert. Zur Phänomenologie der Täuschungen. Inaug. Diss. Halle, 1913.

Phil 5460.2.3   Leyendecker, Herbert. Zur Phänomenologie der Täuschungen. 1. Teil. Halle, 1913.

Phil 5460.3   Mayer, A. Die Sinnestäuschungen. Wien, 1869.

Phil 5460.4   Svenson, Frey. Vanföreställningarnas och sinnesvillornas psykologi. Stockholm, 1919.

Phil 5460.5   Kandinsky, V. Kritische und klinische Betrachtungen im Gebiete der Sinnestäuschungen. Berlin, 1885.

Phil 5460.6   Parish, E. Hallucinations and illusions. London, 1897.

Phil 5460.7   Kraft-Ebing, R. Die Sinnesdelirien. Erlangen, 1864.

Phil 5460.8   Leubuscher, R. Uber die Entstehung der Sinnestäuschung. Berlin, 1852.

Phil 5460.9   Etchart, Carlos R. La ilusion. Buenos Aires, 1948.

Phil 5460.10   Quercy, Pierre. L'hallucination. Paris, 1930. 2v.

Phil 5460.10.2   Faure, Henri. Études sur l'hallucination. Thèse. Paris, 1930. 2v.

Phil 5460.10.5   Faure, Henri. Les hallucinations. Paris, 1936.

Phil 5460.11   Bosch, G. Alucinaciones. Buenos Aires, 1935.

Phil 5460.12   Ward, R.H. A drug-taker's notes. London, 1957.

Phil 5460.13   Walter, W.G. The neurophysiological aspects of hallucinations and illusory experience. London, 1960.

Phil 5460.14   Faure, Henri. Hallucinations et réalité. Paris, 1964.

Phil 5460.14.5   Faure, Henri. Les objets dans la folie. Paris, 1965. 2v.

Phil 5460.14.10   Faure, Henri. Les appartenances du délirant. Paris, 1965.

Phil 5460.14.15   APA-AAAS Symposium on Hallucinations. Hallucinations. N.Y., 1962.

Phil 5465   Psychology - Treatises on special topics - Imagination

Phil 5465   Pamphlet box. Psychology. Special. Imagination.

Phil 5465.1   Bonstetten, K.V. von. Recherches sur la nature et les lois de l'imagination. Genève, 1807. 2v.

Phil 5465.2   Muratori, L.A. Trattato della forza della fantasia umana. Napoli, 1783.

Phil 5465.2.5   Muratori, L.A. Della forza della fantasia umana. Venezia, 1740.

Phil 5465.4   Ambrosi, L. La psicologia della immaginazione. Roma, 1898.

Phil 5465.4.5   Ambrosi, L. Saggio sulla immaginazione. Roma, 1892.

Phil 5465.4.10   Ambrosi, L. La psicologia dell'immaginazione nella storia della filosofia. Padova, 1959.

Phil 5465.5   Ribot, T. Essai sur l'imagination créatrice. Paris, 1900.

Phil 5465.5.3   Ribot, T. Essai sur l'imagination créatrice. 6. éd. Paris, 1921.

Phil 5465.5.4   Ribot, T. Essai sur l'imagination créatrice. 4. éd. Paris, 1914.

Phil 5465.5.5   Ribot, T. Essay on the creative imagination. Chicago, 1906.

Phil 5465.6   Brittain, H.L. A study in imagination. n.p., 1907.

Phil 5465.7   Betts, G.H. The distribution and functions of mental imagery. N.Y., 1909.

Phil 5465.9   Biuso, C. La fantasia. Catania, 1903.

Phil 5465.10   Dugas, L. L'imagination. Paris, 1903.

Phil 5465.12   Philippe, Jean. L'image mentale; évolution et dissolution. Paris, 1903.

Phil 5465.13   Lucka, Emil. Die Phantasie. Wien, 1908.

Phil 5465.14   Giachetti, Apriano. La fantasia. Torino, 1912.

Phil 5465.15   Leuchtenberger, G. Die Phantasie ihr Wesen. Erfurt, 1894.

Phil 5465.16   Glogan, Gustav. Die Phantasie. Halle, 1884.

Phil 5465.17   Sourian, Paul. L'imagination de l'artiste. Paris, 1901.

Phil 5465.18   Erdmann, Benno. Die Funktionen der Phantasie im wissenschaftlichen Denken. Berlin, 1913.

Phil 5465.19   Joly, Henri. L'imagination. 2. éd. Paris, 1883.

Phil 5465.20   Strang, W. Imagination and fancy. London, 1913.

Phil 5465.21   Daudet, Léon. Le monde des images; suite de l'hérédo. Paris, 1919.

Phil 5465.22   Nielsen, Rasmus. Om phantasiens magt. Kjøbenhavn, 1876.

Phil 5465.23   Leeming, B.C. Imagination, mind's dominant power. N.Y., 1926.

Phil 5465.24   Hammer, Bertil. Fantasien. Uppsala, 1916.

Phil 5465.25   Zeller, E. Uber den Einfluss des Gefühls auf die Thätigkeit der Phantasie. Tübingen, 1900.

Phil 5465.26   Griffitts, Charles H. Individual differences in imagery. Diss. n.p., 1919?

Phil 5465.27.2   Jaensch, Erich. Die Eidetik und typologische Forschungsmethode in ihrer Bedeutung für die Jugendpsychologie. 2e Aufl. Leipzig, 1927.

Phil 5465.27.4   Jaensch, Erich. Eidetic imagery and typological methods of investigation. London, 1930.

Phil 5465   Psychology - Treatises on special topics - Imagination - cont.

Phil 5465.27.5   Jaensch, Erich. Die Streitfrage zwischen Assoziation. Berlin, 1927.

Phil 5465.28   Baïtch, Baïa. La psychologie de la rêverie. Thèse. Paris, 1927.

Phil 5465.29   Ölzelt-Newin, A. Über Phantasie-Vorstellungen. Graz, 1889.

Phil 5465.31   Spearman, Charles. Creative mind. London, 1930.

Phil 5465.31.5   Spearman, Charles. Creative mind. Cambridge, Eng., 1931.

Phil 5465.32   Bundy, Murray W. The theory of imagination in classical and mediaeval thought. Urbana, 1927.

Phil 5465.33   Bouthoul, G. L'invention. Paris, 1930.

Phil 5465.33.10   Centre International de Synthèse, Paris. Neuvième semaine internationale de synthèse. L'invention. Paris, 1938.

Phil 5465.34   Welch, Livingston. Imagination and human nature. London, 1935.

Phil 5465.35   Sartre, Jean P. L'imagination. Paris, 1936.

Phil 5465.35.5   Sartre, Jean P. L'imagination; psychologie. Paris, 1940.

Phil 5465.35.10   Sartre, Jean P. L'imaginaire. Paris, 1940.

Phil 5465.35.15   Sartre, Jean P. Imagination. Ann Arbor, 1962[1960]

Phil 5465.36   Harding, R.E.M. Towards a law of creative thought. London, 1936.

Phil 5465.37   Biervliet, J.J. van. La part de l'imagination. Paris, 1937.

Phil 5465.38   Lacroze, René. La fonction de l'imagination. Paris, 1938.

Phil 5465.38.5   Lacroze, René. La fonction de l'imagination. Paris, 1938.

Phil 5465.39   Nussberger, M. Die künstlerische Phantasie. München, 1935.

Phil 5465.40   Cadman, S. Parkes. Imagination. N.Y., 1930.

Phil 5465.41   Rumpf-Thevenot, Theodor Richard. Phantasie - ewiger Born. Zürich, 1943.

Phil 5465.42   Curry, S.S. Imagination and dramatic instinct. Boston, 1896.

Phil 5465.44   Gore, W.C. The imagination in Spinoza and Hume. Chicago, 1902.

Phil 5465.46   Reeb, Eugène. Les images de Taine à Binet. Thèse complementaire. Nancy, 1938.

Phil 5465.48   Schmidt, Otto. Zur revision der Eidetek. Marburg, 1933.

Phil 5465.50   Chicago. University. Committee on Social Thought. The works of the mind. Chicago, 1947.

Phil 5465.52A   Gordon, Kate. Studies in the theory of imagination. Los Angeles, 1941.

Phil 5465.52B   Gordon, Kate. Studies in the theory of imagination. Los Angeles, 1941.

Phil 5465.54   Hutchinson, E.D. How to think creatively. N.Y., 1949.

Phil 5465.56   Bachelard, G. L'eau et les rêves. Paris, 1942.

Phil 5465.56.10   Bachelard, G. La terre et les rêveries de la volonté. Paris, 1948.

Phil 5465.56.20   Bachelard, G. L'air et les songes. Paris, 1943.

Phil 5465.56.30   Bachelard, G. La terre et les rêveries du repos. Paris, 1948.

Phil 5465.56.42   Bachelard, G. La flamme d'une chandelle. 2. éd. Paris, 1962.

Phil 5465.57   Osborn, A.F. Your creative power. N.Y., 1951.

Phil 5465.57.10   Osborn, A.F. Wake up your mind. N.Y., 1952.

Phil 5465.58   Gilson, E. L'école des muses. Paris, 1951.

Phil 5465.59   Osborn, A.F. Applied imagination. N.Y., 1953.

Phil 5465.60   Industrial Research Institute, New York. The nature of creative thinking. N.Y., 1952?

Phil 5465.65   Galimberti, A. L'imaginazione. Torino, 1954.

Phil 5465.70   Zwicker, Heinz. Seelisches Leben und schöpferische Leistung. Bern, 1954.

Phil 5465.75   Weinberg, J.R. Die Dynamik des schoepferischen Akts. Göttingen, 1954.

Phil 5465.80   McKellar, Peter. Imagination and thinking. London, 1957.

Phil 5465.85   Henry, W.E. The analysis of fantasy. N.Y., 1956.

Phil 5465.90   Interdisciplinary Symposium on Creativity, Michigan State University of Agriculture. Creativity and its cultivation. N.Y., 1959.

Phil 5465.95   Armstrong, Frank A. Idea-tracking. N.Y., 1960.

Phil 5465.100   Stein, Morris. Creativity and the individual. Glencoe, 1960.

Phil 5465.100.2   Stein, Morris. Creativity and the individual. Glencoe, 1964.

Phil 5465.105   Durand, G. Les structures anthropologiques de l'imaginaire. Grenoble, 1960.

Phil 5465.105.2   Durand, G. Les structures anthropologiques de l'imaginaire. 2. éd. Paris, 1963.

Phil 5465.110   Greenacre, P. Estudios psicoanalíticos sobre la actividad creadora. 1. ed. México, 1960.

Phil 5465.115   Naksianowicz-Gołaszewska, M. Twórczość a osobowość twórcy. Lublin, 1958.

Phil 5465.120   Furlong, E.J. Imagination. London, 1961.

Phil 5465.121   Metzger, Wolfgang. Schöpferische Freiheit. 2. Aufl. Frankfurt, 1962.

Phil 5465.124   Gruber, Howard E. Contemporary approaches to creative thinking. N.Y., 1962.

Phil 5465.126   Eiseley, Loren. The mind as nature. 1. ed. N.Y., 1962.

Phil 5465.128   Mueller, Robert E. Inventivity. N.Y., 1963.

Phil 5465.130   Maire, Gilbert. Les instants privilégiés. Aubier, 1962.

Phil 5465.132   Dracoulidès, N.N. Psychanalyse de l'artiste et de son oeuvre. Genève, 1952.

Phil 5465.133   Przyluski, J. Créer. Paris, 1943.

Phil 5465.134   Štraus, T. Umelecké myslenie. Bratislava, 1962.

Phil 5465.136   Taylor, C.W. Scientific creativity. N.Y., 1963.

Phil 5465.137   Koestler, Arthur. The act of creation. London, 1964.

Phil 5465.137.5   Koestler, Arthur. The act of creation. N.Y., 1969.

Phil 5465.138   Schuhl, P.M. Imaginer et réaliser. Paris, 1963.

Phil 5465.139   Taylor, C.W. Creativity, progress and potential. N.Y., 1964.

Phil 5465.140   Boston Institute. Conference on creativity as a process. Boston, 1957-58.

Phil 5465.141   Utah Creativity Research Conference. Proceedings of the fifth conference, 1964. N.Y., n.d. 2v.

Phil 5465.142   Hatterer, Lawrence J. The artist in society. N.Y., 1965.

Phil 5465.143   Ruitenbeek, Hendrik M. The creative imagination. Chicago, 1965.

Phil 5465.144   Razik, Jaher A. Bibliography of creativity; studies and related areas. Buffalo, 1965.

Phil 5465.145   Fried, Edrita. Artistic productivity and mental health. Springfield, Ill., 1964.

Phil 5465.146   Seidel, George Joseph. The crisis of creativity. Notre Dame, 1966.

Phil 5465.147   Crawford, Robert Platt. The techniques of creative thinking. 1. ed. N.Y., 1954.

Phil 5465.148   Lefebve, Maurice Jean. L'image fascinante et le surréel. Paris, 1965.

Phil 5465   Psychology - Treatises on special topics - Imagination - cont.

Phil 5465.149   Caillois, Roger. Images, images, essais sur le rôle et les pouvoirs de l'imagination. Paris, 1966.

Phil 5465.150   Piaget, Jean. L'image mentale chez l'enfant, étude sur le développement. Paris, 1966.

Phil 5465.151   Piaget, Jean. Mental imagery in the child; a study of the development of imaginal representation. London, 1971.

Phil 5465.155   Kagan, Jerome. Creativity and learning. Boston, 1967.

Phil 5465.158   Mooney, Ron Lawler. Explorations in creativity. 1. ed. N.Y., 1967.

Phil 5465.160   Patron Miranda, Joaquin R. La tecnica divina: el movimiento. Campeche, 1945.

Phil 5465.162   De Ropp, Robert S. The master game; pathways to higher consciousness beyond the drug experience. N.Y., 1968.

Phil 5465.163   Havelka, Jaroslav. The nature of the creative process in art. The Hague, 1968.

Phil 5465.166   Wiart, Claude. Expression picturale et psychopathologie. Paris, 1967.

Phil 5465.168   Ehrenzweig, Anton. The hidden order of art; a study in the psychology of artistic imagination. Berkeley, 1967.

Phil 5465.170   Le Men, Jean. L'espace figuratif et les structures de la personnalité, une épreuve clinique originale. Paris, 1966. 2v.

Phil 5465.171   Egen, Horst. Kinderzeichnungen und Umwelt. Bonn, 1967.

Phil 5465.172   Meerloo, Joost Abraham Maurits. Creativity and eternization. Assen, 1967.

Phil 5465.173   Arasteh, A. Reza. Creativity in the life-cycle. Leiden, 1968-

Phil 5465.175   Lehmann, Günther Kurt. Phantasie und Künstlerische Arbeit. Berlin, 1966.

Phil 5465.178   Ewert, Otto Maximilian. Phantasie und Intelligenz bei Jugendlichen. Weinheim, 1967.

Phil 5465.180   Lehman, Harvey Christian. Age and achievement. Princeton, 1953.

Phil 5465.182   Richardson, Alan. Mental imagery. London, 1969.

Phil 5465.182.1   Richardson, Alan. Mental imagery. N.Y., 1969.

Phil 5465.182.5   Horowitz, Mardi Jon. Image formation and cognition. N.Y., 1970.

Phil 5465.184   Groch, Judith. The right to create. 1. ed. Boston, 1970.

Phil 5465.186   Strzałecki, Andrzej. Wybrane zagadnienia psychologii twórczości. Wyd. 1. Warszawa, 1969.

Phil 5465.188   Burnshaw, Stanley. The seamless web; language thinking. N.Y., 1970.

Phil 5465.190   Maass, Johann Gebhard Ehrenreich. Versuch über die Einbildungskraft. Bruxelles, 1969.

Phil 5465.192.1   Ghiselin, Brewster. The creative process; a symposium. N.Y., 1955.

Phil 5465.194   Braeuer, Gottfried. Das Finden als Moment des Schöpferischen. Tübingen, 1966.

Phil 5465.196   Moustakas, Clark E. Creativity and conformity. N.Y., 1967.

Phil 5465.198   Nobel Conference, 6th, Gustavus Adolphus College, 1970. Creativity. Amsterdam, 1970.

Phil 5465.200   Vernon, Philip Ewart. Creativity: selected readings. Harmondsworth, 1970.

Phil 5465.202   Astruc, Louis. Créativité et sciences humaines. Paris, 1970.

Phil 5465.204   Shouksmith, George. Intelligence, creativity and cognitive style. London, 1970.

Phil 5465.206   Mironov, Alekseĭ V. Minuty poeticheskikh vdokhnovenii. Iavoslavl', 1970.

Phil 5465.208   Talejko, Eugeniusz. Zagadnienie psychologii twórezoju technĭvznej. Poznań, 1971.

Phil 5465.210   Markov, Mark E. Iskusstvo nak protsess. Moskva, 1970.

Phil 5465.212   Kaufmann, Arnold. L'inventique. Paris, 1970.

Phil 5465.214   Smith, Frederick Madison. The higher powers of man. Thesis. Lamoni, Ia., 1918.

Phil 5465.216   Fernald, Mabel Ruth. The diagnosis of mental imagery. Thesis. Princeton, N.J., 1912.

Phil 5465.218   Thomas de Saint-Laurent, Raymond de. L'imagination, son importance, sa nature. Avignon, 1970.

Phil 5465.220   Problemy nauchnogo tvorchestva v sovremennoi psikhologii. Moskva, 1971.

Phil 5467   Psychology - Treatises on special topics - Imitation

Phil 5467.01   Pamphlet box. Imitation.

Phil 5467.1   Steel, R. Imitation or mimetic force. London, 1900.

Phil 5467.2   Pistolesi, G. L'imitazione; studio di psicologia. Torino, 1910.

Phil 5467.3   Utitz, Emil. Psychologie der Simulation. Stuttgart, 1918.

Phil 5467.4   Lejins, Peter P. The concept of imitation. Part of thesis. Chicago, 1942.

Phil 5467.5   Deahl, J.N. Imitation in education. N.Y., 1900.

Phil 5467.6   Tarde, Gabriel. Les lois de l'imitation; étude sociologique. 4. éd. Paris, 1904.

Phil 5467.7   Ramsey, I.T. Models and mystery. London, 1964.

Phil 5467.8   Miami. University. Symposium on Social Behavior, 1st, 1967. Social formation and imitative behavior. Boston, 1968.

Phil 5467.10   Lueck, Helmut E. Soziale Aktivierung. Köln, 1969.

Phil 5470   Psychology - Treatises on special topics - Impulse

Phil 5470.1   Pamphlet box. Impulse.

Phil 5470.5   Bergler, Edmund. The psychology of gambling. N.Y., 1957.

Phil 5475   Psychology - Treatises on special topics - Influence

Phil 5475.12   Portmann, Adolf. Manipulation des Menschen als Schicksal und Bedrohung. Zürich, 1969.

Phil 5477   Psychology - Treatises on special topics - Inhibition

Phil 5477.01   Pamphlet box. Innate ideas.

Phil 5477.5   Skaggs, Ernest B. Major forms of inhibition in man. Chicago, 1931.

Phil 5477.10   Junker, Erika. Über unterschiedliches Behalten eigener Leistungen. Frankfurt, 1960.

Phil 5477.12   Diamond, Solomon. Inhibition and choice. N.Y., 1963.

Phil 5477.14   Hövmann, H. Konflikt und Entscheidung. Göttingen, 1960.

Phil 5477.16   Greeff, Etienne de. L'homme et son juge. Paris, 1962.

Phil 5478   Psychology - Treatises on special topics - Inhibition - Special [Discontinued]

Phil 5478.5   Frustration and aggression. New Haven, 1943.

Phil 5478.5.6   Frustration and aggression. New Haven, 1947.

Phil 5478.14   Birney, Robert Charles. Fear of failure. N.Y., 1969.

Phil 5480   Psychology - Treatises on special topics - Innate ideas
Phil 5480.1   Gall, F.J. Des dispositions innées de l'âme. Paris, 1811.
Phil 5480.2   Spruijt, C.B. Proeve van eene geschiedenis van de leer der aangeboren begrippen. Leiden, 1879.

Phil 5485   Psychology - Treatises on special topics - Intelligence
Phil 5485.2   Lienert, Gustav Adolf. Belastung und Regression. Meisenheim am Glan, 1964.
Phil 5485.4   Raaheim, Kjell. Opplevelse, erfaring og intelligens. Bergen, 1969.
Phil 5485.6   Sheinin, Iulian M. Integral'nyi intelleks. Moskva, 1970.
Phil 5485.8   Cattell, Raymond Bernard. Abilities: their structure, growth, and action. Boston, 1971.

Phil 5490   Psychology - Treatises on special topics - Intuition
Phil 5490.5   Losskii, Nikolai O. Sensory, intellectual and mystical intuition. v.1-2. n.p., n.d.

Phil 5500   Psychology - Treatises on special topics - Judgment
Phil 5500.01   Pamphlet box. Judgment.
Phil 5500.1   Ruyssen, T. Essai sur l'évolution psychologique du jugement. Nimes, 1904.
Phil 5500.2   Schrader, E. Elemente der Psychologie des Urteils. Leipzig, 1905.
Phil 5500.2.5   Schrader, E. Die bewusste Beziehung. Leipzig, 1893.
Phil 5500.3   Jerusalem, W. Die Urtheilsfunction. Wien, 1895.
Phil 5500.4   Pfordten, O.F. von. Versuch einer Theorie von Urteil und Begriff. Heidelberg, 1906.
Phil 5500.5   Lask, E. Die Lehre vom Urteil. Tübingen, 1912.
Phil 5500.6   Lewis, T.A. Judgment as belief. Baltimore, 1910.
Phil 5500.7   Brunschvicg, Léon. La modalité du jugement. Thèse. Paris, 1897.
Phil 5500.7.3   Brunschvicg, Léon. La modalité du jugement. 3.éd. Paris, 1964.
Phil 5500.8   Cornelius, Hans. Versuch einer Theorie der Existentialurteile. München, 1894.
Phil 5500.9   Rosinski, A. Das Urteil und die Lehre vom synthetischen Charakter desselben. Leipzig, 1889.
Phil 5500.10   Augier, E. De l'action à la connaissance. Paris, 1924.
Phil 5500.11   Katona, G. Psychologie der Relationserfassung und des Vergleichens. Leipzig, 1924.
Phil 5500.12   Gordin, Jakob. Untersuchungen zur Theorie des unendlichen Urteils. Berlin, 1929.
Phil 5500.13   Sharp, F.C. Goodwill and ill will. Chicago, 1950.
Phil 5500.14   Buchler, J. Toward a general theory of human judgment. N.Y., 1951.
Phil 5500.14.5   Buchler, J. Nature and judgment. N.Y., 1955.
Phil 5500.15   Drozdov, A.V. Voprosy klassifikatsii suzhdenii. Leningrad, 1956.
Phil 5500.16   Newell, Allen. Elements of a theory of human problem solving. Santa Monica, 1957.
Phil 5500.16.5   Newell, Allen. Human problem solving. Englewood Cliffs, 1972.
Phil 5500.18   Wasserman, Paul. Decision-making. Ithaca, 1958.
Phil 5500.20   Dijkhuis, J.H.M. Het beoordelen in de psychologie. Utrecht, 1960.
Phil 5500.22   Sherif, Muzafer. Social judgment. New Haven, 1961.
Phil 5500.24   Friedrich-Ebert-Stiftung. Überwindung von Vorurteilen. 2. Aufl. Hannover, 1960.
Phil 5500.26   Klein, Burton Harold. The decision-making problem in development. Santa Monica, 1960.
Phil 5500.28   Jordan, Nehemiah. Decision-making under uncertainty and problem solving. Santa Monica, 1960.
Phil 5500.30   Sadacca, Robert. Dimensions of response consistency in paired comparisons. Princeton, 1962.
Phil 5500.31   Festinger, L. Conflict, decision and dissonance. Stanford, 1964.
Phil 5500.32   Jones, William. On decision-making in large organizations. Santa Monica, 1964.
Phil 5500.33   Geer, J.P. van de. A psychological study of problem solving. Amsterdam, 1957.
Phil 5500.34   Siegel, S. Decision and choice. N.Y., 1964.
Phil 5500.35   Cohen, J. Behavior in uncertainty and its social implications. London, 1964.
Phil 5500.36   Fulcher, Gordon Scott. Common sense decision-making. Evanston, Ill., 1965.
Phil 5500.37   Buron, Robert. Decision-making in the development field. Paris, 1966.
Phil 5500.40   Downs, Anthony. Bureaucratic structure and decision-making. Santa Monica, 1966.
Phil 5500.41   Helmer, Olaf. A use of sumulation for the study of future values. Santa Monica, 1966.
Phil 5500.42   Symposium on Cognition, 1st, Pittsburgh, 1965. Problem solving: research, method and theory. N.Y., 1966.
Phil 5500.44   Clinical and social judgment: the discrimination of behavioral information. N.Y., 1966.
Phil 5500.45   Pears, David Francis. Predicting and deciding. London, 1964.
Phil 5500.48   Churchman, Charles West. Prediction and optimal decision. Englewood Cliffs, 1961.
Phil 5500.50   De Bono, Edward. The five-day course in thinking. N.Y., 1967.
Phil 5500.55   Symposium on Cognition, 3rd, Carnegie Institute of Technology, 1967. Formal representation of human judgment. N.Y., 1968.
Phil 5500.60   Johnsen, Erik. Studies in multiobjective decision models. Lund, 1968.
Phil 5500.65   Hofstee, Willem Karel Bernard. Method effects in absolute and comparative judgment. Proefschrift. Groningen, 1967.
Phil 5500.70   Cohen, Rudolf. Systematische Tendenzen bei Persönlichkeitsbeurteilungen. Bern, 1969.

Phil 5520   Psychology - Treatises on special topics - Language and thought
Phil 5520.01   Pamphlet box. Psychology. Language and thought.
Phil 5520.05   Pamphlet box. General semantics.
Phil 5520.1   Egger, V. La parole intérieure. Paris, 1881.
Phil 5520.2   Gaskell, J. Sense and sound. Philadelphia, 1854.
Phil 5520.3   Müller, F.M. Science of thought. London, 1887.
Phil 5520.3.5   Müller, F.M. Science of thought. v.2. N.Y., 1887.
Phil 5520.4   Ferrero, G. Les lois psychologiques du symbolisme. Paris, 1895.
Phil 5520.6   Martinak, E. Psychologische Untersuchungen zur Bedeutungslehre. Leipzig, 1901.
Phil 5520.7   Erdmann, Karl O. Die Bedeutung des Wortes. Leipzig, 1900.
Phil 5520.7.2   Erdmann, Karl O. Die Bedeutung des Wortes. 2. Aufl. Leipzig, 1910.
Phil 5520.8   Bruchmann, K. Psychologische Studien. Leipzig, n.d.
Phil 5520.9   Sutro, Emil. Duality of voice. N.Y., 1899.

Phil 5520   Psychology - Treatises on special topics - Language and thought - cont.
Phil 5520.9.2   Sutro, Emil. Das Doppelwesen der Menschlichen Stimme. Berlin, 1902.
Phil 5520.9.3   Sutro, Emil. Duality of thought and language. N.Y., 1904.
Phil 5520.9.5   Sutro, Emil. The basic law of vocal utterance. N.Y., 1894.
Phil 5520.9.9   Sutro, Emil. Das Doppelwesen in die Religion der Vernunft. Berlin, n.d.
Phil 5520.10   Finck, F.N. Die Aufgabe und Gliederung der Sprachwissenschaft. Halle, 1905.
Phil 5520.11   Rozwadowski, J. von. Wortbildung und Wortbedeutung. Heidelberg, 1904.
Phil 5520.12   Dittrich, O. Grundzüge der Sprachpsychologie. Halle, 1903- 2v.
Phil 5520.12.5   Dittrich, O. Die Probleme der Sprachpsychologie. Leipzig, 1913.
Phil 5520.13   Sechehaye, C.A. Programme et méthodes de la linguistique théorique. Paris, 1908.
Phil 5520.14   Ginneken, J. van. Principes de linguistic psychologique. Paris, 1907.
NEDL Phil 5520.15.7   Funke, O. Innere Sprachform. Reichenberg, 1924.
Phil 5520.16   MacNamara, N.C. Human speech; its physical basis. N.Y., 1909.
Phil 5520.17   Leroy, E.B. Le langage. Paris, 1905.
Phil 5520.18   Quantz, J.O. Problems in the psychology of reading. Chicago, 1897.
Phil 5520.18.5   Schmidt, William A. An experienced study in the psychology of reading. Theses. Chicago, 1917.
Phil 5520.19   Sechrist, F.K. The psychology of unconventional language. n.p., n.d.
Phil 5520.20   Sheffield, A.D. Grammar and thinking. N.Y., 1912.
Phil 5520.21.15   Landauer, Gustav. Skepsis und Mystik. Berlin, 1903.
Phil 5520.22   Gmelin, J.G. Zur Psychologie der Aussage. Hannover, 1909.
Phil 5520.23   Welby, Victoria. What is meaning. London, 1903.
Phil 5520.23.5   Welby, Victoria. Significs and language. London, 1911.
Phil 5520.24   Haig, James. Symbolism or mind matter, language as elements of thinking. Edinburgh, 1869.
Phil 5520.25   Mauthner, Fritz. Beiträge zu einer Kritik der Sprache. 2. Aufl. Stuttgart, 1906.
Phil 5520.25.1   Weiler, Gershon. Mauthner's Critique of language. Cambridge, Eng., 1970.
Phil 5520.26   Rowland, Eleanor H. The psychological experiences connected with the different parts of speech. Lancaster, 1907.
Phil 5520.27.2   Kussmaul, A. Die Störungen der Sprache. Leipzig, 1887.
Phil 5520.28   Wilson, William D. The influence of language on thought. Albany, 1879.
Phil 5520.29   Garlanda, Fedérico. La filosofia delle parole. 3. ed. Roma, 1905?
Phil 5520.30   Saint-Paul, Georges. Le langage intérieur et les paraphasies. Paris, 1904.
Phil 5520.30.5   Fruttchey, Frank. Voice, speech, thinking. 2. ed. Detroit, Mich., 1920.
Phil 5520.31   Häberlin, Paul. Symbol in der Psychologie. Bern, 1916.
Phil 5520.32   Noiré, Ludwig. Logos; Ursprung und Wesen der Begriffe. Leipzig, 1885.
Phil 5520.32.5   Noiré, Ludwig. Origin of language and logos theory. 2. ed. Chicago, 1899.
Phil 5520.32.7   Berg, Anton. Die Anschauungen Ludwig Noirés über Ursprung und Wesen von Sprache und Vernunft. Diss. Darmstadt, 1918
Phil 5520.33   Oltuszewski, W. Psychologie und Philosophie der Sprache. Berlin, 1901.
Phil 5520.34   Clark, Ruth S. An experimental study of silent thinking. N.Y., 1922.
Phil 5520.35   Ogden, Charles K. The meaning of meaning. London, 1923.
Phil 5520.35.3   Ogden, Charles K. The meaning of meaning. 3. ed. N.Y., 1930.
Phil 5520.35.5   Ogden, Charles K. The meaning of meaning. 5. ed. N.Y., 1938.
Phil 5520.35.7   Ogden, Charles K. The meaning of meaning. 5. ed. London, 1938.
Phil 5520.35.8   Ogden, Charles K. The meaning of meaning. 7. ed. N.Y., 1945.
Phil 5520.35.9   Ogden, Charles K. The meaning of meaning. 8. ed. N.Y., 1953.
Phil 5520.35.10   Ogden, Charles K. The meaning of meaning. N.Y., 1936.
Phil 5520.35.12   Ogden, Charles K. The meaning of meaning. 8. ed. N.Y., 1956.
Phil 5520.35.15.5   Ogden, Charles K. Opposition; a linguistic and psychological analysis. Bloomington, 1967.
Phil 5520.37   Lourié, Ossip. Le langage et la verbomanie. Paris, 1912.
Phil 5520.37.5   Lourié, Ossip. La graphomanie. Paris, 1920.
Phil 5520.38   Schmieder, A. Anregungen zur psychologischen Betrachtung der Sprache. Langensalza, 1902.
Phil 5520.39   Beck, Ernst H.F. Die Impersonalien in sprachpsychologischer, logischer und linguistischer Hinsicht. Leipzig, 1922.
Phil 5520.40   Bechtel, F. Über die Bezeichnungen der sinnlichen Wahrnehmungen. Weimar, 1879.
Phil 5520.41   Delacroix, H. Le langage et la pensée. Paris, 1924.
Phil 5520.41.3   Delacroix, H. Le langage et la pensée. 2. éd. Paris, 1930.
Phil 5520.41.5   Delacroix, H. L'analyse psychologique de la fonction linguistique. Oxford, 1926.
Phil 5520.42   Vailati, G. Alcune osservazioni sulle questioni di parole. Torino, 1899.
Phil 5520.43   Mouchet, Enrique. El lenguaje interior y los trastornos de la palabra. La Plata, 1923.
Phil 5520.44   Ammann, H.J.F. Die menschliche Rede. Lahr, 1925-28. 2v.
Phil 5520.45   Laguna, Grace A. de. Speech; its function and development. New Haven, 1927.
Phil 5520.46   Dodge, Raymond. Die motorischen Wortvorstellungen. Halle, 1896.
Phil 5520.47   Smart, B.H. Thought and language: an essay on...Locke's philosophy. London, 1855.
Phil 5520.48   Dugas, L. Le psittacisme et la pensée symbolique. Paris, 1896.
Phil 5520.49   Fröschels, E. Psychologie der Sprache. Leipzig, 1925.
Phil 5520.50   Owen, E.T. Interrogative thought and the means of its expression. Madison, 1904.
Phil 5520.51A   Pillsbury, Walter B. The psychology of language. N.Y., 1928.
Phil 5520.51B   Pillsbury, Walter B. The psychology of language. N.Y., 1928.
Phil 5520.52   Stöhr, Adolf. Umriss einer Theorie der Namen. Leipzig, 1889.
Phil 5520.53.2   Lorimer, F. The growth of reason. N.Y., 1929.

Phil 5520   Psychology - Treatises on special topics - Language and thought - cont.

Phil 5520.54   Buyssens, T. Langage et pensée, vie et matière. Brasschaat, 1928.

Phil 5520.55   Schölkopf, H. Sinn; eine philosophische Untersuchung. Inaug. Diss. Metzingen, 1931.

Phil 5520.56   Jordan, Leo. Die Kunst des begrifflichen Denkens. München, 1926.

Phil 5520.56.10   Jordan, Leo. Schule der Abstraktion und der Dialektik. München, 1932.

Phil 5520.57   Werner, Heinz. Grundfragen der Sprachphysiognomik. Leipzig, 1932.

Phil 5520.58   Groddeck, Georg. Der Mensch als Symbol. Wien, 1933.

Phil 5520.59   Psychologie du langage. Paris, 1933.

Phil 5520.60   Paulhan, F. La double fonction du langage. Paris, 1929.

Phil 5520.61   Serrus, Charles. Le parallélisme logico-grammatical. Thèse. Paris, 1933.

Phil 5520.61.10   Serrus, Charles. La langue, le sens, la pensée. Paris, 1941.

Phil 5520.62   Blumenfeld, W. Sinn und Unsinn. München, 1933.

Phil 5520.63   Latif, Israil. The physiological basis of linguistic development. Diss. Lancaster, Pa., 1934.

Phil 5520.64   Mannoury, G. Les deux pôles de l'esprit. Amsterdam, 1932.

Phil 5520.65   Zipf, G.K. The psycho-biology of language. Boston, 1935.

Phil 5520.66   Pita, Enrique B. La frase infantil monopalábrica y la intelligencia. Buenos Aires, 1935.

Phil 5520.67   Bruns, L. Metaphysik des Wortes. Inaug. Diss. Bonn, 1937.

Phil 5520.68.3   Chase, Stuart. The tyranny of words. N.Y., 1938.

Phil 5520.68.7   Chase, Stuart. Power of words. 1. ed. N.Y., 1954.

Phil 5520.68.10   Chase, Stuart. Danger: man talking! N.Y., 1969.

Phil 5520.69   Britton, Karl. Communication. London, 1939.

Phil 5520.70   Eisenson, J. Psychology of speech. N.Y., 1938.

Phil 5520.70.5   Eisenson, J. The psychology of communication. N.Y., 1963.

Phil 5520.71   Norris, Tom C. Thought and speech. London, 1938.

Phil 5520.72   Stinchfield, S.M. The psychology of speech. Boston, 1928.

Phil 5520.73   Kunz, H. Zur Phänomenologie und Analyse des Ausdrucks. Basel, 1934.

Phil 5520.74   Müller, H. Experimentelle Beiträge zur Analyse des Verhältnisses von Laut und Sinn. Berlin, 1935.

Phil 5520.75   Hayakawa, S.I. Language in action. N.Y., 1941.

Phil 5520.75.2   Hayakawa, S.I. Language in action. N.Y., 1941.

Phil 5520.75.5A   ETC., a Review of General Semantics. Language, meaning and maturity. 1. ed. N.Y., 1954.

Phil 5520.75.5B   ETC., a Review of General Semantics. Language, meaning and maturity. 1. ed. N.Y., 1954.

Phil 5520.75.10   Hayakawa, S.I. Symbol, status. 1. ed. N.Y., 1963.

Phil 5520.76A   Lee, Irving J. Language habits in human affairs. N.Y., 1941.

Phil 5520.76B   Lee, Irving J. Language habits in human affairs. N.Y., 1941.

Phil 5520.77   American Congress on General Semantics. Papers from the second American congress on general semantics, August, 1941. Chicago, 1943.

Phil 5520.78   Beyer, Alfred. Der Sieg des Denkens. Berlin, 192-.

Phil 5520.80   Burke, Kenneth. A grammar of motives. N.Y., 1945.

Phil 5520.82   Fauré-Frémiet, P. La recréation du réel et l'équivoque. Paris, 1940.

Phil 5520.84A   Morris, Charles W. Signs, language and behavior. N.Y., 1946.

Phil 5520.84B   Morris, Charles W. Signs, language and behavior. N.Y., 1946.

Phil 5520.85   Johnson, Wendel. People in guandaries. N.Y., 1946.

Phil 5520.86   Dobrogaev, S.M. Charl'z Darvin o proiskhozhdenii rechi. Leningrad, 1945.

Phil 5520.86.10   Dobrogaev, S.M. Rechevye refleksy. Moskva, 1947.

Phil 5520.88   Lewis, Morris M. Language in society. London, 1947.

Phil 5520.90   Kainz, Friedrich. Einführung in die Sprachpsychologie. Wien, 1946.

Phil 5520.92   Lipps, Hans. Die Verbindlichkeit der Sprache. Frankfurt, 1944.

Phil 5520.94   Wasmuth, E. Sophie, oder Über die Sprache. Berlin, 1943.

Phil 5520.96.01   Pamphlet box. Korzybski, Alfred. Language and thought.

Phil 5520.96.10   Korzybski, Alfred. Science and sanity. Lakeville, Conn., 1958.

Phil 5520.96.15   Korzybski, Alfred. General semantics seminar, 1937. 2. ed. Lakeville, Conn., 1964.

Phil 5520.96.80   Bulla de Villaret, H. Une nouvelle orientation. Paris, 1965.

Phil 5520.97A   Black, M. Language and philosophy. Ithaca, 1949.

Phil 5520.97B   Black, M. Language and philosophy. Ithaca, 1949.

Phil 5520.97C   Black, M. Language and philosophy. Ithaca, 1949.

Phil 5520.98   Stein, Leopold. The infancy of speech and the speech of infancy. London, 1949.

Phil 5520.99   Woodworth, Hugh. The nature and technique of understanding. Vancouver, B.C., 1949.

Phil 5520.100   Flew, A.G.N. Essays on logic and language. Oxford, 1951.

Phil 5520.100.10   Flew, A.G.N. Logic and language. 2. ser. Oxford, 1953.

Phil 5520.101   Holloway, J. Language and intelligence. London, 1951.

Phil 5520.102   Flesch, R.F. The art of clear thinking. 1. ed. N.Y., 1951.

Phil 5520.103   Winkler, R. Kritik der Wissenschaft. Wien, 1950.

Phil 5520.104   Prasod, Kali. The psychology of meaning. Lucknon, 1949.

Phil 5520.105   General semantics bulletin. Lakeville, Conn. 1-13

Phil 5520.106   Meerloo, A.M. Conversation and communication. N.Y., 1952.

Phil 5520.106.5   Meerloo, A.M. Het web van menselijke en sociale relaties. Den Haag, 1962.

Phil 5520.107   Vinacke, W.E. The psychology of thinking. 1. ed. N.Y., 1952.

Phil 5520.108   California. University. Philosophical Union. Meaning and interpretation. Berkeley, 1950.

Phil 5520.109   Lee, I.J. How to talk with people. N.Y., 1952.

Phil 5520.110   Gusdorf, George. La parole. 1. éd. Paris, 1955.

Phil 5520.110.5   Gusdorf, George. Speaking (La parole). Evanston, Ill., 1965.

Phil 5520.111A   Price, H.H. Thinking and experience. Cambridge, Mass., 1953.

Phil 5520.111B   Price, H.H. Thinking and experience. Cambridge, Mass., 1953.

Phil 5520.112   Haerber, W.L. A scientific foundation of philosophy. Los Angeles, 1952.

Phil 5520.112.1   Haerber, W.L. A scientific foundation of philosophy. Los Angeles, 1952.

Phil 5520.113   Miller, G.A. Language and communication. 1. ed. N.Y., 1951.

Phil 5520.114   Madinier, G. Conscience et signification. 1. éd. Paris, 1953.

Phil 5520.115   Rapoport, A. Operational philosophy. 1. ed. N.Y., 1953.

Phil 5520.116   Filosofia e linguaggio. Padova, 1950.

Phil 5520   Psychology - Treatises on special topics - Language and thought - cont.

Phil 5520.117   Lintsbakh, Ia. Printsipy filosofskogo iazyka. Petrograd, 1916.

Phil 5520.119   Sandman, M. Subject and predicate. Edinburgh, 1954.

Phil 5520.120   Carnap, Rudolf. Testability and meaning. New Haven, 1950.

Phil 5520.121.2   Carnap, Rudolf. Meaning and necessity. Chicago, 1964.

Phil 5520.122   Preti, Giulio. Linguaggia comune e linguaggi scientifici. Roma, 1953.

Phil 5520.124A   Wheelwright, Phillip Ellis. The burning fountain. Bloomington, 1954.

Phil 5520.124B   Wheelwright, Phillip Ellis. The burning fountain. Bloomington, 1954.

Phil 5520.124.2   Wheelwright, Phillip Ellis. The burning fountain. Bloomington, 1964.

Phil 5520.124.3   Wheelwright, Phillip Ellis. The burning fountain. Bloomington, 1968.

Phil 5520.126   Révész, G. Thinking and speaking. Amsterdam, 1954.

Phil 5520.128   Johnson, D.McE. The psychology of thought and judgment. N.Y., 1955.

Phil 5520.130   Clark University, Worcester, Massachusetts. Conference on Expressive Language Behavior. On expressive language. Worcester, Mass., 1955.

Phil 5520.135A   Linsky, Leonard. Semantics and the philosophy of language. Urbana, Ill., 1952.

Phil 5520.135B   Linsky, Leonard. Semantics and the philosophy of language. Urbana, Ill., 1952.

Phil 5520.137   Linsky, Leonard. Refering. London, 1967.

Phil 5520.140   Pike, Kenneth Lee. Language in relation to a unified theory of the structure of human behavior. Glendale, Calif., 1954.

Phil 5520.140.2   Pike, Kenneth Lee. Language in relation to a unified theory of the structure of human behavior. 2. ed. The Hague, 1967.

Phil 5520.145   Richards, Ivor Armstrong. Speculative instruments. Chicago, 1955.

Phil 5520.145.5   Richards, Ivor Armstrong. So much nearer; essays toward a world English. 1. ed. N.Y., 1968.

Phil 5520.145.10   Richards, Ivor Armstrong. Design for escape; world education through modern media. 1. ed. N.Y., 1968.

Phil 5520.145.15   Richards, Ivor Armstrong. Interpretation in teaching. N.Y., 1938.

Phil 5520.150   Archivo di Filosofia. Semantica. Roma, 1955.

Phil 5520.155   Nesbit, F.L. Language meaning. 1. ed. N.Y., 1955.

Phil 5520.160   Wilson, John. Language and the pursuit of truth. Cambridge, Eng., 1956.

Phil 5520.165   Wolard, M.R. Thinking about thinking. N.Y., 1955.

Phil 5520.170   Naess, Arne. Interpretation and preciseness. Oslo, 1953.

Phil 5520.175   Bois, Joseph S. Explorations in awareness. N.Y., 1957.

Phil 5520.180   Guiraud, P. La sémantique. 1. éd. Paris, 1955.

Phil 5520.185   Narskii, I.S. Kritika semanticheskogo idealizma. Moskva, 1956.

Phil 5520.190   Osgood, C.E. The measurement of meaning. Urbana, 1957.

Phil 5520.195   Greenwood, David. Truth and meaning. N.Y., 1957.

Phil 5520.200   Beiträge zur Psychologie der Sprache und des Denkens. Berlin, 1955.

Phil 5520.205   Bartlett, F.C. Thinking. London, 1958.

Phil 5520.210   Stegmüller, W. Das Wahrheitsproblem und die Idee der Semantik. Wien, 1957.

Phil 5520.215   Ushenko, A.P. The field theory of meaning. Ann Arbor, 1958.

Phil 5520.220   Rutt, Theodor. Vom Wesen der Sprache. Ratingen, 1957.

Phil 5520.225   Brown, Roger William. Words and things. Glencoe, Ill., 1958.

Phil 5520.225.2   Brown, Roger William. Words and things. N.Y., 1958.

Phil 5520.230   Raevskii, A.N. Psikhologiia rechi v sovetskoi psikhologicheskoi nauke za 40 let. Kiev, 1958.

Phil 5520.235   Pear, T.H. Personality, appearance and speech. London, 1957.

Phil 5520.240   Language. N.Y., 1957.

Phil 5520.245   ETC., a Review of General Semantics. Our language and our world. 1. ed. N.Y., 1959.

Phil 5520.250   Spirkin, A.G. Myshlenie i iazyk. Moskva, 1958.

Phil 5520.255   Longebaugh, T. General semantics. 1. ed. N.Y., 1957.

Phil 5520.260   Feldman, Sandor S. Mannerisms of speech and gestures in everyday life. N.Y., 1959.

Phil 5520.265   Mandler, George. The language of psychology. N.Y., 1959.

Phil 5520.270   Vieira de Almeida, F. Aspectos de filosofia da linguagen. Coimbra, 1959.

Phil 5520.275   Mayer, Felix. Schöpferische Sprache und Rhythmus. Berlin, 1959.

Phil 5520.280   Cuatrecasas, Juan. Psicobiologia del lenguaje. 2. ed. Buenos Aires, 1958.

Phil 5520.285   Reznikov, Lazar' O. Poniatie i slovo. Leningrad, 1958.

Phil 5520.286   Reznikov, Lazar' O. Gnoseologicheskie voprosy semiotiki. Leningrad, 1964.

Phil 5520.288   Martynov, Viktor V. Kibernetika, semiotika, lingvistika. Minsk, 1966.

Phil 5520.290   Wilson, Neil. The concept of language. Toronto, Canada, 1959.

Phil 5520.295   Thomsen, Robert. The psychology of thinking. Harmondsworth, 1959.

Phil 5520.300   Weinberg, Harry. Levels of knowing and existence. N.Y., 1959.

Phil 5520.305   Achkov, P.A. Myshlenie i iazyk. Moskva, 1959.

Phil 5520.310   Nordisk Sommeruniversitet. Betydningsproblemer. Oslo, 1954.

Phil 5520.311   Caton, Charles. Philosophy and ordinary language. Urbana, Ill., 1963.

Phil 5520.315   Brutian, G.A. Teoriia poznaniia obshchei semantiki. Erevan, 1959.

Phil 5520.320   Pfeil, Alfred. Lesen und Benennen in Reaktionsversuch. Frankfurt, 1959.

Phil 5520.325   Schaff, Adam. Wstęp do semantyki. Warszawa, 1960.

Phil 5520.325.1   Schaff, Adam. Einführung in die Semantik. Frankfurt, 1969.

Phil 5520.325.2   Schaff, Adam. Introduction to semantics. N.Y., 1962.

Phil 5520.325.3   Schaff, Adam. Język a poznanie. Warszawa, 1964.

Phil 5520.325.5   Schaff, Adam. Szkice z filozofii języka. Warszawa, 1967.

Phil 5520.325.7   Schaff, Adam. Essays über die Philosophie der Sprache. Frankfurt, 1968.

Phil 5520.325.10   Schaff, Adam. Language et connaissance. Paris, 1969.

Phil 5520.330   Simonis, Hans. Die Sprachphilosophie O.F. Guppe's und G. Gerber's. Bonn, 1959.

Phil 5520.335.2A   Ziff, Paul. Semantic analysis. Ithaca, 1962.

Phil 5520.335.2B   Ziff, Paul. Semantic analysis. Ithaca, 1962.

Phil 5520.340   Mueller, Heinz A. Die Psychologie des Lesens. Lörrach, 1958.

Phil 5520.345   Weyers, Gertrud. Das Sichbeswien auf Wörber. Köln, 1958.

Classified Listing

Phil 5520   Psychology - Treatises on special topics - Language and thought - cont.

Phil 5520.351   Church, Joseph. Language and the discovery of reality; a developmental psychology of cognition. N.Y., 1961.

Phil 5520.355   Szewczuk, W. Badania eksperymentalne nad rozumieniem zdán. Kraków, 1960.

Phil 5520.360   Barbara, Dominick A. Psychological and psychiatric aspects of speech and hearing. Springfield, 1960.

Phil 5520.365   Saporta, Sol. Psycnlinguistics. N.Y., 1961.

Phil 5520.370   Bunge, Mario. Antologia semantica. Buenos Aires, 1960.

Phil 5520.374   Upton, Albert. Design for thinking. Whittier, Calif, 1948.

Phil 5520.375   Upton, Albert. Design for thinking. Stanford, 1961.

Phil 5520.376   Upton, Albert. Creative analysis. Whittier, Calif., 1961.

Phil 5520.380   Slama-Cazacu, T. Langage et contexte. 's-Gravenhage, 1961.

Phil 5520.385   Cohen, Laurence Jonathan. The diversity of meaning. London, 1962.

Phil 5520.385.2   Cohen, Laurence Jonathan. The diversity of meaning. 2. ed. London, 1966.

Phil 5520.390   Segerstedt, T. Torgnysson. Die Macht des Wortes. Zürich, 1946.

Phil 5520.395   Turbayne, C.M. The myth of metaphor. New Haven, 1962.

Phil 5520.397   Riverso, Emmanuele. La costruzione interpretative del mondo analizzata dal l'epistenrologia genetica. Napoli, 1956.

Phil 5520.399   Antal, Laszló. Questions of meaning. The Hague, 1963.

Phil 5520.401   Ortigues, E. Le discours et le symbole. Paris, 1962.

Phil 5520.402   Lewis, Hywel D. Clarity is not enough. London, 1963.

Phil 5520.402.2   Lewis, Hywel D. Clarity is not enough. N.Y., 1963.

Phil 5520.403   Siewerth, Gustav. Philosophie der Sprache. Einsiedeln, 1962.

Phil 5520.404   Neubert, Q. Semantischer Positivismus in den USA. Halle, 1962.

Phil 5520.405   Wein, Hermann. Sprachphilosophie der Gegenwart. Den Haag, 1963.

Phil 5520.406   Izutsu, T. Language and magic. Tokyo, 1956.

Phil 5520.407   Vildomec, V. Multilingualism. Leyden, 1963.

Phil 5520.407.5   Studies in multilingualism. Leiden, 1969.

Phil 5520.408   Fredriksson, G. Det politiska språket. 2. uppl. Uppsala, 1963.

Phil 5520.409   Association de Psychologie Scientifique de Langue Française. Problèmes de psycholinguistique. Paris, 1963.

Phil 5520.410   Bennett, J.F. Rationality. London, 1964.

Phil 5520.411   Bottotini, Gianfranco. Il segno dalla fino al cinema. Milano, 1963.

Phil 5520.412   Christian, W.A. Meaning and truth in religion. Princeton, 1964.

Phil 5520.413   Martin, R.M. Intension and decision. Englewood Cliffs, N.J., 1963.

Phil 5520.414   Werner, H. Symbol formation. N.Y., 1963.

Phil 5520.415   Conference on Paralinguistics and Kinesics. Approaches to semiotics. The Hague, 1964.

Phil 5520.416   Zhinkin, N.I. Myshlenie i rech'. Moskva, 1963.

Phil 5520.417   Morric, C.W. Signification and significance. Cambridge, 1964.

Phil 5520.418   Alston, W. Philosophy of language. Englewood Cliffs, N.J., 1964.

Phil 5520.419   Oleron, P. Les activités intellectuelles. Paris, 1964.

Phil 5520.420   Fodor, J.A. The structure of language. Englewood Cliffs, N.J., 1964.

Phil 5520.421   Lenneberg, E.H. New directions in the study of language. Cambridge, 1964.

Phil 5520.422   Jánoska, G. Die sprachlichen Grundlagen der Philosophie. Graz, 1962.

Phil 5520.423   Carroll, John B. Language and thought. Englewood Cliffs, N.J., 1964.

Phil 5520.424   Grodziński, Eugeniusz. Znaczenie słowa w języku naturalnym. Warszawa, 1964.

Phil 5520.425   Liebrucks, Bruno. Sprache und Bewusstsein. Frankfurt, 1964. 5v.

Phil 5520.426   Titone, Renzo. La psicolinguistica oggi. Zürich, 1964.

Phil 5520.427   Rossi-Landi, Ferruccio. Significato comunicazioni e parlare comune. Padova, 1961.

Phil 5520.428A   Social Science Research Committee on Linguistics and Psychology. Psycholinguistics; a survey of theory and research problems. Bloomington, 1965.

Phil 5520.428B   Social Science Research Committee on Linguistics and Psychology. Psycholinguistics; a survey of theory and research problems. Bloomington, 1965.

Phil 5520.429   Berlyne, Daniel E. Structure and direction in thinking. N.Y., 1965.

Phil 5520.430   Hotopf, W.H.N. Language, thought and comprehension. London, 1965.

Phil 5520.431   Rosenberg, Sheldon. Directions in psycholinguistics. N.Y., 1965.

Phil 5520.432   Hayden, Donald E. Classics in semantics. N.Y., 1965.

Phil 5520.433   Laffal, Julius. Pathological and normal language. N.Y., 1965.

Phil 5520.434   Mancini, Italo. Linguaggio e salvezza. Milano, 1964.

Phil 5520.435   Thurman, Kelly. Semantics. Boston, 1960.

Phil 5520.436   Cornforth, Maurice Campbell. Marxism and the linguistic philosophy. N.Y., 1965.

Phil 5520.436.5   Cornforth, Maurice Campbell. Marxism and the linguistic philosophy. London, 1965.

Phil 5520.437   Guilhot, Jean. La dynamique de l'expression et de la communication. Paris, 1962.

Phil 5520.438   Graumann, Carl F. Denken. Köln, 1965.

Phil 5520.439   Keller, Benjamin. Toward an informal and creative conference method. Santa Monica, 1965.

Phil 5520.440   Pasquinelli, Alberto. Linguaggio, scienza e filosofia. 2. ed. Bologna, 1964.

Phil 5520.441   Sendel, Bess Selher. The humanity of words. Cleveland, 1958.

Phil 5520.442   Fay, Warren H. Temporal sequence in the perception of speed. The Hague, 1966.

Phil 5520.443   Pittau, Massimo. Filosofia e linguaggio. Pisa, 1962.

Phil 5520.443.5   Pittau, Massimo. Problemi di filosofia del linguaggio. Cagliari, 1967.

Phil 5520.444   Begiashvili, Archil. Sovremennaia angliiskaia lingvisticheskaia filosofiia. Tbilisi, 1965.

Phil 5520.445   Creelman, Marjorico Broer. The experimental investigation of meaning. N.Y., 1966.

Phil 5520.446   Bocheński, Innocentius M. The logic of religion. N.Y., 1965.

Phil 5520.447   Katz, Jerrold J. The philosophy of language. N.Y., 1966.

Phil 5520.448   Drange, Theodore. Type crossings. The Hague, 1966.

Phil 5520.449A   Chomsky, Noam. Cartesian linguistics. N.Y., 1966.

Phil 5520.449B   Chomsky, Noam. Cartesian linguistics. N.Y., 1966.

Phil 5520   Psychology - Treatises on special topics - Language and thought - cont.

Phil 5520.449.5   Chomsky, Noam. Linguistica cartesiana. Madrid, 1969.

Phil 5520.450   Pollio, Howard R. The structural basis of word association behavior. Paris, 1966.

Phil 5520.451   Dienes, Zoltau Paul. Thinking in structures. London, 1965.

Phil 5520.452   Smith, Huston. Condemned to meaning. 1. ed. N.Y., 1965.

Phil 5520.453   Centro di Studi Filosofici de Gallarate. 9. Convegno Annuale. Il problema filosofico del linguaggio. Padova, 1965.

Phil 5520.455   Kastein, Shulamith. The birth of language; the case history of a non-verbal child. Springfield, 1966.

Phil 5520.457   Moscow. Pervyi Moskovskii Gosudarstvennyi Pedagogicheskii Institut Inostrannykh iazykov. Materialy kolloKviuma po eksperimental'noi fonetiki i psikhologii rechi. Moskva, 1966.

Phil 5520.458   Wit, Gerard Antonius de. A psychological study of symbolism in word association and symbolic meaning of words. Eindhoven, 1962.

Phil 5520.459   Spoerri, Theodor. Sprachphänomene und Psychose. Basel, 1964.

Phil 5520.460   Walters, Theodore W. The Georgetown bibliography of studies contributing to the psycholinguistics of language learning. Washington, 1965.

Phil 5520.461   Soehingen, Gottlieb. Analogie und Metapher. Freiburg, 1962.

Phil 5520.462   Edinburgh. University. Faculty of Social Sciences. Research Board. Conference on Psycholinguistics, 1966. Psycholinguistics papers. Edinburgh, 1966.

Phil 5520.463   Rorty, Richard. The linguistic turn; recent essays in philosophical method. Chicago, 1967.

Phil 5520.465   Schmidt, Franz. Zeichen und Wirklichkeit. Stuttgart, 1966.

Phil 5520.466   Clauss, Karl. General semantics. pt.1. Berlin, 1966. 2v.

Phil 5520.477   Clarke, Bowman L. Language and natural theology. The Hague, 1966.

Phil 5520.478   Thass-Thienemann, Théodore. The subconscious language. N.Y., 1967.

Phil 5520.480.2   Mauro, Tullio de. Introduzione alla semantica. 2. ed. Bari, 1966.

Phil 5520.480.5   Anderson, Richard Chase. Readings in the psychology of cognition. N.Y., 1965.

Phil 5520.481   Horálek, Karel. Filosofie jazyku. Praha, 1967.

Phil 5520.482   Iazyk i myshlenie. Moskva, 1967.

Phil 5520.486   Barfield, Owen. Speaker's meaning. 1. ed. Middletown, 1967.

Phil 5520.487   Ventler, Zeno. Linguistics in philosophy. Ithaca, 1967.

Phil 5520.488   Waldron, R.A. Sense and sense development. London, 1967.

Phil 5520.489   Ong, Walter Jackson. The presence of the word. New Haven, 1967.

Phil 5520.490   Research in verbal behavior and some neurophysiological implications. Papers presented at a conference in New York, 1965. N.Y., 1967.

Phil 5520.491   Saunders, John Turk. The private language problem. N.Y., 1967.

Phil 5520.492   Hoermann, Hans. Psychologie der Sprache. Berlin, 1967.

Phil 5520.492.2   Hoermann, Hans. Psychologie der Sprache. Berlin, 1970.

Phil 5520.493   De Bono, Edward. The use of lateral thinking. London, 1968.

Phil 5520.495   Bacchin, Giovanni Romano. I fondamenti della filosofia del linguaggio. Assisi, 1965.

Phil 5520.498   Hoeffe, Wilhelm Laziar. Sprachlicher Ausdrucksgehalt und akustische Struktur. Ratingen bei Düsseldorf, 1966.

Phil 5520.499   Brandt, Elmar. Der theoretische Bedeutungbegriff. Inaug. Diss. München, 1964.

Phil 5520.500   Wagner, Geoffrey A. On the wisdom of words. Princeton, 1968.

Phil 5520.502   Ulshoefer-Heinloth, Elisabeth. Studien zur sprachkommunikativen Orientierung. Inaug. Diss. Passau, 1964.

Phil 5520.504   Sinclair-de Zwart, Hermina. Acquisition du langage et développement de la pensée, sous-systèmes, et opérations concrètes. Paris, 1967.

Phil 5520.505   Delius, Harald. Untersuchungen zur Problematik der sogenannten synthetischen Sätze apriori. Göttingen, 1963.

Phil 5520.506   Yolton, John W. Metaphysical analysis. Toronto, 1967.

Phil 5520.507   Verhaar, John W.M. Some relations between perception, speech and thought. Proefschrift. Assen, 1963.

Phil 5520.508   Hartogs, Renatas. Four-letter word games. N.Y., 1967.

Phil 5520.509   Materialy k konferentsii "Iazyk kak znakovaia sistema osobogo roda. Moskva, 1967.

Phil 5520.510   Leont'ev, Aleksei A. Psikholingvistika. Leningrad, 1967.

Phil 5520.512   Kamrath, Gerhard. Vernunft und Sprache. Heidelberg, 1964.

Phil 5520.513   Logicheskaia semantika i modal'naia logika. Moskva, 1967.

Phil 5520.514   Black, Max. The labyrinth of language. N.Y., 1968.

Phil 5520.515   Schérer, René. Structure et fondement de la communication humaine, essai critique sur les théories contemporaines de la communication. Thèse. Paris, 1965.

Phil 5520.520   Derrida, Jacques. De la gammatologie. Paris, 1967.

Phil 5520.525   Lacan, Jacques. The language of the self. Baltimore, 1968.

Phil 5520.530   Wiener, Morton. Language within language; immediacy, a channel in verbal communication. N.Y., 1968.

Phil 5520.535A   Rommetreit, Ragnar. Words, meanings, and messages. N.Y., 1968.

Phil 5520.535B   Rommetreit, Ragnar. Words, meanings, and messages. N.Y., 1968.

Phil 5520.542   Klaus, Georg. Spezielle Erkenntnistheorie. 2. Aufl. Berlin, 1966.

Phil 5520.545   Thass-Thienemann, Théodore. Symbolic behavior. N.Y., 1968.

Phil 5520.550   Levin, Poul. Semantik. København, 1968.

Phil 5520.551   Bense, Max. Semiotik. Baden-Baden, 1967.

Phil 5520.552   Hançerlioglu, Oshan. Başlan-gicindan bugüne erdem açisindan düsünce. 2. b. Istanbul, 1966.

Phil 5520.555   Chappell, Vere Claiborne. Ordinary language; essays in philosophical method. Englewood Cliffs, N.J., 1964.

Phil 5520.560   Eisler, Frieda Goldman. Psycholinguistics: experiments in spontaneous speech. London, 1968.

Phil 5520.565   Eco, Umberto. La strutture assente. Milano, 1968.

Phil 5520.570   Terwilliger, Robert F. Meaning and mind. N.Y., 1968.

Phil 5520.571   Lewis, David Kellogg. Convention; a philosophical study. Cambridge, 1969.

Phil 5520.575   Santoni, Ronald E. Religious language and problem of religious knowledge. Bloomington, 1968.

Phil 5520.576   Teoriia rechevoi deiatel'nosti. Moskva, 1968.

Classified Listing

Phil 5520   Psychology - Treatises on special topics - Language and thought - cont.

Phil 5520.577   Vetrov, Anatolii A. Semiotika i ee osnovnye problemy. Moskva, 1968.

Phil 5520.578   Lévy-Valensi, Eliane Amado. La communication. 1.éd. Paris, 1967.

Phil 5520.580   Schmidt, Siegfried J. Die Beschreibung des Zusammenhangs von Sprache und Denken in der Sprachphilosophie von Locke bis Wittgenstein. n.p., 1965.

Phil 5520.580.5   Schmidt, Siegfried J. Bedeutung und Begriff. N.Y., 1969.

Phil 5520.581   Rossi, Eduard. Das menschliche Begreifen und seine Grenzen. Bonn, 1968.

Phil 5520.582   Kaminsky, Jack. Language and ontology. Carbondale, 1969.

Phil 5520.584   Schiller, Jerome Paul. I.A. Richard's theory of literature. New Haven, 1969.

Phil 5520.586   Grava, Arnolds. A structural inquiry into the symbolic representation of ideas. The Hague, 1969.

Phil 5520.588   De Bono, Edward. The mechanism of mind. N.Y., 1969.

Phil 5520.590   Simon, Josef. Sprache und Raum. Berlin, 1969.

Phil 5520.592   Stoep, F. van der. Taalanalise en taalevaluering as pedagogies-didaktiese diagnostiseungsmetode. Pretoria, 1965.

Phil 5520.594   Siddiqi, J.A. Experimentelle Untersuchungen über den Zusammenhang von Sprachgestalt und Bedeutung. Meisenheim, 1969.

Phil 5520.595   Leont'ev, Aleksei A. Psikholingvisticheskie edinitsy v porozhdenie rechevogo vyskazyvaniia. Moskva, 1969.

Phil 5520.596   Sotnikian, Pogos A. Osnovnye problemy iazyka i myshleniia. Erevan, 1968.

Phil 5520.598   Parain, Brice. Petite métaphysique de la parole. Paris, 1969.

Phil 5520.600   Welterfahrung in der Sprache. Freiburg, 1968-

Phil 5520.605   Gilson, Etienne. Linguistique et philosophie. Paris, 1969.

Phil 5520.610   Ehrlich, Stéphane. Les mécanismes du comportement verbal. Paris, 1968.

Phil 5520.615   Wierzbicka, Anna. Dociekania semantyczne. Wrocław, 1969.

Phil 5520.616   Wierzbicka, Anna. Kocha, lubi, szanuje. Wyd. 1. Warszawa, 1971.

Phil 5520.618   Psikhologiia grammatiki. Moskva, 1968.

Phil 5520.620   Oldfield, Richard Charles. Language: selected readings. Harmondsworth, 1968.

Phil 5520.622   Chernokov, Petr V. Osnovnye edinitsy iazyka i myshleniia. Rostov-na-Donu, 1966.

Phil 5520.624   Savigny, Eike von. Die Philosophie der normalen Sprache. Frankfurt, 1969.

Phil 5520.626   Deese, James Earle. Psycholinguistics. Boston, 1970.

Phil 5520.628   Komlev, Nikolai G. Komponenty soderzhatel'noi struktury slova. Moskva, 1969.

Phil 5520.630A   Cognition and the development of language. N.Y., 1970.

Phil 5520.630B   Cognition and the development of language. N.Y., 1970.

Phil 5520.632   Engel, S. Morris. Language and illumination. The Hague, 1969.

Phil 5520.634   Cowan, Joseph Lloyd. Studies in thought and language. Tucson, 1970.

Phil 5520.636   Ertel, Suitbert. Psychophonetik; Untersuchungen über Lautsymbolik und Motivation. Göttingen, 1969.

Phil 5520.638   George, Frank Honywill. Models of thinking. London, 1970.

Phil 5520.640   Lehrer, Adrienne. Theory of meaning. Englewood Cliffs, N.J., 1970.

Phil 5520.642   Brkić, Jovan. Norm and order; an investigation into logic, semantics, and the theory of law and morals. N.Y., 1970.

Phil 5520.644   Problema znaka i znacheniia. Moskva, 1969.

Phil 5520.646   Herriot, Peter. An introduction to the psychology of language. London, 1970.

Phil 5520.648   Hintikka, Kaarlo Jaakko Juhani. Information and inference. Dordrecht, 1970.

Phil 5520.650   Bervi, Vasilii V. Kritika osnovnykh idei estestvoznaniia. Photoreproduction. Sankt-Peterburg, 1904.

Phil 5520.652   Osnovnye podkhody k modelirovaniia psikhiki i evristicheskomu programmirovaniiu. Moskva, 1968.

Phil 5520.654   Juliard, Pierre. Philosophies of language in eighteenth-century France. The Hague, 1970.

Phil 5520.656   Kybernetische Analysen geistigen Prozesse. Berlin, 1968.

Phil 5520.658   Konczewski, C. La psychologie dynamique et la pensée vécue. Paris, 1970.

Phil 5520.660   Testa, Aldo. La struttura dialogica del linguaggio. Bologna, 1967.

Phil 5520.665   Hoepp, Gerhard. Evolution der Sprache und Vernunft. Berlin, 1970.

Phil 5520.670   Coseriu, Eugenio. Die Geschichte der Sprachphilosophie von der Antike bis zur Gegenwart. Stuttgart, 1969.

Phil 5520.675   Colli, Giorgio. Filosofia dell'espressione. Milano, 1969.

Phil 5520.680   Goessmann, Wilhelm. Glaubwürdigkeit im Sprachgebrauch. 1. Aufl. München, 1970.

Phil 5520.685   Rundle, Clement William Kennedy. A critique of linguistic philosophy. Oxford, 1970.

Phil 5520.690   Das Jagannath, Prasad. Verbal conditioning and behavior. 1. ed. Oxford, 1969.

Phil 5520.695   Wettler, Manfred. Syntaktische Faktoren im verbalen Lernen. Bern, 1970.

Phil 5520.698   Psikhologicheskie i psikholingvisticheskie problemy vladeniia i ovladeniia iazykom. Moskva, 1969.

Phil 5520.700   Schaefer, Wolfgang von. Was geht uns Noah an? München, 1968.

Phil 5520.702   De Vito, Joseph A. The psychology of speech and language. N.Y., 1970.

Phil 5520.704   Tikhomirov, Oleg K. Struktura myslitel'noi deiatel'nosti cheloveka. Moskva, 1969.

Phil 5520.706   Kochergin, Al'bert N. Modelirovanie myshleniia. Moskva, 1969.

Phil 5520.707   Leont'ev, Aleksei A. Iazyk, rech', rechevaia deiatel'nost'. Moskva, 1969.

Phil 5520.708   Ismailov, B. Iazyk i poznanie mira. Tashkent, 1969.

Phil 5520.710   Smerud, Warren B. Can there be a private language? The Hague, 1970.

Phil 5520.712   Faccani, Remo. I sistemi di segni e lo strutturalismo sovietico. Milano, 1969.

Phil 5520.714   Bourne, Lyle Eugene. The psychology of thinking. Englewood Cliffs, N.J., 1971.

Phil 5520.716   Seuphor, Michel. Le don de la parole. Saint-Aguilin-de-Pacy, 1970.

Phil 5520.718   Peterfalvi, Jean Michel. Introduction à la psycholinguistique. 1. éd. Paris, 1970.

Phil 5520.720   Marmy, Emile. La philosophie du signe. Fribourg, 1969.

Phil 5520.722   Brushlinskii, Andrei V. Psikhologiia myshleniia i kibernetika. Moskva, 1970.

Phil 5520.724   Studia z dziejów semiotyki. Wrocław, 1971.

Phil 5520   Psychology - Treatises on special topics - Language and thought - cont.

Phil 5520.726   Spasov, Dobrin I. Filosofiia na lingvistikata sreshchu lingvisticheskata filosofiia. Sofiia, 1970.

Phil 5520.728   Blumenthal, Arthur L. Language and psychology. N.Y., 1970.

Phil 5520.730   Stichl, Ulrich. Einführung in die allgemeine Semantik. Bern, 1970.

Phil 5520.732   Peterfalvi, Jean Michel. Recherches experimentales sur le symbolisme phonétique. Paris, 1970.

Phil 5520.734   Cognitive development and epistemology. N.Y., 1971.

Phil 5520.736   Slobin, Dan Isaac. Psycholinguistics. Glenview, Ill., 1971.

Phil 5520.738   Centre Regional de Documentation, Pedagogique de Poitiers. Textes et communications sur le thème: philosophie et langage, 24 avril, 1969. Photoreproduction. Paris, 1969?

Phil 5520.740   Bressanone Conference on Psycholinguistics, University of Padova, 1969. Advances in psycholinguistics. Amsterdam, 1971.

Phil 5520.742   Semanticheskaia struktura slova. Moskva, 1971.

Phil 5520.744   Brisset, Jean Pierre. La grammaire logique. Paris, 1970.

Phil 5520.746   Strawson, Peter Frederick. Meaning and truth: an inaugural lecture delivered before the University of Oxford on 5 November 1969. Oxford, 1970.

Phil 5520.748   Pelc, Jerzy. Semiotyka polska, 1894-1969. Warszawa, 1971.

Phil 5520.748.2   Pelc, Jerzy. Studies in functional logical semiotics of natural language. The Hague, 1971.

Phil 5520.750   Mounin, Georges. Introductions à la sémiologie. Paris, 1971.

Phil 5520.752   Wormnaes, Odd. Semantikk i teori og praksis. Oslo, 1971.

Phil 5520.754.2   Regnell, Hans. Filosofiska och språkvetenskapliga grundfrågor inom betydelseläran. 2. uppl. Stockholm, 1971.

Phil 5520.756   Panfilov, Vladimir Z. Vzaimootnoshenie iazyka i myshleniia. Moskva, 1971.

Phil 5520.758   DeVito, Joseph A. Psycholinguistics. Indianapolis, 1971.

Phil 5520.760   Shands, Harley Cecil. The war with words, structure and transcendence. The Hague, 1971.

Phil 5525   Psychology - Treatises on special topics - Laughter

Phil 5525.01   Pamphlet box. Psychology. Special. Laughter.

Phil 5525.1   Keppler, J.F. Kritische Untersuchungen. Cilli, 1792.

Phil 5525.3   Courdaveaux, V. Études sur la comique. Le rire. Paris, 1875.

Phil 5525.4   Sully, J. An essay on laughter. London, 1902.

Phil 5525.5   Dumas, G. La sourire. Paris, 1906.

Htn   Phil 5525.6*   Freud, Sigmund. Der Witz und seine Beziehung zum Unbewussten. Leipzig, 1905.

Phil 5525.6.3   Freud, Sigmund. Der Witz und seine Beziehung zum Unbewussten. 2. Aufl. Leipzig, 1912.

Phil 5525.6.5A   Freud, Sigmund. Wit and its relation to the unconscious. N.Y., 1916.

Phil 5525.6.5B   Freud, Sigmund. Wit and its relation to the unconscious. N.Y., 1916.

Phil 5525.6.10   Freud, Sigmund. Jokes and their relation to the unconscious. London, 1960.

Phil 5525.7   Jahn, Franz. Das Problem des Komischen. Potsdam, 1904.

Phil 5525.8   Ueberhorst, K. Das Komische. Leipzig, 1896-1900. 2v.

Phil 5525.9   Fleet, F.R. Theory of wit and humor. London, 1890.

Phil 5525.10   Backhaus, W.E. Das Wesen des Humors. Leipzig, n.d.

NEDL   Phil 5525.11.5   Bergson, Henri. Il riso, saggio sul significato del comico. Bari, 1916.

NEDL   Phil 5525.11.10   Bergson, Henri. Le rire. 5. éd. Paris, 1908.

Phil 5525.12   Sidis, B. The psychology of laughter. N.Y., 1913.

Phil 5525.12.3   Sidis, B. The psychology of laughter. N.Y., 1919.

Phil 5525.12.5   Leir, Giulio A. Il comico. Genova, 1913.

Phil 5525.13   Lipps, T. Komik und Humor. Hamburg, 1898.

Phil 5525.15   Roetschi, Robert. Der ästhetische Wert des Komischen und das Wesen des Humors. Bern, 1915.

Phil 5525.16   Philbert, Louis. Le rire. Paris, 1883.

Phil 5525.17   Hecker, Ewald. Die Physiologie und Psychologie des Lachens. Berlin, 1873.

Phil 5525.18   Hoffding, Harald. Humor als Lebensgefühl. Leipzig, 1918.

Phil 5525.19.2   Vasey, George. The philosophy of laughter and smiling. 2. ed. London, 1877.

Phil 5525.20A   Eastman, Max. The sense of humor. N.Y., 1921.

Phil 5525.20B   Eastman, Max. The sense of humor. N.Y., 1921.

Phil 5525.20.5   Eastman, Max. The sense of humor. N.Y., 1922.

Phil 5525.20.15   Eastman, Max. Enjoyment of laughter. N.Y., 1936.

Phil 5525.21   Raulin, J.M. Le rire et les exhilarants. Paris, 1900.

Phil 5525.22   Grieg, J.Y.J. The psychology of laughter and comedy. London, 1923.

Phil 5525.23A   Gregory, J.C. The nature of laughter. London, 1924.

Phil 5525.23B   Gregory, J.C. The nature of laughter. London, 1924.

Phil 5525.24   Dugas, L. Psychologie du rire. Paris, 1902.

Phil 5525.26   Dumont, L. Des causes du rire. Paris, 1862.

Phil 5525.27   Talhouet, J. de. Le rire et l'origine des idées. Rennes, 1923.

Phil 5525.28   Laurentius, A.P. Dialogus pulcherrimus et utilissimus. Marpurgi, 1606.

Phil 5525.29   Gilman, Bradley. A clinic on the comic. Nice, 1926.

Phil 5525.30   Victor, C.R. Der Humor und seine Begründung. Bremen, 1925.

Phil 5525.31   Wallerstein, M. Eine Arbeit über das Lachen und des Komische. Wien, 1925.

Phil 5525.32   Armstrong, M. Laughing: an essay. N.Y., 1928.

Phil 5525.32.5   Armstrong, M. Laughing: an essay. London, 1928.

Phil 5525.33   Ziegler, J. Das Komische. Leipzig, 1900.

Phil 5525.34   Kimmins, G.W. The springs of laughter. London, 1928.

Phil 5525.35   Seward, Samuel S. The paradox of the ludicrous. Stanford, 1930.

Phil 5525.36   Menon, V.K.K. A theory of laughter. London, 1931.

Phil 5525.37   Ludovici, A.M. Secret of laughter. London, 1932.

Phil 5525.38.2   Piddington, Ralph. The psychology of laughter. 2. ed. N.Y., 1963.

Phil 5525.39   Reik, Theodor. Lust und Leid im Witz; sechs psychoanalytische Studien. Wien, 1929.

Phil 5525.39.5   Reik, Theodor. Nachdenkliche Heiterkeit. Wien, 1933.

Phil 5525.40   Victoria, Marcos. Ensayo preliminar sobre lo cómico. Buenos Aires, 1941.

Phil 5525.42   Aubouin, Elie. Les genres du risible. Marseille, 1948.

Phil 5525.42.2   Aubouin, Elie. Les genres du risible. Thèse. Marseille, 1948.

Phil 5525.42.10   Aubouin, Elie. Technique et psychologie du comique. Thèse. Marseille, 1948.

Phil 5525.43   Kalina, J. Bojové poslanie humoru a satiry. Bratislava, 1953.

Phil 5525.44   Monro, David Hector. Argument of laughter. Carlton, Victoria, 1951.

Phil 5525   Psychology - Treatises on special topics - Laughter - cont.

Phil 5525.44.5   Monro, David Hector. Argument of laughter. Notre Dame, 1963.
Phil 5525.46   Senise, T. Il riso in psicologia. Napoli, 1950.
Phil 5525.48   Wolfenstein, M. Children's humor. Glencoe, Ill., 1954.
Phil 5525.50   Esar, Evan. The humor of humor. London, 1954.
Phil 5525.52   Victoroff, D. Le rire et le risible. 1. éd. Paris, 1953.
Phil 5525.54   Bergler, Edmund. Laughter and the sense of humor. N.Y., 1956.
Phil 5525.56   Latour, Marius. Le problème du rire et du réel. Paris, 1956.
Phil 5525.58   Mason, Michael. The centre of hilarity. London, 1959.
Phil 5525.60   Introduction à l'étude scientifique du rire. n.p., n.d.
Phil 5525.61   Fry, W.F. Sweet madness. Palo Alto, 1963.
Phil 5525.62   Ramondt, Marie. Studien über des Lachen. Groningen, 1962.
Phil 5525.63   Hirsch, Wolfgang. Worüber lachen wir? Heidelberg, 1963.
Phil 5525.64   Poinsinet de Sivry, Louis. Psychologische und physiologische Untersuchung über das Lachen. Wolfenbüttel, 1794.
Phil 5525.64.5   Schweizer, Werner R. Der Witz. Bern, 1964.
Phil 5525.64.10   Holm, Søren. Humor; en aesthetisk studie. København, 1964.
Phil 5525.65   Nohain, Jean. Histoire du rure à travers le monde. Paris, 1965.
Phil 5525.65.5   Ruvo, Vincenzo de. Il riso e l'arte di ridere. Bari, 1965.
Phil 5525.68   Luk, Oleksandr N. O chuvstve iumora i ostroumii. Moskva, 1968.
Phil 5525.70   Plessner, Helmuth. Laughing and crying; a study of limits of human behavior. Evanston, 1970.
Phil 5525.72   Borev, Iurii B. Komicheskoe. Moskva, 1970.

Phil 5528   Psychology - Treatises on special topics - Laziness

Phil 5528.2   Sperisen, Walter. Arbeitsschen, eine psychologischpädagogische Studie. Bern, 1946.

Phil 5535   Psychology - Treatises on special topics - Learning

Phil 5535.1   Atkinson, Richard G. An introduction to mathematical learning theory. N.Y., 1965.
Phil 5535.2   Bush, Robert Ray. Stochastic models for learning. N.Y., 1964.
Phil 5535.2.5   Bush, Robert Ray. Studies in mathematical learning theory. Stanford, 1959.
Phil 5535.3   Smith, David D. Mammalian learning and behavior. Philadelphia, 1965.
Phil 5535.4   Foppa, Klaus. Lernen, Gedächtnis, Verhalten. Köln, 1965.
Phil 5535.6   Goss, Albert E. Paired-associates learning; the role of meaningfulness, similarity. N.Y., 1965.
Phil 5535.8   Conference on Acquisition of Skill, New Orleans. Acquisition of skill. N.Y., 1966.
Phil 5535.10.3   Hilgard, Ernest Ropiequet. Theories of learning. 3. ed. N.Y., 1966.
Phil 5535.12   Ponomarev, Iakov A. Znaniia, myshlenie i umstvennoe razvitie. Moskva, 1967.
Phil 5535.14   Rubin, Frederick. Current research in hypnopaedia; a symposium of selected literature. London, 1968.
Phil 5535.16   Wilde, Henricus Andreas Maria. Coalitie formatie in triades. Rotterdam, 1968.
Phil 5535.18   Wictorin, Mauritz. Bidrag till zäknefärdighetens psykologi akademisk. Göteborg, 1952.
Phil 5535.20   Lunzer, Eric Anthony. Development in learning. London, 1968- 3v.
Phil 5535.22   Losifeseu, Marius. Random processes and learning. Berlin, 1969.
Phil 5535.24   Marnet, Otto. Soziales Lernen; das Problem der Lertheorien in der Sozialpsychologie. Zürich, 1968.
Phil 5535.26   Biggs, John Burville. Information and human learning. Melbourne, 1968.
Phil 5535.28   Nuttin, Jozef. Tâche réussite et échec. Louvain, 1953.
Phil 5535.28.5   Nuttin, Jozef. Reward and punishment in human learning: elements of a behavior theory. N.Y., 1968.
Phil 5535.30   Lovejoy, Elijah. Attention in discrimination learning; a point of view and a theory. San Francisco, 1968.
Phil 5535.32   Toğrol, Beğlan. Duygusal anlam sistemlesi. Istanbul, 1967.
Phil 5535.34   Rogers, Carl Ransom. Freedom to learn. Columbus, Ohio, 1969.
Phil 5535.36   On the biology of learning. N.Y., 1969.
Phil 5535.38   Green, Edward J. An annotated bibliography of visual discrimination learning. N.Y., 1969.
Phil 5535.40   Annett, John. Feedback and human behavior. Baltimore, 1969.
Phil 5535.42   Kintsch, Walter. Learning, memory, and conceptual processes. N.Y., 1970.
Phil 5535.44   Sluckin, Wladyslaw. Early learning in man and animal. London, 1970.
Phil 5535.46   Estes, William Kaye. Learning theory and mental development. N.Y., 1970.
Phil 5535.48   Der Lernprozess. Anthropologie, Psychologie, Biologie des Lernens. Freiburg, 1969.
Phil 5535.50   Sahakian, William S. Psychology of learning. Chicago, 1970.
Phil 5535.52   Wendeler, Jürgen. Elementare Lernprinzipien; Darstellung und Modifikation von Postulaten der Hull'schen Theorie. Weinheim, 1969.
Phil 5535.54   Saltz, Eli. The cognitive bases of human learning. Homewood, 1971.
Phil 5535.56   Lawson, Philippe Reed. Learning and behavior. N.Y., 1960.
Phil 5535.58   Goguelin, Pierre. La formation continue des adultes. 1. ed. Paris, 1970.
Phil 5535.60   Dienes, Zoltan Paul. The effects of structural relations on transfer. London, 1970.
Phil 5535.62   Haseloff, Otto Walter. Psychologie des Lernens: Methoden, Ergebnisse, Anwendungen. Berlin, 1970.
Phil 5535.64   Buck, Günther. Lernen und Erfahrung. Stuttgart, 1967.

Phil 5545   Psychology - Treatises on special topics - Memory

Phil 5545.1   Arréat, L. Mémoire et imagination. Paris, 1895.
Phil 5545.2   Biervliet, J.J. von. La mémoire. Gand, 1893.
Phil 5545.2.6   Biervliet, J.J. von. Esquisse d'une éducation de la mémoire. 2. éd. Gand, 19- .
Phil 5545.3   Boucher, J. Des idées innées de la mémoire. Paris, 1867.
Htn   Phil 5545.4*   Butler, S. Unconscious memory. London, 1880.
Phil 5545.5   Ebbinghaus, H. Über das Gedächtnis. Leipzig, 1885.
Phil 5545.5.7A   Ebbinghaus, H. Memory. N.Y., 1913.
Phil 5545.5.7B   Ebbinghaus, H. Memory. N.Y., 1913.
Phil 5545.5.7C   Ebbinghaus, H. Memory. N.Y., 1913.
Phil 5545.5.9   Ebbinghaus, H. Memory. N.Y., 1964.

Phil 5545   Psychology - Treatises on special topics - Memory - cont.

Phil 5545.6   Colegrove, F.W. Memory. N.Y., 1900.
Phil 5545.7   Evans, W.L. Memory training. N.Y., 1889.
Phil 5545.8   Fauth, F. Das Gedächtnis. Gütersloh, 1888.
Phil 5545.9   Feinaigle, G. von. New art of memory. London, 1812.
Phil 5545.10   Fauvel-Gourand, F. Phreno-mnemotechny. v.1-2. N.Y., 1844.
Phil 5545.10.5   Fauvel-Gourand, F. Phreno-mnemotechny dictionary. pt.1. N.Y., 1844.
Phil 5545.10.9   Fauvel-Gourand, F. First fundamental basis of phreno-mnemotechnic principles. N.Y., 1844.
Phil 5545.10.10   Fauvel-Gourand, F. Phreno-mnemotechny. n.p., 1844.
NEDL   Phil 5545.11   Granville, J.M. Secret of a good memory. Boston, 1887.
Phil 5545.11.5   Granville, J.M. Secret of a good memory. n.p., 1906.
Phil 5545.12   Gratacap, A. Théorie de la mémoire. Montpellier, 1866.
Phil 5545.13   Grey, R. Memoria technica. London, 1730.
Phil 5545.13.2   Grey, R. Memoria technica. Dublin, 1796.
Phil 5545.13.3   Grey, R. Memoria technica. London, 1806.
Phil 5545.14   Holbrook, M.S. How to strengthen the memory. N.Y., n.d.
Phil 5545.14.2   Holbrook, M.S. How to strengthen the memory. N.Y., 1886.
Phil 5545.15   Huber, J.N. Psychologische Studien. München, 1878.
Phil 5545.16   Jastrow, J. Statistical study of memory. N.Y., 1891.
Phil 5545.17   Kay, D. Memory. London, 1888.
Phil 5545.17.3   Kay, D. Memory. N.Y., 1888.
Phil 5545.18   Leland, C.G. Mastery of memorizing. Harrisburg, 1890-91.
Phil 5545.19   Miles, Pliny. American mnemotechny. N.Y., 1848.
Phil 5545.19.5   Miles, Pliny. Mnemotechny, or art of memory. 1. English ed. London, 1850.
Phil 5545.20   Miller, Adam. Mental gymnastics. Chicago, 1886.
Phil 5545.20.5   Miller, Adam. Mental gymnastics, or lessons on memory. 4. ed. Chicago, 1886.
Phil 5545.21   Pick, E. Memory and its doctors. London, 1888.
Phil 5545.21.5   Pick, E. Lectures on memory culture. N.Y., 1899.
Phil 5545.22   Ribot, T. Les maladies de la mémoire. Paris, 1881.
Phil 5545.22.2   Ribot, T. Les maladies de la mémoire. Paris, 1881.
Phil 5545.22.5   Ribot, T. Diseases of memory. N.Y., 1882.
Phil 5545.22.6   Ribot, T. Diseases of memory. N.Y., 1883.
Phil 5545.22.10   Ribot, T. Viljans sjukdomar. 6. uppl. Stockholm, 1890.
Phil 5545.23   Stokes, W. Memory. London, 1888.
Phil 5545.24   Thompson, L. Influence of memory. Boston, 1840.
Phil 5545.25   Ward, G.W. Dates by name. Baltimore, 1892.
Phil 5545.26   Art of memory. London, 1823.
Phil 5545.27   Edridge-Green, F.W. Memory and its cultivation. N.Y., 1897.
Phil 5545.28   Fowler, O.G. Fowler on memory, phrenology...cultivation of memory. N.Y., 1842.
Phil 5545.29   Fuller, H.H. The art of memory. St. Paul, Minn., 1898.
Phil 5545.30   Smith, D.T. The philosophy of memory. Louisville, Ky., 1899.
Phil 5545.31   Sollier, P. La problème de la mémoire. Paris, 1900.
Phil 5545.31.5   Sollier, P. Les troubles de la mémoire. Paris, 1901.
Phil 5545.32   Johnson, L.D. Memoria technica. 3. ed. Boston, 1847.
Phil 5545.33   Ogden, R.M. Untersuchungen über den Einfluss der Geschwindigkeit des lauten Lesens. Leipzig, 1903.
Phil 5545.34   Siehl, A. Zum Studium der Merkfähigkeit. Berlin, 1902.
Phil 5545.35   Henderson, E.N. A study of memory. n.p., n.d.
Phil 5545.36   Paulhan, F. La fonction de la mémoire. Paris, 1904.
Phil 5545.37   Hering, Ewald. Über das Gedächtnis. Leipzig, 1905.
Phil 5545.37.5   Hering, Ewald. On memory and specific energies of the nervous system. 2. ed. Chicago, 1897.
Phil 5545.37.10   Hering, Ewald. On memory and the specific energies of the nervous system. 4. ed. Chicago, 1905.
Phil 5545.38   Loisette, A. Assimilative memory. N.Y., 1896.
Phil 5545.38.25   Pamphlet box. Loisette, Alphonse.
Phil 5545.38.26   Fellows, G.S. "Loisette" exposed. N.Y., n.d.
Phil 5545.39   Ephrussi, P. Experimentalle Beiträge...vom Gedächtnis. Leipzig, 1904.
Phil 5545.40   Pohlmann, A. Experimentalle Beiträge zur Lehre vom Gedächtnis. Berlin, 1906.
Phil 5545.41   Ziehen, T. Das Gedächtnis. Berlin, 1908.
Phil 5545.42   Austriacus, J. De memoria artificios a lebellus. Argentorati, 1603.
Phil 5545.44   Peiron, Henri. L'évolution de la mémoire. Paris, 1910.
Phil 5545.46   Meumann, E. Ökonomie und Technik des Gedächtnisses. Leipzig, 1908.
Phil 5545.47   Peillaube, E. Les images. Paris, 1910.
Phil 5545.48   Watt, H.J. Economy and training of memory. N.Y., 1911.
Phil 5545.49.3A   Meumann, E. The psychology of learning. N.Y., 1913.
Phil 5545.49.3B   Meumann, E. The psychology of learning. N.Y., 1913.
NEDL   Phil 5545.50   Middleton, A.E. Memory systems. 1. American ed. N.Y., 1888.
Phil 5545.50.5   Verneuil, Henri. La mémoire au point de vue physiologique. Paris, 1888.
Phil 5545.51   Test of accuracy of testimony of by-standers. n.p., 1912.
Htn   Phil 5545.52*   Romberch, J. Congestorium artificiose. Venetijs, 1533.
Phil 5545.53   D., T.W. Mnemonics. N.Y., 1844.
Phil 5545.54   Semon, R. Die Mneme als erhaltendes Prinzip im Wechsel des organischen Gesehens. 3. Aufl. Leipzig, 1911.
Phil 5545.54.5   Semon, R. Die mnemischen Empfindungen. Leipzig, 1909.
Phil 5545.54.10   Semon, R. The mneme. Leipzig, 1921.
Phil 5545.54.15   Semon, R. Mnemic psychology. N.Y., 1923.
Phil 5545.55   Myers, G.C. Study in incidental memory. N.Y., 1913.
Phil 5545.56   Miles, E.H. How to remember without memory systems or wi them. London, 1901.
Phil 5545.58   Coover, J.E. Formal discipline...experimental psychology. Thesis. Princeton, 1916.
Phil 5545.59   Perrin, F.A.C. An experimental...study of human learning. Princeton, 1914.
Phil 5545.60   Jackson, George. Jackson's new...system of mnemonics. London, 1816.
Phil 5545.61   DeCamp, J.E. Study of retroactive inhibition. Thesis. Princeton, 1915.
Phil 5545.62   Martin, M.A. Transfer effects of practice in cancellation tests. N.Y., 1915.
Phil 5545.63   Offner, Max. Das Gedächtnis. Berlin, 1909.
Phil 5545.63.2   Offner, Max. Das Gedächtnis. 2. Aufl. Berlin, 1911.
Phil 5545.63.5   Offner, Max. Das Gedächtnis. Berlin, 1913.
Phil 5545.64   Mnemosyne, Organ für Gedächtniskunst. Leipzig, 1883-1885.
Phil 5545.65   Dugas, L. La mémoire et l'oubli. Paris, 1917.
Phil 5545.65.10   Dugas, L. Les maladies de la mémoire et de l'imagination. Paris, 1931.
Phil 5545.66   Renda, A. L'oblio; saggio sull'attività selettiva della coscienza. Torino, 1910.
Phil 5545.67   Henry, Charles. Mémoire et habitude. Paris, 1911.
Phil 5545.68   Gallinger, A. Zur Grundlegung einer Lehre von der Erinnerung. Halle, 1914.
Phil 5545.69   Dandolo, Giovanni. La dottrina della "memoria", tedesco. Padova, 1893.
Phil 5545.69.5   Dandolo, Giovanni. La memoria. Messina, 1903.

Classified Listing

Phil 5545 Psychology - Treatises on special topics - Memory - cont.

Phil 5545.69.15 Dandolo, Giovanni. La dottrina della memoria. Réggio nell'Emilia, 1891.

Phil 5545.70 Kjerstad, C.L. The form of the learning curves for memory. Private ed. Chicago, 191-?

Phil 5545.71 Uphues, Goswin K. Über die Erinnerung. Leipzig, 1889.

Phil 5545.72 Leroy, Eugène B. Étude sur l'illusion de fausse reconnaissance. Paris, 1898.

Phil 5545.73 Eichthal, Eugène d'. Du rôle de la mémoire dans nos conceptions. Paris, 1920.

Phil 5545.74 Achilles, E.M. Experimental studies in recall and recognition. N.Y., 1920.

Phil 5545.75 Castillio, A.F. de. Tratado demnemonica. Lisboa, 1851.

Phil 5545.76 Kammel, W. Über die erste Einzelerinnerung. Leipzig, 1913.

Phil 5545.77 Binet, A. Psychologie des grands calculateurs et joueurs d'échecs. Paris, 1894.

Phil 5545.78 Erdmann, E.J.E.T. Vom Vergessen. Berlin, 1869.

Itn Phil 5545.79* Dolce, Lodovico. Dialogo nel quale si ragiona del modo di accrescere e conservar la memoria. Venetia, 1586.

Phil 5545.80 Pike, Robert, Jr. Mnemonics applied to acquisition of knowledge. Boston, 1844.

Phil 5545.81 Pike, Robert. Mnemonics. Boston, 1848.

Phil 5545.85 Gloy, Hans. Gedächtnis-Ausbildung. Berlin, 1913.

Phil 5545.90 Delay, Jean Paul Louis. Les dissolutions de la mémoire. Paris, 1942.

Phil 5545.91 Wallon, H. Les mécanismes de la mémoire en rapport avec ses objects. Paris, 1951.

Phil 5545.92 Suellwold, F. Das umittelbare Behalten. Göttingen, 1964.

tn Phil 5545.93* Doeblin, Alfred. Gedächtnisstörungen bei der Korsakoffschen Psychose. Berlin, 1905.

Phil 5545.94 Conference on Learning, Remembering and Forgetting. Learning, remembering, and forgetting. Palo Alto, 1965-

Phil 5545.95 Yates, Frances Amelia. The art of memory. London, 1966.

Phil 5545.96 Oppenheim, Abraham Naftali. Questionnaire design and attitude measurement. N.Y., 1966.

Phil 5545.97 Breer, Paul E. Task experience as a source of attitudes. Homewood, 1965.

Phil 5545.98 Bongard, Mikhail M. Problema uznavaniia. Moskva, 1967.

Phil 5545.99 Shekhter, Mark S. Psikhologicheskie problemy uznavaniia. Moskva, 1967.

Phil 5545.150 Richards, Lysander. The analysis and cause of existence of memory and The analysis and cause of unconsciousness and sleep. pt.1-2. n.p., 1920.

Phil 5545.155 Pear, T.H. Remembering and forgetting. London, 1922.

Phil 5545.156 Edgell, Beatrice. Theories of memory. Oxford, 1924.

Phil 5545.157 Loewenton, E. Versuche über das Gedächtnis. Inaug. Diss. Dorpat, 1893.

Phil 5545.158 Halbwachs, Maurice. Les cadres sociaux de la mémoire. Paris, 1925.

Phil 5545.158.5 Halbwachs, Maurice. La mémoire collective. 1. éd. Paris, 1950.

Phil 5545.159 Herrlin, Axel. Minuet. Stockholm, 1917.

Phil 5545.160 Mondolfo, R. Memoria e associazione nella scuola cartesiana. Firenze, 1900.

Phil 5545.161 Segno, A.V. The secret of memory. Los Angeles, 1906.

Phil 5545.162 Cuff, N.B. The relation of over-learning to retention. Nashville, 1927.

Phil 5545.163 Fränkl, Ernst. Über Vorstellungs-Elemente und Aufmerksamkeit. Augsburg, 1905.

Phil 5545.164 Brunswig, Alfred. Das Gedächtnis und seine Erziehung. Berlin, 1926.

Phil 5545.165 Pelman, Christopher L. Memory training, its law and their application to practical life. pts.1-5. Chicago, 1903.

Phil 5545.165.25 Pelman Institute of America. Pelmanism. Lesson 1,3-12. N.Y., 1924.

Phil 5545.166 Gamble, E.A.M. A study in memorising various materials by the reconstruction method. Lancaster, Pa., 1909.

Phil 5545.167 Memory. By an ignorant student. London, 1928.

Phil 5545.169 Ranachburg, P. Das kranke Gedachtnis. Leipzig, 1911.

Phil 5545.170 Janet, Pierre. L'évolution de la mémoire. Paris, 1928.

Phil 5545.171 Murden, J.R. The art of memory. N.Y., 1818.

Phil 5545.172 Weinland, J.D. Improving the memory for faces and names. Boston, 1934.

Phil 5545.173 Janet, Pierre. L'amnésie continue. Paris, 1893.

Phil 5545.174 Bartlett, F.C. Remembering. N.Y., 1932.

Phil 5545.174.5 Bartlett, F.C. Remembering. Cambridge, Eng., 1964.

Phil 5545.175 Augier, E. La mémoire et la vie. Paris, 1939.

Phil 5545.176 Hajdu, H. Das mnemotechnische Schrifttum. Wien, 1936.

Phil 5545.177 Hartenbach, E. Dr. Ewald Hartenbach's Kunst. 15. Aufl. Quedlinburg, 1882.

Phil 5545.179 Drees, V.J. The effects of practice on memory performance. Thesis. Washington, 1941.

Phil 5545.180 Furst, Bruno. How to remember. N.Y., 1944.

Phil 5545.181.5 Delay, Jean Paul Louis. Les maladies de la mémoire. 3. éd. Paris, 1961.

Phil 5545.182 Lasson, Adolf. Das Gedächtnis. Berlin, 1894.

Phil 5545.183 Ellenberger, F. Le mystère de la mémoire. Genève, 1947.

Phil 5545.184 Furlong, E.J. A study in memory. London, 1951.

Phil 5545.185 Wieck, H.H. Zur Psychologie und Psychopathologie der Erinnerungen. Stuttgart, 1955.

Phil 5545.186 United States Research and Development Board. Symposium on psychology of learning basic to military training problems. Washington, 1953.

Phil 5545.189 Smedslund, Jan. Multiple-probability learning. Oslo, 1955.

Phil 5545.190 Hunter, I.M.L. Memory. Harmondsworth, 1957.

Phil 5545.192 Bridoux, André. Le souvenir. 2. éd. Paris, 1956.

Phil 5545.193 Nohl, Johanna. Erinnerung und Gedächtnis. Langensalza, 1932.

Phil 5545.200 Kendall, Patricia L. Conflict and mood. Glencoe, Ill., 1954.

Phil 5545.205 Meredith, Patrick. Learning, remembering and knowing. N.Y., 1961.

Phil 5545.210 Rossi, Paolo. Clavis universalis. Milano, 1960.

Phil 5545.215 Antsyferova, L.I. O zakonomernostiakh elementarnoi poznavatel'noi deiatel'nosti. Moskva, 1961.

Phil 5545.220 Laird, Donald. Techniques for efficient remembering. N.Y., 1960.

Phil 5545.222 Gorczyński, S. Sztuka pamietania. Warszawa, 1963.

Phil 5545.223 Włodarski, Z. Pamięc jako właściowość poszczególnych analizatorów. Warszawa, 1964.

Phil 5545.224 Smith, Brian. Memory. London, 1966.

Phil 5545.225 Smirnov, Anatolii A. Problemy psikhologii pamiati. Moskva, 1966.

Phil 5545.227 Richter, Derek. Aspects of learning and memory. N.Y., 1966.

Phil 5545 Psychology - Treatises on special topics - Memory - cont.

Phil 5545.228 Rogovin, Mikhail S. Filosofskie problemy teorii pamiati. Moskva, 1966.

Phil 5545.230 Bousfield, William Robert. The basis of memory. N.Y., 1928.

Phil 5545.232 Young, John Zachary. The memory system of the brain. Berkeley, 1966.

Phil 5545.233 Katzenberger, Lothar Friedrich. Auffassung und Gedächtnis. München, 1967.

Phil 5545.235 Luriiâ, Aleksandr R. The mind of a mnemonist. N.Y., 1968.

Phil 5545.236 Luriiâ, Aleksandr R. Une prodigieuse mémoire. Neuchâtel, 1970.

Phil 5545.238 Rey, André. Les troubles de la mémoire et leur examen psychométrique. Bruxelles, 1966.

Phil 5545.240 Norman, Donald A. Memory and attention. N.Y., 1968[1969]

Phil 5545.242 Piaget, Jean. Mémoire et intelligence. Paris, 1968.

Phil 5545.244 Katzenberger, Lothar Friedrich. Dimensionen des Gedächtnisses. Wurzburg, 1964.

Phil 5545.244.1 Katzenberger, Lothar Friedrich. Gedächtnis oder Gedächtnisse? München, 1967.

Phil 5545.246 John, Erwin Roy. Mechanisms of memory. N.Y., 1967.

Phil 5545.248 Bergon, Annie van. Task interruption. Amsterdam, 1968.

Phil 5545.250 al-Ma'ayirji, Muhammad Ismat. Die postmentalen Erregungen als struktureller Faktor beim Lernen. Thesis. St. Margrethen, 1964.

Phil 5545.252 Postman, Leo Joseph. Verbal learning and memory; selected readings. Baltimore, 1970.

Phil 5545.254.2 International Interdisciplinary Conference on Learning, Remembering and Forgetting. The organization of recall; proceedings. N.Y., 1967.

Phil 5545.254.3 International Interdisciplinary Conference on Learning, Remembering and Forgetting. Readiness to remember; proceedings of the third conference on learning, remembering, and forgetting. N.Y., 1969. 2v.

Phil 5545.254.4 International Interdisciplinary Conference on Learning, Remembering and Forgetting. Experience and capacity; proceedings. N.Y., 1968.

Phil 5545.256 Problemy psikhologii pamiati. Khar'kov, 1969.

Phil 5545.258 Chauchard, Paul. Connaissance et maîtrise de la mémoire. Verviers, 1970.

Phil 5545.260 Association de Psychologie Scientifique de Langue Française. La Mémoire. 1. éd. Paris, 1970.

Phil 5545.262 Urach, Elisabeth Furstin von. Über die strukturelle Eigenart und personate Bedeutsamkeit der Erinnerung. Inaug. Diss. Bamburg, 1965.

Phil 5545.264 Tocquet, Robert. La mémoire, comment l'acquérer, comment la conserver. Paris, 1968.

Phil 5545.266 Blum, Herwig. Die antike Mnemotechnik. Thesis. Hildesheim, 1969.

Phil 5545.269 Salaman, Esther Polianowsky. A collection of moments; a study of involuntary memories. N.Y., 1972.

Phil 5545.800.-.999 Pamphlet box. Memory. Chronological file.

Phil 5548 Psychology - Treatises on special topics - Motivation

Phil 5548.3 Nebraska. University. Department of Psychology. Current theory and research in motivation, a symposium. Lincoln. 1954+ 15v.

Phil 5548.5A McClelland, D.C. The achievement nature. N.Y., 1953.

Phil 5548.5B McClelland, D.C. The achievement nature. N.Y., 1953.

Phil 5548.5.5 McClelland, D.C. The roots of consciousness. Princeton, N.J., 1964.

Phil 5548.10 Fuchs, R. Gewissheit. Meisenheim am Glan, 1954.

Phil 5548.15 United States Research and Development Board. Committee on Human Resources. Symposium on motivation. Washington, 1953.

Phil 5548.20 Olds, James. The growth and structure of motives. Glencoe, Ill., 1956.

Phil 5548.25 Schreier, F.T. Human motivation. Glencoe, Ill., 1957.

Phil 5548.30 Peters, R.S. The concept of motivation. London, 1958.

Phil 5548.30.2 Peters, R.S. The concept of motivation. 2. ed. London, 1967.

Phil 5548.35 Cattell, R.B. Personality and motivation structure and measurement. Yonkers-on-Hudson, N.Y., 1957.

Phil 5548.40 Stacey, Chalmers L. Understanding human motivation. Cleveland, 1958.

Phil 5548.45 Spiegel, Berut. Werbepsychologische Untersuchungsmethoden. Berlin, 1958.

Phil 5548.50 Lindzey, Gardner. Assessment of human motives. N.Y., 1958.

Phil 5548.50.2 Lindzey, Gardner. Assessment of human motives. N.Y., 1964.

Phil 5548.55 Ossowska, M. Motywy postępowania. Warszawa, 1958.

Phil 5548.60 Bindra, Dalbir. Motivation. N.Y., 1959.

Phil 5548.65 Association de Psychologie Scientifique de Langue Française. La motivation. 1. éd. Paris, 1959.

Phil 5548.70 Dollard, John. Scoring human motives. New Haven, 1959.

Phil 5548.75 Toman, Walter. An introduction to psychoanalytic theory of motivation. N.Y., 1960.

Phil 5548.75.5 Toman, Walter. Motivation, Persönlichkeit, Umwelt. Göttingen, 1968.

Phil 5548.80 Brown, J.S. The motivation of behavior. N.Y., 1961.

Phil 5548.83 Iff, Werner. La motivation à l'avancement professionnel. Paris, 1962.

Phil 5548.85A Atkinson, John W. Motives in fantasy, action, and society. Princeton, 1958.

Phil 5548.85B Atkinson, John W. Motives in fantasy, action, and society. Princeton, 1958.

Phil 5548.85.2 Atkinson, John W. Motives in fantasy, action, and society. Princeton, 1968.

Phil 5548.85.5 Atkinson, John W. An introduction to motivation. Princeton, 1964.

Phil 5548.90 Young, Paul Thomas. Motivation and emotion. N.Y., 1961.

Phil 5548.95 Madsen, Kaj Berg. Theories of motivation. Copenhagen, 1959.

Phil 5548.95.4 Madsen, Kaj Berg. Theories of motivation; a comparative study. 4. ed. Kent, Ohio, 1968.

Phil 5548.98 Maslow, Abraham Harold. Motivation and personality. 2. ed. N.Y., 1970.

Phil 5548.100 Maslow, Abraham Harold. Toward a psychology of being. Princeton, 1962.

Phil 5548.100.2 Maslow, Abraham Harold. Toward a psychology of being. 2. ed. Princeton, 1968.

Phil 5548.101 Langkjaer, Asger. Contributions to a general normalogy, or Theory of purpose-setting. København, 1961.

Phil 5548.102 Harvey, O.J. Motivation and social interaction. N.Y., 1963.

Phil 5548   Psychology - Treatises on special topics - Motivation - cont.

Phil 5548.103   Heckhausen, H. Hoffnung und Furcht in der Leistungsmotivation. Meisenheim, 1963.

Phil 5548.103.5   Heckhausen, H. The anatomy of achievement motivation. N.Y., 1967.

Phil 5548.104   Dichter, E. Handbook of consumer motivations. N.Y., 1964.

Phil 5548.105   Thomae, Hans. Die Motivation menschlichen Handelns. Köln, 1965.

Phil 5548.106   Haber, Ralph Norman. Current research in motivation. N.Y., 1966.

Phil 5548.107   Johannesson, Ingvar. Effects of praise and blame. Stockholm, 1967.

Phil 5548.108   Atkinson, John W. A theory of achievement motivation. N.Y., 1966.

Phil 5548.108.5   Atkinson, John W. The dynamics of action. N.Y., 1970.

Phil 5548.110   Teevan, Richard Collier. Theories of motivation in learning. Princeton, 1964.

Phil 5548.112   Kages, Wolfgang. Der menschliche Antrieb. Psychologie und Psychopathologie. Stuttgart, 1967.

Phil 5548.115   DeCharms, Richard. Personal causation. N.Y., 1968.

Phil 5548.120   Litwin, George Henry. Motivation and organizational climate. Boston, 1968.

Phil 5548.125   McClelland, David Clarence. Motivating economic achievement. N.Y., 1969.

Phil 5548.130   Vernon, Magdalen Dorothea. Human motivation. London, 1969.

Phil 5548.135   Reiss, Gretel. Der Einfluss von Erfolgs- und Misserfolgsmotivierung auf das Behalten eigener Leistungen. Inaug. Diss. Münster? 1968?

Phil 5548.140   Ryan, Thomas Arthur. Intentional behavior; an approach to human motivation. N.Y., 1970.

Phil 5548.142   Bloeschl, Lilian. Belohnung und Bestrafung im Lernexperiment. Weinheim, 1969.

Phil 5548.144   Keiler, Peter. Wollen und Wert. Berlin, 1970.

Phil 5548.146   Stückmann, Günther. Der Berufserfolg als Motivationsphänomen. Berlin, 1968.

Phil 5548.148   Vontobel, Jacques. Leistungsbedürfnis und soziale Umwelt. Bern, 1970.

Phil 5548.150   Russell, Wallace Addison. Milestones in motivation; contributions to the psychology of drive and purpose. N.Y., 1970.

Phil 5585   Psychology - Treatises on special topics - Perception

Phil 5585.01   Pamphlet box. Perception.

Phil 5585.02   Pamphlet vol. Time perception. 26 pam.

Phil 5585.05   Pamphlet box. Perception. German dissertations.

Phil 5585.1   Böhmer, H. Die Sinneswahrnehmung. Erlangen, 1868.

Phil 5585.1.5   Vierordt, Karl. Der Zeitsinn nach Versuchen. Tübingen, 1868.

Phil 5585.2   Duttenhofer. Die acht Sinne des Menschen. Nördlingen, 1858.

Phil 5585.3   Helmholtz, Hermann van. Thatsachen in der Wahrnehmung. Berlin, 1879.

Phil 5585.3.5A   Helmholtz, Hermann van. Helmholtz on perception; its physiology and development. N.Y., 1968.

Phil 5585.3.5B   Helmholtz, Hermann van. Helmholtz on perception; its physiology and development. N.Y., 1968.

Phil 5585.4   Lukens, H.T. Die Vorstellungsreihen. Gütersloh, 1892.

Phil 5585.5   Pattern recognition. N.Y. 1,1968+ 3v.

Phil 5585.6   Preyer, W. Über die Grenzen des Empfindungsvermögens und des Willens. Bonn, 1868.

Phil 5585.7   Rau, A. Empfinden und Denken. Giessen, 1896.

Phil 5585.7.5   Rau, A. Das Wesen des menschlichen Verstandus und Bewusstseins. München, 1910.

Phil 5585.8   Redern, S.E. de. Des modes accidentels de nos perceptions. Paris, 1818.

Phil 5585.9   Sergi, G. Teoria fisiologica della percezione. Milano, 1881.

Phil 5585.9.5   Heman, Karl F. Die Erscheinung der Dinge. Leipzig, 1881.

Phil 5585.10   Schwarz, H. Das Wahrnehmungsproblem. Leipzig, 1892.

Phil 5585.10.5   Schwarz, H. Umwälzung der Wahrnehmungshypothesen. Leipzig, 1895.

Phil 5585.11   Uphues, G.K. Wahrnehmung und Empfindung. Leipzig, 1888.

Phil 5585.11.11F   La Rive, Lucien de. Sur la collection des sensations. Genève, 1888.

Phil 5585.12   Pierce, A.H. Studies in auditory and visual space perception. N.Y., 1901.

Phil 5585.13   Pearce, H.J. Über den Einfluss von Nebenreizen. Leipzig, 1903.

Phil 5585.14   Wrinch, F.S. Über das Verhältniss der Ebenmerk...Gebiet des Zeitsinns. Leipzig, 1902.

Phil 5585.15   Meinong, A. Untersuchungen zur Gegenstandstheorie und Psychologie. Leipzig, 1904.

Phil 5585.16   Katz, David. Experimentelle Beiträge zur Psychologie...des Zeitsinns. Leipzig, 1906.

Phil 5585.17   Hamilton, F.M. The perceptual factors in reading. N.Y., 1907.

Phil 5585.18   Downey, June Etta. Control processes in modified hand-writing. Chicago? 1908?

Phil 5585.19   Büttner, A. Zweierlei Denken. Leipzig, 1910.

Phil 5585.20   Siegel, Carl. Entwickelung der Raumvorstellung. Leipzig, 1899.

Phil 5585.21   Stiborius. Die Kategorien der sinnlichen Perception. Leipzig, 1890.

Phil 5585.22   Nichols, H. The psychology of time. N.Y., 1891.

Phil 5585.23   Braude, M. Die Elemente der Reinen Wahrnehmung. Lemberg, 1899.

Phil 5585.24   Claparède, E. Expériences collectives sur le...confrontation. Genève, 1906.

Phil 5585.25   Cyon, Elie von. Das Ohrlabyrinth als Organ der mathematischen Sinne fur Raum und Zeit. Berlin, 1908.

Phil 5585.27   Benussi, Vittorio. Psychologie der Zeitauffassung. Heidelberg, 1913.

Phil 5585.29   Linke, Paul F. Grundlagen der Wahrnehmungslehre. München, 1918.

Phil 5585.29.2   Linke, Paul F. Grundlagen der Wahrnehmungslehre. 2. Aufl. München, 1928.

Phil 5585.31   Steinberg, Wilhelm. Die Raumwahrnehmung der Blinden. München, 1920.

Phil 5585.32   Lavelle, Louis. La dialectique du monde sensible. Strasbourg, 1921.

Phil 5585.32.3   Lavelle, Louis. La dialectique du monde sensible. Thèse. Strasbourg, 1921. 2 pam.

Phil 5585.33   Lavelle, Louis. La perception visuelle de la profondeur. Strasbourg, 1921.

Phil 5585.34   Müller, Georg E. Komplextheorie und Gestalttheorie. Göttingen, 1923.

Phil 5585   Psychology - Treatises on special topics - Perception - cont.

Phil 5585.35   Hazelhoff, F.F. De waarnemingstijd. Proefschrift. Groningen, 1923.

Phil 5585.37   Garrison, W.A. The effect of varied instructions on the perception of distance in terms of arm-movement. Ithaca, 1924.

Phil 5585.38   Müller, Günter. Theorie des Vorstellungsverlaufs. Mannheim, 1925.

Phil 5585.39A   Parsons, John H. An introduction to the theory of perception. Cambridge, 1927.

Phil 5585.39B   Parsons, John H. An introduction to the theory of perception. Cambridge, 1927.

Phil 5585.39C   Parsons, John H. An introduction to the theory of perception. Cambridge, 1927.

Phil 5585.40.2   Jaeusch, Erich. Über den Aufbau der Wahrnehmungswelt. 2. Aufl. Leipzig, 1927-1931. 2v.

Phil 5585.41   Dandolo, G. Le integrazioni psichiche e la percezione. Padova, 1898.

Phil 5585.42   Palágyi, M. Wahrnehmungslehre. Leipzig, 1925.

Phil 5585.43   Hamburger, R. Neue Theorie der Wahrnehmung und des Denkens. Berlin, 1927.

Phil 5585.44   Schapp, W. Beiträge zur Phänomenologie der Wahrnehmung. Halle, 1910.

Phil 5585.44.2   Schapp, W. Beiträge zur Phänomenologie der Wahrnehmung. Erlangen, 1925.

Phil 5585.45   Sachs, H. Die Entstehung der Raumvorstellung. Breslau, 1897.

Phil 5585.46   Weber, Christian. The concept of duration as key to the logical forms of reason. Thesis. Lincoln, 1925.

Phil 5585.47   Messenger, J. Franklin. Perception of number. Thesis. N.Y., 1903.

Phil 5585.48   Jaager, Johan J. de. De physiologische tijd bij psychische processen. Proefschrift. Utrecht, 1865.

Phil 5585.49   Rogers, Anna Sophie. An analytic study of visual perceptions. Thesis. Worcester, Mass., 1917.

Phil 5585.50   Hoisington, Louis B. On the non-visual perception of the length of lifted rods. Thesis. Worcester, Mass., 1920.

Phil 5585.51   Wooster, Margaret. Certain factors in the development of a new spatial co-ordination. Thesis. Princeton, 1923.

Phil 5585.52   Böse, Karl G. Über Sinneswahrnehmung und deren Entwicklung zur Intelligenz. Braunschweig, 1872.

Phil 5585.53   Rohde, F. Sinneswahrnehmungen und Sinnestäuschungen. Braunsberg, 1877.

Phil 5585.54   Duret, René. L'objet de la perception. Thèse. Paris, 1929.

Phil 5585.54.2   Duret, René. L'objet de la perception. Thèse. Paris, 1929.

Phil 5585.54.5   Duret, René. Les facteurs pratiques de la croyance dans la perception. Thèse. Paris, 1929.

Phil 5585.54.7   Duret, René. Les facteurs pratiques de la croyance dans la perception. Paris, 1929?

Phil 5585.55   Dehove, H. La perception exterieure. Lille, 1931.

Phil 5585.56   Fröhlich, F.W. Die Empfindungszeit. Jena, 1929.

Phil 5585.57   Seward, John P. The effect of practice on the visual perception of form. N.Y., 1931.

Phil 5585.58.5   Price, Henry H. Perception. London, 1954.

Phil 5585.58.7   Price, Henry H. Perception. London, 1964.

Phil 5585.59   Brunswick, E. Wahrnehmung und Gegenstandswelt. Leipzig, 1934.

Phil 5585.60   Carr, H.A. An introduction to space perception. N.Y., 1935.

Phil 5585.61   Vernon, M.D. Visual perception. Cambridge, Eng., 1937.

Phil 5585.62   Akishige, Yoshiharu. Experimentelle Untersuchungen über die Struktur des Wahrnehmungsraumes. Fukuoka, 1937.

Phil 5585.63   Cresson, A. La représentation. Paris, 1936.

Phil 5585.64   Nogué, Jean. La signification du sensible. Paris, 1936.

Phil 5585.64.5   Nogué, Jean. La signification du sensible. Thèse. Paris, 1936.

Phil 5585.65   Bender, L. A visual motor gestalt test. N.Y., 1938.

Phil 5585.66   Klages, L. Vom Wesen des Rhythmus. Kampen auf Sylt, 1934.

Phil 5585.67   Sechenov, I.M. Elementy mysli. Moskva, 1943.

Phil 5585.67.5   Sechenov, I.M. Izbrannye filosofskie i psikhologicheskie proizvedeniia. Moskva, 1947.

Phil 5585.68   Thurstone, L.L. A factorial study of perception. Chicago, 1944.

Phil 5585.70   Gibson, J. The perception of the visual world. Boston, 1950.

Phil 5585.71   Paliard, J. Pensée implicite et perception visuelle. Paris, 1949.

Phil 5585.72   Blake, R.R. Perception. N.Y., 1951.

Phil 5585.73   Volkov, N.N. Vospriiatie predmeta i risunka. Moskva, 1950.

Phil 5585.74   Akademiia Nauk, SSSR. Institut Filosofii. Sektsiia Psikhologii. Issledovaniia po psikhologii vospriiatiia; sbornik. Moskva, 1948.

Phil 5585.75   Brain, W.R. Mind, perception and science. Oxford, 1951.

Phil 5585.77   Rausch, E. Struktur und Metrik figuraloptischer Wahrnehmung. Frankfurt, 1952.

Phil 5585.78   Allport, F.H. Theories of perception and the concept of structure. N.Y., 1955.

Phil 5585.80   Association de Psychologie Scientifique de Langue Française. La perception. Paris, 1955.

Phil 5585.81   Smythies, J.R. Analysis of perception. London, 1956.

Phil 5585.82A   Mayo, Elton. Achieving sanity in the modern world. Cambridge, Mass., 194-?

Phil 5585.82B   Mayo, Elton. Achieving sanity in the modern world. Cambridge, Mass., 194-?

Phil 5585.85   Smirnov, M.T. Protsess poznaniia v obuchenii. Moskva, 1956.

Phil 5585.90   Chisholm, R.M. Perceiving. Ithaca, 1957.

Phil 5585.95   Becker, Egon. Mengenvergleich und Übung. Frankfurt, 1957.

Phil 5585.100   Linschoten, J. Strukturanalyse der binokularen Tiefenwahrnehmung. Groningen, 1956.

Phil 5585.105   Schmeidler, G. ESP and personality patterns. New Haven, 1958.

Phil 5585.110   Eysenck, Hans Jurgen. Perceptual processes and mental illness. N.Y., 1957.

Phil 5585.115   Beardslee, D.C. Readings in perception. Princeton, 1958.

Phil 5585.120   Bartley, S.H. Principles of perception. N.Y., 1958.

Phil 5585.125   Tagiuri, Renato. Person perception and interpersonal behavior. Stanford, 1958.

Phil 5585.125.3   Tagiuri, Renato. Person perception and interpersonal behavior. Stanford, 1958.

Phil 5585.130   Ehrenzweig, Anton. The psycho-analysis of artistic vision and hearing. London, 1953.

Phil 5585.130.2   Ehrenzweig, Anton. The psycho-analysis of artistic vision and hearing. 2d ed. N.Y., 1965.

Phil 5585   Psychology - Treatises on special topics - Perception - cont.

Phil 5585.135   Logique et Perception. Logique et perception.
Paris, 1958.

Phil 5585.138   Zoltobrocki, Josefa. Über systematische Fehler bei
wiederholter Schätzung von Zeitintervallen.
Frankfurt, 1965.

Phil 5585.140   Fraisse, Paul. Psychologie du temps. 1. éd. Paris, 1957.

Phil 5585.140.2   Fraisse, Paul. Psychologie du temps. 2. éd. Helsinki, 1967.

Phil 5585.140.3   Fraisse, Paul. The psychology of time. N.Y., 1963.

Phil 5585.140.5   Fraisse, Paul. Les structures rythmiques. Thèse.
Bruxelles, 1956.

Phil 5585.141   Lévy-Valensi, Elaine Amado. Le temps dans la vie
psychologique. Paris, 1965.

Phil 5585.145   Murloo, Abraham. The two faces of man. N.Y., 1954.

Phil 5585.150   Solley, Charles. Development of the perceptual world.
N.Y., 1960.

Phil 5585.155   Johansen, Martin. Voluminalfigurale faenomener.
København, 1959.

Phil 5585.160   Wapner, Seymour. Perceptual development. Worcester,
Mass., 1957.

Phil 5585.165   Kilpatrick, F.P. Explorations in transactional psychology.
N.Y., 1961.

Phil 5585.170   Anan'ev, B.G. Psikhologiia chuvstvennogo poznaniia.
Moskva, 1960.

Phil 5585.170.5   Anan'ev, B.G. Psychologie der sinnlichen Erkenntnis.
Berlin, 1963.

Phil 5585.175   Ames, Adelbert. The morning notes of Adelbert Ames, Jr.
New Brunswick, N.J., 1960.

Phil 5585.180   Hamlyn, David Walter. Sensation and perception.
N.Y., 1961.

Phil 5585.185   Moreau, J. L'horizon des esprits. Paris, 1960.

Phil 5585.190   Ittelson, William H. Perceptual changes in
psychopathology. New Brunswick, N.J., 1961.

Phil 5585.190.5   Ittelson, William H. Visual space perception. N.Y., 1960.

Phil 5585.195   Piaget, Jean. Les mécanismes perceptifs. Paris, 1961.

Phil 5585.195.5   Piaget, Jean. The mechanisms of perception. London, 1969.

Phil 5585.200   Rommetveit, R. Selectivity, intuition and halo effects in
social perception. Oslo, 1960.

Phil 5585.205   Dember, William Norton. The psychology of perception.
N.Y., 1961.

Phil 5585.205.5   Dember, William Norton. Visual perception: the nineteenth
century. N.Y., 1964.

Phil 5585.210   Taylor, James. The behavioral basis of perception. New
Haven, 1962.

Phil 5585.211   Michotte, Albert. Causalité, permanence et réalité
phénoménales. Louvain, 1962.

Phil 5585.212   Smith, Karl. Perception and motion; analysis of
space-structured behavior. Philadelphia, 1962.

Phil 5585.213   Vernon, Magdalen. The psychology of perception.
Harmondsworth, 1962.

Phil 5585.214   Jordan, Nehemiah. Perception. Santa Monica, 1961.

Phil 5585.215   Fisandt, Kai von. Havaitsemisen maailma. Helsinki, 1962.

Phil 5585.216   Thinès, G. Contribution à la théorie de la causalité
perceptive. Louvain, 1962.

Phil 5585.217   Kottenhoff, H. Was ist richtiges Sehen mit Umkehrbillen.
Meisenheim am Glan, 1961.

Phil 5585.218   Galindez, J. El papel del cuerpo en la percepción.
Tucuman, 1963.

Phil 5585.220   Ey, Henri. La conscience. Paris, 1963.

Phil 5585.222   Fauville, A. Perception tachistoscopique et communication.
Louvain, 1963.

Phil 5585.223   Francès, R. Quelques aspects du développement perceptif.
Paris, 1962.

Phil 5585.224   Grauman, C.F. Grundlagen einer Phänomenologie und
Psychologie der Perspektivität. Berlin, 1960.

Phil 5585.225   Sokolov, E.N. Perception and the conditioned reflex.
Oxford, 1963.

Phil 5585.226   Mueller, Kurt. Der Aufbau figural-optischer Phänomene bei
sukzessiver Reizung. Frankfurt, 1963.

Phil 5585.227   Oñativia, O.V. Dimensiones de la percepcion.
Tucuman, 1963.

Phil 5585.228   Mashhour, M. Psychophysical relations in the perception of
velocity. Stockholm, 1964.

Phil 5585.229   Hochberg, Julian E. Perception. Englewood Cliffs,
N.J., 1964.

Phil 5585.230   Smith, Ian Macfarlane. Spatial ability. 1. ed. San Diego,
Calif., 1964.

Phil 5585.231   Garnett, Arthur Campbell. The perceptual process.
London, 1965.

Phil 5585.232   Vekker, Lev M. Vospriiatie i osnovy ego modelirovaniia.
Leningrad, 1964.

Phil 5585.233   Chateau, Jean. Attitudes intellectuelles et spatiales dans
le dessin. Paris, 1965.

Phil 5585.234   Mikhailov, Feliks T. Zagadka chelovecheskogo Ia.
Moskva, 1964.

Phil 5585.235   Weber, Klaus. Wahrnehmung und mnemische Verarbeitung
wertbetonter Reihen. Stuttgart, 1964?

Phil 5585.236   Bach, Marcus. The power of perception. Garden City, 1966.

Phil 5585.237   Hall, Edward Twitchell. The hidden dimension. 1. ed.
Garden City, N.Y., 1966.

Phil 5585.238   Staniland, Alan Charles. Patterns of redundancy.
Cambridge, Eng., 1966.

Phil 5585.240   Forgus, Ronald H. Perception. N.Y., 1966.

Phil 5585.242   Hamlyn, David Walter. The psychology of perception.
London, 1961.

Phil 5585.243   Gibson, James Jerome. The senses considered as perceptual
systems. Boston, 1966.

Phil 5585.244   Kidd, Aline Halstead. Perceptual development in children.
N.Y., 1966.

Phil 5585.245   Business Research Limited, Bangkok. Esthetic perception of
villagers in Northeast Thailand, a pilot study.
Bangkok? 1965.

Phil 5585.246   Ferenczi, Victor. La perception de l'espace projectif.
(Etude réalisée auprès des travailleurs africains
analphabètes en France. Montréal, 1966.

Phil 5585.248   Michon, John Albertus. Timing in temporal tracking.
Proefschrift. Essen, 1967.

Phil 5585.250   Green, David Marvin. Signal detection theory and
psychophysics. N.Y., 1966.

Phil 5585.252   Fellows, Brian S. The discrimination process and
development. 1. ed. Oxford, 1968.

Phil 5585.255   Musatti, Cesare L. Condizioni dell'esperienza e fondazione
della psicologia. Firenze, 1964.

Phil 5585.260   Kolers, Paul A. Recognizing patterns; studies in living
and automatic systems. Cambridge, 1968.

Phil 5585.265   Warr, Peter Bryan. The perception of people and events.
London, 1968.

Phil 5585   Psychology - Treatises on special topics - Perception - cont.

Phil 5585.266   Anan'ev, Boris G. Individual'noe razvitie cheloveka i
konstantnost' vospriiatiia. Moskva, 1968.

Phil 5585.270   Bánfeti Fuchs, Károly Miklás. Problemen der subliminale
perceptie. Assen, 1964.

Phil 5585.275   Richerche sperimentali sulla percezione. Trieste, 1968.

Phil 5585.280   Reese, Hayne Waring. The perception of stimulus relations.
N.Y., 1968.

Phil 5585.285   Zwaan, Evert Joost. Links en rechts in waarneming en
beleving. Proefschrift. Utrecht, 1965.

Phil 5585.290   Laurondeau, Monique. La premières notions spatiales de
l'enfant. Neuchâtel, 1968.

Phil 5585.291   Laurondeau, Monique. The development of the concept of
space in the child. N.Y., 1970.

Phil 5585.295   Gibson, Eleanor Jack. Principles of perceptual learning
and development. N.Y., 1969.

Phil 5585.300   Bowman, Jan C. The figure-ground phenomenon in
experimental and phenomenological psychology. Thesis.
Stockholm, 1968.

Phil 5585.305   Combs, Arthur Wright. Florida studies in the helping
professions. Gainesville, 1969.

Phil 5585.310   Baird, John C. Psychophysical analysis of visual space. 1.
ed. Oxford, 1970.

Phil 5585.311   International Congress of Psychology, 18th, Moscow, 1966.
Vospriiatie prostranstva i vremeni. Leningrad, 1969.

Phil 5585.312   Fisher, Gerald H. The frameworks for perceptual
localization. Newcastle-upon-Tyne, 1968.

Phil 5585.315   Jaspars, Joseph Maria Franciscus. On social perception.
Leiden, 1966.

Phil 5585.315.5   From, Franz. Perception of other people. N.Y., 1971.

Phil 5585.320   Conrad, Theodor. Zur Wesenlehre des psychischen Lebens und
Erlebens. Den Haag, 1968.

Phil 5585.325   Orme, John Edward. Time, experience and behavior.
London, 1969.

Phil 5585.330   Dodwell, P.C. Visual pattern recognition. N.Y., 1970.

Phil 5585.335   Uslar, Detlev von. Die Wirklichkeit des Psychischen.
Pfullingen, 1969.

Phil 5585.340   Lévy, Jean Claude. Le temps psychologique. Paris, 1969.

Phil 5585.345   Sandstroem, Carl Ivar. Iakttagelse och upplevelse.
Stockholm, 1969.

Phil 5585.351   NATO Advanced Study Institute, University of Thessaloniki,
1968. Contemporary problems in perception. London, 1970.

Phil 5585.355   Cappon, Daniel. Technology and perception.
Springfield, 1971.

Phil 5590   Psychology - Treatises on special topics - Personality

Phil 5590.01   Pamphlet box. Personality.

Phil 5590.02   Pamphlet box. Personality.

Phil 5590.1   Abaunza, A. Los valores psicologicos de la personalidad.
Mexico, 1940.

Phil 5590.2   Young, Kimball. Personality and problems of adjustment.
N.Y., 1941.

Phil 5590.2.1   Young, Kimball. Personality and problems of adjustment.
N.Y., 1941.

Phil 5590.3   Brill, A. Individual ascendency. N.Y., 1938.

Phil 5590.4   Schettler, C.H. Problems of personality traits.
Chicago, 1940.

Phil 5590.5   Periot, M. Hippocrate avait raison. Marseille, 1941.

Phil 5590.6   Angyal, Andras. Foundations for a science of personality.
N.Y., 1941.

Phil 5590.7   Studies in personality. Contributions in honor of Lewis M.
Terman. 1. ed. N.Y., 1942.

Phil 5590.8   Sheldon, William H. The varieties of temperament; a
psychology of constitutional differences. N.Y., 1942.

Phil 5590.9.3   Plant, James S. Personality and the cultural pattern.
N.Y., 1939.

Phil 5590.10   Motivation and visual factors; individual studies of
college students. Hanover, 1942.

Phil 5590.11   Landis, Carney. Personality and sexuality of the
handicapped woman. N.Y., 1942.

Phil 5590.12   Studies in the relation of personality to field of work.
Cambridge.

Phil 5590.13.5   Kehl, R. Psicología da personalidade. 2. ed. Rio de
Janeiro, 1941.

Phil 5590.14   Davidson, Helen H. Personality and economic background.
N.Y., 1943.

Phil 5590.15   Murray, Henry A. Thematic apperception test. Cambridge,
Mass., 1943. 2v.

Phil 5590.16   Jennings, Helen H. Leadership and isolation. N.Y., 1943.

Phil 5590.17   Magoun, F.A. Balanced personality. N.Y., 1943.

Phil 5590.18   Myerson, Abraham. The foundations of personality.
Boston, 1926.

Phil 5590.19.1   Linton, Ralph. The cultural background of personality.
N.Y., 196-?

Phil 5590.20   Delgado, Honoria. La personalidad y el carácter.
Lima, 1943.

Phil 5590.21A   Heath, C.W. What people are. Cambridge, Mass., 1945.

Phil 5590.21B   Heath, C.W. What people are. Cambridge, Mass., 1945.

Phil 5590.22   Lecky, Prescott. Self-consistency; a theory of
personality. N.Y., 1945.

Phil 5590.23.2   Sawicki, Franz. Das Ideal der Persönlichkeit. 2. Aufl.
Paderborn, 1922.

Phil 5590.24   Baumann, Emilio. Psico-cinesia, ouvero L'arte di formare
il carattere. Pte. 1. Roma, 1900.

Phil 5590.26A   Liebman, Joshua Loth. Peace of mind. N.Y., 1946.

Phil 5590.26B   Liebman, Joshua Loth. Peace of mind. N.Y., 1946.

Phil 5590.26.5   Liebman, Joshua Loth. Hope for man. N.Y., 1966.

Phil 5590.28   Nédoncelle, M. La personne humaine et la nature. 1. éd.
Paris, 1943.

Phil 5590.30   Raushenbush, E. Psychology for individual education.
N.Y., 1942.

Phil 5590.32   Cattell, Raymond B. Description and measurement of
personality. Yonkers-on-Hudson, 1946.

Phil 5590.34   Pastori, Giuseppina. Il substrato biologico della
personalità. Brescia, 1945.

Phil 5590.36   Murphy, Gardner. Personality. N.Y., 1947.

Phil 5590.38   Tomkins, Silvan S. The thematic apperception test.
N.Y., 1947.

Phil 5590.39   Tomkins, Silvan S. Computer simulation of personality.
N.Y., 1963.

Phil 5590.40   Becker, Josef. Einfuhrung in die Charakterkunde.
Nurnberg, 1942.

Phil 5590.42   Larned, Josephus N. A study of greatness in men.
Boston, 1911.

Phil 5590.45   Eysenck, Hans Jurgen. Dimensions of personality.
London, 1948.

Phil 5590.45.5   Eysenck, Hans Jurgen. Experiments in personality.
London, 1960. 2v.

Classified Listing

Phil 5590   **Psychology - Treatises on special topics - Personality - cont.**

Phil 5590.45.10   Eysenck, Hans Jurgen. The structure of human personality. London, 1953.

Phil 5590.45.13   Eysenck, Hans Jurgen. The structure of human personality. 3. ed. London, 1970.

Phil 5590.45.15   Eysenck, Hans Jurgen. The biological basis of personality. Springfield, 1967.

Phil 5590.45.20   Eysenck, Hans Jürgen. Readings in extraversion-introversion. London, 1970-

Phil 5590.50   Roback, A.A. Personality in theory and practice. Cambridge, Mass., 1950.

Phil 5590.55   Kenmare, D. World invisible. London, 1949.

Phil 5590.60   Deschoux, M. Essai sur la personnalité. 1. éd. Paris, 1949.

Phil 5590.65   Abt, L.E. Projective psychology. 1.ed. N.Y., 1950.

Phil 5590.70   Allport, G.W. The nature of personality. Cambridge, Mass., 1950.

Phil 5590.71   Allport, Gordon Willard. The nature of personality. Cambridge, 1950.

Phil 5590.75   Dürr, Otto. Probleme der Gesinnungsbildung. Heidelberg, 1950.

Phil 5590.80   McClelland, D.C. Personality. N.Y., 1951.

Phil 5590.82.2   McClelland, D.C. Personality. N.Y., 1963.

Phil 5590.85   Pauli, R. Der Pauli-Test. 2. Aufl. München, 1951.

Phil 5590.90   Richard, G. La psychanalyse de l'homme normal. Lausanne, 1951.

Phil 5590.95   Lersch, Philipp. Der Aufbau des Charakters. Leipzig, 1938.

Phil 5590.95.3   Lersch, Philipp. Der Aufbau des Charakters. 3. Aufl. Leipzig, 1948.

Phil 5590.95.6   Lersch, Philipp. Aufbau der Person. 6. Aufl. München, 1954.

Phil 5590.95.7   Lersch, Philipp. Aufbau der Person. 7. Aufl. München, 1956.

Phil 5590.95.9   Lersch, Philipp. Aufbau der Person. 9. Aufl. München, 1964.

Phil 5590.100   Cattell, R.B. An introduction to personality study. London, 1950.

Phil 5590.105   Kluckhohn, Clyde. Personality in nature. 2. ed. N.Y., 1953.

Phil 5590.105.2   Kluckhohn, Clyde. Personality in nature, society and culture. 2. ed. N.Y., 1967.

Phil 5590.110   Harrower, M.R. Appraising personality. 1. ed. N.Y., 1952.

Phil 5590.115A   Greenacre, P. Trauma, growth and personality. London, 1953.

Phil 5590.115B   Greenacre, P. Trauma, growth and personality. London, 1953.

Phil 5590.120   Case, V.S. Your personality. N.Y., 1946.

Phil 5590.125   Overstreet, H.A. The mind alive. N.Y., 1954.

Phil 5590.130   Arnold, M.B. The human person. N.Y., 1954.

Phil 5590.135   Mayo, B. The logic of personality. London, 1952.

Phil 5590.140   Pfahler, G. Der Mensch und sein Lebenswerkzeug. Stuttgart, 1954.

Phil 5590.145   Lipps, Hans. Die menschliche Natur. Frankfurt, 1941.

Phil 5590.150   Remplein, Heinz. Psychologie der Persönlichkeit. München, 1954.

Phil 5590.150.5   Remplein, Heinz. Psychologie der Persönlichkeit. 5. Aufl. München, 1965.

Phil 5590.160   Stefanini, L. Metafisica della persona. Padova, 1950.

Phil 5590.165   Brand, Howard. The study of personality. N.Y., 1954.

Phil 5590.170   Cailliet, E. The dawn of personality. 1. ed. Indianapolis, 1955.

Phil 5590.175   Hawthorn, H.B. Sociology of personality functioning. Sioux City, Iowa, 1955.

Phil 5590.180   Mucchielli, R. Caractères et visages. 1. éd. Paris, 1954.

Phil 5590.185   Bourjade, Jean. Principes de caractérologie. Neuchâtel, 1955.

Phil 5590.190   Haring, D.G. Personal character and cultural milieu. N.Y., 1949.

Phil 5590.195   Ninck, M. Schicksal und Charakter. Wien, 1956.

Phil 5590.200   Phillipson, H. The object relations technique. London, 1955. 2v.

Phil 5590.210B   Smith, M.B. Opinions and personality. N.Y., 1956.

Phil 5590.210.2   Smith, M.B. Opinions and personality. N.Y., 1964.

Phil 5590.215   Hall, Calvin S. Theories of personality. N.Y., 1957.

Phil 5590.215.2   Hall, Calvin S. Theories of personality. N.Y., 1965.

Phil 5590.215.2.2   Hall, Calvin S. Theories of personality. 2. ed. N.Y., 1970.

Phil 5590.220   Leary, Timothy. Interpersonal diagnosis of personality. N.Y., 1957.

Phil 5590.225   Burckhardt, Georg. Charakter und Umwelt. München, 1956.

Phil 5590.230   Arnold, Wilhelm. Person, Charakter, Persönlichkeit. Göttingen, 1957.

Phil 5590.235.2A   Jourard, Sidney Marshall. Personal adjustment. 2. ed. N.Y., 1963.

Phil 5590.235.2B   Jourard, Sidney Marshall. Personal adjustment. 2. ed. N.Y., 1963.

Phil 5590.240   Thorpe, Louis Peter. Personality. Princeton, 1958.

Phil 5590.245   Stern, Erich. Experimentelle Persönlichkeitsanalyse nach dem Murray-Test. 1. Aufl. Zürich, 1952.

Phil 5590.250   Boll, Marcel. La personnalité; sa structure. Paris, 1958.

Phil 5590.255   Spreither, Franz. Verwirklichen. Konstanz, 1958.

Phil 5590.255.2   Spreither, Franz. Verwirklichende Vern-Zentrierung. 2. Aufl. Konstanz, 1959.

Phil 5590.260A   Murphy, Gardner. Human potentialities. N.Y., 1958.

Phil 5590.260B   Murphy, Gardner. Human potentialities. N.Y., 1958.

Phil 5590.265   Guilford, J.P. Personality. N.Y., 1959.

Phil 5590.270   Metelli, Fabio. Le dottrine caratterologiche di Ernest Kretschmer e Gerarhd Pfahler. Padova, 1958.

Phil 5590.272   Fingarette, Herbert. Self-deception. London, 1969.

Phil 5590.275   Janis, Irving L. Personality and persuasibility. New Haven, 1959.

Phil 5590.280   Schachtel, Ernest G. Metamorphosis. N.Y., 1959.

Phil 5590.280.5   Schachtel, Ernest G. Metamorphosis. London, 1963.

Phil 5590.285   Hylander, Ernst. Vom Umgang mit sich Selbst. München, 1958.

Phil 5590.292   White, Robert Winthrop. Lives in progress. 2. ed. N.Y., 1966.

Phil 5590.295   Halsman, Phillipe. Jump book. N.Y., 1959.

Phil 5590.300   Leeper, Robert. Toward understanding human personalities. N.Y., 1959.

Phil 5590.305   Neumann, Erich. Der schöpferische Mensch. Zürich, 1959.

Phil 5590.310   Stern, George G. Methods in personality assessment. Glencoe, Ill., 1956.

Phil 5590.315   Gelbmann, Frederich J. Authoritarianism and temperament. Washington, 1958.

Phil 5590.320   Moustakas, Clark E. The self. N.Y., 1956.

Phil 5590   **Psychology - Treatises on special topics - Personality - cont.**

Phil 5590.325   McCary, James Leslie. Psychology of personality. N.Y., 1956.

Phil 5590.330   Kluckhohn, Clyde. Personality in nature, society, and culture. 1. ed. N.Y., 1948.

Phil 5590.335   Solger, Friedrich. Das überpersönliche Leben. Berlin, 1959.

Phil 5590.340.5   David, Henry Philip. Perspectives in personality research. N.Y., 1960.

Phil 5590.345   Marzi, Alberto. La personalitá nell'etá evolutiva. Firenze, 1959.

Phil 5590.350   Mucchielli, R. La caractérologie à l'âge scientifique. Neuchâtel, 1961.

Phil 5590.355   Waszhewitz, B. Fundamente der Persönlichkeitspsychologie. München, 1960.

Phil 5590.360   Beiträge zur Psychologie der Persönlichkeit. Berlin, 1959.

Phil 5590.365   Wylie, R.C. The self concept. Lincoln, 1961.

Phil 5590.370   Dalton, R.H. Personality and social interaction. Boston, 1961.

Phil 5590.375   Cohen, Yehudi A. Social structure and personality. N.Y., 1961.

Phil 5590.380   Allport, G.W. Pattern and growth in personality. N.Y., 1961.

Phil 5590.385   Ignat'ev, E.I. Voprosy psikhologii lichnosti. Moskva, 1960.

Phil 5590.390   Kleiner, Fritz. Das Problem der Persönlichkeit in der amerikanischen Psychologie. München, 1961.

Phil 5590.395   Wallace, Anthony F.C. Culture and personality. N.Y., 1961.

Phil 5590.400   Sigl-Kiener, I. Über die individuelle Konfiguration des Leitbildes. München, 1960.

Phil 5590.405   Baughman, E.E. Personality. Englewood Cliffs, N.J., 1962.

Phil 5590.410   Sarason, Irwin G. Contemporary research in personality. Princeton, 1962.

Phil 5590.415   Brim, Orville Gilbert. Personality and decision processes. Stanford, 1962.

Phil 5590.416   Tomkins, S.S. Affect, imagery, consciousness. N.Y., 1962. 2v.

Phil 5590.418   Sarnoff, Irving. Personality, dynamics and development. N.Y., 1962.

Phil 5590.420   Saul, Leon J. Emotional maturity. Philadelphia, 1960.

Phil 5590.422   Lazarus, Richard. Adjustment and personality. N.Y., 1961.

Phil 5590.422.5   Lazarus, Richard. Patterns of adjustment and human effectiveness. N.Y., 1968.

Phil 5590.423   Bonner, Hubert. Psychology of personality. N.Y., 1961.

Phil 5590.424   Levine, Louis. Personal and social development. N.Y., 1963.

Phil 5590.426   Smelser, Neil Joseph. Personality and social systems. N.Y., 1963.

Phil 5590.426.2   Smelser, Neil Joseph. Personality and social systems. 2. ed. N.Y., 1970.

Phil 5590.427   Bandura, A. Social learning and personality development. N.Y., 1963.

Phil 5590.428   Boer, J. de. A system of characterology. Assen, 1963.

Phil 5590.429   Gordon, J.E. Personality and behavior. N.Y., 1963.

Phil 5590.430   Thomas, Alexander. Behavioral individuality in early childhood. N.Y., 1963.

Phil 5590.431A   Symposium on Personality Change, University of Texas. Personality change. N.Y., 1964.

Phil 5590.431B   Symposium on Personality Change, University of Texas. Personality change. N.Y., 1964.

Phil 5590.432   Ruitenbeek, H.M. The individual and the crowd. N.Y., 1964.

Phil 5590.434   Wepman, J.M. The concepts of personality. London, 1964.

Phil 5590.435   Neugarten, B.L. Personality in middle and late life. N.Y., 1964.

Phil 5590.436   L'inadaptation, phénomèn social. Paris, 1963.

Phil 5590.437   Kaplan, Bert. Studying personality cross-culturally. N.Y., 1961.

Phil 5590.438   Bischof, Ledford J. Interpreting personality theories. N.Y., 1964.

Phil 5590.439   Ullman, Albert Daniel. Sociocultural foundations of personality. Boston, 1965.

Phil 5590.440   Menaker, Esther. Ego in evolution. N.Y., 1965.

Phil 5590.441   Levitov, Nikolai D. Voprosy psikhologii kharaktera. Moskva, 1952.

Phil 5590.442   Levita, David Joël de. The concept of identity. Paris, 1965.

Phil 5590.443   Dorsey, John Morris. The growth of self-insight. Detroit, 1962.

Phil 5590.444   Edelweiss, Malomar Lund. Personalisation. Wien, 1964.

Phil 5590.445   Sappenfield, Bert Reese. Personality dynamics. N.Y., 1961.

Phil 5590.446   Cattell, Raymond. The scientific analysis of personality. Chicago, 1966.

Phil 5590.447.2   Kovalev, Aleksandr G. Psikhologiia lichnosti. 2. izd. Moskva, 1965.

Phil 5590.448.2   Lazurskii, Aleksandr F. Klassifikatsiis lichnosti. 2. izd. Moskva, 1923.

Phil 5590.449   Kinsella, Noël A. Toward a theory of personality development. Fredericton, N.B., 1966.

Phil 5590.450   Hiese, Manfred. Übertragungsphänomene bei verwahrlosten männlichen Jugendlichen. Erlangen, 1965.

Phil 5590.451   Glaser, Eric Michael. The psysiological basis of habituation. London, 1966.

Phil 5590.452   Lückert, Heinz Rolf. Die Problematik der Persönlichkeitsdiagnostik. München, 1965.

Phil 5590.453   Byrne, Donn Erwin. Personality research; a book of readings. Englewood Cliffs, N.J., 1966.

Phil 5590.454   Nuttin, Jozef. La structure de la personnalité. Paris, 1965.

Phil 5590.455   Tournier, Paul. Le secret d'après une conférence donnée à Athènes en la Salle de la Société d'Archéologie le 12 mai 1963. Genève, 1963.

Phil 5590.455.1   Tournier, Paul. Secrets. Richmond, 1968.

Phil 5590.455.6   Tournier, Paul. Escape from loneliness. Philadelphia, 1962.

Phil 5590.455.11   Tournier, Paul. The adventure of living. N.Y., 1965.

Phil 5590.456   Akademiia Nauk SSSR. Institut Filosofii. Garmonicheskii chelovek. Moskva, 1965.

Phil 5590.457   Megargee, Edwin I. Research in clinical assessment. N.Y., 1966.

Phil 5590.457.5   Mischel, Walter. Personality and assessment. N.Y., 1968.

Phil 5590.458   Robaye, Francine. Niveaux d'aspiration et d'expectation. Paris, 1957.

Phil 5590.460   Arasteh, A. Reza. Final integration in the adult personality. Leiden, 1965.

590   Psychology - Treatises on special topics - Personality - cont.
Phil 5590.462   Argyle, Michael. The psychology of interpersonal behavior. Harmondsworth, 1967.
Phil 5590.463   Association de Psychologie Scientifique de Langue Française. Les modèles de la personnalité en psychologie. 9e symposium de l'association de psychologie scientifique de langue française. Paris, 1965.
Phil 5590.464   Tramer, Moritz. Reifung und Formung von Persönlichkeiten. Erlenbach, 1965.
Phil 5590.465   Diggory, James C. Self-evaluation. N.Y., 1966.
Phil 5590.468   Sarason, Irwin G. Personality. N.Y., 1966.
Phil 5590.470   Weldes, Göran. Psykologi och mentalhygien. Lund, 1969.
Phil 5590.471   Fahrenberg, Jochen. Psychophysiologische Persönlichkeitsforschung. Göttingen, 1967.
Phil 5590.472   Petrilowitsch, Nikolaus. Zur Psychologie der Persönlichkeit. Darmstadt, 1967.
Phil 5590.474   Roth, Erwin. Einstellung als Determination individuellen Verhaltens. Habilitationsschrift. Göttingen, 1967.
Phil 5590.475   Lichnost' pri sotsializme. Moskva, 1968.
Phil 5590.475.5   Filosofsko-sotsiologicheskie problemy seorii lichnosti. Photoreproduction. Moskva, 1969. 2v.
Phil 5590.476   Zurabashvili, Avlipii. Problemy psikhologii i patopsikholozii lichnosti. Tbilisi, 1967.
Phil 5590.477   Zurabashvili, Avlippi. Aktual'nye problemy persondogii i klinicheskoi psikhiatrii. Tbilisi, 1970.
Phil 5590.480   Galli, Norberto. La caratterologia di G. Heymans e di R. LeSenne. Zürich, 1965.
Phil 5590.483   Mehrabian, Albert. An analysis of personality theories. Englewood Cliffs, N.J., 1968.
Phil 5590.485   Lidz, Theodore. The person: his development throughout the life cycle. N.Y., 1968.
Phil 5590.486   Bueva, Liudmila P. Sotsial'naia sreda i soznanie lichnosti. Moskva, 1968.
Phil 5590.488   Williams, Roger J. You are extraordinary. N.Y., 1967.
Phil 5590.490   Reuter, Jürgen Paul. Die Persönlichkeitsveränderung im Sinne der Deformierung noch schwerer Hungerdystrophie. Bonn, 1966.
Phil 5590.492   Thomae, Hans. Das Idividuum und seine Welt. Göttingen, 1968.
Phil 5590.492.5   Thomae, Hans. Vita humana. Frankfurt, 1969.
Phil 5590.494   Chapman, Arthur Harry. Put-offs and come-ons. London, 1968.
Phil 5590.496   Stoller, Robert J. Sex and gender; on the development of masculinity and feminity. London, 1968.
Phil 5590.498   Borgatta, Edgar. Handbook of personality theory and research. Chicago, 1968.
Phil 5590.500   The study of personality. N.Y., 1968.
Phil 5590.502   Aarts, Josephus Franciscus Maria Carolus. Zelfbeoordelingen. Tilburg, 1964.
Phil 5590.504   Bouman, Jan C. Psykologi för Erl. Stockholm, 1968.
Phil 5590.506   Lundin, Robert William. Personality; a behavioral analysis. N.Y., 1969.
Phil 5590.508   Salber, Wilhelm. Charakterentwicklung. Wuppertal, 1969.
Phil 5590.510   Aamark, Curt. Individ, persenlighet och medmänsklig miljö. Stolkholm, 1969.
Phil 5590.512   Myers, Gerald E. Self; an introduction to philosophical psychology. N.Y., 1969.
Phil 5590.514   Bannister, Donald. The evaluation of personal constructs. London, 1968.
Phil 5590.514.5   Bannister, Donald. Perspectives in personal construct theory. London, 1970.
Phil 5590.516   Gschwind, Martin. Die Wertfunktion des Menschen. Mainz, 1969.
Phil 5590.518   Sanford, Nevitt. Issues in personality theory. 1. ed. San Francisco, 1970.
Phil 5590.520   Mahrer, Alvin. New approaches to personality classification. N.Y., 1970.
Phil 5590.522   Wolberg, Lewis Robert. The dynamics of personality. N.Y., 1970.
Phil 5590.524   Pervin, Lawrence A. Personality: theory, assessment, and research. N.Y., 1970.
Phil 5590.526   Pieter, Józef. Wstęp do nauki o osobowości. Katowice, 1969.
Phil 5590.528   Duesberg, Hans. Person und Gemeinschaft. Bonn, 1970.
Phil 5590.530.3   Levitov, Nikolai D. Psikologiia kharaktera. 3. izd. Moskva, 1969.
Phil 5590.532   Wimersma Greidanus, H.T. Instinct en karakter proeve eener characterologie op instinct-psychologisch grondalag. Proefschrift. Zeist, 1933.
Phil 5590.534   Herrmann, T. Lehrbuch der empirischen Persönlichkeitsforschung. Göttingen, 1969.
Phil 5590.536.4   Wallon, Henri. Les origines du caractère chez l'enfant. 4. éd. Paris, 1970.
Phil 5590.538   Klimov, Evgenii A. Individual'nyi stil' deiatel'nosti v zavisimosti ot tipologicheskikh svoistv nervnoi sistemy. Kazan', 1969.
Phil 5590.540   Levy, Leon Harris. Conception of personality; theories and research. N.Y., 1970.
Phil 5590.542   Fel'dshtein, David I. Psikhologicheskie problemy formirovaniia nravstvennykh kachestv lichnosti v podrostkovom vozraste. Dushanbe, 1969.
Phil 5590.544   Kucher, Volodymyr. Zorzumiite samykh sebe. Kanada, 1969.
Phil 5590.548   Tournier, Paul. The meaning of persons. N.Y., 1957.
Phil 5590.550   Ozgü, Halis. Şahsiyet. 2. b. Istanbul, 1969.
Phil 5590.552   Hançerlioğlu, Orhan. Başlangicindan bugüne erdem açisindan düşünce. Istanbul, 1966.
Phil 5590.554   Knowles, Henry P. Personality and leadership behavior. Reading, Mass., 1971.
Phil 5590.556   Zawadski, Bohdan. Wstęp do seorii osobowosci. Wyd. 1. Warszawa, 1970.
VPhil 5590.558   Gerstmann, Stanisław. Osobowość. Wyd. 1. Warszawa, 1970.
Phil 5590.560   Ravzvitie lichnosti v usloviiakh stroitel'stva kommunizma. Cheboksary, 1970.
Phil 5590.562   Sotsializm i lichnost'. Volgograd, 1970.
Phil 5590.563   Anufriev, Evgenii A. Sotsial'naia vol' i aktivnost' lichnosti. Moskva, 1971.
Phil 5590.564   Dantov, Tasbolat M. Lichnost' kak sotsiologicheskaia problema. Alma-Ata, 1970.
Phil 5590.566   Nekotorye problemy sormirovaniia lichnosti. Krasnoiarsk, 1968.
Phil 5590.568.1   Jourard, Sidney Marshall. The transparent self. N.Y., 1971.
Phil 5590.570.2   Huth, Albert. Diagnose der Person. 2. Aufl. Bern, 1963.
Phil 5590.572.4   Hiebsch, Hans. Sozialpsychologische Grundlagen der Persönlichrechtsformung. 4. Aufl. Berlin, 1969.
Phil 5590.574   Gilligan, Sonja Carl. The heterosexuals are coming; the fusion strategy. N.Y., 1971.

Phil 5590   Psychology - Treatises on special topics - Personality - cont.
Phil 5590.576   Satura, Vladimir. Struktur und Genese der Person. Innsbrück, 1970.
Phil 5590.578.1   Bloom, Benjamin Samuel. Stability and change in human characteristics. N.Y., 1966.

Phil 5592   Psychology - Treatises on special topics - Personality tests and testing - General works
Phil 5592.5   Koch, Charles. The tree test. Bern, 1952.
Phil 5592.10   Koch, Karl. Der Baumtest. 2. Aufl. Bern, 1954.
Phil 5592.10.3   Koch, Karl. Der Baumtest. 3. Aufl. Bern, 1957.
Phil 5592.15   Cotte, S. Utilisation du dessin comme test psychologique chez les enfants. 3. éd. Marseille, 1951.
Phil 5592.20   Furrer, Walter. Die Farbe in des Persönlichkeitsdiagnostik. Basel, 1953.
Phil 5592.25   Frieling, H. Der Farbenspiegel. Göttingen, 1955.
Phil 5592.30   DuMas, F.M. Manifest structure analysis. Missoula, Montana, 1955.
Phil 5592.35   Porteus, Stanley David. The Porteus maze test manual. London, 1952.
Phil 5592.37   Proteus, Stanley David. Porteus maze test. Palo Alto, 1965.
Phil 5592.40   Engels, Helma. Der Scenotest. Münster, 1957.
Phil 5592.45   Shuey, Audrey Mary. The testing of Negro intelligence. Lynchburg, 1958.
Phil 5592.45.2   Shuey, Audrey Mary. The testing of Negro intelligence. 2. ed. N.Y., 1966.
Phil 5592.50   Zulliger, Hans. Der Diapositiv-Z-Test. Bern, 1955?
Phil 5592.55   Allen, Robert M. Personality assessment procedures. N.Y., 1958.
Phil 5592.60   Lennep, Johanna Elisabeth van. Beleving en verbeelding in het tekenen. Amsterdam, 1958.
Phil 5592.65A   Karon, Bertram P. The Negro personality. N.Y., 1958.
Phil 5592.65B   Karon, Bertram P. The Negro personality. N.Y., 1958.
Phil 5592.70   Edwards, A.L. The social desirability variable in personality assessment and research. N.Y., 1957.
Phil 5592.75   Frederiksen, Norman Oliver. Response set as a measure of personality. Princeton, 1958.
Phil 5592.80   Rey, André. L'examen clinique en psychologie. Paris, 1958.
Phil 5592.85   Maistriaux, Robert. L'intelligence et le caractère. Paris, 1959.
Phil 5592.95   Palmés, F.M. Como informar sobre la personalidad propria. Barcelona, 1958.
Phil 5592.100   Wallis, Ingeborg. Formen und Ausprägung der seelischen Nachreifung. Berlin, 1959.
Phil 5592.105   Gauchet, F. La caracterologie d'Heymans. Paris, 1959.
Phil 5592.110   Doebeli, Peter. Beiträge zur Psychodiagnostik. Zürich, 1959.
Phil 5592.115   Biedma, Carlos. Die Sprache der Zeichnung. Bern, 1959.
Phil 5592.125   Sormani, Jacques. Contribution à l'étude pratique. Marseille, 1958.
Phil 5592.130   Hills, J.R. The influence of instructions of repeated measurement on personality inventory scores. Princeton, 1959.
Phil 5592.135   Pittenger, R.E. The first five minutes. Ithaca, 1960.
Phil 5592.140   Zazzo, René. Manuel pour l'examen psychologique de l'enfant. Neuchâtel, 1960.
Phil 5592.145   Anzieu, D. Les méthodes projectives. Paris, 1960.
Phil 5592.148   Anzieu, D. Les méthodes projectives. 3e éd. Paris, 1970.
Phil 5592.150   Rohde, Amanda R. The sentence completion method. N.Y., 1957.
Phil 5592.155   Dahlstrom, W.G. An MMPI handbook. Minneapolis, 1960.
Phil 5592.155.5   Block, Jack. The challenge of response sets. N.Y., 1965.
Phil 5592.160   Dureman, I. Psykometriska och experimentalpsykologiska metoder för klinisk tillämpning. Stockholm, 1959.
Phil 5592.165   Max Luescher-Institut für Medizinsche Psychologie. Der Lüscher Test. Hergiswil, 1960.
Phil 5592.170   Gross, Martin L. The brain watchers. N.Y., 1962.
Phil 5592.171   Messick, S. Measurement in personality and cognition. N.Y., 1962.
Phil 5592.172   Zuest, R. Das Dorfspiel. Bern, 1963.
Phil 5592.173   Mields, J. Diagnostische Möglichkeiten der Intelligenz-Beurteilung. Heidelberg, 1962.
Phil 5592.174   Ong, Jin. The opposite form procedure in inventory construction and research. 1. ed. N.Y., 1965.
Phil 5592.175   Smits, Willem C.M. Onderzoek naar de kleurintentionaliteit. Nijmegen, 1964.
Phil 5592.176   Murstein, Bernard. Theory and research in projective techniques, emphasizing the TAT. N.Y., 1965.
Phil 5592.176.5   Kahn, Samuel. T.A.T. and understanding people. N.Y., 1966.
Phil 5592.177   Bonner, Hubert. On being mindful of man, essay toward a proactive psychology. Boston, 1965.
Phil 5592.178   Conference on Contemporary Issues in Thematic Apperceptive Methods. Contemporary issues in thematic apperceptive methods. Springfield, Ill., 1961.
Phil 5592.179   Gilberstadt, Harold. A handbook for clinical and actuarial MMPI interpretation. Philadelphia, 1965.
Phil 5592.180   Gough, Harrison Gould. The adjective checklist manual. Palo Alto, 1965.
Phil 5592.181   Kempf, H.E. Der Bild-Test. Inaug. Diss. Marburg, 1964?
Phil 5592.182   Debaty, Pol. La mésure des attitudes. Paris, 1965.
Phil 5592.184   Guillaumin, Jean. La dynamique de l'examen psychologique. Paris, 1965.
Phil 5592.186   Albou, Paul. Les questionnaires psychologiques. Paris, 1968.
Phil 5592.190   Allison, Joel. The interpretation of psychological tests. N.Y., 1968.
Phil 5592.192   Busemann, Adolf. Weltanschauung in psychologischer Sicht. München, 1967.
Phil 5592.194   Horst, Paul. Personality; measurement of dimensions. 1. ed. San Francisco, 1968.
Phil 5592.196   Eysenck, Hans Jurgen. Personality structure and measurement. London, 1969.
Phil 5592.198   Hauss, Kurt. Emotionalität und Wahrnehmung. Göttingen, 1969.
Phil 5592.202   Gaestrin, Jan Emanuel. Den svårfångade intelligensen. 2. uppl. Stockholm, 1968.

Phil 5593   Psychology - Treatises on special topics - Personality tests and testing - Special tests - Rorschach (By date, e.g. .60 for 1960)
Phil 5593.1   Pamphlet box. Rorschach test.
Phil 5593.10   Rorschach, Hermann. Gesammelte Aufsätze. Bern, 1965.
Phil 5593.41   Fosberg, I.A. An experimental study of the rehability of the Rorschach psychodiagnostic technique. N.Y., 1941.

Phil 5593 Psychology - Treatises on special topics - Personality tests and testing - Special tests - Rorschach (By date, e.g. .60 for 1960) - cont.

Phil 5593.42.5 — Klopfer, Bruno. The Rorschach technique; a manual for a projective method of personality diagnosis. Yonkers-on-Hudson, 1942.

Phil 5593.45 — Erickson, Mary R. Large scale Rorschach techniques. 1. ed. Springfield, Ill., 1945.

Phil 5593.45.5 — Maslow, Paul. Rorschach psychology. Brooklyn, 1945.

Phil 5593.45.10 — Munroe, R.L. Prediction of the adjustment and academic performance of college students. Stanford, 1945.

Phil 5593.45.20 — Alcock, T. The Rorschach in practice. Philadelphia, 1964[1963]

Phil 5593.46 — Ford, Mary E.N. The application of the Rorschach test to young children. Minneapolis, 1946.

Phil 5593.47 — Mons, Walter E. Principles and practise of the Rorschach personality test. London, 1947.

Phil 5593.50 — Broek, P. van den. De Behn-Rorschach-test. 's Gravenhage, 1950.

Phil 5593.51 — Kijm, J.M. De varianten der intentionaliteit bij de Rorschachtest. Nijmegen, 1951.

Phil 5593.52 — Pergola, Elio de. Il metodo psicodiagnostico de Rorschach. Roma, 1952.

Phil 5593.53 — Phillips, L. Rorschach interpretation. N.Y., 1953.

Phil 5593.54 — Klapfer, Bruno. Developments in the Rorschach technique. Yonkers-on-Hudson, 1954. 2v.

Phil 5593.54.5 — Kuhn, Roland. Maskendeutungen im Rorschachschen Versuch. 2. Aufl. Basel, 1954.

Phil 5593.54.10 — Ames, Louise Bates. Rorschach responses in old age. 1. ed. N.Y., 1954.

Phil 5593.54.15 — Sarason, S.B. The clinical interaction (with specific reference to Rorschach). N.Y., 1954.

Phil 5593.54.20 — Schofer, Roy. Psychoanalytic interpretation in Rorschach testing. N.Y., 1954.

Phil 5593.57 — Bohm, E.B. Lehrbuch der Rorschach-Psychodiagnostik. 2. Aufl. Bern, 1957.

Phil 5593.57.5 — Piotrowski, Z. Perceptanalysis. N.Y., 1957.

Phil 5593.58 — Chiari, Silvano. Bibliografica italiana. Firenze, 1958.

Phil 5593.58.5 — Chiari, Silvano. Introduzione alla psicodiagnosi di Rorschach. Firenze, 1958.

Phil 5593.60 — Bahm, Ewald B. Psychodiagnostisches Vademecum. Bern, 1960.

Phil 5593.60.5 — Rickers-Ovsiankiua, Maria A. Rorschach psychology. N.Y., 1960.

Phil 5593.62 — Hirt, Michael. Rorschach science; readings in theory and method. N.Y., 1962.

Phil 5593.63 — Künsler, W. Über Blutdeutungen im Rorschachschen Formdeutversuch. Bern, 1963.

Phil 5593.63.5 — Brückner, Peter. Konflikt und Konfliktschicksal. Bern, 1963.

Phil 5593.65 — International Congress of Rorschach and Projective Methods. Comptes rendus. Paris, 1967-68. 4v.

Phil 5593.65.5 — Scholtz, Walter. Zur Frage der Persönlichkeitsveränderung nach stereotaktischen Operationen. Inaug. Diss. Freiburg, 1965?

Phil 5593.66 — Schachtel, Ernest G. Experiential foundations of Rorschach's test. N.Y., 1966.

Phil 5593.66.5 — Lang, Alfred. Rorschach-Bibliographie, 1921-1964. Bern, 1966.

Phil 5593.66.10 — Zulliger, Hans. Praxis des Zulliger-Tafeln- und Diapositiv-Tests und ausgewählte Aufsätze. Bern, 1966.

Phil 5593.66.15 — Beizmann, Cécile. Livret de cotation des formes dans le Rorschach d'après une compilation des cotations de H. Rorschach. Paris, 1966.

Phil 5593.66.20 — Riemsdijk, Jan van. Geschiedenis en perspectieven van de Rorschach. Proefschrift. Utrecht, 1966.

Phil 5593.68 — Matejek, Georg. Zur Frage quantitativer und qualitativer Änderungen einiger Rorschach-Kategorien im Schulalter. Weinheim, 1968.

Phil 5593.69 — Exner, John E. The Rorschach system. N.Y., 1969.

Phil 5593.70 — Rausch de Traubenberg, Nina. La pratique du Rorschach. 1. éd. Paris, 1970.

Phil 5594 Psychology - Treatises on special topics - Personality tests and testing - Special tests - Q methodology (By date, e.g. .165 for 1965)

Phil 5594.153.2 — Stephenson, William. The study of behavior. Chicago, 1964.

Phil 5594.154 — Hector, H. Der 7-Quadrate-Test. Paderborn, 1954.

Phil 5594.156A — Lindquist, Everet F. Design and analysis of experiments in psychology and education. Boston, 1956.

Phil 5594.156B — Lindquist, Everet F. Design and analysis of experiments in psychology and education. Boston, 1956.

Phil 5594.158 — Maxwell, A.E. Experimental design in psychology and the medical sciences. London, 1958.

Phil 5594.161 — Block, J. The Q-sort method in personality assessment. Springfield, Ill., 1961.

Phil 5599 Psychology - Treatises on special topics - Personality tests and testing - Special tests - Other special (99 scheme, A-Z, by name of test)

Phil 5599.39 — Zeppelin, Ilka Sigried von. Die Variablen der Holtzman Inkblot Technique in ihrer Beziehung zur Introversion und Extraversion. Bern, 1966.

Phil 5599.39.10 — Rosenstiel, Lutz von. Zur Validität von Formdeutverfahren. München, 1967.

Phil 5599.52 — Luescher, Max. The Lüscher color test. N.Y., 1969.

Phil 5599.80 — Snider, James G. Semantic differential technique; a sourcebook. Chicago, 1969.

Phil 5599.85 — Ombredane, André. L'exploration de la mentalité des noirs, le Congo T.A.T. Paris, 1969.

Phil 5599.85.5 — Backes-Thomas, Madeleine. Le test des trois personnages. Neuchâtel, 1969.

Phil 5599.93 — Dahl, Gerhard. Übereinstimmungsvalidität des HAWE und Entwicklung einer reduzierten Testform. Meisenheim am Glan, 1968.

Phil 5599.95 — Bowyer, Laura Ruth. The Lowenfeld world technique. 1. ed. Oxford, N.Y., 1970.

Phil 5599.98 — Zulliger, Hans. Der Tafeln-Z-Test für individuelle psychologische Prüfungen, ein abgekürztes Rorschach-Verfahren. Bern, 1954.

Phil 5599.98.5 — Zulliger, Hans. The Zulliger individual and group test. N.Y., 1969.

Phil 5610 Psychology - Treatises on special topics - Public speaking

Phil 5610.1 — Scott, W.D. The psychology of public speaking. Philadelphia, 1907.

Phil 5610.1.15 — Scott, W.D. The psychology of public speaking. N.Y., 1926.

Phil 5610 Psychology - Treatises on special topics - Public speaking - cont.

Phil 5610.2 — Neil, C.E. Sources of effectiveness in public speaking. Philadelphia, 1920.

Phil 5620 Psychology - Treatises on special topics - Reason and reasoning

Phil 5620.01 — Pamphlet box. Reason and reasoning.

Phil 5620.1A — Binet, A. La psychologie du raisonnement. Paris, 1886.

Phil 5620.1B — Binet, A. La psychologie du raisonnement. Paris, 1886.

Phil 5620.1.5 — Binet, A. The psychology of reasoning. Chicago, 1899.

Phil 5620.1.7 — Binet, A. The psychology of reasoning. Chicago, 1907.

Phil 5620.2 — Keller, J. Der Ursprung der Vernunft. Heidelberg, 1884.

Phil 5620.3 — Magy, F. La raison et l'âme. Paris, 1877.

Phil 5620.4 — Mivart, S.G. Origin of human reason. London, 1889.

Phil 5620.5 — Thurot, J.F. De l'entendement de la raison. Paris, 1830. 2v.

Phil 5620.6 — Keary, C.F. The pursuit of reason. Cambridge, 1910.

Phil 5620.7 — Pillsbury, W.B. The psychology of reasoning. N.Y., 1910.

Phil 5620.8 — Jonsson, K.G. Undersökningar...problemräkningens förutsättningar och förlopp. Uppsala, 1919.

Phil 5620.9 — Rignano, Eugenio. Psychologie du raisonnement. Paris, 1920.

Phil 5620.9.7 — Rignano, Eugenio. Psychology of reasoning. N.Y., 1927.

Phil 5620.10 — Grandjean, F. La raison et la vue. Paris, 1920.

Phil 5620.11 — Vacherot, Étienne. De rationis autoritate. Cadomi, 1836.

Phil 5620.12 — Dunn, Miriam Frances. The psychology of reasoning. Diss. n.p., 1926.

Phil 5620.13.3 — Ollé-Laprune, L. La raison et le rationalisme. 3. éd. Paris, 1906.

Phil 5620.14B — Whitehead, A.N. The function of reason. Princeton, 1929.

Phil 5620.14C — Whitehead, A.N. The function of reason. Princeton, 1929.

Phil 5620.15 — Jönsson, A. Om den förnuftiga känslan. Lund, 1868.

Phil 5620.16 — Whittaker, T. Reason. Cambridge, Eng., 1934.

Phil 5620.17 — Macmurray, John. Reason and emotion. London, 1935.

Phil 5620.18 — Zoul, L. On the origin of reason. N.Y., 1938.

Phil 5620.22 — Kogan, Zuce. Essentials in problem solving. Chicago, 1951.

Phil 5620.24 — Lalande, A. La raison et les normes. Paris, 1948.

Phil 5620.26 — Perelman, Chaim. Rhétorique et philosophie pour une théorie de l'argumentation en philosophie. 1. éd. Paris, 1952.

Phil 5620.28 — Macmurray, John. Reason and emotion. 2. ed. N.Y., 1962.

Phil 5620.29 — Gauthier, Daniel Peter. Practical reasoning. Oxford, 1963.

Phil 5620.29.2 — Gauthier, Daniel Peter. Practical reasoning. Oxford, 1966.

Phil 5620.30 — Dar, B.A. Studies in reason and faith. Lahore, 1957.

Phil 5620.31 — Larrabee, H.A. Reliable knowledge. Boston, 1964.

Phil 5620.32 — Kolenda, K. The freedom of reason. San Antonio, 1964.

Phil 5620.33 — Shurter, Robert. Critical thinking. N.Y., 1966.

Phil 5620.34 — Scivoletto, Angelo. Il segno della ragione. Padova, 1963.

Phil 5620.35 — Edgley, Roy. Reason in theory and practice. London, 1969.

Phil 5620.36 — Lee, Wayne. Decision, theory and human behavior. N.Y., 1971.

Phil 5625 Psychology - Treatises on special topics - Reflex action

Phil 5625.01 — Pamphlet box. Nervous system (reflex action).

Phil 5625.02F — Pamphlet box. Nervous system (reflex action).

Phil 5625.1 — Podkopaev, N.A. Die Methodik der Enforschung der bedingten Reflexe. München, 1926.

Phil 5625.1.5.3 — Podkopaev, N.A. Metodika izucheniia uslovnykn refleksov. 3. izd. Moskva, 1952.

Phil 5625.69 — Patrizi, M.L. I riflessi vascolari nelle membra e nel cervello dell'uomo. Reggio-Emilia, 1897.

Phil 5625.75A — Pavlov, Ivan P. Conditioned reflexes. Oxford, 1927.

Phil 5625.75B — Pavlov, Ivan P. Conditioned reflexes. Oxford, 1927.

Phil 5625.75.2 — Pavlov, Ivan P. Polnoe sobranie trudov. v.2-5. Moskva, 1946. 4v.

Phil 5625.75.3 — Pavlov, Ivan P. Conditioned reflexes. London, 1928.

Phil 5625.75.5 — Pavlov, Ivan P. Izbrannye trudy. Moskva, 1950.

Phil 5625.75.7 — Akademiia Nauk SSSR. Arkhiv. Rukopisnye materialy I.P. Pavlova. Moskva, 1949.

Phil 5625.75.10 — Pavlov, Ivan P. Les reflexes conditionelles. Paris, 1927.

Phil 5625.75.15 — Pavlov, Ivan P. Selected works. Moscow, 1955.

Phil 5625.75.20 — Pavlov, Ivan P. Experimental psychology. N.Y., 1957.

Phil 5625.75.25 — Pavlov, Ivan P. Vorlesungen über die Arbeit der Grosshirnhemisphären. Lenogiz, 1932.

Phil 5625.75.30 — Pavlov, Ivan P. The work of the digestive glands. London, 1910.

Phil 5625.75.35 — Pavlov, Ivan P. Psychopathology and psychiatry. Moscow, 1962?

Phil 5625.75.40 — Pavlov, Ivan P. Essays in psychology and psychiatry. N.Y., 1962.

Phil 5625.75.80 — Dontchef-Dezeuze, M. L'image et les réflexes conditionnels dans les travaux de Pavlov. Paris, 1914.

Phil 5625.75.85 — Frolov, I.P. I.P. Pavlovs i ego uchenie ob uslovnykh refleksakh. Moskva, 1936.

Phil 5625.75.87 — Frolov, I.P. Pavlov and his school. London, 1937.

Phil 5625.75.90 — Kiselinchev, A. Die marxistisch-leninistische Widerspiegelungstheorie und die Lehre Pawlows. Berlin, 1957.

Phil 5625.75.95 — Frolov, I.P. Ivan Petrovich Pavlov. 2. izd. Moskva, 1953.

Phil 5625.75.100 — Gray, Jeffrey Alan. Pavlov's typology. N.Y., 1964.

Phil 5625.75.105 — Orbeli, Leon A. Vospominaniia o I.P. Pavlove. Leningrad, 1966.

Phil 5625.75.110 — I.P. Pavlov v vospominaniiakh sovremennikov. Leningrad, 1967.

Phil 5625.75.115 — Letopis' zhizni i deiatel'nosti akademika I.P. Pavlova. Leningrad, 1969.

Phil 5625.79 — Veraguth, Otto. Das psychogalvanische Reflexphänomen. Berlin, 1909.

Phil 5625.80 — Hamel, I.A. A study and analysis of the conditioned reflex. Diss. Washington, 1918.

Phil 5625.81 — Wendt, George R. An analytical study of the conditioned knee-jerk. N.Y., 1930.

Phil 5625.82 — Razran, G.H.S. Conditioned responses in children. Thesis. N.Y., 1933.

Phil 5625.83 — Fearing, F. Reflex action. Baltimore, 1930.

Phil 5625.85 — Tullio, P. I riflessi orientative nella studio delle attività mentali. Bologna, 1938.

Phil 5625.86 — Gellhorn, Ernst. Autonomic regulations. N.Y., 1943.

Phil 5625.86.5 — Gellhorn, Ernst. Autonomic imbalance and the hypothalamus. Minneapolis, 1957.

Phil 5625.87 — Householder, A.S. Some notes for simple Pavlovian learning. Santa Monica, 1951.

Phil 5625.90 — Canguilhem, G. La formation du concept de reflexe aux XVII et XVIII siècles. Paris, 1955.

Phil 5625.92 — Spence, K.W. Behavior theory and conditioning. New Haven, 1956.

Phil 5625 Psychology - Treatises on special topics - Reflex action - cont.

Phil 5625.95 Association de Psychologie Scientifique de Langue Française. Le conditionnement et l'apprentissage. Strasbourg, 1956.
Phil 5625.97 Ferster, Charles B. Schedules of reinforcement. N.Y., 1957.
Phil 5625.99 Wieser, S. Das Schreckverhalten des Menschen. Bern, 1961.
Phil 5625.101 Le Ny, Jean François. Le conditionnement. Paris, 1961.
Phil 5625.101.5 Le Ny, Jean François. Apprentissage et activités psychologiques. Paris, 1967.
Phil 5625.103 Medvedev, N.M. Teoriia otrazheniia i ee estestvenno-nauchnoe obosnovanie. Moskva, 1963.
Phil 5625.104 Ban, Thomas A. Conditioning and psychiatry. Chicago, 1964.
Phil 5625.105 Prokasy, William Frederick. Classical conditioning, a symposium. N.Y., 1965.
Phil 5625.106 Schneersohn, Fischel. Der Weg zum Menschen. Berlin, 1928.
Phil 5625.107 Abramian, Lev. Signal i uslovnyi refleks. Erevan, 1961.
Phil 5625.108 Notterman, Joseph M. Dynamics of response. N.Y., 1965.
Phil 5625.110 Kimble, Gregory A. Foundations of conditioning and learning. N.Y., 1967.
Phil 5625.112 Beritashvili, Ivan S. Neural mechanisms of higher vertebrate behavior. 1st English ed. Boston, 1965.
Phil 5625.114 Ferster, Charles B. Behavior principles. N.Y., 1968.
Phil 5625.115 Petrushevskii, Stefan A. Dialektika reflektornykh protsessov. Moskva, 1967.
Phil 5625.116 Martin, Irene. The genesis of the classical conditioned response. 1. ed. Oxford, 1969.
Phil 5625.117 Reinforcement and behavior. N.Y., 1969.
Phil 5625.120 Skinner, B.F. Contingencies of reinforcement. N.Y., 1969.
Phil 5625.122 Conference on Punishment. Punishment and aversive behavior. N.Y., 1969.
Phil 5625.123 Brush, Franklin Robert. Aversive conditioning and learning. N.Y., 1971.
Phil 5625.124 Miami Symposium on the Prediction of Behavior. Aversive stimulation. Coral Gables, Fla., 1968.
Phil 5625.126 Conditioned reinforcement. Homewood, Ill., 1969.
Phil 5625.128 Baumstimler, Yves. Automatisation du comportement et commutation. Paris, 1969.

Phil 5627 Psychology - Treatises on special topics - Religion - General works (By date, e.g. .265 for 1965)

Phil 5627.01 Pamphlet box. Religious psychology.
Phil 5627.05 Pamphlet box. Religious psychology. German dissertations.
Phil 5627.1 Starbuck, E.D. The psychology of religion. London, 1899.
NEDL Phil 5627.1 Starbuck, E.D. The psychology of religion. London, 1899.
Phil 5627.1.5 Starbuck, E.D. A study of conversion. n.p., 189-?
Phil 5627.1.10 Starbuck, E.D. Some aspects of religious growth. n.p., 1897.
Phil 5627.3A Hylan, J.P. Public worship. Chicago, 1901.
Phil 5627.3B Hylan, J.P. Public worship. Chicago, 1901.
Phil 5627.5 Everett, C.C. The psychological elements of religious faith. N.Y., 1902.
Htn Phil 5627.6.1* James, William. Varieties of religious experience. N.Y., 1902.
Htn Phil 5627.6.2* James, William. Varieties of religious experience. N.Y., 1902.
Phil 5627.6.2.4 James, William. Varieties of religious experience. N.Y., 1902.
Phil 5627.6.2.5 James, William. Varieties of religious experience. N.Y., 1902.
Phil 5627.6.3 James, William. Varieties of religious experience. London, 1915.
Phil 5627.6.4A James, William. Varieties of religious experience. N.Y., 1928.
Phil 5627.6.4B James, William. Varieties of religious experience. N.Y., 1928.
EDL Phil 5627.6.5 James, William. Varieties of religious experience. N.Y., 1903.
Phil 5627.6.5.10 James, William. Varieties of religious experience. N.Y., 1904.
Phil 5627.6.5.15 James, William. Varieties of religious experience. N.Y., 1936.
Phil 5627.6.5.16 James, William. Varieties of religious experience. London, 1960.
Phil 5627.6.6 James, William. L'expérience religieuse. 2. éd. Paris, 1908.
Phil 5627.6.7 James, William. L'expérience religieuse. Paris, 1906.
Phil 5627.6.8 James, William. Religiøs røynsle i sine ymse former. Øslo, 1920.
Phil 5627.6.10 James, William. Den religiösa erfarenheten. Stockholm, 1906.
Phil 5627.6.11 James, William. Den religiösa erfarenheten. Stockholm, 1923.
Phil 5627.6.12A James, William. Religiøse erfaringer. København, 1906.
Phil 5627.6.12B James, William. Religiøse erfaringer. København, 1906.
Phil 5627.6.12.25 James, William. Die religiöse Erfahrung. Leipzig, 1907.
Phil 5627.6.13 James, William. Die religiöse Erfahrung. Leipzig, 1914.
Phil 5627.6.14 James, William. La varie forme della coscienza religiosa. n.p., n.d.
Phil 5627.6.20A Busch, K.A. William James als Religionsphilosoph. Göttingen, 1911.
Phil 5627.6.20B Busch, K.A. William James als Religionsphilosoph. Göttingen, 1911.
Phil 5627.6.85 Morelli, G. La realtà dello spirito. Milano, n.d.
Phil 5627.6.95A Porret, J.A. Au sujet de la conversion...théorie de Wm. James. Genève, 1907.
Phil 5627.6.95B Porret, J.A. Au sujet de la conversion...théorie de Wm. James. Genève, 1907.
Phil 5627.7.5 Bois, Henri. Sentiment religieux et sentiment moral. Paris, 1903.
DL Phil 5627.7.8 Davenport, F.M. Primitive traits in religious revivals. N.Y., 1905.
Phil 5627.9 Vorbrodt, G. Beiträge zur religiösen Psychologie. Leipzig, 1904.
Phil 5627.10 King, Irving. The differentiation of the religious consciousness. N.Y., 1905.
Phil 5627.10.3 King, Irving. The differentiation of the religious consciousness. N.Y., 1905.
Phil 5627.11 Moses, J. Pathological aspects of religions. Worcester, 1906.
Phil 5627.12 Revault D'Allonnes, G. Psychologie d'une religion. Paris, 1908.
Phil 5627.13 Geelkerken, J.G. De empirische godsdienstpsychologie. Amsterdam, 1909.
Phil 5627.14 Strong, A.L. The psychology of prayer. Chicago, 1909.
Phil 5627.14.2 Strong, A.L. A consideration of prayer. Chicago, 1908.

Phil 5627 Psychology - Treatises on special topics - Religion - General works (By date, e.g. .265 for 1965) - cont.

Phil 5627.15 Begbie, H. Twice-born men, a clinic in regeneration. N.Y., 1909.
Phil 5627.15.3 Begbie, H. Souls in action. N.Y., 1911.
Phil 5627.15.9 Begbie, H. More twice-born men. N.Y., 1923.
Phil 5627.15.11 Begbie, H. Life changers. N.Y., 1927.
Phil 5627.16 Cutten, G.B. The psychological phenomenon of Christianity. N.Y., 1908.
Phil 5627.17 Ames, E.S. Psychology of religious experience. Boston, 1910.
Phil 5627.18A Ideler, K.W. Versuch einer Theorie des religiösen Wahnsinns. Halle, 1848-50. 2v.
Phil 5627.18B Ideler, K.W. Versuch einer Theorie des religiösen Wahnsinns. Halle, 1848-50. 2v.
Phil 5627.19 Segond, J. La prière-étude de psychologie religieuse. Paris, 1911.
Phil 5627.20 Leuba, J.H. A psychological study of religion. N.Y., 1912.
Phil 5627.20.5 Leuba, J.H. The psychological origin and the nature of religion. London, 1909.
Phil 5627.20.6 Leuba, J.H. The psychological origin and the nature of religion. London, 1921.
Phil 5627.20.7 Leuba, J.H. The psychology of religious mysticism. London, 1925.
Phil 5627.20.10 Leuba, J.H. Studies in the psychology of religious phenomena. Worcester, 1896.
Phil 5627.21 Cornelison, I.A. The natural history of religious feeling. N.Y., 1911.
Phil 5627.22 Binet-Sangle, Charles. Les lois psychophysiologique du développement des religions. Paris, 1907.
Phil 5627.24 Gill, E.H.K. Psychological aspects of Christian experience. Boston, 1915.
Phil 5627.25 Garban, Louis. Deviations morbides du sentiment religieux. Paris, 1911.
Phil 5627.26 Coe, George A. The spiritual life; studies in the science of religion. Chicago, 1914.
Phil 5627.26.2 Coe, George A. The spiritual life; studies in the science of religion. N.Y., 1900.
Phil 5627.26.5 Coe, George A. The psychology of religion. Chicago, 1917.
Phil 5627.27 Mainage, T. La psychologie de la conversion. Paris, 1915.
Phil 5627.27.5 Mainage, T. Introduction à la psychologie des convertis. Paris, 1913.
Phil 5627.27.15 Runze, George. Essays zur Religionspsychologie. Berlin, 1913.
Phil 5627.28 Stalker, James. Christian psychology. 3. ed. N.Y., 1914.
Phil 5627.29 Roback, A.A. The psychology of confession. Montreal, 1917.
Phil 5627.30 McComas, Henry Clay. Psychology of religious sects. N.Y., 1912.
Phil 5627.31 Burr, Anna Robeson. Religious confessions and confessants. Boston, 1914.
Phil 5627.32 Finot, Jean. Saints, initiés et possédés modernes. Paris, 1918.
Phil 5627.33 Hébert, Marcel. Le divin. Paris, 1907.
Phil 5627.34 Perrier, Louis. Le sentiment religieux. Paris, 1912.
Phil 5627.34.5 Perrier, Louis. Les obsessions dans la vie religieuse. Thèse. Montpellier, 1905.
Phil 5627.35 Sears, Annie L. The drama of the spiritual life. N.Y., 1915.
Phil 5627.36 Kato, Katsuji. The psychology of oriental religious experience. Menaska, Wis., 1915.
Phil 5627.37 Henke, Frederick G. A study in the psychology of ritualism. Diss. Chicago, 1910.
Phil 5627.38 Pamphlet box. Schroeder, Theodore.
Phil 5627.39 Schroeder, Theodore. Erotogenesis of religion. N.Y., 1916.
Phil 5627.40 Schroeder, Theodore. Erotogenesis of religion. St. Louis, 1913.
Phil 5627.41 Heavenly bridegrooms...erotogenetic...religion. N.Y., 1918.
Phil 5627.50 Sankey-Jones, N.E. Bibliography of Theodore Schroeder on the psychology of religion. Cos Cob, Conn., 1934.
Phil 5627.55 Pennock, Gilbert L. The consciousness of communion with God. New Brunswick, N.J., 1919.
Phil 5627.55.5 Cohen, Chapman. Religion and sex. London, 1919.
Phil 5627.56 Pratt, James B. The religious consciousness. N.Y., 1920.
Phil 5627.56.3A Pratt, James B. The religious consciousness. N.Y., 1927.
Phil 5627.56.3B Pratt, James B. The religious consciousness. N.Y., 1927.
Phil 5627.56.4 Pratt, James B. The psychology of religious belief. N.Y., 1907.
Phil 5627.56.5 Swisher, Walter. Religion and the new psychology. Boston, 1920.
Phil 5627.56.7 Howley, John. Psychology and mystical experience. London, 1920.
Phil 5627.57 Wells, W.R. The biological foundations of belief. Boston, 1921.
Phil 5627.58 Pacheu, Jules. L'expérience mystique et l'activité subconciente. Paris, 1911.
Phil 5627.59 Thouless, Robert H. An introduction to the psychology of religion. N.Y., 1923.
Phil 5627.59.5 Thouless, Robert H. An introduction to the psychology of religion. 2. ed. Cambridge, Eng., 1928.
Phil 5627.60 Underhill, E. The life of the spirit and the life of today. 3d ed. London, 1923.
Phil 5627.60.5 Underhill, E. The life of the spirit and the life of today. N.Y., 1926.
Phil 5627.60.7 Underhill, E. The life of the spirit and the life of today. London, 1922.
Phil 5627.60.10 Underhill, E. The golden sequence. 2. ed. London, 1932.
Phil 5627.60.20 Underhill, E. The spiritual life. N.Y., 1937.
Phil 5627.61 Delacroix, H. La religion et la foi. Paris, 1922.
Phil 5627.62 Waterhouse, E.S. The philosophy of religious experience. Thesis. London, 1923.
Phil 5627.62.10 Waterhouse, E.S. Psychology and religion. London, 1930.
Phil 5627.63 Mudge, E.L. The God-experience. Cincinnati, 1923.
Phil 5627.65 Flower, John C. Psychological studies of religious questions. London, 1924.
Phil 5627.65.5 Flower, John C. An approach to the psychology of religion. London, 1927.
Phil 5627.66 Wunderle, G. Einführung in die moderne Religionspsychologie. Kempten, 1923.
Phil 5627.67 Kaltenbaach, J. Étude psychologique des plus anciens reveils religieux aux États-Unis. Thèse. Genève, 1905.
Phil 5627.68 Léo, A. Étude psychologique sur la prière d'après deux enquêtes américaines. Thèse. Cahors, 1905.
Phil 5627.69 Kriebel, O.S. Conversion and religious experience. Pennsburg, Pa., 1907.

Classified Listing

Phil 5627   Psychology - Treatises on special topics - Religion - General works (By date, e.g. .265 for 1965) - cont.

Phil 5627.70   Dupain, J.M. Étude clinique sur le délire religieux. Thèse. Paris, 1888.

Phil 5627.71   Oesterreich, T.K. Einfürung in die Religionspsychologie. Berlin, 1917.

Phil 5627.72   Stead, W.T. The revival in the West. 4. ed. London, 19- .

Phil 5627.73   Flournoy, T. Le génie religieux. Neuchâtel, 1904.

Phil 5627.74.2   Joly, H. Psychologie des saints. 2. éd. Paris, 1897.

Phil 5627.75   Leroy, E.B. Interprétation psychologique des visions intellectuelles. Paris, 1907.

Phil 5627.76   Collins, F.P. My religious experience. Kansas City, Mo., 1901.

Phil 5627.77   Daniels, A.H. The new life. Worcester, 1893.

Phil 5627.78   Foster, R.S. Philosophy of Christian experience. 3d series. N.Y., 1890.

Phil 5627.79   Kaplan, J.H. Psychology of prophecy. Philadelphia, 1908.

Phil 5627.80   Koch, E. Die Psychologie in der Religionswissenschaft. Freiburg, 1896.

Phil 5627.81   Thompson, J.B. The other paraclete. n.p., 1897.

Phil 5627.82   Schneider, E. Les raisons du coeur. Paris, 1907.

Phil 5627.83   Swetenham, L. Religious genius. London, 1905.

Phil 5627.84   Park, M. Remarkable vision and death bed experience of Ada Park. Pulaski, N.Y., 1882.

Phil 5627.85   Dryden, S.H. Daisy Dryden. 3. ed. Boston, 1909.

Phil 5627.86   Köllner, G. Histoire de la vie et de la conversion de Guillaume Köllner. Genève, 1823.

Phil 5627.87.2   Scherr, J. Die Gekreuzigte. 2. Aufl. Leipzig, 1874.

Phil 5627.88   Wells, Mary. Memoir of Mrs. Joanna Turner. 1. American ed. N.Y., 1827.

Phil 5627.90   Upham, Thomas C. Principles of the interior or hidden life. London, 1874.

Phil 5627.91   Slocum, Phebe B. Akin. Witnessing. Brattleboro, 1899.

Phil 5627.92   Chevalier, J. Pour une science de l'individuel. Paris, 1923.

Phil 5627.93   Edward, Kenneth. Religious experience; its nature and truth. Edinburgh, 1926.

Phil 5627.94   Girgensohn, K. Der seelische Aufbau des religiösen Erlebens. Leipzig, 1921.

Phil 5627.94.5   Girgensohn, K. Der seelische Aufbau des religiösen Erlebens. 2. Aufl. Gütersloh, 1930.

Phil 5627.95   Mensching, Gustav. Die heilige Schweigen. Giessen, 1926.

Phil 5627.95.5   Mensching, Gustav. Das heilige Wort. Bonn, 1937.

Phil 5627.95.10   Mensching, Gustav. Die Idee der Sünde. Leipzig, 1931.

Phil 5627.95.15   Mensching, Gustav. Gut und Böse im Glauben der Völker. Leipzig, 1941.

Phil 5627.95.17   Mensching, Gustav. Gut und Böse im Glauben des Völker. 2. Aufl. Stuttgart, 1950.

Phil 5627.96.5   Trumbull, Charles G. Taking men alive. N.Y., 1912.

Phil 5627.97   Allier, Raoul. La psychologie de la conversion chez les peuples noncivilisés. Paris, 1925. 2v.

Phil 5627.98   Hardman, Oscar. Psychology and the church. London, 1925.

Phil 5627.99   Dimond, S.G. The psychology of the Methodist revival. London, 1926.

Phil 5627.100   Bruehn, W. Religionspsychologie. Breslau, 1926.

Phil 5627.101   Josey, C.C. The psychology of religion. N.Y., 1927.

Phil 5627.102   Reik, Theodor. Probleme der Religionspsychologie. 1. Teil. Leipzig, 1919.

Phil 5627.102.5   Reik, Theodor. Der eigene und der fremde Gott; zur Psychoanalyse der religiösen Entwicklung. Leipzig, 1923.

Phil 5627.102.10   Reik, Theodor. Dogma und Zwangsidee eine psychoanalytische Studie zur Entwicklung der Religion. Leipzig, 1927.

Phil 5627.103   Bohne, G. Die religiöse Entwicklung der Jugend in der Reifezeit. Leipzig, 1922.

Phil 5627.104   Rohrbaugh, L.G. The science of religion: an introduction. N.Y., 1927.

Phil 5627.105   Jordan, G.J. A short psychology of religion. N.Y., 1927.

Phil 5627.106   A letter of a friend. Chicago, 1928.

Phil 5627.107   Sanctis, S. de. Religious conversion. London, 1927.

Phil 5627.107.5   Underwood, A.C. Conversion: Christian and non-Christian. N.Y., 1925.

Phil 5627.107.10   Collins, Joyce. The sparrow hath found herself a house. Dublin, 1943.

Phil 5627.107.15   Sargant, W.W. Battle for the mind. Melbourne, 1957.

Phil 5627.107.20   Behanna, Gertrude Florence. The late Liz. N.Y., 1957.

Phil 5627.107.20.5   Behanna, Gertrude Florence. The late Liz. N.Y., 1968.

Phil 5627.107.25   Gordon, Albert. The nature of conversion. Boston, 1967.

Phil 5627.107.30   Frossard, Amdre. Díos existe, yo me la encontre. Madrid, 1969.

Phil 5627.108   Clark, Glenn. Fishers of men. Boston, 1928.

Phil 5627.108.15   Clark, Glenn. The soul's sincere desire. Boston, 1926.

Phil 5627.108.25   Clark, Glenn. I will lift up mine eyes. 9. ed. N.Y., 1937.

Phil 5627.109   Chansou, J. Étude de psychologie religieuse sur...la prière. Thèse. Toulouse, 1927. 2 pam.

Phil 5627.110   Heinsius, Wilhelm. Krisen katholischer Frömmigkeit. Berlin, 1925.

Phil 5627.111   Clemen, Carl. Die Anwendung der Psychoanalyse auf Mythologie und Religionsgeschichte. Leipzig, 1928.

Phil 5627.112   Pfennigsdorf, Emil. Der religiöse Wille. 2. Aufl. Leipzig, 1927.

Phil 5627.113   Wijnaendts Francken, C.J. Wereldbeschouwing en Godsdienstig bewustzyn. Haarlem, 1923.

Phil 5627.113.95   Selbie, W.B. Psychology of religion. Oxford, 1924.

Phil 5627.115   Kupky, Oscar. The religious development of adolescents. N.Y., 1928.

Phil 5627.116   Schjelderup, K. von. Die Askese; eine religionspsychologische Untersuchung. Berlin, 1928.

Phil 5627.117   Bry, Carl Christian. Verkappte Religionen. Gotha, 1925.

Phil 5627.118   Dresser, Horatio W. Outlines of the psychology of religion. N.Y., 1929.

Phil 5627.119   Meige, Henry. Les possédées noires. Paris, 1894.

Phil 5627.120   Morgan, William Joseph. La psychologie de la religion dans l'Amérique. Thèse. Paris, 1928.

Phil 5627.121   Uren, A.R. Recent religious psychology. Edinburgh, 1928.

Phil 5627.122   Yellowlees, David. Psychology's defence of the faith. London, 1930.

Phil 5627.123   Marie, Auguste. Mysticisme et folie. Paris, 1907.

Phil 5627.124   Leitner, Hans. Psychologie jugendlicher Religiosität innerhalb des deutschen Methodismus. München, 1930.

Phil 5627.124.5   Leitner, Hans. Psychologie jugendlicher Religiosität innerhalb des deutschen Methodismus. Inaug. Diss. München, 1930.

Phil 5627.124.20   Williamson, G. Inside Buchmanism. London, 1954.

Phil 5627.125   Brabant, F.H. Religion and the mysterious. London, 1930.

Phil 5627.126   Fourrier, Maurice. Une expérience religieuse. Paris, 1931.

Phil 5627   Psychology - Treatises on special topics - Religion - General works (By date, e.g. .265 for 1965) - cont.

Phil 5627.127   Hodge, Alexander. Prayer and its psychology. Thesis. London, 1931.

Phil 5627.128   Trout, David McC. Religious behavior. N.Y., 1931.

Phil 5627.129   Bolley, Alphons. Gebetsstimmung und Gebet. Düsseldorf, 1930.

Phil 5627.130   Swarts, G. Salut par la foi et conversion brusque. Paris, 1931.

Phil 5627.130.2   Swarts, G. Salut par la foi et conversion brusque. Thèse. Paris, 1931.

Phil 5627.130.10   Swarts, G. Le banc des pénitents. Paris, 1931.

Phil 5627.130.12   Swarts, G. Le banc des pénitents. Thèse. Paris, 1931.

Phil 5627.131   Lang, Wyatt. A study of conversion. London, 1931.

Phil 5627.132.3   Heiler, Friedrich. Das Gebet. 5. Aufl. München, 1923.

Phil 5627.132.5   Heiler, Friedrich. Prayer. London, 1932.

Phil 5627.132.7   Heiler, Friedrich. Prayer. N.Y., 1958.

Phil 5627.132.10   Heard, Gerald. A preface to prayer. 1. ed. N.Y., 1944.

Phil 5627.133   Pyon, T.W. Psychology of the Christian life. N.Y., 1922.

Phil 5627.134   Henson, H.H. The Oxford group movement. N.Y., 1933.

Phil 5627.134.4   Russell, Arthur J. For sinners only. N.Y., 1932.

Phil 5627.134.10   What is the Oxford Group? N.Y., 1933.

Phil 5627.134.12   Russell, A.J. One thing I know. N.Y., 1933.

Phil 5627.134.15   The Oxford Group international house party. Oxford, 1934.

Phil 5627.134.20   Kitchen, V.C. I was a pagan. N.Y., 1934.

Phil 5627.134.25   Foot, Stephen. Life began yesterday. N.Y., 1935.

Phil 5627.134.30F   Oxford Group. The march of events, Oxford, 1935. Oxford, 1935.

Phil 5627.134.32   Buchman, Frank. Remaking the world. London, 1961.

Phil 5627.134.33   Buchman, Frank. Remaking the world. N.Y., 1949.

Phil 5627.134.34   Frank Buchman. London, 1958.

Phil 5627.134.35   Slattery, Sarah L. A year with the Oxford Group. Cambridge, 193-?

Phil 5627.134.40   Benson, C.I. The eight points of the Oxford Group. Melbourne, 1936.

Phil 5627.134.45   Winslow, J.C. Why I believe in the Oxford Group. 3. ed. London, 1934.

Phil 5627.134.50F   Rising tide. Chicago, 1938.

Phil 5627.134.54   Howard, Peter. Design for dedication. Chicago, 1964.

Phil 5627.134.55   Howard, Peter. Innocent men. London, 1941.

Phil 5627.134.55.5   Howard, Peter. Innocent men. London, 1941.

Phil 5627.134.56   Howard, Peter. The world rebuilt...Frank Buchman. London, 1951.

Phil 5627.134.56.5   Howard, Peter. The world rebuilt. N.Y., 1952.

Phil 5627.134.57   Wolrige Gordon, Anne. Peter Howard: life and letters. London, 1969.

Phil 5627.134.60   Spencer, F.A.M. The meaning of the groups. London, 1934.

Phil 5627.134.65   Shoemaker, S.M. The conversion of the church. N.Y., 1932.

Phil 5627.134.70   Sangster, W.E. God does guide us. N.Y., 1934.

Phil 5627.134.75   Howard, Peter. Ideas have legs. London, 1945.

Phil 5627.134.76   Howard, Peter. Ideas have legs. N.Y., 1946.

Phil 5627.134.77   Howard, Peter. Frank Buchman's secret. Garden City, N.Y., 1962.

Phil 5627.134.80   Jones, Olivin Mary. Inspired children. 1. ed. N.Y., 1933.

Phil 5627.134.85A   Eester, Allen W. Drawing-room conversion; Oxford Group movement. Durham, 1950.

Phil 5627.134.85B   Eester, Allen W. Drawing-room conversion; Oxford Group movement. Durham, 1950.

Phil 5627.134.90   Driberg, Tom. The mystery of moral re-armament. N.Y., 1964.

Phil 5627.134.100   Pamphlet box. Oxford Group movement.

Phil 5627.134.105   Ekman, Nils Gösta. Experiment med Gud. Stockholm, 1971.

Phil 5627.135   Wauer, G.A. Studien zur Religionspsychologie. Plauen, 1909.

Phil 5627.137.5   Johnsen, T. Heart and spirit. Oslo, 1934.

Phil 5627.138   Anderson, J.B. Applied religious psychology. Boston, 1919.

Phil 5627.139   Nagle, Urban. An empirical study of the development of religious thinking in boys from twelve to sixteen years old. Washington, 1934.

Phil 5627.140   Whitehead, George. Religion and woman. London, 1928.

Phil 5627.142   Ligon, E.M. The psychology of Christian personality. N.Y., 1936.

Phil 5627.143   Forsyth, D. Psychology and religion. London, 1935.

Phil 5627.144.1   Macmurray, John. The structure of religious experience. Hamden, Conn., 1971.

Phil 5627.145   Bonnaire, L. de. Examen critique, physique et théologique des convulsions. n.p., 1733.

Phil 5627.146   Alm, Ivar. Den religiösa funktionen i människosjälen. Akademisk abhandling. Stockholm, 1936.

Phil 5627.147.5   Lindworsky, J. The psychology of asceticism. London, 1936.

Phil 5627.148   Knudson, A.C. The vaiidity of religious experience. N.Y., 1937.

Phil 5627.149   Ferm, V. Religion in transition. London, 1937.

Phil 5627.150   Fuglsang-Damgaard, H. Religionspsykologi. København, 1933.

Phil 5627.151   L'homme et le péché. Paris, 1938.

Phil 5627.153   Jones, W.L. A psychological study of religious conversion. London, 1937.

Phil 5627.154   Moore, J.M. Theories of religious experience. Thesis. N.Y., 1938.

Phil 5627.155   Trueblood, D.E. The trustworthiness of religious experience. London, 1939.

Phil 5627.156   Norborg, S. Varieties of Christian experience. Minneapolis, 1938.

Phil 5627.160   Hellpach, W. Übersicht der Religionspsychologie. Leipzig, 1939.

Phil 5627.161   McKenzie, J.G. Psychology, psychotherapy and evangelicalism. London, 1940.

Phil 5627.162   Harms, Ernst. Psychologie und Psychiatrie der Conversion. Leiden, 1939.

Phil 5627.163   Pear, T.H. Religion and contemporary psychology. London, 1937.

Phil 5627.164   Clark, E.T. The psychology of religious awakening. N.Y., 1929.

Phil 5627.165   Thornhill, Alan. One fight more. London, 1943.

Phil 5627.166   Lunn, Arnold. Now I see. N.Y., 1933.

Phil 5627.168   Pfister, Oskar. Das Christentum und die Angst; eine religions-psychologische, historische und religionshygienische Untersuchung. Zürich, 1944.

Phil 5627.169   Dumas, Georges. Le surnaturel et les dieux d'après les maladies mentales. Paris, 1946.

Phil 5627.170   Jahn, Ernst. Religion und Individualpsychologie. Wien, 1933.

5627 Psychology - Treatises on special topics - Religion - General works (By date, e.g. .265 for 1965) - cont.

Phil 5627.172	Webb, Clement C.J. Religious experience; a public lecture. London, 1945.
Phil 5627.174	Witwicki, Władysław. La foi des éclairés. Paris, 1939.
Phil 5627.176	Festugière, André M.J. La sainteté. 1. éd. Paris, 1942.
Phil 5627.178	Berguer, Georges. Traité de psychologie de la religion. Lausanne, 1946.
Phil 5627.180.5	Frost, Bede. The art of mental prayer. London, 1935.
Phil 5627.185	Morrish, Furze. The ritual of higher magic. London, 1947?
Phil 5627.187	Martin, Everett D. The mystery of religion. N.Y., 1924.
Phil 5627.189	Allport, Gordon W. The individual and his religion. N.Y., 1950.
Phil 5627.189.3	Allport, Gordon W. The individual and his religion. N.Y., 1951.
Phil 5627.190	Jung, C.G. Arin. Zürich, 1951.
Phil 5627.192	Grensted, L.W. The psychology of religion. N.Y., 1952.
Phil 5627.194	Hellpach, Willy. Grundriss der Religionspsychologie. Stuttgart, 1951.
Phil 5627.196	Van Buskirk, J.D. Religion, healing and health. N.Y., 1952.
Phil 5627.198	Trillhaas, W. Die innere Welt. 2. Aufl. München, 1955.
Phil 5627.200	Amstutz, J. Stuxen des Gebets. Bern, 1954.
Phil 5627.201	Murisier, Ernest. Les maladies du sentiment religieux. Paris, 1901.
Phil 5627.205	Ruemke, H.C. The psychology of unbelief. London, 1952.
Phil 5627.210	Strauss, H.A. Psychologie und astrologische Symbolis. Zürich, 1953.
Phil 5627.215	Gruehn, W. Die Frommigkeit der Gegenwart. Münster, 1956.
Phil 5627.215.10	Moretti-Costanzi, Teodorice. L'estetica pia. Bologna, 1966.
VPhil 5627.215.15	Czakó, Ambrosius. A vallás lelektana, irta Czakó Ambró. Pécs, 1915.
Phil 5627.220	Neeser, Maurice. Du protestantisme au catholicisme. Paris, 1926.
Phil 5627.225	Magie des extremes. Bruges, 1952.
Phil 5627.230	Koerner, Margot. Religionspsychopathologische Untersuchungen. Mainz, 1959.
Phil 5627.231.2	Pauls, Theodor. Pietismus. 2. Aufl. Frankfurt, 1931.
Phil 5627.232	Bucke (R.M.) Memorial Society for the Study of Religious Experience. Newsletter-review. Montreal. 1,1966+
Phil 5627.236.2	Siegmend, Georg. Psychologie des Gottesglaubens auf Grund literarischer Selbstzeugnisse. 2. Aufl. Münster, 1965.
Phil 5627.241	Duguid, Julian. I am persuaded. N.Y., 1941.
Phil 5627.245.1	Tournier, Paul. Technik und Glaube. Basel, 1945.
Phil 5627.245.2	Tournier, Paul. The person reborn. N.Y., 1966.
Phil 5627.247.1	Tournier, Paul. The whole person in a broken world. N.Y., 1964.
Phil 5627.248.1	Tournier, Paul. The strong and weak. Philadelphia, 1963.
Phil 5627.257	Frankl, V.E. The doctor and the soul. N.Y., 1957.
Phil 5627.257.5	Baudouin, Charles. Psychanalyse du symbole religieux. Paris, 1957.
Phil 5627.257.10	Sanson, Henri. Spiritualité de la vie active. Le Puy, 1957.
Phil 5627.258	Argyle, Michael. Religious behavior. London, 1958.
Phil 5627.258.5	Potempa, Rudolf. Persönlichkeit und Religiosität. Göttingen, 1958.
Phil 5627.259	Cox, David. Jung and St. Paul. N.Y., 1959.
Phil 5627.259.5	Vetter, George. Magic and religion. London, 1959.
Phil 5627.259.10	Lindenberg, Wladimir. Mysterium der Begegnung. München, 1959.
Phil 5627.259.15	Sundén, Hjalmar. Religionen och rollerna. Stockholm, 1959.
Phil 5627.259.20	Clark, W.H. The psychology of religion. N.Y., 1959.
Phil 5627.260	White, Victor. Soul and psyche. London, 1960.
Phil 5627.260.5	Graneris, Giuseppe. La vita della religion e nella storia delle religioni. Torino, 1960.
Phil 5627.260.13	Carrier, Hervé. Psycho-sociologie de l'appartenance religieuse. 3. ed. Rome, 1966.
Phil 5627.261	Bitter, W. Zur Rettung des Menschlichen in unserer Zeit. Stuttgart, 1961.
Phil 5627.261.5	Schulz, Johannes Josef. Bionome Geschlechtsentfaltung. München, 1961.
Phil 5627.261.10	Brezzi, Paolo. L'experienza della prehiera. Firenze, 1961.
Phil 5627.261.15	Muñoz, Jesu. Psychologia philosophica. Santander, 1961.
Phil 5627.262	Rochedieu, Edmond. Personnalité et vie religieuse chez l'adolescent. Neuchâtel, 1962.
Phil 5627.262.5	Hopkins, Pryns. The social psychology of religious experience. N.Y., 1962.
Phil 5627.262.10	Nédoncelle, M. Prière humaine, prière divine. Bruges, 1962.
Phil 5627.262.15	Cvekl, Jiří. Člověk a světový názor. Praha, 1962.
Phil 5627.263	Bowers, M.K. Conflicts of the clergy. Edinburgh, 1963.
Phil 5627.264	Berg, J.H. Psychologie en theologische antropologie. Nijkerk, 1964.
Phil 5627.264.5	Maslow, Abraham Harold. Religions, values and peak-experiences. Columbus, Ohio, 1964.
Phil 5627.264.10	Hick, John. Faith and the philosophers. N.Y., 1964.
Phil 5627.264.15	Müller-Eckhard, Hans. Das Unzerstörbare. Stuttgart, 1964.
Phil 5627.264.20	McLaughlin, Barry. Nature, grace and religious development. N.Y., 1964.
Phil 5627.264.25	Fortmann, Henricus Martinus Maria. Als zienda onzienlijke. v.1-3. Hilversum, 1964- 4v.
Phil 5627.265	Bindl, Maria Frieda. Das religiöse Erleben im Spiegel der Bildgestaltung. Freiburg, 1965.
Phil 5627.265.5	Pöll, Wilhelm. Religionspsychologie. München, 1965.
Phil 5627.266	Goldbrunner, Josef. Realisation; Anthropologie in Seelsorge und Erziehung. Greiburg, 1966.
Phil 5627.266.5	Vergote, Antoine. Psychologie religieuse. Bruxelles, 1966.
Phil 5627.266.6	Vergote, Antoine. The religious man. Dublin, 1969.
Phil 5627.266.10	Bakan, David. The duality of human existence. Chicago, 1966.
Phil 5627.266.15	Griesl, Gottfried. Pastoralpsychologische Studien. Innsbruck, 1966.
Phil 5627.266.20	Tournier, Paul. L'homme et son lieu. Psychologie et foi. Neuchâtel, 1966.
Phil 5627.266.21	Tournier, Paul. A place for you; psychology and religion. 1st U.S. ed. N.Y., 1968.
Phil 5627.266.25	Bjoerkhen, John. Människan och makterna. Stockholm, 1966.
Phil 5627.266.30	Hartler, Josef. Religiös roll och Kristusliv. Lund, 1966.
Phil 5627.267	Platonev, Konstantin K. Psikhologiia religii. Moskva, 1967.
Phil 5627.267.5	Pohier, Jacques Marie. Psychologie et théologie. Paris, 1967.
Phil 5627.267.15	Banfi, Antonio. Esperienza religiosa e coscienza religiosa e coscienza filosofica. Urbino, 1967.

Phil 5627 Psychology - Treatises on special topics - Religion - General works (By date, e.g. .265 for 1965) - cont.

Phil 5627.268	Fobry, Joseph B. The pursuit of meaning. Boston, 1968.
Phil 5627.268.5	Smolenaars, A.J. Kerkelijkheid en persoonlijkheidskenmerken in twee Zuiderzeepolders. Amsterdam, 1968.
Phil 5627.268.10	Pruyser, Paul W. A dynamic psychology of religion. N.Y., 1968.
Phil 5627.268.18	Rokeach, Milton. Beliefs, attitudes and values; a theory of organization and change. San Francisco, 1969.
Phil 5627.269	Rabut, Olivier A. L'expérience religieuse fondamentale. Paris, 1969.
Phil 5627.269.5	Bukin, Viktor R. Psikhologiia veruiushchikh i ateisticheskoe vospitanie. Moskva, 1969.
Phil 5627.269.10	Johoda, Gustav. The psychology of superstition. London, 1969.
Phil 5627.269.15	Amon, Jesus. Prejuicio antiprotestante y religiosidad utilitaria. Madrid, 1969.
Phil 5627.270	Homans, Peter. Theology after Freud; an interpretive inquiry. Indianapolis, 1970.
Phil 5627.270.5	Anderson, George Christian. Your religion: neurotic or healthy? 1st ed. Garden City, 1970.
Phil 5627.270.10	Scheibe, Karl Edward. Beliefs and values. N.Y., 1970.
Phil 5627.271.5	Mensching, Gustav. Topos und Typos; Motive und Strukturen religiösen Lebens. Bonn, 1971.

Phil 5628 Psychology - Treatises on special topics - Religion - Special topics

Phil 5628.5	Cutten, George Barton. Speaking with tongues, historically and psychologically considered. New Haven, 1927.
Phil 5628.5.5	Horton, Wade H. The glossolalia phenomenon. 1st ed. Cleveland, 1966.
Phil 5628.10	Vernier, André. L'extase et la personalité. Thèse. Montauban, 1901.
Phil 5628.10.5.1	Buber, Martin. Ekstatische Konfessionen. Leipzig, 1921.
Phil 5628.10.10	Baumann, Evert Dirk. De goddelijke waanzin. Assen, 1932.
Phil 5628.10.15	Arbman, Ernst. Ecstasy or religious trance. Stockholm, 1963-70. 3v.
Phil 5628.10.20	Busson, Claude Ignace. Premières [-secondes] lettres sur l'extatique de Niéderbronn et sur ses révélations. Besançon, 1849.
Phil 5628.11.1	Puccini, Vincenzo. The life of St. Mary Magdalene of Pazzi, a Carmelite nun. London, 1687.
Phil 5628.11.6	Mary Minima, Sister. Seraph among angels; the life of St. Mary Magdalene de' Pazzi. Chicago, 1958.
Phil 5628.12	Perales y Gutiérrez, Arturo. El supernaturalismo de Santa Teresa y la filosofia médica. Madrid, 1894.
Phil 5628.13	Petrus de Dacia. Vita Christinae Stumbelensis edibit Johannes Paukon. Gotoburgi, 1896.
Phil 5628.50	Ostermann, Petrus. Commentarius iuridicus ad L. Stigmata, C. de Fabricensibus. Coloniae Agripinae, 1629.
Phil 5628.50.5	Jordanaeus, Johann. Disputatio brevis ad categorica de proba stigmata utrum scilicet ea licita sit, necne. Coloniae Agrippinae, 1630.
Phil 5628.50.10	Charbonnier, Nestor. Maladies et facultés diverses des mystiques. Bruxelles, 1875.
Phil 5628.50.15	Marin, Paul. Coup d'oeil sur les thaumaturges et les médiums du XIXe siècle. Paris, 1891.
Phil 5628.50.20	Imbert-Gourbeyre, Antoine. La stigmatisation, l'extase divine, et les miracles de Lourdes. Clermont-Ferrand, 1894. 2v.
Phil 5628.50.25	Höcht, Johannes Maria. Träger der Wundmale Christi. Wiesbaden, 1951-52. 2v.
Phil 5628.51	Warlomont, Évariste. Louise Lateau. Bruxelles, 1875.
Phil 5628.51.5	Bourneville, Désiré Magloire. Science and miracle. Louise Lateau ou la stigmatisée belge. Paris, 1875.
Phil 5628.51.10	Rohling, August. Louise Lateau: her stigmas and ecstasy. N.Y., 1879.
Phil 5628.52	Die Stigmatisirten des neunzehnten Jahrhunderts: Anna Katharina Emmerich, Maria von Mörl, Domenico Lazzari. Regensburg, 1874.
Phil 5628.52.5	Schmöger, Karl Erhard. Leben der Gottseligen Anna Katharina Emmerich. Freiburg, 1885.
Phil 5628.53	Merkt, Josef. Die Wundmale des heiligen Franziskus von Assisi. Leipzig, 1910.
Phil 5628.54.4	Lauer, Nikolaus. Barbara Pfister, eine pfälzische Stigmatisierte. 4. Aufl. Speyer, 1964.
Phil 5628.55	Gerlich, Fritz. Die Stigmatisierte Therese Neumann von Konnersreuth. München, 1929. 2v.
Phil 5628.55.6	Lama, Friedrich. Therese Neumann; a stigmatist of our days. Milwaukee, 1929.
Phil 5628.55.11	Teodorowicz, Józef. Mystical phenomena in the life of Theresa Neumann. St. Louis, Mo., 1940.
Phil 5628.55.15	Graef, Hilda Charlotte. The case of Therese Neumann. Cork, 1951.
Phil 5628.55.21	Siwek, Paul. The riddle of Konnersreuth; a psychological and religious study. Dublin, 1954.
Phil 5628.55.25	Rinser, Luise. Die Wahrheit über Konnersreuth. Einsiedeln, 1954.
Phil 5628.55.30	Roessler, Max. Therese Neumann von Konnersreuth. Wurzburg, 1963.
Phil 5628.55.35	Steiner, Johannes. Therese Neumann von Konnersreuth. München, 1963.

Phil 5630 Psychology - Treatises on special topics - Rumor

Phil 5630.3	Chadwick, Thomas. The influence of rumour on human thought and action. Manchester, 1932.
Phil 5630.5A	Allport, G.W. The psychology of rumor. N.Y., 1947.
Phil 5630.5B	Allport, G.W. The psychology of rumor. N.Y., 1947.
Phil 5630.5C	Allport, G.W. The psychology of rumor. N.Y., 1947.
Phil 5630.5.2	Allport, G.W. The psychology of rumor. N.Y., 1948.
Phil 5630.10	Jacobson, David J. The affairs of Dame Rumor. N.Y., 1948.

Phil 5635 Psychology - Treatises on special topics - Sensation

Phil 5635.01	Pamphlet vol. Sensations. German dissertations. 2 pam.
Phil 5635.02	Pamphlet box. Sensation.
Phil 5635.1	Delabarre, E.B. Über Bewegungsempfindungen. Freiburg, 1891.
Phil 5635.2	Delboeuf, J.R.L. Théorie générale de la sensibilité. Bruxelles, 1876.
Phil 5635.4	Guillaume, J.A.M. Nouveau traité des sensations. Paris, 1876. 2v.
Phil 5635.5.2	Mach, Ernst. Contributions to the analysis of the sensations. Chicago, 1897.
Phil 5635.5.4	Mach, Ernst. Beiträge zur Analyse de Empfindungen. Jena, 1886.
Phil 5635.5.5	Mach, Ernst. Die Analyse der Empfindungen. Jena, 1900.
Phil 5635.5.6	Mach, Ernst. Die Analyse der Empfindungen. 6. Aufl. Jena, 1911.

Phil 5635   Psychology - Treatises on special topics - Sensation - cont.

Phil 5635.5.7   Mach, Ernst. Grundlinien der Lehre vom den Bewegungsempfindungen. Leipzig, 1875.
Phil 5635.5.8   Mach, Ernst. The analysis of sensations on the relation of the physical to the psychical. N.Y., 1959.
Phil 5635.5.9   Mach, Ernst. The analysis of sensations. Chicago, 1914.
Phil 5635.5.10   Mach, Ernst. Contributions to the analysis of the sensations. Chicago, 1910.
Phil 5635.5.11   Hell, B. Ernst Mach's Philosophie. Stuttgart, 1907.
Phil 5635.7   Féré, C. Sensation et mouvement. Paris, 1900.
Phil 5635.8   Paulsen, J. Das Problem der Empfindung. Giessen, 1907.
Phil 5635.9   Woodrow, H. Quantitative study of rhythm. N.Y., 1909.
Phil 5635.10   Lippmann, F. Du déterminisme psychologique. Strasbourg, 1909.
Phil 5635.11   Henry, Charles. Sensation et énergie. Paris, 1911.
Phil 5635.12   Murray, E. Organic sensation. n.p., 1909.
Phil 5635.13   De Seze, V. Recherches...sur la sensibilité. Paris, 1786.
Phil 5635.14   Rahn, Carl. Relation of sensation to other categories in contemporary psychology. Princeton, 1914.
Phil 5635.15   Desvaux, Antoine. Introduction à une étude du courant de chaleur. Thèse. Paris, 1914.
Phil 5635.17   Weidensall, C.J. Studies in rhythm. Cincinnati, 1916.
Phil 5635.17.5   Hiriartborde, Edmond. Les aptitudes rythmiques. Paris, 1968.
Phil 5635.18   Beaunis, H. Les sensations internes. Paris, 1889.
Phil 5635.19F   Peirce, C.S. On small differences of sensation. n.p., 18-?
Phil 5635.20   Holt, Edwin B. An experimental study of sensation. Cambridge, Mass., 1903.
Phil 5635.21   Schneider, G.H. Über die Empfindung der Ruhe. Zürich, 1876.
Phil 5635.22   Henmon, V.A.C. The time of perception as a measure of differences in sensations. N.Y., 1906.
Phil 5635.23   Nitsche, Adolf. Versuch einer einheitlichen Lehre von der Gefühlin. Innsbruck, 1886.
Phil 5635.24   Fernberger, Samuel W. Relation of methods of just perceptible differences and constant stimuli. n.p., 1912.
Phil 5635.25   Kessler, Jacob. Untersuchungen über den Temperatursinn. Inaug. Diss. Bonn, 1884.
Phil 5635.26   Deichmann, Ludwig. Erregung secundärer Empfindungen im Gebiete der Sinnesorgane. Inaug. Diss. Greifswald, 1889.
Phil 5635.27   Oppenheimer, Z. Physiologie des Gefühls. Heidelberg, 1899.
Phil 5635.30   Heilig, G. Die sinnlichen Gefühle des Menschen. Jena, 1919.
Phil 5635.31   Richet, Charles. Recherches experimentales et cliniques sur la sensibilité. Paris, 1877.
Phil 5635.32   Stopford, J.S.B. Sensation and the sensory pathway. London, 1930.
Phil 5635.33   Besser, L. Was ist Empfindung? Bonn, 1881.
Phil 5635.34   Pradines, M. Philosophie de la sensation. Paris, 1928-34. 3v.
Phil 5635.35   Hartshorne, C. The philosophy and psychology of sensation. Chicago, 1934.
Phil 5635.36   Salzi, Piierre. La sensation. Paris, 1934.
Phil 5635.36.5   Salzi, Pierre. La sensation, étude de sa genèse et de son rôle dans la connaissance. Thèse. Paris, 1934.
Phil 5635.37   Brentano, Franz. Untersuchungen zur Sinnespsychologie. Leipzig, 1907.
Phil 5635.38   Steige, R. Gefühl und Affekt. Inaug. Diss. Breslau? 1937.
Phil 5635.39   Wolff, E.M. La senation et l'image. Thèse. Carcassonne, 1943.
Phil 5635.40   Boulogne, C.D. My friends. N.Y., 1953.
Phil 5635.45   Kovalgin, V.M. Problema oshchushchenii i reflektornaia teoriia. Minsk, 1959.
Phil 5635.45.5   Kovalgin, V.M. Reflektornaia teoriia oskchushchenii. Minsk, 1963.
Phil 5635.46   Armstrong, David Malet. Bodily sensations. London, 1962.
Phil 5635.48   Christman, Raymond John. Sensory experience. Scranton, 1971.

Phil 5640   Psychology - Treatises on special topics - Senses - General works

Phil 5640.2   Bernstein, J. Five senses of man. N.Y., 1876.
Phil 5640.2.3   Bernstein, J. Die fünf Sinne des Menschen. Leipzig, 1875.
Phil 5640.2.4   Bernstein, J. Five senses of man. N.Y., 1890.
Phil 5640.2.5   Bernstein, J. Les sens. 5e éd. Paris, 1893.
Phil 5640.3.5   M'Kendrick, J.G. The physiology of the senses. N.Y., 1907.
Phil 5640.4   Wilson, G. Five gateways of knowledge. Philadelphia, 1857.
Phil 5640.4.7   Wilson, G. The five gateways of knowledge. 7th ed. London, 1881.
Phil 5640.5   Wyld, R.S. Physics and philosophy of the senses. London, 1875.
Phil 5640.6.25   Brühl, P.N. Die specifischen Sinnesenergien nach John Müller. Fulda, 1915.
Phil 5640.7   Thomson, W. The six gateways of knowledge. N.Y., 1884.
Phil 5640.8   Le Cat, C.N. A physical essay on the senses. London, 1750.
Phil 5640.8.5   Le Cat, C.N. Traité des sens. Rouen, 1740.
Phil 5640.9   Genzmer, A.O.H. Untersuchungen über die Sinneswahrnehmungen des neugeborenen Menschen. Halle, n.d.
Phil 5640.9.2   Genzmer, A.O.H. Untersuchungen über die Sinneswahrnehmungen des neugeborenen Menschen. Halle, 1882.
Phil 5640.10   Williams, C.H. Vision: color, sense and hearing. Chicago, 1902.
Phil 5640.11   Henmon, V.A.C. Time of perception as a measure of differences in sensations. N.Y., 1906.
Phil 5640.12   Pamphlet vol. Psychology. Senses. 16 pam.
Phil 5640.12.2   Pamphlet vol. Psychology. Senses. 10 pam.
Phil 5640.13   George, L. Die fünf Sinne. Berlin, 1846.
Phil 5640.15   Elliott, John. Philosophical observations on the senses. London, 1780.
Phil 5640.15   Wells, G.R. Influence of stimulus...duration on reaction time. Princeton, 1913.
Phil 5640.16   Dell, J.A. The gateways of knowledge. Cambridge, 1912.
Phil 5640.17   Aitken, E.H. The five windows of the soul. London, 1913.
Phil 5640.17.5   Aitken, E.H. Le va del l'anima. Torino, 1913.
Phil 5640.18   Kries, J. von. Allgemeine Sinnesphysiologie. Leipzig, 1923.
Phil 5640.19   Abrutz, Sydney. Om sinnesrörelsernas fysiologi och psykologi. Upsala, 1901.
Phil 5640.20   Nordvall, A.L. Psykologiska studier. Stockholm, 1885.
Phil 5640.21   Goering, W. Raum und Stoff. Berlin, 1876.
Phil 5640.22   Semon, R. Bewusstseinsvorgang und Gehirnprozess. Wiesbaden, 1920.
Phil 5640.23   Rubinstein, S. Aus der Innenwelt. Leipzig, 1888.

Phil 5640   Psychology - Treatises on special topics - Senses - General works - cont.

Phil 5640.24   Dreher, E. Beiträge zu einer exacten Psycho-Physiologie. Halle, 1880.
Phil 5640.25   Hillebrand, F. Ewald Hering ein Gedenkwort der Psychophysik. Berlin, 1918.
Phil 5640.26   Lemaire, J. Étude sur la connaissance sensible des objets extérieurs. Liege, 1921.
Phil 5640.27   Plessner, H. Die Einheit der Sinne grundlinien einer Asthesiologie. Bonn, 1923.
Phil 5640.28   Drbal, M.A. Über Natur der Sinne. Linz, 1860.
Htn   Phil 5640.29*   Mayne, Zachary. Two dissertations concerning sense and the imagination. London, 1728.
Phil 5640.30   Watt, Henry J. The sensory basis and structure of knowledge. London, 1925.
Phil 5640.31   Schwertschlager, J. Die Sinneserkenntnis. München, 1924.
Phil 5640.32   Skramlik, E. von. Handbuch der Physiologie der niederen Sinne. Leipzig, 1926.
Phil 5640.33   Brown, Warner. The judgment of very weak sensory stimuli. Berkeley, 1914.
Phil 5640.34   Grotenfelt, A. Das Webersche Gesetz und die psychische Relativität. Helsingfors, 1888.
Phil 5640.35   Handbuch der Physiologie des Menschen. v.3. Braunschweig, 1905.
Phil 5640.35.5   Handbuch der Physiologie des Menschen. v.3-4. Braunschweig, 1904-09. 3v.
Phil 5640.36   Wolters, A.W.P. The evidence of our senses. London, 1933.
Phil 5640.37   Phusis, Maurice (pseud.). Classification universelle systématique et coordonnée des connaissances humaines. Paris, 1934.
Phil 5640.38   Greenwood, Major. Physiology of the special senses. London, 1910.
Phil 5640.39   Taylor, C.F. Sensation and pain. N.Y., 1881.
Phil 5640.40   Rawdon-Smith, A.F. Theories of sensation. Cambridge, 1938.
Phil 5640.41   Nogué, Jean. Esquisse d'un système des qualités sensibles. Paris, 1943.
Phil 5640.42   Brunswik, Egon. Experimentelle Psychologie in Demonstrationen. Wien, 1935.
Phil 5640.43   Piéron, Henri. Aux sources de la connaissance la sensation. 3. éd. Paris, 1945.
Phil 5640.45   Jeffress, Lloyd A. Cerebral mechanisms in behavior. N.Y., 1951.
Phil 5640.50   Geldard, Frank A. The human senses. N.Y., 1962.
Phil 5640.125   Kreibig, Josef K. Die Sinne des Menschen. 3. Aufl. Leipzig, 1917.
Phil 5640.125.5   Pikler, Gyula. Sinnesphysiologische Untersuchungen. Leipzig, 1917.
Phil 5640.125.7   Pikler, Gyula. Hypothesenfreie Theorie der Gegenfarben. Leipzig, 1919.
Phil 5640.125.8   Pikler, Gyula. Theorie der Konsonanz und Dissonanz. Leipzig, 1919.
Phil 5640.125.9   Pikler, Gyula. Theorie der Empfindungsstärke und Insbesondere des Weberschen Gesetzes. Leipzig, 1920.
Phil 5640.125.10   Pikler, Gyula. Theorie der Empfindungsqualität als Abbildes des Reizes. Leipzig, 1922.
Phil 5640.125.15   Pikler, Gyula. Theorie des Gedächtnisses. Leipzig, 1926.
Phil 5640.127   Hurst, A.F. The Croonian lectures. London, 1920.
Phil 5640.129B   Adrian, E.D. The basis of sensation. N.Y., 1928.
Phil 5640.130.2   Piéron, Henri. La sensation. 2. éd. Paris, 1957.
Phil 5640.132   Juritsch, M. Sinn und Geist. Freiburg, 1961.
Phil 5640.133   Symposium on Principles of Sensory Communication. Sensory communication...Symposium...July 19-Aug. 1, 1959, M.I.T. Cambridge, 1961.
Phil 5640.135   Anan'ev, B.G. Teoriia oshchushchenii. Leningrad, 1961.
Phil 5640.136   Symposium on Sensory Deprivation. Sensory deprivation. Cambridge, 1961.
Phil 5640.136.5   Šváb, L. Bibliography of sensory deprivation and social isolation. Prague, 1966.
Phil 5640.136.10   Hatwell, Yvette. Privation sensorielle et intelligence. Paris, 1966.
Phil 5640.136.15   Zuber, John Peter. Sensory deprivation: fifteen years of research. N.Y., 1969.
Phil 5640.137   Schultz, Duane P. Sensory restriction. N.Y., 1965.
Phil 5640.138   Brownfield, Charles A. Isolation; clinical and experimental approaches. N.Y., 1965.
Phil 5640.139   Mykytenko, Danylo A. Vidchuttia i diisnist'. Kyïv, 1966.
Phil 5640.140   Békésy, Georg von. Sensory inhibition. Princeton, 1967.
Phil 5640.142   Corso, John F. The experimental psychology sensory behavior. N.Y., 1967.
Phil 5640.144   Milne, Lorus J. The senses of animals and men. N.Y., 1962.
Phil 5640.146   Pitcher, George Willard. A theory of perception. Princeton, N.J., 1971.
Phil 5640.148   Cain, William S. Stimulus and sensation; readings in sensory psychology. Boston, 1971.

Phil 5642   Psychology - Treatises on special topics - Senses - Synaesthesia

Phil 5642.01   Pamphlet box. Psychology. Senses. Synaesthesia.
Phil 5642.7   Suarez de Mendoza, Ferdinand. L'audition colorée. 2. éd. Paris, 1899.
Phil 5642.9   Millet, J. Audition colorée. Paris, 1892.
Phil 5642.11   Flournoy, T. Des phénomènes de synopsie. Paris, 1893.
Phil 5642.13   Lemaitre, A. Audition colorée et phénomènes connexes. Paris, 1901.
Phil 5642.15   Wheeler, R.H. The synaesthesia of a blind subject. Eugene, 1920.
Phil 5642.17   Benoist, Émilien. Contribution à l'étude de l'audition colorée. Paris, 1899.
Phil 5642.18   Argelander, A. Das Farbenhören und der synäthetische Faktor der Wahrnehmung. Jena, 1927.
Phil 5642.19   Ellinger, A. Über Doppelempfindung. Diss. Stuttgart, 1889.
Phil 5642.20   Anschütz, Georg. Kurze Einführung in die Farbe-Ton-Forschung. Leipzig, 1927.
Phil 5642.22   Schroder, Ludwig. Sinne und Sinnesverknüpfungen. Heidelberg, 1969.

Phil 5643   Psychology - Treatises on special topics - Senses - Special senses - Sight, Vision

Phil 5643.01   Pamphlet vol. Psychology. Vision. 16 pam.
Phil 5643.02   Pamphlet vol. Psychology. Vision. German dissertations. 20 pam.
Phil 5643.03   Pamphlet vol. Psychology. Vision. German dissertations. 14 pam.
Phil 5643.04   Pamphlet box. Psychology. Vision. German dissertations.
Phil 5643.07   Pamphlet vol. Psychology. Vision. 19 pam.
Phil 5643.08   Pamphlet box. Psychology. Vision.
Phil 5643.1   Abbott, T.K. Sight and touch. London, 1864.

Phil 5643   Psychology - Treatises on special topics - Senses - Special senses - Sight, Vision - cont.

Phil 5643.2   Angelucci, A. Untersuchungen über die Sehthätigkeit. Giessen, 1890.
Phil 5643.3   Aubert, H.R. Physiologie der Netzhaut. Breslau, 1865.
Phil 5643.4   Classen, A. Über das Schlussverfahren der Sehactes. Rostock, 1863.
Phil 5643.5   Classen, A. Physiologie des Gesichtssinnes. Braunschweig, 1876.
Phil 5643.6   Déal, J.N. Nouvel essai sur la lumière et les couleurs. Paris, 1827.
Phil 5643.7   Goblet, H.F. A theory of sight, or How we see. London, 1869.
Phil 5643.8*   Helmholtz, H. Physiologischen Optik. v.1 and Atlas. Leipzig, 1867. 2v.
Phil 5643.8.5   Helmholtz, H. Handbuch der physiologischen Optik. Hamburg, 1896.
Phil 5643.8.10   Helmholtz, H. Optique physiologique. Paris, 1867.
Phil 5643.8.12   Helmholtz, H. Treatise on physiological optics. Rochester, N.Y., 1924-25. 3v.
Phil 5643.8.30   Tscherning, M. Herman von Helmholtz und der Akkommodationstheorie. Leipzig, 1910.
Phil 5643.9   Egger, V. L'oeil et l'oreille. Paris, 1886.
Phil 5643.11   Hering, E. Beiträge zur Physiologie. v.1-5. Leipzig, 1861-
Phil 5643.11.5   Hering, E. Zur Lehre vom Lichtsinne. Wien, 1878.
Phil 5643.11.9   Hering, E. Grundzüge zur Lehre vom Lichtsinne. Leipzig, 1920.
Phil 5643.11.10   Hering, E. Outline of a theory of the light sense. Cambridge, 1964.
Phil 5643.12   Hoppe, J.F. Die Schein-Bewegungen. Würzburg, 1879.
Phil 5643.12.5   Hoppe, J.F. Psychologish-physiologische Optik. Leipzig, 1881.
Phil 5643.12.9   Hoppe, J.F. Die Drehbare Bilderscheibe. Leipzig, 1884.
Phil 5643.13   Jaesche, E. Das räumliche Sehen. Stuttgart, 1879.
Phil 5643.14   Kaiser, H. Compendium der physiologische Optik. Wiesbaden, 1872.
Phil 5643.15   Le Conte, J. Sight. N.Y., 1881.
Phil 5643.16   Bleuler, E. Zwangsmässige Lichtemfindungen. Leipzig, 1881.
Phil 5643.17   Monck, W.H.S. Space and vision. Dublin, 1872.
Phil 5643.18   Stellwag, K. von C. Die Accommodationsfehler des Auges. n.p., 1855.
Phil 5643.19   Wüllner, F.H.A. Einleitung in die Dioptrik des Auges. Leipzig, 1866.
Phil 5643.21   Bowditch, H.P. Optical illusions of motion. Cambridge, 1882.
Phil 5643.22   Dix, J.H. Treatise...nature, treatment, morbid sensibility...retina. Boston, 1849.
Phil 5643.23   Mauthner, L. Gehirn und Auge. Wiesbaden, 1881.
Phil 5643.24   Clark, J.H. Sight and hearing. N.Y., 1856.
Phil 5643.25.2   Franz, Shepherd I. After images. N.Y., 1899.
Phil 5643.26   Bourdon, B. La perception visuelle de l'espace. Paris, 1902.
Phil 5643.27   Kohler, J. Der simultane Farben- und Helligkeitskontrast. Leipzig, 1903.
Phil 5643.28   Seyfert, R. Über die Auffassung einfachster Raumformen. Leipzig, 1902.
Phil 5643.29   Konig, Arthur. Gesammelte Abhandlungen der physiologischen Optik. Leipzig, 1903.
Phil 5643.30   Nuel, J.P. La vision. Paris, 1904.
Phil 5643.31   Zehender, W. Über optische Täuschung. Leipzig, 1902.
Phil 5643.32   Listing, J.B. Beitrag zur physiologischen Optik. Leipzig, 1905.
Phil 5643.33.2   Carr, Harvey. A visual illusion of motion during eye closure. Lancaster, 1906.
Phil 5643.34   Ruediger, W.C. The field of distinct vision. n.p., 1907.
Phil 5643.36   Burrow, N.J. The determination of the position. Baltimore, 1909.
Phil 5643.37   Poffenberger, A.T. Reaction time to retinal stimulation. N.Y., 1912.
Phil 5643.38   Adams, H.F. Autokinetic sensations. Chicago, 1912.
Phil 5643.39   Panum, P.L. Physiologische Untersuchungen über das Sehen mit zwei Augen. Kiel, 1858.
Phil 5643.40   Fearn, John. Rational of the cause of cerebral vision. London, 1830? 4 pam.
Phil 5643.41   Clifford, W.K. Seeing and thinking. London, 1879.
Phil 5643.42   Wilbrand, H. Die Seelenblindheit als Herderscheinung. Wiesbaden, 1887.
Phil 5643.43   Dodge, Raymond. An experimental study of visual fixation. Lancaster, 1907.
Phil 5643.43.5   Bader, Paul. Augentauschungen. Leipzig, 1907.
Phil 5643.44   Hinshelwood, J. Letter, word, and mind blindness. London, 1900.
Phil 5643.45   Dor, Louis. La fatigue oculaire et le surmenage visuel. Paris, 1906.
Phil 5643.46   Ritter, Sarah M. The vertical-horizontal illusion. Princeton, 1917.
Phil 5643.47   Urbantschitsch, V. Über subjektive optische Anschauungsbilder. Leipzig, 1907.
Phil 5643.48   Stilling, Jacob. Psychologie der Gesichtsvorstellung. Berlin, 1901.
Phil 5643.49   Ueberhorst, Karl. Die Entstehung der Gesichtswahrnehmung. Göttingen, 1876.
Phil 5643.50   Pauwels, Friedrich. Beiträge zur Lehre vom optischen Zeitsinn. Inaug. Diss. Frieburg, 1911?
Phil 5643.51   Drott, Anton. Die Aussengrenzen des Gesichtsfeldes für weisse und farbige Objecte beim normalen Auge. Inaug. Diss. Breslau, 1894?
Phil 5643.52A   Gould, George M. Biographic clinics. Philadelphia, 1903-05. 6v.
Phil 5643.52B   Gould, George M. Biographic clinics. v.1. Philadelphia, 1903-05.
Phil 5643.53   Raehlman, E.Zur vergleichenden Physiologie des Gesichtsinnes. Jena, 1907.
Phil 5643.55   Witasek, Stephan. Psychologie der Raumwahrnehmung des Auges. Heidelberg, 1910.
Phil 5643.56   Kries, Johannes von. Die Gesichts-Empfindungen und ihre Analyse. Leipzig, 1882.
Phil 5643.57   Daublebsky, Storneck von. Der Sehraum auf grund der Erfahrung. Leipzig, 1907.
Phil 5643.58   Kolbenheyer, E.G. Die sensorielle Theorie der optischen Raumempfindung. Leipzig, 1905.
Phil 5643.67   Dittler, Rudolf. Stereoskopisches Sehen und Messen. Leipzig, 1919.
Phil 5643.68   Rubin, Edgar. Visuell wahrgenommene figuren. København, 1921.
Phil 5643.68.5   Rubin, Edgar. Synsoplevedefigurer. København, 1915.

Phil 5643   Psychology - Treatises on special topics - Senses - Special senses - Sight, Vision - cont.

Phil 5643.69   Troland, L.T. The present status of visual science. Washington, 1922.
Phil 5643.71   Winkler, F. Studien über Wahrnehmungstauschungen. Leipzig, 1915.
Phil 5643.72   Karplus, S. Beitrag zur Lehre von den Geschichtsempfindungen. Inaug. Diss. Berlin, 1902.
Phil 5643.73   Janet, P. La durée des senstaions visuelles élémentaires. Paris, 1904.
Phil 5643.74   Holsopple, J.Q. Factors involved in the reduction of post-rotation nystagmus time. Baltimore, 1924.
Phil 5643.75   Pollak, G.F.X. Über den Einfluss der Gesichtsschärfe. Inaug. Diss. Dillingen, 1829.
Phil 5643.76   Metz, Bernhard. Uber die pseudoskopische Ablenkung paralleler Linien. Marburg, 1882.
Phil 5643.77   Déjean, Renée. Les conditions objectives de la perception visuelle. Thèse. Paris, 1926. 2 pam.
Phil 5643.77.5   Déjean, Renée. La perception visuelle. Paris, 1926.
Phil 5643.78   Leeser, Otto. Über Linien- und Flächenvergleichung. Inaug. Diss. Leipzig, 1915.
Phil 5643.79   Berger, E. Beiträge zur Psychologie des Sehens. München, 1925.
Phil 5643.80   Neiglick, H. Zur Psychophysik des Lichtsinns. Leipzig, 1887.
Phil 5643.81   Hasenclever, R. Die Raumvorstellung aus der Gesichtssinne. Berlin, 1842.
Phil 5643.82   Stöhr, Adolf. Grundfragen der psychophysiologischen Optik. Leipzig, 1904.
Phil 5643.83   Wirth, Wilhelm. Zur psychophysischen Analyse der repsoldschen Mikrometerrigistrierung von Sterndurchgängen. Leipzig, 1915.
Phil 5643.84   Maxfield, F.N. An experiment in linear space perception. Princeton, 1913.
Phil 5643.85   Rutten, F.J.T. Psychologie der waarneming. Diss. Nijmegen, 1929.
Phil 5643.86   Ames, Adelbert. Collection of papers. n.p., n.d. 6 pam.
Phil 5643.87   Ames, Adelbert. Depth in pictorial art. N.Y., 1925.
Phil 5643.88   Wentworth, H.A. A quantitative study of achromatic and chromatic sensitivity from censes to periphery of the visual field. Diss. Princeton, 1930.
Phil 5643.89.80   Krudewig, M. Die Lehren von der visuelfen Wahrnehmung und Vorstellung. Meisenheim, 1953.
Phil 5643.90   Schmülling, Wilhelm. Aufdeckung latenter eidetischer Anlagen und des integrierton Typus mit der Intermittenz-Methode. Inaug. Diss. Marburg, 1927.
Phil 5643.91   Botelho de Oliveyra, B. Escudo apologetico, physico, optico occidental. Lisboa, 1720.
Phil 5643.92   Ferree, C.E. Studies in physiological optics, Dec. 1928-Oct. 1934. Baltimore, 1934. 2v.
Phil 5643.93   Nahm, E. Über den Vergleich von Komplexen geometrischen Gebilde und tontfreier Farben. Inaug. Diss. Frankfurt, 1930?
Phil 5643.94   Physical Society of London. Report of a joint discussion on vision. London, 1933.
Phil 5643.95F   Pseudoptics, the science of optical illusions. Charts. n.p., n.d.
Phil 5643.96   Duret, René. Les aspects de l'image visuelle. Paris, 1936.
Phil 5643.97   Metzger, W. Gesetze des Sehens. Frankfurt, 1936.
Phil 5643.98   Piéron, Henri. La connaissance sensorielle et les problèmes de la vision. Paris, 1936.
Phil 5643.99   Donders, F.C. Rapport aangaande het onderzoek van het gezichtsvermongen. Utrecht, 1877. 2 pam.
Phil 5643.100   Grant, V.W. Psychological optics. Chicago, 1938.
Phil 5643.101   Gramont, A. Problèmes de la vision. Paris, 1939.
Phil 5643.102   Bröns, N.J. The blind sport of Mariotte. Copenhagen, 1939.
Phil 5643.103   Bartley, S. Howard. Vision. N.Y., 1941.
Phil 5643.104A   McFarland, R.A. Studies of visual fatigue. Boston, 1942.
Phil 5643.104B   McFarland, R.A. Studies of visual fatigue. Boston, 1942.
Phil 5643.105   Kluver, H. Visual mechanisms. Lancaster, 1942.
Phil 5643.106   Peskin, James Charles. The regeneration of visual purple in the living animal. Thesis. N.Y., 1942.
Phil 5643.107   Brandt, Herman F. The psychology of seeing. N.Y., 1945.
Phil 5643.108   Carmichael, Leonard. Reacting and visual fatigue. Boston, 1947.
Phil 5643.109   Romains, Jules. Eyeless sight, a study of extra-retinal vision and the paroptic sense. N.Y., 1924.
Phil 5643.115   Kiefer, Theodor. Der visuelle Mensch. München, 1956.
Phil 5643.120   Meer, H.C. von der. Die Links-Rechts-Polarisation des phaenomenalen Raumes. Groningen, 1959.
Phil 5643.121   Koenig, E. Experimentelle Beiträge zur Theorie des binokularen Einfach- und Tefensehens. Meisenheim, 1962.
Phil 5643.122   Lamy, P. Le mystere de la vision. Paris, 1964.
Phil 5643.123   Piéron, Henri. La vision en lumière intermittente. Paris, 1961.
Phil 5643.124   Jolansky, Samuel. Optical illusion. N.Y., 1964.
Phil 5643.125   Spigel, Irwin Myron. Readings in the study of visually perceived movement. N.Y., 1965.
Phil 5643.126   Gregory, Richard Langton. Eye and brain. N.Y., 1966.
Phil 5643.127   Holland, Harry C. The spiral after-effect. Oxford, 1965.
Phil 5643.128   Hurvich, Leo Maurice. The perception of brightness and darkness. Boston, 1966.
Phil 5643.130   Soltis, Jonas Francis. Seeing, knowing, and believing. Reading, Mass., 1966.
Phil 5643.132   Ákos, Károly. The critical flicker frequency series effect. Budapest, 1966.
Phil 5643.133   Weber, Renate. Experimentelle Untersuchung über die anschauliche Grösse. Inaug. Diss. Tübingen? 1963?
Phil 5643.134   Segall, Marshall H. The influence of culture on visual perception. Indianapolis, 1966.
Phil 5643.136   Vurpillot, Eliane. L'organisation perceptive: son rôle dans l'évolution des illusion optico-géométrique. Paris, 1966.
Phil 5643.138   Rock, Irvin. The nature of perceptual adaptation. N.Y., 1966.
Phil 5643.140   Models for the perception of speech and visual form; proceedings of a symposium. Cambridge, 1967.
Phil 5643.145   Perception; a seminar conducted by the Philosophy Department of Sri Venkateswara University, 1964. Bombay, 1966.
Phil 5643.148   Parmenter, Ross. The awakened eye. 1. ed. Middletown, Conn., 1968.
Phil 5643.150   Haber, Ralph Norman. Contemporary theory and research in visual perception. N.Y., 1968.
Phil 5643.155   Kleinhans, Walter H. Stufen der ganzheitlichen Auffassung bei 2- bis 7 järigen Kindern. Thesis. Weinheim, 1966.

Phil 5643   Psychology - Treatises on special topics - Senses - Special senses - Sight, Vision - cont.

Phil 5643.160   Mandy-van Moerbeke, Marie Paule. Movement apparent et préparation perceptive. Louvain, 1967.

Phil 5643.163   Hoeth, Friedrich. Gesetzlichkeit bei stroboskopischen Alternattivbewegungen. Frankfurt, 1966.

Phil 5643.165   Leeuwerberg, Emanuel Laurens Jan. Structural information of visual pattern. The Hague, 1968.

Phil 5643.168   Sanders, Andries Frans. The selective process in the functional visual field. Assen, 1963.

Phil 5643.170   Cohen, Ronald L. Problems in motion perception. Uppsala, 1964.

Phil 5643.172   Spiekers, Rudolf. Über die optische Unterscheidbarkeit einfacher Zeichen. Thesis. Meisenheim am Glan, 1969.

Phil 5643.174   Pastore, Nicholas. Selective history of theories of visual perception: 1650-1950. N.Y., 1971.

Phil 5643.176   Hillebrand, Franz. Lehre von den Gesichtsempfindungen auf Grund hinterlassener Aufzeichnungen. Wien, 1929.

Phil 5643.178   Zinchenko, Vladimir P. Formirovanie zritel'nogo obraza. Moskva, 1969.

Phil 5643.180   Schmidt, Udo. Figurale Nachwirkungen auf Kinästhetischen Gebeit bei Lageveränderung von Objekt und tastender Hand. Frankfurt, 1970.

Phil 5645   Psychology - Treatises on special topics - Senses - Special senses - Color sense

Phil 5645.01   Pamphlet box. Psychology. Senses. Sight.

Phil 5645.05   Pamphlet box. Psychology. Senses. Sight. German dissertations.

Phil 5645.1   Burnett, S.M. Theories of color-perception. Philadelphia, 1884.

Phil 5645.2   Allen, G. Colour-sense. London, 1879. 2v.

Phil 5645.3   Dove, H.W. Darstellung der Farbenlehre. Berlin, 1853.

X Cg   Phil 5645.4   Goethe, J.W. von. Zur Farbenlehre. Tübingen, 1810. 3v.

Htn   Phil 5645.4.2*   Goethe, J.W. von. Zur Farbenlehre. Tübingen, 1810. 2v.

Phil 5645.4.8   Goethe, J.W. von. Theory of colours. London, 1840.

Phil 5645.4.25   Ostwald, Wilhelm. Goethe, Schopenhauer und die Farbenlehre. Leipzig, 1918.

Phil 5645.4.27   Barthel, Ernst. Goethes Relativitätstheorie der Farbe. Bonn, 1923.

Phil 5645.5   Head, J.F. Color blindness. Boston, 1881.

Phil 5645.6   Jeffries, B.J. Color blindness. Boston, 1879.

Phil 5645.6.5   Jeffries, B.J. Report of the examination of school children for color blindness. Boston, 1880.

Phil 5645.6.10   Jeffries, B.J. Color blindness. Boston, 1878. 3 pam.

Phil 5645.6.15   Jeffries, B.J. Color-names, color-blindness. Boston, 1882.

Phil 5645.7   Hall, G.S. Color-perception. n.p., 1878.

Phil 5645.8   Abney, W. de W. Colour vision. London, 1895.

Phil 5645.8.5   Abney, W. de W. Researches in colour vision. London, 1913.

Phil 5645.9   Allen, Frank. Persistence of vision in color blind subjects. n.p., 1902.

Phil 5645.10   Baker, Emma S. Experiments on tne aesthetics of light and colour. Toronto, 1903.

Phil 5645.11A   Baird, J.W. The color sensitivity of the peripheral retina. Washington, 1905.

Phil 5645.11B   Baird, J.W. The color sensitivity of the peripheral retina. Washington, 1905.

Phil 5645.14   Rand, G. Factor...sensitivity of retina to color. Princeton, 1913.

Phil 5645.15   Parsons, J.H. Introduction to study of colour vision. Cambridge, 1915.

Phil 5645.16   Luckiesh, M. The language of color. N.Y., 1918.

Phil 5645.18   Geuter, Peter. Der Farbensinn und seine Störungen. Leipzig, 1914.

Phil 5645.19   Souriau, Paul. L'esthétique de la lumière. Paris, 1913.

Phil 5645.20   Ostwald, Wilhelm. Die Farbenlehre. v.1-2,4. Leipzig, 1918-22. 3v.

Phil 5645.20.2   Ostwald, Wilhelm. Die Farbenlehre. 2. Aufl. Leipzig, 1921.

Phil 5645.21   Lucky, Bertha. The specific brightness of colors. Lincoln, 1916.

Phil 5645.22   Utitz, Emil. Grundzüge der ästhetischen Farbenlehre. Stuttgart, 1908.

Phil 5645.23   Sergi, Giuseppe. Fisiologia e psicologia del colore. Milano, 1881.

Phil 5645.24   Lehmann, A. Farvernes elementaere aestetik. Kjøbenhavn, 1884.

Phil 5645.25   Schenck, F. Über die physiologischen Grundlagen des Farbensinns. Marburg, 1906.

Phil 5645.26   Collins, Mary. Colour-blindness. London, 1925.

Phil 5645.28   Höllner, Hans. Die Störungen des Farbensinnes ihre klinische Bedeutung und ihre Diagnose. Berlin, 1912.

Phil 5645.29   Brown, J.H. Spectropia. 3. ed. London, 1864.

Phil 5645.30   Sloan, Louise L. The effect of intensity of light...eye and size...on the visibility curve. Diss. n.p., 1926?

Phil 5645.31   Nagel, W.A. Der Lichtsinn augenloser Tiere. n.p., 1896-1908. 7 pam.

Phil 5645.32.2   Franklin, Christine L. Colour and colour theories. London, 1929.

Phil 5645.33.5   Katz, David. Der Aufbau der Farbwelt. 2. Aufl. Leipzig, 1930.

Phil 5645.34   Weidlich, Karl. Farben und Farben-Empfindung. Stettin, 1930.

Phil 5645.34.3   Weidlich, Karl. Farben und Farben-Empfindung. Stettin, 1933.

Phil 5645.35   MacLeod, R.B. An experimental investigation of brightness constancy. N.Y., 1932.

Phil 5645.36   Henneman, R.H. A photometric study of the perception of object color. N.Y., 1935.

Phil 5645.37   Müller, G.E. Kleine Beiträge zur Psychophysik der Farbenempfindungen. Leipzig, 1934.

Phil 5645.38   Peddie, William. Colour vision. London, 1922.

Phil 5645.39   Jerrentrup, F. Allgemein Orientierende experimental psychologische Untersuchungen über den zeitlichen Verlauf von Farbwandelspielen. Inaug. Diss. Bochum, 1936.

Phil 5645.40   Olsson, G.F. Experimentelle Untersuchungen. Stockholm, 1938.

Phil 5645.41   Steinfels, W. Farbe und Dasein. Jena, 1926.

Phil 5645.42   Honoré, Paul. Color light and vision. Detroit, 1938.

Phil 5645.43   Weaver, H.B. A study of discriminative serial action. Thesis. Philadelphia, 1942.

Phil 5645.44   Lindberg, Bengt J. Experimental studies of colour and non-colour attitudes in school children and adults. Copenhagen, 1938.

Phil 5645   Psychology - Treatises on special topics - Senses - Special senses - Color sense - cont.

Phil 5645.45   Wellmer, E.N. Retinal structure and colour vision. Cambridge, Eng., 1946.

Phil 5645.46   Ishihara, S. The series of plates designed as tests for colour-blindness. 8. ed. Tokyo, 1939.

Phil 5645.47   Rouwer, B. Colors and their characters. The Hague, 1949.

Phil 5645.48   Lüscher, Max. Die Farbe als psychologisches Untersuchungsmittel. St. Gallen, 1949.

Phil 5645.49   Kravkou, S.V. Tsvetovoe zrenie. Moskva, 1951.

Phil 5645.50   Wal, T.O. Proeve ener practische kleurenpsychologie. Amsterdam, 1954.

Phil 5645.52   Nederlandse. Kleurendag. Verslag. Den Haag. 6-11

Phil 5645.53   Paris. Ecole Pratique des Hautes Études. Problèmes. Paris, 1957.

Phil 5645.54   Rosseau, René L. Les couleurs. Paris, 1959.

Phil 5645.55   Brandt, Ernest. Form kolarisme. København, 1958.

Phil 5645.56   Teevan, R.C. Color vision. Princeton, 1961.

Phil 5645.57   Heimendahl, E. Licht und Farbe. Berlin, 1961.

Phil 5645.58   Evans, Ralph. Introduction to color. N.Y., 1961.

Phil 5645.59   Burnham, R.W. Color. N.Y., 1963.

Phil 5645.60   Smits, Willem Canisius Maria. Symboliek van de kleut. Amsterdam, 1967.

Phil 5645.65   Schoenborn-Buchheim, Elisabeth. Experimentelle Untersuchüngen den Eindruckscharakter von Einzelfarben. Freiburg, 1963?

Phil 5645.70   Rattleff, Anker. Form, farve og emotioner. København, 1958.

Phil 5647   Psychology - Treatises on special topics - Senses - Special senses - Temperature sense

Phil 5647.5   Cowan, Edwina Abbott. The effect of adaptation on the temperature difference linien. Thesis. Princeton, N.J. 1914.

Phil 5647.7   Sandovici, Constantin. Les sensations de température. Thèse. Montpellier, 1936.

Phil 5648   Psychology - Treatises on special topics - Senses - Special senses - Touch

Phil 5648.01   Pamphlet box. Psychology. Senses.

Phil 5648.1   Kammler, A. Experimenta de variarum cutis. Vratislav, 1858.

Phil 5648.2   Lemon, J.S. The skin considered as an organ of sensation. Gardner, Mass., 1896.

Phil 5648.3   Sobeski, M. Über Täuschungen des Tastsinns. Breslau, 1903.

Phil 5648.4   Weber, E.H. Tastsinn und Gemeingefühl. Leipzig, 1905.

Phil 5648.4.5   Foucault, Marcel. L'illusion paradoxale et le seuil de Weber. Montpelier, 1910.

Phil 5648.5   Spearman, C. Normaltäuschungen in der Lagewahrnehmung. Leipzig, 1905.

Phil 5648.6   Kobylecki, S Wahrnehmbarkeit plötzlicher Drückveranderungen. Leipzig, 1905.

Phil 5648.7   Henri, V. Raumwahrnehmungen des Tastsinnes. Berlin, 1898.

Phil 5648.7.2   Henri, V. Raumwahrnehmungen des Tastsinnes. Berlin, 1898.

Phil 5648.9   Griffing, H. On sensations from pressure and impact. N.Y., 1895.

Phil 5648.10   Cook, H.D. Die taktile Schätzung von Ausgefüllten und leeren Strecken. Leipzig, 1910.

Phil 5648.11   Book, W.F. The psychology of skill. Missoula, Mont., 1908.

Phil 5648.11.5   Book, W.F. The psychology of skill. N.Y., 1925.

Phil 5648.11.25   Ackerson, Luton. A correlational analysis of proficiency in typing. N.Y., 1926.

Phil 5648.12   Hayes, M.H.S. A study of cutaneous after-sensations. Chicago, 1912.

Phil 5648.14   Goudge, Mabel E. A qualitative and quantitative study of Weber's illusion. Thesis. Worcester, Mass., 1918.

Phil 5648.15   Klinkenberg, E. Der Raumsinn der Haut. Inaug. Diss. Bonn, 1883.

Phil 5648.16   Judd, Charles H. Über Reumwahrnehmungen im Gebiet des Tastsinnes. Inaug. Diss. Leipzig, 1896.

Phil 5648.17   Boring, Edwin G. Cutaneous sensation after nerve-division. London, 1916.

Phil 5648.19   Piéron, Henri. Les sensibilités cutanées. v.1-3. Paris, 1928-32.

Phil 5648.20   Révész, Géza. Die Formenwelt des Tastsinnes. Haag, 1938. 2v.

Phil 5648.22   Betz, Dieter. Untersuchungen im haptischen Raum. Diss. Hamburg, 1964.

Phil 5649   Psychology - Treatises on special topics - Senses - Special senses - Muscular sense

Phil 5649.01   Pamphlet box. Psychology. Muscular sense.

Phil 5649.2   Gourgeon, J. L'exploration physiologique...du sens musculaire. Paris, 1901.

Phil 5649.5   Storey, Thomas Andrew. Studies in voluntary muscular contraction. Palo Alto, Calif., 1904.

Phil 5649.6   Woodworth, R.S. Le mouvement. Paris, 1903.

Phil 5649.7   Barnes, J.C. Voluntary isolation of control in a natural muscle group. Diss. Princeton, 1916.

Phil 5649.8   Souriau, Paul. L'esthétique du mouvement. Paris, 1889.

Phil 5649.8.5   Schäfer, Karl. Die Erklärung der Bewegungsempfindungen. Inaug. Diss. Jena, 1889.

Phil 5649.9   Browne, George H. The esthetics of motion. New Ulm, 1917

Phil 5649.10   Schultze, Ernst. Über die Umwandlung willkürlicher Bewegungen in unwillkürliche. Leipzig, 1898.

Phil 5649.11.3   Ribot, Théodule. La vie inconsciente et les mouvements. 3. éd. Paris, 1914.

Phil 5649.12   Bastian, H.C. The "muscular sense". London, 1887.

Phil 5649.13   Fullerton, G.S. On the perception of small differences. Philadelphia, 1892.

Phil 5649.14   Moore, T.V. A study in reaction time and movement. Diss. Washington, 1904.

Phil 5649.15   Froeberg, Sven. Relation between magnitude of stimulus and the time of reaction. Diss. N.Y., 1907.

Phil 5649.16   Waller, A.D. The sense of effort. n.p., 1891?

Phil 5649.18   Bogen, H. Gang und Charakter. Leipzig, 1931.

Phil 5649.19A   Allport, G.W. Studies in expressive movement. N.Y., 1933.

Phil 5649.19B   Allport, G.W. Studies in expressive movement. N.Y., 1933.

Phil 5649.20   Cox, John William. Manual skill. Cambridge, Eng., 1934.

Phil 5649.21   Weigand, E. Analyse der Handgeschicklichkeit. Inaug. Diss. Würzburg, 1936.

Phil 5649.22   McNeill, H. Motor adaptation and accuracy. Louvain, 1934.

Phil 5649.23   Covaciu-Ulmeanu. Effort volontaire et chronaxie. Thèse. Paris, 1936.

Phil 5649.24   Bujeau, L.V. Le schematisme, psychologie de l'action. Paris, 1941.

Classified Listing

Phil 5649 Psychology - Treatises on special topics - Senses - Special senses -
Muscular sense - cont.

Phil 5649.25   Kohl, Kurt. Zum Problem der Sensumotorik.
       Frankfurt, 1956.

Phil 5649.26   Buyteuddigk, Frederik J.J. Attitudes et mouvements.
       Paris, 1957.

Phil 5649.28   Berning, A. Experimentelle Untersuchungen von
       Bewegungsstilen. Inaug. Diss. Bonn, 1960.

Phil 5649.29   Brichcín, Milan. Teoretické a metodologické problémy
       výzkumů průběhu volních pohybu. Praha, 1966.

Phil 5649.30   Bergès, Jean. Les gestes et la personnalité. Paris, 1967.

Phil 5649.32   Metheny, Eleanor. Movement and meaning. N.Y., 1968.

Phil 5649.34   Both, Frans Jacob. Manuele varrdigheid; cen oriëntatie.
       Proefschrift. Groningen, 1967.

Phil 5649.36   Buytendijk, Frederik Jacobus Johannes. Algemene theorie
       der menselijke houding en beweging als verbinding en
       tegenstelling van de fysiologische en de psychologische
       beschouwig. 3. Druk. Utrecht, 1964.

Phil 5649.38   Zweig, Adam. Grundzüge einer tensor-algebraischen
       Psycho-Dynamik. v.1-2. Zürich, 1965.

Phil 5649.40   Cratty, Bryant J. Psychology and physical activity.
       Englewood Cliffs, 1968.

Phil 5649.42   Cratty, Bryant J. Social dimensions of physical activity.
       Englewood Cliffs, 1967.

Phil 5649.44   Roze, Nina A. Psikhomotorika vzroslogo cheloveka.
       Leningrad, 1970.

Phil 5649.46   Lézine, Iréne. Les étopes de l'intelligence
       sensori-motrice. Paris, 1969.

Phil 5650 Psychology - Treatises on special topics - Senses - Special senses -
Hearing

Phil 5650.01   Pamphlet box. Psychology. Hearing.

Phil 5650.05   Pamphlet box. Psychology. Hearing. German dissertations.

Phil 5650.1   Höring, Adolf. Versuche über das Unterscheidungsvermögen
       des Hörsinnes für Zeitgrössen. Inaug. Diss.
       Tübingen, 1864.

Phil 5650.2   Bezold, Friedrich. Über die funktionelle Prüfung des
       menschlichen Gehörorgans. Wiesbaden, 1897.

Phil 5650.3   Mentz, P. Die Wirkung akustischer Sinnesreize auf Puls und
       Athmung. Leipzig, 1895.

Phil 5650.4   Wells, F.L. Linguistic lapses. N.Y., 1906.

Phil 5650.5   Bruner, A.G. The hearing of primitive peoples.
       N.Y., 1908.

Phil 5650.6   Peterson, J. Combination tones and other related auditory
       phenomena. Chicago, 1908.

Phil 5650.9A   Watt, Henry J. Psychology of sound. Cambridge, 1917.

Phil 5650.9B   Watts, Henry J. Psychology of sound. Cambridge, 1917.

Phil 5650.11   Bonnier, Pierre. L'audition. Paris, 1901.

Phil 5650.12   Brücke, Ernst. Über die Wahrnehmung. Wien, 1884.

Phil 5650.13   Ogden, Robert M. Hearing. N.Y., 1924.

Phil 5650.14   Starch, D. Perimetry of the localization of sound. Pt.1-2.
       Thesis. n.p., 1906.

Phil 5650.15   Wilkinson, G. The mechanism of the cochlea. London, 1924.

Phil 5650.17   Kucharski, P. Recherches sur l'exitabilité auditive.
       Thèse. Paris, 1928.

Phil 5650.18   Tullio, Pietro. L'orecchio. Bologna, 1928.

Phil 5650.19   Deenik, Arie. Het onderscheidingsvermogen voor
       toonintensiteiten. Leiden, 1906.

Phil 5650.20   Beatty, R.T. Hearing in man and animals. London, 1932.

Phil 5650.21   Bartlett, F.C. The problem of noise. Cambridge, 1934.

Phil 5650.22   McLachlan, Norman W. Noise. London, 1935.

Phil 5650.22.10   Sader, Manfred. Lautheit und Lärn. Göttingen, 1966.

Phil 5650.23   New York (City). Noise Abatement Commission. City noise.
       N.Y., 1930.

Phil 5650.24   Stevens, Stanley S. Hearing; its psychology and
       physiology. N.Y., 1938.

Phil 5650.25   Harvard University. Psycho-Acoustic Laboratory.
       Bibliography on hearing. Cambridge, 1955.

Phil 5650.26   Kennedy, Helen. A study of children's hearing as it
       relates to reading. Thesis. n.p., 1942.

Phil 5650.30   Harvard University. Psycho-Acoustic Laboratory. A
       bibliography on hearing. v.1-2. Cambridge, 1950.

Phil 5650.32   Kostelijk, P.J. Theories of hearing. Leiden, 1950.

Phil 5650.34   Broadbent, D.E. Perception and communication. N.Y., 1958.

Phil 5650.36   Akademiia Nauk SSSR. Biblioteka. Fiziologicheskaia
       akustika. Moskva, 1960.

Phil 5650.38   Békésy, Georg von. Experiments in hearing. N.Y., 1960.

Phil 5650.40   Wever, Ernest. Theory of hearing. N.Y., 1957.

Phil 5650.42   Hirsh, Ira Jean. The measurement of hearing. N.Y., 1952.

Phil 5650.43   Schouteu, Jan F. Five articles on the perception of sound,
       1938-1940. Eindhoven, 1960.

Phil 5650.45   Furth, Hans G. Thinking without language. N.Y., 1966.

Phil 5650.50   Burns, William. Noise and man. London, 1968.

Phil 5650.52   Denes, Peter B. The speech chain; the physics and biology
       of spoken language. Baltimore? 1968.

Phil 5650.54   Zenatti, Arlette. Le développement génétique de la
       perception musicale. Paris, 1969.

5651 Psychology - Treatises on special topics - Senses - Special senses -
Orientation

Phil 5651.1   Aubert, H.R. Physiologische Studien...Orientierung.
       Tübingen, 1888.

Phil 5651.2   Verworn, M. Gleichgewicht und Otolithenorgan. Bonn, 1891.

Phil 5651.3   Hartmann, F. Die Orientierung; die Physiologie.
       Leipzig, 1902.

Phil 5651.4   Bomier, Pierre. L'orientation. Paris, 1900.

Phil 5651.6   Grasset, Joseph. Les maladies de l'orientation et de
       l'equilibre. Paris, 1901.

Phil 5651.7   Jaccard, Pierre. Le sens de la direction et l'orientation
       lointaine chez l'homme. Paris, 1932.

Phil 5651.8   Oster, Wilhelm. Struktur-psychologische Untersuchungen
       über die Leistung des Zeitsinns. Inaug. Diss.
       Würzburg, 1937.

Phil 5651.9   Lynn, Richard. Attention, arousal, and the orientation
       reaction. 1. ed. Oxford, 1966.

Phil 5651.77   Garten, S. Die Bedeutung unserer Sinne für die
       Orientierung in Luftraume. Leipzig, 1917.

5653 Psychology - Treatises on special topics - Senses - Special senses -
Taste

Phil 5653.1   Pamphlet box. Psychology. Taste.

Phil 5653.5   Hollingworth, H.L. The sense of taste. N.Y., 1917.

Phil 5653.6   Brillat-Savarin, A. Physiologie des Geschmacks.
       Leipzig, 18-.

Phil 5653.7   Marchand, L. Le goût. Paris, 1903.

Phil 5653.8   Kare, M.R. Physiological and behavioral aspects of taste.
       Chicago, 1961.

Phil 5655 Psychology - Treatises on special topics - Senses - Special senses -
Smell

Phil 5655.01   Pamphlet box. Psychology. Smell.

Phil 5655.1   Duméril, A.H.A. Des odeurs. Paris, 1843.

Phil 5655.2   Folsom, N. Essay on the senses of smell and taste.
       Boston, 1863.

Phil 5655.3F   Heyninx, Albert. Essai d'olfactique physiologique.
       Bruxelles, 1919.

Phil 5655.4   Kenneth, J.H. Osmics; the science of smell.
       Edinburgh, 1922.

Phil 5655.5   Henning, H. Der Geruch. Leipzig, 1916.

Phil 5655.5.2   Henning, H. Der Geruch. 2e Aufl. Leipzig, 1924.

Phil 5655.6   McKenzie, Dan. Aromatics and the soul. London, 1923.

Phil 5655.7   Zwaardemaker, H. L'odorat. Paris, 1925.

Phil 5655.9   Airkem, Inc. Odors and the sense of smell. N.Y., 1952.

Phil 5655.10   Jellinek, Paul. Die psychologischen Grundlagen der
       Parfümerie. 2. Aufl. Heidelberg, 1965.

Phil 5655.15   NATO Advanced Study Institute on Theories of Odor and Odor
       Measurement, Istanbul, 1966. Theories of odor and odor
       measurement. Bebek, Istanbul, 1966.

Phil 5685 Psychology - Treatises on special topics - Stage fright

Phil 5685.5   Kielblock, A. The stage fright. Boston, 1891.

Phil 5690 Psychology - Treatises on special topics - Stereotype

Phil 5690.2   Bergler, Reinhold. Psycologie stereotyper Systeme.
       Bern, 1966.

Phil 5695 Psychology - Treatises on special topics - Subliminal perception

Phil 5695.2   Dixon, Norman F. Subliminal perception. London, 1971.

Phil 5700 Psychology - Treatises on special topics - Symbolism

Phil 5700.2   Rosolato, Guy. Essais sur le symbolique. Paris, 1969.

Phil 5700.4   Lorenzer, Alfred. Kritik des psychoanalytischen
       Symbolbegriffs. 1. Aufl. Frankfurt, 1970.

Phil 5700.6   Kadinsky, David. Der Mythos der Maschine. Bern, 1969.

Phil 5710 Psychology - Treatises on special topics - Temperament

Phil 5710.01   Pamphlet box. Psychology. Temperament.

Phil 5710.5.2   Jaques, D.H. The temperaments. N.Y., 1879.

Phil 5710.6   Stevenson, J.G. Religion and temperament. London, 1913.

Phil 5710.7   Ewald, G. Temperament und Charakter. Berlin, 1924.

Phil 5710.8.3   Mercier, C.A. Human temperaments; studies in character. 3.
       ed. London, 1923?

Phil 5710.9   Stewart, A. Our temperaments; their study and teaching. 2.
       ed. London, 1892.

Phil 5710.10   Baxter, M.F. An experimental study of...temperaments.
       Diss. Ithaca, N.Y., 1927.

Phil 5710.11   Bloor, Constance. Temperament, a survey of psychological
       theories. London, 1928.

Phil 5710.12   Allendy, R. Les tempéraments. Paris, 1922.

Phil 5710.13   Alfonso, Nicolo R. La dottrina dei temperamenti
       nell'antichità e ai nostri giorni. Roma, 1902.

Phil 5710.14   Stewart, A. Our temperaments. London, 1887.

Phil 5710.15   Schaer, K.F. Charakter, Blutgruppe und Konstitution.
       Zürich, 1941.

Phil 5710.16   Kretschmer, Ernst. Körperbau und Charakter. 20. Aufl.
       Berlin, 1951.

Phil 5710.18   Kretschmer, Ernst. Körperbau und Charakter. Berlin, 1961.

Phil 5710.20   Sacherl, Karl. Die Pedanterie. Göttingen, 1957.

Phil 5710.21   Merlin, V.S. Ocherk teori temperamenta. Moskva, 1964.

Phil 5710.22   Klibansky, R. Saturn and melancholy. London, 1964.

Phil 5722 Psychology - Treatises on special topics - Unconscious cerebration

Phil 5722.01   Pamphlet box. Psychology. Unconscious cerebration.

Phil 5722.1   Half-hour Recreations. Half-hour recreations in popular
       science. no.6. Boston, 1871.

Phil 5722.2   Schuster, P.R. Gibtesunbewusste und vererbte
       Vorstellungen? Leipzig, 1879.

Phil 5722.3A   Butler, S. Unconscious memory. N.Y., 1911.

Phil 5722.3B   Butler, S. Unconscious memory. N.Y., 1911.

Phil 5722.4.5   Chabaneix, P. Essai sur le subconscient dans les oeuvres.
       Bordeaux, 1897.

Phil 5722.5   Abramowski, Édouard. Le subconscient normal. Paris, 1914.

Phil 5722.6   Martin, L. Ein experimenteller Beitrag zur Erforschung.
       Leipzig, 1915.

Phil 5722.7   Bradley, M.K. The logic of the unconscious mind.
       London, 1920.

Phil 5722.8   Dwelshauvers, G. L'inconscient. Paris, 1916.

Phil 5722.8.5   Dwelshauvers, G. Les mécanismes subconscients.
       Paris, 1925.

Phil 5722.9   Pierce, Frederick. Our unconscious mind and how to use it.
       N.Y., 1922.

Phil 5722.10   Levine, I. The unconscious. N.Y., 1923.

Phil 5722.11   Hesnard, A. L'inconscient. Paris, 1923.

Phil 5722.12   Münsterberg, Hugo. Subconscious phenomena. Boston, 1910.

Phil 5722.13   Nortbridge, W.L. Modern theories of the unconscious.
       London, 1924.

Phil 5722.14   Bumke, O. Das Unterbewusstsein, eine Kritik.
       Berlin, 1922.

Phil 5722.14.2   Bumke, O. Das Unterbewusstsein, eine Kritik. 2. Aufl.
       Berlin, 1926.

Phil 5722.15   Jastrow, J. The subconscious. Boston, 1906.

Phil 5722.16   Schofield, A.T. The unconscious mind. London, 1898.

Phil 5722.16.2   Schofield, A.T. The unconscious mind. 2. ed.
       London, 1899.

Phil 5722.17   Petraschek, K.O. Die Logik des Unbewussten.
       München, 1926. 2v.

Phil 5722.18   Jung, C.G. Die Beziehungen zwischen dem ich und dem
       Unbewussten. Darmstadt, 1928.

Phil 5722.18.5   Jung, C.G. Die Beziehungen zwischen dem ich und dem
       Unbewussten. Zürich, 1935.

Phil 5722.18.15   Jung, C.G. Über die Archetypen. Zürich, 1935.

Phil 5722.19   Wenzl, Aloys. Das unbewusste Denken. Karlsruhe, 1927.

Phil 5722.20   Grau, Kurt Joachim. Bewusstsein, Unbewussts,
       Unterbewusstes. München, 1922.

Phil 5722.21.9   The unconscious: a symposium. N.Y., 1927.

Phil 5722.22   The unconscious: a symposium. N.Y., 1928.

Phil 5722.23.2   Montmasson, J.M. Le rôle de l'inconscient dans l'invention
       scientifique. Thèse. Bourg, 1928.

Phil 5722.23.10   Montmasson, J.M. Invention and the unconscious.
       London, 1931.

Phil 5722.24   Lubac, Émile. Les niveaux de conscience et d'inconscient
       et leurs intercommunications. Paris, 1929.

Phil 5722.24.5   Lubac, Émile. Le cycle de l'inconscient. Paris, 1934.

Phil 5722.24.10   Lubac, Émile. Présent conscient et cycles de durée.
       Paris, 1936.

Phil 5722.25   Miller, James G. Unconsciousness. N.Y., 1942.

Phil 5722   Psychology - Treatises on special topics - Unconscious cerebration - cont.
Phil 5722.26   Sadler, W.S. The mind at mischief. N.Y., 1929.
Phil 5722.27   Brinkmann, Donald. Probleme des Unbewussten. Zürich, 1943.
Phil 5722.28   Spiess, Emil Jakob. Rätsel der Seele. Olten, 1946.
Phil 5722.29   Casey, D.M. La théorie du subconscient de Morton Prince. Paris, 1945.
Phil 5722.30   Tucci, Giuseppe. Teoria e practica del Mandala. Roma, 1949.
Phil 5722.30.5   Tucci, Giuseppe. The theory and practice of the Mandala. London, 1961.
Phil 5722.30.6   Tucci, Giuseppe. The theory and practice of the Mandala. London, 1969.
Phil 5722.32   Simon, C.W. Considerations for research in a sleep-learning program. Santa Monica, 1954.
Phil 5722.32.2   Simon, C.W. Considerations for research in a sleep-learning program. Santa Monica, 1954.
Phil 5722.32.5   Simon, C.W. Responses to material presented during various levels of sleep. Santa Monica, 1954.
Phil 5722.32.10   Simon, C.W. The EEG. Santa Monica, 1955.
Phil 5722.35   Martin, P.W. Experiment in depth. London, 1955.
Phil 5722.38.1   Waldstein, Louis. The subconscious self and its relation to education and health. N.Y., 1902.
Phil 5722.38.2   Waldstein, Louis. The subconscious self and its relation to education and health. N.Y., 1926.
Phil 5722.40   Seifert, F. Tiefenpsychologie. Düsseldorf, 1955.
Phil 5722.42   Whyte, Lancelot. The unconscious before Freud. N.Y., 1960.
Phil 5722.42.2   Whyte, Lancelot. The unconscious before Freud. London, 1967.
Phil 5722.45   Gonseth, J.P. Théâtre de veille et théâtre de songe. Neuchâtel, 1950.
Phil 5722.50   Helsdingen, R.J. van. Beelden uit het onbewuste. Arnhem, 1957.
Phil 5722.55   Tauber, Edward. Prelogical experience. N.Y., 1959.
Phil 5722.60   Kankeleit, Otto. Des Unbewusste als Keimstätte des Schöpferischen. München, 1959.
Phil 5722.65   Cazaux, Jean. Surréalisme et psychologie. Paris, 1958.
Phil 5722.70   Bochorishvili, A.T. Problema bessoznatel'nogo v psikhologii. Tbilisi, 1961.
Phil 5722.71   Martins, D. Do inconsciente. Braga, 1964.
Phil 5722.72   Blyznychenko, Leonid A. Vvod i zakreplenre informatsii v pamiati cheloveka vo vremia estestvennogo sna. Kiev, 1966.
Phil 5722.74   Ey, Henri. L'inconscient, 6e Colloque de Bonneval [1960] sous la direction de Henri Ey. Paris, 1966.
Phil 5722.76   Flottes, Pierre. L'histoire et l'inconscient humain. Genève, 1965.
Phil 5722.78   Williams, John K. The knack of using your subconscious mind. Scarsdale, N.Y., 1952.
Phil 5722.80   Drews, Arthur. Psychologie des Unbewussten. Berlin, 1924.
RRC   Phil 5722.81   Bassin, Filipp. Problema bessoznatel'nogo. Moskva, 1968.
Phil 5722.83   Sheroziia, Apollon E. K probleme soznaniia i bessoznatel'nogo psikhicheskogo. v.1-. Tbilisi, 1969.

Phil 5725   Psychology - Treatises on special topics - Understanding
Phil 5725.1   Ellis, W. Outlines of the history and formation of...understanding. London, 1847.
Phil 5725.2   Wedgwood, H. On development of the understanding. London, 1848.
Phil 5725.4   Reichner, H. Experimentelle und kritische Beiträge zur Psychologie des Verstehens. Inaug. Diss. Leipzig, 1927.
Phil 5725.5   Międzynarodowego Sympozjum Poświęcone Psychologia Rozumienia, Krakow, 1965. Psychologia rozumienia. Warszawa, 1968.

Phil 5750 - 5775   Psychology - Treatises on special topics - Volition - General works (A-Z)
Phil 5750.001   Fellin, J. Die Willensfreiheit; zur Bibliographie. Graz, 1928.
Phil 5750.01   Pamphlet vol. Psychology. Volition. 6 pam.
Phil 5750.05   Pamphlet box. Psychology. Volition. German dissertations.
Phil 5750.1   Allyn, J. Philosophy of mind in volition. Oberlin, 1851.
Phil 5750.3   Ach, Narziss. Über den Willensakt und das Temperament. Leipzig, 1910.
Phil 5750.3.2   Ach, Narziss. Über die Willenstätigkeit und das Denken. Göttingen, 1905.
Phil 5750.3.10   Ach, Narziss. Analyse des Willens. Berlin, 1935.
Phil 5750.4   Ahlberg, Alf. Viljans frihet från transcendental-filosofiens ståndpunkt. Stockholm, 1915.
Phil 5750.5   Ahlander, J.A. De libertate. Disquisitio. Lundae, 1852.
Phil 5750.6   Allendy, René F. Le problème de la destinée. Paris, 1927.
Phil 5750.7   Aveling, Francis. Personality and will. N.Y., 1931.
Phil 5750.8   Auer, Johannes. Die menschliche Willensfreiheit im Lehrsystem des Thomas von Aquin und Johannes Duns Scotus. München, 1938.
Phil 5750.9   Antweiler, A. Das Problem der Willensfreiheit. Freiburg, 1955.
Phil 5750.10   Azzalini, Mario. La necessità del volere e la reattività sociale. Padova, 1931.
Phil 5750.12   Ayres, Michel Richard. The refutation of determinism. London, 1968.
Phil 5751.1   Bockshammer, G.F. On the freedom of the human will. Andover, 1835.
Phil 5751.1.5   Bockshammer, G.F. Die Freyheit des menschlichen Willens. Stuttgart, 1821.
Phil 5751.3   Barrett, Edward Boyd. Strength of will. N.Y., 1915.
Phil 5751.4   Bussey, Gertrude C. Typical recent conceptions of freedom. Thesis. Greenfield, 1917.
Phil 5751.5   Bolliger, Adolf. Die Willensfreiheit. Berlin, 1903.
Phil 5751.6   Brulez, Lucien. Het vrijheidsbegrip. 's Gravenhage, 1920.
Phil 5751.7.3   Bray, Charles. The philosophy of necessity. 3. ed. London, 1889.
Phil 5751.8   Ballard, F. Determinism: false and true. London, 1911.
Phil 5751.9   Bessmer, Julius. Das menschliche Wollen. Freiburg, 1915.
Phil 5751.10   Bolin, W. Problemet om viljans frihet, kritiskt och logiskt undersökt. Helsingfors, 1868.
Htn   Phil 5751.11*   Bossuet, J.B. Traitez du libre-arbitre. Paris, 1731.
Phil 5751.12   Bermann, G. El determinismo en la ciencia y en la vida. Buenos Aires, 1920.
Phil 5751.13   Boufflers, S. Le libre arbitre. Paris, 1808.
Phil 5751.14   Benda, Clemens E. Der Wille zum Geist. Berlin, 1932.
Phil 5751.15   Broad, C.D. Determinism, indeterminism, and libertarianism. Cambridge, Eng., 1934.
Phil 5751.16   Barwis, J. Three dialogues. London, 1776.
Phil 5751.17   Bianca, Giovanni. L'autonomia della volontà. Firenze, 1937.
Phil 5751.18   Baudry, L. La querelle des futurs contingents. Paris, 1950.

Phil 5750 - 5775   Psychology - Treatises on special topics - Volition - General works (A-Z) - cont.
Phil 5751.19   Bourke, Vernon. Will in Western thought. N.Y., 1964.
Phil 5751.20   Berofsky, Bernard. Free will and determinism. N.Y., 1966.
Phil 5751.21   Brehm, Jack Williams. A theory of psychological reactance. N.Y., 1966.
Phil 5752.1   Carleton, H. Liberty and necessity. Philadelphia, 1857.
Phil 5752.2A   Collins, A. Philosophical inquiry...human liberty. London, 1717.
Phil 5752.2B   Collins, A. Philosophical inquiry...human liberty. London, 1717.
Phil 5752.2.3   Collins, A. Philosophical inquiry...human liberty. London, 1735.
Phil 5752.2.10   Collins, A. Philosophical inquiry...human liberty. London, 1890.
Phil 5752.2.15   Clarke, S. Remark on philosophical inquiry...human liberty. London, 1717. 2 pam.
Phil 5752.3   Corry, W. Reflections upon liberty and necessity. London, 1761.
Phil 5752.3.2   Corry, W. Reflections upon liberty and necessity. London, 1759-63. 5 pam.
Phil 5752.4   Crombie, A. Essay on philosophical necessity. London, 1893.
Phil 5752.5   Cudworth, R. A treatis of freewill. London, 1838.
Phil 5752.6   Carr, Herbert W. The freewill problem. London, 1928.
Phil 5752.7   Cohen, Chapman. Determinism or free-will? London, 1919.
Phil 5752.8   Cavallo, V. La libertà umana nella filosofia contemporanea. Napoli, 1933.
Phil 5752.9   Cioffari, Vincenzo. Fortune and fate from Democritus to St. Thomas Aquinas. N.Y., 1935.
Phil 5752.10   Compton, Arthur H. The freedom of man. New Haven, 1935.
Phil 5752.11   Cesari, P. Les déterminismes et les êtres. Thèse. Paris, 1938.
Phil 5752.12   Cahn, Steven. Fate, logic, and time. New Haven, 1967.
Phil 5752.14   Capizzi, Antonio. La difesa del libero arbitrio da Erasmo a Kant. 1. ed. Firenze, 1963.
Phil 5753.1   Desdouits, T. De la liberté et des lois de la nature. Paris, 1868.
Phil 5753.2   Drobisch, M.W. Die moralische Statistik. Leipzig, 1867.
Phil 5753.3   Dearborn, G.V.N. Neurology of Apraxia. Boston, 1911.
X Cg   Phil 5753.4   Day, Jeremiah. An inquiry...power of the will. New Haven, 1838. 4v.
Phil 5753.5   Duchatel, Edmond. Les miracles de la volonté. Paris, 1914.
Phil 5753.6   Dallemagne, Jules. Physiologie de la volonté. Paris, 1898.
Phil 5753.7.2   Demeny, Georges. L'éducation de l'effort psychologie-physiologie. 2. éd. Paris, 1916.
Phil 5753.8.2   Driesch, H. Das Problem der Freiheit. 2. Aufl. Darmstadt, 1920.
Phil 5753.9   Daub, Carl. Des Dr. C. Daub Darstellung und Beurtheilung des Hypothesen in Betreff dei Willensfreiheit. Altona, 1834.
Phil 5753.10   Dandolo, G. Le integrazioni psichiche e la volontà. Padova, 1900.
Phil 5753.11   Duprat, G.L. L'éducation de la volonté et des facultés logiques. Paris, 1920.
Phil 5753.12   Dwelshauvers, G. L'exercice de la volonté. Paris, 1935.
Phil 5753.13   Davidson, M. The free will controversy. London, 1942.
Phil 5753.14   Daudin, H. La liberté de la volonté. 1. éd. Paris, 1950.
Phil 5753.15   Davidovich, Vsevolod E. Problemy chelovechskoi svobody. L'vov, 1967.
Phil 5753.16   Danner, Manfred. Gibt es einen freien Willen? Hamburg, 1967.
Phil 5753.17   D'Angelo, Edward. The problem of freedom and determinism. Columbia, 1968.
Phil 5754.1.2   Edwards, Jonathan. A carefull and strict enquiry...freedom of will. 3. ed. London, 1768.
Phil 5754.1.4   Edwards, Jonathan. A careful and strict enquiry...freedom of will. Glasgow, 1790.
Htn   Phil 5754.1.6*   Edwards, Jonathan. A careful and strict enquiry...freedom of will. Albany, 1804.
Phil 5754.1.8   Edwards, Jonathan. Careful and strict enquiry into the modern...freedom of will. Boston, 1762.
Htn   Phil 5754.1.10*   Edwards, Jonathan. Careful and strict enquiry into the modern...freedom of will. Boston, 1754.
Phil 5754.1.12   Edwards, Jonathan. Careful and strict enquiry into the modern...freedom. N.Y., 1828.
Phil 5754.1.18   Pamphlet box. Edwards, Jonathan. Freedom of the will.
Htn   Phil 5754.1.19*   Dana, J. Examination...Edward's...freedom of will. Boston, 1770.
Htn   Phil 5754.1.20*   Dana, J. Examination...Edward's...freedom of will. New Haven, 1773.
Htn   Phil 5754.1.22*   West, Samuel. Essay on moral agency...remarks on Dana's Examination. New Haven, 1772.
Htn   Phil 5754.1.23*   West, Samuel. Essay on moral agency...remarks on Dana's Examination. Salem, 1794.
NEDL   Phil 5754.1.25   Tappan, H.P. Review of Edward's inquiry...freedom. N.Y., 1839.
Phil 5754.1.27   Stewart, J.G. Freedom of the will vindicated. Glasgow, 1876.
Phil 5754.1.29   A preservative against the doctrine of fate. Boston, 1770.
Phil 5754.1.31   West, Samuel. Essays on liberty and necessity. Boston, 1793.
Phil 5754.1.33   West, Samuel. Essays on liberty and necessity. New Bedford, 1795.
Htn   Phil 5754.1.101*   Edwards, Jonathan. A dissertation concerning liberty and necessity. Worcester, 1797.
Phil 5754.2   Espy, J.P. The human will. Cincinnati, 1860.
Phil 5754.3   Zickendraht, K. Der Streit zwischen Erasmus und Luther über die Willensfreiheit. Leipzig, 1909.
Phil 5755.1   Fischer, J.C. Über die Freiheit des menschlichen Willens und die Einheit der Naturgesetze. Leipzig, 1858.
Phil 5755.1.3   Fischer, J.C. Die Freiheit des menschlichen Willens und die Einheit der Naturgesetze. 2. Aufl. Leipzig, 1871.
Phil 5755.2A   Fischer, E.K.B. Über die menschliche Freiheit. Heidelberg, 1888.
Phil 5755.2B   Fischer, E.K.B. Über die menschliche Freiheit. Heidelberg, 1888.
Phil 5755.3   Fouillée, A. La liberté et le déterminisme. Paris, 1872.
Phil 5755.3.2   Fouillée, A. La liberté et le déterminisme. 2. éd. Paris, 1884.
Phil 5755.4   Fiamingo, G. Individual determinism and social science. Philadelphia, 1896.
Phil 5755.5   Holt, E.B. The Freudian wish and its place in ethics. N.Y., 1915.
Phil 5755.5.2   Holt, E.B. The Freudian wish and its place in ethics. N.Y., 1915.

5750 - 5775 Psychology - Treatises on special topics - Volition - eneral works (A-Z) - cont.

Phil 5755.6 Fonsegrive, G. Essai sur le libre arbitre. Paris, 1887.
Phil 5755.7 Froehlich, Joseph Anselm. Freiheit und Notwendigkeit als elemente einer einheitlichen Weltanschauung. Leipzig, 1908.
Phil 5755.8 Froehlich, Joseph Anselm. Der Wille zu höheren Einheit. Heidelberg, 1905.
Phil 5755.9 Forti, E. La décisión; essai d'analyse psychologique. Thèse. Paris, 1926.
Phil 5755.10 Fröschels, E. Wille und Vernunft. Leipzig, 1925.
Phil 5755.11 Fahrion, Karl. Das Problem der Willensfreiheit. Heidelburg, 1904.
Phil 5755.12 Fernkorn, C.M. Willensfreiheit und Verantwortlichkeit. Greifswald, 1927.
Phil 5755.13 Fruit, John P. Determinism from Hobbes to Hume. Inaug. Diss. Leipzig, 1895.
Phil 5755.14A Farrer, A.M. The freedom of the will. London, 1958.
Phil 5755.14B Farrer, A.M. The freedom of the will. London, 1958.
Phil 5755.14.2 Farrer, A.M. The freedom of the will. 2. ed. London, 1963.
Phil 5755.15.1 Farber, Leslie H. The ways of the will. N.Y., 1966.
Phil 5755.16 Földesi, Tamás. The problem of free will. Budapest, 1966.
Phil 5755.18 Franklin, Richard Langdon. Freewill and determinism: a study of rival conceptions of man. London, 1968.
Phil 5755.20.2 Fassbender, Martin. Wollen; eine königliche Kunst. 2. und 3. Aufl. Freiburg, 1916.
Phil 5756.1 Guthrie, M. Causational and free will. London, 1877.
Phil 5756.3 Goldscheid, R. Grundlinien zu einer Kritik der Willenskraft. Wien, 1905.
Phil 5756.4 Gomperz, Heinrich. Das Problem der Willensfreiheit. Jena, 1907.
Phil 5756.5 Günther, Carl. Die Willensfreiheit. Berlin, 1909.
Phil 5756.6.2 Gutberlet, C. Die Willensfreiheit und ihre Gegner. 2. Aufl. Fulda, 1907.
Phil 5756.7 Göring, Carl. Über die Menschlichefreiheit. Leipzig, 1876.
Phil 5756.8 Gjerdsjø, O. Determinismen og dens konsekvenser. Kristiania, 1907.
Phil 5756.9 Gaede, Udo. Etwas vom Begriff des Willens in der neueren Psychologie. Berlin, 1911.
Phil 5756.11 Gille, Paul. Esquisse d'une philosophie de la dignité humaine. Paris, 1924.
Phil 5756.12 Groos, Helmut. Die Konsequenzen und Inkonsequenzen des Determinismus. München, 1931.
Phil 5756.13 Gehlen, A. Theorie der Willensfreiheit. Berlin, 1933.
Phil 5756.14 Gardet, Louis. La mesure de notre liberté. Tunis, 1946.
Phil 5756.16 Glover, Jonathan. Responsibility. London, 1970.
Phil 5757.1.2 Hazard, R.G. Freedom of mind in willing. N.Y., 1865.
Phil 5757.1.4 Hazard, R.G. Freedom of mind in willing. Boston, 1889.
Phil 5757.1.6 Hazard, R.G. Two letters on causation and freedom. Boston, 1869.
Phil 5757.1.7 Hazard, R.G. Zwei Briefe über Verursachung und Freiheit im Wollen Gerichtet. N.Y., 1875.
Phil 5757.2 Heman, C.F. Zur Geschichte der Lehre von der Freiheit des menschlichen Willens. Leipzig, 1887.
Phil 5757.3 Hughes, T. The human will. London, 1867.
Phil 5757.4 Huber, Johannes. Über die Willensfreiheit. München, 1858.
Phil 5757.5 Horne, H.H. Free will and human responsibility. N.Y., 1912.
Phil 5757.6 Henle, Rudolf. Vorstellungs- und Willentheorie. Leipzig, 1910.
Phil 5757.7 Hilber, H. (pseud.). Über Willenseinheit bei Arbeitsgehmeinschaft. Leipzig, 1914.
Phil 5757.8 Hebler, Karl. Elemente einer philosophischen Freiheitslehre. Berlin, 1887.
Phil 5757.9 Hight, G.A. The unity of will. London, 1906.
Phil 5757.10 Hansen, H.C. Om begrebet frihed en filosofisk afhandling. Kristiania, 1896.
Phil 5757.11 Heinzel, G. Versuch einer Lösung des Willensproblems. Inaug. Diss. Breslau, n.d.
Phil 5757.12.6 Haddock, F.C. Power of will. 55th ed. Meriden, 1915.
Phil 5757.13 Heuer, Wilhelm. Kausalität und Willensfreiheit. Heidelberg, 1924.
Phil 5757.14.2 Herrick, C.J. Fatalism or freedom. N.Y., 1926.
Phil 5757.15 Heiberg, J.L. Om den menneskelige Frihed. Kiel, 1824.
Phil 5757.16 Hooper, Charles E. The fallacies of fatalism. London, 1930.
Phil 5757.17 Hilbert, Gerhard. Moderne Willensziele. Leipzig, 1911.
Phil 5757.18 Hampshire, Stuart. Freedom of the individual. N.Y., 1965.
Phil 5759.1.2 James, W. The dilemma of determinism. n.p. 1884.
Phil 5759.2 Joël, Karl. Der freie Wille, eine Entwicklung in Gesprächen. München, 1908.
Phil 5759.3 Joss, Hermann. Der Wille. Bern, 1921.
Phil 5759.4 Joyau, Emmanuel. Essai sur la liberté morale. Paris, 1888.
Phil 5759.5 Jäkel, Josef. Die Freiheit des menschlichen Willens. Wien, 1906.
Phil 5759.6 Jakubisiak, A. La pensée et le libre arbitre. Paris, 1936.
Phil 5760.1 Kahl, W. Die Lehre von Primat des Willens. Strassburg, 1886.
Phil 5760.2 Klippel, T. Determinismus und Strafe. Berlin, 1890.
Phil 5760.3 Kurt, N. Die Willesnprobleme. Weimar, 1902.
Phil 5760.4 Kulew, T. Das Probleme der Willensfreiheit und der Grundbegriffe der Strafrechts. Sofia, 1906.
Phil 5760.6 Kneib, Philipp. Die Willensfreiheit und die innere Verantwortlichkeit. Mainz, 1898.
Phil 5760.7 Kuntz, Leo F. Education of the will in the light of modern research. Diss. Washington, D.C., 1927.
Phil 5760.8 Knox, Howard V. The will to be free. London, 1928.
Phil 5760.9 Konczewska, H. Contingence, liberté et la personnalité humaine. Paris, 1937.
Phil 5760.9.5 Konczewska, H. Contingence, liberté et la personnalité humaine. Thèse. Paris, 1937.
Phil 5760.10 Keller, W. Psychologie und Philosophie des Wollens. München, 1954.
Phil 5760.12 Kircher, Veronica. Die Freiheit des körpergebundenen Willens. Freiburg, 1957.
Phil 5760.13 Kohnstamm, Philipp A. Vrije wil of determinisme. Haarlem, 1947.
Phil 5760.14 Kurtz, Paul W. Decision and the condition of man. Seattle, 1965.
Phil 5761.1 La Placette, J. Eclaircissemens...difficultez...liberté. Amsterdam, 1709.
Phil 5761.2 Liebmann, O. Über den individuellen Beweis für die Freiheit. Stuttgart, 1866.
Phil 5761.3 Leland, C.G. Have you a strong will? London, 1899.

Phil 5750 - 5775 Psychology - Treatises on special topics - Volition - General works (A-Z) - cont.

Phil 5761.3.2 Leland, C.G. Have you a strong will? London, 1902.
Phil 5761.3.3 Leland, C.G. Have you a strong will? London, 1903.
Phil 5761.3.5 Leland, C.G. The mystic will. Chicago, 1907.
Phil 5761.3.7 Leland, C.G. The mystic will. Chicago, 1907.
Phil 5761.3.10 Leland, C.G. Have you a strong will? N.Y., 1919.
Phil 5761.4.2 Lapie, P. Logique de la volonté. Paris, 1902.
Phil 5761.5 Lipps, G.F. Das Problem der Willensfreiheit. Leipzig, 1912.
Phil 5761.6 Loewenthal, N. Physiologie des freien Willens. Leipzig, 1843.
Phil 5761.7 Luthardt, C.E. Die Lehre vom freien Willen. Leipzig, 1863.
Phil 5761.8 Lutosławski, W. Volenté et liberté! Paris, 1913.
Phil 5761.8.5 Lutosławski, W. Rozwójpotęgi woli przez psychofizyczne ćiviczenią. Warszawa, 1910.
Phil 5761.9 Lévy, Paul Émile. L'éducation rationelle de la volonté. 10e éd. Paris, 1917.
Phil 5761.9.5 Lévy, Paul Émile. The rational education of the will. 9. ed. Philadelphia, 1920.
Phil 5761.9.12 Lévy, Paul Émile. Le traitement moral. Paris, 1927.
Phil 5761.10 Lindworsky, J. Der Wille, seine Erscheinung und seine Beherrschung. Leipzig, 1919.
Phil 5761.10.2 Lindworsky, J. Der Wille, seine Erscheinung und seine Beherrschung. 2. Aufl. Leipzig, 1921.
Phil 5761.10.15 Lindworsky, J. The training of the will. Milwaukee, 1929.
Phil 5761.11 Landquist, J. Viljan. Stockholm, 1908.
Phil 5761.12 Lipps, Theodor. Vom Fühlen, Wollen und Denken. Leipzig, 1902.
Phil 5761.12.3 Lipps, Theodor. Vom Fühlen, Wollen und Denken. 3. Aufl. Leipzig, 1926.
Phil 5761.13 La Luzerne, C.G. de. Dissertation sur la liberté de l'homme. Langres, 1808.
Phil 5761.14 Lewin, Kurt. Vorsatz Wille und Bedürfnis. Berlin, 1926.
Phil 5761.14.10 Lewin, Kurt. Die Entwicklung des experimentellen Willenspsychologie. Leipzig, 1929.
Phil 5761.15 Loewe, Johann H. Die speculative Idee der Freiheit. Prag, 1890.
Phil 5761.16 Leenhardt, Henry. Le déterminisme des lois de la nature et la réalité. Thèse. Montpellier, 1930.
Phil 5761.17.5 Lossky, N.O. Freedom of will. London, 1932.
Phil 5761.18 Lacape, R.S. La notion de liberté et la crise du déterminisme. Paris, 1935.
Phil 5761.19 Leuridan, Charles. L'idée de la liberté morale. Paris, 1936.
Htn Phil 5761.20* Luzac, E. Essai sur la liberté de produire ses sentimens. n.p., 1749.
Phil 5761.21 Laird, John. On human freedom. London, 1947.
Phil 5761.22 Levitskii, S.H. Tragediia svobody. Frankfurt, 1958.
Phil 5761.23 Lebacqz, Joseph. Libre arbitre et jugement. Paris, 1960.
Phil 5761.24 Lamont, Corliss. Freedom of choise affirmed. N.Y., 1967.
Phil 5761.24.1 Lamont, Corliss. Freedom of choice affirmed. Boston, 1969.
Phil 5761.25 Lehrer, Keith. Freedom and determinism. N.Y., 1966.
Phil 5762.1 Maudsley, H. Body and will. London, 1883.
Phil 5762.2 Müffelmann, L. Das Problem der Willensfreiheit. London, 1902.
Phil 5762.3 Münsterberg, H. Die Willenshandlung. Freiburg, 1888.
Phil 5762.4 Mack, Joseph. Kritik der Freiheitstheorien. Leipzig, 1906.
Phil 5762.5 Martin, E. Psychologie de la volonté. Paris, 1913.
Phil 5762.6 Meyer, W. Die Wahlfreiheit des Willens in ihrer Nichtigkeit. Gotha, 1886.
Phil 5762.7 Mahan, Asa. Doctrine of the will. N.Y., 1846.
Phil 5762.8 Marucci, Achille. La volontà. Roma, 1903.
Phil 5762.9 Meumann, Ernst. Intelligenz und Wille. 3. Aufl. Leipzig, 1920.
Phil 5762.9.4 Meumann, Ernst. Intelligenz und Wille. 4. Aufl. Leipzig, 1925.
Phil 5762.10 Milesi, G.B. La negazione del libero arbitrio ed il criterio del giusto. Milano, 1894.
Phil 5762.11 Messer, August. Das Problem der Willensfreiheit. 2. Aufl. Göttingen, 1918.
Phil 5762.11.2 Messer, August. Das Problem der Willensfreiheit. Göttingen, 1911.
Phil 5762.12.5 Mach, F.J. Die Willensfreiheit des Menschen. Paderborn, 1894.
Phil 5762.13 Martin, Alfred H. An experimental study of the factors and types of voluntary choice. N.Y., 1922.
Phil 5762.14 Manno, R. Heinrich Hertz - für die Willensfreiheit? Leipzig, 1900.
Phil 5762.15 Mally, Ernst. Grundgesetze des Sollens. Graz, 1926.
Phil 5762.16 Medicus, Fritz. Die Freiheit des Willens und ihre Grenzen. Tübingen, 1926.
Phil 5762.17 McCarthy, R.C. The measurement of conation. Chicago, 1926.
Phil 5762.19 Miller, David L. Modern science and human freedom. Austin, 1959.
Phil 5762.20 Maillant, Claude. Cultivez votre volonté. Paris, 1960.
Phil 5762.22 Munn, Allan M. Free will and determinism. Toronto, 1960.
Phil 5762.23 Moreau, J. Problèmes et pseudo-problèmes du déterminisme physique, biologique, psychologique. Paris, 1964.
Phil 5762.24 Melden, Abraham Irving. Free action. London, 1964.
Phil 5762.26 Mazzantini, Carlo. Il problema filosofico del "libero arbitrio" nelle controversie teologiche del secolo XIII. Torino, 1965.
Phil 5762.28 Mueller, Heinz Alfred. Spontaneität und Gesetzlichkeit. Bonn, 1967.
Phil 5762.32 Marx, Otto. Leben ist Willkür. Hamburg, 1962.
Phil 5762.34 Martinetti, Piero. La libertà. Torino, 1965.
Phil 5762.36 Margenau, Henry. Scientific indeterminism and human freedom. Latrobe, Pa., 1968.
Phil 5763.1 Naville, E. Le libre arbitre. Genève, 1898.
Phil 5763.2 Natorp, Paul. Sozialpädagogik. Theorie der Willenserziehung. 3. Aufl. Stuttgart, 1909.
Phil 5763.2.5 Natorp, Paul. Sozialpädagogik. Theorie der Willenserziehung. 6. Aufl. Stuttgart, 1925.
Phil 5763.3 Nabert, Jean. L'expérience intérieure de la liberté. Thèse. Paris, 1923.
Phil 5763.3.5 Nabert, Jean. L'expérience intérieure de la liberté. Paris, 1924.
Phil 5764.1 Otto, F.W. Die Freiheit des Menschen. Gütersloh, 1872.
Phil 5764.3 Offner, Max. Willensfreiheit, Zurechnung, und Verantwortung. Leipzig, 1904.
Phil 5764.4 Ofstad, H. An inquiry into the freedom of decision. Oslo, 1961.

Phil 5750 - 5775 Psychology - Treatises on special topics - Volition - General works (A-Z) - cont.

Htn Phil 5765.1* Porzio, S. An homun bonus v. malus volens fiat. Florentiae, 1551.
Htn Phil 5765.1.5* Porzio, S. Se l'huomo diventa buono o cattivo volontariamente. Fiorenza, 1551.
Phil 5765.2 Payot, Jules. L'éducation de la volonté. Paris, 1900.
Phil 5765.2.3 Payot, Jules. L'éducation de la volonté. Paris, 1912.
Phil 5765.2.4 Payot, Jules. L'éducation de la volonté. Paris, 1941.
Phil 5765.2.5 Payot, Jules. Die Erziehung des Willens. Leipzig, 1901.
Phil 5765.2.9 Payot, Jules. The education of the will. N.Y., 1909.
Phil 5765.2.9.5 Payot, Jules. The education of the will. N.Y., 1910.
Phil 5765.2.10 Payot, Jules. Le travail intellectuel et la volonté. Paris, 1919.
Phil 5765.2.11 Payot, Jules. Le travail intellectuel et la volonté. Paris, 1920.
Phil 5765.2.20 Payot, Jules. Will-power and work. 2. ed. N.Y., 1921.
Phil 5765.3 Pfänder, A. Phänomenologie des Wollens. Leipzig, 1900.
Phil 5765.4A Palmer, G.H. The problem of freedom. Boston, 1911.
Phil 5765.4B Palmer, G.H. The problem of freedom. Boston, 1911.
Phil 5765.5 Pfister, Oskar. Die Willensfreiheit. Berlin, 1904.
Phil 5765.6 Piat, Clodius. La liberté. Paris, 1894-95. 2v.
Phil 5765.7 Peterson, Julius. Willensfreiheit, moral und strafrecht. München, 1905.
Phil 5765.8 Pelikán, F. Entstehung und Entwicklung der Kontingentismus. Berlin, 1915.
Phil 5765.9 Planck, Max. Kansalgesetz und Willensfreiheit. Berlin, 1923.
Phil 5765.11 Pears, D.F. Freedom and the will. London, 1966.
Phil 5765.12 Popper, Karl R. Of clouds and clocks. St. Louis, 1966.
Phil 5766.5 Qu'est-ce que vouloir? Paris, 1958.
Phil 5767.1 Ribot, T. Les maladies de la volonté. Paris, 1883.
Phil 5767.1.10 Ribot, T. The diseases of the will. 3. ed. Chicago, 1903.
Phil 5767.1.12 Ribot, T. The diseases of the will. Chicago, 1894.
Phil 5767.2 Romang, T.P. Über Willensfreiheit und Determinismus. Bern, 1835.
Phil 5767.2.3A Rickaby, Joseph. Free will and four English philosophers. London, 1906.
Phil 5767.2.3B Rickaby, Joseph. Free will and four English philosophers. London, 1906.
Phil 5767.3 Rehmke, Johanes. Die Willesfreiheit. Leipzig, 1911.
Phil 5767.4 Rieger, Conrad. Experimentelle Untersuchungen. Jena, 1885.
Phil 5767.5 Rée, Paul. Die Illusion der Willensfreiheit. Berlin, 1885.
Phil 5767.6 Riezler, Kurt. Gestalt und Gesetz. München, 1924.
Phil 5767.7 Reiff, J.F. Das System der Willensbestimmungen. Tübingen, 1842.
Phil 5767.8 Roretz, Karl von. Der Zweckbegriff im psychologischen und erkenntnistheoretischen Denken. Leipzig, 1910.
Phil 5767.9 Ruesch, Arnold. Die Unfreiheit des Willens. Darmstadt, 1925.
Phil 5767.10.5 Reiner, Hans. Freiheit, Wollen und Aktivität. Leipzig, 1927.
Phil 5767.11A Ricoeur, Paul. Philosophie de la volonté. Photoreproduction. Paris, 1950. 2v.
Phil 5767.11B Ricoeur, Paul. Philosophie de la volonté. Photoreproduction. Paris, 1950.
Phil 5767.11.5 Ricoeur, Paul. Philosophy of the will. v.2, pt. 1. Chicago, 1965-
Phil 5767.11.10 Ricoeur, Paul. Freedom and nature. Evanston, Ill., 1966.
Phil 5767.12 Ramm, T. Die Freiheit der Willensbildung. Stuttgart, 1960.
Phil 5767.14 Rankin, K. Choice and chance. Oxford, 1961.
Phil 5767.15 Rohner, Peter. Das Phänomen des Wollens. Bern, 1964.
Phil 5768.1 Schneider, G.H. Der menschliche Wille. Berlin, 1882.
Phil 5768.2 Scholten, J.H. Der freie Wille. Berlin, 1874.
Phil 5768.3 Seth, J. Freedom as an ethical postulate. Edinburgh, 1891.
Phil 5768.4 Tübingen, Germany. Universität. Verzeichnies der Doctoren: Begriff der Wollens...von C. Sigwart. Tübingen, 1879.
Phil 5768.5 Schwarz, H. Psychologie des Willens. Leipzig, 1900.
Phil 5768.6 Salzbrunner, B. Das Gesetz der Freiheit. Ein Beiträg zur Reinigung der Volksreligion. Nürnberg, 1869.
Phil 5768.8 Surbled, G. La volonté. 5. éd. Paris, n.d.
Htn Phil 5768.9* Sepulveda, J.G. De fato i libris arbitrio libero tres. Roma, 1526.
Phil 5768.9.95 Steiner, Rudolf. Die Philosophie der Freiheit. Berlin, 1894.
Phil 5768.10 Steiner, Rudolf. The philosophy of freedom. London, 1916.
Phil 5768.10.3 Steiner, Rudolf. The philosophy of freedom. London, 1964.
Phil 5768.10.5 Steiner, Rudolf. Die Philosophie der Freiheit. Berlin, 1921.
Phil 5768.10.30 Steiner, Rudolf. Frihedens filosofi. København, 1924.
Phil 5768.10.35 Steiner, Rudolf. Rudolf Steiner über seine "Philosophie der Freiheit". Stuttgart, 1966.
Phil 5768.11 Solly, Thomas. The will divine and human. Cambridge, 1856.
Phil 5768.12 Schuch, Hermann. Kant, Schopenhauer, Ihering. München, 1907.
Phil 5768.13 Slosson, P.W. Fated or free? Boston, 1914.
Phil 5768.14 Sartorius, E. Die Lutherische Lehre vom Unvermögen des Freyen Willens zur Höheren. Göttingen, 1821.
Phil 5768.15 Sommer, H. Über das Wesen und die Bedeutung. Berlin, 1885.
Phil 5768.16 Snider, Denton J. The will and its world. St. Louis, 1899.
Phil 5768.17 Schwartzkopff, P. Die Freiheit des Willens als Grundlage der Sittlichkeit. Leipzig, 1885.
Phil 5768.18 Solly, J.R. Free will and determinism. London, 1922.
Phil 5768.19 Stammler, Gerhard. Notwendigkeit in Natur- und Kulturwissenschaft. Halle, 1926.
Phil 5768.20 Schellwien, R. Der Wille, die Lebensgrundmacht. Berlin, 1879.
Phil 5768.20.15 Schellwien, R. Wille und Erkenntnis. Hamburg, 1899.
Phil 5768.22 Simon, Yves. Freedom of choice. N.Y., 1969.
Phil 5769.1.2 Tappan, H.P. Doctrine of the will. N.Y., 1840.
Phil 5769.1.5 Tappan, H.P. Doctrine of the will. N.Y., 1841.
Phil 5769.2 Thomsen, H. Die rechtliche Willens Bestimmung. Kiel, 1882.
Phil 5769.3 Travis, H. Moral freedom reconciled with causation. London, 1865.
Phil 5769.4 Turner, G.L. Wish and will. London, 1880.
Phil 5769.5 Traeger, L. Wille, Determinismus, Strafe. Berlin, 1895.
Phil 5769.6 Theory of agency...an essay on moral freedom. Boston, 1771.
Htn Phil 5769.6.5* Theory of agency...an essay on moral freedom. Boston, 1771.

Phil 5750 - 5775 Psychology - Treatises on special topics - Volition - General works (A-Z) - cont.

Phil 5769.7 Teisen, N. Om viljens frihed. København, 1904.
Phil 5769.8 Tarozzi, G. La libertà umana e la critica del determinismo. Bologna, 1936.
Phil 5770.1 Uphan, T.C. A philosophical and practical treatise on the will. Portland, 1834.
Phil 5771.1 Van Peyma, P.W. The why of the will. Boston, 1910.
Phil 5771.2 Valla, Lorenzo. De libero arbitrio. Firenze, 1934.
Htn Phil 5771.2.5* Valla, Lorenzo. De libero arbitrio. Basileae, 1518.
Phil 5771.3 Vivanti, L. Il concetto della indeterminazione. Firenze, 1938.
Phil 5771.4 Vaz Ferreira, C. Los problemas de la libertad y los del determinismo. Buenos Aires, 1957.
Phil 5772.1 Whedon, D.D. Freedom of the will. N.Y., 1864.
Phil 5772.2.4 Wiese, L. Die Bildung des Willens. Berlin, 1879.
Phil 5772.4 Wolański, L.T. Die Lehre von der Willensfreiheit des Menschen. Münster, 1868.
Phil 5772.5 Windelband, Wilhelm. Über Willensfreiheit. 3. Aufl. Tübingen, 1918.
Phil 5772.5.2 Windelband, Wilhelm. Über Willensfreiheit. Tübingen, 1904.
Phil 5772.6 Wodehouse, Helen. The logic of will. London, 1908.
Phil 5772.7 Witte, J.H. Über Freiheit des Willens. Bonn, 1882.
Phil 5772.8 Werner, S. Das Problem von der menschlichen Willensfreiheit. Berlin, 1914.
Phil 5772.9 Wichmann, O. Wille und Freiheit. München, 1922.
Phil 5772.10 Wiesner, Johann. Die Freihert des menschlichen Willens. Wien, 1920.
Phil 5772.11 Wijnaendts Francken, C.J. Het vraagstuk vanden vrijen wil. Haarlem, 1912.
Phil 5772.12 Weidenbach, Oswald. Ethos contra Logos. München, 1948.
Phil 5774.1 Young, G.P. The ethics of freedom. Toronto, 1911.

Phil 5780 Psychology - Treatises on special topics - Volition - Special topics

Phil 5780.01 Pamphlet box. Psychology. Movement.
Phil 5780.2 Hollingworth, H.L. The inaccuracy of movement. N.Y., 1909.
Phil 5780.2.5 Hollingworth, H.L. The inaccuracy of movement. N.Y., 1909.
Phil 5780.3 Rowe, E.C. Voluntary movement. n.p., 1910.
Phil 5780.6 Washburn, M.F. Movement and mental imagery. Boston, 1916.
Phil 5780.7 Spitta, H. Die Willensbestimmungen und ihr Verhältniss zu den Impulsiven. Tübingen, 1881.
Phil 5780.8 Roback, Abraham A. The interference of will-impulses. Lancaster, Pa., 1918.
Phil 5780.9 Conrad, H. Psychologie und Besteuerung. Stuttgart, 1928.
Phil 5780.10 Dupuis, Léon. Les aboulies sociales, le scrupule, la timidité, la susceptibilité, l'autoritarisme. Paris, 1940.
Phil 5780.12 Trey, M. de. Der Wille in der Handschrift. Bern, 1946.
Phil 5780.14 Vedenov, A.V. Vospitanie voli u rebenka v sem'e. Moskva, 1952.
Phil 5780.15 Hunter, Edward. Brainwashing. N.Y., 1956.
Phil 5780.15.2 Hunter, Edward. Brainwashing. N.Y., 1960.
Phil 5780.15.10 United States. Congress. House. Communist psychological warfare. Washington, 1958.
Phil 5780.15.15 Waechter, Michael. Hjärntvätt. Stockholm, 1965.
Phil 5780.15.20 Thomas, Klaus. Die künstlich gesteuerte Seele. Stuttgart, 1970.
Phil 5780.16 Meerlo, A.M. The rape of the mind. 1. ed. Cleveland, 1956.
Phil 5780.17 Christoff, Daniel. Recherche de la liberté. 1. éd. Paris, 1957.
Phil 5780.18 Reik, Theodor. The compulsion to confess. N.Y., 1959.
Phil 5780.20 Rogge, Oetje G. Why men confess. N.Y., 1959.
Phil 5780.22A Lifton, Robert. Thought reform and the psychology of totalism. N.Y., 1961.
Phil 5780.22B Lifton, Robert. Thought reform and the psychology of totalism. N.Y., 1961.
Phil 5780.23 Klausner, Samuel Z. The quest for self-control. N.Y., 1965.
Phil 5780.24 Julius, Fritz Hendrik. Tierkreis. v.1-2. Freiburg, 1964-
Phil 5780.25 London, Perry. Behavior control. 1. ed. N.Y., 1969.
Phil 5780.27 Kiesler, Charles A. The psychology of commitment. N.Y., 1971.

Phil 5790 Psychology - Treatises on special topics - Miscellaneous minor topics

Phil 5790.2 Rheingold, Joseph Cyrus. The mother, anxiety, and death: the catastrophic death complex. London, 1967.
Phil 5790.2.5 Moriarty, David M. The loss of loved ones. Springfield, 1967.
Phil 5790.2.10 Munnichs, Jozef M.A. Ouderdom en eindigheid. Assen, 1964.
Phil 5790.2.15 Kuebler-Ron, Elisabeth. On death and dying. N.Y., 1969.
Phil 5790.2.20 Caruso, Igor A. Die Trennung der Liebenden. Bern, 1968.
Phil 5790.2.25 Hahn, Alois. Einstellungen zum Tod und ihre soziale Bedingtheit. Stuttgart, 1968.
Phil 5790.5 Jerphagnon, Lucien. De la banalité. Paris, 1965.
Phil 5790.10 Knight, James Allen. For the love of money. Philadelphia, 1968.
Phil 5790.15 Evrim, Selmin. Psikoloji açisindan şahsiyette bir buud olarak içedönükluk-Dişadönüklük. Istanbul, 1967.
Phil 5790.25 Neff, Walter Scott. Work and human behavior. 1. ed. N.Y., 1968.
Phil 5790.30 Langenheder, Werner. Ansatz zu einer allgemeinen Verhaltenstheorie in der Sozialwissenschaften. Köln, 1968.
Phil 5790.35 Lucas, Rex H. Men in crisis; a study of a mine disaster. N.Y., 1969.
Phil 5790.35.5 Stoddard, Ellwyn R. Conceptual models of human behavior in disaster. El Paso, 1968.
Phil 5790.40 Klebelsberg, Dieter von. Risikoverhalten als Persönlichkeitsmerkmal. Bern, 1969.
Phil 5790.45 Latané, Bibb. The unresponsive bystander: why doesn't he help? N.Y., 1970.
Phil 5790.50 Tournier, Paul. The meaning of gifts. Richmond, Va., 1970.

Phil 5808.00 - 5809.99 Psychology - Comparative psychology - Pamphlet volumes

Phil 5808.00.-.99 Pamphlet box. Comparative psychology. Chronological file.
Phil 5809.00.-.99 Pamphlet box. Comparative psychology. Chronological file.

Phil 5809.100 - .999 Psychology - Comparative psychology - General works - Collected authors

Phil 5809.102 Man and beast: comparative social behavior. Washington, 1971.

Phil 5810 - 5835   Psychology - Comparative psychology - General works -
   Individual authors (A-Z)
   Phil 5810.1   Allen, J.B. The associative processes of the guinea pig.
                    Granville, Ohio, 1904.
   Phil 5810.2   Appleton, L.E. A comparative study of the play activities
                    of adult savages and civilized children. Chicago, 1910.
   Phil 5810.3.2   Avebury, John L. On the senses, instincts, and
                    intelligence of animals. 2nd ed. London, 1889.
   Phil 5810.3.3   Avebury, John L. Die Sinne und das geistige Leben der
                    Thiere. Leipzig, 1889.
   Phil 5810.4   Alsberg, M. Die Grundlagen des Gedächtnisses, der
                    Vererbung und der Instinkte. München, 1906.
   Phil 5810.5   Adams, Donald K. Experimental studies of adaptive behavior
                    in cats. Diss. Baltimore, 1929.
   Phil 5810.6   Allesch, G.J. von. Zur nichteuklidischen Struktur des
                    Phänomenalen Raumes. Jena, 1931.
   Phil 5810.7.5   Alverdes, F. The psychology of animals in relation to
                    human psychology. London, 1932.
   Phil 5810.8   Alm, O.W. The effect of habit interference upon
                    performance in maze learning. Worcester, 1931.
NEDL Phil 5811.1   Bascomb, J. Comparative psychology. N.Y., 1878.
   Phil 5811.2   Boullier, D.R. Essai philosophique sur l'âme des bêtes.
                    Amsterdam, 1728.
   Phil 5811.2.2   Boullier, D.R. Essai philosophique sur l'âme des bêtes.
                    Amsterdam, 1737. 2v.
   Phil 5811.3   Bourbon del Monte, J.B.F. L'homme et les animaux.
                    Paris, 1877.
   Phil 5811.4   Brougham, H. Dialogues on instinct. London, 1844.
   Phil 5811.4.2   Brougham, H. Dialogues on instinct. Philadelphia, 1845.
   Phil 5811.5   Büchner, L. Mind in animals. London, 1880.
   Phil 5811.5.5   Büchner, L. Liebe und Leibes- Leben in der Thierwelt.
                    Berlin, 1879.
   Phil 5811.5.10   Büchner, L. Aus dem Geistesleben der Thiere oder Staaten
                    und Thaten der Kleinen. Berlin, 1876.
   Phil 5811.5.12   Büchner, L. Aus dem Geistesleben der Tiere. Leipzig, 18-
                    ?
   Phil 5811.5.20   Büchner, L. La vie psychique des bêtes. Paris, 1881.
   Phil 5811.6   Bushnan, J.S. The philosophy of instinct and reason.
                    Edinburgh, 1837.
   Phil 5811.7   Beard, G.M. Trance and trancoidal states in the lower
                    animals. N.Y., 1881.
   Phil 5811.8   Boujeant, G.H. Amusement philosophique sur le langage des
                    bestes. Paris, 1739.
   Phil 5811.8.5   Hildrop, John. Free thoughts upon the brute-creation:
                    wherein Father Bougeant's Philosophical amusement is
                    examined. London, 1751.
   Phil 5811.9   Buchan, P. Scriptural and philosophical arguments.
                    Peterhead, 1824.
   Phil 5811.10   Bohn, Georges. La nouvelle psychologie animale.
                    Paris, 1911.
   Phil 5811.10.5   Bohn, Georges. Die neue Tierpsychologie. Leipzig, 1912.
   Phil 5811.10.7   Bohn, Georges. La naissance de l'intelligence.
                    Paris, 1920.
   Phil 5811.10.10 Bohn, Georges. Die Entstehung des Denkvermögens.
                    Leipzig, 1911?
   Phil 5811.11   Brun, Rudolf. Die Raumorientierung der Ameisen.
                    Jena, 1914.
   Phil 5811.12   Bauke, Leopold. Ist das tier Unvernünftig? 31. Aufl.
                    Stuttgart, 191-?
   Phil 5811.12.5   Bauke, Leopold. Unterscheidet das tier Mann und Frau?
                    Berlin, 1908.
   Phil 5811.12.10 Bauke, Leopold. Tierfabeln und andere Irrtümer in der
                    Tierkunde. 19. Aufl. Stuttgart, 19- ?
   Phil 5811.13   Baudouin, Charles. Das Lernen des Hundes. Inaug. Diss.
                    Berlin, 1909.
   Phil 5811.15   Buytendijk, Frederik Jacobus Johannes. Psychologie der
                    dieren. Haarlem, 1920.
   Phil 5811.15.5   Buytendijk, Frederik Jacobus Johannes. Psychologie des
                    animaux. Paris, 1928.
   Phil 5811.15.10A Buytendijk, Frederik Jacobus Johannes. The mind of the
                    dog. Boston, 1936.
   Phil 5811.15.10B Buytendijk, Frederik Jacobus Johannes. The mind of the
                    dog. Boston, 1936.
   Phil 5811.15.15 Buytendijk, Frederik Jacobus Johannes. Wege zum
                    Verständnis der Tiere. Zürich, 1940?
   Phil 5811.15.20 Buytendijk, Frederik Jacobus Johannes. Wesen und Sinn des
                    Spiels. Berlin, 1933.
   Phil 5811.15.25 Buytendijk, Frederik Jacobus Johannes. Mensch und Tier.
                    Hamburg, 1958.
   Phil 5811.16   Bretegnier, Louis. L'activité psychique chez les animaux.
                    Paris, 1930.
   Phil 5811.16.5   Bretegnier, Louis. L'activité psychique chez les animaux.
                    Thèse. Toulouse, 1930.
   Phil 5811.17   Brenes Mesén, Roberto. La voluntad en los microorganismos.
                    Costa Rica, 1905.
   Phil 5811.18   Bierens de Haan, J.A. Die tierpsychologische Forschung,
                    ihre Ziele und Wege. Leipzig, 1935.
   Phil 5811.19   Bally, Gustav. Vom Ursprung und von den Grenzen der
                    Freiheit. Basel, 1945.
   Phil 5811.19.12 Bally, Gustav. Vom Spielraum der Freiheit. 2. Aufl.
                    Basel, 1966.
   Phil 5811.20   Beniest-Noirot, Eliane. Analyse du comportement dit
                    maternel chez la souris. Paris, 1958.
   Phil 5811.24   Blancheteau, Marc. L'orientation spatiale chez l'animal,
                    ses indices et ses repères. Paris, 1969.
   Phil 5812.1   Chadbourne, P.A. Instinct. 2nd ed. N.Y., 1883.
   Phil 5812.1.2   Chadbourne, P.A. Instinct. 2nd ed. N.Y., 1872.
   Phil 5812.2   Clevenger, S.V. Comparative physiology and psychology.
                    Chicago, 1885.
   Phil 5812.3   Chesnel, A. Animaux raisonnent. Paris, 1845.
   Phil 5812.4   Foveau de Courmelles, F.V. Les facultés mentales des
                    animaux. Paris, 1890.
   Phil 5812.5   Carus, Carl Gustav. Vergleichende Psychologie.
                    Wien, 1866.
   Phil 5812.6   Choisnard, Paul. Introduction à la psychologie comparée.
                    Paris, 1924.
   Phil 5812.7A   Comparative psychology. N.Y., 1934.
   Phil 5812.7B   Comparative psychology. N.Y., 1934.
   Phil 5812.7.10   Comparative psychology. 3rd ed. N.Y., 1951.
   Phil 5812.8   Claremont, C.A. The innumerable instincts of man.
                    London, 1940.
   Phil 5812.9   Chauvin, R. Le comportement social chez les animaux.
                    Paris, 1961.
   Phil 5812.10   Chauchard, Paul. Des animaux a l'homme. Paris, 1961.
   Phil 5812.10.5   Chauchard, Paul. Psychisme humain et psychisme animal. 2e
                    ed. Paris, 1961.
   Phil 5812.12   Cuny, Hilaire. Sur la psychologie animale. Paris, 1966.
   Phil 5812.14   Crile, George J. A naturalistic view of man. N.Y., 1969.

Phil 5810 - 5835   Psychology - Comparative psychology - General works -
   Individual authors (A-Z) - cont.
   Phil 5813.1   Dean, R. An essay on the future life of brute creatures.
                    v.1-2. London, 1768.
   Phil 5813.2   Davis, H.B. The raccoon: a study in animal intelligence.
                    London, 1907.
   Phil 5813.3   Drever, James. Instinct in man. Cambridge, Eng., 1917.
   Phil 5813.4   Desmoulins, A. Anatomie des systèmes nerveux des animaux.
                    pt.1-2. Atlas. Paris, 1825. 3v.
   Phil 5813.5   Debblee, George B. Instinct and intuition. London, 1929.
   Phil 5814.1   Evans, E.P. Evolutional ethics and animal psychology.
                    N.Y., 1898.
   Phil 5814.2   Espinas, Alfred. Die Thierischen Gesellschaften; eine
                    vergleichend- psychologische Untersuchung. 2. Aufl.
                    Braunschweig, 1879.
   Phil 5814.3   Edinger, Ludwig. Über Tierpsychologie. Leipzig, 1909.
   Phil 5814.4   Erhard, H. Hypnose bei Tieren. Giessen, 1914.
   Phil 5814.5   Ettlinger, Max. Beiträge zur Lehre von der Tierseele und
                    ihrer Entwicklung. Münster, 1925.
   Phil 5814.6   Eichler, Walter. Über die Erregbarkeitsmessung. Inaug.
                    Diss. München, 1929.
   Phil 5815.1   Fée, A.L.A. Études philosophiques...animaux.
                    Strasburg, 1853.
   Phil 5815.2   Flourens, Pierre. De l'instinct et de l'intelligence des
                    animaux. 4e éd. Paris, 1861.
   Phil 5815.2.5.2 Flourens, Pierre. Psychologie comparée. 2e éd.
                    Paris, 1864.
   Phil 5815.3   Fluegel, Otto. Das Seelenleben der Tiere. 3e Aufl.
                    Langensalza, 1897.
   Phil 5815.4   Falco, Francesco. I fatti psichici della vita animale.
                    Lucca, 1880.
   Phil 5815.5   Fjeld, Harriett A. The limits of learning ability in
                    rhesus monkeys. Thesis. Worcester, Mass., 1934.
   Phil 5815.6   Fraenkel, G.S. The orientation of animals. Oxford,
                    Eng., 1940.
   Phil 5815.8   Filloux, Jean Claude. Le psychisme animal. Paris, 1959.
   Phil 5815.8.3   Filloux, Jean Claude. Psychologie des animaux. 3. éd.
                    Paris, 1960.
   Phil 5815.10.2   Fischel, Werner. Vom Leben zum Erleben. 2. Aufl.
                    München, 1967.
   Phil 5816.1   Gregory, J. A comparative view...man...animal world.
                    London, 1766.
   Phil 5816.1.2   Gregory, J. A comparative view...man...animal world.
                    London, 1765.
   Phil 5816.2   Guer, S.A. Histoire critique de l'âme des bêtes. v.1-2.
                    Amsterdam, 1749.
   Phil 5816.3   Groos, K. Die Spiele der Thiere. Jena, 1896.
   Phil 5816.3.5   Groos, K. Die Spiele der Menschen. Jena, 1899.
   Phil 5816.4   Graeser, Kurt. Die Vorstellungen der Tiere. Berlin, 1906.
   Phil 5816.5   Gentry, Thomas G. Life and immortality.
                    Philadelphia, 1897.
   Phil 5816.5.3   Gentry, Thomas G. Intelligence in plants and animals.
                    N.Y., 1900.
   Phil 5816.6   Gesellschaft für Tierpsychologie. Die Seele des Tieres.
                    Berlin, 1916.
   Phil 5816.7   Gay, Henri. Observations sur les instincts de l'homme et
                    l'intelligence des animaux. Paris, 1878.
   Phil 5816.8   Geraud, Petrus J. Dissertatio philosophica de principio
                    actionum. Trajecti ad Rhenum, 1724.
   Phil 5816.9   Garnett, Arthur C. Instinct and personality.
                    London, 1928.
   Phil 5816.10   Griffith, C.R. An historical survey of vestibular
                    equilibration. Urbana, 1922.
   Phil 5816.11   Grindley, G.C. The intelligence of animals. London, 1937.
   Phil 5816.12   Garratt, G. Marvels and mysteries of instinct. 3rd ed.
                    London, 1862.
   Phil 5816.13   Guillaume, P. La psychologie animale. Paris, 1940.
   Phil 5817.1   Hancock, J. Essay on instinct. London, 1824.
   Phil 5817.2   Hazard, R.G. Animals, not automata. N.Y., 1875.
   Phil 5817.3   Henslow, G. Mind in man and animals. London, 1853-81.
                    2 pam.
   Phil 5817.4   Hoffman, S. Thier-Psychologie. Stuttgart, 1881.
   Phil 5817.5   Hobhouse, L.T. Mind in evolution. London, 1901.
   Phil 5817.5.2   Hobhouse, L.T. Mind in evolution. London, 1915.
   Phil 5817.5.5   Hobhouse, L.T. Mind in evolution. 3d ed. London, 1926.
   Phil 5817.6   Hachet-Souplet, P. Examen psychologique des animaux.
                    Paris, 1900.
   Phil 5817.6.5   Hachet-Souplet, P. De l'animal a l'enfant. Paris, 1913.
   Phil 5817.6.9   Hachet-Souplet, P. La genèse des instincts. Paris, 1912.
   Phil 5817.7   Hunter, W.S. The delayed reaction in animals and children.
                    Cambridge, n.d.
   Phil 5817.8   Houzeau, Jean C. Études sur les facultés mentales des
                    animaux. Mons, 1872. 2v.
   Phil 5817.9.5   Holmes, S.J. Evolution of animal intelligence.
                    N.Y., 1911.
   Phil 5817.10   Hubbert, Helen B. Effect of age on habit formation in the
                    albino rat. Baltimore, 1915.
   Phil 5817.11   Hamilton, Gilbert V. A study of perseverance reactions.
                    N.Y., 1916.
   Phil 5817.12   Hement, Felix. De l'instinct et de l'intelligence.
                    Paris, 1880.
   Phil 5817.13   Hempelmann, F. Tierpsychologie vom Standpunkte des
                    Biologen. Leipzig, 1926.
   Phil 5817.15.3   Herrick, C. Judson. Brains of rats and men.
                    Chicago, 1930.
   Phil 5817.16   Hingston, R.W.G. Problems of instinct and intelligence.
                    London, 1928.
   Phil 5819.1   Jarrold, T. Instinct and reason...science of education.
                    London, 1736.
   Phil 5819.2   Joly, H. L'homme et l'animal. Paris, 1877.
   Phil 5819.2.5   Joly, H. L'instinct. Paris, 1869.
   Phil 5819.2.7   Joly, H. L'instinct; ses rapports. 2. éd. Paris, 1873.
   Phil 5819.3   Josey, Charles C. The role of instinct in social
                    psychology. N.Y., 1921.
   Phil 5819.3.5   Josey, Charles C. The social philosophy of instinct.
                    N.Y., 1922.
   Phil 5819.4   Jenkins, Marion. The effect of segregation on the sex
                    behavior of the white rat as measured by the abstraction
                    method. Worcester, Mass., 1928.
   Phil 5819.5   Jarmer, Karl. Das Seelenleben der Fische. München, 1928.
   Phil 5819.6   Jackson, T.A. General factors in transfer of training in
                    the white rat. Worcester, 1932.
   Phil 5819.7   Janssens, E. Études de psychologie animale. Paris, 1939.
   Phil 5819.10   Joffe, J.M. Prenatal determinants of behaviour. 1. ed.
                    Oxford, 1969.
   Phil 5820.1   Körner, F. Instinkt und freier Wille. Leipzig, 1875.
   Phil 5820.1.5   Körner, F. Instinkt und freier Wille. 2. Aufl.
                    Leipzig, 1878.

Phil 5820.2	Kafka, Gustav. Einführung in die Tierpsychologie auf experimenteller und ethnologischer Grundlage. Leipzig, 1914.
Phil 5820.2.5	Kafka, Gustav. Handbuch der vergleichenden Psychologie. München, 1922. 3v.
Phil 5820.3	Kindermann, H. Lola, or The thought and speech of animals. London, 1922.
Phil 5820.4.5	Köhler, Wolfgang. The mentality of apes. London, 1925.
Phil 5820.4.10	Köhler, Wolfgang. Intelligenzprüfungen an Menschenaffen. 2. Aufl. Berlin, 1921.
Phil 5820.4.15	Köhler, Wolfgang. L'intelligence des singes supérieurs. Paris, 1927.
Phil 5820.5	Klüver, H. Behavior mechanisms in monkeys. Chicago, 1933.
Phil 5820.7	Klee, James Butt. Problems of selective behavior. Lincoln, 1951.
Phil 5821.1	Leroy, Charles Georges. Lettres sur les animaux. Paris, 1862.
Phil 5821.1.5	Leroy, Charles Georges. Lettres philosophiques sur l'intelligence et la perfectibilité des animaux. Paris, 1802.
Phil 5821.1.10	Leroy, Charles Georges. Lettres sur les animaux. Nuremberg, 1781.
Phil 5821.1.15	Marx, Moses. Charles Georges Leroy und seine "Lettres philosophiques." Strassburg, 1898.
Phil 5821.2	Lindsay, W.L. Mind in the lower animals. London, 1879. 2v.
Phil 5821.2.3	Lindsay, W.L. Physiology and pathology of mind in the lower animals. Edinburgh, 1871.
Phil 5821.4	Loeb, J. Einleitung...Gehirnphysiologie...Psychologie. Leipzig, 1899.
Phil 5821.4.5	Loeb, J. Comparative physiology of the brain and comparative psychology. N.Y., 1900.
Phil 5821.5	Lukas, F. Psychologie der niedersten Tiere. Wien, 1905.
Phil 5821.6	Lewandowsky, M. Die Funktionen des zentralen Nervensystems. Jena, 1907.
Phil 5821.8	Lazarus, M. Uber die Reize des Spiels. Berlin, 1883.
Phil 5821.9	Langfeldt. Tier- und Menschenverstand. München, 1909.
Phil 5821.10	Leuret, F. Anatomie comparée du système nerveux. Paris, 1839.
Htn Phil 5821.11*	Legrand, A. Dissertatio de carentia sensus et cognitionis in brutis. London, 1675.
Phil 5821.12	Ligon, Ernest M. A comparative study of certain incentives in the learning of the white rat. Diss. Baltimore, 1929.
Phil 5821.14	Loeser, Johann A. Die Psychologie des Emotionalen. Berlin, 1931.
Phil 5821.16	Lovenz, Konrad Zacharias. Antriebe tierischen und menschlichen Verhaltens. München, 1968.
Phil 5822.1A	Morgan, C.L. Introduction to comparative psychology. London, 1884.
Phil 5822.1B	Morgan, C.L. Introduction to comparative psychology. London, 1884.
Phil 5822.1C	Morgan, C.L. Introduction to comparative psychology. London, 1884.
Phil 5822.1.3	Morgan, C.L. Introduction to comparative psychology. London, 1894.
Phil 5822.1.10A	Morgan, C.L. Habit and instinct. London, 1896.
Phil 5822.1.10B	Morgan, C.L. Habit and instinct. London, 1896.
Phil 5822.1.15	Morgan, C.L. Animal behaviour. London, 1900.
Phil 5822.1.20	Morgan, C.L. The animal mind. N.Y., 1930.
Phil 5822.1.25	Morgan, C.L. Instinct and experience. N.Y., 1912.
Phil 5822.2	Mills, W. The nature and development of animal intelligence. London, 1898.
Phil 5822.3	Matthes, B. Betrachtungen über Wirbelthiere. Dresden, 1861.
Phil 5822.4A	Máday, Stefan. Psychologie des Pferdes und der Dressur. Berlin, 1912.
Phil 5822.4B	Máday, Stefan. Psychologie des Pferdes und der Dressur. Berlin, 1912.
Phil 5822.4.3	Muan, N.L. Psychological development. Boston, 1938.
Phil 5822.4.10	Messner, J. Widersprüche in der menschlichen Existenz. Innsbruck, 1952.
Phil 5822.5	Mangold, Ernst. Hypnose und Katalepsie bei Tieren. Jena, 1914.
Phil 5822.6	McCabe, Joseph. The evolution of mind. London, 1910.
Phil 5822.7	McAllister, W.G. A further study of the delayed reaction in the albino rat. Baltimore, 1932.
Phil 5822.8	Munn, Norman L. An introduction to animal psychology. Boston, 1933.
Phil 5822.9	Maier, Norman Raymond Frederick. Principles of animal psychology. N.Y., 1935.
Phil 5822.9.2	Maier, Norman Raymond Frederick. Principles of animal psychology. N.Y., 1964.
Phil 5822.9.10	Maier, Norman Raymond Frederick. Studies of abnormal behavior in the rat. N.Y., 1939.
Phil 5822.10	MacNamara, N.C. Instinct and intelligence. London, 1915.
Phil 5822.12	Miatto, A. Istinto e società animale. Firenze, 195-?
Phil 5822.14	Morris, Desmond. The biology of art. London, 1962.
Phil 5822.14.5	Morris, Desmond. The biology of art. N.Y., 1962.
Phil 5823.1	Nicolaÿ, Fernand. L'âme et l'instinct; l'homme et l'animal. Paris, 1922.
Phil 5823.2	Nadaillac, J.F.A. Intelligence et instinct. Paris, 1892.
Phil 5825.1	Perty, J.A.M. Uber das Seelenleben der Thiere. Leipzig, 1876.
Phil 5825.2	Pfungst, Oskar. Das Pferd des Herrn von Osten. Leipzig, 1907.
Phil 5825.2.5	Pfungst, Oskar. Clever Hans; the horse of Mr. von Osten. N.Y., 1965.
Phil 5825.3	Parmelee, M. The science of human behavior. N.Y., 1913.
Phil 5825.4	Peterson, Joseph. The effect of length of blind alleys on maze learning. N.Y., 1917.
Phil 5825.5	Patten, Charles J. The passing of the phantoms. London, 1924.
Phil 5825.6.4	Pardies, Ignace. Discours de la connaissance des bestes. 4. éd. Paris, 1896.
Phil 5825.7.2	Perez, Bernard. Mes deux chats. 2. éd. Paris, 1900.
Phil 5825.8	Pitt, Frances. The intelligence of animals. London, 1931.
Phil 5825.9	Piéron, Henri. De l'actinie à l'homme. Paris, 1958. 2v.
Phil 5826.5	Quarelli, Elena. Socrate e le bestie. Cuneo, 1958.
Phil 5827.1	Romanes, G.J. Mental evolution in animals. London, 1883.
Phil 5827.1.3A	Romanes, G.J. Mental evolution in animals. N.Y., 1884.
Phil 5827.1.3B	Romanes, G.J. Mental evolution in animals. N.Y., 1884.
Phil 5827.1.5	Romanes, G.J. Mental evolution in man. London, 1888.
Phil 5827.1.6	Romanes, G.J. Mental evolution in man, origin of human faculty. N.Y., 1889.
Phil 5827.1.13	Romanes, G.J. Animal intelligence. N.Y., 1888.

Phil 5827.1.28	Romanes, G.J. Die geistige Entwicklung im Tierreich. Leipzig, 1885.
Htn Phil 5827.2*	Rorario, G. Quôd animalia bruta ratione utantur meliùs homine. Paris, 1648.
Phil 5827.3	Rendu, V. L'intelligence des bêtes. Paris, 1863.
Phil 5827.4	Reimarus, Hermann Samuel. Observations physiques et morales sur l'instinct des animaux. Amsterdam, 1770. 2v.
Phil 5827.4.5	Reimarus, Hermann Samuel. Allgemeine Betrachtungen über die Triebe der Thiere. 2. Ausg. Hamburg, 1762.
Htn Phil 5827.4.6*	Reimarus, Hermann Samuel. Allgemeine Betrachtungen über die Triebe der Thiere. Hamburg, 1760.
Phil 5827.4.7	Reimarus, Hermann Samuel. Allgemeine Betrachtungen über die Triebe der Thiere. 3. Ausg. Hamburg, 1773. 2 pam.
Phil 5827.5	Richardson, F. A study of sensory control in the rat. n.p., 1909.
Phil 5827.5.2	Robinson, R. (Mrs.). A study of sensory control in the rat. Lancaster, Pa., 1909.
Phil 5827.6	Reuter, Odo M. Die Seele der Tiere im Lichte der Forschung. Leipzig, 1908.
Phil 5827.7	Reeves, Cora Daisy. Discrimination of light of different wave-lengths by fish. N.Y., 1919.
Phil 5827.8	Rabaud, E. How animals find their way about. Leipzig, 1928.
Phil 5827.8.5	Rabaud, E. L'orientation lointaine et la reconnaissance des lieux. Paris, 1927.
Phil 5827.9	Rizzolo, Attilio. Études expérimentales sur l'exitabilité de l'écorce cérébrale du chien. Thèse. Paris, 1928.
Phil 5827.10	Rowley, Jean B. Discrimination limens of pattern and size in the goldfish, Carassius auratus. Thesis. Worcester, Mass., 1934.
Phil 5827.11	Riess, Bernard F. Limits of learning ability in the white rat and the guinea pig. Diss. Worcester, Mass., 1934.
Phil 5827.12	Rubin, E. Mennesker og Høns. København, 1937.
Phil 5828.1	Santlus, J.C. Zur Psychologie der menschlichen Triebe. Neuwied, 1864.
Phil 5828.2	Scheitlin, P. Versuch einer vollständigen Thierseelenkunde. Stuttgart, 1840. 2v.
Phil 5828.3	Schneider, G.H. Der thierische Will. Leipzig, 1880.
Phil 5828.4	Strumpell, L. Die Geisteskräfte der Menschen. Leipzig, 1878.
Phil 5828.5	Strassen, O.Z. Die neuere Tierpsychologie. Leipzig, 1908.
Phil 5828.6	Schneider, K.C. Vorlesungen über Tierpsychologie. Leipzig, 1909.
Phil 5828.6.5	Schneider, K.C. Tierpsychologisches Praktikum. Leipzig, 1912.
Phil 5828.7	Smith, E.M. The investigation of mind in animals. Cambridge, 1915.
Phil 5828.7.2	Smith, E.M. The investigation of mind in animals. 2. ed. Cambridge, 1923.
Phil 5828.8	Schultz, F. Vergleichende Seelenkunde. Leipzig, 1892-97. 2v.
Phil 5828.9	Schmarda, L.K. Andeutungen aus dem Seelenleben der Thiere. Wien, 1846.
Phil 5828.10	Skowronnek, Fritz. Seelenleben der Tiere. Berlin, 1911.
Phil 5828.11	Sokolowsky, A. Beobachtungen über die Psyche. Frankfurt, 1908.
Phil 5828.11.5	Sokolowsky, A. Aus dem Seelenleben höherer Tiere. Leipzig, 1910.
Phil 5828.12	Sorel, C.L.F. De l'intelligence chez l'animal. Paris, 19-
Phil 5828.13	Söderhjelm, H. Instinkterna och det mänskliga känslolivet. Helsingfors, 1913.
Phil 5828.14	Sommer, R. Tierpsychologie. Leipzig, 1925.
Phil 5828.15	Shepherd, James. Instinct. Kirkcaldy, 1884.
Phil 5828.16	Schmid, Bastian. Das Tier und Wir. Leipzig, 1916.
Phil 5828.16.5	Schmid, Bastian. Das Tier in seinen Spielen. Leipzig, 1919.
Phil 5828.17	Shuey, A.M. The limits of learning ability in kittens. Worcester, 1931.
Phil 5828.18	Sire, Marcel. L'intelligence des animaux. Paris, 1954.
Phil 5828.19	Schiller, C.H. Instinctive behavior. N.Y., 1957.
Phil 5828.20	Scott, J.P. Animal behavior. Garden City, 1963.
Phil 5828.21	Sluchin, Wladyslaw. Imprinting and early learning. Chicago, 1965.
Phil 5829.1	Tissot, C.J. Psychologie comparée. Paris, 1878.
Phil 5829.3.2	Toussenel, A. L'esprit des bêtes; zoologie passionnelle. 2. éd. Paris, 1855.
Phil 5829.3.4	Toussenel, A. L'esprit des bêtes; zoologie passionnelle. Paris, 1884.
Phil 5829.5	Toenjes, H. Principles of animal understanding. N.Y., 1905.
Phil 5829.6	Thierseelen-Kunde auf thatsachen Begrundet. Berlin, 1804-05. 2v.
Phil 5829.7	Thompson, E.L. An analysis of the learning process in the snail. Cambridge, 1917.
Phil 5829.8	Thorlakson, B.C. Le fondement physiologique des instincts des systèmes nutritif. Thèse. Paris, 1926.
Phil 5829.9	Thomas, Maurice. L'instinct: théories - réalité. Paris, 1929.
Phil 5829.9.5	Thomas, Maurice. La notion de l'instinct et ses bases scientifiques. Paris, 1936.
Phil 5829.10	Tolman, Edward C. Purposive behavior in animals and men. N.Y., 1932.
Phil 5829.10.2	Tolman, Edward C. Purposive behavior in animals and men. Berkeley, 1951.
Phil 5829.11	Thorpe, W.H. Learning and instinct in animals. London, 1956.
Phil 5829.14	Thinès, Georges. Psychologie des animaux. Bruxelles, 1966.
Phil 5829.16	Tukh, Nina A. Predystoniia obshchestva. Leningrad, 1970.
Phil 5831.1	Vignoli, Tito. Über das Fundamentalgesetz der Intelligenz im Thierreiche. Leipzig, 1879.
Phil 5831.1.3	Vignoli, Tito. Della legge fondamentale dell'intelligenza nell regno animali. Milano, 1877.
Phil 5831.2	Verworn, M. Die sogenannte Hypnose der Thiere. Jena, 1898.
Phil 5831.3	Vincent, S.B. The function of the vibrissae in the behavior of the white rat. Chicago, 1912.
Phil 5831.4	Volkelt, Johannes. Über die vorstellungen Deutiere. v.2. Leipzig, 1914.
Phil 5831.5	Vues sur la psychologie animale. Paris, 1930.
Phil 5831.6	Verlaine, Louis. L'âme des bêtes. Paris, 1931.
Phil 5831.6.5	Verlaine, Louis. Histoire naturelle de la connaissance chez le singe inférieur; le concret. Paris, 1935-36. 3v.

Phil 5810 - 5835   Psychology - Comparative psychology - General works -
Individual authors (A-Z) - cont.

Phil 5832.1   Watson, John S. The reasoning power in animals.
London, 1867.

Phil 5832.1.4   Watson, John S. The reasoning power in animals. 2. ed.
London, 1870.

Phil 5832.2   Wilson, W.D. Lectures...psychology: thought, action.
Ithaca, 1871.

Phil 5832.3   Wasmann, E. Vergleichende Studien über das Seelenleben der
Ameisen und der höheren Thiere. Freiburg, 1897.

Phil 5832.3.4   Wasmann, E. Instinct und Intelligenz im Thierreich.
Freiburg, 1899.

Phil 5832.3.9   Wasmann, E. Menschen und Tierseele. Köln, 1906.

Phil 5832.3.13   Wasmann, E. Menschen und Tierseele. 5. Aufl. Köln, 1910.

Phil 5832.4   Wood, J.G. Man and beast, here and hereafter. N.Y., n.d.

Phil 5832.5   Walse, C.S. Chapters on man...comparative psychology.
London, 1868.

Phil 5832.6   Weir, J. The dawn of reason. N.Y., 1899.

Phil 5832.7.5   Watson, John B. Animal education; an experimental study on
the psychological development of the white rat.
Chicago, 1903.

Phil 5832.8   Washburn, M.F. The animal mind. N.Y., 1908.

Phil 5832.8.5   Washburn, M.F. The animal mind. 2. ed. N.Y., 1917.

Phil 5832.8.7   Washburn, M.F. The animal mind. 3. ed. N.Y., 1926.

Phil 5832.9   Watson, John B. Behavior. N.Y., 1914.

Phil 5832.9.2A   Watson, John B. Behavior. N.Y., 1914.

Phil 5832.9.2B   Watson, John B. Behavior. N.Y., 1914.

Phil 5832.9.5   Watson, John B. Kinaesthetic and organic sensations.
Lancaster, 1907.

Phil 5832.10   Wiltbank, R.T. Transfer of training in white rats upon
various series of mazes. Chicago, 1919.

Phil 5832.11   Wolff, Gustav. Zur Psychologie des Erkennens.
Leipzig, 1897.

Phil 5832.13   Warden, C.J. A short outline of comparative psychology.
N.Y., 1927.

Phil 5832.13.10   Warden, C.J. Animal motivation. N.Y., 1931.

Phil 5832.13.15   Warden, C.J. Comparative psychology. N.Y., 1935-40.
3v.

Phil 5832.14   Wyman, Eva May. On instinct and intelligence. Thesis.
Philadelphia, 1931.

Phil 5832.15A   Werner, Heinz. Comparative psychology of mental
development. N.Y., 1940.

Phil 5832.15B   Werner, Heinz. Comparative psychology of mental
development. N.Y., 1940.

Phil 5832.15.5   Werner, Heinz. Comparative psychology of mental
development. N.Y., 1948.

Phil 5832.15.10   Werner, Heinz. Comparative psychology of mental
development. N.Y., 1957.

Phil 5832.15.12   Werner, Heinz. Comparative psychology of mental
development. N.Y., 1966.

Phil 5832.16   Wimersama Greidanus, H.T. van. De hormische psychologie
van den mensch. Leiden, 1946.

Phil 5832.20   Waters, Rolland. Principles of comparative psychology.
N.Y., 1960.

Phil 5832.25   Winkelstraeter, K.H. Das Betteln der Zoo-Tiere.
Bern, 1960.

Phil 5834.1   Yerkes, R.M. The dancing mouse. N.Y., 1907.

Phil 5834.1.5   Yerkes, R.M. Methods of studying vision in animals.
Cambridge, n.d.

Phil 5834.1.9A   Yerkes, R.M. Mental life of monkeys and apes.
Cambridge, 1916.

Phil 5834.1.9B   Yerkes, R.M. Mental life of monkeys and apes.
Cambridge, 1916.

Phil 5834.1.13   Yerkes, R.M. Chimpanzee intelligence. Baltimore, 1925.

Phil 5834.1.15   Yerkes, R.M. The mind of a gorilla. Worcester,
Mass., 1926.

Phil 5834.1.20   Yerkes, R.M. Reaction of entomostraca to...light.
n.p., 1899-1916. 44 pam.

Phil 5834.1.25   Yerkes, R.M. Chimpanzees; a laboratory colony. New
Haven, 1943.

Phil 5835.1.3   Ziegler, H.E. Der Begriff des Instinktes einst und jetzt.
3. Aufl. Jena, 1920.

Phil 5835.2   Zürn, Friedrich A. Die intellectuellen Eigenschaften der
Pferde. Stuttgart, 1899.

Phil 5835.3   Zweig, Adam. Tierpsychologische Beiträge zur Psylogenese
der ich-über-ich-instanzen. Bern, 1959.

Phil 5835.3.5   Zweig, Adam. Tierpsychologische Beiträge zur Psylogenese
der ich-über-ich-instanzen. Bern, 1959.

Phil 5835.10   Zajonc, Robert Boleslaw. Animal social psychology.
N.Y., 1969.

Phil 5838   Psychology - Comparative psychology - Special topics - Instinct (By
date, e.g. .260 for 1960)

Phil 5838.256   L'instinct dans le comportement des animaux et de l'homme.
Paris, 1956.

Phil 5838.257   Fletcher, Ronald. Instinct in man in the light of recent
work in comparative psychology. N.Y., 1957.

Phil 5838.259   Viaud, Gaston. Les instincts. Paris, 1959.

Phil 5838.261   Birney, Robert C. Instinct, an enduring problem in
psychology. Princeton, 1961.

Phil 5838.266   Palmeri, R. The sources of instinctive life, and A theory
of mental functioning. N.Y., 1966.

Phil 5838.269   Glickman, Stephen E. The neurological basis of motivation.
N.Y., 1969.

Phil 5841   Psychology - Sex psychology - General works

Phil 5841.01   Pamphlet box. Sex psychology.

Phil 5841.2   Maxey, Wallace de Ortega. Man is a sexual being. Fresno,
Calif., 1958.

Phil 5841.4   Guérin, Daniel. Essai sur la révolution sexuelle.
Paris, 1969.

Phil 5841.6   Holter, Harriet. Sex roles and social structure.
Oslo, 1970.

Phil 5841.8   Sexualité humaine. Paris, 1970.

Phil 5841.10   Richardson, Herbert Warren. Nun, witch, playmate; the
Americanization of sex. 1st ed. N.Y., 1971.

Phil 5841.12   Christenson, Cornelia Vos. Kinsey, a biography.
Bloomington, 1971.

Phil 5841.14   Loewenfeld, Leopold. Sexualleben und Nervenleiden.
Wiesbaden, 1906.

Phil 5841.16   Stoll, Otto. Die Geschlechtsleben in der
Völkerpsychologie. Leipzig, 1908.

Phil 5841.18.2   Rank, Otto. Der Künstler; Ansatze zu einer
Sexualpsychologie. 2. - 3. Aufl. Wien, 1918.

Phil 5841.18.4   Rank, Otto. Der Künstler. 4. Aufl. Leipzig, 1925.

Phil 5841.18.10   Rank, Otto. Sexualität und Schuldgefühl. Leipzig, 1926.

Phil 5841.20.5   Jung, Emma. Animus und Anima. Zürich, 1967.

Phil 5841.20.8   Jung, Emma. Animus and Anima. N.Y., 1957.

Phil 5841   Psychology - Sex psychology - General works - cont.

Phil 5841.22   Rosenfels, Paul. Love and power. N.Y., 1966.

Phil 5841.24   Heimler, Adolf. Reifung und Geschlecht. München, 1966.

Phil 5841.26   Stern, Karl. The flight from woman. N.Y., 1965.

Phil 5845   Psychology - Applied psychology - Bibliographies

Phil 5845.2   Descloitres, Claudine. La psychologie applique en Afrique;
bibliographie. Aix-en-Provence, 1968.

Phil 5850   Psychology - Applied psychology - General works (299 scheme, A-Z)

Phil 5850.02   Pamphlet box. Psychology. Applied.

Phil 5850.102   Acilles, P.S. Psychology at work. N.Y., 1932.

Phil 5850.108   Alexander, James. Thought-control in everyday life.
N.Y., 1928.

Phil 5850.108.5   Alexander, James. Mastering your own mind. N.Y., 1931.

Phil 5850.111   Anastasi, A. Fields of applied psychology. N.Y., 1964.

Phil 5850.127   Band, Francis. La science des caractères. Paris, 1944.

Phil 5850.127.5   Battegay, Raymond. Der Mensch in der Gruppe. Bern, 1967-
3v.

Phil 5850.128   Beck, Samuel. Reflexes to intelligence. Glencoe, 1959.

Phil 5850.130   Beuesch, H. Wissenschaft der Menschenbehandlung.
Heidelberg, 1958.

Phil 5850.131   Bertine, Eleanor. Human relationships. 1. ed. N.Y., 1958.

Phil 5850.135   Bingham, W.V. Psychology applied. n.p., 1923.

Phil 5850.135.10   Bingham memorial lecture. Pittsburgh. 1961

Phil 5850.135.15   Bertine, Eleanor. How to interview. N.Y., 1931.

Phil 5850.135.20   Bertine, Eleanor. How to interview. 2. ed. N.Y., 1934.

Phil 5850.135.30   Bingham, Walter van Dyke. How to interview. 3. ed.
N.Y., 1941.

Phil 5850.136   Binois, René. La psychologie appliquée. 3. éd.
Paris, 1952.

Phil 5850.138   Bogen, Helmuth. Psychologische Grundlegung der praktischen
Berufsberatung. Langensalza, 1927.

Phil 5850.138.5   Bodalev, Aleksei A. Formirovanie poniatiia o drugom
cheloveke kak lichnosti. Leningrad, 1970.

Phil 5850.140   Bonnardel, Raymond. L'adaption de l'homme à son métier. 1.
éd. Paris, 1946.

Phil 5850.143   Bromberg, R. Toegepaste psychologie. Leiden, 1926.

Phil 5850.145   Brown, William. Oxford essays on psychology.
London, 1948.

Phil 5850.145.50   Burtt, H.E. Applied psychology. N.Y., 1948.

Phil 5850.145.50.5   Burtt, H.E. Applied psychology. 2. ed. Englewood
Cliffs, 1957.

Phil 5850.148.5   Caner, George C. It's how you take it. N.Y., 1946.

Phil 5850.149   Capps, Ora L. Developing and using your inner powers.
Denver, 1932.

Phil 5850.149.5   Capps, Ora L. Controlling your circumstances and affairs
of life. Denver, 1932.

Phil 5850.157.5   Cheatham, T.A. I believe in life. Pinehurst, N.C., 1941.

Phil 5850.161   Coetsier, Leo. Toegepaste psychologie. Gent, 1965.

Phil 5850.162   Collins, Mary. Psychology and practical life.
London, 1936.

Phil 5850.166   Crane, G.W. Psychology applied. Chicago, 1933.

Phil 5850.171   Defares, Peter Bernard. Grondvormen van menselijke
relaties. Assen, 1963.

Phil 5850.176   Dunlap, Knight. Personal adjustment. 1. ed. N.Y., 1946.

Phil 5850.188   Erismann, T. Angewandte Psychologie. Berlin, 1916.

Phil 5850.191.5   Ewer, B.C. Applied psychology. N.Y., 1925.

Phil 5850.196   Fenlason, Anne. Essentials in interviewing. N.Y., 1962.

Phil 5850.200   Fisher, V.E. Dissatisfied worker. N.Y., 1931.

Phil 5850.205   Frankard, Paul. Analyse critique de la notion de validité.
Louvain, 1958.

Phil 5850.211   Garrett, A.M. Interviewing, its principles and methods.
N.Y., 1942.

Phil 5850.214   Giese, Fritz. Theorie der Psychotechnik: Grundzüge der
praktischen Psychologie. Braunschweig, 1925.

Phil 5850.214.10   Giese, Fritz. Arbeits- und Berufspsychologie.
Halle, 1928.

Phil 5850.214.15   Giese, Fritz. Psychoanalytische Psychotechnik.
Leipzig, 1924.

Phil 5850.219   Glidewell, John C. Choice points. Cambridge, Mass., 1970.

Phil 5850.221   Gray, John S. Psychology in use. N.Y., 1941.

Phil 5850.221.10   Goersdorf, Kurt. Arbeitsfreude - Leistungsanstrengungen.
München, 1958.

Phil 5850.221.15   Goude, G. On fundamental measurement in psychology.
Stockholm, 1962.

Phil 5850.221.20   Gorden, Raymond L. Interviewing: strategy, techniques, and
tactics. Homewood, Ill., 1969.

Phil 5850.222   Griffith, C.R. An introduction to applied psychology.
N.Y., 1936.

Phil 5850.226   Gŭrdev, Dinó. Strukturen analiz na obshtestvenoto
Sŭznanie. Sofiia, 1970.

Phil 5850.227   Hayward, C.N. Re-creating human nature. N.Y., 1914.

Phil 5850.227.14   Haernqvist, Kjell. Tillämpad psykologi. 4. uppl.
Stockholm, 1966.

Phil 5850.228   Helke, J.W. Korrelation oder Wertigkeit? Inaug. Diss.
Leipzig, 1934.

Phil 5850.228.15   Hepner, Harry W. Psychology applied to life and work.
N.Y., 1942.

Phil 5850.228.20   Heider, Fritz. The psychology of interpersonal relations.
N.Y., 1958.

Phil 5850.228.20.5   Heider, Fritz. The psychology of interpersonal relations.
N.Y., 1967.

Phil 5850.230   Hollingworth, H.L. Applied psychology. N.Y., 1923.

Phil 5850.230.11   Hollingworth, H.L. Vocational psychology and character
analysis. N.Y., 1931.

Phil 5850.230.15   Hollingworth, H.L. The psychology of the audience.
N.Y., 1935.

Phil 5850.230.100   Holzschuher, L. von. Praktische Psychologie. 2. Aufl.
Seebruck am Chiemsee, 1955.

Phil 5850.231   Huth, Albert. Exakte Persönlichkeitsforschung.
Leipzig, 1930.

Phil 5850.232   Husband, R.W. Applied psychology. N.Y., 1934.

Phil 5850.235   Harwood, Sumner. How to work with people.
Cambridge, 1940.

Phil 5850.244   Jastrow, Joseph. Keeping mentally fit, a guide to everyday
psychology. N.Y., 1928.

Phil 5850.244.5   Jastrow, Joseph. Keeping mentally fit. N.Y., 1928.

Phil 5850.247   Jung, Carl G. Aufsätze zur Zeitgeschichte. Zürich, 1946.

Phil 5850.247.5   Jung, Carl G. Essays on contemporary events.
London, 1947.

Phil 5850.250   Kandhi, S. The winning of wealth. Boston, 1932.

Phil 5850.250.10   Kahn, Robert L. The dynamics of interviewing. N.Y., 1958.

Phil 5850.250.15   Kantor, J.R. Interbehavioral psychology.
Bloomington, 1958.

Phil 5850   Psychology - Applied psychology - General works (299 scheme, A-Z) - cont.

Phil 5850.251   Taylor, F.K. The analysis of therapeutic groups. London, 1961.

Phil 5850.253   Laird, Donald A. Increasing personal efficiency. N.Y., 1925.

Phil 5850.253.5   Laird, Donald A. Increasing personal efficiency. N.Y., 1925.

Phil 5850.253.10   Laird, Donald A. The dynamics of personal efficiency. 1. ed. N.Y., 1961.

Phil 5850.254   Lainz, Ronald David. Interpersonal perception. London, 1966.

Phil 5850.255   Langer, W.C. Psychology and human living. N.Y., 1943.

Phil 5850.256   Lehmann, A. Størst unbytte af legemligt og aandeligt arbejde. København, 1919.

Phil 5850.258.4   Link, Henry C. The return to religion. N.Y., 1937.

Phil 5850.258.5   Link, Henry C. The way to security. Garden City, 1951.

Phil 5850.259   Lombard, G.F.F. Behavior in a selling group. Boston, 1955.

Phil 5850.260   Lurton, D.E. Make the most of your life. London, 1945.

Phil 5850.264   Maier, Norman Raymond Frederick. Psychology in industry. Boston, 1946.

Phil 5850.264.25   Magoun, F.A. The teaching of human relations. Boston, 1959.

Phil 5850.267   Maryland. Conference on Military Contributions to Methology. New methods in applied psychology. College Park, 1947.

Phil 5850.271   Merton, R.K. The focused interview. Glencoe, Ill., 1956.

Phil 5850.274   Moede, Walther. Lehrbuch der Psychotechnik. Berlin, 1930.

Phil 5850.277   Moss, F.A. Applications of psychology. Boston, 1929.

Phil 5850.278   Münsterberg, H. Grundzüge der Psychotechnik. Leipzig, 1914.

Phil 5850.278.5   Münsterberg, H. Psychologie und Wirtschaftsleben. Leipzig, 1912.

Phil 5850.278.7   Münsterberg, H. Psychology and industrial efficiency. Boston, 1913.

Phil 5850.278.13   Münsterberg, H. Psicologia de la actividad industrial. Madrid, 1914.

Phil 5850.278.15   Münsterberg, H. Business psychology. Chicago, 1915.

Phil 5850.279   Myers, Charles S. Present-day applications of psychology. 2nd ed. London, 1918.

Phil 5850.279.7   Myers, Charles S. Mind and work. London, 1920.

Phil 5850.279.13   Myers, Charles S. Psychological conceptions in other sciences. Oxford, 1929.

Phil 5850.279.17   Myers, Charles S. In the realm of mind. Cambridge, Eng., 1937.

Phil 5850.281   National Research Council. Psychology for the returning serviceman. 1st ed. Washington, 1945.

Phil 5850.288.5   O'Connor, Johnson. Psychometrics. Cambridge, Mass., 1934.

Phil 5850.291   Oldfield, R.C. The psychology of the interview. London, 1941.

Phil 5850.291.3   Oldfield, R.C. The psychology of the interview. 3rd ed. London, 1947.

Phil 5850.299   Overstreet, H.A. Influencing human behavior. N.Y., 1925.

Phil 5850.299.5   Overstreet, H.A. Influencing human behavior. N.Y., 1925.

Phil 5850.304   Pascal, Gerald. Behavorial change in the clinic. N.Y., 1959.

Phil 5850.305A   Peale, N.V. The power of positive thinking. N.Y., 1955.

Phil 5850.305B   Peale, N.V. The power of positive thinking. N.Y., 1955.

Phil 5850.306   Pelman Institute of America. Scientific mind training. N.Y., 1924.

Phil 5850.306.5   Pelman Institute of America. Scientific mind training. N.Y., 1927.

Phil 5850.308   Peters, C.C. Human conduct. N.Y., 1918.

Phil 5850.309   Petersohn, F. Projektive Tests und Fahrtüchtigkeit. Hamburg, 1962.

Phil 5850.310   Piéron, Henri. Traité de psychologie appliquée. Paris, 1949- 7v.

Phil 5850.311   Piorkowski, C. Beiträge zur psychologischen Methodologie der wirtschaftlichen Berufseignung. Leipzig, 1915.

Phil 5850.314   Poffenberger, A.T. Applied psychology; its principles and methods. N.Y., 1927.

Phil 5850.314.5   Poffenberger, A.T. Principles of applied psychology. N.Y., 1942.

Phil 5850.326   Roback, A.A. The moral issues involved in applied psychology. n.p., 1917.

Phil 5850.326.5F   Roback, A.A. Course in business psychology assignment. v.1-8. n.p., n.d.

Phil 5850.326.9   Roback, A.A. Getting more out of life. n.p., 1937.

Phil 5850.326.12   Roback, A.A. Aspects of applied psychology and crime. Cambridge, 1964.

Phil 5850.328   Roethlisberger, F.J. Training for human relations. Boston, 1954.

Phil 5850.328.10   Rotter, Julian. Social learning and clinical psychology. Englewood Cliffs, N.J., 1958.

Phil 5850.330   Russell, W.L. Peace and power within. Houston, Texas, 1951.

Phil 5850.330.5   Russell, W.L. Peace and power within. N.Y., 1954.

Phil 5850.331   Sachs, Hildegard. Zur Organisation der Eignungspsychologie. Leipzig, 1920.

Phil 5850.332F   Sasha, A.W. Condensed outline of "The laws of life". Oakland, Cal., 1932.

Phil 5850.335   Schweizerische Stiftung für Angewandte Psychologie. Angewandte Psychologie in der Schweiz. Bern, 1959.

Phil 5850.335.10   Schwartz, David J. The magic of psychic power. West Nyack, N.Y., 1965.

Phil 5850.337   Seabury, David. Unmasking our minds. N.Y., 1924.

Phil 5850.337.9   Seabury, David. Unmasking our minds. N.Y., 1929.

Phil 5850.338   Selling, L.S. Studies on the problem driver. Detroit, 1941.

Phil 5850.340   Shaw, Charles G. Short talks on psychology. N.Y., 1920.

Phil 5850.340.50   Smith, E.D. Psychology for executives. N.Y., 1928.

Phil 5850.341   Smith, May. An introduction to industrial psychology. London, 1943.

Phil 5850.341.5   Smith, May. Handbook of industrial psychology. N.Y., 1944.

Phil 5850.342   Sollier, Paul. La psychotechnique. Bruxelles, 1935.

Phil 5850.343   Sonnet, André. Lerne menschen Kennen und Behandeln. Freiburg, 1959.

Phil 5850.347   Stern, Louis W. Angewandte Psychologie. n.p., 1903. 2 pam.

Phil 5850.347.5   Stern, Louis W. Zur Psychologie der Aussage. Berlin, 1902.

Phil 5850.348   Super, D.E. The psychology of careers. 1st ed. N.Y., 1957.

Phil 5850.349   Symonds, P.M. Diagnosing personality and conduct. N.Y., 1931.

Phil 5850.349.25   Allport, G.W. Review of P.M. Symonds' Diagnosing personality. Cambridge, Mass., 1932.

Phil 5850   Psychology - Applied psychology - General works (299 scheme, A-Z) - cont.

Phil 5850.349.50   Swift, Edgar J. Psychology and the day's work. N.Y., 1924.

Phil 5850.354.5   Thouless, R.H. The control of the mind. London, 1928.

Phil 5850.356   Torgerson, Warren S. Theory and methods of scaling. N.Y., 1958.

Phil 5850.356.5   Touraine, Alain. La conscience ouvrière. Thèse. Paris, 1966.

Phil 5850.356.10   Matalon, Benjamin. L'analyse hiérarchique. Paris, 1965.

Phil 5850.385   Wallas, Graham. The art of thought. N.Y., 1926.

Phil 5850.385.15   Wallon, Henri. Principes de psychologie appliquée. Paris, 1930.

Phil 5850.385.19   Walsh, W.S. Making our minds behave. N.Y., 1935.

Phil 5850.385.28   Weimer, H. Psychologie der Fehler. 2e Aufl. Leipzig, 1929.

Phil 5850.385.30   Weimer, H. Fehlerbehandlung und Fehlerbewertung. Leipzig, 1926.

Phil 5850.385.40   Webb, Ewing T. Strategy in handling people. Chicago, 1931.

Phil 5850.385.60   Weber, Wilhelm. Die praktische Psychologie im Wirtschaftsleben. Leipzig, 1927.

Phil 5850.385.65   West, P.V. Psychology for religious and social workers. N.Y., 1930.

Phil 5850.385.70   Weston, Sidney A. Finding your way in life. N.Y., 1942.

Phil 5850.385.80   White, Wendell. The psychology of dealing with people. N.Y., 1936.

Phil 5850.385.82   White, Wendell. The psychology of dealing with people. N.Y., 1941.

Phil 5850.385.85   White, Wendell. The psychology of making life interesting. N.Y., 1939.

Phil 5850.385.86   White, Wendell. Psychology in living. 3rd ed. N.Y., 1955.

Phil 5850.385.87   Wehowski, D. Ein allgemeines Modell für die Skalierung von Meinungen. Münster? 1961.

Phil 5850.386.5   Wiggam, A.E. The marks of a clear mind. N.Y., 1933.

VPhil 5850.386.10   Wheeler, Elmer. Word magic; tested answers to 100 everyday situations. N.Y., 1939.

Phil 5850.387.5   Wilner, D.M. Human relations in interracial housing. Minneapolis, 1955.

Phil 5850.391   Yates, Dorothy H. Psychological racketeers. Boston, 1932.

Phil 5853   Psychology - Applied psychology - Special topics

Phil 5853.2   Hruschka, Erna. Versuch einer theoretischen Grundlegung des Beratungsprozesses. Habilitationsschrift. Meisenheim am Glan, 1969.

Phil 5853.4   Gauquelin, François. Savoir communiquer. Paris, 1970.

Phil 5853.6   Saint-Arnaud, Yves. La consultation pastorale d'orientation Rogérienne. Paris, 1969.

Phil 5853.6.5   Johnson, Paul Emanuel. Person and counselor. Nashville, 1967.

Phil 5853.8   Blocher, Donald H. Developmental counseling. N.Y., 1966.

Phil 5853.10.3   Tyler, Leona Elizabeth. The work of the counselor. 3d ed. N.Y., 1969.

Phil 5853.12   Dexter, Lewis Anthony. Elite and specialized interviewing. Evanston, 1970.

Phil 5853.14   Carkhuff, Robert R. Helping and human relations. N.Y., 1969. 2v.

Phil 5856   Psychology - Differential psychology - General works

Phil 5856.5.2   Ekman, Gösta. Differentiell psykologi. Stockholm, 1966.

Phil 5856.10   Reuchlin, Maurice. La psychologie différentielle. Paris, 1969.

Phil 5858   Psychology - Differential psychology - Special topics - Other special

Phil 5858.5   Branden, Nathaniel. The psychology of self-esteem. Los Angeles, 1969.

Phil 5865   Psychology - Genetic psychology - General works

Phil 5865.2   Grinder, Robert Eugene. A history of genetic psychology. N.Y., 1967.

Phil 5865.4   Bollinger, Heinz. Das Werden der Person. München, 1967.

Phil 5865.5   Psycologie et épistémologie génétiques, thèmes piagétiens. Paris, 1966.

Phil 5865.5.4   Piaget, Jean. La psychologie de l'enfant. Paris, 1966.

Phil 5865.5.5   Piaget, Jean. The psychology of the child. N.Y., 1969.

Phil 5865.5.6   Piaget, Jean. Six études de psychologie. Genève, 1964.

Phil 5865.5.7   Piaget, Jean. Six psychological studies. N.Y., 1967.

Phil 5865.5.9   Piaget, Jean. On the development of memory and identity. Worcester, 1968.

Phil 5865.5.10   Desbiens, Jean Paul. Introduction à un examen philosophique de la psychologie de l'intelligence chez Jean Piaget. Québec, 1968.

Phil 5865.5.16   Brearley, Molly. A guide to reading Piaget. N.Y., 1967.

Phil 5865.5.20   Piaget, Jean. Genetic epistomology. N.Y., 1970.

Phil 5865.5.22   Piaget, Jean. The child's conception of time. London, 1969.

Phil 5865.5.25   Furth, Hans G. Piaget and knowledge. Englewood Cliffs, 1969.

Phil 5865.5.30   Helmore, Geoffrey Anthony. Piaget: a practical consideration. 1st ed. N.Y., 1969.

Phil 5865.5.35   Boyle, D.G. A student's guide to Piaget. 1st ed. Oxford, 1969.

Phil 5865.5.40   Elkind, David. Children and adolescents. N.Y., 1970.

Phil 5865.5.45   Montada, Leo. Die Lernpsychologie Jean Piagets. Stuttgart, 1970.

Phil 5865.6.2   Oerter, Rolf. Moderne Entwicklungspsychologie. 2. Aufl. Donauwörth, 1968.

Phil 5865.7   Trends and issues in developmental psychology. N.Y., 1969.

Phil 5865.8   Nash, John. Developmental psychology. Englewood Cliffs, N.J., 1970.

Phil 5865.10   Kriekemans, Albert. Genetische Psychologie, systematischen historisch. v.1,7,9,12. Tielt, 1965- 4v.

Phil 5865.12   Life-span developmental psychology. N.Y., 1970.

Phil 5867   Psychology - Genetic psychology - General special

Phil 5867.5   Slovenko, Ralph. Motivations in play, games and sports. Springfield, 1967.

Phil 5867.10   Heidemann, Ingeborg. Der Begriff des Spieles und das ästhetische Weltbild in der Philosphie der Gegenwart [play]. Berlin, 1968.

Phil 5867.15   Thetmark, J.C. Barnesprog. København, 1964.

Phil 5867.20   Gilles, Brigitte. Untersuchungen zur Periodik im Spielverhalten 6-10 jähriger Kinder. Bonn, 1965.

Phil 5867.25   Neale, Robert Edward. In praise of play; toward a psychology of religion. N.Y., 1969.

Phil 5867.30   Miller, David LeRoy. Gods and games; toward a theology of play. N.Y., 1970.

Phil 5867.35   Fried, Edrita. Active/passive: the crucial psychological dimension. N.Y., 1970.

Phil 5867 Psychology - Genetic psychology - General special - cont.

Phil 5867.40 Herron, R.E. Child's play. N.Y., 1971.

Phil 5870 Psychology - Genetic psychology - Child psychology - General works

Phil 5870.5 The psychoanalytic study of the child. N.Y. 1,1945+ 23v.

Phil 5870.6 Minnesota. Symposia on Child Psychology. Papers. Minneapolis. 1,1967+ 3v.

Phil 5870.10 Gästrin, Jan Emanuel. Teoretisk barnpsykologi. Stockholm, 1966.

Phil 5870.15 Talbot, Toby. The world of the child. Garden City, 1967.

Phil 5870.17 Söderling, Bertil. Barn av samma stam. Stockholm, 1967.

Phil 5870.20 Sandels, Stina. Utvecklingsykologiska beteendestudier hos barn i aldern 1 1/2 - 8 1/2 år. Thesis. Uppsala, 1956.

Phil 5870.25 Hetzer, Hildegard. Zur Psychologie des Kindes. Darmstadt, 1967.

Phil 5870.28 Tran-Thong. Stades et concept de stade de développement de l'enfant dans la psychologie contemporaine. Paris, 1967.

Phil 5870.30 Smirnoff, Victor. La psychanalyse de l'enfant. Paris, 1966.

Phil 5870.35 Bruun, Ulla-Britta. Förskoleålderns psykologi. Göteborg, 1968.

Phil 5870.40 Pfahler, Gerhard. Die zwölf wichtigsten Jahre des Lebens. München, 1967.

Phil 5870.45 Studies in cognitive development. N.Y., 1969.

Phil 5870.50 Fordham, Michael Scott Montague. Children as individuals. London, 1969.

Phil 5870.55 Zulliger, Hans. Das Kind in der Entwicklung. Bern, 1969.

Phil 5870.60 Isaacs, Susan (Fairhurst). The nursery years. N.Y., 1968.

Phil 5870.65 Psychologen over het kind. Groningen, 1968.

Phil 5870.70 Rogers, Dorothy. Issues in child psychology. Belmont, 1969.

Phil 5870.75 Freud, Anna. Research at the Hampstead Child-Therapy Clinic and other papers, 1956-1965. London, 1970.

Phil 5870.80.2 Stone, Lawrence Joseph. Childhood and adolescence. 2nd ed. N.Y., 1968.

Phil 5870.85.3 Carmichael, Leonard. Carmichael's manual of child psychology. 3rd ed. N.Y., 1970. 2v.

Phil 5870.90 Clauser, Günter. Die moderne Elternschule. Freiburg, 1969.

Phil 5870.95 Baldwin, Alfred Lee. Behavior and development in childhood. N.Y., 1955.

Phil 5870.100 Ratcliffe, Tom A. The child and reality. London, 1970.

Phil 5870.107 Ausubel, David Paul. Theory and problems of child development. 2nd ed. N.Y., 1970.

Phil 5870.110 Murphy, Lois Barclay. The widening world of childhood. N.Y., 1962.

Phil 5870.117 Nitschke, Alfred. Das verwaiste Kind der Natur. 2. Aufl. Tübingen, 1968.

Phil 5870.120.5 Reymond-Rivier, Berthe. Le développement social de l'enfant et de l'adolescent. 5. ed. Bruxelles, 1965.

Phil 5871 Psychology - Genetic psychology - Child psychology - General special

Phil 5871.2 Skasa-Weiss, Eugen. Mütter-Schicksal grosser Söhne. Oldenburg, 1966.

Phil 5871.5 Scheinfeld, Amram. Twins and supertwins. Philadelphia, 1967.

Phil 5871.5.5 Lindeman, Bard. The twins who found each other. N.Y., 1969.

Phil 5871.10 Erni, Margrit. Das Vaterbild den Tocher. Diss. n.p., 1965.

Phil 5871.15 Dechêne, Hans C. Geschwisterkonstellation und psychische Fehlentwicklung. München, 1967.

Phil 5871.20 Mannoni, Maud. L'enfant arriéré et sa mère. Paris, 1964.

Phil 5871.25 Ziv, Avner. La vie des enfants en collectivité. Paris, 1965.

Phil 5871.30 Harris, Irving D. The promised seed; a comparative study of eminent first and later sons. N.Y., 1964.

Phil 5871.35 Savioz, Esther. Die Anfänge der Geschwisterbeziehung. Bern, 1968.

Phil 5871.40 Bettelheim, Bruno. The children of the dream. N.Y., 1969.

Phil 5871.45 Vernon, Philip Ewart. Intelligence and cultural environment. London, 1969.

Phil 5871.50 Landolf, Peter. Kind ohne Vater. Bern, 1968.

Phil 5871.55 Mahler, Margaret S. On human symbiosis and the vicissitudes of individuation. London, 1969-

Phil 5871.60 Escalona, Sibylle Korsch. The roots of individuality. Chicago, 1968.

Phil 5871.65 Rifbjerg, Sofie. Psykologisk iagttagelse of børn. København, 1966.

Phil 5871.72 Richter, Horst Eberhard. Eltern, Kind und Neurose. 2. Aufl. Stuttgart, 1967.

Phil 5871.75 Wolff, Sula. Children under stress. London, 1969.

Phil 5871.80 Baroni, Christophe. Les parents, les inconnus. Genève, 1969.

Phil 5871.85 Bronfenbrenner, Urie. Two worlds of childhood: U.S. and U.S.S.R. N.Y., 1970.

Phil 5871.90 Hunt, David. Parents and children in history. N.Y., 1970.

Phil 5871.95 Sutton-Smith, Brian. The sibling. N.Y., 1970.

Phil 5871.100 Westley, William A. The silent majority; families of emotionally healthy college students. San Francisco, 1970.

Phil 5871.105.2 Ruehle, Otto. Zur Psychologie des proletarischen Kindes. 2. Aufl. Frankfurt, 1970.

Phil 5871.106 Ulrich, Ferdinand. Der Mensch als Anfang. Benziger, 1970.

Phil 5871.108 Biller, Henry B. Father, child, and sex role. Lexington, 1971.

Phil 5871.110 Cacciagierra, Francesco. I sentimenti del fanciullo nell'ambito familiare. Milano, 1968.

Phil 5871.112.2 Graber, Gustav Hans. Ursprung, Einheit und Zwiespalt der Seele. München, 1970.

Phil 5871.114 Lynn, David Brandon. Parental and sex-role identification. Berkeley, Calif., 1969.

Phil 5871.116 Evans, Judith L. Children in Africa: a review of psychological research. N.Y., 1970.

Phil 5871.118 Förälder i 70-talet. Stockholm, 1971.

Phil 5873 Psychology - Genetic psychology - Child psychology - Emotions

Phil 5873.2 Malrieu, Philippe. Les émotions et la personnalité de l'enfant. Thèse. Paris, 1952.

Phil 5873.2.2 Malrieu, Philippe. Les émotions et la personnalité de l'enfant. 2. éd. Paris, 1967.

Phil 5873.4 Zulliger, Hans. Die Angst unserer Kinder. Frankfurt, 1969.

Phil 5875 Psychology - Genetic psychology - Child psychology - Other special topics

Phil 5875.5 Lambert, Wallace E. Children's views of foreign peoples. N.Y., 1966.

Phil 5875.10 Roecker, Doris. Sprachfreie Kategorisierung bei Kleinkindern. Diss. Tübingen, 1965.

Phil 5875.15 Lévy-Schoen, Ariane. L'image d'autrui chez l'enfant. Paris, 1964.

Phil 5875.20 Lévy-Schoen, Ariane. Sur le développement de la connaissance d'autrui. Thèse. Paris, 1964.

Phil 5875.25 Pongratz, Josa Maria. Zur Ontogenese des sittlichen Urteils in besonderer Antinüpfung and die einschlägige Theorie Piaget's. Inaug. Diss. Heidelberg? 1964.

Phil 5875.30 Kreitler, Hans. Die kognitive Orientierung des Kindes. München, 1967.

Phil 5875.30.5 Sigel, Irving Edward. Logical thinking in children; research based on Piaget's theory. N.Y., 1968.

Phil 5875.50 Coopersmith, Stanley. The antecedents of self-esteem. San Francisco, 1967.

Phil 5875.60 Burton, Lindy. Vulnerable children; three studies of children in conflict. London, 1968.

Phil 5875.62 Fonzi, Ada. Disegno e linguaggio el bambino. Torino, 1968.

Phil 5875.62.5 De Bono, Edward. The dog exercising machine. London, 1970.

Phil 5875.64 Muehling, Ursel. Erstellung eines Projektiven Verfahrens zur psychologischen Untersuchung nichtsprechender und hochgradig sprechbehinderter Kinder. Köln, 1968.

Phil 5875.65 Raffler Engel, Walburga von. Il prelinguaggio infantile. Paideia, 1964.

Phil 5875.65.5 Brandis, Walter. Social class language and communication. London, 1970.

Phil 5875.65.10 Menýuk, Paula. The acquisition and development of language. Englewood Cliffs, 1971.

Phil 5875.70 Kay, William. Moral development: a psychological study of moral growth from childhood to adolescence. London, 1968.

Phil 5875.75 Koupernir, Cyrille. Développement neuro-psychique du nourrisson. 1. ed. Paris, 1968.

Phil 5875.80 Millar, Susanna. The psychology of play. Harmondsworth, 1968.

Phil 5875.90 Nooteboom, Wilhelmina E. Some psychological aspects of the chorcatiform syndrome: development of the intelligence. Assen, 1967.

Phil 5875.100 Andriessen, H. De groei van het geweten. Zeist, 1965.

Phil 5875.110 Debienne, Marie Claire. Le dessin chez l'enfant. Paris, 1968.

Phil 5875.110.5 Tuvo, Fulvio. Il disegno nella psicopatologia dell'età evolutiva. Trieste, 1966.

Phil 5875.115 Gondolatsch, Karl Heinz. Untersuchung der Sympathieäbhangigkeit von Aussageleiustungen bei Kindern und Jugendlichen. Köln, 1958.

Phil 5875.120 Aebli, Hans. Über den Egozentrismus des Kindes. Stuttgart, 1968.

Phil 5875.125 Rieder, Oskar. Die Entwicklung des kindlichen Fragens. München, 1968.

Phil 5875.130 Mecham, Merlin J. Development of audiolinguistic skills in children. St. Louis, 1969.

Phil 5875.140 Mueller, Rudolf. Entwicklung des sozialen Wertbewusstseins; eine empirische Untersuchung des sittlichen Beuresstseins bei Kindern und Jugendlichen. Thesis. Weinheim, 1968.

Phil 5875.145 Mauco, Georges. L'inconscient et la psychologie de l'enfant. 1. éd. Paris, 1970.

Phil 5875.150 Pareek, Udai Narain. Developmental patterns in reactions to frustration. N.Y., 1965.

Phil 5875.155 Sexuality and aggression in maturation: new facets. London, 1969.

Phil 5875.160 Stimulation in early infancy. London, 1969.

Phil 5875.170 Grotloh-Amberg, Heidi. Beeinflussung des Verhaltens durch den Schuleintritt. Bern, 1971.

Phil 5875.175 Piaget, Jean. Psychologie et épistémologie. Paris, 1970.

Phil 5876 Psychology - Genetic psychology - Adolescence, Youth - General works

Phil 5876.5.5 Asklund, Lis. Brytningstid, en bok om ungdom och samlernad. 5. uppl. Stockholm, 1964.

Phil 5876.10 Piel, Jacques. Analyse des formes prises par la socialité des adolescent dans le cadre de leurs loisis. Bruxelles, 1968.

Phil 5876.10.5 Hertzman-Ericson, Merit. Svåra unga år. Stockholm, 1967.

Phil 5876.10.10 Deutsch, Thelene. Selected problems of adolescence; with special emphasis on group formation. N.Y., 1967.

Phil 5876.15 Caplan, Gerald. Adolescence: psychosocial perspectives. N.Y., 1969.

Phil 5876.18 Offer, Daniel. The psychological world of the teen-ager. N.Y., 1969.

Phil 5876.20 Lorimier, Jacques de. Le projet de vie de l'adolescent, identité psychosociale et vocation. Paris, 1967.

Phil 5876.22 Hudson, Liam. Frames of mind. London, 1968.

Phil 5876.25.3 Horrocks, John Edwin. The psychology of adolescence; behavior and development. 3rd ed. Boston, 1969.

Phil 5876.30 Gattegno, Caleb. The adolescent and his will. N.Y., 1971.

Phil 5876.35 Bernard, Harold Wright. Adolescent development. Scranton, 1971.

Phil 5878 Psychology - Genetic psychology - Adolescence, Youth - Special topics

Phil 5878.5 Hauser, Stuart T. Black and white identity formation: studies in the psychosocial development of lower socioeconomic class adolescent boys. N.Y., 1971.

Phil 5878.10 Pearson, Gerald Hamilton Jeffrey. Adolescence and the conflict of generations. N.Y., 1958.

Phil 5880 Psychology - Genetic psychology - Adulthood

Phil 5880.5 Roscam Abbing, Pieter Johan. Volwassenheid. Hilversum, 1968.

Phil 5886 Psychology - Genetic psychology - Old age

Phil 5886.5 Psychological functioning in the normal aging and senile aged. Basel, 1968.

Phil 5886.10 Williams, Richard Hays. Lives through the years. 1st ed. N.Y., 1965.

Phil 5886.15 Birren, James Emmett. Handbook of aging and the individual. Chicago, 1960.

Phil 5886.20 Duke University. Center for the Study of Aging and Human Development. Normal aging: reports from the Duke longitudinal study, 1955-1969. Durham, N.C., 1970.

Phil 5890   Psychology - Genetic psychology - Class psychology in general
Phil 5890.2   McDaniel, James Winnard. Physical disability and human
                        behavior. N.Y., 1969.
Phil 5890.3.1   Pintner, Rudolf. The psychology of the physically
                        handicapped. N.Y., 1945.

Phil 5893   Psychology - Genetic psychology - Race and ethnic psychology in general
Phil 5893.2   Schoene, Wolfgang. Uber die Psychoanalyse in der
                        Ethnologie. Dortmund, 1966.
Phil 5893.4   Porter, Judith Deborah Revitch. Black child, white child;
                        the development of racial attitudes. Cambridge, 1971.
Phil 5893.6   Abraham, Karl. Dreams and myths; a study in race
                        psychology. N.Y., 1913.

Phil 5896   Psychology - Genetic psychology - Psychology of nations in general
Phil 5896.5   Lynn, Richard. Personality and national character. 1. ed.
                        Oxford, 1971.

Phil 5910   Psychology - Quasi-psychological systems - Phrenology - Pamphlet volumes
Phil 5910.2   Epps, J. Horae phrenologicae. London, 1829-1836.
                        6 pam.
Phil 5910.3   Watson, H.C. Statistics of phrenology. London, 1836-1837.
                        2 pam.
Phil 5910.5   Pamphlet vol. Phrenology pamphlets. London, 1821.
                        3 pam.
Phil 5910.15F   Pamphlet box. Phrenology. Charts, numbered I, II, IV-XXI.
                        Descriptions in German.

**Phil 5917.101   -   .399   Psychology - Quasi-psychological systems -
Phrenology - Biographies of phrenologists - Individual (A-Z, 299 scheme,
by person)**
Phil 5917.168   Carnicer, Ramón. Entre la ciencia y la magia. 1. ed.
                        Barcelona, 1969.

**Phil 5918.00   -   5919.99   Psychology - Quasi-psychological systems -
Phrenology - Pamphlet file**
Phil 5918.00.-.99 Pamphlet box. Phrenology. 19th century.
Phil 5919.00.-.99 Pamphlet box. Phrenology. 20th century.

**Phil 5920   -   5945   Psychology - Quasi-psychological systems - Phrenology -
General treatises - Individual authors (A-Z)**
Phil 5920.1   Azais, P.H. De la phrénologie. Paris, 1839. 2v.
Phil 5921.1   Broussais, F.J.V. Cours de phrénologie. Paris, 1836.
Phil 5921.1.5   Broussais, F.J.V. Lectures on phrenology. London, 1847.
Phil 5921.2.5   Combe, A. Observations on Dr. Barclay's ojections.
                        Edinburgh, 1823.
Phil 5921.3F   Bossard, H. Practische Phrenologie. Berlin, 1851.
Phil 5921.4   Buchanan, J.R. Sketches of Buchanan's discoveries in
                        neurology. Louisville, 1842.
Phil 5921.5   Boston Phrenological Society. A catalogue of specimens.
                        Boston, 1835.
Phil 5922.1   Caldwell, C. Phrenology vindicated and antiphrenology
                        unmasked. N.Y., 1838.
Htn   Phil 5922.2*   Calvert, G.H. Illustrations of phrenology.
                        Baltimore, 1832.
Phil 5922.3.3   Combe, George. A system of phrenology. Boston, 1838.
Phil 5922.3.5   Combe, George. A system of phrenology. N.Y., 1841.
Phil 5922.3.7   Combe, George. A system of phrenology. Boston, 1835.
Phil 5922.4   Combe, George. Lectures on phrenology. N.Y., 1839.
Phil 5922.4.3   Combe, George. Lectures on phrenology. 3. ed. N.Y., 1847.
Phil 5922.4.5   Combe, George. Essays on phrenology. Philadelphia, 1822.
Phil 5922.4.6   Combe, George. The constitution of man. Boston, 1829.
Phil 5922.4.6.5   Combe, George. The constitution of man. 5. American ed.
                        Boston, 1835.
Phil 5922.4.9   Combe, George. The constitution of man. N.Y., 1845.
Phil 5922.4.11   Combe, George. The constitution of man. 11th American ed.
                        Boston, 1841.
Phil 5922.4.12   Combe, George. The constitution of man. Boston, 1839.
Phil 5922.4.13   Combe, George. The constitution of man. 15. American ed.
                        Boston, 1847.
Phil 5922.4.14   Combe, George. The constitution of man. Hartford, 1847.
                        6 pam.
Phil 5922.4.15   Combe, George. Letter...Francis Jeffrey.
                        Edinburgh, 1826-29. 2 pam.
Phil 5922.4.20   Combe, George. Testimonials. Edinburgh, 1836. 3 pam.
Phil 5922.4.25   Combe, George. Elements of phrenology.
                        Philadelphia, 1826.
Phil 5922.4.40   Combe, George. Lectures on moral philosophy.
                        Boston, 1836.
Phil 5922.4.41   Combe, George. Lectures on moral philosophy.
                        Boston, 1840.
Phil 5922.4.50   Gibbon, C. The life of George Combe. London, 1878.
                        2v.
Phil 5922.4.51   Combe, George. The suppressed documents. Glasgow, 1836.
Phil 5922.5   Cox, R. Selections from the Phrenological Journal.
                        Edinburgh, 1836.
Phil 5922.6.8   Hammond, L.M. (Mrs.). Trials and triumphs of an orphan
                        girl; biography. Cortland, N.Y., 1859.
Phil 5923.1   Drummond, D. Objections to phrenology. Calcutta, 1829.
Phil 5923.2   Dean, Amos. Lectures on phrenology. Albany, 1834.
Phil 5923.3   Davies, John D. Phrenology. New Haven, 1955.
Phil 5924.1   Ellis, G.W. Synopsis of phrenology. Boston, 1844.
Phil 5924.2   Epps, John. Internal evidences of Christianity deduced
                        from phrenology. 2. ed. London, 1836.
Phil 5924.2.2   Epps, John. Internal evidences of Christianity deduced
                        from phrenology. Boston, 1837.
Phil 5925.1   Flourens, M.J. Examen de la phrenologie. Paris, 1842.
Phil 5925.1.5   Flourens, M.J. De la phrénologie et des études vraies sur
                        la cerveau. Paris, 1863.
Phil 5925.2   Fowler, O.S. Education and self-improvement.
                        N.Y., 1843-45. 7 pam.
Phil 5925.2.2   Fowler, O.S. Physiology, animal and mental. N.Y., 1853.
                        3 pam.
Phil 5925.2.3   Pamphlet box. Fowler, O.S. Minor writings.
Phil 5925.2.5   Fowler, O.S. Practical phrenology. N.Y., 1844.
                        2 pam.
Phil 5925.2.13   Fowler, O.S. Life: its science, laws...improvement.
                        Boston, 1871.
Phil 5925.2.16   Fowler, O.S. Religion: natural and revealed. 3. ed.
                        N.Y., 1844.
Phil 5925.2.16.10 Fowler, O.S. Religion: natural and revealed. 10. ed.
                        N.Y., 1848.
Phil 5925.2.18   Fowler, O.S. Self-culture and the perfection of character.
                        N.Y., 1868.
Phil 5925.3   Fowler, O.S. The illustrated self-instructor in
                        phrenology. N.Y., 1855.
Phil 5925.3.1   Fowler, O.S. The illustrated self-instructor in
                        phrenology. N.Y., 1853.

**Phil 5920   -   5945   Psychology - Quasi-psychological systems - Phrenology -
General treatises - Individual authors (A-Z) - cont.**
Phil 5925.3.3   Fowler, O.S. The illustrated self-instructor in
                        phrenology. N.Y., 1859.
Phil 5925.3.4   Fowler, O.S. The illustrated self-instructor in
                        phrenology. N.Y., n.d.
Phil 5925.3.6   Fowler, L.N. The principles of phrenology and physiology.
                        N.Y., 1842.
Phil 5925.3.10   Fowler, O.S. Phrenology proved. N.Y., 1839.
Phil 5925.3.11   Fowler, O.S. Phrenology proved. N.Y., 1838.
Phil 5925.3.15   Fowler, O.S. Sexuality restored. Boston, 1870.
Phil 5925.3.20   Fowler, O.S. Matrimony. Philadelphia, 1841.
Phil 5925.3.25   Fowler, O.S. Sexual science; including manhood, womanhood
                        and their mutual interrelations. Philadelphia, 1870.
Phil 5925.4   Fletcher, J. The mirror of nature...science of phrenology.
                        Boston, 1838.
Phil 5925.4.2   Pamphlet box. Fletcher, J. The mirror of nature.
Phil 5925.5   Forman, J.G. Elements of phrenology. Cincinnati, 1844.
Phil 5925.6   Fowler, J.A. A manual of mental science for teachers and
                        students. London, 1897.
Phil 5925.7   Fowler, L. (Mrs.). Familiar lessons on phrenology. v.2.
                        N.Y., 1847.
Phil 5926.1.6   Gall, F.J. On the functions of the brain. Boston, 1835.
                        6v.
Phil 5926.1.10   Manual of phrenology...system of Dr. Gall.
                        Philadelphia, 1835.
Phil 5926.1.18   Blondell, Charles. La psycho-physiologie de Gall. Thèse.
                        Paris, 1913.
Phil 5926.1.28   David, A. Le petit Docteur Gall. Paris, 1869?
Phil 5926.1.35   Ottin, N.J. Précis analytique et raisonné du système du
                        docteur Gall. Bruxelles, 1835.
Phil 5926.2.2   Gessmann, G.W. Katechismus der Kopfformkunde. 2. Aufl.
                        Berlin, 1921.
Phil 5927.1   Howe, S.G. A discourse on the social relations of man.
                        Boston, 1837.
Phil 5927.2   Hecker, J. Scientific basis of education demonstrated.
                        N.Y., 1867.
Phil 5929.1   Jones, S. Practical phrenology. Boston, 1836.
NEDL Phil 5929.2.5   How to read character. N.Y., 1870.
Phil 5931.1   Lélut, L.F. Qu'est-ce que la phrénologie...Gall.
                        Paris, 1836.
Phil 5932.1   A challenge to phrenologists. London, 1939.
Phil 5932.2   Miles, L. Phrenology. Philadelphia, 1835.
Phil 5932.3   Möbius, P.J. Uber die Anlage zur Mathematik.
                        Leipzig, 1900.
Phil 5933.1   Noble, Daniel. An inquiry into the claims of phrenology,
                        to rank among the sciences. Manchester, 1846.
Phil 5935.1   Pierpont, J. Phrenology and the scriptures. N.Y., 1850.
Phil 5938.1   Scott, W. The harmony of phrenology with scripture.
                        Edinburgh, 1837.
Phil 5938.2   Sewall, T. An examination of phrenology.
                        Washington, 1837.
Phil 5938.2.2   Sewall, T. An examination of phrenology. Boston, 1839.
Phil 5938.3   Shurtleff, N.R. An epitome of phrenology. Boston, 1835.
Phil 5938.4   Simesen, R.J. Om den nöiagtige bestemmelse.
                        Kjöbenhavn, 1846.
Phil 5938.5   Slade, J. Colloquies. Imaginary conversations between a
                        phrenologist and the shade of Dugald Stewart.
                        London, 1838.
Phil 5938.6   Spurzheim, Johann Gaspar. Outlines of phrenology.
                        Boston, 1832.
Phil 5938.6.2   Spurzheim, Johann Gaspar. Outlines of phrenology. 2nd ed.
                        Boston, 1833.
Phil 5938.6.3   Spurzheim, Johann Gaspar. Outlines of phrenology. 3rd ed.
                        Boston, 1834.
Phil 5938.6.5   Spurzheim, Johann Gaspar. Outlines of phrenology. 3rd ed.
                        Boston, 1834.
Phil 5938.6.10   Spurzheim, Johann Gaspar. Phrenology. v.1-2.
                        Boston, 1832.
Phil 5938.6.11   Spurzheim, Johann Gaspar. Phrenology. Boston, 1834.
                        2v.
Phil 5938.6.12   Spurzheim, Johann Gaspar. Phrenology. 5th American ed.
                        Boston, 1838.
Phil 5938.6.18   Spurzheim, Johann Gaspar. A view of the philosophical
                        principles of phrenology. 3rd ed. London, 18- .
Phil 5938.6.23   Spurzheim, Johann Gaspar. Phrenology. London, 1825?
Phil 5938.6.24   Spurzheim, Johann Gaspar. Phrenology. pt.1. London, 1826.
Phil 5938.6.30   Spurzheim, Johann Gaspar. Phrenology, in connection with
                        the study of physiognomy. Boston, 1833.
Phil 5938.6.43   Spurzheim, Johann Gaspar. Philosophical catechism of the
                        natural laws of man. Boston, 1833.
Phil 5938.7   Bartlett, E. An address of the birth of Spurzheim.
                        Boston, 1838.
Phil 5938.7.5   Follen, Charles. Funeral oration. v.1-3.
                        Boston, 1832-1840.
Phil 5938.7.10   Follen, Charles. Funeral oration. Boston, 1832.
Phil 5938.7.15   Capen, N. Reminiscences of Dr. Spurzheim and George Combe.
                        N.Y., 1881.
Phil 5938.7.20   Carmichael, A. A memoir of the life and philosophy of
                        Spurzheim. 1st American ed. Boston, 1833.
Phil 5938.8   Struve, Gustav von. Phrenologie in und ausserhalb
                        Deutschland. Heidelberg, 1843.
Phil 5938.9   Scheve, G. Phrenologische Bilder. Leipzig, 1874.
NEDL Phil 5938.10   Sizer, N. Heads and faces. N.Y., 1890.
Phil 5938.10.5   Sizer, Nelson. Forty years in phrenology. N.Y., 1891.
Phil 5938.10.10   Sizer, Nelson. How to teach according to temperament and
                        mental development. N.Y., 1877.
Htn   Phil 5938.11F*   Saunders, R. Saunders physiognomie. 2nd ed.
                        London, 1670-71.
Phil 5938.12   Severn, J.M. Life story and experiences of a phrenologist.
                        Brighton, Eng., 1929.
Phil 5938.12.5   Phrenological Institution, Brighton. The boy - what will
                        he become? Hove, 1929.
Phil 5938.13   Stevens, Enos. Rudiments of metal philosophy and
                        phrenological chart. Lampeter, Pa., 1839.
Phil 5940.1   Uncle Sam (pseud.). Uncle Sam's recommendation of
                        phrenology. N.Y., 1842.
Phil 5940.1.3   Uncle Sam's letters on phrenology. N.Y., 1896.
Phil 5942.1   Weaver, G.S. Lectures on mental science. N.Y., 1852.
Phil 5942.1.5   Weaver, G.S. Lectures on mental science according to the
                        philosophy of phrenology. N.Y., 1852.
Phil 5942.2   Williams, N.M. A vindication of phrenology. London, 1894.
Phil 5942.3F   Warren, J.C. The collection of the Boston Phrenological
                        Society, a retrospect. N.Y., 1921.

Classified Listing

Phil 6000   Psychology - Quasi-psychological systems - Physiognomy - Folios [Discontinued]

Htn   Phil 6000.1*   Porta, G.B. De humana physiognomonia. Francofurti, 1586.
Htn   Phil 6000.2*   Duchenne, Guillaume B. Mécanisme de la physionomie humaine. Paris, 1876.
       Phil 6000.3   Rudolph, H. Der Ausdruck der Gemütsbewegungen. Dresden, 1903. 2v.
       Phil 6000.4   Hughes, Henry. Die Mimik des Menschen auf grundvoluntarischer Psychologie. Frankfurt, 1900.

Phil 6005   Psychology - Quasi-psychological systems - Physiognomy - Pamphlet volumes

       Phil 6005.1   Pamphlet box. Psychology. Physiognomy.

Phil 6010   -   6035   Psychology - Quasi-psychological systems - Physiognomy - General treatises - Individual authors (A-Z)

       Phil 6011.5   Bühler, Karl. Ausdruckstheorie. Jena, 1933.
       Phil 6012.1   Cuyer, E. La mimique. Paris, 1902.
       Phil 6012.2   Cross, John. Attempt to establish physiognomy upon scientific principles. Glasgow, 1817.
       Phil 6012.3   Cooke, Thomas. A practical and familiar view of science of physiognomy. London, 1819.
Htn   Phil 6012.4*   Clubbe, J. Physiognomy. London, 1763.
       Phil 6012.5F   Cardano, Girolamo. Metoposcopia libris tredecim. Lutetiae, 1658.
Htn   Phil 6012.6.5* Cureau de la Chambre, Marin. The art how to know men. London, 1665.
       Phil 6012.7   Carus, Karl G. Über Grund und Bedeutung der verschiedenen formenen der hand in verschiedenen Personen. Berlin, 1927.
       Phil 6012.8   Corman, Louis. Visages et caractères. Paris, 1932.
Htn   Phil 6012.9*   Cocles, Bartolommeo della Rocca. In disem Biechlin wurt erfunden von Coplexion der Menschen. Strassburg, 1516.
       Phil 6013.3   Denis, Robert. Le visage de l'homme. Paris, 1961.
       Phil 6015.1   Fosbroke, Gerald Eltac. Character reading through analysis of the features. N.Y., 1914.
       Phil 6015.1.5   Fosbroke, Gerald Eltac. Character qualities outlined and related. N.Y., 1923.
       Phil 6015.2   Fischer, G.H. Ausdruck und Persönlichkeit. Leipzig, 1934.
       Phil 6016.1   Goclenius, R. Physiognomica et chiromantica specialia. Marpurgi Cattorum, 1621.
       Phil 6016.1.5   Goclenius, R. Besonderephysiognomische und chromantische Anmerkungen. Hamburg, 1692.
Htn   Phil 6016.2*   Grisaldi, Paolo. Guidicio di fisionomia. Trevigi, 1620.
       Phil 6017.1.2   Hartenberg, Paul. Physionomie et caractère. Paris, 1911.
       Phil 6017.3   Herland, Leo. Gesicht und Charakter. 2. Aufl. Zürich, 1956.
       Phil 6020.1   Die Kunst in der Liebe und Freundschaft. Pesth, 1816.
       Phil 6020.2.3   Krukenberg, H. Der Gesichtsausdruck des Menschen. 3. und 4. Aufl. Stuttgart, 1923.
       Phil 6020.3   Klages, L. Ausdrucksbewegung von Gestaltungskraft. Leipzig, 1923.
       Phil 6020.3.5   Klages, L. Grundlegung der Wissenschaft von Ausdruck. Leipzig, 1936.
       Phil 6020.4   Kassner, Rudolf. Die Grundlagen der Psysiognomik. Leipzig, 1922.
       Phil 6020.4.5   Kassner, Rudolf. Physiognomik. München, 1932.
       Phil 6020.4.6   Kassner, Rudolf. Physiognomik. Wiesbaden, 1951.
       Phil 6020.5   Kirchhoff, Robert. Allgemeine Ausdruckslehre. Göttingen, 1957.
       Phil 6021.1   Landsberg, I. Wahrsagekunst aus der menschlichen Gestalt. Berlin, 1895.
       Phil 6021.2   Lavater, Johann Caspar. Essays on physiognomy. London, 1789. 3v.
       Phil 6021.2.1F* Lavater, Johann Caspar. Essays on physiognomy. London, 1789-98. 5v.
       Phil 6021.2.2   Lavater, Johann Caspar. Essays on physiognomy. London, 1797. 3v.
       Phil 6021.2.3   Lavater, Johann Caspar. Essays on physiognomy. London, 1840.
       Phil 6021.2.4   Lavater, Johann Caspar. Essays on physiognomy. London, n.d.
       Phil 6021.2.5* Lavater, Johann Caspar. Essays on physiognomy. 1st American ed. Boston, 179-?
       Phil 6021.2.6   Lavater, Johann Caspar. Physiognomy. London, 1792.
       Phil 6021.2.8* Lavater, Johann Caspar. Physiognomische Fragmente. Winterthur, 1783.
       Phil 6021.2.10 Lavater, Johann Caspar. La physiognomonie. Paris, 1841.
       Phil 6021.2.12 Lavater, Johann Caspar. Essays on physiognomy. 17th ed. London, 18- .
       Phil 6021.2.15 Lavater, Johann Caspar. Physionomie portative. Paris, 1806. 2v.
       Phil 6021.2.18 Lavater, Johann Caspar. Physiognomische Fragmente zur Beförderung der Menschenkenntnis und Menschenliebe. Zürich, 1968- 4v.
       Phil 6021.2.50 David, Alexandre. Le petit Lavater français. Paris, 1857.
       Phil 6021.2.53 Pocket Lavater. n.p., n.d.
       Phil 6021.2.55 Lavater, Johann Caspar. The pocket Lavater. Hartford, 18-
       Phil 6021.2.59 Lavater, Johann Caspar. The physiognomist's own book. Philadelphia, 1841.
       Phil 6021.2.80* Gradation de la tête de grenouille jusqu'au profil d'Appollon, d'après les idées du célèbre Lavater. Paris, 17- ?
       Phil 6021.2.85 Steinbrucker, C. Lavaters physiognomische...Kunst. Berlin, 1915.
       Phil 6021.2.87 Janentzky, C.J.C. Lavaters physiognomische Fragmente. Halle, 1916.
       Phil 6021.3   Lemoine, A. De la physiognomie et de parole. Paris, 1865.
       Phil 6021.4   LeClerc, S. Caractères des passions. Paris, n.d.
       Phil 6021.5   La Bellière, C. de. La physionomie raisonnée. Lyon, 1681.
       Phil 6021.6*   Le Brun, Charles. Conference sur l'expression générale et particuliere des passions. Verone, 1751.
       Phil 6021.10   Lima Fulza, G. La faccia e l'anima. Milano, 1875.
       Phil 6021.15   Leonhard, Karl. Der menschliche Ausdruck. Leipzig, 1968.
       Phil 6022.1   Mantegazza, P. La physionomie. Paris, 1885.
       Phil 6022.1.7.5 Mantegazza, P. Physiognomy and expression. 3rd ed. London, 1904.
       Phil 6022.1.8   Mantegazza, P. Physiognomik und Mimik. v.1-2. Leipzig, 1890.
       Phil 6022.2   Martin, William W. Our noses. London, 1893.
       Phil 6022.4   Märker, Friedrich. Symbolik der Gesichtsformen. Erlenbach, 1933.
       Phil 6022.4.5   Märker, Friedrich. Autokraten und Demokraten. Erlenbach, 1931.
       Phil 6022.4.10 Märker, Friedrich. Typen; Grundlagen der Charakterkunde. Erlenbach, 1931.
       Phil 6022.5   Muhammad ibn Umar, Fakhr al-Din. La physiognomonie arabe. Thèse. Paris, 1939.

Phil 6010   -   6035   Psychology - Quasi-psychological systems - Physiognomy - General treatises - Individual authors (A-Z) - cont.

       Phil 6023.1   Nicefaro, A. La fisonomia nell'arte e nella scienza. Firenze, 1952.
       Phil 6025.1   Piderit, Leo. Mimik und Physiognomik. Detmold, 1886.
       Phil 6025.2   Pernetti, J. Lettres philosophiques sur les physionomies. La Haie, 1746.
Htn   Phil 6025.4*   Porta, G.B. De humana physiognomia libri. Hanoviae, 1593.
       Phil 6025.4.3   Porta, G.B. Physiognomoniae collestis libri sex. Argentorati, 1606. 2 pam.
       Phil 6025.4.5   Porta, G.B. Physiognomoniae collestis libri sex. Ursellis, 1601-08. 2 pam.
Htn   Phil 6025.4.6F* Porta, G.B. Della fisonomia dell'huomo. Libri quattro. Napoli, 1598.
Htn   Phil 6025.4.6.5* Porta, G.B. Della fisonomia dell'huomo. Vicenza, 1615.
       Phil 6025.4.7   Porta, G.B. Della fisonomia di tutto il corpo humano. Roma, 1637.
NEDL   Phil 6025.4.8   Porta, G.B. Della fisonomia dell'huomo. Venetia, 1644.
       Phil 6025.4.9   Porta, G.B. Fisonomia dell'huomo. Venetia, 1652.
       Phil 6025.4.15 Porta, G.B. La chirofisonomia overo di quelle parte della humana fisonomia. Napoli, 1677.
Htn   Phil 6025.4.25* Porta, G.B. La physionomie humaine. Rouen, 1655.
       Phil 6025.6   Philosophical letters on physiognomy. London, 1751.
Htn   Phil 6025.7*   Physiognomisches Cabinet für Freunde und Schüler der Menschenkenntniss. pt.1-2. Leipzig, 1777-78.
Htn   Phil 6025.8*   Pellegrini, A. I segni di la natura ne l'humano. Venetia, 1569.
       Phil 6025.9   Picard, Max. Das Menschengesicht. 2. Aufl. München, 1929.
       Phil 6025.9.5   Picard, Max. The human face. London, 1931.
       Phil 6025.9.10 Picard, Max. Die Grenzen der Physiognomik; mit 30 Bildtafeln. Erlenbach, 1937.
       Phil 6025.10   Petit-Douxciel, A. Speculum physionomicum. Langres, 1648.
       Phil 6027.1   Redfield, J.W. Comparative physiognomy. N.Y., 1852.
       Phil 6027.1.5   Redfield, J.W. Outlines...physiognomy. N.Y., 1849.
       Phil 6027.1.8   Redfield, J.W. The twelve qualities of mind...physiognomy. no. 11. N.Y., 1850.
       Phil 6027.2   Rutz, Ottmar. Vom Ausdruck des Menschen. Celle, 1925.
       Phil 6028.1   Simms, J. Human faces. N.Y., 1887.
       Phil 6028.1.5   Simms, J. Physiognomy illustrated. N.Y., 1887.
       Phil 6028.2   Stanton, M.O. A system...physiognomy. Philadelphia, 1890. 2v.
       Phil 6028.3   Schack, S. Physiognomische Studien. Jena, 1881.
       Phil 6028.3.2   Schack, S. Physiognomische Studien. 2e Aufl. Jena, 1890.
       Phil 6028.3.10 Schack, S. Physiognomische chez l'homme. Paris, 1887.
       Phil 6028.4   Spadon, N. Studio di curiosita. Venetia, 1663.
X Cg   Phil 6028.4.5   Spadon, N. Scuola di fisionomia, chiromantia. Macerata, 1654.
       Phil 6028.5   Sanctis, Sante de. Die Mimik des Denkens. Halle, 1906.
       Phil 6028.6   Spontane, Ciro. La metoposcopia, overo comensuratione delle linea della fronte. Venetia, 1626.
       Phil 6028.7   Streble, Hermann. Analyse des Gebarens. Inaug. Diss. Berlin, 1934.
       Phil 6028.8   Stoehr, Coelestinus. Phisiognomik. Coburg, 1804. 2v.
       Phil 6032.1   Warner, F. Physical expression its modes. N.Y., 1886.
       Phil 6032.2   Wolff, Werner. Selbstbeurteilung und Frembdeurteilung im wissentlichen und Unwissentlichen Versuch. Inaug. Diss. Berlin, 1932.
       Phil 6032.5   Waldemar, Charles. Lavater, der Menschenkenner. 1. Aufl. Zürich, 1960.
       Phil 6032.6   Woolnoth, Thomas. The study of the human face. London, 1865.
       Phil 6032.8   Weber, F. Aptitudes et caractère par la physiognomonie. Genève, 1970.
       Phil 6035.1   Zirwes, Ernest. Gesichtsausdruck und Wertraum. Inaug. Diss. Würzburg, 1935.

Phil 6040   Psychology - Quasi-psychological systems - Palmistry, Chiromancy - Pamphlet volumes

       Phil 6040.1   Pamphlet box. Psychology. Palmistry.

Phil 6045   -   6050   Psychology - Quasi-psychological systems - Palmistry, Chiromancy - General works (By date)

Htn   Phil 6045.17F* Cocles, B. Chyromantie ac physionomie anastasis. Bononiae, 1517.
       Phil 6045.19   Corvi, Andreas. Ein schönes Büchlin der kunst Chiromantia dess Wolgelrten Magistri Andree Corvi von Mivandula. Strassburg, 1964.
Htn   Phil 6045.22.7* Indagine, Joannes. Chiromantia. Paris, 1543.
       Phil 6045.22.9 Indagine, Joannes. Chiromantia. Argentorati, 1531.
Htn   Phil 6045.22.13* Indagine, Joannes. Chiromantia. Paris, 1547.
Htn   Phil 6045.22.15* Indagine, Joannes. Introductiones apostelesmaticae in physiognomiam. Argentorati, 1622.
       Phil 6045.22.17 Indagine, Joannes. Introductiones apotelesmaticae in physiognomiam. Argentorati, 1630.
       Phil 6045.22.19 Indagine, Joannes. Introductiones apotilesmaticae in physiognomiam. Argentorati, 1672.
Htn   Phil 6045.22.21* Indagine, Joannes. The book of palmestry and physiognomy. London, 1683.
Htn   Phil 6045.22.25* Indagine, Joannes. Chiromance et physiognomonie. Lyon, 1549.
Htn   Phil 6045.22.35* Indagine, Joannes. La chiromance et phisiognomie. Rouen, 1638.
       Phil 6045.22.40 Indagine, Joannes. La chiromance et phisionomie. Paris, 1662?
Htn   Phil 6045.46*   Cocles, B. Le compendium et brief enseignement de physiognomie and chiromancie. Paris, 1546.
Htn   Phil 6045.55*   Cocles, B. Physiognomiae et chiromantiae compendium. Argentorati, 1555.
Htn   Phil 6045.60*   Tricasso, Patricio. Enarratio pulcherrima principiorum chyromantiae. Noribergae, 1560.
Htn   Phil 6045.61.5* Tricasso, Patricio. La chiromance. Paris, 1583.
Htn   Phil 6045.61.7* Tricasso, Patricio. La chiromance. Paris, 1583.
Htn   Phil 6045.62F* Taisnier, Joannes. Opus mathematicum octs libros complectens. Coloniae, 1562.
Htn   Phil 6045.83F* Taisnier, Joannes. Opus mathematicum cheiromantis. Coloniae, 1583.
Htn   Phil 6045.95*   Rothmann, J. Chiromantiae. Erphordiae, 1595.
       Phil 6046.55   Azzi, G. L'idea del futuro rappresentato dalle linee della mano. Lucca, 1655.
       Phil 6046.57   Peruchio. La chiromance. Paris, 1657.
       Phil 6046.57.5 Peruchio. La chiromance. Paris, 1663.
       Phil 6046.61   Praetorius, J. Ludicrum chiromanticum praetorii sen thesaurus chiromantiae. Jenae, 1661.
       Phil 6046.65   Mey, Philipp. La chiromancie medicinale. La Haye, 1665.
       Phil 6046.77   Praetonius, J. Philologemata abstrusa de pollice. v.1-2. Quedlinburgi, 1677.
       Phil 6046.91   Schulty, Christoph. Dissertatio academica, de chiromantiae vanitate. Regiomonti, 1691?

Classified Listing

Phil 6045 - 6050   Psychology - Quasi-psychological systems - Palmistry, Chiromancy - General works (By date) - cont.

Phil 6048.59.5	Desbarrolles, A. Chiromancie nouvelle...les mystères de la main, revélés et expliqués. 14e ed. Paris, 186-.
Phil 6048.83.2	Metz, V. de. Handbook of modern palmistry. 2. ed. N.Y., 1883.
Phil 6048.85.1	Heron-Allen, Edward. A manual of cheirosophy. 10th ed. London, 1885.
Phil 6048.89.7	Gessmann, G.W. Katechismus der Handelskunst. Berlin, 1921.
Phil 6048.94.5	Hamon, Louis. Cheiro's language of the hand. N.Y., 1894.
Phil 6048.94.7	Hamon, Louis. Cheiro's language of the hand. N.Y., 1895.
X Cg Phil 6048.94.9	Hamon, Louis. Cheiro's language of the hand. 9th ed. N.Y., 1897.
Phil 6048.94.10	Hamon, Louis. Comfort's palmistry guide by Cheiro (pseud.) palmist. Augusta, 1894.
Phil 6048.95	Henderson, Eliza Easter. A guide to palmistry. Boston, 1895.
Phil 6048.97.4	Gessmann, G.W. Katechismus der Handflächenkunde. 4. Aufl. Berlin, 1922.
Phil 6048.97.9	Saint-Germain, C. de. The practice of palmistry. Chicago, 1897. 2v.
Phil 6048.97.13	Saint-Germain, C. de. Practical palmistry illustrated. Chicago, 1897.
Phil 6048.99.5	St. Hill, K. The grammar of palmistry. Philadelphia, 19-
Phil 6049.00.7	Benham, W.G. The laws of scientific hand reading. N.Y., 1912.
Phil 6049.01	Smith, R.C. Cheirosophy, the hand. London, 1901.
Phil 6049.01.5	Hargett, Joseph Bryant. New discoveries in palmistry. N.Y., 1901.
X Cg Phil 6049.05	Lawrence, E. The science of palmistry. London, 1905.
Phil 6049.09	Gratz, Thomas Donelson. Palmistry made easy. Philadelphia, 1909.
Phil 6049.17	Bouchet, G. Cosmogonie humaine. Vichy, 1917.
Phil 6049.31.2	Hamon, Louis. Fate in the making; revelations of lifetime. N.Y., 1931.
Phil 6049.33	Jaquin, Noel. The hand of man. London, 1933.
Phil 6049.34	Jaquin, Noel. Our revealing hands. N.Y., 1934.
Phil 6049.40	Sigurðson, J.S. Hördin min og höndin ín. Reykjavík, 1940.
Phil 6049.42	Jennings, Alice D. Your hand tells all; a manual of simplified palmistry. N.Y., 1942.
Phil 6049.42.8A	Wolff, C. The human hand. N.Y., 1943.
Phil 6049.42.8B	Wolff, C. The human hand. N.Y., 1943.
Phil 6049.57	Jursch, Hanna. Hände als Symbol und Gestalt. 7. Aufl. Stuttgart, 1957.
Phil 6049.61	Mangoldt, Ursula von. Zeichen des Schicksals im Bild der Hand. Olten, 1961.
Phil 6049.62	Kiener, Franz. Hans, Gebärde und Charakter. München, 1962.
Phil 6049.65	Gettings, Fred. The book of the hand. London, 1965.
Phil 6049.67	Mangoldt, Ursula von. Das grosse Buch der Hand. Weilheim, 1967.

Phil 6051   Psychology - Quasi-psychological systems - Palmistry, Chiromancy - Miscellany [Discontinued]

Phil 6051.01	Pamphlet box. Psychology. Palmistry.
Phil 6051.3	Metz, V. de. Hand-book of modern palmistry. N.Y., 1885?
Phil 6051.7	Oxenford, I. The complete palmist. Chicago, 1902.
Phil 6051.11	Phanos (pseud.). Elements of hand-reading. London, 1903.
Phil 6051.15	La Seer, E.J. Illustrated palmistry. N.Y., 1904.
Phil 6051.18	Zancing, Julius. Twentieth century guide to palmistry. Chicago, n.d.
Phil 6051.21	Benham, William G. The law of scientific hand reading. N.Y., 1901.

Phil 6053   Psychology - Quasi-psychological systems - Palmistry, Chiromancy - Special topics

Phil 6053.2.1	Arpentigny, Casimir Stanislas d'. La science de la main. The science of the hand. London, 1886.
Phil 6053.4	Oxenford, Ina. Life studies in palmistry. London, 1899.
Phil 6053.6	St. Hill, Katharine. Hands of celebrities. Westminster, 1889?
Phil 6053.8	Cerchiari, G. Luigi. Chiromanzia e tatuaggio. Milano, 1903.
Phil 6053.10	Vaschide, Nicolas. Essai sur la psychologie de la main. Paris, 1909.
Phil 6053.12	Hamon, Louis. Cheiro's memoirs. Philadelphia, 1912.
Phil 6053.12.10	Nelson, Edith Halforel. Out of the silence. London, 194-?

Phil 6055   Psychology - Quasi-psychological systems - Graphology - Bibliographies

Phil 6055.2.2	Mueller, Alfred Eugen. Weltgeschichte graphologisch Gesehen. Köln, 1965.

Phil 6060   Psychology - Quasi-psychological systems - Graphology - General works

Phil 6060.01	Pamphlet box. Psychology. Graphology.
Phil 6060.03	Pamphlet box. Psychology. German dissertations.
Phil 6060.1	Crepieux-Jamin, J. Traite de graphologie. Paris, 1885.
Phil 6060.1.4	Crepieux-Jamin, J. L'ecriture et le caractère. 6e ed. Basel, 189-?
Htn Phil 6060.1.10*	Crepieux-Jamin, J. La graphologie en exemples. Paris, 1899.
Phil 6060.1.15	Crepieux-Jamin, J. Les éléments de l'écriture descanailles. Paris, 1923.
Phil 6060.1.17	Crepieux-Jamin, J. Les bases fondamentales de la graphologie. Paris, 1921.
Phil 6060.1.25	Crepieux-Jamin, J. The psychology of the movements of handwriting. London, 1926.
Phil 6060.2	Deschamps, L. La philosophie de l'écriture. Paris, 1892.
Phil 6060.3	Lombroso, C. Grafologia. Milano, 1895.
Phil 6060.5	Schneidemühl, Georg. Handschrift und Charakter. Leipzig, 1911.
Phil 6060.5.2	Schneidemühl, Georg. Die Handschriftenbeurteilung. 2e Aufl. Leipzig, 1918.
Phil 6060.6	Preyer, William. Zur Psychologie des Schreibens. Hamburg, 1895.
Phil 6060.6.3	Preyer, William. Zur Psychologie des Schreibens. Leipzig, 1919.
Phil 6060.7.7	Michon, J.H. Méthode pratique de graphologie. Paris, 1899.
Phil 6060.8	Salamanca, F. de. The philosophy of handwriting. London, 1879.
Phil 6060.9	Desbarrolles, A. Les mystères de l'écriture; art de juger les hommes. Paris, 1872.
Phil 6060.10	Binet, Alfred. Les révélations de l'écriture d'après un controle scientifique. Paris, 1906.
Phil 6060.11	Henze, A. Die Chirogrammatonamtie. Leipzig, 1862.

Phil 6060   Psychology - Quasi-psychological systems - Graphology - General works - cont.

Phil 6060.12	Klages, Ludwig. Die Probleme der Graphologie. Leipzig, 1910.
Phil 6060.12.5	Klages, Ludwig. Handschrift und Charakter. 2e Aufl. Leipzig, 1920.
Phil 6060.12.5.20	Klages, Ludwig. Handschrift und Charakter. 23. Aufl. Bonn, 1949.
Phil 6060.12.10	Klages, Ludwig. Handschrift und Charakter. 3. und 4. Aufl. Leipzig, 1921.
Phil 6060.12.16	Klages, Ludwig. Einführung in die Psychologie der Handschrift. 2. Aufl. Heidelberg, 1928.
Phil 6060.12.20	Klages, Ludwig. Graphologisches lesebuch. Bonn, 1930.
Phil 6060.12.25	Klages, Ludwig. Graphologie. 4. Aufl. Heidelberg, 1949.
Phil 6060.12.30	Klages, Ludwig. Was die Graphologie nicht kann. Zürich, 1949.
Phil 6060.12.50	Wollnik, H. Probleme der Graphologie. Inaug. Diss. Leipzig, 1933.
Phil 6060.12.55	Schuerer, Wilhelm. Hestia, 1960-61...Ludwig Klages. Bonn, 1960.
Phil 6060.13	Stoll, Jakob. Zur Psychologie der Schreibfehler. Zürich, 1913.
Phil 6060.15A	Downey, June E. Graphology and the psychology of handwriting. Baltimore, 1919.
Phil 6060.15B	Downey, June E. Graphology and the psychology of handwriting. Baltimore, 1919.
Phil 6060.16	Kronsbein, W. Die physiologischen und psychologischen Beziehungen zwischen Sprache und Schrift. Weinsberg, 191-?
Phil 6060.17.3	Gessmann, G.W. Katechismus der Handschriften-Deutung. 3. Aufl. Berlin, 1922.
Phil 6060.18	Saudek, R. The psychology of handwriting. London, 1925.
Phil 6060.18.10	Saudek, R. Experiments with handwriting. London, 1928.
Phil 6060.18.15	Saudek, R. Experimentelle Graphologie. Berlin, 1929.
Phil 6060.18.20	Saudek, R. Schrift und Mensch. Berlin, 1928.
Phil 6060.19	Keene, John H. The mystery of handwriting. Boston, 1896.
Phil 6060.20	Joire, Paul. Traité de graphologie scientifique. 2d ed. Paris, 1921.
Phil 6060.22	French, William L. The psychology of handwriting. N.Y., 1922.
Phil 6060.23	Smith, Albert J. Applied graphology. N.Y., 1920.
Phil 6060.24	Rexford, John. What handwriting indicates. N.Y., 1904.
Phil 6060.25	Rice, L.G. (Mrs.). Who is your mate? N.Y., 1930.
Phil 6060.25.10	Rice, L.G. (Mrs.). Practical graphology. Chicago, 1910.
Phil 6060.26	Bobertag, Otto. Ist die Graphologie zuverlässig? Heidelberg, 1929.
Phil 6060.27.5	Lungspeer, A.S.L. Lehrbuch der wissenschaftlichen Graphologie. Leipzig, 1929.
Phil 6060.28	Menard, Pierre. L'écriture et le subsconsient. Paris, 1931.
Phil 6060.29	Pulver, Max. Symbolik der Handschrift. Zürich, 1931.
Phil 6060.29.5	Pulver, Max. Auf Spuren des Menschen. Zürich, 1942.
Phil 6060.29.15	Pulver, Max. Trieb und Verhrechen in der Handschrift. 2e Aufl. Zürich, 1934.
Phil 6060.30	Jacoby, Hans. Analysis of handwriting. London, 1939.
VPhil 6060.30.5	Jacoby, Hans. Self-knowledge through handwriting. London, 1941.
Phil 6060.31	Margadant, S.V. Eine tiefenpsychologische Grundlage zur Klages'chen Graphologie. Amsterdam, 1938.
Phil 6060.32	Lewinson, T.S. Handwriting analysis. N.Y., 1942.
Phil 6060.33	Olyanova, N. What does your handwriting reveal? N.Y., 1929.
Phil 6060.34	Graphologie. v.1-2,3-4. Bern, 1945. 2v.
Phil 6060.36	Trillat, Raymond. Eléments de graphologie pratique. Paris, 1944.
Phil 6060.38	Mendel, A.O. Personality in handwriting. N.Y., 1947.
Phil 6060.40.5	Sonnemann, Ulrich. Handwriting analysis. N.Y., 1953.
Phil 6060.40.10	Sonnemann, Ulrich. Handwriting analysis as a psychodiagnostic tool. N.Y., 1964.
Phil 6060.42	Bunker, M.N. What handwriting tells about yourself. Cleveland, 1951.
Phil 6060.44	Wolff, Wermer. Diagrams of the unconscious. N.Y., 1948.
Phil 6060.45	Sievers, A. Gestaltwandel und Gestaltzerfall. Bonn, 1962.
Phil 6060.46	Rand, H.A. Graphology. Cambridge, Mass., 1947.
Phil 6060.48	Ras, M. Los artistas escriben. 1. ed. Madrid, 1954.
Phil 6060.50	Klages, Ludwig. Zur Ausdruckslehre und Charaklerkunde. Heidelberg, 1927.
Phil 6060.52	Wintermantel, F. Bibliographia graphologica. Stuttgart, 1958.
Phil 6060.54	Fervers, Hans. Wie man Menschen beurteilt. Neuwied, 1959.
Phil 6060.56	Dubouchet, Jeanne. L'analogie des phenomenes physiques et psychiques et l'écriture. Bruxelles, 1960.
Phil 6060.56.5	Dubouchet, Jeanne. L'écriture des adolescents, étude psycho-pédagogique. Paris, 1967.
Phil 6060.57.2	Teillard, Ania. Handschriftendeutung auf tiefenpsychologischen Grundlage. 2. Aufl. Bern, 1963.
Phil 6060.58	Reichert, G. Männlichkeit und Weiblichkeit im Spiegel. Heidelberg, 1962.
Phil 6060.60	Broeren, Wilhelm. Über die Zuverlässigkeit der Beschreibung von Sprechstimme und Handschrift. Inaug. D n.p., 1964.
Phil 6060.65	Pokorny, Richard Raphael. Psychologie der Handschrift. Basel, 1968.
Phil 6060.70	Roman, Klara Goldzieher. Encyclopedia of the written word. N.Y., 1968.
Phil 6060.72	Salberg, Renée de. Nouvelle graphologie pratique. Paris, 1967?
Phil 6060.74	Jansen, Abraham. Toetsing van grafologische uitspraken. Amsterdam, 1963.
Phil 6060.76	Schermann, Rafael. Die Schrift lügt nicht! Berlin, 1929.
VPhil 6060.78	Saudek, Robert. What your handwriting shows. London, 1932.
Phil 6060.80	Pophal, Rudolf. Graphologie in Vorlesungen. Stuttgart, 1965- 3v.
Phil 6060.82	Bresard, Suzanne. Empreintes. Neuchâtel, 1968.
Phil 6060.84	Schneevoigt, Ihno. Die graphologische Intelligenzdiagnose. Bonn, 1968.
Phil 6060.86	Kroeber-Keneth, Ludwig. L. Kroeber-Keneth's Buch der Graphologie. 1. Aufl. Düsseldorf, 1968.
Phil 6060.88	Stern, Martin. Entwicklungshemmungen und Graphologie. Thesis. Zürich, 1958.
Phil 6060.90	Wieser, Roda. Grundriss der Graphologie. München, 1969.
Phil 6060.92	Vetter, August. Die Zeichensprache von Schrift und Traum. Freiburg, 1970.

6100 Psychology - Mind and body - Folios [Discontinued]

Phil 6100.1 Mayo, H. A series of engravings...brain...in man. London, 1827.
Phil 6100.10* Kronthal, P. Schnitte durch das centrale Nervensystem des Menschen. Berlin, 1892.
Phil 6100.11* Monro, A. Three treatises. On the brain, the eye and the ear. Edinburgh, 1797.
Phil 6100.12* Bell, C. The anatomy of the brain. London, 1802.
Phil 6100.13* Luys, J. Iconographie photographique des centres nerveux. Texte et atlas. Paris, 1873. 2v.
Phil 6100.14 Blackburn, I.W. Illustrations of the gross morbid anatomy of the brain in the insane. Washington, 1908.
Phil 6100.15 Weed, L.H. Reconstruction of the nuclear masses in the lower portion of the human brain-stem. Washington, 1914.
Phil 6100.17 Sager, O. Recherches sur la somatotopie sensitive dans le thalamus des singes. Harlem, 1933.
Phil 6100.18 Odette, Laffoneriere. L'ame et le corps. Paris, 1961.

6103 Psychology - Mind and body - Pamphlet volumes

Phil 6103 Pamphlet box. Mind and body.
Phil 6103.2 Pamphlet vol. Mind and body. 23 pam.
Phil 6103.3 Pamphlet box. Mental hygiene, mind cure.
Phil 6103.5* Pamphlet vol. Mind and body. 5 pam.
Phil 6103.8* Pflüger, E. Die sensorischen Functionen des Rückenmarks. Berlin, 1853. 5 pam.
Phil 6103.10 Pamphlet box. Mind and body. German dissertations.

6105.101 - .399 Psychology - Mind and body - World Federation for ental Health - Monographs (A-Z, 299 scheme, by title)

Phil 6105.233 Soddy, Kenneth. Identity. Mental health and value systems. London, 1961.
Phil 6105.314 World Federation for Mental Health. Population and mental health. Berne, 1964.

6109 Psychology - Mind and body - General works - Collected authors

Phil 6109.2 Borst, Clive Vernon. The mind-brain identity theory. N.Y., 1970.
Phil 6109.4 Schoenpflug, Wolfgang. Methoden der Aktivierungsforschung. Bern, 1969.

6110 - 6135 Psychology - Mind and body - General works - Individual thors (A-Z)

Phil 6110.1 Anton, G. Bau, Leistung und Erkrankung des menschlichen Stirnhirnes. T.1. Graz, 1902.
Phil 6110.3 Alexander, F.M. Man's supreme inheritance. London, 1910.
Phil 6110.3.1 Alexander, F.M. Man's supreme inheritance. N.Y., 1918.
Phil 6110.3.2 Alexander, F.M. Constructive conscious control of the individual. N.Y., 1923.
Phil 6110.3.10 Alexander, F.M. The use of the self. N.Y., 1932.
Phil 6110.3.15 Alexander, F.M. The universal constant in living. N.Y., 1941.
Phil 6110.6 Arnett, L.D. The soul, a study of past and present beliefs. n.p., 1904.
Phil 6110.8 Alaux, J.E. Théorie de l'âme humaine. Paris, 1896.
Phil 6110.9 Allen, James. As a man thinketh. N.Y., 19- .
Phil 6110.9.3 Allen, James. As a man thinketh. N.Y., 19- .
Phil 6110.9.5 Allen, James. As a man thinketh. N.Y., 19- .
Phil 6110.10.10 Adler, Alfred. Über den nervösen Charakter. München, 1922.
Phil 6110.10.11 Adler, Alfred. Über den nervösen Charakter. 4. Aufl. München, 1928.
Phil 6110.11 Abel, J.F. Einleitung in die Seelenlehre. Stuttgart, 1786.
Phil 6110.12 Aeby, C.T. Schema des Faserverlaufes im menschlichen Gehirn und Rückenmark. Bern, 1883.
Phil 6110.13 Abrutz, Sydney. Till nervsystems dynamik. Stockholm, 1917.
Phil 6110.14 The Arcane formulas, or Mental alchemy. Chicago, 1909.
Phil 6110.15 Arnason, A. Apoplexie und ihre Vererbung. Kopenhagen, 1935.
Phil 6110.16 Althaus, J. On failure of brain-power. London, 1883.
Phil 6110.17 Association for Research in Nervous and Mental Diseases. The hypothalamus and central levels of autonomic function. Baltimore, 1940.
Phil 6110.18 Association for Research in Nervous and Mental Diseases. The interrelationship of mind and body. Baltimore, 1939.
Phil 6110.19 Alexander, R. The doctor alone can't cure you. Overton, 1943.
Phil 6110.20 Arai, T. Mental fatique. N.Y., 1912.
Phil 6110.21 American Academy of Political and Social Science. Mental health in the United States. Philadelphia, 1953.
Phil 6110.22 Ashby, William R. Design for a brain. N.Y., 1952.
Phil 6110.22.2 Ashby, William R. Design for a brain. 2. ed. N.Y., 1960.
Phil 6110.24 Akademiia Pedagogicheskikh Nauk RSFSR, Moscow. Institut Psikhologii. Pogranichnye problemy psikhologii i fiziologii. Moskva, 1961.
Phil 6110.26 Akademiia Nauk SSSR. Institut Filosofii. Filosofskie voprosy fiziologii vysshei nervnoi deiatel'nosti. Moskva, 1963.
Phil 6110.28 Adám, György. Interoception and behaviour. Budapest, 1967.
Phil 6110.30 Psychological aspects of stress. Springfield, Ill., 1970.
Phil 6111.1 Bain, A. Mind and body. London, 1873.
Phil 6111.1.2 Bain, A. Mind and body. N.Y., 1873.
Phil 6111.1.5 Bain, A. Mind and body. N.Y., 1874.
Phil 6111.1.9 Bain, A. Geist und Körper. 2. Aufl. Leipzig, 1881.
Phil 6111.1.20 Bain, A. L'esprit et le corps. 3. ed. Paris, 1878.
Phil 6111.2 Beaunie, H.E. Recherches...l'activité cérébrale. v.1-2. Paris, 1884-86.
Phil 6111.3 Bertrand de Saint-Germain, Guillaume Scipion. Des manifestations de la vie et de l'intelligence. Paris, 1848.
Phil 6111.4 Bouiller, F. Du principe vital. Paris, 1862.
Phil 6111.4.2 Bouiller, F. De l'unité de l'ame pensante et du principe vital. Paris, 1858.
Phil 6111.5 Brigham, Amariah. Remarks on the influence of mental cultivation upon health. Hartford, 1832.
Phil 6111.5.2 Brigham, Amariah. Remarks on the influence of mental cultivation upon health. Boston, 1833.
Phil 6111.6 Brittan, S.B. Man and his relations:...influence of the mind on the body. N.Y., 1868.
Phil 6111.6.2 Brittan, S.B. Man and his relations:...influence of the mind on the body. N.Y., 1864.
Phil 6111.7 Brodie, B. Mind and matter. N.Y., 1857.
Phil 6111.9 Brown-Séquard, C.E. Experimental and clinical researches. Richmond, 1855.
Phil 6111.9.5 Brown-Séquard, C.E. Course...physiology and pathology of central nervous system. Philadelphia, 1860.

Phil 6110 - 6135 Psychology - Mind and body - General works - Individual authors (A-Z) - cont.

Phil 6111.10.2 Bastian, H.C. The brain as an organ of mind. N.Y., 1880.
Phil 6111.10.3 Bastian, H.C. Das Gehirn als Organ des Geistes. Leipzig, 1882.
Phil 6111.10.5 Bastian, H.C. Le cerveau organe de la pensée chez l'homme et chez les animaux. 2. ed. Paris, 1888.
Phil 6111.10.15 Bastian, H.C. On the neural processes underlying attention and volition. London, 1893.
X Cg Phil 6111.12 Bergson, Henri. Matière et mémoire. Paris, 1900.
NEDL Phil 6111.12.15 Bergson, Henri. Materie und Gedächtnis. Jena, 1919.
Phil 6111.13 Busse, L. Geist und Körper, Seele und Leib. Leipzig, 1903.
Phil 6111.13.2 Busse, L. Geist und Körper, Seele und Leib. 2. Aufl. Leipzig, 1913.
Phil 6111.14 Binet, A. L'ame et le corps. Paris, 1905.
Phil 6111.14.3 Binet, A. L'ame et le corps. Paris, 1913.
Phil 6111.14.6 Binet, A. The mind and the brain. London, 1907.
Phil 6111.15 Björnson, B. Wise-Kunst. N.Y., 1909.
Phil 6111.16 Bechterew, W. von. Die Funktionen der Nervencentra. Jena, 1908. 3v.
Phil 6111.16.5 Bechterew, W. von. Die Leitungsbahnen im Gehirn und Rückenmark. Leipzig, 1899.
Phil 6111.16.12 Bechterew, W. von. Psyche und Leben. Wiesbaden, 1908.
Phil 6111.16.20 Dmitriev, V.D. Vydaiushchiisia russkii uchenyi V.M. Bekhterev. Cheboksary, 1960.
Phil 6111.17 Burnett, C.M. Philosophy of spirits in relation to matter. London, 1850.
Phil 6111.18 Bruce, H.A. Scientific mental healing. Boston, 1911.
Phil 6111.18.5 Bruce, H.A. Nerve control and how to gain it. N.Y., 1918.
Phil 6111.19 Becher, E. Gehirn und Seele. Heidelberg, 1911.
Phil 6111.21 Bischoff, T.L.W. von. Das Hirngewicht des Menschen. Bonn, 1880.
Phil 6111.22 Burdach, K.F. Bau und Leben des Gehirns. Leipzig, 1819-26. 3v.
Phil 6111.24 Bidder, Friedrich. Zur Lehre von dem Verhältniss der Ganglienkörper zu den Nerwenfasern. Leipzig, 1847.
Phil 6111.24.5 Bidder, Friedrich. Die Selbständigkeit des sympathischen Nervensystems. Leipzig, 1842.
Phil 6111.24.9 Bidder, Friedrich. Untersuchungen über die Textur des Rückenmarks. Leipzig, 1857.
Phil 6111.26 Barker, L.F. The nervous system and its constituent neurones. N.Y., 1899.
Phil 6111.27.2 Brackett, Anna C. The technique of rest. N.Y., 1893.
Phil 6111.29 Bevan, J.O. The genesis and evolution of the individual soul. London, 1909.
Phil 6111.30 Baylor, Courtenay. Remaking a man...mental refitting. N.Y., 1919.
Phil 6111.32 Butler, Hiram Erastus. Practical methods to insure success. 33rd ed. Applegate, Calif., 1920.
Phil 6111.32.5 Butler, Hiram Erastus. Practical methods to insure success. 31st ed. Applegate, Calif., 1915.
Phil 6111.33 Bastide, Jules. La pensée et le cerveau. Paris, 1886.
Phil 6111.34 Brandler-Pracht, Karl. Geheime Seelenkräfte. Berlin, 1921.
Phil 6111.35 Bianchi, L. The mechanism of the brain. Edinburgh 1922.
Phil 6111.36 Biervliet, J.J. L'homme droit et l'homme gauche. Gand, 1901.
Phil 6111.37 Boyd, T.P. The voice eternal. 2nd ed. San Francisco, 1912-14.
Phil 6111.38 Babbitt, E.D. Human culture and cure. pt.3-4. Los Angeles, 1898.
Phil 6111.40 Butts, Bryan J. Hints on metaphysics. Boston, 1885.
Phil 6111.41 Brown, William. Talks on psychotherapy. London, 1923.
Phil 6111.42 Bell, Charles. Idee einer neuen Hirnanatomie (1811). Leipzig, 1911.
Phil 6111.43 Bürker, Karl. Neueres über die Zentralisation der Funktionen. Giessen, 1926.
Phil 6111.44.5 Berry, Richard J.A. Your brain and its story. London, 1939.
Phil 6111.45 Bianchi, L. Foundations of mental health. N.Y., 1930.
Phil 6111.46 Bowman, Karl M. Personal problems for men and women. N.Y., 1931.
Phil 6111.47 Benedict, F.G. Mental effort. Washington, 1933.
Phil 6111.48 Bowman, A. Mind and brain in thought and reason process. London, 1930.
Phil 6111.49 Bassett, Clara. Mental hygiene in the community. N.Y., 1934.
Phil 6111.50 Batten, L.W. The relief of pain by mental suggestion. N.Y., 1917.
Phil 6111.51 Barker, L.F. A description of the brains...of two brothers dead of hereditary ataxia. Chicago, 1903.
Phil 6111.52 Boston Mental Hygiene Survey. Report of the Boston mental hygiene survey, 1930. Boston, 1930.
Phil 6111.53.2 Brown, Charles R. Faith and health. 2. ed. N.Y., 1910.
Phil 6111.54 Bianchini, M.L. La igiene mentale ed it potenziamento della stirpe. Roma, 1937.
Phil 6111.55 Beck, L.J. Manual skills and the measurement of handedness. Worcester, 1936.
Phil 6111.56 Barcroft, J. The brain. New Haven, 1938.
Phil 6111.56.10 Barcroft, Joseph. The dependence of the mind on its physical environment. Newcastle upon Tyne? 1938?
Phil 6111.57 Bier, A. Die Seele. 3. Aufl. München, 1939.
Phil 6111.58 Buzzard, E.F. An outline of neurology and its outlook. London, 1929.
Phil 6111.59 Baker, R.S. New ideals in healing. N.Y., 1909.
Phil 6111.60 Bills, A.G. The psychology of efficiency. N.Y., 1943.
Phil 6111.61.1 Bartley, Samuel Howard. Fatigue and impairment in man. 1. ed. N.Y., 1947.
Phil 6111.62 Bankoff, G.A. The conquest of brain mysteries. London, 1947.
Phil 6111.63 Blum, Gerald S. A model of the mind. N.Y., 1961.
Phil 6111.64 Beloff, John. The existence of mind. London, 1962.
Phil 6111.65 Boiko, E. Studies in higher neurodynamics as related to problems of psychology. Jerusalem, 1961.
Phil 6111.66 Braden, C.S. Spirits in rebellion. Dallas, 1963.
Phil 6111.67 Brun, J. La main et l'esprit. Paris, 1963.
Phil 6111.70 Barsley, Michael. The other hand; an investigation into the sinister history of left-handedness. 1st ed. N.Y., 1967.
Phil 6111.70.5 Barsley, Michael. Left-handed man in a right-handed world. London, 1970.
Phil 6111.75 Brickner, Richard Max. The intellectual functions of the frontal lobes. N.Y., 1936.
Phil 6111.80 Buytendijk, Frederik Jacobus Johannes. Prolegomena van een antropologische fysiologie. Utrecht, 1965.
Phil 6111.80.5 Buytendijk, Frederik Jacobus Johannes. Prolegomena einer antropologischen Physiologie. Salzburg, 1967.

Phil 6110 - 6135   Psychology - Mind and body - General works - Individual authors (A-Z) - cont.

Phil 6111.85   Bruaire, Claude. Philosophie du corps. Paris, 1968.
Phil 6.11.88   Baumer, Franz. Vom Zauberkult zur Psychoanalyse. München, 1970.
Phil 6112.1   Calderwood, H. The relations of mind and brain. London, 1879.
Phil 6112.1.3   Calderwood, H. The relations of mind and brain. 3d ed. London, 1884.
Phil 6112.2.2   Call, A.P. As a matter of course. Boston, 1894.
Phil 6112.2.4   Call, A.P. Power through repose. Boston, 1891.
Phil 6112.2.5   Call, A.P. Power through repose. Boston, 1893.
Phil 6112.2.8.7   Call, A.P. Power through repose. Boston, 1934.
Phil 6112.2.9   Call, A.P. Freedom of life. Boston, 1905.
Phil 6112.2.11   Call, A.P. How to live quietly. Boston, 1914.
Phil 6112.2.15   Call, A.P. Brain power for business men. Boston, 1911.
Phil 6112.3   Catlow, P. On the principles of aesthetic medicine. London, 1867.
Phil 6112.4.2   Carpenter, W.B. Principles of mental psychology. London, 1881.
Htn   Phil 6112.4.3*   Carpenter, W.B. Principles of mental psychology. London, 1881.
Phil 6112.4.3.5   Carpenter, W.B. Principles of mental psychology. N.Y., 1874.
Phil 6112.4.9   Carpenter, W.B. Principles of mental psychology. 4th ed. N.Y., 1887.
Phil 6112.4.20   Carpenter, W.B. The doctrine of human automatism. London, 1875.
Phil 6112.5.5   Charcot, J.M. La foi qui guérit. Paris, 1897.
Phil 6112.6   Cooke, W. A comentary...mind and the emotions. Philadelphia, 1853.
Phil 6112.7   Cornelius, K.S. Über die Wechselwirkung zwischen Leib und Seele. Halle, 1875.
Phil 6112.7.5   Cornelius, K.S. Zur Theorie der Wechselwirkung zwischen Leib und Seele. Halle, 1880.
Phil 6112.8   Corning, J.L. Brain exhaustion. N.Y., 1884.
Phil 6112.8.5   Corning, J.L. Brain rest. N.Y., 1885.
Phil 6112.9   Courmont, F. Le cervelet et ses fonctions. Paris, 1891.
Phil 6112.9.4   Courmont, F. Le cervelet et ses fonctions. Paris, 1894.
Phil 6112.10   Carus, P. The soul of man. Chicago, 1891.
Phil 6112.11   Clavel, Adolphe. Le corps et l'ame. Paris, 1851.
Phil 6112.12   Cutter, G.B. Three thousand years of mental healing. N.Y., 1911.
Phil 6112.13   Carter, R.B. Influence of education and training in preventing diseases of nervous system. London, 1855.
Phil 6112.14   Clements, J. Metaphysics of the nature and in the conception of the soul. Boston, 1909.
Phil 6112.15.5   Combe, G. On the functions of the cerebellum. Edinburgh, 1838.
Phil 6112.17   Clark, Susie C. A look upward. Boston, 1899.
Phil 6112.19   Colville, W.W.J. Spiritual therapeutics. Chicago, 1890.
Phil 6112.19.5   Colville, W.W.J. Glints of wisdom. N.Y., 1910.
Phil 6112.20   Carroll, Robert S. The mastery of nervousness based upon self-reeducation. N.Y., 1917.
Phil 6112.20.2   Carroll, Robert S. The mastery of nervousness based upon self-reeducation. 2nd ed. N.Y., 1918.
Phil 6112.20.5   Carroll, Robert S. Our nervous friends. N.Y., 1919.
Phil 6112.21   Christison, J.S. Brain in relation to mind. Chicago, 1899.
Phil 6112.22   Christiani, A. Zur Physiologie des Gehirnes. Berlin, 1885.
Phil 6112.23   Cleland, J. The relation of brain to mind. Glasgow, 1882.
Phil 6112.24   Cappie, James. Intra-cranial circulation and its relation to physiology of brain. Edinburgh, 1890.
Phil 6112.25.6   Clouston, T.S. Hygiene of mind. 6th ed. London, 1912.
Phil 6112.26.5   Cheney, A.C.P. (Mrs.). What it is that heals. London, 1912.
Phil 6112.29   Curtis, A.M. Of meditation and health. London, 1910.
Phil 6112.31   Chappell, M.N. In the name of common sense. N.Y., 1938.
Phil 6112.32   Clarke, Eric K. Mental hygiene for community nursing. Minneapolis, 1942.
Phil 6112.33   Courtney, J.W. The conquest of nerves. N.Y., 1919.
Phil 6112.34   Cuny, Louis. Contribution à l'étude de l'action vasomotrice. Thèse. Paris, 1942.
Phil 6112.35   Chauchard, P. L'influx nerveux et la psychologie. Paris, 1950.
Phil 6112.36   Culbertson, J.T. Consciousness and behavior. Dubugue, 1950.
Phil 6112.37   Clausen, John A. Sociology and the field of mental health. N.Y., 1956.
Phil 6112.38   Cumming, Elaine. Clased ranks. Cambridge, 1957.
Phil 6112.40   Sugrue, Thomas. There is a river; the story of Edgar Cayce. N.Y., 1959.
Phil 6112.40.5   Stearn, Jess. Edgar Cayce, the sleeping prophet. Garden City, 1967.
Phil 6112.40.10   Bro, Harmon Hartzell. Edgar Cayce on dreams. N.Y., 1968.
Phil 6112.40.12   Bro, Harmon Hartzell. Dreams in the life of prayer: the approach of Edgar Cayce. 1st ed. N.Y., 1970.
Phil 6112.40.15   Kahn, David E. My life with Edgar Cayce. 1. ed. Garden City, 1970.
Phil 6112.40.20   Cayce, Edgar Evans. The outer limits of Edgar Cayce's power. 1. ed. N.Y., 1971.
Phil 6112.42   California. University Medical Center. Man and civilization: control of the mind. N.Y., 1961.
Phil 6112.43   Caplan, Gerald. An approach to community mental health. N.Y., 1961.
Phil 6112.44   Coval, Samuel Charles. Scepticism and the first person. London, 1966.
Phil 6113.1   Durand, P.J. Electro-dynamisme vital. Paris, 1855.
Phil 6113.2.3   Donaldson, H.H. The growth of the brain. London, 1897.
Phil 6113.3.5   Dexter, E.G. Weather influences. N.Y., 1904.
Phil 6113.4   Dorland, W.A.N. The age of mental virility. N.Y., 1908.
Phil 6113.5   Dogiel, A.S. Der Bau der Spinalganglien des Menschen und der Säugetiere. Jena, 1908.
Phil 6113.6   Dressler, J.G. Beneke oder die Seelenlehre als Naturwissenschaft. Bautzen, 1840.
Phil 6113.6.5   Dressler, J.G. Ist Beneke Materialist? Berlin, 1862.
Phil 6113.7   Dearborn, G.V.N. Influence of joy. Boston, 1916.
Phil 6113.8.5   Dubois, Paul. The influence of the mind on the body. N.Y., 1906.
Phil 6113.8.20   Dubois, Paul. De l'influence de l'esprit sur le corps. 9. éd. Berne, 1910.
Phil 6113.9   Dudley, L. Egyptian elements in the legend of the body and soul. Baltimore, 1911.
Phil 6113.10   Dimmler, H. System der Psychologie. München, n.d.
Phil 6113.11   Dunlap, Knight. An outline of psychobiology. Baltimore, 1914.

Phil 6110 - 6135   Psychology - Mind and body - General works - Individual authors (A-Z) - cont.

Phil 6113.11.2   Dunlap, Knight. An outline of psychobiology. 2d ed. Baltimore, 1917.
Phil 6113.13.3   Dewey, J.H. The way, the truth and the life...Christian theosophy. 3d ed. NY., 1888.
Phil 6113.14F   Dean, J. Microscopic anatomy...of the spinal cord. Cambridge, 1861.
Phil 6113.15   Domrich, O. Die psychischen Zustände. Jena, 1849.
Phil 6113.17   Dorman, Marcus. From matter to mind. London, 1895.
Phil 6113.19   Driesch, Hans. Leib und Seele. Leipzig, 1916.
Phil 6113.19.3   Driesch, Hans. Leib und Seele. 3. Aufl. Leipzig, 1923.
Phil 6113.19.9   Driesch, Hans. Mind and body. N.Y., 1927.
Phil 6113.21   Dulley, William. Body, soul and spirit. London, 1923.
Phil 6113.22   Dorm, T. G. Heymans' psychischer Monismus. Tübingen, 1922.
Phil 6113.23   De Voe, W. Healing currents from the battery of life. 2. ed. Chicago, 1905.
Phil 6113.27   Dyer, V.A. You can have it, personality. Long Beach, 1937.
Phil 6113.28.5   Dercum, F.X. The psychology of mind. 2. ed. Philadelphia, 1925.
Phil 6113.29   Ducasse, C.J. Nature, mind and death. La Salle, Ill., 1951.
Phil 6113.30   Doran, F.S.A. Mind, a social phenomenon. N.Y., 1953.
Phil 6113.32   Deutsch, Felix. On the mysterious leap from the mind to the body. N.Y., 1959.
Phil 6113.33   Davis, James Allen. Education for positive mental health. Chicago, 1965.
Phil 6113.34   Dubrovskii, David I. Psikhicheskie iavleniia i mozg. Moskva, 1971.
Phil 6114.2   Ecker, A. Cerebral convolutions of man. N.Y., 1873.
Phil 6114.4   Eisler, R. Leib und Seele. Leipzig, 1906.
Phil 6114.4.5   Eisler, R. Geist und Körper. Göttingen, 1911.
Phil 6114.5   Evans, W.F. Esoteric Christianity and mental therepeutics. Boston, n.d.
Phil 6114.5.4   Evans, W.F. Mental medicine. 6. ed. Boston, 1881.
Phil 6114.5.7   Evans, W.F. Mental medicine. 15th ed. Boston, 1885.
Phil 6114.5.8   Evans, W.F. Soul and body. Boston, 1876.
Phil 6114.5.12   Evans, W.F. A mental-cure illustrated influence of the mind on the body. Boston, 1884.
Phil 6114.5.16   Evans, W.F. The divine law of cure. Boston, 1881.
Phil 6114.6   Erdmann, B. Wissenschaftliche Hypothesen über Leib und Seele. Köln, 1908.
Phil 6114.8   Ennemoser, Joseph. Historisch-psychologische Untersuchungen...den Ursprung. 2. Aufl. Stuttgart, 1851.
Phil 6114.9   Ebbecke, Ulrich. Die kortikalen Erregungen. Leipzig, 1919.
Phil 6114.10   Erhardt, Franz. Die Wechselwirkung zwischen Leib und Seele. Leipzig, 1897.
Phil 6114.11   Erdmann, J.E. Leib und Seele nach ihrem Begriff und ihrem Verhaltniss zur Einander. Halle, 1837.
Phil 6114.11.10   Erdmann, B. Wissenschaftliche Hypothesen über Leib und Seele. Köln, 1907.
Phil 6114.12   Exner, Sigmund. Entwurf zu einer psychologischen Erklärung der psychischen Erscheinungen. Leipzig, 1894.
Phil 6114.12.5   Exner, Sigmund. Untersuchungen über die Localisation der Functionen. Wien, 1881.
Phil 6114.13   Eschricht, D.F. Om de uvilkaarlige livsyttringers forhold til de vilkaarlige. Kjøbenhavn, 1845.
Phil 6114.14   Ellsworth, P. Health and power. Holyoke, Mass., 1915.
Phil 6114.15   Eccles, J.C. The neurophysiological basis of mind. Oxford, 1953.
Phil 6114.15.3   Eccles, J.C. The neurophysiological basis of mind. Oxford, 1960.
Phil 6114.15.5   Eccles, J.C. Facing reality; philosophical adventures by a brain scientist. London, 1970.
Phil 6114.16   Ellis, Albert. How to line with a neurotic. N.Y., 1957.
Phil 6114.17   Espenschied, Richard. Der Leistungs kräftige Mensch. Hamburg, 1957.
Phil 6114.18   Ebertin, B. Gehirn und Seele. Aalen, 1961.
Phil 6114.20   Estabrooks, George Hoben. The future of the human mind. 1st ed. N.Y., 1961.
Phil 6114.23   Edwards, Henry James. The evidence for spirit healing. London, 1953.
Phil 6115.1   Falconer, W. A dissertation...passions...disorders of the body. London, 1796.
Phil 6115.2.2   Farges, A. Le cerveau, l'âme et les facultés. Paris, 1890.
Phil 6115.3   Ferrier, D. The Croonian lectures on cerebral localisation. London, 1890.
Phil 6115.3.5   Ferrier, D. The functions of the brain. N.Y., 1876.
Phil 6115.3.6   Ferrier, D. The functions of the brain. 2d ed. London, 1886.
Phil 6115.4   Ferrière, E. L'âme est la fonction du cerveau. Paris, 1883. 2v.
Phil 6115.5   Fisher, W.S. Observations on mental phenomena. Philadelphia, 1851.
Phil 6115.6   Flechsig, P. Plan des menschlichen Gehirns. Leipzig, 1883.
Phil 6115.6.5   Flechsig, P. Localisation der geistigen Vorgänge. Leipzig, 1896.
Phil 6115.6.7   Flechsig, P. Gehirn und Seele. 2e Ausg. Leipzig, 1896.
Phil 6115.6.8   Jacobi, M.P. (Mrs.). Considerations on Flechsig's "Gehirn und Seele". N.Y., 1897.
Phil 6115.6.9   Flechsig, P. Die Leitungsbahnen im Gehirn und Rückenmark. Leipzig, 1876.
Phil 6115.6.12   Flechsig, P. Meine myelogenetische Hirnlehre. Berlin, 1927.
Phil 6115.7   Folsom, C.F. The relation of our public schools to the disorders of the nervous system. Boston, 1886.
Phil 6115.8   François-Franck, C. Leçons sur les fonctions motrices du cerveau et sur l'épilepsie cérébrale. Paris, 1887.
Phil 6115.9   Fromentel, Henry de. Les synalgies et les synesthésies. Paris, 1888.
Phil 6115.10   Fullom, S.W. The human mind. v.1-2. London, 1858.
Phil 6115.11   Feuchtersleben, E.F.V. Zur Diätetik der Seele. Wien, 1867.
Phil 6115.11.2   Feuchtersleben, E.F.V. Zur Diätetik der Seele. Hamburg, 1880.
Phil 6115.11.4   Feuchtersleben, E.F.V. Zur Diätetik der Seele. 9. Aufl. Wien, 1852.
Phil 6115.11.6   Feuchtersleben, E.F.V. Zur Diätetik der Seele. 2. Aufl. Halle, 1893.
Phil 6115.11.8   Feuchtersleben, E.F.V. Hygiene de l'âme. Paris, 1860.
Phil 6115.11.12   Feuchtersleben, E.F.V. Lehrbuch der ärtlichen Seelenkunde. Wien, 1845.

311
Classified Listing

Phil 6110 - 6135 Psychology - Mind and body - General works - Individual authors (A-Z) - cont.

Phil 6115.11.14 Feuchtersleben, E.F.V. Ein Dienst zur Nacht ist unser Leben. Graz, 1958.
Phil 6115.11.15 Feuchtersleben, E.F.V. The dietetics of the soul. N.Y., 1858.
Phil 6115.11.17 Feuchtersleben, E.F.V. The dietetics of the soul. London, 1873.
Phil 6115.11.19 Feuchtersleben, E.F.V. Health and suggestion: the dietetics of the mind. N.Y., 1910.
Phil 6115.11.20 Eltz-Hoffmann, L. Feuchtersleben. Salzburg, 1956.
Phil 6115.11.28 Pollak, G. The hygiene of the soul; the memoir of a physician and philosopher. N.Y., 1910.
Htn Phil 6115.12* Farr, Samuel. A philosophical enquiry into the nature, origin, and extent of animal motion. London, 1771.
Phil 6115.13 Fleury, D.M. de. Medicine and the mind. London, 1900.
Phil 6115.13.6 Fleury, D.M. de. Introduction à la médicine de l'esprit. 6. éd. Paris, 1900.
Phil 6115.17 Fletcher, E.A. Law of rhythmic breath. N.Y., 1908.
Phil 6115.18 Fletcher, Horace. Optimism; a real remedy. Chicago, 1908.
Htn Phil 6115.18.5* Fletcher, Horace. Emancipation. Chicago, 1895.
Phil 6115.18.6.5 Fletcher, Horace. Menticulture, or The ABC of true living. Chicago, 1897.
Phil 6115.18.7 Fletcher, Horace. Menticulture. Chicago, 1898.
Phil 6115.18.7.5 Fletcher, Horace. Menticulture. Chicago, 1898.
Phil 6115.18.9 Fletcher, Horace. The new menticulture. London, 1905.
Phil 6115.18.10 Fletcher, Horace. The new menticulture. N.Y., 1903.
Phil 6115.19 Feuchtwanger, E. Die Funktionen des Stirnhirns. Berlin, 1923.
Phil 6115.20 Fitch, Michael H. The physical basis of mind and morals. Chicago, 1914.
Phil 6115.21 Forel, A. Hygiene of nerves and mind in health and disease. London, 1907.
Phil 6115.21.3 Forel, A. Gehirn und Seele. 4. Aufl. Bonn, 1894.
Phil 6115.21.4 Forel, A. Gehirn und Seele. 5. und 6. Aufl. Bonn, 1899.
Phil 6115.21.5 Forel, A. Gehirn und Seele. 12. Aufl. Leipzig, 1914.
Phil 6115.22 Fairburn, W.A. Mentality and freedom. N.Y., 1917.
Phil 6115.23 Frany, Shepherd I. On the functions of the cerebrum. N.Y., 1907.
Phil 6115.23.5 Frany, Shepherd I. The evolution of an idea. 2d ed. Los Angeles, 1929.
Phil 6115.24 Foville, A. Traite complet de l'anatomie, de la physiologie et de la pathologie du système nerveux. Pt.1. Paris, 1844.
Phil 6115.25 Ferrari, G.C. Ricerche ergografiche nella donna. Reggio Emilia, 1898.
Phil 6115.26 Freeman, G.L.V. Introduction to physiological psychology. N.Y., 1934.
Phil 6115.27 Fulton, J.F. Physiology of the nervous system. London, 1938.
Phil 6115.27.5 Fulton, J.F. Physiology of the nervous system. London, 1939.
VPhil 6115.27.7 Fulton, J.F. Physiology of the nervous system. 2. ed. London, 1943.
Phil 6115.27.15 Fulton, J.F. Physiology of the nervous system. 3. ed. N.Y., 1949.
Phil 6115.29 Fink, David H. Release from nervous tension. N.Y., 1943.
Phil 6115.30 Feldenkrais, M. Body and mature behavior. N.Y., 1949.
Phil 6115.31 Funkenstein, D.H. Mastery of stress. Cambridge, Mass., 1957.
Phil 6115.32 Fisher, Seymour. Body image and personality. Princeton, N.J., 1958.
Phil 6115.32.5 Fisher, Seymour. Body experience in fantasy and behavior. N.Y., 1970.
Phil 6115.33 Fair, Charles. The physical foundations of the psyche. Middletown, 1963.
Phil 6115.34 Fritsch, Vilma. La gauche et la droite. Paris, 1967.
Phil 6116.1 Glen, J. Theory of the influence exerted by the mind over the body. London, 1855.
Cg Phil 6116.2 Golgi, C. Sulla fina anatomia degli organi centrali. Napoli, 1886.
Phil 6116.3 Granville, J.M. The secret of a clear head. Salem, 1879.
Phil 6116.3.5 Granville, J.M. Common mind troubles. Salem, 1879.
Phil 6116.4 Grimes, J.S. The mysteries of human nature. Boston, 1860.
Phil 6116.5 Goltz, F.L. Über die Verrichtungen. Bonn, 1881.
Phil 6116.5.85 Soury, Jules. Les fonctions du cerveau, doctrines de F. Goltz. Paris, 1866.
Phil 6116.6 Gould, G.M. Righthandedness and lefthandedness. Philadelphia, 1908.
Phil 6116.7 Gulick, L.H. Mind and work. N.Y., 1908.
Phil 6116.8 Giss, A.J. Die menschliche Geistestätigkeit in der Weltentwicklung. Leipzig, 1910.
Phil 6116.9.5 Grasset, Joseph. Introduction physiologique à l'étude de la philosophie. Paris, 1908.
Phil 6116.10 Gehuchten, Arthur van. Anatomie du système nerveux de l'homme. Louvain, 1900. 2v.
Phil 6116.11F Gavoy, E.A. L'encephale; structure et description inconographique du cerveau. Paris, 1886. 2v.
Phil 6116.12 Goldscheider, A. Gesammette Abhandlungen. v.1-2. Leipzig, 1898.
Phil 6116.13F Grashey, H. Experimentelle Beiträge zur Lehre von der Blut-Circulation in der Schädel-Rückgratshöhle. München, 1892.
Phil 6116.14 Grimké, S.S. Personified unthinkables, an argument against physical causation. Ann Arbor, 1884.
Phil 6116.15 Gorton, D.A. The monism of man. N.Y., 1893.
Phil 6116.16F Gotch, Francis. On the mammalian nervous system. London, 1891.
Phil 6116.17 Gaskell, Walter H. The involuntary nervous system. London, 1916.
Phil 6116.18 Gehring, J.G. The hope of the variant. N.Y., 1923.
Phil 6116.20 Greene, John G. The emmanuel movement, 1906-1929. n.p., 1934.
Phil 6116.21 Groves, E.R. Readings in mental hygiene. N.Y., 1936.
Phil 6116.21.5 Groves, E.R. Introduction to mental hygiene. N.Y., 1930.
Phil 6116.22 Gibson, Van R. The faith that overcomes the world. N.Y., 1926.
Phil 6116.23 Gorton, D.A. Essay on the principles of mental hygiene. Philadelphia, 1873.
Phil 6116.24PF Gibbs, F.A. Atlas of electroencephalography. Cambridge, Mass., 1941.
Phil 6116.25 Guillain, Georges. Travaux neurologiques de guerre. Paris, 1920.
Phil 6116.28 Gurin, Gerald. Americans view their mental health. N.Y., 1960.
Phil 6116.30 Goër de Herve, Jacques de. Mécanisme et intelligence. Paris, 1969.

Phil 6110 - 6135 Psychology - Mind and body - General works - Individual authors (A-Z) - cont.

Phil 6117.1 Herzen, A. Grundlinien einer allgemeinen Psychophysiologie. Leipzig, 1889.
Phil 6117.1.5 Herzen, A. Les conditions physiques de la conscience. Genève, 1886.
Phil 6117.3 Holbrook, M.L. Hygiene of the brain. N.Y., 1878.
Phil 6117.4 Hill, A. The plan of the central nervous system. Chicago, 1885.
Htn Phil 6117.5*A Holmes, O.W. Mechanism in thought and morals. Boston, 1871.
Htn Phil 6117.5*B Holmes, O.W. Mechanism in thought and morals. Boston, 1871.
Phil 6117.5.6 Holmes, O.W. Mechanism in thought and morals. Boston, 1882.
Phil 6117.5.7 Holmes, O.W. Mechanism in thought and morals. Boston, 1879.
Phil 6117.6 Hyslop, T.B. Mental physiology. Philadelphia, 1895.
X Cg Phil 6117.7 Holland, H. Chapters on mental physiology. London, 1852.
Phil 6117.8A Horsley, V. The brain and spinal cord. London, 1892.
Phil 6117.8B Horsley, V. The brain and spinal cord. London, 1892.
Phil 6117.9 Héger, P. La mission de la physiologie expérimentale. Bruxelles, 1899.
Phil 6117.10 Hellpach, W. Die Grenzwissenschaften der Psychologie. Leipzig, 1902.
Phil 6117.10.3 Hellpach, W. Die geopsychischen Erscheinungen. Leipzig, 1911.
Phil 6117.10.5 Hellpach, W. Die geopsychischen Erscheinungen. 2. Aufl. Leipzig, 1917.
Phil 6117.11 Huguenin, G. Allgemeine Pathologie der Krankheiten des Nervensystems. Zürich, 1873.
Phil 6117.12 Huckel, O. Mental medicine. N.Y., 1909.
Phil 6117.13 Henry, M. Charles. Psycho-biologie et energétique. Paris, 1909.
Phil 6117.14 Harris, D.F. Nerves. London, 1913.
Phil 6117.15 Holland, G.C. The psychology of animated nature. London, 1848.
Phil 6117.18 Hill, Leonard. Physiology and pathology of cerebral circulation. London, 1896.
Phil 6117.19 Hannover, A. Recherches microscopiques sur le système nerveux. Copenhagne, 1844.
Phil 6117.20 Herrick, C.J. An introduction to neurology. Philadelphia, 1916.
Phil 6117.20.5 Herrick, C.J. An introduction to neurology. 3. ed. Philadelphia, 1924.
Phil 6117.20.10 Herrick, C.J. An introduction to neurology. 5th ed. Philadelphia, 1934.
Phil 6117.22 Holmes, F.L. The law of mind in action. N.Y., 1919.
Phil 6117.23 Hering, Ewald. Zur Theorie der Nerventhätigkeit. Leipzig, 1899.
Phil 6117.24 Hirth, George. Lokalisations-Psychologie. Die Lokalisationstheorie. 2. Aufl. München, 1895.
Phil 6117.25 Hollingworth, H.L. The influence of caffein on mental and motor efficiency. N.Y., 1912.
Phil 6117.27 Herz, H. Energie und seelische Rechtkräfte. Leipzig, 1909.
Phil 6117.30 Head, Henry. Studies in neurology. London, 1920. 2v.
Phil 6117.31 Hollander, Bernard. In search of the soul and the mechanism of thought, emotion and conduct. London, 1920. 2v.
Phil 6117.31.10 Hollander, Bernard. Brain, mind and the external signs of intelligence. London, 1931.
Phil 6117.32 Hall, H.J. The untroubled mind. Boston, 1915.
Phil 6117.33 Hadfield, J.A. The psychology of power. N.Y., 1923.
Phil 6117.33.5 Hadfield, J.A. The psychology of power. N.Y., 1924.
Phil 6117.34 Han, S.J. The problem of mind and body. n.p., 1922.
Phil 6117.35 Hitzig, E. Untersuchungen über das Gehirn. Berlin, 1874.
Phil 6117.36 Hallervorden, E. Arbeit und Wille. pt.1-2. Würzburg, 1897.
Phil 6117.37 Horn, Paul. Über nervöse Erkraukungen nach Eisenbahnunfällen. Bonn, 1913.
Phil 6117.38 Häberlin, Paul. Leib und Seele. Bern, 1927.
Phil 6117.39 Hollen, Aura May. Consciousness and the purpose. Hollywood, 1931.
Phil 6117.40 Haanel, C.F. The master key. St. Louis, 1919.
Phil 6117.41 Helwig, Paul. Seele als Ausserung. Leipzig, 1936.
Phil 6117.42 Hudson, T.J. The law of mental medicine. Chicago, 1903.
Phil 6117.43 Herrick, C.J. Introduction to neurology. Philadelphia, 1918.
Phil 6117.44 Hathaway, S.R. Physiological psychology. N.Y., 1942.
Phil 6117.45 Holmes, Ernest R. New thought terms and their meanings. N.Y., 1942.
Phil 6117.45.5 Holmes, E.S. This thing called life. N.Y., 1948.
Phil 6117.45.50 Homaday, William H.D. The inner light. N.Y., 1964.
Phil 6117.46 Halstood, W.C. Brain and intelligence. Chicago, 1947.
Phil 6117.47 Roon, K. The new way to relax. N.Y., 1949.
Phil 6117.48 Hutschnecker, A.A. The will to line. London, 1952.
Phil 6117.49 Highet, G. Man's unconquerable mind. N.Y., 1954.
Phil 6117.50 Hofmann, H. Religion and mental health. N.Y., 1961.
Phil 6117.52 Hécaen, Henry. Les gauchers. Paris, 1963.
Phil 6118.1 Ingalese, R. The history and power of mind. N.Y., 1903.
Phil 6118.1.3 Ingalese, R. The history and power of mind. 8th ed. N.Y., 1905.
Phil 6118.2 Ioteyko, Josefa. La fatigue. Paris, 1920.
Phil 6118.4 Ingraham, F.D. Spina bifida and cranium bifidum. Boston, 1944.
Phil 6118.5 International Conference on the Development of the Nervous System. Genetic neurology. Chicago, 1950.
Phil 6118.6 International Conference on Student Mental Health. The student and mental health. London, 1959.
Phil 6118.8 Symposium on Interdisciplinary Research, University of Wisconsin. Biological and biochemical basis of behavior. Madison, Wis., 1958.
Phil 6118.9 Isaacson, R.L. Basic readings in neuropsychology. N.Y., 1964.
Phil 6119.1.5 Jackson, J.H. Observations on the localisation of movements in the cerebral hemispheres. n.p., n.d.
Phil 6119.2 Jaeger, G. Die Neuralanalyse. Leipzig, 1881.
Phil 6119.3 Jakob, L.H. Grundriss der Erfahrungs-Seelenlehre. Halle, 1791.
Phil 6119.4 Jones, E.E. Influence of bodily posture on mental activities. N.Y., 1907.
Phil 6119.5 Jacoby, G.W. Suggestion and psychotherapy. N.Y., 1912.
Phil 6119.6 Jewett, F.G. Control of body and mind. Boston, 1908.
Phil 6119.7 Jones, Wallace Franklin. A study of handedness. Vermillion, S.D., 1918.
Phil 6119.8 Jakob, C. Elementos de neurobiología. Buenos Aires, 1923.
Phil 6119.9 Jones, F. Wood. The matrix of the mind. Honolulu, 1928.

Classified Listing

Phil 6110 - 6135   **Psychology - Mind and body - General works - Individual authors (A-Z) - cont.**

Phil 6119.10	Jacobson, Edmund. Progressive relaxation. Chicago, 1931.
Phil 6119.10.5	Jacobson, Edmund. You must relax. N.Y., 1934.
Phil 6119.11	Jackson, Josephine Agnes. Outwitting our nerves. N.Y., 1921.
Phil 6119.11.5	Jackson, Josephine Agnes. Outwitting our nerves. 2d ed. N.Y., 1932.
Phil 6119.12	Jackson, A.S. The answer is...your nerves. Madison, Wis., 1942.
Phil 6119.14	Jahoda, Marie. Current concepts of positive mental health. N.Y., 1959.
Phil 6120.1	Klein, A. Die modernen Theorien über Verhältnis von Leib und Seele. Breslau, 1906.
Phil 6120.5	Kostyleff, N. Mécanisme cérébral de la pensée. Paris, 1914.
Phil 6120.6	Kenilworth, W.W. Le contrôle psychique. Paris, 1914.
Phil 6120.6.5	Kenilworth, W.W. Thoughts on things psychic. N.Y., 1911.
Phil 6120.8	Kretschmer, E. Körperbau und Charakter. 3. Aufl. Berlin, 1922.
Phil 6120.8.7	Kretschmer, E. Physique and character. N.Y., 1926.
Phil 6120.8.10	Kretschmer, E. Physique and character. 2d ed. N.Y., 1970.
Phil 6120.8.25	Braat, J.P. De experimenteele psychologie en Kretschmer's constitutietypen. Amsterdam, 1934.
Phil 6120.9	Knapp, Sheldon. Towards a new era in healing. London, 1926.
Phil 6120.10	Keiller, William. Nerve tracts of the brain and cord. N.Y., 1927.
Phil 6120.11	Knowlton, C. Two remarkable lectures. Boston, 1833.
Phil 6120.12	King, D.M. Nerves and personal power. N.Y., 1922.
Phil 6120.13	Kirkpatrick, E.A. Mental hygiene for effective living. N.Y., 1934.
Phil 6120.14	Kuntz, A. The autonomic nervous system. Philadelphia, 1934.
Phil 6120.15	Kenyon, F. The myth of the mind. London, 1941.
Phil 6120.16	Krieg, Wendell J.S. Functional neuroanatomy. Philadelphia, 1942.
Phil 6120.18	Klatt, F. Lebensmächte. Jena, 1939.
Phil 6120.19	Kraines, S.H. Managing your mind. N.Y., 1943.
Phil 6120.20	Klein, David B. Mental hygiene. N.Y., 1944.
Phil 6120.21	Kupper, H.I. Back to life. N.Y., 1945.
Phil 6120.22	Kent, Caron. Man's hidden resources. Melbourne, Arkansas, 1962?
Phil 6120.23	Klier, Sol. Effects of induced stress on learning and performance. n.p., 1962.
Phil 6120.24	Konorski, Jerzy. Integrative activity of the brain; an interdisciplinary approach. Chicago, 1967.
Phil 6121.2	Laugel, A. Les problèmes de l'âme. Paris, 1868.
Phil 6121.2.10	Laugel, A. Om själens problemer. Stockholm, 1869.
Phil 6121.3.2	Laycock, T. Mind and brain. Edinburgh, 1860. 2v.
Phil 6121.3.3	Laugel, T. Mind and brain. N.Y., 1869. 2v.
Phil 6121.4	Lemoine, A. L'âme et le corps. Paris, 1862.
Phil 6121.6	Luciani, L. Die Functions-Localisation die Grosshirnrinde. Leipzig, 1886.
Phil 6121.6.5	Luciani, L. Das Keinhirn. Leipzig, 1893.
Phil 6121.7	Luys, J. The brain and its functions. N.Y., 1882.
Phil 6121.7.3	Luys, J. Le cerveau et ses fonctions. Paris, 1876.
Phil 6121.7.5	Luys, J. Recherches sur le système nerveux. Paris, 1865. 2v.
Phil 6121.7.9	Luys, J. Des actions réflexes du cerveau. Paris, 1874.
Phil 6121.7.12	Luys, J. Das Gehirn. Leipzig, 1877.
Phil 6121.7.21	Luys, J. Leçons sur la structure et les maladies du système nerveux. Paris, 1875.
Phil 6121.9	Lueddeckens, F. Rechts und Linkshändigkeit. Leipzig, 1900.
Phil 6121.10	Lipps, G.F. Grundriss der psychophysik. Leipzig, 1909.
Phil 6121.10.5	Lipps, G.F. Die psychischen Massmethoden. Braunschweig, 1906.
Phil 6121.11	Lindsay, A.A. Mind the transformer, the new psychology. 7. ed. Los Angeles, 1911.
Phil 6121.12.5	Lickley, J.D. The nervous system. N.Y., 1919.
Phil 6121.13	Lussana, F. Fisiologia dei centri nervosi encefalici. Padova, 1871. 2v.
Phil 6121.14.5	Lucas, Keith. The conduction of the nervous impulse. London, 1917.
Phil 6121.15	Lyon, I.L.R. The wonders of life. N.Y., 1910.
Phil 6121.16	Lenhossék, Mihaly. Untersuchungen über Leidenschaften und Gemüthsaffekten als Ursachen. Pesth, 1804.
Phil 6121.17	Lewis, W. Bevan. The human brain. London, 1882.
Phil 6121.18	Loomis, E. Seven essays on the subject of your practical forces on the subject of practical occultism. Chicago, 1897.
Phil 6121.18.5	Loomis, E. Occult science library; seven essays. Chicago, 1898.
Phil 6121.20	La Forge, Louis de. Traité de l'esprit de l'homme. Amsterdam, n.d.
Phil 6121.20.3	La Forge, Louis de. Traité de l'esprit de l'homme. Paris, 1666.
Phil 6121.20.5	La Forge, Louis de. Traité de l'esprit de l'homme. Genève, 1725.
Phil 6121.22.2	Lélut, L.F. Physiologie de la pensée. 2. éd. Paris, 1862. 2v.
Phil 6121.23	Laird, John. Our minds and their bodies. London, 1925.
Phil 6121.24	Lhermitte, J. Les fondements biologiques de la psychologie. Paris, 1925.
Phil 6121.25	Leavitt, C.F. Leavitt-science. Chicago, 19- .
Phil 6121.26	Lenhossék, Mihaly. Der Feinere bau des Nervensystems im Lichte neuester Forschungen. Berlin, 1893.
Phil 6121.27	Lashley, K.S. Integrative functions of the cerebral cortex. Baltimore, 1933.
Phil 6121.28	Lashley, K.S. Experimental analysis of instinctive behavior. Lancaster, Pa., 1938.
Phil 6121.29	Liber, B. Your mental health. N.Y., 1940.
Phil 6121.30	Larson, Christian I. Your forces and how to use them. N.Y., 1912.
Phil 6121.34	Lechuga, Z.G. La higiene mental en México. México, 1937.
Phil 6121.36	Langdon-Davies, I. Man: the known and unknown. London, 1960.
Phil 6121.38	La Rivière, A. L'homme et le complexe normal. Paris, 1961.
Phil 6121.39A	Lashley, Karl S. Brain mechanisms and intelligence. N.Y., 1963.
Phil 6121.39B	Lashley, Karl S. Brain mechanisms and intelligence. N.Y., 1963.
Phil 6121.40	Leiderman, P.H. Psychological approaches to social behavior. Manford, 1964.
Phil 6121.41	Lazarus, Richards. Psychological stress and the coping process. N.Y., 1966.

Phil 6110 - 6135   **Psychology - Mind and body - General works - Individual authors (A-Z) - cont.**

Phil 6121.42	Langer, Susanne K. Mind; an essay on human feeling. Baltimore, 1967-
Phil 6121.45.2	Luria, Aleksandr Romanovich. Higher cortical functions in man. N.Y., 1966.
Phil 6121.45.5	Luria, Aleksandr Romanovich. Human brain and psychological processes. N.Y., 1966.
Phil 6121.50	Locke, Don. Myself and others; a study in our knowledge of minds. Oxford, 1968.
Phil 6121.55	Laszlo, Ervin. System, structure, and experience. N.Y., 1969.
Phil 6121.60	Lewis, Hywel David. The elusive mind; based on the first series of the Gifford lectures. London, 1969.
Phil 6121.62.1	Lilly, John Cunningham. Programming and metaprogramming in the human biocomputer. Berkeley, 1970.
Phil 6122.1	Maudsley, H. Body and mind. London, 1870.
Phil 6122.1.3	Maudsley, H. Body and mind. N.Y., 1871.
Phil 6122.1.4	Maudsley, H. Body and mind. N.Y., 1895.
Phil 6122.1.5	Maudsley, H. Body and mind. N.Y., 1873.
Phil 6122.1.10	Maudsley, H. The physiology and pathology of the mind. 2. ed. London, 1868.
Phil 6122.1.11	Maudsley, H. The physiology and pathology of the mind. N.Y., 1867.
Phil 6122.1.13	Maudsley, H. The physiology of mind. N.Y., 1878.
Phil 6122.1.14	Maudsley, H. The physiology of mind. N.Y., 1872.
Phil 6122.1.15	Maudsley, H. The physiology of mind. 3d ed. pt.1. London, 1876.
Phil 6122.1.17	Maudsley, H. Natural causes and supernatural seemings. London, 1897.
Phil 6122.1.19	Maudsley, H. Organic to human; psychology and sociology. London, 1916.
Phil 6122.2	Mello Moraes, Alexandre José de. Physiologia das paixões e affeçôes. Rio de Janeiro, 1854-55. 3v.
Phil 6122.3	Meyer, J.B. Zum streit über Leib und Seele. Hamburg, 1856.
Phil 6122.4	Mills, C.K. Toner lectures, IX. Mental overwork. Washington, 1885.
Phil 6122.5	Moore, G. The use of the body in relation to the mind. N.Y., 1847.
Phil 6122.5.3	Moore, G. Der Beruf des Körpers in Beziehung auf den Geist. Leipzig, 1850.
Phil 6122.7	Mosso, A. La fatigue intellectuelle et physique. Paris, 1894.
Phil 6122.7.3.5	Mosso, A. Fatique. N.Y., 1904.
Phil 6122.7.4	Mosso, A. Die Ermüdung. Leipzig, 1892.
Phil 6122.7.5	Mosso, A. Psychic processes and muscular exercise. n.p., 1899. 2 pam.
Phil 6122.7.9	Mosso, A. Über den Kreislauf des Blutes. Leipzig, 1881.
Phil 6122.7.15	Mosso, A. La température du cerveau, études thermometriques. Turin, 1895.
Phil 6122.8.5	Se sia l'anima o il cervello che pente e pensa. Firenze, 1881.
Phil 6122.9	Marique, J.M.L. Recherches expérimentales sur le mécanisme de fonctionnement des centres psychomoteurs du Cerveau. Bruxelles, 1885.
Phil 6122.10	Möbius, P.J. Das Nervensystem des Menschen. Leipzig, 1880.
Phil 6122.11	Munk, H. Über die Funktionen der Grosshirnrinde. Berlin, 1881.
Phil 6122.11.2	Munk, H. Über die Funktionen der Grosshirnrinde. 2. Aufl. Berlin, 1890.
Phil 6122.11.5	Munk, H. Untersuchungen über das Wesen. Leipzig, 1868.
Phil 6122.12	Mitchell, S.W. Fat and blood. Philadelphia, 1884.
Phil 6122.13.3	McDougall, William. Physiological psychology. London, 1918.
Phil 6122.13.5	McDougall, William. Body and mind. N.Y., 1911.
Phil 6122.13.11	McDougall, William. Body and mind. 4th ed. London, 1918.
Phil 6122.13.13	McDougall, William. Body and mind. 6th ed. London, 1923.
Phil 6122.14	Morat, J.P. Physiology of the nervous system. Chicago, 1906.
Phil 6122.16	Marsh, H.D. Diurnal course of efficiency. N.Y., 1906.
Phil 6122.16.2	Marsh, H.D. Diurnal course of efficiency. N.Y., 1906.
Phil 6122.17	MacDonald, R. Mind, religion and health. N.Y., 1908.
Phil 6122.19	Pamphlet vol. Psychology. Mind and body. 15 pam.
Phil 6122.20	Mills, A.W. Practical metaphysics. Chicago, 1896.
Phil 6122.21	Marston, L.M. Essentials of mental healing. Boston, 1887.
Phil 6122.22	Meyer, G.H. Untersuchungen Psychologie der Nervenfaser. Tübingen, 1843.
Phil 6122.23	Mulford, P. Your forces and how to use them. N.Y., 1904. 2v.
Phil 6122.23.1	Mulford, Prntice. Your forces and how to use them. N.Y., 1888-92. 6v.
Phil 6122.24	Massalongo, Robert. Mielopatia da fulmine. Napoli, 1891.
Phil 6122.25FA	Monro, Alexander. Observations on the structure of the nervous system. Edinburgh, 1783. 2v.
Phil 6122.25FB	Monro, Alexander. Observations on the structure of the nervous system. Edinburgh, 1783. 2v.
Phil 6122.26	Mott, Frederick Walker. Nature and nurture in mental development. N.Y., 1915.
Phil 6122.27	Maule, G.E. Life and law. 1st ed. Ogden, 1908.
Phil 6122.28	Marschik, S. Geist und Seele. Berlin, 1906.
Phil 6122.29	Müller, Wilhelm. Rede Gehalten zur Feier der akademischen Preisverteilung am 23 Juni 1898. Jena, 1898.
Phil 6122.30	McComb, Samuel. The power of self suggestion. N.Y., 1909.
Phil 6122.31	Mercier, Charles A. The nervous system and the mind. London, 1888.
Phil 6122.34.3	Marden, Orison S. Peace, power and plenty. N.Y., 1909.
Phil 6122.35	Marden, Orison S. Every man a king. N.Y., 1906.
Phil 6122.39	Mills, James P. Illumination; spiritual healing. N.Y., 1916.
Phil 6122.40	Müller, A. Bismarck, Nietzsche, Scheffel, Mörike; der Einfluss nervöser Zustände auf ihr Leben und Schaffen. Bonn, 1921.
Phil 6122.41	Micklem, E.R. Miracles and the new psychology. Oxford, 1922.
Phil 6122.42	Matisse, Georges. L'intelligence et le cerveau. Paris, 1909.
Phil 6122.43	Marguardt, H. Der Mechanismus der Seele. Holstein, 1921.
Phil 6122.44	Meynert, T. Zur Mechanik des Gehirnbaues. Wien, 1874.
Phil 6122.47	Murray, William J. The Astor lectures. N.Y., 1917.
Phil 6122.48	Mohr, Fritz. Psychophysische Behandlungs-Methoden. Leipzig, 1925.
Phil 6122.49.3	Monrad-Krohn, G. The clinical examination of the nervous system. 3d ed. London, 1926.
Phil 6122.52	Merriman, H.B. (Mrs.). What shall make us whole? Boston, 1888.

313

Classified Listing

Phil 6110 - 6135 Psychology - Mind and body - General works - Individual authors (A-Z) - cont.

Phil 6122.53 Myers, C.S. The absurdity of any mind-body relation. London, 1932.
Phil 6122.54 Mainini, Carlos. Téorica del sistema nervioso. n.p., 1901.
Phil 6122.55 Morgan, John J.B. Keeping a sound mind. N.Y., 1934.
Phil 6122.56 Miller, A.G. Train development. N.Y., 1909.
Phil 6122.57 Murray, J.A.C. An introduction to a Christian psycho-therapy. Edinburgh, 1938.
Phil 6122.58 Mikesell, W.H. Mental hygiene. N.Y., 1939.
Phil 6122.59 McCarthy, R.C. Safeguarding mental health. N.Y., 1937.
Phil 6122.60.5 McKinney, Fred. Psychology of personal adjustment. 2d ed. N.Y., 1949.
Phil 6122.61 Meng, H. Seelischer Gesundheitschutz. Basel, 1939.
Phil 6122.61.5 Meng, H. Praxis der seelischen Hygiene. Basel, 1943.
Phil 6122.63 Miller, W.H. How to relax. N.Y., 1944.
Phil 6122.64 Muhlbery, W. Mental adjustments. Cincinnati, O., 1944.
Phil 6122.65 Mabille, P. Initiation à la connaissance de l'homme. Paris, 1949.
Phil 6122.66 Monnier, Marcel. L'organisation des fonctions psychiques. Neuchâtel, 1951.
Phil 6122.68 Moser, Ulrich. Psychologie der Arbeitswahl und der Arheitsstörungen. Bern, 1953.
Phil 6122.70 Mott, Francis. The nature of the self. London, 1959.
Phil 6122.75 MacConaill, Michael A. Bodily structure and the will. London, 1960.
Phil 6122.80 Mikhailov, S. Likvidiraneto na protivopolozhnostta mezhdu umstveniia i fizicheokiia trud. Sofiia, 1959.
Phil 6122.85 Mueller, Johannes. Physiologie du système nerveux. 3. éd. Paris, 1840. 2v.
Phil 6122.95 The Midtown Manhattan study. N.Y., 1962. 2v.
Phil 6122.96.2 Magnun, Horace. The waking brain. 2. ed. Springfield, Ill., 1963.
Phil 6122.97 Mardersptein, I.G. Otrazhenie v khudozhestvennoi literature ucheniia o fiziologii golovnogo mozga. Tashkent, 1962.
Phil 6123.1 Newnham, W. The reciprocal influence of body and mind. London, 1842.
Phil 6123.1.5 Newnham, W. Essay on superstition. London, 1830.
Phil 6123.2 Noble, D. The brain and its physiology. London, 1846.
Phil 6123.3 Neff, S.S. Power through perfected ideas. Philadelphia, 1911.
Phil 6123.4 Nothnagel, H. Topische Diagnostik der Gehirnkrankheiten. Berlin, 1879.
Phil 6123.5 Newcomb, C.B. All's right with the world. Boston, 1897.
Itn Phil 6123.5.2* Newcomb, C.B. All's right with the world. Boston, 1897.
Phil 6123.5.5 Newcomb, C.B. Discovery of a lost trail. Boston, 1900.
Phil 6123.6 Nisbet, J.F. The human machine. London, 1899.
Phil 6123.7 Nicolai, J.F. Psicogenesis. Santiago, 1935.
Phil 6123.8 National Committee for Mental Hygiene, Inc. Division on Rehabilition. Bibliography. Mental hygiene in industry. N.Y., 1945.
Phil 6123.10 New York (City). University. Institution of Philosophy. Dimensions of mind. N.Y., 1960.
Phil 6124.1 Obersteiner, H. Anleitung beim Studium des Baues der nervösen Centratorgane. Leipzig, 1888.
Phil 6124.2 Orth, H. Disputatio philosophica. Jenae, 1674.
Phil 6124.4 Tilney, Frederick. The brain from ape to man. N.Y., 1928. 2v.
Phil 6124.5 Overstreet, H.A. The mature mind. N.Y., 1949.
Phil 6124.6 Ochs, Sidney. Elements of neurophysiology. N.Y., 1965.
Phil 6124.7 O'Connor, John. Modern materialism; readings on mind-body identity. N.Y., 1969.
Phil 6125.1 Piderit, T. Gehirn und Geist. Leipzig, 1868.
Phil 6125.5 Psychotherapeutics; a symposium. Boston, 1910.
Phil 6125.5.5 Psychotherapeutics. Boston, 1912.
Phil 6125.6 Poincaré, E.L. Leçons sur la physiologie...du système nerveux. Paris, 1873-6. 3v.
Phil 6125.7.5 Paulhan, F. La physiologie de l'esprit. 5. éd. Paris, 1910.
Phil 6125.8 Polak, A.J. Gedachten over geest. n.p., 1894.
Phil 6125.9 Patrick, G.T.W. The psychology of relaxation. Boston, 1916.
Phil 6125.9.3 Patrick, G.T.W. The psychology of relaxation. Boston, 1916.
Phil 6125.10 Pupin, Charles. Le neurone et les hypothèses. Paris, 1896.
Phil 6125.11 Powell, Hyman R. The Emmanuel movement in a New England town. N.Y., 1909.
Phil 6125.12 Panizza, M. Le metodo nello studio del fenomeno biopsichio. Roma, 1901.
Phil 6125.12.3 Panizza, M. La fisiologia del sistema nervoso. Roma, 1897.
Phil 6125.13 Pratt, J.B. Matter and spirit. N.Y., 1922.
Phil 6125.14 Paton, Stewart. Signs of sanity and the principles of mental hygiene. N.Y., 1922.
Phil 6125.15 Parson, B.S. Lefthandedness. N.Y., 1924.
Phil 6125.16 Pitres, A. Recherches sur les lésions du centre ovale des hémisphères cérébraux. Paris, 1877.
Phil 6125.17 Patterson, C.B. Dominion and power. 2d ed. N.Y., 1902.
Phil 6125.17.5 Patterson, C.B. The will to be well. 5th ed. N.Y., 1906.
Phil 6125.18 Piéron, Henri. Le cerveau et la pensée. Paris, 1923.
Phil 6125.18.5 Piéron, Henri. Thought and the brain. London, 1927.
Phil 6125.19 Pieper, Gustav. Das geistige Heilverfahren. Magdeburg, 1929.
Phil 6125.20 Polen, Laura. Körperbau und Charakter. Inaug. Diss. Leipzig, 1928.
Phil 6125.21 Pierce, S.W. The layman looks at doctors. N.Y., 1929.
Phil 6125.22 Perin, George L. Self healing simplified. N.Y., 1922.
Phil 6125.23 Pratt, George K. Your mind and you. N.Y., 1924.
DL Phil 6125.23.5 Pratt, George K. Your mind and you. N.Y., 1924.
Phil 6125.24.4 Pickford, Mary. Why not try God? N.Y., 1934.
Phil 6125.25 Preston, G.H. The substance of mental health. N.Y., 1943.
Phil 6125.25.5 Preston, G.H. The substance of mental health. London, 1944.
Phil 6125.26 Pitkin, W.B. Take it easy. N.Y., 1935.
Phil 6125.27 Portman, Adolf. Don Quijote und Sancho Pansa vom gegenwartigen Stand der Typenlehre. Basel, 1957.
Phil 6125.28 Penfield, Wilder. Speech and brain-mechanisms. N.J., 1959.
Phil 6125.29 Germany. Heer Inspection des Personalprüfwesens. Menschen Formen. Berlin, 1941.
Phil 6125.30 Perron, Roger. Niveaux de tension et contrôle de l'activité. Paris, 1961.
Phil 6125.31 Peursen, Cornelis Anthonie van. Body, soul, spirit; a survey of the body-mind problem. London, 1966.

Phil 6110 - 6135 Psychology - Mind and body - General works - Individual authors (A-Z) - cont.

Phil 6125.32 Pribram, Karl H. Languages of the brain. Englewood Cliffs, 1971.
Phil 6126.5 Quackenbos, J.D. Body and spirit. N.Y., 1916.
Phil 6127.1 Ray, J. Mental hygiene. Boston, 1863.
Phil 6127.2 Redford, G. Body and soul. London, 1847.
Phil 6127.3 Rohon, J.V. Bau und Verrichtungen des Gehirns. Heidelburg, 1887.
Phil 6127.4 Rubenstein, S. Zur Natur der Bewegungen. Leipzig, 1890.
Phil 6127.6 Rehmke, J. Aussenwelt und Innenwelt, Leib und Seele. Griefswald, 1898.
Phil 6127.7 Ramón y Cajal, S. Comparative study of the sensory areas. Human cortex. n.p., 1899?
Phil 6127.7.5 Ramón y Cajal, S. Textura del sistema nervioso del hombre y de los Vertebrados. V.1-2. Madrid, 1899. 3v.
Phil 6127.7.10 Ramón y Cajal, S. Les nouvelles idées sur la structure du système nerveux. Paris, 1895.
Phil 6127.7.20 Ramón y Cajal, S. El pensamiento vivo de Cajal. Buenos Aires, 1941.
Phil 6127.8 Rogers, A.K. Parallelism of mind and body. Chicago, 1899.
Phil 6127.8.5 Rogers, A.K. Parallelism of mind and body. Chicago, 1899.
Phil 6127.9 Ranvier, L. Leçons sur l'histologie du système nerveux. pt.1-2. Paris, 1878.
Phil 6127.11 Rabbow, Paul. Antik Schriften über Seelenheilung und Seelenleitung. Leipzig, 1914.
Phil 6127.13 Randall, F.H. Psychology. London, 1905.
Phil 6127.14 Rivers, W.H.R. Mind and medicine. 2d ed. Manchester, 1920.
Phil 6127.15 Rüdinger, N. Über die Wage und Ziele. München, 1893.
Phil 6127.15.5 Rüdinger, N. Ein Beitrag zur Anatomie des Sprach-Centrums. Stuttgart, 1882.
Phil 6127.16 Reich, E. Der Mensch und die Seele. Berlin, 1872.
Phil 6127.17 Rieger, Conrad. Über Apparate in dem Hirn. Jena, 1909.
Phil 6127.18 Riggs, A.F. Intelligent living. Garden City, 1929.
Phil 6127.18.10 Riggs, A.F. Just nerves. Boston, 1922.
Phil 6127.18.12 Riggs, A.F. Talks to patients. n.p., 1924-27.
Phil 6127.19 Rees, John R. The health of the mind. Cambridge, Eng., 1929.
Phil 6127.20 Rosett, J. Intercortical systems. N.Y., 1933.
Phil 6127.21 Rasmussen, A.T. The principal nervous pathways. N.Y., 1939.
Phil 6127.22 Rogers, Carl R. Counseling and psychotherapy; newer concepts in practice. Boston, 1942.
Phil 6127.22.10A Rogers, Carl R. Counseling with returned servicemen. 1. ed. N.Y., 1946.
Phil 6127.22.10B Rogers, Carl R. Counseling with returned servicemen. 1. ed. N.Y., 1946.
Phil 6127.23 Rathbone, J.L. Relaxation. N.Y., 1943.
Phil 6127.24 Ray, Marie B. Lyons. How never to be tired, or Two lifetimes in one. Indianapolis, Ind., 1944.
Phil 6127.25 Rennie, T.A.C. Mental health in modern society. N.Y., 1948.
Phil 6127.26 Ryle, Gilbert. The concept of mind. London, 1949.
Phil 6127.26.5 Ryle, Gilbert. The concept of mind. London, 1963.
Phil 6127.28 Russel, Roger. Frontiers in physiological psychology. N.Y., 1966.
Phil 6127.30 Reimann, Helga. Die Mental Health Bewegung. Tübingen, 1967.
Phil 6128.1 Scervini, P. Anatomia dei centri nervosi. Napoli, 1892.
Phil 6128.2 Schaller, J. Leib und Seele. Weimar, 1858.
Phil 6128.2.2 Schaller, J. Leib und Seele. 2. Aufl. Weimar, 1856.
Phil 6128.3 Smith, J.M. A discourse on the influence of diseases on the intellectual and moral powers. N.Y., 1848.
Phil 6128.4 Smith, J.A. Select discourses on the functions of the nervous system. N.Y., 1840.
Phil 6128.5 Spurzheim, J.K. The anatomy of the brain. London, 1826.
Phil 6128.6 Swan, J. The brain in relation to the mind. London, 1854.
Phil 6128.7 Swedenborg, E. The brain. London, 1882-87.
Phil 6128.8 Sweetser, W. Mental hygiene. N.Y., 1850.
Phil 6128.8.3 Sweetser, W. Mental hygiene. N.Y., 1843.
Phil 6128.9 Strömberg, J.D. Undersökningar i läran om själ och kropp. Lund, 1897.
Phil 6128.10 Smee, Alfred. Elements of electrobiology. London, 1849.
Phil 6128.10.2 Smee, Alfred. Principle of the human mind, sequel to elements of electrobiology. London, 1849.
Phil 6128.10.3 Smee, Alfred. Principle of the human mind, deduced from physical laws. N.Y., 1850.
Phil 6128.11 Strong, C.A. Why the mind has a body. N.Y., 1903.
Phil 6128.11.2 Strong, C.A. Why the mind has a body. N.Y., 1903.
Phil 6128.11.9 Strong, C.A. Reply to Bakewell. n.p., 1904.
Phil 6128.11.15 Strong, C.A. Essays on the natural origin of the mind. London, 1930.
Phil 6128.12 Stumpf, C. Leib und Seele. Der Entwicklungs gedanke. Leipzig, 1903.
Phil 6128.13 Sherrington, C.S. The integrative action of the nervous system. N.Y., 1906.
Phil 6128.13.7A Sherrington, C.S. The integrative action of the nervous system. New Haven, 1926.
Phil 6128.13.8 Sherrington, C.S. The integrative action of the nervous system. Cambridge, Eng., 1948.
Phil 6128.13.9A Sherrington, C.S. Man on his nature. Cambridge, 1940.
Phil 6128.13.9B Sherrington, C.S. Man on his nature. Cambridge, 1940.
Phil 6128.13.10 Sherrington, C.S. Man on his nature. Cambridge, Eng., 1946.
Phil 6128.13.11 Sherrington, C.S. Man on his nature. N.Y., 1941.
Phil 6128.13.12 Swazey, Judith Pound. Reflexes and motor integration; Sherrington's concept of integrative action. Cambridge, 1969.
Phil 6128.14 Saleeby, C.W. Worry; the disease of the age. N.Y., 1907.
Phil 6128.15.3 Schofield, A.T. The force of mind. N.Y., 1903.
Phil 6128.16 Sermyn, W.C. de. Contribution à l'étude de certaines facultés cérébrales méconnues. Sawsanne, 1910.
Phil 6128.17F Ramström, M. Emmanuel Swedenborg's investigations in natural science and the basis for his statements concerning the functions of the brain. Uppsala, 1910.
Phil 6128.17.5 Jonsson, Inge. Swodenborgs konespondenslära. Stockholm, 1969.
Phil 6128.18 Sapolini, G. Un tredicesimo nervo craniale. Milano, 1881.
Phil 6128.19 Simson, T. An inquiry how far the vital and animal actions of the more perfect animals can be accounted for independent of the brain. Edinburgh, 1752.
Phil 6128.20 Swan, Joseph. Observations on nervous system. London, 1822.
Phil 6128.21 Soury, Jules. Histoire des doctrines...les fonctions du cerveau. Paris, 1891.
Phil 6128.21.5 Soury, Jules. Le système nerveux centrale. Paris, 1899. 2v.

Phil 6110 - 6135   Psychology - Mind and body - General works - Individual authors (A-Z) - cont.

Phil 6128.22   Sankey, Dora J. Bible authority for metaphysical healing. Boston, 1912.

Phil 6128.24   Sheppard, E.E. The thinking universe. Los Angeles, 1915.

Phil 6128.25   Sherman, J.C. The stunted saplings. Boston, 1911.

Phil 6128.26   Schroeder van der Kolk, J.L.C. Seele und Leib in Wechselbeziehung zu Einander. Braunschweig, 1865.

NEDL Phil 6128.26.5   Schroeder van der Kolk, J.L.C. On the minute structure and functions of the spinal cord. London, 1859.

Phil 6128.27   Scheffler, H. Körper und Geist. Braunschweig, 1862.

Phil 6128.28   Schreber, D.G.M. Das Buch der Erziehung an Leib und Seele. 2. ed. Leipzig, 1882.

Phil 6128.29   Surbled, Georges. L'âme et le cerveau. 3. éd. Paris, 1908.

Phil 6128.30   Starrett, D.W. The last lap. Boston, 1915.

Phil 6128.31.5   Stiles, Percy G. The nervous system and its conservation. Philadelphia, 1915.

Phil 6128.32   Snyder, John Jacob. How to obtain happiness and health. Chicago, 1905.

Phil 6128.33   Sarjant, L.G. Is the mind a coherer? London, 1912.

Phil 6128.34   Sommer, George. Leib und Seele in ihrem verhältnis Zueinander. Leipzig, 1920.

Phil 6128.35   Scheidemacher, C.B. Das Seelenleben und die Behirnthatigkeit. Regensburg, 1876.

Phil 6128.36   Spamer, Karl. Physiologie der Seele. Stuttgart, 1877.

Phil 6128.37   Schiff, M. Leziomi di fisiologia sperimentale sul sistema nervoso. 2. ed. Firenze, 1873.

Phil 6128.38.2   Spinney, W.A. Health through self-control in thinking, breathing, eating. Boston, 1907.

Phil 6128.39   Seward, T.F. The Don't Worry movement. N.Y., 1898.

Phil 6128.40.6   Sunner, Paul. The brain and the mind. N.Y., 1926.

Phil 6128.41   Segno, A.V. The law of mentalism. 26th ed. Los Angeles, 1902.

Phil 6128.42   Sadler, William S. The truth about mind cure. Chicago, 1928.

Phil 6128.43   Sömmerring, S.T. Über das Organ der Seele. Königsberg, 1796.

Phil 6128.44   Saunders, R.H. Health; its recovery and maintanance, by Abduhl Latif. London, 1928.

Phil 6128.45   Simmons, D.A. Cosmicology. N.Y., 1931?

Phil 6128.46   Seabury, David. How to worry successfully. Boston, 1936.

Phil 6128.46.7   Seabury, David. Growing into life. N.Y., 1928.

Phil 6128.46.12   Seabury, David. Help yourself to happiness. N.Y., 1937.

Phil 6128.47.7   Shinn, F.S. (Mrs.). The game of life and how to play it. 7th ed. N.Y., 1927.

Phil 6128.49   Shaffer, Laurance F. Psychology of adjustment. Boston, 1936.

Phil 6128.49.2   Shaffer, Laurance F. The psychology of adjustment. 2d ed. Boston, 1956.

Phil 6128.50   Strecker, E.A. Beyond the clinical frontiers. N.Y., 1940.

Phil 6128.53   Swedenborg, Emanuel. Three transactions on the cerebrum; a posthumous work. V.1-2 and atlas. Philadelphia, 1938-40. 3v.

Phil 6128.54   Swindle, Percy Ford. Quantum reactions and associations; a theory of physical and physiological units or quanta. Boston, 1922.

Phil 6128.55   Social aspects of mental hygiene. New Haven, 1925.

Phil 6128.56   Siddall, R.B. Towards understanding our minds. N.Y., 1951.

Phil 6128.57A   Silverberg, W.V. Childhood experience and personal destiny. N.Y., 1952.

Phil 6128.57B   Silverberg, W.V. Childhood experience and personal destiny. N.Y., 1952.

Phil 6128.58A   Seyle, Hans. The stress of life. N.Y., 1956.

Phil 6128.58B   Seyle, Hans. The stress of life. N.Y., 1956.

Phil 6128.59   Schroedinger, Erwin. Mind and matter. Cambridge, Eng., 1958.

Phil 6128.59.5   Schroedinger, Erwin. Geist und Materie. Braunschweig, 1959.

Phil 6128.60   Steenberghen, F. van. Psychology, morality and education. London, 1958.

Phil 6128.62   Simonian, G.A. Soderzhanie i sushchnost' antagonizma mezhdu fizicheskim i umstvennym trudom. Baku, 1958.

Phil 6128.65   Schottlaender, Felix. Das ich und seine Welt. Stuttgart, 1959.

Phil 6128.66   Stuttgart. Institut für Psychotherapie und Tiefenpsychologie. Felix Schottlaender zum Gedächtnis. Stuttgart, 1959.

Phil 6128.70   Stuttgart. Institut für Psychotherapie und Tiefenpsychologie. Nervose. Stuttgart, 1960.

Phil 6128.75   Sartakov, S.V. Krasota truda. Moskva, 1961.

Phil 6128.76   Scher, Jordan. Theories of the mind. N.Y., 1962.

Phil 6128.77   Schneiders, Alexander A. Personality dynamics and mental health. N.Y., 1965.

Phil 6128.78   Smythies, John Raymond. Brain and mind. London, 1965.

Phil 6128.79   Sadhu, Mouni. Ways to self-realization. N.Y., 1962.

Phil 6128.80   Schur, Max. The id and the regulatory principles of mental functioning. London, 1967.

Phil 6128.81   Stalpers, Jacobus Antonius. Zelfbehoud, aanpassing en cultuur. Arnhem, 1964.

Phil 6128.82   Schmidtke, Heinz. Die Ermüdung; Symptome, Theorien, Messversache. Bern, 1965.

Phil 6128.83   Shontz, Frank C. Perceptual and cognitive aspects of body experience. N.Y., 1969.

Phil 6128.84   Scott, Donald Fletcher. The psychology of work. London, 1970.

Phil 6129.1   Phomson, W.H. Medical aspects of mental dicipline. N.Y., 1890.

Phil 6129.1.4   Thomson, W.H. Brain and personality. N.Y., 1906.

Phil 6129.1.4.2   Pamphlet box. Thomson, W.H. Letters.

Phil 6129.1.8   Thomson, W.H. Brain and personality. N.Y., 1914.

Phil 6129.2   Thoughts on the mental functions. Edinburgh, 1843.

Phil 6129.3   Tuke, D.H. Illustration of the mind upon the body. London, 1872.

Phil 6129.3.2   Tuke, D.H. Illustration of the mind upon the body. 2d ed. Philadelphia, 1884.

Phil 6129.3.3   Tuke, D.H. Geist und Körper. Jena, 1888.

Phil 6129.4   Thompson, J.J. Mirage of the nervous system. n.p., 1914.

Phil 6129.5   Thomas, André. Localisations cérébelleuses. Paris, 1914.

Phil 6129.6   Taylor, E.W. The mental element in the treatment of disease. Boston, 1891.

Phil 6129.6.5   Taylor, E.W. Psychotherapy. Cambridge, 1926.

Phil 6129.7   Trumper, Henry. The message of mysticism in spiritual healing. London, 1933.

Phil 6129.8   Travis, L.E. Personal problems of everyday life. N.Y., 1941.

Phil 6129.9   Tepp, Max. Vom Sinn des Körpers. Hamburg, 1919.

Phil 6110 - 6135   Psychology - Mind and body - General works - Individual authors (A-Z) - cont.

Phil 6129.10   Taniguchi, Masaham. Recovery from all diseases. Tokyo, 1963.

Phil 6130.1   Uschakoff, J. Das Lokalisationsgesetz. Helsingfors, 1900.

Phil 6130.1.2   Uschakoff, J. Das Lokalisationsgesetz. Leipzig, 1900.

Phil 6131.1   Varigny, H.C. de. Recherches expérimentales sur l'excitabilité électrique. Paris, 1884.

Phil 6131.2   Valentin, G.G. Versuch einer physiologischen Pathologie der Nerven. Leipzig, 1864.

Phil 6131.3   Verworn, M. Die Mechanik des Geisteslebens. Leipzig, 1910.

Phil 6131.3.5   Verworn, M. Die Entwicklung des menschlichen Geistes. Jena, 1910.

Phil 6131.4   Von Boeckmann P. Nerve force. N.Y., 1919.

Phil 6131.5   Vere, James A. Physical and moral enquiry. London, 1778.

Phil 6131.6   Vasil'ev, Leonid L. Tainstvennye iavleniia chelov psikhiki. Moskva, 1963.

Phil 6131.6.3   Vasil'ev, Leonid L. Tainstvennye iavleniia chelovecheskoi psikhiki. Izd. 3. Moskva, 1964.

Phil 6131.6.5   Vasil'ev, Leonid L. Mysterious phenomena of the human psyche. New Hyde Park, N.Y., 1965.

Phil 6131.7   Van Kaam, Adrian. Existential foundations and psychology. Pittsburgh, 1966.

Phil 6131.10   Vesey, Godfrey Norman A. The embodied mind. London, 1965.

Phil 6132.2   Wood, H.C. Brain-work and overwork. Philadelphia, 1885.

Phil 6132.3   Wilson, D. The right hand. Left handedness. London, 1891.

Phil 6132.4   Worcester, Elwood. Religion and medicine. N.Y., 1908.

Phil 6132.4.7   Worcester, Elwood. Christian religion as a healing power. N.Y., 1809.

Phil 6132.4.13   Worcester, Elwood. Body, mind and spirit. Boston, 1931.

Phil 6132.4.20   Worcester, Elwood. Making life better. N.Y., 1933.

Phil 6132.5   Religion and medicine. v.1-2,4,6-7. v.3,5 lost. Boston, 1908. 5 pam.

Phil 6132.6   Whipple, L.E. Mental healing. N.Y., 1907.

Phil 6132.6.5   Whipple, L.E. The philosophy of mental healing. N.Y., 1893.

Phil 6132.6.10   Whipple, L.E. Practical health. N.Y., 1907.

Phil 6132.7   Walton, G.L. Why worry? Philadelphia, 1908.

Phil 6132.7.2   Walton, G.L. Why worry? 2d ed. Philadelphia, 1919.

Phil 6132.7.6   Walton, G.L. Peg along. Philadelphia, 1915.

Phil 6132.7.10   Walton, G.L. Those nerves. Philadelphia, 1909.

Phil 6132.7.15   Walton, G.L. Calm yourself. Boston, 1913.

Phil 6132.8   Willman, R. Errors of mind healing. St. Joseph, 1909.

Phil 6132.9   Weaver, E.E. Mind and health. N.Y., 1913.

Phil 6132.10   Wilson, A. Brain and body: the nervous system. 2d ed. London, 1900.

Phil 6132.11   Wichmann, R. Die Rückenmarksnewen über ihre Segmentbezüge. Berlin, 1900.

Phil 6132.12   Wagner, J.R. Neurologische Untersuchungen. Göttingen, 1854.

Phil 6132.13   Walters, J.G. Plates of the thoracic and abdominal nerves. London, 1804.

Phil 6132.14   Wörner, Ernst. Biblische Anthropologie. Stuttgart, 1887.

Phil 6132.15   Walsh, J.J. Psychotherapy. London, 1912.

Phil 6132.16   Wilmans, Helen. Back numbers Wilmans express, condensed. n.p., 18- ?

Phil 6132.17.9   Wood, Henry. Ideal suggestion through mental photography. 9. ed. Boston, 1899.

Phil 6132.17.15   Wood, Henry. The new old healing. Boston, 1908.

Phil 6132.18   Wells, D.W. Psychology applied to medicine. Philadelphia, 1907.

Phil 6132.19   Wilson, H.B. Does Christ still heal? N.Y., 1917.

Phil 6132.20   Winbigler, C.F. Handbook of instructions for healing and helping others. Los Angeles, 1918.

Phil 6132.21   Winkler, H. Die Monotonie der Arbeit. Leipzig, 1922.

Phil 6132.22   Wahle, R. Gehirn und Bewusstsein. Wien, 1884.

Phil 6132.24   White, H.P. The philosophy of health. no.1-3. Kalamazoo, Mich., 1901.

Phil 6132.25   Waylen, H. An apostle of healing...Pastor Richard Howton. London, 1928.

Phil 6132.26   Williams, Frankwood Earl. Some social aspects of mental hygiene. Philadelphia, 1930.

Phil 6132.27   Wilder, Alexander. Mind, thought and cerebration. n.p., 188-?

Phil 6132.28   Wilson, Floyd B. Paths to power. N.Y., 1901.

Phil 6132.29   Wenzl, Aloys. Das Leib-Seele-Problem. Leipzig, 1933.

Phil 6132.31   Wile, Ira S. Handedness, right and left. Boston, 1934.

Phil 6132.32   Welsh, F.G. (Mrs.). Can we live forever? Chicago, 1938.

NEDL Phil 6132.33   Wood, H. Brain-work. Philadelphia, 1880.

Phil 6132.34   Wallin, J.E.W. Minor mental maladjustments in normal people. Durham, N.C., 1939.

Phil 6132.35   Winkler, J.K. Mind explorers. N.Y., 1939.

Phil 6132.36   Wertham, F. The brain as an organ. N.Y., 1934.

Phil 6132.37   Williams, Roger J. The human frontier. N.Y., 1946.

Phil 6132.38   Wedge, Bryant M. Psychosocial problems of college men. New Haven, 1958.

Phil 6132.40   Wright, B.A. Physical disability; a psychological approach. N.Y., 1960.

Phil 6132.41   Wooldridge, Dean E. The machinery of the brain. N.Y., 1963.

Phil 6132.41.5   Wooldridge, Dean E. Mechanical man. N.Y., 1968.

Phil 6132.42   Worrall, Ambrose A. The gift of healing. 1st ed. N.Y., 1965.

Phil 6132.43   White, William Alanson. An introduction to the study of the mind. Washington, 1924.

Phil 6134.1   Youmans, E.L. Observations on scientific study of human nature. N.Y., 1867.

Phil 6134.2   Yoakum, C.S. Experimental study of fatique. Chicago, 1909.

Phil 6134.3A   Yogananda, Swami. Descriptive outline. 9th ed. Los Angeles, 1928.

NEDL Phil 6134.3B   Yogananda, Swami. Descriptive outline. 9th ed. Los Angeles, 1928.

Phil 6134.4A   Young, J.Z. Doubt and certainty in science. Oxford, 1951.

Phil 6134.4B   Young, J.Z. Doubt and certainty in science. Oxford, 1951.

Phil 6135.1   Zukrigl, J. Kritische Untersuchung über das Wesen der vernünstigen Geist-Seele. Regensburg, 1854.

Phil 6135.2   Zuckerkandl, E. Über das Riechcentrum. Stuttgart, 1887.

Phil 6135.3   Ziehen, Theodore. Über die allgemeinen Beziehungen. Leipzig, 1902.

Phil 6135.4.5A   Zweig, Stefan. Mental healers. N.Y., 1932.

Phil 6135.4.5B   Zweig, Stefan. Mental healers. N.Y., 1932.

Phil 6135.5   Zitex, Edward. A research in report on mental hygiene, brain, exercises, sanitation and foods. New Orleans, La., 1935.

Phil 6135.8   Zaneiwski, R. Les théories des milieux et la pédagogie mesologique. Tournai, 1952.

Classified Listing

Phil 6110 - 6135 Psychology - Mind and body - General works - Individual authors (A-Z) - cont.

Phil 6135.9 Ziskind, Robert. Viewpoint on mental health; transcripts, 1963-1965. N.Y., 1967.

Phil 6140 Psychology - Mind and body - Special topics - Community mental health programs and services

Phil 6140.2 Golann, Stuart E. Coordinate index reference guide to community mental health. N.Y., 1969.
Phil 6140.5 The politics of mental health; organizing community mental health in metropolitan areas. N.Y., 1968.
Phil 6140.6 Research Seminar on the Evaluation of Community Mental Health Programs. Community mental health; an international perspective. San Francisco, 1968.
Phil 6140.10 Shore, Milton F. Mental health and the community; problems, programs and strategies. N.Y., 1969.
Phil 6140.15 Bindman, Arthur J. Perspectives in community mental health. Chicago, 1969.
Phil 6140.20 Klein, Donald Charles. Community dynamics and mental health. N.Y., 1968.
Phil 6140.25 Community life for the mentally ill; an alternative to institutional care. Chicago, 1969.

hil 6155 Psychology - Psychopharmacology - General works

Phil 6155.2 Durr, R.A. Poetic vision and the psychedelic experience. 1st ed. Syracuse, 1970.
Phil 6155.4 Leary, Timothy Francis. Psychedelic prayers after the tao te ching. Kerhonkson, 1966.
Phil 6155.4.5 Leary, Timothy Francis. The politics of ecstasy. N.Y., 1968.
Phil 6155.4.10 Leary, Timothy Francis. The psychedelic experience. New Hyde Park, 1964.
Phil 6155.6 Masters, Robert E.L. The varieties of psychedelic experience. 1st ed. N.Y., 1966.
Phil 6155.8 Marshall, William. The art of ecstasy. Don Mills, 1967.
Phil 6155.10 Clark, Walter Houston. Chemical ecstasy. N.Y., 1969.
Phil 6155.12 Hallucinogenic drug research; impact on science and society. Beloit, Wis., 1970.
Phil 6155.14 Polland, John C. Drugs and phantasy: the effects of LSD, psilocykin and Sernyl on college students. 1st ed. Boston, 1965.
Phil 6155.16 McGlothlin, William Herschel. Hallucinogenic drugs: a perspective with special reference to peyote and cannalis. Santa Monica, 1964.
Phil 6155.18 Essai sur l'expérience hallucinogène. Paris, 1969.
Phil 6155.20 Psychedelic drugs. N.Y., 1969.
Phil 6155.22 Mystification and drug misuse; hazards in using psychoactive drugs. 1st ed. San Francisco, 1971.
Phil 6155.24 Psychedelic review. Cambridge, Mass. 1,1963+ 2v.
Phil 6155.26 Legewie, Heiner. Persönlichkeitstheorie und Psychopharmaka. Meisenheim, 1968.

il 6158 Psychology - Psychopharmacology - Special drugs - LSD

Phil 6158.5 Solomon, David. LSD: the consciousness-expanding drug. N.Y., 1964.
Phil 6158.10 Cohen, Sidney. The beyond within; the LSD story. N.Y., 1965.
Phil 6158.15 Braden, William. The private sea; LSD and the search for God. Chicago, 1967.
Phil 6158.20 LSD, man and society. 1st ed. Middletown, 1967.
Phil 6158.25 Dossier LSD. Paris, 1967.
Phil 6158.30 The problems and prospects of LSD. Springfield, 1968.
Phil 6158.35 Bishop, Malden Grange. The discovery of love; a psychedelic experience with LSD-25. N.Y., 1963.
Phil 6158.40 Blum, Richard H. Utopiates; the use and users of LSD-25. N.Y., 1966.
Phil 6158.45 Alpert, Richard. LSD. N.Y., 1966.
Phil 6158.50 Lilly, John Cunningham. The center of the cyclone. N.Y., 1972.

l 6159 Psychology - Psychopharmacology - Special drugs - Others

Phil 6159.5 Solier, René de. Curandera; les champignons hallucinogènes. Paris, 1965.
Phil 6159.10 Kreppel, Gisela Richters. Die psychischen Phänomene im Schwellenbereich des Meshalin. Inaug. Diss. Bonn, 1964.
Phil 6159.15 Roseman, Bernard. The peyote story. Hollywood, Calif., 1966.
Phil 6159.16.1 La Barre, Weston. The peyote cult. Hamden, 1964.

6302 Psychology - Abnormal psychology - Congresses

Phil 6302.5 Life history research in psychopathology. Minneapolis, 1970.
Phil 6302.10 American Psychiatric Association. Committee on Relations with the Social Science. Proceedings...colloquium on personality investigation. 1st - 2nd, 1928-1929. Baltimore, 1929.

6304 Psychology - Abnormal psychology - Reference works - Dictionaries and ncyclopedias

Phil 6304.2 Moor, Lise. Glossaire de psychiatrie. Paris, 1966.

6305 Psychology - Abnormal psychology - Pamphlet volumes

Phil 6305.5 Pamphlet vol. Abnormal psychology. 1891-1912. 9 pam.
Phil 6305.5.5 Pamphlet box. Psychopathological references. English and American.
Phil 6305.9 Pamphlet box. Abnormal psychology. German dissertations.

6306 Psychology - Abnormal psychology - History - General works

Phil 6306.5 Progoff, Ira. The death and rebirth of psychology. N.Y., 1956.

6307 Psychology - Abnormal psychology - History - Local (Geographic Table A)

Phil 6307.332 Graham, Thomas F. Medieval minds; mental health in the Middle Ages. London, 1967.
Phil 6307.408 David, Michel. La psicoanalisi nella cultura italiana. Torino, 1966.
Phil 6307.452 Denmark. Statens Andssvageforsorg. Ti ars andssvageforsorg, 1, oktober, 1969. København, 1969.

6309 Psychology - Abnormal psychology - General treatises - Collected authors

Phil 6309.2 Massachusetts Commission on Lunacy. Insanity and idiocy in Massachusetts; report of the Commission on lunacy, 1855. Cambridge, 1971.
Phil 6309.4 Petrilowitsch, Nikolaus. Psychologie der abnormen Persönnlichkeiten. Darmstadt, 1968.
Phil 6309.6 Seelische Störungen. Frankfurt am Main, 1969.
Phil 6309.8 Psychoanalyse; zum 60. Geburtstag von Alexander Mitscherlich. Frankfurt am Main, 1968.

Phil 6310 - 6335 Psychology - Abnormal psychology - General treatises - Individual authors (A-Z)

Phil 6310.1 Adler, A. The neurotic constitution; individualistic psychology. N.Y., 1917.
Phil 6310.1.3 Adler, A. Problems of neurosis. London, 1930.
Phil 6310.1.5 Adler, A. The practice and theory of individual psychology. London, 1924.
Phil 6310.1.6 Adler, A. The practice and theory of individual psychology. N.Y., 1932.
Phil 6310.1.9 Adler, A. Praxis und Theorie der Individual-Psychologie. 2. Aufl. München, 1924.
Phil 6310.1.11 Adler, A. Die Technik der Individual-Psychologie. Teil 1-2. München, 1928-30.
Phil 6310.1.15 Adler, A. Die Theorie der Organminderwertigkeit. Leipzig, 1908.
Phil 6310.1.20 Adler, A. The science of living. Garden City, N.Y., 1929.
Phil 6310.1.21 Adler, A. The science of living. N.Y., 1929.
Phil 6310.1.22 Adler, A. Social interest. London, 1938.
Phil 6310.1.25A Adler, A. The case of Miss R. N.Y., 1929.
Phil 6310.1.25B Adler, A. The case of Miss R. N.Y., 1929.
Phil 6310.1.27A Adler, A. The individual psychology of Alfred Adler. 1st ed. N.Y., 1956.
Phil 6310.1.27C Adler, A. The individual psychology of Alfred Adler. 1st ed. N.Y., 1956.
Phil 6310.1.30 Adler, Gerhard. Entdeckung der Seele. Zürich, 1934.
Phil 6310.1.35 Adler, A. What life should mean to you. N.Y., 1931.
Phil 6310.1.36 Adler, A. What life should mean to you. Boston, 1931.
Phil 6310.1.37 Adler, Gerhard. Studies in analytical psychology. London, 1948.
Phil 6310.1.38 Adler, A. Der Sinn des Lebens. Wien, 1933.
Phil 6310.1.39 Adler, A. Heilen und Bilden. München, 1922.
Phil 6310.1.40 Adler, A. Heilen und Bilden. München, 1914.
Phil 6310.1.42 Adler, A. The problem child. N.Y., 1963.
Phil 6310.1.45 Adler, A. Superiority and social interest. Evanston, Ill., 1964.
Phil 6310.1.90 Ganz, M. La psychologie d'Alfred Adler. Neuchâtel, 1935.
Phil 6310.1.91 Ganz, M. Adlers psykologi. Stockholm, 1939.
Phil 6310.1.93 Orgler, Hertha. Alfred Adler, the man and his work. London, 1939.
Phil 6310.1.95 Oliver Brachfield, F. Les sentiments d'infériorité. Genève, 1945.
Phil 6310.1.98 Way, Lewis M. Alfred Adler. Harmondsworth, 1956.
Phil 6310.1.99 Rattner, J. Individualpsychologie. München, 1963.
Phil 6310.1.100 Orgler, Hertha. Alfred Adler. Wien, 1956.
Phil 6310.1.102 Internationale Vereinegung für Individualpsychologie, Vienna. Alfred Adler zum Gedenken. Wien, 1957.
Phil 6310.1.103 Orgler, Hertha. Alfred Adler, the man and his work. 3d ed. London, 1963.
Phil 6310.1.104 Selbsterziehung der charakters; Alfred Adler zum 60. geburtstage. Leipzig, 1930.
Phil 6310.1.106 Adler, Gerhard. The living symbol. N.Y., 1961.
Phil 6310.1.110 Sperker, Manès. Alfred Adler oder das Elénd der Psychologie. 1. Aufl. Wien, 1970.
Phil 6310.2.8 Abraham, Karl. Klinische Beitrage zur Psychoanalyse aus den Jahren 1907-1926. Leipzig, 1921.
Phil 6310.2.14 Abraham, Karl. Clinical papers and essays on psychoanalysis. London, 1955.
Phil 6310.2.16 Abraham, Karl. Psychoanalytische Studien zur Charakterbildung und andere Schriften. Frankfurt, 1969. 2v.
Phil 6310.3 Aster, E. Die Psychoanalyse. Berlin, 1930.
Phil 6310.4.4 Alexander, Franz G. Psychoanalyse der Gesamtpersönlichkeit. Leipzig, 1927.
Phil 6310.4.5 Alexander, Franz G. The psychoanalysis of the total personality. N.Y., 1930.
Phil 6310.4.9 Alexander, Franz G. Roots of crime. N.Y., 1935.
Phil 6310.4.10 Alexander, Franz G. The medical value of psychoanalysis. N.Y., 1936.
Phil 6310.4.15.5A Alexander, Franz G. Our age of unreason. Philadelphia, 1951.
Phil 6310.4.15.5B Alexander, Franz G. Our age of unreason. Philadelphia, 1951.
Phil 6310.4.20 Alexander, Franz G. Psychoanalytic threapy. N.Y., 1946.
Phil 6310.4.25 Alexander, Franz G. The western mind in transition. N.Y., 1960.
Phil 6310.4.30 Alexander, Franz G. The scope of psychoanalysis. N.Y., 1961.
Phil 6310.4.35 Alexander, Franz G. Psychoanalytic pioneers. N.Y., 1966.
Phil 6310.6 Adler, Alexandra. Guiding human misfits. N.Y., 1938.
Phil 6310.6.2 Adler, Alexandra. Guiding human misfits. N.Y., 1939.
Phil 6310.8 Bottome, P. Alfred Adler; a biography. N.Y., 1939.
Phil 6310.8.5 Bottome, P. Alfred Adler. 3rd ed. London, 1957.
Phil 6310.9 Allen, Frederick H. Psychotherapy with children. N.Y., 1942.
Phil 6310.10 Anthony, Joseph. The invisible curtain. N.Y., 1957.
Phil 6310.12 Anderson, C.M. Beyond Freud. London, 1958.
Phil 6310.14 Allwohn, Adolf. Das heilende Wort. Göttingen, 1958.
Phil 6310.16 Adler, Kurt. Essays in individual psychology. N.Y., 1959.
Phil 6310.18 Amidieu du Clos-Vinarie-Paule. Les interréactions des facteurs religieux et psychologiques en hygiène mentale. Thèse. Québec, 1958.
Phil 6310.20 American Psychopathological Association. Psychopathology of communication. N.Y., 1958.
Phil 6310.21 Angyal, András. Neurosis and treatment. N.Y., 1965.
Phil 6310.22 Axline, Virginia Mae. Dibs: in search of self. Boston, 1965.
Phil 6310.23 Abraham, Karl. On character and libido development. N.Y., 1966.
Phil 6311.1.2 Brill, A.A. Psychanalysis; its theories. Philadelphia, 1914.
Phil 6311.1.3 Brill, A.A. Psychanalysis. 2. ed. Philadelphia, 1917.
Phil 6311.1.5 Brill, A.A. Fundamental conceptions of psychoanalysis. N.Y., 1921.
Phil 6311.2 Bjerre, P. The history of psychanalysis. Boston, 1919.
Phil 6311.2.2 Bjerre, P. The history and practice of psychanalysis. Boston, 1920.
Phil 6311.2.5 Bjerre, P. Von der Psychoanalyse zur Psychosynthese. Halle, 1925.
Phil 6311.2.10 Bjerre, P. Wie deine Seele geheilt wird. Halle, 1925.
Phil 6311.3 Bridges, J.W. An outline of abnormal psychology. Columbus, 1919.
Phil 6311.3.2 Bridges, J.W. An outline of abnormal psychology. 2d ed. Columbus, 1921.
Phil 6311.3.3 Bridges, J.W. An outline of abnormal psychology. 3rd ed. Columbus, 1925.
Phil 6311.4.2 Brown, William. Psychological methods of healing. London, 1938.

Phil 6310 - 6335 Psychology - Abnormal psychology - General treatises - Individual authors (A-Z) - cont.

Phil 6311.5 Bousfield, Paul. The elements of practical psychoanalysis. London, 1920.
Phil 6311.5.5 Bousfield, Paul. The omnipotent self. London, 1923.
Phil 6311.6 Baudouin, C. Studies in psychoanalysis. London, 1922.
Phil 6311.6.5 Baudouin, C. Studies in psychoanalysis. N.Y., 1922.
Phil 6311.7 Bopp, L. Modern Psychoanalyse, katholische, beichte und pädagogik. Kempten, 1923.
Phil 6311.8 Blondel, C. La psychanalyse. Paris, 1924.
Phil 6311.9 Bohn, W. Ein Fall von doppeltem Bewusstsein. Inaug. Diss. Breslau, 1923.
Phil 6311.10 Birnbaum, Karl. Der Aufbau der Psychose. Berlin, 1923.
Phil 6311.10.15 Birnbaum, Karl. Handwörterbuch der medizinischen Psychologie. Leipzig, 1930.
Phil 6311.11 Boas, J.M. La défense psychique. Thèse. Paris, 1924.
Phil 6311.11.2 Boas, J.M. La défense psychique. Thèse. Paris, 1924.
Phil 6311.12 Baker, A.E. Psychoanalysis explained and criticized. London, 1926.
Phil 6311.13 Barbour, C.E. Sin and the new psychology. London, 1931.
Phil 6311.14 Bumke, Oswald. Die Psychoanalyse; eine Kritik. Berlin, 1931.
Phil 6311.15 Barrett, E.B. Absolution. London, 1932.
Phil 6311.16 Boven, William. L'anxiété. Neuchâtel, 1934.
Phil 6311.17 Bull, Titus. The imperative conquest. N.Y., 1936.
Phil 6311.18 Binet, Alfred. Les altérations de la personnalité. Paris, 1892.
Phil 6311.18.5 Binet, Alfred. Alteration of personality. N.Y., 1896.
Phil 6311.18.6 Binet, Alfred. Alterations of personality. London, 1896.
Phil 6311.19 Brown, William. Mind, medicine and metaphysics. London, 1936.
Phil 6311.20 Bisch, L.E. Be glad you're neurotic. N.Y., 1936.
Phil 6311.20.5 Bisch, L.E. Why be shy? N.Y., 1941.
Phil 6311.21 Bailey, Pearce. Diseases of the nervous system resulting from accident and injury. N.Y., 1906.
Phil 6311.22 Burrow, T. The biology of human conflict. N.Y., 1937.
Phil 6311.22.5 Burrow, T. Preconcious foundations of human experience. N.Y., 1964.
Phil 6311.23 Bluemel, C.S. The troubled mind. Baltimore, 1938.
Phil 6311.23.5 Bluemel, C.S. War, politics, and insanity. Denver, 1948.
Phil 6311.24 Barker, L.F. Psychotherapy. N.Y., 1940.
Phil 6311.26 Bergler, Edmund. Talleyrand, Napoleon, Stendhal, Grabbe, psychoanalytisch-biographishe essays. Wien, 1935.
Phil 6311.26.5 Bergler, Edmund. The superego. N.Y., 1952.
Phil 6311.27 Bowlby, John. Personality and mental illness, psychiatric diagnosis. N.Y., 1942.
Phil 6311.28 Bridger, A.E. Minds in distress. London, 1913.
Phil 6311.29 Buckley, James M. Faith-healing. N.Y., 1900.
Phil 6311.30.5 Berg, Charles. Deep analysis. 1st American ed. N.Y., 1947.
Phil 6311.31 Baynes, H. Analytical psychology and the English mind. London, 1950.
Phil 6311.32 Bonaventura, E. La psicoanalisi. 4. ed. Milano, 1950.
Phil 6311.33 Brierley, Marjorie Ellis. Trends in psycho-analysis. London, 1951.
Phil 6311.34 Bonaparte, Marie. Introduction à la théorie des instincts. 1. éd. Paris, 1951.
Phil 6311.34.5 Bonaparte, Marie. Psychanalyse et anthropologie. Paris, 1952.
Phil 6311.34.6 Bonaparte, Marie. Treis dialexeis eisagōgēs eis tēn psychanalēse. Athenai, 1950.
Phil 6311.34.10 Bonaparte, M. Psychanalyse et biologie. 1. éd. Paris, 1952.
Phil 6311.34.12 Bonaparte, Marie. Stratiotikoi kai koinōnikoi polemoi. Manchester, N.H., 1929.
Phil 6311.35 Baruk, Henri. La désorganisation de la personnalité. Paris, 1952.
Phil 6311.36 Balint, Michael. Primary love, and psycho-analytic technique. London, 1952.
Phil 6311.36.2 Balint, Michael. Primary love, and psycho-analytic technique. N.Y., 1965.
Phil 6311.37 Boss, Medard. Psychoanalyse und Daseinsanalytik. Bern, 1957.
Phil 6311.37.5 Boss, Medard. Psychoanalysis and daseinsanalysis. N.Y., 1963.
Phil 6311.38 Bertine, Eleanor. Menschliche Beziehungen. Zürich, 1957.
Phil 6311.39 Brown, Norman Oliver. Life against death. 1st ed. Middletown, Conn., 1959.
Phil 6311.40 Balint, Michael. Thrills and regressions. London, 1959.
Phil 6311.45 Burton, Arthur. Case studies in counseling and psychotherapy. Englewood Cliffs, N.J., 1959.
Phil 6311.46 Benoit, Hubert. Métaphysique et psychanalyse. 2. éd. Paris, 1964.
Phil 6311.47 Brown, Norman Oliver. Love's body. N.Y., 1966.
Phil 6311.48 Bachelard, Gaston. La psychanalyse du feu. Paris, 1965.
Phil 6311.52 Bouvet, Maurice. Oeuvres psychanalytiques. Paris, 1967-68. 2v.
Phil 6311.54 Becker, Raymond de. Bilan de la psychologie des profondeurs. Paris, 1968.
Phil 6311.56 Bodamer, Joachim. Der gefährdete Mensch. Freiburg, 1968.
Phil 6312.1 Coriat, I.H. Abnormal psychology. London, 1911.
Phil 6312.1.3 Coriat, I.H. Abnormal psychology. N.Y., 1910.
Phil 6312.1.5 Coriat, I.H. Abnormal psychology. 2. ed. N.Y., 1914.
Phil 6312.1.7 Coriat, I.H. Repressed emotions. N.Y., 1920.
Phil 6312.3 Culpin, Millais. Psychoneuroses of war and peace. Cambridge, Eng., 1920.
Phil 6312.4 Core, D.E. Functional nervous disorders. Bristol, 1922.
Phil 6312.5 Collins, J. Letters to a neurologist. 2nd series. N.Y., 1910.
Phil 6312.5.10 Collins, J. The doctor looks at life and death. N.Y., 1931.
Phil 6312.6 Crichton-Brown, J. The Cavendish lecture on dreamy mental states. London, 1895.
Phil 6312.7 Coster, Geraldine. Psycho-analysis for normal people. London, 1926.
Phil 6312.7.5 Coster, Geraldine. Psycho-analysis for normal people. 3. ed. N.Y., 1932.
Phil 6312.10 Chicago. Institute for Psychoanalysis. Five-year report. Chicago, 1937. 2v.
Phil 6312.11.5 Cameron, Donald E. Objective and experimental psychiatry. 2. ed. N.Y., 1941.
Phil 6312.12 Cobb, S. Borderlands of psychiatry. Cambridge, 1943.
Phil 6312.13 Cebola, Luiz. As grandes crises do homen ensaio de psicopatologia individual e colectiva. Lisboa, 1945.
Phil 6312.14 Clerambault, G.G. Oeuvre psychiatrique. v.1-2. Paris, 1942. 2v.
Phil 6312.15 Geikie Cobb, W.J. Spiritual healing. London, 1914.

Phil 6310 - 6335 Psychology - Abnormal psychology - General treatises - Individual authors (A-Z) - cont.

Phil 6312.16 Cameron, N. The psychology of behavior disorders. Boston, 1947.
Phil 6312.16.5 Cameron, N. Personality development and psychopathology. Boston, 1963.
Phil 6312.17 Crow, Lester D. Understanding our behavior. 1st ed. N.Y., 1956.
Phil 6312.18 Corsini, R.J. Methods of group psychotherapy. N.Y., 1957.
Phil 6312.20 Caruso, Igor A. Bios, Psyche, Person. Freiburg, 1957.
Phil 6312.20.5 Caruso, Igor A. Existential psychology. N.Y., 1964.
Phil 6312.22 Cain, Jacques. Le problème des névroses experimentales. Paris, 1959.
Phil 6312.24 Cattell, Raymond. The meaning and measurement of neuroticism and anxiety. N.Y., 1961.
Phil 6312.25 Columbia. University. Psychoanalytic Clinic for Training and Reaserch. New perspectives in psychoanalysis. N.Y., 1965.
Phil 6312.28 Carp, Eugène Antoine Desiré Émile. De dubbelganger. Utrecht, 1964.
Phil 6312.30 Centro di Studi Filosofici di Gallarate. Psicanalisi e filosofia. Padova, 1968.
Phil 6312.32 Choisy, Maryse. Mais la terre est sacrée. Genève, 1968.
Phil 6313.1 Delbrück, A. Gerichtliche psychopathologie. Leipzig, 1897.
Phil 6313.1.5 Delbrück, A. Die pathologische Lüge und die psychisch abnormen Schwindler. Stuttgart, 1891.
Phil 6313.2 Durand, J.P. Le merveilleux scientifique. Paris, 1894.
Phil 6313.3 Dubois, Paul. Les psychonévroses et leur traitement moral. 3e éd. Paris, 1909.
Phil 6313.4.3 Dessoir, Max. Vom Jenseits der Seele. 3. Aufl. Stuttgart, 1919.
Phil 6313.5 Dunlap, K. Mysticism, Freudianism and scientific psychology. St. Louis, 1920. 2v.
Phil 6313.6 Deschamps, Albert. Les maladies de l'esprit et les asthénies. Paris, 1919.
Phil 6313.7 Delmas, F. Achille. La personalité humaine. Paris, 1925.
Phil 6313.8 Deutsch, Helene. Psycho-analysis of the neuroses. London, 1932.
Phil 6313.8.5 Deutsch, Helene. Psychoanalyse der Neurosen. Wien, 1930.
Phil 6313.8.10 Deutsch, Helene. Neuroses and character types. London, 1965.
Phil 6313.9 Dorer, M. Historische Grundlagen der Psychoanalyse. Leipzig, 1932.
Phil 6313.10 Dorcus, Roy M. Textbook of abnormal psychology. Baltimore, 1934.
Phil 6313.10.2 Dorcus, Roy M. Textbook of abnormal psychology. 2d ed. Baltimore, 1944.
Phil 6313.11 Drake, R.M. Outline of abnormal psychology. N.Y., 1936.
Phil 6313.12 Dupré, E. Pathologie de l'imagination et de l'émotivité. Paris, 1925.
Phil 6313.13 Dicks, H.V. Clinical studies in psychopathology. London, 1939.
Phil 6313.14 Deutsch, Felix. The clinical interview. v.1-2. N.Y., 1955. 2v.
Phil 6313.14.5 Deutsch, Felix. Applied psychoanalysis. N.Y., 1949.
Phil 6313.15 De Mille, A. Introduction to scientology. 2d ed. Los Angeles, 1953.
Phil 6313.16 Dempsey, P.J.R. Freud. Cork, 1956.
Phil 6313.17 Dignwall, E.J. Very peculiar people. London, 1950.
Phil 6313.18 Deshaies, Gabriel. Psychopathologie générale. Paris, 1959.
Phil 6313.20 Dallard, John. Personality and psychotherapy. 1st ed. N.Y., 1950.
Phil 6313.22 Dieren, E. van. Professor Freud. Baarn, 1932.
Phil 6313.23 David, H.P. International resources in clinical psychology. N.Y., 1964.
Phil 6313.24 Dorsey, John Morris. Illness or allness; conversations of a psychiatrist. Detroit, 1965.
Phil 6313.25 Dienelt, Karl. Von Freud zu Frankel. Wien, 1967.
Phil 6313.26 Dejung, Beat. Regressionen im Verhalten des Menschen. Zürich, 1967.
Phil 6314.1 Emerson, L.E. Nervousness; its causes, treatment and prevention. Boston, 1918.
Phil 6314.3 Elam, C. A physician's problems. London, 1869.
Phil 6314.3.2 Elam, C. A physician's problems. Boston, 1869.
Phil 6314.4 Edson, D.O. Getting what we want. N.Y., 1921.
Phil 6314.5 Egyedi, H. Die Irrtümer der Psychoanalyse. Wien, 1933.
Phil 6314.6 Ebaugh, Franklin Gessford. Psychiatry in medical education. N.Y., 1942.
Phil 6314.7 English, Oliver Spurgeon. Common neuroses of children and adults. N.Y., 1937.
Phil 6314.7.4 English, Oliver Spurgeon. Emotional problems of living. N.Y., 1945.
Phil 6314.7.5 English, Oliver Spurgeon. Emotional problems of living. N.Y., 1955.
Phil 6314.8 Hobman, J.B. David Eder; memoirs of a modern pioneer. London, 1945.
Phil 6314.9 Eidelberg, L. Take off your mask. N.Y., 1948.
Phil 6314.10 Evans, Jean. Three men. 1st ed. N.Y., 1954.
Phil 6314.11 Eysenck, Hans J. Behaviour therapy and the neuroses. Oxford, 1960.
Phil 6314.11.5 Eysenck, Hans J. Handbook of abnormal psychology. N.Y., 1961.
Phil 6314.11.10 Eysenck, Hans J. The causes and cures of neurosis. London, 1965.
Phil 6314.12 Erikson, Eric H. Insight and responsibility. N.Y., 1964.
Phil 6314.12.5A Erikson, Eric H. Identity; youth and crisis. 1st ed. N.Y., 1868.
Phil 6314.12.5B Erikson, Eric H. Identity; youth and crisis. 1st ed. N.Y., 1968.
Phil 6315.1 Ferenczi, Sandor. Contributions to psycho-analysis. Boston, 1916.
Phil 6315.1.5 Ferenczi, Sandor. Psycho-analysis and the war neurosis. Photoreproduction. London, 1921.
Phil 6315.1.7 Ferenczi, Sandor. Versuch einer Genitaltheorie. Leipzig, 1924.
Phil 6315.1.10 Ferenczi, Sandor. Sex in psychoanalysis. N.Y., 1950.
Phil 6315.1.13 Ferenczi, Sandor. Further contributions to the theory and technique of psycho-analysis. N.Y., 1927.
Phil 6315.1.14 De Forest, Izette. The leaven of love. London, 1926.
Phil 6315.1.15 Ferenczi, Sandor. Final contributions to the problems and methods of psychoanalysis. London, 1955.
Phil 6315.1.16 Ferenczi, Sandor. Bausteine zur Psychoanalyse. Leipzig, 1927-39. 4v.
Phil 6315.1.17 Ferenczi, Sandor. The development of psychoanalysis. N.Y., 1925.

Phil 6310 - 6335   Psychology - Abnormal psychology - General treatises - Individual authors (A-Z) - cont.

Phil 6315.1.18A   Ferenczi, Sandor. First contributions to psychoanalysis. London, 1952.
Phil 6315.1.18B   Ferenczi, Sandor. First contributions to psychoanalysis. London, 1952.
Phil 6315.1.20   Ferenczi, Sandor. Populäre vorträge über Psychoanalyse. Leipzig, 1922.
Phil 6315.1.80   De Forest, Izette. The leaven of love. Hamden, Conn., 1954.
Phil 6315.2   Freud, Sigmund. Gesammelte Werke. v. 1-14,16-18. London, 1940-46. 16v.
Phil 6315.2.2   Freud, Sigmund. Gesammelte Schriften. Leipzig, 1924-34. 12v.
Htn   Phil 6315.2.3*   Zur Geschichte der psychoanalytischen Bewegung. Leipzig, 1924.
Phil 6315.2.3.5   Freud, Sigmund. History of the psychoanalytic movement. N.Y., 1917.
Phil 6315.2.3.10A   Freud, Sigmund. The standard edition of the complete psychological works. v.1-20,22-23. London, 1953-64. 22v.
Phil 6315.2.3.10B   Freud, Sigmund. The standard edition of the complete psychological works. London, 1953-64. 23v.
Phil 6315.2.4A   Freud, Sigmund. Über Psychoanalyse. 5e Aufl. Leipzig, 1920.
Phil 6315.2.4B   Freud, Sigmund. Über Psychoanalyse. 5e Aufl. Leipzig, 1920.
Htn   Phil 6315.2.4.5*   Freud, Sigmund. Über Psychoanalyse. Leipzig, 1910.
Phil 6315.2.5B   Freud, Sigmund. General introduction to psychoanalysis. N.Y., 1920.
Phil 6315.2.5.5   Freud, Sigmund. A general introduction to psycho-analysis. N.Y., 1935.
Phil 6315.2.5.6A   Freud, Sigmund. A general introduction to psycho-analysis. Garden City, 1938.
Phil 6315.2.5.6B   Freud, Sigmund. A general introduction to psycho-analysis. Garden City, 1938.
Phil 6315.2.5.7   Freud, Sigmund. A general introduction to psycho-analysis. N.Y., 1937.
Phil 6315.2.6   Freud, Sigmund. Introductory lecture on psycho-analysis. London, 1922.
Phil 6315.2.6.5   Freud, Sigmund. Über Psychoanalyse. 6e Aufl. Leipzig, 1922.
Phil 6315.2.6.10   Freud, Sigmund. Über Psychoanalyse. 2e Aufl. Leipzig, 1912.
Phil 6315.2.7   Freud, Sigmund. Über Psychoanalyse. 7e Aufl. Leipzig, 1924.
Phil 6315.2.7.5   Freud, Sigmund. Über Psychoanalyse. 9e Aufl. Wien, 1946.
Phil 6315.2.8   Freud, Sigmund. Over psychoanalyse. Leiden, 1912.
Phil 6315.2.8.20   Freud, Sigmund. An outline of psychoanalysis. 1st. ed. N.Y., 1949.
Phil 6315.2.8.30A   Freud, Sigmund. Collected papers. London, 1949. 5v.
Phil 6315.2.8.30B   Freud, Sigmund. Collected papers. v.2. v.5 lost. London, 1949.
Phil 6315.2.8.31   Freud, Sigmund. Collected papers. N.Y., 1959. 5v.
Phil 6315.2.8.40A   Freud, Sigmund. Aus den Anfänger der Psychoanalyse. London, 1950.
Phil 6315.2.8.40B   Freud, Sigmund. Aus den Anfänger der Psychoanalyse. London, 1950.
Phil 6315.2.9   Freud, Sigmund. Cinq leçons sur la psychoanalyse. Paris, 1923.
Phil 6315.2.9.10   Freud, Sigmund. Vorlesungen zur Einführung. 2. Aufl. Leipzig, 1918.
Phil 6315.2.10A   Freud, Sigmund. Vorlesungen zur Einführung in die Psychoanalyse. 2. Aufl. Leipzig, 1922.
Phil 6315.2.10B   Freud, Sigmund. Vorlesungen zur Einführung in die Psychoanalyse. 2. Aufl. Leipzig, 1922.
Phil 6315.2.10.5A   Freud, Sigmund. Vorlesungen zur Einführung in die Psychoanalyse. 4. Aufl. Leipzig, 1922.
Phil 6315.2.10.5B   Freud, Sigmund. Vorlesungen zur Einführung in die Psychoanalyse. 4. Aufl. Leipzig, 1922.
Phil 6315.2.10.10   Freud, Sigmund. Vorlesungen zur Einführung in die Psychoanalyse. Berlin, 1933.
Phil 6315.2.12   Freud, Sigmund. The origin and development of psychoanalysis. Chicago, 1955.
Phil 6315.2.14   Freud, Sigmund. Das Unbewusste. Frankfurt, 1960.
Phil 6315.2.18   Freud, Sigmund. Studien zur Psychoanalyse der Neurosen aus den Jahren 1913-25. Wien, 1926.
Cg   Phil 6315.2.19   Freud, Sigmund. Selected papers on hysteria and other psychoneuroses. N.Y., 1912.
Phil 6315.2.20*   Freud, Sigmund. Sammlung kleiner Schriften zur Neurosenlehre. 2e, 4e, 5e Folge. Leipzig, 1909-22. 3v.
Phil 6315.2.20.5   Freud, Sigmund. Sammlung kleiner Schriften zur Neurosenlehre aus den Jahren 1893-1906. 2. Aufl. 1e, 2e Folge. Leipzig, 1911-21. 2v.
Phil 6315.2.20.7   Freud, Sigmund. Sammlung kleiner Schriften. 3. Aufl. 1e, 2e Folge. Leipzig, 1920-21. 2v.
Phil 6315.2.20.15   Freud, Sigmund. On war, sex and neurosis. N.Y., 1947.
Phil 6315.2.21   Freud, Sigmund. On creativity and the unconscious. N.Y., 1958.
Phil 6315.2.22   Freud, Sigmund. New introductory lectures on psycho-analysis. N.Y., 1964.
Phil 6315.2.24B   Freud, Sigmund. New introductory lectures on psycho-analysis. N.Y., 1933.
Phil 6315.2.24C   Freud, Sigmund. New introductory lectures on psycho-analysis. N.Y., 1933.
Phil 6315.2.25   Freud, Sigmund. Reflections on war and death. N.Y., 1918.
Phil 6315.2.26   Freud, Sigmund. Briefwechsel. Frankfurt, 1968.
Phil 6315.2.26.5   Freud, Sigmund. The letters of Sigmund Freud and Arnold Zweig. N.Y., 1970.
Phil 6315.2.26.6   Freud, Sigmund. The letters of Sigmund Freud and Arnold Zweig. London, 1970.
Phil 6315.2.28   Freud, Sigmund. A psycho-analytic dialogue. London, 1965.
Phil 6315.2.29   Freud, Sigmund. Essais de psychanalyse. Paris, 1948.
Phil 6315.2.33   Freud, Sigmund. Psychopathology of everyday life. London, 1914.
Phil 6315.2.33.5   Freud, Sigmund. Psychopathology of everyday life. London, 1917.
Phil 6315.2.33.6   Freud, Sigmund. Psychopathology of everyday life. N.Y., 1917.
Phil 6315.2.33.8   Freud, Sigmund. The psychopathology of everyday life. N.Y., 1966.
Phil 6315.2.34   Freud, Sigmund. Collected papers. London, 1957-69. 4v.
Phil 6315.2.35   Freud, Sigmund. Collected papers. N.Y., 1924-5.
Phil 6315.2.36   Freud, Sigmund. A general selection from the works of Sigmund Freud. London, 1937.
Phil 6315.2.37.1   Freud, Sigmund. The ego and the id. N.Y., 1961.
Phil 6315.2.37.3   Freud, Sigmund. The ego and the id. London, 1950.
Phil 6315.2.37.4   Freud, Sigmund. The ego and the id. London, 1957.

Phil 6310 - 6335   Psychology - Abnormal psychology - General treatises - Individual authors (A-Z) - cont.

Phil 6315.2.37.5   Freud, Sigmund. Das Ich und das Es. Leipzig, 1923.
Phil 6315.2.37.6   Freud, Sigmund. The ego and the id. N.Y., 1962.
Phil 6315.2.38   Freud, Sigmund. A general selection from the works of Sigmund Freud. N.Y., 1957.
Phil 6315.2.40   Freud, Sigmund. Studienausgabe. v.1,4,6,8,10. Frankfurt, 1969. 6v.
Phil 6315.2.42.5A   Freud, Sigmund. Inhibitions, symptoms and anxiety. London, 1961.
Phil 6315.2.42.5B   Freud, Sigmund. Inhibitions, symptoms and anxiety. London, 1961.
Phil 6315.2.42.5C   Freud, Sigmund. Inhibitions, symptoms and anxiety. London, 1961.
Phil 6315.2.43A   Freud, Sigmund. The problem of anxiety. N.Y., 1936.
Phil 6315.2.43B   Freud, Sigmund. The problem of anxiety. N.Y., 1936.
Phil 6315.2.44   Freud, Sigmund. Massenpsychologie und Ich-Analyse. Leipzig, 1921.
Phil 6315.2.45   Freud, Sigmund. The psychologie collective et analyse du moi. Paris, 1924.
Phil 6315.2.46A   Freud, Sigmund. The problem of lay analysis. N.Y., 1927.
Phil 6315.2.46B   Freud, Sigmund. The problem of lay analysis. N.Y., 1927.
Phil 6315.2.46.10   Freud, Sigmund. The question of lay analysis. 1. ed. N.Y., 1950.
Phil 6315.2.47   Freud, Sigmund. Die Frage der Laienanalyse. Wien, 1926.
Phil 6315.2.51   Freud, Sigmund. Civilization and its discontents. N.Y., 1930.
Phil 6315.2.51.5A   Freud, Sigmund. Civilization and its discontents. N.Y., 1962.
Phil 6315.2.51.5B   Freud, Sigmund. Civilization and its discontents. N.Y., 1962.
Phil 6315.2.52   Freud, Sigmund. The living thoughts of Freud. N.Y., 1941.
Phil 6315.2.53   Freud, Sigmund. The basic writings of Sigmund Freud. N.Y., 1938. 3v.
Phil 6315.2.56   Freud, Sigmund. On the history of the psychoanalytic movement. N.Y., 1966.
Phil 6315.2.57   Freud, Sigmund. Psychoanalysis and faith. London, 1963.
Phil 6315.2.57.1   Freud, Sigmund. Psychoanalysis and faith. N.Y., 1964.
Phil 6315.2.58   Freud, Sigmund. Schriften aus dem Nachlass 1892-1938. London, 1941.
Phil 6315.2.59.3   Freud, Sigmund. Jenseits des Lustprinzips. 3. Aufl. Leipzig, 1923.
Phil 6315.2.59.10   Freud, Sigmund. Beyond the pleasure principle. N.Y., 1950.
Htn   Phil 6315.2.60*   Freud, Sigmund. Hemmung, Symptom und Angst. Leipzig, 1926.
Htn   Phil 6315.2.61*   Freud, Sigmund. Die Zukunft einer Illusion. Wien, 1927.
Phil 6315.2.62.5   Freud, Sigmund. Delusion and dream. N.Y., 1917.
Phil 6315.2.62.7   Freud, Sigmund. Delusion and dream, and other essays. Boston, 1968.
Phil 6315.2.62.10   Freud, Sigmund. Délire et rêves dans la "gradiva" de Jenson. 8. éd. Paris, 1949.
Phil 6315.2.62.15A   Freud, Sigmund. Dreams in folklore. N.Y., 1958.
Phil 6315.2.62.15B   Freud, Sigmund. Dreams in folklore. N.Y., 1958.
Phil 6315.2.64   Freud, Sigmund. Das Unbehagen in der Kultur. Wien, 1931.
Htn   Phil 6315.2.64.1*   Freud, Sigmund. Das Unbehagen in der Kultur. Wien, 1930.
Phil 6315.2.65   Freud, Sigmund. Vier psychoanalytische Krankengeschichten. Wien, 1932.
Phil 6315.2.66   Freud, Sigmund. Briefe 1873-1939. Frankfurt, 1960.
Phil 6315.2.66.5   Freud, Sigmund. Briefe 1909-39. Frankfurt, 1963.
Phil 6315.2.66.10   Freud, Sigmund. Briefe 1873-1939. 2. Aufl. Frankfurt, 1968.
Phil 6315.2.67   Freud, Sigmund. Letters. 1st. ed. N.Y., 1960.
Phil 6315.2.68   Freud, Sigmund. Group psychology and the analysis of the ego. N.Y., 192-?
Phil 6315.2.68.5A   Freud, Sigmund. Group psychology and the analysis of the ego. N.Y., 1967.
Phil 6315.2.68.5B   Freud, Sigmund. Group psychology and the analysis of the ego. N.Y., 1967.
Phil 6315.2.69   Freud, Sigmund. Briefe 1907-1926. Sigmund Freud and Karl Abraham. Frankfurt, 1965.
Phil 6315.2.70   Freud, Sigmund. Beyond the pleasure principle. N.Y., 1924.
Phil 6315.2.72   Freud, Sigmund. Selbstdarstellung. London, 1946.
Phil 6315.2.72.5   Freud, Sigmund. Selbstdarstellung. 2. Aufl. Wien, 1936.
Phil 6315.2.73   Freud, Sigmund. Ma vie et la psychanalyse. 23. éd. Paris, 1949.
Htn   Phil 6315.2.74*   Freud, Sigmund. Aus der Geschichte einer infantilen Neurose. Leipzig, 1924.
Phil 6315.2.75.8   Freud, Sigmund. Drei Abhandlungen zur Sexualtheorie. Leipzig, 1910.
Phil 6315.2.75.10   Freud, Sigmund. Drei Abhandlungen zur Sexualtheorie. 7. Aufl. Wien, 1946.
Phil 6315.2.75.11   Freud, Sigmund. Trois essais sur la théorie de le sexualité. 23e éd. Paris, 1925.
Phil 6315.2.75.12   Freud, Sigmund. Trois essais sur la théorie de la sexualité. 51. éd. Paris, 1949.
Phil 6315.2.75.14   Freud, Sigmund. Three contributions to the theory of sex. 4th ed. N.Y., 1948.
Phil 6315.2.75.15   Freud, Sigmund. Three essays on the theory of sexuality. 1st English ed. London, 1949.
Phil 6315.2.75.17   Freud, Sigmund. Three essays on the theory of sexuality. London, 1962.
Htn   Phil 6315.2.76*   Freud, Sigmund. Zeitgemässes über Krieg und Tod. Leipzig, 1924.
Htn   Phil 6315.2.77*   Pamphlet vol. Studies by Freud. 3 pam.
Phil 6315.2.78   Freud, Sigmund. Dictionary of psychoanalysis. N.Y., 1950.
Phil 6315.2.79   Freud, Sigmund. An autobiographical study. London, 1935.
Phil 6315.2.79.5   Freud, Sigmund. An autobiographical study. 2d ed. London, 1946.
Phil 6315.2.79.10   Freud, Sigmund. Moïse et la monothéisme. 8 éd. Paris, 1948.
Phil 6315.2.79.15   Freud, Sigmund. On aphasia. London, 1953.
Phil 6315.2.79.20A   Freud, Sigmund. The origins of psycho-analysis. 1st ed. N.Y., 1954.
Phil 6315.2.79.20B   Freud, Sigmund. The origins of psycho-analysis. 1st ed. N.Y., 1954.
Phil 6315.2.79.25   Freud, Sigmund. Psychanalyse. 2. éd. Paris, 1965.
Phil 6315.2.79.30   Freud, Sigmund. Brautbriefe. Frankfurt, 1968.
Phil 6315.2.80   Pamphlet box. Freud, Sigmund.
Phil 6315.2.81   Tannenbaum, S.A. The psychology of accidents and "symtomatic actions". N.Y., 1924.
Phil 6315.2.82   Hesmard, Angelo. La psychanalyse; theorie sexuelle de Freud. Paris, 1924.

Classified Listing

Phil 6310 - 6335   Psychology - Abnormal psychology - General treatises -
Individual authors (A-Z) - cont.

Phil 6315.2.82.10   Hesnard, Angelo. Freud dans la société d'après guerre. Genève, 1946.
Phil 6315.2.82.15   Hesnard, Angelo. De Freud à Lacan. Paris, 1970.
Phil 6315.2.83   Schultze, J.H. Sigmund Freud's Sexualpsychoanalyse. Berlin, 1917.
Phil 6315.2.85   Hermann, István. Sigmund Freud. Budapest, 1964.
Phil 6315.2.86   Schmidt, Wilhelm. Der Ödipus-Komplex der Freudschen Psychoanalyse. Berlin, 1929.
Phil 6315.2.87   Wittels, Fritz. Sigmund Freud. N.Y., 1924.
Phil 6315.2.88   Wittels, Fritz. Freud and his time. N.Y., 1931.
Phil 6315.2.88.3   Wittels, Fritz. Freud and his time. N.Y., 1931.
Phil 6315.2.89   Bonsfield, William A. A neglected complex and its relation to Freudian psychology. London, 1924.
Phil 6315.2.90.2   Hitschmann, Eduard. Freud's Neurosenlehre. 2. Aufl. Leipzig, 1913.
Phil 6315.2.90.5   Hitschmann, Eduard. Freud's theories of the neuroses. N.Y., 1913.
Phil 6315.2.90.6   Hitschmann, Eduard. Freud's theories of the neuroses. N.Y., 1913.
Phil 6315.2.91   Laumonier, J. Le freudisme; exposé et critique. Paris, 1925.
Phil 6315.2.93   Michaëlis, Edgar. Die Menschkeitsproblematik der Freudschen Psychoanalyse. Leipzig, 1925.
Phil 6315.2.94   Michaëlis, Edgar. Die Menschkeitsproblematik der Freudschen Psychoanalyse. 2. Aufl. Leipzig, 1931.
Phil 6315.2.95   Bodin, Jean. Contre Freud. Paris, 1926.
Phil 6315.2.96   Delgado, H. Sigmund Freud. Lima, 1926.
Phil 6315.2.99   Maylan, Charles E. Freuds tragischer Komplex. 2e Aufl. München, 1929.
Phil 6315.2.101A   Jastrow, Joseph. The house that Freud built. N.Y., 1932.
Phil 6315.2.101B   Jastrow, Joseph. The house that Freud built. N.Y., 1932.
Phil 6315.2.103   Schelts van Kloosterhuis, E. Freud als ethnoloog. Proefschrift. Amsterdam, 1933.
Phil 6315.2.107   Roback, A.A. Freudiana. n.p., n.d. 3 pam.
Phil 6315.2.109   McDougall, William. Psycho-analysis and social psychology. London, 1936.
Phil 6315.2.111   Dalbiez, R. La méthode psychanalytique et la doctrine freudienne. v.1-2. Thèse. Paris, 1936.
Phil 6315.2.111.5   Dalbiez, R. Psychoanalytical method and the doctrine of Freud. v.1. v.2 lost. N.Y., 1941.
Phil 6315.2.112   Bartlett, Francis H. Sigmund Freud. Photoreproduction. London, 1938.
Phil 6315.2.113.2   Freud, Sigmund. Civilisation. London, 1953.
Phil 6315.2.114   Allers, R. The successful error; a critical study of Freudian psychoanalysis. N.Y., 1940.
Phil 6315.2.115A   Reik, Theodor. From thirty years with Freud. N.Y., 1940.
Phil 6315.2.115B   Reik, Theodor. From thirty years with Freud. N.Y., 1940.
Phil 6315.2.115.5   Reik, Theodor. Freud als Kulturkritiker. Mit einem Briefe S. Freuds. Wien, 1930.
Phil 6315.2.116   Seguin, C.A. Freud, un gran explorador del alma. Buenos Aires, 1940.
Phil 6315.2.118   Andreas-Salomé, L. Mein Dank an Freud; offener Brief an S. Freud zu seinem 75. Geburtstag. Wien, 1931.
Phil 6315.2.120   Castellano, Filemón. El psicoanalisis de Freud. Buenos Aires, 1941.
Phil 6315.2.122   Sears, R.R. Survey of objective studies of psychoanalytic concepts. N.Y., 1942.
Phil 6315.2.124   Brill, A.A. Freud's contribution to psychiatry. N.Y., 1944.
Phil 6315.2.127A   Sacho, H. Freud, master and friend. Cambridge, Mass., 1944.
Phil 6315.2.127B   Sacho, H. Freud, master and friend. Cambridge, Mass., 1944.
Phil 6315.2.129   Cové, M. L'oeuvre paradoxale de Freud. 1. éd. Paris, 1945.
Phil 6315.2.131   Ludwig, Emil. Der entzauberte Freud. 9. Aufl. Zürich, 1946.
Phil 6315.2.132   Ludwig, Emil. Doctor Freud. N.Y., 1947.
Phil 6315.2.134   Pruner, Helen W. Freud, his life and his mind. N.Y., 1947.
Phil 6315.2.136   Hollitscher, W. Sigmund Freud; an introduction. London, 1947.
Phil 6315.2.138   Hollitscher, W. Sigmund Freud; an introduction. N.Y., 1947.
Phil 6315.2.140   Pesch, Edgar. La pensée de Freud et la psychanalyse. Paris, 1946.
Phil 6315.2.140.5   Pesch, Edgar. La pensée de Freud. Paris, 1960.
Phil 6315.2.140.8   Pesch, Edgar. Pour connaître la pensée de Freud. Évreux, 1970.
Phil 6315.2.141A   Glover, E. Freud or Jung. N.Y., 1950.
Phil 6315.2.141B   Glover, E. Freud or Jung. N.Y., 1950.
Phil 6315.2.142   Glover, E. Freud or Jung. London, 1950.
Phil 6315.2.144   Carlemans, A. Development of Freud's conception of anxiety. Amsterdam, 1949.
Phil 6315.2.146   Zilboorg, G. Sigmund Freud. N.Y., 1951.
Phil 6315.2.146.5   Zilboorg, G. Freud - 1956. N.Y., 1956.
Phil 6315.2.148   Spehlmann, Rainer. Sigmund Freuds neurologische Schriften. Berlin, 1953.
Phil 6315.2.150A   Jones, Ernest. The life and work of Sigmund Freud. 1st ed. N.Y., 1953. 3v.
Phil 6315.2.150B   Jones, Ernest. The life and work of Sigmund Freud. 1st ed. v.1-2. N.Y., 1953. 2v.
Phil 6315.2.151   Jones, Ernest. The life and work of Sigmund Freud. London, 1961.
Phil 6315.2.152   Wortis, J. Fragments of an analysis with Freud. N.Y., 1954.
Phil 6315.2.155   Natenberg, M. The case history of Sigmund Freud. 1. ed. Chicago, 1955.
Phil 6315.2.157A   Trilling, L. Freud and the crisis of our culture. Boston, 1955.
Phil 6315.2.157B   Trilling, L. Freud and the crisis of our culture. Boston, 1955.
Phil 6315.2.160   Schoenwald, R.L. Freud. 1st ed. N.Y., 1956.
Phil 6315.2.165   Aldington, H.D. Tribute to Freud. N.Y., 1956.
Phil 6315.2.170   Mette, Alexander. Sigmund Freud. Berlin, 1956.
Phil 6315.2.170.3   Mette, Alexandre. Sigmund Freud. 3. Aufl. Berlin, 1958.
Phil 6315.2.175   Philp, Howard Littleton. Freud and religious belief. London, 1956.
Phil 6315.2.180   Marcuse, L. Sigmund Freud. Hamburg, 1956.
Phil 6315.2.185   Roback, A.A. Freudiana. Cambridge, Mass., 1957.
Phil 6315.2.190   Riemann, Fritz. Lebendige Psychoanalyse. München, 1956.
Phil 6315.2.195   Guatemala (city). Universidad Nacional. Primer centenario del racimiento. Guatemala, 1956.
Phil 6315.2.200   Casa de Cultura Ecuatoriana. Sigmund Freud; homenaje. Cuenca, 1956.
Phil 6315.2.205   Freud in der Gegenwart. Frankfurt, 1957.

Phil 6310 - 6335   Psychology - Abnormal psychology - General treatises -
Individual authors (A-Z) - cont.

Phil 6315.2.210   Freud, Martin. Glory reflected. London, 1957.
Phil 6315.2.215   Relgis, Eugen. Freud, Freudismo y las verdades sociales [a las cieñanos de su nacimiento, 6 de mayo, 1856-1956]. Montevideo, 1956.
Phil 6315.2.220A   Nelson, B.N. Freud and the 20th century. N.Y., 1958.
Phil 6315.2.220B   Nelson, B.N. Freud and the 20th century. N.Y., 1958.
Phil 6315.2.225A   Binswanger, Ludwig. Sigmund Freud. N.Y., 1957.
Phil 6315.2.225B   Binswanger, Ludwig. Sigmund Freud. N.Y., 1957.
Phil 6315.2.226   Binswanger, Ludwig. Erinnerungen an Sigmund Freud. Bern, 1956.
Phil 6315.2.230   Bakan, David. Sigmund Freud and the Jewish mystical tradition. Princeton, N.J., 1958.
Phil 6315.2.235A   Fromm, Erich. Sigmund Freud's mission. 1st ed. N.Y., 1959.
Phil 6315.2.235B   Fromm, Erich. Sigmund Freud's mission. 1st ed. N.Y., 1959.
Phil 6315.2.240   Rieff, Philip. Freud; the mind of the moralist. N.Y., 1959.
Phil 6315.2.245   Loewenstein, Rudolph Maurice. Freud. N.Y., 1951.
Phil 6315.2.250   Revue Francaise de Psychanalyse. Hommage à Sigmund Freud. Paris, 1956.
Phil 6315.2.255   Stoodley, Bartlett. The concepts of Sigmund Freud. Glencoe, 1959.
Phil 6315.2.260   Anzieu, Didier. L'auto-analyse. Paris, 1959.
Phil 6315.2.265   Gicklhorn, Josef. Sigmund Freuds akademische Laufbahn im. Wien, 1960.
Phil 6315.2.270   Bally, Gustav. Einführung in die Psychanalyse Sigmund Freuds. Hamburg, 1961.
Phil 6315.2.275   Vennes, Gaston. Inconscient freudien et problèmes de liberté. Trois Rivières, 1960.
Phil 6315.2.280   Madison, P. Freud's concept of repression and defense, its theoretical and observational language. Minneapolis, 1961.
Phil 6315.2.285   Brown, J.A.C. Freud and the post-Freudians. Baltimore, 1961.
Phil 6315.2.290F   Bentz, Hans Willi. Sigmund Freud in Übersetzungen. Frankfurt, 1961.
Phil 6315.2.295   Mikhailov, Feliks T. Za porogom soznaniia; kriticheskii ocherk freidizma. Moskva, 1961.
Phil 6315.2.300   Choisy, Maryse. Sigmund Freud. N.Y., 1963.
Phil 6315.2.305   Arlow, J.A. The legacy of Sigmund Freud. N.Y., 1956.
Phil 6315.2.310.3   Marcuse, Herbert. Eros and civilization. N.Y., 1962.
Phil 6315.2.310.5   Marcuse, Herbert. Eros and civilization; a philosophical inquiry into Freud. Boston, 1966.
Phil 6315.2.310.10   Marcuse, Herbert. Eros et civilization. Paris, 1963.
Phil 6315.2.315   Koenig, K. Die Schicksale Sigmund Freuds und J. Breners. Stuttgart, 1962.
Phil 6315.2.325   Kronfeld, A. Über die psychologischen Theorien Freuds und verwandte Anschauungen. Leipzig, 1912.
Phil 6315.2.330   Spengler, Ernst. Das Gewissen bei Freud und Jung. Zürich, 1964.
Phil 6315.2.335   Costigan, Giovanni. Sigmund Freud, a short biography. N.Y., 1965.
Phil 6315.2.340   Johnston, Thomas E. Freud and political thought. 1st. ed. N.Y., 1965.
Phil 6315.2.345   Bayen, Jeanne Françoise. Sigmund Freud. Paris, 1964.
Phil 6315.2.350   Freud, Sigmund. The collected papers of Sigmund Freud. (Studies in parapsychology, v.10). N.Y., 1963.
Phil 6315.2.355   Bailey, Percival. Sigmund the unserene. Springfield, Ill., 1965.
Phil 6315.2.360   Grollman, Earl Alan. Judaism in Sigmund Freud's world. N.Y., 1965.
Phil 6315.2.365   Ricoeur, Paul. De l'interprétation. Paris, 1965.
Phil 6315.2.370   Ruitenbeek, Hendrik Marinus. Heirs to Freud. N.Y., 1966.
Phil 6315.2.375   Ruitenbeek, Hendrik Marinus. Freud and America. N.Y., 1966.
Phil 6315.2.380   Robert, Marthe. La révolution psychanalytique. Paris, 1964. 2v.
Phil 6315.2.382   Robert, Marthe. The psychoanalytic revolution. London, 1966.
Phil 6315.2.383   Eissler, Kurt Robert. Sigmund Freud und die Wiener Universität. Bern, 1966.
Phil 6315.2.385   Weiss-Rosmarin, Trude. The Hebrew Moses; an answer to Sigmund Freud. N.Y., 1939.
Phil 6315.2.390   Roazen, Paul. Freud; political and social thought. 1. ed. N.Y., 1968.
Phil 6315.2.395   Reich, Wilhelm. Reich speaks of Freud. N.Y., 1967.
Phil 6315.2.400   Freijo Balsebre, Enrique. El problema religioso en la historia de la psicologia médica contemporánea. Vitoria, 1966.
Phil 6315.2.405   Brome, Vincent. Freud and his early circle; the struggles of psychoanalysis. London, 1967.
Phil 6315.2.410   Stewart, Walter A. Psychoanalysis; the first ten years. N.Y., 1967.
Phil 6315.2.415   Marc-Wogan, Konrad. Freuds psykoanalys, presentation och kritik. Stockholm, 1967.
Phil 6315.2.420   Brandell, Gunnar. Freud; enfant de son siècle. Paris, 1967.
Phil 6315.2.425   Kushner, Martin D. Freud, a man obsessed. Philadelphia, 1967.
Phil 6315.2.430   Schoenan, Walter. Sigmund Freuds Prosa. Stuttgart, 1968.
Phil 6315.2.435   Plé, Albert. Freud et la religion. Paris, 1968?
Phil 6315.2.440   Vansina, M.J. Het super-ego. Antwerpen, 1969.
Phil 6315.2.442   Scharfenberg, Joachim. Sigmund Freud und sein Religionskritik als Herausforderung für den christlichen Glauben. Göttingen, 1968.
Phil 6315.2.444   Ricoeur, Paul. Freud and philosophy. New Haven, 1970.
Phil 6315.2.450   Hall, Calvin S. A primer of Freudian psychology. London, 1956.
Phil 6315.2.455   Hesnard, Angelo. L'oeuvre de Freud et son importance pour le monde moderne. Paris, 1960.
Phil 6315.2.460   Herwig, Hedda Juliane. Therapie der Menscheit. München, 1969.
Phil 6315.2.465   Mannoni, O. Freud. 1st American ed. N.Y., 1971.
Phil 6315.2.470   Fougeyrollas, Pierre. La révolution freudienne. Paris, 1970.
Phil 6315.2.475   Stoev, Stoiu G. Froidizmat i preodoliavaneto ma v Bulgariia. Sofiia, 1969.
Phil 6315.2.480   Birk, Kasimir. Sigmund Freud und die Religion. Münsterschwarzach, 1970.
Phil 6315.3   Frink, H.W. Morbid fears and compulsions, their psychology. N.Y., 1918.
Phil 6315.3.2   Frink, H.W. Morbid fears and compulsions, their psychology. London, 1921.
Phil 6315.4   Friedländer, A. Der Morphinismus, Kokainismus, Alkoholismus und Saturnismus. Jena, 1913.

Phil 6315.5   Furtmüller, Carl. Psychoanalyse und ethik. München, 1912.
Phil 6315.6   Forel, Auguste. L'activité psychique. Genève, 1919.
Phil 6315.9.2   Fuchs, R.F. Phisiologische Praktikum für Mediziner. 2. Aufl. Wiesbaden, 1912.
Phil 6315.11   Flournoy, Henri. La psychanalyse, les médecins et le public. Neuchâtel, 1924.
Phil 6315.12   Forel, O.L. La psychologie des névroses. Genève, 1925.
Phil 6315.13   Fielding, W.J. The caveman within us. N.Y., 1922.
Phil 6315.14   Fisher, Vivian E. An introduction to abnormal psychology. N.Y., 1929.
Phil 6315.15   Flügel, G.C. Men and their motives. London, 1934.
Phil 6315.16.8   Fenichel, Otto. Collected papers. N.Y., 1953-54. 2v.
Phil 6315.16.10   Fenichel, Otto. The psychoanalytic theory of neurosis. N.Y., 1945.
Phil 6315.17.8   Freud, Anna. Psychoanalysis for teachers and parents. Boston, 1960.
Phil 6315.17.10   Freud, Anna. The ego and the mechanisms of defence. N.Y., 1950.
Phil 6315.17.12   Freud, Anna. The ego and the mechanisms of defence. London, 1954.
Phil 6315.17.14   Freud, Anna. Writings of Anna Freud. v.2,4-6. N.Y., 1967. 4v.
Phil 6315.17.16   Freud, Anna. Indications for child analysis, and other papers, 1945-56. London, 1969.
Phil 6315.17.30   Freud, Anna. Difficulties in the path of psychoanalysis. N.Y., 1969.
Phil 6315.18   Federn, Paul. Das psychoanalytische Volksbuch. Bern, 1939.
Phil 6315.18.4   Federn, Paul. Das psychoanalytische Volksbuch. 5. Aufl. Bern, 1957.
Phil 6315.18.5   Federn, Paul. Ich-psychologie und die Psychosen. Bern, 1956.
Phil 6315.18.10   Federn, Paul. Ego psychology and the psychoses. N.Y., 1955.
Phil 6315.19   Fromm, Erich. Escape from freedom. N.Y., 1941.
Phil 6315.19.5   Schaar, John H. The fear of freedom. London, 1942.
Phil 6315.19.10   Fromm, Erich. Die Entwicklung des Christusdogmas. Wien, 1931.
Phil 6315.19.16   Fromm, Erich. Psychoanalysis and religion. New Haven, 1971.
Phil 6315.19.20   Schaar, John H. Escape from authority. N.Y., 1961.
Phil 6315.19.25   Torres, M. El irracionalismo en Erich Fromm. México, 1960.
Phil 6315.19.30   Fromm, Erich. The dogma of Christ. 1. ed. N.Y., 1963.
Phil 6315.19.35   Catemario, A. La società malata. Napoli, 1962.
Phil 6315.19.41   Fromm, Erich. The heart of man. 1st ed. N.Y., 1968.
Phil 6315.19.45   Evans, Richard Isadore. Dialogue with Erich Fromm. 1. ed. N.Y., 1966.
Phil 6315.20   Fishbein, M. Why men fail. N.Y., 1928.
Cg Phil 6315.22   Franz, Shepherd I. Collected papers. n.p., 1911-13.
Phil 6315.24   Fliess, R. The psycho-analytic reader. London, 1950.
Phil 6315.26A   Fromm-Reichmann, F. Principles of intensive psychotherapy. Chicago, 1950.
Phil 6315.26B   Fromm-Reichmann, F. Principles of intensive psychotherapy. Chicago, 1950.
Phil 6315.28   Fischer, S. Principles of general psychopathology. N.Y., 1950.
Phil 6315.30   Freeman, L. Fight against fears. N.Y., 1951.
Phil 6315.32   Marcuse, Herbert. Eros and civilization. Boston, 1955.
Phil 6315.38   Feuer, L.S. Psychoanalysis and ethics. Springfield, 1955.
Phil 6315.44   New York. Academy of Medicine. Freud and contemporary culture. N.Y., 1957.
Phil 6315.46   Fordham, M.S.M. New developments in analytical psychology. London, 1957.
Phil 6315.50   Faithfull, Theodore. The mystery of the androgyne. London, 1938.
Phil 6315.52   Frank, J.D. Persuasion and healing. London, 1961.
Phil 6315.54   Fingrette, H. The self in transformation. N.Y., 1964.
Phil 6315.55   Frost, M. Erzieherliebe als Heilmittel. Bern, 1920.
Phil 6315.56   Fernandez, M. The horizons of the mind. N.Y., 1964.
Phil 6315.58   Friedemann, Adolf. Die Begegnung mit dem kranken Menschen. Bern, 1967.
Phil 6315.60   Ferdinand, Theodore N. Typologies of delinquency. N.Y., 1966.
Phil 6315.62   Zetzel, Elizabeth R. The capacity for emotional growth. London, 1970.
Phil 6315.64   Freeman, Erika. Insights: conversations with Theodor Reik. Englewood Cliffs, 1971.
Phil 6315.66   Frankenstein, Carl. Die Ausserlichkeit des Lebensstils. Amsterdam, 1959.
Phil 6316.1   Gley, E. Etudes de psychologie. Paris, 1903.
Phil 6316.2   Goldscheider, A. Die Bedeutung der Reize für Pathologie und Therapie. Leipzig, 1898.
Phil 6316.3   Gérard, J. La grande névrose. Paris, 1889.
Phil 6316.4   Gregor, Adalbert. Leitfaden der experimentellen Psychopathologie. Berlin, 1910.
Phil 6316.6   Gadelius, Bror. Det mänskliga själslivet i belysning av sinnessjukläkarens erfarenhet. Stockholm, 1921-24. 4v.
Phil 6316.7   Gordon, R.G. The neurotic personality. London, 1927.
Phil 6316.8   Groddeck, Georg. Exploring the unconscious. London, 1933.
Phil 6316.8.8   Groddeck, Georg. Das Buch vom Es; psychoanalytische Briefe an eine Freuden. 3. Aufl. Leipzig, 1934.
Phil 6316.8.10   Groddeck, Georg. Psychoanalytische Schriften zur Psychosomatik. Wiesbaden, 1966.
Phil 6316.8.12   Groddeck, Georg. Das Buch vom Es. Wiesbaden, 1961.
Phil 6316.8.13   Groddeck, Georg. The look of the life. N.Y., 1961.
Phil 6316.8.15   Groddeck, Georg. Au fond de l'homme cela. Paris, 1963.
Phil 6316.8.20   Groddeck, Georg. Psychoanalytische Schriften zur Literatur und Kunst. Wiesbaden, 1964.
Phil 6316.8.25   Taylor, H.M. Life's unknown ruler...teaching of George Groddeck. London, 1935. 2v.
Phil 6316.8.30   Grossman, Carl M. The wild analyst. N.Y., 1965.
Phil 6316.9   Gard, W.L. Some neurological and psychological aspects of shock. Thesis. n.p., 1908.
Phil 6316.10   Guthrie, E.R. The psychology of human conflict. N.Y., 1938.
Phil 6316.11A   Gontard, G.V. In defense of love; a protest against "soul surgery" N.Y., 1940.
Phil 6316.11B   Gontard, G.V. In defense of love; a protest against "soul surgery" N.Y., 1940.
Phil 6316.12   Glover, Edward. An investigation of the technique of psycho-analysis. Baltimore, 1940.
Phil 6316.12.5   Glover, Edward. The technique of psycho-analysis. London, 1955.
Phil 6316.12.10   Glover, Edward. Selected papers on psycho-analysis. London, 1956- 2v.

Phil 6316.12.15   Glover, Edward. The birth of the ego; a nuclear hypothesis. N.Y., 1968.
Phil 6316.12.20   Glover, Edward. Psycho-analysis; a handbook for medical practitioners and students of comparitive psychology. 2d ed. London, 1949.
Phil 6316.13   Gratton, Henri. Psychoanalyses d'hier et d'aujourd'hui comme thérapeutiques. Paris, 1955.
Phil 6316.14   Guntrip, H.J.S. Personality structure and human interaction. London, 1961.
Phil 6316.14.5   Guntrip, H.J.S. Personality structure and human interaction. N.Y., 1961.
Phil 6316.14.10   Guntrip, Henry James Samuel. Psychoanalytic theory, therapy, and the self. N.Y., 1971.
Phil 6316.15   Goerres, Albert. The methods and experience of psychoanalysis. London, 1962.
Phil 6316.15.5   Goerres, Albert. An den Grenzen der Psychoanalyse. München, 1968.
Phil 6316.20   Garfield, Sol. Introductory clinical psychology. N.Y., 1961.
Phil 6316.22   Goldstein, M. The experience of anxiety. N.Y., 1963.
Phil 6316.23   Greenfield, Norman S. Psychoanalysis and current biological thought. Madison, 1965.
Phil 6316.25   Goraber, Gustav Hans. Die Not des Lebens und ihre Überwindung. Bern, 1966.
Phil 6316.27   Greenson, Ralph R. The technique and practice of psychoanalysis. London, 1967.
Phil 6316.30   Gottschalk, Louis. The measurement of psychological states through the content analysis of verbal behavior. Berkeley, 1969.
Phil 6316.32   Coeppert, Hans. Das Ich. München, 1968.
Phil 6317.1   Hammond, W.A. On certain conditions of nervous derangement. N.Y., 1881.
Phil 6317.1.2   Hammond, W.A. On certain conditions of nervous derangement. 3d ed. N.Y., 1883.
Phil 6317.2   Hadfield, J.A. Psychology and morals. London, 1923.
Phil 6317.2.7   Hadfield, J.A. Psychology and morals. N.Y., 1928.
Phil 6317.2.8   Hadfield, J.A. Psychology and morals. 8th ed. London, 1930.
Phil 6317.2.10   Hadfield, J.A. Psychologi och moral. 2a uppl. Stockholm, 1923.
Phil 6317.4   Hélat, C. Névroses et possessions diaboliques. 2. éd. Paris, 1898.
Phil 6317.5   Tridon, André. Psychoanalysis, its history, theory and practice. N.Y., 1919.
Phil 6317.6   Hallingworth, H.L. The psychology of functional neuroses. N.Y., 1920.
Phil 6317.6.10   Hallingworth, H.L. Abnormal psychology. N.Y., 1930.
Phil 6317.7   Hingley, R.H. Psycho-analysis. London, 1921.
Phil 6317.9A   Hoop, J.H. van der. Character and the unconscious. London, 1923.
Phil 6317.9B   Hoop, J.H. van der. Character and the unconscious. London, 1923.
Phil 6317.9.5   Hoop, J.H. van der. Bewusstseinstypen und ihre Beziehung zur Psychopathologie. Bern, 1937.
Phil 6317.9.10   Hoop, J.H. van der. Conscious orientation. London, 1939.
Phil 6317.10   Hinkle, Beatrice. The re-creating of the individual. N.Y., 1923.
Phil 6317.11   Herbert, S. The unconscious mind. London, 1923.
Phil 6317.11.9   Herbert, S. The unconscious in life and art. London, 1932.
Phil 6317.12   Herrlin, Axel. Själslifvets underjordiska verld. Malmo, 1901.
Phil 6317.13   Halberg, F. Om det abnorme. København, 1907.
Phil 6317.14   Heinroth, D.F.C.A. Lehrbuch der Storungen des Seelenlehre. v.1-2. Leipzig, 1818.
Phil 6317.15   Hamilton, Gilbert V. An introduction to objective psychopathology. St. Louis, 1925.
Phil 6317.16   Hoeberlin, Carl. Grundlinien der Psychoanalyse. München, 1925.
Phil 6317.17.2   Hart, Bernard. Psychopathology. N.Y., 1927.
Phil 6317.17.5   Hart, Bernard. Psychopathology; its development and place in medicine. Cambridge, 1939.
Phil 6317.18.2   Healy, William. The structure and meaning of psychoanalysis as related to personality and behavior. N.Y., 1953.
Phil 6317.18.10   Healy, William. Personality information and action. N.Y., 1938.
Phil 6317.19   Howden, R.A. The mind in conflict. London, 1931.
Phil 6317.19.5   Howden, R.A. The man in the street and the new psychology. London, 1935.
Phil 6317.20   Hendrick, Ives. Facts and theories of psychoanalysis. N.Y., 1934.
Phil 6317.20.5A   Hendrick, Ives. Facts and theories of psychoanalysis. 2d ed. N.Y., 1944.
Phil 6317.20.5B   Hendrick, Ives. Facts and theories of psychoanalysis. 2d ed. N.Y., 1944.
Phil 6317.20.8   Hendrick, Ives. Facts and theories of psychoanalysis. 3rd ed. N.Y., 1958.
Phil 6317.20.15   Hendrick, Ives. The birth of institute. Freeport, 1961.
Phil 6317.21.5   Heyer, Gustav R. The organism of the mind. N.Y., 1934.
Phil 6317.21.104   Heyer, Gustav R. Der Organism der Seele. 4. Aufl. München, 1959.
Phil 6317.22A   Horney, Karen. The neurotic personality of our time. N.Y., 1937.
Phil 6317.22B   Horney, Karen. The neurotic personality of our time. N.Y., 1937.
Phil 6317.22.5A   Horney, Karen. New ways in psychoanalysis. N.Y., 1939.
Phil 6317.22.5B   Horney, Karen. New ways in psychoanalysis. N.Y., 1939.
Phil 6317.22.10A   Horney, Karen. Self-analysis. N.Y., 1942.
Phil 6317.22.10B   Horney, Karen. Self-analysis. N.Y., 1942.
Phil 6317.22.20   Horney, Karen. Our inner conflict. N.Y., 1945.
Phil 6317.22.25   Horney, Karen. Feminine psychology. N.Y., 1967.
Phil 6317.22.80   Murray, M. The concepts of self acceptance and self respect in Karen Horney's theory of neurosis. n.p., n.d.
Phil 6317.22.85   Brés, Yvon. Freud et la psychanalyse américaine Karen Horney. Paris, 1970.
Phil 6317.23   Hopkins, P. The psychology of social movements. London, 1938.
Phil 6317.24   Henderson, D.K. Psychopathic states. N.Y., 1939.
Phil 6317.25   Harrington, M. Biological approach to the problem of abnormal behavior. Lancaster, Pa., 1938.
Phil 6317.26   Hartmann, Heinz. Die Grundlagen der Psychoanalyse. Leipzig, 1927.
Phil 6317.26.9   Hartmann, Heinz. Essays on ego psychology. London, 1964.
Phil 6317.26.10   Hartmann, Heinz. Essays on ego psychology. N.Y., 1964.
Phil 6317.27   Hermann, Imre. Psychoanalyse und Logik. Leipzig, 1924.

Phil 6310 - 6335 Psychology - Abnormal psychology - General treatises -
Individual authors (A-Z) - cont.

Phil 6317.28 — Howe, Eric Graham. The triumphant spirit. London, 1943.
Phil 6317.29 — Howe, Eric Graham. Invisible anatomy. London, 1944.
Phil 6317.30 — Halliday, James. Psychosocial medicine. N.Y., 1948.
Phil 6317.31 — Harding, M.E. Psychic energy, its source and goal. N.Y., 1947.
Phil 6317.31.2 — Harding, M.E. Psychic energy. 2. ed. N.Y., 1963.
Phil 6317.32 — Hubbard, L. Ron. Dianetics. N.Y., 1950.
Phil 6317.32.2 — Hubbard, L. Ron. Dianetics. Johhannesburg, 1958.
Phil 6317.32.5 — Hubbard, L. Ron. Scientology. London, 1956.
Phil 6317.33 — Hitschmann, E. Great men. N.Y., 1956.
Phil 6317.34 — Heiss, Robert. Allgemeine, Tiefenpsychologie. Bern, 1956.
Phil 6317.34.5 — Heiss, Robert. Allgemeine Tiefenpsychologie. Bern, 1964.
Phil 6317.35 — Hilgard, E.R. Psychoanalysis as science. N.Y., 1956.
Phil 6317.36 — Hoff, Hans. Die Zeit und ihre Neurose.ien, 1956.
Phil 6317.38 — Hook, Sidney. Psychoanalysis. N.Y., 1959.
Phil 6317.42 — Harding, Mary Esther. The "I" and the "not-I"; a study in the development of consciousness. N.Y., 1965.
Phil 6317.45 — Hendin, Herbert. Psychoanalysis and social research; the psychoanalytic study of the non-patient. Garden City, 1965.
Phil 6317.48 — Hernfeld, Fred Farau. La psychologie des profondeurs, des origines à nos jours. Paris, 1960.
Phil 6317.50 — Henderson, Joseph. Thresholds of initiation. 1. ed. Middletown, 1967.
Phil 6317.52 — Holmes, David S. Reviews of research in behavior pathology. N.Y., 1968.
Phil 6317.54 — Harris, Thomas Anthony. I'm OK, you are OK: a practical guide to transactional analysis. N.Y., 1969.
Phil 6318.1 — Israeli, Nathan. Abnormal personality and time. Photoreproduction. N.Y., 1936.
Phil 6319.1 — Jung, C.G. The theory of psychoanalysis. N.Y., 1915.
Phil 6319.1.01 — Pamphlet box. Jung, C.G. Psychology.
Phil 6319.1.5A — Jung, C.G. Collected papers on analytical psychology. London, 1916.
Phil 6319.1.5B — Jung, C.G. Collected papers on analytical psychology. London, 1916.
Phil 6319.1.5.5 — Jung, C.G. Collected papers on analytical psychology. London, 1922.
Phil 6319.1.5.6 — Jung, C.G. Collected works. v.7. 2nd ed. N.Y., 1966. 2v.
Phil 6319.1.5.7A — Jung, C.G. Collected works. v.1,3-5,7-9,11-17. N.Y., 1953-63. 14v.
Phil 6319.1.5.7B — Jung, C.G. Collected works. v.12. N.Y., 1953-63.
Phil 6319.1.5.8 — Jung, C.G. Collected works. v.1,3-17. London, 1953-63. 15v.
Phil 6319.1.5.9 — Jung, C.G. Praxis der Psychotherapie. v.1,3-4,6-8,11,14-16. Zürich, 1958.
Phil 6319.1.5.10 — Jung, C.G. Basic writings. N.Y., 1959.
Phil 6319.1.6 — Jung, C.G. Analytical psychology. N.Y., 1916.
Phil 6319.1.7 — Jung, C.G. Über die Energetik der Seele und andere psychologische Abhandlungen. Zürich, 1928.
Phil 6319.1.7.9 — Jung, C.G. Wandlungen und Symbole der Libido. Leipzig, 1912.
Phil 6319.1.8 — Jung, C.G. Wandlungen und Symbole der Libido. 2. Aufl. Leipzig, 1925.
Phil 6319.1.8.2 — Jung, C.G. Symbole der Wandlung. Zürich, 1952.
Phil 6319.1.9A — Jung, C.G. Psychology of the unconscious. N.Y., 1916.
Phil 6319.1.9B — Jung, C.G. Psychology of the unconscious. N.Y., 1916.
Phil 6319.1.9.5 — Jung, C.G. Psychology of the unconscious. London, 1916.
Phil 6319.1.10.5 — Jung, C.G. Die Psychologie der Übertragung. Zürich, 1946.
Phil 6319.1.11 — Jung, C.G. Analytische Psychologie und Erziehung. Heidelberg, 1926.
Phil 6319.1.13 — Jung, C.G. Two essays on analytical psychology. London, 1928.
Phil 6319.1.14 — Jung, C.G. Two essays on analytical psychology. N.Y., 1928.
Phil 6319.1.15 — Jung, C.G. Studies in word association. London, 1918.
Phil 6319.1.16 — Jung, C.G. Diagnostische Assoziationstudien. v.1-2. Leipzig, 1915.
Htn Phil 6319.1.25* — Jung, C.G. Zur Psychologie und Pathologie sogenannter occulter Phänomene. Inaug. Diss. Leipzig, 1902.
Phil 6319.1.30 — Jung, C.G. Bewusstes und Unbewusstes. Frankfurt, 1957.
Phil 6319.1.32 — Jung, C.G. Erinnerungen. Zürich, 1962.
Phil 6319.1.34 — Jung, C.G. Neurosis, dreams, reflections. N.Y., 1963.
Phil 6319.1.35 — Jung, C.G. Das Unbewusste im normalen und kranken. Zürich, 1926.
Phil 6319.1.36 — Jung, C.G. Über die Psychologie des Unbewussten. 5. Aufl. Zürich, 1943.
Phil 6319.1.36.2 — Jung, C.G. Über die Psychologie des Unbewussten. 7 Aufl. Zürich, 1960.
Phil 6319.1.37 — Jung, C.G. Seelenprobleme der Gegenwart. Zürich, 1932.
Phil 6319.1.43 — Jung, C.G. Modern man in search of a soul. N.Y., 1947.
Phil 6319.1.45 — Jung, C.G. Wirklichkeit des Seele. Zürich, 1934.
Phil 6319.1.47 — Jung, C.G. Die Bedeutung des Vaters für das Schicksal des Einzelnen. 4. Aufl. Zürich, 1962.
Phil 6319.1.49 — Jung, C.G. Die Beziehungen der Psychotherapie zur Seelsorge. Zürich, 1932.
Phil 6319.1.56 — Jung, C.G. Psychology and religion. New Haven, 1955.
Phil 6319.1.57 — Schär, Hans. Religion and the cure of souls in Jung's psychology. N.Y., 1950.
Phil 6319.1.60 — Jung, C.G. Integration of the personality. N.Y., 1939.
Phil 6319.1.62.1 — Jung, C.G. The undiscovered self. N.Y., 1958.
Phil 6319.1.65 — Jung, C.G. Der Inhalt der Psychose. Leipzig, 1908.
Phil 6319.1.67 — Jung, C.G. Der Inhalt der Psychose. 2. Aufl. Leipzig, 1914.
Phil 6319.1.68 — Jung, C.G. Psyche and symbol. Garden City, 1958.
Phil 6319.1.69 — Jung, C.G. Gestaltungen des Unbewussten. Zürich, 1950.
Phil 6319.1.70 — Jung, C.G. Versuch einer Darstellung der psycho analytischen Theorie. Leipzig, 1913.
Phil 6319.1.71A — Jung, C.G. Man and his symbols. London, 1964.
Phil 6319.1.71B — Jung, C.G. Man and his symbol. Lonson, 1964.
Phil 6319.1.72 — Jung, C.G. Psychologische Abhandlungen. Leipzig, 1914.
Phil 6319.1.73 — Jung, C.G. Gegenwart und Zukunft. Zürich, 1957.
Phil 6319.1.74 — Jung, C.G. Psychotherapeutische Zeitfragen. Leipzig, 1914.
Phil 6319.1.76 — Jung, C.G. Von den Wurzeln des Bewusstsens. Zürich, 1954.
Phil 6319.1.78 — Jung, C.G. Welt der Psyche. Zürich, 1954.
Phil 6319.1.80 — Jung-Institut, Zürich, Studien zur analytischen Psychologie. Zürich, 1955. 2v.
Phil 6319.1.85 — Read, Herbert. Zum 85. Geburtstag von Professor Dr. Carl Gustav Jung. Zürich, 1960.
Phil 6319.1.180 — Jacobi, Jolan. The psychology of C.G. Jung. London, 1942.
Phil 6319.1.181 — Jacobi, Jolan. Komplex. Zürich, 1957.
Phil 6319.1.181.2 — Jacobi, Jolan. Complex, archetype. N.Y., 1959.
Phil 6319.1.181.3 — Jacobi, Jolan. Complex, archtype. London, 1959.

Phil 6310 - 6335 Psychology - Abnormal psychology - General treatises -
Individual authors (A-Z) - cont.

Phil 6319.1.182 — Jacobi, Jolan. Die Psychologie von C.G. Jung. Zürich, 1945.
Phil 6319.1.183 — Jacobi, Jolan. Die Psychologie von C.G. Jung. 4. Aufl. Zürich, 1959.
Phil 6319.1.183.6 — Jacobi, Jolan. The psychology of C.G. Jung. New Haven, 1962.
Phil 6319.1.183.10 — Jacobi, Jolan. Der Weg zur Individuation. Zürich, 1965.
Phil 6319.1.184 — Schär, Hans. Religion und Seele in der Psychologie C.G. Jung. Zürich, 1946.
Phil 6319.1.185 — Jacobi, Jolan. The psychology of C.G. Jung. 5th ed. London, 1951.
Phil 6319.1.186 — Walder, P. Mensch und Welt bei C.G. Jung. Zürich, 1951.
Phil 6319.1.188 — Fordham, F. An introduction to Jung's psychology. London, 1953.
Phil 6319.1.190 — Hostie, Raymond. Analytische Psychologie en Godsdienst. Utrecht, 1954.
Phil 6319.1.190.5 — Hostie, Raymond. Du mythe à la religion. Bruges, 1955.
Phil 6319.1.192 — Rath, Paul. Anima und Animus in der Psychologie C.G. Jung. Winterthur, 1954.
Phil 6319.1.195 — Gemelli, A. Psicologia e religione nella concezione analitica di C.G. Jung. Milano, 1955.
Phil 6319.1.196 — Goldbrunner, Josef. Individuation. London, 1955.
Phil 6319.1.196.3 — Goldbrunner, Josef. Individuation. 3. Aufl. Freiburg, 1966.
Phil 6319.1.197 — Progoff, Ira. Jung's psychology and its social meaning. London, 1953.
Phil 6319.1.200 — Gruesen, J.J. The philosophical implication of C.G. Jung's individuation process. Washington, 1956.
Phil 6319.1.202 — Philip, Howard Littleton. Jung and the problem of evil. London, 1958.
Phil 6319.1.204 — Fordham, M.S.M. The objective psyche. London, 1958.
Phil 6319.1.205 — Fordham, M.S.M. Contact with Jung. London, 1963.
Phil 6319.1.206 — Wolff, Toni. Studien zu C.G. Jungs Psychologie. Zürich, 1959.
Phil 6319.1.208 — Meier, Carl A. Jung and analytical psychology. Newton, Mass., 1959.
Phil 6319.1.209 — Meier, Carl A. Lehrbuch der komplexen Psychologie C.G. Jungs. Zürich, 1968.
Phil 6319.1.210 — Winckel, Erna van de. De l'inconscient à Dieu. Paris, 1959.
Phil 6319.1.212 — Bennet, E.A. C.G. Jung. N.Y., 1962.
Phil 6319.1.214 — Dry, Avis Mary. The psychology of Jung. London, 1961.
Phil 6319.1.216 — Philipson, M.H. Outline of a Jungian aesthetics. Evanton, 1963.
Phil 6319.1.220 — Baudouin, C. L'oeuvre de Jung. Paris, 1963.
Phil 6319.1.221 — Helsdingen, R.J. van. Jung. Den Haag, 1964.
Phil 6319.1.225 — Serreano, Miguel. C.G. Jung and Hermann Hesse. London, 1966.
Phil 6319.1.230 — Evans, Richard Isadore. Conversation with Carl Jung and reactions from Ernest Jones. Princeton, 1964.
Phil 6319.1.235 — Jaffé, Aniela. Der Mythus vom Sinn in Werk von C.G. Jung. Zürich, 1967.
Phil 6319.1.236 — Jaffé, Aniela. The myth of meaning in the work of C.G. Jung. London, 1970.
Phil 6319.1.240 — Bertine, Eleanor. Jung's contribution to our time. N.Y., 1968.
Phil 6319.1.245 — Kaune, Fritz Jürgen. Selbstverwirklichung. München, 1967.
Phil 6319.1.250 — Pintacuda, Luigi. La psicologia religiosa di Karl Jung. Roma, 1965.
Phil 6319.1.255 — Jung, C.G. Analytical psychology: its theory and practice. London, 1968.
Phil 6319.1.260 — Hochheimer, Wolfgang. The psychotherapy of C.G. Jung. N.Y., 1969.
Phil 6319.1.265 — Wehr, Gerhard. C.G. Jung in Selbstzeugnissen und Bilddokumenten. Reinbek, 1969.
Phil 6319.1.266 — Wehr, Gerhard. Portrait of Jung; an illustrated biography. N.Y., 1971.
Phil 6319.1.270 — Jaffé, Aniela. Aus Leben und Werkstatt von C.G. Jung. Zürich, 1968.
Phil 6319.2.1 — Jones, Ernest. Papers on psycho-analysis. N.Y., 1919.
Phil 6319.2.2 — Jones, Ernest. Papers on psycho-analysis. London, 1918.
Phil 6319.2.4 — Jones, Ernest. Papers on psycho-analysis. 4th ed. Baltimore, 1938.
Phil 6319.2.4.5 — Jones, Ernest. Papers on psycho-analysis. 5th ed. Boston, 1961.
Phil 6319.2.4.6 — Jones, Ernest. Papers on psycho-analysis. 5th ed. Boston, 1967.
Phil 6319.2.5.5 — Jones, Ernest. Essays in applied psycho-analysis. London, 1951. 2v.
Phil 6319.2.5.7 — Jones, Ernest. Essays in applied psycho-analysis. N.Y., 1964. 2v.
Phil 6319.2.6 — Jones, Ernest. Papers on psycho-analysis. N.Y., 1913.
Phil 6319.3 — Joffroy, A. Fugues et vagabondage. Paris, 1909.
Phil 6319.4 — Journal of abnormal psychology. Boston. 1919?
Phil 6319.5 — Jackson, Josephine A. Outwitting our nerves. N.Y., 1921.
Phil 6319.6 — Jelliffe, S.E. Psychoanalysis and the drama. N.Y., 1922.
Phil 6319.7 — Jaensch, W. Grundzuge einer Physiologie und Klinik der psychophysischen Persönlichkeit. Berlin, 1926.
Phil 6319.8 — Zolowicz, E. Die Persönlichkeitsanalyse. Leipzig, 1926.
Phil 6319.9 — Jahn, Ernst. Machtwille und Minderwertigkeitsgefuhl. Berlin, 1931.
Phil 6319.10 — Journal of Mental Science. Recent progress in psychiatry. London. 1944
Phil 6319.11 — Jones, Maxwell. Social psychiatry. London, 1952.
Phil 6319.12 — Jacob, Hans. Western psychotherapy and Hindu-Sādhanā. London, 1961.
Phil 6319.13 — Jacobsen, Edith. The self and the object world. London, 1965.
Phil 6319.15 — Janse de Jonge, Adriaan Leendert. Psychopathologie en mensbeschouwing. Kampen, 1968.
Phil 6319.18 — Johnson, Adelaide McFadyne. Experience, affect and behavior: psychoanalytic explorations of Adelaide McFadyn Johnson. Chicago, 1969.
Phil 6319.20 — Jacobson, Edith. Psychotic conflict and reality. N.Y., 1967.
Phil 6320.1 — Kempf, E.J. The autonomic functions and the personality. N.Y., 1918.
Phil 6320.1.5 — Kempf, E.J. Psychopathology. St. Louis, 1921.
Phil 6320.1.9 — Kempf, E.J. Physiology of attitude. n.p., 1935.
Phil 6320.2 — Kaplan, Leo. Psychoanalytische Probleme. Leipzig, 1916.
Phil 6320.3 — Kollarits, Jenö. Charakter und Nervosität. Berlin, 1912.
Phil 6320.4 — Kortsen, K.K. De psykiske spaltninger. København, 1916.
Phil 6320.5 — Krishaber, M. De la névropathie cérébro-cardiaque. Paris, 1873.

321

Classified Listing

Phil 6310 - 6335 Psychology - Abnormal psychology - General treatises - Individual authors (A-Z) - cont.

Phil 6320.6.3 Kretschmer, E. Medizinische Psychologie. 3. Aufl. Leipzig, 1926.
Phil 6320.6.15 Kretschmer, E. A text book of medical psychology. London, 1934.
Phil 6320.6.20 Kretschmer, E. Mensch und Lebensgrund. Tübingen, 1966.
Phil 6320.7 Kohnstamm, O. Erscheinungsformen der Seele. München, 1927.
Phil 6320.8 Kahn, Eugen. Psychopathic personalities. New Haven, 1931.
Phil 6320.9.5 Kranefeldt, W.M. Secret ways of the mind. N.Y., 1932.
Phil 6320.10 Künkel, Fritz. Conquer yourself. N.Y., 1936.
Phil 6320.10.5 Künkel, Fritz. Die Arbeit am Charakter. Schwerin, 1939.
Phil 6320.11 Klein, M. Love, hate and reparation. London, 1937.
Phil 6320.11.5 Klein, M. Die Psychoanalyse des Kindes. Wien, 1932.
Phil 6320.11.10 Klein, M. New directions in psycho-analysis. London, 1955.
Phil 6320.11.17A Klein, M. Contributions to psycho-analysis. London, 1950.
Phil 6320.11.17B Klein, M. Contributions to psycho-analysis. London, 1950.
Phil 6320.11.19 Klein, M. Contributions to psycho-analysis, 1921-1945. London, 1968.
Phil 6320.11.25 Klein, M. Our adult world. N.Y., 1963.
Phil 6320.11.80 Segal, H. Introduction to the work of M. Klein. N.Y., 1964.
Phil 6320.12 Kahn, S. Psychological and neurological definitions and the unconcious. Boston, 1940.
Phil 6320.13 Kaminski, Gerhard. Das Bild vom Ander. Berlin, 1959.
Phil 6320.14 Kaplan, Oscar J. Mental disorders in later life. Stanford, Calif., 1945.
Phil 6320.15 Klapman, J.W. Group psychotherapy; theory and practice. N.Y., 1946.
Phil 6320.17A Kubie, L.S. Neurotic distortion of the creative process. Lawrence, 1958.
Phil 6320.17B Kubie, L.S. Neurotic distortion of the creative process. Lawrence, 1958.
Phil 6320.19 Kramer, Charles. La frustration. Neuchâtel, 1959.
Phil 6320.20 Kelman, Harold. New perspectives in psychoanalysis. N.Y., 1965.
Phil 6320.25 Kalmar, Jacques M. Anti-pensée et monde des conflits. Neuchâtel, 1967.
Phil 6320.30 Kruse, Friedrich. Die Anfänge des menschlichen Seelenlebens. Stuttgart, 1969.
Phil 6321.1 Lattimore, E.L. Some illustrative clinic cases. Thesis. Menasha, 1916.
Phil 6321.2.3 Lay, Wilfrid. Man's unconcious conflict. N.Y., 1919.
Phil 6321.2.5 Lay, Wilfrid. Man's unconcious conflict. N.Y., 1921.
Cg Phil 6321.3.2 Low, Barbara. Psycho-analysis. London, 1920.
Phil 6321.4 Loewenfeld, L. Pathologie und Therapie de Neurasthenie und Hysterie. Wiesbaden, 1894.
Phil 6321.5A Lawrence, David Herbert. Psycho-analysis and its unconscious. N.Y., 1921.
Phil 6321.5B Lawrence, David Herbert. Psycho-analysis and its unconscious. N.Y., 1921.
Phil 6321.5.8.2 Lawrence, David Herbert. Fantasia of the unconscious and Psychoanalysis and the unconscious. London, 1971.
Phil 6321.5.10 Lawrence, David Herbert. Fantasia of the unconscious. N.Y., 1930.
Phil 6321.6 Long, C.E. Collected papers on the psychology of phantasy. N.Y., 1921.
Phil 6321.7.5 La Rue, D.W. Mental hygiene. N.Y., 1930.
Phil 6321.8 Lanteirès, André. Essai descriptif sur les troubles psychopathiques avec lucidités d'esprit. Paris, 1885.
Phil 6321.9.6 Lasswell, H.D. Psychology and politics. Chicago, 1934.
Phil 6321.9.8 Lasswell, H.D. Psychopathology and politics. N.Y., 1960.
Phil 6321.10 Laignel-Lavastine, Maxime. Concentric method in the diagnosis of psychoneurotics. London, 1931.
Phil 6321.11 Lorand, Sándor. Psycho-analysis today. London, 1933.
Phil 6321.11.10 Lorand, Sándor. Psycho-analysis today. N.Y., 1944.
Phil 6321.11.15 Lorand, Sándor. Technique of psychoanalytic therapy. N.Y., 1946.
Phil 6321.12.5 Laforgue, R. Clinical aspects of psychoanalysis. London, 1938.
Phil 6321.12.10 Laforgue, R. Psychopathologie de l'échec. Paris, 1944.
Phil 6321.12.15 Laforgue, R. Au dela du scientisme. Genève, 1963.
Phil 6321.13 Leconte, M. Conflits sociaux et psychoses. Paris, 1938.
Phil 6321.14 L'hermitte, J.J. L'image de notre corps. Paris, 1939.
Cg Phil 6321.15 London, L.S. Mental therapy. N.Y., 1937. 2v.
Phil 6321.16 Laburu, J.A. de. Anormalidades del caracter. Montevideo, 1941.
Phil 6321.17 Low, A.A. Secret of self-help in psychiatric aftercare. v.1-3. Chicago, 1943.
Phil 6321.18 Levine, M. Psychotherapy in medical practice. N.Y., 1942.
Phil 6321.20 Lowy, Samuel. New directions in psychology toward individual happiness and social progress. N.Y., 1945.
Phil 6321.25 Landis, Carney. Text book of abnormal psychology. N.Y., 1946.
Phil 6321.30 Loewenstein, R. Psychoanalyse de l'antisémitisme. 1. éd. Paris, 1952.
Phil 6321.30.5 Loewenstein, R. Drives, affects, behavior. N.Y., 1953.
Phil 6321.30.10 Loewenstein, R. Christians and Jews. N.Y., 1951.
Phil 6321.35 Lindner, R.M. Prescription for rebellion. London, 1953.
Phil 6321.40 Lindner, R.M. The fifty minute hour. N.Y., 1955.
Phil 6321.43 Lévy-Valensi, E. Le dialoge psychanalytique. Paris, 1962.
Phil 6321.45 Langstroth, Lovell. Structure of the ego. Stanford, Calif., 1955.
Phil 6321.46 Lertora, A.C. Re-fundamentacion de la psiquiatria. Buenos Aires, 1963.
Phil 6321.47 Lévy-Valensi, E. Les rapports intersubjectifs en psychanalyse. Paris, 1962.
Phil 6321.48 Lyons, Joseph. Psychology and the measure of man. N.Y., 1963.
Phil 6321.49 Lampl de Groot, Jeanne. The development of the mind. N.Y., 1965.
Phil 6321.49.2 Lampl de Groot, Jeanne. The development of the mind. London, 1966.
Phil 6321.50 Levitas, G.B. The world of psychoanalysis. N.Y., 1965.
Phil 6321.51 Lacan, Jacques. Ecrits. Paris, 1966.
Phil 6321.51.10 Palmier, Jean Michel. Lacan, le symbolique et l'imaginaire. Paris, 1969.
Phil 6321.51.15 Fages, Jean Baptiste. Comprendre Jacques Lacan. Toulouse, 1971.
Phil 6321.53 Laing, Roland David. The politics of experience. N.Y., 1967.
Phil 6321.53.10 Laing, Roland David. Knots. London, 1970.
Phil 6321.55 Leclaire, Serge. Psychanalyser, un essai sur l'ordre de l'inconscient et la pratique de la lettre. Paris, 1968.
Phil 6321.56 Lowe, Gordon Robb. Personal relationships in psychological disorders. Harmondsworth, 1969.

Phil 6310 - 6335 Psychology - Abnormal psychology - General treatises - Individual authors (A-Z) - cont.

Phil 6321.58 Laughlin, Henry Prather. The ego and its defenses. N.Y., 1970.
Phil 6321.60 Laplanche, Jean. Vie et mort en psychanalyse. Paris, 1970.
Phil 6322.1 Möbius, P.J. Stachyologie, weitere vermischte Aufsätze. Leipzig, 1909.
Phil 6322.1.5 Mobius, P.J. Vermischte Aufsätze. Leipzig, 1898.
Phil 6322.1.10 Mobius, P.J. Über den Begriff der Hysterie und andere Vorwürfe vorwegend psychologischer Art. Leipzig, 1894.
Phil 6322.1.15 Möbius, P.J. Die Nervosität. 3e Aufl. Leipzig, 1906.
Phil 6322.2 Müller, F.C. Psychologie des Bewusstseins. Leipzig, 1889.
Phil 6322.3 Marie, Auguste. Traité international de psychologie pathologique. Paris, 1910-12. 3v.
Phil 6322.4 Miller, Hugh C. Functional nerve disease. London, 1920.
Phil 6322.4.5 Miller, Hugh C. The new psychology and the parent. N.Y., 1923.
Phil 6322.4.7 Miller, Hugh C. The new psychology and the preacher. London, 1924.
Phil 6322.4.15 Miller, Hugh C. Psycho-analysis and its derivations. London, 1933.
Phil 6322.5 Maeder, Alphonse. Heilung und Entwicklung im Seelenleben. Zürich, 1918.
Phil 6322.6 Mitchell, T.W. The psychology of medicine. London, 1921.
Phil 6322.6.5 Mitchell, T.W. Medical psychology and psychological research. London, 1922.
Phil 6322.6.10 Mitchell, T.W. Problems in psychopathology. London, 1927.
Phil 6322.8 MacCurdy, J.T. Problems in dynamic psychology. Cambridge, 1923.
Phil 6322.8.5 MacCurdy, J.T. The psychology of emotion; morbid and normal. London, 1925.
Phil 6322.10 MacDonald, A. Abnormal man. Washington, D.C., 1893.
Phil 6322.11 Mitchell, S.W. Lecture on diseases of the nervous system. Philadelphia, 1881.
Phil 6322.12 Moreau, J.J. La psychologie morbide. Paris, 1859.
Phil 6322.13 Muralt, Alexander von. Ein Pseudoprophet. München, 1920.
Phil 6322.13.5 Muralt, Alexander von. Wahnsinniger oder Prophet? Zürich, 1946.
Phil 6322.14A McDougall, W. Outline of abnormal psychology. N.Y., 1926.
Phil 6322.14B McDougall, W. Outline of abnormal psychology. N.Y., 1926.
Phil 6322.14.25 McDougall, W. Psychopathologie funktioneller Störungen. Leipzig, 1931.
Phil 6322.15 Mullen, J.J. Psychological factors in the pastoral treatement of scruples. n.p., 1927.
Phil 6322.16.5 Morgan, John J.B. The psychology of abnormal people with educational applications. N.Y., 1935.
Phil 6322.16.9 Morgan, John J.B. The psychology of abnormal people. 2d ed. N.Y., 1936.
Phil 6322.17 Meyer, Max F. Abnormal psychology. Columbia, 1927.
Phil 6322.18A Murphy, Gardiner. An outline of abnormal psychology. N.Y., 1929.
Phil 6322.18B Murphy, Gardiner. An outline of abnormal psychology. N.Y., 1929.
Phil 6322.18C Murphy, Gardiner. An outline of abnormal psychology. N.Y., 1929.
Phil 6322.19 Menninger, Karl Augustus. The human mind. N.Y., 1930.
Phil 6322.19.2 Menninger, Karl Augustus. The human mind. N.Y., 1930.
Phil 6322.19.5 Menninger, Karl Augustus. The human mind. 2d ed. N.Y., 1937.
Phil 6322.19.7 Menninger, Karl Augustus. The human mind. 3d ed. N.Y., 1945.
Phil 6322.19.10 Menninger, Karl Augustus. Love against hate. 1st ed. N.Y., 1942.
Phil 6322.19.15 Menninger, Karl Augustus. The vital balance. N.Y., 1963.
Phil 6322.20 Mitchell, John K. Self help for nervous women. Philadelphia, 1909.
Phil 6322.21 Monakow, Constantin von. Introduction biologique à l'étude de la neurologie et de la psychopathologie. Paris, 1928.
Phil 6322.22 Mauerhofer, Hugo. Der schizoid-dämonische Charakter. Leipzig, 1930.
Phil 6322.23.5 Myerson, A. The nervous housewife. Boston, 1929.
Phil 6322.24 Mason, E.C. Why we do it? St. Louis, 1937.
Phil 6322.25 Marin, J. Ensayos freudianos. Santiago de Chile, 1938.
Phil 6322.26 Money-Kyrle, R.E. Superstition and society. London, 1939.
Phil 6322.26.5 Money-Kyrle, R.E. Man's picture of his world. London, 1961.
Phil 6322.27A Maslow, A.H. Principles of abnormal psychology. N.Y., 1941.
Phil 6322.27B Maslow, A.H. Principles of abnormal psychology. N.Y., 1941.
Phil 6322.28 Mira y López, E. Psychiatry in war. 1st ed. N.Y., 1943.
Phil 6322.28.5 Mira y López, E. Doctrinas psicoanaliticas. Buenos Aires, 1963.
Phil 6322.29 McFarland, R.A. Miscellaneous papers on abnormal psychology. n.p., n.d.
Phil 6322.29.3 McFarland, R.A. Psycho-physiological studies at high altitude in the Andes. Baltimore, 1937.
Phil 6322.29.5 MacFadden, B. StrengtheningThe nerves. N.Y., 1928.
Phil 6322.30 Moncrieff, A.A. Psychology in general practice. London, 1945.
Phil 6322.31 Mullahy, Patrick. Oedipus. 1st ed. N.Y., 1948.
Phil 6322.31.1 Mullahy, Patrick. Oedipus myth and complex. 1st ed. N.Y., 1948.
Phil 6322.31.2 Mullahy, Patrick. Oedipus. N.Y., 1955.
Phil 6322.32 Menninger, W.C. Social change and scientific progress. Portland, 1951.
Phil 6322.32.5 Menningen, Karl Augustus. Theory of psychoanalytic technique. N.Y., 1958.
Phil 6322.33 Mayer, Felix. Dynamische Tiefenspsychologie. Bern, 1953.
Phil 6322.35 Munroe, R.L. Schools of psychoanalytic thought. N.Y., 1955.
Phil 6322.38 Mitscherlich, A. Entfaltung des Psychoanalyse. Stuttgart, 1956.
Phil 6322.40 Matthew, A.V. Depth psychology and education. Kolhapur, 1944.
Phil 6322.41 Vandendriessche, Gaston. The parapraxis in the Haizmann case of Sigmund Freud. Louvain, 1955.
Phil 6322.42A Macalpine, Ida. Schizophrenia, 1677. London, 1956.
Phil 6322.42B Macalpine, Ida. Schizophrenia, 1677. London, 1956.
Phil 6322.44 Miasishchev, V.N. Lichnost' i nevrozy. Leningrad, 1960.
Phil 6322.45 Masterson, Jenny Gove. Letters from Jenny. N.Y., 1965.
Phil 6322.46 Marmorston, Jessie. Psychoanalysis and the human situation. 1st ed. N.Y., 1964.
Phil 6322.47 Michel, André. L'école freudienne devant la musique. Paris, 1965.
Phil 6322.48 Moscovici, Serge. La psychanalyse, son image et son public. Paris, 1961.

322

Classified Listing

Phil 6310 - 6335 Psychology - Abnormal psychology - General treatises - Individual authors (A-Z) - cont.

Phil 6322.50	Modell, Arnold H. Object love and reality. N.Y., 1968.
Phil 6322.51	Modell, Arnold H. Object love and reality: an introduction to a psychoanalytic theory of object relations. London, 1969.
Phil 6322.55	Marcuse, Herbert. Psychoanalyse und Politik. Frankfurt, 1968.
Phil 6322.60	Minkowski, Eugène. Le temps vécu. Neuchâtel, 1968.
Phil 6322.65	Milner, Marion Blackett. The hands of the living god. London, 1969.
Phil 6322.70	Monroe, Russell R. Episodic behavioral disorders. Cambridge, 1970.
Phil 6323.1	Neue Arbeiten zur Ärztlichen Psychoanalyse. Leipzig. 1-6,1924-1927 5v.
Phil 6323.2	Naegeli, Otto. Über den Einfluss von Rechtsansprüchen bei Neurosen. Leipzig, 1913.
Phil 6323.3	Nathan, Marcel. Les malades dits imaginaires. Paris, 1931.
Phil 6323.4.5	Nicole, J.E. Psychopathology. 2d ed. Baltimore, 1934.
Phil 6323.4.6	Nicole, J.E. Psychopathology. 4. ed. Baltimore, 1947.
Phil 6323.5	Nunberg, Hermann. Allgemeine Neurosenlehre auf psychoanalytischer Gundlage. Bern, 1932.
Phil 6323.5.3	Nunberg, Hermann. Allgemeine Neurosenlehre. Bern, 1959.
Phil 6323.5.6	Nunberg, Hermann. Practice and theory of psychoanalysis. N.Y., 1961. 2v.
Phil 6323.6	Neustatter, W.L. Modern psychology in practice. Philadelphia, 1937.
Phil 6323.7.2	Noyes, Arthur P. Modern clinical psychiatry. 2d ed. Philadelphia, 1939.
Phil 6323.7.5	Noyes, Arthur P. Modern clinical psychiatry. 5th ed. Philadelphia, 1958.
Phil 6323.8	Nacht, Sacha. Le masochisme. 2. éd. Paris, 1948.
Phil 6323.10	Nuttin, Jozef. Psychanalyse et conception spiritualiste de l'homme. 2. ed. Louvain, 1955.
Phil 6323.12	Nuttin, Jozef. Psychoanalyse und Personlichkeit. Freiburg, 1956.
Phil 6323.15	Nelson, John. Look before you leap. Washington, D.C., 1954.
Phil 6323.18	Nemiah, J.C. Foundations of psychopathology. N.Y., 1961.
Phil 6323.20	Nacht, Sacha. La présence du psychanalyste. Paris, 1963.
Phil 6323.21	Nacht, Sacha. Traité de psychanalyse. Paris, 1965.
Phil 6323.24	Novey, Samuel. The second look: the reconstruction of personal history in psychiatry and psychoanalysis. Baltimore, 1968.
Phil 6323.26	Nolte, Helmut. Psychoanalyse und Soziologie. Bern, 1970.
Phil 6324.1	O'Higgins, H. The secret springs. N.Y., 1920.
Phil 6324.2	Odier, Charles. Étude psychoanalytique. Le complex d'Oedipe. Genève, 1925.
Phil 6324.4	Oberndorf, Clarence. A history of psychoanalysis in America. N.Y., 1953.
Phil 6324.6	Oston, Mortimer. Drugs in psychoanalysis and psychopathology. N.Y., 1962.
Phil 6324.7	Osbert, Reuben. Marxism and psycho-analysis. London, 1965.
Phil 6324.8	Örgü, Halis. Kampleksler ve insanlar. Istanbul, 1969.
Phil 6325.1	Pfister, Oskar. The psychoanalytic method. N.Y., 1917.
Phil 6325.1.3	Pfister, Oskar. The psychoanalytic method. London, 1915.
Phil 6325.1.5	Pfister, Oskar. Wahrheit und Schönheit in der Psychoanalyse. Zürich, 1918.
Phil 6325.1.10	Pfister, Oskar. Psycho-analysis in the service of education. London, 1922.
Phil 6325.1.16	Pfister, Oskar. Expressionism in art. N.Y., 1923.
Phil 6325.1.17	Pfister, Oskar. Some applications of psychoanalysis. London, 1923.
Phil 6325.1.20	Pfister, Oskar. Psychoanalyse und Weltanschauung. Leipzig, 1928.
Phil 6325.1.25	Pfister, Oskar. Religiosität und Hysterie. Leipzig, 1928.
Phil 6325.1.30	Pfister, Oskar. Zum Kampf um die Psychoanalyse. Wien, 1920.
Phil 6325.1.35	Pfister, Oskar. Die Behandlung schwer erziehlbarer und abnormer Kinder. Bern, 1921.
Phil 6325.1.40	Pfister, Oskar. Vermeintliche Nullen und angebliche Musterkinder. Bern, 1921.
Phil 6325.2A	Putnam, J.J. Addresses on psycho-analysis. London, 1921.
Phil 6325.2B	Putnam, J.J. Addresses on psycho-analysis. London, 1921.
Phil 6325.3	Pontoppidan, Knud. Psychiatriske foreläsinger. Kjobenhavn, 1892-95.
Phil 6325.6	Pressey, Sidney L. Mental abnormality and deficiency. N.Y., 1926.
Phil 6325.7	Pagès, Louis. Affectivité et intelligence: étude psycho-pathologique. Paris, 1926.
Phil 6325.7.2	Pagès, Louis. Affectivité et intelligence: étude psycho-pathologique. Thèse. Paris, 1926.
Phil 6325.8	Prince, Morton. Miscellaneous pamphlets on psychology. 11 pam.
Phil 6325.8.5	Prince, Morton. The unconscious. N.Y., 1914.
Phil 6325.8.6	Prince, Morton. The unconscious. N.Y., 1916.
Phil 6325.8.7	Prince, Morton. The unconscious. 2d ed. N.Y., 1921.
Phil 6325.8.8	Prince, Morton. The unconscious. 2d ed. N.Y., 1929.
Phil 6325.8.15	Prince, Morton. Clinical and experimental studies in personality. Cambridge, Mass., 1929.
Phil 6325.8.16	Prince, Morton. Clinical and experimental studies in personality. Cambridge, Mass., 1939.
Phil 6325.8.80	Taylor, William Sentman. Morton Prince and abnormal psychology. N.Y., 1928.
Phil 6325.9	Pelman, Carl. Psychische Grenzzustände. 3. Aufl. Bonn, 1912.
Phil 6325.10	Prinzhorn, Hans. Psychotherapie. Leipzig, 1929.
Phil 6325.10.5	Prinzhorn, Hans. Gespräch über Psychoanalyse zwischen Frau, Dichter und Arzt. Heidelberg, 1927.
Phil 6325.11	Peck, Martin W. The meaning of psychoanalysis. N.Y., 1931.
Phil 6325.12	Pillsbury, Walter B. An elementary psychology of the abnormal. 1. ed. N.Y., 1932.
Phil 6325.13	Peters, W. Die Beziehungen der Psychologie zur Medizin. Würzburg, 1913.
Phil 6325.14	Porteus, S.D. The practice of clinical psychology. N.Y., 1941.
Phil 6325.15	Pennsylvania. University. Bicentennial Conference. Therapeutic advances in psychiatry. Philadelphia, 1941.
Phil 6325.16	Paschal, Franklin C. The Witmer cylinder test. Hershey, Pa., 1918.
Phil 6325.17	Palmer, H.A. The philosophy of psychiatry. N.Y., 1952.
Phil 6325.18	Problèmes de psychanalyse. Paris, 1957.
Phil 6325.18.5	Problems in psychoanalysis. London, 1961.
Phil 6325.20	Psykoanalytisk diskussionsklub. Psykoanalyse er to ting. København, 1960.

Phil 6310 - 6335 Psychology - Abnormal psychology - General treatises - Individual authors (A-Z) - cont.

Phil 6325.21	Paul, Louis. Psychoanalytic clinical interpretation. N.Y., 1963.
Phil 6325.22	Platonov, K.I. The word as a physiological and therapeutic factor. Moscow, 1959.
Phil 6325.23	Parker, B. My language is me. N.Y., 1962.
Phil 6325.24	Pontalis, J.B. Après Freud. Paris, 1965.
Phil 6325.25	Podolsky, Edward. Encyclopedia of aberrations. N.Y., 1953.
Phil 6325.26	Perry, Stewart Edmond. The human nature of science; researchers at work in psychiatry. N.Y., 1966.
Phil 6325.27	Petrilowitsch, Nikolaus. Charakterstudien. Basel, 1969.
Phil 6325.28.1	Putnam, James Jackson. James Jackson Putnam and psychoanalysis. Cambridge, 1971.
Phil 6325.30	Peterson, Donold Robert. The clinical study of social behavior. N.Y., 1968.
Phil 6325.32	Plé, Albert. Freud et la morale. Paris, 1969.
Phil 6327.1	Regnard, P. Sorcellerie, magnètisme, morphinisme. Paris, 1887.
Phil 6327.2	Raynier, Julien. Les états dépresifs...chez les militaires. Thèse. Paris, 1915.
Phil 6327.3	Rogues de Fursac, J. Manuel de psychiatrie. Paris, 1917.
Phil 6327.4	Rank, Otto. Die Bedeutung der Psychoanalyse. Wiesbaden, 1913.
Phil 6327.4.5A	Rank, Otto. Das Trauma der Geburt. Leipzig, 1924. 2v.
Phil 6327.4.5B	Rank, Otto. Das Trauma der Geburt. Leipzig, 1924. 2v.
Phil 6327.4.6A	Rank, Otto. The trauma of birth. London, 1929.
Phil 6327.4.6B	Rank, Otto. The trauma of birth. London, 1929.
Phil 6327.4.7	Rank, Otto. The trauma of birth. N.Y., 1952.
Phil 6327.4.9	Rank, Otto. Technik der Psychoanalyse. Leipzig, 1926-31. 3v.
Phil 6327.4.13	Rank, Otto. Grundzüge einer genetischen Psychologie. v.1-2. Wien, 1927-28.
Phil 6327.4.19	Rank, Otto. Wahrheit und Wirklichkeit. Leipzig, 1929.
Phil 6327.4.21A	Rank, Otto. Truth and reality. N.Y., 1936.
Phil 6327.4.21B	Rank, Otto. Truth and reality. N.Y., 1936.
Phil 6327.4.23A	Rank, Otto. Beyond psychology. Camden, 1941.
Phil 6327.4.23B	Rank, Otto. Beyond psychology. Camden, 1941.
Phil 6327.4.25	Rank, Otto. Die don Juan-Gestalt. Leipzig, 1924.
Phil 6327.4.30	Rank, Otto. Will therapy and truth and reality. N.Y., 1945.
Phil 6327.4.32	Rank, Otto. Will therapy and truth and reality. N.Y., 1936.
Phil 6327.4.33	Rank, Otto. Will therapy and truth and reality. N.Y., 1950.
Phil 6327.4.35	Rank, Otto. Der Doppelganger. Zürich, 1925.
Phil 6327.4.36	Rank, Otto. The double: a psychoanalytic study. Chapel Hill, 1971.
Phil 6327.4.40A	Rank, Otto. Psychology and the soul. Philadelphia, 1950.
Phil 6327.4.40B	Rank, Otto. Psychology and the soul. Philadelphia, 1950.
Phil 6327.4.40C	Rank, Otto. Psychology and the soul. Philadelphia, 1950.
Phil 6327.4.60	Otto Rank Association. Journal. Doylestown. 1,1966+ 2v.
Phil 6327.4.80	Karpf, Jay B. The psychology and psychotherapy of Otto Rank. N.Y., 1953.
Phil 6327.5A	Rivers, W.H.R. Instinct and the unconscious. Cambridge, Eng., 1920.
Phil 6327.5B	Rivers, W.H.R. Instinct and the unconscious. Cambridge, Eng., 1920.
Phil 6327.5.5	Rivers, W.H.R. Instinct and the unconscious. 2. ed. Cambridge, Eng., 1924.
Phil 6327.5.15	Rivers, W.H.R. L'instinct et l'inconscient. Paris, 1926.
Phil 6327.6	Rinaldo, Joel. Psychoanalysis of the "reformer". N.Y., 1921.
Phil 6327.9	Reid, J. Essays on hypochondriacal and other nervous affections. Philadelphia, 1817.
Phil 6327.10	Raimann, Emil. Zur psychoanalyse. 2. Aufl. Berlin, 1925.
Phil 6327.11	Rickman, J. Index psychoanalyticus, 1893-1926. London, 1928.
Phil 6327.11.5	Rickman, J. Selected contributions to psychoanalysis. London, 1957.
Phil 6327.11.10	Grinstein, A. The index of psychoanalytic writings. N.Y., 1956-60. 10v.
Phil 6327.12.5	Reik, Theodor. Ritual; psycho-analytical studies. London, 1931.
Phil 6327.12.7	Reik, Theodor. Ritual, psycho-analytical studies. N.Y., 1958.
Phil 6327.12.9	Reik, Theodor. Aus Leiden Freuden. London, 1940.
Phil 6327.12.13	Reik, Theodor. Der überraschte Psychologie. Leiden, 1935.
Phil 6327.12.15	Reik, Theodor. Surprise and the psycho-analyst. London, 1936.
Phil 6327.12.20	Reik, Theodor. Wir Freud-Schüler. Leiden, 1936.
Phil 6327.12.25	Reik, Theodor. Wie man psychologe wird. Leipzig, 1927.
Phil 6327.12.30	Reik, Theodor. Der Schrecken und andere psychoanalytische Studien. Wien, 1929.
Phil 6327.12.35	Reik, Theodor. The search within. N.Y., 1956.
Phil 6327.12.36	Reik, Theodor. The search within; the inner experience of a psychoanalyst. N.Y., 1968.
Phil 6327.12.40	Reik, Theodor. Fragment of a great confession. N.Y., 1949.
Phil 6327.12.45	Reik, Theodor. The secret self. N.Y., 1953.
Phil 6327.12.50	Reik, Theodor. Voices from the inaudible. N.Y., 1964.
Phil 6327.12.55	Reik, Theodor. Curiosities of the self. N.Y., 1965.
Phil 6327.12.60	Reik, Theodor. The many faces of sex. N.Y., 1966.
Phil 6327.13	Roberts, Harry. The troubled mind. N.Y., 1939.
Phil 6327.14	Reese, W. L'idée de l'homme dans la neurologie contemporaine. Paris, 1938.
Phil 6327.15	Rado, Sandor. Die Kastrationsangst des Weibes. Wien, 1934.
Phil 6327.15.5	Rado, Sandor. Psychoanalysis of behavior; collected papers. N.Y., 1956.
Phil 6327.16	Ray, Marie B. Doctors of the mind; the story of the psychiatry. Boston, 1942.
Phil 6327.16.7	Ray, Marie B. Doctors of the mind, what psychiatry can do. Boston, 1946.
Phil 6327.17.5	Ross, Thomas Arthur. The common neuroses. 2. ed. London, 1942.
Phil 6327.17.10	Ross, Thomas Arthur. Lectures on war neuroses. London, 1941.
Phil 6327.17.15	Ross, Thomas Arthur. An enquiry into prognosis in the neuroses. Cambridge, Eng., 1936.
Phil 6327.18	Roheim, Geza. The origin and function of culture. N.Y., 1943.
Phil 6327.20	Radzinowicz, Leon. Mental abnormality and crime. London, 1944.

Phil 6310 - 6335   Psychology - Abnormal psychology - General treatises -
    Individual authors (A-Z) - cont.

Phil 6327.21.10   Reich, Wilhelm. Character analysis. 3. ed. N.Y., 1949.
Phil 6327.21.13   Reich, Wilhelm. Character analysis. 3. ed. N.Y., 1970.
Phil 6327.21.20   Reich, Wilhelm. The murder of Christ: the emotional plague
        of mankind. N.Y., 1953.
Phil 6327.21.25   Reich, Wilhelm. Wilhelm Reich, biographical material. v.2.
        Rangeley, Me., 1953-
Phil 6327.21.26   Reich, Wilhelm. Wilhelm Reich, biographical material. v.1.
        Rangeley, Me., 1953-
Phil 6327.21.30   Reich, Wilhelm. Listen little man. N.Y., 1948.
Phil 6327.21.35   Reich, Wilhelm. Cosmic superimposition. Rangeley,
        Me., 1951.
Phil 6327.21.40   Reich, Wilhelm. Die sexuelle Revolution. Frankfurt am
        Main, 1970.
Phil 6327.21.41   Reich, Wilhelm. The sexual revolution. N.Y., 1971.
Phil 6327.21.46   Reich, Wilhelm. The invasion of compulsory sex-morality.
        N.Y., 1971.
Phil 6327.21.80   Baker, Elsworth. Man in the trap. N.Y., 1967.
Phil 6327.21.85   Reich, Ilse Ollendorff. Wilhelm Reich. N.Y., 1969.
Phil 6327.21.90   Robinson, Paul Arnold. The Freudian left: Wilhelm Reich,
        Geza Roheim, Albert Marcuse. 1st ed. N.Y., 1969.
Phil 6327.21.95   Cattier, Michel. La vie et l'oeuvre der docteur Wilhelm
        Reich. Lausanne, 1969.
Phil 6327.21.100   Rycroft, Charles. Wilhelm Reich. N.Y., 1972.
Phil 6327.22   Rühle, Alice G. Freud und Adler. Dresden, 1924.
Phil 6327.23   Rylander, G. Personality changes after operations on the
        frontal lobes. Copenhagen, 1939.
Phil 6327.24   Rohitsek, A. Der Katillon. Zürich, 1925.
Phil 6327.25   Reviere, Joan. Developments in psycho-analysis.
        London, 1952.
Phil 6327.26   Reed, C.F. Psychopathology. Cambridge, Mass., 1958.
Phil 6327.28   Rogers, Carl Ransom. Client-centered therapy.
        Boston, 1951.
Phil 6327.28.80   Braaten, Leif Johan. Klient-sentrert rådgivning og
        terapi...Carl R. Rogers' psykologi. Oslo, 1967.
Phil 6327.28.85   Dijkhuis, Johannes Josephus. De procestheorie van C.R.
        Rogers. Hilversum, 1964.
Phil 6327.30   Rapoport, Robert N. Community as doctor. London, 1960.
Phil 6327.32   Ruitenbeek, H.M. Psychoanalysis and social science.
        N.Y., 1962.
Phil 6327.34   Ruitenbeek, H.M. Psychoanalysis and existential
        philosophy. N.Y., 1962.
Phil 6327.35   Rochman, S. Critical essays on psychoanalysis.
        N.Y., 1963.
Phil 6327.36A   Riessman, Frank. Mental health of the poor. London, 1964.
Phil 6327.36B   Riessman, Frank. Mental health of the poor. London, 1964.
Phil 6327.37.1   Rosenfeld, Herbert A. Psychotic states. N.Y., 1966.
Phil 6327.38   Reich-Dörr, Marta. Zur Psychologie der falschen
        Anschuldigung und falschen Selbstbezichtigung.
        Hamburg, 1962.
Phil 6327.40   Racker, Heinrich. Transference and counter transference.
        London, 1968.
Phil 6327.42   Ree, Frank van. Botsende Generaties. Assen, 1968.
Phil 6327.42.5   Ree, Frank van. Colliding generations. Varanasi, 1970.
Phil 6327.45   Rattner, Josef. Der nervöse Mensch und seine Heilung.
        Zürich, 1965.
Phil 6327.46   Ribot, Théodule. Les maladies de la personnalité.
        Paris, 1885.
Phil 6327.46.7   Ribot, Théodule. Les maladies de la personnalité. 7. éd.
        Paris, 1897.
Phil 6327.46.10   Ribot, Théodule. The diseases of personality.
        Chicago, 1891.
Phil 6327.46.14   Ribot, Théodule. The diseases of personality. 4th ed.
        Chicago, 1906.
Phil 6327.46.18   Ribot, Théodule. Personlighetens sjukdomar.
        Stockholm, 1892.
Phil 6327.46.20   Ribot, Théodule. Le malattie della personalità.
        Milano, 1923.
Phil 6328.1   Sjobring, H. Den individual psykologiska frage ställungen
        inom psykistrien. Uppsala, 1913.
Phil 6328.2   Stekel, Wilhelm. Nervöse Angstzustände und ihre
        Behandlung. Berlin, 1908.
Phil 6328.2.4A   Stekel, Wilhelm. Conditions of nervous anxiety.
        London, 1923.
Phil 6328.2.4B   Stekel, Wilhelm. Conditions of nervous anxiety.
        London, 1923.
Phil 6328.2.5   Stekel, Wilhelm. The beloved ego. London, 1921.
Phil 6328.2.10   Stekel, Wilhelm. Impulshandlungen. Berlin, 1922.
Phil 6328.2.15   Stekel, Wilhelm. The depth of the soul. London, 1921.
Phil 6328.2.17   Stekel, Wilhelm. Was im Grund der seele Ruht. 4e. Aufl.
        Wien, 1909?
Phil 6328.2.20   Stekel, Wilhelm. Peculiarities of behavior. N.Y., 1924.
        2v.
Phil 6328.2.22   Stekel, Wilhelm. Technik der analyschen Psychotherapie.
        Bern, 1938.
Phil 6328.2.25   Stekel, Wilhelm. Technique of analytical psychotherapy.
        London, 1939.
Phil 6328.2.28   Stekel, Wilhelm. Erziehung derEltern. Wien, 1934.
Phil 6328.2.31   Stekel, Wilhelm. Autobiography. N.Y., 1950.
Phil 6328.2.35   Stekel, Wilhelm. Das liebe Ich. Berlin, 1913.
Phil 6328.2.40   Stekel, Wilhelm. Zwang und Zweifel. Berlin, 1927-28.
        2v.
Phil 6328.2.45   Stekel, Wilhelm. Der Seelenarzt. Leipzig, 1933.
Phil 6328.3   Scholz, F. Die Diätetik des Geistes. Leipzig, 1887.
Phil 6328.5   Silberer, Herbert. Problems of mysticism and its
        symbolism. N.Y., 1917.
Phil 6328.5.5   Silberer, Herbert. Probleme der Mystik und ihrer Symbolik.
        Wien, 1914.
Phil 6328.5.10   Silberer, Herbert. Der Zufall und die Kaboldstreiche.
        Bern, 1921.
Phil 6328.6   Sando, I.J. Abnormal behavior. N.Y., 1923.
Phil 6328.7   Slade, T. Kenrick. Our phantastic emotions. London, 1923.
Phil 6328.9   Simonin, A.H. Les sentiments, les passions et la folie
        explications des phénomènes de la pensée et des sensations.
        Paris, 1885.
Phil 6328.10   Schilder, Paul. Seele und Leben. Berlin, 1923.
Phil 6328.10.10   Schilder, Paul. Das Körperschema...Bewusstsein des eigenen
        Körpers. Berlin, 1923.
Phil 6328.10.20   Schilder, Paul. Entwurf zu einer Psychiatrie auf
        psychoanalysischer Grundlage. Leipzig, 1925.
Phil 6328.10.21   Schilder, Paul. Introduction to a psychoanalytic
        psychiatry. N.Y., 1928.
Phil 6328.10.30   Schilder, Paul. Goals and desires of man, a psychological
        survey of life. N.Y., 1942.
Phil 6328.10.40   Schilder, Paul. The image and appearance of the human
        body. N.Y., 1950.

Phil 6310 - 6335   Psychology - Abnormal psychology - General treatises -
    Individual authors (A-Z) - cont.

Phil 6328.11   Stollenhoff, H. Kurzes Lehrbuch der Psychoanalyse.
        Stuttgart, 1926.
Phil 6328.12   Schmitz, O.A.H. Psychoanalyse und Yoga. Darmstadt, 1923.
Phil 6328.13   Schultz-Hencke, Harald. Enführung in die Psychoanalyse.
        Jena, 1927.
Phil 6328.14.2   Schneider, Kurt. Die psychopathischen Personlichkeiten. 2.
        Aufl. Leipzig, 1928.
Phil 6328.15   Schnell, János. Eredmények a magyar kiaérleti
        gyógypedagógiai és orvosi psychologia. Budapest, 1929.
Phil 6328.16   Stephen, Karin. Psychoanalysis and medicine. Cambridge,
        Eng., 1933.
Phil 6328.17   Sachs, Wulf. Psychoanalysis. London, 1934.
Phil 6328.18   Seabury, David. What makes us seem so queer? N.Y., 1934.
Phil 6328.18.10   Seabury, David. Adventures in self discovery. N.Y., 1938.
Phil 6328.19.5   Starr, Moses A. Familiar forms of nervous disease. 2d ed.
        N.Y., 1891.
Phil 6328.20   Szalai, Alex. Philosophische Grundprobleme der
        psychoanalytischen Psycholgie. Budapest, 1935.
Phil 6328.21   Sterba, Richard. Handwörterbuch der Psychoanalyse.
        Wien, 1936-37.
Phil 6328.21.8   Sterba, Richard. Introduction to the psychoanalytic theory
        of the libido. 3d ed. N.Y., 1968.
Phil 6328.22   Smith, J.C. Psykiatriske forelaesninger. København, 1939.
Phil 6328.23   Sandström, T. Ist die aggressivität ein übel?
        Stockholm, 1939.
Phil 6328.24   Sperber, Alice. Über die seelischen Ursachen des Alterns,
        der Jugendlichkeit und der Schönheit. Leipzig, 1925.
Phil 6328.25   Sachs, Hanns. Gemeinsame Tagträume. Leipzig, 1924.
Phil 6328.25.5   Sachs, Hanns. The creative unconscious. Cambridge, 1942.
Phil 6328.26   Stolz, Karl R. The church and psychotherapy. N.Y., 1943.
Phil 6328.27   Speer, Ernst. Die Liebesfähigkeit. 2e Aufl.
        München, 1937.
Phil 6328.28   Sladen, F.J. Psychiatry and the war. 1st ed.
        Baltimore, 1943.
Phil 6328.29   Strecker, E.A. Fundamentals of psychiatry. London, 1944.
Phil 6328.29.10   Strecker, E.A. Psychiatry in modern warfare. N.Y., 1945.
Phil 6328.30   Strachey, Alix. A new German-English psycho-analytical
        vocabulary. Baltimore, 1943.
Phil 6328.31   Schwarz, Theodor. Zur Kritik der Psychoanalyse.
        Zürich, 1945.
Phil 6328.32   Sharpe, E.F. Collected papers on psycho-analysis.
        London, 1950.
Phil 6328.33A   Scheidlinger, S. Psychoanalysis and group behavior. 1st
        ed. N.Y., 1952.
Phil 6328.33B   Scheidlinger, S. Psychoanalysis and group behavior. 1st
        ed. N.Y., 1952.
Phil 6328.34   Schnetze-Niemann, M. Schöpferische Gestaltung aus dem
        Unbewussten. München, 1953.
Phil 6328.35   Sarason, S.B. Psychological problems in mental deficiency.
        N.Y., 1949.
Phil 6328.35.5   Sarason, S.B. Psychological problems in mental deficiency.
        3d ed. N.Y., 1959.
Phil 6328.36   Stern, Erich. Handbuch der klinischen Psychologie. v.1-2.
        Zürich, 1954. 3v.
Phil 6328.38   Stuttgart. Institut für Psychotherapie und
        Tiefenpsychologie. Wiedergeburt des Einzelnen.
        Stuttgart, 1956.
Phil 6328.40   Szondi, Lipot. Triebpathologie. Bern, 1956. 2v.
Phil 6328.40.5   Szondi, Lipot. Kain, Gestalten des Bösen. Bern, 1969.
Phil 6328.42   Sachs, Hanns. Masks of love and life. London, 1957.
Phil 6328.44   Sutherland, John D. Psycho-analysis and contemporary
        thought. London, 1958.
Phil 6328.46   Sechehaye, Marguerte Albert. Diagnosties psychologiques.
        Berne, 1949.
Phil 6328.48   Spitz, René. A genetic field theory of ego formation.
        N.Y., 1959.
Phil 6328.50   Stone, Leo. The psychoanalytic situation. N.Y., 1961.
Phil 6328.52   Sarbin, T.R. Studies in behavior pathology. N.Y., 1961.
Phil 6328.54   Salzman, Leon. Modern concepts of psychoanalysis.
        N.Y., 1962.
Phil 6328.55   Sundberg, N.D. Clinical psychology. N.Y., 1962.
Phil 6328.56   Schläfer-Wolfram, E. Und du wirst Getrieben.
        Berlin, 1933.
Phil 6328.57   Szumowski, W. Névroses et psychoses au moyen age et au
        début des temps modernes. Paris, 1939.
Phil 6328.58   Sherman, Murray Herbert. Psychoanalysis in America.
        Springfield, 1966.
Phil 6328.59   Seifert, Friedrich. Bilder und Urbilder;
        Erscheinungsformen des Arrhetypus. München, 1965.
Phil 6328.60   Saada, Denise. L'héritage de Freud. Paris, 1966.
Phil 6328.62   Szasz, Thomas Stephen. Ideology and insanity. Garden
        City, 1970.
Phil 6328.62.5   Szasz, Thomas Stephen. The ethics of psychoanalysis; the
        theory and method of autonomous psychotherapy. N.Y., 1965.
Phil 6328.64   Silverman, Samuel. Psychologic cues in forecasting
        physical illness. N.Y., 1970.
Phil 6328.66   Small, Saul Mouchly. Symptoms of personality disorder.
        N.Y., 1944.
Phil 6329.1.3   Tridon, André. Psychoanalysis and behavior. N.Y., 1920.
Phil 6329.1.8   Tridon, André. Easy lessons in psychoanalysis.
        N.Y., 1921.
Phil 6329.1.9   Tridon, André. Psychoanalysis; its history, theory and
        practice. N.Y., 1923.
Phil 6329.1.10   Tridon, André. Psychoanalysis; its history, theory and
        practice. N.Y., 1920.
Phil 6329.1.12   Tridon, André. Psychoanalysis and man's unconscious
        motives. N.Y., 1924.
Phil 6329.2.5   Turco, Natale. Il trattamento morale dello scrupole e
        dell'ossessione morbossa. Torino, 1919-20. 2v.
Phil 6329.3   Taylor, W.S. Readings in abnormal psychology. N.Y., 1926.
Phil 6329.4   Turner, Julia. The psychology of self-consciousness.
        London, 1923.
Phil 6329.5   Tissi, Silvio. La psicanalisi. Milano, 1929.
Phil 6329.6   Tuinstra, C.L. Het symbool in de psychoanalyse.
        Amsterdam, 1933.
Phil 6329.7   Trog, H. Die Religionstheorie der Psychoanalyse. Diss.
        Hamburg, 1914.
Phil 6329.8   Tomkins, S.S. Contemporary psychopathology.
        Cambridge, 1943.
Phil 6329.10   Tramer, Moritz. Lehrbuch der allgemeinen
        Kinderpsychiatrie. Basel, 1945.
Phil 6329.12   Turel, Adrien. Bachofen-Freud. Bern, 1939.
Phil 6329.12.5.2   Turel, Adrien. Selbsterlösung. 1. und 2. Aufl.
        Berlin, 1919.
Phil 6329.14   Trüb, Hans. Heilung aus der Begegnung. Stuttgart, 1951.
Phil 6329.15   Tashman, H.F. Today's neurotic family. N.Y., 1957.

Classified Listing

Phil 6310 - 6335   Psychology - Abnormal psychology - General treatises -
Individual authors (A-Z) - cont.

Phil 6329.16   Thorpe, Louis P. The psychology of abnormal behavior. N.Y., 1961.

Phil 6329.17   This, Bernard. La psychanalyse. Paris, 1960.

Phil 6329.18   Schulze, H. Der progressiv, domesticierte Mensch und seine Neurosen. München, 1964.

Phil 6329.19   Thompson, Clara M. Interpersonal psychoanalysis. N.Y., 1964.

Phil 6329.20   Taylor, Frederick K. Psychopathology. London, 1966.

Phil 6329.22   Roazen, Paul. Brother animal; the story of Freud and Tausk. 1st ed. N.Y., 1969.

Phil 6329.22.5   Eissler, Kurt Robert. Talent and genius. N.Y., 1971.

Phil 6330.1   Urbantschitsch, R. Psycho-analysis for all. London, 1928.

Phil 6330.2   Ullmann, Leonard P. A psychological approach to abnormal behavior. Englewood, Cliffs, 1969.

Phil 6331.1   Valentine, C.W. Dreams and the unconscious; an introduction to the study of psycho-analysis. London, 1921.

Phil 6331.1.5   Valentine, C.W. The new psychology of the unconscious. London, 1932.

Phil 6331.2   Vivante, Leone. Note sopra la originalitá del pensiero. Roma, 1924?

Phil 6331.2.3   Vivante, Leone. Note sopra la originalità del pensiero. Roma, 1925.

Phil 6331.2.5   Vivante, Leone. Notes on the originality of thought. London, 1927.

Phil 6331.3   Verband der Vereine Katholischer Akademiker, Kevalaer. Religion und Seelenleiden. v. 1,2,3,6. Düsseldorf, 1926. 4v.

Phil 6331.4   Vittoz, Roger. Treatment of neurasthenia by teaching of brain control. London, 1911.

Phil 6331.4.5   Vittoz, Roger. Le docteur Roger Vittoz et l'angoisse de l'homme moderne. Paris, 1965.

Phil 6331.5   Van Teslaar, J.S. An outline of psychoanalysis. N.Y., 1925.

Phil 6331.6   Van der Veldt, J.H. Psychiatry and Catholicism. 1st ed. N.Y., 1952.

Phil 6331.6.2   Van der Veldt, J.H. Psychiatry and Catholicism. 2nd ed. N.Y., 1957.

Phil 6331.7   Viard, Marcel. Le noeu suprême de Socrate. Paris, 1953.

Phil 6331.8   Viane, Andre. Psychologie van het onheilsvoorspellen. Gent, 1963.

Phil 6331.10   Vandendriessche, Gaston. The parapraxis in the Haizmann case of Sigmund Freud. Louvain, 1965.

Htn   Phil 6332.1*   Weir, J. The psychical correlation of religious emotion and sexual desire. 2d ed. Louisville, Ky., 1897.

Phil 6332.1.2   Weir, J. The psychical correlation of religious emotion and sexual desire. 2d ed. Louisville, Ky., 1897.

Phil 6332.2.7   Wells, F.L. Mental adjustments. N.Y., 1920.

Phil 6332.2.9   Wells, F.L. Mental adjustments. N.Y., 1922.

Phil 6332.3   Williams, Edward H. Increasing your mental efficiency. N.Y., 1914.

Phil 6332.4.3   Watts, Frank. Abnormal psychology and its educational applications. London, 1921.

Phil 6332.5   Wolfram, E. Gegen Psycho-Analyse. Leipzig, 1918.

Phil 6332.6   Williams, T.A. Dreads and besetting fears. Boston, 1923.

Phil 6332.7   Wohlgemuth, A. A critical examination of psycho-analysis. N.Y., 1923.

Phil 6332.8   Wallon, H. Psychologie pathologique. Paris, 1926.

Phil 6332.9   Whitehead, George. Psycho-analysis and art. London, 1930.

Phil 6332.9.15   Whitehead, George. Gods, devils, and men. London, 1928.

Phil 6332.10   Wallin, John E.W. Personality maladjustments and mental hygiene. 1st ed. N.Y., 1935.

Phil 6332.11   Wickes, F.G. Inner world of man. N.Y., 1938.

Phil 6332.11.5   Wickes, F.G. The inner world of choice. N.Y., 1963.

Phil 6332.12   Wittels, Fritz. Die Technik der Psychoanalyse. München, 1926.

Phil 6332.13   Wolberg, Lewis R. Hypoanalysis. N.Y., 1945.

Phil 6332.14   Wartis, Joseph. Soviet psychiatry. Baltimore, 1950.

Phil 6332.15   Walker, Nigel. A short history of psychotherapy in theory and practice. London, 1957.

Phil 6332.16   Wolff, Konrad. Psychologie und Sittlichkeit. Stuttgart, 1958.

Phil 6332.18   Waelder, Robert. Basic theory of psychoanalysis. N.Y., 1960.

Phil 6332.19   White, Robert. The abnormal personality. 2. ed. N.Y., 1956.

Phil 6332.19.3   White, Robert. The abnormal personality. 3d ed. N.Y., 1964.

Phil 6332.20   Wyrsch, J. Gesellschaft, Kultur und psychische Störung. Stuttgart, 1960.

Phil 6332.22   Wyss, Dieter. Die tiefenpsychologischen Schulen von der Anfanger bis zur Gegenwart. Göttingen, 1961.

Phil 6332.22.2   Wyss, Dieter. Depth psychology, a critical history. N.Y., 1966.

Phil 6332.23   Wolstein, B. Irrational despair. N.Y., 1962.

Phil 6332.24   Weinschenk, Curt. Die erbliche Lese- rechtsssch Reiheschwäche. Bern, 1962.

Phil 6332.26   Wenar, Charks. Origins of psychosomatic and emotional disturbances. N.Y., 1962.

Phil 6332.28   Winch, R.F. Identification and its familial determinants. Indianapolis, 1962.

Phil 6332.30   Wells, Harry K. The failure of psychoanalysis. N.Y., 1963.

Phil 6332.31   Weinberg, Henry. Case book in abnormal psychology. N.Y., 1964.

Phil 6332.32   Weisman, A.D. The existential core of psychoanalysis. Boston, 1965.

Phil 6332.33   Wolberg, Lewis Robert. Psychotherapy and the behavoral sciences. N.Y., 1966.

Phil 6332.34   Wanke, Georg. Psychoanalyse: Geschichte, Wesen. 2. Aufl. Halle, 1926.

Phil 6332.40   Winnicott, Donald Woods. The maturational processes and the facilitating environment. London, 1965.

Phil 6332.45   Whitmont, Edward. The symbolic quest. N.Y., 1969.

Phil 6332.50   Weigert, Edith. The courage to love. New Haven, 1970.

Phil 6332.55   Wiesenhuetter, Eckhart. Grundbegriffe der Tiefenpsychologie. Darmstadt, 1969.

Phil 6334.5   Yellowlees, H. A manuel of psychotherapy. London, 1923.

Phil 6334.10A   Yankelovich, Daniel. Ego and instinct; the psychoanalytic view of human nature. N.Y., 1970.

Phil 6334.10B   Yankelovich, Daniel. Ego and instinct; the psychoanalytic view of human nature. N.Y., 1970.

Phil 6335.5   Zander, R. Vom Nervensystem. 3. Aufl. Leipzig, 1918.

Phil 6335.10   Zweig, S. Die heilung durch den Geist; Mesmer, Mary Baker, Eddy, Freud. Wien, 1936.

Phil 6335.15   Zilboorg, Gregory. Mind, medicine and man. N.Y., 1943.

Phil 6310 - 6335   Psychology - Abnormal psychology - General treatises -
Individual authors (A-Z) - cont.

Phil 6335.15.5   Zilboorg, Gregory. Psychoanalysis and religion. N.Y., 1962.

Phil 6335.20   Zeigarnik, B.V. Patologiia myshleniia. Moskva, 1962.

Phil 6350   Psychology - Abnormal psychology - General special treatises -
Psychodiagnosis in general

Phil 6350.2   Buerli, Alois. Indikation zur analytischen Psychotherapie mit Hilfe des "Experimentellen Triebdiagnostik". Bern, 1970.

Phil 6360   Psychology - Abnormal psychology - General special treatises -
Psychopathology in children

Phil 6360.2   Browning, Robert Mitchell. Behavior modification in child treatment. Chicago, 1971.

Phil 6360.5   Rie, Herbert E. Perspectives in child psychopathology. Chicago, 1971.

Phil 6360.6   Lempp, Reinhart. Eine Pathologie der psychischen Entwicklung. Bern, 1967.

Phil 6360.8   Eckensberger, Diethnd. Sozialisationsbedingungen der öffentlichen Erziehung. 1. Aufl. Frankfurt am Main, 1971.

Phil 6360.10   Manual of child psychopathology. N.Y., 1972.

Phil 6360.12   Quay, Herbert Callister. Psychopathological disorders of childhood. N.Y., 1972.

Phil 6360.14   Aspects of autism. London, 1968.

Phil 6390   Psychology - Abnormal psychology - General special treatises -
Neuroses - General works

Phil 6390.2   Landmann, S. Die Mehrheit geistiger Persönlichkeiten in einem Individuum. Stuttgart, 1894.

Phil 6390.4   Bagby, English. The psychology of personality. N.Y., 1928.

Phil 6400   Psychology - Abnormal psychology - Conditions of a mixed nature - Speech
and language disorders - General works

Phil 6400.01   Pamphlet box. Philosophy. Aphasia.

Phil 6400.1   Ballet, G. Le langage intérieur. Paris, 1886.

Phil 6400.1.3   Ballet, G. Die innerliche Sprache und die verschiedenen Formen der Aphasie. Leipzig, 1890.

Phil 6400.2   Bernard, D. De l'aphasie. Paris, 1885.

Phil 6400.2.2   Bernard, D. De l'aphasie. Paris, 1889.

Htn   Phil 6400.3*   Freud, S. Zur Auffassung der Aphasien. Leipzig, 1891.

Phil 6400.4   Meringer, R. Versprechen und Verlesen. Stuttgart, 1895.

Phil 6400.5.5   Bulin, René. Eine besondere Art der Wortblindhut, Dyslehre. Wiesbaden, 1887.

Phil 6400.6   Wernicke, C. Der aphasische Symptomencomplex. Photoreproduction. Breslau, 1874.

Phil 6400.7   Bernheim, Hippolyte. Doctrine de l'aphasie. Paris, 1907.

Phil 6400.8   Bianchi, Leonardo. Licções sobre as localisações cerebraes. Rio de Janeiro, 1899.

Phil 6400.9   Mirallie, C. De l'aphasie sensorielle. Paris, 1896.

Phil 6400.11   Ferrand, Auguste. Le langage, la parole et les aphasies. Paris, 1894.

Phil 6400.12   Pick, A. Über das Sprachverständnis. Leipzig, 1909.

Phil 6400.13   Bastian, H.C. The Lumleian lectures on some problems in connection with aphasia and new speech defects. n.p., 1897.

Phil 6400.14   Head, Henry. Aphasia and kindred disorders of speech. Cambridge, Eng., 1926. 2v.

Phil 6400.15   Legroux, A. De l'aphasie. Thèse. Paris, 1875.

Phil 6400.16   Weisenburg, T. Aphasia. N.Y., 1935.

Phil 6400.17   Goldstein, Kurt. The problem of the meaning of words based upon observation of aphasic patients. Worcester, 1936.

Phil 6400.18   Granich, L. Aphasia: a guide to retraining. N.Y., 1947.

Phil 6400.19   Wepman, J.M. Recovery from aphasia. N.Y., 1951.

Phil 6400.20.2   Goldstein, Kurt. Language and language disturbances. N.Y., 1948.

Phil 6400.21   Forsboom, Bernhard. Das Buch Emanuel. München, 1957.

Phil 6400.22   Osgood, Charles E. Approaches to the study of aphasia. Urbana, 1963.

Phil 6400.23   Hekaen, Henry. Pathologie du langage. Paris, 1965.

Phil 6400.24   Winkler, Carl. Abnormal speech. Orange, Conn., 1932.

Phil 6400.25   Hein, Leopold. Speech and voice. London, 1942.

Phil 6400.30.2   Brain, Walter Russell. Speech disorders; aphasia, apraxia and agnosia. 2d ed. London, 1965.

VPhil 6400.31   Maruszewski, Mariusz. Afazja. Wyd. 1. Warszawa, 1966.

Phil 6400.32   Lubin, Carl Kenneth. Language disturbance and intellectual functioning. The Hague, 1969.

Phil 6400.33   Travis, Lee E. Speech pathology. N.Y., 1931.

Phil 6400.33.5   Travis, Lee E. Handbook speech pathology. N.Y., 1957.

Phil 6400.34   Luriia, Aleksandr Romanovich. Traumatic aphasia. The Hague, 1970.

Phil 6400.35   Heese, Gerhard. Sprachpflege kurs für Schwerhörige und Ertaubte. Berlin, 1963.

Phil 6400.36   Vetter, Harold J. Language behavior and psychopathology. Chicago, 1969.

Phil 6400.38   Durieu, Colette. La rééduction des aphasiques. Bruxelles, 1969.

Phil 6405   Psychology - Abnormal psychology - Conditions of a mixed nature - Speech
and language disorders - Agraphia, disorders of writing

Phil 6405.2   Myklebust, Helmer R. Development and disorders of written language. N.Y., 1965.

Phil 6420   Psychology - Abnormal psychology - Conditions of a mixed nature - Speech
and language disorders - Stammering and stuttering

Phil 6420.01   Pamphlet box. Stammering.

Phil 6420.2   Beech, H.R. Research and experiment in Stuttering. Oxford, 1968.

Phil 6420.4   Greenbaum, Ferdinand. Erklärung des Stotterns, dessèn Heilung und Verhütung. Leipzig, 1897.

Phil 6420.6   Thorpe, Eliza Jane Ellery. Speech hesitation. N.Y., 1900.

Phil 6420.8   Rosenberg, William L. Stuttering, its cause and remedy. Cleveland, 19- ?

Phil 6420.10   Lewis, George Andrew. The practical treatment of stammering and stuttering. Detroit, 1902.

Phil 6420.12   Bluemel, Charles Sidney. Stammering and cognate defects of speech. N.Y., 1913. 2v.

Phil 6420.12.5   Blumel, Charles Sidney. Stammering and allied disorders. N.Y., 1935.

Phil 6420.14   Fletcher, John Madison. An experimental study of stuttering. Thesis. Worcester, 1914.

Phil 6420.14.5   Fletcher, John Madison. The problem of stuttering. N.Y., 1928.

Phil 6420.16.5   Bogue, Benjamin N. Stammering; its cause and cure. Indianapolis, 1926.

Phil 6420   Psychology - Abnormal psychology - Conditions of a mixed nature - Speech and language disorders - Stammering and stuttering - cont.

Phil 6420.16.9   Bogue, Benjamin N. Stammering; its cause and correction. Indianapolis, 1939.

Phil 6420.18   Froeschels, Emil. Das Stottern: assoziative Aphasie. Leipzig, 1925.

Phil 6420.20   Robbins, Samuel D. Stammering and its treatment. Boston, 1926.

Phil 6420.22   Trumper, Max. A hemato-respiratory study of 101 consecutive cases of stammering. Thesis. Philadelphia, 1928.

Phil 6420.24   Coriat, Isador H. Stammering; a psychoanalytic interpretation. N.Y., 1928.

Phil 6420.26   Fogerty, Elsie. Stammering. N.Y., 1930.

Phil 6420.28   Greene, James S. I was a stutterer; stories from life. N.Y., 1932.

Phil 6420.30   Wolfe, Paul J. A home study course in the correction of stuttering and stammering. n.p., 1932.

Phil 6420.32   Blanton, Smiley. For stutterers. N.Y., 1936.

Phil 6420.34   McAllister, Anne H. Clinical studies in speech therapy. London, 1937.

Phil 6420.36.1   Gifford, Mabel F. Correcting nervous speech disorders. N.Y., 1940.

Phil 6420.36.5   Gifford, Mabel F. How to overcome stammering. N.Y., 1940.

Phil 6420.38   Heltman, Harry J. First aide for stutterers. Boston, 1943.

Phil 6420.40   Pellman, Charles. Overcoming stammering. N.Y., 1947.

Phil 6420.42   Eisenson, John. Stuttering; a symposium. N.Y., 1958.

Phil 6440   Psychology - Abnormal psychology - Conditions of a mixed nature - Memory disorders - General works

Phil 6440.5   Delay, Jean. Les maladies de la mémoire. 5e ed. Paris, 1970.

Phil 6480   Psychology - Abnormal psychology - Conditions of a mixed nature - Dreaming [Discontinued]

Htn   Phil 6480.15*   Tryon, T. A treatise of dreams and visions. London, 168-.

Htn   Phil 6480.23*   Freud, Sigmund. Die Traumdeutung. Leipzig, 1909.

X Cg   Phil 6480.23.5   Freud, Sigmund. The interpretation of dreams. 4th ed. London, 1915. 2v.

X Cg   Phil 6480.23.6   Freud, Sigmund. The interpretation of dreams. London, 1932.

Htn   Phil 6480.23.7*   Freud, Sigmund. Über den Traumdeutung. Wiesbaden, 1901.

Phil 6480.23.13   Freud, Sigmund. On dreams. London, 1924.

Phil 6480.23.18   Freud, Sigmund. The interpretation of dreams. N.Y., 1950.

Htn   Phil 6480.26*   Goodwin, P. The mystery of dreames. London, 1658.

Phil 6480.55&   moral reflections in a dreams. London, 1708. 50v.

Phil 6480.125   Walsh, William S. The psychology of dreams. N.Y., 1920.

Phil 6480.160   Baynes, H.G. Mythology of the soul. Baltimore, 1940.

Phil 6480.167   Dream dictionary. Cincinnati, 1919.

Phil 6480.192   Mozzuchelli, M. I sogni. Milano, 1954.

Phil 6480.194   Roheim, Geza. The gates of the dream. N.Y., 1952.

Phil 6480.200.5   Becker, Raymond de. Les machinations de la nuit. Paris, 1965.

Phil 6480.213   Hall, Calvin Springer. The content analysis of dreams. N.Y., 1966.

Phil 6480.236   Bruller, Jean. Ce que tout rêveur doit savoir de la méthode psychanalytique d'interprétation des rêves. Paris, 1934.

Phil 6480.265   Caligor, Leopold. Dreams and symbols. N.Y., 1969.

Phil 6520   Psychology - Abnormal psychology - Organic psychoses - Ecstacy [Discontinued]

Phil 6520.01   Pamphlet box. Philosophy. Ecstasy and stigmatism.

Phil 6520.7   Wollersheim, T. Das Leben der ekstatischen und stigmatischen Christina von Stommeln. Köln, 1859.

Phil 6520.7.9   Zoepf, L. Die Mystikerin Margaretha Ebner. Leipzig, 1914.

Phil 6520.14   Christiany, L. Eva von Buttler die Messaline und Muckerin...Mysterien des Pietismus. Stuttgart, 1870.

Phil 6535   Psychology - Abnormal psychology - Organic psychoses - Epilepsy - Reports

Phil 6535.7   Charity Organization Society, London. The epileptic and crippled child and adult. Photoreproduction. London, 1893.

Phil 6536   Psychology - Abnormal psychology - Organic psychoses - Epilepsy - Monographs

Phil 6536.01   Pamphlet box. Philosophy. Epilepsy.

Phil 6536.5   Ninde, F.W. The application of the auditory memory test to two thousand institut'l epileptics. West Chester, 1924?

Phil 6536.6   Wreschner, A. Psychologische Untersuchungen an Normalen, Schwachbegabten und Epileptikern. Leipzig, 1927.

Phil 6536.7   Vogt, Heinrich. Die Epilepsie im Kindesalter mit besonderer Berücksichtigung erzieherischer, unterrichtlicher und forensischer Fragen. Berlin, 1910.

Phil 6536.8   Tracy, Edward A. The basis of epilepsy. Boston, 1930.

Phil 6536.9   Lennox, W.G. Science and seizures. N.Y., 1941.

Phil 6536.10   Lundborg, Herman B. Die progressive myoklonus-epilepsie. Upsala, 1903.

Phil 6536.11   Penfield, W. Epilepsy and cerebral localization. 1st ed. Springfield, 1941.

Phil 6536.13   Putnam, T.J. Convulsive seizures; how to deal with them. 2d. ed. Philadelphia, 1945.

Phil 6536.14   Rows, R.G. Epilepsy, a functional mental illness. N.Y., 1926.

Phil 6540   Psychology - Abnormal psychology - Organic psychoses - Paresis

Phil 6540.2   Hollós, Stefom. Psychoanalysis and the psychic disorder of general paresis. N.Y., 1925.

Phil 6615   Psychology - Abnormal psychology - Psychoneurotic disorders - Hysteria - General works

Phil 6615.2   Guinon, Georges. Les agents provocateurs de l'hystérie. Paris, 1889.

Phil 6615.4   Bastian, Henry Charlton. Various forms of functional paralysis. London, 1893.

Phil 6615.6   Janet, Pierre. Etat mental des hystériques. Paris, 1893-94. 2v.

Phil 6615.6.7   Janet, Pierre. The major symptoms of hysteria. 2. ed. N.Y., 1920.

Phil 6615.6.8   Janet, Pierre. The major symptoms of hysteria. 2. ed. N.Y., 1929.

Phil 6615.8   Hellpach, Willy. Grundlinien einer Psychologie der Hysterie. Leipzig, 1904.

Phil 6615.10   Fox, Charles Daniel. Psychopathology of hysteria. Boston, 1913.

Phil 6615.12   Kretschmer, Ernst. Über hysterie. Leipzig, 1923.

Phil 6615   Psychology - Abnormal psychology - Psychoneurotic disorders - Hysteria - General works - cont.

Phil 6615.12.3   Kretschmer, Ernst. Hysterie, reflex und instikt. 3. Aufl. Leipzig, 1944.

Phil 6615.12.5   Kretschmer, Ernst. Hysteria. N.Y., 1926.

Phil 6615.14   Ranschburg, Pál. Neue Beiträg zur Psychologie des hysterischen Geisteszustandes. Leipzig, 1897.

Phil 6615.16   Schleich, Carl Ludwig. Gedankenmacht und Hysterie. Berlin, 1922.

Phil 6615.18   Buess, Heinrich. Die Wandlungen des Psychogenie- Begriffs. Inaug. Diss. Hölstein, 1940.

Phil 6615.20.5   Breuer, Josef. Studies on hysteria. London, 1956.

Phil 6615.20.6   Breuer, Josef. Studies on hysteria. N.Y., 1957.

Phil 6615.20.7   Breuer, Josef. Studies in hysteria. Boston, 1961.

Phil 6615.22   Veith, Ilza. Hysteria; the history of a disease. Chicago, 1965.

Phil 6619   Psychology - Abnormal psychology - Psychoneurotic disorders - Hysteria - Special topics

Phil 6619.2   Pitres, Albert. Leçons cliniques sur l'hystérie et l'hypnotisme faites à l'hôpital Saint André de Bordeaux. Paris, 1891. 2v.

Phil 6619.2.5   Pitres, Albert. Des anesthésies hystériques. Bordeaux, 1887.

Phil 6619.4.2   Richer, Paul. Etudes cliniques sur la grande hystérie ou hystéro-épilepsie. 2. ed. Paris, 1885.

Phil 6619.4.5   Sanctis, Sante de. I sogni e il sonno nell'isterismo e nella epilessia. Roma, 1896.

Phil 6619.6   Cattani, Giuseppe. Isterismo e sentimento. 19. ed. Milano, 1894.

Phil 6619.8.5   Ingenieros, José. Histeria y sugestión 5. ed. Buenos Aires, 1919.

Phil 6619.10   Ingenieros, José. Le langage musical et ses troubles hystériques. Paris, 1907.

Phil 6619.12   Grafé, A. Etude sur quelques paralysies d'origine psychique. Bruxelles, 1889.

Phil 6619.14   Godefroy, Jan C.L. Onderzoekingen over de aandachtsbepaling bij gezonden en zielszieken. Groningen, 1915?

Phil 6625   Psychology - Abnormal psychology - Psychoneurotic disorders - Psychogenic depression - General works

Phil 6625.2   Dumas, Georges. Les états intellectuels dans la mélancolie. Paris, 1895.

Phil 6625.4   Semal. De la sensibilité générale et de ses altérations dans les affections mélancoliques. Paris, 1875.

Phil 6625.6   Bright, Timothy. A treatise of melancholie. N.Y., 1940.

Phil 6625.8   Beck, Aaron T. Depression: clinical, experimental, and theoretical aspects. N.Y., 1967.

Phil 6625.10   Greenacre, Phyllis. Affective disorders. N.Y., 1961.

Phil 6629   Psychology - Abnormal psychology - Psychoneurotic disorders - Psychogenic depression - Other special

Phil 6629.2   Fawcett, Benjamin. Über Melankolie. Leipzig, 1785.

Phil 6631   Psychology - Abnormal psychology - Psychoneurotic disorders - Obsessive-compulsive states - Tic

Phil 6631.5   Meige, Henry. Der Tic. Leipzig, 1903.

Phil 6634   Psychology - Abnormal psychology - Psychoneurotic disorders - Obsessive-compulsive states - Other special

Phil 6634.5   Kuijper, Siem. Einge especten vom vrij en dwangmatig herhalen. Hilversum, 1963.

Phil 6640   Psychology - Abnormal psychology - Psychoneurotic disorders - Occupational neuroses - General works

Phil 6642.5   Barbizet, Jacques. Pathologie de la mémoire. 1. éd. Paris, 1970.

Phil 6659   Psychology - Abnormal psychology - Psychoneurotic disorders - Other psychoneuroses

Phil 6659.2   Binger, Carl A.L. Personality in arterial hypertension. N.Y., 1945.

Phil 6660 - 6695   Psychology - Abnormal psychology - Hypnotism [Discontinued]

Phil 6668.1   Pamphlet vol. Letter to Brigham on animal magnetism. 7 pam.

Phil 6668.3   Robiano, Comte de. Neururgie oder der thierische Magnetismus. Stuttgart, 1849.

Htn   Phil 6668.4*   Lettres sur le magnetis. n.p., 178-. 3 pam.

Phil 6668.800.-.999   Pamphlet box. Philosophy. Hypnotism.

Htn   Phil 6669.01PF*   Pamphlet box. Philosophy. Hypnotism.

Phil 6669.1   Bertrand, A. Du magnetisme animal en France. Paris, 1826.

Htn   Phil 6669.4*   Hervier, C. Lettre sur la découverte du magnetisme. Pekin, 1784.

Phil 6669.11   Wolfe, Bernard. Hypnotism comes of age. 1st ed. Indianapolis, 1948.

Phil 6670.1   Ashburner, J. Notes and studies... philosophy of animal magnetism. London, 1867.

Phil 6670.2   Abrutz, Sydney. Hypnos och suggestion. Stockholm, 1925.

Phil 6671.1   Babbitt, E.D. Vital magnetism. N.Y., n.d.

Phil 6671.2   Barety, A. Le magnetisme animal. Paris, 1887.

Phil 6671.3   Bennett, J.H. The mesmeric mania. Edinburgh, 1851.

Phil 6671.4   Bérillon, E. Hypnotisme experimental. Paris, 1884.

Phil 6671.4.5   Bérillon, E. De la suggestion. Paris, 1886.

Phil 6671.4.9   Bérillon, E. Historie de l'hypnotisme expérimental. Paris, 1902.

Phil 6671.5   Bernheim, H. Hypnotisme. Paris, 1891.

Phil 6671.5.3   Bernheim, H. Hypnotisme and suggestion. Paris, 1910.

Phil 6671.5.4   Bernheim, H. Die Suggestion und ihre Heilwirkung. Leipzig, 1888.

Phil 6671.5.5   Bernheim, H. De la suggestion. Paris, 1884.

Phil 6671.5.9   Bernheim, H. Automatisme et suggestion. Paris, 1917.

Phil 6671.6   Bersot, P.E. Mesmer, le magnétism animal. Paris, 1879.

Phil 6671.7   Binet, A. Le magnetisme animal. Paris, 1887.

Phil 6671.7.5   Binet, A. Animal magnetism. N.Y., 1888.

Phil 6671.8   Bourru, H. La suggestion mentale. Paris, 1887.

Phil 6671.9   Bottey, F. Le magnétisme animal. Paris, 1886.

Htn   Phil 6671.10*   Braid, James. Electro-biological phenomena. Edinburgh, 1851.

Htn   Phil 6671.10.5*   Braid, James. Power of the mind over the body. London, 1846.

Phil 6671.10.10   Braid, James. Magic, witchcraft, animal magnetism. London, 1852.

X Cg   Phil 6671.10.15   Braid, James. Neurypnology. London, 1899.

Phil 6671.10.20   Braid, James. Neurypnologie. Paris, 1883.

Phil 6660 - 6695   Psychology - Abnormal psychology - Hypnotism [Discontinued] - cont.

Phil 6671.11   Buchanan, A. On darlingism, misnamed electro-biology. London, 1851.

Phil 6671.12   Bush, G. Mesmer and Swedenborg. N.Y., 1847.

Phil 6671.13   Barnes, W.A. Personal magnetism and clairvoyance. 4th ed. Boston, 1900.

Phil 6671.13.5   Barnes, W.A. Personal influence. Boston, 1906.

Phil 6671.13.7   Barnes, W.A. Psychology, hypnotism, personal magnetism and clairvoyance. Boston, 1898.

Htn   Phil 6671.14*   Baader, F. Uber die Extase oder das Verzücktseyn der magnetischen Schlafredner. Leipzig, 1817.

Phil 6671.15   Bramwell, J.M. Hypnotism. 2nd ed. London, 1906.

Phil 6671.15.6   Bramwell, J.M. Hypnotism: its history, practice, and theory. N.Y., 1956.

Phil 6671.16   Beaunis, H. Der künstlich Hervorgerufene Somnambulismus. Leipzig, 1889.

Phil 6671.17   Belfiore, Giulio. Magnetismo e ipnotismo. 2. ed. Milano, 1903.

Phil 6671.18   Burdin, C. Historie académique du magnétisme animal. Paris, 1841.

Phil 6671.19.3   Brown, William. Suggestion and mental analysis. 3. ed. London, 1923.

Phil 6671.20   Benussi, V. La suggestione e l'ipnosi come mezzi di analisi psichisa reale. Bologna, 1925.

Phil 6671.21   Billot, G.P. Recherches psychologiques...magnétisme vital. v.1-2. Paris, 1839.

Phil 6671.22.5   Baragnon, Petrus. Étude magnétisme animal sous le point de vue d'une exacte pratique. 2. éd. Paris, 1853.

Phil 6671.23   Bormes, Baron de. Lettre de M.L.B.D.B....sur l'existence du magnétisme animal. Genève, 1784.

Htn   Phil 6671.24*   Bergasse, N. Lettre d'un médicin. Bordeaux, 1784.

Phil 6671.25   Björnström, F.J. Hypnotism. 1889.

Phil 6671.27   Kline, M.V. A scientific report on the search for Bridey Murphy. N.Y., 1956.

Phil 6671.28   Bernstein, Morey. The search for Bridey Murphy. London, 1956.

Phil 6671.28.5   Bernstein, Morey. The search for Bridey Murphy. 1. ed. Garden City, N.Y., 1956.

Phil 6671.28.6   Bernstein, Morey. The search for Bridey Murphy. Garden City, N.Y., 1965.

Phil 6672.1   Calcutta Mesmeric Hospital. Second half-yearly report. London, 1850.

Phil 6672.2   Chardel, C. Esquisse de la nature humaine. Paris, 1826.

Phil 6672.3   Chazarain, L.T. Découverte de la polarité humaine. Paris, 1886.

Phil 6672.4   Colquhoun, J.C. Isis Revelata: an inquiry into animal magnetism. London, 1836. 2v.

Phil 6672.5   Congrès Internationale de L'Hypnotisme. Comptes rendue. Paris, 1889.

Phil 6672.6   Coste, P. Marie Léon. L'inconscient étude sur l'hypnotisme. Paris, 1889.

Phil 6672.7   Crocq, Jean J. L'hypnotisme scientifique. Paris, 1896.

Phil 6672.8   Caperu, T. Mighty curative powers of mesmerism. London, 1851.

Phil 6672.9   Cahagnet, L. Magnétisme, arcanes de vie future. Paris, 1848.

Phil 6672.9.5   Cahagnet, L. Celestial telegraph. 1. American ed. N.Y., 1855.

Phil 6672.9.15   Cahagnet, L. Magnétisme; encyclopédie magnétique. v.1-6. Paris, 1854-62. 3v.

Htn   Phil 6672.9.17*   Cahagnet, L. Magnetic magic. n.p., 1898.

Phil 6672.10   Charpignon, J. Physiologie, médecine et métaphysique. Paris, 1848.

Htn   Phil 6672.11*   Cambry, Jacques. Traces du magnétisme. La Haye, 1784. 2 pam.

Phil 6672.12   Cullere, A. Magnétisme et hypnotisme. Paris, 1886.

Phil 6672.13   Claparède, Édouard. Recherches expérimentales sur quelques processus psychiques simples dans un cas d'hypnose. Genève, 1909.

Phil 6672.14A   Cannon, A. Sleeping through space. 1st ed. N.Y., 1939.

Phil 6672.14B   Cannon, A. Sleeping through space. 1st ed. N.Y., 1939.

Phil 6672.16   Chertok, León. Hypnosis. 1st ed. Oxford, 1966.

Phil 6673.1   Delaage, M.H. Le monde prophétique. Paris, 1853.

Phil 6673.2   Deleuze, J.P.F. Histoire critique du magnétisme animal. Paris, 1819. 2v.

Phil 6673.2.3   Deleuze, J.P.F. Histoire critique du magnétisme animal. Paris, 1813. 2v.

Phil 6673.2.5   Deleuze, J.P.F. Instruction pratique sur le magnétisme animal. Paris, 1825.

Phil 6673.2.8   Deleuze, J.P.F. Practical instruction in animal magnetism Providence, 1837.

Phil 6673.2.15   Deleuze, J.P.F. Lettre à l'auteur d'un ouvrage intitulé: superstitions et prestiges des philosophies du dix-huitième siècle. Paris, 1818.

Phil 6673.3   Dods, J.B. Six lectures on philosophy of mesmerism. Boston, 1843.

Phil 6673.3.5   Dods, J.B. The philosophy of electrical psychology. N.Y., 1850.

Phil 6673.3.6   Dods, J.B. The philosophy of electrical psychology. N.Y., 1852.

Phil 6673.4.3   Du Potet, J. de S. Traité complet de magnétisme animal. 5e éd. Paris, 1894.

Phil 6673.4.5   Du Potet, J. de S. Manuel de l'étudiant magnétiseur. 3e éd. Paris, 1854.

Phil 6673.4.7   Du Potet, J. de S. Manuel de l'étudiant magnétiseur. 5e éd. Paris, 1887.

Phil 6673.4.10   Du Potet, J. de S. Cours de magnétisme en sept leçons. Paris, 1840.

Phil 6673.4.11   Du Potet, J. de S. Cours de magnétisme animal. Paris, 1834.

Phil 6673.4.15   Du Potet, J. de S. Exposé des expériences sur le magnétisme. Paris, 1821.

Phil 6673.4.17   Du Potet, J. de S. L'université de Montpellier et le magnétisme animal. Beziers, 1836.

Phil 6673.4.19   Du Potet, J. de S. An introduction to the study of animal magnetism. London, 1838.

Phil 6673.4.21   Du Potet, J. de S. Le magnétisme opposé a la médecine. Paris, 1840.

Phil 6673.4.22   Du Potet, J. de S. Essai sur l'enseignement philosophique du magnétisme. Paris, 1845.

Phil 6673.5   Durant, C.F. Exposition, or A new theory animal magnetism. N.Y., 1837.

Phil 6673.6   Durand, J.P. Cours théorique et C. de Braidisme. Paris, 1860.

Phil 6673.7   Despine, P. Étude scientifique sur le somnambulisme. Paris, 1880.

Phil 6673.8   Davey, William. The illustrated practical mesmerist. 6th ed. London, 1862?

Phil 6660 - 6695   Psychology - Abnormal psychology - Hypnotism [Discontinued] - cont.

Phil 6673.9   Donati, Alberto. I misteri svelati dello ipnotismo. Roma, 1886.

Phil 6673.10   Dupau, Jean A. Lettres physiologiques...sur le magnétisme. Paris, 1826.

Phil 6673.12   Darly, Joseph. Day visions and clairvoyant night dreams. London, 1892.

Phil 6673.13   Dixon, Jacob. Hygienic clairvoyance. London, 1859.

Phil 6673.14   Dubor, G. de. The mysteries of hypnosis. N.Y., 1923.

Phil 6673.15   Du Prel, Carl. Experimentalpsychologie und Experimentalmetaphysik. Leipzig, 1891.

Phil 6673.16   Durville, H. Magnétisme personnel ou psychique. Paris, 1905.

Phil 6673.16.5   Durville, H. The theory and practice of human magnetism. Chicago, 1900.

Phil 6673.17   Delboeuf, J. Magnétiseurs et médecins. Paris, 1890.

Phil 6673.17.10   Delboeuf, J. Le magnétime animal. Paris, 1889.

Phil 6673.18   Delaudine, Antoine François. De la philosophie corpusculaire. Paris, 1785.

Htn   Phil 6673.19*   Doppet, F.A. Traité théorique. Turin, 1784.

Phil 6674.1   Ennemoser, J. Der Magnetismus in Verhältnisse zur Natur und Religion. Stuttgart, 1842.

Phil 6674.2   Eschenmayer, C.A. Versuch der scheinbare Magie der thierischen Magnetismus. Stuttgart, 1816.

Phil 6674.3   Estlin, John B. Remarks on mesmerism in 1845. London, 1845.

Phil 6674.3.5   Estlin, John B. An address...medical profession of Bristol and Bath. London, 1843.

Phil 6674.4   Esdaile, James. Mesmerism in India. Hartford, 1847.

Phil 6674.4.2K   Esdaik, James. Mesmerism in India. London, 1846.

Phil 6674.5   Elliotson, John. The Harveian oration. London, 1846.

Phil 6674.6   Entreties sur le magnétisme animal. Paris, 1823.

Phil 6674.7   Edgerley, W.J. Lessons in the mechanics of personal magnetism. Washington, D.C., 1888.

Phil 6674.7.15   Edgerley, W.J. Cultivation of personal magnetism. 11. ed. Meriden, Conn., 1923.

Phil 6674.8   Estabrooks, G.H. Hypnotism. N.Y., 1943.

Phil 6675.1A   Fahnestock, W.B. Statu volism. Chicago, 1871.

Phil 6675.1B   Fahnestock, W.B. Statu volism. Chicago, 1871.

Phil 6675.2   Féré, C. La médecine d'imagination. Paris, 1886.

Phil 6675.3   Foissac, P. Rapports...sur magnétisme animal. Paris, 1833.

Phil 6675.4   Académie des Sciences, Paris. Report on experiments on animal magnetism. Edinburgh, 1833.

Phil 6675.5   Fusinieri, A. von. La dinamica molecolare. Foligno, 1866.

Phil 6675.6   Forel, A. Hypnotism and cerebral activity. Worcester, 1899.

Phil 6675.6.5   Forel, A. Hypnotism or suggestion and psychotherapy. N.Y., 1907.

Phil 6675.6.7   Forel, A. Der Hypnotismus. 2. Aufl. Stuttgart, 1891.

Phil 6675.7   Foveau de Courmelles, F.V. L'hypnotisme. Paris, 1890.

Phil 6675.8   Fischer, E.L. Der sogenante Lebensmagnetismus oder Hypnotismus. Mainz, 1883.

Phil 6675.9   Fonvielle, W. de. Les endormeurs. Paris, n.d.

Phil 6675.10   Feyrer, E.C. Practical psychology. Springfield, Mass., 1913.

Phil 6675.12   France. Commissaires Chargée de l'Examen du Magnétisme Animal. Rapport des commissaires chargée par le roi de l'examen du magnétisme animal. Paris, 1784.

Phil 6675.13   Fox, Alfred J. Mind "magic". N.Y., 1937.

Phil 6676.1   Gessman, G. Magnetismus und Hypnotismus. Wien, 1887.

Phil 6676.2   Gauthier, A. Histoire du somnambulisme. Paris, 1842. 2v.

Phil 6676.3   Grimes, J.S. Etherology and the phreno-philosophy. Boston, 1850.

Phil 6676.4   Gibbes, R.W. Lecture on the magnetism of the human body. Columbia, 1843.

Phil 6676.5   Gregary, William. Letters to a candid inquirer on animal magnetism. London, 1851.

Phil 6676.6   Grásset, J. L'hypnotisme et la suggestion. 4. éd. Paris, 1916.

Phil 6676.7   Grossmann, J. Die Bedeutung der hypnotischen Suggestion als Heilmittel. Berlin, 1894.

Phil 6676.8   Guidi, Franc. Il magnetismo animale. Milano, 1860.

Phil 6676.9   Garrett, Thomas L. Hypnotism. N.Y., 1934.

Phil 6676.10   Goldsmith, M. Franz Anton Mesmer. Photoreproduction. London, 1934.

Phil 6677.1   Hart, E. Hypnotism, mesmerism. N.Y., 1893.

Phil 6677.1.5   Hart, E. Hypnotism, mesmerism and the new witchcraft. London, 1896.

Phil 6677.2   Heidenhain, R.P.H. Animal magnetism. London, 1880.

Phil 6677.3A   Husson, H.M. Report on the magnetical experiments. Boston, 1836.

Phil 6677.3B   Husson, H.M. Report on the magnetical experiments. Boston, 1836.

Phil 6677.5   Haberman, J.V. Hypnosis. N.Y., 1910.

Phil 6677.7   Hall, Spencer T. Mesmeric experiences. London, 1845.

Htn   Phil 6677.8*   Histoire véritable du magnétisme animal. La Haye, 1785.

Phil 6677.9   Hall, Charles R. Mesmerism. 1st American ed. N.Y., 1845.

Phil 6677.10   Hilgu, Wilhelm. Die Hypnose und die Suggestion. Jena, 1909.

Phil 6677.11.2   Haddock, J.W. Somnolism and psycheism. 2d ed. London, 1851.

Phil 6677.12.2   Hélot, C. L'hypnotisme franc et l'hypnotisme vrai. Paris, 1909.

Phil 6677.13   Howard, W.L. Hypnotism as a therapeutic agent. Baltimore, 1893.

Phil 6677.14   Hodson, Geoffrey. The science of seership. Philadelphia, 1930.

Phil 6677.15   Hull, C.L. Hypnosis and suggestibility. N.Y., 1933.

Phil 6677.16   Holsbéek, H. von. Lettres sur le magnétisme animal. Bruxelles, 1863.

Phil 6677.17   Harraden, L.A. Complete illustrated course of twenty lessons in magnetic healing. n.p., 1899.

Phil 6677.18   Hénin de Cuvillers, E.T. Exposition critique du système et de la doctrine mystique des magnétistes. Paris, 1822.

Phil 6677.19   Hont, D. La lumière sur le magnétisme. Neuchâtel, 1880.

Phil 6677.20   Hammerschlag, Heinz F. Hypnotism and crime. Hollywood, Calif., 1957.

Phil 6678.1   Imbert-Gourbeyre, A. L'hypnotisme et la stigmatisation. Paris, 1899.

Phil 6679.1   James, John. Mesmerism, with hints for beginners. London, 1879.

Phil 6679.2   Janin de Combe Blanche, J. Reponse au discours. Genève, 1784.

Phil 6679.3   Janis, I.L. Are the cominform countries using hypnotic techniques to elicit confessions. Santa Monica, Calif., 1949.

Phil 6660 - 6695   Psychology - Abnormal psychology - Hypnotism [Discontinued] - cont.

Htn Phil 6680.1*   Kerner, J. Die Seherin von Prevorst. Stuttgart, 1829. 2v.

Phil 6680.1.4   Kerner, J. Die Seherin von Prevorst. 4. Aufl. Stuttgart, 1746.

Phil 6680.1.4.5   Kerner, J. Die Seherin von Prevorst. 2. Aufl. Stuttgart, 1746.

Phil 6680.1.5   Kerner, J. The Seeress of Prevorst. N.Y., 1855.

Phil 6680.1.6   Kerner, J. Die Seherin von Prevorst. Leipzig, 18- .

Phil 6680.1.25   Kretschmar, F. Die Seherin von Prevorst. Weinsberg, 1929.

Phil 6680.1.30   Sopp, Erich. Auf den Spuren der Seheim. Sersheim, 1953.

Phil 6680.2   Krafft-Ebing, R. von. Eine experimentelle Studie. Stuttgart, 1888.

Phil 6680.2.3   Kraft-Ebing, R. von. Hypnotische Experimente. Stuttgart, 1893.

Phil 6680.3   Kiesewetter, C. Mesmer's Leben und Lehre. Leipzig, 1893.

Phil 6680.4   Kaplan, Leo. Hypnotismus, animismus. Leipzig, 1917.

Phil 6680.5.2   Kauffmann, M. Suggestion und Hypnose. 2. Aufl. Berlin, 1923.

Phil 6680.6.3   Kluge, C.A.F. Versuch einer Darstellung dis animalischen Magnetismus. Berlin, 1818.

Phil 6680.7A   Kahn, S. Suggestion and hypnosis made practical. Boston, 1945.

Phil 6680.7B   Kahn, S. Suggestion and hypnosis made practical. Boston, 1945.

Phil 6680.8   Kluge, G. Zhivotnyi magnitizm. Sankt Peterberg, 1818.

Phil 6681.1   Ladame, P. La névrose hypnotique. Paris, 1881.

Phil 6681.2   Lafontaine, C. L'art de magnétiser. Paris, 1886.

Phil 6681.2.5   Lafontaine, C. Mémoires d'un magnétiseur. Paris, 1866. 2v.

Phil 6681.3   Lehmann, A. Die Hypnose. Leipzig, 1890.

Phil 6681.4   Liébeault, A.A. Du sommeil et des états analogues. Paris, 1866.

Phil 6681.4.5   Liébeault, A.A. Le sommeil provoqué et les etats analogues. Paris, 1889.

Phil 6681.4.10   Liébeault, A.A. Thérapeutique suggestive, son mécanisme, propriétés du sommeil provoqué. Paris, 1891.

Phil 6681.4.15   Liébeault, A.A. Étude sur le zoomagnétisme. Paris, 1883.

Phil 6681.5   Leger, J. Animal magnetism. N.Y., 1846.

Phil 6681.6.3   Lapponi, Guiseppe. Iypnotismo e spiritismo. 3. ed. Roma, 1907.

Phil 6681.6.5   Lapponi, Guiseppe. Hypnotism and spiritism...travel. 2. ed. N.Y., 1915.

Phil 6681.7   Lonbert, J.B. Le magnétisme et le sommambulisme. Paris, 1844.

Phil 6681.8   Lassaigne, Auguste. Memoires d'un magnétism. Paris, 1851.

Phil 6681.9   Lee, Edwin. Animal magnetism. 3d ed. London, 1843. 2 pam.

Phil 6681.9.2   Lee, Edwin. Animal magnetism. London, 1849.

Phil 6681.10   Lutzebourg. Nouveaux extraits des journaux d'un magnétiseur. Strasbourg, 1788.

Phil 6681.11   Lombard, A. Les dangers du magnétisme animal. Paris, 1819.

Phil 6681.12   Luys, J. Leçons cliniques sur les principaux phenomènes de l'hypnotisme. Paris, 1890.

Phil 6681.13   Leonidas (pseud.). Stage hypnotism. Chicago, 1901.

Phil 6681.14   Leadbeater, C.W. Clairvoyance. 2d ed. London, 1903.

Phil 6681.15   Lloyd, B. Layton. Hypnotism in the treatment of disease. London, 1934.

Phil 6681.16.5   Le Cron, L.M. Experimental hypnosis. N.Y., 1954.

Phil 6682.1   Magnin, P. Etude clinique et expérimentale sur l'hypnotisme. Paris, 1884.

Phil 6682.2   Martineau, H. Letters on mesmerism. N.Y., 1845.

Phil 6682.3   Mesmer, F.A. Mesmerismus. Berlin, 1814.

Phil 6682.3.2   Mesmer, F.A. Mesmerismus. London, 1948.

Phil 6682.3.4   Mesmer, F.A. Mémoire du magnetisme animal. n.p., 1781. 4 pam.

Phil 6682.3.5   Mesmer, F.A. Précis historique des faits relatifs au magnétisme. Paris, 1781.

n Phil 6682.3.7*   Mesmer, F.A. Mémoire sur la dicouverte du magnetisme animal. Genève, 1799.

Phil 6682.3.10   Mesmer, F.A. Aphorismes de Mesmer. 3. éd. Paris, 1785.

n Phil 6682.3.11*   Mesmer, F.A. Lettres à messieure les auteurs du journal de Paris et à M. Franklin. n.p., 1784.

n Phil 6682.3.12*   Mesmer, F.A. Letters à M. Vicq-d'Azyr. Bruxelles, 1784.

n Phil 6682.3.13*   Mesmer, F.A. Lettres guéri. London, 1784.

n Phil 6682.3.14*   Mesmer, F.A. Lettre à M. le comte de C. Paris? 1784.

Phil 6682.3.80   Jensen, Ann. Franz Anton Mesmer. N.Y., 1967.

Phil 6682.3.85   Look, Maria van. Franz Anton Mesmer, Reinhold Schneider. Freiburg, 1969.

Phil 6682.4   Mesnet, E. Outrages à la pudeur...Somnambulisme. Paris, 1894.

Phil 6682.5   Meyer, J.A.G. Natur. Gotha, 1839.

Phil 6682.6.3   Moll, Albert. Hypnotism. London, 1892.

Phil 6682.6.4   Moll, Albert. Hypnotism. 4th ed. London, 1898.

Phil 6682.6.9   Moll, Albert. Hypnotism. London, 1909?

Phil 6682.6.15   Moll, Albert. Hypnotism. 2. ed. London, 1890.

Phil 6682.7   Morin, A.S. Du magnétisme. Paris, 1860.

Phil 6682.8   Morselli, E.A. Il magnetismo animale. Torino, 1886.

Phil 6682.9   Marin, Carmen. Endemoniada de Santiago. Valparaiso, 1857.

Phil 6682.10   Melvelle, John. Crystal-gazing and the wonders of clairvoyance. London, 1910.

Phil 6682.10.2   Melvelle, John. Crystal-gazing and the wonders of clairvoyance. London, 1910.

Phil 6682.11   Mason, Rufus O. Hypnotism and suggestion in theraputics. N.Y., 1911.

Phil 6682.12   Morand, J.S. Le magnétisme animal. Paris, 1889.

Phil 6682.13*   Montjore, C.F.L. Lettre sur le magnétisme animal. Philadelphia, 1784.

Phil 6682.14   Millington, T.S. A lecture on the phenomena of dreams, mesmerism, clairvoyance. London, 1852?

Phil 6682.15   Le magnétisme traduit en cour d'assises. Paris, 1845.

Phil 6682.16   Reymond, Mine. Vve. Cours de magnétisme. Paris, 1886.

Phil 6682.17   Moreau, R.C. L'hypnotisme. Paris, 1891.

Phil 6682.18   Medeiros e Albuquerque, J.J. de C. da C. O hypnotismo. 3. ed. Rio de Janeiro, 1926.

Phil 6682.19   Mialle, S. Exposé par ordre alphabétique des cures. Paris, 1826. 2v.

Phil 6682.20   Mercier, A.D. La vérité du magnétisme, prouvée par les faits. Paris, 1829.

Phil 6682.21   Moutin, Lucien. Le magnétisme humain. Paris, 1907.

Phil 6682.22   Magnia, E. L'art et hypnose. Genève, 1905?

Phil 6682.24   Marcuse, F.L. Hypnosis through the world. Springfield, Ill., 1964.

Phil 6683.1   Newman, J.B. Fascination. N.Y., 1847.

Phil 6683.2   Newman, W. Human magnetism. London, 1845.

Phil 6683.2.2   Newman, W. Human magnetism. N.Y., 1845.

Phil 6660 - 6695   Psychology - Abnormal psychology - Hypnotism [Discontinued] - cont.

Phil 6683.3   Nani, Giacomo D. Trattato teorico-pratico sul magnetismo animale. Torino, 1850.

Phil 6684.1   Ochorowicz, J. De la suggestion mentale. Paris, 1887.

Phil 6684.1.5   Ochorowicz, J. Mental suggestion. v.1-4. N.Y., 1891.

Phil 6684.2.3   Osgood, H. Therapeutic value of suggestion. Boston, 1890.

Phil 6684.3   Ottolenghi, S. Nuovo studi sull'ipnotismo. Torino, 1889.

Phil 6684.4   Olivier, J. Traité de magnétisme. Paris, 1854.

Phil 6685.1   Passavant, J.K. Untersungen und der Lebensmagnetismus. Frankfurt, 1821.

Phil 6685.2   Peabody, J.R. World of wonders. Boston, 1838.

Phil 6685.3   Petri, J.G. Der thierische magnetismus. Tlmenau, 1824.

Phil 6685.4   Peyen, C. Progress of animal magnetism. Boston, 1837.

Phil 6685.5   Preyer, W. Der Hypnotismus. Wien, 1890.

Phil 6685.6   Putnam, A. Mesmerism, spiritualism. Boston, 1872.

Phil 6685.7   Podmore, F. Mesmerism and christian science...history of mental healing. Philadelphia, 1909.

Phil 6685.7.5   Podmore, F. From Mesmer to Christian Science. N.Y., 1964.

Phil 6685.8   Pigeaire, Jules. Puissance de l'électricité animale. Paris, 1839.

Phil 6685.9   Puységur, Armand Marie Jacques de Chastenet. Du magnétisme animal. Paris, 1807.

Phil 6685.9.5   Puységur, Armand Marie Jacques de Chastenet. Mémoires pour servir à l'histoire et à l'establissement du magnétisme animal. 3. éd. Paris, 1820.

Htn Phil 6685.10*   Paulet, J.J. Mesmer justifié. Constance, 1784.

Htn Phil 6685.10.5*   Paulet, J.J. L'antimagnétisme, ou origine. Loudres, 1784.

Htn Phil 6685.11*   The philosophy of animal magnetism. Philadelphia, 1837.

Phil 6685.12   Petetin, J.H.D. Electricité animale. Paris, 1808.

Phil 6685.13   Purtscher, Nora. Doctor Mesmer. London, 1947.

Phil 6685.14   Philippe, Anthelme Philippe. Vie et paroles du maitre. Lyon, 1959.

Phil 6686.1.5   Quackenbos, J.D. Hypnotic therapeutics. N.Y., 1908.

Phil 6687.1.2   Reichenback, C. Physico-physiological researches. N.Y., 1851.

Phil 6687.1.3   Reichenback, C. Researches on magnetism, electricity. London, 1850.

Phil 6687.1.6   Reichenback, C. Der sensitive Mensch. Leipzig, 1910. 2v.

Phil 6687.1.9   Reichenback, C. Odisch-magnetische Briefe. Stuttgart, 1852.

Phil 6687.1.15   Reichenback, C. Le fluide des magnétiseurs. Paris, 1891.

Phil 6687.2   Richter, J.A.L. Betrachtungen und der animal Magnetismus. Leipzig, 1817.

Phil 6687.3   Rieger, C. Der Hypnotismus. Jena, 1884.

Phil 6687.4   Recollection of a society clairvoyant. London, 1911.

Phil 6687.5   Randolph, P.B. Seership. The magnetic mirror. Toledo, 1875.

Phil 6687.6   Rochas, d'Aiglun, A. L'extériorisation de la sensibilité. 6e éd. Paris, 1909.

Phil 6687.6.2   Rochas d'Aiglun, A. L'extériorisation de la sensibilité. 2e éd. Paris, 1895.

Phil 6687.6.9   Rochas d'Aiglun, A. de. Les forces non définies. Paris, 1887.

Phil 6687.7   Roullier, A. Exposition physiologique des phénomènes du magnétisme animal. Paris, 1817.

Phil 6687.8   Rosenmüller, J.G. Lettre à la société exegétique...magnétisme animal. Leipzig, 1788.

Phil 6687.9   Ricard, J.J.A. Letters d'un magnétiseur. Paris, 1843.

Phil 6687.10   Regnier, L.R. Hypnotisme et croyances anciennes. Paris, 1891.

Phil 6687.11   Rossi-Pagnoni, F. Quelques essais de médiumnité hypnotique. Paris, 1889.

Phil 6687.12   Rouxel. Histoire et philosophie du magnétisme. Paris, 1895. 2v.

Phil 6687.13   Recueil des pieces les plus interessantes sur le magnétisme animal. n.p., 1784.

Phil 6687.14   Rodriquez, Rafael E. Psicoterapia por medio de la hipnosis. Montevideo, 1944.

Phil 6688.1   Schaffer, K. Suggestion und Reflex. Jena, 1895.

Phil 6688.2   Sinnett, A.P. The relationale of mesmerism. Boston, 1892.

Phil 6688.4   Steinbeck, F.A. Der Dichter ein Seher. Leipzig, 1856.

Phil 6688.5   Stone, W.L. Letter to Dr. Brigham on animal magnetism. N.Y., 1837.

Phil 6688.6   Sage, X.L. Hypnotism as it is. N.Y., 1897.

Phil 6688.6.2   Sage, X.L. Hypnotism as it is. Rochester, 1899.

Phil 6688.8   Sandby, G. Mesmerism and its opponents. 2. ed. London, 1848.

Phil 6688.8.2   Sandby, G. Mesmerism and its opponents. London, 1844.

Phil 6688.9   Schrenck von Notzing, A.P. Die Traumtänzerin Magdeleine G. Stuttgart, 1904.

Phil 6688.10   Stephenson, Charles Y. (Mrs.). Clairvoyance and crystal gazing. London, 1918.

Phil 6688.11   Sunderland, La Roy. "Confessions of a magnetiser" exposed. Boston, 1845.

Phil 6688.12   Sturm, G. Mesmerismus und Hypnotismus. Leipzig, n.d.

Phil 6688.13   Szapary, Franz von. Magnétisme et magnétothérapie. Paris, 1853.

Phil 6688.14   Scoresby, William. Zoistic magnetism. London, 1849.

Phil 6688.15.2   Ségouin, A. Les mystères de la magie ou les secrets du magnetisme. 2e éd. Paris, 1853.

Phil 6688.16   Staite, Opie. Mesmerism, or The new school of arts. London, 1844.

Phil 6688.17   Satow, Louis. Hypnotism and suggestion. London, 1923.

Phil 6688.18   Schilder, Paul. Lehrbuch der Hypnose. Wien, 1926.

Phil 6688.19   Schilder, Paul. Uber das Wesen derHypnose. 2. Aufl. Berlin, 1922.

Phil 6688.21   Segnitz, F.L. Specimen inaugurale medicum de electricitate. Jenae, 1790.

Phil 6688.22   Schrenck von Notzing, A. Ein Beitrag zur therapeutischen Verwerthung des Hypnotismus. n.p., 1888-97. 18 pam.

Phil 6688.23.2   Scobardi, R.P. Rapport confidentiel sur le magnétisme animal. 2. éd. Paris, 1839.

Phil 6688.24   Sheldon, William. The millennium: the goodtime coming. Springfield, 1862.

Phil 6688.25   Sarrazin de Montferrier, A.A.V. Der principes et des procédés du magnetisme animal. Paris, 1819. 2v.

Phil 6688.26   Sousselier, de la Tour. L'âmi de la nature, ou Manière de traiter les maladies. Dijon, 1784.

Phil 6688.27   Société Harmonique des Amis-Reunis de Strasbourg. Exposé de différentes cures. Strasbourg, 1786.

Phil 6688.28   Servan, J.M.A. Questions adressées. Padova, 1784.

Phil 6688.29   Salter, Andrew. What is hypnosis. N.Y., 1944.

Phil 6688.30   Shor, Ronald E. The nature of hypnosis. N.Y., 1965.

Phil 6689.1   Tarkhanof, J.R. Hypnotisme, suggestion.

Phil 6689.2   Townehend, C.H. Facts in mesmerism. Boston, 1841.

Phil 6689.2.2   Townehend, C.H. Facts in mesmerism. N.Y., 1841.

Phil 6689.2.5   Townehend, C.H. Mesmerism proved true. London, 1854.

Phil 6660 - 6695   Psychology - Abnormal psychology - Hypnotism [Discontinued] - cont.

Phil 6689.3   Tuckey, C.L. Psycho-therapeutics. London, 1890.
Phil 6689.3.5   Tuckey, C.L. Treatment by hypnotism and suggestion. 6. ed. London, 1913.
Phil 6689.4   Teste, A. A practical manual of animal magnetism. London, 1843.
Phil 6689.5   Thomas, Northcote W. Crystal gasping. London, 1905.
Phil 6689.6   Tardy de Montravel, A.A. Journal du traitement magnétique. London, 1786. 2 pam.
Phil 6689.6.3   Tardy de Montravel, A.A. Journal du traitement magnétique. Strasbourg, 1787.
Phil 6689.6.15   Tardy de Montravel, A.A. Essai sur la théorie du somnambulisme magnétique. Londres, 1787.
Phil 6689.7.3   Trömner, Ernst. Hypnotismus und Suggestion. 3e Aufl. Leipzig, 1919.
Phil 6689.8   Thouret. Recherches et doutes sur le magnetisme animal. Paris, 1784.
Phil 6689.9   Tartaruga, U. Aus dem Reiche der Hellsehwunders. Pfullingen, 1924.
Phil 6689.10   Tischner, Rudolf. Franz Anton Mesmer. München, 1928.
Phil 6689.11   Tamburini, A. Anleitung zur experimentellen Untersuchung des Hypnotismus. Wiesbaden, 1882-85.
Phil 6690.1   L'union Protectrice. Appel à tous les partisans et amis du magnétisme. 2e éd. Paris, 1850.
Phil 6691.1   Vincent, R.H. Elements of hypnotism. London, 1893.
Phil 6691.2   Vinchon, Jean. Mesmer et son secret. Paris, 1936.
Phil 6692.1   Ware, J. Animal magnetism. n.p., 1851.
Phil 6692.2.2   What is mesmerism? 2nd ed. London, 1862.
Phil 6692.3   Wetterstrand, O.G. Hypnotism and its application to practical medecine. N.Y., 1899.
Phil 6692.5   Wolff, C. Hipnotisms teatral. Barcelona, 19- .
Phil 6692.6   Wendler, C.A. De magnetisms animali. Diss. Lipsiae, 1805.
Phil 6692.6.5   Wendler, C.A. De magnetismi animalis efficacia rite diiudicanda. Lipsiae, 1818.
Phil 6692.7   Wiener, M. Selma, die jüdische Seherin. Berlin, 1838.
Phil 6692.8B   Winn, Ralph B. Scientific hypnotism. Boston, 1939.
Phil 6692.9   Wesermann, N.M. Der Magnetismus und die allgemeine Weltsprache. Creveld, 1822.
Phil 6692.10   Weitzenhoffer, André M. Hypnotism. N.Y., 1953.
Phil 6692.10.5   Weitzenhoffer, André M. Stanford hypnotic suseptibility scale. Palo Alto, 1959.
Phil 6694.1   Yeshilian, M.A. Hypnotism and telepathy. N.Y., 1917.
Phil 6694.2   Young, Paul C. An experimental study of mental and physical functions in the normal and hypnotic states. Thesis. n.p., 1923.
Phil 6694.2.5   Young, Paul C. An experimental study of mental and physical functions in the normal and hypnotic states. Ithaca, 1925.
X Cg   Phil 6694.3   Younger, D. Full, concise instructions in mesmerism. 3. ed. London, 1887.
Phil 6695.1   Zilboorg, G. A history of medical psychology. N.Y., 1941.

Phil 6720   Psychology - Abnormal psychology - Hysteria [Discontinued]

Phil 6720.01   Pamphlet box. Philosophy. Hysteria.
Htn   Phil 6720.6*A   Breuer, Josef. Studien über Hysterie. Leipzig, 1895.
Htn   Phil 6720.6*B   Breuer, Josef. Studien über Hysterie. Leipzig, 1895.
Htn   Phil 6720.6.10* Breuer, Josef. Studien über Hysterie. Leipzig, 1909.

Phil 6750   Psychology - Abnormal psychology - Mental deficiency - Idiocy, Imbecility - Monographs (By date, e.g. .260 for 1960)

Phil 6750.01   Pamphlet box. Philosophy. Feebleminded.
Phil 6750.1   Brown, B. Treatment, cure, cretins, idiots. Boston, 1847-62. 4 pam.
Phil 6750.2   Colquhoun, L. Report of the proceedings...of idiotry. Edinburgh, 1837.
Phil 6750.3   Howe, S.G. Report to the legislature. Boston, 1847.
Phil 6750.3.5   Howe, S.G. Report to the legisture of Massachusetts upon idiocy. Boston, 1848.
Phil 6750.3.7   Howe, S.G. Causes and prevention of idiocy. Boston, 1874.
Phil 6750.5   Moreau, P. Fous et Bouffons. Paris, 1888.
Phil 6750.6   Noir, J. Étude sur les tics. Paris, 1893.
Phil 6750.7   Seguin, E. Idiocy and its treatment. N.Y., 1866.
Phil 6750.7.5   Seguin, E. New facts and remarks concerning idiocy. N.Y., 1870.
Phil 6750.7.10   Seguin, E. Idiocy. Albany, 1907.
Phil 6750.8   Sollier, P. Psychologie de l'idiot. Paris, 1891.
Phil 6750.9   Voisin, J. L'idiotie. Paris, 1893.
Phil 6750.10   Davis, C.H.S. The classification...feeble minded, imbecile and idiotic. N.Y., 1883.
Phil 6750.11   Sherlock, E.B. Feeble minded, guide to study. London, 1911.
Phil 6750.12   Virginia. State Board of Charities and Corrections. Mental defectives in Virginia. Richmond, 1915.
Phil 6750.13   Key, Wilhelmine E. Feeble-minded citizens in Pennsylvania. Philadelphia, 1915.
Phil 6750.14   Munro, Caroline S.G. The blight of the feeble-minded. Boston, 191-?
Phil 6750.15   National Conference of Charities and Corrections. Feeble-mindedness and insanity. Chicago, 1916?
Phil 6750.16   Pennsylvania. Commission on Segregation, Care and Treatment of the Feebleminded and Epileptic Persons. Report of the commission. Harrisburg, 1913.
Phil 6750.17   Sheffield, Herman B. The backward baby. N.Y., 1915.
Phil 6750.18   Tredgold, A.F. Mental deficiency (Amentia). N.Y., 1908.
Phil 6750.18.5   Tredgold, A.F. Mental deficiency (Amentia). 2d ed. N.Y., 1914.
Phil 6750.18.12 Tredgold, A.F. Mental deficiency (Amentia). 4.ed. N.Y., 1922.
Phil 6750.18.15 Tredgold, A.F. Mental deficiency (Amentia). 5th ed. N.Y., 1929.
Phil 6750.25   Wallin, John E.W. Problems of subnormality. Yonkers-on-Hudson, 1917.
Phil 6750.26   Nöll, Heinrich. Intentionalität, Reaktivität und Schwachsinn. Halle, 1926.
Phil 6750.27   Pamphlet vol. Defective and delinquent classes. 32 pam.
Phil 6750.216   Binet, Alfred. The intelligence of the feeble-minded. Baltimore, 1916.
Phil 6750.220   MacMurchy, H. The almosts, a study of the feeble minded. Boston, 1920.
Phil 6750.222   Porteus, S.D. Studies in mental deviations. Vineland, 1922.
Phil 6750.223   Davies, S.P. Social control of the feebleminded. N.Y., 1923.
Phil 6750.223.10 Davies, S.P. Social control of the mentally deficient. N.Y., 1930.
Phil 6750.223.15 Davies, S.P. The mentally retarded in society. N.Y., 1959.

Phil 6750   Psychology - Abnormal psychology - Mental deficiency - Idiocy, Imbecility - Monographs (By date, e.g. .260 for 1960) - cont.

Phil 6750.224   Morrison, B.M. A study of the major emotions in persons of defective intelligence. Berkeley, 1924.
Phil 6750.231   Wembridge, Eleanor H.R. Life among the lowbrows. Boston, 1931.
Phil 6750.234   Penrose, Lionel S. Mental defect. N.Y., 1934.
Phil 6750.235   Town, C.H. Familial feeblemindedness. Buffalo, 1939.
Phil 6750.259   Busemann, Adolf. Psychologie der intelligenz defekte. München, 1959.
Phil 6750.259.2 Busemann, Adolf. Psychologie der intelligenz Defekte. München, 1963.
Phil 6750.262   United States. President's Panel on Mental Retardation. Report of the mission to Denmark and Sweden. Washington, D.C., 1962.
Phil 6750.263   United States. Presdent's Panel on Mental Retardation. Report of the task force education and rehabilitation. Washington, D.C., 1963.
Phil 6750.265   Keblon, Lars. The structure of abilities at lower levels of intelligence. Stockholm, 1965.
Phil 6750.267   Edgerton, Robert B. The look of competence; stigma in the lives of the mentally retarded. Berkeley, 1967.
Phil 6750.267.5 Maire, Luce. Les enfants de nulle part. Paris, 1967.
Phil 6750.269   Heggland, Ruth. Ti år med Erik; en mors beretning om sin hjerneskadede sønn. Oslo, 1969.

Phil 6760   Psychology - Abnormal psychology - Mental deficiency - States due to injury - Mongolism

Phil 6760.5   Gjedde, Georg. Bogen om Jesper. København, 1971.

Phil 6805   Psychology - Abnormal psychology - Personality disorders - General works

Phil 6805.2   Dugas, Laurent. La dépersonnalisation. Paris, 1911.
Phil 6805.4   Sherman, Mandel. Mental conflicts and personality. N.Y., 1938.
Phil 6805.6   Cattell, Raymond Bernard. Crooked personalities in childhood and after. N.Y., 1940.
Phil 6805.8   Strecker, Edward Adam. Their mother's sons. Philadelphia, 1951.
Phil 6805.10   Ohm, August. Persönlichkeitswandlung unter Freiheitsentzug. Berlin, 1964.

Phil 6816   Psychology - Abnormal psychology - Personality disorders - Adult maladjustment - Inferiority complex

Phil 6816.5   Kahn, Samuel. Make inferiorities and superiorities work for you. Ossining, N.Y., 1954.
Phil 6816.10.2   Natale, Nicola G. Vita segreta del complesso d'inferiorita. 2. ed. Bologna, 1961.

Phil 6819   Psychology - Abnormal psychology - Personality disorders - Adult maladjustment - Other special

Phil 6819.6   Rheingold, Joseph Cyrus. The fear of being a woman; a theory of maternal destructiveness. N.Y., 1964.

Phil 6825   Psychology - Abnormal psychology - Personality disorders - Psychopathic personality - General works

Phil 6825.2.2   Cleckley, Hervey Milton. The mask of sanity. 2. ed. St. Louis, 1950.

Phil 6830   Psychology - Abnormal psychology - Personality disorders - Sexual deviations - General works

Phil 6830.4   Venturi, Silvio. Li digenerazioni psico-sessuali. Torino, 1892.
Phil 6830.6.4   Rau, Hans. Die Grausamkeit mit besonder Bezugnahme auf sexuale Factoren. 4. Aufl. Berlin, 1921.

Phil 6834   Psychology - Abnormal psychology - Personality disorders - Sexual deviations - Homosexuality

Phil 6834.1   Millett, Antony P.U. Homosexuality; a bibliography of literature published since 1959 and available in New Zealand. Wellington, 1967.
Phil 6834.2   Carpenter, Edward. Intermediate types among primitive folk. N.Y., 1914.
Phil 6834.3   Welter, Ernst Günther. Bibliographie Freundschaftseros; einschliesslich Homoerotik, Homosexualität und der verwandten und vergleichenden Gebiete. Frankfurt, 1964.
Phil 6834.4   Emde Boas, Coenrad van. Essays in erotiek. Amsterdam, 1969.
Phil 6834.5   Bovet, Théodore. Sinnerfülltes Anders-sein. Tübingen, 1959.
Phil 6834.6   Hutton, Robert. Of those alone. London, 1958.
Phil 6834.8   Dacguino, Giacomo. Diario di un omosessuale. Milano, 1970.
Phil 6834.10   Murphy, John. Homosexual liberation; a personal view. N.Y., 1971.
Phil 6834.15   Parker, William. Homosexuality: a selective bibliography of over 3000 items. Metuchen, N.J., 1971.
Phil 6834.20   Freedman, Mark. Homosexuality and psychological functioning. Belmont, Calif., 1971.

Phil 6836   Psychology - Abnormal psychology - Personality disorders - Sexual deviations - Lesbianism

Phil 6836.2   Frederics, Diana. Diana; a strange autobiography. N.Y., 1939.

Phil 6840   Psychology - Abnormal psychology - Personality disorders - Sexual deviations - Masochism

Phil 6840.2   Gagey, Roland. La volupté dans la souffrance. Paris, 1970?

Phil 6842   Psychology - Abnormal psychology - Personality disorders - Sexual deviations - Sadism

Phil 6842.2   Dawes, C.R. The marquis de Sade. London, 1927.
Phil 6842.2.5   Cleugh, James. The Marquis and the Chevalier. London, 1951.

Phil 6844   Psychology - Abnormal psychology - Personality disorders - Sexual deviations - Transvestism

Phil 6844.2   Raynor, Darrell G. A year among the girls. N.Y., 1966.

Phil 6849   Psychology - Abnormal psychology - Personality disorders - Sexual deviations - Other special

Phil 6849.2   Schumann, Hans Joachim von. Liebesunfähigkeit bie Frauen und ihre Behandlung. München, 1969.
Phil 6849.4   Bell, Alan P. The personality of a child molester. Chicago, 1971.

Phil 6854   Psychology - Abnormal psychology - Personality disorders - Special compulsions - Homicidal and suicidal compulsion

Phil 6854.2 — Leonard, Calista V. Understanding and preventing suicide. Springfield, Ill., 1967.

Phil 6854.4 — Shneidman, Edwin S. The psychology of suicide. N.Y., 1970.

Phil 6854.6 — Masaryk, Tomáš Gottigue. Der Selbstmord als sociale Massenerscheinung des modernen Civilisation. Wien, 1881.

Phil 6854.6.5 — Masaryk, Tomáš Gottigue. Suicide and the meanings of civilization. Chicago, 1970.

Phil 6854.8 — Tetaz, Numa. Du darfst Leben. Zürich, 1970.

Phil 6854.10 — Retterstøl, Nils. Selvmord. Oslo, 1970.

Phil 6854.12 — Jacobs, Jerry. Adolescent suicide. N.Y., 1971.

Phil 6854.14 — Choran, Jacques. Suicide. N.Y., 1972.

Phil 6854.16 — Alvarez, Alfred. The savage god: a study of suicide. London, 1972.

Phil 6859   Psychology - Abnormal psychology - Personality disorders - Special compulsions - Others

Phil 6867.30 — Binswanger, Ludwig. Drei Formen missglückten : Verstiegenheit, Verschrobenheit, Maineriertheit. Tübingen, 1956.

Phil 6903   Psychology - Abnormal psychology - Mental disease - Reference works - Bibliographies

Phil 6903.5 — Driver, Edwin D. The sociology and anthropology of mental illness, a reference guide. Amherst, 1965.

Phil 6903.10 — Tavistock Institute of Human Relations, London. Annotated list of publications, 1946-1970. London, 1970?

Phil 6906   Psychology - Abnormal psychology - Mental disease - History of psychiatry - General works

Phil 6906.5 — Schneck, Jerome M. A history of psychiatry. Springfield, Ill., 1960.

Phil 6906.10 — Ellenberger, Henri F. The discovery of the unconscious. N.Y., 1970.

Phil 6906.15 — Doerner, Klaus. Bürger und Irre. Frankfurt, 1969.

Phil 6930   Psychology - Abnormal psychology - Mental disease - Melancholia [Discontinued]

Phil 6930.01 — Pamphlet box. Psychology. Melancholia.

Phil 6930.7 — Boieldiev, M.J.A. Discours sur la mélancolie. Paris, 1808.

Phil 6940   Psychology - Abnormal psychology - Mental disease - Law and legislation

Phil 6940.5 — Eugenics Society, London. Family council law in Europe. London, 1930.

Phil 6945   Psychology - Abnormal psychology - Mental disease - Hospitals - General works

Phil 6945.1 — Earle, P. History description...Bloomingdale. N.Y., 1848-67. 21 pam.

Phil 6945.2 — Leech, J. Suggestion of the law of the lunacy. London, 1852.

Phil 6945.3 — Kirkbride, T.S. On the construction, organization and general arrangements of hospitals for the insane. Philadelphia, 1854.

Phil 6945.4 — American Psychiatric Association. Propositions and resolutions of the Association of Medical Superintendents of American Institutions for the insane. Philadelphia, 1876.

Phil 6945.5 — Curwen, J. A manual for attendants in hospitals for the insane. Philadelphia, 1851.

Phil 6945.6 — Eddy, T. Hints for introducing an improved mode of treating the insane in the asylum. N.Y., 1815.

Phil 6945.7 — Galt, J.M. Essays on asylums for persons of unsound mind. v.1-2. Richmond, 1850-53.

Phil 6945.8 — Beard, G.M. The asylums of Europe. Cambridge, 1881.

Phil 6945.9 — Seguin, E.C. Lunacy reform. v.1-4. N.Y., 1879-

Phil 6945.10 — Ray, Isaac. Ideal characters of officers of a hospital for the insane. Philadelphia, 1873.

Phil 6945.11 — Pamphlet vol. Dix D.L. Memorials on insane and feebleminded. 15 pam.

Phil 6945.11.5 — Pamphlet vol. Reports of asylums...with mention of Miss Dix. 5 pam.

Phil 6945.11.10 — United States. Congress. Senate. Commission on Public Lands. Report to accompany Bill S44; include memorial of Miss D.L. Dix, January 23, 1848. Washington, 1854.

Phil 6945.12 — Ruggles, A.H. Mental health. Baltimore, 1934.

Phil 6945.14 — Treadway, Walter L. Mental hygiene with special reference to the migration of the people. Washington, 1925.

Phil 6945.15 — Bryan, William A. Administrative psychiatry. N.Y., 1936.

Phil 6945.16 — Clayton, J.M. Speech on the veto message of the President on the bill for the benefit of the indigent insane. Washington, 1854.

Phil 6945.17.2 — Deutsch, Albert. The mentally ill in America. 2. ed. N.Y., 1960.

Phil 6945.17.3 — Deutsch, Albert. The mentally ill in America. 2. ed. N.Y., 1962.

Phil 6945.18 — Grines, J.M. Institutional care of mental patients in the United States. Chicago, 1934.

Phil 6945.20 — Kirkbride, T.S. On the construction, organization and general arrangements of hospitals for the insane. 2. ed. Philadelphia, 1880.

Phil 6945.25 — Hurd, Henry M. The institutional care of the insane in the United States and Canada. Baltimore, 1916-17. 4v.

Phil 6945.30 — Deutsch, Albert. The shame of the States. 1. ed. N.Y., 1948.

Phil 6945.35 — Martin, Denis V. Adventure in psychiatry. Oxford, 1962.

Phil 6945.40 — Programmation, architecture et psychiatrie. Paris, 1967.

Phil 6945.45 — Stanton, Alfred Hodgin. The mental hospital. N.Y., 1954.

Phil 6945.50 — Krause, Elliott Arthur. Factors related to length of mental hospital stay. Boston, 1966?

6946   Psychology - Abnormal psychology - Mental disease - Hospitals - Local (By special scheme) - United States and Canada

Phil 6946.1.5 — Joint Commission on Mental Illness and Health. Action for mental health. N.Y., 1961.

Phil 6946.1.10 — Ridenour, Nina. Mental health in the United States. Cambridge, 1961.

Phil 6946.1.15 — Goffman, E. Asylums. Garden City, 1961.

Phil 6946.1.16 — Goffman, Erving. Asylums: essays on the social situation of mental patients and other inmates. Chicago, 1970.

Phil 6946.1.20 — Felix, Robert Hanna. Mental illness; progress and prospects. N.Y., 1967.

Phil 6946.1.25 — Conolly, John. The construction and government of lunatic asylums. London, 1968.

Phil 6946   Psychology - Abnormal psychology - Mental disease - Hospitals - Local (By special scheme) - United States and Canada - cont.

Phil 6946.38 — Blatt, Burton. Exodus from pandemonium; human abuse and a reformation of public policy. Boston, 1970.

Phil 6946.40 — Parker, Seymour. Mental illness in the urban Negro community. N.Y., 1966.

Phil 6946.42 — U.S. President's Task Force on the Mentally Handicapped. Action against mental disability; the report. Washington, 1970.

Htn Phil 6946.8420* — Dix, D.L. Memorial to Legislative Assembly of Nova Scotia (concerning confinement of insane persons). Halifax? 1850.

Phil 6947   Psychology - Abnormal psychology - Mental disease - Hospitals - Local (By special scheme) - Other countries

Phil 6947.1.5 — Great Britain. Commissioners in Lunacy. Further report. London, 1847.

Phil 6947.1.10 — Robb, Barbara. Sans everything; a case to answer. London, 1967.

Htn Phil 6947.1.893* — Account of the rise and progress of the asylum. Philadelphia, 1814. 2 pam.

Phil 6947.1854 — Amsterdam. Valerius-Kliniek. Een halve eeuw arbeid op psychiatrisch-neurologischgen, terrein 1910-1960. Wagenin, 1960.

Phil 6947.1940 — Venray, Netherlands. Psychiatrisch Ziekenhuis Sint Anna. Een halve eeuw. Venray, 1961?

Phil 6948   Psychology - Abnormal psychology - Mental disease - Pamphlet volumes

Htn Phil 6948.25* — Pamphlet box. Psychology. Insanity. Broadsides.

Phil 6949   Psychology - Abnormal psychology - Mental disease - General treatises - Collected authors (By date, e.g. .360 for 1960)

Phil 6949.363 — Hunter, Richard A. Three hundred years of psychiatry, 1535-1860; a history presented in selected English texts. London, 1963.

Phil 6949.366 — Society of Medical Psycho-Analysts. The etiology of neuroses. Palo Alto, Calif., 1966.

Phil 6949.368 — International Colloquium of Psychopathology of Expression, 4th, Washington, 1966. Psychiatry and art. Basel, 1968.

Phil 6949.369 — Laiblin, Wilhelm. Märchenforschung und Tiefenpsychologie. Darmstadt, 1969.

Phil 6950 - 6975   Psychology - Abnormal psychology - Mental disease - General treatises - Individual authors (A-Z)

Phil 6950.1 — Arnold, T. Observation...insanity, lunacy or madness. v.1-2. Leicester, 1782-86.

Phil 6950.2 — Audiffret, G. Des maladies du cerveau. Paris, 1874.

Phil 6950.3 — Abercrombie, J. Pathological, practical researches, diseases...brain. Philadelphia, 1831.

Phil 6950.4 — Pamphlet box. Amsden, G.S. Minor writings.

Phil 6950.5 — Abby, Carl. Is anyone sane. Boston, 1935.

Phil 6950.6 — Cassinelli, B. Histoire de la folie. Paris, 1939.

Phil 6950.7 — Arieti, S. Interpretation of schizophrenia. N.Y., 1955.

Phil 6950.7.6 — Arieti, S. Interpretation of schizophrenia. N.Y., 1955.

Phil 6950.10 — Symposium on Schizophrenia. Schizophrenia. N.Y., 1959.

Phil 6950.12 — Alvarez, W.C. Minds that came back. Philadelphia, 1961.

Phil 6950.14 — American Psychiatric Association. Comperative psycholinguistic analysis of two psychotherapeutic interviews. N.Y., 1961.

Phil 6951.1 — Bakewell, T. The domestic guide in cases of insanity. Newcastle, 1809.

Phil 6951.2 — Ball, B. La morphinomanie. Paris, 1888.

Phil 6951.3 — Blandford, G.F. Insanity and its treatment. Edinburgh, 1892.

Phil 6951.4.5 — Bucknill, J.C. A manual psychological medicine...insanity. London, 1858.

Phil 6951.4.6 — Bucknill, J.C. A manual psychological medicine...insanity. London, 1879.

NEDL Phil 6951.5.2 — Beers, C.W. A mind that found itself. 2. ed. N.Y., 1912.

Phil 6951.5.3 — Beers, C.W. A mind that found itself. N.Y., 1908.

Phil 6951.5.4.2 — Beers, C.W. A mind that found itself. 4. ed. N.Y., 1920.

Phil 6951.5.5 — Beers, C.W. A mind that found itself. 5. ed. N.Y., 1921.

Phil 6951.5.5.7 — Beers, C.W. A mind that found itself. Garden City, 1925.

Phil 6951.5.6 — Beers, C.W. A mind that found itself. Garden City, 1929.

Phil 6951.5.7 — Beers, C.W. A mind that found itself. Garden City, 1933.

Phil 6951.5.8 — Beers, C.W. A mind that found itself. Garden City, 1937.

Phil 6951.5.10 — Farrar, C.B. The autopathography of C.W. Beers. n.p., 1908.

Phil 6951.5.12 — Farrar, C.B. Twenty-five years of mental hygiene; a tribute to C.W. Beers. n.p., 1933.

Phil 6951.5.15 — Beers, C.W. The mental hygiene movement. N.Y.? 1921.

Phil 6951.5.17 — Beers, C.W. A new project; the first International Congress on Mental Hygiene. N.Y., 1924.

Phil 6951.5.50 — A mind that found itself and its author. N.Y., 1924.

Phil 6951.5.52 — American Foundation for Mental Hygiene, Inc. A mind that found itself and its author. N.Y., 193-.

Phil 6951.5.53 — National Committee for Mental Hygiene. The mental hygiene movement. N.Y., 1938.

Phil 6951.6 — Broussais, F.J.V. In irritation and insanity. Columbia, 1831.

Phil 6951.6.5 — Broussais, F.J.V. De l'irritation et de la folie. Paris, 1839. 2v.

Phil 6951.7 — Barrus, C. Nursing the insane. N.Y., 1908.

Phil 6951.8 — Bayle, A.L.J. Traité des maladies du cerveau. Paris, 1826.

Phil 6951.9 — Burr, Colonel Bell. Handbook of psychology and mental disease. 4. ed. Philadelphia, 1915.

Phil 6951.9.5 — Burr, Colonel Bell. Practical psychology and psychiatry. 5. ed. Philadelphia, 1922.

Phil 6951.10 — Beck, Theodric R. An inaugural dissertation on insanity. Thesis. N.Y., 1811.

Phil 6951.11 — Bleuler, E. Affektivität, Suggestibilität, Paranoia. Halle, 1906.

Phil 6951.11.2 — Bleuler, E. Affektivität, Suggestibilität, Paranoia. 2. Aufl. Halle, 1926.

Phil 6951.11.5 — Bleuler, E. Textbook of psychiatry. N.Y., 1924.

Phil 6951.12 — Beard, G.M. Psychology of the Salem witchcraft...1697. Photoreproduction. N.Y., 1882.

Phil 6951.12.3 — Beard, G.M. Practical treatise on nervous exhaustion. 2. ed. N.Y., 1880.

Phil 6951.12.4 — Beard, G.M. Practical treatise on nervous exhaustion. 2. ed. N.Y., 1880.

Phil 6951.12.5 — Beard, G.M. Die Nervenschwäche. 2. Aufl. Leipzig, 1883.

Phil 6951.12.10A — Beard, G.M. American nervousness. N.Y., 1881.

Phil 6951.12.10B — Beard, G.M. American nervousness. N.Y., 1881.

Phil 6951.12.15 — Beard, G.M. Neurasthenia (nerve exhaustion), with remarks on treatment. n.p., 1879?

Phil 6951.13 — Böttger, H. Die Nahrungsverweigerung der Irren. Leipzig, 1878.

330

Classified Listing

Phil 6950 - 6975 Psychology - Abnormal psychology - Mental disease - General treatises - Individual authors (A-Z) - cont.

Phil 6951.14 Bergmann, W. Die Seelenleiden der Nervösen. 2. und 3. Aufl. Freiburg, 1922.
Phil 6951.15 Bouveret, L. La neurasthénie. 2. éd. Paris, 1891.
Phil 6951.16 Bennett, C. The modern malady. London, 1890.
Phil 6951.17 Belbèze, Raymond. La neurasthénie ruale. Paris, 1911.
NEDL Phil 6951.17 Blondel, C. La conscience morbide. Thèse. Paris, 1913.
Phil 6951.18 Bastian, H.C. On paralysis from brain disease. N.Y., 1875.
Phil 6951.19 Boulenger. Association des idées chez les idiots. Gand, 1906.
Phil 6951.20 Burrow, T. The structure of insanity. London, 1932.
Phil 6951.22 Brown, H.C. A mind mislaid. N.Y., 1937.
Phil 6951.23 Bromberg, W. The mind of man. N.Y., 1937.
Phil 6951.24 Braatøy, T. Männer zwischen 15 und 25. Oslo, 1934.
Phil 6951.25 Boss, M. Körperliches Kranksein als Folge seelescher Gleichgewichtsstörungen. Bern, 1940.
Phil 6951.26 Brown, Carlton. Brainstorm. N.Y., 1944.
Phil 6951.27 Bergler, E. Money and emotional conflicts. 1. ed. Garden City, 1951.
Phil 6951.28 Babcock, H. Dementia praecox. N.Y., 1933.
Phil 6951.29 Brody, E.B. Psychotheraphy with schizophrenia. N.Y., 1952.
Phil 6951.30 Binswanger, Ludwig. Schizophrenie. Pfullingen, 1957.
Phil 6951.30.5 Binswanger, Ludwig. Wahn; Beiträge zu seiner phanomenologischen und daseinsanalytischen Erforschung. Pfullingen, 1965.
Phil 6951.31 Battie, William. A treatise on madness. London, 1962.
Phil 6951.32 Bastide, Roger. Soziologie des maladies mentales. Paris, 1965.
Phil 6952.1 Calmeil, J.L.F. De la folie. Paris, 1845. 2v.
Phil 6952.2A Carnochan, J.M. Cerebral localization...insanity. N.Y., 1884.
Phil 6952.2B Carnochan, J.M. Cerebral localization...insanity. N.Y., 1884.
Phil 6952.3 Castiglioni, C. Sulle alterazioni delle pupille nei pazzi. Milano, 1863-65. 2 pam.
Phil 6952.4 Chambers, J. A mad world and its inhabitants. N.Y., 1877.
Phil 6952.5 Channing, W. The mental status of guiteau. Cambridge, 1882.
Phil 6952.6A Clouston, T.S. Clinical lectures on mental diseases. Philadelphia, 1884.
Phil 6952.6B Clouston, T.S. Clinical lectures on mental diseases. Philadelphia, 1884.
Phil 6952.7 Conolly, John. The treatment of the insane without mechanical restraints. London, 1856.
Phil 6952.7.5 Conolly, John. An inquiry concerning the indications of insanity. London, 1964.
Phil 6952.7.30 Clark, James. A memoir of John Conolly. London, 1869.
Phil 6952.7.35 James, E. A memoir of John Conolly. London, 1869?
Phil 6952.8 Constans, A. Relation sur un épidémie d'hystéro-démonopathie en 1861. Paris, 1863.
Phil 6952.9 Cotard, J. Études sur les maladies cérébrales et mentales. Paris, 1891.
Phil 6952.10 Cowles, E. Insistent and fixed ideas. Baltimore, 1888.
Phil 6952.10.2 Cowles, E. Neurasthenia and its mental symptoms. Boston, 1891.
Phil 6952.10.25 Pamphlet box. Cowles, E. Minor writings.
Phil 6952.11 Cox, J.M. Practical observations on insanity. London, 1806.
Phil 6952.11.2 Cox, J.M. Practical observations on insanity. Philadelphia, 1811.
Phil 6952.12 Crichton, A. An inquiry...nature, origin, mental derangement. London, 1798. 2v.
Phil 6952.14 Chiara, D. Les diables de morzine en 1861. n.p., 1861.
Phil 6952.15 Clark, L.P. Neurological and mental diagnosis. N.Y., 1908.
Phil 6952.16 Cruden, Alexander. The London-citizen...sent...to...madhouse. 2. ed. London, 17-
Phil 6952.17 Chaslin, Philippe. La confusion mentale primitive. Paris, 1895.
Phil 6952.18.25 Robinson, Victor. The Don Quixote of psychiatry. N.Y., 1919.
Phil 6952.20 Cotton, Henry A. The defective delinquent and insane. Princeton, 1921.
Phil 6952.21A Campbell, C.M. A present-day conception of mental disorders. Cambridge, 1924.
Phil 6952.21B Campbell, C.M. A present-day conception of mental disorders. Cambridge, 1924.
Phil 6952.21.5 Campbell, C.M. Delusion and belief. Cambridge, 1926.
Phil 6952.21.6 Campbell, C.M. Delusion and belief. Cambridge, 1927.
Phil 6952.21.10 Campbell, C.M. Towards mental health. Cambridge, 1933.
Phil 6952.21.15 Campbell, C.M. Destiny and disease in mental disorders. N.Y., 1935.
Phil 6952.23 Charcot, J.M. Leçons sur les localisations dans les maladies du cerveau. Paris, 1876.
Phil 6952.23.5 Charcot, J.M. Lectures on localization in diseases of the brain. N.Y., 1878.
Phil 6952.23.10 Charcot, J.M. Étude critique et clinique de la doctrine des localisations motrices. Paris, 1883.
Phil 6952.23.20 Charcot, J.M. Clinique des maladies du système nerveaux. Paris, 1892-93. 2v.
Phil 6952.23.80 Guillain, Georges. J.M. Charcot, 1825-1893. N.Y., 1959.
Phil 6952.24 Cobb, Stanley. An outline of neuropathology for students of general medicine. Cambridge, 1929.
Phil 6952.24.15 Cobb, Stanley. Foundations of neuropsychiatry. 2. ed. Baltimore, 1941.
Phil 6952.25 Cebold, Luis. Psiquiatria social. Lisboa, 1931.
Phil 6952.26 Hanover Bank, New York. The mental hygiene movement from the philanthropic standpoint. N.Y., 1939.
Phil 6952.27 Crutcher, H.B. Foster home care for mental patients. N.Y., 1944.
Phil 6952.28 Caravedo, B. Tratamiento social de los enfermos de la mente. Lima, 1943.
Phil 6952.29 Custance, J. Wisdom, madness, and folly. N.Y., 1952.
Phil 6952.32 Cotti, Edelweiss. Contro la psichiatria. 1.ed. Firenze, 1970.
Phil 6953.1 Dallemagne, J. Dégénérés et déséquilibrés. Bruxelles, 1895.
Htn Phil 6953.2* DeRenne, G.W.J. Theory concerning the nature of insanity. Wormsloe, 1847.
Phil 6953.3 Derby, J.B. Life among lunatics. Boston, 1839.
Phil 6953.4 Descourtis, G. Du fractionnement des opérations cérébrales. Paris, 1882.
Phil 6953.4.2 Descourtis, G. Du fractionnement des opérations cérébrales. Paris, 1882.

Phil 6950 - 6975 Psychology - Abnormal psychology - Mental disease - General treatises - Individual authors (A-Z) - cont.

Phil 6953.5 Dupuy, Paul. De l'automatisme psychologique. Bordeaux, 1894.
Phil 6953.6 Delgado, Honorio F. La psiquiatría psicológica. Lima, 1919.
Phil 6953.7 Despine, Prosper. De la folie au point de vue philosophique. Paris, 1875.
Phil 6953.8 Dromard, Gabriel. La mimique ches les aliénés. Paris, 1909.
Phil 6953.9 Duprat, G.L. L'instabilité mentale. Paris, 1898.
Phil 6953.10 Dantas, J. Pintores e poetas de Rilhafolles. Liboa, 1900.
Phil 6953.11 Dejerine, J. L'hérédité dans les maladies du système nerveux. Paris, 1886.
Phil 6953.12.5 Dubois, Paul. Psychic treatment of nervous disorders. N.Y., 1905.
Phil 6953.13 Damaye, Henri. Psychiatrie et civilisation. Paris, 1934.
Phil 6953.14 Davis, J.E. Principles and practice of recreational theraphy for the mentally ill. N.Y., 1936.
Phil 6953.14.5 Davis, J.E. Principles and practice of rehabilatation. N.Y., 1943.
Phil 6953.15 Dunlap, K. Research in methods of adjustment. Berkeley, 1941.
Phil 6953.16.3 The autobiography of David. London, 1946.
Phil 6953.18 Louisiana. Southeast Louisiana Hospital, Mandeville. Psychotherapy with schizophrenics. Baton Rouge, 1961.
Phil 6953.19 Dain, Norman. Concepts of insanity in the United States, 1789-1865. New Brunswick, N.J., 1964.
Phil 6953.20 Dunham, Henry Warren. Community and schizophrenia. Detroit, 1965.
Phil 6954.1 Earle, P. The curability of insanity. Philadelphia, 1887.
Phil 6954.1.5 Earle, P. A visit to thirteen asylums...insane, Europe. Philadelphia, 1841.
Phil 6954.1.25 Pamphlet box. Psychology. Mental disease.
Phil 6954.2 Emminghaus, H. Die psychischen Störungen. Tübingen, 1887.
Phil 6954.2.5 Emminghaus, H. Allgemeine Psychopathologie. Leipzig, 1878.
Phil 6954.3 Esquirol, Etienne. Mental maladies. Philadelphia, 1845.
Phil 6954.3.5 Esquirol, Etienne. Des maladies mentales. v.1,2 and atlas. Paris, 1838. 3v.
Phil 6954.3.10 Esquirol, Etienne. Von den Geisteskrankheiten. Bern, 1968.
Phil 6954.4 Evensen, Hans. Dementia praecox. Kristiania, 1904.
Phil 6954.5A Erb, Wilhelm. Handbuch der Krankheiten des Nervensystems. 2e Aufl. Leipzig, 1876-78. 2v.
Phil 6954.5B Erb, Wilhelm. Handbuch der Krankheiten des Nervensystems. v.2. 2. Aufl. Leipzig, 1876.
Phil 6954.6 Ey, Henri. Hallucinations et délire. Paris, 1934.
Phil 6954.7 Ellery, Reginald S. Schizophrenia, the Cinderella of psychiatry. Sidney, 1941.
Phil 6954.7.5 Ellery, Reginald S. Schizophrenia, the Cinderella of psychiatry. Sydney, 1944.
Phil 6955.1 Falret, J.P. Des maladies mentales. Paris, 1864.
Phil 6955.1.5 Falret, J.P. Études cliniques sur les maladies mentales et nerveuses. Paris, 1890.
Phil 6955.2 Familiar views of lunacy and lunatic life. London, 1850.
Phil 6955.3 Fisher, T.W. Plain talk about insanity. Boston, 1872.
Phil 6955.3.25 Pamphlet box. Psychology. Mental disease.
Phil 6955.4 Folsom, C.F. Four introductory lectures on insanity. Cambridge, 1875-80. 4 pam.
Phil 6955.4.5 Folsom, C.F. Mental disease. n.p., 1886.
Phil 6955.4.25 Pamphlet box. Psychology. Mental disease.
Phil 6955.5 Foville, A. Étude clinique de la folie. Paris, 1871.
Phil 6955.6 Franzolini, F. L'epidemia di istero-demonopatie. Reggio, 1879.
Phil 6955.8 Friedreich, H.B. Historisch-kritische Darstellung der Theorien über das Wesen und den Sitz der psychischen Krankheiten. Leipzig, 1836.
Phil 6955.9 Folsom, C.F. Abstract of the statutes of the United States, and of the several territories relating to the custody of the insane. Philadelphia, 1884.
Phil 6955.10 Fechner, Gustav. In Sachen der Psychophysik. Leipzig, 1877.
Phil 6955.11 Franz, S.I. Handbook of mental examining methods. 2. ed. N.Y., 1919.
Phil 6955.12 Friedmann, M. Über den Wahn. v.1-2. Wiesbaden, 1894.
Phil 6955.13 Fleury, M. de. Les grands symptômes neurasthéniques. Paris, 1901.
Phil 6955.13.10 Fleury, M. de. Manuel pour l'étude des maladies du système nerveaux. Paris, 1904.
Phil 6955.14 Fox, E.L. Pahological anatomy of nervous centres. London, 1874.
Phil 6955.15 Frostig, Jakób. Das schizophrene Denken. Leipzig, 1929.
Phil 6955.16 Filho, Roch. Psychiatria e hygiene mental. Maceló, 1936.
Phil 6955.17 Feber, G.H.A. Beschouwingen over Psychopathenstrafrecht. Zwolle, 1932.
Phil 6955.18 Freeman, Thomas. Chronic schizophrenia. London, 1958.
Phil 6955.20 Fein, Rashi. Economics of mental illness. N.Y., 1958.
Phil 6955.22 Foucault, Michel. Folie et déraison. Paris, 1961.
Phil 6955.23 Foucault, Michel. Madness and civilization. N.Y., 1965.
Phil 6956.1 Gowers, W.R. Lectures on the diagnosis of disease of the brain. London, 1885.
Phil 6956.2 Griesinger, W. Die Pathologie und Therapie der psychischen Krankheiten. Braunschweig, 1871.
Htn Phil 6956.2.2* Griesinger, W. Die Pathologie und Therapie der psychischen Krankheiten. Stuttgart, 1867.
Phil 6956.2.5 Griesinger, W. Mental pathology and therapeutics. London, 1867.
Phil 6956.3 Guislain, J. Leçons orales phrénopathies. Paris, 1880. 2v.
Phil 6956.4 Gross, Otto. Über psychopatische Minderwertigkuten. Wien, 1909.
Phil 6956.5.2 Grasset, Joseph. Demifous et demiresponsables. 2. éd. Paris, 1908.
Phil 6956.5.5 Grasset, Joseph. The semi-insane and semi-responsible. N.Y., 1907.
Phil 6956.6 Grant-Smith, Rachel. The experiences of an asylum patient. London, 1922.
Phil 6956.7 Garnier, P.E. Des idées de grandeur dans le délire des persécutions. Paris, 1878.
Phil 6956.8 Guimares, A. De hygiene mental e sua importancia em mosso meio. San Paulo, 1926.
Phil 6956.10 Gotewood, Lee C. An experimental study of dermentia preacox. Lancaster, 1909.
Phil 6956.11 Grasset, Joseph. Le psychisme inférieur. 2. éd. Paris, 1913.
Phil 6956.12 Graves, Alonzo. The eclipse of a mind. N.Y., 1942.
Phil 6956.13 Grinker, Roy. War neuroses in North Africa. N.Y., 1943.

Phil 6950 - 6975   Psychology - Abnormal psychology - Mental disease - General
treatises - Individual authors (A-Z) - cont.

Phil 6956.15   Green, Sidney L. A manual of first aid for mental health.
N.Y., 1955.
Phil 6956.16   Goldfarb, W. Childhood schizophrenia. Cambridge, 1961.
Phil 6956.17   Guntrip, Henry James Samuel. Schizoid phenomena, object
relations and the self. London, 1968.
Phil 6956.18   Gebhard, Erwin. Psychiatrie in unserer Zeit.
Göttingen, 1969.
Phil 6957.1   Hallaran, W.G. Practical observations, causes, cure
insanity. Cork, 1818.
Phil 6957.2   Hammond, W.A. Cerebral hyperaemia. N.Y., 1878.
Phil 6957.2.5   Hammond, W.A. A treatise on insanity in its medical
relations. N.Y., 1891.
Phil 6957.2.9   Hammond, W.A. A treatise on the diseases of the nervous
system. 6. ed. N.Y., 1876.
Phil 6957.3   Hill, R.G. Lunacy: Its past and its present.
London, 1870.
Phil 6957.4   Hunt, J.H. Astounding disclosures. n.p., 1851.
Phil 6957.5   Hamon, A. La responsabilité. Lyon, 1897.
Phil 6957.6   Harrison, G.L. Legisation on insanity.
Philadelphia, 1884.
Phil 6957.7   Hart, Bernard. The psychology of insanity.
Cambridge, 1914.
Phil 6957.7.3   Hart, Bernard. The psychology of insanity.
Cambridge, 1921.
Phil 6957.7.4   Hart, Bernard. The psychology of insanity.
Cambridge, 1925.
Phil 6957.7.4.7   Hart, Bernard. The psychology of insanity. 4. ed.
N.Y., 1937.
Phil 6957.7.4.10   Hart, Bernard. The psychology of insanity.
Cambridge, 1962.
Phil 6957.7.5   Hart, Bernard. The modern treatment of mental disorders.
Manchester, 1918.
Phil 6957.8   Haskell, E. The trial of Ebenezer Haskell in lunacy.
Philadelphia, 1869.
Phil 6957.9   Hoch, August. Benign stupors. N.Y., 1921.
Phil 6957.10   Hellpach, W. Grundgedanken zur Wissenschaftslehre der
Psychopathologie. Leipzig, 1906.
Phil 6957.10.5   Hellpach, W. Die Hysterie und die moderne Schule.
n.p., 1905-1913. 11 pam.
Phil 6957.11   Hitzig, E. Über den Quärulantenwahnsinn. Leipzig, 1895.
Phil 6957.12   Hyslop, T.B. The great abnormals. London, 1925.
Phil 6957.12.7   Hyslop, T.B. The borderland, some of the problems of
insanity. N.Y., 1925.
Phil 6957.13   Highmore, N. Exercitationes duae...histerica. 2. ed.
Amstelodami, 1660.
Phil 6957.14   Henry, Jules. Du délire des negations (Syndrome de Cotard)
dans la paralysie générale. Paris, 1896.
Phil 6957.15   Hartenberg, P. La névrose d'angoisse. Paris, 1902.
Phil 6957.16   Herz, M. Versuch über den Schwindel. Berlin, 1786.
Phil 6957.17.5   Henderson, D.K. A text-book of psychiatry for students and
practitioners. 2. ed. London, 1930.
Phil 6957.17.7   Henderson, D.K. A text-book of psychiatry for students and
practitioners. 3. ed. London, 1933.
Phil 6957.17.20   Henderson, D.K. A text-book of psychiatry for students and
practitioners. Oxford, 1947.
Phil 6957.18   Hamilton, A.M. Recollections of an alienist. N.Y., 1916.
Phil 6957.19   Hanes, E.L. The minds and nerves of soldiers. Pasadena,
Calif., 1941.
Phil 6957.20   Hanfmann, E. Conceptual thinking in schizophrenia.
N.Y., 1942.
Phil 6957.22   Hoskins, Roy G. The biology of schizophrenia. 1. ed.
N.Y., 1946.
Phil 6957.25   Hollingshead, A. de B. Social class and mental illness.
N.Y., 1958.
Phil 6957.28   Hinsie, Leland. The treatment of schizophrenia.
Baltimore, 1930.
Phil 6957.30   Myers, Jerome Keeley. A decade later: a follow-up of
social class and mental illness. N.Y., 1968.
Phil 6957.35   Hagnell, Olle. A prospective study of the incidences of
mental disorder. Stockholm, 1966.
Phil 6958.1   Ireland, W.W. The blot upon the brain. Edinburgh, 1885.
Phil 6958.1.2*   Pamphlet box. Psychology. Mental disease. Letters.
Phil 6958.1.3   Ireland, W.W. The blot upon the brain. N.Y., 1886.
Phil 6958.1.5   Ireland, W.W. Through the ivory gate. Edinburgh, 1889.
Phil 6958.2   Ingenieros, José. Simulación de la locura. 8. ed. Buenos
Aires, 1918.
Phil 6958.3   Imianitoff, Mme. Contribution à l'étude du rôle des
emotions. Thèse. Paris, 1917.
Phil 6958.4   Ilberg, Georg. Geisteskrankheiten. Leipzig, 1907.
Phil 6958.4.2   Ilberg, Georg. Geisteskrankheiten. 2. Aufl.
Leipzig, 1918.
Phil 6958.5   Ideler, K.W. Biographieen Geisteskranker. Berlin, 1841.
Phil 6958.6   International Congress of Charities, Corrections and
Philanthrophy, Chicago, 1893. Commitment, detention care,
and treatment of the insane. Baltimore, 1894.
Phil 6959.1   Janet, Pierre. L'automatisme psychologique. Paris, 1889.
Phil 6959.1.3   Janet, Pierre. L'automatisme psychologique. 2. ed.
Paris, 1894.
Phil 6959.1.5   Janet, Pierre. Névroses et idées fixes. Paris, 1898.
2v.
Phil 6959.1.9A   Janet, Pierre. Les obsessions et la psychasthénie.
Paris, 1903. 2v.
Phil 6959.1.9B   Janet, Pierre. Les obsessions et la psychasthénie. v.1.
Paris, 1903.
Phil 6959.1.12   Janet, Pierre. Les névroses. Paris, 1909.
Phil 6959.1.15   Janet, Pierre. Les médications psychologiques.
Paris, 1919. 3v.
Phil 6959.1.18   Janet, Pierre. Psychological healing. N.Y., 1925.
2v.
Phil 6959.1.20   Janet, Pierre. La médecine psychologique. Paris, 1923.
Phil 6959.1.25   Janet, Pierre. Principles of psychotherapy. N.Y., 1924.
Phil 6959.1.29   Janet, Pierre. La force et la faiblesse psychologiques.
Paris, 1932.
Phil 6959.2   Jarvis, E. Insanity and insane asylums. Louisville,
Ky., 1841.
Phil 6959.3   Jacobi, M.P. The prevention of insanity. Boston, 1882.
Phil 6959.3.2   Jacobi, M.P. The prevention of insanity. Boston, 1880-82.
3 pam.
Phil 6959.4   Jaspers, K. Allgemeine Psychopathologie. Berlin, 1913.
Phil 6959.4.17   Jaspers, K. General psychopathology. Manchester, 1963.
Phil 6959.4.18   Jaspers, K. General psychopathology. Chicago, 1967.
Phil 6959.4.25   Jaspers, K. The nature of psychotherapy.
Manchester, 1964.
Phil 6959.5   Jahrmärker, M. Zur Frage der Dementia Praecox.
Halle, 1903.

Phil 6950 - 6975   Psychology - Abnormal psychology - Mental disease - General
treatises - Individual authors (A-Z) - cont.

Phil 6959.6   Jones, Kathleen. Mental health and social policy.
London, 1960.
Phil 6959.7   Jong, Herman H. de. Experimental catatonia, a general
reaction form of the central nervous system.
Baltimore, 1945.
Phil 6959.8   Jung, C.G. Über die Psychologie der Dementia Praecox.
Halle, 1907.
Phil 6959.9   Jaco, E.G. The social epidemiology of mental disorders.
N.Y., 1960.
Phil 6959.10   Jackson, Donald. The etiology of schizophrenia.
N.Y., 1960.
Phil 6959.11   Jensen, Susanne. Ein Versuch zur quantitativen Analyse des
gruppenpsychotherapeutischen Prozesses mit schizophrenen
Patienten. Bonn, 1965.
Phil 6960.1   Knapp, P.C. The insanity of doubt. Baltimore, 1890.
Phil 6960.2   Knight, P.S. Beobachtungen...des Irrseyns. Koln, 1829.
Phil 6960.3   Koch, J.L.A. Die psychopathischen Minderwertigkeiten.
Ravensburg, 1891-93. 3v.
Phil 6960.4   Krafft-Ebing, R. von. Lehrbuch der Psychiatrie.
Stuttgart, 1893.
Phil 6960.4.3   Krafft-Ebing, R. von. Lehrbuch der Psychiatrie. 3. Aufl.
Stuttgart, 1888.
Phil 6960.5   Kraepelin, E. Psychiatrie. Leipzig, 1896.
Phil 6960.5.3   Kraepelin, E. Psychiatrie. Leipzig, 1909-15. 4v.
Phil 6960.5.5   Kraepelin, E. Clinical psychiatry. N.Y., 1902.
Phil 6960.5.7   Kraepelin, E. Clinical psychiatry. N.Y., 1904.
Phil 6960.5.11   Kraepelin, E. Einfuhrung in die psychiatrische Klenik
dreissez Vorlesungen. Leipzig, 1901.
Phil 6960.5.12   Kraepelin, E. Einfuhrung in die psychiatrische Klenik.
Leipzig, 1905.
Phil 6960.5.15   Kraepelin, E. One hundred years of psychiatry.
N.Y., 1962.
Phil 6960.6   Kronfeld, Arthur. Das Wesen der psychiatrischen Erkenn.
Berlin, 1920.
Phil 6960.6.5   Kronfeld, Arthur. Psychotherapie. Berlin, 1924.
Phil 6960.6.7   Kronfeld, Arthur. Psychotherapie, Charakterlehre,
Psychoanalyze, Hynose, Psychogogik. 2. Aufl. Berlin, 1925.
Phil 6960.7   Kretschmer, E. Der sensitive Beziehungwahn. Berlin, 1918.
Phil 6960.8   Kirehhoff. Beziehungen das Dämonen- und Hexenwesens zur
deutschen Irrenpflege. Berlin, 1888.
Phil 6960.9   Kaan, Hanns. Der neurasthenische Angstaffect bei
Zwangsvorstellungen und der primordiale Grübelzwang.
Wien, 1892.
Phil 6960.10   Kallmann, F.J. Genetics of schizophrenia. N.Y., 1938.
Phil 6960.12   Kasanin, J.S. Language and thought in schizophrenia.
Berkeley, 1944.
Phil 6960.13   King, H.E. Psychomotor aspects of mental disease.
Cambridge, Mass., 1954.
Phil 6960.15   Kahn, Theodore. Psychological techniques in diagnosis and
evaluation. N.Y., 1960.
Phil 6960.16   Kreitler, Hans. Die wellanscharlie Orienterung der
Schizophrenen. München, 1965.
Phil 6961.1   Legrain, M. Du délire chez les dégénérés. Paris, 1886.
Phil 6961.2   Lemoine, A. L'aliéné devant la philosophie, la morale et
la societé. Paris, 1865.
Phil 6961.3.2   Letchworth, W.P. The insane in foreign countries.
N.Y., 1889.
Phil 6961.4   Lunt, Adeline T.P. Behind the bars. Boston, 1871.
Phil 6961.5   Luys, J. Traité clinique et pratique des maladies
mentales. Paris, 1881.
Phil 6961.6.2   Lincoln, D.F. Sanity of mind. N.Y., 1901.
Phil 6961.7   Lauze, Charles A. La psychose hallucinatoire chronique.
Thèse. Paris, 1914.
Phil 6961.8   Lurié, Aron. Multiple Sklerose mit amnestischer Aphasie.
Inaug. Diss. Königsberg, 1914.
Phil 6961.9.5   Liepmann, Hugo. Drei Aufsätze aus dem Aprariegebut.
Berlin, 1908.
Phil 6961.10   Lewis, W.B. A text-book of mental diseases.
Philadelphia, 1890.
Phil 6961.11   Levillain, F. La neurasthénie. Paris, 1891.
Phil 6961.12   Loosmore, W.C. Nerves and the man. N.Y., 1921.
Phil 6961.13   Lundholm, Helge. Schizophrenia. Durham, N.C., 1932.
Phil 6961.14   Lundholm, Helge. The manic-depressive pychosis. Durham,
N.C., 1931.
Phil 6961.15   Lugaro, E. La psichiatria tedesca. Firenze, 1916.
Phil 6961.16   Landis, C. Modern society and mental diseases.
N.Y., 1938.
Phil 6961.17   Langfeldt, G. The schizophreniform states.
Copenhagen, 1939.
Phil 6961.17.5   Langfeldt, G. The prognosis in schizophrenia.
Copenhagen, 1937.
Phil 6961.18   Leibbrand, Werner. Der Wahnsinn. Freiburg, 1961.
Phil 6961.19   Laing, Ronald David. The self and others. London, 1961.
Phil 6961.19.2   Laing, Ronald David. Self and others. 2. ed.
London, 1969.
Phil 6961.19.5   Laing, Ronald David. The divided self; a study.
Chicago, 1960.
Phil 6961.20   Levinson, Daniel Jacob. Patienthood in the mental
hospital. Boston, 1964.
Phil 6961.22   Loechen, Yngvar. Idealer og realiteter i et psykiatrisk
sykehus. Oslo, 1970.
Phil 6962.1   Magnan, V. Leçons cliniques sur les maladies mentales.
Paris, 1882-91.
Phil 6962.1.2   Magnan, V. Leçons cliniques sur les maladies mentales. 2.
éd. Paris, 1893.
Phil 6962.1.3   Magnan, V. Psychiatische Vorlesungen. v.2-6.
Leipzig, 1892-93.
Phil 6962.1.5   Magnan, V. Recherches sur les centres nerveux. 2. série.
Paris, 1893.
Phil 6962.1.10   Magnan, V. Le délire chronique à évolution systématique.
Paris, 1892.
Phil 6962.2   Maudsley, H. Responsibility in mental disease.
N.Y., 1874.
Phil 6962.2.3   Maudsley, H. Die Zurechnungsfähigkeit der Geisteskranken.
Leipzig, 1875.
Phil 6962.2.6   Maudsley, H. The pathology of mind. London, 1895.
Phil 6962.2.9A   Maudsley, H. The pathology of mind. N.Y., 1880.
Phil 6962.2.9B   Maudsley, H. The pathology of mind. N.Y., 1880.
Phil 6962.3   Mayo, T. Elements of pathology of human mind.
London, 1838.
Phil 6962.4   Mercier, C.A. Sanity and insanity. London, 1890.
Phil 6962.4.4   Mercier, C.A. A text-book of insanity. London, 1902.
Phil 6962.4.5   Mercier, C.A. A text-book of insanity. London, 1914.
Phil 6962.5   Meynert, T. Psychiatrie. Wien, 1884.
Phil 6962.5.5   Meynert, T. Klinische Vorlesungen über Psychiatrie. v.1-2.
Wien, 1889-90.

Phil 6962.6	Moreau-Christopie, L.M. De la mortalité et de la folie. Paris, 1839.
Phil 6962.7	Moreau, P. Les excentriques. Paris, 1894.
Phil 6962.9	Meyerhof, O. Beiträge zur psychologischen Theorie der Geistesstörungen. Göttingen, 1910.
Phil 6962.10	Mendel, Emanuel. Text-book of psychiatry. Philadelphia, 1907.
Phil 6962.10.5	Mendel, Emanuel. Leitfaden der Psychiatrie. Stuttgart, 1902.
Phil 6962.11	Morison, A. Physiognomik der Geisteskrankheiten. Leipzig, 1853.
Phil 6962.12	Pamphlet box. Mills, C.K. Minor writings.
Phil 6962.13	Monakow, Constantin von. Gehirnpathologie. 2. Aufl. Wien, 1905. 2v.
Phil 6962.14	Marie, A. La demence. Paris, 1906.
Phil 6962.15	Myerson, Abraham. The psychology of mental disorders. N.Y., 1927.
Phil 6962.16	Moreau, J.J. Un chapitre oublié de la pathologie mentale. Paris, 1850.
Phil 6962.17	Mathieu, A. Neurasthénie. Paris, 1892.
Phil 6962.18	Mignard, Maurice. L'unité psychique et les troubles mentaux. Paris, 1928.
Phil 6962.19	Morgenthaler, Walter. Die Pflege der Gemüts- und Geisteskranken. Bern, 1930.
Phil 6962.19.5	Morgenthaler, Walter. Die Pflege der Gemüts- und Geisteskranken. 4. Aufl. Bern, 1941.
Phil 6962.20	Moss, Fred August. Foundations of abnormal psychology. N.Y., 1932.
Phil 6962.21	Moore, T.V. The essential psychoses and their fundamental syndromes. Baltimore, 1933.
Phil 6962.22	Mondain, Paul. Les fous satisfaits. Paris, 1933.
Phil 6962.23	Mallet, Raymond. La démence. Paris, 1935.
Phil 6962.25	Miller, E. The neurosis in war. N.Y., 1940.
Phil 6962.28	McAuley, W.F. The concept of schizophrenia. N.Y., 1954.
Phil 6962.30	Malzberg, Benjamin. Migration and mental disease. N.Y., 1956.
Phil 6962.32	Meyer, Henry F. An experiment in mental patient rehabilitation. N.Y., 1959.
Phil 6962.34	Myers, Jerome K. Family and class dynamics in mental illness. N.Y., 1959.
Phil 6962.35	Moses, Paul Joseph. Die Stimme der Neurose. Stuttgart, 1956.
Phil 6962.35.1	Moses, Paul Joseph. The voice of neurosis. N.Y., 1954.
Phil 6962.36	Mills, Enid. Living with mental illness. London, 1962.
Phil 6962.37	Moore, W.L. The mind in chains. N.Y., 1955.
Phil 6962.38	Macnab, Francis A. Estrangement and relationship. Bloomington, 1966.
Phil 6963.1	National association for the protection of the insane, 1880-1882. Boston, 1880. 2v.
Phil 6963.2	Noyes, W. Paranoia. Baltimore, 1888-89.
Phil 6963.3	Neumann, H. Über die Knochenbrüche bei Geisteskranken. Berlin, 1883.
Phil 6963.5	Nothnagel, H. Über die Localisation der Gehirnkrankheiten. Wiesbaden, 1887.
Phil 6963.7	Nathan, M. Manuel élémentaire de psychiatrie. Paris, 1930.
Phil 6963.8	National Conference on Social Welfare. Mental health and social welfare. N.Y., 1961.
Phil 6964.1.6	Oppenheim, H. Lehrbuch der Nervenkrankheiten. 6. Aufl. Berlin, 1913. 2v.
Phil 6964.2	Oliver, John R. Pastoral psychiatry and mental health. N.Y., 1932.
Phil 6964.2.6	Oliver, John R. Psychiatry and mental health. N.Y., 1933.
Phil 6964.3.5	O'Brien, John D. An outline of psychiatry. 2. ed. St. Louis, Mo., 1935.
Phil 6964.4	Ogdon, J.A.H. The kingdom of the lost. London, 1947.
Phil 6964.6	O'Brien, Barbara (pseud.). Operators and things: the inner life of a schizophrenic. Cambridge, Mass., 1958.
Phil 6965.1	Parkman, G. Management of lunatics. Boston, 1817-18. 2 pam.
Phil 6965.2	Philip, A.P.W. Treatise on the more obscure affections of the brain. London, 1835.
Phil 6965.3	Pinel, Philippe. Traité médico-philosophique sur l'aliénation mentale. Paris, 1809.
Phil 6965.3.5	Pinel, Philippe. Treatise on insanity. Sheffield, 1806.
Phil 6965.3.80	Pamphlet box. Pinel, Philippe.
Phil 6965.3.90	Lechler, Walther Helmut. Neue Ergebnisse in der Forschung über Philippe Pinel. München, 1960.
Phil 6965.3.95	Riese, Walter. The legacy of Philippe Pinel. N.Y., 1969.
Phil 6965.4	Prichard, J.C. Treatise on insanity and other disorders. Philadelphia, 1837.
X Cg Phil 6965.5	Paton, Stewart. Psychiatry. Philadelphia, 1905.
Phil 6965.6	Provost, Maurice. Aliénation mentale, chez les employés de chemins de fer et de transports publics. Thèse. Paris, 1914.
Phil 6965.8	Peters, John C. A treatise on nervous derangements. N.Y., 1854.
Phil 6965.9	Pargeter, William. Observations on maniacal disorders. Reading, Eng., 1792.
Phil 6965.10	Pick, Arnold. Studien über motorische Apraxie. Leipzig, 1905.
Phil 6965.11	Putnam, J.J. Studies in neurological diagnosis. Boston, 1902.
Phil 6965.12	Pottier, Claude. Réflexions sur les troubles du langage dans les psychoses paranoïdes. Thèse. Paris, 1930.
Phil 6965.14	Paris. Université. Faculté de Medecine. Rapport de Mm. Cosnier, Maloet, Darcet, [and others]...nouveau méthode d'adminstrer l'électricité...maladies nerveuses. Paris, 1783.
Phil 6965.15	Preu, P.W. Outline of psychiatric case-study. N.Y., 1939.
Phil 6965.16	Preston, G.H. Psychiatry for the curious. N.Y., 1940.
Phil 6965.17	Psychoanalytic orientation in case work. N.Y., 1944.
Phil 6965.18	Prinzhorn, H. Bildnerei der Geisteskranken. Berlin, 1922.
Phil 6965.20	Plunkett, Richard. Epidemiology and mental illness. N.Y., 1960.
Phil 6965.22	Perceval, J. Perceval's narrative. Stanford, 1961.
Phil 6965.24	Plokker, J.H. Geschonden feeld. 's-Gravenhage, 1962.
Phil 6965.26	Poljak, Leo. Graphologische Untersuchungen an den Handelschriften von Schizophren-Paranoiden und Epileptikern. Abhandlung. Tübingen, 1957.
Phil 6965.28	Pesso, Albert. Movement in psychotherapy; psychomotor techniques and training. N.Y., 1969.
Phil 6967.1	Regis, E. Practical manual of mental medicine. Philadelphia, 1894.
NEDL Phil 6967.1.5	Regis, E. La psychoanalyse des névroses. Paris, 1914.
Phil 6967.2	Reynolds, J.R. The diagnosis of diseases. London, 1855.

Phil 6967.3.2	Rush, B. Medical inquiries...diseases...mind. Philadelphia, 1830.
Phil 6967.3.5	Rush, B. Medical inquiries...diseases...mind. 5. ed. Philadelphia, 1835.
Phil 6967.3.25	Mills, Charles K. Benjamin Rush and American psychiatry. n.p., 1886.
Htn Phil 6967.4*	Randall, J.R. On the treatment of the insane. n.p., n.d.
Phil 6967.5	Ray, Isaac. Contributions to mental pathology. Boston, 1873.
Phil 6967.5.4	Ray, Isaac. Treatise of medical jurisprudence of insanity. Boston, 1838.
Phil 6967.5.5	Ray, Isaac. Treatise on the medical jurisprudence of insanity. 2. ed. Boston, 1844.
Phil 6967.5.8	Ray, Isaac. Treatise on the medical jurisprudence of insanity. 5. ed. Boston, 1871.
Phil 6967.5.10	Ray, Isaac. A treatise on the medical jurisprudence of insanity. Cambridge, 1962.
Phil 6967.6	Revault D'Allounes, G. Thèse pour le doctorat en médecine. Paris, 1971.
Phil 6967.7	Ross, T.A. The common neuroses, their treatment by psychotherapy. London, 1923.
Phil 6967.8	Revere, John. Disputatio medica inauguralis de insania. Edinburgh, 1811.
Phil 6967.10	Read, C. Stanford. Military psychiatry in peace and war. London, 1920.
Phil 6967.10.2	Read, C. Stanford. Abnormal mental strain. London, 1920.
Phil 6967.11.6	Rogues de Fursac, J. Manuel de psychiatrie. 6. éd. Paris, 1923.
Phil 6967.11.15	Rogues de Fursac, J. Manual of psychiatry. 3. ed. N.Y., 1913.
Phil 6967.12	Romberg, M.H. Manual of the nervous diseases. London, 1853. 2v.
Phil 6967.13	Ruiz Maya, M. Psiquiatria penal y civil. Madrid, 1931.
Phil 6967.14.5	Rostan, L. Untersuchungen über die Erweichung des Gehirns. 2. Aufl. Leipzig, 1824.
Phil 6967.15	Ruesch, Jurgen. Chronic disease and psychological individualism. N.Y., 1946.
Phil 6967.16	Ringel, Erwin. Einführung in die Grundprobleme der Neurose. Wien, 1959.
Phil 6967.18.2	Rogers, C.R. Psychothérapie et relations humaines. Louvain, 1965. 2v.
Phil 6967.19	Rokeach, M. The three Christs of Ypsilanti. N.Y., 1964.
Phil 6967.20	Rattner, Josef. Das Wesen der schizophrenen Reaktion. München, 1963.
Phil 6967.21	Rogler, Lloyd H. Trapped: families and schizophrenia. N.Y., 1965.
Phil 6967.22	Rosenthal, David. The Genain quadruplets. N.Y., 1963.
Phil 6967.25	Rosen, George. Madness in society. London, 1968.
Phil 6968.1	Saury, H. Etude clinique sur la folie héréditaire. Paris, 1886.
Phil 6968.2	Schramm, F. Über die Zweifelsucht und Berührungsangst. Berlin, 1888.
Phil 6968.3	Schubert, G.H. von. Die Krankheiten, Storüngen, menschlichen Seele. Stuttgart, 1845.
Phil 6968.4	Schüle, H. Handbuch der Geisteskrankheiten. Leipzig, 1880.
Phil 6968.4.3	Schüle, H. Klinische Psychiatrie. 3. Aufl. Leipzig, 1886.
Phil 6968.5	Séglas, J. Paranoia, systematized delusions. N.Y., 1888.
Phil 6968.5.5	Séglas, J. Des troubles du langage...aliénés. Paris, 1892.
Phil 6968.5.10	Séglas, J. Leçons cliniques sur les maladies. Paris, 1895.
Phil 6968.5.15	Séglas, J. Le délire des négations. Paris, 189-.
Phil 6968.6	Sémérie, E. Des symptomes intellectuels de la folie. Paris, 1867.
Phil 6968.7	Spitzka, E.C. Insanity, its classification. N.Y., 1887.
Phil 6968.8	Spurzheim, J.K. Beobashtungen über den Wahnsinn. Hamburg, 1818.
Phil 6968.8.5	Spurzheim, J.K. Observations...mind...insanity. London, 1817.
Phil 6968.8.6	Spurzheim, J.K. Observations...mind...insanity. Boston, 1833.
Phil 6968.9	Stearns, H.P. Lectures on mental disease. Philadelphia, 1893.
Phil 6968.10	Storer, H.R. The causation...reflex insanity in women. Boston, 1871.
Phil 6968.11	Stedman, H.R. Case of moral insanity. Boston, 1904.
Phil 6968.12	Sidis, Boris. Psychopathological researches. N.Y., 1902.
Phil 6968.12.5	Sidis, Boris. Symptomatology, psychognosis, and diagnosis of psychopathic diseases. Boston, 1914.
Phil 6968.12.7	Sidis, Boris. The causation and treatment of psychopathic diseases. Boston, 1916.
Phil 6968.12.9	Sidis, Boris. Nervous ills; their cause and cure. Boston, 1922.
Phil 6968.12.15	Sidis, Boris. An inquiry into the nature of hallucination. n.p., 1904-12. 10 pam.
Phil 6968.13	Schaefer, H. Allgemeine Gerichtliche Psychiatrie. Berlin, 1910.
Phil 6968.14	Smith, S. Who is insane? N.Y., 1916.
Phil 6968.15	Sailo, Francesco. La patologia mentale im rapporto. Milano, 1908.
Phil 6968.16	Storring, Gustav. Vorlesungen über Psychopathologie. Leipzig, 1900.
Phil 6968.17	Stekel, Wilhelm. Compulsion and doubt. N.Y., 1949.
Phil 6968.19	Souhard, E.E. The kingdom of evils. N.Y., 1922.
Phil 6968.20	Schroeder van der Kolk, J.L.K. The pathology and therapeutics of mental diseases. London, 1870.
Phil 6968.21	Sondén, Tarsten. A study of somatic conditions in manic-depressive psychosis. Inaug. Diss. Uppsala, 1927.
Phil 6968.22	Sommer, Robert. Lehrbuch der psychopathologischen untersuchungs Methoden. Berlin, 1899.
Phil 6968.23	Schneider, Carl. Die Psychologie der Schizophrenen und ihre Bedeutung für die Klinik der Schizophrenie. Leipzig, 1930.
Phil 6968.24	Small, Victor R. I knew 3000 lunatics. N.Y., 1935.
Phil 6968.25	Schou, H.J. Religiösitet og sygelige sindstilstande. 3. udg. København, 1928.
Phil 6968.26	Stern, Edith M. Mental illness. N.Y., 1942.
Phil 6968.28	Sharp, A.A. Dynamic era of court psychiatry, 1914-44. Chicago, 1944.
Phil 6968.30	Straus, Erwin. On obsession, a clinical and methodological study. N.Y., 1948.
Phil 6968.32	Schreben, Daniel P. Memoirs of my nervous illness. London, 1955.
Phil 6968.34	Sullivan, Harry Stack. Schizophrenia as human process. N.Y., 1962.

6950 - 6975 Psychology - Abnormal psychology - Mental disease - General eatises - Individual authors (A-Z) - cont.

Phil 6968.35 Searles, Harold F. Collected papers on schizophrenia and related subjects. London, 1965.
Phil 6968.36 Stefan, Gregory. In search of sanity. New Hyde Park, 1966.
Phil 6968.37 Shapiro, David. Neurotic styles. N.Y., 1965.
Phil 6968.39 Shands, Harley C. Semiotic approaches to psychiatry. The Hague, 1970.
Phil 6969.1 Talcott, S.H. Mental diseases...modern treatment. N.Y., 1901.
Phil 6969.2 Town, C.H. The train of thought. Philadelphia, 1909.
Phil 6969.4 Thuillier-Landry, L. Études sur les délires d'évolution démentielle précoce. Thèse. Paris, 1916.
Phil 6969.5 Tuke, Daniel H. Insanity in ancient and modern life. London, 1878.
Phil 6969.6 Thalbitzer, S. Emotion and insanity. London, 1926.
Phil 6969.7 Targowla, René. L'intuition délirante. Paris, 1931.
Phil 6969.10 Tramer, Moritz. Technisches Schaffen Geisteskranker. München, 1926.
Phil 6969.12 Tweedie, D.F. Logotherapy and the Christian faith. Grands Rapids, 1961.
Phil 6969.14 The transmission of schizophrenia: proceedings of the second research conference of the Foundations' Fund for Research in Psychiatry. Oxford, 1968.
Phil 6971.2 Voisin, F. Des causes...maladies mentales. Paris, 1826.
Phil 6971.3 Voisin, A. Lecons cliniques...maladies mentales. Paris, 1883.
Phil 6971.4 Villey, G. La psychiatrie et les sciences de l'homme. Paris, 1938.
Phil 6971.5 Vetter, Harold T. Language behavior in schizophrenia. Springfield, Ill., 1968.
Phil 6972.1 Wepferi, J.J. Observationes...affectibus capitis. Scaphusii, 1727.
Phil 6972.2 Wernicke, C. Lehrbuch der Gehirnkrankheiten. v.1-2. Kassel, 1881.
Phil 6972.2.5 Wernicke, C. Gesammelte Aufsätze und kritische Riferate. Berlin, 1893.
Phil 6972.2.10 Wernicke, C. Grundriss der Psychiatrie in klinischen Vorlesungen. v.1-2. Leipzig, 1894.
Phil 6972.2.15 Wernicke, C. Über den wessenschaftlichen Standpunkt. Cassel, 1880.
Phil 6972.3 Wigan, A.L. A new view of insanity. The duality of the mind. London, 1844.
Phil 6972.4 Winslow, F. The case of Luigi Buranelli. London, 1855.
Phil 6972.4.5 Winslow, F. The plea of insanity in criminal cases. Boston, 1843.
Phil 6972.5 Winslow, E. On obscure diseases of the brain. London, 1860.
Phil 6972.5.2 Winslow, F. On obscure diseases of the brain. Philadelphia, 1860.
Phil 6972.6 Wright, T.L. Some points connected with the questions of responsibility as it relates to the partially insane. n.p., 18- .
Phil 6972.7 Wynter, A. The borderlands of insanity. N.Y., 1875.
Phil 6972.7.2 Wynter, A. The borderlands of insanity (with 5 new chpaters). London, 1877.
Phil 6972.8 White, A.D. New chapters in the warfare of science. v.1-2. N.Y., 1889.
Phil 6972.9 Wallaschek, R. Psychologie und Pathologie der Vorstellung. Leipzig, 1905.
Phil 6972.10.4 Wharton, F. Treatise on mental unsoundness. 4. ed. Philadelphia, 1882.
Phil 6972.11 Pamphlet box. Wells, F.L. Minor writings.
Phil 6972.12 White, H.W. Demonism verified and analyzed. Shanghai, 1922.
Phil 6972.13 Wildermuth, H. Seele und Seelenkrankheit. Berlin, 1926.
Phil 6972.14.13 White, William Alanson. Outlines of psychiatry. 13. ed. Washington, 1932.
Phil 6972.14.20 White, William Alanson. Foundations of psychiatry. N.Y., 1921.
Phil 6972.14.25 White, William Alanson. Essays in psychopathology. N.Y., 1925.
Phil 6972.14.30 White, William Alanson. Lectures in psychiatry. N.Y., 1928.
Phil 6972.14.50 White, William Alanson. William Alanson White, the autobiography of a purpose. Garden City, 1938.
Phil 6972.15 Wertheimer, F.I. The significance of the physical constitution in mental disease. Baltimore, 1926.
Phil 6972.16 Wechsler, Israel S. The neuroses. Philadelphia, 1929.
Phil 6972.17 Whitwell, James Richard. Historical notes on psychiatry. Photoreproduction. Philadelphia, 1937.
Phil 6972.18 West, Charles. On some disorders. Philadelphia, 1871.
Phil 6972.19.5 Wells, Frederick L. Mental examiners handbook. 2. ed. N.Y., 1945.
Phil 6972.20 Wolfe, Walter Béran. Nervous breakdown; its cause and cure. N.Y., 1933.
Phil 6975.1 Ziehen, T. Psychiatrie. Berlin, 1894.
Phil 6975.5.2 Zaglul, Antonio. Mis quinientos locos; memorias del director de un manicomio. 2. ed. Santo Domingo, 1966.

6976 Psychology - Abnormal psychology - Mental disease - Special diseases and ates - Schizophrenia

Phil 6976.5 Society of Medical Psychoanalysts. Schizophrenia in psychoanalytic office practice. N.Y., 1957.
Phil 6976.10 Buss, Arnold H. Theories of schizophrenia. N.Y., 1969.
Phil 6976.17 Laing, Ronald David. Sanity, madness and family: families of schizophrenics. 2. ed. London, 1970.
Phil 6976.20 Flegel, Horst. Schizophasie in linguistischer Deutung. Berlin, 1965.
Phil 6976.25 Wolfson, Louis. Le schizo et les langues. Paris, 1970.
Phil 6976.30 Binswanger, Ludwig. Drei Formen missglückten Daseins: Verstiegenheit, Verschrobenheit, Manieriertheit. Tübingen, 1956.
Phil 6976.35 Wechsler, James Arthur. In a darkness. 1. ed. N.Y., 1972.

6978 Psychology - Abnormal psychology - Mental disease - Special diseases and ates - Other special

Phil 6978.5 Straub, Richard Ralph. A view of the levels of perceptual development in autistic syndromes. Academisch proefschrift. n.p., 1964.
Phil 6978.5.5 Fryes, F.B.M. Fremdes unter uns. Meppel, 1968.
Phil 6978.10 Bricout, Jacques. L'homme et la douleur. Paris, 1969.
Phil 6978.12 Kraussold, Karl. Melancholie und Schuld. Stuttgart, 1884.
Phil 6978.12.5 Raubinovitch, Jacques. La mélancolie. Paris, 1897.
Phil 6978.12.10 Krafft-Ebing, Richard. Die Melancholie. Erlangen, 1874.
Phil 6978.12.15 Binswanger, Ludwig. Melancholie und Manie. Pfullingen, 1960.

Phil 6978 Psychology - Abnormal psychology - Mental disease - Special diseases and states - Other special - cont.

Phil 6978.12.20 Biran, Sigmund. Melancholie und Todestriebe. München, 1961.

Phil 6980.1 - .799 Psychology - Abnormal psychology - Mental disease - Psychotherapy - General works (800 scheme, A-Z)

Phil 6980.14.100 Ackerknecht, E.H. Kurge Geschichte der Psychiatrie. Stuttgart, 1957.
Phil 6980.14.102 Ackerknecht, E.H. A short history of psychiatry. N.Y., 1959.
Phil 6980.32 Albee, George. Mental health manpower trends. N.Y., 1959.
Phil 6980.33 Alexander, F. Dynamic psychiatry. Chicago, 1952.
Phil 6980.34 Allers, Rudolf. Existentialism and psychiatry. Springfield, 1961.
Phil 6980.36 Altschule, Mark David. Roots of modern psychiatry. N.Y., 1957.
Phil 6980.36.2 Altschule, Mark David. Roots of modern psychiatry. 2. ed. N.Y., 1965.
Phil 6980.38.2 American Psychiatric Association. One hundred years of American psychiatric Association, 1844-1944. N.Y., 1945.
Phil 6980.38.5 American Psychiatric Association. Application of basic science techniques to psychiatric research. Washington, 1957.
Phil 6980.38.10 American Psychiatric Association. Biographical directory of fellows and members of the American Psychiatric Association. N.Y., 1941.
Phil 6980.40 American Psychiatric Association. Approaches to the study of human personality. Washington, 1956.
Phil 6980.43 Aucelin Schoetzenberger, Anne. Précis de psychodrame, introduction. 1. éd. Paris, 1966.
Phil 6980.45 Annell, A.L. Elementär barrpsykiatri. Stockholm, 1958.
Phil 6980.58 Arieti, Silvano. American handbook of psychiatry. N.Y., 1959. 3v.
Phil 6980.93 Barahona Fernandes, Henrique João de. Filosofia e psiquiatria. Coimbra, 1966.
Phil 6980.102 Bellak, L. Contemporary European psychiatry. N.Y., 1961.
Phil 6980.102.5 Bellman, Richard. A simulation of the initial psychiatric interview. Santa Monica, Calif., 1966.
Phil 6980.105 Berne, Eric. The mind in action. N.Y., 1947.
Phil 6980.105.5 Berne, Eric. Transactional analysis in psychotherapy. N.Y., 1961.
Phil 6980.105.10 Berge, André. Les psychothérapies. 1. éd. Paris, 1968.
Phil 6980.106 Bettelheim, Bruno. The empty fortress. N.Y., 1967.
Phil 6980.112 Bingham, J. The inside story. 1. ed. N.Y., 1953.
Phil 6980.112.10 Binger, C.A.L. More about psychiatry. Chicago, 1949.
Phil 6980.112.20 Binswanger, L. Der Mensch in der Psychiatrie. Pfullingen, 1957.
Phil 6980.112.50 Bion, Wilfrid R. Experiences in groups. London, 1961.
Phil 6980.113 Bittner, Günther. Psychoanalyse und soziale Erziehung. München, 1967.
Phil 6980.114 Bitter, Wilhelm. Magie und Wunder in der Heilkunde. Stuttgart, 1959.
Phil 6980.124 Bogdanovich, L.A. Carnets d'une psychiatre soviétique. Paris, 1963.
Phil 6980.127 Bond, Earl Clanford. One mind. N.Y., 1958.
Phil 6980.130 Baur, Pierre. Le psychodrame et la vie. Paris, 1968.
Phil 6980.132 Bratz, Emil. Humor in der Neurologie und Psychiatrie. Berlin, 1930.
Phil 6980.133 Alexander, Franz G. The history of psychiatry. N.Y., 1966.
Phil 6980.135 Brill, Abraham A. Lectures on psychoanalytic psychiatry. N.Y., 1946.
Phil 6980.141 Bry, Adelaide. Inside psychotherapy. N.Y., 1972.
Phil 6980.148 Burton, A. Case histories in clinical and abnormal psychology. v.2. N.Y., 1947.
Phil 6980.157 Campbell, John D. Everyday psychiatry. Philadelphia, 1945.
Phil 6980.182 Ciba Foundation. Ciba foundation symposium [on] transcultural psychiatry. Boston, 1965.
Phil 6980.198 Cooke, Elliot D. All but me and thee. Washington, 1946.
Phil 6980.210 Cumming, John. Ego and milieu. N.Y., 1962.
Phil 6980.222 Devereaux, G. Reality and dream. N.Y., 1951.
Phil 6980.224 Dick, Samuel. Psychotherapy. Minneapolis? 1909.
Phil 6980.241 Dumas, A.G. A psychiatric primer for the veteran's family and friends. Minneapolis, 1945.
Phil 6980.254 Ehrenwald, Jan. From medicine man to Freud. N.Y., 1956.
Phil 6980.259 Ellery, R.S. Psychiatric aspects of modern warfare. Melbourne, 1945.
Phil 6980.263 Enoch, M. David. Some uncommon psychiatric syndromes. Bristol, 1967.
Phil 6980.263.5 Enfance aliénée. Paris, 1967.
Phil 6980.286 Fedotov, D.D. Ocherki po istorii otechestvennoi psikhiatrii, vtoria polovina XVIII. Moskva, 1957.
Phil 6980.289 Fenichel, Otto. Problemas de ténica psicoanalitica. México, 1960.
Phil 6980.289.5 Fenichel, Otto. Perversionen, Psychosen, Charakterstörungen. Darmstadt, 1967.
Phil 6980.292 Findl, Fritz. Die psychiatriochen Theorien Rudolf Arndt's. München, 1960.
Phil 6980.293 Fisher, Vivian Ezra. The meaning and practice of psychotherapy. N.Y., 1950.
Phil 6980.305 Frankenstein, C. Persönlichkeitswandel. München, 1964.
Phil 6980.308 Freud, Anna. The pscyho-analytical treatment of children. London, 1946.
Phil 6980.309 Fromm-Reichmann, Frieda. Progress in psychotherapy. N.Y., 1956.
Phil 6980.309.5 Fromm-Reichmann, Frieda. Psychoanalysis and psychotherapy. Chicago, 1959.
Phil 6980.319 Gebsattel, V.E.F. von. Imago Hominis. Schweinfurt, 1964.
Phil 6980.321 Gesellschaft zur Orderung Tiefenpsychologischer und Psychotherapeutischer Forschung und Weiterbildung in München. Möglichkeiten moderner Psychotherapien. Göttingen, 1967.
Phil 6980.326 Ginsburg, S.W. A psychiatrist's views on social issues. N.Y., 1963.
Phil 6980.328 Glasser, William. Mental health or mental illness? N.Y., 1960.
Phil 6980.328.5 Glasser, William. Reality therapy, a new approach to psychiatry. N.Y., 1965.
Phil 6980.335 Graber, Gustav. Seelenspiegel des Kindes. Zürich, 1946.
Phil 6980.335.20 Greenberg, Ira A. Psychodrama and audience attitude change. Beverly Hills, 1968.
Phil 6980.336.5 Grinker, Roy R. Men under stress. Philadelphia, 1945.
Phil 6980.346 Haakanson, Kaj. Psykisk sjukdom: illusioner och realiteter; en teoretisk studie. Uppsala, 1968.
Phil 6980.347 Haley, Jay. The power tactics of Jesus Christ and other essays. N.Y., 1969.

Phil 6980.1 - .799   Psychology - Abnormal psychology - Mental disease - Psychotherapy - General works (800 scheme, A-Z) - cont.

Phil 6980.348   Hartmann, Heinz. La psicología del yo y el problema de la adaptación. México, 1961.

Phil 6980.348.10   Hartmann, Heinz. Psychoanalysis and moral values. N.Y., 1960.

Phil 6980.348.50   Harms, Ernest. Origins of modern psychiatry. Springfield, 1967.

Phil 6980.350   Held, Fritz. Jugendpsychiatrische Studien. Berlin, 1966.

Phil 6980.350.25   Henry, William Earl. The fifth profession. 1st ed. San Francisco, 1971.

Phil 6980.351.5   Herzberg, Alexander. Active psychotherapy. N.Y., 1946.

Phil 6980.354   Hoffer, Abram. Niacin therapy in psychiatry. Springfield, Ill., 1962.

Phil 6980.355   Holmberg, Gunnar. Modern svensk psykiatri under redaktion av Gunnar Holmberg. Stockholm, 1908.

Phil 6980.362   Institute on Preventive Psychiatry, State University of Iowa. Proceedings. Iowa City. 1-4 2v.

Phil 6980.363.5   Iudin, Tikhon I. Ocherki istorii otechestvennoi psikhiatrii. Moskva, 1951.

Phil 6980.363.20   Isserlin, Max. Psychotherapie. Berlin, 1926.

Phil 6980.365   Jakab, Irene. Zeichnungen und Gemälde der Geisteskranken. Budapest, 1956.

Phil 6980.367A   Johnson, James A. Group therapy. N.Y., 1963.

Phil 6980.367B   Johnson, James A. Group therapy. N.Y., 1963.

Phil 6980.372   Kalff, Dora M. Sandspiel. Zürich, 1966.

RRC   Phil 6980.383   Kiev, Ari. Psychiatry in the Communist world. N.Y., 1968.

Phil 6980.398   Krapf, E. Eduardo. Tomas de Aquino y la psicopatología. Buenos Aires, 1943.

Phil 6980.398.20   Kramer, Edith. Art therapy in a children's community. Springfield, 1958.

Phil 6980.398.40   Kraft, Thomas. De jeudgpsychiatriche diensten in Nederland. Utrecht, 1960.

Phil 6980.400   Krout, M.H. Psychology. Minneapolis, 1956.

Phil 6980.403   Kugelmass, I.N. The management of mental deficiency in children. N.Y., 1954.

Phil 6980.413   Lazarus, Arnold A. Behavior therapy and beyond. N.Y., 1971.

Phil 6980.416   Lennard, H.L. The anatomy of psychotherapy. N.Y., 1960.

Phil 6980.419   Lewis, Nolan don Carpentier. A short history of psychiatric achievement. N.Y., 1941.

Phil 6980.419.5   Lewis, Nolan don Carpentier. Wartime psychiatry; a compendium. N.Y., 1954.

Phil 6980.424   Lippman, Hyman. Treatment of the child in emotional conflict. N.Y., 1956.

Phil 6980.429   Loewnau, H.W. Reifungskrisen im Kindes- und Jugendalter. Göttingen, 1961.

Phil 6980.429.5   Loebsacu, T. Die unheimlichen Moglichkeiten oder die Manipulierte Seele. Düsseldorf, 1967.

Phil 6980.431   López Ibor, Juan. La agonía del psicoanalisis. 3. ed. Madrid, 1961.

Phil 6980.433   Lowrey, Lawson G. Psychiatry for social workers. N.Y., 1946.

Phil 6980.433.2   Lowrey, Lawson G. Psychiatry for social workers. 2. ed. N.Y., 1952.

Phil 6980.447   Maeder, Alphonse. Der Psychotherapeut als Paktnei. Zürich, 1957.

Phil 6980.458   Marlet, J.J.C. De psychiater en zijn pratkijk. Utrecht, 1962.

Phil 6980.458.5   Margolis, Joseph. Psychotherapy and morality. N.Y., 1966.

Phil 6980.459   Masserman, Jules Hymen. Principles of dynamic psychiatry. London, 1946.

Phil 6980.460   Matte Blanco, Ignacio. Estudios de psicología dinámica. Santiago de Chile, 1955.

Phil 6980.464   McDougall, Joyce. Dialogue with Sammy; a psycho-analytical contribution to the understanding a child psychosis. London, 1969.

Phil 6980.466   Meltzoff, Julian. Research in psychotherapy. 1. ed. N.Y., 1970.

Phil 6980.482   Mowrer, O.H. The crisis in psychiatry and religion. Princeton, N.J., 1961.

Phil 6980.484   Münsterberg, Hugo. Psychotherapy. N.Y., 1909.

Phil 6980.485   Mullahy, Patrick. A study of interpersonal relations. N.Y., 1957.

Phil 6980.489   Meyer, Adolf. Psychobiology. Springfield, 1957.

Phil 6980.504   New York Academy of Medicine. Modern attitudes in psychiatry. N.Y., 1946.

Phil 6980.516   Noveck, Simon. Judaism and psychiatry. N.Y., 1956.

VPhil 6980.518   Levi, Vladimir L'. Okhota za mysl'iu. Moskva, 1967.

Phil 6980.518.2   Levi, Vladimir L'. Okhota za mysl'iu. Izd. 2. Moskva, 1971.

Phil 6980.557   Ortigues, Marie. Oedipe africain. Paris, 1966.

Phil 6980.573   Pan-African Psychiatric Conference, 1st, Abeokuta, 1961. First Pan-African psychiatric conference. Ibadan, 1962?

Phil 6980.573.5   Pankow, Gisela. Gesprengte Fesseln der Psychose. München, 1968.

Phil 6980.575   Patterson, Charles H. Counseling and psychotherapy. N.Y., 1959.

Phil 6980.575.5   Paterson, A.S. Electrical and drug treatment in psychiatry. Amsterdam, 1963.

Phil 6980.583.2   Petrilowitsch, Nikolaus. Probleme der Psychotherapie alternder Menschen. 2. Aufl. Basel, 1968.

Phil 6980.587   Phillips, Ewing. Psychotherapy. Englewood Cliffs, 1956.

Phil 6980.598   National Committee for Mental Hygiene. Directory of psychiatric clinics in the United States. 1. ed. N.Y., 1932.

Phil 6980.606   Pollak, Otto. Social science and psychotherapy for children. N.Y., 1952.

Phil 6980.606.5   Pollak, Otto. Integrating sociological and psychoanalytic concepts. N.Y., 1956.

Phil 6980.611   Prick, Joseph Jules Guillaume. Human moods. Assen, 1968.

Phil 6980.614   Psychiatric research papers read at the dedication of the laboratory. Cambridge, 1947.

Phil 6980.631   Rapaport, David. Diagnostic psychological testing. Chicago, 1945. 2v.

Phil 6980.632   Rattner, Josef. Tiefenpsychologie und Humanismus. Zürich, 1967.

Phil 6980.635.5   Rees, J.R. The shaping of psychiatry by war. London, 1945.

Phil 6980.635.25   Reitman, F. Psychotic art. N.Y., 1951.

Phil 6980.635.26   Reitman, F. Insanity, art and culture. N.Y., 1959.

Phil 6980.635.40   Reik, T. The need to be loved. N.Y., 1963.

Phil 6980.644   Riese, Hertha. Heal the hurt child. Chicago, 1962.

Phil 6980.650   Rogow, Arnold A. The psychiatrists. N.Y., 1970.

Phil 6980.650.35   Rogers, Carl Ransom. On becoming a person. Boston, 1961.

Phil 6980.650.40   Rogers, Carl Ransom. Psychothérapie et relations humaines. Louvain, 1962. 2v.

Phil 6980.652.8   Rosanoff, A.J. Manuel of psychiatry. 6. ed. N.Y., 1927.

Phil 6980.1 - .799   Psychology - Abnormal psychology - Mental disease - Psychotherapy - General works (800 scheme, A-Z) - cont.

Phil 6980.653   Rotthaus, Erich. Das sittliche, eine Kraft des menschlichen Unbewussten. Stuttgart, 1949.

Phil 6980.661   Rycroft, Charles. Imagination and reality; psycho-analytical essays, 1951-1961. London, 1968.

Phil 6980.666   Sahakian, William S. Psychotherapy and counselling; studies in technique. Chicago, 1969.

Phil 6980.668   San Francisco, Department of Public Health. An experiment in the psychiatric treatment of promiscuous girls. San Francisco, 1945.

Phil 6980.668.10   Santer-Weststrate, Henrietta Cornelia. Gedragstherapie in het bijzonder de methode van wedenkerige remming. Assen, 1964.

Phil 6980.674   Schelder, Paul. Psychotherapy. N.Y., 1951.

Phil 6980.674.10   Schneider, Ulment Victor. Music and medicine; inaugural lecture. Johannesburg, 1964. 2v.

Phil 6980.674.25   Schofield, William. Psychotherapy. Englewood Cliffs, N.J., 1964.

Phil 6980.679   Seidmann, Peter. Der Weg der Tiefenpsychologie in geistesgeschichtlicher Perspektive. Zürich, 1959.

Phil 6980.685   Shepard, Martin. Games analysts play. N.Y., 1970.

Phil 6980.687   Phillips, J.H. Psychoanalyse und Symbolik. Bern, 1962.

Phil 6980.699   Snyder, William U. The psychotherapy relationship. N.Y., 1961.

Phil 6980.704   Spotnitz, Hyman. The couch and the circle. N.Y., 1961.

Phil 6980.707   Stein, Morris. Contemporary psychotherapies. N.Y., 1961.

Phil 6980.709   Storr, Anthony. The integrity of the personality. N.Y., 1961.

Phil 6980.710   Strauss, E.B. Psychiatry in the modern world. London, 1958.

Phil 6980.710.63   Stocker, Arnold. De la psychoanalyse à la psychosynthese. Paris, 1957.

Phil 6980.710.80   Strupp, Hans Herman. Psychotherapy and the modification of abnormal behavior. N.Y., 1971.

Phil 6980.712   Sullivan, Harry Stack. The interpersonal theory of psychiatry. 1. ed. N.Y., 1953. 4v.

Phil 6980.712.1   Sullivan, Harry Stack. Collected works. N.Y., 1965. 2v.

Phil 6980.712.5   Sullivan, Harry Stack. The psychiatric interview. N.Y., 1954.

Phil 6980.712.10   Sullivan, Harry Stack. The fusion of psychiatry and social science. N.Y., 1964.

Phil 6980.712.100   Blisten, D.R. The social theories of Harry Stack Sullivan. N.Y., 1953.

Phil 6980.712.105   Rattner, Josef. Psychologie der zwischenmenschlichen Beziehungen. Olten, 1969.

Phil 6980.717   Szondi, Lipot. Heilwege der Tiefenpsychologie. Bern, 1956.

Phil 6980.717.25   Szasz, Thomas Stephen. The myth of mental illness. N.Y., 1961.

Phil 6980.717.30   Szasz, Thomas Stephen. The manufacture of madness. 1st ed. N.Y., 1970.

Phil 6980.721   Tarachow, S. An introduction to psychotherapy. N.Y., 1963.

Phil 6980.732   Thomas, Alexander. Temperament and behavior disorders in children. N.Y., 1969.

Phil 6980.734   Redlich, Fredrick. The theory and practice of psychiatry. N.Y., 1966.

Phil 6980.744   Török, Stephan. Thymotherapie. Göttingen, 1967.

Phil 6980.759   Ungersma, Aaron J. The search for meaning. Philadelphia, 1961.

Phil 6980.760   United States. Children's Bureau. Residential treatment centers for emotional disturbed children. Washington, 1953.

Phil 6980.760.10   Urban challenges to psychiatry. 1. ed. Boston, 1969.

Phil 6980.768   Verster, Justus. Psychische bijwerkings verschijnselen van moltergan. Assen, 1967.

Phil 6980.770   Vinchon, Jean. La magie du dession. Paris, 1959.

Phil 6980.772   Volmat, R. L'art pyschopathologique. Paris, 1956.

Phil 6980.775   Wechsler, Israel S. The neurologist's point of view. N.Y., 1945.

Phil 6980.775.20   Weinstein, E.A. Cultural aspects of delusion. N.Y., 1962.

Phil 6980.775.50   Weiss, Edward. The structure and dynamics of the human mind. N.Y., 1960.

Phil 6980.776   Westman, H. The springs of creativity. N.Y., 1961.

Phil 6980.776.10   Werner, Reiner. Das verhaltensgestörte Kind. 1. Aufl. Berlin, 1967.

Phil 6980.777   Whittington, H.G. Psychiatry on the college campus. N.Y., 1963.

Phil 6980.779   Witmer, Helen L. Psychiatric interviews with children. N.Y., 1946.

Phil 6980.780   Wolpe, Joseph. Psychotherapy by reciprocal inhibition. Stanford, 1958.

Phil 6980.780.5   Wolpe, Joseph. The conditioning therapies. N.Y., 1964.

Phil 6980.780.10   Wolpe, Joseph. Behavior therapy techniques. Oxford, 1967.

Phil 6980.780.15.2   Wolberg, Lewis Robert. The technique of psychotherapy. 2. ed. N.Y., 1967. 2v.

Phil 6980.780.20   Wolpe, Joseph. The practice of behavior therapy. 1. ed. N.Y., 1969.

Phil 6980.794   Zander, A.F. Role relations in the mental health professions. Ann Arbor, 1957.

Phil 6983   Psychology - Abnormal psychology - Mental disease - Psychotherapy - Chemotherapy

Phil 6983.2   Caldwell, William Vernon. LSD psychotherapy; an explosion of psychedelic and psycholytic therapy. N.Y., 1968.

Phil 6985   Psychology - Abnormal psychology - Mental disease - Psychotherapy - Group therapy

Phil 6985.5   Sigrell, B. Group psychotherapy. Stockholm, 1968.

Phil 6985.10   Mann, John Harvey. Encounter; a weekend with intimate strangers. N.Y., 1970.

Phil 6985.15   Shepard, Martin. Marathon 16. N.Y., 1970.

Phil 6985.20A   Powdermaker, Florence. Group psychotherapy. Cambridge, 1953.

Phil 6985.20B   Powdermaker, Florence. Group psychoterapy. Cambridge, 1953.

Phil 6985.25   Bach, George Robert. Intensive group psychotherapy. N.Y., 1954.

Phil 6985.30   Howells, John Gwilym. Theory and practice of family psychiatry. N.Y., 1971.

Phil 6985.35   Therapy with families of sexually acting-out girls. N.Y., 1971.

Phil 6985.40   Berne, Eric. Principles of group treatment. N.Y., 1966.

Phil 6985.45   Barrucand, Dominique. La catharsis dans le théâtre. Paris, 1970.

Phil 6990   Psychology - Abnormal psychology - Mental disease - Psychotherapy -
Miraculous cures

Phil 6990.01	Pamphlet box. Psychology. Miraculous cures.
Phil 6990.1	Carre, L.B. La verité des miracles. n.p., 1737-41. 2v.
Phil 6990.1.2	Carré, L.B. La verité des miracles. Utrecht, 1737-41.
Phil 6990.2	Marx, J. History of the robe of Jesus Christ. Philadelphia, 1845.
Phil 6990.3	Lasserre, H. Les épisodes miraculeux de Lourdes. Paris, 1884.
Phil 6990.3.5	Lasserre, H. Our lady of Lourdes. N.Y., 1904.
Phil 6990.3.7	Lasserre, H. Notre-Dame de Lourdes. Paris, 1869.
Phil 6990.3.9	Huysmans, J.K. Les foules de Lourdes. 21. éd. Paris, 1906.
Phil 6990.3.15	Fourcade, M. l'abbé. L'apparition...grotté de Lourdes en 1858. Tarbes, 1862.
Phil 6990.3.19	Benson, R.F.O. Lourdes. St. Louis, 1914.
Phil 6990.3.20	Rebsomen, A. Notre-Dame de Lourdes. Paris, 1925.
Phil 6990.3.25	Boissarie, P.G. Lourdes und seine Geschichte vom medizinischen Standpunkte. 2. ed. Augsburg, 1892.
Htn Phil 6990.3.27*	Boissarie, P.G. Lourdes depuis 1858 jusqu'à nos jours. Paris, 1894.
Phil 6990.3.29	Shanley, W.J. The story of Lourdes. Hartford, 1908.
Phil 6990.3.31	Bonnières, L. de. Dans la lumière de Lourdes. Paris, 1920.
Phil 6990.3.33	Senna Freitas, José J. de. O milagre e a critica moderna on a immaculada conceição de Lourdes. Braga, 1873.
Phil 6990.3.35	Estrade, J.B. Les apparitions de Lourdes. Tours, 1899.
Phil 6990.3.38	Saint-Pierre, M. de. Bernadette and Lourdes. N.Y., 1954.
Phil 6990.3.40	Storer, M.L. (Mrs.). The story of a miracle at Lourdes, Aug., 1907. N.Y., 1908.
Phil 6990.3.42	Grandmaison de Bruno, F. Twenty cures at Lourdes. St. Louis, 1912.
Phil 6990.3.43	Martin, Stuart. The secret of Lourdes. London, 1926.
Phil 6990.3.50	Müller, G.A. Nach Lourdes. Luzern, 1909.
Phil 6990.3.52	Mayer, L. Lourdes, Konnersreuth oder Gallspach? Schopfheim, 1932.
Phil 6990.3.54	Barbé, Daniel. Lourdes: yesterday, today and tomorrow. Baden, 1893.
Phil 6990.3.55	Barbé, Daniel. Lourdes: hier, aujourd'hui, demain. Paris, 1893.
Phil 6990.3.60	Groneman, William. Bernadette Soubirous. Leuven, 1933.
Phil 6990.3.65	Carrel, A. The voyage to Lourdes. 1. ed. N.Y., 1950.
Phil 6990.3.70	Trouch, F. Sainte Bernadette Soubirous. Lyon, 1953.
Phil 6990.3.75	Deery, Joseph. Our Lady of Lourdes. Dublin, 1958.
Phil 6990.3.80	Trois écrivains devant Lourdes. Paris, 1958.
Phil 6990.3.85	Combes, André. Pilerinage spirituel à Lourdes. Paris, 1959.
Phil 6990.3.88	Guynot, Ernest. Sainte Bernadette. Paris, 1959.
Phil 6990.3.90	Laurentin, René. Lourdes. Paris, 1961. 6v.
Phil 6990.3.92	Laurentin, René. Lourdes. 2. ed. Paris, 1957. 7v.
Phil 6990.3.95	Stolarek, Z. Gorod chudes svoimi i chuzhimi glazami. Moskva, 1961.
Phil 6990.3.100	Izard, Francis. The meaning of Lourdes. London, 1939.
Phil 6990.3.105	Stafford, Ann (pseud.). Bernadette and Lourdes. London, 1967.
Phil 6990.3.106	Neame, Alan. The happening at Lourdes. London, 1968.
Phil 6990.3.110	Laurentin, René. Les apparitions de Lourdes. Paris, 1966.
Phil 6990.3.112	Gerloff, Hans. Die Heilungen von Lourdes im Lichte der Parapsychologie. Büdingen-Gettenbach, 1959.
Phil 6990.3.114	Cassagnard, Jean Marie. Carrel et Zola devant le miracle à Lourdes. Lourdes, 1958.
Phil 6990.3.116	Bettez, Norbert Marie. Lourdes et Fatima. Montréal, 1967.
Phil 6990.4	Mathieu, P.F. Histoire des miracules et des convulsionnaires de Saint-Médard. Paris, 1864.
Phil 6990.4.2	Bonnaire, Louis de. Observations. n.p., 1773. 2 pam.
Phil 6990.5	Hamilton, M. Incubation....Pagan...Christian Churches. London, 1906.
Phil 6990.6	Vialard, Felix. Recueil des pieces...sur les miracles. Nancy, 1735.
Phil 6990.7	Duffel, O.L.V. van. Ofte van Goeden Will. Antwerpen, 1717.
n Phil 6990.8*	Maillard, Mary. A true relation of the wonderful cure of Mary Maillard. London, 1694.
Phil 6990.8.5	Maillard, Mary. An exact relation of the wonderful cure of Mary Maillard. London, 1730.
Phil 6990.11	Waddle, C.W. Miracles of healing. n.p., 1909.
Phil 6990.12	Saintyves, P. La simulation du merveilleux. Paris, 1912.
Phil 6990.12.5	Saintyves, P. Le discernement du miracle. Paris, 1909.
Phil 6990.13	Mir y Noguera, Juan. El milagro. 2. ed. Barcelona, 1915. 3v.
Phil 6990.14	LaVausserie. Apparitions de la St. Vierge à deux jeunes enfants. Paris, 1873.
Phil 6990.15	Joyce, G.H. The question of miracles. St. Louis, 1914.
Phil 6990.16	Myers, J. Narrative of two wonderful cures. Baltimore, 1831.
Phil 6990.17	Huelster, A. Miracles in the light, science and history. Chicago, 19- .
Phil 6990.18	Nanz, C.F. Die Besessenen im neuen Testament. Reutlingen, 1840.
Phil 6990.19.5	Abbott, E.A. Philomythus, an antidote against credulity. London, 1891.
Phil 6990.20	Poulpiquet, E. Le miracle et ses suppléances. Paris, 1914.
Phil 6990.21	Pamphlet vol. Miracles of Prince Hohenlohe. 10 pam.
Phil 6990.21.3	A brief disclosure to the people of England of the liberality of the Irish Roman Catholics. London, 1824.
Phil 6990.21.5	Sebastian, L. Fürst Alexander von Hohenlohe-Schillings. Inaug. Diss. Kempten, 1918.
Phil 6990.21.10	Pamphlet vol. Guerisons du P. de Hohenlohe. 4 pam.
Phil 6990.22	Romagne, M. l'abbe de. Dictionnaire historique des miracles. Paris, 1824.
Phil 6990.23	Taylor, William F. Miracles; their physical possibility. Liverpool, 1868.
Phil 6990.24	Daurelle. Etude des manifestations surnaturelles au XIX siècle. Rome, 1878.
Phil 6990.25	Bushenskii, N. Kniga chudes. Pesch', 1860.
Phil 6990.26	Wonderful works of God. Irvington, N.J., 1858.
Phil 6990.26.5	Wonderful works of God. Fall River, Mass., 1877.
Phil 6990.27	Blumhardt, C.G. Vertheidigungsschrift. Reutlingen, 1850.
Phil 6990.28	Tennant, F.R. Miracle and its philosophical presuppositions. Cambridge, 1925.
Phil 6990.29	Milner, John. Authentic documents relative to the cure of Winefrid White. 3. ed. London, 1806.
Phil 6990.30	Grellety, L. Du merveilleux, des miracles et des pelerinages au point de vue medical. Paris, 1876.
Phil 6990.31	Regnault, Félix. La genèse des miracles. Paris, 1910.
Phil 6990.32	Allen, Simeon C. Miracles and medicine. Boston, 1929.

Phil 6990   Psychology - Abnormal psychology - Mental disease - Psychotherapy -
Miraculous cures - cont.

Phil 6990.33	Brewer, E.C. A dictionary of miracles. Philadelphia, 1884.
Phil 6990.33.5	Brewer, E.C. Dictionary of miracles. Philadelphia, 188-?
Phil 6990.34.5	Touquédec, J. de. Introduction a l'étude du merveilleux et du miracle. 3. éd. Paris, 1923.
Phil 6990.35	Vilar, Albert. Réflexions sur le miracle et les lois naturelles. Clamecy, 1934.
Htn Phil 6990.36*	Morry, A. de. Discours d'un miracle avenu en la Basse Normandie. Paris, 1598.
Phil 6990.37	Le Quien de la Neufville, Charles Jacques. Nouvelles prennes contre le faux miracle de migne approuvé à Rome. Paris, 1828.
Phil 6990.37.5	Le Quien de la Neufville, Charles Jacques. Vains efforts de plusieurs évêques. Paris, 1830.
Htn Phil 6990.38*	Luquet, J.P. Abrege de la notice sur la vie et les vertus d'Anna Maria Taigi. Rome, 1851.
Phil 6990.39	Schreiber, G. Deutsche Mirakelbücher. Dusseldorf, 1938.
Htn Phil 6990.40*	Blount, Charles. Miracles, no violations of the law of nature. London, 1683.
Htn Phil 6990.40.5*	Browne, T. Miracles work's. London, 1683.
Phil 6990.41	Keyes, F.P.W. (Mrs.). The sublime shepherdess; the life of St. Bernadette of Lourdes. N.Y., 1940.
Phil 6990.42	Saunders, E. Lourdes. N.Y., 1940.
Phil 6990.43	Major, R.H. Faiths that healed. N.Y., 1940.
Phil 6990.44	Blanton, M.G. Bernadette of Lourdes. London, 1939.
Phil 6990.44.20	Barbet, Jean. La dame plus belle que tout. Paris, 1957.
Phil 6990.45	Boyle, J.L. A pictorial history of Lourdes. Philadelphia, 1940.
Phil 6990.46	Olden, R. Propheten in deutscher Krise. Berlin, 1932.
Phil 6990.47.5	Virchow, R. Über Wunder. 2. Aufl. Frankfurt, 1908.
Phil 6990.48	García Aceituno, José Luis. Esquípulas. 1. ed. Jalapa, 1940.
Phil 6990.48.2	García Aceituno, José Luis. Esquípulas. 2. ed. Guatemala? 1954.
Phil 6990.50	Mousset, Albert. L'étrange histoire des convulsionnaires de Saint-Medard. Paris, 1953.
Phil 6990.52	Meist, Paul. Les cinquant-quatre miracles de Lourdes au jugement du drait canon. Paris, 1958.
Phil 6990.55	Rairer, A. Essai sur la spiritualité de Bernadette. Nevers, 1958.
Phil 6990.58	Celma, Bernal. Curaciones milagrosas. Zaragoza, 1961.
Phil 6990.60	Marert, Léonce. Nouvelle histoire de Lourdes. Paris, 1955.
Phil 6990.61	Bach, H. Mirakelbücker bayerischer Wallfahrtsorte. Möhrendorf, 1963.
Phil 6990.62	Smith, Robert D. Comparative miracles. St. Louis, 1965.
Phil 6990.65	Sherman, Harold Morrow. Wonder healers of the Philippines. London, 1967.
Phil 6990.68	Bishop, George Victor. Faith healing; God or fraud? Los Angeles, 1967.

Phil 6992   Psychology - Abnormal psychology - Mental disease - Psychotherapy -
Suggestion therapy

| Phil 6992.2 | Cohen, Jacques J. Psychotherapy. London, 1936. |
| Phil 6992.4 | Frétigny, Roger. L'imagerie mentale; introduction à l'onirothérapie. Genève, 1968. |

Phil 6996   Psychology - Abnormal psychology - Mental disease - Psychotherapy -
Surgery

| Phil 6996.5 | Freeman, Walter. Psychosurgery. Springfield, 1942. |

Phil 6998   Psychology - Abnormal psychology - Mental disease - Psychotherapy -
Other special

Phil 6998.2	Perls, Frederick S. Ego, hunger, and aggression; the beginning of Gestalt therapy. N.Y., 1969.
Phil 6998.2.5	Perls, Frederick S. In and out the garbage pail. Lafayette, Calif., 1969.
Phil 6998.2.11	Perls, Frederick S. Gestalt therapy. N.Y., 1969.
Phil 6998.3	Brockton Symposium and Workshop on Behavior Therapy. Proceedings. Nutley, N.J. 1,1970+
Phil 6998.4.2	Axline, Virginia Mae. Play therapy. N.Y., 1969.
Phil 6998.4.5	Ginott, Haim G. Group psychotherapy with children. N.Y., 1961.
Phil 6998.6	Kanfer, Frederick H. Learning foundations of behavior therapy. N.Y., 1970.
Phil 6998.8	Aubin, Henri. Art et magie chez l'enfant. Toulouse, 1971.

Phil 7003   Psychology - Parapsychology - Reference works - Bibliographies

| Phil 7003.2 | A bibliography and index of psychic research and related topics. Chicago. 1962-1964// |
| Phil 7003.5 | Zorab, George. Bibliography of parapsychology. N.Y., 1957. |

Phil 7009.101   - .399   Psychology - Parapsychology - History - Biographies
of researchers, etc. - Individual (A-Z, 299 scheme, by person)

| Phil 7009.145.1 | Byrd, Elizabeth. A strange and seeing time. London, 1971. |
| Phil 7009.210 | Gandee, Lee R. Strange experience; the autobiography of a hexenmeister. Englewood Cliffs, 1971. |

Phil 7010   Psychology - Parapsychology - General treatises - Collected authors

Phil 7010.5	Bender, Hans. Parapsychologie. Entwicklung, Ergebnisse, Probleme. Darmstadt, 1966.
Phil 7010.5.1	Bender, Hans. Parapsychologie; ihre Ergebnisse und Probleme. Bremen, 1970.
Phil 7010.7	Knight, David C. The ESP reader. N.Y., 1969.
Phil 7010.10	Rhine, Joseph Banks. Parapsychology today. 1. ed. N.Y., 1968-

Phil 7011   - 7036   Psychology - Parapsychology - General treatises -
Individual authors (A-Z)

Phil 7011.2.2	Abhedánanda, Swami. The science of psychic phenomena. 2. ed. Calcutta, 1966.
Phil 7012.2	Bathurst, James. Atomic-consciousness. Exeter, 1892.
Phil 7012.2.5	Bathurst, James. Atomic consciousness reviewed. Bristol, 190-?
Phil 7012.4	Bender, Hans. Unser sechster Sinn. Stuttgart, 1971.
Phil 7016.2	Frei, Gebhard. Probleme der Parapsychologie. München, 1969.
Phil 7020.2	Jacobson, Nils-Olof. Liv efter döden? Salna, 1971.
Phil 7026.2	Pratt, Joseph G. Parapsychology. N.Y., 1966.
Phil 7028.2	Rýzl, Milan. Parapsychology. N.Y., 1970.
Phil 7028.4	Rouxel. Rapports du magnétisme et du spiritisme. Paris, 1892.
Phil 7030.2	Tenhaeff, Wilhelm H.C. Parapsychologie. Antwerpen, 1968.

Phil 7039 Psychology - Parapsychology - Reports of commissions, investigations, etc. - Special cases

Phil 7039.2.2 — Mais, Charles. The surprising case of Rachel Baker who prays and preaches in her sleep. v.1-2. 2d ed. N.Y., 1814.

Phil 7039.4.1 — Prince, Morton. The dissociation of a personality. N.Y., 1906.

Phil 7039.4.3 — Prince, Morton. The dissociation of a personality. N.Y., 1910.

Phil 7039.4.6 — Prince, Morton. The dissociation of a personality. N.Y., 1925.

Phil 7039.4.8 — Prince, Morton. The dissociation of a personality. N.Y., 1957.

Phil 7039.4.15 — Prince, Morton. My life as a dissociated personality. Boston, 1909.

Phil 7039.6A — Mitchell, Silas Weir. Mary Reynolds: a case of double consciousness. Philadelphia, 1889.

Phil 7039.6B — Mitchell, Silas Weir. Mary Reynolds: a case of double consciousness. Philadelphia, 1889.

Phil 7039.8 — Stevens, E. Winchester. The Watseka wonder. Chicago, 1879.

Phil 7039.8.2 — Stevens, E. Winchester. The Watseka wonder. Chicago, 1887.

Phil 7039.10 — Prince, Walter Franklin. The Doris case of multiple personality. York, Pa., 1915-16. 2v.

Phil 7039.12 — Lancaster, Evelyn. The final face of Eve. N.Y., 1958.

Phil 7040 Psychology - Parapsychology - General special - Disorders of personality [Discontinued]

Phil 7040 — Pamphlet box. Psychology. Abnormal. Personality.

Phil 7040.01 — Pamphlet box. Psychology. Abnormal. Personality.

Phil 7040.2.5 — Ribot, T. Diseases of personality. Photoreproduction. N.Y., 1887.

Phil 7040.6.60 — Pamphlet box. Prince, Morton. Criticism.

Phil 7040.22A — Hunt, Joseph M. Personality and the behavior disorders. N.Y., 1944. 2v.

Phil 7040.22B — Hunt, Joseph M. Personality and the behavior disorders. N.Y., 1944. 2v.

Phil 7040.29 — Thigpen, C.H. The three faces of Eve. N.Y., 1957.

Phil 7040.39 — Craft, Michael. Ten studies into psychopathic personality. Bristol, 1965.

Phil 7040.40 — Claridge, Gordon S. Personality and arousal; a psychophysiological study of psychiatric disorder. Oxford, 1967.

Phil 7040.43 — Gaylin, Willard. The meaning of despair. N.Y., 1968.

Phil 7042 Psychology - Parapsychology - General special - Multiple consciousness, Dissociation of personality

Phil 7042.2 — Dessoir, Max. Das Doppel-Ich. Leipzig, 1890.

Phil 7042.2.2 — Dessoir, Max. Das Doppel-Ich. 2e Aufl. Leipzig, 1896.

Phil 7042.4 — Binet, Alfred. On double consciousness. Chicago, 1890.

Phil 7042.4.1 — Binet, Alfred. On double consciousness. Chicago, 1896.

Phil 7042.4.2 — Binet, Alfred. On double consciousness. Chicago, 1905.

Phil 7042.6A — Sidis, Boris. Multiple personality: an experimental investigation. N.Y., 1905.

Phil 7042.6B — Sidis, Boris. Multiple personality: an experimental investigation. N.Y., 1905.

Phil 7042.8.2 — Berg, Jan Hendrik van den. Leven in meervoud. 2. druk. Nijkerk, 1963.

Phil 7050 Psychology - Parapsychology - Spiritualism - Folios [Discontinued]

Htn Phil 7050.3PF* — Pamphlet box. Newspaper clippings.

Htn Phil 7050.4* — Pamphlet vol. Spiritism. 7 pam.

Htn Phil 7050.5* — Pamphlet vol. Spiritism. 8 pam.

Htn Phil 7050.6* — Pamphlet vol. Spiritism. 18 pam.

Phil 7050.8 — Pamphlet vol. Spiritism. 13 pam.

Phil 7050.10 — Diotrephes. The "knockings" Exposed. N.Y., 1850. 3 pam.

Phil 7050.11 — Guillard, J.-C.A. Table qui douse et table qui répond. Paris, 1853. 3 pam.

Htn Phil 7050.12* — Pamphlet vol. Spiritism. 1852-1868.

Phil 7050.800.-.999 — Pamphlet boxes. Spiritism. Chronological file by year.

Phil 7050.800.-.999F — Pamphlet boxes. Spiritism. Chronological file by year.

Phil 7052 Psychology - Parapsychology - Spiritualism - History - General works

Phil 7052.5 — Home, D.D. Lights and shadows of spiritualism. London, 1878.

Phil 7052.6 — Kiesewetter, Karl. Die Entwickelungsgeschichte des Spiritismus. Leipzig, 1893.

Phil 7052.7 — Abbott, D.P. Behind the scenes with the mediums. Chicago, 1907.

Phil 7052.7.5 — Abbott, D.P. The history of a strange case. Chicago, 1908.

Phil 7052.8 — Rochas d'Aiglun, Albert de. L'extériorisation de la motricité. Paris, 1896.

Phil 7052.9 — Howitt, William. The history of the supernatural. Philadelphia, 1863. 2v.

Phil 7052.10 — Spicer, Henry. Sights and sounds. London, 1853.

Phil 7052.10.2 — Spicer, Henry. Facts and fantasies, a sequel to Sights and sounds. London, 1853.

Phil 7052.15.2 — Aldrete y Soto, Luis de. Aldrete ó Los espiritistas españoles. 2. ed. Barcelona, 1881.

Phil 7052.20 — Brown, Slater. The heyday of spiritualism. N.Y., 1970.

Phil 7053 Psychology - Parapsychology - Spiritualism - History - Local (Geographic Table A)

Phil 7053.344 — Norman, Diana. Tom Corbett's stately ghosts of England. N.Y., 1970.

Phil 7054 Psychology - Parapsychology - Spiritualism - History - Miscellany [Discontinued]

Phil 7054.1 — Francis, John R. The encyclopaedia of death and life in the spirit world. Chicago, 1985-1900. 3v.

Phil 7054.2 — Danskin, W.A. How and why I became a spiritualist. 4th ed. Baltimore, 1869.

Phil 7054.3 — Farnese, A. A wanderer in the spirit lands. Chicago, 1901.

Phil 7054.4.9 — Whiting, Lilian. After her death. Boston, 1898.

Phil 7054.4.15 — Whiting, Lilian. The spiritual significance. Boston, 1900.

Phil 7054.5 — Sweet, Elizabeth. The future life as described...by spirits. 4th ed. Boston, 1873.

Phil 7054.6.05 — Pamphlet box. Davis, A.J. Minor writings.

NEDL Phil 7054.6.3 — Davis, A.J. The magic staff; an autobiography. N.Y., 1857.

Phil 7054.6.5 — Davis, A.J. The philosophy of spiritual intercourse. N.Y., 1851.

Phil 7054 Psychology - Parapsychology - Spiritualism - History - Miscellany [Discontinued] - cont.

Phil 7054.6.6 — Davis, A.J. The present age and inner life. N.Y., 1855.

Phil 7054.6.8 — Davis, A.J. The present age and inner life. 3d ed. Boston, 1870.

Phil 7054.6.9 — Davis, A.J. The great harmonia. 4th ed. Boston, 1870. 5v.

Phil 7054.6.18 — Davis, A.J. The penetralia, being harmonial answers. 3. ed. Boston, 1857.

Phil 7054.6.30 — Davis, A.J. The principles of nature, her divine revelations. 12. ed. N.Y., 1855.

Phil 7054.6.35 — Davis, A.J. The fountain. 1st ed. Boston, 1870.

Phil 7054.6.50 — Davis, A.J. Introduction to the writings of Andrew J. Davis. Boston, 1930.

Phil 7054.6.55 — Davis, A.J. The harmonial man. Boston, 1853.

NEDL Phil 7054.7 — Underhill, A. Leah. The missing link in modern spiritualism. N.Y., 1885.

Phil 7054.7.5 — Davenport, R.B. The death blow to spiritualism...true story of the Fox sisters. N.Y., 1888.

Phil 7054.8 — Moses, William S. Higher aspects of spiritualism. London, 1880.

Phil 7054.8.5 — Moses, William S. Spirit identity. London, 1879.

Phil 7054.9 — Giles. A.E. English and parental versions of Bible...in the light of modern spiritualism. Boston, 1897.

Phil 7054.10 — Holland, C. Spiritual or magnetic forces. 2. ed. N.Y., 1882.

Phil 7054.11 — Shelhamer, M.F. Life and labor in the spirit world. Boston, 1885.

Phil 7054.13 — Stevenson. William G. Does spiritualism transcend natural law? Poughkeepsie, 1880.

Phil 7054.14 — Arnold, H. Wie errichtet und leitet man spiritistische Zirkel in der Familie? Leipzig, 1894.

Phil 7054.15 — Mayer, John (Mrs). Further communications from the world of spirits. N.Y., 1861.

Phil 7054.17 — Pridham, A. The spirits tried. London, 1874.

Phil 7054.18 — Ford, S.L. Interwoven. Letters from a son to his mother. Boston, 1905.

Phil 7054.19 — Fritz, (pseud.). Where are the dead? or Spiritualism explained. Manchester, 1873.

Phil 7054.20 — Light on the hidden way. Boston, 1886.

Phil 7054.21 — Lewis, H.C. The alleged physical phenomena of spiritualism. Boston, 1887.

Phil 7054.22 — Stead, William T. After death or Letters from Julia. 3. ed. Chicago, 1910.

Phil 7054.22.5 — Stead, William T. After death; a personal narrative. N.Y., 1914.

Phil 7054.23 — Mattison, H. The rappers. N.Y., n.d.

Phil 7054.23.3 — Mattison, H. Spirit rapping unveiled. N.Y., 1953.

Phil 7054.23.5 — Mattison, H. Spirit-rapping unveiled. N.Y., 1855.

Phil 7054.24 — Helleberg, C.C. A book written by the spirits of the so-called dead. Cincinnati, 1883.

Phil 7054.25 — Brown, Robert. Demonology and witchcraft. London, 1889.

Phil 7054.26 — Golden light angels's visits to my farm in Florida. N.Y., 1892.

Phil 7054.27 — Putnam, A. Flashes of light from the spirit land. Boston, 1892.

Phil 7054.27.5 — Putnam, A. Agassiz and spiritualism. Boston, n.d.

Phil 7054.27.7 — Putnam, A. Natty, a spirit; his portrait and his life. Boston, 1856.

Phil 7054.27.9 — Putnam, A. Tipping his tables. Boston, 1873.

Phil 7054.27.11 — Putnam, A. Bible marvel workers. Boston, 1873.

Phil 7054.28 — Kiddle, H. Spiritual communications. Boston, 1879.

Phil 7054.29 — Tindall, A.F. Occult revelations in prose and verse. London, n.d.

Phil 7054.30 — Rifts in the veil. London, 1878.

Phil 7054.31 — Zillah, the child medium. N.Y., 1857.

Phil 7054.32 — Clerk, A.M. Spiritism; the keystone of Christianity. London, 1894.

Phil 7054.33 — Samson, G.W. The physical in spiritualism. Philadelphia, 1880.

Phil 7054.33.5 — Samson, G.W. "To daemoion" or The spiritual medium. Boston, 1852.

Phil 7054.33.7 — Samson, G.W. Spiritualism tested. Boston, 1860.

Phil 7054.34 — Sargent, Epes. The scientific basis of spiritualism. Boston, 1880.

Phil 7054.34.5 — Sargent, Epes. Planchette; or, The despair of science. Boston, 1869.

Phil 7054.34.8 — Sargent, Epes. The proof palpable of immortalty. Boston, 1875.

Phil 7054.34.10 — Sargent, Epes. The proof palpable of immortality. 3. ed. Boston, 1881.

Phil 7054.35 — Henke, O. Der Gespensterglaube der Gegenwart. Mülheim, 1881.

Phil 7054.36 — Fichet, I.H. von. Der neuere Spiritualismus; sein Werth. Leipzig, 1878.

Phil 7054.37 — Rivail, H.L.D. Le livre des esprits. Paris, 1857.

Phil 7054.37.15 — Rivail, H.L.D. Le livre des esprits. 15. ed. Paris, 1866.

Phil 7054.37.25 — Rivail, H.L.D. El evangelio segun el espiritismo. Barcelona, 1875.

Phil 7054.37.30 — Rivail, H.L.D. El cielo y el infierno. 4. ed. Barcelona, 1871.

Phil 7054.37.33 — Rivail, H.L.D. El génesis, los milagros. Barcelona, 1871.

Phil 7054.37.35 — Rivail, H.L.D. El génesis. San Martin de Provensals, 1887.

Phil 7054.37.40 — Rivail, H.L.D. Spiritizm v samom prostom ego vyrazhenii. Leiptsig, 1864.

Phil 7054.38 — Spirit rapping in England and America. London, 1853.

Phil 7054.39 — Gibier, P. Le spiritisme. Paris, 1887.

Phil 7054.40 — Hall, T.B. Modern spiritualism; or Opening way. Boston, 1883.

Phil 7054.40.5 — Hall, T.B. Three articles on modern spiritualism. Boston, 1863.

Phil 7054.41 — Webber, C.W. Spiritual vampirism. Philadelphia, 1853.

Phil 7054.42 — Peebles, J.M. The practical of spiritualism. Chicago, 1868.

Phil 7054.43 — Bartlett, G.C. The Salem seer. N.Y., 1891.

Phil 7054.43.3A — Bartlett, G.C. The Salem seer. N.Y., n.d.

Phil 7054.43.3B — Bartlett, G.C. The Salem seer. N.Y., n.d.

Phil 7054.43.15 — Senillosa, Felipe. Concordancia del espiritismo con la ciencia. v.1-2. Buenos Aires, 1891.

Phil 7054.43.20 — Pioda, Alfredo. Memorabilia. Bellinzona, 1891.

Phil 7054.45 — Home, Daniel Dunglas (Mrs.). The gift of D.D. Home. London, 1890.

Phil 7054.45.5 — Home, Daniel Dunglas (Mrs.). D.D. Home, his life and mission. London, 1888.

Phil 7054.45.9 — Home, Daniel Douglas. Incidents in my life. N.Y., 1863.

Phil 7054.45.11 — Home, Daniel Dunglas. Incidents in my life. London, 1863.

Classified Listing

Phil 7054 Psychology - Parapsychology - Spiritualism - History - Miscellany [Discontinued] - cont.

Phil 7054.45.14 Home, Daniel Dunglas. Incidents in my life. 5th ed. N.Y., 1864.
Phil 7054.45.50 Gardy, Louis. Le médium D.D. Home. Genève, 189-.
Phil 7054.45.55 Dunraven, W.T.W.-Q. Experiences in spiritualism with D.D. Home. Glasgow, 1924.
Phil 7054.45.60 Tischner, R. Das medium D.D. Home. Leipzig, 1925.
Phil 7054.46 Chase, W. The gist of spiritualism. 3. ed. Boston, 1867.
Phil 7054.47 Olcott, H.S. People from the other world. Hartford, 1875.
Phil 7054.48 Weil, Samuel. The religion of the future. Boston, 1894.
Phil 7054.49.4 Waggoner, J.H. The nature and tendency of modern spiritualism. 4. ed. Battle creek. Mich., 1872.
Phil 7054.50 Lillie, Arthur. Modern mystics and modern magic. N.Y., 1894.
Phil 7054.50.2 Lillie, Arthur. The worship of Satan in modern France. London, 1896.
Phil 7054.51.5 Werner, H. Guardian spirits. N.Y., 1847.
Phil 7054.51.10 Werner, H. Die Schutzgeister. Stuttgart, 1839.
Phil 7054.52 Edmonds, J.W. Spiritualism. N.Y., 1855. 2v.
Phil 7054.52.4 Edmonds, J W. Spiritualism. 4th ed. N.Y., 1853.
Phil 7054.53 Wolfe, N.B. Startling facts in modern spiritualism. Cincinnati, 1874.
Phil 7054.54.5 Linton, Charles. The healing of the nations. 2. ed. N.Y., 1855.
Phil 7054.54.7 Linton, Charles. The healing of the nations. 2. series. Philadelphia, 1864.
Phil 7054.56 Adams, John Quincy. Twelve messages from the spirit. Boston, 1859.
Phil 7054.57 Brownson, O.A. The spirit-rapper. Boston, 1854.
Phil 7054.57.5 Brownson, O.A. The spirit-rapper, an autobiography. Detroit, 1884.
Phil 7054.58 Williamson, M.J. Modern diabolism; commonly called modern spiritualism. N.Y., 1873.
Phil 7054.59 Redman, G.A. Mystic hours, or spiritual experience. N.Y., 1859.
Phil 7054.60.4 Beecher, Charles. A review of the spiritual manifestations. N.Y., 1853.
Phil 7054.60.5 Beecher, Charles. A review of the spiritual manifestations. London, 1853.
Phil 7054.61 Brittan, S.B. A review of Rev. Charles Beecher's report. N.Y., 1853.
Phil 7054.61.3 Brittan, Samuel B. The tables turned. N.Y., 1854.
Phil 7054.61.5 Brittan, Samuel B. A discussion of the facts of...ancient and modern spiritualism. N.Y., 1853.
Phil 7054.61.7 Brittan, Samuel B. The telegraph's answer. N.Y., 1855.
Phil 7054.61.8 Spiritual telegraph. The telegraph papers. N.Y., 1853. 8v.
Phil 7054.61.9 The Shekinah. N.Y., 1853. 3v.
Phil 7054.61.12 Brittan, Samuel B. The battleground of the spiritual reformation. N.Y., 1882.
Phil 7054.62 Hammond, Charles. Pilgrimage of Thos. Paine. N.Y., 1852.
Phil 7054.62.2 Hammond, Charles. Light from the spirit world. N.Y., 1852.
Phil 7054.62.5 Hammond, Charles. Philosophy of the spirit world. N.Y., 1853.
Phil 7054.63.4 Hare, Robert. Experimental investigation of the spirit manifestations. N.Y., 1856.
Phil 7054.64 Hall, S.C. The use of spiritualism? Glasgow, 1876.
Phil 7054.65 Fairfield, F.G. Ten years with spiritual mediums. N.Y., 1875.
Phil 7054.66 Ferguson, J.B. A record of communications from the spirit-spheres. Nashville, 1854.
Phil 7054.67 White, N.F. Voices from spirit-land. N.Y., 1854.
Phil 7054.68 Gleason, S.W. The spirit home: a closet companion. Boston, 1852.
Phil 7054.69 Gridley, J.A. Astounding facts from the spirit world. South Hampton, 1854.
Phil 7054.70 Crosland, N. Light in the valley: my experience of spiritualism. London, 1857.
Phil 7054.71 Cridge, A. Epitome of spirit-intercourse. Boston, 1854.
Phil 7054.72 Essays on various subjects. N.Y., 1861.
Phil 7054.73 A history of the recent developments in spiritual manifestations. Philadelphia, 1851.
Phil 7054.73.9 Observations on the theological mystery...spirit rappings. Hartford, 1851.
Phil 7054.74 Wilson, R.P. Discourses from the spirit-world. N.Y., 1855.
Phil 7054.75 Monroe, L.B. A revelation from heaven. Boston, 1851.
Phil 7054.76 Cooke, P. Necromancy; or a rap for the rappers. Boston, 1857 .
Phil 7054.77F Kidder, L. A spiritual communicating diagram. n.p., n.d.
Phil 7054.78 Child. A.B. The bouquet of spiritual flowers. Boston, 1856.
Phil 7054.79 Hewitt, S.C. Messages from the superior state. Boston, 1853.
Phil 7054.80 Robinson, J.H. The religion of manhood. Boston, 1854.
Phil 7054.81 Modern Christian spiritualism. Philadelphia, 1863.
Phil 7054.81.15 Guppy, Samuel. Mary Jane; or spiritualism chemically explained. London, 1863.
Phil 7054.81.19 De Morgan, Sophia Elisabeth. From matter to spirit. London, 1863.
Phil 7054.82 Grimes, J.S. Great discussion of modern spritualism. Boston, 1860.
Phil 7054.83 Lunt, George. Boston Courier report of the proceedings of professed spiritual agents and mediums. Boston, 1859. 2 pam.
Phil 7054.84 Randolph, P.B. The unveiling: or What I think of spiritualism. Newburyport, 1860.
Phil 7054.85 Platt, L.L. Spiritual experience. New Haven, 1852. 2 pam.
Phil 7054.86 Hatch, Cora L.V. Two lectures on the present crisis. N.Y., 1860.
Phil 7054.87 Pierce, David. The revelation...twenty-one days' entrancement. Bangor, 1857.
Phil 7054.88 Pierce, A.P. Extracts from unpublished volumes. Boston, 1868.
Phil 7054.89 Adams, J.S. A rivulet from the ocean of truth. Boston, 1854.
Phil 7054.90 Constantine, T.C. Modern spiritualism. Manchester, 1858.
Phil 7054.90.5 Auguez, Paul. Spiritualisme; faits curieux. Paris, 1858.
Phil 7054.91 Parisi, G. Two appeals to the leaders of spiritualism. Florence, 1871.
Phil 7054.92 Courtney, W.S. A review of J.B. Dods...theory of spiritual manifestations. N.Y., 1855.
Phil 7054.92.5 Dods, John B. Spirit manifestations. N.Y., 1854.
Phil 7054.93 Dewey, D.M. History of the strange sounds or rappings. Rochester, 1850.

Phil 7054 Psychology - Parapsychology - Spiritualism - History - Miscellany [Discontinued] - cont.

Phil 7054.94 Warren, O.G. Supernal theology and life in the spheres. N.Y., 1852.
Phil 7054.95 Pond, E. Familiar spirits and spiritual manifestations. Boston, 1852.
Phil 7054.96 Post, S. An exposition of modern spiritualism. N.Y., 1861.
Phil 7054.97 Pamphlet vol. Spiritualism. 6 pam.
Phil 7054.98 Ramsey, William. Spiritualism, a satanic delusion. Rochester, N.Y., 1857.
Phil 7054.98.3 Ramsey, William. Spiritualism, a satanic delusion. Peace Dale, R.I., 1856.
Phil 7054.99 Phenomena of the "spiritual rappings". Boston, 1852.
Phil 7054.100 Coggshall, W.T. The signs of the times. Cincinnati, 1851.
Phil 7054.101 Rouband, F. La danse des tables. Paris, 1853.
Phil 7054.102.2 Hayden, William B. On the phenomena of modern spiritualism. 2. ed. Boston, 1855. 2 pam.
Phil 7054.103 Shufeldt, G.A., Jr. History of the Chicago artesian well. Chicago, 1867. 2 pam.
Phil 7054.104 Snow, H. Spirit-intercourse containing incidents of personal experience. Boston, 1853.
Phil 7054.105 Ballou, Adin. An exposition of views...spirit manifestations. Boston, 1852.
Phil 7054.105.2 Ballou, Adin. An exposition of views...spirit manifestations. 2. ed. Boston, 1853.
Phil 7054.106 Hazard, T.R. Mediums and mediumship. Boston, 1872.
Phil 7054.106.2 Hazard, T.R. Mediums and mediumship. Boston, 1873.
Phil 7054.106.5 Hazard, T.R. Eleven days at Moravia. Boston, 1872.
Phil 7054.107 Mahan, A. Modern mysteries explained and exposed. Boston, 1855.
Phil 7054.109 King, M.M. The spiritual philosophy vs. diabolism. Boston, 1871.
Phil 7054.110 Ewer, F.C. The eventful nights of August 20th. N.Y., 1855.
Phil 7054.111.2 Fowler, J.H. New Testament "miracles". 2. ed. Boston, 1856.
Phil 7054.111.5 Fowler, J.H. New Testament "miracles". 2. ed. Boston, 1859.
Phil 7054.112 Everett, J. A book for skeptics being communications from angels. Columbus, 1853.
Phil 7054.113 Corning, W.H. The infidelity of the times. Boston, 1854.
Phil 7054.114 Glass, C.E. Advance thought. London, 1876.
Phil 7054.115 Capron, Eliab W. Modern spiritualism: its facts and fanaticisms. Boston 1855.
Phil 7054.115.5 Capron, Eliab W. Explanation and history of the mysterious communion with spirits. 2. ed. Auburn, N.Y., 1850.
Phil 7054.116.2 Tuttle, H. Arcana of nature. London, 1909.
Phil 7054.116.5 Tuttle, H. Scenes in the spirit world. N.Y., 1855.
Phil 7054.116.7 Tuttle, H. Arcana of spiritualism. Chicago, 1934.
Phil 7054.117 Woodman, J.C. A reply to Wm. T. Dwight, D.D., on spiritualism. Portland, 1857.
Phil 7054.118 Danmar, William. Modern nirvanaism. N.Y., 1914.
Phil 7054.118.5 Danmar, William. Modern nirvanaism. Jamaica, 1921.
Phil 7054.119 Truesdell, J.W. The bottom facts...science of spiritualism. N.Y., 1883.
Phil 7054.120 Emmons, S.B. The spirit land. Philadelphia, 1857.
Phil 7054.121 Leymarie, P.G. Proces des spirites. Paris, 1875.
Phil 7054.122 Philosophy of modern miracles. N.Y., 1850.
NEDL Phil 7054.123 Britten, Emma H. Modern American spiritualism. N.Y., 1870.
Phil 7054.123.2 Britten, Emma H. Modern American spiritualism. 4th ed. N.Y., 1870.
Phil 7054.123.5 Britten, Emma H. Ghostland. Boston, 1876.
Htn Phil 7054.124* Knaggs, Samuel T. Human fads, foibles, fallacies. Sydney, 1898.
Phil 7054.126 Richards, L.S. The beginning of man and what becomes of him. Boston, 1815.
Phil 7054.127 Davies, Charles M. The great secret, and its unfoldment in occultism. 2. ed. London, 1896.
Phil 7054.128 Henry, T.S. "Spookland", a record of research. Chicago, 1902.
Phil 7054.128.5 Lo spiritismo e la scienza di Ateo e Trinacrio. Trecastagne, 1902.
Phil 7054.129 Wright, Alfred A. Spiritual science, universal religion. N.Y., 1917.
Phil 7054.131 Schultze, F. Die Grundgedanken des Spiritismus und die Kritik derselben. Leipzig, 1883.
Phil 7054.132 Hill, J. Arthu. Spiritualism. N.Y., 1919.
Phil 7054.136 Hafed, prince of Persia. London, 1876.
Phil 7054.137 Tiffany, Joel. Lectures on spiritualism. Cleveland, 1851.
Phil 7054.137.3 Tiffany, Joel. Modern spiritualism compared with Christianity. Warren, Ohio, 1855.
Phil 7054.137.5 Tiffany, Joel. Spiritualism explained. 2. ed. N.Y., 1856.
Phil 7054.138 Green, Frances H. Biography of Mrs. Semantha Mettler. N.Y., 1853.
Phil 7054.139 Daniels, J.W. Spiritualism versus Christianity. N.Y., 1856.
Phil 7054.140 Rogers, E.C. Philosophy of mysterious agents. Boston, 1853.
Phil 7054.141.5 Cooper, Robert. Spiritual experiences. London, 1867.
Phil 7054.142 Gordon, William R. A three-fold test of modern spiritualism. N.Y., 1856.
Phil 7054.143 Lum, Dyer D. The "spiritual" delusion. Philadelphia, 1873.
Phil 7054.144 Horn, Henry J. Strange visitors. N.Y., 1869.
Phil 7054.146 Ramsdell, Elizabeth. Spirit life of Theodore Parker. Boston, 1870.
Phil 7054.146.5 Ramsdell, Sarah. Spirit life of Theodore Parker. Boston, 1876.
Phil 7054.147 Campbell, Z. The spiritual telegraphic opposition line. Springfield, 1853.
Phil 7054.148 Judson, Abby A. The bridge between two worlds. Minneapolis, 1894.
Phil 7054.149 Brown, John. Mediumistic experiences of John Brown. 3. ed. San Francisco, 1897.
Phil 7054.150 Henck, E.C. Spirit voices. Philadelphia, 1853.
Phil 7054.151 Morrison, A.B. Spiritualism and necromancy. Cincinnati, 1873.
Phil 7054.152 Brofferio, Angelo. Per lo spiritismo. 2. ed. Milano, 1893.
Phil 7054.153 The book of spirits. London, n.d.
Phil 7054.153.15 Tales of the horrible, or The book of spirits. London, 1837.
Phil 7054.154 Spiritualism and other signs. London, n.d.
Phil 7054.156 Von Ravens, Clara I. The scribe of a soul. Seattle, 1901.
Phil 7054.157 Delanne, Gabriel. Le phénomène spirite. 5. ed. Paris, 1897.

338

Classified Listing

Phil 7054 Psychology - Parapsychology - Spiritualism - History - Miscellany [Discontinued] - cont.

Phil 7054.157.5 Delanne, Gabriel. L'évolution animique. Paris, 1897.
Phil 7054.159 Maxwell, Joseph. Un récent procès spirite. Bordeaux, 1904.
Phil 7054.160 Tappan, Cora L.V. Discourses through the mediumship of Mrs. C. Tappan. London, 1875.
Phil 7054.160.5 Tappan, Cora L.V. What is the use of spiritualism? London, 1874.
Phil 7054.161 Berg. J.T. Abaddon and Mahanaim...guardian angels. Philadelphia, 1856.
Phil 7054.162 Clark, Uriah. Plain guide to spiritualism. Boston, 1863.
Phil 7054.163 Petersilea, Carlyle. Mary Anne Carew; wife, mother, spirit. London, 1893.
Phil 7054.164 Gasparin, Agénov. Science vs. modern spiritualism. N.Y., 1857. 2v.
Phil 7054.166 Longley, Mary. Teachings...from the spirit world. Chicago, 1908.
Phil 7054.167 Peebles, J.M. Seers of the ages, embracing spiritualism. Boston, 1869.
Phil 7054.167.10 Peebles, J.M. Spirit mates, their origin and destiny. Battle Creek, 1909.
Phil 7054.168 Sherman, M.L. The gospel of nature. Chicago, 1877.
Phil 7054.169 Budington, Henry A. Death is birth. Springfield, Mass., 1897.
Phil 7054.170 Dawburn, Charles. The science of spirit return. Springfield, Mass., 188-.
Phil 7054.171 Grant, Miles. Spiritualism unveiled. Boston, 1866.
Phil 7054.172 Nichols, T.L. Supramundane facts. London, 1865.
Phil 7054.173 McComb, Samuel. The future life in the light of modern inguiry. N.Y., 1919.
Phil 7054.173.10 Forster, David. The vital choice, Endor or Calvary. London, 1919.
Phil 7054.173.15 Meyer, F.B. The modern craze of spiritualism. London, 1919.
Phil 7054.174 Raupert, J.G. The new black magic. N.Y., 1920.
Phil 7054.174.5 Bazett, L.M. After-death communications. London, 1920.
Phil 7054.175 Knapp, C. Richard. The newest Bible demonstrated by nature. Grass Valley, Calif., n.d.
Phil 7054.175.10 Doyle, Arthur Conan. The wanderings of a spiritualist. London, 1921.
Phil 7054.175.11 Doyle, Arthur Conan. The wanderings of a spiritualist. N.Y., 1921.
Phil 7054.175.15 Cooke, I. The return of Arthur Conan Doyle. 2. ed. Liss, 1963.
Phil 7054.176 Richmond, Cora L. Spiritual sermons [delivered in 1886-1889]. n.p., n.d.
Phil 7054.177 Bonfiglioli, Casimiro. Lo spiritismo nella unianità. Bologna, 1888.
Phil 7054.178 Azzi, Gaetano. Idea vera dello spiritismo. Torino, 1895.
Phil 7054.179 Back to the father's house. London, 18- . 2v.
Phil 7054.180 Henslow, G. Proofs of the truth of spiritualism. London, 1919.
Phil 7054.181.15 Leslie, John. Nature and super-nature. Aberdeen, 1820.
Phil 7054.182 Grimard, Edouard. Une échappée sur l'infini. Paris, 1899.
Phil 7054.184 Lawrence, E. Spiritualism among civilised and savage races. London, 1921.
Phil 7054.185 Oxley, William. Angelic revelations concerning the origin, ultimation and destiny of the human spirit. Manchester, 1875-83. 4v.
Phil 7054.186 Simon, Otto J. The message of Anne Simon. Boston, 1920.
Phil 7054.187 Cadwallader, Mary E. Mary S. Vanderbilt, a twentieth century seer. Chicago, 1921.
Phil 7054.188 Eriksen, R. Sjaelens gaade. Kristiania, 1893.
Phil 7054.190 Holmes, W.H.G. Memories of the supernatural in east and west. London,, 1941.

Phil 7055.101 - .399 Psychology - Parapsychology - Spiritualism - History - Biographies of mediums - Individual (299 scheme, A-Z, by person)

Phil 7055.101 Aakerblom, Lilly. Bortom mänsklig horisont. Stockholm, 1966.
Phil 7055.108 Mathias, Julio. Don Luis de Alderete y Soto. Málaga, 1965.
Phil 7055.156 Weldon, Warren. A happy medium: the life of Caroline Randolph Chapman. Englewood Cliffs, 1970.
Phil 7055.173 Leroy, Roger. Un voyant au XXe siècle: Dieudonné. Paris, 1965.
Phil 7055.205 Serrano, Geraldo. Arigó, desafio à ciência. Rio de Janeiro, 1967.
Phil 7055.205.7 Pires, José. Arigó: vida, mediunidade e martírio. 2. ed. São Paulo, 1966.
Phil 7055.211 Garrett, Eileen Jeanette Lyttle. Many voices; the autobiography of a medium. N.Y., 1968.
Phil 7055.251 Drage, Charles. William King's profession. London, 1960.
Phil 7055.256 Smith, Susy. The mediumship of Mrs. Leonard. New Hyde Park, N.Y., 1964.
Phil 7055.310 Pike, James Albert. The other side. Garden City, 1968.
Phil 7055.310.25 Holzer, Hans W. The psychic world of Bishop Pike. N.Y., 1970.
Phil 7055.338 Eisenbud, Jule. The world of Ted Serios. N.Y., 1967.
Phil 7055.341 Smith, Susy. Confessions of a psychic. N.Y., 1971.
Phil 7055.386 Woods, Margaret. Mosaic; a psychic autobiography. London, 1968.
Phil 7055.388 Barbosa, Elia. No mundo de Chico Xavier. São Paulo, 1968.

Phil 7057 Psychology - Parapsychology - Spiritualism - Spirit writing [Discontinued]

Phil 7057.8.15 Burke, Jane Revere. Messages on healing understood to have been dictated by William James. N.Y., 1936.

Phil 7059.1 - .99 Psychology - Parapsychology - Spiritualism - Miscellany [Discontinued]

Phil 7059.5 Revelations of the great modern mystery planchette. Boston, 1868.
Phil 7059.6 Buchanan, J.R. Manual of psychometry. Boston, 1885.
Phil 7059.7 Denton, William. The soul of things. Boston, 1863.
Phil 7059.8 Rebman, F.J. The human aura. Storm Lake, Iowa, 1912.
Phil 7059.9 Arnold, L.M. History of the origin of all things. n.p., 1852.
Phil 7059.10 Walrath, M.E. History of the earth's formation. N.Y., 1868.
Phil 7059.11.2 Bland, T.A. In the world celestial. 2. ed. Chicago, 1902.
Phil 7059.12 Hull, Moses. The question settled. Boston, 1869.
Phil 7059.12.5 Hull, Moses. Two in one...spiritualism of the Bible settled. Chicago, 1895.
Phil 7059.12.9 Hull, Moses. The spiritual Alps and how we ascend them. 5th ed. Chicago, 1895.

Phil 7059.1 - .99 Psychology - Parapsychology - Spiritualism - Miscellany [Discontinued] - cont.

Phil 7059.12.11 Hull, Moses. Jesus and the mediums. Chicago, 1890.
Phil 7059.12.13 Hull, Moses. All about devils. Chicago, 1890.
Phil 7059.12.15 Hull, Moses. Which: spiritualism or Christianity? N.Y., 1873.
Phil 7059.15 Atkinson, Lulu Hurst. Lulu Hurst...writes her biography. Rome, Ga., 1897.
Phil 7059.16 Ambler, R.P. Spiritual teacher. N.Y., 1852.
Phil 7059.18 Gallion, D.A. Know thyself, o man! Keokuk, Iowa, 1865.
Phil 7059.19 King, Maria M. Real life in the spirit land. 5. ed. Hammonton,N.J., 1892.
Phil 7059.20 Denis, Léon. Pourquoi la vie! Paris, 1892.
Phil 7059.21 Whytt, James. Disembodied spirits. London, 1840.
Phil 7059.22 Our unseen guest. N.Y. 1920.

Phil 7059.500 - .999 Psychology - Parapsychology - Spiritualism - Pamphlet volumes

Phil 7059.800.-.999 Pamphlet boxes. Psychical research. Chronological file by year.

Phil 7060 Psychology - Parapsychology - Spiritualism - General works [Discontinued]

Phil 7060.01 Pamphlet box. Philosophy. Ghosts and hypnotism.
Phil 7060.1 Taillepied, F.N. Traité de l'apparition des esprits. Roven, 1602.
Phil 7060.1.5 Taillepied, Noël. Psichologie ou traité de l'apparition des esprits. Paris, 1588.
Htn Phil 7060.2* Lavater, L. De spectris. Genevae, 1580.
Phil 7060.2.2 Lavater, L. De spectris. Lugduni Batavorum, 1659.
Phil 7060.2.3 Lavater, L. De spectris. Lugduni Batavorum, 1687.
Htn Phil 7060.2.5* Lavater, L. Of ghostes and spirites walking by night. London, 1572.
Htn Phil 7060.2.7* Lavater, L. Of ghostes and spirites walking by night. London, 1596.
Phil 7060.2.15 Lavater , L. Of ghostes and spirites walking by nyght. London, 1929.
Phil 7060.3 Spectriana. Paris, 1817.
Phil 7060.5 Lenglet, Dufresnoy N. Traité historique et dogmatique...apparitions. Avignon, 1751. 2v.
Phil 7060.5.5 Calmet, Augustin. Recueil de dissertations...sur les apparitions. Avignon, 1751. 2v.
Htn Phil 7060.6* Le Loyer, P. Des spectres ou apparitions et visions. Angers, 1586.
Phil 7060.6.3 Le Loyer, P. Discours et histoires des spectres, visions et apparitions des spirits. Paris, 1605.
Htn Phil 7060.6.5* Le Loyer, P. Treatise of specters. London, 1605.
Phil 7060.6.7 Le Loyer, P. Discours des spectres, ou visions. Paris, 1608.
Phil 7060.7 Thyraeus, Petrus. De apparitionibus spirituum tractatus duo. Coloniae Agrippinae, 1600.
Htn Phil 7060.7.5* Thyraeus, P. Loca infesta, hoc est, de infestes. London, 1599.
Phil 7060.8 View of the invisible world. London, 1752.
Phil 7060.9 Oldenburg, F. Om gjenfard eller gjengangere. Kjobenhavn, 1818.
Phil 7060.10 Jung Stilling, J.H. Theory of pneumatology. London, 1834.
Htn Phil 7060.10.7* Jung Stilling, J.H. Theorie der Geister-Kunde. Nürnberg, 1808 .
Phil 7060.10.80 Geiger, M. Aufklärung und Erweckung. Zürich, 1963.
Phil 7060.11 Taylor, J. Apparitions. London, 1815.
Phil 7060.12 Ackermann, G. Über die Entwickelung von Wahnideen. Weimar, 1892.
Htn Phil 7060.13.5* A most strange and dreadful apparition. London, 1680.
Phil 7060.14.3 Brierre de Boismont, A. Des hallucinations, ou histoire raisonnée. 3. ed. Paris, 1862.
Phil 7060.14.5 Brierre de Boismont, A. Des hallucinations. 2. ed. Paris, 1852.
Phil 7060.14.9 Brierre de Boismont, A. Hallucinations. 1st American ed. Philadelphia, 1853.
Phil 7060.15 Ferriar, J. Essay towards a theory of apparitions. London, 1813.
Phil 7060.16 Clarke, E.H. Visions: study of false sight. Boston, 1878.
Phil 7060.17 Hibbert, S. Sketches of the philosophy of apparitions. Edinburgh, 1824.
Phil 7060.17.2 Hibbert, S. Sketches of the philosophy of apparitions. London, 1825.
Phil 7060.18 Hoppe, J.F. Erklärung der Sinnestäuschungen. Würzburg, 1888.
Htn Phil 7060.20* Müller, J. Über die phantastischen Gesichteserscheinungen. Coblenz, 1826.
Phil 7060.21 Paterson, Robert. On illusions of the senses. Photoreproduction. Edinburgh, 1867.
Phil 7060.22 Vulpius, W. Über den psychischen Mechanismus der Sinnestäuschungen. Jena, 1885.
Phil 7060.23 Sunderland, L. Book of human nature. N.Y. 1853.
Phil 7060.23.5 Sunderland, L. Book of psychology. N.Y. 1853.
Phil 7060.24 Dendy, W.B. Philosophy of mystery. London, 1841.
Phil 7060.24.5 Dendy, W.B. Philosophy of mystery. N.Y., 1845.
Phil 7060.25 Blakeman. R. Philosophical essay on credulity and superstition. N.Y., 1849.
Phil 7060.26 Dennis, J. Subversion of materialism. Bath, n.d.
Phil 7060.27.3 Owen, R.D. Footfalls on the boundary of another world. Philadelphia, 1865.
Phil 7060.27.5 Owen, R.D. The debatable land between this world and the next. N.Y., 1872.
Phil 7060.28 Hudson, T.J. Law of psychic phenomena. Chicago, 1893.
Phil 7060.28.10 Hudson, T J. The evolution of the soul and other essays. Chicago, 1904.
Phil 7060.30 Blackburn, D. Thought-reading. London, 1884.
Phil 7060.31 Lombroso, C. Inchiesta sulla trasmissione del pensiero. Torino., 1891.
Phil 7060.33 Preyer, W. Die Erklärung des Gedankenlesens. Leipzig, 1886.
Phil 7060.34 Du Prel, C.F. Die monistische Seelenlehre. Leipzig, 1888.
Phil 7060.35 Johnson, F. The new psychic studies. N.Y., 1887.
Phil 7060.36 Crowe, C.S. Night side of nature. London, n.p.
Phil 7060.36.5 Crowe, C.S. Nacht Seite der Natur. v.1-2. Stuttgart, 1849.
Phil 7060.36.7 Crowe, C.S. The night-side of nature. N.Y., 1853.
Phil 7060.37 Rauschink, Gottfried Peter. Gespenstersagen. Rudolstadt, 1817.
Phil 7060.37.15 Savile, B.W. Apparitions; a narrative of facts. 2. ed. London, 1880.
Phil 7060.38 Ingram, J.H. Haunted homes. London, 1884.
Phil 7060.38.2 Ingram, J.H. Haunted homes. London, 1884.

Classified Listing

Phil 7060.38.3 — Ingram, J.H. The haunted homes and family traditions of Great Britain. 3. ed. London, 1886.

NEDL Phil 7060.38.5 — Ingram, J.H. The haunted homes and family traditions of Great Britain. 5. ed. London, 1901.

Phil 7060.38.9 — Ingram, J.H. The haunted homes and family traditions of Great Britain. 5th ed. London, 1901.

NEDL Phil 7060.38.15 — Ingram, J.H. The haunted homes and family traditions of Great Britain. London, 1912.

Phil 7060.39 — Schelwig, Samuel. De apparitionibus. Lipziae, 1709.

Phil 7060.42 — Dyer, T.F.T. The ghost world. London, 1893.

Phil 7060.43.5 — Goodrich-Freer, A. The alleged haunting of B-- house. London, 1899.

Phil 7060.44 — Ermacora, G.B. La telepatia. Padova, 1898.

Phil 7060.45 — Kleinpaul, R. Die Lebendigen und die Toten. Leipzig, 1898.

Phil 7060.45.5 — Kleinpaul, R. Volkspsychologie. Berlin, 1914.

Phil 7060.46 — Puls, G. Spuls-Geschichten. Berlin, n.d.

Phil 7060.47 — Francisci, Erasmus. Der höllischen Proteus...Erscheinder Gespenster. Nürnberg, 1695.

Phil 7060.48 — Harris, J. Inferences from haunted houses. London, 1901.

Phil 7060.49 — Ghost stories. Philadelphia 1854.

Phil 7060.52 — Nichols, T.L. A biography of the brothers Davenport. London, 1864.

Phil 7060.52.5 — The Davenport brothers...spiritual mediums. Boston, 1869.

Phil 7060.54 — Funk, Isaac Kaufmann. The widow's mite and other psychic phenomena. N.Y., 1904.

Phil 7060.56 — Hilscher, M.P.C. Nachricht von einem gewissen Monche in Dresden. Dresden, 1729.

Phil 7060.59 — Bissel, J. Incolorum alterius mundi phenoemena. Dillingen, 1685.

Phil 7060.60 — M'Leod, D. Treatise on the second sight. Edinburgh, 1763.

Phil 7060.61 — La merveilleuse hystorie de l'esprit de Lyon. Paris, 1887.

Phil 7060.62 — Frazer, John. Deuteroskopia; or, A brief discourse concerning the second sight. Edinburgh, 1820

Phil 7060.63 — Colton, C. Sampford ghost. Tiverton, 1810.

Phil 7060.64* — Defoe, D. Essay on the history...of apparitions. London, 1727.

Phil 7060.64.5 — Defoe, D. The secrets of the invisible world laid open. London, 1770.

Phil 7060.65 — Moreton, A. Secrets of the invisible world disclos'd. London, 1735.

Phil 7060.65.5 — Moreton, A. Secrets of the invisible world disclos'd. London, 1740.

Phil 7060.66 — Diederich, Benno. Von Gespenstergeschichten. Leipzig, 1903.

Phil 7060.67.5 — Flammarion, C. L'inconnu et les problèmes psychiques. Paris, 1900.

Phil 7060.68 — Bruce, Henry Addington Bayley. Historic ghosts and ghost hunters. N.Y., 1908.

Phil 7060.68.5 — Bruce, Henry Addington Bayley. Adventurings in the psychical. Boston, 1914.

Phil 7060.69 — Grasset, J. L'occultisme: hier et aujourd'hui. Montpelier, 1908.

Phil 7060.70 — Badaud, U.N. Coup d'oeil sur la magie au XIXe siècle. Paris, 1891.

Phil 7060.72.7 — Raupert, J.G. The supreme problem. Buffalo, 1910.

Phil 7060.73* — Cruikshank, G. Discovery concerning ghosts. 2d ed. London, 1864.

Phil 7060.74 — Boucher, G. Une séance de spiritisme. Niort, 1908.

Phil 7060.75.5 — Carrington, H. True ghost stories. N.Y., 1915.

Phil 7060.76 — Jacolliot, Louis. Occult science in India. N.Y., 1908.

Phil 7060.77 — Alderson, J. Essay on apparitions. London, 1823.

Phil 7060.78 — Lewes, M.L. Stranger than fiction. London., 1911.

Phil 7060.78.5 — Lewes, M.L. The queer side of things. London, 1923.

Phil 7060.79 — Ludwig, W. Spaziergänge eines Wahrheitssuchers. Leipzig, 1899.

Phil 7060.80.9 — Flournoy, J. Des Indes à la planète Mars. Paris, 1900.

Phil 7060.81 — Reichel, W. Occult experiences. London. n.d.

Phil 7060.82.4 — Barrett, W.F. On the threshold of the unseen. London, 1917.

Phil 7060.82.5 — Barrett, W.E. On the threshold of the unseen. 3. ed. London, 1918.

Phil 7060.83 — Jarvis, T.M. Accredited ghost stories. London, 1823.

Phil 7060.84 — Welby, H. Signs before death. London, 1825.

Phil 7060.85 — Signs before death. London, 1875.

Phil 7060.86 — Lee, F.G. Glimpses of the supernatural. London, 1875.

Phil 7060.86.5 — Lee, F.G. Lights and shadows. London, 1894.

Phil 7060.87 — Crosland, N. Apparitions. London, 1873.

Phil 7060.88 — The unseen world: communications. London, 1847.

Phil 7060.89 — Welby, H. Mysteries of life, death and futurity. London, 1861.

Phil 7060.89.5 — Timbs, John. Mysteries of life, death and futurity. N.Y., 1863.

Phil 7060.90 — Ollier, Charles. Fallacy of ghosts, dreams and omens. London, 1848.

Phil 7060.90.11 — Day, Clarence S. Remarkable apparitions and ghost-stories. N.Y., 1848.

Phil 7060.91 — Robbins, Anne M. Both sides of the veil. Boston, 1911.

Phil 7060.91.5 — Tuckett, I.L. The evidence for the supernatural. London, 1911.

Phil 7060.92.5 — O'Donnell, Elliot. Some haunted houses. London, 1908.

Phil 7060.92.9 — O'Donnell, Elliot. Ghostly phenomena. London, n.d.

Phil 7060.92.15 — O'Donnell, Elliot. Haunted houses of London. London, 1909.

Phil 7060.92.19 — O'Donnell, Elliot. Animal ghosts. London, 1913.

Phil 7060.92.20 — O'Donnell, Elliot. By ways of ghost-land. London, 1911.

Phil 7060.92.25 — O'Donnell, Elliot. Haunted highways and byways. London, 1914.

Phil 7060.92.29 — O'Donnell, Elliot. Bona-fide adventures with ghosts. Bristol, 1908.

Phil 7060.92.35 — O'Donnell, Elliot. Haunted places in England. London, 1919.

Phil 7060.92.41 — O'Donnell, Elliot. Twenty years' experience as a ghost hunter. London, 1916.

Phil 7060.92.45 — O'Donnell, Elliot. More haunted houses of London. London, 1920.

Phil 7060.92.47 — O'Donnell, Elliot. The Banshee. London, 1920.

Phil 7060.92.55 — O'Donnell, Elliot. Confessions of a ghost hunter. London, 1928.

Phil 7060.92.57 — O'Donnell, Elliot. Ghosts of London. London, 1932.

Phil 7060.92.60 — O'Donnell, Elliot. Family ghosts and ghostly phenomena. 1st ed. N.Y., 1934.

Phil 7060.92.61 — O'Donnell, Elliot. Phantoms of the night. London, 1956.

Phil 7060.93 — Harper, C.G. Haunted houses. London, 1907.

Phil 7060.94 — Capper, Alfred. A rambler's recollections and reflections. London, 1915.

Phil 7060.95 — Hauréau, M.B. Mémoire sur les récits d'apparitions. Paris, 1875.

Htn Phil 7060.96* — The comparative study of ghost stories. n.p., n.d.

Phil 7060.97 — Zöllner, J.C.F. Transcendental physics. London, 1880.

Phil 7060.97.3 — Zöllner, J.C.F. Transcendental physics. 2. ed. Boston, 1881.

Phil 7060.98 — Life after death. London, 1758.

Phil 7060.99 — Tuttle, H. Studies in outlying fields of psychic science. N.Y., 1889.

Phil 7060.100 — Holt, H. On the cosmic relations. Boston, 1914. 2v.

Phil 7060.101 — Schneider, Wilhelm. Der neuere Geisterglaube. Paderborn, 1882.

Phil 7060.102 — Pennsylvania. University. Seybert Commission for Investigating Modern Spiritualism. Preliminary report. Philadelphia, 1887.

Phil 7060.102.2 — Pennsylvania. University. Seybert Commission for Investigating Modern Spiritualism. Preliminary report. Philadelphia, 1887.

Phil 7060.102.9 — Richmond, Almon B. What I saw at Cassadaga lake: Seybert Commission report. Boston, 1888.

Phil 7060.103 — Hartmann, K.R.E. von. Der Spiritismus. Leipzig, 1885.

Phil 7060.103.5 — Aksakov, Aleksandr N. Animismus und spiritismus...als Entgegnung auf Dr. Ed. V. Hartmann's Werk "Der Spiritismus". Leipzig, 1890.

Phil 7060.103.7 — Aksakov, Aleksandr N. Animisme et spiritisme. Paris, 1895.

Phil 7060.104 — Wallace, A.R. On miracles and modern spiritualism. London, 1875.

Phil 7060.104.5 — Wallace, A.R. A defense of modern spiritualism. Boston, 1874.

Phil 7060.104.9 — Wallace, A.R. If a man die shall he live again? San Francisco, 1888.

Phil 7060.105 — Berthelen, K.A. Die Klopf- und Spussgeister. Zittau, 1864.

Phil 7060.106 — Aksakov, Aleksandr N. Vorläuser des Spiritismus. Leipzig, 1898.

Phil 7060.107 — Cox, E.W. Spiritualism answered by science. London, 1871.

Phil 7060.108 — Crookes, William. Researches in the phenomenena of spiritualism. London, 1874.

Phil 7060.108.5 — Crookes, William. Recherches sur les phénomènes du spiritualisme. Paris, 1886.

Phil 7060.109 — Johnson, Samuel. Spiritualism tested by science. New Haven, 1858.

Phil 7060.110 — Seymour, S.J.D. True Irish ghost stories. Dublin, 1914.

Phil 7060.111.15 — Middleton, Jessie A. The grey ghost book. London, 1915.

Phil 7060.111.19 — Middleton, Jessie A. Another grey ghost book. London, 1915.

Phil 7060.113 — Willson, Beckles. Occultism and common sense. London, 1908.

Phil 7060.114 — The lawyer's ghost. London, 17- ?

Phil 7060.116 — Batchel, R. The stoneground ghost tales. Cambridge, Eng., 1912.

Phil 7060.117 — Tregortha, John. News from the invisible world. Burslem, 1813.

Phil 7060.119 — Baring-Gould, S. Book of ghosts. London, 1904.

Phil 7060.120 — Decker, Johann H. Spectrologia, h. e. Discursus ut plurimum philosophicus de spectris. Hamburgi, 1690.

Phil 7060.122 — Hoffman, Frank S. Psychology and common life. N.Y., 1912.

Phil 7060.126 — Richet, C. Experimentelle Studien. Stuttgart, 1891.

Phil 7060.129 — Boirac, Émile. L'avenir des sciences psychiques. Paris, 1917.

Phil 7060.129.9 — Boirac, Émile. La psychologie inconnue. 2. ed. Paris, 1917.

Phil 7060.130 — Davis, H.P. Expose of Newburyport excentricities. n.p., 1873.

Phil 7060.131 — Osty, Eugène. Lucidité et intuition. Paris, 1913.

Phil 7060.132 — Crawford, W. J. The reality of psychic phenomena. N.Y., 1918.

Phil 7060.133 — McDonald, Neil T. The Belledoon mysteries, 1830-40. 3. ed. Wallaceburg, Ont., n.d.

Phil 7060.134 — Thomasius, C. Dissertatio iuridica de non rescindendo contractu conductionis ob natura spectrorum. Halle, 1711.

Phil 7060.135 — Etchart, Carlos R. Psychologie énergétique. Paris, 1914.

Phil 7060.136 — The compleat wizzard. London, 1770.

Phil 7060.137 — Mayo, Herbert. Popular superstitions. 3. ed. Philadelphia, 1852.

Phil 7060.138 — The drummer of Tedworth...story of that demon. London, 1716.

Phil 7060.139.5 — Hubbell, Walter. The great Amherst mystery. 10th ed. N.Y., 1916.

Phil 7060.141 — Duchâtel, Edmond. La vue à distance...des cas de psychomètrie. Paris, 1910.

Phil 7060.142 — Constable, Frank C. Telergy, the communion of souls. London, 1918.

Phil 7060.143 — Taillepied, Noël. Traicté de l'apparition des esprits. Paris, 1917.

Phil 7060.144 — Liljencrants, Johan. Spiritism and religion. Diss. Lynchburg, Va., 1918.

Phil 7060.145 — Fair and fatal warnings. London, 1800?

Phil 7060.147 — Alexandre Bisson, J. Les phénomènes dits de matérialisation. Paris, 1914.

Phil 7060.149 — Duroy de Bruignac, A. Satan et la magie de nos jours. Paris, 1864.

Phil 7060.151 — Tweedale, V.C. Ghosts I have seen. N.Y., 1919.

Phil 7060.151.5 — Tweedale, C.L. Man's survival after death. 2. ed. London, 1920.

Phil 7060.151.20 — Wickwar, J.W. The ghost world. London, 1919.

Phil 7060.152 — Fontenay, G. de. La photographie et l'étude des phénomènes psychiques. Paris, 1912.

Phil 7060.154 — Kaarsberg, H.S. Om satanism. Kjøbenhavn, 1896.

Phil 7060.156 — Moser, F. Spuk. Baden bei Zürich, 1950.

Phil 7060.250 — Bland, Oliver. The adventures of a modern occultist. N.Y., 1920.

Phil 7060.253 — Turvey, Vincent N. The beginnings of seership. London, 1911.

Phil 7060.254 — Stead, William T. Real ghost stories. N.Y., 1921.

Phil 7060.255 — Wasielewski, W. Telepathie und Hellsehen. Halle, 1922.

Phil 7060.256 — Kummerich, M. Gespenster und Spuk. Ludwigshafenam Bodensee, 1921.

Phil 7061   Psychology - Parapsychology - Spiritualism - Bibliographies

Phil 7061.5 — Society for Psychical Research, London. Library catalogue of the Society for Psychical Research. Glasgow, 1927.

Phil 7061.10 — National Laboratory of Psychical Research, London. Short title catalogue of works...from c.1450 to 1929. London, 1929.

Phil 7061   Psychology - Parapsychology - Spiritualism - Bibliographies - cont.
Phil 7061.15   Spiritual and Ethical Society, N.Y. Publications.
N.Y., 19- .

Phil 7064   -   7070   Psychology - Parapsychology - Spiritualism - General treatises - Individual authors (By date)
Htn   Phil 7065.09*   Van Arnolt Boschmä und Herich syme alde vader.
Collen, 1509.
Htn   Phil 7066.72*   Pye, John. A true and perfect account of a strange and dreadful apparition. London, 1672.
Htn   Phil 7066.74*   News from Puddle-Dock in London. London, 1674.
Phil 7067.00   Stryk, Johann S. Disputatio iuridica inauguralis de iure spectrorum...Andreas Becker. Halae Magdeburgicae, n.d.
Phil 7067.00.5   Stryk, Johann S. Disputatio iuridica inauguralis de iure spectrorum...Andreas Becker. Jenae, 1745.
Phil 7067.04   Der Veilfoermige Hintzelmann. Göttingen, 1965.
Phil 7067.29   Das Gespenst auf dem Klapperfeld. Frankfurt, 1729.
Phil 7067.46.5   Calmet, Augustin. Dissertations sur les apparitions. Paris, 1746.
Phil 7067.46.10   Calmet, Augustin. Traité sur les apparitions des esprits. Paris, 1751. 2v.
Htn   Phil 7067.46.10*   Calmet, Augustin. Traité sur les apparitions des esprits. Paris, 1751. 2v.
Phil 7067.46.15   Calmet, Augustin. Gelehrte Verhandlung der Materi von Erscheinungen der Geisteren. 3. Aufl. Augspurg. 1751.
Phil 7067.46.16   Calmet, Augustin. Gelehrte Verhandlung der Materi von Erscheinungen der Geisteren. 3. Aufl. Augspurg. 1757.
Phil 7067.46.18   Calmet, Augustin. Dissertazioni sopra le apparizioni de spiriti. Venezia, 1756.
Phil 7067.46.20   Calmet, Augustin. Disertazioni sopra le apparizioni de spiriti. Venezia, 1770.
Phil 7067.46.25   Calmet, Augustin. The phantom world. London, 1850.
Phil 7067.46.26   Calmet, Augustin. The phantom world. Philadelphia. 1850.
Phil 7067.47   Wegner, George W. Philosophische Abhandlung von Gespenstern. Berlin, 1747.
Phil 7067.48   Sucro, J.G. Widerlegung der Gedancken von Gespenstern. Halle im Magdeburgischen, 1748.
Phil 7067.48.10   Meier, George F. Vertheidigung der Gedanken von Gespenstern. Halle im Magdeburgischen, 1748.
Phil 7067.91   Visits from the world of spirits. London, 1791.
Phil 7068.09   The supernatural magazine. Dublin, 1809.
Phil 7068.10   Colton, C.C. Sampford ghost. Tiverton, 1810.
Phil 7068.36   Kerner, J. Eine Erscheinung aus dem Nachtgebiete der Natur. Stuttgart, 1826.
Phil 7068.36.20   Ottway, T. The spectre. London, 1836.
Phil 7068.37   Calmet, Augustin. Des benediktiner-abtes zu Senones. München. 1837.
Phil 7068.47   Davis, A.J. The principles of nature. 3. ed. N.Y., 1847.
Phil 7068.52   Davis, A.J. The approaching crisis. N.Y., 1852.
Phil 7068.53.5   Goupy, Louis. Explication des tables parlantes. 1st ed. Paris, 1860.
Phil 7068.54   Mirville, J.E. Pneumatologie des esprits. 3. ed. Paris, 1854.
Phil 7068.55   Mirville, J.E. Questions des esprits; ses progrès dans la science. Paris, 1855.
Phil 7068.55.14   Mahan, A. Modern mysteries, explained and exposed. Boston, 1885.
Phil 7068.56   Newton, Alonzo E. Answer to charges of belief in modern revelations. Boston, 1856. 2 pam.
Phil 7068.59.10   Footsteps of spirits. London, 1859.
Phil 7068.61   Bible. New Testament. English. New Testament of our Lord...as revised and corrected by the spirits. N.Y., 1861.
Phil 7068.63   Mirville, J.E. Pneumatologie. Des esprits. v. 2-6. Paris, 1863-68. 5v.
Phil 7068.63.5   Mirville, J.E. Question des esprits et de leurs manifestations diverses. Paris, 1863.
Phil 7068.63.25   Denton, W. Nature's secrets or psychometric researches. Photoreproduction. London, 1863.
Phil 7068.63.35   Gougenot des Mousseaux, H.R. Les médiateurs et les moyens de la magie. Paris, 1863.
Phil 7068.64   Bertolacci, W.R. Christian spiritualism. London, 1864.
Phil 7068.65.2   Blanc, H. Le merveilleux dans le Jansénisme, le magnétisme, le méthodisme et le baptisme américains. Paris, 1865.
Phil 7068.65.4   Chase, Warren. The gist of spiritualism. 4th ed. Boston, 1865.
Phil 7068.66.80   Tissandier, J.B. Des sciences occultes et du spiritisme. Paris, 1866.
Phil 7068.70.33   Güldinstubbe, J. von. Positive Pneumatologie. 2. Aufl. Bern, n.d.
Phil 7068.71.2   Cox, E.W. Spiritualism answered by science. N.Y., 1872.
Phil 7068.71.8   Massey, G. Concerning spiritualism. London, 1871.
Phil 7068.72   Müller, M. Triumph of the blessed sacrament or History of Nicola Aubry. Baltimore, 1872.
Phil 7068.72.20   Hoppe, I. Hellsehen des Unbewussten. Freiburg., 1872.
Phil 7068.73.10   London Dialectical Society. Report on spiritualism of the committee of the London Dialectical Society. London, 1873.
Phil 7068.74.10   Lawrence, Jas. Angel voices from the spirit world. Cleveland, 1874.
Phil 7068.74.15   Polak, M.S. Het materialismus, het spiritismus. 2. druk. Amsterdam, 1874.
Phil 7068.74.26   Crookes, W. Researches in the phenomena of spiritualism. London, 1874.
Phil 7068.74.26.5   Crookes, W. Researches in the phenomena of spiritualism. London, 1874.
Phil 7068.74.40   Ritti, A. Théorie psychologique de l'hallucination Paris, 1874.
Phil 7068.76.10   Wilson, Ebenezer V. The truths of spiritualism. Chicago, 1876.
Phil 7068.77   Carpenter, William B. Mesmerism, spiritualism,...historically and scientifically considered. N.Y., 1877.
Phil 7068.77.1   Carpenter, William B. Mesmerism, spiritualism,...historically and scientifically considered. London, 1877.
Phil 7068.79   Zöllner, J.K.F. Die transcendentale Physik und die sogenannte Philosophie. Leipzig, 1879.
NEDL   Phil 7068.82.5   Confessions of a medium. London, 1882.
Phil 7068.83.6   Gay, Susan E. John William Fletcher, clairvoyant. London, 1883.
Phil 7068.83.12   Sociedad de Estudios Espiritistas de Key West. Contestatión a los detractores del espiritismo. Key West, 1883.
Phil 7068.84   Truesdell, J.W. The bottom facts concerning the science of spiritualism. N.Y., 1884.
Phil 7068.84.10   Reminiscences and memories of Henry Thomas Butterworth and Nancy Irvin Wales. Lebanon, Ohio, 1886.

Phil 7064   -   7070   Psychology - Parapsychology - Spiritualism - General treatises - Individual authors (By date) - cont.
Phil 7068.84.15   Crookes, William. Der Spiritualismus und die Urssenschaft. 2. Aufl. Leipzig, 1884.
Phil 7068.86.10F   Farmer, John S. Twixt two worlds. London, 1886.
Phil 7068.86.11   Franco, P.G. Die Geister der Finsterniss. Ausburg, 1886.
Phil 7068.86.20A   Gurney, Edmund. Phantasms of the living. London, 1886. 2v.
Htn   Phil 7068.86.20*B   Gurney, Edmund. Phantasms of the living. London, 1886. 2v.
Phil 7068.86.40   Brackett, E.A. Materialized apparitions. Boston, 1886.
Phil 7068.86.50   Maudsley, H. Natural causes and supernatural seemings. London, 1886.
Phil 7068.86.60A   Putman, A. Post-mortem confessions. Boston, 1886.
Phil 7068.86.60B   Putman, A. Post-mortem confessions. Boston, 1886.
Phil 7068.87.5   Assier, Adolphe d'. Posthumous humanity. London, 1887.
Phil 7068.87.9.5   Pennsylvania. University. Seybert Commission for Investigating Modern Spiritualism. Preliminary report. Philadelphia, 1895.
Phil 7068.87.10   Theobald, Morell. Spirit workers in the home circle. London, 1887.
Phil 7068.87.20   Massey, C.C. Zöllner. London, 1887.
Phil 7068.88   Pamphlet vol. Spiritism, psychical rescarch. 9 pam.
Phil 7068.88.10   Cumberland, Stuart. A thought-reader's thoughts. London, 1888.
Phil 7068.88.20   Lippitt, F.J. Physical proof of another life. Washington, 1888.
Phil 7068.89.3   Müller, Egbert. Enthüllung des Spukes von Resau. 3. Aufl. Berlin, 1889.
Phil 7068.90.10   Haven, Gilbert. Heavenly messenger. Washington, 1890.
Phil 7068.91.4   Dénis, Léon. Après la mort. Paris, 1891.
Phil 7068.91.10   Sargent, Epes. The scientific basis of spiritualism. 6th ed. Boston, 1891.
Phil 7068.91.15   Weatherly, L.A. The supernatural? Bristol, 1891.
Phil 7068.91.25   Revelations of a spirit medium. St. Paul, 1891.
Phil 7068.92.25   Daniels, Cora Linn Morrison. As it is to be. 5. ed. Franklin, Mass., 1892.
Phil 7068.92.35   Gurney, Edmund. Les hallucinations télépathiques. 2. ed. Paris, 1892.
Phil 7068.92.45   Some account of the vampires of onset, past and present. Boston, 1892.
Phil 7068.92.55   Du Prel, K.L.A.F.M.A. Das Rätsel des Menschen. Leipzig, 1892.
Phil 7068.92.65   Ermacora, G.B. I fatti spiritici e le ipotesi affrettate. Padova, 1892.
Phil 7068.93.10   Rivail, H.L.D. Spiritualist philosophy. Boston, 1893.
Phil 7068.93.15   Savage, Minot J. Psychics; facts and theories. Boston, 1893.
Phil 7068.93.26   Coste, A. Les phénomèmes psychiques occultes. 2. ed. Montpellier, 1895.
Phil 7068.94.5   Lang, Andrew. Cock Lane and common-sense. London, 1894.
Phil 7068.94.10   Podmore, Frank. Apparitions and thought-transference. London, 1894.
Phil 7068.94.15   Parish, Edmond. Über die Trugwahrnehmung. Leipzig, 1894.
Phil 7068.94.25   Wilmot, T.S. Twenty photographs of the risen dead. Lonon, 1894.
Phil 7068.94.35   Pettis, O.G. Autobiography by Jesus of Nazareth. Washington, 1894.
Phil 7068.94.45   Moses, W.S. Spirit teachings. London, 1894.
Phil 7068.94.50   Borderland; a quarterly review and index. London. 1893-1897 3v.
Phil 7068.95   Tindall, A.F. Spiritual Christianity revealed by occultism. London, 189-.
Phil 7068.95.10   Barrett, Harrison D. Life work of Mrs. Cora L.V. Richmond. Chicago, 1895.
Phil 7068.95.15   Erny, Alfred. Le psychisme expérimental. Paris, 1895.
Phil 7068.95.20   Judson, Abby A. Why she became a spiritualist. 3. ed. Cincinnati, 1895.
Phil 7068.95.27   Desertis, V.C. Psychic philosophy as the foundation of a religion of natural law. 2. ed. London, 1901.
Phil 7068.96.7.9   Hudson, Thomson J. The law of psychic phenomena. 30. ed. Chicago, 1905.
Phil 7068.96.10   Wallace, Alfred R. Miracles and modern spiritualism. London, 1896.
Phil 7068.96.15   Underwood, Sara A. Automatic or spirit writing, with other psychic experiences. Chicago, 1896.
Phil 7068.96.20   Wilson, Ebenezer V. The truths of spiritualism. Chicago, 1896.
Phil 7068.96.30   Hubbard, H.S. Beyond. Boston, 1896.
Phil 7068.96.35   Pribytkov, V von. Aufrichtige Unterhaltungen über den Spiritismus. Leipzig, 1896?
Phil 7068.96.40   Mery, Gaston. La voyante de la rue de Paradis. Paris, 1896.
Phil 7068.97.5   Lang, Andrew. The book of dreams and ghosts. London, 1897.
Phil 7068.97.10   Podmore, Frank. Studies in psychical research. London, 1897.
Phil 7068.97.11   Podmore, Frank. Studies in psychical research. N.Y., 1897.
Phil 7068.97.20   Watch Tower Bible and Tract Society. What say the scriptures about spiritualism? Allegheny, Pa., 1897.
Phil 7068.97.22   Watch Tower Bible and Tract Society. What say the scriptures about spiritualism? Brooklyn, 1897.
Phil 7068.97.30   Mason, R.O. Telepathy and the subliminal self. N.Y., 1897.
Phil 7068.97.34   Mason, R.O. Telepathy and the subliminal self. N.Y., 1899.
Phil 7068.97.42   Dippel, Joseph. Der neuere Spiritismus in seinem Wesen dargelegt und nach seinem Werte geprüft. 2. Aufl. München, 1897.
Phil 7068.98.5   Baudidi Vesme, C. Geschichte des Spiritismus. Leipzig, 1898-1900.
Phil 7068.98.10   Fontenay, Guillaume de. A propos d'Eusapia Paladino. Paris, 1898.
Phil 7068.98.15   Robinson, William E. Spirit state writing and kindred phenomena. N.Y., 1898.
Phil 7068.98.20   Falcomer, M.T. Contributo di fatti pella soluzione del problema di psicologia. Selessandria, 1898.
Phil 7068.98.30   Fitler, C.H. New thoughts. Philadelphia, 1898.
Htn   Phil 7068.99*   Spoer, Adela Goodrich-Freer. Essays in psychical research. London, 1899.
Phil 7068.99.4   Dheur, P. Les hallucinations volontaires. Paris, 1899.
Phil 7068.99.20   Spoer, Adela Goodrich-Freer. Essays in psychical research. 2. ed. London, 1899.
Phil 7068.99.33   Gibier, P. Psychism; analysis of things existing. 3. ed. N.Y., 1899.
Phil 7068.99.40   Hall, T.B. The purity and destiny of modern spiritualism. Boston, 1899.

Phil 7064 - 7070   Psychology - Parapsychology - Spiritualism - General
treatises - Individual authors (By date) - cont.

Phil 7068.99.60	Pamphlet vol. Spiritism, psychical research. 6 pam.
Phil 7069.00.1	Pamphlet box. Spiritualism.
Phil 7069.00.2	Pamphlet vol. Spiritualism. 4 pam.
Phil 7069.00.10	Cooper, William Earnshaw. Spiritual manifestations. Exeter, 19- .
Phil 7069.00.20	Daniels, Cora L. As it is to be. Exeter, 1900.
Phil 7069.00.28	Flammarion, C. L'inconnu, The unknown. N.Y., 1900.
Phil 7069.00.30	Flournoy, Théodore. From India to the planet Mars. N.Y., 1900.
Phil 7069.00.32	Gaffield, E.C. A series of meditations on the ethical and physical relation of spirit to the human organism. Syracuse,.N.Y., 1900.
Phil 7069.00.35	News from the invisible world. 3. ed. London, 1900.
Phil 7069.00.37	Omni Victis (pseud.). Super-physical projection. n.p., 19- ?
Phil 7069.00.40	Tuttle, Hudson. Arcana of spiritualism. Manchester, 1900.
Phil 7069.00.53	Tuttle, Hudson. Mediumship and its laws. 3. ed. Chicago, 1900.
Phil 7069.00.60	Rayon, M. The mystic self. Chicago, 1900.
Phil 7069.00.65	Berndt, G.H. Das Buch der Wunder und der Geheimwissenschaften. 2. Aufl. v.1-2. Leipzig, 1900.
Phil 7069.00.80	Personal magnetism...by a diplomat. n.p., 19- ?
Phil 7069.01	Pamphlet box. The Society for Psychical Research.
Phil 7069.01.5	The occultist's handbook. Chicago, 1901.
Phil 7069.01.10	Atkinson, W.W. Thought-force in business and everyday life. 2. ed. Chicago, 1901.
Phil 7069.02.5	Gaffield, E.C. A celestial message. Boston, 1902.
Phil 7069.02.11	Podmore, Frank. Modern spiritualism. London, 1902. 2v.
Phil 7069.02.12	Podmore, Frank. Mediums of the 19th century. N.Y., 1963. 2v.
Phil 7069.02.17	Richardson, J.E. The great psychological crime. 11th ed. Chicago, 1912.
Phil 7069.02.20	Savage, Minot J. Can telepathy explain? N.Y., 1902.
n Phil 7069.02.30*	Searching the truth. N.Y., 1902.
Phil 7069.03.10	Myers, Frederic William Henry. Human personality and its survival of bodily death. N.Y., 1903. 2v.
Phil 7069.03.25	Sollier, P. Les phénomènes d'autoscopie. Paris, 1903.
Phil 7069.03.35	Maxwell, J. Les phénomènes psychiques. Paris, 1903.
Phil 7069.03.45	Spivey, T.S. Lavius Egyptus. Cincinnati, 1903. 2v.
Phil 7069.04.10	Bell, Clark. Spiritism, hypnotism and telepathy. 2. ed. N.Y., 1904.
Phil 7069.04.35	Grasset, J. Le spiritisme devant la science. Montpellier, 1904.
Phil 7069.04.60	Peebles, J.M. The demonism of the ages. Battle Creek, Mich., 1904.
Phil 7069.05.10	Hyslop, James Hervey. Science and a future life. Boston, 1905.
Phil 7069.05.12	Kvaran, E.H. Samband viðframlíða menn. Reykjavik, 1905.
Phil 7069.05.15	Rayon, M. Fads or facts. Chicago, 1905.
Phil 7069.05.20	Thomas, Northcote W. Thought transference. N.Y., 1905.
Phil 7069.05.30	Bennett, E.T. Automatic speaking and writing. London, 1905.
Phil 7069.05.35	Hennig, R. Wunder und Wissenschaft. Hamburg, 1905.
Phil 7069.06.5	Flugrit gegn andatrúnni. Reykjavik, 1906.
Phil 7069.06.7	Hennig, R. Die moderne Spuk- und Geisterglaube. Hamburg, 1906.
Phil 7069.06.10	Hyslop, James Hervey. Borderland of psychical research. 2. ed. Boston, 1906.
Phil 7069.06.11	Hyslop, James Hervey. Enigmas of psychical research. Boston, 1906.
Phil 7069.06.11.5	Hyslop, James Hervey. Problem der Seelenforschung. Stuttgart, 1909.
Phil 7069.06.13	Jónsson, G. Ur dularheimum. Reykjavik, 1906.
Phil 7069.06.15	Kvaran, E.H. Dularfull fyrirbrigð Reykjavik, 1906.
Phil 7069.06.20	Raupert, John G. The dangers of spiritualism. 2. ed. London, 1906.
Phil 7069.06.35	Richardson, J.E. The great work. 12. ed. Chicago, 1911.
Phil 7069.07.9	Bois, Jules. Le miracle moderne. 4. ed. Paris, 1907.
Phil 7069.07.10	Carrington, Hereward. The physical phenomena of spiritualism. Boston, 1907.
Phil 7069.07.12	Carrington, Hereward. The physical phenomena of spiritualism. 2. ed. Boston, 1908.
Phil 7069.07.13	Carrington, Hereward. The physical phenomena of spiritualism. 3. ed. N.Y., 1920.
Phil 7069.07.17	Flammarion, C. Les forces naturelles inconnues. Paris, 1907.
Phil 7069.07.18	Flammarion, C. Mysterious psychic forces. Boston, 1907.
Phil 7069.07.21	Funk, Isaac K. The psychic riddle. N.Y., 1907.
Phil 7069.07.25	Myers, F.W.H. Human personality. N.Y., 1907.
Phil 7069.07.32	La vita di Gesù. 2. ed. Roma, 1907.
Phil 7069.07.35	Edgerly, Webster. Book of the Psychic Society. Washington, 1907.
Phil 7069.08.10	Bennett, E.T. The direct phenomena of spirtualism. London, 1908.
Phil 7069.08.12	Brackett, E.A. Materialized apparitions. Boston, 1908.
Phil 7069.08.15	Carrington, Hereward. The coming science. Boston, 1908.
Phil 7069.08.16	Carrington, Hereward. The physical phenomena of spiritualism. Boston, 1908.
Phil 7069.08.20	Garland, Hamlin. The shadow world. N.Y., 1908.
Phil 7069.08.22	Hyslop, James Hervey. Psychical research and the resurrection. Boston, 1908.
Phil 7069.08.24	Macrae, Norman. Highland second-sight. Dingwall., 1908?
Phil 7069.08.27	Podmore, Frank. The naturalisation of the supernatural. N.Y., 1908.
Phil 7069.08.30	Reichel, Willy. An occultist's travels. N.Y., 1908.
Phil 7069.08.40	Morselli, E. Psicologia e "spiritismo". Torino, 1908. 2v.
Phil 7069.08.45	The twice-born. London, 1906.
Phil 7069.08.50	Kotik, N. Die Emanation der psychophysischen Energie. Wiesbaden, 1908.
Phil 7069.09.2	Bormann, W. Der Schotte Home. Leipzig, 1909.
Phil 7069.09.3	Carrington, Hereward. Eusapia Palladino and her phenomena. N.Y., 1909.
Phil 7069.09.5A	James, William. Report on Mrs. Piper's Hodgson-control. n.p., 1909.
Phil 7069.09.5B	James, William. Report on Mrs. Piper's Hodgson-control. n.p., 1909.
Phil 7069.09.5C	James, William. Report on Mrs. Piper's Hodgson-control. n.p., 1909.
Phil 7069.09.7	Lonbroso, Cesare. After death - what? Boston, 1909.
Phil 7069.09.10	Paget, Walburga v.H. Colloquies with an unseen friend. London, 1909.
Phil 7069.09.17	Raupert, John G. Modern spiritism. 2. ed. St. Louis, 1909.
Phil 7069.09.20	Rider, Fremont. Are the dead alive? N.Y., 1909.

Phil 7064 - 7070   Psychology - Parapsychology - Spiritualism - General
treatises - Individual authors (By date) - cont.

Phil 7069.09.30	Willson, Beckles. Occultism and common-sense. N.Y., 1908?
Phil 7069.09.40	Robbins, A.M. Both sides of the veil. Boston, 1909.
Phil 7069.09.70	Wiltse, May B. Theorem or teleology of spiritualism. New-Rockford, N. Dak., 1909.
Phil 7069.10.3	Gook, Arthur. Andatrúin. Akureyri, n.d.
Phil 7069.10.5	Hyslop, James Hervey. Science and a future life. 5. ed. Boston, 1910.
Phil 7069.10.10	Jones, Amanda T. A psychic autobiography. N.Y., 1910.
Phil 7069.10.19	Lodge, Oliver Joseph. The survival of man. N.Y., 1909.
Phil 7069.10.20	Lodge, Oliver Joseph. The survival of man. 3. ed. London, 1910.
Phil 7069.10.30	Myers, Gustavus. Beyond the borderline of life. Boston 1910.
Phil 7069.10.40	Podmore, Frank. The newer spiritualism. London, 1910.
Phil 7069.11.10	Barrett, William F. Psychical research. N.Y., 1911.
Phil 7069.11.15	Flournoy, Théodore. Esprits et médiums. Genève, 1911.
Phil 7069.11.20	Flournoy, Theodore. Spiritism and psychology. N.Y., 1911.
Phil 7069.11.30	Greene, Anvernetta (pseud.). Psychisms through Anvernetta Greene. Newark, 1911.
Phil 7069.11.40	Hill, John A. New evidences in psychical research. London, 1911.
Htn Phil 7069.11.45*	Moberly, C.A.E. An adventure. London, 1911.
Phil 7069.11.48	Moberly, C.A.E. An adventure. 4th ed. London, 1931.
Phil 7069.11.49	Iremonger, L. The ghosts of Versailles. London, 1957.
Phil 7069.11.50	Moore, William U. Glimpses of the next state (the education of an agnostic). London, 1911.
Phil 7069.11.70	Russel, Fox. Hugsíminn. Reykjavik, 1911.
Phil 7069.12.10	Fish, Eben. Voices from the open door. Cleveland, 1912.
Phil 7069.12.51	Lodge, Oliver Joseph. La survivance humaine. 3. ed. Paris, 1912.
Phil 7069.12.98	Zingaropoli, F. Telepatia e sogno. Napoli, 1912.
Phil 7069.13.5	Carrington, Hereward. Death, its causes and phenomena. 2. ed. London, 1913
Phil 7069.13.10	Colville, William J. Mystic light essays. 1st ed. N.Y., 1913.
Phil 7069.13.15	Dallas, Helen A. Across the barrier. London, 1913.
Phil 7069.13.20	Hude, Fru Anna. The evidence for communication with the dead. London, 1913.
Phil 7069.13.30	Moore, William U. The voices. London, 1913.
Phil 7069.13.32	Nielsson, H. Hví slaer pú mig? v.1-2. Reykjavik, 1913.
Phil 7069.13.40	Station, Horace C. Telepathy of the celestial world. N.Y., 1913.
Phil 7069.14.5	Carrington, Hereward. The problems of psychical research. London, 1914.
Phil 7069.14.10	Colville, William J. Light and colors. N.Y., 1914.
Phil 7069.14.20	Comstock, William C. Will higher of God and free will of life. Boston, 1914.
Phil 7069.14.30	Cooper, William E. Where two worlds meet. London, 1914.
Phil 7069.14.40	D'Aute-Hooper, T. Spirit-psychometry and trance communications by unseen agencies. London, 1914.
Phil 7069.14.50	Primot, Alphonse. La psychologie d'une conversion du positivisme au spiritualisme. Paris, 1914.
Phil 7069.14.58	Schrenck von Notzing, Albert. Die Kampf und die Materialisationsphänomene. München, 1914.
Phil 7069.14.60	Schrenck von Notzing, Albert. Materialisationsphaenomene. München, 1914.
Phil 7069.14.61	Schrenck von Notzing, Albert. Materialisationsphaenomene. 2. ed. München, 1923.
Phil 7069.15.10	Barker, Elsa. War letters from the living dead man. N.Y., 1915.
Phil 7069.15.20	Crawford, Mary MacDermont. Peeps into the psychic world. Philadelphia, 1915.
Phil 7069.15.28	Gravies, L.C. The natural order of spirit. Boston, 1915.
Phil 7069.15.30	Holt, Henry. On the cosmic relations. Boston, 1915. 2v.
Phil 7069.15.40	Philpott, Anthony J. The quest for Dean Bridgman Conner. London, 1915.
Phil 7069.15.50	Richmond, Cora L. My experiences while out of my body and my return after many days. Boston, 1915.
Phil 7069.15.53	Richmond, Cora L. Psychosophy. Chicago, 1915.
Phil 7069.15.60	Sigfússon, S. Dulsýnir. Reykjavik, 1915.
Phil 7069.16.10	Churchill, Lida A. The truth about our dead told by those who know. 1st ed. N.Y., 1916.
Phil 7069.16.17	Finnbogason, Gudmundr. Þörfin á vinnuvísindum. Reykjavik, 1916.
Phil 7069.16.20	Fuller, George A. Wisdom of the ages. 2. ed. Boston, 1916.
Phil 7069.16.25	Grabinski, B. Neuere mystik. Hildesheim, 1916.
Phil 7069.16.30	Kates, George W. The philosophy of spiritualism. Boston, 1916.
Phil 7069.16.40	Lodge, Oliver Joseph. Raymond. N.Y., 1916.
Phil 7069.16.41	Lodge, Oliver Joseph. The survival of man. 7. ed. London, 1916.
Phil 7069.16.50	Parker, Frank E. Christian wisdom. Cambridge, Mass., 1916.
Phil 7069.16.60	Worth, Patience. Patience Worth; a psychic mystery. N.Y., 1916.
Phil 7069.16.63	Prince, W.F. The case of Patience Worth. Boston, 1927.
Phil 7069.16.65	McKenzie, J.H. Spirit intercourse. 5th ed. London, 1916.
Phil 7069.17.10	Bates, Emily K. Our living dead. London, 1917.
Phil 7069.17.13	Boirac, Emile. Our hidden forces. N.Y., 1917.
Phil 7069.17.20	Cadwallader, Mary E. Hydesville in history. Chicago, 1917.
Phil 7069.17.23	Clodd, Edward. The question: "If a man die, shall he live again?" London, 1917.
Phil 7069.17.24	Cook, Walter. Reflections on "Raymond". London, 1917.
Phil 7069.17.25	Coover, John Edgar. Experiments in psychical research at Leland Stanford Jr. University. n.p. 1917.
Phil 7069.17.26	Hill, John Arthur. Psychical investigations. N.Y., 1917.
Phil 7069.17.27	Joire, Paul. Psychical and supernormal phenomena. N.Y., 1917.
Phil 7069.17.29	Kvaran, E.H. Líf og daudi. Reykjavik, 1917.
Phil 7069.17.30	Light on the future. London, 1917.
Phil 7069.17.31	Mercier, Charles A. Spiritualism and Sir Oliver Lodge. London, 1917.
Phil 7069.17.31.15	Piper, Otto. Der Spuk. 2. Aufl. München, 1922.
Phil 7069.17.32	Randall, Edward Caleb. The dead have never died. N.Y., 1917.
Phil 7069.17.40	Robertson, Helen F. The letters of a woman who wa. Minneapolis, 1917.
Phil 7069.17.45	Troland, L.T. A technique for the experimental study of telepathy. Albany, N.Y., 1917.
Phil 7069.17.50	White, Mary Blount. Letters from Harry and Helen. N.Y., 1917.
Phil 7069.18.10	Barker, Elsa. Letters from a living dead man. N.Y., 1918.

Classified Listing

Phil 7064 - 7070 Psychology - Parapsychology - Spiritualism - General treatises - Individual authors (By date) - cont.

Phil 7069.18.20   Boirac, Émile. The psychology of the future. N.Y., 1918.

Phil 7069.18.21   Boirac, Émile. Psychic science. London, 1918.

Phil 7069.18.40   Bryan, William J. The truth about spiritualism. N.Y., 1918.

Phil 7069.18.50   Cameron, Margaret. The seven purposes. N.Y., 1918.

Phil 7069.18.60   Clodd, Edward. The question: "If a man die, shall he live again?" N.Y., 1918.

Phil 7069.18.70   Comstock, William C. Thought for help from those who know men's need. Boston, 1918.

Phil 7069.18.80   Crawford, William J. Hints and observations for those investigating the phenomena of spiritualism. N.Y., 1918.

Phil 7069.18.90   Cushman, Emma Crow. Insight. Boston, 1918.

Phil 7069.18.95   Doyle, Arthur Conan. The new revelation. N.Y., 1918.

Phil 7069.18.95.6   Doyle, Arthur Conan. The new revelation. 6th ed. London, 1918.

Phil 7069.18.97   God's world. Chicago, 1918.

Phil 7069.18.98   Gook, Arthur. Andatrúin afhjúpuð Akureyri, 1918.

Phil 7069.18.100   Gurney, Edmund. Phantasms of the living. London, 1918.

Phil 7069.18.110   Hicks, Betsey B. The bugle. N.Y., 1918.

Phil 7069.18.112   Hill, John Arthur. Man is a spirit. N.Y. 1918.

Phil 7069.18.120   "I heard a voice."N.Y., 1918.

Phil 7069.18.130A   Maeterlinck, Maurice. The light beyond. N.Y., 1918.

Phil 7069.18.130B   Maeterlinck, Maurice. The light beyond. N.Y., 1918.

Phil 7069.18.132   Martin, Alfred Wilhelm. Psychic tendencies of to-day. N.Y., 1918.

Phil 7069.18.140   Sciens, (pseud.). How to speak with the dead. N.Y., 1918.

Phil 7069.18.150   Thy son liveth. Boston, 1918.

Phil 7069.18.159   Werner-Hagen. Gedankenlesen und Hellsehen. Berlin, 1918.

Phil 7069.18.160   Whiting, Lilian. After her death. Boston, 1918.

Phil 7069.19.5   Aksakov, A.N. Animus und Spsiritismus. Leipzig 1919. 2v.

Phil 7069.19.10   Barker, Elsa. Last letters from the living dead man. N.Y., 1919.

Phil 7069.19.15   Barrett, William F. On the threshold of the unseen. N.Y., 1919.

Phil 7069.19.20   Boyce, Adam. The great beyond and its inhabitants. London, 1919.

Phil 7069.19.27   Bozzano, E. Les phénomènes de hantise. Paris, 1920.

Phil 7069.19.30   Cameron, Margaret. Twelve lessons from the seven purposes. N.Y., 1919.

Phil 7069.19.40   Carrington, Hereward. Modern psychical phenomena. N.Y., 1919.

Phil 7069.19.45   Carrington, Hereward. Psychical phenomena. N.Y., 1919.

Phil 7069.19.50   Corson, Hiram. Spirit messages. Boston, 1919.

Phil 7069.19.55   Christ in you. N.Y., 1919.

Phil 7069.19.60   Crawford, William J. Experiments in psychical science. N.Y., 1919.

Phil 7069.19.65   Crawford, William J. The reality of psychic phenomena, raps, levitations. N.Y., 1919.

Phil 7069.19.70   Curtiss, Harriette A. Realms of the living dead. N.Y., 1919.

Phil 7069.19.80   Dallas, Helen A. Death the gate of life? N.Y., 1919.

Phil 7069.19.90   Denis, Léon. Life and destiny. N.Y., 1919.

Phil 7069.19.92   Doyle, Arthur Conan. The vital message. N.Y., 1919.

Phil 7069.19.93   Doyle, Arthur Conan. The vital message. London, 1919.

Phil 7069.19.100   Grove, Harriet McC. Gone west, by a soldier doctor. N.Y., 1919.

Phil 7069.19.110   Hardy, Thomas J. Spiritism in the light of the faith. London, 1919.

Phil 7069.19.120   Henslow, George. The proofs of the truths of spiritualism. 2. ed. London, 1919.

Phil 7069.19.130   Herbine, Charlotte G. The meeting of the spheres. N.Y., 1919.

Phil 7069.19.140   Holt, Henry. The cosmic relations and immortality. Boston, 1919. 2v.

Phil 7069.19.147   Hyslop, James H. Contact with the other world. N.Y., 1919.

Phil 7069.19.150   King, Basil. The abolishing of death. N.Y., 1919.

Phil 7069.19.152   Kvaran, E.H. Trú og sannanir. Reykjavik, 1919.

Phil 7069.19.155   Leaf, Horace. What is this spiritualism? N.Y., 1919.

Phil 7069.19.160   Living waters. N.Y., 1919.

Phil 7069.19.163   Mann, Walter. The follies and frauds of spiritualism. London, 1919.

Phil 7069.19.165   Mercier, C.A. Spirit experiences. London, 1919.

Phil 7069.19.170   Myers, Fred W.H. Human personality and its survival of bodily death. London, 1919.

Phil 7069.19.173   Myers, Fred W.H. Human personality and its survival of bodily death. London, 1919.

Phil 7069.19.180   Private Dowding. N.Y., 1919.

Phil 7069.19.190   Randall, Edward Caleb. The dead have never died. N.Y., 1919.

Phil 7069.19.200   Smith, Hester T. Voices from the void. N.Y., 1919.

Phil 7069.19.210   "So saith the spirit." London, 1919.

Phil 7069.19.215   Spiritual reconstruction. N.Y., 1919.

Phil 7069.19.220   Thy son liveth. Boston, 1919.

Phil 7069.19.225   Vold, Karl. Andatrú vorra tíma. Reykjavik, 1919.

Phil 7069.19.230   Wallace, Mary B. The thinning of the veil. N.Y., 1919.

Phil 7069.19.240   Watson, Albert D. The twentieth plane. Philadelphia, 1919.

Phil 7069.20   Almasque, Jose A. Memorias de un fraile. Habana, 192-?

Phil 7069.20.10   Balfour, Gerald W. The ear of Dionysius. N.Y., 1920.

Phil 7069.20.20   Bamber, L. Kelway. Claude's second book. N.Y., 1920.

Phil 7069.20.30   Bazter, Francis K. Does telepathy explain spiritualism? N.Y., 1920.

Phil 7069.20.40   Bond, Frederick B. The gate of remembrance. 3. ed. Boston, 1920.

Phil 7069.20.42   Bond, Frederick B. The gate of remembrance. 4th ed. N.Y., 1921.

Phil 7069.20.50   Carrington, Hereward. The coming science. N.Y., 1920.

Phil 7069.20.53A   Carrington, Hereward. Your psychic powers and how to develop them. N.Y., 1920.

Phil 7069.20.53B   Carrington, Hereward. Your psychic powers and how to develop them. N.Y., 1920.

Phil 7069.20.61   Carter, Huntly. Spiritualism, its present-day meaning. Philadelphia, 1920.

Phil 7069.20.70   Chevreuil, L. Proofs of the spirit world. N.Y., 1920.

Phil 7069.20.80   Crockett, Albert Stevens. Revelations of Louise. N.Y., 1920.

Phil 7069.20.82   Culpin, Millais. Spiritualism and the new psychology. London, 1920.

Phil 7069.20.90   Davis, Andrew J. A stellar key to the summer land. 6th ed. Los Angeles, 1920.

Phil 7069.20.100   Dearmer, Nancy K. The fellowship of the picture. N.Y., 1920.

Phil 7069.20.110   De Koven, Anna F. A cloud of witnesses. N.Y., 1920.

Phil 7064 - 7070 Psychology - Parapsychology - Spiritualism - General treatises - Individual authors (By date) - cont.

Phil 7069.20.115   Doyle, Arthur Conan. Verbatim report of a public debate on "The truth of spiritualism" between A.C. Dolye and Joseph McCabe. London, 1920.

Phil 7069.20.120   Dresser, Horatio W. The open vision. N.Y., 1920.

Phil 7069.20.130   Flammarion, Camille. La mort et son mystère. Paris, 1920-1921. 2v.

Phil 7069.20.140   Gray, James M. Spiritism and the fallen angels in the light of the Old and New Testaments. N.Y., 1920.

Phil 7069.20.145   Grunewald, F. Physikalisch-mediumistische Untersuchungen. Pfullingen, 1920.

Phil 7069.20.150   Haldeman, Isaac M. Can the dead communicate with the living? N.Y., 1920.

Phil 7069.20.160   Hill, John A. Psychical miscellanea. N.Y., 1920.

Phil 7069.20.162   Hill, John A. Psychical miscellanea. London, 1919.

Phil 7069.20.170   Humphreys, Eliza Margaret J.G. The truth of spiritualism. Philadelphia, 1920.

Phil 7069.20.180   Kernahan, Coulson. Spiritualism. N.Y., 1920.

Phil 7069.20.190   King, John S. Dawn of the awakened mind. N.Y., 1920.

Phil 7069.20.192   Kingsford, S.M. Psychical research for the plain man. London, 1920.

Phil 7069.20.200   Lane, Anne W. To walk with God. N.Y., 1920.

Phil 7069.20.205   Lane, Anne W. Life in the circles. N.Y., 1920.

Phil 7069.20.210   Lees, Robert James. Through the mists. London, 1920.

Phil 7069.20.220   McCabe, J. Spiritualism. N.Y., 1920.

Phil 7069.20.230   McEvilly, Mary A. Meslom's messages from the life beyond. N.Y., 1920.

Phil 7069.20.232   McEvilly, Mary A. To woman from Meslom. N.Y., 1920.

Phil 7069.20.240   Magnusson, Julius. God's smile. N.Y., 1920.

Phil 7069.20.250   Maturin, Edith Money. Rachel comforted. N.Y., 1920.

Phil 7069.20.259   Occult diary. Chicago, 1920.

Phil 7069.20.260   O'Donnell, Elliot. The menace of spiritualism. Chicago, 1920.

Phil 7069.20.261   O'Donnell, Elliot. The menace of spiritualism. London, 1920.

Phil 7069.20.270   Pennsylvania. University. Seybert Commission for Investigating Modern Spiritualism. Preliminary report. Philadelphia, 1920.

Phil 7069.20.272   Platts, J. The witness. London, 1920.

Phil 7069.20.280   Raynor, Frank C. Through jewelled windows. London, 1920.

Phil 7069.20.290   Robertson, Mabel N. "The other side of God's door". London, 1920.

Phil 7069.20.298   Schofield, A.T. Modern spiritism. London, 1920.

Phil 7069.20.300   Sewell, May Wright. Neither dead nor sleeping. Indianapolis, 1920.

Htn   Phil 7069.20.300*   Sewell, May Wright. Neither dead nor sleeping. Indianapolis, 1920.

Phil 7069.20.301   Schrenck von Notzing, Albert. Physikalische Phaenomene des Mediumismus. München, 1920.

Phil 7069.20.303   Schrenck von Notzing, Albert. Phenomena of materialisation; a contribution to the investigation of mediumistic telepastics. London, 1920.

Phil 7069.20.310   Smith, Walter W. The foundations of spiritualism. N.Y., 1920.

Phil 7069.20.320   Tertium Quid (pseud.). The verdict:-? London, 1920.

Phil 7069.20.330   Thiébault, Jules. The vanished friend. N.Y., 1920.

Phil 7069.20.340   Williams, Gail. Fear not the crossing. N.Y., 1920.

Phil 7069.20.350   Wright, George E. The church and psychical research. London, 1920.

Phil 7069.20.352   Wright, George E. Practical views on psychic phenomena. N.Y., 1920.

Phil 7069.20.360   Zymonidas, Allessandro. The problems of mediumship. London, 1920.

Phil 7069.20.365   Carrington, H. The psychic world. N.Y., 1937.

Phil 7069.20.370   Roberts, W. Adair. A spiritual interpretation of some psychic happenings. London, 1932.

Phil 7069.21.10   Abbott, Anne. The two worlds of attraction. Boston, 1921.

Phil 7069.21.20   Cornillier, PE. The survival of the soul and its evolution after death. London, 1921.

Phil 7069.21.30   Flammarion, Camille. Death and its mystery. pt.1,3. N.Y., 1921-23. 2v.

Phil 7069.21.31   Flammarion, C. Imod døden. Kjøbenhavn, 1921.

Phil 7069.21.33   Flournoy, Theodor. Spiritismus und experimental-psychologie. Leipzig, 1921.

Phil 7069.21.35   Glenconner, Pamela. The earthen vessel. London, 1921.

Phil 7069.21.37   Green, H.L. Think on these things. Pasadena, 1921.

Phil 7069.21.40   Ingalese, Richard. Fragments of truth. N.Y., 1921.

Phil 7069.21.43   Kirchhoff, P. Der moderne Okkultismus im Lichte des Experiments! Köln, 1921.

Phil 7069.21.45   Oesterreich, T.K. Der Okkultismus im modernen Weltbild. 3. Aufl. Dresden, 1923.

Phil 7069.21.47   Oesterreich, T.K. Occultism and modern science. London, 1923.

Phil 7069.21.50   Randall, John H. The new light on immortality. N.Y., 1921.

Phil 7069.21.57   Mukerji, S. Indian ghost stories. Allahabad, 1921.

Phil 7069.21.60   Tweedale, Charles L. Man's survival after death. N.Y., 1921?

Phil 7069.21.70   Danils, H. Anden. Stockholm, 1921.

Phil 7069.21.90   Warcollier, R. La télépathie, recherches experimentales. Paris, 1921.

Phil 7069.22.3   Chevreuil, L. Le spiritisme dans l'église. Paris, 1922.

Phil 7069.22.5   Doyle, Arthur Connan. Our American adventure. N.Y., 192

Phil 7069.22.10   Godard, André. Le surnaturel contemporain. Paris, 1922.

Phil 7069.22.11   Grabinski, B. Spuk und Geistererscheinungen oder was sonst? 2. Aufl. Hildesheim, 1922.

Phil 7069.22.12   Hein, Rudolf. Der Fluidalkörper des Menschen...okkulten Erscheinungen. Leipzig, 1922.

Phil 7069.22.14   Hellberg, E. Telepathie. Prien, 1922.

Phil 7069.22.17   Milburn, L.M. The classic of spiritism. N.Y., 1922.

Phil 7069.22.20   Richet, Charles R. Traité de métapsychique. Paris, 1922.

Phil 7069.22.30   Jesus' teachings; by Shakespeare's spirit. N.Y., 1922.

Phil 7069.22.40   Tenhaeff, W.H.C. Supernormale vermogens. Amsterdam, 19

Phil 7069.22.45   Nielsson, H. Kirken og den psykiske Forskning. København, 1922.

Phil 7069.22.91   Wulff, E. Okkultismus. Dresden, 1922.

Phil 7069.23.2   Brid, J. Malcolm. My psychic adventures. London, 1923.

Phil 7069.23.5   Brandt, J.v.W. The red octopus. London, 1923?

Phil 7069.23.6   Dumanjó, L. Daniel. Habana, 1923.

Phil 7069.23.7   The Glastonbury scripts. Glastonbury. 1-9

Phil 7069.23.8   How I know that the dead do live. Boston, 1923.

Phil 7069.23.9   Cavanagh, M.R. A strange manuscript. N.Y., 1923.

Phil 7069.23.10   Osty, Eugène. La connaissance supra-normale. Paris, 1923.

Phil 7069.23.11   Osty, Eugène. Supernormal faculties in man. London, 1923

Phil 7069.23.15   Richet, Charles. Thirty years of psychical research. N.Y., 1923.

Classified Listing

Phil 7064 - 7070 Psychology - Parapsychology - Spiritualism - General treatises - Individual authors (By date) - cont.

Phil 7069.23.16 Richet, Charles. Traité de métaphysique. 2. ed. Paris, 1923.
Phil 7069.23.17 Rowe, Lucien. Le spiritisme d'aujourd'hui et d'hier. 2. ed. Paris, 1923.
Phil 7069.23.19 Rutot, A. Le mécanisme de la survie. Paris, 1923.
Phil 7069.23.20 Simon, Gustave. Chez Victor Hugo. Les tables tournantes de Jersey. Paris, 1923.
Phil 7069.23.21 Wilkins, H.J. A further criticism of the psychical claims concerning Glastonbury Abbey. Bristol, 1923.
Phil 7069.23.25 Wasylewski, S. Pod urokiem zaświatów. Lwów, 1923.
Phil 7069.23.45 Wright A.A. Momentous memoirs. Boston, 1923.
Phil 7069.24.5 Doyle, Arthur Conan. Our second American adventure. Boston, 1924.
Phil 7069.24.10 Eínar Níelsen, midíll. Reykjavik, 1924.
Phil 7069.24.12 Fischer, Oskar. Experimente mit Raphael Schermann. Berlin, 1924.
Phil 7069.24.15 Flammarion, Camille. Haunted houses. London, 1924.
Phil 7069.24.15.2 Flammarion, Camille. Haunted houses. N.Y., 1924.
Phil 7069.24.18 Geschichte der okkultischen (metapsychischen) Forschung von der Antike bis zur Gegenwart. Pfullingen, 1922.
Phil 7069.24.21 Geley, Gustave. L'ectoplasmie et la clairvoyance. Paris, 1924.
Phil 7069.24.22 Geley, Gustave. Clairvoyance and materialisation, a record of experiments. London, 1927.
Phil 7069.24.24 Hill, J.A. From agnosticism to belief. London, 1924.
Phil 7069.24.25 Houdini, Harry. A magician among the spirits. N.Y., 1924.
Phil 7069.24.28 James, William. Études et réflexions d'un psychiste. Paris, 1924.
Phil 7069.24.29 Kemmerich, M. Wunderbare Tatsachen aus dem Reich des Übersinnlichen. Kempten im Allgäu, 1924.
Phil 7069.24.31 Murray, O. The spiritual universe. London, 1924.
Phil 7069.24.33 Sigurgeirsson, Oddur. Andatrúin. Reykjavik, 1924.
Phil 7069.24.35 Walbrook, L. The case of Lester Coltman. London, 1924.
Phil 7069.24.40 Wickland, C.A. Thirty years among the dead. Los Angeles, 1924.
Phil 7069.24.42 Giese, F. Die Lehre von den Gedankenwellen. 2.-3. Aufl. Leipzig, 1924.
Phil 7069.24.44 Schrenck von Notzing, Albert. Experimente der Fernbewegung. Stuttgart, 1924.
Phil 7069.24.50 Besterman, T. Crystal-gazing: a study in the history, distribution, theory, and practice of scrying. London, 1924.
Phil 7069.25.3 Baerwald, R. Die intellektuellen Phänomene. Berlin, 1925.
Phil 7069.25.4 Danmar, William. Geisterkenntnis. Leipzig, 1925.
Phil 7069.25.5A Bird, J. Malcolm. "Margery" the medium. Boston, 1925.
Phil 7069.25.5B Bird, J. Malcolm. "Margery" the medium. Boston, 1925.
Phil 7069.25.9A Richardson, Mark Wyman. Margery - Harvard - Veritas; a study in psychics. Boston, 1925.
Phil 7069.25.9B Richardson, Mark Wyman. Margery - Harvard - Veritas; a study in psychics. Boston, 1925.
Phil 7069.25.10 Richardson, Mark Wyman. Margery, Harvard veritas. Boston, 1925.
Phil 7069.25.11 Prince, Walter Franklin. A review of the Margery case. Ithaca, 1926.
Phil 7069.25.11.5 Crandon, Le R.G. The Margery mediumship. n.p., 1930.
Phil 7069.25.12 Tillyard, R.J. Some recent personal experiences with Margery. N.Y., 1926.
Phil 7069.25.12.5 The "Margery" mediumship. N.Y., 1931.
Phil 7069.25.12.10 The "Margery" mediumship. N.Y., 1932. 2 pam.
Phil 7069.25.13 Guyard, J. The door of death wide open. Boston, 1925.
Phil 7069.25.14 Gulat-Wellenburg, W.K.H. Der physikalische Mediumismus. Berlin, 1925.
Phil 7069.25.15 Gruber, K. Parapsychologische Erkenntnisse. München, 1925.
Phil 7069.25.20 Moll, A. Der Spiritismus. Stuttgart, 1925.
Phil 7069.25.25 Tischner, R. Telepathy and clairvoyance. London, 1925.
Phil 7069.25.30 Wilson, T.S. Thought transference. London, 1925..
Phil 7069.26.2 Barrett, W. Death-bed visions. London, 1926.
Phil 7069.26.4 Cornillier, P.E. La prédiction de l'avenir. Paris, 1926.
Phil 7069.26.5 Doyle, Arthur Conan. The history of spiritualism. N.Y., 1926. 2v.
Phil 7069.26.9 Hellwig, A. Okkultismus und Wissenschaft. Stuttgart, 1926.
Phil 7069.26.10 Halford, J. The voice. London, 1926.
Phil 7069.26.12 Luther, F. Der Okkultismus. Leipzig, 1926.
Phil 7069.26.13A Murchison, C. The case for and against psychical belief. Worcester, 1927.
Phil 7069.26.13B Murchison, C. The case for and against psychical belief. Worcester, 1927.
Phil 7069.26.15 Owen, G.V. The life beyond the veil. London, 1926. 2v.
Phil 7069.26.25 Prince, Walter Franklin. The psychic in the house. Boston, 1926.
Phil 7069.26.30 Seymour, S.J.D. True Irish ghost stories. 2. ed. Dublin, 1926.
Phil 7069.26.35 Stobart, M.A. Torchbearers of spiritualism. N.Y., 1926.
Phil 7069.26.40 Sudre, R. Introduction à la métapsychique humaine. Paris, 1926.
Phil 7069.26.50 Heuzé P. Où en est la métapsychique. Paris, 1926.
Phil 7069.26.60 Heuzé, P. Fakirs, fumistes et Cie. Paris, 1926.
Phil 7069.26.70 Tenhaeff, W.H.C. Beknopte Handleiding der psychical research. 's Gravenhage, 1926. 3v.
Phil 7069.26.80 Baerwald, R. Okkultismus und Spiritismus. Berlin, 1926.
Phil 7069.26.85 Pamphlet vol. Spiritism, psychical research. 6 pam.
Phil 7069.26.90 Feerhow, F. Die menschliche Aura und ihre experimentelle Erforschung. 2.-3. Aufl. Leipzig, 1926.
Phil 7069.27.5 Bateman, A.B. Christianity and spiritualism. London, 1927.
Phil 7069.27.10 Bennett, E.N. Appolonius. London, 1927?
Phil 7069.27.11 Bret, Thomas. Précis de métapsychic. Paris, 1927. 2v.
Phil 7069.27.12 Chevalier, F. Albert Chevalier comes back. London, 1927.
Phil 7069.27.15 Dallas, H.A. Leaves from a psychic note-book. London, 1927.
Phil 7069.27.17 Daily News, London. Warnings from beyond. London, 1927.
Phil 7069.27.18 Daily News, London. Uncanny stories. London, 1927.
Phil 7069.27.19 Daily News, London. Ghosts in the Great War. London, 1927.
Phil 7069.27.20 Robotton. Realms of light and healing. London, 1927.
Phil 7069.27.23 Saunders, R.H. Healing through spirit agency. London, 1927.
Phil 7069.27.25 Speer, W.H. Companions still. London, 1927?
Phil 7069.27.27 Sinel, J. The sixth sense. London, 1927.
Phil 7069.27.30 Owen, G.V. Problems which perplex. London, 1927.
Phil 7069.27.33 Palmer, E.C. The riddle of spiritualism. London, 1927.

Phil 7064 - 7070 Psychology - Parapsychology - Spiritualism - General treatises - Individual authors (By date) - cont.

Phil 7069.27.38 Sherrill, E.P. The mechanism of death. Boston, 1927.
Phil 7069.27.40 Holms, A.C. The fundamental facts of spiritualism. London, 1927.
Phil 7069.27.45 Harper, C.G. Haunted houses. 3. ed. London, 1927.
Phil 7069.27.50 Doyle, Arthur Conan. Phineas speaks. London, 1927.
Phil 7069.27.55 Wells, H.B. Spiritual America. Boston, 1927.
Phil 7069.27.60 Snipes, Joseph F. Fifty years in psychic research. Boston, 1927.
Phil 7069.28.4 Bird, J. Malcolm. The Margery mediumship. N.Y., 1928.
Phil 7069.28.10 Richardson, Mark Wyman. The thumbprint and cross correspondence experiments made with the medium Margery during 1927-1928. n.p., 1928.
Phil 7069.28.12 Haynes, Frederick H. The book of spiritual wisdom by "Cuno". London, 1928.
Phil 7069.28.16 Doyle, Arthur Conan. A word of warning. London, 1928.
Phil 7069.28.20 Dudley, O.F. The abomination in our midst. London, 1928.
Phil 7069.28.35 Jaeschke, Willy K. Die parapsychologischen Erscheinungen. 2. Aufl. Leipzig, 1928.
Phil 7069.28.40 Johnson, G.L. The great problem and the evidence. London, 1928.
Phil 7069.28.45 Lambert, Helen C.S. A general survey of psychical phenomena. N.Y., 1928.
Phil 7069.28.50 Leroy, O. La lévitation. Paris, 1928.
Phil 7069.28.70 Thomas, Charles D. Life beyond death, with evidence. 1st ed. London, 1937.
Phil 7069.28.75 Thurston, Herbert. Modern spiritualism. St-Louis, 1928.
Phil 7069.28.85 Prince, Walter Franklin. Noted witnesses for psychic occurrences. N.Y., 1963.
Phil 7069.28.90 Valdry, Luma. Living secrets. London, 1928.
Phil 7069.28.95 Whitehead, George. Spiritualism explained. London, 1928.
Phil 7069.28.100 Underhill, Margaret. Your infinite possibilities. London, 1928.
Phil 7069.29.5 Allison, Lydia W. Leonard and Soule experiments in psychical research. Boston, 1929.
Phil 7069.29.7 Beatty, Mabel. Man made perfect. Lonodon, 1929.
Htn Phil 7069.29.20* Doyle, Arthur Conan. The Roman Catholic church, a rejoinder (to Herbert Thurston). London, 1929.
Phil 7069.29.40 Fullwood, A.M. The song of Sano Tarot. N.Y., 1929.
Phil 7069.29.45 Hack, Gwendolyn Kelley. Modern psychic mysteries. London, 1929.
Phil 7069.29.50 Lascelles, (pseud.). Beyond, a continuation of the seekers. London, 1929.
Phil 7069.29.61 Muldoon, Sylvan J. The projection of the astral body. London, 1961.
Phil 7069.29.70 O'Donnell, Elliot. Famous curses. London, 1929.
Phil 7069.29.80 Purchas, T.A.R. The spiritual adventures of a business man. 2. ed. London, 1930.
Phil 7069.29.90 Spiritual and Ethical Society, New York. How do the dead communicate. n.p., 1929.
Phil 7069.29.100 Þórðardóttir, Théodóra. Arangur reynslu minnar í dulraenum afnum. Akureyri, 1929.
Phil 7069.29.105 Sage, Michel. Frú Piper og Ensk-Vestraena Salarransóknarfjelagid Reykjavik, 1929.
Phil 7069.30 Behr, Hermann. Letters from eternity. N.Y., 1930.
Phil 7069.30.1 Besterman, T. Some modern mediums. London, 1930.
Phil 7069.30.2 Battersby, Henry F.P. Psychic certainties. London, 1930.
Phil 7069.30.2.15 Bozzano, Ernesto. Letteratura d'Oltretomba. Città della Pieve, 1930.
Phil 7069.30.4 Cummins, G.D. Paul in Athens (the scripts of Cleophas). London, 1930.
Phil 7069.30.5 Dallas, Helen A. Comrades on the homeward way. Lonodon, 1930.
Phil 7069.30.6 Dingwall, E.J. Ghosts and spirits in the ancient world. London, 1930.
Phil 7069.30.7 Friedländer, A.A. Telepathie und Hellsehen. Stuttgart, 1930.
Phil 7069.30.8 Grant, Isabel. Conversations with the other world. London, 1930.
Phil 7069.30.8.15 Guénon, R. L'erreur spirite. Paris, 1930.
Phil 7069.30.9 Hinchliffe, Emilie. The return of Captain W.G.R. Hinchliffe. London, 1930.
Phil 7069.30.10 Kernaham, C. "Black objects". London, 1930.
Phil 7069.30.11 Livingston, Marjorie. The new Nuctemeron (The twelve hours of Apollonius of Tyana). London, 1930.
Phil 7069.30.12 Lodge, Oliver Joseph. Conviction of survival. London, 1930.
Phil 7069.30.12.5 Lodge, Oliver Joseph. Phantom walls. N.Y., 1930.
Phil 7069.30.13 Lovejoy, H.T. Talks with the invisible. Sunderland, 1930.
Phil 7069.30.14 Matla, J.L.W.P. La solution du mystère de la mort. La Haye, 1930.
Phil 7069.30.15 Mühl, Anita M. Automatic writing. Dresden, 1930.
Phil 7069.30.17 MacGregor, Helen. The psychic faculties and their development. London, 1930.
Phil 7069.30.25 Piper, Alta L. Life and work of Mrs. Piper. London, 1929.
Phil 7069.30.26 Price, Harry. Rudi Schneider; a scientific example of his mediumship. London, 1930.
Phil 7069.30.28 Prince, Walter Franklin. The enchanted boundary;...psychical phenomena 1820-1930. Boston, 1930.
Phil 7069.30.30 Sinclair, Upton B. Mental radio. N.Y., 1930.
Phil 7069.30.30.2 Sinclair, Upton B. Mental radio. N.Y., 1930.
Phil 7069.30.32 Stallard, C.L. Beyond our ken. London, 1930.
Phil 7069.30.35 Thompson, C.J.S. Mystery and love of apparitions. London, 1930.
Phil 7069.30.45 Wells, Helen. The hidden path. Floral Park, N.Y., 1930. 4 pam.
Phil 7069.30.46F Wells, Helen B. The hidden path. v.2. N.Y., 1934.
Phil 7069.31.5 Cook, Ellen A.P. The voice triumphant, the revelations of a medium. N.Y., 1931.
Phil 7069.31.6 Dahl, Ludwig. We are here. London, 1931.
Phil 7069.31.7 Findlay, J.A. Á landmaerum annars heims. Reykjavik, 1934?
Phil 7069.31.8 Firth, Violet M. Spiritualism in the light of occult science. London, 1931.
Phil 7069.31.10 Hunt, H. Ernest. Spiritualism for the enquirer. London, 1931.
Phil 7069.31.20 Jacoby, Samuel A. The immortality of the soul. Los Angeles, 1931.
Phil 7069.31.25 The light and the word. London, 1931.
Phil 7069.31.27 Lyttelton, Edith B. Our superconscious mind. London, 1931.
Phil 7069.31.28 Lyttelton, Edith B. Our superconscious mind. N.Y., 1931.
Phil 7069.31.31 Prince, Walter Franklin. Human experiences. Boston, 1931.
Phil 7069.31.32 Whymant, A.N.J. Psychic adventures in New York. Boston, 1931.
Phil 7069.31.37 Talks with spirit friends, bench and bar. London, 1931.
Phil 7069.31.40 Trespioli, Gino. "Ultrafamia", esegesi della fenomenologia intellettuale dello spiritismo moderno. Milano, 1931.

Phil 7064 - 7070 Psychology - Parapsychology - Spiritualism - General
treatises - Individual authors (By date) - cont.

Phil 7069.31.50   Wells, Helen B. Law governing mediumship. N.Y., 1931.
Phil 7069.31.55   Jónsdóttir, J. Bréf frá Ingu. Winnipeg, 1931.
Phil 7069.32.10   Bull, Titus. Analysis of unusual experiences in healing
                   relative to diseased minds. N.Y., 1932.
Phil 7069.32.12   Christie, Anne. The opening of the door. Boston, 1932.
Phil 7069.32.13   Drouet, Bessie Clarke. Station Astral. N.Y., 1932.
Phil 7069.32.15   Dudley, E.E. Fingerprint demonstrations. Boston, 1932.
Phil 7069.32.20   Breitfield, R. Your psychic self. N.Y., 1932.
Phil 7069.32.30   Osty, E. Les pouvoirs inconnus de l'esprit sur la matière.
                   Paris, 1932.
Phil 7069.32.40   Taylor, Sarah E.L. Fox - Taylor automatic writing,
                   1869-1892. Minneapolis, 1932.
Phil 7069.32.45   Taylor, Sarah E.L. Fox - Taylor automatic writing,
                   1969-1892. Boston, 1936.
Phil 7069.32.50   Lawton, George. The drama of life after death.
                   N.Y., 1932.
Phil 7069.33.10   Benedict, Anna Louise. Continuity of life. Boston, 1933.
Phil 7069.33.15   Bull, Titus. Nature, man and destiny. N.Y., 1933.
Phil 7069.33.40   Reality. Boston, 1933.
Phil 7069.33.43   Taillepied, N. A treatise of ghosts. London, 1933.
Phil 7069.33.45   Tenhaeff, W.H.C. Paragnosie en "Einfuehlen". Proefschrift.
                   Bussum, N.H., 1933.
Phil 7069.33.46   Taylor, William G.L. Katie Fox, epochmaking medium.
                   N.Y., 1933.
Phil 7069.33.50   Wells, Helen B. Lessons in etheric and electric vibratory
                   law. N.Y., 1933. 6 pam.
Phil 7069.33.52   Wells, Helen B. Flower-life in ethic. N.Y., 1933.
                   2 pam.
Phil 7069.33.54   Wells, Helen B. Collection mimeographs. N.Y., 1933.
                   8 pam.
Phil 7069.33.56   Fodor, Nandor. Encyclopaedia of psychic science.
                   London, 1933?
Phil 7069.33.57   Fodor, Nandor. Encyclopaedia of psychic science. New Hyde
                   Park, N.Y., 1966.
Phil 7069.33.60   Driesch, Hans. Psychical research. London, 1933.
Phil 7069.34.5   Besterman, T. Inquiry into the unknown. London, 1934.
Phil 7069.34.7   Cannon, Alexander. Powers that be (the Mayfair lectures).
                   London, 1934.
Phil 7069.34.8   Cannon, Alexandre. Powers that be (the Mayfair lectures).
                   N.Y., 1935.
Phil 7069.34.9   Clark, R. A spiritual spiritualism. London, 1934.
Phil 7069.34.15   Jónsson, J. Framhaldslif og nútímaþekking.
                   Reykjavik, 1934.
Phil 7069.34.25A   Rhine, Joseph B. Extra-sensory perception. Boston, 1934.
Phil 7069.34.25B   Rhine, Joseph B. Extra-sensory perception. Boston, 1934.
Phil 7069.34.25.2A
                   Rhine, Joseph B. Extra-sensory perception. Boston, 1935.
Phil 7069.34.25.2B
                   Rhine, Joseph B. Extra-sensory perception. Boston, 1935.
Phil 7069.34.25.2C
                   Rhine, Joseph B. Extra-sensory perception. Boston, 1935.
Phil 7069.34.26   Rhine, Joseph B. Extra-sensory perception. Boston, 1964.
Phil 7069.34.35   Streamline (pseud.). Foretold; stories of modern
                   second-sight. Stirling 1934.
Phil 7069.34.41   Vilanova, María. El tesoro de la ciencia eterna de Dios.
                   Barcelona, 1933-34. 2v.
Phil 7069.34.43   Vilanova, María. Va siguiendo la tercera parte de el radio
                   de luz del regentador del mundo solar. Barcelona, 1934.
                   8 pam.
Phil 7069.34.45   Vilanova, María. Un drama del espacio. Año 1932. Dictado
                   por el espiritu de Blasco Ibáñez. Barcelona, 1934.
Phil 7069.34.47   Vilanova, María. El regentador del mondo solar os da un
                   radio de luz...julio de 1934. Barcelona, 1934.
Phil 7069.34.47.2 Vilanova, Maria. La segunda parte que ha dado el
                   regentador del mondo solar, para que los lectores lo leau
                   que va siquiendo su lectura. Barcelona, 1934.
Phil 7069.34.50   Wells, Helen B. Pythagoras speaks. N.Y., 1934.
Phil 7069.34.55   Wells, Helen B. The song of the seven seas. N.Y., 1934.
Phil 7069.34.60   Wells, Helen B. The intelligence of the spaces.
                   N.Y., 1934.
Phil 7069.34.62   Wells, Helen B. As in a mirror. N.Y., 1934. 2 pam.
treatises 7069.34.63 Wells, Helen B. Ribbons of the sky. v.1-3. N.Y., 1934-35.
Phil 7069.35   Tubby, G.O. Psychics and mediums. Boston, 1935.
Phil 7069.35.7   Burton, Eva. A natural bridge to cross. N.Y., 1935.
Phil 7069.35.10   Haley, P.S. Modern loaves and fishes. San
                   Francisco, 1935.
Phil 7069.35.15   Herodius (pseud.). Show me the way; spirit counsels for
                   right living. Boston, 1935.
Phil 7069.35.20   O'Hare, Elizabeth. Universal knowledge; the road home.
                   N.Y., 1935.
Phil 7069.35.25   Spivey, T.S. The awakening of the sixth sense; a look into
                   the great unknown. Shawneetown, Ill., 1935.
Phil 7069.35.45   Pamphlet box. Wells, Helen B. Psychic books.
Phil 7069.35.50   Wells, Helen B. Key to the spaces...dictated by A.P.
                   Mathewson. N.Y., 1935.
Phil 7069.35.51F   Wells, Helen B. Linking the spaces. N.Y., 1935.
                   2 pam.
Phil 7069.35.52   Wells, Helen B. Some laws of materialization. Dictated by
                   John King. N.Y., 1935.
Phil 7069.35.54   Wells, Helen B. "Whom the gods love". Dictated by Ernest
                   Wells. N.Y., 1935.
Phil 7069.35.56   Wells, Helen B. Through the gates of time. v.1.
                   N.Y., 1935.
Phil 7069.35.60   Wells, Helen B. The progressive Pllgrim's progress.
                   N.Y., 1935.
Phil 7069.35.65   Hegy, Reginald. A witness through the centuries.
                   N.Y., 1935.
Phil 7069.35.70   Parkman, Frances. Dedication; being later letters from the
                   writer of "Reality". Boston, 1935.
Phil 7069.35.75   Walter Franklin Prince, a tribute to his memory.
                   Boston, 1935.
Phil 7069.36.5   Garland, Hamlin. Forty years of psychic research; a plain
                   narrative of fact. N.Y., 1936.
Phil 7069.36.7   Glardon, R. Le spiritisme en face de l'historie.
                   Lausanne, 1936.
Phil 7069.36.10   Price, Harry. Confessions of a ghost-hunter.
                   London, 1936.
Phil 7069.36.13   Price, Harry. The haunting of Cashen's Gap. London, 1936.
Phil 7069.36.15   Sergeant, P.W. Historic British ghosts. London, 1936.
Phil 7069.36.20   Halifax, Charles L.W. Lord Halifax's ghost book. 3. ed.
                   London, 1936.
Phil 7069.36.50   Thomas, C.D. An amazing experiment. London, 1936.
Phil 7069.37   Cole, M.A. Isaiah as read by a clairvoyant. Boston, 1937.
Phil 7069.37.5A   Rhine, Joseph B. New frontiers of the mind. N.Y., 1937.
Phil 7069.37.5B   Rhine, Joseph B. New frontiers of the mind. N.Y., 1937.
Phil 7069.37.12   Thomas, J.F. Beyond normal cognition. Boston, 1937.

Phil 7064 - 7070 Psychology - Parapsychology - Spiritualism - General
treatises - Individual authors (By date) - cont.

Phil 7069.37.45   Taylor, William G.L. Immortality. Boston, 1937.
Phil 7069.37.50   Vivante, Leone. Studi sulle precognizioni. Firenze, 1937.
Phil 7069.38.4   Bozzano, E. Discarnate influence. London, 1938.
Phil 7069.38.5A   Warcollur, R. Experimental telepathy. Boston, 1939.
Phil 7069.38.5B   Warcollur, R. Experimental telepathy. Boston, 1939.
Phil 7069.38.30   Mulholland, J. Beware familiar spirits. N.Y., 1938.
Phil 7069.38.50   Richmond, Z. Evidence of purpose. London, 1939.
Phil 7069.38.58   Thomas, Charles D. In the dawn beyond death.
                   London, 1938?
Phil 7069.38.58.5 Thomas, Charles D. In the dawn beyond death.
                   London, 194-.
Phil 7069.38.59   Thomas, Charles D. Beyond life's sunset. London, 194-.
Phil 7069.38.60   Tyrrell, G.N.M. Science and psychical phenomena.
                   London, 1938.
Phil 7069.38.65   Parkman, Frances. Vision, being the continuation of
                   "Reality" and "Dedication". Boston, 1938.
Phil 7069.39.4   Bennett, E.N. Apparitions and haunted houses.
                   London, 1939.
Phil 7069.39.9   Carrington, H. Laboratory investigations into psychic
                   phenomena. Philadelphia, 1939.
Phil 7069.39.19   Garrett, Eileen Jeanette Lyttle. My life as a search for
                   the meaning of mediumship. London, 1939.
Phil 7069.39.45   Poortman, Johannes J. Drei Forträge über Philosophie und
                   Parapsychologie. Leiden, 1939.
Phil 7069.39.50   Richmond, K. Evidence of identity. London, 1939.
Phil 7069.39.52   Salminen, I. Essence of life in psychic phenomena.
                   Brooklyn, 1938.
Phil 7069.39.55   Thompson, L.S. Geometric telepathy. Los Angeles, 1939.
Phil 7069.39.57   Labadié, Jean. Aux frontières de l'au-dela. Paris, 1939.
Phil 7069.40.4   Hettinger, John. The ultra-perceptive faculty.
                   London, 1940.
Phil 7069.40.6A   Extra-sensory perception after 60 years. N.Y., 1940.
Phil 7069.40.6B   Extra-sensory perception after 60 years. N.Y., 1940.
Phil 7069.40.7   Sitwell, S. Poltergeists. London, 1940.
Phil 7069.40.8   Tweedale, C.L. News from the next world. London, 1940.
Phil 7069.40.10   Seymour, C.J. This spiritualism. London, 1940.
Phil 7069.40.11   Redemptor Spiritual Center. Rational and scientific
                   (Christian) spiritualism. Rio de Janeiro, n.d.
Phil 7069.40.12   Eaton, A.K. A message to a troubled world. Clarmont,
                   Calif., 1940.
Phil 7069.40.13   White, S.E. The unobstructed universe. N.Y., 1940.
Phil 7069.40.14   Hort, Gertrude M. Three famous occultists: Dr. John Dee.
                   Photoreproducton. Philadelphia, 1940.
Phil 7069.40.15   Palmstierna, E.K. Widening horizons. London, 1940.
Phil 7069.40.16   Hole, C. Haunted England. London, 1940.
Phil 7069.40.17   Wood, E.C. The "how" of divine revelation. Camden,
                   N.J., 1940.
Phil 7069.40.19   Hendrickson, R.J. Divine science and metaphysics.
                   N.Y., 1940.
Phil 7069.41.4   Edwards, Harry. The mediumship of Jack Webber.
                   N.Y., 1941.
Phil 7069.41.5   Price, Harry. The most haunted house in England.
                   London, 1941.
Phil 7069.41.6   Temple, Laurence. The shining brother. London, 1941.
Phil 7069.41.7   Garrett, Eileen Jeanette Lyttle. Telepathy in search of a
                   lost faculty. N.Y., 1941.
Phil 7069.42.5   Hamilton, T. Glen. Intention and survival. Toronto, 1942.
Phil 7069.42.10   Tyrrell, George N.M. Apparitions. London, 1942?
Phil 7069.42.12   Tyrrell, George N.M. Apparitions. London, 1953.
Phil 7069.43   Garrett, Eileen Jeanette Lyttle. Awareness. N.Y., 1943.
Phil 7069.43.5   Allen, Maurice. Our invisible friends. N.Y., 1943.
Phil 7069.43.10   Dowding, H.C.T. Many mansions. London, 1943.
Phil 7069.43.15   Wade, A.M. Evidences of immortality. N.Y., 1943.
Phil 7069.43.20   Driesch, Hans. Parapsychologie. Zürich, 1943.
Phil 7069.43.22   Driesch, Hans. Parapsychologie. 3. Aufl. Zürich, 1952.
Phil 7069.44   Burton, Jean. Heyday of a wizard. 1. ed. N.Y., 1944.
Phil 7069.44.5   Cummins, G.D. After Pentecost; the Alexandrian chronicle
                   of Cleophas. London, 1944.
Phil 7069.44.10   Moore, M.G. Things I can't explain. London, 1944.
Phil 7069.44.17   Bendit, L.J. Paranormal cognition in human psychology.
                   London, 1944.
Phil 7069.44.20   Butterworth, G.W. Spiritualism and religion.
                   London, 1944.
Phil 7069.44.25   Desmond, S. Love after death. London, 1944.
Phil 7069.44.30   Seymour, C.J. Curiosities of psychical research.
                   London, 1944.
Phil 7069.44.35   Baird, A.T. One hundred cases for survival after death.
                   N.Y., 1944.
Phil 7069.44.40   O'Neill, Herbert V. Spiritualism as spiritualists have
                   written of it. London, 1944.
Phil 7069.44.45   Abhedânanda. Life beyond death. Calcutta, 1944.
Phil 7069.45   Barnes, M.S. Long distance calling. N.Y., 1945.
Phil 7069.45.5   Clark, Ida C.G. Men who wouldn't stay dead. N.Y., 1945.
Phil 7069.45.10   Sherwood, Jane. The country beyond; a study of survival
                   and rebirth. London, 1945.
Phil 7069.45.15   Price, Harry. Poltergeist over England; three centuries of
                   mischievous ghosts. London, 1945.
Phil 7069.45.20   Edwards, H.J. The science of spirit healing.
                   London, 1945.
Phil 7069.45.25   Dowding, H.C.T. Lychgate. London, 1945.
Phil 7069.45.30   Dowden, Hester. The book of Johannes, by Peter Fripp.
                   London, 1945.
Phil 7069.45.35   Stevens, William O. Unbidden guests, a book of real
                   ghosts. N.Y., 1945.
Phil 7069.45.45   Carington, Whately. Telepathy. 2. ed. London, 1945.
Phil 7069.45.50   Duncan, V.H.M. The trial of Mrs. Duncan. London, 1945.
Phil 7069.45.55   Keith, Cassius C. The dawn of a new day, a revelation.
                   Kansas City, Mo., 1945.
Phil 7069.45.60   Swaffer, Hannen. My greatest story. London, 1945.
Phil 7069.45.65   Jordan, Alfred McKay, (Mrs.). Science from the unseen.
                   N.Y., 1945.
Phil 7069.46   White, Stewart E. The stars are still there. 1. ed.
                   N.Y., 1946.
Phil 7069.46.5   Cannon, A. The shadow of destiny. London, 1946?
Phil 7069.46.15   Desmond, Shaw. Spiritualism. London, 1946?
Phil 7069.46.25   Carington, Whately. Thought transference. N.Y., 1946.
Phil 7069.47   White, S.E. With folded wings. 1. ed. N.Y., 1947.
Phil 7069.47.5A   Rhine, Joseph B. The reach of the mind. N.Y., 1947.
Phil 7069.47.5B   Rhine, Joseph B. The reach of the mind. N.Y., 1947.
Phil 7069.47.10   Pond, Mariam B. Time is kind. N.Y., 1947.
Phil 7069.47.15   Soal, Samuel G. The experimental situation in psychical
                   research. London, 1947.
Phil 7069.47.20   Ehrenwald, Jan. Telepathy and medical psychology.
                   London, 1947.
Phil 7069.47.30   Tyrrell, George N.M. The personality of man. W.
                   Drayton, 1948.

Classified Listing

Phil 7064 - 7070   Psychology - Parapsychology - Spiritualism - General
treatises - Individual authors (By date) - cont.

Phil 7069.47.35   Anspacher, L.K. Challenge of the unknown. N.Y., 1947.
Phil 7069.47.40   Estabrooks, George Hoben. Spiritism. 1. ed. N.Y., 1947.
Phil 7069.48   Warcollier, R. Mind to mind. N.Y., 1948.
Phil 7069.48.5   Keith, C.C. Worlds beyond. Hastings, Neb., 1948.
Phil 7069.48.12   Roberts, Ursula. Mary Baker Eddy, her communications from beyond the grave to Harold Horwood. London, 1964.
Phil 7069.49   Garrett, Eileen Jeanette Lyttle. Adventures in the supernormal. N.Y., 1949.
Phil 7069.49.5   Westwood, Horace. There is a psychic world. N.Y., 1947.
Phil 7069.49.12   Rosenthal, Eric. They walk by night; true South African ghost stories and tales of the supernormal. Cape Town, 1965.
Phil 7069.49.15   Bendit, Phoebe Daphne Payne. The psychic sense. N.Y., 1949.
Phil 7069.50   Garrett, Eileen Jeanette Lyttle. The sense and nonsense of prophecy. N.Y., 1950.
Phil 7069.50.6   Silva Mello, Antonio da. Mysteries and realities of this world and the next. London, 1960.
Phil 7069.50.10   Marion, Frederick. In my mind's eye. 1. ed. N.Y., 1950.
Phil 7069.51   Carrington, H. Haunted people. 1. ed. N.Y., 1951.
Phil 7069.51.5   O'Donnell, Elliot. Ghosts with a purpose. London, 1951.
Phil 7069.51.10   Aron, Robert. Mors et vita. Paris, 1951.
Phil 7069.51.15   Sabine, Waldo. Second sight in daily life. London, 1951.
Phil 7069.51.25   Muldoon, Sylvan Joseph. The phenomena of astral projection. London, 1962.
Phil 7069.52   Hettinger, John. Telepathy and spiritualism. N.Y., 1952.
Phil 7069.53   Rhine, Joseph B. New world of the mind. N.Y., 1953.
Phil 7069.54   Thurston, Herbert. Ghosts and poltergeists. Chicago, 1954.
Phil 7069.54.5   Soal, Samuel G. Modern experiments in telepathy. New Haven, 1954.
Phil 7069.54.10   West, D.J. Psychical research today. London, 1954.
Phil 7069.54.15   Amadou, Robert. La parapsychologie. Paris, 1954.
Phil 7069.54.20   Alexander, Rolf. Creative realism. 1. ed. N.Y., 1954.
Phil 7069.54.25   Porten, Harry. The miracle on the wall. Eastbourne, Eng., 1954.
Phil 7069.55   Jung Institute, Zürich. The interpretation of nature and the psyche. N.Y., 1955.
Phil 7069.55.2A   Jung Institute, Zürich. The interpretation of nature and the psyche. London, 1955.
Phil 7069.55.2B   Jung Institute, Zürich. The interpretation of nature and the psyche. London, 1955.
Phil 7069.55.15   Ehrenwald, Jan. New dimensions of deep analysis. N.Y., 1955.
Phil 7069.55.20   Saint-Clair, Simone. The heart aflame. London, 1955.
Phil 7069.55.25   Bodin, Edward Longstreet. Upper purgatory. Daytona Beach, Fla., 1955.
Phil 7069.56   Johnson, R.C. Psychical research. N.Y., 1956.
Phil 7069.56.5   Gibt es Geister? Bern, 1956.
Phil 7069.56.10   Ciba Foundation. Symposium on extrasensory perception. London, 1956.
Phil 7069.56.15   Dietz, Paul A. Parapsychologische woordentolk. Den Haag, 1956.
Phil 7069.56.20   Davis, S.E. Man being revealed. 1. ed. N.Y., 1956.
Phil 7069.56.25   Omez, Réginald. Supranormal ou surnaturel. Paris, 1956.
Phil 7069.57   Parapsychology, F. Proceedings of four conferences. N.Y., 1957.
Phil 7069.57.5   O'Donnell, Elliot. Haunted waters. London, 1957.
Phil 7069.57.10   Stirling, A.M.W.P. Ghosts vivisected. London, 1957.
Phil 7069.57.15   Rhine, Joseph B. Parapsychology. Springfield, Ill., 1957.
Phil 7069.57.16   Rhine, Joseph B. Parapsychology, frontier science of the mind. 2. ed. Springfield, 1962.
Phil 7069.58   Jaffe, Aniela. Geistererscheinungen und Vorzeichen. Zürich, 1958.
Phil 7069.58.2   Jaffe, Aniela. Apparitions and precognition. New Hyde Park, N.Y., 1963.
Phil 7069.58.5   Amadou, Robert. La télépathie. Paris, 1958.
Phil 7069.58.10   Ford, Arthur. Nothing so strange. 1. ed. N.Y., 1958.
Phil 7069.59   Puharich, A. The sacred mushroom. Garden City, 1959.
Phil 7069.59.5   Heywood, Rosalind. The sixth sense. London, 1959.
Phil 7069.59.10   Soal, Samuel G. The mind readers. London, 1959.
Phil 7069.59.15   Visser, B.J.J. Parapsychologie, paragnosie. Roermond, 1959.
Phil 7069.59.20   Huber, Guido. Übersinnliche Gaben. 1. Aufl. Zürich, 1959.
Phil 7069.59.25   Sonnet, Andre. Der Mensch ist voller Geheimnisse. Berlin, 1959.
Phil 7069.59.30   Imbert-Nergal, R. Les sciences occultes ne sont pas des sciences. Paris, 1959.
Phil 7069.59.35   Castellan, Yvonne. Le spiritisme. 2. ed. Paris, 1959.
Phil 7069.59.40   Long, Max Freedom. Psychometric analysis. Vista, Calif., 1959.
Phil 7069.59.45   Durand, M. Technique et panthéon des mediums viêtnamiens. Paris, 1959.
Phil 7069.59.50   Steinour, Harold Heiges. Exploring the unseen world. 1. ed. N.Y., 1959.
Phil 7069.60   Nagel, E.W. Mind power. 1. ed. N.Y., 1960.
Phil 7069.60.5   Sudre, René. Treatise on parapsychology. London, 1960.
Phil 7069.60.10   East, John. Man the immortal. London, 1960.
Phil 7069.60.15   Heine, Hilda G. The vital sense. London, 1960.
Phil 7069.60.20   Pole, W.T. The silent road in the light of personal experience. London, 1960.
Phil 7069.60.25   Abreu Filho, Julio. Rosa dos ventos; artigos e palestras. São Paulo, 1960.
Phil 7069.61A   Murphy, Gardner. Challenge of psychical research. 1. ed. N.Y., 1961.
Phil 7069.61B   Murphy, Gardner. Challenge of psychical research. 1. ed. N.Y., 1961.
Phil 7069.61.5   Teillard, A. Spiritual dimensions. London, 1961.
Phil 7069.61.10   Rhine, Louisa E. Hidden channels of the mind. N.Y., 1961.
Phil 7069.61.15   Roberts, D.O. Elizabethan episode. London, 1961.
Phil 7069.61.20   Salter, William Henry. Zoar, or The evidence of psychical research concerning survival. London, 1961.
Phil 7069.61.30   Harlow, Samuel R. A life after death. 1. ed. Garden City, 1961.
Phil 7069.61.35   Van der Huok, P. Psychic. Indianapolis, 1961.
Phil 7069.61.40   Haynes, Renée. The hidden springs. London, 1961.
Phil 7069.62   Banks, Frances. Frontiers of revelation. London, 1962.
Phil 7069.62.5   Hall, Trevor. The spiritualists; story of F. Cook and Wm. Crookes. London, 1962.
Phil 7069.62.10   Sidgwick, Eleanor Mildred. Phantasms of the living. N.Y., 1962.
Phil 7069.62.15   Broad, Charlie. Lectures on physical research. London, 1962.
Phil 7069.62.20   Vasil'ev, L.L. Vnushenie na rasstoianii. Moskva, 1962.
Phil 7069.62.25   Koernev, E.M. Wege Zum Licht; Erlebnisse und Gespräche mit mystikern. Garmisch-Partenkirchen, 1962.

Phil 7064 - 7070   Psychology - Parapsychology - Spiritualism - General
treatises - Individual authors (By date) - cont.

Phil 7069.62.30   Schjelderup, Harald Krabbe. Det skjulte menneske. Köbenhavn, 1962.
Phil 7069.63   Hankey, M. James Hewat McKenzie, pioneer of psychical research. Londnon, 1963.
Phil 7069.63.5   Stearn, J. The door to the future. Garden City, 1963.
Phil 7069.63.10   Feilding, Everard. Sittings with Eussapia Palladino and other studies. New Hyde Park, 1963.
Phil 7069.64   Juegenson, F. Rosterna från rymden. Stockholm, 1964.
Phil 7069.64.5   Heywood, R. ESP: a personal memoir. 1. ed. N.Y., 1964.
Phil 7069.64.10   Stone, W.C. The other side of the mind. Englewood Cliffs, 1964.
Phil 7069.64.15   Fornell, Earl W. The unhappy medium. Austin, 1964.
Phil 7069.64.20   Fodor, Nandor. Between two worlds. West Nyack, 1966.
Phil 7069.64.27   Hunt, Douglas. A handbook on the occult. London, 1967.
Phil 7069.64.30   Maple, Eric. The realm of ghost. London, 1967.
Phil 7069.64.35   Cayce, Hugh Lynn. Venture inward. N.Y., 1964.
Phil 7069.65.5   Gerloff, Hans. The crisis in parapsychology. Tittmoning, 1965.
Phil 7069.65.6   Gerloff, Hans. The crisis in parapsychology. 2. supplement. Tittmoning, 1966.
Phil 7069.65.7   Gerloff, Hans. The crisis in parapsychology. 3. supplement. Bayerisch Gmain, 1967.
Phil 7069.65.10   Parapsychology Foundation. Ten years of activities. N.Y., 1965.
Phil 7069.65.15   Rhine, Joseph B. Parapsychology from Duke to FRNM. Durham, 1965.
Phil 7069.65.20   Maudiut, Jacques A. Aux fontières de l'irrationnel. Paris, 1965.
Phil 7069.65.25   Crouzet, Jean-Philippe. Les merveilles du spiritualisme. Paris, 1965.
Phil 7069.65.30   Hall, Trevor H. New light on old ghosts. London, 1965.
Phil 7069.65.37   Byrne, Patrick. Irish ghost stories. Cork, 1968.
Phil 7069.65.40   Richard, Hermann. La tradition ésotérique et la science. Paris, 1965.
Phil 7069.66.5   Osborn, Arthur Walter. The meaning of personal existence. London, 1966.
Phil 7069.66.15   Lance, Pierre. Le spiritualisme athée. Paris, 1966.
Phil 7069.66.20   Du Plessis, Izak David. Poltergeists of the south. Cape Town, 1966.
Phil 7069.66.25   Mackenzie, Andrew. The unexplained; some strange cases in psychical research. London, 1966.
Phil 7069.66.30   Beard, Paul. Survival of death: for and against. London, 1966.
Phil 7069.66.35   Edmunds, Simeon. Spiritualism: a critical survey. London, 1966.
Phil 7069.66.40   Schult, Arthur. Vom übersinnlichen Wesen des Menschen. Bietigheim, 1966.
Phil 7069.66.45   Vallberg, Viktor. Den kära okunnigheten, eller, Den fördolda kunskapen. Stockholm, 1966.
Phil 7069.67   Manning, A.G. Helping yourself with E.S.P. West Nyack, 1967.
Phil 7069.67.5   Bayless, Raymond. The enigma of the poltergeist. West Nyack, 1967.
Phil 7069.67.10   Lethbridge, Thomas. A step in the dark. London, 1967.
Phil 7069.67.15   Spraggett, Allen. The unexplained. N.Y., 1967.
Phil 7069.67.20   Cohen, Daniel. Myths of the space age. N.Y., 1967.
Phil 7069.67.25   Smythies, John Raymond. Science and the E.S.P. London, 1967.
Phil 7069.67.30   Bradley, Dorothy Bomar. Psychic phenomena, revelations and experiences. West Nyack, 1967.
Phil 7069.67.40   McCreery, Charles. Science, philosophy and E.S.P. London, 1967.
Phil 7069.67.50   Andreas, Peter. Between heaven and earth, adventures in the search of the nature of man. Toronto, 1967.
Phil 7069.67.50.2   Andreas, Peter. Was niemand glauben will. Berlin, 1967.
Phil 7069.67.55   Ludlam, Harry. The restless ghosts of Ladye Place, and other true hauntings. London, 1967.
Phil 7069.67.60   Lots-Poole, Marietta. Strange dreams and their portents and other reflections Brentwood, 1967.
Phil 7069.67.65   McDougall, William. William McDougall: explorer of the mind. N.Y., 1967.
Phil 7069.67.75   Ebon, Martin. Beyond space and time. N.Y., 1967.
Phil 7069.67.80   Dollo, Corrado. Momenti e problemi dello spiritualismo. Padova, 1967.
VPhil 7069.68   Swanson, Mildred Burris. God bless U, daughter. Independance, 1968.
Phil 7069.68.5   Gauld, Alan. The founders of psychical research. London, 1968.
Phil 7069.68.10   Holzer, Hans W. Ghosts of the Golden West. Indianapolis, 1968.
Phil 7069.68.15   Appleman, John A. Your psychic powers and immortality. N.Y., 1968.
Phil 7069.68.20   Holzer, Hans W. Psychic investigator. 1st ed. N.Y., 1968.
Phil 7069.68.25   MacKenzie, Andrew. Frontiers of the unknown: the insights of psychical research. London, 1968.
Phil 7069.68.30   Holzer, Hans W. The lively ghosts of Ireland. London, 1968.
Phil 7069.68.35   Federmann, Reinhard. Botschaft aus dem Jenseits. Tübingen, 1968.
Phil 7069.68.40   Campbell, John Lorne. Strange things: the story of Fr. Allan McDonald, Ada Goodrich Freer, and the Society for Psychical Research's enquiry into Highland second sight. London, 1968.
Phil 7069.68.50   Bunge, H. Meesters van het verborgene. Amsterdam, 1968.
Phil 7069.68.55   Piccardt, Karel. De bovenzinnelijke wereld. Amsterdam, 1968.
Phil 7069.68.60   Daurado, Alzira Guanaes. Igrejas reunidas, plano divino. 1. ed. Rio de Janeiro, 1968.
Phil 7069.68.65   Lietaert, Peerbolte, Maarten. Psychocybernetica. Amsterdam, 1968.
Phil 7069.69   Holzer, Hans W. Window to the past. Garden City, 1969.
Phil 7069.69.5   Nelson, Geoffrey K. Spiritualism and society. London, 1969.
Phil 7069.69.10   Agee, Doris. Edgar Cayce on E.S.P. 1st ed. N.Y., 1969.
Phil 7069.69.20   Stearn, Jess. Adventures into the psychic. N.Y., 1969.
Phil 7069.69.25   Cayce, Edgar. The Edgar Cayce reader. N.Y., 1969.
Phil 7069.69.40   Laubscher, Barend Jacob Frederick. In quest of the unseen. 1st ed. N.Y., 1969.
Phil 7069.70   Ebon, Martin. Test your E.S.P. N.Y., 1970.
Phil 7069.70.5   Worrall, Ambrose A. Explore your psychic world. N.Y., 1970.
Phil 7069.70.10   Ostrander, Sheila. Psychic discoveries behind the Iron Curtain. Englewood Cliffs, 1970.
Phil 7069.70.15   Burke, Clara Baker. The ghosts about us. Philadelphia, 1969.

Phil 7072 Psychology - Parapsychology - Spiritualism - Physical phenomena of spiritualism - Special topics

Phil 7072.2 Alberg, Albert. Frost flowers on the windows. Chicago, 1899.
Phil 7072.3 Shirley, Ralph. The mystery of the human double. N.Y., 1965.
Phil 7072.4 Alexander, Rolf. The power of the mind. London, 1965.
Phil 7072.5 Smith, Susy. The enigma of out-of-body travel. N.Y., 1965.
Phil 7072.6 Gerry, Elbridge T. The number "spirit" photograph case. N.Y., 1869.
Phil 7072.6.5 Glendinning, Andrew. The veil lifted; modern developments of spirit photography. London, 1894.
Phil 7072.6.10 Morse, James Johnson. Spirit photography. Manchester, 1909.
Phil 7072.10 Mahony, Patrick. Unsought visitors; a book of visitations. v.1-2. N.Y., 1953. 2v.
Phil 7072.15 Langley, Noel. Edgar Cayce on reincarnation. N.Y., 1968.
Phil 7072.20 Crawford, William Jackson. The psychic structures at the Goligher Circle. London, 1921.
VPhil 7072.21 Shakhnovich, Mikhail I. Primety v svete nauki. 2. izd. Leningrad, 1969.
Phil 7072.22 Raudive, Konstantins. Unhorbares wird Hörbar. Ramagen, 1968.
Phil 7072.22.5 Raudive, Konstantins. Breakthrough. N.Y., 1971.

Phil 7074 Psychology - Parapsychology - Spiritualism - Mediumship, Psychometry - Spirit messages - Special topics

Phil 7074.5 Laval. L'heure des révélations; le livre des temps. Montpellier, 1969.
Phil 7074.10 Brown, Rosemary. Unfinished symphonies; voices from the beyond. N.Y., 1971.
Phil 7074.16 Cummins, Geraldine Dorothy. Swan on a black sea: a study in automatic writing, the Cummins-Willet scripts. London, 1970.
Phil 7074.20 Burke, Jane R. The one way. N.Y., 1922.
Phil 7074.20.1 Burke, Jane R. The one way. N.Y., 1923.
Phil 7074.20.5 Burke, Jane R. Let us in. 1st ed. N.Y., 1931.
Phil 7074.20.6 Burke, Jane R. Let us in. N.Y., 1931.
Phil 7074.20.10 Burke, Jane R. The bundle of life. 1st ed. N.Y., 1934.

Phil 7075 Psychology - Parapsychology - Spiritualism - Sexual perversion [Discontinued]

Htn Phil 7075.5.2* Moreau, P. Des aberrations du sens génésique. 2. ed. Paris, 1880.
Htn Phil 7075.6.3* Orsi, Alberto. La donna nuda. 3. ed. Milano, 1912.
Htn Phil 7075.6.7* Orsi, Alberto. Lussuria e castità. Milano, 1913.
Htn Phil 7075.7.8* Krafft-Ebing, Richard von. Psychopathia sexualis. Stuttgart, 1893.
Htn Phil 7075.8* Moll, Albert. Die conträre Sexualempfindung. Berlin, 1891.
X Cg Phil 7075.8.3 Moll, Albert. Die conträre Sexualempfindung. Berlin, 1899.
X Cg Phil 7075.9 Bloch, Iwan. Le Marquis de Sade et son temps. Berlin, 1901.
X Cg Phil 7075.9.5 Bloch, Iwan. Neue Forschungen über den Marquis de Sade. Berlin, 1904.
Htn Phil 7075.10* Ball, B. La folie erotique. Paris, 1888.
Htn Phil 7075.11.5* Mantegazza, P. Gli amori degli uomeni. Milano, 1886.
X Cg Phil 7075.127 Money-Kyrle, R.E. The development of the sexual impulses. London, 1932.
X Cg Phil 7075.130 Individual psychology and sexual difficulties. pt.1-2. London, 1932-34.
X Cg Phil 7075.131 Stekel, William. Der Fetischismus dargestellt für Ärzte und Kriminalogen. Berlin, 1923.
X Cg Phil 7075.132 Bergler, E. Die psychische Importenz des Mannes. Bern, 1937.
X Cg Phil 7075.135 Cleugh, James. The marquis and the chevalier. London, 1951.
X Cg Phil 7075.137 Reik, T. Psychology of sex relations. N.Y., 1945.
X Cg Phil 7075.139 Hartwell, S.W. A citizen's handbook of sexual abnormalities and the mental hygiene approach to their prevention. Washington, 1951.
X Cg Phil 7075.140 Linsert, Richard. Kabale und Liebe. Berlin, 1931.
X Cg Phil 7075.144 Fliess, Robert. Erogeneity and libido. N.Y., 1957.
X Cg Phil 7075.146 Cleckley, H.M. The caricature of love. N.Y., 1957.
X Cg Phil 7075.152 Luvandowski, Herbert. Ferne Lände, fremde Sitten. 1. Aufl. Stuttgart, 1958.
Phil 7075.154 Hunt, Morton M. The natural history of love. N.Y., 1959.

Phil 7076 Psychology - Parapsychology - Spiritualism - Trance states - General works

Phil 7076.2.2 Benneville, George de. Some remarkable passages in the life of Dr. George de Benneville. Germantown, Pa., 1870.
Phil 7076.5 Boyer, Onesimas Alfred. She wears a crown of thorns; Marie Rose Perron, 1902-1936. N.Y., 1951.
Phil 7076.10 Isou, Isidore. Histoire et rénovation de l'automatismé spirituel. Paris, 1967.
Phil 7076.12 Bertrand, Alexandre Jacques François. Extase. Paris, 1826.
Phil 7076.14 Mantegazza, Paolo. Die Ekstasen des Menschen. Jena, 1888.
Phil 7076.16 Achelis, Thomas. Die Ekstase in ihrer kulturellen Bedeutung. Berlin, 1902.
Phil 7076.18 Beck, Paul. Die Ekstase. Bad Sachsa, 1906.
Phil 7076.20 Janet, Pierre. De l'angoisse à l'extase. Paris, 1926-28. 2v.
Phil 7076.20.5 Janet, Pierre. Une extatique. Paris, 1901.
Phil 7076.22 Morrison, Paul Guerrant. The place of the ecstatic trance in the ideal of the good life. Chicago, 1932.
Phil 7076.24 Pagenstecher, Gustav. Aussersinnliche Wahrnehmung. Halle, 1924.

Phil 7077 Psychology - Parapsychology - Spiritualism - Trance states - Automatic communication

Phil 7077.2 Montgomery, Ruth Shick. A world beyond. N.Y., 1971.
Phil 7077.3 Devotional somnium. N.Y., 1815.
Phil 7077.4 Moses, William S. Psychography. London, 1878.
Phil 7077.4.2 Moses, William S. Psychography. 2d ed. London, 1882.

Phil 7080 Psychology - Parapsychology - Sleep phenomena - General works

Phil 7080.01 Pamphlet box. Philosophy. Sleep.
Phil 7080.1 Cappie, J. Causation of sleep. Edinburgh, 1872.
Phil 7080.2 Dupuy, P. Étude psycho-physiologique. Bordeaux, 1879.
Phil 7080.3 Fosgate, B. Sleep. N.Y., 1850.
Phil 7080.4 Granville, J.M. Sleep and sleeplessness. Boston, 1881.
NEDL Phil 7080.5.2 Hammond, W.A. Sleep and its derangements. Philadelphia, 1869.
Phil 7080.5.5 Hammond, W.A. On wakefulness. Philadelphia, 1866.

Phil 7080 Psychology - Parapsychology - Sleep phenomena - General works - cont.

Phil 7080.6 Lyman, H.M. Insomnia and other disorders of sleep. Chicago, 1885.
Phil 7080.7 Macnish, R. Philosophy of sleep. N.Y., 1834.
Phil 7080.8 Marvaud, J.L.A. Le sommeil et l'insomnie. Paris, 1881.
Phil 7080.9 Maury, L.F.A. Le sommeil et les rêves. Paris, 1861.
Phil 7080.9.3 Maury, L.F.A. Le sommeil et les rêves. Paris, 1865.
Phil 7080.10 More, C.H. On going to sleep. London, 1868.
NEDL Phil 7080.11 Radestock, P. Schlaf und Traum. Leipzig, 1879.
Phil 7080.12 Yung, E. Le sommeil normal. Paris, 1883.
Phil 7080.13 Manaceïne, M. de. Sleep, its physiology, pathology, hygiene and psychology. London, 1897.
Phil 7080.14 Hennings, Justus Christian. Von den Träumen und Nachtwandlern. Weimar, 1784.
Phil 7080.15 Spitta, H. Die Schlaf- und Traumzustände der menschlichen Seele. Tübingen, 1878.
Phil 7080.15.2 Spitta, H. Die Schlaf- und Traumzustände der menschlichen Seele. 2. Aufl. Tübingen, 1882.
Phil 7080.16 Bigelow, John. The mystery of sleep. N.Y., 1903.
Phil 7080.16.5 Bigelow, John. Mystery of sleep. N.Y., 1924.
Phil 7080.17 Thomasius, C. De jure circa somnum et somnia. Regiomonti, 1712.
Phil 7080.18.5 Relação de dous extraordinar[ios] e notaveis successos. Lisbon, 1789.
Phil 7080.19 Sawyer, James. Insomnia: its causes and cure. Birmingham, 1904.
Phil 7080.20 Oliver, William. A relation of a very extraordinary sleeper. London, 1707.
Phil 7080.21 Powell, S.P. The art of natural sleep. N.Y., 1908.
Phil 7080.23 Trömmer, E. Das Problem des Schlafes. Wiesbaden, 1912.
Phil 7080.24 Shepard, J.F. The circulation and sleep. Text and atlas. N.Y., 1914. 2v.
Phil 7080.25 Pieron, H. Le problème physiologique du sommeil. Paris, 1912.
Phil 7080.26 Bruce, H.A. Sleep and sleeplessness. Boston, 1915.
Phil 7080.27 Delboeuf, Joseph. Le sommeil et les rêves. Paris, 1885.
Phil 7080.28 Vaschide, Nicolas. Le sommeil et les rêves. Paris, 1914.
Htn Phil 7080.29* Binns, E. The anatomy of sleep. London, 1842.
Phil 7080.30 Lemoine, Albert. Du sommeil au point de vue physiologique et psychologique. Paris, 1855.
Phil 7080.31 Cox, E. William. A monograph on sleep and dream. London, 1878.
Phil 7080.32 Michaelis, A.O. Der Schlaf nach seinerBedeutung. Leipzig, 1894.
Phil 7080.33 Preyer, William. Über die Ursache des Schlafes. Stuttgart, 1877.
Phil 7080.34 Veronese, F. Versuch einer Physiologie des Schlafes und des Traumes. Leipzig, 1910.
Phil 7080.35 Poyer, G.P. Contribution à la pathologie du sommeil. Le sommeil automatique. Thèse. Paris, 1914.
Phil 7080.36 Pfaff, E.R. Das Traumleben und seine Deutung. Leipzig, 1868.
Phil 7080.37 Dandolo, G. La coscienza nel sonno. Padova, 1889.
Phil 7080.38 Fraser-Harris, D.F. Morpheus, or The future of sleep. London, 1928.
Phil 7080.39 MacFarlane, A.W. Insomnia and its therapeutics. N.Y., 1891.
Phil 7080.40A Thorlákson, Björg Caritas. Svefn og draumar. Reykjavík, 1926.
Phil 7080.40B Thorlákson, Björg Caritas. Svefn og draumar. Reykjavík, 1926.
Phil 7080.41 Schenk, Paul. Versuch einer psychologischen Theorie des Schlafes. Inaug. Diss. Leipzig, 1928.
Phil 7080.42 Lhermitte, J.J. Le sommeil. Paris, 1931.
Phil 7080.43 Zambeccari, G. Il sonne e la vigilia. Firenze, 1928.
Phil 7080.44 Fish, Luther S. Knowledge exchanged; phenomenon of sleep. Cheveland, 1920.
Phil 7080.45 Collins, Joseph. Insomnia, how to combat it. N.Y., 1930.
Phil 7080.46 Weschcke, Charles. Overcoming sleeplessness. St. Paul, 1935.
Phil 7080.47 Scholz, F. Sleep and dreams. N.Y., 1893.
Phil 7080.49.5 Jacobson, Edmund. You can sleep well. N.Y., 1938.
Phil 7080.50 Garvey, Chester R. Activity of young children during sleep. Minneapolis, 1939.
Phil 7080.51 Stekel, W. Der Wille zum Schlaf! Wiesbaden, 1915.
Phil 7080.52 Cassina, U. Congetture su i sogni. Parma, 1783.
Phil 7080.53 Wiedemann, Fritz. Müde Menschen. Heidenheim, 1953.
Phil 7080.54 Foulkes, David. The psychology of sleep. N.Y., 1966.
Phil 7080.55 Othmer, Ekkehard. Persönlichkeit und Schlafverhalten. Meisenheim, 1965.
Phil 7080.56 Luce, Gay Gaer. Sleep. N.Y., 1966.
Phil 7080.58 Murray, Edward. Sleep, dreams, and arousal. N.Y., 1965.

Phil 7081 Psychology - Parapsychology - Sleep phenomena - Dreaming - Bibliographies

Phil 7081.2 Weiss, Harry Bischoff. Oneirocritica Americana. N.Y., 1944.

Phil 7082 Psychology - Parapsychology - Sleep phenomena - Dreaming - General works

Phil 7082.2 Michaux, Henri. Façons d'endormi, façons d'éveillé. Paris, 1969.
Phil 7082.4.3 Schubert, Gotthilf Heinrich von. Die Symbolik des Traumes. 3. Aufl. Leipzig, 1840.
Phil 7082.4.5 Schubert, Gotthilf Heinrich von. Die Symbolik des Traumes. Heidelberg, 1968.
Phil 7082.6 Arthurs, André. Répertoire des images et symboles oniriques rencontrés au cours des analyses psychotherapiques. Genève, 1967.
Phil 7082.8.2 Freud, Sigmund. Über den Traum. 2. Aufl. Wiesbaden, 1911.
Phil 7082.8.5 Freud, Sigmund. On dreams. N.Y., 1952.
Phil 7082.8.14 Freud, Sigmund. Die Traumdeuting. 4. Aufl. Leipzig, 1914.
Phil 7082.8.20 Freud, Sigmund. The interpretation of dreams. London, 1954.
Phil 7082.10 Grinstein, Alexander. On Sigmund Freud's dreams. Detroit, 1968.
Phil 7082.12 Jones, Richard Matthew. Ego synthesis in dreams. Cambridge, 1962.
Phil 7082.12.5 Jones, Richard Matthew. The new psychology of dreaming. N.Y., 1970.
Phil 7082.14 Diamond, Edwin. The science of dreams. 1st ed. Garden City, 1962.
Phil 7082.16 Gutheil, Emil Arthur. The handbook of dream analysis. N.Y., 1951.
Phil 7082.18 Bossard, Robert. Psychologie des Traumbewustseins. Zürich, 1951.
Phil 7082.20 Hill, Brian. Gates of horn and ivory. N.Y., 1968.
Phil 7082.21 Grunebaum, Gustave Edmund von. The dream and human societies. Berkeley, 1966.

Phil 7082 **Psychology - Parapsychology - Sleep phenomena - Dreaming - General works - cont**

Phil 7082.22 — Caillois, Roger. Le rêve et les sociétés humaines. Paris, 1967.

Phil 7082.22.5 — Caillois, Roger. L'incertitude qui vient des rêves. Paris, 1956.

Phil 7082.24.5 — Beradt, Charlotte. The third Reich of dreams. Chicago, 1968.

Phil 7082.26 — Tissié, Philippe. Les rêves. Paris, 1890.

Phil 7082.28 — Weygandt, Wilhelm. Entstehung der Träume. Leipzig, 1893.

Phil 7082.30 — Grant, Alexander Henley. Extraordinary and well-authenticated dreams. London, 18- ?

Phil 7082.30.5 — Grant, Alexander Henley. The literature and curiosities of dreams. London, 1865. 2v.

Phil 7082.32.2 — Surbled, Georges. Le rêve. 2e éd. Paris, 1898.

Phil 7082.34 — Traugott, Richard. Der Traum. Würzburg, 1913.

Phil 7082.36 — Volkelt, Johannes. Die Traum-Phantasie. Stuttgart, 1875.

Phil 7082.38 — Stekel, Wilhelm. Die Sprache des Traumes. Wiesbaden, 1911.

Phil 7082.38.2 — Stekel, Wilhelm. Die Sprache des Traumes. 2e Aufl. München, 1922.

Phil 7082.38.3 — Stekel, Wilhelm. Die Sprache des Traumes. 3e Aufl. München, 1927.

Phil 7082.38.5 — Stekel, Wilhelm. Fortschritte und Technik der Traumdeutung. Wien, 1935.

Phil 7082.38.6 — Stekel, Wilhelm. The interpretation of dreams. N.Y., 1943. 2v.

Phil 7082.40 — Uslar, Detlev von. Der Traum als Welt. Pfullingen, 1964.

Phil 7082.42 — Sanford, John A. Dreams; God's forgotten language. Philadelphia, 1968.

Phil 7082.44.1 — Miller, Gustavus Hindman. Ten thousand dreams interpreted; or, What's in a dream. Chicago, 1931.

Phil 7082.45 — Símonardottir, Helga. Draumur. Reykjavík, 1916.

Phil 7082.46 — Jónasson, Hermann. Draumar. Reykjavík, 1912.

Phil 7082.46.5 — Jónasson, Hermann. Dulrímir. Reykjavík, 1914.

Phil 7082.48 — Jónsson, Brynjólfur. Dulraenar smásögur. Bessastadir, 1907.

Cg Phil 7082.50 — Andrésson, Fridik. Draumur Fridiks Andréssonar. Reykjavík, 1904. (Changed to XM 1329)

Phil 7082.51 — Thorleifsdóttir, Elízabet. Draumur. Reykjavík, 1892.

Phil 7082.51.1 — Thorleifsdóttir, Elízabet. Draumur. Reykjavík, 1905.

Phil 7082.52 — Jóhannsson, Jón. Draumur. Akureyri, 1882.

Phil 7082.52.2 — Jóhannsson, Jón. Draumur. 2. Utgáfa. Reykjavík, 1916.

Phil 7082.54 — Einarsson, Gudmundur. Draumvitran Gudmundar Einarssonar. n.p., 1913?

Phil 7082.56 — Austmann, S.J. Sögur af ýmsu tagi. Winnipeg, 1915.

Phil 7082.58 — Hedenius, Per. Om drömmen. Stockholm, 1880.

Phil 7082.59 — Wijnaendtsfrancken, Cornelis Johannes. Die psychologie van het droomen. Haarlem, 1907.

Phil 7082.60 — Sveinsson, Ingimundur. 2 draumur. Reykjavík, 1914.

Phil 7082.62 — Bjarnason, Halldór. Draumur. Reykjavík, 1879.

Phil 7082.64 — Combes, Marguerite. Le rêve et la personnalité. Paris, 1932.

Phil 7082.64.5 — Pierce, Frederick. Dreams and personality. N.Y., 1931.

Phil 7082.66 — Cutting, Mary Stewart. What dreams mean to you. London, 1928.

Phil 7082.68 — Brander, Robert. Der Schlaf und das Traumleben. Leipzig, 1884.

Phil 7082.70 — Hoche, Alfred. Das Träumende ich. Jena, 1927.

Phil 7082.72 — Hutchinson, Horace Gordon. Dreams and their meanings. London, 1901.

Phil 7082.72.5 — Graves, Robert. The meaning of dreams. London, 1924.

Phil 7082.72.10 — Roback, Abraham Aaron. The meaning of dreams. n.p., 193-

Phil 7082.72.15 — Coriat, Isador Henry. The meaning of dreams. Boston, 1915.

Phil 7082.72.20 — Hall, Calvin Springer. The meaning of dreams. N.Y., 1953.

Phil 7082.74 — Archer, William. On dreams. London, 1935.

Phil 7082.76 — Cohen, G. Das Wesen der Träume. Dresden, 1925.

Phil 7082.78 — L'art de se rendre heureux par les songes. Francfort, 1746.

Phil 7082.80 — Baudouin, Charles. Introduction à l'analyse des rêves. Genève, 1945.

Phil 7082.80.1 — Baudouin, Charles. Introduction à l'analyse des rêves. Paris, 1950.

Phil 7082.82.2 — Rogers, Louis William. Dreams and premonitions. 2d ed. Chicago, 1923.

Phil 7082.84 — Wood, Clement. Dreams. N.Y., 1931.

Phil 7082.86 — Sanctis, Sante de. I sogni. Torino, 1899.

Phil 7082.88 — Siemens, Otto. Wissenschaftliche Traum de Terei. Leipzig, 1919?

Phil 7082.90 — Spiller, Gustav. A contribution towards a science of dreams. London, 1934.

Phil 7082.92 — Stumpf, E.J.G. Der Traum und seine Dentung. Leipzig, 1899.

Phil 7082.94 — Mégroz, Rodolphe Louis. The dream world. N.Y., 1939.

Phil 7082.96 — Stevens, William Oliver. The mystery of dreams. London, 1950.

Phil 7082.98 — Stiles, Percy Goldthwait. Dreams. Cambridge, 1927.

Phil 7082.100 — Westerfield, Jonathan B. The scientific dream book and dictionary of dream symbols. N.Y., 1932.

Phil 7082.102 — Romsche, Heinrich. Unsere Träume und Traumzustände. Stuttgart, 1926.

Phil 7082.104.4 — La vera spiegazione numerica dei sogni. 4a ed. Palermo, 1886.

Phil 7082.106 — Lomer, Georg. Der Traumspiegel. München, 1918.

Phil 7082.108 — Monteith, Mary E. A book of true dreams. London, 1929.

Phil 7082.110 — Narayan, Ram. The dream problem. Delhi, 1917?-22. 2v.

Phil 7082.112 — Arnold-Forster, Mary Story-Maskelyne. Studies in dreams. N.Y., 1921.

Phil 7082.112.1 — Arnold-Forster, Mary Story-Maskelyne. Studies in dreams. London, 1921.

Phil 7082.114 — Cavallin, Paul. Dröm och vaka. Stockholm, 1901.

Phil 7082.116 — Henning, Hans. Der Traum. Wiesbaden, 1914.

Phil 7082.118 — Dietz, Paul Antoine. Mensch en droom. Leiden, 1935.

Phil 7082.120 — Foucault, Marcel. De somniis observationes et cogitationes. Thesis. Paris, 1901.

Phil 7082.122 — Meseguer, Pedro. El secreto de los sueños. Madrid, 1956.

Phil 7082.124 — Richardson, Phelps. A book on the interpretation of dreams. Worcester, 1904-05.

Phil 7082.126.1 — Saalfeld, Adam Friedrich William. Philosophical discourse on the nature of dreams. London, 1764.

Phil 7082.128 — Otaola, J.R. de. El análisis de los sueños. Barcelona, 195-?

Phil 7082.130 — What are dreams? N.Y., 1900.

Phil 7082.132 — Giessler, Carl Max. Aus den Tiefen des Traumlebens. Halle-Saale, 1890.

Phil 7082.134 — Scheruer, Karl Albert. Das Leben des Traums. Berlin, 1861.

Phil 7082 **Psychology - Parapsychology - Sleep phenomena - Dreaming - General works - cont**

Phil 7082.136 — Gray, Robert. The theory of dreams: in which an inquiry is made into the powers and faculties of the human mind. v.1-2. London, 1808.

Phil 7082.138 — Vold, John Mourly. Über den Traum. Leipzig, 1910-1912. 2v.

Phil 7082.140 — Ježower, Ignaz. Das Buch der Träume. Berlin, 1928.

Phil 7082.142 — Malcolm, Norman. Dreaming. London, 1959.

Phil 7082.142.5 — Lewis, Hywel David. Dreaming and experience. London, 1968.

Phil 7082.144 — Andreas-Friedrich, Ruth. Ursprung und Sinn der Träume. Zürich, 1958.

Phil 7082.146 — Simpson, David. A discourse on dreams and night-visions. Macclesfield, 1791.

Phil 7082.148 — Vaschide, Nicolas. La psychologie du rêve au point de une médical. Paris, 1902.

Phil 7082.150 — Siebenthal, Walter von. Die Wissenschaft vom Traum, Ergebnisse und Probleme. Berlin, 1953.

Phil 7082.152.2 — Simon, Paul Max. Le monde des rêves. 2. éd. Paris, 1888.

Phil 7082.154 — Maeder, Alphonse. The dream problem. N.Y., 1916.

Phil 7082.156 — Woods, Ralph Louis. The world of dreams. N.Y., 1947.

Phil 7082.158 — Dendy, Walter Cooper. On the phenomena of dreams. London, 1832.

Phil 7082.160 — Ellis, Havelock. The world of dreams. Boston, 1911.

Phil 7082.162 — Strümpell, Ludwig. Die Natur und Entstehung der Träume. Leipzig, 1874.

Phil 7082.164 — Delage, Yves. Le rêve. Paris, 1924.

Phil 7082.166A — Ratcliff, Arthur James John. A history of dreams. Boston, 1923.

Phil 7082.166B — Ratcliff, Arthur James John. A history of dreams. Boston, 1923.

Phil 7082.168 — Craig, Katherine Taylor. The fabric of dreams. N.Y., 1918.

Phil 7082.170 — Baege, Max Hermann. Naturgeschichte des Traums. Leipzig, 1928.

Phil 7082.172 — Daudet, Léon. Le rêve éveillé. Paris, 1926.

Phil 7082.174A — Fromm, Erich. The forgotten language. N.Y., 1951.

Phil 7082.174B — Fromm, Erich. The forgotten language. N.Y., 1951.

Phil 7082.176 — Klages, Ludwig. Vom Traumbewusstsein. Hamburg, 1952.

Phil 7082.178 — Becker, Raymond de. Les songes. Paris, 1958.

Phil 7082.180 — De Martino, Manfred F. Dreams and personality dynamics. Springfield, 1959.

Phil 7082.182 — Pongracz, Marion. Das Königreich der Träume. Wien, 1963.

Phil 7082.184 — French, Thomas Morton. Dream interpretation, a new approach. N.Y., 1964.

Phil 7082.186 — Nicoll, Maurice. Dream psychology. London, 1917.

Phil 7082.188.1 — Lowy, Samuel. Psychological and biological foundations of dream-interpretation. London, 1946.

Phil 7082.190 — Teillard, Ania. Le rêve, une porte sur le réel. Paris, 1951.

Phil 7082.190.5 — Teillard, Ania. Ce que disent les rêves. Paris, 1970.

Phil 7082.192 — Graevenitz, Jutta von. Bedeutung und Deutung des Traumes in der Psychotherapie. Darmstadt, 1968.

Phil 7082.194 — Mackenzie, Norman Jan. Dreams and dreaming. N.Y., 1965.

Phil 7082.196 — Boss, Medard. Des Traum und seine Auslegung. Bern, 1953.

Phil 7082.196.5 — Boss, Medard. The analysis of dreams. N.Y., 1958.

Phil 7082.198 — Il sogno e le civiltà umane. Bari, 1966.

Phil 7084 **Psychology - Parapsychology - Sleep phenomena - Dreaming - Special topics**

Phil 7084.2 — Fliess, Robert. The revival of interest in the dream. N.Y., 1953.

Phil 7084.4 — Garma, Ángel. Psicoanálisis de los sueños. Buenos Aires, 1940.

Phil 7084.4.5 — Sharpe, Ella Freeman. Dream analysis: a practical handbook for psycho-analysts. London, 1937.

Phil 7084.4.10 — Tridon, André. Psychoanalysis, sleep and dreams. N.Y., 1921.

Phil 7084.4.15 — Laforgue, René. Le rêve et la psychanalyse. Paris, 1926.

Phil 7084.4.20 — Micheloud, Pierrette. Dictionnaire psychanalytique des rêves. Paris, 1957.

Phil 7084.6 — Diepgen, Paul. Traum und Traumdeutung im medizinisch-naturwissenschaftliches Problem im Mittelalter. Berlin, 1912.

Phil 7084.8 — Kimmins, Charles William. Children's dreams. London, 1920.

Phil 7084.10 — Teillard, Ania. Traumsymbolik. Zürich, 1944.

Phil 7084.12.1 — Schultz-Hencke, Harald. Lehrbuch der Traumanalyse. 1. Aufl. Stuttgart, 1968.

Phil 7084.14 — Mahoney, Maria F. The meaning in dreams and dreaming. 1st ed. N.Y., 1966.

Phil 7084.14.8 — Wickwar, John William. Dreams: what they are and what they mean. 3d ed. London, 1918.

Phil 7084.16 — Green, George Henry. The terror-dream. London, 1927.

Phil 7084.18 — Klein, David Ballin. The experimental production of dreams during hypnosis. Austin, 1930.

Phil 7084.20 — Bjerre, Paul. Das Träumen als Heilungsweg der Seele. Zürich, 1936.

Phil 7084.22 — Allendy, René Félix. Les rêves et leur interpretation psychanalytique. Paris, 1926.

Phil 7084.24 — Layard, John Willoughby. The lady of the hare, being a study in the healing power of dreams. London, 1944.

Phil 7084.26 — Rivers, William Halse Rivers. Conflict and dream. London, 1923.

Phil 7084.28 — Rivers, William Halse Rivers. Dreams and primitive culture. Manchester, 1917-18.

Phil 7084.28.5 — Lincoln, Jackson Steward. The dream in primitive cultures. London, 1935.

Phil 7084.30.2 — Cook, John. A true relation of Mr. Justice Cook's passage by sea from Wexforel to Kinsaile, and of the great storm. 2d ed. London, 1652?

Phil 7084.32 — Moral reflections in a real dream. London, 1708.

Phil 7084.34 — Lewin, Bertram David. Dreams and the uses of regression. N.Y., 1958.

Phil 7084.36 — Abu Schirin. Das goldene ägyptisch-arabische Traumbuch. Heidenheim, 1960.

Phil 7084.38 — Hyppolite, Michelson Paul. La mentalité haitienne et le domaine du rêve. Port-au-Prince, 1965.

Phil 7084.40 — Loehrich, Rolf Rudolf. Oneirics and psychosomatics. McHenry, Ill., 1953.

Phil 7084.42 — Schumann, Hans Joachim von. Träume der Blinden vom Standpunkt der Phänomenologie. Basel, 1959.

Phil 7084.44 — Boehm, Arthur. Rätsel des Traumes und des Zufalls. Leipzig, 1920.

Phil 7084.46 — Stekel, Wilhelm. Die Träume der Dichter. Wiesbaden, 1912.

Phil 7084.48 — Becker, Raymond de. Rêve et sexualité. Paris, 1965.

Phil 7085   Psychology - Parapsychology - Sleep phenomena - Somnambulism - General works
Phil 7085.1   Mesnet, E. De l'automatisme. Paris, 1874.
Phil 7085.2   Belden, L.W. Account of Jane E. Rider somnambulist. Springfield, 1834.
Phil 7085.3   Wienholt, A. Seven lectures on somnambulism. Edinburgh, 1845.
Phil 7085.4   Reichenbacn, C.A. Somanmbulism and cramp. N.Y., 1860.
Phil 7085.5   Levade, L. A true account of a natural sleep walker. Edinburgh, 1792.
Phil 7085.6   Puysegur, A. M.J. Recherches...sur l'homme dans l'état de somnambulisme naturel. Paris, 1811.
Phil 7085.7   Bertrand, A. Traité du somnabulisme. Paris, 1823.
Phil 7085.8   Perry, L. de. Les somnambules extra-lucides. Paris, 1897.
Phil 7085.9   Steffanius, J.J. Dissertatio medica inauguralis de somnambulis. Basileae, 1701.
Phil 7085.10   Sadger, Isidor. Sleep walking and moon walking. N.Y., 1920.
Phil 7085.10.1   Sadger, Isidor. Über Nachtwandeln und Mondsucht. Nendeln, 1970.
Phil 7085.11.5   Debay, A. Mystères du sommeil et du magnétisme. 4. ed. Paris, 1845.

Phil 7103   Psychology - Parapsychology - Hypnotism - Bibliographies
Phil 7103.2   Dessoir, Max. Bibliographie des modernen Hypnotismus. Berlin, 1888.
Phil 7103.2.1   Dessoir, Max. Bibliographie des modernen Hypnotismus. Nachtrag. Berlin, 1890.
Phil 7103.4   Dureau, Alexis. Histoire de la médicine et des sciences occultes. Paris, 1869.

Phil 7106   Psychology - Parapsychology - Hypnotism - History - General works
Phil 7106.2   Bergasse, Nicolas. Considérations sur le magnétisme animal. La Hague, 1784.
Phil 7106.4   South, Thomas. Early magnetism in its higher relations to humanity. London, 1846.
Phil 7106.5   Marks, Robert. The story of hypnotism. N.Y., 1947.
Phil 7106.6   Harte, Richard. Hypnotism and the doctors. London, 1903.
Phil 7106.10   Abnormal hypnotic phenomena, a survey of nineteenth century cases. London, 1967[1968] 4v.

Phil 7108   Psychology - Parapsychology - Hypnotism - History - Local (Geographic Table A)
Phil 7108.372   Darnton, Robert. Mesmerism and the end of the Enlightenment in France. Cambridge, 1968.
Phil 7108.388   Avé-Lallemant, F.C.B. Der Magnetismus mit seinen mystischen Verirrungen. Leipzig, 1881.

Phil 7109.101 - .399   Psychology - Parapsychology - Hypnotism - History - Biographies of hypnotists - Individual (A-Z, 299 scheme, by person)
Phil 7109.195   Moniz, Egas. O padre Faria na história do hipnotismo. Lisboa, 1925.

Phil 7111 - 7136   Psychology - Parapsychology - Hypnotism - General treatises - Individual authors (A-Z)
Phil 7112.5   Bernstien, Abraham Emmanuel. Explorations of a hypnotist. London, 1959.
Phil 7113.5   Clements, John. Hypnotism; masterpiece of myths. Manchester, 1966.
Phil 7118.5   Hollander, Bernard. Methods and uses of hypnosis and self-hypnosis. Hollywood, Calif. 1966.
Phil 7118.10   Hilgard, Josephine Rohrs. Personality and hypnosis. Chicago, 1970.
Phil 7120.2   Jagot, Paul Clément. Traité méthodique de magnétisme personnel. Paris, 1969.
Phil 7123.2   Mabru, G. Les magnetiseurs, jugés par eux-mêmes. Paris, 1858.

Phil 7140   Psychology - Parapsychology - Hypnotism - Special topics - Suggestion and autosuggestion
Phil 7140.01   Pamphlet box. Psychology. Suggestion.
Phil 7140.1   Souriau, P. La suggestion dans l'art. Paris, 1893.
Phil 7140.2A   Sidis, B. The psychology of suggestion. N.Y., 1898.
Phil 7140.2B   Sidis, B. The psychology of suggestion. N.Y., 1898.
Phil 7140.3   Stoll, O. Suggestions und Hypnotismus...Volkerpsychologie. Leipzig, 1894.
Phil 7140.4   Binet, A. La suggestibilité. Paris, 1900.
Phil 7140.5   Lévy, Alfred. La psychose d'influence. Thèse. Paris, 1914.
Phil 7140.6   Loryea, J.H. Is man a free agent? London, 1902.
Phil 7140.8   Schrenck-Notzing, Albert. Die Suggestions-Therapie. Stuttgart, 1892.
Phil 7140.8.5   Schmidkung, Hans. Psychologie der Suggestion. Stuttgart, 1892.
Phil 7140.10   Barrows, C.M. Suggestion instead of medicine. Boston, 1900.
Phil 7140.11   Tietjens, E. Die Desugestion; ihre Bedeutung und Auswertung. Berlin, 1928.
Phil 7140.11.5   Tietjens, E. Desugestion for the attainment of health. London, 1931.
Phil 7140.12   Ebbard, R.J. How to acquire and strengthen will-power. London, 1905.
Phil 7140.105   Bekhterev, W.M. Die Bedeutung der Suggestion. Wiesbaden, 1905.
Phil 7140.106   Krebs, Stanley le Fevre. The law of suggestion. 1st ed. Chicago, 1906.
Phil 7140.107   Brügelmann, W. Die Behandlung der kranken durch Suggestion. Leipzig, 1906.
Phil 7140.110   Gaupp, Robert. Wahn und Irrtum im Leben der Völker. Tübingen, 1916.
Phil 7140.113   Meijer, A.F. Experimenten omtrent suggestibilteit bij senuw- en zielszieken. Amsterdam, 1919.
Phil 7140.115   Baudouin, C. Suggestion and autosuggestion. London, 1920.
Phil 7140.115.3   Baudouin, C. Suggestion and autosuggestion. London, 1921.
Phil 7140.115.5   Baudouin, C. Suggestion and autosuggestion. N.Y., 1921.
Phil 7140.115.15   Baudouin, C. Suggestion und autosuggestion. Dresden, 1924.
Phil 7140.115.20   Baudouin, C. Suggestion et autosuggestion. 5. ed. Neuchâtel, 1938.
Phil 7140.116   Coué, Émile. Selfmastery through conscious autosuggestion. N.Y., 1922.
Phil 7140.116.5   Coué, Émile. My method. Garden City, 1923.
Phil 7140.116.7   Coué, Émile. How to practice suggestion and autosuggestion. N.Y., 1923.
Phil 7140.116.9   Coué, Émile. Ce que j'ai fait. Nancy, 1924.
Phil 7140.116.11   Coué, Émile. Conscious auto-suggestion. London, 1924.
Phil 7140.116.13   Coué, Émile. Conscious auto-suggestion. N.Y., 1924.

Phil 7140   Psychology - Parapsychology - Hypnotism - Special topics - Suggestion and autosuggestion - cont.
Phil 7140.116.15   Coué, Émile. The world's greatest power. pt.3-6. London, 192-. 2 pam.
Phil 7140.116.50   Macnaghten, H. Emile Coué, the man and his work. N.Y., 1922.
Phil 7140.116.51   Baudouin, C. Emile Coué and his life-work. N.Y., 1923.
Phil 7140.116.55   Baudouin, C. Der Couéismus. Darmstadt, 1926.
Phil 7140.116.70   Brooks, C.H. The practice of autosuggestion by the method of Emile Coué. N.Y., 1922.
Phil 7140.116.71   Brooks, C.H. The practice of autosuggestion by the method of Emile Coué. London, 1922.
Phil 7140.116.72   Brooks, C.H. The practice of autosuggestion by the method of Emile Coué. N.Y., 1922.
Phil 7140.116.73A   Brooks, C.H. The practice of autosuggestion by the method of Emile Coué. N.Y., 1922.
Phil 7140.116.73B   Brooks, C.H. The practice of autosuggestion by the method of Emile Coué. N.Y., 1922.
Phil 7140.116.75   Seeling, Otto. Der Couéismus. Diss. Giessen, 1926.
Phil 7140.116.80   Émile Coué: sa méthode, son esprit, son influence. Paris, 1928.
Phil 7140.118   Thamiry, E. De l'influence: étude psychologique. Thèse. Lille, 1921.
Phil 7140.118.2   Thamiry, E. De l'influence: étude psychologique, métaphysique, pédagogique. Lille, 1922.
Phil 7140.119   Vigouroux, A. Le contagion mentale. Paris, 1905.
Phil 7140.120   Dolonne, A. Self healing by autosuggestion. London, 1923.
Phil 7140.121.5   Gulat-Wellenburg. Das Wunder der Autosuggestion. Kempten im Allgäu, 1925.
Phil 7140.122   Yoritomo-Tashi. Influence; how to exert it. N.Y., 1916.
Phil 7140.123   Straus, Erwin. Wesen und Vorgang der Suggestion. Berlin, 1925.
Phil 7140.124   Friedrichs, T. Zur Psychologie der Hypnose und der Suggestion. Stuttgart, 1922.
Phil 7140.125   Lestchinski, A. Essai médico-psychologique sur l'autosuggestion. Neuchâtel, 1924.
Phil 7140.126   Graeter, Karl. Menschenleiden als Lebensgeheimnis...Autosuggestion. Kandern, 1926.
Phil 7140.127   Baerwald, Richard. Psychologie der Selbstverteidigung in Klampf-, Not- und Krankheitzeiten. Leipzig, 1927.
Phil 7140.128   Arnold, Hans. Schulmedizin und Wunderkuren. Leipzig, 1892.
Phil 7140.131   Ferri, N.A. The behavior of health. Boston, 1937.
Phil 7140.132   Pierce, Frederick. Mobilizing the mid-brain. N.Y., 1924.
Phil 7140.133   Pöll, Wilhelm. Die Suggestion. München, 1951.
Phil 7140.134   Liebetrau, H. Macht und Geheimnis der Suggestion. Basel, 1951.
Phil 7140.140   Slavson, S.R. An introduction to group therapy. N.Y., 1943.
Phil 7140.140.6   Slavson, S.R. An introduction to group therapy. N.Y., 1954.

Phil 7149   Psychology - Parapsychology - Hypnotism - Special topics - Other special
Phil 7149.2   Duckworth, J. Herbert. Autosuggestion and its personal application. N.Y., 1922.

Phil 7150   Psychology - Parapsychology - Suicide [Discontinued]
Phil 7150.01   Pamphlet box. Suicide.
Phil 7150.1   Brierre de Boismont, A.J.F. Du suicide. Paris, 1856.
Phil 7150.1.2   Brierre de Boismont, A.J.F. Du suicide et la folie suicide. 2. éd. Paris, 1865.
Phil 7150.2   Geiger, K.A. Der Selbstmord. Augsburg, 1888.
Phil 7150.3   Strahan, S.A.K. Suicide and insanity. London, 1893.
Phil 7150.5   Winslow, F. Anatomy of suicide. London, 1840.
Phil 7150.6   Motta, Emilio. Bibliografia del suicidio. Bellinzona, 1890.
Phil 7150.8   La Rue, F.A.H. Du suicide. Québec, 1859.
Phil 7150.9.5   Morsell, H. Suicide. N.Y., 1882.
Phil 7150.10   Hertog, Mattheus M. De zedelijke waardeering den zelfmoord. 's Gravenhage, 1913.
Phil 7150.11   Douay, Edmond. Suicide, ou La mort volontaire. Paris, 1870.
Phil 7150.12   Dabadie, F. Les suicidés illustrés. Paris, 1859.
Phil 7150.13   Taverni, Romeo. Del suicidio massime In Italia nel quinquennio 1866-70. Roma, 1873.
Phil 7150.14   Kürten, O. Statistik des Selbstmordes im Königreich Sachsen. Leipzig, 1913.
Phil 7150.15   Baker, W.E. Diary of a suicide. N.Y., 1913.
Phil 7150.16   Moreau, Jacques. Du suicide chez les enfants. Thèse. Paris, 1906.
Htn   Phil 7150.17*   Adams, John. An essay concerning self-murther. London, 1700.
Phil 7150.18   Altavilla, Enrico. La psicologia del suicidio. Napoli, 1910.
Phil 7150.19   Tapia, Ambrosios. Los suicidios en Cataluña y en general en toda España. Barcelona, 1900.
Htn   Phil 7150.20*   Lathrop, Joseph. Two sermons on the atrocity of suicide. Suffield, 1805.
Phil 7150.21.2   Bayet, Albert. Le suicide et la morale. Thèse. Paris, 1922.
Phil 7150.22   Frenay, A.D. The suicide problem in the United States. Diss. Boston, 1927.
Phil 7150.23   Rost, Hans. Bibliographie des Selbstmords. Augsburg, 1927.
Phil 7150.24   Cavan, R.S. Suicide. Chicago, 1928.
Phil 7150.25   Hoffman, F.L. Suicide problems. Newark, 1927.
Phil 7150.26   Halbwachs, M. Les causes du suicide. Paris, 1930.
Phil 7150.27.5   Durkheim, É. Le suicide. Paris, 1930.
Phil 7150.27.15   Durkheim, É. Le suicide. Paris, 1960.
Phil 7150.27.20   Durkheim, É. Suicide; a study in sociology. Glencoe, 1962.
Phil 7150.28   Relaçaõ de hum notavel caso. Lisboa, 1755?
Phil 7150.29   Blondel, Charles. Le suicide. Strasbourg, 1933.
Phil 7150.30   Bula, C.A. Analisis estadistico del suicidio. Rosario, 1934.
Phil 7150.31   Menninger, Karl Augustus. Man against himself. N.Y., 1938.
Phil 7150.32   Fedden, Henry R. Suicide, a social and historical study. London, 1938.
Phil 7150.33   Less, G. Vom Selbstmorde. Göttingen, 1786.
Phil 7150.34   Berdiaev, N.A. O samoubiistvie. Paris, 1931.
Phil 7150.35   Palazzo, D. Il suicidio sotto l'aspetto fisiopatologico. Napoli, 1953.
Phil 7150.36   Szittya, E. Selbstmörder. Leipzig, 1925.
Phil 7150.38   Shneidman, Edwin S. Clues to suicide. N.Y., 1957.
Phil 7150.38.5   Shneidman, Edwin S. Essays in self-destruction. N.Y., 1967.
Phil 7150.40   Meyuard, L. Le suicide. Paris, 1958.

Phil 7150   Psychology - Parapsychology - Suicide [Discontinued] - cont.

Phil 7150.42   Kruijt, Cornuijtus Simon. Zilfmoord. Assen, 1960.
Phil 7150.44   Touraine, Yves. Le suicide ascétique. Paris, 1960.
Phil 7150.46   Berdiaev, N.A. Le suicide. Paris, 1953?
Phil 7150.47   Spain. Instituto Nacional de Estadística. El suicidio en
                España durante medio siglo. Madrid, 1959.
Phil 7150.48   Fondazione Piero Varenna, Milan. Assistenza medico sociale
                ai tenfati suicide. Milano, 1959.
Phil 7150.49   Aarberon, Norman. The cry for help. N.Y., 1961.
Phil 7150.50   Ringel, Erwin. Neue Untersuchungen zum Selbstmordproblem.
                Wien, 1961.
Phil 7150.51   Fuellkrug, Gerhard. Der Selbstmord. Schwerin, 1919.
Phil 7150.52   Siegmund, Georg. Sein oder Nichtsein. Trier, 1961.
Phil 7150.53   Dublin, L.I. Suicide. N.Y., 1963.
Phil 7150.54   Thakur, Upendra. The history of suicide in India. 1st ed.
                Delhi, 1963.
Phil 7150.55   Gibbs, J.P. Status integration and suicide. Eugene,
                Oreg., 1964.
Phil 7150.57   Hendin, H. Suicide and Scandinavia. N.Y., 1964.
Phil 7150.58   Kobler, Arthur. The end of hope. N.Y., 1964.
Phil 7150.59   Ellis, E.R. Traitor within: our suicide problem. 1st ed.
                Garden City, N.Y., 1961.
Phil 7150.60   Porterfield, Austin Larimore. Cultures of violence; a
                study of the tragic man in society. Fort Worth,
                Texas, 1965.
Phil 7150.61   Balluseck, Lothar von. Selbstmord. Bad Godesberg, 1965.
Phil 7150.62   Thomas, Klaus. Handbuch der Selbstmordverhütung.
                Stuttgart, 1964.
Phil 7150.63F   Meer, Fatima. Suicide in Durban. Durban, 1964.
Phil 7150.64   Douglas, Jack D. The social meanings of suicide.
                Princeton, 1967.
Phil 7150.65   Centro Nazionale di Prevenzione e Difesa Sociale. Suicidio
                e tentato suicidio. Milano, 1967.
Phil 7150.65.10 Convegno di Studio su Suicidio eTentato Suicidio in
                Italia, Milan, 1967. Suicidio e tentato suicidio in
                Italia. Milano, 1968.
Phil 7150.70   Farber, Maurice. Theory of suicide. N.Y., 1968.
Phil 7150.75   Ghysbrecht, Paul. Der Doppelselbstmord. München, 1967.
Phil 7150.80   Haffter, Carl. Selbstmordversuche bei Kindern und
                Jugendlichen. Basel, 1966.
Phil 7150.85   Poeldinger, Walter. Die Abschätzung der Suizidalität.
                Bern, 1968.
Phil 7150.90   Bulletin of suicidology. Washington. 1,1967+
Phil 7150.95   Maris, Ronald W. Social forces in urban suicide.
                Homewood, 1969.
Phil 7150.98   Hendin, Herbert. Black suicide. N.Y., 1969.
Phil 7150.100   Speijer, Nico. Het zelfmoordvraagstuk. Arnhem, 1969.
Phil 7150.105   On the nature of suicide. 1st ed. San Francisco, 1969.

**Phil 7158   Psychology - Parapsychology - Extrasensory perception - History - Local
(Geographic Table A)**
Phil 7158.715   MacDermot, Violet. The cult of the seer in the ancient
                Middle East. Berkeley, 1971.

**Phil 7159.1 - .99   Psychology - Parapsychology - Extrasensory perception -
History - Biographies - Collected**
Phil 7159.8   Bjornstad, James. Twentieth century prophecy: Jeane Dixon,
                Edgar Cayce. Minneapolis, 1969.

**Phil 7159.101 - .399   Psychology - Parapsychology - Extrasensory
perception - History - Biographies - Individual (A-Z, 299 scheme, by
person)**
Phil 7159.152   Millard, Joseph. Edgar Cayce, mystery man of miracles.
                N.Y., 1956.
Phil 7159.173   Montgomery, Ruth S. A gift of prophecy: the phenomenal
                Jeane Dixon. N.Y., 1965.
Phil 7159.260   Logan, Daniel. The reluctant prophet. 1st ed. Garden
                City, N.Y., 1968.

**Phil 7160   Psychology - Parapsychology - Extrasensory perception - General
treatises - Collected authors**
Phil 7160.5   Schmeidler, Gertrude R. Extra-sensory perception.
                N.Y., 1969.

**Phil 7162   Psychology - Parapsychology - Extrasensory perception - General
treatises - Individual authors (By date, e.g. .265 for 1965)**
Phil 7162.261.1 Walker, Kenneth M. The extra-sensory mind. N.Y., 1965.
Phil 7162.265   Lethbridge, Thomas C. E.S.P.; beyond time and distance.
                London, 1965.
Phil 7162.266   Hansel, C.E.M. E.S.P.; a scientific evaluation.
                N.Y., 1966.
Phil 7162.267.1 Holzer, Hans W. ESP and you. 1st ed. N.Y., 1968.
Phil 7162.267.5 Rhine, Louisa E. ESP in life and lab. N.Y., 1967.

**Phil 7180   Psychology - Parapsychology - Extrasensory perception - Special types -
Precognition**
Phil 7180.2   Frankenau, Rasmus. Tildragelser under ahnelser.
                Kjøbenhavn, 1804.

Phil 7225   Psychology - Parapsychology - Daydreams - General works
Phil 7225.2A   Varendonck, Julien. The psychology of day-dreams.
                London, 1921.
Phil 7225.2B   Varendonck, Julien. The psychology of day-dreams.
                London, 1921.

Phil 7230   Psychology - Parapsychology - Trance [Discontinued]
Phil 7230.1*   Braid, J. Observations on trance. London, 1850.
Phil 7230.2   Mitchell, G.W. X+Y=Z, or The sleeping preacher.
                N.Y., 1877.
Phil 7230.4.2* Devotional somnium. N.Y., 1815.
Phil 7230.7   Bucke (R.M.) Memorial Society for the Study of Religious
                Experience. Trance and possession states. Montreal? 1968.

Phil 8001 - 8026   Esthetics - Periodicals (A-Z)
Phil 8002.3   British journal of aesthetics. London. 2,1962+ 9v.
Phil 8003.2   Chronika aisthētikès. Athēna. 1,1962+ 2v.
Phil 8005.5   Estetika. Praha. 2,1965+ 6v.
Phil 8005.7   Esztetikai fuzetek. Budapest. 1,1934
Phil 8005.8   Esztetikai szemle. Budapest. 1-9,1935-1943 3v.
Phil 8005.9   Estetiku, v zhizn'. Sverdlovsk. 2,1967+
Phil 8005.10   Estetika i zhizn! Moskva. 1,1971+
Phil 8010.3   Journal of aesthetics and art criticism. N.Y. 6,1947+
                20v.
Phil 8010.5   The journal of aesthetic education. Champaigne, Ill.
                1,1966+ 5v.
Phil 8015.2   O sovremennoi burzhuaznoi estetike. Moskva. 2,1965+
Phil 8019.5   Studia estetyczne. Warszawa. 2,1965+ 6v.
Phil 8019.10   Studi di estetica. Bologna. 1,1965+

Phil 8001 - 8026   Esthetics - Periodicals (A-Z) - cont.
Phil 8019.15   Sotsialisticheskii realizm i problemy estetiki. Moskva.
                1,1967+
Phil 8022.5   Voprosy estetiki [sbornik statei]. Saratov. 1,1963+
Phil 8026.5   Zur Kritik der bürgerlichen Ideologie. Berlin. 1,1971+

Phil 8030   Esthetics - Reference works - Bibliographies
Phil 8030.2   Chandler, A.R. A bibliography of experimental aesthetics,
                1865-1932. Columbus, 1933.
Phil 8030.3   Chandler, A.R. A bibliography of psychology and
                experimental aesthetics, 1864-1937. Berkeley, 1938.
Phil 8030.4   Gayley, Charles. A guide to the literature of aesthetics.
                Berkeley, 1890.
Phil 8030.5   Hammond, W.A. A bibliography of aesthetics and of the
                philosophy of the fine arts from 1900-1932. N.Y., 1934.
Phil 8030.6   Apresian, Z.G. Estetika; bibliografiia, 1956-60.
                Moskva, 1963.
Phil 8030.7   Mandel'shtam, Roza S. Marksistskoe iskusstvovedenie.
                Moskva, 1929. Ann Arbor, 1965.
Phil 8030.8   Kiell, Norman. Psychiatry and psychology in the visual
                arts and aesthetics. Madison, 1965.

Phil 8050   Esthetics - History of esthetic theory - General works
Phil 8050.5   Geschichte der Ästhetik. Köln, 1962.
Phil 8050.10   Akademiia Nauk SSSR. Institut Filosofii. Iz istorii
                esteticheskoi mysli srednevekov'ia.
                Moskva, 1961.
Phil 8050.15   Akademiia Nauk SSSR. Institut Filosofii. Iz istorii
                esteticheskoi mysli novogo vremeni. Moskva, 1959.
Phil 8050.20   Akademiia Khudozhestv SSSR. Institut Teorii i Istorii
                Iskusstva. Istoriia estetiki. Moskva, 1962- 5v.
Phil 8050.21   Ovsiannikov, M.F. Ocherki istorii esteticheskikh uchenii.
                Moskva, 1963.
Phil 8050.21.2 Ovsiannikov, M.F. Kurze Geschichte der Ästhetik.
                Berlin, 1966.
Phil 8050.22   Croce, Benedetto. Storia dell'estetica per saggi.
                Bari, 1942.
Phil 8050.23   Trudu, Luciano. Soggettività e oggettività del bello.
                Padova, 1963.
Phil 8050.24   Buyer, Raymond. Histoire de l'esthétique. Paris, 1961.
Phil 8050.26   Tatarkiewicz, Władysław. Historia estetyki.
                Wrocław, 1960. 2v.
Phil 8050.28   Chambers, Frank. The history of taste. N.Y., 1932.
Phil 8050.28.5 Chambers, Frank. Cycles of taste. Cambridge, 1928.
Phil 8050.30   Utitz, Emil. Geschichte der Ästhetik. Berlin, 1932.
Phil 8050.32   Weisbach, Werner. Stilbegriffe und Stilphänomene.
                Wien, 1957.
Phil 8050.34   Friedlaender, L. Über die Entstehung und Entwicklung des
                Gefühls für das Romantische in der Natur. Leipzig, 1873.
Phil 8050.36   Bergmann, E. Geschichte der Ästhetik und Kunstphilosophie.
                Leipzig, 1914.
Phil 8050.38   Bosanquet, B. A history of aesthetic. London, 1892.
Phil 8050.38.5 Bosanquet, B. A history of aesthetic. London, 1922.
Phil 8050.40   Schulemann, G. Ästhetik. Breslau, 1930.
Phil 8050.41   Ljunggren, G. Framställning af de förnämsta esthetiska
                systemerna. Lund, 1856. 2v.
Phil 8050.43   Ljunggren, G. Några punkter ur läran om det natursköna.
                Lund, 1852.
Phil 8050.44   Kampanēs, Aristos. Historia tōn aisthētikōn theōrion.
                Athēna, 1936.
Phil 8050.46   Hermann, C. Die Ästhetik in ihrer Geschichte und als
                wissenschaftliches System. Leipzig, 1876.
Phil 8050.47   Begg, W.P. The development of taste, and other studies in
                aesthetics. Glasgow, 1887.
Phil 8050.48   Burger, Fritz. Weltanschauungsprobleme und Lebenssysteme in
                der Kunst der Vergangenheit. München, 1918.
Phil 8050.49   Baer, Hans. Grundriss eines Systems. Strassburg, 1913.
Phil 8050.50   Egger, Alais. Vorschule der Ästhetik. Wien, 1872.
Phil 8050.51   Gauckler, T.G. Le beau et son histoire. Paris, 1873.
Phil 8050.52   Fasola, Guista Nicco. Della critica. Firenze, 1941.
Phil 8050.53   Frey, Dagobert. Grundlegung zu einer vergleichenden
                Kunstwissenschaft. Innsbruck, 1949.
Phil 8050.54   Flaccus, L.W. Artists and thinkers. N.Y., 1916.
Phil 8050.55   Gori, Gino. Studi di estetica dell'irrazionale.
                Milano, 1921.
Phil 8050.56   Fischer, Ernest. Von der Notwendigkeit der Kunst.
                Dresden, 1959.
Phil 8050.57   Hauch, J.C. Afhandlinger og aesthetiske betragtninger.
                Kjøbenhavn, 1855.
Phil 8050.57.5 Hauch, J.C. Aesthetiske afhandlinger og recensioner.
                Kjøbenhavn,1869. 1861.
Phil 8050.57.10 Hauch, J.C. Afhandlinger og aesthetiske betragtninger.
                Kjøbenhavn, 1869.
Phil 8050.58   Bruyne, E. de. Geschiedenis van de aesthetica.
                Antwerpen, 1951. 5v.
Phil 8050.59   Spitzer, Hugo. Kritische studien zur Ästhetik der
                Gegenwart. Wien, 1897.
Phil 8050.60   Spoerri, T. Die Struktur der Existenz. Zürich, 1951.
Phil 8050.61   Voigtländer, E. Zur Gesetzlichkeit der abendländischen
                Kunst. Bonn, 1921.
Phil 8050.63   Propris, A de. Storia degli orientamenti artistici.
                Roma, 1953.
Phil 8050.64   Krestovskaia, L.A. La laideur dans l'art à travers les
                âges. Paris, 1947.
Phil 8050.65.5 Kayser, W. The grotesque in art and literature.
                Bloomington, 1963.
Phil 8050.67   Howard, W.G. Ut pictura poesis; a historical
                investigation. Cambridge, 1909.
Phil 8050.68   Zonta, Giuseppe. Manualetto d'estetica. Torino, 1925.
Phil 8050.69   Vlaanderen, Andre. Het zien van kunst en de kunst van het
                zien. Amsterdam, 1952.
Phil 8050.70   Kallen, H.M. Art and freedom; a historical and
                biographical interpretation. N.Y., 1942. 2v.
Phil 8050.72   McMahon, Amos. Preface to an American philosophy of art.
                Chicago, 1945.
Phil 8050.73   Nauwelaerts, M.A.M.E. Uren van schoonheid.
                Antwerpen, 1946.
Phil 8050.74   Melchers, H. Von Kunst und Künstlern. München, 1953.
Phil 8050.75   Nohl, H. Die ästhetische Wirklichkeit; eine Einfuhrung. 2.
                Aufl. Frankfurt, 1954.
Phil 8050.76   Mascello, Leonardo. Aestheticà di silencio. Rio de
                Janeiro, 1919.
Phil 8050.77   Utitz, Emil. Aesthetik. Berlin, 1923.
Phil 8050.78   Gilbert, Mesk. A history of aesthetics. N.Y., 1939.
Phil 8050.79   Panofsky, E. Idea. 2. Aufl. Berlin, 1960.
Phil 8050.80   Ramos, S. Estudios de estetica. México, 1963.
Phil 8050.81   Ekman, Rolf. Estetikens historia från sjuttonhundratalets
                början till och med Goethe. Lund, 1963.

Phil 8050   Esthetics - History of esthetic theory - General works - cont.

Phil 8050.82 — Giacchelti, Vincenzo. Il giardino della mala biscia. Firenze, 1965.
Phil 8050.83 — Novák, Mirko. Otázky estetiky v přítainnosti i minulosti. Praha, 1963.
Phil 8050.84 — Miele, Franco. Teoria e storia dell'estetica. Milano, 1965.
Phil 8050.85 — Beardsley, Monroe Curtis. Aesthetics from classical Greece to the present. 1. ed. n.p., n.d.
Phil 8050.86 — Trofimov, Pavel S. Estetika i iskusstvo. Moskva, 1966.
Phil 8050.90 — Gehrig, Hans. Wesen und Bestand ästhetischer Bildung in Geschichte und Begenwart. Zürich, 1964.
Phil 8050.91 — Fazio-Allmayer, Bruna. Richerche di estetica e il guidizio stoico. Bologna, 1968.
VPhil 8050.92 — Kelecsényi, János. Az esztétika alapvetí elvei. Budapest, 1913.
Phil 8050.95 — Tatarkiewicz, Wladysław. History of aesthetics. The Hague, 1970.

Phil 8060   Esthetics - History of esthetic theory - Special periods - Ancient - General

Phil 8060.2 — Müller, Eduard. Geschichte der Theorie der Kunst. v.1-2. Breslau, 1834-37.
Phil 8060.3 — Lapcević, Draguicha. La philosophie de l'art classique. Paris, 1927.
Phil 8060.4 — Asmus, V.F. Antichnye mysliteli ob iskusstve. 2. izd. Moskva, 1938.
Phil 8060.5 — O'Callaghan, J. Las tres categorías estétecas de la cultura clásica. Madrid, 1960.
Phil 8060.6 — Standinger, J. Das schöne als Weltanschauung. Wien, 1948.
Phil 8060.7 — Motz, H. Über die Empfindung der Naturschönheit bei den Alten. Leipzig, 1865.
Phil 8060.8 — Krueger, J. Ästhetik der Antike. Berlin, 1964.

Phil 8062   Esthetics - History of esthetic theory - Special periods - Ancient - Greek

Phil 8062.2 — Warry, John Gibson. Greek aesthetic theory...in...Plato and Aristotle. London, 1962.
Phil 8062.3 — Grand, Y. Recherche des principes d'une philosophie des arts, dits d'imitation chez Platon, Aristote et Plotin. Lausanne, 1952.
Phil 8062.4 — Walter, Julius. Die Geschichte der Ästhetik im Altertum. Leipzig, 1893.
Phil 8062.5 — Taine, H.A. Philosophie de l'art en Grèce. Paris, 1869.
Phil 8062.6 — Utitz, Emil. Bemerkungen zur altgriechischen Kunsttheorie. Berlin, 1959.
Phil 8062.7 — Perpeet, Wilhelm. Antike Ästhetik. Freiburg, 1961.
Phil 8062.8 — Losev, Aleksei F. Istoriia antichnoi estetiki. Moskva, 1969.
Phil 8062.9 — Schaper, Eva. Prelude to aesthetics. London, 1968.

Phil 8064   Esthetics - History of esthetic theory - Special periods - Ancient - Roman

Phil 8064.2 — Wiseman, N. On the perception of natural beauty by the ancients and moderns. London, 1856.

Phil 8070   Esthetics - History of esthetic theory - Special periods - Medieval - General

Phil 8070.2 — Bruyne, Edgar de. Études d'esthétique médiévale. Brugge, 1946. 3v.
Phil 8070.2.10 — Bruyne, Edgar de. The esthetics of the Middle Ages. N.Y., 1969.

Phil 8080   Esthetics - History of esthetic theory - Special periods - Modern - General

Phil 8080.2 — Oribe, Emilia. Tres ideales esteticos. Montevideo, 1958.
Phil 8080.3 — Meumann, Ernst. Einführung in die Ästhetik der Gegenwart. Leipzig, 1908.
Phil 8080.4 — Listowel, William Francis Hare. A critical history of modern aesthetics. London, 1933.
Phil 8080.4.5 — Listowel, William Francis Hare. Modern aesthetics. N.Y., 1967.
Phil 8080.6 — Anceschi, Luciano. Autonomia ed eteronomia dell'arte. Firenze, 1936.
Phil 8080.7 — Ballo, Guido. I miti delle Poetiche. Milano, 1959.
Phil 8080.8 — Cossio del Pomar, F. Critica de arte de Baudelaire à Malraux. México, 1956.
Phil 8080.9 — Anceschi, Luciano. D. Hume e i presupposti empiristici della estetica kantiana. Milano, 1956.
Phil 8080.10 — Farnsworth, E.C. The ideales and tendencies of modern art. Portland, 1917.
Phil 8080.11 — Kayser, Wolfgang. Das Groteske, seine Gestaltung in Malerei und Dichtung. Oldenburg, 1957.
Phil 8080.11.1 — Kayser, Wolfgang. Das Groteske in Malerei und Dichtung. Reinbek, 1960.
Phil 8080.12 — Hurtado, L. Espacio y tiempo en el arte actual. Buenos Aires, 1941.
Phil 8080.13 — Redeker, Horst. Die Klassische Kulturkritik und das Dilemma der Dekadenz. Berlin, 1958.
Phil 8080.14 — Ludács, G. Adalékok az estétika történetehez. Budapest, 1953.
Phil 8080.14.5 — Ludács, G. Beitrage zur Geschichte der Ästhetik. Berlin, 1954.
Phil 8080.15 — Plebe, Armando. Processo all'estetica. Firenze, 1959.
Phil 8080.16 — Meumann, Ernst. A estética contemporânea. 3. ed. Coimbia, 1930.
Phil 8080.17 — Hannay, Howard. Roger Fry and other essays. London, 1937.
Phil 8080.18 — Grenier, Jean. L'imitation et les principes de l'esthétique classique. Paris, 1963.
Phil 8080.20 — Hermann, Rolf-Dieter. Künstler und Interpret; zur Modernen Ästhetik. Bern, 1967.
Phil 8080.24 — Kreis, Friedrich. Die Autonomie des Ästhetischen in der neuren Philosophie. Tübingen, 1922.

Phil 8082   Esthetics - History of esthetic theory - Special periods - Modern - Renaissance

Phil 8082.2 — Rocio, Montano. L'estetica del rinascimento e del Barocco. Napoli, 1962.
Phil 8082.4 — Ossola, Carlo. Autunno del Rinascimento. Firenze, 1971.

Phil 8084   Esthetics - History of esthetic theory - Special periods - Modern - 16th century

Phil 8084.2F — Prodi, Paolo. Ricerche sulla teorica delle arti figurative nella riforma cattalica. Roma, 1962.

Phil 8088   Esthetics - History of esthetic theory - Special periods - Modern - 18th century

Phil 8088.2 — Alfieri, V. L'estetica dall'illuminismo. Milano, 1957.
Phil 8088.3 — Folkierski, W. Entre le classicisme et le romantisme. Cracovie, 1925.
Phil 8088.4 — Will, F. Intelligible beauty in aesthetic thought. Tübingen, 1958.
Phil 8088.6 — Assunto, Rosario. Stagionie ragioni nell'estetica del settecento. Milano, 1967.
Phil 8088.8 — Morawski, Stefan. Studia z historii myśli estetycznej XVII:i XIX wieku. Warszawa, 1961.

Phil 8090   Esthetics - History of esthetic theory - Special periods - Modern - 19th century

Phil 8090.2 — Zabel, M.D. The romantic idealism of art, 1800-1848. Chicago, 1938.
Phil 8090.3 — Needham, Harold. Le développement de l'esthétique sociologique en France et en Angleterre au XIX siècle. Paris, 1926.
Phil 8090.4 — Trofimov, P.S. Ocherki istorii marksistskoi estetiki. Moskva, 1963.
Phil 8090.5 — Johnson, Robert Vincent. Aestheticism. London, 1969.
Phil 8090.8 — Volpe, Galvo della. Crisi dell'estetica romantica. Roma, 1963.
Phil 8090.10 — Koopmann, Helmut. Beiträge zur Theorie der Künste im 19. Jahrhundert. Frankfurt, 1971-

Phil 8092   Esthetics - History of esthetic theory - Special periods - Modern - 20th century

Phil 8092.2 — Koch, Hans. Marxismus und Ästhetik. Berlin, 1962.
Phil 8092.4 — Assunto, Rosario. Teoremi e problemi di estetica contemporanea. Milano, 1960.
Phil 8092.5 — Gunzenhaeuser, R. Ästhetisches Mass und Ästhetische Information. Hamburg, 1962.
Phil 8092.6 — Bayer, R. L'esthétique mondiale au XXe siècle. Paris, 1961.
Phil 8092.7 — Gilbert, Katherine Everett. Studies in recent aesthetic. Chapel Hill, 1927.
Phil 8092.8 — Zum Felde, A. Estetica del novecientos. Buenos Aires, 1928?
Phil 8092.9 — Moholy-Nagy, L. Vision in motion. Chicago, 1956.
Phil 8092.10 — Morpurgo Taghabue, G. L'esthétique contemporaine. Milan, 1960.
Phil 8092.11 — Duplessis, V. Surrealism. N.Y., 1963.
Phil 8092.12 — Barilli, Renato. Per un'estetica mondana. Bologna, 1964.
Phil 8092.13 — Fischer, Ernst. Kunst und Koexistenz. Reinbek, 1966.
Phil 8092.13.5 — Fischer, Ernst. Art against ideology. London, 1969.
Phil 8092.13.10 — Fischer, Ernst. Auf den Spuren der Wirklichkeit. Reinbek, 1968.
Phil 8092.14 — Bianco, Giovanni A. Il rifiuto del mondo nell'arte comtemporanea. Bari, 1964.
Phil 8092.15 — Damnjanović, Milan. Strujanja u savremenoj estetici. Zagreb, 1966.
Phil 8092.16 — Gus, Mikhail S. Modernizm bez maski. Moskva, 1966.
Phil 8092.17 — Matsa, Ivan L. Problemy khudozhestvennoi kul'tury XX veka. Moskva, 1966.
Phil 8092.18 — Realizm i khudozhestvennye iskaniia XX veka. Moskva, 1969.
Phil 8092.19 — Klivar, Miroslav. Estetika nových umění. Vyd. 1. Praha, 1970.
Phil 8092.20 — Arvon, Henri. L'esthétique marxiste. Paris, 1970.
Phil 8092.22 — Bignami, Ariel. Notas para la polémica sobre realismo. Buenos Aires, 1969.
Phil 8092.24 — Mozhniagun, Sergei E. O modernizme. Moskva, 1970.
Phil 8092.26 — Kalelin, Eugene Francis. Art and existence: a phemomenological aesthetics. Lewisburg, Pa. 1971.
Phil 8092.28 — Dorfles, Gillo. Comunicazione e struttura nell'analisi di alcumi linguaggi artistici. Milano, 1970.
Phil 8092.30 — Esteticheskoe nasledie V.I. Lenina i problemy iskusstva. Moskva, 1971.
Phil 8092.31 — Esteticheski idei V.I. Lenina i sovremennost'. Kalinin, 1970.
Phil 8092.32 — Chiari, Joseph. The aesthetics of modernism. London, 1970.

Phil 8110 - 8350   Esthetics - History of esthetic theory - Local history - Other countries, etc. (Geographic Table B, starting at 10)

Phil 8110.2 — Ladd, H.A. With eyes of the past. N.Y., 1928.
Phil 8110.3 — Monk, S.H. The sublime; a study of critical theories in 18th century England. Ann Arbor, 1960.
Phil 8110.4 — Thielke, K.L.F. Literatur- und Kunstkritik in ihren Wechselbeziehungen. Halle, 1935.
Phil 8110.5 — Allen, B.S. Tides in English taste (1619-1800); a background for the study of literature. Cambridge, Mass., 1937. 2v.
Phil 8110.6 — Wallace, H.B. Die Kritik der rationalcn Ästhetik in England im achtzehnten Jahrhundert. Jena, 1912.
Phil 8110.8 — Ogden, Henry. English taste in landscape. Washington, 1955.
Phil 8110.9 — Anceschi, L. L'estetica dell'empirismo inglese. Bologna, 1959.
Phil 8110.10 — Brunius, Teddy. Pionjärer och fullföjare. Stockholm, 1952.
Phil 8110.11 — Hipple, W.J. The beautiful, the sublime, and the picturesque in eighteenth-century British aesthetic theory. Carbondale, 1957.
Phil 8110.12 — Smith, A.C. Theories of the nature and standard of taste in England, 1700-1790. Chicago, 1937.
Phil 8110.13 — Mirabent, F. La estética inglesa del siglo XVIII. Barcelona, 1927.
Phil 8110.14 — Formigari, Lia. L'estetica del gusto nel settecento inglesa. 1. ed. Firenze, 1962.
Phil 8110.16 — Mainusch, Herbert. Romantische Ästhetik. Habilitationsschrift. Bad Homburg, 1969.
Phil 8120.2 — Soreil, A. Introduction à l'histoire de l'esthétique. Bruxelles, 1930.
Phil 8120.3 — Soreil, A. Introduction à l'histoire de l'esthétique française. Bruxelles, 1955.
Phil 8120.4 — König, René. Die naturalitistische Ästhetik in Frankreich und ihre Auflösung. Borna, 1931.
Phil 8120.5 — König, René. Die naturalistische Ästhetik in Frankreich und ihre Auflösung. Leipzig, 1930.
Phil 8120.6A — Mustoxidi, T.M. Histoire de l'esthétique française, 1700-1900. Paris, 1920.
Phil 8120.6B — Mustoxidi, T.M. Histoire de l'esthétique française, 1700-1900. Paris, 1920.
Phil 8120.7 — Feldman, V. L'esthétique française contemporaine. Paris, 1936.
Phil 8120.8 — Traz, Georges de. Diderot à Valéry. Paris, 1926.

Phil 8110 - 8350   Esthetics - History of esthetic theory - Local history - Other countries, etc. (Geographic Table B, starting at 10) - cont.

Phil 8120.9   Bopp, Léon. Philosophie de l'art; ou, Alchimie contre histoire. Paris, 1954.

Phil 8120.10   Brincourt, A. Les oeuvres et les lumières. Paris, 1955.

Phil 8120.10.5   Coleman, Francis X.J. The aesthetic thought of the French Enlightenment. Pittsburgh, 1971.

Phil 8120.11   Traz, Georges. De Diderot à Valéy. Paris, 1960.

Phil 8120.12   Simches, S.O. Le romantisme et le goût esthétique du XVIIIe siècle. Paris, 1964.

Phil 8120.13   Saisselin, Rémy Gilbert. Taste in eighteenth century France. Syracuse, 1965.

Phil 8125.02   Pamphlet vol. German esthetics. German. L-W. 6 pam.

Phil 8125.04   Pamphlet vol. German esthetics. German. A-K. 6 pam.

Phil 8125.2   Guerrero, Luis. Panorama de la estética clásica-romántica alemana. La Plata, 1934.

Phil 8125.4   Flemming, Willi. Der Wandel des deutschen Naturgefühls. Halle, 1931.

Phil 8125.6   Vorholz, Gerhard. Der Begriff des Tragischen. Halle, 1932.

Phil 8125.8   Denk, Ferdinand. Das Kunstschone und chacaktivstische von Winckelmann bis Friedrich Schlegel. Inaug. Diss. München, 1925.

Phil 8125.10   Bite-Palevitch. Essai sur les tendances critiques. Paris, 1925.

Phil 8125.12   Moos, Paul. Die deutsche Ästhetik der Gegenwart. Berlin, 1919.

Phil 8125.12.5   Moos, Paul. Die deutsche Ästhetik der Gegenwart. Berlin, 1931.

Phil 8125.14   Stöcker, Helene. Zur Kunstanschauung des XVIII. Jahrhunderts. Berlin, 1904.

Phil 8125.16   Volbehr, Theodor. Das Verlangen nach einer neuen deutschen Kunst. Leipzig, 1901.

Phil 8125.18   Betgmann, Ernst. Die Begrundung der deutschen Ästhetik durch...Baumgarten und...Mejer. Leipzig, 1911.

Phil 8125.20   Harnack, Otto. Die klassische Asthetik der Deutschen. Leipzig, 1892.

Phil 8125.22   Grucker, Emile. Histoire des doctrines litteraires. Paris, 1883.

Phil 8125.24   Lotze, Hermann. Geschichte der Aesthetik in Deutschland. München. 1848.

Phil 8125.26   Morawski, Stefan. Rozwáj myśli. Warszawa, 1957.

Phil 8125.28   Birt, Theodor. Laienurtheil über bildende Kunst bei den Alten. Marburg, 1902.

Phil 8125.30   Neudecher, Georg. Studien zur Geschichte des deutschen Asthetik seit Kant. Wurzburg, 1878.

Phil 8125.32   Begennu, Siegfried. Zur Theorie des Schönen. Berlin, 1956.

Phil 8125.34   Wilhelm, Richard. Friedrich Justus Riedel. Heidelberg, 1933.

Phil 8125.36   Krudewig, B. Das Groteske in der Ästhetik seit Kant. Bergisch, 1934.

Phil 8125.37   Nivelle, A. Kunst- und Dichtungstheorien zwischen Aufklärung und Klassik. Berlin, 1960.

Phil 8125.37.2   Nivelle, A. Kunst- und Dichtungstheorien zwischen Aufklärung und Klassik. 2. Aufl. Berlin, 1971.

Phil 8125.37.5   Nivelle, A. Les théories esthétiques en Allemagne de Baumgarten à Kant. Paris, 1955.

Phil 8125.38   Lotze, H. Geschichte der Aesthetik in Deutschland. München, 1868.

Phil 8125.40   Asmus, V.F. Nemetskaia estetika XVIII veka. Moskva, 1962.

Phil 8140.2   Sgroi, Carmelo. Gli studi estetici in Italia nel primo trantennio del'900. Firenze, 1932.

Phil 8140.3   Rolla, Alfredo. Storia delle idee estetiche in Italia. Torino, 1905.

Phil 8140.4   Blunt, A. Artistic theory in Italy, 1450-1600. Oxford, 1956.

Phil 8140.5   Napoli, Paolo. Arte e architettura in regime fascista. Roma, 1938.

Phil 8140.6   Giraldi, Giovanni. L'estetica italiana nella prima metà del secolo XX. Pisa, 1963.

Phil 8140.7   Pesce, Domenico. L'estetica dopo Croce. Firenze, 1962.

Phil 8140.8   Sinnonini, Augusto. Storia dei movimenti estetici nella cultura italiana. Firenze, 1968.

Phil 8140.10   Plebe, Armando. L'estetica italiana dopo Croce. Padova, 1968.

Phil 8141.2   Kőszegi, L. Präparation zu einer Rom-zentrischen Ästhetik. Detmold, 1959.

DL Phil 8145.2   Menendez y Pelayo. Historia de las ideas. Madrid, 1890.

Phil 8146.2   Querolgavaldá, M. La escuela estetica catalana contemporanea. Madrid, 1953.

Phil 8170.2   Reve, K. van het. Sovjet-annexatie der klassieken. Amsterdam, 1954.

Phil 8170.3   Sakharova, E.M. Osnovy marksistsko-leninskoi estetiki. Moskva, 1961.

Phil 8170.4   Matsa, Ivan. Khudozhestvennoe nasledie i estetickeskoe vospitanie. Moskva, 1959.

Phil 8170.5   Rappoport, S.Kh. Tvorit' mir po zakonam krasoty. Moskva, 1962.

Phil 8170.5.9   Pavlov, T.D. Osnovni vuprosi na estetikata. 2. izd. Sofiia, 1949-

Phil 8170.6   Pavlov, T.D. Osnovni vuprosi na marksistko-leninskata estetika. 3. izd. Sofiia, 1958.

Phil 8170.7   Honcharenko, M.V. Mystetstvo i estetichne vychovannia. Kyïv, 1963.

Phil 8170.8   Morawski, Stefan. Miedzy tradycja a wizja przyszłości. Warszawa, 1964.

Phil 8170.9   Iz istorii sovetskoi esteticheskoi mysli. Moskva, 1967.

Phil 8170.10   Asmus, Valenti F. Voprosy teorii i istorii esteiki. Moskva, 1968.

Phil 8171.5   Apresian, Grant Z. Krasota i dobro. Moskva, 1966.

Phil 8171.5.5   Apresian, Grant Z. Esteticheskaia mysl' narodov Zakavkaz'ia. Moskva, 1968.

Phil 8171.100   Konan, Uladzimir M. Razvitstsio estetychnai dumki u Belarusi. Minsk, 1968.

Phil 8171.100.5   Konan, Uladzimir M. Demokraticheskaia estetika Belorussii (1905-1917 gg.) Minsk, 1971.

Phil 8171.200   Kazykhanova, Batish R. Rol' khudozhestvennogo naslediia v esteticheskom vospitanii. Alma-ata, 1967.

Phil 8171.300   Ivan'o Ivan V. Spetsyfika mystetstva. Kyïv, 1970.

Phil 8176.2   Novák, Mirko. Ceská estetika. Praha, 1941.

Phil 8177.5   Mitrovics, Gyula. A magyar esztétikai irodolan történeto. Debrecen, 1928.

Phil 8181.2   Tsenkov, Boris. Iz istoriiata na esteticheskata misul v Bulgariia. Sofiia, 1964.

Phil 8182.2   Lukić, Sveta. Umetnost i kriterijumi. Beograd, 1964.

Phil 8190.2   Coomaraswamy, Ananda. The transformation of nature in art. Cambridge, Mass., 1934.

Phil 8110 - 8350   Esthetics - History of esthetic theory - Local history - Other countries, etc. (Geographic Table B, starting at 10) - cont.

Phil 8220.5   Zemlianova, L.M. Sovremennaia estetika v SShA. Moskva, 1962.

Phil 8228.2   Tobias, José Antônio. História das idéias estéticas no Brasil. São Paulo, 1967.

Phil 8277.2   Huonder, Quirin. Das Unsterblichkeitsproblem in der abendländischenPhilosophie. Stuttgart, 1970.

Phil 8328.2.2   Mello, Mario Vieira de Mello. Desenvolvimento e cultura. 2. ed. Rio de Janeiro, 1970.

Phil 8350.2   Rankin, D.H. The development and philosophy of Australian aestheticism. Melbourne, 1949.

Phil 8400   Esthetics - Treatises on esthetics - General works - Collected authors

Phil 8400.1   Pamphlet vol. Esthetics. 4 pam.

Phil 8400.1.1   Pamphlet vol. Esthetics. 5 pam.

Phil 8400.1.2   Pamphlet vol. Esthetics. 5 pam.

Phil 8400.1.3   Pamphlet vol. Esthetics. 3 pam.

Phil 8400.1.4   Pamphlet vol. Esthetics. 4 pam.

Phil 8400.2   Concinnitas. Basel, 1944.

Phil 8400.3A   Carritt, E.F. Philosophies of beauty, from Socrates to R. Bridges. N.Y., 1931.

Phil 8400.3B   Carritt, E.F. Philosophies of beauty, from Socrates to R. Bridges. N.Y., 1931.

Phil 8400.4   Archivio di Filosofia. Filosofia dell'arte. Roma, 1953.

Phil 8400.4.5   Archivio di Filosofia. Surrealismo e simbolismo. Padova, 1965.

Phil 8400.6   Voprosy estetiki. Moscow, 1958- 8v.

Phil 8400.8   Akademiia Nauk SSSR. Institut Filosofii. Nekotorye voprosy marksistsko-leninskoi estetiki. Moskva, 1954.

Phil 8400.10   Akademiia Nauk SSSR. Institut Filosofii. Voprosy marksistsko-leninskoi estetiki. Moskva, 1956.

Phil 8400.12   Arata, Rodolfo. I fondamenti del giudizio estetico. Bologna, 1960.

Phil 8400.13   Akademiia Khudozhestv SSSR. Institut Teorii i Istorii Iskusstva. Ocherki marksistsko-leninskoi estetiki. Moskva, 1956.

Phil 8400.14A   Burgum, E.B. The new criticism; an anthology of modern aesthetics. N.Y. , 1930.

Phil 8400.14B   Burgum, E.B. The new criticism; an anthology of modern aesthetics. N.Y., 1930.

Phil 8400.15   Akademiia Khudozhestv SSSR. Institut Teorii i Istorii Iskusstva. Ocherki marksistsko-leninskoi estetiki. Moskva, 1960.

Phil 8400.16   Philipson, Morris. Aesthetics today. Cleveland, 1961.

Phil 8400.17   Berestnev, V.F. Osnovy marksistsko-leninskoi estetiki. Moskva, 1960.

Phil 8400.18   Elton, William. Aesthetics and language. Oxford, 1954.

Phil 8400.20   Gerard, Alex. An essay on taste. London, 1759.

Phil 8400.21   Kaloshen, F.I. Protiv revizionizma v estetike. Moskva, 1960.

Phil 8400.22   Jahn, Johannes. Die Kunstwissenschaft der Gegenwart in Selbstdarstellungen. Leipzig, 1924.

Phil 8400.23   Bases of artistic creation essays by Maxwell Anderson, Rhys Carpenter and Roy Harris. New Brunswick, 1942.

Phil 8400.24A   Genteno, A. The intent of the artist. Princeton, 1941.

Phil 8400.24B   Genteno, A. The intent of the artist. Princeton, 1941.

Phil 8400.25   Mon, Franz. Movens; Dokumente und Analysen zur Dichtung. Wiesbaden, 1960.

Phil 8400.26   Pastore, A. Introduzione alla metafisica della poesia. Padova, 1957. 2 pam.

Phil 8400.27   Prieger, E. Anregung und metaphysische Grundlagen der Aesthetik von Alex Gottbeb Baumgarten. Berlin, 1875. 3 pam.

Phil 8400.28.3   Rader, M.M. A modern book of esthetics. 3. ed. N.Y., 1962.

Phil 8400.29   Margolis, J. Philosophy looks at the arts. N.Y., 1962.

Phil 8400.30A   Vivas, Eliseo. The problems of aesthetics. N.Y., 1953.

Phil 8400.30B   Vivas, Eliseo. The problems of aesthetics. N.Y., 1953.

Phil 8400.31   Weitz, M. Problems in aesthetics. N.Y., 1959.

Phil 8400.32   Leningrad. Gosudarstvennyi Institut Istorii Iskusstv. Zadachi i metody izucheniia iskusstv. Peterburg, 1924.

Phil 8400.33   Lukin, Iu.B. Prekrasnoe i zhizn'. Moskva, 1962.

Phil 8400.34   Levich, M. Aesthetics and the philosophy of criticism. N.Y., 1963.

Phil 8400.35   Gallatin, A.E. Of art: Plato to Picasso. N.Y., 1945.

Phil 8400.36   International Congress on Aesthetics, 1st, Berlin, 1913. Bericht. Stuttgart, 1913.

Phil 8400.36.2   International Congress on Aesthetics, 2nd, Paris, 1937. Deuxième congrès international d'esthétique. Paris, 1937. 2v.

Phil 8400.36.3   International Congress on Aesthetics, 3rd, Venice, 1956. Proceedings of the third international congress on aesthetics. v. 1-2. Torino, 1957.

Phil 8400.36.4   International Congress on Aesthetics, 5th, Amsterdam, 1964. Actes du cinquième congrès international d'esthétique, Amsterdam, 1964. La Haye, 1969.

Phil 8400.37   Razumnyi, V.A. Esteticheskoe sbornik statei. Moskva, 1964.

Phil 8400.39   The nature of beauty. Lahore, 1962.

Phil 8400.40   Akademiia Nauk SSSR. Institut Istorii Iskusstv. Sovremennoe iskusstvoznanie za rubezhom; ocherki. Moskva, 1964.

Phil 8400.41   Kagan, Moisei S. Lektsii po marksistsko-leninskoi estetike. Leningrad, 1963- 3v.

Phil 8400.41.2   Kagan, Moisei S. Lektsii po marksistsko-leninskoi estetike. Izd. 2. Leningrad, 1971.

Phil 8400.42   Baskin, Mark P. Protiv sovremennogo abstraktsionizma i formalizma. Moskva, 1964.

Phil 8400.43   Sesonske, Alexander. What is art? N.Y., 1965.

Phil 8400.44   Astakhov, Ivan B. Estetika i sovremennost'. Moskva, 1965.

Phil 8400.45   Barrett, Cyril. Collected papers on aesthetics. N.Y., 1966.

Phil 8400.46   New York University. Institute of Philosophy, 7th, 1964. Art and philosophy. N.Y., 1966.

Phil 8400.47   Akademiia Nauk SSSR. Institut Filosofii. Estetika: kategorii i iskusstvo. Moskva, 1965.

Phil 8400.48   Estetika. Moskva, 1966.

VPhil 8400.49   Bakalov, Georgi. Izkustvo i kritika. Sofiia, 1906.

Phil 8400.50   Internationale Hegelkongress, 5th, Salzburg, 1964. Bor'ba idei v estetike. Moskva, 1966.

Phil 8400.51   Iskusstvo i narod. Moskva, 1966.

Phil 8400.52   Die nicht mehr schönen Künste; Grenzphänomene des Asthetischen. München, 1968.

Phil 8400.53   Voprosy zarubezhnoi literatury i estetiki. Moskva, 1967.

Phil 8400.54   Kepes, Gyorgy. Structure in art and in science. N.Y., 1965.

Phil 8400.54.5   Keper, Gyorgy. The nature and art of motion. N.Y., 1965.

Phil 8400   Esthetics - Treatises on esthetics - General works - Collected authors - cont.

Phil 8400.55   Kritika sovremennoi burzhuaznoi estetiki. Moskva, 1968.
Phil 8400.56   Estetika segodnia. Moskva, 1968- 2v.
Phil 8400.57   Kul'tura chuvstv. Moskva, 1968.
VPhil 8400.58   Některé otázky kulturní politiky a marxistické estetiky. 1. vyd. Praha, 1965.
Phil 8400.59   Iskusstvo revoliutsiei prizvannoe. Moskva, 1969.
Phil 8400.60   Priroda i funktsii esteticheskogo. Moskva, 1968.
Phil 8400.61   Ovsiannikov, Mkikhail F. Marksistsko-leninskaia estetika. Moskva, 1966.
Phil 8400.63   Trud i esteticheskoe vospitanie. Riga, 1969.
Phil 8400.65   Estetika i chelovek. Moskva, 1967.
Phil 8400.65.5   Revoliutsiia, prekrasnoe, chelovek. Moskva, 1968.
Phil 8400.66   Voprosy teorii esteticheskogo vospitaniia. Moskva, 1970.
Phil 8400.69   Aesthetische Aufsätze. Budapest, 1966.

Phil 8401 - 8426   Esthetics - Treatises on esthetics - General works - Individual authors (A-Z)

Phil 8401.2   Alison, Archibald. Essays on the nature and principles of taste. Edinburgh, 1790.
Phil 8401.2.2   Alison, Archibald. Essays on the nature and principles of taste. 2. ed. Edinburgh, 1811.
Phil 8401.2.3   Alison, Archibald. Essays on the nature and principles of taste. Boston, 1812. 2v.
Phil 8401.2.4   Alison, Archibald. Essays on the nature and principles of taste. 4th ed. Edinburgh, 1815. 2v.
Phil 8401.2.5   Alison, Archibald. Essays on the nature and principles of taste. Hartford, 1821.
Phil 8401.2.10   Fedeles, Constantin. Versuch über Alison's Ästhetik, Darstellung und Kritik. München, 1911.
Phil 8401.4   Alvard, Julien. L'art moral. Paris, 1957.
VPhil 8401.6   Arréat, Lucien. Art et psychologie individuelle. Paris, 1906.
Phil 8401.8   Alt, Theodor. Die Grenzen der Kunst und die Buntfarbigkeit der Antike. Berlin, 1886.
Phil 8401.10   Alexander, Samuel. Art and the material. London, 1925.
Phil 8401.12   Aranio, Ruiz. Umanità dell'arte. Firenze, 1954.
Phil 8401.14   André, Yves, Essai sur le beau. Amsterdam, 1760.
Phil 8401.14.5   André Yves. Essai su le beau. Paris, 1924.
Phil 8401.16   Appin, Adolph. L'oeuvre d'art vivant. Genève, 1921.
Phil 8401.18   Allen, Grant. Physiological aesthetics. N.Y., 1877.
Phil 8401.20   Adam, Charles. Essai sur le jugement. Paris, 1885.
Phil 8401.22   Alexander, Samuel. Artistic creation and cosmic creation. London, 1927.
Phil 8401.22.5   Alexander, Samuel. Art and instinct. Oxford, 1927.
Phil 8401.22.10   Alexander, Samuel. Beauty and other forms of value. London, 1933.
Phil 8401.23   Adamian, Arshag. Stat'i ob iskusstve. Moskva, 1961.
Phil 8401.23.5   Adamian, Arshag. Stat'i ob estetike. Erevan, 1967.
Phil 8401.24   Adams, E.K. The aesthetic experience: its meaning in a functional psychology. Chicago, 1907.
Phil 8401.25   Antoni, Carlo. Chiose all'estetica, con un profile dell'autore a cura di G. Calogero. Roma, 1960.
Phil 8401.25.5   Antoni, Carlo. Scritti di estetica. Napoli, 1968.
Phil 8401.26   Alvarez, Villar A. Filosofia del arte. Madrid, 1962.
Phil 8401.27   Antonio de ia Virgen del Carmen. Al arte por el dolor. Burgos, 1952.
Phil 8401.28   Apollonio, M. Ontologia dell'arte. Brescia, 1961.
Phil 8401.29   Assunto, Rosario. L'integrazione estetica, studi e ricerche. Milano, 1959.
Phil 8401.29.10   Assunto, Rosario. L'automobile di Mallarmé e altri ragionamenti intorno, alla vocazione odierna delle arti. Roma, 1968. 10v.
Phil 8401.30   Anceschi, Luciano. Autonomia ed eteronomia dell'arte. 2. ed. Firenze, 1959.
Phil 8401.30.5   Anceschi, Luciano. Progetto di una sistematica dell'arte. Milano, 1962.
Phil 8401.30.7   Anceschi, Luciano. Progetto di una sistematica dell'arte. 2. ed. Milano, 1966.
Phil 8401.31   Astakhov, I.B. Iskusstvo i problema prekrasnogo. Moskva, 1963.
Phil 8401.31.5   Astakhov, I.B. Estetika. Moskva, 1971.
Phil 8401.32   Alexander, C.W.J. Notes on the synthesis of form. Cambridge, 1964.
Phil 8401.33   Assunto, Rosario. Guidizio estetico critica e censura. Firenze, 1963.
Phil 8401.34   Apresian, Zorii Grantovich. Svoboda khudozhestvennogo tvorchestva. Moskva, 1965.
Phil 8401.34.5   Apresian, Zorii Grantovich. Freedom and the artist. Moscow, 1968.
Phil 8401.35   Apresian, Grant Z. Cheloveku byt' khudozhnikom. Moskva, 1965.
Phil 8401.36   Angelov, Valentin. Groznoto. Sofiia, 1964.
Phil 8401.37   Adorno, Theodor W. Ohne Leitbild. Frankfurt, 1967.
Phil 8401.40   Arnheim, Rudolf. Toward a psychology of art. Berkeley, 1967.
Phil 8401.40.5   Arnheim, Rudolf. Art and visual perception. Berkeley, 1966.
Phil 8401.40.10   Arnheim, Rudolf. Visual thinking. Berkeley, 1969.
Phil 8401.41   Avramov, Dimitur. Estetika na modernoto izkustvo. Sofiia, 1969.
Phil 8402.2   Buzin, Germain. Le crépuscule des images. Paris, 1946.
Phil 8402.4   Biese, Alfred. Das Associationsprincip und der Anthropomorphismus in der Asthetik. Kiel, 1890.
Phil 8402.5.1   Bascom, J. Aesthetics or the science of beauty. Boston, 1867.
Phil 8402.5.2   Bascom, J. Aesthetics or the science of beauty. N.Y., 1874.
Phil 8402.6   Bergmann, J. Über das Schöne. Berlin, 1887.
Phil 8402.7   Blackie, J.S. On beauty; three discourses delivered in the University of Edinburgh. Edinburgh, 1858.
Phil 8402.8   Bayer, Raymond. Traité d'esthétique. Paris, 1956.
Phil 8402.8.5   Bayer, Raymond. Von der Methode der Ästhetik. Darmstadt, 1960.
Phil 8402.8.10   Bayer, Raymond. L'esthétique de la grâce. Paris, 1933. 2v.
Phil 8402.8.15   Bayer, Raymond. L'esthétique de la grâce. Paris, 1933. 2v.
Phil 8402.8.20   Bayer, Raymond. Essais sur la méthode en esthétique. Paris, 1953.
Phil 8402.9   Burton, W. The scenery-shower, with word-paintings of the beautiful. Boston, 1844.
Phil 8402.10   Bouterwek, F. Ideen zur Metaphysik des Schönen. Leipzig, 1807.
Phil 8402.10.5   Bouterwek, F. Aesthetik. 2. ed. Göttingen, 1815. 2v.
Phil 8402.12F   Birkhoff, G.D. Aesthetic measure. Cambridge, 1933.
Phil 8402.12.5   Birkhoff, G.D. Medida estetica. Rosario, 1945.

Phil 8401 - 8426   Esthetics - Treatises on esthetics - General works - Individual authors (A-Z) - cont.

Phil 8402.13   Bosanquet, B. Three lectures on aesthetic. London, 1915.
Phil 8402.14A   Burke, E. A philosophical enquiry into the origin of our ideas of the sublime and beautiful. 6th ed. London, 1770.
Phil 8402.14B   Burke, E. A philosophical enquiry into the origin of our ideas of the sublime and beautiful. 6th ed. London, 1770.
Phil 8402.14.2   Burke, E. A philosophical enquiry into the origin of our ideas. 3rd ed. London, 1761.
Phil 8402.14.5   Burke, E. A philosophical enquiry into the origin of our ideas of the sublime and beautiful. N.Y., 1829.
Phil 8402.14.7   Burke, E. A philosophical enquiry into the origin of our ideas of the sublime and beautiful. Philadelphia, 1806.
Phil 8402.14.10   Burke, E. A philosophical enquiry into the origin of our ideas of the sublime and beautiful. Baltimore, 1833.
Phil 8402.14.15   Burke, E. Philosophische Untersuchungen über den Ursprung unsrer Begriffe vom Erhaben und Schönen. Riga, 1773.
Phil 8402.14.20   Burke, E. A philosophical inquiry into the origin of our ideas of the sublime and beautiful. London, 1958.
Phil 8402.16   Bartlett, E.M. Types of aesthetic judgment. London, 1937.
Phil 8402.18   Balet, Leo. Synthetische Kunstwissenschaft. Stuttgart? 1938.
Phil 8402.20   Bernard, Charles. Esthétique et critique. Paris, 1946.
Phil 8402.22   Balfour, A.J. Criticism and beauty. Oxford, 1910.
Phil 8402.24   Banfi, Antonio. Vita dell'arte. Milano, 1947.
Phil 8402.25.3   Batteux, Charles. Einschränkung des schonen Künste auf einen einzigen Grundsatz. 3. Aufl. Leipzig, 1770.
Phil 8402.26   Burov, A.I. Esteticheskaia sushchnost' iskusstva. Moskva, 1956.
Phil 8402.26.5A   Burov, A.I. Das ästhetische Wesen. Berlin, 1958.
Phil 8402.26.5B   Burov, A.I. Das ästhetische Wesen. Berlin, 1958.
Phil 8402.26.5C   Burov, A.I. Das ästhetische Wesen. Berlin, 1958.
Phil 8402.28   Babbitt, Irving. The new Laocoon. Boston, 1910.
Phil 8402.28.5   Babbitt, Irving. The new Laocoon. Boston, 1910.
Phil 8402.28.10   Babbitt, Irving. The new Laocoon; an essay on the confusion of the arts. Boston, 1913.
Phil 8402.29   Bruno, F. Il problema estetica contemporanea. Lanclano, 1928.
Phil 8402.30   Bruyne, Edgar. Esquisse d'une philosphie de l'art. Bruxelles, 1930.
Phil 8402.32   Ballard, Edward. Art and analysis. The Hague, 1957.
Phil 8402.33   Baudauin, Paul. La beauté et la vie. Paris, 1959.
Phil 8402.34   Batteux, Charles. Les beaux arts reduits. Paris, 1747.
Phil 8402.35   Blümner, Hugo. Laokoon-studien. Freiburg, 1881-82.
Phil 8402.36   Baratono, A. Il monda sensbile. Milano, 1934.
Phil 8402.37   Besenbruch, Walter. Zum Problem des Typischen in der Kunst. Weimar
Phil 8402.38   Boldrini, M. Alla ricerca del tempo nell'arte. 1. ed. Milano, 1954.
Phil 8402.39   Brunius, Teddy. Estetik. Stockholm, 1961.
Phil 8402.39.5   Brunius, Teddy. Theory and taste. Uppsala, 1969.
Phil 8402.40   Buermeyer, L. The aesthetic experience. Merion, Pa., 1924.
Phil 8402.41   Bruhn, Karl. De växandes estetiska liv. Vasa, 1720-21. 2v.
Phil 8402.42   Bobrik, Eduard. Freie vorträge über Ästhetik. Zürich, 1834.
Phil 8402.42.5   Fiebig, Ernst. Bobriks Ästhetik; Beiträge zur Lehre des ästhetischen Formalismus. Bonn, 1930.
Phil 8402.43   Byk, S. Physiologie des Schönen. Leipzig, 1878.
Phil 8402.44   Bayer, Josef. Asthetik in Umrissen. Prag, 1856. 2v.
Phil 8402.45   Bendavid, L. Versuch einer Geschmackslehre. Berlin, 1799.
Phil 8402.46   Bendavid, L. Beytrage zur Kritik des Geschmacks. Wien, 1797.
Phil 8402.47   Bray, Lucien. Du beau. Paris, 1902.
Phil 8402.48   Berestnev, V.F. Problemy estetiki. Moskva, 1958.
Phil 8402.49   Brinkmann, D. Natur und Kunst. Zürich, 1938.
Phil 8402.51   Baumgarten, A. Aesthetica. Bari, 1936.
Phil 8402.52A   Boas, George. A primer of cities. Baltimore, 1937.
Phil 8402.52B   Boas, George. A primer for cities. Baltimore, 1937.
Phil 8402.52.5   Boas, George. The heaven of invention. Baltimore, 1962.
Phil 8402.53   Bodensohn, A. Uber das Wesen des Asthetischen. Frankfurt, 1961.
Phil 8402.54   Bernheimer, Richard. The nature of representation. N.Y., 1961.
Phil 8402.55   Bullough, E. Aesthetics; lectures and essays. London, 1957.
Phil 8402.56   Bense, Max. Asthetica. v.1,2-4. Stuttgart, 1954- 2v.
Phil 8402.56.5   Bense, Max. Ungehorsam der Ideen. Köln, 1965.
Phil 8402.57   Beardsley, Monroe Curtis. Aesthetics; problems in the philosophy of criticism. N.Y., 1958.
Phil 8402.57.5A   Beardsley, Monroe Curtis. Aesthetic inquiry: essays on art criticism and the philosophy of art. Belmont, Calif., 1967.
Phil 8402.57.5B   Beardsley, Monroe Curtis. Aesthetic inquiry: essays on art criticism and the philosophy of art. Belmont, Calif., 1967.
Phil 8402.58   Bizzarri, R. Il problema estetico. Brescia, 1954.
Phil 8402.59   Battaglia, F. Il valore estetico. Brescia, 1949.
Phil 8402.60   Belik, Aleksandr P. Estetika i sovremennost'. Moskva, 1963.
Phil 8402.60.2   Belik, Aleksandr P. Estetika i sovremennost'. Izd. 2. Moskva, 1967.
Phil 8402.61   Berthelemy, J. Traité d'esthétique. Paris, 1964.
Phil 8402.62A   Bense, Max. Aesthetica. Baden-Baden, 1965.
Phil 8402.62B   Bense, Max. Aesthetica. Baden-Baden, 1965.
Phil 8402.63   Borev, Iurii B. Vvedenie v estetiku. Moskva, 1965.
Phil 8402.64   Bianca, Giovanni A. Discussioni sull'arte e sulla condizione dell'uomo. Messina, 1965.
Phil 8402.65   Banach, Andrzej. O kiczu. Wyd. 6. Kraków, 1968.
Phil 8402.66   Baekkelund, Kjell. Kunst eller kaos? Oslo, 1969.
Phil 8402.68   Brissoni, Armando. Pagine di estetica. Padova, 1968.
Phil 8402.70   Berlyne, Daniel Ellis. Aesthetics and psychology. N.Y., 1971.
Phil 8403.2   Camón Aznar, J. El tiempo en el arte. Madrid, 1958.
Phil 8403.4   Cherbuliez, V. L'art et la nature. Paris, 1892.
Phil 8403.6   Cooper, John G. Letters concerning taste. 3. ed. London, 1757.
Phil 8403.6.4   Cooper, John. Letters concerning taste. 4th ed. London, 1771.
Phil 8403.8   Cousin, Victor. Du vrai, du beau et du bien. Paris, 1853.
Phil 8403.8.6   Cousin, Victor. Du vrai, du beau et du bien. 18. éd. Paris, 1873.
Phil 8403.8.10   Cousin, Victor. The philosophy of the beautiful. N.Y., 1849.
Phil 8403.10.2   Carriere, Moriz. Aesthetik. Leipzig, 1873. 2v.

Classified Listing

Phil 8401 - 8426 Esthetics - Treatises on esthetics - General works -
  Individual authors (A-Z) - cont.

Phil 8403.10.3   Carriere, Moriz. Aesthetik. 3. Aufl. Leipzig, 1885. 2v.

Phil 8403.10.5   Carriere, Moriz. Aesthetik. Leipzig, 1859. 2v.

Phil 8403.12   Chernyshevskii, N.G. Esteticheskie otnosheniia iskusstva k deistvitel'nosti. Moskva, 1945.

Phil 8403.12.5   Chernyshevskii, N.G. N.G. Chernyshevskii ob iskusstve. Moskva, 1950.

Phil 8403.12.10   Chernyshevskii, N.G. Stat'i po estetike. Moskva, 1938.

Phil 8403.13   Canitt, Edgar. An introduction to aesthetics. London, 1949.

Phil 8403.13.5   Canitt, Edgar. The theory of beauty. London, 1914.

Phil 8403.13.10   Canitt, Edgar. What is beauty. Oxford, 1932.

Phil 8403.14   Ciaccio, G. Il vera interiore. Sarzana, 1921.

Phil 8403.15   Carus, Paul. The principles of art. Boston, 1886.

Phil 8403.16   Cameron, Charles. Two essays. London, 1835.

Phil 8403.17   Cabrisas y Madero. El sentido del dolor en el arte. La Habana, 1937.

Phil 8403.18   Coculesco, P. Principes d'esthétique. Paris, 1935.

Phil 8403.19   Coen, Augusto. L'estetica sperimentale. Roma, 1920.

Phil 8403.20   Church, Ralph. An essay on critical appreciation. London, 1938.

Phil 8403.21   Collingwood, Robin George. The principles of art. Oxford, 1938.

Phil 8403.21.7   Collingwood, Robin George. The principles of art. Oxford, 1967.

Phil 8403.22   Clay, Felix. The origin of the sense of beauty. London, 1908.

Phil 8403.23   Chartier, Émile. Système des beaux-arts. Paris, 1926.

Phil 8403.23.5   Chartier, Émile. Préliminaires à l'esthétique. Paris, 1939.

Phil 8403.23.10   Chartier, Émile. Propos sur l'esthetique. paris, 1923.

Phil 8403.24   Conti, Augusto. Il bello nel vero o estetica. Firenze, 1872. 2v.

Phil 8403.24.5   Conti, Auguso. Il bell nel vero o estetic. 4. ed. Firenze, 1901. 2v.

Phil 8403.25   Castelfranco, G. Lineamenti di estetica. 1. ed. Firenze, 1950.

Phil 8403.26   Capasso, Aldo. Arte e sentimento. Firenze, 1957.

Phil 8403.27   Challaye, F. Esthétique. Paris, 1929.

Phil 8403.27.5   Challaye F. L'art et la beauté. Paris, 1929.

Phil 8403.28   Chaignet, A. Les principes de la science du beau. Paris, 1860.

Phil 8403.29   Cartalano, F. La filosofia dell'arte. Torino, 1875.

Phil 8403.30   Carey, Arthur. The majority report on art. Newport, R.I., 1927.

Phil 8403.31   Cohn, Jonas. algemeine Ästhetik. Leipzig, 1910.

Phil 8403.32   Cabat, Walter. The place of beauty in American life. N.Y., 1911.

Phil 8403.33   Cevallos García, G. Del arte actual y de su existencia. Cuenca, 1950.

Phil 8403.34   Cochofel, J.J. Iniciação estética. Lisboa, 1958.

Phil 8403.35   Caudwell, H. The creative impulse in writing and painting. London, 1951.

Phil 8403.36   Camón, Aznar J. El arte desde su esencia. Zaragoza, 1940.

Phil 8403.37   Carbonara, C. Ricerche per un'estetica del contenuto. Napoli, 1960.

Phil 8403.37.5   Carbonara, C. Del bello e dell'arte. 2. ed. Napoli, 1953

Phil 8403.38   Chiari, Joseph. Realism and imagination. London, 1960.

Phil 8403.39   Chaudhury, P.J. Studies in comparative aesthetics. Santiniketan, 1953.

Phil 8403.39.5   Chaudhury, P.J. Studies in aesthetics. Calcutta, 1964.

Phil 8403.40   Calderaro, José. La dimensión estetica del hombre. Buenos Aires, 1961.

Phil 8403.41   Coomaraswamy, A.K. Figures of speech or figures of thought. London, 1946.

Phil 8403.42   Chandler, A.R. Beauty and human nature. N.Y., 1934.

Phil 8403.45   Coutinho, Afrânio. Por uma crítica estética. Rio de Janeiro, 1959.

Phil 8403.46   Crousaz, Jean Pierre de. Traité du beau, où l'on montre en quoi consiste ce que l'on nomme ainsi, Amsterdam, 1715. Genève, 1970.

Phil 8404.2   Danz, Louis. The psychologist looks at art. London, 1937.

Phil 8404.3   Dorfles, Gillo. Discurso tecnico delle arti. Pisa, 1952.

Phil 8404.3.5   Dorfles, Gillo. Le ascillazioni del gusto. Milano, 1958.

Phil 8404.3.10   Dorfles, Gillo. Il divinire delle arti. Torino, 1959.

Phil 8404.3.15   Dorfles, Gillo. Simbolo. Torino, 1962.

Phil 8404.3.20   Dorfles, Gillo. Artificio e natura. Torino, 1968.

Phil 8404.4   Dufrenne, Michel. Phénoménologie de l'expérience esthétique. Paris, 1953.

Phil 8404.4.5   Dufrenne, Michel. Esthétique et philosophie. Paris, 1967.

Phil 8404.5   Day, Henry. The science of aesthetics. New Haven, 1872.

Phil 8404.6   Diano, Carlo. Linee per una fenomenologia dell'arte. Venezia, 1956.

Phil 8404.7   Deren, Maya. An anagram of ideas on art. N.Y., 1946.

Phil 8404.8   Ducasse, Curt. Art, the critics and you. N.Y., 1944.

Phil 8404.8.5   Ducasse, Curt. The philosophy of art. Toronto, 1929.

Phil 8404.9   Daneo, G. Alcune considerazioni sul bello. Torino, 1877.

Phil 8404.10   Dittes, Friedrich. Das Asthetische nach seinem eigenthümlichen Grundwesen. Leipzig, 1854.

Phil 8404.11   Delacroix, Henri. Psychologie de l'art. Paris, 1927.

Phil 8404.12   Delville, Jean. La mission de l'art. Bruxelles, 1900.

Phil 8404.13   Diez, Max. Algemeine ästhetik. Leipzig, 1906.

Phil 8404.13.5   Diez, Max. Theorie des Gefühls zur Begrundung des Asthetik. Stuttgart, 1892.

Phil 8404.14   Dubos, Jean B. Critical reflections on poetry. London, 1748. 3v.

Phil 8404.14.5   Dubos, J.B. Reflexions critiques sur la poésie et sur la peinture. 6. éd. Paris, 1755. 3v.

Phil 8404.15   Dessior, Max. Asthetik und allgemeine Kunstwissenschaft. Stuttgart, 1923.

Phil 8404.15.2   Dessoir, Max. Asthetik und allgemeine Kunstwissenschaft in den Grundzügen dargestellt. Stuttgart, 1906.

Phil 8404.15.5   Dessoir, Max. Beiträge zur allgemeinen Kunstwissenschaft. Stuttgart, 1929.

Phil 8404.16   Durdík. Josef. Všeobecna aesthetika. Praha, 1875.

Phil 8404.17   De Selincourt, O. Art and morality. London, 1935.

Phil 8404.18   Dmitrieva, N.A. Izobrazhenie i slovo. Moskva, 1962.

Phil 8404.19A   Dewey, J. Art as experience. N.Y., 1934.

Phil 8404.19B   Dewey, J. Art as experience. N.Y., 1934.

Phil 8404.20   Dyroff, Adolf. Asthetik des tätigen Geistes. Bonn, 1948.

Phil 8404.21   Doucher, Hans. Künstlerisches und rationalisiertes Sehen. München, 1967.

Phil 8404.22   Dunham, Barrows. The artist in society. N.Y., 1960.

Phil 8404.23   Davydov, Iurii N. Iskusstvo i elita. Moskva, 1966.

VPhil 8404.24   Dimitrov, D.N. Život i umetnosta. Skopje, 1967.

Phil 8401 - 8426 Esthetics - Treatises on esthetics - General works -
  Individual authors (A-Z) - cont.

Phil 8404.25   Defrenza, Giuseppe. Il problema della bellezza e dell'arte. Roma, 1967.

Phil 8404.26   Dzhibladze, Georgii N. Iskustvo i deistoitel'nost'. Tbilisi, 1971.

Phil 8405.2   Ehrlich, Walter. Aphorismen zur Philosophie der Kunst. Tübingen, 1962.

Phil 8405.2.5   Ehrlich, Walter. Asthetik. Chur, 1947.

Phil 8405.3   Evans, W.V. Belief and art. Chicago, 1939.

Phil 8405.4   Eberhard, Johann. Handbuch der Asthetik. Halle, 1803-04.

Phil 8405.5   Eleutheropoulos, Abrolelàs. Das Schöne. Berlin, 1905.

Phil 8405.6   Eddy, Arthur. Delight, the soul of art. Philadelphia, 1902.

Phil 8405.7   Egorov, A.G. O reaktsionnoi sushchnosti. Moskva, 1961.

Phil 8405.8   Ekman, Rolf. Estetiska problem. Lund, 1954.

Phil 8405.8.2   Ekman, Rolf. Estetiska problem. 2. uppl. Lund, 1960.

Phil 8405.8.5   Ekman, Rolf. Problems and theories in modern aesthetics. Lund, 1960.

Phil 8405.9   Estève, Pierre. L'esprit des beaux-arts. v.1-2. Paris, 1753.

Phil 8405.10   Edwards, A.T. The things which are seen. London, 1947.

Phil 8405.12   Eco, Umberto. La definizione dell'arte. Milano, 1968.

Phil 8406.2   Fuerstenberg, Hans. Les sources de la création artistique. Monaco, 1962.

Phil 8406.4   Formaggio, Dino. L'idea di artisticita. Milano, 1962.

Phil 8406.4.5   Formaggio, Dino. L'arte come comunicazione. Milano, 1953.

Phil 8406.5   Frauenstädt, J. Aesthetische Fragen. Dessau, 1853.

Phil 8406.6F   Fry, R.E. Transformations; critical and speculative essays on art. N.Y., 1927.

Phil 8406.7   Fischer, Kuno. Diotima; die Idee des Schönen. Stuttgart, 1852.

Phil 8406.7.5   Fischer, Kuno. Diotima; die Idee des Schönen. Leipzig, 1928.

Phil 8406.8   Frothingham, A.L. The philosophy of art. Princeton, 1894.

Phil 8406.9   Federn, Karl. Das aesthetische Problem. Hannover, 1928.

Phil 8406.10   Fontaine, André. Essai sur le principe et les lois de la critique d'art. Paris, 1903.

Phil 8406.11   Feltkamp, W.C. Zien en verstaan. Amsterdam, 1946.

Phil 8406.12   Farnell, Lewis R. Hedonism and art. London, 1928.

Phil 8406.13   Frey, Dagobert. Kunstwissenschaftliche Grundfragen. Wien, 1946.

Phil 8406.14   Friedländer, Max J. On art and connoisseurship. London, 1942.

Phil 8406.14.5   Friedländer, Max J. Von Kunst und Kennerschaft. Zürich, 1946.

Phil 8406.15   Figari, Pedro. Art, esthétique, idéal. Paris, 1920.

Phil 8406.16   Ferrant, Angel. La eseneia humana de las formos. Santander, 1952.

Phil 8406.17   Fremling, M. Dissertatio philosophica. Lundae, 1789.

Phil 8406.18   Focillon, Henri. Vita delle forme, di Henri Focillon. Padova, 1945.

Phil 8406.18.5   Focillon, Henri. Vie des formes. 3. ed. Paris, 1947.

Phil 8406.19   Feibleman, J. Aesthetics. N.Y., 1949.

Phil 8406.20   Flaccus, L.W. The spirit and substance of art. N.Y., 1926.

Phil 8406.20.5   Flaccus, L.W. The spirit and substance of art. N.Y., 1931.

Phil 8406.20.8   Flaccus, L.W. The spirit and substance of art. N.Y., 1941.

Phil 8406.20.9   Flaccus, L.W. The spirit and substance of art. N.Y., 1947.

Phil 8406.21   Fasola, Giusta Nicco. L'arte nella vita dell'uomo. Pisa, 1956.

Phil 8406.22   Fanciulli, G. La coscienza estetica. Torino, 1906.

Phil 8406.23   Friche, V.M. Problemy iskusstvovedeniia: sbornik statei. Moskva, 1930.

Phil 8406.24   Fallico, A.B. Art and existentialism. Englewood Cliffs, 1962.

Phil 8406.25   Fariña Nuñez, Eloy.Conceptos estéticos mitos guaraníes. Buenos Aires, 1926.

Phil 8406.26   Fanizza, Franco. Estetica problematica. Manduria, 1963.

Phil 8406.28   Fiedler, Konrad. Schriften zur Kunst. München, 1971. 2v.

Phil 8406.30   Farner, Konrad. Der Aufstand der Abstrakt-Konkreten. Neuwied, 1970.

Phil 8407.1   Gromov, Evgenii S. Esteticheskii ideal. Moskva, 1961.

Phil 8407.1.5   Gromov, Evgenii S. Khudozhestvennoe tvorchestvo. Moskva, 1970.

Phil 8407.2   Gerard, Alexander. An essay on taste (1759). Facsimile. Gainesville, Fla., 1963.

Phil 8407.3   Guyau, M. Les problèmes de l'esthétique comtemporaine. Paris, 1884.

Phil 8407.4   Griveau, Maurice. Histoire esthétique de la nature. Paris, 1927-30. 3v.

Phil 8407.5   Grudin, Louis. A primer of aesthetics. N.Y., 1930.

Phil 8407.6   Gentile, G. La filosofia dell'arte in compendio, ad uso delle scuole. Firenze, 1934.

Phil 8407.6.5   Gentile, G. La filosofia dell'arte. Milano, 1931.

Phil 8407.6.10   Gentile, G. Philosophie der Kunst. Berlin, 1934.

Phil 8407.7   Griveau, Maurice. La sphère de beauté, lois d'évolution. Paris, 1901.

Phil 8407.8   Guastalla, Pierre. Esthétique. Paris, 1925.

Phil 8407.8.5   Guastalla, Pierre. L'esthetique et l'art. Paris, 1928.

Phil 8407.9   Gioberti, V. Essai sur le beau, ou Eléments de philosophie esthétique. Bruxelles, 1843.

Phil 8407.9.5   Gioberti, V. Del bello. 2. ed. Firenze, 1845.

Phil 8407.10   Groos, Karl. Der ästhetische Genuss. Giessen, 1902.

Phil 8407.10.5   Groos, Karl. Einleitung in die Asthetik. Giessen, 1892.

Phil 8407.10.10   Groos, Karl. Beiträge zur Asthetik. Tübingen, 1891.

Phil 8407.11   Ghyka, M.C. Esthétique des proportions dans la nature et dans les arts. Paris, 1927.

Phil 8407.12   Greswell, R. On education in the principles of art. Oxford, 1844.

Phil 8407.13   Göller, Adolf. Das ästhetische Gefühl. Stuttgart, 1905.

Phil 8407.14.4   Gaultier, Paul. Le sens de l'art. 4. éd. Paris, 1911.

Phil 8407.14.10   Gaultier, Paul. The meaning of art. Philadelphia, 1914.

Phil 8407.15   Gordon, Kate. Esthetics. N.Y., 1922.

Phil 8407.16   Grzegorzewska, M. Essai sur le développement du sentiment esthétique. Paris, 1916.

Phil 8407.16.2   Grzegorzewska, M. Essai sur le développement du sentiment esthétique. Paris, 1916.

Phil 8407.17   Gadmann, E. Subjekt und Objekt des ästischen Aktes. Halle, 1917.

Phil 8407.18   Gleichen-Russwurm, A. Sieg der Freude. Stuttgart, 1913.

Phil 8407.18.5   Gleichen-Russwurm, A. Die Schönheit. Stuttgart, 1916?

Phil 8407.19   Görland, Albert. Asthetik; kritische Philosophie des Stils. Hamburg, 1937.

Classified Listing

Phil 8401 - 8426 Esthetics - Treatises on esthetics - General works -
Individual authors (A-Z) - cont.

Phil 8407.20   Guillou, R. L'art invincible. Paris, 1948.
Phil 8407.21   Grosse, Ernst. Kunstwissenschaftliche Studien. Tübingen, 1900.
Phil 8407.22   Goudal, Jean. Volontés de l'art moderne. Paris, 1927.
Phil 8407.23   Geiger, M. Zugänge zur Ästhetik. Leipzig, 1928.
Phil 8407.24   Griggs, Edward. The philosophy of art. N.Y., 1913.
Phil 8407.25   Gilbert, K. Aesthetic studies: architecture and poetry. Durham, 1952.
Phil 8407.26   Galli, E. L'estetica e i suoi problemi. Napoli, 1936.
Phil 8407.27   Guardo, V. L'estetica e i suoi problemi. Siracusa, 1955.
Phil 8407.28   Gargiulo, A. Scritti di estetica. Firenze, 1952.
Phil 8407.29   Goffin, Peter (pseud.). The realm of art. London, 1946.
Phil 8407.30   Green, Peter. The problem of art; a text book of aesthetics. London, 1937.
Phil 8407.31   Guggenheimer, R.H. Creative vision in artist and audience. N.Y., 1950.
Phil 8407.31.5   Guggenheimer, R.H. Sight and insight, a prediction of new perceptions in art. N.Y., 1945.
Phil 8407.32   Giesz, L. Phänomenologie des Kitsches. Heidelberg, 1960.
Phil 8407.33   Ghelli, Nino. Problematica dell'arte. Roma, 1958.
Phil 8407.34   Gornfel'd, A.G. Puti tvorchestva. Peterburg, 1922.
Phil 8407.35   Goranov, Krusto. Sudurzhanie i forma v izkustvoto. Sofiia, 1958.
Phil 8407.35.5   Goranov, Krusto. Istoricheskiias zhivos na izkustvoto. Sofiia, 1970.
Phil 8407.36   A memoir of the late Rev. William Gilpin. Lymington, 1851.
Phil 8407.37   Greenough, H. Form and function; remarks on art. Berkeley, 1947.
Phil 8407.38   Panofsky, E. Galileo as a critic of the arts. The Hague, 1954.
Phil 8407.39   Gatecki, L. Problematyka estetiki. Kraków, 1962.
Phil 8407.40   Gacher, Dmitrii I. Studii, statii, pisma i spomeni. Sofiia, 1964.
Phil 8407.41   Gilson, Étienne. Matiéres et formes. Paris, 1964.
Phil 8407.41.5   Gilson, Étienne. The arts of the beautiful. N.Y., 1965.
Phil 8407.42   Garcia Prado, Carlos, Teorías estéticas. Madrid, 1962.
Phil 8407.43   Gol'dentrikht, Semen S. O prirode esteticheskogo tvorchestva. Moskva, 1966.
Phil 8407.44   Grenier, Jean. Vicissitudes de l'esthétique et révolutions du gout. Paris, 1966.
Phil 8407.44.5   Grenier, Jean. L'art et ses problèmes. Lausanne, 1970.
Phil 8407.46   Guerrero, Luis Juan. Estética operatoria en sus tres direcciones. Buenos Aires, 1956-67. 3v.
Phil 8407.48   Giorgi, Rubina. Simbolo e schema. Padova, 1968.
Phil 8407.50   Geel, Jacobus. Onderzoek en phantasie. Leiden, 1838.
Phil 8408.3   Hawkins, Denis John B. The concepts of aesthetics. London, 1962.
Phil 8408.4   Heyl, Bernard. New bearings in esthetics and art criticism. New Haven, 1957.
Phil 8408.5   Hirth, Georg. Aufgaben der Kunstphysiologie. München, 1891.
Phil 8408.6   Hildebrand, A. The problem of form in painting and sculpture. N.Y., 1907.
Phil 8408.6.5   Hildebrand, A. Das Problem der Form in der Bildendenkunst. 6. Aufl. Strassburg, 1908.
Phil 8408.7   Hartman, H.G. Aesthetics: a critical theory of art. Columbus, 1919.
Phil 8408.8   Hart, Julius. Revolution der Ästhetik als Einleitung zu einer Revolution der Wissenschaft. Berlin, 1909.
Phil 8408.9   Hillebrand, K. Zwölf Briefe eines ästhetischen Ketzer's. 2. Aufl. Berlin, 1874.
Phil 8408.10   Haecker, T. Schönheit; ein Versuch. 3. Aufl. München, 1953.
Phil 8408.11   Haecker, T. Schönheit; ein Versuch. Leipzig, 1936.
Phil 8408.12   Hogarth, William. The analysis of beauty. Pittsfield, 1909.
Phil 8408.12.5   Hogarth, William. The analysis of beauty. Oxford, 1955.
Phil 8408.13   Hirsch, W. Die Gültigkeit der Kunst. Köln, 1957.
Phil 8408.14   Hammond, Robert. Lineamenti d'estetica fondati sul problema gnoseologico. Aleppo, 1926.
Phil 8408.15   Heimann, B. Uber den Geschmack. Berlin, 1924.
Phil 8408.16   Häberlin, Paul. Allgemeine Ästhetik. Basel, 1929.
Phil 8408.17   Heller, R. Das Wesen der Schönheit. Wein, 1936.
Phil 8408.18   Hartmann, N. Ästhetik. Berlin, 1953.
Phil 8408.19   Hiriyanna, M. Art experience. Mysore, 1954.
Phil 8408.20   Haezrahi, P. The contemplative activity; a study in aesthetics. N.Y., 1958.
Phil 8408.21   Hirsch, W. Substanz und Thema in der Kunst. Amsterdam, 1961.
Phil 8408.22   Huyghe, René. L'art et l'âme. Paris, 1960.
Phil 8408.23   Huisman, Denis. L'esthétique. 3. éd. Paris, 1959.
Phil 8408.24   Hamann, J.G. Scritti e frammenti di estetica. Roma, 1938.
Phil 8408.25   Hartford, H. Has God been insulted here? Chicago, 1952.
Phil 8408.26   Howell, A.R. Gems of wisdom from the writings of A.R. Howell. Sussex, 1958.
Phil 8408.27   Huber, Kurt. Ästhetik. Ettal, 1954.
Phil 8408.28   Heller-Heinzelmann, R. L'immaginazione e la vita estetica. Firenze, 1933.
Phil 8408.29   Hogarth, William. Zergliederung der Schönheit, die schwankendenBegriffe von dem geschmack Festzusetzen. Berlin, 1754.
Phil 8408.30   Hostinsky, Otakar. O umění. Praha, 1956.
Phil 8408.30.5   Sádecký, Z. O některých otázkách estetiky Otakara Hostinskéko. Praha, 1956.
Phil 8408.30.10   Hostinský, Otakar. Otakara Hostinského esthetika. Praha, 1921.
Phil 8408.30.15   Profesor Dr. Otakar Hostinský, 1847-1907. Praha, 1907.
Phil 8408.31   Hermann, C. Grundriss einer allgemeinen Ästhetik. Leipzig, 1857.
Phil 8408.32   Herzog, J.A. Was ist Ästhetisch? Leipzig, 1900.
Phil 8408.33   Hamann, R. Ästhetik. 2. Aufl. Leipzig, 1919.
Phil 8408.34   Herz, Marcus. Versuch über den Geschmach und die ursachen seiner Verschiednheit. Leipzig, 1776.
Phil 8408.35   Howes, E.D. (Mrs.). The psychology of beauty. Boston, 1905.
Phil 8408.36   Haspers, John. Meaning and truth in the arts. Chapel Hill, 1947.
Phil 8408.36.2   Haspers, John. Meaning and truth in the art. Hamden, Connecticut, 1946.
Phil 8408.37   Hirn, Yrjö. Förstudier till en konstfilosofi på psykologisk grundval. Helsingfors, 1896.
Phil 8408.38   Halder, A. Kunst und Kult. Freiburg, 1964.
Phil 8408.39   Havryliuk, P.J. Spetsyfichni osoblynosti zmistu i formy v mystetstvi. Kyïv, 1969.
Phil 8408.40   Hofstsdter, Albert. Truth and art. N.Y., 1965.
Phil 8408.41   Hadživasilev, Mito. Odraz, izraz. Skopje, 1958.

Phil 8401 - 8426 Esthetics - Treatises on esthetics - General works -
Individual authors (A-Z) - cont.

Phil 8408.42   Hordiienko, Anatolii. Mystetstvo, diisnist' i svoboda khudozhn'oï tvorchosti. Kyïv, 1966.
Phil 8408.45   Harries, Karsten. The meaning of modern art. Evanston, 1968.
Phil 8408.48   Hussain, Fakhir. Le jugement esthétique. Paris, 1968.
Phil 8408.50   Hogg, James. Psychology and the visual arts: selected readings. Harmondsworth, 1969.
Phil 8408.52   Havryliuk, Pedro I. Problema estetychnoko i teoriia upravlinnia. Kyïv, 1970.
Phil 8408.54   Hopf, Andreas. Die Struktur des östhetischen Urteils. München, 1968.
Phil 8409.2   Ingarden, R. Untersuchungen zur Ontologie der Kunst. Tübingen, 1962.
Phil 8409.3   Iastrebova, Nataliia. Konflikti v estetichnogo. Sofiia, 1968.
Phil 8409.4   Ivanov, Pavel L. O sushchnosti krasoty. Moskva, 1967.
Phil 8410.2   Jarett, J.L. The quest for beauty. Englewood Cliffs, 1957.
Phil 8410.3   Jordan, E. The aesthetic object; an introduction to the philosophy of value. Bloomington, 1937.
Phil 8410.4   Julianez Islas, L. El culto di lo bello. La Plata, 1929.
Phil 8410.5   Jacques, A. A system of aesthetics. Dublin, 1921.
Phil 8410.6   Jordán de Urríes y Azara, José. Resumen de teoría general del arte. 1. ed. Madrid, 1933.
Phil 8410.7   Jouffroy, T.S. Cours d'esthétique suivi de la thèse de l'art. 1. éd. Paris, 1843.
Phil 8410.7.5   Jouffroy, T.S. Cours d'esthétique. 2. éd. Paris, 1863.
Phil 8410.8   Jenkins, I. Art and the human enterprise. Cambridge, 1958.
Phil 8410.9   Joffe, Jeremiia I. Kul'tura i stil'. Leningrad, 1927.
Phil 8411.2   Kubler, George. The shape of time; remarks on the history of things. New Haven, 1962.
Phil 8411.3   Köstlin, K. Ästhetik. pt.1-2. Tübingen, 1869.
Phil 8411.3.5   Köstlin, K. Prolegomena zur Ästhetik. Tübingen, 1889.
Phil 8411.5   Krause, K.C.F. Karl Christian Friedrich Krause's Abriss der Ästhetik oder der Philosophie des schönen Kunst. Göttingen, 1837.
Phil 8411.5.5   Krause, K.C.F. Compendio de estética traducido del aleman. Sevilla, 1874.
Phil 8411.7   Mayoux, J.J. Richard Payne Knight et le pittoresque essai sur une phase esthétique. Paris, 1932.
Phil 8411.7.5   Knight, R.P. An analytical inquiry into the principles of taste. 2. ed. London, 1805.
Phil 8411.7.6   Knight, R.P. An analytical inquiry into the principles of taste. 3. ed. London, 1806.
Phil 8411.7.10   Knight, R.P. An analytical inquiry into the principles of taste. 4. ed. London, 1808.
Phil 8411.7.15   Knight, W. The philosophy of the beautiful. N.Y., 1891-93. 2v.
Phil 8411.8   Kahlert, August. System der Ästhetik. Leipzig, 1846.
Phil 8411.9   Kohnstamm, O. Kunst als Ausdruckstätigkeit; biologische Voraussetzungen der ästhetik. München, 1907.
Phil 8411.10   Keussler, G. von. Die Grenzen der Ästhetik. Leipzig, 1902.
Phil 8411.11   Kirstein, Anton. Entwurf einer Ästhetik der Natur und Kunst. Paderborn, 1896.
Phil 8411.12   Kirchmann, J.H. von. Ästhetik auf realistischer Grundlage. Berlin, 1868. 2v.
Phil 8411.13   Külpe, O. Grundlagen der Ästhetik. Leipzig, 1921.
Phil 8411.14   Kaplan, Leo. Versuch einer Psychologie der Kunst. Baden-Baden, 1930.
Phil 8411.16   Kornfeld, M. L'énigme du beau. Paris, 1942.
Phil 8411.17   Katann, O. Ästhetisch-literarische Arbeiten. Wien, 1918.
Phil 8411.18   Kallen, H.M. Indecency and the seven arts, and other adventures of a pragmatist in aesthetics. N.Y., 1930.
Phil 8411.19   Kulke, Eduard. Kritik der Philosophie des Schönen. Leipzig, 1906.
Phil 8411.20   Kainz, F. Vorlesungen über Ästhetik. Wien, 1948.
Phil 8411.20.5   Kainz, F. Vorlesungen über Ästhetik. Detroit, 1962.
Phil 8411.21   Kuznitzky, G. Die Seinssymbolik des Schönen und die Kunst. Berlin, 1932.
Phil 8411.22   Kuhr, Victor. Ästhetisches Erleben und kunstlerisches Schaffen. Stuttgart, 1929.
Phil 8411.23   Kublanov, B.G. Esteticheskoe chuvstvo i iskusstvo. L'vov, 1956.
Phil 8411.23.5   Kulvanov, B.G. Gnoseologicheskaia priroda literatury i iskusstva. L'vov, 1958.
Phil 8411.23.10   Kaublanov, B.G. Mystetstvo iak forma piznannia diisnosti. Kyïv, 1867.
Phil 8411.24   Kaloshin, F.I. Soderzhanie odforma v proizvedeniiakh iskusstva. Leningrad, 1953.
Phil 8411.25   Krug, W.T. Geschmackslehre oder Ästhetik. Wien, 1818. 2v.
Phil 8411.26   Koebner, R. Vom Schönen und seiner Wahrheit. Berlin, 1957.
Phil 8411.27   Kaufmann, F. Das Reich des Schönen. Stuttgart, 1960.
Phil 8411.28   Kuhn, Helmut. WesenUnd Wirken des Kunstwerks. München, 1960.
Phil 8411.28.5   Kuhn, Helmut. Schriften zur Ästhetik. München, 1966.
Phil 8411.29A   Kris, Ernst. Psychoanalytic exploration in art. London, 1953.
Phil 8411.29B   Kris, Ernst. Psychoanalytic exploration in art. London, 1953.
Phil 8411.29C   Kris, Ernst. Psychoanalytic exploration in art. London, 1953.
Phil 8411.30   Kornienko, V.S. O sushchnosti esteticheskogo poznaniia. Novosibirsk, 1962.
Phil 8411.32   Kahnweiller, D. Confessions esthétiques. Paris, 1963.
Phil 8411.33   Kupareo, Raimundo. Tratado de estetica. v.1- Santiago de Chile, 1964-
Phil 8411.34   Krivskovskii, Nikolai I. Logika krasoty. Minsk, 1965.
Phil 8411.36.2   Kassil', Lev A. "Delo vkusa". Izd. 2. Moskva, 1964.
Phil 8411.37   Kucherenko, Georgii A. Esteticheskoe mnogoobrazie iskusstva sotsialisticheskogo realizma. Moskva, 1966.
Phil 8411.38   Kogan, Lev Naumovich. Khudozhestvennyi vkus. Moskva, 1966.
Phil 8411.38.5   Kogan, Lev Naumovich. Iskusstvo i my. Moskva, 1970.
Phil 8411.39   Kuncheva, L.I. Esteticheskoe i eticheskoe v zhizni i v iskusstve. Moskva, 1968.
Phil 8411.40   Kollen, Horace Meyer. Liberty, laughter, and tears. De Kalb, 1968.
Phil 8411.41   Kuczyńska, Alicja. Przemiany wyobraźni. Wyd. 1. Warszawa, 1969.
Phil 8411.42   Kornienko, Vasilii S. O zakonakh krasoty. Khar'kov, 1970.
Phil 8411.43.80   Haase, Rudolf. Hans Kayser. Basel, 1968.
Phil 8412.3   Lefrancq, J. Oser penser. Neuchâtel, 1961.

Classified Listing

Phil 8401 - 8426   Esthetics - Treatises on esthetics - General works -
Individual authors (A-Z) - cont.

Phil 8412.4 — Laprade, Victor de. Histoire du sentiment de la nature. Paris, 1882.

Phil 8412.5 — Lévêque, C. La science du beau, ses principes, ses applications et son histoire. 2. éd. Paris, 1872. 2v.

Phil 8412.6 — Lalo, Charles. Notions d'esthétique. Paris, 1925.

Phil 8412.6.5 — Lalo, Charles. L'expression de la vie dans l'art. Paris, 1933.

Phil 8412.6.10 — Lalo, Charles. L'art et la vie. Paris, 1946-47. 3v.

Phil 8412.7 — Lechalas, G. Études esthétiques. Paris, 1902.

Phil 8412.8 — Laurila, K.S. Versuch einer Stellungnahme zu den Hauptfragen der Kunstphilosophie. Helsingfors, 1903.

Phil 8412.8.5 — Laurila, K.S. Asthetische Streitfragen. Helsinki, 1934.

Phil 8412.8.10 — Laurila, K.S. Estetiikhan peruskysymyksia. Porvoo, 1919.

Phil 8412.9 — Landmann, E. Grundzüge einer Lehre vom Schönen. Basel, 1940.

Phil 8412.9.5 — Landmann, E. Die Lehre vom Schönen. Wien, 1952.

Phil 8412.10 — Lipps, Theodor. Asthetik; Psychologie des Schönen und der Kunst. Hamburg, 1903-06. 2v.

Phil 8412.10.5 — Lipps, Theodor. Von der Form des ästhetischen Apperception. Halle, 1902.

Phil 8412.10.80 — Remos, y Rubio, J.J. Las ideas estéticas de Lipps. Habana, 1925.

Phil 8412.11 — Loewenberg, J. Dialogues from Delphi. Berkeley, 1949.

Phil 8412.14 — Lundholm, H. The aesthetic sentiment. Cambridge, 1941.

Phil 8412.15 — Lindholm, C. Konsten och tiden. Stockholm, 1950.

Phil 8412.16 — La Via, Vincenzo. L'umanità dell'arte. Roma, 1924.

Phil 8412.17 — Lesparre, A. de G. Essai sur le sentiment esthétique. Paris, 1921.

Phil 8412.18 — Lukács, György. A különösség mintesztétikai kategória. Budapest, 1957.

Phil 8412.18.5 — Lukács, Georg. Über die (Beson derheit) als Kategorie der Asthetik. Neuwied, 1967.

Phil 8412.19 — Lotze, Hermann. Grundzuge der Ästhetik. 3. Aufl. Leipzig, 1906.

Phil 8412.19.5 — Lotze, Hermann. Grundzüge der Ästhetik; Diktate aus den Vorlesungen. 2. Aufl. Leipzig, 1888.

Phil 8412.19.10 — Lotze, Hermann. Über den Begriff der Schonhëit. Göttingen, 1845.

Phil 8412.19.15 — Lotze, Hermann. Über Bedingungen der Kunstschönheit. Göttingen, 1847.

Phil 8412.20 — Lee, H.L. Perception and aesthetic value. N.Y., 1938.

Phil 8412.21 — Lippold, F. Bausteine zu einer Ästhetik der inneren Form. München, 1920.

Phil 8412.22 — Lange, K. von. Das Wesen der Kunst. Berlin, 1907.

Phil 8412.23.2 — Langfeld, Herbert Sidney. The aesthetic attitude. N.Y., 1920.

Phil 8412.23.3 — Langfeld, Herbert Sidney. The aesthetic attitude. Port Washington, N.Y., 1967.

Phil 8412.24 — Lemcke, Carl von. Populäre Ästhetik. Leipzig, 1879.

Phil 8412.25 — Lemke, Carl von. Populäre Ästhetik. 4. Aufl. Leipzig, 1873.

Phil 8412.26 — Laprade, V. Questions d'art et de morale 2. éd. Paris, 1861.

Phil 8412.27 — Little, J.S. What is art? London, 1884.

Phil 8412.28 — Lundegårdh, H. Ludvig sju dialoger om idé. Stockholm, 1913.

Phil 8412.29 — Lion, Ferdinand. Die Geburt der Aphrodite. Heidelberg, 1955.

Phil 8412.30 — Lamouche, A. Esthétique. Paris, 1961.

Phil 8412.31 — Lange, K. von. Das Wesen der Kunst. Berlin, 1901. 2v.

Phil 8412.32 — Lechner, R. The aesthetic experience. Chicago, 1953.

Phil 8412.33 — Lange, A.K. Problems of art. N.Y., 1957.

Phil 8412.35 — Logroscimo, G. Teoria dell'arte e della critica. Padova, 1962.

Phil 8412.36 — Lier, Henri. Les arts de l'espace. 3. éd. Tournai, 1963.

Phil 8412.37 — Librizzi, Carmelo. Conoscenza e arte. Padova, 1962.

Phil 8412.38 — L'Andelyn, Charles de. Esthétique. Neuchâtel, 1964.

Phil 8412.39 — Losev, Aleksei F. Istoriia esteticheskikh kategorii. Moskva, 1965.

Phil 8412.40 — Langer, Susanne Katherina Knauth. Feeling and form; a theory of art developed from philosophy in a new key. N.Y., 1953.

Phil 8412.42 — Leijonhiel, Christer. Colours, forms and art. Studies in differential aesthetic psychology. Akademisk avhandling. Stockholm, 1967.

Phil 8412.43 — Lunacharskii, Anatolii V. Osnovy pozitivnoi estetiki. Moskva, 1923.

Phil 8413.2 — Merle, Pierre. Pour une clinique d'art. Paris, 1962.

Phil 8413.4 — Martano, Guiseppe. La conoscenza sensible nel razionalismo moderno. Napoli, 1960.

Phil 8413.5 — Moore, T.S. Armour for aphrodite. London, 1929.

Phil 8413.6 — M'Dermot, Martin. A critical dissertation on nature and principles of taste. London, 1823.

Phil 8413.7 — Munro, Thomas. Scientific method in aesthetics. N.Y., 1928.

Phil 8413.7.5 — Munro, Thomas. Toward science in aesthetics. N.Y., 1956.

Phil 8413.8 — Manzari, A. Principii di estetica. Napoli, 1908.

Phil 8413.9 — McMahon, Amos. The meaning of art. N.Y., 1930.

Phil 8413.10 — MacVicar, John. The philosophy of the beautiful. Edinburgh, 1855.

Phil 8413.11 — Marshall, Henry. Aesthetic principles. N.Y., 1895.

Phil 8413.11.5 — Marshall, Henry. The beautiful. London, 1924.

Phil 8413.12 — McAlpen, Colin. Hermara, a study in compatative aesthetics. London, 1915.

Phil 8413.13 — Muller, Josef. Eine Philosophie des Schönen in Natur und Kunst. Mainz, 1897.

Phil 8413.14 — Medicus, Fritz. Grundfragen der Ästhetik. Jena, 1917.

Phil 8413.15 — Monrad, M.J. Ästhetik. Christiania, 1889-90. 2v.

Phil 8413.16 — Mundt, Ernest. Art, form, and civilization. Berkeley, 1952.

Phil 8413.17 — Mormone, R. Avviamento alla critica d'arte. Napoli, 1954.

Phil 8413.18 — MacKenzie, G.S.B. An essay on some subjects connected with taste. Edinburgh, 1817.

Phil 8413.19 — Mather, F.J. Concerning beauty. Princeton, 1935.

Phil 8413.20 — Mantegazza, P. Epikur; Physiologie des Schönen. Jena, 1891.

Phil 8413.21 — McDowall, S.A. Beauty and the beast; an essay in evolutionary aesthetic. Cambridge, Mass., 1920.

Phil 8413.22 — Moffat, J.C. An introduction to the study of aesthetics. Cincinnati, 1856.

Phil 8413.23 — Martha, C. La délicatesse dans l'art. Paris, 1884.

Phil 8413.24 — Moerth, L. Was ist Schön? Eine ästhetische Studie. München, 1913?

Phil 8413.25 — Meyer, T.A. Ästhetik. Stuttgart, 1923.

Phil 8413.26 — Morris, B. The aesthetic process. Evanston, 1943.

Phil 8413.27 — Martini, Miro. La deformazione estetica. Milano, 1955.

Phil 8413.28 — Müller-Freienfels, R. Psychologie der Kunst. Leipzig, 1923-33. 3v.

Phil 8413.29 — Mueller, A.E. The world as spectacle, an aesthetic view of philosophy. N.Y., 1944.

Phil 8413.30 — Mauron, C. Aesthetics and psychology. London, 1935.

Phil 8413.31 — Mirabent, F. De la bellesa. v.5. Barcelona, 1936.

Phil 8413.32 — Mottier, G. Le phémomène de l'art. Parisè 1936.

Phil 8413.33 — Maritain, J. Art and scholasticism. N.Y., 1962.

Phil 8413.34 — Malraux, Q. The voices of silence. Garden City, 1935.

Phil 8413.35 — Medlöe, Jon. Kunst og idé. Oslo, 1965.

Phil 8413.36 — Margolis, Joseph. The language of art and art criticism. Detroit, 1965.

Phil 8413.37 — Murian, Vasim M. Esteticheskii ideal. Moskva, 1966.

Phil 8413.38 — Molchanova, Albina S. Na vkus, na tsvet. Moskva, 1966.

Phil 8413.39 — Malygin, Vladimir A. O vozvyshennom v mire estetiki. Leningrad, 1966.

Phil 8413.40 — Mundt, Theodor. Asthetik. Göttingen, 1966.

Phil 8413.41 — Morkrejs, Antonín. Umění, skutečnost, poznání. Praha, 1966.

Phil 8413.42 — Michelés, Panagiótés Andreau. Études d'esthétique. Paris, 1967.

Phil 8413.44 — Malecki, Herbert. Spielräume. Frankfurt, 1969.

Phil 8414.5 — Natev, A. Tsel ili samotselnost na izkustvoto. Sofiia, 1960.

Phil 8414.6 — Nüsslein, F.A. Lehrbuch der Kunstwissenschaft zum Gebrance bei Vorlesungen. Landshut, 1819.

Phil 8414.7 — Nolte, Fred O. Art and reality. Lancaster, 1942.

Phil 8414.8 — Nahm, Milton Charles. The artist as creator; an essay of human freedom. Baltimore, 1956.

Phil 8414.8.11 — Nahm, Milton Charles. Aesthetic experience and its presuppositions. N.Y., 1968.

Phil 8414.9 — Nadiani, A. Fra kaos til form. Oslo, 1949.

Phil 8414.10 — Nédoncelle, M. Introduction à l'esthétique. Paris, 1953.

Phil 8414.11 — Neumann, E. Kunst und schöpferisches Unbewusstes. Zürich, 1954.

Phil 8414.12 — Nunez de Arenas, I. Elementos filosóficos de la literatura. Madrid, 1858.

Phil 8414.13 — Novak, Mirko. Základy vidy o umění, se zvláštním zřením k vědeckému studiu hudby. Praha, 1928.

Phil 8414.14 — Novák, Mirko. Od skutečnosti ku umění. Praha, 1965.

Phil 8414.15.2 — Noyes, Carleton E. The gate of appreciation. Boston, Mass., 1922.

Phil 8415.2 — Ossowski, S. U podstaw estetyki. Wyd. 3. Warszawa, 1958.

Phil 8415.3 — Odebrecht, R. Gefühl und schöpferische Gestaltung. Berlin, 1929.

Phil 8415.3.5 — Odebrecht, R. Grundlegung einer ästhetischen Werttheorie. Berlin, 1927-

Phil 8415.4 — Osborne, H. Theory of beauty; an introduction to aesthetics. N.Y., 1953.

Phil 8415.5A — Ogden, C.K. The foundations of aesthetics. London, 1922. 2v.

Phil 8415.5B — Ogden, C.K. The foundations of aesthetics. London, 1922. 2v.

Phil 8415.6 — Ozzòla, L. L'arte come conoscenza degli individuali. Roma, 1928.

Phil 8415.7.4 — Oeser, C. Briefe an eine Jungfrau über die Hauptgegenstände der Asthetik. 4. Aufl. Leipzig, 1852.

Phil 8415.7.13 — Oeser, C. Briefe an eine Jungfrau über die Hauptgegenstände der Asthetik. 13. Aufl. Leipzig, 1872.

Phil 8415.8A — Ogden, R.M. The psychology of art. N.Y., 1938. 2v.

Phil 8415.8B — Ogden, R.M. The psychology of art. N.Y., 1938. 2v.

Phil 8415.9 — Oberti, Elisa, Contributi all'analisi estetica. Milano, 1962.

Phil 8415.9.5 — Oberti, Elisa. Estetica teoria dell'oggetto artistico come presenz evidenziata. Milano, 1962.

Phil 8415.9.10 — Oberti, Elisa. Per una fondazione fenomenologica della conoscitività dell'arte. Milano, 1968.

Phil 8415.10.3 — Ottaviano, Carmelo. La legge della come legge universale della natura. 3. ed. Padova, 1970.

Phil 8416.5 — Papennyi, Z.S. O khudozhestvennom obraze. Moskva, 1961.

Phil 8416.6 — Piemonteal, Filippo. Problemi di filosofia dell'arte. Torino, 1945.

Phil 8416.8 — Pareyson, Luigi. L'estetica e i suoi problemi. Milano, 1961.

Phil 8416.8.5 — Pareyson, Luigi. Theoria dell'arte; saggi di estetica. Milano, 1965.

Phil 8416.8.12 — Pareyson, Luigi. I problemi dell'estetica. 2. ed. Milano, 1966.

Phil 8416.8.15 — Pareyson, Luigi. Conversazioni di estetica. Milano, 1966.

Phil 8416.9 — Pepper, Stephen. The work of art. Indiana, 1955.

Phil 8416.10 — Portnoy, Julius. A psychology of art creation. Philadephia, 1942.

Phil 8416.11 — Plekhanov, Georgii Valentinovich. Iskusstvo i literatura. Moskva, 1948.

Phil 8416.11.5 — Plekhanov, Georgii Valentinovich. Literatura i estetika. Moskva, 1958.

Phil 8416.11.10 — Plekhanov, Georgii Valentinovich. Kunst und Literatur. Berlin, 1955.

Phil 8416.11.15 — Plekhanov, Georgii Valentinovich. Iskusstvo i obshchestvennaia zhizn'. Moskva, 1922.

Phil 8416.11.20 — Plekhanov, Georgii Valentinovich. Art and society. N.Y., 1936.

Phil 8416.11.22 — Plekhanov, Georgii Valentinovich. Art and social life. London, 1953.

Phil 8416.11.25 — Plekhanov, Georgii Valentinovich. L'art et de vie sociale (quatorze études). Paris, 1950.

Phil 8416.12 — Pareyson, Luigi. Estetica. Torino, 1954.

Phil 8416.13 — Pagano, José L. Motivos de estética. 2. ed. Buenos Aires, 1941.

Phil 8416.14 — Perls, Hugo. Das Geheimnis der Kunst. Zürich, 1959.

Phil 8416.15 — Ponze, Francis. Le murmure condition et destin de l'artiste. Lyon, 1956.

Phil 8416.16 — Petruzzellis, N. Filosofia dell'arte. 2. ed. Mazara, 1952.

Phil 8416.16.2 — Petruzzellis, N. Filosofia dell'arte. 3. ed. Napoli, 1964.

Phil 8416.17 — Pro, Diezo F. Tres aspectos de la cultura. Mendoza, 1942.

Phil 8416.18 — Propris, A. de. Brevario della nuova estetica. Roma, 1951.

Phil 8416.18.5 — Propris, A. de. Problemi di estetica e critica. Roma, 1954.

Phil 8416.19 — Piemontese, F. L'intelligenza nell'arte. Milano, 1955.

Phil 8416.21 — Purser, J.W.R. Art and truth. Glasgow, 1937.

Phil 8416.22 — Pudor, H. Laokoon; kunstheoretische Essays. Leipzig, 1902.

Phil 8401 - 8426 Esthetics - Treatises on esthetics - General works - Individual authors (A-Z) - cont.

Phil 8416.23 Porena, M. Che cos'é il bello? Schema d'un estetica psicologica. Milano, 1905.
Phil 8416.24 Parkhurst, H.H. Beauty; an interpretation of art and the imaginative life. 1st ed. N.Y., 1930.
Phil 8416.25 Prölss, Robert. Ästhetik; Belehrungen über die Wissenschaft vom Schönen und der Kunst. 3. Aufl. Leipzig, 1904.
Phil 8416.26 Pap, Julius. Kunst und Illusion. Leipzig, 1914.
Phil 8416.27 Perès, Jean. L'art et le reel; essai de metaphysique fondée sur l'esthétique. Paris, 1897.
Phil 8416.28 Prall, D.W. Aesthetic judgment. N.Y., 1929.
Phil 8416.29 Parker, de W.H. The principles of aesthetics. Boston, 1920.
Phil 8416.30 Parker, H.W. The spirit of beauty; essays, scientific and aesthetic. N.Y., 1888.
Phil 8416.31 Pierson, A. Schöhiedszon en levenswijsheid. Arnhem, 1886.
Phil 8416.32 Pirenne, H.E. Essai sur le beau. Paris, 1924.
Phil 8416.33 Pilo, Mario. Estetica lexioni sur bello. 2. ed. Milano, 1921.
Phil 8416.34 Pepper, S.C. Aesthetic quality, a contextualistic theory of beauty. N.Y., 1938.
Phil 8416.34.5 Pepper, S.C. The basis of criticism in the arts. Cambridge, 1945.
Phil 8416.35 Piccardt, K.L. Het wezen der kunst. Amsterdam, 1937.
Phil 8416.36 Pereira, M.A. Vida e morte das formas. Lisboa, 1962.
Phil 8416.37 Poggioli, Renato. Teoria dell'arte d'avanguardia. Bologna, 1962.
Phil 8416.37.5 Poggioli, Renato. The theory of the avant-garde. Cambridge, 1968.
Phil 8416.38 Pospelov, Gennadii N. Esteticheskoe i khudozhestvennoe. Moskva, 1965.
Phil 8416.39 Pimienta, Gustave. Évidences. Paris, 1965.
Phil 8416.40 Pilar, Ivo. Secesija. Zagreb, 1898.
Phil 8416.42 Prestipino, Giuseppe. Lavovo e conoscenza nell'arte. Napoli, 1967.
Phil 8416.44 Pasi, Isak. Esteticheski studii. Sofiia, 1970.
Phil 8417.2 Quadri, G. La vita estetica, e lo sviluppo della coscienza. Firenze, 1953.
Phil 8417.3 Quatremère de Quincy, Antoine C. Essai sur la nature, le but et les moyens de l'imitation dans les beaux-arts. Paris, 1823.
Phil 8417.3.5 Quatremère de Quincy, Antoine C. An essay on the nature, the end, and the means of imitation in the fine arts. London, 1837.
Phil 8417.3.15 Schneider, René. L'esthétique classique chez Quatremère. Paris, 1910.
Phil 8417.3.20 Schneider, René. Quatremère de Quincy et son intervention dans les arts, 1788-1830. Paris, 1910.
Phil 8418.2 Ratzal, Friedrich. Uber Naturschilderung. München, 1904.
Phil 8418.4 Raymond, G.L. The representative significance of form. N.Y., 1900.
Phil 8418.4.2 Raymond, G.L. The representative significance of form. 2. ed. N.Y., 1909.
Phil 8418.5 Raymond, G.L. Art theory; an introduction to the study of comparative aesthetics. N.Y., 1894.
Phil 8418.5.2 Raymond, G.L. Art in theory; an introduction to the study of comparative aesthetics. 2. ed. N.Y., 1909.
Phil 8418.6 Raymond, G.L. The essentials of aesthetics in music. N.Y., 1911.
Phil 8418.6.3 Raymond, G.L. The essentials of aesthetics in music. 3.ed. N.Y., 1921.
Phil 8418.6.10 Raymond, G.L. An art philosopher's cabinet. N.Y., 1915.
Phil 8418.7 Rogerio Sanchez, J. Estética general. Madrid, 1907.
Phil 8418.8 Rusu, Liviu. Essai sur la création artistique comme révélation du sens de l'éxistence. Paris, 1935.
Phil 8418.8.5 Rusu, Liviu. Essai sur la création artistique. Paris, 1935.
Phil 8418.10 Rensi, G. La scepsi estetica. Bologna, 1919.
Phil 8418.11 Rosenkranz, K. Ästhetik des Hässlichen. Königsberg, 1853.
Phil 8418.12 Roussel-Despierres, F. L'idéal esthétique. Paris, 1904.
Phil 8418.13 Ruskin, J. Frondes agrestes. N.Y., 1875.
Phil 8418.14 Rogger, K. Essai sur la valeur expressive de l'art. Dijon, 1929.
Phil 8418.15 Russo, S. Arte e libertá e altri saggi. Padova, 1960.
Phil 8418.16 Russi, Antonio. L'arte et le arti. Pisa, 1960.
Phil 8418.17.5 Reimers, N.A. Le concept du beau; essaie d'une théorie. Paris, 1930.
Phil 8418.18 Redeker, Horst. Geschichte und Gesetze des Ästhetischen. Berlin, 1960.
Phil 8418.19 Roux, J. Le sentiment de la beauté; étude de psychologie. Paris, 1908.
Phil 8418.20 Read, Herbert. The forms of things unknown. London, 1960.
Phil 8418.20.5 Read, Herbert. Icon and idea. Harvard, 1955.
Phil 8418.20.10 Read, Herbert. Art and alienation: the role of the artist in society. London, 1967.
Phil 8418.21 Reid, L.A. A study in aesthetics. London, 1931.
Phil 8418.22 Ruefenacht, E. Lebensstufe und Kunstwerk, ihre Symbolik und ihre Foringesetze. 1. Aufl. Zürich, 1960.
Phil 8418.24 Reynolds, J. Discourses. London, 1884.
X Cg Phil 8418.24.5 Reynolds, J. Discourses. London, 1842.
Phil 8418.25 Rouart, Eugène. L'artiste et la société. Paris, 1902.
Phil 8418.30.2 Ruvo, Vincenzo de. Il bello. 2. ed. Napoli, 1965.
Phil 8418.35 Ruschioni, Ada. Lineamenti di una storia della poetica e dell'estetica. Milano, 1966.
Phil 8418.40 Rubert de Ventós, Xavier. Teoría de la sensibilidad. 1. ed. Barcelona, 1969.
Phil 8418.42 Razummyi, Vladimir A. Esteticheskoe vospitanie. Moskva, 1969.
Phil 8418.43 Rochlitz, Manfred. Einige philosophische und informationstheoretische Aspekte der moralisch-ästhetischen Verhaltensdetermination der Persönlichkeit. Diss. Leipzig? 1967?
Phil 8419.2 Sacchetti, E. Che cos è l'arte. Firenze, 1961.
Phil 8419.3 Sturmfels, W. Grundprobleme der Ästhetik. München, 1963.
Phil 8419.4 Schasler, Max. Ästhetik, Grundzüge der Wissenschaft des Schönen und der Kunst. Leipzig, 1886. 2v.
Phil 8419.6F Salisbury, Edward. Principles of domestic taste. New Haven, 1877.
Phil 8419.7 Solger, K.W.F. K.W.F. Solger's Vorlesungen über Ästhetik. Leipzig, 1829.
Phil 8419.8 Scheffler, K. Form als Schicksa. 2. Aufl. Erlenbach, 1943.
Phil 8419.9 Stange, Alfred. Die Welt als Gestalt. Köln, 1952.
Phil 8419.10 Siebeck, H. Das Wesen der ästhetischen Anschauung. Berlin, 1875.
Phil 8419.11 Schneider, E. Aesthetic motive. N.Y., 1939.

Phil 8401 - 8426 Esthetics - Treatises on esthetics - General works - Individual authors (A-Z) - cont.

Phil 8419.12 Stein, Leo. Appreciation: painting, poetry and prose. N.Y., 1947.
Phil 8419.12.5 Stein, Leo. The ABC of aesthetics. N.Y., 1927.
Phil 8419.13 Spalletti, G. Saggio sopra la bellezza. Firenze, 1933.
Phil 8419.14 Shishkov, G. Erschopfte Kunst oder Kunstformalismus? Schlehdorf, 1952.
Phil 8419.15 Schulze-Soelde, W. Das Gesetz der Schönheit. Darmstadt, 1925.
Phil 8419.16 Schmied, W. Das Poetische in der Kunst. Nürnburg, 1960.
Phil 8419.17 Sewell, Arthur. The physiology of beauty. London, 1931.
Phil 8419.18 Stefanini, Luigi. Trattado di estetica. Brescia, 1955-
Phil 8419.19 Stolovich, L.N. Predmet estetiki. Moskva, 1961.
Phil 8419.19.5 Esteticheskoe v deistvitel'nosti i v iskusstve. Moskva, 1959.
Phil 8419.20 Stubbe, Achilles. Het zien en genieten van schilderkunst. 4. druk. Hasselt, 1960.
Phil 8419.21 Šimat, Žarko. Sotto il velame; aspetti psicologici dell'arte. 1.ed. Roma, 1959.
Phil 8419.22 Stolnitz, Jerome. Aesthetics and philosophy of art criticism. Boston, 1960.
Phil 8419.23 Simmel, Georg. Zur Philosophie der Kunst. Potsdam, 1922.
Phil 8419.24 Symonds, J.A. The principles of beauty. London, 1857.
Phil 8419.25 Streignart, Joseph. Trente-trois oeuvres d'art. v.1-2. Gembloux, 1953?
Phil 8419.26 Spence, Joseph. Crito, or A dialogue on beauty. Edinburgh, 1885.
Phil 8419.26.1 Spence, Joseph. Crito, or A dialogue on beauty. Edinburgh, 1885.
Phil 8419.26.5 Howard, W.G. Reiz ist Schönheit in Bewegung; a Rettung of Joseph Spence. n.p., 1909.
Phil 8419.27 Santangelo, P.E. Discorso sull'arte. Milano, 1956.
Phil 8419.28 Stace, W.T. The meaning of beauty, a theory of aesthetics. London, 1929.
Phil 8419.29 Schumacher, F. Die Sprache der Kunst. Stuttgart, 1942.
Phil 8419.30 Silcock, Arnold. A background for beauty. London, 1951.
Phil 8419.31 Siunerberg, K.A. Iskusstvo i narod; sbornik. Peterburg, 1922.
Phil 8419.32 Schimmelpenninck, Mary Anne. The principles of beauty as manifested in nature, art, and human character. London, 1859.
Phil 8419.33 Saitschick, R. Kunstschöpfer und Kunstschaffen. Marburg, 1957.
Phil 8419.34 Sobeski, M. Mýsl a marmur, i inne szkice estetyczne. Wyd. 1. Warszawa, 1959.
Phil 8419.35A Salinger, H. Über das Schöne als Sinnbild und Wegweisung. Köln, 1960.
Phil 8419.35B Salinger, H. Über das Schöne als Sinnbild und Wegweisung. Köln, 1960.
Phil 8419.36 Sébag, Henri. Anatomie de l'âme; essai de psych-esthétique. Paris, 1952. 3v.
Phil 8419.37 Stoeckl, A. Grundriss der Ästhetik. Mainz, 1871.
Phil 8419.38 Severgnini, D. La inevitabile illusione; rilievi modali dell'estetica. Torino, 1960.
Phil 8419.39 Wili, Hans. Johann G. Sulzer; Personlichkeit und Kunstphilosophie. St. Gallen, 1945.
Phil 8419.39.5 Tumarkin, Anna. Der Ästhetiker Johann G. Sulzer. Frauenfeld, 1933.
Phil 8419.40 Santayana, G. The sense of beauty, being the outlines of aesthetic theory. N.Y., 1955.
Phil 8419.40.5 Santayana, G. The sense of beauty, being the outlines of aesthetic theory. N.Y., 1898.
Phil 8419.40.6A Santayana, G. The sense of beauty. N.Y., 1896. 3v.
Phil 8419.40.6B Santayana, G. The sense of beauty. N.Y., 1896. 3v.
Phil 8419.40.6C Santayana, G. The sense of beauty. N.Y., 1896. 3v.
Phil 8419.41 Sully Prudhomme, R.F.A. L'expression dans les beaux-arts. Paris, 1883.
Phil 8419.42 Stein, H. von. Vorlesungen über Ästhetik. Stuttgart, 1897.
Phil 8419.43 Solger, K.W.F. Erwin; vier Gespräche über das Schöne une die Kunst. Berlin, 1815. 2v.
Phil 8419.43.2 Solger, K.W.F. Erwin. München, 1971.
Phil 8419.43.80 Grunert, B. Solgers Lehre vom Schönen in ihrem Verhältnis zur Kunstlehre. Marburg, 1960.
Phil 8419.44 Séailles, G. Essai sur le génie dans l'art. Paris, 1883.
Phil 8419.45 Schoen, Max. Art and beauty. N.Y., 1932.
Phil 8419.46 Stone, W.F. Questions on the philosophy of art. London, 1897.
Phil 8419.47 Shaw, T.L. Art reconstructed, a new theory of aesthetics. Boston, 1937.
Phil 8419.48 Souriau, E. L'avenir de l'esthétique essai sur l'objet d'une science naissante. Paris, 1929.
Phil 8419.50 Şindelář, Dušan. Smysl věcí. Praha, 1963.
Phil 8419.50.5 Şindelář, Dušan. Estetické vnémáné. Praha, 1961.
Phil 8419.50.10 Šindelář, Dušan. Tržiště estetiky. Vyd. 1. Praha, 1969.
Phil 8419.51 Schneiderfranken, J.A. Aus Meiner Malerwerkstatt. Basel, 1932.
Phil 8419.52 Saarinen, E. Search for form. N.Y., 1948.
Phil 8419.53 Schillinger, J. The mathematical basis of the arts. N.Y., 1948.
Phil 8419.54 Schneiderfranken, J.A. Das Reich der Kunst. Basel, 1933.
Phil 8419.55 Sesti, Luigi. Quattro dialoghi sull'arte. Milano, 1963.
Phil 8419.56 Sparshott, F.E. The structure of aesthetics. Toronto, 1963.
Phil 8419.57 Spirito, Ugo. Critica dell'estetica. Firenze, 1964.
Phil 8419.60 Sandstroem, Sven. Konstforskning. Stockholm, 1965.
Phil 8419.61 Santinello, Giovanni. Estetica della forma. Padova, 1962.
Phil 8419.62 Shamota, Mykolaz. O svobode tvorchestva. Moskva, 1966.
Phil 8419.63 Shudria, Kateyna P. Estetychnyi ideal myttsia. Kyïv, 1967.
Phil 8419.64 Şokolov, Aleksandr N. Teoriia stilia. Moskva, 1968.
Phil 8419.65 Šabouk, Sáva. Jazyk umění. Praha, 1969.
Phil 8419.66 Stolovich, Leonid N. Kategoriia prekrasnogo i obshchestvennyi ideal. Moskva, 1969.
Phil 8419.67 Schmidt, Siegfried Josef. Ästhetische Prozesse. Köln, 1971.
Phil 8419.68 Séran de la Tour. L'art de sentir et de juger en matière de goût. v.1-2. Genève, 1970.
Phil 8419.70 Slattery, Mary Francis. Hazard, form, and value. Detroit, 1971.
Phil 8420.5 Tolstykh, V. Iskusstvo i moral'. Moskva, 1962.
Phil 8420.7 Trudu, Luciano. La legge del bello. Padova, 1962.
Phil 8420.9 Todd, John. The arts, artists and thinkers. London, 1959.
Phil 8420.11 Tafts, James. On the genesis of the aesthetic categories. Chicago, 1902.
Phil 8420.12 Thorburn, J.M. Art and the unconscious; a psychological approach to a problem of philosophy. London, 1925.

357

Classified Listing

Phil 8401 - 8426 Esthetics - Treatises on esthetics - General works - Individual authors (A-Z) - cont.

Phil 8420.13 Torres-García, J. Universalismo constructivo. Buenos Aires, 1944.
Phil 8420.13.5 Torres-García, J. La recuperacion del objeto. v.1-2. Montevideo, 1965.
Phil 8420.14 Tilgher, A. Primi scritti de estetica. Roma, 1931.
Phil 8420.14.5 Tilgher, A. Estetica; teoria generale dell'attività artistica. Roma, 1931.
Phil 8420.15 Talia, G.B. Principi di estetica. Venezia, 1827-28. 2v.
Phil 8420.16 Torrey, J. A theory of fine art. N.Y., 1874.
Phil 8420.17 Teige, Karel. Stavba a báseň; umĕnídues a zítra. Praha, 1927.
Phil 8420.18 Tari, Antonio. Saggi di estetica e metafisica. Bari, 1911.
Phil 8420.19 Testa, Aldo. Filosofia dell'arte. Bologna, 1959.
Phil 8420.20 Trahndorff, K.F.E. Ästhetik, oder Lehre von der Weltauschauung und Kunst. v.1-2. Berlin, 1827.
Phil 8420.21 Tatarkiewicz, W. Skupienie i marzenie. Kraków, 1951.
Phil 8420.22 Treves, Marco. Trattato d'estetica. Firenze, 1938.
Phil 8420.23 Tollemonde, G. de. Du juste milieu; traité général de philosophie et d'art. Paris, 1910.
Phil 8420.24 Torossian, A. A guide to aesthetics. Stanford, 1937.
Phil 8420.25 Trofimov, Pavel S. Estetika marksizma-leninizma. Moskva, 1964.
Phil 8420.26 Tartalja, Ivo. Djure Daničića lekcije iz estetike. Beograd, 1968.
Phil 8420.28 Tilghman, Benjamin R. The expression of emotion in the visual arts: a philosophical inquiry. The Hague, 1970.
Phil 8421.2 Ulricus Engelberti, Argentinensis. Des Ulricus Engelberti von Strassburg O. Pr. (+1277) Abhandlung de Pulchro. München, 1926.
Phil 8421.3 Usher, James. Clio, or A discourse on taste. 2. ed. London, 1769.
Phil 8421.4 Ushenko, A.P. Dynamics of art. Indiana, 1953.
Phil 8422.2 Volbehr, Theodor. Gibt es Kunstgesetze. Esslingen, 1906.
Phil 8422.3 Vieira de Almeida, F. Filosofia da arte; ensaio. Coimbra, 1942.
Phil 8422.4 Vanslov, V.V. Problema prekrasnogo. Moskva, 1957.
Phil 8422.4.5 Vanslov, V.V. Soderzhanie i forma v iskusstve. Moskva, 1956.
Phil 8422.5 Volkelt, J. System der Ästhetik. München, 1905-14. 3v.
Phil 8422.6 Valdes Rodriguez, Manuel. Relaciones entre lo bueno, lo bello y lo verdadero. Tesis, 1888.
Phil 8422.7A Vischer, F.T. Ästhetik. Reutlingen, 1846-57. 3v.
Phil 8422.7B Vischer, F.T. Ästhetik. Reutlingen, 1846-57.
Phil 8422.7.2 Vischer, F.T. Ästhetik Vollständiges, Inhaltsverzeichniss, Namen und Sachregister. Stuttgart, 1858.
Phil 8422.7.5 Vischer, F.T. Ästhetik; oder, Wissenschaft des Schönen. München, 1922-23. 6v.
Phil 8422.7.10 Vischer, F.T. Das Schöne und die Kunst. Stuttgart, 1898.
Phil 8422.7.15 Vischer, F.T. Über das Erhabene und konische Einleitung. Frankfurt, 1967.
Phil 8422.7.30 Oelmueller, W. Friedrich T. Vischer und das Problem der nachhegelschen Ästhetik. Stuttgart, 1959.
Phil 8422.8 Carmella, S. I problemi del gusto e dell'arte nella mente di Pietro Verri. Napoli, 1926.
Phil 8422.9 Vendéen, E. Principes du beau. Paris, 1912.
Phil 8422.10 Vascoucelos, J. Estética. 2. ed. México, 1936.
Phil 8422.11 Vogt, T. Form und Gehalt in der Ästhetik. Wien, 1865.
Phil 8422.12 Vedel, V. Liv og kunst. København, 1949. 2v.
Phil 8422.13 Volpe, G. della. Fondamenti di una filosofia dell'espressione. Bologna, 1936.
Phil 8422.14A Véron, Eugène. Aesthetics. London, 1879.
Phil 8422.14B Véron, Eugène. Aesthetics. London, 1879.
Phil 8422.15 Volkelt, Johannes. Das ästhetische Bewusstsein. Photoreproduction. München, 1920.
Phil 8422.15.5 Volkelt, Johannes. Ästhetische Zeitfragen. München, 1895.
Phil 8422.16 Vischer, R. Drei Schriften zum ästhetischen Formproblem. Halle, 1927.
Phil 8422.17 Volek, Jaroslav. O předmětu a metodě estetáky a obecne teorie umění. Praha, 1963.
Phil 8422.17.5 Volek, Jaroslav. Základy obecné teorie umění. Praha, 1968.
Phil 8422.18 Vaiman, Semen T. Marksistskaia estetika i problemy realizma. Moskva, 1964.
Phil 8423.2 Weber, J. Paul. La psychologie de l'art. Paris, 1961.
Phil 8423.3 Wernaer, R.M. Das ästhetische Symbol. Leipzig, 1907.
Phil 8423.4 Witasek, Stephan. Grundzüge der allgemeinen Ästhetik. Leipzig, 1904.
Phil 8423.5 Wright, W.H. The creative will, studies in the philosophy and syntax of aesthetics. N.Y., 1916.
Phil 8423.6 Wize, K.F. Abriss einer Wissenschaftslehre der Ästhetik. Berlin, 1909.
Phil 8423.7 Wulf, M. de. L'oeuvre d'art et la beauté. Louvain, 1920.
Phil 8423.8 Wienbarg, Ludolf. Ästhetische Feldzüge. 2. Aufl. Hamburg, 1919.
Phil 8423.8.2 Wienbarg, Ludolf. Ästhetische Feldzüge. Berlin, 1964.
Phil 8423.8.25 Schweizer, V. Ludolf Wienbarg als jungdeutscher Ästhetiker und Kunstkritiker. Leipzig, 1896.
Phil 8423.9 Waelhem, M. de. Quelques réflexions sur la conception du beau. Paris, 1958.
Phil 8423.10 Walsh, Dorothy. The objectivity of the judgment of aesthetic value. Lancaster, 1936.
Phil 8423.11 Weiss, Paul. Nine basic arts. Carbondale, 1961.
Phil 8423.12 Wieckberg, W. Grundwissenschaftliche Unterlage der Kunstwissenschaft. Charlottenburg, 1922.
Phil 8423.13 Wilkens, Claudius. Aesthetik i ømrids. Kjøbenhavn, 1888.
Phil 8423.14 Waetzoldt, W. Das Kunstwerk als Organismus. Leipzig, 1905.
Phil 8423.15 Weisbach, W. Von Geschmack und seinen Wandlungen. Basel, 1947.
Phil 8423.16 Winckelmann, Johann Joachim. Johann Winckelmann, G. Ephraim Lessing klassische Schönheit. Jena, 1906.
Phil 8423.16.5 Winckelmann, Johann Joachim. Kleine Schriften, Vorreden, Entwürfe. Berlin, 1968.
Phil 8423.16.10 Winckelmann, Johann Joachim. Werke in einem Band. Berlin, 1969.
Phil 8423.16.15 Winckelmann, Johann Joachim. Gedanken über die Nachahmung der griechischen Werke in der Malerei und Bildhauerkunst. Stuttgart, 1969.
Phil 8423.16.80 Spengler, Walter Eckehart. Der Begriff des Schönen bei Winckelmann. Göppingen, 1970.
Phil 8423.17 Werner, Alfred. Impressionismus und Expressionismus. Leipzig, 1917.
Phil 8423.18 Wembridge, Eleanor Harris Rowland. The significance of art. Boston, 1913.
Phil 8423.19 Wyneken, Karl. Der Aufbau der Form beim naturlichen Werden und kunstlerischen Schoffen. Freiburg, 1903- 2v.
Phil 8423.19F Wyneken, Karl. Der Aufbau der form beim natürlichen Werden und kunstlerischen Schoffen. Atlas. Freiburg, 1903-
Phil 8423.20 Levy, Hanna. Henri Wölfflin; sa théorie, ses prédécesseurs. Rottweil, 1936.
Phil 8423.21 Worringer, W. Abstraktion und Einfühlung. München, 1959.
Phil 8423.22 Weitz, M. Philosophy of the arts. Cambridge, 1950.
Phil 8423.23 Woelfflin, H. Das Erklären von Kunstwerken. Köln, 1940.
Phil 8423.24 Wind, Edgar. Art and anarchy, and other essays. London, 1963.
Phil 8423.25 Wahl, Marcelle. Création picturale et ordre cérébral. Paris, 1964.
Phil 8423.26.2 Weisse, Christian H. System der Ästhetik als Wissenschaft von der Idee der Schönheit, reprografischer Nachdruck von 1830. Hildesheim, 1966.
VPhil 8423.27 Wallis, Mieczysław. Przeżycie i wartość. Wyd. 1. Kraków, 1968.
Phil 8423.28 Wiegand, Anke. Die Schönheit und das Böse. München, 1967.
Phil 8425.2 Young, E. Art: its constitution and capacities. Bristol, 1854.
Phil 8426.2 Zeising, Adolf. Ästhetische Forschungen. Frankfurt, 1855.
Phil 8426.3 Ziegenfuss, W. Die phänomenologische Ästhetik nach Grundsätzen und bisherigen Ergebnissen kritisch Dargestellt. Borna, 1927.
Phil 8426.4 Zimmermann, R. Ästhetik. Wien, 1858-65. 2v.
Phil 8426.5 Ziehen, T. Vorlesungen über Ästhetik. Halle, 1923-25. 2v.
Phil 8426.6 Zotov, Ivan A. Priroda prekrasnogo. Moskva, 1965.
Phil 8426.7 Ziff, Paul. Philosophic turnings. Ithaca, N.Y., 1966.
Phil 8426.8 Zis', Avner Ia. Iskusstvo i estetika. Moskva, 1967.
Phil 8426.9 Zykmund, Václav. K základní otázce estetiky. Praha, 1957.
Phil 8426.11 Zelenov, L.A. Protsess esteticheskogo otrazheniia. Moskva, 1969.

Phil 8430 Esthetics - Treatises on esthetics - Special topics - Relations of esthetics to other disciplines, etc.

Phil 8430.3 Moles, Abraham A. Théorie de l'information et perception esthétique. Paris, 1958.
Phil 8430.3.5 Moles, Abraham A. Information theory and esthetic perception. Urbana, 1966.
Phil 8430.5 Eversople, Finley. Christian faith and the contemporary arts. N.Y., 1962.
Phil 8430.6 Benaz, Manuel. Lo bello y la buena a la luz. Buenos Aires, 1933.
Phil 8430.7 Burckhard, M. Ästhetik und Sozialwissenschaft. Stuttgart, 1895.
Phil 8430.8 Carpenter, Edward. Angels' wings. London, 1898.
Phil 8430.8.5 Carpenter, Edward. The religious influence of art. Cambridge, 1870.
Phil 8430.9 Coculesco, P. Esthétique. Paris, 1953.
Phil 8430.10 Caillais, Roger. Meduse et cie. Paris, 1960.
Phil 8430.11A Dudley, Louise. The humanities. 1. ed. N.Y., 1940. 2v.
Phil 8430.11B Dudley, Louise. The humanities. 1. ed. N.Y., 1940. 2v.
Phil 8430.11.2 Dudley, Louise. The humanities. 2. ed. N.Y., 1951.
Phil 8430.12 Dreher, Eugen. Die KunstIn ihrer Beziehung. Berlin, 1878.
Phil 8430.13 Castelnuovo, E. El arte y las masas, ensayos sobre una nueva teoría della actividad estética. Buenos Aires, 1935.
Phil 8430.14 Calcara, A. Discorsi di letteratura e d'arte. Marcianise, 1961.
Phil 8430.15 Fazio-Allmayer, V. Moralità dell'arte. Firenze, 1953.
Phil 8430.16 Gleizes, A. Vers une conscience plastique; la forme et l'histoire. Paris, 1932.
Phil 8430.17 Hay, D.R. The science of beauty, as developed in nature. Edinburgh, 1856.
Phil 8430.18 Lalo, C. L'art et la morale. Paris, 1922.
Phil 8430.18.5 Lalo, C. L'arte et la vie sociale. Paris, 1921.
Phil 8430.19 Loisel, A. L'expérience esthétique et l'ideal chrétien. Paris, 1909.
Phil 8430.20 Lénström, C.J. Om konstens förhållande till religionen. Upsala, 1842.
Phil 8430.22 Raymond, G.L. The genesis of art form. N.Y., 1893.
Phil 8430.23 Robertson, A. Contrasts: the arts and religion. London, 1947.
Phil 8430.24 Taylor, Harold. Art and the intellect. N.Y., 1960.
Phil 8430.25 Walston, C. Harmonism and conscious evolution. London, 1922.
Phil 8430.26 Salicrú Puigvert, C. Moray y arte. Barcelona, 1960.
Phil 8430.27 Ruefenacht, E. Mächte der Gestaltung; vom künstlerischen, philosophischen und religiösen Sein. Zürich, 1957.
Phil 8430.28 Riverso, M. L'esperienza estetica e la vita del fanciullo. Napoli, 1958.
Phil 8430.29A Raphael, Max. Provalon, Marx, Picasso. Paris, 1933.
Phil 8430.29B Raphael, Max. Provalon, Marx, Picasso. Paris, 1933.
Phil 8430.30 Jaszi, Oszhai. Muveszet és erkölcs. Budapest, 1908.
Phil 8430.31 Kunzle, Magnus. Ethik und Ästhetik. Freiburg, 1910.
Phil 8430.32 Gotshalk, D.W. Art and the social order. Chicago, 1947.
Phil 8430.34 Raymond, G.L. The genesis of art form. N.Y., 1893.
Phil 8430.35 Vogel, Heinrich. Der Christ und das Schöne. 1. Aufl. Berlin, 1955.
Phil 8430.36 Michel, E. Der Weg zum Mythos. Jena, 1919.
Phil 8430.37 Mumford, L. The role of the creative arts in comtemporary society. Durham, 1958.
Phil 8430.38 Nebel, G. Das Ereignis es Schönen. Stuttgart, 1953.
Phil 8430.39 Meier, N.C. Art in human affairs. N.Y., 1942.
Phil 8430.40 Thode, H. Kundt und Sittlichkeit. Heidelberg, 1906.
Phil 8430.41 Thielicke, H. Das verhältnis zwischen demethischen und dem ästhetischen. Leipzig, 1932.
Phil 8430.42 Souriau, Étienne. La correspondance des arts. Paris, 1947.
Phil 8430.42.1 Souriau, Étienne. La correspondance des arts, éléments d'esthétique comparée. Paris, 1969.
Phil 8430.43 Freyre, G. Arte, ciêncis e trópico. São Paulo, 1962.
Phil 8430.44 Leeuw, G. van der. Sacred and profane beauty. N.Y., 1963. 10v.
Phil 8430.45 Vučković, Vojislav. Umetnost i umetničko delo. Beograd, 1962.
Phil 8430.45.5 Vučković, Vojislav. Studije, eseji, kritike. Beograd, 1968. 2v.
Phil 8430.46 Adler, Mortimer Jerome. Poetry and politics. Pittsburgh, 1965.

Classified Listing

Phil 8430   Esthetics - Treatises on esthetics - Special topics - Relations of esthetics to other disciplines, etc. - cont.

Phil 8430.47   Ladyhina, Aryadna B. Iskusstvo i sovremennost'. Minsk, 1964.
Phil 8430.48   Eremeev, Arkadii F. Vek nauki i iskusstvo. Moskva, 1965.
Phil 8430.49   Stardelov, Georgi. Esci. Skopje, 1958.
Phil 8430.50   Problemi na khudozhestvenoto tvorchestvo. Sofiia, 1968.
Phil 8430.51   Naksianowicz-Golaszewska, Maria. Odbiorca sztuki jako krytyk. Wyd.1. Kraków, 1967.
Phil 8430.53   Pesce, Domenico. Apollineo e dionisiaco nella storia del classicismo. Napoli, 1968.
Phil 8430.55.2   Kayser, Hans. Akróasis, die Lehre von der Harmonik der Welt. 2. Aufl. Basel, 1964.
Phil 8430.57   Vian, Boris. En avant la zizique...et par ici les gros sous. Paris, 1966.
VPhil 8430.58   Iastrebova, Nataliia A. Esteticheski paraleli. Sofiia, 1968.
Phil 8430.60   Frances, Robert. Psychologie de l'esthétique. Paris, 1968.
Phil 8430.62   John, Erhard. Probleme der marxistisch-leninistischen Ästhetik. Halle, 1968.
Phil 8430.63   Plebe, Armando. Che cosa è l'estetica sovietica. Roma, 1969.
Phil 8430.64   Dorfles, Gillo. L'estetica del mito. Milano, 1967.
Phil 8430.66   Evans, Joan. Taste and temperament. London, 1939.
Phil 8430.68   Hanslick, Eduard. Vom Musikalisch-Schönen. 16. Aufl. Wiesbaden, 1966.
Phil 8430.70   Bolam, David Whielden. Art and belief. N.Y., 1970.
Phil 8430.72   Iakovlev, Eugenii G. Esteticheskoe soznanie iskusstvo i religiia. Moskva, 1969.
Phil 8430.74   Iuldashev, Lekal G. Esteticheskoe chuvstvo i proizvedenie iskusstva. Moskva, 1969.
Phil 8430.76   Tagliaferri, Aldo. L'estetica dell'oggettivo. Milano, 1968.
Phil 8430.77   Sikors'kyi, Qurii P. Estetychna tsinnist' tekhniky. Kyïv, 1970.
Phil 8430.79   Thiele, Joachim. Verfahren der statistischen Ästhetik. Hamburg, 1966.
Phil 8430.81   Klein, Robert. La forme et l'intelligible. Paris, 1970.
Phil 8430.83   Estetika i proizvodstvo. Moskva, 1969.
Phil 8430.85   Novozhilova, Larisa I. Sotsiologiia iskusstva. Leningrad, 1968.
Phil 8430.86   Pracht, Erwin. Sozialistischer Realismus-Positionen, Probleme, Perspektiven. 1. Aufl. Berlin, 1970.
Phil 8430.87   Problemy estetiki i esteticheskogo vospitaniia. Moskva, 1967.
Phil 8430.89   Kofman, Sarah. L'enfance de l'art. Paris, 1970.
Phil 8430.90   Pavlovskii, Boris V. U istokov sovetskoi khudozhestvennoi kritiki. Leningrad, 1970.
Phil 8430.92   Afasizhev, Marat Nurbievich. Freĭdizm i burzhuaznoe iskusstvo. Moskva, 1971.
Phil 8430.94   Bono, Pierluigi. La morale dell'artista. Milano, 1969.

Phil 8432   Esthetics - Treatises on esthetics - Special topics - Inspiration

Phil 8432.2   Heidsieck, F. L'inspiration. 1. éd. Paris, 1961.

Phil 8434   Esthetics - Treatises on esthetics - Special topics - Landscape, nature, etc.

Htn Phil 8434.2*   Gilpin, W. Remarks on forest scenery, and other woodland views. London, 1791. 2v.
Htn Phil 8434.2.5*   Gilpin, W. Three essays: on picturesque beauty. London, 1792.
Phil 8434.2.10   Gilpin, W. Remarks on forest scenery, and other woodland views. 3. ed. London, 1808. 2v.
Phil 8434.2.15   Gilpin, W. Observations on forest scenery. Edinburgh, 1834.
Phil 8434.3.5   Van Dyke, J.C. Nature for its own sake. 5th ed. N.Y., 1908.
Phil 8434.4   Hussey, C. The picturesque. London, 1927.
Phil 8434.5   Tea, Eva. Il corpo umano. Brescia, 1949.
Phil 8434.6   Shepard, Paul. Man in the landscape. N.Y., 1967.

Phil 8436   Esthetics - Treatises on esthetics - Special topics - Grotesque, ugliness, etc.

Phil 8436.5   Gori, Gino. Il grottesco nell'arte e nella letteratura. Roma, 1926.

Phil 8440   Esthetics - Treatises on esthetics - Special topics - Symbolism

Phil 8440.5   Hermeren, Göran. Representation and meaning in the visual arts. Lund, 1969.

Phil 8444   Esthetics - Treatises on esthetics - Special topics - The Comic, the Tragic, etc.

Phil 8444.2   Cantoni, Remo. Il significato del tragico. Milano, 1970.

Phil 8446   Esthetics - Treatises on esthetics - Special topics - Irony

Phil 8446.2   Pagliaro, Antonino. Ironia e verità. Milano, 1970.

Phil 8448   Esthetics - Treatises on esthetics - Special topics - Other special

Phil 8448.5   Ästhetik und Gewalt. Gütersloh, 1970.
Phil 8448.11   Dorfles, Gillo. Kitsch: an anthology of bad taste. London, 1969.
Phil 8448.11.7   Giesz, Ludwig. Phanomenologie des Kitsches. 2. Aufl. München, 1971.
Phil 8448.15   Richter, G. Erbauliches, Belehrendes, wie auch Vergnügliches kitsch Lexion. Gütersloh, 1970.
Phil 8448.20   Introspection: the artist looks at himself. Tulsa, 1971.
Phil 8448.25   Eriksson, Ole. Estetisk upplevelse. Stockholm, 1970.

Phil 8500   Philosophy of religion - Folios [Discontinued]

Htn Phil 8500.1*   Grew, N. Cosmologia sacra. London, 1701.
Phil 8500.12   Feigel, F.K. Die französische Neokriticismus. Tübingen, 1913.

Phil 8505   Philosophy of religion - Societies

Phil 8505.1   Report...National Liberal League. Boston, 1876.
Phil 8505.2   Potter, W.J. The Free Religious Association. Boston, 1892.
Phil 8505.3   Pamphlet box. Cambridge Conferences. Announcements.
Phil 8505.4   Humanist. American Humanist Association. Yellow Springs, Ohio. 10,1950+ 7v.
Phil 8505.5   Humanist pamphlet. Yellow Springs, Ohio.
Phil 8505.6   International Congress on Humanism and Ethical Culture. Proceedings. Utrecht.
Phil 8505.7   International Humanist and Ethical Union Regional Conference, Antwerp. Proceedings.
Phil 8505.8   Leningrad. Muzei Istorii Religii i Ateizma. Ezhegodnik. Moskva. 1,1957+ 6v.

Phil 8505   Philosophy of religion - Societies - cont.

Phil 8505.8.5   Butinova, M.S. Estestvoznanie i religiia. Moskva, 1957.
Phil 8505.8.10   Leningrad. Muzei Istorii Religii i Ateizma. Istoriia papstva i inkvizitsii. Moskva, 1959.
Phil 8505.8.15   Leningrad. Muzei Istorii Religii i Ateizma. Nauka i religiia. Moskva, 1961.
Phil 8505.8.20   Leningrad. Muzei Istorii Religii i Ateizma. Proiskhozhdenie religii. Moskva, 1962.
Phil 8505.8.25   Leningrad. Muzei Istorii Religii i Ateizma. Muzei istorii religii i ateizma. Leningrad, 1965.
Phil 8505.9   Pax Romana, International Catholic Movement for Intellectual and Cultural Affairs. Foi et technique. Paris, 1960.
Phil 8505.10   New York University. Institute of Philosophy. Religious experience and truth. N.Y., 1961.
Phil 8505.15   American Scientific Affiliation. Journal. Mankato. 1,1949+ 6v.
Phil 8505.20   The ethical record. London. 55,1950+ 8v.

Phil 8510   Philosophy of religion - Pamphlet volumes

Phil 8510   Pamphlet box. Philosophy of religion.
Phil 8510.1   Pamphlet vol. Philosophy of religion. 6 pam.
Htn Phil 8510.2*   Pamphlet vol. Philosophy of religion. 13 pam.
Htn Phil 8510.2.2*   Pamphlet vol. Philosophy of religion. 13 pam.
Phil 8510.3   Pamphlet vol. Philosophy of religion. German dissertations. 13 pam.
Htn Phil 8510.5*   Pamphlet vol. Philosophy of religion. 9 pam.
Htn Phil 8510.6*   Pamphlet vol. Philosophy of religion. 1883-1912. 6 pam.
Phil 8510.6.1   Pamphlet vol. Philosophy of religion. 1848-1929. 19 pam.
Phil 8510.7   Pamphlet box. Philosophy of religion.
Phil 8510.8   Pamphlet vol. Philosophy of religion. German dissertations.
Phil 8510.9   Pamphlet vol. Communism and religion. Serbocroatian and Slovenian. 4 pam.
Phil 8510.15   Pamphlet vol. Philosophy of religion. 12 pam.
Phil 8510.20   Pamphlet vol. Philosophy of religion. 6 pam.
Phil 8510.25   Larsen, H. Martensen. Jesus und die Religionsgeschichte. Freiburg, 1898. 3 pam.

Phil 8520   Philosophy of religion - History - General works

Phil 8520.1   Hicks, L.E. A critique of design-arguments. N.Y., 1883.
Phil 8520.2   Müller, F.M. Theosophy or psychological religion. London, 1893.
Phil 8520.3   Pünjer, G.C.B. Geschichte der christlichen Religionsphilosophie seit der Reformation. Braunschweig, 1880-83. 2v.
Phil 8520.4A   Lechler, G.V. Geschichte des Englischen Deismus. Stuttgart, 1881.
Phil 8520.4B   Lechler, G.V. Geschichte des Englischen Deismus. Stuttgart, 1881.
Phil 8520.5   Leland, J. A view of the principal deistical writers. London, 1754-56. 3v.
Phil 8520.5.2   Leland, J. A view of the principal deistical writers. London, 1954.
Htn Phil 8520.5.3*   Leland, J. A view of the principal deistical writers. London, 1757. 2v.
Phil 8520.5.3.10   Leland, J. A view of the principal deistical writers. 5. ed. London, 1766. 2v.
Phil 8520.5.4   Leland, J. A view of the principal deistical writers. 5. ed. London, 1798. 2v.
Phil 8520.6   Rémusat, C.F.M. Philosophie religieuse de la théologie naturelle. Paris, 1864.
Phil 8520.8   Caldecott, Alfred. The philosophy of religion in England and America. N.Y., 1901.
Phil 8520.9   Anzoletti, Luisa. La fede nel soprannaturale. Milano, 1894.
Phil 8520.11   Cooke, George W. The social evolution of religion. Boston, 1920.
Phil 8520.13   Maier, Heinrich. An der Grenze der Philosophie. Photoreproduction. Tübingen, 1909.
Phil 8520.14   Wolff, Karl. Schillers Theodizee bis zum Beginn der Kantischen Studien. Leipzig, 1909.
Phil 8520.15   Richter, Johannes. Die Religionsphilosophie der fichteschen Schule. Berlin, 1931.
Phil 8520.15.3   Carriere, Moriz. Die philosophische Weltanschauung. 2. Aufl. Leipzig, 1887. 2v.
Phil 8520.16   Wegener, R. Das Problem der Theodicee. Halle, 1909.
Phil 8520.17   Monod, Albert. De Pascal à Chateaubriand. Paris, 1916.
Phil 8520.18.2   Moore, Edward C. An outline of the history of Christian thought since Kant. London, 1912.
Phil 8520.19   Geyser, Joseph. Das philosophische Gottesproblem in seinen wichtigsten Auffassungen. Bonn, 1899.
Phil 8520.20   Nirenstein, S. The problem of the existence of God, in Maimonides, Alanus and Averroes. Philadelphia, 1924.
Phil 8520.21.2   Hessen, J. Die Religionsphilosophie des Neukantianismus. 2. Aufl. Freiburg, 1924.
Phil 8520.22   Gardner, P. The growth of Christianity. London, 1907.
Phil 8520.23   Straubinger, H. Die Religion und ihre Grundwahrheiten in der deutschen Philosophie seit Leibniz. Freiburg, 1919.
Phil 8520.24   Wobbermin, G. Religions Philosophie. Berlin, 1924.
Phil 8520.25   Lindau, Hans. Die Theodicee im 18 Jahrhundert. Leipzig, 1911.
Phil 8520.28A   Wieman, H.N. American philosophies of religion. Chicago, 1936.
Phil 8520.28B   Wieman, H.N. American philosophies of religion. Chicago, 1936.
Phil 8520.29   Lewkowitz, A. Religiöse Denker der Gegenwart. Berlin, 1923.
Phil 8520.31   Gillett, C.R. The McAlpin collection of British history and theology. N.Y., 1924.
Phil 8520.32   Pünjer, G.C.B. History of the Christian philosophy of religion. Edinburgh, 1887.
Phil 8520.33   Gross, J. La divinisation du chrétien d'après les pères grecs. Paris, 1938.
Phil 8520.34   Horton, Walter M. Contemporary English theology; an American interpretation. N.Y., 1936.
Phil 8520.34.3   Horton, Walter M. Contemporary continental theology. 2. ed. N.Y., 1938.
Phil 8520.36   Bieler, Ludwig. Theios. Wien, 1935-36. 2v.
Phil 8520.37   Sertillanges, R.P. Le christianisme et les philosophies. Paris, 1939-41. 2v.
Phil 8520.39   Adam, Antoine. Sur le problème religieux dans la première moitié du XVIIe siècle. Oxford, 1959.
Phil 8520.40   Tresmontant, C. Les origines de la philosophie chrétienne. Paris, 1962.
Phil 8520.42   Zampetti, Pier L. Il problema della giustizia nel protestantesimo contemporaneo. Milano, 1962.
Phil 8520.44   Macquarrie, J. Twentieth century religious thought. London, 1963.

Classified Listing

Phil 8520   **Philosophy of religion - History - General works - cont.**

Phil 8520.50   Catholic University of America. Workshop on Christian Philosophy and Religious Renewal, 1964. Christian philosophy in the college and seminary. Washington, 1966.

Phil 8520.55   Feiereis, Konrad. Die Umprägung der natürlichen Theologie in Religionsphilosophie. Leipzig, 1965.

Phil 8520.60   Krieger, Evelina. Grenzwege. Freiburg, 1968.

Phil 8520.65   Philipp, Wolfgang. Das Zeitalter der Ausklärung. Bremen, 1967.

Phil 8520.70   Kryvelev, Iosif A. Religioznaia kartina mira i ee bogoslovskaia modernizatsiia. Moskva, 1968.

Phil 8520.80   Joussain, André. Temps présent et religion. Toulouse, 1967.

Phil 8525   **Philosophy of religion - History - Special topics**

Phil 8525.5   Heimbeck, Raeburne Seeley. Theology and meaning: a critique of metatheological scepticism. Stanford, 1969.

Phil 8525.10   Tribe, David H. One hundred years of freethought. London, 1967.

Phil 8525.15   Ot Erazma Potterdamskogo do Bertrana Rassela. Moskva, 1969.

Phil 8525.20   Sokolov, Nikolai P. Istoriia svobodo mysliia i ateizma v Evrope. Moskva, 1966.

Phil 8550   **Philosophy of religion - History - Local (Geographical Table A)**

Phil 8550.342   Webb, Clement C.J. A study of religious thought in England from 1850. Oxford, 1933.

Phil 8550.342.5   Nédoncelle, Maurice. La philosophie religieuse en Grand-Bretagne de 1850 à nos jours. Paris, 1934.

Phil 8550.342.10   Curtis, Lewis P. Anglican moods of the eighteenth century. Hamden, Conn., 1966.

Phil 8550.388   Siebert, Otto. Die Religionsphilosophie in Deutschland in ihren gegenwärtigen Hauptvertretern. Langensalza, 1906.

Phil 8550.420   Martins, Mário. Correntes da filosofia religiosa em Braga dos séculos IV-VII. Porto, 1950.

Phil 8550.508   Lossky, Nikolai O. Slavonic religious philosophy. n.p., n.d.

Phil 8575   **Philosophy of religion - General treatises - Collected authors**

Phil 8575.5   Plantinga, Alvin. Faith and philosophy; philosophical studies in religion and ethics. Grand Rapids, 1964.

Phil 8575.7   New themes in Christian philosophy. Notre Dame, 1968.

Phil 8575.10   Philosophy and contemporary man. Washington, 1968.

Phil 8575.12   Cockshut, Anthony Oliver John. Religious controversies of the nineteenth century: selected documents. London, 1966.

Phil 8575.14   Reardon, Bernard M.G. Religious thought in the nineteenth century. Cambridge, Eng., 1966.

Phil 8575.16   Die Zeit Jesu. Freiburg, 1970.

Phil 8580 - 8605   **Philosophy of religion - General treatises - Individual authors (A-Z)**

Phil 8580.1   Abbot, F.E. The way out of agnosticism. Boston, 1890.

Phil 8580.3*   Allen, E. Reason, the only oracle of man. Bennington, Vt., 1784.

Phil 8580.3.2   Allen, E. Reason, the only oracle of man. N.Y., 1940.

Phil 8580.3.5   Allen, E. Reason, the only oracle of man. N.Y., 1836.

Phil 8580.3.25   Anderson, George P. Who wrote "Ethan Allen's Bible"? n.p., 1937.

Phil 8580.4   Allen, S.M. Religion and science; the letters of "Alpha". Boston, 1875.

Phil 8580.5   Alliott, R. Psychology and theology. London, 1855.

Phil 8580.6   Andrews, W.S. A treatise upon theological subjects. Cambridge, 1829.

Phil 8580.7   Goblet d'Alviella, E. L'évolution religieuse contemporaine chez les anglais, les américains, et les hindous. Paris, 1884.

Phil 8580.7.15   Goblet d'Alviella, E. The contemporary evolution of religious thought in England. London, 1885.

Phil 8580.9   Abbot, F.L. Faith built on reason. Boston, 1902.

Phil 8580.10   Abranches, J. dos Santos. Questões fundamentaes. Coimbra, 1891.

Phil 8580.11   Asher, David. Der religiöse Glaube. Leipzig, 1860.

Phil 8580.12.2   Allen, J.H. Positive religion. Boston, 1894. 5v.

Phil 8580.13   Annet, Peter. A collection of the tracts of a certain free thinker. London, 1739-1749.

Phil 8580.14   Alvarez, Joachim. Lectiones philosophiae. v.2. Vallisoleti, 1868-69. 3 pam.

Phil 8580.15   Abbetmeyer, Theo. Das Gralsreich als Streiter wider den Untergang des Abendlandes. Heilbronn, 1926.

Phil 8580.16   Atkins, Gaius G. Pilgrims of the lonely road. N.Y., 1913.

Phil 8580.16.10   Atkins, Gaius G. Modern religious cults. N.Y., 1923.

Phil 8580.17   Ames, Edward S. Religion. N.Y., 1929.

Phil 8580.17.10   Ames, Edward S. Humanism. Chicago, 1931.

Phil 8580.18   Araiztegui, R.M. Bosquejo de un paralelo de la relation catholica. Habana, 1872.

Phil 8580.19   Alstrin, Erico. Dissertatio philosophica. Upsaliae, 1728.

Phil 8580.20   Alexander, Mikhailovich. The religion of love. N.Y., 1929.

Phil 8580.21   Alexander, H.B. Truth and the faith. N.Y., 1929.

Phil 8580.21.5   Alexander, H.B. God and man's destiny. 1. ed. N.Y., 1936.

Phil 8580.22.5*   Amyraut, M. A treatise concerning religions. London, 1660.

Phil 8580.24A   Auer, J.A.C.F. Humanism states its case. Boston, 1933.

Phil 8580.24B   Auer, J.A.C.F. Humanism states its case. Boston, 1933.

Phil 8580.25   Auvergne, D. Regards catholiques sur le monde. Paris, 1938.

Phil 8580.27   Aldwinckle, M.R.F. The object of Christian worship. Thesis. Strasbourg, 1938.

Phil 8580.28   Arbousse-Bastide, A.F. Le christianisme et l'esprit moderne. Paris, 1862.

Phil 8580.29   Adam, J.D. Under the highest leadership. N.Y., 1918.

Phil 8580.30A   Attwater, D. Modern Christian revolutionaries. N.Y., 1947.

Phil 8580.30B   Attwater, D. Modern Christian revolutionaries. N.Y., 1947.

Phil 8580.31   Amorim de Carvalho. Deus e o homem na poesia e na filosofia. Porto, 195-.

Phil 8580.32   Aggebo, Anker. Jeg er nemlig ikke religiøs. København, 1959.

Phil 8580.33   Archivio di Filosofia. Il problema della demitizzazione. Padova, 1961.

Phil 8580.33.5   Archivio di Filosofia. Demitizzazione e immagine. Padova, 1962.

Phil 8580.34   Arata, C. Persona ed evidenza nella prospettiva classica. Milano, 1963.

Phil 8580.35   Abbagnano, N. La religione. Torino, 1961.

Phil 8580.36   Augereau, Joseph. La chance suprême de l'homme. Paris, 1964.

Phil 8580 - 8605   **Philosophy of religion - General treatises - Individual authors (A-Z) - cont.**

Phil 8580.37   Aubert, Jean-Marie. Philosophie de la nature. Paris, 1965.

Phil 8580.38   Alston, William P. Religious belief and philosophical thought. N.Y., 1963.

Phil 8580.40   Armaner, Neda. İnanç ve hareket bütünlüğü bakimindan din terbiyesi. Istanbul, 1967.

Phil 8581.1   Barthel, N. Religion scientifique de l'humanité. Paris, 1859.

Phil 8581.2   Basedow, J.B. Neue Aussichten in die Wahrheiten und Religion der Vernunft. Altona, 1764. 2v.

Phil 8581.2.10   Basedow, J.B. Examen in der allernatürlichsten Religion. Leipzig, 1784.

Phil 8581.3   Beale, L.S. Life theories. London, 1871.

Phil 8581.4   Beard, J.R. Letters on the grounds and objects of religious knowledge. London, 1856. 2v.

Phil 8581.5.7   Beecher, C.E. Common sense applied to religion. N.Y., 1857.

Phil 8581.6   Bender, W. Das Wesen der Religion. Bonn, 1886.

Phil 8581.6.4   Bender, W. Das Wesen der Religion. 4. Aufl. Bonn, 1888.

Phil 8581.9   Braithwaite, H.T. Esse and posse. London, 1872.

Phil 8581.10   Chalmers, T. Bridgewater treatises [1,8]. On the power, wisdom, and goodness of God. Philadelphia, 1836.

Phil 8581.10.2   Kidd, J. Bridgewater treatises [2]. On the adaptation of external nature to the physical condition of man. Philadelphia? 1836?

Phil 8581.10.4.5   Bell, Charles. Bridgewater treatises [4]. The hand, its mechanism and vital endowments. N.Y., 1840.

Phil 8581.10.4.10   Bell, Charles. Bridgewater treatises [4]. The hand, its mechanism and vital endowments. 7. ed. London, 1865.

Phil 8581.10.5   Roget, P.M. Bridgewater treatises [5]. Animal, vegetable physiology. Philadelphia, 1836. 2v.

Phil 8581.10.6   Buckland, W. Bridgewater treatises [6]. Geology and mineralogy. Philadelphia, 1837. 2v.

Phil 8581.10.7   Kirby, W. Bridgewater treatises [7]. On the power...God. Philadelphia, 1837.

Phil 8581.10.8   Prout, William. Bridgewater treatises [8]. Chemistry, meteorology. London, 1855.

Phil 8581.10.9   Babbage, C. The ninth Bridgewater treatise. 2. ed. London, 1838.

Phil 8581.11   Babbage, C. The ninth Bridgewater treatise. 2. ed. London, 1838.

Phil 8581.12   Brinton, D.G. The religious sentiment. N.Y., 1876.

Phil 8581.13   Brougham, H. A discourse of natural theology. Philadelphia, 1835.

Phil 8581.13.3   Brougham, H. A discourse of natural theology. 4. ed. London, 1835.

Phil 8581.13.5   Brougham, H. Dissertations on the subjects of science. London, 1839. 2v.

Phil 8581.13.15   Wallace, T. Observations...natural theology by H. Lord Brougham. London, 1835.

Phil 8581.13.16   Wallace, T. Additional observations...natural theology by H. Lord Brougham. Dublin, 1835.

Phil 8581.14   Browne, Peter. Things divine and supernatural. London, 1733.

Phil 8581.14.5   Browne, Peter. A letter in answer to a book...entitled Christianity not mysterious. London, 1697.

Phil 8581.14.9   Browne, Peter. The procedure, extent and limits of human understanding. London, 1728.

Phil 8581.14.10   Browne, Peter. The procedure, extent and limits of human understanding. London, 1737.

Phil 8581.16   Bushnell, H. Nature and the supernatural. N.Y., 1858.

Phil 8581.16.2   Bushnell, H. Nature and the supernatural. N.Y., 1859.

Phil 8581.17   Byles, J.B. Foundations of religion in the mind and heart of man. London, 1875.

Phil 8581.18   Balguy, J. A letter to a deist. London, 1730-38. 7 pam.

Phil 8581.18.7   Silvester, Tipping. A sermon containing some reflections upon Mr. Balguy's essay on moral goodness. London, 1734.

Phil 8581.18.8   Jones, H.D. John Balguy, an English moralist of the 18th century. Leipzig, 1907.

Htn   Phil 8581.19*   Barrington, J.S. A discourse of natural and revealed religion. n.p., n.d.

Phil 8581.20   Bascom, J. Philosophy of religion. N.Y., 1876.

Phil 8581.21   Bowker, R.R. Of religion. Boston, 1903.

Phil 8581.22   Blamires, W.L. Studies and speculation in natural history. London, 1901.

Phil 8581.23   Ballard, A. From talk to text. N.Y., 1904.

Phil 8581.24   Brierley, J. Religion and experience. N.Y., 1906.

Phil 8581.24.5   Brierley, J. Ourselves and the universe. N.Y., 1905.

Phil 8581.24.18   Brierley, J. Självlifvet. Stockholm, 1904.

Phil 8581.24.20   Brierley, J. Vårt gemensamma lif. Stockholm, 1907.

Phil 8581.24.25   Brierley, J. Vi och världsalltet. Stockholm, 1903.

Phil 8581.25   Burris, M.A. Creation's way. Smithville, Ohio, 1911.

Phil 8581.26   Bonnefon, C. Dialogue sur la vie et sur la mort. 3. éd. Paris, 1911.

Phil 8581.27   Biroth, H. Tolerance in religion; liberal thoughts of modern thinkers. Rome, 1913.

Phil 8581.28   Brent, C.H. Presence. N.Y., 1914.

Phil 8581.29   Bukaty, A. Polska w apostazii cryli wtak zwanym russo-sławianismie. Paryż, 1842.

Phil 8581.30.4   Bretschneider, K.G. Die religiöse Glaubenslehre. 4. ed. Halle, 1846.

Phil 8581.31   Bierer, E. The evolution of religions. N.Y., 1906.

Phil 8581.32   Balmforth, R. The new reformation...moral and social problems. London, 1893.

Phil 8581.33   Beach, D.N. The newer religious thinking. Boston, 1893.

Phil 8581.34   Bremond, Henri. L'inquiétude religieuse. 2nd series. Paris, 1909. 2v.

Phil 8581.35   Bridges, H.J. Criticisms of life. Boston, 1915.

Phil 8581.36   Brown, Charles R. Modern man's religion. N.Y., 1911.

Phil 8581.37   Bowne, Borden P. Essence of religion. Boston, 1910.

Phil 8581.37.5   Bowne, Borden P. Studies in Christianity. Boston, 1909.

Phil 8581.38   Baumann, J. Religionsphilosophie auf modernwissenschaftlicher Grundlage. Leipzig, 1886.

Phil 8581.39   Barnes, Earl. Where knowledge fails. N.Y., 1907.

Phil 8581.40   Benett, W. Religion and free will. Oxford, 1913.

Phil 8581.41   Benitez de Lugo, A. El cristianismo y la filosofia. Sevilla, 1882.

Phil 8581.42   Burroughs, John. Accepting the universe. Boston, 1920.

Phil 8581.43   Brod, M. Heidentum, Christentum, Judentum. München, 1922. 2v.

Phil 8581.43.2   Brod, M. Heidentum, Christentum, Judentum. München, 1921. 2v.

Phil 8581.43.3   Brod, M. Paganism, Christianity, Judaism; a confession of faith. University, 1970.

Phil 8581.44   Bois, Henri. De la connaissance religieuse. Paris, 1894.

Phil 8580 - 8605   Philosophy of religion - General treatises - Individual
authors (A-Z) - cont.

Phil 8581.45   Buonaiuti, Ernesto. Verso la luce. Foligno, 1924.
Phil 8581.45.10   Buonaiuti, Ernesto. La religione nella vito dello spirito.
                      Roma, 1926.
Phil 8581.45.15   Buonaiuti, Ernesto. Escursioni spirituali. Roma, 1921.
Phil 8581.45.20   Buonaiuti, Ernesto. Pellegrino di Roma. Bari, 1964.
Phil 8581.46   Brochner, Hans. Om det religiöse i dets enhed met det
                      humane. Kjöbenhavn, 1869.
Phil 8581.47   Bergstedt, C.F. Hvad vi veta, hvad vi tro och hvad vi
                      vilja. Stockholm, 1878.
Phil 8581.48   Bridges, J.H. Five discourses on positive religion.
                      London, 1882.
Phil 8581.49   Bolliger, A. Drei ewige Lichter. Berlin, 1903.
Phil 8581.50   Burlingame, E.L. Current discussion. N.Y., 1878.
                      2v.
Phil 8581.51   Bouquet, A.C. The Christian religion and its competitors
                      today. Cambridge, Eng., 1925.
Phil 8581.52   Baillie, John. The roots of religion in the human soul.
                      London, 1926.
Phil 8581.52.10   Baillie, John. The interpretation of religion.
                      N.Y., 1928.
Phil 8581.52.20   Baillie, John. Invitation to pilgrimage. London, 1942.
Phil 8581.52.30   Baillie, John. The sense of the presence of God.
                      London, 1962.
Phil 8581.53   Brown, William A. Beliefs that matter. N.Y., 1928.
Phil 8581.53.5   Brown, William A. Pathways to certainty. N.Y., 1930.
Phil 8581.54   Bulgakov, S. Sviet nevechernii. Moskva, 1917.
Phil 8581.54.5   Bulgakov, C. Dva grada. Moskva, 1911.
Phil 8581.55   Bolland, G.J.P.J. Wijsbegeerte van den godsdienst bewerkt
                      naar dictaten. Amsterdam, 1923.
Phil 8581.56   Bruhn, Wilhelm. Der Vernunftcharakter der Religion.
                      Leipzig, 1921.
Phil 8581.57   Bell, Bernard I. Beyond agnosticism, a book for tired
                      mechanists. N.Y., 1929.
Phil 8581.58   Barrow, George A. The validity of the religious
                      experience. Boston, 1917.
Phil 8581.59   Bauer, Joachim M. The modern notion of faith. Diss.
                      Washington, 1930.
Phil 8581.60   Burkart, Anna D. The person in religion. Thesis.
                      Philadelphia, 1930.
Phil 8581.61   Bauhofer, O. Das Metareligiöse. Leipzig, 1930.
Phil 8581.62   Bosanquet, Bernard. What religion is. London, 1920.
Phil 8581.63   Bennett, Charles A. The dilemma of religious knowledge.
                      New Haven, 1931.
Phil 8581.64   Blood, B.P. Optimism, the lesson of ages. Boston, 1860.
Phil 8581.65   Blair, P. Thoughts on nature and religion. London, 1774.
Phil 8581.66.15   Bergson, Henri. The two sources of morality and religion.
                      N.Y., 1946.
Phil 8581.67   Brightman, E.S. Personality and religion. N.Y., 1934.
Phil 8581.67.5   Brightman, E.S. A philosophy of religion. N.Y., 1940.
Phil 8581.67.10   Brightman, E.S. Nature and values. N.Y., 1945.
Phil 8581.68.5   Broglie, Paul. Religion et critique. 3. éd. Paris, 1906.
Phil 8581.68.10   Broglie, Paul. La définition de la religion. Paris, 1882.
Phil 8581.68.15   Broglie, Paul. Les fondements intellectuels de la foi
                      chrétienne. Paris, 1905.
Phil 8581.68.20   Broglie, Paul. Les conditions modernes. Paris, 1910.
Phil 8581.69A   Berdyaev, N.A. Freedom and the spirit. N.Y., 1935.
Phil 8581.69B   Berdyaev, N.A. Freedom and the spirit. N.Y., 1935.
Phil 8581.69.3   Berdiaev, N.A. Filosofiia svobodnogo dukha. v.1-2.
                      Parizh, 1927.
Phil 8581.69.5   Berdiaev, N.A. God, man and the church. London, 1937.
Phil 8581.69.7   Berdiaev, N.A. Samopoznanie: opyt filosofskoi
                      avtobiografii. Parizh, 1949.
Phil 8581.69.10   Berdiajew, N.A. Von der Würde des Christentums und der
                      Unwürde der Christen. 4. Aufl. Luzern, 1937.
Phil 8581.70   Blanchard, Pierre. Catéchisme de la nature, ou religion et
                      morale naturelles. Paris, n.d.
Phil 8581.71   Bezzant, J.S. Aspects of belief. N.Y., 1938.
Phil 8581.72   Bevan, E.R. Symbolism and belief. London, 1938.
Phil 8581.73   Ballou, Robert O. The glory of God. N.Y., 1938.
Phil 8581.74   Bowman, Archibald Allan. Studies in the philosophy of
                      religion. London, 1938. 2v.
Phil 8581.75   Bell, E.T. Man and his lifebelts. N.Y., 1938.
Phil 8581.76   Burtt, Edwin A. Types of religious philosophy. 1. ed.
                      N.Y., 1939.
Phil 8581.77A   Brémond, H. Introduction à la philosophie de la prière.
                      Paris, 1929.
Phil 8581.77B   Brémond, H. Introduction à la philosophie de la prière.
                      Paris, 1929.
Phil 8581.78   Bixler, J.S. Religion for free minds. N.Y., 1939.
Phil 8581.78.5   Bixler, J.S. Conversations with an unrepentant liberal.
                      New Haven, 1946.
Phil 8581.79   Bewkes, E.G. Experience, reason and faith. N.Y., 1940.
Phil 8581.80   Baillie, James. Spiritual religion. London, 1940.
Phil 8581.81A   Bellamy, E. The religion of solidarity. Yellow
                      Springs, 1940.
Phil 8581.81B   Bellamy, E. The religion of solidarity. Yellow
                      Springs, 1940.
Phil 8581.81.80   Morgan, A.E. The philosophy of Edward Bellamy.
                      N.Y., 1945.
Phil 8581.82   Buckham, J.W. The inner world...philosophy of
                      Christianity. N.Y., 1941.
Phil 8581.83   Brown, Oswald E. God and the new knowledge.
                      Nashville, 1926.
Phil 8581.84   Bradshaw, M.J. Philosophical foundations of faith.
                      N.Y., 1941.
Phil 8581.85   Boodin, J.E. Religion of tomorrow. N.Y., 1943.
Phil 8581.86   Brightman, E.S. The spiritual life. N.Y., 1942.
Phil 8581.87   Barnes, H.E. The twilight of Christianity. N.Y., 1929.
Phil 8581.88   Brown, C.R. A working faith. Chapel Hill, 1926.
Phil 8581.89   Baker, A.E. Prophets for a day of judgment. London, 1944.
Phil 8581.90   Bandeira de Mello, L.M. Teoria do destino. Gazeta de
                      Leopoldina, 1944.
Phil 8581.91   Bosley, Harold A. The philosophical heritage of the
                      Christian faith. Chicago, 1944.
Phil 8581.91.10   Bosley, Harold A. A firm faith for today. 1. ed.
                      N.Y., 1950.
Phil 8581.92   Baumann, J. Die Grundfrage der Religion. Stuttgart, 1895.
Phil 8581.93   Brownell, B. Earth is enough. N.Y., 1933.
Phil 8581.94   Berdiaev, N.A. Khristanstvo i aktivnaia uslovnost'.
                      Parizh, 194-.
Phil 8581.95   Blondel, Maurice. La philosophie et l'esprit chrétien.
                      Paris, 1944.
Phil 8581.95.10   Blondel, Maurice. Exigences philosophiques du
                      christianisme. 1. éd. Paris, 1950.
Phil 8581.96   Brunner, Heinrich Emil. Christianity and civilisation.
                      N.Y., 1949. 2v.

Phil 8580 - 8605   Philosophy of religion - General treatises - Individual
authors (A-Z) - cont.

Phil 8581.96.2   Brunner, Heinrich Emil. Christianity and civilization.
                      N.Y., 1949.
Phil 8581.98   Brunschvicg, Léon. De la vraie et de la fausse conversion.
                      1. éd. Paris, 1951.
Phil 8581.98.5   Brunschvicg, Léon. La raison et la religion. Paris, 1964.
Phil 8581.100   Brunner, August. Die Religion. Freiburg, 1956.
Phil 8581.102   Barthel, Ernst. Der Mensch und die ewigen Hintergründe.
                      München, 1939.
Phil 8581.105   Beck, Lewis W. Six secular philosophers. 1. ed.
                      N.Y., 1960.
Phil 8581.106A   Burke, K. The rhetoric of religion. Boston, 1961.
Phil 8581.106B   Burke, K. The rhetoric of religion. Boston, 1961.
Phil 8581.108   Broglie, Guy de. Les signes de crédibilité de la
                      révélation chrétienne. Paris, 1964.
Phil 8581.109   British Broadcasting Corporation. Religion and humanism.
                      London, 1964.
Phil 8581.110   Hermans, Francis. L'humanisme religieux de l'abbé Henri
                      Bremond, 1865-1933. Paris, 1965.
Phil 8581.112   Basilius, Harold Albert. Contemporary problems in
                      religion. Detroit, 1956.
Phil 8581.113   Bošnjak, Branko. Filozofija i kršćanstvo. Zagreb, 1966.
Phil 8581.113.5   Bošnjak, Branko. Marksist i kršćanin. Zagreb, 1969.
Phil 8581.114   Başgil, Ali Fuad. Din ve Lâiklik. Istanbul, 1962.
Phil 8581.115   Bellet, Maurice. Essai d'une critique de la foi.
                      Paris, 1968.
Phil 8581.120   Bloch, Ernst. Man on his own. N.Y., 1970.
Phil 8581.127   Blanc de Saint-Bonnet, Antoine Joseph Elisée Adolphe. De
                      l'affaiblissement de la raison et de la décadence en
                      Europe. 2. éd. Paris, 1854.
Phil 8582.1.2   Caird, J. An introduction to the philosophy of religion.
                      N.Y., 1880.
Phil 8582.1.5   Caird, J. The fundamental ideas of Christianity.
                      Glasgow, 1899. 2v.
Phil 8582.2   Campbell, A. The necessity of revelation. London, 1739.
Phil 8582.3.1   Argyll, G.D.C. The reign of law. 5. ed. N.Y., 1869.
Phil 8582.3.3   Argyll, G.D.C. The reign of law. London, 1871.
Phil 8582.3.5   Argyll, G.D.C. The reign of law. 4. ed. London, 1867.
Phil 8582.3.6   Argyll, G.D.C. The unity of nature. London, 1884.
Phil 8582.3.7   Argyll, G.D.C. The unity of nature. N.Y., 1884.
Phil 8582.4   Caumont, G. Jugements d'un mourant sur la vie.
                      Paris, 1876.
Phil 8582.5   Chadbourne, P.A. Lectures on natural theology.
                      N.Y., 1867.
Phil 8582.7   Chalybäus, H.M. Philosophie und Christenthum. Kiel, 1853.
Phil 8582.8   Cheyne, G. Philosophical principles of religion. v.1-2.
                      London, 1915-16.
Phil 8582.10   Claubergii, J. De cognitione dei et nostri.
                      Franequerae, 1685.
Phil 8582.11   Colliber, S. An impartial enquiry. v.1-2.
                      London, 1728-29.
Phil 8582.13   Crabbe, G. An outline of a system of natural theology.
                      London, 1840.
Phil 8582.14   Crombie, A. Natural theology. London, 1829. 2v.
Phil 8582.15   Crosskey, H.W. A defense of religion. London, 1854.
Htn Phil 8582.16* Culverwel, N. An elegant and learned discourse...light of
                      nature. London, 1652.
Phil 8582.17   Culverwel, N. Of the light of nature. Edinburgh, 1857.
Phil 8582.18A   Campagnac, E.T. The Cambridge Platonists. Oxford, 1901.
Phil 8582.18B   Campagnac, E.T. The Cambridge Platonists. Oxford, 1901.
Phil 8582.19   Carver, T.N. The religion worth having. Boston, 1912.
Phil 8582.19.2A   Carver, T.N. The religion worth having. Boston, 1912.
Phil 8582.19.2B   Carver, T.N. The religion worth having. Boston, 1912.
Phil 8582.19.5   Carver, T.N. The religion worth having. Los
                      Angeles, 1940.
Phil 8582.20   Cornford, F.M. From religion to philosophy. London, 1912.
Phil 8582.21   Caulfield, An essay on the immateriality and immortality
                      of the soul. London, 1778.
Phil 8582.22   Coan, T.M. Topics of the time. Questions of belief.
                      N.Y., 1883.
Phil 8582.23.3   Common sense. Philadelphia, 1795.
Phil 8582.24   Craufurd, A.H. Christian instincts and modern doubt.
                      London, 1897.
Phil 8582.25   Carson, Capshaw, (pseud.). A witness testifies.
                      Chicago, 1918.
Phil 8582.25.5   Carson, Capshaw, (pseud.). An appeal to the real leaders
                      of men. Chicago, 1918.
Phil 8582.26   Collingwood, Robin George. Religion and philosophy.
                      London, 1916.
Phil 8582.26.5   Collingwood, Robin George. Faith and reason.
                      Chicago, 1968.
Phil 8582.27   Chandler, Arthur. Faith and experience. 2. ed.
                      London, 1912.
Phil 8582.28   Claraz, Jules. La faillité des religions. Paris, 1912.
Phil 8582.29   Coxe, A. Cleveland. Holy writ and modern thought.
                      N.Y., 1892.
Htn Phil 8582.30* Collins, Anthony. Examen des prophéties qui servient de
                      fondement de la religion chrétienne. Londres, 1768.
Phil 8582.31   Cremer, Herman. Das Wesen des Christentums. 3. Aufl.
                      Gütersloh, 1902.
Phil 8582.32   Cunow, Heinrich. Ursprung der Religion und des
                      Gottesglaubens. Berlin, 1913.
Phil 8582.33.2   Charbonnel, Victor. La volonté de vivre. 2. éd.
                      Paris, 1898.
Phil 8582.33.5   Charbonnel, Victor. The victory of will. Boston, 1907.
Phil 8582.34   Carabellese, P. L'essere e il problema religioso.
                      Bari, 1914.
Phil 8582.35   Cobbe, F.P. Broken lights; an inquiry into the present
                      condition and future prospects of religious faith.
                      London, 1864.
Phil 8582.35.5   Cobbe, F.P. Broken lights; an inquiry into the present
                      condition and future prospects of religious faith.
                      London, 1864.
Phil 8582.35.9   Cobbe, F.P. The peak in Darien...an octave of essays.
                      Boston, 1882.
Phil 8582.35.15   Cobbe, F.P. The religious demands of the age.
                      Boston, 1863.
Phil 8582.36   Crane, A.M. A search after ultimate truth. Boston, 1910.
Phil 8582.37   Cherix, Robert B. L'arche d'alliance. Paris, 1923.
Phil 8582.38   Chiocchetti, E. Religione e filosofia. Milano, 1921.
Phil 8582.39   Cordovani, M. Rivelazione e filosofia. Milano, n.d.
Phil 8582.40   Clarke, M. Traités de l'existence et des attributs de
                      Dieu, des devoirs de la religion naturelle. n.p., 1744.
                      3v.
Phil 8582.41   Crawford-Frost, W.A. The philosophy of integration.
                      Boston, 1906.
Phil 8582.42   Cadman, S.P. Imagination and religion. N.Y., 1926.

Phil 8580 - 8605 Philosophy of religion - General treatises - Individual authors (A-Z) - cont.

Phil 8582.43 Carr, Herbert W. Changing backgrounds in religion and ethics. N.Y., 1927.
Phil 8582.44 Colas, Émile. La mystique et la raison. Paris, 1922.
Phil 8582.45.3 Capron, F.H. The anatomy of truth. 3. ed. London, 1927.
Phil 8582.46 Castelli, Enrico. Filosofia e apologetica. Roma, 1929.
Phil 8582.47 Caramella, S. Religione, teosofia e filosofia. Messina, 1931.
Phil 8582.48 Clark, E.H. This world and the next. Boston, 1934.
Phil 8582.49 Creed, J.M. Religious thought in the eighteenth century. Cambridge, Eng., 1934.
Phil 8582.50 Chartier, E. Les dieux. Paris, 1934.
Phil 8582.50.5 Chartier, E. Propos sur la religion. Paris, 1938.
Phil 8582.51 Chaning-Pearce, Melville. Religion and reality. London, 1937.
Phil 8582.51.10 Chaning-Pearce, Melville. The terrible crystal; studies in Kierkegaard and modern Christianity. London, 1940.
Phil 8582.52 Coqueret, H. Théosophie ou science de Dieu. Paris, 1803.
Phil 8582.53 Churchill, W. The uncharted way. Philadelphia, 1940.
Phil 8582.54 Chauvet-Dusoul, F. Philosophie et religion. Paris, 1941-42. 5v.
Phil 8582.55 Cailliet, Émile. The life of the mind. N.Y., 1942.
Phil 8582.56 Chamberlain, H.S. Mensch und Gott. München, 1921.
Phil 8582.57 Crawford, Benjamin F. The political faith of our fathers. Carnegie, Pa., 1943.
Phil 8582.58 Cave, S. The Christian estimate of man. London, 1944.
Phil 8582.59 Christlieb, M.L. How can I bear suffering? London, 1944.
Phil 8582.60 Cullmann, Oscar. Christus und die Zeit. Zollikon-Zürich, 1946.
Phil 8582.62 Cleobury, F.H. God, man and the absolute. London, 1947?
Phil 8582.64 Caird, John. An introduction to the philosophy of religion. N.Y., 1881.
Phil 8582.65 Chédel, André. Pour un humanisme laïc. Neuchâtel, 1963.
Phil 8582.66 Carrier, Hervé. The sociology of religious belonging. N.Y., 1965.
Phil 8582.72 Caracciolo, Alberto. La religione come struttura e come modo autonomo della coscienza. Milano, 1965.
Phil 8582.75 Colish, Marcia L. The mirror of language. New Haven, 1968.
Phil 8582.78 Corvez, Maurice. L'être et la conscience morale. Louvain, 1968.
Phil 8582.80 Cimić, Esad. Drama ateizacije. Religija, ateizam i odgoj. Sarajevo, 1971.
Phil 8583.1 Damiron, J.P. Souvenirs de vingt ans d'enseignement. Paris, 1859.
Phil 8583.2 Davesiès de Pontès, L. Études morales et religieuses. Paris, 1869.
Htn Phil 8583.3* DeVere, Aubrey. Proteus and Amadeus. London, 1878.
Phil 8583.3.5 DeVere, Aubrey. The subjective difficulties in religion. n.p., n.d.
Phil 8583.4 Dick, T. The philosophy of religion. Brookfield, Mass., 1829.
Phil 8583.4.2 Dick, T. On the improvement of society by the diffusion of knowledge. Glasgow, 1833.
Phil 8583.4.3 Dick, T. On the improvement of society by the diffusion of knowledge. N.Y., 1836.
Phil 8583.4.5.-.9 Dick, T. Works. Philadelphia, 1836. 5v.
Phil 8583.4.15 Dick, T. Works. v.1-4. Hartford, 1839.
Phil 8583.4.16 Dick, T. The works of Thomas Dick. Hartford, 1851.
Phil 8583.4.18 Dick, T. The philosophy of religion. v.1-2. Philadelphia, 1845.
Phil 8583.5 Disdier, H. Conciliation rationnelle du droit et du devoir. Genève, 1859. 2v.
Phil 8583.6 Drobisch, M.W. Grundlehren der Religionsphilosophie. Leipzig, 1840.
Phil 8583.7 Dühring, E.K. Der Werth des Lebens. Leipzig, 1881.
Phil 8583.7.3 Dühring, E.K. Der Werth des Lebens. 6. Aufl. Leipzig, 1902.
Phil 8583.7.5 Dühring, E.K. Der Ersatz der Religion. Karlsruhe, 1883.
Phil 8583.8 Duncan, H. Sacred philosophy of the Seasons. Boston, 1839. 2v.
Phil 8583.8.2 Duncan, H. Sacred philosophy. v.3. Boston, 1839?
Phil 8583.9 Dole, Charles F. Theology of civilization. N.Y., 1899.
Phil 8583.9.5 Dole, Charles F. The smoke and the flame. Boston, 1892.
Phil 8583.9.10 Dole, Charles F. A religion for the new day. N.Y., 1920.
Phil 8583.10A Dickinson, G.L. Religion, a criticism and a forecast. N.Y., 1905.
Phil 8583.10B Dickinson, G.L. Religion, a criticism and a forecast. N.Y., 1905.
Phil 8583.11 Dorner, A. Grundriss der Religionsphilosophie. Leipzig, 1903.
Phil 8583.11.5 Dorner, A. Grundprobleme der Religionsphilosophie. Berlin, 1903.
Phil 8583.11.15 Dorner, A. Pessimismus...Nietzsche und Naturalismus. Leipzig, 1911.
Phil 8583.11.90 Lau, Paul. August Dorners Religionsphilosophie. Inaug. Diss. Königsberg, 1928.
Phil 8583.12 Drustowitz, H. Moderne Versuche eines Religionsersatzes. Heidelberg, 1886.
Phil 8583.14 Drake, Durant. Problems of religion. Boston, 1916.
Phil 8583.15 Dodge, Ebenezer. Evidences of Christianity. Boston, 1872.
Phil 8583.16 Deussen, Paul. Die Philosophie der Bibel. 2. Aufl. Leipzig, 1919.
Phil 8583.16.8 Deussen, Paul. Bibelns filosofi. Stockholm, 1916.
Phil 8583.17 Delany, Selden P. The ideal of Christian worship. Milwaukee, 1909.
Phil 8583.17.5 Delany, Selden P. Christian practice. N.Y., 1920.
Phil 8583.18.2 Durkheim, É. Les formes élémentaires de la vie religieuse. 2. éd. Paris, 1925.
Phil 8583.18.5 Durkheim, É. Les formes élementaires de la vie religieuse. 5e éd. Paris, 1968.
Phil 8583.19 Dunkmann, D.K. Religionsphilosophie. Gütersloh, 1917.
Phil 8583.20 Denkmann, D.K. Metaphysik der Geschichte. Leipzig, 1914.
Phil 8583.21 Drown, E.S. Religion or God? Cambridge, 1927.
Phil 8583.22 Descamps, E. Le génie des religions. Paris, 1923.
Phil 8583.23 Dugard, Marie. Sur les frontières de la foi. Paris, 1928.
Phil 8583.24 Deyo, M.L. A modern conception of religion. Binghamton, 1933.
Phil 8583.25 Dewey, John. A common faith. New Haven, 1934.
Phil 8583.26* De Costa, J.H. Reason and faith. Philadelphia, 1791.
Phil 8583.27 Draghicesco, D. Vérité et révélation. Paris, 1934. 2v.
Phil 8583.28 Schlesinger, Bruno P. Christopher Dawson and the modern political crisis. Notre Dame, 1949.
Phil 8583.28.2 Dawson, Christopher H. Religion and the modern state. London, 1935.

Phil 8580 - 8605 Philosophy of religion - General treatises - Individual authors (A-Z) - cont.

Phil 8583.28.4 Dawson, Christopher H. Religion and the modern state. London, 1936.
Phil 8583.28.5 Dawson, Christopher H. The judgment of the nations. N.Y., 1942.
Phil 8583.28.10 O'Connor, D.A. The relation between religion and culture according to C. Dawson. Montreal, 1952.
Phil 8583.28.15 Schlagberger, Frans Xavier. Die Geschichts- und Kulturphilosophie Christopher Dawson. München, 1965?
Phil 8583.28.20 Dawson, Christopher H. Beyond politics. London, 1939.
Phil 8583.29 De Burgh, William George. The relations of morality to religion. London, 1935.
Phil 8583.29.5 De Burgh, William George. Towards a religious philosophy. London, 1937.
Phil 8583.30 Desquiron de Saint Agnan, A.T. Dieu, la nature et la loi. Paris, 1814.
Phil 8583.31 Dutoit-Mombrini, P. La science du Christ et de l'homme. n.p., 1810. 3v.
Phil 8583.32 De Pauley, W.C. The candle of the Lord. London, 1937.
Phil 8583.33 Delitzsch, Friedrich. Zur Weiterbildung der Religion. Stuttgart, 1908.
Phil 8583.33.15 Delitzsch, Friedrich. Whose son is Christ? Boston, 1908.
Phil 8583.34 Dennert, E. Klassiker du religiösen Weltanschauung. Bd.1. Hamburg, 1909.
Phil 8583.35 D'Arcy, M.C. Mirage and truth. N.Y., 1935.
Phil 8583.35.5 D'Arcy, M.C. The meeting of love and knowledge. 1. ed. N.Y., 1957.
Phil 8583.36 Dynamic religion, a personal experience. N.Y., 193-.
Phil 8583.37 Dent, Phyllis. The growth of the spiritual life. London, 1944.
Phil 8583.38 Dimond, S.G. Heart and mind. London, 1945.
Phil 8583.39 Dunlap, Knight. Religion. N.Y., 1946.
Phil 8583.40 Dunham, J.H. The religion of philosophers. Philadelphia, 1947.
Phil 8583.41 Duméry, Henry. Critique et religion. Paris, 1957.
Phil 8583.41.5 Duméry, Henry. Phénoménologie et religion. 1. éd. Paris, 1958.
Phil 8583.41.20 Luijk, Henk van. Philosophie du fait chrétien. Paris, 1964.
Phil 8583.43 Dessauer, Philipp. Die naturale Meditation. München, 1961.
Phil 8583.43.5 Dessauer, Philipp. Meditation im christlichen Dasein. München, 1968.
Phil 8583.44 Dallago, Carl. Der Begriff des Absoluten. Innsbruck, 1964.
Phil 8583.45.2 Denzinger, Heinrich. Vier Bücher von der religiösen Erkenntniss. Frankfurt, 1967. 2v.
Phil 8583.46 Damiani, Raoul. Cristianesimo-marxismo. Milano, 1969.
Phil 8584.1 Eddy, J. Thoughts on religion and morality. Providence, R.I., 1891.
Phil 8584.2 Ellis, J. The knowledge of divine things from revelation. London, 1743.
Phil 8584.2.2 Ellis, J. The knowledge of divine things from revelation. London, 1747.
Phil 8584.2.3 Ellis, J. The knowledge of divine things from revelation. London, 1771.
Phil 8584.3 Eschenmayer, C.A. Religionsphilosophie. v.1-3. Tübingen, 1818-24. 2v.
Htn Phil 8584.4* An estimate of the profit and loss of religion. Edinburgh, 1753.
Phil 8584.5 Eucken, Rudolf. Das Wesen der Religion, philosophisch Betrachtet. Leipzig, 1901.
Phil 8584.5.3 Eucken, Rudolf. The truth of religion. N.Y., 1911.
Phil 8584.5.5 Eucken, Rudolf. Christianity and the new idealism. London, 1909.
Phil 8584.5.7 Eucken, Rudolf. Der religiöse Wahrheitsbegriff in der Philosophie Rudolf Euckens. Göttingen, 1910.
Phil 8584.5.14 Eucken, Rudolf. Der Wahrheitsgehalt der Religion. Leipzig, 1901.
Phil 8584.5.15 Eucken, Rudolf. Der Wahrheitsgehalt der Religion. Leipzig, 1901.
Phil 8584.5.15.4 Eucken, Rudolf. Der Wahrheitsgehalt der Religion. 4. Aufl. Berlin, 1927.
Phil 8584.5.16 Eucken, Rudolf. Hauptprobleme der Religionsphilosophie der Gegenwart. Berlin, 1912.
Phil 8584.6 Ellwood, C.A. The reconstruction of religion. N.Y., 1922.
Phil 8584.7 Eliot, C.W. The religion of the future. Berlin, 1909.
Phil 8584.7.5 Eliot, C.W. The religion of the future. Boston, 1935.
Phil 8584.8 Edfeldt, Hans. Filosofisk religionslära. Uppsala, 1903.
Phil 8584.9 Eberhardt, Paul. Von der Möglichkeit und der Notwendigkeit der reinen Religion. Gotha, 1916.
Phil 8584.10 Edwards, D.M. The philosophy of religion. N.Y., 1924.
Phil 8584.11.2 Evans, Robert C.T. Man. What? Whence? Whither? 2. ed. Chatham, 1923.
Phil 8584.12 Evelyn, John. The history of religion. London, 1850. 2v.
Phil 8584.13 Emge, Carl A. Der philosophische Gehalt der religiösen Dogmatik. München, 1929.
Phil 8584.14 Elving, S. Five books of Joses, a catechism of rational religion. Newllano, La., 1930.
Phil 8584.15A Einstein, Albert. Cosmic religion. N.Y., 1931.
Phil 8584.15B Einstein, Albert. Cosmic religion. N.Y., 1931.
Phil 8584.16 Enckendorff, M.L. Kindschaft zur Welt. Jena, 1927.
Phil 8584.17 Éléments de la philosophie du ciel. Paris, 1806.
Phil 8584.18 Eustace, C.J. Mind and the mystery. N.Y., 1937.
Phil 8584.19 Espinosa, G. La mascarada cristiana. Santiago de Chile, 1940.
Phil 8584.21 Eryshev, A.A. Religiia, vrag ravnopraviia i druzhby narodov. Kiev, 1962.
Phil 8584.22 Eley, A.S. God's own image. Luton, Eng., 1963.
Phil 8585.1 Fairbairn, A.M. Studies...philosophy of religion and history. London, 1877.
Phil 8585.1.2 Fairbairn, A.M. Studies...philosophy of religion and history. 4. ed. N.Y., 1876.
Phil 8585.1.5 Fairbairn, A.M. The philosophy of the Christian religion. London, 1905.
Phil 8585.3 Fellowes, R. The religion of the universe. London, 1836.
Phil 8585.3.2 Fellowes, R. The religion of the universe. London, 1836.
Phil 8585.4 Ferrières, C.E. Le théisme. 2. éd. v.1-2. Paris, 1790.
Phil 8585.5 The first day in heaven. London, 1820.
Phil 8585.6 Fisher, G.P. The grounds of theistic and Christian belief. N.Y., 1883.
Phil 8585.6.3 Fisher, G.P. The grounds of theistic and Christian belief. N.Y., 1885.
Phil 8585.6.5 Fisher, G.P. Faith and rationalism. N.Y., 1879.
Phil 8585.6.6 Fisher, G.P. Faith and rationalism. N.Y., 1885.

Phil 8580 - 8605 Philosophy of religion - General treatises - Individual authors (A-Z) - cont.

Phil 8585.8   Foster, J. Discourses...natural religion and social virtue. London, 1749-52.
Phil 8585.9   Fowle, T.W. A new analogy. London, 1881.
Phil 8585.10   Fownes, G. Chemistry as exemplifying the wisdom and beneficence of God. N.Y., 1844.
Phil 8585.10.2   Fownes, G. Chemistry as exemplifying the wisdom and beneficence of God. London, 1849.
Phil 8585.11   Fox, W.J. On the religious ideas. London, 1849.
Phil 8585.12   Franck, A. Philosophie et religion. Paris, 1869.
Phil 8585.13   Fauenstädt, C.M.J. Briefe über natürliche Religion. Leipzig, 1858.
Phil 8585.13.10   Frauestädt, C.M.J. Studien und Kritiken zur Theologie und Philosophie. Berlin, 1840.
Phil 8585.13.15   Frauestädt, C.M.J. Blicke in die intellectuelle, physische und moralische Welt. Leipzig, 1869.
X Cg   Phil 8585.14   Free Religious Association. Freedom and fellowship. Boston, 1875.
Phil 8585.15   Frohschammer, J. Das neue Wissen und der neue Glaube. Leipzig, 1873.
Phil 8585.16   Frothingham, O.B. The religion of humanity. N.Y., 1873.
Phil 8585.17   Fiske, J. Through nature to God. Boston, 1899.
Phil 8585.17.5   Fiske, J. Studies in religion. Boston, 1902.
Phil 8585.18   Ferguson, G. The religion of democracy. N.Y., 1900.
Phil 8585.19   Fielding-Hall, H. The hearts of men. N.Y., 1901.
Phil 8585.19.3   Fielding-Hall, H. The hearts of men. 3rd ed. London, 1904.
Phil 8585.19.5   Fielding-Hall, H. The world soul. N.Y., 1913.
Phil 8585.20   Forsyth, P.T. Principle of authority in relation to certainty. London, 1912.
Phil 8585.20.80   Foakes-Jackson, F.J. The faith and the war; a series of essays. London, 1915.
Phil 8585.22   Frothingham, E.L. Christian philosophy. Baltimore, 1888-1890. 2v.
Phil 8585.23.5   Figgis, J.N. Civilisation at the cross roads. N.Y., 1912.
Phil 8585.24   Fernandes de Santanna, Manuel. Apologetica. Lisboa, 1901.
Phil 8585.25   Furman, R.T. What a man told his son. N.Y., 1924.
Phil 8585.26   Flügel, O. Zur philosophie des Christentums. Langensalza, 1899.
Phil 8585.27A   Fosdick, Harry E. Adventurous religion and other essays. 1st ed. N.Y., 1926.
Phil 8585.27B   Fosdick, Harry E. Adventurous religion and other essays. 1st ed. N.Y., 1926.
Phil 8585.28A   Freud, Sigmund. The future of an illusion. London, 1928.
Phil 8585.28B   Freud, Sigmund. The future of an illusion. London, 1928.
Phil 8585.28.2   Freud, Sigmund. The future of an illusion. London, 1949.
Phil 8585.28.3   Freud, Sigmund. The future of an illusion. N.Y., 1928.
Phil 8585.29   Friend, Nellie E. God and you. N.Y., 1929.
Phil 8585.30   Floyd, William. Our gods on trial. N.Y., 1931.
Phil 8585.31   Franken, J.C. Kritische Philosophie und Dialektischen Theologie. Proefschrift. Amsterdam, 1932.
Phil 8585.32   Feldman, R.V. The domain of selfhood. London, 1934.
Phil 8585.33   Fornerod, A. Religion et théologie. Lausanne, 1932.
Phil 8585.35A   Frank, Erich. Philosophical understanding and religious truth. 1st ed. London, 1945.
Phil 8585.35B   Frank, Erich. Philosophical understanding and religious truth. 1st ed. London, 1945.
Phil 8585.36   Fries, Heinrich. Die Katholische religions philosophie der Gegenwart. Heidelberg, 1949.
Phil 8585.37   Ferrière, A. L'essentiel. Lausanne, 1952.
Phil 8585.40   Filosofia. Palmi, 1956.
Phil 8585.45   Fedorov, N.I. U tserkovnoi ogrady. Buenos Aires, 1955.
Phil 8585.47   Fatone, Vicente. Temas de mistica y religion. Bahía Blance, 1963.
Phil 8585.48   Feiner, Johannes. Mysterium salutis. Einsiedeln, 1965. 4v.
Phil 8585.50   Feaver, J. Clayton. Religion in philosophical and cultural perspective. Princeton, 1967.
Phil 8585.55   Faggiotto, Agostino. La religione nell'esperienza umana. Padova, 1967.
Phil 8586.1   Gastrell, F. The certainty and necessity of religion. London, 1697.
Phil 8586.1.2   Gastrell, F. The certainty and necessity of religion. London, 1703.
Phil 8586.2   Gordon, T. A new method of demonstrating...the four fundamental points of religion. London, 1756.
Phil 8586.3   Gisborne, T. The testimony of natural theology to Christianity. London, 1818.
Phil 8586.4   Gould, George M. The meaning and method of life. N.Y., 1893.
Phil 8586.5   Graham, W. The creed of science, religious, moral and social. London, 1881.
Phil 8586.6   Gréard, Mlle. Du doute. Paris, 1867.
Phil 8586.7   Gresley, W. Thoughts on religion and philosophy. London, 1875.
Phil 8586.8.3   Guyau, M.J. L'irréligion de l'avenir. 18. éd. Paris, 1912.
Phil 8586.8.5   Guyau, M.J. The non-religion of the future. London, 1897.
Phil 8586.8.10   Guyau, M.J. Framtidens irreligion. Stockholm, 1907.
Phil 8586.8.15   Guyau, M.J. Die irreligion der Zukunft. Leipzig, 192-?
Phil 8586.9   Gallaudet, T.H. The class-book of natural theology. 2nd ed. Hartford, 1843.
Phil 8586.10   Galloway, G. Studies in the philosophy of religion. Edinburgh, 1904.
Phil 8586.10.5   Galloway, G. Principles of religious development. London, 1909.
Phil 8586.10.9   Galloway, G. Religion and modern thought. Edinburgh, 1922.
Phil 8586.10.17   Galloway, G. The philosophy of religion. N.Y., 1927.
Phil 8586.10.25   Galloway, G. Faith and reason in religion. London, 1927.
Phil 8586.11   Gourd, J.J. Philosophie de la religion. Paris, 1911.
Phil 8586.12   Gérard, Philippe Louis. Le Comte de Valmont ou les égaremens de la raison. Paris, 1775.
Phil 8586.13   George, J.F.L. Mythus und Sage. Berlin, 1837.
Phil 8586.14   Guilbert, A.V.F. La divine synthèse. Paris, 1875. 3v.
Phil 8586.15   Graham, Bothwell. Philosophy of Christianity. Columbia, 1917.
Phil 8586.16   Gese, Paul. Einleitung in die Religionsphilosophie über die verschiedenen Standpunkt und Methoden zur Enforchung des Wesens der Religion. Göttingen, 1918.
Phil 8586.17   Gentile, G. Discorsi di religione. Firenze, 1920.
Phil 8586.17.2   Gentile, G. Discorsi di religione. 2. ed. Firenze, 1924.
Phil 8586.18   Girgensohn, Karl. Die religion. Leipzig, 1903.
Phil 8586.19   Grane, Georg. Selbstbwusstsein und Willensfreiheit. Berlin, 1904.

Phil 8580 - 8605 Philosophy of religion - General treatises - Individual authors (A-Z) - cont.

Phil 8586.20   Leuchtende fakel zum allgemeinen Glaubensbekenntniss aller Religionen. Frankfurt, 1784.
Phil 8586.21   Gebete eines Weisen. Thal Ehrenbreitstein, 1786.
Phil 8586.22   Gabriel, R.H. Christianity and modern thought. New Haven, 1924.
Phil 8586.23   Gould, Gerald. The helping hand. London, 1922.
Phil 8586.24   Goeschel, C.F. Beiträge zur Spekulativen philosophie. Berlin, 1838.
Phil 8586.25   Grundler, O. Elemente zu einer religionsphilosophie auf Phänomenonologischer Grundlage. Kempten, 1922.
Phil 8586.26   Güttler, C. Wissen und Glauben. 2e Aufl. München, 1904.
Phil 8586.27   Grimm, D. Die zwei Wege im religiösen Denken. Göttingen, 1922.
Phil 8586.28   Ghose, J.C. The positive religion. Calcutta, n.d.
Phil 8586.29   Giovanni, V. di. Critica religiosa e filosofia lettere e saggi. Palermo, 1897. 2v.
Phil 8586.30   Gentile, P. Sommario d'un filosofia della religione. Bari, 1923.
Phil 8586.31   Gehring, Albert. The religion of thirty great thinkers. Boston, 1925.
Phil 8586.32   Gardner, P. Modernity and the churches. London, 1909.
Phil 8586.33   Graf, A. Per una fede. Milano, 1906.
Phil 8586.34   Guizot, F.P.G. Méditations sur l'essence de la religion chrétienne. 1e série. Paris, 1864.
Phil 8586.34.2   Guizot, F.P.G. Méditations sur l'essence de la religion chrétienne. 1e série. Paris, 1864.
Phil 8586.34.3   Guizot, F.P.G. Méditations sur l'essence de la religion. Paris, 1866.
Phil 8586.34.5   Guizot, F.P.G. Méditations sur la religion chrétienne. Paris, 1866-1868. 3v.
Phil 8586.35   Grohmann, W. Lutherische Metaphysik. Leipzig, 1904.
Phil 8586.36   Gogarten, Friedrich. Ich Glaube an den dreieinigen Gott. Jena, 1926.
Phil 8586.36.5   Gogarten, Friedrich. Glaube und Wirklichkeit. Jena, 1928.
Phil 8586.36.10   Gogarten, Friedrich. Die Frage nach Gott. Tübingen, 1968.
Phil 8586.36.50   Schräter, Fritz. Glaube und Geschichte bei Friedrich Gogarten und Wilhelm Hermann. Inaug. Diss. Kothenanhalt, 1932?
Phil 8586.36.60   Runte, H. Glaube und Geschichte. Festschrift für Friedrich Gogarten. Giessen, 1948.
Phil 8586.36.65   Strohm, Theodor. Konservative politische Romantik. Berlin, 1961.
Phil 8586.36.66   Strohm, Theodor. Theologie im Schatten politischer Romantik. Mainz, 1970.
Phil 8586.36.70   Weth, Rudolf. Gott in Jesus; der Ansatz der Christologie Friedrich Gogartens. München, 1968.
Phil 8586.36.80   Nievergelt, Hans-Ulrich. Hutorität und Begegnung. Zürich, 1963.
Phil 8586.37   Greg, William R. The creed of Christendom. London, 1851.
Phil 8586.37.10   Greg, William R. The creed of Christendom. 5th ed. London, 1877. 2v.
Phil 8586.38   Grensted, L.W. Philosophical implications of Christianity. Oxford, 1930.
Phil 8586.39   Grant, Malcolm. A new argument for God. London, 1934.
Phil 8586.40   Gröbner, Wolfgang. Der Weg Aufwärts. Wien, 1935.
Phil 8586.41   Gill, Eric. The necessity of belief. London, 1936.
Phil 8586.42   Gunther, G. Christliche Metaphysik und das Schicksal des modernen Bewusstseins. Leipzig, 1937.
Phil 8586.43   Genlis, S.F. La religion considérée comme l'unique base du bonheur et de la véritable philosophie. Orleans, 1787.
Phil 8586.43.5   Genlis, S.F. La religion considérée comme l'unique base du bonheur et de la véritable philosophie. Maestricht, 1787.
Phil 8586.44   Guisan, René. Reliquiae. Lausanne, 1535.
Phil 8586.45   Gilson, Étienne. God and philosophy. New Haven, 1941.
Phil 8586.45.5   Gilson, Étienne. Les tribulations de Sophie. Paris, 1967.
Phil 8586.47   Garnett, A.C. A realistic philosophy of religion. Chicago, 1942.
Phil 8586.48   Griffith, G.O. Interpreters of man. London, 1943.
Phil 8586.49   Gillett, H.T. The spiritual basis of democracy. Oxford, 1952.
Phil 8586.50   Gregg, R.B. Self-transcendence. London, 1956.
Phil 8586.52   Guirdham, A. Christ and Freud. London, 1959.
Phil 8586.54   Guardini, Romano. Religion und Offenbarung. Würzburg, 1958.
Phil 8586.55   Guerin, Pierre. Vérité et religion; essai le problème. Paris, 1962.
Phil 8586.55.5   Guerin, Pierre. Pensée constructive et réalités spirituelle. Paris, 1934.
Phil 8586.56   Galitskaia, I.A. Mysli o religii. Moskva, 1962.
Phil 8586.57   Goedt, Michel de. Foi au Christ et dialogues du Chrétien. Bruges, 1967.
Phil 8586.60   Grillo, Friedrich. Aphoristische Darstellung der Religion. Bruxelles, 1968.
Phil 8586.62   Gibson, Alexander Boyce. Theism and empiricism. London, 1970.
Phil 8586.64.80   Mitchell, Phillip Marshall. Vilhelm Grønbech. En indføring. København, 1970.
Phil 8587.1   Hannotin, E. Nouvelle théologie philosophique. Paris, 1846. 2v.
Phil 8587.1.5   Hannotin, E. Les grandes questions. Paris, 1867.
Phil 8587.2.2   Harris, J. The pre-Adamite earth. London, 1849.
Phil 8587.2.3   Harris, J. The pre-Adamite earth. Boston, 1850.
Phil 8587.2.5   Harris, J. Man primeval. Boston, 1849.
Phil 8587.5   Hecker, I.T. Aspirations of nature. N.Y., 1857.
Phil 8587.6   Hedge, F.H. Reason in religion. Boston, 1865.
Phil 8587.6.5   Hedge, F.H. Ways of the spirit. Boston, 1877.
Phil 8587.6.15   Bowen, D. Assumed authority:...Hedge's address. Boston, 1864.
Phil 8587.8   Helmersen, A. von. Die Religion. Graz, 1875.
Htn   Phil 8587.9*   Hemsterhuis, F. Aristée ou de la divinité. Paris, 1778-79. 2 pam.
Phil 8587.10   Hennell, S.S. Present religion. v.1-2. London, 1865-87. 3v.
Phil 8587.10.5   Hennell, S.S. Comparativism. London, 1869.
Phil 8587.10.10   Hennell, S.S. Thoughts in aid of faith. London, 1860.
Phil 8587.10.15   Hennell, S.S. Christianity and infidelity. London, 1857.
Phil 8587.11   Henslow, G. The theory of evolution of living things. London, 1873.
Phil 8587.12   Hehn, Johannes. Wege zum Monotheismus. Würzburg, 1913.
Phil 8587.13   Herrmann, W. Die Religion. Halle, 1879.
Phil 8587.13.90   Herrmann, R. Christentum und Geschichte bei W. Herrmann. Leipzig, 1914.
Phil 8587.14   Heydenreichs, K.H. Betrachtungen über die Religion. v.1-2. Leipzig, 1904.
Phil 8587.14.3   Heydenreichs, K.H. Beträchtungen über die Philosophie. Leipzig, 1790-91. 2 pam.

Phil 8580 - 8605   Philosophy of religion - General treatises - Individual
     authors (A-Z) - cont.

	Phil 8587.14.10	Heydenreichs, K.H. Grundsätze der moralischen Gotteslehre. Leipzig, 1792.
	Phil 8587.15	Higginson, T.W. The sympathy of religions. Boston, 1876.
	Phil 8587.15.2	Higginson, T.W. The sympathy of religions. Chicago, 1893.
Htn	Phil 8587.15.5*	Higginson, T.W. L'affinité des religions. Paris, n.d.
	Phil 8587.15.6	Higginson, T.W. L'affinité des religions. Paris, n.d.
	Phil 8587.16	Hill, T. Geometry and faith. N.Y., 1849.
	Phil 8587.16.2	Hill, T. Geometry and faith. Boston, 1882.
	Phil 8587.17	Hitchcock, E. The religion of geology...connected sciences. Boston, 1851.
	Phil 8587.17.5	Hitchcock, E. Religious truth. Boston, 1857.
	Phil 8587.19	Huber, M. The world unmasked. London, 1736.
	Phil 8587.19.10	Huber, M. The divine instinct recommended to men. London, 1781.
	Phil 8587.21.2	Huntington, F.D. Human society: Graham lectures. N.Y., 1860.
	Phil 8587.24	Huntington, F.W. Cué bono? or What shall it profit. London, 1912.
	Phil 8587.25	Hyndman, F.A. The time of transition. London, 1900.
	Phil 8587.26	Harnack, Adolf. Das Wesen des Christentums. 4. Aufl. Leipzig, 1901.
	Phil 8587.26.3	Harnack, Adolf. Das Wesen des Christentums. Leipzig, 1903.
	Phil 8587.26.12	Harnack, Adolf. What is Christianity? London, 1901.
	Phil 8587.26.13	Harnack, Adolf. What is Christianity? 2. ed. N.Y., 1904.
	Phil 8587.26.16	Harnack, Adolf. What is Christianity? 2. ed. N.Y., 1903.
	Phil 8587.26.80	Rolffs, Ernst. Harnack's Wesen des Christentums und die religiösen Strömmungen der Gegenwart. Leipzig, 1902.
	Phil 8587.27.3	Huntington, William R. Four key-words of religion. 2. ed. N.Y., 1899.
	Phil 8587.28	Hoppe, Edmund. Natur und Offenbarung. 2. Aufl. Hannover, 1904.
	Phil 8587.28.5	Hoppe, Edmund. Glauben und Wissen. 2. Aufl. Gütersloh, 1922.
	Phil 8587.29	Hunzinger, A.W. Das Christentum im Weltanschauungskampf. 3. Aufl. Leipzig, 1919.
	Phil 8587.29.10	Hunzinger, A.W. Hunzinger. Hamburg, 1921-22. 2v.
	Phil 8587.30	Horneffer, Ernst. Die künftige Religion. Leipzig, 1909.
	Phil 8587.31	Horneffer, Ernst. Das klassische Ideal. 2-3. Aufl. Leipzig, 1909.
	Phil 8587.32	Hügel, Friedrich von. Essays and addresses on the philosophy of religion. London, 1921.
	Phil 8587.32.5	Hügel, Friedrich von. Essays and addresses on the philosophy of religion. London, 1926.
	Phil 8587.32.25	Hügel, Friedrich von. Reading from Friedrich von Hügel. London, 1928.
	Phil 8587.32.85	Hügel, Friedrich von. Selected letters 1896-1924. London, 1928.
	Phil 8587.32.87	Hügel, Friedrich von. Some letters. London, 1925.
	Phil 8587.32.91	Lester-Garland, L.V. The religious philosophy of Baron F. von Hügel. N.Y., 1933.
	Phil 8587.32.95	Dakiri, A.H., Jr. Von Hügel and the supernatural. London, 1934.
	Phil 8587.32.99	Nédoncelle, M. La pensée religieuse de F. von Hügel, 1852-1925. Paris, 1935.
	Phil 8587.32.101	Nédoncelle, M. La pensée religieuse de F. von Hügel, 1852-1925. Thèse. Paris, 1935.
	Phil 8587.32.109	Zari, A. Frederico von Hügel. Pinerolo, 1935.
	Phil 8587.32.112	Hügel, Friedrich. Baron von Hügel, man of God. London, 1947.
	Phil 8587.32.115	Bedoyere, M. de la. The life of Baron von Hügel. London, 1951.
	Phil 8587.32.117	Steinmann, J. Friedrich von Hügel. Paris, 1962.
	Phil 8587.33	Horn, E.F.B. Tolv forebaesninger over tro og taenkning. Kristiania, 1896.
	Phil 8587.33.3	Hoppe, J.I. Die Erforschung der Gefühle und moralischen Begriffe. 3. Aufl. Regensburg, 1876.
	Phil 8587.34.2	Hauter, Charles. Religion et réalité. Thèse. Strasbourg, 1922.
	Phil 8587.34.5	Hauter, Charles. Essai sur l'objet religieux. Thèse. Strasbourg, 1928.
	Phil 8587.35	Heinzelmann, G. Die erkenntnistheoretische Begründung der Religion. Basel, 1915.
	Phil 8587.36	Hegenwald, H. Gegenwartsphilosophie und christliche Religion. Leipzig, 1913.
	Phil 8587.37	Hocking, W.E. Illicit naturalizing of religion. Chicago, 1923.
	Phil 8587.38	Heegaard, P.S.V. Om intolerance, isaer i henseende til religios overbevisning. Kjobenhavn, 1878.
	Phil 8587.39	Heiberg, J.L. Religion og moral. 2. oplag. Kjobenhavn, 1911.
	Phil 8587.40	Hallock, C. Luminous bodies here and hereafter (the shining ones). N.Y., 1906.
	Phil 8587.41	Hatch, D.P. Om twentieth century Christ. Boston, 1906.
	Phil 8587.42	Hering, Jean. Phénoméologie et philosophie religieuse. Thèse. Strasbourg, 1925.
	Phil 8587.43	Hervey, Jacob. Ausserlesene Briefe über verschiedne Gegenstände aus der Sittenlehre und Religion. Hamburg, 1762.
	Phil 8587.44	Harkness, George E. Conflicts in religious thought. N.Y., 1929.
	Phil 8587.44.5	Harkness, George E. The resources of religion. N.Y., 1936.
	Phil 8587.44.10	Harkness, George E. Religious living. N.Y., 1937.
	Phil 8587.44.15	Harkness, George E. The recovery of ideals. N.Y., 1937.
	Phil 8587.45	Hamburger, Leo. Die Religion in ihrer dogmatischen und ihrer reinen Form. München, 1930.
	Phil 8587.46	Hyde, Laurence. The prospects of humanism. London, 1931.
	Phil 8587.47	Heard, Gerald. Social substance of religion. London, 1931.
	Phil 8587.47.5	Heard, Gerald. The recollection. Palo Alto, 1944.
	Phil 8587.48	Huxley, J.S. Religion without revelation. N.Y., 1927.
	Phil 8587.48.2	Huxley, J.S. Religion without revelation. N.Y., 1957.
	Phil 8587.49	Houf, Horace T. What religion is and does. N.Y., 1935.
	Phil 8587.50	Harper, W.A. Personal religious beliefs. Boston, 1937.
	Phil 8587.51	Haecker, T. Christentum und Kultur. München, 1927.
	Phil 8587.51.5	Haecker, T. Der Christ und die Geschichte. Leipzig, 1935.
	Phil 8587.51.10	Haecker, T. Opuscula. Olten, 1949.
	Phil 8587.53	Heering, H.J. De religienze toekomstverwachting. Amsterdam, 1937.
	Phil 8587.54	Hanse, H. "Gott haben." Berlin, 1939.
	Phil 8587.55	Hughes, T.H. Psychology and religious truth. London, 1942.
	Phil 8587.56	Hough, Lynn Harold. Whither Christianity. N.Y., 1929.
	Phil 8587.57	Hutchinson, Paul. The ordeal of western civilization. Boston, 1933.

Phil 8580 - 8605   Philosophy of religion - General treatises - Individual
     authors (A-Z) - cont.

	Phil 8587.58	Hallimond, J.G. The miracle of answered prayers. N.Y., 1916.
	Phil 8587.60	Huxley, Aldous. The perennial philosophy. 1. ed. N.Y., 1945.
	Phil 8587.60.5	Huxley, Aldous. The perennial philosophy. 5. ed. N.Y., 1945.
	Phil 8587.60.7	Huxley, Aldous. The perennial philosophy. N.Y., 1964.
	Phil 8587.62	Hirschmann, Eva. Phänomenologie der Religion. Proefschrift. Würzburg, 1940.
	Phil 8587.65	Hessen, Johannes. Religionsphilosophie. v.1-2. Essen, 1948.
	Phil 8587.65.3	Hessen, Johannes. Platonismus und Prophetismus. 2. Aufl. München, 1955.
	Phil 8587.65.5	Hessen, Johannes. Religionsphilosophie. 2. Aufl. v.1-2. München, 1955.
	Phil 8587.65.10	Hessen, Johannes. Griechische oder biblische Theologie. München, 1962.
	Phil 8587.66	Hägerström, A.A.T. Religionsfilosofi. Stockholm, 1949.
	Phil 8587.67	Hermans, F. Histoire doctrinale de l'humanisme chrétien. Tournai, 1948. 4v.
	Phil 8587.68	Heins, Karl. Die Wandlung im naturwissenschaftlicher Weltbild. 2. Aufl. Hamburg, 1951.
	Phil 8587.69	Hodges, H.A. Languages, standpoints, attitudes. London, 1953.
	Phil 8587.70	Hutchison, J.A. Faith. N.Y., 1956.
	Phil 8587.71	Herberg, Will. Four existentialist theologians. Garden City, N.Y., 1958.
	Phil 8587.72	Hedenius, I. Tro och roetande. Stockholm, 1949.
	Phil 8587.73	L'homme au regard de la foi. Paris, 1959.
	Phil 8587.74	Hayward, John. Existentialism and religious liberalism. Boston, 1962.
	Phil 8587.76	Haegerstroem, Axel. Philosophy and religion. London, 1964.
	Phil 8587.78	Hançerlioğlu, Orhan. Fel sefe sölüğü. Istanbul, 1967.
	Phil 8587.80	Heering, Herman Johan. Dogmatische verkenningen. 's-Gravenhage, 1968.
	Phil 8587.82	Hildebrand, Alice M. (Jourdain) von. Introduction to a philosophy of religion. Chicago, 1971.
	Phil 8588.1	Ibarreta, R.H. La religion al alcance de todos. 5. ed. Madrid, 1884.
	Phil 8588.1.5	Ibarreta, R.H. La religion al alcance de todos. 35. ed. Barcelona, 1912.
	Phil 8588.2	Inge, W.R. The eternal values. London, 1933.
	Phil 8588.2.5	Inge, W.R. Personal religion and the life of devotion. London, 1924.
	Phil 8588.4	Immanuel, ein Buch für Christum und Juden. Bruxelles, 1968.
	Phil 8589.1	Jackson, W. The philosophy of natural theology. London, 1874.
	Phil 8589.2	Jerusalem, J.F.W. Betrachtungen über die vornehmsten Wahrheiten der Religion. 5. Aufl. Braunschweig, 1776-91. 3v.
	Phil 8589.2.10	Jerusalem, J.F.W. Nachgelassene Schriften. Braunschweig, 1792-93. 2v.
Htn	Phil 8589.4*	Johnson, F.H. What is reality? Boston, 1891.
	Phil 8589.5	James, H. Lectures and miscellanies. Redfield, N.Y., 1852.
	Phil 8589.5.5A	James, H. Literary remains. Boston, 1885.
	Phil 8589.5.5B	James, H. Literary remains. Boston, 1885.
	Phil 8589.5.10A	James, H. Society, the redeemed form of man. Boston, 1879.
	Phil 8589.5.10B	James, H. Society, the redeemed form of man. Boston, 1879.
	Phil 8589.5.15	James, H. Moralism and Christianity, or Man's experience and destiny, in three lectures. N.Y., 1850.
	Phil 8589.5.20	James, H. Christianity, the logic of creation. N.Y., 1857.
	Phil 8589.5.30	Young, F.H. The philosophy of Henry James, Sr. N.Y., 1951.
	Phil 8589.5.40	Kellogg, J.A. Philosophy of Henry James. N.Y., 1883.
	Phil 8589.5.45	Hoover, Dwight W. Henry James. Grand Rapids, 1969.
	Phil 8589.6	Jones, William T. Spiritual ascent of man. N.Y., 1917.
	Phil 8589.7	Jevons, Frank B. Religion in evolution. London, 1906.
	Phil 8589.9	Joussain, André. Romantisme et religion. Paris, 1910.
	Phil 8589.10	Jones, David A. Philosophic thought and religion. London, 1919.
	Phil 8589.11	Jeanette, Agnes. The seventh seal. Philadelphia, 1920.
	Phil 8589.12	Jones, Henry. A faith that enquires. N.Y., 1922.
	Phil 8589.13	Jones, R.M. Religious foundations. N.Y., 1923.
	Phil 8589.14.5	Jacks, L.P. A living universe (Hibbert lectures, 1923). N.Y., 1924.
	Phil 8589.14.9	Jacks, L.P. The revolt against mechanism. N.Y., 1934.
	Phil 8589.14.12	Jacks, L.P. The revolt against mechanism. London, 1934.
	Phil 8589.15	Jacobsson, M. Om förhallandet mellan religion och moral. Stockholm, 1917.
	Phil 8589.16	Johnson, J.W. Fundamentalism versus modernism. N.Y., 1925.
	Phil 8589.17	Joad, Cyril E.M. Present and future of religion. London, 1930.
	Phil 8589.17.10	Joad, Cyril E.M. Counter attack from the East. London, 1933.
	Phil 8589.17.15A	Joad, Cyril E.M. Counter attack from the East. 1. Indian ed. Bombay, 1951.
	Phil 8589.17.15B	Joad, Cyril E.M. Counter attack from the East. 1. Indian ed. Bombay, 1951.
	Phil 8589.18	James, E.O. Social functions of religion. Nashville, 1940.
	Phil 8589.19.8	Jones, E.S. The Christ of the Mount. N.Y., 1935.
	Phil 8589.20	Jung, Carl Gustav. Antwort auf Hiob. Zürich, 1952.
	Phil 8589.20.3	Jung, Carl Gustav. Answer to Job. Cleveland, 1964.
	Phil 8589.21	Jaspers, Karl. Die Frage der Entmythologisierung. München, 1954.
	Phil 8589.21.2	Jaspers, Karl. Myth and Christianity. N.Y., 1958.
	Phil 8589.25	Jankélévetch, V. Láusterité et la vie morale. Paris, 1956.
	Phil 8589.30	Jordan, Placidus. Antwort auf Wort. München, 1969.
X Cg	Phil 8590.2	Kidd, J. On the adaption of external nature, physical condition of man. London, 1852.
	Phil 8590.2.2	Kidd, J. On the adaption of external nature, physical condition, Man. Philadelphia, 1883.
	Phil 8590.3	Kemp, J.T. van der. Tentamen theologiae dunatscopicae. Lugdunum Batavorum, 1775.
	Phil 8590.4	Koenig, Julius. Religion a curse! Why? N.Y., 1915.
	Phil 8590.7	King, I. The development of religion. N.Y., 1910.
	Phil 8590.9	Knowles, E.R. The supremacy of the spiritual. Boston, 1895.

Phil 8580 - 8605 Philosophy of religion - General treatises - Individual authors (A-Z) - cont.

Htn	Phil 8590.9.2*	Pamphlet box. Knowles, E.R. The supremacy of the spiritual.
	Phil 8590.10	King, Henry C. Religion as life. N.Y., 1913.
	Phil 8590.10.5	King, Henry C. Seeing life whole; a Christian philosophy of life. N.Y., 1923.
	Phil 8590.10.7	King, Henry C. Letters on the greatness and simplicity of the Christian faith. Boston, 1906.
	Phil 8590.10.9	King, Henry C. Reconstruction in theology. N.Y., 1901.
	Phil 8590.10.15	King, Henry C. Seeming unreality of the spiritual life. N.Y., 1911.
	Phil 8590.11.2	Kneib, Philipp. Wissen und Glauben. 2. Aufl. Mainz, 1905.
	Phil 8590.12	Köhler, Friedrich. Kulturwege und Erkenntnisse. Leipzig, 1916. 2v.
	Phil 8590.13.5	Krarup, F.C. Religionsfilosofi. København, 1921.
	Phil 8590.14	Köhler, R. Der Begriff a priori in der modernen Religionsphilosophie. Leipzig, 1920.
	Phil 8590.15	Kesseler, Kurt. Kritik der neukantischen religionsphilosophie der Gegenwart. Leipzig, 1920.
	Phil 8590.15.5	Kesseler, Kurt. Religionsphilosophie. Leipzig, 1927.
	Phil 8590.16	Key, Ellen. Der Lebensglaube. Berlin, 1906.
	Phil 8590.17	Kreiss. Theophilosophie. Berlin, 1880.
	Phil 8590.18.3	King, Basil. The conquest of fear. Garden City, 1921.
	Phil 8590.18.20	King, Basil. Faith and success. Garden City, 1928.
	Phil 8590.18.25	King, Basil. Adventures in religion. Garden City, 1929.
	Phil 8590.19	Knittermeyer, Heinrich. Die philosophie und das Christentum. Jena, 1927.
	Phil 8590.20	Knox, Raymond C. Religion and the American dream. N.Y., 1934.
	Phil 8590.21	Keller, Aaron. Das Prinzip der Dialektik in der Theologie. Inaug. Diss. Erlangen-Bruck, 1934.
	Phil 8590.22	Keilbach, W. Die Problematik der Religionen. Paderborn, 1936.
	Phil 8590.23	Kuhlmann, G. Theologische Anthropologie im Abriss. Tübingen, 1935.
	Phil 8590.24A	Keppler, P.W. von. Wahre und falsche Reform. Freiburg, 1903.
	Phil 8590.24B	Keppler, P.W. von. Wahre und falsche Reform. Freiburg, 1903.
	Phil 8590.25	Koppelmann, W. Der Erlösungs- und Heilsgedanke von freisinnig protestantischen Standpunkt. Bonn, 1925.
	Phil 8590.26.5	Kaftan, Julius. Das Christentum und die Philosophie. 3. Aufl. Leipzig, 1896.
	Phil 8590.27.10	Clemens, Franz J. Die Wahrheit in dem von J. von Kuhn in Tübingen. Münster, 1860.
	Phil 8590.28	Knudson, A.C. Present tendencies in religious thought. N.Y., 1924.
	Phil 8590.29	Kimpel, B.F. The symbols of religious faith. N.Y., 1954.
	Phil 8590.30	Kristensen, William. The meaning of religion. The Hague, 1960.
	Phil 8590.31	Die katholische Glaubenswelt. v.3. Freiburg, 1961.
	Phil 8590.32	Kazhdan, Al.P. Proiskhozhdenie khristianstva i ego sushchnost'. Moskva, 1962.
	Phil 8590.33	Kasch, Wilhelm. Atheistischer Humanismus und christliche Existenz in der Gegenwart. Tübingen, 1964.
	Phil 8590.34	Kerényi, Karoly. Umgang mit Göttlichem. Göttingen, 1955.
	Phil 8590.34.2	Kerényi, Karoly. Umgang mit Göttlichem. 2. Aufl. Göttingen, 1961.
	Phil 8590.35	Krieger, Evelina. Abgrund und Gründe. Versuch einer Philosophie christlicher Positivität. Graz, 1966.
	Phil 8590.37	Koehler, Hans. Theologische Anthropologie; die biblische Sicht des Menschen und der Mensch der Gegenwart. München, 1967.
	Phil 8590.40	Kroeger, Athanasius. Mensch und Person. Recklinghausen, 1968.
	Phil 8590.42	Kahraman, Ahmet. Dinber tarihi. Istanbul, 1965.
	Phil 8590.44	Kamlah, Wilhelm. Der Ruf des Steuermanns. Stuttgart, 1954.
	Phil 8591.1	Law, E. Considerations...theory of religion. Cambridge, 1755.
	Phil 8591.1.2	Law, E. Considerations...theory of religion. Cambridge, 1765.
	Phil 8591.1.3	Law, E. Considerations...theory of religion. Cambridge, 1765.
NEDL	Phil 8591.3	Leifchild, J.R. The higher ministry of nature. London, 1872.
Htn	Phil 8591.4*	Leroux, Pierre. De l'humanité. Paris, 1860. 2v.
	Phil 8591.4.5	Leroux, Pierre. Du christianisme et de son origine democratique. pt.1-2. Boussac, 1848.
	Phil 8591.6	Levallois, J. Deisme et christianisme. Paris, 1866.
	Phil 8591.7	Liddon, H.P. Some elements of religion. London, 1872.
	Phil 8591.7.10	Liddon, H.P. Some elements of religion. 10. ed. London, 1894.
	Phil 8591.8	Lilly, W.S. The great enigma. N.Y., 1892.
	Phil 8591.8.5	Lilly, W.S. Ancient religion and modern thought. 2. ed. London, 1885.
	Phil 8591.10	Löwenhardt, E. Über Gott, Geist und Unsterblichkeit. Wolgast, 1875.
Htn	Phil 8591.11*	Lyons. The infallibility of human judgement. London, 1724.
	Phil 8591.12	Lang, Albert. Making of religion. London, 1898.
	Phil 8591.12.2	Lang, Albert. Making of religion. 2. ed. London, 1900.
	Phil 8591.12.5	Lang, Albert. Wesen und Wahrheit der Religion. München, 1957.
	Phil 8591.13	LeGallienne, R. The religion of a literary man. N.Y., 1893.
	Phil 8591.14	Sadd, G.T. The philosophy of religion. N.Y., 1905. 2v.
	Phil 8591.16	La Grasserie, R. de. De la psychologie des religions. Paris, 1899.
Htn	Phil 8591.17.8*	Lessius, Leonardus. Sir Walter Rawleigh's ghost. London, 1651.
	Phil 8591.18	Lindsay, James. Recent advances in theistic philosophy of religion. Edinburgh, 1897.
	Phil 8591.19	Lamanna, E.P. La religione nella vita dello spirito. Firenze, 1914.
	Phil 8591.20	Loisy, Alfred. La religion. Paris, 1917.
	Phil 8591.20.2	Loisy, Alfred. La religion. 2. éd. Paris, 1924.
	Phil 8591.20.5	Loisy, Alfred. Autour d'un petit livre. Paris, 1903.
	Phil 8591.20.9	Loisy, Alfred. Religion et l'humanité. Paris, 1926.
	Phil 8591.20.12	Loisy, Alfred. Autres mythes à propos de la religion. Paris, 1938.
	Phil 8591.21	Landmark, J.D. Erkjendelses-teortisk religionsfilosofi. København, 1908.
	Phil 8591.22	La Belle, Alfred. Essai sur l'origine des cults. Paris, 1880.
	Phil 8591.23	Lee, Gerald S. The shadow Christ. N.Y., 1896.

Phil 8580 - 8605 Philosophy of religion - General treatises - Individual authors (A-Z) - cont.

	Phil 8591.24	Leighton, J.A. Religion, and the mind of to-day. N.Y., 1924.
	Phil 8591.25.2	Lévy, L.G. Une religion rationnelle et laïque. 2. éd. Dijon, 1904.
	Phil 8591.26	Lambek, C. Religionen och nutidsmänniskan. Stockholm, 1924.
	Phil 8591.27	Laberthonnière, L. Le réalisme chrétien et l'idealisme grec. Paris, 1904.
	Phil 8591.27.5	Laberthonniere, Lucien. Il realismo cristiano e l'idealismo greco. Firenze, 1922.
	Phil 8591.27.6	Laberthonniere, Lucien. Le réalisme chrétien, précédé de essais de philosophie religieuse. Paris, 1966.
	Phil 8591.28	Lavollée, R. Raison et foi. Paris, 1926.
	Phil 8591.29	Lönborg, Sven. Religion och vetenskap. Stockholm, 1914.
	Phil 8591.30	Lewis, John. The passion for life. New Haven, 1928.
	Phil 8591.32	Lütgert, Wilhelm. Natur und geist Gottes; Vorträge zur Ethik. Leipzig, 1910.
	Phil 8591.33	Labanca, B. Della religione e della filosofia cristiana. Pt.2. Torino, 1888.
	Phil 8591.34	Le Prince de Beaumont, Marie. Les americaines, ou La preuve de la religion chrétienne par les lumières naturelles. 1. éd. Lyon, 1770. 6v.
	Phil 8591.35	Lion, Aline. The idealistic conception of religion. Oxford, 1932.
	Phil 8591.36	Lyman, E.W. The meaning and truth of religion. N.Y., 1933.
	Phil 8591.36.10	Lyman, E.W. Religion and the issues of life. N.Y., 1943.
	Phil 8591.37	Lupus, J. Le traditionalisme et le rationalisme. Liége, 1858. 3v.
	Phil 8591.38	Lindsay, Eric. Losing religion to find it. London, 1935.
	Phil 8591.39	Leufvén, E. Det religiösa kunskapsproblemet. Uppsala, 1914.
	Phil 8591.40	Lupton, D. Religion says you can. Boston, 1938.
	Phil 8591.41	Litt, Theodor. Protestantisches Geschichtswussteins. Leipzig, 1939.
	Phil 8591.42	Lamm, H. The relation of concept and demonstration in the ontological argument. Chicago, 1940.
	Phil 8591.43	Ludendorff, Mathilde S. Aus der Gotterkenntnis meinerwerke. München, 1935.
	Phil 8591.43.5	Ludendorff, Mathilde S. In den Gegilden der Gottoffenbarung. Pähl, 1959.
	Phil 8591.44.5A	Lewis, Clive Staples. The screwtape letters. N.Y., 1943.
	Phil 8591.44.5B	Lewis, Clive Staples. The screwtape letters. N.Y., 1943.
	Phil 8591.44.6	Lewis, Clive Staples. The screwtape letters and Screwtape proposes a toast. London, 1961.
	Phil 8591.44.8	Lewis, Clive Staples. The screwtape letters. N.Y., 1969.
	Phil 8591.44.10	Lewis, Clive Staples. The case for Christianity. N.Y., 1944.
	Phil 8591.44.11	Lewis, Clive Staples. The case for Christianity. N.Y., 1945.
	Phil 8591.44.12	Lewis, Clive Staples. More Christianity. N.Y., 1960.
	Phil 8591.44.15A	Lewis, Clive Staples. The great divorce. N.Y., 1946.
	Phil 8591.44.15B	Lewis, Clive Staples. The great divorce. N.Y., 1946.
	Phil 8591.44.20	Lewis, Clive Staples. Transposition, and other addresses. London, 1949.
	Phil 8591.44.25	Lewis, Clive Staples. The weight of glory. N.Y., 1949.
	Phil 8591.44.30	Lewis, Clive Staples. The world's last night. 1. ed. N.Y., 1960.
	Phil 8591.44.35	Lewis, Clive Staples. They asked for a paper. London, 1962.
	Phil 8591.44.45	Lewis, Clive Staples. Christian reflections. London, 1967.
	Phil 8591.45	Leh, L.L. Christianity reborn. N.Y., 1928.
	Phil 8591.50	Lunn, Arnold. Good gorilla. London, 1944.
	Phil 8591.55	Lee, Atkinson. Groundwork of the philosophy of religion. London, 1946.
	Phil 8591.60	Leese, Kurt. Ethische und religiöse Grundfragen im Denken der Gegenwart. Stuttgart, 1956.
	Phil 8591.65	Loewith, Karl. Wissen, Glaube und Skepsis. Göttingen, 1956.
	Phil 8591.65.5	Loewith, Karl. Zur Kritik der Christlichen Überlieferung. Stuttgart, 1966.
	Phil 8591.70	Bonafede, Giulio. Luciano Laberthomière. Palermo, 1958.
	Phil 8591.75	Laurila, K.S. Vapaamielisyys. Helsingissä, 1912.
	Phil 8591.80	Lewis, Hywel David. Philosophy of religion. London, 1965.
	Phil 8591.81	Lings, Martin. Ancient beliefs and modern superstitions. London, 1964.
	Phil 8591.82	Lofland, John. Doomsday Cult; a study of conversion proselytization, and maintenance of faith. Englewood Cliffs, 1966.
	Phil 8591.83	Lings, Martin. Ancient beliefs and modern superstitions. 1. ed. London, 1965.
	Phil 8591.84	Ling, Trevor Oswald. Buddha, Marx, and God: some aspects of religion in the modern world. N.Y., 1966.
	Phil 8591.86	Libizzi, Carmelo. Religione e vita. Padova, 1966.
	Phil 8591.87	Lotz, Johannes Baptist. Neue Erkenntnisprobleme in Philosophie und Theologie. Freiburg, 1968.
	Phil 8592.2	McConnell, S. Christianity. N.Y., 1912.
	Phil 8592.3	Macdonald, L.B. Life in the making. Boston, 1911.
	Phil 8592.4.5	Maurice, F.D. Sequel to the inquiry, what is revelation? Cambridge, 1860.
	Phil 8592.5	Margerie, A. de. Théodicée. Paris, 1865. 2v.
	Phil 8592.6	Martineau, James. Study of religion. Oxford, 1888. 2v.
	Phil 8592.6.2	Martineau, James. Study of religion. London, 1900. 2v.
	Phil 8592.6.3	Martineau, James. A study of religion. Oxford, 1888. 2v.
	Phil 8592.6.4	Martineau, James. A study of religion. 1. American ed. Oxford, 1888. 2v.
	Phil 8592.6.6	Sunderland, J.T. James Martineau and his Great Book. Toronto, 1905.
	Phil 8592.6.8	Martineau, James. Inter Amicos. London, 1901.
	Phil 8592.6.11	Martineau, James. The new affinities of faith. London, 1869.
	Phil 8592.6.12	Martineau, James. The new affinities of faith. Boston, 1869.
	Phil 8592.6.15	Upton, Charles B. Doctor Martineau's philosophy; a survey. London, 1905.
	Phil 8592.6.20	Martineau, James. The relation between ethics and religion. London, 1881.
	Phil 8592.6.80	Jones, Henry. The philosophy of Martineau in relation to the idealism of the present day. London, 1905.
	Phil 8592.7	Matter, J. La philosophie de la religion. Paris, 1857. 2v.
	Phil 8592.8	Maret, H.L.C. Théodicée chrétienne. Paris, 1844.

Phil 8580 - 8605 Philosophy of religion - General treatises - Individual authors (A-Z) - cont.

Phil 8592.9	Meyer, J.F. von. Wahrnehmungen einer Seherin. v.1-2. Hamburg, 1827-28.
Phil 8592.10	Miles, J.W. Philosophic theology. Charleston, 1849.
Phil 8592.11	Mills, B.F. Twentieth century religion. Boston, 1898.
Phil 8592.12	Momerie, A.W. The basis of religion. Edinburgh, 1886.
Phil 8592.13	Miller, Andrew. The problem of theology in modern thought. London, 1909.
Phil 8592.14	Morell, J.D. The philosophy of religion. N.Y., 1849.
Phil 8592.14.2	Morell, J.D. The philosophy of religion. London, 1849.
Phil 8592.15	Müller, F.M. Lectures on the origin and growth of religion. London, 1880.
Phil 8592.15.2	Müller, F.M. Lectures on the origin and growth of religion. N.Y., 1879.
Phil 8592.15.4	Müller, F.M. Lectures on the origin and growth of religion. 2. ed. London, 1878.
Phil 8592.15.5	Müller, F.M. Natural religion. London, 1889.
Phil 8592.16.2	Murphy, J.J. The scientific basis of faith. London, 1873.
Phil 8592.17	Marshall, H.K. Instinct and reason. N.Y., 1898.
Phil 8592.18	Merriman, H.B. Religio pictoris. Boston, 1899.
Phil 8592.19	Morison, J.C. The service of man. London, 1887.
Phil 8592.20	Monaco, C. La ragione naturale. Caserta, 1888.
Phil 8592.21.5	McTaggart, J.M.E. Some dogmas of religion. London, 1930.
Phil 8592.22	Mach, Franz. Das religions- und Weltproblem. 2. Aufl. Dresden, 1904. 2v.
Phil 8592.22.6	Mach, Franz. Die Krisis im Christentum. 2. Aufl. Dresden, 1908.
Phil 8592.23	Mehlis, Goerg. Einfuhrung in ein System...Religions. Tübingen, 1917.
Phil 8592.26	Marillier, Léon. La liberté de conscience. Paris, 1890.
Phil 8592.27	Mead, G.R.S. Quests old and new. London, 1913.
Phil 8592.28	Mellor, Stanley. Religion as effected by modern science philosophy. London, 1914.
Phil 8592.30	Mansel, H.L. A second letter to professor Goldwin Smith. Oxford, 1862.
Phil 8592.31	Matthews, W.R. Studies in Christian philosophy. London, 1921.
Phil 8592.32	McGiffert, A.C. The rise of modern religous ideas. N.Y., 1922.
Phil 8592.33	Møller, Otto. Noget om determinisme og frihed. Kjøbenhavn, 1893.
Phil 8592.34	Myers, J.H. Philosophy of faith. Syracuse, N.Y., 1896.
Phil 8592.35	Milburn, R.G. The theology of the real. London, 1925.
Phil 8592.35.10	Milburn, R.G. The logic of religious thought. London, 1929.
Phil 8592.36	Moore, Willis L. Spiritual gravity of the cosmist. Pasadena, 1926.
Phil 8592.37	Münzenberger, H.C. Über die Entstehung religiöser Volksbegriffe. Göttingen, 1791.
Phil 8592.38	Mariavé, Henry. Le philosophe suprême. v.2. Montpellier, 1925-26. 2v.
Phil 8592.39	Medina, Juan J. Cuadros disolventes. Sevilla, 1881.
Phil 8592.40	Pamphlet box. Martsynkovskii, V.F. Philosophy of religion.
Phil 8592.41	Mellone, S.H. Back to realities. London, 1928.
Phil 8592.42	Medina. Conjunto de las doctrinas y filosofías del siglo comparadas con los conocimientos modernos. Madrid, 1872.
Phil 8592.43	Hinrichs, B. Die religionsphilosophischen Elemente in J. David Michaelis' Dogmatik. Diss. Göttingen, 1911.
Phil 8592.44	Masci, Filippo. L'idealismo indeterminista. Napoli, 1898.
Phil 8592.45	Montague, W.P. Belief unbound. New Haven, 1930.
Phil 8592.45.6	Montague, W.P. Belief unbound. Freeport, N.Y., 1970.
Phil 8592.46	Mortier, Lowis. Le problème de la vie. Paris, 1872.
Phil 8592.47	McCabe, Joseph. Story of religious controversy. Boston, 1929.
Phil 8592.48	Macintosh, D.C. Religious realism. N.Y., 1931.
Phil 8592.48.3	Macintosh, D.C. Theology as an empirical science. N.Y., 1919.
Phil 8592.48.5	Macintosh, D.C. The problem of religious knowledge. N.Y., 1940.
Phil 8592.48.7	Macintosh, D.C. The reasonableness of Christianity. N.Y., 1926.
Phil 8592.48.10	Macintosh, D.C. The reaction against metaphysics in theology. Chicago, 1911.
Phil 8592.49	McCormac, H. Aspirations from the inner, the spiritual life. London, 1860.
Phil 8592.50.5	Molinari, G. de. Religion. 2. ed. London, 1894.
Phil 8592.52.5	Mason, Francis. The contents of the history of ancient paganism. London, 1747.
Phil 8592.53	Mitchell, H.B. Talks on religion. N.Y., 1908.
Phil 8592.55A	Moore, Edward C. The nature of religion. N.Y., 1936.
Phil 8592.55B	Moore, Edward C. The nature of religion. N.Y., 1936.
Phil 8592.57	Masaryk, T.G. Moderní člověk a náboženství. Praha, 1934.
Phil 8592.57.5	Masaryk, T.G. Modern man and religion. London, 1938.
n Phil 8592.58*	M'Farland, Asa. An oration, produced before the Phi Beta Kappa,...Hanover, Aug. 25, 1802. Hanover, 1802.
n Phil 8592.59*	Morgan, Caesar. A demonstration that true philosophy has no tendency to undermine divine revelation. Cambridge, 1787.
Phil 8592.60	Martin, Cecil Percy. The decline of religion. London, 1940.
Phil 8592.61	Man unfit to govern man, by a citizen of London. London, 1833.
Phil 8592.62	Magre, M. Le livre des certitudes admirables. Avignon, 1941.
Phil 8592.63	Morris, Charles W. Paths of life, prepace to a world religion. N.Y., 1942.
Phil 8592.63.10	Morris, Charles W. The open self. N.Y., 1948.
Phil 8592.64	Mackay, J.A. Heritage and destiny. N.Y., 1943.
Phil 8592.65	Murray, R. Time and the timeless. London, 1942.
Phil 8592.66	Miller, Hugh. Christian truth in history. N.Y., 1941.
Phil 8592.67	Marvin, D.E. The church and her prophets. N.Y., 1909.
Phil 8592.68	Mathews, B. Through tragedy to triumph. N.Y., 1939.
Phil 8592.69	Matthes, H. Christus-Religion oder philosophische Religion? Göttingen, 1925.
Phil 8592.70	Moffatt, J. The thrill of tradition. London, 1944.
Phil 8592.71	Myers, E.D. Christianity and reason. N.Y., 1951.
Phil 8592.72	Marain, L. Humanism as the next step. Boston, 1954.
Phil 8592.73	MacLeish, Norman. The nature of religious knowledge. N.Y., 1938.
Phil 8592.75	McMurrin, S.M. The patterns of our religious faiths. Salt Lake City, 1954.
Phil 8592.80	Mouroux, Jean. The meaning of man. N.Y., 1952.
Phil 8592.81	Mouroux, Jean. Sens chrétien de l'homme. Paris, 1953.
Phil 8592.85	Meyer, Hans. Weltanschauungsprobleme der Gegenwart. 1. Aufl. Recklinghausen, 1956.
Phil 8592.90	Mascall, E.L. The importance of being human. N.Y., 1958.
Phil 8592.100	Martin-Deslias, N. L'invention divine. Paris, 1957.

Phil 8580 - 8605 Philosophy of religion - General treatises - Individual authors (A-Z) - cont.

Phil 8592.105	MacGregor, Geddes. Introduction to religious philosophy. London, 1960.
Phil 8592.106	MacGregor, Geddes. The hemlock and the cross. Philadelphia, 1963.
Phil 8592.108	MacKinnon, D.M. The borderlands of theology. Cambridge, Eng., 1961.
Phil 8592.110	Martin, C.B. Religious belief. Ithaca, N.Y., 1959.
Phil 8592.112	Magnino, B. Illuminismo e cristianesimo. Brescia, 1960. 3v.
Phil 8592.113	Mehl, R. The condition of the Christian philosopher. London, 1963.
Phil 8592.114	Molina, Antonio de. Excercicios espirituales de las excelencias, provecho y necesidad. Barcelona, 1702.
Phil 8592.115	Muck, Otto. Christliche Philosophie. Kevelaer, 1964.
Phil 8592.116	McPherson, Thomas. The philosophy of religion. London, 1965.
Phil 8592.117	Munson, Thomas N. Reflective theology; philosophical orientations in religion. New Haven, 1968.
Phil 8592.118	Mainberger, G. Widerspruch und Zuversicht. Olten, 1967.
Phil 8592.119	Mitchell, Basil. Neutrality and commitment: an inaugural lecture delivered before the University of Oxford on 13 May, 1968. Oxford, 1968.
Phil 8592.120	Meinvielle, Julio. Un progresismo vergonzante. Buenos Aires? 1967.
Phil 8592.122	Meslier, Jean. Oeuvres complètes. Paris, 1970- 2v.
Phil 8592.122.5	Meslier, Jean. Le testament de Jean Meslier. Amsterdam, 1864. 3v.
Phil 8592.122.10	Sociètè des Études Robespierristes. Études sur le curé Meslier. Paris, 1966.
Phil 8592.122.15	Dommanget, Maurice. Le curé Meslier, athée. Paris, 1965.
Phil 8592.122.20	Marchal, Jean. L'étrange figure du curé Meslier, 1664-1729. Charleville, 1957.
Phil 8592.122.25	Kucherenko, Gennadii S. Sud'ba "Zaveshchaniia" zhana mel'e v XVIII veke. Moskva, 1968.
Phil 8592.122.30	Porshnev, Boris F. Mel'e. Moskva, 1964.
Phil 8592.124	Morra, Gianfranco. Dio senza Dio. Bologna, 1970.
Phil 8593.1	The new philosophy. London, 1847-49. 3v.
Phil 8593.2	Newman, F.W. Hebrew Theism, common basis of Judaism, Christianity and Mohammedism. London, 1874.
Phil 8593.2.5	Newman, F.W. The soul. London, 1849.
Phil 8593.2.6	Newman, F.W. The soul. London, 1853.
Phil 8593.2.8	Newman, F.W. The soul. London, 1858.
Phil 8593.2.9	Newman, F.W. Soul, its sorrows and its aspirations. 3. ed. London, 1852.
Phil 8593.2.10	Newman, F.W. Phases of faith. London, 1850.
Phil 8593.2.11	Newman, F.W. Phases of faith. 3. ed. London, 1853.
Phil 8593.2.13	Newman, F.W. Phases of faith. 5. ed. London, 1858.
Phil 8593.3	Nichols, I. A catechism of natural theology. Portland, 1829.
Phil 8593.3.2	Nichols, I. A catechism of natural theology. Boston, 1831.
Phil 8593.3.3	Nichols, I. A catechism of natural theology. Boston, 1839.
Phil 8593.4	Nichols, J.R. From whence, what, where? Boston, 1882.
Phil 8593.4.10	Nichols, J.R. Whence, what, where? Boston, 1886.
NEDL Phil 8593.5	Nieuwentyt, B. The religious philosopher. London, 1719. 3v.
Phil 8593.5.2	Nieuwentyt, B. The religious philosopher. London, 1730. 3v.
Phil 8593.5.7	Nieuwentyt, B. Het regt gebruik der werelt beschouwingen. 4. druk. Amsterdam, 1725.
Phil 8593.6	Noyes, R.K. Views of religion. Boston, 1906.
Phil 8593.7	Nonnotte, Claude. Dictionnaire philosophique de la religion. n.p., 1772. 4v.
Phil 8593.8.2	Natorp, Paul. Religion inneralb der Grenzen. Tübingen, 1908.
Phil 8593.9	Nygren, A. Religiöst apriori. Lund, 1921.
Phil 8593.10	Nielsen, Rasmus. Om hindringer og betingelser for det aandelige liv i nutiden. Kjøbenhavn, 1867.
Phil 8593.11	A new departure. Boston, 1895.
Phil 8593.12	Nyström, A. Gyldene ord ur mensklighetens allmänna religion. 2. uppl. Stockholm, 1880.
Phil 8593.13	Nikolai, Pavel N. Mozhet-li sovremennyi obrazovannyi, mysliashchii cheloviek vierit' v bozhectvo Iisusa Khrista. 3. izd. Praga, 1923.
Phil 8593.14	Nyblaeus, Axel. Om religionens betydelse och förhållande till philosophen. pt.1-4. Upsala, 1853.
Phil 8593.15	The necessity of some of the positive institutions of ch---ty consider'd, in a letter to the minister of Moffat. London, 1731.
Phil 8593.16	Nuñez Regueiro, Manuel. Suma contra una nueva edad media. Rosario, 1938.
Phil 8593.17	The nature of religious experience. N.Y., 1937.
Phil 8593.18	Nicodemus (pseud.). Renaissence; an essay in faith. London, 1943.
Phil 8593.19	Nass, R.B. Two popular philosophic-scientific essays in the spirit of faith and religion. Brooklyn, N.Y., 1943.
Phil 8593.20	Nigg, Walter. Religiöse Denker. Bern, 1942.
Phil 8593.20.2	Nigg, Walter. Religiöse Denker. Berlin, 1952.
Phil 8593.20.5	Nigg, Walter. Prophetische Denker. Zürich, 1957.
Phil 8593.21	Nestle, Wilhelm. Die Krisis des Cristentums. Stuttgart, 1947.
Phil 8593.22	Nilsson, M.P. Fondamenti di scienza delle religioni. 1. ed. Firenze, 1950.
Phil 8593.23	Neill, T.P. Religion and culture. Milwaukee, 1952.
Phil 8593.24	Noack, H. Sprache und Offenbarung. Gütersloh, 1960.
Phil 8593.25	Novak, Michael. Ascent of the mountain. 1. ed. N.Y., 1971.
Phil 8594.1	Ohlert, A.L.J. Religionsphilosophie. Leipzig, 1835.
Phil 8594.2	Opzoomer, C.W. Die Religion. Elberfeld, 1868.
Phil 8594.2.5	Opzoomer, C.W. De godsdienst. Amsterdam, 1864.
Phil 8594.2.9	Opzoomer, C.W. Onze godsdienst. Amsterdam, 1874.
Phil 8594.2.15	Opzoomer, C.W. De vrucht der godsdienst. 3. druk. Amsterdam, 1868.
Phil 8594.3	Opzoomer, C.W. Order. n.p., 1885.
Phil 8594.3.2	Opzoomer, C.W. Order. n.p., 1885.
Phil 8594.4	Orr, J. The theory of religion. London, 1762.
Phil 8594.5.2	Oliphant, L. Scientific religion. 2. ed. Edinburgh, 1888.
Phil 8594.5.5	Oliphant, L. Scientific religion. Buffalo, 1889.
Phil 8594.6	Ollé-Laprune, L. La vitalite chrétiene. Paris, 1914.
Phil 8594.7	Opitz, H.G. Das Christentum im Freilichte. Leipzig, 1911.
Phil 8594.8	Ormond, A.T. The philosophy of religion. Princeton, N.J., 1922.
Phil 8594.10	Otto, Walter F. Der Geist der Antike und die christliche Welt. Bonn, 1923.

Phil 8580 - 8605   Philosophy of religion - General treatises - Individual authors (A-Z) - cont.

Phil 8594.11 — Oltramare, P. La religion et la vie de l'esprit. Paris, 1925.
Phil 8594.13 — Oman, John. The natural and the supernatural. N.Y., 1931.
Phil 8594.13.10 — Oman, John. Honest religion. Cambridge, Eng., 1941.
Phil 8594.14 — Ortegat, Paul. Philosophie de la religion. Bruxelles, 1938.
Phil 8594.14.5 — Ortegat, Paul. Philosophie de la religion. Gembloux, 1948. 2v.
Phil 8594.15 — Orr, J. The Christian view of God and the world. 8. ed. N.Y., 1907.
Phil 8594.16.80 — Benz, Ernst. Rudolf Otto's Bedeutung für die Religionswissenschaft und die Theologie. Leiden, 1971.
Phil 8595.1 — Parker, T. A discourse of matters pertaining to religion. Boston, 1847.
Phil 8595.1.2 — Parker, T. A discourse of matters pertaining to religion. Boston, 1856.
Phil 8595.1.3 — Parker, T. A discourse of matters pertaining to religion. Boston, 1842.
Phil 8595.1.4A — Parker, T. A discourse of matters pertaining to religion. Boston, 1907.
Phil 8595.1.4B — Parker, T. A discourse of matters pertaining to religion. Boston, 1907.
Phil 8595.1.6 — Parker, T. Sermons of Theism, Atheism, and the popular theology. Boston, 1853.
Phil 8595.1.7 — Parker, T. Sermons of Theism, Atheism, and the popular theology. Boston, 1856.
Phil 8595.2 — Peabody, A.P. Christianity the religion of nature. Boston, 1864.
Phil 8595.3 — Perrin, R.S. The religion of philosophy. N.Y., 1885.
Phil 8595.4 — Pfleiderer, O. Die Religion. Leipzig, 1869. 2v.
Phil 8595.4.2 — Pfleiderer, O. Religionsphilosophie. Berlin, 1878.
Phil 8595.4.2.2 — Pfleiderer, O. Religionsphilosophie. 2. Aufl. Berlin, 1883-84. 2v.
Phil 8595.4.3 — Pfleiderer, O. Religionsphilosophie. 3. Aufl. Berlin, 1896.
Phil 8595.4.5 — Pfleiderer, O. Die Religion. 2. Aufl. v.1-2. Leipzig, 1878.
Phil 8595.4.10 — Pfleiderer, O. The philosophy of religion. London, 1886-88. 4v.
Phil 8595.4.11 — Pfleiderer, O. Philosophy and development of religion. N.Y., 1894. 2v.
Phil 8595.4.12 — Pfleiderer, O. Religion und Religionen. München, 1906.
Phil 8595.4.13 — Pfleiderer, O. Religion and historic faiths. N.Y., 1907.
Phil 8595.4.15 — Pfleiderer, O. Über das Verhältnis der Religionsphilosophie. Berlin, 1906.
Phil 8595.4.113 — Gastrow, Paul. Pfleiderer als Relionsphilosophie. Berlin, 1913.
Phil 8595.5 — Poiret, P. Cogitationum rationalium. Amsterdam, 1715.
Phil 8595.7 — Powell, B. The order of nature. London, 1859.
Phil 8595.8 — Prevost, J.M.C. De la déomanie au XIXe siècle. Toulouse, 1860.
Phil 8595.9 — Pritchard, C. Occasional thoughts...astronomer, nature, revelation. London, 1889.
Phil 8595.10 — Prout, W. Chemistry, meteorology...natural theology. London, 1855.
Phil 8595.11 — Phillips, S.L. The testimony of reason. Washington, 1903.
Phil 8595.12 — Perry, R.B. Religion and mere morality. Boston, 1906.
Phil 8595.13 — Pritchett, H.S. What is religion. Boston, 1906.
Phil 8595.14 — Piercy, B.H. Facts and fancies. London, 1913.
Phil 8595.14.5 — Piercy, B.H. Superstition and common sense. London, 1912.
Phil 8595.15.2 — Paine, Thomas. Theological works. London, 1824.
Phil 8595.15.2.5 — Paine, Thomas. The theological works. London, 1827.
Phil 8595.15.3.5 — Paine, Thomas. The theological works. Boston, 1834.
Phil 8595.15.4 — Paine, Thomas. Theological works. Boston, 1858.
Phil 8595.15.4.3 — Paine, Thomas. Theological works. Chicago, 19- ?
Phil 8595.15.4.5 — Paine, Thomas. Theologische Werke. v.1-4,6. Philadelphia, 1851.
Phil 8595.15.4.10 — Paine, Thomas. Theological works. London, 1819.
Htn Phil 8595.15.5* — Paine, Thomas. Age of reason. Investigation of true and fabulous theology. Boston, 1794. 4 pam.
Htn Phil 8595.15.6* — Paine, Thomas. The age of reason. Pt.1. Paris, 1794.
Phil 8595.15.7 — Paine, Thomas. Age of reason. Investigation of true and fabulous theology. pt.1-2. 2d ed. Boston, 1795.
Htn Phil 8595.15.8* — Paine, Thomas. Age of reason. Investigation of true and fabulous theology. pt.1-2. London, 1796.
Phil 8595.15.9A — Paine, Thomas. Age of reason. Investigation of true and fabulous theology. London, 1852.
Phil 8595.15.9B — Paine, Thomas. Age of reason. Investigation of true and fabulous theology. London, 1852.
Htn Phil 8595.15.16* — Paine, Thomas. Age of reason. Investigation of true and fabulous theology. n.p., n.d. 5 pam.
Phil 8595.15.17 — Paine, Thomas. Age of reason. Investigation of true and fabulous theology. Boston, 1875. 2 pam.
Phil 8595.15.18 — Paine, Thomas. The age of reason. N.Y., 1896.
Phil 8595.15.19 — Paine, Thomas. Age of reason. N.Y., 1898.
Phil 8595.15.23 — Paine, Thomas. Age of reason. N.Y., 194-?
Phil 8595.15.24 — Paine, Thomas. Age of reason. N.Y., 1951.
Htn Phil 8595.15.28* — Paine, Thomas. La siècle de la raison. Paris, 1794.
Phil 8595.15.30 — Paine, Thomas. Siècle de la raison. pt.2. Paris, 1795-96.
Phil 8595.15.50 — Paine, Thomas. Letter of Thomas Paine to lawyer Erskine. n.p., 18-.
Phil 8595.15.65 — Drew, Samuel. Remarks on the 1st part of book entitled "The age of reason." 2. ed. N.Y., 1831.
Phil 8595.16 — Paine, Thomas. Age of reason. London, 1795.
Phil 8595.16.3 — Dutton, Thomas. A vindication of the age of reason, by Thomas Paine. London, 1795.
Htn Phil 8595.16.5* — Patten, William. Christianity the true theology. Warren, 1795.
Phil 8595.16.7 — Wakefield, Gilbert. An examination of the age or reason. 2. ed. London, 1794.
Phil 8595.16.9 — Estlin, John P. Evidences of revealed religion. Bristol, 1796?
Htn Phil 8595.16.11* — Winchester, E. A defence of revelation. N.Y., 1796.
Htn Phil 8595.16.13* — Tytler, James. Paine's second part of The age of reason answered. Salem, 1796.
Htn Phil 8595.16.15* — Levi, David. Defence of Old Testament. N.Y., 1797.
Htn Phil 8595.16.19* — Scott, Thomas. Vindication of divine inspiration. London, 1797.
Htn Phil 8595.16.20* — Scott, Thomas. Treatises on various theological subjects. Middletown, Conn., 1815.
Phil 8595.16.21 — Scott, Thomas. Treatises on various theological subjects. Middletown, Conn., 1824. 5v.
Phil 8595.16.23 — Watson, R. An apology for the Bible. Cambridge, 1828.
Htn Phil 8595.16.24* — Watson, R. An apology for Christianity. Philadelphia, 1796.

Phil 8595.16.24.2 — Watson, R. An apology for Christianity. 2. ed. Cambridge, 1777.
Htn Phil 8595.16.25* — Watson, R. Christian panoply. Sheperdstown, 1797. 2 pam.
Phil 8595.16.26 — Watson, R. Apology for the Bible. 7. ed. London, 1796.
Phil 8595.16.26.5 — Watson, R. An apology for the Bible. London, 1796.
Htn Phil 8595.16.27* — Watson, R. Apology for the Bible. N.Y., 1796.
Htn Phil 8595.16.27.3* — Watson, R. Apology for Christianity. 1st American ed. Providence, 1794.
Phil 8595.16.27.5 — Watson, R. Apology for the Bible. 2. ed. Philadelphia, 1796.
Phil 8595.16.27.7 — Watson, R. Two apologies, one for Christianity. London, 1818.
Phil 8595.16.27.8 — Watson, R. Watson refuted: being an answer to the apology for the Bible. London, 1819.
Phil 8595.16.27.10 — Watson, R. Apologies for Christianity and the Bible. London, 1824.
Phil 8595.16.27.25 — Watson, R. An apology for the Bible. Nashville, 1855.
Phil 8595.16.28.5 — Watson, R. An apology for the Bible. N.Y., 1835. 8 pam.
Phil 8595.16.29 — Thomson, Robert. Divine authority of the Bible. Boston, 1807.
Phil 8595.16.35 — Christianity the only true theology. London, 179-?
Phil 8595.17 — Seth Prugle Pattison, A. The idea of God. Aberdeen, 1917.
Phil 8595.18 — Perovsky-Petrovo, Solovovo. Le sentiment religieux, base logique de la morale? Paris, 1913.
Phil 8595.19 — Plekhanov, G. O religii. Moskva, 1923.
Phil 8595.20 — Pariser, E. Einführung in die Religions-Psychologie. Halle, 1914.
Phil 8595.21 — Parker, S. A demonstration of the divine authority of the law of nature. London, 1681.
Phil 8595.22 — Phelps, William L. Adventures and confessions. N.Y., 1926.
Phil 8595.23A — Powicke, F.J. The Cambridge Platonists; a study. London, 1926.
Phil 8595.23B — Powicke, F.J. The Cambridge Platonists; a study. London, 1926.
Phil 8595.23.5A — Powicke, F.J. The Cambridge Platonists. Cambridge, 1926.
Phil 8595.23.5B — Powicke, F.J. The Cambridge Platonists. Cambridge, 1926.
Phil 8595.24 — Penel, Raymond. Qu'est-ce que la vérité? Paris, 1926.
Phil 8595.25A — Philips Brooks House Association. Harvard University. Religion and modern life. N.Y., 1927.
Phil 8595.25B — Philips Brooks House Association. Harvard University. Religion and modern life. N.Y., 1927.
Phil 8595.26 — Perronet, V. Some enquiries, chiefly related to spiritual beings. London, 1740.
Phil 8595.27 — Pontanilles, E. Los dos grandes problemas de la humanidad. N.Y., 1882.
Phil 8595.28 — Potter, Charles F. Humanism; a new religion. N.Y., 1930.
Phil 8595.29 — Prideaux, Sherburne P.T. Man and his religion. London, 1930.
Phil 8595.30F — Persons, Lee C. The religion of the beautiful. Miami, 1932?
Phil 8595.31 — Przywara, Erich. Plarity; a German Catholic's interpretation of religion. London, 1935.
Phil 8595.32 — Philips, Vivian. The churches and modern thought. London, 1906.
Phil 8595.32.5 — Philips, Vivian. Concerning progressive revelation. London, 1936.
Phil 8595.32.7 — Philips, Vivian. Concerning progressive revelation. London, 1936.
Phil 8595.33 — Padovani, U.A. La filosofia della religione e il problema della vita. Milano, 1937.
Phil 8595.33.5 — Padovani, U.A. Cultura e critianesimo. Milano, 1964.
Phil 8595.34A — Pennsylvania. University. Bicentennial Conference. Religion and the modern world. Philadelphia, 1941.
Phil 8595.34B — Pennsylvania. University. Bicentennial Conference. Religion and the modern world. Philadelphia, 1941.
Phil 8595.35 — Palmstierna, E.K. The world's crisis and faiths. London, 1942.
Phil 8595.36 — Pesch, T. Christliche Lebensphilosophie. 20. bis 22. Aufl. Freiburg, 1923.
Phil 8595.37 — Persons, Stow. Free religion. New Haven, 1947.
Phil 8595.38 — Paul, Leslie A. The meaning of human existence. London, 1949.
Phil 8595.39 — Le problème de la philosophie chrétienne. Paris, 1949.
Phil 8595.40 — Paton, H.J. The modern predicament. London, 1955.
Phil 8595.41 — Pavelkin, P.A. Chto takoe religiia; besedy. Moskva, 1956.
Phil 8595.45 — Philosophies chrétiennes. Paris, 1955.
Phil 8595.50 — Panese, Roberto. Necessità e sufficienza del principio cristiano. Padova, 1958.
Phil 8595.55 — Pegis, Anton C. Christian philosophy and intellectual freedom. Milwaukee, 1960.
Phil 8595.56 — Pozov, A. Osnovy drevne-tserkovnoi antropologii. Madrid, 1965. 2v.
Phil 8595.56.5 — Pozov, A. Logos-meditatsiia drevnei tserkvi. Miunkhen, 1964.
Phil 8595.57 — Paggiaro, Luigi. L'esperienza religiosa. Padova, 1964.
Phil 8595.58 — Paus, Ansgar. Religiöser Erkenntnisgrund. Leiden, 1966.
Phil 8595.60 — Penelhum, Terence. Religion and rationality. 1. ed. N.Y., 1971.
Phil 8595.62 — Patterson, Robert Leet. A philosophy of religion. Durham, 1970.
Phil 8596.1 — Quetin, M.A. L'origine de la religion. Montauban, 1903.
Phil 8596.2 — Quick, O.C. Philosophy and the cross. London, 1931.
Phil 8597.1 — Ramsay, A.M. The philosophical principles of natural and revealed religion. Glasgow, 1748-49. 2v.
Phil 8597.2 — Ray, J. Three physico-theological discourses. London, 1721.
Phil 8597.3A — Reimarus, H.S. Abhandlungen von den vornehmsten Wahrheiten der natürlichen Religion. 6. Aufl. Hamburg, 1791.
Phil 8597.3B — Reimarus, H.S. Abhandlungen von den vornehmsten Wahrheiten der natürlichen Religion. 6. Aufl. Hamburg, 1791.
Phil 8597.3.3 — Reimarus, H.S. Die Vornehmstenwahrheiten der natürlichen Religion. 3. Aufl. Hamburg, 1766.
Phil 8597.3.4 — Reimarus, H.S. Die Vornehmstenwahrheiten der natürlichen Religion. 4. Aufl. Hamburg, 1772.
Phil 8597.3.8 — Reimarus, H.S. The principal truths of natural religion. London, 1766.
Phil 8597.3.10 — Reimarus, Johann Albert Heinrich. Über die Grunde der menschlichen Erkenntniss und der natürlichen Religion. Hamburg, 1787.

Phil 8580 - 8605   Philosophy of religion - General treatises - Individual authors (A-Z) - cont.

Phil 8597.3.11   Remarus, Johann Albert Heinrich. Über die Gründe der menschlichen Erkentniss und der natürlichen Religion. Bruxelles, 1968.
Phil 8597.3.12   Reimarus, H.S. Von dem Zwecke Jesu und seiner Jünger. Braunschweig, 1778.
Phil 8597.3.13   Reimarus, H.S. Von dem Zwecke Jesu und seiner Jünger. Berlin, 1784.
Phil 8597.3.15   Blasche, J.C. Kurze auch dem Laien verstandliche Verantwortung wider die Beschuldigungen. Jena, 1778.
Phil 8597.3.18   Schettler, R. Samuel Reimarus zur Religion. Leipzig, 1904.
Phil 8597.3.21   Reimarus, Johann Albert Heinrich. Von dem daseyn Gottes und der menschlichen Seele. Hamburg, 1781.
Phil 8597.4   Die Religion des Zweiflers. Leipzig, 1874.
Phil 8597.5   Religion one, even the self-same thing in all ages. London, 1741.
Phil 8597.6   Reinhold, E. Das Wesen der Religion. Jena, 1846.
Phil 8597.7   Rennie, J. Alphabet of natural theology. London, 1834.
Phil 8597.8   Reynaud, J.E. Philosophie religiuse terre et ciel. Paris, 1854.
Phil 8597.8.2   Reynaud, J.E. Philosophie religieuse terre et ciel. Paris, 1858.
Phil 8597.9   Riddle, A.G. Alcastor. n.p., 1883.
Phil 8597.10   Robles, M. Bigotry, superstition, hypocrasy...Atheism. London, 1742.
Phil 8597.11.4   Rogers, H. The eclipse of faith. 8. ed. Boston, 1863.
Phil 8597.11.7   Rogers, H. A defence of the eclipse of faith. London, 1854.
Phil 8597.11.8   Rogers, H. A defence of the eclipse of faith. Boston, 1856.
Phil 8597.11.12   Rogers, H. Reason and faith. London, 1850.
Phil 8597.11.15   Rogers, H. Reason and faith. Boston, 1853.
Phil 8597.12   Romanes, G.J. Thoughts on religion. London, 1895.
Phil 8597.12.5   Romanes, G.J. Thoughts on religion. Chicago, 1895.
Phil 8597.12.8   Romanes, G.J. Thoughts on religion. Chicago, 1898.
Phil 8597.13   Romang, J.P. Über Wichtigere Fragen der Religion. Heidelberg, 1870.
Phil 8597.14*   Rust, G. A discourse...reason in matters of religion. London, 1683.
Phil 8597.15   Robinson, E.K. The religion of nature. London, 1906.
Phil 8597.16   Rogers, A.K. The religious conception of the world. N.Y., 1907.
Phil 8597.17   Rowland, E.H. Right to believe. Boston, 1909.
Phil 8597.18   Religion of the spiritual evolution of man. Chicago, 1910.
Phil 8597.19A   Royce, Josiah. The sources of religious insight. N.Y., 1912.
Phil 8597.19B   Royce, Josiah. The sources of religious insight. N.Y., 1912.
Phil 8597.20A   Royce, Josiah. The problem of Christianity. N.Y., 1913. 2v.
Phil 8597.20B   Royce, Josiah. The problem of Christianity. N.Y., 1913.
Phil 8597.20C   Royce, Josiah. The problem of Christianity. N.Y., 1913.
Phil 8597.20.2   Royce, Josiah. The problem of Christianity. N.Y., 1914.
Phil 8597.20.5   Royce, Josiah. What is vital in Christianity? N.Y., 1909.
Phil 8597.20.10   Royce, Josiah. The sources of religious insight. Edinburgh, 1912.
Phil 8597.21   Rámanthán, P. The culture of the soul. N.Y., 1906.
Phil 8597.22   Religio universalis et naturalis. Paris, 1818.
Phil 8597.23   Reisner, Edward H. Religious values and intellectual consistency. N.Y., 1915.
Phil 8597.23.5   Reisner, Edward H. Faith in an age of fact. N.Y., 1937.
Phil 8597.24   Runze, Georg. Katechismus der Religionsphilosophie. Leipzig, 1901.
Phil 8597.25   Rade, Martin. Die Stellung des Christentums zum Geschlechtsleben. Tübingen, 1910.
Phil 8597.26   Rabus, Leonhard. Philosophie und Theologie. Erlangen, 1876.
Phil 8597.27   Rignano, Eugenio. Religione, materialismo, socialismo. Bologna, 1920.
Phil 8597.28   Richmond, W. Philosophy and the Christian experience. Oxford, 1922.
Phil 8597.29   Religion and life; the foundations of personal religion. N.Y., 1923.
Phil 8597.30   The religion of the future and other essays. London, 1911.
Phil 8597.31   Richter, R. Religionsphilosophie. Leipzig, 1912.
Phil 8597.32.5   Rauwenhoff, D.L.W.E. Religionsphilosophie. 2. Aufl. Braunschweig, 1894.
Phil 8597.33   Reischle, Max. Die Frage nach dem Wesen der Religion. Freiburg, 1889.
Phil 8597.34   Romberg, P.A. Filosofi och religion. Karlskrona, 1881.
Phil 8597.35   Reese, Curtis W. Humanism. Chicago, 1926.
Phil 8597.35.10   Reese, Curtis W. Humanist sermons. Chicago, 1927.
Phil 8597.36   Raven, Charles E. The creator spirit. Cambridge, 1927.
Phil 8597.36.5   Raven, Charles E. Jesus and the gospel of love. London, 1931.
Phil 8597.38   Radhakrishnan, S. An idealist view of life. N.Y., 1932.
Phil 8597.38.10   Radhakrishnan, S. East and West in religion. London, 1933.
Phil 8597.38.15   Radhakrishnan, S. The world's unborn soul. Oxford, 1936.
Phil 8597.39   Rattray, R.F. Fundamentals of modern religion. London, 1932.
Phil 8597.40   Rogeri, G. Iddio, l'uomo e la religione. Revere, 1887.
Phil 8597.41   Réflexions sur la religion, ou L'on établit d'une manière générale. Londres, 1801.
Phil 8597.42   Robinson, D.F. In search of a religion. Chester, 1938.
Phil 8597.43   Rudin, W. Om det personligas betydelse. Upsala, 1885?
Phil 8597.44   Roth, J. Der antichrist. Amsterdam, 1934.
Phil 8597.45   Rüssel, H.W. Gestalt eines christlichen Humanismus. Amsterdam, 1940.
Phil 8597.46   Richardson, Robert D. Christian belief and practice. London, 1940.
Phil 8597.48   Rocafuerte, Vicente. Ensayo sobre tolerancia religiosa. 2. ed. México, 1831.
Phil 8597.49   Ross, John Elliot. Truths to live by. N.Y., 1929.
Phil 8597.50   Roetschi, R. Humanität und Idealismus. Bern, 1943.
Phil 8597.51   Reade, W.H.V. The Christian challenge and philosophy. London, 1951.
Phil 8597.52   Religion, humanism. Stockholm, 1942.
Phil 8597.53   Rabut, Olivier A. Valeur spirituelle du profane. Paris, 1963.
Phil 8597.54   Riva, C. Pensiero e coerenza cristiana. Brescia, 1963.
Phil 8597.55   Robinson, John Arthur Thomas. The new reformation? London, 1965.
Phil 8597.56   Reischauer, August K. The nature and truth of the great religions. Tokyo, 1966.

Phil 8580 - 8605   Philosophy of religion - General treatises - Individual authors (A-Z) - cont.

Phil 8597.58   Rahner, Karl. Offenarung und Uberlieferung. Freiburg, 1965.
Phil 8597.60.2   Radbruch, Gustav. Religionsphilosophie der Kultur. 2. Aufl. Darmstadt, 1968.
Phil 8597.62   Ruyer, Raymond. Dieu des religious, dieu de la science. Paris, 1970.
Phil 8597.64   Rohrmoser, Günter. Emanzipation und Freiheit. München, 1970.
Phil 8597.66   Riet, Georges van. Philosophie et religion. Louvain, 1970.
Phil 8598.1   Saint Pierre, J.H.B. de. Vindication of divine providence. Worcester, 1797.
Phil 8598.2   Saisset, E. Essais sur la philosophie et la religion. Paris, 1845.
Phil 8598.3   Schaumann, J.C.G. Philosophie der Religion. Halle, 1793.
Phil 8598.5   Schwarz, C.H.W. Das Wesen der Religion. Halle, 1847.
Phil 8598.6   Sedgwick, Adam. A discourse on the studies of the university of Cambridge. Cambridge, 1850.
Phil 8598.6.2   Sedgwick, Adam. A discourse on the studies of the university of Cambridge. 2. ed. Cambridge, 1834.
Phil 8598.6.4   Sedgwick, Adam. A discourse on the studies of the university of Cambridge. 3. ed. Cambridge, 1834.
Phil 8598.6.10   Sedgwick, Adam. A discourse on the studies of the university. N.Y., 1969.
Phil 8598.7   Seeley, R. Natural religion. London, 1882.
Phil 8598.7.3   Seeley, R. Natural religion. Boston, 1882.
Phil 8598.8   Serious thoughts...Brougham's discourse of natural theology. London, 1836-31. 2 pam.
Phil 8598.9   Siebeck, Hermann. Lehrbuch der Religionsphilosophie. Freiburg, 1893.
Phil 8598.9.5   Siebeck, Hermann. Zur Religionsphilosophie. Tübingen, 1907.
Phil 8598.10   Simon, J. La religion naturelle. 3. éd. Paris, 1857.
Phil 8598.10.5   Simon, J. Natural religion. London, 1857.
Phil 8598.11   Slack, David B. The celestial magnet. Providence, R.I., 1820-21. 2 pam.
Phil 8598.12   Smith, Goldwin. Sermons and speeches. N.Y., 1861.
Phil 8598.12.3   Smith, Goldwin. Rational religion. Oxford, 1861.
Phil 8598.12.5   Smith, Goldwin. Inquest of light. N.Y., 1906.
Phil 8598.12.9   Smith, Goldwin. No refuge but in truth. N.Y., 1909.
Phil 8598.12.15   Smith, Goldwin. Guesses at the riddle of existence. N.Y., 1897.
Phil 8598.13   Snell, M.M. One hundred theses, foundations of human knowledge. Washington, 1891.
Phil 8598.14   Snow, G.D. A theologico-political treatise. London, 1874.
Phil 8598.15   Stäudlin, C.F. Beiträge zur Philosophie und Geschichte der Religion und Sittenlehre überhaupt und verschiedenen Glaubensarten und kirchen Insbesondere. Lübeck, 1797-98. 4v.
Phil 8598.16   Statham, F. From old to new. London, 1872.
Phil 8598.18   Straus-Durckheim, H.E. Théologie de la nature. Paris, 1852. 3v.
Phil 8598.19   Sulivan, R.J. A view of nature. London, 1794. 6v.
Phil 8598.20   Summer, J.B. A treatise...records of the creation. London, 1816. 2v.
Phil 8598.20.2   Sumner, J.B. A treatise...records of the creation. London, 1818. 2v.
Phil 8598.21   Sykes, A.A. The principles and connexion of natural and revealed religion distinctly considered. London, 1740.
Phil 8598.22   Sprague, F.H. Spiritual consciousness. Wollaston, 1898.
Phil 8598.23   Savage, M.J. Passing and permanent in religion. N.Y., 1901.
Phil 8598.24.2   Sabatier, Auguste. Esquisse d'une philosophie de la religion. Paris, 1897.
Phil 8598.24.3   Sabatier, Auguste. Esquisse d'une philosophie de la religion d'après la psychologie et l'histoire. 10. éd. Paris, 1937.
Phil 8598.24.7   Sabatier, Auguste. Outlines of a philosophy of religion. N.Y., 1902.
Phil 8598.24.9   Sabatier, Auguste. Philosophie de l'effort. Paris, 1908.
Phil 8598.26   Scot, David. Discourses on...subjects of natural and revealed religion. Edinburgh, 1825.
Phil 8598.27   Schinz, Max. Wahrheit der Religion nach den neuesten Vertretern der Religionsphilosophie. Zürich, 1908.
Phil 8598.28   Stapfer, P. L'inquiétude religieuse du temps présent. Paris, 1912.
Phil 8598.29   Spencer, F.A.M. The meaning of Christianity. 2. ed. London, 1914.
Phil 8598.30   Shaw, Charles G. The precinct of religion in culture of humanity. London, 1908.
Phil 8598.31   Shotwell, James T. The religious revolution of to-day. Boston, 1913.
Phil 8598.33   Simmel, G. Die Religion. 2. Aufl. Frankfurt, 1912.
Phil 8598.33.3   Simmel, G. Die Religion. Frankfurt, 1906.
Phil 8598.34   Shebbeare, Charles J. Challenge of the universe. London, 1918.
Phil 8598.34.5   Shebbeare, Charles J. The design argument reconsidered. London, 1923.
Phil 8598.34.6   Shebbeare, Charles J. The design argument reconsidered. London, 1923.
Phil 8598.35.15   Sellars, Roy W. Religion coming of age. N.Y., 1928.
Phil 8598.36   Pamphlet box. Smith, Gerrit. Pamphlets on religion.
Phil 8598.37   Storrs, Richard S. The recognition of the supernatural. N.Y., 1881.
Phil 8598.38   Satterlee, Henry Y. A creedless Gospel and the Gospel creed. N.Y., 1895.
Phil 8598.39   Seydel, Rudolf. Religionsphilosophie im Umriss. Freiburg, 1893.
Phil 8598.40   Secretan, Charles. Recherches de la méthode qui conduit à la vérité sur nos plus grands intérêts. Neuchâtel, 1857.
Phil 8598.41   Stern, Adolf. Die religiöse Stellung der vornehmsten Denker. Berlin, 1911.
Phil 8598.43   Schrempf, C. Gegen den Strom. Stuttgart, 1922. 5v.
Phil 8598.44   Schwarz, Hermann. Das Ungegebene; eine Religions- und Wertphilosophie. Tübingen, 1921.
Phil 8598.45   Sanders, Frederic W. Religio doctoris; meditations upon life and thought. Boston, 1913.
Phil 8598.45.5   Sanders, Frederic W. A reasonable religion (Religio doctoris). Boston, 1913?
Phil 8598.46.2   Scheler, Max. Vom Ewigen im Menschen. 2e Aufl. Leipzig, 1923. 2v.
Phil 8598.47   Stegenga, P. Twijfel als psychologisch verschijnsel in het religieuse leven. Amsterdam, 1924.
Phil 8598.48   Svensson, P.K. Religionsfilosofi. Lund, 1904.
Phil 8598.49   Segerstedt, T.K. Gammal och my religiositet. Stockholm, 1915.

368

Classified Listing

Phil 8580 - 8605 Philosophy of religion - General treatises - Individual authors (A-Z) - cont.

Phil 8598.49.5 Segerstedt, T.K. Det religiösa sanningsproblemet. Stockholm, 1912.
Phil 8598.50 Scholz, H. Die Religionsphilosophie des Als-Ob. Leipzig, 1921.
Phil 8598.51 Scudder, D. The passion for reality. N.Y., 1910.
Phil 8598.52 Steffes, J.P. Religionsphilosophie. München, 1925.
Phil 8598.53 Snaith, John. The philosophy of spirit. London, 1914.
Phil 8598.55.2 Stange, Carl. Christentum und moderne Weltanschauung. Leipzig, 1913-14. 2v.
Phil 8598.56 Störring, G. Die Frage der Wahrheit der christlichen Religion. Leipzig, 1920.
Phil 8598.57 Streeter, Burnett. Reality; a new correlation of science and religion. N.Y., 1926.
Phil 8598.57.8 Streeter, Burnett. Reality; a new correlation of science and religion. N.Y., 1926.
Phil 8598.58 Steffens, H. Von der falschen Theologie und der wahren Glauben. Breslau, 1823.
Phil 8598.58.5 Steffens, H. Christliche Religionsphilosophie. Pt.1-2. Breslau, 1839. 2v.
Phil 8598.59 Supernatural religion. 5th ed. London, 1875. 2v.
Phil 8598.59.5 Cassels, W.R. Supernatural religion. London, 1874-77. 3v.
Phil 8598.59.10 Cassels, W.R. Supernatural religion. London, 1879. 3v.
Phil 8598.60 Speculum religionis, being essays, presented to C.G. Montefiore. Oxford, 1929.
Phil 8598.61 Strachan, Robert H. The authority of Christian experience. London, 1929.
Phil 8598.62 Seth Pringle-Pattison, Andrew. Studies in the philosophy of religion. Oxford, 1930.
Phil 8598.63 Selbie, W.B. Religion and life. Cambridge, 1930.
Phil 8598.64 Stuart-Glennie, John S. In the morningland. London, 1873.
Phil 8598.65.5 Sorel, G. La religione d'oggi. Lanciani, 1911.
Phil 8598.66 Strakhov, F.A. Voprosy zhizni. Christchurch, Hants, Eng., 1903.
Phil 8598.67 Stepanov, I. Mysli o religii. Moskva, 1922.
Phil 8598.67.5 Skvortsov-Stepanov, I.I. Izbra mye ateisticheskie proizve - deniia. Moskva, 1959.
Phil 8598.68 Silver, Abba H. Religion in a changing world. N.Y., 1930.
Phil 8598.69 Saint René-Taillandier, R.G.E. Histoire et philosophie religieuse. Paris, 1859.
Phil 8598.70 Slack, Robert. Old truths and modern progress. London, 1856.
Phil 8598.71 Saggio sulla religione in generale. Torino, 1866.
Phil 8598.72 Stocks, J.L. On the nature and grounds of religious belief. London, 1934.
Phil 8598.73 Shumaker, E.E. God and man. N.Y., 1909.
Phil 8598.74 Sekendorf, V.L. von. Christen-Staat. Leipzig, 1716.
Phil 8598.75 Smith, Abbot Edes. Philosophy of life; with an appendix on the Bible. Norwood, 1938.
Phil 8598.76 Sibbern, F.C. Meddelelser af indholdet af et skrivt fra aaret. v.1-2. Kjøbenhavn, 1858-72.
Phil 8598.77 Schmidt, H.W. Zeit und Ewigkeit. Gutersloh, 1927.
Phil 8598.78 Schneider, H.W. Meditations in season on the elements of Christian philosophy. N.Y., 1938.
Phil 8598.79.5 Shestov, L. Athènes et Jerusalem. Paris, 1938.
Phil 8598.79.5.10 Shestov, L. Afiny i Ierusalim. Parizh, 1951.
Phil 8598.79.5.15 Shestov, L. Athens and Jerusalem. Athens, 1966.
Phil 8598.80 Silen, S. Den kristna människouppfattningen. Stockholm, 1938.
Phil 8598.81 Steckelmacher, M. Die Gottesidee der Offenbarung. Mannheim, 1890.
Phil 8598.82 Sayers, Dorothy L. The mind of the maker. London, 1941.
Phil 8598.82.5 Sayers, Dorothy L. The mind of the maker. N.Y., 1941.
Phil 8598.83 Sperry, Willard L. The disciplines of liberty. New Haven, 1921.
Phil 8598.83.5A Sperry, Willard L. The disciplines of liberty. New Haven, 1923.
Phil 8598.83.5B Sperry, Willard L. The disciplines of liberty. New Haven, 1923.
Phil 8598.83.10 Sperry, Willard L. Signs of these times. Garden City, N.Y., 1929.
Phil 8598.84 Sheldon, Henry Clay. The essentials of Christianity. N.Y., 1922.
Phil 8598.85 Shoemaker, S.M. The church can save the world. N.Y., 1938.
Phil 8598.86 Schmidt, K. From science to God. 1. ed. N.Y., 1944.
Phil 8598.88.2 Solov'ev, Vladimir Sergeevich. Lectures on Godmanhood. London, 1948.
Phil 8598.90.5 Schulze-Gaevernitz, G. Zur Wiedergeburt des Abendlandes. 2. Aufl. Berlin, 1934.
Phil 8598.92 Spann, Othmar. Religions-Philosophie auf geschichtlicher Grundlage. Wien, 1947.
Phil 8598.92.2 Spann, Othhmar. Religionsphilosophie auf geschichtlicher Grundlage. 2. Aufl. Graz, 1970.
Phil 8598.94 Sanders, B.G. Christianity after Freud. London, 1949.
Phil 8598.96 Sellmair, Josef. Humanitas Christiana. München, 1950.
Phil 8598.96.5 Sellmair, Josef. Der Mensch in der Fragik. München, 1948.
Phil 8598.98 Sheen, Fulton John. Philosophy of religion. Dublin, 1952.
Phil 8598.100 Stace, W.T. Religion and the modern mind. 1. ed. Philadelphia, 1952.
Phil 8598.102 Straubinger, H. Religionsphilosophie mit Theodizee. 2. Aufl. Freiburg, 1949.
Phil 8598.104 Sagesse. Bruges, 1951.
Phil 8598.106 Spalding, K.J. Essays on the evolution of religion. Oxford, 1954.
Phil 8598.108 Studi di filosofia della religione. Roma, 1955.
Phil 8598.110 Schuon, Frithjof. Sentien de gnose. Paris, 1957.
Phil 8598.110.5 Schuon, Frithjof. Gnosis. London, 1959.
Phil 8598.110.10 Schuon, Frithjof. Spiritual perspectives and human facts. London, 1954.
Phil 8598.110.15A Schuon, Frithjof. Stations of wisdom. London, 1961.
Phil 8598.110.15B Schuon, Frithjof. Stations of wisdom. London, 1961.
Phil 8598.110.20 Schuon, Frithjof. Language of the self. Madras, 1959.
Phil 8598.110.25 Schuon, Frithjof. Transcendent unity of religions. N.Y., 1953.
Phil 8598.115 Schlesinger, Ruth. Probleme seines religiösen Apriori. Berlin, 1959.
Phil 8598.120 Schulz-Angern, Karl Friedrich. Ewiges-Vergängliches. Berlin, 1958.
Phil 8598.125 Sukhov, Andrei D. Sotsial'nye i gnoseologicheskie korni religii. Moskva, 1961.
Phil 8598.125.5 Sukhov, Andrei D. Filosofskie problemy proiskhozhdeniia religii. Moskva, 1967.
Phil 8598.130 Smith, J.E. Reason and God. New Haven, 1961.

Phil 8580 - 8605 Philosophy of religion - General treatises - Individual authors (A-Z) - cont.

Phil 8598.131 Smart, Ninian. Historical selections in the philosophy of religion. London, 1962.
Phil 8598.133 Smith, W.C. The meaning and end of religion. N.Y., 1963.
Phil 8598.134 Schoell, F. Heimkehr Gottes in seine Wirklichkeit. Erbstetten, 1962.
Phil 8598.135 Schlette, Heinz Robert. Die Religionen als Thema der Theologie. Freiburg, 1963.
Phil 8598.135.5 Schlette, Heinz Robert. Towards a theology of religions. Freiburg, 1966.
Phil 8598.135.10 Schlette, Heinz Robert. Philosophie, Theologie, Ideologie. Köln, 1968.
Phil 8598.135.15 Schlette, Heinz Robert. Aporie und Glaube. München, 1970.
Phil 8598.136 Schneider, Louis. Religion, culture and society. N.Y., 1964.
Phil 8598.137 Smith, John E. Philosophy of religion. N.Y., 1965.
Phil 8598.138 Saher, Purvezji Jamshedji. Indische Weisheit und das Abendland. Meisenheim, 1965.
Phil 8598.138.1 Saher, Purvezji Jamshedji. Easten wisdom and Western thought. London, 1969.
Phil 8598.138.5 Saher, Purvezji Jamshedji. Evolution und Gottesidee. Ratigen, 1967.
Phil 8598.139 Serrand, A.Z. Evolution technique et théologies. Paris, 1965.
Phil 8598.140 Sahakian, William S. Philosophies of religion. Cambridge, 1965.
Phil 8598.141 Smith, John Edwin. Religion and empiricism. Milwaukee, 1967.
Phil 8598.143 Stenson, Sten H. Sense and nonsense in religion. Nashville, 1969.
Phil 8598.144 Standinger, Hugo. Gott: Fehlanzeige? Tries, 1968.
Phil 8599.1 Thoughts on recent scientifc conclusions. London, 1872.
Phil 8599.2 Thring, E. Thoughts on life science. London, 1871.
Phil 8599.3 Tiberghien, G. Estudios sobre religion. Madrid, 1873.
Htn Phil 8599.4* Tindall, M. Christianity as old as the creation. London, 1730. 2v.
Phil 8599.4.2 Tindall, M. Christianity as old as the creation. London, 1732.
Htn Phil 8599.4.7* Conybeare, J. A defence of revealed religion against the exceptions of a late writer in his book intituled, Christianity as old as the creation. London, 1732.
Phil 8599.4.95 Leland, John. An answer to a late book intituled, Christianity as old as the creation. Dublin, 1733. 2v.
Phil 8599.4.97 Leland, John. An answer to a book intituled, Christianity as old as the creation. 2. ed. London, 1740. 2v.
Phil 8599.5 Tittmann, J.A.H. Über Supranaturalismus. Leipzig, 1816.
Phil 8599.6 Töllner, J.G. Beweis dass Gott die menschen bereits durch seine Offenbarung in der Natur zur seligkeit führt. Züllichau, 1766.
Phil 8599.7 Tulloch, J. Theism. Edinburgh, 1855.
Phil 8599.8 Tunstall, J. Lectures on natural and revealed religion. London, 1765.
Phil 8599.9 Turton, Thomas. Natural theology considered with reference to Lord Brougham's discourse on that subject. 2. ed. Cambridge, 1836.
Phil 8599.9.5 Turton, Thomas. Natural theology considered with reference to Lord Brougham's discourse on that subject. 2. ed. London, 1836.
Phil 8599.10 Tyler, Charles Mellon. The study of the history and philosophy of religion. Ithica, N.Y., 1891.
Phil 8599.10.6 Tyler, Charles Mellen. Bases of religious belief. N.Y., 1897.
Phil 8599.11 Tiele, C.P. Elements of the science of religion. Edinburgh, 1897-99. 2v.
Phil 8599.11.5 Tiele, C.P. Grundzüge der Religionswissenschaft. Tübingen, 1904.
Phil 8599.12 Tulloch, John. Rational theology and Christian philosophy in England in the 17th century. Edinburgh, 1872. 2v.
Phil 8599.13 Teichmüller, Gustav. Religionsphilosophie. Breslau, 1886.
Phil 8599.13.80 Posselt, H. Die Religionsphilosophie Gustav Teichmüllers. Marburg, 1960.
Phil 8599.14 Torrey, D.C. Protestant modernism. Boston, 1910.
Phil 8599.14.2 Torrey, D.C. Protestant modernism. N.Y., 1910.
Phil 8599.15 Troward, T. The Doré lectures. N.Y., 1909.
Phil 8599.15.5 Troward, T. The Doré lectures. N.Y., 1919.
Htn Phil 8599.16.5* De Tribus Impostoribus. De tribus impostoribus. Paris, 1861.
Phil 8599.16.6 De Tribus Impostoribus. De tribus impostoribus. Paris, 1861.
Phil 8599.16.9 De Tribus Impostoribus. De tribus impostoribus. 2. Aufl. Heilbronn, 1876.
Phil 8599.16.10 De Tribus Impostoribus. De tribus impostoribus. Berlin, 1960.
Phil 8599.16.80 Presser, Jacob. Das Buch De tribus impostoribus. Amsterdam, 1926.
Phil 8599.17 Temple, William. Mens creatrix. v.1-2. London, 1917.
Phil 8599.17.10 Temple, William. Nature, man and God. London, 1935.
Phil 8599.18 Thompson, L. Buckland. Exact science of Christianity. Garden City, N.Y., 1916.
Phil 8599.19.2 Troeltsch, Ernst. Die Absolutheit des Christentums. 2. Aufl. Tübingen, 1912.
Phil 8599.19.5 Sleigh, R.S. The sufficiency of Christianity and Ernst Troeltsch. London, 1923.
Phil 8599.19.10 Troeltsch, Ernst. Psychologie und Erkenntnistheorie in der Religionswissenschaft. Tübingen, 1905.
Phil 8599.19.15 Troeltsch, Ernst. Zur religiösen Lage. 2. Aufl. Tübingen, 1922.
Phil 8599.19.20 Troeltsch, Ernst. Der Historismus und seine Überwindung; fünf Vorträge. Berlin, 1924.
Phil 8599.19.21 Troeltsch, Ernst. Christian thought, its history and application. London, 1923.
Phil 8599.19.90 Spiess, Emil. Die Religionstheorie von Ernst Troeltsch. Paderborn, 1927.
Phil 8599.19.95 Fellner, Karl. Das überweltliche Gut und die innerweltlichen Güter. Diss. Leipzig, 1927.
Phil 8599.19.100 Leidreiter, Erich. Troeltsch und die Absolulheit des Christentums. Inaug. Diss. Mahrungen, 1927.
Phil 8599.19.105 Wieneke, Friedrich. Die Entwicklung des philosophischen Gottesbegriffs bei Ernst Troeltsch. Inaug. Diss. Berlin, 1929.
Phil 8599.19.107 Spaleck, G. Religionssoziologische Grundbegriffe bei Troeltsch. Bleichersde, 1937.
Phil 8599.19.109 Köhler, Walther. Ernst Troeltsch. Tübingen, 1941.
Phil 8599.19.115 Bodenstein, Walter. Neige des Historismus. Gütersloh, 1959.
Phil 8599.19.120 Drescher, H.G. Glaube und Vernuft bei Ernst Troeltsch. Marburg, 1957.

Phil 8580 - 8605	**Philosophy of religion - General treatises - Individual authors (A-Z) - cont.**	
Phil 8599.20	Tyler, W.F. The dimensional idea as an aid to religion. N.Y., 1910.	
Phil 8599.20.2	Tyler, W.F. The dimensional idea as an aid to religion. London, 1907.	
Phil 8599.21	Tennant, F.R. Philosophical theology. Cambridge, 1928-30. 2v.	
Phil 8599.21.5	Tennant, F.R. The nature of belief. London, 1943.	
Phil 8599.21.90	Scudder, D.L. Tennant's philosophical theology. New Haven, 1740.	
Phil 8599.22	Taylor, Alfred E. Faith of a moralist. London, 1930. 2v.	
Phil 8599.23	Turner, J.E. Essentials in the development of religion. London, 1934.	
Phil 8599.24	Tarenne, G. La théologie naturelle, histoire, philosophique, critique et morale, ou Les pensées d'un homme sur l'être-Suprême. Paris, 1800?	
Phil 8599.25	Teichmüller, Gustav. G. Teichmüllers Philosophie des Christentums von E. Tennmann. Tartu, 1931.	
Phil 8599.26	Thielicke, H. Geschichte und Existenz. Gütersloh, 1935.	
Phil 8599.27	Thomas, E.E. The political aspects of religious development. London, 1937.	
Phil 8599.28	Tampoe, A.McG. Coomarasamy. Life negation; an Indian study of Christ. London, 19- .	
Phil 8599.29	Tanquerey, A. The spiritual life. 2. ed. Tournai, 1932.	
Phil 8599.30	Taylor, I. Essay on the application of abstract reasoning to the Christian doctrines. 1. American ed. Boston, 1832.	
Phil 8599.31	Taft, Charles Phelps. Do we still need religion? N.Y., 1942.	
Phil 8599.32	Tsanoff, R.A. Religious corssroads. N.Y., 1942.	
Phil 8599.33	Trueblood, D.E. The logic of belief. 1. ed. N.Y., 1942.	
Phil 8599.34	Thomas, George Finger. The vitality of the Christian tradition. N.Y., 1944.	
Phil 8599.34.5	Thomas, George Finger. Philosophy and religious belief. N.Y., 1970.	
Phil 8599.35	Trautmann, O. Die wiederkehr Göttes. Stuttgart, 1950.	
Phil 8599.36	Thomas, George Finger. Poetry, religion, and the spiritual life. Houston, 1951.	
Phil 8599.37	Todoli, José. Filosofía de la religion. Madrid, 1955.	
Phil 8599.38	Tarasov, A.A. Sotsial'naia religiia. Miunkhen, 1959.	
Phil 8599.40	Le Trocquer, René. Homme, qui suis-je? Paris, 1957.	
Phil 8599.42	Thévenaz, Pierre. La condition de la raison philosophique. Neuchâtel, 1960.	
Phil 8599.44	Tresmontant, Claude. La métaphysique du christianisme. Paris, 1961.	
Phil 8599.44.2	Tresmontant, Claude. Les idées maîtresses de la métaphysique chrétienne. Paris, 1962.	
Phil 8599.44.10	Tresmontant, Claude. La métaphysique du christianisme. Paris, 1964.	
Phil 8599.46	Toro, Antonio del. La crisis del pensamiento cristiano en el siglo XVI. Madrid, 1961.	
Phil 8599.48	Toinet, Paul. Existence chrétienne et philosophie. Paris, 1965.	
Phil 8599.50	Tillich, Paul. What is religion? 1. ed. N.Y., 1969.	
Phil 8599.52	Theill-Wunder, Hella. Die archaische Verborgenheit. München, 1970.	
Phil 8600.1	Upton, C.B. Lectures on the bases of religious belief. London, 1894.	
Phil 8600.2	Union de Libres Penseurs et de Libres Croyants pour la Culture Morale. Le sentiment religieux à l'heure actuelle. Paris, 1919.	
Phil 8600.3	Underhill, E. Man and the supernatural. N.Y., 1928.	
Phil 8600.3.5	Underhill, E. Man and the supernatural. London, 1927.	
Phil 8600.4	Usher, E.P. The Greek gospel; an interpretation of the coming faith. Grafton, Mass., 1909.	
Phil 8600.5	Urban, W.M. Humanity and deity. London, 1951.	
Phil 8600.6	Ugrinovich, Dimitrii M. Filosofskie problemy Kritiki religii. Moskva, 1965.	
Phil 8601.1	Vacherot, E. La religion. Paris, 1869.	
Phil 8601.2	Véry, P. Philosophie de la religion (Eléments). Paris, 1858.	
Phil 8601.3	Vidal, F. Théologie de la religion naturelle. Paris, 1859.	
Phil 8601.4	Vallis, R. Die Naturgeschichte der Göttes. Leipzig, 1875.	
Phil 8601.6	Vilenkin, N.M. Religiia budushchago. Sankt Peterburg, 1905.	
Phil 8601.7	Vogel, W. La religion de l'évolutionisme. Bruxelles, 1912.	
Phil 8601.8	Vignoli, Tito. Mito e scienza saggio. Milano, 1879.	
Phil 8601.9	Voysey, C. Religion for all mankind. London, 1903.	
Phil 8601.10	Vrooman, H. Religion rationalized. Philadelphia, 1910.	
Phil 8601.11	Veiga, Antonio D.A. Lei das contrastes. Porto, 1928.	
Phil 8601.12	Vann, Gerald. On being human; St. Thomas and Mr. Aldous Huxley. N.Y., 1934.	
Phil 8601.13A	Voegelin, Eric. Die politischen religionen. Stockholm, 1939.	
Phil 8601.13B	Voegelin, Eric. Die politischen religionen. Stockholm, 1939.	
Phil 8601.15	Vogeler, H. Friede. Bremen, 1922.	
Phil 8601.16	Varadachari, K. Idea of God. Tirupati, 1950.	
Phil 8601.17	Vancourt, Raymond. Pensée moderne et philosophie chrétienne. Paris, 1957.	
Phil 8601.20	Vattimo, Gianni. Poesia e ontologia. Milano, 1967.	
Phil 8602.1	Ward, D.J.H. How religion arises. Boston, 1888.	
Phil 8602.1.5	Ward, D.J.H. The biography of God as men have told it. Denver, 1924?	
Phil 8602.2*	Ward, S. A philosophical essay. Oxford, 1667.	
Phil 8602.3	Ware, H. An inquiry...religion. Cambridge, 1842. 2v.	
Phil 8602.3.2	Ware, H. An inquiry...religion. Cambridge, 1842. 2v.	
Phil 8602.4	Weiss, J. American religion. Boston, 1871.	
Phil 8602.5	Wette, W.M.L. de. Über die Religion. Berlin, 1827.	
Phil 8602.6	Whewell, W. Of the plurality of worlds. London, 1853.	
Phil 8602.6.2	Whewell, W. The plurality of worlds. Boston, 1854.	
Phil 8602.6.3	Whewell, W. The plurality of worlds. Boston, 1855.	
Phil 8602.7*	Wilkins, J. Of the principles and duties of natural religion. 1698-99.	
Phil 8602.7.2*	Wilkins, J. Of the principles and duties of natural religion. 1710.	
Phil 8602.8	Wilson, G. Religio chemici. London, 1862.	
Phil 8602.9	Wilson, W.D. The foundations of religious belief. N.Y., 1883.	
Phil 8602.11	Wollaston, W. The religion of nature delineated. London, 1724.	
Phil 8602.11.2.5*	Wollaston, W. The religion of nature delineated. London, 1724.	
Phil 8602.11.3*	Wollaston, W. The religion of nature delineated. London, 1726.	

	Phil 8580 - 8605	**Philosophy of religion - General treatises - Individual authors (A-Z) - cont.**	
Htn	Phil 8602.11.4*	Wollaston, W. The religion of nature delineated. London, 1738.	
	Phil 8602.11.5	Wollaston, W. The religion of nature delineated. London, 1759.	
Htn	Phil 8602.11.7*	Wollaston, W. The religion of nature delineated. London, 1725.	
	Phil 8602.11.8	Wollaston, W. Ebauche de la religion naturelle...avec un supplément. La Haye, 1756. 3v.	
	Phil 8602.12	Wright, H.C. The living present and the dead past. Boston, 1865.	
	Phil 8602.13	Woods, J.H. The value religious facts. N.Y., 1899.	
	Phil 8602.14	Wallace, W. Lectures and essays on natural theology and ethics. Oxford, 1898.	
	Phil 8602.15	Watson, J. The philosophical basis of religion. Glasgow, 1907.	
	Phil 8602.15.9	Watson, J. The interpretation of religious experience. Glasgow, 1912. 2v.	
	Phil 8602.16	Waterhouse, E.S. Modern theories of religion. London, 1910.	
	Phil 8602.16.5	Waterhouse, E.S. The philosophical approach to religion. London, 1933.	
	Phil 8602.17	Wilm, Emil Carl. Problem of religion. Boston, 1912.	
	Phil 8602.18	Webb, C.C.J. Group theories of religion and the individual. London, 1916.	
	Phil 8602.18.5	Webb, C.C.J. Studies in the history of natural theology. Oxford, 1915.	
	Phil 8602.18.7	Webb, C.C.J. Problems in the relations of God and man. London, 1915.	
	Phil 8602.18.15	Webb, C.C.J. Natural and comparative religion. Oxford, 1912.	
	Phil 8602.18.20	Webb, C.C.J. Philosophy and the Christian religion. Oxford, 1920.	
	Phil 8602.19	Wright, H.W. Faith justified by progress. N.Y., 1916.	
	Phil 8602.20	Wallis, Louis. Egoism. Chicago, 1905.	
	Phil 8602.22	Watson, A.C. The logic of religion. Diss. Chicago, 1918.	
	Phil 8602.23	Wunderle, Georg. Grundzüge der Religionsphilosophie. Paderborn, 1918.	
	Phil 8602.24	Wittels, Fritz. Über den Tod und über den Glauben an Gott. Wien, 1914.	
	Phil 8602.26	Wilson, D.A. The faith of all sensible people. London, 1913.	
	Phil 8602.27	Wood, Herbert G. Living issues in religious thought. London, 1924.	
	Phil 8602.27.10	Wood, Herbert G. Christianity and the nature of history. Cambridge, Eng., 1934.	
	Phil 8602.28	Wimmer, Richard. Hrad är sanning? Stockholm, 1894.	
	Phil 8602.28.5	Wimmer, Richard. Im Kampf um die Weltanschauung. 3. und 4. Aufl. Freiburg, 1888.	
	Phil 8602.29	Wishart, A.W. Primary facts in religious thought. Chicago, 1905.	
	Phil 8602.30	Wood, Henry. Life more abundant. Boston, 1905.	
	Phil 8602.30.3	Wood, Henry. God's image in man. Boston, 1905.	
	Phil 8602.31	Wienel, H. Die Wirkungen Des Geistes und der Glister. Freiburg, 1899.	
	Phil 8602.32	Wright, William K. A student's philosophy of religion. London, 1922.	
	Phil 8602.33A	Whitehead, A.N. Religion in the making. N.Y., 1926.	
	Phil 8602.33B	Whitehead, A.N. Religion in the making. N.Y., 1926.	
	Phil 8602.33C	Whitehead, A.N. Religion in the making. N.Y., 1926.	
	Phil 8602.33.2	Whitehead, A.N. Religion in the making. N.Y., 1926.	
	Phil 8602.33.5	Whitehead, A.N. Religion in the making. N.Y., 1926.	
	Phil 8602.33.10	Whitehead, A.N. Religion in the making. N.Y., 1960[1954]	
	Phil 8602.34	Wobbermin, G. Zwei akademische Vorlesungen über Grundprobleme der systematischen Theologie. Berlin, 1899.	
	Phil 8602.34.10	Wobbermin, G. The nature of religion. N.Y., 1933.	
	Phil 8602.35	Wieman, Henry Nelson. The wrestle of religion with truth. N.Y., 1927.	
	Phil 8602.35.10	Wieman, Henry Nelson. Religious inquiry; some explorations. Boston, 1968.	
	Phil 8602.36	Winkler, R. Phänomenologie und Religion. Tübingen, 1921.	
	Phil 8602.37	Waggoner, John G. The beautiful sunset of life. Boston, 1928.	
	Phil 8602.38	Welby-Gregory, Victoria. Echoes of larger life. London, 1929.	
	Phil 8602.38.10	Welby-Gregory, Victoria. Other dimensions. London, 1931.	
	Phil 8602.39	Webb, c.C.J. Religion and the thought of today. London, 1929.	
	Phil 8602.40	Widney, J.P. The faith that has come to me. Los Angeles, 1932.	
	Phil 8602.41	Walsh, Walter. The world rebuilt. London, 1917.	
	Phil 8602.42	Walker, Joseph. Humanism as a way of life. N.Y., 1932.	
	Phil 8602.43	Werner, Max. Das Christentum und die monistische Religion. Berlin, 1908.	
	Phil 8602.44	Weber, H.E. Das Geisteserbe der Gegenwart und die Theologie. Leipzig, 1925.	
	Phil 8602.45	Wiley, H.O. Christian theology. Kansas City, 1940-41. 2v.	
	Phil 8602.46	Wolfson, H.A. The double faith theory in Clement, Saadia, Averroes and St. Thomas. Philadelphia, 1942.	
	Phil 8602.46.5A	Wolfson, H.A. Religious philosophy. Cambridge, 1961.	
	Phil 8602.46.5B	Wolfson, H.A. Religious philosophy. Cambridge, 1961.	
	Phil 8602.47.5	Wright, Ronald S. Asking them questions. Second series. London, 1938.	
	Phil 8602.47.10	Wright, Ronald S. Asking why. London, 1939.	
	Phil 8602.49	Wheeler, F. What do Christians believe? London, 1944.	
	Phil 8602.50	Walker, K.M. Meaning and purpose. London, 1944.	
	Phil 8602.51	Werfel, Franz. Zwischen Oben und Unten. Stockholm, 1946.	
	Phil 8602.52	Wilson, Colin. Religion and the rebel. London, 1957.	
	Phil 8602.53	Watts, Alan W. The wisdom of insecurity. N.Y., 1958.	
	Phil 8602.55	Witcutt, W.P. The rise and fall of the individual. N.Y., 1958.	
	Phil 8602.60	Wild, John. Human freedom and social order. Darban, N.C., 1959.	
	Phil 8602.65	Wilson, J. Philosophy and religion. London, 1961.	
	Phil 8602.70	Wynne-Tyson, Esmé. The philosophy of compassion. London, 1962.	
	Phil 8602.75	Woods, George. Theological explanation. Welwyn, 1958.	
	Phil 8602.77	Woelger, Hans I. Religion ohne Entscheidung. 2. Aufl. Göttingen, 1960.	
	Phil 8602.78	Weiss, P. The God we seek. Carbondale, 1964.	
	Phil 8602.80	Waldmann, Günter. Christliches Glauben und christliche Glaubenslosigkeit. Tübingen, 1968.	
	Phil 8604.1	Young, J. The providence of reason: criticism. N.Y., 1860.	
	Phil 8604.1.2	Young, J. The providence of reason: criticism. London, 1860.	

Phil 8580 - 8605 Philosophy of religion - General treatises - Individual authors (A-Z) - cont.

	Phil 8604.2	Younghusband, F.E. Vital religion. London, 1940.
	Phil 8605.1	Zweifel, H. Die gesetze Göttes. München, 1876.
	Phil 8605.2	Zoppola, G. Il pensiero religioso. Lugano, 1911. 2 pam.
	Phil 8605.2.5	Zoppola, G. A vapore. Firenze, 1914.
	Phil 8605.3.5	Zacchi, P.A. L'uomo. Roma, 1921. 2v.
	Phil 8605.4	Zethraeus, A.G. Isätalät-ordens (sanningssökarnes) vishetslära. Stockholm, 1900.
	Phil 8605.5	Zuver, Dudley. Salvation by laughter. N.Y., 1933.
	Phil 8605.7	Zuurdeeg, Willem. An analytical philosophy of religion. N.Y., 1958.
	Phil 8605.8	Zen'kovskii, V.V. Apologetika. 2. izd. Parizhe, 195-? 3 pam.
	Phil 8605.10	Zen'kovskii, V.V. Osnovy khristianskoi filosofii. Frankfurt, 1960.
	Phil 8605.15	Žrvotić, Milad. Aktuelni problemi odnosa prema religiji. Beograd, 1961.

Phil 8610 Philosophy of religion - Treatises on special topics - Agnosticism (By date, e.g. .960 for 1960)

	Phil 8610.171	Psychologie van het ongeloof. Amsterdam. 3,193?+
Htn	Phil 8610.713*	Collins, Anthony. A discourse of free thinking occasioned by the rise and growth of a sect call'd free-thinker. London, 1713. 3 pam.
	Phil 8610.713.5	Collins, Anthony. A discourse of free-thinking. Stuttgart, 1965.
Htn	Phil 8610.713.10*	Collins, Anthony. Discours sur la liberté de penser. Londres, 1714.
Htn	Phil 8610.713.20*	Bentley, Richard. Remarks upon a late discourse of free-thinking. London, 1713. 3 pam.
	Phil 8610.713.30	Bentley, Richard. Remarks upon a late discourse of free-thinking. pt.3. 8th ed. Cambridge, Eng., 1743.
	Phil 8610.713.40	Bentley, Richard. La friponnerie laïque des pretendus esprits forts d'Angleterre. Amsterdam, 1738.
	Phil 8610.759	Trinius, Johann Anton. Freydenker-Lexicon. Leipzig, 1759.
	Phil 8610.759.5F	Trinius, Johann Anton. Freydenker-Lexicon. Torino, 1966.
	Phil 8610.776	Recueil nécessaire avec l'évangile de la raison. Londres, 1776.
	Phil 8610.798	Le catéchisme des Christicoles. Paris, 1798.
	Phil 8610.798.10	Gradis, David. Réponse à divers contradicteurs sur la coéternelle existence de la matière. Paris, 1798-99.
	Phil 8610.798.11	Gradis, David. Discussions philosophiques sur l'athéisme. Paris, 1803.
	Phil 8610.801.5	Hall, Robert. Modern infidelity considered. Philadelphia, 1853.
	Phil 8610.804	Piestre, J.L. Les crimes de la philosophie. Paris, 1804.
	Phil 8610.821	Philanthropos [pseud.]. The character of a priest. London, 1821. 2 pam.
	Phil 8610.828.5	Taylor, Robert. Syntagma of the evidences of the Christian religion. Boston, 1828.
	Phil 8610.829.5	Taylor, Robert. The diegesis. Boston, 1832.
	Phil 8610.829.10	Taylor, Robert. The diegesis. 3. ed. London, 1845.
	Phil 8610.829.15	Taylor, Robert. The diegesis. Boston, 1873.
	Phil 8610.831.3	Taylor, Robert. The devil's pulpit. Boston, 1866.
	Phil 8610.831.5	Taylor, Robert. The devil's pulpit. v.1, no.1-15,17-23; v.2, no.1. London, 1879.
	Phil 8610.831.20	Taylor, Robert. The devil's pulpit. London, 1882. 2v.
	Phil 8610.832	Aldred, G.A. The devil's chaplain. (Robert Taylor, 1784-1844). Glasgow, 1942.
	Phil 8610.834.5	Kneeland, A. National hymns. Boston, 1836.
	Phil 8610.837	Criticisms on current theology as they appeared in the 18th century. London, 1837. 4 pam.
	Phil 8610.841	The oracle of reason. Bristol, Eng. 1-2,1841-1843 2v.
	Phil 8610.841.3	The oracle of reason. Bristol, Eng. 1-18
	Phil 8610.842	The Library of reason. London. 1-22
	Phil 8610.846	Balmes, Jaime. Cartas á un escéptico en materia de religion. Barcelona, 1846.
	Phil 8610.851	Wright, B.W. Sketches of modern irreligion and infidelity. London, 1851.
	Phil 8610.853	Noack, L. Die Freidenker in der Religion. pt.3. Bern, 1853-55.
	Phil 8610.853.10	Grant, B. Christianity and secularism. London, 1853.
	Phil 8610.854.2	Davis, A.J. Free thoughts concerning religion. 2. ed. Boston, 1854.
	Phil 8610.854.15	Pearson, Thomas. Infidelity. N.Y., 1854.
	Phil 8610.856	Post, T.M. The skeptical era in modern history. N.Y., 1856.
	Phil 8610.857	Taylor, Robert. The astronomico-theological lectures. Boston, 1857.
	Phil 8610.858.5	Bradlaugh, Charles. Biographies of ancient and modern celebrated freethinkers. Boston, 1877.
	Phil 8610.859	Taylor, Robert. Who is the Holy Spirit? N.Y., 1859.
	Phil 8610.870	Was, H. Geschichiedenis van het scepticisme der zeventiende eeuw in de voornaamste europeesche staten. 1e aflevering. Utrecht, 1870.
	Phil 8610.870.10	Bradlaugh, Charles. Theological essays. London, 1883.
	Phil 8610.870.25	Boston lectures, 1870-1871. Christianity and scepticism. Boston, 1871. 2v.
	Phil 8610.871	Pamphlet vol. Scott's tracts. v.1. 21 pam.
	Phil 8610.871.2	Pamphlet vol. Scott's tracts. v.2. 7 pam.
	Phil 8610.871.4	Pamphlet vol. Scott's tracts. v.4. 28 pam.
	Phil 8610.871.5	Pamphlet vol. Scott's tracts. v.5. 21 pam.
	Phil 8610.871.6	Pamphlet vol. Scott's tracts. v.6. 25 pam.
	Phil 8610.871.7	Pamphlet vol. Scott's tracts. v.7. 8 pam.
	Phil 8610.871.8	Pamphlet vol. Scott's tracts. v.8. 19 pam.
	Phil 8610.871.9	Pamphlet vol. Scott's tracts. v.9. 20 pam.
	Phil 8610.871.10	Pamphlet vol. Scott's tracts. v.10. 21 pam.
	Phil 8610.871.11	Pamphlet vol. Scott's tracts. v.11. 16 pam.
	Phil 8610.871.12	Pamphlet vol. Scott's tracts. v.12. 18 pam.
	Phil 8610.871.25	Viardot, L. Libre examen. 5. éd. Paris, 1877.
	Phil 8610.872	Somerset, Edward Adolphus. Christian theology and modern scepticism. London, 1872.
	Phil 8610.872.2	Somerset, Edward Adolphus. Christian theology and modern scepticism. N.Y., 1872.
	Phil 8610.873	Stephen, Leslie. Essays on freethinking and plain-speaking. London, 1873.
	Phil 8610.875	Ménard, Louis. Catéchisme religieux des libres penseurs. Paris, 1875.
	Phil 8610.875.10	Guild, E.E. The pro and con of supernatural religion...together with a sketch of the life of the author. N.Y., 1876.
X Cg	Phil 8610.875.20	National Secular Society. The secular song and hymn book. London, 1875?
	Phil 8610.875.25	Pullen, H.W. Modern Christianity, a civilized heathenism. Boston, 1875.

Phil 8610 Philosophy of religion - Treatises on special topics - Agnosticism (By date, e.g. .960 for 1960) - cont.

Phil 8610.875.27	Pullen, H.W. Modern Christianity, a civilized heathenism. N.Y., 1879.
Phil 8610.875.30	Pullen, H.W. Modern Christianity, a civilized heathenism. N.Y., 1901.
Phil 8610.876	Truth seeker tracts upon a variety of subjects by different authors. v.2-4. N.Y., 1876-77. 3v.
Phil 8610.876.10	Bennett, D.M. Thirty discussions, Bible stories, essays and lectures. N.Y., 1876.
Phil 8610.877.5	Humphrey, G.H. Christianity and infidelity. N.Y., 1877.
Phil 8610.877.15	Monteil, Edgar. The freethinker's catechism. N.Y., 19- ?
Phil 8610.877.17	Monteil, Edgar. The freethinker's catechism. N.Y., 19- ?
Phil 8610.878	Chronicles of Simon Christianus and his manifold and wondrous adventures in the land of Cosmos. N.Y., 1878.
Phil 8610.878.10	Tuttle, Hudson. Career of religious ideas. N.Y., 1878.
Phil 8610.878.15	Underwood, B.F. The Underwood-Marples debate. N.Y., 1878.
Phil 8610.880.14	Congrès Universel de la Libre Pensée, 14th, Prague, 1907. Světový kongres volné myšlenky v Praze 8,9,10,11 a 12 září 1907. Podrobná Zpráva. Praha, 1908.
Phil 8610.880.18	Congrès Universel de la Libre Pensée, 18th, Prague, 1920. XVIII. Světový kongres volné myšlenky v Praze od 5-9 září, 1920. Přípravy. Praha, 1920?
Phil 8610.881	Cairns, John. Unbelief in the eighteenth century as contrasted with its earlier and later history. Edinburgh, 1881.
Phil 8610.881.10	Bennett, D.M. An infidel abroad. N.Y., 1881.
Phil 8610.881.20	Gibson, Ellen E. The godly women of the Bible. N.Y., 1881.
Phil 8610.881.25	Rodenhausen, C. Christenthum ist Heidenthum. Hamburg, 1881.
Phil 8610.881.30	The conflicts of the age. N.Y., 1881.
Phil 8610.881.35	Corresspondance d'un sceptique et d'un croyant. Genève, 1881.
Phil 8610.882	Ellis, John. Skepticism and divine relation. N.Y., 1882.
Phil 8610.883	Greg, Percy. Without God. London, 1883.
Phil 8610.883.10	Berthet, André. Les débats de la conscience, catéchisme laïque. Paris, 1883.
Phil 8610.884.10	Momerie, A.W. Agnosticism. 2. ed. Edinburgh, 1887.
Phil 8610.884.20	Hardwicke, H.J. Popular faith unveiled. n.p., 1884.
Phil 8610.888	Pearson, Karl. The ethic of freethought. London, 1888.
Phil 8610.888.3A	Pearson, Karl. The ethic of freethought. 2. ed. London, 1901.
Phil 8610.888.3B	Pearson, Karl. The ethic of freethought. 2. ed. London, 1901.
Phil 8610.888.10	Foote, G.W. The Bible handbook of freethinkers and inquiring Christians. London, 1900.
Phil 8610.888.12	Pamphlet vol. Free thought. 14 pam.
Phil 8610.889	Christianity and agnosticism. N.Y., 1889.
Phil 8610.889.5	Bradlaugh, C. Humanity's gain from unbelief. London, 1889.
Phil 8610.889.7	Bradlaugh, C. Humanity's gain from unbelief. London, 1929.
Phil 8610.889.10	Hart, William. The candle from under the bushel. N.Y., 1889.
Phil 8610.889.15	Wheeler, Joseph Mazzini. A bibliographical dictionary of freethinkers of all ages and nations. London, 1889.
Phil 8610.890	Fitzgerald, P.F. (Mrs.). A protest against agnosticism. London, 1890.
Phil 8610.890.10	Contra el altar y el trono; artículos varios, publicados en "El Progreso" de 1884-85 por su director, R. Verea. N.Y., 1890.
Phil 8610.890.20	Kelso, John R. The real blasphemers. N.Y., 189-?
Phil 8610.890.30	Holyoake, G.J. What would follow on the effacement of Christianity. Buffalo, 1890.
Phil 8610.890.35	La dea ragione. Milano, 1890.
Phil 8610.890.42	Abbot, Francis Ellingwood. The way out of agnosticism, or The philosophy of free religion. 2. ed. Ann Arbor, 1962.
Phil 8610.891.5	Bradlaugh, Charles. Doubts in dialogue. London, 1909.
Phil 8610.891.10	Putnam, S.P. My religious experience. N.Y., 1891.
Phil 8610.892	Wheeler, J.M. Bible studies. London, 1892.
Phil 8610.893	Putnam, S.P. Why don't he lend a hand? N.Y., 1893.
Phil 8610.894	Hartmann, J. God and sin in the appetites. N.Y., 1894.
Phil 8610.894.5	Putnam, S.P. Four hundred years of freethought. N.Y., 1894.
Phil 8610.895	Landers, C.M. The skeptics defense against all Christian or other priests. Rochester, 1895.
Phil 8610.896	Schurman, J.G. Agnosticism and religion. N.Y., 1896.
Phil 8610.896.5	Roselli, G. Confutazione degli argomenti teologici. Foggia, 1896.
Phil 8610.897	Taber, H.M. Faith or fact. N.Y., 1897.
Phil 8610.898	D'Arusmont, Frances Wright. Six lectures on the nature of knowledge, free enquiry, the more important divisions and essentials of knowledge, religion, morals, opinions. London, 1898.
Phil 8610.899	Robertson, J.M. A short history of freethought, ancient and modern. London, 1899.
Phil 8610.899.5	Robertson, J.M. A short history of freethought, ancient and modern. 2. ed. London, 1906. 2v.
Phil 8610.899.15	Ward, James. Naturalism and agnosticism. London, 1899. 2v.
Phil 8610.899.17	Ward, James. Naturalism and agnosticism. v.1. v.2 lost. N.Y., 1899.
Phil 8610.899.25	Mackenzie, G.L. Brimstone ballads and other verse. London, 1899.
Phil 8610.899.30	Sirai and Olympus. N.Y., 1899.
Phil 8610.899.55	Turner, M.M. (Mrs.). The Bible God, Bible teachings. N.Y., 1899.
Phil 8610.900	Cooley, P.J. Evolution; an exposition of Christian dogmas and pagan myths. N.Y., 1900.
Phil 8610.900.5	Roberts, G.L. Rational agnosticism. n.p., n.d.
Phil 8610.902	Brooklyn Philosophical Association. Facts worth knowing. N.Y., 1902.
Phil 8610.902.5	Greenwood, Granville George. The faith of an agnostic. 2. ed. London, 1919.
Phil 8610.902.15	Adams, R.C. Good without God. N.Y., 1902.
Phil 8610.902.25	Mortimer, G. The new morality. London, 1902.
Phil 8610.902.36	Mangasarian, M.M. A new catechism. 2. ed. Chicago, 1902.
Phil 8610.903	Flint, Robert. Agnosticism. Edinburgh, 1903.
Phil 8610.903.10	Hawley, J.S. Tradition versus truth. N.Y., 1903.
Phil 8610.904	Hedderwick, J.A. Do we believe? London, 1904.
Phil 8610.905	Haeckel, Ernst. A universal monistic alliance. Los Angeles, 1905.
Phil 8610.907	Hunt, E.J. The evolution of faith; an essay. London, 1907.
Phil 8610.911	Indiana Rationalist Association. The light of reason. Indianapolis, Ind., 1911.
Phil 8610.911.4	Bongini, V. Il pregiudizio religioso. Roma, 1911.

Classified Listing

Phil 8610   Philosophy of religion - Treatises on special topics - Agnosticism (By date, e.g. .960 for 1960) - cont.

Phil 8610.912   Thomas, J.C. The darkness, the dawn and the day. London, 1912.
Phil 8610.913A   Bury, J.B. A history of freedom of thought. N.Y., 1913.
Phil 8610.913B   Bury, J.B. A history of freedom of thought. N.Y., 1913.
Phil 8610.913.5A   Bury, J.B. A history of freedom of thought. 2. ed. London, 1952.
Phil 8610.913.5B   Bury, J.B. A history of freedom of thought. 2. ed. London, 1952.
Phil 8610.913.10   Stansbury, H. In quest of truth. London, 1917.
Phil 8610.913.20   Whyte, A.G. The religion of the open mind. London, 1913.
Phil 8610.913.25   The new New England primer. Newport, Vt., 1913.
Phil 8610.914   Griggs, H.S. The book of truth. Brooklyn, 1914.
Phil 8610.915   Coughlin, D.R. Review of the Bibles. East Aurora, N.Y., 1915.
Phil 8610.916   Ricker, M.M. I don't know, do you? East Aurora, N.Y., 1916.
Phil 8610.917   Ricker, M.M. I am not afraid, are you? East Aurora, N.Y., 1917.
Phil 8610.917.10   Secular Society, Ltd. A fight for right. London, 1917.
Phil 8610.918   Riley, Isaac W. Early free thinking societies in America. N.Y., 1918.
Phil 8610.919   Bonner, Hypatia Bradlaugh (Mrs.). Christianity and conduct. London, 1919.
Phil 8610.919.20   Gorham, C.T. A plain man's plea for rationalism. London, 1919.
Phil 8610.919.30   Lyttleton, Edward. The parson and the atheist. London, 1919.
Phil 8610.921   Cohen, Chapman. A grammar of freethought. London, 1921.
Phil 8610.922   Costa, U. da. Die Schriften. Amsterdam, 1922.
Phil 8610.923   Cohen, Chapman. Essays in freethinking. Series 1. London, 1923.
Phil 8610.923.10   McCabe, Joseph. The twilight of the gods. London, 1923.
Phil 8610.924   Reid, W.N. The supremacy of reason. London, 1924.
Phil 8610.925   Hughes, R. Why I quit going to church. N.Y., 1925.
Phil 8610.925.10   Powers, H.H. The religion of to-morrow...correspondence between H.H. Powers and William Archer. London, 1925.
Phil 8610.925.30   Schott, Walter E. The immaculate deception. Sausahto, Calif., 1925.
Phil 8610.926   Freeman, C.R.B. Towards the answer. Derbyshire, 1926.
Phil 8610.927.7   Russell, Bertrand Russell. Why I am not a Christian. Girard, Kansas, 1929.
Phil 8610.927.8   Russell, Bertrand Russell. Why I am not a Christian. N.Y., 1957.
Phil 8610.927.10   Russell, Bertrand Russell. Pourquoi je ne suis pas chrétien. Paris, 1964.
Phil 8610.927.20   Cohen, Chapman. Essays in freethinking. 2. series. London, 1927.
Phil 8610.929   Robertson, J.M. A history of freethought in the nineteenth century. London, 1929.
Phil 8610.929.5   Robertson, J.M. A history of freethought in the nineteenth century. N.Y., 1930. 2v.
Phil 8610.929.9   Robertson, J.M. A history of freethought in the nineteenth century. 4. ed. London, 1936. 2v.
Phil 8610.929.15   MacDonald, G.E. Fifty years of freethought. v.1. pt.1-2. N.Y., 1929-31. 2v.
Phil 8610.929.20   Darrow, C. Infidels and heretics. Boston, 1929.
Phil 8610.929.25   Cohen, Chapman. Four lectures on freethought and life. London, 1929.
Phil 8610.929.35   Housman, L. The religious advance toward rationalism, delivered at Conway Hall on Sept. 25, 1929. London, 1929.
Phil 8610.929.40   Berdiaev, N.A. Marksizm i religiia. Paris, 1929.
Phil 8610.933   Cohen, C. Bradlaugh and Ingersoll. London, 1933.
Phil 8610.940.1   Cohen, C. Almost an autobiography. London, 1940.
Phil 8610.940.5   Richberg, Donald. G. Hovah explains. Washington, 1940.
Phil 8610.941   Floyd, W. Christianity cross-examined. N.Y., 1941.
Phil 8610.955   Wood, Herbert. Belief and unbelief since 1850. Cambridge, 1955.
Phil 8610.958   Szczesny, Gerhard. Die Zukunft des Unglaubens. München, 1958.
Phil 8610.958.5   Buri, Fritz. Die Substanz des christlichen Glaubens, ihr Verlust und ihre Neugewinnung. Tübingen, 1960.
Phil 8610.959   Bayet, Albert. Histoire de la libre-pensée. Paris, 1959.
Phil 8610.960   Kotarbiński, Tad. Przykład indywidualny kształtowania sie postawy wolnomyślicielskiej. Warszawa, 1960.
Phil 8610.963   Lahoz Lainez, Bienvenido. El destino humano en el realismo introspectivo. Madrid, 1963.
Phil 8610.964   Ekmalian, A. Agnostitsizm i problema znaniia i very v burzhuaznoi filosofii. Erevan, 1964.
Phil 8610.964.5   Crekshut, A.O.J. The unbelievers. London, 1964.
Phil 8610.964.10   Mason, Gabriel Richard. What I believe. v.1-2. N.Y., 1964?
Phil 8610.967.5   Ratnathicam, Daniel S. Honest to man. Colombo, 1967.

8612   Philosophy of religion - Treatises on special topics - Death

Phil 8612.01   Pamphlet box. Philosophy. Religion.
Phil 8612.5   Alden, Henry M. A study of death. N.Y., 1895.
Phil 8612.6   Wilson, J.K. Death; the meaning and result. N.Y., 1901.
Phil 8612.7   LeDantec, F. Le problème de la mort et la conscience universelle. Paris, 1917.
Phil 8612.7.5   LeDantec, F. Le problème de la mort et la conscience universelle. Paris, 1917.
Phil 8612.10   Mercer, Edward. Why do we die? London, 1919.
Phil 8612.11.2   Aurelj, T. La vita e la morte. 2. ed. Roma, 1904.
Phil 8612.12.2   Bourdeau, L. Le problème de la mort. 2. éd. Paris, 1896.
Phil 8612.13   Müller, J. Vom Leben und Sterben. 3. Aufl. München, 1913.
Phil 8612.15   Unger, Rudolf. Herder, Novalis und Kleist. Frankfurt, 1922.
Phil 8612.20   Block, Oscar. Om døden; en almenfattelig fremstilling. København, 1903. 2v.
Phil 8612.20.5   Block, Oscar. Döden; populär framställning. Stockholm, 1904. 2v.
Phil 8612.21   Lovatelli, E. Thanatos. Roma, 1888.
Phil 8612.22   Fox, W.J. Reports of lectures delivered at the chapel So. Place, Finsburg. Nos. 9,10,12. London, 1838.
Phil 8612.23*   Tasso, Ercole. Il confortatore. Bergamo, 1595.
Phil 8612.24   Schleich, Carl L. Das Problem des Todes. Berlin, 1921.
Phil 8612.25   Marminia, A. L'idée de la mort et de l'eternité. Paris, 1865.
Phil 8612.26   Baghdigian, B.K. The forgotten purpose. Kansas City, 1934.
Phil 8612.28   Husemann, F. Vom Bild und Sinn des Todes. Dresden, 1938.
Phil 8612.28.5   Husemann, F. Vom Bild und Sinn des Todes. 2. Aufl. Stuttgart, 1954.
Phil 8612.29   Gómez de la Serna, R. Los muertos, las muertas y otras fantasmagarias. Madrid, 1935.
Phil 8612.30   Feier, I. Essais sur la mort. Bucarest, 1939.

Phil 8612   Philosophy of religion - Treatises on special topics - Death - cont.

Phil 8612.31   Landsberg, P.L. Die Erfahrung des Todes. Luzern, 1937.
Phil 8612.32   Ziegler, L. Vom Tod; essay. Leipzig, 1937.
Phil 8612.33   Bürgel, B.H. Saat und Ernte. Berlin, 1942.
Phil 8612.33.5   Bürgel, B.H. Anfang und Ende. Berlin, 1947.
Phil 8612.34   Jolivet, Régis. Le problème de la mort chez M. Heidegger et J.P. Sartre. Paris, 1950.
Phil 8612.35   Wach, Joachim. Das Problem des Todes in der Philosophie unserer Zeit. Tübingen, 1934.
Phil 8612.36   Fischer, J.A. Studien zum Todesgedanken in der Alten Kirche. München, 1954.
Phil 8612.37   Berlinger, R. Das Nichts und der Tod. Frankfurt, 1954.
Phil 8612.38   Echeverria, José. Réflexions métaphysiques sur la mort et la problème du sujet. Paris, 1957.
Phil 8612.40   Mangoldt, Ursula von. Der Tod als Antwort auf das Leben. München, 1957.
Phil 8612.42   Schoepf, Bernhard. Das Tötungsrecht bei den frühchristlichen Schriftstellern. Regensburg, 1958.
Phil 8612.44B   Feifel, Herman. The meaning of death. N.Y., 1959.
Phil 8612.45   Marin, Edgar. L'homme et la mort dans l'histoire. Paris, 1951.
Phil 8612.45.2   Morin, Edgar. L'homme et la mort. Paris, 1970.
Phil 8612.47   Sikken, Willem. Midden in het leven. Kampen, 1960.
Phil 8612.49   Wasmuth, E. Vom Sinn des Todes. Heidelberg, 1959.
Phil 8612.51   Schachtel, H.J. The shadowed valley. N.Y., 1962.
Phil 8612.52   Boros, Ladislaus. Mysterium mortis. Olten, 1962.
Phil 8612.52.5   Boros, Ladislaus. L'homme et son ultime option, Mysterium mortis. Paris, 1966.
Phil 8612.52.10   Lepp, Ignace. La mort et ses mystères. Paris, 1966.
Phil 8612.53   Brunner, S. Büchlein gegen die Todesfurcht. Wien, 1856.
Phil 8612.54   Rahner, Karl. On the theology of death. Freiburg, 1964.
Phil 8612.54.5   Rahnez, Karl. Zur Theologie des Todes. 5. Aufl. Freiburg, 1958.
Phil 8612.55   Fulton, Robert Lester. Death and identity. N.Y., 1965.
Phil 8612.56   Ferrater Mora, José. Being and death. Berkeley, Calif., 1965.
Phil 8612.56.5   Ferrater Mora, José. El ser la muerte. Madrid, 1962.
Phil 8612.57   Boros, Ladislaus. The moment of truth. London, 1965.
Phil 8612.58   Zoepfl, Werner. Der Tod im Phänomen der Bildung und Erziehung. Thesis. München, 1963.
Phil 8612.58.1   Zoepfl, Helmut. Bildung und Erziehung angesichts der Endlichkeit des Menschen. Donauwörth, 1967.
Phil 8612.59   Montanden, Raoul. La mort, cette in connue. Neuchâtel, 1948.
Phil 8612.60   Zinker, Joseph Chaim. Rosa Lee; motivation and the crisis of dying. Painesville, Ohio, 1966.
Phil 8612.61   Jankélévitch, Valdimir. La mort. Paris, 1966.
Phil 8612.62   Foss, Martin. Death, sacrifice, and tragedy. Lincoln, 1966.
Phil 8612.64   Man's concern with death. London, 1968.
Phil 8612.65   Gaboriau, Florent. Interview sur la mort avec Karl Rabner. Paris, 1967.
Phil 8612.67   Halldén, Sören. Universum, döden och den logiska analysen. Lund, 1967.
Phil 8612.68   Pieper, Josef. Tod und Vusterblichkeit. München, 1968.
Phil 8612.68.5   Pieper, Josef. Death and immortality. N.Y., 1969.
Phil 8612.70   Badawï, Abdurrahmän. Le problème de la mort dans la philosophie existentielle. Le Claire, 1964.
Phil 8612.72   Fagerberg, Holsten. Om rätten att dö. Stockholm, 1967.
Phil 8612.74   Guiomar, Michel. Principes d'une esthétique de la mort. Paris, 1967.
Phil 8612.76   Fuchs, Werner. Todesbilder in der modernen Gesellschaft. Frankfurt, 1969.
Phil 8612.78   Fink, Eugen. Metaphysik und Tod. Stuttgart, 1969.
Phil 8612.80   Johann, Horst Theodor. Trauer und Trost. München, 1968.
Phil 8612.82   Bordoni, Marcello. Dimensioni antropologiche della morte. Roma, 1969.
Phil 8612.84   Vernon, Glenn M. Sociology of death; an analysis of death-related behavior. N.Y., 1970.
Phil 8612.86   Bornscheuer, Lothar. Miseriae regum. Diss. Berlin, 1968.
Phil 8612.88   Wiplinger, Fridolin. Der personal verstandene Tod. Freiburg, 1970.
Phil 8612.90   Moos, Peter von. Consolatio; Studien zur mittellateinischen Trostliteratur über den Tod und zum Problem der christlichen Trauer. München, 1971-

Phil 8615   Philosophy of religion - Treatises on special topics - Ethical Culture Movement

Phil 8615.01   Pamphlet box. Ethical movement.
Phil 8615.1   Salter, W.M. Ethical religion. Boston, 1889.
Phil 8615.1.3   Salter, W.M. Ethical religion. London, 1905.
Phil 8615.1.5   Salter, W.M. Der Religion der Moral. Leipzig, 1885.
Phil 8615.1.7   Salter, W.M. On a foundation for religion. Boston, 1879. 17 pam.
Phil 8615.1.15   Salter, W.M. Moral aspiration and song. Philadelphia, 1905.
Phil 8615.1.20   Salter, W.M. Christmas from an ethical standpoint. Chicago, 1888.
Phil 8615.2   Sheldon, Walter L. An ethical movement. N.Y., 1896.
Phil 8615.2.3   Sheldon, Walter L. The meaning of the ethical movement, fifth anniversary address. St. Louis, 1891.
Phil 8615.2.7   Sheldon, Walter L. Ethical culture; its threefold attitude. St. Louis, Mo? 188-?
Phil 8615.3   Society of Ethical Propagandists. Ethics and religion. London, 1900.
Phil 8615.4   Sidgwick, H. Practical ethics. London, 1898.
Phil 8615.5   Adler, Felix. The religion of duty. N.Y., 1905.
Phil 8615.5.4   Adler, Felix. Vágen till målet. Stockholm, 1925.
Phil 8615.5.5   Adler, Felix. Life and destiny. N.Y., 1905.
Phil 8615.5.9   Adler, Felix. Creed and deed. N.Y., 1894.
Phil 8615.5.10   Adler, Felix. The essentials of spirituality. N.Y., 1905.
Phil 8615.5.15   Adler, Felix. An ethical philosophy of life. N.Y., 1918.
Phil 8615.5.20   Adler, Felix. The reconstruction of the spiritual ideal. N.Y., 1924.
Phil 8615.5.23   Adler, Felix. Our part in this world. N.Y., 1946.
Phil 8615.5.50   Bridges, Horace J. Aspects of ethical religion; essays in honor of Felix Adler...fiftieth anniversary...Ethical movement, 1876. N.Y., 1926.
Phil 8615.6   New York Society for Ethical Culture. Year book. N.Y. 1905
Phil 8615.6.5   New York Society for Ethical Culture. Ethical pamphlets. N.Y.
Phil 8615.6.9   New York Society for Ethical Culture. Ethical addresses. Philadelphia. 2v.
Phil 8615.7   Desjardins, P. The present duty. Philadelphia, 1893.
Phil 8615.8   Mourik Broekman, M.C. von. De "Deutsche Gesellschaft für ethische Kultur". n.p., 1909.

Phil 8615   **Philosophy of religion - Treatises on special topics - Ethical Culture**
Movement - cont.

Phil 8615.8.15   Jodl, Friedrich. Über das Wesen und die Aufgabe der
     ethischen Gesellschaft. 2. Aufl. Wien, 1903.

Phil 8615.9.2   Coit, Stanton. The spiritual nature of man.
     Bayswater, 1910.

Phil 8615.10   Hoffmann, P. La religion basée sur la morale. 2. éd.
     Bruxelles, 1901.

Phil 8615.11   Gannett, W.C. The religion of the "ethical culture
     societies." Chicago, 1885.

Phil 8615.12   Spiller, G. The ethical movement in Great Britain.
     London, 1934.

Phil 8615.13   Bacon, S.F. An evaluation of the philosophy and pedagogy
     of ethical culture. Diss. Washington, 1933.

Phil 8615.14   Martin, Alfred W. Deity, duty, destiny; selections from
     addresses. N.Y., 1916.

Phil 8615.14.5   Martin, Alfred W. Consolations. N.Y., 1931.

Phil 8615.14.15   Martin, Alfred W. What human life is for. n.p., 19- .

Phil 8615.15   Chubb, Percival. On the religious frontier. N.Y., 1931.

Phil 8615.16   Fiftieth anniversary of the Ethical movement. N.Y., 1926.

Phil 8615.17   Sheldon, Walter L. Ethics and the belief in a God. St.
     Louis, 1892.

Phil 8615.18   Petrović, E. U znaku preporoda. Odjek Vivodićevoj pokreta.
     Sarajevo, 1928.

Phil 8615.19   Cabot, P. The conversion of a sinner. Boston, 1923.

Phil 8615.20   Muzzey, David S. Ethical religion. N.Y., 1943.

Phil 8615.20.10   Muzzey, David S. Ethics as a religion. N.Y., 1951.

Phil 8615.20.12   Muzzey, David S. Ethics as a religion. N.Y., 1967.

Phil 8615.21   Jacobs, Leo. Three types of practical ethical movements.
     N.Y., 1922.

Phil 8615.23   Hohoff, Tay. A ministry to man. 1. ed. N.Y., 1959.

Phil 8615.25   Ethisch-socialwissenschaftliche Vortragskurse. Bern.
     1,1897

Phil 8615.28   Radest, Howard B. Toward common ground; the study of the
     ethical societies in the United States. N.Y., 1969.

Phil 8620   **Philosophy of religion - Treatises on special topics - Evil**

Phil 8620.1   Bledsoe, A.T. A theodicy. N.Y., 1856.

Phil 8620.2   Burton, W. Cheering views of man and providence.
     Boston, 1832.

Phil 8620.3   Daub, C. Judas Ischariot. v.1-2. Heidelberg, 1816-18.

Phil 8620.4   Evil and evolution. London, 1896.

Phil 8620.5   James, H. The nature of evil. N.Y., 1855.

Htn   Phil 8620.6*   Jenyns, Soame. A free inquiry into the nature and origin
     of evil. London, 1761.

Phil 8620.6.5   Jenyns, Soame. Essai sur la nécessité du mal.
     Paris, 1791.

Phil 8620.7.2   King, William. An essay on the origin of evil.
     London, 1758. 2v.

Phil 8620.7.3   King, William. An essay on the origin of evil.
     London, 1781.

Phil 8620.7.8   King, Gulielmo. De origine mali. Dublinii, 1702.

Phil 8620.8   Naville, E. Le problème du mal. Genève, 1869.

Phil 8620.9   The philosophy of evil. Philadelphia, 1845.

Phil 8620.10   Ritter, H. Über das Böse und seine Folgen. Cotha, 1869.

Phil 8620.10.5   Ritter, H. Über das Böse und seine Folgen. Kiel, 1839.

Phil 8620.11   Thompson, D.G. The problem of evil. London, 1887.

Phil 8620.12   Young, J. The mystery; or evil and God.
     Philadelphia, 1856.

Phil 8620.13A   Carus, D.P. History of the devil and idea of evil.
     Chicago, 1900.

Phil 8620.13B   Carus, D.P. History of the devil and idea of evil.
     Chicago, 1900.

Phil 8620.14   Bonniot, P.J. de. Le problème du mal. 3. éd. Paris, 1911.

Phil 8620.15   Carver, T.N. The economic basis of the problem of evil.
     Cambridge, 1908.

Phil 8620.16   Villaume, P. Von dem Ursprung und der Absichten des Übels.
     Leipzig, 1784. 3v.

Phil 8620.17   Read, H. The foot-prints of Satan. N.Y., 1874.

Phil 8620.19   Willcox, I.L. The psychological aspect of...sin and
     salvation. Oxford, 1910.

Phil 8620.20   Burton, Marion LeRoy. The problem of evil. Chicago, 1909.

Phil 8620.21   Bruyssel, Ernest van. Mal et ses origines. Paris, 1911.

Phil 8620.22   Beard, J.R. Autobiography of Satan. London, 1872.

Phil 8620.23   Bradlaugh, Charles. A few words about the devil.
     N.Y., 1874.

Phil 8620.24   Gree, Peter. The problem of evil. London, 1920.

Phil 8620.24.5   Heyl, Paul R. The mystery of evil. Chicago, 1920.

Phil 8620.25   Nagel, E. Das Problem der Erlösung. Basel, 1901.

Phil 8620.26   Kym, Arnold L. Das Problem des Bösen. München, 1878.

Phil 8620.31   Fischer, Engelbert Lorenz. Das Problem des Ubels und die
     Theodicee. Mainz, 1883.

Phil 8620.32   Lasbax, Émile. Le problème du mal. Paris, 1919.

Phil 8620.34   Worcester, Noah. Some difficulties proposed for solution.
     Newbury-Port, 1786.

Phil 8620.35   Keppler, Paul. Das Problem des Leidens in der Moral.
     Freiburg im Breisgau, 1894.

Phil 8620.36   Kühler, Hans. Das Problem der Theodizee. Inaug. Diss.
     Bonn, 1929.

Phil 8620.37   Tsanoff, R.A. The nature of evil. N.Y., 1931.

Phil 8620.38   Homo (pseud.). Essais. Le don des langues. Paris, 1931.

Phil 8620.39   Samuel, H. The tree of good and evil. London, 1933.

Phil 8620.40   Whyte, A.G. The natural history of evil. London, 1920.

Phil 8620.41   Bond, C.J. The nature and meaning of evil. London, 1937.

Phil 8620.42   Steinhausen, H. Die Rolle des Bösen. Stockholm, 1939.

Phil 8620.43   Rougemont, Denis de. La part du diable. N.Y., 1942.

Phil 8620.43.3   Rougemont, Denis de. La part du diable. N.Y., 1944.

Phil 8620.43.7   Rougemont, Denis de. The devil's share. 2. ed.
     N.Y., 1945.

Phil 8620.44   Joad, C.E.M. God and evil. London, 1943.

Phil 8620.44.5   Headlam, A.C. Why I am satisfied; an open letter to Prof.
     C.E.M. Joad. Oxford, 1944.

Phil 8620.46   Billicsich, F. Das Problem des Übels in der Philosophie.
     Wien, 1952. 3v.

Phil 8620.47   Metzger, A. Freiheit und Tod. Tübingen, 1955.

Phil 8620.48   Borne, Étienne. Le problème du mal. 1. éd. Paris, 1958.

Phil 8620.49   Petit, François. Le problème du mal. Paris, 1958.

Phil 8620.50   Häberlin, P. Das Böse. Bern, 1960.

Phil 8620.51   Journet, C. The meaning of evil. N.Y., 1963.

Phil 8620.52   Gillen, Louis Bertrand. La théorie des oppositions et la
     théologie du péché, au XIIIe siècle. Paris, 1937.

Phil 8620.53   Pike, Nelson. God and evil. Englewood Cliffs, 1764.

Phil 8620.54   Ling, Trevor. The significance of Satan. London, 1961.

Phil 8620.60   Kluger, Rivkah Schärf. Satan in the Old Testament.
     Evanston, 1967.

Phil 8620.62   Murdoch, Iris. The sovereignty of good over other
     concepts. London, 1967.

Phil 8620.62.5   Murdoch, Iris. The sovereignty of good. London, 1970.

Phil 8620   **Philosophy of religion - Treatises on special topics - Evil - cont.**

Phil 8620.64   Barreau, Jean Claude. Oú est le mal? Paris, 1969.

Phil 8622   **Philosophy of religion - Treatises on special topics - Faith**

Phil 8622.2   Kroner, Richard. The primacy of faith. N.Y., 1943.

Phil 8622.2.5   Kroner, Richard. Between faith and thought: reflections
     and suggestions. N.Y., 1966.

Phil 8622.4   Waylen, B. Creators of the modern spirit. N.Y., 1951.

Phil 8622.8   Kimpel, B.F. Religious faith, language, and knowledge.
     N.Y., 1952.

Phil 8622.10   MacGregor, G. Doubt and faith. London, 1951.

Phil 8622.12   Jakob, J. Der Konflikt. Basel, 1952.

Phil 8622.14   Radhakrishnan, S. Recovery of faith. 1. ed. N.Y., 1955.

Phil 8622.20   Duméry, Henry. La tentation de faire du bien.
     Paris, 1957.

Phil 8622.25   Interiorité et vie spirituelle. Paris, 1954.

Phil 8622.30   d'Arcy, M.C. The nature of belief. Dublin, 1958.

Phil 8622.35   Cirne-Lima, Carlos. Der personale Glaube.
     Innsbruck, 1959.

Phil 8622.40   Heer, Friedrich. Glaube und Unglaube. München, 1959.

Phil 8622.45   Glaube und Unglaube. Zürich, 1959.

Phil 8622.50   Hailsham, Quinten McG. The need for faith in a scientifc
     age. Glasgow, 1961.

Phil 8622.55   Tülilä, Osmo. Epäilyksistä uskoon. Helsinki, 1963.

Phil 8622.56   Buhr, H. Der Glaube - was ist das? Pfullingen, 1963.

Phil 8622.57   Lutzenberger, H. Das Glaubensproblem in der
     Religionsphilosophie. München? 1962.

Phil 8622.58   Pruefung der Secte die an allem zweifelt. Göttingen, 1751.

Phil 8622.59   Broglic, Guy de. Pour une théorie rationnelle de l'acte de
     foi. Paris, 1963. 2v.

Phil 8622.60   Morgan, E.K. The ordeal of wonder. London, 1964.

Phil 8622.62   Rahner, Karl. Intellektuelle Redlichkeit und christlicher
     Glaube. Wien, 1966.

Phil 8622.64   Colloque International sur Mythe et Foi, Rome, 1966. Mythe
     et foi. Paris, 1966.

Phil 8622.66   Barruffo, Antonio. Dinamismo e maturità della fede.
     Roma, 1968.

Phil 8622.68   Buri, Fritz. Denkender Glaube. Bern, 1966.

Phil 8622.70   Molevez, Léopold. Pour une théologie de la foi.
     Paris, 1969.

Phil 8622.72   Kanellopoulos, Panagiōtēs. Ascent to faith. 1st ed.
     N.Y., 1966.

Phil 8622.74   Amb o sense fe; mots de conversa. Barcelona, 1968.

Phil 8622.76   McKinnon, Alastair. Falsification and belief. The
     Hague, 1970.

Phil 8622.78   Duss-von Werdt, Josef. Theologie aus Glaubenserfahrung.
     Zürich, 1969.

Phil 8622.80   Fede e mondo moderno. Roma, 1969.

Phil 8622.82.2   Ratzinger, Joseph. Glaube und Zukunft. 2. Aufl.
     München, 1971.

Phil 8622.84   Dobraczyński, Jan. W co wierze. Wyd. 1. Warszawa, 1970.

Phil 8622.86   Parker, Francis H. Reason and faith revisited.
     Milwaukee, 1971.

Phil 8622.88   Scoppio, Domenico. Fede e verità nel Cristianesimo
     contemporaneo. Bari, 1968.

Phil 8624   **Philosophy of religion - Treatises on special topics - Future life -**
Pamphlet volumes; Collected authors

Phil 8624   Pamphlet vol. Philosophy. On immortality. 3 pam.

Htn   Phil 8624.1*   Overton, R. Man's mortallitie. Amsterdam, 1644-97.
     7 pam.

Htn   Phil 8624.2*   Layton, Henry. A search after souls. n.p., 1706.

Htn   Phil 8624.3*   Layton, Henry. Arguments and replies. London, 1703.
     7 pam.

Phil 8624.4   Agnosticism and the future life. n.p., n.d.

Phil 8624.5   Pamphlet box. Future life.

Phil 8624.100   Archivio di Filosofia. Il problema dell'immortalità.
     Roma, 1946.

Phil 8624.105   The future as the presence of shared hope. N.Y., 1968.

Phil 8625 - 8650   **Philosophy of religion - Treatises on special topics -**
Future life - Individual authors (A-Z)

Phil 8625.1   Alger, W.R. A critical history of the doctrine of a future
     life. Philadelphia, 1864.

Phil 8625.1.5   Alger, W.R. A critical history of the doctrine of a future
     life. N.Y., 1871.

Phil 8625.2   Abbot, Ezra. Literature of the doctrine of a future life.
     Cambridge? 1862?

Phil 8625.2.5   Abbot, Ezra. The literature of the doctrine of a future
     life. N.Y., 1871.

Phil 8625.3   Andresen, Karl. Die Unsterblichkeitsfrage. Leipzig, 1906.

Phil 8625.3.15   Andresen, Karl. Wir werden wieder geboren. Hamburg, 1894.

Phil 8625.4   Arjuna. The single eye. N.Y., 1921.

Phil 8625.5.15   Arnold, Edwin. Death and afterwards. London, 1907.

Phil 8625.5.17   Arnold, Edwin. Death and afterwards. N.Y., 1901.

Phil 8626.1   Baguenault de Puchesse, F. L'immortalité, la mort et la
     vie. Paris, 1868.

Phil 8626.1.10   Baguenault de Puchesse, F. A immortalidade, a morte e a
     vida. Porto, 1903.

Phil 8626.2   Bakewell, F.C. Natural evidence of a future life.
     London, 1835.

Phil 8626.3   Blanche, C.I. Le surnaturel. Paris, 1872.

Phil 8626.4   Baxter, A. The evidence of reason in proof of the
     immortality of the soul. London, 1779.

Phil 8626.5   Browne, I.H. The immortality of the soul.
     Cambridge, 1795.

Phil 8626.6   Bolzano, B. Athanasia oder Gründe für die Unsterblichkeit
     der Seele. Sulzbach, 1827.

Phil 8626.6.2.5   Bolzano, B. Anhang zur zweiten Auflage der Athanasia.
     Sulzbach, 1838.

Phil 8626.7   Blackwell, A.B. Physical basis of immortality.
     N.Y., 1876.

Phil 8626.8   Björklund, Gustaf. Death and resurrection. London, 1910.

Phil 8626.8.5   Björklund, Gustaf. Om döden och uppstandeken fran
     cellärans synpunkt. London, 1910.

Phil 8626.9   Ball, J.W. Absolute idealism and immortality.
     Lincoln, 1906.

Phil 8626.10   Bernies, V. Spiritualité et immortalité. Paris, 1901.

Phil 8626.11   Blades, Franklin. Is the life of man eternal? N.Y., 1911.

Phil 8626.12   Berry, J.B.N. Some assurances of immortality. N.Y., 1909.

Phil 8626.13   Brightman, E.S. Immortality in post-Kantian idealism.
     Cambridge, 1925.

Phil 8626.14   Björkman, E.A. Det bortkastade helvetet. Stockholm, 1864.

Phil 8626.15.5   Burnet, Thomas. De statu mortuorum et resurgentium
     tractatus of the state of the dead. London, 1728. 5 pam.

Phil 8626.15.7   Burnet, Thomas. Burnett's state of the dead.
     London, 1725-28. 4 pam.

Phil 8626.15.9　Burnet, Thomas. A treatise concerning the state of the departed souls. London, 1633.

Phil 8626.15.12　Burnet, Thomas. A treatise concerning the state of the departed souls. 2. ed. London, 1739.

Phil 8626.16　Bennett, F.S.M. Expecto, an essay towards a biology of the world to come. Chester, 1926.

Phil 8626.17　Bromberg, F.G. Man's immortality proved by study of his natural constitution. Mobile, Ala., 1929.

Phil 8626.18　Bavan, Edwyn R. The hope of a world to come underlying Judaism and Christianity. London, 1930.

Phil 8626.19　Budgett, H.M. The avenue of beeches. London, 1930.

Phil 8626.20　Barbarin, Georges. L'après-mort. Paris, 1958.

Phil 8626.21　Bonner, H.B. (Mrs.). The Christian hell. London, 1913.

Phil 8626.22　Brecher, G. Die Unsterblichkeitslehre des israelitischen Volkes. Leipzig, 1857.

Phil 8626.23　Beecher, E. History of opinions on the scriptural doctrine of retribution. N.Y., 1878.

Phil 8626.24　Baillie, John. And the life everlasting. N.Y., 1933.

Phil 8626.25　Barnes, C.T. The duration of mind. Salt Lake City, 1955.

Phil 8626.28　Borgia, Anthony V. Life in the world unseen. London, 1956.

Phil 8626.28.5　Borgia, Anthony V. More about life in the world unseen. London, 1958.

Phil 8627.2　Cobbe, F.P. The hope of the human race. London, 1880.

Phil 8627.2.2　Cobbe, F.P. The hope of the human race. London, 1874.

Phil 8627.3　Charles, R.H. A critical history of the doctrine of a future life in Israel. London, 1899.

Phil 8627.3.5　Charles, R.H. A critical history of the doctrine of a future life in Israel. 2. ed. London, 1913.

Phil 8627.3.10　Charles, R.H. Eschatology. N.Y., 1963.

Phil 8627.5　Curtis, L.Q. Immortal life. N.Y., 1901.

Phil 8627.7　Cheney, William A. Can we be sure of mortality? N.Y., 1910.

Phil 8627.8　Clarke, W.N. Immortality. New Haven, 1920.

Phil 8627.9　Chambers, A. Man and the spiritual world. Philadelphia, 1900.

Phil 8627.9.3　Chambers, A. Our life after death. Philadelphia, 1902.

Phil 8627.9.5　Chambers, A. Thoughts of the spiritual. London, 1905.

Phil 8627.9.7　Chambers, A. Problems of the spiritual. Philadelphia, 1907.

Phil 8627.9.9　Chambers, A. Ourself after death. Chicago, 191-.

Phil 8627.10*　Charleton, W. The immortality of the human soul. London, 1657.

Phil 8627.11　Chiappelli, A. Amore, morte ed immortalità. Milano, 1913.

Phil 8627.12　Carmichael, A. An essay...man's ultimate destination. Dublin, 1830.

Phil 8627.13　Cohen, Chapman. The other side of death. London, 1922.

Phil 8627.14　Carpenter, Joseph E. The place of immortality in religious belief. London, 1898.

Phil 8627.15　Cojazzi, Antonio. L'anima umana non muore. Torino, 1944.

Phil 8627.20　Cerný, Ladislav. The day of Yahweh and some relevant problems. Praha, 1943.

Phil 8628.1　Dedekind, G.E.W. Dokimion, oder praktischen Versuch über ein reales Verhältniss der Geister der Verstorbenen. Hannover, 1797.

Phil 8628.1.5　Dedekind, G.E.W. Über Geisternähe und Geisterwirkung oder über die Wahrscheinlichkeit das die Geister der Verstorbenen den Lebenden sowohl nahe seyn, als auch auf sie wirken können. Hannover, 1797.

Phil 8628.2　Dick, T. The philosophy of a future state. N.Y., 1829.

Phil 8628.2.2　Dick, T. The philosophy of a future state. Philadelphia, 1843.

Phil 8628.2.5　Dick, T. The philosophy of a future state. N.Y., 1831.

Phil 8628.3*　Digby, K. Two treatises. London, 1658-57.

Phil 8628.3.2F*　Digby, K. Two treatises...nature of bodies...nature of man's soul. Paris, 1644.

Phil 8628.3.3*　Ross, Alexander. Philosophical touchstone. London, 1645.

Phil 8628.3.4*　Digby, K. Two treatises. London, 1645. 2 pam.

Phil 8628.3.5*　Digby, K. Demonstratio immortalitatis animae. Francofurti, 1664.

Phil 8628.3.8F*　Digby, K. Demonstratio immortalitatis animae. Parisiis, 1651.

Phil 8628.3.9F*　Digby, K. Demonstratos immortalitatis animae rationalis. Paris, 1655.

Phil 8628.4　Drew, Samuel. An original essay on the immateriality and immortality of the human soul. London, 1819.

Phil 8628.4.2*　Drew, Samuel. An original essay on the immateriality and immortality of the human soul. 1st American ed. Baltimore, 1810.

Phil 8628.5　Drossbach, M. Die Harmonie der Ergebnisse der Naturforschung. Leipzig, 1858.

Phil 8628.6　Dumesnil, A. L'immortalite. Paris, 1861.

Phil 8628.7　Dickinson, G.L. Religion and immortality. London, 1911.

Phil 8628.7.5　Dickinson, G.L. Religion and immortality. Boston, 1911.

Phil 8628.8　Desmond, Shaw. How you live when you die. London, 1942.

Phil 8628.10　Des Georges, A. La réincarnation des âmes selon les traditions orientales et occidentales. Paris, 1966.

Phil 8628.15　Delgado Varela, J.M. Supervivencia del hombre. Madrid, 1966.

Phil 8629.1　Enfantin, B.P. La vie éternelle. Paris, 1861.

Phil 8629.2　English, C.D. The philosophy of a future state. Philadelphia, 1885.

Phil 8629.3　Elliott, W.H. Rendezvous; the life that some call death. London, 1942.

Phil 8629.4　Eschatologie et cosmologie. Bruxelles, 1969.

Phil 8630.1　Farlin, J.W. A primer on the origin of knowledge. Saratoga Springs, 1835.

Phil 8630.3　Fiske, J. The destiny of man. Boston, 1884.

L Phil 8630.3C　Fiske, J. The destiny of man. Boston, 1885.

L Phil 8630.3D　Fiske, J. The destiny of man. Boston, 1884.

L Phil 8630.3E　Fiske, J. The destiny of man. Boston, 1893.

L Phil 8630.3G　Fiske, J. The destiny of man. Boston, 1899.

L Phil 8630.3J　Fiske, J. The destiny of man. Boston, 1884.

Phil 8630.3.6A　Fiske, J. Life everlasting. Boston, 1901.

Phil 8630.3.6B　Fiske, J. Life everlasting. Boston, 1901.

Phil 8630.4　Flammarion, C. Récits de l'infini. Paris, 1873.

Phil 8630.4.5　Flammarion, C. Stories of infinity. Boston, 1873.

Phil 8630.5A　Frazer, J.G. Belief in immortality. London, 1913-24. 3v.

Phil 8630.5B　Frazer, J.G. Belief in immortality. London, 1913-24. 2v.

Phil 8630.6.4　Figuier, L. Le lendemain de la mort. 4e éd. Paris, 1872.

Phil 8630.7　Frank, Henry. Modern light on immortality. 2. ed. Boston, 1909.

Phil 8630.7.5　Frank, Henry. Psychic phenomena; science and immortality. 2. ed. Boston, 1916.

Phil 8630.7.9　Frank, Henry. The challenge of the war. Boston, 1919.

Phil 8630.9　Fosdick, H.E. Spiritual values and eternal life. Cambridge, 1927.

Phil 8630.9.10　Fosdick, H.E. The assurance of immortality. N.Y., 1916.

Phil 8630.10　Franck, K. Wie wird's sein? Halle, 1901.

Phil 8630.11　Foerster Lecture. On immortality of the soul. N.Y. 1933+

Phil 8630.12　The future life of the good. Boston, 1839.

Phil 8630.13　Farrar, F.W. Mercy and judgment. London, 1881.

Phil 8630.13.5　Farrar, F.W. Future retribution. N.Y., 1885.

Phil 8630.14　Foerst-Crato, Ilse. Ausblicke ins Paradies. München, 1958.

Phil 8630.15　Findlay, Stephen. Immortal longings. London, 1961.

Phil 8631.1　Göschel, C.F. Von den Beweisen für die Unsterblichkeit der Menschlichen Seele. Berlin, 1835.

Phil 8631.1.5　Göschel, C.F. Der Mensch nach Leib, Seele und Geist. Leipzig, 1856.

Phil 8631.2　Gross, J.B. The belief in immortality. Philadelphia, 1882.

Phil 8631.3　Gordon, G.A. The witness to immortality. Boston, 1900.

Phil 8631.4　Gilbert, L. Side-lights on immortality. London, 1903.

Phil 8631.6　Giraudet, Jules. Y a-t-il une vie future? Paris, 1864.

Phil 8631.8　Genung, John F. The life indeed. Boston, 1921.

Phil 8631.10　Girard, Victor. La transmigration des âmes. Paris, 1888.

X Cg　Phil 8631.11　Graves, Hiram A. Attractions of heaven. Boston, 1846?

Phil 8631.12　Griffin, N.E. The farther shore; an anthology...on the immortality of the soul. Boston, 1934.

Phil 8631.13　Grenfell, W.T. On immortality. Boston, 1912.

Phil 8631.14　Ghyvelde, F. de. Le ciel, séjour des élus. Montréal, 1912.

Phil 8631.15　Guardini, R. The last things. London, 1954.

Phil 8632.1.12　Hudson, T.J. A scientific demonstration...future life. 12th ed. Chicago, 1922.

Phil 8632.2　Höffding, H. The philosophy of religion. London, 1906.

Phil 8632.5　Holmes, John H. Is death the end? N.Y., 1915.

Phil 8632.6　Harris, J.C. The inevitable future. 4. ed. Sydney, 1917.

Phil 8632.7　Hall, Charles A. They do not die. London, 1918.

Phil 8632.8.5　Hyslop, J.H. Life after death. N.Y., 1919.

Phil 8632.9　Harrison, Frederic. A modern symposium. Detroit, 1878.

Phil 8632.10　Hunt, Jasper B. Existence after death implied by science. London, 1910.

Phil 8632.11　Heagle, David. Do the dead still live? Philadelphia, 1920

Phil 8632.12　Hirn, G.A. La vie future et la science moderne. Colmar, 1890.

Htn　Phil 8632.13*　Hoddesdon, H. A treatise, concerning the death and resurrection of our bodies. London, 1606.

Phil 8632.14　Harris, J. Immortality. London, 1927.

Phil 8632.16　Hall, G.S. Thanataphobia and immortality. n.p., 1915.

Phil 8632.17　Hardenberg, H. Wir sollen nicht sterben. Darmstadt, 1920.

Phil 8632.18　Halsey, Don Peters. The evidence for immortality. N.Y., 1932.

Phil 8632.19　Haynes, E.S.P. The belief in personal immortality. N.Y., 1913.

Phil 8632.20　Head, Joseph. Reincarnation. N.Y., 1961.

Phil 8632.21　Heiler, Friedrich. Unsterblichkeitsglaube und Jenseitshoffnung in der Geschichte der Religionen. München, 1950.

Phil 8632.25　Huber, Johannes. Die Idee der Unsterblichkeit. München, 1864.

Phil 8633.1　Gordon, G.A. Immortality and the new theodicy. Boston, 1896.

Phil 8633.1.2A　James, W. Human immortality. Two supposed objections. Boston, 1897. 2v.

Phil 8633.1.2B　James, W. Human immortality. Two supposed objections. Boston, 1897. 2v.

Phil 8633.1.3　Wheeler, B.I. Dionysos and immortality. Boston, 1898.

Phil 8633.1.4　Royce, J. The conception of immortality. Boston, 1900.

Phil 8633.1.5　Fiske, J. Life everlasting. Boston, 1900.

Phil 8633.1.6.5　Osler, W. Science and immortality. Boston, 1904.

Phil 8633.1.7　Crothers, S.M. The endless life. Boston, 1905.

Phil 8633.1.8　Ostwald, W. Individuality and immortality. Boston, 1906.

Phil 8633.1.8.5　Ostwald, W. Personlighet och odödlighet. Stockholm, 1911.

Phil 8633.1.9　Dole, C.F. The hope of immortality, our reasons. N.Y., 1906.

Phil 8633.1.11　Bigelow, W.S. Buddhism and immortality. Boston, 1908.

Phil 8633.1.12　Dickinson, G.L. Is immortality desirable? Boston, 1909.

Phil 8633.1.14　Reisner, George A. The Egyptian conception of immortality. Boston, 1912.

Phil 8633.1.15　Palmer, George H. Intimations of immortality in the sonnets of Shakespeare. Boston, 1912.

Phil 8633.1.17　Moore, G.F. Metempsychosis. Cambridge, 1914.

Phil 8633.1.18　Moore, Clifford H. Pagan ideas of immortality. Cambridge, 1918.

Phil 8633.1.20　Brown, Charles R. Living again. Cambridge, 1920.

Phil 8633.1.22　Lake, Kirsopp. Immortality and the modern mind. Cambridge, 1922.

Phil 8633.1.22.3　Lake, Kirsopp. Immortality and the modern mind. Cambridge, 1922.

Phil 8633.1.23　Horr, George E. The Christian faith and eternal life. Cambridge, 1923.

Phil 8633.1.24　Cabot, Philip. The sense of immortality. Cambridge, 1924.

Phil 8633.1.26　Krüger, G. Immortality of man. Cambridge, 1927.

Phil 8633.1.28　Lyman, E.W. The meaning of selfhood and faith in immortality. Cambridge, 1928.

Phil 8633.1.29　Mackenzie, W.D. Man's consciousness of immortality. Cambridge, 1929.

Phil 8633.1.30　Falconer, Robert A. The idea of immortality. Cambridge, 1930.

Phil 8633.1.31　Bixler, Julius S. Immortality and the present mood. Cambridge, 1931.

Phil 8633.1.32　Montague, W.P. The chances of surviving death. Cambridge, 1934.

Phil 8633.1.33　Matthews, Shailer. Immortality and the cosmic process. Cambridge, 1933.

Phil 8633.1.34　Clark, W.E. Indian conceptions of immortality. Cambridge, 1934.

Phil 8633.1.35　Dodd, Charles H. The communion of saints. Cambridge, 1936.

Phil 8633.1.36　Hocking, W.E. Thoughts on death and life. N.Y., 1937.

Phil 8633.1.36.5　Hocking, W.E. The meaning of immortality in human experience. N.Y., 1957.

Phil 8633.1.37　Kittredge, George L. The old Teutonic idea of the future life. Cambridge, 1937.

Phil 8633.1.42　Steere, Douglas. V. Death's illumination of life. Cambridge, 1942.

Phil 8633.1.47　Thurman, Howard. The negro spiritual speaks of life and death. N.Y., 1947.

Phil 8625 - 8650   Philosophy of religion - Treatises on special topics -
Future life - Individual authors (A-Z) - cont.

Phil 8633.1.50   James, William. Human immortality. Boston, 1900.
Phil 8633.2   In after days; thoughts on the future life. N.Y., 1910.
Phil 8633.3   Immortality; an essay. N.Y., 1917.
Phil 8633.4   Irvine, M.C. The friendly disputants. London, 1859.
Phil 8633.5   Ismard, M. De l'immortalité de l'âme. Paris, 1802.
Phil 8634.2.5   James, William. Människans odödlighet. Stockholm, 1908.
Phil 8634.2.7   James, William. Menneskets udødelighed. Kjøbenhavn, 1918.
Phil 8634.4   Johnston, R.F. Letters to a missionary. London, 1918.
Phil 8634.5   Jones, John Daniel. Our life beyond. Boston, 1914.
Phil 8634.7   Jaeger, Paul. Innseits; zur Verständigung über die Jenseitsfrage. Tübingen, 1917.
Htn   Phil 8635.1*   Kenrick, W. The grand question debated. Dublin, 1751. 2 pam.
Phil 8635.2   Kirk, H.C. The possibility of not dying. N.Y., 1883.
Phil 8635.3   Kaufmann, H. Die Unsterblichkeitsbeweise. Paderborn, 1912.
Phil 8635.4   Keyserling, Hermann. Unsterblichkeit. 2. Aufl. München, 1911.
Phil 8635.4.5   Keyserling, Hermann. Immortality. London, 1938.
Phil 8635.6   Kneib, P. Die Beweise für die Unsterblichkeit der Seele. Freiburg, 1903.
Phil 8635.7   Kast, J. Ernster Blick. Würzburg, 1818.
Phil 8635.8   Knight, W.A. Aspects of theism. London, 1893.
Phil 8635.9   Kretzenbacher, Leopold. Die Seelenwaage. Klagenfurt, 1958.
Phil 8635.12   Kelsey, Denys. Many lifetimes. 1. ed. Garden City, N.Y., 1967.
Phil 8636.05   Lodge, Oliver Joseph. The immortality of the soul. Boston, 1908.
Phil 8636.2   Leuba, James H. The belief in God and immortality. Boston, 1916.
Phil 8636.4   Lathbury, C. The great morning. Minneapolis, 1911.
Phil 8636.5.5   Lescoeur, Louis. A vida futura; conferencias. Lisboa, 1877.
Phil 8636.6   Le Long, Jean. Saint Athanase, ou Traité de la nature. Middelburg, 1645.
Phil 8636.7   Lewis, Jason. The anastasis of the dead. Boston, 1860.
Phil 8636.8   Lamont, Corliss. Issues of immortality. N.Y., 1932.
Phil 8636.8.5   Lamont, Corliss. The illusion of immortality. N.Y., 1935.
Phil 8636.8.7   Lamont, Corliss. The illusion of immortality. 2. ed. N.Y., 1950.
Phil 8636.8.10   Lamont, Corliss. The illusion of immortality. 3. ed. N.Y., 1959.
Htn   Phil 8636.9*   Lyttelton, W.H. Scripture revelations of the life of man after death. 3. ed. London, 1876.
Phil 8636.10   Lindhardt, P.G. Helvedes strategi. n.p., 1958.
Phil 8637.1   Martin, T.H. La vie future. Paris, 1870.
Phil 8637.2   Meister, J.H. Euthanasie. Paris, 1809.
Phil 8637.3   Mendelsohn, M. Phädon oder über die Unsterblichkeit der Seele. Berlin, 1821.
Phil 8637.4   Moody, L. The problem of life and immortality. Boston, 1872.
Phil 8637.5   Muzzey, A.B. Man a soul. Boston, 1842.
Phil 8637.6.5   McConnell, S.D. The evolution of immortality. N.Y., 1902.
Phil 8637.7   Münsterberg, S. The eternal life. Boston, 1905.
Phil 8637.8   Miller, J. Are souls immortal? 3rd ed. Princeton, N.J., 1887.
Htn   Phil 8637.9*   Montagu, H. Contemplatio mortis, and immortalitatis. London, 1638.
Htn   Phil 8637.9.3*   Montagu, H. Contemplatio mortis, and immortalitatis. London, 1631.
Phil 8637.10   Mellone, S.H. The immortal hope. Edinburgh, 1910.
Phil 8637.11   Milne, J. Napier. The dream that comes true. London, 1919.
Phil 8637.12   Moore, Justin H. The world beyond. N.Y., 1920.
Phil 8637.13   Martin, A.W. Faith in a future life. N.Y., 1916.
Phil 8637.14   Mazzantini, C. La speranza nell'immortalità. Torino, n.d.
Phil 8637.15   Moore, Clifford Herschel. Ancient beliefs in the immortality of the soul. N.Y., 1931.
Phil 8637.16   Mamiani della Rovere, T. Mario Pagano, ovvero Della immortalità. Parigi, 1845.
Phil 8637.17   McDonald, N.T. The dawn beyond the sunset. London, 1929.
Phil 8637.18   Mifflin, Mildred. Out of darkness into light. Shelbyville, 1888.
Phil 8637.19   Murphy, R.W. A key to the secret vault. San Francisco, 1890.
Phil 8637.20.5   Mattison, H. The immortality of the soul. 2d ed. Philadelphia, 1866.
Phil 8637.21   McGavin, E.C. Paradise revisited. Boston, 1937.
Phil 8637.22   Martin, E. Reincarnation, the ring of return. New Hyde Park, N.Y., 1963.
Phil 8637.23   Manthey, Franz. Das Problem der Erlösung in den Religionen der Menschheit. Hildesheim, 1964.
Phil 8637.24.2   Muderspach, L. Bag død og grav. 2. udg. København, 1927.
Phil 8638.1   Noel, R. Philosophy of immortality. London, 1882.
Phil 8638.2   Nicoll, N.R. Reunion in eternity. N.Y., 1908.
Phil 8638.3   Norris, John. A philosophical discourse...natural immortality. London, 1708.
Htn   Phil 8640.1*   Pomponazzi, P. Tractatus de immortalitate animae. Paris, 1534.
Phil 8640.1.5   Pomponazzi, P. Trattato sull'immortalità dell'anima. Roma, 1914.
Phil 8640.1.10   Pomponazzi, P. De immortalitate animae. Messina, 1925.
Phil 8640.1.12   Pomponazzi, P. Tractatus de immortalitate animae. Haverford, Pa., 1938.
Htn   Phil 8640.1.15*   Pomponazzi, P. Tractatus de immortalitate animae. Paris, 161-?
Phil 8640.2   Perdelwitz, R. Die Lehre von der Unsterblichkeit der Seele. Leipzig, 1900.
Phil 8640.3   Petavel-Ollief, E. Le problème de l'immortalité. Paris, 1891-92. 2v.
Phil 8640.4   Phelps, E.S. The struggle for immortality. Boston, 1889.
Phil 8640.5   Palmer, Fred. Winning of immortality. London, 1910.
Phil 8640.6   Perrois, A. Les preuves de l'immortalité de l'âme. Paris, 1866.
Phil 8640.7.2   Piat, A. La destinée de l'homme. 2. éd. Paris, 1912.
Phil 8640.8   Peters, M.C. After death - what? N.Y., 1908.
Phil 8640.9   Polak, M.S. Die Unsterblichkeitsfrage. Amsterdam, 1857.
Phil 8640.10   Philipson, J. The natural history of hell. N.Y., 1894.
Phil 8640.11   Ponton, M. Glimpses of the future life. London, 1873.
Phil 8640.12   Pickford, M. My rendezvous with life. N.Y., 1935.
Phil 8640.13   Pilcher, C.V. The hereafter in Jewish and Christian thought. London, 1940.
Phil 8640.14   Petry, Ray C. Christian eschatology and social thought. N.Y., 1956.

Phil 8625 - 8650   Philosophy of religion - Treatises on special topics -
Future life - Individual authors (A-Z) - cont.

Phil 8640.16   Penelhum, Terence. Survival and disembodied existence. London, 1970.
Phil 8642.1   Richter, J.P.F. Das Kampaner Thal. Erfurt, 1797.
Phil 8642.3   Rogers, C.F. Immortality. London, 1930?
Phil 8642.4   Reid, William. Everlasting punishment and modern speculation. Edinburgh, 1874.
Phil 8642.5.5   Ritter, Heinrich. Unsterblichkeit. Leipzig, 1866.
Phil 8642.6   Rogers, E.H. National life in the spirit world. Chelsea? 1891.
Phil 8642.7   Rovighi, S.V. L'immortalità dell'anima nei maestri francescani del secolo XIII. Milano, 1936.
Phil 8642.8   Richmond, I. Archaeology. London, 1950.
Phil 8642.9   Rey Altuna, Luis. La inmortalidad del alma a la luz de los filósofos. Madrid, 1959.
Phil 8642.10   Robinson, John Arthur Thomas. In the end, God. 1. ed. N.Y., 1968.
Phil 8643.1   Schneider, L. Die Unsterblichkeitsidee im Glauben. Regensburg, 1870.
Phil 8643.2   Schutz, L. Vernunf-Beweis...Unsterblichkeit der menschlichen Seele. Paderborn, 1874.
Phil 8643.3   Sintenis, F. Immortality or annihilation? London, 1827.
Phil 8643.3.10   Sintenis, F. Elpizon, oder Über meine Fortdauer im Tode. 3. Aufl. Köln, 1811. 6v.
Phil 8643.4   Stockwell, C.T. The evolution of immortality. Chicago, 1887.
Phil 8643.5   Straub, J. The consolations of science. Chicago, 1884.
Phil 8643.6   Seebach, E. Die Lehre von der bedingten Unsterblichkeit in ihren Entstehung geschichtlichen Entwickelung. Krefeld, 1898.
Phil 8643.7   Spitta, H. Mein Recht auf Leben. Tübingen, 1900.
Phil 8643.8   Sopote, M. Grades of life. Letters on immortality. Oxford, 1909.
Phil 8643.9   Schwarz, H. Der Gottesgedanke in der Geschichte der Philosophie. Heidelberg, 1913.
Phil 8643.11   Savage, M.J. Life beyond death. N.Y., 1899.
Phil 8643.12   Slattery, C.L. The gift of immortality. Boston, 1916.
Phil 8643.13   Slater, J.R. Living for the future. Boston, 1916.
Phil 8643.14.5   Snowden, J.F. Can we believed in immortality. N.Y., 1919.
Phil 8643.15   Shaw, Fred G. Our future existence. London, 1912.
Phil 8643.16   Stanley, T.P. The gift of immortality. Collingswood, 1919.
Phil 8643.17   Spiegler, Julius. Die Unsterblichkeit der Seele. 3. Aufl. Leipzig, 1909.
Phil 8643.18.2   Steinmann, Theophil. Der religiose Unsterblichkeitsglaube. 2. Aufl. Göttingen, 1912.
Phil 8643.19   Smyth, John P. The gospel of the hereafter. N.Y., 1910.
Phil 8643.19.10   Smyth, John P. The gospel of the hereafter. N.Y., 1930.
Phil 8643.20.3   Sabatier, Armand. Essai sur l'immortalité au point de vue du naturalisma évolutionniste. 3. éd. Paris, 1911.
Phil 8643.21   Stanton, H.C. The starry universe the Christian's future empire. N.Y., 1909.
Phil 8643.22   Seth Pringle-Pattison, A. The idea of immortality. Oxford, 1922.
Phil 8643.23   Simpson, J.Y. Man and the attainment of immortality. 2. ed. London, 1923.
Phil 8643.24   Smith, O. Tho material, why not immortal? Boston, 1921.
Phil 8643.25.4   Seeberg, R. Ewiges Leben. Leipzig, 1920.
Phil 8643.26   Stern-Gwiazdowski, H. von. Leben wir nach unseren Tode weiter? Leipzig, 1896.
Phil 8643.27   Schleich, Carl L. Bewusstsein und Unsterblichkeit. Berlin, 1922.
Phil 8643.28.7   Stewart, Balfour. The unseen universe. 7. ed. London, 1878.
Phil 8643.29   Spencer, Frederick A.M. The future life. 1. ed. London, 1935.
Phil 8643.30   Smyth, Newman. Modern belief in immortality. N.Y., 1910.
Phil 8643.31   Litwell, Constance. Seek paradise. London, 1948.
Phil 8643.32   Siwek, Paul. The enigma of the hereafter. N.Y., 1952.
Phil 8643.35   Streeter, B.H. Immortality. London, 1925.
Phil 8643.38   Spazier, Karl. Antiphädon. Berlin, 1961.
Phil 8643.39   Stendahl, Krister. Immortality and resurrection. N.Y., 1965.
Phil 8643.40   Staudinger, Josef. Die letzte Zeit. Innsbruck, 1955.
Phil 8644.1   Tait, P.G. The unseen universe. N.Y., 1875.
Phil 8644.1.2   Tait, P.G. The unseen universe. N.Y., 1875.
Phil 8644.1.5   Tait, P.G. Paradoxical philosophy. London, 1879.
Phil 8644.2   Taylor, Isaac. Physical theory of another life. N.Y., 1836.
Phil 8644.2.2   Taylor, Isaac. Physical theory of another life. 2. ed. N.Y., 1836.
Phil 8644.2.3   Taylor, Isaac. Physical theory of another life. 3. ed. London, 1847.
Phil 8644.3   Turner, F.H. Beside the new-made grave. Boston, 1906.
Phil 8644.4   Taylor, D. The composition of matter and the evolution of the mind. London, 1912.
Phil 8644.5   Teed, Cyrus R. The immortal manhood. 2. ed. Estero, 1909
Phil 8644.6.2   Teichmüller, G. Über die Ansterblichkeit der Seele. 2. Aufl. Leipzig, 1879.
Phil 8644.7   Thompson, R.J. The proofs of life after death. Paris, 1906.
Phil 8644.8   Tucker, C.C. On the doctrine of personal identity. London, 1909.
Phil 8644.9   Tsanoff, R.A. The problem of immortality. N.Y., 1924.
Phil 8644.10   Turlot, F.C. Études sur la théorie de l'avenir. Paris, 1810. 2v.
Phil 8644.11   Taylor, Alfred E. The Christian hope of immortality. London, 1938.
Phil 8644.12.5   Turk, Morris H. They live and are not far away. N.Y., 1923.
Phil 8647.1   Weiss, J. The immortal life. Boston, 1880.
Phil 8647.2   Woods, J.H. Practice and science of religion. London, 1906.
Phil 8647.3   Warren, William F. Religions of the world and the world religion. N.Y., 1911.
Phil 8647.4   Wright, T.F. Life eternal. Boston, 1885.
Phil 8647.5   Florenzi Waddington, M. Della immortalita dell'anima. Firenzi, 1868.
Phil 8647.6   Woodruff, J.L.M. The king's garden. N.Y., 1902.
Phil 8647.8   Willink, Arthur. The world of the unseen. N.Y., 1893.
Phil 8647.9   Weir, J.F. Human destiny in the light of revelation. Boston, 1903.
Phil 8647.10   Where are the dead? London, 1928.
Phil 8647.11   Ware, Mary G.C. Death and life. Boston, 1864.
Phil 8647.12   Wenzl, Aloys. Unsterblichkeit. Berlin, 1951.
Phil 8647.13   Walker, Daniel P. The decline of hell. London, 1964.

Phil 8625 - 8650 Philosophy of religion - Treatises on special topics - Future life - Individual authors (A-Z) - cont.

Phil 8647.14 Wood, Frederic Herbert. Through the psychic door. Houston, 1964?
Phil 8649.1 Yeiser, J.O. Immortality established through science. Omaha, n.d.
Phil 8649.1.2 Yeiser, J.O. Evolution proving immortality. Omaha, 1917.
Phil 8650.1 Zucca, A. Essere e non essere. Roma, 1920.

Phil 8654 Philosophy of religion - Treatises on special topics - God - Pamphlet volumes; Collected authors

Phil 8654.01 Pamphlet box. Philosophy of religion. God.
Phil 8654.100 De la connaissance de Dieu. Paris, 1958.
Phil 8654.105 Journées Universitaires, 44th, Pau, France, 1967. Qui est notre Dieu? n.p., n.d.
Phil 8654.114 Dio é morto? 4. ed. Milano, 1968.
Phil 8654.115 Problemy lichnosti v religii i ateizme. Moskva, 1969.
Phil 8654.116 O bogu i o czlowieku. Warszawa, 1968.
Phil 8654.118 L'analis del linguaggio teologico: il nome di Dio. Padova, 1969.
Phil 8654.120 Dibattito sull'ateismo. Brescia, 1967.

Phil 8655 - 8680 Philosophy of religion - Treatises on special topics - God - Individual authors (A-Z)

Phil 8655.1.3 Abernethy, J. Discourses concerning...God. Dublin, 1743. 2v.
Phil 8655.1.6 Abernethy, J. Discourses concerning...God. Aberdeen, 1778. 2v.
Phil 8655.2 Ancillon, L.F. Judicium de judiciis. Berolini, 1792.
Phil 8655.3 Anderson, J.H. God or no God. Osceola, Neb., 1889.
Phil 8655.4 Allen, G. Evolution of the idea of God. N.Y., 1897.
Phil 8655.5 Abbot, F.E. Scientific theism. Boston, 1885.
Phil 8655.5.5 Abbot, F.E. Scientifc theism. 2. ed. Boston, 1886.
Phil 8655.6 Alden, H.M. God in his world. N.Y., 1890.
Phil 8655.8 American Association for the Advancement of Atheism, Inc. Annual report. N.Y. 1,1926
Phil 8655.8.10 Pamphlet box. Philosophy of religion. God.
Phil 8655.9 The American antitheistical catechism. London, 1830?
Phil 8655.10 Armstrong, R.A. Man's knowledge of God. London, 1886.
Phil 8655.11 Albright, W.F. From the stone age to Christianity. Baltimore, 1940.
Phil 8655.12 L'athéisme contemporain. Genève, 1956.
Phil 8655.13 Allen, D.C. Doubt's boundless sea. Baltimore, 1964.
Phil 8655.14 L'ateismo contemporaneo. Torino, 1967- 4v.
Phil 8655.15 Algermissen Konrad. Die Gottlosenbewegung der Gegenwart. 1. und 2. Aufl. Hannover, 1933.
Phil 8655.16 Anonimnye ateisticheskie traktaty. Moskva, 1969.
Phil 8655.18 Akademiia Nauk SSSR. Muzei Istorii Religii i Ateizma. Istoriia pravoslaviia i russkogo ateizma. Leningrad, 1960.
Phil 8655.19 Akademiia Nauk SSSR. Institut Filosofii. Filosofskie problemy ateizma. Moskva, 1963.
Phil 8655.20 Akademiia Nauk SSSR. Institut Filosofii. Osnovy nauchnogo ateizma. 3. izd. Moskva, 1964.
Phil 8655.22 Amor Ruibal, Angel Maria. Cuatro manuscritos inéditos: Los principios de donde recibe el ente la existencia. Madrid, 1964.
Phil 8655.24 Aubry, Joseph. L'ateismo oggi. 1. ed. Torino, 1968.
Phil 8656.1 Barclay, J. Without faith, without God. London, 1836.
Phil 8656.2 Beckett, E. The origin of the laws of nature. London, 1879.
Phil 8656.3 Blackie, J.S. The natural history of atheism. London, 1877.
Phil 8656.3.2 Blackie, J.S. The natural history of atheism. N.Y., 1878.
EDL Phil 8656.4 Brown, W.L. An essay on the existence...supreme creator. Aberdeen, 1816. 2v.
Phil 8656.5 Buchanan, J. Faith in God. London, 1857. 2v.
Phil 8656.6 Buckland, W. Geology and mineralogy...natural theology. London, 1837. 2v.
Phil 8656.6.2 Buckland, W. Geology and mineralogy...natural theology. Philadelphia, 1841. 2v.
Phil 8656.6.5 Buckland, W. Geologie und Mineralogie. Neufchatel, 1838-39. 2v.
Phil 8656.7 Buddeus, J.F. Theses theologicae de atheismo. Traiecti ad Rhenum, 1737.
Phil 8656.7.10 Buddeus, J.F. Traité de l'athéisme et de la superstition. Amsterdam, 1740.
Phil 8656.7.20 Buddeus, J.F. Lehr-Sätze von der Atheisterey und dem Aberglauben mit gelehrten Anmerckungen erläutert. 2. Aufl. Jena, 1723.
Phil 8656.8 Bowne, B.P. Studies in theism. N.Y., 1879.
Phil 8656.8.5 Bowne, B.P. Philosophy of theism. N.Y., 1887.
Phil 8656.8.7 Bowne, B.P. Theism. N.Y., 1902.
Phil 8656.9.2 Bruce, A.B. The moral order of the World. N.Y., 1899.
Phil 8656.10 Baynes, H. The idea of God...in the light of language. London, 1895.
n Phil 8656.11* Butler, Samuel. God the known and God the unknown. London, 1909.
Phil 8656.12 Barbour, G.F. Ethical approach to theism. Edinburgh, 1913.
Phil 8656.13 Balfour, A.J.B. Theism and humanism. N.Y., 1915.
Phil 8656.13.3 Balfour, A.J.B. L'idée de Dieu et l'esprit humain. 4. éd. Paris, 1916.
Phil 8656.13.5 Balfour, A.J.B. Theism and thought. London, 1923.
Phil 8656.13.7 Balfour, A.J.B. Theism and thought. N.Y., 1924.
Phil 8656.14 Beecher, E. The conflict of the ages. 5. ed. Boston, 1854.
Phil 8656.14.25 King, Thomas S. A short review of Edward Beecher's work on the conflict of ages. 2. ed. Boston, 1854.
Phil 8656.14.27 Blain, Jacob. A review, giving the main ideas in E. Beecher's Conflict of ages. Buffalo, 1856.
Phil 8656.15 Brewster, F.C. God; revelation by Christianity and astronomical science. Newport, 1922.
Phil 8656.16 Bouyssonie, A. Batailles d'idées sur les problèmes de Dieu, du bien, du vrai. Paris, 1923.
Phil 8656.17 Blatchford, R. God and my neighbor. Chicago, 1919.
Phil 8656.17.5 Blatchford, R. God and my neighbor. London, 1904.
Phil 8656.18 Burman, E.O. Om teismen. Upsala, 1886.
Phil 8656.19 Beysens, J.T. Theodicee of natuurlijke godsleer. 2. druk. Bussum, 1919.
Phil 8656.20 Bornträger, J.C.F. Über das Daseyn Gottes in Beziehung auf Kantische und Mendelssonnsche Philosophie. Hannover, 1788.
Phil 8656.21 Brentano, Franz. Vom Dasein Gottes. Leipzig, 1929.
Phil 8656.22 Brightman, E.S. The problem of God. N.Y., 1930.
Phil 8656.23 Ballou, Moses. The divine character vindicated. N.Y., 1854.
Phil 8656.24 Baker, Rannie B. Concept of a limited God. Washington, 1934.

Phil 8655 - 8680 Philosophy of religion - Treatises on special topics - God - Individual authors (A-Z) - cont.

Phil 8656.25 Box, Hubert S. The world and God. Thesis. London, 1934.
Phil 8656.26 Bocheńske, I.M. De cognitione existential Dei per niam causalitatis relate ad fidem catholicam. Poznań, 1936.
Phil 8656.27 Bertocci, Peter Anthony. The empirical argument for God in late British thought. Cambridge, 1938.
Phil 8656.27.5 Bertocci, Peter Anthony. The person God is. N.Y., 1970.
Phil 8656.30 Bandeira de Mello, L.M. Próva matemático da existencia de Deus. Leopoldina, 1942.
Phil 8656.31 Baskfield, G.T. The idea of God in British and American personal idealism. Thesis. Washington, 1933.
Phil 8656.35 Bulgakov, S.N. Filosofiia imeni. Parizh, 1953.
Phil 8656.37 Borne, Étienne. Dieu n'est pas mort. Paris, 1959.
Phil 8656.40 Balbontín, José A. A la busca del Dios perdido. Madrid, 1969.
VPhil 8656.42 Békassy, Árpád. Az analógia je lentősége a tudomángos es vallásos világismeret kialakulásában. Budapest, 1936.
Phil 8656.44 Barbotin, Edmond. Humanité de Dieu. Paris, 1970.
Phil 8656.46.2 Ratschow, Carl Heinz. Atheismus im Christentum? 2. Aufl. Gütersloh, 1971.
Phil 8657.1 Caro, E.M. L'idée de Dieu. Paris, 1868.
Phil 8657.1.2 Caro, E.M. L'idée de Dieu et ses nouveaux critiques. Paris, 1864.
Phil 8657.2 Chalmers, T. The power, wisdom and goodness of God. N.Y., 1834.
Phil 8657.4 Cocker, B.F. The theistic conception of the world. N.Y., 1875.
Phil 8657.5 Coke, H. Creeds of the day. London, 1883. 2v.
Phil 8657.6 Cazenove, J.G. Historic aspects...being attributes of God. London, 1886.
Phil 8657.7 Clarke, W.N. Can I believe in God the Father. N.Y., 1899.
Phil 8657.7.6 Clarke, W.N. The Christian doctrine of God. N.Y., 1910.
Phil 8657.8 Clarke, J.C.C. Man and his Divine Father. Chicago, 1900.
Phil 8657.9 Cyon, E. von. Gott und Wissenschaft. v.1-2. Leipzig, 1912.
Phil 8657.10 Conversations on the attributes of God. Boston, 1831.
Htn Phil 8657.11* Croswell, A. A letter to the Rev. A. Cumming attempting to show him that it is not blasphemy to say, no man can love God. Boston, 1831. 2 pam.
Phil 8657.12 Candlish, J.S. The kingdom of God. Edinburgh, 1884.
Phil 8657.14 Cieszkowski, August D. Ojcze-nasz. Paryż, 1848.
Phil 8657.14.5 Cieszkowski, August D. Notre Père. Paris, 1906.
Phil 8657.14.10 Cieszkowski, August D. Ojcze-nasz. v.1-3. Poznań, 1922-23.
Phil 8657.14.15 Cieszkowski, August D. Ojcze-nasz. Poznań, 1899-1906. 4v.
Phil 8657.14.20 Cieszkowski, August D. Bóg i palingenezya. Poznań, 1912.
Htn Phil 8657.15* Church, Henry. Miscellanea philo-theologica, or God and man. London, 1937.
Htn Phil 8657.15.3* Church, Henry. Miscellanea philo-theologica, or God and man. London, 1638.
Phil 8657.16 Cohen, Chapman. Theism or atheism. London, 1921.
Phil 8657.17 Corte, P.A. Elementi di filosofia. v.2. 4. ed. Torino, 1862.
Htn Phil 8657.18* Charleton, W. The darkness of atheism dispelled by the light of native. London, 1652.
Phil 8657.19 Christiansen, Broder. Der neue Gott. München, 1934.
Phil 8657.20 Cohen, Chapman. Socialism, atheism and Christianity. London, 1908.
Phil 8657.21 Collins, J.D. God in modern philosophy. Chicago, 1959.
Phil 8657.22 Congar, M.J. Le mystère du temple. 2. éd. Paris, 1963.
Phil 8657.23 Coffy, Robert. Dieu des athées: Marx, Sartre, Camus. Lyon, 1965.
Phil 8657.25 Des chrétiens interrogent l'athéisme. Paris, 1967- 2v.
Phil 8657.30 Coseglia, Raffaele. L'ateismo contemporaneo [l'aberrante avventura dello spirito] relazioni, studi, esperienze. Napoli, 1965.
Phil 8657.32 Capizzi, Antonio. Dall'ateismo all'umanismo. Roma, 1967.
Phil 8657.34 Cottier, Georges. Horizons de l'athéisme. Paris, 1969.
Phil 8658.1 Damiron, J.P. Petits traites...de la providence. Paris, 1849.
Phil 8658.1.5 Damiron, J.P. Memoire sur Naigeon et accessoirement sur Sylvain Maréchal et Delalande. Paris, 1857.
Phil 8658.2 Davis, A.J. The philosophy of special providences. Boston, 1856.
Htn Phil 8658.3* Dove, J. Atheism defined and confuted. London, 1656.
Htn Phil 8658.4* Derham, W. Astro-theology. London, 1715.
Phil 8658.4.2 Derham, W. Astro-theology. London, 1719.
Phil 8658.4.5 Derham, W. Astro-theology. Hamburg, 1728.
Phil 8658.4.6 Derham, W. Physico-theology. London, 1714.
Phil 8658.4.7 Derham, W. Physico-theology. London, 1716.
Phil 8658.4.9 Derham, W. Physico-theology. 7. ed. London, 1727.
Phil 8658.5 Diman, J.L. The theistic argument as affected by recent theories. Boston, 1881.
Phil 8658.6 D'Arcy, C.F. Idealism and theology. London, 1899.
Phil 8658.7 Dole, C.F. From agnosticism to theism. Boston, n.d.
Phil 8658.8 Davidson, W.L. Theism as grounded in human nature. London, 1893.
Htn Phil 8658.9* Divine oracles; the true antidote against deism and false Christianity. Providence, 1797.
Phil 8658.10 Dotterer, R.H. The argument for a finitist theology. Diss. Lancaster, Pa., 1917.
Phil 8658.11 Dayton, A.C. Emma Livingston, infidel's daughter. Nashville, Tenn., 1861.
Phil 8658.12.2 Doedes, J.I. Inleidung tot de leer van God. Utrecht, 1880.
Phil 8658.13 Davenport, S.F. Immanence and incarnation. Cambridge, 1925.
Phil 8658.14 Dyroff, Adolf. Probleme der Gotteserkenntnis. Münster, 1928.
Phil 8658.15 Descoqs, Pedro. Praelectiones theologiae naturalis. Paris, 1932. 2v.
Phil 8658.16 De Dieu. Par M***. Paris, 1811.
Phil 8658.17 Duméry, Henry. Le problème de Dieu en philosophie de la religion. Bruges, 1957.
Phil 8658.17.3 Duméry, Henry. The problem of God in philosophy of religion. Evanston, Ill., 1964.
Phil 8658.17.10 Duméry, Henry. Raison et religion dans la philosophie de l'actin. Paris, 1963.
Phil 8658.17.80 Malevez, Léopold. Transcendence de Dieu et création des valeurs. Paris, 1958.
Phil 8658.22 Delanglade, Jean. Le probleme de Dieu. Paris, 1960.
Phil 8658.24 Durandeaux, Jacques. Question vivante a un Dieu mort. Paris, 1967.
Phil 8658.25 Dewart, Leslie. The future of belief; theism in a world come of age. N.Y., 1966.

Phil 8655 - 8680 Philosophy of religion - Treatises on special topics - God - Individual authors (A-Z) - cont.

	Phil 8658.26	Duquesne, Jacques. Dieu pour l'homme d'aujourd'hui. Paris, 1970.
	Phil 8658.27	Duluman, Evgraf K. Ideiia boga. Moskva, 1970.
	Phil 8659.2	Edwards, John. A demonstration of the existence and providence of God. London, 1696.
Htn	Phil 8659.3*	Elis, C. The folly of atheism. London, 1692.
	Phil 8659.4	Ercole, P. d'. Il teismo filosofico cristiano. pt.1. Torino, 1884.
	Phil 8659.5	Evans, Joseph. Theistic monism. London, 1928.
	Phil 8659.7	Elliot, George. God is spirit, God is love. London, 1895.
	Phil 8660.2.7	Fiske, J. The idea of God. Boston, 1891.
	Phil 8660.2.10	Shanahan, E.T. John Fiske on the idea of God. Washington, 1897.
	Phil 8660.3	Flammarion, C. Dieu dans la nature. Paris, 1867.
	Phil 8660.3.7	Flammarion, C. Dieu dans la nature. 7. ed. Paris, 1871.
	Phil 8660.4	Flint, R. Theism. (Baird lectures for 1876). Edinburgh, 1877.
	Phil 8660.4.4	Flint, R. Theism (Baird lectures for 1876). 10. ed. London, 1902.
	Phil 8660.4.5	Flint, R. Anti-theistic theories. (Baird lectures for 1877). Edinburgh, 1879.
	Phil 8660.5	Fraser, A.C. Philosophy of theism. 2. ed. Edinburgh, 1899.
	Phil 8660.5.2	Fraser, A.C. Philosophy of theism. N.Y., 1895.
	Phil 8660.5.3	Fraser, A.C. Philosophy of theism. 2. series. N.Y., 1896.
	Phil 8660.6	Faber, F.W. The creator and the creature. London, 1889.
	Phil 8660.7.2	Faber, G.S. The difficulties of infidelity. 2. ed. London, 1833.
	Phil 8660.8.5	Wüchner, J.G. Frohschammers Stellung zum Theismus. Paderborn, 1913.
	Phil 8660.9	Fischer, K.P. Die Idee der Gottheit. Stuttgart, 1839.
	Phil 8660.10	Farnell, Lewis R. The attributes of God. Oxford, 1925.
	Phil 8660.12	Flügel, Otto. Das Wunder und die Erkennbarkeit Gottes. Langensalza, 1869.
	Phil 8660.13	Fitzpatrick, M.S. Mind and the universal frame. Dublin, 1935.
	Phil 8660.14	Farmer, H.H. The world and God. London, 1935.
	Phil 8660.15	Fox, Adam. God is an artist. London, 1957.
	Phil 8660.16	Fishler, Max. What the great philosophers thought about God. Los Angeles, 1958.
	Phil 8660.20	Fuerstenberg, E. Der Selbstwiderspruch des philosophischen Atheismus. Regensburg, 1960.
	Phil 8660.21	Fabro, Conelio. Introduzione all'ateismo moderno. Roma, 1964.
	VPhil 8660.22	Flam, Leopold. Geschiedenis van het atheisme. 1. uitg. Brussel, 1964. 4v.
	Phil 8660.23	Flew, Antony. God and philosophy. 1st American ed. N.Y., 1966.
	Phil 8660.25	Frontistès, Mario. Il est un Dieu. Padova, 1964.
	Phil 8660.26	Faith in the face of doubt. N.Y., 1968.
	Phil 8661.1	Goblet D'Alviella, E. Lectures on the origin and growth of the conception of God. London, 1892.
	Phil 8661.2	Godwin, B. Lectures on the atheistic controversy. London, 1834.
	Phil 8661.2.3	Godwin, B. Lectures on the atheistic controversy. Boston, 1835.
	Phil 8661.3	Guilbert, A.V.F. Monde et Dieu. Paris, 1879.
	Phil 8661.5	Garrigou-Lagrange, R. Dieu, son existence et sa nature. Paris, 1914.
	Phil 8661.5.5	Garrigou-Lagrange, R. God, His existence and His nature. St. Louis, 1934-36. 2v.
	Phil 8661.6	Gomer, A. de. Journée solitaire de l'homme sensible. Paris, 1800.
	Phil 8661.7	Groddeck, G. Hin zu Gottnatur. 2. Aufl. Leipzig, 1909.
	Phil 8661.8.30	Gillespie, W.H. The necessary existence of God. Edinburgh, 1843.
	Phil 8661.8.35	Barrett, R.H. A refutation of Mr. U.H. Gillespie's argument a priori for the existence of a great first cause. London, 1968.
	Phil 8661.8.80	Urquhart, James. William Honyman Gillespie. Edinburgh, 1920.
	Phil 8661.9	Gratry, A. De la connaissance de Dieu. 9. éd. Paris, 1918. 2v.
	Phil 8661.9.2	Gratry, A. De la connaissance de Dieu. 2. éd. Paris, 1854. 2v.
	Phil 8661.11	Griffths, Rees. God in idea and experience. Edinburgh, 1931.
	Phil 8661.12.5	Godfrey, W.S. Theism found wanting. London, 1920.
Htn	Phil 8661.13*	Gildon, Charles. The deist's manual. London, 1705.
	Phil 8661.14	Greene, K.C. The evolution of the conception of God. Boston, 1934.
	Phil 8661.15	Graham, Bothwell. The self-evolution of God and His creation of nature. Greenville, S.C., 1923.
	Phil 8661.17	Gururmurti, D. God and progress. Madras, 1945.
	Phil 8661.18	Gonzalez Alvarez, Angel. El tema de Dios en la filosofía existencial. Madrid, 1945.
	Phil 8661.19	Gregoire, A. Immanence et transcendance. Bruxelles, 1939.
	Phil 8661.20	Grison, M. Théologie naturelle, ou théodicée. Paris, 1959.
	Phil 8661.21	Goldstein, Walter Benjamin. Glaube oder Unglaube. Jerusalem, 1964.
	Phil 8661.22	Gent, Werner. Untersuchungen zum Problem des Atheismus. Hildesheim, 1964.
	Phil 8661.23	Gay, Peter. Deism, an anthology. Princeton, 1968.
	Phil 8661.25	Gaboriau, Florent. Dieu dans le débat des hommes. Paris, 1964.
	Phil 8661.28	Guilhot, Jean. La psychiatrie morale et le problème de Dieu. Thesis. La Haye, 1967.
	Phil 8661.28.2	Guilhot, Jean. La psychiatrie morale et le problème de Dieu. Paris, 1967.
	Phil 8661.30	Gutiérrez, Antonio José. La providencia y España. San Sebastián, 1941.
	Phil 8661.33	Gironella, José María. Cien españoles y Dios. 3. ed. Barcelona, 1969.
	Phil 8661.35	Girardi, Giulio. Dialogue et révolution. Paris, 1969.
	Phil 8661.35.5	Girardi, Giulio. Credenti e non credenti per un mondo nuovo. Firenze, 1969.
	Phil 8661.40	Giannini, Giorgio. L'ateismo nella filosofia italiana contemporanea. Roma, 1969.
	Phil 8661.45	Guérard des Lauriers, Michel L. La preuve de Dieu et les cinq voies. Roma, 1966.
	Phil 8662.1	Hamilton, Hugh. An attempt to prove the existance...of the supreme unoriginated being. London, 1785.
Htn	Phil 8662.2*	Hancock, J. Arguments to prove the being of God. London, 1707.
	Phil 8662.3	Harris, S. The philosophical basis of Theism. N.Y., 1883.

Phil 8655 - 8680 Philosophy of religion - Treatises on special topics - God - Individual authors (A-Z) - cont.

	Phil 8662.4	Hiller, T.O.P. God manifest. London, 1858.
	Phil 8662.5	Holyoake, George Jacob. Secularism, scepticism and atheism. London, 1870.
	Phil 8662.5.5	Holyoake, George Jacob. The report of the four nights' public discussion...on the truth of Christianity. London, 1850.
	Phil 8662.5.9	Holyoake, George Jacob. The last trial for atheism in England. 5. ed. London, 1878.
	Phil 8662.5.10	Holyoake, George Jacob. Why do the clergy avoid discussion. London, 1852.
	Phil 8662.5.25	Collet, S.D. George Jacob Holyoake and modern atheism. London, 1855.
	Phil 8662.6	Henri, P.E. Religion d'amour ou Dieu existe. Marseille, 1910.
	Phil 8662.7	Hocking, W.E. The meaning of God in human experience. New Haven, Conn., 1912.
	Phil 8662.7.5	Hocking, W.E. The meaning of God in human experience. New Haven, 1923.
	Phil 8662.7.6A	Hocking, W.E. The meaning of God in human experience. New Haven, Conn., 1924.
	Phil 8662.7.6B	Hocking, W.E. The meaning of God in human experience. New Haven, Conn., 1924.
	Phil 8662.8	Hill, J. Thoughts concerning God and nature. London, 1755.
	Phil 8662.9	Hood, John. The beauty of God. Baltimore, 1908.
	Phil 8662.10	Harris, T.L. God's breath in man. Santa Rosa, 1891.
	Phil 8662.12	Huhn, Friedrich. Der Beweis vom dasein Gottes. Berlin, 1927.
	Phil 8662.13	Horton, Walter M. Theism and the modern mood. N.Y., 1930.
	Phil 8662.14	Hudson, T.J. Divine pedigree of man. Chicago, 1899.
	Phil 8662.15	Heim, Karl. God transcendent. London, 1935.
	Phil 8662.15.80	Allen, E. Jesus, our leader...Karl Heim. London, 1950.
	Phil 8662.16	Hicks, G.D. The philosophical bases of theism. London, 1937.
	Phil 8662.17	Hartshorne, Charles. Man's vision of God, and the logic of theism. Chicago, 1941.
	Phil 8662.18	Heydon, J.K. The God of reason. N.Y., 1942.
	Phil 8662.19	Hawkins, D.J. The essentials of theism. London, 1949.
	Phil 8662.20	Heer, Freidrich. Alle Moglichkeit liegt bei uns. Nürnberg, 1958.
	Phil 8662.22	Hills, Ernest. Philosophie et athéisme. Paris, 1923.
	Phil 8662.24	Henrich, Dieter. Der ontologische Gottesbeweis. Tübingen, 1960.
	Phil 8662.25	Hubbeling, H.G. Is the Christian God-conception philosophically inferior? Assen, 1963.
	Phil 8662.26	Hidding, Klaas Albert Hendrik. De evolutie van het godsdienstig bewustzijn. Utrecht, 1965.
	Phil 8662.27	Humanism, atheism; principles and practice. Moscow, 1966?
	Phil 8662.30	Humanism, atheism; principles and practice. Moscow, 1968?
	Phil 8663.1	Irons, W.J. On the whole doctrine of final causes. London, 1836.
	Phil 8663.2	Illingworth, J. Divine immanence. London, 1868.
	Phil 8663.3.06	Pamphlet vol. Ingersoll, Robert G. 6 pam.
	Phil 8663.3.07	Pamphlet vol. Ingersoll, Robert G. 1884-1922. 25 pam.
	Phil 8663.3.2	Ingersoll, Robert G. Ingersollia. Chicago, 1899.
	Phil 8663.3.3	Ingersoll, Robert G. The works. N.Y., 1900-02. 12v.
	Phil 8663.3.12	Ingersoll, Robert G. Collection of Robert G. Ingersoll's famous speeches. N.Y., 1906.
Htn	Phil 8663.3.31*	Ingersoll, Robert G. An oration on the Gods. Peoria, 1872.
	Phil 8663.3.32	Ingersol, Robert G. The Christian religion. n.p., 1851?
	Phil 8663.3.33	Ingersoll, Robert G. The Christian religion. Manchester, 1882.
	Phil 8663.3.34	Ingersoll, Robert G. The ghosts, and other lectures. Peoria, Ill., 1878.
	Phil 8663.3.35	Ingersoll, Robert G. The limits of toleration. N.Y., 1889.
	Phil 8663.3.37	Ingersoll, Robert G. Ingersoll to the clergy. N.Y., 1897.
	Phil 8663.3.40	Ingersoll, Robert G. The Christian religion. N.Y., 1882.
	Phil 8663.3.45	Ingersoll, Robert G. The house of death. London, 1897.
	Phil 8663.3.75	Ingersoll, Robert G. Letters. N.Y., 1951.
	Phil 8663.3.80	Pamphlet box. Ingersoll, Robert G. Biography and Criticism.
	Phil 8663.3.83	The great Ingersoll controversy. Photoreproduction. N.Y., 189-?
	Phil 8663.3.85	Bertron, Ottilie. Review of Col. Ingersoll's attacks upon Christianity. Philadelphia, 1889.
	Phil 8663.3.86.2	Pringle, Allen. Ingersoll in Canada. 2. ed. Toronto, 1880.
	Phil 8663.3.87	Edgett, G.W. The mistakes of R.G. Ingersoll on nature and God. Boston, 1881.
	Phil 8663.3.88	Lambert, L.A. Ingersoll's Christmas sermon delivered by Rev. L.A. Lambert. Akron, 1898.
	Phil 8663.3.89	Lucas, H.M. View of Lambert's "Notes on Ingersoll." N.Y., 1909.
	Phil 8663.3.90	Lambert, L.A. Tactics of infidels. Buffalo, 1887.
	Phil 8663.3.91	McDonald, E.M. Col. Robert G. Ingersoll as he is. N.Y., 1910?
	Phil 8663.3.93	Homo (pseud.). Analogy, or The theology of nature. New Haven, 1885.
	Phil 8663.3.95	Lewis, Joseph. Ingersoll the magnificent. N.Y., 1957.
	Phil 8663.3.96	Cramer, C.H. Royal Bob. 1. ed. Indianapolis, 1952.
	Phil 8663.3.97	Larson, O.P. American infidel. 1. ed. N.Y., 1962.
	Phil 8663.3.100	Stein, Gordon. Robert G. Ingersoll; a checklist. 1. ed. Kent, Ohio? 1969.
	Phil 8663.4	In search of God and immortality. Boston, 1961.
	Phil 8663.5	Information Catholiques Internationales. L'athéisme. Paris, 1963.
	Phil 8663.6	Illanes, José L. Hablar de Dios. Madrid, 1970.
	Phil 8664.1	Jack, R. Mathematical principles of theology. London, 1747.
	Phil 8664.2	Jakob, L.H. Über die Beweise für das Daseyn Gottes. Liebau, 1798.
Htn	Phil 8664.3*	Jaquelot, I. Dissertations sur l'existence de Dieu. La Haye, 1697.
	Phil 8664.4	Jolivet, R. Études sur la problème de Dieu dans la philosophie contemporaine. Lyon, 1932.
	Phil 8664.5	Jernegan, P.F. Man and his God. n.p., 1927.
	Phil 8664.6	James, E.O. The concept of deity. London, 1950.
	Phil 8664.7	Johann, Robert O. The pragmatic meaning of God. Milwaukee, 1966.
	Phil 8664.9	Javaux, J. Prouver Dieu? Paris, 1968.
	Phil 8664.10	Jüchen, Aurel von. Atheismus in West und Ost. 1. Aufl. Berlin, 1968.
	Phil 8664.12	Journet, Charles. Connaissance et inconnaissance de Dieu. Paris, 1969.
	Phil 8665.1	Knight, H. The being and attributes of God. London, 1747.

Phil 8655 - 8680 Philosophy of religion - Treatises on special topics - God - Individual authors (A-Z) - cont.

Phil 8665.2 Kernahan, C. The lonely God. London, n.d.
Phil 8665.3 Keyser, L.S. A system of natural theism. Burlington, Ia., 1917.
Phil 8665.4 Kawaguchi, U. The bearing of the evolutionary theory on the conception of God. Thesis. Menasha, Wis., 1916.
Phil 8665.5 Klostermann, E. Späte Vergeltung aus der Geschichte der Theodicee. Strassburg, 1916.
Phil 8665.7 Kent, G. Det absolute gudshegreb. Kristiania, 1886.
Phil 8665.8 Kleutgen, J. Praeter introductionem continens partem primamque est De ipso deo. Ratisbonae, 1881.
Phil 8665.9 Koch, H.G. Abschaffung Tottes? Stuttgart, 1961.
Phil 8665.9.5 Koch, H.G. The abolition of God. Philadelphia, 1963.
Phil 8665.10 Krejčí, Jaroslav. Teleologický, kosmologický, a etický důkaz existence Boha v neotomismu. Vyd. 1. Praha, 1967.
Phil 8665.18.1 Kahl, Joachim. Das Elend des Christentums. Reinbek bei Hamburg, 1969.
Phil 8665.20 Karliak, A.S. Ocherki po nauchnomu ateizmu. Minsk, 1961.
Phil 8665.23 Karpushin, Vladimir A. Populiarnye lektsii po ateizmu. 2. izd. Moskva, 1965.
Phil 8665.25 Kryvelev, A.I. O dokazatel'stvakh bytiia Bozhiia. Moskva, 1960.
Phil 8665.27 Kromer, Klaus. Gott und Welt in der klassischen Metaphysik. Stuttgart, 1969.
Phil 8665.30 Kruger, Klaus. Der Gottesbegriff der spekulativen Theologie. Berlin, 1970.
Phil 8666.1 Lacordaire, P.J.B.H.D. God. London, 1870.
Phil 8666.2 Lesser, F.C. Testaceo-Theologia. Leipzig, 1756.
Phil 8666.2.5 Lesser, F.C. Theologie des insects. La Hague, 1742.
Htn Phil 8666.4* Leslie, Charles. A short and easie method with the deists. 8. ed. v.1-3. London, 1723.
Phil 8666.5 Leighton, J.A. Typical modern conceptions of God. N.Y., 1901.
Phil 8666.6.5 Le Dantec, Felix. L'athéisme. Paris, 1912.
Phil 8666.7 La Paquerie, J. Les arguments de l'athéisme. Paris, 1909.
Phil 8666.8 Leitch, A. Ethics of theism. Edinburgh, 1868.
Phil 8666.9 Lacour, J.B. Dieu et la création. Paris, 1866.
Phil 8666.11 Le Roy, Edouard. Le problème de Dieu. Paris, 1930.
Phil 8666.12 Lattey, Cuthbert. God. London, 1931.
Phil 8666.13 Laird, John. Theism and cosmology. London, 1940.
Phil 8666.14 Laird, John. Mind and deity. London, 1941.
Phil 8666.15 Lederer, Julius. Gott und Teufel im 20. Jahrhundert. 4. Aufl. Berlin, 1910?
Phil 8666.16.5 Lewis, Clive Staples. Beyond personality; the Christian idea of God. London, 1945.
Phil 8666.17.6 Lubac, Henri de. Le drame de l'humanisme athée. 6. éd. Paris, 1959.
Phil 8666.17.7 Lubac, Henri de. Le drame de l'humanisme athée. Paris, 1963.
Phil 8666.17.10 Lubac, Henri de. Le drame de l'humanisme athée. 3. éd. Paris, 1945.
Phil 8666.17.11 Lubac, Henri de. The drama of atheist humanism. Cleveland, 1969.
Phil 8666.18 Lewis, Hymel D. Our experience of God. London, 1959.
Phil 8666.19 Lelong, Michel. Pour un dialogue avec les athées. Paris, 1965.
Phil 8666.21.5 Lacroix, Jean. The meaning of modern atheism. N.Y., 1966.
Phil 8666.22 Lepp, Ignace. Psychoanalyse de l'atéisme moderne. Paris, 1961.
Phil 8666.23 Lunacharskii, Anatolii V. Pochemu nel'zia verit' v boga. Moskva, 1965.
Phil 8666.24.2 Librizzi, Carmelo. Immanenza e trascendenza. 2. ed. Padova, 1966.
Phil 8667.2 Macculloch, J. Proofs and illustrations of the attributes of God. London, 1837. 3v.
Htn Phil 8667.3* Mendelssohn, M. Morgenstunden oder Vorlesungen uber das Daseyn Gottes. Berlin, 1785.
Htn Phil 8667.4* Mather, C. The Christian philosopher. London, 1721.
Phil 8667.5 Mendelssohn, M. Morgenstunden. Berlin, 1786.
Phil 8667.6 Momerie, A.W. Belief in God. Edinburgh, 1888.
Phil 8667.7 Moisant, Xavier. Dieu. Paris, 1907.
Htn Phil 8667.8* More, G. A demonstration of God in his workes. London, 1598.
Phil 8667.9 Michelet, Georges. Dieu et l'agnosticisme contemporaine. 3. éd. Paris, 1912.
Phil 8667.10 Mallock, William H. Atheism and the value of life. London, 1884.
Phil 8667.11 Medina, Juan J. La cruzada del error. Sevilla, 1879.
Phil 8667.12 Mayer, P. Der teleologische Gottesbeweis und der Darwinismus. Mainz, 1901.
Phil 8667.13 Monod, W. Un athée. Neuchâtel, 1904.
Phil 8667.14 Micrandu, J. Disputatio philosophica de contemplatione mortis. Stockholmiae, 1684.
Phil 8667.15 McCabe, J. The existence of God. London, 1913.
Phil 8667.16 Miller, T.A. The mind behind the universe. N.Y., 1928.
Phil 8667.17 Matthews, W.R. God in Christian experience. N.Y., 193-?
Phil 8667.17.7 Matthews, W.R. The purpose of God. London, 1935.
Phil 8667.18 Monod, Victor. Dieu dans l'univers. Thèse. Paris, 1933.
Phil 8667.19 McAuliffe, A.T. Some modern non-intellectual approaches to God. Washington, D.C., 1934.
Phil 8667.20 Morais, H.M. Deism in eighteenth century America. N.Y., 1934.
Phil 8667.20.5 Morais, H.M. Deism in eighteenth century America. N.Y., 1960.
Phil 8667.21 Maréchal, P.S. La fable de Christ dévoilée. Paris, 1794.
Phil 8667.22 Mascall, E.L. He who is; a study in traditional theism. London, 1943.
Phil 8667.22.10 Mascall, E.L. Existence and analogy. London, 1949.
Phil 8667.23 Murry, John M. God, being an introduction to the science of metabiology. London, 1929.
Phil 8667.25 Mauthner, F. Der Atheismus und seine Geschichte im Abendlande. Stuttgart, 1922-23. 4v.
Phil 8667.26 Martins, Diamantino. O problema de Deus. Braga, 1957.
Phil 8667.27 Murray, J.C. The problem of God. New Haven, 1964.
Phil 8667.29 Moscow. Gosudarstvennaia Biblioteka SSSR Imeni V.I. Lenina. Osnovy nauchnogo ateizma. Moskva, 1966.
Phil 8667.30 MacIntyre, Alasdair C. The religious significance of atheism. N.Y., 1969.
Phil 8667.35 Masi, Giorgio. Dalla religione degli dei alla religione dell'uomo. Milano, 1967.
Phil 8667.40 Morel, Georges. Problèmes actuels de religion. Paris, 1968.
Phil 8667.45 Moderner Atheismus und Moral. Freiburg, 1968.
Phil 8667.50 Mavrodes, George I. Belief in God; a study in the epistemalogy of religion. N.Y., 1970.
Phil 8667.52 Maréchal, Pierre. Culte et loix d'une societé d'hommes sans Dieu. Paris, 1967.

Phil 8655 - 8680 Philosophy of religion - Treatises on special topics - God - Individual authors (A-Z) - cont.

Phil 8667.54 Mizor, Nikolai. Metadologicheski problemi na ateizma. Sofiia, 1970.
Phil 8668.1 Naville, E. Le père céleste. Genève, 1866.
Phil 8668.1.5 Naville, E. The heavenly father. Boston, 1867.
Phil 8668.1.10 Naville, E. Det ondas problem. Stockholm, 1872.
Phil 8668.2 Nieuwentijt, B. L'existence de Dieu. Paris, 1725.
Phil 8668.3 Norlin, C. Étude laique de la notion de Dieu. Paris, 1906.
Phil 8668.4.5 Newton, J.F. My idea of God. Boston, 1927.
Phil 8668.5 Noyes, A. The unknown god. London, 1937.
Phil 8668.6 Nink, Gaspar. Philosophische Gotteslehre. München, 1948.
Phil 8668.7 Noto, Antonio di. L'evidenza di Dio nella filosofia del secolo XIII. Padova, 1958.
Phil 8668.8 Noce, Augusto del. Il problema dell'ateismo. 2. ed. Bologna, 1964.
Phil 8668.9 Nabert, Jean. Le désir de Dieu. Paris, 1966.
Phil 8668.10 Nastol'naia Kniga ateista. Moskva, 1968.
Phil 8669.1 Orr, John. Theism. London, 1857.
Phil 8669.1.5 Orr, John. English deism. Grand Rapids, 1934.
Phil 8669.2 Franklin, Maria. Observations on the chronology of scripture. N.Y., 1795.
Phil 8669.3.5 Otto, Rudolf. The idea of the holy. London, 1928.
Phil 8669.3.25 Geyser, Joseph. Intellekt oder Gemüt? Eine philosophische Studie über Rudolf Ottos Buch "Das Heilige". Freiburg, 1922.
Phil 8669.3.29 Seifert, P. Die Religionsphilosophie bei Rudolf Otto. Inaug. Diss. Dusseldorf, 1936.
Phil 8669.4 Oursler, F. Why I know there is a God. 1. ed. Garden City, N.Y., 1950.
Phil 8669.5 O'Connor, William R. The natural desire for God. Milwaukee, 1948.
Phil 8669.6 O'Brien, Thomas C. Metaphysics and the existence of God. Washington, 1960.
Phil 8669.7 O religii; khrestomatiia. Moskva, 1963.
Phil 8669.8 Yaroslavl', Russia (City). Gosudarstvennyi Pedagogicheskii Institut. Kafedra Filosofii. Osnovy nauchnogo ateizma. Iaroslavl', 1963.
Phil 8669.9 Ortuzar Arriaga, Martin. Los prenotandos del conocimiento natural de Dios. Madrid, 1963.
Phil 8670.3 Parker, S. Disputationes de Deo. London, 1678.
Htn Phil 8670.4* Pelling, E. A discourse concerning the existence of God. London, 1696.
Phil 8670.5 Philipps, J.T. Dissertatio historico-philosophica de atheismo. London, 1716.
Phil 8670.5.5 Philipps, J.T. Dissertationes historicae quatuor. London, 1735.
Phil 8670.5.10 Philipps, J.T. Historia atheismi. Altdorfi Noricorum, 1713. 3 pam.
Phil 8670.6 Poetter, F.C. Der persönliche Gott und Welt. Elberfeld, 1875.
Phil 8670.7 Prout, W. Chemistry, meteorology and the function of digestion considered with reference to natural theology. London, 1834.
Phil 8670.7.2 Prout, W. Chemistry, meteorology and the function of digestion considered with reference to natural theology. Philadelphia, 1834.
Phil 8670.8 Prolegomena to theism. N.Y., 1910.
Phil 8670.9 Rigou, Arthur C. The problem of theism. London, 1908.
Phil 8670.10 Pereira de Sampaio, José. A idéa de Deus. Porto, 1902.
Phil 8670.11 Pounder, R.M. Some thoughts about God. Toronto, 1923.
Phil 8670.12.5 Platner, E. Über den Atheismus. Leipzig, 1783.
Phil 8670.13 Petty, Orville A. Common sense and God. New Haven, 1936.
Phil 8670.14 Pythian-Adams, W.J. The people and the presence. London, 1942.
Phil 8670.15 Parkes, J.W. God and human progress. Harmondsworth, Eng., 1944.
Phil 8670.16 Papini, G. The memoirs of God. Boston, 1926.
Phil 8670.17 Picard, Max. Die Flucht vor Gott. 2. Aufl. Erlenbach, 1935.
Phil 8670.17.2 Picard, Max. The flight from God. London, 1951.
Phil 8670.18 Przywara, Erich. Was ist Gott; cinc Summula. Nürnberg, 1953.
Phil 8670.19 Pinto, Raphael de Souza. Deus, pensamento e universo. Curitiba, 1959.
Phil 8670.20 Pantskhawa, I.D. Osnovnye voprosy nauchnogo ateizma. Moskva, 1962.
Phil 8670.20.2 Moscow. Universitet. Kafedra Istorii i Teorii Ateizma. Osnovnye voprosy nauchnogo ateizma. 2. izd. Moskva, 1966.
Phil 8670.20.5 Pantskhawa, I.D. Istoriia i teoriia ateizma. Moskva, 1962.
Phil 8670.21 Plantinga, Alvin. The ontological argument. Garden City, N.Y., 1965.
Phil 8670.21.5 Plantinga, Alvin. God and other minds. Ithaca, 1967.
Phil 8670.22 Pike, Nelson craft. God and timelessness. N.Y., 1970.
Phil 8670.24 Pita Carpenter, Tomás. El ateismo de las masas. Madrid, 1969.
Phil 8672.1 Randles, M. First principles of faith. London, 1884.
Htn Phil 8672.2* Ray, J. The wisdom of God manifested in the works of the creation. v.1-2. London, 1714.
Phil 8672.2.2 Ray, J. The wisdom of God manifested in the works of the creation. v.1-2. London, 1717.
Htn Phil 8672.2.3*A Ray, J. The wisdom of God manifested in the works of the creation. v.1-2. London, 1704.
Htn Phil 8672.2.3*B Ray, J. The wisdom of God manifested in the works of the creation. v.1-2. London, 1704.
Htn Phil 8672.2.5* Ray, J. The wisdom of God manifested in the works of the creation. London, 1691.
Phil 8672.3 Ritter, H. Über die Erkenntniss Gottes in der Welt. Hamburg, 1836.
Phil 8672.4 Robertson, A. The laws of thought. London, 1865.
Phil 8672.5 Romanes, J. A candid examination of theism. London, 1878.
Phil 8672.6 Royce, J. The conception of God. Berkeley, 1895.
Phil 8672.6.4A Royce, J. The conception of God. N.Y., 1898.
Phil 8672.6.4B Royce, J. The conception of God. N.Y., 1898.
Phil 8672.6.5 Royce, J. The conception of God. N.Y., 1894.
Phil 8672.6.6 Royce, J. The conception of God. N.Y., 1902.
Phil 8672.7 Runze, G. Der ontologische Gottesbeweis. Halle, 1882.
Phil 8672.8 Reinhard, J. Gott und die Seele. Inaug. Diss. Erlangen, 1908.
Phil 8672.9 Read, E.A. The idea of God in relation to theology. Chicago, 1900.
Phil 8672.10 Religion and life;...address by...faculty of Meadville Theological School. Boston, 1909.
Phil 8672.11 Richards, William. Reflections on French atheism. 2. ed. Lynn, n.d.

Classified Listing

Phil 8655 - 8680   Philosophy of religion - Treatises on special topics -
God - Individual authors (A-Z) - cont.

Phil 8672.12 — Richard, Gaston. L'athéisme dogmatique en sociologie religieuse. Strasbourg, 1923.
Phil 8672.13 — Rensi, G. Apologia dell'ateismo. Roma, 1925.
Phil 8672.14 — Raven, Charles E. Evolution and the Christian concept of God. London, 1936.
Phil 8672.18.3 — Reusner, M.A. Nuzhna li vera v Boga. 3. izd. Moskva, 1923.
Phil 8672.19 — Kostenne, P. La foi des athées. Paris, 1953.
Phil 8672.20 — Ricciotti, G. Dio nella ricerca umana. 3. ed. Roma, 1954.
Phil 8672.22 — Rohde, Hubert. Mensch ohne Gott. Freiburg, 1961.
Phil 8672.24 — Riazantsev, N.I. Chto takoe ateizm. Moskva, 1961.
Phil 8672.25 — Robinson, R. An atheist's values. Oxford, 1964.
Phil 8672.26 — Romanov, Aleksandr A. Dorogami zemli. Moskva, 1965.
Phil 8672.28 — Rizzacasa, Aurelio. Il problema di Dio nella filosofia occidentale. Viterbo, 1969?
Phil 8672.30 — Ritti, Jean Marie Paul. De la notion de Dieu d'après la méthode sentimentale. Paris, 1930.
Phil 8673.1 — Saisset, E.E. Essai de philosophie religieuse. Paris, 1859.
Phil 8673.1.5 — Saisset, E.E. Essay on religious philosophy. Edinburgh, 1863. 2v.
Phil 8673.2 — Samuelson, J. Views of the deity. London, 1871.
Phil 8673.4 — Staab, K. Die Gottesbeweise. Paderborn, 1909.
Phil 8673.5 — Schwab, L.H. The kingdom of God. N.Y., 1897.
Phil 8673.6.2 — Pattison, A. The idea of God. 2. ed. N.Y., 1920.
Phil 8673.6.7 — Gallagher, Denis Maria. Pringle-Pattison's idea of God. Washington, D.C., 1933.
Phil 8673.7 — Schmidt, Wilhelm. L'origine de l'idée de Dieu. pt.1. Paris, 1910.
Phil 8673.8 — Specker, Gideon. Versuch eines neuen Gottesbegriffs. Stuttgart, 1902.
Phil 8673.9 — Sacchi, Gaetano. Esistenza di Dio. Roma, 1919.
Phil 8673.10 — Savage, M.J. Belief in God. 2. ed. Boston, 1881.
Phil 8673.11 — Sheen, F.J. God and intelligence in modern philosophy. London, 1925.
Phil 8673.12 — Smith, N.K. Is divine existence credible? London, 1931.
Phil 8673.13 — Schock, Adolph. The problem of God's identity in cosmic change. Chicago, 1932.
Htn   Phil 8673.14* — Stephens, William. An account of the growth of deism in England. London, 1696.
Phil 8673.15 — Streeter, B.H. The God who speaks. N.Y., 1936.
Phil 8673.16 — Schütz, A. Gott in der Geschichte. Salzburg, 1936.
Phil 8673.17 — Seth, A. Two lectures on theism delivered on the occasion of the sesquicentennial celebration of Princeton University. N.Y., 1897.
Phil 8673.18 — Saitta, G. Il problema di Dio e la filosofia della immanenza. Bologna, 1953.
Phil 8673.19 — Steenberghen, Fernand van. Dieu caché. Louvain, 1961.
Phil 8673.20 — Sputnik ateista. 2. izd. Moskva, 1961.
Phil 8673.20.5 — The atheist's handbook. n.p., 196-.
Phil 8673.21 — Sertillanges, Antonio Gilbert. Dieu ou rien? Paris, 1965.
Phil 8673.23 — Steenberghen, Fernand van. Hidden God; how do we know that God exists? Saint Louis, 1966.
Phil 8673.26 — Schoonbrood, C.A. Wijsgerige teksten over het absolute. Arnhem, 1967.
Phil 8673.27 — Shekhterman, Efim I. Vera ili zhanie. Alme-Ata, 1967.
Phil 8673.30 — Schmucker, Josef. Die primären Quellen des Gottesglaubens. Freiburg, 1967.
Phil 8673.32 — Il senso dell'ateismo contemporaneo. Bologna, 1967.
Phil 8673.34 — Ivanov, Ivan G. Rol' estestvornaniia v razvitii ateisticheskogo miroponimaniia. Moskva, 1969.
Phil 8673.36 — Seidlitz, Carl Siegmund von. Briefe über Gott und Unsterblichkeit. Bruxelles, 1968.
Phil 8673.38 — Sencer, Muammer. Allah neden var. Istanbul, 1970.
Phil 8674.1 — Tait, J. Mind in matter. London, 1884.
Phil 8674.2 — Taylor, G. The indications of the creator. N.Y., 1852.
Phil 8674.3 — Thompson, R.A. Christian theism. N.Y., 1856.
Phil 8674.4 — Tyerman, D. Essays on the wisdom of God. London, 1818.
Phil 8674.5 — Pamphlet box. Theistic Endeavour Society.
Phil 8674.6 — Tuttle, Hudson. Evolution of the God and Christ ideas. Berlin, 1906.
Phil 8674.7 — Trap, William M. Divine personality. Ann Arbor, 1925.
Phil 8674.8 — Turner, J.E. Personality and reality. N.Y., 1926.
Phil 8674.8.7 — Turner, J.E. The nature of deity; a sequel to Personality and reality. London, 1927.
Phil 8674.8.15 — Turner, J.E. The revelation of deity. London, 1931.
Phil 8674.9 — Trattner, Ernest R. The autobiography of God. N.Y., 1930.
Phil 8674.10 — Thoughts on theism with suggestions towards a public religious service. London, 1880.
Phil 8674.11 — Thornton, L.S. The incarnate Lord. London, 1928.
Phil 8674.12 — Trueblood, D.E. Knowledge of God. N.Y., 1939.
Phil 8674.13 — Tresmoutant, Claude. Essai sur la connaissance de Dieu. Paris, 1959.
Phil 8674.14 — Tugov, Iu.M. Osnovy nauchnogo ateizma. Moskva, 1959.
Phil 8674.16 — Tvethoworn, Illtyd. Absolute value: a study in Christian theism. London, 1970.
Htn   Phil 8676.1* — Vanino, G.C. Amphitheatrum. Lugdunum, 1615.
Phil 8676.2 — Vorstius, Conrad. Tractatus theologicus dedeo. Steinfursti, 1610. 2 pam.
Phil 8676.3 — Voysey, C. Theism as a science of natural theology. London, 1895.
Phil 8676.3.5 — Voysey, C. Sermons preached at St. George's Hall, Laugham Place. London, 1872-77. 4v.
Phil 8676.3.10 — Pamphlet box. Collected sermons.
Phil 8676.3.80 — Pamphlet box. Voysey, Charles.
Phil 8676.3.85 — Pamphlet box. Voysey establishment fund publications.
Phil 8676.4 — Vance, J.G. The sovereignty of God. Oxford, 1934.
Phil 8676.5 — Verret, Michel. Les marxistes et la religion. Paris, 1961.
Phil 8676.5.3 — Verret, Michel. Les marxistes et la religion. 3. éd. Paris, 1966.
Phil 8676.6 — Voronitsyn, I.P. Istoriia ateizma. 3. izd. Moskva, 1930.
Phil 8676.7 — Voprosy nauchnogo ateizma. Moskva. 1,1966+ 12v.
Phil 8677.1 — Ward, W.G. Essays on the philosophy of theism. London, 1884. 2v.
Phil 8677.2 — Wesley, J. A survey...wisdom of God in the creation. Bristol, 1770. 3v.
Phil 8677.3 — Whewell, William. Astronomy and general physics, considered with reference to natural theology. London, 1833.
Phil 8677.3.2 — Whewell, William. Astronomy and general physics, considered with reference to natural theology. London, 1834.
Phil 8677.3.3 — Whewell, William. Astronomy and general physics, considered with reference to natural theology. N.Y., 1841.

Phil 8655 - 8680   Philosophy of religion - Treatises on special topics -
God - Individual authors (A-Z) - cont.

Phil 8677.3.6 — Whewell, William. Astronomy and general physics, considered with reference to natural theology. 7. ed. London, 1852.
Phil 8677.4 — Whish, J.C. The first cause. London, 1855.
Phil 8677.5 — Wise, Thomas. A confutation of the reason and philosophy of atheism. London, 1706. 2v.
Phil 8677.6 — Weener, J. Scheping en voorzienigheid. Utrecht, 1899.
Phil 8677.7 — Walcott, G.D. Kantian and Lutheran elements in Ritschl's conception of God. N.Y., 1904.
Phil 8677.8 — Ward, James. The realm of ends, or Pluralism and theism. Cambridge, 1911.
Phil 8677.8.2 — Ward, James. The realm of ends, or Pluralism and theism. 2. ed. Cambridge, 1912.
Phil 8677.8.3 — Ward, James. The realm of ends, or Pluralism and theism. 3. ed. Cambridge, 1920.
Phil 8677.9 — Wells, H.G. God the invisible king. N.Y., 1917.
Phil 8677.9.5 — Wells, H.G. God the invisible king. London, 1917.
Phil 8677.9.80 — Archer, William. God and Mr. Wells. N.Y., 1917.
Phil 8677.10 — Wobbermin, George. Christian belief in God. New Haven, 1918.
Phil 8677.11 — Weill, Alexandre. L'athéisme déraciné de la science...démocratie. Paris, 1878.
Phil 8677.11.5 — Weill, Alexandre. Lois et mystères de la création. Paris, 1896.
Phil 8677.11.10 — Weill, Alexandre. Gesetze und Mysterien der Liebe. 1. Aufl. Berlin, 1895.
Phil 8677.12.2 — Walter von Walthoffen, Hippolyt. Die Gottesidee in religiöser und spekulativer Richtung. Wien, 1904.
Phil 8677.13 — Wyneken, G.A. Amor dei intellectualis. Greifswald, 1898.
Phil 8677.14 — Willink, M.D.R. The holy and the living God. London, 1931.
Phil 8677.15 — Walmarans, H.P. Die mens naar die beeld van God. Purmerend, 1932.
Phil 8677.16 — Whitehead, George. The case against theism. London, 1922.
Phil 8677.17 — Walker, L.J. The return to God. London, 1933.
Phil 8677.18 — Werfel, Franz. Können wir ohne Gottesglauben Leben? Berlin, 1932.
Phil 8677.19 — Williams, Charles. He came down from heaven. London, 1938.
Phil 8677.20 — Watts, A.W. The supreme identity. London, 1950.
Phil 8677.21 — Wolfson, H.A. The Muslim attributes and the Christian trinity. Cambridge, Mass., 1956.
Phil 8680.5 — Zuver, Dudley. Retreat to reality. N.Y., 1959.

Phil 8685   Philosophy of religion - Treatises on special topics - Pantheism

Phil 8685.1 — Daniélo, J. Du panthéisme. Paris, 1848.
Phil 8685.2 — DeConcilio, J. Catholicity and pantheism. pt.1. N.Y., 1874.
Phil 8685.3 — Hittell, J.S. A plea for pantheism. N.Y., 1857.
Phil 8685.4 — Jäsche, G.B. Der Pantheismus. Berlin, 1826-32. 3v.
Phil 8685.4.5 — Pitter, A.H. Die Halb-Kantianer und der Pantheismus (veranlasst durch Jäsche's Pantheismus). Berlin, 1827.
Phil 8685.5 — Manning, J.M. Half truths and the truth. Boston, 1872.
Phil 8685.6 — Maret, H.L.C. Essai sur le panthéisme. Paris, 1841.
Phil 8685.7 — Martha-Beker, F. Spiritualisme et panthéisme. Paris, 1867.
Phil 8685.8 — Mill, W.H. Observations...pantheistic principles. Cambridge, 1855.
NEDL   Phil 8685.9 — Plumptre, C.E. General sketch...history of pantheism. London, 1881. 2v.
Phil 8685.11 — Picton, J.A. The religion of the universe. London, 1904.
Phil 8685.11.5 — Picton, J.A. Pantheism, its story and significance. London, 1905.
Phil 8685.12 — Jundt, A. Histoire du panthéisme populaire. Strasbourg, 1875.
Phil 8685.13 — Pike, G.R. The divine drama; the manifestation of God. N.Y., 1899.
Phil 8685.14 — Amryc, C. Pantheism. n.p., 1898.
Phil 8685.15 — Urquhart, W.S. Pantheism, and the value of life. Thesis. London, 1919.
Phil 8685.16 — Klockhoff, D. Om den pantheistiska esthetiken. Academisk ävhandling. Upsala, 1864.
Phil 8685.17 — Weissenborn, G. Vorlesungen über Pantheismus und Theismus. Marburg, 1859.
Phil 8685.18 — Rosenkranz, K. Die Naturreligion. Iserlohn, 1831.
Phil 8685.19 — Günther, A. Thomas a Scrupulis. Wien, 1835.
Phil 8685.20 — Hugenholtz, P.H. Ethisch pantheisme. Amsterdam, 1903.
Phil 8685.21 — Bersot, E. Du spiritualisme et de la nature. Paris, 1846.
Phil 8685.22 — Masferrer, A. Helios. San Salvador, 1963.

Phil 8689   Philosophy of religion - Treatises on special topics - Religion and science - Pamphlet volumes; Collected authors

Phil 8689.1 — Pamphlet vol. Religion and science. 1874-1926. 32 pam.
Phil 8689.2 — Pamphlet box. Religion and science.
Phil 8689.100 — Zimmerman, Paul A. Darwin, evolution, and creation. Saint Louis, 1959.
Phil 8689.105 — Science et théologie: méthode et langage. Paris, 1970.

Phil 8690 - 8715   Philosophy of religion - Treatises on special topics - Religion and science - Individual authors (A-Z)

Phil 8690.2 — Agassiz, L.J.R. The structure of animal life. N.Y., 1866.
Phil 8690.3 — Anzoletti, Luisa. Per un nuovo patto fra la scienze e la religione. Milano, 1899.
Phil 8690.4 — Anthony, H.D. Relativity and religion. London, 1927.
Phil 8690.5 — Alstrin, Eric. Exercitium academicum. Upsaliae, 1727.
Phil 8690.6 — Anderson, Paul R. Science in defense of liberal religion. N.Y., 1933.
Phil 8690.12 — Abelé, Jean. Le christianisme se désintéressé-t-il de la science? Paris, 1960.
Phil 8690.14 — Akademiia Nauk SSSR. Institutii Filosofii. Dostizheniia estestvoznaniia i religiia. Moskva, 1960.
X Cg   Phil 8691.2 — Beecher, H.W. Evolution and religion. pt.1. N.Y., 1885.
Phil 8691.3 — Bixby, J.T. Similarities of physical and religious knowledge. N.Y., 1876.
Phil 8691.4 — Burr, E.F. Pater mundi. 1st series. Boston, 1870.
Phil 8691.4.2 — Burr, E.F. Pater mundi. 2nd series. Boston, 1873.
Htn   Phil 8691.5* — Boyle, R. Some considerations about the reconcileablness of reason and religion. London, 1675.
NEDL   Phil 8691.6.1 — Boutroux, E. Science et religion. Paris, 1908.
Phil 8691.6.5 — Boutroux, E. Science and religion in contemporary philosophy. London, 1909.
Phil 8691.6.10 — Boutroux, E. Wissenschaft und Religion in der Philosophie unserer Zeit. Leipzig, 1910.
Phil 8691.7 — Buckland, William. Vindiciae geologicae. Oxford, 1820.

379

Classified Listing

Phil 8690 - 8715 Philosophy of religion - Treatises on special topics - Religion and science - Individual authors (A-Z) - cont.

Itn Phil 8691.8F* Burnet, Thomas. The theory of the earth. v.1-4. London, 1684-90.

Itn Phil 8691.8.2F* Burnet, Thomas. The theory of the earth. 2. ed. London, 1690-91. 4 pam.

Phil 8691.8.4 Burnet, Thomas. The sacred theory of the earth. London, 1719. 2v.

Itn Phil 8691.8.5* Burnet, Thomas. Telluris theoria sacra. v.1-2. London, 1681-89.

Phil 8691.8.7 Burnet, Thomas. The sacred theory of the earth. London, 1722-26. 2v.

Phil 8691.8.9 Burnet, Thomas. The sacred theory of the earth. Glasgow, 1753. 2v.

Phil 8691.8.12 Burnet, Thomas. The sacred theory of the earth. 7. ed. London, 1759. 2v.

Phil 8691.8.15 Burnet, Thomas. The sacred theory of the earth. London, 1965.

Phil 8691.9 Bonney, T.G. Christian doctrines and modern thought. London, 1892.

Phil 8691.10 Brookshire, E.V. The law of human life; scriptures in the light of science. N.Y., 1916.

Phil 8691.11 Buisson, F. La religion, la morale, et la science...quatre conference. 3. éd. Paris, 1904.

Phil 8691.12.5 Chalmers, Thomas. On the power, wisdom and goodness of God. London, 1865.

Phil 8691.12.5.5 Chalmers, Thomas. On the power, wisdom and goodness of God. London, 1839. 2v.

Phil 8691.13 Borrows, Samuel Jure. Science and immortality. Boston, 1887.

Phil 8691.14 Borrero Echeverria, E. La vieja ortodoxia y la ciencia moderna. Habana, 1879.

Phil 8691.15 Bach, W.H. Big Bible stories. Lilly Dale, N.Y., 1897.

Phil 8691.16 Broglie, Paul. La science et la religion. Paris, 1885.

Phil 8691.17 Bell, A.J. Whence comes man; from nature or from God? London, 1888.

Phil 8691.18 Barthélemy-Saint-Hilaire, J. La philosophie dans ses rapports avec les sciences et la religion. Paris, 1889.

Phil 8691.19 Barry, W. The triumph of life. London, 1928.

Phil 8691.20 Bruhn, Wilhelm. Glauben und Wissen. Leipzig, 1921.

Phil 8691.21 Bond, Walter G. Three things that matter; religion, philosophy, science. London, 1931.

Phil 8691.22 Bavink, B. Science and God. London, 1933.

Phil 8691.23 Boorman, W.R. Independent young thinkers. Boston, 1933.

Phil 8691.24 Barnes, E.W. Scientific theory and religion. Cambridge, Eng., 1933.

Phil 8691.24.2 Barnes, E.W. Scientifc theory and religion. N.Y., 1934.

Phil 8691.25 Beckett, Lucile C. The world breath. London, 1935.

Phil 8691.25.2 Beckett, Lucile C. Everyman and the infinite. London, n.d.

Phil 8691.26 Bragg, W. Science and faith. London, 1941.

Phil 8691.27 Baker, Albert E. Science, Christianity and truth. London, 1943.

Phil 8691.28 Brockman, R.W. Het vraagteken achter de horizon van ons Leven. Assen, 1957.

Phil 8691.30 Boveri, Walter. Ethik und Atomzeitalter. Zürich, 1958.

Phil 8691.31 Bayne, Stephen. Space age to Christianity. N.Y., 1963.

Phil 8691.32 Booth, E.P. Religion ponders science. 1. ed. N.Y., 1964.

Phil 8691.33 Barbour, Ian G. Issues in science and religion. Englewood Cliffs, N.J., 1966.

Phil 8691.34 Babosov, Evgenii M. Nauckno-teknicheskaia revoliutsiia i modernizatsiia katolitsizma. Minsk, 1971.

Phil 8692.1 Cook, J. Christ and modern thought. Boston, 1881.

Phil 8692.2.1 Cooke, J.P. The credentials of science, the warrant of faith. 2. ed. N.Y., 1888.

Phil 8692.2.2 Cooke, J.P. The credentials of science the warrent of faith. N.Y., 1893.

Phil 8692.2.4 Cooke, J.P. Religion and chemistry. N.Y., 1864.

Phil 8692.2.5 Cooke, J.P. Religion and chemistry. N.Y., 1880.

Phil 8692.3 Coutts, John. The divine wisdom...nature, man and bible. London, 1907.

Phil 8692.3.5 Coutts, John. Old lamps and new light of science. London, 1911.

Phil 8692.3.7 Coutts, John. Homely thoughts on the city of God and way to find it. London, 1921.

Phil 8692.3.9 Coutts, John. The harmony and unity of the kingdom of God. London, 1922.

Phil 8692.3.10 Coutts, John. A prospective view of the new age. London, 1923.

Phil 8692.4 Crofton, D. Genesis and geology. Boston, 1857.

Phil 8692.5.3 Chalmers, Thomas. Series of discourses on the Christian revelation, viewed in connexion with modern astronomy. N.Y., 1817.

Phil 8692.5.5 Chalmers, Thomas. Series of discourses on the Christian revelation, viewed in connexion with modern astronomy. N.Y., 1818. 2 pam.

Phil 8692.5.7 Chalmers, Thomas. Series of discourses on the Christian revelation, viewed in connexion with modern astronomy. Hartford, 1818.

Phil 8692.5.12 Chalmers, Thomas. Series of discourses on the Christian revelation, viewed in connexion with modern astronomy. N.Y., 18- .

Phil 8692.5.15 Chalmers, Thomas. Series of discourses on the Christian revelation, viewed in connexion with modern astronomy. 12th ed. Glasgow, 1834.

Phil 8692.6 Crosby, H. The bible on the side of science. N.Y., 1875.

Phil 8692.7 Carpenter, W.B. Doctine of evolution in its relation to theism. London, 1882.

Phil 8692.8 Cotterill, H. On true relations of scientific thought and religious belief. London, 1878.

Phil 8692.9 Christmas, H. The world of matter and its testimony. London, 1848.

Phil 8692.10 Carus, Paul. The dawn of a new era. Chicago, 1899.

Phil 8692.10.15 Carus, Paul. The religion of science. Chicago, 1893.

Phil 8692.11 Cyon, Elie de. Dieu et science. 2. éd. Paris, 1912.

Phil 8692.12 Ceballos Dosamantes, J. Ciencia y religion del porvenir. México, 1897.

Phil 8692.13.8 Capron, F.H. The conflict of truth. 8. ed. London, 1927.

Phil 8692.14 Cotton, Edward. Has science discovered God? N.Y., 1931.

Phil 8692.15 Cohen, Chapman. God and evolution. London, 1925.

Phil 8692.17 Chicherin, Boris N. Nauka i religiia. Moskva, 1901.

Phil 8692.19 Chauvin, Rémy. God of the scientists. Baltimore, 1960.

Phil 8692.20A Coulson, C.A. Science and Christian belief. Chapel Hill, 1955.

Phil 8692.20B Coulson, C.A. Science and Christian belief. Chapel Hill, 1955.

Phil 8692.22 Chauchard, Paul. La création évolutive. Paris, 1957.

Phil 8692.24 Coggin, Philip. Art, science, and religion. London, 1962.

Phil 8690 - 8715 Philosophy of religion - Treatises on special topics - Religion and science - Individual authors (A-Z) - cont.

Phil 8692.26 Čížek, Fr. Od víry k vědě. Praha, 1961.

Phil 8692.27 Chicherin, Boris N. Nauka i religiia. Moskva, 1817.

Phil 8692.28 Clark, Cecil Henry Douglas. The scientist and the supernatural: a systematic examination of the relation between Christianity and humanism. London, 1966.

Phil 8693.1 Dick, T. The Christian philosopher. N.Y., 1827.

Phil 8693.1.2 Dick, T. The philosophy of a future state. Philadelphia, 1845. 2 pam.

Phil 8693.2 Davies, T.A. Answer to Hugh Miller and theoretic geologists. N.Y., 1860.

Phil 8693.2.5 Davies, T.A. Cosmogony, or The mysteries of creation. N.Y., 1857?

Phil 8693.3 Dove, J. A vindication of the divine authority. n.p., 1888.

Phil 8693.4.3 Draper, J.W. History of the conflict between religion and science. N.Y., 1875.

Phil 8693.4.3.10 Draper, J.W. History of the conflict between religion and science. N.Y., 1897.

Phil 8693.4.5 Draper, J.W. Historia de los conflictos entre la religion y la ciencia. Madrid, 1876.

Phil 8693.4.6 Draper, J.W. Los conflictos entre la ciencia y la religion. Madrid, 1876.

Phil 8693.5.2 Drummond, H. Natural law in the spiritual world. 17th ed. London, 1885.

Phil 8693.5.3 Drummond, H. Natural law in the spiritual world. Philadelphia, 1892.

Phil 8693.5.10A Drummond, H. Natural law in the spiritual world. N.Y., 1885.

Phil 8693.5.10B Drummond, H. Natural law in the spiritual world. N.Y., 1886.

Phil 8693.5.11 Drummond, H. Natural law in the spiritual world. N.Y., 1887.

Phil 8693.5.14 Drummond, H. Natural law in the spiritual world. N.Y., 189-.

Phil 8693.5.20 Drummond, H. Naturens lagar och andens verld. Stockholm, 1888.

Phil 8693.5.40 Drummond, H. Lowell lectures on the ascent of man. 13th ed. N.Y., 1906.

Phil 8693.5.70 Cockburn, S. The laws of nature...reply to Professor Drummond. London, 1886.

Phil 8693.6 Dwight, T. Thoughts of a catholic anatomist. London, 1911.

Phil 8693.7 Deyo, M.L. Spiritual evolution. Binghamton, N.Y., 1913.

Phil 8693.8 Dana, J.D. Creation or biblical cosmogony. Oberlin, 1885.

Phil 8693.9 Dale, T. Nelson. The outskirts of physical science. Boston, 1884.

Phil 8693.11 Doane, George W. The word of God to be studied with his works. Burlington, 1839.

Phil 8693.12 Dadson, Arthur J. Evolution and religion. London, 1893.

Phil 8693.12.5 Dadson, Arthur J. Evolution, and its bearing on religions. London, 1901.

Phil 8693.13 Dalin, C.O. Infor de stora varldsproblemen. Stockholm, 1912.

Phil 8693.14 Dessauer, F. Leben, Natur, Religion. 2. Aufl. Bonn, 1926.

Phil 8693.15 Dewart, E.H. (Mrs.). The march of life. Boston, 1929.

Phil 8693.16 Donat, Josef. Die Freiheit der Wissenschaft. 3. Aufl. Innsbruck, 1925.

Phil 8693.17 Davidson, M. The heavens and faith. London, 1936.

Phil 8693.20 Dessauer, F. Am Rande der Dinge. 2. Aufl. Frankfurt, 1952.

Phil 8693.20.5 Dessauer, F. Religion im Lichte der heutigen Naturwissenschaft. 3. Aufl. Frankfurt, 1952.

Phil 8693.20.10 Dessauer, F. Auf den Spuren der Unendlichkeit. Frankfurt, 1954.

Phil 8693.20.15 Tuchel, K. Die Philosophie der Technik. Frankfurt, 1964.

Phil 8693.25 Dubarle, D. Humanisme scientifique et raison chrétienne. Paris, 1953.

Phil 8694.1 Eucken, R. Wissenschaft und Religion. München, 1906.

Phil 8694.2 Elder, William. Ideas from nature. Philadelphia, 1898.

Phil 8694.3 Emery, J.A. Quelques lettres au physicien G.L. Le Sage. Paris, 1916.

Phil 8694.4A Eddington, Arthur. Science and the unseen world. N.Y., 1929.

Phil 8694.4B Eddington, Arthur. Science and the unseen world. N.Y., 1929.

Phil 8694.4.5 Eddington, Arthur. Science and the unseen world. N.Y., 1930.

Phil 8694.5 Ewald, Günter. Naturgestez und Schöpfung. Wuppertal, 1966.

Phil 8695.2 Fowle, T.W. The reconciliation of religion and science. London, 1873.

Phil 8695.3 Frankland, F.W. Thoughts on ultimate problems. 4. ed. London, 1911.

Phil 8695.4 Froehlich, J. Das Gesetz von der Erhaltung der Kraft und der Geist des Christentums. Leipzig, 1903.

Phil 8695.5 Ferreira da Silva, A.J. O ideal religioso e a cultura scientifica. Porto, 1908.

Phil 8695.5.3 Ferreira da Silva, A.J. A cultura das sciencias e os ensinamentos da igreja. Porto, 1908.

Phil 8695.5.5 Ferreira da Silva, A.J. Duas allocuçōs; a religiaõ, amparo do homen na vida. Porto, 1911.

Phil 8695.6 Frémont, G. Que l'orgueil de l'esprit est le grand écueil de la foi. Paris, 1900.

Phil 8695.7 Fulton, William. Nature and God. Edinburgh, 1927.

Phil 8695.8 Fargues, Paul. Transformisme et christianisme. Paris, 1909.

Phil 8695.9 Frohschammer, J. Über die Freiheit der Wissenschaft. München, 1861.

Phil 8695.10 Farrar, Adam Storey. Science in theology: sermons. Philadelphia, 1860.

Phil 8695.11 Feibleman, James. The pious scientist. N.Y., 1958.

Phil 8696.1 Gibson, S.T. Religion and science. London, 1875.

Phil 8696.2 Grote, A.R. The new infidelity. N.Y., 1881.

Phil 8696.3 Gardiner, F. Occasional papers. Middletown, Conn., 1881. 3 pam.

Phil 8696.4 Poole, R.S. Genesis of the earth and of man. 2. ed. London, 1860.

Phil 8696.5 Guyot, Arnold. Creation. N.Y., 1884.

Phil 8696.6 Gulliver, John P. Christianity and science. Andover, 1880.

Phil 8696.7 Gray, Asa. Natural science and religion. N.Y., 1880.

Phil 8696.8 Goodwin, H. Walks in the regions of science and faith. London, 1883.

Phil 8696.9 Gridley, Albert L. First chapter of Genesis as the rock foundation for science and religion. Boston, 1913.

Phil 8696.10 Gemelli, Agostino. Religione e scienza. Milano, 1920.

Phil 8690 - 8715   Philosophy of religion - Treatises on special topics -
Religion and science - Individual authors (A-Z) - cont.

Phil 8696.10.5   Gemelli, Agostino. Scienza ed apologetica. Milano, 1920.

Phil 8696.11   Goldsmith, W.M. Evolution or Christianity, God or Darwin? St. Louis, 1924.

Phil 8696.12   Gager, C.S. The relation between science and theology. Chicago, 1925.

Htn   Phil 8696.13*   Glanvill, Joseph. Philosophia pia. London, 1671.
Phil 8696.15   Gaulter, A. The riddle of nature. London, 1929.
Phil 8696.16   Gibbs, Jessie W. Evolution and Christianity. Memphis, 1930.

Phil 8696.17   Gregory, R.A. Religion in science and civilization. London, 1940.

Phil 8696.18   Gaskell, A. (Mrs.). Whence? Whither? Why? N.Y., 1939.
Phil 8696.19   Gordon, Ronald G. The philosophy of a scientist. London, 1947.

Phil 8696.20A   Gillispie, C.C. Genesis and geology. Cambridge, Mass., 1951.

Phil 8696.20B   Gillispie, C.C. Genesis and geology. Cambridge, Mass., 1951.

Phil 8696.20.5   Gillispie, C.C. Genesis and geology. Cambridge, 1969.
Phil 8696.21   Greene, J.C. Darwin and the modern world view. Baton Rouge, 1961.

Phil 8696.22   Gurev, Grigorii. Velikii konflikt. Moskva, 1965.
Phil 8696.23   Geloof en natuurwetenschap; studies over de verhouding van christelijk geloof en moderne natuurwetenschap. 's-Gravenhage, 1965-67. 2v.

Phil 8696.24   Gilch, Gerhard. Gebrochemes Weltbild. 1. Aufl. Stuttgart, 1966.

Phil 8696.25   Giret, André. L'astronomie et le sentiment religieux. Paris, 1965.

Phil 8696.26   Gilkey, Langdon Brown. Religion and the scientific future; reflections on myth, science, and theology. 1. ed. N.Y., 1970.

Phil 8696.27   Garadzha, Vikton I. Neotomizm. Razum. Nauka. Moskva, 1969.

Phil 8696.28   Giesswein, Sándor. Vilagegyetem es a lélek világa. Budapest, 1913.

NEDL   Phil 8697.1   Hutton, R.H. Aspects of religious and scientific thought. London, 1899.

Phil 8697.2   Hark, J.M. The unity of truth in Christianity and evolution. N.Y., 1888.

Phil 8697.4   Hitchcock, C.H. The relations of geology to theology. Andover, 1867.

Phil 8697.5   Huxley, T.H. Essays upon some controverted questions. N.Y., 1892.

Phil 8697.5.3   Huxley, T.H. Essays upon some controverted questions. N.Y., 1893.

Phil 8697.5.15   Huxley, T.H. Science and Christian tradition; essays. N.Y., 1898.

Phil 8697.5.20   Huxley, T.H. Science and Christian tradition; essays. N.Y., 1913.

Phil 8697.6   Hall, F.J. Recent work of angelican theologians. Chicago, 1912.

Phil 8697.7   Hodgson, Leonard. Theology in an age of science. Oxford, 1944.

Phil 8697.8   Hamlin, G.S. Human nature. N.Y., 1917.
Phil 8697.9   Hardwick, J.C. Religion and science. London, 1920.
Phil 8697.10   Hand, J.E. Ideals of science and faith. N.Y., 1904.
Phil 8697.11   Hoffmann, J.G. Kurtze Fragen von den natürlichen Dingen. Halle, 1757.

Phil 8697.13   Huxley, Julian S. What dare I think? London, 1931.
Phil 8697.13.5   Huxley, Julian S. What dare I think? N.Y., 1931.
Phil 8697.14   Hill, Mabel. Wise men worship. 1. ed. N.Y., 1931.
Phil 8697.15   Hayden, W.B. Science and revelation. Boston, 1852.
Phil 8697.16   Harrison, A.J. The ascent of faith. N.Y., 1894.
Phil 8697.17   Hocking, W.E. Science and the idea of God. Chapel Hill, 1944.

Phil 8697.18   Heim, Karl. The transformation of the scientific world view. N.Y., 1953.

Phil 8697.19   Hengstenberg, Hans E. Sein und Ursprünglichkeit. München, 1958.

Phil 8697.20   Hanaghan, J. Society, evolution and revelation. Dublin, 1957.

Phil 8697.21   Harris, Errol E. Revelation through reason. New Haven, 1958.

Phil 8697.23   Hennemann, Gerhard. Philosophie, Religion, moderne Naturwissenschaft. Witten, 1955.

Phil 8697.25   Habgood, J.S. Religion and science. London, 1964.
Phil 8697.25.2   Habgood, J.S. Truths in tension. 1. ed. N.Y., 1965.
Phil 8697.26   High, Dallas M. New essays on religious language. N.Y., 1969.

Phil 8697.28   Howe, Günter. Die Christenheit im Atomzeitalter. Stuttgart, 1970.

Phil 8698.1   Inge, W.P. Science and ultimate truth. London, 1926.
Phil 8698.5   Irkolin, N.E. Vera i znanie; o Boge, religii. Muinkhen, 1961.

Phil 8698.10   Ikeda, Daisaku. Science and religion. Tokyo, 1965.
Phil 8698.15   Schueppe, Otto. Gott sprach-es-ward. Bern, 1970.
Phil 8699.1   Jones, Richard U. The scientifc eye of faith. Boston, 1935.

Phil 8699.5   Joad, Cyril E.M. The recovery of belief. London, 1952.
Phil 8700.1   Keyser, C.J. Science and religion, rational and superrational. New Haven, 1914.

Htn   Phil 8700.2*   Keill, J. Examination of Dr. Burnett's theory of the earth. Oxford, 1698.

Phil 8700.2.2   Keill, J. Examination of Dr. Burnett's theory of the earth. Oxford, 1734. 2 pam.

Phil 8700.2.6   Keill, J. Examination of the reflections on the theory of the earth. Oxford, 1699.

Phil 8700.7   Keebler, R.S. The Tennessee evolution case. Memphis, 1925.

Phil 8700.8   King, David. The principles of geology explained. N.Y., 1851.

Phil 8700.9   Klyce, S. Sins of science. Boston, 1925.
Phil 8700.12   Kettner, F. The synthesis of science and religion. N.Y., 1939.

Phil 8700.14   Kocher, Paul Harold. Science and religion in Elizabethan England. San Marino, Calif., 1955.

Phil 8700.14.5   Kocher, Paul Harold. Science and religion in Elizabethan England. N.Y., 1969.

Phil 8700.16   Kryvelev, I.A. Sovremennoe bogoslov'e i nauka. Moskva, 1959.

Phil 8700.18   Klotz, John William. Genes. Saint Louis, 1959.
Phil 8701.1   Lord, D.N. Geognosy, or The facts and principles of geology against theories. N.Y., 1855.

Phil 8701.2.2   Lewis, Tayler. Six days of creation. 2nd ed. Schenectady, 1855.

Phil 8690 - 8715   Philosophy of religion - Treatises on special topics -
Religion and science - Individual authors (A-Z) - cont.

Phil 8701.2.4   Lewis, Tayler. Faith, the life of science. Albany, 1838.
Phil 8701.2.7   Dana, J.D. Science and the bible, a review of the Six days of creation. Andover, 1856.

Phil 8701.2.15   Lewis, Tayler. Nature, progress, ideas. Schenectady, 1850.

Phil 8701.3   Troels Lund, Troels Frederik. Himmelsbild und Weltanschauung. Leipzig, 1900.

Phil 8701.3.4   Troels Lund, Troels Frederik. Himmelsbild und Weltanschauung. 4. Aufl. Leipzig, 1913.

Phil 8701.3.6   Troels Lund, Troels Frederik. Himmelsbild und Weltanschauung. 5. Aufl. Leipzig, 1929.

Phil 8701.4   Lodge, Oliver Joseph. Science and immortality. N.Y., 1908.

Phil 8701.4.2   Lodge, Oliver Joseph. Science and immortality. N.Y., 1914.

Phil 8701.4.3   Lodge, Oliver Joseph. Man and the universe. 9. ed. London, 1911.

Phil 8701.4.3.5   Lodge, Oliver Joseph. Man and the universe. N.Y., 1920.
Phil 8701.4.4   Lodge, Oliver Joseph. The substance of faith allied with science. N.Y., 1907.

Phil 8701.4.5   Lodge, Oliver Joseph. The substance of faith allied with science. London, 1915.

Phil 8701.4.7   Lodge, Oliver Joseph. Reason and belief. N.Y., 1910.
Phil 8701.4.9   Lodge, Oliver Joseph. Reason and belief. 5. ed. London, 1911.

Phil 8701.4.13   Lodge, Oliver Joseph. Faith and knowledge, April, 1902. London, 19- .

Phil 8701.4.50   McCabe, Joseph. The religion of Sir Oliver Lodge. London, 1914.

Phil 8701.5   Le Conte, J. Religion and science. N.Y., 1874.
Phil 8701.6   Lang, O. Am Wendepunkt der Ideen. Wien, 1909.
Phil 8701.7.2   Laing, Samuel. Modern science and modern thought. 2. ed. London, 1885.

Phil 8701.8   Loisy, Alfred. De la discipline intellectuelle. Paris, 1919.

Phil 8701.9   Lamy, Bernard. Entretiens sur les sciences dans lesquels on apprend comment l'on doit étudier les sciences. Lyon, 1724.

Htn   Phil 8701.9.5*   Lamy, Bernard. Entretiens sur les sciences dans lesquels on apprend comment l'on doit étudier les sciences. Bruxelles, 1684.

Phil 8701.9.7   Lamy, Bernard. Entretiens sur les sciences dans lesquels on apprend comment l'on doit étudier les sciences. 3. éd. Lyon, 1706.

Phil 8701.9.9   Lamy, Bernard. Entretiens sur les seiences dans lesquels on apprend comment l'on doit étudier les sciences. Paris, 1966.

Phil 8701.10   Leslie, John. Revelation and science. Aberdeen, 1921.
Phil 8701.11   Lane, H.H. Evolution and Christian faith. Princeton, 1923.

Phil 8701.12   Luckey, L.W.A. Whence comest thou? Whither goest thou? Boston, 1927.

Phil 8701.13   Lorbeer, Floyd Irwing. A message of light, containing scientifc foundation for religion. Los Angeles, 1927.

Phil 8701.13.5   Lorbeer, Floyd Irwing. Philosophy of light. Los Angeles, 1932.

Phil 8701.14   Loewenberg, B.J. The controversy over evolution in New England, 1859-1873. n.p., 1935.

Phil 8701.15   Ladd, H.O. The trade of scientific thought away from religious beliefs. Boston, 1909.

Phil 8701.16   Lunn, Arnold. Science and the supernatural; a correspondence between Arnold Lunn and J.B.S. Haldane. N.Y., 1935.

Phil 8701.17   Lord, Eleazar. The epoch of creation. N.Y., 1851.
Phil 8701.18   Laffey, C. Religion and science. London, 1940.
Phil 8701.19   Lindsay, A.D. Religion, science, and society in the modern world. New Haven, 1943.

Phil 8701.20   Lee, John H. Are science and religion at strife? Evanston, 1945.

Phil 8701.21   Lecomte du Nouy, Pierre. Human destiny. N.Y., 1947.
Phil 8701.22   Lubac, H. de. The discovery of God. N.Y., 1960.
Phil 8701.23   Lemonnyer, Antoine. La révélation primitive, et les données actuelles de la science. Paris, 1914.

Phil 8701.24   Lindroth, Hjalmer. Filosofiska och teologiska essayer. Stockholm, 1965.

Phil 8702.1   Macbriar, R.M. Geology and geologists. London, 1843.
Phil 8702.2   McCausland, D. Sermons in stones. London, 1873.
Phil 8702.2.5   McCausland, D. Shinar. London, 1867.
Phil 8702.2.9   McCausland, D. Adam and the adamite. London, 1872.
Phil 8702.3   Mackenzie, H. Evolution illuminating the Bible. London, 1891.

Phil 8702.3.5   Mackenzie, H. Modern science unlocking the Bible. London, 1892.

Phil 8702.4   MacQueary, H. The evolution of man and Christianity. N.Y., 1890.

Phil 8702.5   Martin, J.L. Anti-evolution: Girardeau vs. Woodrow. Memphis, Tenn.? 1888.

Phil 8702.6   Miller, H. The testimony of the rocks. Boston, 1857.
Phil 8702.6.25   Miller, H. The two records: The mosaic and the geological. Boston, 1854.

Phil 8702.7.2   Mallock, W.H. Religion as a credible doctrine. N.Y., 1903.

Phil 8702.7.5   Mallock, W.H. The reconstruction of belief. London, 1905.
Phil 8702.7.7   Mallock, W.H. The reconstruction of religious belief. N.Y., 1905.

Phil 8702.8   Moore, W.U. The cosmos and the creeds. London, 1903.
Phil 8702.9   Merz, J.T. Religion and science. Edinburgh, 1915.
Phil 8702.10   Mason, Henry M. The relation between religion and science. n.p., 1839.

Phil 8702.11   Moigno, F.N.M. Un pequeño libro de actualidad. Puerto Rico, 1884.

Phil 8702.12.5   Moreux, T. Les confins de la science et de la foi. Paris, 1925. 2v.

Phil 8702.13   Millikan, R.A. Evolution in science and religion. New Haven, 1927.

Phil 8702.14   Mir, Miguel. Harmonia entre a sciencia a fé. v.2. Coimbra, 1892.

Phil 8702.15   Mikos, J. Eine wissenschaftliche Wellanschauung auf religiöser Grundlage. Leipzig, 1895.

Phil 8702.16A   Mather, K.F. Science in search of God. N.Y., 1928.
Phil 8702.16B   Mather, K.F. Science in search of God. N.Y., 1928.
Phil 8702.16.2   Mather, K.F. Science in search of God. N.Y., 1928.
Phil 8702.16.5   Mather, K.F. Crusade for life. Chapel Hill, N.C., 1949.
Phil 8702.17   Maria, R. de. Religione e scienza. Palermo, 1936.
Phil 8702.18   Metzger, H. Atraction universelle et religion naturelle. Paris, 1938. 3v.

Phil 8690 - 8715 **Philosophy of religion - Treatises on special topics -**
Religion and science - Individual authors (A-Z) - cont.

Phil 8702.19.5   Morrison, Abraham C. Man does not stand alone. N.Y., 1946.

Phil 8702.20   Miller, C.W. A scientist's approach to religion. N.Y., 1947.

Phil 8702.21   Morris, D.L. Possibilities unlimited. 1. ed. N.Y., 1952.

Phil 8702.22   Monsma, John C. The evidence of God in an expanding universe. N.Y., 1958.

Phil 8702.24   Mouiren, Trophine. La création. Paris, 1961.

Phil 8702.26   Masi, R. Religione. Brescia, 1958.

Phil 8702.28   MacMurray, John. Religion, art, and science. Liverpool, 1961.

Phil 8702.30   Muller, C. Science and faith, co-existence or synthesis? Louvain, 1962.

Phil 8702.32   Moretti, Jean. Biologie et réflexion chrétienne. Paris, 1967.

Phil 8702.34   Miller, Samuel Howard. Religion in a technical age. Cambrjdge, 1968.

Phil 8702.36   Mairlot, Édouard. Science et foi chrétienne. Bruxelles, 1968.

Phil 8703.1   Netto. F.J. Sociabilidade natural do homem. Povoa de Varzim, 1914.

Phil 8703.2   Needham, Joseph. Science, religion and reality. N.Y., 1928.

Phil 8703.2.5   Needham, Joseph. The great amphibium; four lectures. London, 1931.

Phil 8703.2.10   Needham, Joseph. Time: the refreshing river; essays and addresses, 1932-1942. London, 1943.

Phil 8703.2.15   Needham, Joseph. History is on our side. London, 1946.

Phil 8703.3   The naturalist: a dialogue. London, 1749. 2 pam.

Phil 8703.4   Nauka protiv religii. v.1- Moskva, 1967. 2v.

Phil 8703.5   Nasr, Segyed Hossein. The encounter of man and nature; the spiritual crisis of modern man. London, 1968.

Phil 8704.1.5   Otto, Rudolf. Naturalism and religion. London, 1907.

Phil 8704.2   Osborn, H.F. Evolution and religion. N.Y., 1923.

Phil 8704.2.5   Osborn, H.F. The earth spaks to Bryan. N.Y., 1925.

Phil 8704.3   Ostwald, Wilhelm. Wissenschaft contra Gottesglauben. Leipzig, 1960.

Phil 8705.1   Paine, M. A discourse on the soul and the principle of instinct. N.Y., 1848. 4 pam.

Phil 8705.1.2   Paine, M. A discourse on the soul and the principle of instinct. N.Y., 1848. 4 pam.

Phil 8705.1.5   Paine, M. A review of theoretical geology. N.Y., 1856.

Phil 8705.2   Pendleton, W.N. Science a witness for the Bible. Philadelphia, 1860.

Phil 8705.3   Perce, W.R. Geneses and modern science. N.Y., 1897.

Phil 8705.4.2   Powell, E.P. Our heredity from God. 2. ed. N.Y., 1888.

Phil 8705.4.5   Powell, E.P. Liberty and life. Chicago, 1889.

Phil 8705.5   Pye, S. The mosaic theory of the solar or planetary system. London, 1766.

Phil 8705.7   Phillips, S.L. Agreement of evolution and Christianity. Washington, 1904.

Phil 8705.8   Penn, G. A comparative estimate of the mineral and mosaical geology. London, 1822.

Phil 8705.9   Pike, S. Philosopha sacra: or The principles of natural philosophy. London, 1753.

Phil 8705.10   Plea for candor in Bible-reading. Jackson, 1878.

Phil 8705.11   Parker, Benjamin. A survey of six days work of creation. London, 1745.

Phil 8705.12   Pollach, Friedrich. Gesetz von der Erhaltung der Energie und christliche Glaube. Fulda, 1913.

Phil 8705.13   Panin, Ivan. The writings of Ivan Panin. New Haven, 1918.

Phil 8705.14   Prepin, Michael T. The new reformation. N.Y., 1927.

Phil 8705.15   Pedder, Henry C. Issues of the age. N.Y., 1874.

Phil 8705.16   Pensée scientifique et foi chrétienne. Paris, 1953.

Phil 8705.17   Perego, Angelo S.J. La creazione. Brescia, 1958.

Phil 8705.18   Pilkington, Roger. World without end. London, 1961.

Phil 8705.20   Perlman, Robert Odehyah. Science and religion for modern man. Jerusalem, 1964.

Phil 8705.22   Pégand, Georges. Ascèse et science. Paris, 1963.

Phil 8706.1   Quarterman, J. The mosaic cosmogony. n.p., n.d.

Phil 8706.3   Queffélec, H. La technique contre la foi? Paris, 1962.

Phil 8706.4   Quevremont, Pierre. Dieu et l'homme créateur. Paris, 1965.

Phil 8707.1   Reichenbach, H.G.L. Blicke in das Leben der Gegenwart. Dresden, 1856.

Phil 8707.2   Reusch, F.H. Nature and the Bible. Edinburgh, 1886. 2v.

Phil 8707.3   Rudder, W. The mutual relations of natural science and theology. Philadelphia, 1869.

Phil 8707.4   Rhind, W. The age of the earth. Edinburgh, 1838.

Phil 8707.5   Raymond, G.L. The psychology of inspiration. N.Y., 1908.

Phil 8707.6   Remarks on the religious sentiments of...eminent laymen. London, 1790. 2 pam.

Phil 8707.7   Rice, William N. Christian faith in an age of science. N.Y., 1903.

Phil 8707.7.3   Rice, William N. The return to faith. N.Y., 1916.

Phil 8707.7.5   Rice, William N. The poet of science and other addresses. N.Y., 1919.

Phil 8707.7.9   Rice, William N. Science and religion. Cincinnati, 1925.

Phil 8707.8   Rawson, F.L. The evolution of the world; or, Science from a religious point of view. Garden City, 1909.

Phil 8707.9   The relations of Christianity and science. N.Y., 1863.

Phil 8707.10   Russell, H.N. Fate and freedom. New Haven, 1927.

Phil 8707.11.2   Riley, W.B. Inspiration or evolution. 2. ed. Cleveland, 1926.

Phil 8707.12   Rahn, Carl. Science and the religious life. New Haven, 1928.

Phil 8707.13   Reuterdahl, A. The God of science. Minneapolis, 1928.

Phil 8707.14   Rigdon, Jonathan. Science and religion as they look to a layman. Danville, Ind., 1928.

Phil 8707.15   Rodger, James George. Passages from the scientist's Bible. Washington, 1931.

Phil 8707.16.5   Russell, Bertrand Russell. Religion and science. London, 1968.

Phil 8707.17   Ransom, J.C. God without thunder. N.Y., 1930.

Phil 8707.18   Regard, G. Etude biologique. Lausanne, 1937.

Phil 8707.19   Riba Elichabe, R. La ciencia confirma a Cristo. Rosario, 1939.

Phil 8707.20   Ross, W.D. Foundations of ethics. Oxford, 1939.

Phil 8707.21   Raven, C.E. Science, religion, and the future. Cambridge, Eng., 1943.

Phil 8707.21.5A   Raven, C.E. Natural religion and Christian theology. Cambridge, Eng., 1953. 2v.

Phil 8707.21.5B   Raven, C.E. Natural religion and Christian theology. v.2. Cambridge, Eng., 1953.

Phil 8707.22   Rowland, J. One man's mind. London, 1952.

Phil 8690 - 8715 **Philosophy of religion - Treatises on special topics -**
Religion and science - Individual authors (A-Z) - cont.

Phil 8707.24   Randall, John Herman. The role of knowledge in western religion. Boston, 1958.

Phil 8707.25   Roth, A. Stiinta si religie. Bucaresti, 1960.

Phil 8707.27   Robert, M.D. Approche contemporaine d'une affirmation de Dieu. Bruges, 1962.

Phil 8707.28   Ramsey, I.T. Religion and science: conflict and synthesis. London, 1964.

Phil 8707.29   Rotureau, G. Conscience religieuse et mentalité technique. Paris, 1962.

Phil 8707.30   Rust, Eric C. Science and faith. N.Y., 1967.

Phil 8707.32   Rueff, Jacques. Les Dieux et les rois, regards sur le pouvoir créateur. Paris, 1967.

Phil 8707.34   Rohrbach, Hans. Naturwissenschaft, Weltbild, Glaube. Wuppertal, 1967.

Phil 8707.36   Roqueplo, Philippe. La foi d'un mal-eroyant ou mentalité scientifique et vie de foi. Paris, 1969.

Phil 8707.38   Reusch, Franz Heinrich. Die biblische Schöpfungsgesichte und ihr Verhältniss zu den Ergebnissen der Naturforschung. Bonn, 1877.

Phil 8708.1   Savage, M.J. Evolution and religion. Philadelphia, 1886.

Phil 8708.2.7   Shaler, N.S. The interpretation of nature. 2. ed. Boston, 1893.

Phil 8708.4   Stokes, G.G. On the absence of real opposition between science and revelation. London, 1884?

Phil 8708.6   Sacred geology. London, 1847.

Phil 8708.7   The stars and the angels. London, 1858.

Phil 8708.8   Smyth, Newman. Through science to faith. N.Y., 1902.

Phil 8708.10   Simpson, James Y. The spiritual interpretation of nature. 2. ed. London, 1912.

Phil 8708.10.5   Simpson, James Y. Landmarks in the struggle between science and religion. N.Y., 1925?

Phil 8708.10.9   Simpson, James Y. Nature. New Haven, 1929.

Phil 8708.11   Sedgwick, William. Man's position in the universe. London, 1902.

Phil 8708.12   Sampson, H.E. Progressive creation. London, 1909. 2v.

Phil 8708.12.5   Sampson, H.E. Theou sophia...divine mysteries. London, 1918.

Phil 8708.13   Shafer, Robert. Christianity and naturalism. New Haven, 1926.

Phil 8708.14A   Shipley, Maynard. The war on modern science. N.Y., 1927.

Phil 8708.14A   Shipley, Maynard. The war on modern science. N.Y., 1927.

Phil 8708.15   Spaulding, E.G. What am I? N.Y., 1928.

Phil 8708.16   Snowden, J.H. Old faith and new knowledge. N.Y., 1928.

Phil 8708.17   Smith, Orlando Jay. Balance the fundamental verity. Boston, 1904.

Phil 8708.18   Singer, Charles. Religion and science considered in their historical relations. N.Y., 1929.

Phil 8708.19   Sanford, Hugh W. Science and faith, or The spiritual side of science. N.Y., 1930. 2v.

Phil 8708.20   Science and religion; a symposium. N.Y., 1931.

Phil 8708.21   Silliman, B. Suggestions relative to the philosophy of geology. New Haven, 1839.

Phil 8708.22   Smith, Nathan A. Through science to God. N.Y., 1936.

Phil 8708.24   Science and religion. London, 1931.

Phil 8708.25   Strömberg, G. The searchers. Philadelphia, 1948.

Phil 8708.26   Sinnott, Edmund Ware. Two roads to truth. N.Y., 1953.

Phil 8708.27   Sabine, P.E. Atoms, men and God. N.Y., 1953.

Phil 8708.28   Sinnott, Edmund Ware. Matter. 1. ed. N.Y., 1957.

Phil 8708.28.2   Sinott, Edmund Ware. Matter, mind and man. N.Y., 1962.

Phil 8708.29   Ginger, Ray. Six days or forever? Boston, 1958.

Phil 8708.29.5   Tompkins, Jerry R. D-days at Dayton. Baton Rouge, La., 1965.

Phil 8708.29.10   De Camp, Lyon Sprague. The great monkey trial. 1. ed. Garden City, 1968.

Phil 8708.30   Simonsson, Tord. Face to face with Darwinism. Lund, 1958.

Phil 8708.31   Scopes, John Thomas. Center of the storm. N.Y., 1967.

Phil 8708.32   Schumann, F.K. Uberwindung des Säkularismus in der Wissenschaft. Gladbeck, 195-.

Phil 8708.34   Samuel, Herbert S. A threefold cord. London, 1961.

Phil 8708.36   Schilling, Harold K. Science and religion. N.Y., 1962.

Phil 8708.37   Semmelroth, O. Die Welt als Schöpfung. Frankfurt, 1962.

Phil 8708.38   Science and revelation: a series of lectures. Belfast, 1875.

Phil 8708.40   Schiffers, Norbert. Fragen der Physik an die Theologie. 1. Aufl. Düsseldorf, 1968.

Phil 8708.42   Spülbeck, Otto. Zur Begegnung von Naturwissenschaft und Theologie. Einsiedeln, 1969.

Phil 8708.42.5   Spülbeck, Otto. Grenzfragen zwischen Naturwissenschaft und Glaube. München, 1970.

Phil 8708.44   Semeria, Giovanni. Scienza e fede e il liro preteso conflitto. Roma, 1903.

Phil 8709.1   Townsend, L.T. The Bible and other ancient literature in the nineteenth century. N.Y., 1888.

Phil 8709.1.5   Townsend, L.T. Credo. Boston, 1870.

Phil 8709.2   Tyndall, John. Address. Cambridge, 1874. 2 pam.

Phil 8709.2.4   Tyndall, John. Address...before British association. N.Y., 1875.

Phil 8709.2.9   Tyndall, John. Address. N.Y., 1874.

Phil 8709.2.13   Tyndall, John. Advancement of science. N.Y., 1874.

Phil 8709.2.14   Tyndall, John. Advancement of science. N.Y., 1874.

Phil 8709.2.50   McCosh, James. Ideas in nature overlooked by Dr. Tyndall. N.Y., 1875.

Phil 8709.3   Topinard, P. Science and faith. Chicago, 1899.

Phil 8709.4   Tucker, G.M. A layman's apology. Boston, 1913.

Phil 8709.5   Tupper, Martin F. Probabilities; an aid to faith. N.Y., 1847.

Phil 8709.6   Temple, William. The faith and modern thought. London, 1913.

Phil 8709.7   Thomson, S.H. Geology as an interpreter of scripture. Cincinnati, 1858.

Phil 8709.8   Tuttle, Hudson. Religion of man and ethics of science. Chicago, 1902.

X Cg   Phil 8709.9.5   Allen, Leslie H. Bryan and Darrow at Dayton. N.Y., 1925.

Phil 8709.11   Talamo, S. Il rinnovamento...tomistico e la scienza. Roma, 1927.

Phil 8709.11   Thallackson, E. Science, evolution, religion. Boston, 1927.

Phil 8709.12   Trumbull, William. Evolution and religion. N.Y., 1907.

Phil 8709.13   Taylor, Robert O.P. Universe within us. N.Y., 1931.

Phil 8709.14.5   Turner, Sharon. The sacred history of the world. 3. ed. London, 1833. 2v.

Phil 8709.14.6   Turner, Sharon. The sacred history of the world. v.1. N.Y., 1832.

Phil 8709.14.8   Turner, Sharon. The sacred history of the world. N.Y., 1835-39. 3v.

Phil 8690 - 8715   Philosophy of religion - Treatises on special topics -
Religion and science - Individual authors (A-Z) - cont.

Phil 8709.14.10	Turner, Sharon. The sacred history of the world. N.Y., 1835-36. 2v.
Phil 8709.15	Teller, Woolsey. The atheism of astronomy. N.Y., 1938.
Phil 8709.15.5	Teller, Woolsey. Essays of an atheist. N.Y., 1945.
Phil 8709.16	Thomas, J.B. The old Bible and the new science. 2. ed. N.Y., 1877.
Phil 8709.17	Thomson, J.A. Science and religion; being the Morse lecture for 1924. N.Y., 1925.
Phil 8709.18.5	Tóth, T. God's amazing world. N.Y., 1935.
Phil 8709.19	Tute, Richard C. After materialism - what? 1. ed. N.Y., 1945.
Phil 8709.20	Taylor, F.S. Man and matter. N.Y., 1953?
Phil 8709.21	Thomas, W. On the resolution of science and faith. N.Y., 1946.
Phil 8709.22	Temperley, H.N.V. A scientist who believes in God. London, 1961.
Phil 8709.23	Akademiia Nauk SSSR. Institut Filosofii. Uspekhi sovremennoi nauki i religiia. Moskva, 1961.
Phil 8709.24	Talafous, Camillus D. Readings in science and spirit. Englewood Cliffs, N.J., 1966.
Phil 8709.25	Tancher, Volodymyr K. Nauka oprovergaet religioznye dogmaty. Kiev, 1970.
Phil 8709.26	Torrance, Thomas Forsyth. God and rationality. London, 1971.
Phil 8710.1	Upham, F.W. The debate between the church and science. Andover, 1860.
Phil 8711.2	Vignon, Paul. Au sauffle de l'esprit créatur. Paris, 1946.
Phil 8712.05	Wayland, Francis. A discourse delivered at...dedication of...the chapel. Providence, 1835.
Phil 8712.1	Weaver, G.O. Moses and modern science. Cincinnati, 1872.
Phil 8712.3.3	White, Andrew Dickson. New chapters in the warfare of science. (Meteorology). N.Y., 1887.
Phil 8712.3.4	White, Andrew Dickson. New chapters in the warfare of science. (Geology). N.Y., 1888.
Phil 8712.3.5	White, Andrew Dickson. History of the warfare of science with theology in Christendem. N.Y., 1896. 2v.
NEDL Phil 8712.3.9	White, Andrew Dickson. History of the warfare of science with theology in Christendem. N.Y., 1901. 2v.
Phil 8712.3.10	White, Andrew Dickson. History of the warfare of science with theology in Christendem. N.Y., 1910. 2v.
Phil 8712.3.11	White, Andrew Dickson. History of the warfare of science with theology in Christendem. N.Y., 1920. 2v.
Phil 8712.3.12	White, Andrew Dickson. A history of the warfare of science with theology in Christendem. N.Y., 1965.
Phil 8712.3.15	White, Andrew Dickson. Histoire de la lutte entre la science et la théologie. Paris, 1899.
Phil 8712.4	Woodrow, J. An examination of certain recent assaults on physical science. Columbia, S.C., 1873-74.
Phil 8712.4.5	Woodrow, J. Evolution. Columbia, S.C., 1884.
Phil 8712.5	Wright, George F. Recent works bearing on the relation of science to religion. New Haven, 1877-78. 2 pam.
Phil 8712.5.5	Wright, George F. Studies in science and religion. Andover, 1882.
Phil 8712.5.9	Wright, George F. Scientific aspects of Christian evidences. N.Y., 1898.
Phil 8712.5.18	Wright, George F. Story of my life and work. Oberlin, 1916.
Phil 8712.6	Wright, T.S. Science and revelation. Bellefontaine, 1878.
Phil 8712.9	Whiston, W. Theory of the earth, from its original. London, 1755.
Phil 8712.10	Wenley, R.M. Modern thought and crisis in belief. N.Y., 1909.
Phil 8712.11	Walsh, J.J. The popes and science. N.Y., 1911.
Phil 8712.11.2	Walsh, J.J. The popes and science. N.Y., 1915.
Phil 8712.12	Wessenberg, J.G. von. Die falsche Wissenschaft. Stuttgart, 1844.
Phil 8712.13.1	Wiseman, N.P.S. Twelve lectures on the connexion between science and revealed religion. Andover, 1837.
Phil 8712.13.2	Wiseman, N.P.S. Twelve lectures on the connexion between science and revealed religion. 2. ed. London, 1842.
Phil 8712.13.8	Wiseman, N.P.S. Twelve lectures on the connexion between science and revealed religion. 4. ed. Baltimore, 1852. 2v.
Phil 8712.14	Woodburne, A.S. The relation between religion and science. Chicago, 1920.
Phil 8712.15	Westaway, F.W. Science and theology. London, 1920.
Phil 8712.16	Webber, G.P. Tro och vebande. Stockholm, 1915. 3v.
Phil 8712.17	Wieman, H.N. Religious experience and scientific method. N.Y., 1926.
Phil 8712.18	Wood, A. In pursuit of truth. London, 1927.
Phil 8712.19	Weygoldt, G.P. Darwinismus, Religion, Sittlichkeit. Leiden, 1878.
Phil 8712.20	Wahrmund, L. Katholische Weltanschauung und freie Wissenschaft. München, 1908.
Phil 8712.21	Wittstein, T. Der Streit zwischen glauben. Hannover, 1884.
Phil 8712.22	Warring, C.B. The mosaic account of creation. N.Y., 1875.
Phil 8712.23	Walker, L.J. Science and revelation. London, 1932.
Phil 8712.24	Winchell, A. Reconciliation of science and religion. N.Y., 1877.
Phil 8712.25	Wilson, Robert M. The witness of science. 1. ed. London, 1942.
Phil 8712.26	Williston, A.L. Beyond the horizon of science. Boston, 1944.
Phil 8712.27	White, E.A. Science and religion in American thought. Stanford, 1952.
Phil 8712.30	Whitehouse, Walter. Order, goodness, glory. London, 1960.
Phil 8712.32	Wood, John Karl. The nature of conflicts between science and religion. Logan, 1962.
Phil 8712.35	Weil, Simone. On science, necessity, and the love of God. London, 1968.
Phil 8714.1	Yorke, J.F. Notes on evolution and Christianity. N.Y., 1883.
Phil 8715.1	Zahm, John Augustine. Bible, science and faith. Baltimore, 1895.
Phil 8715.1.10	Zahm, John Augustine. The Catholic church and modern science. Notre Dame, Ind., 1886.
Phil 8715.2	Zart, G. Bibel und Naturwissenschaft. Berlin, 1878.
Phil 8715.3	Zöllner, J.F.K. Naturwissenschaft und christliche Offenbarung. Leipzig, 1881.
Phil 8715.4	Zocher, Rudolf. Philosophie in Begegnung mit Religion und Wissenschaft. München, 1955.
Phil 8715.5	Zum Felde, Alberto. Croisto y nosotros. Montevideo, 1959.

Phil 8725   Philosophy of religion - Treatises on special topics - Secularism

Phil 8725.1	Bonham, J. Secularism; its progress and morals. N.Y., 1894.
Phil 8725.2	Coulet. Catholicisme et laïcité. Paris, 1932.
Phil 8725.5	Vahanian, G. The death of God. N.Y., 1961.
Phil 8725.6	Luebbe, Hermann. Säkularisierung. Freiburg, 1965.
Phil 8725.8	Alvarez, Lili. El seglarismo y su integridad. Madrid, 1959.
Phil 8725.10	Edwards, David Lawrence. Religion and change. London, 1969.
Phil 8725.12	Martin, David. The religious and the secular. London, 1969.
Phil 8725.14	Christelijk bestaan in een seculaire cultuur. Roermond, 1969.
Phil 8725.16	Werhahn, Hans. Das Vorschreiten der Säkularisierung. Bonn, 1969.
Phil 8725.18	Marty, Martin E. The modern schism. 1. ed. N.Y., 1969.
Phil 8725.20	Jouguelet, Pierre. Laïcité, liberté et vérité. Tournai, 1969.

Phil 8735   Philosophy of religion - Treatises on special topics - Teleology

	Phil 8735.01	Pamphlet box. Philosophy of religion.
	Phil 8735.1	Call, W.M.W. Final causes. London, 1891.
Htn	Phil 8735.2*	Boyle, R. A disquisition...final causes of natural things. London, 1688.
	Phil 8735.3	Sully-Prudhomme, René F.A. Le problème de causes finales. Paris, 1903.
	Phil 8735.4	Cossmann, P.N. Elemente der empirischen Teleologie. Stuttgart, 1899.
	Phil 8735.5	Desdouits, M. L'homme et la création. 2. éd. Paris, 1846.
	Phil 8735.6A	Henderson, L.J. The order of nature. Cambridge, 1917.
	Phil 8735.6B	Henderson, L.J. The order of nature. Cambridge, 1917.
	Phil 8735.6C	Henderson, L.J. The order of nature. Cambridge, 1917.
	Phil 8735.6.5A	Henderson, L.J. The order of nature. Cambridge, 1925.
	Phil 8735.6.5B	Henderson, L.J. The order of nature. Cambridge, 1925.
	Phil 8735.7	Pflüger, E.F.W. Die teleologische Mechanik der lebendigen Natur. 2. Aufl. Bonn, 1877.
	Phil 8735.8	Eisler, Rudolf. Der Zweck; seine Bedeutung für Natur und Geist. Berlin, 1914.
	Phil 8735.9	Prandtl, Antonin. Über Teleologie des Geistes und über Teleologie überhaupt. Leipzig, 1915.
	Phil 8735.10	Baerenbach, Friedrich von. Gedanken über die Teleologie in der Natur. Berlin, 1878.
	Phil 8735.11	Elkus, S.A. The concept of control. N.Y., 1907.
	Phil 8735.12	Domet de Vorges, E. Cause efficiente et cause finale. Paris, 1888.
	Phil 8735.13	Erhart, Franz. Mechanismus und Teleologie. Leipzig, 1890.
	Phil 8735.15	Becher, Erich. Die fremddienliche Zweckmässigkeit der Pflanzgallen und dieHypothese eines überindividuellen Seelischen. Leipzig, 1917.
	Phil 8735.16	Étrillard, E. Études philosophiques sur les causes premières et les causes finales. Paris, 1900.
	Phil 8735.17	Lesparre, A. de G. L'idée de finalité. Paris, 1916.
	Phil 8735.18	Lasson, A. De causis finalibus. Berolini, 1876.
	Phil 8735.19	Garrigou-Lagrange, Reginaldo. Le réalisme du principe de finalité. Paris, 1932.
	Phil 8735.20.5	Ziegenhagen, F.H. Lehre vom richtigen Verhältniss zu den Schöpfungswerken und die durch öffentliche Einführung derselben allein zu bewürkende allgemeine Menschenbeglückung. Braunschweig, 1799.
	Phil 8735.21	Ferrière, Émile. La cause première d'après les données experimentales. Paris, 1897.
	Phil 8735.22	Cogni, G. Lo spirito assoluto. Firenze, 1937.
	Phil 8735.23	Van Nuys, K. Science and cosmic purpose. 1. ed. Thesis. N.Y., 1949.
	Phil 8735.24	Ruyer, R. Néo-finalisme. 1. éd. Paris, 1952.
	Phil 8735.25	D'Arcy, M.C. The pain of this world and the providence of God. London, 1952.
	Phil 8735.30	Wasmuth, E. Sokrates und der Engel. Olten, 1948.
	Phil 8735.35	Dolch, Heimo. Kausalität im Verständnis des Theologen und der Begründer neuzeitlicher Physik. Freiburg, 1954.
	Phil 8735.40	Fondazione Giorgio Cini, Venice. Centro de Cultura e Civiltà. Il valore del fine nel mondo. Firenze, 1955.
	Phil 8735.40.5	Fondazione Giorgio Cini, Venice. Centro de Cultura e Civiltà. Causalità e finalità. Firenze, 1959.
	Phil 8735.50	Schmitz, Josef. Disput über das teleologische Denken. Mainz, 1960.
	Phil 8735.52	Ward, L.R. God and world order. Saint Louis, 1961.
	Phil 8735.55	Frolov, I.T. O prichinnosti i tselesoobraznosti v zhivoi prirode. Moskva, 1961.
	Phil 8735.56	Meyers, A.M. Die Ursachen aller geschaffenen Dinge. Limburg, 1963?
	Phil 8735.57	Hurlbutt, Robert H. Hume, Newton, and the design argument Lincoln, 1965.
	Phil 8735.58	Canfield, John V. Purpose in nature. Englewood Cliffs, N.J., 1966.
VPhil	Phil 8735.59	Trubnikov, Nikolai N. O kategoriiakh "tsel'", "sredstvo", "rezul'tat". Moskva, 1968.
	Phil 8735.60	De Angelis, Enrico. La critica del finalismo nella cultura cartesiana. Firenze, 1967.
	Phil 8735.61	Kazakevich, Tat'iana A. Tselesoobraznost' i tsel' v obshchestvennom razvitii. Leningrad, 1969.

Phil 8740   Philosophy of religion - Treatises on special topics - Worship

Phil 8740.1	Suggestions for a public religious service. London, 1876.
Phil 8740.2	Goodale, E. Extracts concerning the importance of religion and public worship. Hallowell, 1820.
Phil 8740.3	Will, Robert. Le culte. Thèse. Strasbourg, 1925.
Phil 8740.4	Dun, Angus. Not by bread alone. 2. ed. N.Y., 1942.
Phil 8740.5	De Pierrefeu, Elsa (Tudor). Unity in the spirit. Rindge, N.H., 1955.
Phil 8740.8	Graef, Hilda C. The light and the rainbow. London, 1959.
Phil 8740.10	Gilson, Étienne. Théologie et histoire de la spiritualité. Paris, 1943.

Phil 8800   Ethics - Folios [Discontinued]

	Phil 8800.1	Hyde, E. The miscellaneous works. London, 1751.
Htn	Phil 8800.3*	Vincent de Beauvais. Speculum morale. Venetiis, 1493.
Htn	Phil 8800.6*	Feltham, Owen. Resolves. London, 1661.
Htn	Phil 8800.6.2*	Feltham, Owen. Resolves. London, 1677.
Htn	Phil 8800.6.5*	Feltham, Owen. Resolves. London, 1696.
	Phil 8800.7	Ferguson, A. Principles of moral and political science. Edinburgh, 1792. 2v.
	Phil 8800.8	Gisborne, T. An enquiry into the duties of men. London, 1794.

Phil 8805   Ethics - Pamphlet volumes
Phil 8805   Pamphlet box. Ethics.
Phil 8805.1   Pamphlet vol. Ethics. 12 pam.
Phil 8805.1.2   Pamphlet vol. Ethics. 7 pam.
Phil 8805.2   Pamphlet vol. Ethics. German dissertations, 1908-1921.
                 11 pam.
Phil 8805.3   Pamphlet vol. Ethics. 1876-1910. 9 pam.
Phil 8805.4   Pamphlet box. Ethics.
Phil 8805.5   Pamphlet box. Ethics. German dissertations.

Phil 8815   Ethics - Reference works - Dictionaries and encyclopedias
Phil 8815.5   Hoermann, Karl. Lexikon der christlichen Moral.
                 Innsbruck, 1969.

Phil 8820   Ethics - History - General works - Collected authors
Phil 8820.5   Eifler, Günter. Ritterliches Tugendsystem.
                 Darmstadt, 1970.

Phil 8825   -   8850   Ethics - History - General works - Individual authors (A-Z)
Phil 8825.5   Akarsu, Bedia. Ahlâk öprelileri. Istanbul, 1965.
Phil 8825.10   Attisam, Adelchi. Saggi di etica e di filosofia del
                 diritto. Napoli, 1970.
Phil 8826.1   Becker, J.H. Ursprung...Sittlichkeit. Leipzig, 1888.
Phil 8826.2   Blackie, J.S. Four phases of morals. Edinburgh, 1871.
Phil 8826.2.5   Blackie, J.S. Four phases of morals; Socrates, Aristotle,
                 Christianity, Utilitarianism. 2nd ed. Edinburgh, 1874.
Phil 8826.3   Blakey, R. History of moral science. Edinburgh, 1836.
                 2v.
Phil 8826.4   Bastian, Adolf. Zur ethnischen Ethik. Berlin, 1889.
Phil 8826.5   Bayet, Albert. La morale des gaulois. Paris, 1930.
Phil 8826.5.10   Bayet, Albert. La morale paienne a l'époque gallo-romaine.
                 Paris, 1931.
Phil 8826.6   Baumgardt, D. Der Kampf um den Lebenssinn den Vorläufern
                 der modernen Ethik. Leipzig, 1933.
Phil 8826.7   Banning, Willem. Typen van zedelee. Haarlem, 1965.
Phil 8826.8   Bourke, Vernon Joseph. History of ethics. Garden
                 City, 1968.
Phil 8827.1   Courtney, W.L. Constructive ethics. London, 1886.
EDL Phil 8827.2 Cousin, V. Cours d'histoire de la philosophie morale au
                 dix-huitième siècle. Paris, 1839-42. 3v.
Phil 8827.3   Caro, E.M. Études morales sur le temps présent.
                 Paris, 1855.
Phil 8827.3.2   Caro, E.M. Études morales sur le temps présent.
                 Paris, 1869.
Phil 8827.3.7   Caro, E.M. Nouvelles études morales sur le temps présent.
                 Paris, 1869.
Phil 8827.5   Cabot, R.C. What men live by. Boston, 1914.
Phil 8827.6   Cohn, Frederick. Evolutionism and idealism in ethics.
                 Thesis. Omaha, Nebr., 1909.
Phil 8827.7   Chandavarkar, G.A. A manual of Hindu ethics. 3rd ed.
                 Poona, 1925.
Phil 8827.8   Cresson, André. Le problème moral et les philosophes.
                 Paris, 1933.
Phil 8827.9   Crocker, L. Nature and culture. Baltimore, 1963.
Phil 8827.10   Ciarletta, Nicola. Eticità e cultura. 1. ed.
                 Milano, 1960.
Phil 8828.1   Dupuy, Paul. La question morale à la fin du XIXe siècle.
                 Paris, 1897.
Phil 8828.2   Du sage antique au citoyen moderne. Paris, 1921.
Phil 8828.3   Dittrich, Ottmar. Systeme der moral. Bd. 1-3.
                 Leipzig, 1923-26. 3v.
Phil 8828.3.5A   Dittrich, Ottmar. Geschichte der Ethik. Leipzig, 1926-32.
                 4v.
Phil 8828.3.5B   Dittrich, Ottmar. Geschichte der Ethik. v.4.
                 Leipzig, 1926-32.
Phil 8828.4   Dempf, Alois. Ethik des Mittelalters. München, 1927.
Phil 8828.5   Drobnitskii, Oleg G. Kritika sovremennykh burzhuaznykh
                 eticheskikh kontseptsii. Moskva, 1967.
Phil 8828.6   Dubois, Pierre. Le problème moral dans la philosophie
                 anglaise de 1900 à 1950. Paris, 1967.
Phil 8828.8   Du Plessis, Pieter Gert Wessel. Opskorting van die etiese?
                 Thesis. Potchefstroom, 1965.
Phil 8828.10   Dzhafarli, Teimuraz M. Iz istorii domarksistskoi
                 eticheskoi mysli. Tbilisi, 1970.
Phil 8829.1   England, G. An enquiry into the morals of the ancients.
                 London, 1735.
Phil 8829.2   Eucken, Rudolf. Die Lebensanschauungen der grossen Denker.
                 Leipzig, 1890.
Phil 8829.2.2   Eucken, Rudolf. Die Lebensanschauungen der grossen Denker.
                 Leipzig, 1897.
Phil 8829.2.5   Eucken, Rudolf. Die Lebensanschauungen der grossen Denker.
                 Leipzig, 1905.
Phil 8829.2.7   Eucken, Rudolf. Die Lebensanschauungen der grossen Denker.
                 12. Aufl. Leipzig, 1918.
Phil 8829.2.8   Eucken, Rudolf. Der Lebensanschauungen der grossen Denker.
                 13e und 14e Aufl. Berlin, 1919.
Phil 8829.2.8.2 Eucken, Rudolf. Die Lebensanschauungen der grossen Denker.
                 20. Aufl. Berlin, 1950.
Phil 8829.2.9   Eucken, Rudolf. Grundlinien einer neuen Lebensanschauung.
                 Leipzig, 1907.
Phil 8829.2.10   Eucken, Rudolf. Grundlinien einer neuen Lebensanschauung.
                 2e Aufl. Leipzig, 1913.
Phil 8829.2.12   Eucken, Rudolf. The problem of human life. N.Y., 1909.
Phil 8829.2.20   Eucken, Rudolf. The problem of human life. N.Y., 1924.
Phil 8829.3   Engelhardt, Paulus. Sein und Ethos. Mainz, 1963.
Phil 8830.1   Feuerlein, E. Die philosophische Sittenlehre. v.1-2.
                 Tübingen, 1857-59.
Phil 8830.3   Fouillée, A. Critique; systèmes de morale contemporaine.
                 Paris, 1883.
Phil 8830.4   Faquet, Émile. La démission de la morale. Paris, 1910.
Phil 8831.1   Guyau, M.J. La morale anglaise contemporaine.
                 Paris, 1878.
Phil 8831.2   Goedewaagen, T. Die logische rechtvaadiging der
                 zedelijkheid bij Fichte, Schelling en Hegel. Proefschrift.
                 Amsterdam, 1923.
Phil 8831.3   Garve, Christian. Übersicht der vornehmsten Principien der
                 Sittenlehre. Breslau, 1798.
Phil 8831.4   Gore, Charles. Philosophy of the good life. London, 1930.
Phil 8831.5   Ginsberg, M. Moral progess; being the Frazer lecture
                 delivered within the University of Glasgow on 18th April
                 1944. Glasgow, 1944.
Phil 8831.6   Gent, W. Der sittliche Mensch. Meisenheim, 1950.
Phil 8831.7   Gentile, Marino. I grandi moralisti. Torino, 1955.
Phil 8831.8   Graaf, Johannes de. De bezinning over goed en kwaad in de
                 geschiedenis van het menselijk denken. Utrecht, 1957- 3v.
Phil 8831.10   Garnett, Arthur. Ethics. N.Y., 1960.
Phil 8831.12   Grégoire, François. Leo grandes doctrines morales.
                 Paris, 1958.

Phil 8825   -   8850   Ethics - History - General works - Individual authors (A-Z) - cont.
Phil 8831.14   Geschichte der Ethik. v.2. Gütersloh, 1967.
Phil 8832.1   Hentsch, Alice Adele. De la littérature didactique du Moyen
                 Age. Photoreproduction. Halle, 1903.
Phil 8832.2   Hoekstra, S. Geschiedenis van de zedenleer.
                 Amsterdam, 1896. 2v.
Phil 8832.3.5   Hobhouse, L.T. Morals in evolution. 5th ed. London, 1925.
Phil 8832.4A   Hibino, Yutaka. Nippon shindo ron; or, The national ideals
                 of the Japanese people. Cambridge, Eng., 1928.
Phil 8832.4B   Hibino, Yutaka. Nippon shindo ron; or, The national ideals
                 of the Japanese people. Cambridge, Eng., 1928.
Phil 8832.5   Hall-Quest, A.L. It's not our fault. N.Y., 1929.
Phil 8832.6   Heard, Gerald. Morals since 1900. London, 1950.
Phil 8832.7   Harkness, G.E. The sources of western culture.
                 London, 1955.
Phil 8832.8   Held, Virginia. The bewildered age. N.Y., 1962.
Phil 8834.1   Janet, P. Histoire de la philosophie morale. Paris, 1858.
                 2v.
Phil 8834.2   Jodl, Friedrich. Geschichte der Ethik. v.1-2.
                 Stuttgart, 1882-1889.
Phil 8834.2.5   Jodl, Friedrich. Geschichte der Ethik. 4. Aufl.
                 Stuttgart, 1923-30. 2v.
Phil 8834.2.10   Jodl, Friedrich. Ethik und Moralpädagogik.
                 Stuttgart, 1913.
Phil 8834.4   Judge, M.H. The ethical movement in England, 1902.
                 London, 1902.
Phil 8835.1   Köstlin, K.R. Geschichte der Ethik. Tübingen, 1887.
Phil 8835.2.5   Kropotkin, Petr Alekseevich. Ethics; origin and
                 development. N.Y., 1924.
Phil 8835.2.6   Kropotkin, Petr Alekseevich. Ethics; origin and
                 development. N.Y., 1968.
Phil 8835.3   Keller, M. Ethik als Wissenschaft ein methodologischer
                 Versuch. Zürich, 1925.
Phil 8835.5   Krook, Dorothea. Three traditions of moral thought.
                 Cambridge, Eng., 1959.
Phil 8835.6   Kerner, George. The revolution in ethical theory.
                 N.Y., 1966.
Phil 8836.1   Laurie, S.S. Notes, expository and critical, on certain
                 British theories of morals. Edinburgh, 1868.
Phil 8836.2   Lecky, W.E.H. History of European morals. London, 1869.
                 2v.
Phil 8836.2.5   Lecky, W.E.H. History of European morals. v.1.
                 N.Y., 1876.
Phil 8836.2.6   Lecky, W.E.H. History of European morals. 3. ed.
                 N.Y., 1897. 2v.
Phil 8836.2.11   Lecky, W.E.H. History of European morals. N.Y., 1913.
                 2v.
Phil 8836.2.13   Lecky, W.E.H. History of European morals. N.Y., 1926.
Phil 8836.2.15   Lecky, W.E.H. A survey of English ethics. London, 1903.
Phil 8836.2.18   Lecky, E. A memoir of W.E.H. Lecky. London, 1909.
Phil 8836.2.20   Lecky, W.E.H. A Victorian historian. London, 1947.
Phil 8836.2.80   Auchmuty, J.J. Lecky. London, 1945.
Phil 8836.4   Lessona, Marco. La storia della filosofia morale; studio.
                 Torino, 1888.
Phil 8837.1.2   Mackintosh, James. A general view of the progress of
                 ethical philosophy. Philadelphia, 1832.
Phil 8837.1.3   Mackintosh, James. A general view of the progress of
                 ethical philosophy. Philadelphia, 1834.
Phil 8837.1.4   Mackintosh, James. A general view of the progress of
                 ethical philosophy. Edinburgh, 1837.
Phil 8837.1.15   Mill, James. A fragment on Mackintosh. London, 1835.
Phil 8837.1.16   Mill, James. A fragment on Mackintosh. London, 1870.
Phil 8837.2   Martin, L.A. Histoire de la morale. Paris, 1859.
Phil 8837.3   Meiners, C. Allgemeine kritische Geschichte der ältern und
                 neuern Ethik. Göttingen, 1800-01. 2v.
Phil 8837.5   Myers, P.V. History as past ethics. Boston, 1913.
Phil 8837.6   Moore, T.V. Historical introduction to ethics.
                 N.Y., 1915.
Phil 8837.7   Mayer, Gottlob. Die Lehre vom Erlaubten in der Geschichte
                 der Ethic seit Schleier Macher. Leipzig, 1899.
Phil 8837.8   McKenzie, John. Hindu ethics. London, 1922.
Phil 8837.9   Meyer, R.M. Le mouvement moral vers 1840. Paris, 1913.
Phil 8837.10   Maitra, Sushil Kumar. The ethics of the Hindus.
                 Calcutta, 1925.
Phil 8837.11   Markum, Leo. Mrs. Grundy. N.Y., 1930.
Phil 8837.12   Muirhead, J.H. Rule and end in morals. London, 1932.
Phil 8837.13   Mencken, H.L. Treatise on right and wrong. N.Y., 1934.
Phil 8837.14   Miloyévitch, Voukossava. La théorie des passions du P.
                 Senault et la morale chrétienne en France au XVIIe siècle.
                 Thèse. Paris, 1934.
Phil 8837.15   Masson-Ourel, Paul. La morale et l'histoire. 1. éd.
                 Paris, 1955.
Phil 8837.16   Méautis, Georges. Mes pélerinages de l'âme. Paris, 1959.
Phil 8837.17   MacIntyre, Alasdair C. A short history of ethics.
                 N.Y., 1966.
Phil 8839.5   Ocherk istorii etiki. Moskva, 1969.
Phil 8840.1.8   Prévost-Paradol, L.A. Etudes sur les moralistes français.
                 8e éd. Paris, 1895.
Phil 8840.2   Paton, H.J. Fashion and philosophy. Oxford, 1937.
Phil 8840.3   Prell, H.H. Das Unmittelbare in der Philosophie der Moral.
                 Amsterdam, 1941.
Phil 8840.4   Perelman, Chaim. Philosophie morale. Bruxelles, 1967.
Phil 8842.1   Rod, E. Les idées morales du temps present. Paris, 1891.
Phil 8842.3   Rees, D. Contemporary English ethics. Leipzig, 1892.
Phil 8842.4   Robertson, J.M. A short history of morals. London, 1920.
Phil 8842.5   Reybekiel, A. Das biologische Prinzip in den
                 moralphilosophischen Anschauungen W. Rolph's, M. Guyau's
                 und Fr. Nietzsches. Krakau, 1906.
Phil 8842.6   Rogers, A.K. Morals in review. N.Y., 1927.
Phil 8842.7   Riley, Isaac. Men and morals. Garden City, 1929.
Phil 8842.8   Romagnosi, G.D. L'antica morale filosofia. Prato, 1838.
Phil 8842.9   Richard, Gaston. L'évolution des moeurs. Paris, 1925.
Phil 8842.10   Rohmer, J. La finalité morale. Paris, 1939.
Phil 8842.10.5   Rohmer, J. La finalité morale chez les théologiens de
                 Saint Augustin à Duns Scot. Thèse. Paris, 1938.
Phil 8842.11   Robertson, Archibald M.A. Morals in world history.
                 London, 1945.
Phil 8843.1.5   Sidgwick, Henry. Lectures on the ethics of T.H. Green.
                 London, 1902.
Phil 8843.1.7   Sidgwick, Henry. Outlines of history of ethics for English
                 readers. Boston, 1960.
Phil 8843.1.10   Sidgwick, Henry. Prime livee di una storia della morale.
                 Torino, 1922.
Phil 8843.2   Selby-Bigge, L.A. British moralists. v.1-2. Oxford, 1897.
Phil 8843.2.2   Selby-Bigge, L.A. British moralists. v.1-2.
                 Indianapolis, 1964.
Phil 8843.3   Samson, G.W. Outlines of the history of ethics.
                 Washington, 1861.

Phil 8825 - 8850   Ethics - History - General works - Individual authors (A-Z) - cont.

Phil 8843.4   Sutherland, A. The origin and growth of moral instinct. London, 1898. 2v.

Phil 8843.5   Sorley, W.R. Recent tendencies in ethics. Edinburgh, 1904.

Phil 8843.6   Scotti, Giulio. La metafisica nella morale moderna. Milano, 1903.

Phil 8843.8   Stieglitz, T. Über den Ursprung des Sittlichen und die Formen seiner Erscheinung. Wien, 1894.

Phil 8843.9   Stoops, J.D. Ideals of conduct. N.Y., 1926.

Phil 8843.10   Stefanini, L. Il problema morale nello stoicismo e nel cristianesimo. Torino, 1926.

Phil 8843.11   Sneath, E.H. Evolution of ethics...in great religions. New Haven, 1927.

Phil 8843.12   Sheriff, W.S. Religion and ethics. Thesis. Philadelphia, 1933.

Phil 8843.13   Saunders, K.J. The ideals of East and West. Cambridge, Eng., 1934.

Phil 8843.13.2   Saunders, K.J. The ideals of East and West. N.Y., 1934.

Phil 8843.14   Smith, Wilson. Professors and public ethics. Ithaca, N.Y., 1956.

Phil 8843.15   Sparshott, F.E. An enquiry into goodness. Chicago, 1958.

Phil 8843.16   Shishkin, A.F. Iz istorii eticheskikh uchenii. Moskva, 1959.

Phil 8843.17   Swabey, W.C. Ethical theory. N.Y., 1961.

Phil 8843.18   Sahakian, W. Systems of ethics and value theory. N.Y., 1963.

Phil 8843.20   Sena, Cemil. Insanlar ve ahlâklar. Istanbul, 1970.

Phil 8844.1   Thamin, R. Extraits des moralistes. Paris, 1897.

Phil 8844.2   Turner, Arthur T. A new morality. London, 1904.

Phil 8844.3   Tufts, J.H. The individual and his relation to society. N.Y., 1904.

Phil 8844.4   Tsanoff, R.A. The moral ideals of our civilization. N.Y., 1942.

Phil 8846.1   Voltz, H. Die Ethik als Wissenschaft. Strassburg, 1886.

Phil 8846.2   Vorländer, F. Geschichte der philosophischen Moral. Marburg, 1855.

Phil 8846.3   Vidari, Giovanni. L'individualismo nelle dottrine morali del secolo XIX. Milano, 1909.

Phil 8846.4   Vázquez, Francisco. Tres éticas del siglo XX. Madrid, 1970.

Phil 8847.1   Whewell, W. History of moral philosophy in England. London, 1852.

Phil 8847.2   Wake, Charles S. The evolution of morality. London, 1878. 2v.

Phil 8847.3   Ward, Stephen. Ethics. London, 1924.

Phil 8847.4   Winter, F.J. Der Individualismus. Leipzig, 1880.

Phil 8847.5   Wentscher, Max. Geschichte der Ethik. Berlin, 1931.

Phil 8847.10   Wieman, H.N. The directive in history. Boston, 1949.

Phil 8847.12   Wedar, S. Duty and utility. Lund, 1952.

Phil 8847.14   Winkler, Paul. Les sources mystiques des concepts moraux de l'occident. Paris, 1957.

Phil 8847.15   Warnock, Mary. Ethics since 1900. London, 1960.

Phil 8847.15.2   Warnock, Mary. Ethics since 1900. 2nd ed. London, 1966.

Phil 8847.17   Whiteley, Charles Henry. The permissive morality. London, 1964.

Phil 8850.1   Ziegler, T. Geschichte der Ethik. Bonn, 1881-86. 2v.

Phil 8850.2   Zangenberg, Therese. Asthetische Gesichtspunkte in der englischen Ethik des 18. Jahrhunderts. Langensalza, 1918.

Phil 8850.3   Zucker, Friedrich. Syneidesis-conscientia. Jena, 1928.

Phil 8855   Ethics - History - Special topics

Phil 8855.2   Ussel, Jozef Maria Willem van. Sociogenese en evolutie van het probleem der seksuele propaedeuse tussen de 16 de en 18 de eeuw. Gent, 1967. 2v.

Phil 8855.4   Höffe, Otfried. Praktische Philosophie. München, 1971.

Phil 8865   Ethics - History - Local (Geographical Table A)

Phil 8865.342   Austin, Eugene M. The ethics of the Cambridge Platonists. Philadelphia, 1935.

Phil 8865.342.5   Willey, Basil. The English moralists. London, 1964.

Phil 8865.372   Levi, Anthony. French moralists; the theory of the passions, 1585-1649. Oxford, 1964.

Phil 8865.534   Geiushev, Ziiaddin B. Eticheskaia mysl' v Azerbaidzhane. Baku, 1968.

Phil 8865.636   Tiwari, Brij Gopal. Secularism and materialism in modern India. Delhi, 1964?

Phil 8865.636.5   Sharma, Ishwar Chandra. Ethical philosophies of India. London, 1965.

Phil 8865.660   Suyematsu, Kencho. The ethics of Japan. Washington, 1907.

Phil 8870   Ethics - General treatises - Collected authors

Phil 8870.5   Coit, Stanton. The message of man. London, 1905.

Htn   Phil 8870.7*   Pirckheimer, W. Theatrum virtutis et honoris. Nürnberg, 1606.

Phil 8870.8   Larned, J.N. A multitude of counselors. Boston, 1901.

Phil 8870.9   Larned, J.N. A primer of right and wrong. Boston, 1902.

Phil 8870.11   Felseneer, Jean. Morale de savants d'Hippocrate à Einstein. Bruxelles, 1946.

Phil 8870.12   Institute for Religious Studies, Jewish Theological Seminary of America. Conflict of loyalties. N.Y., 1952.

Phil 8870.13   Anshen, R.N. Moral principles of action. 1st ed. N.Y., 1952.

Phil 8870.14   Miscellanea moralia in honorem eximii domini Arthur Janssen. v.1-2. Leuven, 1949.

Phil 8870.15.2   Melden, A.I. Ethical theories. 2nd ed. N.Y., 1955.

Phil 8870.16   Wagner, J. Was soll ich tun? Braunschweig, 1953.

Phil 8870.17   Johnson, Oliver A. Ethics. N.Y., 1958.

Phil 8870.18   Thomson, Judith J. Ethics. N.Y., 1968.

Phil 8870.20   Clair, F.F. The ultimate defense. 1st ed. Rutland, 1959.

Phil 8870.23   Dewey, Robert E. Problems of ethics. N.Y., 1961.

Phil 8870.24   Castaneda, H. Morality and the language of conduct. Detroit, 1963.

Phil 8870.25   Ethische verkenningen. Nijkerk, 1961. 10v.

Phil 8870.26   The ethics of change; a symposium. Toronto, 1969.

Phil 8870.27   Hume, Rolando. Etica inspirado o exterminio. Santa Fe, Argentina, 1960.

Phil 8870.28   De George, Richard T. Ethics and society. Garden City, 1966.

Phil 8870.29   Boeckle, Franz. Moral zwischen Anspruch und Verantwortung. Düsseldorf, 1964.

Phil 8870.30   Rosenberg, Stuart E. A humane society. Toronto, 1962.

Phil 8870.31   Raphael, David Daiches. British moralists, 1650-1800. Oxford, 1969. 2v.

Phil 8870.32   Studies in moral philosophy. Oxford, 1968.

Phil 8870.34   Wallace, Gerald. The definition of morality. London, 1970.

Phil 8870.36   Wetenschappelijke moraalstudie. Ledeberg, 1966.

Phil 8870   Ethics - General treatises - Collected authors - cont.

Phil 8870.38   Sellars, Wilfrid. Readings in ethical theory. N.Y., 1952.

Phil 8870.40   Struktura morali. Sverdlovsk, 1970.

Phil 8870.42   La fondazione del giudizio morale. Padova, 1968.

Phil 8875 - 8900   Ethics - General treatises - Individual authors (A-Z)

Phil 8875.1   Abercrombie, J. The philosophy of the moral feelings. N.Y., 1833.

Phil 8875.1.3   Abercrombie, J. The philosophy of the moral feelings. N.Y., 1839.

Phil 8875.2   Adams, J. Elements of moral philosophy. Cambridge, 1837.

Phil 8875.3   Agrippa von Nettesheim, Heinrich Cornelius. De incertitudine et vanitate omnium scientiarum et artium liber. Lugduni Batavorum, 1643.

Htn   Phil 8875.3.2*   Agrippa von Nettesheim, Heinrich Cornelius. De incertitudine et vanitate omnium scientiarum et artium liber. n.p., 1544.

Htn   Phil 8875.3.4*   Agrippa von Nettesheim, Heinrich Cornelius. De incertitudine et vanitate omnium scientiarum et artium liber. Ealf, 1531.

Phil 8875.3.5   Agrippa von Nettesheim, Heinrich Cornelius. The vanity of arts and sciences. London, 1676.

Htn   Phil 8875.3.8*   Agrippa von Nettesheim, Heinrich Cornelius. Della vanitate delle scienze. Venetia, 1552.

Phil 8875.3.15   Agrippa von Nettesheim, Heinrich Cornelius. Paradoxe sur l'incertitude vanité et abus des sciences. n.p., 1603.

Phil 8875.3.16   Agrippa von Nettesheim, Heinrich Cornelius. Paradoxe sur l'incertitude vanité et abus des sciences. n.p., 1603.

Phil 8875.4   Alexander, A. A theory of conduct. N.Y., 1890.

Phil 8875.4.15   Alexander, A. Outlines of moral science. N.Y., 1858.

Phil 8875.5   Alexander, S. Moral order and progress. London, 1889.

Phil 8875.7   Ancillon, J.P.F. Zur Vermittlung der Extreme. Berlin, 1831-38. 2v.

Phil 8875.8   Abbadie, J. L'Art de se connoitre soy-même. v.1-2. La Haye, 1711.

Phil 8875.9   Albertson, Ralph. Little Jeremiads. Lewiston, 1903.

Phil 8875.10   Altgeld, J.P. The cost of something for nothing. Chicago, 1904.

Phil 8875.11   Alvarez, Agustín. Creación del mundo moral. 2a ed. Buenos Aires, 1915.

Phil 8875.12   Alaux, J.E. Philosophie morale et politique. Paris, 1893.

Phil 8875.13   Ayres, Clarence E. The nature of the relationship between ethics and economics. Chicago, Ill., n.d.

Phil 8875.14   Aars, K.B.R. Gut und Böse. Christiania, 1907.

Phil 8875.15   Allihn, Friedrich H. Grundriss der Ethik. 2e Aufl. Langensalza, 1898.

Phil 8875.16   Aall, Anathon. Macht und Pflicht. Leipzig, 1902.

Phil 8875.17   Allen, James. From poverty to power. N.Y., 1907.

Phil 8875.18   Antieh, José. Egoismo y altruismo. Barcelona, 1906.

Phil 8875.19   Åberg, L.H. Filosofisk sedelära. v.1-4. Uppsala, 1893-94.

Phil 8875.20   D'Acquisto, P.B. Corso di filosofia morale. 2. ed. Palermo, 1855.

Phil 8875.21   Achelis, J. Ethik. Leipzig, 1910.

Phil 8875.21.5   Achelis, J. Ethik. 2nd ed. Leipzig, 1900.

Phil 8875.22   D'Acol. La reduction de toutes les sciences en la connaissance de l'homme. Paris, 1668.

Phil 8875.23   Alstrin, Eric. Dissertatio philosophica. Upsala, 1723.

Phil 8875.24   Alger, W.R. The school of life. Boston, 1881.

Phil 8875.25   Alquié, F. Notions de morale générale. Paris, 1933.

Phil 8875.25.5   Alquié, F. Le problème moral. Paris, 1933.

Phil 8875.26   Astrada, C. La ética formal. La Plata, 1938.

Phil 8875.27   Adler, Mortimer Jerome. A dialectic of morals. Notre Dame, 1941.

Phil 8875.27.5   Adler, Mortimer Jerome. The time of our lives. 1st ed. N.Y., 1970.

Phil 8875.28   American Academy of Political and Social Science, Philadelphia. Ethical standards and professional conduct. Philadelphia, 1955.

Phil 8875.30   Aichen, Henry D. Reason and conduct. N.Y., 1962.

Phil 8875.31   Aleksandrov, R.N. Pis'ma k neizvestnomu drugu. Frankfurt, 1951.

Phil 8875.32   Akademiia Nauk SSSR. Institut Filosofii. Protiv sovremennoi burzhuaznoi etiki. Moskva, 1965.

Phil 8875.33   Albert, Henri. Les dangers du moralisme. n.p., 1896?

Phil 8875.34   Alisjahbana, Sutan Takdir. Values as integrating forces in personality society and culture. Kuala Lumpur, 1966.

Phil 8875.36   Androutsos, Chrèstos. Systèma ēthikēs. Athènai, 1925.

Phil 8876.1   Bagshaw, W. On man. London, 1833. 2v.

NEDL   Phil 8876.2   Bain, A. Moral science. N.Y., 1869.

Phil 8876.3   Balfour, J. A delineation...nature. Obligations. Morality. Edinburgh, 1753.

Phil 8876.3.2   Balfour, J. A delineation of the nature and obligation of morality. Edinburgh, 1763.

Phil 8876.4   Barni, J. La morale dans la démocratie. Paris, 1868.

Phil 8876.5   Barratt, A. Physical ethics. London, 1869.

Phil 8876.6   Bartlett, J. Aphorisms. Boston, 1823.

Phil 8876.6.3   Bartlett, J. Aphorisms. Portsmouth, 1810.

Htn   Phil 8876.6.4*   Bartlett, J. Aphorisms. Portsmouth, 1810.

Phil 8876.7   Bartolommeo, F. Ammaestramenti degli antighi. Milan, 1808.

Phil 8876.8   Basedow, J.B. Practische Philosophie für alle Stande. v.1-2. Dessau, 1777.

Phil 8876.9   Basford, J.L. Sparks from the philosophers stone. London, 1882.

Phil 8876.9.5   Basford, J.L. Seven seventy seven sensations. Boston, 1897.

Phil 8876.10   Baudrillart, H. Études de philosophie morale. Paris, 1858. 2v.

Phil 8876.11   Baumann, Julius. Sechs Vorträge aus dem Gebiete der praktischen Philosophie. Leipzig, 1874.

Phil 8876.11.5   Baumann, Julius. Handbuch der Moral. Leipzig, 1879.

Phil 8876.11.10   Baumann, Julius. Realwissenschaftliche Begründung der Moral. Leizpig, 1898.

Phil 8876.12   Bautain, L.E.M. Manuel de philosophie morale. Paris, 1866.

Phil 8876.12.5   Bautain, L.E.M. Philosophie morale. Paris, 1842. 2v.

Htn   Phil 8876.13*   Bryskett, Lodowick. Discourse of civil life. London, 1606.

Phil 8876.14.2   Baldwin, W. The sayings of the wise. London, 1908.

Htn   Phil 8876.14.3*   Baldwin, W. A treatise of morall phylosophye. London, n.d.

Htn   Phil 8876.14.5*   Baldwin, W. A treatise of morall philosophie. London, 1640.

Htn   Phil 8876.14.8*   Baldwin, W. A treatise of morall philosophie. London, n.d.

Phil 8876.15   Bersot, D.P.E. Un moraliste. Paris, 1882.

Phil 8875 - 8900 Ethics - General treatises - Individual authors (A-Z) - cont.

Phil 8876.17 Birks, T.R. First principles of moral science. London, 1873.
Phil 8876.18 Blakey, R. An essay...good and evil. Edinburgh, 1831.
Htn Phil 8876.19* Bodenham, John. Politeuphuia, wits common-wealth. London, 1688.
Htn Phil 8876.19.2* Bodenham, John. Politeuphuia, wits common-wealth. London, 1655.
Htn Phil 8876.19.3* Bodenham, John. Wits commonwealth. London, 1722.
Htn Phil 8876.19.5* Bodenham, John. Politeuphuia. London, 1598.
Htn Phil 8876.19.6* Bodenham, John. Politeuphuia, wits common-wealth. London, 1650.
Htn Phil 8876.19.7* Bodenham, John. Politeuphuia, wits common-wealth. London, 1653.
Htn Phil 8876.19.13* Bodenham, John. Politeuphuia, wits common-wealth. London, 1674.
Phil 8876.20 Bolton, R. On the employment of time. London, 1754.
X Cg Phil 8876.21 Bonnaire, L. de. Les leçons de la sagesse. Paris, 1750-51. 3v.
Phil 8876.22 Bösch, I.M. Das menschliche Mitgefühl. Winterthur, 1891.
Phil 8876.23 Boussinesq, J. Conciliation du véritable déterminisme mécanique. Paris, 1878.
Phil 8876.24 Bovee, C.N. Thoughts, feelings, and fancies. N.Y., 1857.
Phil 8876.24.5 Bovee, C.N. Intuitions and summaries of thought. Boston, 1862. 2v.
Phil 8876.25 Bowne, B.P. The principles of ethics. N.Y., 1892.
Phil 8876.25.5 Bowne, B.P. The principles of ethics. N.Y., 1893.
Phil 8876.26 Boyd, J.R. Eclectic moral philosophy. N.Y., 1846.
Phil 8876.27.7 Bradley, Francis Herbert. Ethical studies. 2nd ed. Oxford, 1927.
Phil 8876.27.12 Bradley, Francis Herbert. Ethical studies. N.Y., 1951.
Phil 8876.27.15 Bradley, Francis Herbert. Ethical studies. 2nd ed. London, 1969.
Phil 8876.27.16A Bradley, Francis Herbert. Ethical studies. 2nd ed. Oxford, 1967.
Phil 8876.27.16B Bradley, Francis Herbert. Ethical studies. 2nd ed. Oxford, 1967.
Phil 8876.28 Brandis, J.D. Überhumanes Leben. Schleswig, 1825.
Phil 8876.29 Brown, H.S. Lectures for the people. Philadelphia, 1859.
Phil 8876.30 Brown, John. An estimate of the manners and principles of the times. v.1-2. London, 1758.
tn Phil 8876.30.5* Brown, John. An estimate of the manners and principles of the times. 2nd ed. London, 1757.
Phil 8876.31 Brown, T. Redivivus. An exposition of vulgar and common errors. Philadelphia, 1846.
Phil 8876.32 Brown, W.L. An essay on the natural equality of men. London, 1794.
Phil 8876.33 Bruce, J. Elements of the science of ethics. London, 1786.
Phil 8876.34 Bucke, R.M. Man's moral mature. N.Y., 1879.
n Phil 8876.35* Burgersdyck, F. Idea philosophiae tum moralis. Oxoniae, 1631.
Phil 8876.35.3 Burgersdyck, F. Idea philosophiae tum moralis. 2a ed. Lugduni, 1629.
Phil 8876.36 Burgh, J. The dignity of human nature. London, 1754.
Phil 8876.36.3 Burgh, J. The dignity of human nature. London, 1767. 2v.
n Phil 8876.36.4* Burgh, J. The dignity of human nature. Boston, 1794.
n Phil 8876.36.5* Burgh, J. The dignity of human nature. Hartford, 1802.
Phil 8876.36.6 Burgh, J. The dignity of human nature. N.Y., 1812.
Phil 8876.37 Buys, J. De statibus hominum. Moguntiae, 1613.
Phil 8876.38 Browne, I.H. Essays on subjects of important enquiry. London, 1822.
Phil 8876.39 Bon, Fred. Über das Sollen und das Gute. Leipzig, 1898.
Phil 8876.39.5 Bon, Fred. Grundzüge der wissenschaftlichen und technischen Ethik. Leipzig, 1896.
Phil 8876.40 Bodnai, Zsigmond. Az orkölcsi törvény alkalmazása. Budapest, 1896.
Phil 8876.41 Brentano, Franz. Origin of knowledge of right and wrong. London, 1902.
Phil 8876.41.6 Brentano, Franz. Vom Ursprung sittlicher Erkenntnis. Leipzig, 1889.
Phil 8876.41.7A Brentano, Franz. Vom Ursprung sittlicher Erkenntnis. 2e Aufl. Leipzig, 1921.
Phil 8876.41.7B Brentano, Franz. Vom Ursprung sittlicher Erkenntnis. 2e Aufl. Leipzig, 1921.
Phil 8876.41.9 Brentano, Franz. Vom Ursprung sittlicher Erkenntnis. Hamburg, 1955.
Phil 8876.42 Brent, C.H. The splendor of the human body. N.Y., 1904.
Phil 8876.43 Beveridge, A.J. Work and habits. Philadelphia, 1908.
Phil 8876.44 Belot, G. Études de morale positive. Paris, 1907.
Phil 8876.44.2 Belot, G. Études de morale positive. 2e éd. Paris, 1921. 2v.
Phil 8876.44.5 Belot, G. Études sur philosophie morale au XIXeme siècle. Paris, 1904.
Phil 8876.45 Beary, H.R. Individual development of man. N.Y., 1909.
Phil 8876.46 Bligh, S.M. The desire for qualities. London, n.d.
Phil 8876.47 Black, Hugh. Culture and restraint. N.Y., 1901.
Phil 8876.48 Benedict, W.R. World views and their ethical implications. Cincinnati, 1902.
Phil 8876.49 Bunge, E.O. Il diritto. 3. ed. Torino, 1909.
Phil 8876.50 Bosanquet, B. Some suggestions in ethics. London, 1918.
Phil 8876.51 Bayet, Albert. La morale scientifique. 2e ed. Paris, 1907.
Phil 8876.51.5 Bayet, Albert. L'ideé de bien. Paris, 1908.
Phil 8876.51.9 Bayet, Albert. Le mirage de la vertu. Paris, 1912.
Phil 8876.51.13 Bayet, Albert. La science des faits moraux. Paris, 1925.
Phil 8876.51.19 Bayet, Albert. La morale laïque et ses adversaires. 4e éd. Paris, 1925.
Phil 8876.52 Berge, Vincent. La vraie morale basée sur l'étude de la nature. 3. ed. Paris, 1913.
Phil 8876.53 Bonet-Maury, G. L'unité morale des religions. Paris, 1913.
Phil 8876.54 Blondel, Maurice. L'action. Paris, 1893.
Phil 8876.54.5 Blondel, Maurice. L'azione. Firenze, 1921. 2v.
Phil 8876.54.10 Blondel, Maurice. L'action. Paris, 1936.
Phil 8876.54.25 Crippa, R. Profilo della critica blondeliana. Milano, 1962.
Phil 8876.55 Bennett, Arnold. How to live on 24 hours a day. N.Y., 1910.
Phil 8876.55.5 Bennett, Arnold. The reasonalbe life, being hints for men and women. London, 1907.
Phil 8876.55.7 Bennett, Arnold. How to make the best of life. N.Y., 1923.
Phil 8876.55.13A Bennett, Arnold. The human machine. N.Y., 1911.
Phil 8876.55.13B Bennett, Arnold. The human machine. N.Y., 1911.
Phil 8876.55.20 Bennett, Arnold. The human machine. London, 1920.
Phil 8876.56 Becher, Erich. Die Grundfrage der Ethik. Köln, 1908.

Phil 8875 - 8900 Ethics - General treatises - Individual authors (A-Z) - cont.

Phil 8876.57 Beaussire, Émile. Les principes de la morale. Paris, 1885.
Phil 8876.58 Bender, Hedwig. Über das Wesen der Sittlichkeit. Halle, 1891.
Phil 8876.59 Böhmer, Gustav. Ein Buch von der deutschen Gesinnung fünf ethische Essays. München, 1897.
Phil 8876.60 Benett, William. Freedom and liberty. London, 1920.
Phil 8876.61 Balsillie, David. The ethic of nature and its practical bearings. Edinburgh, 1889.
Phil 8876.62.3 Barbier, Louise. La loi morale fondée sur l'etude comparée des deux natures de l'homme. Paris, 1884.
Phil 8876.63 Baets, Maurice de. Les bases de la morale et du droit. Paris, 1892.
Phil 8876.64 Biedermann, Karl. Zeit- und Lebensfragen aus dem Gebiete der Moral. Breslau, 1899.
Phil 8876.65 Bonnaire, L. de. La regle des devoirs. Paris, 1758. 3v.
Phil 8876.66 Broglie, Paul. Instruction morale. 10e éd. Paris, 18- .
Phil 8876.67 Bowker, R.R. The arts of life. Boston, 1900.
Phil 8876.68 Bohlin, F. Das Grundproblem der Ethik. Uppsala, 1923.
Phil 8876.69 Bouillier, F. Questions de morale pratique. Paris, 1889.
Phil 8876.72 Beysens, J.T. Ethiek of natuurlijke zedenleer. Leiden, 1913.
Phil 8876.73 Bang, N.H. Begrebet moral; analyse og kritik. København, 1897.
Phil 8876.74 Bolliger, Adolf. Beiträge zur Dogmatik und Ethik. Aaran, 1890.
Phil 8876.75 Bergemann, Paul. Ethik als Kulturphilosophie. Leipzig, 1904.
Phil 8876.76 Braileanu, T. Die Grundlegung zur einer Wissenschaft der Ethik. Wien, 1919.
Phil 8876.78 Barry, John D. Intimations. San Francisco, 1913.
Phil 8876.79 Bizyenos, Georgios. Psychologikai meletai apo tou kalou. Athens, 1885.
Phil 8876.80 Baumgarten, O. Praktische Sittenlehre. Tübingen, 1921.
Phil 8876.81 Bellaigue, A. La science morale. Paris, 1904.
Phil 8876.82 Bonucci, A. L'orientazione psicologica dell'etica e della filosofia del diritto. Perugia, 1907.
Phil 8876.83 Bentley, Joseph. How to sleep on a windy night. Philadelphia, 1928.
Phil 8876.84 Bonatelli, Paolo. Spunti di dottrina etica. Bologna, 1928.
Phil 8876.85 Bertauld, Alfred. L'ordre social et l'ordre moral. Paris, 1874.
Phil 8876.86 Bergmann, J. Über das Richtige. Berlin, 1883.
Phil 8876.87 Bullock, Arthur B. The supreme human tragedy and other essays. London, 1920.
Phil 8876.88 Broad, C.D. Five types of ethical theory. London, 1930.
Phil 8876.88.5 Broad, C.D. Five types of ethical theory. London, 1951.
Phil 8876.89 Bonar, J. Moral sense. London, 1930.
Phil 8876.90 Bouterwek, F. Praktische Aphorismen. Leipzig, 1808.
Phil 8876.91 Berdiaev, N.A. O naznachenii cheloveka. Parizh, 1931.
Phil 8876.91.5 Berdiaev, N.A. Von der Bestimmung des Menschen. Bern, 1935.
Phil 8876.91.11 Berdiaev, N.A. The destiny of man. N.Y., 1960.
Phil 8876.91.12A Berdiaev, N.A. The destiny of man. London, 1959.
Phil 8876.91.12B Berdiaev, N.A. The destiny of man. London, 1959.
Phil 8876.91.15 Berdiaev, N.A. De la destination de l'homme. Paris, 1935.
Phil 8876.92 Barclay, Thomas. The wisdom of Lang-Sin. N.Y., 1927.
Phil 8876.93 Brightman, E.S. Moral laws. N.Y., 1933.
Phil 8876.94 Barrett, C.L. Ethics; an introduction to the philosophy of moral values. N.Y., 1933.
Phil 8876.95 Baumgarten, Arthur. Der Weg des Menschen. Tübingen, 1933.
Phil 8876.96 Barnett, M.J. The five redeemers. Boston, 1890.
Phil 8876.97 Bell, F.O. The minor moralist. London, 1903.
Phil 8876.98 Bauch, Bruno. Grundzüge der Ethik. Stuttgart, 1935.
Phil 8876.99 Bouffleis, Stanislas de. Discours sur la vertu. 2e éd. Paris, 1800.
Phil 8876.100 Baudin, E. Cours de philosophie morale. Paris, 1936.
Phil 8876.101 Borle, Charles A. The art of living. Boston, 1936.
Phil 8876.102 Briel, C. L'homme moral, ou Règles de conduite prises dans sa propre nature. Sens, 179-
Phil 8876.103 Brooklyn Ethical Association. Life and the conditions of survival. Chicago, 1895.
Phil 8876.104 Blanchard, Mme. Common sense. N.Y., 1916.
Phil 8876.105 Blanchard, Mme. Timidity. N.Y., 1916.
Phil 8876.106 Barrett, J.W. How to overcome your 7 deadly enemies. N.Y., 1939.
Phil 8876.107 Börner, W. Politsche Zeitfragen in ethischer Beleuchtung. Wien, 1935.
Phil 8876.107.5 Börner, W. Zur ethischen Lebensgestaltung. Wien, 1937?
Phil 8876.108 Beauvoir, Simone de. The ethics of ambiguity. N.Y., 1949.
Phil 8876.108.5A Beauvoir, Simone de. Pour une morale de l'ambiguité. Paris, 1947.
Phil 8876.108.5B Beauvoir, Simone de. Pour une morale de l'ambiguité. Paris, 1947.
Phil 8876.108.7 Beauvoir, Simone de. Pour une morale de l'ambiguité suivi de Pyraus et Cinéas. Paris, 1944.
Phil 8876.110 Barboza, E. Etica. Lima, 1936.
Phil 8876.112 Brentano, F. Grundlegung und Anfban der Ethik. Bern, 1952.
Phil 8876.115 Barbour, R.R.P. Ethical theory. Adelaide, 1933.
Phil 8876.117 Baier, Kurt. The moral point of view. Ithaca, 1958.
Phil 8876.117.2 Baier, Kurt. The moral point of view. N.Y., 1967.
Phil 8876.118.2 Bollnow, Otto Friedrich. Einfache Sittlichkeit. 2. Aufl. Göttingen, 1957.
Phil 8876.119 Baylis, C.A. Ethics. N.Y., 1958.
Phil 8876.120 Brock, Erich. Befreiung und Erfüllung. Zürich, 1958.
Phil 8876.121 Bowes, Pratima. The concept of morality. London, 1959.
Phil 8876.123 Berlin, Isaiah. Two concepts of liberty. Oxford, 1958.
Phil 8876.125 Brandt, Richard. Ethical theory. Englewood Cliffs, N.J., 1959.
Phil 8876.130 Blegvad, Mogeus. Den naturalistiske sejlslutning. København, 1959.
Phil 8876.135A Blanshard, Brand. Reason and goodness. London, 1961.
Phil 8876.135B Blanshard, Brand. Reason and goodness. London, 1961.
Phil 8876.140 Binkley, Luther J. Contemporary ethical theories. N.Y., 1961.
Phil 8876.145 Berge, André. Les maladies de la vertu. Paris, 1960.
Phil 8876.150 Bersandius, J. Venatio hominum. Francofonte, 1677.
Phil 8876.155 Bastide, Georges. Traite de l'action morale. Paris, 1961. 2v.
Phil 8876.156 Bertocci, Peter. Personality and the good. N.Y., 1963.
Phil 8876.157 Biroud, K. Manevi limler metadu olorok anlama. Ankara, 1960.
Phil 8876.160 Banner, William Augustus. Ethics: an introduction to moral philosophy. N.Y., 1968.

Phil 8875 - 8900   Ethics - General treatises - Individual authors (A-Z) - cont.

Phil 8876.162   Blumenfeld, Walter. Vom sittlichen Bewusstsein. Bonn, 1968.

Phil 8876.164   Beardsmore, R.W. Moral reasoning. London, 1969.

Phil 8876.166   Baader, Franz von. Über die Begründung der Ethik durch die Physik und andere Schriften. Stuttgart, 1969.

Phil 8877.1   Calderwood, H. Handbook of moral philosophy. London, 1884.

Phil 8877.1.2   Calderwood, H. Handbook of moral philosophy. London, 1872.

Phil 8877.1.3   Calderwood, H. Handbook of moral philosophy. 6th ed. London, 1879.

Phil 8877.1.5   Calderwood, H. Handbook of moral philosophy. London, 1895.

Phil 8877.4   Capel, A. Excellent contemplations divine and moral. London, 1683.

Phil 8877.5.2   Champlin, J.T. First principles of ethics. N.Y., n.d.

Phil 8877.6   Chaney, G.L. Every day life and every day morals. Boston, 1885.

Phil 8877.7   Charma, A. Essai...bases...développmens de la moralité. Paris, 1834.

Phil 8877.8   Chipman, G. The American moralist. Wrentham, Mass., 1801.

X Cg   Phil 8877.10   Clap, T. An essay...nature. Foundation. Moral virtue. New Haven, 1765.

Phil 8877.11   Clark, S.D. The faithful steward. Boston, 1853.

NEDL   Phil 8877.12   Cobbe, F.P. An essay on intuitive morals. London, 1855-57. 2v.

Phil 8877.12.2   Cobbe, F.P. An essay on intuitive morals. pt.1. Boston, 1859.

Phil 8877.13   Cockburn, C. Works. London, 1751. 2v.

Phil 8877.14   Cogan, T. Ethical questions. London, 1817.

Phil 8877.15   Collier, Jeremy. Essays upon several moral subjects. v.1-4. London, 1702-09. 3v.

Phil 8877.15.2   Collier, Jeremy. Essays upon several moral subjects. 5th ed. pt. 1-2. London, 1703.

Phil 8877.15.4   Collier, Jeremy. Essays upon several moral subjects. 7th ed. pt. 1-2. London, 1732.

Htn   Phil 8877.15.5*   Collier, Jeremy. Miscellanies in five essays. London, 1694.

Phil 8877.16   Collignon, A. L'art et la vie. Metz, 1866.

Phil 8877.18   Compayré, J.G. Eléments d'instruction morale et civique. Paris, 1882.

Phil 8877.18.2   Compayré, J.G. Lectures morales et civiques. Paris, 1883.

Phil 8877.18.10   Compayré, J.G. Cours de morale theorique et pratique. 19th ed. Paris, n.d.

Phil 8877.19   Coignet, C. La morale indépendante. Paris, 1869.

Phil 8877.20   Counsel, E. Maxims. Melbourne, 188-?

Phil 8877.20.2   Counsel, E. Maxims. 2nd ed. Melbourne, 1892.

Phil 8877.21   Cowdery, M.F. Elementary moral lessons. Sandusky, 1855.

Phil 8877.21.2   Cowdery, M.F. Elementary moral lessons. Philadelphia, 1856.

Phil 8877.22   Campbell, A. An enquiry...original of moral virtue. London, 1734.

Phil 8877.24.5   Curtis, G.W. Aves recte vivendi. N.Y., 1899.

Phil 8877.25   Crell, J. Ethica aristotelica. Selenoburgi, n.d.

Phil 8877.26   Clark, T.M. Lectures on the formation of character. Hartford, 1852.

Phil 8877.27   Craufurd, A.H. Enigmas of the spiritual life. London, 1888.

Phil 8877.28   Curbipet. Fragments of the elements and principles of the life of man. Bombay, 1904.

Phil 8877.29   Cresson, Andre. La morale de la raison theorique. Paris, 1903.

Phil 8877.30   Cole, W.M. The American hope. N.Y., 1910.

Phil 8877.31   Crane, F. Human confessions. Chicago, 1911.

Phil 8877.32   Carpenter, T.E. The doctrines of life. Boston, 1913.

Phil 8877.33.5   Callieres, F. de. The knowledge of the world and the attainments. Dublin, 1774.

Phil 8877.34   Croce, Benedetto. Cultura e vita morale. Bari, 1914.

Phil 8877.34.2   Croce, Benedetto. Cultura e vita morale. 2a ed. Bari, 1926.

Phil 8877.34.4   Croce, Benedetto. Filosofia della pratica; economica ed etica. Bari, 1909.

Phil 8877.34.5   Croce, Benedetto. Filosofia della pratica; economia ed etica. 2a ed. Bari, 1915.

Phil 8877.34.6   Croce, Benedetto. Filosofia della pratica; economia ed etica. 6. ed. Bari, 1950.

Phil 8877.34.8   Croce, Benedetto. Frammenti di etica. Bari, 1922.

Phil 8877.34.9   Croce, Benedetto. Fragmente zur Ethik; übersetzt von J. Schlosser. Zürich, 1922.

Phil 8877.35   Carpenter, W.B. Life's tangled thread. London, 1912.

Phil 8877.36   Coffin, J.H. The socialized conscience. Baltimore, 1913.

Phil 8877.37   Caso, Antonio. Filósofos y doctrinas morales. Mexico, 1915.

Phil 8877.38   Cooke, H.P. Maurice, the philosopher. Cambridge, 1912.

Phil 8877.39   Culp, C.J. The ethical ideal of renunciation. Thesis. N.Y., 1914.

Phil 8877.41   Carus, Paul. The ethical problem. Chicago, 1890.

Phil 8877.42   Carus, Paul. The ethical problem. 3rd ed. Chicago, 1910.

Phil 8877.43   Coppens, Charles. A brief text-book of moral philosophy. N.Y., 1895.

Phil 8877.44.5   Calkins, Mary W. The good man and the good. N.Y., 1928.

Phil 8877.47   Cope, Henry F. The friendly life. N.Y., 1909.

Phil 8877.48   Cutler, Carroll. The beginnings of ethics. N.Y., 1889.

Phil 8877.49   Castellotti, G. de. Saggi di etica e di diritto. Ser. 1-2,3-5. Ascoli Piceno, 1903-06. 2v.

Phil 8877.50.5   Cathrein, Victor. Die Einheit des sittlichen Bewusstseins der Menschheit. Freiburg, 1914. 3v.

Phil 8877.50.15   Cathrein, Victor. Moralphilosophie. Leipzig, 1924. 2v.

Phil 8877.51   Cohen, C. An outline of evolutionary ethics. London, 1896.

Phil 8877.52   Class, Gustav. Ideale und Güter; Untersuchungen zur Ethik. Erlangen, 1886.

Phil 8877.53   Chalybäus, Heinrich. System der speculativen Ethik. Leipzig, 1850. 2v.

Phil 8877.54   Cox, George C. The public conscience. N.Y., 1922.

Phil 8877.55   Cronin, Michael. The science of ethics. Dublin, 1909.

Phil 8877.55.2   Cronin, Michael. The science of ethics. 2nd ed. Dublin, 1920-22. 2v.

Phil 8877.56   Courcelle-Seneuil, J.G. Précis de morale rationnelle. Paris, 1875.

Phil 8877.58   Challaye, F. Les principes généraux de la science et de la morale. Paris, 1920.

Phil 8877.58.5   Challaye, F. Philosophie scientifique et philosophie morale. 3. ed. Paris, 1927.

Phil 8877.58.15   Challaye, F. Cours de morale, a l'usuge des écoles primaires superieures. Paris, 1927.

Phil 8877.59   Clemmens, H.W. Moralische Betrachtungen. Stuttgart, 1761.

Phil 8877.60   Chabot, Charles. Nature et moralité. Paris, 1896.

Phil 8877.60.10   Chabot, Charles. Morale théorique et notions historiques. 10e éd. Paris, 1925.

Phil 8877.61   Christ, Paul. Die sittliche Weltordnung. Leiden, 1894.

Phil 8877.62   Carneri, B. Entwicklung und Glückseligkeit. Stuttgart, 1886.

Phil 8877.62.12   Carneri, B. Grundlegung der Ethik. Stuttgart, 19- .

Phil 8877.63   Cohn, Georg. Etik og sociologi. Kjøbenhavn, 1913.

Phil 8877.64   Coudenhove-Kalergi, R.N. Ethik und Hyperethik. Leipzig, 1923.

Phil 8877.64.5   Coudenhove-Kalergi, R.N. Krise der Weltanschauung. Wien, 1923.

Phil 8877.65   Cabot, Richard C. Adventures on the borderlands of ethics. N.Y., 1926.

Phil 8877.65.8   Cabot, Richard C. What men live by. Boston, 1914.

Phil 8877.65.20A   Cabot, Richard C. The meaning of right and wrong. N.Y., 1933.

Phil 8877.65.20B   Cabot, Richard C. The meaning of right and wrong. N.Y., 1933.

Phil 8877.65.22   Cabot, Richard C. The meaning of right and wrong. N.Y., 1936.

Phil 8877.65.30   Cabot, Richard C. Prescriptions. Boston, 1915.

Phil 8877.66   Crane, Anker. Lykkens smil. København, 1922.

Phil 8877.67   Campos Gimenez, J. La voz de la virtud. Habana, 1868.

Phil 8877.68   Carritt, Edgar F. Theory of morals. London, 1928.

Phil 8877.68.5   Carritt, Edgar F. An ambiguity of the word "good". London, 1937.

Phil 8877.68.10   Carritt, Edgar F. Ethical and political thinking. Oxford, 1947.

Phil 8877.68.15   Carritt, Edgar F. The theory of beauty. London, 1962.

Phil 8877.69   Copeland, Edwin B. Natural conduct. Stanford, Calif., 1928.

Phil 8877.70   Carlos, M. Moral e economia politica. Rio de Janeiro, 1941.

Phil 8877.71   Clark, Gordon H. Reading in ethics. N.Y., 1931.

Phil 8877.71.15   Clark, Gordon H. Reading in ethics. 2nd ed. N.Y., 1943.

Phil 8877.72   Crothers, S.McC. Three lords of destiny. Boston, 1913.

Phil 8877.73   Clarke, F. (Mrs.). Give yourself a new deal. Boston, 1933.

Phil 8877.74   Cushman, H.E. Ten lessons in ethics. Newton, 1924.

Phil 8877.75   Clifford, William K. The scientific basis of morals, and other essays. N.Y., 1884.

Phil 8877.75.5   Clifford, William K. The ethics of belief. London, 1947.

Phil 8877.76   Colesanti, Giulio. Esiste una morale? Catania, 1937.

Phil 8877.76.5   Colesanti, Giulio. La morale supérieure. Paris, 1940.

Phil 8877.77   Coltman, J. Everyman's monitor. Philadelphia, 1815.

Phil 8877.78.3   Conwell, Russell H. Acres of diamonds. N.Y., 1943.

Phil 8877.79   Chevalier, J. La vie morale et l'audelà. Paris, 1938.

Phil 8877.80   Casserley, J.V.L. Morals and man in the social sciences. London, 1951.

Phil 8877.82   Childs, M.W. Ethics in a business society. 1st ed. N.Y., 1954.

Phil 8877.84   Coornhert, D.V. Zedekunst. Leiden, 1942.

Phil 8877.86   Castell, Alhurey. An elementary ethics. Englewood Cliffs, 1955.

Phil 8877.90   Cysarz, Herbert. Individuelle und collektive Ethik. Tübingen, 1958.

Phil 8877.91   Casamayor, Louis. La justice, l'homme et la liberté. Paris, 1964.

Phil 8877.94   Campbell, Charles Arthur. In defense of free will. London, 1967.

Phil 8877.95   Creasey, John. Good, God and man; an outline of the philosophy of self-ism. London, 1967.

VPhil 8877.96   Čáda, F. Cádova etika individualní. Praha, 1920.

Phil 8877.100   Casey, John. Morality and moral reasoning; five essays in ethics. London, 1971.

Phil 8877.102   Coste, René. Une morale pour un monde en mutation. Gembloux, 1969.

Phil 8878.1   Dameth, C.M.H. Le juste et l'utile. Paris, 1859.

Phil 8878.2   Damiron, P. Cours de philosophie, morale. Paris, 1834.

Phil 8878.4A   Davies, J.L. Theology and morality. London, 1873.

Phil 8878.4B   Davies, J.L. Theology and morality. London, 1873.

Htn   Phil 8878.4.5*   Davies, J.L. Order and growth. London, 1891.

Phil 8878.5   Davy, H. Consolations in travel. Philadelphia, 1831.

Phil 8878.5.4   Davy, H. Consolations in travel. 4th ed. London, 1838.

Phil 8878.5.5   Davy, H. Consolations in travel. London, 1851.

Phil 8878.5.7   Davy, H. Consolations in travel. Philadelphia, 1830.

Phil 8878.5.8   Davy, H. Consolations in travel. London, 1830.

Phil 8878.6   Davy, C.W. The maxims...of Agogos. Boston, 1844.

Phil 8878.7   Delisle de Sales, J.B.C.I. De la philosophie de la nature. London, 1777. 6v.

Phil 8878.7.10   Delisle de Sales, J.B.C.I. De la philosophie du bonheur. Paris, 1796. 2v.

Phil 8878.7.20   Delisle de Sales, J.B.C.I. Memoire en faveur de Dieu. Paris, 1802.

Phil 8878.7.25   Delisle de Sales, J.B.C.I. Defense d'un homme. n.p., 1802.

Phil 8878.7.27   Delisle de Sales, J.B.C.I. Defense d'un homme. Paris, 1803.

Phil 8878.8   Dewar, D. Elements of moral philosophy. London, 1826. 2v.

Phil 8878.9   Dewey, O. Moral views of commerce, society and politics. N.Y., 1838.

Phil 8878.10   Disney, J. A second essay...execution...laws against immorality. London, 1710.

Phil 8878.10.5   Disney, J. Essay upon execution of laws vs. immorality and prophaneness. London, 1708.

Phil 8878.11.2   Dewey, John. Outlines of a critical theory of ethics. N.Y., 1957.

Phil 8878.11.3   Dewey, John. Outlines of a critical theory of ethics. N.Y., 1969.

Phil 8878.11.7   Dewey, John. The study of ethics, a syllabus. Photoreproduction. Ann Arbor, 1897.

Phil 8878.11.8   Dewey, John. Ethics [lecture]. N.Y., 1908.

Phil 8878.11.9A   Dewey, John. Ethics. N.Y., 1908.

Phil 8878.11.9B   Dewey, John. Ethics. N.Y., 1908.

Phil 8878.11.12   Dewey and Tufts. Ethics. N.Y., 1929.

Phil 8878.11.13   Dewey, John. Logical conditions of a scientific treatment of morality. Chicago, 1903.

Phil 8878.11.15B   Dewey, John. Ethics. N.Y., 1926.

Phil 8878.11.20A   Dewey, John. Ethics. N.Y., 1932.

Phil 8878.11.20B   Dewey, John. Ethics. N.Y., 1932.

Phil 8878.11.20C   Dewey, John. Ethics. N.Y., 1932.

Phil 8878.11.20D   Dewey, John. Ethics. N.Y., 1932.

Phil 8878.12   Doddridge, P. A course of lectures...pneumatology, ethics. London, 1794.

387

Classified Listing

Phil 8875 - 8900 Ethics - General treatises - Individual authors (A-Z) - cont.

Htn Phil 8878.13* Dodsley, R. The economy of human life. v.1-2. Philadelphia, 1786.
Htn Phil 8878.13.2* Dodsley, R. The economy of human life. Leominster, Mass., 1797.
Phil 8878.13.3 Dodsley, R. The economy of human life. v.1-2. Manchester, 1801.
Phil 8878.13.3.10 Dodsley, R. The economy of human life. London, 1806.
Phil 8878.13.3.25 Dodsley, R. The economy of human life. Chisnick, 1825.
Phil 8878.13.4 Dodsley, R. The economy of human life. Chicago, 1827.
Phil 8878.13.4.15 Dodsley, R. The economy of human life. Philadelphia, 1845.
Phil 8878.13.5 Dodsley, R. The duties of human life. West Killingly, Conn., 1858.
Htn Phil 8878.13.7* Dodsley, R. The economy of human life. Norwich, 1795.
Phil 8878.13.8 Dodsley, R. Economia della vita umana. N.Y., 1825.
Phil 8878.13.9 Dodsley, R. The economy of human life. London, 1751.
Htn Phil 8878.13.9.5* Dodsley, R. The economy of human life. n.p., 1769.
Phil 8878.13.10 Dodsley, R. The economy of human life. pt. 1-2. London, 1795.
Htn Phil 8878.13.12* Dodsley, R. The economy of human life. N.Y., 1793.
Htn Phil 8878.13.15* Dodsley, R. The economy of human life. Salem, 1795.
Htn Phil 8878.15* Drexelius, H. Nicetas feu triumphata incontinentia. Colonia Agrippina, 1631.
Phil 8878.16 Durand Desormeaux, F. Etudes philosophiques. Paris, 1884. 2v.
Phil 8878.17 Dusch, J.J. Moralische Briefe. Leipzig, 1772. 2v.
Phil 8878.17.5 Dusch, J.J. Moralische Briefe. v.2. Wien, 1771.
Phil 8878.18 Dymond, J. Essays...principles of morality. London, 1867.
Phil 8878.18.2 Dymond, J. Essays...principles of morality. N.Y., 1844.
Phil 8878.18.4 Dymond, J. Essays...principles of morality. N.Y., 1834.
Phil 8878.18.5 Dymond, J. Essays...principles of morality. Philadelphia, 1896.
Phil 8878.18.7 Dix, A. Der Egoismus. Leipzig, 1899.
Phil 8878.19 Darell, W. The gentleman instructed. London, 1738.
Phil 8878.20 Durand, J.P. Nouvelles recherches sur l'esthetique et la morale. Paris, 1900.
Phil 8878.21 Davis, Noals K. Elements of ethics. Boston, 1900.
Phil 8878.22 Duprat, G.L. Morals: a treatise on the psycho-sociological bases of ethics. London, 1903.
Phil 8878.22.2 Duprat, G.L. La morale. Théorie psycho-sociologique d'une conduite rationnelle. 2. ed. Paris, 1912.
Phil 8878.23.4 Dickinson, G.L. The meaning of good. 4th ed. N.Y., 1907.
Phil 8878.24 DuBois, P. The culture of justice. N.Y., 1907.
Phil 8878.24.5 DuBois, P. Self-control and how to secure it. N.Y., 1909.
Phil 8878.24.7 DuBois, P. The education of self. N.Y., 1911.
Phil 8878.24.10 DuBois, P. L'éducation de soi-même. Paris, 1913.
Phil 8878.25 Davies, A.E. The moral life; a study in genetic ethics. Baltimore, 1909.
Phil 8878.26 Döring, A. Philosophische Güterlehre. Berlin, 1888.
Phil 8878.27 DeMotte, J.B. The secret of character building. Chicago, 1893.
Phil 8878.28.2 Drake, Durant. Problems of conduct. Boston, 1921.
Phil 8878.28.10 Drake, Durant. The new morality. N.Y., 1928.
Phil 8878.29 Dumont, Arsène. La morale basée sur la démographie. Paris, 1901.
Phil 8878.30 Dittes, F. Über die sittliche Freiheit. Leipzig, 1860.
Phil 8878.30.2 Dittes, F. Über die sittliche Freiheit. 2e Aufl. Leipzig, 1892.
Phil 8878.31 Dalmau y Gratacós, F. Elementos de filosofia. Barcelona, 1911.
Phil 8878.32 DuRoussaux, L. Ethique; traité de philosophie morale. Bruxelles, 1907.
Phil 8878.33 Dupuy, Paul. Les fondements de la morale. Paris, 1900.
Phil 8878.34 Dugas, L. Cours de morale thérique et pratique. v.1-2. Paris, 1905-06.
Phil 8878.35 Davies, William. The pilgrim of the infinite. London, 1894.
Phil 8878.36 Deshumbert, Marius. An ethical system based on the laws of nature. Chicago, 1917.
Phil 8878.36.8 Deshumbert, Marius. Morale fondée sur les lois de la nature. 3e éd. Paris, 191-.
Phil 8878.37 Dürr, Ernst. Das Gute und das Sittliche. Heidelberg, 1911.
Phil 8878.37.5 Dürr, Ernst. Grundzüge der Ethik von Dr. E. Dürr. Heidelberg, 1909.
Phil 8878.38 Dorner, August. Individuelle und sozial Ethik. Berlin, 1906.
Phil 8878.39 Duboc, Julius. Grundriss einer Einheitlichen. Leipzig, 1892.
Phil 8878.40 Dugard, Marie. La culture morale. 8e éd. Paris, 1919.
Phil 8878.41 Dessaignes, J.P. Études de l'homme moral. Paris, 1882. 3v.
Phil 8878.42 Del Mar, E. The divinity of desire. N.Y., 1906.
Phil 8878.43 Droz, J. De la philosophie morale. 2e éd. Paris, 1824.
Phil 8878.44 Dam, Axel. Livets vardiproblemer. København, 1921.
Phil 8878.45 Dresser, H.W. Ethics in theory and application. N.Y., 1925.
Phil 8878.46 Donati, G. La morale. Forli, 1918.
Phil 8878.47 Driesch, Hans. Die sittliche Tat. Leipzig, 1927.
Phil 8878.47.5 Driesch, Hans. Ethical principles in theory and practice. N.Y., 1927.
Phil 8878.48 Dumesnil, L.A.L. Examen politique, philosophique et moral. Caen, 1805.
Phil 8878.49 Dunham, James. Principles of ethics. N.Y., 1929.
Phil 8878.50 Dupréel, Eugène. Traité de morale. Bruxelles, 1932. 2v.
Phil 8878.50.1 Dupréel, Eugène. Traité de morale. Bruxelles, 1967. 2v.
Phil 8878.51.5 Dimnet, Ernest. What we live by. N.Y., 1932.
Phil 8878.51.8 Dimnet, Ernest. What we live by. London, 1932.
Phil 8878.52 Dyer, W.A. The richer life. Garden City, 1911.
Phil 8878.53 Dingler, Hugo. Das Handeln im Sinne des Höchsten Zieles. (Absolute Ethik). München, 1935.
Phil 8878.54 Das, Ras-Vihari. The self and the ideal. Calcutta, 1935.
Phil 8878.55 DeBoer, Cecil. The if's and ought's of ethics. Grand Rapids, Mich., 1936.
Phil 8878.57 Burgh, W.G. de. From morality to religion. London, 1938.
Phil 8878.58* Dodsley, R. The economy of human life. Exeter, 1788.
Phil 8878.59 Delvolvé, J. La fonchion morale. Paris, 1951.
Phil 8878.60 D'Arcy, E. Human acts. Oxford, 1963.
Phil 8878.61 Devlin, Patrick. The enforcement of morals. London, 1965.
Phil 8878.62 Dupleix, Scipion. L'ethique, ou Philosophie morale. Paris, 1610.
Phil 8879.2A Eliot, C.W. The happy life. N.Y., 1896-97.
Phil 8879.2B Eliot, C.W. The happy life. N.Y., 1896-97.
Phil 8879.2.3 Eliot, C.W. The happy life. N.Y., 1896.
Phil 8879.2.5 Eliot, C.W. The happy life. N.Y., 1896.

Phil 8875 - 8900 Ethics - General treatises - Individual authors (A-Z) - cont.

Phil 8879.2.9 Eliot, C.W. The happy life. N.Y., 1896.
Phil 8879.2.12 Eliot, C.W. The happy life. N.Y., 1905.
Phil 8879.3 Ellis, S.S. The women of England. v.1-4. N.Y., 1843.
Phil 8879.3.2 Ellis, S.S. The women of England. v.1-2. Philadelphia, 1839.
Phil 8879.3.5 Ellis, S.S. Guide to social happiness. v.1-4. N.Y., 1844-47.
Phil 8879.4 Ellis, S.S. At our best. Boston, 1873.
Phil 8879.5 Ensor, G. The principles of morality. London, 1801.
Phil 8879.6A Erasmus, D. Lingua, sive, de linguae. Lugdunum Batavorum, 1641.
Phil 8879.6B Erasmus, D. Lingua, sive, de linguae. Lugdunum Batavorum, 1641.
Htn Phil 8879.6.2* Erasmus, D. Lingua, sive, de linguae. Basileae, 1547.
Phil 8879.6.5 Erasmus, D. Civilitas morum. Goslariae, 1733.
Phil 8879.6.6 Erasmus, D. De civilitate morum. Rostochi, 1632.
Phil 8879.7 Eschenmayer, C.A.A. System der Moralphilosophie. Stuttgart, 1818.
Phil 8879.8 Estlin, J.P. Familiar lectures on moral philosophy. London, 1818. 2v.
Phil 8879.10 Everett, C.C. The ultimate facts of ethics. Boston, 1887.
Phil 8879.10.5 Everett, C.C. Theism and the Christian faith. N.Y., 1909.
Phil 8879.10.8 Everett, C.C. Ethics for young people. Boston, 1891.
Phil 8879.11 Ephemeriden der Menschkeit. v.1-4,5-8,9-12. Basel, 1777. 3v.
Phil 8879.12 Ehrenfels, C. System der Werttheorie. Leipzig, 1897.
Phil 8879.13 Eucken, R.C. Einführung...Philosophie des Geisteslebens. Leipzig, 1908.
Phil 8879.13.5 Eucken, R.C. Present-day ethics. London, 1913.
Phil 8879.13.10 Eucken, R.C. Ethics and modern thought. N.Y., 1913.
Phil 8879.14 Ehrenberg, F. Reden uber wichtige Gegenstande. Leipzig, 1804.
Phil 8879.15 Everett, W.G. Moral values. N.Y., 1918.
Phil 8879.16.2 Eisler, Julius. Lehrbuch der allgemeinen Ethik. 2e Aufl. Wien, 1912.
Phil 8879.17 Eleutheropoulos, A. Die Sittlichkeit und der philosophische Sittlichkeitswahn. Berlin, 1899.
Phil 8879.18 Edgeworth, F.Y. New and old methods of ethics. Oxford, 1877.
Phil 8879.19 Edfeldt, Hans. Om de etiska grundbegreppen. Upsala, 1894.
Phil 8879.20 Enberg, L.M. Moralfilosofiens elementer. Stockholm, 1831.
Phil 8879.21 Eberhard, J.A. Sittenlehre der Vernunft. Berlin, 1786.
Phil 8879.22 Edfeldt, H. Om begreppet sedlighet. Upsala, 1877.
Phil 8879.23 Edgell, B. Ethical problems. London, 1929.
Phil 8879.24 Eby, L.S. The quest for moral law. N.Y., 1944.
Phil 8879.25 Everett, M.S. Ideals of life. N.Y., 1954.
Phil 8879.26 Edel, A. Ethical judgement. Glencoe, 1955.
Phil 8879.27 Erismann, T. Sein und Wollen. Wien, 1953.
Phil 8879.28 Edwards, Paul. The logic of moral discourse. Glencoe, Ill., 1955.
Phil 8879.29 Easton, L.D. Ethics. Dubuque, Iowa, 1955.
Phil 8879.30 Ehrlich, Walter. Ethik. Tübingen, 1956.
Phil 8879.31 Endres, Josef. Menschliche Grundhaltungen. Salzubrg, 1958.
Phil 8879.32 Ewing, Alfred. Ethics. London, 1960.
Phil 8879.33 Engst, Jaroslav. Nekotorye problemy nauchnoi etiki. Moskva, 1960.
Phil 8879.34 Edel, A. Method in ethical theory. London, 1963.
Phil 8879.35 Elken, Robert. Konsequenzen der Naturwissenschaft. Kassel, 1963.
Phil 8879.35.5 Elken, Rober. Ethik naturwissenschaftlich Fundiert und Kirche. Kassel, 1968.
Phil 8879.36 Egemen, Bedi Ziya. Terkiye ilminin problemlen. Ankara, 1965.
Phil 8879.38 Eichhorn, Wolfgang. Wie ist Ethik als Wissenschaft möglich? Berlin, 1965.
Phil 8879.40 Emmet, Dorothy Mary. Rules, roles, and relations. N.Y., 1966.
Htn Phil 8880.1* Feltham, O. Resolves. London, 1636.
Phil 8880.1.2 Feltham, O. Resolves. London, 1806.
Phil 8880.1.3 Feltham, O. Resolves. London, 1840.
Htn Phil 8880.1.3.2* Feltham, O. Resolves. London, 1840.
Phil 8880.1.4 Feltham, O. Resolves. Cambridge, 1832.
Phil 8880.1.7 Feltham, O. Resolves. London, 1904.
Htn Phil 8880.1.8* Feltham, O. Resolves. 2nd ed. London, 1628. 2 pam.
Htn Phil 8880.1.9* Feltham, O. Resolves. 3rd ed. London, 1628.
Htn Phil 8880.1.10* Feltham, O. Resolves. 4th ed. London, 1631.
Htn Phil 8880.1.11* Feltham, O. Resolves. 5th ed. London, 1634.
Htn Phil 8880.1.12* Feltham, O. Resolves. London, 1670.
Phil 8880.1.15 Feltham, O. The beauties of Owen Felltham. N.Y., 1803.
Phil 8880.2 Ferris, S. Mental perceptions. London, 1807.
Phil 8880.3 Ferguson, Adam. Grundsätze der Moralphilosophie. Leipzig, 1772.
Phil 8880.3.5 Ferguson, Adam. Institutes of moral philosophy. Edinburgh, 1769.
Phil 8880.4 Fiddes, R. A general treatise of morality. London, 1724.
Phil 8880.5 Fiske, N. The moral monitor. v.2. Worcester, Mass., 1801.
Phil 8880.6 Fitzgerald, P.F. The rational, or scientific ideal of morality. London, 1897.
Htn Phil 8880.7* Fleming, C. A scale of first principles. London, 1755.
Phil 8880.8 Fleming, W. A manual of moral philosophy. London, 1867.
Phil 8880.8.2 Fleming, W. A manual of moral philosophy. London, 1870.
Phil 8880.10 Fordyce, D. The elements of moral philosophy. v.1-3. London, 1758.
Phil 8880.11 Forsyth, R. The principles of moral science. Edinburgh, 1805.
Phil 8880.12.25 Foster, John. An essay on the improvement of time. N.Y., 1866.
Phil 8880.13 Fowler, O.S. Self culture and perfection of character. N.Y., 1856.
Phil 8880.14 Fowler, T. The principles of moral. v.1-2. Oxford, 1886-87.
NEDL Phil 8880.15 Franklin, B. Saggi di morale. v.1-2. Volterre, 1834.
Phil 8880.16 Fry, Caroline. The listner. Philadelphia, 1833. 2v.
Phil 8880.16.2 Fry, Caroline. The listner. Philadelphia, 1832. 2v.
Phil 8880.16.5 Fry, Caroline. A word to women. Philadelphia, 1840.
Phil 8880.17 Fuller, T. The holy state and the profane state. London, 1840.
Phil 8880.17.2 Fuller, T. The holy state and the profane state. London, 1840.
Phil 8880.18.2 Fite, Warner. An introductory study of ethics. N.Y., 1906.
Phil 8880.18.5 Fite, Warner. Moral philosophy. N.Y., 1925.
Phil 8880.18.9 Fite, Warner. An adventure in moral philosophy. London, 1926.
Phil 8880.18.10 Fite, Warner. The examined life. Bloomington, Ind., 1957.

Phil 8875 - 8900   Ethics - General treatises - Individual authors (A-Z) - cont.

	Phil 8880.19	Farr, Lorin G. Ideal and real; the students calendar. Portland, Maine, 1904.
	Phil 8880.20	Fuller, J. Introductio ad prudentiam, or Directions. London, 1731.
	Phil 8880.20.5	Fuller, J. Introductio ad prudentiam, or Directions. pt.2. London, 1727.
	Phil 8880.20.10	Fuller, J. Introductio ad prudentiam, or Directions. London, 1787. 2v.
	Phil 8880.21	Fulliquet, G. Essai l'obligation morale. Paris, 1898.
	Phil 8880.23	Fairbairn, R.B. Of the doctrine of morality in its relation to grace of redemption. N.Y., 1887.
	Phil 8880.24	Fouillée, Alfred. Les elements sociologiques de la morale. Paris, 1905.
	Phil 8880.25	Fonsegrive, George. Morale et societé. 4e ed. Paris, 1908.
	Phil 8880.26	Fleuriau, A. de. L'activité réfléchie. Paris, 1911.
	Phil 8880.27	Faguet, Émile. Les préjugés nécessaires. Paris, 1911.
	Phil 8880.28	Frins, Victor. De actibus humanis. Friburgi Brisgoviae, 1897-1911.
	Phil 8880.29	Flügel, Otto. Das Ich und die sittlichen Ideen im Leben. 5e Aufl. Langensalza, 1912.
	Phil 8880.29.5	Flügel, Otto. Das Ich und die sittlichen Ideen im Leben der Völker. Langensalza, 1885.
	Phil 8880.30	Friso, Luigi. Filosofia morale. 3a ed. Milano, 1913.
	Phil 8880.31	Franze, Paul. Idealistische Sittenlehre. Leipzig, 1909.
	Phil 8880.32	Franze, Paul. Das höchste Gut. Berlin, 1912.
	Phil 8880.33	Frauenstädt, Julius. Das sittliche Leben. Leipzig, 1866.
	Phil 8880.34	Fuchs, Emil. Gut und Böse. Tübingen, 1906.
	Phil 8880.35	Fullerton, G.S. Handbook of ethical theory. N.Y., 1922.
	Phil 8880.36	Field, G.C. Moral theory. An introduction to ethics. London, 1922.
	Phil 8880.37.3	Freyer, Hans. Antäus. Jena, 1922.
	Phil 8880.38	Fowler, Thomas. Progressive morality; an essay in ethics. London, 1884.
	Phil 8880.39	Ferrari, G.M. Il problema etico. Rome, 1902.
	Phil 8880.40	Feder, J.G.H. Lehrbuch der praktischen Philosophie. Göttingen, 1770.
	Phil 8880.41	Flake, Otto. Die moralische Idee. München, 1921.
	Phil 8880.42	Franck, A. Menniskans sedliga lif. Stockholm, 1870.
	Phil 8880.43.5	Fairchild, J.H. Moral philosophy. Oberlin, Ohio, 1869.
	Phil 8880.44.5	Forbes, Alexander. Essays, moral and philosophical. London, 1734.
	Phil 8880.45	Falco, Francesco. L'ordine ed i fatti morali. Alessandria, 1874.
	Phil 8880.46	Freudenberg, G. Grenzen der Ethik. Leipzig, 1927.
	Phil 8880.47.10	Field, Joanna. An experiment in leisure. London, 1937.
	Phil 8880.48A	Fromm, Erich. Man for himself. N.Y., 1947.
	Phil 8880.48B	Fromm, Erich. Man for himself. N.Y., 1947.
	Phil 8880.49	Fagathey, Austin. Right and reason. St. Louis, 1953.
	Phil 8880.49.2	Fagathey, Austin. Right and reason. 2nd ed. St. Louis, 1959.
	Phil 8880.50	Findlay, John Niemayer. Values and intentions. London, 1961.
	Phil 8880.52	Frankena, W. Ethics. Englewood, 1963.
	Phil 8880.53	Fruchon, Pierre. Création ou consentement. Paris, 1963.
	Phil 8880.54	Ferraro, L. Dell'egoismo. Novara, 1963.
	Phil 8880.55	Feibleman, James. Moral strategy. The Hague, 1967.
	Phil 8880.56	Fourastié, Jean. Essais de morale prospective. Paris, 1967.
	Phil 8880.58	Forrest, John K. Reality or preachment; the moral crisis of our time. Boston, 1967.
	Phil 8880.60	Fernand-Laurent, Camille J. Morale et tyrannies. Paris, 1967.
	Phil 8880.63	Finance, Joseph de. Grundlegung der Ethik. Freiburg, 1968.
	Phil 8880.66	Fried, Charles. An anatomy of values; problems of personal and social choice. Cambridge, 1970.
	Phil 8880.68	Fink, Hans. Moralbegrundelse og logik. København, 1970.
	Phil 8880.70	Fallot, Jean. Pouvoir et morale. Thèse. Saverne, 1967.
	Phil 8881.1	G., W.A. The contrast: duty and pleasure, right and wrong. London, 1890.
	Phil 8881.3	Géhant, J.B.V. Science du bien et du mal. Paris, 1848. 2v.
	Phil 8881.4	Gellert, C.F. Leçons de morale. Utrecht, 1772. 2v.
Htn	Phil 8881.4.5*	Gellert, C.F. Moralische Vorlesungen. v. 1-3. Leipzig, 1770.
	Phil 8881.4.9	Douglas, M. The life of Professor C.F. Gellert. London, 1810. 3v.
	Phil 8881.6	Gerando, J.M. Self-education. Boston, 1830.
	Phil 8881.6.2	Gerando, J.M. Self-education. 2nd ed. Boston, 1832.
	Phil 8881.6.4	Gerando, J.M. Self-education. 3rd ed. Boston, 1860.
	Phil 8881.6.5	Gerando, J.M. Du perfectionnement moral. Paris, 1826. 2v.
	Phil 8881.7	Giles, A.E. Moral pathology. London, 1895.
	Phil 8881.8	Gilliot, A. Physiologie du sentiment. Paris, 1848. 2v.
	Phil 8881.9	Gilson, B. Manuel de philosophie morale. Louvain, 1883.
	Phil 8881.10	Gilman, N.P. Conduct as a fine art. Boston, 1891.
	Phil 8881.11	Gisborne, T. An enquiry into the duties of men. London, 1800. 2v.
	Phil 8881.11.2	Gisborne, T. An enquiry into the duties of men. London, 1824. 2v.
	Phil 8881.11.6	Gisborne, T. The principles of moral philosophy. London, 1790.
	Phil 8881.12A	Gizycki, G. Grundzüge der Moral. Leipzig, 1883.
	Phil 8881.12B	Gizycki, G. Grundzüge der Moral. Leipzig, 1883.
	Phil 8881.12.5	Gizycki, G. Students manual of ethical philosophy. London, 1889.
	Phil 8881.12.10	Gizycki, G. Moralphilosophie. Leipzig, n.d.
	Phil 8881.13A	Godwin, W. Thoughts on man. London, 1831.
	Phil 8881.13B	Godwin, W. Thoughts on man. London, 1831.
Htn	Phil 8881.14*	Government of the tongue. Oxford, 1675.
Htn	Phil 8881.14.2*	Government of the thoughts. Longon, 1700.
	Phil 8881.15.5	Gow, A.M. Good morals and gentle manners. N.Y., 1873.
	Phil 8881.16	Gratry, A.J.A. La morale et la loi de l'histoire. Paris, 1871. 2v.
	Phil 8881.17	Grote, J. The moral ideals. Cambridge, 1876.
	Phil 8881.18	Gross, J.B. What makes us unhappy? Philadelphia, 1882.
	Phil 8881.19	Grote, G. Fragments on ethical subjects. London, 1876.
	Phil 8881.20	Greg, W.R. Enigmas of life. London, 1883.
	Phil 8881.20.2	Greg, W.R. Enigmas of life. Boston, 1873.
	Phil 8881.21	Grove, H. A system of moral philosophy. London, 1749.
	Phil 8881.21.4	Grove, H. A system of moral philosophy. London, 1755. 2v.
	Phil 8881.22	Guilly, E.P. La nature et la morale. Paris, 1884.
	Phil 8881.23.15	Guizot, F.P.G. Méditations et études morales. Paris, 1864.

	Phil 8881.24	Garrison, W.P. Parables for school and home. N.Y., 1897.
	Phil 8881.25	Gladden, W. Plain thoughts on the art of living. Boston, 1868.
	Phil 8881.26	Guyau, M. Esquisse d'une morale. Paris, 1896.
	Phil 8881.26.5	Guyau, M. A sketch of morality. London, 1898.
	Phil 8881.26.18	Aslan, G. La morale selon Guyau. Paris, 1906.
	Phil 8881.26.21	Fouillée, A. La morale, l'art...d'après Guyau. Paris, 1909.
	Phil 8881.26.28	Schwartz, E.J. M. Guyaus Moral. Inaug. Diss. Strassburg, 1909.
	Phil 8881.27	Gleed, J.W. Real life. n.p., 1899.
	Phil 8881.28	Gorton, D.A. Ethics civil and political. N.Y., 1902.
	Phil 8881.29	Gibson, W.R.B. A philosophical introduction to ethics. London, 1904.
	Phil 8881.31	Gerkrath, E. Grundlinien der Ethik. Charlottenburg, 1912.
	Phil 8881.32	Grossmann, L. The real life. N.Y., 1914.
	Phil 8881.33	Gorodenskii, N. Nravstvennoe soznanie cheloviechestva. Sergiev, 1903.
	Phil 8881.34	Görland, Albert. Ethik als Kritik der Weltgeschichte. Leipzig, 1914.
	Phil 8881.34.5	Görland, Albert. Neubegründung der Ethik aus ihrem Verhältnis zu den besonderen Gemeinschaftswissenschaften. Berlin, 1918.
	Phil 8881.35	González y Martinez de Pinillos. Ética. Madrid, 1911.
	Phil 8881.36	Gehring, Albert. Shadows and realities. Cleveland, 1912.
	Phil 8881.37	Gaultier, Jules de. La dépendance de la morale et l'indépendance des moeurs. Paris, 1907.
	Phil 8881.38	Godwin, John H. Active principles, or Elements of moral science. London, 1885.
	Phil 8881.39	Guyot, Yves. La morale: la moralé théologique. Paris, 1883.
	Phil 8881.40	Gottschick, Johannes. Ethik. Tübingen, 1907.
	Phil 8881.41	Goldscheid, Rudolf. Zur Ethik des Gesamtwellens. Leipzig, 1902.
	Phil 8881.42.3	Gaultier, Paul. L'ideal moderne. Paris, 1911.
	Phil 8881.42.9	Gaultier, Paul. Les moeurs du temps. 3e éd. Paris, 1928.
	Phil 8881.42.15	Gaultier, Paul. La leçon des moeurs contemporaines. 2e éd. Paris, 1930.
	Phil 8881.43	Gutberlet, C. Ethik und Religion. Münster, 1892.
	Phil 8881.44	Gomperz, Heinrich. Über den Begriff des sittlichen Ideals. Bern, 1902.
	Phil 8881.45	Gomer, A. de. L'obligation morale raisonnée. Paris, 1913.
	Phil 8881.46	Garello, Luigi. Levjathan; ricerche sulla natura morale dell'uomo. Torino, 1910.
	Phil 8881.47	Givler, R.C. The ethics of Hercules. N.Y., 1924.
	Phil 8881.48	Galli, E. Alle radici della morale. Milano, 1919.
	Phil 8881.49	Gerlach, G.W. Grundriss der philosophischen Lugendlehre. Halle, 1829.
	Phil 8881.50	Gibson, R.W. The morality of nature. N.Y., 1923.
	Phil 8881.51	Gasté, Marude. Réalités imaginatives. Paris, 1911.
	Phil 8881.52	Garve, Christian. Eigene Betrachtungen über die allgemeinsten Grundsätze der Sittenlehre. Bresslau, 1798.
	Phil 8881.53	Girini Corio, Gioseffo. L'antropologie. n.p., 1761. 2v.
	Phil 8881.54	Genberg, Paul. De principio philosophiae moralis. Diss. Lundae, 1846.
	Phil 8881.55	Griggs, Edward H. The use of the margin. N.Y., 1907.
	Phil 8881.57	Giamboni, Bono. Della miseria dell'uomo. Milano, 1847.
	Phil 8881.57.5	Giamboni, Bono. Della miseria dell'uomo. Firenze, 1836.
	Phil 8881.58	Goddard, H.C. Morale. N.Y., 1918.
	Phil 8881.59	Goodman, R.M. The philosophy of life. Marietta, Ga., 1863.
	Phil 8881.60	Gabelli, Aristide. L'uomo e le scienze morali. Torino, 1920.
	Phil 8881.61.5	Glenn, Paul J. Ethics. 4th ed. St. Louis, Mo., 1934.
	Phil 8881.62	Govi, Mario. Etica rinnovata su basi scientifiche. Pte.I. Firenze, 1935.
	Phil 8881.63	Gordon, John. A new estimate of manners and principles. pt.1-2. Cambridge, Eng., 1760.
	Phil 8881.64	Gurvitch, Georges. Morale théorique et science des moeurs. Paris, 1937.
	Phil 8881.64.2	Gurvitch, Georges. Morale théorique et science des moeurs. 2. éd. Paris, 1948.
	Phil 8881.65	Geiger, George R. Towards an objective ethics. Yellow Springs, 1938.
	Phil 8881.66	Groos, R. Wertethik oder religiöse Sittlichkeit? München, 1933.
Htn	Phil 8881.67*	Gros, J.D. Natural principles of rectitude. N.Y., 1795.
	Phil 8881.68	Gaussault, Abbe. Le portrait d'un honneste homme. 2e éd. Paris, 1694.
	Phil 8881.69	Garnett, C.B. Wisdom in conduct. N.Y., 1940.
	Phil 8881.70	García Máynez, E. Etica: etica empirica; etica de bienes; etica formal; etica valorativa. México, 1944.
	Phil 8881.71	Gilbert, Headley B. Temptation. Dallas, Texas, 1949.
	Phil 8881.72A	Gusdorf, Georges. Traité de l'existence morale. Paris, 1949.
	Phil 8881.72B	Gusdorf, Georges. Traité de l'existence morale. Paris, 1949.
	Phil 8881.72.5	Gusdorf, Georges. La vertu de force. 1. éd. Paris, 1957.
	Phil 8881.73	Ginsberg, Morris. Reason and experience in ethics. London, 1956.
	Phil 8881.74	Gobry, Ivan. Les niveaux de la vie morale. 1. éd. Paris, 1956.
	Phil 8881.75	Garvin, Lucius. A modern introduction to ethics. Boston, 1953.
	Phil 8881.77	Gobry, Ivan. Le modèle en morale. Paris, 1962.
	Phil 8881.78	Grice, Geoffry R. The grounds of moral judgement. Cambridge, 1967.
	Phil 8881.80	Gupta, Rajender Kumas. Studien zur Ethik. Bonn, 1967.
	Phil 8881.82	Gehlen, Arnold. Moral und Hypemoral. Frankfurt, 1969.
NEDL	Phil 8882.1	Hall, A. A manual of morals. Andover, 1848.
	Phil 8882.1.2	Hall, A. A manual of morals. Boston, 1850.
	Phil 8882.2A	Hamilton, E. A series of popular essays. Boston, 1817. 2v.
	Phil 8882.2B	Hamilton, E. A series of popular essays. Boston, 1817. 2v.
	Phil 8882.3	Hampden, R.D. A course of lectures...study, moral philosophy. London, 1835.
	Phil 8882.4	Harris, G. Moral evolution. Boston, 1896.
	Phil 8882.5.2	Haven, J. Moral philosophy. Boston, 1874.
	Phil 8882.6	Hazlitt, W. Essays on the principles of human action. London, n.d.
NEDL	Phil 8882.7.25*	Heinroth, J.C.A. Der Schlüssel zu Himmel und Hölle. Leipzig, 1839.
Htn	Phil 8882.7.25*	Herle, Charles. Wisdomes tripos. London, 1655.
Htn	Phil 8882.8*	Herle, Charles. Wisdom's tripos. London, 1670.

Classified Listing

Phil 8875 - 8900   Ethics - General treatises - Individual authors (A-Z) - cont.

Phil 8882.9	Hickok, L.P. A system of moral science. Schenectady, 1853.
Phil 8882.9.3	Hickok, L.P. A system of moral science. 3rd ed. N.Y., 1873.
Phil 8882.9.5	Hickok, L.P. A system of moral science. Boston, 1880.
Phil 8882.10	Hildreth, R. Theory of morals. Boston, 1844.
Phil 8882.10.15	Hildreth, R. Letter. Boston, 1844.
Phil 8882.11	Hill, W.H. Ethics, or Moral philosophy. Baltimore, 1884.
Phil 8882.12	Hilty, K. Glück. Frauenfeld, 1894.
Phil 8882.12.3	Hilty, K. Glück. Frauenfeld, 1900.
Phil 8882.12.5	Hilty, K. Happiness. N.Y., 1903.
Phil 8882.12.9	Hilty, K. Steps of life, further essays on happiness. N.Y., 1907.
Htn Phil 8882.13*	The hive. Worcester, Mass., 1795.
Htn Phil 8882.13.2*	The hive. Worcester, Mass., 1796.
Phil 8882.14	Hodgson, S.H. The theory of practice. London, 1870. 2v.
Phil 8882.15	Hoefer, F. L'homme devant ses oeuvres. Paris, 1872.
Phil 8882.16	Höffding, H. Ethik. Leipzig, 1888.
Phil 8882.16.3	Höffding, H. Etik. København, 1913.
Phil 8882.16.5	Höffding, H. Etik. 5te udg. København, 1926.
Phil 8882.18.2	Holland, J.G. Gold foil. 5th ed. N.Y., 1859.
Phil 8882.18.5	Holland, J.G. Lessons in life. N.Y., 1861.
Phil 8882.18.9	Holland, J.G. Letters to the Joneses. N.Y., 1863.
Phil 8882.19	Holyoke, E.A. An ethical essay. Salem, 1830.
Phil 8882.20	Home, H. Introduction to the art of thinking. Edinburgh, 1764.
Phil 8882.21	Hopkins, M. The connexion between taste and morals. Boston, 1842.
Phil 8882.21.2	Hopkins, M. The connexion between taste and morals. Boston, 1841.
Phil 8882.21.3	Hopkins, M. The connexion between taste and morals. Boston, 1841.
Phil 8882.21.5.3	Hopkins, M. Lectures on moral science. Boston, 1865.
Phil 8882.21.12	Hopkins, M. The law of love and love as a law. 3rd ed. N.Y., 1871.
Phil 8882.21.15	Hopkins, M. The law of love and love as a law. N.Y., 1885.
Phil 8882.22	Hughes, H. Principles, natural and supernatural morals. London, 1890-91. 2v.
Phil 8882.23	Hurd, R. Moral and political dialogues. London, 1760.
Phil 8882.24	Hyde, W. De W. Practical ethics. N.Y., 1892.
Phil 8882.24.8	Hyde, W. De W. Self-measurement. N.Y., 1912.
Phil 8882.24.9	Hyde, W. De W. The cardinal virtues. N.Y., 1902.
Phil 8882.24.15	Hyde, W. De W. Are you human? N.Y., 1916.
Phil 8882.25	Hyslop, J.H. The elements of ethics. N.Y., 1895.
Phil 8882.26	Hillis, N.D. Great books as life teachers. Edinburgh, 1900.
Phil 8882.26.5	Hillis, N.D. Right living as a fine art. N.Y., 1899.
Phil 8882.26.9	Hillis, N.D. A man's value to society. Edinburgh, 1901.
Phil 8882.27	Hamilton, E.J. The moral law - theory and practice of duty. N.Y., 1902.
Phil 8882.28	Henderson, C.H. The children of good fortune. N.Y., 1905.
Phil 8882.29	Hall, B. Life and love and peace. N.Y., 1909.
Phil 8882.30	Hobhouse, L.T. Morals in evolution. London, 1908. 2v.
Phil 8882.30.10	Hobhouse, L.T. The rational good. London, 1947.
Phil 8882.31	Huntington, F.D. Good talking and good manners. Syracuse, 1887.
Phil 8882.31.5	Huntington, F.D. Good talking a fine art. Syracuse, 1892.
Phil 8882.32	Hensel, P. Hauptprobleme der Ethik. 2e aufl. Leipzig, 1913.
Phil 8882.32.5	Hensel, P. Ethisches Wissen und ethisches Handeln. Freiburg, 1889.
Phil 8882.33	Hirst, E.W. Self and neighbor. London, 1919.
Phil 8882.34	Heymans, Gerardus. Einführung in die Ethik auf Grundlage der Erfahrung. Leipzig, 1914.
Phil 8882.35	Hansen, Søren. Etikens begrundelse. København, 1903.
Phil 8882.36	Harms, F. Ethik. Leipzig, 1889.
Phil 8882.37	Hoffmann, A. Ethik. Freiburg, 1897.
Phil 8882.38	Handyside, John. The historical method in ethics and other essays. Liverpool, 1920.
Phil 8882.39	Hall, G. Stanley. Morale. N.Y., 1920.
Phil 8882.40	Hamilton, William E. Studies in moral science. Chicago, 1916.
Phil 8882.41	Herrmann, W. Ethik. Tübingen, 1901.
Phil 8882.41.5	Herrmann, W. Ethik. 5e Aufl. Tübingen, 1921.
Phil 8882.42	Hill, Owen. Ethics, general and special. London, 1921.
Phil 8882.43	Hansen, Hans C. Moral, religion og videnskab. Kjøbenhavn, 1890.
Phil 8882.44	Hoekstra, S. Zedenleer. Amsterdam, 1894. 3v.
Phil 8882.45	Hansen, Osvald. Etikkens grundlag. Kobenhavn, 1916.
Phil 8882.46	Horn, E.F.B. Mennesket og moralen. Malling, 1877.
Phil 8882.47	Heegaard, P.C.V. Indledning til den rationelle ethik. Kjøbenhavn, 1866.
Phil 8882.48	Häberlin, Paul. Das Gute. Basel, 1926.
Phil 8882.49	Hartenstein, G. Die Grundbegriffe der ethischen Wissenschaften. Leipzig, 1844.
Phil 8882.50	Hartmann, N. Ethik. Berlin, 1926.
Phil 8882.50.5	Hartmann, N. Ethics. London, 1932. 3v.
Phil 8882.50.7	Hartmann, N. Ethik. 3. Aufl. Berlin, 1949.
Phil 8882.51	Horne, H.H. Jesus as a philosopher, and other radio talks. N.Y., 1927.
Phil 8882.52	Hlucka, J.F. Entwurf eines geschlossenen Systems der ethischen Formen. Wien, 1924.
Phil 8882.53	Horwicz, Adolf. Moralische Briefe. Magdebourg, 1878.
Phil 8882.54	Hollander, A.G. Om praktiska filosofiens grundbegrepp och deras inre förhållande till hvarandra. Lund, 1855.
Phil 8882.55	Haldane, J.B.S. Science and ethics. London, 1928.
Phil 8882.56	Hochfelder, J. The supreme law of the future man. 2nd ed. N.Y., 1909.
Phil 8882.57	Howe, E.G. Morality and reality. London, 1934.
Phil 8882.58	Heard, G. The third morality. London, 1937.
Phil 8882.59	Habas, R.A. Morals for moderns. N.Y., 1939.
Phil 8882.60	Hires, H. For my children. N.Y., 1943.
Phil 8882.64	Huxley, Thomas H. Touchstone for ethics. 1st ed. N.Y., 1941.
Phil 8882.66A	Hill, Thomas E. Contemporary ethical theories. N.Y., 1950.
Phil 8882.66B	Hill, Thomas E. Contemporary ethical theories. N.Y., 1950.
Phil 8882.66.5	Hill, Thomas E. Ethics in theory and practice. N.Y., 1956.
Phil 8882.68	Hare, Richard Mervyn. The language of morals. Oxford, 1952.
Phil 8882.68.5	Hare, Richard Mervyn. Freedom and reason. Oxford, 1963.
Phil 8882.68.10	Hare, Richard Mervyn. Descriptivism. London, 1965?

Phil 8875 - 8900   Ethics - General treatises - Individual authors (A-Z) - cont.

Phil 8882.69	Hesnard, Angelo. Morale sans péché. Paris, 1954.
Phil 8882.70	Hourani, G.F. Ethical value. London, 1956.
Phil 8882.71	Hessen, J. Ethik. Leiden, 1954.
Phil 8882.73	Hawkins, Denis J.B. Man and morals. London, 1960.
Phil 8882.75	Hytten, E. The concept of morality. Stockholm, 1959.
Phil 8882.80	Hospers, John. Human conduct. N.Y., 1961.
Phil 8882.85	Haezrahi, P. The price of morality. London, 1961.
Phil 8882.87	Henningsen, N. Moral-hvad er det? København, 1962.
Phil 8882.88	Hazlitt, H. The foundations of morality. Princeton, N.J., 1964.
Phil 8882.90	Hedenius, Ingemar. Sjn studier i praktish filosof. Uppsala, 1968.
Phil 8882.90.5	Hedenius, Ingemar. Den omoraliska anständigheten. Stockholm, 1969.
Phil 8882.95	Haering, Herman Johan. Ethiek der voorlopigheid. Nijkerk, 1969.
Phil 8882.100	Hemming, James. Individual morality. London, 1969.
Phil 8882.102	Hoffbauer, Johann C. Untersuchungen über die wichtigsten Gegenstände. Dortmund, 1799-
Phil 8882.105	Hudson, William Donald. The is-ought question. London, 1969.
Phil 8882.108	Hengstenberg, Hans Eduard. Grundlegung der Ethik. Stuttgart, 1969.
Phil 8882.110	Hirsch, Maximilian. Das Problem der Vernunftherrschaft. Leipzig, 1913.
Phil 8882.115	Harrison, Jonathan. Our knowledge of right and wrong. London, 1971.
Htn Phil 8883.1*	Israel, L.S. d'. Talmudic maxims. Boston, 1848.
Phil 8883.2	Irons, D. Study in psychology of ethics. Edinburgh, 1903.
Phil 8883.3.2	Ingenieros, José. Hacia una moral sin dogmas. 2a ed. Buenos Aires, 1919.
Phil 8883.3.7	Ingenieros, José. Las fuerzas morales. Obra póstuma. Buenos Aires, 1926.
Phil 8883.4	Isbyam, I.C. (pseud.). The self-seeker and his search. London, 1926.
Phil 8884.1A	James, William. Is life worth living? Philadelphia, 1896.
Phil 8884.1B	James, William. Is life worth living? Philadelphia, 1896.
Phil 8884.1.5	James, William. Is life worth living? Philadelphia, 1904.
Phil 8884.1.6	James, William. Is life worth living? Philadelphia, 1904.
Phil 8884.2	Jevons, W. Systematic morality. v.1-2. London, 1827.
Phil 8884.4	Jordan, W.G. Kingship of self-control individual problems. N.Y., 1901.
Phil 8884.4.2	Jordan, W.G. Kingship of self-control individual problems. N.Y., 1899.
Phil 8884.4.5	Jordan, W.G. Self-control, its kingship and majesty. N.Y., 1905.
Phil 8884.4.9	Jordan, W.G. The power of truth. N.Y., 1902.
Phil 8884.4.13	Jordan, W.G. The power of purpose. N.Y., 1910.
Phil 8884.4.17	Jordan, W.G. The majesty of calmness. N.Y., 1900.
Phil 8884.5	Jackson, A.W. Deafness and cheerfulness. Boston, 1901.
Phil 8884.7	Janssens, E. La morale de l'impératif catégorique et la morale du bonheur. Louvain, 1921.
Phil 8884.11	Joussain, A. Le fondement psychologique de la morale. Paris, 1909.
Phil 8884.12	Jackson, John. The sinfulness of little sins. 5th ed. London, 1851.
Phil 8884.13	Johnston, George A. An introduction to ethics, for training colleges. London, 1915.
Phil 8884.14	Jeudon, L. La morale de l'honneur. Paris, 1911.
Phil 8884.15	Juvalta, E. Il vecchio e il nuovo problema della morale. Bologna, 1914.
Phil 8884.15.5	Juvalta, E. Il metodo dell'economica pura nell'etica. Pavia, 1907.
Phil 8884.15.15	Juvalta, E. Prolegomeni a una morale distinta dalla metafisica. Pavia, 1901.
Phil 8884.16	Jodl, Friedrich. Allgemeine Ethik. 1. und 2. Aufl. Stuttgart, 1918.
Phil 8884.17.3	Jahn, Max. Ethik als Grundwissenschaft. Leipzig, 1905.
Phil 8884.17.10	Jahn, Max. Ethik als Grundwissenschaft. 4. Aufl. Leipzig, 1925. 2v.
Phil 8884.18	Joad, Cyril E.M. Common-sense ethics. N.Y., 1921.
Phil 8884.18.6	Joad, Cyril E.M. Thrasymachus; or The future of morals. London, 1925.
Phil 8884.18.7	Joad, Cyril E.M. Thrasymachus. N.Y., 1926.
Phil 8884.19	Jelgersma, D.G. De ontkening der moraal. Amsterdam, 1896.
Phil 8884.20	Jakob, L.H. Philosophische sittenlehre. Halle, 1794.
Phil 8884.21	Janet, Paul. Elements of morals. N.Y., 1884.
Phil 8884.22	Joseph, H.W.B. Some problems of ethics. Oxford, 1931.
Phil 8884.23	Jordan, Furneaux. Moral nerve and the error of literary verdicts. London, 1901.
Phil 8884.24	Jordan, E. The good life. Chicago, 1949.
Phil 8884.25	Johnson, Oliver Adolph. Moral knowledge. Hague, 1966.
Phil 8884.25.5	Johnson, Oliver Adolph. The moral life. London, 1969.
Phil 8885.1	Kaulich, W. System der Ethik. Prag, 1877.
Phil 8885.2	Kendall, J. Eccentricity. London, 1859.
Phil 8885.4	Kidd, J. Morality and religion. Edinburgh, 1895.
Phil 8885.5	Kies, M. The ethical principle. Ann Arbor, 1892.
Phil 8885.6	Kirchmann, J.H. von. Die Grundbegriffe des Rechts und der Moral. Berlin, 1873.
Phil 8885.7	Knox, V. Essays, moral and literary. London, 1808. 3v.
Phil 8885.8	Koerner, H.J.A. Natur-Ethik. Hamburg, 1873. 2v.
Phil 8885.9	Kedney, J.S. Problems in ethics. N.Y., 1900.
Phil 8885.10.5	King, H.C. National living. N.Y., 1912.
Phil 8885.11	Kirn, O. Sittliche Lebens anschauungen der Gegenwart. 2. Aufl. Leipzig, 1911.
Phil 8885.11.5	Kirn, O. Vårtids etiska Lifsåskådningar. Stockholm, 1909.
Phil 8885.12	Koppelmann, W. Kritik des sittlichen Bewusstzeins vom philosophische und historische Standpunkt. Berlin, 1904.
Phil 8885.15	Ein Katechismus der moral und Politik für das deutsche Volk. 2e Aufl. Leipzig, 1891.
Phil 8885.16	Keyser, Leander S. A system of general ethics. Burlington, 1918.
Phil 8885.17	Knigge, Adolf. Practical philosophy of social life. 1st American ed. Lansingburgh, 1805.
Phil 8885.18	Kroman, Krist. Etik I. København, 1904.
Phil 8885.18.5	Koröman, Kristian. Ethik. Leipzig, 1904.
Phil 8885.18.20	Koröman, Kristian. Begrebet "det etiske". København, 1903.
Phil 8885.19	Kautsky, Karl. Ethik und materialistische Geschichtsauffassung. Stuttgart, 1919.
Phil 8885.19.5	Kautsky, Karl. Ethics and the materialist conception of history. Chicago, 1918.
Phil 8885.19.7	Kautsky, Karl. Ethics and the materialist conception of history. Chicago, 1906.

Phil 8875 - 8900   Ethics - General treatises - Individual authors (A-Z) - cont.

Phil 8885.19.8   Kautsky, Karl. Ethics and the materialist conception of history. Chicago, 1907.

Phil 8885.19.9   Kautsky, Karl. Ethik und materialistische Geschichtsauffassung. Stuttgart, 1906.

Phil 8885.20   Kerler, Dietrich H. Jenseits von Optimismus und Pessimismus. Ulm, 1914.

Phil 8885.21.2   Kirchner, F. Ethik; Katechismus der Sittenlehre. 2e Aufl. Leipzig, 1898.

Phil 8885.22   Kittel, Rudolf. Sittliche fragen. Stuttgart, 1885.

Phil 8885.23   Kellerwessel, Josef. Beitrage zur Theorie der sittlichen Erkenntnis. Münster, 1919.

Phil 8885.24   Kutna, G. Egoismus und Altruismus als Grundlage des Sittlichen. Berlin, 1903.

Phil 8885.25   Kane, Robert. Worth lectures. London, 1920.

Phil 8885.26   Kleffler, Henri. Philosophie du sens commun. Paris, 1894-95. 3v.

Phil 8885.27   Kirckner, F. Ethik. Leipzig, 1881.

Phil 8885.28   Kiesewetter, J.G.C. Über der ersten Grundsatz der Moralphilosophie. Berlin, 1790-1791. 2v.

Phil 8885.29   Krueger, Felix. Der Begriff des absolut Wertvollen. Leipzig, 1898.

Phil 8885.30   Klug, J. Die Tiefen der Seele. Paderborn, 1926.

Phil 8885.31   Kronenberg, Moritz. Ethische Präludien. München, 1905.

Phil 8885.32   Kramer, Morris. Song of the optimist. N.Y., 1926.

Phil 8885.33   Koch, Gregor. Das menschliche Leben. Ensiedeln, 1916.

Phil 8885.34   Kant, Otto. Zur Biologie der Ethik. Wien, 1932.

Phil 8885.35   Kirkham, S.D. Where dwells the soul serene. 3rd ed. San Francisco, 1907.

Phil 8885.36   Kirk, K.E. Personal ethics. Oxford, 1934.

Phil 8885.37   Katô, Hiroyuke. Der Kampf ums recht des Stärkeren und seine Entwickelung. Tokyô, 1893.

Phil 8885.38   Kresge, E.E. The search for a way of life. N.Y., 1950.

Phil 8885.39   Kamiat, A.H. The ethics of civilization. Washington, 1954.

Phil 8885.40   Kettner, F. Biosophy and spiritual democracy. N.Y., 1954.

Phil 8885.41   Kaelin, Bernard. Einführung in die Ethik. 2. Aufl. Sarnen, 1954.

Phil 8885.42   Kimpel, B.F. Principles of moral philosophy. N.Y., 1960.

Phil 8885.45   Kron, Helmut. Ethos und Ethik. Frankfurt, 1960.

Phil 8885.46   Kemp, J. Reason, action and morality. London, 1964.

Phil 8885.47   Kattsoff, Louis Osgood. Making moral decisions. The Hague, 1965.

Phil 8885.48   Klácel, František M. Dobrowĕda. Praha, 1847.

VPhil 8885.49   Kangrga, Milan. Etika i ploboda. Zagreb, 1966.

Phil 8885.49.5   Kangrga, Milan. Razmisljanja o etici. Zagreb, 1970.

Phil 8885.52   Knox, Malcolm. Action. London, 1968.

Phil 8885.54   Kalinowski, Jerzy. Querelle de la science normative, une contribution à la théorie de la science. Paris, 1969.

Phil 8885.56   Kupperman, Joel J. Ethical knowledge. London, 1970.

Phil 8886.1   Lalor, J. Money and morals. London, 1852.

Phil 8886.2   Lambert, C. Le système du monde moral. Paris, 1862.

Phil 8886.3   Landmann, R. Hauptfragen der Ethik. Leipzig, 1874.

Phil 8886.4   Lange, J. Medicina mentis. London, 1715.

Phil 8886.5   Laurie, S.S. On the philosophy of ethics. Edinburgh, 1866.

Phil 8886.5.5   Laurie, S.S. Ethica: or The ethics of reason. London, 1885.

Htn   Phil 8886.6*   Lavater, J.C. Aphorisms on man. Boston, 1790.

Phil 8886.6.10   Laycock, F.U. Motives of mankind. London, 1907.

Phil 8886.7   Lessons on the subject of right and wrong. Boston, 1864.

Phil 8886.8   Letourneau, C. L'évolution de la morale. Paris, 1894.

Phil 8886.8.2   Letourneau, C. L'évolution de la morale. Paris, 1887.

Phil 8886.8.10   Key, Ellen. Moralens utveckling: fri bearbetning efter Letourneau. Stockholm, 1903.

Phil 8886.9   Lloyd, J. Duty and faith. Manchester, 1884.

Phil 8886.10   Lombarès, M. de. Du gout ou de la passion du bien-être matériel. Montauban, 1860?

Phil 8886.11   Lowell, A.C. (Mrs.). Seed-grain for thought and discussion. Boston, 1856. 2v.

Phil 8886.12.5   Avebury, John Lubbock. The use of life. N.Y., 1900.

Phil 8886.13   Leadbeater, M. Cottage dialogues. Richmond, 1811.

Phil 8886.14   Lecky, W.E.H. The map of life. N.Y., 1899.

Phil 8886.14.2   Lecky, W.E.H. The map of life. N.Y., 1901.

Phil 8886.14.5   Lecky, W.E.H. The map of life. London,1899.

Phil 8886.15   Lipps, T. Die ethischen Grundfragen. Hamburg, 1899.

Phil 8886.15.6   Lipps, T. Die ethischen Grundfragen. 2e Aufl. Hamburg, 1905.

Phil 8886.17   Ladd, G.T. Philosophy of conduct. N.Y., 1902.

Phil 8886.18   Lilly, W.S. On right and wrong. London, 1892.

Phil 8886.19   Lagerborg, R. La morale publique. Paris, 1903.

Phil 8886.19.5   Lagerborg, R. Moralens vasen. Helsingfors, 1900.

Phil 8886.20   Lefèvre, G. Obligation morale et idéalisme. Paris, 1894.

Htn   Phil 8886.21*   La Primaudaye, P. de. The French Academie. London, 1586.

Htn   Phil 8886.21.2*   La Primaudaye, P. de. L'Académie française. 3. ed. Paris, 1582.

Htn   Phil 8886.21.3*   La Primaudaye, P. de. L'Académie française. 3. ed. London, 1594. 2v.

Phil 8886.21.5   La Primaudaye, P. de. L'Académie française. v.1-4. Saumur, 1613.

Htn   Phil 8886.21.7*   La Primaudaye, P. de. Suite de l'Académie française. Paris, 1580.

Htn   Phil 8886.21.12*   La Primaudaye, P. de. The third volume of the French Academie. London, 1601.

Phil 8886.22   Leith, W.C. Apologia diffidentis. London, 1908.

Phil 8886.23   Leclère, A. La morale rationnelle. Paris, 1908.

Phil 8886.23.5   Leclère, A. L'éducation morale rationnelle. Paris, 1909.

Phil 8886.24   Lanessan, J.I. de. La morale naturelle. Paris, 1908.

Phil 8886.24.5   Lanessan, J.I. de. La morale des religions. Paris, 1905.

Phil 8886.24.9   Lanessan, J.I. de. L'idéal moral du matérialisme et la guerre. Paris, 1918.

Phil 8886.25   Laguna, T. de. Introduction to the science of ethics. N.Y., 1914.

Phil 8886.26   Lawätz, H.W. Über die Tugenden und Laster...des Menschen. Flensburg, 1789-1792. 3v.

Phil 8886.27   Laplaigne, H. Morale d'un égoiste; essai de morale sociale. Paris, 1900.

Phil 8886.28   Lewis, George Edward. Pay your fare. N.Y., 1914.

Phil 8886.29   Lévy-Bruhl, L. Ethics and moral science. London, 1905.

Phil 8886.29.5   Lévy-Bruhl, L. La morale et la science des moeurs. 5. ed. Paris, 1913.

Phil 8886.30   Leathes, Stanley. The foundations of morality. London, 1882.

Phil 8886.31   La Hautière, E. de. Cours élémentaire de philosophie morale. 2. ed. Paris, 18- .

Phil 8886.32   Limentani, Ludovico. I presupposti formali...etica. Genova, 1913.

Phil 8875 - 8900   Ethics - General treatises - Individual authors (A-Z) - cont.

Phil 8886.33   Lessona, Marco. L'utilità e il senso morale. Torino, 1886.

Phil 8886.34   Lynch, Arthur. Ethics, an exposition of principles. London, 1922.

Phil 8886.35   Laing, B.M. A study in moral problems. London, 1922.

Phil 8886.36   Lilly, William S. An invisible kingdom. London, 1919.

Phil 8886.37   Lalande, André. Précis raisonné de morale pratique. 2. ed. Paris, 1909.

Phil 8886.37.5   Lalande, André. Précis raisonné de morale pratique. 3. ed. Paris, 1930.

Phil 8886.38   Loisy, Alfred. La morale humaine. Paris, 1923.

Phil 8886.38.5   Loisy, Alfred. La morale humaine. 2. ed. Paris, 1928.

Phil 8886.38.8   Loisy, Alfred. La crise morale. Paris, 1937.

Phil 8886.39   Landau, L.R. System der gesammten Ethik. Band 1-2. Berlin, 1877-78.

Phil 8886.40   Laudatio, Giorgio. La giustizia e la morale. Trani, 1902.

Phil 8886.41   Landry, Adolph. Principes de morale rationnelle. Paris, 1906.

Phil 8886.43   Liebert, Arthur. Ethik. Berlin, 1924.

Phil 8886.44   Leuba, J.H. The psycho-physiology of the moral imperative. n.p., 1897.

Phil 8886.45   Laird, John. A study in moral theory. N.Y., 1926.

Phil 8886.45.10   Laird, John. Morals and western religion. London, 1931.

Phil 8886.45.15   Laird, John. An enquiry into moral nations. London, 1935.

Phil 8886.47   Levine, Israel. Reasons and morals. Glasgow, 1924.

Phil 8886.48   Longo, P. Etica umana. Torino, 1924.

Phil 8886.49   Lamblardie. Traité élémentaire de métaphysique et de morale. Brunswick, 1801.

Phil 8886.50   Lippmann, W. A preface to morals. N.Y., 1929.

Phil 8886.50.3   Lippmann, W. A preface to morals. N.Y., 1929.

Phil 8886.50.5   Lippmann, W. A preface to morals. N.Y., 1931.

Phil 8886.50.6   Lippmann, W. A preface to morals. London, 1931.

Phil 8886.51.5   Levesque, M. Cours élémentaire de morale. Paris, 1801.

Phil 8886.52   Lowell, Abbot L. Conflicts of principle. Cambridge, 1932.

Phil 8886.53   Lemarie, O. La morale privée. Paris, 1932.

Phil 8886.54   Lenglart, Marcel. Essai sur les conditions du progrès moral. Paris, 1934.

Phil 8886.56   Lombardi, F. Il mondo degli uomini. Firenze, 1935.

Phil 8886.57   Lagresille, Henry. Monde moral, l'ordre des fins et des progrès. Paris, 1911.

Phil 8886.58   Livry, Hypolite. Reflexions morales et probablement fort inutiles. Paris, 1807.

Phil 8886.59   Lancre, P. de. Tableau de l'inconstance et instabilité de toutes choses. Paris, 1607.

Phil 8886.60   Lee, James W. The making of a man. St. Louis, 1899.

Phil 8886.61   Leys, W.A.R. Ethics and social policy. N.Y., 1941.

Phil 8886.61.5   Leys, W.A.R. Ethics and policy decisions. N.Y., 1952.

Phil 8886.62   Lanz, H. In quest of morals. Stanford, 1941.

Phil 8886.63   Larroyo, F. Los principios de la ética social. 4. ed. Mexico, 1941.

Phil 8886.64   Le Senne, René. Traité de morale générale. 1. ed. Paris, 1942.

Phil 8886.65   Lamont, William D. The principles of moral judgement. Oxford, 1946.

Phil 8886.66   Leake, C.D. Can we agree? Austin, 1950.

Phil 8886.67   Löwith, K. Das Individuum in der Rolle des Mitmenschen. München, 1928.

Phil 8886.68   Leighton, J.A. The individual and the social order. N.Y., 1927.

Phil 8886.69   Losskii, N.O. Usloviia absoliutnogo dobra. Parizh, 1949.

Phil 8886.72   Lillie, William. An introduction to ethics. 3. ed. London, 1957.

Phil 8886.73   López Aranguren, José Luis. Etica. Madrid, 1958.

Phil 8886.73.2   López Aranguren, José Luis. Etica. 2. ed. Madrid, 1959.

Phil 8886.73.5   López Aranguren, José Luis. Lo que sabemos de moral. Madrid, 1967.

Phil 8886.73.10   López Aranguren, José Luis. Teoria y sociedad. Barcelona, 1970.

Phil 8886.74   Leclercq, Francois. Propos sur la morale et la science. Paris, 1959.

Phil 8886.76   Loegstrup, K.E.C. Kunst og etik. Kobenhavn, 1961.

Phil 8886.78   Lamouche, André. D'une morale de l'amour à une sociologie de la raison. Paris, 1963. 2v.

Phil 8886.79   Lepp, Ignance. La morale nouvelle. Paris, 1963.

Phil 8886.80.2   Lunn, Arnold. The new morality. London, 1967.

Phil 8886.82   Libnizzi, Carmelo. Il pro e il contro: considerazioni morali. Padova, 1967.

Phil 8886.84   Lévy-Valensi, Eliane Amado. Le temps dans la vie morale. Paris, 1968.

Phil 8886.86   Lewis, Clarence I. Values and imperatives. Stanford, Calif., 1969.

Phil 8886.86.5   Saydah, J. Roger. The ethical theory of Clarence Irving Lewis. Athens, Ohio, 1969.

Phil 8886.90   Loiser, Burton M. Custom, law, and morality: conflict and continuity in social behavior. 1st ed. Garden City, 1969.

Phil 8886.91   Lauth, Reinhard. Ethik in ihrer Grundlage aus Prinzipien entfaltet. Stuttgart, 1969.

Phil 8887.1.3   Mackenzie, J.S. A manual of ethics. 3rd ed. London, 1897.

Phil 8887.1.4   Mackenzie, J.S. A manual of ethics. 4th ed. N.Y., 1901.

Phil 8887.1.15   Mackenzie, J.S. A manual of ethics. 6th ed. London, 1948.

Phil 8887.2   Marion, H. De la solidarité morale. Paris, 1880.

Phil 8887.2.5   Marion, H. Leçons de morale. 17. ed. Paris, 1917.

Phil 8887.3   Martineau, H. How to observe. Morals and manners. London, 1838.

Phil 8887.3.2   Martineau, H. How to observe. Morals and manners. N.Y., 1838.

Phil 8887.3.3   Martineau, H. How to observe. Morals and manners. N.Y., 1838.

Phil 8887.4   Martineau, J. Types of ethical theory. Oxford, 1885.

Phil 8887.4.2   Martineau, J. Types of ethical theory. 2. ed. Oxford, 1886. 2v.

Phil 8887.4.3   Martineau, J. Types of ethical theory. 2. ed. Oxford, 1886. 2v.

Phil 8887.4.5   Martineau, J. Types of ethical theory. v.1-2. 3. ed. Oxford, 1891.

Phil 8887.4.10   Martineau, J. Types of ethical theory. 3. ed. Oxford, 1901. 2v.

Phil 8887.4.13   Martineau, J. Tides of the spirit. Boston, 1905.

Phil 8887.4.18   Wilkinson, J.J. James Martineau Ethik...Kritik. Inaug. Diss. Leipzig, 1898.

Phil 8887.5   Martinelli, V. Istoria critica della vita civile. Napoli, 1764. 2v.

Phil 8887.6   Mason, J. Self-knowledge. London, 1745.

Phil 8887.6.2   Mason, J. Self-knowledge. London, 1753.

Phil 8887.6.3   Mason, J. Self-knowledge. London, 1755.

Htn   Phil 8887.6.4*   Mason, J. Self-knowledge. Worcester, Mass., 1789.

Phil 8887.6.4.5   Mason, J. Self-knowledge. London, 1794.

Classified Listing

Phil 8875 - 8900 Ethics - General treatises - Individual authors (A-Z) - cont.

Phil 8887.6.5 Mason, J. Self-knowledge. Portland, 1807.
Phil 8887.6.6 Mason, J. A treatise on self-knowledge. Boston, 1809.
Htn Phil 8887.6.6.5* Mason, J. A treatise on self-knowledge. Newburyport, 1812.
Phil 8887.6.7 Mason, J. A treatise on self-knowledge. Montpelier, 1813.
Phil 8887.6.9 Mason, J. A treatise on self-knowledge. London, 1821.
Phil 8887.6.9.5 Mason, J. A treatise on self-knowledge. 3. ed. Boston, 1822.
Phil 8887.6.10 Mason, J. Self-knowledge. London, 1824.
Phil 8887.6.12 Mason, J. A treatise on self knowledge. 4th ed. Boston, 1826.
Phil 8887.6.15 Mason, J. A treatise on self-knowledge. N.Y., 1943.
Phil 8887.6.25 Mason, J. Peri tou gnōthi sauton. Korphoi, 1821.
Phil 8887.7.2 Mather, C. Essays to do good. Dover, 1826.
Phil 8887.7.4 Mather, C. Essays to do good. London, 1816.
Phil 8887.8 Matter, J. La morale, ou La philosophie des moeurs. Paris, 1860.
Phil 8887.8.5 Matter, J. De l'affaiblissement des idées. Paris, 1841.
Phil 8887.9 Maude, J.E. The foundations of ethics. N.Y., 1887.
Phil 8887.10 Maurice, F.D. Social morality. London, 1869.
Phil 8887.11 Mercer, M. Popular lectures on ethics. Petersburg, 1841.
Phil 8887.12 Mercier, A.D. Méditations philogiques et morales. Paris, 1835.
tn Phil 8887.13* Meres, F. Wits commonwealth. pt. 2. London, 1634.
Phil 8887.13.5 Meres, F. Palladis tamia. N.Y., 1938.
Phil 8887.14 Metcalf, D. An enquiry into...moral obligation. Boston, 1860.
Phil 8887.16 The moral library. Boston, 1796.
Phil 8887.17 The moral mirror. Philadelphia, 1813.
Phil 8887.18 Morgan, T. The moral philosopher. London, 1737-39. 2v.
Phil 8887.18.3 Morgan, T. The moral philosopher. v.1, 2. ed. London, 1738-40. 3v.
Phil 8887.18.5 Morgan, T. Physico-theology. London, 1741.
Phil 8887.18.9 Pamphlet vol. Ethics. 4 pam.
Phil 8887.19 Morgan, T.C. Sketches of the philosophy of morals. London, 1822.
Phil 8887.20 More, H. Moral sketches. Boston, 1819.
Phil 8887.20.3 More, H. Moral sketches. London, 1819.
Phil 8887.21.2 Moore, George Edward. Principia ethica. Cambridge, Eng., 1922.
EDL Phil 8887.21.2 Moore, George Edward. Principia ethica. Cambridge, Eng., 1922.
Phil 8887.21.3 Moore, George Edward. Principia ethica. Cambridge, Eng., 1929.
Phil 8887.21.4 Moore, George Edward. Principia ethica. Cambridge, Eng., 1954.
Phil 8887.21.6 Moore, George Edward. Principia ethica. Cambridge, Eng., 1959.
Phil 8887.21.7 Moore, George Edward. Ethics. N.Y., 1912.
Phil 8887.21.10 Moore, George Edward. Ethics. N.Y., 1965.
Phil 8887.22 Morton, E. A key to true happiness. Hudson, Ohio, 1854.
Phil 8887.23 Mosby, E.F. The ideal life. Cincinnati, Ohio, 1877.
Phil 8887.24 Moustalon. La morale des poètes. Paris, 1816.
Phil 8887.25 Muirhead, J.H. The elements of ethics. N.Y., 1892.
Phil 8887.25.6 Muirhead, J.H. The elements of ethics. London, 1910.
Phil 8887.25.9 Muirhead, J.H. Philosophy and life. London, 1902.
Phil 8887.26 Murray, J.C. An introduction to ethics. Paisley, 1891.
Phil 8887.27 Muzzey, A.B. The moral teacher. N.Y., 1839.
Phil 8887.28 Montlosier, F.D. de R. Des mysteres de la vie humaine. v.1-2. Bruxelles, 1829. 2v.
n Phil 8887.29* Montlosier, F.D. de R. The management of the tongue. Boston, 1814.
Phil 8887.30 Mallock, W.H. Is life worth living? N.Y., 1879.
Phil 8887.30.5 Aveling, E.B. "The value of this earthly life": a reply. London, 1879.
n Phil 8887.31* Muzéo, G. La polvere del mutio. n.p., n.d.
Phil 8887.32 Matthia, C. Systema ethicum. Marpurgi, 1626.
Phil 8887.34 Mezes, S.E. Ethics descriptive and explanatory. N.Y., 1901.
Phil 8887.35 Mercer, A.G. Notes of an outlook on life. London, 1899.
Phil 8887.36 Münsterberg, H. Der Ursprung der Sittlichkeit. Freiburg, 1889.
Phil 8887.37 McConnell, R.M. Duty of altruism. N.Y., 1910.
Phil 8887.37.90 Mabie, H.W. The life of the spirit. N.Y., 1900.
Phil 8887.38.5 Mabie, H.W. Works and days. N.Y., 1902.
Phil 8887.39 Murdoch, J.G. Economics as the basis of living ethics. Troy, 1913.
Phil 8887.40 Mudie, Robert. Man as a moral and accountable being. London, 1840.
Phil 8887.40.5 Mudie, Robert. Man in his relations to society. London, 1840.
Phil 8887.41 Meakin, J.P. A man worth while. Rahway, N.J., 1913.
Phil 8887.41.5 Meakin, F. Function, feeling, and conduct. N.Y., 1910.
Phil 8887.43 Merrington, E.N. Morales et religions. Paris, 1909.
Phil 8887.44 Mitra, Ambika C. The elements of morals. 2. ed. Calcutta, 1914.
Phil 8887.45 Mazumdar, A.K. Outlines of moral philosophy. Culcutta, 1915.
Phil 8887.46 MacDonald, Normand. Maxims and moral reflections. N.Y., 1827.
Phil 8887.48 Marshall, H.R. Mind and conduct. N.Y., 1919.
Phil 8887.49 Mauxion, Marcel. Essai sur les éléments et l'évolution. Paris, 1904.
Phil 8887.50 Müller, Johannes. Neue Wegweiser; Aufsätze und Reden. München, 1920.
Phil 8887.50.10 Müller, Johannes. Hemmungen des Lebens. München, 193-?
Phil 8887.50.11 Müller, Johannes. Hemmungen des Lebens. München, 1956.
Phil 8887.50.12 Müller, Johannes. Hindrances of life. N.Y., 1909.
Phil 8887.51 Mecklin, John M. An introduction to social ethics. N.Y., 1920.
Phil 8887.52 Mehlis, Georg. Probleme der ethik. Tübingen, 1918.
Phil 8887.53 Messer, A. Ethik. Leipzig, 1918.
Phil 8887.53.4 Messer, A. Ethik. Leipzig, 1925.
Phil 8887.53.10 Messer, A. Sittenlehre. Leipzig, 1920.
Phil 8887.54 McNair, G.H. Timely lessons on today's living. Newport, Vt., 1922.
Phil 8887.55 Moore, J.H. The new ethics. London, 1909.
Phil 8887.56.5 Martin, A.W. A philosophy of life and its spiritual values. N.Y., 1923.
Phil 8887.57 McDougall, William. Ethics and some modern world problems. N.Y., 1924.
Phil 8887.58 Marcus, E. Das Gesetz der Vernunft und die ethischen Strömungen der Gegenwart. Herford, 1907.
Phil 8887.58.10 Marcus, E. Das Rätsel der Sittlichkeit und seine Lösung. München, 1932.
Phil 8887.59 Mackenzie, J.S. A manual of ethics. 4. ed. London, 1910.

Phil 8875 - 8900 Ethics - General treatises - Individual authors (A-Z) - cont.

Phil 8887.59.10 Mackenzie, G. Essays upon several moral subjects. London, 1713.
Phil 8887.60 McGinley, A.A. The profit of love. N.Y., 1907.
Phil 8887.61 Mersch, Émile. L'obligation morale, principe de liberté. Louvain, 1927.
Phil 8887.62 Masci, F. Coscienza, volontà, libertà. Lanciano, 1884.
Phil 8887.63 Mutschelle, S. Vermischte Schriften, oder philosophischen Gedanken. 2. Aufl. München, 1799. 4v.
Phil 8887.64 MacKaye, James. Convictionism versus non-convictionism. n.p., 1928.
Phil 8887.65 Mancini, F.O. Riflessioni per la vita morale civile. Parma, 1706.
Phil 8887.67 Menger, Karl. Moral, Wille und Weltgestaltung. Wien, 1934.
Phil 8887.68 Michel, Virgil. Philosophy of human conduct. Minneapolis, 1936.
Phil 8887.69 Margolius, Hans. Grundlegung zur Ethik. Berlin, 1936.
Phil 8887.70 Molé, L.M. Essai de morale et de politique. Paris, 1791.
Phil 8887.71 Maurois, André. The art of living. 5. ed. N.Y., 1940.
Phil 8887.71.5 Maurois, André. Un art de vivre. Paris, 1939.
Phil 8887.71.10 Maurois, André. Sentiments et coutumes. 56. ed. Paris, 1934.
Phil 8887.72 Mukenje, D.G. Daily meditations. N.Y., 1933.
Phil 8887.73 Michaud, Félix. Science et morale. Paris, 1941.
Phil 8887.74 Martínez de Trujillo, Maria. Meditaciones morales. México, 1948.
Phil 8887.74.5 Martínez de Trujillo, Maria. Moral meditations. N.Y., 1954.
Phil 8887.75 Messner, J. Social ethics; natural law in the modern world. St. Louis, 1949.
Phil 8887.75.5 Messner, J. Kulturethik. Innsbruck, 1954.
Phil 8887.75.10 Messner, J. Ethik. Innsbruck, 1955.
Phil 8887.76 Messner, J. Das Naturrecht. Innsbruck, 1950.
Phil 8887.77 Melden, A.I. Essays in moral philosophy. Seattle, 1958.
Phil 8887.77.5 Melden, A.I. Essays in moral philosophy. Seattle, 1958.
Phil 8887.78 MacBeath, A. Experiments in living. London, 1952.
Phil 8887.80 MacGregor, G. Les frontières de la morale et de la religion. Thèse. Paris, 1952.
Phil 8887.85 Mandelbaum, M.H. The phenomenology of moral experience. Glencoe, Ill., 1955.
Phil 8887.90 Mayer, Charles L. La morale de l'avenir. Paris, 1953.
Phil 8887.91 Mayer, Charles L. In quest of a new ethics. Boston, 1954.
Phil 8887.95 Mackinnon, D.M. A study in ethical theory. London, 1957.
Phil 8887.100 Mayo, Bernard. Ethics and the moral life. London, 1958.
Phil 8887.105 Meyer, Arthur E. Mind, matter, and morals. 1st. ed. N.Y., 1957.
Phil 8887.110.5 Montefiore, Alan. A modern introduction to moral philosophy. N.Y., 1959.
Phil 8887.110.10 Montefiore, Alan. A modern introduction to moral philosophy. London, 1964.
Phil 8887.115 Molitor, Arnulf. Zum Formalismus in der neueren Ethik. Wien, 1960.
Phil 8887.120 Morris, B. Philosophical aspects of culture. Yellow Springs, Ohio, 1961
Phil 8887.121 Margenau, H. Ethics and science. Princeton, 1964.
Phil 8887.122 Munz, Peter. Relationship and solitude. 1st. American ed. Middletown, Conn., 1965.
Phil 8887.123 Monro, David Hector. Empiricism and ethics. Cambridge, Eng., 1967.
Phil 8887.124 Mabbott, John David. An introduction to ethics. London, 1966.
Phil 8887.125 McGrath, Patrick. The nature of moral judgement: a study in contemporary moral philosophy. London, 1967.
Phil 8887.127 Moser, Shia. Absolutism and relativism in ethics. Springfield, 1968.
Phil 8887.129 Margolius, Hans. System der Ethik. Freiburg, 1967.
Phil 8887.132 Melsen, Andreas Gerardus Maria van. Physical science and ethics. Pittsburgh, 1967.
Phil 8887.134 McCloskey, H.J. Meta-ethics and normative ethics. The Hague, 1969.
Phil 8887.135 Momov, Vasil M. Nravstvenata norma i neinata realizatsiia. Sofiia, 1969.
Phil 8887.136 Margolis, Joseph Zalman. Values and conduct. Oxford, 1971.
Phil 8887.138 McGann, Thomas F. Ethics: theory and practice. Chicago, 1971.
Phil 8888.1 Nahlowsky, J.W. Allgemeine praktische Philosophie. Leipzig, 1871.
Phil 8888.1.3 Nahlowsky, J.W. Allgemeine Ethik. 2. Aufl. Pleizig, 1885.
Phil 8888.1.6 Nahlowsky, J.W. Die ethischen Ideen als die Waltenden Mächte. Langensalza, 1904.
Phil 8888.2 Nicole, P. Moral essayes. London, 1696. 2v.
Phil 8888.3 Nihell, L. Rational self-love. Limerick, 1770.
NEDL Phil 8888.4 Nettleton, T. A treatise on virtue. London, 1759.
Phil 8888.4.2 Nettleton, T. A treatise on virtue. Edinburgh, 1774.
Phil 8888.5 Nicoll, W.R. Letters on life. N.Y., 1901.
Phil 8888.6 Nelson, Leonard. Kritik der praktischen Vernunft. Leipzig, 1917.
Phil 8888.6.1 Nelson, Leonard. Critique of practical reason. Scarsdale, 1970?
Phil 8888.6.2 Nelson, Leonard. System der philosophischen Ethik und Pädagogik. Göttingen, 1932.
Phil 8888.6.3 Nelson, Leonard. System der philosophischen Rechtslehre und Politik. Leipzig, 1924.
Phil 8888.6.25 Nelson, Leonard. Ethische Methodenlehre. Leipzig, 1915.
Phil 8888.6.27 Nelson, Leonard. Ethischer Realismus. Leipzig, 1921.
Phil 8888.6.30 Nelson, Leonard. System of ethics. New Haven, 1956.
Phil 8888.7 Nordau, Max. Morals and the evolution of man. London, 1922.
Phil 8888.7.10 Nordau, Max. La biologie de l'éthique. Paris, 1930.
Phil 8888.8 Nolan, Preston M. Pertinent and impertinent. Chicago, 1923.
Phil 8888.9 Nobili-Vitelleschi, F. Morale induttiva. Roma, 1882-91. 4v.
Phil 8888.10 Nordwall, Adolf L. Om ethikens problem och de vigtigaste försäken att lösa detsamma. Upsala, 1852.
Phil 8888.11 Nivard, M. Ethica. Paris, 1928.
Phil 8888.12 Nevins, W.N. The meaning of the moral life. N.Y., 1930.
Phil 8888.13 Nabert, Jean. Éléments pour une éthique. 1st ed. Paris, 1943.
Phil 8888.14 Neumam, Erich. Tiefenpsychologie und neue Ethik. Zürich, 1949.
Phil 8888.14.1 Neumann, Erich. Depth psychology and a new ethic. London, 1969.
Phil 8888.15 Nowell-Smith, P.H. Ethics. Melbourne, 1954.
Phil 8888.17 Nedeljković, Dušan. Etika. 2. izd. Beograd, 1969.
Phil 8888.18 Nagel, Thomas. The possibility of altruism. Oxford, 1970.

Phil 8875 - 8900 Ethics - General treatises - Individual authors (A-Z) - cont.

Phil 8888.20 Nassent, Georges. Joie, souffrance et vie morale. Paris, 1968.
Phil 8889.1 Ollé-Laprune, L. De la certitude morale. Paris, 1880.
Phil 8889.1.10 Ollé-Laprune, L. Les sources de la paix intellectuelle. 7. ed. Paris, 1916.
Phil 8889.1.15 Ollé-Laprune, L. Le prix de la vie. 43. ed. Paris, 1921.
Phil 8889.2 Oxenstjerna, J.T. Pensées sur divers sujets. Francfort, 1736. 2v.
Phil 8889.2.2 Oxenstjerna, J.T. Pensées, réflexions et maximes morales. Paris, 1825. 2v.
Phil 8889.2.3 Oxenstjerna, J.T. Pensées. v.1-2. Paris, 1774.
Phil 8889.2.4 Oxenstjerna, J.T. Pensées. v.1-2. Rouen, 1782.
Phil 8889.3 Orestano, F. I valori umani. Milan, 1907.
Phil 8889.3.7 Orestano, Francesco. Prolegomeni alla scienza del bene e del mali. Roma, 1915.
Phil 8889.4 Ogden, John. Elements of ethical science. Bismarck, N.D., 1891.
Phil 8889.5 Oesterle, J.A. Ethics. Englewood Cliffs, N.J., 1957.
Phil 8889.7 Osbert, Reuben. Humanism and moral theory. London, 1959.
Phil 8889.8 Ossowska, Maria. Socjologia moralności. Warszawa, 1963.
Phil 8889.8.2 Ossowska, Maria. Socjologia moralności 2. wyd. Warszawa, 1969.
Phil 8889.8.5 Ossowska, Maria. Social determinants of moral ideas. Philadelphia, 1970.
Phil 8889.8.10 Ossowska, Maria. Normy moralne. Warszawa, 1970.
Phil 8889.9F Ofstad, Harald. Innføring i moralfilosofi. Stockholm, 1964.
Phil 8889.10 Olson, Robert Goodwin. The morality of self-interest. N.Y., 1965.
Htn Phil 8890.1* Palfreyman, T. A treatise of moral philosophy. London?, 1564?
Phil 8890.2 Palmer, T.H. The moral instructor. pt.1. Philadelphia, 1841.
NEDL Phil 8890.2.2 Palmer, T.H. The moral instructor. pt. 2. Boston, 1846.
Phil 8890.2.3 Palmer, T.H. The moral instructor. pt.3. Boston, 1874.
Phil 8890.2.4 Palmer, T.H. The moral instructor. pt.4. Boston, 1851.
Phil 8890.2.5 Palmer, T.H. The moral instructor. pt.1. Boston, 1853.
Phil 8890.3 Paolino. Trattato de regimine rectoris. Vienna, 1868.
Phil 8890.4 Parkhurst, J.L. Elements of moral philosophy. Boston, 1832.
Phil 8890.5 Patterson, J.S. Conflict in nature and life. N.Y., 1883.
Phil 8890.5.50 Patterson, C.H. Moral standards. 2. ed. N.Y., 1957.
Phil 8890.6 Paulsen, F. Symbolae ad systemata philosophiae moralis. Berolini, 1871.
Phil 8890.6.5 Paulsen, F. System der Ethik. Berlin, 1889.
Phil 8890.6.5.8 Paulsen, F. System der Ethik. 2. Aufl. Berlin, 1891.
Phil 8890.6.5.9 Paulsen, F. System der Ethik. 3. Aufl. Berlin, 1894. 2v.
Phil 8890.6.6 Paulsen, F. System der Ethik. Berlin, 1896-97. 2v.
Phil 8890.6.7 Paulsen, F. System der Ethik. Stuttgart, 1903. 2v.
Phil 8890.6.8 Paulsen, F. System der Ethik. 11. und 12. Aufl. Stuttgart, 1921. 2v.
Phil 8890.6.9 Paulsen, F. System of ethics. N.Y., 1899.
Phil 8890.6.11 Paulsen, F. System of ethics. N.Y., 1899.
Phil 8890.6.12 Paulsen, F. Zur Ethik und Politik. v.1-2. Berlin, n.d.
Phil 8890.6.15 Paulsen, F. Zur Ethik und Politik. Berlin, 19- . 2v.
Phil 8890.6.17 Paulsen, F. Zur Ethik und Politik. Berlin, 19- ? 2v.
Htn Phil 8890.7* Pavonio, F. Summa ethicae. Oxonii, 1633.
Phil 8890.8 Payne, G. Elements of mental and moral science. London, 1828.
Phil 8890.9 Peabody, A.P. A manual of moral philosophy. N.Y., 1873.
Phil 8890.9.2 Peabody, A.P. Moral philosophy. Boston, 1887.
Phil 8890.9.5 Peabody, A.P. The immutable right. Boston, 1858.
Phil 8890.10 Penn, W. Fruits of solitude, in reflections and maxims. N.Y., 1813.
Phil 8890.10.5 Penn, W. Früchte der Einsamkeit. Friedensthal, 1803.
Phil 8890.11 Penrose, John M.A. An inquiry chiefly on principles of religion. London, 1820.
Phil 8890.12 Percival, T. Moral and literary dissertations. Warrington, 1784.
Phil 8890.12.2 Percival, T. Moral and literary dissertations. Dublin, 1786.
Phil 8890.12.3 Percival, T. Moral and literary dissertations. Philadelphia, 1806.
Phil 8890.13 Pestel, F.G. Fundamenta jurisprudentae naturalis. Lugdunum Batavorum, 1777.
Phil 8890.15 Pezzani, A. Principes supérieurs de la morale. Paris, 1859.
Phil 8890.16 Placette, J. Essais de morale. Amsterdam, 1716-32 6v.
Phil 8890.17 Platt, J. Life. N.Y., 1889.
Phil 8890.19 Polier de St. Germain, A. de. Du gouvernement des moeurs. Lausanne, 1785.
Phil 8890.20 Porter, N. Elements of moral science. N.Y., 1885.
Phil 8890.20.1 Porter, N. Elements of moral science. N.Y., 1885.
Htn Phil 8890.21* Piccolomini, A. Della institutione morale, libri XII. Venetia, 1560. (Transferred to Houghton Library 31/1/72)
Htn Phil 8890.21.5* Piccolomini, A. Della institutione morale, libri XII. Venetia, 1594. (Transferred to Houghton Library 31/1/72)
Htn Phil 8890.22* Piccolomini, A. Della institutione morale. Venetia, 1575. (Transferred to Houghton Library 31/1/72)
Htn Phil 8890.22.10* Piccolomini, A. Della institutione di tutta la vita. Vinegia, 1552.
Phil 8890.23 Palmer, G.H. The glory of the imperfect. Boston, 1891.
Phil 8890.23.3 Palmer, G.H. The glory of the imperfect. N.Y., 1898.
Phil 8890.23.5 Palmer, G.H. The glory of the imperfect. Boston, 1915.
Phil 8890.23.7A Palmer, G.H. The field of ethics. Boston, 1901.
Phil 8890.23.7B Palmer, G.H. The field of ethics. Boston, 1901.
Phil 8890.23.9 Palmer, G.H. Field of ethics. Boston, 1902.
Phil 8890.23.16 Palmer, G.H. The nature of goodness. Boston, 1904.
Phil 8890.23.21 Palmer, George H. Altruism. N.Y., 1920.
Htn Phil 8890.24* Pater, W. Conclusion: an essay. N.Y., 1898.
Phil 8890.25 Pitcairn, E.H. Unwritten laws of active careers. London, 1899.
Phil 8890.26 Perry, R.B. Conception of moral goodness. n.p., 1907.
Phil 8890.26.5 Perry, R.B. The moral economy. N.Y., 1909.
Phil 8890.27 Everything bought with a price, or Moral commerce. Salem, 1820.
Phil 8890.28 Palhoriès, F. Nouvelles orientations de la morale. Paris, 1911.
Phil 8890.29 Payot, Jules. Cours de morale. 9. ed. Paris, 1914.
Phil 8890.30 Ecole des Hautes Études Sociales. Morale religieuse et morale laïque. Paris, 1914.
Phil 8890.32 Pascot, Giovanni. Scienze ausiliarie della morale. Udine, 1903.

Phil 8875 - 8900 Ethics - General treatises - Individual authors (A-Z) - cont.

Phil 8890.33 Pitt-Rivers, Goerge. Conscience and fanaticism. London, 1919.
Phil 8890.34 Pardines, Maurice. Critique des conditions de l'action. Paris, 1909. 2v.
Phil 8890.34.5 Piccolomineus, F. Universa philosophia de moribus. Francofurti, 1627.
Htn Phil 8890.35F* Piccolomineus, F. Universa philosophia de moribus. Venetiis, 1583.
Phil 8890.36 Pichler, Hans. Grundzüge einer Ethik. Graz, 1919.
Phil 8890.37 Petrone, Igino. Etica. Milano, 1918.
Phil 8890.37.5 Petrone, Igino. Ascetica. Milano, 1918.
Phil 8890.38 Pfordten, O. Ethik. Berlin, 1919.
Phil 8890.39 Pascal, G. de. Philosophie morale et sociale. Paris, 1894.
Phil 8890.40 Pörschke, K.L. Einleitung in die Moral. Libau, 1797.
Phil 8890.41 Parodi, D. Le problème morale et la pensée contemporaine. 2. ed. Paris, 1921.
Phil 8890.41.10 Parodi, D. Les bases psychologiques de la vie morale. Paris, 1928.
Phil 8890.42 Paton, H.J. The good will. London, 1927.
Htn Phil 8890.43* Palmieri, Matteo. Libro della vita civile. n.p., 15- .
Phil 8890.44 Pauler, Ákós. Az ethikai megismerés természete. Budapest, 1907.
Phil 8890.45 Patten, Simon N. Economic causes of moral progress. Philadelphia, 1892.
Phil 8890.46 Palmer, E. Principles of nature. London, 1823.
Phil 8890.46.5 Palmer, E. Principles of nature. 3. ed. N.Y., 1806.
Phil 8890.47 Pratt, James B. Reason in the art of living. N.Y., 1949.
Phil 8890.48 Prior, A.N. Logic and the bases of ethics. Oxford, 1949.
Phil 8890.49 Popov I.V. Estestvennyi nravstvennyi zakon. Sergiev, 1897.
Phil 8890.52 Pepper, Stephen Coburn. Ethics. N.Y., 1960.
Phil 8890.54 Pons, Walter. Steht uns der Himmel offen. Wiesbaden, 1960.
Phil 8890.54.2 Pons, Walter. Steht uns der Himmel offen. 2. Aufl. Wiesbaden, 1960.
Phil 8890.56 Padovani, U.A. Filosofia e morale. Padova, 1960.
Phil 8890.58 Palazzini, Pietro. Morale generale. Brescia, 1961.
Phil 8890.59 Polzer, Ignatius. Praelectiones ethicae. Olomuc, 1770.
Phil 8890.60 Perelman, Chaim. The idea of justice and the problem of argument. London, 1963.
Phil 8890.60.1 Perelman, Chaim. Justice et raison. Bruxelles, 1963.
Phil 8890.61 Pohl, Hermann Paul Albert. Das Gesetz. Der Morgen der Menschheit. Berlin, 1966.
Phil 8890.62 Pieper, Josef. Reality and the good. Chicago, 1967.
Phil 8890.63 Petrov, Erik F. Egoizm. Moskva, 1969.
Phil 8890.64 Punzo, Vincent C. Reflective naturalism. N.Y., 1969.
Phil 8890.66 Phillips, Dewi Zephaniah. Moral practices. London, 1966[1970]
Phil 8890.68 Pontara, Giuliano. Does the end justify the means? Stockholm, 1967.
Phil 8891.1 Quarles, F. Enchiridion. 1658. Reprint. London, 1568.
Phil 8891.1.2 Quarles, F. Enchiridion. London, 1856.
Phil 8891.2 Questions de morale. Paris, 1900.
Phil 8891.3 Quinby, L.J. Natural basis of moral and ethics. Boston, 1936.
Phil 8891.4 Quillian, W.F. The moral theory of evolutionary naturalism. New Haven, 1945.
Phil 8892.1 Randolph, R. Sober thoughts on staple themes. Philadelphia, 1889.
Phil 8892.3 Rolph, W.H. Biologische Probleme. Leipzig, 1882.
Phil 8892.3.3 Rolph, W.H. Biologische Probleme. 2. Aufl. Leipzig, 1884.
Phil 8892.4 Roberty, E. de. Constitution de l'éthique. Paris, 1900.
Phil 8892.4.5 Roberty, E. de. L'éthique. Les fondements de l'éthique. 2. ed. Paris, 1899.
Phil 8892.4.10 Roberty, E. de. L'éthique. Le bien et le mal. Paris, 1896.
Phil 8892.5 Ratzenhofer, G. Positive Ethik. Leipzig, 1901.
Phil 8892.6 Rowe, E.S. Friendship in death. London, 1733-34.
Htn Phil 8892.6.2* Rowe, E.S. Friendship in death. Philadelphia, 1805.
Htn Phil 8892.6.3* Rowe, E.S. Friendship in death. N.Y., 1795.
Htn Phil 8892.6.5* Rowe, E.S. Friendship in death. New Haven, 1802.
Phil 8892.7 Rosteri, P.L. Sentenze e massime morali. London, 1842.
Phil 8892.8 Rush, Benjamin. An oration...enquiry into the influence of physical causes upon the moral faculty. Philadelphia, 1786.
Phil 8892.8.2 Rush, Benjamin. An inquiry into the influence of physical causes upon the moral faculty. Philadelphia, 1839.
Phil 8892.9 Ryland, F. Ethics. London, 1893.
Phil 8892.10 The rule of life. Springfield, 1800.
Phil 8892.11 Rutherforth, T. An essay on the nature and obligations of virtue. Cambridge, 1744.
Phil 8892.12.2B Royce, J. The philosophy of loyalty. N.Y., 1908.
Phil 8892.12.4 Royce, J. The philosophy of loyalty. N.Y., 1908.
Phil 8892.12.5A Royce, J. Race questions, provincialism and other American problems. N.Y., 1908.
Phil 8892.12.5B Royce, J. Race questions, provincialism and other American problems. N.Y., 1908.
Phil 8892.12.5C Royce, J. Race questions, provincialism and other American problems. N.Y., 1908.
Phil 8892.12.9 Royce, J. The philosophy of loyalty. N.Y., 1908.
Phil 8892.12.10 Royce, J. The philosophy of loyalty. N.Y., 1908.
Phil 8892.12.15A Royce, J. The philosophy of loyalty. N.Y., 1920.
Phil 8892.12.15B Royce, J. The philosophy of loyalty. N.Y., 1920.
Phil 8892.12.20A Royce, J. The philosophy of loyalty. N.Y., 1924.
Phil 8892.12.20B Royce, J. The philosophy of loyalty. N.Y., 1924.
Phil 8892.13 Rashdall, Hastings. The theory of good and evil. Oxford, 1907. 2v.
Phil 8892.13.2 Rashdall, Hastings. The theory of good and evil. 2. ed. Oxford, 1924. 2v.
Phil 8892.13.4 Rashdall, Hastings. The theory of good and evil. 2. ed. London, 1948. 2v.
Phil 8892.13.5 Rashdall, Hastings. Ethics. London, 1913.
Phil 8892.14 Read, Carveth. Natural and social morals. London, 1909.
Phil 8892.15 Roosevelt, T. Applied ethics being one of the Wm.B. Noble lectures for 1910. Cambridge, 1911.
Phil 8892.15.2 Roosevelt, T. Applied ethics being one of the Wm.B. Noble lectures for 1910. Cambridge, 1911.
Phil 8892.17 Rodrigues, G. Le problème de l'action. Paris, 1909.
Phil 8892.18 Rauh, F. Études de morale. Paris, 1911.
Phil 8892.19 Richards, C.H.B. Springs of action. N.Y., 1863.
Phil 8892.20 Riego, Julio del. Nociones fundamentales de ética ó filosofía moral. Madrid, 1903.
Phil 8892.21 Robert, A. Leçons de morale. Quebec, 1915.
Phil 8892.23 Royer, Clémence. Le bien et la loi morale; éthique. Paris, 1881.
Phil 8892.24 Raymond, George L. Ethics and natural law. N.Y., 1920.

Phil 8875 - 8900   Ethics - General treatises - Individual authors (A-Z) - cont.

Phil 8892.24.5   Raymond, George L. Ethics and natural law. 2. ed. N.Y., 1920.
Phil 8892.25   Rogers, A.K. The theory of ethics. N.Y., 1922.
Phil 8892.25.15   Rogers, A.K. Ethics and moral tolerance. N.Y., 1934.
Phil 8892.26.8   Rayot, E. Précis de morale. 8. ed. Paris, 1906.
Phil 8892.27   Ryner, J.H. Le subjectivisme. Paris, 1923.
Phil 8892.28   Rueff, Jacques. Des sciences physiques aux sciences morales. Paris, 1922.
Phil 8892.29.7   Ritter, P.H. Ethische fragmenten. 7. druk. Haarlem, 1924.
Phil 8892.29.15   Ritter, P.H. Etiske fragmenter. København, 1896.
Phil 8892.30   Ritter, Eli F. Moral law and civil law; parts of the same thing. N.Y., 1896.
Phil 8892.30.2   Ritter, Eli F. Moral law and civil law; parts of the same thing. Westerville, Ohio, 1910.
Phil 8892.31   Ritter, T.H. Lifvets konst. Stockholm, 1906.
Phil 8892.32   Rensi, Giuseppe. Introduzione alla scepsi etica. Firenze, n.d.
Phil 8892.32.5   Rensi, Giuseppe. Critica dello morale. Catania, 1935.
Phil 8892.34   Renauld, J.F. Manuel de morale. Paris, 1920.
Phil 8892.35   Renard, G. Des sciences physiques aux sciences morales. Paris, 1922.
Phil 8892.36   Rush, Jacob. Charges, and extracts of charges on moral and religious subjects. Philadelphia, 1803.
Phil 8892.37   Russell, Bertrand Russell. What I believe. London, 1925.
Phil 8892.37.3   Russell, Bertrand Russell. What I believe. N.Y., 1925.
Phil 8892.37.10   Russell, Bertrand Russell. What I believe. N.Y., 1928.
Itn   Phil 8892.38F*   Roback, A.A. The status of ethics. n.p., 1914.
Phil 8892.39   Rehmke, J. Ethik als Wissenschaft. 3. Aufl. Greifswald, 1925.
Phil 8892.39.5   Rehmke, J. Grundlegung der Ethic als Wissenschaft. Leipzig, 1925.
Itn   Phil 8892.40*   Romei, A. Discori...in sette giornate. Verona, 1586.
Itn   Phil 8892.40.5*   Romei, A. The courtiers academie. London, 1598.
Phil 8892.41   Roth, Leon. The science of morals; an essay in method. London, 1928.
Phil 8892.42   Rolffs, Ernst. Politische Ethik und ethische Weltanschauung. Leipzig, 1923.
Phil 8892.43   Ruiz Gómez, J.E. El nuevo mundo moral ó La nueva vida del hombre. Madrid, 1892.
Phil 8892.44   Rée, Paul. Der Ursprung der moralischen Empfindungen. Chemnitz, 1877.
Phil 8892.45   Rignano, E. Il fine dell'uomo. Bologna, 1928.
Phil 8892.46   Ross, W.D. The right and the good. Oxford, 1930.
Phil 8892.47   Regras da vida. n.p., n.d.
Phil 8892.48   Reiner, Hans. Der Grund der sittlichen Bindung und das sittlich Gute. Halle, 1932.
Phil 8892.49   Roberts, G.L. The domain of utilitarian ethics. Philadelphia, 1903.
Phil 8892.50   Rines, George E. Getting the most out of life. Boston, 1935.
Phil 8892.51   Rigerus, Johannes. Ethicorum liber. v.1-2. n.p., 16-?
Phil 8892.52   Rivarol, E.F. de. Encyclopédie morale. Paris, 1803.
Phil 8892.53   Rainsford, F.B. The Isle of Good Intent. Boston, 1936.
Phil 8892.54   Reid, L.A. Creative morality. London, 1937.
Phil 8892.55   Roche, J. Le gouvernement de soi. Paris, 1938.
Phil 8892.56   Reininger, Robert. Wertphilosophie und Ethik. Leipzig, 1939.
Phil 8892.56.5   Reininger, Robert. Wertphilosophie und Ethik. 3. Aufl. Wien, 1947.
Phil 8892.57   Ruvo, Vincenzo de. I valori morali. Bari, 1942.
Phil 8892.57.2   Ruvo, Vincenzo de. I valori morali. 2. ed. Padora, 1970.
Phil 8892.58   Raphael, D. Daiches. The moral sense. London, 1947.
Phil 8892.59   Rodriguez, G.H. Etica y jurisprudencia. Mexico, 1947.
Phil 8892.60   Reding, Marcel. Metaphysik der sittlichen Werte. 1. Aufl. Düsseldorf, 1949.
Phil 8892.62   Russell, Bertrand Russell. Human society in ethics and politics. London, 1954.
Phil 8892.62.5   Russell, Bertrand Russell. Human society in ethics and politics. N.Y., 1955.
Phil 8892.65   Raphael, D. Daiches. Moral judgement. London, 1955.
Phil 8892.68   Richards, David A.J. A theory of reasons for action. Oxford, 1971.
Phil 8892.70   Rosmini-Serbati, Antonio. Principi della scienza morale. Roma, 1959.
Phil 8892.72   Rubert y Candau, José M. Fundamento constitutivo de la moral. Madrid, 1956.
Phil 8892.74   Roys, F.X. Ethica et jus naturae in usum auditorum. Viennae, 1755.
Phil 8892.75   Rader, M.M. Ethics and the human community. N.Y., 1964.
Phil 8892.76   Reiner, Hans. Die philosophische Ethik. Heidelberg, 1964.
Phil 8892.76.5   Reiner, Hans. Gut und Böse. Freiburg, 1965.
Phil 8892.77   Roschacher, E. Das Recht und die Rechtssätze. Winterthur, 1963.
Phil 8892.79   Rašovský, Adolf. Ethos und Naturrecht. Wien, 1964.
Phil 8892.80   Ross, Alf. Directives and norms. London, 1968.
Phil 8892.82   Roscam Abbing, Pieter Johan. Om de mens. Leiden, 1968.
Phil 8892.84   Roubiczek, Paul. Ethical values in the age of science. Cambridge, Eng., 1969.
Phil 8892.86   Reyer, Wilhelm. Anthropologische Ethik. Köln, 1963.
Phil 8892.88   Rotter, Hans. Strukturen sittlichen Handelns. Mainz, 1970.
Phil 8893.1A   Salter, W.M. What can ethics do for us? Chicago, 1891.
Phil 8893.1B   Salter, W.M. What can ethics do for us? Chicago, 1891.
Phil 8893.2   Sandona, G. Della filosofia morale. Firenze, 1847. 2v.
Phil 8893.3   Schuppe, W. Grundzüge der Ethik und Rechtsphilosophie. Breslau, 1881.
Phil 8893.4*   Sculteti, A. Ethicorum. Argentinae, 1614.
Phil 8893.5.5   Secrétan, C. Le principe de la morale. Lausanne, 1883.
Phil 8893.6   Sedgwick, C.M. A short essay to do good. Stockbridge, 1828.
Phil 8893.7   Sewall, F. The new ethics. N.Y., 1881.
Phil 8893.8   Seth, J. A study of ethical principles. Edinburgh, 1894.
Phil 8893.8.2   Seth, J. A study of ethical principles. 5th ed. N.Y., 1899.
Phil 8893.8.3   Seth, J. A study of ethical principles. 8. ed. N.Y., 1905.
Phil 8893.8.5   Seth, J. A study of ethical principles. 12. ed. N.Y., 1911.
Phil 8893.8.10   Seth, J. A study of ethical principles. 17. ed. N.Y., 1926.
Phil 8893.8.15   Seth, J. Essays in ethics and religion with other papers. Edinburgh, 1926.
Phil 8893.9   Seydel, R. Ethik. Leipzig, 1874.
Phil 8893.10   Sharp, F.C. Das aesthetische Element in der Moral. Berlin, 1892.

Phil 8875 - 8900   Ethics - General treatises - Individual authors (A-Z) - cont.

Phil 8893.10.5   Sharp, F.C. The aesthetic element in morality. N.Y., 1893.
Phil 8893.10.10   Sharp, F.C. A study of the influence of custom. Madison, Wis., 1908.
Phil 8893.10.15   Sharp, F.C. Ethics. N.Y., 1928.
Phil 8893.11   Sidgwick, H. The methods of ethics. London, 1874.
Phil 8893.11.2   Sidgwick, H. The methods of ethics. London, 1874.
Phil 8893.11.6   Sidgwick, H. The methods of ethics. 6. ed. London, 1801.
Phil 8893.11.10   Sidgwick, H. The methods of ethics. Supplement to 1. ed. Photoreproduction. London, 1877.
Phil 8893.11.15   Sidgwick, H. The methods of ethics. London, 1922.
Phil 8893.11.17   Sidgwick, H. The methods of ethics. 7. ed. London, 1930.
Phil 8893.11.18   Hayward, F.H. The ethical philosophy of Sidgwick. Photoreproduction. London, 1901.
Phil 8893.11.22   Sidgwick, H. Die Methoden der Ethick. v.1-2. Leipzig, 1909.
Phil 8893.12   Sigwart, C. Vorfragen der Ethik. Freiburg, 1886.
Phil 8893.12.15   Flaig, Josef. Christoph Sigwarts Beiträge zu Grundlegung und Aufbau der Ethik. Stuttgart, 1912.
Phil 8893.13   Simcox, E. Natural law. London, 1877.
Phil 8893.14   Smiles, Samuel. Life and labour. London, 1887.
Phil 8893.14.2   Smiles, Samuel. Life and labour. N.Y., 1888.
Phil 8893.14.3   Smiles, Samuel. Life and labour. Chicago, 1891.
Phil 8893.14.4   Smiles, Samuel. Self-help. N.Y., 1860.
Phil 8893.14.6.5   Smiles, Samuel. Self-help. N.Y., 1875.
Phil 8893.14.7   Smiles, Samuel. Self-help. Chicago, 1890.
NEDL   Phil 8893.14.8   Smiles, Samuel. Self-help. N.Y., 1870.
Phil 8893.14.8.20   Smiles, Samuel. Self-help. N.Y., 1915.
Phil 8893.14.8.25   Smiles, Samuel. Self-help. London, 1958.
Phil 8893.14.9   Smiles, Samuel. Aýudate! Self-help. 5. ed. Paris, 1900.
Phil 8893.14.11   Smiles, Samuel. Thrift. Toronto, 1876.
Phil 8893.14.13   Smiles, Samuel. Thrift. Chicago, 1890.
Phil 8893.14.15   Smiles, Samuel. The art of living. Boston, 1887.
Phil 8893.15   Smith, Alexander. The philosophy of morals. London, 1835. 2v.
Phil 8893.16.5   Smith, Sydney. Elementary sketches of moral philosophy. N.Y., 1850.
Phil 8893.18   Speece, C. The mountaineer. Staunton, 1823.
Phil 8893.19   Spir, A. Moralität und Religion. Leipzig, 1874.
Phil 8893.20   Sprague, W.B. Letters on practical subjects. Hartford, 1822.
Phil 8893.21   Spurzheim, J.K. Philosophical catechism...natural laws of man. Boston, 1832.
Phil 8893.21.2   Spurzheim, J.K. Philosophical catechism...natural laws of man. Boston, 1835.
Phil 8893.21.3   Spurzheim, J.K. The natural laws of man. N.Y., 1849.
Phil 8893.23   Steinthal, H. Allgemeine Ethik. Berlin, 1885.
NEDL   Phil 8893.23.2   Stephen, L. The science of ethics. N.Y., 1882.
Phil 8893.23.5   Stephen, L. Social rights and duties. London, 1896. 2v.
X Cg   Phil 8893.24   Stewart, J. The book of nature. London, n.d.
Phil 8893.25   Stinson, J.H. Ethica. N.Y., 1860.
Phil 8893.26   The student's companion. London, 1748.
Phil 8893.27   Sturman, E.A. Inaugural dissertation, moral philosophy. London, 1871.
Phil 8893.28   Sullivan, W. The moral class book. Boston, 1831.
Phil 8893.28.3   Sullivan, W. The moral class book. Boston, 1833.
Phil 8893.28.8   Sullivan, W.R. Morality as a religion. London, 1898.
Phil 8893.29   Schmid, G.L. Traités sur divers sujets. n.p., 1760.
Phil 8893.30   Senac de Meilhan, G. Considérations sur l'esprit et les moeurs. London, 1787.
Phil 8893.30.3   Senac de Meilhan, G. Considérations sur l'esprit et les moeurs. Paris, 1905.
Phil 8893.31.5   Savage, M.J. The morals of evolution. Boston, 1881.
Phil 8893.32   Strümpell, L. Abhandlungen aus dem Gebiete der Ethik, der Staatswissenschaft, der Asthetik und der Theologie. Leipzig, 1895.
Phil 8893.32.5   Strümpell, L. Die Vorschule der Ethik. Mitau, 1844.
Phil 8893.33   Séailles, G. Les affirmations de la conscience moderne. Paris, 1903.
Phil 8893.34   Stanton, S.B. The essential life. N.Y., 1908.
Phil 8893.34.10   Stanton, S.B. The hidden happiness. N.Y., 1917.
Phil 8893.35   Spínola, R. Moral razonada. Guatemala, 1900.
Phil 8893.36   Smith, J.A. Knowing and acting. Oxford, 1910.
Phil 8893.37   Sorley, W.R. The moral life and moral worth. Cambridge, Eng., 1911.
Phil 8893.38   Stockwell, Joseph. A sermon preach'd at Faringdon...opening a charity school. Oxford, 1717.
Phil 8893.39   Schwarz, Hermann. Das sittliche Leben, eine Ethik auf psychologischer Grundlage. Berlin, 1901.
Phil 8893.39.5   Schwarz, Hermann. Grundzüge der Ethik. Leipzig, 1896.
Phil 8893.39.10   Schwarz, Hermann. Ethik. Breslau, 1925.
Phil 8893.40   Severn, Elizabeth. The psychology of behavior. N.Y., 1917.
Phil 8893.41   Simmel, G. Einleitung in die Moralwissenschaft. Berlin, 1892-93. 2v.
Phil 8893.42   Schubert-Soldern, R. von. Grundlagen zu einer Ethik. Leipzig, 1887.
Phil 8893.43   Sarlo, Francisco de. Principii di scienza etica. Milano, 1907.
Phil 8893.43.5   Sarlo, Francisco de. L'altività pratica e la coscienza morale. Firenze, 1907.
Phil 8893.43.10   Sarlo, Francisco de. Metafisica, scienza e moralità. Roma, 1898.
Phil 8893.44   Sugimori, K. The principles of the moral empire. London, 1917.
Phil 8893.45   Solov'ev, Vladimir. The justification of the good. N.Y., 1918.
Phil 8893.46   Salvadori, Guglielmo. Saggio di uno studio sui sentimenti morali. Firenze, 1903.
Phil 8893.47.2   Schneider, Wilhelm. Göttliche Weltordnung und religionslose Sittlichkeit. Paderborn, 1909.
Phil 8893.48   Schneider, H.W. Science and social progress. Lancaster, Pa., 1920.
Phil 8893.49   Stern, Wilhelm. Das Wesen des Mitleids. Berlin, 1903.
Phil 8893.50   Staudinger, Franz. Das Sittengesetz. 2. Aufl. Berlin, 1897.
Phil 8893.50.5   Staudinger, Franz. Wirtschaftliche Grundlagen der Moral. Darmstadt, 1907.
Phil 8893.51   Stange, Karl. Einleitung in die Ethik. Leipzig, 1901.
Phil 8893.52   Steudel, F. Alte und neue Tafeln. Berlin, 1912?
Phil 8893.53   Störring, Gustav. Ethische Grundfragen. Leipzig, 1906.
Phil 8893.53.5   Störring, Gustav. Moralphilosophische Streitfragen. Leipzig, 1903.
Phil 8893.53.7   Störring, Gustav. Die sittlichen Forderungen und die Frage ihrer Gultigkeit. Leipzig, 1919.

Phil 8875 - 8900   Ethics - General treatises - Individual authors (A-Z) - cont.

Phil 8893.53.10   Störring, Gustav. Grundfragen der philosophischen Ethik. Meisenheim, 1967.

Phil 8893.55.2   Seu, Mohit C. The elements of moral philosophy. 2. ed. London, 1913.

Phil 8893.56   Silva Cordeira, J.A. da. A crise em seus aspectos morals. Coimbra, 1896.

Phil 8893.57   Sturt, Henry. Human value. Cambridge, 1923.
Phil 8893.57.10   Sturt, Henry. Moral experience, an outline of ethics for class-teaching. London, 1928.

Phil 8893.58   Seta, Ugo della. Filosofia morale. Roma, 1917-19. 2v.
Phil 8893.58.10   Seta, Ugo della. I valori morali. 3. ed. Roma, 1925.
Phil 8893.59   Svensson, P.K. Om autonoma och heteronoma moralprinciper. Lund, 1904.

Phil 8893.60   Stein, F.J. Historisch-kritische Darstellung der pathologischen Moralprincipien. Wien, 1871.

Phil 8893.61   Schmid, C.C.E. Versuch einer Moralphilosophie. 2. Ausg. Jena, 1792.

Phil 8893.61.5   Schmid, C.C.E. Versuch einer Moralphilosophie. Jena, 1790.

Phil 8893.62   Schwalb, Carl J. Ethische und philosophische Betrachtungen auf empirischer Grundlage. Zürich, 1897.

Phil 8893.63   Sera, L.G. Sulle tracce della vita. Roma, 1907.
Htn   Phil 8893.64*   Shannon, F.B. Moral essays and discourses upon several subjects. London, 1690.

Phil 8893.65   Sourian, M. La fonction pratique de la finalité. Paris, 1925.

Phil 8893.65.2   Sourian, M. La fonction pratique de la finalité. Thèse. Paris, 1925.

Htn   Phil 8893.66*   Sensi, Lodovico. La historia dell'huomo. Perugia, 1577.
Phil 8893.67   Stumpf, Karl. Vom ethischen Skeptizismus. Leipzig, 1909.
Phil 8893.67.5   Stumpf, Karl. Vom ethischen Skeptizismus; Rede. Berlin, 1908.

Phil 8893.68   Sherman, C.L. The moral self: an introduction to the science of ethics. Boston, 1927.
Phil 8893.69   Schulze, K.E. Ethik der Dekadenz. Leipzig, 1925.
Phil 8893.70   Sallwürk, E v. Ethik in entwickelnder Darstellung. Langensalza, 1920.

Phil 8893.71   Seidel, A. Wegweiser zum moralischen Handeln. Leipzig, 1914.

Phil 8893.72   Skala, Richard. Der Stachel der Ethik. Wien, 1927.
Htn   Phil 8893.73*   Selva, Lorenzo. Della metamorfosi...del virtuoso. Orvieto, 1582.

Htn   Phil 8893.73.5*   Selva, Lorenzo. Della metamorfosi...del virtuoso. Firenze, 1583.

Htn   Phil 8893.73.10*   Selva, Lorenzo. Della metamorfosi...del virtuoso. Firenze, 1615.

Phil 8893.74   Sandström, A. Modern; romantik och etik. Stockholm, 1898.
Phil 8893.75   Say, J.B. Olbie, ou Essai sur les moyens de reformer. Paris, 1799-1800.

Phil 8893.76   Saturday Review. Studies in conduct. London, 1867.
Phil 8893.77   Sahlin, Karl Y. Om vilkoren för möjligheten al praktisk philosophi. Lund, 1855.

Phil 8893.78   Streeter, Burnett. Moral adventure. N.Y., 1929.
Phil 8893.79   Stapledon, W.O. A modern theory of ethics. London, 1929.
Phil 8893.80   Strain, J. The postulates of the moral life. Cambridge, 1929.

Phil 8893.81   Sockman, R.W. Morals of tomorrow. N.Y., 1931.
Phil 8893.82   Snell, C.W. Die sittlichkei Verbindung mit der Glükseligkeit einzelner Menschen und gauzer Staaten. Frankfurt, 1790.

Phil 8893.83   Salat, Jakob. Die Moralphilosophie. 3. Aufl. München, 1821.

Phil 8893.83.10   Salat, Jakob. Grundlinien der Moralphilosophie. München, 1819.

Phil 8893.83.15   Salat, Jakob. Auch die Aufklärung hat ihre Gefahren. München, 1801.

Phil 8893.83.15.5   Salat, Jakob. Auch ein paar Worte über die Fräge. München, 1802.

Phil 8893.83.16   Salat, Jakob. Die Philosophie mit obskuranten und Sophisten in Kampfe. Nachtrag: Auch die Aufklärung. Ulm, 1802.

Phil 8893.83.20   Salat, Jakob. Winke über das Verhältniss der intellektuellen und der verfeinernden Kultur zur Sittlichen. München, 1802.

Phil 8893.83.25   Salat, Jakob. Die literarische Stellung des Protestanten zu dem Katholiken. Laudshut, 1831.

Phil 8893.84   Schlick, Moritz. Fragen der Ethik. Wien, 1930.
Phil 8893.84.8A   Schlick, Moritz. Problems of ethics. N.Y., 1962.
Phil 8893.84.8B   Schlick, Moritz. Problems of ethics. N.Y., 1962.
Phil 8893.85   Stone, M.A. The philosophy of indifference. Providence, 1931.

Phil 8893.86.5   Scheler, Max. Der formalismus in der Ethik und die materiale Wertethik. 2. Aufl. Halle, 1921.

Phil 8893.87   Sibecas, S. Factores morales. Habana, 1926.
Phil 8893.88   Schulze, G.E. Philosophische Tugendlehre. Göttingen, 1817.

Phil 8893.89   Samuel, Herbert. Practical ethics. London, 1935.
Phil 8893.90   Staehr, V. von. Logische Struktur des emotionalen Ich. Diss. Saalfeld, 1934.

Phil 8893.91   Sargent, Porter E. The new immoralities. Boston, 1935.
Phil 8893.91.90   Sinclair, Upton. The book of life. Chicago, 1921.
Phil 8893.92A   Sinclair, Upton. The book of life. 4th ed. v.1-2. Long Beach, 1926.

Phil 8893.92B   Sinclair, Upton. The book of life. 4th ed. v.1-2. Long Beach, 1926.

Phil 8893.93   Schwarz, O.L. Unconventional ethics. Washington, 1936.
Phil 8893.94   Stoce, W.J. The concept of morals. N.Y., 1937.
Phil 8893.95.5   Schrempf, C. Die Grundlage der Ethik. Stuttgart, 1936.
Phil 8893.96   Saltzmann, C.G. Elements of morality. Baltimore, 1811.
Phil 8893.97   Smith, F.B. Men wanted. N.Y., 1911.
Phil 8893.98   Seaverns, A.S. Thoughts for the thoughtful. N.Y., 1893.
Phil 8893.99   Sacheli, C.A. Ragion pratica. Firenze, 1938.
Phil 8893.100   Boissière, P. La morale fouillée dans ses fondements. Paris, 1866.

Phil 8893.101   Stebbing, L.S. Ideals and illusions. London, 1941.
Phil 8893.102   Stevenson, Charles Leslie. Ethics and language. New Haven, 1944.

Phil 8893.102.2   Stevenson, Charles Leslie. Ethics and language. New Haven, 1946.

Phil 8893.102.5   Stevenson, Charles Leslie. Ethics and language. New Haven, 1948.

Phil 8893.102.15   Stevenson, Charles Leslie. Facts and values. New Haven, 1963.

Phil 8893.103A   Sorokin, Pitirim Aleksandrovich. Altruistic love. Boston, 1950.

Phil 8893.103B   Sorokin, Pitirim Aleksandrovich. Altruistic love. Boston, 1950.

Phil 8893.103.2   Sorokin, Pitirim Aleksandrovich. Altruistic love. N.Y., 1969.

Phil 8893.104   Sorokin, Pitirim Aleksandrovich. Explorations in altruistic love and behavior. Boston, 1950.

Phil 8893.104.3   Sorokin, Pitirim Aleksandrovich. Explorations in altruistic love and behavior. N.Y., 1970.

Phil 8893.104.5   Sorokin, Pitirim Aleksandrovich. Forms and techniques of altruistic and spiritual growth. Boston, 1954.

Phil 8893.104.6   Sorokin, Pitirim Aleksandrovich. Forms and techniques of altruistic and spiritual growth. Boston, 1954. N.Y., 1971.

Phil 8893.105   Sambarino, Mario. Investigaciones sobre la estructura aporético-dialéctica. Montevideo, 1959-60.

Phil 8893.110   Schneider, Herbert W. Morals for mankind. Columbia, 1960.
Phil 8893.115A   Singer, M.G. Generalization in ethics. 1. ed. N.Y., 1961.
Phil 8893.115B   Singer, M.G. Generalization in ethics. 1. ed. N.Y., 1961.
Phil 8893.120   Schoellgen, W. Konkrete Ethik. Düsseldorf, 1961.
Phil 8893.125   Shvartsman, Klara Aronovna. Kritika sovremennykh burzhuaznykh filosofsko-esteticheskikh system. Moskva, 1961.

Phil 8893.127   Shvartsman, Klara Aronovna. Etika...bez morali. Moskva, 1964.

Phil 8893.127.5   Shvartsman, Klara Aronovna. Ethik ohme Moral. Berlin, 1967.

Phil 8893.130   Selivanov, F.A. Etika. Tomsk, 1961.
Phil 8893.135   Sathaye, S.G. A philosophy of living. N.Y., 1963.
Phil 8893.136   Simon, Yves. The tradition of natural law. N.Y., 1965.
Phil 8893.137   Shirk, Evelyn Urban. The ethical dimension. N.Y., 1965.
Phil 8893.138   Sibben, Frederik Christian. Moralphilosophie. Kjobenhavn, 1878.

Phil 8893.139   Selsam, Howard. Ethics and progress. N.Y., 1965.
Phil 8893.140   Simonsen, Andreas. Erkendelse og lidenskab. København, 1966.

Phil 8893.142   Satyananda, Swami. World ethics. Calcutta, 1967.
Phil 8893.145   Schmoebz, Franz Martin. Das Naturgesetz und seine dynamische Kraft. Freiburg, 1959.

Phil 8893.147   Sen Gupta, Santosh Chandra. Good, freewill and God. Calcutta, 1963.

Phil 8894.1   Taylor, H. Notes from life. Boston, 1853.
Phil 8894.2   Taylor, Jane. The contributions of Q.Q. Philadelphia, 1830.

Phil 8894.2.5   Taylor, Jane. The contributions of Q.Q. to a periodical work. 6. ed. London, 1831.

Phil 8894.3   Thiess, J.O. Vorlesungen über die Moral. Leipzig, 1801-03. 2v.

Phil 8894.4   Thomassen, J.H. Das Evangelium der Wahrheit und Freiheit. Leipzig, 1871.

Phil 8894.5   Tiberghien, G. Éléments de morale universelle. Bruxelles, 1879.

Phil 8894.5.5   Tiberghien, G. Elementos de ética ó filosofía moral. Madrid, 1873.

Phil 8894.5.10   Tiberghien, G. Esquisse de philosophie morale. Bruxelles, 1854.

Phil 8894.6   Tissot, Joseph. Éthique ou science des moeurs. Paris, 1840.

Phil 8894.6.5   Tissot, Joseph. Méditations morales. Paris, 1860.
Phil 8894.6.10   Tissot, Joseph. Décadence du sentiment moral et religieux. Paris, 1878.

Phil 8894.6.15   Tissot, Joseph. Principes de la morale. Paris, 1866.
Htn   Phil 8894.8*   Toussaint, F.V. Les moeurs. 4th ed. n.p., 1749.
Phil 8894.8.2   Toussaint, F.V. Les moeurs. Amsterdam, 1763.
Htn   Phil 8894.8.3*   Toussaint, F.V. Les moeurs. pt.1-2,3. Aux Indes, 1749.
Htn   Phil 8894.8.5*   Toussaint, F.V. Les moeurs. pt. 3. Amsterdam, 1748.
Htn   Phil 8894.8.6*   Toussaint, F.V. Eclaircissement sur les moeurs. Amsterdam, 1762.

Phil 8894.8.15   Toussaint, F.V. Manners. 2d ed. London, 1752.
Phil 8894.10   Turnbull, G. The principles of moral philosophy. London, 1740. 2v.

Phil 8894.11.5   Thilly, F. Introduction to ethics. N.Y., 1913.
Phil 8894.12   Taylor, A.E. The problem of conduct. London, 1901.
Phil 8894.13   Tomkins, D.B. The individual and society. Thesis. Somerville, N.J., 1915.

Phil 8894.14   Troufleau, L, Morale pratique. 3e éd. Paris, 1913.
Phil 8894.15   Thouverez, Emile. Eléments de morale théoretique et pratique appliquéé a la pédagogie. 2. éd. Paris, 1911.

Phil 8894.16   Tille, A. Von Darwin bis Nietzsche. Leipzig, 1895.
Phil 8894.17.3   Trine, Ralph W. In tune with the infinite. N.Y., 1897.
Phil 8894.17.4   Trine, Ralph W. Set synliga i samklang med det o synliga. Stockholm, 1910.

Phil 8894.17.5   Trine, Ralph W. Auf dem Wege zur Wahrheit. Stuttgart, 1909.

Phil 8894.17.15   Trine, Ralph W. On the open road. N.Y., 1908.
Phil 8894.17.20   Trine, Ralph W. The greatest thing ever known. N.Y., 1898.

Phil 8894.17.22   Trine, Ralph W. What all the world's a-seeking. N.Y., 1896.

Htn   Phil 8894.17.23*   Trine, Ralph W. What all the world's a-seeking. Boston, 1897.

Phil 8894.18   Tarantino, Giuseppe. Il principio dell'ética e la crisi morale contemporanea; memoria. Napoli, 1904.

Phil 8894.18.5   Tarantino, Giuseppe. Il problema della morale di fronte al positivismo ed alla metafisica. Pisa, 1901.

Phil 8894.19   Tönnies, Ferdinand. Die Sitte. Frankfurt, 1909.
Phil 8894.19.5   Tönnies, Ferdinand. Custom. N.Y., 1961.
Phil 8894.20   Trojano, Paolo R. Ethica. Napoli, 1897.
Phil 8894.20.10   Trojano, Paolo R. La filosofia morale. Torino, 1902.
Phil 8894.21   Traub, Friedrich. Die sittliche Weltordnung. Freiburg, 1892.

Phil 8894.22   Trivero, Camillo. Saggi di etica. Milano, 1917.
Phil 8894.23   Tarozzi, G. Filosofia morale e nozioni affini. Bologna, 1911.

Phil 8894.23.5   Tarozzi, G. La virtù contemporanea. Torino, 1900.
Phil 8894.23.15   Tarozzi, G. Idea di una scienza del bene. Firenze, 1901.
Phil 8894.24   Turner, J.E. The philosophic basis of moral obligation; a study in ethics. London, 1924.

Htn   Phil 8894.25.5*   Torrey, Jesse, Jr. The moral instructor. 2d ed. Albany, 1819.

Phil 8894.26   Titus, H.H. Ethics for today. Boston, 1936.
Phil 8894.26.5   Titus, H.H. What is mature morality. N.Y., 1943.
Phil 8894.27   Tilgher, A. Filosofia delle morali. Roma, 1937.
Phil 8894.28   Thwing, C.F. The best life; an address. N.Y., 1898.
Phil 8894.29   Tuker, M.A.R. Past and future of ethics. London, 1938.
Phil 8894.30   Taeusch, C.F. Professional and business ethics. N.Y., 1926.

Phil 8894.31   Törngren, P.H. Moralsjukdomen. Stockholm, 1940.
Phil 8894.32   Tsanoff, Radoslov A. Ethics. N.Y., 1947.
Phil 8894.32.5   Tsanoff, Radoslov A. Ethics. N.Y., 1955.

Phil 8875 - 8900   Ethics - General treatises - Individual authors (A-Z) - cont.

Phil 8894.33   Toulmin, S. An examination of the place of reason in ethics. Cambridge, England, 1950.

Phil 8894.34   Timur, Mohammed. The theory of morals. London, 1956.

Phil 8894.36   Turner, Dean. The autonomous man. St. Louis, 1970.

Phil 8895.1   Uloth, L. Begriff, Wesen...Darstellung der Ethik. Göttingen, 18- .

Phil 8895.2   Unold, J. Grundlegung für eine moderne praktisch-ethische Lebensanschauung. Leipzig, 1896.

Phil 8895.3   Urban, W.M. Fundamentals of ethics. N.Y., 1930.

Phil 8895.4   Urwick, Edward. The values of life. Toronto, 1948.

Phil 8896.1   Vincent, G.G. The appendix to volumes I. and II. of the moral system, or Law of human nature. London, 1850.

Phil 8896.2A   Voluseno, F. De animi tranquillitate dialogus. Edinburg, 1751.

Phil 8896.2B   Voluseno, F. De animi tranquillitate dialogus. Edinburg, 1751.

Htn   Phil 8896.3*   Vives, Juan Luis. De disciplinis. Lugdunum Batavorum, 1636.

Phil 8896.3.5   Vives, Juan Luis. Introducción á la sabiduria. Valencia, 1779.

Phil 8896.3.10   Vives, Juan Luis. Vives' introduction to wisdom. N.Y., 1968.

Phil 8896.4.3   Vidari, Giovanni. Elementi di etica. 3. ed. Milano, 1911.

Phil 8896.4.4   Vidari, Giovanni. Elementi di etica. 4. ed. Milano, 1917.

Phil 8896.4.5   Vidari, Giovanni. Elementi di etica. 5. ed. Milano, 1922.

Phil 8896.4.9   Vidari, Giovanni. Problemi generali di etica. Milano, 1901.

Phil 8896.5   Vietinghoff, Jeanne de. La liberté intérieure. Paris, 1912.

Phil 8896.6   Varona, E.J. Conferencias sobre el fundamento de la moral. N.Y., 1913.

Phil 8896.7   Vallier, C.A. De l'intention morale. Paris, 1883.

Phil 8896.8   Verplanck, G.C. The influence of moral causes upon opinion. N.Y., 1834.

Phil 8896.9   Véron, Eugène. La morale. Paris, 1884.

Phil 8896.10   Vecchia, Paolo. Elementi di morale e cenni di economia politica. 8. ed. Torino, 1917?

Phil 8896.11   Vivante, Lello. Principii di etica. Roma, 1920.

Phil 8896.12   Vinet, Alexandre. Essais de philosophie morale et de moral e religieuse. Paris, 1837.

Phil 8896.13   Vermilye, T.E. An introductory address to the course of lectures before the young men's Association for Mutual Improvement in the city of Albany. Albany, 1837.

Phil 8896.14   Vesper, Noël. Anticipations à une morale du risque. Paris, 1914.

Phil 8896.15   Vysheslavtsev, V. Etika preobrazhennago erosa. Paris, 1931.

Phil 8896.16   Virey, J.J. L'art de perfectionner l'homme. Paris, 1808. 2v.

Phil 8896.17   Volney, C.F.C. The law of nature, or Principles of morality. Philadelphia, 1796.

Phil 8896.17.5   Volney, C.F.C. La loi naturelle. Paris, 1934.

Phil 8896.18   Valentine, M. Theoretical ethics. Chicago, 1897.

Phil 8896.19   Vasconcelos, J. Etica. 2. ed. Mexico, 1939.

Phil 8896.20   Vivas, E. The moral life and the ethical life. Chicago, 1950.

Phil 8896.21   Veatch, Henry B. Rational man; a modern interpretation. Bloomington, 1962.

Phil 8896.22   Vernet, Maurice. L'homme, maître de sa destinée. Paris, 1956.

Phil 8897.1   Walker, S. Reformation of manners. London, 1711.

Phil 8897.1.5   Walker, S. Familiar introduction to the knowledge of ourselves. London, 1761.

Phil 8897.2   Wallace, R. Various prospects of mankind. London, 1761.

Phil 8897.4   Waters, R. Intellectual pursuits. N.Y., 1892.

Phil 8897.4.2   Waters, R. Culture by self-help in a literary, an academic or an oratorical career. N.Y., 1909.

Phil 8897.5   Waterson, R.C. Thoughts on moral and spiritual culture. Boston, 1844.

Phil 8897.6   Wayland, F. Elements of moral science. Boston, 1835.

Phil 8897.6.2   Wayland, F. The elements of moral science. N.Y., 1835.

Phil 8897.6.3   Wayland, F. The elements of moral science. Boston, 1838.

Phil 8897.6.5   Wayland, F. The elements of moral science. Boston, 1859.

Phil 8897.6.7   Wayland, F. The elements of moral science. Boston, 1872.

Phil 8897.6.10   Wayland, F. The elements of moral science. Abridged. Boston, 1848.

Phil 8897.6.15   Wayland, F. The elements of moral science. Cambridge, Mass., 1963.

Phil 8897.6.20   Wayland, F. The elements of moral science. Rangoon, 1885.

Phil 8897.7   Wedgwood, J. The moral ideal. London, 1888.

Phil 8897.7.2   Wedgwood, J. The moral ideal. London, 1889.

Phil 8897.8   Weishaupt, A. Die Leuchte des Diogenes. Regensburg, 1804.

Phil 8897.8.10   Weishaupt, A. Ueber die Selbstkenntniss. Regensburg, 1794.

Phil 8897.9   Weiss, F.R. de. Principes philosophiques. Bruxelles, 1832. 2v.

Phil 8897.10   Wells, K.G. Lessons in ethics. pt.1. Boston, 1882.

Phil 8897.12   Wette, W.M.L. de. Vorlesungen über die Sittenlehre. v. 1-2. Berlin, 1823-24.

Phil 8897.12.5A   Wette, W.M.L. de. Human life; or Practical ethics. Boston, 1842. 2v.

Phil 8897.12.5B   Wette, W.M.L. de. Human life: or Practical ethics. Boston, 1842. 2v.

Phil 8897.12.9   Wette, W.M.L. de. Human life; or Practical ethics. Boston, 1856. 2v.

Phil 8897.13   Whately, R. Introductory lessons on morals. Cambridge, 1856.

Phil 8897.13.3   Whately, R. Introductory lessons on morals. Cambridge, 1860.

Phil 8897.13.5   Whately, R. Introductory lessons on morals. London, 1855.

Phil 8897.13.10   Whately, R. Thoughts and apophthegms. Philadelphia, 1856.

Phil 8897.14.1   Whewell, W. Elements of morality. N.Y., 185-? 2v.

Phil 8897.14.2   Whewell, W. Elements of morality. N.Y., 1854. 2v.

DL   Phil 8897.14.5   Whewell, W. Elements of morality. 4th ed. Cambridge, 1864.

Phil 8897.14.9   Whewell, W. Lectures on systematic morality. London, 1846.

Phil 8897.14.15   Whewell, W. On the foundations of morals. N.Y., 1839.

Phil 8897.14.16   Whewell, W. On the foundations of morals. Cambridge, n.d.

Phil 8897.15   Whitby, D. Ethices compendium. London, 1713.

Phil 8897.17   Wiart, J.J. De principe de la morale. Paris, 1862.

Phil 8897.19   Winslow, H. Elements of moral philosophy. N.Y., 1856.

Phil 8897.20   Witherspoon, J. Lectures on moral philosophy. Philadelphia, 1822.

Phil 8897.20.5   Witherspoon, J. Lectures on moral philosophy. Princeton, 1912.

Phil 8897.21   Woillez, C.T.R. Les médecins moralistes. Paris, 1862.

Phil 8875 - 8900   Ethics - General treatises - Individual authors (A-Z) - cont.

Htn   Phil 8897.22*   Woodward, Josiah. An account of the societies for reformation of manners. London, 1699.

Phil 8897.23.3   Wright, T. A good life. Boston, 1837.

Phil 8897.24   Wright, F. Course of popular lectures. N.Y., 1829.

Phil 8897.24.5   Wright, F. Course of popular lectures. v.2. Philadelphia, 1836.

Phil 8897.25   When to say no. London, n.d.

Phil 8897.26   Woltmann, L. System der moralischen Bewusstseins. Düsseldorf, 1898.

Phil 8897.27   Watson, John. The homely virtues. N.Y., 1902.

Phil 8897.28   Westermarck, E. The origin and development...moral ideas. 2nd ed. London, 1906-17. 2v.

Phil 8897.28.3   Westermarck, E. The origin and development...moral ideas. London, 1908-12. 2v.

Phil 8897.28.5   Westermarck, E. Moralens uppkomst och utveckling. Stockholm, 1916.

Phil 8897.28.15   Westermarck, E. Ethical relativity. N.Y., 1932.

Phil 8897.28.20   Westermarck, E. The origin and development of the moral ideas. 2nd ed. London, 1924-26.

Phil 8897.29A   Washington, B.T. Putting the most into life. N.Y., 1906.

Phil 8897.29B   Washington, B.T. Putting the most into life. N.Y., 1906.

Phil 8897.29.8   Washington, B.T. Sowing and reaping. Boston, 1900.

Phil 8897.30   Wentscher, M. Ethik. Leipzig, 1902.

Phil 8897.31   Wood, W. Ideals of life - symposium on the coming man. N.Y., 1892.

Phil 8897.32   Wittman, M. Die Grundfragen der Ethik. Kempten, 1909.

Phil 8897.32.5   Wittman, M. Ethik. München, 1923.

Phil 8897.33   Wolff, H. Handbuch der Ethik. Leipzig, n.d.

Phil 8897.34   Wallace, A.R. Social environment and moral progress. N.Y., 1913.

Phil 8897.35   Wentscher, E. Grundzüge der Ethik. Leipzig, 1913.

Phil 8897.36   Wilbois, J. Devoir et durée. Paris, 1912.

Phil 8897.37   Whittaker, Thomas. Theory of abstract ethics. Cambridge, 1916.

Phil 8897.38   Wallaschek, R. Ideen zur praktischen Philosophie. Tübingen, 1886.

Phil 8897.38.5   Wallaschek, R. Studien zur Rechtsphilosophie. Leipzig, 1889.

Phil 8897.39   Werner, Charles. Études de philosophie morale. Genève, 1917.

Phil 8897.40   Walcott, Gregory. Tsing Hua lectures on ethics. Boston, 1919.

Phil 8897.41   Ward, Stephen. The ways of life. London, 1920.

Phil 8897.41.3   Ward, Stephen. The ways of life. N.Y., 1920.

Phil 8897.42   Wyneken, Ernst F. Das Naturgestz der Seele und...Freiheit. Heidelberg, 1906.

Phil 8897.43   Van Wesep, H.B. The control of ideals. N.Y., 1920.

Phil 8897.44   Woffny, F. Leitfaden der Moral. 2. Aufl. Leipzig, 1903.

Phil 8897.45   Witte, J.H. Grundzüge der Sittenlehre. Bonn, 1882.

Phil 8897.46   Wiggam, A.E. The new decalogue of science. Indianapolis, 1923.

Phil 8897.46.5   Wiggam, A.E. The new decalogue of science. Garden City, 1925.

Phil 8897.47   Weigelin, Ernst. Sitte, Recht und Morale. Berlin, 1919.

Phil 8897.47.5   Weigelin, Ernst. Einführung in die Moral- und Rechtsphilosophie. Leipzig, 1827.

Phil 8897.48   Wirpel, Aaron. Observations of a progressive religionist. Cleveland, 1923.

Phil 8897.49   White, A.K. The moral self; its nature and development. London, 1925.

Phil 8897.50.2   Weiss, Berthold. Die ethische Aufgabe des Menschen. Berlin, 1893.

Phil 8897.52   Wilkens, C. Etisk vurdering. København, 1916.

Phil 8897.52.5   Wilkens, C. Livets grundvardier. København, 1909.

Phil 8897.53   Wijnaendts Francken, C.J. Ethische studien. Haarlem, 1903.

Phil 8897.54   Wirth, J.U. System der speculativen Ethik. v.1-2. Heilbronn, 1841-42.

Phil 8897.55   Wiggin, F.A. Cubes and spheres in human life. Boston, 1899.

Phil 8897.56   Wright, Henry W. Self realization. N.Y., 1913.

Phil 8897.57   Wintzer, Wilhelm. Der Sinn und Zweck des Lebens. Stuttgart, 1922.

Phil 8897.58   Wright, William K. General introduction to ethics. N.Y., 1929.

Phil 8897.59   Wilson, M.H. Vocational guidance. Boston, 1916.

Phil 8897.60   Wiedling, Hans. Die Wirklichkeit der Ethik. Leipzig, 1931.

Phil 8897.61   Winsor, F. The art of behaviour. Boston, 1932.

Phil 8897.62.3   Whiting, Lilian. The world beautiful. Boston, 1897.

Phil 8897.62.5   Whiting, Lilian. The world beautiful. 3rd ser. Boston, 1898.

Phil 8897.63.5   Wilson, Woodrow. When a man comes to himself. N.Y., 1915.

Phil 8897.64   Whitehead, George. What is morality? London, 1925.

Phil 8897.65   Wheelwright, P. A critical introduction to ethics. Garden City, N.Y., 1935.

Phil 8897.65.5   Wheelwright, P. A critical introduction to ethics. N.Y., 1949.

Phil 8897.66   Whitney, R.E. Morality in the making. N.Y., 1929.

NEDL   Phil 8897.67   Walsh, Robert. Didactics. Philadelphia, 1836. 2v.

Phil 8897.69   Westermarck, E. Christianity and morals. N.Y., 1939.

Phil 8897.70   Winternitz, M. Religion und Moral. Prag, 1922.

Phil 8897.72   Wijnaendts Francken, C.J. Vier moralisten. Amsterdam, 1946.

Phil 8897.73   Wellman, Carl. The language of ethics. Cambridge, 1961.

Phil 8897.73.5   Wellman, Carl. Challenge and response. Carbordale, 1971.

Phil 8897.74   Weiss, Richard. World without frontiers. Sydney, 1950.

Phil 8897.76   Weil, Simone. L'enracinement. 3. éd. Paris, 1949.

Phil 8897.76.5   Weil, Simone. The need for roots. N.Y., 1952.

Phil 8897.78   Williams, G. Humanistic ethics. N.Y., 1951.

Phil 8897.80   Wilson, John. Reason and morals. Cambridge, Eng., 1961.

Phil 8897.82   Witwicki, W. Pogadanki obczajowe. Warszawa, 1960.

Phil 8897.83   Weil, Eric. Philosophie morale. Paris, 1961.

Phil 8897.84   Wright, G.H. von. The logic of preference, an essay. Edinburgh, 1963.

Phil 8897.85   Wright, G.H. von. Norm and action. London, 1963.

Phil 8897.88   Weiss, Paul. Right and wrong; a philosophical dialogue between father and son. N.Y., 1967.

Phil 8897.90   Warnock, Geoffrey James. Contemporary moral philosophy. N.Y., 1967.

Phil 8897.90.5   Warnock, Geoffrey James. The object of morality. London, 1971.

Phil 8897.92   William, Bernard Arthur Owen. Morality and the emotions: an inaugural lecture. London, 1966.

Phil 8897.94   Wyss, Dieter. Strukturen der Moral. Göttingen, 1968.

Phil 8897.94.2   Wyss, Dieter. Strukturen der Moral. 2. Aufl. Göttingen, 1970.

Phil 8875 - 8900   Ethics - General treatises - Individual authors (A-Z) - cont.

Phil 8897.96   Winch, Peter. Moral integrity: inaugural lecture in the Chair of Philosophy delivered at King's College, London, 9 May 1968. Oxford, 1968.

Phil 8897.98   Wertheimer, Roger. The significance of sense. Ithaca, 1972.

Phil 8900.1   Zeigler, T. Sittliches Sein und sittliches Werden. 2. Aufl. Strassburg, 1890.

Phil 8900.1.5   Zeigler, T. Social ethics. London, 1892.

Phil 8900.2   Zini, Zino. Il pentimento e la morale ascentica. Torino, 1902.

Phil 8900.3   Zweifel, Hans. Die sittliche Weltordnung. München, 1875.

Phil 8900.4   Ziller, T. Allgemeine philosophische Ethik. Langensalza, 1880.

Phil 8900.5   Zinninger, E.D. Ethical philosophy and civilization. Los Angeles, 1935.

Htn   Phil 8900.6*   Zuccolo, G. I discorsi mi quali si tratta della nobilità. Venetia, 1575.

Phil 8900.7   Zen'kovskii, V.V. Dar svobody. Paris, 193-?

Phil 8900.8   Zink, Sidney. The concepts of ethics. N.Y., 1962.

Phil 8900.9   Zdotusskii, Igor P. Faust i fiziki. Moskva, 1968.

Phil 8900.10   Ziemba, Zdzisław. Logika deontyczna jako formalizacja rozumowań normalywnych. Wyd. 1. Warszawa, 1969.

Phil 8905   Ethics - General special treatises - Relations of ethics to other disciplines

Phil 8905.5   Coulson, Charles Alfred. Faith and technology; being the inaugural lecture of the Luton Industrial College. London, 1969.

Phil 8905.10   Utz, Arthur Fridolin. Ethik und Politik. Stuttgart, 1970.

Phil 8905.15   Iskusstvo uravstvennoe i bezuravstvennoe. Moskva, 1969.

Phil 8905.22   Odier, Charles. Les deux sources, consciente et inconsciente, de la vie morale. 2. éd. Neuchâtel, 1968.

Phil 8905.25   Hudon, Louis-Nazaire. Le corps humain dans la pensée de Dieu. Alma, 1947.

Phil 8905.28   Eticheskoe i esteticheskoe. Leningrad, 1971.

Phil 8905.30   Friedmann, Georges. La puissance et la sagesse. Paris, 1971.

Phil 8905.32   Nome, John. Kritisk forskerholdning i etikk og religionsfilosofi. Oslo, 1970.

Phil 8905.34   Nauka i nravstvennost'. Moskva, 1971.

Phil 8910   Ethics - General special treatises - Comparative ethics

Phil 8910.2   Behn, Siegfried. Ethik; ein Repetitorium. Bonn, 1948.

Phil 8950 - 8975   Ethics - General special treatises - Religious ethics - Christian (A-Z)

Phil 8950.1   Andreae, J.V. Civis Christianus. Lipsiae, 1706.

Htn   Phil 8950.2*   Ariadne mystica. Monachij, 1698. 2 pam.

Phil 8950.3   Alstrin, Eric. Ethica theologiae ministra. Upsaliae, 1725.

Phil 8950.4   Anderson, L.D. The business of living. N.Y., 1923.

Phil 8950.5   Anglican and International Christian Moral Science Association. Science and the gospel. London, 1870.

Phil 8950.6   Arregui, Antonio M. Summarium theologiae morales. Bilbao, 1922.

Phil 8950.6.2   Arregui, Antonio M. Summarium theologiae morales. Bilbao, 1919.

Phil 8950.7   Antnenko, V.H. Sotsialistychnyi humanizm i khrystianskyi bubov do blyzhiv'oho. Kyïv, 1961.

Phil 8950.8   Arrese y Ontiveros, Pedro Alexandro de. Modo para vivir eternamento. Madrid, 1710.

Phil 8950.10   Aula, Olari. Kristikunnan kouluss. Porvoo, 1964.

Phil 8950.12   Anciaux, Paul. Le dynamisme de la morale chrétienne. Gembloux, 1968-69.

Phil 8951.1   Bestmann, H.J. Geschichte der christlichen Sitte. Nödling, 1880-85. 2v.

Htn   Phil 8951.2*   Browne, T. Christian morals. 2. ed. London, 1756.

Phil 8951.3   Boutteville, M.L. La morale de l'église et la morale naturelle. Paris, 1866.

Phil 8951.4   Barbour, G.F. Philosophical study of Chrisian ethics. Edinburgh, 1911.

Phil 8951.4.5   Barbour, G.F. Essays and addresses. Edinburgh, 1949.

Phil 8951.5   Bruch, J.F. Lehrbuch der christlichen Sittenlehre. v.1-2. Strassburg, 1829-32.

Htn   Phil 8951.6*   Barlow, Thomas. Several miscellaneous and mighty cases of conscience. London, 1692.

Phil 8951.7.9   Benedictus XIV. Casus conscientiae de mandato. Augustae Vindelicorum, 1772.

Phil 8951.7.10   Benedictus XIV. Casus conscientiae de mandato. Appendix. v.1-5. Augustae Vindelicorum, 1772. 3v.

Phil 8951.8   Babrovnitzki, I. Sushchestvennyia cherty pravoslavnago. Elisavetgrad, 1897.

Phil 8951.9   Brown, William L. Comparative view of Christianity. Edinburgh, 1826. 2v.

Phil 8951.10   Bindi, Enrico. Religione e morale, scritti varii. Firenze, 1904.

Phil 8951.11   Bautain, Louis E. La morale de l'évangile comparée. Paris, 1855. 2 pam.

Phil 8951.11.5   Bautain, Louis E. Philosophie du Christianisme. Paris, 1835. 2v.

Phil 8951.11.80   Prupard, Paul. L'abbé Louis Bautain. Tournai, 1961.

Phil 8951.12   Broglie, L'abbé de. La morale sans Dieu. Paris, 1903.

Phil 8951.13   Ballerini, A. Opus theologicum morale in Busernbaum Medullam. 3.ed. Prati, 1898-1901. 7v.

Phil 8951.14   Beysens, J.T. Hoofdstukken uit de bijzondere ethiek. v.1-5. Bussum, 1917-19-.

Phil 8951.15   Bruce, William S. Social aspects of Christian morality. London, 1905.

Phil 8951.17   Birchard, Ford G. Out of the rut, a layman's point of view. Boston, 1931.

Phil 8951.18   Buddeus, J.F. Institutiones theologiae moralis. Lipsiae, 1719.

Phil 8951.19.2   Pamphlet vol. Busch, F. Découvertes d'un bibliophile. 5 pam.

Phil 8951.19.5   Busch, F. Découvertes d'un bibliophile. 2. éd. Strassburg, 1843.

Phil 8951.20   Brown, Charles R. Dreams come true. N.Y., 1944.

Phil 8951.21A   Brunner, Heinrich E. Justice and the social order. London, 1945.

Phil 8951.21B   Brunner, Heinrich E. Justice and the social order. London, 1945.

Phil 8951.22   Braun, K. Justice and the law of love. London, 1950.

Phil 8951.23   Bennett, J. Christian ethics and social policy. N.Y., 1946.

Phil 8951.24   Allen, E. Creation and grace...Ernie Brunner. London, 1950.

Phil 8951.24.5   Valken, L. Der Glaube bei Emil Brunner. Freiburg, 1947.

Phil 8950 - 8975   Ethics - General special treatises - Religious ethics - Christian (A-Z) - cont.

Phil 8951.25   Barrett, E.B. Life begins with love. Dublin, 1953.

Phil 8951.26   Christian values and economic life. 1st ed. N.Y., 1954.

Phil 8951.27   Bourke, V.J. Ethics. N.Y., 1959.

Phil 8951.28   Berthélemy, Jean. Structure et dimensions de la liberté. Paris, 1956.

Phil 8951.29   Borowski, A. Teologia moralna. Wyd. 2. Lublin, 1960.

Phil 8951.30   Brungs, Robert A. Building the city. N.Y., 1967.

VPhil 8951.31   Brumen, Vinko. Iskanja. Buenos Aires, 1967.

Phil 8951.32   Boeckman, Peter Wilhelm. Liv, fellesskap, tjeneste. Oslo, 1970.

Phil 8952.1   Chalmers, T. Application of Christianity to...ordinary affairs of life. Glasgow, 1820.

Phil 8952.1.2   Chalmers, T. Application of Christianity to...ordinary affairs of life. Glasgow, 1821.

Phil 8952.1.5   Chalmers, T. Application of Christianity to...ordinary affairs of life. N.Y., 1821.

Phil 8952.1.6   Chalmers, T. Application of Christianity to...ordinary affairs of life. 3d American ed. Hartford, 1821.

Phil 8952.2   Croslegh, C. Christianity judged by its fruits. London, 1884.

Phil 8952.3   The cost of living; a personal reflection and its outcome. n.p., 1919.

Phil 8952.4   Christianity and problems of today. N.Y., 1922.

Phil 8952.5   Crawford, F.G. The Christ ideal for world peace. San Francisco, 1925.

Phil 8952.6   Cunningham, W. The gospel of work. Cambridge, 1902.

Phil 8952.7   Christian ethics. Philadelphia, 1927.

Phil 8952.8   Christianity and the present moral unrest. London, 1926.

Phil 8952.9   Corte, P.A. Primi elementi di antropologia e di scienza morale. Torino, 1867.

Phil 8952.10   Chassanis. La morale universale. Paris, 1791.

Phil 8952.11   Constantino, S.A. Amen, amen. N.Y., 1944.

Phil 8952.12   Cary-Elwes, C.F. Law, liberty and love. N.Y., 1951.

Phil 8952.13   Cattani de Menasce, Giovanni. Saggi di analisi dell'atto morale. Roma, 1957.

Phil 8952.14   Cathrein, Victor. Philosophia moralis in usum scholarum. Friburgi, 1959.

Phil 8952.15   Crofts, Ambrose M. Moral philosophy. Dublin, 1960.

Phil 8952.20   Carpenter, Edward. Common sense about Christian ethics. London, 1961.

Phil 8952.21   Chauchard, P. Morale du cerveau. Paris, 1962.

Phil 8952.22   Curran, Charles E. A new look at Christian morality. Notre Dame, 1968.

Phil 8952.22.5   Curran, Charles E. Contemporary problems in moral theology. Notre Dame, 1970.

Phil 8952.23   Comitato Cattolico Docenti Universitari. Il problema morale, oggi. Bologna, 1969.

Phil 8952.25   Cunningham, Robert L. Situationism and the new morality. N.Y., 1970.

Phil 8953.1   Döllinger, J.J.I. von. Geschichte der Moralstreitigheiten. v.1-2. Nordlingen, 1889.

Phil 8953.2   Davidson, William L. Christian ethics. London, 1899.

Phil 8953.3   Dawbarn, C.Y.C. Applied philosophy. London, 1923.

Phil 8953.4   Dyroff, A. Religion und Moral. Berlin, 1925.

Phil 8953.5   Dorner, I.A. System of Christian ethics. N.Y., 1887.

Phil 8953.6   Donat, J. Summa philosophiae christianae. v.7-8. Oeniponte, 1920-21.

Phil 8953.7   Davis, H. Moral and pastoral theology. 3. ed. N.Y., 1938. 4v.

Phil 8953.8   D'Arcy, Martin Cyrile. The mind and heart of love. London, 1945.

Phil 8953.8.2   D'Arcy, Martin Cyrile. The mind and heart of love, lion and unicorn. N.Y., 1947.

Phil 8953.8.3   D'Arcy, Martin Cyrile. The mind and heart of love, lion and unicorn. London, 1954.

Phil 8953.8.6   D'Arcy, Martin Cyrile. La double nature de l'amour. Paris, 1948.

Phil 8953.9   Dodd, C.H. Gospel and law. Cambridge, Eng., 1951.

Phil 8953.10   Demoulin, Jérôme. Critiques; á la bona consciència dels christians. Barcelona, 1963.

Phil 8953.15   Dunphy, William. The new morality. N.Y., 1967.

Phil 8954.2   Everett, E.L. Impossible things and other essays. Philadelphia, 1932.

Phil 8954.3   Eddy, S. Maker of men. N.Y., 1941.

Phil 8954.4   Elliot, W.H. As I was saying. London, 1944?

Phil 8954.4.5   Elliot, W.H. Bring me my bow. London, 1946.

Phil 8954.5   Eisenstadt, Shmuel Noah. The Protestant ethic and modernization. N.Y., 1968.

Phil 8954.10   Ellul, Jacques. Violence. N.Y., 1969.

VPhil 8955.1   Fox, J.J. Religion and morality. N.Y., 1899.

Phil 8955.2   Frank, F.H.R. System du christliche Sittlichkeit. Erlangen, 1884-87. 2v.

Phil 8955.3   Fassler, A. A new gospel. N.Y., 1908.

Phil 8955.4   Flynn, V.S. The norm of morality. Diss. Washington, 1928.

Phil 8955.5   Ford, J.C. Contemporary moral theology. Westminster, Md., 1958-63. 2v.

Phil 8955.6   Frodl, Ferdinand. Gesellschaftslehre. Wien, 1936.

Phil 8955.7   Fuchs, Emil. Christliche und marxistische Ethik. Leipzig, 1958. 2v.

Phil 8955.8   Fletcher, Joseph Francis. Situation ethics. Philadelphia, 1966.

Phil 8955.8.80   Cox, Harvey G. The situation ethics debate. Philadelphia, 1968.

Phil 8955.9   Furger, Franz. Gewissen und Klugheit in der katholischen Moraltheologie der letzten Jahrzehnte. Luzern, 1965.

Phil 8955.11   Fotion, Nicholas G. Moral situation. Yellow Springs, 1968.

Phil 8955.13   Furfey, Paul Hanly. The morality gap. N.Y., 1968.

Phil 8955.13.5   Fuchs, Josef. Le renouveau de la théologie morale selon Vatican II. Paris, 1968.

Phil 8955.13.5   Fuchs, Josef. Moral und Moraltheologie nach dem Konzil. Freiburg, 1969.

Phil 8955.14   al Faruqi, Ismàil Ragi A. Christian ethics: a historical and systematic analysis of its dominant ideas. Montreal, 1967.

Phil 8956.1A   Gass, F.W.H.J. Geschichte der christlichen Ethik. Berlin, 1881-87. 2v.

Phil 8956.1B   Gass, F.W.H.J. Geschichte der christlichen Ethik. Berlin, 1881.

Phil 8956.2   Gladden, Washington. Ruling ideas of the present age. Boston, 1895.

Phil 8956.3   Gregory, Daniel. Christian ethics. Philadelphia, 1875.

Phil 8956.4   Gooding, W.M. A philosophy of the moral nature of man. Newark, 1877.

Phil 8956.5   Gallwitz, Hans. Das Problem der Ethik...Gegenwart. Göttingen, 1891.

Classified Listing

Phil 8956.6 — Geismar, E. Etik. København, 1926.

Phil 8956.7 — Green, Peter. The problem of right conduct. London, 1931.

Phil 8956.8 — Cenicot, Edouard. Institutiones theologiae moralis quas in Collegio Lovaniensi Societatis Jesu. 12. ed. Louvain, 1931.

Phil 8956.8.15 — Genicot, Edouard. Casus conscientiae propositi ac soluti. 6. ed. Louvain, 1928.

Phil 8956.9 — Göransson, N.J. Utkast till en undersökning af religionen. Sköfde, 1899.

Phil 8956.10 — Gilleman, Gérard. The primacy of charity in moral theology. Westminster, 1959.

Phil 8956.12 — Guitton, Jean. Rapport de Jean Guitton sur les prix de vertu. Paris, 1964.

Phil 8956.18 — Gaboury, Placide. Un monde ambigu. Montréal, 1968.

Phil 8956.20.80 — Derungs, Ursicin. Der Moraltheologe Joseph Geishüttner (1763-1805), I. Kant und J.G. Fichte. Regensburg, 1969.

Phil 8956.22 — Greet, Kenneth. The art of moral judgement. London, 1970.

Phil 8956.24 — Guenthöe, Anselm. Entscheidung gegen das Gesetz. Freiburg, 1969.

Phil 8956.26.2 — Gruendel, Johannes. Wandelbares und Unwandelbares in der Moraltheologie. 2. Aufl. Düsseldorf, 1971.

Phil 8957.1 — Hovey, A. Christian ethics. Boston, 1875.

Phil 8957.2 — Harless, G.C.A. System of Christian ethics. Edinburgh, 1868.

Phil 8957.3 — Holt, A.E. The function of Christian ethics. Chicago, 1904.

Phil 8957.4 — Hall, T.C. History of ethics...Christianity. N.Y., 1910.

Phil 8957.5 — Hill, Thomas. The hydrostatic paradox in morals. Portland, 1880.

Phil 8957.5.5 — Hill, Thomas. The postulates of revelation and of ethics. Boston, 1895.

Phil 8957.6 — Hocking, William J. Modern problems and Christian ethics. London, 1898.

Phil 8957.7 — Hermanns, W. Über den Begriffs der Mässigung. Inaug. Diss. Aachen, 1913.

Phil 8957.8 — Heppe, H. Christliche Sittenlehre. Elberfeld, 1882.

Phil 8957.9 — Hirst, E.W. Jesus and the moralists. London, 1935.

Phil 8957.9.5 — Hirst, E.W. Studies in Christian love. London, 1944.

Phil 8957.10 — Henson, Herbert H. Christian morality; natural, developing, final. Oxford, 1936.

Phil 8957.11 — Handbuch der katholischen Sittenlehre. v.1-5. Düsseldorf, 1938. 7v.

Phil 8957.12 — Hildebrand, D. von. Christian ethics. N.Y., 1953.

Phil 8957.12.5 — Hildebrand, D. von. Sittliche Grundhaltungen. Mainz, 1954.

Phil 8957.12.7 — Hildebrand, D. von. True morality and i.. counterfeits. N.Y., 1955.

Phil 8957.12.10 — Hildebrand, D. von. Transformation in Christ. Baltimore, 1960.

Phil 8957.13 — Haering, Bernhard. Macht und Ohnmacht der Religion. Salzburg, 1956.

Phil 8957.13.5 — Haering, Bernhard. Das Gesetz Christi. 4. Aufl. Freiburg, 1957.

Phil 8957.13.10 — Haering, Bernhard. Die Gegenwärtige Heilsstunde. Freiburg, 1964.

Phil 8957.13.15 — Haering, Bernhard. Toward a Christian moral theology. Notre Dame, 1966.

Phil 8957.13.20 — Haering, Bernhard. Morality is for persons. N.Y., 1971.

Phil 8957.14 — Hoermann, Karl. Handbuch der christlichen Moral. Innsbruck, 1958.

Phil 8957.15 — Harding, A.L. Religion, morality, and law. Dallas, 1956.

Phil 8957.16 — Hofmann, Rudolf. Moraltheologisch Erkenntniss- und Methodenlehre. München, 1963.

Phil 8957.18 — Huemmeler, Hans. Jugend an der Maschine. Freiburg, 1932.

Phil 8957.20 — Heinen, Wilhelm. Liebe als sittliche Grundkraft und ihre Fehlformen. 3. Aufl. Basel, 1968.

Phil 8957.22 — Hermanson, Robert Fredrik. Oikeus ja uskonnolliset totuudet. Porvoossa, 1921.

Phil 8958.1 — Ideström, A. Kristendomen och det etiska behovet. Stockholm, 1918.

Phil 8958.2 — Inge, W.R. Christian ethics and modern problems. London, 1930.

Phil 8958.3 — Inge, W.R. Freedom, love and truth. Boston, 1939?

Phil 8958.5 — Izu Loiteque, Gofronia. Libertad. Venezuela, 1944.

Phil 8958.6 — Ioann, Bishop of San Francisco. Vremia very. N'iu-Iork, 1954.

Phil 8958.7 — Ioann, Bishop of San Francisco. Beloe inochestvo. Berlin, 1932.

Phil 8958.9 — Iorio, Tommaso Angelo. Theologia moralis. 5. ed. Neapolis, 1960-64. 3v.

Phil 8959.3 — Joly, C. Traité des restitutions des grands. Amsterdam, 1665.

Phil 8959.4 — Jessof, T.E. Law and love. London, 1940.

Phil 8959.6 — Jonsen, Albert R. Responsibility in modern religious ethics. Washington, 1968.

Phil 8959.8 — Juva, Mikko. Tästa on kysymys. Söderström, 1965.

Phil 8960.1 — Kirn, Otto. Zur Feier des Reformationsfestes. Leipzig, 1906.

Phil 8960.2 — Kachnik, Josef. Ethica catholica. Olomucii, 1910-12. 3v.

Phil 8960.3 — Kent, Charles F. Fundamentals of Christianity. Philadelphia, 1925.

Phil 8960.4 — Kirk, Kenneth E. Conscience and its problems. London, 1927.

Phil 8960.6 — Kramer, H.G. The indirect voluntary, or Voluntarium in causa. Diss. Washington, 1935.

Phil 8960.7 — Kramer, J.W. The right road. N.Y., 1891.

Phil 8960.8 — Kenmare, D. (pseud.). The philosophy of love. London, 1942.

Phil 8960.9 — Knight, F.H. The economic order and religion. N.Y., 1945.

Phil 8960.10 — Kalmeyer, D. En bog om religion og moral. København, 1956.

Phil 8960.12 — Klomps, Heinrich. Tradition und Fortschritt in der Moraltheologie: die grundsätzliche Bedeutung der Kontroverse zwischen Jansenismus und Probabilismus. Köln, 1963.

Phil 8960.14 — Keeling, Michael. Morals in free society. London, 1967.

Phil 8960.15 — Kongress der Deutschsprachigen Moraltheologen, Freiburg, Germany, 1963. Moraltheologie und Bibel. Paderborn, 1964.

Phil 8960.20 — Kleber, Karl-Heinz. De parvitate materiae in sexto. Regensburg, 1971.

g Phil 8961.1 — Less, G. Kompendium der theologischen Moral. Göttingen, 1767.

Phil 8961.2 — Lobstein, P. Die Ethik Calvins. Strassburg, 1877.

Phil 8961.3 — Luthardt, C.E. Geschichte der christlichen Ethik. Leipzig, 1888-93. 2v.

Phil 8961.4 — La Serre. La vie heureuse, ou L'homme content. Paris, 1693.

Phil 8961.5 — La Barre, A. La morale d'après St. Thomas. Paris, 1911.

Phil 8961.6 — Lahy, J.M. La morale de Jésus. Paris, 1911.

Phil 8961.7 — Le Bosquet, John E. The war within. Boulder, Col., 1911.

Phil 8961.8 — Lindwurm, A. Die metaphysische Wurzel die christlichen Ethik. 1872.

Phil 8961.10 — Lachmann, J.J. Religion og ethik. Kjobenhavn, 1897.

Phil 8961.11 — Lehmkuhl, A. Theologia moralis. Freiburg, 1888. 2v.

Phil 8961.12 — Lindsay, A.D. The two moralities: our duty to God and society. London, 1940.

Phil 8961.13 — Lewis, Clive Staples. Christian behaviour. London, 1943.

Phil 8961.13.10 — Lewis, Clive Staples. Christian behaviour. N.Y., 1944.

Phil 8961.15 — Łapicki, B. Etyczna kultura starożytnego Rzymu. Łódź, 1958.

Phil 8961.16 — Lottin, O. Etudes de morale histoire et doctrine. Gembloux, 1961.

Phil 8961.17 — Lehmann, P.L. Ethics in a Christian context. 1. ed. N.Y., 1963.

Phil 8961.18 — Lemme, Ludwig. Christliche Ethik. Berlin, 1905. 2v.

Phil 8961.19 — Lorenz, Willy. Der Gentleman und der Christ. Wien, 1967.

Phil 8961.21 — Langfeldt, Gabriel. Den gylne regel og andre humanisticke moralnormer. Oslo, 1966.

Phil 8962.1 — Martensen, H.L. Christian ethics. Edinburgh, 1873.

Phil 8962.1.5 — Martensen, H.L. Christian ethics. Edinburgh, 1881. 2v.

Phil 8962.2 — Maushach, J. Christentum und Weltmoral. Münster, 1897.

Phil 8962.3 — Maurice, F.D. Epistles of Saint John. London, 1867.

Htn Phil 8962.4.5* — More, Hannah. Christian morals. 1st American ed. N.Y., 1813.

Htn Phil 8962.4.6* — More, Hannah. Christian morals. 2nd American ed. N.Y., 1813.

Phil 8962.5 — Murray, J.C. A handbook of Christian ethics. Edinburgh, 1908.

Phil 8962.6 — Montgomery, G.R. The unexplored self. N.Y., 1910.

Phil 8962.7 — Moren, Thorbjörn. Sedeläran i sammandrag. Stockholm, 1823.

Phil 8962.9 — Miltner, C.C. The elements of ethics. N.Y., 1931.

Phil 8962.10 — Muratori, L.A. Della carita cristiana in quanto essa è amore del prossimo. Venezia, 1736.

Phil 8962.11 — Magoon, E.L. Proverbs for the people. Boston, 1849.

Phil 8962.12 — Masaryk, J.G. The immortal soul in danger. London, 1941.

Phil 8962.13 — Massimi, Massimo. Catholic morality. Paterson, 1943.

Phil 8962.14 — Munby, D.L. Christianity and economic problems. London, 1956.

Phil 8962.15 — Morale sans péché? Paris, 1955.

Phil 8962.16 — McLaughlin, P.J. The church and modern science. N.Y., 1957.

Phil 8962.17 — Morale chrétienne et morale marxiste. Paris, 1960.

Phil 8962.18 — Morale cristiana ed esigenre contemporanee. Milano, 1957.

Phil 8962.20 — Maclagan, W.G. The theological frontier of ethics. N.Y., 1961.

Phil 8962.21 — Mohr, R. Die christliche Ethik im Lichte der Ethnologie. München, 1954.

Phil 8962.22 — Marck, Wilhelm Henricus Marie van der. Toward a Christian ethic. Westminster, 1967.

Phil 8962.22.5 — Marck, Wilhelm Henricus Marie van der. Grundzüge einer christlichen Ethik. Düsseldorf, 1967.

Phil 8962.24 — Manaranche, André. Y a-t-il une éthique sociale chrétienne? Paris, 1969.

Phil 8962.26 — Morals, law and authority. Dayton, Ohio, 1969.

Phil 8962.26.1 — Morals, law and authority. Dublin, 1969.

Phil 8962.28 — Maehl, Sibylle. Quadriga virtutum. Köln, 1969.

Phil 8962.30 — Mehl, Roger. Éthique catholique et éthique protestante. Neuchâtel, 1970.

Phil 8962.32 — Milhaven, John Giles. Toward a new Catholic morality. Garden City, 1970.

Phil 8962.34 — Murray, Michael V. Problems in conduct. N.Y., 1963.

Phil 8963.1 — Necker, J. Cours de morale religieuse. Paris, 1800. 3v.

Phil 8963.2 — Neander, A. Vorlesungen über Geschichte der christlichen Ethik. Berlin, 1864.

Phil 8963.3 — Niebuhr, R. Interpretation of Chirstian ethics. N.Y., 1935.

Phil 8963.4 — Nepliuev, N.N. Polnoe sobranie sochinenii. Sankt Peterburg, 1901. 2v.

Phil 8963.5 — Nygren, A. Agape and Eros. London, 1953.

Phil 8964.1 — Ottley, Robert L. Christian ideas and ideals. London, 1916.

Phil 8964.2 — Oddone, Andrea. Teoria degli atti umani. Milano, 1933.

Phil 8964.3 — Osborne, A.R. Christian ethics. London, 1940.

Phil 8964.4 — O'Rahilly, Alfred. Moral principles. Cork, 1948.

Phil 8964.5 — Oyen, Hendrik van. Evangelische Ethik. Basel, 1952. 2v.

Phil 8964.6 — Oesterreichisches Seelsorge-Institut. Weihnachts-Seelsorgertagung, 1959. Der Christ und die Weltwirklichkeit. Wien, 1960.

Phil 8964.7 — Olejnik, Stanisław. Moralność życia Społecznego. Warszawa, 1970.

Phil 8965.1 — Pfeiderer, O. Moral und Religion. Leipzig, 1872.

Phil 8965.2 — University of Pennsylvania. The Boardman Lectureship in Christian ethics. Philadelphia, 1900.

Phil 8965.2.5 — Mabie, H.W. Ethics and the Garger neighborhood, 1914. Philadelphia, 1914.

Phil 8965.3 — Peabody, F.G. Jesus Christ and the Christian character. N.Y., 1905.

Phil 8965.4.5 — Palmer, Herbert. Lord Bacon not the author of The Christian paradoxes. Edinburgh, 1865.

Phil 8965.6 — Pictet, Benedict. Morale chrétienne. Genève, 1710. 2v.

Phil 8965.7 — Powell, John W. What is a Christian? N.Y., 1915.

Phil 8965.8 — Piat, Clodius. Idées directrices de la morale chrétienne. Paris, 1917.

Phil 8965.9 — Porret, James A. Les philosophies morales du temps présent. Genève, 1897.

Phil 8965.10 — Peabody, A.P. Christian morals. Boston, 1886.

Phil 8965.11 — Peabody, F.G. The Christian life in the modern world. N.Y., 1914.

Phil 8965.12 — Piper, Otto. Die Grundlagen der evangelischen Ethik. Gütersloh, 1928.

Phil 8965.13 — Pieper, Josef. Prudence. N.Y., 1959.

Phil 8965.13.5 — Pieper, Josef. Über die Gerechtigkeit. 1. Aufl. München, 1953.

Phil 8965.13.10 — Pieper, Josef. Justice. London, 1957.

Phil 8965.13.15 — Pieper, Josef. The four cardinal virtues. N.Y., 1965.

Phil 8950 - 8975 Ethics - General special treatises - Religious ethics - Christian (A-Z) - cont.

Phil 8965.13.15.5   Pieper, Josef. Das Viergespann; Klugheit, Gerechtigkeit, Tapferkeit, Mass. München, 1964.

Phil 8965.13.20   Pieper, Josef. Missbrauch der Sprache, Missbrauch der Macht. Zürich, 1970.

Phil 8965.15   Pike, James A. The next day. 1st ed. Garden City, 1959.

Phil 8965.16   Piergiovanni, Enzo. La metamorfosi dell'etica medioevale. Bologna, 1967.

Phil 8965.17   Palazzini, Pietro. Casus conscientiae. Torino, 1958. 2v.

Phil 8965.17.2   Palazzini, Pietro. Casus conscientiae. 2. ed. Torino, 1964. 2v.

Phil 8965.18   Pinckaers, Servais. Le renouveau de la morale. Tournai, 1964.

Phil 8965.20   Peschke, Karlheinz. Naturrecht in der Kontroverse. Salzburg, 1967.

Phil 8965.25   Potterie, I. de. La vie selon l'Esprit, condition du chrétien. Paris, 1965.

Phil 8966.2   Quacquarelli, Antonio. Il triplice frutto della vita cristiana. Roma, 1953.

Phil 8967.1   Rothe, R. Theologische Ethik. Wittenberg, 1845-48. 3v.

NEDL Phil 8967.1   Rothe, R. Theologische Ethik. Wittenberg, 1845-48. 3v.

Phil 8967.1.3   Rothe, R. Theologische Ethik. Wittenberg, 1869-71. 5v.

Phil 8967.1.10   Rothe, R. Uebersicht der theologischen Ethik. Bremen, 1895.

Phil 8967.1.85   Roltzmann, H.J. R. Rothe's speculatives System. Freiburg, 1899.

Phil 8967.2   Row, C.A. The moral teaching of the New Testament. London, 1873.

Phil 8967.3   Rashdall, H. Conscience and Christ; six lectures. London, 1916.

Phil 8967.4   Rau, Albrecht. Die Ethik jesu. Giessen, 1899.

Phil 8967.5.4   Reinhard, Franz V. System der christlichen Moral. Wittenberg, 1802-05. 3v.

Phil 8967.5.10   Reinhard, Franz V. System der christlichen Moral. Wittenberg, 1814. 5v.

Phil 8967.6   Reid, A.C. Christ and the present crisis. Wake Forest, 1936.

Phil 8967.7   Ramsey, Paul. Basic Christian ethics. N.Y., 1950.

Phil 8967.7.5   Ramsey, Paul. Nine modern moralists. Englewood, 1962.

Phil 8967.8   Rademacher, A. Religion und Leben. Freiburg, 1926.

Phil 8967.10   Ranwez, E. Morale et perfection. Tournai, 1959.

Phil 8967.15   Rahner, Karl. Das Dynamische in der Kirche. Freiburg, 1958.

Phil 8967.15.5   Rahner, Karl. The dynamic element in the church. Freiburg, 1964.

Phil 8967.20   Reiners, Hermann. Grundintention und sittliches Tun. Freiburg, 1966.

Phil 8968.1   Sewell, W. Christian morals. London, 1841.

Phil 8968.2   Stäudlin, C.F. Geschichte der christlichen Moral. Göttingen, 1808.

Phil 8968.2.5   Stäudlin, C.F. Neues Lehrbuch der Moral. Göttingen, 1813.

Phil 8968.4   Smyth, N. Christian ethics. N.Y., 1892.

Phil 8968.5   Scullard, H.H. Early Christian ethics in the West. London, 1907.

Phil 8968.6   Stern, M.L. Monistische Ethik. Leipzig, 1911.

Phil 8968.8   Sanderson, R. Christian ethics. London, 1833.

Phil 8968.8.20   Soe, N.H. Christliche Ethik. München, 1949.

Phil 8968.9   Smart, G.T. Studies in conduct. N.Y., 1909.

Phil 8968.10   Scharling, C. Henrik. Christliche Sittenlehre nach evangesischlutherischer Auffassung. Bremen, 1892.

Phil 8968.11   Schwellenbach, R. Die Erneuerung des Abendlandes. Berlin, 1922.

Phil 8968.12   Scott, Charles A.A. New Testament ethics. Cambridge, Eng., 1930.

Phil 8968.13   Schilling, Otto. Apologie der katholischen Moral. Paderborn, 1936.

Phil 8968.14   Slattery, M. Thy kingdom come...but not now. N.Y., 1938.

Phil 8968.15   Steinbüchel, T. Zerfall des christlichen Ethos im XIX. Jahrhundert. Frankfurt, 1951.

Phil 8968.15.80   Alcalá, M. La etica de situación y T. Steinbüchel. Barcelona, 1963.

Phil 8968.15.85   Balle, Theo. Dialogische Existenz. Bamberg, 1967.

Phil 8968.16   Smith, G.B. Social idealism and the changing theology. N.Y., 1913.

Phil 8968.17   Stelzenberger, J. Synderesis. Paderborn, 1963.

Phil 8968.18   Sellers, James. Theological ethics. N.Y., 1966.

Phil 8968.20   Sidorov, D.I. Khristianstvo i pravstvennost'. Moskva, 1962.

Phil 8968.22   Semaine des Intellectuels Catholiques, 1966. Morale humaine, morale chrétienne. Paris, 1966.

Phil 8968.22.5   Semaine des Intellectuels Catholiques, 1967. La violenza. Roma, 1968.

Phil 8969.1   Thamin, R. Saint Ambroise et la morale chrétienne au IV siècle. Paris, 1895.

Phil 8969.2   Tenney, E.P. Jubilee essays. Boston, 1862.

Phil 8969.3   Traherne, Thomas. Of magnanimity and charity. N.Y., 1942.

Phil 8969.3.5   Traherne, Thomas. Christian ethicks. Ithaca, 1968.

Phil 8969.4   Thielicke, Helmut. Theologische Ethik. v.1-3. Tübingen, 1951. 4v.

Phil 8969.5   Thibon, G. What God has joined together. Chicago, 1952.

Phil 8969.10   Thielicke, Helmut. Die Atomwaffe als Frage an die christliche Ethik. Tübingen, 1958.

Phil 8969.11   Tillich, Paul. Morality and beyond. N.Y., 1963.

Phil 8969.15   Tournier, Paul. The seasons of life. Richmond, Va., 1970[1963]

Phil 8969.16   Theiner, Johann. Die Entwicklung der Moraltheologie zur eigenständigen Disziplin. Regensburg, 1970.

Phil 8969.18.3   Trillhaas, Wolfgang. Ethik. 3. Aufl. Berlin, 1970.

Phil 8971.1   Van Dyke, Henry. The gospel for a world of sin. N.Y., 1899.

Phil 8971.2   Vann, Gerald. The water and the fire. London, 1953.

Phil 8971.2.5   Vann, Gerald. Morals and man. N.Y., 1960.

Phil 8971.4   Vandenbroucke, Francois. La morale monastique du XIe au XVIe siècle. Louvain, 1966.

Phil 8971.6   La violenza die cristiani. Assisi, 1969.

Phil 8971.8   Van der Poel, Cornelius J. The search for human values. N.Y., 1971.

Phil 8972.1   Wuttke, K.F.A. Handbuch der christlichen Sittenlehre. Leipzig, 1874-75. 2v.

Phil 8972.1.5   Wuttke, K.F.A. Christian ethics. Boston, 1873. 2v.

Phil 8972.2   Wardlaw, R. Christian ethics. London, 1833.

Phil 8972.2.2   Wardlaw, R. Christian ethics. N.Y., 1835.

Phil 8950 - 8975 Ethics - General special treatises - Religious ethics - Christian (A-Z) - cont.

Phil 8972.2.8   Dewey, Orville. A review on the Calvinistic views of moral philosophy. N.Y., 1835.

Phil 8972.3   Walker, James. Government of the thoughts. Boston, 1899.

Phil 8972.4   Werner, Karl. System der christlichen Ethik. Regensburg, 1888. 2v.

Phil 8972.5   Walter, Franz. Der Leib und sein Recht im Christentum. Donauwörth, 1910.

Phil 8972.6   Wahre Philosophie des praktischen Christenthums. Frankfurt, 1782.

Htn Phil 8972.7*   Wales, Ebenezer. Counsels and directions of Ebenezer Wales to his children. Boston, 1813.

Phil 8972.8   Webb, C.J. The contribution of Christianity to ethics. Calcutta, 1932.

Phil 8972.9   Widgery, A.G. Christian ethics in history and modern life. N.Y., 1940.

Phil 8972.10   Wyse, Alexander. Moral and social questions arranged for high school religious discussion groups and study clubs. Paterson, 1943.

Phil 8972.11   Ward, H.F. Which way religion? N.Y., 1931.

Phil 8972.12   Warner, F.E. Future of man. London, 1944.

Phil 8975.1   Zwicker, Heinz. Reich Gottes. Bern, 1948.

Phil 8980 Ethics - General special treatises - Ethics of political and social systems - Communist (800 scheme, A-Z)

Phil 8980.01   Pamphlet box. Communist ethics.

Phil 8980.02   Pamphlet vol. "Communist ethics". 4 pam.

Phil 8980.03   Pamphlet vol. "Communist ethics". 6 pam.

Phil 8980.04   Pamphlet vol. "Communist ethics". Russian. 6 pam.

Phil 8980.05   Pamphlet vol. "Communist ethics". Russian. 6 pam.

Phil 8980.06   Pamphlet vol. "Communist ethics". Russian. 3 pam.

Phil 8980.07   Pamphlet vol. "Communist ethics". Russian. 4 pam.

Phil 8980.1   Pamphlet vol. "Communist ethics". 4 pam.

NEDL Phil 8980.2   Drobnitskii, Oleg G. Kratkii slovar' po etike. Moskva, 1965.

Phil 8980.3   Drobnitskii, Oleg G. Slovar po etike. Izd. 2. Moskva, 1970.

Phil 8980.5   Über Kommunistische Moral. Berlin, 1953.

Phil 8980.8   Akademiia nauk SSSR. Kafedra Filosofii. Moral'nye oblik stroitelia kommunizma. Moskva, 1964.

Phil 8980.10   Boldyrev, N.I. Vospitanie kommunistecheskoi morali u shkol nikov. Izd. 2. Moskva, 1956.

Phil 8980.15   Berlin. Institut für Gesellschaftswissenschaften. Neues Leben. 1. Aufl. Berlin, 1957.

Phil 8980.126   Agapov, B.N. My ne odin na svete. Moskva, 1961.

Phil 8980.126.10   Pamphlet vol. "Communist ethics". 8 pam.

Phil 8980.131   Akademiia Nauk SSSR. Institut Filosofii. Nravstvennost' i religiia. Moskva, 1964.

Phil 8980.131.5   Anisimov, Sergei F. Nravstvennyi progressi religiia. Moskva, 1965.

Phil 8980.131.10   Akademiia Nauk SSSR. Institut Filosofii. Problemy etiki. Moskva, 1964.

Phil 8980.131.15   Akmambeton, Galikhan G. Problemy nravstvennogo razvitiia lichnosti. Alma-Ata, 1971.

Phil 8980.159   Arkhangel'skii, Leonid M. Kategorii marksistskoi etiki. Moskva, 1963.

Phil 8980.159.5   Arkhangel'skii, Leonid M. Lektsii po marksistskoi etike. v.1-. Sverdlovsk, 1969.

Phil 8980.162   Artač, Marija. Gradiva za pouk temeljev socialistične morale. Ljubljana, 1969.

Phil 8980.165   Ash, William F. Marxism and moral concepts. N.Y., 1964.

Phil 8980.180   Avraamov, D. Kommunist nravstvennost'. Moskva, 1963.

Phil 8980.191   Bandzeladze, Gela. Aktual'nye problemy marksistskoi etiki. Tbilisi, 1967.

Phil 8980.191.5   Bandzeladze, Gela. Opyt izlozheniia sistemy marksistskoi etiki. Tbilisi, 1963.

Phil 8980.193   Barton, William Ernest. The moral challenge of Communism. London, 1966.

Phil 8980.208   Bezuglov, A.A. Eto kasaetsia usekh. Moskva, 1956.

Phil 8980.213   Bittighoefer, Bernd. Moral und Gesellschaft. Berlin, 1968.

Phil 8980.213.5   Bittighoefer, Bernd. Die Rind dir andere neben Dir. Berlin, 1965.

Phil 8980.220   Bludov, Iakov S. Prostota i skromnost'. Kiev, 1968.

Phil 8980.248   Burdiva, Alla I. Formuvannia komunistychnoi idei nosti osoby. Kyïv, 1970.

Phil 8980.252   Bychkova, N.V. Moral' kak ee ponimaiut kommunisty. Moskva, 1960.

Phil 8980.252.2   Bychkova, N.V. Moral' kak ee ponimaiut kommunisty. 2. izd. Moskva, 1960.

Phil 8980.252.3   Bychkova, N.V. Moral' kak ee ponimaiut kommunisty. Izd. 3. Moskva, 1966.

Phil 8980.275   Chelovek budushchego rozhdaetsia segodnia. Novosibirsk, 1962.

Phil 8980.275.10   Chevkashyn, D.S. Kommunistychnyi ideal i diisnist'. Kharkiv, 1970.

Phil 8980.276   Chelovek budushchego rozhdaetsia segodnia. Moskva, 1959.

Phil 8980.316   Danielian, Mal'feda. Nekotorye voprosy marksistsko-leninskoi etiki. Erevan, 1962.

Phil 8980.320A   De George, Richard T. Soviet ethics and morality. Ann Arbor, 1969.

Phil 8980.320B   De George, Richard T. Soviet ethics and morality. Ann Arbor, 1969.

Phil 8980.329   Dmitrenko, A.P. Kommunisticheskaia moral' i voinskii dolg. Moskva, 1960.

RRC Phil 8980.330   Dodon, Larisa L. Kul'tura povedeniia sovetskogo molodogo cheloveka. Izd. 3. Leningrad, 1957.

Phil 8980.330.5   Dobrovol'skii, Eugenii N. Osoboe mnenie. Moskva, 1967.

Phil 8980.346   Dzhafarli, Teimuraz M. Byt' chelovekom na zemle. Moskva, 1968.

Phil 8980.346.5   Dzhafarli, Teimuraz M. Besedy o kommunisticheskoi morali. Moskva, 1970.

Phil 8980.386   Fedorenko, I.H. Kommunisticheskaia nravntvennost'. Kiev, 1958.

Phil 8980.386.5   Fedorenko, I.H. Osnovy marksistsko-leninskoi etiki. Kiev, 1969.

Phil 8980.392   Filonovich, Pavel G. O kommunisticheskoi morali. Moskva, 1963.

Phil 8980.403   Formirovanie moral'nogo oblika sovetskogo rabochego. Moskva, 1961.

Phil 8980.416   Galdiaev, P.K. Eto ukrashaet cheloveka. Moskva, 1962.

Phil 8980.417   Garaudy, R. Qu'est-ce que la morale marxiste. Paris, 1963.

Phil 8980.428   Glebova, Tamara G. Pis'ma k tebe. Moskva, 1965.

Phil 8980.432   Golovan, I.P. Po dolgu grazhdanina. Moskva, 1962.

Phil 8980.435   Graaf, Johannes de. Moraal, marxisme en ethiek in de sowietunie. Hilversum, 1967.

Phil 8980   Ethics - General special treatises - Ethics of political and social
    systems - Communist (800 scheme, A-Z) - cont.
    Phil 8980.456   Hott, V.S. Dva svity, dvi morali. Kyiv, 1959.
    Phil 8980.459   Iakuba, Elena A. Pravoi nravstvennost'kak reguliatory
        obshchestvennykh otnoshenii pri sotsializme.
        Khav'kov, 1970.
    Phil 8980.463   Ivanov, Vladimir G. Ocherki marksistsko-leninskoi etiki.
        Leningrad, 1963.
    Phil 8980.472   Kánský, Jiří. Čo je zmyslom našho života?
        Bratislava, 1961.
    Phil 8980.472.5   Kánský, Jiří. Morálka dnes a zajtra. Bratislava, 1963.
    Phil 8980.481   Khmara, V.V. Cheloveku nado verit. Moskva, 1960.
    Phil 8980.485   Kiknadze, Dmitrii A. Potrebnosti, povedenie, vospitanie.
        Moskva, 1968.
    Phil 8980.486   Kiselev, Askol'd A. V.I. Lenin i voprosy etiki.
        L'vov, 1969.
    Phil 8980.495   Kon, I.S. Moral kommunisticheskaia i moral' burzhvaznaia.
        Moskva, 1960. 2 pam.
    Phil 8980.495.5   Kolbanovskii, Viktor N. Kommunisticheskaia moral' i byt.
        Moskva, 1955.
    Phil 8980.495.10   Kommunizm i lichnost! Moskva, 1964.
    Phil 8980.496   Kononenko, E.V. O krasote dushevnoi. Moskva, 1959.
    Phil 8980.496.5   Kosolapov, S.M. Voprosy vospitaniia trudiashchikhsia v
        dukhe kommunisticheskoi nravstvennosti. Moskva, 1961.
    Phil 8980.496.10   Kosolapov, S.M. Nravstvennye printsipy stroitelia
        kommunizma. Moskva, 1962.
    Phil 8980.497   Kotov, L.I. Razuitie nravstvennykh ubezhdenii i privychek
        v protsesse kommunisticheskogo vospitaniia. Moskva, 1961.
    Phil 8980.497.20   Kovalev, S.M. Rabotat' i zhit' po kommunisticheski.
        Moskva, 1961.
    Phil 8980.498   Krasnor, Iu. M. O kul'ture povedeniia molodogo cheloveka.
        Moskva, 1962.
    Phil 8980.498.25   Krešić, Ljubinka. Etičko-humanisticki problemi
        socijalizma. Beograd, 1964.
    Phil 8980.501   Krutova, Ol'ga Natanouna. Chelovek i moral'.
        Moskva, 1970.
    Phil 8980.516   Leninskoe eticheskoe nasledstvo i sovremennost.
        Tambov, 1971.
    Phil 8980.529   Loeser, Franz. Deontik, Planung und Leitung der
        moralischen Entwicklung. Berlin, 1966.
    Phil 8980.537   Lushchytski, I.N. Osnovy marksistsko-leninskoi etiki.
        Minsk, 1965.
    Phil 8980.546   Machovec, Milan. Smysl lidského života. Praha, 1965.
    Phil 8980.552   Makarova, N.F. Pogovorim o zhizni i sehe. Moskva, 1961.
    Phil 8980.564   Medynskii, Grigorii A. Trudnaia kniga. Moskva, 1964.
    Phil 8980.566   Mende, Georg. Treiheit und Verantwortung. Berlin, 1958.
    Phil 8980.572   Mikhalevich, Aleksandr Vl. Izmeniat'sia. Moskva, 1964.
    Phil 8980.572.5   Mikhalevich, Aleksandr Vl. Sporiu. Moskva, 1968.
    Phil 8980.572.10   Mikhalevich, Aleksandr Vl. Front dushi. Kiev, 1970.
    Phil 8980.572.15   Milovidov, Arsenii S. Kommunisticheskaia moral' i voinskii
        dolg. Moskva, 1971.
    Phil 8980.572.30   Miladinović, Milan M. Moralno-politicki lik komunista
        Vojvodine u NOR-u i revoluciji. Beograd, 1971.
    Phil 8980.579   Moral'nyi rodeks stroitelia kommunizma. Moskva, 1964.
    Phil 8980.580   Moscow. Gosudavstvennaia Bibiblioteka SSSR. Imeni V.I.
        Lenina. Chto chitat' o kommunisticheskoi morali.
        Moskva, 1955.
    Phil 8980.581   Moscow. Akademiia Obshchestvennykh Nauk. Voprosy
        marksistko-leninskoi etiki. Moskva, 1962.
    Phil 8980.581.10   Moscow. Vsesoiuznyi Zaochnyi Politekhunicheskii Institut.
        Marksistsko-leninskaia filosofiia. Moskva, 1965.
    Phil 8980.602   Nemtsov, V.I. Volneniia, radosti, nadezoidy.
        Moskva, 1961.
    Phil 8980.604   Nesteroo, Vladimir G. Trud i moral' v sovetskom
        doshchestve. Moskva, 1969.
    Phil 8980.610F   Nivison, A. S. Communist ethics and Chinese tradition.
        Cambridge, Mass., 1954.
    Phil 8980.616   Kommunisticheskaia Partiia Sovetskogo Soiuza.
        Novosibirskaia Vysshaia Partiinaia Shkola. Kategorii
        marksistsko-leninskoi etiki. Moskva, 1965.
    Phil 8980.616.5   Nravstvennoe razvitie lichnosti. Moskva, 1969.
    Phil 8980.630   Obshchestvo pro Rasprostran. O kommunisticheskoi etike.
        London, 1962.
    Phil 8980.659   Osnovy marksysts'ko-leninśkoi etyky. Chernivtsi, 1962.
    Phil 8980.673   Panferov, F.I. O moral'nom oblike sovetskogo cheloveka.
        Moskva, 1960.
    Phil 8980.676   Pavlova, Liia Jakovlevna. Nravstvennye tsennosti nachego
        sovremennika. Moskva, 1971.
    Phil 8980.697   Platonov, Rostislav P. Vospitanie kommunisticheskoi
        soznatel'nosti. Minsk, 1970.
    Phil 8980.707   Popelová, J. Etika. Praha, 1962.
    Phil 8980.712   Prokof'ev, V.I. Dve morali; moral' religioznaia i moral'
        kommunisticheskaia. Moskva, 1961.
    Phil 8980.712.20   Protopopova, A.N. V sem'e; vzaimnoe uvazhenie, zabota o
        detiakh. Moskva, 1962.
    Phil 8980.712.50   Problemy razvitiia kommunisticheskogo soznaniia.
        Moskva, 1965.
    Phil 8980.712.60   Problemy formirovaniia kommunisticheskogo soznaniia.
        Ivanovo, 1969.
    Phil 8980.712.65   Problemy dukhovnoi kul'tury i formirovaniia lichnosti.
        Sverdlovsk, 1970.
    Phil 8980.759   Rutkovs'kyi, Borys O. Katehoriia dovir'ia v marksysts'kii
        etytsi. Kyiv, 1970.
    Phil 8980.770   Sarich, A.L. Obshchie metody nravstvennogo vospitaniia.
        Moskva, 1956.
    Phil 8980.770.5   Savez Komunista Srbije. Univerzitetski Komitet. O
        socijalističkom moralu. Beograd, 1964.
    Phil 8980.780   Semov, Mois I. Prichini za ostatutsite ot burzhoazniia
        moral v nasheto obshchestvo. Sofiia, 1965.
    Phil 8980.780.5   Semenov, Mikhail N. O moral'nom avtoritete.
        Alma-Ata, 1967.
    Phil 8980.782   Sevrikov, Konstantin I. Prostye istiny. Moskva, 1969.
    Phil 8980.785   Shariia, P.A. O nekotorykh voprosakh kommunisticheskoi
        morali. Moskva, 1951.
    Phil 8980.785.20   Shcherbak, F.N. Nravstvennyi oblik razvedchikov
        budushchego. Leningrad, 1961.
    Phil 8980.787   Shishkin, Aleksandr F. Osnovy kommunisticheskoi morali.
        Moskva, 1955.
    Phil 8980.787.5   Shishkin, Aleksandr F. Die Grundlagen der kommunistischen
        Moral. Berlin, 1958.
    Phil 8980.787.10   Soveshchanie po Voprosam Marksistko-Leninskoi Etiki,
        Leningrad, 1959. Voprosy marksistsko-leninskoi etiki.
        Moskva, 1960.
    Phil 8980.787.15   Shishkin, Aleksandr F. Marksistskoi etiki.
        Moskva, 1961.
    Phil 8980.787.20   Russia (1917-). Upravlenie Prepodavaniia
        Obshchestvennykh Nauk. Marksistskaia etika; khrestomatiia.
        Moskva, 1961.

    Phil 8980   Ethics - General special treatises - Ethics of political and social
    systems - Communist (800 scheme, A-Z) - cont.
    Phil 8980.787.25   Shishkin, Aleksandr F. Dvadtsatyi vek i moral'nye
        tsennosti chelovechestva. Moskva, 1968.
    Phil 8980.790   Simpozium Posviashchennyi 100-letiiu so Dnia Rozhdeniia
        V.I. Lenina, Novosibirsk? 1968? Problemy kategorii
        marksistsko-leninskoi etiki. Novosibirsk, 1968.
    Phil 8980.792   Schaff, Adam. Spór o zagadnienie moralnosci.
        Warszawa, 1958.
    Phil 8980.795   Slovak, Emil. Desat prikazani. Bratislava, 1968.
    Phil 8980.801   Sokolov, Andrei V. Filosofiia bor'by. Moskva, 1909.
    Phil 8980.802   Sorokin, K.F. Za leninskii stil' v rabote. Kiev, 1960.
    Phil 8980.827   Terekhov, S.S. Za kommunisticheskuiu nravstvennost'.
        Leningrad, 1964.
    Phil 8980.838   Titarenko, Aleksandr I. Kriterii nravstvennogo progressa.
        Moskva, 1967.
    Phil 8980.839   Tkachenko, Vera M. Vernost'. 2. izd. Moskva, 1965.
    Phil 8980.850   Tselikova, Ol'ga P. Kommunisticheskii ideal i nravstvennoe
        razvitie lichnosti. Moskva, 1970.
    Phil 8980.851   Tugarinov, Vasilii P. O tsennostiakh zhizni i kul'tury.
        Leningrad, 1960.
    Phil 8980.851.5   Tugarinov, Vasilii P. Lichnost' i obshchestvo.
        Moskva, 1965.
    Phil 8980.861   Utkin, S.S. Ocherki po marksistsko-leninskoi etike.
        Moskva, 1962.
    Phil 8980.866   Vagovič, Stefano. Etica comunista. Roma, 1959.
    Phil 8980.866.5   Vagovič, Stefano. L'etica comunista. Roma, 1966.
    Phil 8980.872   Vokrug tebia, khoroshie liudi. Moskva, 1961.
    Phil 8980.872.5   Vstupaia v zhizn'. Moskva, 1967.
    Phil 8980.872.10   Voprosy marsistko-leninskoi etiki i kommunisticheskogo
        vospitaniia. Sverdlovsk, 1970.
    Phil 8980.873   Zapovedi tvoei zhizni. Moskva, 1963.
    Phil 8980.895   Zemlianskii, D.S. U istokov zhiznennogo puti.
        Moskva, 1962.
    Phil 8980.895.5   Zhuravkov, M.G. Moral'nyi oblik sovetskogo rabochego.
        Moskva, 1966.
    Phil 8980.895.10   Zhuravkov, M.G. Nravstvennye printsipy stroitelia
        kommunizma. Moskva, 1965.
    Phil 8980.896.5   Ziuziukin, Ivan I. Uznaiu cheloveka. Mosva, 1970.
    Phil 8980.898   Leninskoe teoreticheskoe nasledie i nekotorye voprosy
        marksistkoi etiki. Moskva, 1970.

    Phil 8982   Ethics - General special treatises - Ethics of political and social
    systems - Socialist
    Phil 8982.2   Vega, Rafael de la. Marxismus und Ethik. 1. Aufl.
        Frankfurt am Main, 1970.

    Phil 9005   Ethics - Treatises on special topics - Ambition
    Htn   Phil 9005.1*   Burges, T. The art of excelling. Providence, 1799.
    Phil 9005.2   Sacy, M.L. de. Traité de la gloire. La Haye, 1745.

    Phil 9010   Ethics - Treatises on special topics - Amusements
    Phil 9010.01   Pamphlet box. Amusements.
    Phil 9010.2   Sawyer, F.W. A plea for amusements. N.Y., 1847.
    Phil 9010.2.2   Sawyer, F.W. A plea for amusements. N.Y., 1847.
    Phil 9010.8   Testimony of Progressive Friends. Amusements.
        N.Y., 1856-59. 3 pam.
    Phil 9010.11   Mattison, H. Popular amusements. N.Y., 1867?
    Htn   Phil 9010.14*   Mather, Cotton. A serious address. Boston, 1726.
    Phil 9010.17   Dix, M. The drift of the age. Springfield, 1888.
    Phil 9010.18   Fowler, Montague. The morality of social pleasures.
        London, 1910.
    Phil 9010.19   Burder, George. Lawful amusements. London, 1805.
    Phil 9010.20   The pulpit and rostrum...unchristian amusement.
        N.Y., 1858.
    Phil 9010.21   Vincent, Marvin. Amusement. Troy, 1867.
    Phil 9010.22   Clark, Martha. Victims of amusements. Philadelphia, n.d.
    Phil 9010.23   Henry, Charlton. An inquiry into the consistency of
        popular amusements. Charleston, S.C., 1825.
    Phil 9010.24   Vaes, Lachlan. Amusements and the Christian life.
        Philadelphia, 1884.
    Phil 9010.25   Corning, James L. The Christian law of amusements.
        Buffalo, 1859.
    Phil 9010.26.2   Crane, J.T. Popular amusements. Cincinnati, n.d.
    Phil 9010.27   Hill, Richard. An address to persons of fashion.
        Baltimore, 1807.
    Phil 9010.27.2   Hill, Richard. An address to persons of fashions. 6th ed.
        Shrewsbury, 1771.
    Phil 9010.28   Thiers, Jean B. Traité des jeux et des divertissements.
        Paris, 1686.
    Phil 9010.29   Andrews, Charles W. Religious novels; an argument against
        their use. 2d ed. N.Y., 1856.
    Phil 9010.30   Brooke, Iris. Pleasures of the past. London, 1955.
    Phil 9010.32   Renard, Hubert. L'automobiliste et la morale chrétienne.
        Paris, 1967.

    Phil 9030   Ethics - Treatises on special topics - Chance
    Phil 9030.3   Revel, Camille. Le hasard. Paris, 1905.
    Htn   Phil 9030.5.5*   Garimberto, G. Della fortuna libri sei. Vinetia, 1550.
    Phil 9030.7   Bartoš, Jaromír. Kategorie nahodilého v dějinách
        filosofického myšlení. Praha, 1965.

    Phil 9035   Ethics - Treatises on special topics - Character
    Phil 9035.01   Pamphlet box. Character.
    Phil 9035.1   Azam, E. Le caractère. Paris, 1887.
    Phil 9035.2   Bain, A. On the study of character. London, 1861.
    Phil 9035.3   Hyde, T.A. How to study character. N.Y., 1884.
    Phil 9035.4   Jordan, F. Character as seen in body and parentage.
        London, 1890.
    Phil 9035.5   Lazarus, M.E. Comparative psychology and universal
        analogy. Vegetable portraits of character. N.Y., 1851.
    Phil 9035.6   Peabody, A.P. Building a character. Boston, 1887.
    Phil 9035.7   Smiles, S. Character. N.Y., 1880?
    Phil 9035.7.5   Smiles, S. Character. Chicago, 1890.
    Phil 9035.7.13   Smiles, S. El carácter; version española. Paris, 1892.
    Phil 9035.8.2   Ware, M.G. Chandler. The elements of character.
        Boston, 1854.
    Phil 9035.9   Taylor, S. Character essential to success in life.
        Canandaigua, 1821.
    Phil 9035.10   Fouillée, A. Tempérament et caractère. Paris, 1895.
    Phil 9035.12   Washington, B.S. Character building. N.Y., 1902.
    Phil 9035.14   Foster, John. Essays on decision of character.
        Burlington, 1830.
    Phil 9035.14.5   Foster, John. Decision of character. N.Y., 19- .
    Phil 9035.15   Ribery, C. Essai de classification naturelle des
        caracteres. Paris, 1902.
    Phil 9035.16   Jastrow, J. The qualities of men. Boston, 1910.
    Phil 9035.16.5   Jastrow, J. Character and temperament. N.Y., 1915.

Phil 9035   Ethics - Treatises on special topics - Character - cont.

Phil 9035.17   Rehmeké, J. Zur Lehre vom Gemüt. Leipzig, 1911.

Phil 9035.18   Lemmon, G.J. Eternal building, or The making of manhood. N.Y., 1899.

Phil 9035.19   King, Henry C. How to make a rational fight for character. N.Y., 1911.

Phil 9035.20   Vogler, M. Die Verwahrlosung der modernen Charakters. Leipzig, 1884.

Phil 9035.21   Shand, A.F. The foundations of character. London, 1914.

Phil 9035.21.2   Shand, A.F. The foundations of character. London, 1920.

Phil 9035.21.15   Stout, G.F. Alexander Faulkner Shand, 1858-1936. London, 1936?

Phil 9035.22   Bucke, Charles. The book of human character. London, 1837. 2v.

Phil 9035.23   White, William A. Mechanisms of character formation. N.Y., 1916.

Phil 9035.24   Sisson, E.O. The essentials of character. N.Y., 1915.

Phil 9035.25   Adickes, E. Charakter und Weltanschauung. Tübingen, 1907.

Phil 9035.26   Malapert, P. Le caractère. Paris, 1902.

Phil 9035.26.2   Malapert, P. Les éléments du caractère. 2e éd. Paris, 1906.

Phil 9035.27   Hocking, W.E. Human nature and its remaking. New Haven, 1918.

Phil 9035.27.5   Hocking, W.E. Human nature and its remaking. New Haven, 1923.

Phil 9035.27.12   Hocking, W.E. Human nature and its remaking. New Haven, 1932.

Phil 9035.28   Gaston, William. An address delivered before the American Whig and Cliosophic Societies. 2d ed. Princeton, 1835.

Phil 9035.29.3   Ingegnieros, José. El hombre mediocre. 3d ed. Buenos Aires, 1917.

Phil 9035.30   Jones, A.J. Character in the making. London, 1913.

Phil 9035.31   Ekenhans, Theodor. Charakterbildung. Leipzig, 1908.

Phil 9035.32   Norton, Carol. Studies in character. Boston, 1906.

Phil 9035.33   Wolff, Hermann. Gemüth und Charakter sechs Vorträge. Leipzig, 1882.

Phil 9035.34   Newfang, Oscar. The development of character. N.Y., 1921.

Phil 9035.35   Colville, N.J. Fate mastered, destiny fulfilled. London, 1903.

Phil 9035.36   Jones, W. Tudor. The training of mind and will. London, 1920.

Phil 9035.37   Parlette, R.A. The university of hard knocks. Chicago, 1917.

Phil 9035.38   Churchill, L.A. The magnet. N.Y., 1903.

Phil 9035.39   Pierce, Edgar. The philosophy of character. Cambridge, 1924.

Phil 9035.40   Apfelbach, H. Der Aufbau des Charakters. Wien, 1924.

Phil 9035.41   Perez, Bernard. Le caractère à l'homme. Paris, 1892.

Phil 9035.42   Häberlin, Paul. Der Charakter. Basel, 1925.

Phil 9035.43   Utitz, Emil. Charakterologie. Charlottenburg, 1925.

Phil 9035.44   Bryant, S.W. Short studies in character. London, 1894.

Phil 9035.45   Roback, A.A. The psychology of character. London, 1927.

Phil 9035.45.2   Roback, A.A. The psychology of character. N.Y., 1927.

Phil 9035.45.3   Roback, A.A. The psychology of character. N.Y., 1927.

Phil 9035.45.4   Roback, A.A. Psicologia del caracter. Traduccion de Santo Rubiano. Madrid, 192-?

Phil 9035.45.5   Roback, A.A. A bibliography of character. Cambridge, Mass., 1927.

Phil 9035.45.10   Roback, A.A. The psychology of character. 3. ed. Cambridge, Mass., 1952.

Phil 9035.45.15   Allport, G.W. The psychology of character by A.A. Roback. Princeton, 1927.

Phil 9035.45.20   Todoranu, D. O conceptie americana despre caracter. Cluj, 1933.

Phil 9035.47   Hoffmann, H. Das Problem des Charakteraufbaus. Berlin, 1926.

Phil 9035.47.5   Hoffmann, H. Charakter und Umwelt. Berlin, 1928.

Phil 9035.48   Falconnet de la Bellonie. La psycantropie ou nouvelle théorie de l'homme. v.1-3. Avignon, 1748.

Phil 9035.49   McDougall, W. Character and the conduct of life. N.Y., 1927.

Phil 9035.50   Vance, J.G. A mirror of personality. London, 1927.

Phil 9035.51   Hagemann, C.L.A. Was ist Charakter und wie Kann er durch die Erziehung gebildet? Dorpat, 1881.

Phil 9035.52   Lasurski, A. Uber das Studium der Individualität. Leipzig, 1912.

Phil 9035.53   Adler, Alfred. Understanding human nature. N.Y., 1927.

Phil 9035.53.2A   Adler, Alfred. Understanding human nature. Garden City, N.Y., 1927.

Phil 9035.53.2B   Adler, Alfred. Understanding human nature. Garden City, N.Y., 1927.

Phil 9035.53.4   Adler, Alfred. Understanding human nature. N.Y., 1928.

Phil 9035.53.5   Adler, Alfred. Menschenkenntnis. 2. Aufl. Leipzig, 1928.

Phil 9035.53.6   Adler, Alfred. Menschenkenntnis. 5. Aufl. Zürich, 1947.

Phil 9035.53.10   Adler, Alfred. Understanding human nature. N.Y., 1946.

Phil 9035.54   Stipriaan Luiscius, J.M. van. Karakter. Haag, 1925.

Phil 9035.55   Wahle, Richard. Entstehung der Charakters. München, 1928.

Phil 9035.57   McDonough, M.R. The empirical study of character. Diss. Washington, 1929.

Phil 9035.58   Künkel, Fritz. Let's be normal! N.Y., 1929.

Phil 9035.59.5   Künkel, Fritz. Einfuhrung in die Charakterkunde auf individualpsychologischer Grundlage. 2. Aufl. Leipzig, 1929.

Phil 9035.59.7   Künkel, Fritz. Einfuhrung in die Charakterkunde auf individualpsychologischer Grundlage. 8. Aufl. Leipzig, 1939.

Phil 9035.59.9   Künkel, Fritz. Charakter, Wachstum und Erziehung. 2. Aufl. Leipzig, 1934.

Phil 9035.59.15   Künkel, Fritz. Charakter, Einzelmensch und Gruppe. Leipzig, 1933.

Phil 9035.59.20   Künkel, Fritz. Charakter. Leipzig, 1932.

Phil 9035.59.30   Künkel, Fritz. Vitale Dialektik. Leipzig, 1929.

Phil 9035.60   Priddle, Oamer D. Procedures in developing character controls through instructions. Thesis. Philadelphia, 1929.

Phil 9035.61.5   Allers, Rudolf. Psychology of character. N.Y., 1931.

Phil 9035.61.9   Allers, Rudolf. Practical psychology in character development. N.Y., 1934.

Phil 9035.61.12   Allers, Rudolf. Das Werden der settlichen Person. 4. Aufl. Freiburg, 1935.

Phil 9035.62   Seiterich, Eugen. Die logische Struktur des Typusbegriffes. Inaug. Diss. Freiburg, 1930.

Phil 9035.63   Boven, William. La science du caractère. Neuchâtel, 1931.

Phil 9035.64   Kronfeld, Arthur. Lehrbuch der Charakterkunde. Berlin, 1932.

Phil 9035.65   Aulich, Werner. Untersuchungen über das charakterologische Rhythmusproblem. Inaug. Diss. Halle, 1932.

Phil 9035.67   Neumann, Johannes. Die Entwicklung zur sittlichen Persönlichkeit. Gütersloh, 1931.

Phil 9035   Ethics - Treatises on special topics - Character - cont.

Phil 9035.68   Whitby, Charles J. The logic of human character. London, 1905.

Phil 9035.68.5   Whitby, Charles J. Makers of man, a study of human initiative. London, 1911.

Phil 9035.69   Lichtenfels, H. Die christliche Religion in ihrer Bedeutung für dieCharaktererziehung. Kallmünz, 1934.

Phil 9035.70   Elliot, H.S.R. Human character. London, 1922.

Phil 9035.71   Peillaube, E. Caractère et personnalité. Paris, 1935.

Phil 9035.72   Heiss, Robert. Die Lehre vom Charakter. Berlin, 1936.

Phil 9035.73   Volkmann, E. Uber die Formkraft des Vorbildes für die Charakterprägung in der Reifezeit. Inaug. Diss. Würzburg, 1936.

Phil 9035.75   Hartshore, H. Studies in deceit. N.Y., 1928.

Phil 9035.76   Columbia University. Teachers College. Character Education Inquiry. Studies in the nature of character. v.2. N.Y., 1929.

Phil 9035.77   Hartshore, H. Studies in the organization of character. N.Y., 1930.

Phil 9035.78   Helwig, Paul. Charakterologie. Leipzig, 1936.

Phil 9035.78.5   Helwig, Paul. Charakterlogie. 2. Aufl. Stuttgart, 1951.

Phil 9035.79   Nohl, Herman. Charakter und Schicksal. Frankfurt, 1938.

Phil 9035.80   Cheley, Frank H. After all it's up to you. Boston, 1935.

Phil 9035.81   Boston. The will to win. Boston, 1938.

Phil 9035.82   Piwowarczyk, W. Charakter. Kielce, 1938.

Phil 9035.83   Muñoz, Juan A. El caracter. México, 1912.

Phil 9035.84.10   King, Henry C. How to make a rational fight for character. N.Y., 1916.

Phil 9035.85   Carr, Wells. Know thyself. N.Y., 1944.

Phil 9035.86   Burloud, Albert. Le caractère. Paris, 1942.

Phil 9035.88   Troth, D.C. Selected readings in character education. Boston, 1930.

Phil 9035.90   Hellek, A. Die Polarität im Aufbau des Charakters. Bern, 1950.

Phil 9035.92   Vbbink, G. Karakterkundig woordenbock des Nederlands taal. Baarn, 1951.

Phil 9035.94   Wheelis, Allen. The quest for identity. 1st ed. N.Y., 1958.

Phil 9035.96   Betzendahl, Walter. Der menschliche Charakter in Wertung und Forschung. Paderborn, 1956.

Phil 9035.98   Wolff, Edgar Maurice. Le individualisme radical fondé sur la caractérologie. Paris, 1955.

Phil 9035.100   Taulemonde, Jean. Les extériorises. Lyon, 1958[1959]

Phil 9035.101   Norakidze, Vladimir. Tipy kharaktera i fiksirovannaia ustanovka. Tbilisi, 1966.

Phil 9035.105   Rogers, Raymond. Coming into existence. Cleveland, 1967.

Phil 9035.110   Granell Mañiz, Manuel. La recindad humana. Madrid, 1969.

Phil 9035.111   Norakidze, Vladimir G. Temperament lichnosti i fiksiorovannaia ustanovka. Tbilisi, 1970.

Phil 9045   Ethics - Treatises on special topics - Citizens and citizenship

Phil 9045.1   Ceba, A. The citizen of a republic. N.Y., 1845.

Phil 9045.2   Bahrdt, C.F. Handbuch der Moral für den Bürgerstand. Halle, 1790.

Phil 9045.3   Brewer, D.J. American citizenship. Yale lectures. N.Y., 1902.

Phil 9045.4   Potte, Henry Codman. Citizen in relation in his relationship to the industrial situation. N.Y., 1902.

Phil 9045.5   Cleveland, G. Good citizenship. Philadelphia, 1908.

Phil 9045.6   Bryce, J. The hindrances to good citizenship. New Haven, 1909.

Phil 9045.6.2   Bryce, J. The hindrances to good citizenship. New Haven, 1909[1919]

Phil 9045.7   Tucker, W.J. Public mindedness, an aspect of citizenship. Concord, 1910.

Phil 9045.8   Brinley, C.A. Citizenship. Philadelphia, 1893.

Phil 9045.9   Varela, Alfredo. Patria! Livro da Mocidade. Rio de Janeiro, 1900.

Phil 9045.10   Carpenter, L. Discourse on Christian patriotism. London, 1838.

Phil 9045.11   Sowdon, A.J.C. Political duties. Boston, 1878.

Phil 9045.12   Chojeckiego, E. Patrjotyzm i objawy Jego u niektórych narodów. Paryz, 1870.

Phil 9045.13   Defoy, H. Le citoyen. Paris, 1912.

Phil 9045.14   MacCunn, John. Ethics of citizenship. Glasgow, 1894.

Phil 9045.15   Baldwin, S.E. The relations of education to citizenship. New Haven, 1912.

Phil 9045.16   Krogh, Matthias B. Om Kierlighed til faedrenelandet. Trondhiem, 1801.

Phil 9045.17   Lequinio, J.M. Philosophie du peuple. Paris, 1796.

Phil 9045.18   Fox, William J. Reports of lecture on morality. London, 1836.

Phil 9045.18.5   Fox, William J. Reports of lectures delivered. London, 1838.

Phil 9045.19   Klausen, Gottlieb E. Rede über den Gemeingeist. Altona, 1797.

Phil 9045.20   Siveking, Gustav A. Rede über einige Hauptregeln zum wohlthätigen Einwirken auf das Zeitalter. Hamburg, 1814.

Phil 9045.21   Sighele, Seipio. Morale privata e morale politica. Milano, 1913.

Phil 9045.75   Reidenbach, Clarence. A critical analysis of patriotism as an ethical concept. Indianpolis? 1920.

Phil 9050   Ethics - Treatises on special topics - City life and country life

Phil 9050.1   Bates, E. Rural philosophy. London, 1803.

Phil 9050.1.2   Bates, E. Rural philosophy. London, 1804.

Phil 9050.1.3   Bates, E. Rural philosophy. Philadelphia, 1807.

Phil 9050.2   Scott, Rev. Dr. A lecture...on the influences of great cities. San Francisco, 1854.

Phil 9050.3   Hubert, P.G. Liberty and a living. 2nd ed. N.Y., 1904.

Phil 9050.4.5   Bailey, L.H. The outlook to nature. N.Y., 1911.

Phil 9050.5.5   Thorsch, Berthold. Der Einzelne und die Gesellschaft. Dresden, 1907.

Phil 9050.6   Chapin, E.H. Moral aspects of city life. 2d ed. N.Y., 1854.

Htn   Phil 9050.7*   Nash, T. Quaternio, or A fourfold way to a happy life. London, 1636.

Htn   Phil 9050.7.5*   Nash, T. Quaternio, or A fourfold way to a happy life. London, 1633.

Phil 9050.8   Todd, John. The moral influence, dangers and duties connected with great cities. Northampton, 1841.

Phil 9050.9   Fitch, R.E. A certain blind man. N.Y., 1944.

Phil 9060   Ethics - Treatises on special topics - Compensation

Phil 9060.1   Azaïs, P.H. Des compensations dans destinées humaines. Paris, 1825. 3v.

Phil 9060.1.2   Azaïs, P.H. Des compensations dans les destinées humaines. Paris, 1846.

Phil 9065 Ethics - Treatises on special topics - Compromise

Phil 9065.1 Morley, J. On compromise. London, 1877.
Phil 9065.1.5 Morley, J. On compromise. London, 1898.
Phil 9065.1.15 Morley, J. On compromise. London, 1933.
Phil 9065.2 Sikken, William. Het compromis als zedelijk vraagstuk. Academie proefachaft. Assen, 193-.
Phil 9065.3 Steubing, Hans. Der Kompromiss als ethisches Problem. Gütersloh, 1955.
Phil 9065.4 Joehr, W.A. Der Kompromiss als Problem der Gesellschaft. Tübingen, 1958.
Phil 9065.5 Ülken, Hilmi Ziyoi. Telifcilipin tenokurlan. Istanbul, 1933.

Phil 9070 Ethics - Treatises on special topics - Conduct of life

Phil 9070.01 Pamphlet box. Ethics. Conduct of life.
Phil 9070.1 Lappin, M.M. Let us talk about you. N.Y., 1940.
Phil 9070.2 Perley, R.N. Today you are a man. Omaha, 1940.
Phil 9070.3 Smith, G.W. Constructive human relationship. Kutztown, Pa., 1940.
Phil 9070.4 Tomlison, W.W. Time out to live. N.Y., 1939.
Phil 9070.5 Wilson, F.T. These three alone. N.Y., 1940.
Phil 9070.6 Wolfe, W.B. How to be happy though human. N.Y., 1931.
Phil 9070.7 Bartlett, A.C. Find your own frontier. Boston, 1940.
Phil 9070.8 Kern, J.H. Do something about it! N.Y., 1940.
Phil 9070.9 Shurtleft, A.D.K. Lighted candles. Boston, 1939.
Phil 9070.10 Wilson, M. Make up your mind. N.Y., 1940.
Phil 9070.11 Hostel, G. Out of the wilderness. N.Y., 1940.
Phil 9070.12 Manchester, R.E. The Saturday letters. Cuyahooga Falls, 1941.
Phil 9070.13 Pereira Alves, A. Fe y valor. El Paso, 1937?
Phil 9070.13.5 Pereira Alves, A. La utilidad de la honradez. Buenos Aires, 1942.
Phil 9070.14 Dowry, S.S. The thoughts of youth. N.Y., 1932.
Phil 9070.15 Robert, B.R. The glorious game. N.Y., 1929.
Phil 9070.16 Goldmann, R.L. The good fight. N.Y., 1935.
Phil 9070.17 Ellis, William J. Studies of man. London, 1874.
Phil 9070.18 A letter to my son. By a solider's mother. 1st ed. N.Y., 1942.
Phil 9070.19.2 Oliver, J.R. The ordinary difficulties of everyday people. N.Y., 1935.
Phil 9070.20 Greenbie, M.L.B. The art of living in wartime. N.Y., 1943.
Phil 9070.21 Landau, Rom. Letter to Andrew. London, 1943.
Phil 9070.21.10 Landau, Rom. Human relations. London, 1948.
Phil 9070.22 Cole, Walton E. Standing up to life. Boston, 1943.
Phil 9070.22.5 Cole, Walton E. The three R's of religion. Boston, 1945.
Phil 9070.23 Bisch, Louis Edward. The conquest of self. Garden City, 1923.
Phil 9070.24 Spillman, Harry Collins. Personality. N.Y., 1919.
Phil 9070.25 Young, Vashni. A fortune to share. Indianapolis, 1931.
Phil 9070.26 Fairbanks, Douglas. Youth points the way. N.Y., 1924.
Phil 9070.27 Lansing, Florence. The builder. N.Y., 1936.
Phil 9070.28 Wilkins, Ernest Hatch. Living in crisis. Boston, 1937.
Phil 9070.29 Danforth, William Henry. I dare you! Four fold development. 8. ed. St. Louis, Mo., 1938.
Phil 9070.30 Major, Clare Tree. How to develop your will-power. N.Y., 1920.
Phil 9070.31 Grenfell, W.T. The prize of life. N.Y., 1914.
Phil 9070.32 Perlaky, Lajos. A ma életművészete. Budapest, 193-?
Phil 9070.33 Banning, M.C. Conduct yourself accordingly. N.Y., 1944.
Phil 9070.34.5 Wilson, W. On being human. N.Y., 1916.
Phil 9070.35 Eskartshausen, K. von. Klugheit vereind mit Tugend. Brünn, 1791.
Phil 9070.36 Garcia, Garia. Modelando el porvenir. Lima, 1944.
Phil 9070.38 Hopkinson, A.W. Pastor's psychology. London, 1944.
Phil 9070.39 Zúñiga, Pallais M. Golpes en cantera reflexiva. San José, 1931.
Phil 9070.40 Katterhenry, E.A. Can you take it? St. Louis, Mo., 1944.
Phil 9070.41 Roche, A. Knots and crosses. Dublin, 1943.
Phil 9070.42 Nash, R.S.J. Label your luggage. Dublin, 1943.
Phil 9070.43 Onis y Sanchez, F. de. Disciplina y rebeldia. San José, Costa Rica, 1917.
Phil 9070.44 Chamberlain, F.E. The lighted pathway. Los Angeles, Calif., 1945.
Phil 9070.45 Spezzafumo de Faucamberge, S. Se suffire à soi-même. Paris, 1941.
Phil 9070.47.5 Ashton, M.O. To whom it may concern. 2. ed. Salt Lake City, 1946.
Phil 9070.48 Meehan, Francis Joseph D. The temple of the spirit. N.Y., 1948.
Phil 9070.48.5 Iranschähr, H.K. Der Meister und sein Jünger. Olten, 1948-1950. 2v.
Phil 9070.49.5 Odier, Charles. Les deux sources consciente et inconsciente de la vie morale. 2d éd. Neuchâtel, 1947.
Phil 9070.50 Ross, William. It's up to you A way to a better life. N.Y., 1950.
Phil 9070.50.5 Nicolson, Harold Georg. Good behaviour; being a study of certain types of activity. Garden City, 1956.
Phil 9070.51 Rencontres Internationales. Les droits de l'esprit et les exigences sociales. Neuchâtel, 1951.
Phil 9070.51.5A Mumford, Lewis. The conduct of life. 1st ed. N.Y., 1951.
Phil 9070.51.5B Mumford, Lewis. The conduct of life. 1st ed. N.Y., 1951.
Phil 9070.52 Carrel, Alexis. Réflexions sur la conduite de la vie. Paris, 1950.
Phil 9070.53 Holzamer, Karl. Grundriss einer praktischen Philosophie. Frankfurt am Main, 1951.
Phil 9070.54 Wicks, R.R. The reason for living. N.Y., 1934.
Phil 9070.55 Murrow, E.R. This I believe. N.Y., 1952. 2v.
Phil 9070.56 Kates, J.W. The use of life. 1st ed. N.Y., 1953.
Phil 9070.57 Nicolson, Harold Georg. Good behavior. London, 1955.
Phil 9070.58 Kuehne, O. Lebenskunst und Lebensgemeinschaft in Gesellschaft und Wirtschaft. Berlin, 1954[1958] 2v.
Phil 9070.59 Ashley Montagu, M.F. How to find happiness and keep it. 1st ed. Garden City, 1942.
Phil 9070.60 Arnoux, André. La voie du bonheur. Paris, 1957.
Phil 9070.62 Bartek, Edward. A treasury of parables. N.Y., 1959.
Phil 9070.65 Kraines, S.H. Live and help live. N.Y., 1951.
Phil 9070.67 Schmidt, Karl Otto. Wunder der Lebenskunst. Büdingen, 1959.
Phil 9070.70 Melden, Abraham. Rights and right conduct. Oxford, 1959.
Phil 9070.75 Mueller-Eckhard, Hans. Weltbewältigung. Stuttgart, 1959.
Phil 9070.80 Corts Grau, José. El hombre en vilo. Madrid, 1958.
Phil 9070.85 Way, Joseph. Happiness for you now. 2d ed. Adyar, 1959.
Phil 9070.90 Sullivan, Aloysius Michael. The three-dimensional man. N.Y., 1956.
Phil 9070.95 Wright, L.B. Advise to a son. Ithaca, N.Y., 1962.
Phil 9070.100 Moeller, Orla. At vaere ung. København, 1962.

Phil 9070 Ethics - Treatises on special topics - Conduct of life - cont.

Phil 9070.102 Brunswik, E. Wunsch und Pflicht im Auflau des menschlichen Lebens. Wien, 1937.
Phil 9070.103 Il'in, Ivan A. Die ewigen Grundlagen des Lebens. Zürich, 1943.
Phil 9070.103.5 Il'in, Ivan A. Put' dukhovnago obnovleniia. Miunkhen, 1962.
Phil 9070.104F Bergstroem, L. Imperatives and ethics. Stockholm, 1962.
Phil 9070.105 Weber, Johann Adam. Annulus memoriae ex dictaminibus ethicis et politicis. Salisburgi, 1679.
Phil 9070.106 Jørgensen, T.G. Livsforståelse moralloven livets ophør. København, 1964.
Phil 9070.107 Huxley, Laura. You are not the target. N.Y., 1965.
Phil 9070.108 Peale, Norman Vincent. Sin, sex and self control. 1st ed. Garden City, 1965.
Phil 9070.109 Kuczyński, Janusz. Filozofia życia. Wyd. 1. Warszawa, 1965.
Phil 9070.110 Oraison, Marc. Une morale pour notre temps. Paris, 1964.
Phil 9070.111 McGee, Charles Douglas. The recovery of meaning; an essay on the good life. N.Y., 1966.
Phil 9070.112 Feofanov, Iurii V. Lichnoe dostoianie i lichnoe destoinstvo. Moskva, 1966.
Phil 9070.113 Brihat, Denise. Risque et prudence. Paris, 1966.
Phil 9070.114 Margolius, Hans. Aphorismen zur Ethik. Heidelberg, 1957.
Phil 9070.114.5 Margolius, Hans. Notes on ethics. Miami, 1947.
Phil 9070.116 Simon, Pierre Henri. Pour un garçon de vingt ans, essai. Paris, 1967.
Phil 9070.117 Windisch, Konrad. Revolution der Satten. Wolfsburg, 1967.
Phil 9070.118 Mandelbaum, Bernard. Choose life. N.Y., 1968.
Phil 9070.119 Onimus, Jean. Lettres à mes fils. 5. éd. Paris, 1965.
Phil 9070.120 Halldén, Söken. Handbok för Tveksamma. Solna, 1968
Phil 9070.121 Green, Celia Elizabeth. The human evasion. London, 1969.
Phil 9070.122 Starcke, Walter. The ultimate revolution. 1st ed. N.Y., 1969.
VPhil 9070.124 Almásy, József. A tizparancsalat a közéletben. Budapest, 1942.
Phil 9070.126 Husén, Torsten. Livsåskådning och religion. Stockholm, 1968.
Phil 9070.128 Banowsky, William Slater. It's a playboy world. Old Tappan, 1969.
VPhil 9070.130 Schneiderfranken, Joseph Anton. Der Weg meiner Schüler. Basel, 1932.
Phil 9070.134 Carus, Karl Gustav. Die Lebenskunst nach den Inschriften des Tempels zu Delphi. Stuttgart, 1968.
Phil 9070.136 Frank, Hannelore. Auf der Suche nach dem eigenen Ich. Stuttgart, 1969.
Phil 9070.138 Kemelman, Haim. How to live in the present tense. South Brunswick, 1970.
Phil 9070.140 United States. Department of the Army. Character guidance discussion topics; duty, honor, country. Washington. 1951+ 2v.
Phil 9070.142 Mayeroff, Milton. On caring. 1st American ed. N.Y., 1971.
Phil 9070.144 Watts, Alan Wilson. Does it matter? N.Y., 1970.
Phil 9070.146 Natesan, B. The sympathy of life. Madras, 1967.
Phil 9070.148 Montapert, Alfred Armand. The supreme philosophy of man; the laws of life. Englewood Cliffs, N.J., 1970.
Phil 9070.150 Dilman, Ilhman. Sense and delusion. London, 1971.

Phil 9075 Ethics - Treatises on special topics - Conscience

Phil 9075.1 Bautain, L.E.M. La conscience. Paris, 1861.
Phil 9075.2 Bouillier, F.C. La vraie conscience. Paris, 1882.
Phil 9075.3.5 Gasparin, A.E. La conscience. 3. éd. Paris, 1873.
Phil 9075.5 Labbé, J. La conscience. Paris, 1868.
Phil 9075.6 Maurice, J.F.D. The conscience. London, 1872.
Phil 9075.7 Robertson, J.D. Conscience. London, 1894.
Phil 9075.8 Vacherot, E. La science et la conscience. Paris, 1870.
Phil 9075.9 Waddington, C.T. Dieu et la conscience. Paris, 1870.
Phil 9075.10 Delvolve, Jean. L'organisation de la conscience morale. Paris, 1906.
Phil 9075.11 Huckel, O. Modern study of conscience. Philadelphia, 1907.
Phil 9075.12 Sharp, F.C. Study of influence, of custom on world judgment. Madison, 1908.
Phil 9075.13 Rashdall, H. Is conscience an emotion? Boston, 1914.
Htn Phil 9075.14.5* Dyke, J. Good conscience. 5. ed. London, 1632. 2 pam.
Phil 9075.15 Bauer, Arthur. La conscience collective et la morale. Paris, 1912.
Phil 9075.16 Rée, Paul. Die Entstehung des Gewissens. Berlin, 1885.
Phil 9075.17 Jeffs, Harry. Concerning conscience. London, 1912.
Phil 9075.18 Coquerel, A. La conscience et la foi. Paris, 1867.
Phil 9075.19 Gillet, Marie S. L'éducation de la conscience. Paris, 1913.
Phil 9075.20 Carrau, Ludovic. La conscience psychologique et morale. Paris, 1888.
Phil 9075.21 Sollier, Paul. Morale et moralité. Paris, 1912.
Phil 9075.22 Knowlton, Pitt G. Origin and nature of conscience. Oberlin, 1897.
Phil 9075.23 Schmidt, W. Das Gewissen. Leipzig, 1889.
Phil 9075.24 Hasenclever, K.H. Die Berührung und Verwerthung der Gewissens. Karleruhe, 1877.
Phil 9075.25 Vogt, Fritz. Das Wesen des Gewissens. Inaug. Diss. Greifswald, 1908.
Phil 9075.26 Pauly, Karl. Zur Theorie des Gewissens. Inaug. Diss. Greifswald, 1913.
Phil 9075.27 Friedmann, J. Die Lehre vom Gewissen in den Systemen des ethischen Idealismus. Budapest, 1904.
Phil 9075.28 Stoker, H.G. Das Gewissen, Erscheinungsformen und Theorie. Bonn, 1925.
Phil 9075.29 Wohlrabe, W. Über Gewissen und Gewissensbildung. Gotha, 1883.
Phil 9075.30 Hassel, H. De conscientia theses morales. Diss. Aboae, 1738.
Phil 9075.31 Anderson, Louis F. Die Seele und das Gewissens. Leipzig, 1929.
Phil 9075.32.10 Marchal, Victor. La coscienza quale dev'essere. Torino, 1932.
Phil 9075.34 Gorham, C.T. Why we do right. London, 1924.
Phil 9075.35 Jankélévitch, Vladimir. Valeur et signification de la mauvais conscience. Thèse. Paris, 1933.
Phil 9075.35.5 Jankélévitch, Vladimir. La mauvaise conscience. Paris, 1933.
Phil 9075.36 Smith, T.V. Beyond conscience. N.Y., 1934.
Phil 9075.37 Merrington, E.N. The possibility of a science of casuistry. Sydney, 1902.
Phil 9075.38 Kabisch, R. Das Gewissen. Göttingen, 1906.
Phil 9075.39 Meyer, Rudolf. Der Protest der Gewissens in der Philosophie. Zürich, 1941.

Phil 9075 Ethics - Treatises on special topics - Conscience - cont.
Phil 9075.40 Bergler, Edmund. The battle of the conscience. Washington, D.C., 1948.
Phil 9075.45 Madinier, G. La conscience morale. Paris, 1954.
Phil 9075.50 Bastide, G. Meditations pour une éthique de la personne. 1st éd. Paris, 1953.
Phil 9075.55 Chauchord, Paul. Les mécanismes cerebraux de la prise de conscience. Paris, 1956.
Phil 9075.60 Chaperd, Marc. La révolution originelle. Paris, 1958.
Phil 9075.65 Crippa, Romeo. Studi nella coscienza etica e religiosa del seicento. Brescia, 1960. 3v.
Phil 9075.70 D'Arcy, Eric. Conscience and its right to freedom. N.Y., 1961.
Phil 9075.71 Hylkema, G.W. Homo duplex. Haarlem, 1963.
Phil 9075.73.2 Wermlund, Sven. Samvetets uppkomst. 2. Uppl. Stockholm, 1966.
Phil 9075.74 Jankélévitch, Vladimir. La mauvaise conscience. Paris, 1966.
Phil 9075.77 Mönks, Franz. Gewetens groei en gewetens functie. Nijmogen, 1967.
Phil 9075.80 Ziegler, Josef Georg. Vom Gesetz zum Gewissen. Freiburg, 1968.
Phil 9075.82 Geweten en vrijheid. Utrecht, 1968.
Phil 9075.84 Flither, Andreas. Wirklichkeit und Mass des Menschen. München, 1967.
Phil 9075.86 Bertola, Ermenegildo. Il problema della coscienza nella téologia Monastica del XII secolo. Padova, 1970.
Phil 9075.88 Baumhauer, Otto. Das Vor-Urteil des Gewissens. Limburg, 1970.
Phil 9075.94 Scholl, Robert. Das Gewissen des Kindes. 2. Aufl. Stuttgart, 1970.

Phil 9120 Ethics - Treatises on special topics - Duty
Phil 9120.1 Ferraz, M. Philosophie du devoir. Paris, 1869.
Phil 9120.2 Seelye, J.H. Duty. Boston, 1891.
Phil 9120.3 Simon, J. Le devoir. Paris, 1854.
Phil 9120.3.2 Simon, J. Le devoir. Paris, 1855.
Phil 9120.4 Smiles, S. Duty. N.Y., 1881.
Phil 9120.4.3 Smiles, S. Duty. London, 1880.
Phil 9120.4.5 Smiles, S. Duty. Chicago, 1890.
Phil 9120.4.13 Smiles, S. El deber; versión española. Paris, 1898.
Phil 9120.5 Dole, C.F. The problem of duty. N.Y., n.d.
Phil 9120.7 Ladd, G.T. What ought I to do? N.Y., 1915.
Phil 9120.8 Sérol, Maurice. Le besoin et la devoir religieux. Paris, 1908.
Phil 9120.9 Wendt, Hans H. Die sittliche Pflicht. Göttingen, 1916.
Phil 9120.10 Cederschiöld, F. Allmän inledning till apriorisk. Lund, 1821.
Phil 9120.10.5 Cederschiöld, F. Menniskors aprioriska. Lund, 1828.
Phil 9120.157 Radcke, Fritz. Pflicht oder Lust? Langensalza, 1917.
Phil 9120.160 Hofmann, Paul. Eigengesetz oder Pflichtgebot? Berlin, 1920.
Phil 9120.161 Prichard, H.A. Duty and interest. Oxford, 1928.
Phil 9120.161.10 Prichard, H.A. Duty and ignorance of fact. London, 1932.
Phil 9120.161.20 Prichard, H.A. Moral obligations. Oxford, 1949.
Phil 9120.162 Le Senne, René. Le devoir. Paris, 1930.
Phil 9120.165 Hopmann, W. Essai d'une nouvelle explication utilitariste du sentiment d'obligation. Genève, 1941.
Phil 9120.170 Barker, E. The values of life. Glasgow, 1939.
Phil 9120.175 Hollingworth, H.L. Psychology and ethics. N.Y., 1949.
Phil 9120.180 Henriot, Jacques. Existence et obligation. Paris, 1967.
Phil 9120.185 Ross, Ralph Gilbert. Obligation; a social theory. Ann Arbor, 1970.

Phil 9145 Ethics - Treatises on special topics - Etiquette
Phil 9145.5 Friends for Pennsylvania, New Jersey and Delaware. Address on some growing evils of the day. Philadelphia, 1882.
Phil 9145.6 Eyre, L.L. Fashionable society. Philadelphia, 1889.
Phil 9145.7.5 Montegazza, P. The Tartuffian age. Boston, 1890.
Phil 9145.8 Estienne, Antoine Minim. A charitable remonstrance. Edinburgh, 1887.

Phil 9150 Ethics - Treatises on special topics - Evolution
Phil 9150.01 Pamphlet box. Ethics.
Phil 9150.1.2 Kelly, E. Evolution and effort. N.Y., 1895.
Phil 9150.1.5 Kelly, E. Evolution and effort. 2. ed. N.Y., 1900.
Phil 9150.2 Morgan, C.L. The springs of conduct. London, 1885.
Phil 9150.3 Schurman, J.G. The ethical import of Darwinism. N.Y., 1887.
Phil 9150.3.2 Schurman, J.G. The ethical import of Darwinism. N.Y., 1888.
Phil 9150.4 Sorley, W.R. On the ethics of naturalism. London, 1885.
Phil 9150.4.3 Sorley, W.R. On the ethics of naturalism. 2. ed. London, 1904.
Phil 9150.4.9 Pagnone, Annibale. L'eredità organica e la formazione delle idealità morale. Torino, 1904.
NEDL Phil 9150.5 Huxley, T.H. Evolution and ethics. London, 1893.
Phil 9150.6 Carneri, B. Sittlichkeit und Darwinismus. Wien, 1871.
Phil 9150.7 Read, M.S. English evolutionary ethics. N.Y., 1902.
Phil 9150.8 Smith, A.W. A new theory of evolution. N.Y., 1901.
Phil 9150.9.2 Bixby, James T. The crisis in morals. Boston, 1891.
Phil 9150.9.3 Bixby, James T. The ethics of revolution. Boston, 1900.
Phil 9150.10 Benett, W. Ethical aspects of evolution. Oxford, 1908.
Phil 9150.11 Funk, I.K. The next step in evolution. N.Y., 1902.
Phil 9150.12 Franklin, C.K. What nature is. Boston, 1911.
Phil 9150.13 Bruneteau, E. La doctrine morale de l'évolution. Paris, 1911.
Phil 9150.14 Sanderson, J.R. The relation of evolutionry theory to ethical problem. Toronto, 1912.
Phil 9150.15 Kies, Marietta. Institutional ethics. Boston, 1894.
Phil 9150.17 Jaeger, Gustav. Die Darwin'sche Theorie und ihre Stellung. Stuttgart, 1869.
Phil 9150.18 Massebieau, Eugéne. De principe de la morale. Thèse. Alençon, 1886.
Phil 9150.19 Folkmar, D. L'anthropologie philosophique. Thèse. Paris, 1899.
Phil 9150.21 Hanssen, Andreas. Etiken og evolutionslaeren. København, 1915.
Phil 9150.22 Lingle, T.W. Die Bedeutung der Entwickelungsgeschichte. Leipzig, 1899.
Phil 9150.23 Dawson, M. Nineteenth century evolution and after. N.Y., 1923.
Phil 9150.24 Sarolea, Charles. La liberté et le déterminisme rapports avec la théorie de l'évolution. Thèse. Bruxelles, 1893.
Phil 9150.26 Bartholomew, I.G. The cause of evil. London, 1927.
Phil 9150.27 Jensen, J.V. Evolution og moral. Kjøbenhavn, 1925.
Phil 9150.28 Ritter, William E. The natural history of our conduct. N.Y., 1927.

Phil 9150 Ethics - Treatises on special topics - Evolution - cont.
Phil 9150.29 Williams, C.M. A review of the systems of ethics founded on the theory of evolution. N.Y., 1893.
Phil 9150.30 Gantz, K.F. The beginnings of Darwinian ethics: 1859-1871. Chicago, 1939.
Phil 9150.31 Keith, Arthur. Evolution and ethics. N.Y., 1947.
Phil 9150.32 Ferabino, Aldo. Storia dell'uomo avantie dopo Cristo. Assisi, 1957.
Phil 9150.33 Waddington, C.H. The ethical animal. London, 1960.
Phil 9150.34 Volkova, Emma V. Determinatsaia evoliutsionnogo professor. Minsk, 1971.

Phil 9160 - 9185 Ethics - Treatises on special topics - Family - Individual authors (A-Z)
Phil 9160.1 Abbott, Jacob. The Rollo code of morals. Boston, 1841.
Phil 9160.1.5 Abbott, Jacob. A primer of ethics. Boston, 1891.
Htn Phil 9160.1.9* Abbott, Jacob. Parental duties in the promotion of early piety. London, 1836.
Phil 9160.2.5 Abbott, Jacob. The school-girl. Boston, 1840.
Phil 9160.2.8 Abbott, Jacob. The child at Howe. 2. ed. Boston, 1834.
Phil 9160.2.15 Abbott, Jacob. The child at Howe. N.Y., 1871.
NEDL Phil 9160.3 Alcott, W.A. The young husband. Boston, 1839.
Phil 9160.3.7 Alcott, W.A. The young wife. Boston, 1837.
Phil 9160.3.10 Alcott, W.A. The boy's guide. Boston, 1844.
Phil 9160.4 Allen, N. The New England family. New Haven, 1882.
Phil 9160.6 Anderson, C. Book for parents. The genius and design of the domestic constitution. Boston, 1834.
Htn Phil 9160.7* The American spectator. A collection of essays relating to the married state. Boston, 1797.
Phil 9160.8 Alcalde Prieto, D. Cuadros de familia. Valladolid, 1890.
NEDL Phil 9161.1 Bean, James. The Christian minister's affectionate advice to a new married couple. London, 1814.
X Cg Phil 9161.1.3 Bean, James. The Christian minister's affectionate advice to a new married couple. London, 1814.
Phil 9161.2 Beleze, G.L.G. Livre de lecture courante des devoirs des enfants. Paris, 1855.
Phil 9161.4 Bulkeley, H.W. A word to parents. Philadelphia, 1858?
Phil 9161.5 Brière, L. de la. La jeune mariée. Paris, 1896.
Phil 9161.6 Blair, H. On the duties of the young. London, 1794.
Phil 9161.7 Beck, Frank O. Marching manward. N.Y., 1913.
Phil 9161.8 Byford, W.H. The philosophy of domestic life. Boston, 1869.
Phil 9161.10 Broendum, L.C. Familielivets etik. København, 1963.
Htn Phil 9162.1* Carr, Roger. A godlie forme of household government. London, 16- ?
Htn Phil 9162.1.5* Carr, Roger. A godly forme of household government. London, 1621.
Htn Phil 9162.2* Courtin, A. de. Traité de la jalousie. Paris, 1685.
Phil 9162.3 Clowes, John. The golden wedding ring...marriage. Boston, 1832.
Phil 9162.4 Chassay, F.E. Les devoirs des femmes dans la famille. Paris, 1852.
Htn Phil 9162.5* La civilité puerile et honneste pour l'instruction des enfans. Troyes, 1677.
Phil 9162.6 Cramer, W.M.A. Unterhaltungen zur Beförderung der häuslichen Glückseligkeit. Berlin, 1781.
Phil 9162.7 Cox, S. Friendly counsel for girls. N.Y., 1868.
Phil 9163.1 De Foe, D. Religious courtship. London, 1762.
Phil 9163.2 Doumer, P. Livre de mes fils. Paris, 1906.
Phil 9163.3 Diggle, J.W. Home life. London, 1908.
Phil 9164.1 Ellis, S. Stickney. The wives of England. N.Y., 1843.
Phil 9164.1.2 Ellis, S. Stickney. The wives of England. N.Y., 1843.
Phil 9164.2 Encontro Latino Americano, 3d, Rio de Janeiro, 1963. Tercero encontro Latino-Americano. Rio de Janeiro, 1963.
Phil 9165.1 The family book. N.Y., 1835.
Phil 9165.2 Foster, J. The married state. Hartford, 18- .
Phil 9165.3 Foerster, F.W. Lebenskunde, ein Buch für Knaben und Mädchen. Berlin, 1907.
Phil 9165.3.6 Foerster, F.W. Lebensführung. Berlin, 1922.
Phil 9165.4.2 Foster, F. Thoughts on the times. London, 1779.
Phil 9165.5 Forsyth, P.T. Marriage, its ethic and religion. London, 1912.
Phil 9165.6.5 Fowler, O.S. Love and parentage. 40th ed. N.Y., 1869.
Phil 9166.1 A good wife God's gift. Boston, 1796.
Phil 9166.2 Gibson, W.S. An essay on the filial duties. London, 1848.
Htn Phil 9166.3* Glasse, S. Advice from a lady of quality to her children. 3. ed. Newbury Port, 1778. 2v.
Htn Phil 9166.3.5* Glasse, S. Advice from a lady of quality to her children. Boston, 1796.
Phil 9166.4 Gasparin, A.E. La famille. Paris, 1867. 2v.
Phil 9166.4.5 Gasparin, A.E. Le mariage au point de vue chrétien. 2. éd. Paris, 1844.
Phil 9166.5 Godimus, Z.J. L'esprit de famille étude morale. Paris, 1870.
Phil 9166.6 Girault, A. Le foyer, scènes de la vie de famille aux États Unis. Paris, 1875.
Phil 9166.7 Grossman, J.S. Do you know your daughter? N.Y., 1944.
Phil 9166.8 Guardini, R. Neue Jugend und katholischer Geist. Mainz, 1924.
Phil 9167.1 Hale, M. A letter of advice to his grandchildren. Boston, 1817.
Phil 9167.2 Hopkins, E. The family, a religious institution. Troy, N.Y., 1840.
Phil 9167.3 Hallifax, de M. Airs d'un père à sa fille. London, 1757.
Phil 9167.3.9F Halifax, G.S. The lady's new-years gift, or Advice to a daughter. Kensington, 1927.
Phil 9167.4 Hyde, William de W. The quest of the best. N.Y., 1913.
Phil 9167.5 Hodges, George. The happy family. N.Y., 1906.
Phil 9167.6 Heydenreich, K.H. Vesta; kleine Schriften zur Philosophie des Lebens. v.1-5. Leizpig, 1798-1803. 4v.
Phil 9169.1 James, J.A. The family monitor. Concord, N.H., 1829.
Phil 9169.1.1 James, J.A. The family monitor. Boston, 1829.
Phil 9169.1.2 James, J.A. The family monitor. Boston, 1833.
Phil 9169.1.5 James, J.A. The marriage ring. Boston, 1842?
Phil 9169.2 Jay, W. Thoughts on marriage. Boston, 1833.
Phil 9170.1 K., J.P.A. Bildungslehre...zum ehelichen Glücke. Düsseldorf, 1807.
Phil 9170.2 Kinney, A. The conquest of death. N.Y., 1893.
Phil 9171.1 De Lambert, A.T. de M. de C. A mother's advice to her son and daughter. London, 1800.
Phil 9171.1.2 De Lambert A.T. de M. de C. A mother's advice to her son and daughter. Boston, 1814.
Phil 9171.1.5 De Lambert, A.T. de M. de C. A mother's advice to her son and daughter. Haverhill, 1814.
Phil 9171.1.9 De Lambert, A.T. de M. de C. De l'éducation des jeunes gens. Paris, 1896.
Phil 9171.2 Letters on the moral and religious duties of parents. Boston, 1860.

Phil 9160 - 9185 Ethics - Treatises on special topics - Family - Individual authors (A-Z) - cont.

Phil 9171.2.3	Letters on the moral and religious duties of parents. Boston, 1844.
Phil 9171.3	Letters to a mother. Boston, 1831.
Phil 9171.4.8	Legouvé, E. Les pères et les enfants. Enfance et adolescence. 16. éd. Paris, 1867.
Phil 9171.4.12	Legouvé, E. Les pères et les enfants. La jeunesse. 13. éd. Paris, 1869.
Phil 9171.5	Lawton, R.O. The making of a home. Boston, 1914.
Phil 9171.6	Levi, G. Autobiografia di un padre di famiglia. Firenze, 1868.
tn Phil 9171.7.5*	Luján, Pedro de. Colo os matrimoniales. Toledo, 1563.
Phil 9171.8	Lofthouse, William F. Ethics and the family. London, 1912.
Cg Phil 9172.1	Moody, C.C.P. Lights and shadows of domestic life. Boston, 1846.
Phil 9172.2	The moral class book. Photoreproduction. London, 1856.
Phil 9172.3	Muzzey, A.B. The fireside: an aid to parents. Boston, 1854.
Phil 9172.4.2	Moncrieff, A.H. A book about boys. 2. ed. Edinburgh, 1868.
Phil 9172.5	Means without living. Boston, 1837.
Phil 9173.1	Newcomb, H. How to be a man: a book for boys. Boston, 1850.
n Phil 9173.2*	Nevizanis, J. de. Sylva nuptialis. n.p., 1602.
Phil 9174.1	Osgood, S. The hearth-stone. N.Y., 1854.
Phil 9174.1.2	Osgood, S. The hearth-stone. N.Y., 1876.
EDL Phil 9174.1.3	Osgood, S. The hearth-stone. N.Y., 1854.
Phil 9174.1.8	Osgood, S. American boys and girls. N.Y., 1867.
Phil 9175.1	Pandolfini, A. Trattato del governo della famiglia. Milano, 1802.
Phil 9175.1.8	Pandolfini, A. Trattato del governo della famiglia. Milano, 1829.
Phil 9175.2	Percival, T. A father's instructions to his children. Dublin, 1790.
Phil 9175.3	Parkes, W. Domstic duties. N.Y., 1829.
Phil 9175.4	Pacheco, R. Cartas a mi esposa. Santiago de Chile, 1878.
Phil 9175.5	Porter, Ann E. Uncle Jerry's letters to young mothers. Boston, 1854.
Phil 9175.6	Pimentel Castello-Branco, B.B. Regimento saudavel. Lisboa, 1750.
Phil 9177.1	Randall, M. Reflections...duty of masters, mistresses and servants. London, 1725.
Phil 9177.2	The refuge. New Haven, 1805. 2 pam.
Phil 9177.3	Grimaldi Robbio, Pelegro de. Discorsi de...ne'quali si ragiona compiutamente. Genova, 1585.
Phil 9177.4	Rowntree, Constance M. The right relationship between parents and children. Bannisdale, 19- ?
Phil 9178.1	Sanders, C.E. The little family. v.1-2. Haverhill, n.d.
Phil 9178.2	Sigourney, L.H. Letters to mothers. N.Y., 1839.
Phil 9178.2.2	Sigourney, L.H. Letters to mothers. Hartford, 1838.
Phil 9178.3	Smith, D.D. Lectures on domestic duties. Portland, 1837.
Phil 9178.4	Steel, D. A system of moral philosophy. Boston, 1847.
Phil 9178.5	Seymour, A. Home, the basis of the state. Boston, 1869.
Phil 9178.6.5	Somerville, E. A birthday present. Boston, 1803.
Phil 9178.6.6	Somerville, E. A birthday present. Boston, 1805.
Phil 9178.7	Stephens, John. Advantages which man derives from woman. N.Y., 1815.
Phil 9178.8	Sherwood, M.E.W. Amenities of home. N.Y., 1881.
Phil 9178.9	Stopes, M.C.C. Radiant motherhood. N.Y., 1932.
Phil 9178.10	Schapp, Wilhelm. Zur Metaphysik des Muttertums. Den Haag, 1965.
Phil 9179.1	Taylor, A. Hinton. Practical hints to young females. London, 1815.
Phil 9179.1.2	Taylor, A. Hinton. Practical hints to young females. Boston, 1816.
Phil 9179.1.5	Taylor, A. Hinton. Reciprocal duties of parents and children. Boston, 1825.
Phil 9179.3	Toner, J.M. Maternal instinct, or Love. Baltimore, 1864.
Phil 9179.4	Thayer, W.M. Hints for the household. Photoreproduction. Boston, 1853.
Phil 9179.5	Théry, A.F. Conseils aux mères. Paris, 1859. 2v.
Phil 9179.6	Thorburn, Grant. Sketches from the notebook of Laurie Todd on marriage. N.Y., 1847.
Phil 9179.7	Townsend, S. A practical essay designed for general use. Boston, 1783.
Phil 9179.8	Todd, J. Nuts for boys to crack. N.Y., n.d.
Phil 9179.9.4	Taylor, Isaac. Advice to the teens. Boston, 1820.
Phil 9179.10	Thomson, John. The domestic circle. Edinburgh, n.d.
Phil 9179.11	Tommaséo, N. Consigli ai giovani. Milano, 1869.
Phil 9182.1	Weaver, G.S. The Christian household. Boston, 1856.
Phil 9182.1.2	Weber, M.W. Über die Sozalen-Pflichten der Familie. 2. Aufl. Berlin, 1886.
Phil 9182.2	Wright, H.C. A kiss for a blow. Boston, 1858. (Changed to XP 9413)
Phil 9182.2.5	Wright, H.C. The unwelcome child. Boston, 1860.
Phil 9182.3	Ware, J.F.W. Home life: what it is, and what it needs. Boston, 1864.
Phil 9182.4	Wagner, Charles. Auprès du foyer. Paris, 1898.
Phil 9182.4.5	Wagner, Charles. By the fireside. N.Y., 1904.
Phil 9182.4.6	Wagner, Charles. La vie simple. 2. éd. Paris, 1895.
Phil 9182.4.9	Wagner, Charles. The simple life. N.Y., 1904.
Phil 9182.4.10	Wagner, Charles. The simple life. N.Y., 1904.
Phil 9182.4.12	Wagner, Charles. Why appeal to America. N.Y., 1905.
Phil 9182.4.15	Wagner, Charles. The better way. N.Y., 1903.
Phil 9182.5	Wise, D. Bridal greetings: a marriage gift. N.Y., 1852.
Phil 9182.6	Wallace, Henry. Uncle Henry's letters to the farm boy. 4. ed. N.Y., 1906.
Phil 9182.7	Wicks, Robert R. One operation and another. N.Y., 1939.
Phil 9182.8	Weber, L.M. Mysterium magnum. Freiburg, 1963.
Phil 9184.1	More, H. The young bride at home. Boston, 1836.

Phil 9200   Ethics - Treatises on special topics - Fanaticism

Phil 9200.1	Taylor, Isaac. Fanaticism. N.Y., 1834.
Phil 9200.1.5	Taylor, Isaac. Fanaticism. London, 1833.
Phil 9200.1.10	Taylor, Isaac. Fanaticism. London, 1853.
Phil 9200.2.5	Heer, Friedrich. Sieben Kapitel aus der Geschichte des Schreckens. Zürich, 1957.
Phil 9200.3	Rudin, Josef. Fanaticismus. Olten, 1965.

Phil 9215   Ethics - Treatises on special topics - Freedom of the will

Phil 9215.2	Norman, Richard. Reasons for actions: a critique of utilitarian rationality. Oxford, 1971.

Phil 9220   Ethics - Treatises on special topics - Friendship

Phil 9220.1	Staudlin, C.F. Geschichte der Vorst...Freundschaft. Hannover, 1826.
Phil 9220.2.20	King, H.C. Laws of friendship human and devine. N.Y., 1919.
Phil 9220.3A	Taylor, Jeremy. A discourse of friendship. Cedar Rapids, 1913.
Phil 9220.3B	Taylor, Jeremy. A discourse of friendship. Cedar Rapids, 1913.
Htn Phil 9220.3.5*	Taylor, Jeremy. A discourse of the nature...of friendship. London, 1671. 2 pam.
Phil 9220.4.3	Carpenter, Edward. Ioläus; anthology of friendship. 3d ed. London, 1915.
Phil 9220.5	Streamer, Volney. What makes a friend? 9th ed. N.Y., 1904.
Phil 9220.5.5	Streamer, Volney. In friendship's name. Chicago, 1891.
Phil 9220.5.6	Streamer, Volney. In friendship's name. 10th ed. N.Y., 1899.
Phil 9220.5.9	Streamer, Volney. In friendship's name. 14th ed. N.Y., 1904.
Phil 9220.5.11	Streamer, Volney. In friendship's name. 16th ed. N.Y., 1909.
Phil 9220.6	Friendship: two essays by Cicero and Emerson. N.Y., n.d.
Phil 9220.7	Bacon, Francis. For friendship's sake. N.Y., 1900.
Phil 9220.8	Friendship; Cicero, Bacon, Emerson. Chicago, 1890.
Phil 9220.9	Eglinger, Ruth. Der Begriff der Freundschaft in der Philosophie. Inaug. Diss. Basel, 1916.
Phil 9220.10.9	Gleichen-Russwurm, Alexander von. Freundschaft. Stuttgart, 1918?
Phil 9220.11	Trumbull, H.C. Friendship the master-passion. Philadelphia, 1894.
Phil 9220.12	Price, W.J. Between friends. Norwood, Mass., 1934.
Phil 9220.13	Gonçalves Viana, M. Psicolgia da Amizade. Porto, 1943.
Phil 9220.14	Kennell, Earl. This is friendship. N.Y., 1949.
Phil 9220.15	Brelting, Rudolf. Die Freundschaft. Düsseldorf, 1956.
Phil 9220.18	Fentener van Vlissingen, Johannes. Een psychologische theorie van de vriendschap. Proefschrift. Arnhem, 1966.

Phil 9230   Ethics - Treatises on special topics - Gaming

Phil 9230.1	Joostens, P. Alea, sive de curanda ludendi in pecuniam cupiditate. Amsterodami, 1642.
Phil 9230.2	Convocation of the Province of York. Report of the committee on betting and gambling. London, 1890.
Phil 9230.3	Hey, R. A dissertation...gaming. Cambridge, 1784-85. 3 pam.
Phil 9230.3.7	Hey, R. Three dissertations on...gaming. Cambridge, 1812.
Htn Phil 9230.4*	Gataker, T. Of the nature and use of lots. London, 1627.
Htn Phil 9230.4.5*	Gataker, T. Of the nature and use of lots. London, 1619.
Phil 9230.5	Barbeyrac, J. Traité du jeu. Amsterdam, 1737. 3v.
Phil 9230.6	Gataker, T. Antithesis de sorte. Lugdunum Batavorum, 1659-60. 3 pam.
Phil 9230.7	Venault de charmilly. Letter...to Lieutenant General B. Tarleton. London, 1810.
Phil 9230.8	Gordon, G.W. A lecture before Boston young men's societies on the subject of lotteries. Boston, 1833.
Phil 9230.10A	Walker, Gilbert. A manifest detection of the most vyle and detestable use of dice play. London, 1850.
Phil 9230.10B	Walker, Gilbert. A manifest detection of the most vyle and detestable use of dice play. London, 1850.
Phil 9230.11	Labrousse, Louis. De l'exception de jeu. Paris, 1897.
Htn Phil 9230.12*	Collier, Jeremy. An essay upon gaming. London, 1713. (Transferred to Houghton Library 14/1/72)
Phil 9230.12.5	Collier, Jeremy. An essay upon gaming. Edinburgh, 1885.
Phil 9230.13	Great Britain. Commission on Lotteries and Betting, 1932-33. Final report. London, 1933.
Phil 9230.13.5F	Great Britain. Commission on Lotteries and Betting, 1932-33. Minutes of evidence...first 24 days, Thursday, 30 June, 1932-Thursday, 23 February, 1933. Pt.1-24. London, 1932-33.
Phil 9230.14	Green, Peter. Betting and gambling. London, 1927.
Phil 9230.15	Peterson, V.W. Gambling, should it be legalized? Chicago, Ill., 1945.
Phil 9230.20	Allen, David D. The nature of gambling. N.Y., 1952.
Phil 9230.25	Olmsted, Charlotte. Heads, I win; tails, you lose. N.Y., 1962.
Phil 9230.30	Borély, Joseph. Discours prononcé devant la cour royale d'Aix à l'audience solenelle de rentrée. Aix, 1836.

Phil 9240   Ethics - Treatises on special topics - Good and evil

Phil 9240.1	Lloyd, R.B. The mastery of evil. London, 1941.
Phil 9240.2.5	Simard, Georges. Maux présents et foi chrétienne. 2. éd. Montréal, 1941.
Phil 9240.3	Skinner, Clarence R. Human nature, or The nature of evil. Boston, 1939.
Phil 9240.4	Clamageran, J.J. La lutte contre le mal. Paris, 1897.
Phil 9240.5	Lindsay, A.D. The good and the clever. Cambridge, 1945.
Phil 9240.6	Ewing, Alfred C. The definition of good. N.Y., 1947.
Phil 9240.6.5	Ewing, Alfred C. Second thoughts in moral philosophy. London, 1959.
Phil 9240.7	Palmer, G.H. The nature of goodness. Boston, 1903.
Phil 9240.8	Sertellanges, A.G. Le problème du mal. Paris, 1948-1951. 2v.
Phil 9240.9	Whale, J.S. The Christian answers to the problem of evil. 2. ed. London, 1948.
Phil 9240.10.5	Camus, Albert. L'homme révolté. 94. éd. Paris, 1952.
Phil 9240.12	Salmon, E.G. The good in existential metaphysics. Milwaukee, 1953.
Phil 9240.13	Rice, P.B. On the knowledge of good and evil. N.Y., 1955.
Phil 9240.14	Grenier, Jean. L'existence malheureuse. Paris, 1957.
Phil 9240.15	Siewerth, Gustav. Die Freiheit und das Gute. Freiburg, 1959.
Phil 9240.16	Macht und Wirklichkeit des Bösen. München, 1958.
Phil 9240.18	Dessauer, F.J. Prometheus und die Weltübel. Frankfurt, 1959.
Phil 9240.20	Welte, Bernhard. Über das Böse. Basel, 1959.
Phil 9240.22	Farrer, Austin. Love almighty and ills unlimited. 1st ed. Garden City, N.Y., 1961.
Phil 9240.24	Walsh, V.C. Scarcity and evil. Englewood Cliffs, N.J., 1961.
Phil 9240.26	Journet, Charles. Le mal. Bruges? 1961.
Phil 9240.28	Child, A. Bemis. Whatever is, is right. 2d ed. Boston, 1861.
Phil 9240.30	Veloso, Agostinho. O homem em face da dor. Lisboa, 1961.
Phil 9240.31	Wright, Georg. The varieties of goodness. London, 1963.
Phil 9240.31.5	Wright, Georg. The varieties of goodness. N.Y., 1963.
Phil 9240.32	Gotshalk, D.W. Patterns of good and evil. Urbana, 1963.
Phil 9240.34	Simon, Ulrich Ernest. A theology of Auschwitz. London, 1967.

Classified Listing

Phil 9240   Ethics - Treatises on special topics - Good and evil - cont.
Phil 9240.36   Brod, Viktor. Die Ich-du-Beziehung als Erfahrungsgrundlage der Ethik. München, 1967.

Phil 9245   Ethics - Treatises on special topics - Happiness
Phil 9245.1   Droz, F.X.J. The art of being happy. Boston, 1832.
Phil 9245.1.5   Droz, F.X.J. The art of being happy. London, 18- ?
Phil 9245.2   Forbes, J. Of happiness in its relations to work and knowledge. London, 1850.
Phil 9245.3   Gasparin, A.E. Le bonheur. Paris, 1874.
Htn   Phil 9245.4*   Lucas, R. An enquiry after happiness. London, 1704.
NEDL   Phil 9245.4.2   Lucas, R. An enquiry after happiness. London, 1717. 2v.
Phil 9245.4.3   Lucas, R. An enquiry after happiness. London, 1753. 2v.
Phil 9245.4.4   Lucas, R. An enquiry after happiness. pt.1. Edinburgh, 1754.
Phil 9245.4.5   Lucas, R. An enquiry after happiness. v.1-2. London, 1764.
Phil 9245.5   Macmillan, M. The promotion of general happiness. London, 1890.
Phil 9245.6   Oliver, B.L. Hints for an essay on the pursuit of happiness. Chicago, 1818.
Phil 9245.7   Sigaud de la Fond, J.R. L'école du bonheur. Paris, 1785.
Phil 9245.8   Pfleiderer, E. Eudämonismus und Egoismus. Leipzig, 1880.
Phil 9245.8.5   Pfleiderer, E. Zur Ehrenrettung des Eudämonismus. Tübingen, 1879.
Phil 9245.9.1   Avebury, John Lubbock. The pleasures of life. N.Y., 1887.
Phil 9245.9.2.3   Avebury, John Lubbock. The pleasures of life. London, 1889.
Phil 9245.9.3   Avebury, John Lubbock. The pleasures of life. N.Y., 1893.
Phil 9245.9.4   Avebury, John Lubbock. The pleasures of life. v.1-2. London, 1913-14.
Phil 9245.9.7   Avebury, John Lubbock. The pleasures of life. London, 1893.
Phil 9245.9.50   Avebury, John Lubbock. Duty of happiness. Philadelphia, 1896.
Phil 9245.9.55   Avebury, John Lubbock. Le bonheur de vivre. v.1-2. Paris, 1897-98.
Phil 9245.9.75   Avebury, John Lubbock. Peace and happiness. N.Y., 1909.
Phil 9245.10   Grasset, B. Sur le plaisir. Paris, 1954.
Phil 9245.11.3   Brinton, Daniel G. The pursuit of happiness. Philadelphia, 1893.
Phil 9245.12   Harris, J. Three treatises. London, 1744.
Phil 9245.12.2   Harris, J. Three treatises. London, 1765.
Htn   Phil 9245.12.2*   Harris, J. Three treatises. London, 1765.
Phil 9245.12.3   Harris, J. Three treatises. London, 1772.
Phil 9245.13   Hamerton, P.G. The quest of happiness. Boston, 1897.
Phil 9245.14   Watson, J. Hedonistic theories. Glasgow, 1895.
Phil 9245.15   Schwarz, H. Glück und Sittlichkeit. Halle, 1902.
Phil 9245.16.2   Hillis, N.D. Quest of happiness. N.Y., 1902.
Phil 9245.17   Wright, W.K. Ethical significances of pleasure. Chicago, 1906.
Phil 9245.18   Joslyn, R. The philosophy of happiness. Elgin, n.d.
Phil 9245.19   Laserre, J.P. de. Le tombeau des délices du monde. Brusselles, 1632.
Phil 9245.20   Souriau, Paul. Les conditions du bonheur. Paris, 1908.
Phil 9245.21   Finot, Jean. Progrès et bonheur. Paris, 1914. 2v.
Phil 9245.22   Dickson, Henry S. An oration...before...Phi Beta Kappa Society. New Haven, 1842.
Phil 9245.24   Fletcher, Horace. Happiness. N.Y., 1898.
Phil 9245.24.3   Fletcher, Horace. Happiness as found in forethought minus fearthought. Chicago, 1897.
Phil 9245.25   Ramsey, George. An inquiry into the principles of human happiness and human duty. London, 1843.
Phil 9245.26   Dudoc, J. Die Lust als socialethisches Entwickelungsprincip. Leipzig, 1900.
Phil 9245.27   Zerbst, Max. Die Philosophie der Freude. Leipzig, 191-.
Phil 9245.28   Marden, Orison S. The joys of living. N.Y., 1913.
Phil 9245.28.10   Marden, Orison S. Arbetsglädje-livsglädje. Stockholm, 1912.
Phil 9245.29   Lescoeur, Louis. La science du bonheur. Paris, 1873.
Phil 9245.30   Gomperz, H. Kritik des Hedonismus. Stuttgart, 1898.
Phil 9245.31   Holmes, E. The secret of happiness. London, 1919.
Phil 9245.32   Piat, Clodius. La morale du bonheur. Paris, 1910.
Phil 9245.33   Payot, Jules. La conquête du bonheur. Paris, 1921.
Phil 9245.33.10   Payot, Jules. Erövringen av lyckan. Stockholm, 1923.
Phil 9245.34   Beausobre, Louis de. Essai sur le bonheur. Berlin, 1758.
Phil 9245.35   Der neue Epikur, oder die Philosophie der Sittlichenwollust. Prag, 1779.
Phil 9245.36.5   Deslandes, A.F.B. The art of being easy at all times and in all places. London, 1724.
Htn   Phil 9245.37*   Phelps, William L. Happiness. N.Y., 1927.
Phil 9245.37.2   Phelps, William L. Happiness. N.Y., 1927.
Phil 9245.38   Grimanelli, P. La morale positive et le bonheur. Paris, 1924.
Phil 9245.39   Nobile, Flamineo. De hominis felicitate libri treo. Lucae, 1563.
Phil 9245.40   Steele, Mary D. A happy life. Dayton, Ohio, 1895.
Phil 9245.41   Miltenberger, W.F. De felicitate. Washington, D.C., 1914.
Phil 9245.42   The art of employing time to the greatest advantage. London, 1822.
Phil 9245.43A   Russell, B.A.W. The conquest of happiness. N.Y., 1930.
Phil 9245.43B   Russell, B.A.W. The conquest of happiness. N.Y., 1930.
Phil 9245.43.1   Russell, B.A.W. The conquest of happiness. N.Y., 1930.
Phil 9245.43.2   Russell, B.A.W. The conquest of happiness. London, 1930.
X Cg   Phil 9245.44   Calder, Alexander. The man of the future. London, 1872.
Phil 9245.45   Lush, Samuel Beryl. Six roads to happiness. N.Y., 1930.
Phil 9245.46.5   Pitkin, W.B. The psychology of happiness. N.Y., 1929.
Phil 9245.47   Powys, Llwelyn. Impassioned day. London, 1931.
Phil 9245.48   Hodge, George. The pursuit of happiness. N.Y., 1906.
Phil 9245.49   Russell, Dora. The right to be happy. N.Y., 1927.
Phil 9245.50.5   Powys, J.C. The art of happiness. N.Y., 1935.
Phil 9245.50.10   Powys, J.C. In defense of sensuality. N.Y., 1930.
Phil 9245.51   Patter, Charles F. Technique of happiness. N.Y., 1935.
Phil 9245.52   Andrus, F.N. The evolution of happiness. Boston, 1936.
Phil 9245.53   Somer, Marcelle de. Le rythme de la vie, le bonheur. Gand, 1933.
Phil 9245.54.5   Chartier, E. Propos sur le bonheur. 18e éd. Paris, 1928.
Phil 9245.55A   Trinkhaus, C.E. Adversity's noblemen. N.Y., 1940.
Phil 9245.55B   Trinkhaus, C.E. Adversity's noblemen. N.Y., 1940.
Phil 9245.56   Schauffler, Robert H. The joyful heart. Boston, 1914.
Phil 9245.57   Cadman, Samuel P. Adventure for happiness. N.Y., 1935.
Phil 9245.58   Marcuse, L. Die Philosophie des Glücks. Zürich, 1949.
Phil 9245.59   Gumpert, M. The anatomy of happiness. N.Y., 1951.
Phil 9245.60A   MacIver, R.M. The pursuit of happiness. N.Y., 1955.
Phil 9245.60B   MacIver, R.M. The pursuit of happiness. N.Y., 1955.

Phil 9245   Ethics - Treatises on special topics - Happiness - cont.
Phil 9245.62   Rencontres Internationales, Genève, 1961. Les conditions du bonheur. Neuchâtel, 1961.
Phil 9245.63   Delessert, Benjamin Guron. Le guide du bonheur. 2. éd. Paris, 1840.
Phil 9245.64   Polin, Raymond. Le bonheur considéré comme l'un des beaux-arts. Paris, 1965.
Phil 9245.115   Tatarkiewicz, W. A szczęściu. Wyd. 3. Warszawa, 1962.
Phil 9245.116   Fernández, Julio F. Proyecciónes espirituales del sufrimiento radiografia del dolor. San Salvador, 1964.
Phil 9245.117   Bradburn, Norman Marshall. Reports on happiness. Chicago, 1965.
Phil 9245.118   Novikov, Mikhail I. O schast'e. Moskva, 1965.
Phil 9245.119   Naguib, Mohammad. Full happiness. Cairo, n.d.
Phil 9245.120   McGill, Vivian Jerauld. The idea of happiness. N.Y., 1967.
VPhil 9245.125   Curry, Samuel Silas. The smile. Boston, 1915.
Phil 9245.128   Maggal, Moshe M. Acres of happiness. 1st ed. N.Y., 1967.
Phil 9245.130   Harper, Ralph. The path of darkness. Cleveland, 1968.
Phil 9245.132   Kramp, Willy. Über die Freude; zwei Betrachtungen. Hamburg, 1968.
Phil 9245.134   Boelen, Bernard J. Eduaimonie en het wezen der ethiek. Leuven, 1949.
Phil 9245.136   Bradburn, Norman Marshall. The structure of psychological well-being. Chicago, 1969.
Phil 9245.138   Gosling, Justin Cyril Bertrand. Pleasure and desire: the case for hedonism reviewed. Oxford, 1969.
Phil 9245.140   Korneva, Mariia N. Kommunizm i problema schast'ia. Moskva, 1970.
Phil 9245.142   Hancerlioğlu, Orhan. Başlangicidan bugüne mutluluk düsüncesi. Istanbul, 1969.
Phil 9250.34   Volkova, Emma V. Determinatsiia evoliutsionnogo protsessa. Minsk, 1971.

Phil 9255   Ethics - Treatises on special topics - Irony
Phil 9255.5   Paulhan, Frederic. La morale de l'ironie. 2. éd. Paris, 1914.
Phil 9255.15   Jancke, Rudolf. Das Wesen der Ironie. Leipzig, 1929.
Phil 9255.17   Sedgewick, Garrett G. Of irony, especially in drama. Toronto, 1935.
Phil 9255.17.5   Sedgewick, Garrett G. Of irony, especially in drama. Toronto, 1948.
Phil 9255.19   Jankélévitch, Vladimir. L'ironie. Paris, 1936.
Phil 9255.25   Staecker, Karlheinz. Ironie und Ironiker. Diss. Mainz? 1963.
Phil 9255.30   Dikkers, S.J. Ironie als vorm van communicatie. Den Haag, 1969.

Phil 9290   Ethics - Treatises on special topics - Labor
Phil 9290.1   Quill, C. The American mechanic. Philadelphia, 1838.
Phil 9290.2   Nagel, O. Die Welt als Arbeit. Stuttgart, 1909.
Phil 9290.3   Martinet, J.F. Zeemans handboek. Amsterdam, 1781.
Phil 9290.4   Bryson, Lyman. The use of the radio in leisure time. N.Y., 1935?
Phil 9290.5   Prevet, François. La moralité professionnelle des origines à nos jours. Paris, 1956. 2v.
Phil 9290.6   Donohue, John W. Work and education. Chicago, 1959.
Phil 9290.8   Arvon, Henri. La philosophie du travail. Paris, 1961.
Phil 9290.9   Overstreet, Harry A. A guide to civilized loafing. N.Y., 1934.
Phil 9290.10   Simnett, William E. Leisure, how to enjoy it. London, 1946.

Phil 9320   Ethics - Treatises on special topics - Meditative life
Phil 9320.7   Duerckheim-Montmartin, Karlfried. Der Alltag als Übung vom Weg zur Verwandlung. 2. Aufl. Bern, 1966.
Phil 9320.10   Desjardins, Arnaud. Les chemins de la sagesse. Paris, 1969- 2v.

Phil 9330   Ethics - Treatises on special topics - Melancholy
Phil 9330.1   Smith, Garnet. The melancholy of Stephen Allard. N.Y., 1895.
Phil 9330.10   Lepenies, Wolf. Melancholie und Gesellschaft. Thesis. Frankfurt, 1969.

Phil 9339   Ethics - Treatises on special topics - Men and women - Pamphlet volumes; Collected authors
Phil 9339.01   Pamphlet box. Ethics for men and women.

Phil 9340 - 9365   Ethics - Treatises on special topics - Men and women - Individual authors (A-Z)
Phil 9340.1   Aikin, J. Letters from a father to his son. London, 1794-1800. 2v.
Htn   Phil 9340.1.2*   Aikin, J. Letters from a father to his son. Philadelphia, 1794.
Htn   Phil 9340.1.5*   Aikin, J. Letters from a father to his son. Philadelphia, 1796.
Phil 9340.2.5   Alcott, William Alex. Young woman's guide to excellence. Boston, 1847.
Phil 9340.3   Austin, J.M. Voice to youth. N.Y., 1847.
Phil 9340.4   Abbott, John S. The school-boy. Boston, 1839.
Phil 9340.5   Ancourt, Abbe d'. The lady's preceptor. London, 1743.
Htn   Phil 9340.6*   Allestree, Richard. The ladies calling. Oxford, 1673.
Htn   Phil 9340.7*   Advice to a young lord, written by his father. London, 1691.
Phil 9340.8   Angell, Frances. Compete Philadelphia, 1935.
Htn   Phil 9340.9*   Advice to the fair sex. Philadelphia, 1803.
Phil 9340.10   Adams, (Mrs.). Daily duties inculcated in a series of letters. Boston, 1835.
Phil 9340.12   Andreas-Salomé, Lou. Die Erotik. Frankfurt, 1910.
Phil 9341.1   Beecher, C.E. Duty of American women to their country. N.Y., 1845.
Phil 9341.2.2   Beecher, H.W. Lectures to young men. Boston, 1850.
Phil 9341.2.5   Beecher, H.W. Lectures to young men. Salem, 1846.
Phil 9341.2.6   Beecher, H.W. Lectures to young men. N.Y., 1856.
Phil 9341.2.10   Beecher, H.W. Lectures to young men. Edinburgh, 1887.
Phil 9341.3   Berens, E. Advice to young man...Oxford. London, 1832.
Phil 9341.4   Burnap, G.W. Lectures on the sphere and duties of woman. Baltimore, 1841.
Phil 9341.4.5   Burnap, G.W. Lectures to young men. Baltimore, 1840.
Phil 9341.5   Bell, J.D. A man. Philadelphia, 1860.
Phil 9341.6   Butler, C. The American gentleman. Philadelphia, 1836.
Phil 9341.6.9   Butler, C. The American lady. Philadelphia, 1841.
Phil 9341.7   Bennett, J. Letters to a young lady. Philadelphia, 1818.
Phil 9341.7.5   Bennett, J. Letters to a young lady. London, 1803. 2v.
Phil 9341.8   Blair, H. Advice to youth. n.p., n.d.
Phil 9341.9   Brown, C.R. The young man's affairs. N.Y., 1909.

Phil 9340 - 9365   Ethics - Treatises on special topics - Men and women -
Individual authors (A-Z) - cont.

Phil 9341.9.5   Brown, C.R. Yale talks. New Haven, 1919.
Phil 9341.9.20   Brown, C.R. What is your name? New Haven, 1931.
Phil 9341.10A   Batchelder, S. The young men of America. N.Y., 1858.
Phil 9341.10B   Batchelder, S. The young men of America. N.Y., 1858.
Phil 9341.11   Burgh, J. Directions prudential, moral, religious.
                     London, 1750.
Phil 9341.12   Bennett, Arnold. Mental efficiency. N.Y., 1911.
Phil 9341.12.5   Bennett, Arnold. Mental efficiency and other hints to men
                     and women. London, 1912.
Phil 9341.13.5   Bourn, Benjamin. A sure guide to hell, in seven sections.
                     London, 1785.
Phil 9341.15   Bouilly, J.N. Conseils à ma fille. Paris, 18- ?
Phil 9341.16   Beveridge, Albert J. The young man and the world.
                     N.Y., 1906.
Phil 9341.17   Beale, Dorothea. A few words to girls at school.
                     n.p., 18- .
Phil 9342.1   Chapin, E.H. Duties of young men. Boston, 1846.
EDL Phil 9342.1.5   Chapin, E.H. Duties of young men. Boston, 1848.
Phil 9342.1.10   Chapin, E.H. Duties of young women. Boston, 1850.
Phil 9342.2   Chapone, H. (Mrs.). Letters on the improvement of the
                     mind. London, 1830.
tn   Phil 9342.2.2* Chapone, H. (Mrs.). Letters on the improvement of the
                     mind. v.1-2. N.Y., 1793.
tn   Phil 9342.2.3* Chapone, H. (Mrs.). Letters on the improvement of the
                     mind. v.1-2. Hagerstown, 1819.
Phil 9342.2.4   Chapone, H. (Mrs.). Letters on the improvement of the
                     mind. London, 1822.
Phil 9342.2.5   Chapone, H. (Mrs.). Letters on the improvement of the
                     mind. 2. ed. London, 1773. 2v.
Cg   Phil 9342.2.6   Chapone, H. (Mrs.). Letters on the improvement of the
                     mind. Philadelphia, 1816.
n   Phil 9342.2.7* Chapone, H. (Mrs.). Letters on the improvement of the
                     mind. Philadelphia, 1786.
Phil 9342.2.8   Chapone, H. (Mrs.). Letters on the improvement of the
                     mind. N.Y., 1827.
Phil 9342.2.9   Chapone, H. (Mrs.). Letters on the improvement of the
                     mind. London, 1815.
Phil 9342.2.10   Chapone, H. (Mrs.). Letters on the improvement of the
                     mind. London, 1819.
ı   Phil 9342.2.11* Chapone, H. (Mrs.). Letters on the improvement of the
                     mind. Portland, 17- ?
Phil 9342.2.12   Chapone, H. (Mrs.). Letters on the improvement of the
                     mind. Boston, 1809.
Phil 9342.3A   Farrar, Eliza W.R. Young lady's friend. Boston, 1836.
ı   Phil 9342.3*B   Farrar, Eliza W.R. Young lady's friend. Boston, 1836.
Phil 9342.4   Cobbett, W. Advice to young men. N.Y., 1831.
Phil 9342.4.2   Cobbett, W. Advice to young men. London, 1887.
Phil 9342.4.10   Cobbett, W. Advice to young men. London, 1906.
Phil 9342.4.12   Cobbett, W. Advice to young men. London, 1926.
Phil 9342.4.15   Cobbett, W. Advice to young men. London, 1930.
Phil 9342.5   Collyer, S. Talks to young men. Boston, 1888.
Phil 9342.7   Cummings, A.I. Lady's present. Boston, 1856.
Phil 9342.8*   Cautious lady, or Religion the chief happiness in a married
                     state. London, 1760.
Phil 9342.9   Cary, V. (Mrs.). Letters on female character.
                     Richmond, 1830.
Phil 9342.11   Charpentier, Louis. Décence em elle-même. Paris, 1767.
Phil 9342.12.5   Cobbe, F.P. The duties of women. Boston, 1881.
Phil 9342.13   Carlisle, Isabella (Byron) Howard. Thoughts in the forms
                     of maxims. London, 1790.
Phil 9342.14   Coxe, Margaret. The young lady's companion.
                     Columbus, 1839.
Phil 9342.15*   Cleland, James. Erō-paideia, or The institution of a young
                     noble man. Oxford, 1607.
Phil 9342.16   Callet, P. L'écolier chŕetien. Lyon, 1776.
Phil 9342.17.5   Campe, J.H. Vaterlicher Rath für meine Tochter. 2. Aufl.
                     Tübingen, 1789.
Phil 9342.18   Cunningham, W. True womanhood. N.Y., 18- .
Phil 9343.2   Darell, W. Gentleman instructed. London, 1723.
Phil 9343.2.2   Darell, W. Gentleman instructed. London, 1707. 2v.
Phil 9343.2.3   Darell, W. A supplement to the first part of the G.I.
                     London, 1708.
Phil 9343.3   Daughter's own book. Philadelphia, 1836.
Phil 9343.5   Davis, William. Friendly advice to industrious persons.
                     4th ed. London, 1817.
Phil 9343.6   Deems, C.F. What now? N.Y., 1852.
Phil 9343.7   Dodge, Grace H. A bundle of letters to busy girls.
                     N.Y., 1887.
Phil 9343.7.6   Dodge, Grace H. Thoughts of busy girls. N.Y., 1892.
Phil 9343.8*   Dorrington, T. The excellent woman described.
                     London, 1692.
Phil 9343.9   Paige, Elbridge G. Short patent sermons. N.Y., 1845.
Phil 9343.10   Dupuy, La Chapelle. Instruction d'un père à sa fille. 3e
                     éd. Paris, 1731.
Phil 9343.10.5   Dupuy, La Chapelle. Instruction d'un père à sa fille. 3e
                     éd. Paris, 1750.
Phil 9343.11   Drury, Samuel S. Backbone; the development of character.
                     N.Y., 1923.
Phil 9343.12*   Dare, Josiah. Counsellor Manners, his last legacy to his
                     son. London, 1673.
Phil 9343.12.5   Dare, Josiah. Counsellor Manners, his last legacy to his
                     son. London, 1710.
Phil 9343.14   Dentico, Salvatore. Gioventu atea? Palermo, 1967.
Phil 9344.1   Eddy, A.D. Addresses on duties of youth. N.Y., 1836.
Phil 9344.2   Eliot, W.G. Lectures to young men. St. Louis, 1852.
Phil 9344.2.3   Eliot, W.G. Lectures to young men. 6th ed. Boston, 1856.
Phil 9344.2.5   Eliot, W.G. Lectures to young women. Boston, 1860.
Phil 9344.3   Ellis, S.S. Daughters of England. N.Y., 1843.
Phil 9344.3.5   Ellis, S.S. Mothers of England. N.Y., 1844. 7 pam.
Phil 9344.3.7   Ellis, S.S. The woman of England. N.Y., 1843.
Phil 9344.5*   Evening amusement for the ladies. Boston, 1796.
Phil 9344.6   Ellis, John. Deterioration of the Puritan stock.
                     N.Y., 1884.
Phil 9344.7*   Ellis, Clement. The gentile sinner. Oxford, 1660.
Phil 9344.8   Ehrenberg, F. Der Charakter und die Bestimmung des Mannes.
                     Leipzig, 1808.
Phil 9344.9   Everett, G. Ethics for young people. Boston, 1893.
Phil 9344.10   Elson, F.S. Quiet hints to ministers' wives.
                     Boston, 1934.
Phil 9345.1   Fathers gift to his son. N.Y., 1821.
Phil 9345.2   Female aegis. London, 1798.
Phil 9345.4*   Forrester, J. Polite philosopher. London, 1758.
Phil 9345.5*   Foster, H. (Webster). Boarding school. Boston, 1829.
Phil 9345.6*   Fergurson, F. The young man. Nashua, N.H., 1848.
Phil 9345.7   Fortin, P. Testament, ou Conseils fideles d'un bon pere.
                     Leide, 1653.

Phil 9340 - 9365   Ethics - Treatises on special topics - Men and women -
Individual authors (A-Z) - cont.

Phil 9345.8   Fischer, E.L.C. Heart and soul culture.
                     Philadelphia, 1912.
Phil 9345.9   Farrar, Eliza W. The young lady's friend. Boston, 1837.
Phil 9345.10   A father's advice to his son. London, n.d.
Phil 9345.11   Friend, N.E. (Mrs.). Love and you. N.Y., 1933.
Phil 9345.12   Folliet, Joseph. Adam et Eve. Lyon, 1965.
Phil 9346.2   Girot. Le moraliste de la jeunesse. London, 1801.
Phil 9346.3.2   Gisborne, T. Enquiry...duties of the female sex.
                     London, 1798.
Phil 9346.5   Gratry. A.J. Les sources. v.1-2. Paris, 1862-69.
Phil 9346.5.5   Gratry, A.J. Les sources. 16. éd. Paris, 1921.
Phil 9346.6   Gregory, John. A father's legacy to his daughters.
                     London, 1822.
Htn Phil 9346.6.2* Gregory, John. A father's legacy to his daughters.
                     Philadelphia, 1781.
X Cg Phil 9346.6.3   Gregory, John. A father's legacy to his daughters.
                     Albany, 1821.
Htn Phil 9346.6.5* Gregory, John. A father's legacy to his daughters.
                     N.Y., 1775.
Htn Phil 9346.6.7* Chesterfield, Philip Dormer Stanhope. Principles of
                     politeness. Portsmouth, N.H., 1786.
Phil 9346.7   The gentleman's library. 2d ed. London, 1722.
Phil 9346.8   Gulick, L.H. The dynamic of manhood. N.Y., 1917.
Htn Phil 9346.9*   Gauden, John. A discourse of auxiliary beauty.
                     n.p., 1656.
Phil 9346.10A   Gray, Arthur Herbert. Men, women and God. N.Y., 1922.
Phil 9346.11   Gizycki, Paul von. Vom Baume der Erkenntnis.
                     Berlin, 1897.
Htn Phil 9346.12*   Gailhard, J. The compleat gentleman. Savoy, 1678.
Phil 9346.13   The gentleman and lady of pleasure's amusement.
                     London, 1759.
Phil 9346.15   Garabedian, John H. Eastern religions in the electric age.
                     N.Y., 1969.
Phil 9347.1   Hawes, J. Lectures to young men. Boston, 1856.
Phil 9347.1.2   Hawes, J. Lectures to young men. Hartford, 1832.
Phil 9347.2   Hubbard, E. A message to Garcia. N.Y., 1900.
Phil 9347.2.3   Hubbard, E. A message to Garcia. East Aurora, 1899.
Htn Phil 9347.2.5* Hubbard, E. A message to Garcia. N.Y., 1906.
Phil 9347.2.13   Hubbard, E. A message to Garcia. n.p., 192-.
Phil 9347.2.25   Hubbard, E. Health and wealth. East Aurora, 1908.
Phil 9347.3   Hersey, H.E. To girls. A budget of letters. Boston, 1901.
Phil 9347.4   The history of man. 3d ed. Dublin, 1791.
Phil 9347.5   Hood, E.P. Self formation. 3d ed. London, 1878.
Phil 9347.6   Hall, John. Familiar talks to boys. N.Y., n.d.
Phil 9347.7   Hepworth, G. Rocks and shoals. Boston, 1870.
Phil 9347.8   Hall, S.S. Bliss of marriage; or How to get a rich wife.
                     New Orleans, 1858.
Phil 9347.9   Hill, James L. The worst boys in town. Boston, 1919.
Phil 9347.10   Hackley, E.A. (Mrs.). The colored girl beautiful. Kansas
                     City, 1916.
Phil 9347.11.2   Hicks, S. Difficulties; an attempt to help. London, 1922.
Phil 9347.12   Higford, William. Institutions: or Advice to his grandson.
                     London, 1818.
Phil 9347.13   Harris, Erdman. Twenty-one. N.Y., 1931.
Phil 9347.14   The harmonium. Chicago, 1881.
Phil 9347.15   Hewitt, M.E.G. High school lectures. London, 1889.
Htn Phil 9347.16*   Hassen, Martin. De noncommutando sexus habitu.
                     Vitembergae, 1714.
Phil 9348.1   The institution of a gentleman. London, 1839.
Phil 9349.1   James, J.A. Young man from home. N.Y., 1839.
Phil 9349.2   Johnson, F. True womanhood. Cambridge, 1882.
Phil 9349.3   Jacks, William. Singles from life's gathering.
                     Glasgow, 1902.
Phil 9349.4   Joly, Henri. Pour les jeunes. Paris, 1919.
Phil 9349.5   Jamin, F. Conseils aux jeunes de France après la victoire.
                     2e éd. Paris, 1921.
Phil 9349.6   Jumigny, de. Le père gouverneur de Son fils.
                     Bourbes, 1780.
Phil 9350.1   Knott, Laura A. Vesper talks to girls. Boston, 1916.
Phil 9350.2   Kittredge, H.C. Ten minute talks to boys. Concord,
                     N.H., 1917.
Phil 9350.3.7   Keddie, H. Papers for thoughtful girls. Boston, 1864.
Phil 9350.3.8   Keddie, H. Sweet counsel. Boston, 1866.
Phil 9350.3.15   Keddie, H. Heroines in obscurity. London, 1871.
Phil 9351.1   Ladies library. London, 1722.
NEDL Phil 9351.1.2   Ladies library. London, 1751. 3v.
NEDL Phil 9351.1.3   Ladies library. London, 1714. 3v.
Htn Phil 9351.2*   Lectures to young men. N.Y., 1892.
Phil 9351.3   Lieber, F. Character of the gentleman.
                     Philadelphia, 1864.
Phil 9351.4   Lemontey, P.E. Raison, folie. Bruxelles, 1830. 2v.
Phil 9351.5   Linsley, J.H. Lectures on relations and middle aged.
                     Hartford, 1828.
Phil 9351.6   Livermore, A.A. Lectures to young men. Boston, 1846.
Phil 9351.7   Lady's pocket library. Philadelphia, 1797.
Phil 9351.7.2   Lady's pocket library. Philadelphia, 1792.
Phil 9351.7.4   Lady's pocket library. 4th ed. Philadelphia, 1809.
Htn Phil 9351.8*A   Letters from an elder to a younger brother. Boston, 1810.
Htn Phil 9351.8*B   Letters from an elder to a younger brother. Boston, 1810.
Phil 9351.9   Le Roup, Hugues. Nos filles qu'en ferons-nous? 5. ed.
                     Paris, 1898.
Phil 9351.10   Lewis, D. Our girls. N.Y., 1871.
Phil 9351.11   Lingard, R. A letter of advice to a young gentleman.
                     N.Y., 1907.
Htn Phil 9351.12*   Lindsley, Philip. Baccalaureaute address.
                     Nashville, 1827.
Phil 9351.13   The ladies' companion...politeness of manners. 2d. ed.
                     Brookfield, 1826.
Phil 9351.14   Llonu, Lastenia Lurriva de. Cartas a mi hijo. Lima, 1919.
Phil 9351.15   Lanfear, (Mrs.). Letters to young ladies on their entrance
                     into the world. London, 1824.
Phil 9351.16.2   Lindsay, A.R.B. What is worth while? N.Y., 1893.
Htn Phil 9352.1*   Mackenzie, G. Moral gallantry. Edinburgh, 1669.
                     2 pam.
Phil 9352.1.5   Mackenzie, G. Moral gallantry. London, 1685.
Htn Phil 9352.2*   Mather, C. Daughters of Zion. n.p., 1691?
Phil 9352.4   Moore, J.H. Young gentleman and lady's monitor.
                     London, 1794.
Phil 9352.5   Muzzey, A.B. The blade and the ear. Boston, 1865.
Phil 9352.5.4   Muzzey, A.B. The young maiden. Boston, 1840.
Phil 9352.5.5   Muzzey, A.B. The young maiden. Boston, 1841.
Phil 9352.5.6   Muzzey, A.B. The young maiden. London, 1843.
Phil 9352.5.10   Muzzey, A.B. Young man's friend. Boston, 1836.
Phil 9352.5.11   Muzzey, A.B. Young man's friend. Boston, 1838.
Phil 9352.6   My daughter's manual. N.Y., 1837.
Phil 9352.6.7   My son's book. N.Y., 1841.

Phil 9340 - 9365   Ethics - Treatises on special topics - Men and women -
Individual authors (A-Z) - cont.

	Phil 9352.7.3	Marden, O.S. Pushing to the front. Boston, 1895.
	Phil 9352.7.7	Marden, O.S. Pushing to the front. Petersburg, N.Y., 1911.
	Phil 9352.7.15	Marden, O.S. Architects of fate. Boston, 1895.
	Phil 9352.7.17	Marden, O.S. The optimistic life. N.Y., 1907.
	Phil 9352.8.3	Munger, Theodore T. On the threshold. Boston, 1884.
	Phil 9352.8.7	Munger, Theodore T. On the threshold. 26th ed. Boston, 1893.
	Phil 9352.10	Mowry, William A. Talks with my boys. Boston, 1885.
	Phil 9352.10.5	Mowry, William A. Talks with my boys. 5th ed. N.Y., 1909.
	Phil 9352.11	Moxom, P.S. The aim of life. Boston, 1894.
	Phil 9352.12	Mather, Persis (pseud.). The counsels of a worldly godmother. Boston, 1905.
	Phil 9352.13	Manchester, R.E. The Saturday letters. Cuyahoga Falls, 1937.
	Phil 9352.13.5	Manchester, R.E. The Saturday letters. Cuyahoga Falls, 1938.
	Phil 9352.14	Miller, James R. Girls: faults and ideals. N.Y., 1892.
	Phil 9353.1	Newcomb, H. How to be a lady. Boston, 1850.
	Phil 9353.2	Niemeyer, J.F. Vermaechtniss an Helene von ihrem Vater. Bremen, 1794.
	Phil 9353.3	Notes for boys...on morals, mind and manners. London, 1885.
	Phil 9354.1	Olcott, Gage. Meditations of a young man. Boston, 1914.
	Phil 9354.2.5	O'Reilly, B. True men as we need them. 4th ed. N.Y., 1882.
	Phil 9355.1	Pilkington, M. A mirror for the female sex. London, 1804.
	Phil 9355.1.2	Pilkington, M. A mirror for the female sex. London, 1798.
Htn	Phil 9355.1.5*	Pilkington, M. A mirror for the female sex. Hartford, 1799.
	Phil 9355.2	Peacham, Henry. The worth of a penny. London, 1667.
	Phil 9355.2.5	Peachman, Henry. The compleat gentleman. London, 1906.
	Phil 9355.2.7	Peacham, Henry. The complete gentleman. N.Y., 1962.
Htn	Phil 9355.2.9*	Peacham, Henry. The truth of our times. London, 1638.
	Phil 9355.2.10	Peacham, Henry. The truth of our times. N.Y., 1942.
	Phil 9355.4	Potter, Horatio. The importance of liberal tastes and good intellectual habits. Troy, N.Y., 1837.
	Phil 9355.5	Pomeroy, Marcus. Sense. N.Y., 1871.
	Phil 9355.6	Purinton, E.E. The triumph of the man who acts. N.Y., 1920.
	Phil 9355.7	Phillips, John H. Old tales and modern ideals. N.Y., 1905.
	Phil 9355.8	Paine, Harriet E. Girls and women. Boston, 1890.
	Phil 9355.9	Park, John Edgar. New horizons. Norton, 1929.
Htn	Phil 9355.10*	Pasquier, N. Le gentilhomme. Paris, 1611. 3 pam.
	Phil 9355.11	A present to youth and young men. Birmingham, Eng., 1891. 2v.
	Phil 9355.12	Parting advice to a youth on leaving his Sunday school. N.Y., 1833.
	Phil 9355.13	Postovoitov, V.K. O kul'ture molodogo rabochego. Moskva, 1960.
	Phil 9357.2	Rozan, C. Le jeune homme. Paris, 1878.
	Phil 9357.3	Readings for young men. Boston, 1859.
	Phil 9357.4	Rowland, James. Ruin and restoration. Albany, 1862.
	Phil 9357.4.2	Rowland, James. Ruin and restoration. Albany, 1860.
	Phil 9357.5	Reed, James. Man and woman, equal but different. Boston, 1870.
	Phil 9357.6	Reclus, Elisée. L'ideal et la jeunesse. Bruxelles, 1894.
	Phil 9357.7	Rudd, John C. A series of discourses...to young men. 2d ed. Auburn, 1831.
	Phil 9357.8.5	Rack, E. Mentor's letters, addresses to youth. 3d ed. Bath, 1778.
X Cg	Phil 9358.1	Sargent, J.A. Letters from a mother...daughter. Boston, n.d.
	Phil 9358.2	Sedgwick, C. Talks with my pupils. N.Y., n.d.
Htn	Phil 9358.2.5*	Sedgwick, C. Means and ends, or Self-training. Boston, 1839.
	Phil 9358.3	Smith, S.R. Words to young gentlemen and ladies. Boston, n.d.
	Phil 9358.4	Strong, J. The times and young men. N.Y., 1901.
Htn	Phil 9358.5*	Scott, William. An essay of drapery. London, 1635.
	Phil 9358.6	Shearer, W.J. Morals and manners. N.Y., 1904.
Htn	Phil 9358.7*	Shannon, F. Discourses...useful for vain modish ladies and their gallants. London, 1696.
Htn	Phil 9358.7.5*	Shannon, F. Several discourses and characters. London, 1689.
	Phil 9358.8.2	Sprague, W.B. Letters to young men. 2d ed. Albany, 1845.
	Phil 9358.9	Saint-Jacques, F. Lettres à Claude. Québec, 1916.
	Phil 9358.10	St. Lambert, J.F. de. Principes des moeurs chez toutes les nations. Paris, 1798. 3v.
Htn	Phil 9358.11*	Sprigg, William. Philosophicall essayes...advises to ladyes. London, 1657.
	Phil 9358.12	Southwick, Solomon. Five lessons for young men. Albany, 1837.
	Phil 9358.13	A present for an apprentice. 3d ed. London, 1807.
	Phil 9358.14	Stearns, Alfred E. The challenge of youth. Boston, 1923.
	Phil 9358.14.5	Stearns, Alfred E. To him that overcometh. Boston, 1935.
	Phil 9358.15.5	Starrett, H.E. (Mrs.). The charm of fine manners. Philadelphia, 1921.
	Phil 9358.16	Strickland, C.J. Stray thoughts. Charlotte, N.C., 1931.
	Phil 9358.17	Seabury, Samuel. Self government and the power of an ideal. n.p., 1931.
	Phil 9358.18	Swan, John N. Four lives. Boston, 1935.
	Phil 9358.19	Semaines Sociales de France. 48th, Reims, 1961. La montée des jeunes dans la communauté des générations. Lyon, 1962.
	Phil 9359.2	Thayer, W.M. Poor girl and true woman. Boston, 1859.
	Phil 9359.3	Thurston, D. Letters from a father to a son. Portland, 1858.
	Phil 9359.4	Todd, J. Hints addressed to the young men of the United States. 2d ed. Northampton, 1845.
Htn	Phil 9359.5*	Trenchfield, C. A cap of gray hairs for a green head. London, 1688.
	Phil 9359.6.5	Holland, Josiah G. Titcomb's letters to young people, single and married. 15th ed. N.Y., 1859.
	Phil 9359.6.25	Holland, Josiah G. Titcomb's letters to young people. 50th ed. N.Y., 1884.
Htn	Phil 9359.7*	Tuke, Thomas. A discourse against painting...of women. London, 1616.
Htn	Phil 9359.7.5*	Tuke, Thomas. A treatise against painting...of men and women. London, 1616.
	Phil 9359.8	Tenow, Elsa. Kärlek och lycka af Elsa Törne, [Pseud.]. Stockholm, 1916.
Htn	Phil 9359.9*	The true conduct of persons of quality. London, 1694.
	Phil 9361.1	Vincent. Les caracteres de l'honnete homme et de l'homme chrestien. Paris, 1690.

Phil 9340 - 9365   Ethics - Treatises on special topics - Men and women -
Individual authors (A-Z) - cont.

	Phil 9361.2	Valenca, Francisco P. de. Instruccam. Lisboa, 1745. 3 pam.
	Phil 9361.3.6	Vertua-Gentile, Anna. Come devo compotarmi? 6. ed. Milano, 1909.
	Phil 9362.1	Weaver, G.S. Hopes and helps for the young. N.Y., 1855.
Htn	Phil 9362.2*	West, J. (Mrs.). Letters to a young lady. N.Y., 1806.
Htn	Phil 9362.2.2*	West, J. (Mrs.). Letters to a young man. Charlestown, 1803.
	Phil 9362.3	Whitman, J. Young lady's aid. Portland, 1845.
	Phil 9362.3.2	Whitman, J. Young lady's aid. 2d ed. Portland, 1839.
	Phil 9362.3.5	Whitman, J. Young man's assistant. Portland, 1838.
	Phil 9362.4	Kendrick, William. Whole duty of woman. Walpole, 1797.
	Phil 9362.4.6	The whole duty of woman. n.p., 1821.
	Phil 9362.5	Wise, D. Young lady's counsellor. N.Y., 1852.
	Phil 9362.5.2	Wise, D. Young man's counsellor. N.Y., 1852.
	Phil 9362.6	Winslow, H. Young man's aid. Boston, 1837.
	Phil 9362.6.2	Winslow, H. Young man's aid. Boston, 1839.
Htn	Phil 9362.8*	Wisdom in miniature. Worcester, 1796.
	Phil 9362.9	Woman's worth; or Hints to raise the female character. N.Y., 1844.
	Phil 9362.10	Woodbury, A. Plain words to young men. Concord, 1858.
Htn	Phil 9362.12*	Waterhoues, E. The gentleman's monitor. London, 1665.
	Phil 9362.13	Waterman, Nixon. The girl wanted. Chicago, 1910.
	Phil 9362.14	Wilson, Calvin D. Making the most of ourselves. Chicago, 1909.
	Phil 9362.15.5	Weininger, Otto. Gedanken über Geschlechtsprobleme. Berlin, 1922.
	Phil 9362.16.5	Wagner, C. Youth. N.Y., 1893.
	Phil 9362.16.6	Wagner, C. Jeunesse. 8e ed. Paris, 1893.
	Phil 9362.17	Weston, S.A. Social and religious problems and young people. N.Y., 1934.
	Phil 9362.18.5	Wakefield, P. Bell (Mrs.). Leisure hours. 3d ed. London, 1798-1801. 2v.
	Phil 9362.19	Watts, Alan W. Nature, man and woman. N.Y., 1958.
	Phil 9362.20	Wylie, Max. Career girl, watch your step. N.Y., 1964.
	Phil 9364.1	Young lady's own book. Philadelphia, 1832.
	Phil 9364.1.3	Young lady's own book. Philadelphia, 1842.
	Phil 9364.2.6	Young man's own book. Philadelphia, 1833.
	Phil 9364.3	Young lady's Sunday book. Philadelphia, 1834.
	Phil 9364.4	The youth's guide. Worcester, 1836.
	Phil 9364.5	The young husband's book. Philadelphia, 1839.

Phil 9375   Ethics - Treatises on special topics - Merchants

	Phil 9375.1	Hints to young trademen. Boston, 1838.
	Phil 9375.2	Hunt, F. Worth and wealth. N.Y., 1857.
	Phil 9375.3.2	Pomeroy, R.W. The young merchant. 2d ed. Boston, 1840.
	Phil 9375.4	Hillard, G.S. Dangers and duties of the mercantile profession. Boston, 1850.
	Phil 9375.5	Platt, J. Business. London, 1876.
	Phil 9375.6	Wood, H.A.W. Money hunger. N.Y., 1908.
	Phil 9375.7	Mis'c., or Sundry discourses concerning trade. London, 1712.

Phil 9380   Ethics - Treatises on special topics - Morale

	Phil 9380.01	Pamphlet box. Philosophy. Morale.
	Phil 9380.02	Pamphlet box. Philosophy. Morale.
	Phil 9380.1	Munson, E.L. The management of men. N.Y., 1921.
	Phil 9380.2A	Glover, E. The psychology of fear and courage. Harmondsworth, Eng., 1940.
	Phil 9380.2B	Glover, E. The psychology of fear and courage. Harmondsworth, Eng., 1940.
	Phil 9380.3	American Psychiatric Association. Military Mobilization Committee. Psychiatric aspects of civilian morale. N.Y., 1942.
	Phil 9380.4	Nash, Jay Bryan. Building morale. N.Y., 1942.
	Phil 9380.5A	Society for the Psychological Study of Social Issues. Civilian morale. N.Y., 1942.
	Phil 9380.5B	Society for the Psychological Study of Social Issues. Civilian morale. N.Y., 1942.
	Phil 9380.6	MacCurdy, J.T. The structure of morale. Cambridge, Eng., 1943.
	Phil 9380.7	Harvard University. Department of Psychology. Worksheets on morale. Cambridge, 1943.
	Phil 9380.8	Miller, D.C. The morale of adults. Thesis. Menasha, Wis., 1940.
	Phil 9380.9	English, Raymond. The pursuit of purpose. London, 1947.
	Phil 9380.10	Hurvich, L.M. Beginnings of a bibliography on psychological factors in morale. n.p., n.d.

Phil 9390   Ethics - Treatises on special topics - Oaths and swearing

	Phil 9390.01	Pamphlet box. Philosophy. Oaths.
Htn	Phil 9390.1*	Herport, B. Essay on truths of importance. London, 1768.
Htn	Phil 9390.1.2*	Herport, B. Essay on truths of importance. London, 1768.
	Phil 9390.2	Lewis, E. Dissertation on oaths. Philadelphia, 1838.
	Phil 9390.2.5	Lewis, E. Observations on legal and judicial oaths. v.1-2. Philadelphia, 1846-59.
	Phil 9390.6	Douglas, Robert. Observations on the nature of oaths. Edinburgh, 1783.
	Phil 9390.8	Huad en falsk eed alvorlig oc forfaerlig betyde effter som den hellige scrifft udviser. n.p., 1605.
	Phil 9390.9 ⁻	The wickedness of a disregard of oaths. London, 1723.
Htn	Phil 9390.10*	A warning to sinners. London, 1660.
	Phil 9390.12	Bauernfeind, O. Eid und Frieden. Stuttgart, 1956.
	Phil 9390.14	Hoffman, H.B. Loyalty by oath. Wallingford, 1957.

Phil 9400   Ethics - Treatises on special topics - Old age

	Phil 9400.01	Pamphlet box. Philosophy. Old age.
	Phil 9400.1	Bernard, T. Spurinna...comforts of old age. London, 1816.
Htn	Phil 9400.1.3*	Bernard, T. Comforts of old age. N.Y., 1818.
	Phil 9400.1.4	Bernard, T. Comforts of old age. London, 1820.
	Phil 9400.2	Paine, Harriet E. Old people. Boston, 1910.
	Phil 9400.3	Bishop, E.M. Seventy years young. N.Y., 1907.
	Phil 9400.4A	Lionberger, I.H. The felicities of sixty. Boston, 1922.
	Phil 9400.4B	Lionberger, I.H. The felicities of sixty. Boston, 1922.
	Phil 9400.5	Lathrop, S.G. Fifty years and beyond. Chicago, 1881.
	Phil 9400.6	Peabody, F.G. The privileges of old age. Cambridge, 1931.
	Phil 9400.7	Vorse, M.H. (Mrs.). Autobiography of an elderly woman. Boston, 1911.
	Phil 9400.8	Brigham, H. The youth of old age. Boston, 1934.
	Phil 9400.9	Poweys, J.C. The art of growing old. London, 1944.
	Phil 9400.10	Perry, Ralph B. Plea for an age movement. N.Y., 1942.
	Phil 9400.11	Flake, A. Life at eighty as I see it. Nashville, 1945.
	Phil 9400.12	De Gruchy, C. Creative old age. San Francisco, 1946.
	Phil 9400.13	Lawton, George. Aging successfully. N.Y., 1946.
	Phil 9400.14	Industrial Relations Research Association. The aged and society. Champaign, 1950.

9400   Ethics - Treatises on special topics - Old age - cont.

Phil 9400.15   American Academy of Political and Social Science, Philadelphia. Social contribution by the aging. Philadelphia, 1952.

Phil 9400.16   Buckley, J.C. The retirement handbook. 1st ed. N.Y., 1953.

Phil 9400.17   United States. Federal Security Agency. Committee on Aging and Geriatrics. Fact book on aging. Washington, D.C., 1952.

Phil 9400.18   Heller, Edward. Spiegel des Altes. Affoltern, 1956.

Phil 9400.20   Smith, E.S. The dynamics of aging. 1st ed. N.Y., 1956.

Phil 9400.22   New York (State). Legislature. Joint Committee on Problems for the Aging. New channels for the golden years. Albany? 1956.

Phil 9400.23   Cavan, R.S. Personal adjustments in old age. Chicago, 1949.

Phil 9400.25   Pax, Schweyerische Lebensmensecherungsgesellschaft, Basel. Der Weg, ins Altern. Basel, 1958.

Phil 9400.26   Gonçalves Viana, Mário. Psicologia da maturidade e da velhice. Porto, 196-.

Phil 9400.27   Bartholody, E Mendelssohn. Der Lebensabend. 1. Aufl. Gütersloh, 1958.

Phil 9400.30   Blanton, S. Now or never. Englewood Cliffs, N.J., 1959.

Phil 9400.35   Wijngaarden, H.M. Hoofdproblemen der volwassenheid. Utrecht, 1950.

Phil 9400.40   Pennsylvania. Governor's White House Conference Committee on Aging. Subcommittee reports. Harrisburg, 1960.

Phil 9400.41   Williams, R.H. Processes of aging. N.Y., 1963. 2v.

Phil 9400.45   Brøndsted, Holger Valdemar. Tanker til overvejelse for os aeldre. København, 1969.

9410   Ethics - Treatises on special topics - Optimism

Phil 9410.1   Duboc, K.J. Der Optimismus als Weltanschauung. Bonn, 1881.

Phil 9410.2   Keller, Helen. Optimism. N.Y., 1903.

Phil 9410.3   Prantl, Carl von. Uber die Berechtigung des Optimismus. München, 1879.

Phil 9410.5.3   Loomis, Charles. The knack of it. 2. ed. N.Y., 1908.

Phil 9410.6.2   Landesmann, H. Der grundlose Optimismus. Dresden, 1897.

Phil 9410.7   Lovejoy, Arthur O. Optimism and romanticism. n.p., 1927.

Phil 9410.8   Nutrimento, L. La definizione del bene in relazione al problema dell'ottimismo. Padova, 1936.

Phil 9410.9   Sarrazin, N.J. Le véritable optimisme. Nancy, 18- ?

9415   Ethics - Treatises on special topics - Pain and suffering

Phil 9415.5   Mueller-Lyer, Franz. Soziologie der Leiden. München, 1914.

Phil 9415.10   Rowley, Harold H. Submission in suffering. Cardiff, 1942.

Phil 9415.12   Wilds, Louis T. Why good people suffer. Richmond, Va., 1944.

Phil 9415.14   Bowker, John. Problems of suffering in religions of the world. Cambridge, 1970.

9420   Ethics - Treatises on special topics - Passions

Phil 9420.1*   Bragge, F. A practical treatise...regulation...passions. London, 1708.

Phil 9420.2   Cogan, T. A treatise on the passions and affections of the mind. v.2-5. v.1 lost. London, 1813. 4v.

Phil 9420.2.5   Cogan, T. Philosophical treatise...passions. v.1-2. Bath, 1802.

Phil 9420.2.6   Cogan, T. Philosophical treatise...passions. v.1-2. London, 1813.

Phil 9420.2.7   Cogan, T. Philosophical treatise...passions. v.1-2. Boston, 1821.

Phil 9420.2.9   Cogan, T. An ethical treatise...passions. Bath, 1807-10. 2v.

Phil 9420.3   Enquiry into the origin of the human appetites and affections. Lincoln, 1747.

Phil 9420.4   Schneider, G.H. Freud und Leid des Menschengeschlechte. Stuttgart, 1883.

Phil 9420.5   Essais sur les passions et sur leurs caracteres. v.2. La Haye, 1748.

Phil 9420.6   Carrau, L. Théorie des passions. Strasbourg, 1870.

Phil 9420.7   Walters, H.G. The wisdom of passion. Boston, 1901.

Phil 9420.8   Gardair, J. Philosophie de Saint Thomas. Les passions et la volonté. Paris, 1892.

Phil 9420.9   Thiroux d'Arconville, M. Des passions. Londres, 1764.

Phil 9420.10   Siegfried, R. Lettres et discours sur les passions. Paris, 1925.

Phil 9420.11   Pensieri di un solitario. Torino, 1826.

Phil 9420.12   Lewis, C.S. The four loves. London, 1960.

Phil 9420.13   Plack, A. Die Stellung der Liebe. Landshut, 1962.

9425   Ethics - Treatises on special topics - Peace

Phil 9425.5   Ironside, Henry A. The way of peace. N.Y., 1940.

Phil 9425.10   Wollgast, Siegfried. Zur Friedensidee in der Reformationszeit. Berlin, 1968.

9430   Ethics - Treatises on special topics - Pessimism

L Phil 9430.1   Bacmeister, A. Der Pessimismus und die Sittenlehre. Gütersloh, 1882.

Phil 9430.2   Bourchenin, D. La trace du pessimisme dans la société. Paris, 1892.

Phil 9430.3   Caro, E.M. Le pessimisme au XIX siècle. 4. éd. Paris, 1889.

Phil 9430.3.1   Caro, E.M. Le pessimisme au XIX siècle. 2. éd. Paris, 1880.

Phil 9430.3.2   Caro, E.M. El pesimismo en el siglo XIX. Madrid, 1878.

Phil 9430.3.10   Caro, E.M. Pessimismen i nittonde arhundradet. Stockholm, 1880.

Phil 9430.4   Huber, J.W. Der Pessimismus. München, 1876.

Phil 9430.5   Plümacher, O. Der Pessimismus. Heidelberg, 1888.

Phil 9430.6   Küssner, G. Kritk des Pessimismus. Halle, 1888.

Phil 9430.7   Barlow, J.W. The ultimatum of pessimism. London, 1882.

Phil 9430.8   Lloyd, R.J. Pessimism, a study in contemporary sociology. Liverpool, 1880.

Phil 9430.9   Rehmke, J. Der Pessimismus und die Sittenlehre. Leipzig, 1882.

Phil 9430.10.4   Saltus, Edgar. The philosophy of disenchantment. N.Y., 1885.

Phil 9430.10.10 Saltus, Edgar. The anatomy of negation. N.Y., 1925?

Phil 9430.11   Schädelin, K.F.E. Der moderne Pessimismus. Bern, 1878.

Phil 9430.12   Sully, J. Pessimism. London, 1877.

Phil 9430.12.2   Sully, J. Pessimism. 2. ed. N.Y., 1891.

Phil 9430.13   Trautz, D. Pessimismus. Karlsruhe, 1876.

Phil 9430.14   Weygoldt, G.P. Kritik des philosophischen Pessimismus der neuesten Zeit. Leiden, 1875.

Phil 9430   Ethics - Treatises on special topics - Pessimism - cont.

Phil 9430.15   Hartsen, F.A. von. Die Moral des Pessimismus. Leipzig, n.d.

Phil 9430.15.5   Hartsen, F.A. von. Die Moral des Pessimismus. Nordhausen, 1874.

Phil 9430.16   Taubert, A. Der Pessimismus. Berlin, 1873.

Phil 9430.17   Paulsen, F. Schopenhauer und Naturgeschichte des Pessimismus. Berlin, 1900.

Phil 9430.18   Jordan, D.S. The philosophy of despair. San Francisco, 1902.

Phil 9430.21   Vögele, Albert. Der Pessimismus und das Tragische in Kunst und Leben. Freiburg, 1910.

Phil 9430.22   Palante, Georges. Pessimisme et individualisme. Paris, 1914.

Phil 9430.23   Scheffer, Wessel. Het wijsgeerig pessimisme van den jongstentijd. Leiden, 1875.

Phil 9430.24.2   Sommer, Hugo. Der Pessimismus und der Sittenlehre. Berlin, 1883.

Phil 9430.25   Wentscher, M. Über den Pessimismus und seine Wurzeln. Bonn, 1877.

Phil 9430.26   Goldschmidt, Kurt Walter. Der Wert des Lebens. Berlin, 1908.

Phil 9430.27   Voigt, G. Der moderne Pessimismus. Heilbronn, 1889.

Phil 9430.28   Jouvin, Léon. Le pessimisme. Paris, 1892.

Phil 9430.29   Golther, L. von. Der moderne Pessimismus. Leipzig, 1878.

Phil 9430.30   Gass, W. Optimismus und Pessimismus. Berlin, 1876.

Phil 9430.31   Weng, Gustav. Schopenhauer-Darwin, Pessimismus oder Optimismus? Berlin, 1911.

Phil 9430.32   Stein, Ludwig. Evolution and optimism. N.Y., 1926.

Phil 9430.33   Petraschek, K.O. Die Rechtsphilosophie des Pessimismus. München, 1929.

Phil 9430.34   Lacy, B.F. Pessimism. Philadelphia, 1920.

Phil 9430.35   Marcuse, L. Pessimismus. Hamburg, 1953.

Phil 9430.36   Zdziechowski, M. Pessymizm romantyzm a podstawy chrześcijaństwa. v.1-2. Krakow, 1915.

Phil 9435   Ethics - Treatises on special topics - Poverty

Phil 9435.2   Bok, Edward. Why I believe in poverty. Boston, 1915.

Phil 9440   Ethics - Treatises on special topics - Professional ethics

Phil 9440.1   Med ideali in resniônostjo. Ljubljana, 1970.

Phil 9450   Ethics - Treatises on special topics - Public morals

Phil 9450.1   Lieber, F. Manual of political ethics. Boston, 1838-39. 2v.

Phil 9450.1.2   Lieber, F. Manual of political ethics. Boston, 1839. 2v.

Phil 9450.2   Matter, J. De l'influence des moeurs sur le lois. Paris, 1832.

Phil 9450.3   Harcourt, W.G.G.V.V. The morality of public men. London, 1852.

Phil 9450.3.2   Harcourt, W.G.G.V.V. The morality of public men. 2. ed. London, 1853.

Phil 9450.4   Ruemelin, G. Politics, and the moral law. N.Y., 1901.

Phil 9450.5   Ferencz I Rakoczi, Prince of Transylvania. Testament politique et moral. La Haye, 1751.

Phil 9450.6   Post, Louis F. Ethics of democracy. N.Y., 1903.

Phil 9450.7   Hadley, A.T. Standards of public morality. N.Y., 1907.

Phil 9450.8   Coit, S. Ethical democracy. London, 1900.

Phil 9450.9   Christensen, A. Politics and crowd-morality. London, 1915.

Phil 9450.9.5   Christensen, A. Politik og massemoral. København, 1911.

Phil 9450.10   Pensa, Henri. De la morale politique. Paris, 1910.

Phil 9450.11   Martin, Félix. La morale républicaine. Paris, 1912.

Phil 9450.12   Deschamps, Louis. Principes de morale sociale. Paris, 1903.

Phil 9450.14   Cook, Silas A. The essence and the ethics of politics. N.Y., 1915.

Phil 9450.15   Trattato sulla unione della morale colla politica. Torino, 1846.

Phil 9450.16   Joad, C.E.M. Guide to the philosophy of morals and politics. N.Y., 1938.

Phil 9450.17   Joklík, J. Naše dějinné poslání; čaovas úvaha politicko-ethická. Praha, 1919?

Phil 9450.18   Oppler, A.C. Ethics in public administration. Cambridge, 1942.

Phil 9450.20   Gogartin, F. Politische Ethik. Jena, 1932.

Phil 9450.22   Simon, Yves. Community of the free. N.Y., 1947.

Phil 9450.23   Claparède, Edouard. Morale et politique. Neuchâtel, 1947.

Phil 9450.24   Money-Kyrle, R.E. Psychoanalysis and politics. N.Y., 1951.

Phil 9450.25   Künneth, W. Politik zwischen Dämon und Gott. 1. Aufl. Berlin, 1954.

Phil 9450.26   Pieper, J. Über del Gerechtigkeit. München, 1953.

Phil 9450.27   Freund, Ludwig. Politik und Ethik. Frankfurt, 1955.

Phil 9450.27.2   Freund, Ludwig. Politik und Ethik. 2. Aufl. Gütersloh, 1961.

Phil 9450.28   Schneider, H.W. Three dimensions of public morality. Bloomington, Ind., 1956.

Phil 9450.30   Northrop Filmer, Stuart C. The complexity of legal and ethical experience. 1. ed. Boston, 1959.

Phil 9450.32   Union Internationale d'Études Sociales. Code de morale politique. Bruxelles, 1957.

Phil 9450.35   Selekman, Sylvia Kopald. Power and morality in a business society. N.Y., 1956.

Phil 9450.40   Speer, James. For what purpose? Washington, 1960.

Phil 9450.45   Nitze, P.H. The recovery of ethics. N.Y., 1960.

Phil 9450.50   Gordis, R. Politics and ethics. Santa Barbara, Calif., 1961.

Phil 9450.55   Freyer, Hans. Pallas athene. Jena, 1935.

Phil 9450.56   López Aranguren, J.L. Etica y política. Madrid, 1963.

Phil 9450.57   Tri-ennial Congress of the International Union for the Protection of Public Morality, 3rd, London, 1961. International public morals. Rushden, 1951?

Phil 9450.58   Inglis, B. Private conscience - public mortality. London, n.d.

Phil 9450.59   Chiavacci, Enrico. Etica politica. Roma, 1964.

Phil 9450.60   Schmölz, Franz Martin. Chance und Dilemma der politischen Ethik. Köln, 1966.

Phil 9450.61   Rus, Vojan. Kultura, politika in morala. Maribor, 1969.

Phil 9450.62   Hauser, Richard. Was des Kaisers ist. 1. Aufl. Frankfurt, 1968.

Phil 9450.64   Wendland, Heinz Dietrich. Politik und Ethik. Darmstadt, 1969.

Phil 9450.66   Hamelin, Jacques. Entretiens sur la justice contemporaire. Paris, 1970.

Phil 9450.68   Haring, Philip S. Political morality; a general theory of politics. Cambridge, Mass., 1970.

Phil 9455 Ethics - Treatises on special topics - Public opinion

Phil 9455.4 Lowell, A.L. Public opinion in war and peace. Cambridge, 1923.
Phil 9455.5 Lewis, G.C. An essay on the influence of authority in matters of opinion. London, 1894.
Phil 9455.7 Metcalf, Thomas. An address to the Phi Beta Kappa Society of Brown University, Sept. 5, 1832. Boston, 1833.
Phil 9455.8 Howe, M.A. de Wolfe. Public opinion,...an oration...Connecticut Beta of Phi Beta Kappa Society, July 28, 1852. Hartford, 1852.
Phil 9455.12 Wright, Quincy. Public opinion and world politics. Chicago, 1933.
Phil 9455.17 Rühlmann, Paul. Kulturpropaganda. Charlottenburg, 1919.
Phil 9455.20 Gallup, G.H. A guide to public opinion polls. Princeton, 1944.

Phil 9470 Ethics - Treatises on special topics - Responsibility

Phil 9470.1 Wayland, F. The limitations of human responsibility. Boston, 1838.
Phil 9470.1.2 Wayland, F. The limitations of human responsibility. N.Y., 1838.
Phil 9470.2 Lévy-Bruhl, L. L'idée de responsabilité. Paris, 1884.
Phil 9470.3 Oliveira Guimarães, José Joaquim d'. De morali responsabilitate. Conimbrigae, 1901.
Phil 9470.4 Taylor, Isaac. Man responsible for his dispositions, opinions, and conduct. London, 1840.
Phil 9470.5 Wieschedel, W. Versuch über das Wesen der Verantwortung. Inaug. Diss. Heppenheim, 1932.
Phil 9470.6 Jordan, Rudolf. Homo sapiens socialis, principles of the philosophy of responsibility. Johannesburg, 1944.
Phil 9470.8 Sears, L. Responsibility. N.Y., 1932.
Phil 9470.10 Semerari, Giuseppe. Responsabilitá e comunitá umana. Manduria, 1960.
Phil 9470.12 Roberts, Moira. Responsibility and practical freedom. Cambridge, Eng., 1965.
Phil 9470.14 Fingarette, Herbert. On responsibility. N.Y., 1967.
Phil 9470.16 Ingarden, Roman. Über die Verantwortung. Stuttgart, 1970.

Phil 9480 Ethics - Treatises on special topics - Ridicule

Phil 9480.1 Gay, M.F.S. Physiologie du ridicule. Bruxelles, 1833.

Phil 9490 Ethics - Treatises on special topics - Scholars

Phil 9490.1 Adams, C.K. The present obligations of the scholar. Madison, Wis., 1897.
Phil 9490.2 Olney, R. The scholar in politics. Philadelphia, 1896.
Phil 9490.3 Curtis, G.W. The public duty of educated men. Albany, N.Y., 1878.
Phil 9490.5 Tucker, W.J. Personal power counsels to college men. Boston, 1910.
Phil 9490.6 Forbes, W.C. Letter to an undergraduate. n.p., 1904.
Phil 9490.7.2 Hart, J.S. Mistakes of educated men. Philadelphia, 1862.
Phil 9490.8 Eliot, C.W. The training for an effective life. Boston, 1915.
Phil 9490.9 Trisca, P.C. Die Pflichten der Intelligenten. Jena, 1911.
Phil 9490.10 Osler, W. A way of life. London, 1918.
Phil 9490.15 Vaz Ferreira, C. Moral para intelectuales. La Plata, 1957.
Phil 9490.20 Frye, Northrop. The morality of scholarship. Ithaca, 1967.

Phil 9495 Ethics - Treatises on special topics - Sexual ethics. (By date, e.g. .160 for 1960)

Phil 9495.01 Pamphlet vol. Ethics. Sexual.
Phil 9495.1.8 Stall, Sylvanus. What a young boy ought to know. Philadelphia, 1897.
Phil 9495.2 Lyttelton, E. Training of the young in laws of sex. London, 1900.
Phil 9495.3.2 Sperry, L.B. Confidential talks with young men. N.Y., 1892.
Phil 9495.4.5 Warren, M.A. Almost fourteen. N.Y., 1897.
Phil 9495.5 Willson, R.N. Social evil in university life. N.Y., 1904.
Phil 9495.5.6 Wilson, Robert N. The American boy and the social evil. Philadelphia, 1905.
Phil 9495.8 Drossbach, M. Objecte der sinnlichen Wahrnehmung. Halle, 1865.
Phil 9495.9 Portland (Oregon). Social Hygiene Society. Annual report. Portland, Ore. 1-4
Phil 9495.10 Willard, E.O.G. (Mrs.). Sexology as philosophy of life. Chicago, 1867.
X Cg Phil 9495.11 Hall, W.S. Biological, physiological and sociological reproduction, also sexual hygiene. 14. ed. Chicago, 1913.
Phil 9495.12 Friedlander, B. Die liebe Platons. Berlin, 1909.
Phil 9495.14 Foerster, F.W. Marriage and the sex problem. N.Y., n.d.
Phil 9495.14.2 Foerster, F.W. Marriage and the sex problem. London, 1911.
Phil 9495.15.4 Storer, H.R. Is it D? A book for every man. Boston, 1867.
Phil 9495.16 Colom, P.M. La chasteté. Paris, 1847.
Phil 9495.17 Fowler, O.S. Love and parentage. N.Y., 1855.
Phil 9495.17.15 Fowler, O.S. Private lectures on perfect men, women and children. N.Y., 1880.
Phil 9495.18.5 Fowler, O.S. The physiology of marriage. Boston, 1860.
Phil 9495.20.2 Ware, J. Hints to young men. Boston, 1879.
Phil 9495.21 Karsch-Haach, F. Das gleichgeschlechtliche Leben der Naturvölker. München, 1911.
Phil 9495.22 Foster, W.T. The social emergency. Boston, 1914.
Phil 9495.23 International Congress on School Hygiene, 4th, Buffalo, 1913. Report of sex education sessions. N.Y., 1913.
Phil 9495.24 New York. Homeopathic Medical Society. Communication on Public Education. Second communication. Albany? 1905.
Phil 9495.25 Woodruff, C.S. Legalized prostitution. Boston, 1862.
Phil 9495.27 Cansinos Assens, Rafael. Etica y estética de los sexos. Madrid, 1920.
Phil 9495.28 Exner, M.J. The physician's answer. N.Y., 1913.
Phil 9495.28.5 Exner, M.J. Problems and principles of sex education. N.Y., 1915.
Phil 9495.29 Ellis, Havelock. Essays in war-time. 1st series. Boston, 1917.
Phil 9495.29.5 Ellis, Havelock. The philosophy of conflict. 2nd series. London, 1919.
Phil 9495.29.10 Ellis, Havelock. The philosophy of conflict. 2nd series. Boston, 1919.
Phil 9495.30 Public Morals Conference, London, 1910. The nation's morals. London, 1910.
Phil 9495.33 Debreyne, P.J.C. Moechialogie, traité des péchés contre les sixième et neuvième commandements du décalogue. 4th ed. Paris, 1868.
Htn Phil 9495.35* Robie, W.F. Rational sex ethics. Boston, 1916.

Phil 9495 Ethics - Treatises on special topics - Sexual ethics. (By date, e.g. .160 for 1960) - cont.

Phil 9495.35.15 Macfadden, B.A. The virile powers of superb manhood. London, 1896.
Htn Phil 9495.36* Symonds, J.A. A problem in modern ethics. London, 1896.
Phil 9495.37 Young Women's Christian Association, United States. National Board. War Council Work. Social Morality Committee. Report...Je. 1917 to Jl. 1919. N.Y.? 1919?
Phil 9495.37.15 National Council of Public Morals for Great and Greater Britain. Campaigns of peace. N.Y., 1919.
Htn Phil 9495.38* Drouet de Maupertny, J. Le commerce dangereux entre les deux sexes. Bruxelles, 1715.
Phil 9495.39 Northcote, Hugh. Christianity and sex problems. 2d ed. Philadelphia, 1916.
Phil 9495.39.5 Northcote, Hugh. Christianity and sex problems. Philadelphia, 1906.
Phil 9495.40 Chauvin, A. De la préservation morale de l'enfant. Paris, 1912.
Phil 9495.41 Revue de morale sociale. Paris. 1899-1903 4v.
Phil 9495.42 Oregon Social Hygiene Society. Bulletin. Portland.
Phil 9495.43 Forel, Auguste. Sexuelle Ethik. München, 1908.
Phil 9495.68 Grindon, Leopold Hartley. The sexuality of nature. Boston, 1868.
Phil 9495.72 The truth about love. N.Y., 1872.
Phil 9495.115 Dourães Castro. O racionalismo atrevido do Snr. Frederico de Ancede. Porto, 1915.
Phil 9495.120 United States. Public Health Service. Fighting venereal diseases. Washington, 1920.
Phil 9495.123 Royden, A.M. Sex and common-sense. N.Y., 1922.
Phil 9495.124 Stockham, A.B. (Mrs.). Karezza, ethics of marriage. Chicago, 1903.
X Cg Phil 9495.124.2 Stockham, A.B. (Mrs.). Karezza, ethics of marriage. Chicago, 1898.
X Cg Phil 9495.125 Bloch, Iwan. The sexual life of our time. London, 1910?
Htn Phil 9495.126* Lawrence, D.H. Pornography and obscenity. N.Y., 1930.
Phil 9495.127 Dennett, M.W. (Mrs.). Who's obscene? N.Y., 1930.
Phil 9495.127.5 Hildebrand, Dietrich von. Reinheit und Jungfräulichkeit. Köln, 1927.
Phil 9495.127.6 Hildebrand, Dietrich von. In defence of purity. Chicago, 1920.
X Cg Phil 9495.127.15 Dennett, M.W. (Mrs.). The sex side of life; an explanation for young people. Astoria, 1928.
Phil 9495.128 Wylm, Antoine. La morale sexuelle. Paris, 1907.
Phil 9495.129 Muller, J.P. Kønsmoral og livslykke. 3. opl. København, 1910.
Phil 9495.130 Schmalhausen, S.D. Why we misbehave. Garden City, N.Y., 1928.
Phil 9495.130.7 Schmalhausen, S.D. Why we misbehave. N.Y., 1929.
Phil 9495.130.10 Kolnai, Aurel. Sexualethik. Paderborn, 1930.
Phil 9495.131 Sicard de Plauzales, J. La fonction sexuelle au point de vue de l'éthique et de l'hygiène sociales. Paris, 1908.
Phil 9495.132 Wexberg, Erwin. The psychology of sex. N.Y., 1931.
Phil 9495.133.5 Weatherhead, L.D. Mastery of sex through psychology and religion. 2d ed. London, 1931.
Phil 9495.133.10 Weatherhead, L.D. Mastery of sex through psychology and religion. N.Y., 1934.
Phil 9495.134 Newsom, G.E. The new morality. N.Y., 1933.
Phil 9495.135.5 Buschke, A. Sex habits. N.Y., 1933.
Phil 9495.138 Cabot, R.C. The Christian approach to social morality. N.Y., 1913.
Phil 9495.138.5 Cabot, R.C. Christianity and sex. N.Y., 1937.
Phil 9495.139 Galloway, T.W. Sex and life. N.Y., 1920.
X Cg Phil 9495.141 Hitschmann, E. Frigidity in women. Washington, 1936.
Phil 9495.142 Wolf, J. Die neue Sexualmoral und das Geburtenproblem unserer Tage. Jena, 1928.
Phil 9495.143 Walton, A.H. New vistas...religion, sex and morals. London, 1943.
Phil 9495.146 Dawson, C. Christianity and sex. London, 1930.
Phil 9495.148 Comfort, A. Barbarism and sexual freedom. London, 1948.
Phil 9495.149 Glasgow, M. Problems of sex. Boston, 1949.
Phil 9495.154 Kardiner, A. Sex and morality. 1st ed. Indianapolis, Ind., 1954.
Phil 9495.155 Langdon Davies, J. Sex, sin and sanity. London, 1954.
Phil 9495.155.5 Zenkovskii, V.V. Na poroge zrelosti. 2. izd. Parizh, 1955.
Phil 9495.155.10 Williamson, Geoffrey. Morality fair. London, 1955.
Phil 9495.155.15 Cole, William G. Sex in Christianity and psychoanalysis. N.Y., 1955.
Phil 9495.156A Sorokin, P.A. The American sex revolution. Boston, 1956.
Phil 9495.156B Sorokin, P.A. The American sex revolution. Boston, 1956.
Phil 9495.159.2 Fuchs, Josef Jesuit. De castitate et ordine sexuali. 2nd ed. Roma, 1960.
Phil 9495.160 Wojtyka, Karol. Milość i odpowiedzialność. Lublin, 1960.
Phil 9495.160.5 Marchi, L. de. Sesso e cività. 2. ed. Bari, 1960.
Phil 9495.160.15 Koehn-Behrens, Charlotte. Eros at bay; the illusion of modern love. London, 1962.
Phil 9495.162.1 Trobisch, Walter. I loved a girl (including I loved a young man); young Africans speak. N.Y., 1965.
Phil 9495.163 Exner, Adam. The amplexus reservatus seen in the history of Catholic doctrine on the use of marriage. Ottawa, 196[illegible]
Phil 9495.163.5 Sexualité et limitation des naissances. Paris, 1963.
Phil 9495.164 Thielicke, H. The ethics of sex. 1st ed. N.Y., 1964.
Phil 9495.164.5 Klomps, H. Ehemoral und Jansenismus. Köln, 1964.
Phil 9495.164.10 Rhymes, D.A. No new morality. Indianapolis, Ind., 1964.
Phil 9495.165 Acland, Richard. Sexual morality. London, 1965.
Phil 9495.166 British Council of Churches. Sex and morality: a report to the British Council of Churches. London, 1966.
Phil 9495.166.5 Aquinas Institute of Philosophy and Theology. Institute of Spiritual Theology. Sex, love and the life of the spirit. Chicago, 1966.
Phil 9495.167 Ryan, Mary Perkins. Love and sexuality. 1st ed. N.Y., 1967.
Phil 9495.167.5 Bjerg, Kresten. Moralpsykologi og sexualmoral. København, 1967.
Phil 9495.167.10 Plack, Arno. Die Gesellschaft und das Böse. München, 1967.
Phil 9495.168 Callahan, Sidney Cornelia. Beyond birth control; the Christian experience of sex. N.Y., 1968.
Phil 9495.168.5 Walker, Brooks R. The new immorality. 1st ed. Garden City, 1968.
Phil 9495.168.10 O'Neil, Robert P. Sexuality and moral responsibility. Washington, 1968.
Phil 9495.168.15 Müller, Michael. Grundlagen der Katholischen Sexualethik. Regensburg, 1968.
Phil 9495.168.20 Evely, Louis. Lovers in marriage. N.Y., 1968.
Phil 9495.168.25 Gagey, Roland. La révolution sexuelle. Paris, 1968.
Phil 9495.168.30 Barra, Giovanni. Castità: problema o liberazione? Torino, 1968.

Classified Listing

Phil 9495   Ethics - Treatises on special topics - Sexual ethics. (By date, e.g. .160 for 1960) - cont.

Phil 9495.169   Schaetzing, Eberhard. Schön wieder ein Aufklärungsbuch? Hamburg, 1969.
Phil 9495.169.5   Trillhaas, Wolfgang. Sexualethik. Göttingen, 1969.
Phil 9495.169.10   Speicher, Günter. Die grossen Tabus. Düsseldorf, 1969.
Phil 9495.170.5   Geets, Claude. Psychanalyse et morale sexuelle. Paris, 1970.
Phil 9495.170.10   Caraco, Albert. L'ordre et le sexe. Lausanne, 1970.
Phil 9495.170.15   Schlegelberger, Bruno. Vor- und ausserehelicher Geschlechtsverkehr. Remscheid, 1970.

Phil 9500   Ethics - Treatises on special topics - Sickness

Phil 9500.1   Martineau, H. Life in the sick-room. Boston, 1844.
Phil 9500.1.2   Martineau, H. Life in the sick-room. 2d American ed. Boston, 1845.
Phil 9500.2   Townsend, F. Mutterings and musings of an invalid. N.Y., 1851.
Phil 9500.3   Anderson, Maggie P. Sick-room thoughts and gleanings. Saint John, N.B., 1897.
Phil 9500.4   Benjamin, F.N. (Mrs.). The sunny side of shadow. Boston, 1887.
Phil 9500.5   Lindenberg, Wladimir. Gespräche am Krankenbett. München, 1959.
Phil 9500.8   Berg, Jan Hendrik van den. The psychology of the sickbed. Pittsburgh, 1966.
Phil 9500.10.5   Hárdi, István. Psychologie am Krankenbett. Budapest, 1968.

Phil 9510   Ethics - Treatises on special topics - Slander

NEDL Phil 9510.1   Opie, A.A. (Mrs.). Detraction displayed. Philadelphia, 1828.
Phil 9510.1.5   Opie, A.A. (Mrs.). Detraction displayed. N.Y., 1828.
Phil 9510.2   Tonna, C.E.B.P. Backbiting. N.Y., 1842. 2 pam.
Htn Phil 9510.3*   Le Mercier, A. A treatise against detraction. Boston, 1733.
Phil 9510.4   Barrow, I. Sermons on evil-speaking. N.Y., 1887.
Htn Phil 9510.5*   Boreman, R. An antidote against swearing. London, 1662.
Phil 9510.6   Colonéri, L.J. La dénonciation et les dénonciateurs. 4. éd. Paris, 1948.

Phil 9513   Ethics - Treatises on special topics - Society, Social ethics

NEDL Phil 9513.1   Dole, C.F. The citizen and the neighbor. Boston, 1884.
Phil 9513.2   Knigge, A. von. Über den Umgang mit Menschen. Pt.1-3. Hildburghausen, 1830.
Phil 9513.2.5   Knigge, A. von. Über den Umgang mit Menschen. 3. Aufl. pt.1-3. Hannover, 1790.
Phil 9513.3   Ross, E.A. Sin and society. Boston, 1907.
Phil 9513.4   Batchelor, George. Social equilibrium. Boston, 1887.
Phil 9513.5   Coleman, George William. Searchlights. Boston, 1910.
Phil 9513.5.5   Coleman, George William. This business of living. Boston, 1936.
Phil 9513.5.6   Coleman, George William. This business of living. Boston, 1936.
Phil 9513.6   Rouger, G. Spécialisation et évolution. Paris, 1935.
Phil 9513.7   Wiese, Leopold von. Ethik in der Schauweise der Wissenschaften. Bern, 1947.
Phil 9513.7.2   Wiese, Leopold von. Ethik in der Schauweise der Wissenschaften. 2. Aufl. Bern, 1960.
Phil 9513.8   Wiese, Leopold von. Das Soziale im Leben und im Denken. Köln, 1956.
Phil 9513.9   Angell, Robert Cooley. Free society and moral crisis. Ann Arbor, 1958.
Phil 9513.12   Fröhlich, C.W. Über den Menschen und seine Verhältnisse. Berlin, 1960.
Phil 9513.14   Sheremetev, Vl.Vl. Dukh vremeni. Shankai, 1937.
Phil 9513.16   Wilson, Matthew Hale. An inductive study of standards of right. Boston, 1916.
Phil 9513.18   Hanis, Robert T. Social ethics. Philadelphia, 1962.
Phil 9513.19   Berg, Ludwig. Sozialethik. München, 1959.
Phil 9513.20   Lopez, Aranguren, José Luis. Moral y sociedad. Madrid, 1965.
Phil 9513.22   Kirche, Bekenntnis und Sozialethos. Genf, 1934.
Phil 9513.25   Carbonara, Cleto. L'esperienza e la prassi. Napoli, 1964.
Phil 9513.30   Niebuhr, Reinhold. Faith and politics. N.Y., 1968.
Phil 9513.35   Huant, Ernest. Masses, morale et machines. Paris, 1967.
Phil 9513.40   Rice, Charles E. The vanishing right to live. 1st ed. Garden City, N.Y., 1969.
Phil 9513.41   Titarenko, Aleksandr I. Nravstvennyi progress. Moskva, 1969.
Phil 9513.42   Lichnost i sotsial'no-nravstvennye otnosheniia vobshchestve. Photoreproduction. Pskov, 1968.
Phil 9513.44   Sozialethik im Umbruch der Gesellschaft. Göttingen, 1969.
Phil 9513.46   Polishchuk, Nina P. Problema moral'noho idealn. Kyív, 1970.
Phil 9513.48   Aukrust, Tor. Mennesket i samfunnet. En sosialetikk. Oslo, 1965-
Phil 9513.50   Angers, France (Diocese). Conferences ecclesiastiques du Diocese d'Angers. Angers, 1737.

Phil 9515   Ethics - Treatises on special topics - Solitude

Phil 9515.1*   Burges, T. Solitude and society contrasted. Providence, 1797.
Phil 9515.2   Alger, W.R. The solitudes of nature and of man. 4. ed. Boston, 1867.
Phil 9515.2.5   Alger, W.R. Solitudes of nature and of man. 5th ed. Boston, 1867.
Phil 9515.3   Zimmermann, J.G. Über die Einsamkeit. Leipzig, 1784-85. 4v.
Phil 9515.3.3   Zimmermann, J.G. Solitude. 2d ed. London, 1792.
Phil 9515.3.5   Zimmermann, J.G. Solitude. Dublin, 1800.
OL Phil 9515.3.6   Zimmermann, J.G. Solitude. London, 1800-02.
Phil 9515.3.6.5   Zimmermann, J.G. Solitude. London, 1800.
Phil 9515.3.7*   Zimmermann, J.G. Solitude. 1st ed. N.Y., 1801.
Phil 9515.3.7.2*   Zimmermann, J.G. Solitude. 1st ed. N.Y., 1801.
Phil 9515.3.8   Zimmermann, J.G. Solitude. v.1-2. Exeter, 1836.
Phil 9515.3.9   Zimmermann, J.G. Solitude. N.Y., 1813.
Phil 9515.3.80   Bahrat, Karl F. Mit dem Herrn [von] Zimmermann. n.p., 1790.
Phil 9515.3.83   Bodemann, E. J.G. Zimmermann. Hannover, 1878.
Phil 9515.3.88   Ischer, Rudolf. J.G. Zimmermann's Leben und Werke. Bern, 1893.
Phil 9515.3.90   Melzer, Friso. J.G. Zimmermann's "Einsamkeit". Inaug. Diss. Breslau, 1930.
Phil 9515.3.95   Maduschka, Leo. Das Problem des Einsamkeit in 18 Jahrhundert. Inaug. Diss. Murnan, 1932.
Phil 9515.3.96   Maduschka, Leo. Das Problem des Einsamkeit in 18 Jahrhundert. Weimar, 1933.
Phil 9515.3.99   Milch, W. Die Einsamkeit. Frauenfeld, 1937.

Phil 9515   Ethics - Treatises on special topics - Solitude - cont.

Htn Phil 9515.4*   Mackenzie, George. Moral essay, preferring solitude to public employment. London, 1685.
Htn Phil 9515.5*   Evelyn, John. Publick employment and active life prefered. London, 1667.
Phil 9515.6   Powys, J.C. A philosophy of solitude. N.Y., 1933.

Phil 9520   Ethics - Treatises on special topics - Sorrow

Phil 9520.1   Gasparin, V.B. Human sadness. London, 1864.
Phil 9520.2.1   Hinton, James. The mystery of pain. London, 1879.
Phil 9520.2.2   Hinton, James. The mystery of pain. Boston, 1886.
Phil 9520.2.3   Hinton, James. The mystery of pain. London, 1866.
Phil 9520.2.5   Hinton, James. The mystery of pain. N.Y., 1914.
Phil 9520.3   Fierens-Gevaert, H. La tristesse contemporaine. Paris, 1899.
Phil 9520.4.8   Keppler, Paul W. Das Problem des Leidens. 8. und 9. Aufl. Freiburg, 1919.

Phil 9528   Ethics - Treatises on special topics - Students

Phil 9528.1   Not in the curriculum. N.Y., 1903.
Phil 9528.2   Miller, S. Letters from a father to his son in college. Philadelphia, 1852.
Phil 9528.3.5A   Gellert, C.F. Instructions from a father to his son. Boston, 1823.
Phil 9528.3.5B   Gellert, C.F. Instructions from a father to his son. Boston, 1823.
Phil 9528.5   Oppermann, W. Schulfeierstunden. Leipzig, 1923.
Phil 9528.6   Cooper, John M. Religion outlines for colleges. Washington, D.C., 1928.

Phil 9530   Ethics - Treatises on special topics - Success

Phil 9530.01   Pamphlet box. Success.
Phil 9530.1   Butler, B.F. How to get rich. Boston, 1888.
Phil 9530.2   Carnegie, A. How to win fortune. N.Y., 1890.
Phil 9530.3   Cleveland, G. The self-made man. N.Y., 1897.
Htn Phil 9530.5*   Franklin, B. The way to wealth. Paris, 1795.
Phil 9530.5.2   Franklin, B. The way to wealth. N.Y., 1848.
Phil 9530.5.5   Franklin, B. Hē epistēmē tou kalou richardou. Paris, 1823.
Phil 9530.8   Schmidt, F.L. An object in life. N.Y., 1889.
Phil 9530.9   Thayer, W.M. Ethics of success. Boston, 1893.
Phil 9530.10   Tilley, W.J. Masters of the situation. Chicago, 1887.
Phil 9530.11   Whipple, E.P. Success and its conditions. Boston, 1880.
Phil 9530.12   Fowler, M.C. The boy! How to help him succeed. Boston, 1902.
Phil 9530.15   Durant, E.E. How to make your mark in life. Boston, 1917.
Phil 9530.17   Rice, Elwood E. Rice leaders of the world association, its inspiration, realization and objects. N.Y., 1914.
Phil 9530.18.4   Bligh, Stanley M. The direction of desire. London, 1910.
Phil 9530.19   Great men being the substance of a lecture. Calcutta, 1868.
Phil 9530.20   Wyckoff, Isaac N. Stability, an indispensable element of usefulness and greatness. Albany, 1840.
Phil 9530.21   Dayton, William L. Address delivered before the American Whig and Cliosophic societies of the college of New Jersey, Sept. 26, 1843. Princeton, 1843.
Phil 9530.22   Babcock, M.D. The success of defeat. N.Y., 1905.
Phil 9530.24   Waterman, Nixon. Boy wanted. Chicago., 1906.
Phil 9530.25   Marden, Orison S. He can who thinks he can. N.Y., 1908.
Phil 9530.25.5   Marden, Orison S. Prosperity, how to attract it. N.Y., 1922.
Phil 9530.25.10   Marden, Orison S. Success. Boston, 1897.
Phil 9530.26   Parlette, R.A. A book of rejoicing, big business. Chicago, 1917.
Phil 9530.27   Lyons, Albert E. The self-starter. Boston, 1924.
Phil 9530.28   Practical wisdom! letters. N.Y., 1902.
Phil 9530.29   Tapper, Thomas. Youth and opportunity. N.Y., 1912.
Phil 9530.31   Pitkin, Walter B. The psychology of achievement. N.Y., 1930.
Phil 9530.31.5   Pitkin, Walter B. Life begins at forty. N.Y., 1932.
Phil 9530.32   Laurie, Ossip. L'arrivisme. Paris, 1929.
Phil 9530.33   Emmel, Paul W. Experience, or A post-graduate course in life. Philadelphia, 1931.
Phil 9530.35   Kleiser, Grenville. How to succeed in life. N.Y., 1934.
Phil 9530.36.5   Beaverbrook, W.M.A. Success. 2. ed. London, 1921.
Phil 9530.36.8   Beaverbrook, W.M.A. The three keys to success. N.Y., 1956.
Phil 9530.37   Alexander, James. Through failure to success. N.Y., 1934.
Phil 9530.38.15   Carnegie, Dale. How to win friends and influence people. N.Y., 1937.
Phil 9530.38.28   Carnegie, Dale. How to win friends and influence people. 28th ed. N.Y., 1937.
Phil 9530.38.50   Roback, A.A. I am winning friends. Cambridge, 1938.
Phil 9530.39.5   Popplestone, C.E. Every man a winner. N.Y., 1936.
Phil 9530.40   Reilly, William J. How to improve your human relations, by straight thinking. N.Y., 1942.
Phil 9530.41   Babson, Roger Ward. Storing up triple reserves. N.Y., 1929.
Phil 9530.42   Ranson, J.C. The successful man. Richmond, 1887.
Phil 9530.43   Barton, Bruce. More power to you. N.Y., 1917.
Phil 9530.44   Platt, C. The essence of success. London, 19- ?
Phil 9530.45.5   Panzer, Martin. It's your future. N.Y., 1943.
Phil 9530.46   Sherman, Ray W. If you want to get ahead. Boston, 1934.
Phil 9530.47   Coffee, John R. Personal achievements. N.Y., 1932.
Phil 9530.48   Friedländer, Max. Wie Rationalisiert man sein Leben. Zürich, 1943?
Phil 9530.50   Halle, L.J. On facing the world. N.Y., 1950.
Phil 9530.52   Orage, A.R. The active mind. N.Y., 1954.
Phil 9530.54   Lebhar, G.M. The use of time. 3. ed. N.Y., 1958.
Phil 9530.55   Lamprecht, H. Erfolg und Gesellschaft. München, 1964.
Phil 9530.56   Ginzberg, Eli. Talent and performance. N.Y., 1964.
Phil 9530.57   Conklin, Bob. The power of a magnetic personality. West Ryack, N.Y., 1965.
Phil 9530.58   Darvas, Nicolas. The anatomy of success. Indianapolis, 1966.
Phil 9530.60.2   Grossmann, Gustav. Meine Daktor-Dissertation...die Revolution der Begabten. 2. Aufl. München, 1964.
Phil 9530.62   Schuller, Robert. Move ahead with possibility thinking. 1. ed. Garden City, 1967.
Phil 9530.65   Getty, Jay Paul. The golden age. N.Y., 1968.
Phil 9530.66   Huber, Richard M. The American idea of success. 1st ed. N.Y., 1971.

Phil 9540   Ethics - Treatises on special topics - Toleration
Phil 9540.1   Van Loon, H.W. Tolerance. N.Y., 1939.
Phil 9540.1.5   Van Loon, H.W. Tolerance. N.Y., 1925.
Phil 9540.1.10   Van Loon, H.W. Tolerance. Garden City, 1927.
Phil 9540.2   Wise, J.W. From bigotry to brotherhood. N.Y., 1953?
Phil 9540.5   Trevelyan, G.M. De haeretico comburendo. Cambridge,
                     Eng., 1914.
Phil 9540.8   Smith, Thomas Vernor. The ethics of compromise and the art
                     of containment. Boston, 1956.
Phil 9540.9   Freie Akademie Nüremberg. Toleranz eine Grundforderung
                     geschichtlicher Existenz. Nürnberg, 1960.
Phil 9540.10   Wolff, Robert Paul. A critique of pure tolerance.
                     Boston, 1965.
Phil 9540.12   Moore, Katharine. The spirit of tolerance. London, 1964.

Phil 9550   Ethics - Treatises on special topics - Utilitarianism
Phil 9550.1   Birks, T.R. Modern utilitarianism. London, 1874.
Phil 9550.2   Grote, J. An examination of the utilitarian philosophy.
                     Cambridge, 1870.
Phil 9550.3   Meinong, A. Psychologisch-ethische Untersuchungen zur
                     Werth-Theorie. Graz, 1874.
Phil 9550.3.5   Meinong, A. Zur Grundlegung der allgemeinen Werth-Theorie.
                     Graz, 1923.
Phil 9550.4   Krueger, F. Der Begriff des Absolut Wertvollen.
                     Leipzig, 1898.
Phil 9550.5   Albee, Ernest. A history of English utilitarianism.
                     London, 1902.
Phil 9550.5.2   Albee, Ernest. A history of English utilitarianism.
                     London, 1957.
Phil 9550.6   Parris, M. Total utility and the economic judgment.
                     Philadelphia, 1909.
Phil 9550.7   Bernard, L.L. Transition to an objective standard of
                     social control. Chicago, 1911.
Phil 9550.8   Mackaye, J. The happiness of nations. N.Y., 1915.
Phil 9550.9   Kaler, Emil. Der Ethik des Utiliarismus. Inaug. Diss.
                     Hamburg, 1885.
Phil 9550.10   Bergmann, Julius. Über den Utilitarianismus.
                     Marburg, 1883.
Phil 9550.11   Carran, Ludovic. La morale utilitaire. Paris, 1875.
Phil 9550.11.5   Cantoni, C. Una critica dell'utilitarismo. Roma, 1876.
Phil 9550.12   Marchesini, G. La teoria dell'utile. Milano, 1900.
Phil 9550.13   Keim, Albert. L'épicurisme, l'ascétisme et la morale
                     utilitaire. Paris, 1924.
Phil 9550.14   Manzoni, A. Del sistema che fonda la morale sull'utilità.
                     Firenze, 1925.
Phil 9550.15A   Bentham, J. Utilitarianism. London, 1890.
Phil 9550.15B   Bentham, J. Utilitarianism. London, 1890.
Phil 9550.16   Plamenatz, J.P. Mills' utilitarianism. Oxford, 1949.
Phil 9550.16.5   Plamenatz, J.P. The English utilitarians. 2. ed.
                     Oxford, 1958.
Phil 9550.17   Ofstad, Harald. Upartiskhet og utilitarisme.
                     Stockholm, 1962.
Phil 9550.18   Lyons, David. Forms and limits of utilitarianism.
                     Oxford, 1965.
Phil 9550.20   Narveson, Jan. Morality and utility. Baltimore, 1967.
Phil 9550.22   Hodgson, D.H. Consequences of utilitarianism.
                     Oxford, 1967.
Phil 9550.24   Rescher, Nicholas. Distributive justice; a constructive
                     critique of the utilitarian theory of distribution.
                     Indianapolis, 1966.

Phil 9558   Ethics - Treatises on special topics - Vice and vices
Phil 9558.01   Pamphlet box. Vices.
Phil 9558.1   Heinroth, J.C.A. Die Lüge. Leipzig, 1834.
Phil 9558.2   Beecher, H.W. Industry and idleness. Philadelphia, 1850.
Phil 9558.2.5   Beecher, H.W. Industry and idleness. Philadelphia, 1896.
Phil 9558.3   Ellinger, G. Verhältniss der offentlichen Meinung zu
                     Wahrheit und Lüge. Berlin, 1884.
Phil 9558.4   Villiers, Pierre. Reflexions sur les défauts d'autruy.
                     Paris, 1904.
Phil 9558.5   Rogues de Fursac, J. L'avarice. Paris, 1911.
Phil 9558.5.10   Relaçam historia das vidas dos avarentos em que se escreve
                     todos os seus costumes vicios. Lisboa, 17- .
Phil 9558.6   An introduction to the art of lying. London, 1744.
Phil 9558.7   Grayson, P.W. Vice unmasked; an essay. N.Y., 1830.
Phil 9558.8   Jakobovits, J. Lüge im Urteil der neuesten deutschen
                     Ethiker. Inaug. Diss. Paderborn, 1914.
Phil 9558.9   Paulhan, F. Les mensonges du caractère. Paris, 1905.
Phil 9558.10   Zyromski, Ernest. L'orgueil humain. 2. éd. Paris, 1905.
Phil 9558.10.5   Payne, Robert. Hubris. N.Y., 1960.
Phil 9558.10.10   Aires Ramos da Silva de Eca, M. Reflexões sobre a vaidade
                     dos homens. Facsimile. Rio de Janeiro, 1921.
Phil 9558.10.12   Aires Ramos da Silva de Eca, M. Reflexões sobre a vaidade
                     dos homens. São Paulo, 1942.
Phil 9558.10.14   Aires Ramos da Silva de Eca, M. Reflexões sobre a vaidade
                     dos homens. Rio de Janeiro, 1962.
Phil 9558.10.15   Grau, Kurt J. Eitelkeit und Schamgefühl. Leipzig, 1928.
Phil 9558.10.20   Payne, R. The wanton nymph. London, 1951.
Phil 9558.11   Walston, C. Truth; an essay in moral reconstruction.
                     Cambridge, 1919.
Phil 9558.12   Wenzel, Siegfried. The sin of sloth. Chapel Hill, 1967.
NEDL Phil 9558.13 Opie, Amelia A. (Mrs.). Illustrations of lying, in all its
                     branches. 2. ed. Boston, 1826.
Phil 9558.14   Küppers, L. Psychologische Untersuchungen über die Lüge.
                     Inaug. Diss. Bedburg-Erft, 1928.
Phil 9558.15   Le Senne, René. Le mensonge et la caractère. Paris, 1930.
Phil 9558.15.2   Le Senne, René. Le mensonge et la caractère. Thèse.
                     Paris, 1930.
Phil 9558.20   Guyon, René. La cruauté. Paris, 1927.
Htn Phil 9558.21* Abaddon's steam engine. Philadelphia, 1817.
Phil 9558.23   Dunn, Ellen Catherine. The concept of ingratitude in
                     renaissance English moral philosophy. These. Washington,
                     D.C., 1946.
Phil 9558.25   Jullian, T. Dictionnaire du snobisme. Paris, 1958.
Phil 9558.27   DuPuy de Clinchamps, Philippe. Le snobisme. Paris, 1964.
Phil 9558.30   Larrañaga, T. De materia gravi in furto apud theologos
                     saeculorum XVI et XVII. Romae, 1960.
Phil 9558.35   Berg, Robert Frederik. Liegen met en zonder opzet.
                     Utrecht, 1961.
Phil 9558.40   Walker, James L. The philosophy of egoism. Denver, 1905.
Phil 9558.41   Van der Schaar, P.J. Dynamik der Pseudologie.
                     München, 1964.
Phil 9558.42   Ludwig, Arnold M. The importance of lying. Springfield,
                     Ill, 1965.
Phil 9558.45   Lipmann, Otto. Die Lüge Sprach- und
                     literaturwissenschaftlicher und entwicklungsgeschichtlicher
                     Betrachtung. Leipzig, 1927.
Phil 9558.48   Kraus, Annie. Über den Hochmut. Frankfurt, 1966.

Phil 9558   Ethics - Treatises on special topics - Vice and vices - cont.
Phil 9558.50   Hallie, Phillip Paul. The paradox of cruelty. 1. ed.
                     Middletown, Conn., 1969.

Phil 9560   Ethics - Treatises on special topics - Virtue and virtues
Phil 9560.01   Pamphlet box. Ethics. Virtues.
Phil 9560.1   De Britaine, W. Human prudence. Dedham, 1806.
Phil 9560.1.5   Essay on prudence, by a lover of peace. n.p., 1839.
Phil 9560.2   Hughes, T. True manliness. Boston, 1880?
Phil 9560.3   Montgomery, G.w. Illustrations of the law of kindness.
                     Utica, 1841.
Phil 9560.4   Morley, C. The power of kindness. N.Y., 1851.
Phil 9560.5   Storrs, R.S. Manliness in the scholar. N.Y., 1883.
Phil 9560.7   Terraillon, E. L'honneur sentiment et principle moral.
                     Paris, 1912.
Phil 9560.7.5   Gay, Antoine. L'honneur, sa place dans la morale.
                     Paris, 1913.
Phil 9560.7.7   Pescetti, Orlando. Dell'onore dialoghi tre. Verona, 1624.
Phil 9560.7.9   Maarse, Jan. Een psychologische en zebekundige studie over
                     de hegrippen eer en eergevoel. Proefschrift.
                     Amsterdam, 1936.
Phil 9560.7.13   Weidauer, F. Die Wahrung der Ehre und die sittliche Tat.
                     Leipzig, 1936.
Phil 9560.8   Stearne, J. De obstinatione. Dublin, 1672.
Phil 9560.9   Tschubrovitz, P. Die Entwicklung der Moraltugenden.
                     Leipzig, 1911.
Phil 9560.10   Courtenay, Charles. The empire of silence. N.Y., 1916.
Phil 9560.10.20   Picard, Max. The world of silence. London, 1948.
Phil 9560.11   Caracciolli, L. De la gaieté. Paris, 1782.
Phil 9560.12   Gardair, J. Philosophie de Saint Thomas. Les passions et
                     la volonté. Paris, 1901.
Phil 9560.13   Robbins, C. Force of right purpose. Boston, 1859.
Phil 9560.14   Fiore di virtù historiato. Vinegia, 1545.
Phil 9560.14.5   Fiore di virtù. Firenze, 1856.
Phil 9560.14.10   Fiore di Virtù. The Florentine Fior di virtù of 1491.
                     Philadelphia, 1953.
Phil 9560.14.18   Cartojan, N. Fiore di virtù in literature româneasca.
                     Bucarsti, 1928.
Phil 9560.14.20   Cartojan, N. Fiore di virtù dans la litterature roamaine.
                     n.p., n.d.
Phil 9560.15   Zuccolo, L. Nobilita commune, et heroica penser nuova é
                     curiosa. Venetia, 1625.
Htn Phil 9560.16* Mackenzie, George. The moral history of frugality.
                     London, 1691.
Htn Phil 9560.17* Baldacchini, F. Dyalogo de patientia. Perosia, 1525.
Htn Phil 9560.18* Nenna, Giovanni B. Il nennio, nel quale si ragiona di
                     nobilita. Colophon, 1542.
Htn Phil 9560.18.5* Nenna, Giovanni B. Nennio, or A treatise of nobility.
                     London, 1595.
Phil 9560.18.6   Nenna, Giovanni B. Nennio, or A treatise of nobility.
                     Facsimile. Jerusalem, 1967.
Phil 9560.19   Rosini, G. Introduzione alle virtù. Firenze, 1810.
Htn Phil 9560.22* Hartcliffe, John. A treatise of moral and intellectual
                     virtues. London, 1691.
Phil 9560.23   Mensing, C. An activity analysis of the four cardinal
                     virtues. Diss. Washington, 1929.
Htn Phil 9560.24* Pasquali, C. Virtutes et vitia. Parisiis, 1615.
Htn Phil 9560.25* Pocaterra, A. Due dialogi della vergogna. Ferrara, 1592.
                     2v.
Phil 9560.26   Herault de Séchelles, M.J. Théorie de l'ambition.
                     Paris, 1802.
Phil 9560.27.5   Martinus, Dumiensis. Volgarizzamento della forma di onesta
                     vita. Napoli, 1863.
Phil 9560.28   Heron, Grace. What word will you choose? Chicago, 1932.
Phil 9560.29   Miller, J.R. The beauty of kindness. N.Y., 1905.
Htn Phil 9560.30* Possevino, G.B. Dialogo dell'honore. Venice, 1553.
Phil 9560.31   Baumrann, W. Vertu. Berlin, 1939.
Phil 9560.32   Braithwaite, R.B. Theory of games as a tool for the moral
                     philosopher. Cambridge, Eng., 1955.
Phil 9560.32.5   Braithwaite, R.B. Theory of games. Cambridge, Eng., 1963.
Phil 9560.33   Cleghorn, S.N. The seamless robe; the religion of loving
                     kindness. N.Y., 1945.
Phil 9560.35   Ashley, Robert. Of honour. San Marino, 1947.
Phil 9560.38   Barrett, E.B. The guest of honour. Dublin, 1954.
Phil 9560.40   Baden, H.J. Ende und Anfang der Humanität.
                     Gütersloh, 1955.
Phil 9560.42   Schottlaender, Rudolf. Theorie des Vertrauens.
                     Berlin, 1957.
Phil 9560.44   Johnson, Oliver A. Rightness and goodness. The
                     Hague, 1959.
Phil 9560.50   Bollnow, O.F. Wasen und Wandel der Tugenden.
                     Frankfurt, 1958.
Phil 9560.52   Morisset, B. Le syllogisme prudentiel. Laval, 1961.
Phil 9560.54   Mackenzie, C. On moral courage. London, 1962.
Phil 9560.56   Sinko, Tadeuz. Od filantropii do human i humanizmu. 2.
                     wyd. Warszawa, 1960.
Phil 9560.57   Klubertanz, George Peter. Habits and virtues. N.Y., 1965.
Phil 9560.60   Korff, Wilhelm. Ehre, Prestige, Gewissen. Köln, 1966.
Phil 9560.62   Abicht, Johann Heinrich. Neues System einer
                     philosophischen Tugendlehre. Leipzig, 1970.
Phil 9560.64   Kuş, Nuri. Güneş batidan doğmustur. Kütahya, 1970.
Phil 9560.66   Pieper, Josef. Auskunft über die Tugenden. Zürich, 1970.
Phil 9560.68   Heyst, Jacques. Hypothèse de la vérité. Versailles, 1960.

Phil 9575   Ethics - Treatises on special topics - Wealth
Phil 9575.01   Pamphlet box. Ethics of wealth.
Phil 9575.1   Arnot, W. The race for riches. Philadelphia, 1853.
Phil 9575.2   Eliot, C.W. Great riches. N.Y., 1906.
Phil 9575.3   Jenks, J.W. Great fortunes: The winning, the using.
                     N.Y., 1906.
Phil 9575.4   Hensel, W.U. Wealth and worth. South Bethlehem,
                     Pa., 1907.
Phil 9575.5   Lee, G.S. Inspired millionaires...America.
                     Northampton, 1908.
Phil 9575.6   Remsen, D.S. Post-Mortem use of wealth. N.Y., 1911.
Phil 9575.7   Ebersberg, Luise. Der Mensch und das Geld. Wien, 1826.
Phil 9575.8   Atwood, Albert W. The mind of the millionaire.
                     N.Y., 1926.
Phil 9575.9   Gallegas Rocafull, J.M. Un aspecto del orden cristiano.
                     México, 1943.
Phil 9575.10   Du Lassage, Henri. A moral e o capitalismo. Pôrto, 19- .
Phil 9575.15   Masani, Rustom Pestonji. The role of wealth in society.
                     Bombay, 1956.

Phil 9590   Miscellany

Phil 9590.1   Alder, V.S. The fifth dimension. London, 1940.
Phil 9590.2   Moore, J.H. The law of biogenesis. Chicago, 1914.
Phil 9590.3   García, E.A. Negación de la nueva verdad. Buenos
                   Aires, 1929.
Phil 9590.4   Bonnard, L.C. Entufhrôn. Paris, 1933.
Phil 9590.5   Bryan, G.B. Psychic dictatorship in America. Los
                   Angeles, 1940.
Phil 9590.6   Hudson, J.W. The old faiths perish. N.Y., 1939.
Phil 9590.7   Wood, F.H. This Egyptian miracle. Philadelphia, 1939.
Phil 9590.8   Spallazani, L. The devil laughs. Boston, 1937.
Phil 9590.9   Cosgrave, J.O. The academy for souls. N.Y., 1931.
Phil 9590.10   Symes, (Mrs.). Character reading. Akron, O., 1903.
Phil 9590.11   Brewster, E.T. The understanding of religion.
                   Boston, 1923.
Phil 9590.12   Greene, Alice. The philosophy of silence. N.Y., 1940.
Phil 9590.13   Menendez Samara, A. Fanatismo y misticismo. México, 1940.
X Cg Phil 9590.14 Spetien Montero y Austri, P.A. Meximas de buena educación.
                   México, 1828.
Phil 9590.17   Krol', L.I. Vvedenie v biosofiia. Kaunas, 1937.
Phil 9590.17.5   Krol', L.I. Osnovaniia biosofii. v.1-2. Kaunas, 1937.
Phil 9590.18   Waddington, C.H. Science and ethics. London, 1942.
Phil 9590.19   Bok, E.W. Dollars only. N.Y., 1926.
Phil 9590.20   Reinhardt, K.F. A realistic philosophy. Milwaukee, 1944.
Phil 9590.21   Drummond, D.D. Today we think of our tomorrows. Richmond,
                   Va., 1945.
Phil 9590.22.3   Fearon, Arthur D. How to think. San Francisco, 1944.
Phil 9590.23   Steiner, L.R. (Mrs.). Where do people take their troubles?
                   Boston, 1945.
Phil 9590.24   Milum, John P. Man and his meaning. London, 1945.
Phil 9590.25   Shishkin, A.F. Burzhuaznaia moral' - oruzhie
                   imperialisticheskoi reaktsii. Moskva, 1951.
Phil 9590.25.5   Shishkin, A.F. Die bürgerliche Moralinwaffe der
                   imperialistischen Reaktion. Berlin, 1952.
Phil 9590.26   Carr, H.W. Life and finite individuality. London, 1918.
Phil 9590.27   Riazantsev, N.I. Sushchestovet li sud'ba? Moskva, 1959.
Phil 9590.28   Masferrer, A. Ensayo sobre el destino. San
                   Salvador, 1963.
Phil 9590.29   Sanders, Willy. Glück. Köln, 1965.
VPhil 9590.30   De Condé, Minerva E. Forever into the past and future.
                   Boston, 196-.
Phil 9590.32   Sendy, Jean. Les Dieux nous sont nées. Paris, 1966-
Phil 9590.32.5   Sendy, Jean. L'ére du verseau. Paris, 1970.
VPhil 9590.34   Bergel, Bernard. Von der Krankheit und Genesung des
                   Seienden, oder Der zweite Sündenfall. Tel-Aviv, 1966.
VPhil 9590.37   Lagrange, Charles Henri. Mathématique de l'histoire,
                   géométrie et cinématique. Bruxelles, 1900.
Phil 9590.40   Spalding, Baird Thomas. Life and teaching of the masters
                   of the Far East. Los Angeles, California, 1944. 5v.

WIDENER LIBRARY SHELFLIST, 42

PHILOSOPHY
AND
PSYCHOLOGY

CHRONOLOGICAL LISTING

Chronological Listing

No date

Phil 8624.4   Agnosticism and the future life. n.p., n.d.
Phil 575.91.5   Allport, G.W. The field of personality. n.p., n.d.
Phil 10.88.5   The American journal of psychoanalysis. Cumulative index. v.1-17,1941-1957. n.p., n.d.
Phil 5643.86   Ames, Adelbert. Collection of papers. n.p., n.d. 6 pam.
Phil 1020.11   Anderson, M.B. Arabian philosophy. n.p., n.d.
Phil 3425.112   Archambault, P. Hegel. Paris, n.d.
Phil 3552.108   Archambault, P. Leibniz. Paris, n.d.
Phil 2805.103   Archambault, P. Pascal. Paris, n.d.
Phil 2138.92   Archambault, P. Stuart Mill. Paris, n.d.
Phil 4751.1.30   Arsen'ev, N.S. Zhazhda podlinnago Bytiia. Berlin, n.d.
Phil 10.59.5   Australian journal of psychology. Cumulative index, 1-10,1949-1958. Melbourne, n.d.
Phil 8875.13   Ayres, Clarence E. The nature of the relationship between ethics and economics. Chicago, Ill., n.d.
Phil 6671.1   Babbitt, E.D. Vital magnetism. N.Y., n.d.
Phil 5525.10   Backhaus, W.E. Das Wesen des Humors. Leipzig, n.d.
Htn   Phil 8876.14.8*   Baldwin, W. A treatise of morall philosophie. London, n.d.
Htn   Phil 8876.14.3*   Baldwin, W. A treatise of morall phylosophye. London, n.d.
Phil 176.5.13   Balfour, A.J. Familiar belief and transcendent reason. London, n.d.
Phil 3425.113   Barrès, M. De Hegel aux cantines du nord. Paris, n.d.
Htn   Phil 8581.19*   Barrington, J.S. A discourse of natural and revealed religion. n.p., n.d.
Phil 7054.43.3A   Bartlett, G.C. The Salem seer. N.Y., n.d.
Phil 4265.1.81   Baudouin, A. Histoire critique de Jules César Vanini. Toulouse, n.d.
Phil 1504.10.5   Bauer, H. Die Psychologie Alhazens. v.10, pt.5. Münster, n.d.
Phil 1504.4.2   Baur, L. Gundissalinus de divisione philosophiae. v.4, pt.2-3. Münster, n.d. 2v.
Phil 1504.18.4   Baur, L. Die Philosophie des Robert Grosseteste. v.18, pt.4-6. Münster, n.d.
Phil 8050.85   Beardsley, Monroe Curtis. Aesthetics from classical Greece to the present. 1. ed. n.p., n.d.
Phil 8691.25.2   Beckett, Lucile C. Everyman and the infinite. London, n.d.
Phil 1106.3.10   Benn, A.W. Early Greek philosophy. N.Y., n.d.
Phil 176.50   Bernès, M. Cours élémentaire de philosophie. Paris, n.d.
Phil 9341.8   Blair, H. Advice to youth. n.d.
Phil 2733.84   Blampignon, Emile Antoine. Bibliographie de Malebranche. Montbéliard, n.d.
Phil 8581.70   Blanchard, Pierre. Catéchisme de la nature, ou religion et morale naturelle. Paris, n.d.
Phil 1504.18.2   Bliemetzrieder, P. Anselms von Laon systematische Sentenzen. v.18, pt.2-3. Münster, n.d.
Phil 8876.46   Bligh, S.M. The desire for qualities. London, n.d.
Phil 476.5   Bliven, Eliza M. Materialism. n.p., n.d.
Phil 2053.81   Boerma, N.W. De Leer van den Zedelijken zin bij Hutcheson.
Phil 7054.153   The book of spirits. London, n.d.
Phil 3001.6.5   Borelius, J.J. Blicke auf den Gegenwärtigen Standpunkt der Philosophie in Deutschland und Frankreich. Berlin, n.d.
Phil 2270.90   Bowne, B.P. The philosophy of Herbert Spencer. N.Y., n.d.
Phil 11.2.11   British journal of statistical psychology. Cumulative index, 1-14. n.p., n.d.
Phil 3640.95   Broene, J. Philosophy of Friedrich Nietzsche. n.p., n.d.
Phil 5520.8   Bruchmann, K. Psychologische Studien. Leipzig, n.d.
Phil 4065.31   Bruno, Giordano. Caudelaio. Strasburgo, n.d.
Phil 1106.5.6*   Burley, W. Vita omnium philosophorum et poetarum. n.p., n.d.
Phil 1900.60.5   Butler, Joseph. Fifteen sermons and six sermons. 5th ed. London, n.d.
Phil 2480.20A   Cabanis, P.J.G. Choix de textes. Paris, n.d.
Phil 2050.92A   Calderwood, H. David Hume. Edinburgh, n.d.
Phil 3484.7   Cantecor, G. Kant. Paris, n.d.
Phil 720.8   Carr, H.W. The problem of truth. London, n.d.
Phil 9560.14.20   Cartojan, N. Fiore di virtù dans la litterature roamaine. n.p., n.d.
Phil 8877.5.2   Champlin, J.T. First principles of ethics. N.Y., n.d.
Phil 2515.2.34*   Charron, P. Charron on wisdom. London? n.d.
Phil 1200.8   Chollet, A. La morale stoïcienne. Paris, n.d.
Phil 802.9   Claeson, Gustaf. Filosofiens historia i sammandrag. n.p., n.d.
Phil 9010.22   Clark, Martha. Victims of amusements. Philadelphia, n.d.
Phil 7060.96*   The comparative study of ghost stories. n.p., n.d.
Phil 8877.18.10   Compayré, J.G. Cours de morale theorique et pratique. 19th ed. Paris, n.d.
Phil 802.6.5   Conti, Augusto. Histoire de la philosophie. Paris, n.d. 2v.
Phil 978.15.2   Cook, M.C. Light on the path. Chicago, Ill., n.d.
Phil 8582.39   Cordovani, M. Rivelazione e filosofia. Milano, n.d.
Phil 3484.3.5   Cousin, V. Philosophy of Kant. London, n.d.
Phil 9010.26.2   Crane, J.T. Popular amusements. Cincinnati, n.d.
Phil 8877.25   Crell, J. Ethica aristotelica. Selenoburgi, n.d.
Phil 1870.93   David, M. Berkeley. Paris, n.d.
Phil 2520.112   Debricon, L. Descartes. Paris, n.d.
Phil 7060.26   Dennis, J. Subversion of materialism. Bath, n.d.
Phil 2520.35.9   Descartes, René. Discours de la méthode pour bien conduire sa raison et chercher la vérité dans les sciences. Strasbourg, n.d.
Phil 2520.17   Descartes, René. Oeuvres morales et philosophiques. Paris, n.d.
Phil 2520.32   Descartes, René. Philosophische Werke. v.1-2. n.p., n.d.
Phil 803.4.15   Deussen, P. Discours de la méthode pour bien étudier l'histoire de la philosophie. Paris, n.d.
Phil 8583.3.5   DeVere, Aubrey. The subjective difficulties in religion. n.p., n.d.
Phil 3900.1.81   Dilthey, W. Zum Andenken an Friedrich Ueberweg. n.p., n.d.
Phil 6113.10   Dimmler, H. System der Psychologie. München, n.d.
Phil 8658.7   Dole, C.F. From agnosticism to theism. Boston, n.d.
Phil 9120.5   Dole, C.F. The problem of duty. N.Y., n.d.
Phil 178.20   Domecq, J.B. Études analytiques sur les auteurs philosophiques. Tours, n.d.
Phil 3415.89.5   Drews, A. Das Lebens Werk Eduard von Hartmanns. Leipzig, n.d.
Phil 3552.233   Eberhard, J.A. Charakteristik des Leibnitz. Leipzig, n.d.
Phil 3486.3   Edmunds, J. Kant's ethics: the Clavis to an index. Louisville, n.d.
Phil 804.2.4   Enfield, W. History of philosophy. London, n.d. 2v.
Phil 623.19   Enriques, F. Scienza e razionalismo. Bologna, n.d.
Phil 5244.9.15   Erismann, T. Die Eigenart des Geistigen. Leipzig, n.d.

No date - cont.

Htn   Phil 2115.36.33*   Essay concerning human understanding. Editor's ms. for edition of 1931. n.p., n.d.
Phil 179.3.28.2   Eucken, R. Geistesprobleme und Lebensfragen. 2e Aufl. Leipzig, n.d.
Phil 6114.5   Evans, W.F. Esoteric Christianity and mental therepeutics. Boston, n.d.
Phil 9345.10   A father's advice to his son. London, n.d.
Phil 5545.38.26   Fellows, G.S. "Loisette" exposed. N.Y., n.d.
Phil 4260.99   Ferrari, G.M. Il Leibnitz gindicato da G.B. Vico. n.p., n.d.
Phil 3246.55.5   Fichte, Johann Gottlieb. Reden an die deutsche Nation. Leipzig, n.d.
Phil 9495.10   Foerster, F.W. Marriage and the sex problem. N.Y., n.d.
Phil 336.5   Fonsegrive, G. Essais sur la connaissance. 2. ed. n.p., n.d. 2v.
Phil 6675.9   Fonvielle, W. de. Les endormeurs. Paris, n.d.
Phil 5925.3.4   Fowler, O.S. The illustrated self-instructor in phrenology. N.Y., n.d.
Phil 2115.90.4   Fowler, T. Life of Locke. N.Y., n.d.
Phil 1885.81   Francis Herbert Bradley, 1846-1924. London, n.d.
Phil 5400.7   Frédault, F. Les passions. Paris, n.d.
Phil 9220.6   Friendship: two essays by Cicero and Emerson. N.Y., n.d.
Phil 3487.5   Fromm, E. Das Kantbildnis der grafen Keyserling. n.p., n.d.
Phil 978.12   Fullerton, Alex. The Wilkesbarre letters on theosophy. N.Y., n.d.
Phil 1504.12   Gaul, L. Alberts des Grossen Verhältnis zu Palto. v.12, pt.1. Münster, n.d.
Phil 4114.45   Genovesi, Antonio. Della diceosina o sia della filosofia sul religione. Napoli, n.d. 3v.
Phil 5640.9   Genzmer, A.O.H. Untersuchungen über die Sinneswahrnehmungen des neugeborenen Menschen. Halle, n.d.
Phil 974.3.60   Geyer, C.K.L. Rudolf Steiner und die Religion. München, n.d.
Phil 8586.28   Ghose, J.C. The positive religion. Calcutta, n.d.
Htn   Phil 181.24*   Gifford, A. Lectures. Frankfurt, n.d.
Phil 8881.12.10   Gizycki, G. Moralphilosophie. Leipzig, n.d.
Phil 181.28   Godlover, H.B. Science of minds. n.p., n.d.
Phil 7069.10.3   Gook, Arthur. Andartrúin. Akureyri, n.d.
Phil 1504.14   Graf, G. Des Theodor Abû Kurra Traktat. v.14, pt.1. Münster, n.d.
Phil 337.1   Grimm, E. Zur Geschichte der Erkenntnis Problems. Leipzig, n.d.
Phil 806.3   Grosse Denker. Leipzig, n.d. 2v.
Phil 7068.70.33   Güldinstubbe, J. von. Positive Pneumatologie. 2. Aufl. Bern, n.d.
Htn   Phil 5246.16.2*   Gurley, R.R. Skeleton project of a science of psychology. n.p., n.d.
Htn   Phil 5246.16*   Gurley, R.R. Skeleton project of a science of psychology. n.p., n.d.
Phil 1990.80   Haldane, E.S. Ferrier James Frederick. London, n.d.
Phil 182.35.5   Haldane, Richard B. The doctrine of degrees in knowledge, truth, and reality. London, n.d.
Phil 9347.6   Hall, John. Familiar talks to boys. N.Y., n.d.
Phil 3850.1.86   Harrauss, K. David Friedrich Strauss. Leipzig, n.d.
Phil 182.5.5   Harris, W.T. A collection of philosophical and psychological essays; extracts from periodicals. n.p., n.d.
Phil 3415.68   Hartmann, Eduard von. Die Geisterhypothese des Spiritismus und seine Phantome. Leipzig, n.d.
Phil 5247.3.300   Hartmann, George W. A collection of miscellaneous papers. n.p., n.d.
Phil 9430.15   Hartsen, F.A. von. Die Moral des Pessimismus. Leipzig, n.d.
Phil 288.5   Hartung, G. Philosophie und Naturwissenschaft. n.p., n.d.
Phil 3100.83   Hauffe, G. Professor Dr. Eduard Beneckes Psychologie als Naturwissenschaft. Borna, n.d.
Phil 8882.6   Hazlitt, W. Essays on the principles of human action. London, n.d.
Phil 3425.34.35   Hegel, Georg Wilhelm Friedrich. Essence. n.p., n.d.
Phil 5757.11   Heinzel, G. Versuch einer Lösung des Willensproblems. Inaug. Diss. Breslau, n.d.
Phil 5545.35   Henderson, E.N. A study of memory. n.p., n.d.
Phil 5374.16   Herbertz, R. Bewusstsein und Unbewusstes. Köln, n.d.
Htn   Phil 8587.15.5*   Higginson, T.W. L'affinité des religions. Paris, n.d.
Phil 8587.15.6   Higginson, T.W. L'affinité des religions. Paris, n.d.
Phil 3850.3.80   Hildenbrand, R. Gotthilf Samuel Steinbart. Herne, n.d.
Phil 338.7   Hodgson, S.H. Some cardinal points in knowledge. London, n.d.
Phil 338.13   Höfler, Alois. Erkenntnis Probleme und Erkenntnistheorie. Leipzig, n.d.
Htn   Phil 2648.60*   Holbach, Paul Henri T. Examen impartial des principales religions. n.p., n.d.
Phil 5545.14   Holbrook, M.S. How to strengthen the memory. N.Y., n.d.
Phil 5047.27   Holman, H. A key to Holman and Irvine's questions on logic. London, n.d.
Phil 21.6   Hubbard, Elbert. Little journeys to the homes of great philosophers. East Aurora, n.d.
Phil 2050.34   Hume, David. Essays and treatises on several subjects. n.p., n.d.
Phil 5817.7   Hunter, W.S. The delayed reaction in animals and children. Cambridge, n.d.
Phil 9380.10   Hurvich, L.M. Beginnings of a bibliography on psychological factors in morale. n.p., n.d.
Htn   Phil 4938.2.30*   Hus, J. Liber egregius de unitate ecclesiae. n.p., n.d.
Phil 665.21   Hygiene del alma. n.p., n.d.
Phil 1870.103   Ikbal Kishen, Shargha. A critical essay on Berkeley's theory of perception. Allababad, n.d.
Phil 4759.1.30   Il'in, I.A. Religioznyi smysl filosofii. Paris,, n.d.
Phil 9450.58   Inglis, B. Private conscience - public mortality. London, n.d.
Phil 18.7.5   International journal of psycho-analysis. Index. v.1-10. London, n.d.
Phil 5525.60   Introduction à l'étude scientifique du rire. n.p., n.d.
Phil 3552.247   Ivaldi, I.G. Il platonismo di Plotino, Sant'Agosinto, Cartesio, Leibniz. Napoli, n.d.
Phil 6119.1.5   Jackson, J.H. Observations on the localisation of movements in the cerebral hemispheres. n.p., n.d.
Phil 5627.6.14   James, William. La varie forme della coscienza religiosa. n.p., n.d.
Phil 2045.88   Jodl, F. Studien...über Ursprung des Sittlichen; Hobbes. München, n.d.
Phil 705.2   Johnson, S. Transcendentalism. n.p., n.d.
Phil 184.9   Joly, H. Nouveau cours de philosophie. Paris, n.d.
Phil 9245.18   Joslyn, R. The philosophy of happiness. Elgin, n.d.
NEDL   Phil 19.1.5   Journal of mental science. Index. London, n.d.

Chronological Listing

No date - cont.

Phil 8654.105 — Journées Universitaires, 44th, Pau, France, 1967. Qui est notre Dieu? n.p., n.d.

Phil 2270.137 — Juvalta, Erminio. La dottrina delle due etiche di H. Spencer, e la morale come scienza. n.p., n.d.

Phil 1133.19.10 — Kafka, Gustav. Der Ausklang der antiken Philosophie und das Erwachen einer neuen Zeit. n.p., n.d.

Phil 310.375 — Kechov, B.M. O povtoriaemosti v protsesse razoitiia. Moskva, n.d.

Phil 8665.2 — Kernahan, C. The lonely God. London, n.d.

Phil 7054.77F — Kidder, L. A spiritual communicating diagram. n.p., n.d.

Phil 7054.175 — Knapp, C. Richard. The newest Bible demonstrated by nature. Grass Valley, Calif., n.d.

Phil 2070.93 — Kortsen, K.K. William James' filosofi. København, n.d.

Phil 1200.24 — Lafon, R. Les stoïciens. Paris, n.d.

Phil 6121.20 — La Forge, Louis de. Traité de l'esprit de l'homme. Amsterdam, n.d.

Phil 2725.2.73 — Lamennais, F.R. de. Les erreurs. Bruxelles, n.d.

Phil 2725.2.54 — Lamennais, F.R. de. Il libro del popolo. n.p., n.d. 2 pam.

Phil 2730.88 — Lang, Albert. Maine de Biran und die neuere Philosophie. Köln, n.d.

Phil 1504.6.2 — Lappe, J. Nicolaus von Autrecourt. v.6, pt.2. Münster, n.d.

Phil 4600.2.33 — Larsson, Hans. Nagot om den fria viljan. n.p., n.d.

Phil 6021.2.4 — Lavater, Johann Caspar. Essays on physiognomy. London, n.d.

Phil 6021.4 — LeClerc, S. Caractères des passions. Paris, n.d.

Phil 3552.78.25 — Leibniz, Gottfried Wilhelm. Leibniz' bref till Sparfrenfelt. n.p., n.d.

Phil 3552.67.5 — Leibniz, Gottfried Wilhelm. La monadologie. 5. éd. Paris, n.d.

Phil 978.72.5 — Ljumgström, O. Theosophy. n.p., n.d. 6 pam.

Phil 2115.27 — Locke, J. The beauties of Locke. London, n.d.

Htn — Phil 2115.77.5F* — Locke, J. Catalogue of Locke's library. Ms. photostat. n.p., n.d.

Htn — Phil 2115.77F* — Locke, J. Catalogus librorum. Ms. photostat. n.p., n.d.

Htn — Phil 2115.75.11* — Locke, J. Correspondence of John Locke and Edward Clarke. Editor's ms. for Cambridge edition. n.p., n.d.

Htn — Phil 2115.36.32* — Locke, J. Essay concerning human understanding. Photostat copy of Locke's original ms. n.p., n.d.

Phil 186.156 — Losskii, N.O. Types of world views; an introduction to metaphysics. Typescript. n.p., n.d.

Phil 5490.5 — Losskii, Nikolai O. Sensory, intellectual and mystical intuition. v.1-2. n.p., n.d.

Phil 4762.1.37 — Losskii, Nikolai Onufrievich. Svoboda voli. Paris, n.d.

Phil 8550.508 — Lossky, Nikolai O. Slavonic religious philosophy. n.p., n.d.

Phil 7060.133 — McDonald, Neil T. The Belledoon mysteries, 1830-40. 3. ed. Wallaceburg, Ont., n.d.

Phil 6322.29 — McFarland, R.A. Miscellaneous papers on abnormal psychology. n.p., n.d.

Phil 187.6 — Makowski, J. Metaphysica. n.p., n.d.

Phil 978.41 — Mason, E.L. The discovery of discoveries. n.p., n.d.

Phil 7054.23 — Mattison, H. The rappers. N.Y., n.d.

Phil 8637.14 — Mazzantini, C. La speranza nell'immortalità. Torino, n.d.

Phil 2520.143 — Meier, M. Descartes und die Renaissance. München, n.d.

Phil 5252.55 — Meier, M. Der Seelenbegriff in der modernen Psychologie. München, n.d.

Phil 3625.1.39.15 — Mendelssohn, Moses. Phädon. London, n.d. 2 pam.

Phil 3625.1.31A — Mendelssohn, Moses. Philosophische Schriften. Carlsruhe, n.d.

Phil 52.8 — Metaphysical Club, Boston. Calendar. Boston, n.d.

Phil 1517.1 — Mignon, A. Les origines de la scolastique. Paris, n.d. 2v.

Phil 3494.23 — Moog, Willy. Kants Ansichten über Krieg und Frieden. Leipzig, n.d.

Phil 5627.6.85 — Morelli, G. La realtà dello spirito. Milano, n.d.

Htn — Phil 187.54.9F* — Motion, George. Diagram of the celestial city. n.p., n.d.

Phil 2150.6.01 — Münsterberg, H. The library of H. Münsterberg. n.p., n.d.

Phil 6317.22.80 — Murray, M. The concepts of self acceptance and self respect in Karen Horney's theory of neurosis. n.p., n.d.

Htn — Phil 8887.31* — Muzéo, G. La polvere del mutio. n.p., n.d.

Phil 9245.119 — Naguib, Mohammad. Full happiness. Cairo, n.d.

Phil 188.9.5 — Nelson, L. Die neue Reformation. v.1-2,4. n.p., n.d. 3v.

Phil 3640.77.25 — Nietzsche, Friedrich. The joyful wisdom. London, n.d.

Phil 23.18.5 — Nordisk Psykologi. Register, 1949-1960. København, n.d.

Phil 7060.92.9 — O'Donnell, Elliot. Ghostly phenomena. London, n.d.

Htn — Phil 8595.15.16* — Paine, Thomas. Age of reason. Investigation of true and fabulous theology. n.p., n.d. 5 pam.

Htn — Phil 2225.3.35* — Paine, Thomas. Examination of...passages in the New Testament. N.Y., n.d.

Phil 2205.30.6 — Paley, W. Natural theology. N.Y., n.d. 2 pam.

Phil 510.01 — Papers from the Monist. n.p., n.d.

Phil 2270.100 — Parisot, E. Herbert Spencer. Paris, n.d.

Htn — Phil 190.67* — Parité de la vie et de la mort. n.p., n.d.

Phil 2805.30.19 — Pascal, Blaise. Les provinciales. Strasbourg, n.d.

Phil 8890.6.12 — Paulsen, F. Zur Ethik und Politik. v.1-2. Berlin, n.d.

Phil 5360.7 — Peillaube, E. Théorie des concepts. Paris, n.d.

Phil 25.77.5 — Pensamiento, revista de investigacion filosofica. Indices generales, 1945-60. Madrid, n.d. 2v.

Phil 815.5 — Perry, Rufus L. Sketch of philosophical systems. n.p., n.d.

Phil 25.55.3 — Philosophia reformata. Register, v.1-20,1936-1955. n.p., n.d.

Phil 25.66.2 — Philosophic abstracts. Index, 1-2,1939-1950. N.Y., n.d.

Phil 25.1.5 — The philosophical review. Index, 1892-1926. N.Y., n.d.

Phil 25.5.5 — Philosophische Studien. Index, 1-20. Leipzig, n.d.

Phil 25.37F — Philosophischer Weltanzeiger. Berlin, n.d.

Phil 25.62 — Philosophiskt archiv og repertorium. Kjöbenhavn, n.d.

Phil 3497.6 — Piat, C. L'idée ou Critique du Kantisme. Paris, n.d.

Phil 5055.1 — Pierce, C.S. Logical papers. n.p., n.d.

Phil 6021.2.53 — Pocket Lavater. n.p., n.d.

Phil 5643.95F — Pseudoptics, the science of optical illusions. Charts. n.p., n.d.

Phil 25.9.9 — Psychlogical review. Psychological index, 1894-1935. Lancaster, N.Y., n.d. 24v.

Phil 25.67.2 — Psychoanalytic quarterly. Cumulative index, 1-35,1932-1966. n.p., n.d.

Phil 25.16.3 — Psychoanalytic review. Subject author index, v.1-18,1913-1931. Washington, n.d.

Phil 25.9.12 — Psychological index. Abstrast references of volumes 1-35,1894-1928. Colombia, n.d. 2v.

Phil 25.71.5 — Psychometrika. Topical and author indexes, 1936-1945. n.p., n.d.

Phil 7060.46 — Puls, G. Spuls-Geschichten. Berlin, n.d.

No date - cont.

Phil 7054.27.5 — Putnam, A. Agassiz and spiritualism. Boston, n.d.

Phil 8706.1 — Quarterman, J. The mosaic cosmogony. n.p., n.d.

Phil 5425.20 — Ramos Mejia, J.M. Los simuladores del talento. Barcelona, n.d.

Htn — Phil 6967.4* — Randall, J.R. On the treatment of the insane. n.p., n.d.

Phil 400.53 — Ranzoli, C. L'idealismo e la filosofia. n.p., n.d.

Phil 7069.40.11 — Redemptor Spiritual Center. Rational and scientific (Christian) spiritualism. Rio de Janeiro, n.d.

Phil 1850.130 — Réfutation de l'ouvrage intitulé; ou Reponse à un ecclésiastique sur cet ouvrage. n.p., n.d.

Phil 8892.47 — Regras da vida. n.p., n.d.

Phil 7060.81 — Reichel, W. Occult experiences. London, n.d.

Phil 3525.89 — Reiff, F. Über Krause's Philosophie. n.p., n.d.

Phil 1504.8.5 — Reiners, J. Der Nominalismus in der Frühscholastik. v.8, pt.5. Münster, n.d.

Phil 4080.15.81 — Renauld, J.F. L'oeuvre inachevée de Mario Calderoni. n.p., n.d.

Phil 75.29 — Renoir, Edmund. Bibliography of recent French philosophy, 1920. n.p., n.d.

Phil 8892.32 — Rensi, Giuseppe. Introduzione alla scepsi etica. Firenze, n.d.

Phil 27.45.3 — The review of metaphysics. Index, 1947-1967. New Haven, n.d.

Phil 27.6 — Revue des sciences psychologiques. Paris, n.d.

Phil 27.34.5 — Ricerche filosofiche. Index to 1-10 (1931-1940). Messina, n.d.

Phil 8672.11 — Richards, William. Reflections on French atheism. 2. ed. Lynn, n.d.

Phil 7054.176 — Richmond, Cora L. Spiritual sermons [delivered in 1886-1889]. n.p., n.d.

Phil 3791.40 — Riehl, Alois. Führende Denker und Forscher. Leipzig, n.d.

Phil 1817.9 — Riley, I.W. La philsophie française en Amérique. Paris, n.d.

Phil 5057.18 — Ritschl, Otto. Program zur Feier des Gedächtnisses. Bonn, n.d.

Phil 27.11.5 — Rivista di psicologia. Indice generale, 1905-1936. Bologna, n.d. 2v.

Phil 5850.326.5F — Roback, A.A. Course in business psychology assignment. v.1-8. Boston, n.d.

Phil 6315.2.107 — Roback, A.A. Freudiana. n.p., n.d. 3 pam.

Phil 8610.900.5 — Roberts, G.L. Rational agnosticism. n.p., n.d.

Phil 9178.1 — Sanders, C.E. The infant family. v.1-2. Haverhill, n.d.

Phil 193.49.4 — Santayana, G. The life of reason. v.3. N.Y., n.d.

X Cg — Phil 9358.1 — Sargent, J.A. Letters from a mother...daughter. Boston, n.d.

Phil 3800.59 — Schelling, F.W.J. von. Darlegung des wahren Verhältnisses der Naturphilosophie zu der verbesserten Fichte'schenLehre. n.p., n.d. 4 pam.

Phil 1718.9 — Schjelderup, Harald K. Hauptlinien der Entwicklung der Philosophie von mitte des 19. Jahrhunderts bis zur Gegenwart. n.p., n.d.

Phil 3808.24.14 — Schopenhauer, Arthur. Arthur Schopenhauer. n.p., n.d.

Phil 3808.76 — Schopenhauer, Arthur. Brieftasche, 1822-1823. Berlin, n.d.

Phil 3808.44 — Schopenhauer, Arthur. The essays of Arthur Schopenhauer. N.Y., n.d.

Phil 3808.74 — Schopenhauer, Arthur. Zur Ästhetik der Poesie, Musik und der bildend en Künste. Leipzig, n.d.

Phil 193.94 — Schulte-Tigges, A. Philosophische Propadeutik. n.p., n.d. 3 pam.

Phil 343.4.9 — Schultz, R. Die Machsche Erkenntnistheorie. Berlin, n.d.

Phil 193.62 — Schuyler, A. Critical history of philosophical theories. Boston, n.d.

Phil 5058.8 — Schuyler, A. The principles of logic. Cincinnatti, n.d.

Phil 5520.19 — Sechrist, F.K. The psychology of unconventional language. n.p., n.d.

Phil 9358.2 — Sedgwick, C. Talks with my pupils. N.Y., n.d.

Phil 600.34 — Senna Freitas, J.J. de. A doutrina positivista. Póvoa de Varzim, n.d.

Phil 4769.1.82A — Séverac, B. Vladimir Soloviev. Paris, n.d.

Phil 2494.82A — Séverac, J.B. Condorcet. Paris, n.d.

Phil 2636.81 — Séverac, J.B. Helvétius. Paris, n.d.

Phil 3500.103 — Shcherbina, A.M. Uchenie Kanta o veshchi vě sebe. n.p., n.d.

Phil 9358.3 — Smith, S.R. Words to young gentlemen and ladies. Boston, n.d.

Phil 193.61 — Sopote, M. Mind and brain with other studies. Oxford, n.d.

Phil 1850.97 — Sortain, J. The life of Francis Lord Bacon. London, n.d.

Phil 3270.1.82 — Sosnoioski, M.E.V. Kuno Fischer. Breslau, n.d.

Phil 2270.45.7 — Spencer, Herbert. First principles. N.Y., n.d.

Phil 7054.154 — Spiritualism and other signs. London, n.d.

Phil 978.49.130 — Steiner, R. Anthroposophy. n.p., n.d. 5 pam.

Phil 1818.2.6 — Stephen, L. The English Utilitarians. n.p., n.d.

Phil 3500.37 — Stern, Albert. Über die Beziehungen Garve's zu Kant. Inaug. Diss. n.p., n.d.

Phil 3195.6.103 — Steuzel, J. Über Diltheys Verhaltnis zu Hegel. n.p., n.d.

Phil 2275.40 — Stewart, D. Philosophie des facultés actives et morales de l'homme. v.1-2. Paris, n.d.

X Cg — Phil 8893.24 — Stewart, J. The book of nature. London, n.d.

Phil 7067.00 — Stryk, Johann S. Disputatio iuridica inauguralis de iure spectrorum...Andreas Becker. Halae Magdeburgicae, n.d.

Phil 6688.12 — Sturm, G. Mesmerismus und Hypnotismus. Leipzig, n.d.

Phil 5768.8 — Surbled, G. La volonté. 5. éd. Paris, n.d.

Phil 5520.9.9 — Sutro, Emil. Das Doppelwesen in die Religion der Vernunft. Berlin, n.d.

Phil 5058.38 — Switalski, B.W. Vom Denken und Erkennen. Kempten, n.d.

Phil 5258.81 — Syrkin, N. Was muss man von der Psychologie wissen? Berlin, n.d.

Phil 3839.2 — Thomas, C. Spinoza systema philosophicum adumbratum. Borussorum, n.d.

Phil 9179.10 — Thomson, John. The domestic circle. Edinburgh, n.d.

Phil 7054.29 — Tindall, A.F. Occult revelations in prose and verse. London, n.d.

Phil 9179.8 — Todd, J. Nuts for boys to crack. N.Y., n.d.

Phil 194.15 — Tounissoux, M. L'Abbé. L'homme dan sa triple vie. n.p., n.d.

Phil 2725.14.85 — Union pour l'Action Morale, Paris. Jules Lagneau. Paris, n.d.

Phil 5465.141 — Utah Creativity Research Conference. Proceedings of the fifth conference, 1964. N.Y., n.d. 2v.

Phil 3915.105.5 — Vannérus, Allen. Zur Kritik des Seelenbegriffs. n.p., n.d.

Phil 2733.92 — Vidgrain, J. Le Christianisme dans la philosophie de Malebranche. Paris, n.d.

Phil 2733.78.2 — Vidgrain, Joseph. Malebranche. Paris, n.d.

Chronological Listing

No date - cont.

Phil 302.1 — Vinogradoff, I. Theory of cosmic reason. n.p., n.d.
Phil 2125.81 — Volbeda, S. De intuitieve philosophie van James McCosh. Grand Rapids, n.d.
Phil 600.9 — Ward, W. The clothes of religion. London, n.d.
Htn Phil 5400.5.6* — Watts, I. The doctrine of the passions. Trenton, n.d.
Phil 5003.6A — Weiss, Paul. A preliminary draft of a bibliography of contributions to modern logic. Supplement. n.p., n.d.
Phil 197.21 — Wendelino, M.F. Philosophia moralis. v.2. n.p., n.d.
Phil 8897.25 — When to say no. London, n.d.
Phil 8897.14.16 — Whewell, W. On the foundations of morals. Cambridge, n.d.
Phil 5062.19 — Williams, S. Principles of logic. London, n.d.
Phil 3504.6 — Wirgman, T. Kants works and life. n.p., n.d.
Phil 8897.33 — Wolff, H. Handbuch der Ethik. Leipzig, n.d.
Phil 197.11 — Wolff, Hermann. Zusammenhang unserer Vorstellungen. Leipzig, n.d.
Phil 5832.4 — Wood, J.G. Man and beast, here and hereafter. N.Y., n.d.
Phil 197.66 — Woods, A. The great quest. n.p., n.d.
Phil 3915.3 — Wundt, Wilhelm. Collected papers; articles. n.p., n.d.
Phil 64.1 — Yale Psychological Studies. The psychological review and studies from Yale psychological laboratory. v.1., no.1-2 and supplement. New Haven, n.d. 3v.
Phil 8649.1 — Yeiser, J.O. Immortality established through science. Omaha, n.d.
Phil 5834.1.5 — Yerkes, R.M. Methods of studying vision in animals. Cambridge, n.d.
Phil 6051.18 — Zancing, Julius. Twentieth century guide to palmistry. Chicago, n.d.
Phil 35.30.2 — Zeitschrift für diagnostische Psychologie und Persönlichkeitsforschung. Beiheft. n.p., n.d.
Phil 3428.86 — Ziechner, A. Herbarts Asthetik. n.p., n.d.

1490-1499

Htn Phil 5058.23* — Strode, R. Consequentie. Venice, 1493.
Htn Phil 8800.3* — Vincent de Beauvais. Speculum morale. Venetiis, 1493.

15-

tn Phil 8890.43* — Palmieri, Matteo. Libro della vita civile. n.p., 15- .

1500-1509

tn Phil 4934.2.30* — Dionysius Areopagita. Theologia vivificans. Argĕtine, 1502.
Phil 4195.3F — Pico della Mirandola, Giovanni. Opera omnia. Reggio, 1506.
tn Phil 4932.2.30F* — Bernard de Clairvaux, St. Opera. n.p., 1508.
tn Phil 186.54* — Landino, C. Disputationum Camaldulensium. Bk. 4. Argentoraci, 1508.
tn Phil 4196.5* — Pico, G.F. Opera. n.p., 1508.
tn Phil 7065.09* — Van Arnolt Boschmã und Herich syme alde vader. Collen, 1509.

1510-1519

n Phil 5000.3* — Monti, Panfilo. Logica pamph. v.1-3. Venice, 1512.
n Phil 6012.9* — Cocles, Bartolommeo della Rocca. In disem Biechlin wurt erfunden von Cöplexion der Menschen. Strassburg, 1516.
n Phil 6045.17F* — Cocles, B. Chyromantie ac physionomie anastasis. Bononiae, 1517.
n Phil 1105.2* — Agricola, R. De inventione. Libri III. Coloniae, 1518.
n Phil 2150.5.30* — More, Thomas. De optimo reipublicae statu, deque nova insula Utopia. Basileae, 1518.
n Phil 5771.2.5* — Valla, Lorenzo. De libero arbitrio. Basileae, 1518.
n Phil 1106.5* — Burley, W. Von dem Leben, sitten und freyen Sprüchen der alten Philosophie. Ausburg, 1519.
n Phil 3585.4.30* — Luther, Martin. Theologia Deütsch. n.p., 1519.

1520-1529

Phil 1135.26F* — Picodella Mirandola, G.F. Examen vanitatis doctrinae gentium et veritatis Christianae disciplinae. Mirandulae, 1520.
Phil 4934.1.30* — Diogenes Laertius. De vita et moribus philosophorum. Basiliae, 1524.
Phil 9560.17* — Baldacchini, F. Dyalogo de patientia. Perosia, 1525.
Phil 250.2* — Giorgio, F. De harmonia mundi totius. Venice, 1525.
Phil 5768.9* — Sepulveda, J.G. De fato i libris arbitrio libero tres. Roma, 1526.
Phil 4931.2.30F* — Alexander, A. In Aristotelis meteorolicus libros commentaria. n.p., 1527.
Phil 3585.4.31* — Luther, Martin. Wie man für dem Sterben fliehen muge. Wittenberg, 1527.
Phil 1020.4.1* — Averroës. Destructio destructionú. Lugduni, 1529.

1530-1539

Phil 8875.3.4* — Agrippa von Nettesheim, Heinrich Cornelius. De incertitudine et vanitate omnium scientiarum et artium liber. Ealf, 1531.
Phil 6045.22.9 — Indagine, Joannes. Chiromantia. Argentorati, 1531.
Phil 3585.4.32* — Luther, Martin. Vermanug an die Geistlichen. Wittemberg, 1531.
Phil 3085.1.30* — Agrippa von Nettesheim, H.C. De nobilitate. n.p., 1532.
Phil 4195.30* — Pico della Mirandola, Giovanni. Conclusiones nongentae. n.p., 1532.
Phil 3085.1.36* — Agrippa von Nettesheim, H.C. Apologia aduersus calumnias proptes declamationem. n.p., 1533.
Phil 3585.4.33* — Luther, Martin. Etliche schöne Predigten. n.p., 1533.
Phil 5545.52* — Romberch, J. Congestorum artificiose. Venetijs, 1533.
Phil 8640.1* — Pomponazzi, P. Tractatus de immortalitate animae. Paris, 1534.
Phil 1105.2.5* — Agricola, R. De inventione dialectica. pt.3. Parisiis, 1535.
Phil 8586.44 — Guisan, René. Reliquiae. Lausanne, 1535.

1540-1549

Phil 4200.3.30* — Pasi, Bartholomeo. Tariffa. Vinetia, 1540.
Phil 4075.31* — Cardano, Girolamo. De consolatione. Venetijs, 1542.
Phil 9560.18* — Nenna, Giovanni B. Il nennio, nel quale si ragiona di nobilita. Colophon, 1542.
Phil 6045.22.7* — Indagine, Joannes. Chiromantia. Paris, 1543.
Phil 8875.3.2* — Agrippa von Nettesheim, Heinrich Cornelius. De incertitudine et vanitate omnium scientiarum et artium liber. n.p., 1544.

1540-1549 - cont.

Phil 9560.14 — Fiore di virtù historiato. Vinegia, 1545.
Htn Phil 293.4* — Memma, G.M. Sostanza et forma del mondo. Venice, 1545. 4v.
Htn Phil 6045.46* — Cocles, B. Le compendium et brief enseignement de physiognomie and chiromancie. Paris, 1546.
Htn Phil 8879.6.2* — Erasmus, D. Lingua, sive, de linguae. Basileae, 1547.
Htn Phil 6045.22.13* — Indagine, Joannes. Chiromantia. Paris, 1547.
Htn Phil 6045.22.25* — Indagine, Joannes. Chiromance et physiognomonie. Lyon, 1549.

1550-1559

Htn Phil 3085.1.32* — Agrippa von Nettesheim, H.C. De occulta philosophia. Lugduni, 1550.
Htn Phil 9030.5.5* — Garimberto, G. Della fortuna libri sei. Vinetia, 1550.
Htn Phil 5765.1* — Porzio, S. An homun bonus v. malus volens fiat. Florentiae, 1551.
Htn Phil 5765.1.5* — Porzio, S. Se l'huomo diventa buono o cattivo volontariamente. Fiorenza, 1551.
Phil 4372.1.45 — Vives, Juan Luis. De veritate fidei christianae libri quinque. Lupluni, 1551.
Htn Phil 8875.3.8* — Agrippa von Nettesheim, Heinrich Cornelius. Della vanitate delle scienze. Venetia, 1552.
Htn Phil 4060.2.33* — Leo Hebraeus. Dialoghi di amore. Vinegia, 1552.
Htn Phil 8890.22.10* — Piccolomini, A. Della institutione di tutta la vita. Vinegia, 1552.
Htn Phil 9560.30* — Possevino, G.B. Dialogo dell'honore. Venice, 1553.
Htn Phil 2340.4.30* — Wilson, Thomas. The use of reason. n.p., 1553.
Htn Phil 4946.1.30* — Philo Iudaeus. De vita Mosis. Paris, 1554.
Htn Phil 6045.55* — Cocles, B. Physiognomiae et chiromantiae compendium. Argentorati, 1555.
Phil 4195.32 — Pico della Mirandola, Giovanni. Le sette sposizioni. Pescia, 1555.
Htn Phil 3585.4.34* — Luther, Martin. Warnung. Nürnberg, 1556.
Htn Phil 4075.40* — Cardano, Girolamo. De libris propriis, eorumque ordinis et usu. Lugduni, 1557.
Htn Phil 4170.1.30* — Manuzio, Paolo. De gli elementi. Venetia, 1557.
Htn Phil 2150.5.10* — More, Thomas. Workes. London, 1557.
Phil 176.123 — Baldini, Bernardino. Dialogi duo in quorum altero agitur de multitudine rerum. Mediolani, 1558. 3 pam.
Htn Phil 5052.31* — Melanchthon, Philipp. Erotemata dialectices. Lipsiae, 1559. 2 pam.

1560-1569

Htn Phil 8890.21* — Piccolomini, A. Della institutione morale, libri XII. Venetia, 1560. (Transferred to Houghton Library 31/1/72)
Htn Phil 6045.60* — Tricasso, Patricio. Enarratio pulcherrima principiorum chyromantiae. Noribergae, 1560.
Htn Phil 5055.19* — Piccolomini, A. L'instrumento de la filosofia. Roma, 1561.
Htn Phil 6045.62F* — Taisnier, Joannes. Opus mathematicum octs libros complectens. Coloniae, 1562.
Htn Phil 283.9* — Cattani da Diacceto, F. L'essamerone. Florenza, 1563.
Htn Phil 9171.7.5* — Luján, Pedro de. Colo os matrimoniales. Toledo, 1563.
Phil 9245.39 — Nobile, Flamineo. De hominis felicitate libri treo. Lucae, 1563.
Htn Phil 283.8* — Camilla, G. Enthosiasmo, de'misterii e maravigliose cause della compositione del mondo. Vinegia, 1564.
Htn Phil 8890.1* — Palfreyman, T. A treatise of moral philosophy. London?, 1564?
Htn Phil 4200.1.10* — Pomponazzi, Pietro. Opera. Basileae, 1567.
Htn Phil 4060.2.35* — Leo Hebraeus. Los dialogos de amor. Venetia, 1568.
Phil 8891.1 — Quarles, F. Enchiridion. 1658. Reprint. London, 1568.
Htn Phil 6025.8* — Pellegrini, A. I segni de la natura ne l'huomo. Venetia, 1569.
Htn Phil 193.149* — Salicino, A. In lode della filosofia. Fiorenza, 1569.

1570-1579

Htn Phil 4939.1.30* — Iamblichus. Iamblichus de mysteriis. Lugduni, 1570.
Phil 4235.1.30 — Telesius, B. Consentini de rerum. Neapoli, 1570.
Htn Phil 1845.2.30* — Ascham, Roger. The scholemaster. London, 1571.
Phil 5049.15.10 — Alcala, P. de. Petri hispani summulae logicales. Venetiis, 1572.
Htn Phil 7060.2.5* — Lavater, L. Of ghostes and spirites walking by night. London, 1572.
Htn Phil 4060.2.37* — Leo Hebraeus. Los dialogos de amor. Venetia, 1572.
Htn Phil 5051.19* — Lever, Ralph. The arte of reason. London, 1573.
Htn Phil 176.123.5* — Maffei, G.C. Scala naturale. Venice, 1573.
Htn Phil 4195.5* — Pico della Mirandola, Giovanni. Opera omnia. Basileae, 1573. 2v.
Htn Phil 3085.1.35* — Agrippa von Nettesheim, H.C. Henrici Cornelii Agrippae. Coloniae, 1575.
Htn Phil 8890.22* — Piccolomini, A. Della institutione morale. Venetia, 1575. (Transferred to Houghton Library 31/1/72)
Htn Phil 8900.6* — Zuccolo, G. I discorsi mi quali si tratta della nobilità. Venetia, 1575.
Htn Phil 283.6* — Contarini, N. De perfectione rerum, libri sex. Venetiis, 1576.
Htn Phil 4110.1.30F* — Ficino, Marsilio. Opera. Basileae, 1576. 2v.
Htn Phil 8893.66* — Sensi, Lodovico. La historia dell'huomo. Perugia, 1577.
Htn Phil 5412.3* — Wier, Johann. Ioannis VVieri De ira morbo. Basileae, 1577.

1580-1589

Htn Phil 5247.13.22* — Huarte de San Juan, J. Anacrise, ou Parfait jugement et examen. Lyon, 1580.
Htn Phil 8886.21.7* — La Primaudaye, P. de. Suite de l'Académie française. Paris, 1580.
Htn Phil 7060.2* — Lavater, L. De spectris. Genevae, 1580.
Htn Phil 5041.11* — Beurhusius, F. In P. Rami. London, 1581.
Htn Phil 4065.32.5* — Bruno, Giordano. De umbris idearum. Paris, 1582.
Htn Phil 4065.30* — Bruno, Giordano. Philothei Jordani. Paris, 1582.
Htn Phil 8886.21.2* — La Primaudaye, P. de. L'Académie française. 3. ed. Paris, 1582.
Htn Phil 8893.73* — Selva, Lorenzo. Della metamorfosi...del virtuoso. Orvieto, 1582.
Htn Phil 8890.35F* — Piccolomineus, F. Universa philosophia de moribus. Venetiis, 1583.
Htn Phil 8893.73.5* — Selva, Lorenzo. Della metamorfosi...del virtuoso. Firenze, 1583.
Htn Phil 6045.83F* — Taisnier, Joannes. Opus mathematicum cheiromantis. Coloniae, 1583.
Htn Phil 6045.61.5* — Tricasso, Patricio. La chiromance. Paris, 1583.

1580-1589 - cont.

Htn	Phil 6045.61.7*	Tricasso, Patricio. La chiromance. Paris, 1583.
Htn	Phil 4065.58*	Bruno, Giordano. De gl'heroici furori. Parigi, 1585.
	Phil 9177.3	Grimaldi Robbio, Pelegro de. Discorsi de...ne'quali si ragiona compiutamente. Genova, 1585.
Htn	Phil 296.10*	Piccolomini, A. Della filosofia naturale. Venetia, 1585. 2v.
Htn	Phil 5545.79*	Dolce, Lodovico. Dialogo nel quale si ragiona del modo di accrescere e conservar la memoria. Venetia, 1586.
Htn	Phil 8886.21*	La Primaudaye, P. de. The French Academie. London, 1586.
Htn	Phil 7060.6*	Le Loyer, P. Des spectres ou apparitions et visions. Angers, 1586.
Htn	Phil 6000.1*	Porta, G.B. De humana physiognomonia. Francofurti, 1586.
Htn	Phil 8892.40*	Romei, A. Discori...in sette giornate. Verona, 1586.
Htn	Phil 4065.35*	Bruno, Giordano. Camoeracensis acrotismus. Vitebergae, 1588.
Htn	Phil 4080.4.30*	Castilio, Baldessa. The courtier. London, 1588.
Htn	Phil 2120.3.30*	Lyly, John. Euphues and his England. London, 1588.
	Phil 7060.1.5	Taillepied, Noël. Psichologie ou traité de l'apparition des esprits. Paris, 1588.

1590-1599

Htn	Phil 4065.55*	Bruno, Giordano. De monade, numero et figura. Franco, 1591.
Htn	Phil 9560.25*	Pocaterra, A. Due dialogi della vergogna. Ferrara, 1592. 2v.
Htn	Phil 4200.2.10*	Patrizzi, F. Nova de universis philosophia. Venetiis, 1593.
Htn	Phil 6025.4*	Porta, G.B. De humana physiognomia libri. Hanoviae, 1593.
Htn	Phil 5247.13.7*	Huarte de San Juan, J. Examen de ingenios. London, 1594.
Htn	Phil 8886.21.3*	La Primaudaye, P. de. L'Académie française. 3. ed. London, 1594. 2v.
Htn	Phil 8890.21.5*	Piccolomini, A. Della institutione morale, libri XII. Venetia, 1594. (Transferred to Houghton Library 31/1/72)
Htn	Phil 2515.2.45*	Charron, P. Les trois veritez. 2e éd. Bordeaux, 1595.
Htn	Phil 2750.5.30*	Montaigne, Michel de. Les essais. Lyon, 1595.
Htn	Phil 9560.18.5*	Nenna, Giovanni B. Nennio, or A treatise of nobility. London, 1595.
Htn	Phil 6045.95*	Rothmann, J. Chiromantiae. Erphordiae, 1595.
Htn	Phil 8612.23*	Tasso, Ercole. Il confortatore. Bergamo, 1595.
Htn	Phil 5247.13.5*	Huarte de San Juan, J. The examination of men's wits. London, 1596.
Htn	Phil 7060.2.7*	Lavater, L. Of ghostes and spirites walking by night. London, 1596.
	Phil 5049.15	Joannes XXI, Pope. Summulae logicales. Venetiis, 1597.
Htn	Phil 1535.14*	Zabarella, J. De rebus naturalibus. Coloniae, 1597.
Htn	Phil 8876.19.5*	Bodenham, John. Politeuphuia. London, 1598.
Htn	Phil 8667.8*	More, G. A demonstration of God in his workes. London, 1598.
Htn	Phil 6990.36*	Morry, A. de. Discours d'un miracle avenu en la Basse Normandie. Paris, 1598.
Htn	Phil 6025.4.6F*	Porta, G.B. Della fisonomia dell'huomo. Libri quattro. Napoli, 1598.
Htn	Phil 8892.40.5*	Romei, A. The courtiers academie. London, 1598.
Htn	Phil 7060.7.5*	Thyraeus, P. Loca infesta, hoc est, de infestes. London, 1599.

16-

Htn	Phil 9162.1*	Carr, Roger. A godlie forme of household government. London, 16- ?
	Phil 2045.61.9	Hobbes, Thomas. Elementa philosophica de cive. n.p., 16-
	Phil 8892.51	Rigerus, Johannes. Ethicorum liber. v.1-2. n.p., 16- ?

1600-1609

	Phil 182.29.10	Heidfeld, J. Sphinx philosophica. Herbornae Nassoviorum, 1600.
	Phil 900.4	Heurnius, O. Barbaricae philosophiae. Lugdunum Batavorum, 1600.
	Phil 5190.4.15F	Piccolomineus, F. De rerum definitionibus liber unus. Venetiis, 1600.
	Phil 7060.7	Thyraeus, Petrus. De apparitionibus spirituum tractatus duo. Coloniae Agrippinae, 1600.
Htn	Phil 2515.2.49*	Charron, P. De la sagesse. Bordeaux, 1601.
Htn	Phil 8886.21.12*	La Primaudaye, P. de. The third volume of the French Academie. London, 1601.
	Phil 4195.6F	Pico della Mirandola, Giovanni. Opera quae extant omnia. Basileae, 1601.
	Phil 6025.4.5	Porta, G.B. Physiognomoniae collestis libri sex. Ursellis, 1601-08. 2 pam.
Htn	Phil 9173.2*	Nevizanis, J. de. Sylva nuptialis. n.p., 1602.
	Phil 7060.1	Taillepied, F.N. Traité de l'apparition des esprits. Roven, 1602.
	Phil 8875.3.16	Agrippa von Nettesheim, Heinrich Cornelius. Paradoxe sur l'incertitude vanité et abus des sciences. n.p., 1603.
	Phil 8875.3.15	Agrippa von Nettesheim, Heinrich Cornelius. Paradoxe sur l'incertitude vanité et abus des sciences. n.p., 1603.
	Phil 5545.42	Austriacus, J. De memoria artificios a lebellus. Argentorati, 1603.
Htn	Phil 5247.13*	Huarte de San Juan, J. Examen de ingenios para las sciencias. Antwerp? 1603.
Htn	Phil 2515.2.47*	Charron, P. De la sagesse. v.1-3. Paris, 1604.
Htn	Phil 5247.13.9*	Huarte de San Juan, J. Examen de ingenios. London, 1604.
	Phil 1200.1	Lipsius, J. Manuductionis ad stoicam philosophiam. Antverpriae, 1604.
Htn	Phil 2725.7.30*	Lipsius, Justus. Manuductionis ad stoicam. Antverpiae, 1604.
Htn	Phil 5400.10*	Wright, Thomas. The passions of the minde in generall. London, 1604.
Htn	Phil 5400.10.2*	Wright, Thomas. The passions of the minde in generall. London, 1604.
	Phil 5000.4F	Zabarella, Giacomo. Opera logica. 16a ed. Tarvisii, 1604.
Htn	Phil 1850.31*	Bacon, Francis. The two books of proficience and advancement of learning. London, 1605.
	Phil 9390.8	Huad en falsk eed alvorlig oc forfaerlig betyde effter som den hellige scrifft udviser. n.p., 1605.
	Phil 7060.6.3	Le Loyer, P. Discours et histoires des spectres, visions et apparitions des spirits. Paris, 1605.
Htn	Phil 7060.6.5*	Le Loyer, P. Treatise of specters. London, 1605.
Htn	Phil 8876.13*	Bryskett, Lodowick. Discourse of civil life. London, 1606.
Htn	Phil 8632.13*	Hoddesdon, H. A treatise, concerning the death and resurrection of our bodies. London, 1606.
Htn	Phil 5050.2*	Keckermann, B. Systema logicae minus. Hanoviae, 1606.

1600-1609 - cont.

	Phil 5525.28	Laurentius, A.P. Dialogus pulcherrimus et utilissimus. Marpurgi, 1606.
Htn	Phil 8870.7*	Pirckheimer, W. Theatrum virtutis et honoris. Nürnberg, 1606.
	Phil 6025.4.3	Porta, G.B. Physiognomoniae collestis libri sex. Argentorati, 1606. 2 pam.
Htn	Phil 9342.15*	Cleland, James. Erö-paideia, or The institution of a young noble man. Oxford, 1607.
	Phil 5247.13.13	Huarte de San Juan, J. Examen des esprits et naiz aux sciences. Rouen, 1607.
	Phil 8886.59	Lancre, P. de. Tableau de l'inconstance et instabilité de toutes choses. Paris, 1607.
Htn	Phil 182.29.15*	Heidfeld, J. Quintum renata. Herbornae Nassoviorum, 1608.
	Phil 7060.6.7	Le Loyer, P. Discours des spectres, ou visions. Paris, 1608.

1610-1619

Htn	Phil 8640.1.15*	Pomponazzi, P. Tractatus de immortalitate animae. Paris, 161-?
Htn	Phil 4931.1.30*	Augustinus, S. Of the citie of God. London, 1610.
	Phil 2835.80	Downame, G. Commentarii in P. Rami Dialecticam. Francofurti, 1610.
	Phil 8878.62	Dupleix, Scipion. L'ethique, ou Philosophie morale. Paris, 1610.
Htn	Phil 187.5*	Magirus, J. Physiologiae peripateticae. Francofurti, 1610.
	Phil 8676.2	Vorstius, Conrad. Tractatus theologicus dedeo. Steinfursti, 1610. 2 pam.
	Phil 5050.2.5	Keckermann, B. Systema logicae. Coloniae, 1611. 2 pam.
	Phil 250.1	Nancel, N. de. Analogia microcosmi. Paris, 1611.
Htn	Phil 9355.10*	Pasquier, N. Le gentilhomme. Paris, 1611. 3 pam.
	Phil 8876.37	Buys, J. De statibus hominum. Moguntiae, 1613.
	Phil 5000.2	Keckermanni, B. Systema systematum. Hanoviae, 1613.
	Phil 8886.21.5	La Primaudaye, P. de. L'Académie française. v.1-4. Saumur, 1613.
	Phil 5040.12	Alstedius, J.H. Logicae systema harmonicum. Herbonae Nassoviorum, 1614.
Htn	Phil 2515.2.27*	Charron, P. De la sagesse, trois livres. 3e éd. Paris, 1614.
Htn	Phil 2515.2.48*	Charron, P. De la sagesse. Rouen, 1614.
Htn	Phil 8893.4*	Sculteti, A. Ethicorum. Argentinae, 1614.
Htn	Phil 4950.1.30F*	Thomas Aquinas, St. Summa theologica. Duaci, 1614.
	Phil 3000.1	Adam, M. Vitae germanorum superiori. Franefort, 1615.
Htn	Phil 9560.24*	Pasquali, C. Virtutes et vitia. Parisiis, 1615.
Htn	Phil 6025.4.6.5*	Porta, G.B. Della fisonomia dell'huomo. Vicenza, 1615.
Htn	Phil 8893.73.10*	Selva, Lorenzo. Della metamorfosi...del virtuoso. Firenze, 1615.
Htn	Phil 8676.1*	Vanino, G.C. Amphitheatrum. Lugdunum, 1615.
Htn	Phil 9359.7*	Tuke, Thomas. A discourse against painting...of women. London, 1616.
Htn	Phil 9359.7.5*	Tuke, Thomas. A treatise against painting...of men and women. London, 1616.
Htn	Phil 4265.1.30*	Vanini, Lucilio, afterwards Giulio Cesare. De admirandis naturae reginae deaeque mortalium arcanis. Lutetieae, 1616.
Htn	Phil 1535.13*	Mendoza, P.H. de. Disputationes de universa philosophia. Lugduni, 1617.
Htn	Phil 5041.52.5*	Blundeville, Thomas. The arte of logicke. London, 1619.
Htn	Phil 9230.4.5*	Gataker, T. Of the nature and use of lots. London, 1619.

1620-1629

Htn	Phil 1850.56*	Bacon, Francis. De Verulamio summi angliae. London, 1620.
Htn	Phil 6016.2*	Grisaldi, Paolo. Guidicio di fisionomia. Trevigi, 1620.
Htn	Phil 1850.27.10*	Bacon, Francis. Essays politiques et moraux. Paris, 1621.
Htn	Phil 9162.1.5*	Carr, Roger. A godly forme of household government. London, 1621.
	Phil 6016.1	Goclenius, R. Physiognomica et chiromantica specialia. Marpurgi Cattorum, 1621.
Htn	Phil 182.29*	Heidfeld, J. Octavum renata. Herbornae Nassoviorum, 1621.
Htn	Phil 3890.3.30F*	Tauler, J. Des heilige Lerers Predigfast. Basel, 1621.
Htn	Phil 1850.57*	Bacon, Francis. The historie of the raigne of...Henry VII. London, 1622.
Htn	Phil 1850.73*	Bacon, Francois. Historia naturalis. Londini, 1622.
Htn	Phil 177.53*	Carpenter, Nathaniel. Philosophia libera. Ed. 2a. Oxoniae, 1622.
Htn	Phil 5042.17*	Crakanthorp, R. Logicae, libri quinque. London, 1622.
Htn	Phil 5043.12*	DuMoulin, Pierre. Elementa logica. Breamae, 1622.
Htn	Phil 6045.22.15*	Indagine, Joannes. Introductiones apostelesmaticae in physiognomiam. Argentorati, 1622.
Htn	Phil 2225.4.30*	Peacham, Henry. The compleat gentleman. London, 1622.
	Phil 185.15	Keckermann, B. Systema physicum. Hanoviae, 1623.
Htn	Phil 1850.31.15*	Bacon, Francis. De dignitate et augmentis scientiarum. Libri IX. Paris, 1624.
Htn	Phil 1850.37*	Bacon, Francis. Les progrez et avancement aux sciences divines et humaines. Paris, 1624.
Htn	Phil 2040.30*	Herbert, E. De veritate. Paris, 1624.
	Phil 9560.7.7	Pescetti, Orlando. Dell'onore dialoghi tre. Verona, 1624.
Htn	Phil 1850.39*	Bacon, Francis. The essayes or counsels. London, 1625.
	Phil 9560.15	Zuccolo, L. Nobilita commune, et heroica penser nuova é curiosa. Venetia, 1625.
	Phil 8887.32	Matthia, C. Systema ethicum. Marpurgi, 1626.
	Phil 6028.6	Spontane, Ciro. La metoposcopia, overo comensuratione delle linea della fronte. Venetia, 1626.
Htn	Phil 1850.71*	Bacon, Francis. Sylva Sylvarum. London, 1627.
Htn	Phil 9230.4*	Gataker, T. Of the nature and use of lots. London, 1627.
	Phil 8890.34.5	Piccolomineus, F. Universa philosophia de moribus. Francofurti, 1627.
Htn	Phil 8880.1.8*	Feltham, O. Resolves. 2nd ed. London, 1628. 2 pam.
Htn	Phil 8880.1.9*	Feltham, O. Resolves. 3rd ed. London, 1628.
Htn	Phil 184.1*	Jack, G. Primae philosophiae institutiones. Lugdunum Batavorum, 1628.
Htn	Phil 1850.59*	Bacon, Francis. The use of the law. London, 1629.
	Phil 8876.35.3	Burgersdyck, F. Idea philosophiae tum moralis. 2a ed. Lugduni, 1629.
	Phil 5628.50	Ostermann, Petrus. Commentarius iuridicus ad L. Stigmata, C. de Fabricensibus. Coloniae Agripinae, 1629.

1630-1639

Htn	Phil 1850.55*	Bacon, Francis. A collection of some principall rules and maximes of the common laws of England. London, 1630.
Htn	Phil 2515.2.33*	Charron, P. Of wisdome. London, 1630.

Chronological Listing

1630-1639 - cont.

Phil 6045.22.17 Indagine, Joannes. Introductiones apotelesmaticae in physiognomiam. Argentorati, 1630.

Phil 5628.50.5 Jordanaeus, Johannes. Disputatio brevis ad categorica de proba stigmata utrum scilicet ea licita sit, necne. Coloniae Agrippinae, 1630.

Htn Phil 5400.10.5* Wright, Thomas. The passions of the minde in generall. London, 1630.

Htn Phil 1850.75.5* Bacon, Francis. Histoire naturelle. Paris, 1631.
Htn Phil 5041.23* Brerewood, E. Tractatus guidam logici. Oxoniae, 1631. 3 pam.

Htn Phil 8876.35* Burgersdyck, F. Idea philosophiae tum moralis. Oxoniae, 1631.

Htn Phil 8878.15* Drexelius, H. Nicetas feu triumphata incontinentia. Colonia Agrippina, 1631.

Htn Phil 8880.1.10* Feltham, O. Resolves. 4th ed. London, 1631.
Phil 5247.13.26 Guibelet, J. Examen de l'examen des esprits. Paris, 1631.
Htn Phil 8637.9.3* Montagu, H. Contemplatio mortis, and immortalitatis. London, 1631.

Htn Phil 190.7* Pemble, W. De Formarum origine. Cantabrigia, 1631.
Htn Phil 1850.38* Bacon, Francis. Neuf livres de la dignité et de l'accroissement des sciences. Paris, 1632.

Htn Phil 9075.14.5* Dyke, J. Good conscience. 5. ed. London, 1632. 2 pam.
Phil 8879.6.6 Erasmus, D. De civilitate morum. Rostochi, 1632.
Htn Phil 4120.7.30* Galilei, Galileo. Dialogo. Fiorenza, 1632.
Phil 9245.19 Laserre, J.P. de. Le tombeau des délices du monde. Brusselles, 1632.

Htn Phil 2750.5.35* Montaigne, Michel de. Essayes or Morall, politike, and militarie discourses. 3d ed. London, 1632.

Htn Phil 3110.80* Werdenhagen, I.G. Psychologia. Amsterdam, 1632.
Htn Phil 1850.27.5* Bacon, Francis. Les oeuvres morales et politiques. Paris, 1633. 2v.

Phil 8626.15.9 Burnet, Thomas. A treatise concerning the state of the departed souls. London, 1633.

Htn Phil 2040.30.3* Herbert, E. De veritate. London, 1633.
Htn Phil 2040.30.2* Herbert, E. De veritate. London, 1633.
Htn Phil 9050.7.5* Nash, T. Quaternio, or A fourfold way to a happy life. London, 1633.

Htn Phil 8890.5* Pavonio, F. Summa ethicae. Oxonii, 1633.
Htn Phil 8880.1.11* Feltham, O. Resolves. 5th ed. London, 1634.
Htn Phil 8887.13* Meres, F. Wits commonwealth. pt. 2. London, 1634.
Htn Phil 5058.15.3* Smith, Samuel. Aditus ad logicam. Oxoniae, 1634.
Phil 1535.15.5 Bonaventura, St., Cardinal. Summa totius philosophiae Aristotelicae. pt.1-2. Romae, 1635. 2v.

Phil 4075.45 Cardano, Girolamo. Arcana politica. Lugduni, 1635.
Htn Phil 9358.5* Scott, William. An essay of drapery. London, 1635.
Htn Phil 1850.63* Bacon, Francis. Historia vitae et mortis. Lugdunum Batavorum, 1636.

Htn Phil 4073.35* Campanella, Tommaso. Ludovico iusto XIII; Atheismus Tsiumphatus. Parisiis, 1636.

Htn Phil 3200.1.30* Erasmus, D. Colloquia. Lugdunum Batavorum, 1636.
Htn Phil 8880.1* Feltham, O. Resolves. London, 1636.
Htn Phil 9050.7* Nash, T. Quaternio, or A fourfold way to a happy life. London, 1636.

Htn Phil 8896.3* Vives, Juan Luis. De disciplinis. Lugdunum Batavorum, 1636.

Htn Phil 4372.1.31* Vives, Juan Luis. I.L. Vivis Valentini, de disciplinis libri XII. Batavorum Lugduni, 1636.

Htn Phil 1850.64* Bacon, Francis. Historia vitae et mortis. Lugdunum Batavorum, 1637.

Htn Phil 1850.27* Bacon, Francis. Les oeuvres morales et politiques. Paris, 1637.

Htn Phil 1850.27.3* Bacon, Francis. Les oeuvres morales et politiques. Paris, 1637.

Htn Phil 2520.35.1* Descartes, René. Discours de la méthode pour bien conduire sa raison et chercher la vérité dans les sciences. Leyde, 1637.

Phil 6025.4.7 Porta, G.B. Della fisonomia di tutto il corpo humano. Roma, 1637.

Htn Phil 1850.1.10* Bacon, F. Operum moralium et civilium tomus. London, 1638.

Htn Phil 1850.1.11F* Bacon, Francis. Francisci Baconi operum moralium. Londini, 1638. 2 pam.

Htn Phil 1850.74* Bacon, Francis. Historia naturalis et experimentalis de ventis. Lugdunum Batavorum, 1638.

Htn Phil 1850.64.5* Bacon, Francis. Historie of life and death. London, 1638.
Htn Phil 1850.64.7* Bacon, Francis. History naturall and experimentall, of life and death. London, 1638.

Htn Phil 8657.15.3* Church, Henry. Miscellanea philo-theologica, or God and man. London, 1638.

Htn Phil 170.2.5F* Fludd, Robert. Philosophia moysaica. Goudae, 1638.
Htn Phil 6045.22.35* Indagine, Joannes. La chiromance et phisiognomie. Rouen, 1638.

Htn Phil 8637.9* Montagu, H. Contemplatio mortis, and immortalitatis. London, 1638.

Htn Phil 9355.2.9* Peacham, Henry. The truth of our times. London, 1638.
Htn Phil 193.7* Scheiblero, C. Philosophia compendiosa. Oxonii, 1639.
Htn Phil 193.7.2* Scheiblero, C. Philosophia compendiosa. Oxonii, 1639.

1640-1649

Phil 1850.3.3* Bacon, Francis. Advancement and proficience of learning. Oxford, 1640.

Phil 1850.3.2* Bacon, Francis. Advancement and proficience of learning. Oxford, 1640.

Phil 8876.14.5* Baldwin, W. A treatise of morall philosophie. London, 1640.

Phil 720.11* Brooke, R.G. Nature of truth. London, 1640.
Phil 1535.4.5* Eustachius a S. Paulo. Summa philosophiae quadripartita. Cantabrigiae, 1640.

Phil 1535.4.4* Eustachius a S. Paulo. Summa philosophiae quadripartita. Cantabrigiae, 1640.

Phil 665.11* Reynolds, E. Treatise of the passions and faculties of the soule of man. London, 1640.

Phil 4369.1.30* Sebon, Raymond. La theologie naturelle. 2. ed. Paris, 1640.

Phil 1850.72* Bacon, Francis. The confession of faith. London, 1641.
Phil 1850.61* Bacon, Francis. A wise and moderate discourse concerning church affaires. n.p., 1641.

Phil 8879.6A Erasmus, D. Lingua, sive, de linguae. Lugdunum Batavorum, 1641.

Phil 3110.32 Böhme, J. Bedrachtingh vande goddelycke openbaringh. n.p., 1642.

g Phil 176.37 Burgersdijck, F.P. Collegium physicum disputationibus XXXII absolutum. Lugdunum Batavorum, 1642.

Phil 176.37.6 Burgersdijck, F.P. Institutionum metaphyricarum libri II. Lugdunum Batavorum, 1642.

1640-1649 - cont.

Htn Phil 5041.25* Burgersdijck, Franco. Institutionum logicarum. Lugdunum Batavorum, 1642-60. 2 pam.

Htn Phil 2520.52.17* Descartes, René. Meditationes de prima philosophia. 2a ed. Amstelodami, 1642. 2 pam.

Phil 9230.1 Joostens, P. Alea, sive de curanda ludendi in pecuniam cupiditate. Amsterodami, 1642.

Phil 303.5 White, T. De mundo dialogi tres quibus. Paris, 1642.
Phil 8875.3 Agrippa von Nettesheim, Heinrich Cornelius. De incertitudine et vanitate omnium scientiarum et artium liber. Lugduni Batavorum, 1643.

Htn Phil 4075.79* Cardano, Girolamo. De propria vita liber. Parisiis, 1643.
Phil 2515.2.90 Chanet, P. Considérations sur la Sagesse de Charron. Paris, 1643.

Htn Phil 2520.77* Descartes, René. Epistola...ad celeberrimum virum D. Gisbertum Voetium. Amsterodami, 1643.

Phil 2520.150 Schoock, Martin. Admiranda methodus novae philosophiae Renati des Cartes. Waesberge, 1643.

Phil 2520.52.20 Descartes, René. Meditationes de prima philosophia. Amstelodami, 1644.

Htn Phil 2520.10.5* Descartes, René. Principia philosophiae. Amsterdam, 1644. 2 pam.

Htn Phil 8628.3.2F* Digby, K. Two treatises...nature of bodies...nature of man's soul. Paris, 1644.

Htn Phil 2555.3.30* DuRefuge, E. Aulicus inculpatus. Amsterdam, 1644.
Htn Phil 2520.182* Gassendi, Pierre. Disquisitio metaphysica. Amstelodami, 1644.

Htn Phil 3110.87* The life of one Jacob Boehmen. London, 1644.
Phil 1200.1.5 Lipsius, J. Manuductionis ad stoicam philosophiam. Lugduni Batavorum, 1644.

Htn Phil 8624.1* Overton, R. Man's mortallitie. Amsterdam, 1644-97. 7 pam.

NEDL Phil 6025.4.8 Porta, G.B. Della fisonomia dell'huomo. Venetia, 1644.
Htn Phil 177.16* CJ.A. Physicae. Amsterdam, 1645.
Htn Phil 8628.3.4* Digby, K. Two treatises. London, 1645. 2 pam.
Htn Phil 2040.31* Herbert, E. De causis errorum. London, 1645.
Phil 8636.6 Le Long, Jean. Saint Athanase, ou Traité de la nature. Middelburg, 1645.

Htn Phil 8628.3.3* Ross, Alexander. Philosophical touchstone. London, 1645.
Htn Phil 2515.2.30* Charron, P. De la sagesse. Leide, 1646.
Htn Phil 3110.30* Böhme, J. Questions concerning the soul. London, 1647.
Htn Phil 3120.3.30* Burgeridicii, F. Institutionum logicarum. Cantabrigiae, 1647. 2 pam.

Phil 176.37.10 Burgersdijck, F.P. Instituionum metaphysicarum libri II. n.p., 1647.

Htn Phil 5041.25.2* Burgersdijck, Franco. Institutionum logicarum. Cantabrigiae, 1647-80. 3 pam.

Htn Phil 2520.52.7* Descartes, René. Les méditations métaphysics. Paris, 1647.

Htn Phil 2520.39.8* Descartes, René. Les principes de la philosophie. Paris, 1647.

Htn Phil 2045.60.25* Hobbes, Thomas. Elementa philosophica de cive. Amsterdam, 1647.

Htn Phil 1850.18* Bacon, Francis. Remaines, being essayes and severall letters. London, 1648.

Htn Phil 3110.35* Böhme, J. Concerning the three principles of divine essence. London, 1648.

Phil 6025.10 Petit-Douxciel, A. Speculum physionomicum. Langres, 1648.
Htn Phil 5827.2* Rorario, G. Quôd animalia bruta ratione utantur meliùs homine. Paris, 1648.

Htn Phil 3110.23* Böhme, J. Epistles. London, 1649-50.
Htn Phil 2520.35.10* Descartes, René. A discours of a method. London, 1649.
Htn Phil 184.1.2* Jack, G. Primae philosophiae institutiones. Cantabrigia, 1649.

1650-1659

Htn Phil 1850.50.6* Bacon, Francis. Novum organum. Lugdunum Batavorum, 1650. 2 pam.

Htn Phil 8876.19.6* Bodenham, John. Politeuphuia, wits common-wealth. London, 1650.

Phil 2520.52.25 Descartes, René. Meditationes de prima philosophia. Amstelodami, 1650. 3 pam.

Htn Phil 2520.60.1* Descartes, René. Passiones animae. Amstelodami, 1650.
Htn Phil 2520.60* Descartes, René. Passiones animae. Amstelodami, 1650.
Htn Phil 2520.10* Descartes, René. Principia philosophiae. Amsterdam, 1650.
Htn Phil 4938.1.30* Hermes Trismegistus. The divine Pymander. London, 1650.
Phil 2045.59* Hobbes, Thomas. Human nature. London, 1650.
Phil 193.32.3 Stahli, D. Metaphysicae. Bredae, 1650.
Htn Phil 2515.2.40* Charron, P. Of wisdom, three books. London, 1651.
Phil 177.16.9 Comenius, J.A. Natural philosophie reformed by divine light. London, 1651.

Htn Phil 2520.61.12* Descartes, René. Les passions de l'âme. Rouen, 1651.
Htn Phil 2520.39* Descartes, René. Les principes de la philosophie. Paris, 1651.

Htn Phil 8628.3.8F* Digby, K. Demonstratio immortalitatis animae. Parisiis, 1651.

Phil 2045.61.30 Hobbes, Thomas. Elemens philosophiques du bon citoyen. Paris, 1651.

Htn Phil 2045.48.5F* Hobbes, Thomas. Leviathan. London, 1651.
Htn Phil 2045.48* Hobbes, Thomas. Leviathan. London, 1651.
Htn Phil 2045.60* Hobbes, Thomas. Philosophical rudiments concerning goverment and society. London, 1651.

Htn Phil 8591.17.8* Lessius, Leonardus. Sir Walter Rawleigh's ghost. London, 1651.

Phil 187.6.2 Makowski, J. Metaphysica. Amsterdam, 1651.
Htn Phil 2150.4.30* Milton, Joannis. Angli pro populo anglicano defensio. Londini, 1651.

Htn Phil 193.32* Stahli, D. Axiomata philosophica. Amsterdam, 1651.
Htn Phil 1850.32* Bacon, Francis. De augmentis scientiarum. Libri IX. Lugduni, 1652.

Phil 665.15 Carpenter, A. Pseuchographia anthropomagica. London, 1652.

Htn Phil 8657.18* Charleton, W. The darkness of atheism dispelled by the light of native. London, 1652.

Phil 7084.30.2 Cook, John. A true relation of Mr. Justice Cook's passage by sea from Wexforel to Kinsaile, and of the great storm. 2d ed. London, 1652.

Htn Phil 8582.16* Culverwel, N. An elegant and learned discourse...light of nature. London, 1652.

Phil 6025.4.9 Porta, G.B. Fisonomia dell'huomo. Venetia, 1652.
Phil 2520.80 Andrea, T. Brevis replicatia...notis Cartesii. Amstelodami, 1653.

Htn Phil 1850.74.5* Bacon, Francis. The naturall and experimentall history of winds. London, 1653.

Phil 1850.30 Bacon, Francis. Scripta in naturali...philosophia. Amsterdam, 1653.

1650-1659 - cont.

Htn Phil 8876.19.7* Bodenham, John. Politeuphuia, wits common-wealth. London, 1653.

Htn Phil 2520.65* Descartes, R. Excellent compendium of musik. London, 1653.

Phil 9345.7 Fortin, P. Testament, ou Conseils fideles d'un bon pere. Leide, 1653.

Htn Phil 2145.65* More, Henry. Antidote against atheisme. London, 1653.

Htn Phil 2045.87* Rosse, A. Leviathan drawn out with a hook. London, 1653.

Phil 1850.32.8 Bacon, Francis. De dignitate et augmentis scientarum. Libri IX. Argentorari, 1654.

Htn Phil 3110.39* Böhme, J. Musterium magnum. London, 1654.

Phil 4075.78 Cardano, Girolamo. Hieronymi Cardani mediolanensis. Amstelaedami, 1654.

Phil 2520.52.26 Descartes, René. Meditationes de prima philosophia. Amstelodami, 1654.

Htn Phil 2045.63* Hobbes, Thomas. Of libertie and necessity. London, 1654.

X Cg Phil 6028.4.5 Spadon, N. Scuola di fisionomia, chiromantia. Macerata, 1654.

Htn Phil 5062.5* Wendelin, M.F. Logicae institutiones. Amstelrodami, 1654.

Phil 6046.55 Azzi, G. L'idea del futuro rappresentato dalle linee della mano. Lucca, 1655.

Htn Phil 8876.19.2* Bodenham, John. Politeuphuia, wits common-wealth. London, 1655.

Htn Phil 3110.40* Böhme, J. Concerning the election of grace. London, 1655.

Htn Phil 8628.3.9F* Digby, K. Demonstratos immortalitatis animae rationalis. Paris, 1655.

Htn Phil 8882.7.25* Herle, Charles. Wisdomes tripos. London, 1655.

Htn Phil 6025.4.25* Porta, G.B. La physionomie humaine. Rouen, 1655.

Htn Phil 665.6* Woolnor, H. The extraction of man's soul. London, 1655.

Htn Phil 3110.36.2* Böhme, J. High and deep searching out. London, 1656.

Htn Phil 5405.6* Casaubon, M. A treatise concerning enthusiasme. 2. ed. London, 1656.

X Cg Phil 2520.11 Descartes, René. Opera philosophica. Francofurti, 1656-58.

Phil 2520.35.2 Descartes, René. Specimina philosophiae. Amsterdam, 1656.

Phil 8658.3* Dove, J. Atheism defined and confuted. London, 1656.

Htn Phil 9346.9* Gauden, John. A discourse of auxiliary beauty. n.p., 1656.

Htn Phil 2045.62* Hobbes, Thomas. Elements of philosophy. London, 1656.

Htn Phil 5058.15* Smith, Samuel. Aditis at logicam. Oxoniae, 1656-1657.

Phil 1123.3.1 Stanley, T. History of philosophy. v.1-3. London, 1656-60. 2v.

Htn Phil 1123.3.2* Stanley, T. History of philosophy. v.1-3. London, 1656-60. 2v.

Htn Phil 1850.75.10* Bacon, Francis. Resuscitatio, or Bringing into public light. London, 1657.

Phil 176.119 Baron, K. Metaphysica generalis. Londini, 1657?

X Cg Phil 176.37.5 Burgersdijck, F.P. Institutionum metaphyricarum libri II. Hagae Comitis, 1657.

Htn Phil 8627.10* Charleton, W. The immortality of the human soul. London, 1657.

Phil 1210.15 Cornaeus, Melchior. Curriculm philosophiae peripateticae. v.1-2. Herbipoli, 1657.

Htn Phil 2520.76.3* Descartes, René. Lettres ou sont traitées les plusieurs belles questions de la morale. Paris, 1657.

Phil 2520.52.60 Descartes, René. Meditationes de prima philosophia. Amsterdam, 1657. 5 pam.

Htn Phil 2045.61* Hobbes, Thomas. Elementa philosophica de cive. Amsterdam, 1657.

Htn Phil 2045.104* Lawson, George. An examination of the political part of Mr. Hobbs his Leviathan. London, 1657.

Htn Phil 2805.28* Pascal, Blaise. Les provinciales. Cologne, 1657.

Htn Phil 2805.30.16* Pascal, Blaise. Les provinciales. Cologne, 1657.

Htn Phil 2805.32.11* Pascal, Blaise. Les provinciales. Cologne, 1657.

Phil 6046.57 Peruchio. La chiromance. Paris, 1657.

Htn Phil 9358.11* Sprigg, William. Philosophicall essayes...advises to ladyes. London, 1657.

Htn Phil 1850.76* Bacon, Francis. Opuscula varia posthuma, philosophica, civilia, et theologica. Londini, 1658.

Phil 2045.105 Bramhall, J. Castigations of Mr. Hobbes. London, 1658.

Phil 6012.5F Cardano, Girolamo. Metoposcopia libris tredecim. Lutetiae, 1658.

Htn Phil 2515.2.31* Charron, P. De la sagesse. Leide, 1658?

Phil 5042.12 Clauberg, Johann. Logica vetus et nova. 2a ed. Amsterdam, 1658.

Htn Phil 8628.3* Digby, K. Two treatises. London, 1658-57.

Htn Phil 6480.26* Goodwin, P. The mystery of dreames. London, 1658.

Htn Phil 2805.32.12* Pascal, Blaise. Les provinciales. London, 1658.

Phil 5058.39 Smiglecki, Marcin. Logica Martini. Oxonii, 1658.

Phil 1850.59.50 Bacon, Francis. Sermones fidelis, ethici, politici, o economici, sive interiora rerum. Lugdunum Batavorum, 1659.

Htn Phil 2520.39.10* Descartes, René. Les principes de la philosophie. Paris, 1659.

Htn Phil 170.2* Fludd, Robert. Mosaicall philosophy. London, 1659.

Phil 9230.6 Gataker, T. Antithesis de sorte. Lugdunum Batavorum, 1659-60. 3 pam.

Phil 7060.2.2 Lavater, L. De spectris. Lugduni Batavorum, 1659.

Phil 2115.1.6F Locke, J. Works. London, 1659. 3v.

Htn Phil 2150.5.31* More, Henry. The immortality of the soul. London, 1659.

Htn Phil 2145.70* More, Henry. The immortality of the soul. London, 1659.

1660-1669

Htn Phil 1845.1.25* Allestree, Richard. The gentleman's calling. London, 1660.

Htn Phil 8580.22.5* Amyraut, M. A treatise concerning religions. London, 1660.

Htn Phil 1850.50.7* Bacon, Francis. Novum organum. 2a ed. Amsterdam, 1660.

Htn Phil 3120.3.31* Burgeridicii, F. Institutionum logicarum. Libri duo. Cantabrigiae, 1660.

Phil 2520.11.5 Descartes, René. Les principes de la philosophie. 2e éd. Paris, 1660.

Htn Phil 9344.7* Ellis, Clement. The gentile sinner. Oxford, 1660.

Phil 6957.13 Highmore, N. Exercitationes duae...histerica. 2. ed. Amstelodami, 1660.

Phil 3450.3.90 Stearne, John. Adriani Heereboordi. Dublinii, 1660.

Htn Phil 9390.10* A warning to sinners. London, 1660.

Htn Phil 1850.5.2F* Bacon, Francis. Resuscitatio. 2nd ed. London, 1661.

Phil 4075.45.15 Cardano, Girolamo. La science du monde. 4e ed. Paris, 1661.

Phil 2520.52.8 Descartes, René. Les méditations métaphysiques. 2e éd. Paris, 1661.

Htn Phil 8800.6* Feltham, Owen. Resolves. London, 1661.

Htn Phil 337.4* Glanvill, Joseph. The vanity of dogmatizing. London, 1661. 2 pam.

1660-1669 - cont.

Phil 5247.13.15 Huarte de San Juan, J. L'examen des esprits pour les sciences. Paris, 1661.

Phil 6046.61 Praetorius, J. Ludicrum chiromanticum praetorii sen thesaurus chiromantiae. Jenae, 1661.

Htn Phil 665.4* Ramesey, W. Man's dignity. London, 1661.

Htn Phil 1850.32.5* Bacon, Francis. De augmentis scientiarum. Libri IX. Amsterdam, 1662.

Htn Phil 1850.75* Bacon, Francis. Historia naturalis et experimentalis de ventis. Amstelodami, 1662. 3 pam.

Htn Phil 1850.60* Bacon, Francis. Sermones fidelis. Amsterdam, 1662.

Htn Phil 3110.15* Böhme, J. Remainder of books. London, 1662.

Htn Phil 9510.5* Boreman, R. An antidote against swearing. London, 1662.

Htn Phil 2515.2.32* Charron, P. De la sagesse. Amsterdam, 1662.

Htn Phil 2520.34.2* Descartes, René. De homine, figuris, et latinitate donatus. Lugduni Batavorum, 1662.

Htn Phil 665.12* Glanvill, Joseph. Lux orientalis. London, 1662.

Htn Phil 2045.64* Hobbes, Thomas. Mr. Hobbes considered in his loyalty, religion, reputation and manners. London, 1662.

Phil 6045.22.40 Indagine, Joannes. La chiromance et phisionomie. Paris, 1662?

Htn Phil 2145.1* More, Henry. Collection...philosophical writings. London, 1662.

Phil 5059.8 Trieu, A.R.P.P.D. Manuductio ad logicam. Oxoniae, 1662.

Htn Phil 2045.97* Wallis, John. Hobbius Heauton-timorumenos. Oxford, 1662.

Htn Phil 3000.1.2 Adam, M. Vitae germanorum philosophorum. Franefort, 1663.

Htn Phil 1850.65* Bacon, Francis. Historia vitae et mortis. Amstelodami, 1663.

Htn Phil 1850.62* Bacon, Francis. True peace; or A moderate discourse. London, 1663.

Phil 4075.1F Cardano, Girolamo. Opera. Lugduni, 1663. 10v.

Htn Phil 2520.76* Descartes, René. Lettres ou sont traitées les plusieurs belles questions touchant la morale. Paris, 1663. 2v.

Phil 5047.4 Heereboord, Adriano. Ermhneia logica...burgersdicianae. Cantabridgiae, 1663.

Htn Phil 3552.50* Leibniz, Gottfried Wilhelm. Disputatio metaphysica. Lipsiae, 1663.

Htn Phil 294.4F* Newcastle, M.L.C. Philosophical and physical opinions. London, 1663.

Htn Phil 2805.60* Pascal, Blaise. Traitez de l'equilibre. Paris, 1663.

Phil 6046.57.5 Peruchio. La chiromance. Paris, 1663.

Phil 6028.4 Spadon, N. Studio di curiosita. Venetia, 1663.

Htn Phil 2520.163.20* Spinoza, B. de. Renati des Cartes principiorum philosophiae pars I, et II. Amstelodami, 1663.

VPhil 1850.1F Bacon, F. Opera omnia. Frankfort, 1664-68.

Htn Phil 2520.34.3* Descartes, René. De homine...Schuye a Florentio Schuye. Lugduni Batavorum, 1664.

Phil 2520.34* Descartes, René. L'homme et un traitte de la formation du Foetus. Paris, 1664.

Htn Phil 2520.62.5* Descartes, René. Le monde. Paris, 1664.

Htn Phil 2520.10.9* Descartes, René. Opera philosophica. 4a ed. Amsterdam, 1664.

Phil 2520.10.10 Descartes, René. Opera philosophica. 4a ed. Amsterdam, 1664.

Phil 2520.10.8 Descartes, René. Opera philosophica. 4a ed. Amsterdam, 1664.

Htn Phil 2520.60.5* Descartes, René. Passiones animae. Amstelodami, 1664.

Htn Phil 8628.3.5* Digby, K. Demonstratio immortalitatis animae. Francofurti, 1664.

Phil 2805.29 Pascal, Blaise. Litterae provinciales. Helmaestadt, 1664.

Htn Phil 2520.163.15* Spinoza, B. de. Renatus des Cartes beginzelen der wijsbegeerte. Amsterdam, 1664.

VPhil 1850.1.2F Bacon, F. Opera omnia. Frankfort, 1665.

Htn Phil 6012.6.5* Cureau de la Chambre, Marin. The art how to know men. London, 1665.

Htn Phil 2030.1.30* Glanvill, Joseph. Scepsis scientifica. London, 1665.

Htn Phil 182.10.3* Heereboort, A. Meletemata philosophica. Amsterdam, 1665.

Phil 8959.3 Joly, C. Traité des restitutions des grands. Amsterdam, 1665.

Phil 6046.65 Mey, Philipp. La chiromancie medicinale. La Haye, 1665.

Phil 665.22 Scheibler, Christoph. Liber de anima. Francofurti, 1665.

Htn Phil 9362.12* Waterhoues, E. The gentleman's monitor. London, 1665.

Htn Phil 2520.76.5* Descartes, René. Lettres ou sont traitées les plusieurs belles questions touchant la morale. v.1-3. Paris, 1666-67.

Phil 3455.2 Isendoorn, Gisbert. Cursus logicus systematicus et agonisticus. Francofurti, 1666.

Phil 6121.20.3 La Forge, Louis de. Traité de l'esprit de l'homme. Paris, 1666.

Htn Phil 2805.29.6* Pascal, Blaise. Les provinciales. 6. éd. Cologne, 1666.

Htn Phil 3120.3.35* Burgeridicii, F. Idea philosophiae. Oxonii, 1667.

Htn Phil 9515.5* Evelyn, John. Publick employment and active life prefered. London, 1667.

Phil 2045.49 Hobbes, Thomas. Leviathan. Amsterdam, 1667.

Phil 9355.2 Peacham, Henry. The worth of a penny. London, 1667.

Htn Phil 8602.2* Ward, S. A philosophical essay. Oxford, 1667.

Htn Phil 665.5* Warren, E. No praeexistence. London, 1667.

Htn Phil 5041.25.3* Burgersdijck, Franco. Institutionum logicarum. Cantabrigiae, 1668-1670. 3 pam.

Phil 8875.22 D'Acol. La reduction de toutes les sciences en la connaissance de l'homme. Paris, 1668.

Htn Phil 2520.35.12* Descartes, René. Discours de la méthode pour bien conduire sa raison et chercher la vérité dans les sciences. Paris, 1668.

Htn Phil 2520.35.13* Descartes, René. Discours de la méthode pour bien conduire sa raison et chercher la vérité dans les sciences. Paris, 1668.

Phil 2520.35.3 Descartes, René. Discours de la méthode pour bien conduire sa raison et chercher la vérité dans les sciences. Paris, 1668.

Htn Phil 2520.75.3* Descartes, René. Epistolae. v.1-2. Amstelodami, 1668.

Htn Phil 2520.75.5* Descartes, René. Epistolae. v.1-2. Londini, 1668.

Phil 2520.39.3 Descartes, René. Les principes de la philosophie. Paris, 1668.

NEDL Phil 2610.15 Gassendi, P. Institutio logica, et Philosophiae Epicuri syntagma. London, 1668.

Htn Phil 2045.3* Hobbes, Thomas. Opera philosophica. Amstelodami, 1668. 2v.

Htn Phil 2045.4* Hobbes, Thomas. Works in Latin. Amsterdam, 1668-70.

Htn Phil 2145.60* More, Henry. Divine dialogues. London, 1668. 2v.

Htn Phil 294.4.2F* Newcastle, M.L.C. Grounds of natural philosophy. 2. ed. London, 1668.

Htn Phil 177.15* Casaubon, M. Letter...concerning natural experimental philosophy. Cambridge, 1669.

Htn Phil 1955.3.30* Digby, Kenelm. Of bodies and of man's soul. London, 1669.

Htn Phil 2045.61.5* Hobbes, Thomas. Elementa philosophica de cive. Amsterdam, 1669.

Chronological Listing

1660-1669 - cont.

	Phil 2045.58	Hobbes, Thomas. Quadratura circuli. n.p., 1669.
	Phil 2725.20	Lamy, G. De principiis rerum. Paris, 1669.
Htn	Phil 9352.1*	Mackenzie, G. Moral gallantry. Edinburgh, 1669. 2 pam.
Htn	Phil 2805.30.18*	Pascal, Blaise. Les provinciales. 7. éd. Cologne, 1669.
Htn	Phil 2835.30*	Ramus, P. Dialecticae libri duo. London, 1669.
Htn	Phil 2045.97.5*	Wallis, John. Thomae Hobbes quadratura circuli. 2. ed. Oxoniae, 1669.

1670-1679

Htn	Phil 1850.5.5F*	Bacon, Francis. The second part of the Resuscitatio. London, 1670.
Htn	Phil 2515.2.41*	Charron, P. Of wisdome. London, 1670.
	Phil 5042.17.3	Crakanthorp, R. Logicae libri quinque. 3a ed. Oxoniae, 1670.
Htn	Phil 8880.1.12*	Feltham, O. Resolves. London, 1670.
Htn	Phil 8882.8*	Herle, Charles. Wisdom's tripos. London, 1670.
	Phil 2045.49.5	Hobbes, Thomas. Leviathan. Amstelodami, 1670.
Htn	Phil 2805.39*	Pascal, Blaise. Pensées...sur la religion. Paris, 1670.
Htn	Phil 2805.39.5*	Pascal, Blaise. Pensées. Paris, 1670.
Htn	Phil 2805.39.2*	Pascal, Blaise. Pensées. Paris, 1670.
Htn	Phil 5938.11F*	Saunders, R. Saunders physiognomie. 2nd ed. London, 1670-71.
Htn	Phil 2045.107*	Tenison, Thomas. The creed of Mr. Hobbes examined. London, 1670.
	Phil 1210.16F	Weis, Georg. Nexus philosophiae theorico-politécae pecipatentica. Prague, 1670.
Htn	Phil 8696.13*	Glanvill, Joseph. Philosophia pia. London, 1671.
Htn	Phil 2145.40*	More, Henry. Enchiridion metaphysicum. London, 1671.
	Phil 126.2	Stier, J. Praecepta doctrinae logicae. London, 1671.
Htn	Phil 9220.3.5*	Taylor, Jeremy. A discourse of the nature...of friendship. London, 1671. 2 pam.
Htn	Phil 2340.3.30*	Waring, Robert. Amoris effigies. 4th ed. London, 1671.
Htn	Phil 4075.51*	Cardano, Girolamo. De utilitate-ex adversis capienda libri. Amsterdam, 1672.
Htn	Phil 2515.2.35*	Charron, P. La sagesse de Charron. Paris, 1672.
	Phil 1928.30.2	Cumberland, R. De legibus naturae. London, 1672.
Htn	Phil 2520.10.15*	Descartes, René. Opera philosophica. 5a ed. Amsterdam, 1672.
Htn	Phil 2520.10.16*	Descartes, René. Opera philosophica. 5a ed. Amsterdam, 1672.
	Phil 6045.22.19	Indagine, Joannes. Introductiones apotilesmaticae in physiognomiam. Argentorati, 1672.
Htn	Phil 7066.72*	Pye, John. A true and perfect account of a strange and dreadful apparition. London, 1672.
	Phil 2520.204	Rochon, Antoine. Lettre d'un philosophie à un cartesien de ses amis. Paris, 1672.
	Phil 9560.8	Stearne, J. De obstinatione. Dublin, 1672.
Htn	Phil 5262.16*	Willis, T. De anima Brutorum. Oxonii, 1672.
Htn	Phil 9340.6*	Allestree, Richard. The ladies calling. Oxford, 1673.
Htn	Phil 1845.1.30*	Allestree, Richard. The ladies calling. Oxford, 1673.
Htn	Phil 1850.29*	Bacon, Francis. Essays or counsels, civil and moral...where unto is added the wisdom of the ancients. London, 1673.
Htn	Phil 9343.12*	Dare, Josiah. Counsellor Manners, his last legacy to his son. London, 1673.
	Phil 2520.52.10	Descartes, René. Les méditationes métaphysiques. 3e éd. Paris, 1673.
Htn	Phil 2045.103*	Eachard, John. Some opinions of Mr. Hobbs. London, 1673.
Htn	Phil 1850.33.5*	Bacon, Francis. Of the advancement and proficiencie of learning. London, 1674.
Htn	Phil 8876.19.13*	Bodenham, John. Politeuphuia, wits common-wealth. London, 1674.
Htn	Phil 5400.2*	Charleton, W. Natural history of the passions. London, 1674.
	Phil 3832.15	Mansveld, R. Adversus anonymun theologs-politicum. Amstelaedami, 1674.
Htn	Phil 7066.74*	News from Puddle-Dock in London. London, 1674.
	Phil 6124.2	Orth, H. Disputatio philosophica. Jenae, 1674.
Htn	Phil 8691.5*	Boyle, R. Some considerations about the reconcileablness of reason and religion. London, 1675.
Htn	Phil 5242.18.2*	Charleton, Walter. Two discourses. 2. ed. London, 1675.
Htn	Phil 2733.32*	Foucher, Simon. Critique de la recherche de la verité. Paris, 1675.
Htn	Phil 2610.7.5*	Gassendi, P. Abregé de la philosophie de Mr. Gassendi. Paris, 1675.
	Phil 8881.14*	Government of the tongue. Oxford, 1675.
	Phil 5049.1*	Jack, Gilbert. Grammatica rationis sive institutiones logicos. Oxonii, 1675.
	Phil 5821.11*	Legrand, A. Dissertatio de carentia sensus et cognitionis in brutis. London, 1675.
	Phil 2733.29.20	Malebranche, Nicolas. De la recherche de la vérité. 2e éd. Paris, 1675. 2v.
	Phil 8875.3.5	Agrippa von Nettesheim, Heinrich Cornelius. The vanity of arts and sciences. London, 1676.
	Phil 2045.84.2*	Clarendon, Edward Hyde. A brief view and survey of the...errors...in Mr. Hobbes's book, entitled Leviathan. Oxford, 1676.
	Phil 2045.84*	Clarendon, Edward Hyde. A brief view and survey of the...errors...in Mr. Hobbes's book, entitled Leviathan. Oxford, 1676.
	Phil 3200.1.35*	Erasmus, D. Stultitiae laus. Basiliae, 1676.
	Phil 181.32*	Gale, Theophilus. Philosophia generalis in duas partes disterminata. London, 1676.
	Phil 181.11.2	Glanvill, J. Essays...philosophy and religion. London, 1676.
	Phil 181.11*	Glanvill, J. Essays...philosophy and religion. London, 1676.
	Phil 5047.4.5	Heereboord, Adriano. Ermhneia logica...burgersdicianae. London, 1676.
	Phil 3450.15.85	Hirnhaim, H. De typho generis humani. Prague, 1676.
	Phil 2733.29	Malebranche, Nicolas. De la recherche de la vérité. Paris, 1676-78. 3v.
	Phil 187.101	Marci von Kronland, J.M. Philosophia vetus restituta. Francofurti, 1676.
	Phil 1200.2*	Thomasius, J. Exercitatio de stoica mundi exustione. Leipzig, 1676.
	Phil 8876.150	Bersandius, J. Venatio hominum. Francofonte, 1677.
	Phil 9162.5*	La civilité puerile et honneste pour l'instruction des enfans. Troyes, 1677.
	Phil 2520.34.10*	Descartes, René. L'homme de René Descartes et la formation du Foetus. Paris, 1677.
	Phil 2520.10.20	Descartes, René. Opera philosophica. 5a ed. Amsterdam, 1677-78. 2v.

1670-1679 - cont.

	Phil 2520.34.5	Descartes, René. Tractatus de homine et de formatione Foetus. Amsterdam, 1677.
Htn	Phil 2005.4.30F*	Felltham, Owen. Resolves: Divine, moral, political. London, 1677.
Htn	Phil 8800.6.2*	Feltham, Owen. Resolves. London, 1677.
	Phil 6025.4.15	Porta, G.B. La chirofisonomia overo di quelle parte della humana fisonomia. Napoli, 1677.
	Phil 6046.77	Praetonius, J. Philologemata abstrusa de pollice. v.1-2. Quedlinburgi, 1677.
Htn	Phil 3819.10.11*	Spinoza, Benedictus de. Opera posthuma. Pt.2. Amstelodami, 1677.
	Phil 2520.127	Vincentius, Joannes. Discussio perysatitica. Tolosae, 1677.
Htn	Phil 176.31*	Browne, R. Liber...vetaribus rarum principia. London, 1678.
Htn	Phil 1925.1.2*	Cudworth, R. True intellectual system of the universe. London, 1678.
	Phil 1925.1	Cudworth, R. True intellectual system of the universe. London, 1678.
Htn	Phil 1925.1.3*	Cudworth, R. True intellectual system of the universe. London, 1678.
	Phil 2520.52.27	Descartes, René. Meditationes de prima philosophia. Amstelodami, 1678.
Htn	Phil 9346.12*	Gailhard, J. The compleat gentleman. Savoy, 1678.
Htn	Phil 2045.70*	Hobbes, Thomas. Decameron physiologicum. London, 1678.
Htn	Phil 2045.47.5*	Hobbes, Thomas. Leviathan, sive de materia civitatis. London, 1678.
Htn	Phil 2045.31*	Hobbes, Thomas. Tracts. London, 1678-82. 2 pam.
Htn	Phil 2725.3.35*	LeGrand, A. Institutio philosophiae. London, 1678.
	Phil 8670.3	Parker, S. Disputationes de Deo. London, 1678.
Htn	Phil 192.6*	Reflections upon ancient and modern philosophy. London, 1678.
Htn	Phil 2145.48.5*	More, Henry. Enchiridion ethicum. Amstelodami, 1679.
	Phil 9070.105	Weber, Johann Adam. Annulus memoriae ex dictaminibus ethicis et politicis. Salisburgi, 1679.

1680-1689

Htn	Phil 6480.15*	Tryon, T. A treatise of dreams and visions. London, 168-.
Htn	Phil 5041.25.4*	Burgersdijck, Franco. Institutionum logicarum libri duo. Cantabrigiae, 1680. 3 pam.
Htn	Phil 2520.52.15*	Descartes, René. Six metaphysical meditations. London, 1680.
Htn	Phil 2005.5.30*	Filmer, Robert. Patriarcha. London, 1680.
Htn	Phil 3450.3.30*	Heereboord, Adriani. Meletemata philosophica. Amsterdam, 1680.
	Phil 182.10A	Heereboort, A. Meletemata philosophica. Amsterdam, 1680.
Htn	Phil 2045.77F*	Hobbes, Thomas. Last sayings. London, 1680.
Htn	Phil 2045.78.5F*	Hobbes, Thomas. Life. London, 1680.
Htn	Phil 2045.30*	Hobbes, Thomas. Vita. Carolopoli, 1680-8-? 4 pam.
Htn	Phil 2725.3.30*	LeGrand, A. Institutio philosophiae. London, 1680.
Htn	Phil 2733.55.5*	Malebranche, Nicolas. Traité de la nature et de la grace. Amsterdam, 1680. 2 pam.
Htn	Phil 7060.13.5*	A most strange and dreadful apparition. London, 1680.
Htn	Phil 2045.95*	Blackburne, Richard. Thomae Hobbes angli malmesburiensis vita. Carolopoli, 1681.
Htn	Phil 8691.8.5*	Burnet, Thomas. Telluris theoria sacra. v.1-2. London, 1681-89.
	Phil 2520.11.10	Descartes, René. Les principes de la philosophie. 4e éd. Paris, 1681.
Htn	Phil 2045.31.5*	Hobbes, Thomas. Tracts. London, 1681.
Htn	Phil 2045.30.2*	Hobbes, Thomas. Vita. Carolopoli, 1681.
	Phil 6021.5	La Bellière, C. de. La physionomie raisonnée. Lyon, 1681.
	Phil 8595.21	Parker, S. A demonstration of the divine authority of the law of nature. London, 1681.
Htn	Phil 2045.95.2*	Blackburne, Richard. Magni philosophi Thomae Hobbes malmesburiensis vita. London, 1682.
	Phil 3110.55	Böhme, J. Der weeg zu Christo. Amsterdam, 1682.
	Phil 3110.39.5	Böhme, J. Mysterium magnum. Amsterdam, 1682.
	Phil 3110.41	Böhme, J. Von der Genaden-Wahl. Amsterdam, 1682.
	Phil 2520.66	Descartes, René. De Verhandeling van den Mensch, en de Makinge de Vrugt. Middeleburg, 1682.
	Phil 2520.13.16	Descartes, René. Epistolae, Pars prima-tertia. Amsterdam, 1682-83. 3v.
	Phil 2520.75	Descartes, René. Epistolae. Amstelodami, 1682-83.
Htn	Phil 665.12.2*	Glanvill, Joseph. Two choice and useful treatises: Lux orientalis and A discourse of truth, by Dr. Rust. London, 1682.
Htn	Phil 2045.32*	Hobbes, Thomas. Tracts. London, 1682-84. 2 pam.
	Phil 720.22	Arnauld, A. Des vrayes et des fausses idées. Cologne, 1683.
Htn	Phil 6990.40*	Blount, Charles. Miracles, no violations of the law of nature. London, 1683.
Htn	Phil 6990.40.5*	Browne, T. Miracles work's. London, 1683.
	Phil 8877.4	Capel, A. Excellent contemplations divine and moral. London, 1683.
	Phil 2520.13.12	Descartes, René. Geometria. 3a ed. Amsterdam, 1683. 2v.
Htn	Phil 6045.22.21*	Indagine, Joannes. The book of palmestry and physiognomy. London, 1683.
Htn	Phil 8597.14*	Rust, G. A discourse...reason in matters of religion. London, 1683.
Htn	Phil 2520.103*	Boyle, Pierre. Recueil de quelques...philosophie de Descartes. Amsterdam, 1684.
Htn	Phil 8691.8F*	Burnet, Thomas. The theory of the earth. v.1-4. London, 1684-90.
	Phil 5042.6	Cuffelaer, A.J. Specimen artes ratiocinandi. v.1-3. Hamburgi, 1684.
	Phil 2610.7	Gassendi, P. Abregé de la philosophie de Gassendi. 2e ed. v.1-7. Lyon, 1684. 6v.
Htn	Phil 8701.9.5*	Lamy, Bernard. Entretiens sur les sciences dans lesquels on apprend comment l'on doit étudier les sciences. Bruxelles, 1684.
Htn	Phil 2733.50*	Malebranche, Nicolas. Traité de morale. pt.1-2. Rotterdam, 1684.
	Phil 8667.14	Micrandu, J. Disputatio philosophica de contemplatione mortis. Stockholmiae, 1684.
Htn	Phil 192.82*	Roas, A. Den amsteldamsen diogenes. Utrecht, 1684.
	Phil 7060.59	Bissel, J. Incolorum alterius mundi phenoemena. Dillingen, 1685.
	Phil 8582.10	Claubergii, J. De cognitione dei et nostri. Franequerae, 1685.
Htn	Phil 9162.2*	Courtin, A. de. Traité de la jalousie. Paris, 1685.
	Phil 2520.13.14	Descartes, René. Meditationeo de prima philosophia. Amsterdam, 1685.

Chronological Listing

1680-1689 - cont.

Phil 2520.14 Descartes, René. Meditationes de prima philosophia. Amsterdam, 1685.
Phil 2520.13.11 Descartes, René. Principia philosophiae. Amsterdam, 1685. 3 pam.
Htn Phil 182.13* Helmont, F.M. van. Macrocosm and microcosm. London, 1685.
Phil 9352.1.5 Mackenzie, G. Moral gallantry. London, 1685.
Htn Phil 9515.4* Mackenzie, George. Moral essay, preferring solitude to public employment. London, 1685.
Phil 2733.61 Malebranche, Nicolas. Conversations chrêtiennes. Rotterdam, 1685.
Htn Phil 2733.30.6* Malebranche, Nicolas. De inquirenda veritate. Genevae, 1685.
Htn Phil 2733.56* Malebranche, Nicolas. Trois lettres...la defense de Mr. Arnauld. Rotterdam, 1685.
Htn Phil 2805.29.5* Pascal, Blaise. Les provinciales. Cologne, 1685.
Htn Phil 1915* Clarke, Samuel. Miscellaneous pamphlets on Dr. Clarke. London, 1686-1834. 4 pam.
Phil 2520.13.15 Descartes, René. Tractatus de homine et de formatione foetus. Amsterdam, 1686.
Phil 9010.28 Thiers, Jean B. Traité des jeux et des divertissements. Paris, 1686.
Phil 7060.2.3 Lavater, L. De spectris. Lugduni Batavorum, 1687.
Phil 5628.11.1 Puccini, Vincenzo. The life of St. Mary Magdalene of Pazzi, a Carmelite nun. London, 1687.
Htn Phil 1123.3* Stanley, T. History of philosophy. London, 1687.
Htn Phil 8876.19* Bodenham, John. Politeuphuia, wits common-wealth. London, 1688.
Htn Phil 8735.2* Boyle, R. A disquisition...final causes of natural things. London, 1688.
Htn Phil 2045.75* Hobbes, Thomas. Historia ecclesiastica. Augustae, 1688.
Phil 2733.29.10 Malebranche, Nicolas. De la recherche de la vérité. 4e éd. v.1-2. Amsterdam, 1688.
Htn Phil 4363.2.30* Molinos, M. de. The spiritual guide. Venice, 1688.
Htn Phil 2175.2.30* Norris, John. The theory and regulation of love. Oxford, 1688.
Htn Phil 2805.41* Pascal, Blaise. Thoughts, meditations, and prayers, touching matters moral and divine. London, 1688.
Htn Phil 9359.5* Trenchfield, C. A cap of gray hairs for a green head. London, 1688.
Htn Phil 2520.91* Huetii, P.D. Censura philosophiae Cartesianae. Paris, 1689.
Htn Phil 2115.70* Locke, J. Letter concerning toleration. London, 1689.
Htn Phil 2805.32.15* Pascal, Blaise. The mystery of jesuitism. London, 1689[1679].
Htn Phil 9358.7.5* Shannon, F. Several discourses and characters. London, 1689.
Phil 3819.50 Spinoza, Benedictus de. A treatise partly theological, and partly political. London, 1689.

1690-1699

Htn Phil 8691.8.2F* Burnet, Thomas. The theory of the earth. 2. ed. London, 1690-91. 4 pam.
Htn Phil 2520.88.5* Daniel, Gabriel. Voiage du monde de Descartes. Paris, 1690.
Phil 7060.120 Decker, Johann H. Spectrologia, h. e. Discursus ut plurimum philosophicus de spectris. Hamburgi, 1690.
Phil 182.13.5 Helmont, F.M. van. Eenige gedagten. Amsterdam, 1690.
Htn Phil 2725.6.31* LeClerc, Jean. Five letters concerning the inspiration of the Holy Scriptures. London, 1690.
Htn Phil 3552.55* Leibniz, Gottfried Wilhelm. Ars Combinatoria. Francofurti, 1690.
Htn Phil 2115.2* Locke, J. An essay concerning humane understanding. London, 1690.
Htn Phil 2115.2.1F* Locke, J. An essay concerning humane understanding. London, 1690.
Htn Phil 2115.74* Locke, J. Two treatises of government. London, 1690.
Htn Phil 2175.2.49* Norris, John. Reflections on the conduct of human life. London, 1690.
Htn Phil 8893.64* Shannon, F.B. Moral essays and discourses upon several subjects. London, 1690.
Phil 9558.4 Villiers, Pierre. Reflexions sur les défauts d'autruy. Paris, 1690.
Phil 9361.1 Vincent. Les caracteres de l'honneste homme et de l'homme chrestien. Paris, 1690.
Htn Phil 9340.7* Advice to a young lord, written by his father. London, 1691.
Htn Phil 2520.81.2* Baillet, A. La vie de Monsieur Des-Cartes. Paris, 1691. 2v.
Phil 2520.81 Baillet, A. La vie de Monsieur Des-Cartes. Paris, 1691.
Phil 2520.88.7 Daniel, Gabriel. Voiage du monde de Descartes. Paris, 1691.
Htn Phil 2520.166* Geulincx, A. Annotata majora in principia philosophiae R. Des Cartes. Dordraci, 1691.
Htn Phil 9560.22* Hartcliffe, John. A treatise of moral and intellectual virtues. London, 1691.
Phil 185.2 Kessler, R. Praktische Philosophie. Leipzig, 1691.
Htn Phil 9560.16* Mackenzie, George. The moral history of frugality. London, 1691.
Htn Phil 9352.2* Mather, C. Daughters of Zion. n.p., 1691?
Htn Phil 2175.2.45* Norris, John. Reflections on the conduct of human life. 2nd ed. London, 1691-93. 2 pam.
Htn Phil 8672.2.5* Ray, J. The wisdom of God manifested in the works of the creation. London, 1691.
Htn Phil 2520.146* Regis, P.S. Response au livre qui a pour titre P. Danielis Huetii. Paris, 1691.
Phil 6046.91 Schulty, Christoph. Dissertatio academica, de chiromantiae vanitate. Regiomonti, 1691?
Htn Phil 3110.25*A Taylor, Edward. Jakob Böhme's theosophick philosophy. London, 1691.
Htn Phil 2520.81.5* Baillet, A. La vie de Monsieur Des-Cartes. Paris, 1692.
Htn Phil 8951.6* Barlow, Thomas. Several miscellaneous and mighty cases of conscience. London, 1692.
Phil 80.1 Chauvin, E. Lexicon rationale. Rotterdam, 1692.
Phil 2520.75.2 Descartes, René. Epistolae. Francofurti ad Moenum, 1692.
Phil 2520.13.20 Descartes, René. Opera omnia, novem tomis comprehensa. Amstelodami, 1692. 9v.
Phil 2520.10.25 Descartes, René. Opera philosophica. Francofurti, 1692.
Phil 2520.67 Descartes, René. Principia philosophiae. Amstelodami, 1692.
Htn Phil 9343.8* Dorrington, T. The excellent woman described. London, 1692.
Htn Phil 8659.3* Elis, C. The folly of atheism. London, 1692.
Phil 6016.1.5 Goclenius, R. Besonderephysiognomische und chromantische Anmerkungen. Hamburg, 1692.

1690-1699 - cont.

Phil 186.5.5 LeClerc, J. Logica, sive Ars ratiocinandi. London, 1692. 3 pam.
Htn Phil 3552.64* Leibniz, Gottfried Wilhelm. De la tolérance des religions. Paris, 1692.
Htn Phil 2115.70.2* Locke, J. A third letter for toleration. London, 1692.
Phil 3890.8.30 Thomasius, Christian. Von der Kunst vernünftig und tugendhafft zu Lieben als dem eintzigen Mittel zu einen Glückseligen. Halle, 1692.
Phil 2520.88.30 Daniel, Gabriel. Nouvelles difficultez proposees par un peripateticien. Paris, 1693.
Phil 8961.4 La Serre. La vie heureuse, ou L'homme content. Paris, 1693.
Htn Phil 2115.71* Locke, J. Some thoughts concerning education. London, 1693.
VPhil 1850.1.7F Bacon, F. Opera omnia. Hafniae, 1694.
VPhil 1850.1.8F Bacon, F. Opera omnia. Lipsiae, 1694.
Htn Phil 1905.9.9* Burthogge, R. An essay upon reason. London, 1694. 3 pam.
Htn Phil 2115.107* Burthogge, Richard. An essay upon reason and the nature of spirits. London, 1694-1755. 3 pam.
Htn Phil 8877.15.5* Collier, Jeremy. Miscellanies in five essays. London, 1694.
Htn Phil 1928.30.5* Cumberland, R. De legibus naturae. 3d ed. Lubecae, 1694.
Phil 2520.88.25 Daniel, Gabriel. Iter per mundum Cartesii. Amesteledami, 1694.
Htn Phil 2520.88.20* Daniel, Gabriel. Voyage to the world of Cartesius. London, 1694.
Phil 8881.68 Gaussault, Abbe. Le portrait d'un honneste homme. 2e éd. Paris, 1694.
Htn Phil 2725.3* LeGrand, A. An entire body of philosophy. London, 1694.
Htn Phil 2115.2.3F* Locke, J. An essay concerning humane understanding. 2nd ed. London, 1694.
Htn Phil 2115.2.2*A Locke, J. An essay concerning humane understanding. 2nd ed. London, 1694.
Htn Phil 186.30* Lowde, James. A discourse concerning the nature of man. London, 1694.
Htn Phil 6990.8* Maillard, Mary. A true relation of the wonderful cure of Mary Maillard. London, 1694.
Htn Phil 2733.31* Malebranche, Nicolas. Search after truth. London, 1694-95. 2v.
Htn Phil 2733.6.1F* Malebranche, Nicolas. Treatise...Search for truth. Oxford, 1694.
Htn Phil 9359.9* The true conduct of persons of quality. London, 1694.
Phil 7060.47 Francisci, Erasmus. Der höllischen Proteus...Erscheinder Gespenster. Nürnberg, 1695.
Htn Phil 2115.2.5F* Locke, J. An essay concerning humane understanding. 3rd ed. London, 1695.
Htn Phil 2115.58* Locke, J. The reasonableness of Christianity. London, 1695.
Phil 2733.55 Malebranche, Nicolas. A treatise of nature and grace. London, 1695. 2 pam.
Htn Phil 2145.49.5* More, Henry. Enchiridion ethicum. Amstelodami, 1695.
Htn Phil 2145.49* More, Henry. Enchiridion ethicum. Amstelodami, 1695.
Phil 3890.2.30 Tschirnhaus, E.W. von. Medicina mentis. Lipsiae, 1695.
Htn Phil 2115.153* Barbon, N. A discourse...in answer to Mr. Lock. London, 1696.
Htn Phil 2295.86* Beverley, Thomas. Christianity the great mystery; answer to a late treatise. Dondon, 1696.
Phil 8659.2 Edwards, John. A demonstration of the existence and providence of God. London, 1696.
Htn Phil 8800.6.5* Feltham, Owen. Resolves. London, 1696.
Htn Phil 2115.44* Locke, J. An abridgment of Mr. Locke's Essay concerning humane understanding. London, 1696.
Phil 8888.2 Nicole, P. Moral essayes. London, 1696. 2v.
Htn Phil 8670.4* Pelling, E. A discourse concerning the existence of God. London, 1696.
Phil 5058.2.2 Sargent, J. The method to science. London, 1696.
Htn Phil 9358.7* Shannon, F. Discourses...useful for vain modish ladies and their gallants. London, 1696.
Htn Phil 8673.14* Stephens, William. An account of the growth of deism in England. London, 1696.
Phil 3890.8.35 Thomasius, Christian. Von der Artzeney widner die Unvernunfftige Lieben und der zuvorher Nöthigen Erkäntniss sein Sellst. Halle, 1696.
Htn Phil 2295.34* Toland, John. Christianity not mysterious. v.1-3. London, 1696.
Htn Phil 2295.35* Toland, John. Christianity not mysterious. 2nd ed. London, 1696.
Htn Phil 2115.140* Animadversions on a late book entituled The reasonableness of Christianity. Oxford, 1697.
Phil 8581.14.5 Browne, Peter. A letter in answer to a book...entitled Christianity not mysterious. London, 1697.
Htn Phil 5041.26* Burgersdijck, Franco. Monitio logica, or An abstract and translation of Burgersdicius his Logick. London, 1697.
Htn Phil 2115.129* Burnet, Thomas. Remarks upon an essay concerning humane understanding. London, 1697. 3 pam.
Phil 2805.101.15 Daniel, Gabriel. Entretiens de Cléandre et d'Eudoxe sur les lettres au provincial. 10. éd. Pierre Marteau, 1697.
Phil 2805.101 Daniel, Gabriel. Réponse aux lettres provinciales. Amsterdam, 1697.
Htn Phil 3824.3* Earbery, Matthias. Deism examin'd and confuted in...Tractatus Theologico Politicus. London, 1697.
Phil 8586.1 Gastrell, F. The certainty and necessity of religion. London, 1697.
Htn Phil 8664.3* Jaquelot, I. Dissertations sur l'existence de Dieu. La Haye, 1697.
Htn Phil 2115.64* Locke, J. A common-place book to the Holy Bible. London, 1697.
Htn Phil 2115.73* Locke, J. A letter to Edward, Lord Bishop of Worcester. London, 1697.
Htn Phil 2115.73.5* Locke, J. Reply to the Lord Bishop of Worcester's answer to his letter. London, 1697.
Htn Phil 2733.50.3* Malebranche, Nicolas. Traité de morale. Lyon, 1697. 2v.
Htn Phil 2805.205* Petit-Didier, M. Apologie des lettres provinciales de Louis de Montalte. Delft, 1697-98.
Htn Phil 2805.205.5* Petit-Didier, M. Apologie des lettres provinciales de Louis de Montalte. Pt.1-4. Delft, 1697-98. 2v.
Htn Phil 530.11.16* Philadelphian Society, London. Propositions. London, 1697.
Htn Phil 2115.85* Sergeant, J. Solid philosophy asserted. London, 1697.
Htn Phil 2115.83* Stillingfleet, E. Answer to Mr. Locke's letter. London, 1697.
Htn Phil 8950.2* Ariadne mystica. Monachij, 1698. 2 pam.
Phil 2805.402 Daniel, Gabriel. Lettre de Mr. l'abbé...à Eudoxe. Cologne, 1698-99.

Chronological Listing

1690-1699 - cont.

Phil 2805.101.5 — Daniel, Gabriel. Réponse aux lettres provinciales. Bruxelles, 1698.

Phil 2520.52.28 — Descartes, René. Meditationes de prima philosophia. Amstelodami, 1698. 3 pam.

Phil 2520.39.12 — Descartes, René. Les principes de la philosophie. Rouen, 1698.

Htn Phil 1535.4* — Eustachius a S. Paulo. Summa philosophiae quadripartita. Cantabrigiae, 1698.

Phil 5247.13.17 — Huarte de San Juan, J. Examen de ingenios. London, 1698.

Htn Phil 8700.2* — Keill, J. Examination of Dr. Burnett's theory of the earth. Oxford, 1698.

Phil 186.5 — LeClerc, J. Opera philosophica. v.1-4. Amsterdam, 1698. 3v.

Htn Phil 2280.4.30F* — Sidney, Algernon. Discourses concerning government. London, 1698.

Htn Phil 2115.83.3* — Stillingfleet, E. Answer to Mr. Locke's second letter. London, 1698.

Htn Phil 8602.7* — Wilkins, J. Of the principles and duties of natural religion. London, 1698-99.

Phil 585.142 — Wölcker, Joannes. Amussis vitae humanae. Olomucii, 1698.

Phil 1905.9.30 — Burthogge, R. Of the soul of the world of particular souls. London, 1699.

Htn Phil 2610.35* — Gassendi, P. Three discourses of happiness, virtue and liberty. London, 1699.

Phil 2605.9.80 — Hugo, C.L. Refutation du sistème de Monsr. Faidy. Luxemburg, 1699.

Phil 8700.2.6 — Keill, J. Examination of the reflections on the theory of the earth. Oxford, 1699.

Htn Phil 2115.73.7* — Locke, J. Reply to the Lord Bishop of Worcester's answer to his second letter. London, 1699.

Htn Phil 2115.130* — Lowde, J. Moral essays; wherein some of Mr. Locks and Monsir. Malbranch's opinions are briefly examin'd. York, 1699.

Htn Phil 2733.50.5* — Malebranche, Nicolas. A treatise of morality. pt.1-2. London, 1699.

Htn Phil 8897.22* — Woodward, Josiah. An account of the societies for reformation of manners. London, 1699.

17-

Htn Phil 9342.2.11* — Chapone, H. (Mrs.). Letters on the improvement of the mind. Portland, 17- ?

Phil 6952.16 — Cruden, Alexander. The London-citizen...sent...to...madhouse. 2. ed. London, 17-

Htn Phil 6021.2.80* — Gradation de la tête de grenouille jusqu'au profil d'Appollon, d'après les idées du célèbre Lavater. Paris, 17- ?

Phil 7060.114 — The lawyer's ghost. London, 17- ?

Phil 9558.5.10 — Relaçam historia das vidas dos avarentos em que se escreve todos os seus costumes vicios. Lisboa, 17- .

Phil 2262.30.2 — Shaftesbury, A.A.C. Characteristicks. v.3. London, 17- .

Phil 2750.8.91 — Tressan, Louis Elisabeth de la Vergne. Éloge de M. Moreau de Maupertuis. Nancy, 17- .

Phil 5062.4.25 — Watts, S. Logic. London, 17- .

1700-1709

Phil 7150.17* — Adams, John. An essay concerning self-murther. London, 1700.

Phil 8881.14.2* — Government of the thoughts. Longon, 1700.

Phil 2040.35.2 — Herbert, E. De religione gentilium. Amsterdam, 1700.

Phil 2115.45* — Locke, J. An abridgment of Mr. Locke's Essay concerning human understanding. London, 1700.

Phil 2115.78A — Locke, J. An account of Mr. Lock's religion. London, 1700.

Phil 2115.48.2 — Locke, J. Essai philosophique concernant l'entendement humaine. Amsterdam, 1700.

Phil 2115.2.7F* — Locke, J. An essay concerning humane understanding. 4th ed. London, 1700.

Phil 2733.6.2 — Malebranche, Nicolas. Father Malebranche, his treatise...Search after truth. 2d ed. London, 1700.

Phil 2805.29.3 — Pascal, Blaise. Ludovici Montaltii Litterae provinciales. 6. éd. Coloniae, 1700. 2v.

Phil 193.6 — Sargent, J. Transnatural philosophy, or Metaphysicks. London, 1700.

Phil 1850.29.10* — Bacon, Francis. Essays or counsels, civil and moral...and discourse of the wisdom of the ancients. London, 1701.

Phil 2520.30 — Descartes, René. Opuscula posthuma. Amsterdam, 1701.

Phil 8500.1* — Grew, N. Cosmologia sacra. London, 1701.

Phil 2520.131* — Howard, E. Remarks on...new philosophy of Descartes. London, 1701.

Phil 1810.1 — Kortholti, C. De tribus impostoribus magnis liber. Hamburgi, 1701.

Phil 2115.29.125F — Locke, J. De intellectu humano. Ed. 4a. London, 1701.

Phil 188.5.2 — Norris, J. Essay towards the theory of the world. London, 1701-1704. 2v.

Phil 2175.2.55* — Norris, John. An essay towards the theory of the ideal or intelligible world. pt.1-2. London, 1701-04. 2v.

Phil 2175.2.40* — Norris, John. An essay towards the theory of the world. London, 1701. 2v.

Phil 1123.3.3 — Stanley, T. History of philosophy. London, 1701.

Phil 7085.9 — Steffanius, J.J. Dissertatio medica inauguralis de somnambulis. Basileae, 1701.

Phil 3890.8.6 — Thomasius, Christian. Allerhand bissher Publicirte Kleine deutsche Schriften. Halle, 1701.

Phil 5040.4 — Arnauld, Antoine. Logik, or The art of thinking. London, 1702.

Phil 1050.1 — Buddeus, J.F. Introductio ad historia philosophiae ebraeorum. Halae, 1702.

Phil 8877.15 — Collier, Jeremy. Essays upon several moral subjects. v.1-4. London, 1702-09. 3v.

Phil 2520.88.2 — Daniel, Gabriel. Voyage du monde de Descartes. Paris, 1702.

Phil 665.50* — E., T. Vindiciae mentis. London, 1702.

Phil 8620.7.8 — King, Gulielmo. De origine mali. Dublinii, 1702.

Phil 2115.4F — Lee, Henry. Anti-scepticism: or notes upon...Mr. Lock's essay. London, 1702.

Phil 2733.61.2 — Malebranche, Nicolas. Conversations chrêtiennes. Paris, 1702.

Phil 8592.114 — Molina, Antonio de. Excercicios espirituales de las excelencias, provecho y necesidad. Barcelona, 1702.

Phil 2295.75* — Toland, John. Vindicius liberius. London, 1702.

Phil 2295.75.2* — Toland, John. Vindicius liberius. London, 1702.

Phil 8877.15.2 — Collier, Jeremy. Essays upon several moral subjects. 5th ed. pt. 1-2. London, 1703.

1700-1709 - cont.

Phil 2520.88.9 — Daniel, Gabriel. Voyage du monde de Descartes. Paris, 1703.

Phil 8586.1.2 — Gastrell, F. The certainty and necessity of religion. London, 1703.

Phil 5046.37 — Grosser, S. Pharus intellectus, sive logica. Lipsiae, 1703.

Phil 182.96 — Heydenreich, K.H. Encyclopädische Einleitung in das Studium der Philosophie. Leipzig, 1703.

Htn Phil 8624.3* — Layton, Henry. Arguments and replies. London, 1703. 7 pam.

Htn Phil 477.4* — Coward, W. Grand essay. London, 1704.

Htn Phil 665.3* — Coward, William. Second thoughts concerning human souls. London, 1704.

Phil 2805.101.25 — Daniel, Gabriel. The discourses of Cleander and Eudoxe. London, 1704.

Phil 186.5.6 — LeClerc, J. Logica, ontologia, et pneumatologia. 4. ed. Cambridge, 1704.

Htn Phil 9245.4* — Lucas, R. An enquiry after happiness. London, 1704.

Htn Phil 2733.57* — Malebranche, Nicolas. Réponse du Père Malebranche à la troisième lettre de Mr. Arnauld. Amsterdam, 1704.

Htn Phil 2805.42.4* — Pascal, Blaise. Thoughts on religion. London, 1704.

Htn Phil 8672.2.3*A — Ray, J. The wisdom of God manifested in the works of the creation. v.1-2. London, 1704.

Htn Phil 2295.24* — Toland, John. Letters to Serena. London, 1704.

Phil 3822.4.10 — Colerus, Johannes. Korte, dog waaragtige levens-beschrijving van Benedictus de Spinoza. Amsterdam, 1705[1910]

Htn Phil 665.3.3* — Coward, William. Just scrutiny...modern notions of the soul. London, 1705?

Htn Phil 8661.13* — Gildon, Charles. The deist's manual. London, 1705.

Phil 8950.1 — Andreae, J.V. Civis Christianus. London, 1706.

Phil 2520.81.6 — Baillet, A. La vie de Monsieur Des-Cartes. Paris, 1706.

Htn Phil 2115.141* — Bold, S. A collection of tracts. London, 1706.

Phil 801.6 — Budeus, J.F. Analecta historiae philosophicae. Halle, 1706.

Htn Phil 2115.80* — Carroll, William. A dissertation upon the tenth chapter of the fourth book of Mr. Locke's Essay concerning human understanding. London, 1706.

Phil 1915.60.4 — Clarke, Samuel. Discourse...attributes of God. London, 1706. 2 pam.

Phil 3822.4.6A — Colerus, Johannes. The life of Benedict de Spinoza. London, 1706.

Htn Phil 3822.4.5* — Colerus, Johannes. The life of Benedict de Spinoza. London, 1706.

Phil 3822.4 — Colerus, Johannes. La vie de Benoit de Spinoza. La Haye, 1706.

Phil 2520.88.10 — Daniel, Gabriel. Voyage du monde de Descartes. v.1-2. Amsterdam, 1706.

Phil 2520.39.9 — Descartes, René. Les principes de la philosophie. Rouen, 1706.

Phil 2045.121 — A dissertation...according to the principles of Mr. Hobbes. London, 1706.

Phil 8701.9.7 — Lamy, Bernard. Entretiens sur les sciences dans lesquels on apprend comment l'on doit étudier les sciences. 3. éd. Lyon, 1706.

Htn Phil 8624.2* — Layton, Henry. A search after souls. n.p., 1706.

Htn Phil 2115.82.1* — LeClerc, J. The life and character of Mr. John Locke. London, 1706.

Phil 2115.82* — LeClerc, J. The life and character of Mr. John Locke. London, 1706-13.

Htn Phil 2115.2.9F* — Locke, J. An essay concerning humane understanding. 5th ed. London, 1706.

Htn Phil 2115.15.5* — Locke, J. Posthumous works. London, 1706.

Htn Phil 2115.15* — Locke, J. Posthumous works. London, 1706.

Phil 8887.65 — Mancini, F.O. Riflessioni per la vita morale civile. Parma, 1706.

Phil 8677.5 — Wise, Thomas. A confutation of the reason and philosophy of atheism. London, 1706. 2v.

Phil 2515.2.39 — Charron, P. Charron on wisdom. London, 1707. 2v.

Phil 9343.2.2 — Darell, W. Gentleman instructed. London, 1707. 2v.

Htn Phil 8662.2* — Hancock, J. Arguments to prove the being of God. London, 1707.

Phil 2115.62.2* — Locke, J. A paraphrase and notes on epistle of St. Paul. London, 1707.

Htn Phil 2733.39* — Malebranche, Nicolas. Meditations chrétiennes et métaphysiques. Lyon, 1707.

Htn Phil 2733.65.1* — Malebranche, Nicolas. Traité de l'amour de Dieu. Lyon, 1707.

Phil 5054.1 — Oldfield, J. An essay towards the improvement of reason. London, 1707.

Phil 7080.20 — Oliver, William. A relation of a very extraordinary sleeper. London, 1707.

Htn Phil 9420.1* — Bragge, F. A practical treatise...regulation...passions. London, 1708.

Htn Phil 1915.70* — Clarke, Samuel. Letter to Dodwell. London, 1708-13. 9 pam.

Phil 9343.2.3 — Darell, W. A supplement to the first part of the G.I. London, 1708.

Phil 8878.10.5 — Disney, J. Essay upon execution of laws vs. immorality and prophaneness. London, 1708.

Phil 2115.74.50 — Locke, J. Some familiar letters between Mr. Locke and his friends. London, 1708.

Phil 2733.60 — Malebranche, Nicolas. Entretien d'un philosophe chrétien. Paris, 1708.

Phil 7084.32 — Moral reflections in a real dream. London, 1708.

Phil 8638.3 — Norris, John. A philosophical discourse...natural immortality. London, 1708.

Htn Phil 2262.76* — Shaftesbury, A.A.C. Letter concerning enthusiasm. London, 1708-09. 4 pam.

Phil 1870.60.1.2 — Berkeley, G. Essay towards a new theory. Dublin, 1709.

Htn Phil 1870.60* — Berkeley, G. Essay towards a new theory of vision. Dublin, 1709.

Htn Phil 1870.60.1* — Berkeley, G. Essay towards a new theory of vision. 2d ed. Dublin, 1709.

Phil 3280.50 — Geulincx, A. Gnôthi Seauton, sive ethica. Amsterdam, 1709.

Phil 5761.1 — La Placette, J. Eclaircissemens...difficultez...liberté. Amsterdam, 1709.

Phil 2115.49.20 — Locke, J. Libri IV de intellectu humano. Lipsiae, 1709.

Htn Phil 4946.2.30F* — Philostratus. Quae supersunt omnia. Lipsiae, 1709.

Phil 7060.39 — Schelwig, Samuel. De apparitionibus. Lipziae, 1709.

Htn Phil 2262.49* — Shaftesbury, A.A.C. The moralists. London, 1709.

Htn Phil 2262.62* — Shaftesbury, A.A.C. Sensus communis. London, 1709.

Phil 1500.3 — Vinas, M. de. Philosophia scholastica. Genuae, 1709. 3v.

1710-1719

	Phil 8950.8	Arrese y Ontiveros, Pedro Alexandro de. Modo para vivir eternamente. Madrid, 1710.
Htn	Phil 1870.40.1*	Berkeley, G. Treatise...principles of human knowledge. Dublin, 1710.
	Phil 9343.12.5	Dare, Josiah. Counsellor Manners, his last legacy to his son. London, 1710.
	Phil 8878.10	Disney, J. A second essay...execution...laws against immorality. London, 1710.
Htn	Phil 3552.60*	Leibniz, Gottfried Wilhelm. Essai de Theodicée. Amsterdam, 1710. 3 pam.
Htn	Phil 2115.20*	Locke, J. Oeuvres diverses. Rotterdam, 1710.
	Phil 8965.6	Pictet, Benedict. Morale chrétienne. Genève, 1710. 2v.
	Phil 2262.63	Shaftesbury, A.A.C. Soliloquy. London, 1710.
Htn	Phil 2262.63*	Shaftesbury, A.A.C. Soliloquy. Photoreproduction. London, 1710.
Htn	Phil 8602.7.2*	Wilkins, J. Of the principles and duties of natural religion. London, 1710.
	Phil 8875.8	Abbadie, J. L'Art de se connoitre soy-même. v.1-2. La Haye, 1711.
	Phil 1915.60.5	Clarke, Samuel. Discourse...attributes of God. London, 1711. 2 pam.
	Phil 2145.50	More, Henry. Enchiridion ethicum. London, 1711.
Htn	Phil 2262.29*	Shaftesbury, A.A.C. Characteristicks. London, 1711. 3v.
	Phil 1123.3.4	Stanley, T. Historia philosophiae. Lipsiae, 1711.
	Phil 7060.134	Thomasius, C. Dissertatio iuridica de non rescindendo contractu conductionis ob natura spectrorum. Halle, 1711.
	Phil 8897.1	Walker, S. Reformation of manners. London, 1711.
Htn	Phil 2725.6.30*	An account of the life and writings of Mr. John LeClerc. London, 1712. 2 pam.
Htn	Phil 4265.1.90*	Arpe, P.F. Apologia J. Caesare Vanino neapolitano. Csmomopoli, 1712.
	Phil 1915.61	Clarke, Samuel. The scripture-doctrine of the Trinity. London, 1712.
	Phil 2733.55.10	Malebranche, Nicolas. Traité de la nature et de la grace. Rotterdam, 1712. 2 pam.
	Phil 9375.7	Mis'c., or Sundry discourses concerning trade. London, 1712.
Htn	Phil 2145.2.2*	More, Henry. Collection...philosophical writings. London, 1712.
	Phil 2145.2	More, Henry. Collection...philosophical writings. 4th ed. London, 1712.
	Phil 7080.17	Thomasius, C. De jure circa somnum et somnia. ...giomonti, 1712.
Htn	Phil 8610.713.20*	Bentley, Richard. Remarks upon a late discourse of free-thinking. London, 1713. 3 pam.
Htn	Phil 1870.45.1*	Berkeley, G. Three dialogues...Hylas and Philonous. London, 1713.
Htn	Phil 1930.4.30*	Collier, Arthur. Clavis universalis. London, 1713. 2 pam.
Htn	Phil 9230.12*	Collier, Jeremy. An essay upon gaming. London, 1713. (Transferred to Houghton Library 14/1/72)
Htn	Phil 8610.713*	Collins, Anthony. A discourse of free thinking occasioned by the rise and growth of a sect call'd free-thinker. London, 1713. 3 pam.
	Phil 2520.88	Daniel, Gabriel. Voyage du monde de Descartes...Suite du voyage du monde de Descartes. Amsterdam, 1713.
	Phil 8887.59.10	Mackenzie, G. Essays upon several moral subjects. London, 1713.
Htn	Phil 2145.61*	More, Henry. Divine dialogues. London, 1713.
	Phil 8670.5.10	Philipps, J.T. Historia atheismi. Altdorfi Noricorum, 1713. 3 pam.
	Phil 8897.15	Whitby, D. Ethices compendium. London, 1713.
	Phil 5041.33	Buffier, Claude. Les principis du raisonnent exposez en deux logiques nouvéles. Paris, 1714.
Htn	Phil 8610.713.10*	Collins, Anthony. Discours sur la liberté de penser. Londres, 1714.
	Phil 8658.4.6	Derham, W. Physico-theology. London, 1714.
	Phil 2520.75.15	Descartes, René. Epistolae. v.1-2. Amstelodami, 1714.
	Phil 1915.82.2	A full account of the late proceedings in convocation relating to Dr. Clarke's writings about the Trinity. London, 1714.
Htn	Phil 9347.16*	Hassen, Martin. De noncommutando sexus habitu. Vitembergae, 1714.
NEDL	Phil 9351.1.3	Ladies library. London, 1714. 3v.
	Phil 2115.48.5	Locke, J. Essai philosophique concernant l'entendement humaine. La Haye, 1714.
	Phil 2115.1	Locke, J. Works. 1st ed. v.1,3. London, 1714. 2v.
Htn	Phil 2128.27*	Mandeville, B. Fable of the bees. London, 1714.
Htn	Phil 8672.2*	Ray, J. The wisdom of God manifested in the works of the creation. v.1-2. London, 1714.
Htn	Phil 2262.29.5*	Shaftesbury, A.A.C. Characteristicks. 2nd ed. London, 1714. 3v.
Htn	Phil 8658.4*	Derham, W. Astro-theology. London, 1715.
Htn	Phil 9495.38*	Drouet de Maupertny, J. Le commerce dangereux entre les deux sexes. Bruxelles, 1715.
	Phil 8886.4	Lange, J. Medicina mentis. London, 1715.
Htn	Phil 2733.66*	Malebranche, Nicolas. Reflections sur la primation physique. Paris, 1715.
	Phil 8595.5	Poiret, P. Cogitationum rationalium. Amsterdam, 1715.
	Phil 4265.1.83	Schramm, J.M. De vita et scriptis...Julii Caesaris Vanini. 2. ed. Ciistrini, 1715.
	Phil 5062.3	Wallis, J. Institutio logicae. Oxonii, 1715.
	Phil 2805.101.8	Daniel, Gabriel. Réponse aux lettres provinciales. La Haye, 1716.
	Phil 8658.4.7	Derham, W. Physico-theology. London, 1716.
	Phil 7060.138	The drummer of Tedworth...story of that demon. London, 1716.
	Phil 75.7	Jonsius, Johannes. De scriptoribus historiae philosophicae. Jena, 1716.
	Phil 1200.25	Karg, F. Stoicos' Aëatheiae falso suspectos. Lipsiae, 1716.
	Phil 2115.30.3	Locke, J. Essay concerning human understanding. London, 1716. 2v.
	Phil 8670.5	Philipps, J.T. Dissertatio historico-philosophica de atheismo. London, 1716.
	Phil 8890.16	Placette, J. Essais de morale. Amsterdam, 1716-32 6v.
	Phil 8598.74	Sekendorf, V.L. von. Christen-Staat. Leipzig, 1716.
	Phil 5040.4.2	Arnauld, Antoine. Logic, or The art of thinking. London, 1717.
	Phil 5752.2.15	Clarke, S. Remark on philosophical inquiry...human liberty. London, 1717. 2 pam.
	Phil 5752.2A	Collins, A. Philosophical inquiry...human liberty. London, 1717.

1710-1719 - cont.

	Phil 6990.7	Duffel, O.L.V. van. Ofte van Goeden Will. Antwerpen, 1717.
Htn	Phil 186.33*	Lau, Theodor L. Meditationes philosophicae de Deo, mundo, homine. Frankfurt, 1717.
Htn	Phil 3552.71.1*	Leibniz, Gottfried Wilhelm. A collection of papers. London, 1717.
	Phil 3552.71	Leibniz, Gottfried Wilhelm. A collection of papers. London, 1717.
NEDL	Phil 9245.4.2	Lucas, R. An enquiry after happiness. London, 1717. 2v.
	Phil 8672.2.2	Ray, J. The wisdom of God manifested in the works of the creation. v.1-2. London, 1717.
	Phil 8893.38	Stockwell, Joseph. A sermon preach'd at Faringdon...opening a charity school. Oxford, 1717.
	Phil 4265.1.84	Vie et les sentimens de Lucilio Vanini. Rotterdam, 1717.
Htn	Phil 3552.29.2*	Leibniz, Gottfried Wilhelm. Otium hanoueranum sive Miscellanea. Lipsiae, 1718.
Htn	Phil 3552.29*	Leibniz, Gottfried Wilhelm. Otium hanoueranum sive Miscellanea. Lipsiae, 1718.
Htn	Phil 2295.27*	Toland, John. Historical account of life. London, 1718-22. 3 pam.
	Phil 176.103.3	Buddeus, J.F. Elementa philosophiae instrumentalis. v.1-2. Halae-Saxonum, 1719-20.
	Phil 8951.18	Buddeus, J.F. Institutiones theologiae moralis. Lipsiae, 1719.
	Phil 8691.8.4	Burnet, Thomas. The sacred theory of the earth. London, 1719. 2v.
	Phil 1915.60	Clarke, Samuel. Discourse...attributes of God. London, 1719. 2 pam.
	Phil 1915.60.2	Clarke, Samuel. Discourse...attributes of God. London, 1719.
	Phil 1915.61.2	Clarke, Samuel. The scripture-doctrine of the Trinity. 2d ed. London, 1719.
	Phil 8658.4.2	Derham, W. Astro-theology. London, 1719.
	Phil 3552.63.20	Leibniz, Gottfried Wilhelm. Tentamina theodicaeae de bonitate Dei libertate hominis et origine mali. Francofurti, 1719.
NEDL	Phil 8593.5	Nieuwentyt, B. The religious philosopher. London, 1719. 3v.

1720-1729

	Phil 5643.91	Botelho de Oliveyra, B. Escudo apologetico, physico, optico occidental. Lisboa, 1720.
	Phil 8402.41	Bruhn, Karl. De växandes estetiska liv. Vasa, 1720-21. 2v.
	Phil 5042.5.5	Crousaz, J.P. de. La logique. 2e éd. Amsterdam, 1720. 3v.
Htn	Phil 1928.30*	Cumberland, R. De legibus naturae. Dublin, 1720.
	Phil 3552.61	Leibniz, Gottfried Wilhelm. Essais de Theodicée. Paris, 1720.
	Phil 3552.60.5	Leibniz, Gottfried Wilhelm. Essais de Theodicée sur la bonté de Dieu. Amsterdam, 1720.
	Phil 3552.54	Leibniz, Gottfried Wilhelm. Lehr-Satze über die Monadologie. Franckfurt, 1720.
Htn	Phil 2115.25*	Locke, J. Collection of several pieces. London, 1720.
Htn	Phil 2128.65*	Mandeville, B. Free thoughts on religion. London, 1720.
Htn	Phil 2295.39*	Toland, John. Pantheisticon, sive formula celebrandae sodalitatis Socraticae. Cosmopoli, 1720.
	Phil 5051.40	Lossada, Luis de. Institutiones dialecticae, vulgo summulae, ad primam partem philosophici cursus pertinentes. Salmanticae, 1721.
	Phil 2733.29.3	Malebranche, Nicolas. De la recherche de la verité. 7e éd. v.1-2. Paris, 1721.
	Phil 2733.36.4	Malebranche, Nicolas. Entretiens sur la métaphysique. Paris, 1721. 2v.
Htn	Phil 8667.4*	Mather, C. The Christian philosopher. London, 1721.
	Phil 8597.2	Ray, J. Three physico-theological discourses. London, 1721.
Htn	Phil 8876.19.3*	Bodenham, John. Wits commonwealth. London, 1722.
	Phil 8691.8.7	Burnet, Thomas. The sacred theory of the earth. London, 1722-26. 2v.
	Phil 4073.80	Cyprian, E. Vita T. Campanella. Amstelodami, 1722.
	Phil 9346.7	The gentleman's library. 2d ed. London, 1722.
	Phil 9351.1	Ladies library. London, 1722.
	Phil 186.5.2	LeClerc, J. Opera philosophica. Amsterdam, 1722. 4v.
	VPhil 2115.1.1	Locke, J. Works. 2nd ed. London, 1722. 3v.
Htn	Phil 2280.3.30*	Stoddard, Solomon. An answer to some cases of conscience. Boston, 1722.
	Phil 5040.1.7	Aldrich, H. Artis logicae rudimenta. Oxonae, 1723.
	Phil 8875.23	Alstrin, Eric. Dissertatio philosophica. Upsala, 1723.
	Phil 5040.4.3	Arnauld, Antoine. Logic, or The art of thinking. London, 1723.
	Phil 332.10	Brucker, Jacob. Historia philosophica doctrinae de ideis. Augustae Vindelicorum, 1723.
	Phil 8656.7.20	Buddeus, J.F. Lehr-Sätze von der Atheisterey und dem Aberglauben mit gelehrten Anmerckungen erläutert. 2. Aufl. Jena, 1723.
	Phil 9343.2	Darell, W. Gentleman instructed. London, 1723.
	Phil 2520.11.13	Descartes, René. Les principes de la philosophie. Paris, 1723.
	Phil 2520.61.5	Descartes, René. Tractat von den Leidenschafften der Seele. Franckfurth, 1723.
Htn	Phil 8666.4*	Leslie, Charles. A short and easie method with the deists. 8. ed. v.1-3. London, 1723.
Htn	Phil 2128.28*	Mandeville, B. Fable of the bees. London, 1723.
	Phil 2262.30	Shaftesbury, A.A.C. Characteristicks. London, 1723. 3v.
	Phil 9390.9	The wickedness of a disregard of oaths. London, 1723.
	Phil 3910.59.5	Wolff, Christian von. Vernunfftige Gedancken von der Menschen. 2. Aufl. Halle, 1723.
	Phil 1500.2	Bobenstuber, P.L. Philosophia thomistica salisburgensis. Augusta Vindelicorum, 1724.
	Phil 176.103	Buddeus, J.F. Elementa philosophiae instrumentalis. Halae Saxonum, 1724-25.
	Phil 176.103.5	Buddeus, J.F. Elementa philosophiae instrumentalis. v.1-2. Halae Saxonum, 1724-25.
	Phil 176.103.10	Buddeus, J.F. Elementa philosophiae practicae. Halaeo Magdeburgical, 1724.
	Phil 801.6.2	Budeus, J.F. Analecta historiae philosophicae. 2. ed. Halle, 1724.
Htn	Phil 1930.5.30*	Collins, Anthony. A discourse of the grounds and reasons of the Christian religion. London, 1724-37.
Htn	Phil 1930.5.29*	Collins, Anthony. A discourse of the grounds and reasons of the Christian religion. v.1-2. London, 1724.

1720-1729 - cont.

Phil 5042.5 — Crousaz, J.P. de. New treatise...art of thinking. London, 1724. 2v.

Htn Phil 2128.82* — Dennis, John. Vice and luxury publick mischiefs. London, 1724.

Phil 2520.76.55 — Descartes, René. Lettres de Descartes. Paris, 1724-25. 6v.

Phil 2520.52.35 — Descartes, René. Les méditations métaphysiques. Paris, 1724. 2v.

Phil 2520.39.6 — Descartes, René. Les principes de la philosophie. Paris, 1724.

Phil 2520.39.5 — Descartes, René. Les principes de la philosophie. Paris, 1724.

Phil 9245.36.5 — Deslandes, A.F.B. The art of being easy at all times and in all places. London, 1724.

Phil 8880.4 — Fiddes, R. A general treatise of morality. London, 1724.

Phil 5816.8 — Geraud, Petrus J. Dissertatio philosophica de principio actionum. Trajecti ad Rhenum, 1724.

Phil 8701.9 — Lamy, Bernard. Entretiens sur les sciences dans lesquels on apprend comment l'on doit étudier les sciences. Lyon, 1724.

Phil 2128.80.5 — Law, William. Remarks on...the fable of the bees. London, 1724.

Phil 850.1 — Levesque de Bruiquy, J. Histoire de la philosophie payenne. La Haye, 1724.

Htn Phil 8591.11* — Lyons. The infallibility of human judgement. London, 1724.

Phil 2128.29 — Mandeville, B. Fable of the bees. 3rd ed. London, 1724.

Phil 8602.11 — Wollaston, W. The religion of nature delineated. London, 1724.

Htn Phil 8602.11.2.5* — Wollaston, W. The religion of nature delineated. London, 1724.

Htn Phil 1845.1.35F* — Allestree, Richard. The whole duty of man. London, 1725.

Phil 5190.23 — Alstrin, Eric. Dissertatio gradualis. Upsaliae, 1725.

Phil 8950.3 — Alstrin, Eric. Ethica theologiae ministra. Upsaliae, 1725.

Phil 2128.81 — Bluet. An enquiry whether a general practice of virtue tends to the wealth or poverty...of a people. London, 1725.

Htn Phil 1930.5.95* — Bullock, T. The reasoning of Christ and his Apostles...sermons...Nov. and Dec., 1724. London, 1725.

Phil 8626.15.7 — Burnet, Thomas. Burnett's state of the dead. London, 1725-28. 4 pam.

Phil 1915.60.7 — Clarke, Samuel. Discourse...attributes of God. 6th ed. London, 1725. 2 pam.

Htn Phil 2053.50* — Hutcheson, F. Inquiry into...beauty and virtue. London, 1725.

Phil 6121.20.5 — La Forge, Louis de. Traité de l'esprit de l'homme. Genève, 1725.

Phil 2115.64.20 — Locke, J. A common-place book to the Holy Bible. 3d ed. London, 1725.

Htn Phil 2128.60.2* — Mandeville, B. Enquiry into the origin of honour. v.1-2. London, 1725-32.

Phil 2128.30 — Mandeville, B. Fable of the bees. London, 1725.

Phil 8668.2 — Nieuwentijt, B. L'existence de Dieu. Paris, 1725.

Phil 8593.5.7 — Nieuwentyt, B. Het regt gebruik der werelt beschouwingen. 4. druk. Amsterdam, 1725.

Phil 2805.40.10 — Pascal, Blaise. Pensées...sur la religion. Paris, 1725.

Phil 9177.1 — Randall, M. Reflections...duty of masters, mistresses and servants. London, 1725.

Phil 4630.3.37 — Rydelius, Anders. Dissertatio metaphysica de novis...axiomatibus...Leibnitus et Volfius. Lundini et Volfius. Lundini, 1725.

n Phil 5062.4.2* — Watts, S. Logick. London, 1725.

n Phil 8602.11.7* — Wollaston, W. The religion of nature delineated. London, 1725.

n Phil 2340.5.30* — Wollaston, William. The religion of nature. London, 1725.

Phil 1900.60 — Butler, Joseph. Fifteen sermons preached at the Rolls Chapel. London, 1726.

Phil 2520.61.15 — Descartes, René. Les passions de l'âme. Paris, 1726.

Phil 2053.50.2 — Hutcheson, F. Inquiry into...beauty and virtue. London, 1726.

Phil 3552.62 — Leibniz, Gottfried Wilhelm. Theodicaea. Paris, 1726.

Phil 2115.30 — Locke, J. Essay concerning human understanding. London, 1726. 2v.

Phil 2115.74.15 — Locke, J. O forgripelize. Stockholm, 1726.

n Phil 9010.14* — Mather, Cotton. A serious address. Boston, 1726.

n Phil 2150.5.80* — More, Thomas. Life of Sir Thomas More, by his great-grandson. London, 1726.

Phil 4630.3.39 — Rydelius, Anders. Aphorismi philosophici de moderamine libertatis philosophicae. Diss. Lundini, 1726.

Phil 4630.3.44 — Rydelius, Anders. Dissertatio philosophica, fidelem praeceptorem...privatum adumbrans. Diss. Lundini, 1726.

Phil 4630.3.42 — Rydelius, Anders. Dissertatio philosophica, gradualis de tempore. Diss. Lundini, 1726.

Phil 4630.3.35 — Rydelius, Anders. Dissertatio philosophica mepi...seu de excessu subtilitatis in philosophicae. Lund, 1726.

Phil 2295.10 — Toland, John. Collection of several pieces. London, 1726. 2v.

Phil 8602.11.3* — Wollaston, W. The religion of nature delineated. London, 1726.

Phil 2520.171 — Alstrin, Eric. Dissertationis academicae. Holmiae, 1727.

Phil 8690.5 — Alstrin, Eric. Exercitium academicum. Upsaliae, 1727.

Phil 1930.5.51 — Collins, Anthony. The scheme of literal prophecy considered. London, 1727.

Phil 1930.5.50* — Collins, Anthony. The scheme of literal prophecy considered. London, 1727.

Phil 1928.33* — Cumberland, R. A treatise of the laws of nature. London, 1727.

Phil 7060.64* — Defoe, D. Essay on the history...of apparitions. London, 1727.

Phil 8658.4.9 — Derham, W. Physico-theology. 7. ed. London, 1727.

Phil 8880.20.5 — Fuller, J. Introductio ad prudentiam, or Directions. pt.2. London, 1727.

Phil 2610.1 — Gassendi, P. Opera omnia. Florentiae, 1727. 6v.

VPhil 2115.1.2 — Locke, J. Works. 3rd ed. London, 1727. 3v.

Phil 4630.3.46 — Rydelius, Anders. Dissertatio philosophica de vera rationis humanae definitione. Diss. Lund, 1727.

Phil 2262.30.3 — Shaftesbury, A.A.C. Characteristicks. v.2,3. London, 1727. 2v.

Phil 2262.30.4 — Shaftesbury, A.A.C. Characteristicks. 4th ed. n.p., 1727. 3v.

Phil 6972.1 — Wepferi, J.J. Observationes...affectibus capitis. Scaphusii, 1727.

Phil 3910.34* — Wolff, Christian von. Meinung von dem Wesen der Seele. Leipzig, 1727.

Phil 175.36 — Alstrin, Eric. Dissertationes academicae. pt.1-2. Upsaliae, 1728.

1720-1729 - cont.

Phil 8580.19 — Alstrin, Erico. Dissertatio philosophica. Upsaliae, 1728.

Phil 5811.2 — Boullier, D.R. Essai philosophique sur l'âme des bêtes. Amsterdam, 1728.

Phil 8581.14.9 — Browne, Peter. The procedure, extent and limits of human understanding. London, 1728.

Phil 8626.15.5 — Burnet, Thomas. De statu mortuorum et resurgentium tractatus of the state of the dead. London, 1728. 5 pam.

Phil 850.2 — Burnett, T. Archaeologiae philosophicae. v.1-2. London, 1728-33.

Phil 1915.60.3 — Clarke, Samuel. Discourse...attributes of God. London, 1728.

Phil 8582.11 — Colliber, S. An impartial enquiry. v.1-2. London, 1728-29.

Phil 8658.4.5 — Derham, W. Astro-theology. Hamburg, 1728.

Phil 4582.6.30 — Hermansson, J. Quaestio philosophica an philosophus passit errare? Upsaliae, 1728.

Phil 2651.40 — Huet, Pierre Daniel. Philosophical treatise concerning the weakness of human understanding. London, 1728.

Htn Phil 2053.60.2* — Hutcheson, F. Essay on nature and conduct of passions. London, 1728. 2 pam.

Phil 2053.60 — Hutcheson, F. Essay on nature and conduct of passions. London, 1728.

Htn Phil 3552.30.5* — Leibniz, Gottfried Wilhelm. Principia philosophica. Lipsiae, 1728.

Phil 2128.31 — Mandeville, B. Fable of the bees. London, 1728-29. 2v.

Htn Phil 5640.29* — Maync, Zachary. Two dissertations concerning sense and the imagination. London, 1728.

Phil 3665.4.30 — Nieuwenlijt, B. Gronden van zekerheid of Die regte betooguyse der wiskundigen. Amsterdam, 1728.

Phil 672.7 — Place, C. That space is necesary being. London, 1728.

Phil 585.60 — Sabuco de Nantes Barrera, O. Nueva filosofía de la naturaleza del hombre. Madrid, 1728.

Phil 2515.2.36 — Charron, P. Charron on wisdom. London, 1729. 3v.

Phil 7067.29 — Das Gespenst auf dem Klapperfeld. Frankfurt, 1729.

Phil 1535.31 — Guerinois, J.C. Clypeus philosophiae Thomisticae. Venetiis, 1729. 7v.

Phil 7060.56 — Hilscher, M.P.C. Nachricht von einem gewissen Monche in Dresden. Dresden, 1729.

Htn Phil 2053.50.3* — Hutcheson, F. Inquiry into...beauty and virtue. London, 1729.

Htn Phil 2120.2.30* — Law, William. A serious call to a devout and holy life. London, 1729.

Phil 2128.32 — Mandeville, B. Fable of the bees. London, 1729-32. 2v.

1730-1739

Phil 4513.4.31 — Asp, Matthia. Disputatio gradualis de philosopho curioso. Upsaliae, 1730.

Phil 1850.1.4F — Bacon, F. Opera omnia. London, 1730. 2v.

VPhil 1850.1.3F — Bacon, F. Opera omnia. London, 1730 4v.

Phil 8581.18 — Balguy, J. A letter to a deist. London, 1730-38. 7 pam.

Phil 1915.63.2 — Clarke, Samuel. An exposition of the church catechism. 2d ed. London, 1730.

Phil 5545.13 — Grey, R. Memoria technica. London, 1730.

Phil 6990.8.5 — Maillard, Mary. An exact relation of the wonderful cure of Mary Maillard. London, 1730.

Phil 2128.33.5 — Mandeville, B. Fable of the bees. Pt.II. London, 1730.

Phil 4363.11 — Martinez, Martin. Philosophia sceptica. Madrid, 1730.

Phil 8593.5.2 — Nieuwentyt, B. The religious philosopher. London, 1730. 3v.

Htn Phil 8599.4* — Tindall, M. Christianity as old as the creation. London, 1730. 2v.

Phil 1915.80 — Whiston, W. Historical memoires of...Dr. S. Clarke. London, 1730.

Phil 3910.29 — Wolff, Christian von. Philosophia prima. Francofurti, 1730.

Phil 3552.285 — Alstrin, Eric. Meditationes philosophicas. Upsala, 1731.

Htn Phil 5751.11* — Bossuet, J.B. Traité du libre-arbitre. Paris, 1731.

Phil 801.5.15 — Brucker, J. Kurtze Fragen aus der philosophischen Historie. Ulm, 1731-36. 7v.

Phil 1915.70.5 — Clarke, Samuel. Letters to Mr. Dodwell. London, 1731.

Htn Phil 1925.55* — Cudworth, R. Eternal and immutable morality. London, 1731.

Phil 9343.10 — Dupuy, La Chapelle. Instruction d'un père a sa fille. 3e éd. Paris, 1731.

Phil 8880.20 — Fuller, J. Introductio ad prudentiam, or Directions. London, 1731.

Htn Phil 2100.1.30* — King, William. An essay on the origin of evil. 1st ed. and additions. London, 1731. 2v.

Phil 8593.15 — The necessity of some of the positive institutions of ch---ty consider'd, in a letter to the minister of Moffat. London, 1731.

Phil 270.35 — Alstrin, Eric Praeses. Dissertatio philosophica, de concursu caussaé primaé cum secundis. Upsaliae, 1732.

Phil 4513.4.33 — Asp, Matthia. Dissertatio academica potiores antiquorum. Upsaliae, 1732.

Phil 4513.4.35 — Asp, Matthia. Dissertatio gradualis de vera perfectionis idea. Upsaliae, 1732.

Phil 4513.4.39 — Asp, Matthia. Stylus character animi. Upsaliae, 1732.

Htn Phil 1870.29* — Berkeley, G. Alciphron. Dublin, 1732.

Htn Phil 1870.30* — Berkeley, G. Alciphron. London, 1732. 2v.

Htn Phil 1870.30.1* — Berkeley, G. Alciphron. 2d ed. London, 1732. 2v.

Phil 176.34.9F — Buffier, Claude. Cours de science. Paris, 1732.

Phil 4363.3.90 — Cardenas, Juan. Breve relacion de la muerte. Sevilla, 1732.

Phil 1915.77 — Clarke, J. Defence of Dr. Clarke's...attributes. v.1-3. London, 1732-33.

Phil 1915.61.3 — Clarke, Samuel. The scripture-doctrine of the Trinity. 3d ed. London, 1732.

Phil 8877.15.4 — Collier, Jeremy. Essays upon several moral subjects. 7th ed. pt. 1-2. London, 1732.

Htn Phil 8599.4.7* — Conybeare, J. A defence of revealed religion against the exceptions of a late writer in his book intituled, Christianity as old as the creation. London, 1732.

Htn Phil 2100.1.30.2* — King, William. An essay on the origin of evil. London, 1732. 2v.

Phil 2128.60 — Mandeville, B. Enquiry into the origin of honour. London, 1732.

Htn Phil 1870.81* — Mandeville, B. A letter to Dion Bp. Berkeley on Alciphron. London, 1732.

Htn Phil 525.10* — Phelipeaux, J. Relation de l'origine, du progrès...du quiétisme. Ste. Ménehould, 1732.

1730-1739 - cont.

Phil 2262.30.7 Shaftesbury, A.A.C. Characteristicks. London, 1732. 3v.
Phil 2262.31.2 Shaftesbury, A.A.C. Characteristicks. 5th ed. London, 1732. 3v.
Phil 8599.4.2 Tindall, M. Christianity as old as the creation. London, 1732.
Phil 3910.35 Wolff, Christian von. Psychologia empirica. Francofurti, 1732.
Phil 4513.4.41 Asp, Matthia. Dissertatio academica de caussis obscuritatis philosophorum. Upsaliae, 1733.
Phil 4513.4.37 Asp, Matthia. Exercitium academicum de philosophia parabolica. Upsaliae, 1733.
Phil 4513.4.43 Asp, Matthia. Mexethma philosophicum de subordinatione veritatum. Upsaliae, 1733.
Phil 5627.145 Bonnaire, L. de. Examen critique, physique et théologique des convulsions. n.p., 1733.
Phil 8581.14 Browne, Peter. Things divine and supernatural. London, 1733.
Phil 3822.4.15 Colerus, Johannes. Das Leben des Benedict von Spinoza. Frankfurt, 1733.
Phil 1180.5F Crousaz, J.P. Examen du Pyrrhonisme. La Haye, 1733.
VPhil 1925.49F Cudworth, R. Systema intellectuale huius universi. Jenae, 1733.
Phil 8879.6.5 Erasmus, D. Civilitas morum. Goslariae, 1733.
Phil 182.103.5 Heineccius, J.G. Elementa philosophiae rationalis et moralis. Amstelodami, 1733.
Phil 4582.6.35 Hermansson, J. Speciminis academici. Upsaliae, 1733.
Phil 8599.4.95 Leland, John. An answer to a late book intituled, Christianity as old as the creation. Dublin, 1733. 2v.
Htn Phil 9510.3* Le Mercier, A. A treatise against detraction. Boston, 1733.
Phil 8892.6 Rowe, E.S. Friendship in death. London, 1733-34.
Htn Phil 197.3* Watts, T. Philosophical essays. London, 1733.
Phil 3910.56 Wolff, Christian von. Der Vernunftigen Gedancken von Gott. 2. Aufl. Pt.2. Franckfurt, 1733.
Htn Phil 1870.40.2* Berkeley, G. Treatise...principles of human knowledge. London, 1734.
Phil 8877.22 Campbell, A. An enquiry...original of moral virtue. London, 1734.
Phil 1915.25 Clarke, Samuel. XVIII sermons. 3rd ed. London, 1734.
Phil 665.2 Colliber, S. Free thoughts concerning souls. London, 1734.
Phil 8880.44.5 Forbes, Alexander. Essays, moral and philosophical. London, 1734.
Phil 8700.2.2 Keill, J. Examination of Dr. Burnett's theory of the earth. Oxford, 1734. 2 pam.
Htn Phil 3552.74* Leibniz, Gottfried Wilhelm. Epistolae ad diversos. Cum annotationibus suis primum divulgavit christian. Lipsiae, 1734-42. 4v.
Htn Phil 2750.6.30* Montesquieu, Charles Louis de Secondat. Considerations sur les causes de la grandeur des Romains et de leur décadence. Amsterdam, 1734.
Phil 2805.40.11 Pascal, Blaise. Pensées...sur la religion. Paris, 1734.
Phil 2805.30.9 Pascal, Blaise. Les provinciales. Amsterdam, 1734. 3v.
Phil 8581.18.7 Silvester, Tipping. A sermon containing some reflections upon Mr. Balguy's essay on moral goodness. London, 1734.
Htn Phil 4635.1.30* Swedenborg, E. Prodromus philosophiae. Dresdae, 1734.
Htn Phil 3910.40* Wolff, Christian von. Psychologia rationalis. Francofurti, 1734.
Phil 3095.51 Baumgarten, A.G. Meditationes philosophicae de nonnullis ad poema pertinentibus. Halae, 1735.
Phil 5752.2.3 Collins, A. Philosophical inquiry...human liberty. London, 1735.
Phil 8829.1 England, G. An enquiry into the morals of the ancients. London, 1735.
Phil 179.27 Ewast, John-Bart. Disquisitio philosophica de contingentia rerum. Aboae, 1735.
Phil 2115.48.7 Locke, J. Essai philosophique concernant l'entendement humaine. Amsterdam, 1735.
Phil 2115.30.4 Locke, J. Essay concerning human understanding. v.2. London, 1735.
Phil 7060.65 Moreton, A. Secrets of the invisible world disclos'd. London, 1735.
Phil 8670.5.5 Philipps, J.T. Dissertationes historicae quatuor. London, 1735.
Phil 6990.6 Vialard, Felix. Recueil des pieces...sur les miracles. Nancy, 1735.
Phil 3910.1 Wolff, Christian von. Philosophia rationalis suie logica. Veronae, 1735.
Phil 3910.57 Wolff, Christian von. Vernunfftige Gedancken von Gott. 7. Aufl. Frankfurt, 1735.
Phil 850.2.5 Burnett, T. Doctrina antigua. London, 1736. 3 pam.
Htn Phil 1900.30* Butler, Joseph. Analogy of religion. London, 1736.
Htn Phil 1900.30.2* Butler, Joseph. Analogy of religion. London, 1736.
Phil 181.29 Gravesande, G.J. Introductio ad philosophiam. Leidae, 1736.
Phil 4582.6.40 Hermansson, J. Dissertatio philosophica. Upsaliae, 1736.
Phil 8587.19 Huber, M. The world unmasked. London, 1736.
Phil 182.24 Huber, M. World unmasked. London, 1736.
Phil 5819.1 Jarrold, T. Instinct and reason...science of education. London, 1736.
Phil 8962.10 Muratori, L.A. Della carita cristiana in quanto essa è amore del prossimo. Venezia, 1736.
Phil 8889.2 Oxenstjerna, J.T. Pensées sur divers sujets. Francfort, 1736. 2v.
Htn Phil 2115.126* Perronet, Vincent. A vindication of Mr. Locke. London, 1736.
NEDL Phil 5062.4.3 Watts, S. Logick. 6th ed. London, 1736.
Phil 3910.10 Wolff, Christian von. Gesammlete kleine Philosophie Schrifften. Magdeburg, 1736-40. 6v.
Phil 3910.30 Wolff, Christian von. Philosophia prima suie ontologia. Francofurti, 1736.
Phil 3910.35.5F Wolff, Christian von. Psychologia empirica. Veronae, 1736.
Phil 3910.50 Wolff, Christian von. Theologia naturalis. Francofurti, 1736-41. 2v.
Phil 9513.50 Angers, France (Diocese). Conferences ecclesiastiques du Diocese d'Angers. Angers, 1737.
Phil 4513.4.47 Asp, Matthia. Dissertatio academica de syncretismo philosophico. Upsaliae, 1737.
Phil 4513.4.45 Asp, Matthia. Dissertatio gradualis de usu philosophiae in convertendis gentilibus. Upsaliae, 1737.
Phil 1850.10 Bacon, Francis. Philosophical works. London, 1737. 3v.
Phil 9230.5 Barbeyrac, J. Traité du jeu. Amsterdam, 1737. 3v.

1730-1739 - cont.

Phil 2610.83 Bougerel, J. Vie de Pierre Gassendi. Paris, 1737.
Phil 5811.2.2 Boullier, D.R. Essai philosophique sur l'âme des bêtes. Amsterdam, 1737. 2v.
Phil 8581.14.10 Browne, Peter. The procedure, extent and limits of human understanding. London, 1737.
Phil 8656.7 Buddeus, J.F. Theses theologicae de atheismo. Traiecti ad Rhenum, 1737.
Phil 6990.1 Carre, L.B. La verité des miracles. n.p., 1737-41. 2v.
Phil 6990.1.2 Carré, L.B. La verité des miracles. Utrecht, 1737-41.
Htn Phil 1930.5.37* Collins, Anthony. A discourse of the grounds and reasons of the Christian religion. London, 1737. 2 pam.
Phil 1930.5.35 Collins, Anthony. A discourse of the grounds and reasons of the Christian religion. London, 1737. 2 pam.
Htn Phil 2055.4.30F* Harrington, James. The oceana of James Harrington. Dublin, 1737.
Phil 3552.90 Ludovici, C.G. Ausfuhrlicher...Historie der leibnitzischen Philosophie. Leipzig, 1737. 2v.
Phil 3910.84 Ludovici, Karl G. Sammlung Auszüge der sämmtlichen Wegen der Wolffischen Philosophie. Pt.1-2. Leipzig, 1737-38.
Phil 8887.18 Morgan, T. The moral philosopher. London, 1737-39. 2v.
Phil 4630.3.31 Rydelius, Anders. Förnufts-öfningar. Linköping, 1737.
Phil 2262.32 Shaftesbury, A.A.C. Characteristicks. 6th ed. London, 1737. 3v.
Phil 3910.58 Wolff, Christian von. Cosmologia generalis methodo scientifica. Francofurti, 1737.
Phil 3910.40.5 Wolff, Christian von. Psychologia rationalis. Veronae, 1737.
Phil 8610.713.40 Bentley, Richard. La friponnerie laïque des pretendus esprits forts d'Angleterre. Amsterdam, 1738.
Htn Phil 1870.72* Berkeley, G. A discourse addressed to magistrates and men in authority. Dublin, 1738.
Htn Phil 1915.10.2F* Clarke, Samuel. Works. London, 1738. 2v.
VPhil 1915.10F Clarke, Samuel. Works. London, 1738. 4v.
Phil 8878.19 Darell, W. The gentleman instructed. London, 1738.
Phil 9075.30 Hassel, H. De conscientia theses morales. Diss. Aboae, 1738.
Phil 2053.50.4 Hutcheson, F. Inquiry into...beauty and virtue. London, 1738.
Phil 2115.64.25 Locke, J. A common-place book to the Holy Bible. 4th ed. London, 1738.
Phil 8887.18.3 Morgan, T. The moral philosopher. v.1, 2. ed. London, 1738-40. 3v.
Htn Phil 2115.127* Perronet, Vincent. A second vindication of Mr. Locke. London, 1738.
Phil 3910.54 Wolff, Christian von. Philosophia practica. Francofurti, 1738-39. 2v.
Phil 3910.50.5 Wolff, Christian von. Theologia naturalis. Veronae, 1738. 2v.
Htn Phil 8602.11.4* Wollaston, W. The religion of nature delineated. London, 1738.
Phil 8580.13 Annet, Peter. A collection of the tracts of a certain free thinker. London, 1739-1749.
Phil 3095.35.5 Baumgarten, A.G. Metaphysica. Halae, 1739.
Phil 5811.8 Boujeant, G.H. Amusement philosophique sur le langage des bestes. Paris, 1739.
Phil 8626.15.12 Burnet, Thomas. A treatise concerning the state of the departed souls. 2. ed. London, 1739.
Phil 8582.2 Campbell, A. The necessity of revelation. London, 1739.
Phil 181.26.3 Gottsched, J.C. Erste Gründe. 3. Aufl. v.1-2. Leipzig, 1739.
Phil 3910.54.5 Wolff, Christian von. Philosophia practica. Veronae, 1739-42. 2v.

1740-1749

VPhil 1850.1.15F Bacon, Francis. Works. London, 1740. 4v.
Phil 8656.7.10 Buddeus, J.F. Traité de l'athéisme et de la superstition. Amsterdam, 1740.
Phil 1900.31 Butler, Joseph. Analogy of religion. London, 1740.
Phil 1980.5 Experimental philosophy asserted and defended against some late attempts to undermine it. London, 1740.
Phil 3552.294 Lamprecht, J.F. Leben des Freyherrn Gottfried Wilhelm von Leibnitz au das licht Gestellet. Berlin, 1740.
Phil 5640.8.5 Le Cat, C.N. Traité des sens. Rouen, 1740.
Phil 3552.21 Leibniz, Gottfried Wilhelm. Kleinere philosophische Schriften. Jena, 1740.
Phil 8599.4.97 Leland, John. An answer to a book intituled, Christianity as old as the creation. 2. ed. London, 1740. 2v.
VPhil 2115.1.3 Locke, J. Works. 4th ed. v.1,3. London, 1740. 2v.
Phil 2115.1.3 Locke, J. Works. 4th ed. v.2. London, 1740.
Phil 7060.65.5 Moreton, A. Secrets of the invisible world disclos'd. London, 1740.
Phil 5465.2.5 Muratori, L.A. Della forza della fantasia umana. Venezia, 1740.
Phil 8595.26 Perronet, V. Some enquiries, chiefly related to spiritual beings. London, 1740.
Phil 296.4 Pluche, N.A. The history of the heavens. London, 1740. 2v.
Phil 8599.21.90 Scudder, D.L. Tennant's philosophical theology. New Haven, 1740.
Phil 75.9 Struve, B.G. Bibliothecae philosphicae. Göttingen, 1740.
Phil 8598.21 Sykes, A.A. The principles and connexion of natural and revealed religion distinctly considered. London, 1740.
Phil 8894.10 Turnbull, G. The principles of moral philosophy. London, 1740. 2v.
Phil 3910.77.10 Baumeister, F.C. Historiam doctrinae recentius controversae de mundo optimo. Lipsiae, 1741.
Phil 3910.77.3 Baumeister, F.C. Institutiones philosophiae rationalis methodo Wolfii conscriptae. 5. ed. Vitembergae, 1741.
Phil 3552.82 Bilfingeri, G.B. Harmonia...praestabilita...Leibnitii. Tubingae, 1741.
Phil 334.3 Della certitude des connaissance humaines. Londres, 1741.
Phil 2651.30 Huet, Pierre Daniel. Traité philosophique de la faiblesse. London, 1741.
Htn Phil 2050.34.50* Hume, David. Essays moral and political. Edinburgh, 1741.
Phil 2115.48.10 Locke, J. Essai philosophique concernant l'entendement humaine. Abrégé. Genève, 1741.
Phil 2115.49.25 Locke, J. Libri IV de intellectu humano. Lipsiae, 1741.
Phil 8887.18.5 Morgan, T. Physico-theology. London, 1741.
Phil 8597.5 Religion one, even the self-same thing in all ages. London, 1741.
Phil 5058.1 Sandersono, R. Logicae artis compend. Oxoniae, 1741.
Htn Phil 1535.15* Bonaventura, St., Cardinal. Cursus philosophicus. n.p., 1742.

Chronological Listing

1740-1749 - cont.

	Phil 801.5	Brucker J. Historia critica philosophiae. Lipsiae, 1742-67. 6v.
	Phil 177.25.30	Canz, Israel Gottlieb. Theologia naturalis thetico-polemica. Dresdae, 1742.
	Phil 1915.12F	Clarke, Samuel. Works. London, 1742. 2v.
	Phil 803.1	Deslandes, A.F.B. Histoire critique de la philosophie. London, 1742. 3v.
	Phil 2045.61.10	Hobbes, Thomas. Elementa philosophica de cive. Amsterdam, 1742.
Htn	Phil 2050.34.55*	Hume, David. Essays moral and political. 2nd ed. Edinburgh, 1742.
	Phil 2053.52	Hutcheson, F. Metaphysicae synopsis. n.p., 1742.
	Phil 2053.40	Hutcheson, F. Philosophiae moralis. v.1-3. Glasgow, 1742.
	Phil 8666.2.5	Lesser, F.C. Theologie des insects. La Hague, 1742.
	Phil 2115.48.11	Locke, J. Essai philosophique concernant l'entendement humaine. 4e éd. Amsterdam, 1742.
	Phil 2115.75	Locke, J. Familiar letters. London, 1742.
	Phil 2115.75.2	Locke, J. Familiar letters. London, 1742.
	Phil 3625.8.55	Meier, Georg Friedrich. Beweiss: das keine Materie dencken Könne. Halel, 1742.
Htn	Phil 2115.116*	Memoirs of the life...of Mr. John Locke. London, 1742.
	Phil 4170.13	Monti, G.F. Anima brutorum secundum sanioris. Neapoli, 1742.
	Phil 8597.10	Robles, M. Bigotry, superstition, hypocrasy...Atheism. London, 1742.
	Phil 8655.1.3	Abernethy, J. Discourses concerning...God. Dublin, 1743. 2v.
	Phil 9340.5	Ancourt, Abbe d'. The lady's preceptor. London, 1743.
	Phil 8610.713.30	Bentley, Richard. Remarks upon a late discourse of free-thinking. pt.3. 8th ed. Cambridge, Eng., 1743.
	Phil 4080.24	Corsini, Edoardo. Institutiones philosophicae. Venetius, 1743.
Htn	Phil 1925.30.2*	Cudworth, R. The true intellectual system of the universe. 2d ed. London, 1743. 2v.
	Phil 3910.82	Des Champs, J. Cours abrégé de la philosophie Wolffienne. Amsterdam, 1743-47. 2v.
	Phil 8584.2	Ellis, J. The knowledge of divine things from revelation. London, 1743.
	Phil 184.8.5	Johnson, Samuel. Introduction to the study of philosophy. 2. ed. London, 1743.
	Phil 193.1	Saint-Hyacinth, T. Recherches philosophiques. Rotterdam, 1743.
	Phil 1123.3.5	Stanley, T. Historia philosophiae. Lipsiae, 1743.
Itn	Phil 1870.65*	Berkeley, G. Siris: a chain of...reflexions. Dublin, 1744.
	Phil 8582.40	Clarke, M. Traités de l'existence et des attributs de Dieu, des devoirs de la religion naturelle. n.p., 1744. 3v.
	Phil 1928.31	Cumberland, R. Traité philosophique des loix naturelles. Amsterdam, 1744.
	Phil 9245.12	Harris, J. Three treatises. London, 1744.
	Phil 9558.6	An introduction to the art of lying. London, 1744.
	Phil 665.58.5	Knutzen, Martin. Philosophische Abhandlung von der immateriellen Natur der Seele. Königsberg, 1744.
	Phil 3552.62.10	Leibniz, Gottfried Wilhelm. Theodicée. Hannover, 1744.
	Phil 2115.45.5	Locke, J. An abridgment of Mr. Locke's Essay concerning human understanding. Glasgow, 1744.
tn	Phil 2175.2.35*	Norris, John. The picture of love unveil'd. 4. ed. London, 1744.
	Phil 8892.11	Rutherforth, T. An essay on the nature and obligations of virtue. Cambridge, 1744.
	Phil 3819.30.50	Spinoza, Benedictus de. Sittenlehre. Frankfurt, 1744.
tn	Phil 4260.33*	Vico, G.B. Principi di scienza nuova. v.1-2. Napoli, 1744.
tn	Phil 2340.3.31*	Waring, Robert. The picture of love. 4th ed .v.1-2. London, 1744.
tn	Phil 665.1.2*	Baxter, A. An enquiry into nature of human soul. London, 1745. 2v.
	Phil 282.5.5	Baxter, A. Matho, or, The cosmotheoria puerilis. London, 1745. 2v.
	Phil 1870.65.5	Berkeley, G. Recherches sur les vertus de l'eau de goudron. Amsterdam, 1745.
	Phil 3552.362	Gruber, J.D. Commercii epistolici Leibnitiani. Hanoverae, 1745. 2v.
tn	Phil 2705.40*	La Mettrie, Julien Offray de. Histoire naturelle de l'ame. La Haye, 1745.
	Phil 8887.6	Mason, J. Self-knowledge. London, 1745.
	Phil 8705.11	Parker, Benjamin. A survey of six days work of creation. London, 1745.
	Phil 9005.2	Sacy, M.L. de. Traité de la gloire. La Haye, 1745.
	Phil 7067.00.5	Stryk, Johann S. Disputatio iuridica inauguralis de iure spectrorum...Andreas Becker. Jenae, 1745.
	Phil 9361.2	Valenca, Francisco P. de. Instrucçam. Lisboa, 1745. 3 pam.
	Phil 5062.4.3.5	Watts, S. Logick. 8th ed. London, 1745.
	Phil 7082.78	L'art de se rendre heureux par les songes. Francfort, 1746.
	Phil 282.5	Baxter, A. Matho; sive, Cosmotheoria puerilis. London, 1746.
	Phil 3120.4.31	Bilfinger, G.B. Dilucidationes philosophicae de Deo. 3. ed. Tubingae, 1746.
	Phil 7067.46.5	Calmet, Augustin. Dissertations sur les apparitions. Paris, 1746.
1	Phil 2530.30*	Diderot, Denis. Pensées philosophiques. La Haye, 1746.
1	Phil 3480.34*	Kant, Immanuel. Gedanken von der wahren Schätzung des lebendigen Kräfte. Königsberg, 1746.
	Phil 6680.1.4	Kerner, J. Die Seherin von Prevorst. 4. Aufl. Stuttgart, 1746.
	Phil 3625.8.38	Meier, Georg Friedrich. Gedancken von der Ehre. Halle, 1746.
	Phil 6025.2	Pernetti, J. Lettres philosophiques sur les physionomies. La Haie, 1746.
	Phil 5055.15	Plenning, J. Logica, usui juniorum. Holmiae, 1746.
	Phil 3910.2	Wolff, Christian von. Philosophia rationalis suie logica. Helmstadia, 1746.
	Phil 3910.70.5	Wolff, Christian von. Vernunfftige Gedancken von dem Würckungen der Natur. 5. Aufl. Halle, 1746.
	Phil 8402.34	Batteux, Charles. Les beaux arts reduits. Paris, 1747.
	Phil 801.5.7	Brucker, J. Institutiones historiae philosophicae. Lipsiae, 1747.
	Phil 8584.2.2	Ellis, J. The knowledge of divine things from revelation. London, 1747.
	Phil 9420.3	Enquiry into the origin of the human appetites and affections. Lincoln, 1747.
	Phil 2115.113	Gerdil, G.S. L'immatérialité de l'âme...contre Locke. Turin, 1747.

1740-1749 - cont.

	Phil 8664.1	Jack, R. Mathematical principles of theology. London, 1747.
	Phil 8665.1	Knight, H. The being and attributes of God. London, 1747.
	Phil 5050.15	Knutzen, M. Elementa philosophiae rationalis seu logicae. Regiomonti, 1747.
	Phil 8592.52.5	Mason, Francis. The contents of the history of ancient paganism. London, 1747.
	Phil 2295.15	Toland, John. Miscellaneous works. London 1747. 2v.
	Phil 7067.47	Wegner, George W. Philosophische Abhandlung von Gespenstern. Berlin, 1747.
	Phil 3910.68.6	Wolff, Christian von. Vernunfftige Gedancken von dem gesellschafftlichen. 6. Aufl. Franckfurt, 1747.
	Phil 1870.65.8	Berkeley, G. Recherches sur les vertus de l'eau de goudron. Genève, 1748.
	Phil 801.5.20	Brucker, J. Miscellanea historiae philosophicae literariae criticae. Augustae Vindelicorum, 1748.
	Phil 8404.14	Dubos, Jean B. Critical reflections on poetry. London, 1748. 3v.
	Phil 9420.5	Essais sur les passions et sur leurs caracteres. v.2. La Haye, 1748.
	Phil 9035.48	Falconnet de la Bellonie. La psycantropie ou nouvelle théorie de l'homme. v.1-3. Avignon, 1748.
	Phil 2733.95	Gerdil, G.S. Défense du sentiment du P. Malebranche. Turin, 1748.
Htn	Phil 2050.15*	Hume, David. Essays. v.3-4. London, 1748-53. 2v.
Htn	Phil 2705.30*	La Mettrie, Julien Offray de. L'homme machin. v.1-2. Leyde, 1748.
	Phil 5402.4	Levesque de Pouilly, L.J. Theorie des sentimens agreables. Paris, 1748.
	Phil 2115.30.2	Locke, J. Essay concerning human understanding. London, 1748. 2v.
Htn	Phil 2705.85*	Luface, Elie. L'homme plus que machine. Londres, 1748.
	Phil 293.8	Maillet, Benoît de. Telliamed. v.1-2. Amsterdam, 1748.
	Phil 7067.48.10	Meier, George F. Vertheidigung der Gedanken von Gespenstern. Halle im Magdeburgischen, 1748.
	Phil 2805.40.12	Pascal, Blaise. Pensées...sur la religion. Paris, 1748.
	Phil 8597.1	Ramsay, A.M. The philosophical principles of natural and revealed religion. Glasgow, 1748-49. 2v.
	Phil 8893.26	The student's companion. London, 1748.
	Phil 7067.48	Sucro, J.G. Widerlegung der Gedancken von Gespentern. Halle im Magdeburgischen, 1748.
Htn	Phil 8894.8.5*	Toussaint, F.V. Les moeurs. pt. 3. Amsterdam, 1748.
	Phil 175.9.5	Argens, J.B. The impartial philosopher. London, 1749. 2v.
	Phil 176.11.3	Baumeister, F.C. Institutiones metaphysicae. Wittenbergae, 1749.
Htn	Phil 1870.65.9*	Berkeley, G. Extrait des recherches sur les vertus de l'eau de goudron. Amsterdam, 1749.
	Phil 1900.60.4	Butler, Joseph. Fifteen sermons and six sermons. 4th ed. London, 1749.
	Phil 177.25.10	Canz, Israle Gottlieb. Philosophicae Leibnitianae. Francofurti, 1749.
	Phil 2493.50	Condillac, Étienne Bonnot. Traité des sistêmes. La Haye, 1749.
Htn	Phil 2530.35*	Diderot, Denis. Lettre sur les aveugles. Londres, 1749.
	Phil 8585.8	Foster, J. Discourses...natural religion and social virtue. London, 1749-52.
	Phil 181.26.5	Gottsched, J.C. Erste Grunder der Weltweisheit. Leipzig, 1749. 2v.
	Phil 8881.21	Grove, H. A system of moral philosophy. London, 1749.
	Phil 5816.2	Guer, S.A. Histoire critique de l'âme des bêtes. v.1-2. Amsterdam, 1749.
Htn	Phil 2038.30*	Hartley, D. Observations on man. London, 1749. 2v.
Htn	Phil 3552.58*	Leibniz, Gottfried Wilhelm. Summi polyhistoris Godefridi Guilielmi Leibntii Protogaea. Goettingae, 1749.
Htn	Phil 5761.20*	Luzac, E. Essai sur la liberté de produire ses sentimens. n.p., 1749.
	Phil 2750.8.35	Maupertuis, P.L.M. de. Essai de philosophie morale. Berlin, 1749.
	Phil 3625.8.65	Meier, Georg Friedrich. Vertheidigung der christlichen Religion. 2e Aufl. Halle, 1749.
	Phil 8703.3	The naturalist: a dialogue. London, 1749. 2 pam.
	Phil 2805.42.5	Pascal, Blaise. Thoughts on religion and other curious subjects. London, 1749.
Htn	Phil 2262.32.5*	Shaftesbury, A.A.C. Characteristicks. London, 1749. 3v.
Htn	Phil 8894.8.3*	Toussaint, F.V. Les moeurs. pt.1-2,3. Aux Indes, 1749.
Htn	Phil 8894.8*	Toussaint, F.V. Les moeurs. 4th ed. n.p., 1749.
	Phil 3910.45	Wolff, Christian von. Vernunfftige Gedancken. Halle, 1749-53.

1750-1759

Htn	Phil 665.1.5*	Baxter, A. Appendix to 1st pt. An enquiry into nature of human soul. v.3. London, 1750.
X Cg	Phil 8876.21	Bonnaire, L. de. Les leçons de la sagesse. Paris, 1750-51. 3v.
	Phil 9341.11	Burgh, J. Directions prudential, moral, religious. London, 1750.
	Phil 177.25	Canz, Israel Gottlieb. Meditationes philosophicae. Tubingae, 1750.
	Phil 1928.35	Cumberland, R. A philosophical enquiry into the laws of nature. Dublin, 1750.
	Phil 9343.10.5	Dupuy, La Chapelle. Instruction d'un père à sa fille. 3e éd. Paris, 1750.
	Phil 2045.1	Hobbes, Thomas. Moral and political works. London, 1750.
Htn	Phil 2050.34.25*	Hume, David. Philosophical essays concerning human understanding. 2nd ed. London, 1750.
Htn	Phil 2053.70*	Hutcheson, F. Reflections upon laughter. Glasgow, 1750.
	Phil 5640.8	Le Cat, C.N. A physical essay on the senses. London, 1750.
	Phil 293.8.6	Maillet, Benoît de. Telliamed. London, 1750.
Htn	Phil 2128.50*	Mandeville, B. La fable des abeilles. London, 1750. 2v.
	Phil 2115.151	Massie, J. An essay on...Mr. Locke. London, 1750.
	Phil 2750.8.37	Maupertuis, P.L.M. de. Essai de philosophie morale. Londres, 1750.
	Phil 5255.3	Petvin, J. Letters concerning mind. London, 1750.
	Phil 9175.6	Pimentel Castello-Branco, B.B. Regimento saudavel. Lisboa, 1750.
	Phil 2262.75	Shaftesbury, A.A.C. Letters. London, 1750.
	Phil 197.41.5	Wallerius, N. Systema metaphysicum. v.1-4. Stockholmiae, 1750-1752. 2v.
	Phil 3910.55	Wolff, Christian von. Philosophia moralis suie ethica. Halae, 1750-53. 5v.
Htn	Phil 2262.79.1*	Brown, J. Essays on the characteristics. London, 1751.

1750-1759 - cont.

	Phil 2262.79	Brown, J. Essays on the characteristics. 2d ed. London, 1751.
	Phil 7067.46.15	Calmet, Augustin. Gelehrte Verhandlung der Materi von Erscheinungen der Geisteren. 3. Aufl. Augspurg. 1751.
	Phil 7060.5.5	Calmet, Augustin. Recueil de dissertations...sur les apparitions. Avignon, 1751. 2v.
	Phil 7067.46.10	Calmet, Augustin. Traité sur les apparitions des esprits. Paris, 1751. 2v.
Htn	Phil 7067.46.10*	Calmet, Augustin. Traité sur les apparitions des esprits. Paris, 1751. 2v.
	Phil 8877.13	Cockburn, C. Works. London, 1751. 2v.
Htn	Phil 2530.40*	Diderot, Denis. Lettre sur les sourds et muets. n.p., 1751.
	Phil 8878.13.9	Dodsley, R. The economy of human life. London, 1751.
	Phil 9450.5	Ferencz II Rakoczi, Prince of Transylvania. Testament politique et moral. La Haye, 1751.
	Phil 4114.25	Genovesi, Antonio. Elementa metaphysicae mathematicum in morem adornata. 2a ed. Neapoli, 1751-56. 4v.
	Phil 5811.8.5	Hildrop, John. Free thoughts upon the brute-creation: wherein Father Bougeant's Philosophical amusement is examined. London, 1751.
Htn	Phil 2055.1.30*	Home, Henry. Essays on the principles of morality. Edinburgh, 1751.
Htn	Phil 2050.69.2*	Hume, David. An enquiry concerning...morals. London, 1751.
Htn	Phil 2050.34.27*	Hume, David. Philosophical essays concerning human understanding. 2nd ed. London, 1751.
	Phil 8800.1	Hyde, E. The miscellaneous works. London, 1751.
Htn	Phil 8635.1*	Kenrick, W. The grand question debated. Dublin, 1751. 2 pam.
NEDL	Phil 9351.1.2	Ladies library. London, 1751. 3v.
Htn	Phil 2705.15*	La Mettrie, Julien Offray de. Oeuvres philosophiques. London, 1751.
Htn	Phil 6021.6*	Le Brun, Charles. Conference sur l'expression générale et particuliere des passions. Verone, 1751.
	Phil 7060.5	Lenglet, Dufresnoy N. Traité historique et dogmatique...apparitions. Avignon, 1751. 2v.
	Phil 3625.8.57	Meier, Georg Friedrich. Beweis: dass' keine Materie dencken Könne. 2e Aufl. Halle, 1751. 7 pam.
	Phil 3625.8.58	Meier, Georg Friedrich. Beweis dass die menschliche Seele ewig Lebt. Halle, 1751.
	Phil 6025.6	Philosophical letters on physiognomy. London, 1751.
	Phil 490.7	Ploucquet, G. Dissertatio de materialismo. Tubingae, 1751.
	Phil 8622.58	Pruefung der Secte die an allem zweifelt. Göttingen, 1751.
	Phil 8896.2A	Voluseno, F. De animi tranquillitate dialogus. Edinburg, 1751.
NEDL	Phil 5400.5	Watts, I. The doctrine of the passions. London, 1751.
NEDL	Phil 5062.4.4	Watts, S. Logick. 9th ed. London, 1751.
	Phil 2050.204	Adams, William. An essay on Mr. Hume's essay on miracles. London, 1752.
	Phil 1870.70	Berkeley, G. Miscellany containing several tracts on various subjects. London, 1752.
	Phil 3110.55.15	Böhme, J. The way to Christ discovered. Manchester, 1752.
	Phil 2262.79.2	Brown, J. Essays on the characteristics. London, 1752.
	Phil 1158.9	Combes, M. Les vies d'Epicure de Platon et de Pythagore. Amsterdam, 1752.
	Phil 5247.13.21	Huarte de San Juan, J. Prüfung der Köpfe zu den Wissenschaften. Zerbst, 1752.
Htn	Phil 2050.73*	Hume, David. Political discourses. Edinburgh, 1752.
Htn	Phil 184.8.3*	Johnson, Samuel. Elementa philosophica. Philadelphia, 1752.
Htn	Phil 184.8*	Johnson, Samuel. Elementa philosophica. v.1-2. Philadelphia, 1752.
	Phil 2705.31	La Mettrie, Julien Offray de. Man a machine. v.1-2. London, 1752.
	Phil 2750.8.50	Maupertuis, P.L.M. de. Lettres de Mr. de Maupertuis. Dresden, 1752.
	Phil 3625.8.62	Meier, Georg Friedrich. Auszug aus der Vernunftlehre. Halle, 1752.
	Phil 6128.19	Simson, T. An inquiry how far the vital and animal actions of the more perfect animals can be accounted for independent of the brain. Edinburgh, 1752.
	Phil 8894.8.15	Toussaint, F.V. Manners. 2d ed. London, 1752.
	Phil 7060.8	View of the invisible world. London, 1752.
	Phil 3910.72.15	Wolff, Christian von. Vernunfftige Gedancken von dem Absichten. Magdeburgischen, 1752.
	Phil 3910.59.15	Wolff, Christian von. Vernunfftige Gedancken von der Menschen. Magdeburgischen, 1752.
	Phil 3910.57.15	Wolff, Christian von. Vernunfftige Gedancken von Gott. Halle, 1752-40. 2v.
	Phil 175.9.8	Argens, J.B. Philosophical dissertations. London, 1753. 2v.
	VPhil 1850.2F	Bacon, Francis. Works. London, 1753. 3v.
	Phil 8876.3	Balfour, J. A delineation...nature. Obligations. Morality. Edinburgh, 1753.
	Phil 8691.8.9	Burnet, Thomas. The sacred theory of the earth. Glasgow, 1753. 2v.
Htn	Phil 2404.1*	Eloges de trois philosophes. London, 1753.
	Phil 8405.9	Estève, Pierre. L'esprit des beaux-arts. v.1-2. Paris, 1753.
Htn	Phil 8584.4*	An estimate of the profit and loss of religion. Edinburgh, 1753.
Htn	Phil 2053.41*	Hutcheson, F. A short introduction to moral philosophy. v.1-3. Glasgow, 1753.
	Phil 2115.31	Locke, J. Essay concerning human understanding. London, 1753. 2v.
	Phil 9245.4.3	Lucas, R. An enquiry after happiness. London, 1753. 2v.
	Phil 8887.6.2	Mason, J. Self-knowledge. London, 1753.
	Phil 8705.9	Pike, S. Philosopha sacra: or The principles of natural philosophy. London, 1753.
	Phil 3910.73.15	Wolff, Christian von. Vernunfftige Gedancken von dem Gebrauche. Magdeburgischen, 1753.
	Phil 8876.20	Bolton, R. On the employment of time. London, 1754.
	Phil 8876.36	Burgh, J. The dignity of human nature. London, 1754.
Htn	Phil 2493.45*	Condillac, Étienne Bonnot. Traité des sensations. v.1-2. Londres, 1754.
Htn	Phil 1980.1.30*	Edwards, Jonathan. A careful...enquiry. Boston, 1754.
Htn	Phil 5754.1.10*	Edwards, Jonathan. Careful and strict enquiry into the modern...freedom of will. Boston, 1754.
	Phil 8408.29	Hogarth, William. Zergliederung der Schönheit, die schwankendenBegriffe von dem geschmack Festzusetzen. Berlin, 1754.
	Phil 8520.5	Leland, J. A view of the principal deistical writers. London, 1754-56. 3v.
	Phil 9245.4.4	Lucas, R. An enquiry after happiness. pt.1. Edinburgh, 1754.
	Phil 3625.8.30	Meier, Georg Friedrich. Gedanken von Scherzen. Halle, 1754.
	Phil 3910.60	Wolff, Christian von. Oeconomica. Halae, 1754.
	Phil 175.9.2	Argens, J.B. La philosophie du Bon-Sens. La Haye, 1755. 3v.
	Phil 176.11	Baumeister, F.C. Elementa philosophiae. Leipzig, 1755.
	Phil 2493.35	Condillac, Étienne Bonnot. Traité des animaux. Amsterdam, 1755.
	Phil 8404.14.5	Dubos, J.B. Reflexions critiques sur la poésie et sur la peinture. 6. éd. Paris, 1755. 3v.
Htn	Phil 8880.7*	Fleming, C. A scale of first principles. London, 1755.
	Phil 3910.83	Gottsched, J.C. Historische Lobschrift des Herrn C. von Wolf. Halle, 1755.
	Phil 8881.21.4	Grove, H. A system of moral philosophy. London, 1755. 2v.
	Phil 8662.8	Hill, J. Thoughts concerning God and nature. London, 1755.
	Phil 807.3	Hornius, G. Historiae philosophicae. Lugdunum Batavorum, 1755.
	Phil 2053.30	Hutcheson, F. System of moral philosophy. Glasgow, 1755. 2v.
Htn	Phil 2053.30.1*	Hutcheson, F. System of moral philosophy. London, 1755. 2v.
Htn	Phil 3480.69.1*	Kant, Immanuel. Allgemeine Naturgeschichte. Theorie des Himmels. Königsberg, 1755.
	Phil 8591.1	Law, E. Considerations...theory of religion. Cambridge, 1755.
	Phil 2115.48.12	Locke, J. Essai philosophique concernant l'entendement humaine. Amsterdam, 1755.
	Phil 293.8.4	Maillet, Benoît de. Telliamed. La Haye, 1755. 2v.
	Phil 293.8.2	Maillet, Benoît de. Telliamed. La Haye, 1755. 2v.
Htn	Phil 2128.33.12*	Mandeville, B. Fable of the bees. Edinburgh, 1755. 2v.
	Phil 8887.6.3	Mason, J. Self-knowledge. London, 1755.
	Phil 3625.8.31	Meier, Georg Friedrich. Betrachtung über den Fehler der menschlichen Tugenden. Halle, 1755.
	Phil 3625.8.25	Meier, Georg Friedrich. Georg Friedrich Meiers Metaphysik. v.1-4. Halle, 1755-59. 3v.
	Phil 7150.28	Relaçãi de hum notavel caso. Lisboa, 1755?
	Phil 8892.74	Roys, F.X. Ethica et jus naturae in usum auditorum. Viennae, 1755.
	Phil 197.41	Wallerius, N. Compendium metaphysicae. Stockholmiae, 1755.
NEDL	Phil 5062.4.5	Watts, S. Logick. 10th ed. London, 1755.
	Phil 8712.9	Whiston, W. Theory of the earth, from its original. London, 1755.
	Phil 1105.3	Aquilianiis, S. Placitis philosophorum. Lipsiae, 1756.
	Phil 1850.66	Bacon, Francis. Analyse de la philosophie. Leyde, 1756.
Htn	Phil 8951.2*	Browne, T. Christian morals. 2. ed. London, 1756.
	Phil 7067.46.18	Calmet, Augustin. Dissertazioni sopra le apparizioni de spiriti. Venezia, 1756.
	Phil 1915.63.6	Clarke, Samuel. An exposition of the church catechism. 6th ed. London, 1756.
	Phil 1915.20	Clarke, Samuel. Sermons on several subjects and occasions. 8th ed. London, 1756. 8v.
Htn	Phil 2493.40.5*	Contillac, Étienne Bonnot. An essay on the origin of human knowledge. London, 1756.
	Phil 803.1.5	Deslandes, A.F.B. Historie critique de la philosophie. Amsterdam, 1756. 4v.
	Phil 4110.13.30	Fortunato da Brescia. Philosophia sensuum mechanica methodice tractata atque ad usus academicos accommodata. Venetiis, 1756.
	Phil 8586.2	Gordon, T. A new method of demonstrating...the four fundamental points of religion. London, 1756.
	Phil 182.26	Hutcheson, F. Synopsis metaphysicae. Glasguae, 1756.
Htn	Phil 3480.36*	Kant, Immanuel. Metaphysicae cum geometria junctae usus in philosophiam naturicam. Regiomonti, 1756.
	Phil 8666.2	Lesser, F.C. Testaceo-Theologia. Leipzig, 1756.
NEDL	Phil 5051.8	Logical compendium. Glasguae, 1756.
	Phil 5062.24	Wesley, John. A compendium of logic. 2nd ed. London, 1756.
	Phil 8602.11.8	Wollaston, W. Ebauche de la religion naturelle...avec un supplément. La Haye, 1756. 3v.
	Phil 3095.35	Baumgarten, A.G. Metaphysica. Halae, 1757.
Htn	Phil 8876.30.5*	Brown, John. An estimate of the manners and principles of the times. 2nd ed. London, 1757.
	Phil 7067.46.16	Calmet, Augustin. Gelehrte Verhandlung der Materi von Erscheinungen der Geisteren. 3. Aufl. Augspurg. 1757.
	Phil 5042.28.5	Cochet, J. La clef des sciences et des beaux arts, ou La logique. Paris, 1757.
	Phil 8403.6	Cooper, John G. Letters concerning taste. 3. ed. London, 1757.
	Phil 1928.31.2	Cumberland, R. Loix de la nature. Leiden, 1757.
	Phil 9167.3	Hallifax, de M. Airs d'un père à sa fille. London, 1757.
	Phil 8697.11	Hoffmann, J.G. Kurtze Fragen von den natürlichen Dingen. Halle, 1757.
Htn	Phil 2050.30*	Hume, David. Four dissertations. London, 1757.
Htn	Phil 8520.5.3*	Leland, J. A view of the principal deistical writers. London, 1757. 2v.
Htn	Phil 2115.49.5*	Locke, J. Versuch vom menschlichen Verstand. Altenburg, 1757.
	Phil 2412.2	Moreau, Jacob N. Nouveau mémoire pour servir à l'histoire des Cacouacs. Amsterdam, 1757. 2 pam.
Htn	Phil 2340.2.80*	Walker, O. Proposed for the press. Boston, 1757.
	Phil 9245.34	Beausobre, Louis de. Essai sur le bonheur. Berlin, 1758.
	Phil 8876.65	Bonnaire, L. de. La regle des devoirs. Paris, 1758. 3v.
	Phil 8876.30	Brown, John. An estimate of the manners and principles of the times. v.1-2. London, 1758.
	Phil 8880.10	Fordyce, D. The elements of moral philosophy. v.1-3. London, 1758.
Htn	Phil 9345.4*	Forrester, J. Polite philosopher. London, 1758.
Htn	Phil 2636.40*	Helvétius, C.A. De l'esprit. Amsterdam, 1758.
Htn	Phil 2050.43*	Hume, David. Essais philosophiques sur l'entendement humain. Amsterdam, 1758. 2v.
	Phil 2050.1	Hume, David. Essays and treatises. London, 1758.
	Phil 8620.7.2	King, William. An essay on the origin of evil. London, 1758. 2v.
	Phil 7060.98	Life after death. London, 1758.
	Phil 3625.8.35	Meier, Georg Friedrich. Versuch einer Erklärung des Nachtwandelns. Halle, 1758.
Htn	Phil 2215.30*	Price, Richard. A review of the principal questions and difficulties in morals. London, 1758.
	Phil 176.98	Bouillier, D.R. Discours philosophiques. Amsterdam, 1759.

Chronological Listing

1750-1759 - cont.

Phil 8691.8.12 — Burnet, Thomas. The sacred theory of the earth. 7. ed. London, 1759. 2v.
Htn Phil 2915.50* — Candide ou L'optimisme. n.p., 1759.
Phil 5752.3.2 — Corry, W. Reflections upon liberty and necessity. London, 1759-63. 5 pam.
Phil 9346.13 — The gentleman and lady of pleasure's amusement. London, 1759.
Phil 8400.20 — Gerard, Alex. An essay on taste. London, 1759.
Phil 2636.41 — Helvétius, C.A. De l'esprit, or Essays on the mind. London, 1759.
Htn Phil 2636.40.1* — Helvétius, C.A. De l'esprit. Paris, 1759.
Phil 2050.18 — Hume, David. Dissertations sur les passions. Amsterdam, 1759.
Phil 3552.70 — Leibniz, Gottfried Wilhelm. Recueil...Pieces...Leibniz. Lausanne, 1759. 2v.
VPhil 2115.1.5F — Locke, J. Works. 6th ed. London, 1759. 3v.
NEDL Phil 8888.4 — Nettleton, T. A treatise on virtue. London, 1759.
Htn Phil 2266.36* — Smith, Adam. The theory of moral sentiments. London, 1759.
Phil 8610.759 — Trinius, Johann Anton. Freydenker-Lexicon. Leipzig, 1759.
Phil 8602.11.5 — Wollaston, W. The religion of nature delineated. London, 1759.

1760-1769

Phil 8401.14 — André, Yves, Essai sur le beau. Amsterdam, 1760.
Phil 3095.52 — Baumgarten, A.G. Initia philosophiae practicae primae acroamatice. Halae, 1760.
Phil 2465.30 — Bonnet, Charles. Essai analytique sur les facultés de l'âme. Copenhagen, 1760.
Htn Phil 9342.8* — Cautious lady, or Religion the chief happiness in a married state. London, 1760.
Phil 805.1.9 — Formey, J.H.S. Histoire abrégée de la philosophie. Amsterdam, 1760.
Phil 8881.63 — Gordon, John. A new estimate of manners and principles. pt.1-2. Cambridge, Eng., 1760.
Htn Phil 2050.31* — Hume, David. Essays and treatises on several subjects. London, 1760. 4v.
Phil 8882.23 — Hurd, R. Moral and political dialogues. London, 1760.
Phil 2115.152 — Massie, J. Observations. London, 1760.
Htn Phil 5827.4.6* — Reimarus, Hermann Samuel. Allgemeine Betrachtungen über die Triebe der Thiere. Hamburg, 1760.
Phil 8893.29 — Schmid, G.L. Traités sur divers sujets. n.p., 1760.
Htn Phil 2925.2.35* — Vattel, Emmerich. The law of nations. v.1-2. London, 1760[1759].
Phil 8402.14.2 — Burke, E. A philosophical enquiry into the origin of our ideas. 3rd ed. London, 1761.
Phil 8877.59 — Clemmens, H.W. Moralische Betrachtungen. Stuttgart, 1761.
Phil 5752.3 — Corry, W. Reflections upon liberty and necessity. London, 1761.
Phil 8881.53 — Girini Corio, Gioseffo. L'antropologie. n.p., 1761. 2v.
Htn Phil 8620.6* — Jenyns, Soame. A free inquiry into the nature and origin of evil. London, 1761.
Phil 3625.8.50 — Meier, Georg Friedrich. Philosophische Betrachtungen über die chrislichen Religion. v.1-7. Halle, 1761-66. 2v.
Phil 2493.96 — Meoli, Umberto. Il pensiero economico del Condillac. Milano, 1761.
Phil 2805.30.11 — Pascal, Blaise. Les provinciales. Leiden? 1761. 4v.
Phil 2855.7.30 — Robinet, Jean Baptiste René. De la nature. Amsterdam, 1761.
Phil 2262.55 — Shaftesbury, A.A.C. Lettres sur l'enthousiasme de milord Shaftesbury. London, 1761.
Phil 2266.37 — Smith, Adam. The theory of moral sentiments. 2nd ed. London, 1761.
Phil 8897.1.5 — Walker, S. Familiar introduction to the knowledge of ourselves. London, 1761.
Phil 8897.2 — Wallace, R. Various prospects of mankind. London, 1761.
Phil 281.10 — Alvarea de Queiroz, M. Historia da creação do mundo conforme as ideas de Moizes. Porto, 1762.
Phil 1850.28 — Bacon, Francis. Grosskanzlers von England moralische, politische und ökonomische Versuche. Breslau, 1762.
Phil 9163.1 — De Foe, D. Religious courtship. London, 1762.
Phil 2403.3 — DeLuc, J.F. Observations sur les Savans incredules. Genève, 1762.
Phil 5754.1.8 — Edwards, Jonathan. Careful and strict enquiry into the modern...freedom of will. Boston, 1762.
Phil 3450.11.275 — Eley, Lathan. Die Krise des a priori in der Transzendentalen. Den Haag, 1762.
Phil 181.26.7 — Gottsched, J.C. Erste Grunde der Weltweisheit. 7. Aufl. Leipzig, 1762. 2v.
Phil 8587.43 — Hervey, Jacob. Ausserlesene Briefe über verschiedne Gegenstände aus der Sittenlehre und Religion. Hamburg, 1762.
Phil 3625.8.41 — Meier, Georg Friedrich. Gedanken vom philosophischen Predigen. Halle, 1762.
Phil 3625.8.42 — Meier, Georg Friedrich. Philosophische Sittenlehre. Halle, 1762. 2v.
Phil 3625.8.43 — Meier, Georg Friedrich. Philosophische Sittenlehre. 2. Aufl. Halle, 1762-66. 5v.
Phil 3625.8.60 — Meier, Georg Friedrich. Vernenftlehre. 2e Aufl. Halle, 1762.
Phil 8594.4 — Orr, J. The theory of religion. London, 1762.
Phil 5827.4.5 — Reimarus, Hermann Samuel. Allgemeine Betrachtungen über die Triebe der Thiere. 2. Ausg. Hamburg, 1762.
Htn Phil 2855.4.30* — Rousseau, J.J. Principes du droit politique. Amsterdam, 1762.
Htn Phil 8894.8.6* — Toussaint, F.V. Eclaircissement sur les moeurs. Amsterdam, 1762.
Phil 8876.3.2 — Balfour, J. A delineation of the nature and obligation of morality. Edinburgh, 1763.
Htn Phil 6012.4* — Clubbe, J. Physiognomy. London, 1763.
Htn Phil 3480.21* — Kant, Immanuel. Der einzig mögliche Beweisgrund. Königsberg, 1763. 4 pam.
Htn Phil 3480.84.3* — Kant, Immanuel. Versuch den Begriff der negativen Grössen in die Weltweisheit einzuführen. Königsberg, 1763.
Htn Phil 3552.63* — Leibniz, Gottfried Wilhelm. Theodicee. Hannover, 1763.
Phil 7060.60 — M'Leod, D. Treatise on the second sight. Edinburgh, 1763.
Phil 2855.7.32 — Robinet, Jean Baptiste René. De la nature. v.1-2. Amsterdam, 1763.
Phil 8894.8.2 — Toussaint, F.V. Les moeurs. Amsterdam, 1763.
Phil 2300.40* — Tucker, Abraham. Freewill, foreknowledge. v.1-2. London, 1763.
Phil 5062.4.5.2 — Watts, S. Logick. 12th ed. London, 1763.
Phil 8581.2 — Basedow, J.B. Neue Aussichten in die Wahrheiten und Religion der Vernunft. Altona, 1764. 2v.

1760-1769 - cont.

Htn Phil 3110.10.2* — Böhme, J. Works. London, 1764- 4v.
Phil 5043.13 — Duncan, William. The elements of logick. London, 1764.
Phil 8882.20 — Home, H. Introduction to the art of thinking. Edinburgh, 1764.
Phil 2050.34.60 — Hume, David. Essays and treatises on several subjects. London, 1764. 2v.
X Cg Phil 2053.41.2 — Hutcheson, F. A short introduction to moral philosophy. v.1,2-3. Glasgow, 1764. 2v.
Htn Phil 3480.82.1* — Kant, Immanuel. Beobachtungen über das Gefühl des Schönen und Erhabenen. Königsberg, 1764.
Htn Phil 3480.42* — Kant, Immanuel. Untersuchung über die Deutlichkeit der Grundsätze der naturlichen Theologie und der Moral. Berlin, 1764. 2 pam.
Phil 5051.1 — Lambert, J.H. Neues organon Gedanken. Leipzig, 1764. 2v.
Phil 9245.4.5 — Lucas, R. An enquiry after happiness. v.1-2. London, 1764.
Htn Phil 130.1*A — Martin, Benjamin. Biographia philosophica. London, 1764.
Phil 8887.5 — Martinelli, V. Istoria critica della vita civile. Napoli, 1764. 2v.
Phil 8620.53 — Pike, Nelson. God and evil. Englewood Cliffs, 1764.
Phil 1200.38 — Reichard, Elias C. Animi perturbationes ex mente potissimum. Magdeburgi, 1764.
Phil 2240.30A — Reid, Thomas. An inquiry into the human mind. Edinburgh, 1764.
Phil 7082.126.1 — Saalfeld, Adam Friedrich William. Philosophical discourse on the nature of dreams. London, 1764.
Phil 2266.43.5 — Smith, Adam. La métaphysique de l'âme. Paris, 1764. 2v.
Phil 9420.9 — Thiroux d'Arconville, M. Des passions. Londres, 1764.
Phil 3095.83 — Abbt, Thomas. Alexander Gottlieb Baumgartens Leben und Charakter. Halle, 1765.
Phil 175.9 — Argens, J.B. La philosophie du Bon-Sens. La Haye, 1765. 2v.
VPhil 1850.2.1F — Bacon, Francis. Works. London, 1765. 5v.
X Cg Phil 8877.10 — Clap, T. An essay...nature. Foundation. Moral virtue. New Haven, 1765.
Phil 5816.1.2 — Gregory, J. A comparative view...man...animal world. London, 1765.
Phil 9245.12.2 — Harris, J. Three treatises. London, 1765.
Htn Phil 9245.12.2* — Harris, J. Three treatises. London, 1765.
Phil 8591.1.2 — Law, E. Considerations...theory of religion. Cambridge, 1765.
Phil 8591.1.3 — Law, E. Considerations...theory of religion. Cambridge, 1765.
Htn Phil 3552.10.2* — Leibniz, Gottfried Wilhelm. Oeuvres philosophiques. Amsterdam, 1765.
Phil 3552.10 — Leibniz, Gottfried Wilhelm. Oeuvres philosophiques. Amsterdam, 1765.
Phil 2115.31.5 — Locke, J. Essay concerning human understanding. v.2. Edinburgh, 1765.
Htn Phil 2115.70.5* — Locke, J. Letters concerning toleration. London, 1765.
Phil 2805.30.27 — Pascal, Blaise. The life of Mr. Paschal with his letters relating to the Jesuits. London, 1765-66. 2v.
Phil 2240.30.2A — Reid, Thomas. An inquiry into the human mind. 2nd ed. Edinburgh, 1765.
Htn Phil 2520.172* — Thomas, A.L. Eloge de René Descartes. Paris, 1765. 2 pam.
Phil 8599.8 — Tunstall, J. Lectures on natural and revealed religion. London, 1765.
Htn Phil 2915.42* — Voltaire, F.M.A. de. Recueil necessaire. Leipsik, 1765[1766].
Htn Phil 106.1.3* — Voltaire, Francois Marie Arouet de. Dictionnaire philosophique. London, 1765.
Htn Phil 106.1.2* — Voltaire, Francois Marie Arouet de. Dictionnaire philosophique. Londres, 1765.
Htn Phil 106.1* — Voltaire, Francois Marie Arouet de. Dictionnaire philosophique. n.p., 1765.
Phil 2445.3.1 — André, Yves. Oeuvres. Paris, 1766-67. 4v.
Phil 176.11.10 — Baumeister, F.C. Philosophia recens controversa complexa definitiones theoremata. Vratislaviae, 1766.
Phil 3095.45 — Baumgarten, A.G. Metaphysik. Halle, 1766.
Phil 2493.35.2 — Condillac, Etienne Bonnot. Traité des animaux. Amsterdam, 1766.
Phil 178.9 — Dutens, Louis. Recherches. v.1-2. Paris, 1766.
Htn Phil 2605.2.30* — Fontenelle, B. Entretiens sur la pluralité des mondes. Paris, 1766.
Htn Phil 805.1.3* — Formey, J.H.S. A concise history of philosophy. London, 1766.
Htn Phil 805.1* — Formey, J.H.S. History of philosophy. London, 1766.
Phil 4114.23 — Genovesi, Antonio. Elementorum artis logico criticae. n.p., 1766.
Phil 5816.1 — Gregory, J. A comparative view...man...animal world. London, 1766.
Phil 181.23 — Gualberto, G. Raccolta di opuscoli filosofici. Pisa, 1766. 3v.
Phil 5247.14 — Histoire philosophique de l'homme. Londres, 1766.
Htn Phil 2050.78* — Hume, David. Concise and genuine account of dispute between Mr. Hume and Mr. Rousseau. London, 1766.
Htn Phil 3480.53.5* — Kant, Immanuel. Traüme eines Geistersehers. Riga, 1766.
Phil 8520.5.3.10 — Leland, J. A view of the principal deistical writers. 5. ed. London, 1766. 2v.
Phil 2193.30 — Oswald, J. An appeal to common sense in behalf of religion. Edinburgh, 1766-72. 2v.
Phil 8705.5 — Pye, S. The mosaic theory of the solar or planetary system. London, 1766.
Phil 8597.3.8 — Reimarus, H.S. The principal truths of natural religion. London, 1766.
Phil 8597.3.3 — Reimarus, H.S. Die Vornehmstenwahrheiten der naturlichen Religion. 3. Aufl. Hamburg, 1766.
Phil 8599.6 — Töllner, J.G. Beweis dass Gott die menschen bereits durch seine Offenbarung in der Natur zur seligkeit führt. Züllichau, 1766.
Htn Phil 2915.30* — Voltaire, F.M.A. de. Le philosophe ignorant. n.p., 1766.
Phil 3910.77 — Baumeister, F.C. Philosophia definitiva. Vitembergae, 1767.
Phil 8876.36.3 — Burgh, J. The dignity of human nature. London, 1767. 2v.
Phil 177.11 — Changeux, P.J. Traiti des extrêmes. Amsterdam, 1767. 2v.
Phil 9342.11 — Charpentier, Louis. Décence em elle-même. Paris, 1767.
Htn Phil 5425.1* — Duff, W. Essay on original genius. London, 1767.
Phil 805.1.5 — Formey, J.H.S. A concise history of philosophy and philosophers. Glasgow, 1767.
Htn Phil 2648.52.2* — Holbach, Paul Henri T. Le christianisme dévoilé. Londres, 1767.

1760-1769 - cont.

	Phil 2648.52	Holbach, Paul Henri T. Le christianisme dévoilé. Londres, 1767.
	Phil 2648.52.3	Holbach, Paul Henri T. Le christianisme dévoilé. Paris, 1767.
	Phil 2050.37.20	Hume, David. Pensées philosophiques, morales, critiques, littéraires et politiques. Londres, 1767.
X Cg	Phil 8961.1	Less, G. Kompendium der theologischen Moral. Göttingen, 1767.
Htn	Phil 3625.1.38*	Mendelssohn, Moses. Phädon. Berlin, 1767.
	Phil 2915.33	Voltaire, F.M.A. de. The ignorant philosopher. Glasgow, 1767.
	Phil 106.1.12	Voltaire, Francois Marie Arouet de. Dictionnaire philosophique. 6. ed. Londres, 1767. 2v.
	Phil 5062.9	Wijnperse, D. van de. Institutiones logicae. Groningae, 1767.
	Phil 4260.86	Apologia del genere umano. Venezia, 1768.
	Phil 176.118	Balfour, James. Philosophical essays. Edinburgh, 1768.
Htn	Phil 8582.30*	Collins, Anthony. Examen des prophéties qui servient de fondement de la religion chrétienne. Londres, 1768.
	Phil 5813.1	Dean, R. An essay on the future life of brute creatures. v.1-2. London, 1768.
	Phil 5754.1.2	Edwards, Jonathan. A carefull and strict enquiry...freedom of will. 3. ed. London, 1768.
Htn	Phil 9390.1.2*	Herport, B. Essay on truths of importance. London, 1768.
Htn	Phil 9390.1*	Herport, B. Essay on truths of importance. London, 1768.
	Phil 2648.45	Holbach, Paul Henri T. La contagion sacrée. v.1-2. Londres, 1768.
	Phil 2055.1.35	Homes, Henry. Versuche über die ersten Gründe der Sittlichkeit. Braunschweig, 1768.
	Phil 2050.2	Hume, David. Essays and treatises. London, 1768. 2v.
	Phil 3480.88	Kant, Immanuel. Von dem ersten Grunde des Unterschiedes der Gegenden im Raume. Steglitz, 1768[1920]
	Phil 3552.11	Leibniz, Gottfried Wilhelm. Opera omnia. Genevae, 1768. 6v.
	Phil 3625.1.39	Mendelssohn, Moses. Phädon. Berlin, 1768.
	Phil 2193.30.2	Oswald, J. An appeal to common sense in behalf of religion. London, 1768-72. 2v.
Htn	Phil 2262.45*	Shaftesbury, A.A.C. Characteristicks. Leipzig, 1768.
	Phil 3552.256	Sigorgne, P. Institutions léibnitiennes. Lyon, 1768.
Htn	Phil 2295.65*	Toland, John. Lettres philosophiques. London, 1768.
	Phil 3839.6.5	Traité des trois imposteurs. Amsterdam? 1768?
	Phil 2300.30.2	Tucker, Abraham. Light of nature pursued. London, 1768. 5v.
	Phil 2300.30	Tucker, Abraham. Light of nature pursued. London, 1768-77. 7v.
	Phil 282.4	Batteux, C. Histoire des causes premières. Paris, 1769.
	Phil 1930.5.25	Collins, Anthony. Essai sur la nature de l'âme humaine. Londres, 1769.
Htn	Phil 8878.13.9.5*	Dodsley, R. The economy of human life. n.p., 1769.
	Phil 2115.157	An essay on personal identity, in 2 parts. London, 1769.
	Phil 5045.8	Feder, J.G.H. Logik und Metaphysik. Göttingen, 1769.
	Phil 8880.3.5	Ferguson, Adam. Institutes of moral philosophy. Edinburgh, 1769.
Htn	Phil 2045.90*	Graham, C.M. Loose remarks on certain positions to be found in Mr. Hobbes's Philosophical rudiments of government and society. 2nd ed. London, 1769.
Htn	Phil 2648.32.80*	Holbach, Paul Henri T. De la cruauté religieuse. Londres, 1769.
	Phil 2648.54	Holbach, Paul Henri T. L'enfer detruit. Londres, 1769.
	Phil 2053.60.3A	Hutcheson, F. Essay on nature and conduct of passions. Glasgow, 1769.
X Cg	Phil 3625.1.39.3	Mendelssohn, Moses. Phädon. 3. Aufl. Berlin, 1769.
	Phil 2215.30.2	Price, Richard. A review of the principal questions and difficulties in morals. 2d ed. London, 1769.
	Phil 2262.2	Shaftesbury, A.A.C. Les oeuvres. v.1-3. Genève, 1769.
	Phil 8421.3	Usher, James. Clio, or A discourse on taste. 2. ed. London, 1769.

1770-1779

	Phil 8402.25.3	Batteux, Charles. Einschränkung des schonen Künste auf einen einzigen Grundsatz. 3. Aufl. Leipzig, 1770.
	Phil 3095.30	Baumgarten, A.G. Philosophia generalis. Halae, 1770.
Htn	Phil 1860.50*	Beattie, James. Essay on the nature and immutability of truth. Edinburgh, 1770.
	Phil 5011.2	Brevis ad artem cogitandi. London, 1770.
	Phil 8402.14A	Burke, E. A philosophical enquiry into the origin of our ideas of the sublime and beautiful. 6th ed. London, 1770.
	Phil 7067.46.20	Calmet, Augustin. Disertazioni sopra le apparizioni de spiriti. Venezia, 1770.
	Phil 7060.136	The compleat wizzard. London, 1770.
Htn	Phil 5754.1.19*	Dana, J. Examination...Edward's...freedom of will. Boston, 1770.
	Phil 7060.64.5	Defoe, D. The secrets of the invisible world laid open. London, 1770.
Htn	Phil 5425.1.5*	Duff, W. Critical observations. London, 1770.
	Phil 8880.40	Feder, J.G.H. Lehrbuch der praktischen Philosophie. Göttingen, 1770.
	Phil 1135.153	Garve, C. Legendorum philosophorum veterum praecepta nonnulla et exemplum. Leipzig, 1770.
Htn	Phil 8881.4.5*	Gellert, C.F. Moralische Vorlesungen. v. 1-3. Leipzig, 1770.
Htn	Phil 2648.40*	Holbach, Paul Henri T. Essai sur les préjugés. Amsterdam, 1770.
Htn	Phil 2648.29*	Holbach, Paul Henri T. Système de la nature. London, 1770. 2v.
Htn	Phil 2648.30*	Holbach, Paul Henri T. Système de la nature. London, 1770. 2v.
Htn	Phil 2648.56*	Holbach, Paul Henri T. Tableau des saints. Londres, 1770. 2v.
	Phil 2050.19	Hume, David. Le génie de M. Hume. London, 1770.
	Phil 3480.21.3	Kant, Immanuel. Der einzig mögliche Beweis vom Daseyn Gottes. Königsberg, 1770.
Htn	Phil 3625.1.160*	Lavater, J.C. Antwort an den herrn Moses Mendelssohn zu Berlin. Berlin, 1770.
	Phil 8591.34	Le Prince de Beaumont, Marie. Les americaines, ou La preuve de la religion chrétienne par les lumières naturelles. 1. éd. Lyon, 1770. 6v.
Htn	Phil 3625.1.40*	Mendelssohn, Moses. Schreiben an den Herrn Diaconus Lavater. Berlin, 1770-87. 3 pam.
	Phil 8888.3	Nihell, L. Rational self-love. Limerick, 1770.
	Phil 8890.59	Polzer, Ignatius. Praelectiones ethicae. Olomuc, 1770.
	Phil 5754.1.29	A preservative against the doctrine of fate. Boston, 1770.
	Phil 5827.4	Reimarus, Hermann Samuel. Observations physiques et morales sur l'instinct des animaux. Amsterdam, 1770. 2v.

1770-1779 - cont.

	Phil 8677.2	Wesley, J. A survey...wisdom of God in the creation. Bristol, 1770. 3v.
	Phil 197.7	Wijnperse, D. Institutiones metaphysicae. Lugdunum Batavorum, 1770.
	Phil 3910.66	Wolff, Christian von. Logic. London, 1770.
	Phil 476.1	Bergier, N.S. Examen du matérialisme. Paris, 1771. 2v.
	Phil 477.3	Castillon, J. de. Observations sur le livre "Système de la nature". Berlin, 1771.
	Phil 2493.51	Condillac, Étienne Bonnot. Traité des sistèmes. Amsterdam, 1771.
	Phil 8403.6.4	Cooper, John. Letters concerning taste. 4th ed. London, 1771.
	Phil 8878.17.5	Dusch, J.J. Moralische Briefe. v.2. Wien, 1771.
	Phil 8584.2.3	Ellis, J. The knowledge of divine things from revelation. London, 1771.
Htn	Phil 6115.12*	Farr, Samuel. A philosophical enquiry into the nature, origin, and extent of animal motion. London, 1771.
	Phil 182.97	Herz, M. Betrachtungen aus der Spekulativen Weltweisheit. Königsberg, 1771.
	Phil 9010.27.2	Hill, Richard. An address to persons of fashions. 6th ed. Shrewsbury, 1771.
Htn	Phil 3480.82*	Kant, Immanuel. Beobachtungen über das Gefühl des Schönen und Erhabenen. Riga, 1771.
	Phil 3585.1.40	Lambert, Johann Heinrich. Anlage zur Architectonic oder Theorie. Riga, 1771. 2v.
	Phil 3552.63.25	Leibniz, Gottfried Wilhelm. Tentamina theodicaeae de bonitate Dei libertate hominis et origine mali. Tubingae, 1771.
	Phil 3625.1.26	Mendelssohn, Moses. Philosophische Schriften. Verb. Aufl. Berlin, 1771.
Htn	Phil 5769.6.5*	Theory of agency...an essay on moral freedom. Boston, 1771.
	Phil 5769.6	Theory of agency...an essay on moral freedom. Boston, 1771.
	Phil 8951.7.9	Benedictus XIV. Casus conscientiae de mandato. Augustae Vindelicorum, 1772.
	Phil 8951.7.10	Benedictus XIV. Casus conscientiae de mandato. Appendix. v.1-5. Augustae Vindelicorum, 1772. 3v.
	Phil 801.7	Buschings, A.F. Grundriss einer Geschichte de Philosophie. Berlin, 1772-4. 2v.
	Phil 8878.17	Dusch, J.J. Moralische Briefe. Leipzig, 1772. 2v.
	Phil 3552.251	Emery, J.A. Esprit de Leibnitz. Lyon, 1772. 2v.
	Phil 8880.3	Ferguson, Adam. Grundsätze der Moralphilosophie. Leipzig, 1772.
	Phil 8881.4	Gellert, C.F. Leçons de morale. Utrecht, 1772. 2v.
	Phil 9245.12.3	Harris, J. Three treatises. London, 1772.
Htn	Phil 2648.39.3*	Holbach, Paul Henri T. Le bon-sens. Londres, 1772.
	Phil 2648.39.4	Holbach, Paul Henri T. Le bon-sens. Londres, 1772. 2 pam.
	Phil 8593.7	Nonnotte, Claude. Dictionnaire philosophique de la religion. n.p., 1772. 4v.
	Phil 3745.1.50	Platner, E. Anthropologie für Ärzte und Weltweise. Leipzig, 1772.
	Phil 8597.3.4	Reimarus, H.S. Die Vornehmstenwahrheiten der natürlichen Religion. 4. Aufl. Hamburg, 1772.
Htn	Phil 5754.1.22*	West, Samuel. Essay on moral agency...remarks on Dana's Examination. New Haven, 1772.
	Phil 282.4.5	Batteux, C. Geschichte der Meynungen...Grundursachen. Leipzig, 1773.
	Phil 3095.50	Baumgarten, A.G. Acroasis logica. Halae, 1773.
	Phil 1860.50.2	Beattie, James. Essay on the nature and immutability of truth. Dublin, 1773.
	Phil 1860.50.3	Beattie, James. Essay on the nature and immutability of truth. London, 1773.
	Phil 6990.4.2	Bonaire, Louis de. Observations. n.p., 1773. 2 pam.
	Phil 2465.33	Bonnet, Charles. Psychologischer Versuch. Lemgo, 1773.
	Phil 8402.14.15	Burke, E. Philosophische Untersuchungen über den Ursprung unsrer Begriffe vom Erhaben und Schönen. Riga, 1773.
	Phil 9342.2.5	Chapone, H. (Mrs.). Letters on the improvement of the mind. 2. ed. London, 1773. 2v.
	Phil 1925.50	Cudworth, R. Systema intellectuale. Lugduni Batavorum, 1773. 2v.
Htn	Phil 5754.1.20*	Dana, J. Examination...Edward's...freedom of will. New Haven, 1773.
Htn	Phil 2636.32*	Helvétius, C.A. De l'homme. London, 1773. 2v.
	Phil 2648.30.9	Holbach, Paul Henri T. Système social. London, 1773. 3v.
	Phil 2648.30.7	Holbach, Paul Henri T. Système social. v.1-2. London, 1773.
Htn	Phil 2750.3.30*	Marat, Jean Paul. A philosophical essay on man. v.1-2. London, 1773.
	Phil 3625.1.39.4	Mendelssohn, Moses. Phédon. Amsterdam, 1773.
	Phil 5827.4.7	Reimarus, Hermann Samuel. Allgemeine Betrachtungen über die Triebe der Thiere. 3. Ausg. Hamburg, 1773. 2 pam.
Htn	Phil 2262.30.5*	Shaftesbury, A.A.C. Characteristicks. 5th ed. Birmingham, 1773. 3v.
	Phil 3910.77.15	Baumeister, F.C. Institutiones philosophiae naturalis. Olomueii, 1774.
	Phil 1860.50.4	Beattie, James. Essay on the nature and immutability of truth. London, 1774.
	Phil 8581.65	Blair, P. Thoughts on nature and religion. London, 1774.
	Phil 4520.5.25	Boethius, Daniel. Dissertatio philosophica, de angustis rationis humanae limitibus. Upsaliae, 1774.
	Phil 8877.33.5	Callieres, F. de. The knowledge of the world and the attainments. Dublin, 1774.
X Cg	Phil 5425.17	Gerard, Alexander. An essay on genius. London, 1774.
	Phil 5425.17	Gerard, Alexander. An essay on genius. London, 1774.
	Phil 2636.44	Helvétius, C.A. Le vrai sens du système de la nature. Londres, 1774.
	Phil 2648.39.2	Holbach, Paul Henri T. Le bon-sens, ou idées naturelles. Londres, 1774.
	Phil 2648.30.8	Holbach, Paul Henri T. Système social. London, 1774.
	Phil 5402.4.2	Levesque de Pouilly, L.J. Theorie des sentimens agreables. Paris, 1774.
	Phil 8888.4.2	Nettleton, T. A treatise on virtue. Edinburgh, 1774.
	Phil 8889.2.3	Oxenstjerna, J.T. Pensées. v.1-2. Paris, 1774.
	Phil 2520.151	Savérien, A. Vita di Renato Cartesio. Venezia, 1774.
Htn	Phil 2050.96*	Specimen of the Scots Review. n.p., 1774.
Htn	Phil 2915.74*	Voltaire, F.M.A. de. Lettre philosophique. Berlin, 1774.
	Phil 176.11.5	Baumeister, F.C. Institutiones metaphysicae. Wittebergae, 1775.
	Phil 2465.30.5	Bonnet, Charles. Essai analytique sur les facultés de l'âme. v.1-2. 3e éd. Copenhagen, 1775.

1770-1779 - cont.

Phil 8586.12 Gérard, Philippe Louis. Le Comte de Valmont ou les égaremens de la raison. Paris, 1775.

Htn Phil 9346.6.5* Gregory, John. A father's legacy to his daughters. N.Y., 1775.

Phil 182.30 Harris, J. Philosophical arrangements. London, 1775.
Phil 2038.50 Hartley, D. Theory of the human mind. London, 1775.
Phil 182.22 Holland, G. Réflexions philosophiques. Neuchâtel, 1775.

Htn Phil 3480.75.15* Kant, Immanuel. Von der verschiedenen Racen der Menschen. Königsberg, 1775.

Phil 8590.3 Kemp, J.T. van der. Tentamen theologiae dunatscopicae. Lugdunum Batavorum, 1775.

Phil 3552.28 Leibniz, Gottfried Wilhelm. Geist des Herrn von Leibniz. Wittenburg, 1775. 2v.

Phil 1117.3.10 Meiners, C. Vermischte philosophische Schriften. Leipzig, 1775. 3v.

Phil 2218.40 Priestley, Joseph. An examination of Dr. Reid's Inquiry. 2d. ed. London, 1775.

Htn Phil 2880.1.33* Saint-Martin, L.C. Des erreurs et de la vérité. Edimbourg, 1775.

Phil 5751.16 Barwis, J. Three dialogues. London, 1776.
Htn Phil 1865.29* Bentham, Jeremy. A fragment on government. London, 1776.
Htn Phil 1870.40.3 Berkeley, G. Treatise...principles of human knowledge. London, 1776.

Phil 9342.16 Callet, P. L'écolier chrétien. Lyon, 1776.
Phil 5043.13.2 Duncan, William. The elements of logick. Edinburgh, 1776.
Phil 178.9.2 Dutens, Louis. Recherches. 2. éd. Paris, 1776. 2v.
Phil 5244.1 Eberhard, J.A. Allgemeine Theorie des Denkens und Empfindens. Berlin, 1776.

Phil 5245.8 Flögel, C.F. Geschichte des menschlichen Verstandes. Breslau, 1776.

Phil 2636.34 Helvétius, C.A. De l'homme. London, 1776.
Phil 8408.34 Herz, Marcus. Versuch über den Geschmach und die ursachen seiner Verschiednheit. Leipzig, 1776.

Phil 2648.58 Holbach, Paul Henri T. Éthocratie. Amsterdam, 1776.
tn Phil 2648.49* Holbach, Paul Henri T. La morale universelle. Amsterdam, 1776. 3v.

Phil 8589.2 Jerusalem, J.F.W. Betrachtungen über die vornehmsten Wahrheiten der Religion. 5. Aufl. Braunschweig, 1776-91. 3v.

Phil 3625.1.39.5A Mendelssohn, Moses. Phédon. 4. Aufl. Amsterdam, 1776.
Phil 3745.1.31 Platner, E. Philosophische Aphorismen. Leipzig, 1776.
Phil 8610.776 Recueil nécessaire avec l'évangile de la raison. Londres, 1776.

Phil 193.114 Schütz, C.G. Einleitung in die speculative Philosophie. Lemgo, 1776.

:n Phil 2266.68* Smith, Adam. An inquiry into the nature and causes of the wealth of nations. London, 1776. 2v.

Phil 1200.13 Tiedemann, D. System der stoischen Philosophie. Leipzig, 1776. 3v.

Phil 8876.8 Basedow, J.B. Practische Philosophie für alle Stande. v.1-2. Dessau, 1777.

Phil 1860.50.5 Beattie, James. Essay on the nature and immutability of truth. Edinburgh, 1777.

Phil 8878.7 Delisle de Sales, J.B.C.I. De la philosophie de la nature. London, 1777. 6v.

Phil 8879.11 Ephemeriden der Menschheit. v.1-4,5-8,9-12. Basel, 1777. 3v.

Phil 2636.10 Helvétius, C.A. Oeuvres complètes. London, 1777. 2v.

Phil 5325.3 Hissmann, M. Geschichte der Lehre...Association der Ideen. Göttingen, 1777.

Phil 2648.30.14 Holbach, Paul Henri T. Système de la nature. Londres, 1777.

a Phil 2050.82.3* Hume, David. Life. London, 1777. 5 pam.
a Phil 2050.82.2* Hume, David. Life. London, 1777.
a Phil 3585.3.30* Lessing, G.E. Zur Geschichte und Literatur. Braunschweig, 1777.

Phil 2115.1.8F Locke, J. Works. 8th ed. London, 1777. 4v.
Phil 3625.1.30 Mendelssohn, Moses. Philosophische Schriften. Berlin, 1777. 2v.

Phil 8890.13 Pestel, F.G. Fundamenta jurisprudentae naturalis. Lugdunum Batavorum, 1777.

a Phil 6025.7* Physiognomisches Cabinet für Freunde und Schüler der Menschenkenntniss. pt.1-2. Leipzig, 1777-78.

Phil 2050.89* Pratt, Samuel J. An apology for life and writings of D. Hume. London, 1777.

Phil 2218.29 Priestley, Joseph. Disquisitions relating to matter and spirit. 1st ed. London, 1777.

Phil 2218.45* Priestley, Joseph. The doctrine of philosophical necessity. London, 1777.

Phil 811.4 Savérien, A. Histoire des progrès de l'esprit humain dans les sciences et dans les arts que en dépendent. Paris, 1777.

Phil 1870.119 Stock, J. An account of the life of George Berkeley. 2nd ed. Dublin, 1777.

Phil 5259.6 Tetens, J.N. Philosophische Versuche über die menschliche Natur. Leipzig, 1777. 2v.

Phil 3839.6.10* Traité des trois imposteurs. Amsterdam, 1777.
Phil 8595.16.24.2 Watson, R. An apology for Christianity. 2. ed. Cambridge, 1777.

Phil 8655.1.6 Abernethy, J. Discourses concerning...God. Aberdeen, 1778. 2v.

Phil 1850.2.2F Bacon, Francis. Works. London, 1778. 5v.
Phil 8597.3.15 Blasche, J.C. Kurze auch dem Laien verstandliche Verantwortung wider die Beschuldigungen. Jena, 1778.

Phil 8582.21 Caulfield. An essay on the immateriality and immortality of the soul. London, 1778.

Phil 1850.110 Deleyre, A. Analyse de la philosophie du chancelier François Bacon avec sa vie. Leyde, 1778. 2v.

Phil 4114.23.10 Genovesi, Antonio. Elementorum artis logico criticae. Neapoli, 1778.

Phil 9166.3* Glasse, S. Advice from a lady of quality to her children. 3. ed. Newbury Port, 1778. 2v.

Phil 8587.9* Hemsterhuis, F. Aristée ou de la divinité. Paris, 1778-79. 2 pam.

Phil 75.6 Hiszmann, M. Anleitung der Literatur der Philosophie. Göttingen, 1778.

Phil 3625.8.92 Langen, S.G. Leben Georg Friedrich Meiers. Halle, 1778.
Phil 3552.10.15 Leibniz, Gottfried Wilhelm. Philosophische Werke nach Rapspens Sammlung. Halle, 1778-80. 2v.

Phil 2218.30 Priestley, Joseph. Disquisitions relating to matter and spirit. Birmingham, 1778-82. 3v.

Phil 9357.8.5 Rack, E. Mentor's letters, addresses to youth. 3d ed. Bath, 1778.

Phil 8597.3.12 Reimarus, H.S. Von dem Zwecke Jesu und seiner Jünger. Braunschweig, 1778.

1770-1779 - cont.

Phil 4225.23.15 Stellini, J. Opera omnia. Patavii, 1778-79. 4v.
Phil 6131.5 Vere, James A. Physical and moral enquiry. London, 1778.
Phil 1850.41 Bacon, Francis. De dignitate et augmentis scientiarum. Wirceburgi, 1779-80. 2v.

Phil 1850.50.9 Bacon, Francis. Novum organum. Wirceburgi, 1779.
Phil 3095.40 Baumgarten, A.G. Metaphysica. 7th ed. Halae, 1779.
Phil 8626.4 Baxter, A. The evidence of reason in proof of the immortality of the soul. London, 1779.

Phil 1860.45 Beattie, James. Neue philosophische Versuche. Leipzig, 1779-80. 2v.

Phil 3120.16.30 Brastberger, G.U. Philosophische Briefe an meine Schwester. Halle, 1779.

Phil 2515.2.50 Charron, P. Die wahre Weisheit. v.2. München, 1779.
Phil 5045.8.5 Feder, J.G.H. Logik und Metaphysik. Wien, 1779.
Phil 9165.4.2 Foster, F. Thoughts on the times. London, 1779.
Phil 2050.67A Hume, David. Dialogues concerning natural religion. 2nd ed. London, 1779.

Phil 292.1 Luc, J.A. de. Lettres physiques et morales sur l'histoire...terre. Paris, 1779. 6v.

Phil 176.41 Monboddo, James Barnet. Ancient metaphysics. v.1-6. Edinburgh, 1779-99. 7v.

Phil 9245.35 Der neue Epikur, oder die Philosophie der Sittlichenwollust. Prag, 1779.

Phil 2218.84 Palmer, J. Observations. v.1-2. London, 1779.
Phil 2805.10 Pascal, Blaise. Oeuvres. La Haye, 1779. 5v.
Phil 8896.3.5 Vives, Juan Luis. Introducción á la sabiduria. Valencia, 1779.

Phil 2915.35 Voltaire, F.M.A. de. The ignorant philosopher. London, 1779.

178-

Htn Phil 6668.4* Lettres sur le magnetism. n.p., 178-. 3 pam.

1780

Phil 176.34.5 Buffier, Claude. First truths. London, 1780.
Phil 5640.14 Elliott, John. Philosophical observations on the senses. London, 1780.

Phil 9349.6 Jumigny, de. Le père gouverneur de Son fils. Bourbes, 1780.

Phil 3625.1.32 Mendelssohn, Moses. Philosophische Schriften. v.1-2. Carlsruhe, 1780.

Phil 3110.81 Okely, F. Memoris...Jacob Behrnen. Northampton, 1780.
Phil 3850.60 Sander, Heinrich. Von der Güte und Weisheit Gottes in der Natur. Carlsruhe, 1780.

Phil 1124.2 Tiedemann, D. Griechenlands erste Philosophen. Leipzig, 1780.

Phil 3501.3 Troitzsch, J.G. Etwas über den Werth der kritischen Philosophie. Leipzig, 1780-1800. 3 pam.

1781

Phil 9162.6 Cramer, W.M.A. Unterhaltungen zur Beförderung der häuslichen Glückseligkeit. Berlin, 1781.

Htn Phil 9346.6.2* Gregory, John. A father's legacy to his daughters. Philadelphia, 1781.

Htn Phil 2636.10.7* Helvétius, C.A. Oeuvres complètes. v.1-2. London, 1781.
Phil 8587.19.10 Huber, M. The divine instinct recommended to men. London, 1781.

Htn Phil 2050.68.10* Hume, David. Gespräche über natürliche Religion. Leipzig, 1781.

Htn Phil 3480.29* Kant, Immanuel. Critik der reinen Vernunft. Riga, 1781.
Phil 8620.7.3 King, William. An essay on the origin of evil. London, 1781.

Phil 5821.1.10 Leroy, Charles Georges. Lettres sur les animaux. Nuremberg, 1781.

Phil 2115.50.10 Locke, J. The conduct of the understanding. Cambridge, 1781.

Phil 9290.3 Martinet, J.F. Zeemans handboek. Amsterdam, 1781.
Phil 1117.3 Meiners, C. Geschichte des Ursprungs. Lemzo, 1781-82.
Phil 6682.3.4 Mesmer, F.A. Mémoire du magnetisme animal. n.p., 1781. 4 pam.

Phil 6682.3.5 Mesmer, F.A. Précis historique des faits relatifs au magnétisme. London, 1781.

Phil 187.19 Moreau de St. Elier, L. Les songes physiques. Amsterdam, 1781.

Phil 190.14 Ploucquet, W.G. Commentationes philosophicae selectiores. Trajecti ad Rhenum, 1781.

Phil 8597.3.21 Reimarus, Johann Albert Heinrich. Von dem daseyn Gottes und der menschlichen Seele. Hamburg, 1781.

1782

Phil 6950.1 Arnold, T. Observation...insanity, lunacy or madness. v.1-2. Leicester, 1782-86.

Phil 176.30 Brisor de Warville, Jean Pierre. De la vérité. Neuchatel, 1782.

Phil 9560.11 Caracciolli, L. De la gaieté. Paris, 1782.
Phil 1145.3 Collection des moralistes anciens. Paris, 1782-83. 12v.
Htn Phil 3625.1.89* Das forschen Nach licht und recht. Berlin, 1782.
Phil 4114.30 Genovesi, Antonio. Delle scienze metafisiche. Venezia, 1782.

Phil 182.14.5 Hemsterhuis, F. Vermischte philosophische Schriften. Leipzig, 1782. 3v.

Phil 2648.39 Holbach, Paul Henri T. Le bon-sens. London, 1782.
Phil 3585.1.30 Lambert, Johann Heinrich. Logische und philosophische Abhandlungen. Berlin, 1782-87. 2v.

Phil 8889.2.4 Oxenstjerna, J.T. Pensées. v.1-2. Rouen, 1782.
Phil 2218.35 Priestley, Joseph. Institutes of natural and revealed religion. 2nd ed. Birmingham, 1782. 2v.

Phil 2880.1.30 Saint-Martin, L.C. Des erreurs et de la vérité. Edimbourg, 1782.

Phil 8972.6 Wahre Philosophie des praktischen Christenthums. Frankfurt, 1782.

1783

Htn Phil 1860.40* Beattie, James. Dissertations moral and critical. Dublin, 1783.

Phil 1860.40.2 Beattie, James. Dissertations moral and critical. London, 1783.

Phil 7080.52 Cassina, U. Congetture su i sogni. Parma, 1783.
Phil 9390.6 Douglas, Robert. Observations on the nature of oaths. Edinburgh, 1783.

Chronological Listing

1783 - cont.

	Phil 180.46	Fremling, Matthaus. Dissertatio philosophica de ratione praecepta philosophiae theoreticae tradendi. Pt.1-3. Lundae, 1783-1787.
	Phil 4114.47	Genovesi, Antonio. Meditazioni filosofiche sulla religione e sulla morale. Bassano, 1783.
Htn	Phil 3480.57.2*	Kant, Immanuel. Prolegomena zu einer jeden künftigen Metaphysik. Riga, 1783. 2 pam.
Htn	Phil 3480.57.3*	Kant, Immanuel. Prolegomena zu einer jeden künftigen Metaphysik. Riga, 1783.
Htn	Phil 6021.2.8*	Lavater, Johann Caspar. Physiognomische Fragmente. Winterthur, 1783.
	Phil 6122.25FA	Monro, Alexander. Observations on the structure of the nervous system. Edinburgh, 1783. 3v.
	Phil 5465.2	Muratori, L.A. Trattato della forza della fantasia umana. Napoli, 1783.
	Phil 6965.14	Paris. Université. Facultá de Medecine. Rapport de Mm. Cosnier, Maloet, Darcet, [and others]...nouveau méthode d'adminstrer l'électricité...maladies nerveuses. Paris, 1783.
	Phil 8670.12.5	Platner, E. Über den Atheismus. Leipzig, 1783.
	Phil 1135.16	Plessing, F.V.L. Osiris und Sokrates. Berlin, 1783.
	Phil 9179.7	Townsend, S. A practical essay designed for general use. Boston, 1783.

1784

Htn	Phil 8580.3*	Allen, E. Reason, the only oracle of man. Bennington, Vt., 1784.
	Phil 8581.2.10	Basedow, J.B. Examen in der allernatürlichsten Religion. Leipzig, 1784.
Htn	Phil 6671.24*	Bergasse, N. Lettre d'un médicin. Bordeaux, 1784.
	Phil 7106.2	Bergasse, Nicolas. Considérations sur le magnétisme animal. La Hague, 1784.
	Phil 1870.75	Berkeley, G. Memoirs. 2nd ed. London, 1784.
	Phil 6671.23	Bormes, Baron de. Lettre de M.L.B.D.B...sur l'existence du magnétisme animal. Genève, 1784.
Htn	Phil 6672.11*	Cambry, Jacques. Traces du magnétisme. La Haye, 1784. 2 pam.
Htn	Phil 6673.19*	Doppet, F.A. Traité théorique. Turin, 1784.
	Phil 6675.12	France. Commissaires Chargée de l'Examen du Magnétisme Animal. Rapport des commissaires chargée par le roi de l'examen du magnétisme animal. Paris, 1784.
	Phil 2636.11	Helvétius, C.A. Oeuvres complètes. v.3-7. Deuxponts, 1784. 5v.
	Phil 7080.14	Hennings, Justus Christian. Von den Träumen und Nachtwandlern. Weimar, 1784.
Htn	Phil 6669.4*	Hervier, C. Lettre sur la découverte du magnetisme. Pekin, 1784.
	Phil 9230.3	Hey, R. A dissertation...gaming. Cambridge, 1784-85. 3 pam.
	Phil 6679.2	Janin de Combe Blanche, J. Reponse au discours. Genève, 1784.
	Phil 3480.71.2	Kant, Immanuel. Die Religion innerhalb der Grenzen der blossen Vernunft. Königsberg, 1784.
	Phil 8586.20	Leuchtende fakel zum allgemeinen Glaubensbekenntniss aller Religionen. Frankfurt, 1784.
Htn	Phil 6682.3.12*	Mesmer, F.A. Letters à M. Vicq-d'Azyr. Bruxelles, 1784.
Htn	Phil 6682.3.14*	Mesmer, F.A. Lettre à M. le comte de C. Paris? 1784.
Htn	Phil 6682.3.11*	Mesmer, F.A. Lettres à messieure les auteurs du journal de Paris et à M. Franklin. n.p., 1784.
Htn	Phil 6682.3.13*	Mesmer, F.A. Lettres guéri. London, 1784.
	Phil 187.15	Migeot, A. Philosophiae elementa. Carolopoli, 1784. 2v.
Htn	Phil 6682.13*	Montjore, C.F.L. Lettre sur le magnétisme animal. Philadelphia, 1784.
Htn	Phil 6685.10.5*	Paulet, J.J. L'antimagnétisme, ou origine. Loudres, 1784.
Htn	Phil 6685.10*	Paulet, J.J. Mesmer justifié. Constance, 1784.
	Phil 8890.12	Percival, T. Moral and literary dissertations. Warrington, 1784.
	Phil 6687.13	Recueil des pieces les plus interessantes sur le magnétisme animal. n.p., 1784.
	Phil 8597.3.13	Reimarus, H.S. Von dem Zwecke Jesu und seiner Jünger. Berlin, 1784.
	Phil 3500.4.5	Schmid, K.C.E. Critik der reinen Vernunft. Jena, 1784.
	Phil 3500.14.2	Schulze, J. Erläuterungen...Kant Critik der reinen Vernunft. Königsberg, 1784.
	Phil 6688.28	Servan, J.M.A. Questions adressées. Padova, 1784.
	Phil 6688.26	Sousselier, de la Tour. L'âmi de la nature, ou Manière de traiter les maladies. Dijon, 1784.
	Phil 2880.1.90	Suite des erreurs et de la vérité. Salomonapolis, 1784.
	Phil 6689.8	Thouret. Recherches et doutes sur le magnetisme animal. Paris, 1784.
	Phil 8620.16	Villaume, P. Von dem Ursprung und der Absichten des Übels. Leipzig, 1784. 3v.
	Phil 9515.3	Zimmermann, J.G. Über die Einsamkeit. Leipzig, 1784-85. 4v.
	Phil 3625.1.96	Zöllner, J.F. Über Moses Mendelssohn's Jerusalem. Berlin, 1784.

1785

	Phil 9341.13.5	Bourn, Benjamin. A sure guide to hell, in seven sections. London, 1785.
	Phil 1106.14	Büsching, A.F. Vergleichung der griechischen Philosophie mit der Neuern. Berlin, 1785.
	Phil 6673.18	Delaudine, Antoine François. De la philosophie corpusculaire. Paris, 1785.
	Phil 6629.2	Fawcett, Benjamin. Über Melankolie. Leipzig, 1785.
	Phil 4114.25.3	Genovesi, Antonio. Disciplinarum metaphysicarum elementa. Bassani, 1785. 5v.
	Phil 4114.50	Genovesi, Antonio. Lettere filosofiche. Napoli, 1785.
	Phil 8662.1	Hamilton, Hugh. An attempt to prove the existance...of the supreme unoriginated being. London, 1785.
Htn	Phil 6677.8*	Histoire véritable du magnétisme animal. La Haye, 1785.
Htn	Phil 3480.64*	Kant, Immanuel. Grundlegung zur Metaphysik der Sitten. Riga, 1785.
Htn	Phil 8667.3*	Mendelssohn, M. Morgenstunden oder Vorlesungen uber das Daseyn Gottes. Berlin, 1785.
	Phil 6682.3.10	Mesmer, F.A. Aphorismes de Mesmer. 3. éd. Paris, 1785.
Htn	Phil 2205.39*	Paley, W. Principles of moral and political philosophy. London, 1785.
	Phil 2205.1	Paley, W. Principles of moral and political philosophy. London, 1785.
	Phil 8890.19	Polier de St. Germain, A. de. Du gouvernement des moeurs. Lausanne, 1785.

1785 - cont.

Htn	Phil 2240.58*	Reid, Thomas. Essays on the intellectual powers of man. Edinburgh, 1785.
	Phil 2240.31	Reid, Thomas. An inquiry into the human mind. 4th ed. London, 1785.
	Phil 5258.2	Sailer, J.D.M. Vernunftlehre für Menschen, wie sie sind. München, 1785.
	Phil 2262.89	Schlosser, J.G. Über Schaftsbury von der Tugend. Basel, 1785.
	Phil 9245.7	Sigaud de la Fond, J.R. L'école du bonheur. Paris, 1785.

1786

	Phil 6110.11	Abel, J.F. Einleitung in die Seelenlehre. Stuttgart, 1786.
	Phil 5240.25	Abel, Jacob Friedrich von. Einleitung in die Seelenlehre. Stuttgart, 1786. 2 pam.
	Phil 281.9	Almeida, Theodoro de. Recreação filosofica. Lisboa, 1786-1805. 10v.
	Phil 8876.33	Bruce, J. Elements of the science of ethics. London, 1786.
Htn	Phil 9342.2.7*	Chapone, H. (Mrs.). Letters on the improvement of the mind. Philadelphia, 1786.
Htn	Phil 9346.6.7*	Chesterfield, Philip Dormer Stanhope. Principles of politeness. Portsmouth, N.H., 1786.
	Phil 5635.13	De Seze, V. Recherches...sur la sensibilité. Paris, 1786.
Htn	Phil 8878.13*	Dodsley, R. The economy of human life. v.1-2. Philadelphia, 1786.
	Phil 8879.21	Eberhard, J.A. Sittenlehre der Vernunft. Berlin, 1786.
	Phil 8586.21	Gebete eines Weisen. Thal Ehrenbreitstein, 1786.
	Phil 6957.16	Herz, M. Versuch über den Schwindel. Berlin, 1786.
	Phil 182.24.2	Huber, M. World unmasked. London, 1786.
Htn	Phil 3829.3.20*	Jacobi, F.E. Wider Mendelssohns Beschuldigung Betreffend die Briefe über die Lehre des Spinoza. Leipzig, 1786.
Htn	Phil 3625.1.100*	Jakob, Ludwig H. Prüfung der Mendelssohnschen Morgenstunden oder aller spekulativen Beweise für das Daseyn. Leipzig, 1786.
Htn	Phil 3480.64.5*	Kant, Immanuel. Grundlegung zur Metaphysik der Sitten. 2. Aufl. Riga, 1786.
Htn	Phil 3480.55.2*	Kant, Immanuel. Metaphysische Anfangsgründe Naturwissenschaft. Riga, 1786.
	Phil 7150.33	Less, G. Vom Selbstmorde. Göttingen, 1786.
	Phil 8667.5	Mendelssohn, M. Morgenstunden. Berlin, 1786.
Htn	Phil 3625.1.47*	Mendelssohn, Moses. An die Freunde Lessings. Berlin, 1786.
Htn	Phil 3625.1.55*	Mendelssohn, Moses. An die Freunde Lessings. Berlin, 1786.
	Phil 2205.39.5	Paley, W. Principles of moral and political philosophy. London, 1786.
	Phil 8890.12.2	Percival, T. Moral and literary dissertations. Dublin, 1786.
	Phil 2240.59	Reid, Thomas. Essays on the intellectual powers of man. Dublin, 1786. 2v.
	Phil 8892.8	Rush, Benjamin. An oration...enquiry into the influence of physical causes upon the moral faculty. Philadelphia, 1786.
	Phil 6688.27	Société Harmonique des Amis-Reunis de Strasbourg. Exposé de différentes cures. Strasbourg, 1786.
	Phil 6689.6	Tardy de Montravel, A.A. Journal du traitement magnétique. London, 1786. 2 pam.
NEDL	Phil 5062.4.6	Watts, S. Logick. London, 1786.
	Phil 3625.1.133	Wizenmann, T. Die Resultate der Jacobischen und Mendelssohnschen Philosophie. Leipzig, 1786.
	Phil 8620.34	Worcester, Noah. Some difficulties proposed for solution. Newbury-Port, 1786.

1787

	Phil 5240.25.20	Abel, Jakob Friedrich von. Versuch über die Natur der speculativen Vernunft zur Prüfung des Kantischen Systems. Frankfurt, 1787.
	Phil 3487.6	Feder, J.G.H. Ueber Raum und Caussalitat. Göttingen, 1787.
	Phil 8880.20.10	Fuller, J. Introductio ad prudentiam, or Directions. London, 1787. 2v.
	Phil 8586.43.5	Genlis, S.F. La religion considérée comme l'unique base du bonheur et de la véritable philosophie. Maestricht, 1787.
	Phil 8586.43	Genlis, S.F. La religion considérée comme l'unique base du bonheur et de la véritable philosophie. Orleans, 1787.
	Phil 2045.15	Hobbes, Thomas. Oeuvres philosophiques et politiques. Neufchatel, 1787. 2v.
Htn	Phil 2050.189*	Jacobi, F.H. David Hume über den Glauben. Breslau, 1787.
	Phil 3480.29.4	Kant, Immanuel. Critik der reinen Vernunft. 2. Aufl. Riga, 1787.
Htn	Phil 3480.29.2*	Kant, Immanuel. Critik der reinen Vernunft. 2. Aufl. Riga, 1787.
	Phil 3480.55.4	Kant, Immanuel. Metaphysische Anfangsgründe Naturwissenschaft. Riga, 1787.
	Phil 3552.294.5	Lamprecht, J.F. Vita del Signore Barone Goffredo G. di Leibnitz. Roma, 1787.
Htn	Phil 8592.59*	Morgan, Caesar. A demonstration that true philosophy has no tendency to undermine divine revelation. Cambridge, 1787.
	Phil 2205.40.30	Paley, W. Grundsätze der Moral und Politik. Leipzig, 1787. 2v.
	Phil 2215.30.3	Price, Richard. A review of the principal questions in morals. 3d ed. London, 1787.
	Phil 8597.3.10	Reimarus, Johann Albert Heinrich. Über die Grunde der menschlichen Erkenntniss und der natürlichen Religion. Hamburg, 1787.
	Phil 3625.1.90	Schütz, F.W. von. Leben und Meinungen M. Mendelssohn. Hamburg, 1787.
	Phil 8893.30	Senac de Meilhan, G. Considérations sur l'esprit et les moeurs. Paris, 1787.
	Phil 6689.6.15	Tardy de Montravel, A.A. Essai sur la théorie du somnambulisme magnétique. Londres, 1787.
	Phil 6689.6.3	Tardy de Montravel, A.A. Journal du traitement magnétique. Strasbourg, 1787.
Htn	Phil 2305.1.30*	Taylor, Thomas. The mystical initiations. London, 1787.
	Phil 3501.12	Tittel, Gottlob August. Kantischen den Reformen oder Kategorien. Frankfurt, 1787.

1788

	Phil 1850.50.23	Bacon, Francis. Nuovo organo delle scienze. Bassano, 1788.
	Phil 801.31	Bardili, C.G. Epochen der Vorzüglichsten philosophischen Begriffe. Halle, 1788. 2 pam.
	Phil 4520.5.30	Boethius, Daniel. Dissertatio philosophica de origine atque indole nimiae divitiarum aestimationis. Upsaliae, 1788.
	Phil 8656.20	Bornträger, J.C.F. Über das Daseyn Gottes in Beziehung auf Kantische und Mendelssonnsche Philosophie. Hannover, 1788.
	Phil 2493.40	Condillac, Etienne Bonnot. Essai sur l'origine des connaissances humaines. v.1-2. Amsterdam, 1788.
	Phil 2493.45.2	Condillac, Etienne Bonnot. Traité des sensations. v.1-2. Londres, 1788.
Htn	Phil 8878.58*	Dodsley, R. The economy of human life. Exeter, 1788.
	Phil 180.50	Feder, J.G.H. Philosophische Bibliothek. v.1-4. Göttingen, 1788-1791. 2v.
Htn	Phil 3480.44*	Kant, Immanuel. Critik der practischen Vernunft. Riga, 1788.
	Phil 186.83	LaSalle, A. de. La balance naturelle, ou Essai sur une loi universelle appliquée aux sciences. Londres, 1788. 2v.
	Phil 6681.10	Lutzebourg. Nouveaux extraits des journaux d'un magnétiseur. Strasbourg, 1788.
	Phil 3625.1.147	Mirabeau, H.G.R. Sur la réforme politique des Juifs. Bruxelles, 1788.
	Phil 2205.40	Paley, W. Principles of moral and political philosophy. Paris, 1788.
	Phil 1120.1	Plessing, F.V.L. Versuche zur Aufklärung der Philosophie des ältesten Alterthums. Leipzig, 1788-90. 3v.
Htn	Phil 2050.89.10*	Pratt, Samuel J. Curious particulars and genuine anecdotes respecting the late Lord Chesterfield and David Hume. London, 1788.
Htn	Phil 2240.33*	Reid, Thomas. Essays on the active powers of man. Edinburgh, 1788.
	Phil 6687.8	Rosenmüller, J.G. Lettre à la société exegétique...magnétisme animal. Leipzig, 1788.
	Phil 3500.4	Schmid, K.C.E. Wörterbuch zum leichtern Gebrauch der Kantischen Schriften. Jena, 1788.
	Phil 3850.13.25	Schulze, G.E. Grundriss der philosophischen Wissenschaften und Zerbst. Wittenberg, 1788-90. 2v.
	Phil 3500.57.10	Stattler, B. Anti-Kant. München, 1788. 2v.
	Phil 3504.4	Weishaupt, A. Über die Kantischen Anschauungen. Nürnberg, 1788.
	Phil 3504.4.10	Weishaupt, A. Zweifel über die Kantischen Begriffe von Zeit und Raum. Nürnberg, 1788.
	Phil 3504.34	Will, G.A. Vorlesungen über der Kantische Philosophie. Altdorf, 1788.

1789

tn	Phil 1865.49*	Bentham, Jeremy. An introduction to the principles of morals and legislation. London, 1789.
	Phil 9342.17.5	Campe, J.H. Vaterlicher Rath für meine Tochter. 2. Aufl. Tübingen, 1789.
	Phil 2493.30.10	Condillac, Etienne Bonnot. La logique. Paris, 1789.
	Phil 3487.14	Flatt, Johann F. Briefe über den moralischen Erkenntnisgrund der Religion überhaupt. Tübingen, 1789.
	Phil 8406.17	Fremling, M. Dissertatio philosophica. Lundae, 1789.
	Phil 5415.8	Fremling, Mattahaus. Dissertatio philosophica, de sympathia. Lundae, 1789.
	Phil 2648.39.5	Holbach, Paul Henri T. Le bon-sens. Londres, 1789.
	Phil 2050.64	Hume, David. Essays on suicide. London, 1789.
	Phil 3829.3	Jacobi, F.E. Über die Lehre des Spinoza. Breslau, 1789.
	Phil 3492.38	Kleuker, Johann. De libertate morali ex ratione Kantiana. Osnabrugi, 1789.
	Phil 6021.2	Lavater, Johann Caspar. Essays on physiognomy. London, 1789. 3v.
n	Phil 6021.2.1F*	Lavater, Johann Caspar. Essays on physiognomy. London, 1789-98. 5v.
	Phil 8886.26	Lawätz, H.W. Über die Tugenden und Laster...des Menschen. Flensburg, 1789-1792. 3v.
n	Phil 8887.6.4*	Mason, J. Self-knowledge. Worcester, Mass., 1789.
n	Phil 3625.1.35*	Mendelssohn, Moses. Kleine philosophische Schriften. Berlin, 1789.
	Phil 3499.2.10	Reinhold, K.L. Über die bisherigen Schicksale der Kantischen Philosophie. Jena, 1789.
	Phil 5257.5	Reinhold, K.L. Versuch einer neuen Theorie des menschlichen Vorstellungs-Vermögens. Prag, 1789.
	Phil 7080.18.5	Relação de dous extraordinar[ios] e notaveis successos. Lisbon, 1789.
	Phil 3500.52	Schultz, John. Prüfung der Kantischen Critik der reinen Vernunft. v.1-2. Königsberg, 1789-92.
	Phil 3850.13.27	Schulze, G.E. Über den höchsten Zweck des Studiums der Philosophie. Leipzig, 1789.
	Phil 3500.35.5	Snell, F.W.D. Menon oder Versuch in Gesprächen. Mannheim, 1789.
	Phil 5062.4.7*	Watts, S. Logick. 16th ed. Philadelphia, 1789.
	Phil 197.53	Wetterburg, Jacobue. Dissertatio philosophica. Lundae, 1789.

179-

	Phil 8876.102	Briel, C. L'homme moral, ou Règles de conduite prises dans sa propre nature. Sens, 179-
	Phil 8595.16.35	Christianity the only true theology. London, 179-?
	Phil 6021.2.5*	Lavater, Johann Caspar. Essays on physiognomy. 1st American ed. Boston, 179-?

1790

	Phil 5240.25.5	Abel, Jacob Friedrich von. Erläuterungen wichtiger Gegenstände aus der philosophischen und christlichen Moral. Tübingen, 1790.
	Phil 5040.17	Abicht, Johann H. Vom dem Nutzen und der Einrichtung eines zu logischen uebingen Bestimmten Colleginus. Leipzig, 1790.
	Phil 8401.2	Alison, Archibald. Essays on the nature and principles of taste. Edinburgh, 1790.
	Phil 9515.3.80	Bahrat, Karl F. Mit dem Herrn [von] Zimmermann. n.p., 1790.
	Phil 9045.2	Bahrdt, C.F. Handbuch der Moral für den Bürgerstand. Halle, 1790.
	Phil 4520.5.32	Boethius, Daniel. Dissertatio philosophica de morali ordine in eventu rerum jure postulato. Upsaliae, 1790.
	Phil 3483.39.5	Brastberger, G.U. Untersuchungen über Kants Critik der reinen Vernunft. Halle, 1790.

1790 - cont.

	Phil 9342.13	Carlisle, Isabella (Byron) Howard. Thoughts in the forms of maxims. London, 1790.
	Phil 5754.1.4	Edwards, Jonathan. A careful and strict enquiry...freedom of will. Glasgow, 1790.
	Phil 3486.15	Ewald, J.L. Über die Kantische Philosophie. Berlin, 1790.
	Phil 8585.4	Ferrières, C.E. Le théisme. 2. éd. v.1-2. Paris, 1790.
	Phil 4114.40	Genovesi, Antonio. La logica. Napoli, 1790.
	Phil 8881.11.6	Gisborne, T. The principles of moral philosophy. London, 1790.
	Phil 8587.14.3	Heydenreichs, K.H. Beträchtungen über die Philosophie. Leipzig, 1790-91. 2 pam.
Htn	Phil 3480.30*	Kant, Immanuel. Critik der reinen Vernunft. 3. Aufl. Riga, 1790.
Htn	Phil 3480.48*	Kant, Immanuel. Critik der Urtheilskraft. Berlin, 1790.
	Phil 3480.48.2	Kant, Immanuel. Critik der Urtheilskraft. Berlin, 1790. 2 pam.
	Phil 8885.28	Kiesewetter, J.G.C. Über der ersten Grundsatz der Moralphilosophie. Berlin, 1790-1791. 2v.
	Phil 9513.2.5	Knigge, A. von. Über den Umgang mit Menschen. 3. Aufl. pt.1-3. Hannover, 1790.
Htn	Phil 8886.6*	Lavater, J.C. Aphorisms on man. Boston, 1790.
	Phil 2805.43	Pascal, Blaise. Pensamientos. Zaragoza, 1790.
	Phil 9175.2	Percival, T. A father's instructions to his children. Dublin, 1790.
	Phil 3835.5	Philipson, M. Leben Benedikt's von Spinoza. Braunschweig, 1790.
	Phil 2240.49	Reid, Thomas. Essays on the intellectual and active powers of man. v.3. Dublin, 1790.
	Phil 5057.2	Reimarus, H.S. Die Vernunstlehre. Hamburg, 1790.
	Phil 3499.2.5	Reinhold, K.L. Auswahl der besten Aufsätze über die Kantische Philosophie. Frankfurt, 1790.
	Phil 3778.32	Reinhold, K.L. Beyträge zur Berichtigung bisheriger Missverständnisse der Philosophen. Jena, 1790. 2v.
	Phil 3499.2	Reinhold, K.L. Briefe über die Kantische Philosophie. Leipzig, 1790-92. 2v.
	Phil 8707.6	Remarks on the religious sentiments of...eminent laymen. London, 1790. 2 pam.
Htn	Phil 2880.1.40*	Saint-Martin, L.C. L'homme de désir. Lyon, 1790.
	Phil 8893.61.5	Schmid, C.C.E. Versuch einer Moralphilosophie. Jena, 1790.
	Phil 6688.21	Segnitz, F.L. Specimen inaugurale medicum de electricitate. Jenae, 1790.
	Phil 2262.33	Shaftesbury, A.A.C. Characteristicks. Basel, 1790. 3v.
	Phil 8893.82	Snell, C.W. Die sittlichkei Verbindung mit der Glükseligkeit einzelner Menschen und gauzer Staaten. Frankfurt, 1790.

1791

	Phil 331.8	Abicht, J.H. Philosophie der Erkenntnisse. Pt.1-2. Bayreuth, 1791.
	Phil 1105.1	Anderson, W. Philosophy of ancient Greece. Edinburgh, 1791.
Htn	Phil 1865.35*	Bentham, Jeremy. Panopticon. Dublin, 1791.
	Phil 177.94	Carra, J.L. Systême de la raison. 3e éd. Paris, 1791.
	Phil 8952.10	Chassanis. La morale universelle. Paris, 1791.
Htn	Phil 8583.26*	De Costa, J.H. Reason and faith. Philadelphia, 1791.
	Phil 804.2	Enfield, W. History of philosophy. London, 1791. 2v.
	Phil 9070.35	Eskartshausen, K. von. Klugheit vereind mit Tugend. Brünn, 1791.
	Phil 4114.31	Genovesi, Antonio. Delle scienze metafisiche. Napoli, 1791.
Htn	Phil 8434.2*	Gilpin, W. Remarks on forest scenery, and other woodland views. London, 1791. 2v.
	Phil 2038.31	Hartley, D. Observations on man. London, 1791. 3v.
	Phil 3489.9	Herrmann, C.G. Kant und Hemsterhuis in Rüksicht ihrer definitionen der Schönheit. Erfurt, 1791.
	Phil 9347.4	The history of man. 3d ed. Dublin, 1791.
	Phil 2050.60.25	Hume, David. Über die menschliche Natur. Bd.2. Halle, 1791.
	Phil 6119.3	Jakob, L.H. Grundriss der Erfahrungs-Seelenlehre. Halle, 1791.
	Phil 8620.6.5	Jenyns, Soame. Essai sur la nécessité du mal. Paris, 1791.
	Phil 3480.44.3	Kant, Immanuel. Critik der practischen Vernunft. Frankfurt, 1791.
	Phil 3480.30.01	Kant, Immanuel. Critik der reinen Vernunft. 3. Aufl. Frankfurt, 1791.
Htn	Phil 3480.43*	Kant, Immanuel. Über eine Entdeckung, nach der alle neue Critik der reinen Vernunft. Königsberg, 1791-97. 2 pam.
	Phil 5050.5.6	Kiesewetter, J.G.C.C. Grundriss einer reinên allgemeinen Logik nach kantischen Grundsaetzen. Berlin, 1791.
	Phil 2115.32	Locke, J. Essay concerning human understanding. London, 1791. 2v.
	Phil 2115.49.8	Locke, J. Vom menschlichen Verstande. Mannheim, 1791.
	Phil 97.1	Maimon, S. Philosophisches Wörterbuch. Berlin, 1791.
	Phil 8887.70	Molé, L.M. Essai de morale et de politique. Paris, 1791.
	Phil 8592.37	Münzenberger, H.C. Uber die Entstehung religiöser Volksbegriff. Göttingen, 1791.
	Phil 3496.4	Obereit, J.H. Beobachtungen über die Quelle der Metaphysik. Meiningen, 1791.
	Phil 8597.3A	Reimarus, H.S. Abhandlungen von den vornehmsten Wahrheiten der natürlichen Religion. 6. Aufl. Hamburg, 1791.
	Phil 3778.40	Reinhold, K.L. Über das fundament des philosophischen Wissens. Jena, 1791.
	Phil 5258.82	Schmid, C.C.E. Empirische Psychologie. Jena, 1791.
	Phil 3500.14	Schulze, J. Erläuterungen...Kant Critik der reinen Vernunft. Frankfurt, 1791.
	Phil 7082.146	Simpson, David. A discourse on dreams and night-visions. Macclesfield, 1791.
	Phil 2266.42.5	Smith, Adam. Theorie der sittlichen Gefühle. Leipzig, 1791-95. 2v.
	Phil 3500.35	Snell, E.W.D. Darstellung und Erläuterung I. Kant Critik. v.1-2. Mannheim, 1791.
	Phil 4225.5.2	Spedalieri, Nicola. De diritti dell'uomo libri 6. Assisi, 1791.
	Phil 3500.57	Stattler, B. Kurzer Entwurf der unausstehlichen Ungeimtheiten der Kantischen Philosophie. n.p., 1791.
	Phil 819.3	Tiedemann, D. Geschichte der spekulativen Philosophie. Marburg, 1791-97. 6v.
	Phil 7067.91	Visits from the world of spirits. London, 1791.

1792

	Phil 8655.2	Ancillon, L.F. Judicium de judiciis. Berolini, 1792.
	Phil 3625.5.78.2	Atlas, S. Lebensgeschichte. Berlin, 1792-93. 2 pam.
	Phil 1860.60	Beattie, James. Elements of moral science. Philadelphia, 1792-94. 2v.
	Phil 3483.39	Brastberger, G.U. Untersuchungen über Kants Critik der practischen Vernunft. Tübingen, 1792.
	Phil 1900.60.2.6	Butler, Joseph. Fifteen sermons and six sermons. 6th ed. London, 1792.
	Phil 5043.13.3	Duncan, William. The elements of logick. Philadelphia, 1792.
	Phil 284.14	Dupont de Nemours, P.S. Philosophie de l'univers. Paris, 1792.
	Phil 804.2.2	Enfield, W. History of philosophy. Dublin, 1792. 2v.
	Phil 8800.7	Ferguson, A. Principles of moral and political science. Edinburgh, 1792. 2v.
Htn	Phil 3246.30*	Fichte, Johann Gottlieb. Versuch einer Critik aller Offenbarung. Königsberg, 1792.
Htn	Phil 8434.2.5*	Gilpin, W. Three essays: on picturesque beauty. London, 1792.
	Phil 182.14	Hemsterhuis, F. Oeuvres philosophiques. Paris, 1792. 2v.
	Phil 8587.14.10	Heydenreichs, K.H. Grundsätze der moralischen Gotteslehre. Leipzig, 1792.
	Phil 2648.39.6	Holbach, Paul Henri T. Le bon-sens. Rome, 1792.
	Phil 2648.50	Holbach, Paul Henri T. La morale universelle. Tours, 1792. 3v.
	Phil 8589.2.10	Jerusalem, J.F.W. Nachgelassene Schriften. Braunschweig, 1792-93. 2v.
	Phil 3480.20	Kant, Immanuel. Grundlegung zur Metaphysik. Riga, 1792-98. 3 pam.
Htn	Phil 3480.70.80*	Kant, Immanuel. Ueber das radikale Böse in der menschlichen Natur. Pt. 1. n.p., 1792.
	Phil 5525.1	Keppler, J.F. Kritische Untersuchungen. Cilli, 1792.
	Phil 9351.7.2	Lady's pocket library. Philadelphia, 1792.
	Phil 6021.2.6	Lavater, Johann Caspar. Physiognomy. London, 1792.
	Phil 7085.5	Levade, L. A true account of a natural sleep walker. Edinburgh, 1792.
	Phil 2115.48.15	Locke, J. Essai philosophique concernant l'entendement humaine. Abrégé. Upsal, 1792.
	Phil 2115.139	Mellring, J.G. Specimen academicum. Upsaliae, 1792.
	Phil 281.9.10	Palimodia manifesta. Sevilla, 1792?
	Phil 6965.9	Pargeter, William. Observations on maniacal disorders. Reading, Eng., 1792.
Htn	Phil 3800.100*	Schelling, F.W.J. von. Antiquissimi de prima malorum humanorum origine. Tubingae, 1792.
	Phil 8893.61	Schmid, C.C.E. Versuch einer Moralphilosophie. 2. Ausg. Jena, 1792.
	Phil 3850.13.33	Schulze, G.E. Aenesidemus öder über die Fundamenta. Helmstadt, 1792.
	Phil 2266.38	Smith, Adam. The theory of moral sentiments. 7th ed. London, 1792. 2v.
	Phil 2275.30	Stewart, D. Elements of the philosophy of the human mind. London, 1792.
	Phil 9515.3.3	Zimmermann, J.G. Solitude. 2d ed. London, 1792.
	Phil 3507.5.2	Zwanziger, J.C. Commentar über Kant's Kritik der reinen Vernunft. Leipzig, 1792.

1793

	Phil 3483.1	Beck, J.S. Erläuternder Auszug. Riga, 1793-96. 3v.
	Phil 3483.45.5	Bouterwek, F. Aphorismen den Freunden der Vernunftkritik nach Kantischer Lehre. Gottingen, 1793.
Htn	Phil 1900.32.6*	Butler, Joseph. Analogy of religion. Bishop of Gloucester. Boston, 1793.
	Phil 1900.32A	Butler, Joseph. Analogy of religion. Bishop of Gloucester. Boston, 1793.
Htn	Phil 9342.2.2*	Chapone, H. (Mrs.) Letters on the improvement of the mind. v.1-2. N.Y., 1793.
Htn	Phil 8878.13.12*	Dodsley, R. The economy of human life. N.Y., 1793.
	Phil 5045.8.20	Feder, J.G.H. Erklaerung der Logik. Wien, 1793-94. 3v.
Htn	Phil 3246.30.5*	Fichte, Johann Gottlieb. Versuch einer Critik aller Offenbarung. Königsberg, 1793.
Htn	Phil 2030.3.30*	Godwin, William. An enquiry concerning political justice. London, 1793. 2v.
	Phil 3488.20	Goess, G.F.D. Ueber die Critik der reinen Vernunft. Erlangen, 1793.
	Phil 3489.1	Hausius, K.G. Materialen zur Geschichte der critischen Philosophie. Leipzig, 1793. 2v.
	Phil 2636.40.2	Helvétius, C.A. De l'esprit. v.1-4. Paris, 1793. 2v.
	Phil 2636.12	Helvétius, C.A. Oeuvres complètes. Paris, 1793. 5v.
	Phil 2636.12.2	Helvétius, C.A. Oeuvres complètes. Paris, 1793-97. 10v.
	Phil 3489.4	Heydenreich, C.H. Originalität über die kritische Philosophie. Leipzig, 1793.
	Phil 2050.32	Hume, David. Essays and treatises. Edinburgh, 1793. 2v.
	Phil 2050.33	Hume, David. Essays and treatises. v.1-2,3-4. Basel, 1793. 2v.
Htn	Phil 2050.42.12*	Hume, David. Eine Untersuchung über den menschlichen Verstand. Jena, 1793.
Htn	Phil 3480.50*	Kant, Immanuel. Critik der Urtheilskraft. Berlin, 1793.
Htn	Phil 3480.19*	Kant, Immanuel. Kleine Schriften. Neuwied, 1793.
Htn	Phil 3480.71.2.5*	Kant, Immanuel. Die Religion innerhalb der Grenzen der blossen Vernunft. Frankfurt, 1793.
Htn	Phil 3480.71.2.6*	Kant, Immanuel. Die Religion innerhalb der Grenzen der blossen Vernunft. Frankfurt, 1793.
Htn	Phil 3480.70.75*	Kant, Immanuel. Die Religion innerhalb der Grenzen der blossen Vernunft. Königsberg, 1793.
Htn	Phil 3480.75.25*	Kant, Immanuel. Über den Gemeinspruch: Das mag in Theorie richtig sein taugt, aber nicht für die Praxis. Berlin, 1793. 2 pam.
Htn	Phil 3480.19.5*	Kant, Immanuel. Zerstreute Aufsätze. Frankfurt, 1793.
	Phil 3745.1.30A	Platner, E. Philosophische Aphorismen. Leipzig, 1793-1800. 2v.
	Phil 8598.3	Schaumann, J.C.G. Philosophie der Religion. Halle, 1793.
Htn	Phil 3800.105*	Schelling, F.W.J. von. Über Mythen. Leipzig, 1793.
	Phil 2275.31	Stewart, D. Elements of the philosophy of the human mind. Philadelphia, 1793.
Htn	Phil 194.2*	Taylor, B.S. Contemplatio philosophica. London, 1793.
	Phil 3839.6.15	Traité des trois imposteurs. Luisse, 1793.
	Phil 3502.5	Ueber Immanuel Kant's philosophische Religionslehre. Augsburg? 1793.

1793 - cont.

	Phil 3504.35	Weber, Joseph. Versuch, die harten Urtheile über der Kantische Philosophie zu Mildern. Wirzburg, 1793.
	Phil 5754.1.31	West, Samuel. Essays on liberty and necessity. Boston, 1793.

1794

	Phil 9340.1	Aikin, J. Letters from a father to his son. London, 1794-1800. 2v.
Htn	Phil 9340.1.2*	Aikin, J. Letters from a father to his son. Philadelphia, 1794.
	Phil 176.125	Bardili, C.G. Sophylus oder Sittlichkeit und Natur. Stuttgart, 1794.
	Phil 3483.50	Beiträge zur Erläuterung und Prüfung des Kantischen Sistems in sechs Abhandlungen. Gotha, 1794.
	Phil 5402.18	Bendavid, L. Versuch über das Vergnügen. Wien, 1794.
	Phil 9161.6	Blair, H. On the duties of the young. London, 1794.
	Phil 8876.32	Brown, W.L. An essay on the natural equality of men. London, 1794.
Htn	Phil 8876.36.4*	Burgh, J. The dignity of human nature. Boston, 1794.
	Phil 2218.85.5	Cobbett, William. Observations on the emigration of Joseph Priestley. Philadelphia, 1794.
	Phil 1200.31	Conz, C.P. Abhandlungen für die Geschichte und das Eigenthümliche der späteren stoischen Philosophie. Tübingen, 1794.
	Phil 8878.12	Doddridge, P. A course of lectures...pneumatology, ethics. London, 1794.
Htn	Phil 3246.44*	Fichte, Johann Gottlieb. Über den Begriff der Wissenschaftslehre. Weimar, 1794.
	Phil 8800.8	Gisborne, T. An enquiry into the duties of men. London, 1794.
	Phil 3488.20.5	Goess, G.F.D. Systematische Darstellung der Kantischen Vernunftkritik zum gebrauch akademischer Vorlesungen. Nürnberg, 1794.
	Phil 170.3	Hutton, James. Investigation of the principles of knowledge. Edinburgh, 1794. 3v.
	Phil 8884.20	Jakob, L.H. Philosophische sittenlehre. Halle, 1794.
Htn	Phil 3480.19.7*	Kant, Immanuel. Anhang zu den Zerstreuten Aufsatzen. Frankfurt, 1794.
	Phil 3480.30.03	Kant, Immanuel. Critik der reinen Vernunft. Neueste Aufl. Frankfurt, 1794.
	Phil 3480.30.05	Kant, Immanuel. Critik der reinen Vernunft. 4. Aufl. Riga, 1794.
Htn	Phil 3480.30.02*	Kant, Immanuel. Critik der reinen Vernunft. 4. Aufl. Riga, 1794.
	Phil 3480.50.05	Kant, Immanuel. Critik der Urtheilskraft. Frankfurt, 1794.
	Phil 3480.21.5	Kant, Immanuel. Der einzig mögliche Beweisgrund zu einer Demonstration des Daseyns Gottes. Königsberg, 1794.
	Phil 3480.64.7	Kant, Immanuel. Grundlegung zur Metaphysik der Sitten. 4. Aufl. Frankfurt, 1794. 2 pam.
	Phil 3480.55.12	Kant, Immanuel. Metaphysische Anfangsgründe Naturwissenschaft. Frankfurt, 1794.
Htn	Phil 3480.78.5*	Kant, Immanuel. Politische Meinungen. n.p., 1794.
	Phil 3480.57	Kant, Immanuel. Prolegomena zu künftigen Metaphysik. Frankfurt, 1794.
	Phil 3480.71.2.7	Kant, Immanuel. Die Religion innerhalb der Grenzen der blossen Vernunft. Frankfurt, 1794.
Htn	Phil 3480.73.5*	Kant, Immanuel. Vorlesungen über der philosophische Religionslehre. Leipzig, 1794-1817. 2 pam.
	Phil 2115.45.2	Locke, J. An abridgment of Mr. Locke's Essay concerning human understanding. Boston, 1794.
	Phil 3625.5.34	Maimon, Salomon. Versuch einer neuen Logik, oder Theorie. Berlin, 1794.
	Phil 8667.21	Maréchal, P.S. La fable de Christ dévoilée. Paris, 1794.
	Phil 8887.6.4.5	Mason, J. Self-knowledge. London, 1794.
Htn	Phil 3494.15*	Mellin, G.S.A. Marginalien und Register zu Kants Kritik der Erkentnissvermögen. Züllichau, 1794.
	Phil 9352.4	Moore, J.H. Young gentleman and lady's monitor. London, 1794.
	Phil 2115.81	Morell, T. Notes and annotations on Locke. London, 1794.
	Phil 9353.2	Niemeyer, J.F. Vermaechtniss an Helene von ihrem Vater. Bremen, 1794.
	Phil 2218.85	Observations on the emigration of Joseph Priestley. London, 1794.
Htn	Phil 2225.3.30*	Paine, Thomas. The age of reason. Paris, 1794.
Htn	Phil 8595.15.5*	Paine, Thomas. Age of reason. Investigation of true and fabulous theology. Boston, 1794. 4 pam.
Htn	Phil 8595.15.6*	Paine, Thomas. The age of reason. Pt.1. Paris, 1794.
Htn	Phil 8595.15.28*	Paine, Thomas. La siècle de la raison. Paris, 1794.
	Phil 5525.64	Poinsinet de Sivry, Louis. Psychologische und physiologische Untersuchung über das Lachen. Wolfenbüttel, 1794.
	Phil 645.6	Stäudlin, C.F. Geschichte und Geist des Skepticismus. Leipzig, 1794.
	Phil 3500.57.5	Stattler, B. Wahres Verhaltniss der Kantischen Philosophie. München, 1794.
	Phil 2275.50.10	Stewart, D. Anfangsgründe der Philosophie über die menschliche Seele. Berlin, 1794. 2v.
	Phil 3500.13	Storr, D.G.C. Bemerkungen über Kant's Philosophie Religion. Tübingen, 1794.
Htn	Phil 3585.1.50*	Strnadt, A. Gedanken über die schönen und soliden Wissenschaften. Dresden, 1794.
	Phil 8598.19	Sulivan, R.J. A view of nature. London, 1794. 6v.
	Phil 5262.1	Wagner, M. Beyträge zur philosophischen Anthropologie. Wien, 1794-96. 2v.
	Phil 8595.16.7	Wakefield, Gilbert. An examination of the age or reason. 2. ed. London, 1794.
Htn	Phil 8595.16.27.3*	Watson, R. Apology for Christianity. 1st American ed. Providence, 1794.
	Phil 8897.8.10	Weishaupt, A. Ueber die Selbstkenntniss. Regensburg, 1794.
Htn	Phil 5754.1.23*	West, Samuel. Essay on moral agency...remarks on Dana's Examination. Salem, 1794.
	Phil 3507.5	Zwanziger, J.C. Commentar über Kant's Kritik der reinen Vernunft. Leipzig, 1794.

1795

	Phil 175.1	Abicht, J.H. System der Elementarphilosophie. Erlangen, 1795.
	Phil 4520.4.31	Bastholm, Christopher. Philosophie för olarde. Lund, 1795.
	Phil 3483.33.10	Bendavid, L. Vorlesungen über der Critik der reinen Vernunft. Wien, 1795.

Chronological Listing

Phil 8626.5 — Browne, I.H. The immortality of the soul. Cambridge, 1795.

Phil 5041.24 — Buhle, J.G. Einleitung in die allgemeine Logik und die Kritik der reinen Vernunft. Göttingen, 1795.

Phil 8582.23.3 — Common sense. Philadelphia, 1795.

Phil 2493.21 — Condillac, Étienne Bonnot. Oeuvres philosophiques. Paris, 1795. 2v.

Phil 2494.31 — Condorcet, M.J.A.N. Esquisse d'un tableau historique. n.p., 1795.

tn Phil 2494.31.5* — Condorcet, N.J.A.N. Esquisse d'un tableau historique. Paris, 1795.

tn Phil 8878.13.7* — Dodsley, R. The economy of human life. Norwich, 1795.
tn Phil 8878.13.15* — Dodsley, R. The economy of human life. Salem, 1795.
Phil 8878.13.10 — Dodsley, R. The economy of human life. pt. 1-2. London, 1795.

Phil 8595.16.3 — Dutton, Thomas. A vindication of the age of reason, by Thomas Paine. London, 1795.

tn Phil 3246.45.8* — Fichte, Johann Gottlieb. Grundriss des Eigenthümlichen der Wissenschaftslehre. Jena, 1795.

tn Phil 9530.5* — Franklin, B. The way to wealth. Paris, 1795.
Phil 8669.2 — Franklin, Maria. Observations on the chronology of scripture. N.Y., 1795.

n Phil 8881.67* — Gros, J.D. Natural principles of rectitude. N.Y., 1795.
n Phil 8882.13* — The hive. Worcester, Mass., 1795.
Phil 2648.41.2 — Holbach, Paul Henri T. Essai sur les préjugés. Paris, 1795.

Phil 2648.30.5 — Holbach, Paul Henri T. Système social. Paris, 1795. 2v.

Phil 3480.44.5 — Kant, Immanuel. Critik der practischen Vernunft. Frankfurt, 1795.

Phil 3480.30.07 — Kant, Immanuel. Critik der reinen Vernunft. v.1-2,3-4. Grätz, 1795. 2v.

Phil 3480.19.10 — Kant, Immanuel. Frühere nocht nicht Gesammelte Kleine Schriften. Lintz, 1795.

n Phil 3480.19.11* — Kant, Immanuel. Neue Kleine Schriften. Berlin? 1795.
Phil 3480.57.5 — Kant, Immanuel. Prolegomena zu einer jeden künftigen Metaphysik. Grätz, 1795.

n Phil 3480.68* — Kant, Immanuel. Über moralische und politische Gegenstände. Frankfurt, 1795.

n Phil 3480.79* — Kant, Immanuel. Zum ewigen Frieden. Königsberg, 1795.
n Phil 3480.79.3* — Kant, Immanuel. Zum ewigen Frieden. Königsberg, 1795. 2 pam.

Phil 5050.5.2 — Kiesewetter, J.G.C.C. Grundriss einer allgemeinen Logik. 2. Aufl. Berlin, 1795-96. 2v.

Phil 3492.34.15 — Kiesewetter, J.G.K.C. Gedrängter Auszug aus Kants Kritik der reinen Vernunft. Berlin, 1795.

Phil 3492.34 — Kiesewetter, J.G.K.C. Versuch einer...Darstellung der wichtigsten Wahrheiten der neuern Philosophie. Berlin, 1795.

Phil 2115.32.3A — Locke, J. Essay concerning human understanding. v.1-2,3. London, 1795. 2v.

Phil 2115.49.10 — Locke, J. Versuch über den menschlichen Verstand. Jena, 1795. 3v.

Phil 3494.33 — Metz, Andreas. Kurze und deutliche Darstellung des Kantischen Systemes. Bamberg, 1795.

Phil 187.24 — Müller, J.G. Philosophische Aufsäze. Breslau, 1795.
Phil 3495.14.5 — Neeb, Johann. Über Kant's Verdienste um das Interesse der philosophiren den Vernunft. 2. Aufl. Frankfurt, 1795.

Phil 8595.16 — Paine, Thomas. Age of reason. London, 1795.
Phil 8595.15.7 — Paine, Thomas. Age of reason. Investigation of true and fabulous theology. pt.1-2. 2d ed. Boston, 1795.

Phil 8595.15.30 — Paine, Thomas. Siècle de la raison. pt.2. Paris, 1795-96.
Phil 2205.40.2 — Paley, W. Principles of moral and political philosophy. Boston, 1795.

Phil 8595.16.5* — Patten, William. Christianity the true theology. Warren, 1795.

Phil 3745.1.40 — Platner, E. Lehrbuch der Logik und Metaphysik. Leipzig, 1795.

Phil 2218.50 — Priestley, Joseph. A continuation of the letters to the philosophers and politicians of France. Salem, 1795.

Phil 8892.6.3* — Rowe, E.S. Friendship in death. N.Y., 1795.
Phil 3800.120* — Schelling, F.W.J. von. Über die Möglichkeit einer Form der Philosophie überhaupt. Tübingen, 1795.

Phil 3800.120.5* — Schelling, F.W.J. von. Über die Moglichkeit einer Form der Philosophie überhaupt. Tübingen, 1795.

Phil 3800.130* — Schelling, F.W.J. von. Vom ich als Princip der Philosophie. Tübingen, 1795.

Phil 3500.4.3 — Schmid, K.C.E. Wörterbuch zum leichtern Gebrauch der Kantischen Schriften. 3. Ausg. Jena, 1795.

Phil 3500.56 — Schulze, Gottlob E. Einige Bemerkungen über Kants philosophische Religionslehre. Kiel, 1795.

Phil 2266.30 — Smith, Adam. Essays. London, 1795.
Phil 3500.91 — Snell, Christian. Lehrbuch der Kritik des Geschmach. Leipzig, 1795.

Phil 2305.1.35* — Taylor, Thomas. The fable of Cupid and Psyche. London, 1795.

Phil 5754.1.33 — West, Samuel. Essays on liberty and necessity. New Bedford, 1795.

1796

Phil 9340.1.5* — Aikin, J. Letters from a father to his son. Philadelphia, 1796.

Phil 5325.25 — Bardili, C.G. Uber die Geseze der Ideenassoziation. Tübingen, 1796.

Phil 3483.1.15 — Beck, J.S. Grundriss der critischen Philosophie. Halle, 1796.

Phil 3483.33.5 — Bendavid, L. Vorlesungen über der Critik der practischen Vernunft. Wien, 1796.

Phil 3483.33 — Bendavid, L. Vorlesungen über der Critik des Urtheilskraft. Wien, 1796.

Phil 3483.41 — Bernhardi, A.B. Gemeinfassliche Darstellung der Kantischen Lehren über Sittlichkeit, Freyheit, Gottheit und Unsterblichkeit. v.1-2. Freyberg, 1796-97.

Phil 5041.31* — Best, William. A concise system of logics. N.Y., 1796.
Phil 801.8 — Buhle, T.G. Lehrbuch der Geschichte der Philosophie. Göttingen, 1796-1804. 8v.

Phil 5042.2 — Collard, John. The essentials of logic. London, 1796.
Phil 2494.41 — Condorcet, M.J.A.N. Outlines...historical...progress...human mind. Philadelphia, 1796.

Phil 8878.7.10 — Delisle de Sales, J.B.C.I. De la philosophie du bonheur. Paris, 1796.

Phil 178.9.3 — Dutens, Louis. Origine des découvertes. 3e éd. Louvain, 1796.

Phil 8595.16.9 — Estlin, John P. Evidences of revealed religion. Bristol, 1796?

Htn Phil 9344.5* — Evening amusemente for the ladies. Boston, 1796.
Phil 6115.1 — Falconer, W. A dissertation...passions...disorders of the body. London, 1796.

Htn Phil 3246.38* — Fichte, Johann Gottlieb. Grundlage des Naturrechts nach Prinzipien der Wissenschaftslehre. Jena, 1796.

Phil 3487.18 — Flügge, C.W. Versuch einer historisch-kritischen Darstellung. Hannover, 1796-98. 2v.

Phil 3488.21 — Gertanner, Christoph. Ueber das Kantische Prinzip für die Naturgeschichte. Göttingen, 1796.

Htn Phil 9166.3.5* — Glasse, S. Advice from a lady of quality to her children. Boston, 1796.

Phil 9166.1 — A good wife God's gift. Boston, 1796.
Phil 5545.13.2 — Grey, R. Memoria technica. Dublin, 1796.
Htn Phil 8882.13.2* — The hive. Worcester, Mass., 1796.
Phil 2648.52.5 — Holbach, Paul Henri T. Le christianisme dévoilé. Suisse, 1796.

Phil 2648.45.2 — Holbach, Paul Henri T. La contagion sacrée. v.1-2. Paris, 1796-97.

Phil 3491.6 — Jenisch, D. Uber Grundlugen und Werth der Entdeckungen des Herrn Professor Kant. Berlin, 1796.

Phil 3480.64.50 — Kant, Immanuel. Constitutio principii metaphysicae morum zwantziger. Lipsiae, 1796.

Phil 3480.44.8 — Kant, Immanuel. Critik der practischen Vernunft. Grätz, 1796.

Phil 3480.64.10 — Kant, Immanuel. Grundlegung zur Metaphysik der Sitten. Grätz, 1796. 2 pam.

Phil 3480.55.15 — Kant, Immanuel. Metaphysische Anfangsgründe Naturwissenschaft. Grätz, 1796. 3 pam.

Phil 3480.10 — Kant, Immanuel. Opera ad philosophiam criticam. Leipzig, 1796-98. 4v.

Htn Phil 3480.78* — Kant, Immanuel. Politische Meinungen. n.p., 1796.
Htn Phil 3480.72* — Kant, Immanuel. Theorie der Reinmoralischen Religion. Riga, 1796.

Phil 3480.43.5 — Kant, Immanuel. Über eine Entdeckung, nach der alle neue Critik der reinen Vernunft. Grätz, 1796. 2 pam.

Htn Phil 3480.79.4* — Kant, Immanuel. Zum ewigen Frieden. Königsberg, 1796.
Phil 3480.68.5 — Kant, Immanuel. Zwo Abhandlungen über moralische Gegenstände. 2. Aufl. Königsberg, 1796.

Phil 5050.5.3 — Kiesewetter, J.G.C.C. Compendium einer allgemeinen Logik. Berlin, 1796.

Phil 5050.5.4 — Kiesewetter, J.G.C.C. Grundriss einer allgemeinen Logik. Berlin, 1796-1802. 2v.

Phil 341.4 — Krug, W.T. Versuch einer systematischen Enzyklopädie. Whittenberg, 1796.

Phil 9045.17 — Lequinio, J.M. Philosophie du peuple. Paris, 1796.
Phil 3494.34 — Michaelis, C.F. Über die settliche Natur und Bestimmung des Menschen. v.1-2. Leipzig, 1796-97.

Phil 8887.16 — The moral library. Boston, 1796.
Htn Phil 8595.15.8* — Paine, Thomas. Age of reason. Investigation of true and fabulous theology. pt.1-2. London, 1796.

Phil 3497.15 — Promnitz, C.F. Antischrift zur Vertheidigung der Vernunft und Religion. Berlin, 1796.

Phil 3778.6 — Reinhold, K.L. Auswahl vermischter Schriften. Jena, 1796-97. 2v.

Phil 3499.15 — Remer, G.L. Kant's Theorie der reinmoralischen Religion. Rega, 1796.

Phil 3500.5 — Schmidt-Phiseldek, C. Criticae ratien. Purae expositio systematica. Hafniae, 1796.

Phil 3018.1 — Schwab, J.C. Preisschriften...Metaphysik séet Leibnitz. Berlin, 1796.

Phil 2266.70 — Smith, Adam. An inquiry into the nature and causes of the wealth of nations. London, 1796. 3v.

Phil 3500.35.7 — Snell, F.W.D. Menon oder Versuch in Gesprächen. 2. Aufl. Mannheim, 1796.

Phil 6128.43 — Sömmering, S.T. Über das Organ der Seele. Königsberg, 1796.

Htn Phil 5400.4.2* — Stael-Holstein, Anne Louise G. De l'influence des passions. Lausanne, 1796.

Htn Phil 8595.16.13* — Tytler, James. Paine's second part of The age of reason answered. Salem, 1796.

Phil 3503.3 — Venturini, Karl. Geist der kritischen Philosophie. Altona, 1796-97. 2v.

Phil 8896.17 — Volney, C.F.C. The law of nature, or Principles of morality. Philadelphia, 1796.

Htn Phil 8595.16.24* — Watson, R. An apology for Christianity. Philadelphia, 1796.

Phil 8595.16.26.5 — Watson, R. An apology for the Bible. London, 1796.
Htn Phil 8595.16.27* — Watson, R. Apology for the Bible. N.Y., 1796.
Phil 8595.16.27.5 — Watson, R. Apology for the Bible. 2. ed. Philadelphia, 1796.

Phil 8595.16.26 — Watson, R. Apology for the Bible. 7. ed. London, 1796.
Htn Phil 5062.4.8* — Watts, I. Logick. 2nd American ed. Newburyport, 1796.
Htn Phil 2225.3.80* — Williams, Thomas. The age of infidelity...answer to the second part of The age of reason. Philadelphia, 1796.

Htn Phil 8595.16.11* — Winchester, E. A defence of revelation. N.Y., 1796.
Htn Phil 9362.8* — Wisdom in miniature. Worcester, 1796.

1797

Htn Phil 9160.7* — The American spectator. A collection of essays relating to the married state. Boston, 1797.

Phil 3625.5.40 — Atlas, S. Kritische Untersuchungen über den menschlichen Geist. Leipzig, 1797.

Phil 1850.26 — Bacon, Francis. Oeuvres philosophiques et morales. Paris, 1797. 2v.

Phil 3483.1.10 — Beck, J.S. The principles of critical philosophy. London, 1797.

Phil 8402.46 — Bendavid, L. Beytrage zur Kritik des Geschmacks. Wien, 1797.

Phil 3483.31 — Bergk, J. Briefe über Immanuel Kant's metaphysische Anfangsgründe der Rechtslehre. Leipzig, 1797.

Htn Phil 9515.1* — Burges, T. Solitude and society contrasted. Providence, 1797.

Phil 2205.82 — Croft, G. A short commentary, with strictures on certain parts of the moral writings of Dr. Paley and Mr. Gisborne. Birmingham, 1797.

Phil 8628.1 — Dedekind, G.E.W. Dokimion oder praktischen Versuch über ein reales Verhältniss der Geister der Verstorbenen. Hannover, 1797.

Phil 8628.1.5 — Dedekind, G.E.W. Über Geisternähe und Geisterwirkung oder über die Wahrscheinlichkeit das die Geister der Verstorbenen den Lebenden sowohl nahe seyn, als auch auf sie wirken können. Hannover, 1797.

1797 - cont.

Htn Phil 8658.9* Divine oracles; the true antidote against deism and false Christianity. Providence, 1797.

Htn Phil 8878.13.2* Dodsley, R. The economy of human life. Leominster, Mass., 1797.

Htn Phil 5754.1.101* Edwards, Jonathan. A dissertation concerning liberty and necessity. Worcester, 1797.

Phil 5045.8.14 Feder, J.G.H. Institutiones logical et metaphysicae. 4a ed. Gottingae, 1797.

Phil 3489.29.10 Heynig, J.G. Berichtigung der Urtheile des Publikums über Kant und seine Philosophie. Cölln, 1797.

Phil 3480.82.4 Kant, Immanuel. Beobachtungen über das Gefühl des Schönen und Erhabenen. Grätz, 1797.

Htn Phil 3480.45* Kant, Immanuel. Critik der practischen Vernunft. Riga, 1797.

Phil 3480.50.1 Kant, Immanuel. Critik der Urtheilskraft. Grätz, 1797. 2v.

Phil 3480.87 Kant, Immanuel. Die falsche Spitzfindigkeit der vier syllogistischen Figuren. Frankfurt, 1797.

Phil 4520.5.20 Kant, Immanuel. Grundlaggning till metaphysiken för seder. Upsala, 1797.

Phil 3480.65A Kant, Immanuel. Grundlegung zur Metaphysik der Sitten. Riga, 1797.

Htn Phil 3480.63* Kant, Immanuel. Die Metaphysik der Sitten. Königsberg, 1797.

Htn Phil 3480.81* Kant, Immanuel. Metaphysische Anfangsgründe der Jugendlehre. Königsberg, 1797.

Phil 3480.67.50.5 Kant, Immanuel. Metaphysische Anfangsgrunde der Rechtslehre. Frankfurt, 1797.

Htn Phil 3480.67.50* Kant, Immanuel. Metaphysische Anfangsgründe der Rechtslehre. Königsberg, 1797.

Phil 3480.19.12 Kant, Immanuel. Sämmtliche Kleine Schriften. Königsberg, 1797. 3v.

Phil 3480.84 Kant, Immanuel. Versuch den Begriff der negativen Grössen in die Weltweisheit einzuführen. Grätz, 1797.

Phil 9362.4 Kendrick, William. Whole duty of woman. Walpole, 1797.

Phil 9045.19 Klausen, Gottlieb E. Rede über den Gemeingeist. Altona, 1797.

Phil 9351.7 Lady's pocket library. Philadelphia, 1797.

Phil 6021.2.2 Lavater, Johann Caspar. Essays on physiognomy. London, 1797. 3v.

Htn Phil 8595.16.15* Levi, David. Defence of Old Testament. N.Y., 1797.

Htn Phil 293.8.15* Maillet, Benoît de. Telliamed. The world explained. Baltimore, 1797.

Phil 97.2 Mellin, G.S.A. Encyclopädisches Wörterbuch der Philosophie. Leipzig, 1797. 6v.

Htn Phil 6100.11* Monro, A. Three treatises. On the brain, the eye and the ear. Edinburgh, 1797.

Phil 8890.40 Pörschke, K.L. Einleitung in die Moral. Libau, 1797.

Phil 2218.83 Pures, J. Observations. Philadelphia, 1797.

Phil 8642.1 Richter, J.P.F. Das Kampaner Thal. Erfurt, 1797.

Phil 8598.1 Saint Pierre, J.H.B. de. Vindication of divine providence. Worcester, 1797.

Phil 3800.140.2 Schelling, F.W.J. von. Ideen zu einer Philosophie der Natur. v.1-2. Leipzig, 1797.

Htn Phil 3800.140* Schelling, F.W.J. von. Ideen zu einer Philosophie der Natur. v.1-2. Leipzig, 1797.

Phil 3500.5.30 Schmidt-Phiseldek, C. Briefe ästhelischen Inhalts. Altona, 1797.

Htn Phil 8595.16.19* Scott, Thomas. Vindication of divine inspiration. London, 1797.

Phil 8598.15 Stäudlin, C.F. Beiträge zur Philosophie und Geschichte der Religion und Sittenlehre überhaupt und verschiedenen Glaubensarten und kirchen Insbesondere. Lübeck, 1797-98. 4v.

Htn Phil 8595.16.25* Watson, R. Christian panoply. Sheperdstown, 1797. 2 pam.

Phil 3504.39 Wilmans, C.A. Dissertatio philosophica de similitudine. Halis Saxonum, 1797.

1798

Phil 1900.33 Butler, Joseph. Analogy of religion. London, 1798.

Phil 8610.798 Le catéchisme des Christicoles. Paris, 1798.

Phil 2493.40.10 Condillac, Etienne Bonnot. Essai sur l'origine des connaissances humaines. Paris, 1798.

Phil 2493.10 Condillac, Etienne Bonnot. Oeuvres. Paris, 1798. 23v.

Phil 2494.30 Condorcet, M.J.A.N. Esquisse d'un tableau historique. Paris, 1798.

Phil 6952.12 Crichton, A. An inquiry...nature, origin, mental derangement. London, 1798. 2v.

Phil 9345.2 Female aegis. London, 1798.

Phil 2045.102 Feuerbach, P.J.A. Anti-Hobbes. Erfurt, 1798.

Htn Phil 3246.72* Fichte, Johann Gottlieb. Das System der Sittenlehre. Jena, 1798.

Htn Phil 3246.20* Fichte, Johann Gottlieb. Über der Begriff der Wissenschaftslehre. Jena, 1798-1822. 4 pam.

Phil 8881.52 Garve, Christian. Eigene Betrachtungen über die allgemeinsten Grundsätze der Sittenlehre. Bresslau, 1798.

Phil 8831.3 Garve, Christian. Übersicht der vornehmsten Principien der Sittenlehre. Breslau, 1798.

Phil 9346.3.2 Gisborne, T. Enquiry...duties of the female sex. London, 1798.

Phil 8610.798.10 Gradis, David. Réponse à divers contradicteurs sur la coéternelle existence de la matière. Paris, 1798-99.

Phil 9167.6 Heydenreich, K.H. Vesta; kleine Schriften zur Philosophie des Lebens. v.1-5. Leipzig, 1798-1803. 4v.

Phil 3489.29 Heynig, J.G. Herausfoderung an Professor Kant in Königsberg. Leipzig, 1798.

Phil 8664.2 Jakob, L.H. Über die Beweise für das Daseyn Gottes. Liebau, 1798.

Phil 3480.69.3 Kant, Immanuel. Allgemeine Naturgeschichte. Theorie des Himmels. Zeitz, 1798.

Htn Phil 3480.25.15* Kant, Immanuel. Essays and treatises on moral, political and various philosophical subjects. London, 1798-99. 2v.

Htn Phil 3480.67.51* Kant, Immanuel. Metaphysische Anfangsgrunde der Rechtslehre. 2. Aufl. Königsberg, 1798.

Phil 3480.57.7 Kant, Immanuel. Prolegomena zu einer jeden künftigen Metaphysik. Frankfurt, 1798.

Htn Phil 3480.86* Kant, Immanuel. Der streit der Facultaeten. Königsberg, 1798.

Htn Phil 3480.86.2* Kant, Immanuel. Der streit der Facultaeten. Königsberg, 1798.

Htn Phil 3480.72.5* Kant, Immanuel. Theorie der Reinmoralischen Religion. Elberfeld, 1798.

Htn Phil 3480.89* Kant, Immanuel. Über die Büchmacheren. Königsberg, 1798.

1798 - cont.

Htn Phil 3480.54* Kant, Immanuel. Verkündigung des nahen Abschlusses eines Traktats zum ewigen Frieden in der Philosophie. Ulm, 1798.

Phil 3480.85.6.10 Kant, Immanuel. Von der Macht des Gemüths durch den blossen Vorsatz seiner krankhaften Gefühle Meister zu seyn. Königsberg, 1798?

Htn Phil 3480.85.5* Kant, Immanuel. Von der Macht des Gemüths durch den blossen Vorsatz seiner krankhaften Gefühle Meister zu seyn. Jena, 1798.

Htn Phil 3480.85.6* Kant, Immanuel. Von der Macht des Gemüths durch den blossen Vorsatz seiner krankhaften Gefühle Meister zu seyn. Jena, 1798.

Phil 8520.5.4 Leland, J. A view of the principal deistical writers. 5. ed. London, 1798. 2v.

Phil 2115.32.5 Locke, J. Essay concerning human understanding. Edinburgh, 1798. 3v.

Htn Phil 293.11* Marsh, E.G. An oration on the truth of the Mosaic history of the creation. Hartford, 1798.

Phil 97.2.5 Mellin, G.S.A. Kunstsprache der kritischen Philosophie. Jena, 1798.

Phil 3495.13 Nehr, J.G. Kritik über die metaphysischen Aufangsgründe der Rechtslehre des I. Kant. Nürnberg, 1798.

Htn Phil 3801.606* Nicolai, F. Leben und Meinungen Sempronius Gundibert's. Berlin, 1798.

Phil 9355.1.2 Pilkington, M. A mirror for the female sex. London, 1798.

Phil 3778.39 Reinhold, K.L. Verhandlungen über die Grundbegriffe und Grundsätze der Moralität. Lübeck, 1798.

Phil 9358.10 St. Lambert, J.F. de. Principes des moeurs chez toutes les nations. Paris, 1798. 3v.

Htn Phil 3800.150* Schelling, F.W.J. von. Von der Weltseele. Hamburg, 1798.

Htn Phil 3500.17.10* Schwab, J.C. Neun Gespräche zwischen Christian Wolff. Berlin, 1798.

Phil 5400.4 Stael-Holstein, Anne Louise G. Treatise on the influence of the passions. London, 1798.

Phil 819.1 Tennemann, W.G. Geschichte der Philosophie. v.1-11. Leipzig, 1798-1819. 12v.

Phil 9362.18.5 Wakefield, P. Bell (Mrs.). Leisure hours. 3d ed. London, 1798-1801. 2v.

Phil 3504.41 Weiller, K. Über den nachsten Zweck der Erziehung nach Kantischen Grunsätzen. Regensburg, 1798.

Phil 3504.5 Willich, A.F.M. Elements of the critical philosophy...Kant. London, 1798.

1799

Phil 3246.206 Belthusen, J.C. Einige Fragen, veranlasst Durch. Helmstädt, 1799.

Phil 8402.45 Bendavid, L. Versuch einer Geschmackslehre. Berlin, 1799.

Phil 176.53.15 Bouterwek, F. Idee einer Spodiktik. Halle, 1799. 2v.

Htn Phil 9005.1* Burges, T. The art of excelling. Providence, 1799.

Phil 5042.2.5 Collard, John. A praxis of logic. London, 1799.

Phil 3246.192 Eberhard, J.A. Über den Gott des Herrn Professor Fichte. Halle, 1799.

Phil 3246.219 Et was über Herrn Professor Fichte. Hamburg, 1799.

Phil 3246.71.20A Fichte, Johann Gottlieb. Appellation an das Publikum über...atheistischen. Jena, 1799.

Htn Phil 3246.21* Fichte, Johann Gottlieb. Das Herausgeber des philosophischen Journals. Jena, 1799-1815. 4 pam.

Phil 3246.263 Gruner, J.G. Ein paar Worte zur Belehrung. Jena, 1799.

Phil 3246.220 Grusber, J.G. Eine Stimme aus dem Publikum über Gottes Sein und Wesen. Leipzig, 1799.

Phil 3246.218 Heusinger, J.H.G. Über das idealistisch-atheistische System des Professor Fichte in Jena. Dresden, 1799.

Phil 8882.102 Hoffbauer, Johann C. Untersuchungen über die wichtigsten Gegenstände. Dortmund, 1799-

Htn Phil 3460.72* Jacobi, F.H. Jacobi an Fichte. Hamburg, 1799.

Phil 3246.226 Jensen, F.C. Kann man Herrn Professor Fichte mit Recht beschuldigen. Kiel, 1799.

Phil 3480.69.2 Kant, Immanuel. Allgemeine Naturgeschichte. Theorie des Himmels. Frankfurt, 1799.

Phil 3480.40.3 Kant, Immanuel. Anthropologie in pragmatischer Hinsicht Abgefasst. Frankfurt, 1799.

Phil 3480.30.1 Kant, Immanuel. Critik der reinen Vernunft. 5. Aufl. Leipzig, 1799.

Htn Phil 3480.50.2* Kant, Immanuel. Critik der Urtheilskraft. Grätz, 1799.

Phil 3480.67.65 Kant, Immanuel. Eleinenta metaphysica juris doctrinae. Amsteleadami, 1799.

Htn Phil 3480.67.70* Kant, Immanuel. The metaphysic of morals, divided into metaphisical elements of law and of ethics. v.1-2. London, 1799.

Phil 3480.18 Kant, Immanuel. Vermischte Schriften. Halle, 1799-1807. 4v.

Phil 185.32 Kolmark P. Utkast til en systematisk afhandling i theoretiska och practiska philosophien. Stockholm, 1799.

Phil 3549.30 Kosegarten, Christian. Memnens Bildsäule in Briefen au Ida von Kosegarten. Berlin, 1799.

Phil 2115.48.14 Locke, J. Essai philosophique concernant l'entendement humaine. 5e éd. Paris, 1799? 4v.

Phil 1117.3.5 Meiners, C. Histoire de l'origine...des sciences dans la Grèce. Paris, 1799. 5v.

Htn Phil 6682.3.7* Mesmer, F.A. Mémoire sur la dicouverte du magnetisme animal. Genève, 1799.

Phil 8887.63 Mutschelle, S. Vermischte Schriften, oder philosophischen Gedanken. 2. Aufl. München, 1799.

Htn Phil 3495.1* Nicolai, C.F. Über...kritischen Philosophie...Kant. Berlin, 1799.

Htn Phil 9355.1.5* Pilkington, M. A mirror for the female sex. Hartford, 1799.

Phil 3778.36 Reinhold, K.L. Sendschreiben an J.C. Lavater und J.G. Fichte über den Glauben an Gott. Hamburg, 1799. 3 pam.

Phil 3778.35 Reinhold, K.L. Über die Paradoxien der neuesten Philosophie. Hamburg, 1799.

Phil 3499.24 Roos, Andreas Praeses. Dissertatio philosophica de summo bono secundum decreta philosophiae criticae. Lundae, 179

Phil 8893.75 Say, J.B. Olbie, ou Essai sur les moyens de reformer. Paris, 1799-1800.

Phil 3246.222 Schäffer, W.F. Über den Herrn Professor Fichte Appellation an das Publikum. Gotha, 1799.

Phil 3246.223 Schaumann, J.C.G. Erklärung über Fichte's Appellation. Giessen, 1799.

Htn Phil 3800.170* Schelling, F.W.J. von. Einleitung zu seinem Entwurf eines Systems der Naturphilosophie. Jena, 1799.

Htn Phil 3800.170.5* Schelling, F.W.J. von. Einleitung zu seinem Entwurf eines Systems der Naturphilosophie. Jena, 1799. 2 pam.

Htn Phil 3800.160*A Schelling, F.W.J. von. Erster Entwurf eines Systems der Naturphilosophie. Jena, 1799.

Chronological Listing

1799 - cont.

Htn	Phil 3805.30*	Schleiermacher, Friedrich. Über die Religion. Berlin, 1799.
Htn	Phil 3805.34*	Schleiermacher, Friedrich. Über Offenbarung und Mythologie. Berlin, 1799.
	Phil 2266.30.5	Smith, Adam. Essay on philosophical subjects. Basil, 1799.
	Phil 3507.7	Zallinger, J.A. Disquisitionum philosophiae Kantianae. v.1-2. Augustae Vindelicorum, 1799.
	Phil 8735.20.5	Ziegenhagen, F.H. Lehre vom richtigen Verhältniss zu den Schöpfungswerken und die durch öffentliche Einführung derselben allein zu bewürkende allgemeine Menschenbeglückung. Braunschweig, 1799.

18-

	Phil 7054.179	Back to the father's house. London, 18- . 2v.
	Phil 1535.1.5	Balmès, Jaime. Filosofía fundamental. Paris, 18- . 2v.
	Phil 9341.17	Beale, Dorothea. A few words to girls at school. n.p., 18- .
	Phil 9341.15	Bouilly, J.N. Conseils à ma fille. Paris, 18- ?
	Phil 3483.20	Brahn, Max. Die Entwicklung des Seelenbegriffes bei Kant. Inaug. Diss. Leipzig, 18- ?
Cg	Phil 5653.6	Brillat-Savarin, A. Physiologie des Geschmacks. Leipzig, 18- .
	Phil 8876.66	Broglie, Paul. Instruction morale. 10e éd. Paris, 18- .
	Phil 5811.5.12	Büchner, L. Aus dem Geistesleben der Tiere. Leipzig, 18- ?
	Phil 8692.5.12	Chalmers, Thomas. Series of discourses on the Christian revelation, viewed in connexion with modern astronomy. N.Y., 18- .
	Phil 978.15.4.5	Cook, M.C. Light on the path. N.Y., 18- .
	Phil 9342.18	Cunningham, W. True womanhood. N.Y., 18- .
	Phil 9245.1.5	Droz, F.X.J. The art of being happy. London, 18- ?
	Phil 9165.2	Foster, J. The married state. Hartford, 18- .
	Phil 7082.30	Grant, Alexander Henley. Extraordinary and well-authenticated dreams. London, 18- ?
	Phil 288.1.8	Hickok, S.P. Review of rational cosmology. n.p., 18- ?
	Phil 2070.51	James, William. Sentiment of rationality. Aberdeen, 18- .
	Phil 6680.1.6	Kerner, J. Die Seherin von Prevorst. Leipzig, 18- .
	Phil 4761.3.30	Kratkoe poniatie o cheloveke. n.p., 18-?
	Phil 8886.31	La Hautière, E. de. Cours élémentaire de philosophie morale. 2. ed. Paris, 18- .
	Phil 186.18.9	Laugel, Auguste. Los problemas de la naturaleza. Barcelona, 18- ?
	Phil 6021.2.12	Lavater, Johann Caspar. Essays on physiognomy. 17th ed. London, 18- .
	Phil 6021.2.55	Lavater, Johann Caspar. The pocket Lavater. Hartford, 18-
	Phil 5251.7.7	Lindner, G.A. Leerbaek der empirische zielkunde. Zutphen, 18- .
	Phil 2115.65.25	Locke, J. A commonplace book to the Holy Bible. 5th London ed. N.Y., 18- ?
	Phil 8595.15.50	Paine, Thomas. Letter of Thomas Paine to lawyer Erskine. n.p., 18- .
	Phil 5635.19F	Peirce, C.S. On small differences of sensation. n.p., 18-?
	Phil 9410.9	Sarrazin, N.J. Le véritable optimisme. Nancy, 18- ?
	Phil 193.31.17	Spir, A. von. Philosophische Essays. Stuttgart, 18- .
	Phil 5938.6.18	Spurzheim, Johann Gaspar. A view of the philosophical principles of phrenology. 3rd ed. London, 18- .
	Phil 8895.1	Uloth, L. Begriff, Wesen...Darstellung der Ethik. Göttingen, 18- .
	Phil 4655.1.25	Wikner, Pontus. Anteckningar till filosofiens historia efter P. Wikners kollegium af K.S. Upsala, 18- .
	Phil 6132.16	Wilmans, Helen. Back numbers Wilmans express, condensed. n.p., 18- ?
	Phil 6972.6	Wright, T.L. Some points connected with the questions of responsibility as it relates to the partially insane. n.p., 18- .

1800

	Phil 1850.23	Bacon, Francis. Oeuvres. Dijon, 1800. 3v.
	Phil 5041.5	Bardili, C.G. Grundriss der ersten Logik. Stuttgart, 1800.
	Phil 3110.50*	Böhme, J. L'aurore naissante. Paris, 1800. 2v.
	Phil 4520.5.34	Boethius, Daniel. De modo inculcandi veritates morales in concione publica. Diss. Upsaliae, 1800.
	Phil 8876.99	Bouffleis, Stanislas de. Discours sur la vertu. 2e éd. Paris, 1800.
	Phil 1701.3	Buhle, J.G. Geschichte der neueren Philosophie. Göttlieb, 1800-1804. 6v.
	Phil 2493.30.3	Condillac, Etienne Bonnot. Segunda edición de la Lógica puesta. Madrid, 1800.
	Phil 9171.1	De Lambert, A.T. de M. de C. A mother's advice to her son and daughter. London, 1800.
	Phil 7060.145	Fair and fatal warnings. London, 1800?
	Phil 3246.34.2	Fichte, Johann Gottlieb. Die Bestimmung der Menschen. Frankfurt, 1800.
	Phil 3246.34*	Fichte, Johann Gottlieb. Die Bestimmung des Menschen. Berlin, 1800.
	Phil 3246.75*	Fichte, Johann Gottlieb. Der geschlossne Handelsstaat. Tübingen, 1800.
	Phil 5246.5	Gerando, J.M. de. Des signes et de l'art de penser. Paris, 1800. 4v.
	Phil 8881.11	Gisborne, T. An enquiry into the duties of men. London, 1800. 2v.
	Phil 8661.6	Gomer, A. de. Journée solitaire de l'homme sensible. Paris, 1800.
	Phil 2648.41	Holbach, Paul Henri T. Essai sur les préjugés. v.1-2. Paris, 1800.
	Phil 3480.40.2*	Kant, Immanuel. Anthropologie in pragmatischer Hinsicht. 2. Aufl. Königsberg, 1800.
	Phil 3480.70*	Kant, Immanuel. Logik. Königsberg, 1800.
	Phil 3480.81.2*	Kant, Immanuel. Metaphysische Anfangsgründe der Jugendlehre. 2. Aufl. Kreuznach, 1800.
	Phil 3480.81.5	Kant, Immanuel. Metaphysische Anfangsgründe der Jugendlehre. 2. Aufl. Kreuznach, 1800.
	Phil 3480.55	Kant, Immanuel. Metaphysische Anfangsgründe Naturwissenschaft. Leipzig, 1800.
	Phil 3480.19.20*	Kant, Immanuel. Sammlung einiger bisher unbekannt gebliebener kleiner Schriften. Königsberg, 1800.
	Phil 3480.85.7	Kant, Immanuel. Von der Macht des Gemüths durch den blossen Vorsatz seiner krankhaften Gefühle Meister zu seyn. Frankfurt, 1800.

1800 - cont.

	Phil 185.10.30	Krug, W.T. De humanitate in philosophando rite servanda. Vitebergae, 1800.
	Phil 3528.37	Krug, Wilhelm Traugott. Bruchstücke aus meiner Lebensphilosophie. v.1-2. Berlin, 1800-01.
	Phil 3492.33	Kunhardt, H. I. Kants Grundlegung zur Metaphysik der Sitten. Lübeck, 1800.
	Phil 8837.3	Meiners, C. Allgemeine kritische Geschichte der ältern und neuern Ethik. Göttingen, 1800-01. 2v.
	Phil 3625.1.20	Mendelssohn, Moses. Opere filosofiche. Parma, 1800. 2v.
	Phil 8963.1	Necker, J. Cours de morale religieuse. Paris, 1800. 3v.
	Phil 2205.80.5	Pearson, Edward. Remarks on the theory of morals in which is contained an examination of the theoretical part of Dr. Paley's Principles of moral and political philosophy. Ipswich, 1800.
	Phil 3499.13	Rätze, J.G. Herder Gegen Kant. Leipzig, 1800.
	Phil 8892.10	The rule of life. Springfield, 1800.
	Phil 3246.96	Schad, Johann B. Gemeinfassliche Darstellung des Fichteschen Systems and der daraus. Erfurt, 1800-02. 3v.
	Phil 3310.6.90	Schelle, K.G. Briefe über Garve's Schriften und Philosophie. Leipzig, 1800.
Htn	Phil 3800.180.5*	Schelling, F.W.J. von. System des transscendentalen Idealismus. Tübingen, 1800.
Htn	Phil 3800.180*	Schelling, F.W.J. von. System des transscendentalen Idealismus. Tübingen, 1800.
Htn	Phil 3800.190*	Schelling, F.W.J. von. Über die jenaische allgemeine Literaturzeitung. Jena, 1800.
Htn	Phil 3800.190.2*	Schelling, F.W.J. von. Über die jenaische allgemeine Literaturzeitung. Jena, 1800. 3 pam.
	Phil 3805.40	Schleiermacher, Friedrich. Monologen. Berlin, 1800.
	Phil 3018.18	Schod, J.B. Geschichte der Philosophie unserer Zeit. Jena, 1800.
Htn	Phil 3801.778*	Schütz, C.G. Vertheidigung gegen Herren Professor Schellings...Erläuterungen. Jena, 1800. 4v.
Htn	Phil 3500.17*	Schwab, J.C. Vergleichung des Kantischen Moralprinzips. Berlin, 1800.
	Phil 8599.24	Tarenne, G. La théologie naturelle, histoire, philosophique, critique et morale, ou Les pensées d'un homme sur l'être-Suprême. Paris, 1800?
	Phil 29.1	The temple of reason. N.Y., 1800.
	Phil 9515.3.5	Zimmermann, J.G. Solitude. Dublin, 1800.
	Phil 9515.3.6.5	Zimmermann, J.G. Solitude. London, 1800.
NEDL	Phil 9515.3.6	Zimmermann, J.G. Solitude. London, 1800-02.

1801

	Phil 176.16	Belsham, T. Elements of the philosophy of the mind. London, 1801.
	Phil 8877.8	Chipman, G. The American moralist. Wrentham, Mass., 1801.
	Phil 8878.13.3	Dodsley, R. The economy of human life. v.1-2. Manchester, 1801.
	Phil 8879.5	Ensor, G. The principles of morality. London, 1801.
	Phil 3246.35.7	Fichte, Johann Gottlieb. Die Bestimmung des Menschen. 2. Aufl. Berlin, 1801.
	Phil 8880.5	Fiske, N. The moral monitor. v.2. Worcester, Mass., 1801.
	Phil 9346.2	Girot. Le moraliste de la jeunesse. London, 1801.
	Phil 2038.32	Hartley, D. Observations on man. London, 1801. 3v.
Htn	Phil 3801.449*	Hegel, Georg W.F. Differenz des Fichte'schen und Schelling'schen Systems der Philosophie. Jena, 1801.
	Phil 3480.70.1	Kant, Immanuel. Logik. Königsberg, 1801.
	Phil 3480.70.2	Kant, Immanuel. Logik. Reutlingen, 1801.
	Phil 9045.16	Krogh, Matthias B. Öm Kierlighed til faedrenelandet. Trondhiem, 1801.
	Phil 8886.49	Lamblardie. Traité élémentaire de métaphysique et de morale. Brunswick, 1801.
	Phil 8886.51.5	Levesque, M. Cours élémentaire de morale. Paris, 1801.
	Phil 2115.33	Locke, J. Essay concerning human understanding. v.1-3. Edinburgh, 1801.
	Phil 2115.10	Locke, J. Works. London, 1801. 10v.
	Phil 3494.15.10	Mellin, G.S.A. Marginalien und Register zu Kants metaphysichen Anfangsgründen der Sittenlehre. Pt.1-2. Jena, 1801[1800]
	Phil 3494.28.5	Miotti. Uiber die Falschheit und Gottlosigkeit des Kantischen System. Wien, 1801.
	Phil 2205.40.2.5	Paley, W. Principles of moral and political philosophy. Boston, 1801.
	Phil 2205.80	Pearson, Edward. Annotations on the practical part of Dr. Paley's Principles of moral and political philosophy. Ipswich, 1801.
	Phil 8597.41	Réflexions sur la religion, ou L'on établit d'une manière générale. Londres, 1801.
	Phil 8893.83.15	Salat, Jakob. Auch die Aufklärung hat ihre Gefahren. München, 1801.
	Phil 3850.13.30	Schulze, G.E. Kritik der theoritischen Philosophie. Hamburg, 1801. 2v.
	Phil 8893.11.6	Sidgwick, H. The methods of ethics. 6. ed. London, 1801.
	Phil 3110.178	Sillig, J.F. Jakob Böhme. Perna, 1801.
	Phil 8894.3	Thiess, J.O. Vorlesungen über die Moral. Leipzig, 1801-03. 2v.
	Phil 5059.19	Tieftrunk, J.H. Grundriss der Logik. Halle, 1801.
	Phil 3503.2	Villers, C. Philosophie de Kant. v.1-2. Metz, 1801.
NEDL	Phil 5062.4.8.5	Watts, S. Logick. London, 1801.
Htn	Phil 9515.3.7*	Zimmermann, J.G. Solitude. 1st ed. N.Y., 1801.
Htn	Phil 9515.3.7.2*	Zimmermann, J.G. Solitude. 1st ed. N.Y., 1801.

1802

	Phil 5040.17.5	Abicht, Johann H. Verbesserte Logik. Fürth, 1802.
	Phil 1850.11	Bacon, Francis. Works. London, 1802-7. 12v.
Htn	Phil 6100.12*	Bell, C. The anatomy of the brain. London, 1802.
	Phil 332.16	Bendavid, L. Über den Ursprung unserer Erkenntniss. Berlin, 1802.
Htn	Phil 8876.36.5*	Burgh, J. The dignity of human nature. Hartford, 1802.
	Phil 2480.30	Cabanis, P.J.G. Rapports du physique et du moral de l'homme. Paris, 1802. 2v.
	Phil 9420.2.5	Cogan, T. Philosophical treatise...passions. v.1-2. Bath, 1802.
	Phil 2493.30.15	Condillac, Etienne Bonnot. Logique de Condillac à l'usage des élèves des prytanées. v.1-2. Paris, 1802. 2v.
	Phil 2494.42	Condorcet, M.J.A.N. Outlines...historical...progress...human mind. Baltimore, 1802.
	Phil 8878.7.25	Delisle de Sales, J.B.C.I. Defense d'un homme. n.p., 1802.

1802 - cont.

Phil 8878.7.20   Delisle de Sales, J.B.C.I. Memoire en faveur de Dieu.
    Paris, 1802.
Phil 5043.13.4   Duncan, William. The elements of logick. N.Y., 1802.
Phil 3246.45   Fichte, Johann Gottlieb. Grundlage der gesammten
    Wissenschaftslehre. Tübingen, 1802.
Phil 9560.26   Herault de Séchelles, M.J. Théorie de l'ambition.
    Paris, 1802.
Phil 2648.34   Holbach, Paul Henri T. Le bon sens du Curé Meslier.
    Paris, 1802.
Phil 2648.34.3   Holbach, Paul Henri T. Le bon sens du Curé Meslier.
    Paris, 1802.
Phil 2648.34.2   Holbach, Paul Henri T. Le bon sens du Curé Meslier.
    Paris, 1802.
Phil 8633.5   Ismard, M. De l'immortalité de l'âme. Paris, 1802.
Htn   Phil 3480.101*   Kant, Immanuel. Physische Geographie. v.1-2.
    Königsberg, 1802.
Phil 5821.1.5   Leroy, Charles Georges. Lettres philosophiques sur
    l'intelligence et la perfectibilité des animaux.
    Paris, 1802.
Phil 1850.85   Luc, J.A. de. Précis de la philosophie de Bacon.
    Paris, 1802. 2v.
Htn   Phil 8592.58*   M'Farland, Asa. An oration, produced before the Phi Beta
    Kappa,...Hanover, Aug. 25, 1802. Hanover, 1802.
Phil 187.98   Markovics, J.M. Assertiones ex universa philosophia.
    Pestini, 1802? 2 pam.
Phil 5252.150   Mauchart, I.D. Neues allgemeines Repertorium.
    Leipzig, 1802-03.
Phil 3494.33.5   Metz, Andreas. Darstellung der Hauptmomente der
    Elementarlehre der Kantischen Kritik der reinen Vernunft.
    Pt. 1-2. Bamberg, 1802.
Phil 3494.28   Miotti. Uiber die Falschheit und Gottlosigkeit des
    Kantischen System. Augsburg, 1802.
Phil 3494.39   Mortzfeldt, J.C. Fragmente aus Kants Leben.
    Königsberg, 1802.
Phil 9175.1   Pandolfini, A. Trattato del governo della famiglia.
    Milano, 1802.
Phil 8967.5.4   Reinhard, Franz V. System der christlichen Moral.
    Wittenberg, 1802-05. 3v.
Phil 3778.30   Reinhold, K.L. Beyträge zur leichtern Übersicht des
    Zustandes der Philosophie. v.1-6. Hamburg, 1802. 2v.
Htn   Phil 8892.6.5*   Rowe, E.S. Friendship in death. New Haven, 1802.
Phil 8893.83.15.5   Salat, Jakob. Auch ein paar Worte über die Fräge.
    München, 1802.
Phil 8893.83.16   Salat, Jakob. Die Philosophie mit obskuranten und
    Sophisten in Kampfe. Nachtrag: Auch die Aufklärung.
    Ulm, 1802.
Phil 8893.83.20   Salat, Jakob. Winke über das Verhältniss der
    intellektuellen und der verfeinernden Kultur zur
    Sittlichen. München, 1802.
Htn   Phil 3800.200*   Schelling, F.W.J. von. Bruno. Berlin, 1802.
Phil 3819.58   Spinoza, Benedictus de. Adnotationes ad tractatum
    theologico politicum. Hagae, 1802.
Phil 3819.10   Spinoza, Benedictus de. Opera quae supersunt omnia.
    Ienae, 1802. 2v.
Phil 2275.31.5   Stewart, D. Elements of the philosophy of the human mind.
    London, 1802.
NEDL   Phil 5062.4.9   Watts, S. Logic. London, 1802.

1803

Htn   Phil 9340.9*   Advice to the fair sex. Philadelphia, 1803.
Phil 1850.50.10   Bacon, Francis. Novum organum. Glasguae, 1803.
Phil 1850.2.5   Bacon, Francis. Works. London, 1803. 10v.
Phil 9050.1   Bates, E. Rural philosophy. London, 1803.
Phil 9341.7.5   Bennett, J. Letters to a young lady. London, 1803.
    2v.
Htn   Phil 1870.30.2*   Berkeley, G. Alciphron. New Haven, 1803.
Phil 8582.52   Coqueret, H. Théosophie ou science de Dieu. Paris, 1803.
Phil 8878.7.27   Delisle de Sales, J.B.C.I. Defense d'un homme.
    Paris, 1803.
Phil 178.26   Dilthey, Wilhelm. Einleitung in die Geisteswissenschaften.
    Leipzig, 1803.
Phil 8405.4   Eberhard, Johann. Handbuch der Ästhetik. Halle, 1803-04.
Phil 3552.251.5   Emery, J.A. Pensées de Leibnitz sur la religion.
    Paris, 1803. 2v.
Phil 3200.6   Eschenmayer, C.A. Die Philosophie. Erlangen, 1803.
Phil 8880.1.15   Feltham, O. The beauties of Owen Feltham. N.Y., 1803.
Phil 3246.191.5   Fries, Jakob F. Reinhold, Fichte und Schelling.
    Leipzig, 1803.
Htn   Phil 3801.407*   Fries, Jakob F. Reinhold, Fichte und Schelling.
    Leipzig, 1803.
Phil 8610.798.11   Gradis, David. Discussions philosophiques sur l'athéisme.
    Paris, 1803.
Phil 3480.65.5   Kant, Immanuel. Grundlegung zur Metaphysik der Sitten.
    v.1-2. Königsberg, 1803.
Phil 3480.81.3   Kant, Immanuel. Metaphysische Anfangsgründe der
    Jugendlehre. 2. Aufl. Königsberg, 1803.
Phil 3480.101.2   Kant, Immanuel. Physische Geographie. Leipzig, 1803-07.
    2v.
Htn   Phil 3480.75*   Kant, Immanuel. Über des Ausgesetzte Preisfrage.
    Königsberg, 1803-04. 2 pam.
Htn   Phil 3480.74.5*   Kant, Immanuel. Über Pädagogik. Königsberg, 1803.
Htn   Phil 3480.74.7*   Kant, Immanuel. Über Pädagogik. Königsberg, 1803.
Phil 3492.34.2   Kiesewetter, J.G.K.C. Versuch einer...Darstellung der
    wichtigsten Wahrheiten der kritischen Philosophie.
    Berlin, 1803. 2v.
Htn   Phil 3801.494*   Köppen, Friedrich. Schellingslehre. Hamburg, 1803.
Phil 3801.494.2   Köppen, Friedrich. Schellingslehre. Hamburg, 1803.
Phil 3525.60   Krause, K.C.F. Grundriss der historischen Logik.
    Jena, 1803.
Phil 2115.34.2   Locke, J. Essay concerning human understanding. v.1,3: 1st
    American ed. Boston, 1803-06. 3v.
Phil 2115.34   Locke, J. Essay concerning human understanding. 1st
    American ed. Boston, 1803. 3v.
Phil 96.1   Lossius, J.C. Neues Philosophie Real-Lexikon.
    Erfurt, 1803-06. 4v.
Phil 2730.35   Maine de Biran, Pierre. Influence de l'habitude.
    Paris, 1803.
Phil 3494.32   Mutschelle, S. Versuch einer solchen fasslichen
    Darstellung der Kantischen Philosophie. München, 1803.
    2v.
Phil 2205.30.12   Paley, W. Natural theology. Albany, 1803.
Phil 2205.30   Paley, W. Natural theology. London, 1803.
Phil 8890.10.5   Penn, W. Früchte der Einsamkeit. Friedenthal, 1803.
Phil 2240.50   Reid, Thomas. Essays on the powers of the human mind.
    Edinburgh, 1803. 3v.

1803 - cont.

Phil 8892.52   Rivarol, E.F. de. Encyclopédie morale. Paris, 1803.
Phil 8892.36   Rush, Jacob. Charges, and extracts of charges on moral and
    religious subjects. Philadelphia, 1803.
Phil 193.103   Salat, J. Ueber den Geist der Philosophie. München, 1803.
Htn   Phil 3800.140.5*A   Schelling, F.W.J. von. Ideen zu einer Philosophie der
    Natur. 2e Aufl. Landshut, 1803.
Htn   Phil 3800.210*   Schelling, F.W.J. von. Vorlesungen über die Methode des
    academische Studium. Tübingen, 1803.
Phil 3805.35   Schleiermacher, Friedrich. Grundlinien eines
    Kritik...Sittenlehre. Berlin, 1803.
Phil 3500.17.20   Schwab, J.C. Uber die Wahrheit der Kantischen
    Philosophie...Ausehung dieser Philosophie. Berlin, 1803.
Phil 9178.6.5   Somerville, E. A birthday present. Boston, 1803.
Htn   Phil 3801.989*   Uber den neuesten Idealismus der Herren Schelling und
    Hegel. München, 1803.
Htn   Phil 3801.875*   Weiller, K. von. Der Geist der allerneuesten Philosophie
    der Herren Schelling, Hegel. v.1-2. München, 1803-05.
Htn   Phil 9362.2.2*   West, J. (Mrs.). Letters to a young man.
    Charlestown, 1803.

1804

Phil 5240.25.10   Abel, Jacob Friedrich von. Versuch über die Seelenstärke.
    Tübingen, 1804.
Phil 9050.1.2   Bates, E. Rural philosophy. London, 1804.
Htn   Phil 3801.198*   Berg, Franz. Sextus oder über die absolute Erkenntniss von
    Schelling. Würzburg, 1804.
Phil 3483.29   Böckel, C.G.A. Die Todtenfeyer Kant's. 1. Aufl.
    Königsberg, 1804.
Phil 3483.15.5   Borowski, L.E. Darstellung des Lebens und Charakters
    Immanuel Kants. Königsberg, 1804.
Phil 1900.9   Butler, Joseph. Works. Edinburgh, 1804. 2v.
Phil 2218.80   Corry, J. The life of Joseph Priestley. Birmingham, 1804.
Htn   Phil 5754.1.6*   Edwards, Jonathan. A careful and strict enquiry...freedom
    of will. Albany, 1804.
Phil 8879.14   Ehrenberg, F. Reden uber wichtige Gegenstande.
    Leipzig, 1804.
Phil 3270.4.30   Feuerbach, P.J.A. Über Philosophie und Empirie in ihrem
    Verhältnisse zur positiven Rechtswissenschaft.
    Landshut, 1804.
Phil 7180.2   Frankenau, Rasmus. Tildragelser under ahnelser.
    Kjøbenhavn, 1804.
Phil 3260.31   Fries, J.F. System der Philosophie als evidente
    Wissenschaft. Leipzig, 1804.
Phil 3489.26   Hasse, J.G. Lezte aeusserungen Kant's von einem seiner
    Tischgenossen. Königsberg, 1804.
Phil 338.25   Heynig, J.G. Plato und Aristoteles. Amberg, 1804.
Phil 2050.35   Hume, David. Essays and treatises. Edinburgh, 1804.
    2v.
Phil 3491.4   Jackmann, R.B. Immanuel Kant. Königsberg, 1804.
Phil 3480.50.40   Kant, Immanuel. Kritik der Urtheilskraft für
    Uneingeweihte. Berlin, 1804.
Phil 6121.16   Lenhossék, Mihaly. Untersuchungen über Leidenschaften und
    Gemüthsaffekten als Ursachen. Pesth, 1804.
Phil 3494.47   Metzger, J.D. Aeusserungen über Kant. Königsberg, 1804.
Phil 2205.40.3   Paley, W. Principles of moral and political philosophy.
    London, 1804. 2v.
Phil 8610.804   Piestre, J.L. Les crimes de la philosophie. Paris, 1804.
Phil 9355.1   Pilkington, M. A mirror for the female sex. London, 1804.
Htn   Phil 3800.220*   Schelling, F.W.J. von. Philosophie und Religion.
    Tübingen, 1804.
Phil 1730.2   Starck, Johann G. Der Triumph der Philosophie im
    Achtzehnten Jahrhunderts. Germantown, 1804. 2v.
Phil 6028.8   Stoehr, Coelestinus. Phyisiognomik. Coburg, 1804. 2v.
Phil 5829.6   Thierseelen-Kunde auf thatsachen Begrundet.
    Berlin, 1804-05. 2v.
Phil 197.1.7   Wagner, J. System der Idealphilosophie. Leipzig, 1804.
Phil 197.56   Wagner, J.J. Ueber das Wesen der Philosophie.
    Bamberg, 1804.
Phil 6132.13   Walters, J.G. Plates of the thoracic and abdominal nerves.
    London, 1804.
Phil 3504.31.5   Wasianski, E.A.C. Immanuel Kant in seinen letzen
    Lebensjahren. Königsberg, 1804.
Htn   Phil 3801.876.40*   Wegscheider, J.A.L. Über die von der neusten Philosophie.
    Hamburg, 1804.
Phil 8897.8   Weishaupt, A. Die Leuchte des Diogenes. Regensburg, 1804.

1805

Phil 1860.50.6   Beattie, James. Essay on the nature and immutability of
    truth. Edinburgh, 1805.
Phil 3483.45   Bouterwek, F. Immanuel Kant. Hamburg, 1805.
Phil 9010.19   Burder, George. Lawful amusements. London, 1805.
Phil 2480.30.2   Cabanis, P.J.G. Rapports du physique et du moral de
    l'homme. Paris, 1805.
Phil 178.24   Daub, E. Studien. Frankfurt, 1805. 6v.
Phil 178.7   Drummond, W. Academical questions. London, 1805.
Phil 178.7.5   Drummond, W. Academical questions. London, 1805.
Phil 8878.48   Dumesnil, L.A.L. Examen politique, philosophique et moral.
    Caen, 1805.
Phil 8880.11   Forsyth, R. The principles of moral science.
    Edinburgh, 1805.
Phil 3260.32   Fries, J.F. Wissen, Glaube und Ahndung. Jena, 1805.
Phil 900.5   Horn, J. Über die biblische Gnosis. Hannover, 1805.
Phil 8885.17   Knigge, Adolf. Practical philosophy of social life. 1st
    American ed. Lansingburgh, 1805.
Phil 8411.7.5   Knight, R.P. An analytical inquiry into the principles of
    taste. 2. ed. London, 1805.
Htn   Phil 7150.20*   Lathrop, Joseph. Two sermons on the atrocity of suicide.
    Suffield, 1805.
Phil 5400.87   Maas, J.G. Versuch über die Leidenschaften.
    Halle, 1805-07. 2v.
Phil 3494.40   Marheinecke, P. De potiori vi quam ad commutandam.
    Erlangae, 1805.
NEDL   Phil 2205.30.4   Paley, W. Natural theology. 10th ed. London, 1805.
Phil 2218.81   Priestley, Joseph. Memoirs. London, 1805-07. 2v.
Phil 9177.2   The refuge. New Haven, 1805. 2 pam.
Phil 3778.38   Reinhold, K.L. Anleitung zur Kenntniss und Beurtheilung
    der Philosophie in ihren sämmtlichen Lehrgebäuden.
    Wien, 1805.
Phil 3499.26   Rink, Friedrich T. Ansichten aus Immanuel Kant's Leben.
    Königsberg, 1805.
Htn   Phil 8892.6.2*   Rowe, E.S. Friendship in death. Philadelphia, 1805.
Phil 3838.11   Sabatier, A. de Castres. Apologie de Spinoza et du s'isme.
    Altona, 1805.

1805 - cont.

	Phil 5258.12	Scott, R.E. Elements of intellectual philosophy. Edinburgh 1805.
	Phil 9178.6.6	Somerville, E. A birthday present. Boston, 1805.
	Phil 349.26	Suabedissen, D.T.A. Resultate des philosophischen Forschungen über...Erkenntnis. Marburg, 1805.
	Phil 1124.4	Taylor, Thomas. Miscellanies in prose and verse. London, 1805.
	Phil 400.91.25	Thanner, Ignaz. Der Transcendental-Idealismus. München, 1805.
	Phil 2300.30.3	Tucker, Abraham. Light of nature pursued. London, 1805. 7v.
	Phil 6692.6	Wendler, C.A. De magnetisms animali. Diss. Lipsiae, 1805.

1806

X Cg	Phil 1850.59.10	Bacon, Francis. Exemplum tractatus de justitia universali. Metz, 1806. (Changed to XM 1503)
	Phil 8402.14.7	Burke, E. A philosophical enquiry into the origin of our ideas of the sublime and beautiful. Philadelphia, 1806.
	Phil 6952.11	Cox, J.M. Practical observations on insanity. London, 1806.
	Phil 9560.1	De Britaine, W. Human prudence. Dedham, 1806.
	Phil 8878.13.3.10	Dodsley, R. The economy of human life. London, 1806.
	Phil 8584.17	Eléments de la philosophie du ciel. Paris, 1806.
	Phil 179.29	Eschenmayer, C.H. von. Einleitung in Natur und Geschichte. Erlangen, 1806.
	Phil 8880.1.2	Feltham, O. Resolves. London, 1806.
Htn	Phil 3246.49.2*	Fichte, Johann Gottlieb. Die Anweisung zum seeligen Leben. Berlin, 1806.
Htn	Phil 3246.47*	Fichte, Johann Gottlieb. Die Grundzüge des gegenwartigen Zeitalters. Berlin, 1806.
	Phil 4114.32	Genovesi, Antonio. Denoihnsion stoixeia, metafisikis. Vienna, 1806.
	Phil 5545.13.3	Grey, R. Memoria technica. London, 1806.
	Phil 3120.14.90	Grubbe, Samuel. Dissertatio de realismo rationali Bardilii. Upsaliae, 1806.
	Phil 3428.34	Herbart, J.F. Allgemeine Pädagogik. Göttingen, 1806.
	Phil 5050.5.15	Kiesewetter, J.G.C.C. Lärobok i logiken. Abo, 1806.
	Phil 8411.7.6	Knight, R.P. An analytical inquiry into the principles of taste. 3. ed. London, 1806.
	Phil 3528.30.2	Krug, Wilhelm Traugott. System der theoretischen Philosophie. Königsberg, 1806-18. 2v.
	Phil 6021.2.15	Lavater, Johann Caspar. Physionomie portative. Paris, 1806. 2v.
	Phil 186.63	Le Fébure, L.F.H. Essai sur l'organisation du monde physique et moral. Commercy, 1806.
Htn	Phil 2115.34.3*	Locke, J. Essay concerning human understanding. 2nd American ed. Brattleboro, Vt., 1806. 3v.
Htn	Phil 2115*	Locke, J. Essay concerning human understanding. 2nd American ed. Brattleboro, Vt., 1806. 3v.
	Phil 6990.29	Milner, John. Authentic documents relative to the cure of Winefrid White. 3. ed. London, 1806.
	Phil 8890.46.5	Palmer, E. Principles of nature. 3. ed. N.Y., 1806.
	Phil 8890.12.3	Percival, T. Moral and literary dissertations. Philadelphia, 1806.
	Phil 6965.3.5	Pinel, Philippe. Treatise on insanity. Sheffield, 1806.
	Phil 2218.81.2	Priestley, Joseph. Memoirs. London, 1806. 2v.
Htn	Phil 3800.230*A	Schelling, F.W.J. von. Darlegung der wahren Verhältnisses der Naturphilosophie. Tübingen, 1806.
Htn	Phil 3800.240*	Schelling, F.W.J. von. Über das Verhältniss der Realen und Idealen in der Natur. Hamburg, 1806.
Htn	Phil 3800.150.3*	Schelling, F.W.J. von. Von der Weltseele. 2e Aufl. Hamburg, 1806.
	Phil 3805.30.2	Schleiermacher, Friedrich. Über die Religion. Berlin, 1806.
	Phil 3805.50.5	Schleiermacher, Friedrich. Die Weihnachtsfeier. Halle, 1806.
	Phil 193.34	Steffens, H. Grundzüge der philosophischen Naturwissenschaft. Berlin, 1806.
Htn	Phil 5062.4.10*	Watts, S. Logic. 3rd American ed. Exeter, 1806.
Htn	Phil 9362.2*	West, J. (Mrs.). Letters to a young lady. N.Y., 1806.

1807

	Phil 9050.1.3	Bates, E. Rural philosophy. Philadelphia, 1807.
	Phil 801.24	Berthre de Bowinisseaux, P.V.J. La charlatanisme philosophique de tous les ages dévoilé. Paris, 1807.
	Phil 5465.1	Bonstetten, K.V. von. Recherches sur la nature et les lois de l'imagination. Genève, 1807. 2v.
	Phil 8402.10	Bouterwek, F. Ideen zur Metaphysik des Schönen. Leipzig, 1807.
	Phil 1900.10	Butler, Joseph. Works. Oxford, 1807. 2v.
	Phil 9420.2.9	Cogan, T. An ethical treatise...passions. Bath, 1807-10. 2v.
	Phil 850.8	Eberhard, J.A. Der Geist des Urchristenthums. Halle, 1807-08. 3v.
	Phil 8880.2	Ferris, S. Mental perceptions. London, 1807.
	Phil 3801.407.5*	Fries, Jakob F. Fichte's und Schelling's neueste Lehren von Gott und die Welt. Heidelberg, 1807.
	Phil 3246.96.5	Fries, Jakob F. Fichte's und Schelling's neueste Lehren von Gott und die Welt. Heidelberg, 1807.
	Phil 3801.431.2	Goetz, Johann K. Anti-Sextus, oder über das absolute Erkenntniss von Schelling. Heidelberg, 1807.
	Phil 3801.431*	Goetz, Johann K. Anti-Sextus, oder über das absolute Erkenntniss von Schelling. Heidelberg, 1807.
	Phil 2520.173	Grubbe, S. De philosophia Cartesii observationes. Diss. Upsaliae, 1807.
	Phil 3425.72	Hegel, Georg Wilhelm Friedrich. System der Wissenschaft. Bamberg, 1807.
	Phil 9010.27	Hill, Richard. An address to persons of fashion. Baltimore, 1807.
	Phil 9170.1	K., J.P.A. Bildungslehre...zum ehelichen Glücke. Düsseldorf, 1807.
	Phil 8886.58	Livry, Hypolite. Reflexions morales et probablement fort inutiles. Paris, 1807.
	Phil 8887.6.5	Mason, J. Self-knowledge. Portland, 1807.
	Phil 9358.13	A present for an apprentice. 3d ed. London, 1807.
	Phil 6685.9	Puységur, Armand Marie Jacques de Chastenet. Du magnétisme animal. Paris, 1807.
	Phil 2050.86	Ritchie, T.E. Account of life...D. Hume. London, 1807.
	Phil 3800.250*	Schelling, F.W.J. von. Über das Verhältniss der bildenden Künste zur Natur. München, 1807.
	Phil 8595.16.29	Thomson, Robert. Divine authority of the Bible. Boston, 1807.
	Phil 2300.30.15	Tucker, Abraham. An abridgment of the Light of nature pursued. London, 1807.

1807 - cont.

	Phil 5400.3	Vernier, I. Caractère des passions. Paris, 1807. 2v.
NEDL	Phil 5062.4.11	Watts, S. Logic. Edinburgh, 1807.

1808

	Phil 8876.7	Bartolommeo, F. Ammaestramenti degli antighi. Milan, 1808.
	Phil 176.19.5	Berger, J.E. Philosophische Darstellung der Harmonien des Weltalls. Altona, 1808.
	Phil 6930.7	Boieldiev, M.J.A. Discours sur la mélancolie. Paris, 1808.
	Phil 5751.13	Boufflers, S. Le libre arbitre. Paris, 1808.
	Phil 8876.90	Bouterwek, F. Praktische Aphorismen. Leipzig, 1808.
	Phil 5212.1	Carus, F.A. Geschichte der Psychologie. Leipzig, 1808.
	Phil 9344.8	Ehrenberg, F. Der Charakter und die Bestimmung des Mannes. Leipzig, 1808.
Htn	Phil 3246.55.2*	Fichte, Johann Gottlieb. Reden an die deutsche Nation. Berlin, 1808.
	Phil 5090.2	Gambier, J.E. Introduction...moral evidence. v.1-2. London, 1808-1818.
	Phil 8434.2.10	Gilpin, W. Remarks on forest scenery, and other woodland views. 3. ed. London, 1808. 2v.
	Phil 7082.136	Gray, Robert. The theory of dreams: in which an inquiry is made into the powers and faculties of the human mind. v.1-2. London, 1808.
	Phil 3428.36	Herbart, J.F. Allgemeine practische Philosophie. Göttingen, 1808.
Htn	Phil 3801.450*	Herbart, Johann F. Hauptpuncte der Metaphysik. Göttingen, 1808.
Htn	Phil 7060.10.7*	Jung Stilling, J.H. Theorie der Geister-Kunde. Nürnberg, 1808 .
	Phil 3480.69.4	Kant, Immanuel. Allgemeine Naturgeschichte. Theorie des Himmels. 4. Aufl. Zeitz, 1808.
	Phil 8411.7.10	Knight, R.P. An analytical inquiry into the principles of taste. 4. ed. London, 1808.
	Phil 8885.7	Knox, V. Essays, moral and literary. London, 1808. 3v.
	Phil 5761.13	La Luzerne, C.G. de. Dissertation sur la liberté de l'homme. Langres, 1808.
	Phil 2205.31	Paley, W. Theologia naturale. Roma, 1808.
	Phil 6685.12	Petetin, J.H.D. Electricité animale. Paris, 1808.
	Phil 2880.1.42	Saint-Martin, L.C. L'homme de désir. Londres, 1808.
	Phil 8968.2	Stäudlin, C.F. Geschichte der christlichen Moral. Göttingen, 1808.
	Phil 2275.80	Stewart, D. Élémens de la philosophie de l'esprit humain. Genève, 1808. 3v.
	Phil 2275.33	Stewart, D. Elements of the philosophy of the human mind. Brattleborough, 1808.
	Phil 3508.2	Verzeichniss der Bücher des Verstorben Professor Johann Friedrich Gensichen. Königsberg, 1808.
	Phil 8896.16	Virey, J.J. L'art de perfectionner l'homme. Paris, 1808. 2v.

1809

	Phil 175.6.20	Ancillon, F. Mélanges de littérature et de philosophie. Paris, 1809. 2v.
	Phil 3090.31	Baader, Franz von. Beiträge zur dinamischen Philosophie im Gegensaze der Mechanischen. Berlin, 1809.
	Phil 6951.1	Bakewell, T. The domestic guide in cases of insanity. Newcastle, 1809.
	Phil 1860.10	Beattie, James. Dissertations moral and critical. Works 1-3. Philadelphia, 1809. 3v.
	Phil 1860.10.3	Beattie, James. Elements of moral science. Works 7-9. Philadelphia, 1809. 3v.
	Phil 1860.50.7	Beattie, James. Essay on the nature and immutability of truth. Philadelphia, 1809.
	Phil 1860.10.2	Beattie, James. Essays. Works 4-6. Philadelphia, 1809. 3v.
	Phil 1860.10.4	Beattie, James. The minstrel. Works 10. Philadelphia, 1809.
	Phil 1900.34	Butler, Joseph. Analogy of religion. Boston, 1809.
	Phil 177.36	Carus, F.A. Ideen zur Geschichte der Philosophie. Leipzig, 1809.
	Phil 1050.8	Cearus, F.A. Psychologie der Hebräer. Leipzig, 1809.
	Phil 9342.2.12	Chapone, H. (Mrs.). Letters on the improvement of the mind. Boston, 1809.
	Phil 2493.30.6	Condillac, Étienne Bonnot. The logic of Condillac. Philadelphia, 1809.
	Phil 3838.29	Delouit. Lettre d'un ami du sens commun à un Hollandois. Utrecht, 1809.
Htn	Phil 3801.435*	Grohmann, J.C.A. De recentissimae philosophiae vanitate. Vitebergae, 1809.
	Phil 806.10	Grulle, Samuel. Dissertatio stationes successivas philosophiae progredientis abumbrans. Upsaliae, 1809.
	Phil 182.14.1	Hemsterhuis, F. Oeuvres philosophiques. Paris, 1809. 2v.
	Phil 185.6.5	Kirwan, R. Metaphysical essays. London, 1809.
	Phil 185.6	Kirwan, R. Metaphysical essays. London, 1809.
	Phil 9351.7.4	Lady's pocket library. 4th ed. Philadelphia, 1809.
Htn	Phil 2725.5.30*	Lamarck, J.B. Philosophie zoologique. Paris, 1809. 2v.
	Phil 8887.6.6	Mason, J. A treatise on self-knowledge. Boston, 1809.
	Phil 2205.83	Meadley, G.W. Memoirs of William Paley, D.D. Sunderland, 1809. 2 pam.
	Phil 8637.2	Meister, J.H. Euthanasie. Paris, 1809.
	Phil 6965.3	Pinel, Philippe. Traité médico-philosophique sur l'aliénation mentale. Paris, 1809.
Htn	Phil 3800.50*A	Schelling, F.W.J. von. Philosophische Schriften. Landshut, 1809.
	Phil 3800.150.2	Schelling, F.W.J. von. Von der Weltseele. 3e Aufl. Hamburg, 1809.
Htn	Phil 3800.150.6*A	Schelling, F.W.J. von. Von der Weltseele. 3e Aufl. Hamburg, 1809.
	Phil 7068.09	The supernatural magazine. Dublin, 1809.
	Phil 6132.4.7	Worcester, Elwood. Christian religion as a healing power. N.Y., 1809.

1810

	Phil 8876.6.3	Bartlett, J. Aphorisms. Portsmouth, 1810.
Htn	Phil 8876.6.4*	Bartlett, J. Aphorisms. Portsmouth, 1810.
	Phil 7060.63	Colton, C. Sampford ghost. Tiverton, 1810.
	Phil 7068.10	Colton, C.C. Sampford ghost. Tiverton, 1810.

1810 - cont.

	Phil 8881.4.9	Douglas, M. The life of Professor C.F. Gellert. London, 1810. 3v.
Htn	Phil 8628.4.2*	Drew, Samuel. An original essay on the immateriality and immortality of the human soul. 1st American ed. Baltimore, 1810.
	Phil 8583.31	Dutoit-Mombrini, P. La science du Christ et de l'homme. n.p., 1810. 3v.
Htn	Phil 5645.4.2*	Goethe, J.W. von. Zur Farbenlehre. Tübingen, 1810. 2v.
X Cg	Phil 5645.4	Goethe, J.W. von. Zur Farbenlehre. Tübingen, 1810. 3v.
	Phil 4570.1.60	Grubbe, Samuel. Dissertatio de harmonia religionis et moralitatis. Upsaliae, 1810.
	Phil 2636.41.2	Helvétius, C.A. De l'esprit, or Essays on the mind. 2. ed. London, 1810.
	Phil 2636.31.2	Helvétius, C.A. A treatise on man. London, 1810. 2v.
	Phil 5047.7	Hoffbauer, J.C. Unfangsgrunde der Logik. Halle, 1810.
	Phil 2648.43.25	Holbach, Paul Henri T. Cartas á Eugenia. Paris, 1810.
	Phil 185.48	Köppen, Friedrich. Darstellung des Wesens der Philosophie. Nürnberg, 1810.
	Phil 3525.70	Krause, K.C.F. System der Sittenlehre. Bd.1. Leipzig, 1810.
Htn	Phil 9351.8*A	Letters from an elder to a younger brother. Boston, 1810.
	Phil 3200.3.81	Nicolai, Friedrich. Gedächtnisschrift auf Johann August Eberhard. Berlin, 1810.
	Phil 2205.40.4	Paley, W. Principles of moral and political philosophy. Boston, 1810.
	Phil 2205.10	Paley, W. Works. Boston, 1810-12. 5v.
	Phil 9560.19	Rosini, G. Introduzione alle virtù. Firenze, 1810.
	Phil 270.12	Scott, R.E. Inquiry into limits...nature of causation. Edinburgh, 1810.
Htn	Phil 2275.59*	Stewart, D. Philosophical essays. Edinburgh, 1810.
	Phil 8644.10	Turlot, F.C. Etudes sur la théorie de l'avenir. Paris, 1810. 2v.
	Phil 9230.7	Venault de charmilly. Letter...to Lieutenant General B. Tarleton. London, 1810.
	Phil 3504.31	Wasianskì, E.A.C. Immanuel Kant. Upsala, 1810.
	Phil 3504.47	Wendel, J.A. Grundzüge und Kritik der Philosophien Kant's. Coburg, 1810.

1811

	Phil 8401.2.2	Alison, Archibald. Essays on the nature and principles of taste. 2. ed. Edinburgh, 1811.
	Phil 4351.4.10	Alvarado, Francisco. Cartas del filósofo rancio. Sevilla, 1811-14. 3v.
	Phil 1850.26.5	Bacon, Francis. Oeuvres philosophiques, morales et politiques. Paris, 1811.
	Phil 6951.10	Beck, Theodric R. An inaugural dissertation on insanity. Thesis. N.Y., 1811.
	Phil 1865.43	Bentham, Jeremy. Theorie des peines et des récompenses. v.1-2. London, 1811.
	Phil 6952.11.2	Cox, J.M. Practical observations on insanity. Philadelphia, 1811.
	Phil 8658.16	De Dieu. Par M***. Paris, 1811.
	Phil 2520.27	Descartes, René. Pensées de Descartes sur la religion et la morale. Paris, 1811.
	Phil 5043.13.7	Duncan, William. The elements of logick. Albany, 1811.
	Phil 3260.49	Fries, J.F. System der Logik. Heidelberg, 1811.
	Phil 5480.1	Gall, F.J. Des dispositions innées de l'âme. Paris, 1811.
Htn	Phil 3801.419*	Gerlach, G.W. De differentia, quae inter Plotini et Schellingii doctrinam de numine summo intercedit. Thesis. Vitebergae, 1811.
	Phil 3489.32	Herbart, J.F. Immanuel Kants Gedächtnissfeyer zu Königsberg am 22stem April 1812. Königsberg, 1811.
	Phil 8886.13	Leadbeater, M. Cottage dialogues. Richmond, 1811.
Htn	Phil 2115.58.5*	Locke, J. The reasonableness of Christianity. Boston, 1811.
	Phil 2205.40.5	Paley, W. Principles of moral and political philosophy. Boston, 1811.
	Phil 7085.6	Puysegur, A. M.J. Recherches...sur l'homme dans l'état de somnambulisme naturel. Paris, 1811.
	Phil 6967.8	Revere, John. Disputatio medica inauguralis de insania. Edinburgh, 1811.
	Phil 8893.96	Saltzmann, C.G. Elements of morality. Baltimore, 1811.
	Phil 3805.33.10	Schleiermacher, Friedrich. Kurze Darstellung des theologischen Studiums. Berlin, 1811.
	Phil 8643.3.10	Sintenis, F. Elpizon, oder Über meine Fortdauer im Tode. 3. Aufl. Köln, 1811. 6v.
	Phil 2275.60	Stewart, D. Philosophical essays. Philadelphia, 1811.

1812

	Phil 8401.2.3	Alison, Archibald. Essays on the nature and principles of taste. Boston, 1812. 2v.
	Phil 4351.4.20	Alvarado, Francisco. La maza de fraga sobre los filosofastros liberales del día. Madrid, 1812.
	Phil 2477.3.31	Barruel, Augustine. Les Helviennes. 5. éd. Paris, 1812. 4v.
	Phil 1865.19	Bentham, Jeremy. Panopticon. London, 1812-17. 4 pam.
	Phil 5241.20	Buchanan, Joseph. The philosophy of human nature. Richmond, 1812.
	Phil 8876.36.6	Burgh, J. The dignity of human nature. N.Y., 1812.
	Phil 2493.30	Condillac, Étienne Bonnot. La lógica. Caracas, 1812.
	Phil 178.9.4	Dutens, Louis. Origine des découvertes. 4e éd. Paris, 1812.
	Phil 5545.9	Feinaigle, G. von. New art of memory. London, 1812.
	Phil 3246.53.5	Fichte, Johann Gottlieb. Über die Bestimmung des Gelehrten. Berlin, 1812.
Htn	Phil 3801.407.10*	Fries, Jakob F. Von deutscher Philosophie...ein Votum für F.H. Jacobi gegen...Schelling. Heidelberg, 1812.
	Phil 9230.3.7	Hey, R. Three dissertations on...gaming. Cambridge, 1812.
	Phil 3460.10	Jacobi, F.H. Werke. Leipzig, 1812-25. 7v.
	Phil 5402.4.5	Levesque de Pouilly, L.J. Theory of agreeable sensations. Boston, 1812.
	Phil 2115.10.5A	Locke, J. Works. London, 1812. 10v.
Htn	Phil 8887.6.6.5*	Mason, J. A treatise on self-knowledge. Newburyport, 1812.
	Phil 2205.10.5	Paley, W. Works. v.1,3-5. Boston, 1812. 4v.
	Phil 2805.40.16	Pascal, Blaise. Pensées. v.1-2. Paris, 1812.
Htn	Phil 2880.1.50*	Saint-Martin, L.C. Vom Geist und Wesen der Dinge. v.1-2. Leipzig, 1812.
Htn	Phil 3801.763*	Salat, Jakob. Erläuterung einiger Hauptpunkt der Philosophie. Landshut, 1812.

1812 - cont.

Htn	Phil 3801.776*	Schaffroth, J.A.G. Blicke auf die Schellingsch-Jacobi'sche Streitsache. Stuttgart, 1812.
Htn	Phil 3800.260*	Schelling, F.W.J. von. Denkmal der Schrift von den göttlichen Dingen des Herrn F.H. Jacobi. Tübingen, 1812.
	Phil 3800.180.10	Schelling, F.W.J. von. Système de l'idéalisme trancendental. Paris, 1812.
	Phil 3819.30.29	Spinoza, Benedictus de. Ethik nebst Briefen Welche sich auf die Gegenstände der Ethik. Bd.1. Berlin, 1812.
Htn	Phil 3801.812*	Süskind, F.G. von. Prüfung der Schellingischen Lehren von Gott. Tübingen, 1812.
	Phil 4640.1.30	Treschow, N. Om den menneskelige natur. København, 1812.
	Phil 194.34.10	Troxler, I.P.V. Blicke in das Wesen des Menschen. Aarau, 1812.

1813

	Phil 1850.50.11	Bacon, Francis. Novum organum. Oxonii, 1813.
	Phil 1860.60.5	Beattie, James. Elements of moral science. v.1-2. Baltimore, 1813.
	Phil 2480.88	Bigoni, Angelo. Vero rapporto del fisico e del morale dell'uomo. Padova, 1813.
	Phil 9420.2.6	Cogan, T. Philosophical treatise...passions. v.1-2. London, 1813.
	Phil 9420.2	Cogan, T. A treatise on the passions and affections of the mind. v.2-5. v.1 lost. London, 1813. 4v.
	Phil 6673.2.3	Deleuze, J.P.F. Histoire critique du magnétisme animal. Paris, 1813. 2v.
	Phil 7060.15	Ferriar, J. Essay towards a theory of apparitions. London, 1813.
	Phil 3480.19.30	Kant, Immanuel. Kantische Blumenlese. v.1-2. Zittau, 1813-
Htn	Phil 3801.488*	Klein, Georg M. Betrachtungen über den gegenwartigen Zustand der Philosophie...Schellingsche Philosophie. Nürnberg, 1813.
NEDL	Phil 2115.34.5	Locke, J. Essay concerning human understanding. v.2. 2nd American ed. Boston, 1813.
	Phil 8887.6.7	Mason, J. A treatise on self-knowledge. Montpelier, 1813.
	Phil 8887.17	The moral mirror. Philadelphia, 1813.
Htn	Phil 8962.4.5*	More, Hannah. Christian morals. 1st American ed. N.Y., 1813.
Htn	Phil 8962.4.6*	More, Hannah. Christian morals. 2nd American ed. N.Y., 1813.
	Phil 8890.10	Penn, W. Fruits of solitude, in reflections and maxims. N.Y., 1813.
	Phil 2240.10	Reid, Thomas. Works. Charlestown, 1813-15. 4v.
	Phil 185.48.25	Schafberger, F. Kritik der Schrift Darstellung des Wesens der Philosophie. Nürnberg, 1813.
Htn	Phil 3800.210.5*	Schelling, F.W.J. von. Vorlesungen über die Methode des academische Studium. 2e Ausg. Stuttgart, 1813.
	Phil 3850.13.60	Schulze, G.E. Leitfaden der Entwickelung der philosophischen Prinzipien. Göttingen, 1813.
	Phil 8968.2.5	Stäudlin, C.F. Neues Lehrbuch der Moral. Göttingen, 1813.
	Phil 4610.9.85	Steen, H. Problemet om tro og viden. Kjøbenhavn, 1813.
	Phil 2275.33.2	Stewart, D. Elements of the philosophy of the human mind. Brattleborough, 1813.
	Phil 7060.117	Tregortha, John. News from the invisible world. Burslem, 1813.
Htn	Phil 8972.7*	Wales, Ebenezer. Counsels and directions of Ebenezer Wales to his children. Boston, 1813.
	Phil 5062.4.11.5	Watts, S. Logic. London, 1813.
	Phil 9515.3.9	Zimmermann, J.G. Solitude. N.Y., 1813.

1814

Htn	Phil 6947.1.893*	Account of the rise and progress of the asylum. Philadelphia, 1814. 2 pam.
NEDL	Phil 9161.1	Bean, James. The Christian minister's affectionate advice to a new married couple. London, 1814.
X Cg	Phil 9161.1.3	Bean, James. The Christian minister's affectionate advice to a new married couple. London, 1814.
	Phil 9171.1.5	De Lambert, A.T. de M. de C. A mother's advice to her son and daughter. Haverhill, 1814.
	Phil 9171.1.2	De Lambert A.T. de M. de C. A mother's advice to her son and daughter. Boston, 1814.
	Phil 8583.30	Desquiron de Saint Agnan, A.T. Dieu, la nature et la loi. Paris, 1814.
	Phil 3428.65	Herbart, J.F. Über meiner Streit met der Modephilosophie. Königsberg, 1814.
	Phil 7039.2.2	Mais, Charles. The surprising case of Rachel Baker who prays and preaches in her sleep. v.1-2. 2d ed. N.Y., 1814.
	Phil 6682.3	Mesmer, F.A. Mesmerismus. Berlin, 1814.
Htn	Phil 8887.29*	Montlosier, F.D. de R. The management of the tongue. Boston, 1814.
NEDL	Phil 2205.30.11	Paley, W. Natural theology. Philadelphia, 1814.
	Phil 2205.30.2	Paley, W. Natural theology. Philadelphia, 1814.
NEDL	Phil 2205.30.3	Paley, W. Natural theology. Philadelphia, 1814.
	Phil 3790.11.85	Reimarus, J.A.H. Lebensbeschreibung, von ihm selbst. Hamburg, 1814.
	Phil 8967.5.10	Reinhard, Franz V. System der christlichen Moral. Wittenberg, 1814-15. 5v.
	Phil 9045.20	Siveking, Gustav A. Rede über einige Hauptregeln zum wohlthätigen Einwirken auf das Zeitalter. Hamburg, 1814.
	Phil 2275.34	Stewart, D. Elements of the philosophy of the human mind. Boston, 1814-27. 3v.
	Phil 2275.32	Stewart, D. Elements of the philosophy of the human mind. v.2. Boston, 1814.

1815

	Phil 8401.2.4	Alison, Archibald. Essays on the nature and principles of taste. 4th ed. Edinburgh, 1815. 2v.
	Phil 1850.12	Bacon, Francis. Works. v.2. London, 1815.
Htn	Phil 1865.55*	Bentham, Jeremy. A table of the springs of action. London, 1815.
	Phil 4520.2.34	Biberg, N.F. Commentationum Stoicarum. Diss. Upsaliae, 1815-1821.
	Phil 801.27.15	Bjarnason, A. Vesturlönd. Reykjavik, 1815.
	Phil 8402.10.5	Bouterwek, F. Aesthetik. 2. ed. Göttingen, 1815. 2v.
	Phil 9342.2.9	Chapone, H. (Mrs.). Letters on the improvement of the mind. London, 1815.
	Phil 8877.77	Coltman, J. Everyman's monitor. Philadelphia, 1815.
Htn	Phil 7230.4.2*	Devotional somnium. N.Y., 1815.
	Phil 7077.3	Devotional somnium. N.Y., 1815.
	Phil 3790.11.90	Ebeling, C.D. Memoriae J.A.H. Reimari. Hamburgi, 1815.

Chronological Listing

	Phil 6945.6	Eddy, T. Hints for introducing an improved mode of treating the insane in the asylum. N.Y., 1815.
	Phil 5049.17	Johanson, Johan. Apharismi e logica transcendali quas praeside Samuel Grubbs. Upsaliae, 1815.
	Phil 5251.30	Laromiguiere, P. Leçons de philosophie, ou Essai sur les facultés de l'ame. Paris, 1815-18. 2v.
	Phil 4363.5.31	Macedo, J.A. de. Cartas filosoficas a Attico. Lisboa, 1815.
	Phil 2205.40.6	Paley, W. Principles of moral and political philosophy. Boston, 1815.
	Phil 2805.30.15	Pascal, Blaise. Les provinciales. Paris, 1815. 2v.
Htn	Phil 3790.11.87*	Reimarus, J.A.H. De vita sua commentarius. Hamburgi, 1815.
	Phil 7054.126	Richards, L.S. The beginning of man and what becomes of him. Boston, 1815.
Htn	Phil 3800.270.1*	Schelling, F.W.J. von. Über die Gottheiten von Samothrace. Stuttgart, 1815.
Htn	Phil 3800.270.5*	Schelling, F.W.J. von. Über die Gottheiten von Samothrace. Stuttgart, 1815.
Htn	Phil 3800.270*	Schelling, F.W.J. von. Über die Gottheiten von Samothrace. Stuttgart, 1815.
Htn	Phil 8595.16.20*	Scott, Thomas. Treatises on various theological subjects. Middletown, Conn., 1815.
	Phil 8419.43	Solger, K.W.F. Erwin; vier Gespräche über das Schöne une die Kunst. Berlin, 1815. 2v.
	Phil 9178.7	Stephens, John. Advantages which man derives from woman. N.Y., 1815.
	Phil 9179.1	Taylor, A. Hinton. Practical hints to young females. London, 1815.
	Phil 7060.11	Taylor, J. Apparitions. London, 1815.

	Phil 2445.1.30	Azaïs, Pierre H. Manuel du philosophe. Paris, 1816.
	Phil 9400.1	Bernard, T. Spurinna...comforts of old age. London, 1816.
NEDL	Phil 8656.4	Brown, W.L. An essay on the existence...supreme creator. Aberdeen, 1816. 2v.
	Phil 1701.3.5	Buhle, J.G. Histoire de la philosophie moderne. Paris, 1816. 6v.
X Cg	Phil 9342.2.6	Chapone, H. (Mrs.). Letters on the improvement of the mind. Philadelphia, 1816.
	Phil 8620.3	Daub, C. Judas Ischariot. v.1-2. Heidelberg, 1816-18.
	Phil 6674.2	Eschenmayer, C.A. Versuch der scheinbare Magie der thierischen Magnetismus. Stuttgart, 1816.
	Phil 1730.4	Gourju, Pierre. La philosophie du dix-huitième siècle dévoilée par elle-même. Paris, 1816. 2v.
	Phil 3428.43	Herbart, J.F. Lehrbuch zur Psychologie. Königsberg, 1816.
	Phil 5545.60	Jackson, George. Jackson's new...system of mnemonics. London, 1816.
	Phil 6020.1	Die Kunst in der Liebe und Freundschaft. Pesth, 1816.
	Phil 8887.7.4	Mather, C. Essays to do good. London, 1816.
	Phil 8887.24	Moustalon. La morale des poètes. Paris, 1816.
Htn	Phil 189.2*	Ogilvie, J. Philosophical essays. Philadelphia, 1816.
NEDL	Phil 2805.30.12	Pascal, Blaise. Les provinciales. Paris, 1816. 2v.
	Phil 2805.30.7	Pascal, Blaise. Les provinciales. Paris, 1816. 2v.
	Phil 75.8	Schaller, Karl A. Handbuch der klassischen philosophichen Literatur. Halle, 1816.
Htn	Phil 3808.63*	Schopenhauer, Arthur. Über das Sehn und die Farben. Leipzig, 1816.
	Phil 3850.13.40	Schulze, G.E. Psychische Anthropologie. Göttingen, 1816.
	Phil 8598.20	Summer, J.B. A treatise...records of the creation. London, 1816. 2v.
	Phil 9179.1.2	Taylor, A. Hinton. Practical hints to young females. Boston, 1816.
	Phil 8599.5	Tittmann, J.A.H. Über Supranaturalismus. Leipzig, 1816.
	Phil 106.1.4	Voltaire, Francois Marie Arouet de. Dictionnaire philosophique. Paris, 1816. 14v.

Htn	Phil 9558.21*	Abaddon's steam engine. Philadelphia, 1817.
tn	Phil 6671.14*	Baader, F. Über die Extase oder das Verzücktseyn der magnetischen Schlafredner. Leipzig, 1817.
	Phil 176.19	Berger, J.E. Grundzuge zur Wissenschaft. Altona, 1817. 4v.
	Phil 4080.34	Carena, Giacinto. Essai d'un parallèle entre les forces physiques et les forces morales. Turin, 1817.
	Phil 8692.5.3	Chalmers, Thomas. Series of discourses on the Christian revelation, viewed in connexion with modern astronomy. N.Y., 1817.
	Phil 8692.27	Chicherin, Boris N. Nauka i religiia. Moskva, 1817.
	Phil 8887.14	Cogan, T. Ethical questions. London, 1817.
	Phil 6012.2	Cross, John. Attempt to establish physiognomy upon scientific principles. Glasgow, 1817.
	Phil 9343.5	Davis, William. Friendly advice to industrious persons. 4th ed. London, 1817.
	Phil 2523.30	Destutt de Tracy, A.L.C. Élémens d'idéologie. Paris, 1817-18. 4v.
	Phil 2523.31	Destutt de Tracy, A.L.C. Elementi d'ideologia. Milano, 1817-19. 10v.
	Phil 2523.45	Destutt de Tracy, A.L.C. Principes logiques. Paris, 1817. 2 pam.
	Phil 2523.50	Destutt de Tracy, A.L.C. Principes logiques. Paris, 1817.
	Phil 5244.3	Eschenmayer, C.A.A. Psychologie. Stuttgart, 1817.
	Phil 3246.65*	Fichte, Johann Gottlieb. Die Thatsachen des Bewusstseyns. Stuttgart, 1817.
	Phil 181.162	Gley, Gérard. Essai sur les éléments de la philosophie. Paris, 1817.
	Phil 9167.1	Hale, M. A letter of advice to his grandchildren. Boston, 1817.
	Phil 8882.2A	Hamilton, E. A series of popular essays. Boston, 1817. 2v.
	Phil 5425.23	Hancock, Thomas. Essay on capacity and genius. London, 1817.
	Phil 3425.43*	Hegel, Georg Wilhelm Friedrich. Encyclopädie der philosophischen Wissenschaften. Heidelberg, 1817.
	Phil 3428.61	Herbart, J.F. Gespräche über das Böse. Königsberg, 1817.
	Phil 2050.35.85	Hume, David. Philosophical essays. 1st American ed. Philadelphia, 1817. 2v.
	Phil 3246.221	Keyserlingk, H.W.E. von. Vergleich zwischen Fichtens System. Königsberg, 1817.
	Phil 5250.24	Kiesewetter, J.G.C. Fassliche Darstellung der Erfahrungsseelenlehre. Wien, 1817.
	Phil 3528.35	Krug, Wilhelm Traugott. System der praktischen Philosophie. 2. Aufl. Königsberg, 1817-19. 3v.

	Phil 2115.34.9	Locke, J. Essay concerning human understanding. 24th ed. London, 1817.
	Phil 8413.18	MacKenzie, G.S.B. An essay on some subjects connected with taste. Edinburgh, 1817.
	Phil 2205.40.8	Paley, W. Principles of moral and political philosophy. N.Y., 1817.
	Phil 6965.1	Parkman, G. Management of lunatics. Boston, 1817-18. 2 pam.
	Phil 2805.40.13	Pascal, Blaise. Pensées de Blaise Pascal. Paris, 1817. 2v.
	Phil 7060.37	Rauschink, Gottfried Peter. Gespenstersagen. Rudolstadt, 1817.
	Phil 6327.9	Reid, J. Essays on hypochondriacal and other nervous affections. Philadelphia, 1817.
	Phil 6687.2	Richter, J.A.L. Betrachtungen und der animal Magnetismus. Leipzig, 1817.
	Phil 2520.265	Ritter, Heinrich. Welcher Einfluss hat die Philosophie des Cartesius auf die Ausbildung der des Spinoza Gehabt. Leipzig, 1817.
	Phil 6687.7	Roullier, A. Exposition physiologique des phénomènes du magnétisme animal. Paris, 1817.
	Phil 5258.7.3	Schubert, G.H. von. Altes und Neues aus dem Gebiet der innren Seelenkunde. Leipzig, 1817.
	Phil 8893.88	Schulze, G.E. Philosophische Tugendlehre. Göttingen, 1817.
	Phil 2266.41.2	Smith, Adam. The theory of moral sentiments. Philadelphia, 1817.
	Phil 2266.41	Smith, Adam. The theory of moral sentiments. v.1-2. Boston, 1817.
	Phil 193.30	Solger, K.W.F. Philosophische Gespräche. Berlin, 1817.
	Phil 7060.3	Spectriana. Paris, 1817.
	Phil 6968.8.5	Spurzheim, J.K. Observations...mind...insanity. London, 1817.

	Phil 3090.35	Baader, Franz von. Sur la notion du tems. Munic, 1818.
	Phil 1850.12.5	Bacon, Francis. Works. London, 1818. 12v.
	Phil 9341.7	Bennett, J. Letters to a young lady. Philadelphia, 1818.
Htn	Phil 9400.1.3*	Bernard, T. Comforts of old age. N.Y., 1818.
	Phil 4520.2.30	Biberg, N.F. In jus natuarae recentiorum stricturae. Diss. Upsaliae, 1818.
	Phil 2477.4.30	Bonald, L.G.A. Recherches philosophiques sur les premiers objets des connaissances morales. Paris, 1818. 2v.
	Phil 176.53	Bouterwek, F. Kleine schriften philosophichen. Bd.1. Göttingen, 1818.
	Phil 8692.5.7	Chalmers, Thomas. Series of discourses on the Christian revelation, viewed in connexion with modern astronomy. Hartford, 1818.
	Phil 8692.5.5	Chalmers, Thomas. Series of discourses on the Christian revelation, viewed in connexion with modern astronomy. N.Y., 1818. 2 pam.
	Phil 6673.2.15	Deleuze, J.P.F. Lettre à l'auteur d'un ouvrage intitué: superstitions et prestiges des philosophies du dix-huitième siècle. Paris, 1818.
	Phil 8584.3	Eschenmayer, C.A. Religionsphilosophie. v.1-3. Tübingen, 1818-24. 2v.
	Phil 8879.7	Eschenmayer, C.A.A. System der Moralphilosophie. Stuttgart, 1818.
	Phil 8879.8	Estlin, J.P. Familiar lectures on moral philosophy. London, 1818. 2v.
	Phil 5045.9	Fischhaber, G.C.F. Lehrbuch der Logik. Stuttgart, 1818.
	Phil 3260.33A	Fries, J.F. Handbuch der praktischen Philosophie oder der philosophischen Zwecklehre. Heidelberg, 1818-32. 2v.
	Phil 181.10.5	Gioja, M. Elementi di filosofia. Milano, 1818. 2v.
	Phil 8586.3	Gisborne, T. The testimony of natural theology to Christianity. London, 1818.
	Phil 3801.436	Grubbe, Samuel. Animadversiones in constructionem materiae Schellingianam. Pt.1-4. Upsaliae, 1818.
	Phil 6957.1	Hallaran, W.G. Practical observations, causes, cure insanity. Cork, 1818.
	Phil 5047.3.2	Hedge, Levi. Elements of logick. Boston, 1818.
	Phil 6317.14	Heinroth, D.F.C.A. Lehrbuch der Storungen des Seelenlehre. v.1-2. Leipzig, 1818.
	Phil 9347.12	Higford, William. Institutions: or Advice to his grandson. London, 1818.
	Phil 5049.2	Jardine, George. Outlines. Philosophy. Education. Logic. Glasgow, 1818.
Htn	Phil 3480.45.3*	Kant, Immanuel. Critik der practischen Vernunft. 5. Aufl. Leipzig, 1818.
	Phil 3480.30.2.10	Kant, Immanuel. Critik der reinen Vernunft. 6. Aufl. Leipzig, 1818.
	Phil 8635.7	Kast, J. Ernster Blick. Würzburg, 1818.
	Phil 185.1	Keratry, A.H. Inductions. Paris, 1818.
	Phil 185.3.5	Keyserlingh, H. von. Metaphysik. Heidelberg, 1818.
	Phil 6680.6.3	Kluge, C.A.F. Versuch einer Darstellung dis animalischen Magnetismus. Berlin, 1818.
	Phil 6680.8	Kluge, G. Zhivotnyi magnitizm. Sankt Peterberg, 1818.
	Phil 8411.25	Krug, W.T. Geschmackslehre oder Asthetik. Wien, 1818. 2v.
	Phil 3528.35.5	Krug, Wilhelm Traugott. System der praktischen Philosophie. Wien, 1818.
	Phil 5545.171	Murden, J.R. The art of memory. N.Y., 1818.
	Phil 7060.9	Oldenburg, F. Om gjenfard eller gjengangere. Kjobenhavn, 1818.
	Phil 9245.6	Oliver, B.L. Hints for an essay on the pursuit of happiness. Chicago, 1818.
	Phil 5585.8	Redern, S.E. de. Des modes accidentels de nos perceptions. Paris, 1818.
	Phil 8597.22	Religio universalis et naturalis. Paris, 1818.
Htn	Phil 3800.250.5*	Schelling, F.W.J. von. Rede über das Verhältniss der bildenden Künste zu der Natur. Upsala, 1818.
	Phil 4803.799.20	Śniadecki, Jan. Pisma rozmaite. Wilno, 1818-22. 4v.
	Phil 6968.8	Spurzheim, J.K. Beobashtungen über den Wahnsinn. Hamburg, 1818.
Htn	Phil 2275.34.6*	Stewart, D. Elements of the philosophy of the human mind. N.Y., 1818. 2v.
	Phil 2275.34.5	Stewart, D. Elements of the philosophy of the human mind. N.Y., 1818. 2v.
	Phil 8598.20.2	Sumner, J.B. A treatise...records of the creation. London, 1818. 2v.
	Phil 8674.4	Tyerman, D. Essays on the wisdom of God. London, 1818.
	Phil 8595.16.27.7	Watson, R. Two apologies, one for Christianity. London, 1818.
	Phil 6692.6.5	Wendler, C.A. De magnetismi animalis efficacia rite diiudicanda. Lipsiae, 1818.

1819

	Phil 6111.22	Burdach, K.F. Bau und Leben des Gehirns. Leipzig, 1819-26. 3v.
	Phil 9342.2.10	Chapone, H. (Mrs.). Letters on the improvement of the mind. London, 1819.
Htn	Phil 9342.2.3*	Chapone, H. (Mrs.). Letters on the improvement of the mind. v.1-2. Hagerstown, 1819.
	Phil 2523.31.2	Compagnoni, G. Saggio di un trattato di morale. Milano, 1819.
	Phil 6012.3	Cooke, Thomas. A practical and familiar view of science of physiognomy. London, 1819.
	Phil 6673.2	Deleuze, J.P.F. Histoire critique du magnétisme animal. Paris, 1819. 2v.
	Phil 8628.4	Drew, Samuel. An original essay on the immateriality and immortality of the human soul. London, 1819.
	Phil 804.2.3	Enfield, W. History of philosophy. London, 1819. 2v.
	Phil 805.2.5	Fries, J.F. Beträge zur Geschichte der Philosophie. Heidelberg, 1819.
	Phil 3801.437	Groos, Friedrich. Die Schellingische Gottes- und s freiheits - Lehre. Tübingen, 1819.
	Phil 5247.5	Haslam, J. Sound mind. London, 1819.
	Phil 3528.40.5	Krug, Wilhelm Traugott. Fundamentalphilosophie. 2. Aufl. Züllichan, 1819.
	Phil 2725.2.57	Lamennais, F.R. de. Essai sur l'indifférence en matière de religion. Paris, 1819-20. 2v.
	Phil 3552.68	Leibniz, Gottfried Wilhelm. Exposition sur la religion. Paris, 1819.
	Phil 186.7	Lemoine, J.J. Les trois voyageurs. Paris, 1819.
	Phil 6681.11	Lombard, A. Les dangers du magnétisme animal. Paris, 1819.
	Phil 8887.20	More, H. Moral sketches. Boston, 1819.
	Phil 8887.20.3	More, H. Moral sketches. London, 1819.
	Phil 8414.6	Nüsslein, F.A. Lehrbuch der Kunstwissenschaft zum Gebrance bei Vorlesungen. Landshut, 1819.
	Phil 8595.15.4.10	Paine, Thomas. Theological works. London, 1819.
Htn	Phil 2205.30.17*	Paley, W. Natural theology. Hallowell, 1819.
	Phil 2205.30.18	Paley, W. Natural theology. Hallowell, 1819.
	Phil 2805.30.14	Pascal, Blaise. Les provinciales. Paris, 1819. 2v.
	Phil 2805.30.2	Pascal, Blaise. Les provinciales. Paris, 1819. 2v.
	Phil 5057.3	Reinhold, Ernest. Versuch einer Begrundung und neuen Darstellung der logischen Formen. Leipzig, 1819.
	Phil 6688.25	Sarrazin de Montferrier, A.A.V. Der principes et des procédés du magnetisme animal. Paris, 1819. 2v.
	Phil 3460.87	Schlichtegroll, A.H.F. Friedrich Heinrich Jacobi. München, 1819.
Htn	Phil 3808.33*	Schopenhauer, Arthur. Die Welt als Wille und Vorstellung. Leipzig, 1819.
	Phil 3850.13.42	Schulze, G.E. Psychische Anthropologie. 2. Aufl. Göttingen, 1819.
	Phil 193.71	Sketch of a new theory of man. Vivey, 1819.
	Phil 818.16	Snell, P.L. Kurzer Abriss der Geschichte der Philosophie. Giessen, 1819. 2v.
	Phil 5058.44	Storchenau, S. Institutiones logicae. Venetiis, 1819.
	Phil 193.38	Storchenau, S. Metaphysicae. v.1-4. Venice, 1819-1820. 2v.
Htn	Phil 8894.25.5*	Torrey, Jesse, Jr. The moral instructor. 2d ed. Albany, 1819.
	Phil 106.1.6	Voltaire, Francois Marie Arouet de. The philosophical dictionary. v.1-2. London, 1819.
	Phil 197.1.10	Wagner, J. Religion, Wissenschaft, Kunst und Staat in ihren Gegenseitigen Verhältnissen. Erlangen, 1819.
	Phil 8595.16.27.8	Watson, R. Watson refuted: being an answer to the apology for the Bible. London, 1819.
Htn	Phil 5062.4.12*	Watts, S. Logic. 6th American ed. Boston, 1819.

1820

	Phil 3100.52	Beneke, F.E. Erfahrungsseelenlehre als Grundlage alles Wissens in ihren Hauptzügen Dargestellt. Berlin, 1820.
	Phil 1870.10	Berkeley, G. Works. London, 1820. 3v.
	Phil 9400.1.4	Bernard, T. Comforts of old age. London, 1820.
	Phil 176.53.7	Bouterwek, F. Lehrbuch der philosophischen Vorkenntnisse. Göttingen, 1820.
	Phil 176.53.2	Bouterwek, F. Lehrbuch der philosophischen Wissenschaften. Göttingen, 1820. 2v.
	Phil 1890.30	Brown, T. Lectures on philosophy of human mind. Edinburgh, 1820. 4v.
	Phil 1890.30.7	Brown, T. Sketch of a system of human mind. Edinburgh, 1820.
	Phil 8691.7	Buckland, William. Vindiciae geologicae. Oxford, 1820.
	Phil 176.43	Burdon, W. Materials for thinking. London, 1820. 2v.
	Phil 177.2.5	Calker, F. Urgesetzlehre der wahren Guten und Schöne. Berlin, 1820.
	Phil 8952.1	Chalmers, T. Application of Christianity to...ordinary affairs of life. Glasgow, 1820.
	Phil 2515.2.53	Charron, P. De la sagesse. Paris, 1820-24. 3v.
	Phil 1925.31.55	Cudworth, R. The true intellectual system of the universe. London, 1820. 4v.
	Phil 8890.27	Everything bought with a price, or Moral commerce. Salem, 1820.
	Phil 5245.2	Fearn, J. First lines of the human mind. London, 1820.
Htn	Phil 3246.77*	Fichte, Johann Gottlieb. Staatslehre. Berlin, 1820.
	Phil 8585.5	The first day in heaven. London, 1820.
	Phil 7060.62	Frazer, John. Deuteroskopia; or, A brief discourse concerning the second sight. Edinburgh, 1820
	Phil 8740.2	Goodale, E. Extracts concerning the importance of religion and public worship. Hallowell, 1820.
	Phil 5047.29	Hillebrand, J. Grundriss der Logik. Heidelberg, 1820.
	Phil 2648.30.10	Holbach, Paul Henri T. Système de la nature. Paris, 1820. 2v.
	Phil 2050.3A	Hume, David. Private correspondence...1761-76. London, 1820.
	Phil 3480.40	Kant, Immanuel. Anthropologie. Königsberg, 1820.
	Phil 3552.69.30	Leibniz, Gottfried Wilhelm. System der Theologie. Mainz, 1820.
	Phil 7054.181.15	Leslie, John. Nature and super-nature. Aberdeen, 1820.
	Phil 2115.60.2	Locke, J. Essay for the understanding of St. Paul's epistles. Boston, 1820.
Htn	Phil 2115.60*	Locke, J. Essay for the understanding of St. Paul's epistles. Boston, 1820.
	Phil 1865.191	Nuñez, T. Sistema de la ciencia social. Salamanca, 1820.
	Phil 8890.11	Penrose, John M.A. An inquiry chiefly on principles of religion. London, 1820.
	Phil 6685.9.5	Puységur, Armand Marie Jacques de Chastenet. Mémoires pour servir à l'histoire et à l'etablissement du magnétisme animal. 3. éd. Paris, 1820.

1820 - cont.

	Phil 3778.41	Reinhold, K.L. Die alte Frage: was ist die Wahrheit? Altona, 1820.
	Phil 193.28	Sigwart, H.C.W. Handbuch der theoretischen Philosophie. Tübingen, 1820.
	Phil 8598.11	Slack, David B. The celestial magnet. Providence, R.I., 1820-21. 2 pam.
	Phil 9179.9.4	Taylor, Isaac. Advice to the teens. Boston, 1820.
	Phil 819.1.3	Tennemann, W.G. Grundriss der Geschichte der Philosophie. Leipzig, 1820.
	Phil 5062.14	Wyttenback, D. Praecepta philosophiae logicae. Hallae, 1820.

1821

	Phil 8401.2.5	Alison, Archibald. Essays on the nature and principles of taste. Hartford, 1821.
	Phil 1865.18	Bentham, Jeremy. Principios de la ciencia social. Salamanca, 1821.
	Phil 5751.1.5	Bockshammer, G.F. Die Freyheit des menschlichen Willens. Stuttgart, 1821.
	Phil 5241.14	Bonstetten, C.V. de. Études de l'homme. Genève, 1821. 2v.
	Phil 2725.2.68	Bouchitté, Louis Herve. Réfutation de la doctrine. Paris, 1821.
	Phil 177.2	Calker, F. Propädeutik der Philosophie. Bonn, 1821.
	Phil 4075.79.10	Cardano, Girolamo. Vita di Girolamo Cardano. Milano, 1821.
	Phil 9120.10	Cederschiöld, F. Allmän inledning till apriorisk. Lund, 1821.
	Phil 8952.1.2	Chalmers, T. Application of Christianity to...ordinary affairs of life. Glasgow, 1821.
	Phil 8952.1.5	Chalmers, T. Application of Christianity to...ordinary affairs of life. N.Y., 1821.
	Phil 8952.1.6	Chalmers, T. Application of Christianity to...ordinary affairs of life. 3d American ed. Hartford, 1821.
Htn	Phil 1930.2.30*	Channing, William E. A discourse on religion. Boston, 1821.
	Phil 9420.2.7	Cogan, T. Philosophical treatise...passions. v.1-2. Boston, 1821.
	Phil 2493.30.2	Condillac, Etienne Bonnot. Logique. Paris, 1821.
	Phil 6673.4.15	Du Potet, J. de S. Exposé des expériences sur le magnétisme. Paris, 1821.
	Phil 9345.1	Fathers gift to his son. N.Y., 1821.
X Cg	Phil 9346.6.3	Gregory, John. A father's legacy to his daughters. Albany, 1821.
	Phil 4508.2	Hammarsköld, Lorenzo. Historiska antickningar rörande fortgången och utvecklingen af det philosophiska studium i Sverige. Stockholm, 1821.
Htn	Phil 3425.70.1*	Hegel, Georg Wilhelm Friedrich. Grundlinien der Philosophie des Rechts. Berlin, 1821.
	Phil 3428.30.5	Herbart, J.F. Lehrbuch zur Einleitung in die Philosophie. 2. Aufl. Königsberg, 1821.
	Phil 2648.30.12	Holbach, Paul Henri T. Système de la nature. Paris, 1821.
	Phil 1535.19	Institutionum philosophicarum cursus. v.2-3. Besancon, 1821. 2v.
Htn	Phil 3480.59.20*	Kant, Immanuel. Vorlesungen über die Metaphysik. Erfurt, 1821.
	Phil 2115.19	Locke, J. Oeuvres philosophiques de Locke. Paris, 1821-25. 7v.
	Phil 5252.5	Martin, T. Zetemata dianoetika. Liverpool, 1821.
	Phil 8887.6.25	Mason, J. Peri tou gnōthi sauton. Korphoi, 1821.
	Phil 8887.6.9	Mason, J. A treatise on self-knowledge. London, 1821.
	Phil 8637.3	Mendelsohn, M. Phädon oder über die Unsterblichkeit der Seele. Berlin, 1821.
	Phil 3625.1.39.9	Mendelssohn, Moses. Phédon. Amsterdam, 1821.
	Phil 6685.1	Passavant, J.K. Untersungen und der Lebensmagnetismus. Frankfurt, 1821.
	Phil 8610.821	Philanthropos [pseud.]. The character of a priest. London, 1821. 2 pam.
	Phil 5910.5	Pamphlet vol. Phrenology pamphlets. London, 1821. 3 pam.
	Phil 1122.2.10	Ritter, Heinrich. Geschichte der jonischen Philosophie. Berlin, 1821.
	Phil 8893.83	Salat, Jakob. Die Moralphilosophie. 3. Aufl. München, 1821.
	Phil 5768.14	Sartorius, E. Die Lutherische Lehre vom Unvermögen des Freyen Willens zur Höheren. Göttingen, 1821.
	Phil 3805.30.3	Schleiermacher, Friedrich. Uber die Religion. Berlin, 1821.
	Phil 2275.34.11	Stewart, D. Elements of the philosophy of the human mind. v.1-2. Boston, 1821.
	Phil 9035.9	Taylor, S. Character essential to success in life. Canandaigua, 1821.
	Phil 300.3	Tieftrunk, J.H. Das Weltall nach menschlicher Ansicht. Halle, 1821.
	Phil 9362.4.6	The whole duty of woman. n.p., 1821.

1822

	Phil 9245.42	The art of employing time to the greatest advantage. London, 1822.
	Phil 3090.42	Baader, Franz von. Fermenta cognitionis. pt. 1-6. Berlin, 1822-25. 5v.
	Phil 5241.10	Beasley, F. A search of truth. Philadelphia, 1822.
	Phil 3100.42	Beneke, F.E. Grundlegung zur Physik der Sitten. Berlin, 1822.
	Phil 3246.216	Bergbom, F. De ortu et indole idealismi Fichtii. Diss. Aboae, 1822.
	Phil 1890.40.2	Brown, T. Inquiry into relation of cause and effect. Andover, 1822.
	Phil 1890.30.2	Brown, T. Lectures on philosophy of human mind. Andover, 1822. 3v.
	Phil 8876.38	Browne, I.H. Essays on subjects of important enquiry. London, 1822.
	Phil 5042.1	Calker, J.F.A. Denklehre oder Logik und Dialektik...Geschichte und Literatur. Bonn, 1822.
	Phil 9342.2.4	Chapone, H. (Mrs.). Letters on the improvement of the mind. London, 1822.
	Phil 5922.4.5	Combe, George. Essays on phrenology. Philadelphia, 1822.
	Phil 3260.39	Fries, J.F. Die mathematische Naturphilosophie. Heidelberg, 1822.
	Phil 181.4	Genlis, S.F. de. Les diners baron D'Holbach. Paris, 1822.
	Phil 806.1	Gerando, J.M. de. Histoire comparée des systèmes de philosophie. Paris, 1822-23. 4v.
	Phil 5046.17	Gerlach, G.W. Grundriss der Logik. 2e Aufl. Halle, 1822.

1822 - cont.

Phil 4120.1.30   Gioja, Melchiorre. Elementi di filosofia ad uso de'Giovanetti. Milano, 1822. 2v.

Phil 4120.1.40   Gioja, Melchiorre. Ideologia. Milano, 1822-23. 2v.

Phil 9346.6   Gregory, John. A father's legacy to his daughters. London, 1822.

Phil 2030.4   Grote, George. Analysis of the influence of natural religion on the temporal happiness of mankind. London, 1822.

Phil 6677.18   Hénin de Cuvillers, E.T. Exposition critique du système et de la doctrine mystique des magnétistes. Paris, 1822.

Phil 3428.40   Herbart, J.F. De attentionis. Regiomonti, 1822.

Phil 3460.30.2   Jacobi, F.H. Von den göttlichen Dingen und ihrer Offenbarung. Leipzig, 1822.

Phil 2675.5   Jakob, L.H. von. Essais philosophiques sur l'homme. Saint-Pétersbourg, 1822.

Phil 8887.6.9.5   Mason, J. A treatise on self-knowledge. 3. ed. Boston, 1822.

Phil 8887.19   Morgan, T.C. Sketches of the philosophy of morals. London, 1822.

Phil 2205.30.4   Paley, W. Natural theology. London, 1822.

Phil 8705.8   Penn, G. A comparative estimate of the mineral and mosaical geology. London, 1822.

Phil 2240.12   Reid, Thomas. Works. N.Y., 1822. 3v.

Phil 348.2   Reinhold, C.E. Grundzüge...Erkenntnisslehre. Schleswig, 1822.

Phil 8893.20   Sprague, W.B. Letters on practical subjects. Hartford, 1822.

Phil 193.34.3   Steffens, H. Anthropologie. Breslau, 1822. 2v.

Phil 2275.34.15   Stewart, D. Elements of the philosophy of the human mind. v.1-2. Albany, 1822.

Phil 2275.65   Stewart, D. A general view of the progress of...philosophy. Boston, 1822.

Phil 6128.20   Swan, Joseph. Observations on nervous system. London, 1822.

Phil 6692.9   Wesermann, N.M. Der Magnetismus und die allgemeine Weltsprache. Creveld, 1822.

Phil 8897.20   Witherspoon, J. Lectures on moral philosophy. Philadelphia, 1822.

1823

Phil 7060.77   Alderson, J. Essay on apparitions. London, 1823.

Phil 5545.26   Art of memory. London, 1823.

Phil 8876.6   Bartlett, J. Aphorisms. Boston, 1823.

Phil 1860.50.13   Beattie, James. Essay on the nature and immutability of truth. London, 1823.

Phil 3100.43   Beneke, F.E. Schutzschrift für meine Grundlegung zur Physik der Sitten. Leipzig, 1823.

Phil 1865.50.1*   Bentham, Jeremy. Introduction to the principles of morals and legislation. London, 1823. 2v.

Phil 1865.50   Bentham, Jeremy. Introduction to the principles of morals and legislation. v.1-2. London, 1823.

Phil 1865.60.5*   Bentham, Jeremy. Not Paul, but Jesus. London, 1823.

Phil 7085.7   Bertrand, A. Traité du somnabulisme. Paris, 1823.

Phil 4520.2.32   Biber, N.F. Notionum ethicarum quas formales dicunt, dialexis critica. Diss. Pt.1-2. Upsaliae, 1823-24.

Phil 5041.21   Braniss, C.J. Die Logik...Verhaltniss zur philosophische Geschichte betrachter. Berlin, 1823.

Phil 2480.10   Cabanis, P.J.G. Oeuvres. Paris, 1823. 5v.

Phil 5921.2.5   Combe, A. Observations on Dr. Barclay's ojections. Edinburgh, 1823.

Phil 6674.6   Entretiens sur le magnétisme animal. Paris, 1823.

Phil 9530.5.5   Franklin, B. Hē epistēmē tou kalou richardou. Paris, 1823.

Phil 3260.40   Fries, J.F Lehren der Liebe des Glaubens. Heidelberg, 1823.

Phil 9528.3.5A   Gellert, C.F. Instructions from a father to his son. Boston, 1823.

Phil 5047.3.5   Hedge, Levi. Elements of logick. Boston, 1823.

Phil 7060.83   Jarvis, T.M. Accredited ghost stories. London, 1823.

Phil 3492.17   Kératry, A.H. de. Examen philosophique des Considérations sur le sentiment du sublime et du beau. Paris, 1823.

Phil 5627.86   Köllner, G. Histoire de la vie et de la conversion de Guillaume Köllner. Genève, 1823.

Phil 3528.30   Krug, Wilhelm Traugott. System der theoretischen Philosophie. Königsberg, 1823-33. 3v.

Phil 2115.34.15   Locke, J. Essay concerning human understanding. London, 1823. 3v.

Phil 2115.62   Locke, J. A paraphrase and notes on epistle of St. Paul. London, 1823.

Phil 2115.11   Locke, J. Works. London, 1823. 10v.

Phil 8413.6   M'Dermot, Martin. A critical dissertation on nature and principles of taste. London, 1823.

Phil 8962.7   Moren, Thorbjörn. Sedeläran i sammandrag. Stockholm, 1823.

Phil 3665.2.31   Naumann, M.E.A. Über die Grenzen zwischen Philosophie und Naturwissenschaften. Leipzig, 1823.

Phil 2205.13   Paley, W. Works. London, 1823. 5v.

Phil 8890.46   Palmer, E. Principles of nature. London, 1823.

Phil 8417.3   Quatremère de Quincy, Antoine C. Essai sur la nature, le but et les moyens de l'imitation dans les beaux-arts. Paris, 1823.

Phil 192.49   Richter, H. Anrede bey Eröffnung von Vorlesungen über Metaphysik. Leipzig, 1823.

Phil 3850.13.31   Schulze, G.E. Encyklopaedie der philosophischen Wissenschaften. Göttingen, 1823.

Phil 8893.18   Speece, C. The mountaineer. Staunton, 1823.

Phil 8598.58   Steffens, H. Von der falschen Theologie und der wahren Glauben. Breslau, 1823.

Phil 5060.2   Ufford, H.G. Elementary treatise on logic. N.Y., 1823.

Phil 8897.12   Wette, W.M.L. de. Vorlesungen über die Sittenlehre. v. 1-2. Berlin, 1823-24.

1824

Phil 4351.4.15   Alvarado, Francisco. Cartas criticas. Madrid, 1824-25. 5v.

Phil 175.6.9   Ancillon, F. Über Glauben und Wissen in der Philosophie. Berlin, 1824.

Phil 175.30   Azais, H. Cours de philosophie générale. Paris, 1824. 8v.

Phil 1850.12.20   Bacon, Francis. Works. London, 1824. 10v.

Phil 1865.40.2*   Bentham, Jeremy. The book of fallacies. London, 1824.

Phil 3805.158   Braniss, C.J. Über Schleiermachers Glaubenslehre. Berlin, 1824.

1824 - cont.

Phil 6990.21.3   A brief disclosure to the people of England of the liberality of the Irish Roman Catholics. London, 1824.

Phil 1890.30.3   Brown, T. Lectures on philosophy of human mind. Philadelphia, 1824. 3v.

Phil 5811.9   Buchan, P. Scriptural and philosophical arguments. Peterhead, 1824.

Phil 176.66   Burton, Asa. Essays. Portland, 1824.

Phil 2480.30.5   Cabanis, P.J.G. Rapports du physique et du moral de l'homme. Paris, 1824. 3v.

Phil 2520.16   Descartes, René. Oeuvres. Paris, 1824-26. 11v.

Phil 8878.43   Droz, J. De la philosophie morale. 2e éd. Paris, 1824.

Phil 3246.55   Fichte, Johann Gottlieb. Reden an die deutsche Nation. Leipzig, 1824.

Phil 3260.30   Fries, J.F. System der Metaphysik. Heidelberg, 1824.

Phil 4120.1.45   Gioja, Melchiorre. Esercizio logico sugli errori d'ideologia. Milano, 1824.

Phil 8881.11.2   Gisborne, T. An enquiry into the duties of men. London, 1824. 2v.

Phil 5817.1   Hancock, T. Essay on instinct. London, 1824.

Phil 5757.15   Heiberg, J.L. Om den menneskelige Frihed. Kiel, 1824.

Phil 3428.47   Herbart, J.F. Psychologie als Wissenschaft. Königsberg, 1824. 2v.

Phil 7060.17   Hibbert, S. Sketches of the philosophy of apparitions. Edinburgh, 1824.

Phil 2050.194   Howitz, Franz G. Determinismen eller Hume imod Kant. Kjøbenhavn, 1824.

Phil 3480.85.6.15   Kant, Immanuel. Von der Macht des Gemüths durch den blossen Vorsatz seiner krankhaften Gefühle Meister zu seyn. Leipzig, 1824?

Phil 3480.85.9   Kant, Immanuel. Von der Macht des Gemüths durch den blossen Vorsatz seiner krankhaften Gefühle Meister zu seyn. 2. Aufl. Leipzig, 1824.

Phil 5050.5   Kiesewetter, J.G.C.C. Grundriss einer allgemeinen Logik. Leipzig, 1824-25. 2v.

Phil 3492.34.4   Kiesewetter, J.G.K.C. Darstellung der wichtigsten Wahrheiten der kritischen Philosophie. Berlin, 1824.

Phil 5251.2   Lallebasque. Introduzione alla filosofia naturale di pensiero. Lugano, 1824.

Phil 9351.15   Lanfear, (Mrs.). Letters to young ladies on their entrance into the world. London, 1824.

Phil 2115.65   Locke, J. A commonplace book to the Holy Bible. London, 1824.

Phil 2115.35   Locke, J. Essay concerning human understanding. v.1-2. N.Y., 1824.

Phil 8887.6.10   Mason, J. Self-knowledge. London, 1824.

Phil 8595.15.2   Paine, Thomas. Theological works. London, 1824.

Phil 2205.30.14   Paley, W. Natural theology. Trenton, N.J., 1824.

Phil 2205.40.10   Paley, W. Principles of moral and political philosophy. N.Y., 1824.

Phil 6685.3   Petri, J.G. Der thierische magnetismus. Tlmenau, 1824.*

Phil 2240.32   Reid, Thomas. An inquiry into the human mind. N.Y., 1824.

Phil 5057.12   Ritter, Heinrich. Abriss der philosophischen Logik. Berlin, 1824.

Phil 6990.22   Romagne, M. l'abbe de. Dictionnaire historique des miracles. Paris, 1824.

Phil 6967.14.5   Rostan, L. Untersuchungen über die Erweichung des Gehirns. 2. Aufl. Leipzig, 1824.

Phil 3850.13.32   Schulze, G.E. Encyklopaedie der philosophischen Wissenschaften. Göttingen, 1824.

Phil 8595.16.21   Scott, Thomas. Treatises on various theological subjects. Middletown, Conn., 1824. 5v.

Phil 106.1.7   Voltaire, Francois Marie Arouet de. A philosophical dictionary. London, 1824. 6v.

Phil 8595.16.27.10   Watson, R. Apologies for Christianity and the Bible. London, 1824.

Phil 1865.177   Wells, D.B. Saint Paul vindicated, being Part I of a reply...not Paul, but Jesus. Cambridge, 1824.

Htn   Phil 3801.876*   Wendell, Johann A. Grundzüge und Kritik der Philosophien Kant's, Fichte's und Schelling's 2. 2. Aufl. Coburg, 1824.

Phil 3504.6.2   Wirgman, T. Principles Kantesian...philosophy. London, 1824.

1825

Phil 9060.1   Azaïs, P.H. Des compensations dans destinées humaines. Paris, 1825. 3v.

Phil 1850.34.2   Bacon, Francis. The books of Lord Verulam. London, 1825.

Phil 1850.13   Bacon, Francis. Works. v.1-16. London, 1825-34. 17v.

Phil 3100.65   Beneke, F.E. Psychologische Skizzen. Göttingen, 1825-27. 2v.

Phil 8876.28   Brandis, J.D. Überhumanes Leben. Schleswig, 1825.

Phil 5400.1   Burgess, S.W. Historical illustrations of the origin and progress of the passions. London, 1825. 2v.

Htn   Phil 1930.3.30*   Coleridge, S.T. Aids to reflection. London, 1825.

Phil 6673.2.5   Deleuze, J.P.F. Instruction pratique sur le magnétisme animal. Paris, 1825.

Phil 5813.4   Desmoulins, A. Anatomie des systèmes nerveux des animaux. pt.1-2. Atlas. Paris, 1825.

Phil 2523.32   Destutt de Tracy, A.L.C. Élémens d'idéologie. Paris, 1825-27. 5v.

Phil 8878.13.8   Dodsley, R. Economia della vita umana. N.Y., 1825.

Phil 8878.13.3.25   Dodsley, R. The economy of human life. Chisnick, 1825.

Phil 804.8   Ertsei, D. Philosophia historiaja. Debreczen, 1825.

Phil 3270.5.79   Feder, J.G.H. G.J.H. Feder's Lebens Natur und Grundsätze. Leipzig, 1825.

Phil 3246.35   Fichte, Johann Gottlieb. Die Bestimmung der Menschen. Berlin, 1825.

Htn   Phil 3801.392*   Fick, Georg Karl. Vergleichende Darstellung der philosophen Systeme von Kant, Fichte, Schelling. Heilbronn, 1825.

Phil 2725.2.69   Flottes, J.B.M. M. l'abbé F. de Lamennais réfuté. Paris, 1825.

Phil 1112.4   Hammarsköld, L. Grunddragen af philosophiens historia. 1a afd. Stockholm, 1825.

Phil 9010.23   Henry, Charlton. An inquiry into the consistency of popular amusements. Charleston, S.C., 1825.

Phil 7060.17.2   Hibbert, S. Sketches of the philosophy of apparitions. London, 1825.

Phil 4575.10   Höijer, B.C.H. Samlade skrifter. Stockholm, 1825-27. 5v.

Phil 3460.70   Jacobi, F.H. Jacobis auserlesener Briefwechsel. Leipzig, 1825. 2v.

Phil 3525.45   Krause, K.C.F. Abriss des Systemes der Philosophie. Göttingen, 1825.

Phil 2493.87.5   Laromiguiere, P. Paradoxes de Condillac. Paris, 1825.

1825 - cont.

Phil 2115.50   Locke, J. The conduct of the understanding. Boston, 1825.
Phil 2115.35.5 Locke, J. Essay concerning human understanding. 25th ed. London, 1825.
Phil 8889.2.2   Oxenstjerna, J.T. Pensées, réflexions et maximes morales. Paris, 1825. 2v.
Phil 2205.40.8.5 Paley, W. Principles of moral and political philosophy. 11th American ed. Boston, 1825.
Phil 2205.11   Paley, W. Works. London, 1825. 5v.
NEDL Phil 2805.42.7 Pascal, Blaise. Thoughts on religion. London, 1825.
Phil 3778.90   Reinhold, E. Karl Leonhard Reinholds Leben. Jena, 1825.
Phil 5057.5   Richter, Heinrich. Über den Gegenstand und den Umfang der Logik. Leipzig, 1825.
Phil 3625.1.44 Samuels, M. Memoirs of Moses Mendelssohn. London, 1825.
Htn Phil 3800.250.10* Schelling, F.W.J. von. Über das Verhältniss der bildenden Künste zu der Natur. Wien, 1825.
Phil 5258.7   Schubert, G.H. von. Altes und Neues aus dem Gebiet der innren Seelenkunde. Leipzig, 1825-44. 5v.
Phil 8598.26   Scot, David. Discourses on...subjects of natural and revealed religion. Edinburgh, 1825.
Phil 5938.6.23 Spurzheim, Johann Gaspar. Phrenology. London, 1825?
Phil 9179.1.5   Taylor, A. Hinton. Reciprocal duties of parents and children. Boston, 1825.
Phil 7060.84   Welby, H. Signs before death. London, 1825.

1826

Phil 281.6.5   Ayais, H. Explication universelle. Paris, 1826. 2v.
Phil 3090.38   Baader, Franz von. Über die Freiheit der Intelligenz. München, 1826.
Phil 3090.39   Baader, Franz von. Von Segen und Fluch der Creatur. Strassburg, 1826.
Phil 5135.1   Bailey, S. Essays...opinions. London, 1826.
Phil 6951.8   Bayle, A.L.J. Traité des maladies du cerveau. Paris, 1826.
Phil 3100.53   Beneke, F.E. Das Verhältniss von Seele und Leib. Göttingen, 1826.
Phil 6669.1   Bertrand, A. Du magnetisme animal en France. Paris, 1826.
Phil 7076.12   Bertrand, Alexandre Jacques François. Extase. Paris, 1826.
Phil 3110.47   Böhme, J. Clef, ou Explication des divers points et termes principaux. Paris, 1826.
Phil 8951.9   Brown, William L. Comparative view of Christianity. Edinburgh, 1826. 2v.
Phil 6672.2   Chardel, C. Esquisse de la nature humaine. Paris, 1826.
Phil 5922.4.25 Combe, George. Elements of phrenology. Philadelphia, 1826.
Phil 5922.4.15 Combe, George. Letter...Francis Jeffrey. Edinburgh, 1826-29. 2 pam.
Phil 8878.8   Dewar, D. Elements of moral philosophy. London, 1826. 2v.
Phil 6673.10   Dupau, Jean A. Lettres physiologiques...sur le magnétisme. Paris, 1826.
Phil 9575.7   Ebersberg, Luise. Der Mensch und das Geld. Wien, 1826.
Phil 3245.32   Fichte, Immanuel Hermann. Sätze zur Vorschule der Theologie. Stuttgart, 1826.
Phil 8881.6.5   Gerando, J.M. Du perfectionnement moral. Paris, 1826. 2v.
Phil 4570.1.20 Grubbe, Samuel. Bidrag till utredandet af samhällslärans grundbegrepp. 1. delen. Upsala, 1826.
Phil 182.17.15 Hillebrand, J. Lehrbuch der theoretischen Philosophie. Mainz, 1826.
Phil 5047.26   Hinrichs, H.F.W. Grundlinien der Philosophie der Logik. Halle, 1826. 2 pam.
Phil 2648.33   Holbach, Paul Henri T. De la cruauté religieuse. Paris, 1826.
Phil 2050.10   Hume, David. Philosophical works. Edinburgh, 1826. 4v.
Phil 8685.4   Jäsche, G.B. Der Pantheismus. Berlin, 1826-32. 3v.
Phil 7068.36   Kerner, J. Eine Erscheinung aus dem Nachtgebiete der Natur. Stuttgart, 1826.
Phil 9351.13   The ladies' companion...politeness of manners. 2d. ed. Brookfield, 1826.
Phil 811.1   Laurent, P.M. Résumé de l'histoire de la philosophie. Paris, 1826.
Phil 8887.6.12 Mason, J. A treatise on self knowledge. 4th ed. Boston, 1826.
Phil 8887.7.2   Mather, C. Essays to do good. Dover, 1826.
Phil 6682.19   Mialle, S. Exposé par ordre alphabétique des cures. Paris, 1826.
Htn Phil 7060.20* Müller, J. Über die phantastischen Gesichteserscheinungen. Coblenz, 1826.
Phil 400.82   Mussmann, J.G. De idealismo, seu philosophia ideali. Diss. Berolini, 1826.
NEDL Phil 9558.13 Opie, Amelia A. (Mrs.). Illustrations of lying, in all its branches. 2. ed. Boston, 1826.
Phil 9420.11   Pensieri di un solitario. Torino, 1826.
Phil 5057.7   Rösling, C.L. Die Lehren der reinen Logik. Ulm, 1826.
Phil 3805.10   Schleiermacher, Friedrich. Sämmtliche Werke. Berlin, 1826-64. 29v.
Phil 3850.13.44 Schulze, G.E. Psychische Anthropologie. Göttingen, 1826.
Phil 6128.5   Spurzheim, J.K. The anatomy of the brain. London, 1826.
Phil 5938.6.24 Spurzheim, Johann Gaspar. Phrenology. pt.1. London, 1826.
Phil 9220.1   Staudlin, C.F. Geschichte der Vorst...Freundschaft. Hannover, 1826.
Phil 623.12   Staudlin, C.F. Geschichte des Naturalismus. Göttingen, 1826.
Phil 2520.172.5 Thomas, A.L. Eulogy of Descartes. Cheltenham, 1826.
Phil 4260.35   Vico, G.B. Principi di una scienza nuova. Napoli, 1826.
Phil 6971.2   Voisin, F. Des causes...maladies mentales. Paris, 1826.

1827

Phil 5400.36   Alibert, J.L. Physiologie des passions. 2e éd. Paris, 1827. 2v.
Phil 3090.37   Baader, Franz von. Vorlesungen...über religiöse Philosophie. München, 1827.
Htn Phil 5041.37* Bentham, G. Outline of a new system of logic. London, 1827.
Phil 8626.6   Bolzano, B. Athanasia oder Gründe für die Unsterblichkeit der Seele. Sulzbach, 1827.
Phil 4515.48   Boström, C.J. De nexu rerum cum Deo ex ratione pantheismi positiones. Upsaliae, 1827.
Phil 1890.30.6 Brown, T. Treatise on the philosophy of human mind. Cambridge, 1827. 2v.
Phil 1900.35   Butler, Joseph. Analogy of religion. Cambridge, 1827.

1827 - cont.

Phil 1900.60.15 Butler, Joseph. Sermons. Cambridge, 1827.
Phil 1900.9.2   Butler, Joseph. Works. v.1-2. Cambridge, 1827.
Phil 2402.3   Carove, F.M. Philosophie in Frankreich. Göttingen, 1827. 2v.
Phil 9342.2.8   Chapone, H. (Mrs.). Letters on the improvement of the mind. N.Y., 1827.
Phil 2515.2.55 Charron, P. De la sagesse. Paris, 1827. 3v.
Phil 5643.6   Déal, J.N. Nouvel essai sur la lumière et les couleurs. Paris, 1827.
Phil 8693.1   Dick, T. The Christian philosopher. N.Y., 1827.
Phil 8878.13.4 Dodsley, R. The economy of human life. Chicago, 1827.
Phil 179.31   Egaña, Juan. Tractatus de re logica. Santiago, 1827.
Phil 181.1.2   Gabler, G.A. Lehrbuch der philosophischen Propädeutik. Erlangen, 1827.
Phil 181.1   Gabler, G.A. Lehrbuch der philosophischen Propädeutik. Erlangen, 1827.
Htn Phil 4112.39* Gallupi, Pasquale. Lettere filosofiche. Messina, 1827.
Phil 4114.71   Genovesi, Antonio. Opuscoli e lettere familiari. Venezia, 1827.
Phil 182.87   Hammarsköld, L. Strödda afhandlingar öfver ämnen inom philosophiens gebiet. Mariefred, 1827.
Phil 3425.44   Hegel, Georg Wilhelm Friedrich. Encyclopädie der philosophischen Wissenschaften. Heidelberg, 1827.
Phil 5247.39   Heinroth, J.C.A. Die Psychologie als Selbsterkenntnisslehre. Leipzig, 1827.
Phil 5047.6   Hinds, Samuel. Introduction to logic. Oxford, 1827.
Phil 1850.96.3 Hoppus, J. An account of Lord Bacons Novum Organon Scientiarum. London, 1827. 3 pam.
Phil 1850.96.2 Hoppus, J. An account of Lord Bacons Novum Organon Scientiarum. London, 1827. 3 pam.
Phil 1850.96   Hoppus, J. An account of Lord Bacon's Novum Organon Scientiarum. London, 1827-28.
Phil 2520.99   Jammes. Le sens commun de M. Gerbet. Paris, 1827.
Phil 8884.2   Jevons, W. Systematic morality. v.1-2. London, 1827.
Phil 3480.45.5 Kant, Immanuel. Critik der practischen Vernunft. Leipzig, 1827.
Phil 185.3   Keyserlingh, H. von. Menschen-Kenntnis oder Anthropologie. Berlin, 1827.
Phil 1115.2   Krug, W.T. Geschichte der Philosophie alter Zeit. Leipzig, 1827.
Phil 95.2   Krug, Wilhelm Traugott. Allgemeines Handwörterbuch der philosophischen Wissenschaften. Leipzig, 1827. 5v.
Phil 3528.40   Krug, Wilhelm Traugott. Fundamentalphilosophie. Leipzig, 1827.
Htn Phil 9351.12* Lindsley, Philip. Baccalaureaute address. Nashville, 1827.
Phil 8887.46   MacDonald, Normand. Maxims and moral reflections. N.Y., 1827.
Phil 6100.1   Mayo, H. A series of engravings...brain...in man. London, 1827.
Phil 8592.9   Meyer, J.F. von. Wahrnehmungen einer Seherin. v.1-2. Hamburg, 1827-28.
Phil 293.19   Momo, Giovanni. Sulla proposizione il mondo va da se. Lucca, 1827.
Phil 5252.66   Musmann, J.G. Lehrbuch der Seelenwissenschaft. Berlin, 1827.
Phil 8595.15.2.5 Paine, Thomas. The theological works. London, 1827.
Phil 2205.40.11 Paley, W. Principles of moral and political philosophy. Boston, 1827.
Phil 2205.32   Paxton, J. Illustrations of Paley's natural theology. Boston, 1827.
Phil 8685.4.5   Pitter, A.H. Die Halb-Kantianer und der Pantheismus (veranlasst durch Jäsche's Pantheismus). Berlin, 1827.
Phil 25.33.2   Psychologies of 1925. 2d ed. Worcester, 1827.
Phil 5057.3.5   Reinhold, Ernest. Die Logik oder die allgemeine Denkformenlehre. Jena, 1827.
Phil 8893.83.10 Salat, Jakob. Grundlinien der Moralphilosophie. München, 1827.
Phil 3625.1.45 Samuels, M. Memoirs of Moses Mendelssohn. 2. ed. London, 1827.
Htn Phil 3850.10.30* Schlegel, Friedrich von. Die drey ersten Vorlesungen über die Philosophie des Lebens. Wien, 1827.
Htn Phil 193.10.3* Schlegel, Friedrich von. Die drey ersten Vorlesungen über die Philosophie des Lebens. Wien, 1827.
Phil 3552.248   Schulze, G.E. Über die Entdeckung, dass Leibnitz ein Katholik gewesen sey. Göttingen, 1827.
Phil 270.13   Shepherd, M. Essays...doctrine of causation. London, 1827.
Phil 8643.3   Sintenis, F. Immortality or annihilation? London, 1827.
Phil 3850.19.40 Suabedissen, D.T.A. Zur Einleitung in die Philosophie. Marburg, 1827.
Phil 8420.15   Talia, G.B. Principi di estetica. Venezia, 1827-28. 2v.
Phil 8420.20   Trahndorff, K.F.E. Ästhetik, oder Lehre von der Weltauschauung und Kunst. v.1-2. Berlin, 1827.
Phil 5260.1   Upham, T.C. Elements of intellectual philosophy. Portland, 1827.
Phil 4260.36A   Vico, G.B. Principes de la philosophie de l'histoire. Paris, 1827.
Phil 8897.47.5 Weigelin, Ernst. Einführung in die Moral- und Rechtsphilosophie. Leipzig, 1827.
Phil 5627.88   Wells, Mary. Memoir of Mrs. Joanna Turner. 1. American ed N.Y., 1827.
Phil 8602.5   Wette, W.M.L. de. Über die Religion. Berlin, 1827.
Phil 900.1   Windischmann, C.J.H. von. Die Philosophie im Fortgang. v.1-4. Bonn, 1827-34. 3v.

1828

Phil 3090.41   Baader, Franz von. Vorlesungen über speculative Dogmatik. pt. 1-5. Stuttgart, 1828-38.
Phil 5041.1   Bachmann, C.F. System der Logik. Leipzig, 1828.
Phil 1850.34.3 Bacon, Francis. Of the proficience and advancement of learning. London, 1828.
Phil 5241.4   Ballantyne, J. An examination of the human mind. Edinburgh, 1828.
Phil 4520.2.3   Biberg, N.F. Samlade skrifter. Upsala, 1828-30. 3v.
Phil 3821.16   Boumann, L. Explicatio spinozismi. Diss. Berlin, 1828.
Phil 9120.10.5 Cederschiöld, F. Menniskors aprioriska. Lund, 1828.
Phil 802.2.2   Cousin, V. Cours de philosophie. Paris, 1828.
Phil 802.2.1   Cousin, V. Cours d'histoire de la philosophie. Paris, 1828.
Phil 2496.31   Cousin, Victor. Nouveaux fragmens philosophiques. Paris, 1828.
Phil 2403.1.10 Damiron, J.P. Essai sur l'histoire...philosophie en France au dix-neuvième siècle. Paris, 1828. 2v.

Chronological Listing

1828 - cont.

Phil 5243.2	Davies, J. An estimate of the human mind. London, 1828. 2v.
Phil 5754.1.12	Edwards, Jonathan. Careful and strict enquiry into the modern...freedom. N.Y., 1828.
Phil 3246.49A	Fichte, Johann Gottlieb. Die Anweisung zum seeligen Leben. Berlin, 1828.
Phil 482.1	Heinroth, J.C. Über die Hypothese der Materie. Leipzig, 1828.
Phil 3428.35	Herbart, J.F. Allgemeine Metaphysik. Königsberg, 1828-29. 2v.
Phil 3480.30.2	Kant, Immanuel. Critik der reinen Vernunft. 7. Aufl. Leipzig, 1828.
Phil 3425.89	Keil, Oswald T. Einige Bemerkungen über den Standpankt, Welchen die deutsche Philosophie durch Hegel erreicht hat. Leipzig, 1828.
Phil 3525.61	Krause, K.C.F. Abriss des Systemes der Logik. Göttingen, 1828.
Phil 3525.40	Krause, K.C.F. Vorlesungen über das System der Philosophie. Göttingen, 1828.
Phil 185.10	Krug, W.T. Handbuch der Philosophie. Leipzig, 1828.
Phil 2725.2.66	Lamennais, F.R. de. Défense de l'essai sur l'indifférence. Paris, 1828.
Phil 2725.2.59	Lamennais, F.R. de. Essai sur l'indifférence en matière de religion. Paris, 1828. 5v.
Phil 6990.37	Le Quien de la Neufville, Charles Jacques. Nouvelles prennes contre le faux miracle de migne approuvé à Rome. Paris, 1828.
Phil 9351.5	Linsley, J.H. Lectures on relations and middle aged. Hartford, 1828.
Phil 2115.50.2	Locke, J. The conduct of the understanding. v.1-2. Boston, 1828.
Phil 2115.27.5	Locke, J. Philosophical beauties. N.Y., 1828.
Phil 2403.1.50	Massias, N. Lettre à M.P. Damiron sur un article de son essai sur l'histoire de la philosophie en France au dix-neuvième siècle. Paris, 1828.
Phil 2520.94	Mazure, P.A. Études du Cartésianisme. Paris, 1828.
Phil 9510.1.5	Opie, A.A. (Mrs.). Detraction displayed. N.Y., 1828.
NEDL Phil 9510.1	Opie, A.A. (Mrs.). Detraction displayed. Philadelphia, 1828.
Phil 2205.40.13	Paley, W. Paley's moral philosophy. N.Y., 1828.
Phil 2205.40.9	Paley, W. Principles of moral and political philosophy. v.1-2. Boston, 1828.
Phil 2805.32.5	Pascal, Blaise. The provincial letters. N.Y., 1828.
Phil 8890.8	Payne, G. Elements of mental and moral science. London, 1828.
Phil 623.11	Pusey, E.B. An historical enquiry into the probable causes of the rationalist character lately predominant in the theology of Germany. London, 1828.
Phil 2240.20	Reid, Thomas. Oeuvres complètes. Paris, 1828-36. 6v.
Phil 3790.14	Reinwald, J.G. Kultur und Barbarei. 2e Aufl. Mainz, 1828.
Phil 3837.3	Rosenkranz, C. De Spinozae philosophia dissertatio. Halae, 1828.
Htn Phil 193.10.10*	Schlegel, Friedrich von. Philosophie des Lebens. Wien, 1828.
Phil 3805.32	Schleiermacher, Friedrich. Der christliche Glaube. Bd.1-2. Reutlingen, 1828.
Phil 8893.6	Sedgwick, C.M. A short essay to do good. Stockbridge, 1828.
Phil 5058.42	Snell, F.W.D. Erste Grundlinien der Logik oder Verstandeslehre. Gieosen, 1828.
Cg Phil 9590.14	Spetien Montero y Austri, P.A. Meximas de buena educación. México, 1828.
Phil 2275.60.10	Stewart, D. Essais philosophique sur les systèmes de Locke, Berkeley. Paris, 1828.
tn Phil 2275.38*A	Stewart, D. Philosophy of the active and moral powers. Boston, 1828. 2v.
Phil 2275.38.2	Stewart, D. Philosophy of the active and moral powers. v.1-2. Boston, 1828.
Phil 8610.828.5	Taylor, Robert. Syntagma of the evidences of the Christian religion. Boston, 1828.
Phil 194.34	Troxler, I.P.V. Naturlehre dis menschlichen Erkennens. Aarau, 1828.
Phil 4265.2.32	Ventura, J. De methodo philosphandi. Romae, 1828.
Phil 8595.16.23	Watson, R. An apology for the Bible. Cambridge, 1828.

1829

Phil 175.6.15	Ancillon, F. Pensées sur l'homme, ses rapports. Berlin, 1829. 2v.
Phil 8580.6	Andrews, W.S. A treatise upon theological subjects. Cambridge, 1829.
Phil 3090.30	Baader, Franz von. Über den Begriff des Gut-Oderpositiv und der Richtgut-Oder-Negative-Gewordnen. Luzern, 1829.
Phil 176.4A	Bailey, S. Essays on the pursuit of truth. London, 1829.
Phil 8951.5	Bruch, J.F. Lehrbuch der christlichen Sittenlehre. v.1-2. Strassburg, 1829-32.
Phil 8402.14.5	Burke, E. A philosophical enquiry into the origin of our ideas of the sublime and beautiful. N.Y., 1829.
Phil 5922.4.6	Combe, George. The constitution of man. Boston, 1829.
Phil 8582.14	Crombie, A. Natural theology. London, 1829.
Phil 8628.2	Dick, T. The philosophy of a future state. N.Y., 1829.
Phil 8583.4	Dick, T. The philosophy of religion. Brookfield, Mass., 1829.
Phil 2530.15	Diderot, Denis. Oeuvres philosophiques. Bruxelles, 1829. 6v.
Phil 5923.1	Drummond, D. Objections to phrenology. Calcutta, 1829.
Phil 5910.2	Epps, J. Horae phrenologicae. London, 1829-1836. 6 pam.
Phil 5245.2.2	Fearn, J. A manual of the physiology of mind. London, 1829.
Phil 5400.51	Festa, Alfonso. Introduzione alla filosofia dell'affetto. Piacenza, 1829.
Phil 1705.3.5	Fichte, T.H. Beiträge zur Charakteristik der neueren Philosophie. Sulzbach, 1829.
Phil 1135.17	Fortlage, C. Ueber die Denkweise der altesten Philosophen. München, 1829.
Phil 9345.5*	Foster, H. (Webster). Boarding school. Boston, 1829.
Phil 2605.3.30*	Fourier, C. Le nouveau monde. Paris, 1829.
Phil 8881.49	Gerlach, G.W. Grundriss der philosophischen Lugendlehre. Halle, 1829.
Phil 2115.96*	Grenville. Oxford and Locke. London, 1829.
Phil 3625.1.87	Guttenstein, B. M. Mendelssohn's Verdienste und die Bildung seines Volkes. Heidelberg, 1829.
Phil 182.9	Heinroths, J. Pisteodicee. Leipzig, 1829.
Phil 9169.1.1	James, J.A. The family monitor. Boston, 1829.

1829 - cont.

Phil 9169.1	James, J.A. The family monitor. Concord, N.H., 1829.
Htn Phil 3801.471.10*	Kapp, Christian. Über den Ursprung des Menschen und Völker nach der mosaischen Genesis. Nürnberg, 1829.
Htn Phil 6680.1*	Kerner, J. Die Seherin von Prevorst. Stuttgart, 1829. 2v.
Phil 2115.92.90	King, Peter. Life of John Locke. London, 1829.
Phil 6960.2	Knight, P.S. Beobachtungen...des Irrseyns. Koln, 1829.
Phil 2750.7.37	Massias, Nicolas. Principe de la philosophie psycho-physiologique sur lequel repose la science de l'homme. Paris, 1829.
Phil 6682.20	Mercier, A.D. La vérité du magnétisme, prouvée par les faits. Paris, 1829.
Phil 5252.7A	Mill, J. Analysis of the phenomena of human mind. London, 1829. 2v.
Phil 8887.28	Montlosier, F.D. de R. Des mysteres de la vie humaine. v.1-2. Bruxelles, 1829. 2v.
Phil 1075.1	Neumann, C.F. Memoire sur la vie et les ouvrages de David. Paris, 1829.
Phil 8593.3	Nichols, I. A catechism of natural theology. Portland, 1829.
Phil 2205.30.9	Paley, W. Natural theology. Boston, 1829.
Phil 9175.1.8	Pandolfini, A. Trattato del governo della famiglia. Milano, 1829.
Phil 9175.3	Parkes, W. Domstic duties. N.Y., 1829.
Phil 2805.40.13.5	Pascal, Blaise. Pensées de Blaise Pascal. Paris, 1829.
Phil 5643.75	Pollak, G.F.X. Über den Einfluss der Gesichtsschärfe. Inaug. Diss. Dillingen, 1829.
Phil 5257.2.2	Reed, S. Observations on the growth of the mind. Boston, 1829.
Phil 1210.2	Riambourg, Jean B.C. L'école d'Athènes. Paris, 1829.
Phil 3625.1.180	Richter, Johann Andreas Lebrecht. Moses Mendelssohn als Mensch. Dessau, 1829.
Phil 817.2	Ritter, A.H. Geschichte der Philosophie. Hamburg, 1829-45. 12v.
Phil 5057.12.4	Ritter, Heinrich. Abriss der philosophischen Logik. 2. Aufl. Berlin, 1829.
Htn Phil 3800.290*	Schelling, F.W.J. von. Rede zum siebzigsten in öffentlicher Sitzung gefeyerten Jahrestag der K. Akademie der Wissenschaften. München, 1829.
Htn Phil 3800.300*	Schelling, F.W.J. von. Zur öffentlichen Sitzung der k. Academie der Wissenschaften am Vorabend des Ludwigs-Tages 1829. München, 1829.
Phil 8419.7	Solger, K.W.F. K.W.F. Solger's Vorlesungen über Ästhetik. Leipzig, 1829.
Phil 2275.35	Stewart, D. Elements of the philosophy of the human mind. Cambridge, 1829. 2v.
Phil 2275.35.2	Stewart, D. Elements of the philosophy of the human mind. v.1-2. Cambridge, 1829.
Phil 2275.20	Stewart, D. Oeuvres. Bruxelles, 1829. 5v.
Phil 2275.22	Stewart, D. Oeuvres. Paris, 1829. 2v.
Phil 2275.10	Stewart, D. Works. Cambridge, 1829. 7v.
Phil 5258.80	Suabedissen, D.T.A. Von dem Begriffe der Psychologie. Marburg, 1829.
Phil 819.1.5	Tennemann, W.G. Grundriss der Geschichte der Philosophie. 5. Aufl. Leipzig, 1829.
Phil 819.1.7	Tennemann, W.G. Manuel de l'histoire de la philosophie. Paris, 1829. 2v.
Phil 2419.3	Théard. Tableau des trois époques, ou Les philosophes. Paris, 1829.
Phil 5059.9	Troxler, I.P.V. Logik. Stuttgart, 1829-30. 3v.
Phil 3425.285	Weisse, C.H. Über den gegenwärtigen Standpunct der philosophischen Wissenschaft. Leipzig, 1829.
Phil 5062.6	Whately, Richard. Elements of logic. London, 1829.
Phil 8897.24	Wright, F. Course of popular lectures. N.Y., 1829.
Phil 200.4	Zenetti, Jacob. Einfluss der Philosophie auf das Leben. München, 1829.

1830

Phil 8655.9	The American antitheistical catechism. London, 1830?
Phil 175.6.6	Ancillon, F. Essai sur la science. Paris, 1830.
Phil 2477.3.33	Barruel, Augustine. Les Helviennes. 7e éd. Paris, 1830. 4v.
Phil 1865.53	Bentham, Jeremy. Official aptitude maximized. London, 1830.
Htn Phil 1865.50.5*	Bentham, Jeremy. Principles of legislation. Boston, 1830.
Phil 1865.42	Bentham, Jeremy. The rationale of reward. London, 1830.
Phil 5041.21.10	Braniss, C.J. Grundriss der Logik. Breslau, 1830.
Phil 623.6	Bretschneider, K.G. Sendschreiben an einen Staatsmann über die Frage...Rationalismus. Leipzig, 1830.
Phil 4065.10A	Bruno, Giordano. Opere. Lipsia, 1830. 2v.
Phil 1900.35.5	Butler, Joseph. Analogy of religion. 2d ed. Cambridge, 1830.
Phil 177.5	Cardaillac, M. Etudes élémentaires de philosophie. Paris, 1830. 2v.
Phil 8627.12	Carmichael, A. An essay...man's ultimate destination. Dublin, 1830.
Phil 9342.9	Cary, V. (Mrs.). Letters on female character. Richmond, 1830.
Phil 9342.2	Chapone, H. (Mrs.). Letters on the improvement of the mind. London, 1830.
Htn Phil 2490.30*	Comte, Auguste. Cours de philosophie positive. Paris, 1830-42. 6v.
Phil 8878.5.8	Davy, H. Consolations in travel. London, 1830.
Phil 8878.5.7	Davy, H. Consolations in travel. Philadelphia, 1830.
Phil 5044.2	Esser, Wilhelm. System der Logik. Münster, 1830.
Phil 5643.40	Fearn, John. Rational of the cause of cerebral vision. London, 1830? 4 pam.
Phil 3246.82	Fichte, Immanuel Hermann. Johann Gottlieb Fichte's Leben und Ritter. Sulzbach, 1830-31. 2v.
Phil 400.1	Fischer, Friedrich. Über den Begriff der Philosophie. Tübingen, 1830.
Phil 9035.14	Foster, John. Essays on decision of character. Burlington, 1830.
Phil 8881.6	Gerando, J.M. Self-education. Boston, 1830.
Phil 4120.1.32F	Gioja, Melchiorre. Del merito e delle ricompense; trattato storico e filosofico. v. 1-2. 2. ed. Lugano, 1830.
Phil 9558.7	Grayson, P.W. Vice unmasked; an essay. N.Y., 1830.
Phil 3425.45	Hegel, Georg Wilhelm Friedrich. Encyclopädie der philosophischen Wissenschaften. Heidelberg, 1830.
Phil 525.12	Heinroth, J.C.A. Geschichte und Kritik des Mysticismus. Leipzig, 1830.
Phil 182.17.20	Hillebrand, J. Universal-philosophische Prolegomena. Mainz, 1830.
Phil 8882.19	Holyoke, E.A. An ethical essay. Salem, 1830.

1830 - cont.

Phil 3480.73 — Kant, Immanuel. Vorlesungen über der philosophische Religionslehre. Leipzig, 1830.

Htn Phil 3801.471* — Kapp, Christian. Sendschreiben an den...von Schelling. n.p., 1830.

Phil 2115.93A — King, Peter. Life of John Locke. London, 1830. 2v.

Phil 9513.2 — Knigge, A. von. Über den Umgang mit Menschen. Pt.1-3. Hildburghausen, 1830.

Phil 3528.10 — Krug, Wilhelm Traugott. Gesammelte Schriften. Braunschweig, 1830-45. 12v.

Phil 3528.35.2 — Krug, Wilhelm Traugott. System der praktischen Philosophie. Königsberg, 1830-38. 2v.

Phil 1750.1 — Leib, J.R. Lecture on nature and objects of modern philosophy. Philadelphia, 1830-39. 3 pam.

Phil 9351.4 — Lemontey, P.E. Raison, folie. Bruxelles, 1830. 2v.

Phil 6990.37.5 — Le Quien de la Neufville, Charles Jacques. Vains efforts de plusieurs évêques. Paris, 1830.

Phil 2115.75.3 — Locke, J. Familiar letters. London, 1830.

Phil 2750.7.35 — Massias, Nicolas. Traité de philosophie psycho-physiologique. Paris, 1830.

Phil 6123.1.5 — Newnham, W. Essay on superstition. London, 1830.

Phil 2205.40.7 — Paley, W. Principles of moral and political philosophy. Boston, 1830. 2v.

Phil 2205.11.5 — Paley, W. Works. Cambridge, 1830. 6v.

Phil 2805.40 — Pascal, Blaise. Oeuvres; Les pensées. Paris, 1830.

Phil 6967.3.2 — Rush, B. Medical inquiries...diseases...mind. Philadelphia, 1830.

Htn Phil 3800.210.10* — Schelling, F.W.J. von. Vorlesungen über die Methode des academisch Studium. 3e Ausg. Stuttgart, 1830.

Phil 3805.32.5 — Schleiermacher, Friedrich. Der christliche Glaube. 2. Aufl. Berlin, 1830-31. 2v.

Phil 2266.43 — Smith, Adam. Théorie des sentiments moraux. Paris, 1830. 2v.

Htn Phil 2268.1.30* — Smith, Joseph. The book of Mormon. Palmyra, 1830.

Phil 3819.10.2 — Spinoza, Benedictus de. Opera philosophische omnia. v.3. Stuttgardiae, 1830.

Phil 5405.5.2 — Taylor, I. Natural history of enthusiasm. Boston, 1830.

Phil 5405.5.5 — Taylor, I. Natural history of enthusiasm. London, 1830.

Phil 5405.5.3 — Taylor, I. Natural history of enthusiasm. London, 1830.

Phil 8894.2 — Taylor, Jane. The contributions of Q.Q. Philadelphia, 1830.

Phil 5029.1 — Tellbom, J.P. De progressibus desciplinae logicae. Diss. Upsaliae, 1830.

Phil 5620.5 — Thurot, J.F. De l'entendement de la raison. Paris, 1830. 2v.

NEDL Phil 300.1 — Toulmin, G.H. Eternity of the universe. Philadelphia, 1830.

Phil 196.6 — Varas, J. Miguel y Marin. Elementos de ideolojia. Santiago de Chile, 1830.

Phil 2915.70 — Voltaire, F.M.A. de. Philosophical dictionary of M. de Voltaire. N.Y., 1830.

Phil 2205.81 — Wainewright, L. A vindication of Dr. Paley's theory of morals. London, 1830.

1831

Phil 5240.1 — Abercrombie, J. Inquiries...intellectual powers. Edinburgh, 1831.

Phil 6950.3 — Abercrombie, P.E. Pathological, practical researches, diseases...brain. Philadelphia, 1831.

Phil 8875.7 — Ancillon, J.P.F. Zur Vermittlung der Extreme. Berlin, 1831-38. 2v.

Phil 3090.20 — Baader, Franz von. Philosophische Schriften und Aufsätze. v.1-2. Münster, 1831-33.

Phil 5135.1.3 — Bailey, S. Essays...opinions. London, 1831.

Phil 176.4.3 — Bailey, S. Essays on the pursuit of truth. London, 1831.

Phil 8876.18 — Blakey, R. An essay...good and evil. Edinburgh, 1831.

Phil 3910.80 — Breslau. Prussia Magdalinisch-Gymnas. Christian ven Wolf. Breslau, 1831.

Phil 6951.6 — Broussais, F.J.V. In irritation and insanity. Columbia, 1831.

Phil 1890.30.3.5 — Brown, T. Lectures on philosophy of human mind. Hallowell, 1831.

Phil 5242.1 — Carus, C.G. Vorlesungen über Psychologie. Leipzig, 1831.

Phil 9342.4 — Cobbett, W. Advice to young men. N.Y., 1831.

Phil 8657.10 — Conversations on the attributes of God. Boston, 1831.

Htn Phil 8657.11* — Croswell, A. A letter to the Rev. A. Cumming attempting to show him that it is not blasphemy to say, no man can love God. Boston, 1831. 2 pam.

Phil 178.2 — Daumer, G.F. Andeutung eines Systems speculativer Philosophie. Nürnberg, 1831.

Phil 8878.5 — Davy, H. Consolations in travel. Philadelphia, 1831.

Phil 8628.2.5 — Dick, T. The philosophy of a future state. N.Y., 1831.

Phil 8595.15.65 — Drew, Samuel. Remarks on the 1st part of book entitled "The age of reason." 2. ed. N.Y., 1831.

Phil 8879.20 — Enberg, L.M. Moralfilosofiens elementer. Stockholm, 1831.

Phil 8881.13A — Godwin, W. Thoughts on man. London, 1831.

Phil 181.19 — Gruppe, O.F. Antäus. Berlin, 1831.

Phil 4803.454.50 — Hoene-Wroński, Józef Maria. Messianisme, union finale de la philosophie et de la religion. Paris, 1831.

Phil 2648.35 — Holbach, Paul Henri T. Good sense; or natural ideas. N.Y., 1831.

Htn Phil 182.23* — Hope, T. Essay on origin of man. London, 1831. 3v.

Htn Phil 3480.40.49* — Kant, Immanuel. Anweisung zur Menschen und Weltkenntniss. 4. Aufl. Leipzig, 1831.

Htn Phil 3480.40.50* — Kant, Immanuel. Menschenkunde oder philosophische Anthropologie. Leipzig, 1831.

Phil 185.10.15 — Krug, W.T. Handbuch i philosophien. Stockholm, 1831.

Phil 3528.45 — Krug, Wilhelm Traugott. Universalphilosophische Vorlesungen für Gebildete beiderlei Geschlechts. Neustadt, 1831.

Htn Phil 3110.88* — Lamotte-Fouqué, Friedrich. Jakob Böhme. Greiz, 1831.

Phil 9171.3 — Letters to a mother. Boston, 1831.

Phil 2115.50.3 — Locke, J. The conduct of the understanding. v.1-2. Boston, 1831.

Phil 3832.18 — Marbach, G.O. Gedächtnissrede auf Benedict von Spinoza. Halle, 1831.

Phil 6990.16 — Myers, J. Narrative of two wonderful cures. Baltimore, 1831.

Phil 8593.3.2 — Nichols, I. A catechism of natural theology. Boston, 1831.

Phil 5053.2 — Nieuwenhuis, Jacobi. Initia philosophiae logicae. Lugdunum Batavorum, 1831.

Phil 2205.30.13 — Paley, W. Natural theology. Boston, 1831.

Phil 2205.40.14 — Paley, W. The principles of moral and political philosophy. Boston, 1831. 2v.

Phil 1140.7 — Philippson, L. Hylē anthrōpinē. Berolini, 1831.

1831 - cont.

Phil 8597.48 — Rocafuerte, Vicente. Ensayo sobre tolerancia religiosa. 2. ed. México, 1831.

Phil 8685.18 — Rosenkranz, K. Die Naturreligion. Iserlohn, 1831.

Phil 192.17 — Rozaven, J.L. Examen d'un ouvrage intitulé. Avignon, 1831.

Phil 9357.7 — Rudd, John C. A series of discourses...to young men. 2d ed. Auburn, 1831.

Phil 8893.83.25 — Salat, Jakob. Die literarische Stellung des Protestanten zu dem Katholiken. Laudshut, 1831.

Htn Phil 3800.310* — Schelling, F.W.J. von. Rede an die Studierenden der Ludwig-Maximilians-Universität...29 dec. 1830. München, 1831.

Htn Phil 3800.320* — Schelling, F.W.J. von. Rede zum zwei und Siebzigsten...Jahrestag der k. Academie der Wissenschaften. München, 1831.

Phil 3805.30.4 — Schleiermacher, Friedrich. Über die Religion. Berlin, 1831.

Phil 3500.7 — Schön, L.F. Philosophie transcendantale...Kant. Paris, 1831.

Phil 3850.13.55 — Schulze, G.E. Grundsätze der allgemeinen Logik. Göttingen, 1831.

Phil 193.27.5 — Sigwart, H.C.W. Vermischte philosophische Abhandlungen. Tübingen, 1831.

Phil 8893.28 — Sullivan, W. The moral class book. Boston, 1831.

Phil 8894.2.5 — Taylor, Jane. The contributions of Q.Q. to a periodical work. 6. ed. London, 1831.

Phil 2300.30.5 — Tucker, Abraham. Light of nature pursued. Cambridge, 1831. 4v.

Phil 5260.1.2 — Upham, T.C. Elements of mental philosophy. Portland, 1831. 2v.

1832

Phil 5240.1.2 — Abercrombie, J. Inquiries...intellectual powers. N.Y., 1832.

Phil 175.6 — Ancillon, F. Essais de philosophie. Paris, 1832. 4v.

Phil 175.6.2 — Ancillon, F. Essais de philosophie. Paris, 1832. 4v.

Phil 3483.46 — Beneke, F. Eduard. Kant und die philosophische Aufgabe unserer Zeit. Berlin, 1832.

Phil 9341.3 — Berens, E. Advice to young man...Oxford. London, 1832.

Phil 6111.5 — Brigham, Amariah. Remarks on the influence of mental cultivation upon health. Hartford, 1832.

Phil 8620.2 — Burton, W. Cheering views of man and providence. Boston, 1832.

Htn Phil 5922.2* — Calvert, G.H. Illustrations of phrenology. Baltimore, 1832.

Phil 9162.3 — Clowes, John. The golden wedding ring...marriage. Boston, 1832.

Phil 802.2.8 — Cousin, V. Introduction to the history of philosophy. Boston, 1832.

Phil 7082.158 — Dendy, Walter Cooper. On the phenomena of dreams. London, 1832.

Phil 9245.1 — Droz, F.X.J. The art of being happy. Boston, 1832.

Phil 8880.1.4 — Feltham, O. Resolves. Cambridge, 1832.

Phil 3245.40 — Fichte, Immanuel Hermann. Über Gegen satz Wendepunkt und Zeit. Heidelberg, 1832.

Phil 3246.35.9 — Fichte, Johann Gottlieb. Destination de l'homme. Paris, 1832.

Phil 5938.7.10 — Follen, Charles. Funeral oration. Boston, 1832.

Phil 5938.7.5 — Follen, Charles. Funeral oration. v.1-3. Boston, 1832-1840.

Phil 8880.16.2 — Fry, Caroline. The listner. Philadelphia, 1832. 2v.

Phil 4112.50 — Galluppi, Pasquale. Filosofia della volonta. Napoli, 1832-40. 4v.

Phil 4112.31 — Galluppi, Pasquale. Introduzione allo studio della filosofia. Milano, 1832.

Phil 8881.6.2 — Gerando, J.M. Self-education. 2nd ed. Boston, 1832.

Phil 4120.1.10 — Gioja, Melchiorre. Opere minori. Lugano, 1832-37. 17v.

Phil 3425.87 — Goeschel, K.F. Hegel und seine Zeit. Berlin, 1832.

Phil 182.7 — Hassler, K.D. Paragraphen für den Unterricht in der Philosophie. Ulm, 1832.

Phil 9347.1.2 — Hawes, J. Lectures to young men. Hartford, 1832.

X Cg Phil 3425.8 — Hegel, Georg Wilhelm Friedrich. Werke. Berlin, 1832-45. 14v.

Phil 3425.10 — Hegel, Georg Wilhelm Friedrich. Werke. Berlin, 1832-87. 19v.

Phil 2050.103 — Kahle, C.M. De Davidis Humii philosophia. Inaug. Diss. Berolini, 1832?

Phil 5050.5.5 — Kiesewetter, J.G.C.C. Logik zum Gebrauch für Schulen. Leipzig, 1832.

Phil 95.2.2A — Krug, Wilhelm Traugott. Allgemeines Handwörterbuch der philosophischen Wissenschaften. 2e Aufl. Leipzig, 1832-38. 5v.

Phil 5051.9 — Lecomte, A. La logique populaire. Paris, 1832.

Phil 2115.62.10 — Locke, J. A paraphrase and notes on epistle of St. Paul. Cambridge, 1832.

Phil 8837.1.2 — Mackintosh, James. A general view of the progress of ethical philosophy. Philadelphia, 1832.

Phil 9450.2 — Matter, J. De l'influence des moeurs sur le lois. Paris, 1832.

Phil 3425.229.10 — Michelet, C.L. Einleitung in Hegel's philosophische Abhandlungen. Berlin, 1832.

Phil 5052.4 — Mora, J.J. de. Cursos de lojica y etica segun la escuela de Edinburgo. Lima, 1832.

Phil 8890.4 — Parkhurst, J.L. Elements of moral philosophy. Boston, 1832.

Phil 192.7 — Reinhold, C.E. Theorie des menschlichen Erkenntnissvermögens. Gotha, 1832-1835. 2v.

Htn Phil 3800.330* — Schelling, F.W.J. von. Über Faradays neueste Entdlckung. München, 1832.

Phil 3850.13.70 — Schulze, G.E. Ueber die Menschliche Erkenntnis. Göttingen, 1832.

Phil 8893.21 — Spurzheim, J.K. Philosophical catechism...natural laws of man. Boston, 1832.

Phil 5938.6 — Spurzheim, Johann Gaspar. Outlines of phrenology. Boston, 1832.

Phil 5938.6.10 — Spurzheim, Johann Gaspar. Phrenology. v.1-2. Boston, 1832.

Phil 8599.30 — Taylor, I. Essay on the application of abstract reasoning to the Christian doctrines. 1. American ed. Boston, 1832.

Phil 8610.829.5 — Taylor, Robert. The diegesis. Boston, 1832.

Phil 819.1.12 — Tennemann, W.G. Manual of the history of philosophy. Oxford, 1832.

Phil 8709.14.6 — Turner, Sharon. The sacred history of the world. v.1. N.Y., 1832.

Chronological Listing

1832 - cont.

Phil 8897.9 Weiss, F.R. de. Principes philosophiques.
Bruxelles, 1832. 2v.

Phil 5062.6.2 Whately, Richard. Elements of logic. N.Y., 1832.

Htn Phil 3504.6.3* Wirgman, T. Principles Kantesian...philosophy. 2d ed.
London, 1832.

Phil 9364.1 Young lady's own book. Philadelphia, 1832.

1833

Phil 8875.1 Abercrombie, J. The philosophy of the moral feelings.
N.Y., 1833.

Phil 6675.4 Académie des Sciences, Paris. Report on experiments on
animal magnetism. Edinburgh, 1833.

Phil 3090.40 Baader, Franz von. Über das Verhalten des Wissens zum
Glauben. Münster, 1833.

Phil 3425.91.30 Bachmann, C.F. Uber Hegel's System und die Nothwendigkeit.
Leipzig, 1833.

Phil 8876.1 Bagshaw, W. On man. London, 1833. 2v.

Phil 6111.5.2 Brigham, Amariah. Remarks on the influence of mental
cultivation upon health. Boston, 1833.

Phil 8402.14.10 Burke, E. A philosophical enquiry into the origin of our
ideas of the sublime and beautiful. Baltimore, 1833.

Phil 5938.7.20 Carmichael, A. A memoir of the life and philosophy of
Spurzheim. 1st American ed. Boston, 1833.

Phil 4002.4 Colangelo, F. Storia dei filosofi e dei matematici
napolitani. v.1-3. Napoli, 1833-34.

NEDL Phil 960.2 Colebrooke, H.T. Essais sur la philosophie des Hindous.
Paris, 1833.

Phil 177.21 Cory, Isaac P. Metaphysical inquiry. London, 1833-37.

Phil 8583.4.2 Dick, T. On the improvement of society by the diffusion of
knowledge. Glasgow, 1833.

Phil 8660.7.2 Faber, G.S. The difficulties of infidelity. 2. ed.
London, 1833.

Phil 1705.2 Feuerbach. Geschichte der neueren Philosophie.
Ansbach, 1833-37. 2v.

Phil 3245.30 Fichte, Immanuel Hermann. Grundzüge zur System der
Philosophie. Heidelberg, 1833-46. 4v.

Phil 6675.3 Foissac, P. Rapports...sur magnétisme animal.
Paris, 1833.

Phil 8880.16 Fry, Caroline. The listner. Philadelphia, 1833. 2v.

Phil 4112.40 Galluppi, Pasquale. Lettere filosofiche. Firenze, 1833.

Phil 9480.1 Gay, M.F.S. Physiologie du ridicule. Bruxelles, 1833.

Phil 9230.8 Gordon, G.W. A lecture before Boston young men's societies
on the subject of lotteries. Boston, 1833.

Phil 3428.66 Herbart, J.F. Der principio logico exclusi medii.
Gottingae, 1833.

Phil 9169.1.2 James, J.A. The family monitor. Boston, 1833.

Phil 9169.2 Jay, W. Thoughts on marriage. Boston, 1833.

Phil 2672.29 Jouffroy, Théodore S. Mélanges philosophiques.
Paris, 1833.

Phil 3480.40.4 Kant, Immanuel. Anthropologie in pragmatischer Hinsicht.
Leipzig, 1833.

:n Phil 3480.19.15* Kant, Immanuel. Vorzügliche Kleine Schriften und Aufsätze.
Bd.1-2. Leipzig, 1833.

Phil 6120.11 Knowlton, C. Two remarkable lectures. Boston, 1833.

Phil 260.9 Lafaist, M. Dissertation sur la philosophie atomistique.
Paris, 1833.

Phil 5251.30.5 Laromiguiere, P. Leçons de philosophie:sur les principes
de l'intelligence. 5. ed. Paris, 1833. 2v.

Phil 2411.1 Lerminier, E. De l'influence de la philosophie du XVIIIe
siècle. Paris, 1833.

Phil 8592.61 Man unfit to govern man, by a citizen of London.
London, 1833.

Phil 9455.7 Metcalf, Thomas. An address to the Phi Beta Kappa Society
of Brown University, Sept. 5, 1832. Boston, 1833.

Phil 2205.12 Paley, W. Works. Edinburgh, 1833.

Phil 9355.12 Parting advice to a youth on leaving his Sunday school.
N.Y., 1833.

Phil 2880.1.25 Saint-Martin, L.C. NachgelasseneWerke. Münster, 1833.

Phil 8968.8 Sanderson, R. Christian ethics. London, 1833.

Phil 5258.7.5 Schubert, G.H. von. Die Geschichte der Seele.
Stuttgart, 1833.

Phil 6968.8.6 Spurzheim, J.K. Observations...mind...insanity.
Boston, 1833.

Phil 5938.6.2 Spurzheim, Johann Gaspar. Outlines of phrenology. 2nd ed.
Boston, 1833.

Phil 5938.6.43 Spurzheim, Johann Gaspar. Philosophical catechism of the
natural laws of man. Boston, 1833.

Phil 5938.6.30 Spurzheim, Johann Gaspar. Phrenology, in connection with
the study of physiognomy. Boston, 1833.

Phil 8893.28.3 Sullivan, W. The moral class book. Boston, 1833.

Phil 9200.1.5 Taylor, Isaac. Fanaticism. London, 1833.

Phil 8709.14.5 Turner, Sharon. The sacred history of the world. 3. ed.
London, 1833. 2v.

Phil 8972.2 Wardlaw, R. Christian ethics. London, 1833.

Phil 8677.3 Whewell, William. Astronomy and general physics,
considered with reference to natural theology.
London, 1833.

Phil 9364.2.6 Young man's own book. Philadelphia, 1833.

1834

Phil 9160.2.8 Abbott, Jacob. The child at Howe. 2. ed. Boston, 1834.

Phil 9160.6 Anderson, C. Book for parents. The genius and design of
the domestic constitution. Boston, 1834.

Phil 1850.25 Bacon, Francis. Oeuvres philosophiques. Paris, 1834.
3v.

Phil 7085.2 Belden, L.W. Account of Jane E. Rider somnambulist.
Springfield, 1834.

Phil 1865.30.2* Bentham, Jeremy. Deontology. London, 1834. 2v.

Phil 1865.30 Bentham, Jeremy. Deontology. v.1-2. London, 1834.

Phil 5041.13 Blakey, Robert. Essay towards...system of logic.
London, 1834.

Phil 8402.42 Bobrik, Eduard. Freie vorträge über Ästhetik.
Zürich, 1834.

Phil 176.100 Braniss, C.J. System der Metaphysik. Breslau, 1834.

Phil 1900.36 Butler, Joseph. Analogy of religion. London, 1834.

Phil 8657.2 Chalmers, T. The power, wisdom and goodness of God.
N.Y., 1834.

Phil 8692.5.15 Chalmers, Thomas. Series of discourses on the Christian
revelation, viewed in connexion with modern astronomy. 12th
ed. Glasgow, 1834.

Phil 8877.7 Charma, A. Essai...bases...développmens de la moralité.
Paris, 1834.

Phil 2496.50.5 Cousin, Victor. Elements of psychology. Hartford, 1834.

1834 - cont.

Phil 3002.6 Cousin, Victor. Uber französische und deutsche
Philosophie. Stuttgart, 1834.

Htn Phil 3801.293* Cousin, Victor. Uber französische und deutsche
Philosophie...Nebst einer Beurtheilen den Vorrede
des...Schelling. Stuttgart, 1834.

Phil 1150.5 Dähne, A.F. Geschichtliche Darstellung der
jüdisch-alexandrinischen Religions-Philosophie.
Halle, 1834. 2v.

Phil 2403.1.11 Damiron, J.P. Essai sur l'histoire...philosophie en France
au XIXe siècle. Paris, 1834. 2v.

Phil 8878.2 Damiron, P. Cours de philosophie, morale. Paris, 1834.

Phil 178.1 Damiron, P. Cours de philosophie. Bruxelles, 1834.
3v.

Phil 5753.9 Daub, Carl. Des Dr. C. Daub Darstellung und Beurtheilung
des Hypothesen in Betreff dei Willensfreiheit.
Altona, 1834.

Phil 5923.2 Dean, Amos. Lectures on phrenology. Albany, 1834.

Phil 6673.4.11 Du Potet, J. de S. Cours de magnétisme animal.
Paris, 1834.

Phil 8878.18.4 Dymond, J. Essays...principles of morality. N.Y., 1834.

Phil 1704.1 Erdmann, J.E. Versuch...Geschichte der neuern Philosophie.
Riga, 1834-53. 6v.

Phil 3425.272 Eschenmayer, C.A. Die Hegel'sche Religions-Philosophie.
Tübingen, 1834.

Phil 3245.50.2 Fichte, Immanuel Hermann. Die Idee der Persönlichkeit.
Elberfeld, 1834.

Phil 3245.55 Fichte, Immanuel Hermann. Religion und Philosophie.
Heidelberg, 1834.

Phil 180.6.7 Fischer, K.P. Die Wissenschaft der Metaphysik im
Grundrisse. Stuttgart, 1834.

NEDL Phil 8880.15 Franklin, B. Saggi di morale. v.1-2. Volterre, 1834.

Phil 4112.30 Galluppi, Pasquale. Elementi di filosofia. v.1-2.
Firenze, 1834.

Phil 4112.30.5 Galluppi, Pasquale. Elementi di filosofia. v.1-6. 3. ed.
Napoli, 1834-37. 3v.

Phil 8434.2.15 Gilpin, W. Observations on forest scenery.
Edinburgh, 1834.

Phil 181.10 Gioja, M. E. Elementi di filosofia. Lugano, 1834.

Phil 4120.1.50 Gioja, Melchiorre. La causa di Dio e degli uomini difesa
dagl'insulti degli empj e dalle pretensioni dei fanatici.
Lugano, 1834.

Phil 8661.2 Godwin, B. Lectures on the atheistic controversy.
London, 1834.

Phil 1735.2 Gruppe, Otto F. Wendepunkt der Philosophie im neunzehnten
Jahrhundert. Berlin, 1834.

Phil 3310.1.30 Günther, Anton. Janusköpfe zur Philosophie und Theologie.
Wien, 1834.

Phil 2038.33 Hartley, D. Observations on man. London, 1834.

Phil 9558.1 Heinroth, J.C.A. Die Lüge. Leipzig, 1834.

Phil 3450.13.32 Heusde, P.W. De Socratische school of Wijsgeerte.
Utrecht, 1834. v.

Phil 7060.10 Jung Stilling, J.H. Theory of pneumatology. London, 1834.

Phil 3525.20.3 Krause, K.C.F. Handschriftlicher Nachlass;
Religionsphilosophie. Dresden, 1834-43. 2v.

Phil 2725.2.81 Lacordaire, H. Considérations sur le système philosophique
de M. de Lamennais. Paris, 1834.

Phil 2725.2.47 Lamenais, F.R. de. Parole d'un credente. Bruxelles, 1834.
3 pam.

Phil 2725.2.48 Lamenais, F.R. de. Parole d'un credente. Italia, 1834.

Phil 2725.2.37 Lamenais, F.R. de. Paroles d'un croyant. 7. éd.
Paris, 1834.

Phil 2725.2.39 Lamenais, F.R. de. Paroles d'un croyant. 9. éd.
Paris, 1834.

Phil 2725.2.49 Lamenais, F.R. de. The words of a believer. London, 1834.

Phil 2725.2.46 Lamennais, F.R. de. Palabras de un creyente. 8. ed.
Paris, 1834.

Htn Phil 2725.2.40* Lamennais, F.R. de. Paroles d'un croyant.
Bruxelles, 1834.

Htn Phil 2725.2.36* Lamennais, F.R. de. Paroles d'un croyant. Paris, 1834.

Phil 2725.2.43 Lamennais, F.R. de. Worte eines Gläubigen. Hamburg, 1834.

Phil 8837.1.3 Mackintosh, James. A general view of the progress of
ethical philosophy. Philadelphia, 1834.

Phil 7080.7 Macnish, R. Philosophy of sleep. N.Y., 1834.

Phil 2730.50 Maine de Biran, Pierre. Nouvelles considerations sur les
rapports du physique et du moral de l'homme. Paris, 1834.

Phil 4012.1.3 Mamiani di Rovere, T. Del rinnovamento della filosofia
antica italiana. Parigi, 1834.

Phil 187.34 Marin, E. Elementos de la filosofia del espiritu humano.
Santiago, 1834.

Phil 8060.2 Müller, Eduard. Geschichte der Theorie der Kunst. v.1-2.
Breslau, 1834-37.

Phil 8595.15.3.5 Paine, Thomas. The theological works. Boston, 1834.

Phil 2415.3 Portalis, J.E.M. De l'usage et de l'abus de l'esprit
philosophique durant le XVIIE siècle. Paris, 1834.
2v.

Phil 8670.7 Prout, W. Chemistry, meteorology and the function of
digestion considered with reference to natural theology.
London, 1834.

Phil 8670.7.2 Prout, W. Chemistry, meteorology and the function of
digestion considered with reference to natural theology.
Philadelphia, 1834.

Phil 8597.7 Rennie, J. Alphabet of natural theology. London, 1834.

Htn Phil 3800.200.5* Schelling, F.W.J. von. Bruno. Reutlingen, 1834.

Htn Phil 3800.340* Schelling, F.W.J. von. Philosophische Untersuchungen über
das Wesen der menschlichen Freiheit. Reutlingen, 1834.

Htn Phil 3800.350* Schelling, F.W.J. von. Rede zum 75. Jahrestag der k.
Academie der Wissenschaften. München, 1834.

Phil 3850.10.50 Schlegel, Friedrich von. Lifrets philosophie.
Stockholm, 1834.

Phil 3805.94 Schweizer, A. Schleiermachers Wirksamkeit als Prediger.
Halle, 1834.

Phil 8598.6.2 Sedgwick, Adam. A discourse on the studies of the
university of Cambridge. 2. ed. Cambridge, 1834.

Phil 8598.6.4 Sedgwick, Adam. A discourse on the studies of the
university of Cambridge. 3. ed. Cambridge, 1834.

Phil 193.22 Sengler, J. Über das Wesen und speculativen Philosophie.
Mainz, 1834.

Phil 5938.6.3 Spurzheim, Johann Gaspar. Outlines of phrenology. 3rd ed.
Boston, 1834.

Phil 5938.6.5 Spurzheim, Johann Gaspar. Outlines of phrenology. 3rd ed.
Boston, 1834.

Phil 5938.6.11 Spurzheim, Johann Gaspar. Phrenology. Boston, 1834.
2v.

Phil 645.32 Tafel, J.F.I. Geschichte und Kritik des Skepticismus und
Irrationalismus. Tübingen, 1834.

Phil 9200.1 Taylor, Isaac. Fanaticism. N.Y., 1834.

1834 - cont.

Phil 5770.1   Uphan, T.C. A philosophical and practical treatise on the will. Portland, 1834.

Phil 8896.8   Verplanck, G.C. The influence of moral causes upon opinion. N.Y., 1834.

Phil 8677.3.2   Whewell, William. Astronomy and general physics, considered with reference to natural theology. London, 1834.

Phil 9364.3   Young lady's Sunday book. Philadelphia, 1834.

1835

Phil 5240.1.3   Abercrombie, J. Inquiries...intellectual powers. Boston, 1835.

Phil 9340.10   Adams, (Mrs.). Daily duties inculcated in a series of letters. Boston, 1835.

Phil 5040.1.5   Aldrich, H. Artis logicae rudimenta. 5th ed. Oxford, 1835.

Phil 175.35   Atterbom, P.D.A. Inledning till philosphiens system. Upsala, 1835.

Phil 3425.91.28   Bachmann, C.F. Anti-Hegel. Jena, 1835.

Phil 8626.2   Bakewell, F.C. Natural evidence of a future life. London, 1835.

Phil 8951.11.5   Bautain, Louis E. Philosophie du Christianisme. Paris, 1835. 2v.

Phil 3246.210   Bayer, Karl. Zu Fichte's Gedächtniss. Ansbach, 1835.

Phil 176.99   Bayrhoffer, K.T. Die Grundprobleme der Metaphysik. Marburg, 1835.

Htn   Phil 3801.210*   Biedermann, K. Degenetica philosophandi ratione et methods praesertim Fichti, Schellingii, Hegelii. Lipsiae, 1835.

Phil 5751.1   Bockshammer, G.F. On the freedom of the human will. Andover, 1835.

Phil 5921.5   Boston Phrenological Society. A catalogue of specimens. Boston, 1835.

Phil 1106.4   Brandes, C.A. Handbuch der Geschichte der griechisch-römischen Philosophie. Berlin, 1835-60. 5v.

Phil 8581.13   Brougham, H. A discourse of natural theology. Philadelphia, 1835.

Phil 8581.13.3   Brougham, H. A discourse of natural theology. 4. ed. London, 1835.

Phil 2205.30.8   Brougham and Vaux, Henry Brougham. Discourse of natural theology. London, 1835.

Phil 8403.16   Cameron, Charles. Two essays. London, 1835.

Phil 5922.4.6.5   Combe, George. The constitution of man. 5. American ed. Boston, 1835.

Phil 5922.3.7   Combe, George. A system of phrenology. Boston, 1835.

Phil 2520.15   Descartes, René. Oeuvres philosophiques. Paris, 1835. 4v.

Phil 8972.2.8   Dewey, Orville. A review on the Calvinistic views of moral philosophy. N.Y., 1835.

Phil 9165.1   The family book. N.Y., 1835.

Phil 8630.1   Farlin, J.W. A primer on the origin of knowledge. Saratoga Springs, 1835.

Htn   Phil 3801.391*   Fichte, I.H. Über die Bedingungen eines spekulativen Theismus. Elberfeld, 1835.

Phil 5926.1.6   Gall, F.J. On the functions of the brain. Boston, 1835. 6v.

Phil 9035.28   Gaston, William. An address delivered before the American Whig and Cliosophic Societies. 2d ed. Princeton, 1835.

Phil 181.2   Gatien-Arnoult, A. Programe d'un cours de philosophie. Paris, 1835.

Phil 8661.2.3   Godwin, B. Lectures on the atheistic controversy. Boston, 1835.

Phil 8631.1   Göschel, C.F. Von den Beweisen für die Unsterblichkeit der Menschlichen Seele. Berlin, 1835.

Phil 8685.19   Günther, A. Thomas a Scrupulis. Wien, 1835.

Phil 806.2   Guillon, M.N.S. Histoire générale de la philosophie. Paris, 1835. 4v.

Phil 8882.3   Hampden, R.D. A course of lectures...study, moral philosophy. London, 1835.

Phil 5047.3.7   Hedge, Levi. Elements of logick. Boston, 1835.

Phil 3425.9   Hegel, Georg Wilhelm Friedrich. Werke. Berlin, 1835-45. 20v.

Phil 182.17   Hillebrand, J. Philosophie des Geistes. Heidelberg, 1835-1836. 2v.

NEDL   Phil 2520.90   Hock, C.F. Cartesius und seine Gegner. Wien, 1835.

Phil 2648.31   Holbach, Paul Henri T. System of nature. N.Y., 1835.

Phil 5248.1   Ideler, K.W. Grundriss der Seelenheilkunde. Berlin, 1835-38. 2v.

Phil 2672.31   Jouffroy, Théodore S. Cours de droit naturel. Paris, 1835. 3v.

Phil 3480.31.1   Kant, Immanuel. Critique de la raison pure. 1. éd. Paris, 1835. 2v.

Htn   Phil 3801.498*   Krug, W.T. Schelling und Hegel. Leipzig, 1835.

Phil 2725.2.83   Lamennais, F.R. de. Études et notice biographique. Paris, 1835.

Phil 5926.1.10   Manual of phrenology...system of Dr. Gall. Philadelphia, 1835.

Htn   Phil 3801.546*   Marbach, G.O. Schelling, Hegel, Cousin und Krug. Regensburg, 1835.

Phil 8887.12   Mercier, A.D. Méditations philogiques et morales. Paris, 1835.

Phil 5932.2   Miles, L. Phrenology. Philadelphia, 1835.

Phil 8837.1.15   Mill, James. A fragment on Mackintosh. London, 1835.

Phil 189.26   Oegger, G. Nouvelles questions philosophiques. Tubingue, 1835.

Phil 8594.1   Ohlert, A.L.J. Religionsphilosophie. Leipzig, 1835.

Phil 5926.1.35   Ottin, N.J. Précis analytique et raisonné du système du docteur Gall. Bruxelles, 1835.

Htn   Phil 3801.749.10*   Paulus, H.E.G. Entdeckungen über des Entdeckungen unserer neuesten Philosophen. Bremen, 1835.

Phil 6965.2   Philip, A.P.W. Treatise on the more obscure affections of the brain. London, 1835.

Phil 192.5   Redern, S.E. de. Considerations sur la nature de l'homme. Paris, 1835. 2v.

Phil 1122.2   Ritter, Heinrich. Histoire de la philosophie ancienne. Paris, 1835-36. 4v.

Phil 5767.2   Romang, T.P. Über Willensfreiheit und Determinismus. Bern, 1835.

Phil 6967.3.5   Rush, B. Medical inquiries...diseases...mind. 5. ed. Philadelphia, 1835.

Phil 3805.37   Schleiermacher, Friedrich. Entwurf eines Systems der Sittenlehre. Berlin, 1835.

Phil 5938.3   Shurtleff, N.R. An epitome of phrenology. Boston, 1835.

Phil 5058.37.5   Sibbern, F.C. Logik sem taenkelaere. 2. udg. Kjöbenhavn, 1835.

1835 - cont.

Phil 5058.11   Sigwart, H.C.W. Handbuch zu Vorlesungen über Logik. Tübingen, 1835.

Phil 8893.15   Smith, Alexander. The philosophy of morals. London, 1835. 2v.

Phil 8893.21.2   Spurzheim, J.K. Philosophical catechism...natural laws of man. Boston, 1835.

Phil 3805.82   Theil. Friedrich Daniel Ernst Schleiermacher. Berlin, 1835.

Phil 194.34.15   Troxler, I.P.V. Vorlesungen über Philosophie. Bern, 1835.

Phil 8709.14.10   Turner, Sharon. The sacred history of the world. N.Y., 1835-36. 2v.

Phil 8709.14.8   Turner, Sharon. The sacred history of the world. N.Y., 1835-39. 3v.

Phil 4260.25   Vico, G.B. Oeuvres. Paris, 1835. 2v.

Phil 4260.36.5   Vico, G.B. Principes de la philosophie de l'histoire. Bruxelles, 1835.

Phil 8581.13.16   Wallace, T. Additional observations...natural theology by H. Lord Brougham. Dublin, 1835.

Phil 8581.13.15   Wallace, T. Observations...natural theology by H. Lord Brougham. London, 1835.

Phil 8972.2.2   Wardlaw, R. Christian ethics. N.Y., 1835.

Phil 8595.16.28.5   Watson, R. An apology for the Bible. N.Y., 1835. 8 pam.

Phil 8897.6   Wayland, F. Elements of moral science. Boston, 1835.

Phil 8897.6.2   Wayland, F. The elements of moral science. N.Y., 1835.

Phil 8712.05   Wayland, Francis. A discourse delivered at...dedication of...the chapel. Providence, 1835.

Phil 3925.3.31   Weisse, Christian Hermann. Grundzüge der Metaphysik. Hamburg, 1835.

Phil 5264.1   Young, J. Lectures on intellectual philosophy. Glasgow, 1835.

.1836

Htn   Phil 9160.1.9*   Abbott, Jacob. Parental duties in the promotion of early piety. London, 1836.

Phil 5240.2   Ahrens, Heinrich. Cours de psychologie. v.1-2. Paris, 1836-38.

Phil 8580.3.5   Allen, E. Reason, the only oracle of man. N.Y., 1836.

Phil 3001.1   Barchou, A.T.H. Histoire de la philosophie allemande. Paris, 1836. 2v.

Phil 8656.1   Barclay, J. Without faith, without God. London, 1836.

Phil 8826.3   Blakey, R. History of moral science. Edinburgh, 1836. 2v.

Phil 9230.30   Borély, Joseph. Discours prononcé devant la cour royale d'Aix à l'audience solennelle de rentrée. Aix, 1836.

Phil 5921.1   Broussais, F.J.V. Cours de phrénologie. Paris, 1836.

Phil 9341.6   Butler, C. The American gentleman. Philadelphia, 1836.

Phil 9100.69   Butler, Joseph. Fifteen sermons. London, 1836.

Htn   Phil 1930.1.30*   Carlyle, Thomas. Sartor Resartus. Boston, 1836.

Phil 8581.10   Chalmers, T. Bridgewater treatises [1,8]. On the power, wisdom, and goodness of God. Philadelphia, 1836.

Htn   Phil 1930.4.31*   Collier, Arthur. Clavis universalis. Edinburgh, 1836.

Phil 6672.4   Colquhoun, J.C. Isis Revelata: an inquiry into animal magnetism. London, 1836. 2v.

Phil 5922.4.40   Combe, George. Lectures on moral philosophy. Boston, 1836.

Phil 5922.4.51   Combe, George. The suppressed documents. Glasgow, 1836.

Phil 5922.4.20   Combe, George. Testimonials. Edinburgh, 1836. 3 pam.

Phil 2496.40   Cousin, Victor. Cours de philosophie...Du Vrai, Du Bean, Du Bien. Paris, 1836.

Phil 5922.5   Cox, R. Selections from the Phrenological Journal. Edinburgh, 1836.

Phil 5043.1   Damiron, M.J.P. Cours de philosophie. Paris, 1836.

Phil 9343.3   Daughter's own book. Philadelphia, 1836.

Phil 8583.4.3   Dick, T. On the improvement of society by the diffusion of knowledge. N.Y., 1836.

Phil 8583.4.5.-.9   Dick, T. Works. Philadelphia, 1836. 5v.

Phil 6673.4.17   Du Potet, J. de S. L'université de Montpellier et le magnétisme animal. Beziers, 1836.

Phil 9344.1   Eddy, A.D. Addresses on duties of youth. N.Y., 1836.

Htn   Phil 1980.2.30*   Emerson, R.W. Nature. Boston, 1836.

Phil 5924.2   Epps, John. Internal evidences of Christianity deduced from phrenology. 2. ed. London, 1836.

Phil 9342.3A   Farrar, Eliza W.R. Young lady's friend. Boston, 1836.

Phil 3210.67   Fechner, G.T. Das Büchlein vom Leben nach dem Tode. Dresden, 1836.

Phil 8585.3   Fellowes, R. The religion of the universe. London, 1836.

Phil 8585.3.2   Fellowes, R. The religion of the universe. London, 1836.

Phil 9045.18   Fox, William J. Reports of lecture on morality. London, 1836.

Phil 6955.8   Friedreich, H.B. Historisch-kritische Darstellung der Theorien über das Wesen und den Sitz der psychischen Krankheiten. Leipzig, 1836.

Phil 181.1.15   Gabler, G.A. De verae philosophiae erga religionem Christi. Berolini, 1836.

Phil 8881.57.5   Giambioni, Bono. Della miseria dell'uomo. Firenze, 1836.

Phil 525.42   Gorres, J. Die christliche Mystik. Bd.1-2,3,4[1],4[2]. Regensburg, 1836-42.

Phil 182.41   Hartenstein, G. Probleme und Grundlehren der allgemeinen Metaphysik. Leipzig, 1836.

Phil 3090.80.15   Hoffmann, F. Vorhalle zur speculativen Lehre F. Baader's. Aschaffenburg, 1836.

Phil 6677.3A   Husson, H.M. Report on the magnetical experiments. Boston, 1836.

Phil 8663.1   Irons, W.J. On the whole doctrine of final causes. London, 1836.

Phil 5929.1   Jones, T. Practical phrenology. Boston, 1836.

Phil 3480.61   Kant, Immanuel. Metaphysical works. London, 1836.

Phil 3480.85.10   Kant, Immanuel. Von der Macht des Gemüths durch den blossen Vorsatz seiner krankhaften Gefühle Meister zu seyn. 3. Aufl. Leipzig, 1836.

Phil 8581.10.2   Kidd, J. Bridgewater treatises [2]. On the adaptation of external nature to the physical condition of man. Philadelphia? 1836?

Phil 8610.834.5   Kneeland, A. National hymns. Boston, 1836.

Phil 3525.20   Krause, K.C.F. Handschriftlicher Nachlass; Logik. Göttingen, 1836.

Phil 3528.50   Krug, Wilhelm Traugott. Über altes und neues Christenthum. Leipzig, 1836.

Phil 2725.2.82   Lamennais, F.R. de. Catalogue de livres rares et precieux provenant de la bibliothèque de M.F. de la Mennais. Paris, 1836.

Phil 5931.1   Lélut, L.F. Qu'est-ce que la phrénologie...Gall. Paris, 1836.

Chronological Listing

1836 - cont.

Phil 2115.58.9	Locke, J. The reasonableness of Christianity. London, 1836.
Phil 1850.86	Maestre, J. de. Examen de la philosophie de Bacon. Paris, 1836. 2v.
Phil 4012.1	Mamiani di Rovere, T. Del rinnovamento della filosofia antica italiana. Milano, 1836.
Phil 4012.1.4	Mamiani di Rovere, T. Del rinnovamento della filosofia antica italiana. 3. ed. Firenze, 1836.
Phil 9184.1	More, H. The young bride at home. Boston, 1836.
Phil 9352.5.10	Muzzey, A.B. Young man's friend. Boston, 1836.
Phil 7068.36.20	Ottway, T. The spectre. London, 1836.
Phil 2205.30.7.5	Paley, W. Natural theology. London, 1836.
Phil 2205.30.7	Paley, W. Natural theology. London, 1836. 2v.
Phil 2805.42.3	Pascal, Blaise. Thoughts on religion. London, 1836.
Phil 817.2.4	Ritter, A.H. Geschichte der Philosophie. 2e Aufl. Hamburg, 1836-53. 12v.
Phil 8672.3	Ritter, H. Über der Erkenntniss Gottes in der Welt. Hamburg, 1836.
Phil 8581.10.5	Roget, P.M. Bridgewater treatises [5]. Animal, vegetable physiology. Philadelphia, 1836. 2v.
Phil 3805.175	Rosenkranz, Karl. Kritik der Schleiermacherschen Glaubenslehre. Königsberg, 1836.
Phil 4210.22	Rosmini-Serbati, Antonio. Nouovo saggio sull'origine delle idee. Milano, 1836-37. 3v.
Phil 4210.24.5	Rosmini-Serbati, Antonio. Il rinnovamento della filosofia in Italia. Milano, 1836. 3 pam.
Htn Phil 193.10*	Schlegel, Friedrich von. Philosophische Vorlesungen. Bonn, 1836-37. 2v.
Phil 3838.12	Schlüter, C.B. Die Lehre des Spinoza. Münster, 1836.
Phil 193.12	Schmid, J.H. Vorlesungen...Wesen der Philosophie. Stuttgart, 1836.
Htn Phil 3808.65*	Schopenhauer, Arthur. Über den Willen in der Natur. Frankfurt, 1836.
Phil 3018.16	Schram, J. Beitrag zur Geschichte der Philosophie. Bonn, 1836.
Phil 8598.8	Serious thoughts...Brougham's discourse of natural theology. London, 1836-31. 2 pam.
Phil 3850.19.30	Suabedissen, D.T.A. Die Grundzüge der Metaphysik. Marburg, 1836.
Phil 8644.2	Taylor, Isaac. Physical theory of another life. N.Y., 1836.
Phil 8644.2.2	Taylor, Isaac. Physical theory of another life. 2. ed. N.Y., 1836.
Phil 4235.3.31	Testa, Alfonso. Della filosofia della mente. Piacenza, 1836.
Phil 8599.9.5	Turton, Thomas. Natural theology considered with reference to Lord Brougham's discourse on that subject. 2. ed. London, 1836.
Phil 8599.9	Turton, Thomas. Natural theology considered with reference to Lord Brougham's discourse on that subject. 2. ed. Cambridge, 1836.
Phil 5620.11	Vacherot, Étienne. De rationis autoritate. Cadomi, 1836.
EDL Phil 8897.67	Walsh, Robert. Didactics. Philadelphia, 1836. 2v.
Phil 5910.3	Watson, H.C. Statistics of phrenology. London, 1836-1837. 2 pam.
Phil 5062.6.3.5	Whately, Richard. Elements of logic. N.Y., 1836.
Phil 8897.24.5	Wright, F. Course of popular lectures. v.2. Philadelphia, 1836.
Phil 9364.4	The youth's guide. Worcester, 1836.
Phil 9515.3.8	Zimmermann, J.G. Solitude. v.1-2. Exeter, 1836.

1837

Phil 5240.1.12	Abercrombie, J. The culture and discipline of the mind. 6th ed. Edinburgh, 1837.
Phil 8875.2	Adams, J. Elements of moral philosophy. Cambridge, 1837.
Phil 9160.3.7	Alcott, W.A. The young wife. Boston, 1837.
Phil 5135.1.4	Bailey, S. Essays on the formation and publication of opinions. London, 1837.
Phil 3100.60	Beneke, F.E. Grundlinien des natürlichen System der praktischen Philosophie. Berlin, 1837-41. 2v.
Phil 9035.22	Bucke, Charles. The book of human character. London, 1837. 2v.
Phil 8581.10.6	Buckland, W. Bridgewater treatises [6]. Geology and mineralogy. London, 1837. 2v.
Phil 8656.6	Buckland, W. Geology and mineralogy...natural theology. London, 1837. 2v.
Phil 5811.6	Bushnan, J.S. The philosophy of instinct and reason. Edinburgh, 1837.
Phil 7068.37	Calmet, Augustin. Des benediktiner-abtes zu Senones. München. 1837.
Phil 6750.2	Colquhoun, L. Report of the proceedings...of idiotry. Edinburgh, 1837.
Phil 5242.10	Costa, P. Del modo di comporre l'idee. Firenze, 1837. 2 pam.
Phil 8610.837	Criticisms on current theology as they appeared in the 18th century. London, 1837. 4 pam.
Phil 1925.31	Cudworth, R. The true intellectual system of the universe. Andover, 1837-38. 2v.
Phil 5243.1	Damiron, J.P. Cours de philosophie. Paris, 1837. 2v.
Phil 6673.2.8	Deleuze, J.P.F. Practical instruction in animal magnetism. Providence, 1837.
Phil 6673.5	Durant, C.F. Exposition, or A new theory animal magnetism. N.Y., 1837.
Phil 804.2.5	Enfield, W. History of philosophy. London, 1837.
Phil 5924.2.2	Epps, John. Internal evidences of Christianity deduced from phrenology. Boston, 1837.
Phil 6114.11	Erdmann, J.E. Leib und Seele nach ihrem Begriff und ihrem Verhaltniss zur Einander. Halle, 1837.
Phil 9345.9	Farrar, Eliza W. The young lady's friend. Boston, 1837.
Phil 4260.81	Ferrari, G. La mente di Giambattista Vico. Milano, 1837.
Phil 805.2	Fries, J.F. Die Geschichte der Philosophie. Halle, 1837-40. 2v.
Phil 3260.60	Fries, J.F. Handbuch der psychischen Anthropologie. Jena, 1837.
Phil 3260.50	Fries, J.F. System der Logik. Heidelberg, 1837.
Phil 8586.9	Gallaudet, T.H. The class-book of natural theology. 2nd ed. Hartford, 1837.
Phil 4112.30.2	Galluppi, Pasquale. Elementi di filosofia. Bologna, 1837. 3v.
Phil 8586.13	George, J.F.L. Mythus und Sage. Berlin, 1837.
Phil 3805.174	Hartenstein, G. De ethice a Schleiermachero propositae fundamento. Pt.1-2. Lipsiae, 1837.
Phil 3428.30	Herbart, J.F. Lehrbuch zur Einleitung in die Philosophie. Königsberg, 1837.

1837 - cont.

Phil 5927.1	Howe, S.G. A discourse on the social relations of man. Boston, 1837.
Phil 3480.65.20	Kant, Immanuel. Principes métaphysiques de la morale. Paris, 1837.
Phil 3480.67.55	Kant, Immanuel. Principes métaphysiques du droit. Paris, 1837.
Phil 8581.10.7	Kirby, W. Bridgewater treatises [7]. On the power...God. Philadelphia, 1837.
Phil 8411.5	Krause, K.C.F. Karl Christian Friedrich Krause's Abriss der Asthetik oder der Philosophie des schönen Kunst. Göttingen, 1837.
Phil 1850.126	The life and writings of Francis Bacon. Edinburgh, 1837.
Phil 187.1	M'Cormac, H. Philosophy of human nature. London, 1837.
Phil 8667.2	Macculloch, J. Proofs and illustrations of the attributes of God. London, 1837. 3v.
Phil 8837.1.4	Mackintosh, James. A general view of the progress of ethical philosophy. Edinburgh, 1837.
Phil 2733.5	Malebranche, Nicolas. Oeuvres complètes. Paris, 1837. 2v.
Phil 187.12	Matthiae, A.H. Manuel de philosophie. Paris, 1837.
Phil 9172.5	Means without living. Boston, 1837.
Phil 3012.1	Michelet, C.L. Geschichte...Philosophie in Deutschland. Berlin, 1837-38. 2v.
Phil 9352.6	My daughter's manual. N.Y., 1837.
Phil 5933.1	Noble, Daniel. An inquiry into the claims of phrenology, to rank among the sciences. Manchester, 1837.
Phil 1145.15	Oakeley, Frederick. Remarks upon Aristotelian and Platonic ethics. Oxford, 1837.
Phil 190.2	Parr, S. Metaphysical tracts by English philosophers of the 18th century. London, 1837.
Phil 6685.4	Peyen, C. Progress of animal magnetism. Boston, 1837.
Htn Phil 6685.11*	The philosophy of animal magnetism. Philadelphia, 1837.
Phil 9355.4	Potter, Horatio. The importance of liberal tastes and good intellectual habits. Troy, N.Y., 1837.
Phil 6965.4	Prichard, J.C. Treatise on insanity and other disorders. Philadelphia, 1837.
Phil 8417.3.5	Quatremère de Quincy, Antoine C. An essay on the nature, the end, and the means of imitation in the fine arts. London, 1837.
Phil 3195.4.81	Rosenkranz, Karl. Erinnerungen an Karl Daub. Berlin, 1837.
Phil 3780.37	Rosenkranz, Karl. Psychologie oder die Wissenschaft vom subjectiven Geist. Königsberg, 1837.
Phil 4210.8	Rosmini-Serbati, Antonio. Opere edite e inedite. v.5, 11-14, 20, 27-30. Milano, 1837. 10v.
Htn Phil 3801.763.5*	Salat, Jakob. Schelling in München. pt.I. Freiburg, 1837.
Phil 3018.12	Schaller, J. Die Philosophie unserer Zeit. Leipzig, 1837.
Phil 3805.50.10	Schleiermacher, Friedrich. Die Weihnachtsfeier. 3. Ausg. Berlin, 1837.
Phil 5938.1	Scott, W. The harmony of phrenology with scripture. Edinburgh, 1837.
Phil 3018.2	Sengler, J. Ueber das Wesen...Philosophie und Theologie in der gegenwärtigen Zeit...Religionsphilosophie. Heidelberg, 1837.
Phil 5938.2	Sewall, T. An examination of phrenology. Washington, 1837.
Phil 9178.3	Smith, D.D. Lectures on domestic duties. Portland, 1837.
Phil 193.117	Snellman, J.W. Philosophisk elementar-curs. 1. Psychologi; 2. Logik; 3. Rättslära. Stockholm, 1837-1840. 3 pam.
Phil 4803.799.2	Śniadecki, Jan. Dzieła. v.1-7. Warszawa, 1837-39. 3v.
Phil 9358.12	Southwick, Solomon. Five lessons for young men. Albany, 1837.
Phil 6688.5	Stone, W.L. Letter to Dr. Brigham on animal magnetism. N.Y., 1837.
Phil 5059.1	Tagart, Edward. Remarks on mathematical or demonstrative reasoning. London, 1837.
Phil 7054.153.15	Tales of the horrible, or The book of spirits. London, 1837.
Phil 4803.846.30	Trentowski, Bronisław F. Grundlage der universellen Philosophie. Karlsruhe, 1837.
Phil 8896.13	Vermilye, T.E. An introductory address to the course of lectures before the young men's Association for Mutual Improvement in the city of Albany. Albany, 1837.
Phil 8896.12	Vinet, Alexandre. Essais de philosophie morale et de moral e religieuse. Paris, 1837.
Phil 9362.6	Winslow, H. Young man's aid. Boston, 1837.
Phil 8712.13.1	Wiseman, N.P.S. Twelve lectures on the connexion between science and revealed religion. Andover, 1837.
Phil 8897.23.3	Wright, T. A good life. Boston, 1837.
Phil 3120.2.115	Zimmermann, J. Krug und Bolzano. Sulzbach, 1837.

1838

Phil 5240.1.4	Abercrombie, J. Inquiries...intellectual powers. N.Y., 1838.
Phil 8581.11	Babbage, C. The ninth Bridgewater treatise. 2. ed. London, 1838.
Phil 8581.10.9	Babbage, C. The ninth Bridgewater treatise. 2. ed. London, 1838.
Phil 1850.34.5	Bacon, Francis. Of the proficience and advancement of learning. London, 1838.
Phil 1850.21	Bacon, Francis. The works of Lord Bacon. London, 1838. 2v.
Phil 5938.7	Bartlett, E. An address of the birth of Spurzheim. Boston, 1838.
Phil 801.30	Bayrhoffer, K.T. Die Idee und Geschichte der Philosophie. Marburg, 1838.
Phil 176.96	Biunde, F.X. Fundamental-Philosophie. Trier, 1838.
Phil 5041.14	Bobrik, Eduard. Neues praktisches System der Logik. Zürich, 1838.
Phil 3110.60	Böhme, J. Blüthen aus Jakob Böhme's Mystik. Stuttgart, 1838.
Phil 8626.6.2.5	Bolzano, B. Anhang zur zweiten Auflage der Athanasia. Sulzbach, 1838.
Phil 1880.28	Bowen, F. Berkeley and his philosophy. Cambridge, 1838-57. 5 pam.
Phil 176.32	Buchez, P.T.B. Traité de philosophie. Paris, 1838. 3v.
Phil 8656.6.5	Buckland, W. Geologie und Mineralogie. Neufchatel, 1838-39. 2v.
Phil 5922.1	Caldwell, C. Phrenology vindicated and antiphrenology unmasked. N.Y., 1838.
Phil 9045.10	Carpenter, L. Discourse on Christian patriotism. London, 1838.

Phil 5242.3   Chardel, C. Essai de psychologie. Paris, 1838.
Phil 6112.15.5   Combe, G. On the functions of the cerebellum. Edinburgh, 1838.
Phil 5922.3.3   Combe, George. A system of phrenology. Boston, 1838.
Phil 2496.50   Cousin, Victor. Elements of psychology. N.Y., 1838.
Phil 2496.30   Cousin, Victor. Fragments philosophiques. Paris, 1838. 2v.
Phil 5752.5   Cudworth, R. A treatis of freewill. London, 1838.
Phil 178.24.5   Daub, Carl. Philosophische und theologische Vorlesungen. v.1-7. Berlin, 1838-44. 8v.
Phil 8878.5.4   Davy, H. Consolations in travel. 4th ed. London, 1838.
X Cg   Phil 5753.4   Day, Jeremiah. An inquiry...power of the will. New Haven, 1838. 4v.
Phil 8878.9   Dewey, O. Moral views of commerce, society and politics. N.Y., 1838.
Phil 6673.4.19   Du Potet, J. de S. An introduction to the study of animal magnetism. London, 1838.
Phil 6954.3.5   Esquirol, Etienne. Des maladies mentales. v.1,2 and atlas. Paris, 1838. 3v.
Phil 2450.81   Feuerback, L.A. Pierre Bayle. Ansbach, 1838.
Phil 5045.1   Fischer, Friedrich. Lehrbuch der Logik. Stuttgart, 1838.
Phil 5925.4   Fletcher, J. The mirror of nature...science of phrenology. Boston, 1838.
Phil 5925.3.11   Fowler, O.S. Phrenology proved. N.Y., 1838.
Phil 8612.22   Fox, W.J. Reports of lectures delivered at the chapel So. Place, Finsburg. Nos. 9,10,12. London, 1838.
Phil 9045.18.5   Fox, William J. Reports of lectures delivered. London, 1838.
Phil 5015.1   Franck, A. Esquisse d'une histoire de la logique. Paris, 1838.
Phil 4112.40.2   Galluppi, Pasquale. Lettere filosofiche. Napoli, 1838.
Phil 8407.50   Geel, Jacobus. Onderzoek en phantasie. Leiden, 1838.
Phil 4120.1.31   Gioja, Melchiorre. Elementi di filosofia ad uso de'Giovanetti. v.1-2. Milano, 1838.
Phil 4120.1.8   Gioja, Melchiorre. Opere principali. Lugano, 1838-40. 16v.
Phil 8586.24   Goeschel, C.F. Beiträge zur Spekulativen philosophie. Berlin, 1838.
Phil 3006.5   Günther, A. Die Juste-Milieus in der deutschen Philosophie. Wien, 1838.
Phil 3428.160   Hartenstein, G. Über die neuesten Darstellungen und Beurtheilungen der Herbart'schen Philosophie. Leipzig, 1838.
Phil 182.15   Heusde, P.W. Die Socratic Schule. v.1-2. Erlangen, 1838.
Phil 9375.1   Hints to young tradmen. Boston, 1838.
Phil 2672.30   Jouffroy, Théodore S. Mélanges philosophiques. Paris, 1838.
Phil 3480.32   Kant, Immanuel. Critick of pure reason. London, 1838.
Phil 3480.40.52   Kant, Immanuel. Menschenkunde oder philosophische Anthropologie. Quedlinburg, 1838.
Phil 3480.71.5   Kant, Immanuel. Religion within the boundary of Pure reason. Edinburgh, 1838.
Phil 3480.12   Kant, Immanuel. Sämmtliche Werke. Leipzig, 1838-40. 12v.
Phil 3480.19.16   Kant, Immanuel. Vorzügliche Kleine Schriften und Aufsätze. v.1-2. Quedlinburg, 1838.
Phil 3480.11   Kant, Immanuel. Werke. Leipzig, 1838-39. 10v.
Htn   Phil 2725.2.52*   Lamennais, F.R. de. Le livre du peuple. Paris, 1838.
Phil 3552.23.5   Leibniz, Gottfried Wilhelm. Deutsche Schriften. Berlin, 1838-40. 2v.
Phil 9390.2   Lewis, E. Dissertation on oaths. Philadelphia, 1838.
Phil 8701.2.4   Lewis, Tayler. Faith, the life of science. Albany, 1838.
Phil 9450.1   Lieber, F. Manual of political ethics. Boston, 1838-39. 2v.
Phil 342.16   Lubboch, J.W. Remarks on the classification of the different branches of human knowledge. London, 1838.
Phil 4012.1.5   Mamiani di Rovere, T. Sei lettere...intorno al libro filosofia antica italiana. Parigi, 1838.
Phil 812.14   Marbach, G.O. Lehrbuch des Geschichte der Philosophie. v.1-2. Leipzig, 1838-41.
Phil 8887.3   Martineau, H. How to observe. Morals and manners. London, 1838.
Phil 8887.3.2   Martineau, H. How to observe. Morals and manners. N.Y., 1838.
Phil 8887.3.3   Martineau, H. How to observe. Morals and manners. N.Y., 1838.
Phil 6962.3   Mayo, T. Elements of pathology of human mind. London, 1838.
Phil 3625.1.7   Mendelssohn, Moses. Moses Mendelssohn's sämmtliche Werke. Wien, 1838.
Phil 3625.1.5   Mendelssohn, Moses. Sämmtliche Werke. Wien, 1838.
Htn   Phil 2150.3.30*   Miller, William. Evidence from Scripture...the second coming of Christ. Troy, 1838.
Phil 9352.5.11   Muzzey, A.B. Young man's friend. Boston, 1838.
Phil 5053.8   Newman, F.W. Lectures on logic. Oxford, 1838.
Phil 2205.13.15   Paley, W. Works. London, 1838. 4v.
Phil 6685.2   Peabody, J.R. World of wonders. Boston, 1838.
Phil 296.1   Petöcz, M. Ansicht der Welt. Leipzig, 1838.
Phil 9290.1   Quill, C. The American mechanic. Philadelphia, 1838.
Phil 1195.8   Rascher, Wilhelm. De historicae doctrinae apud sophistas maiores vesligus. Inaug. Diss. Gottingae, 1838.
Phil 6967.5.4   Ray, Isaac. Treatise of medical jurisprudence of insanity. Boston, 1838.
Phil 5257.2   Reed, S. Observations on the growth of the mind. Boston, 1838.
Phil 3499.17   Reiche, L.P.A. De Kanti antinomüs. Thesis. Gottingae, 1838.
Phil 8707.4   Rhind, W. The age of the earth. Edinburgh, 1838.
Phil 2417.2A   Ripley, G. Philosophical miscellanies...Cousin, Jouffray. Boston, 1838. 2v.
Phil 817.2.2   Ritter, A.H. Zusätze und Verbesserungen. Hamburg, 1838.
Phil 1122.3   Ritter, Heinrich. Historia philosophiae graeco-romanae. Hamburg, 1838.
Phil 1122.2.6   Ritter, Heinrich. History of ancient philosophy. Oxford, 1838-46. 4v.
Phil 1122.2.5   Ritter, Heinrich. History of ancient philosophy. Oxford, 1838-46. 4v.
Phil 8842.8   Romagnosi, G.D. L'antica morale filosofia. Prato, 1838.
Phil 193.10.9   Schlegel, Friedrich von. Philosophie de la vie. Paris, 1838.
Phil 5258.7.10   Schubert, G.H. von. Lehrbuch der Menschen- und Seelenkunde. Erlangen, 1838.
Phil 9178.2.2   Sigourney, L.H. Letters to mothers. Hartford, 1838.

Phil 5938.5   Slade, J. Colloquies. Imaginary conversations between a phrenologist and the shade of Dugald Stewart. London, 1838.
Phil 5938.6.12   Spurzheim, Johann Gaspar. Phrenology. 5th American ed. Boston, 1838.
Phil 8897.6.3   Wayland, F. The elements of moral science. Boston, 1838.
Phil 9470.1   Wayland, F. The limitations of human responsibility. Boston, 1838.
Phil 9470.1.2   Wayland, F. The limitations of human responsibility. N.Y., 1838.
Phil 9362.3.5   Whitman, J. Young man's assistant. Portland, 1838.
Phil 6692.7   Wiener, M. Selma, die jüdische Seherin. Berlin, 1838.

1839

Phil 9340.4   Abbott, John S. The school-boy. Boston, 1839.
Phil 8875.1.3   Abercrombie, J. The philosophy of the moral feelings. N.Y., 1839.
NEDL   Phil 9160.3   Alcott, W.A. The young husband. Boston, 1839.
Phil 5920.1   Azais, P.H. De la phrénologie. Paris, 1839. 2v.
Phil 1900.80   Bartlett, T. Memoirs...Joseph Butler D.C.L. London, 1839.
Phil 5241.9   Bautain, L.E.M. Psychologie experimentale. Strasbourg, 1839. 2v.
Phil 3100.70   Beneke, F.E. Syllogismorum analyticorum origines et ordinem naturalem. Berolini, 1839.
Phil 6671.21   Billot, G.P. Recherches psychologiques...magnétisme vital. v.1-2. Paris, 1839.
Phil 5041.17   Bosanquet, S.R. A new system of logic. London, 1839.
Phil 8581.13.5   Brougham, H. Dissertations on the subjects of science. London, 1839. 2v.
Phil 6951.6.5   Broussais, F.J.V. De l'irritation et de la folie. Paris, 1839. 2v.
Phil 1900.37   Butler, Joseph. Analogy of religion. N.Y., 1839.
Phil 8691.12.5.5   Chalmers, Thomas. On the power, wisdom and goodness of God. London, 1839. 2v.
Phil 5922.4.12   Combe, George. The constitution of man. Boston, 1839.
Phil 5922.4   Combe, George. Lectures on phrenology. N.Y., 1839.
NEDL   Phil 8827.2   Cousin, V. Cours d'histoire de la philosophie morale au dix-huitième siècle. Paris, 1839-42. 3v.
Phil 9342.14   Coxe, Margaret. The young lady's companion. Columbus, 1839.
Phil 178.29   Dean, Amos. Philosophy of human life. Boston, 1839.
Phil 6953.3   Derby, J.B. Life among lunatics. Boston, 1839.
Phil 8583.4.15   Dick, T. Works. v.1-4. Hartford, 1839.
Phil 8693.11   Doane, George W. The word of God to be studied with his works. Burlington, 1839.
Phil 3120.2.105   Dr. Bolzano und seine Gegner. Sulzbach, 1839.
Phil 8583.8.2   Duncan, H. Sacred philosophy. v.3. Boston, 1839?
Phil 8583.8   Duncan, H. Sacred philosophy of the Seasons. Boston, 1839. 2v.
Phil 8879.3.2   Ellis, S.S. The women of England. v.1-2. Philadelphia, 1839.
Phil 5044.4   Erhard, A. Handbuch der Logik. München, 1839.
Phil 9560.1.5   Essay on prudence, by a lover of peace. n.p., 1839.
Phil 4260.81.5   Ferrari, G. Vico et l'Italie. Paris, 1839.
Phil 4215.1.80   Ferrari, Giuseppe. La mente di G.D. Romagnosi. Prato, 1839.
Phil 3235.52   Feuerbach, Ludwig. Über Philosophie und Christenthum. Mannheim, 1839.
Phil 180.5   Field, G. Outlines of analogical philosophy. London, 1839. 2v.
Phil 8660.9   Fischer, K.P. Die Idee der Gottheit. Stuttgart, 1839.
Phil 5925.3.10   Fowler, O.S. Phrenology proved. N.Y., 1839.
Phil 8630.12   The future life of the good. Boston, 1839.
Phil 5246.2   Garnier, A. La psychologie et la phrénologie comparées. Paris, 1839.
Phil 4120.1.33   Gioja, Melchiorre. Del merito e delle ricompense. Lugano, 1839. 2v.
Phil 5046.4   Gockel, C.F. Propädentische Logik und Hodegetik. Karlsruhe, 1839.
Phil 181.15   Grazia, V. de. Saggio...della scienza umana. Napoli, 1839.
Phil 4570.1.30   Grubbe, Samuel. Filosofisk rätts- och samhälls-lära. Upsala, 1839.
NEDL   Phil 8882.7   Heinroth, J.C.A. Der Schlüssel zu Himmel und Hölle. Leipzig, 1839.
Phil 3428.67   Herbart, J.F. Psychologische Untersuchungen. Göttingen, 1839-40.
NEDL   Phil 2045.11   Hobbes, Thomas. English works. v.1-7,9-11. London, 1839-45. 10v.
Phil 2045.12   Hobbes, Thomas. Opera philosophica. London, 1839-45. 5v.
Phil 2045.10   Hobbes, Thomas. Opera philosophica. London, 1839-45. 5v.
Phil 9348.1   The institution of a gentleman. London, 1839.
Phil 9349.1   James, J.A. Young man from home. N.Y., 1839.
Phil 3450.13.90   Kist, N.C. Memoriam Heusdii. Lugduni Batavorum, 1839.
Phil 2725.2.55   Lamennais, F.R. de. The people's own book. Boston, 1839.
Phil 3552.15   Leibniz, Gottfried Wilhelm. Opera philosophica. v.1-2. Berolini, 1839-40.
Phil 2496.81.2   Leroux, P. Réfutation de l'eclectisme. Paris, 1839.
Phil 5821.10   Leuret, F. Anatomie comparée du système nerveux. Paris, 1839.
Phil 9450.1.2   Lieber, F. Manual of political ethics. Boston, 1839. 2v.
Phil 3525.81   Lindemann, H.S. Uebersichtliche Darstellung des Lebens und der Wissenschaftlehre K.C.F. Krause's. München, 1839.
Phil 2115.48.25   Locke, J. Oeuvres de Locke et Leibnitz. Paris, 1839.
Phil 8702.10   Mason, Henry M. The relation between religion and science. n.p., 1839.
Phil 6682.5   Meyer, J.A.G. Natur. Gotha, 1839.
Htn   Phil 3801.570*A   Michelet, Carl L. Schelling und Hegel. Berlin, 1839.
Phil 3801.570.2   Michelet, Carl L. Schelling und Hegel. Berlin, 1839.
Phil 187.48   Mirbt, Ernst. Was heisst Philosophiren und was 1st Philosophie? Jena, 1839.
Phil 6962.6   Moreau-Christopie, L.M. De la mortalité et de la folie. Paris, 1839.
Phil 8887.27   Muzzey, A.B. The moral teacher. N.Y., 1839.
Phil 8593.3.3   Nichols, I. A catechism of natural theology. Boston, 1839.
Phil 2805.40.13.10   Pascal, Blaise. Pensées de Blaise Pascal. Paris, 1839.
Phil 6685.8   Pigeaire, Jules. Puissance de l'électricité animale. Paris, 1839.
Phil 5257.4   Reinhold, E.C. Lehrbuch der philosophisch propäeutischen Psychologie und der formalen Logik. 2. Aufl. Jena, 1839.

1839 - cont.

Phil 3837.18   Rietz, J.E.   De Spinozismi fonte orientali. Diss. Lundae, 1839.

Phil 8620.10.5   Ritter, H.   Über das Böse und seine Folgen. Kiel, 1839.

Phil 192.12.5   Ritter, Heinrich.   Kleine philosophische Schriften. v.1-3. Kiel, 1839-1840.

Phil 3780.30   Rosenkranz, Karl.   Studien. v.1-5. Berlin, 1839-48. 4v.

Phil 3892.8.2   Rush, Benjamin.   An inquiry into the influence of physical causes upon the moral faculty. Philadelphia, 1839.

Phil 818.12   Schmidt, Edward.   Umrisse zur Geschichte der Philosophie. Berlin, 1839.

Phil 6688.23.2   Scobardi, R.P.   Rapport confidentiel sur le magnétisme animal. 2. éd. Paris, 1839.

Htn   Phil 9358.2.5*   Sedgwick, C.   Means and ends, or Self-training. Boston, 1839.

Phil 5938.2.2   Sewall, T.   An examination of phrenology. Boston, 1839.

Phil 9178.2   Sigourney, L.H.   Letters to mothers. N.Y., 1839.

Phil 3838.2   Sigwart, H.C.W.   Der Spinozismus. Tübingen, 1839.

Phil 8708.21   Silliman, B.   Suggestions relative to the philosophy of geology. New Haven, 1839.

Phil 193.29   Smart, Benjamin Humphrey.   Beginnings of a new school of metaphysics. London, 1839.

Phil 299.18   Snell, Karl.   Philosophische Betrachtungen der Natur. Dresden, 1839.

Phil 5058.16   Solly, T.   A syllabus of logic. Cambridge, 1839.

Phil 8598.58.5   Steffens, H.   Christliche Religionsphilosophie. Pt.1-2. Breslau, 1839. 2v.

Phil 5938.13   Stevens, Enos.   Rudiments of metal philosophy and phrenological chart. Lampeter, Pa., 1839.

Phil 3850.19.50   Suabedissen, D.T.A.   Die Grundzüge der philosophischen Tugend- und Rechtslehre. Marburg, 1839.

Phil 4813.10   Szontagh, Gusztav.   Propylaeumok a' magyar phìlosophiákoz. Budań, 1839.

NEDL   Phil 5754.1.25   Tappan, H.P.   Review of Edward's inquiry...freedom. N.Y., 1839.

Phil 819.1.8   Tennemann, W.G.   Manuel de l'historie de la philosophie. Paris, 1839. 2v.

Phil 5260.1.4   Upham, T.C.   Elements of mental philosophy. 3. ed. Portland, 1839. 2v.

Phil 5440.11   Walker, Alexander.   Intermarriage. N.Y., 1839.

Htn   Phil 5440.11.2*   Walker, Alexander.   Intermarriage. N.Y., 1839.

Phil 197.15   Weber, H.B. von.   Kleine Philosophie und politische Schriften. Stuttgart, 1839.

Phil 7054.51.10   Werner, H.   Die Schutzgeister. Stuttgart, 1839.

Phil 8897.14.15   Whewell, W.   On the foundations of morals. N.Y., 1839.

Phil 9362.3.2   Whitman, J.   Young lady's aid. 2d ed. Portland, 1839.

Phil 9362.6.2   Winslow, H.   Young man's aid. Boston, 1839.

Phil 9364.5   The young husband's book. Philadelphia, 1839.

1840

Phil 9160.2.5   Abbott, Jacob.   The school-girl. Boston, 1840.

Phil 281.6.10   Ayais, H.   Constitution de l'univers. Paris, 1840.

Phil 8581.10.4.5   Bell, Charles.   Bridgewater treatises [4]. The hand, its mechanism and vital endowments. N.Y., 1840.

Phil 3100.30   Beneke, F.E.   System der Metaphysik and Religionsphilosophie. Berlin, 1840.

Phil 176.93   Bexell, Carl E.   Samvetet i forhallaude till natur. Jönköping, 1840.

Phil 9341.4.5   Burnap, G.W.   Lectures to young men. Baltimore, 1840.

Phil 4215.1.95   Cantù, Cesare.   Notizia di G.D. Romagnosi. 2a ed. Prato, 1840.

Phil 3002.1.9   Chalybäus, H.   Phänomenologische Blätter. Kiel, 1840.

Phil 5042.16   Charma, A.   Leçons de logique. Paris, 1840.

Phil 5922.4.41   Combe, George.   Lectures on moral philosophy. Boston, 1840.

Phil 1107.1   Cousin, Victor.   Fragments philosophiques. Paris, 1840.

Phil 2496.5   Cousin, Victor.   Oeuvres de Victor Cousin. Bruxelles, 1840-41. 3v.

Phil 8582.13   Crabbe, G.   An outline of a system of natural theology. London, 1840.

Phil 9245.63   Delessert, Benjamin Guron.   Le guide du bonheur. 2. éd. Paris, 1840.

Phil 6113.6   Dressler, J.G.   Beneke oder die Seelenlehre als Naturwissenschaft. Bautzen, 1840.

Phil 8583.6   Drobisch, M.W.   Grundlehren der Religionsphilosophie. Leipzig, 1840.

Phil 2725.2.87   Du Plessis de Grenédan, L.   Examen des Paroles d'un croyant et du Livre du peuple. Rennes, 1840.

Phil 6673.4.10   Du Potet, J. de S.   Cours de magnétisme en sept leçons. Paris, 1840.

Phil 6673.4.21   Du Potet, J. de S.   Le magnétisme opposé a la médecine. Paris, 1840.

Phil 285.2   Erdmann, J.E.   Natur oder Schöpfung? Leipzig, 1840.

Htn   Phil 8880.1.3.2*   Feltham, O.   Resolves. London, 1840.

Phil 8880.1.3   Feltham, O.   Resolves. London, 1840.

Phil 480.3   Forichon, L.   Le matérialisme et la phrénologie. Paris, 1840.

Phil 8585.13.10   Frauestädt, C.M.J.   Studien und Kritiken zur Theologie und Philosophie. Berlin, 1840.

Phil 8880.16.5   Fry, Caroline.   A word to women. Philadelphia, 1840.

Phil 8880.17.2   Fuller, T.   The holy state and the profane state. London, 1840.

Phil 8880.17   Fuller, T.   The holy state and the profane state. London, 1840.

Phil 2240.80   Garnier, A.   Critique de la philosophie de Thomas Reid. Paris, 1840.

Phil 181.7   Géruzez, E.   Cours de philosophie. Paris, 1840.

Phil 4115.33   Gioberti, V.   Introduzione allo studio della filosofia. v.1-2. Brusselle, 1840. 3v.

Phil 5645.4.8   Goethe, J.W. von.   Theory of colours. London, 1840.

Phil 2035.60   Hamilton, William.   Fragments de philosophie. Paris, 1840.

Phil 1707.4A   Hegel, E.W.F.   Vorlesungen und der Geschichte der Philosophie. Berlin, 1840. 3v.

Phil 3425.56   Hegel, Georg Wilhelm Friedrich.   Cours d'esthétique. Paris, 1840-43. 2v.

Phil 3425.60.10   Hegel, Georg Wilhelm Friedrich.   Vorlesungen über die Philosophie der Religion. Berlin, 1840. 2v.

Phil 9167.2   Hopkins, E.   The family, a religious institution. Troy, N.Y., 1840.

Phil 2672.35   Jouffroy, Théodore S.   Introduction to ethics. Boston, 1840. 2v.

Phil 3480.70.5   Kant, Immanuel.   Logique. Paris, 1840.

Phil 1135.18   Krische, A.B.   Die theologischen Lehren der griechischen Denker. Göttingen, 1840.

1840 - cont.

Phil 2725.2.30   Lamennais, F.R. de.   Esquisse d'une philosophie. Paris, 1840-1846. 4v.

Phil 2725.2.70   Lamennais, F.R. de.   Questions politiques et philosophiques. v.1-2. Paris, 1840.

Phil 6021.2.3   Lavater, Johann Caspar.   Essays on physiognomy. London, 1840.

Phil 187.65   Merten, J.   Die Hauptfragen der Metaphysik in Verbindung mit der Speculation. Trier, 1840.

Phil 5252.54   Michelet, C.L.   Anthropologie und Psychologie. Berlin, 1840.

Phil 8887.40   Mudie, Robert.   Man as a moral and accountable being. London, 1840.

Phil 8887.40.5   Mudie, Robert.   Man in his relations to society. London, 1840.

Phil 6122.85   Mueller, Johannes.   Physiologie du système nerveux. 3. éd. Paris, 1840. 2v.

Phil 9352.5.4   Muzzey, A.B.   The young maiden. Boston, 1840.

Phil 6990.18   Nanz, C.F.   Die Besessenen im neuen Testament. Reutlingen, 1840.

Phil 1750.27   Nicolas, M.   De l'eclectisme. Paris, 1840.

Phil 3805.168   Petrelli, C.M.J.   In Schleiermacherianam christianae fidei expositionem. Diss. Upsaliae, 1840.

Phil 9375.3.2   Pomeroy, R.W.   The young merchant. 2d ed. Boston, 1840.

Phil 5257.1   Rauch, F.A.   Psychology. N.Y., 1840.

Phil 1133.5   Reesema, W.S.   Parmenidas, anaxagore, protagore principia. Lugduni, 1840.

Phil 192.35   Reiff, J.F.   Der Anfang der Philosophie. Stuttgart, 1840.

Phil 2805.200   Reuchlin, H.   Pascal's Leben und der Geist seiner Schriften. Stuttgart, 1840.

Phil 3425.91   Rosenkranz, K.   Kritische Erläuterungen des Hegel's...Systems. Königsberg, 1840.

Phil 4210.15   Rosmini-Serbati, Antonio.   Breve esposizione della filosofia di Melchiorre Gioja. Milano, 1840. 8 pam.

Phil 1522.2   Rousselot, X.   Etudes sur la philosophie...moyen âge. Paris, 1840-42. 3v.

Phil 5828.2   Scheitlin, P.   Versuch einer vollständigen Thierseelenkunde. Stuttgart, 1840. 2v.

Htn   Phil 3808.59*   Schopenhauer, Arthur.   Kan menneskets frie villie bevises af dets selvebevidsthed. Trodhjem, 1840.

Phil 193.15   Schubert, G. von.   Ansichten von der Nachseite der Naturwissenschaft. Dresden, 1840.

Phil 7082.4.3   Schubert, Gotthilf Heinrich von.   Die Symbolik des Traumes. 3. Aufl. Leipzig, 1840.

Phil 3552.95   Secretan, C.   La philosophie de Leibnitz. Genève, 1840.

Phil 818.8.5   Sigwart, H.C.W.   Die Propädeutik der Geschichte. Tübingen, 1840.

Phil 1135.15   Simon, J.   Etudes sur la Théodicée de Platon. Paris, 1840.

Phil 6128.4   Smith, J.A.   Select discourses on the functions of the nervous system. N.Y., 1840.

Phil 3428.97   Strümpell.   Die Hauptpuncte der Herbartschen Metaphysik. Braunschweig, 1840.

Phil 5769.1.2   Tappan, H.P.   Doctrine of the will. N.Y., 1840.

Phil 9470.4   Taylor, Isaac.   Man responsible for his dispositions, opinions, and conduct. London, 1840.

Phil 3501.2   Thomas, K.   Kant und Herbart. Berlin, 1840-69. 2 pam.

Phil 3839.1   Thomas, K.   Spinoza als Metaphysiker. Königsberg, 1840.

Phil 5545.24   Thompson, L.   Influence of memory. Boston, 1840.

Phil 194.6   Tissot, C.J.   Cours élémentaire de philosophie. Dijon, 1840.

Phil 819.4   Tissot, C.J.   Histoire de la philosophie. Paris, 1840.

Phil 8894.6   Tissot, Joseph.   Ethique ou science des moeurs. Paris, 1840.

Phil 4210.93.10   Tommaseo, N.   Esposizione sul sistema filosofico del nuovo saggio. Torino, 1840?

Phil 194.8   Tommaseo, N.   Studii filosofici. Venezia, 1840. 2v.

Phil 3425.293   Trahndorff, K.F.E.   Wie kann der Supernaturalismus sein Recht gegen Hegel's Religionsphilosophie behaupten? Berlin, 1840.

Phil 3890.1.42   Trendelenburg, A.   Logische Untersuchungen. Berlin, 1840. 2v.

Phil 5059.10   True, C.K.   The elements of logic. Boston, 1840.

Phil 4260.12   Vico, G.B.   Opere. v.1-4. Napoli, 1840-41. 5v.

Phil 5062.2   Waitz, F.H.W.   Die Hauptlehren der Logic. Erfurt, 1840.

Phil 5062.6.5   Whately, Richard.   Elements of logic. London, 1840.

Phil 7059.21   Whytt, James.   Disembodied spirits. London, 1840.

Phil 7150.5   Winslow, F.   Anatomy of suicide. London, 1840.

Phil 9530.20   Wyckoff, Isaac N.   Stability, an indispensable element of usefulness and greatness. Albany, 1840.

1841

Phil 9160.1   Abbott, Jacob.   The Rollo code of morals. Boston, 1841.

Phil 3090.64   Baader, Franz von.   Über die Nothwendigkeit einer Revision der Wissenschaft natürlicher. Erlanzen, 1841.

Phil 4515.45   Boström, C.J.   Dissertatio de notionibus religionis. Upsala, 1841.

Phil 705.9   Bradford, Alden.   Human learning favorable to true religion. Boston, 1841.

Phil 8656.6.2   Buckland, W.   Geology and mineralogy...natural theology. Philadelphia, 1841. 2v.

Phil 6671.18   Burdin, C.   Historie académique du magnétisme animal. Paris, 1841.

Phil 9341.4   Burnap, G.W.   Lectures on the sphere and duties of woman. Baltimore, 1841.

Phil 9341.6.9   Butler, C.   The American lady. Philadelphia, 1841.

Phil 177.87   Cavour, G.B. de.   Fragments philosophiques. Turin, 1841.

Phil 177.12   Charma, Antoine.   Réponses aux questions de philosophie. Paris, 1841.

Phil 5922.4.11   Combe, George.   The constitution of man. 11th American ed. Boston, 1841.

Phil 5922.3.5   Combe, George.   A system of phrenology. N.Y., 1841.

Phil 802.2.3   Cousin, V.   Cours de l'histoire de la philosophie. Paris, 1841.

Phil 1702.1.2   Cousin, Victor.   Cours de l'histoire de la philosophie, XVIIIe siècle. Paris, 1841. 2v.

Phil 1702.1.3   Cousin, Victor.   Cours de l'histoire de la philosophie moderne. Paris, 1841.

Phil 7060.24   Dendy, W.B.   Philosophy of mystery. London, 1841.

Phil 6954.1.5   Earle, W.B.   A visit to thirteen asylums...insane, Europe. Philadelphia, 1841.

Htn   Phil 1980.2.35*   Emerson, R.W.   Essays. London, 1841.

Phil 3235.45.2   Feuerbach, Ludwig.   Das Wesen des Christenthums. Leipzig, 1841.

Phil 1705.3   Fichte, T.H.   Beiträge zur Charakteristik der neueren Philosophie. Sulzbach, 1841.

Phil 5925.3.20   Fowler, O.S.   Matrimony. Philadelphia, 1841.

1841 - cont.

Phil 5047.3.12 Hedge, Levi. Elements of logick. N.Y., 1841.
Phil 3425.73.2 Hegel, Georg Wilhelm Friedrich. Phänomenologie des Geistes. 2. Aufl. Berlin, 1841.
Phil 3428.37 Herbart, J.F. Kurze Encyklopädie der Philosophie. Halle, 1841.
Phil 8882.21.3 Hopkins, M. The connexion between taste and morals. Boston, 1841.
Phil 8882.21.2 Hopkins, M. The connexion between taste and morals. Boston, 1841.
Phil 2050.76 Hume, David. Letters. Edinburgh, 1841.
Phil 6958.5 Ideler, K.W. Biographieen Geisteskranker. Berlin, 1841.
Phil 6959.2 Jarvis, E. Insanity and insane asylums. Louisville, Ky., 1841.
Phil 2672.35.1 Jouffroy, Théodore S. Introduction to ethics. Boston, 1841. 2v.
Phil 185.1.2 Keratry, A.H. Inductions. Paris, 1841.
Phil 2725.2.35 Lamennais, F.R. de. Discussions critiques, et pensées diverses sur la religion et la philosophie. Paris, 1841.
Phil 2725.2.31 Lamennais, F.R. de. Grundriss einer Philosophie. v.1-3. Paris, 1841. 3v.
Phil 2725.2.34 Lamennais, F.R. de. M. Lamennais réfuté par lui-même. Paris, 1841.
X Cg Phil 6021.2.59 Lavater, Johann Caspar. The physiognomist's own book. Philadelphia, 1841.
Phil 6021.2.10 Lavater, Johann Caspar. La physiognomonie. Paris, 1841.
Phil 2496.81 Leroux, P. Réfutation de l'eclectisme. Paris, 1841.
Phil 3493.2 Lorquet, N.H.A. Discussion des Antinomies Kantiennes. Paris, 1841.
Phil 3565.45 Lotze, Hermann. Metaphysik. Leipzig, 1841.
Phil 2730.10 Maine de Biran, Pierre. Oeuvres philosophiques. Paris, 1841. 4v.
Phil 2733.40 Malebranche, Nicolas. Méditations métaphysiques. Paris, 1841.
Phil 4170.7.35 Mamiani della Rovere, Terenzio. Dell'ontologia e del metodo. Parigi, 1841.
Phil 8685.6 Maret, H.L.C. Essai sur le panthéisme. Paris, 1841.
Phil 8887.8.5 Matter, J. De l'affaiblissement des idées. Paris, 1841.
Phil 8887.11 Mercer, M. Popular lectures on ethics. Petersburg, 1841.
Phil 3494.5 Mirbt, E.S. Kant und seine Nachfolger. Jena, 1841.
Phil 9560.3 Montgomery, G.w. Illustrations of the law of kindness. Utica, 1841.
Phil 9352.5.5 Muzzey, A.B. The young maiden. Boston, 1841.
Phil 9352.6.7 My son's book. N.Y., 1841.
Phil 4215.1.10 Opere di G.D. Romagnosi. Pt. 1-2. Milano, 1841. 16v.
Phil 8890.2 Palmer, T.H. The moral instructor. pt.1. Philadelphia, 1841.
Phil 2805.30.21 Pascal, Blaise. Les provinciales. Mexico, 1841.
Phil 5257.1.2 Rauch, F.A. Psychology. N.Y., 1841.
Phil 4210.45 Rosmini-Serbati, Antonio. Opuscali morali. Milano, 1841.
Phil 623.7 Saintes, A. Histoire critique du rationalisme en Allemagne. Paris, 1841.
Phil 5058.3 Schaden, E.A. System der Positiven Logik. Erlangen, 1841.
Phil 1718.3 Schaller, J. Geschichte der Naturphilosophie, Bacon. pt.1-2. Leipzig, 1841-6.
Htn Phil 3800.380*A Schelling, F.W.J. von. Erste Vorlesung in Berlin, 15 nov. 1841. Stuttgart, 1841.
Htn Phil 3801.743* Schellings religiongeschichtliche Ansicht. Berlin, 1841.
Htn Phil 3801.801*A Schellings religionsgechichtliche Ansicht. Berlin, 1841.
Phil 3805.36.5 Schleiermacher, Friedrich. Grundriss der philosophischen Ethik. Berlin, 1841.
Htn Phil 3808.70* Schopenhauer, Arthur. Die beiden Grundprobleme der Ethik. Frankfurt, 1841.
Phil 8968.1 Sewell, W. Christian morals. London, 1841.
Phil 3425.276 Steinhart, C. Hegel und sein Werk. Naumburg, 1841.
Phil 3018.3 Steininger, F. Examen critique de la philosophie allemande. Trèves, 1841.
Phil 4210.77 Sulla difesa del...A. Rosmini-Serbai. Firenze, 1841.
Phil 5769.1.5 Tappan, H.P. Doctrine of the will. N.Y., 1841.
Phil 9050.8 Todd, John. The moral influence, dangers and duties connected with great cities. Northampton, 1841.
Phil 6689.2 Townehend, C.H. Facts in mesmerism. Boston, 1841.
Phil 6689.2.2 Townehend, C.H. Facts in mesmerism. N.Y., 1841.
Phil 3425.219 Ulrici, Hermann. Über Princip und Methode der hegelschen Philosophie. Halle, 1841.
Phil 5260.1.5 Upham, T.C. Elements of mental philosophy. N.Y., 1841.
Phil 5261.13 Vorländer, F. Grundlinien einer organischen Wissenschafte der menschlichen Seele. Berlin, 1841.
Phil 3425.309 Werder, K. Logik. Als Commentar und Ergänzung zu Hegels Wissenschaft der Logik. Berlin, 1841.
Phil 8677.3.3 Whewell, William. Astronomy and general physics, considered with reference to natural theology. N.Y., 1841.
Phil 8897.54 Wirth, J.U. System der speculativen Ethik. v.1-2. Heilbronn, 1841-42.
Phil 3910.76 Wolff, Christian von. Eigene Lebensbeschreibung. Leipzig, 1841.

1842

Phil 1870.83 Bailey, S. Review of Berkeley's theory of vision. London, 1842.
Phil 1106.15 Bakhuizen Van Den Brink, R.C. Varias lectiones ex historia philosophiae antiquae. Lugduni-Batavorum, 1842.
Phil 8876.12.5 Bautain, L.E.M. Philosophie morale. Paris, 1842. 2v.
Phil 3100.40 Beneke, F.E. System der Logik. Berlin, 1842. 2v.
Htn Phil 1865.65* Bentham, Jeremy. Auto-icon. London, 1842?
Phil 6111.24.5 Bidder, Friedrich. Die Selbständigkeit des sympathischen Nervensystems. Leipzig, 1842.
Phil 3001.2 Biedermann, F.C. Die deutsche Philosophie. Leipzig, 1842. 2v.
Htn Phil 7080.29* Binns, E. The anatomy of sleep. London, 1842.
Phil 1880.25 Bowen, F. Critical essays. Boston, 1842.
Phil 1701.2 Braniss, C.J. Übersecht des Entwicklungsganges der Philosophie. Breslau, 1842.
Phil 5921.4 Buchanan, J.R. Sketches of Buchanan's discoveries in neurology. Louisville, 1842.
Phil 8581.29 Bukaty, A. Polska w apostazii cryli wtak zwanym russo-sławianismie. Paryż, 1842.
Phil 176.36 Burdach, K.F. Blicke ins Leben. v.1-4. Leipzig, 1842. 2v.
Phil 2496.50.2 Cousin, Victor. Elements of psychology. 3e éd. N.Y., 1842.
Phil 9245.22 Dickson, Henry S. An oration...before...Phi Beta Kappa Society. New Haven, 1842.
Phil 5243.10 Drobisch, M.W. Empirische Psychologie. Leipzig, 1842.
Phil 3552.84 Encke, J.F. Rede...G.W. Leibnitz. Berlin. 1842.

1842 - cont.

Phil 6674.1 Ennemoser, J. Der Magnetismus im Verhältnisse zur Natur und Religion. Stuttgart, 1842.
Phil 3425.82 Erner, F. Die Psychologie der Hegelschen Schule. Leipzig, 1842-44. 2v.
Phil 705.1 Essay on transcendentalism. Boston, 1842.
Phil 5925.1 Flourens, M.J. Examen de la phrenologie. Paris, 1842.
Phil 5925.3.6 Fowler, L.N. The principles of phrenology and physiology. N.Y., 1842.
Phil 5545.28 Fowler, O.G. Fowler on memory, phrenology...cultivation of memory. N.Y., 1842.
Htn Phil 3801.405* Frauenstädt, J. Schelling's Vorlesungen in Berlin. Berlin, 1842.
Phil 3801.405.5 Frauenstädt, J. Schelling's Vorlesungen in Berlin. Berlin, 1842.
Phil 4112.39.5 Galluppi, Pasquale. Lettere filosofiche. Firenze, 1842.
Phil 6676.2 Gauthier, A. Histoire du somnambulisme. Paris, 1842. 2v.
Phil 3425.85 George, L. Princip und Methode der Philosophie. Berlin, 1842.
Phil 181.8 Gibon, A.E. Cours de philosophie. Paris, 1842. 2v.
Htn Phil 3801.428* Glaser, Johann K. Differenz der Schelling'schen und Hegel'schen Philosophie. Leipzig, 1842.
Phil 5046.13 Gruber, F.X. Philosophie des Denkens. Bern, 1842.
Phil 3552.87 Guhrauer, G.E. Gottfried Willhelm Freiherr von Leibnitz. Breslau, 1842. 2v.
Phil 5643.81 Hasenclever, R. Die Raumvorstellung aus der Gesichtssinne. Berlin, 1842.
Htn Phil 3801.447* Hast, Johann. Andeutungen über Glauben und Wissen. Münster, 1842.
Phil 3425.294 Hegels Lehre von der Religion und Kunst von dem Standpuncte des Glauhens ausbeurtheilt. Leipzig, 1842.
Phil 525.41 Helfferich, A. Die christliche Mystik. Gotha, 1842. 2v.
Phil 3428.15 Herbart, J.F. Kleinere philosophische Schriften und Abhandlungen. Leipzig, 1842-43. 3v.
Phil 182.17.10 Hillebrand, J. Der Organismus der philosophischen Idee. Dresden, 1842.
Phil 4803.454.40 Hoene-Wroński, Józef Maria. Le destin de la France, de l'Allemagne, et de la Russie, comme prolégomènes du messianisme. Paris, 1842.
Phil 8882.21 Hopkins, M. The connexion between taste and morals. Boston, 1842.
Phil 4582.3.31 Hwasser, Israel. Om vår tids ungdom. Upsala, 1842.
Phil 9169.1.5 James, J.A. The marriage ring. Boston, 1842?
Phil 184.7 Johnson, Edward. Nuces philosophicae, or The philosophy of things. London, 1842.
Phil 2672.30.2 Jouffroy, Théodore S. Nouveaux mélanges philosophiques. Paris, 1842.
Phil 3480.71.21 Kant, Immanuel. Theorie de Kant sur la religion dans limites. Paris, 1842.
Phil 3552.16 Leibniz, Gottfried Wilhelm. Oeuvres. Paris, 1842-45. 2v.
Phil 8430.20 Lénström, C.J. Om konstens förhållande till religionen. Upsala, 1842.
Phil 1145.78 Märcker, F.A. Das Princip des Bösen nach den Begriffen den Griechen. Berlin, 1842.
Phil 2733.4 Malebranche, Nicolas. Oeuvres. Paris, 1842. 2v.
Phil 1117.4 Mallet, Charles. Histoire de la philosophie ionienne. Paris, 1842.
Phil 4012.1.7 Mamiani di Rovere, T. Sei lettere...intorno al libro filosofia antica italiana. 2. ed. Firenze, 1842.
Phil 3425.273 Marheineke, Philipp. Einleitung in die öffentlichen Vorlesungen über die Bedeutung der hegelschen Philosophie in der christlichen Theologie. Berlin, 1842.
Phil 3012.4 Murdock, J. Sketches of modern philosophy. Hartford, 1842.
Phil 8637.5 Muzzey, A.B. Man a soul. Boston, 1842.
Phil 6123.1 Newnham, W. The reciprocal influence of body and mind. London, 1842.
Phil 4215.1.81 Nova, Alessandro. Delle censure dell'abate A. Rosmini-Serbati contro la dottrina religiosa di G.D Romagnosi. Milano, 1842.
Phil 8595.1.3 Parker, T. A discourse of matters pertaining to religion. Boston, 1842.
Phil 2805.30.6 Pascal, Blaise. Lettres écrites à un provincial. Paris, 1842.
Phil 2805.40.13.15 Pascal, Blaise. Pensées. Paris, 1842.
Htn Phil 3801.734* Reichlin-Meldegg, C.A. von. Bedenken eines süddeutschen Krebsfeindes über Schellings erste Vorlesung in Berlin. Stuttgart, 1842.
Phil 5767.7 Reiff, J.F. Das System der Willensbestimmungen. Tübingen, 1842.
Phil 192.8 Remusat, C. de. Essais de philosophie. Paris, 1842. 2v.
Phil 1717.1 Renouvier, C.B. Manuel de philosophie moderne. Paris, 1842.
X Cg Phil 8418.24.5 Reynolds, J. Discourses. London, 1842.
Phil 4210.10 Rosmini-Serbati, Antonio. Opere. v.1, 9-10, 11-12, 15. Napoli, 1842-47. 4v.
Phil 8892.7 Rosteri, P.L. Sentenze e massime morali. London, 1842.
Phil 3838.1 Saintes, A. Histoire...ouvrages de B. de Spinoza. Paris, 1842.
Htn Phil 3801.763.10* Salat, Jacob. Schelling und Hegel. Heidelberg, 1842.
Htn Phil 3801.185* Schelling, der Philosoph in Christo. Berlin, 1842.
Phil 3800.200.11A Schelling, F.W.J. von. Bruno. 2. Aufl. Berlin, 1842.
Htn Phil 3800.200.10* Schelling, F.W.J. von. Bruno. 2e Aufl. Berlin, 1842.
Phil 3801.982 Schelling und die Offerbarung. Leipzig, 1842.
Phil 5258.6 Schmucker, S.S. Psychology. N.Y., 1842.
Phil 3819.12 Spinoza, Benedictus de. Oeuvres. Paris, 1842.
Phil 9510.2 Tonna, C.E.B.P. Backbiting. N.Y., 1842. 2 pam.
Htn Phil 3801.846* Trahndorff, Karl F.E. Schelling und Hegel. Berlin, 1842.
Phil 5940.1 Uncle Sam (pseud.). Uncle Sam's recommendation of phrenology. N.Y., 1842.
Phil 4265.1.15 Vanini, Lucilio, afterwards Giulio Cesare. Oeuvres philosophiques. Paris, 1842.
Phil 8602.3 Ware, H. An inquiry...religion. Cambridge, 1842. 2v.
Phil 8602.3.2 Ware, H. An inquiry...religion. Cambridge, 1842. 2v.
Phil 3925.3.45 Weisse, Christian Hermann. Das philosophische Problem der Gegenwart. Leipzig, 1842.
Phil 8897.12.5A Wette, W.M.L. de. Human life; or Practical ethics. Boston, 1842. 2v.
Phil 8712.13.2 Wiseman, N.P.S. Twelve lectures on the connexion between science and revealed religion. 2. ed. London, 1842.
Phil 9364.1.3 Young lady's own book. Philadelphia, 1842.

Chronological Listing

1843

	Phil 3425.203	Afzelius, F.G. Hegelska philosophien. Upsala, 1843.
	Phil 3801.125	Afzelius, F.G. Von Schelling's nya lära. Upsala, 1843.
	Phil 2445.3.3	André, Yves. Oeuvres philosophiques. Paris, 1843.
	Phil 2438.16	Arnauld, Antoine. Oeuvres philosophiques. Paris, 1843.
	Phil 2438.15	Arnauld, Antoine. Oeuvres philosophiques. Paris, 1843.
	Phil 1865.25A	Bentham, Jeremy. Benthamiana. Edinburgh, 1843.
	Phil 1865.10	Bentham, Jeremy. Works. Edinburgh, 1843. 11v.
	Phil 3552.254	Bertereau, A. Leibnitz considéré comme historien de la philosophie. Thèse. Paris, 1843.
	Phil 176.23	Blein, A. Essais philosophiques. Paris, 1843.
	Phil 2520.82	Bordas-Demoulin, J.B. Le Cartésianisme. Paris, 1843. 2v.
	Phil 176.34	Buffier, Claude. Oeuvres philosophiques. Paris, 1843.
	Phil 1865.80	Burton, J.H. Introduction to study of Bentham's works. Edinburgh, 1843.
	Phil 8951.19.5	Busch, F. Découvertes d'un bibliophile. 2. éd. Strassburg, 1843.
	Phil 1900.37.3	Butler, Joseph. Analogy of religion. N.Y., 1843.
	Phil 2480.31	Cabanis, P.J.G. Rapports du physique et du moral de l'homme. Paris, 1843.
	Phil 1915.14	Clarke, Samuel. Oeuvres philosophiques. Paris, 1843.
	Phil 4080.7.31	Colecchi, O. Sopra alcune quistioni...della filosofeia. Napoli, 1843.
	Phil 5242.5	Collineau, J.C. Analyse physiologique. Paris, 1843-44. 2 pam.
	Phil 2805.80	Cousin, Victor. Des pensées de Pascal. Paris, 1843.
	Phil 9530.21	Dayton, William L. Address delivered before the American Whig and Cliosophic societies of the college of New Jersey, Sept. 26, 1843. Princeton, 1843.
	Phil 8628.2.2	Dick, T. The philosophy of a future state. Philadelphia, 1843.
	Phil 6673.3	Dods, J.B. Six lectures on philosophy of mesmerism. Boston, 1843.
	Phil 5655.1	Duméril, A.H.A. Des odeurs. Paris, 1843.
	Phil 9164.1	Ellis, S. Stickney. The wives of England. N.Y., 1843.
	Phil 9164.1.2	Ellis, S. Stickney. The wives of England. N.Y., 1843.
	Phil 9344.3	Ellis, S.S. Daughters of England. N.Y., 1843.
	Phil 9344.3.7	Ellis, S.S. The woman of England. N.Y., 1843.
	Phil 8879.3	Ellis, S.S. The women of England. v.1-4. N.Y., 1843.
	Phil 5044.5.2	Erdmann, J.E. Grundriss der Logik und Metaphysik. 2e Aufl. Halle, 1843.
	Phil 6674.3.5	Estlin, John B. An address...medical profession of Bristol and Bath. London, 1843.
	Phil 3235.25	Feuerbach, Ludwig. Grundsätze der Philosophie der Zukunft. Zürich, 1843.
	Phil 3246.40	Fichte, Johann Gottlieb. Doctrine de la science...de la connaissance. Paris, 1843.
	Phil 5925.2	Fowler, O.S. Education and self-improvement. N.Y., 1843-45. 7 pam.
	Phil 3425.84	Gabler, G.A. Die hegelsche Philosophie. Berlin, 1843.
	Phil 6676.4	Gibbes, R.W. Lecture on the magnetism of the human body. Columbia, 1843.
	Phil 8661.8.30	Gillespie, W.H. The necessary existence of God. Edinburgh, 1843.
	Phil 8407.9	Gioberti, V. Essai sur le beau, ou Éléments de philosophie esthétique. Bruxelles, 1843.
	Phil 4115.12	Gioberti, V. Opere edite ed inedite. v. 1-7, 13. Brusselle, 1843-44. 6v.
	Phil 3425.22	Hegel, Georg Wilhelm Friedrich. Philosophie in wörtlichen Auszügen. Berlin, 1843.
	Phil 2636.40.6	Helvétius, C.A. De l'esprit. Paris, 1843.
	Phil 1210.5	Henne, Désiré. École de Mégare. Paris, 1843.
	Phil 8410.7	Jouffroy, T.S. Cours d'esthétique suivi de la thèse de l'art. 1. éd. Paris, 1843.
	Phil 3480.60	Kant, Immanuel. Leçons de metaphysique. Paris, 1843.
	Phil 3801.470.2	Kapp, Christian. F.W.J. von Schelling. Leipzig, 1843.
tn	Phil 3801.470*	Kapp, Christian. F.W.J. von Schelling. Leipzig, 1843.
	Phil 2725.2.61	Lamennais, F.R. de. Essai sur l'indifférence en matière de religion. Paris, 1843. 4v.
	Phil 6681.9	Lee, Edwin. Animal magnetism. 3d ed. London, 1843. 2 pam.
	Phil 186.6	Lemaire, C. Initiation à la philosophie. Paris, 1843. 2v.
	Phil 3831.14	Lénström, C.J. De principiis philosophiae practicae Spinozae. Gevaliae, 1843.
	Phil 2672.81	Leroux, Pierre. De la mutilation d'un écrit posthume de Théodore Jouffroy. Paris, 1843.
	Phil 4210.93	Lettere intorno al nuovo paggio sull'origine delle idea dell'ab. A. Rosmini-Serbati. Modena, 1843. 2 pam.
	Phil 5761.6	Loewenthal, N. Physiologie des freien Willens. Leipzig, 1843.
	Phil 3565.64	Lotze, Hermann. Logik. Leipzig, 1843.
	Phil 8702.1	Macbriar, R.M. Geology and geologists. London, 1843.
	Phil 3425.203.5	Mager, K.W.E. Popular framstallning af Hegelska philosofeska. Stockholm, 1843.
	Phil 4170.7.36	Mamiani della Rovere, Terenzio. Dell'ontologia e del metodo. 2a ed. Firenze, 1843.
n	Phil 3801.545*	Marheineke, P. Zur Kritik der Schellingschen Offenbarungsphilosophie. Berlin, 1843.
	Phil 3625.1.10	Mendelssohn, Moses. Gesammelte Schriften. Leipzig, 1843-45. 8v.
	Phil 6122.22	Meyer, G.H. Untersuchungen Psychologie der Nervenfaser. Tübingen, 1843.
	Phil 3012.1.5	Michelet, C.L. Entwickelungsgeschichte der neuesten deutschen Philosophie. Berlin, 1843.
	Phil 3801.570.10*	Michelet, Carl L. Entwickelungsgeschichte der neuesten deutschen Philosophie...Schelling. Berlin, 1843.
	Phil 2138.35.1*	Mill, John S. A system of logic. London, 1843. 2v.
	Phil 9352.5.6	Muzzey, A.B. The young maiden. London, 1843.
	Phil 3834.1	Orelli, J.C. von. Spinoza's Leben und Lehre. Aurau, 1843.
	Phil 3801.669.2	Paulus, H.E.G. Die endlich offenbar Gewordene positive Philosophie der Offenbarung. Darmstadt, 1843.
	Phil 3801.669*	Paulus, H.E.G. Die endlich offenbar Gewordene positive Philosophie der Offenbarung. Darmstadt, 1843.
	Phil 3801.669.10*	Paulus, H.E.G. Vorläufige Appellation...Contra das Philosophie...Schelling. Darmstadt, 1843.
	Phil 25.20	The phreno-magnet and mirror of nature. London, 1843.
	Phil 9245.25	Ramsey, George. An inquiry into the principles of human happiness and human duty. London, 1843.
	Phil 192.4	Rattier, M.S. Cours complet de philosophie. Paris, 1843-1844. 4v.
	Phil 2240.25	Reid, Thomas. Essays on the active powers of the human mind. London, 1843.
	Phil 6687.9	Ricard, J.J.A. Letters d'un magnétiseur. Paris, 1843.
	Phil 1522.1.5	Ritter, A.H. Histoire de la philosophie chretienne. Paris, 1843-4. 2v.

1843 - cont.

Htn	Phil 3801.749*	Rosenkranz, J.K.F. Schelling Vorlesungen. Danzig, 1843.
	Phil 3801.749.2	Rosenkranz, J.K.F. Schelling Vorlesungen. Danzig, 1843.
Htn	Phil 3801.749.6*	Rosenkranz, J.K.F. Über Schelling und Hegel. Königsberg, 1843. 2 pam.
Htn	Phil 3801.749.5*	Rosenkranz, J.K.F. Über Schelling und Hegel. Königsberg, 1843.
	Phil 3425.91.35	Rosenkranz, K. Hegel; Sendschreiben an...Carl Friedrich Bachmann. Königsberg, 1843.
	Phil 3425.91.40	Rosenkranz, K. Über Schelling und Hegel. Königsberg, 1843.
	Phil 192.18	Ruge, Arnold. Anekdota. Zürich, 1843. 2v.
Htn	Phil 3800.250.15*	Schelling, F.W.J. von. Über das Verhältniss der bildenden Künste zu der Natur. Berlin, 1843.
Htn	Phil 3801.979*	Schellings Offenbarungsphilosophie. Drei Briefe. Berlin, 1843.
Htn	Phil 3801.774*	Schmidt, A. Beleuchtung der neuen Schellingschen Lehre. Berlin, 1843.
	Phil 4635.8.31	Sibbern, F.C. Om philosophiens begreb. Kjøbenhavn, 1843.
	Phil 3819.10.3	Spinoza, Benedictus de. Opera quae supersunt omnia. Lipsiae, 1843-46. 3v.
	Phil 3819.25	Spinoza, Benedictus de. Renati des Cartes et Benedicti de Spinoza praecipua opera. Lipsiae, 1843.
	Phil 2275.36	Stewart, D. Elements of the philosophy of the human mind. London, 1843.
	Phil 5938.8	Struve, Gustav von. Phrenologie in und ausserhalb Deutschland. Heidelberg, 1843.
	Phil 6128.8.3	Sweetser, W. Mental hygiene. N.Y., 1843.
	Phil 104.1	Taylor, I. Elements of thought. London, 1843.
	Phil 6689.4	Teste, A. A practical manual of animal magnetism. London, 1843.
	Phil 6129.2	Thoughts on the mental functions. Edinburgh, 1843.
Htn	Phil 3801.831*	Thürmer, J. Versuch die Anhänger Hegel's und Schelling's. Berlin, 1843.
	Phil 5259.4	Tissot, C.J. Anthropologie. Paris, 1843. 2v.
	Phil 3425.270	Trendelenburg, A. Die logische Frage in Hegel's System. Leipzig, 1843.
	Phil 4803.846.45	Trentowski, Bronisław F. Stosunek filozofii do cybernetyki czyli sztuki rządzenia narodem. Poznań, 1843.
	Phil 4080.6.80	Varchi, B. Vita di Francesco Cattani da Diacceto. Ancona, 1843.
Htn	Phil 3801.872*	Vogel, Emil F. Schelling oder Hegel oder Keiner von Beyden? Leipzig, 1843.
	Phil 1850.109	Welhelmy, Gerrit. De vita et philosophia F. Baconi. Groningae, 1843.
	Phil 6972.4.5	Winslow, F. The plea of insanity in criminal cases. Boston, 1843.

1844

	Phil 9160.3.10	Alcott, W.A. The boy's guide. Boston, 1844.
	Phil 5040.1.8	Aldrich, H. Artis logicae compendium. Oxonii, 1844.
	Phil 281.6.15	Ambacher, Michel. Le précurseur philosophique. Paris, 1844.
	Phil 2400.1	André, Y.M. Documents...l'histoire...philosophie. Caen, 1844-56. 2v.
	Phil 2998.1	Anthologie aus F.W.J. von Schelling's Werken. Berlin, 1844-57. 8 pam.
	Phil 3425.56.35	Bartsch, Heinrich. Register zu Hegel's Vorlesungen über die Ästhetik. Mainz, 1844.
	Phil 1195.3	Baumhauer, T.C.M. Disputatio literaria. Rhenum, 1844.
	Phil 1100.7	Baumhauer, Theodor C.M. Disputatia literaria. Trajuti ad Rhinum, 1844. 4 pam.
	Phil 3110.24	Böhme, J. Die Lehre des deutschen Philosophen J. Böhme. München, 1844.
	Phil 176.26	Bouillier, F. Theorie de la raison impersonnelle. Paris, 1844.
	Phil 5041.18	Bouttier, M.Z. Essai de philosophie française. Paris, 1844.
	Phil 5811.4	Brougham, H. Dialogues on instinct. London, 1844.
	Phil 4803.454.100	Bukaty, Antoni. Hoene-Wroński i jego udział w rozwinięciu ostatecznem wiedzy ludzkiej. Paryz, 1844.
	Phil 8402.9	Burton, W. The scenery-shower, with word-paintings of the beautiful. Boston, 1844.
	Phil 1900.9.5	Butler, Joseph. Works. Oxford, 1844. 2v.
	Phil 2480.31.5	Cabanis, P.J.G. Rapports du physique et du moral de l'homme. 8e éd. Paris, 1844.
	Phil 2490.53A	Comte, Auguste. Discours sur l'esprit positif. Paris, 1844.
	Phil 1133.9	Cornwallis, C.F. Brief view of Greek philosophy. London, 1844.
	Phil 2496.45.3	Cousin, Victor. Défense de l'université et de la philosophie. Paris, 1844.
	Phil 2496.45.2	Cousin, Victor. Défense de l'université et de la philosophie. 2e éd. Paris, 1844.
	Phil 2805.80.2	Cousin, Victor. Des pensées de Pascal. Paris, 1844.
	Phil 5545.53	D., T.W. Mnemonics. N.Y., 1844.
	Phil 8878.6	Davy, C.W. The maxims...of Agogos. Boston, 1844.
	Phil 2520.19.4	Descartes, René. Oeuvres. Paris, 1844.
	Phil 8878.18.2	Dymond, J. Essays...principles of morality. N.Y., 1844.
	Phil 5924.1	Ellis, G.W. Synopsis of phrenology. Boston, 1844.
	Phil 8879.3.5	Ellis, S.S. Guide to social happiness. v.1-4. N.Y., 1844-47.
	Phil 9344.3.5	Ellis, S.S. Mothers of England. N.Y., 1844. 7 pam.
Htn	Phil 3801.923*	Die Enthullte Geheimlehre des Herren von Schelling. Schaffhausen, 1844.
	Phil 5545.10.9	Fauvel-Gourand, F. First fundamental basis of phreno-mnemotechnic principles. N.Y., 1844.
	Phil 5545.10.10	Fauvel-Gourand, F. Phreno-mnemotechny. n.p., 1844.
	Phil 5545.10	Fauvel-Gourand, F. Phreno-mnemotechny. v.1-2. N.Y., 1844.
	Phil 5545.10.5	Fauvel-Gourand, F. Phreno-mnemotechny dictionary. pt.1. N.Y., 1844.
	Phil 5925.5	Forman, J.G. Elements of phrenology. Cincinnati, 1844.
	Phil 6115.24	Foville, A. Traite complet de l'anatomie, de la physiologie et de la pathologie du système nerveux. Pt.1. Paris, 1844.
	Phil 5925.2.5	Fowler, O.S. Practical phrenology. N.Y., 1844. 2 pam.
	Phil 5925.2.16	Fowler, O.S. Religion: natural and revealed. 3. ed. N.Y., 1844.
	Phil 8585.10	Fownes, G. Chemistry as exemplifying the wisdom and beneficence of God. N.Y., 1844.
	Phil 90.2	Franck, Adolphe. Dictionnaire des sciences philosophiques. Paris, 1844. 6v.
	Phil 4112.41	Galluppi, Pasquale. Lettres philosophiques. Paris, 1844.
	Phil 9166.4.5	Gasparin, A.E. Le mariage au point de vue chrétien. 2. éd. Paris, 1844.

1844 - cont.

Phil 4114.75 — Genovesi, Antonio. Lettere familiari. Venezia, 1844. 2v.

Phil 3310.3.31 — George, L. System der Metaphysik. Berlin, 1844.

Phil 4115.96 — Gioberti, V. Réponse à un article. Bruxelles, 1844.

Phil 806.20 — Gladisch, August. Einleiteug in das Verständriss der Weltgeschichte. Posen, 1844.

Phil 8407.12 — Greswell, R. On education in the principles of art. Oxford, 1844.

Phil 5246.10 — Gruyer. L.A. Les causes...phénomènes de l'âme. Paris, 1844.

Phil 6117.19 — Hannover, A. Recherches microscopiques sur le système nerveux. Copenhagne, 1844.

Phil 8882.49 — Hartenstein, G. Die Grundbegriffe der ethischen Wissenschaften. Leipzig, 1844.

Phil 8882.10.15 — Hildreth, R. Letter. Boston, 1844.

Phil 8882.10 — Hildreth, R. Theory of morals. Boston, 1844.

Phil 665.20 — Kirk, Edward N. The greatness of the human soul. Boston, 1844.

Phil 185.8 — Koenig, E. La science du vrai. Paris, 1844.

Phil 5050.7 — Krause, K.H. Versuchplanmässiger und Naturgemässer unmittelbarer Denkübungen. Halle, 1844. 3v.

Phil 2128.80 — Law, William. Remarks on...the fable of the bees. Cambridge, 1844.

Htn Phil 2128.80.2* — Law, William. Remarks on...the fable of the bees. Cambridge, 1844.

Phil 3552.78.10 — Leibniz, Gottfried Wilhelm. Sechzehn ungedruckte Briefe. Zürich, 1844.

Phil 9171.2.3 — Letters on the moral and religious duties of parents. Boston, 1844.

Phil 186.14 — Lindemann, H.S. Die Lehre vom Menschen. Zürich, 1844.

Phil 6681.7 — Lonbert, J.B. Le magnétisme et le sommambulisme. Paris, 1844.

Phil 1135.56 — Lwellengrebel, J.G.H. Veterum de Elementis Placita. Rhenum, 1844.

Phil 187.7 — Mallet, C.A. Études philosophiques. Paris, 1844. 2v.

Phil 8592.8 — Maret, H.L.C. Théodicée chrétienne. Paris, 1844.

Phil 9500.1 — Martineau, H. Life in the sick-room. Boston, 1844.

Phil 187.85 — Mehring, G. Grundzüge der speculativen Kritik. Heilbronn, 1844.

Phil 187.23 — Mercier, E. De la certitude. Paris, 1844.

Phil 3425.90 — Ott, A. Hegel et la philosophie allemande. Paris, 1844.

Phil 2805.40.2A — Pascal, Blaise. Pensées, fragments et lettres. Paris, 1844. 2v.

Phil 2480.82 — Peisse, L. Notice historique et philosophique sur la vie. Paris, 1844.

Phil 5545.80 — Pike, Robert, Jr. Mnemonics applied to acquisition of knowledge. Boston, 1844.

Phil 6967.5.5 — Ray, Isaac. Treatise on the medical jurisprudence of insanity. 2. ed. Boston, 1844.

Phil 1122.1 — Renouvier, C.B. Manuel de philosophie ancienne. Paris, 1844. 2v.

Phil 5057.6 — Rion, J. Gemeinfassliche Darstellung der Denklehre. Reutlingen, 1844.

Phil 1020.16 — Ritter, H. Uber unsere Kenntniss der arabischen Philosophie. Göttingen, 1844.

Phil 3425.91.10 — Rosenkranz, K. Georg Wilhelm F. Hegel's Leben. Berlin, 1844.

Phil 4210.25 — Rosmini-Serbati, Antonio. Trattato della coscienza morale. Milano, 1844.

Phil 3500.1 — Saintes, A. Histoire de la vie et de la philosophie de Kant. Paris, 1844.

Phil 6688.8.2 — Sandby, G. Mesmerism and its opponents. London, 1844.

Phil 3805.157 — Schaller, Julius. Vorlesungen über Schleiermacher. Halle, 1844.

Htn Phil 3800.51* — Schelling, F.W.J. von. Anthologie aus Schelling's Werken. Berlin, 1844.

Phil 3801.959.2 — Schelling, F.W.J. von. Der neue Reineke Fuchs in acht philosophischen Fabeln. Stuttgart, 1844.

Htn Phil 3801.959* — Schelling, F.W.J. von. Der neue Reineke Fuchs in acht philosophischen Fabeln. Stuttgart, 1844.

Htn Phil 3801.772* — Schleiden, M.J. Schelling's und Hegel's Verhältniss zur Naturwissenschaft. Leipzig, 1844.

Htn Phil 3801.773* — Schwarz, J.L. Schelling's alte und neue Philosophie. Berlin, 1844.

Phil 818.8 — Sigwart, H.C.W. Geschichte der Philosophie. v.1-3. Stuttgart, 1844.

Phil 6688.16 — Staite, Opie. Mesmerism, or The new school of arts. London, 1844.

Phil 3425.93 — Staudenmaier, F. Darstellung und Kritik des Hegelschen Systems. Mainz, 1844.

Phil 3850.1.43 — Strauss, D.F. The opinions of Professor D.F. Strauss. London, 1844.

Phil 8893.32.5 — Strümpell, L. Die Vorschule der Ethik. Mitau, 1844.

Phil 5059.2 — Tappan, H.P. Elements of logic. N.Y., 1844.

Phil 819.2 — Tiberghien, G. Essai théorique et historique. Bruxelles, 1844.

Phil 4803.846.40 — Trentowski, Bronisław F. Myślini czyli catoksztalt loiki narodowéj. Poznań, 1844. 2v.

Phil 1850.89 — Tyler, S. Discourse of the Baconian philosophy. Frederick City, 1844.

Phil 4260.35.5 — Vico, G.B. La science nouvelle. Paris, 1844.

Phil 8897.5 — Waterson, R.C. Thoughts on moral and spiritual culture. Boston, 1844.

Phil 8712.12 — Wessenberg, J.G. von. Die falsche Wissenschaft. Stuttgart, 1844.

Phil 5062.6.6 — Whately, Richard. Elements of logic. London, 1844.

Phil 6972.3 — Wigan, A.L. A new view of insanity. The duality of the mind. London, 1844.

Phil 9362.9 — Woman's worth; or Hints to raise the female character. N.Y., 1844.

1845

Phil 1150.1 — Barthélemy, H.J. De l'ecole d'Alexandrie. Paris, 1845.

Phil 9341.1 — Beecher, C.E. Duty of American women to their country. N.Y., 1845.

Phil 176.17 — Bénard, Charles. Précis de philosophie. Paris, 1845.

Phil 3100.50.2 — Beneke, F.E. Die neue Psychologie. 2. Aufl. Berlin, 1845.

Phil 176.97 — Biese, Franz. Philosophie Propädeutik für Gymnasien und höhere Bildungsanstalten. Berlin, 1845.

Phil 801.9 — Blainville, H. de. Historie des sciences de l'organisation. Paris, 1845. 3v.

Phil 801.4 — Bouillier, F. Manuel de l'histoire de la philosophie. Paris, 1845.

Phil 1880.25.5 — Bowen, F. Critical essays. 2nd ed. Boston, 1845.

1845 - cont.

Phil 5811.4.2 — Brougham, H. Dialogues on instinct. Philadelphia, 1845.

Phil 6952.1 — Calmeil, J.L.F. De la folie. Paris, 1845. 2v.

NEDL Phil 2402.1 — Caraman, V.A.C. Histoire des révolutions de la philosophie. Paris, 1845-48. 3v.

Phil 9045.1 — Ceba, A. The citizen of a republic. N.Y., 1845.

Phil 5812.3 — Chesnel, A. Animaux raisonnent. Paris, 1845.

Phil 5922.4.9 — Combe, George. The constitution of man. N.Y., 1845.

Phil 2520.86 — Cousin, V. Fragments de philosophie Cartésienne. Paris, 1845.

Phil 2496.45.4 — Cousin, Victor. Defense de l'université et de la philosophie. 4e éd. Paris, 1845.

Phil 1925.32 — Cudworth, R. The true intellectual system of the universe. London, 1845. 3v.

Phil 7085.11.5 — Debay, A. Mystères du sommeil et du magnétisme. 4. ed. Paris, 1845.

Phil 7060.24.5 — Dendy, W.B. Philosophy of mystery. N.Y., 1845.

Phil 8693.1.2 — Dick, T. The philosophy of a future state. Philadelphia, 1845. 2 pam.

Phil 8583.4.18 — Dick, T. The philosophy of religion. v.1-2. Philadelphia, 1845.

Phil 8878.13.4.15 — Dodsley, R. The economy of human life. Philadelphia, 1845.

Phil 6673.4.22 — Du Potet, J. de S. Essai sur l'enseignement philosophique du magnétisme. Paris, 1845.

Phil 6114.13 — Eschricht, D.F. Om de uvilkaarlige livsyttringers forhold til de vilkaarlige. Kjøbenhavn, 1845.

Phil 6954.3 — Esquirol, Etienne. Mental maladies. Philadelphia, 1845.

Phil 6674.3 — Estlin, John B. Remarks on mesmerism in 1845. London, 1845.

Phil 6115.11.12 — Feuchtersleben, E.F.V. Lehrbuch der ärtlichen Seelenkunde. Wien, 1845.

Phil 3246.50 — Fichte, Johann Gottlieb. Méthode...a la vie bienheureuse. Paris, 1845.

Phil 3246.53 — Fichte, Johann Gottlieb. Nature of the scholar. London, 1845.

Phil 3246.10 — Fichte, Johann Gottlieb. Sämmtliche Werke. Berlin, 1845-46. 8v.

Phil 3246.11 — Fichte, Johann Gottlieb. Sämmtliche Werke. Berlin, 1845-46. 11v.

Phil 3100.84 — Freimuth, F.W. Die wichtigsten Grundlehren und Vorzüge der Psychologie Dr. Beneke's. Bautzen, 1845.

Phil 481.1 — Galitzine, E. De l'analyse de la force. v.1-3. Paris, 1845. 3v.

Phil 4112.45 — Galluppi, Pasquale. Lezioni di logica e metafisica. v.1-4. Milano, 1845-46. 2v.

Phil 1190.18 — Geffers, A. De arcesilae successoribus disputatio. Göttingen, 1845.

Phil 8407.9.5 — Gioberti, V. Del bello. 2. ed. Firenze, 1845.

Phil 4115.35 — Gioberti, V. Introduction à l'étude de la philosophie. Moulins, 1845-47. 2v.

Phil 4115.33.5 — Gioberti, V. Introduzione allo studio della filosofia. 2a ed. v.1-4. Capolago, 1845-46. 2v.

Phil 2725.2.95 — Gioberti, V. Lettera intorno alle dottrine filosofiche e politiche del sig. di Lamennais. Lucca, 1845. 2 pam.

Phil 4115.14 — Gioberti, V. Opere. v. 1-16. Napoli, 1845- 7v.

Phil 4210.92 — Gioberti, Vincenzo. Degli errori filosofici di Antonio Rosmini. Napoli, 1845.

Phil 181.14 — Goodrich, Samuel G. A glance at philosophy. Boston, 1845.

Phil 6677.9 — Hall, Charles R. Mesmerism. 1st American ed. N.Y., 1845.

Phil 6677.7 — Hall, Spencer T. Mesmeric experiences. London, 1845.

Phil 3007.1 — Harms, F. Der Anthropologismus. Leipzig, 1845.

Phil 3425.45.4 — Hegel, Georg Wilhelm Friedrich. Encyclopädie der philosophischen Wissenschaften. 4. Aufl. Berlin, 1845.

Phil 3425.74 — Hegel, Georg Wilhelm Friedrich. Hegels philosophiska propädentik. Helsingfors, 1845.

Phil 2672.35.2 — Jouffroy, Théodore S. Introduction to ethics. Boston, 1845. 2v.

Phil 3480.31 — Kant, Immanuel. Critique de la raison pure. 2. éd. Paris, 1845. 2v.

Phil 3552.20 — Leibniz, Gottfried Wilhelm. Opusculum adscititio titulo Systema theologicum inscriptum. Lutetiae Parisiorum, 1845.

Phil 811.3 — Lewes, G.H. A biographical history of philosophy. v.1-4. London, 1845-46. 2v.

Phil 600.7 — Littré, Émile. De la philosophie positive. v.1-2. Paris, 1845.

Phil 8412.19.10 — Lotze, Hermann. Über den Begriff der Schonhëit. Göttingen, 1845.

Phil 3552.91 — Mackie, J.M. Life of Godfrey William von Leibnitz. Boston, 1845.

Phil 6682.15 — Le magnétisme traduit en cour d'assises. Paris, 1845.

Phil 1210.6 — Mallet, Charles. Histoire de l'école de Mégare et des écoles d'Elis et d'Érétrie. Paris, 1845.

Phil 8637.16 — Mamiani della Rovere, T. Mario Pagano, ovvero Della immortalità. Parigi, 1845.

Phil 6682.2 — Martineau, H. Letters on mesmerism. N.Y., 1845.

Phil 9500.1.2 — Martineau, H. Life in the sick-room. 2d American ed. Boston, 1845.

Phil 6990.2 — Marx, J. History of the robe of Jesus Christ. Philadelphia, 1845.

Phil 3801.544.2 — Matter, Jacques. Schelling, ou La philosophie de la nature. Paris, 1845.

Htn Phil 3801.544* — Matter, Jacques. Schelling, ou La philosophie de la nature. Paris, 1845.

Phil 5252.8 — Moore, G. Power of the soul. London, 1845.

Phil 6683.2 — Newman, W. Human magnetism. London, 1845.

Phil 6683.2.2 — Newman, W. Human magnetism. N.Y., 1845.

Phil 188.2 — Nicole, P. Oeuvres philosophiques et morales. Paris, 1845.

Phil 3425.263 — Noack, Ludwig. Der Religions begriff Hegel's. Darmstadt, 1845.

Phil 9343.9 — Paige, Elbridge G. Short patent sermons. N.Y., 1845.

Phil 530.20.5 — Pfeiffer, Franz. Deutsche Mystiker des vierzehnten Jahrhunderts. Leipzig, 1845. 2v.

Phil 8620.9 — The philosophy of evil. Philadelphia, 1845.

Phil 817.1 — Reinhold, C.E.G. Geschichte der Philosophie. Jena, 1845. 2v.

Phil 3017.1 — Rémusat, C. de. De la philosophie allemande. Paris, 1845.

Phil 3425.91.7 — Rosenkranz, K. Aus Hegels Leben. Leipzig, 1845.

NEDL Phil 8967.1 — Rothe, R. Theologische Ethik. Wittenberg, 1845-48. 3v.

Phil 8967.1 — Rothe, R. Theologische Ethik. Wittenberg, 1845-48. 3v.

Phil 28.1 — The Saint Louis magnet. v.1-2. St. Louis, 1845.

Phil 8598.2 — Saisset, É. Essais sur la philosophie et la religion. Paris, 1845.

Phil 2915.80 — Saisset, E.E. Renaissance du Voltairianisme. Paris, 1845.

1845 - cont.

Phil 3801.763.7   Salat, Jacob. Schelling in München. pt.1-2. Heidelberg, 1845.

Phil 3801.764*   Saldanha, J.C. de S. de B.D. de. Concordancia das sciencas naturaes. Vienna, 1845.

Phil 3800.200.20   Schelling, F.W.J. von. Bruno. Paris, 1845.

Phil 3800.250.50   Schelling, F.W.J. von. The philosophy of art. London, 1845.

Phil 3801.564*   Schelling und die Theologie. Berlin, 1845.

Phil 3801.564.2   Schelling und die Theologie. Berlin, 1845.

Phil 6968.3   Schubert, G.H. von. Die Krankheiten, Storüngen, menschlichen Seele. Stuttgart, 1845.

Phil 3801.779*   Seuberg, J.A. Ob Schelling? ob Schmitt? Mainz, 1845.

Phil 1150.2   Simon, J. Histoire de l'ecole d'Alexandrie. Paris, 1845. 2v.

Phil 9358.8.2   Sprague, W.B. Letters to young men. 2d ed. Albany, 1845.

Phil 6688.11   Sunderland, La Roy. "Confessions of a magnetiser" exposed. Boston, 1845.

Phil 5405.5.10   Taylor, I. Natural history of enthusiasm. 10th ed. London, 1845.

Phil 8610.829.10   Taylor, Robert. The diegesis. 3. ed. London, 1845.

Phil 9359.4   Todd, J. Hints addressed to the young men of the United States. 2d ed. Northampton, 1845.

Phil 3895.45   Ulrici, H. Das Grundprincip der Philosophie. Leipzig, 1845-46. 2v.

Phil 3425.95   Véra, A. Introduction à la philosophie de Hegel. Paris, 1845-55. 3 pam.

Phil 9362.3   Whitman, J. Young lady's aid. Portland, 1845.

Phil 7085.3   Wienholt, A. Seven lectures on somnambulism. Edinburgh, 1845.

1846

Phil 9060.1.2   Azaïs, P.H. Des compensations dans les destinées humaines. Paris, 1846.

Phil 8610.846   Balmes, Jaime. Cartas á un escéptico en materia de religion. Barcelona, 1846.

Phil 5241.6   Barlow, J. Connection. Physiology. Intellectual philosophy. 2. ed. Philadelphia, 1846.

Phil 4065.80   Bartholmess, C. Jordano Bruno. Paris, 1846-47. 2v.

Phil 4065.80.5   Bartholmess, C. Jordano Bruno. Paris, 1846-47. 2v.

Phil 9341.2.5   Beecher, H.W. Lectures to young men. Salem, 1846.

Phil 8685.21   Bersot, E. Du spiritualisme et de la nature. Paris, 1846.

Phil 4001.2   Bertinaria, F. Sull'indole e le vicende della filosofia italiana. Torino, 1846.

Phil 176.25   Bordas-Demoulin, Jean B. Mélanges philosophiques. Paris, 1846.

Phil 8876.26   Boyd, J.R. Eclectic moral philosophy. N.Y., 1846.

Phil 6671.10.5*   Braid, James. Power of the mind over the body. London, 1846.

Phil 8581.30.4   Bretschneider, K.G. Die religiöse Glaubenslehre. 4. ed. Halle, 1846.

Phil 1890.30.4   Brown, T. Lectures on philosophy of human mind. Edinbrugh, 1846. 4v.

Phil 8876.31   Brown, T. Redivivus. An exposition of vulgar and common errors. Philadelphia, 1846.

Phil 2050.80A   Burton, J.H. Life and correspondence of Hume. Edinburgh, 1846. 2v.

Phil 5242.1.5   Carus, C.G. Psychologie zur Entwicklungsgeschichte der Seele. Pforzheim, 1846.

Phil 9342.1   Chapin, E.H. Duties of young men. Boston, 1846.

Phil 1133.9.3   Cornwallis, C.F. Brief view of Greek philosophy. Philadelphia, 1846.

Phil 177.20   Cornwallis, C.F. Philosophical theories. Philadelphia, 1846.

Phil 1850.100A   Craik, G.L. Bacon; his writings and his philosophy. London, 1846.

Phil 2403.1   Damiron, J.P. Essai sur l'histoire...philosophie en France. Paris, 1846. 2v.

Phil 178.81   Delavigne, A. Manual de filosofíe. Buçuresti, 1846.

Phil 8735.5   Desdouits, M. L'homme et la création. 2. éd. Paris, 1846.

Phil 284.1   Durfee, J. The Panidèa. Boston, 1846.

Phil 6674.5   Elliotson, John. The Harveian oration. London, 1846.

Phil 179.22   Erdmann, J.E. Vermischte Aufsätze. Leipzig, 1846.

Phil 3210.42   Fechner, G.T. Über das höchste Gut. Leipzig, 1846.

Phil 3235.10   Feuerbach, Ludwig. Sämmtliche Werke. Leipzig, 1846-90. 10v.

Phil 3245.60   Fichte, Immanuel Hermann. Die speculative Theologie der Allgemeine Religionslehre. Heidelberg, 1846.

Phil 3246.35.5   Fichte, Johann Gottlieb. Destination of man. London, 1846.

Phil 4112.35   Galluppi, Pasquale. Saggio filosofico. v.1-6. 1a ed. Milano, 1846-47. 3v.

Phil 5246.3   Garreau, P. Essai sur les bases ontologiques...l'homme. Paris, 1846.

Phil 3425.215   Genberg, P. Belysning och granskning af Hegelska philosophiens. Lund, 1846.

Phil 8881.54   Genberg, Paul. De principio philosophiae moralis. Diss. Lundae, 1846.

Phil 5640.13   George, L. Die fünf Sinne. Berlin, 1846.

Phil 4115.33.10   Gioberti, V. Introduzione allo studio della filosofia. v.1-4. Napoli, 1846-47.

Phil 4210.92.2   Gioberti, Vincenzo. Degli errori filosofici di Antonio Rosmini. 2a ed. Capolago, 1846. 3v.

Phil 2733.97   Glaser, J.C. Vergleichung der Philosophie des Malebranche und Spinoza. Berlin, 1846.

Phil 8631.11   Graves, Hiram A. Attractions of heaven. Boston, 1846?

Phil 8587.1   Hannotin, E. Nouvelle théologie philosophique. Paris, 1846. 2v.

Phil 3552.250   Hartenstein, G. De materiae apud Leibnitium notione et ad monadas relatione. Lipsiae, 1846.

Phil 182.11.10   Helfferich, A. Die Metaphysik als Grundwissenschaft. Hamburg, 1846.

Phil 3827.5   Helfferich, A. Spinoza und Leibniz. Hamburg, 1846.

Phil 8411.8   Kahlert, August. System der Asthetik. Leipzig, 1846.

Phil 3480.51   Kant, Immanuel. Critique du jugement. Paris, 1846. 2v.

Phil 6681.5   Leger, J. Animal magnetism. N.Y., 1846.

Phil 3552.78   Leibniz, Gottfried Wilhelm. Briefwechsel zwischen Leibniz, Arnould, und dem Landgrafen Earnst von Hessen-Rheinfels. Hannover, 1846.

Phil 2805.83   Lelut, L.F. L'amulette de Pascal. Paris, 1846.

Phil 9390.2.5   Lewis, G.T. Observations on legal and judicial oaths. v.1-2. Philadelphia, 1846-59.

Phil 4803.522.20   Libelt, Karol. Feleton polityczno-literacki. Poznań, 1846.

1846 - cont.

Phil 5051.4   Lindemann, H.S. Die Denkkunde oder die Logik. Solothurn, 1846.

Phil 9351.6   Livermore, A.A. Lectures to young men. Boston, 1846.

Phil 5762.7   Mahan, Asa. Doctrine of the will. N.Y., 1846.

Phil 4170.7.46   Mamiani della Rovere, Terenzio. Dialoghi di scienza prima. Parigi, 1846.

Phil 187.8   Mancino, S. Elementi di filosofia. Palermo, 1846. 2v.

X Cg   Phil 9172.1   Moody, C.C.P. Lights and shadows of domestic life. Boston, 1846.

Phil 1712.1   Morell, J.D. Historical and critical...philosophy, XIX century. London, 1846. 2v.

Phil 6123.2   Noble, D. The brain and its physiology. London, 1846.

Phil 3525.91   Opzoomer, C.W. De leer van God bij Schelling, Hegel en Krause. Leiden, 1846.

Phil 189.15   Opzoomer, C.W. De wijsbegeerte, den mensch met zich zelven verzoenende. Leiden, 1846.

NEDL Phil 8890.2.2   Palmer, T.H. The moral instructor. pt. 2. Boston, 1846.

Phil 2805.35   Pascal, Blaise. Las celebres cartas provinciales. Madrid, 1846.

Htn   Phil 2855.3.30*   Ravaisson-Mollien, Felix. Essai sur la métaphysique. Paris, 1846.

Phil 8597.6   Reinhold, E. Das Wesen der Religion. Jena, 1846.

Phil 192.9   Riambourg, J.B. Oeuvres philosophiques. Paris, 1846. 3v.

Phil 5057.24   Rosenkranz, Karl. Die Modification en des Logik. Leipzig, 1846.

Phil 900.3   Roth, E. Geschichte und abendländischen Philosophie. Mannheim, 1846.

Phil 3500.2   Schaller, J. Darstellung Kantscher Philosophie. Halle, 1846.

Htn   Phil 3800.385.5*   Schelling, F.W.J. von. Vorwort zu H. Steffens Nachgelassenen Schriften. Berlin, 1846.

Phil 5828.9   Schmarda, L.K. Andeutungen aus dem Seelenleben der Thiere. Wien, 1846.

Phil 4635.8.33   Sibbern, F.C. Speculativ kosmologie med grundlag. Kjøbenhavn, 1846.

Phil 5938.4   Simesen, R.J. Om den nöiagtige bestemmelse. Kjöbenhavn, 1846.

Phil 3246.84   Smith, W. Memoir. Boston, 1846.

Phil 7106.4   South, Thomas. Early magnetism in its higher relations to humanity. London, 1846.

Htn   Phil 3800.385*   Steffens, Henrik. Nachgelassene Schriften...Vorwort von Schelling. Berlin, 1846.

Phil 5058.18   Strümpell, L. Entwurf der Logik. Mitau, 1846.

Phil 9450.15   Trattato sulla unione della morale colla politica. Torino, 1846.

Phil 3890.1.30   Trendelenburg, A. Historische Beiträge zur Philosophie. Berlin, 1846-67. 3v.

Phil 1850.89.2   Tyler, S. Discourse of the Baconian philosophy. Frederick City, 1846.

Phil 1150.3   Vacherot, E. Histoire critique de l'ecole d'Alexandrie. Paris, 1846-51. 3v.

Phil 8422.7A   Vischer, F.T. Asthetik. Reutlingen, 1846-57. 3v.

Phil 5262.2   Waitz, T. Grundlegung der Psychologie. Hamburg, 1846.

Phil 8897.14.9   Whewell, W. Lectures on systematic morality. London, 1846.

Phil 3022.2   Willm, J. Histoire de la philosophie allemande. Paris, 1846-49. 4v.

1847

Phil 9340.2.5   Alcott, William Alex. Young woman's guide to excellence. Boston, 1847.

Phil 9340.3   Austin, J.M. Voice to youth. N.Y., 1847.

Phil 3090.25   Baader, Franz von. Kleine Schriften. Würzburg, 1847.

Phil 6111.24   Bidder, Friedrich. Zur Lehre von dem Verhältniss der Ganglienkörper zu den Nerwenfasern. Leipzig, 1847.

Phil 4115.90   Bonnetty, A. Examen critique de la philosophie de Gioberti. Paris, 1847-49. 2 pam.

Phil 5921.1.5   Broussais, F.J.V. Lectures on phrenology. London, 1847.

Phil 6750.1   Brown, B. Treatment, cure, cretins, idiots. Boston, 1847-62. 4 pam.

Phil 6671.12   Bush, G. Mesmer and Swedenborg. N.Y., 1847.

Phil 1900.15   Butler, Joseph. Whole works. London, 1847.

Phil 177.3   Calinich, E.A.E. Philosophische Propädeutik. Dresden, 1847.

Phil 4065.81   Clemens, F.J. Giordano Bruno und Nicolaus von Cusa. Bonn, 1847.

Phil 9495.16   Colom, P.M. La chasteté. Paris, 1847.

Phil 5922.4.14   Combe, George. The constitution of man. Hartford, 1847. 6 pam.

Phil 5922.4.13   Combe, George. The constitution of man. 15. American ed. Boston, 1847.

Phil 5922.4.3   Combe, George. Lectures on phrenology. 3. ed. N.Y., 1847.

Phil 4112.86   Cursi, C.M. Onori funebri che alla memoria di Pasquale Galluppi. Napoli, 1847.

Phil 7068.47   Davis, A.J. The principles of nature. 3. ed. N.Y., 1847.

Htn   Phil 1955.2.30*   De Morgan, Augustus. Formal logic. London, 1847.

Phil 5043.5   DeMorgan, Augustus. Formal logic. London, 1847.

Htn   Phil 6953.2*   DeRenne, G.W.J. Theory concerning the nature of insanity. Wormsloe, 1847.

Phil 5725.1   Ellis, W. Outlines of the history and formation of...understanding. London, 1847.

Phil 6674.4   Esdaile, James. Mesmerism in India. Hartford, 1847.

Phil 5245.4   Feuchtersleben, E. von. Principles of medical psychology. London, 1847.

Phil 3245.75   Fichte, Immanuel Hermann. Grundsätze für die Philosophie der Zukunft. Stuttgart, 1847.

Phil 180.14   Flourens, P. Fontenelle. Paris, 1847-1851. 5 pam.

Phil 5925.7   Fowler, L. (Mrs.). Familiar lessons on phrenology. v.2. N.Y., 1847.

Phil 5090.5   Franck, A. De la certitude. Paris, 1847.

Phil 2496.86   Fuchs, C.E. Die Philosophie Victor Cousins. Berlin, 1847.

Phil 8881.57   Giambioni, Bono. Della miseria dell'uomo. Milano, 1847.

Phil 4115.36   Gioberti, V. Introduction à l'étude de la philosophie. Paris, 1847. 3v.

Phil 6947.1.5   Great Britain. Commissioners in Lunacy. Further report. London, 1847.

Phil 3801.934.2   Die Grundlehren der neu- Schelling'schen und der Hegel'schen Philosophie. Berlin, 1847.

Htn   Phil 3801.934*   Die Grundlehren der neu- Schelling'schen und der Hegel'schen Philosophie. Reutlingen, 1847.

Phil 181.21   Gruyer, L.A. Méditations critiques. Paris, 1847.

Phil 4803.454.66   Hoene-Wroński, Józef Maria. Adresse aux nations slaves sur les destinées du monde. Paris, 1847.

1847 - cont.

Phil 4803.454.30 — Hoene-Wroński, Józef Maria. Messianisme; ou Réforme absolue du savoir humain. Paris, 1847. 3v.

Phil 6750.3 — Howe, S.G. Report to the legislature. Boston, 1847.

Phil 184.6 — Javary, L.A. La certitude. Paris, 1847.

Phil 5545.32 — Johnson, L.D. Memoria technica. 3. ed. Boston, 1847.

Phil 8885.48 — Klácel, František M. Dobrowěda. Praha, 1847.

Phil 3552.78.5 — Leibniz, Gottfried Wilhelm. Leibniz und Landgraf E. von Hessen-Rheinfels...Briefwechsel. v.1-2. Frankfurt, 1847.

Phil 3552.73 — Leibniz, Gottfried Wilhelm. Leibnizens geschichtliche Aufsätze und Gedichte. Hannover, 1847.

Phil 3552.67.15 — Leibniz, Gottfried Wilhelm. Monadologie. Wien, 1847.

Phil 8412.19.15 — Lotze, Hermann. Über Bedingungen der Kunstschönheit. Göttingen, 1847.

Phil 5252.2 — Mahan, A. System of intellectual philosophy. N.Y., 1847.

Phil 6122.5 — Moore, G. The use of the body in relation to the mind. N.Y., 1847.

Phil 8593.1 — The new philosophy. London, 1847-49. 3v.

Phil 6683.1 — Newman, J.B. Fascination. N.Y., 1847.

Phil 8595.1 — Parker, T. A discourse of matters pertaining to religion. Boston, 1847.

Phil 190.116 — Pezzani, André. Exposé d'un nouveau système philosophique. Paris, 1847.

Phil 6127.2 — Redford, G. Body and soul. London, 1847.

Phil 850.18 — Ritter, Heinrich. Über die Unanationslehre im Übergange aus der Alterhümlichen in die christlicheDenkeweise. Göttingen, 1847.

Phil 4115.80.5 — Rosmini-Serbati, A. Vincenzo Gioberti e il panteismo. Milano, 1847.

Phil 4115.80.10 — Rosmini-Serbati, A. Vincenzo Gioberti e il panteismo. Napoli, 1847.

Phil 4210.26 — Rosmini-Serbati, Antonio. Antropologia. Novara, 1847.

Phil 8708.6 — Sacred geology. London, 1847.

Phil 8893.2 — Sandona, G. Della filosofia morale. Firenze, 1847. 2v.

Phil 9010.2.2 — Sawyer, F.W. A plea for amusements. N.Y., 1847.

Phil 9010.2 — Sawyer, F.W. A plea for amusements. N.Y., 1847.

Phil 3235.113 — Schaller, Julius. Darstellung und Kritik der Philosophie Ludwig Feuerbach's. Leipzig, 1847.

Htn Phil 3800.33.2* — Schelling, F.W.J. von. Écrits philosophiques. Paris, 1847.

Phil 3800.33 — Schelling, F.W.J. von. Écrits philosophiques. Paris, 1847.

Phil 193.10.6 — Schlegel, Friedrich von. Philosophy of life. London, 1847.

Phil 1350.10 — Schmidt, W.A. Geschichte der Denk- und Glaubensfreiheit. Berlin, 1847.

Htn Phil 3808.48* — Schopenhauer, Arthur. Über die vierfache Wurzel des Satzes vom zureichen den Grunde. 2. Aufl. Frankfurt, 1847.

Phil 8598.5 — Schwarz, C.H.W. Das Wesen der Religion. Halle, 1847.

Phil 9178.4 — Steel, D. A system of moral philosophy. Boston, 1847.

Phil 5258.26 — Sunderland, La Ray. Pathetism. Boston, 1847.

Phil 8644.2.3 — Taylor, Isaac. Physical theory of another life. 3. ed. London, 1847.

Phil 9179.6 — Thorburn, Grant. Sketches from the notebook of Laurie Todd on marriage. N.Y., 1847.

Phil 194.6.2 — Tissot, C.J. Cours élémentaire de philosophie. Paris, 1847.

Phil 4803.846.35 — Trentowski, Bronisław F. Wizerunki duszy narodowej s końca ostatniego szesnastolecia. Paryż, 1847.

Phil 8709.5 — Tupper, Martin F. Probabilities; an aid to faith. N.Y., 1847.

Phil 7060.88 — The unseen world: communications. London, 1847.

Phil 352.2 — Vorlaender, F. Wissenschaft der Erkenntniss. Leipzig, 1847.

Phil 3805.86 — Weissenborn, G. Vorlesungen über Schleiermacher's Dialektik und Dogmatik. v.1-2. Leipzig, 1847-49.

Phil 7054.51.5 — Werner, H. Guardian spirits. N.Y., 1847.

1848

Phil 4352.1.40 — Balmes, Jaime. Filosofia fundamental. 2. ed. Barcelona, 1848. 4v.

Phil 6111.3 — Bertrand de Saint-Germain, Guillaume Scipion. Des manifestations de la vie et de l'intelligence. Paris, 1848.

NEDL Phil 801.3 — Blakey, R. History of the philosophy of the mind. London, 1848. 4v.

Phil 176.130 — Buscalioni, C.M. Carolus Michael Buscalioni Monregalensis ut philosophiae rationalis professor crearetur. Turin? 1848.

Phil 1900.37.3.5A — Butler, Joseph. Analogy of religion. 20th ed. N.Y., 1848.

Phil 6672.9 — Cahagnet, L. Magnétisme, arcanes de vie future. Paris, 1848.

NEDL Phil 9342.1.5 — Chapin, E.H. Duties of young men. Boston, 1848.

Phil 6672.10 — Charpignon, J. Physiologie, médecine et métaphysique. Paris, 1848.

Phil 8692.9 — Christmas, H. The world of matter and its testimony. London, 1848.

Phil 8657.14 — Cieszkowski, August D. Ojcze-nasz. Paryż, 1848.

Phil 177.67 — Cleve, Z.J. De principio philosophiae. Helsingfors, 1848.

Phil 2805.81 — Collet, F. Fait inédit de la vie de Pascal. Paris, 1848.

Htn Phil 2490.51* — Comte, Auguste. Discours sur l'ensemble du positivisme. Paris, 1848.

Phil 2496.35 — Cousin, Victor. Philosophie populaire. Paris, 1848.

Phil 2496.40.15 — Cousin, Victor. The philosophy of the beautiful. London, 1848.

Phil 8685.1 — Daniélo, J. Du panthéisme. Paris, 1848.

Phil 7060.90.11 — Day, Clarence S. Remarkable apparitions and ghost-stories. N.Y., 1848.

Phil 3460.81 — Deyks, F. F.H. Jacobi im Verhaltniss zu seinen Zeitgenossen. Frankfurt, 1848.

Phil 6945.1 — Earle, P. History description...Bloomingdale. N.Y., 1848. 21 pam.

Htn Phil 9345.6* — Ferguson, F. The young man. Nashua, N.H., 1848.

Phil 2450.81.2 — Feuerback, L.A. Pierre Bayle. 2. Aufl. Leipzig, 1848.

Phil 3246.53.2 — Fichte, Johann Gottlieb. Nature of the scholar. 2nd ed. London, 1848.

Phil 3246.68 — Fichte, Johann Gottlieb. Vocation of man. London, 1848.

Phil 180.6 — Fischer, K.P. Grundzüge des Systems der Philosophie. Frankfurt, 1848-1855. 3v.

Phil 5925.2.16.10 — Fowler, O.S. Religion: natural and revealed. 10. ed. N.Y., 1848.

Phil 9530.5.2 — Franklin, B. The way to wealth. N.Y., 1848.

Phil 4352.1.120 — Garcia de Los Santos, B. Vida de Balmes. Madrid, 1848.

Phil 8881.3 — Géhant, J.B.V. Science du bien et du mal. Paris, 1848. 2v.

1848 - cont.

Phil 9166.2 — Gibson, W.S. An essay on the filial duties. London, 1848.

Phil 8881.8 — Gilliot, A. Physiologie du sentiment. Paris, 1848. 2v.

Phil 4115.30.5 — Gioberti, V. Del buono. Napoli, 1848.

Phil 4115.65 — Gioberti, V. Grundzüge eines Systems der Ethik. Mainz, 1848.

Phil 4210.92.15 — Gioberti, Vincenzo. Risposta agli attachi di G. di Cavour. Torino, 1848.

Phil 5203.3 — Grässe, J.G.T. Bibliotheca psychologica. Leipzig, 1848.

NEDL Phil 8882.1 — Hall, A. A manual of morals. Andover, 1848.

Phil 5047.1 — Halle, H.F. Exact philosophy. London, 1848.

Phil 4803.454.74F — Hoene-Wroński, Józef Maria. Odezwa do narodóv slawianskii wzgledem przeznaczeń świata. Paryz, 1848.

Phil 6117.15 — Holland, G.C. The psychology of animated nature. London, 1848.

Phil 6750.3.5 — Howe, S.G. Report to the legistature of Massachusetts upon idiocy. Boston, 1848.

Phil 5627.18A — Ideler, K.W. Versuch einer Theorie des religiösen Wahnsinns. Halle, 1848-50. 2v.

Htn Phil 8883.1* — Israel, L.S. d'. Talmudic maxims. Boston, 1848.

Phil 3480.46 — Kant, Immanuel. Critique de la raison pratique. Paris, 1848.

Phil 3525.20.2 — Krause, K.C.F. Handschriftlicher Nachlass; Anthropologie. Göttingen, 1848.

Phil 2725.2.33 — Lamennais, F.R. de. De la famille et de la propriété. Paris, 1848.

Phil 2725.2.53 — Lamennais, F.R. de. Il libro del popolo. v.1-2. Firenze, 1848.

Phil 8591.4.5 — Leroux, Pierre. Du christianisme et de son origine democratique. pt.1-2. Boussac, 1848.

Phil 8125.24 — Lotze, Hermann. Geschichte der Aesthetik in Deutschland. München. 1848.

Phil 4170.7.37 — Mamiani della Rovere, Terenzio. Dell'ontologia e del metodo. 2a ed. Firenze, 1848.

Phil 187.65.5 — Merten, J. Grundriss der Metaphysik. Trier, 1848.

Phil 5545.19 — Miles, Pliny. American mnemotechny. N.Y., 1848.

Phil 5052.7 — Moberly, Charles Edward. Lectures on logic. Photoreproduction. Oxford, 1848.

Phil 1712.1.2 — Morell, J.D. Historical and critical...philosophy, XIX century. N.Y., 1848.

Phil 187.20 — Morell, J.O. Philosophical tendencies of the age. London, 1848.

Phil 7060.90 — Ollier, Charles. Fallacy of ghosts, dreams and omens. London, 1848.

Phil 8705.1.2 — Paine, M. A discourse on the soul and the principle of instinct. N.Y., 1848. 4 pam.

Phil 8705.1 — Paine, M. A discourse on the soul and the principle of instinct. N.Y., 1848. 4 pam.

Phil 1520.4 — Patru, G.A. De la philosophie du moyen âge. Paris, 1848.

Phil 5545.81 — Pike, Robert. Mnemonics. Boston, 1848.

Phil 346.9 — Portius, K.N. Ueber den Ursprung der Begriffe. Leipzig, 1848.

Phil 6688.8 — Sandby, G. Mesmerism and its opponents. 2. ed. London, 1848.

Phil 193.10.7 — Schlegel, Friedrich von. Philosophy of life. N.Y., 1848.

Phil 6128.3 — Smith, J.M. A discourse on the influence of diseases on the intellectual and moral powers. N.Y., 1848.

Phil 3425.275 — Springer, Anton T.H. Die Hegel'sche Geschichtsanschauung. Tübingen, 1848.

Phil 410.4.5 — Swedenborg, E. The philosophy of the infinite. Boston, 1848.

Phil 2805.91.1 — Vinet, A. Études sur Blaise Pascal. Paris, 1848.

Phil 2915.40 — Voltaire, F.M.A. de. La philosophie. Paris, 1848.

Phil 8897.6.10 — Wayland, F. The elements of moral science. Abridged. Boston, 1848.

Phil 5725.2 — Wedgwood, H. On development of the understanding. London, 1848.

Phil 3425.217 — Wennerberg, G. Num recte et vere de Spinozismo judicavit Hegelius? Upsaliae, 1848.

Phil 4115.82 — Zarelli, T. Il sistema filosofico di V. Gioberti. Paris, 1848.

Phil 35.2 — The zoist. London, 1848. 2v.

1849

Phil 5010.2 — Ahlander, J.A. De prascipuis philosophorum recentioris aevi logicam tractandi rationibus. Diss. Lundae, 1849.

Phil 4235.1.80 — Bartholmes, C. De Bernardino Telesio. Paris, 1849.

Phil 5241.12 — Bishop, D. An introduction...study...mind. London, 1849.

Phil 7060.25 — Blakeman. R. Philosophical essay on credulity and superstition. N.Y., 1849.

Phil 4352.1.85 — Blanche-Raffin, A. de. Jacques Balmes, sa vie et ouvrages. Paris, 1849.

Phil 1880.43.2 — Bowen, F. Lowell lectures...metaphysics...science. Boston, 1849.

Phil 1880.43 — Bowen, F. Lowell lectures...metaphysics...science. Boston, 1849.

Phil 2050.80.9A — Burton, J.H. Letters of eminent persons to Hume. Edinburgh, 1849.

Phil 5628.10.20 — Busson, Claude Ignace. Premières [-secondes] lettres sur l'extatique de Niéderbronn et sur ses révélations. Besançon, 1849.

Phil 1900.37.3.6 — Butler, Joseph. Analogy of religion. Cincinnati, 1849.

Phil 1900.75 — Butler, Joseph. Six sermons on moral subjects. Cambridge, 1849.

Phil 1900.9.9 — Butler, Joseph. Works. Oxford, 1849-50. 2v.

Phil 5425.14 — Carus, Karl G. Über ungleiche Befähigung der verschiedenen Menschheitstämme. Leipzig, 1849.

Phil 8403.8.10 — Cousin, Victor. The philosophy of the beautiful. N.Y., 1849.

Phil 7060.36.5 — Crowe, C.S. Nacht Seite der Natur. v.1-2. Stuttgart, 1849.

Phil 8658.1 — Damiron, J.P. Petits traites...de la providence. Paris, 1849.

Phil 490.1 — Discourse on the soul and instinct. N.Y., 1849.

Phil 5643.22 — Dix, J.H. Treatise...nature, treatment, morbid sensibility...retina. Boston, 1849.

Phil 6113.15 — Domrich, O. Die psychischen Zustände. Jena, 1849.

Phil 1730.6 — Erdmann, Karl. Die theologische und philosophische Aufklärung des achtzshuten und neunzehuten Jahrhunderts. Leipzig, 1849.

Phil 3246.50.5 — Fichte, Johann Gottlieb. The way toward the blessed life. London, 1849.

Phil 8585.10.2 — Fownes, G. Chemistry as exemplifying the wisdom and beneficence of God. London, 1849.

Phil 8585.11 — Fox, W.J. On the religious ideas. London, 1849.

Chronological Listing

1849 - cont.

Htn Phil 705.26*   Greene, William B. Transcendentalism. West Brookfield, 1849.

Phil 8587.2.5   Harris, J. Man primeval. Boston, 1849.

Phil 8587.2.2   Harris, J. The pre-Adamite earth. Boston, 1849.

Phil 5247.9   Hickok, L.P. Rational psychology. Auburn, 1849.

Phil 8587.16   Hill, T. Geometry and faith. N.Y., 1849.

Phil 270.10   Journeyman (pseud.). Beneficence design in problem of evil...causation. N.Y., 1849.

Phil 6681.9.2   Lee, Edwin. Animal magnetism. London, 1849.

Phil 5135.2   Lewis, G.C. An essay on the influence of authority opinion. London, 1849.

Phil 4803.522.10   Libelt, Karol. Pisma promniejsze. Poznań, 1849-51. 6v.

Phil 2115.35.15   Locke, J. Essay concerning human understanding. Philadelphia, 1849.

Phil 8962.11   Magoon, E.L. Proverbs for the people. Boston, 1849.

Phil 293.3   Martin, T.H. Philosophie spiritualiste de la nature. Paris, 1849. 2v.

Phil 8592.10   Miles, J.W. Philosophic theology. Charleston, 1849.

Phil 2138.35.12   Mill, John S. Die inductive Logik. Braunschweig, 1849.

Phil 8592.14.2   Morell, J.D. The philosophy of religion. London, 1849.

Phil 8592.14   Morell, J.D. The philosophy of religion. N.Y., 1849.

Phil 8593.2.5   Newman, F.W. The soul. London, 1849.

Phil 813.4   Nicolas, Michel. Introduction à l'étude de l'histoire de la philosophie. Paris, 1849-50. 2v.

Phil 2805.36   Pascal, Blaise. Cartas escritas a un provincial. Paris, 1849.

Phil 2805.42.6A   Pascal, Blaise. Miscellaneous writings. London, 1849.

Phil 5055.5A   Prantl, C. Die Bedeutung der Logik. München, 1849.

Phil 6027.1.5   Redfield, J.W. Outlines...physiognomy. N.Y., 1849.

Phil 6668.3   Robiano, Comte de. Neururgie oder der thierische Magnetismus. Stuttgart, 1849.

Phil 623.7.5   Saintes, A. Critical history of rationalism in Germany. 2nd ed. London, 1849.

Phil 6688.14   Scoresby, William. Zoistic magnetism. London, 1849.

Phil 193.21   Secrétan, C. La philosophie de la liberté. Paris, 1849. 2v.

Phil 6128.10   Smee, Alfred. Elements of electrobiology. London, 1849.

Phil 6128.10.2   Smee, Alfred. Principle of the human mind, sequel to elements of electrobiology. London, 1849.

Phil 8893.21.3   Spurzheim, J.K. The natural laws of man. N.Y., 1849.

Phil 672.14.7   The stars and the earth. Boston, 1849.

Phil 2275.39   Stewart, D. Philosophy of the active and moral poweers. Cambridge, 1849.

Phil 5059.4   Thomson, W. Outline of the necessary laws of thought. London, 1849.

EDL Phil 29.6   The truth promotor. v.1-3. London, 1849-55.

Phil 5262.2.5   Waitz, T. Lehrbuch der Psychologie. Braunschweig, 1849.

Phil 5125.4   Whewell, W. Of induction. London, 1849.

Phil 3428.155.15   Zimmerman, R. Leibnitz und Herbart. Wien, 1849.

185-

Phil 2115.35.19A   Locke, J. Essay concerning human understanding. Philadelphia, 185-?

Phil 2115.35.17   Locke, J. Essay concerning human understanding. Philadelphia, 185-?

Phil 2915.31   Voltaire, F.M.A. de. The ignorant philosopher. N.Y., 185-?

Phil 8897.14.1   Whewell, W. Elements of morality. N.Y., 185-? 2v.

1850

Phil 5040.1.6   Aldrich, H. Artis logicae rudimenta. 6th ed. Oxford, 1850.

Phil 5040.4.4   Arnauld, Antoine. Logic, or The art of thinking. Edinburgh, 1850.

Phil 175.18   Arndt, Julius. Des Bewusstwerden der Menschheit. Halle, 1850.

Phil 4210.139   Ballarini. Principj della scuola Rosminiana. Milano, 1850. 2v.

Phil 3483.9   Barni, J. Philosophie de Kant. Examen de la Critique du jugement. Paris, 1850.

Phil 2651.82   Bartholmess, B.J.W. Huet, évêque d'Avranches. Paris, 1850.

Phil 3001.4   Bartholmiss, C.J.W. Histoire philosophique de l'academie de Prusse. Paris, 1850. 2v.

DL Phil 5041.7   Baynes, T.S. Essay...new analytic. Logical forms. Edinburgh, 1850.

Phil 9558.2   Beecher, H.W. Industry and idleness. Philadelphia, 1850.

Phil 9341.2.2   Beecher, H.W. Lectures to young men. Boston, 1850.

Phil 3100.45   Beneke, F.E. Pragmatische Psychologie. v.1-2. Berlin, 1850.

Phil 801.3.2   Blakey, R. History of the philosophy of the mind. London, 1850. 4v.

Phil 6990.27   Blumhardt, C.G. Vertheidigungsschrift. Reutlingen, 1850.

Phil 3110.55.20   Böhme, J. The way to Christ discovered. N.Y., 1850. (Changed to XM 710, 1971)

Phil 7230.1*   Braid, J. Observations on trance. London, 1850.

Phil 6111.17   Burnett, C.M. Philosophy of spirits in relation to matter. London, 1850.

Phil 6672.1   Calcutta Mesmeric Hospital. Second half-yearly report. London, 1850.

Phil 7067.46.25   Calmet, Augustin. The phantom world. London, 1850.

Phil 7067.46.26   Calmet, Augustin. The phantom world. Philadelphia, 1850.

Phil 7054.115.5   Capron, Eliab W. Explanation and history of the mysterious communion with spirits. 2. ed. Auburn, N.Y., 1850.

Phil 8877.53   Chalybäus, Heinrich. System der speculativen Ethik. Leipzig, 1850. 2v.

Phil 9342.1.10   Chapin, E.H. Duties of young women. Boston, 1850.

Phil 3822.8   Cleve, Z.J. De cognitionis generibus Spinozae. Thesis. Helsingforsiae, 1850.

Phil 3425.225   Collan, F. De notione necessitatis Hegeliana. Diss. Helsingforsiae, 1850.

Phil 2520.38   Descartes, René. Discourse on the method of rightly conducting the reason. Edinburgh, 1850.

Phil 2520.19.4.5   Descartes, René. Oeuvres. Paris, 1850.

Phil 7054.93   Dewey, D.M. History of the strange sounds or rappings. Rochester, 1850.

Phil 7050.10   Diotrephes. The "knockings" Exposed. N.Y., 1850. 3 pam.

Phil 6946.8420*   Dix, D.L. Memorial to Legislative Assembly of Nova Scotia (concerning confinement of insane persons). Halifax? 1850.

Phil 6673.3.5   Dods, J.B. The philosophy of electrical psychology. N.Y., 1850.

1850 - cont.

Phil 5243.10.2   Drobisch, M.W. Erste Grundlehren der mathematischen Psychologie. Leipzig, 1850.

Phil 8584.12   Evelyn, John. The history of religion. London, 1850. 2v.

Phil 6955.2   Familiar views of lunacy and lunatic life. London, 1850.

Phil 3235.50   Feuerbach, Ludwig. Qu'est-ce que la religion. Paris, 1850.

Phil 3245.65   Fichte, Immanuel Hermann. System der Ethik. Leipzig, 1850-51. 2v.

Phil 180.6.2   Fischer, K.P. Grundzüge des Systems der Philosophie. v.2,3. Erlangen, 1850-1855. 2v.

Phil 9245.2   Forbes, J. Of happiness in its relations to work and knowledge. London, 1850.

Phil 7080.3   Fosgate, B. Sleep. N.Y., 1850.

Phil 6945.7   Galt, J.M. Essays on asylums for persons of unsound mind. v.1-2. Richmond, 1850-53.

Phil 75.4   Geissler, C.A. Bibliographisches Handbuch der philosophischer Literatur. Leipzig, 1850.

Phil 4115.30   Gioberti, V. Del buono, del bello. Firenze, 1850.

Phil 4115.34   Gioberti, V. Introduzione allo studio della filosofia. Milano, 1850. 2v.

Phil 4115.50   Gioberti, V. Teorica del sovranaturale. Capolago, 1850. 2v.

Phil 4115.50.5   Gioberti, V. Teorica del sovranaturale. Venezia, 1850.

Phil 6676.3   Grimes, J.S. Etherology and the phreno-philosophy. Boston, 1850.

Phil 8882.1.2   Hall, A. A manual of morals. Boston, 1850.

Phil 850.15   Hanus, G.J. Geschichte der Philosophie von ihren Uranfängen. Olmütz, 1850.

Phil 8587.2.3   Harris, J. The pre-Adamite earth. Boston, 1850.

Phil 1512.1   Haureau, B. De la philosophie scolastique. Paris, 1850. 2v.

Phil 3827.10   Hebler, Carl. Spinoza's Lehre vom Verhältniss der Substanz zu ihren Bestimmtheiten Dargestellt. Bern, 1850.

Phil 182.14.2   Hemsterhuis, F. Oeuvres philosophiques. v.3. Leuwarde, 1850.

Phil 3428.10   Herbart, J.F. Sämmtliche Werke. Leipzig, 1850-52. 12v.

Phil 9375.4   Hillard, G.S. Dangers and duties of the merchantile profession. Boston, 1850.

Phil 3090.80.5   Hoffmann, F. Franz von Baader in seinem Verhällnitz zu Hegel und Schelling. Leipzig, 1850.

Phil 8662.5.5   Holyoake, George Jacob. The report of the four nights' public discussion...on the truth of Christianity. London, 1850.

Phil 8589.5.15   James, H. Moralism and Christianity, or Man's experience and destiny, in three lectures. N.Y., 1850.

Phil 3492.14   Kinker, Johannes. Le dualisme de la raison humaine; ou, Le criticisme de E. Kant. Amsterdam, 1850-52. 2v.

Phil 2725.2.75   Lamennais, F.R. de. Una voce di prigione. Genova, 1850.

Phil 292.10   Lecouturier, H. La cosmosphie. Paris, 1850.

Phil 3552.69   Leibniz, Gottfried Wilhelm. A system of theology. London, 1850.

Phil 2465.81   Lemoine, Albert. Charles Bonnet de Genève. Thèse. Paris, 1850.

Phil 8701.2.15   Lewis, Tayler. Nature, progress, ideas. Schenectady, 1850.

Phil 6690.1   L'union Protectrice. Appel à tous les partisans et amis du magnétisme. 2e éd. Paris, 1850.

Phil 2125.65.7   McCosh, James. Method of divine government. 2nd ed. Edinburgh, 1850.

Phil 4170.7.50   Mamiani della Rovere, Terenzio. Discorso proemiale letto li 10 nov. 1850. Genova, 1850.

Phil 812.3   Maurice, J.F.D. Moral and metaphysical philosophy. London, 1850.

Phil 2805.84   Maynard, M.U. Pascal, sa vie et son charactère. Paris, 1850. 2v.

Phil 5545.19.5   Miles, Pliny. Mnemotechny, or art of memory. 1. English ed. London, 1850.

Phil 6122.5.3   Moore, G. Der Beruf des Körpers in Beziehung auf den Geist. Leipzig, 1850.

Phil 6962.16   Moreau, J.J. Un chapitre oublié de la pathologie mentale. Paris, 1850.

Phil 6683.3   Nani, Giacomo D. Trattato teorico-pratico sul magnetismo animale. Torino, 1850.

Phil 188.17   Nevin, J.W. Human freedom and a plea for philosophy. Mercersburg, 1850.

Phil 9353.1   Newcomb, H. How to be a lady. Boston, 1850.

Phil 9173.1   Newcomb, H. How to be a man: a book for boys. Boston, 1850.

Phil 8593.2.10   Newman, F.W. Phases of faith. London, 1850.

Phil 189.4.10   Oersted, H.C. Der Geist in der Natur. München, 1850-1851. 2v.

Phil 189.4   Oersted, H.C. Gesammelte Schriften. Leipzig, 1850-1851. 6v.

Phil 2205.14   Paley, W. Works. Philadelphia, 1850.

Phil 2805.32.4   Pascal, Blaise. The provincial letters. N.Y., 1850.

Phil 4210.142.5   Pestalozza, A. Le postille di un anonimo. Milano, 1850.

Phil 7054.122   Philosophy of modern miracles. N.Y., 1850.

Phil 5935.1   Pierpont, J. Phenology and the scriptures. N.Y., 1850.

Phil 6027.1.8   Redfield, J.W. The twelve qualities of mind...physiognomy. no. 11. N.Y., 1850.

Phil 6687.1.3   Reichenbach, C. Researches on magnetism, electricity. London, 1850.

Phil 2240.60   Reid, Thomas. Essays on the intellectual powers of man. Cambridge, 1850.

Phil 8597.11.12   Rogers, H. Reason and faith. London, 1850.

Phil 3780.38   Rosenkranz, Karl. System der Wissenschaft. Königsberg, 1850.

Phil 4210.20   Rosmini-Serbati, Antonio. Introduzione alla filosofia. Casalle, 1850.

Phil 3805.33.20   Schleiermacher, Friedrich. Brief outline of the study of theology. Edinburgh, 1850.

Phil 1750.11   Schmidt, H.J. Geschichte der Romantik...philosophische Geschichte. Leipzig, 1850. 2v.

Phil 5258.7.6   Schubert, G.H. von. Die Geschichte der Seele. Stuttgart, 1850.

Phil 8598.6   Sedgwick, Adam. A discourse on the studies of the university of Cambridge. Cambridge, 1850.

Phil 5090.6   Smedley, E.A. Treatise on moral evidence. Cambridge, 1850.

Phil 6128.10.3   Smee, Alfred. Principle of the human mind, deduced from physical laws. N.Y., 1850.

Phil 8893.16.5   Smith, Sydney. Elementary sketches of moral philosophy. N.Y., 1850.

Chronological Listing

Phil 4115.100   Sordi, Serafino. I misteri di Demofilo. Milano, 1850. 3 pam.

Phil 672.14   The stars and the earth. 4th ed. London, 1850.

Phil 6128.8   Sweetser, W. Mental hygiene. N.Y., 1850.

Phil 1850.89.3   Tyler, S. Discourse of the Baconian philosophy. N.Y., 1850.

Phil 8896.1   Vincent, G.G. The appendix to volumes I. and II. of the moral system, or Law of human nature. London, 1850.

Phil 9230.10A   Walker, Gilbert. A manifest detection of the most vyle and detestable use of dice play. London, 1850.

Phil 5062.28   Weissborn, G. Logik und Metaphysik. Halle, 1850.

Phil 5262.6   Winslow, H. Elements of intellectual philosophy. Boston, 1850.

Phil 303.3   Wuttke, A. Abhandlung über die Cosmogonie. Haag, 1850.

Phil 200.7   Zarcone, O. Il genio dell'uomo. 2a ed. Palermo, 1850.

1851

Phil 5750.1   Allyn, J. Philosophy of mind in volition. Oberlin, 1851.

Phil 5240.3.2   Atkinson, H.G. Letters...laws of man's nature. Boston, 1851.

Phil 5240.3   Atkinson H.G. Letters...laws of man's nature. London, 1851.

Phil 3090.10   Baader, Franz von. Sämmtliche Werke. Leipzig, 1851-60. 16v.

Phil 1850.35A   Bacon, Francis. Of the proficience and advancement of learning. London, 1851.

Phil 5041.2.5   Bailey, Samuel. The theory of reasoning. London, 1851.

Phil 1535.1.10   Balmes, Giacomo. La filosofia fondamentale. v.1-2. Napoli, 1851.

Phil 3483.9.10   Barni, J. Philosophie de Kant. Examen des fondements de la métaphysique des moeurs. Paris, 1851.

Phil 6671.3   Bennett, J.H. The mesmeric mania. Edinburgh, 1851.

Phil 5011.1   Blakey, R. Historical sketch of logic. London, 1851.

Phil 3425.200.5   Borelius, J.J. I hvad afseende är Hegel Pantheist? Upsala, 1851.

Phil 5921.3F   Bossard, H. Practische Phrenologie. Berlin, 1851.

Htn   Phil 6671.10*   Braid, James. Electro-biological phenomena. Edinburgh, 1851.

Phil 6671.11   Buchanan, A. On darlingism, misnamed electro-biology. London, 1851.

Phil 6672.8   Caperu, T. Mighty curative powers of mesmerism. London, 1851.

Phil 5545.75   Castillio, A.F. de. Tratado demnemonica. Lisboa, 1851.

Phil 6112.11   Clavel, Adolphe. Le corps et l'ame. Paris, 1851.

Phil 7054.100   Coggshall, W.T. The signs of the times. Cincinnati, 1851.

Phil 177.22.5A   Cournot, A.A. Essai sur les fondations de nos connaissances. Paris, 1851. 2v.

Phil 6945.5   Curwen, J. A manual for attendants in hospitals for the insane. Philadelphia, 1851.

Phil 7054.6.5   Davis, A.J. The philosophy of spiritual intercourse. N.Y., 1851.

Phil 8878.5.5   Davy, H. Consolations in travel. London, 1851.

Phil 3003.6   Deutschlands Denker seit Kant. Dessan, 1851.

Phil 8583.4.16   Dick, T. The works of Thomas Dick. Hartford, 1851.

Phil 5043.10   Drobisch, Moritz Wilhelm. Neue Darstellung der Logik. Leipzig, 1851.

Phil 6114.8   Ennemoser, Joseph. Historisch-psychologische Untersuchungen...den Ursprung. 2. Aufl. Stuttgart, 1851.

Phil 4110.5.28   Ferrari, G. Filosofia della rivoluzione. v.1-2. Londra, 1851.

Phil 6115.5   Fisher, W.S. Observations on mental phenomena. Philadelphia, 1851.

Phil 5400.86.5   Fourier, C. The passions of the human soul. London, 1851. 2v.

Phil 4115.82.5   Gioberti e Zarellj. Pisa, 1851.

Phil 1750.14   Gratry, A.J.A. Etude sur la sophistique contemporaine. Paris, 1851.

Phil 8586.37   Greg, William R. The creed of Christendom. London, 1851.

Phil 6676.5   Gregary, William. Letters to a candid inquirer on animal magnetism. London, 1851.

Phil 1135.28   Gruppe, O.F. Die kosmischen Systeme der Griechen. Berlin, 1851.

Phil 181.21.5   Gruyer, L.A. Opuscules philosophiques. Bruxelles, 1851.

Phil 75.5   Gumposh, V.P. Die philosophische Literatur der Deutschen. Regensburg, 1851.

Phil 6677.11.2   Haddock, J.W. Somnolism and psycheism. 2d ed. London, 1851.

Phil 7054.73   A history of the recent developments in spiritual manifestations. Philadelphia, 1851.

Phil 8587.17   Hitchcock, E. The religion of geology...connected sciences. Boston, 1851.

Phil 4803.454.72   Hoene-Wroński, Józef Maria. Épitre secrète à son altesse le Prince Louis-Napoléon sur les destinées de la France. Metz, 1851.

Phil 2205.84.5   Holyoake, G.J. Paley's natural theology refuted in his own words. London, 1851.

Phil 3827.4   Horn, J.F. Spinoza's Staatslehre. Dessau, 1851.

Phil 1170.9   Hultkrantz, C.A. Historisk framställning och granskning utaf hufvudpunkterna i Plotini theoretiska philosophi. Thesis. Stockholm, 1851.

Phil 6957.4   Hunt, J.H. Astounding disclosures. n.p., 1851.

Phil 8663.3.32   Ingersol, Robert G. The Christian religion. n.p., 1851?

Phil 8884.12   Jackson, John. The sinfulness of little sins. 5th ed. London, 1851.

Phil 3475.4   Jacobi, Maximilian. Naturleben und Geistesleben. Leipzig, 1851.

Phil 8700.8   King, David. The principles of geology explained. N.Y., 1851.

Phil 3525.50   Krause, K.C.F. Das Urbild der Menschheit. Göttingen, 1851.

Phil 6681.8   Lassaigne, Auguste. Memoires d'un magnétism. Paris, 1851.

Phil 9035.5   Lazarus, M.E. Comparative psychology and universal analogy. Vegetable portraits of character. N.Y., 1851.

Phil 8701.17   Lord, Eleazar. The epoch of creation. N.Y., 1851.

Htn   Phil 6990.38*   Luquet, J.F.O. Abrege de la notice sur la vie et les vertus d'Anna Maria Taigi. Rome, 1851.

Phil 2125.65   McCosh, James. Method of divine government. N.Y., 1851.

Phil 2130.35   Mansel, H.L. Prolegomena logica. Oxford, 1851.

Phil 8407.36   A memoir of the late Rev. William Gilpin. Lymington, 1851.

NEDL   Phil 2138.35.2   Mill, John S. A system of logic. 3rd ed. London, 1851. 2v.

Phil 3494.5.5   Mirbt, E.S. Kant's Philosophie. Jena, 1851.

Phil 7054.75   Monroe, L.B. A revelation from heaven. Boston, 1851.

Phil 9560.4   Morley, C. The power of kindness. N.Y., 1851.

Phil 3833.5   Norinder, A.V. Försök till en framställning, af Spinozismens nufvidsatser. Upsala, 1851.

Phil 3425.251   Nyblaeus, Axel. Bidrag till granskning af den Hegelska dialektiken och dess princip "Motsägelsen". Upsala, 1851.

Phil 7054.73.9   Observations on the theological mystery...spirit rappings. Hartford, 1851.

Phil 189.1   O'Connell, J. Vestiges of civilization. N.Y., 1851.

Phil 189.4.2   Oersted, H.C. Samlede og efterladte skrifter. v.1-3, 4-6, 7-9. Kjøbenhavn, 1851-1852. 3v.

Phil 8595.15.4.5   Paine, Thomas. Theologische Werke. v.1-4,6. Philadelphia, 1851.

Phil 2205.15   Paley, W. Works. London, 1851.

Phil 8890.2.4   Palmer, T.H. The moral instructor. pt.4. Boston, 1851.

Phil 2805.30.13   Pascal, Blaise. Les provinciales. Paris, 1851. 2v.

Phil 6687.1.2   Reichenback, C. Physico-physiological researches. N.Y., 1851.

Phil 192.76   Rosa, Gabriele. Le meraviglio del mondo. Milano, 1851.

Phil 4210.22.5   Rosmini-Serbati, Antonio. Ideologia (Nuovo saggio sull'origine delle idee). Torino, 1851-52. 3v.

Phil 4210.25.20   Rosmini-Serbati, Antonio. Sul principio: Pa legge dubia non obliga. Milano, 1851.

Phil 3425.252   Sahlin, C. Yngve. Har Hegel öfvervunnit dualismen? Upsala, 1851.

Phil 3808.60.2   Schopenhauer, Arthur. Parerga und Paralipomena. v.1-2. Berlin, 1851.

Phil 818.2   Smyth, C.B. Christian metaphysics. London, 1851.

Phil 2270.55.2   Spencer, Herbert. Social statics. London, 1851.

Phil 2270.55   Spencer, Herbert. Social statics. London, 1851.

Phil 2270.55.3   Spencer, Herbert. Social statics. London, 1851.

Htn   Phil 2270.55.1*   Spencer, Herbert. Social statics. London, 1851.

Phil 104.1.9   Taylor, I. Elements of thought. 2nd American ed. N.Y., 1851.

Phil 7054.137   Tiffany, Joel. Lectures on spiritualism. Cleveland, 1851.

Phil 9500.2   Townsend, F. Mutterings and musings of an invalid. N.Y., 1851.

Phil 3805.100   Vorlander, Franz. Schleiermachers Sittenlehre ausführlich. Marburg, 1851.

Phil 5062.1.5   Waddington, C. De l'utilité des études logiques. Paris, 1851.

Phil 197.1   Wagner, J. Organon der menschlichen Erkenntniss. Ulm, 1851.

Phil 6692.1   Ware, J. Animal magnetism. n.p., 1851.

Phil 8610.851   Wright, B.W. Sketches of modern irreligion and infidelity. London, 1851.

1852

Phil 5040.11   Afzelius, F.G. Lärobok i logiken for elementar-undervisningen. Upsala, 1852.

Phil 5750.5   Ahlander, J.A. De libertate. Disquisitio. Lundae, 1852.

Phil 5040.1   Aldrich, H. Artis logicae rudimenta. Oxford, 1852.

Phil 3425.269   Allihn, F.H.T. Der verderbliche Einfluss der Hegelschen Philosophie. Leipzig, 1852.

Phil 7059.16   Ambler, R.P. Spiritual teacher. N.Y., 1852.

Phil 7059.9   Arnold, L.M. History of the origin of all things. n.p., 1852.

Phil 5041.2   Bailey, Samuel. The theory of reasoning. London, 1852.

Phil 7054.105   Ballou, Adin. An exposition of views...spirit manifestations. Boston, 1852.

Phil 4352.1.33   Balmes, Jaime. Art d'arriver au vrai. Paris, 1852.

Phil 1535.1   Balmès, Jaime. Philosophie fondamentale. Paris, 1852. 3v.

Phil 4001.4.5   Bonavino, C. La filosofia delle scuole italiane. Capolago, 1852.

Phil 4001.4   Bonavino, C. L'introduzione alla filosofia delle scuole italiane. Italia, 1852.

Phil 3425.200.10   Borelius, J.J. Om filosofiens supremati enligt Hegelska systemet. Lund, 1852.

Phil 2733.99   Bouillier, F. Mémoire sur la vision en Dieu de Malebranche. Orleans, 1852?

Phil 6671.10.10   Braid, James. Magic, witchcraft, animal magnetism. London, 1852.

Phil 7060.14.5   Brierre de Boismont, A. Des hallucinations. 2. ed. Paris, 1852.

Phil 1900.25   Butler, Joseph. Analogy of religion and sermons. London, 1852.

Phil 2880.1.80   Caro, E.M. Essai sur la vie et la doctrine de St. Martin. Paris, 1852.

Phil 9162.4   Chassay, F.E. Les devoirs des femmes dans la famille. Paris, 1852.

Phil 8877.26   Clark, T.M. Lectures on the formation of character. Hartford, 1852.

Phil 2490.55   Comte, Auguste. Catèchisme positiviste. Paris, 1852.

Phil 7068.52   Davis, A.J. The approaching crisis. N.Y., 1852.

Phil 9343.6   Deems, C.F. What now? N.Y., 1852.

Phil 2520.18A   Descartes, René. Oeuvres philosophiques publiées. Paris, 1852.

Phil 3310.1.85   Dischinger, J.N.P. Die Günther'sche Philosophie. Schaffhausen, 1852.

Phil 6673.3.6   Dods, J.B. The philosophy of electrical psychology. N.Y., 1852.

Phil 5043.9   Dressler, J.G. Praktisch Denklehre. Bautzen, 1852.

Phil 9344.2   Eliot, W.G. Lectures to young men. St. Louis, 1852.

Phil 179.1   Engel, G.E. System der metaphysischen Grundbegriffe. Berlin, 1852.

Phil 179.22.10   Erdmann, J.E. Wir leben Nicht auf der Erde. Berlin, 1852-71. 5 pam.

Phil 6115.11.4   Feuchtersleben, E.F.V. Zur Diätetik der Seele. 9. Aufl. Wien, 1852.

Phil 8406.7   Fischer, Kuno. Diotima; die Idee des Schönen. Stuttgart, 1852.

Phil 3005.1   Fortlage, K. Genetische Geschichte der Philosophie seit Kent. Leipzig, 1852.

Phil 5245.16.3   Friedreich, J.B. System der gerichtlichen Psychologie. 3e Aufl. Regensburg, 1852.

Phil 1200.34   Gidionsen, W. De es quad stoici naturae comienienter vivendum esse, principium ponunt. Lipsiae, 1852.

Phil 7054.68   Gleason, S.W. The spirit home: a closet companion. Boston, 1852.

Phil 2035.30   Hamilton, William. Discussions on philosophy and literature. London, 1852.

Phil 7054.62.2   Hammond, Charles. Light from the spirit world. N.Y., 1852.

Phil 7054.62   Hammond, Charles. Pilgrimage of Thos. Paine. N.Y., 1852.

Phil 9450.3   Harcourt, W.G.G.V.V. The morality of public men. London, 1852.

1852 - cont.

Phil 182.4 — Harms, F. Prolegomena zur Philosophie. Braunschweig, 1852.

Phil 182.7.2 — Hassler, K.D. Paragraphen für den Unterricht in der Philosophie. 2. Aufl. Ulm, 1852.

Phil 8697.15 — Hayden, W.B. Science and revelation. Boston, 1852.

X Cg Phil 6117.7 — Holland, H. Chapters on mental physiology. London, 1852.

Phil 8662.5.10 — Holyoake, George Jacob. Why do the clergy avoid discussion. London, 1852.

Phil 325.1 — Hoppe, R. Zulänglichkeit des Empirismus...Philosophie. Berlin, 1852.

Phil 9455.8 — Howe, M.A. de Wolfe. Public opinion,...an oration...Connecticut Beta of Phi Beta Kappa Society, July 28, 1852. Hartford, 1852.

Phil 8589.5 — James, H. Lectures and miscellanies. Redfield, N.Y., 1852.

Phil 3480.85.11 — Kant, Immanuel. Von der Macht des Gemüths durch den blossen Vorsatz seiner krankhaften Gefühle Meister zu seyn. 6. Aufl. Leipzig, 1852.

X Cg Phil 8590.2 — Kidd, J. On the adaption of external nature, physical condition of man. London, 1852.

Phil 3425.216 — Lagus, R.E. De Hegeliana philosophiam juris tractandi ratione. Helsingforsiae, 1852.

Phil 8886.1 — Lalor, J. Money and morals. London, 1852.

Phil 6945.2 — Leech, J. Suggestion of the law of the lunacy. London, 1852.

Phil 5460.8 — Leubuscher, R. Über die Entstehung der Sinnestäuschung. Berlin, 1852.

Phil 1535.5 — Liberatore, M. Elementi di filosofia. Livorno, 1852.

Phil 8050.43 — Ljunggren, G. Några punkter ur läran om det natursköna. Lund, 1852.

Htn Phil 3565.68.1* — Lotze, Hermann. Medicinische Psychologie. Leipzig, 1852.

Phil 3565.68 — Lotze, Hermann. Medicinische Psychologie. Leipzig, 1852.

Phil 2125.65.5 — McCosh, James. Method of divine government. Edinburgh, 1852.

Phil 4170.7.52 — Mamiani della Rovere, Terenzio. Nuovo discorso proemiale. Genova, 1852.

Phil 4260.149 — Marini, Cesare. Grambattista Vico al cospetto del secolo XIX. Napoli, 1852.

Phil 7060.137 — Mayo, Herbert. Popular superstitions. 3. ed. Philadelphia, 1852.

Phil 9528.2 — Miller, S. Letters from a father to his son in college. Philadelphia, 1852.

Phil 6682.14 — Millington, T.S. A lecture on the phenomena of dreams, mesmerism, clairvoyance. London, 1852?

Phil 1050.2 — Munk, S. Philosophie und Schriftsteller der Juden. Leipzig, 1852.

Phil 8593.2.9 — Newman, F.W. Soul, its sorrows and its aspirations. 3. ed. London, 1852.

Phil 3833.3 — Nordwall, A.L. De Spinozismi initiis aphorismi. Upsaliae, 1852.

Phil 8888.10 — Nordwall, Adolf L. Om ethikens problem och de vigtigaste försäken att lösa detsamma. Upsala, 1852.

Phil 4070.1.90 — I nuovi auspizi all'Italia e le confessioni di Ausonio Franchi. Genova, 1852.

Phil 4610.6.31 — Nyblaeus, Axel. Om straffrätten. Lund, 1852.

Phil 189.4.12 — Oersted, H.C. The soul in nature. London, 1852.

Phil 8415.7.4 — Oeser, C. Briefe an eine Jungfrau über die Hauptgegenstände der Asthetik. 4. Aufl. Leipzig, 1852.

Phil 8595.15.9A — Paine, Thomas. Age of reason. Investigation of true and fabulous theology. London, 1852.

Phil 2805.40.37 — Pascal, Blaise. Pensées. Paris, 1852.

Phil 7054.99 — Phenomena of the "spiritual rappings". Boston, 1852.

Phil 7054.85 — Platt, L.L. Spiritual experience. New Haven, 1852. 2 pam.

Phil 7054.95 — Pond, E. Familiar spirits and spiritual manifestations. Boston, 1852.

Phil 190.19 — Prantl, Karl. Die gegenwärtige Aufgabe der Philosophie. München, 1852. 8 pam.

Phil 6027.1 — Redfield, J.W. Comparative physiognomy. N.Y., 1852.

Phil 6687.1.9 — Reichenbach, C. Odisch-magnetische Briefe. Stuttgart, 1852.

Phil 2240.60.3 — Reid, Thomas. Essays on the intellectual powers of man. 3rd ed. Cambridge, 1852.

Phil 1020.4.5 — Renan, E. Averrose et l'Averroisme. Paris, 1852.

Phil 4630.1.35 — Ribbing, Sigurd. Eristiska blad. Upsala, 1852.

Phil 3780.79 — Rosenkranz, Karl. Meine Reform der hegelschen Philosophie. Königsberg, 1852.

Phil 7054.33.5 — Samson, G.W. "To daemoion" or The spiritual medium. Boston, 1852.

Phil 3805.78 — Schleiermacher, Friedrich. Briefwechsel mit J.C. Gass. Berlin, 1852.

Phil 5062.6.55 — Smart, B.H. A letter to Dr. Whately. London, 1852.

Phil 3819.37 — Spinoza, Benedictus de. Tractatus de Deo et homine eiusque felicitate lineamenta atque adnotationes ad tractatum theologico politicum. Halae, 1852.

Phil 8598.18 — Straus-Durckheim, H.E. Théologie de la nature. Paris, 1852. 3v.

Phil 8674.2 — Taylor, G. The indications of the creator. N.Y., 1852.

Phil 819.1.13A — Tennemann, W.G. Manual of the history of philosophy. London, 1852.

Phil 3895.49 — Ulrici, H. System der Logik. Leipzig, 1852.

Phil 7054.94 — Warren, O.G. Supernal theology and life in the spheres. N.Y., 1852.

Phil 5942.1 — Weaver, G.S. Lectures on mental science. N.Y., 1852.

Phil 5942.1.5 — Weaver, G.S. Lectures on mental science according to the philosophy of phrenology. N.Y., 1852.

Phil 303.2 — Werther, C.A. Die Kräfte der unorganischen Natur. Dessau, 1852.

Phil 5062.6.7.5 — Whately, Richard. Elements of logic. Boston, 1852.

Phil 5062.6.7.7 — Whately, Richard. Logic. 2nd ed. London, 1852.

Phil 8847.1 — Whewell, W. History of moral philosophy in England. London, 1852.

Phil 8677.3.6 — Whewell, William. Astronomy and general physics, considered with reference to natural theology. 7. ed. London, 1852.

g Phil 9182.5 — Wise, D. Bridal greetings: a marriage gift. N.Y., 1852.

Phil 9362.5 — Wise, D. Young lady's counsellor. N.Y., 1852.

Phil 9362.5.2 — Wise, D. Young man's counsellor. N.Y., 1852.

Phil 8712.13.8 — Wiseman, N.P.S. Twelve lectures on the connexion between science and revealed religion. 4. ed. Baltimore, 1852. 2v.

Phil 3552.292 — Zimmermann, R. Das Rechtsprinzip bei Leibnitz. Wien, 1852.

Phil 200.3.12 — Zimmermann, R. Was Erwarten wir von der Philosophie? Prag, 1852.

1853

Phil 5040.2 — Allihn, F.H.T. Des antibarbarus logicus. Halle, 1853.

Phil 281.1 — Ambler, R.P. Birth of the universe. N.Y., 1853.

Phil 9575.1 — Arnot, W. The race for riches. Philadelphia, 1853.

Phil 4210.87.5 — Avogadro della Motta, Emiliano. Sul valore scientifico e sulle pratiche consequenze. Napoli, 1853.

Phil 7054.105.2 — Ballou, Adin. An exposition of views...spirit manifestations. 2, ed. Boston, 1853.

Phil 6671.22.5 — Baragnon, Petrus. Étude magnétisme animal sous le point de vue d'une exacte pratique. 2. éd. Paris, 1853.

Phil 7054.60.5 — Beecher, Charles. A review of the spiritual manifestations. London, 1853.

Phil 7054.60.4 — Beecher, Charles. A review of the spiritual manifestations. N.Y., 1853.

Phil 3100.46 — Beneke, F.E. Lehrbuch der pragmatischen Psychologie. Berlin, 1853.

Phil 1870.11.5 — Berkeley, G. Works. London, 1853. 2v.

Phil 3425.200 — Borelius, J.J. Det hegelska systemet och den spekulativa ethiken. Lund, 1853.

Phil 7060.14.9 — Brierre de Boismont, A. Hallucinations. 1st American ed. Philadelphia, 1853.

Phil 7054.61 — Brittan, S.B. A review of Rev. Charles Beecher's report. N.Y., 1853.

Phil 7054.61.5 — Brittan, Samuel B. A discussion of the facts of...ancient and modern spiritualism. N.Y., 1853.

Phil 7054.147 — Campbell, Z. The spiritual telegraphic opposition line. Springfield, 1853.

Phil 8582.7 — Chalybäus, H.M. Philosophie und Christenthum. Kiel, 1853.

Phil 8877.11 — Clark, S.D. The faithful steward. Boston, 1853.

Phil 2490.41.1.5 — Comte, Auguste. The positive philosophy. N.Y., 1853. 2v.

Phil 6112.6 — Cooke, W. A comentary...mind and the emotions. Philadelphia, 1853.

Phil 1702.1.9 — Cousin, Victor. Course of the history of modern philosophy. N.Y., 1853. 2v.

Phil 8403.8 — Cousin, Victor. Du vrai, du beau et du bien. Paris, 1853.

Phil 7060.36.7 — Crowe, C.S. The night-side of nature. N.Y., 1853.

Phil 7054.6.55 — Davis, A.J. The harmonial man. Boston, 1853.

Phil 6673.1 — Delaage, M.H. Le monde prophétique. Paris, 1853.

Phil 5645.3 — Dove, H.W. Darstellung der Farbenlehre. Berlin, 1853.

Phil 7054.52.4 — Edmonds, J W. Spiritualism. 4th ed. N.Y., 1853.

Phil 7054.112 — Everett, J. A book for skeptics being communications from angels. Columbus, 1853.

Phil 5815.1 — Fée, A.L.A. Etudes philosophiques...animaux. Strasburg, 1853.

Phil 3270.4.79 — Feuerbach, P.J.A. Biographischer Nachlass. v.1-2. Leipzig, 1853.

Phil 480.4 — Fischer, K.P. Die Unwahrheit des Sensualismus und Materialismus. Erlangen, 1853.

Phil 5925.3.1 — Fowler, O.S. The illustrated self-instructor in phrenology. N.Y., 1853.

Phil 5925.2.2 — Fowler, O.S. Physiology, animal and mental. N.Y., 1853. 3 pam.

Phil 8406.5 — Frauenstädt, J. Aesthetische Fragen. Dessau, 1853.

Phil 90.3 — Furtmair, M. Philosophisches Real-Lexikon. Augsburg, 1853.

Phil 4115.30.2 — Gioberti, V. Del buono, del bello. Firenze., 1853.

Phil 4120.1.35 — Gioja, Melchiorre. Del merito e delle ricompenae. Torino, 1853. 2v.

Phil 8610.853.10 — Grant, B. Christianity and secularism. London, 1853.

Phil 7054.138 — Green, Frances H. Biography of Mrs. Semantha Mettler. N.Y., 1853.

Phil 7050.11 — Guillard, J.-C.A. Table qui douse et table qui répond. Paris, 1853. 3 pam.

Phil 8610.801.5 — Hall, Robert. Modern infidelity considered. Philadelphia, 1853.

Phil 2035.30.2 — Hamilton, William. Discussions on philosophy and literature. N.Y., 1853.

Phil 2035.30.1 — Hamilton, William. Discussions on philosophy and literature. 2nd ed. London, 1853.

Phil 2035.20 — Hamilton, William. Philosophy. N.Y., 1853.

Phil 7054.62.5 — Hammond, Charles. Philosophy of the spirit world. N.Y., 1853.

Phil 9450.3.2 — Harcourt, W.G.G.V.V. The morality of public men. 2. ed. London, 1853.

Phil 7054.150 — Henck, E.C. Spirit voices. Philadelphia, 1853.

Phil 5817.3 — Henslow, G. Mind in man and animals. London, 1853-81. 2 pam.

Phil 7054.79 — Hewitt, S.C. Messages from the superior state. Boston, 1853.

Phil 8882.9 — Hickok, L.P. A system of moral science. Schenectady, 1853.

Phil 1112.1 — History of Greek and Roman philosophy. London, 1853.

Phil 340.3 — Jacob, T. Allgemeiner Theil der Erkenntnislehre. Berlin, 1853.

Phil 3480.67.60 — Kant, Immanuel. Éléments métaphysique de la doctrine du droit. Paris, 1853.

Phil 3480.30.8 — Kant, Immanuel. Kritik der reinen Vernunft. Leipzig, 1853.

Phil 3310.1.127 — Knoodt, Peter. Günther und Blemens. Wien, 1853-54.

Phil 2490.81 — Lewes, G.H. Comte's philosophy of the sciences. London, 1853.

Phil 3625.1.145 — Mirabeau, H.G.R. Sur Moses Mendelssohn. Leipzig, 1853.

Phil 5252.9 — Morell, J.D. Elements of psychology. pt. 1. Photoreproduction. London, 1853.

Phil 6962.11 — Morison, A. Physiognomik der Geisteskrankheiten. Leipzig, 1853.

Phil 5053.1 — Neil, Samuel. The art of reasoning. London, 1853.

Phil 8593.2.11 — Newman, F.W. Phases of faith. 3. ed. London, 1853.

Phil 8593.2.6 — Newman, F.W. The soul. London, 1853.

Phil 8610.853 — Noack, L. Der Freidenker in der Religion. pt.3. Bern, 1853-55.

Phil 813.3 — Noack, L. Geschichte der Philosophie. Weimar, 1853.

Phil 525.12.7 — Noack, Ludwig. Die christliche Mystik. Königsberg, 1853.

Phil 8593.14 — Nyblaeus, Axel. Om religionens betydelse och förhällande till philosophen. pt.1-4. Upsala, 1853.

Phil 575.3 — Oginski, T. Die Idee der Person. Breslau, 1853.

Phil 1714.1 — Oischinger, J.N.P. Speculative Entwicklung...neueren Philosophie. Schaffhaussen, 1853-4. 2v.

Phil 8890.2.5 — Palmer, T.H. The moral instructor. pt.1. Boston, 1853.

Phil 8595.1.6 — Parker, T. Sermons of Theism, Atheism, and the popular theology. Boston, 1853.

Phil 2805.30.25 — Pascal, Blaise. Les provinciales. Paris, 1853.

Phil 490.2 — Perty, M. Über die Bedeutung der Anthropologie. Bern, 1853.

Htn Phil 6103.8* — Pflüger, E. Die sensorischen Functionen des Rückenmarks. Berlin, 1853. 5 pam.

1853 - cont.

Phil 3425.227   Quist, C.J. De philosophia juris Hegeliana. Thesis. Helsingforsiae, 1853.

Htn   Phil 2240.60.4*   Reid, Thomas. Essays on the intellectual powers of man. 4th ed. Cambridge, 1853.

Phil 2240.14   Reid, Thomas. Works. Edinburgh, 1853. 2v.

Phil 4265.2.94   Rémusat, Charles. Il padre Ventura e la filosofia. Milano, 1853.

Phil 4265.2.93   Rémusat, Charles. Il padre Ventura e la filosofia. Milano, 1853.

Phil 3017.2   Ritter, A.H. Versuch zur neueste deutsche Philosophie...Kant. Braunschweig, 1853.

Phil 7054.140   Rogers, E.C. Philosophy of mysterious agents. Boston, 1853.

Phil 8597.11.15   Rogers, H. Reason and faith. Boston, 1853.

Phil 6967.12   Romberg, M.H. Manual of the nervous diseases. London, 1853. 2v.

Phil 8418.11   Rosenkranz, K. Ästhetik des Hässlichen. Königsberg, 1853.

Phil 4115.80   Rosmini-Serbati, A. Vincenzo Gioberti. Lucca, 1853.

Phil 4210.23.2   Rosmini-Serbati, Antonio. Logica. Torino, 1853.

Phil 7054.101   Rouband, F. La danse des tables. Paris, 1853.

Phil 6688.15.2   Ségouin, A. Les mystéres de la magie ou les secrets du magnetisme. 2e éd. Paris, 1853.

Phil 7054.61.9   The Shekinah. N.Y., 1853. 3v.

Phil 1200.26   Sibbern, G. Den stoiske og epikuraeiske moral. Kjobenhavn, 1853.

Phil 7054.104   Snow, H. Spirit-intercourse containing incidents of personal experience. Boston, 1853.

Phil 7052.10.2   Spicer, Henry. Facts and fantasies, a sequel to Sights and sounds. London, 1853.

Phil 7052.10   Spicer, Henry. Sights and sounds. London, 1853.

Phil 7054.38   Spirit rapping in England and America. London, 1853.

Phil 7054.61.8   Spiritual telegraph. The telegraph papers. N.Y., 1853. 8v.

Phil 7060.23   Sunderland, L. Book of human nature. N.Y. 1853.

Phil 7060.23.5   Sunderland, L. Book of psychology. N.Y. 1853.

Phil 6688.13   Szapary, Franz von. Magnétisme et magnétothérapie. Paris, 1853.

Phil 8894.1   Taylor, H. Notes from life. Boston, 1853.

Phil 9200.1.10   Taylor, Isaac. Fanaticism. London, 1853.

Phil 9179.4   Thayer, W.M. Hints for the household. Photoreproduction. Boston, 1853.

Phil 2520.125   Ventura de Raulica, G. Essai sur l'origine des idées...sur le carthésianisme. Paris, 1853.

Phil 7054.41   Webber, C.W. Spiritual vampirism. Philadelphia, 1853.

Phil 8602.6   Whewell, W. Of the plurality of worlds. London, 1853.

Phil 303.4   Winslow, C.F. Cosmography. Boston, 1853.

1854

Phil 7054.89   Adams, J.S. A rivulet from the ocean of truth. Boston, 1854.

Phil 5125.1   Apelt, E.F. Die Theorie der Induction. Leipzig, 1854.

Phil 5040.3.5   Arnauld, Antoine. Logique de Port Royal. Paris, 1854.

Phil 3820.1   Auerbach, B. Spinoza. Mannheim, 1854.

Phil 5135.1.5   Bailey, S. Essays on opinions and truth. Boston, 1854.

Phil 8656.23   Ballou, Moses. The divine character vindicated. N.Y., 1854.

Phil 1535.1.15   Balmes, Giacomo. Corso di filosofia elementare. v.1-4. Firenze, 1854.

Phil 8656.14   Beecher, E. The conflict of the ages. 5. ed. Boston, 1854.

Phil 3100.51   Beneke, F.E. Neue Seelenlehre. Bautzen, 1854.

Phil 8581.127   Blanc de Saint-Bonnet, Antoine Joseph Elisée Adolphe. De l'affaiblissement de la raison et de la décadence en Europe. 2. éd. Paris, 1854.

Phil 4070.1.35   Bonavino, Cristoforo. Studi filosofici e religiosi; del sentimento. 1. ed. Torino, 1854.

Phil 4070.1.36   Bonavino, Cristoforo. Studi filosofici e religiosi; del sentimento. 2. ed. Torino, 1854.

Htn   Phil 5041.15.1*   Boole, George. The laws of thought. London, 1854.

Phil 5041.15   Boole, George. The laws of thought. London, 1854.

Phil 2520.83.5   Bouillier, F. Histoire de la philosophie Cartésienne. Paris, 1854. 2v.

Phil 7054.61.3   Brittan, Samuel B. The tables turned. N.Y., 1854.

Phil 5241.16   Brodie, B.C. Psychological inquiries. London, 1854.

Phil 7054.57   Brownson, O.A. The spirit-rapper. Boston, 1854.

Phil 6672.9.15   Cahagnet, L. Magnétisme; encyclopédie magnétique. v.1-6. Paris, 1854-62. 3v.

Phil 410.1   Calderwood, H. The philosophy of the infinite. Edinburgh, 1854.

Phil 3002.1.6   Chalybäus, H. Historical development of speculative philosophy. Edinburgh, 1854.

Phil 3002.1.7   Chalybäus, H. Historical survey of speculative philosophy. Andover, 1854.

Phil 3002.1.5   Chalybäus, H. Historical survey of speculative philosophy. London, 1854.

Phil 9050.6   Chapin, E.H. Moral aspects of city life. 2d ed. N.Y., 1854.

Phil 6945.16   Clayton, J.M. Speech on the veto message of the President on the bill for the benefit of the indigent insane. Washington, 1854.

Phil 7054.113   Corning, W.H. The infidelity of the times. Boston, 1854.

Phil 1702.1.8   Cousin, Victor. Course of the history of modern philosophy. N.Y., 1854. 2v.

Phil 2496.40.10   Cousin, Victor. Lectures on the true, the beautiful and the good. N.Y., 1854.

Phil 2496.40.5   Cousin, Victor. Lectures on the true, the beautiful and the good. N.Y., 1854.

Phil 7054.71   Cridge, A. Epitome of spirit-intercourse. Boston, 1854.

Phil 8582.15   Crosskey, H.W. A defense of religion. London, 1854.

Phil 8610.854.2   Davis, A.J. Free thoughts concerning religion. 2. ed. Boston, 1854.

Phil 2651.80   DeGournay, M.F.A. Huet. Caen, 1854.

Phil 5043.6   Devey, Joseph. Logic; or The science of inference. London, 1854.

Phil 8404.10   Dittes, Friedrich. Das Ästhetische nach seinem eigenthümlichen Grundwesen. Leipzig, 1854.

Phil 7054.92.5   Dods, John B. Spirit manifestations. N.Y., 1854.

Phil 6673.4.5   Du Potet, J. de S. Manuel de l'étudiant magnétiseur. 3e éd. Paris, 1854.

Phil 3200.7   Erdmann, J.E. Über den Naturalismus. Halle, 1854.

Phil 5244.4   Esser, W. Psychologie. Münster, 1854.

Phil 7054.66   Ferguson, J.B. A record of communications from the spirit-spheres. Nashville, 1854.

Phil 1990.30   Ferrier, J.F. Institutes of metaphysic. Edinburgh, 1854.

1854 - cont.

Phil 1705.4   Fischer, K. Geschichte der neueren Philosophie. v.1-6. Mannheim, 1854-77. 7v.

Phil 3270.1.31   Fischer, Kuno. Die Apologie meiner Lehre. Mannheim, 1854.

Phil 3270.1.32   Fischer, Kuno. Das Interdict meiner Vorlesungen. Mannheim, 1854.

Phil 3808.82   Frauenstädt, C.M.J. Briefe über des Schopenhauerische Philosophie. Leipzig, 1854.

Phil 5520.2   Gaskell, J. Sense and sound. Philadelphia, 1854.

Phil 5246.4   George, S. Lehrbuch der Psychologie. Berlin, 1854.

Phil 7060.49   Ghost stories. Philadelphia 1854.

Htn   Phil 4006.3.10*   Giovanni, V. Sullo stato attuale...filosofici in Sicilia. Palermo, 1854.

Phil 4006.3.12   Giovanni, V. Sullo stato attuale...filosofici in Sicilia. Palermo, 1854.

Phil 8661.9.2   Gratry, A. De la connaissance de Dieu. 2. éd. Paris, 1854. 2v.

Phil 7054.69   Gridley, J.A. Astounding facts from the spirit world. South Hampton, 1854.

Phil 1735.4   Guepin, Anec. Philosophie du XIXe siècle. Paris, 1854.

Phil 3425.35   Hegel, Georg Wilhelm Friedrich. Logique subjective. Paris, 1854.

Phil 5247.9.7   Hickok, L.P. Empirical psychology. 2. ed. N.Y., 1854.

Phil 2050.11A   Hume, David. Philosophical works. Edinburgh, 1854. 4v.

Phil 3480.65.23   Kant, Immanuel. Principes métaphysiques de la morale. 3. éd. Paris, 1854.

Phil 8656.14.25   King, Thomas S. A short review of Edward Beecher's work on the conflict of ages. 2. ed. Boston, 1854.

Phil 1150.4   Kingsley, C. Alexandria and her schools. Cambridge, 1854.

Phil 6945.3   Kirkbride, T.S. On the construction, organization and general arrangements of hospitals for the insane. Philadelphia, 1854.

Phil 185.11   Kym, A.L. Die Weltanschauungen. Zürich, 1854.

Phil 3552.19.5   Leibniz, Gottfried Wilhelm. Lettres et opuscules inédits. Paris, 1854.

Htn   Phil 3552.45*   Leibniz, Gottfried Wilhelm. Réfutation inédite de Spinoza. Paris, 1854.

Phil 4803.522.5   Libelt, Karol. Estetyka czyli umnictwo piękne. v.1-2. Petersburg, 1854. 3v.

Phil 2115.12   Locke, J. Works. London, 1854. 2v.

Phil 2130.50   Mansel, H.L. Man's conception of eternity. London, 1854.

Phil 812.2   Matter, J. Histoire de la philosophie. Paris, 1854.

Phil 812.3.2   Maurice, J.F.D. Moral and metaphysical philosophy. 2d ed. London, 1854.

Phil 6122.2   Mello Moraes, Alexandre José de. Physiologia das paixões e affeções. Rio de Janeiro, 1854-55. 3v.

Phil 8702.6.25   Miller, H. The two records: The mosaic and the geological. Boston, 1854.

Phil 7068.54   Mirville, J.E. Pneumatologie des esprits. 3. ed. Paris, 1854.

Phil 4075.80   Morley, H. Jerome Cardan. v.2. London, 1854.

Phil 8887.22   Morton, E. A key to true happiness. Hudson, Ohio, 1854.

Phil 9172.3   Muzzey, A.B. The fireside: an aid to parents. Boston, 1854.

Phil 188.3   Noack, L. Propädeutik der Philosophie. Weimar, 1854.

Phil 6684.4   Olivier, J. Traité de magnétisme. Paris, 1854.

NEDL   Phil 9174.1.3   Osgood, S. The hearth-stone. N.Y., 1854.

Phil 9174.1   Osgood, S. The hearth-stone. N.Y., 1854.

Phil 2205.30.5   Paley, W. Natural theology. Boston, 1854.

Phil 3835.8   Parkinson, G.H.R. Spinoza's theory of knowledge. Oxford, 1854.

Phil 2805.40.3   Pascal, Blaise. Pensées. Paris, 1854.

Phil 1850.122   Patru, G.A. Esprit et méthode de Bacon en philosophie. Paris, 1854.

Phil 8610.854.15   Pearson, Thomas. Infidelity. N.Y., 1854.

Phil 6965.8   Peters, John C. A treatise on nervous derangements. N.Y., 1854.

Phil 9175.5   Porter, Ann E. Uncle Jerry's letters to young mothers. Boston, 1854.

Phil 1120.2   Prantl, K. Übersicht der griech-römischen Philosophie. Stuttgart, 1854.

Phil 5055.6   Püllenberg, Johann. Kurze Darstellung des Hauptinhalts der Logik. Coblenz, 1854.

Phil 192.7.2   Reinhold, C.E. System der Metaphysik. Jena, 1854.

Phil 2840.40   Renouvier, C.B. Essais de critique générale. Paris, 1854-64. 4v.

Phil 8597.8   Reynaud, J.E. Philosophie religiuse terre et ciel. Paris, 1854.

Phil 7054.80   Robinson, J.H. The religion of manhood. Boston, 1854.

Phil 8597.11.7   Rogers, H. A defence of the eclipse of faith. London, 1854.

Phil 193.8   Schildener, H. Progress der Weltgeschichte. Greifswald, 1854.

Phil 3805.25   Schleiermacher, Friedrich. Ideen, Reflexionen und Betrachtungen aus Schleiermachers Werken. Berlin, 1854.

Phil 5058.4   Schlötel, W. Die Logik. Göttingen, 1854.

Htn   Phil 3808.65.5*   Schopenhauer, Arthur. Über den Willen in der Natur. Frankfurt, 1854.

Phil 3850.6.79   Schubert, G.H. Der Erwerb aus...Leben: eine Selbstbiographie. Erlangen, 1854-56. 3v.

Phil 9050.2   Scott, Rev. Dr. A lecture...on the influences of great cities. San Francisco, 1854.

Phil 9120.3   Simon, J. Le devoir. Paris, 1854.

Phil 2275.11   Stewart, D. Collected works. v.1-4, 6-10, and supplement. Edinburgh, 1854-60. 10v.

X Cg   Phil 2275.11   Stewart, D. Collected works. v.5. Edinburgh, 1854-60.

Phil 2275.50   Stewart, D. Elements of the philosophy of the human mind. Boston, 1854.

Phil 1123.6   Strümpell, L. Die Geschichte der griechischen Philosophie zur Übersicht. pts.1-2. Leipzig, 1854-61.

Phil 6128.6   Swan, J. The brain in relation to the mind. London, 1854.

Phil 8894.5.10   Tiberghien, G. Esquisse de philosophie morale. Bruxelles, 1854.

Phil 6689.2.5   Townehend, C.H. Mesmerism proved true. London, 1854.

Phil 3428.90.5   Trendelenburg, A. Über Herbart's Metaphysik. Berlin, 1854.

Phil 6945.11.10   United States. Congress. Senate. Commission on Public Lands. Report to accompany Bill S44; include memorial of Miss D.L. Dix, January 23, 1848. Washington, 1854.

Phil 4265.2.30   Ventura da Raulica, G. Della vera e della falsa filosofia. Napoli, 1854.

Phil 196.2.5   Ventura de Raulica, G. La raison philosophique et la raison catholique. Paris, 1854-1864. 4v.

Phil 4260.15   Vico, G.B. Opere. v.1-6. Milano, 1854- 3v.

Phil 197.1.5   Wagner, J. Erläuterungen zur Organon der menschlichen Erkenntniss. Ulm, 1854.

1854 - cont.

Phil 6132.12 Wagner, J.R. Neurologische Untersuchungen.
Göttingen, 1854.
Phil 497.2 Wagner, R. Menschenschöpfung und Seelensubstanz.
Göttingen, 1854.
Phil 497.2.5 Wagner, R. Über Wissen und Glauben. Göttingen, 1854.
Phil 2496.82 Wallon, J. Du livre de M. Cousin. Paris, 1854.
Phil 525.16.9 Walton, C. Notes and materials for an adequate biography
of...William Law. London, 1854.
Phil 9035.8.2 Ware, M.G. Chandler. The elements of character.
Boston, 1854.
Phil 5262.4 Wayland, F. Elements of intellectual philosophy.
Boston, 1854.
Phil 8897.14.2 Whewell, W. Elements of morality. N.Y., 1854. 2v.
Phil 8602.6.2 Whewell, W. The plurality of worlds. Boston, 1854.
Phil 7054.67 White, N.F. Voices from spirit-land. N.Y., 1854.
Phil 3246.188 Widmark, Elof. Historisk öfversigt af Fichtes naturrält
och Babergs outik deraf. Upsala, 1854.
Phil 8425.2 Young, E. Art: its constitution and capacities.
Bristol, 1854.
Phil 6135.1 Zukrigl, J. Kritische Untersuchung über das Wesen der
vernünstigen Geist-Seele. Regensburg, 1854.

1855

Phil 3000.2 Allihn, F.H.T. Die Umkehr der Wissenschaft in Preussen.
Berlin, 1855.
Phil 8580.5 Alliott, R. Psychology and theology. London, 1855.
Phil 1850.51 Bacon, Francis. The novum organon. Oxford, 1855.
Phil 5241.1 Bailey, S. Letters...philosophy...human mind.
London, 1855.
Phil 5241.2.20 Bain, A. The senses and the intellect. London, 1855.
Phil 1750.9 Barthoemiss, C. Histoire critique des doctrines
religieuses et philosophiques. Paris, 1855. 2v.
Phil 8951.11 Bautain, Louis E. La morale de l'évangile comparée.
Paris, 1855. 2 pam.
Htn Phil 3801.197* Beckers, Hubert. F.W.J. von Schelling. München, 1855.
Phil 9161.2 Beleze, G.L.G. Livre de lecture courante des devoirs des
enfants. Paris, 1855.
Phil 1535.25 Bensa, A.M. Manuel de logique. Paris, 1855.
Phil 1850.94 Biechy, A. Essai sur la méthode de Bacon. Toulon, 1855.
Phil 530.20.10 Böhringer, F. Die deutschen Mystiker. Zürich, 1855.
Phil 623.2.15 Bonarino, Cristoforo. Le rationalisme. Bruxelles, 1855.
Phil 4514.1.40 Borelius, J.J. Menniskans naturlif i dess förhållande in
till det andliga lifvet. Stockholm, 1855.
Phil 1880.40 Bowen, F. Principles of metaphysical and ethical science.
Boston, 1855.
Phil 1535.2 Boylesve, M. de. Cursus philosophie. Paris, 1855.
Phil 7054.61.7 Brittan, Samuel B. The telegraph's answer. N.Y., 1855.
Phil 1801.1 Brougham, H. Lives of philosophers of the time of George
III. London, 1855.
Phil 6111.9 Brown-Séquard, C.E. Experimental and clinical researches.
Richmond, 1855.
Phil 476.3.1 Büchner, L. Kraft und Stoff. Frankfurt, 1855.
Phil 1900.70 Butler, Joseph. Ethical discourses. Philadelphia, 1855.
Phil 6672.9.5 Cahagnet, L. Celestial telegraph. 1. American ed.
N.Y., 1855.
Phil 7054.115 Capron, Eliab W. Modern spiritualism: its facts and
fanaticisms. Boston 1855.
Phil 8827.3 Caro, E.M. Études morales sur le temps présent.
Paris, 1855.
Phil 6112.13 Carter, R.B. Influence of education and training in
preventing diseases of nervous system. London, 1855.
EDL Phil 8877.12 Cobbe, F.P. An essay on intuitive morals.
London, 1855-57. 2v.
Phil 8662.5.25 Collet, S.D. George Jacob Holyoake and modern atheism.
London, 1855.
Phil 2490.57 Comte, Auguste. Appel aux conservateurs. Paris, 1855.
Phil 2490.41.1 Comte, Auguste. The positive philosophy. N.Y., 1855.
Phil 7054.92 Courtney, W.S. A review of J.B. Dods...theory of spiritual
manifestations. N.Y., 1855.
Phil 2496.50.4 Cousin, Victor. Elements of psychology. N.Y., 1855.
Phil 2496.40.6 Cousin, Victor. Lectures on the true, the beautiful, and
the good. N.Y., 1855.
Phil 2496.55.3 Cousin, Victor. Premiers essais de philosophie. 3e éd.
Paris, 1855.
Phil 8877.21 Cowdery, M.F. Elementary moral lessons. Sandusky, 1855.
Phil 477.5 Czolbe, H. Neue Darstellung des Sensualismus.
Leipzig, 1855.
Phil 8875.20 D'Acquisto, P.B. Corso di filosofia morale. 2. ed.
Palermo, 1855.
Phil 7054.6.6 Davis, A.J. The present age and inner life. N.Y., 1855.
Phil 7054.6.30 Davis, A.J. The principles of nature, her divine
revelations. 12. ed. N.Y., 1855.
Phil 178.4.2 Dennys, E.N. The alpha. London, 1855.
Phil 178.4 Dennys, E.N. The alpha. London, 1855.
Phil 2496.85 Deschamps, A.F. Reflexions sur l'instruction synodale de
Mgr. l'évêque de Poitiers. Paris, 1855.
Phil 6113.1 Durand, P.J. Electro-dynamisme vital. Paris, 1855.
Phil 5043.14 Duval-Jouve, J. Traité de logique. Paris, 1855.
Phil 7054.52 Edmonds, J.W. Spiritualism. N.Y., 1855. 2v.
Phil 7054.110 Ewer, F.C. The eventful nights of August 20th.
N.Y., 1855.
Phil 3210.34 Fechner, G.T. Über die physikalische und philosophische
Atomenlehre. Leipzig, 1855.
Phil 3235.72 Feuerbach, Ludwig. The essence of Christianity.
N.Y., 1855.
Phil 3245.50 Fichte, Immanuel Hermann. Die Idee der Persönlichkeit.
Leipzig, 1855.
Phil 5245.9.5 Fortlage, A.R.K. System der Psychologie. Leipzig, 1855.
2v.
Phil 5925.3 Fowler, O.S. The illustrated self-instructor in
phrenology. N.Y., 1855.
Phil 9495.17 Fowler, O.S. Love and parentage. N.Y., 1855.
Phil 5046.6.2 Gatry, A.J.A. Philosophie. Logique. Paris, 1855.
2v.
Phil 6116.1 Glen, J. Theory of the influence exerted by the mind over
the body. London, 1855.
Phil 181.12 Gockel, C.F. Encyklopädische Einleitung in die
Philosophie. Karlsruhe, 1855.
Phil 3006.1 Gruppe, O.F. Gegenwart und Philosophie in Deutschland.
Berlin, 1855.
Phil 3090.81.5 Hamberger, Julius. Die Cardinalpunkte der F. Baader'schen
Philosophie. Stuttgart, 1855.
Phil 2035.30.3 Hamilton, William. Discussions on philosophy and
literature. N.Y., 1855.
Phil 2035.65 Hamilton, William. Philosophy. N.Y., 1855.

1855 - cont.

Phil 8050.57 Hauch, J.C. Afhandlinger og aesthetiske betragtninger.
Kjøbenhavn, 1855.
Phil 7054.102.2 Hayden, William B. On the phenomena of modern
spiritualism. 2. ed. Boston, 1855. 2 pam.
Phil 3425.36 Hegel, Georg Wilhelm Friedrich. The subjective logic of
Hegel. London, 1855.
Phil 3090.80.10 Hoffmann, F. Zur Würdigung des Vorurthelie über die Lehre
Baaders. Leipzig, 1855.
Phil 8882.54 Hollander, A.G. Om praktiska filosofiens grundbegrepp och
deras inre förhållande till hvarandra. Lund, 1855.
Phil 5247.13.19 Huarte de San Juan, J. Essai sur l'ouvrage. Paris, 1855.
Phil 184.25 Jacob, T. Aus der Lehre vom Ganzen. Berlin, 1855.
Phil 184.2 Jacques, A. Manuel de philosophie. Paris, 1855.
Phil 8620.5 James, H. The nature of evil. N.Y., 1855.
Phil 5249.10.5 Jessen, Peter. Versuch einer wissenschaftlichen Begründung
der Psychologie. Berlin, 1855.
Phil 3480.32.2 Kant, Immanuel. Critique of pure reason. London, 1855.
Htn Phil 3480.32.3* Kant, Immanuel. Critique of pure reason. London, 1855.
Phil 6680.1.5 Kerner, J. The Seeress of Prevorst. N.Y., 1855.
Phil 3801.495 Kotzias, Nikolaos. Skellighios iti oligha tina peri ton
vion ke tis filosofias aftou. Athena, 1855.
Phil 1730.8 Lanfrey, Pierre. L'église et les philosophes au
dix-huitième siècle. Paris, 1855.
Phil 3831.2 Leibnitz, G.W. A refutation...Spinoza. Edinburgh, 1855.
Phil 7080.30 Lemoine, Albert. Du sommeil au point de vue physiologique
et psychologique. Paris, 1855.
Phil 8701.2.2 Lewis, Tayler. Six days of creation. 2nd ed.
Schenectady, 1855.
Phil 7054.54.5 Linton, Charles. The healing of the nations. 2. ed.
N.Y., 1855.
Phil 8701.1 Lord, D.N. Geognosy, or The facts and principles of
geology against theories. N.Y., 1855.
Phil 186.15 Lyall, W. Intellect, the emotions and moral nature.
Edinburgh, 1855.
Phil 2125.65.4 McCosh, James. Method of divine government. N.Y., 1855.
Phil 8413.10 MacVicar, John. The philosophy of the beautiful.
Edinburgh, 1855.
Phil 7054.107 Mahan, A. Modern mysteries explained and exposed.
Boston, 1855.
Phil 2130.33 Mansel, H.L. Psychology; the test of moral and
metaphysical philosophy. Oxford, 1855.
Phil 7054.23.5 Mattison, H. Spirit-rapping unveiled. N.Y., 1855.
Phil 8685.8 Mill, J.S. Observations...pantheistic principles.
Cambridge, 1855.
Phil 7068.55 Mirville, J.E. Questions des esprits; ses progrès dans la
science. Paris, 1855.
Phil 487.1.3 Moleschott, M. Der Kreislauf des Lebens. Mainz, 1855.
Phil 3425.204 Nyblaeus, Axel. Ar en praktisk philosophi möjlig efter
Hegels verldsäsigt? Lund, 1855.
Phil 5190.1 Oesterlen, F. Medical logic. London, 1855.
Phil 4210.94 Pestalozza, A. La mente di Antonio Rosmini. Milano, 1855.
Phil 5025.1 Prantl, Carl von. Geschichte der Logik. Leipzig, 1855-70.
3v.
Phil 5025.1.1 Prantl, Carl von. Geschichte der Logik. v.2. 2e Aufl.
Leipzig, 1855-1885.
X Cg Phil 5025.1 Prantl, Carl von. Geschichte der Logik. v.4.
Leipzig, 1855-70.
Phil 8595.10 Prout, W. Chemistry, meteorology...natural theology.
London, 1855.
Phil 8581.10.8 Prout, William. Bridgewater treatises [8]. Chemistry,
meteorology. London, 1855.
Phil 2240.60.6A Reid, Thomas. Essays on the intellectual powers of man.
6th ed. Boston, 1855.
Phil 6967.2 Reynolds, J.R. The diagnosis of diseases. London, 1855.
Phil 8893.77 Sahlin, Karl Y. Om vilkoren för möjligheten al praktisk
philosophi. Lund, 1855.
Phil 5258.10 Schultz-Schultzenstein, K.H. Die Bildung der menschlichen
Geistes. Berlin, 1855.
Phil 9120.3.2 Simon, J. Le devoir. Paris, 1855.
Phil 5520.47 Smart, B.H. Thought and language: an essay on...Locke's
philosophy. London, 1855.
Phil 2270.70.2 Spencer, Herbert. Principles of psychology. London, 1855.
Phil 2270.70 Spencer, Herbert. Principles of psychology. London, 1855.
Phil 5643.18 Stellwag, K. von C. Die Accommodationsfehler des Auges.
n.p., 1855.
Phil 2275.50.2 Stewart, D. Elements of the philosophy of the human mind.
Boston, 1855.
Phil 2115.86 Tagart, E. Locke's writings and philosophy. London, 1855.
Phil 3525.23 Tiberghien, G. De la doctrine de Krause. Bruxelles, 1855.
Phil 7054.137.3 Tiffany, Joel. Modern spiritualism compared with
Christianity. Warren, Ohio, 1855.
Phil 5829.3.2 Toussenel, A. L'esprit des bêtes; zoologie passionnelle.
2. éd. Paris, 1855.
Phil 8599.7 Tulloch, J. Theism. Edinburgh, 1855.
Phil 7054.116.5 Tuttle, H. Scenes in the spirit world. N.Y., 1855.
Phil 8846.2 Vorländer, F. Geschichte der philosophischen Moral.
Marburg, 1855.
Phil 2835.81 Waddington, C. Ramue (Pierre de la Ramée). Paris, 1855.
Phil 497.1 Wagner, J.A. Naturwissenschaft und Bibel.
Stuttgart, 1855.
Phil 8595.16.27.25 Watson, R. An apology for the Bible. Nashville, 1855.
Phil 9362.1 Weaver, G.S. Hopes and helps for the young. N.Y., 1855.
Phil 1722.1 Weigelt, G. Zur Geschichte der neueren Philosophie.
Hamburg, 1855.
Phil 3925.3.35 Weisse, Christian Hermann. Philosophische Dogmatik oder
Philosophie des Christenthums. Leipzig, 1855-62. 3v.
Phil 197.5 Werner, K. Grundlinien de Philosophie. Regensburg, 1855.
Phil 8897.13.5 Whately, R. Introductory lessons on morals. London, 1855.
Phil 8602.6.3 Whewell, W. The plurality of worlds. Boston, 1855.
Phil 8687.4 Whish, J.C. The first cause. London, 1855.
Phil 497.6 Wilson, A.S. The unity of matter. London, 1855.
Phil 7054.74 Wilson, R.P. Discourses from the spirit-world.
N.Y., 1855.
Phil 6972.4 Winslow, F. The case of Luigi Buranelli. London, 1855.
Phil 8426.2 Zeising, Adolf. Aesthetische Forschungen. Frankfurt, 1855.

1856

Phil 5040.1.2 Aldrich, H. Artis logicae rudimenta. Oxford, 1856.
Phil 9010.29 Andrews, Charles W. Religious novels; an argument against
their use. 2d ed. N.Y., 1856.
Phil 281.2 Atkinson, J. Universe powers of nature revealed.
London, 1856.
Phil 5041.8 Barron, William. Elements of logic. N.Y., 1856.

1856 - cont.

Phil 8402.44   Bayer, Josef. Ästhetik in Umrissen. Prag, 1856. 2v.

Phil 8581.4   Beard, J.R. Letters on the grounds and objects of religious knowledge. London, 1856. 2v.

Phil 9341.2.6   Beecher, H.W. Lectures to young men. N.Y., 1856.

Phil 7054.161   Berg. J.T. Abaddon and Mahanaim...guardian angels. Philadelphia, 1856.

Phil 8656.14.27   Blain, Jacob. A review, giving the main ideas in E. Beecher's Conflict of ages. Buffalo, 1856.

Phil 8620.1   Bledsoe, A.T. A theodicy. N.Y., 1856.

Htn   Phil 3801.234*   Brandis, Christian A. Gedächtnissrede auf Friedrich Wilhelm Joseph von Schelling. Berlin, 1856.

Phil 7150.1   Brierre de Boismont, A.J.F. Du suicide. Paris, 1856.

Phil 5241.16.2   Brodie, B.C. Psychological inquiries. London, 1856.

Phil 8612.53   Brunner, S. Büchlein gegen die Todesfurcht. Wien, 1856.

Phil 476.3.2.10   Büchner, L. Der Humor in Kraft und Stoff. Darmstadt, 1856.

Phil 1106.7   Butler, W.A. Lectures on the history of ancient philosophy. Cambridge, 1856. 2v.

Phil 333.1   Carus, C.G. Organon der Erkenntniss. Leipzig, 1856.

Phil 7054.78   Child. A.B. The bouquet of spiritual flowers. Boston, 1856.

Phil 5643.24   Clark, J.H. Sight and hearing. N.Y., 1856.

Phil 2490.60   Comte, Auguste. Synthèse subjective. Paris, 1856.

Phil 6952.7   Conolly, John. The treatment of the insane without mechanical restraints. London, 1856.

X Cg   Phil 3808.160   Cornill, Adolph. Arthur Schopenhauer. Heidelberg, 1856.

Phil 2496.50.3   Cousin, Victor. Elements of psychology. N.Y., 1856.

Phil 2496.32   Cousin, Victor. Fragments de philosophie moderne. Paris, 1856.

Phil 8877.21.2   Cowdery, M.F. Elementary moral lessons. Philadelphia, 1856.

Phil 9342.7   Cummings, A.I. Lady's present. Boston, 1856.

Phil 5374.34   Czolbe, Heinrich. Entstehung des Selbstbewusstseins. Leipzig, 1856.

Phil 8701.2.7   Dana, J.D. Science and the bible, a review of the Six days of creation. Andover, 1856.

Phil 7054.139   Daniels, J.W. Spiritualism versus Christianity. N.Y., 1856.

Phil 8658.2   Davis, A.J. The philosophy of special providences. Boston, 1856.

Phil 2750.8.85   De la Beaumelle, Laurent A. Vie de Maupertuis. Paris, 1856.

Phil 1145.5   Denis, J. Histoire des theories...dans l'Antiquité. Paris, 1856. 2v.

Phil 2490.54   Edger, Henry. The positivist calendar. Long Island, N.Y., 1856.

Phil 3425.205   Edman, Alfred. Hegels lära om konstformerna. Helsingfors, 1856.

Phil 9344.2.3   Eliot, W.G. Lectures to young men. 6th ed. Boston, 1856.

Phil 5244.2   Erdmann, J.E. Psychologische Briefe. Leipzig, 1856.

Phil 1990.30.2   Ferrier, J.F. Institutes of metaphysic. 2nd ed. Edinburgh, 1856.

Htn   Phil 3800.715*   Fichtes and Schellings philosophischer Briefwechsel. Stuttgart, 1856.

Phil 9560.14.5   Fiore di virtù. Firenze, 1856.

Phil 1850.82.10   Fischer, K, Franz Bacon von Verulam. Leipzig, 1856.

Phil 2520.155   Fog, B.J. Cartesius. Kjøbenhavn, 1856.

Phil 7054.111.2   Fowler, J.H. New Testament "miracles". 2. ed. Boston, 1856.

Phil 8880.13   Fowler, O.S. Self culture and perfection of character. N.Y., 1856.

Phil 476.3.50   Frauenstadt, J. Der Materialismus. Leipzig, 1856.

Phil 4115.51   Gioberti, V. Della filosofia della rivelazione. Torino, 1856.

Phil 8631.1.5   Göschel, C.F. Der Mensch nach Leib, Seele und Geist. Leipzig, 1856.

Phil 7054.142   Gordon, William R. A three-fold test of modern spiritualism. N.Y., 1856.

Phil 7054.63.4   Hare, Robert. Experimental investigation of the spirit manifestations. N.Y., 1856.

Phil 3246.235   Hase, K. von. Jenaisches Fichte - Büchlein. Leipzig, 1856.

Phil 9347.1   Hawes, J. Lectures to young men. Boston, 1856.

Phil 8430.17   Hay, D.R. The science of beauty, as developed in nature. Edinburgh, 1856.

Phil 182.11   Helfferich, A. Der Organismus der Wissenschaft. Leipzig, 1856.

Phil 807.6   Henry, C.S. An epitome of the history of philosophy. N.Y., 1856. 2v.

Phil 2648.35.9   Holbach, Paul Henri T. Der gesunde Menschenverstand. 2e Aufl. Baltimore, 1856.

Phil 182.74   Hugonin, F. Ontologie. Paris, 1856-1857. 2v.

Phil 4582.3.32   Hwasser, Israel. Mannens ynglingaålder. Upsala, 1856.

Phil 5048.1   Ingleby, C.M. Outlines of theoretical logic. Cambridge, 1856.

Phil 3625.1.195   Kayserling, Meyer. Moses Mendelssohn's philosophische und religiöse Grundsätze mit Hinblick auf Lessing. Leipzig, 1856.

Phil 5050.4   Kidd, R.B. A deliniation, primary principal reasoning. London, 1856.

Phil 5051.3   Latham, R.G. Logic..application to language. London, 1856.

Phil 8050.41   Ljunggren, G. Framställning af de förnämsta esthetiska systemerna. Lund, 1856. 2v.

Phil 4210.83.2   Lockhart, W. An outline of the life of...Antonio Rosmini. London, 1856.

Phil 8886.11   Lowell, A.C. (Mrs.). Seed-grain for thought and discussion. Boston, 1856. 2v.

Phil 812.1   Maret, H.S.C. Philosophie et religion. Paris, 1856.

Phil 3494.3   Maurial, E. Le scepticisme...Scepticisme de Kant. Montpellier, 1856.

Phil 6122.3   Meyer, J.B. Zum streit über Leib und Seele. Hamburg, 1856.

Phil 8413.22   Moffat, J.C. An introduction to the study of aesthetics. Cincinnati, 1856.

Phil 487.1.5   Moleschott, J. Licht und Leben. Frankfurt, 1856.

Phil 9172.2   The moral class book. Photoreproduction. London, 1856.

Phil 1712.1.6   Morell, J.D. Historical and critical...philosophy, XIX century. N.Y., 1856.

Phil 7068.56   Newton, Alonzo E. Answer to charges of belief in modern revelations. Boston, 1856. 2 pam.

Phil 4610.9.35   Nielsen, R. Om personlig sanning och sann personlighet. Upsala, 1856.

Phil 8705.1.5   Paine, M. A review of theoretical geology. N.Y., 1856.

1856 - cont.

Phil 8595.1.2   Parker, T. A discourse of matters pertaining to religion. Boston, 1856.

Phil 8595.1.7   Parker, T. Sermons of Theism, Atheism, and the popular theology. Boston, 1856.

Phil 2805.32.6   Pascal, Blaise. The provincial letters. N.Y., 1856.

Phil 8610.856   Post, T.M. The skeptical era in modern history. N.Y., 1856.

Phil 7054.27.7   Putnam, A. Natty, a spirit; his portrait and his life. Boston, 1856.

Phil 8891.1.2   Quarles, F. Enchiridion. London, 1856.

Phil 7054.98.3   Ramsey, William. Spiritualism, a satanic delusion. Peace Dale, R.I., 1856.

Phil 8707.1   Reichenbach, H.G.L. Blicke in das Leben der Gegenwart. Dresden, 1856.

Phil 4363.2.82   Reynier, Frédéric. Étude sur la doctrine de Molinos. Thèse. Strasbourg, 1856.

Phil 192.12   Ritter, Heinrich. System der Logik und der Metaphysik. Göttingen, 1856. 2v.

NEDL   Phil 5257.8   Röse, F. Die Psychologie. Göttingen, 1856.

Phil 8597.11.8   Rogers, H. A defence of the eclipse of faith. Boston, 1856.

Phil 4210.21   Rosmini-Serbati, Antonio. Filosofia del diritto. Napoli, 1856. 2v.

Phil 3801.765   Sandberg, Sven. Några anteckningar om Schellings philosophi. Lund, 1856.

Phil 6128.2.2   Schaller, J. Leib und Seele. 2. Aufl. Weimar, 1856.

Htn   Phil 3800.30.5*   Schelling, F.W.J. von. Sämmtliche Werke. v.1. pt.1-10, v.2. pt.1-4. Stuttgart, 1856-61. 14v.

Phil 3800.30A   Schelling, F.W.J. von. Sämtliche Werke. v.1. pt.1-10, v.2. pt.1-4. Stuttgart, 1856-61. 14v.

Phil 193.102   Schenach, G. Metaphysik. Innsbruck, 1856.

Phil 818.15   Schwegler, A. Grunddragen of filosofiens historia. Örebro, 1856.

Phil 818.1.5   Schwegler, F.C.A. History of philosophy in epitome. N.Y., 1856.

Phil 5258.77   Sibbern, F.C. Psychologie, indledet ved almindelig biologie, i sammentroengt fremstelling. Kjøbenhavn, 1856.

Phil 8598.70   Slack, Robert. Old truths and modern progress. London, 1856.

Phil 5768.11   Solly, Thomas. The will divine and human. Cambridge, 1856.

Phil 6688.4   Steinbeck, F.A. Der Dichter ein Seher. Leipzig, 1856.

Phil 3245.83   Swahn, F.O.B. Kritiska anmärkningar vid I.H. Fichtes ethiska grundsatzer. Lund, 1856.

Phil 9010.8   Testimony of Progressive Friends. Amusements. N.Y., 1856-59. 3 pam.

Phil 8674.3   Thompson, R.A. Christian theism. N.Y., 1856.

Phil 7054.137.5   Tiffany, Joel. Spiritualism explained. 2. ed. N.Y., 1856.

Phil 3428.90F   Trendelenburg, A. Herbarts praktische Philosophie. Berlin, 1856.

Phil 525.9   Vaughan, R.A. Hours with the mystics. London, 1856. 2v.

Phil 4265.2.10   Ventura da Raulica, G. Opere. v.1-13. Napoli, 1856-64. 11v.

Phil 4265.3.32   Vera, A. In inquiry into speculative and experimental science. London, 1856.

Phil 2805.91   Vinet, A. Études sur Blaise Pascal. Paris, 1856.

NEDL   Phil 497.2.9   Vogt, C. Köhlerglaube und Wissenschaft...Wagner. Giessen, 1856.

Phil 9182.1   Weaver, G.S. The Christian household. Boston, 1856.

Phil 8897.12.9   Wette, W.M.L. de. Human life; or Practical ethics. Boston, 1856. 2v.

Phil 8897.13   Whately, R. Introductory lessons on morals. Cambridge, 1856.

Phil 8897.13.10   Whately, R. Thoughts and apophthegms. Philadelphia, 1856.

Phil 5062.11   Wilson, W.D. Elementary treatise on logic. N.Y., 1856.

Phil 5262.6.3   Winslow, H. Elements of intellectual philosophy. Boston, 1856.

Phil 8897.19   Winslow, H. Elements of moral philosophy. N.Y., 1856.

Phil 8064.2   Wiseman, N. On the perception of natural beauty by the ancients and moderns. London, 1856.

Phil 8620.12   Young, J. The mystery; or evil and God. Philadelphia, 1856.

Phil 1130.1   Zeller, Eduard. Die Philosophie der Griechen. Tubingen, 1856-68. 5v.

1857

Phil 3085.3.31   Apelt, E.F. Metaphysik. Leipzig, 1857.

Phil 175.31   Aquisto, B. d'. Elementi di filosofia fondamentale. Palermo, 1857.

Phil 1300.5   Aubertin, C. De sapientiae doctoribusqui, a ciceronis morte ad neronis principatum. Parisiis, 1857.

Phil 1850.40.4   Bacon, Francis. Essays. 2nd ed. London, 1857.

Phil 1850.40   Bacon, Francis. Essays. 3rd ed. London, 1857.

Phil 1850.14   Bacon, Francis. Works. v.1-7, 9-14. London, 1857-74. 13v.

Phil 8581.5.7   Beecher, C.E. Common sense applied to religion. N.Y., 1857.

Phil 176.17.2   Bénard, Charles. Précis de philosophie. Paris, 1857.

Phil 6111.24.9   Bidder, Friedrich. Untersuchungen über die Textur des Rückenmarks. Leipzig, 1857.

Phil 3255.87   Bischof, Hermann. Sebastian Franck von deutsche Geschichtsschreibung. Tübingen, 1857.

Phil 5241.12.5   Bishop, D. An introduction...study...mind. London, 1857.

Phil 176.24   Blignières, C. Exposition de la philosophie. Paris, 1857.

Phil 4514.1.35   Borelius, J.J. Den dogmatiska rationismens strid mot den spekulativa filosofien. Stockholm, 1857.

Phil 8876.24   Bovee, C.N. Thoughts, feelings, and fancies. N.Y., 1857.

Phil 8626.22   Brecher, G. Die Unsterblichkeitslehre des israelitischen Volkes. Leipzig, 1857.

Phil 6111.7   Brodie, B. Mind and matter. N.Y., 1857.

Phil 3821.18   Bröchner, Hans. Benedict Spinoza. Kjøbenhavn, 1857.

Phil 8656.5   Buchanan, J. Faith in God. London, 1857. 2v.

Phil 476.3.20   Büchner, L. Natur und Geist. Frankfurt, 1857.

Phil 1535.3   Buscarini, G. Discussioni di filosofia razionale. Milano, 1857. 2v.

Phil 1900.37.15   Butler, Joseph. Analogy of religion. London, 1857.

Phil 1900.38   Butler, Joseph. Analogy of religion. Philadelphia, 1857.

Phil 1106.7.5   Butler, W.A. Lectures on the history of ancient philosophy. Philadelphia, 1857. 2v.

Phil 5752.1   Carleton, H. Liberty and necessity. Philadelphia, 1857.

Phil 7054.76   Cooke, P. Necromancy; or a rap for the rappers. Boston, 1857.

Phil 1200.30   Courdaveaux, V. De l'immortalité de l'âme dans le stoïcisme. Paris, 1857.

1857 - cont.

Phil 3484.3 — Cousin, V. Philosophie de Kant. Paris, 1857.
Phil 1802.2 — Cousin, V. Philosophie écossaise. 3e éd. Paris, 1857. 2 pam.
Phil 8692.4 — Crofton, D. Genesis and geology. Boston, 1857.
Phil 7054.70 — Crosland, N. Light in the valley: my experience of spiritualism. London, 1857.
Phil 8582.17 — Culverwel, N. Of the light of nature. Edinburgh, 1857.
Phil 260.8 — Dahlbäck, Carl J. Om atomism. Stockholm, 1857.
Phil 8658.1.5 — Damiron, J.P. Memoire sur Naigeon et accessoirement sur Sylvain Maréchal et Delalande. Paris, 1857.
Phil 6021.2.50 — David, Alexandre. Le petit Lavater français. Paris, 1857.
Phil 8693.2.5 — Davies, T.A. Cosmogony, or The mysteries of creation. N.Y., 1857?
NEDL Phil 7054.6.3 — Davis, A.J. The magic staff; an autobiography. N.Y., 1857.
Phil 7054.6.18 — Davis, A.J. The penetralia, being harmonial answers. 3. ed. Boston, 1857.
Phil 7054.120 — Emmons, S.B. The spirit land. Philadelphia, 1857.
Phil 3801.367 — Erdmann, Johann E. Über Schelling. Halle, 1857.
Htn Phil 3801.367.2* — Erdmann, Johann E. Uber Schelling. Halle, 1857.
Phil 8830.1 — Feuerlein, E. Die philosophische Sittenlehre. v.1-2. Tübingen, 1857-59.
Phil 1850.82 — Fischer, K. Frances Bacon of Verulam. London, 1857.
Phil 90.1.3 — Fleming, William. Vocabulary of philosophy. London, 1857.
Phil 2651.81 — Flottes, J.B.M. Etude sur Pierre Daniel Huet. Montpellier, 1857.
Phil 4112.55.3 — Galluppi, Pasquale. Considerazioni filosofiche sull'idealismo transcendentale. 3a ed. Torino, 1857.
Phil 7054.164 — Gasparin, Agénov. Science vs. modern spiritualism. N.Y., 1857. 2v.
Phil 5046.3.5 — Gilbart, J.W. Logic for the million. 5th ed. London, 1857.
Phil 4115.40 — Gioberti, V. Della protologia. Torino, 1857-58. 2v.
Phil 5246.9 — Gratry, A.J.A. De la connaissance de l'âme. Paris, 1857. 2v.
Phil 3450.41 — Haekstra, Sytze. Oratio de summae veritatis cognoscendae ratione atque via. Amstelodami, 1857.
Phil 3425.88A — Haym, Rudolf. Hegel und seine Zeit. Berlin, 1857.
Phil 8587.5 — Hecker, I.T. Aspirations of nature. N.Y., 1857.
Phil 8587.10.15 — Hennell, S.S. Christianity and infidelity. London, 1857.
Phil 8408.31 — Hermann, C. Grundriss einer allgemeinen Asthetik. Leipzig, 1857.
Phil 8587.17.5 — Hitchcock, E. Religious truth. Boston, 1857.
Phil 8685.3 — Hittell, J.S. A plea for pantheism. N.Y., 1857.
Phil 3090.80 — Hoffmann, F. Biographie Franz von Baader's. Leipzig, 1857.
Phil 9375.2 — Hunt, F. Worth and wealth. N.Y., 1857.
Phil 184.2.2 — Jacques, A. Manuel de philosophie. Paris, 1857.
Phil 8589.5.20 — James, H. Christianity, the logic of creation. N.Y., 1857.
Phil 3552.229 — Kvĕt, F.B. Leibnitz und Comenius. Prag, 1857.
Phil 3552.229.5 — Kvĕt, F.B. Leibnitz'ens Logik. Prag, 1857.
Phil 4363.3.80 — Latour, A. de. Don Miguel de Manara. Paris, 1857.
Phil 3552.76 — Leibniz, Gottfried Wilhelm. Nouvelles lettres. Paris, 1857.
Phil 811.3.2 — Lewes, G.H. A biographical history of philosophy. London, 1857.
Phil 1535.5.15 — Liberatore, M. Institutiones philosophicae. v.1-3. 10th ed. Romae, 1857.
Phil 3565.55 — Lotze, Hermann. Streitschriften. Leipzig, 1857.
Phil 2125.60 — McCosh, James. Typical forms and special ends in creation. Edinburgh, 1857.
Phil 5052.35 — Mahan, Asa. The science of logic. N.Y., 1857.
Phil 6682.9 — Marin, Carmen. Endemoniada de Santiago. Valparaiso, 1857.
Phil 8592.7 — Matter, J. La philosophie de la religion. Paris, 1857. 2v.
Phil 3494.3.2 — Maurial, É. Le scepticisme...Scepticisme de Kant. Supplément. Paris, 1857.
Phil 343.12 — Mayer, J.V. Der welthistorische Prozess als die unzige Grundlage der Philosophie. Freiburg, 1857.
Phil 5252.6 — Mehring, G. Philosophische-Kritische Grundsätze der Selbsterkenntniss. Stuttgart, 1857.
Phil 8702.6 — Miller, H. The testimony of the rocks. Boston, 1857.
Phil 487.1 — Moleschott, J. De Kreislauf des Lebens. Mainz, 1857.
Phil 2730.80 — Naville, E. Maine de Biran. Paris, 1857.
Phil 8669.1 — Orr, John. Theism. London, 1857.
Phil 2205.30.15 — Paley, W. Natural theology. Boston, 1857.
Phil 1535.10 — Pestalozza, A. Elementi di filosofia. Milano, 1857. 2v.
Phil 7054.87 — Pierce, David. The revelation...twenty-one days' entrancement. Bangor, 1857.
Phil 8640.9 — Polak, M.S. Die Unsterblichkeitsfrage. Amsterdam, 1857.
Phil 7054.98 — Ramsey, William. Spiritualism, a satanic delusion. Rochester, N.Y., 1857.
Phil 1122.3.5 — Ritter, Heinrich. Historia philosophiae graeco-romanae. Gotha, 1857.
Phil 7054.37 — Rivail, H.L.D. Le livre des esprits. Paris, 1857.
Phil 2115.128 — Rosell, Anton. Betraktelse af Lockes. Upsala, 1857.
Phil 4210.75 — Rosmini-Serbati, Antonio. Epistolario. pt.1, v.1-2. Torino, 1857. 2v.
Phil 1718.17 — Schaarschmidt, C. Der Entwicklungsgang der neueren Speculation. Bonn, 1857.
Phil 193.15.3 — Schubert, G. von. Vermischte Schriften. Erlangen, 1857-1860. 2v.
Phil 8598.40 — Secretan, Charles. Recherches de la méthode qui conduit à la vérité sur nos plus grands intérêts. Neuchâtel, 1857.
Phil 8598.10.5 — Simon, J. Natural religion. London, 1857.
Phil 8598.10 — Simon, J. La religion naturelle. 3. éd. Paris, 1857.
Phil 5062.7 — Smart, B.H. Easy lessons on reasoning. Boston, 1857.
Phil 5058.17 — Spalding, W. An introduction to logical science. Edinburgh, 1857.
Phil 28.3 — Le spiritualiste de la Nouvelle Orleans. Nouvelle Orleans, 1857.
Phil 4210.88.2 — Stresa, Italy. Istituto della Carità. Cenni biografici di Antonio Rosmini. 2a ed. Milano, 1857.
Phil 8419.24 — Symonds, J.A. The principles of beauty. London, 1857.
Phil 2419.1 — Taine, Hippolyte Adolphe. Les philosophes français du XIXe siècle. Paris, 1857.
Phil 8610.857 — Taylor, Robert. The astronomico-theological lectures. Boston, 1857.
Phil 5059.4.4 — Thomson, W. Outline of the necessary laws of thought. 4th ed. London, 1857.
Phil 5060.1 — Ueberweg, F. System der Logik. Bonn, 1857.
Phil 5260.1.8 — Upham, T.C. Elements of mental philosophy. N.Y., 1857.
Phil 196.2.10 — Ventura de Raulica, G. La tradizione e i semi-Pelagiani della filosofia. pt.1-2. Milano, 1857.

1857 - cont.

Phil 5062.1 — Waddington, C. Essais de logique. Paris, 1857.
Phil 197.1.15 — Wagner, J. Praktische Philosophie enthaltend Religionslehre. Ulm, 1857.
Phil 2115.87 — Webb, T.E. Intellectualism of Locke. London, 1857.
Phil 5640.4 — Wilson, G. Five gateways of knowledge. Philadelphia, 1857.
Phil 7054.117 — Woodman, J.C. A reply to Wm. T. Dwight, D.D., on spiritualism. Portland, 1857.
Phil 7054.31 — Zillah, the child medium. N.Y., 1857.

1858

Phil 8875.4.15 — Alexander, A. Outlines of moral science. N.Y., 1858.
Phil 4060.3.35 — Allievo, G. G. Allievo...per essere aggregato...Universita di Torino. Torino, 1858.
Phil 7054.90.5 — Auguez, Paul. Spiritualisme; faits curieux. Paris, 1858.
Phil 3805.80 — Aus F.D.E. Schleiermacher's Leben. Berlin, 1858-63. 4v.
Phil 1850.40.2 — Bacon, Francis. Essays. 3rd ed. London, 1858.
Phil 176.2 — Bäggesen, Jens. Philosophischer Nachlasz. Zürich, 1858. 2v.
Phil 5241.1.2 — Bailey, S. Letters...philosophy...human mind. London, 1858.
Phil 9341.10A — Batchelder, S. The young men of America. N.Y., 1858.
Phil 8876.10 — Baudrillart, H. Etudes de philosophie morale. Paris, 1858. 2v.
Htn Phil 3801.197.16* — Beckers, Hubert. Historisch-kritische Erläuterungen zu Schelling's Abhandlungen über die Quelle der ewigen Wahrheiten. München, 1858.
Phil 4210.120 — Bianciardi, S. Antonio Rosmini o il filosofo cristiano. Firenze, 1858.
Phil 176.22 — Biederman, G. Wissenschaft des Geistes. Leipzig, 1858.
Phil 8402.7 — Blackie, J.S. On beauty; three discourses delivered in the University of Edinburgh. Edinburgh, 1858.
Phil 6111.4.2 — Bouiller, F. De l'unité de l'ame pensante et du principe vital. Paris, 1858.
Phil 6951.4.5 — Bucknill, J.C. A manual psychological medicine...insanity. London, 1858.
Phil 476.3.2.5 — Büchner, L. Kraft und Stoff. Frankfurt, 1858.
Phil 9161.4 — Bulkeley, H.W. A word to parents. Philadelphia, 1858?
Phil 8581.16 — Bushnell, H. Nature and the supernatural. N.Y., 1858.
Phil 960.2.5 — Colebrooke, H.T. Essays on the religion and philosophy of the Hindus. London, 1858.
X Cg Phil 2490.56 — Comte, Auguste. Catechism of positive religion. London, 1858.
Phil 7054.90 — Constantine, T.C. Modern spiritualism. Manchester, 1858.
Phil 177.19 — Conti, Augusto. Evidenza, amore e fede. Florence, 1858. 2v.
Phil 5042.4 — Coppée, Henry. Elements of logic. Philadelphia, 1858.
Phil 2403.1.5 — Damiron, J.P. Memoires pour servir à l'histoire...philosophie au XVIIIe siècle. Paris, 1858. 2v.
Phil 8878.13.5 — Dodsley, R. The duties of human life. West Killingly, Conn., 1858.
Phil 4195.81 — Dreydorff, Georg. Das System des Johannes Pico. Warburg, 1858.
Phil 8628.5 — Drossbach, M. Die Harmonie der Ergebnisse der Naturforschung. Leipzig, 1858.
Phil 5585.2 — Duttenhofer. Die acht Sinne des Menschen. Nördlingen, 1858.
Phil 5435.6 — Erdmann, J.E. Über Gewohnheiten und Angewohnheiten. Berlin, 1858.
Phil 8585.13 — Fauenstädt, C.M.J. Briefe über natürliche Religion. Leipzig, 1858.
Phil 6115.11.15 — Feuchtersleben, E.F.V. The dietetics of the soul. N.Y., 1858.
Phil 5755.1 — Fischer, J.C. Über die Freiheit des menschlichen Willens und die Einheit der Naturgesetze. Leipzig, 1858.
Phil 90.1 — Fleming, William. Vocabulary of philosophy. London, 1858.
Phil 5245.23.5 — Flourens, Pierre. De la vie et de l'intelligence. 2. éd. Paris, 1858.
Phil 180.9 — Fraser, A.C. Rational philosophy. Edinburgh, 1858.
Phil 75.3 — Freude, C.G.A. Wegweiser. Ebersbach, 1858. 2v.
Phil 180.12 — Frohschammer, J. Einleitung in die Philosophie. München, 1858.
Phil 6115.10 — Fullom, S.W. The human mind. v.1-2. London, 1858.
Phil 181.6 — Gerhart, E.V. An introduction to study of philosophy. Philadelphia, 1858.
Phil 2630.1.20 — Gratry, Auguste. Studien. Regensburg, 1858-1859. 3v.
Phil 9347.8 — Hall, S.S. Bliss of marriage; or How to get a rich wife. New Orleans, 1858.
Phil 3090.81 — Hamberger, Julius. Die Fundamentalbegriffe von Franz von Baader's Ethik. Stuttgart, 1858.
Phil 2035.30.7 — Hamilton, William. Discussions on philosophy and literature, education. N.Y., 1858.
Phil 8662.4 — Hiller, T.O.P. God manifest. London, 1858.
Phil 5757.4 — Huber, Johannes. Über die Willensfreiheit. München, 1858.
Phil 8834.1 — Janet, P. Histoire de la philosophie morale. Paris, 1858. 2v.
Phil 7060.109 — Johnson, Samuel. Spiritualism tested by science. New Haven, 1858.
Phil 2672.35.3 — Jouffroy, Théodore S. Introduction to ethics. v.1-2. Boston, 1858.
Phil 5648.1 — Kammler, A. Experimenta de variarum cutis. Vratislav, 1858.
Phil 185.13 — Kaufmann, P. The temple of truth. Cincinnati, 1858.
NEDL Phil 2115.93.10 — King, Peter. The life and letters of John Locke. London, 1858.
Phil 1540.1 — Koehler, H.O. Realismus und Nominalismus. Gotha, 1858.
Phil 8591.37 — Lupus, J. Le traditionalisme et le rationalisme. Liége, 1858. 3v.
Phil 7123.2 — Mabru, G. Les magnetiseurs, jugés par eux-mêmes. Paris, 1858.
Phil 812.15 — Melillo, F. Preliminari alla storia della filosofia. Napoli, 1858.
Phil 8593.2.13 — Newman, F.W. Phases of faith. 5. ed. London, 1858.
Phil 8593.2.8 — Newman, F.W. The soul. London, 1858.
Phil 813.1 — Nourrisson, J.F. Tableau des progrès de la pensée humaine. Paris, 1858.
Phil 8414.12 — Nunez de Arenas, I. Elementos filosóficos de la literatura. Madrid, 1858.
Phil 8595.15.4 — Paine, Thomas. Theological works. Boston, 1858.
Phil 5643.39 — Panum, P.L. Physiologische Untersuchungen über das Sehen mit zwei Augen. Kiel, 1858.
Phil 2805.12 — Pascal, Blaise. Oeuvres complètes. Paris, 1858. 2v.
Phil 8890.9.5 — Peabody, A.P. The immutable right. Boston, 1858.

1858 - cont.

Htn Phil 3801.697* Planck, Adolf. Schellings nachgelassene Werke. Erlangen, 1858.

Phil 25.26 Psyche; popular-wissenschaftliche Zeitschrift. Leipzig, 1858-63. 3v.

Phil 9010.20 The pulpit and rostrum...unchristian amusement. N.Y., 1858.

Phil 1850.88 Rémusat, Charles de. Bacon. Paris, 1858.

Phil 8597.8.2 Reynaud, J.E. Philosophie religieuse terre et ciel. Paris, 1858.

Phil 1522.1 Ritter, A.H. Die christliche Philosophie. Göttingen, 1858-9.

Phil 3425.91.5 Rosenkranz, K. Apologie Hegel's gegen Dr. R. Haym. Berlin, 1858.

Phil 3780.35.2 Rosenkranz, Karl. Wissenschaft der logischen Idee. Königsberg, 1858-59. 2v.

Phil 3780.35 Rosenkranz, Karl. Wissenschaft der logischen Idee. v.1-2. Königsberg, 1858-59.

Phil 4210.27 Rosmini-Serbati, Antonio. Psicologia. v.1-2. Napoli, 1858.

Phil 2880.1.55 Saint-Martin, L.C. Der Dienst desGeist-Menschen. Münster, 1858.

Phil 6128.2 Schaller, J. Leib und Seele. Weimar, 1858.

Phil 3425.123 Schmid, Aloys. Entwicklungsgeschichte der Hegel'schen Logik. Regensburg, 1858.

Phil 3500.36 Schmidt, H. Immanuel Kants Leben. Halle, 1858.

Phil 349.2 Sengler, J. Erkenntnisslehre. Heidelberg, 1858.

Phil 8598.76 Sibbern, F.C. Meddelelser af indholdet af et skrivt fra aaret. v.1-2. Kjøbenhavn, 1858-72.

Phil 2270.40 Spencer, Herbert. Essays. London, 1858.

Phil 8708.7 The stars and the angels. London, 1858.

Phil 2275.39.2 Stewart, D. Philosophy of the active and moral powers. Boston, 1858.

Phil 850.4 Stöcke, A. Die speculative Lehre vom Menschen. Würzburg, 1858-59. 2v.

Phil 5259.2 Taylor, T. World of mind. N.Y., 1858.

Phil 8709.7 Thomson, S.H. Geology as an interpreter of scripture. Cincinnati, 1858.

Phil 9359.3 Thurston, D. Letters from a father to a son. Portland, 1858.

Phil 3895.30 Ulrici, H. Glauben und Wissen. Leipzig, 1858.

Phil 196.1 Vacherot, E. La métaphysique. Paris, 1858. 2v.

Phil 8601.2 Véry, P. Philosophie de la religion (Éléments). Paris, 1858.

Phil 8422.7.2 Vischer, F.T. Ästhetik Vollständiges, Inhaltsverzeichniss, Namen und Sachregister. Stuttgart, 1858.

Phil 497.4 Weber, A. Die neueste Vergötterung des Stoffs. Giessen, 1858.

Phil 5062.8 Whewell, W. Novum organon renovatum. London, 1858.

Phil 6990.26 Wonderful works of God. Irvington, N.J., 1858.

Phil 9362.10 Woodbury, J. Plain words to young men. Concord, 1858.

X Cg Phil 9182.2 Wright, H.C. A kiss for a blow. Boston, 1858. (Changed to XP 9413)

Phil 3915.53 Wundt, Wilhelm. Die Lehre von der Muskelbewegung. Braunschweig, 1858.

Phil 8426.4 Zimmermann, R. Aesthetik. Wien, 1858-65. 2v.

1859

Phil 7054.56 Adams, John Quincy. Twelve messages from the spirit. Boston, 1859.

Phil 1850.50.5A Bacon, Francis. Novum organum. Rev. A. Johnson. London, 1859.

Phil 8581.1 Barthel, N. Religion scientifique de l'humanité. Paris, 1859.

Phil 5241.9.5 Bautain, L.E.M. L'esprit humain et ses facultés. Paris, 1859. 2v.

Phil 476.2 Böhner, A.N. Naturforschung und Kulturleben. Hannover, 1859.

Phil 176.131 Bonghi, Ruggiero. Delle relazioni della filosofia colla società; prolusione. Milano, 1859.

Phil 4515.96 Borelius, J.J. Kritik öfver den Boströmska filosofien. v.1-2. Stockholm, 1859-60.

Phil 4515.32.5 Boström, C.J. Grundlinier till philosophiska statslärans propaedeutik. Upsala? 1859?

Phil 8876.29 Brown, H.S. Lectures for the people. Philadelphia, 1859.

Phil 665.94 Bruch, Johann Friedrich. Die Lehre von der Präexistenz der Menschlichen Seelen. Strassburg, 1859.

Phil 476.3 Büchner, L. Kraft und Stoff. Frankfurt, 1859.

Phil 8581.16.2 Bushnell, H. Nature and the supernatural. N.Y., 1859.

Phil 4515.89 C.J. Boström och hans filosofi. Orebro, 1859.

Phil 2465.80 Caraman, V.A.C.R. Charles Bonnet. Paris, 1859.

Phil 8403.10.5 Carriere, Moriz. Aesthetik. Leipzig, 1859. 2v.

Phil 8877.12.2 Cobbe, F.P. An essay on intuitive morals. pt.1. Boston, 1859.

Phil 9010.25 Corning, James L. The Christian law of amusements. Buffalo, 1859.

Phil 7150.12 Dabadie, F. Les suicidés illustrés. Paris, 1859.

Phil 8878.1 Dameth, C.M.H. Le juste et l'utile. Paris, 1859.

Phil 8583.1 Damiron, J.P. Souvenirs de vingt ans d'enseignement. Paris, 1859.

Htn Phil 1955.1.30* Darwin, Charles. On the origin of species. London, 1859.

Phil 4003.1 Debrit, M. Histoire des doctrines philosophiques dans l'Italie. Paris, 1859.

Phil 8583.5 Disdier, H. Conciliation rationnelle du droit et du devoir. Genève, 1859. 2v.

Phil 6673.13 Dixon, Jacob. Hygienic clairvoyance. London, 1859.

Phil 4210.86 Ferre, Pietro Maria. Esposizione del principo filosofico di Rosmini. Verona, 1859.

Phil 3245.33 Fichte, Immanuel Hermann. Zur Seelenfrage. Leipzig, 1859.

Phil 7068.59.10 Footsteps of spirits. London, 1859.

Phil 7054.111.5 Fowler, J.H. New Testament "miracles". 2. ed. Boston, 1859.

Phil 5925.3.3 Fowler, O.S. The illustrated self-instructor in phrenology. N.Y., 1859.

Phil 4115.27 Gioberti, V. Pensieri. Torino, 1859-60. 2v.

Phil 2035.40 Hamilton, William. Lectures on metaphysics and logic. Boston, 1859-60. 2v.

Phil 2035.40.3 Hamilton, William. Lectures on metaphysics and logic. Edinburgh, 1859. 4v.

Phil 5922.6.8 Hammond, L.M. (Mrs.). Trials and triumphs of an orphan girl; biography. Cortland, N.Y., 1859.

Phil 3425.31 Hegel, Georg Wilhelm Friedrich. Logique. v.1-2. Paris, 1859.

Phil 1900.89 Hennell, Sara S. Essay on the sceptical tendency of Butler's "analogy". London, 1859.

Phil 182.18 Hinton, J. Man and his dwelling place. N.Y., 1859.

1859 - cont.

Phil 3625.1.175 Holdheim, Samuel. Moses Mendelssohn und die Dink. Berlin, 1859.

Phil 8882.18.2 Holland, J.G. Gold foil. 5th ed. N.Y., 1859.

Phil 9359.6.5 Holland, Josiah G. Titcomb's letters to young people, single and married. 15th ed. N.Y., 1859.

Phil 8633.4 Irvine, M.C. The friendly disputants. London, 1859.

Phil 184.4 Jamieson, G. The essentials of philosophy. Edinburgh, 1859.

Phil 8885.2 Kendall, J. Eccentricity. London, 1859.

Phil 2725.2.15 Laffitte, Pierre. Cours philosophique sur l'histoire générale de l'humanité; discours d'ouverture, ordre et progrès. Paris, 1859.

Phil 7150.8 La Rue, F.A.H. Du suicide. Québec, 1859.

Phil 3552.17 Leibniz, Gottfried Wilhelm. Oeuvres. Paris, 1859-75. 7v.

Phil 3552.59 Leibniz, Gottfried Wilhelm. Protegée; ou De la formation et des révolutions du globe. Paris, 1859.

Phil 811.3.6 Lewes, G.H. The biographical history of philosophy. N.Y., 1859.

Phil 600.7.1 Littré, Émile. Paroles de philosophie positive. Paris, 1859.

Phil 7054.83 Lunt, George. Boston Courier report of the proceedings of professed spiritual agents and mediums. Boston, 1859. 2 pam.

Phil 2730.11 Maine de Biran, Pierre. Oeuvres inédites. Paris, 1859. 3v.

Phil 2733.4.5 Malebranche, Nicolas. Oeuvres. Paris, 1859. 2v.

Phil 2130.45 Mansel, H.L. The limits of religious thought. 1st American ed. Boston, 1859.

Phil 2130.45.5 Mansel, H.L. The limits of religious thought. 3rd ed. London, 1859.

Phil 8837.2 Martin, L.A. Histoire de la morale. Paris, 1859.

Phil 812.3.3 Maurice, J.F.D. Mediaeval philosophy. 2d ed. London, 1859.

Phil 2138.40 Mill, John S. On liberty. London, 1859.

Htn Phil 2138.40.1* Mill, John S. On liberty. London, 1859.

Phil 6322.12 Moreau, J.J. La psychologie morbide. Paris, 1859.

Phil 1050.5 Munk, S. Mélanges de philosophie Juive et Arabe. Paris, 1859.

Htn Phil 3801.612* Noack, Ludwig. Schelling und der Philosophie des Romantik. Berlin, 1859. 2v.

Phil 3801.612.2 Noack, Ludwig. Schelling und der Philosophie des Romantik. v.1-2. Berlin, 1859.

Phil 189.15.5 Opzoomer, C.W. De waarheid en hare kenbronnen. Amsterdam, 1859.

Phil 2205.40.15 Paley, W. Paley's moral philosophy. London, 1859.

Phil 2805.32 Pascal, Blaise. Provincial letters. London, 1859.

Phil 8890.15 Pezzani, A. Principes supérieurs de la morale. Paris, 1859.

Phil 8595.7 Powell, B. The order of nature. London, 1859.

Phil 9357.3 Readings for young men. Boston, 1859.

Phil 7054.59 Redman, G.A. Mystic hours, or spiritual experience. N.Y., 1859.

Phil 5257.2.5 Reed, S. Observations on the growth of the mind. 5th ed. Boston, 1859.

Phil 9560.13 Robbins, C. Force of right purpose. Boston, 1859.

Phil 4210.28 Rosmini-Serbati, Antonio. Teosofia. Torino, 1859-74. 2v.

Phil 8598.69 Saint René-Taillandier, R.G.E. Histoire et philosophie religieuse. Paris, 1859.

Phil 8673.1 Saisset, E.E. Essai de philosophie religieuse. Paris, 1859.

Phil 193.3.5 Saisset, E.E. Mélanges d'histoire, de morale. Paris, 1859.

Phil 8419.32 Schimmelpenninck, Mary Anne. The principles of beauty as manifested in nature, art, and human character. London, 1859.

Phil 2520.115 Schmidt aus Schwarzenberg, X. René Descartes und seine Reform der Philosophie. Nördlingen, 1859.

Htn Phil 3808.35* Schopenhauer, Arthur. Die Welt als Wille und Vorstellung. Leipzig, 1859. 2v.

NEDL Phil 6128.26.5 Schroeder van der Kolk, J.L.C. On the minute structure and functions of the spinal cord. London, 1859.

Phil 1123.2 Schwegler, A. Geschichte der griechischen Philosophie. Tübingen, 1859.

Phil 8610.859 Taylor, Robert. Who is the Holy Spirit? N.Y., 1859.

Phil 9359.2 Thayer, W.M. Poor girl and true woman. Boston, 1859.

Phil 9179.5 Théry, A.F. Conseils aux mères. Paris, 1859. 2v.

Phil 5059.4.2 Thomson, W. Outline of the necessary laws of thought. Cambridge, 1859.

Phil 194.32 Tittmann, F.W. Aphorismen zur Philosophie. Dresden, 1859.

Phil 5260.1.9 Upham, T.C. Elements of mental philosophy. N.Y., 1859.

Phil 8601.3 Vidal, F. Théologie de la religion naturelle. Paris, 1859.

Phil 8897.6.5 Wayland, F. The elements of moral science. Boston, 1859.

Phil 8685.17 Weissenborn, G. Vorlesungen über Pantheismus und Theismus. Marburg, 1859.

Phil 3552.5 Whately, R. Introductory lessons on mind. Boston, 1859.

Phil 5262.5.2 Whately, R. Introductory lessons on mind. London, 1859.

Phil 5062.6.8.5 Whately, Richard. Elements of logic. Boston, 1859.

Phil 6520.7 Wollersheim, T. Das Leben der ekstatischen und stigmatischen Christina von Stommeln. Köln, 1859.

186-

Phil 6048.59.5 Desbarrolles, A. Chiromancie nouvelle...les mystères de la main, revélés et expliqués. 14e ed. Paris, 186-.

Phil 1200.21 Dourif, J. Du stoïcisme et du christianisme considérés dans leurs rapports. Thèse. Paris, 186-?

Phil 2805.40.29 Pascal, Blaise. Pensées. Paris, 186-.

1860

Phil 175.2.5 Alaux, J.E. La raison. Paris, 1860.

Phil 8580.11 Asher, David. Der religiöse Glaube. Leipzig, 1860.

Phil 1850.15.2 Bacon, Francis. Works. v.1,3-15. Paris, 1860-65. 14v.

Phil 2520.178 Baumann, Julius. Doctrina Cartesiana de vero et falso explicata atque examinata. Berolini, 1860?

Phil 9341.5 Bell, J.D. A man. Philadelphia, 1860.

Phil 1870.60.2 Berkeley, G. The theory of vision vindicated. Cambridge, 1860.

Phil 8581.64 Blood, B.P. Optimism, the lesson of ages. Boston, 1860.

Phil 3110.11 Böhme, J. Sämmtliche Werke. v.1-7. Leipzig, 1860. 6v.

Phil 4514.1.80 Boström, C.J. Den specultiva philosophen Johann Jacob Borelius Calmar. Upsala, 1860.

1860 - cont.

Phil 1890.30.5 — Brown, T. Lectures on philosophy of human mind. London, 1860.

Phil 6111.9.5 — Brown-Séquard, C.E. Course...physiology and pathology of central nervous system. Philadelphia, 1860.

Phil 6990.25 — Bushenskii, N. Kniga chudes. Pesch', 1860.

Phil 1900.39 — Butler, Joseph. Analogy of religion. London, 1860.

Phil 1900.39.5 — Butler, Joseph. Analogy of religion. 20th ed. N.Y., 1860.

Phil 1900.28 — Butler, Joseph. Analogy of religion and ethical discourses. Boston, 1860.

Phil 8403.28 — Chaignet, A. Les principes de la science du beau. Paris, 1860.

Phil 3002.1 — Chalybäus, H. Historie entwickelischen der speculativen Philosophie. Leipzig, 1860.

Phil 5242.4 — Champlin, J.T. Text-book in intellectual philosophy. Boston, 1860.

Phil 4525.2.5 — Claeson, Krist. Skrifter. Stockholm, 1860. 2v.

Phil 8590.27.10 — Clemens, Franz J. Die Wahrheit in dem von J. von Kuhn in Tübingen. Münster, 1860.

Phil 5242.6 — Collins, T.W. Humanics. N.Y., 1860.

Phil 5042.4.2 — Coppée, Henry. Elements of logic. Philadelphia, 1860.

Phil 4080.5.31 — Corleo, Simone. Filosofia universale. Palermo, 1860-63. 2v.

Phil 1850.100.5 — Craik, G.L. Bacon; his writings and his philosophy. v.1-3. London, 1860.

Phil 8693.2 — Davies, T.A. Answer to Hugh Miller and theoretic geologists. N.Y., 1860.

Phil 5043.5.5A — DeMorgan, Augustus. Syllabus of a proposed system of logic. London, 1860.

Phil 2520.19.3 — Descartes, René. Oeuvres. Paris, 1860.

Phil 8878.30 — Dittes, F. Über die sittliche Freiheit. Leipzig, 1860.

Phil 5640.28 — Drbal, M.A. Über Natur der Sinne. Linz, 1860.

Phil 5374.3 — Drossbach, M. Genesis des Bewusstseins. Leipzig, 1860.

Phil 1050.4.5 — Dukes, L. Salomo ben Gabirol. Hannover, 1860.

Phil 6673.6 — Durand, J.P. Cours théorique et C. de Braidisme. Paris, 1860.

Phil 9344.2.5 — Eliot, W.G. Lectures to young women. Boston, 1860.

Phil 5754.2 — Espy, J.P. The human will. Cincinnati, 1860.

Phil 8695.10 — Farrar, Adam Storey. Science in theology: sermons. Philadelphia, 1860.

Phil 3210.47 — Fechner, G.T. Elemente der Psychophysik. v.1-2. Leipzig, 1860.

Phil 6115.11.8 — Feuchtersleben, E.F.V. Hygiene de l'âme. Paris, 1860.

Phil 3245.35 — Fichte, Immanuel Hermann. Anthropologie: von der menschlichen Seele. Leipzig, 1860.

Phil 3245.70.5 — Fichte, Immanuel Hermann. Contributions to mental philosophy. London, 1860.

Phil 9495.18.5 — Fowler, O.S. The physiology of marriage. Boston, 1860.

Phil 8881.6.4 — Gerando, J.M. Self-education. 3rd ed. Boston, 1860.

Phil 5046.3 — Gilbart, J.W. Logic for the million. London, 1860.

Phil 7068.53.5 — Goupy, Louis. Explication des tables parlantes. 1st ed. Paris, 1860.

Phil 7054.82 — Grimes, J.S. Great discussion of modern spritualism. Boston, 1860.

Phil 6116.4 — Grimes, J.S. The mysteries of human nature. Boston, 1860.

Phil 181.21.10 — Gruyer, L.A. Observations sur le dieu-monde de M. Vacherot et de M. Tiberghien. Paris, 1860.

Phil 6676.8 — Guidi, Franc. Il magnetismo animale. Milano, 1860.

Phil 2035.40.5 — Hamilton, William. Lectures on metaphysics and logic. Boston, 1860.

Phil 7054.86 — Hatch, Cora L.V. Two lectures on the present crisis. N.Y., 1860.

Phil 8587.10.10 — Hennell, S.S. Thoughts in aid of faith. London, 1860.

Phil 1135.21 — Hoffmann, F. Über die Gottes Idee des Anagoras. Wurzbrug, 1860.

Phil 2648.35.11 — Holbach, Paul Henri T. Der gesunde Menschenverstand. 2e Aufl. Baltimore, 1860.

Phil 8587.21.2 — Huntington, F.D. Human society: Graham lectures. N.Y., 1860.

Phil 530.15.15 — Jacob, A.A. La France mystique. v.1-2. 3e ed. Amsterdam, 1860.

Phil 3010.1 — Kirchner, C.K. Die speculativen Systeme seit Kant. Leipzig, 1860.

Phil 6121.3.2 — Laycock, T. Mind and brain. Edinburgh, 1860. 2v.

Phil 3552.69.20 — Leibniz, Gottfried Wilhelm. Theologisches System. Tübingen, 1860.

Phil 8591.4* — Leroux, Pierre. De l'humanité. Paris, 1860. 2v.

Phil 9171.2 — Letters on the moral and religious duties of parents. Boston, 1860.

Phil 8636.7 — Lewis, Jason. The anastasis of the dead. Boston, 1860.

Phil 3805.81 — The life of F.D.E. Schleiermacher. London, 1860.

Phil 8886.10 — Lombarès, M. de. Du gout ou de la passion du bien-être matériel. Montauban, 1860?

Phil 8592.49 — McCormac, H. Aspirations from the inner, the spiritual life. London, 1860.

Phil 2125.52 — McCosh, James. Intuitions of the mind. London, 1860.

Phil 187.2 — MacMahon, J.H. Treatise on metaphysics. London, 1860.

Phil 4170.7.93 — Mamini, C. Diagnosi comparativa della filosofia di Rosmini e di Mamiani. Bologna, 1860.

Phil 2130.30 — Mansel, H.L. Metaphysics. Edinburgh, 1860.

Phil 2130.35.3 — Mansel, H.L. Prolegomena logica. Boston, 1860.

Phil 2130.35.2A — Mansel, H.L. Prolegomena logica. 2nd ed. Oxford, 1860.

Phil 8887.8 — Matter, J. La morale, ou La philosophie des moeurs. Paris, 1860.

Phil 8592.4.5 — Maurice, F.D. Sequel to the inquiry, what is revelation? Cambridge, 1860.

Phil 1145.11 — Ménard, L. De la morale avant les philosophes. Paris, 1860.

Phil 8887.14 — Metcalf, D. An enquiry into...moral obligation. Boston, 1860.

Phil 2138.40.13 — Mill, John S. Über die Freiheit. Frankfurt, 1860. 4 pam.

Phil 6682.7 — Morin, A.S. Du magnétisme. Paris, 1860.

Phil 960.6 — Mullens, J. Religious aspects of Hindu philosophy. London, 1860.

Phil 188.6 — Nourrison, J.F. Histoire et philosophie. Paris, 1860.

Phil 3552.113 — Nourrisson, M. La philosophie de Leibniz. Paris, 1860.

Phil 3110.84 — Peip, A. Jakob Böhme der deutsche Philosoph. Leipzig, 1860.

Phil 8705.2 — Pendleton, W.N. Science a witness for the Bible. Philadelphia, 1860.

Phil 5055.2 — Perrard, M.J.F. Logique classique. Paris, 1860.

Phil 8696.4 — Poole, R.S. Genesis of the earth and of man. 2. ed. London, 1860.

Phil 8595.8 — Prevost, J.M.C. De la déomanie au XIXe siècle. Toulouse, 1860.

1860 - cont.

Phil 7054.84 — Randolph, P.B. The unveiling: or What I think of spiritualism. Newburyport, 1860.

Phil 7085.4 — Reichenbach, C.A. Somanmbulism and cramp. N.Y., 1860.

Phil 2490.85 — Robinet, J.F. Notice sur l'oeuvre et sur la vie d'Auguste Comte. Paris, 1860.

Phil 4210.76 — Rosmini-Serbati, Antonio. Giovane età e primi studi di Antonio Rosmini-Serbati. Italia, 1860.

Phil 9357.4.2 — Rowland, James. Ruin and restoration. Albany, 1860.

Phil 3838.10 — Saisset, Émile. Introduction critique aux oeuvres de Spinoza. Paris, 1860.

Phil 7054.33.7 — Samson, G.W. Spiritualism tested. Boston, 1860.

Phil 2115.155 — Schärer, E. John Locke. Leipzig, 1860.

Phil 5258.5 — Schaller, J. Das Seelenleben des Menschen. Weimar, 1860.

Phil 3805.75 — Schleiermacher, Friedrich. Aus Schleiermacher's Leben. Berlin, 1860.

Phil 193.13 — Schmid, L. Grundzüge der Einleitung in die Philosophie. Giessen, 1860.

Phil 3808.70.10 — Schopenhauer, Arthur. Die beiden Grundprobleme der Ethik. Leipzig, 1860.

Phil 8893.14.4 — Smiles, Samuel. Self-help. N.Y., 1860.

Phil 8893.25 — Stinson, J.H. Ethica. N.Y., 1860.

Phil 2419.1.2 — Taine, Hippolyte Adolphe. Les philosophes français du XIXe siècle. Paris, 1860.

Phil 4515.90 — Theorell, Sven L. Betraktelser i samhällslären med granskning af Boströmska statslärans grundinier. Stockholm, 1860.

Phil 8894.6.5 — Tissot, Joseph. Méditations morales. Paris, 1860.

Phil 5060.5 — Ubahgs, G.C. Logicae seu philosophiae rationalis elementa. 6. ed. Lovanii, 1860.

Phil 3895.50 — Ulrici, H. Compendium der Logik. Leipzig, 1860.

Phil 8710.1 — Upham, F.W. The debate between the church and science. Andover, 1860.

Phil 525.9.2 — Vaughan, R.A. Hours with the mystics. 2nd ed. London, 1860. 2v.

Phil 5262.3 — Warden, R.B. Familiar forensic view of man and law. Columbus, 1860.

Phil 3801.876.30 — Weber, Alfred. Examen critique de la philosophie religieuse se Schelling. Thèse. Strasbourg, 1860.

Phil 8897.13.3 — Whately, R. Introductory lessons on morals. Cambridge, 1860.

Phil 197.6.5 — Whewell, W. On the philosophy of discovery. London, 1860.

Phil 6972.5 — Winslow, E. On obscure diseases of the brain. London, 1860.

Phil 6972.5.2 — Winslow, F. On obscure diseases of the brain. Philadelphia, 1860.

Phil 3910.75 — Wolff, Christian von. Briefe...aus 1719-1753. St. Petersburg, 1860.

Phil 9182.2.5 — Wright, H.C. The unwelcome child. Boston, 1860.

Phil 8604.1.2 — Young, J. The providence of reason: criticism. London, 1860.

Phil 8604.1 — Young, J. The providence of reason: criticism. N.Y., 1860.

1861

Phil 5040.3.9 — Arnauld, Antoine. Logique de Port Royal. Paris, 1861.

Phil 5040.4.5 — Arnauld, Antoine. The Port Royal logic. Edinburgh, 1861.

Phil 1850.35.1 — Bacon, Francis. Of the proficience and advancement of learning. London, 1861.

Phil 1850.15A — Bacon, Francis. Works. v.1-8, 10-15. Boston, 1861-64. 14v.

Phil 9035.2 — Bain, A. On the study of character. London, 1861.

Phil 1535.1.25 — Balmes, Jaime. Lehrbuch der Elemente der Philosophie. v.1-4. Regensburg, 1861.

Phil 9075.1 — Bautain, L.E.M. La conscience. Paris, 1861.

Htn — Phil 3801.197.10*A — Beckers, Hubert. Über die Bedeutung des Schelling'schen Metaphysik. München, 1861.

Phil 3100.50 — Beneke, F.E. Lehrbuch der Psychologie. Berlin, 1861.

Phil 7068.61 — Bible. New Testament. English. New Testament of our Lord...as revised and corrected by the spirits. N.Y., 1861.

Phil 476.2.5 — Böhner, A.N. Du matérialisme. Genève, 1861.

Phil 2477.2.25 — Bordas-Demoulin, J.B. Oeuvre posthumes. Paris, 1861. 2v.

Phil 801.14 — Brothier, Léon. Histoire populaire de la philosophie. Paris, 1861.

Phil 410.1.2 — Calderwood, H. The philosophy of the infinite. Cambridge, 1861.

Phil 283.2 — Carus, C.G. Natur und Idee. Wien, 1861.

Phil 177.87.5 — Cavour, G.B. di. Discorso. Torino, 1861.

Phil 177.10 — Chalybäur, H. Fundamental Philosophie. Kiel, 1861.

Phil 6952.14 — Chiara, D. Les diables de morzine en 1861. n.p., 1861.

Phil 9240.28 — Child, A. Bemis. Whatever is, is right. 2d ed. Boston, 1861.

Phil 177.22 — Cournot, A.A. Traité des idées fondamentales. Paris, 1861.

Phil 2115.102.4 — Cousin, V. Philosophie de Locke. 4e éd. Paris, 1861.

Phil 8658.11 — Dayton, A.C. Emma Livingston, infidel's daughter. Nashville, Tenn., 1861.

Phil 6113.14F — Dean, J. Microscopic anatomy...of the spinal cord. Cambridge, 1861.

Htn — Phil 8599.16.5* — De Tribus Impostoribus. De tribus impostoribus. Paris, 1861.

Phil 8599.16.6 — De Tribus Impostoribus. De tribus impostoribus. Paris, 1861.

Phil 8628.6 — Dumesnil, A. L'immortalite. Paris, 1861.

Phil 8629.1 — Enfantin, B.P. La vie éternelle. Paris, 1861.

Phil 7054.72 — Essays on various subjects. N.Y., 1861.

Phil 1020.4.7 — Fakhry, Majid. Islamic occasionalism and its critique by Averroës and Aquinas. Paris, 1861.

Phil 3210.45 — Fechner, G.T. Über die Seelenfrage. Leipzig, 1861.

Phil 4065.119 — Fiorentino, F. Il panteismo di Giordano Bruno. Napoli, 1861.

Phil 5245.23 — Flourens, Pierre. De la raison du genié et...folie. Paris, 1861.

Phil 5815.2 — Flourens, Pierre. De l'instinct et de l'intelligence des animaux. 4e éd. Paris, 1861.

Phil 3552.86 — Foucher de Careil, Alexandre. Leibniz la philosophie juive et la cabale. Paris, 1861.

Phil 623.2 — Franchi, A. Il razionalismo del Popolo. Losanna, 1861.

Phil 900.8 — Franck, Adolphe. Études orientales. Paris, 1861.

Phil 2415.3.25 — Frégier, J.C. Portalis, philosophes-chrétien. Paris, 1861.

Phil 286.6 — Frohschammer, J. Über die Aufgabe der Naturphilosophie. München, 1861.

1861 - cont.

Phil 8695.9   Frohschammer, J. Über die Freiheit der Wissenschaft. München, 1861.

Phil 4210.84   Garelli, V. Antonio Rosmini. Torino, 1861.

Phil 181.68   Gatti, Stanislao. Scritti varii di filosofia e letteratura. Napoli, 1861. 2v.

Phil 4803.434.30   Gołuchowski, Józef. Dumania nad najwyzszemi zagadnieniami człowieka. Wilno, 1861. 2v.

Phil 806.5   Grätz, H. von. Geschichte der Philosophie. Langensalza, 1861.

Phil 530.20.15   Greith, Carl. Die deutsche Mystik. Freiburg, 1861.

Phil 338.16   Haig, J. Philosophy, or The science of truth. London, 1861.

Phil 2035.51   Hamilton, William. Metaphysics. Cambridge, 1861.

Phil 2115.5   Hartenstein, G. Locke's Lehre. Leipzig, 1861.

Phil 8050.57.5   Hauch, J.C. Aesthetiske afhandlinger og recensioner. Kjøbenhavn,1869. 1861.

Phil 5643.11   Hering, E. Beiträge zur Physiologie. v.1-5. Leipzig, 1861-

Phil 8882.18.5   Holland, J.G. Lessons in life. N.Y., 1861.

Phil 2477.2.80   Huet, François. Histoire de la vie et des ouvrages de Bordas-Demoulin. Paris, 1861.

Phil 2672.30.3   Jouffroy, Théodore S. Nouveaux mélanges philosophiques. 2e éd. Paris, 1861.

Phil 8412.26   Laprade, V. Questions d'art et de morale 2. éd. Paris, 1861.

Phil 3552.274   Mabilleau, L. De perfectione apud Leibnitium. Thesim. Paris, 1861.

Phil 5822.3   Matthes, B. Betrachtungen über Wirbelthiere. Dresden, 1861.

Phil 7080.9   Maury, L.F.A. Le sommeil et les rêves. Paris, 1861.

Phil 7054.15   Mayer, John (Mrs). Further communications from the world of spirits. N.Y., 1861.

Phil 4525.2.90   Myrberg, Otto F. Om förhållandet mellan teologi och filosofi. v.2. Upsala, 1861.

Phil 3495.8   Noack, L. I. Kant's Auferstehung aus dem Grabe. Leipzig, 1861.

Phil 1870.108   Norton, John N. The life of Bishop Berkeley. N.Y., 1861.

Phil 814.2.5   Ondes Reggio, V. Sulla necessità della instaurazione. 2a ed. Palermo, 1861.

Phil 2520.128   Opzoomer, C.W. Cartesius. Amsterdam, 1861.

Phil 2805.40.30   Pascal, Blaise. Pensées contenant les lettres et opuscules. Paris, 1861.

X Cg   Phil 2805.41.15   Pascal, Blaise. Thoughts, letters, and opuscules. N.Y., 1861.

Phil 525.21   Perty, M. Die mystischen Erscheinungen der menschlichen Natur. With supplement. Leipzig, 1861.

Phil 7054.96   Post, S. An exposition of modern spiritualism. N.Y., 1861.

Phil 4260.107F   Ranieri, A. Discorso recitato il di primo anniversario del plebiscito dell'Italia meridionale. Napoli, 1861.

Phil 1717.2   Ritter, A.H. Histoire de la philosophie moderne. Paris, 1861. 3v.

Phil 5190.5   Rondelet, A. Théorie logique des propositions modales. Paris, 1861.

Phil 8843.3   Samson, G.W. Outlines of the history of ethics. Washington, 1861.

Phil 7082.134   Scheruer, Karl Albert. Das Leben des Traums. Berlin, 1861.

Phil 5258.206   Schleiden, Matthias Jacob. Zur Theorie des Erkennens durch den Gesichtssinn. Leipzig, 1861.

Phil 3805.32.10   Schleiermacher, Friedrich. Der christliche Glaube. 5. Aufl. Berlin, 1861. 2v.

Phil 818.10.5   Scholten, J.H. Manuel d'histoire comparée de la philosophie et de la religion. Paris, 1861.

Phil 193.25   Shields, C.W. Philosophia ultima. Philadelphia, 1861.

Phil 8598.12.3   Smith, Goldwin. Rational religion. Oxford, 1861.

Phil 8598.12   Smith, Goldwin. Sermons and speeches. N.Y., 1861.

Phil 3819.12.2   Spinoza, Benedictus de. Oeuvres. Paris, 1861.

Phil 672.14.5   The star and the earth. 7th ed. London, 1861.

Phil 194.20   Tongiorgi, Salvator. Institutiones philosophicae. Romae, 1861. 3v.

Phil 196.2   Ventura de Raulica, G. La philosophie chrétienne. Paris, 1861. 3v.

Phil 3425.95.12   Véra, A. L'hégélianisme et la philosophie. Paris, 1861.

Phil 4265.3.45   Vera, A. Prolusioni alla storia della filosofia. Milano, 1861.

Phil 7060.89   Welby, H. Mysteries of life, death and futurity. London, 1861.

1862

Phil 8625.2   Abbot, Ezra. Literature of the doctrine of a future life. Cambridge? 1862?

Phil 600.1   Adam, W. Inquiry into theories of history. v.1-10. London, 1862.

Phil 5040.1.3   Aldrich, H. Artis logicae rudimenta. Oxford, 1862.

Phil 8580.28   Arbousse-Bastide, A.F. Le christianisme et l'esprit moderne. Paris, 1862.

Phil 2733.81   Blampignon, Emile Antoine. Étude sur Malebranche. Paris, 1862.

Phil 6111.4   Bouiller, F. Du principe vital. Paris, 1862.

Phil 8876.24.5   Bovee, C.N. Intuitions and summaries of thought. Boston, 1862. 2v.

Phil 7060.14.3   Brierre de Boismont, A. Des hallucinations, ou histoire raisonnée. 3. ed. Paris, 1862.

Phil 5241.10.4   Brodie, B.C. Psychological inquiries. London, 1862.

Phil 8657.17   Corte, P.A. Elementi di filosofia. v.2. 4. ed. Torino, 1862.

Phil 1850.100.7   Craik, G.L. Bacon; his writings and his philosophy. London, 1862.

Phil 6673.8   Davey, William. The illustrated practical mesmerist. 6th ed. London, 1862?

Phil 6113.6.5   Dressler, J.G. Ist Beneke Materialist? Berlin, 1862.

Phil 5525.26   Dumont, L. Des causes du rire. Paris, 1862.

Phil 5244.2.8   Erdmann, J.E. Grundriss der Psychologie. 4. Aufl. Leipzig, 1862.

Phil 3246.98   Erdmann, Johann E. Fichte, der Mann der Wissenschaft und des Katheders. Halle, 1862.

Phil 3246.82.2   Fichte, Immanuel Hermann. Johann Gottlieb Fichte's Leben und Ritter. Leipzig, 1862. 2v.

Phil 3246.78.5   Fichte, Johann Gottlieb. Achtundvierzig Briefe. Leipzig, 1862.

Phil 3246.199   Fischer, Kuno. Johann Gottlieb Fichte. Stuttgart, 1862.

Phil 2520.102.5   Foucher de Careil, A. Descartes et la princesse palatine. Paris, 1862.

1862 - cont.

Phil 3552.86.15   Foucher de Careil, Alexandre. Leibniz, Descartes et Spinoza. Paris, 1862.

Phil 3425.83   Foucher de Careil, L.A. Hegel et Schopenhauer. Paris, 1862.

Phil 6990.3.15   Fourcade, M. l'abbé. L'apparition...grotté de Lourdes en 1858. Tarbes, 1862.

Phil 5816.12   Garratt, G. Marvels and mysteries of instinct. 3rd ed. London, 1862.

Phil 181.67   Giuliani, G. Intorno al principio...della filosofia civile. Napoli, 1862.

Phil 585.154   Goltz, B. Hinter den Feigenblättern. Berlin, 1862-64.

Phil 9346.5   Gratry, A.J. Les sources. v.1-2. Paris, 1862-69.

Phil 3808.86   Gwinner, W. Arthur Schopenhauer. Leipzig, 1862.

Phil 1112.2   Hampden, R.D. The fathers of Greek philosophy. Edinburgh, 1862.

Phil 3246.95   Harms, F. Johann Gottlieb Fichte. Kiel, 1862.

Phil 9490.7.2   Hart, J.S. Mistakes of educated men. Philadelphia, 1862.

Phil 6060.11   Henze, A. Die Chirogrammatonamtie. Leipzig, 1862.

Phil 3246.288   Johann Gottlieb Fichte; ein Vortrag zu Fichtes hundertjährischen Geburtstag. Raiserslauterer, 1862.

Phil 2672.36   Jouffroy, Théodore S. Moral philosophy. N.Y., 1862.

Phil 3480.70.6   Kant, Immanuel. Logique. 2. éd. Paris, 1862.

Phil 3625.1.107   Kayserling, M. Moses Mendelssohn. Leipzig, 1862.

Phil 3246.270   Koestlin, Karl. Fichte; ein Lebensbild. Tübingen, 1862.

Phil 8886.2   Lambert, C. Le système du monde moral. Paris, 1862.

Phil 4600.3.31   Leander, P.J.H. Öm substansbegreppet hos Cartesius, Spinoza och Liebnitz. Akademisk afhandling. Lund, 1862. 2 pam.

Phil 6121.22.2   Lélut, L.F. Physiologie de la pensée. 2. éd. Paris, 1862. 2v.

Phil 6121.4   Lemoine, A. L'âme et le corps. Paris, 1862.

Phil 5821.1   Leroy, Charles Georges. Lettres sur les animaux. Paris, 1862.

Phil 3831.3   Linde, A. van der. Spinoza. Göttingen, 1862.

Phil 3246.95.9   Loewe, Johann H. Die Philosophie Fichte's. Stuttgart, 1862.

Phil 3246.200   Lott, F.C. Festrede zur Saecularfeier Fichtes. Wien, 1862.

Phil 2125.66   McCosh, James. The supernatural in relation to the natural. Cambridge, Eng., 1862.

Phil 5052.1   McGregor, P. A system of logic. N.Y., 1862.

Phil 8592.30   Mansel, H.L. A second letter to professor Goldwin Smith. Oxford, 1862.

Phil 4012.2   Mario, A. I nostri filosofi contemporanei; rivista. Napoli, 1862.

Phil 2880.1.87   Matter, Jacques. Saint-Martin. 2. ed. Paris, 1862.

Phil 812.3.4   Maurice, J.F.D. Modern philosophy. London, 1862.

Phil 4958.210   Mestre, José Manuel. De la filosofia en la Habana. Habana, 1862.

Phil 2138.35.8   Mill, John S. System der deductiven und inductiven Logik. 2e Aufl. Braunschweig, 1862-63. 2v.

Phil 5252.9.5   Morell, J.D. Introduction to mental philosophy. London, 1862.

Phil 3246.203   Noack, Ludwig. Johann Gottlieb Fichte nach seinen Leben, Lehren und Wirken. Leipzig, 1862.

Phil 3110.84.5   Peip, A. Jakob Böhme, der deutsche Philosoph. Hamburg, 1862.

Phil 4015.3   Pennisi, S. Intorno allo stato e ai bisogni attuali della filosofia teoretica in Italia. Firenze, 1862. 3v.

Phil 348.1   Ramsay, G. Instinct and reason. London, 1862.

Phil 298.1   Richard, C. Les lois de Dieu. Paris, 1862.

Phil 192.12.7   Ritter, Heinrich. Encyklopädie der philosophischen Wissenschaften. Göttingen, 1862-1864. 3v.

Phil 850.3   Röth, E. Die Geschichte unserer abendländischen Philosophie. Mannheim, 1862. 2v.

Phil 3780.36   Rosenkranz, Karl. Epilegomena...Wissenschaft der logischen Idee. Königsberg, 1862.

Phil 9357.4   Rowland, James. Ruin and restoration. Albany, 1862.

Phil 2880.1.79   Saint-Martin, L.C. La correspondance inédite de L.C. Saint-Martin dit le philosophe inconnu et Kirchberger. Amsterdam, 1862.

Phil 2520.97.3   Saisset, Emile. Précurseurs et disciples de Descartes. Paris, 1862.

Phil 2520.97   Saisset, Emile. Précurseurs et disciples de Descartes. Paris, 1862.

Phil 5028.1   Sanseverino, G. Philosophia Christiana cum antiqua et nova comparata. Neapoli, 1862-66. 3v.

Phil 5228.4   Sanseverino, G. Philosophia christianacum antiqua et nova comparata. Neapoli, 1862-66. 3v.

Phil 6128.27   Scheffler, H. Körper und Geist. Braunschweig, 1862.

Htn   Phil 3800.390*   Schelling, F.W.J. von. Clara. Stuttgart, 1862.

Phil 3808.60   Schopenhauer, Arthur. Parerga und Paralipomena. Berlin, 1862.

Phil 6688.24   Sheldon, William. The millennium: the goodtime coming. Springfield, 1862.

Phil 2270.45   Spencer, Herbert. First principles. London, 1862.

Htn   Phil 2270.45.2.5*   Spencer, Herbert. First principles. London, 1862.

Htn   Phil 2270.45.1*   Spencer, Herbert. First principles. London, 1862.

Phil 2270.45.2   Spencer, Herbert. First principles. London, 1862.

Phil 3819.10.4   Spinoza, Benedictus de. Opera quae supersunt omnia supplementum. Amstelodami, 1862.

Phil 3246.211   Stahr, Adolf. Fichte, der Held unter der deutschen Denkern. Berlin, 1862.

Phil 3790.1.100   Strauss, D.F. Herman S. Reimarus und seine Schitzschrift für die vernünftigen Verehrer Gottes. Leipzig, 1862.

Phil 5258.24   Struve, H. Zur Entstehung der Seele. Tübingen, 1862.

Phil 8969.2   Tenney, E.P. Jubilee essays. Boston, 1862.

Phil 3890.1.41   Trendelenburg, A. Logische Untersuchungen. 2. Aufl. Leipzig, 1862. 3v.

Phil 3246.193   Trendelenburg, A. Zur Erinnerung an Johann Gottlieb Fichte. Berlin, 1862.

Phil 3502.4   Ueberweg, F. De priore et posteriore forma Kantianae critices. Berolini, 1862.

Phil 3895.40   Ulrici, H. Gott und die Natur. Leipzig, 1862.

Phil 4265.3.37   Vera, A. Mélanges philosophiques. Paris, 1862.

Phil 5262.22   Waddington, Charles. L'âme humaine. 2. série. Paris, 1862.

Phil 5262.22.2   Waddington, Charles. De l'âme humaine. 2. série. Paris, 1862.

Phil 6692.2.2   What is mesmerism? 2nd ed. London, 1862.

Phil 8897.17   Wiart, E. Du principe de la morale. Paris, 1862.

Phil 8602.8   Wilson, G. Religio chemici. London, 1862.

Phil 8897.21   Woillez, C.T.R. Les médecins moralistes. Paris, 1862.

Phil 9495.25   Woodruff, C.S. Legalized prostitution. Boston, 1862.

Phil 3915.52   Wundt, Wilhelm. Beiträge zur Theorie der Sinneswahrnehm. Leipzig, 1862.

Chronological Listing

1863

Phil 801.1 — Bauer, W. Geschichte der Philosophie. Halle, 1863.
Phil 176.46 — Benvenuti, F. Saggi filosofici. Firenze, 1863.
Phil 4001.4.6 — Bonavino, C. La filosofia delle scuole italiane. 2. ed. Firenze, 1863.
Phil 4210.126 — Brogialdi, Adolfo. Elogio di Antonio Rosmini letto l'11 giugno 1863 all'Accademia degli Eutelet. Firenze, 1863.
Phil 86.4 — Brothier, L. Ebauche d'un glossaire du langage philosophique. Paris, 1863.
Phil 476.3.3 — Büchner, L. Force et matière. Paris, 1863.
Phil 6952.3 — Castiglioni, C. Sulle alterazioni delle pupille nei pazzi. Milano, 1863-65. 2 pam.
Phil 170.1 — Chase, P.E. Intellectual symbolism. Philadelphia, 1863.
Phil 7054.162 — Clark, Uriah. Plain guide to spiritualism. Boston, 1863.
Phil 5643.4 — Classen, A. Über das Schlussverfahren der Sehactes. Rostock, 1863.
Phil 8582.35.15 — Cobbe, F.P. The religious demands of the age. Boston, 1863.
Phil 6952.8 — Constans, A. Relation sur un épidémie d'hystéro-démonopathie en 1861. Paris, 1863.
Phil 1145.50 — Curtius, E. Der Freundschafts begriff der Alten. Göttingen, 1863.
Phil 7054.81.19 — De Morgan, Sophia Elisabeth. From matter to spirit. London, 1863.
Phil 7068.63.25 — Denton, W.A. Nature's secrets or psychometric researches. Photoreproduction. London, 1863.
Phil 7059.7 — Denton, William. The soul of things. Boston, 1863.
Phil 3003.5 — Drechsler, Adolf. Charakteristik der philosophischen Systeme seit Kant. Dresden, 1863.
Phil 5244.2.10 — Erdmann, J.E. Psychologische Briefe. 3e Aufl. Leipzig, 1863.
Phil 5245.1 — Fabre d'Envieu, J. Cours de philosophie. Paris, 1863-1866. 2v.
Phil 3210.65A — Fechner, G.T. Drei Motive und Gründe des Glaubens. Leipzig, 1863.
Phil 5925.1.5 — Flourens, M.J. De la phrénologie et des études vraies sur la cerveau. Paris, 1863.
Phil 5655.2 — Folsom, N. Essay on the senses of smell and taste. Boston, 1863.
Phil 1705.8 — Franchi, Ausonio. Letture su la storia della filosofia moderna. Milano, 1863. 2v.
Phil 4120.3.30 — Giovanni, V. di. Principii di filosofia prima. Palermo, 1863. 2v.
Phil 8881.59 — Goodman, R.M. The philosophy of life. Marietta, Ga., 1863.
Phil 8881.59 — Gougenot des Mousseaux, H.R. Les médiateurs et les moyens de la magie. Paris, 1863.
Phil 7054.81.15 — Guppy, Samuel. Mary Jane; or spiritualism chemically explained. London, 1863.
Phil 3808.86.10 — Gwinner, W. Schopenhauer und seine Freunde. Leipzig, 1863.
Phil 7054.40.5 — Hall, T.B. Three articles on modern spiritualism. Boston, 1863.
Phil 2050.177 — Henschen, W.A. Bidrag till kännedomen af David Humes filosofiska betydelse. Upsala, 1863.
Phil 8882.18.9 — Holland, J.G. Letters to the Joneses. N.Y., 1863.
Phil 6677.16 — Holsbéek, H. von. Lettres sur le magnétisme animal. Bruxelles, 1863.
Phil 7054.45.9 — Home, Daniel Douglas. Incidents in my life. N.Y., 1863.
Phil 7054.45.11 — Home, Daniel Dunglas. Incidents in my life. London, 1863.
Phil 7052.9 — Howitt, William. The history of the supernatural. Philadelphia, 1863. 2v.
Phil 1850.95 — Jacquinet, P. Francisci Baconi de re litteraria judicia. Paris, 1863.
Phil 8410.7.5 — Jouffroy, T.S. Cours d'esthétique. 2. éd. Paris, 1863.
Phil 3480.40.5 — Kant, Immanuel. Anthropologie in pragmatischer Hinsicht. Paris, 1863.
Phil 1515.1 — Kaulich, W. Geschichte der scholastischen Philosophie. Prag, 1863.
Phil 3246.227 — Lasson, Adolf. Johann Gottlieb Fichte im Verhältniss zu Kirche und Staat. Berlin, 1863.
Phil 2725.9.86 — LeGoff, François. De la philosophie de l'abbé de Lignac. Paris, 1863.
Phil 3552.28.5 — Leibniz, Gottfried Wilhelm. Leibniz als Denker. Leipzig, 1863.
Phil 186.40.5 — Lichtenfels, Johann. Lehrbuch zur Einleitung in die Philosophie. 5e Aufl. Wien, 1863.
Phil 1850.91F — Liebig, J.F. von. Rede in der...(F. Bacon...Geschichte...Naturwissenschaften). München, 1863.
Phil 3808.93 — Lindner, E.O. Arthur Schopenhauer. Berlin, 1863.
Phil 600.7.2 — Littré, Émile. Paroles de philosophie positive. Paris, 1863.
Phil 486.7 — Löwenthal, E. System und Geschichte des Naturalismus. Leipzig, 1863.
Phil 4265.3.85 — Longoni, L. Il sistema filosofico di Hegel...sulla pena di morte di A. Vera. Milano, 1863.
Phil 5761.7 — Luthardt, C.E. Die Lehre vom freien Willen. Leipzig, 1863.
Phil 9560.27.5 — Martinus, Dumiensis. Volgarizzamento della forma di onesta vita. Napoli, 1863.
Phil 1145.12 — Ménard, L. De la morale avant les philosophes. 2e éd. Paris, 1863.
Phil 2138.40.2.2 — Mill, John S. On liberty. 2nd ed. Boston, 1863.
Phil 2138.50.4* — Mill, John S. Utilitarianism. London, 1863.
Phil 7068.63 — Mirville, J.E. Pneumatologie. Des esprits. v. 2-6. Paris, 1863-68. 5v.
Phil 7068.63.5 — Mirville, J.E. Question des esprits et de leurs manifestations diverses. Paris, 1863.
Phil 7054.81 — Modern Christian spiritualism. Philadelphia, 1863.
Phil 6127.1 — Ray, J. Mental hygiene. Boston, 1863.
Phil 4630.2.38 — Rein, T. Grunddragen af den filosofiska imputationsläran. Helsingfors, 1863.
Phil 8707.9 — The relations of Christianity and science. N.Y., 1863.
Phil 5827.3 — Rendu, V. L'intelligence des bêtes. Paris, 1863.
Phil 1890.85 — Réthoré, François. Critique de la philosophie de Thomas Brown. Paris, 1863.
Phil 8892.19 — Richards, C.H.B. Springs of action. N.Y., 1863.
Phil 8597.11.4 — Rogers, H. The eclipse of faith. 8. ed. Boston, 1863.
Phil 8673.1.5 — Saisset, É.E. Essay on religious philosophy. Edinburgh, 1863. 2v.
Phil 193.11 — Schmid, F.X. Entwurf eines Systems der Philosophie. v.1-3. Wien, 1863-1868. 2v.   Htn
Phil 4115.91 — Spaventa, B. La filosofia di Gioberti. v.1. Napoli, 1863.
Phil 3552.135 — Svahn, Oscar. Monadlärans uppkomst. Lund, 1863.
Phil 104.1.5 — Taylor, I. Elements of thought. London, 1863.
Phil 7060.89.5 — Timbs, John. Mysteries of life, death and futurity. N.Y., 1863.

1863 - cont.

Phil 820.01 — Ueberweg, F. Grundriss der Geschichte der Philosophie. v.1-3. Berlin, 1863.
Phil 196.1.2 — Vacherot, E. La metaphysique et de science. 2d ed. Paris, 1863.
Phil 3460.89 — Wiegand, Wilhelm. Zur Erinnerung an den Denker F.H. Jacobi und seine Weltansicht. Worms, 1863?
Phil 353.5 — Wijck, B.H.C.K. van der. De oorsprong en de grenzen der kennis. 2e Druk. Groningen, 1863.
Phil 4655.1.43 — Wikner, Pontus. Undersökningar om enhet och mängfald. Upsala, 1863.
Phil 5262.6.10 — Winslow, H. Intellectual philosophy. 8th ed. Boston, 1863.
Phil 3915.55 — Wundt, Wilhelm. Vorlesungen über die Menschen- und Thierseele. Leipzig, 1863. 2v.

1864

Phil 1870.82A — Abbot, T.K. Sight and touch...Berkeleian theory. London, 1864.
Phil 5643.1 — Abbott, T.K. Sight and touch. London, 1864.
Phil 2496.80 — Alaux, J.E. La philosophie de M. Cousin. Paris, 1864.
Phil 8625.1 — Alger, W.R. A critical history of the doctrine of a future life. Philadelphia, 1864.
Phil 175.4 — Allibaco, W.A. Philosophic and scientific ultimatum. N.Y., 1864.
Phil 5241.2.21 — Bain, S. The senses and the intellect. 2. ed. London, 1864.
Phil 3450.15.80 — Barach, C.S. Hieronymus Hirnhaim. Wien, 1864.
Phil 3801.197.25* — Beckers, Hubert. Über die Wahre und bleibende Bedeutung der Naturphilosophie Schelling's. München, 1864.   Htn
Phil 176.21.5 — Bersot, P.E. Essais de philosophie et de morale. Paris, 1864. 2v.
Phil 7060.105 — Berthelen, K.A. Die Klopf- und Spussgeister. Zittau, 1864.
Phil 7068.64 — Bertolacci, W.R. Christian spiritualism. London, 1864.
Phil 8626.14 — Björkman, E.A. Det bortkastade helvetet. Stockholm, 1864.
Phil 3552.133 — Bolin, Wilhelm. Leibnitz ett forëbud till Kant. Akademisk afhandling. Helsingfors, 1864.
Phil 4070.1.65 — Bonavino, Cristoforo. Il razionalismo del popolo dei Ausonio Franchi. 3a ed. corretta e aumentata. Milano, 1864.
Phil 1200.33 — Bonnell, Karl E. Programm. Berlin, 1864.
Phil 4515.33 — Boström, C.J. Anmärkningar om helveteslären. 2. uppl. Upsala, 1864.
Phil 8587.6.15 — Bowen, D. Assumed authority:...Hedge's address. Boston, 1864.
Phil 1880.46 — Bowen, F. Treatise on logic. Cambridge, 1864.
Phil 6111.6.2 — Brittan, S.B. Man and his relations:...influence of the mind on the body. N.Y., 1864.
Phil 5645.29 — Brown, J.H. Spectropia. 3. ed. London, 1864.
Phil 8657.1.2 — Caro, E.M. L'idée de Dieu et ses nouveaux critiques. Paris, 1864.
Phil 8582.35.5 — Cobbe, F.P. Broken lights; an inquiry into the present condition and future prospects of religious faith. London, 1864.
Phil 8582.35 — Cobbe, F.P. Broken lights; an inquiry into the present condition and future prospects of religious faith. London, 1864.
Phil 177.18 — Consciousness. Boston, 1864.
Phil 8692.2.4 — Cooke, J.P. Religion and chemistry. N.Y., 1864.
Phil 7060.73* — Cruikshank, G. Discovery concerning ghosts. 2d ed. London, 1864.   Htn
Phil 5043.24 — Dahlbäck, Carl J. Om logikens studium vid elementarläroverken. Umea, 1864.
Phil 7060.149 — Duroy de Bruignac, A. Satan et la magie de nos jours. Paris, 1864.
Phil 5044.5.4 — Erdmann, J.E. Grundriss der Logik und Metaphysik. Halle, 1864.
Phil 6955.1 — Falret, J.P. Des maladies mentales. Paris, 1864.
Phil 3210.35 — Fechner, G.T. Atomenlehre. Leipzig, 1864.
Phil 3245.70 — Fichte, Immanuel Hermann. Psychologie. Leipzig, 1864-73. 2v.
Phil 4110.2.31 — Florenzi Waddington, Marianna. Saggi di psicologia e di logica. Firenze, 1864.
Phil 5815.2.5.2 — Flourens, Pierre. Psychologie comparée. 2e éd. Paris, 1864.
Phil 3825.5 — Forsberg, N.A. Jemförande betraktelse af Spinozas och Malebranches metafysiska principier. Upsala, 1864.
Phil 5045.10 — Friedrich, E.F. Beiträge zur Förderung der Logik. Leipzig, 1864.
Phil 180.10A — Frothingham, Ephraim L. Philosophy as absolute science. Boston, 1864.
Phil 9520.1 — Gasparin, V.B. Human sadness. London, 1864.
Phil 181.2.5 — Gatien-Arnoult, A. Eléments de philosophie. Toulouse, 1864.
Phil 4170.8.90 — Giovanni, V. di. Il Miceli ovvero dell'ente uno e reale. Palermo, 1864.
Phil 8631.6 — Giraudet, Jules. Y a-t-il une vie future? Paris, 1864.
Phil 1750.14.10 — Gratry, A.J.A. Les sophistes et la critique. Paris, 1864.
Phil 8881.23.15 — Guizot, F.P.G. Méditations et études morales. Paris, 1864.
Phil 8586.34 — Guizot, F.P.G. Méditations sur l'essence de la religion chrétienne. 1e série. Paris, 1864.
Phil 8586.34.2 — Guizot, F.P.G. Méditations sur l'essence de la religion chrétienne. 1e série. Paris, 1864.
Phil 2035.51.9 — Hamilton, William. Metaphysics. Cambridge, 1864.
Phil 3808.148 — Haym, R. Arthur Schopenhauer. Berlin, 1864.
Phil 5650.1 — Höring, Adolf. Versuche über das Unterscheidungsvermögen des Hörsinnes für Zeitgrössen. Inaug. Diss. Tübingen, 1864.
Phil 7054.45.14 — Home, Daniel Dunglas. Incidents in my life. 5th ed. N.Y., 1864.
Phil 8632.25 — Huber, Johannes. Die Idee der Unsterblichkeit. München, 1864.
Phil 182.25 — Huet, F. La science de l'esprit. Paris, 1864. 2v.
Phil 3009.1 — Janet, P. Le matérialisme contemporaine...Allem. Paris, 1864.
Phil 2668.60 — Janet, Paul A.R. Philosophie du bonheur. Paris, 1864.
Phil 5049.7 — Jevons, W.S. Pure logic. London, 1864.
Phil 3801.469* — Jung, Alexander. F.W.J. von Schelling. Leipzig, 1864.   Htn
Phil 185.33 — Kaeppelin, E.R. El universo, Dios y el hombre, ó Creador, creacion y criaturas. Paris, 1864.
Phil 3480.31.5 — Kant, Immanuel. Critique de la raison pure. 3. éd. Paris, 1864. 2v.
Phil 9350.3.7 — Keddie, H. Papers for thoughtful girls. Boston, 1864.

1864 - cont.

Phil 8685.16   Klockhoff, D. Om den pantheistiska esthetiken. Academisk ävhandling. Upsala, 1864.

Phil 5460.7   Kraft-Ebing, R. Die Sinnesdelirien. Erlangen, 1864.

Phil 2725.8.82   Lame, D. Etude sur la philosophie de Laromiguiere. Guéret, 1864.

Phil 186.18.5   Laugel, Auguste. Les problèmes de la nature. Paris, 1864.

Phil 5051.13   Leechman, John. Logic. 4th ed. London, 1864.

Phil 3831.13   Lehmans, J.B. Spinoza. Würzburg, 1864.

Phil 3552.13   Leibniz, Gottfried Wilhelm. Die Werke von Leibniz gemäss seinem handschriftlichen Nachlasse in der Königlichen Bibliothek zu Hannover. Hannover, 1864-84. 11v.

Phil 3850.2.80A   Lemoine, A. Le vitalisme et l'animisme de Stahl. Paris, 1864.

Phil 130.2   Lenoël, L. Les philosophes de l'antiquité. Paris, 1864.

Phil 8886.7   Lessons on the subject of right and wrong. Boston, 1864.

Phil 9351.3   Lieber, F. Character of the gentleman. Philadelphia, 1864.

Phil 5403.4   Lindner, Gustav. Das Problem des Glücks. Wien, 1864.

Phil 7054.54.7   Linton, Charles. The healing of the nations. 2. series. Philadelphia, 1864.

Phil 2490.83.2   Littré, M.P.E. Auguste Comte et la philosophie positive. Paris, 1864.

Phil 293.1   Madiis, H. de. Le plan de la creation. Paris, 1864.

Phil 487.9   Materialy dlia razoblacheniia materialisticheskago nigilizma. Photoreproduction. Sankt Peterburg, 1864.

Phil 6990.4   Mathieu, P.F. Histoire des miracules et des convulsionnaires de Saint-Médard. Paris, 1864.

Phil 5325.13   Mervoyer, P.M. Étude sur l'association des idées. Paris, 1864.

Phil 8592.122.5   Meslier, Jean. Le testament de Jean Meslier. Amsterdam, 1864. 3v.

Phil 8963.2   Neander, A. Vorlesungen über Geschichte der christlichen Ethik. Berlin, 1864.

Htn   Phil 2175.1.30*   Newman, John H. Apologia pro vita sua. pt.1-7. London, 1864. 3 pam.

Phil 7060.52   Nichols, T.L. A biography of the brothers Davenport. London, 1864.

Phil 5053.7   Nielsen, R. Grundideernes logik. Kjøbenhavn, 1864-66. 2v.

Phil 8594.2.5   Opzoomer, C.W. De godsdienst. Amsterdam, 1864.

Phil 2805.70   Pascal, Blaise. Opuscules philosophiques. Paris, 1864.

Phil 8595.2   Peabody, A.P. Christianity the religion of nature. Boston, 1864.

Phil 600.7.79   Pellarin, Charles. Essai critique sur la philosophie positive. Paris, 1864.

Phil 2415.2   Poitou, E.L. Les philosophes français contemporains. Paris, 1864.

Phil 8520.6   Rémusat, C.F.M. Philosophie religieuse de la théologie naturelle. Paris, 1864.

Phil 2493.84   Réthoré, François. Condillac. Paris, 1864.

Phil 817.12   Ribbing, Sigurd. Grundlinier till philosophiens historia. Upsala, 1864.

Phil 1122.3.9   Ritter, Heinrich. Historia philosophiae graecae et romanae. Gotha, 1864.

Phil 7054.37.40   Rivail, H.L.D. Spiritizm v samom prostom ego vyrazhenii. Leiptsig, 1864.

Phil 5257.26.2   Rüegg, H.R. Grundriss der Seelenlehre. 2. Aufl. Bern, 1864.

Phil 5258.3   Saisset, E.E. L'âme et la vie. Paris, 1864.

Phil 5828.1   Santlus, J.C. Zur Psychologie der menschlichen Triebe. Neuwied, 1864.

Phil 3808.20   Schopenhauer, Arthur. Aus A. Schopenhauer's handschriftlichen Nachlass. Leipzig, 1864.

Phil 3808.49   Schopenhauer, Arthur. Uber die vierfache Wurzel des Satzes vom zureichen den Grunde. 3. Aufl. Leipzig, 1864.

Phil 818.1.6.5   Schwegler, F.C.A. History of philosophy in epitome. N.Y., 1864.

Phil 5058.10   Shedden, T. The elements of logic. London, 1864.

Phil 3425.282F   Spaventa, B. Le prime categorie della logica di Hegel; memoria. Napoli, 1864.

Htn   Phil 2270.60*   Spencer, Herbert. The classification of the sciences. London, 1864.

Phil 2270.60.3   Spencer, Herbert. The classification of the sciences. N.Y., 1864.

Phil 2270.45.3   Spencer, Herbert. First principles. N.Y., 1864.

Phil 2270.65   Spencer, Herbert. Illustrations of universal progress. N.Y., 1864.

Phil 2270.30.2   Spencer, Herbert. Principles of biology. London, 1864-67. 2v.

Phil 3850.15.31   Staegmann, B.A. von. Die Theorie des Bewusstseyns im Wesen. Berlin, 1864.

Phil 1523.1   Stöckl, A. Geschichte der Philosophie der Mittelalters. Mainz, 1864-6. 3v.

Phil 2138.87   Taine, H.A. Positivisme anglais. Paris, 1864.

Phil 2138.118   Tennant, C. Utilitarianism explained and exemplified in moral and political government. In answer to John Stuart Mill's utilitarianism. London, 1864.

Phil 9179.3   Toner, J.M. Maternal instinct, or Love. Baltimore, 1864.

Phil 196.1.5   Vacherot, E. Essais de philosophie critique. Paris, 1864.

Phil 6131.2   Valentin, G.G. Versuch einer physiologischen Pathologie der Nerven. Leipzig, 1864.

Phil 3425.95.8   Véra, A. Essais de philosophie hégélienne. Paris, 1864.

Phil 3425.95.15   Véra, A. Introduction à la philosophie de Hegel. 2. éd. Paris, 1864.

Phil 4265.3.33   Vera, A. Ricerche sulla scienza speculativa e esperimentale. Parigi, 1864.

Phil 9182.3   Ware, J.F.W. Home life: what it is, and what it needs. Boston, 1864.

Phil 8647.11   Ware, Mary G.C. Death and life. Boston, 1864.

Phil 5772.1   Whedon, D.D. Freedom of the will. N.Y., 1864.

NEDL   Phil 8897.14.5   Whewell, W. Elements of morality. 4th ed. Cambridge, 1864.

Phil 4655.1.52   Wikner, Pontus. Kan philosophien bringa någon välsignelse åt mensklighet? 2. uppl. Upsala, 1864.

Phil 199.1   Young, A. The fractional family. N.Y., 1864.

1865

Phil 5643.3   Aubert, H.R. Physiologie der Netzhaut. Breslau, 1865.

Phil 5241.2.10   Bain, A. The emotions and the will. London, 1865.

Phil 4803.799.95   Baliński, Michał. Pamiętniki o Janie Śniadeckim. Wilno, 1865. 2v.

Phil 2555.1.80   Beaussire, E. Antécédents de l'hégélianisme...Dom Deschamps. Paris, 1865.

Phil 3801.197.20   Beckers, Hubert. Die Unsterblichkeitslehre Schelling's im ganzen Zusammenhange ihrer Entwicklung. München, 1865.

1865 - cont.

Phil 8581.10.4.10   Bell, Charles. Bridgewater treatises [4]. The hand, its mechanism and vital endowments. 7. ed. London, 1865.

Phil 7068.65.2   Blanc, H. Le merveilleux dans le Jansénisme, le magnétisme, le méthodisme et le baptisme américains. Paris, 1865.

Phil 5402.8   Bouillier, F. Du plaisir et de la douleur. Paris, 1865.

Phil 7150.1.2   Brierre de Boismont, A.J.F. Du suicide et la folie suicide. 2. éd. Paris, 1865.

Phil 476.3.15   Büchner, L. Natur und Geist. 2e Aufl. Hamm, 1865.

Phil 8691.12.5   Chalmers, Thomas. On the power, wisdom and goodness of God. London, 1865.

Phil 7068.65.4   Chase, Warren. The gist of spiritualism. 4th ed. Boston, 1865.

Phil 4002.2   Conti, Augusto. La philosophie italienne contemporaine. Paris, 1865.

Phil 333.4.5   Czolbe, H. Die Grenzen und der Ursprung der menschlichen Erkenntniss. Jena, 1865.

Phil 5043.4   Delboéuf, J. Essai de logique scientifique. Liége, 1865.

Phil 2520.19.5   Descartes, René. Oeuvres choisies. Paris, 1865.

Phil 2520.19.11   Descartes, René. Oeuvres choisies. Paris, 1865.

Htn   Phil 2520.19.9*   Descartes, René. Oeuvres choisies. Paris, 1865.

Phil 2477.7.81   Dippel, Joseph. Versuch einer systematischen Darstellung der Philosophie des C. Bovillus. Würzburg, 1865.

Phil 9495.8   Drossbach, M. Objecte der sinnlichen Wahrnehmung. Halle, 1865.

Phil 5043.11.5   Dühring, E.K. Natürliche Dialektik. Berlin, 1865.

Phil 5043.15.2   Duhamel, J.M.C. Des méthodes dans les sciences de raisonnement. pt.1. Paris, 1865.

Phil 5043.15   Duhamel, J.M.C. Des méthodes dans les sciences de raisonnement. v.1-5. Paris, 1865-73. 3v.

Phil 5440.17   Fernald, W.M. View at the foundatiuons...of character. Boston, 1865.

Phil 3090.82   Fischer, K.P. Zur hundertjährigen Geburtsfeier Franz von Baaders. Erlangen, 1865.

Phil 3825.7   Fischer, Kuno. Baruch Spinoza's Leben und Charakter. Mannheim, 1865.

Phil 5045.6.2   Fischer, Kuno. System der Logik und Metaphysik oder Wissenschaftslehre. 2e Aufl. Heidelberg, 1865.

Phil 7059.18   Gallion, D.A. Know thyself, o man! Keokuk, Iowa, 1865.

Phil 1145.8   Garnier, A. De la morale dans l'Antiquité. Paris, 1865.

Phil 5246.2.10   Garnier, A. Traite des facultés de l'âme. Paris, 1865. 3v.

Phil 181.25   Gonçalvez de Magalhães, J.G. Factos do espirito humano. Rio de Janeiro, 1865.

Phil 7082.30.5   Grant, Alexander Henley. The literature and curiosities of dreams. London, 1865. 2v.

Phil 181.16   Green, Joseph Henry. Spiritual philosophy. London, 1865. 2v.

Phil 181.20   Grote, J. Exploratio philosophica. Cambridge, 1865.

Phil 623.10.5   Hagenbach, K.R. German rationalism. Edinburgh, 1865.

Phil 5757.1.2   Hazard, R.G. Freedom of mind in willing. N.Y., 1865.

Phil 8587.6   Hedge, F.H. Reason in religion. Boston, 1865.

Phil 8587.10   Hennell, S.S. Present religion. v.1-2. London, 1865-87. 3v.

Phil 182.19.8   Hodgson, S.H. Time and space. A metaphysical essay. London, 1865.

Phil 8882.21.5.3   Hopkins, M. Lectures on moral science. Boston, 1865.

Phil 623.8.3   Hurst, J.J. History of rationalism. N.Y., 1865.

Phil 5585.48   Jaager, Johan J. de. De physiologische tijd bij psychische processen. Proefschrift. Utrecht, 1865.

Phil 2409.1   Janet, P. La crise philosophique. Paris, 1865.

Phil 2035.82A   Jones, J.H. Know the truth. Hamilton's theory. N.Y., 1865.

Phil 184.21.9   Jourdain, Charles. Notions de philosophie. Paris, 1865.

Phil 3428.81   Lange, F.A. Die Grundlegung der mathematische Psychologie. Duisburg, 1865.

Phil 486.2   Leblais, A. Matérialisme et spiritualisme. Paris, 1865.

Phil 623.1.5   Lecky, W.E.H. History of the rise and influence of the spirit of rationalism in Europe. London, 1865. 2v.

Phil 6961.2   Lemoine, A. L'aliéné devant la philosophie, la morale et la société. Paris, 1865.

Phil 6021.3   Lemoine, A. De la physiognomie et de parole. Paris, 1865.

Phil 4110.2.85   Leonij, Lorenzo. Notizie della vita di Marianna Florenzi Waddington. Todi, 1865.

Htn   Phil 186.8*   Lequier, J. La recherche d'une première vérité. Saint-Cloud, 1865.

Phil 186.9   Lévêque, C. La science de l'invisible. Paris, 1865.

Phil 5070.1   Lowndes, R. Introduction...philosophy of primary beliefs. London, 1865.

Phil 5070.1.2   Lowndes, R. Introduction...philosophy of primary beliefs. London, 1865.

Phil 6121.7.5   Luys, J. Recherches sur le système nerveux. Paris, 1865. 2v.

Phil 293.2   Magy, F. De la science et de la nature. Paris, 1865.

Phil 4170.7.33   Mamiani della Rovere, Terenzio. Confessioni di un metafisico. Firenze, 1865. 2v.

Phil 8592.5   Margerie, A. de. Théodicée. Paris, 1865. 2v.

Phil 8612.25   Marminia, A. L'idée de la mort et de l'eternité. Paris, 1865.

Phil 1812.2.5   Masson, D. Recent British philosophy. London, 1865.

Phil 530.15.37   Matter, Jacques. Le mysticisme en France au temps de Fénelon. 2e éd. Paris, 1865.

Phil 187.78   Maugeri, P. Antonino. Corso di lezioni di filosofia razionale. Catania, 1865-1866. 2v.

Phil 7080.9.3   Maury, L.F.A. Le sommeil et les rêves. Paris, 1865.

Phil 812.7   Michelis, F. Geschichte der Philosophie von Thales. Braunsberg, 1865.

Phil 2035.80.6   Mill, J.S. Examination...Hamilton's philosophy. Boston, 1865. 2v.

Phil 2035.80A   Mill, J.S. Examination...Hamilton's philosophy. London, 1865.

Phil 2138.30A   Mill, John S. An examination of Hamilton's philosophy. Boston, 1865. 2v.

Htn   Phil 2138.30.2*   Mill, John S. An examination of Hamilton's philosophy. London, 1865.

Phil 1350.11   Montée, P. Le stoïcisme à Rome. Paris, 1865.

Phil 4115.83   Morkos, D. Spiegazione analitica della formula ideale di V. Gioberti. Torino, 1865.

Phil 8060.7   Motz, H. Über die Empfindung der Naturschönheit bei den Alten. Leipzig, 1865.

Phil 9352.5   Muzzey, M. The blade and the ear. Boston, 1865.

Phil 7054.172   Nichols, T.L. Supramundane facts. London, 1865.

Phil 5253.3   Nourisson, J.F. La nature humaine. Paris, 1865.

Phil 7060.27.3   Owen, R.D. Footfalls on the boundary of another world. Philadelphia, 1865.

Phil 8965.4.5   Palmer, Herbert. Lord Bacon not the author of The Christian paradoxes. Edinburgh, 1865.

Chronological Listing

1865 - cont.

Phil 815.2 Pompa, R.P. Sommario della storia di filosofia. Napoli, 1865.

Phil 192.3 Rands, W.B. Henry Holbeach. London, 1865. 2v.

Phil 8672.4 Robertson, A. The laws of thought. London, 1865.

Phil 645.5 Saisset, E. Le scepticisme. Paris, 1865.

Phil 193.3 Saisset, E.E. Critique...de la philosophie. Paris, 1865.

Phil 3705.2.80 Sandberg, A.J. Het stelsel der ervaring van Mr. C.W. Opzoomer. Zeist, 1865.

tn Phil 3800.390.5* Schelling, F.W.J. von. Clara. 2e Aufl. Stuttgart, 1865.

Phil 193.14 Schoebel, C. Philosophie de la raison pure. Paris, 1865.

Phil 6128.26 Schroeder van der Kolk, J.L.C. Seele und Leib in Wechselbeziehung zu Einander. Braunschweig, 1865.

Phil 2270.40.2 Spencer, Herbert. Essays. N.Y., 1865.

Phil 2270.45.3.10 Spencer, Herbert. First principles. N.Y., 1865.

Phil 2270.55.4 Spencer, Herbert. Social statics. N.Y., 1865.

Phil 2035.87 Sterling, J.H. Sir W. Hamilton. London, 1865.

Phil 3425.94 Stirling, J.H. The secret of Hegel. London, 1865. 2v.

Phil 193.40 Strada, G.J. de. Essai d'un ultimum organum. Paris, 1865. 2v.

Phil 2885.34.5 Taine, Hippolyte Adolphe. Philosophie de l'art. Paris, 1865.

Phil 350.3 Tauschinski, Hippolyt. Der Begriff. Wien, 1865.

Phil 5059.5 Tibergheim, G. Logique. Paris, 1865. 2v.

Phil 5769.3 Travis, H. Moral freedom reconciled with causation. London, 1865.

Phil 3841.1.2 Vloten, J. van. Baruck d'Espinoza. Amsterdam, 1865.

Phil 8422.11 Vogt, T. Form und Gehalt in der Asthetik. Wien, 1865.

Phil 5262.4.9 Wayland, F. Elements of intellectual philosophy. N.Y., 1865.

Phil 4655.1.53 Wikner, Pontus. Hvad vi behöfva. Upsala, 1865.

Phil 6032.6 Woolnoth, Thomas. The study of the human face. London, 1865.

Phil 8602.12 Wright, H.C. The living present and the dead past. Boston, 1865.

Phil 200.2.5 Zeller, E. Vorträge und Abhandlungen geschichtlichen Inhalts. Leipzig, 1865.

1866

Phil 8690.2 Agassiz, L.J.R. The structure of animal life. N.Y., 1866.

Phil 2138.80 Alexander, P.P. Mill and Carlyle. Edinburgh, 1866.

Phil 4060.3.30 Allievo, G. Saggi filosofici. Milano, 1866.

Phil 1506.1 Barach, C.S. Zur Geschichte des Nominalis von Roscellin. Wien, 1866.

Phil 2445.2.6 Barthélemy-Saint-Hilaire, J. Philosophie des deux Ampère. Paris, 1866.

Phil 2035.81 Battle of the two philosophies. London, 1866.

Phil 8876.12 Bautain, L.E.M. Manuel de philosophie morale. Paris, 1866.

Phil 8893.100 Boissière, P. La morale fouillée dans ses fondements. Paris, 1866.

Phil 4001.4.9 Bonavino, C. Appendice alla filosofia delle scuole italiane. 2. ed. Milano, 1866.

Phil 3428.159 Borelius, J.J. Anmärkningar vid Herbarts filosofiska system. Kalmar, 1866.

Phil 8951.3 Boutteville, M.L. La morale de l'église et la morale naturelle. Paris, 1866.

Phil 1880.46.4 Bowen, F. Treatise on logic. 4th ed. Cambridge, 1866.

Phil 315.4 Brandes, Georg. Dualismus i vor nyeste philosophie. Kjobenhavn, 1866.

Phil 2490.80 Bridges, J.H. The unity of Comte's life and doctrine. London, 1866.

Phil 176.33.5 Büchner, L. Science et nature. v.1-2. Paris, 1866.

Phil 5812.5 Carus, Carl Gustav. Vergleichende Psychologie. Wien, 1866.

Phil 177.78* Cointha, Jean des Boulez. Paradoxo ou Sentença, philosophica contra opinão do vulgo. Lixboa, 1866.

Phil 8877.16 Collignon, A. L'art et la vie. Metz, 1866.

Phil 2494.32 Condorcet, M.J.A.N. Esquisse d'un tableau historique. 2e éd. Paris, 1866.

Phil 4080.8.40 Conti, Augusto. Dio e il male. Prato, 1866.

Phil 1750.12 Cousin, V. Philosophie sensualiste au XVIIIe siècle. Paris, 1866.

Phil 5243.12 Durand, M.J.P. Essais de physiologie philosophique. Paris, 1866.

Phil 4080.10.85 Ercole, P. d'. Notizia degli scritti e del pensiere filosofico di Pietro Ceretti. Torino, 1866.

Phil 5390.2.2 Erdmann, Johann Eduard. Über Dummheit. Berlin, 1866.

Phil 1110.1.5 Ferrier, J.F. Lectures on Greek philosophy. v.2. Edinburgh, 1866.

Phil 1705.4.8 Fischer, K. Kort inledning till nyare filosofia historia. Stockholm, 1866.

Phil 3487.1.5 Fischer, Kuno. Commentary on Kant's Critick of pure reason. London, 1866.

Phil 480.2 Flentje, L. Das Leben und die todte Natur. Cassel, 1866.

Phil 8880.12.25 Foster, John. An essay on the improvement of time. N.Y., 1866.

Phil 2880.1.81 Franck, A. La philosophie mystique...Saint-Martin. Paris, 1866.

Phil 8880.33 Frauenstädt, Julius. Das sittliche Leben. Leipzig, 1866.

Phil 6675.5 Fusinieri, A. von. La dinamica molecolare. Foligno, 1866.

Phil 5246.44 Garvey, M.A. A manual of human culture. London, 1866.

Phil 4215.2.86 Giordano-Zocchi, V. Tommaso Rossi. Napoli, 1866.

Phil 7054.171 Grant, Miles. Spiritualism unveiled. Boston, 1866.

Phil 5545.12 Gratacap, A. Théorie de la mémoire. Montpellier, 1866.

Phil 2655.1.80 Grucker, E. François Hemsterhuis. Paris, 1866.

Phil 8586.34.5 Guizot, F.P.G. Méditations sur la religion chrétienne. Paris, 1866-1868. 3v.

Phil 8586.34.3 Guizot, F.P.G. Méditations sur l'essence de la religion. Paris, 1866.

Phil 7080.5.5 Hammond, W.A. On wakefulness. Philadelphia, 1866.

Phil 8882.47 Heegaard, P.C.V. Indledning til den rationelle ethik. Kjøbenhavn, 1866.

Phil 9520.2.3 Hinton, James. The mystery of pain. London, 1866.

Phil 2668.35.5 Janet, Paul A.R. The materialism of the present day. London, 1866.

Phil 2672.31.5 Jouffroy, Théodore S. Cours de droit naturel. 4. éd. v.2. Paris, 1866.

Phil 2672.30.5 Jouffroy, Théodore S. Mélanges philosophiques. 4e éd. v.1-2. Paris, 1866.

Phil 9350.3.8 Keddie, H. Sweet counsel. Boston, 1866.

Phil 3808.133 Kiy, Victor. Der Pessimismus und die Ethik Schopenhauers. Berlin, 1866.

Phil 8666.9 Lacour, J.B. Dieu et la création. Paris, 1866.

1866 - cont.

Phil 6681.2.5 Lafontaine, C. Mémoires d'un magnétiseur. Paris, 1866. 2v.

Phil 1116.1 Laforet, N.J. Histoire de la philosophie ancienne. Bruxelles, 1866. 2v.

Phil 2490.106 L'Ange-Huet, J. De methode der positieve filosofie volgens Auguste Comte. Leiden, 1866.

Phil 8886.5 Laurie, S.S. On the philosophy of ethics. Edinburgh, 1866.

Phil 623.1A Lecky, W.E.H. History of the rise and influence of the spirit of rationalism in Europe. N.Y., 1866. 2v.

Phil 3552.18 Leibniz, Gottfried Wilhelm. Oeuvres philosophiques. v.2. Paris, 1866.

Phil 8591.6 Levallois, J. Deisme et christianisme. Paris, 1866.

Phil 6681.4 Liébeault, A.A. Du sommeil et des états analogues. Paris, 1866.

Phil 5761.2 Liebmann, O. Über den individuellen Beweis für die Freiheit. Stuttgart, 1866.

Phil 186.13 Lindner, G.A. Einleitung in das Studium der Philosophie. Wien, 1866.

Phil 4115.92 Luciani, P. Gioberti e la filosofia nuova italiana. Napoli, 1866-72. 3v.

Htn Phil 3801.539* Lyng, Georg V. Studier over Schelling. Thesis. Christiania, 1866.

Phil 2138.85 McCosh, James. An examination of Mr. J.S. Mill's philosophy. London, 1866.

NEDL Phil 2138.85.2 McCosh, James. An examination of Mr. J.S. Mill's philosophy. N.Y., 1866.

Phil 2035.84 Mansel, H.L. Philosophy of the conditioned. London, 1866.

Phil 2130.60 Mansel, H.L. Philosophy of the conditioned. London, 1866.

Phil 1350.5 Martha, Constant. Les moralistes sous l'Empire romain. Paris, 1866.

Phil 187.11.2 Martineau, J. Essays. Boston, 1866. 2v.

Phil 187.11 Martineau, J. Essays. Boston, 1866-1868. 2v.

Phil 1812.2 Masson, D. Recent British philosophy. N.Y., 1866.

Phil 530.15.3 Matter, Jacques. Le mysticisme en France au temps de Fénelon. 2e éd. Paris, 1866.

Phil 8637.20.5 Mattison, H. The immortality of the soul. 2d ed. Philadelphia, 1866.

Phil 5252.56 Mayer, A. Zur Seelenfrage. Mainz, 1866.

Phil 487.1.10 Morell, J.D. Handbook of logic. London, 1866.

Phil 5052.41 Moleschott, J. La circulation de la vie. Paris, 1866.

Phil 8668.1 Naville, E. Le père céleste. Genève, 1866.

Phil 3833.1 Nourrisson, J.F. Spinoza et le naturalisme contemporain. Paris, 1866.

Phil 2805.40.4A Pascal, Blaise. Pensées. v.1-2. Paris, 1866.

Phil 2805.40.4.3 Pascal, Blaise. Pensées. 2e éd. v.1-2. Paris, 1866. 2v.

Phil 2805.40.32 Pascal, Blaise. Pensées de Pascal. Paris, 1866.

Phil 8640.6 Perrois, A. Les preuves de l'immortalité de l'âme. Paris, 1866.

Phil 192.3.2 Rands, W.B. Henry Holbeach. London, 1866. 2v.

Phil 817.15 Reichlin-Meldegg, K. Der Parallelismus der Alten und neuen Philosophie. Leipzig, 1866.

Phil 3425.111 Reiff, F. Über die Hegel'sche Dialektik. Tübingen, 1866.

Phil 8642.5.5 Ritter, Heinrich. Unsterblichkeit. Leipzig, 1866.

Phil 7054.37.15 Rivail, H.L.D. Le livre des esprits. 15. ed. Paris, 1866.

Phil 3499.20 Roeder, E. De voce "a priori" in philosophia Kantii. Diss. Bonnae, 1866.

Phil 365.53 Rolle, Friedrich. Der Mensch, seine Abstammung und Gesittung. Frankfurt, 1866.

Phil 3790.5.31 Rosenkrantz, Wilhelm. Die Wissenschaft des Wissens und Begründung der besonderer Wissenschaften durch die allgemeine Wissenschaft. v.1-2. München, 1866-68.

Phil 8598.71 Saggio sulla religione in generale. Torino, 1866.

Phil 5258.10.25 Schultz-Schultzenstein, K.H. Naturstudium und Kultur. Berlin, 1866.

Phil 193.21.2 Secrétan, C. La philosophie de la liberté. 2e ed. Paris, 1866.

Phil 6750.7 Seguin, E. Idiocy and its treatment. N.Y., 1866.

Phil 5058.9 Seydel, R. Logik. Leipzig, 1866.

Phil 3925.3.80 Seydel, R. Christian Hermann Weisse. Leipzig, 1866.

Phil 5058.37 Sibbern, F.C. Taenkelaere eller logik i sammentraengt fremstilling. 3. udg. Kjøbenhavn, 1866.

Phil 3838.16 Sigwart, Christoph von. Spinoza's neuentdeckter Tractat von Gott. Gotha, 1866.

Phil 6116.5.85 Soury, Jules. Les fonctions du cerveau, doctrines de F. Goltz. Paris, 1866.

Phil 2270.45.3.15 Spencer, Herbert. First principles. N.Y., 1866.

Phil 2275.37 Stewart, D. Elements of the philosophy of the human mind. Edinburgh, 1866.

Phil 8610.831.3 Taylor, Robert. The devil's pulpit. Boston, 1866.

Phil 7068.66.80 Tissandier, J.B. Des sciences occultes et du spiritisme. Paris, 1866.

Phil 8894.6.15 Tissot, Joseph. Principes de la morale. Paris, 1866.

Phil 3895.40.5 Ulrici, H. Gott und die Natur. 2. Aufl. Leipzig, 1866.

Phil 5061.1.9 Venn, J. The logic of chance. London, 1866.

Phil 4322.1 Vidart, Louis. La filosofía española. Madrid, 1866.

Phil 303.11 Waddington, M.F. Saggio sulla natura. Firenze, 1866.

Phil 1195.4 Wecklein, N. Die Sophisten und die Sophistik nach den angaben Plato's. Wurzburg, 1866.

Phil 4655.1.67 Wikner, Pontus. Naturens förbannelse. Upsala, 1866.

Phil 5643.19 Wüllner, F.H.A. Einleitung in die Dioptrik des Auges. Leipzig, 1866.

Phil 3915.69 Wundt, Wilhelm. Die physikalischen Axiome und ihre Beziehung zum Causal Princip. Erlangen, 1866.

Phil 3850.1.94 Zeller, Eduard. Strauss and Renan. London, 1866.

1867

Phil 9515.2 Alger, W.R. The solitudes of nature and of man. 4. ed. Boston, 1867.

Phil 9515.2.5 Alger, W.R. Solitudes of nature and of man. 5th ed. Boston, 1867.

Phil 8582.3.5 Argyll, G.D.C. The reign of law. 4. ed. London, 1867.

Phil 6670.1 Ashburner, J. Notes and studies... philosophy of animal magnetism. London, 1867.

Phil 5040.6 Atwater, L.H. Manual of elementary logic. Philadelphia, 1867.

Phil 5040.6.2 Atwater, L.H. Manual of elementary logic. Philadelphia, 1867.

Phil 176.3 Bahnsen, J. Beitrage zur Charakterologie. Leipzig, 1867. 2v.

Phil 8402.5.1 Bascom, J. Aesthetics or the science of beauty. Boston, 1867.

1867 - cont.

Phil 665.43.2   Beskow, B. von. Om själens helsa. 2e uppl. Stockholm, 1867.

Phil 5545.3   Boucher, J. Des idées innées de la mémoire. Paris, 1867.

Phil 801.5.3   Brucker, J. Historia critica philosophiae. Lipsiae, 1867. 6v.

Phil 801.5.2   Brucker, J. Historia critica philosophiae. Lipsiae, 1867. 6v.

Phil 476.3.2   Büchner, L. Kraft und Stoff. Leipzig, 1867.

Phil 75.2   Büchring, Adolph. Bibliotheca philosophica. Nordhausen, 1867.

Phil 4260.80   Cantoni, C. G.B. Vico. Torino, 1867.

Phil 477.2   Caro, E.M. Le matérialisme et la science. Paris, 1867.

Phil 6112.3   Catlow, P. On the principles of aesthetic medicine. London, 1867.

Phil 8582.5   Chadbourne, P.A. Lectures on natural theology. N.Y., 1867.

Phil 7054.46   Chase, W. The gist of spiritualism. 3. ed. Boston, 1867.

Phil 7054.141.5   Cooper, Robert. Spiritual experiences. London, 1867.

Phil 9075.18   Coquerel, A. La conscience et la foi. Paris, 1867.

Phil 8952.9   Corte, P.A. Primi elementi di antropologia e di scienza morale. Torino, 1867.

Phil 802.2.5   Cousin, V. Histoire générale de la philosophie. 8e éd. Paris, 1867.

Phil 1507.1   Cupély. Esprit de la philosophie scolastique. Paris, 1867.

Phil 5043.3   Day, Henry N. Elements of logic. N.Y., 1867.

Phil 5753.2   Drobisch, M.W. Die moralische Statistik. Leipzig, 1867.

Phil 5043.10.3   Drobisch, Moritz Wilhelm. Die moralische Statistik und die menschliche Willens Freiheit. Leipzig, 1867.

Phil 8878.18   Dymond, J. Essays...principles of morality. London, 1867.

Phil 6115.11   Feuchtersleben, E.F.V. Zur Diätetik der Seele. Wien, 1867.

Phil 3245.43   Fichte, Immanuel Hermann. Die Seelenfortdauer und die Weltstellung des Menschen. Leipzig, 1867.

Phil 8660.3   Flammarion, C. Dieu dans la nature. Paris, 1867.

Phil 8880.8   Fleming, W. A manual of moral philosophy. London, 1867.

Phil 4110.2.35   Florenzi Waddington, Marianna. Saggio sulla filosofia dello spirito. Firenze, 1867.

Phil 5045.2   Fowler, Thomas. The elements of deductive logic. Oxford, 1867.

Phil 9166.4   Gasparin, A.E. La famille. Paris, 1867. 2v.

Phil 4115.28   Gioberti, V. Studi filologici. Torino, 1867.

Phil 4170.9.90   Giovanni, V. di. Salvatore Mancino e l'ecletticismo in Sicilia. Palermo, 1867.

Phil 8586.6   Gréard, Mlle. Du doute. Paris, 1867.

Phil 6956.2.5   Griesinger, W. Mental pathology and therapeutics. London, 1867.

Htn   Phil 6956.2.2*   Griesinger, W. Die Pathologie und Therapie der psychischen Krankhejten. Stuttgart, 1867.

Phil 8587.1.5   Hannotin, E. Les grandes questions. Paris, 1867.

Phil 5927.2   Hecker, J. Scientific basis of education demonstrated. N.Y., 1867.

Phil 5643.8.10   Helmholtz, H. Optique physiologique. Paris, 1867.

Htn   Phil 5643.8*   Helmholtz, H. Physiologischen Optik. v.1 and Atlas. Leipzig, 1867. 2v.

Phil 3260.85   Henke, E.L.T. Jakob Friedrich Fries. Leipzig, 1867.

Phil 807.14   Hermann, C. Geschichte der Philosophie. Leipzig, 1867.

Phil 8697.4   Hitchcock, C.H. The relations of geology to theology. Andover, 1867.

Phil 5757.3   Hughes, T. The human will. London, 1867.

Phil 623.8.5   Hurst, J.J. History of rationalism. London, 1867.

Phil 3552.278   Jacoby, Daniel. De Leibnitii studiis Aristotelicis. Berolini, 1867.

Phil 2668.45   Janet, Paul A.R. Le cerveau et la pensée. Paris, 1867.

Phil 3480.13A   Kant, Immanuel. Sämmtliche Werke. Leipzig, 1867-68. 8v.

Phil 8411.23.10   Kaublanov, B.G. Mystetstvo iak forma piznannia diisnosti. Kyiv, 1867.

Phil 5251.4.5   Langel, A. Les problèmes de la vie. Paris, 1867.

Phil 3428.93   Langenbeck, H. Die theoretische Philosophie Herbarts und seiner Schule. Berlin, 1867.

Phil 9171.4.8   Legouvé, E. Les pères et les enfants. Enfance et adolescence. 16. éd. Paris, 1867.

Phil 811.3.3   Lewes, G.H. History of philosophy. 3d ed. London, 1867. 2v.

Phil 486.5   Lucas, F. Le procès du matérialisme. Paris, 1867.

Phil 8702.2.5   McCausland, D. Shinar. London, 1867.

Phil 4265.2.31   Mariano, R. Le bellezze della fede ne misteri. Milano, 1867. 3v.

Phil 8685.7   Martha-Beker, F. Spiritualisme et panthéisme. Paris, 1867.

Phil 1812.2.2   Masson, D. Recent British philosophy. London, 1867.

Phil 9010.11   Mattison, H. Popular amusements. N.Y., 1867?

Phil 6122.1.11   Maudsley, H. The physiology and pathology of the mind. N.Y., 1867.

Phil 8962.3   Maurice, F.D. Epistles of Saint John. London, 1867.

Phil 2035.80.2.5   Mill, J.S. Examination...Hamilton's philosophy. 3rd ed. London, 1867.

Phil 2035.80.2   Mill, J.S. Examination...Hamilton's philosophy. 3rd ed. London, 1867.

Htn   Phil 2138.65*   Mill, John S. Inaugural address to...University of St. Andrews. London, 1867.

Phil 2138.107   Millet, J. An Millius veram mathematicorum axiomatum originem invenerit. Paris, 1867.

Phil 2520.95   Millet, J. Histoire de Descartes avant 1637. Paris, 1867.

Phil 8668.1.5   Naville, E. The heavenly father. Boston, 1867.

Phil 8593.10   Nielsen, Rasmus. Om hindringer og betingelser for det aandelige liv i nutiden. Kjøbenhavn, 1867.

Phil 813.1.2   Nourrisson, J.F. Tableau des progrès de la pensée humaine. Paris, 1867.

Phil 5054.2.2   Opyoomer, C.W. Het weyen der kennis. 2e druk. Amsterdam, 1867.

Phil 9174.1.8   Osgood, S. American boys and girls. N.Y., 1867.

Phil 2805.30.23   Pascal, Blaise. Les provinciales. Paris, 1867.

Phil 2805.30.3   Pascal, Blaise. Texte primitif des Lettres provinciales. Paris, 1867.

Phil 7060.21   Paterson, Robert. On illusions of the senses. Photoreproduction. Edinburgh, 1867.

Phil 600.8   Peabody, A.P. The positive philosophy. Boston, 1867.

Phil 5403.2   Piderit, Theodor. Die Theorie des Glücks. Leipzig, 1867.

Htn   Phil 5055.1.15*   Pierce, C.S. Papers on logic. n.p., 1867?

Htn   Phil 5055.1.9*   Pierce, C.S. Three papers on logic. n.p., 1867?

Phil 2605.5.95   Rabbe, Felix P. L'abbé Simon Foucher. Paris, 1867.

Phil 4630.2.39   Rein, T. Om kunskapens möjlighet. Helsingfors, 1867.

Phil 192.12.15   Ritter, Heinrich. Philosophische Paradoxa. Leipzig, 1867.

Phil 4210.23   Rosmini-Serbati, Antonio. Logica. Intra, 1867.

1867 - cont.

Phil 8893.76   Saturday Review. Studies in conduct. London, 1867.

Phil 493.4   Schilling, G. Beiträge zur Geschichte und Kritik des Materialismus. Leipzig, 1867.

Phil 3808.21   Schopenhauer, Arthur. Lichtstrahlen aus seinen Werken. Leipzig, 1867.

Phil 3808.65.2   Schopenhauer, Arthur. Über den Willen in der Natur. Leipzig, 1867.

NEDL   Phil 818.1.7   Schwegler, F.C.A. Handbook of the history of philosophy. Edinburgh, 1867.

Phil 6968.6   Sémérie, E. Des symptomes intellectuels de la folie. Paris, 1867.

Phil 7054.103   Shufeldt, G.A., Jr. History of the Chicago artesian well. Chicago, 1867. 2 pam.

Phil 9495.15.4   Storer, H.R. Is it D? A book for every man. Boston, 1867.

Phil 2885.33   Taine, Hippolyte Adolphe. De l'ideal dans l'art. Paris, 1867.

Phil 2885.34.12   Taine, Hippolyte Adolphe. The philosophy of art. Photoreproduction. London, 1867.

Phil 820.01.3   Ueberweg, F. Grundriss der Geschichte der Philosophie. 3rd ed. Berlin, 1867.

Phil 3425.95.4   Véra, A. Philosophie de l'esprit. Paris, 1867-69. 2v.

Phil 9010.21   Vincent, Marvin. Amusement. Troy, 1867.

Phil 5832.1   Watson, John S. The reasoning power in animals. London, 1867.

Phil 3925.3.50   Weisse, Christian Hermann. Kleine Schriften zur Aesthetik und ästhetischen Kritik. Leipzig, 1867.

Phil 9495.10   Willard, E.O.G. (Mrs.). Sexology as philosophy of life. Chicago, 1867.

Phil 6134.1   Youmans, E.L. Observations on scientific study of human nature. N.Y., 1867.

Phil 200.3.5   Zimmermann, R. Philosophische Propaedeutik. Wien, 1867.

Phil 3460.80   Zirngiebl, E. F.H. Jacobis Seben, Dichten und Denken. Wien, 1867.

1868

Phil 2035.80.17   Alexander, P.P. Moral causation, or Notes on Mr. Mill's notes to the chapter on freedom in the 3rd edition of his examination of Sir W. Hamilton's philosophy. Edinburgh, 1868.

Phil 3425.237   Allievo, G. L'Hegelianismo, la scienza e la vita. Milano, 1868.

Phil 8580.14   Alvarez, Joachim. Lectiones philosophicae. v.2. Vallisoleti, 1868-69. 3 pam.

Phil 3820.2   Avenarius, R. Ueber die...Spinozischen Pantheismus. Leipzig, 1868.

Phil 8626.1   Baguenault de Puchesse, F. L'immortalité, la mort et la vie. Paris, 1868.

Phil 5241.2   Bain, A. Mental science. N.Y., 1868.

Phil 8876.4   Barni, J. La morale dans la démocratie. Paris, 1868.

Phil 672.1   Baumann, J.J. Die Lehren von Raun, Zeit, und Mathematik. v.1-2. Berlin, 1868-69.

Phil 176.21   Bersot, P.E. Libre philosophie. Paris, 1868.

Phil 5585.1   Böhmer, H. Die Sinneswahrnehmung. Erlangen, 1868.

Phil 5751.10   Bolin, W. Problemet om viljans frihet, kritiskt och logiskt undersökt. Helsingfors, 1868.

Phil 3483.38   Bolin, W. Undersökning af läran om viljans frihet - Kants behandling af problemet. Helsingfors, 1868.

Phil 2520.83.6   Bouillier, F. Histoire de la philosophie Cartésienne. Paris, 1868. 2v.

Phil 6111.6   Brittan, S.B. Man and his relations:...influence of the mind on the body. N.Y., 1868.

Phil 4065.32   Bruno, Giordano. De umbris idearum. Berolini, 1868.

Phil 8877.67   Campos Gimenez, J. La voz de la virtud. Habana, 1868.

Phil 8657.1   Caro, E.M. L'idée de Dieu. Paris, 1868.

Phil 477.2.5   Caro, E.M. Le matérialisme et la science. 2e éd. Paris, 1868.

Phil 1107.2   Caspari, Otto. Die Irrthümer der altclassischen Philosophie. Heidelberg, 1868.

Phil 2490.41.12A   Comte, Auguste. Principes de philosophie positive. Paris, 1868.

Phil 9162.7   Cox, S. Friendly counsel for girls. N.Y., 1868.

Phil 9495.33   Debreyne, P.J.C. Moechialogie, traité des péchés contre les sixième et neuvième commandements du décalogue. 4th Paris, 1868.

Phil 2520.19.7   Descartes, René. Oeuvres. Paris, 1868.

Phil 5753.1   Desdouits, T. De la liberté et des lois de la nature. Paris, 1868.

Phil 5243.6   Despine, P. Psychologie naturelle. Paris, 1868. 3v.

Phil 3823.1.5   Dessauer, M. Spinoza und Hobbes. Breslau, 1868.

Phil 178.6   Dollfus, C. De la nature humaine. Paris, 1868.

Phil 179.23   Edfeldt, Hans. Hvilken verldsförklaring uppfyller fordringarna för möjlighrtin of menniskans praktiska lif? Uppsala, 1868.

Phil 6314.12.5A   Erikson, Eric H. Identity; youth and crisis. 1st ed. N.Y., 1868.

Phil 1350.9.2   Farrar, F.W. Seekers after God. London, 1868.

Phil 1350.9   Farrar, F.W. Seekers after God. Philadelphia, 1868.

Phil 2805.113F   Faugère, Armand P. Défense de Blaise Pascal. Paris, 1868.

X Cg   Phil 3246.58.2   Fichte, Johann Gottlieb. Science of knowledge. Philadelphia, 1868.

Phil 4200.1.82   Fiorentino, F. Pietro Pomponazzi. Firenze, 1868.

Phil 8647.5   Florenzi Waddington, M. Della immortalita dell'anima. Firenzi, 1868.

Phil 5925.2.18   Fowler, O.S. Self-culture and the perfection of character. N.Y., 1868.

Phil 180.13   Funck-Brentano, T. Les sciences humaines: la philosophie. Paris, 1868.

Phil 5046.1   George, L. Die Logik als Wissenschaftslehre Dargestellt. Berlin, 1868.

Phil 4006.3.15   Giovanni, V. Della filosofia moderna in Sicilia libri due. Palermo, 1868.

Phil 4060.6.90   Giovanni, V. di. D'acquisto e la filosofia della creazione in Sicilia. Firenze, 1868.

Phil 8881.25   Gladden, W. Plain thoughts on the art of living. Boston, 1868.

Phil 5046.6   Gratry, A.J.A. Logique. Paris, 1868. 2v.

Phil 9530.19   Great men being the substance of a lecture. Calcutta, 1868.

Phil 9495.68   Grindon, Leopold Hartley. The sexuality of nature. Boston, 1868.

Phil 2035.80.20A   Grote, George. Review of the work of Mr. John Stuart Mill. London, 1868.

Phil 3552.415   Guerrier, V.I. Leibnits i ego vek. Sankt Peterburg, 1868.

1868 - cont.

Phil 8957.2   Harless, G.C.A. System of Christian ethics. Edinburgh, 1868.

Phil 182.4.3   Harms, F. Abhandlungen zur systematischen Philosophie. Berlin, 1868.

Phil 3425.247   Hartmann, E. v. Ueber die dialektische Methode. Berlin, 1868.

Phil 182.52   Hoffmann, Franz. Philosophische Schriften. v.1-2,4. Erlangen, 1868-1877. 3v.

Phil 288.2   Hutchins, S. Theory of the universe. N.Y., 1868.

Phil 8663.2   Illingworth, J. Divine immanence. London, 1868.

Phil 3460.75   Jacobi, F.H. Briefe an Friedrich Bouterwek. Göttingen, 1868.

Phil 5620.15   Jönsson, A. Om den förnuftiga känslan. Lund, 1868.

Phil 484.2   Jones, H.B. Croonian lectures on matter and force. London, 1868.

Phil 4515.97   Kalling, P. Framställning af Boströmska filosofien. Örebro, 1868.

Phil 3625.1.93   Kanngiesser, G. Die Stellung M. Mendelssohn's in der Geschichte der Ästhitik. Frankfurt, 1868.

Phil 3480.30.10   Kant, Immanuel. Kritik der reinen Vernunft. Berlin, 1868-69.

Phil 3480.30.9   Kant, Immanuel. Kritik der reinen Vernunft. Leipzig, 1868.

Phil 8411.12   Kirchmann, J.H. von. Ästhetik auf realistischer Grundlage. Berlin, 1868. 2v.

Phil 1515.2   Kleutgen, R.P. La philosophie scolastique. Paris, 1868-70. 4v.

Phil 3525.35   Krause, K.C.F. Erneute Vernunftkritik. Prag, 1868.

Phil 4160.1.33   Labanca, Baldassare. Della filosofia razionale. 2a ed. Firenze, 1868. 2v.

Phil 9075.5   Labbé, J. La conscience. Paris, 1868.

Phil 6121.2   Laugel, A. Les problèmes de l'âme. Paris, 1868.

Phil 8836.1   Laurie, S.S. Notes, expository and critical, on certain British theories of morals. Edinburgh, 1868.

Phil 8666.8   Leitch, A. Ethics of theism. Edinburgh, 1868.

Phil 5400.6.3   Letourneau, C. Physiologie des passions. Paris, 1868.

Phil 9171.6   Levi, G. Autobiografia di un padre di famiglia. Firenze, 1868.

Phil 8125.38   Lotze, H. Geschichte der Aesthetik in Deutschland. München, 1868.

Phil 187.3   Macvicar, J.G. Sketch of a philosophy. v.1-4. London, 1868-1874.

Phil 4012.3   Mariano, R. La philosophie contemporaine. Paris, 1868.

Phil 6122.1.10   Maudsley, H. The physiology and pathology of the mind. 2. ed. London, 1868.

Phil 2035.80.2.10   Mill, J.S. Examination...Hamilton's philosophy. Boston, 1868. 2v.

Phil 9172.4.2   Moncrieff, A.H. A book about boys. 2. ed. Edinburgh, 1868.

Phil 7080.10   More, C.H. On going to sleep. London, 1868.

Phil 6122.11.5   Munk, H. Untersuchungen über das Wesen. Leipzig, 1868.

Phil 8594.2   Opzoomer, C.W. Die Religion. Elberfeld, 1868.

Phil 8594.2.15   Opzoomer, C.W. De vrucht der godsdienst. 3. druk. Amsterdam, 1868.

Phil 1535.8   P. Institutiones philosophiae. Parisiis, 1868. 2v.

Phil 8890.3   Paolino. Trattato de regimine rectoris. Vienna, 1868.

Phil 7054.42   Peebles, J.M. The practical of spiritualism. Chicago, 1868.

Phil 7080.36   Pfaff, E.R. Das Traumleben und seine Deutung. Leipzig, 1868.

Phil 6125.1   Piderit, T. Gehirn und Geist. Leipzig, 1868.

Phil 7054.88   Pierce, A.P. Extracts from unpublished volumes. Boston, 1868.

Phil 5585.6   Preyer, W. Über die Grenzen des Empfindungsvermögens und des Willens. Bonn, 1868.

Phil 2115.109   Quaebicker, R. Lockii et Liebnitii de cognitione humana. Inaug.-Diss. Halis Saxonium, 1868.

Phil 192.2.5   Rabus, L. Logik und Metaphysik. Erlangen, 1868.

Phil 2417.1   Ravaisson, J.G.F. La philosophie en France au XIXe siècle. Paris, 1868.

Phil 4630.2.40   Rein, T. Om den filosofiska methoden. Helsingfors, 1868.

Phil 7059.5   Revelations of the great modern mystery planchette. Boston, 1868.

Phil 3425.91.22   Rosenkranz, K. Hegel's Naturphilosophie. Berlin, 1868.

Phil 5258.1   Sagra, R. de la. L'âme. Paris, 1868.

Phil 623.18   Scheele, K.H.G. von. Rationalismens förberedelser. Upsala, 1868.

Phil 3805.176   Schenkel, D. Friedrich Schleiermacher, ein Lebens- und Charakterbild. Elberfeld, 1868.

Phil 3805.41   Schleiermacher, Friedrich. Monologen. Berlin, 1868.

Phil 3805.30.5   Schleiermacher, Friedrich. Über die Religion. Leipzig, 1868-69.

Phil 3805.162   Schmidt, P. Spinoza und Schleiermacher. Berlin, 1868.

Phil 3805.92   Schürer, Emil. Schleiermacher's Religionsbegriff. Leipzig, 1868.

Phil 3625.1.109   Schwab, Moise. Mendelssohn, sa vie et ses oeuvres. Paris, 1868.

Phil 818.1.8   Schwegler, F.C.A. Handbook of the history of philosophy. 2d ed. Edinburgh, 1868.

Phil 193.21.5   Secrétan, C. Préis élémentaire de philosophie. Lausanne, 1868.

Phil 3552.284   Sjöberg, Gustaf M. Historisk öfversigt af den på monadlären grundade metafysikens utveckling. Upsala, 1868.

Phil 2270.40.3.5   Spencer, Herbert. Essays. N.Y., 1868.

Phil 2270.39   Spencer, Herbert. Essays. v.1 N.Y., 1868.

Phil 2270.39   Spencer, Herbert. Essays. v.2,3. London, 1868. 2v.

Phil 3819.30.5   Spinoza, Benedictus de. Ethik. Berlin, 1868. 2 pam.

Phil 2419.1.3   Taine, Hippolyte Adolphe. Les philosophes clasiques du XIXe siècle. Paris, 1868.

Phil 6990.23   Taylor, William F. Miracles; their physical possibility. Liverpool, 1868.

Phil 3808.96   Thilo, C.A. Über Schopenhauer's ethischen Atheism. Leipzig, 1868.

Phil 194.5   Tiberghien, G. Introduction a la philosophie. Bruxelles, 1868.

Phil 5059.6   Tissot, C.J. Essai de logique objective. Paris, 1868.

Phil 820.1   Ueberweg, F. Grundriss der Geschichte der Philosophie. v.1-3. Berlin, 1868-71. 2v.

Phil 5585.1.5   Vierordt, Karl. Der Zeitsinn nach Versuchen. Tübingen, 1868.

Phil 7059.10   Walrath, M.E. History of the earth's formation. N.Y., 1868.

Phil 5832.5   Walse, C.S. Chapters on man...comparative psychology. London, 1868.

Phil 1050.15   Weil, Isidore. Philosophie religieuse de Léi-ben-Gerson. Paris, 1868.

1868 - cont.

Phil 5262.28   Wentzke, J.A. Compendium der Psychologie und Logik. Leipzig, 1868.

Phil 5772.4   Wolański, L.T. Die Lehre von der Willensfreiheit des Menschen. Münster, 1868.

Phil 1130.6   Zeller, Eduard. Socrates and the Socratic schools. London, 1868.

1869

Phil 600.2   Angiuli, A. La filosofia e la ricerca positiva. Napoli, 1869.

Phil 4200.1.83   Ardigò, R. Pietro Pomponazzi. Mantova, 1869.

Phil 8582.3.1   Argyll, G.D.C. The reign of law. 5. ed. N.Y., 1869.

Phil 5040.3.12   Arnauld, Antoine. Logique de Port Royal. Paris, 1869.

Phil 175.11   Aulard, A. Eléments de philosophie. Paris, 1869.

Phil 1850.35.2A   Bacon, Francis. The advancement of learning. Oxford, 1869.

NEDL Phil 8876.2   Bain, A. Moral science. N.Y., 1869.

Phil 8876.5   Barratt, A. Physical ethics. London, 1869.

Phil 270.1   Barrett, T.S. Examination of Gillespie's "First Cause". London, 1869.

Phil 5241.7   Bascom, J. The principles of psychology. N.Y., 1869.

Phil 176.17.5   Bénard, Charles. Questions de philosophie. Paris, 1869.

Phil 2115.103   Benoit, G. von. Darstellung der Locke'schen Erkenntnisstheorie. Bern, 1869.

Phil 5125.2   Biéchy, A. L'induction. Paris, 1869.

Phil 176.44.5   Blackwell, A.B. Studies in general science. N.Y., 1869.

Phil 2035.89   Bolton, M.P.W. Examination of the principles of the Scoto-Oxonian philosophy. London, 1869.

Phil 8581.46   Brochner, Hans. Om det religiöse i dets enhed met det humane. Kjøbenhavn, 1869.

Phil 801.18   Brøchner, Hans. Bidrag til opfattelsen of philosophiens historisk Udvikling. Kjøbenhavn, 1869.

Phil 476.3.11   Büchner, L. El hombre segum la ciencia. Barcelona, 1869.

Phil 476.3.4.10   Büchner, L. Kraft och materia. Stockholm, 1869.

Phil 176.35   Bunot, Albert Louis. Eléments de philosophie chretienne. Paris, 1869.

Phil 9161.8   Byford, W.H. The philosophy of domestic life. Boston, 1869.

Phil 477.1   Cahagnet, A. Etudes sur le matérialisme. Argenteuil, 1869.

Phil 8827.3.2   Caro, E.M. Etudes morales sur le temps présent. Paris, 1869.

Phil 8827.3.7   Caro, E.M. Nouvelles études morales sur le temps présent. Paris, 1869.

Phil 177.9   Catara-Lettieri, Antonio. L'omu nun l'usu di la ragiuni. Messina, 1869.

Phil 177.9.5   Catara-Lettieri, Antonio. Sull' uomo; pensieri. Messina, 1869.

Phil 2520.126   Charpentier, T.V. Essai sur la méthode de Descartes. Thèse. Paris, 1869.

Phil 177.26   Choraux, C. La pensée et l'amour. Paris, 1869.

Phil 6952.7.30   Clark, James. A memoir of John Conolly. London, 1869.

Phil 8877.19   Coignet, C. La morale indépandante. Paris, 1869.

Phil 2490.31   Comte, Auguste. Cours de philosophie positive. Paris, 1869. 6v.

Phil 7054.2   Danskin, W.A. How and why I became a spiritualist. 4th ed. Baltimore, 1869.

Phil 7060.52.5   The Davenport brothers...spiritual mediums. Boston, 1869.

Phil 8583.2   Davesiès de Pontès, L. Etudes morales et religieuses. Paris, 1869.

Phil 5926.1.28   David, L. Le petit Docteur Gall. Paris, 1869?

Phil 3552.231   Durdik, Josef. Leibnitz und Newton. Halle, 1869.

Phil 7103.4   Dureau, Alexis. Histoire de la médicine et des sciences occultes. Paris, 1869.

Phil 6314.3.2   Elam, C. A physician's problems. Boston, 1869.

Phil 6314.3   Elam, C. A physician's problems. London, 1869.

Phil 5545.78   Erdmann, E.J.E.T. Vom Vergessen. Berlin, 1869.

Phil 804.3   Erdmann, J.E. Grundriss der Geschichte der Philosophie. Berlin, 1869-70. 2v.

Phil 8880.43.5   Fairchild, J.H. Moral philosophy. Oberlin, Ohio, 1869.

Phil 1020.4.8   Fakhry, Majid. Islamic occasionalism and its critique by Averros and Aquinas. Paris, 1869.

Phil 9120.1   Ferraz, M. Philosophie du devoir. Paris, 1869.

Phil 4005.1   Ferri, L. Essai sur l'histoire de la philosophie en Italie. Paris, 1869. 2v.

Phil 3245.20   Fichte, Immanuel Hermann. Vernuschte Schriften zur Philosophie, Theologie und Ethik. Leipzig, 1869. 2v.

Phil 3246.58   Fichte, Johann Gottlieb. New exposition of the science of knowledge. Saint Louis, 1869.

X Cg Phil 3246.60.5   Fichte, Johann Gottlieb. Science of rights. Philadelphia, 1869.

Phil 3246.60.5   Fichte, Johann Gottlieb. Science of rights. Philadelphia, 1869.

Phil 3246.199.5   Fischer, Kuno. Geschichte der neuern Philosophie. Heidelberg, 1869.

Phil 3487.1.4   Fischer, Kuno. Geschichte der neuern Philosophie. 2. Aufl. Bd.3,4. Heidelberg, 1869. 2v.

Phil 8660.12   Flügel, Otto. Das Wunder und die Erkennbarkeit Gottes. Langensalza, 1869.

Phil 5245.9   Fortlage, A.R.K. Acht psychologische Vorträge. Jena, 1869.

Phil 9165.6.5   Fowler, O.S. Love and parentage. 40th ed. N.Y., 1869.

Phil 8585.12   Franck, A. Philosophie et religion. Paris, 1869.

Phil 8585.13.15   Frauestädt, C.M.J. Blicke in die intellectuelle, physische und moralische Welt. Leipzig, 1869.

Phil 5425.2A   Galton, F. Hereditary genius. London, 1869.

Phil 7072.6   Gerry, Elbridge T. The number "spirit" photograph case. N.Y., 1869.

Phil 5643.7   Goblet, H.F. A theory of sight, or How we see. London, 1869.

Phil 181.31   Graham, W. The true philosophy of mind. Louisville, 1869.

Phil 3552.119.5   Grote, Ludwig. Leibniz und seine Zeit. Hannover, 1869.

Phil 5520.24   Haig, James. Symbolism or mind matter, language as elements of thinking. Edinburgh, 1869.

NEDL Phil 7080.5.2   Hammond, W.A. Sleep and its derangements. Philadelphia, 1869.

Phil 3415.30.1   Hartmann, Eduard von. Philosophie des Unbewussten. Berlin, 1869.

Htn Phil 3801.446*   Hartmann, K.R.E. von. Schelling's positive Philosophie. Berlin, 1869.

Phil 3801.446.2   Hartmann, K.R.E. von. Schelling's positive Philosophie. Berlin, 1869.

Phil 5247.4.10   Hartsen, F.A. Untersuchungen über Psychologie. Leipzig, 1869.

Chronological Listing

Phil 3255.85　Hase, Karl A. Sebastian Frank von Wörd der Schwarmgeist. Leipzig, 1869.

Phil 6957.8　Haskell, E. The trial of Ebenezer Haskell in lunacy. Philadelphia, 1869.

Phil 8050.57.10　Hauch, J.C. Afhandlinger og aesthetiske betragtninger. Kjøbenhavn, 1869.

Phil 5757.1.6　Hazard, R.G. Two letters on causation and freedom. Boston, 1869.

Phil 182.58　Hebler, Carl. Philosophische Aufsätze. Leipzig, 1869.

Phil 3425.74.5　Hegel, Georg Wilhelm Friedrich. Hegel's first principle. Saint Louis, 1869.

Phil 8587.10.5　Hennell, S.S. Comparativism. London, 1869.

Phil 5047.22　Hoppe, James. Die kleine Logik. Paderborn, 1869.

Phil 7054.144　Horn, Henry J. Strange visitors. N.Y., 1869.

Phil 7059.12　Hull, Moses. The question settled. Boston, 1869.

Phil 3460.20　Jacobi, F.H. Nachlass. Ungedruckte Briefe. Leipzig, 1869.

Phil 9150.17　Jaeger, Gustav. Die Darwin'sche Theorie und ihre Stellung. Stuttgart, 1869.

Phil 6952.7.35　James, E. A memoir of John Conolly. London, 1869?

Phil 5049.7.5　Jevons, W.S. The substitution of similars. London, 1869.

Phil 5819.2.5　Joly, H. L'instinct. Paris, 1869.

Phil 3480.31.2　Kant, Immanuel. Critique de la raison pure. Paris, 1869. 2v.

Phil 3480.32.5　Kant, Immanuel. Critique of pure reason. London, 1869.

Phil 3480.50.30　Kant, Immanuel. Immanuel Kant's Kritik der Urteilskraft. Berlin, 1869.

Phil 3480.45.7　Kant, Immanuel. Kritik der praktischen Vernunft. Berlin, 1869.

Phil 3492.1　Kirchmann, J. Erläuterungen zu Kant's Kritik. Berlin, 1869-73. 7 pam.

Phil 3830.1.5　Kirchmann, J.H. von. Erläuterungen zu Benedict von Spinoza's Ethik. Berlin, 1869.

Phil 3492.22　Klinberg, A.G. Kants kritik af heibnizianismen. Upsala, 1869.

Phil 8411.3　Köstlin, K. Asthetik. pt.1-2. Tübingen, 1869.

Phil 3525.30　Krause, K.C.F. Emporleitende Theil der Philosophie. Prag, 1869.

Phil 6990.3.7　Lasserre, H. Notre-Dame de Lourdes. Paris, 1869.

Phil 6121.2.10　Laugel, A. Om själens problemer. Stockholm, 1869.

Phil 6121.3.3　Laugel, T. Mind and brain. N.Y., 1869. 2v.

Phil 8836.2　Lecky, W.E.H. History of European morals. London, 1869. 2v.

Phil 486.3　Lecomte, F.D. L'âme. Paris, 1869.

Phil 9171.4.12　Legouvé, E. Les pères et les enfants. La jeunesse. 13. éd. Paris, 1869.

Phil 5403.4.5　Lindner, Gustav. Lyckans problem. Stockholm, 1869.

Phil 3565.50　Lotze, Hermann. Mikrokosmus. Leipzig, 1869-72. 3v.

Phil 1190.4　Maccoll, N. Greek sceptics from Pyrrho to Sextus. London, 1869.

Phil 2125.40　McCosh, James. Philosophical papers. N.Y., 1869.

Phil 4170.7.60　Mamiani della Rovere, Terenzio. Le meditazioni cartesiane rinnovate nel seccolo XIX. Firenze, 1869.

Phil 187.10　Martin, T.H. Les sciences et la philosophie. Paris, 1869.

Phil 8592.6.12　Martineau, James. The new affinities of faith. Boston, 1869.

Phil 8592.6.11　Martineau, James. The new affinities of faith. London, 1869.

Phil 8887.10　Maurice, F.D. Social morality. London, 1869.

Phil 5460.3　Mayer, A. Die Sinnestäuschungen. Wien, 1869.

Phil 4570.1.83　Meden, Carl. Om Grubbes deduktion af rättsbegreppet. Uppsala, 1869.

Phil 3625.1.39.11　Mendelssohn, Moses. Phédon. Leipzig, 1869.

Phil 2496.83　Mignet, M. Notice historique sur la vie...de Victor Cousin. Paris, 1869.

Phil 5252.7.2　Mill, J. On the mind. London, 1869. 2v.

Phil 2138.2　Mill, John S. Gesammelte Werke. v.1-3, 4-6, 7-9, 10-12. Leipzig, 1869-80. 4v.

Htn　Phil 2138.60*　Mill, John S. The subjection of women. London, 1869.

NEDL　Phil 2138.35.3　Mill, John S. A system of logic. N.Y., 1869.

Phil 5252.13　Murphy, J.J. Habit and intelligence. London, 1869. 2v.

Phil 3665.2.35　Naumann, M.E.A. Die Naturwissenschaften und Materialismus. Bonn, 1869.

Phil 8620.8　Naville, E. Le problème du mal. Genève, 1869.

Phil 2805.40.34　Pascal, Blaise. Pensées. Paris, 1869.

Phil 3497.16　Paul, Ludwig. Kant's Lehre vom Idealen Christus. Kiel, 1869.

Phil 7054.167　Peebles, J.M. Seers of the ages, embracing spiritualism. Boston, 1869.

Phil 8595.4　Pfleiderer, O. Die Religion. Leipzig, 1869. 2v.

Phil 3552.119　Pichler, A. Die Theologie des Leibniz. München, 1869. 2v.

Phil 2840.50　Renouvier, C.B. Science de la morale. Paris, 1869. 2v.

Phil 8620.10　Ritter, H. Über das Böse und seine Folgen. Cotha, 1869.

Phil 2493.85　Robert, Louis. Les théories logiques de Condillac. Thèse. Paris, 1869.

Phil 8967.1.3　Rothe, R. Theologische Ethik. Wittenberg, 1869-71. 5v.

Phil 530.40.5　Rousselot, P. Les mystiques espagnols. Paris, 1869.

Phil 8707.3　Rudder, W. The mutual relations of natural science and theology. Philadelphia, 1869.

Phil 5768.6　Salzbrunner, B. Das Gesetz der Freiheit. Ein Beiträg zur Reinigung der Volksreligion. Nürnberg, 1869.

Phil 7054.34.5　Sargent, Epes. Planchette; or, The despair of science. Boston, 1869.

Phil 3800.720　Schelling, F.W.J. von. Aus Schellings Leben. In briefe. v.1, 2-3. Leipzig, 1869-70. 2v.

Phil 9178.5　Seymour, A. Home, the basis of the state. Boston, 1869.

Phil 4635.6.30　Sjöholm, L.A. Det historiska sammanhanget mellan Humes skepticism och Kants kriticism. Upsala, 1869.

Phil 2266.30.50A　Smith, Adam. Essays on I. Moral sentiment; II. Astronomical inquiries. London, 1869.

Phil 3425.282.5F　Spaventa, B. Studii sull'etica hegeliana; memoria. Napoli, 1869.

Phil 3819.40　Spinoza, Benedictus de. Korte verhandeling van God. Amsterdam, 1869.

Phil 3819.11　Spinoza, Benedictus de. Sämmtliche philosophische Werke. Berlin, 1869-71. 2v.

Phil 193.31.9　Spir, A. von. Forschung nach der Gewissheit. Leipzig, 1869.

Phil 193.31.13　Spir, A. von. Vorschlag an die Freunde einer vernünftigen Lebensführung. Leipzig, 1869.

Phil 3850.12.31　Stoy, Karl J. Philosophische Propädentik. Leipzig, 1869.

Phil 476.3.53　Strohecker, J.R. Die freie Naturbetrachtung. Augsburg, 1869.

Phil 8062.5　Taine, H.A. Philosophie de l'art en Grèce. Paris, 1869.

Phil 9179.11　Tommaséo, N. Consigli ai giovani. Milano, 1869.

Phil 3487.1.10　Trendelenburg, A. Kuno Fischer und sein Kant. Leipzig, 1869.

Phil 1870.102　Ueberweg, F. Berkeley's Abhandlung über Principien der menschlichen Erkenntnis. Berlin, 1869.

Phil 5260.1.3　Upham, T.C. Mental philosophy. N.Y., 1869. 2v.

Phil 8601.1　Vacherot, E. La religion. Paris, 1869.

Phil 2035.88.5　Veitch, J. Memoir of William Hamilton. Edinburgh, 1869.

Phil 3925.3.40　Weisse, Christian Hermann. Psychologie und Unsterblichkeitslehre. Leipzig, 1869.

Phil 3504.48　Wickenhagen, Ernst. Die Logik bei Kant. Inaug. Diss. Jena, 1869.

Phil 4655.1.35　Wikner, Pontus. Kultur och filosofi i deras förhällande till hvarandra. Stockholm, 1869.

Phil 1130.2　Zeller, Eduard. Die Philosophie der Griechen. Leipzig, 1869-79. 3v.

187-

Phil 2520.162　Schmid, Paul J. Die Prinzipien der menschischen Erkenntniss nach Descartes. Leipzig, 187-?

Phil 3842.1　Weise, H. Uber das Erste Buch der Ethik des Spinoza. Salzwede, 187-?

1870

Phil 175.13　Ampère, A.M. Philosophie. Paris, 1870.

Phil 8950.5　Anglican and International Christian Moral Science Association. Science and the gospel. London, 1870.

Phil 3482.3.5　Arnoldt, Emil. Kant's transcendentale idealität des Raumes und der zeit. Pt.1-5. Königsberg, 1870-72.

Phil 1850.50.8　Bacon, Francis. Neues Organon. J.H. Kirchmann. Berlin, 1870.

Phil 1850.15.5　Bacon, Francis. Works. London, 1870-72. 7v.

Phil 176.3.3　Bahnsen, J. Zum Verhältniss Zwischen Wille und Motiv. Lauenburg, 1870.

Phil 5041.3　Bain, Alexander. Logic. London, 1870. 2v.

Phil 7076.2.2　Benneville, George. Some remarkable passages in the life of Dr. George de Benneville. Germantown, Pa., 1870.

Phil 332.1　Bergmann, J. Grundlinien einer Theorie des Bewusstseins. Berlin, 1870.

Phil 476.6　Bertini, G.M. Schiarimenti sulla controversia fra spiritualismo e materialismo. Torino, 1870.

Phil 5041.12　Biedermann, Gustav. Zur logischen Frage. Prag, 1870.

Phil 176.61　Bierbower, A. Principles of a system of philosophy. N.Y., 1870.

Phil 801.4.5　Bouillier, F. Analyses des ouvrages de philosophie. 3. ed. Paris, 1870.

Phil 3821.15　Brasch, Moritz. Spinoza's System der Philosophie. Berlin, 1870.

NEDL　Phil 7054.123　Britten, Emma H. Modern American spiritualism. N.Y., 1870.

Phil 7054.123.2　Britten, Emma H. Modern American spiritualism. 4th ed. N.Y., 1870.

Phil 476.3.6　Büchner, L. L'homme selon la science. Paris, 1870.

Phil 8691.4　Burr, E.F. Pater mundi. 1st series. Boston, 1870.

Phil 177.4　Cantoni, C. Corso elementare di filosofia. Milan, 1870.

Phil 8430.8.5　Carpenter, Edward. The religious influence of art. Cambridge, 1870.

Phil 1850.116　Carrau, L. De sermonibus fidelibus F. Baconi Verulamii. Argentorat, 1870.

Phil 9420.6　Carrau, L. Théorie des passions. Strasbourg, 1870.

Phil 3552.267　Caspari, Otto. Leibniz' Philosophie. Leipzig, 1870.

Phil 9045.12　Chojeckiego, E. Patrjotyzm i objawy Jego u niektórych narodów. Paryz, 1870.

Phil 6520.14　Christiany, L. Eva von Buttler die Messaline und Muckerin...Mysterien des Pietismus. Stuttgart, 1870.

Phil 850.10　Cocker, B.F. Christianity and Greek philosophy. N.Y., 1870.

Phil 2490.73　Comte, Auguste. Lettres d'Auguste Comte à M. Valat. Paris, 1870.

Phil 2493.45.4　Condillac, Etienne Bonnot. Abhandlung über die Empfindungen. Berlin, 1870.

Phil 7054.6.35　Davis, A.J. The fountain. 1st ed. Boston, 1870.

Phil 7054.6.9　Davis, A.J. The great harmonia. 4th ed. Boston, 1870. 5v.

Phil 7054.6.8　Davis, A.J. The present age and inner life. 3d ed. Boston, 1870.

Phil 3805.85　Dilthey, Wilhelm. Leben Schleiermachers. Berlin, 1870.

Phil 7150.11　Douay, Edmond. Suicide, ou La mort volontaire. Paris, 1870.

Phil 2805.89　Dreydorff, J.G. Pascal sein Leben und seine Kämpfe. Leipzig, 1870.

Phil 2885.85　Empart, L. L'empirisme et le naturalisme contemporain. Paris, 1870.

Phil 672.22　Eyfferth, Max. Der Begriff der Zeit. Berlin, 1870.

Phil 180.1　Fabre, J. Cours de philosophie. Paris, 1870.

Phil 180.42　Falco, Francesco. L'uomo:saggio popolare. Piacenza, 1870.

Phil 3270.2.31　Fick, Adolf. Die Welt als Vorstellung. Würzburg, 1870.

Phil 8880.8.2　Fleming, W. A manual of moral philosophy. London, 1870.

Phil 5925.3.25　Fowler, O.S. Sexual science; including manhood, womanhood and their mutual interrelations. Philadelphia, 1870.

Phil 5925.3.15　Fowler, O.S. Sexuality restored. Boston, 1870.

Phil 8880.82　Franck, A. Menniskans sedliga lif. Stockholm, 1870.

Phil 2005.6.31　Friswell, J.H. Hä och der i verlden. Stockholm, 1870.

Phil 9166.5　Godimus, Z.J. L'esprit de famille étude morale. Paris, 1870.

Phil 3488.18　Grapengiesser, C. Kants Lehre von Raum und Zeit, Kuno Fischer und Trendelenburg. Jena, 1870.

Phil 9550.2　Grote, J. An examination of the utilitarian philosophy. Cambridge, 1870.

Phil 182.1　Hagemann, G. Elemente der Philosophie. v.1-3. Münster, 1870.

Phil 3110.89　Harless, G.C.A. von. Jakob Böhme und die Alchymisten. Berlin, 1870.

Phil 182.41.5　Hartenstein, G. Historisch-philosophische Abhandlungen. Leipzig, 1870.

Phil 9347.7　Hepworth, G. Rocks and shoals. Boston, 1870.

Phil 6957.3　Hill, R.G. Lunacy: Its past and its present. London, 1870.

Phil 2055.2.20　Hinton, James. Selections from manuscripts. London, 1870. 4v.

Phil 8882.14　Hodgson, S.H. The theory of practice. London, 1870. 2v.

Phil 2648.43.10　Holbach, Paul Henri T. Letters to Eugenia. Boston, 1870.

1870 - cont.

Phil 8662.5 — Holyoake, George Jacob. Secularism, scepticism and atheism. London, 1870.

NEDL Phil 5929.2.5 — How to read character. N.Y., 1870.

Phil 4110.2.81 — In morte della M. sa Marianna Florenzi Waddington tributo di dolore. Perugia, 1870.

Phil 2668.55 — Janet, Paul A.R. Petits éléments de morale. Paris, 1870.

Phil 5049.4.4.5 — Jevons, W.S. Elementary lessons in logic. London, 1870.

Phil 3829.2 — Joel, Manuel. Spinoza's theologisch-politischen Traktat. Breslau, 1870.

Phil 2138.91 — Jordan, W. Program des königlichen Gymnasiums. Stuttgart, 1870.

Phil 184.14 — Jourdain, Charles. Nociones de filosofia. Valparaiso, 1870.

Phil 3492.10 — Kalich, Karl. Cantii, Schellingii, Fichtii de filio divino sententiam. Diss. Lipsiae, 1870.

Phil 3480.28.12 — Kant, Immanuel. Kleinere Schriften zur Ethik und Religionsphilosophie. Berlin, 1870.

Phil 3480.24.5 — Kant, Immanuel. Kleinere Schriften zur Logik und Metaphysik. Berlin, 1870.

Phil 3480.63.15 — Kant, Immanuel. Metaphysik der Sitten. Leipzig, 1870.

Phil 5250.20 — Kaulich, W. Handbuch der Psychologie. Graz, 1870. 3 pam.

Phil 3830.1 — Kirchmann, J.H. von. Erlauterungen zu Benedict von Spinoza's. Berlin, 1870-72. 5 pam.

Phil 3425.235 — Köstlin, K.R. Hegel. Tübingen, 1870.

Phil 8666.1 — Lacordaire, P.J.B.H.D. God. London, 1870.

Phil 2115.35.25 — Locke, J. Essay concerning human understanding. London, 1870.

Phil 5052.22 — McCosh, James. The laws of discursive thought. London, 1870.

Phil 5052.22.3 — McCosh, James. The laws of discursive thought. N.Y., 1870.

Phil 2412.1 — Margerie, M.A. Philosophie contemporaine. Paris, 1870.

Phil 8637.1 — Martin, T.H. La vie future. Paris, 1870.

Phil 6122.1 — Maudsley, H. Body and mind. London, 1870.

Phil 812.3.3.5 — Maurice, J.F.D. Mediaeval philosophy. London, 1870.

Phil 3494.20 — Meyer, Jürgen B. Kant's Psychologie. Berlin, 1870.

Phil 3425.229.15 — Michelet, C.L. Hegel, der unwiderlegte Weltphilosoph. Leipzig, 1870.

Phil 8837.1.16 — Mill, James. A fragment on Mackintosh. London, 1870.

Cg Phil 2138.37 — Mill, John S. The student's handbook...of Mill's...logic. London, 1870.

Phil 2035.86 — Murray, J.C. Outline of Sir William Hamilton's philosophy. Boston, 1870.

Phil 3552.242.5 — Neff, L. Gottfried Wilhelm Leibniz als Sprachforscher und Etynologie. v.1-2. Heidelburg, 1870-71.

Phil 5090.3A — Newman, J.H. Grammar of assent. N.Y., 1870.

Phil 2733.83 — Ollé-Laprune, L. La philosophie de Malebranche. Paris, 1870. 2v.

Phil 3552.296 — Pfleiderer, Edmund. Gottfried Wilhelm Leibniz. Leipzig, 1870.

Phil 3552.296.10 — Pfleiderer, Edmund. Leibniz als Verfasser von Zwölf Anonymen. Leipzig, 1870.

Phil 5000.5 — Pierce, C.S. Logic of relatives. Cambridge, 1870.

Phil 7054.146 — Ramsdell, Elizabeth. Spirit life of Theodore Parker. Boston, 1870.

Phil 9357.5 — Reed, James. Man and woman, equal but different. Boston, 1870.

Phil 5057.1 — Reichlin-Meldegg, K.A.F. System der Logik. v.1-2. Wien, 1870.

Phil 492.1 — Renaud, H. Le matérialisme et la nature. Paris, 1870.

Phil 4630.1.31 — Ribbing, Sigurd. Grundlinier till anthropololgien. 4. uppl. Upsala, 1870.

Phil 5227.1 — Ribot, T. La psychologie anglaise contemporaine. Paris, 1870.

Phil 3791.45 — Riehl, Alois. Realistische Grundzüge. Graz, 1870.

Phil 8597.13 — Romang, J.P. Über Wichtigere Fragen der Religion. Heidelberg, 1870.

Phil 3425.91.13A — Rosenkranz, K. Hegel als deutscher Nationalphilosoph. Leipzig, 1870.

Phil 4210.62 — Rosmini-Serbati, Antonio. Letteratura e arti belle. pt.1-2. Intra, 1870-73.

Phil 3808.108.5 — Scheffer, Wessel. Arthur Schopenhauer; de philosophie. Leiden, 1870.

Phil 3805.93 — Schleiermacher, Friedrich. Philosophische Sittenlehre. Berlin, 1870.

Phil 8643.1 — Schneider, L. Die Unsterblichkeitsidee im Glauben. Regensburg, 1870.

Phil 3808.63.10 — Schopenhauer, Arthur. Über das Sehn und die Farben. 3. Aufl. Leipzig, 1870.

Phil 6968.20 — Schroeder van der Kolk, J.L.K. The pathology and therapeutics of mental diseases. London, 1870.

Phil 2050.202 — Schultze, W.F. Hume und Kant über den Causalbegriff. Inaug. Diss. Rostock, 1870.

Phil 5058.7.5 — Schuppe, W. Das menschliche Denken. Berlin, 1870.

Phil 818.1 — Schwegler, F.C.A. Geschichte der Philosophie. Stuttgart, 1870.

Phil 6750.7.5 — Seguin, E. New facts and remarks concerning idiocy. N.Y., 1870.

Phil 2262.34 — Shaftesbury, A.A.C. Characteristicks. v.1. London, 1870.

DL Phil 8893.14.8 — Smiles, Samuel. Self-help. N.Y., 1870.

Phil 4115.91.2 — Spaventa, B. La filosofia di Gioberti. Napoli, 1870.

Phil 2270.30 — Spencer, Herbert. First principles. London, 1870.

Phil 2270.30.3 — Spencer, Herbert. Principles of psychology. London, 1870-72. 2v.

Phil 1850.115 — Stapfer, P. Qualis sapientae antiquae laudator qualis interpres Franciscus Baconus exstiterit. Paris, 1870.

Phil 2885.30.5 — Taine, Hippolyte Adolphe. De l'intelligence. 2. éd. v.1-2. Paris, 1870. 2v.

Phil 4120.3.90 — Titoli del professore Vincenzo di Giovanni. Palermo, 1870.

Phil 8709.1.5 — Townsend, L.T. Credo. Boston, 1870.

Phil 3890.1.45A — Trendelenburg, A. Logische Untersuchungen. 3. Aufl. Leipzig, 1870.

Phil 5059.11 — Turrell, H.J. A manual of logic. London, 1870.

Phil 4800.8 — Tyszyński, Aleksander. Piérwsze zasady krytyki powszechnéj. v.1-2. Warszawa, 1870.

Phil 9075.8 — Vacherot, E. La science et la conscience. Paris, 1870.

Phil 5070.2 — Venn, J. On some of the characteristics of belief; scientific and religious. London, 1870.

Phil 9075.9 — Waddington, C.T. Dieu et la conscience. Paris, 1870.

Phil 8610.870 — Was, H. Geschichiedenis van het scepticisme der zeventiende eeuw in de voornaamste europeesche staten. 1e aflevering. Utrecht, 1870.

Phil 5832.1.4 — Watson, John S. The reasoning power in animals. 2. ed. London, 1870.

Phil 4655.1.45 — Wikner, Pontus. Lärobok i anthropologien. Upsala, 1870.

1870 - cont.

Phil 4655.1.64 — Wikner, Pontus. Undersökningar angående den materialistiska verldsåskådningen. Stockholm, 1870.

Phil 3842.2 — Willis, R. Benedict de Spinoza. London, 1870.

Phil 270.53 — Windelband, W. Die Lehren vom Zufall. Berlin, 1870.

Phil 3504.16.5 — Wolff, Hermann. Die metaphysische Grundanschauung Kants. Leipzig, 1870.

Phil 1130.8A — Zeller, Eduard. The Stoics, Epicureans, and Sceptics. London, 1870.

Phil 200.3.7 — Zimmermznn, R. Studien und Kritiken zur Philosophie und Aesthetik. v.1-2. Wien, 1870.

1871

Phil 8625.2.5 — Abbot, Ezra. The literature of the doctrine of a future life. N.Y., 1871.

Phil 9160.2.15 — Abbott, Jacob. The child at Howe. N.Y., 1871.

Phil 8625.1.5 — Alger, W.R. A critical history of the doctrine of a future life. N.Y., 1871.

Phil 8582.3.2 — Argyll, G.D.C. The reign of law. London, 1871.

Phil 3808.80 — Asher, D. Arthur Schopenhauer. Berlin, 1871.

Phil 270.2.5 — Barrett, T.S. A new view of causation. London, 1871.

Phil 176.9 — Bascom, J. Science, philosophy and religion. N.Y., 1871.

Phil 8581.3 — Beale, L.S. Life theories. London, 1871.

Phil 3100.55 — Beneke, F.E. The elements of psychology. London, 1871.

Phil 1870.12A — Berkeley, G. Works. Oxford, 1871. 4v.

Phil 8826.2 — Blackie, J.S. Four phases of morals. Edinburgh, 1871.

Phil 4070.1.50 — Bonavino, Cristoforo. Saggi di critica e polemica per Ausonio Franchi (pseud.). Milano, 1870-72. 3v.

Phil 4070.1.45 — Bonavino, Cristoforo. Su la teoria del giudizio. Milano, 1871. 2v.

Phil 8610.870.25 — Boston lectures, 1870-1871. Christianity and scepticism. Boston, 1871. 2v.

Phil 4515.30.2 — Boström, C.J. Satser om lag och lagstiftning med tillägg och anmärkningar å nyo utgifne. 2e uppl. Upsala, 1871.

Phil 1135.57 — Bouché-Leclerq, A. Placita Graecorum. Paris, 1871.

Phil 9150.6 — Carneri, B. Sittlichkeit und Darwinismus. Wien, 1871.

Phil 3484.2 — Cohen, H. Kant's Theorie der Erfahrung. Berlin, 1871.

Phil 7060.107 — Cox, E.W. Spiritualism answered by science. London, 1871.

Phil 600.6 — Croly, D.G. A positivist primer. N.Y., 1871.

Phil 672.22.5 — Eyfferth, Max. Über die Zeit; philosophische Untersuchung. Berlin, 1871.

Phil 6675.1A — Fahnestock, W.B. Statu volism. Chicago, 1871.

Phil 1158.7 — Ferri, Luigi. L'epicureismo e l'atomismo. Firenze, 1871.

Phil 5755.1.3 — Fischer, J.C. Die Freiheit des menschlichen Willens und die Einheit der Naturgesetze. 2. Aufl. Leipzig, 1871.

Phil 8660.3.7 — Flammarion, C. Dieu dans la nature. 7. ed. Paris, 1871.

Phil 6955.5 — Foville, A. Étude clinique de la folie. Paris, 1871.

Phil 5925.2.13 — Fowler, O.S. Life: its science, laws...improvement. Boston, 1871.

Phil 1870.84.3 — Fraser, Alexander Campbell. Life and letters of George Berkeley. London, 1871.

Phil 3808.83 — Frauenstädt, C.M.J. Schopenhauer-Lexikon. Leipzig, 1871. 2v.

Htn Phil 3808.83.1* — Frauenstädt, C.M.J. Schopenhauer-Lexikon. Leipzig, 1871. 2v.

Phil 5046.5 — Garden, F. An outline of logic or the use of teachers and students. 2nd ed. London, 1871.

Phil 4115.55 — Gioberti, V. Essay on the beautiful. London, 1871.

Phil 3488.18.5 — Grapengiesser, C. Erklärung und Vertheidigung von Kant's Kritik der reinen Vernueft wider die "sogenannten" Erläuterungen des J.H.v. Kirchmann. Jena, 1871.

Phil 8881.16 — Gratry, A.J.A. La morale et la loi de l'histoire. Paris, 1871.

Phil 2270.81 — Greene, W.B. Facts of consciousness and philosophy of Spencer. Boston, 1871.

Phil 6956.2 — Griesinger, W. Die Pathologie und Therapie der psychischen Krankheiten. Braunschweig, 1871.

Phil 5722.1 — Half-hour Recreations. Half-hour recreations in popular science. no.6. Boston, 1871.

Phil 3425.278 — Harms, F. Zur Erinnerungen an Georg W.F. Hegel. Berlin, 1871.

Phil 3415.40 — Hartmann, Eduard von. Das Ding an sich. Berlin, 1871.

Htn Phil 6117.5*A — Holmes, O.W. Mechanism in thought and morals. Boston, 1871.

Phil 8882.21.12 — Hopkins, M. The law of love and love as a law. 3rd ed. N.Y., 1871.

Phil 182.72 — Huber, J. Kleine Schriften. Leipzig, 1871.

Phil 1750.6 — Huet, F. La révolution philosophique. Paris, 1871.

Phil 183.4 — Isola, I.G. Il metodo secondo dialogo filosofico. Modena, 1871.

Phil 3805.91 — Iuäbicke, R. Über Schleiermachers erkenntnisstheoretische Grundausicht. Berlin, 1871.

Phil 5049.4.4.7 — Jevons, W.S. Elementary lessons in logic. London, 1871.

NEDL Phil 3480.66.3 — Kant, Immanuel. The metaphysics of ethics. 3. ed. Edinburgh, 1871.

Phil 9350.3.15 — Keddie, H. Heroines in obscurity. London, 1871.

Phil 7054.109 — King, M.M. The spiritual philosophy vs. diabolism. Boston, 1871.

Phil 5250.1 — Kirchmann, J.H. von. Die Lehre vom Wissen. Berlin, 1871.

Phil 3830.5 — Kratz, H. Spinoza's Ansicht über den Zweckbegriff. Newied, 1871.

Phil 3525.55 — Krause, K.C.F. Ideal de la humanidad para la vida. 2. ed. Madrid, 1871.

Phil 2725.11.30 — Lachelier, Jules. Du fondement de l'induction. Paris, 1871.

Phil 3900.1.82 — Lange, F.A. Friedrich Ueberweg. Berlin, 1871.

Phil 3831.1 — Ledinský, F. Die Philosophie Spinoza's. Budweis, 1871.

Phil 2490.81.5 — Lewes, G.H. Comte's philosophy of the sciences. London, 1871.

Phil 9351.10 — Lewis, D. Our girls. N.Y., 1871.

Phil 3831.5 — Linde, A. van der. Benedictus Spinoza. Gravenhage, 1871.

Phil 5821.2.3 — Lindsay, W.L. Physiology and pathology of mind in the lower animals. Edinburgh, 1871.

Phil 6961.4 — Lunt, Adeline T.P. Behind the bars. Boston, 1871.

Phil 6121.13 — Lussana, F. Fisiologia dei centri nervosi encefalici. Padova, 1871. 2v.

Phil 2125.62.5 — McCosh, James. Christianity and positivism. N.Y., 1871.

Phil 2733.36 — Malebranche, Nicolas. Entretiens sur la métaphysique. Paris, 1871.

Phil 2733.3 — Malebranche, Nicolas. Oeuvres. v.1-4. Paris, 1871. 2v.

Phil 2130.31 — Mansel, H.L. Metaphysics. N.Y., 1871.

Phil 7068.71.8 — Massey, G. Concerning spiritualism. London, 1871.

Phil 6122.1.3 — Maudsley, H. Body and mind. N.Y., 1871.

Phil 3494.4 — Michelis, F. Kant vor und nach dem Jahre 1770. Braunsberg, 1871.

1871 - cont.

Phil 2138.40.2.5 — Mill, John S. On liberty. London, 1871.
Phil 2138.50.5 — Mill, John S. Utilitarianism. 4th ed. London, 1871.
Phil 3494.7 — Montgomery, E. Die Kant'sche Erkenntnisslehre. München, 1871.
Phil 8888.1 — Nahlowsky, J.W. Allgemeine praktische Philosophie. Leipzig, 1871.
Phil 7054.91 — Parisi, G. Two appeals to the leaders of spiritualism. Florence, 1871.
Phil 2805.26.7 — Pascal, Blaise. Pascal de l'esprit géométrique. Paris, 1871.
Phil 8890.6 — Paulsen, F. Symbolae ad systemata philosophiae moralis. Berolini, 1871.
Phil 5255.4.5 — Plank, K.C. Seele und Geist. Leipzig, 1871.
Phil 9355.5 — Pomeroy, Marcus. Sense. N.Y., 1871.
Phil 190.15 — Porter, N. Sciences of nature vs. sciences of man. N.Y., 1871.
Phil 4114.80 — Racioppi, G. Antonio Genovesi. Napoli, 1871.
Phil 817.13 — Ragnisco, P. Storia critica delle categorie dai primordj della filosofia Greca sino ad Hagel. v.1-2. Firenze, 1871.
Phil 192.3.8 — Rands, W.B. Lilliput lectures. London, 1871.
Phil 6967.5.8 — Ray, Isaac. Treatise on the medical jurisprudence of insanity. 5. ed. Boston, 1871.
Phil 3791.06 — Riehl, Alois. Moral und Dogma. n.p., 1871-92. 5 pam.
Phil 7054.37.30 — Rivail, H.L.D. El cielo y el infierno. 4. ed. Barcelona, 1871.
Phil 7054.37.33 — Rivail, H.L.D. El génesis, los milagros. Barcelona, 1871.
Phil 672.8 — Rosanes, J. Über die neuesten Untersuchungen in Betreff unserer Anschauung vom Raume. Breslau, 1871.
Phil 3499.4 — Rowland, D. Essay...unsolved ethical questions in Kant's. London, 1871.
Phil 8673.2 — Samuelson, J. Views of the deity. London, 1871.
Phil 3500.3 — Scherer, G. Kritik über Kant's Subjektivität und Apriorität des Raumes und der Zeit. Frankfurt, 1871.
Phil 193.120 — Schöpfung und Mensch. Hamburg, 1871.
Phil 3850.21.91 — Schroeder, B. Leopold Schmid's Leben und Denken. Leipzig, 1871.
Phil 4018.1 — Siciliani, P. Sul rinnovamento della filosofia positiva in Italia. Firenze, 1871.
Phil 5115.2 — Sigwart, C. Beigefügt sind Beiträge zur Lehre vom hypothetischen Urtheile. Tübingen, 1871.
Phil 2490.86 — Spencer, Herbert. The classification of the sciences...philosophy of M. Comte. London, 1871.
Phil 2270.40.3 — Spencer, Herbert. Essays. N.Y., 1871.
Phil 2270.45.50 — Spencer, Herbert. Les premiers principes. Paris, 1871.
Phil 2270.50.2 — Spencer, Herbert. Recent discussions in science. N.Y., 1871.
Phil 3819.10.14 — Spinoza, Benedictus de. Benedictus de Spinoza's Sämmtliche Werke. Stuttgart, 1871. 2v.
Phil 8893.60 — Stein, F.J. Historisch-kritische Darstellung der pathologischen Moralprincipien. Wien, 1871.
Phil 193.36 — Steudel, A. Philosophie im Umriss. Stuttgart, 1871-1884. 6v.
Phil 8419.37 — Stoeckl, A. Grundriss der Ästhetik. Mainz, 1871.
Phil 6968.10 — Storer, H.R. The causation...reflex insanity in women. Boston, 1871.
Phil 8893.27 — Sturman, E.A. Inaugural dissertation, moral philosophy. London, 1871.
Phil 5258.40 — Sullivan, H. Mediation; the function of thought. Andover, 1871.
Phil 493.3 — Svenson, S.G. Betraktelseröfver den materialistiska och idealistiska verldsåsigten. Stockholm, 1871.
NEDL Phil 2885.31.1 — Taine, Hippolyte Adolphe. On Intelligence. N.Y., 1871.
Phil 2885.31 — Taine, Hippolyte Adolphe. On intelligence. pt. 1-2. London, 1871.
Phil 8894.4 — Thomassen, J.H. Das Evangelium der Wahrheit und Freiheit. Leipzig, 1871.
Phil 8599.2 — Thring, E. Thoughts on life science. London, 1871.
Phil 5060.1.5 — Ueberweg, F. System of logic. London, 1871.
Phil 5230.1 — Ullersperger, J.B. Die Geschichte der Psychologie und der Psychiatrik in Spanien. Würzburg, 1871.
Phil 3841.1.15 — Vloten, J. van. Benedictus de Spinoza. 2. Aufl. Schiedam, 1871.
Phil 497.3 — Weis, L. Anti-Materialismus. v.1-2, 3. Berlin, 1871-73. 2v.
Phil 8602.4 — Weiss, J. American religion. Boston, 1871.
Phil 6972.18 — West, Charles. On some disorders. Philadelphia, 1871.
Phil 4655.1.70 — Wikner, Pontus. Uppsatser i religiösa ämnen. Stockholm, 1871.
Phil 5832.2 — Wilson, W.D. Lectures...psychology: thought, action. Ithaca, 1871.
Phil 3915.44 — Wundt, Wilhelm. Untersuchungen zur Mechanik der Nerven. v.1-2. Erlangen, 1871-76.
Phil 3507.4 — Zimmerman, R. Über Kant's Widerlegung des Idealismus von Berkeley. Wien, 1871.

1872

Phil 175.2 — Alaux, J.E. L'analyse métaphysique. Paris, 1872.
Phil 175.5.5 — Amersin, F. Populäre Philosophie oder leichtfassliche Einfuhrung in die Weisheitslehre. Graz, 1872.
Phil 175.21 — Andrews, S.P. Basic outlines of universology. N.Y., 1872.
Phil 8580.18 — Araiztegui, R.M. Bosquejo de un paralelo de la relation catholica. Habana, 1872.
Phil 5241.2.21.5 — Bain, A. The senses and the intellect. 3. ed. N.Y., 1872.
Phil 270.2 — Barrett, T.S. Philosophy of science...on cause and effect. London, 1872.
Phil 176.10 — Baumann, Julius J. Philosophie. Leipzig, 1872.
Phil 8620.22 — Beard, J.R. Autobiography of Satan. London, 1872.
Phil 8626.3 — Blanche, C.I. Le surnaturel. Paris, 1872.
Phil 5585.52 — Böse, Karl G. Über Sinneswahrnehmung und deren Entwicklung zur Intelligenz. Braunschweig, 1872.
Phil 176.74.5 — Bonatelli, F. La coscienza e il meccanismo interiore. Padova, 1872.
Phil 3890.1.81 — Bonitz, Hermann. Zur Erinnerung an Friedrich Adolf Trendelenburg. Boston, 1872.
Phil 8581.9 — Braithwaite, H.T. Esse and posse. London, 1872.
Phil 476.3.7 — Büchner, L. Man in the past, present and future. London, 1872.
Phil 476.3.5 — Büchner, L. Der Mensch. Leipzig, 1872.
Phil 2115.125 — Burger, D. Locke's bewijs voor het bestaan van God. Amersfoort, 1872.
Phil 4575.93 — Bygdén, Anders L. Benjamin Höijer. Akademisk afhandling. Upsala, 1872.
X Cg Phil 9245.44 — Calder, Alexander. The man of the future. London, 1872.
Phil 8877.1.2 — Calderwood, H. Handbook of moral philosophy. London, 1872.

1872 - cont.

Phil 7080.1 — Cappie, J. Causation of sleep. Edinburgh, 1872.
Phil 177.6 — Carey, H.C. The unity of law. Philadelphia, 1872.
Phil 5812.1.2 — Chadbourne, P.A. Instinct. 2nd ed. N.Y., 1872.
Phil 8403.24 — Conti, Augusto. Il bello nel vero o estetica. Firenze, 1872. 2v.
Phil 7068.71.2 — Cox, E.W. Spiritualism answered by science. N.Y., 1872.
X Cg Phil 5400.18.50 — Darwin, Charles. The expression of the emotions in man and animals. London, 1872.
Phil 8404.5 — Day, Henry. The science of aesthetics. New Haven, 1872.
Phil 1170.10 — Decoster, V. Des antécédents du Néoplatonisme. Bruxelles, 1872.
Phil 178.3 — Dejean de Fonroque, Numd. Croyances philosophiques. Paris, 1872.
Phil 5243.4 — Delaperche, H. Essai de philosophie analytique. Paris, 1872.
Phil 6060.9 — Desbarrolles, A. Les mystères de l'écriture; art de juger les hommes. Paris, 1872.
Phil 8583.15 — Dodge, Ebenezer. Evidences of Christianity. Boston, 1872.
Phil 178.10 — Dressler, J.G. Grundlehren der Psychologie und Logik. Leipzig, 1872.
Phil 8050.50 — Egger, Alais. Vorschule der Ästhetik. Wien, 1872.
Phil 3246.55.3 — Fichte, Johann Gottlieb. Reden an die deutsche Nation. Leipzig, 1872.
Phil 8630.6.4 — Figuier, L. Le lendemain de la mort. 4e éd. Paris, 1872.
Phil 1850.106 — Finch, A. Elley. On the inductive philosophy. London, 1872.
Phil 4235.1.82 — Fiorentino, Francesco. Bernardino Telesio ossia studi storici su l'idea della natura nel risorgimento italiano. Firenze, 1872-74. 2v.
Phil 3415.80 — Fischer, J.C. Hartmann's Philosophie des Unbewussten. Leipzig, 1872.
Phil 6955.3 — Fisher, T.W. Plain talk about insanity. Boston, 1872.
Htn Phil 5245.7* — Fiske, J. The composition of mind. N.Y., 1872. 3 pam.
X Cg Phil 180.21 — Fortlage, Karl. Sechs philosophische Vorträge. 2. Ausg. Jena, 1872.
Phil 5755.3 — Fouillée, A. La liberté et le déterminisme. Paris, 1872.
Phil 180.8 — Franck, A. Moralistes et philosophes. Paris, 1872.
Phil 3487.16 — Frauenstädt, J. Immanuel Kant. Leipzig, 1872.
Phil 3808.84 — Frommann, H. Arthur Schopenhauer. Jena, 1872.
Phil 287.2 — Giera, Jules. Les deux creations. Paris, 1872.
Phil 400.2 — Graham, W. Idealism. London, 1872.
Phil 2035.51.15 — Hamilton, William. The metaphysics of Sir William Hamilton. Boston, 1872.
Phil 3415.38 — Hartmann, Eduard von. Gesammelte philosophische Abhandlungen Philosophie Unbewussten. Berlin, 1872.
Phil 3415.30.1.2 — Hartmann, Eduard von. Philosophie des Unbewussten. 4. Aufl. Berlin, 1872.
Phil 3415.35 — Hartmann, Eduard von. Das Umbewusste...Physiologie. Berlin, 1872.
Phil 5247.4.5 — Hartsen, F.A. Princepes de psychologie. Paris, 1872.
Phil 5047.2.5 — Hartsen, F.A. Principes de logique exposés d'après une méthode nouvelle. Paris, 1872.
Phil 1512.1.2 — Haureau, B. Histoire de la philosophie scolastique. Paris, 1872-80. 3v.
Phil 5247.6.1 — Haven, J. Mental philosophy. Boston, 1872.
Phil 7054.106.5 — Hazard, T.R. Eleven days at Moravia. Boston, 1872.
Phil 7054.106 — Hazard, T.R. Mediums and mediumship. Boston, 1872.
Phil 1135.80 — Heinze, M. Die Lehre vom Logos. Oldenburg, 1872.
Phil 2655.5.30 — Hello, E. L'homme. Paris, 1872.
Phil 8882.15 — Hoefer, F. L'homme devant ses oeuvres. Paris, 1872.
Phil 3007.6 — Høffding, H. Philosophien i Tydskland efter Hegel. Kjøbenhavn, 1872.
Phil 182.20 — Hoffmann, K. Philosophische Propädeutik. Passan, 1872.
Phil 7068.72.20 — Hoppe, I. Hellsehen des Unbewussten. Frieburg., 1872.
Phil 5247.12 — Horwicz, A. Psychologische Analysen. v.1-2. Halle, 1872-78. 3v.
Phil 5817.8 — Houzeau, Jean C. Études sur les facultés mentales des animaux. Mons, 1872. 2v.
Phil 2520.132 — Hunze, Max. Die Sittenlehre des Descartes. Leipzig, 1872.
Htn Phil 8663.3.31* — Ingersoll, Robert G. An oration on the Gods. Peoria, 1872.
Phil 270.9 — Jamieson, G. Causality. London, 1872.
Phil 3808.139 — Jellinck, G. Die Weltanschauungen Leibnitz und Schopenhauer's ihre Gründe und ihre Berechtigung. Wien, 1872.
Phil 3552.88 — Jellinek, G. Die Weltanschauungen Leibnitz' und Schopenhauer's, ihre Gründe und ihre Berechtigung. Wien, 1872.
Phil 5249.10 — Jessen, Peter. Physiologie des menschlichen Denkens. Hannover, 1872.
Phil 2050.83 — Jodl, F. Leben und Philosophie David Hume's. Halle, 1872.
Phil 5643.14 — Kaiser, H. Compendium der physiologische Optik. Wiesbaden, 1872.
Phil 3480.28.15 — Kant, Immanuel. Kleinere Schriften zur Natur- Philosophie. v.1-2. Berlin, 1872-73.
Phil 485.1.5 — Körner, F. Thierseele und Menschengeist. Leipzig, 1872.
Phil 3492.4 — Kroeger, A.E. Immanuel Kant. New Haven, 1872.
Phil 186.1 — Landon, E. Le spiritualisme. Paris, 1872.
Phil 270.25 — L'Ange Huet, J. Niewve oplossing van een oud vraagstuk. Leiden, 1872.
NEDL Phil 2035.83 — Leaves from my writing desk. London, 1872.
Phil 8591.3 — Leifchild, J.R. The higher ministry of nature. London, 1872.
Phil 8412.5 — Lévêque, C. La science du beau, ses principes, ses applications et son histoire. 2. éd. Paris, 1872. 2v.
Phil 8591.7 — Liddon, H.P. Some elements of religion. London, 1872.
Phil 1135.32 — Liebeck, H. Quaestiones Duae de Philosophia Graecorum. Halle, 1872.
Phil 5251.7 — Lindner, G.A. Lehrbuch der empiriochen Psychologie. Wien, 1872.
Phil 8961.8 — Lindwurm, A. Die metaphysische Wurzel die christlichen Ethik. Berlin, 1872.
Phil 2115.49.13 — Locke, J. Versuch über den menschlichen Verstand. Berlin, 1872-73. 2v.
Phil 3831.4 — Loewenhardt, S.E. Benedict von Spinoza. Berlin, 1872.
Phil 8702.2.9 — McCausland, D. Adam and the adamite. London, 1872.
Phil 3494.1 — Mahaffy, J.P. Kant's critical philosophy. v.1,3. London, 1872.
Phil 8685.5 — Manning, J.M. Half truths and the truth. Boston, 1872.
Phil 187.34.5 — Marin, V. Elementos de la filosofia del espiritu humano. 3d ed. Santiago, 1872.
Phil 6122.1.14 — Maudsley, H. The physiology of mind. N.Y., 1872.
Phil 9075.6 — Maurice, J.F.D. The conscience. London, 1872.
Phil 8592.42 — Medina. Conjunto de las doctrinas y filosofías del siglo comparadas con los conocimientos modernos. Madrid, 1872.

1872 - cont.

Phil 3808.99 — Meyer, J.B. Weltelend und Weltschmerz. Bonn, 1872.
Phil 2138.35.10 — Mill, John S. System der deductiven und inductiven Logik. Leipzig, 1872. 3 pam.
Phil 2138.35.3.15A — Mill, John S. A system of logic. 8th ed. London, 1872. 2v.
Phil 5643.17 — Monck, W.H.S. Space and vision. Dublin, 1872.
Phil 8637.4 — Moody, L. The problem of life and immortality. Boston, 1872.
Phil 8592.46 — Mortier, Lowis. Le problème de la vie. Paris, 1872.
Phil 7068.72 — Müller, M. Triumph of the blessed sacrament or History of Nicola Aubry. Baltimore, 1872.
Phil 8668.1.10 — Naville, E. Det ondas problem. Stockholm, 1872.
Phil 8415.7.13 — Oeser, C. Briefe an eine Jungfrau über die Hauptgegenstände der Ästhetik. 13. Aufl. Leipzig, 1872.
Phil 5764.1 — Otto, F.W. Die Freiheit des Menschen. Gütersloh, 1872.
Phil 7060.27.5 — Owen, R.D. The debatable land between this world and the next. N.Y., 1872.
Phil 525.21.2 — Perty, M. Die mystischen Erscheinungen der menschlichen Natur. Bd.1-2. 2e Aufl. Leipzig, 1872.
Phil 190.11 — Pezzani, A. Une philosophie nouvelle. Paris, 1872.
Phil 8965.1 — Pfeiderer, O. Moral und Religion. Leipzig, 1872.
Phil 490.1.6 — Physiology of the soul and instinct. N.Y., 1872.
Phil 490.1.5 — Physiology of the soul and instinct. N.Y., 1872.
Phil 5255.5.9 — Porter, Noah. The elements of intellectual science. N.Y., 1872.
Phil 1750.2 — Price, E.K. Some phases of modern philosophy. Philadelphia, 1872. 2 pam.
Phil 6685.6 — Putnam, A. Mesmerism, spiritualism. Boston, 1872.
Phil 1135.135 — Rechenberg, C.M. Entwickelung des Gottesbegriffes. Leipzig, 1872.
Phil 6127.16 — Reich, E. Der Mensch und die Seele. Berlin, 1872.
Phil 3791.30 — Riehl, Alois. Über Begriff und Form der Philosophie. Berlin, 1872.
Phil 3640.535 — Rohde, Erwin. Afterphilologie. Leipzig, 1872.
Phil 193.5.3 — Sanctis, F. de. La scienza e la vita. Napoli, 1872.
Phil 3500.42 — Sarchi, Charles. Examen de la doctrine de Kant. Paris, 1872.
Phil 103.1 — Signorrello, N. Lexicon peripateticum philosophico theologicum. Neapoli, 1872.
Phil 8610.872 — Somerset, Edward Adolphhus. Christian theology and modern scepticism. London, 1872.
Phil 8610.872.2 — Somerset, Edward Adolphhus. Christian theology and modern scepticism. N.Y., 1872.
Phil 2270.55.7.5 — Spencer, Herbert. Social statics. N.Y., 1872.
Phil 2262.83 — Spicker, G. Die Philosophie des Grafen von Shaftesbury. Freiburg, 1872.
Phil 3819.12.3 — Spinoza, Benedictus de. Oeuvres. Paris, 1872. 3v.
Phil 8598.16 — Statham, H. From old to new. London, 1872.
Phil 3838.20 — Stern, Alfred. Über einen Bisher unbeachteten Brief Spinozas. Göttingen, 1872?
Phil 3850.1.29 — Strauss, D.F. Der alte und der neue Glaube. Leipzig, 1872.
Phil 3850.1.45 — Strauss, D.F. Essais d'histoire religieuse et mélanges littéraires. Paris, 1872.
Phil 8599.1 — Thoughts on recent scientifc conclusions. London, 1872.
Phil 9495.72 — The truth about love. N.Y., 1872.
Phil 6129.3 — Tuke, D.H. Illustration of the mind upon the body. London, 1872.
Phil 8599.12 — Tulloch, John. Rational theology and Christian philosophy in England in the 17th century. Edinburgh, 1872. 2v.
Phil 820.1.8A — Ueberweg, F. History of philosophy. N.Y., 1872-4. 2v.
Phil 3895.53 — Ulrici, H. Compendium der Logik. 2. Aufl. Leipzig, 1872.
Phil 4265.3.35 — Vera, A. Problema dell'assoluto. v.1-4. Napoli, 1872-82.
Phil 8676.3.5 — Voysey, C. Sermons preached at St. George's Hall, Laugham Place. London, 1872-77. 4v.
Phil 7054.49.4 — Waggoner, J.H. The nature and tendency of modern spiritualism. 4. ed. Battle creek. Mich., 1872.
Phil 8897.6.7 — Wayland, F. The elements of moral science. Boston, 1872.
Phil 8712.1 — Weaver, G.O. Moses and modern science. Cincinnati, 1872.
Phil 822.1 — Weber, A. Histoire de la philosophie européenne. Paris, 1872.
Phil 3100.85 — Weber, Adalbert. Kritik der Psychologie von Beneke. Inaug-Diss. Weimar, 1872.
Phil 4655.1.38 — Wikner, Pontus. Om auktoritet och sjelfständighet. Upsala, 1872.
Phil 4655.1.62 — Wikner, Pontus. Promotionspredikan. Upsala, 1872.
Phil 197.8 — Wilson, W.D. Introduction to metaphysics. Ithaca, 1872.
Phil 5062.11.5 — Wilson, W.D. Logic. Ithaca, N.Y., 1872.
Phil 3507.2 — Zango, F. Über das Fundament der Ethik. Leipzig, 1872.
Phil 3428.155 — Zimmerman, R. Über Trendelenburg's Einwürfe gegen Herbarts praktische Ideen. Wien, 1872.

1873

Phil 5240.2.5 — Ahrens, Heinrich. Curso de psicología. Madrid, 1873. 2v.
Phil 175.10 — Asmus, P. Das Ich. Halle, 1873.
Phil 5241.2.2 — Bain, A. Mental science. N.Y., 1873.
Phil 6111.1 — Bain, A. Mind and body. London, 1873.
Phil 6111.1.2 — Bain, A. Mind and body. N.Y., 1873.
Phil 8876.17 — Birks, T.R. First principles of moral science. London, 1873.
Phil 126.1 — Bouscaillou, R.P. Precis de philosophie. Paris, 1873.
Phil 801.18.3 — Bröchner, Hans. Philosophiens historie i Grundrids. Kjøbenhavn, 1873-74.
Phil 8691.4.2 — Burr, E.F. Pater mundi. 2nd series. Boston, 1873.
Phil 1900.40.2 — Butler, Joseph. Analogy of religion. London, 1873.
Phil 8403.10.2 — Carriere, Moriz. Aesthetik. Leipzig, 1873. 2v.
Phil 87.14 — Carrión, Joaquin. Diccionario de sinónimos ó sea la propiedad del lenguage filosófico. Madrid, 1873.
Phil 3425.81 — Chlebik, F. Kraft und Stoff...Hegel'schen Prämissen. Berlin, 1873.
Phil 600.30 — Clavel, Adolphe. La morale positive. Paris, 1873.
Phil 3484.2.30 — Cohen, H. Die systematischen Begriffe. Berlin, 1873.
Phil 2050.109 — Compayré, Gabriel. La philosophie de David Hume. Paris, 1873.
Phil 4080.8.31 — Conti, Augusto. Il buono nel vero. Libri quattro. Firenze, 1873. 2v.
Phil 8403.8.6 — Cousin, Victor. Du vrai, du beau et du bien. 18. éd. Paris, 1873.
Phil 7060.87 — Crosland, N. Apparitions. London, 1873.
Phil 178.25 — Dana, A.H. Inductive inquiries in physiology, ethics, and ethnology. N.Y., 1873.

1873 - cont.

Phil 5400.19 — Darwin, Charles. The expression of the emotions in man and animals. N.Y., 1873.
Phil 8878.4A — Davies, J.L. Theology and morality. London, 1873.
Phil 7060.130 — Davis, H.P. Expose of Newburyport excentricities. n.p., 1873.
Phil 5243.5.10 — Delboeuf, J.R.L. Étude psychophysique. Belgium, 1873.
Phil 5243.8 — Dittes, F. Lehrbuch der Psychology. Wien, 1873.
Phil 5043.7 — Dittes, Friedrich. Praktische Logik. Wien, 1873.
Phil 3823.2 — Dörffling, M. Die Ansichten Spinozas. Leipzig, 1873.
Phil 178.35 — Drossbach, M. Über die Verschiedenengrade. Berlin, 1873.
Phil 803.2 — Dühring, E. Kritische Geschichte der Philosophie. 2d Aufl. Berlin, 1873.
Phil 3415.108 — Ebbinghaus, Hermann. Über die hartmannsche Philosophie des Unbewussten. Düsseldorf, 1873.
Phil 6114.2 — Ecker, A. Cerebral convolutions of man. N.Y., 1873.
Phil 8879.4 — Ellis, S.S. At our best. Boston, 1873.
Phil 179.22.5 — Erdmann, J.E. Filosofiska miniaturer. Stockholm, 1873.
Phil 5244.2.9 — Erdmann, J.E. Grundriss der Psychologie. 5e Aufl. Leipzig, 1873.
Phil 3210.61 — Fechner, G.T. Einige Ideen zur Schöpfungs- und Entwickelungsgeschichte der Organismen. Leipzig, 1873.
Phil 4110.5.30 — Ferrari, G. Filosofia della rivoluzione. v.1-2. 2. ed. Milano, 1873.
Phil 6115.11.17 — Feuchtersleben, E.F.V. The dietetics of the soul. London, 1873.
Phil 3235.73 — Feuerbach, Ludwig. The essence of religion. N.Y., 1873.
Phil 3245.45 — Fichte, Immanuel Hermann. Die theistische Weltansicht. Leipzig, 1873.
Phil 3246.25.5 — Fichte, Johann Gottlieb. Popular works. London, 1873.
Phil 5090.1 — Finch, A.E. The pursuit of truth. London, 1873.
Phil 8630.4 — Flammarion, C. Récits de l'infini. Paris, 1873.
Phil 8630.4.5 — Flammarion, C. Stories of infinity. Boston, 1873.
Phil 4005.6 — Fontana, B. La filosofia della storia nei pensatori italiani. Imola, 1873.
Phil 8695.2 — Fowle, T.W. The reconciliation of religion and science. London, 1873.
Phil 8050.34 — Friedlaender, L. Über die Entstehung und Entwicklung des Gefühls für das Romantische in der Natur. Leipzig, 1873.
Phil 7054.19 — Fritz, (pseud.). Where are the dead? or Spiritualism explained. Manchester, 1873.
Phil 8585.15 — Frohschammer, J. Das neue Wissen und der neue Glaube. Leipzig, 1873.
Phil 8585.16 — Frothingham, O.B. The religion of humanity. N.Y., 1873.
Phil 9075.3.5 — Gasparin, A.E. La conscience. 3. éd. Paris, 1873.
Phil 3826.1 — Gaspary, A. Spinoza und Hobbes. Leipzig, 1873.
Phil 8050.51 — Gauckler, T.G. Le beau et son histoire. Paris, 1873.
Phil 4006.3 — Giovanni, V. Storia della filosofia in Sicilia. Palermo, 1873. 2v.
Phil 4120.3.32 — Giovanni, V. di. Sofismi e buon senso, serati campestri. 2. ed. Palermo, 1873.
Phil 6116.23 — Gorton, D.A. Essay on the principles of mental hygiene. Philadelphia, 1873.
Phil 8881.15.5 — Gow, A.M. Good morals and gentle manners. N.Y., 1873.
Phil 8881.20.2 — Greg, W.R. Enigmas of life. Boston, 1873.
Phil 2520.142 — Grimm, E. Descartes' Lehre von den angeborenen Ideen. Inaug.-Diss. Jena, 1873.
Phil 600.38 — Guthlin, A. Les doctrines positivistes en France. Paris, 1873.
Phil 5247.2 — Hamilton, D.H. Autology...mental science. Boston, 1873.
Phil 3415.30 — Hartmann, Eduard von. Philosophie des Unbewussten. 5. Aufl. Berlin, 1873.
Phil 5047.2 — Hartsen, F.A. Grundzüge der Logik. Berlin, 1873.
Phil 7054.106.2 — Hazard, T.R. Mediums and mediumship. Boston, 1873.
Phil 5525.17 — Hecker, Ewald. Die Physiologie und Psychologie des Lachens. Berlin, 1873.
Phil 3425.25 — Hegel, Georg Wilhelm Friedrich. Populäre Gedanken aus seinen Werker. Berlin, 1873.
Phil 8587.11 — Henslow, G. The theory of evolution of living things. London, 1873.
Phil 3428.63 — Herbart, J.F. Über philosophisches Studium. Leipzig, 1873.
Phil 8882.9.3 — Hickok, L.P. A system of moral science. 3rd ed. N.Y., 1873.
Phil 3489.5 — Hölder, Alfred. Darstellung der Kantischen Erkenntnisstheorie. Tübingen, 1873.
Phil 6117.11 — Huguenin, G. Allgemeine Pathologie der Krankheiten des Nervensystems. Zürich, 1873.
Phil 7059.12.15 — Hull, Moses. Which: spiritualism or Christianity? N.Y., 1873.
Phil 2668.40 — Janet, Paul A.R. Les problèmes du XIXe siècle. 2e éd. Paris, 1873.
Phil 5819.2.7 — Joly, H. L'instinct; ses rapports. 2. Paris, 1873.
Phil 2672.35.10 — Jouffroy, Théodore S. Introduction to ethics. Boston, 1873. 2v.
Phil 3480.18.5 — Kant, Immanuel. Vermischte Schriften und Briefwechsel. Berlin, 1873.
Phil 3492.1.5 — Kirchmann, J. Erläuterungen zu Kant's kleinern Schriften. Berlin, 1873.
Phil 8885.6 — Kirchmann, J.H. von. Die Grundbegriffe des Rechts und der Moral. Berlin, 1873.
Phil 5400.33 — Klencke, P.F.H. Diätetik der Seele. 2e Aufl. Leipzig, 1873.
Phil 3415.83 — Knauer, G. Das Facit aus Eduard von Hartmann's Philosophie des Unbewussten. Berlin, 1873.
Phil 8885.8 — Koerner, H.J.A. Natur-Ethik. Hamburg, 1873. 2v.
Phil 6320.5 — Krishaber, M. De la névropathie cérébro-cardiaque. Paris, 1873.
Phil 486.1 — Lange, F.A. Geschichte des Materialismus. Iserlohn, 1873-75. 2v.
Phil 5251.4 — Langel, A. Les problèmes. Paris, 1873.
Phil 6990.14 — LaVausserie. Apparitions de la St. Vierge à deux jeunes enfants. Paris, 1873.
Phil 8412.25 — Lemke, Carl von. Populäre Ästhetik. 4. Aufl. Leipzig, 1873.
Phil 9245.29 — Lescoeur, Louis. La science du bonheur. Paris, 1873.
Phil 1535.5.10 — Liberatore, M. Della conoscenza intellectuale. 2e ed. Roma, 1873-74. 2v.
Phil 1135.30 — Liebeck, H. Untersuchungen zur Philosophie der Griechen. Halle, 1873.
Phil 600.7.3 — Littré, Émile. La science au point de vue philosophique. Paris, 1873.
Phil 7068.73.10 — London Dialectical Society. Report on spiritualism of the committee of the London Dialectical Society. London, 1873.
Phil 7054.143 — Lum, Dyer D. The "spiritual" delusion. Philadelphia, 1873.

Htn   Phil 6100.13*   Luys, J. Iconographie photographique des centres nerveux. Texte et atlas. Paris, 1873. 2v.

Phil 487.4   Maccall, William. The newest materialism. London, 1873.
Phil 8702.2   McCausland, D. Sermons in stones. London, 1873.
Phil 4170.7.43   Mamiani della Rovere, Terenzio. Critica delle rivelazioni. Roma, 1873.
Phil 2130.40   Mansel, H.L. Letters, lectures and reviews. London, 1873.
Phil 8962.1   Martensen, H.L. Christian ethics. Edinburgh, 1873.
Phil 6122.1.5   Maudsley, H. Body and mind. N.Y., 1873.
Phil 812.3.9   Maurice, J.F.D. Moral and metaphysical philosophy. London, 1873. 2v.
Phil 187.105   Melillo, F. Manuale di filosofia. Napoli, 1873.
Phil 3425.229   Michelet, C.L. Hegel und der Empirismus. Berlin, 1873.
Htn   Phil 2138.79.4*   Mill, John S. Autobiography. London, 1873.
Phil 2138.38.5   Mill, John S. Dissertations and discussions. v.2-5. v.1 rejected 1972. N.Y., 1873-75. 4v.
Phil 2490.84.6   Mill, John Stuart. The positive philosophy of Auguste Comte. N.Y., 1873.
Phil 2490.41.2.2   Mill, John Stuart. The positive philosophy of Auguste Comte. N.Y., 1873.
Phil 4605.1.41   Monrad, M.J. Om det skjønne. Christiania, 1873.
Phil 7054.151   Morrison, A.B. Spiritualism and necromancy. Cincinnati, 1873.
Phil 8592.16.2   Murphy, J.J. The scientific basis of faith. London, 1873.
Phil 5252.130   Murphy, James G. The human mind. Belfast, 1873.
Phil 4610.9.31   Nielsen, R. Natur og aand. Kjøbenhavn, 1873. 2 pam.
Phil 5253.2   Noel, R.R. Physical basis of mental life. London, 1873.
Phil 4508.4   Nyblaeus, Axel. Den filosofiska forskningen i Sverige. Lund, 1873-97. 3v.
Phil 189.18   Ott, Auguste. De la raison. Paris, 1873.
Phil 2705.80   Paquet, H.R.R. Essai sur La Mettrie. Paris, 1873.
Phil 2805.40.33   Pascal, Blaise. Pensées, opuscules et lettres. Paris, 1873. 2v.
Phil 2805.40.6   Pascal, Blaise. Pensées. Tours, 1873.
Phil 2805.40.5   Pascal, Blaise. Pensées. Paris, 1873.
Phil 2805.40.6.5   Pascal, Blaise. Pensées de Blaise Pascal. Paris, 1873.
Phil 8890.9   Peabody, A.P. A manual of moral philosophy. N.Y., 1873.
Phil 190.6   Pellissier, P.A. Précis d'un cours complet de philosophie élémentaire. Paris, 1873. 2v.
Phil 190.12   Picton, J.A. The mystery of matter. London, 1873.
Phil 6125.6   Poincaré, E.L. Leçons sur la physiologie...du système nerveux. Paris, 1873-6. 3v.
Phil 8640.11   Ponton, M. Glimpses of the future life. London, 1873.
Phil 7054.27.11   Putnam, A. Bible marvel workers. Boston, 1873.
Phil 7054.27.9   Putnam, A. Tipping his tables. Boston, 1873.
Phil 4215.2.83   Ragnisco, P. Tommaso Rossi e Benedetto Spinoza, saggio storico-critico. Salerno, 1873.
Phil 6967.5   Ray, Isaac. Contributions to mental pathology. Boston, 1873.
Phil 6945.10   Ray, Isaac. Ideal characters of officers of a hospital for the insane. Philadelphia, 1873.
Phil 3552.268   Reinhardt, Arthur. Sind es Vorzugsweise speculative oder naturwissenschaftliche Gründe. Jena, 1873.
Phil 5227.1.10   Ribot, T. English psychology. London, 1873.
Phil 8967.2   Row, C.A. The moral teaching of the New Testament. London, 1873.
Phil 4369.7   Sanz del Rio, Julián. Cartas ineditas. Madrid, 1873?
Phil 3460.82   Schaumburg, E. Jacobis Garten zu Pempelfort. Aachen, 1873.
Phil 6128.37   Schiff, M. Leziomi di fisiologia sperimentale sul sistema nervoso. 2. ed. Firenze, 1873.
Phil 3808.10   Schopenhauer, Arthur. Sämmtliche Werke. Leipzig, 1873-77. 6v.
Phil 3808.35.2.3   Schopenhauer, Arthur. Die Welt als Wille und Vorstellung. Leipzig, 1873. 2 pam.
Phil 3808.35.2   Schopenhauer, Arthur. Die Welt als Wille und Vorstellung. Leipzig, 1873. 2v.
Phil 3500.62   Schramm, G. Kant's kategorischen Imperativ nach seiner Genesis und Bedeutung für die Wissenschaft. Bamberg, 1873.
Phil 3500.51   Schultheis, P. Kant's Lehre vom radicalen Bösen. Diss. Leipzig, 1873.
Phil 818.1.3   Schwegler, F.C.A. Geschichte der Philosophie. 8e Aufl. Stuttgart, 1873.
Phil 818.1.12   Schwegler, F.C.A. Handbook of the history of philosophy. 5th ed. N.Y., 1873.
Phil 6990.3.33   Senna Freitas, José J. de. O milagre e a critica moderna on a immaculada conceição de Lourdes. Braga, 1873.
Phil 5058.12   Sigwart, H.C.W. Logik. Tübingen, 1873-78. 2v.
Phil 2138.88.86   Spencer, H. John Stuart Mill. Boston, 1873.
Phil 2270.45.4   Spencer, Herbert. First principles. N.Y., 1873.
Phil 2270.50   Spencer, Herbert. Recent discussions in science. N.Y., 1873.
Phil 193.31.6   Spir, A. von. Denken und Wirklichkeit. v.1-2. Leipzig, 1873.
Phil 8610.873   Stephen, Leslie. Essays on freethinking and plain-speaking. London, 1873.
Phil 3850.1.30   Strauss, D.F. Der alte und der neue Glaube. Bonn, 1873. 2v.
Phil 3850.1.36   Strauss, D.F. The old faith and the new. London, 1873.
Phil 3850.1.37   Strauss, D.F. The old faith and the new. v.1-2. N.Y., 1873.
Phil 8598.64   Stuart-Glennie, John S. In the morningland. London, 1873.
Phil 672.13   Stumpf, C. Über den psychologischen Ursprung der Raumvorstellung. Leipzig, 1873.
Phil 7054.5   Sweet, Elizabeth. The future life as described...by spirits. 4th ed. Boston, 1873.
Phil 2885.34.10   Taine, Hippolyte Adolphe. The philosophy of art. Photoreproduction. 2. ed. N.Y., 1873.
Phil 9430.16   Taubert, A. Der Pessimismus. Berlin, 1873.
Phil 7150.13   Taverni, Romeo. Del suicidio massime In Italia nel quinquiennio 1866-70. Roma, 1873.
Phil 8610.829.15   Taylor, Robert. The diegesis. Boston, 1873.
Phil 2138.113   The Examiner, London. John Stuart Mill. London, 1873.
Phil 3805.30.20   Thönes, C. Schleiermacher's handschriftlichen Anmerkungen zur I. Theil der Glaubenslehre. Berlin, 1873.
Phil 194.4   Thornton, W.T. Old-fashioned ethics. London, 1873.
Phil 8894.5.5   Tiberghien, G. Elementos de ética ó filosofía moral. Madrid, 1873.
Phil 8599.3   Tiberghien, G. Estudios sobre religion. Madrid, 1873.
Phil 3895.35   Ulrici, H. Gott und der Mensch. Bd.1. Leipzig, 1873.
Phil 3850.1.83   Ulrici, H. Der Philosoph Strauss. Halle, 1873.
Phil 3808.97   Venetianer, M. Schopenhauer als Scholastiker. Berlin, 1873.
Phil 4265.3.30   Vera, A. Introduction to speculative logic and philosophy. St. Louis, 1873.

Phil 3415.88   Volkelt, J. Das Unbewusste und der Pessimismus. Berlin, 1873.
Phil 3022.1   Weber, T. Die Geschichte der neueren deutschen Philosophie. v.1-3. Münster, 1873.
Phil 1135.50   Weisz, C.O.M. Metaphysische Theorie der griechischen Philosophie. Rostock, 1873.
Phil 3842.9   Wetzel, Paul. Der Zweckbegriff bei Spinoza. Thesis. Leipzig, 1873.
Phil 7054.58   Williamson, M.J. Modern diabolism; commonly called modern spiritualism. N.Y., 1873.
Phil 353.8   Windelband, W. Ueber die Gewissheit der Erkenntniss. Berlin, 1873.
Phil 8712.4   Woodrow, J. An examination of certain recent assaults on physical science. Columbia, S.C., 1873-74.
Phil 8972.1.5   Wuttke, K.F.A. Christian ethics. Boston, 1873. 2v.
Phil 3025.2   Zeller, Eduard. Geschichte der deutschen Philosophie. München, 1873.
Phil 3428.155.5   Zimmerman, R. Über den Einfluss der Tonlehre auf Herbart's Philosophie. Wien, 1873.

1874

Phil 6950.2   Audiffrent, G. Des maladies du cerveau. Paris, 1874.
Phil 6111.1.5   Bain, A. Mind and body. N.Y., 1874.
Phil 8402.5.2   Bascom, J. Aesthetics or the science of beauty. N.Y., 1874.
Phil 8876.11   Baumann, Julius. Sechs Vorträge aus dem Gebiete der praktischen Philosophie. Leipzig, 1874.
Phil 1870.20A   Berkeley, G. Selections. Oxford, 1874.
Phil 8876.85   Bertauld, Alfred. L'ordre social et l'ordre moral. Paris, 1874.
Phil 9550.1   Birks, T.R. Modern utilitarianism. London, 1874.
Phil 8826.2.5   Blackie, J.S. Four phases of morals; Socrates, Aristotle, Christianity, Utilitarianism. 2nd ed. Edinburgh, 1874.
Phil 2520.145   Bordas-Demoulin. Les cartésianisme. Paris, 1874.
Phil 2477.1.30   Boutroux, Émile. De la contingence des lois de la nature. Thèse. Paris, 1874.
Phil 2520.134   Boutroux, Émile. De veritatibus aeternis apud Cartesium. Thesis. Parisiis, 1874.
Phil 8620.23   Bradlaugh, Charles. A few words about the devil. N.Y., 1874.
Phil 176.33   Büchner, L. Aus Natur und Wissenschaft. Leipzig, 1874.
Phil 283.1   Carpenter, S.H. Philosophy of evolution. Madison, 1874.
Phil 6112.4.3.5   Carpenter, W.B. Principles of mental psychology. N.Y., 1874.
Phil 8598.59.5   Cassels, W.R. Supernatural religion. London, 1874-77. 3v.
Phil 575.1   Chantepie, É. Le presonnage humain. Paris, 1874.
Phil 3552.120.10   Class, Gustav. Der Determinismus von Leibnitz. Tübingen, 1874.
Phil 3552.120.5   Class, Gustav. Die metaphysischen Voraussetzungen. Tübingen, 1874.
Phil 8627.2.2   Cobbe, F.P. The hope of the human race. London, 1874.
Phil 2490.59.2   Comte, Auguste. Catèchisme positiviste. Paris, 1874.
Phil 7068.74.26   Crookes, W. Researches in the phenomena of spiritualism. London, 1874.
Phil 7068.74.26.5   Crookes, W. Researches in the phenomena of spiritualism. London, 1874.
Phil 7060.108   Crookes, William. Researches in the phenomena of spiritualism. London, 1874.
Phil 5242.26   Cros, A. Les fonctions supérieures du système nerveux. Paris, 1874.
Phil 283.4   Cuyás, F.G. Unidad del universo. Habana, 1874.
Phil 8685.2   DeConcilio, J. Catholicity and pantheism. pt.1. N.Y., 1874.
Phil 4515.92   Dons, Waldemar. Om Bostrømianismen. Christiania, 1874.
Phil 9070.17   Ellis, William J. Studies of man. London, 1874.
Phil 8880.45   Falco, Francesco. L'ordine ed i fatti morali. Alessandria, 1874.
Phil 3235.75   Feuerbach, Ludwig. Philosophische Charakterentwicklung. v.1-2. Leipzig, 1874.
Phil 5374.26   Fischer, J.C. Das Bewusstsein. Leipzig, 1874.
Phil 286.2.3   Fiske, J. Outlines of cosmic philosophy. Boston, 1874. 2v.
Phil 286.2.2   Fiske, J. Outlines of cosmic philosophy. London, 1874. 2v.
Phil 5245.9.15   Fortlage, A.R.K. Vier psychologische Vorträge. Jena, 1874.
Phil 3552.86.10   Foucher de Careil, Alexandre. Leibniz et Pierre-le-Grand. Paris, 1874.
Phil 6955.14   Fox, E.L. Pahological anatomy of nervous centres. London, 1874.
Phil 5425.2.8   Galton, F. English men of science. London, 1874.
Phil 5246.49   Gaskell, John. New elements from old subjects presented as the basis for a science of mind. Philadelphia, 1874.
Phil 9245.3   Gasparin, A.E. Le bonheur. Paris, 1874.
Phil 1870.106   Gerard, J. D idealismo aprud Berkeleium. Sancti Clodoaldi, 1874.
Phil 4215.1.97   Giorgi, A. de. Biografia di G.D. Romagnosi e catalogo delle sue opere. Parma, 1874.
Phil 181.13   Göring, C. System der kritischen Philosophie. Leipzig, 1874. 2v.
Phil 3826.3   Gordon, A. Spinoza's Psychologie der Affekte mit Rücksicht auf Descartes. Breslau, 1874.
Phil 1135.40   Goring, C. Über den Begriff der Ursache im der griechischen Philosophie. Leipzig, 1874.
Phil 3489.8   Harris, John, of Montreal. Review of Kant's Critique of pure reason. Supplement to Theology and science of goverment. Montreal, 1874.
Phil 3415.36   Hartmann, Eduard von. Erläuterungen zur Metaphysik der Bewussten. Berlin, 1874.
Phil 3415.30.3   Hartmann, Eduard von. Philosophie des Unbewussten. 6. Aufl. Berlin, 1874.
Phil 3415.61   Hartmann, Eduard von. Die Selbstzersetzung des Christenthums. 2. Aufl. Berlin, 1874.
Phil 5247.4   Hartsen, F.A. Grundzüge der Psychologie. Berlin, 1874.
Phil 9430.15.5   Hartsen, F.A. von. Die Moral des Pessimismus. Nordhausen, 1874.
Phil 8882.5.2   Haven, J. Moral philosophy. Boston, 1874.
Phil 3425.32   Hegel, Georg Wilhelm Friedrich. Logic. Oxford, 1874.
Phil 338.15   Heyder, Carl. Die Lehre von den Ideen. Frankfurt am Main, 1874.
Phil 8408.9   Hillebrand, K. Zwölf Briefe eines ästhetischen Ketzer's. 2. Aufl. Berlin, 1874.
Phil 6117.35   Hitzig, E. Untersuchungen über das Gehirn. Berlin, 1874.

Chronological Listing

Phil 1807.1.5   Höffding, H. Den engelke philosophie i vortid. Kjøbenhavn, 1874.

Phil 6750.3.7   Howe, S.G. Causes and prevention of idiocy. Boston, 1874.

Phil 2050.51   Hume, David. Treatise on human nature. London, 1874. 2v.

Phil 8589.1   Jackson, W. The philosophy of natural theology. London, 1874.

Phil 184.11   Jacoby, L. Die Idee der Entwicklung. Berlin, 1874. 2v.

Phil 5249.4   Jardine, R. Elements of the psychology of cognition. London, 1874.

Phil 5049.6   Jevons, W.S. The principles of science. London, 1874. 2v.

Phil 5049.6.2.5   Jevons, W.S. The principles of science. N.Y., 1874.

Phil 185.27   Kaulish, W. System der Metaphysik. Prag, 1874.

Phil 2115.121   Kirchmann, J.H. Erläuterungen zu John Locke's Versuch über den menschlichen Verstand. Abt II. Berlin, 1874.

Phil 3552.120   Kirchner, Friedrich. Leibnitz's Stellung zur katholischen Kirche. Berlin, 1874.

Phil 6978.12.10   Krafft-Ebing, Richard. Die Melancholie. Erlangen, 1874.

Phil 8411.5.5   Krause, K.C.F. Compendio de estética traducido del aleman. Sevilla, 1874.

Phil 3525.20.4   Krause, K.C.F. Handschriftlicher Nachlass; Rechtsphilosophie. Leipzig, 1874.

Phil 185.9   Krönig, Prof. Das Dasein Gottes. Berlin, 1874.

Phil 5051.20   Labanca, B. Della dialettica. v.1-2. Firenze, 1874.

Phil 2725.2.65   Lamennais, F.R. de. Libro per il popolo. Milano, 1874.

Phil 8886.3   Landmann, R. Hauptfragen der Ethik. Leipzig, 1874.

Phil 7068.74.10   Lawrence, Jas. Angel voices from the spirit world. Cleveland, 1874.

Phil 8701.5   Le Conte, J. Religion and science. N.Y., 1874.

Phil 3552.77.20   Leibniz, Gottfried Wilhelm. Correspondance de Leibniz avec l'électrice Sophie de Brunswick-Lunebourg. Hanovre, 1874. 3v.

Phil 5251.6.2.6   Lewes, G.H. Problems of life and mind. 1st series. London, 1874-75. 2v.

Phil 5251.6.3   Lewes, G.H. Problems of life and mind. 1st-3rd series. London, 1874. 5v.

Phil 4803.522.15   Libelt, Karol. Filozofia i krytyka. Wyd. 2. v.1-6. Poznań, 1874-75. 3v.

Phil 3565.30   Lotze, Hermann. System der Philosophie. Leipzig, 1874-79. 2v.

Phil 6121.7.9   Luys, J. Des actions réflexes du cerveau. Paris, 1874.

Phil 2125.62   McCosh, James. Christianity and positivism. N.Y., 1874.

Phil 2125.52.5   McCosh, James. Intuitions of the mind. 3rd ed. N.Y., 1874.

Phil 6962.2   Maudsley, H. Responsibility in mental disease. N.Y., 1874.

Phil 9550.3   Meinong, A. Psychologisch-ethische Untersuchungen zur Werth-Theorie. Graz, 1874.

Phil 7085.1   Mesnet, E. De l'automatisme. Paris, 1874.

Phil 3552.441   Meyer, H.G. Leibniz und Baumgarten als Begründer der deutschen Aesthetik. Halle, 1874.

Phil 187.13   Meyer, J.B. Philosophische Zeitfragen. Bonn, 1874.

Phil 6122.44   Meynert, T. Zur Mechanik des Gehirnbaues. Wien, 1874.

Cg   Phil 2138.79.6   Mill, John S. Autobiography. N.Y., 1874.

Phil 2138.45.12   Mill, John S. Nature, the utility of religion and theism. London, 1874.

Phil 2138.45A   Mill, John S. Nature, the utility of religion and theism. London, 1874.

Phil 2138.40.3   Mill, John S. On liberty. London, 1874.

Phil 2138.35.3.19   Mill, John S. A system of logic. 8th ed. N.Y., 1874.

Phil 2138.45.2   Mill, John S. Three essays on religion. N.Y., 1874.

Phil 3494.6   Monck, W.H.S. Introduction to the critical philosophy. Dublin, 1874.

Phil 2493.82   Mülhaupt, P. Darstellung der Psychologie bei Condillac und Bonnet. Cassel, 1874.

Phil 5330.3   Müller, G.E. Zur Theorie der sinnlichen Aufmerksamkeit. Leipzig, 1874?

Phil 8593.2   Newman, F.W. Hebrew Theism, common basis of Judaism, Christianity and Mohammedism. London, 1874.

Phil 188.4   Noire, L. Die Welt als Entwicklung des Geistes. Leipzig, 1874.

Phil 4610.6.2   Nyblaeus, Axel. Trenne religiousfilosfiska uppsatser. 2. uppl. Lund, 1874.

Phil 8594.2.9   Opzoomer, C.W. Onze godsdienst. Amsterdam, 1874.

Phil 8890.2.3   Palmer, T.H. The moral instructor. pt.3. Boston, 1874.

EDL   Phil 2805.40.14   Pascal, Blaise. Pensées. Paris, 1874.

Phil 8705.15   Pedder, Henry C. Issues of the age. N.Y., 1874.

Phil 2050.84   Pfleiderer, E. Empirismus und Skepsis...Hume's. Berlin, 1874.

Phil 5255.4   Planck, K.C. Anthropologie und Psychologie. Leipzig, 1874.

Phil 815.1   Poetter, F.C. Die Geschichte der Philosophie. Elberfeld, 1874.

Phil 7068.74.15   Polak, M.S. Het materialismus, het spiritismus. 2. druk. Amsterdam, 1874.

Phil 530.20.25   Preger, Wilhelm. Geschichte der deutschen Mystik im Mittelalter. Leipzig, 1874-1893. 3v.

Phil 7054.17   Pridham, A. The spirits tried. London, 1874.

Phil 3497.10   Pünjer, G.C. Die Religionslehre Kants. Jena, 1874.

Phil 8620.17   Read, H. The foot-prints of Satan. N.Y., 1874.

Phil 8642.4   Reid, William. Everlasting punishment and modern speculation. Edinburgh, 1874.

Phil 8597.4   Die Religion des Zweiflers. Leipzig, 1874.

Phil 3850.1.80   Reuschle, C.G. Philosophie und Naturwiss...D.F. Strauss. Bonn, 1874.

Phil 3808.94   Ribot, T. La philosophie de Schopenhauer. Paris, 1874.

Phil 3805.185   Ritschl, Alfrecht. Schleiermachers Reden über die Religion und ihre Nachwirkungen auf die evangelische Kirche Deutschlands. Bonn, 1874.

Phil 7068.74.40   Ritti, A. Théorie psychologique de l'hallucination Paris, 1874.

Phil 3425.91.15   Rosenkranz, K. Hegel as national philosopher of Germany. St.Louis, 1874.

Phil 5627.87.2   Scherr, J. Die Gekreuzigte. 2. Aufl. Leipzig, 1874.

Phil 5938.9   Scheve, G. Phrenological Bilder. Leipzig, 1874.

Phil 3805.34.10   Schleiermacher, Friedrich. Räthsel und Charaden. Berlin, 1874.

Phil 5768.2   Scholten, J.H. Der freie Wille. Berlin, 1874.

Phil 1619.2   Schultze, Fritz. Geschichte der Philosophie der Renaissance. Jena, 1874.

Phil 8643.2   Schutz, L. Vernunf-Beweis...Unsterblichkeit der menschlichen Seele. Paderborn, 1874.

Phil 8893.9   Seydel, R. Ethik. Leipzig, 1874.

Phil 8893.11.2   Sidgwick, H. The methods of ethics. London, 1874.

Phil 8893.11   Sidgwick, H. The methods of ethics. London, 1874.

Htn   Phil 2280.1.30*   Sidgwick, Henry. The methods of ethics. London, 1874.

Phil 8598.14   Snow, G.D. A theologico-political treatise. London, 1874.

Phil 2270.40.4   Spencer, Herbert. Essays. N.Y., 1874.

Phil 3500.9   Spicker, G. Über das Verhältniss...Kantischen. Berlin, 1874.

Phil 8893.19   Spir, A. Moralität und Religion. Leipzig, 1874.

Phil 3500.10   Stadler, A. Kant's Teleologie. Berlin, 1874.

Phil 7082.162   Strümpell, Ludwig. Die Natur und Entstehung der Träume. Leipzig, 1874.

Phil 2885.34.14   Taine, Hippolyte Adolphe. The ideal in art. N.Y., 1874.

Phil 7054.160.5   Tappan, Cora L.V. What is the use of spiritualism? London, 1874.

Phil 1124.1   Teichmüller, G. Studien zur Geschichte der Begriffe. Berlin, 1874.

Phil 1719.1   Thilo, C.A. Kurze pragmatische Geschichte der neueren Philosophie. Göthen, 1874.

Phil 8420.16   Torrey, J. A theory of fine art. N.Y., 1874.

Phil 3839.4   Turbiglio, S. Benedetto Spinoza. v.3. Roma, 1874.

Phil 8709.2   Tyndall, John. Address. Cambridge, 1874. 2 pam.

Phil 8709.2.9   Tyndall, John. Address. N.Y., 1874.

Htn   Phil 2305.2.30*   Tyndall, John. Address before...British association at Belfast. London, 1874.

Phil 8709.2.13   Tyndall, John. Advancement of science. N.Y., 1874.

Phil 8709.2.14   Tyndall, John. Advancement of science. N.Y., 1874.

Phil 820.1.14   Ueberweg, F. History of philosophy. London, 1874-75. 2v.

Phil 820.1.10   Ueberweg, F. History of philosophy. N.Y., 1874. 2v.

Phil 3895.35.2   Ulrici, H. Gott und der Mensch. 2. Aufl. Bd.1-2. Leipzig, 1874. 2v.

Phil 5627.90   Upham, Thomas C. Principles of the interior or hidden life. London, 1874.

Phil 196.9   Venetianer, M. Der allgeist. Grundzüge des Panpsychismus. Berlin, 1874.

Phil 7060.104.5   Wallace, A.R. A defense of modern spiritualism. Boston, 1874.

Phil 1135.90   Walter, J. Die Lehre von der praktischen Vernunft. Jena, 1874.

Phil 6400.6   Wernicke, C. Der aphasische Symptomencomplex. Photoreproduction. Breslau, 1874.

Phil 510.138   Wirth, R. Über Monismus (Pantheismus). Plauen, 1874.

Phil 3504.8   Witte, J.H. Beiträge zum Verständniss Kant's. Berlin, 1874.

Phil 7054.53   Wolfe, N.B. Startling facts in modern spiritualism. Cincinnati, 1874.

Phil 3915.45   Wundt, Wilhelm. Grundzüge der physiologischen Psychologie. Leipzig, 1874.

Phil 8972.1   Wuttke, K.F.A. Handbuch der christlichen Sittenlehre. Leipzig, 1874-75. 2v.

Phil 3850.1.93   Zeller, Eduard. David Friedrich Strauss. London, 1874.

Phil 3850.1.91   Zeller, Eduard. David Friedrich Strauss. 2. Aufl. Bonn, 1874.

Phil 3507.4.5   Zimmerman, R. Kant und die positive Philosophie. Wien, 1874.

1875

Phil 4000.10   Acri, Francesco. Critica di alcune critiche di spaventa. Bologna, 1875.

Phil 2035.80.18   Alexander, P.P. Moral causation. Notes on Mr. Mill's examination. 2nd ed. Edinburgh, 1875.

Phil 8580.4   Allen, S.M. Religion and science; the letters of "Alpha". Boston, 1875.

Phil 5241.2.10.15   Bain, A. The emotions and the will. 3. ed. N.Y., 1875.

Phil 176.113   Barrett, Thomas S. An introduction to the study of logic and metaphysics. London, 1875.

Phil 6951.18   Bastian, H.C. On paralysis from brain disease. N.Y., 1875.

Phil 176.12   Baumgärtner, H. Die Weltzellen. Leipzig, 1875.

Htn   Phil 3801.197.30*A   Beckers, Hubert. Schelling's Geistesentwicklung in Ihrem inneren Zusammenhang. München, 1875.

Phil 1865.66   Bentham, Jeremy. La religion naturelle...d'apres les papiers de J. Bentham. Paris, 1875.

Phil 5640.2.3   Bernstein, J. Die fünf Sinne des Menschen. Leipzig, 1875.

Phil 978.6.3   Besant, Annie. On the nature and the existence of God. London, 1875.

Phil 176.242   Bihari, Péter. A philosophiai tudamányok encyclopaediája. Budapest, 1875.

Phil 2218.82   Birmingham, England. Priestley memorial. Photoreproduction. London, 1875.

Phil 5628.51.5   Bourneville, Désiré Magloire. Science and miracle. Louise Lateau ou la stigmatisée belge. Paris, 1875.

Phil 3821.4   Busolt, Georg. Grundzuge der Erkenntnisztheorie Spinozas. Berlin, 1875.

Phil 8581.17   Byles, J.B. Foundations of religion in the mind and heart of man. London, 1875.

Phil 6112.4.20   Carpenter, W.B. The doctrine of human automatism. London, 1875.

Phil 9550.11   Carran, Ludovic. La morale utilitaire. Paris, 1875.

Phil 8403.29   Cartalano, F. La filosofia dell'arte. Torino, 1875.

Phil 365.10   Cazalles, Emile. Outline of the evolution-philosophy. N.Y., 1875.

Phil 5628.50.10   Charbonnier, Nestor. Maladies et facultés diverses des mystiques. Bruxelles, 1875.

Phil 177.74   Clemens, F. Das Manifest der Vernunft. 3e Aufl. Berlin, 1875.

Phil 1135.22   Cocker, B.F. Christianity and Greek philosophy. N.Y., 1875.

Phil 8657.4   Cocker, B.F. The theistic conception of the world. N.Y., 1875.

Phil 2490.54.20   Comte, Auguste. Framställning öfver den positive anden. Stockholm 1875.

Phil 2490.41.2.4A   Comte, Auguste. The positive philosophy. 2. ed. London, 1875. 2v.

Phil 2490.41.9   Comte, Auguste. Principios de filosofía positiva. Santiago, 1875.

Phil 6112.7   Cornelius, K.S. Über die Wechselwirkung zwischen Leib und Seele. Halle, 1875.

Phil 8877.56   Courcelle-Seneuil, J.G. Précis de morale rationnelle. Paris, 1875.

Phil 5525.3   Courdaveaux, V. Études sur le comique. Le rire. Paris, 1875.

Phil 477.6   Cournot, A.A. Matérialisme, vitalisme, rationalisme. Paris, 1875.

Phil 8692.6   Crosby, H. The bible on the side of science. N.Y., 1875.

Chronological Listing

	Phil 333.4	Czolbe, H. Grundzüge einer extensionalen Erkenntnisstheorie. Plauen, 1875.
	Phil 6953.7	Despine, Prosper. De la folie au point de vue philosophique. Paris, 1875.
	Phil 510.134	Dieterich, K. Philosophie und Naturwissenschaft. Tübingen, 1875.
	Phil 8693.4.3	Draper, J.W. History of the conflict between religion and science. N.Y., 1875.
	Phil 5043.10.4	Drobisch, Moritz Wilehlm. Neue Darstellung der Logik nach ihren einfaschsten Verhältnissen mit Rücksicht auf Mathematik und Naturwissenschaft. 4. Aufl. Leipzig, 1875.
NEDL	Phil 2705.81	Du Bois-Reymond, E. La Mettrie. Berlin, 1875.
	Phil 2705.81.2	Du Bois-Reymond, E. La Mettrie. Berlin, 1875.
	Phil 3195.9.75	Dühring, E. Cursus der Philosophie als streng wissenschaftlicher Weltanschauung und Lebensgestaltung. Leipzig, 1875.
	Phil 5402.1	Dumont, L. Théorie scientifique de la sensibilité. Paris, 1875.
	Phil 178.13	Dupont, A.H.H. Ontologie. Louvain, 1875.
	Phil 8404.16	Durdík, Josef. Všeobecna aesthetika. Praha, 1875.
	Phil 4515.83.10	Edfeldt, Hans. Granskning af kandidaten Waldemar. Upsala, 1875.
	Phil 179.22.15	Erdmann, J.E. Ernste Spiele. 3. Aufl. Berlin, 1875.
	Phil 5244.2.12	Erdmann, J.E. Psychologische Briefe. 5e Aufl. Leipzig, 1875.
	Phil 480.5	Fabié, Antonio M. Exámen del materialismo moderno. Madrid, 1875.
	Phil 7054.65	Fairfield, F.G. Ten years with spiritual mediums. N.Y., 1875.
	Phil 3210.26	Fechner, G.T. Kleine Schriften von Dr. Mises (pseud.). Leipzig, 1875.
	Phil 1110.1.6	Ferrier, J.F. Lectures on Greek philosophy. 2nd ed. Edinburgh, 1875.
	Phil 1990.10A	Ferrier, J.F. Philosophical works. Edinburgh, 1875. 3v.
	Phil 2270.88	Fischer, E.L. Über den Gesetz der Entwicklung. Würzburg, 1875.
	Phil 1850.82.5	Fischer, K. Francis Bacon und seine Nachfolger. 2e Aufl. Leipzig, 1875.
	Phil 1705.4.2	Fischer, K. Geschichte der neueren Philosophie. v.1-9. München, 1875-93. 10v.
Htn	Phil 286.2*A	Fiske, J. Outlines of cosmic philosophy. Boston, 1875. 2v.
	Phil 6955.4	Folsom, C.F. Four introductory lectures on insanity. Cambridge, 1875-80. 4 pam.
	Phil 5245.9.10	Fortlage, A.R.K. Beiträge zur Psychologie. Leipzig, 1875.
	Phil 90.2.3	Franck, Adolphe. Diccionnaire des sciences philosophiques. 2e eéd. Paris, 1875.
	Phil 90.2.2	Franck, Adolphe. Dictionnaire des sciences philosophiques. 2. éd. Paris, 1875.
	Phil 3487.9	Frederichs, F. Ueber Kant's Princip der Ethik. Berlin, 1875.
X Cg	Phil 8585.14	Free Religious Association. Freedom and fellowship. Boston, 1875.
	Phil 672.4A	Funcke, D. Grundlagen der Raumwissenschaft. Hannover, 1875.
	Phil 5425.2.9	Galton, F. English men of science. N.Y., 1875.
	Phil 8696.1	Gibson, S.T. Religion and science. London, 1875.
	Phil 9166.6	Girault, A. Le foyer, scènes de la vie de famille aux Etats Unis. Paris, 1875.
	Phil 8956.3	Gregory, Daniel. Christian ethics. Philadelphia, 1875.
	Phil 8586.7	Gresley, W. Thoughts on religion and philosophy. London, 1875.
	Phil 3280.84	Grimm, Edward. Arnold Geulincx' Erkenntnisstheorie und Occasionalismus. Jena, 1875.
	Phil 8586.14	Guilbert, A.V.F. La divine synthèse. Paris, 1875. 3v.
	Phil 1190.10	Haas, Leander. De philosophorum scepticorum successionibus. Inaug. Diss. Wurciburgi, 1875.
	Phil 182.54	Hallier, Ernst. Die Weltanschauung des Naturforschers. Jena, 1875.
	Phil 3827.1	Hann, F.G. Die Ethik Spinozas und die Philosophie Descartes. Innsbruck, 1875.
	Phil 3549.1.85	Hartmann, E. von. J.H. von Kirchmanns erkentnisstheoretischer Realismus. Berlin, 1875.
	Phil 3415.55	Hartmann, Eduard von. Kritische Grundlegung der trancedentalen Realismus. Berlin, 1875.
	Phil 182.6.5	Hartsen, F.A. Grundiss der Philosophie. Abt. 1. Nordhausen, 1875.
	Phil 7060.95	Hauréau, M.B. Mémoire sur les récits d'apparitions. Paris, 1875.
	Phil 5817.2	Hazard, R.G. Animals, not automata. N.Y., 1875.
	Phil 5757.1.7	Hazard, R.G. Zwei Briefe über Verursachung und Freiheit im Wollen Gerichtet. N.Y., 1875.
	Phil 8587.8	Helmersen, A. von. Die Religion. Graz, 1875.
	Phil 525.76	Heppe, Heinrich. Geschichte der quietistischen Mystik in der katholischen Kirche. Berlin, 1875.
	Phil 3415.81	Hernan, C.F. Edward von Hartmann's Religion der Zukunft. Leipzig, 1875.
	Phil 4803.454.45	Hoene-Wroński, Józef Maria. Propédeutigue messianique. v.2. Paris, 1875.
	Phil 182.32	Holland, Henry. Fragmentary papers on science. London, 1875.
	Phil 182.75	Hollenberg, W. Philosophische Propädeutik. 2. Aufl. Elberfeld, 1875.
	Phil 8957.1	Hovey, A. Christian ethics. Boston, 1875.
	Phil 25.21	The illustrated annual of phrenology, 1882. N.Y., 1875.
	Phil 2668.35	Janet, Paul A.R. Le matérialisme contemporain. Paris, 1875.
	Phil 184.21.15	Jourdain, Charles. Notions de philosophie. 15e ed. Paris, 1875.
	Phil 8685.12	Jundt, A. Histoire du panthéisme populaire. Strasbourg, 1875.
	Phil 4515.88	Kalling, P. Om kunskapen; studier. Upsala, 1875.
	Phil 3480.71.10	Kant, Immanuel. Die Religion innerhalb der Grenzen der blossen Vernunft. 2. Aufl. Leipzig, 1875.
	Phil 3195.2.95	Kastner, Lorenz. Martin Deutinger's Leben und Schriften. München, 1875.
	Phil 3552.94.5	Kirchner, Friedrich. Leibniz's Psychologie. Cöthen, 1875.
	Phil 3808.232	Klee, Hermann. Grundzüge einer Asthetik nach Schopenhauer. Berlin, 1875.
	Phil 3415.82	Kluge, A. Philosophische Fragmente...Hartmann's Philosophie. Breslau, 1875-77. 2v.
	Phil 5820.1	Körner, F. Instinkt und freier Wille. Leipzig, 1875.
	Phil 185.11.5	Kym, A.L. Metaphysische Untersuchungen. München, 1875.

	Phil 600.41	Laffitte, P. Les grandes types de l'humanité. Paris, 1875-76. 2v.
	Phil 7060.86	Lee, F.G. Glimpses of the supernatural. London, 1875.
	Phil 6400.15	Legroux, A. De l'aphasie. Thèse. Paris, 1875.
	Phil 3552.14	Leibniz, Gottfried Wilhelm. Die philosophischen Schriften. Berlin, 1875-90. 7v.
	Phil 811.3.5	Lewes, G.H. The biographical history of philosophy. London, 1875.
	Phil 7054.121	Leymarie, P.G. Proces des spirites. Paris, 1875.
	Phil 5251.9	Lichthorn, C. Die Erforschung der physiologische Naturgesetze. Breslau, 1875.
	Phil 6021.10	Lima Fulza, G. La faccia e l'anima. Milano, 1875.
	Phil 8591.10	Löwenhardt, E. Über Gott, Geist und Unsterblichkeit. Wolgast, 1875.
	Phil 672.26	Luguet, Henry. Étude sur la notion d'espace d'après Descartes. Thèse. Paris, 1875.
	Phil 6121.7.21	Luys, J. Leçons sur la structure et les maladies du système nerveux. Paris, 1875.
	Phil 1812.1	McCosh, J. The Scottish philosophy. N.Y., 1875.
	Phil 8709.2.50	McCosh, James. Ideas in nature overlooked by Dr. Tyndall. N.Y., 1875.
	Phil 5635.5.7	Mach, Ernst. Grundlinien der Lehre vom den Bewegungsempfindungen. Leipzig, 1875.
	Phil 2130.45.10	Mansel, H.L. The limits of religious thought. 1st American ed. Boston, 1875.
	Phil 5252.70	Marconi, A. Oggetto ed ufico della psicologia. Milano, 1875.
	Phil 187.11.9	Martineau, J. Essays. N.Y., 1875. 2v.
	Phil 487.2.6	Martineau, J. Religion affected by modern materialism. N.Y., 1875.
	Phil 6962.2.3	Maudsley, H. Die Zurechnungsfähigkeit der Geisteskranken. Leipzig, 1875.
	Phil 343.1	Mayer, A. Die Lehre von der Erkenntniss. Leipzig, 1875.
	Phil 8610.875	Ménard, Louis. Catéchisme religieux des libres penseurs. Paris, 1875.
	Phil 2138.79.9	Mill, John S. Mes mémoires: histoire de ma vie et de mes idées. 2e éd. Paris, 1875.
	Phil 2138.40.3.2	Mill, John S. On liberty. London, 1875.
	Phil 2138.46	Mill, John S. Über Religion. Berlin, 1875.
	Phil 487.1.4	Moleschott, J. Der Kreislauf des Lebens. Giessen, 1875-87. 2v.
X Cg	Phil 8610.875.20	National Secular Society. The secular song and hymn book. London, 1875?
	Phil 270.20	Noiré, Ludwig. Die Doppelnatur der Causalität. Leipzig, 1875.
	Phil 510.9	Noiré, Ludwig. Der monistische Gedanke. Leipzig, 1875.
	Phil 3495.4	Nolen, D. Critique de Kant. Paris, 1875.
	Phil 3552.281	Nolen, Désiré. Quid Leibniz uis Aristoteli debuerit. Parisiis, 1875.
	Phil 600.37	Nyström, Anton. Den gamla tiden inför den nya. Stockholm, 1875.
	Phil 7054.47	Olcott, H.S. People from the other world. Hartford, 1875.
	Phil 7054.185	Oxley, William. Angelic revelations concerning the origin, ultimation and destiny of the human spirit. Manchester, 1875-83. 4v.
	Phil 8595.15.17	Paine, Thomas. Age of reason. Investigation of true and fabulous theology. Boston, 1875. 2 pam.
	Phil 2805.74	Pascal, Blaise. Entretien avec de Saci sur Epictète et Montaigne. Paris, 1875.
	Phil 2805.24	Pascal, Blaise. Fragments philosophiques. Paris, 1875.
	Phil 3497.3.15	Paulsen, Friedrich. Versuch...Kantischen Erkenntnisstheorie. Leipzig, 1875.
Htn	Phil 3801.685*A	Pfleiderer, Otto. Friedrich Wilhelm Joseph Schelling. Stuttgart, 1875.
	Phil 11.1	Philosophische Gesellschaft zu Berlin. Verhandlungen. v.1-21. Leipzig, 1875-82. 2v.
	Phil 8670.6	Poetter, F.C. Der persönliche Gott und Welt. Elberfeld, 1875.
	Phil 4015.4	Pompa, Raffaele. L'Italia filosofica contemporanea. Salerno, 1875.
	Phil 8400.27	Prieger, E. Anregung und metaphysische Grundlagen der Aesthetik von Alex Gottbeb Baumgarten. Berlin, 1875. 3 pam.
	Phil 8610.875.25	Pullen, H.W. Modern Christianity, a civilized heathenism. Boston, 1875.
	Phil 191.1.5	Quinet, Edgar. L'esprit nouveau. Paris, 1875.
	Phil 191.1	Quinet, Edgar. L'esprit nouveau. 4. éd. Paris, 1875.
	Phil 6687.5	Randolph, P.B. Seership. The magnetic mirror. Toledo, 1875.
	Phil 1817.1	Rémusat, C.F. Histoire de la philosophie en Angleterre. Paris, 1875. 2v.
	Phil 2840.40.2	Renouvier, C.B. Essais de critique générale. v.1. pt.1-3; v.2, pt.1-3. Paris, 1875. 6v.
	Phil 2855.5.31	Richard, C. Esquisse d'une philosophie synthétique. Paris, 1875.
	Phil 2855.5.33	Richard, C. Réponse à Charles Renouvier au sujet de son appreciation de l'Esquisse d'une philosophie synthéiste. Paris, 1875.
	Phil 1122.3.11	Ritter, Heinrich. Historia philosophiae graecae et romanae. 5. ed. Gotha, 1875.
	Phil 7054.37.25	Rivail, H.L.D. El evangelio segun el espiritismo. Barcelona, 1875.
Htn	Phil 2250.30*	Royce, Josiah. The intention of the Prometheus Bound of Aeschylus. Thesis. Berkeley, 1875.
	Phil 8418.13	Ruskin, J. Frondes agrestes. N.Y., 1875.
	Phil 7054.34.8	Sargent, Epes. The proof palpable of immortality. Boston, 1875.
	Phil 9430.23	Scheffer, Wessel. Het wijsgeerig pessimisme van den jongstentijd. Leiden, 1875.
	Phil 3552.93	Schmidt, J. Leibnitz und Baumgarten. Halle, 1875.
	Phil 3808.49.5	Schopenhauer, Arthur. Über die vierfache Wurzel des Satzes vom zureichen den Grunde. 4. Aufl. Leipzig, 1875.
	Phil 3500.29	Schultze, F. Kant und Darwin. Jena, 1875.
	Phil 3415.86	Schwarz, H. Das Ziel der religiösen und wissenschaftlichen Gährung nachgewiesen Hartmann's Pessimismus. Berlin, 187
	Phil 8708.38	Science and revelation: a series of lectures. Belfast, 1875.
	Phil 6625.4	Semal. De la sensibilité générale et de ses altérations dans les affections mélancoliques. Paris, 1875.
	Phil 7060.85	Siebeck, H. Das Wesen der ästhetischen Anschauung. Berlin, 1875.
	Phil 8893.14.6.5	Signs before death. London, 1875.
	Phil 2270.31	Smiles, Samuel. Self-help. N.Y., 1875.
		Spencer, Herbert. System der Synthetische Philosophie: Grundlagen. Stuttgart, 1875.
	Phil 349.3	Spicker, G. Kant, Hume und Berkeley. Berlin, 1875.

Chronological Listing

1875 - cont.

Phil 3819.30   Spinoza, Benedictus de. Die Ethik. Leipzig, 1875.
Phil 2138.88   Stebbing, W. Analysis of Mr. Mill's system of logic. London, 1875.
Phil 8598.59   Supernatural religion. 5th ed. London, 1875. 2v.
Phil 2885.32   Taine, Hippolyte Adolphe. Lectures on art. 1st series. N.Y., 1875.
Phil 2885.34.16A   Taine, Hippolyte Adolphe. Lectures on art. 3d ed. 1st series. N.Y., 1875. 2v.
Phil 2885.31.3   Taine, Hippolyte Adolphe. On intelligence. N.Y., 1875. 2v.
Phil 8644.1.2   Tait, P.G. The unseen universe. N.Y., 1875.
Phil 8644.1   Tait, P.G. The unseen universe. N.Y., 1875.
Phil 7054.160   Tappan, Cora L.V. Discourses through the mediumship of Mrs. C. Tappan. London, 1875.
Phil 3428.82   Thomas, K. Herbart, Spinoza, Kant. Langensalza, 1875.
Phil 194.7   Tobias, W. Grenzen der Philosophie. Berlin, 1875.
Phil 8709.2.4   Tyndall, John. Address...before British association. N.Y., 1875.
Phil 3895.40.2   Ulrici, H. Gott und die Natur. Leipzig, 1875.
Phil 5260.1.15   Upham, T.C. Mental philosophy. v.2. N.Y., 1875.
Phil 8601.4   Vallis, R. Die Naturgeschichte der Göttes. Leipzig, 1875.
Phil 3503.5.5   Volkelt, Johannes. Kant's kategorischer Imperativ. Wien, 1875.
Phil 7082.36   Volkelt, Johannes. Die Traum-Phantasie. Stuttgart, 1875.
Phil 5261.1   Volkmann, W. Lehrbuch der Psychologie. Göthen, 1875-76. 2v.
Phil 2262.86   Waern, L.M. Shaftesbury's dygdelära. Upsala, 1875.
Phil 7060.104   Wallace, A.R. On miracles and modern spiritualism. London, 1875.
Phil 5628.51   Warlomont, Évariste. Louise Lateau. Bruxelles, 1875.
Phil 8712.22   Warring, C.B. The mosaic account of creation. N.Y., 1875.
Phil 9430.14   Weygoldt, G.P. Kritik des philosophischen Pessimismus der neuesten Zeit. Leiden, 1875.
Phil 353.11   Wilkens, Claudius. Erkjendelses problem. København, 1875.
Phil 5062.34   Willcox, J.M. Elementary philosophy. Philadelphia, 1875.
Phil 5640.5   Wyld, R.S. Physics and philosophy of the senses. London, 1875.
Phil 6972.7   Wynter, A. The borderlands of insanity. N.Y., 1875.
Phil 200.2.6   Zeller, E. Vorträge und Abhandlungen Geschichtlichen Inhalts. 1. Aufl. Leipzig, 1875.
Phil 3025.2.2   Zeller, Eduard. Geschichte der deutschen Philosophie seit Leibniz. 2. Aufl. München, 1875.
Phil 3801.896*   Zimmermann, R. Schelling's Philosophie der Kunst. Wien, 1875.
Phil 8900.3   Zweifel, Hans. Die sittliche Weltordnung. München, 1875.

1876

Phil 6945.4   American Psychiatric Association. Propositions and resolutions of the Association of Medical Superintendents of American Institutions for the insane. Philadelphia, 1876.
Phil 331.2.12   Avenarius, R. Philosophie als Denken der Welt Gemäss dem Prinzip des kleinsten Kraftmasses. Leipzig, 1876.
Phil 176.7   Barsalou-Fromenty, Gustave. La philosophie terrestre. Geneva, 1876.
Phil 8581.20   Bascom, J. Philosophy of religion. N.Y., 1876.
Phil 176.40   Batz, P. Philosophie der Erlösung. Berlin, 1876-86. 2v.
Phil 3805.83   Bender, W. Schleiermachers Theologie. v.1-2. Nördlingen, 1876-78.
Phil 8610.876.10   Bennett, D.M. Thirty discussions, Bible stories, essays and lectures. N.Y., 1876.
Phil 5640.2   Bernstein, J. Five senses of man. N.Y., 1876.
Phil 270.3   Bertauld, P.A. Introduction à la recherche des causes premières. Paris, 1876.
Phil 2295.80   Berthold, G. John Toland und der Monismus der Gegenwart. Heidelberg, 1876.
Phil 365.26   Bertinaria, F. La dottrina dell'evoluzione e la fil. Genova, 1876.
Phil 3821.7   Betz, H.J. Levenschets van Baruch de Spinoza. 's Gravenhage, 1876.
Phil 2270.80   Birks, T.R. Modern physical fatalism. London, 1876.
Phil 3625.5.86   Bitte, I.H. Salomon Maimon. Berlin, 1876.
Phil 8691.3   Bixby, J.T. Similarities of physical and religious knowledge. N.Y., 1876.
Phil 8626.7   Blackwell, A.B. Physical basis of immortality. N.Y., 1876.
Phil 3552.110.5   Bodemann, E. G.W. Leibniz. Hannover, 1876.
Phil 2115.91A   Bourne, H.R.F. The life of John Locke. London, 1876. 2v.
Phil 2115.91.2A   Bourne, H.R.F. The life of John Locke. N.Y., 1876. 2v.
Phil 1885.30*   Bradley, Francis H. Ethical studies. London, 1876.
Phil 3120.8.30   Brentano, Franz. Was für ein Philosoph manchmal Epoche macht. Wien, 1876.
Phil 3483.5   Bridel, P. La philosophie de la religion. Lausanne, 1876.
Phil 3483.24   Bring, Gustaf. Immanuel Kants förhallande till den filosofiska teologien. Lund, 1876.
Phil 8581.12   Brinton, D.G. The religious sentiment. N.Y., 1876.
Phil 7054.123.5   Britten, Emma H. Ghostland. Boston, 1876.
Phil 960.1   Brockie, W. Indian thought. Sunderland, 1876.
Phil 5811.5.10   Büchner, L. Aus dem Geistesleben der Thiere oder Staaten und Thaten der Kleinen. Berlin, 1876.
Phil 3552.295   Bussenius, Karl. Über die Theodicee des Leibniz. Halle, 1876.
Phil 1133.15   Byk, S.A. Die vorsokratische Philosophie der Griechen. Leipzig, 1876-77. 2v.
Phil 9550.11.5   Cantoni, C. Una critica dell'utilitarismo. Roma, 1876.
Phil 802.8.10   Carbonel, Pierre. Essai de philosophie classique. Paris, 1876.
Phil 333.2   Caspari, O. Grundprobleme der Erkenntniss. Berlin, 1876. 2v.
Phil 8582.4   Caumont, G. Jugements d'un mourant sur la vie. Paris, 1876.
Phil 6952.23   Charcot, J.M. Leçons sur les localisations dans les maladies du cerveau. Paris, 1876.
Phil 5643.5   Classen, A. Physiologie des Gesichtssinnes. Braunschweig, 1876.
Phil 2805.80.7   Cousin, Victor. Études sur Pascal. Paris, 1876.
Phil 5242.11   Cox, E.W. The mechanism of man. London, 1876. 2v.
Phil 2520.87   Cunningham, William. The influence of Descartes on metaphysical speculation in England. London, 1876.
Phil 5243.3   Day, H.N. Elements of psychology. N.Y., 1876.
Phil 5043.3.10   Day, Henry N. Logical praxis. N.Y., 1876.

1876 - cont.

Phil 5243.5.5   Delboeuf, J.R.L. La psychologie. Paris, 1876.
Phil 5635.2   Delboeuf, J.R.L. Théorie générale de la sensibilité. Bruxelles, 1876.
Phil 2520.35.6   Descartes, René. Discours de la méthode pour bien conduire sa raison et chercher la vérité dans les sciences. Paris, 1876.
Phil 2520.26.2   Descartes, René. Oeuvres choisies. Paris, 1876.
Phil 3485.6   Desdouits, T. La philosophie de Kant. Paris, 1876.
Phil 8599.16.9   De Tribus Impostoribus. De tribus impostoribus. 2. Aufl. Heilbronn, 1876.
Phil 3485.2   Dieterich, K. Kant und Newton. Tübingen, 1876.
Phil 1020.2   Dieterici, F. Die Philosophie der Araber im X. Jahrhunderts. v.1-2,4-6,9,12-13. Leipzig, 1876-1895. 10v.
Phil 5330.19   Dohrn, H. Das Problem der Aufmerksamkeit. Schleswig, 1876.
Phil 8693.4.6   Draper, J.W. Los conflictos entre la ciencia y la religion. Madrid, 1876.
Phil 8693.4.5   Draper, J.W. Historia de los conflictos entre la religion y la ciencia. Madrid, 1876.
Phil 3428.156   Drobisch, M.W. Über die Fortbildung der Philosophie durch Herbart. Leipzig, 1876.
Htn   Phil 6000.2*   Duchenne, Guillaume B. Mécanisme de la physionomie humaine. Paris, 1876.
Phil 5402.1.3   Dumont, L. Vergnügen und Schmerz. Leipzig, 1876.
Phil 3415.103   Ebrard, A. Eduard von Hartmann's Philosophie des Unbewussten. Gütersloh, 1876.
Phil 804.1   Elmendorf, J.J. Outlines of lectures on history of philosophy. N.Y., 1876.
Phil 6954.5A   Erb, Wilhelm. Handbuch der Krankheiten des Nervensystems. 2e Aufl. Leipzig, 1876-78. 2v.
Phil 3549.5.90   Erdmann, B. Martin Knutzen und seine Zeit. Leipzig, 1876.
Phil 6114.5.8   Evans, W.F. Soul and body. Boston, 1876.
Phil 8585.1.2   Fairbairn, A.M. Studies...philosophy of religion and history. 4. ed. N.Y., 1876.
Phil 3210.66   Fechner, G.T. Erinnerungen an die letzten Tage der Odlehre und ihre Urhebers. Leipzig, 1876.
Phil 3210.63   Fechner, G.T. Vorschule der Aesthetik. v.1-2. Leipzig, 1876.
Phil 4200.1.5F   Ferri, L. La psicologia di Pietro Pomponazzi. Roma, 1876.
Phil 6115.3.5   Ferrier, D. The functions of the brain. N.Y., 1876.
Phil 3235.76   Feuerbach, Ludwig. Briefwechsel zwischen L. Feuerbach und C. Kapp, 1832-1848. Leipzig, 1876.
Phil 3005.2   Fichte, T.H. Fragen und Bedenken. Leipzig, 1876.
Phil 4005.2   Fiorentino, F. La filosofia contemporanea in Italia. Napoli, 1876.
Phil 4005.2.5   Fiorentino, F. Scritti varii di letteratura, filosofia e critica. Napoli, 1876.
Phil 180.16   Fiske, J. The unseen world and other essays. Boston, 1876.
Phil 6115.6.9   Flechsig, P. Die Leitungsbahnen im Gehirn und Rückenmark. Leipzig, 1876.
Phil 270.54   Foissac, Pierre. La chance ou la destinée. Paris, 1876.
Phil 3552.86.5   Foucher de Careil, Alexandre. Leibniz et les deux sophies. Paris, 1876.
Phil 5045.2.5   Fowler, Thomas. Inductive logic. Oxofrd, 1876.
Phil 3808.82.5   Frauenstädt, C.M.J. Neue Brief über Schopenhauerische Philosophie. Leipzig, 1876.
NEDL   Phil 705.3   Frothingham, Octavius Brooks. Transcendentalism in New England. N.Y., 1876.
Phil 9430.30   Gass, W. Optimismus und Pessimismus. Berlin, 1876.
Phil 3552.132   Geijer, K.R. Huru förhåller sig Leibnitz' metafysik. Upsala, 1876.
Phil 2730.92   Gérard, J. La philosophie de Maine de Biran. Paris, 1876.
Phil 181.46   Gille, E. Cours de philosophie. Paris, 1876.
Phil 5046.9   Gilmore, J.H. Outlines of logic. Rochester, 1876.
Phil 181.9   Giner, F. Estudios filosoficos y religiosos. Madrid, 1876.
Phil 2262.82   Gizycki, G. von. Die Philosophie Shaftesbury's. Leipzig, 1876.
Phil 365.29   Gizycki, G. von. Philosophische Consequenzen der Lamarck-Darwin. Leipzig, 1876.
Phil 7054.114   Glass, C.E. Advance thought. London, 1876.
Phil 5756.7   Göring, Carl. Über die Menschlichefreiheit. Leipzig, 1876.
Phil 5640.21   Goering, W. Raum und Stoff. Berlin, 1876.
Phil 6990.30   Grellety, L. Du merveilleux, des miracles et des pelerinages au point de vue medical. Paris, 1876.
Phil 181.18   Griffith, J. Behind the veil. London, 1876.
Phil 8881.19   Grote, G. Fragments on ethical subjects. London, 1876.
Phil 8881.17   Grote, J. The moral ideals. Cambridge, 1876.
Phil 4570.1.5   Grubbe, Samuel. Filosofiska skrifter i Urval. v.1-5. Lund, 1876. 7v.
Phil 630.26   Grün, Karl. Die Philosophie in der Gegenwart. Leipzig, 1876.
Phil 8610.875.10   Guild, E.E. The pro and con of supernatural religion...together with a sketch of the life of the author. N.Y., 1876.
Phil 5635.4   Guillaume, J.A.M. Nouveau traité des sensations. Paris, 1876. 2v.
Phil 5046.14   Gustrin, E.F. Några anmarkningar angående den formella logiken. Lund, 1876.
Phil 7054.136   Hafed, prince of Persia. London, 1876.
Phil 7054.64   Hall, S.C. The use of spiritualism? Glasgow, 1876.
Phil 807.13   Hamma, M. Geschichte und Grundfragen der Metaphysik. Freiburg, 1876.
Phil 6957.2.9   Hammond, W.A. A treatise on the diseases of the nervous system. 6. ed. N.Y., 1876.
Phil 3007.1.5   Harms, F. Die Philosophie seit Kant. Berlin, 1876.
Phil 2055.6   Harris, G. A philosophical treatise. London, 1876. 2v.
Phil 3415.48   Hartmann, Eduard von. Gesammelte Studien und Aufsätze. Berlin, 1876.
Phil 3415.62.2   Hartmann, Eduard von. La religion de L'Avenir. Paris, 1876.
Phil 182.6.10   Hartsen, F.A. Die Philosophie als Wissenschaft. Heidelberg, 1876.
Phil 807.1   Haven, J. A history of philosophy. N.Y., 1876.
Phil 3425.60   Hegel, Georg Wilhelm Friedrich. Philosophie de la religion. Paris, 1876-78. 2v.
Phil 182.12   Hellenbach, L.B. Eine Philosophie des gesunden Menschenverstandes. Wien, 1876.
Phil 5247.7   Henle, F.G.J. Anthropologische Vorträge. Braunschweig, 1876-80.
Phil 8050.46   Hermann, C. Die Ästhetik in ihrer Geschichte und als wissenschaftliches System. Leipzig, 1876.

1876 - cont.

Phil 5247.9.5 — Hickok, L.P. Rational psychology. N.Y., 1876.

Phil 8587.15 — Higginson, T.W. The sympathy of religions. Boston, 1876.

Phil 4580.64 — Høffding, Harald. Om grundlaget for den humane ethik. Kjøbenhavn, 1876.

Phil 4803.454.35 — Hoene-Wroński, Józef Maria. Messianisme; philosophie absolue. Paris, 1876.

Phil 8587.33.3 — Hoppe, J.I. Die Erforschung der Gefühle und moralischen Begriffe. 3. Aufl. Regensburg, 1876.

Phil 9430.4 — Huber, J.W. Der Pessimismus. München, 1876.

Phil 3491.9 — Jacobson, Julius. Ueber die Auffindung des Apriori. Berlin, 1876.

Phil 2668.50 — Janet, Paul A.R. Les causes finales. Paris, 1876.

Phil 809.1 — Joel, M. Beiträge zur Geschichte der Philosophie. Bd.1-2. Breslau, 1876.

Phil 3480.70.20 — Kant, Immanuel. Logik. 2. Aufl. Leipzig, 1876.

Phil 3552.94.9 — Kirchner, Friedrich. Gottfried Wilhelm Leibniz. Cöthen, 1876.

Phil 185.5 — Kirkman, T.P. Philosophy without assumptions. London, 1876.

Phil 1710.1 — Knauer, V. Geschichte der Philosophie mit besonderer Berücksichtigung der Neuzeit. Wien, 1876.

Phil 672.12 — Krause, A. Die Gesetze der menschlichen Herzens. Lahr, 1876.

Phil 3493.1 — Laas, E. Kants Analogien der Erfahrung. Berlin, 1876.

Phil 292.22 — Landesmann, Heinrich. Der Naturgenuss. Berlin, 1876.

Phil 486.1.6A — Lange, F.A. Geschichte des Materialismus. 3e Aufl. Iserlohn, 1876-77. 2v.

Phil 5251.3 — Langer, P. Die Grundlagen der Psychophysik. Jena, 1876.

Phil 8735.18 — Lasson, A. De causis finalibus. Berolini, 1876.

Phil 5251.10 — Lazarus, M. Das Leben der Seele. Berlin, 1876. 3v.

Phil 8836.2.5 — Lecky, W.E.H. History of European morals. v.1. N.Y., 1876.

Phil 186.12 — Liebmann, O. Zur Analysis der Wirklichkeit. Strassburg, 1876.

Phil 600.7.5 — Littré, Émile. Fragments de philosophie positive et de sociologie. Paris, 1876.

Phil 2115.13 — Locke, J. Works. London, 1876.

Phil 3565.68.5 — Lotze, Hermann. Principes généraux de psychologie physiologique. Paris, 1876.

Phil 6121.7.3 — Luys, J. Le cerveau et ses fonctions. Paris, 1876.

Htn Phil 8636.9* — Lyttelton, W.H. Scripture revelations of the life of man after death. 3. ed. London, 1876.

Phil 2125.57 — McCosh, James. The laws of discursive thought. N.Y., 1876.

Phil 187.73F — Madiedo, M.M. Una gran revolucion, ó La razon del hombre juzgada por sí misma. Caracas, 1876.

Phil 4170.7.30 — Mamiani della Rovere, Terenzio. Compendio e sintesi della propriafilosofia. Torino, 1876.

NEDL Phil 5300.1 — Mantegazza, P. Atlante della espressione del dolore. Firenze, 1876.

Phil 293.17 — Marin de Carranrais, E. de. Études sur les origines. Paris, 1876.

Phil 487.2.2 — Martineau, J. Modern materialism. Boston, 1876.

Phil 487.2 — Martineau, J. Modern materialism. Boston, 1876.

Phil 487.2.5 — Martineau, J. Religion affected by modern materialism. London, 1876-78. 2 pam.

Phil 6122.1.15 — Maudsley, H. The physiology of mind. 3d ed. pt.1. London, 1876.

Phil 187.14 — Michelet, K.L. Das System der Philosophie. Berlin, 1876-1881. 5v.

Phil 2520.95.5 — Millet, J. Descartes; son histoire depuis 1637. Paris, 1876.

Phil 5465.22 — Nielsen, Rasmus. Om phantasiens magt. Kjøbenhavn, 1876.

Phil 9174.1.2 — Osgood, S. The hearth-stone. N.Y., 1876.

Phil 1715.1 — Papillen, Fernand. Histoire de la philosophie moderne. Paris, 1876. 2v.

Phil 2805.25 — Pascal, Blaise. Fragments philosophiques. Paris, 1876.

Phil 2805.40.21 — Pascal, Blaise. Pensées choisies. 6e éd. Paris, 1876.

Phil 190.5 — Peck, J.S. The ultimate generalization. N.Y., 1876.

Phil 5825.1 — Perty, J.A.M. Über das Seelenleben der Thiere. Leipzig, 1876.

Phil 9375.5 — Platt, J. Business. London, 1876.

Phil 5255.29 — Preyer, W. Über die Grenzen der Tonwahrnehmung. n.p., 1876-89. 9 pam.

Phil 8597.26 — Rabus, Leonhard. Philosophie und Theologie. Erlangen, 1876.

Phil 7054.146.5 — Ramsdell, Sarah. Spirit life of Theodore Parker. Boston, 1876.

Phil 8505.1 — Report...National Liberal League. Boston, 1876.

Phil 5440.4.3 — Ribot, T. Die Erblichkeit. v.1-4. Leipzig, 1876.

Phil 3791.35 — Riehl, Alois. Der philosophischeKriticismus. v.1-2. Leipzig, 1876-1887.

Phil 5257.26.8 — Rüegg, H.R. Lehrbuch der Psychologie. 3. Aufl. Bern, 1876.

Phil 193.45 — Scheffler, H. Die Naturgesetze. v.1-4 and Supplement 1-3. Leipzig, 1876-1883. 7v.

Phil 6128.35 — Scheidemacher, C.B. Das Seelenleben und die Behirnthatigkeit. Regensburg, 1876.

Phil 270.11 — Schellwein, R. Das Gesets der Causalität in der Natur. Berlin, 1876.

Phil 525.14 — Schmidt, C. Les libertins spirituels. Bale, 1876.

Phil 5635.21 — Schneider, G.H. Über die Empfindung der Ruhe. Zürich, 1876.

Phil 5258.83 — Sièrebois, R.P. Psychologie réaliste. Paris, 1876.

Phil 5258.17 — Simonin, A. Traité de psychologie. Paris, 1876.

Phil 8893.14.11 — Smiles, Samuel. Thrift. Toronto, 1876.

Phil 2270.31.2 — Spencer, Herbert. System der synthetischen Philosophie: Biologie. Stuttgart, 1876-77. 2v.

Phil 299.17 — Spiller, P. Die Urkraft des Weltalls. Berlin, 1876.

Phil 3819.70 — Spinoza, Benedictus de. Briefwechsel; Einleitung.

Phil 3018.11 — Spitzer, Hugo. Nominalismus und Realismus in der neuesten deutschen Philosophie. Leipzig, 1876.

Phil 3500.10.15 — Stadler, A. Die Grundsätze der reinen Erkenntnisstheorie in der Kantischen Philosophie. Leipzig, 1876.

Phil 1818.2 — Stephen, Leslie. History of English thought in XVIIIth century. N.Y., 1876. 2v.

Phil 5754.1.27 — Stewart, J.G. Freedom of the will vindicated. Glasgow, 1876.

Phil 1535.11 — Stöckl, A. Lehrbuch der Philosophie. Mainz, 1876. 2v.

Phil 8740.1 — Suggestions for a public religious service. London, 1876.

Phil 1124.1.5 — Teichmüller, G. Neue Studien zur Geschichte der Begriffe. Gotha, 1876-1879. 2v.

Phil 3501.1 — Thiele, G. Kant's intellektuelle Anschauung. Halle, 1876.

1876 - cont.

Phil 2672.90 — Tissot, J. Théodore Jouffroy: sa vie et ses écrits. Paris, 1876.

Phil 9430.13 — Trautz, T. Der Pessimismus. Karlsruhe, 1876.

Phil 8610.876 — Truth seeker tracts upon a variety of subjects by different authors. v.2-4. N.Y., 1876-77. 3v.

Phil 5643.49 — Ueberhorst, Karl. Die Entslehung der Gesichtswahrnehmung. Göttingen, 1876.

Phil 3415.87 — Vaihinger, H. Hartmann, Dühring und Lange. Faerlohn, 1876.

Phil 5061.1.8 — Venn, J. The logic of chance. London, 1876.

Phil 3504.2 — Wangenheim, F. Vertheidigung Kants Gegen Fries. Berlin, 1876.

Phil 1500.1 — Werner, K. Die Entwicklung der mittelalterlicher Psychologie. Wien, 1876.

Phil 1200.35 — Wevers, Friedrich. Quid Paulus, quid stoici de virtute docuerint. Meursae, 1876? 3 pam.

Phil 7068.76.10 — Wilson, Ebenezer V. The truths of spiritualism. Chicago, 1876.

Phil 5232.1 — Windelband, W. Über den...psychologische Forschung. Leipzig, 1876.

Phil 3925.6.06 — Windelband, W. Ueber den Gegenwärtigen stand der Psychologie. n.p., 1876-1914. 12 pam.

Phil 4803.879.06 — Wiszniewski, Michał. Charaktery rozumów ludzkich. Warszawa, 1876. 2 pam.

Phil 3915.36 — Wundt, Wilhelm. Über die Einfluss der Philosophie. Leipzig, 1876.

Phil 3245.80 — Zeller, E. Antwort an...Dr. Immanuel Hermann Fichte. Berlin, 1876.

Phil 1130.2.5 — Zeller, Eduard. Die Philosophie der Griechen. v. 1-2,4-5. Leipzig, 1876-81. 4v.

Phil 1130.7 — Zeller, Eduard. Plato and the older academy. Leipzig, 1876.

Phil 3428.155.10 — Zimmermann, R. Perioden in Herbart's philosophischen Geistesgang. Wien, 1876.

Phil 3808.98 — Zimmern, H. Arthur Schopenhauer. London, 1876.

Phil 8605.1 — Zweifel, H. Die gesetze Göttes. München, 1876.

1877

Phil 1870.82.5 — Abbot, T.K. Bishop Berkeley and Professor Fraser. Dublin, 1877.

Phil 8401.18 — Allen, Grant. Physiological aesthetics. N.Y., 1877.

Phil 175.27 — Anhuth, R.O. Das wahnsinnige Bewusstsein. Halle, 1877.

Phil 3525.80 — Atienza y Medrano, A. El Krausismo. Madrid, 1877.

Phil 4210.87 — Avogadro della Motta, Emiliano. La filosofia dell'abate Antonio Rosmini esaminata. 4a ed. Napoli, 1877.

Phil 176.3.9 — Bahnsen, J. Das tragische als Weltgesetz und der Humor. Lauenburg, 1877.

Phil 5241.5 — Ballardi, L. Die Elemente der Psychologie. Cöthen, 1877.

Phil 3100.50.4 — Beneke, F.E. Die neue Psychologie. 4. Aufl. Berlin, 1877.

Phil 5247.35.5 — Bertinaria, F. La psicologia fisica ed iperfisica di Hoenato Wronski. Torino, 1877.

Phil 3821.7.7 — Betz, H.J. Spinoza en de vrijheid. 's Gravenhage, 1877.

Phil 3483.30 — Biese, Reinhold. Die Erkenntnisslehre des Aristoteles und Kant's. Berlin, 1877.

Phil 8656.3 — Blackie, J.S. The natural history of atheism. London, 1877.

Phil 3235.84.10 — Bolin, Wilhelm. Über Ludwig Feuerbach's Briefwechsel und Nachlass. Helsingfors, 1877.

Phil 5811.3 — Bourbon del Monte, J.B.F. L'homme et les animaux. Paris, 1877.

Phil 1701.1.2 — Bowen, F. Modern philosophy. N.Y., 1877.

Phil 1701.1 — Bowen, F. Modern philosophy. N.Y., 1877.

Phil 1701.1.3 — Bowen, F. Modern philosophy. 2nd ed. N.Y., 1877.

Phil 8610.858.5 — Bradlaugh, Charles. Biographies of ancient and modern celebrated freethinkers. Boston, 1877.

Phil 2280.1.90 — Bradley, F.H. Mr. Sidgwick's hedonism. London, 1877.

Phil 4210.116F — Buroni, Giuseppe. Dell'essere e del conoscere. Torino, 1877.

Phil 3808.81 — Busch, O. Arthur Schopenhauer. Heidelberg, 1877.

Phil 3484.1 — Caird, E. A critical account of the philosophy of Kant. Glasgow, 1877.

Phil 3484.1.2 — Caird, E. A critical account of the philosophy of Kant. London, 1877.

Phil 3822.2 — Camerer, T. Die Lehre Spinoza's. Stuttgart, 1877.

Phil 177.51 — Carneri, Bartolomeo. Der Mensch als Selbstjweck. Wien, 1877.

Phil 7068.77.1 — Carpenter, William B. Mesmerism, spiritualism,...historically and scientifically considered. London, 1877.

Phil 7068.77 — Carpenter, William B. Mesmerism, spiritualism,...historically and scientifically considered. N.Y., 1877.

Phil 6952.4 — Chambers, J. A mad world and its inhabitants. N.Y., 1877.

Phil 3484.2.5A — Cohen, H. Kant's Begrundung der Ethik. Berlin, 1877.

Phil 2490.74 — Comte, Auguste. Lettres d'Auguste Comte à J.S. Mill. Paris, 1877.

Phil 4265.2.91 — Cultrera, Paolo. Della vita e delle opere del Rev. P.D. Geovachino Ventura. Palermo, 1877.

Phil 8404.9 — Daneo, G. Alcune considerazioni sul bello. Torino, 1877.

Phil 2520.26 — Descartes, René. Oeuvres choisies. Paris, 1877.

Phil 3823.1 — Dessauer, M. Der Sokrates der Neuzeit...Spinoza's. Cöthen, 1877.

Phil 178.5.2 — Deussen, P. Die Elemente der Metaphysik. Aachen, 1877.

Phil 5643.99 — Donders, F.C. Rapport aangaande het onderzoek van het gezichtsvermongen. Utrecht, 1877. 2 pam.

Phil 1900.82 — Eaton, J.R.T. Bishop Butler and his critics. Oxford, 1877.

Phil 8879.22 — Edfeldt, H. Om begreppet sedlighet. Upsala, 1877.

Phil 8879.18 — Edgeworth, F.Y. New and old methods of ethics. Oxford, 1877.

Phil 600.22 — Estasén y Cortada, P. El positivismo. Barcelona, 1877.

Phil 8585.1 — Fairbairn, A.M. Studies...philosophy of religion and history. London, 1877.

Phil 3210.49 — Fechner, G.T. In Sachen der Psychophysik. Leipzig, 1877.

Phil 6955.10 — Fechner, Gustav. In Sachen der Psychophysik. Leipzig, 1877.

Phil 2405.1 — Ferraz, Marin. Étude sur la philosophie en France au XIXe siècle. Paris, 1877.

Phil 4110.5.95F — Ferri, Luigi. Cenno su Giuseppe Ferrari e le sul dottrine. Roma, 1877.

Phil 5245.6 — Filachou, J.E. Éléments de psychologie mathématique. Montpelier, 1877.

Phil 4120.6.90 — Fiorentino, F. Della vita e delle opere di Vincenzo de Grazia. Napoli, 1877.

Chronological Listing

Phil 4200.1.6 Fiorentino, F. Luigi Ferri: la psicologia di Pietro Pomponazzi. Napoli, 1877.

Phil 8660.4 Flint, R. Theism. (Baird lectures for 1876). Edinburgh, 1877.

Phil 5245.10 Fournié, E. Essai de psychologie. Paris, 1877.

Phil 5245.12 Frohschammer, J. Die Phantasie als Grundprincip des Weltprocesses. München, 1877.

Phil 4260.93 Galasso, Antonio. Del criterio della verita nella scienza e nella storia secondo G.B. Vico. Milano, 1877.

Phil 5246.6 Giner de los Rios, Francisco. Lecciones sumarias de psicología. Midrid, 1877.

Phil 181.48 Giovanni, V. di. Prelezioni di filosofia. Palermo, 1877.

Phil 8956.4 Gooding, W.M. A philosophy of the moral nature of man. Newark, 1877.

Phil 8586.37.10 Greg, William R. The creed of Christendom. 5th ed. London, 1877. 2v.

Phil 5435.11 Gurney, Joseph J. Thoughts on habit and discipline. Philadelphia, 1877.

Phil 5756.1 Guthrie, M. Causational and free will. London, 1877.

Phil 3900.1.83 Hallmer, Lars. Om Friedrich Ueberwegs "System der logik". Lund, 1877.

Phil 2035.51.19 Hamilton, William. The metaphysics of Sir William Hamilton. Boston, 1877[1861]

Phil 3415.50 Hartmann, Eduard von. Le Darwinisme. Paris, 1877.

Phil 3415.42 Hartmann, Eduard von. Neukantianismus, Schopenhauerianismus. Berlin, 1877.

Phil 3415.31 Hartmann, Eduard von. Philosophie de L'inconscient. Paris, 1877. 2v.

Phil 3415.62 Hartmann, Eduard von. La religion de L'Avenir. Paris, 1877.

Phil 3415.35.2 Hartmann, Eduard von. Das Umbewusste...Physiologie. 2. Aufl. Berlin, 1877.

Phil 3415.39 Hartmann, Eduard von. Verldsprocessens väsen eller det omedvetnas filosofi. Stockholm, 1877-78.

Phil 182.6 Hartsen, F.A. Principes de philosophie. Paris, 1877.

Phil 9075.24 Hasenclever, K.H. Die Berührung und Verwerthung der Gewissens. Karleruhe, 1877.

Phil 8587.6.5 Hedge, F.H. Ways of the spirit. Boston, 1877. 2v.

Phil 2636.31 Helvétius, C.A. A treatise on man. London, 1877. 2v.

Phil 1750.10 Hermann, C. Der Gegensatz...der neueren Philosophie. Leipzig, 1877.

Phil 3827.3 Høffding, H. Spinozas liv og laere. København, 1877.

Phil 8882.46 Horn, E.F.B. Mennesket og moralen. Malling, 1877.

Phil 8610.877.5 Humphrey, G.H. Christianity and infidelity. N.Y., 1877.

Phil 340.4 Jacobson, J. Über die Beziehungen zwischen Kategorien und Urtheilsfarmen. Inaug. Diss. Königsberg, 1877.

Phil 5819.2 Joly, H. L'homme et l'animal. Paris, 1877.

Phil 3480.30.3 Kant, Immanuel. Kritik der reinen Vernunft. 2. Verb. Aufl. Leipzig, 1877.

Phil 3480.62 Kant, Immanuel. Metafisica de Kant. Madrid, 1877.

Phil 8885.1 Kaulich, W. System der Ethik. Prag, 1877.

Phil 810.1 Kirchner, F. Katechismus der Geschichte der Philosophie. Leipzig, 1877.

Phil 5374.27 Koch, Julius L.A. Vom Bewusstsein in Zustanden sogennanten Bewusstlosigkeit. Stuttgart, 1877.

L Phil 1850.105 Laing, F.H. Lord Bacon's philosophy examined. London, 1877.

Phil 8886.39 Landau, L.R. System der gesammten Ethik. Band 1-2. Berlin, 1877-78.

Phil 486.1.5 Lange, F.A. History of materialism. London, 1877. 3v.

Phil 5051.2 Lange, F.A. Logische Studien. Iserlohn, 1877.

Phil 8636.5.5 Lescoeur, Louis. A vida futura; conferencias. Lisboa, 1877.

Phil 600.62 Lesevich, Vladimir V. Opyt kriticheskago izsledovaniia osnovonachal pozitivnoi filosofii. Sanktpeterburg, 1877. 2 pam.

Phil 486.4 Lewins, R. Life and mind. Lewes, 1877.

Phil 8961.2 Lobstein, P. Die Ethik Calvins. Strassburg, 1877.

Phil 2115.14 Locke, J. Philosophical works. London, 1877. 2v.

Phil 6121.7.12 Luys, J. Das Gehirn. Leipzig, 1877.

Phil 186.51 Lyng, G.W. Philosophische Studien. n.p., 1877.

Phil 5620.3 Magy, F. La raison et l'âme. Paris, 1877.

Phil 5400.8 Maillet, E. De l'essence des passions. Paris, 1877.

Phil 3494.27 Mamiani, T. Della psicologia di Kant. Roma, 1877.

Phil 3850.8.81 Michelis, F. Staudenmaier's Wissenschaftliche Leistung. Freiburg, 1877.

Phil 187.52 Michelis, Friedrich. Die Philosophie des Bewusstseins. Bonn, 1877.

Phil 2138.35.6 Mill, John S. System der deductiven und inductiven Logik. 4e Aufl. v.1-2. Braunschweig, 1877.

Phil 187.16 Miller, J. Metaphysics. N.Y., 1877.

Phil 7230.2 Mitchell, G.W. X+Y=Z, or The sleeping preacher. N.Y., 1877.

Phil 9065.1 Morley, J. On compromise. London, 1877.

Phil 8887.23 Mosby, E.F. The ideal life. Cincinnatti, Ohio, 1877.

Phil 1135.70 Müller, E. Die Idee der Menschheit. Leipzig, 1877.

Phil 2730.80.5 Naville, E. Maine de Biran. 3e éd. Paris, 1877.

Phil 3195.2.93 Neudecker, G. Der Philosoph Deutinger und ultramontane Sophistik. Würzburg, 1877.

Phil 510.9.10 Noiré, Ludwig. Einleitung und Begründung einer monistischen Erkenntnis-Theorie. Mainz, 1877.

Phil 5254.4 Oreg, J. Gondolkodastan az eggetemesitö (inductiv) s lehozó (deductiv) módazer alapján. Nagy Körös, 1877.

Phil 2805.40.7 Pascal, Blaise. Les pensées. Paris, 1877-79. 2v.

Phil 190.24 Perreaux, L.-G. Lois de l'univers. Paris, 1877. 2v.

Phil 8735.7 Pflüger, E.F.W. Die teleologische Mechanik der lebendigen Natur. 2. Aufl. Bonn, 1877.

Phil 6125.16 Pitres, A. Recherches sur les lésions du centre ovale des hémisphères cérébraux. Paris, 1877.

Phil 296.3 Pivány, J.A. Entwicklungsgeschichte des Welt...Organismen. Plauen, 1877.

Phil 5055.3 Planck, K.C. Logisches Kausalgesetz. Nördlingen, 1877.

Phil 3850.1.102 Plasman, L.C. de. Lettres à Gambetta...sur le dernier ouvrage de Strauss. Paris, 1877.

Phil 5055.5.5 Prantl, C. Verstehen und Beurtheilen. München, 1877.

Phil 28.2 Preyer, W. Sammlung physiologischer Abhandlungen. Jena, 1877. 2v.

Phil 7080.33 Preyer, William. Über die Ursache des Schlafes. Stuttgart, 1877.

Phil 3010.4 Rannengiesser, P. Dogmatismus und Skepticismus. Elberfeld, 1877.

Phil 8892.44 Rée, Paul. Der Ursprung der moralischen Empfindungen. Chemnitz, 1877.

Phil 3837.1 Rehorn, K.W.A. G.E. Lessing's Stellung zur Philosophie des Spinoza. Frankfurt, 1877.

Phil 3837.8.5 Renan, Ernest. Spinoza; conference tenue à La Haye. Paris, 1877.

Phil 3837.8 Renan, Ernest. Spinoza; Rede...gehalten im Haag. Leipzig, 1877.

Phil 8707.38 Reusch, Franz Heinrich. Die biblische Schöpfungsgesichte und ihr Verhältniss zu den Ergebnissen der Naturforschung. Bonn, 1877.

Phil 5635.31 Richet, Charles. Recherches experimentales et cliniques sur la sensibilité. Paris, 1877.

Phil 5585.53 Rohde, F. Sinneswahrnehmungen und Sinnestäuschungen. Braunsberg, 1877.

Phil 5257.10 Rubinstein, Susanna. Psychologisch-ästhetische Essays. Heidelberg, 1877-88. 2v.

Phil 3805.179 Runze, G. Schleiermacher's Glaubenslehre in ihrer Abhängigkeit von seiner Philosophie. Berlin, 1877.

Phil 3500.18 Sahlin, C.Y. Kants, Schleiermacher's och Bostroms etiska. Upsala, 1877.

Phil 4515.87.2 Sahlin, K.Y. Om menistrarne i den konstitutionela monarkien enligt Boströms statslära. Upsala, 1877.

Phil 4515.87 Sahlin, K.Y. Om ministrarne i den konstitutionela monarkien enligt Boströms statslära. Upsala, 1877.

Phil 8419.6F Salisbury, Edward. Principles of domestic taste. New Haven, 1877.

Phil 193.46 Sanz del Rio, D.J. Analisis del pensamiento racional. Madrid, 1877.

Phil 4260.101 Sarchi, Carlo. Della dottrina di B. Spinoza e di G.B. Vico. Milano, 1877.

Phil 3552.118 Schmarsow, A. Justus-Georgius Schottelius i. Leibniz und Schottelius. Strassburg, 1877.

Phil 3415.85 Schmidt, O. Die naturwissenschaftlichen Grundlagen der Philosophie des Unbewussten. Leipzig, 1877.

Phil 3808.68 Schopenhauer, Arthur. Essai sur le Libre Arbitre. Paris, 1877.

Phil 3808.15 Schopenhauer, Arthur. Sämmtliche Werke. 2. Aufl. Leipzig, 1877. 6v.

Phil 5058.5 Schröder, E. Der Operationskries der Logikkalkuls. Leipzig, 1877.

Phil 7054.168 Sherman, M.L. The gospel of nature. Chicago, 1877.

Phil 193.25.3 Shields, C.W. The final philosophy. N.Y., 1877.

Phil 193.26 Shute, R. A discourse on truth. London, 1877.

Phil 8893.11.10 Sidgwick, H. The methods of ethics. Supplement to 1. ed. Photoreproduction. London, 1877.

Phil 8893.13 Simcox, E. Natural law. London, 1877.

Phil 5938.10.10 Sizer, Nelson. How to teach according to temperament and mental development. N.Y., 1877.

Phil 5258.46 Spamer, K. Physiologie der Seele. Stuttgart, 1877.

Phil 6128.36 Spamer, Karl. Physiologie der Seele. Stuttgart, 1877.

Phil 2050.183 Speckmann, A. Über Hume's metaphysische Skepsis. Bonn, 1877.

Phil 2270.31.4 Spencer, Herbert. System der synthetischen Philosophie: Sociologie. Stuttgart, 1877-97. 4v.

Htn Phil 193.31.5* Spir, A. von. Denken und Wirklichkeit. Leipzig, 1877. 2v.

Phil 349.16 Stein, Heinrich. Ueber Wahrnehmung. Berlin, 1877.

Phil 2275.12 Stewart, D. Collected works. 2nd ed. Edinburgh, 1877. 11v.

Phil 5628.52 Die Stigmatisirten des neunzehnten Jahrhunderts: Anna Katharina Emmerich, Maria von Mörl, Domenico Lazzari. Regensburg, 1877.

Phil 2915.81 Strauss, D.F. Voltaire. 4e Aufl. Bonn, 1877.

Phil 9430.12 Sully, J. Pessimism. London, 1877.

Phil 3501.9 Theodor, J. Der Unendlichkeitsbegriff bei Kant und Aristoteles. Breslau, 1877.

Phil 8709.16 Thomas, J.B. The old Bible and the new science. 2. ed. N.Y., 1877.

Phil 2733.96 Turbiglio, S. Le antitesi...in ispecie nella dottrina...di Malebranche. Roma, 1877.

Phil 1850.89.5 Tyler, S. Discourse of the Baconian philosophy. 3rd ed. Washington, 1877.

X Cg Phil 2138.95 Vasey, George. Individual liberty, legal, moral, and licentious. 2nd ed. London, 1877.

Phil 5525.19.2 Vasey, George. The philosophy of laughter and smiling. 2. ed. London, 1877.

Phil 8610.871.25 Viardot, L. Libre examen. 5. éd. Paris, 1877.

Phil 5831.1.3 Vignoli, Tito. Della legge fondamentale dell'intelligenza nell regno animali. Milano, 1877.

Phil 4260.88 Werner, K. Über Giambattista Vico als Geschichtsphilosophen und begründer der neueren italienischen Philosophie. Wien, 1877.

Phil 672.161 Wiessner, Alexander. Die wesenhafte oder absolute Realität des Raumes. Leipzig, 1877.

Phil 3842.10 Wijck, J. van. Spinoza. Groningen, 1877.

Phil 197.8.5 Wilson, W.D. Five questions in psychology and metaphysics. N.Y., 1877.

Phil 8712.24 Winchell, A. Reconciliation of science and religion. N.Y., 1877.

Phil 353.7 Witte, J.H. Zur Erkenntnistheorie und Ethik. Berlin, 1877.

Phil 6990.26.5 Wonderful works of God. Fall River, Mass., 1877.

Phil 197.12.5A Wright, C. Letters. Cambridge, 1877.

Phil 197.12A Wright, C. Philosophical discussions. N.Y., 1877.

Phil 8712.5 Wright, George F. Recent works bearing on the relation of science to religion. New Haven, 1877-78. 2 pam.

Phil 6972.7.2 Wynter, A. The borderlands of insanity (with 5 new chpaters). London, 1877.

Phil 200.2.7 Zeller, E. Vorträge und Abhandlungen Geschichtlichen Inhalts. 2. Aufl. Leipzig, 1877.

Phil 1130.6.5 Zeller, Eduard. Socrates and the Socratic schools. London, 1877.

1878

NEDL Phil 5040.3.15 Arnauld, Antoine. Logique de Port Royal. Paris, 1878.

Phil 1850.50.2 Bacon, Francis. Novum organum. T. Fowler. Oxford, 1878.

Phil 1850.50.3 Bacon, Francis. Novum organum. T. Fowler. Oxford, 1878.

Phil 8735.10 Baerenbach, Friedrich von. Gedanken über die Teleologie in der Natur. Berlin, 1878.

Phil 6111.1.20 Bain, A. L'esprit et le corps. 3. ed. Paris, 1878.

Phil 176.75 Barach, Carl S. Kleine philosophische Schriften. Wien, 1878.

Phil 600.23 Barzellotti, G. The ethics of positivism. N.Y., 1878.

NEDL Phil 5811.1 Bascomb, J. Comparative psychology. N.Y., 1878.

Phil 8626.23 Beecher, E. History of opinions on the scriptural doctrine of retribution. N.Y., 1878.

1878 - cont.

Phil 8581.47   Bergstedt, C.F. Hvad vi veta, hvad vi tro och hvad vi vilja. Stockholm, 1878.

Phil 1870.40.9   Berkeley, G. Treatise concerning the principles of human knowledge. Chicago, 1878.

Phil 8656.3.2   Blackie, J.S. The natural history of atheism. N.Y., 1878.

Phil 9515.3.83   Bodemann, E. J.G. Zimmermann. Hannover, 1878.

Phil 6951.13   Böttger, H. Die Nahrungsverweigerung der Irren. Leipzig, 1878.

Phil 8876.23   Boussinesq, J. Conciliation du véritable déterminisme mécanique. Paris, 1878.

Phil 8581.50   Burlingame, E.L. Current discussion. N.Y., 1878. 2v.

Phil 4210.116.5   Buroni, Giuseppe. Nozioni di ontologia. 2a ed. Torino, 1878.

Phil 4210.116.10   Buroni, Giuseppe. Risposta 1a al padre Cornoldi in difesa delle nozioni di ontologia. Torino, 1878.

Phil 1900.41   Butler, Joseph. The analogy of religion, natural and revealed, to the constitution and course of nature. London, 1878.

Phil 8402.43   Byk, S. Physiologie des Schönen. Leipzig, 1878.

Phil 4210.80   Calza, G. Esposizione ragionata della filosofia. Intra, 1878-79. 2v.

Phil 4110.5.90   Cantoni, Carlo. Giuseppe Ferrari. Milano, 1878.

Phil 3428.80   Capesius, J. Die Metaphysik Herbarts. Leipzig, 1878.

Phil 9430.3.2   Caro, E.M. El pesimismo en el siglo XIX. Madrid, 1878.

Phil 6952.23.5   Charcot, J.M. Lectures on localization in diseases of the brain. N.Y., 1878.

Phil 177.26.5   Choraux, C. L'ombre de Socrate. Paris, 1878.

Phil 8610.878   Chronicles of Simon Christianus and his manifold and wondrous adventures in the land of Cosmos. N.Y., 1878.

Phil 7060.16   Clarke, E.H. Visions: study of false sight. Boston, 1878.

Phil 177.13   Clemente, A. Le bon sens. Paris, 1878. 2v.

Phil 8692.8   Cotterill, H. On true relations of scientific thought and religious belief. London, 1878.

Phil 7080.31   Cox, E. William. A monograph on sleep and dream. London, 1878.

Phil 9490.3   Curtis, G.W. The public duty of educated men. Albany, N.Y., 1878.

Phil 5300.3   Cyon, E. de. Recherches éxperimentales sur les fonctions des canaux semi-circulaires. Thèse. Paris, 1878.

Phil 6990.24   Daurelle. Étude des manifestations surnaturelles au XIX siècle. Rome, 1878.

Phil 478.2   Dauriac, L. Des notions de matière et de force. Paris, 1878.

Phil 3460.83   Delius, J.F. Darstellung und Hauptgedanken F.H. Jacobi. Halle, 1878.

NEDL Phil 2520.51   Descartes, René. Life and meditations. London, 1878.

Htn Phil 8583.3*   DeVere, Aubrey. Proteus and Amadeus. London, 1878.

Phil 3485.2.5   Dieterich, K. Kant und Rousseau. Tübingen, 1878.

Phil 365.24   Dominicis, S.F. de. La dottrina dell'evoluzione: I. Torino, 1878.

Phil 8430.12   Dreher, Eugen. Die KunstIn ihrer Beziehung. Berlin, 1878.

Phil 803.2.3   Dühring, E. Kritische Geschichte der Philosophie. 3e Aufl. Leipzig, 1878.

Phil 5043.11   Dühring, E.K. Logik und Wissenschaftstheorie. Leipzig, 1878.

Phil 3486.12   Edfeldt, Hans. Kants lära om det moraliskt onda. Upsala, 1878.

Phil 6954.2.5   Emminghaus, H. Allgemeine Psychopathologie. Leipzig, 1878.

Phil 3486.1.5   Erdmann, B. Kant's Kritícismus. Leipzig, 1878. 3 pam.

Phil 804.3.3A   Erdmann, J.E. Grundriss der Geschichte der Philosophie. 3e Aufl. Berlin, 1878. 2v.

Phil 179.3.60   Eucken, R. Geschichte und Kritik der grund Begriffe der Gegenwart. v.1-2. Leipzig, 1878.

Phil 7054.36   Fichet, I.H. von. Der neuere Spiritualismus; sein Werth. Leipzig, 1878.

Phil 665.56   Flügel, O. Die Seelenfrage. Cöthen, 1878.

Phil 6956.7   Garnier, P.E. Des idées de grandeur dans le délire des persécutions. Paris, 1878.

Phil 5816.7   Gay, Henri. Observations sur les instincts de l'homme et l'intelligence des animaux. Paris, 1878.

Phil 4570.2.6   Genberg, P. Valda skrifter. v.1-2. Stockholm, 1878.

Phil 5922.4.50   Gibbon, C. The life of George Combe. London, 1878. 2v.

Phil 181.9.5   Giner, H. Filosofía y arte. Madrid, 1878.

Phil 181.48.5   Giovanni, V. di. Principii di filosofia prima. Palermo, 1878. 3v.

Phil 2050.211   Giżycki, G. von. Die Ethik David Hume's in ihrer geschichtlichen Stellung. Breslau, 1878.

Phil 9430.29   Golther, L. von. Der moderne Pessimismus. Leipzig, 1878.

Phil 3310.5.30   Gutberlet, C. Die Theodicee. Münster, 1878.

Phil 2270.84   Guthrie, M. On Mr. Spencer's formula of evolution. London, 1878.

Phil 1158.5   Guyau, M. La morale d'Epicure. Paris, 1878.

Phil 8831.1   Guyau, M.J. La morale anglaise contemporaine. Paris, 1878.

Phil 3808.86.5   Gwinner, W. Schopenhauer's Leben. Leipzig, 1878.

Phil 5645.7   Hall, G.S. Color-perception. n.p., 1878.

Phil 6957.2   Hammond, W.A. Cerebral hyperaemia. N.Y., 1878.

Phil 807.4   Harms, F. Die Philosophie in ihrer Geschichte. Berlin, 1878-81. 2v.

Phil 8632.9   Harrison, Frederic. A modern symposium. Detroit, 1878.

Phil 3415.30.2   Hartmann, Eduard von. Philosophie des Unbewussten. 8. Aufl. Berlin, 1878. 2v.

Phil 4065.90   Hartung, E.B. Grundlinien einer Ethik bei Giordano Bruno. Leipzig, 1878.

Phil 8587.38   Heegaard, P.S.V. Om intolerance, isaer i henseende til religios overbevisning. Kjobenhavn, 1878.

Phil 5643.11.5   Hering, E. Zur Lehre vom Lichtsinne. Wien, 1878.

Phil 3425.268   Hermann, Conrad. Hegel und die logische Frage der Philosophie in der Gegenwart. Leipzig, 1878.

Phil 182.19.5   Hodgson, S.H. Philosophy of reflection. London, 1878. 2v.

Phil 182.69F   Hoëné Wronski, J.M. Prospectus de la philosophie absolue et son développement. Paris, 1878.

Phil 6117.3   Holbrook, M.L. Hygiene of the brain. N.Y., 1878.

Phil 8662.5.9   Holyoake, George Jacob. The last trial for atheism in England. 5. ed. London, 1878.

Phil 7052.5   Home, D.D. Lights and shadows of spiritualism. London, 1878.

Phil 9347.5   Hood, E.P. Self formation. 3d ed. London, 1878.

Phil 8882.53   Horwicz, Adolf. Moralische Briefe. Magdebourg, 1878.

Phil 5545.15   Huber, J.N. Psychologische Studien. München, 1878.

1878 - cont.

Phil 2050.60   Hume, David. Traité de la nature humaine. Paris, 1878.

Phil 2050.52   Hume, David. Treatise on human nature. v.2. London, 1878.

Phil 8663.3.34   Ingersoll, Robert G. The ghosts, and other lectures. Peoria, Ill., 1878.

Phil 2675.1.31   Jaffre, F.A. Cours de philosophie adapté au programme du baccalauréat ès lettres. Lyon, 1878.

Phil 5645.6.10   Jeffries, B.J. Color blindness. Boston, 1878. 3 pam.

Phil 3480.32.6   Kant, Immanuel. Critique of pure reason. London, 1878.

Phil 3480.30.3.2A   Kant, Immanuel. Kritik der praktischen Vernunft. Leipzig, 1878?

Phil 3480.30.4   Kant, Immanuel. Kritik der reinen Vernunft. Leipzig, 1878.

Phil 3480.50.10A   Kant, Immanuel. Kritik der Urtheilskraft. Leipzig, 1878?

Phil 3552.290   Klopp, O. Zur Ehrenrettung von Leibniz. Berlin, 1878.

Phil 5820.1.5   Körner, F. Instinkt und freier Wille. 2. Aufl. Leipzig, 1878.

Phil 3492.2A   Krause, A. Kant und Helmholtz. Lahr, 1878.

Phil 95.3   Krauth, C.P. Vocabulary of the philosophical sciences. N.Y., 1878.

Phil 2050.94   Kühne, R. Über das Verhältniss der Hume'schen und Kantischen Erkenntnisstheorie. Leipzig, 1878.

Phil 8620.26   Kym, Arnold L. Das Problem des Bösen. München, 1878.

Phil 4285.1.95   Labanca, B. Sopra Giacomo Zabarella. Napoli, 1878.

Phil 186.4   Lazarus, M. Ideale Fragen. Berlin, 1878.

Phil 186.17   Le Conte, J. Man's place in nature. N.Y., 1878.

Phil 5400.6.2   Letourneau, C. Physiologie des passions. 2. éd. Paris, 1878.

Phil 5021.1   Liard, L. Les logiciens anglais contemporains. Paris, 1878.

Phil 4363.3.35   Manara Vincentelo de Leca, M. de. Discurso de la verdad dedicado á la Imperial Majestad de Dios. Madrid, 1878.

Phil 4110.3.80   Marino, L. Gli elementi di filosofia del professore Francesco Fiorentino. Napoli, 1878.

Phil 2115.134.5   Marion, Henri. J. Locke: sa vie et son oeuvre. Paris, 1878.

Phil 6122.1.13   Maudsley, H. The physiology of mind. N.Y., 1878.

Phil 2138.40.4   Mill, John S. On liberty. London, 1878.

Phil 187.20.5   Morell, J.D. Philosophical fragments. London, 1878.

Phil 7077.4   Moses, William S. Psychography. London, 1878.

Phil 8592.15.4   Müller, F.M. Lectures on the origin and growth of religion. 2. ed. London, 1878.

Phil 3495.11   Neide, P.S. Die Kantische Lehre vom Schematismus der reinen Verstandesbegriffe. Diss. Halle, 1878.

Phil 8125.30   Neudecher, Georg. Studien zur Geschichte des deutschen Asthetik seit Kant. Wurzburg, 1878.

Phil 9175.4   Pacheco, R. Cartas a mi esposa. Santiago de Chile, 1878.

Phil 4265.1.80   Palumbo, R. Giulio Cesare Vanini e i suoi tempi. Napoli, 1878.

Phil 3497.20   Panaev, I. Ras"iskateli istinyi: I. Kant. Sankt Peterburg, 1878.

Phil 4210.128   Paoli, A. Lo Schopenhauer e il Rosmini. Roma, 1878.

Phil 3808.120   Paoli, Alessandro. Lo Schopenhauer e il Rosmini. Roma, 1878.

Phil 2805.33   Pascal, Blaise. Les provinciales. Berlin, 1878.

Phil 1870.92   Penjon, A. Etude sur vie et les oeuvres philosophiques de G. Berkeley. Paris, 1878.

Phil 3552.124   Penjon, Auguste. De infinito apud Leibnitium. Thesis. Paris, 1878.

Phil 510.145   Penzler, Martin. Die Monadenlehre und ihre Beziehung zur griechischen Philosophie. Minden, 1878.

Phil 4210.129   Petri, Giuseppe. Lo dottrine di Antonio Rosmini...ed altri esaminate da Giuseppe Petri. Torino, 1878.

Phil 8595.4.5   Pfleiderer, O. Die Religion. 2. Aufl. v.1-2. Leipzig, 1878.

Phil 8595.4.2   Pfleiderer, O. Religionsphilosophie. Berlin, 1878.

Phil 8705.10   Plea for candor in Bible-reading. Jackson, 1878.

Phil 6127.9   Ranvier, L. Leçons sur l'histologie du système nerveux. pt.1-2. Paris, 1878.

Phil 7054.30   Rifts in the veil. London, 1878.

Phil 1122.3.12   Ritter, Heinrich. Historia philosophiae graecae et romanae. 6. ed. Gotha, 1878.

Phil 4983.5.90   Rodriguez, José Ignacio. Vida del presbítero don Félix Varela. N.Y., 1878.

Phil 8672.5   Romanes, J. A candid examination of theism. London, 1878.

Phil 4960.645   Roméro, Sylvio. A philosophia no Brasil. Pôrto Alegre, 1878.

Phil 3017.3   Rosenkranz, K. Neue Studien: IV Geschichte deutschen Philosophie. v.1-2. Leipzig, 1878. 3v.

Phil 9357.2   Rozan, C. Le jeune homme. Paris, 1878.

Phil 260.1.5   Sasswitz, K. Atomistik und Kriticismus. Braunschweig, 1878.

Phil 9430.11   Schädelin, K.F.E. Der moderne Pessimismus. Bern, 1878.

Phil 349.5   Schmitz-Dumont, O. Die mathematischen Elemente der Erkenntnisstheorie. Berlin, 1878.

Phil 5058.7   Schuppe, W. Erkenntnisstheoretische Logik. Bonn, 1878.

Phil 8893.138   Sibben, Frederik Christian. Moralphilosophie. Kjobenhavn, 1878.

Phil 493.1   Simonin, A.H. Le matérialisme de masque. Paris, 1878.

Phil 9045.11   Sowdon, A.J.C. Political duties. Boston, 1878.

Phil 2270.70.4.15   Spencer, Herbert. Principles of psychology. N.Y., 1878. 2v.

Phil 7080.15   Spitta, H. Die Schlaf- und Traumzustände der menschlichen Seele. Tübingen, 1878.

Phil 8643.28.7   Stewart, Balfour. The unseen universe. 7. ed. London, 1878.

Phil 4215.1.82   Stiattesi, Andrea. Notizia storica di Gian Domenico Romagnosi. Firenze, 1878.

Phil 5828.4   Strumpell, L. Die Geisteskräfte der Menschen. Leipzig, 1878.

NEDL Phil 2885.30   Taine, Hippolyte Adolphe. De l'intelligence. Paris, 1878. 2v.

Phil 5059.16   Thiele, G. Grundriss der Logik und Metaphysik. Halle, 1878.

Phil 5829.1   Tissot, C.J. Psychologie comparée. Paris, 1878.

Phil 8894.6.10   Tissot, Joseph. Décadence du sentiment moral et religieux. Paris, 1878.

Phil 4610.6.3   Trenne filosofiska uppsatser. Lund, 1878.

Phil 6969.5   Tuke, Daniel H. Insanity in ancient and modern life. London, 1878.

Phil 2805.86.5   Tulloch, J. Pascal. Edinburgh, 1878.

Phil 2805.86   Tulloch, J. Pascal. Edinburgh, 1878.

Phil 8610.878.10   Tuttle, Hudson. Career of religious ideas. N.Y., 1878.

Phil 3502.2   Ueberhorst, C. Kant's Lehre von dem Verhältnisse der Kategorien zu der Erfahrung. Göttingen, 1878.

Phil 8610.878.15   Underwood, B.F. The Underwood-Marples debate. N.Y., 187

Chronological Listing

Phil 1535.35 — Vallet, Pa. Praelectiones philosophicae. Parisiis, 1878-9. 2v.

Phil 196.11 — Varnbüler, Theodore. Acht Aufsätze zur Apologie der menschlichen Vernunft. Leipzig, 1878.

Phil 3503.7 — Vogt, Carl. Darstellung und Beurtheilung der Kant'schen und Hegel'schen Christologie. Marburg, 1878.

Phil 352.4 — Voit, Carl von. Ueber die Entwicklung der Erkenntniss. München, 1878.

Phil 8847.2 — Wake, Charles S. The evolution of morality. London, 1878. 2v.

Phil 5400.12 — Waldstein, C. Balance of emotion and intellect. London, 1878.

Phil 8677.11 — Weill, Alexandre. L'athéisme déraciné de la science...démocratie. Paris, 1878.

Phil 8712.19 — Weygoldt, G.P. Darwinismus, Religion, Sittlichkeit. Leiden, 1878.

Phil 1722.2A — Windelband, W. Die Geschichte der neueren Philosophie. Leipzig, 1878-80. 2v.

Phil 623.20 — Wolf, Hermann. Spekulation und Philosophie. v.1-2. Berlin, 1878.

Phil 8712.6 — Wright, T.S. Science and revelation. Bellefontaine, 1878.

Phil 8715.2 — Zart, G. Bibel und Naturwissenschaft. Berlin, 1878.

Phil 3246.89 — Zimmer, F. Johann Gottlieb Fichte's Religionsphilosophie. Berlin, 1878.

1879

Phil 4515.91.5 — Åberg, L.H. Försök till en lärobok i allmän samhällslära. Upsala, 1879.

Phil 1845.4.90 — Abbot, F.E. Testimonials to his character. Boston, 1879.

Phil 3482.1 — Adamson, R. Philosophy of Kant. Edinburg, 1879.

Phil 175.2.8 — Alaux, J.E. Métaphysique considérée comme science. Paris, 1879.

Phil 5645.2 — Allen, G. Colour-sense. London, 1879. 2v.

Phil 8887.30.5 — Aveling, E.B. "The value of this earthly life": a reply. London, 1879.

Phil 176.1 — Bärenbach, F. Grundlegung der kritischen Philosophie. Leipzig, 1879.

Phil 5241.2.22 — Bain, A. The senses and the intellect. N.Y., 1879.

Phil 176.5 — Balfour, A.J. Defence of philosophic doubt. London, 1879.

Phil 176.40.5 — Batz, P. Die Philosophie der Erlösung. 2e Aufl. Berlin, 1879.

Phil 8876.11.5 — Baumann, Julius. Handbuch der Moral. Leipzig, 1879.

Phil 6951.12.15 — Beard, G.M. Neurasthenia (nerve exhaustion), with remarks on treatment. n.p., 1879?

Phil 5520.40 — Bechtel, F. Über die Bezeichnungen der sinnlichen Wahrnehmungen. Weimar, 1879.

Phil 8656.2 — Beckett, E. The origin of the laws of nature. London, 1879.

Phil 5041.9 — Bergmann, J. Allgemeine Logik. Berlin, 1879.

Phil 6671.6 — Bersot, P.E. Mesmer, le magnétism animal. Paris, 1879.

Phil 7082.62 — Bjarnason, Halldór. Draumur. Reykjavík, 1879.

Phil 3001.6 — Borelius, J.J. En blick pa den newarande filosofien i Tyshland. Stockholm, 1879.

Phil 8691.14 — Borrero Echeverria, E. La vieja ortodoxia y la ciencia moderna. Habana, 1879.

Phil 1880.50 — Bowen, F. The idea of cause. N.Y., 1879.

Phil 1880.50.2 — Bowen, F. The idea of cause. N.Y., 1879.

Phil 8656.8 — Bowne, B.P. Studies in theism. N.Y., 1879.

Phil 1200.22 — Brochard, Victor. De assensione Stoici quid Senserint. Thesis. Paris, 1879.

Phil 4065.12A — Bruno, Giordano. Opera latine. v. 1-3. Neapoli, 1879-91. 6v.

Phil 8876.34 — Bucke, R.M. Man's moral mature. N.Y., 1879.

Phil 6951.4.6 — Bucknill, J.C. A manual psychological medicine...insanity. London, 1879.

Phil 5811.5.5 — Büchner, L. Liebe und Leibes- Leben in der Thierwelt. Berlin, 1879.

Phil 8877.1.3 — Calderwood, H. Handbook of moral philosophy. 6th ed. London, 1879.

Phil 6112.1 — Calderwood, H. The relations of mind and brain. London, 1879.

Phil 3484.10 — Cantoni, Carlo. Emanuele Kant. v.1,3. Milano, 1879-84. 2v.

Phil 365.1 — Carrau, V.M.J.L. Études sur la théorie de l'evolution. Paris, 1879.

Phil 8598.59.10 — Cassels, W.R. Supernatural religion. London, 1879. 3v.

Phil 177.14A — Clifford, W.K. Lectures and essays. London, 1879. 2v.

Phil 5643.41 — Clifford, W.K. Seeing and thinking. London, 1879.

Phil 1135.22.4 — Cocker, B.F. Christianity and Greek philosophy. N.Y., 1879.

Phil 4080.5.32 — Corleo, Simone. Il sistema della filosofia universale. Roma, 1879.

Phil 2138.82 — Courtney, W.S. Metaphysics of John Stuart Mill. London, 1879.

Phil 1145.6 — Denis, J. Histoire des theories...dans l'Antiquité. Paris, 1879. 2v.

Phil 2520.17.5 — Descartes, René. Oeuvres morales et philosophiques. Paris, 1879.

Phil 3625.1.103 — Dessauer, M. Der deutsche Plato. Berlin, 1879.

Phil 284.2 — Drossbach, M. Uber Kraft und Bewegung. Halle, 1879.

Phil 7080.2 — Dupuy, P. Étude psycho-physiologique. Bordeaux, 1879.

Phil 5814.2 — Espinas, Alfred. Die Thierischen Gesellschaften; eine vergleichend- psychologische Untersuchung. 2. Aufl. Braunschweig, 1879.

Phil 89.2 — Eucken, R. Geschichte der philosophischen Terminologie. Leipzig, 1879.

Phil 3210.30A — Fechner, G.T. Tagesansicht gegenüber der Nachtansicht. Leipzig, 1879.

Phil 3235.28 — Feuerbach, Ludwig. Aussprüche aus seinen Werken. Leipzig, 1879.

Phil 3246.35.3A — Fichte, Johann Gottlieb. Die Bestimmung des Menschen. Leipzig, 1879.

Phil 8585.6.5 — Fisher, G.P. Faith and rationalism. N.Y., 1879.

Phil 8660.4.5 — Flint, R. Anti-theistic theories. (Baird lectures for 1877.) Edinburgh, 1879.

Phil 2520.102 — Foucher de Careil, A. Descartes, la princesse Elizabeth et la reine Christine. Paris, 1879.

Phil 2605.6.31 — Foucou, L. Les preliminaries de la philosophie. Paris, 1879.

Phil 1705.5 — Franck, A. Philosophes modernes. Paris, 1879.

Phil 3801.406 — Frantz, Constantin. Schelling's positive Philosophie. Pt.1-3. Cöthen, 1879-80.

Phil 6955.6 — Franzolini, F. L'epidemia di istero-demonopatie. Reggio, 1879.

Phil 510.22 — Frohschammer, J. Monaden und Weltphantasie. München, 1879.

Phil 3487.4 — Frohschammer, J. Ueber die Bedeutung der Einbildungskraft. München, 1879.

Phil 1750.15 — Funck-Brentano, T. Les sophistes grecs...et contemporains. Paris, 1879.

Htn — Phil 2030.2.30* — George, Henry. Progress and poverty. San Francisco, 1879.

Phil 6116.3.5 — Granville, J.M. Common mind troubles. Salem, 1879.

Phil 6116.3 — Granville, J.M. The secret of a clear head. Salem, 1879.

Phil 3808.207 — Guetzlaff, Victor. Schopenhauer ueber die Thiere und den Tierschutz. Berlin, 1879.

Phil 8661.3 — Guilbert, A.V.F. Monde et Dieu. Paris, 1879.

Phil 3007.1.7 — Harms, F. Die Philosophie seit Kant. Berlin, 1879.

Phil 1512.2 — Harper, Thomas. Metaphysics of the school. London, 1879. 3v.

Phil 3415.65 — Hartmann, Eduard von. Phänomenologie des sittlichen Bewussten. Berlin, 1879.

Phil 3425.56.25 — Hegel, Georg Wilhelm Friedrich. The philosophy of art. N.Y., 1879.

Phil 5585.3 — Helmholtz, Hermann van. Thatsachen in der Wahrnehmung. Berlin, 1879.

Phil 182.18.5 — Henton, J. The art of thinking. London, 1879.

Phil 630.2 — Herbert, T.M. Realistic assumptions of modern science. London, 1879.

Phil 8587.13 — Herrmann, W. Die Religion. Halle, 1879.

Phil 9520.2.1 — Hinton, James. The mystery of pain. London, 1879.

Phil 4508.5 — Höffding, Harald. Filosofien i Sverige. Stockholm, 1879.

Phil 4803.454.21 — Hoene-Wroński, Józef Maria. Sept manuscrits inédits, écrits de 1803 à 1806. Paris, 1879.

Phil 3525.88 — Hohlfeld, P. Die Krause'sche Philosophie. Jena, 1879.

Phil 1200.4.3 — Holland, F.M. The reign of the Stoics. N.Y., 1879.

Phil 6117.5.7 — Holmes, O.W. Mechanism in thought and morals. Boston, 1879.

Phil 5643.12 — Hoppe, J.F. Die Schein-Bewegungen. Würzburg, 1879.

Phil 2050.87 — Huxley, Thomas H. Hume. London, 1879.

Phil 2050.87.3 — Huxley, Thomas H. Hume. N.Y., 1879.

Phil 2050.87.4A — Huxley, Thomas H. Hume. N.Y., 1879.

Phil 182.27 — Hvalgrens, E. Grunddragen. Göteborg, 1879.

Phil 5643.13 — Jaesche, E. Das räumliche Sehen. Stuttgart, 1879.

Phil 8589.5.10A — James, H. Society, the redeemed form of man. Boston, 1879.

Phil 6679.1 — James, John. Mesmerism, with hints for beginners. London, 1879.

Phil 2070.09 — James, William. The sentiment of rationality. n.p., 1879-1907. 8 pam.

Phil 2409.1.5 — Janet, P. La philosophie française contemporaine. Paris, 1879.

Phil 5710.5.2 — Jaques, D.H. The temperaments. N.Y., 1879.

Phil 5645.6 — Jeffries, B.J. Color blindness. Boston, 1879.

Phil 19.1.5 — Journal of mental science. Index. London, 1879-1928.

Phil 5115.3 — Joyau, E. De l'invention dans les arts. Paris, 1879.

Phil 1540.7.2 — Jundt, A. Les anis de Dieu au quatorzième siècle. Thèse. Strasbourg, 1879.

Phil 530.20.30 — Jundt, Auguste. Les amis de Dieu au quatorzième siècle. Paris, 1879.

Phil 7054.28 — Kiddle, H. Spiritual communications. Boston, 1879.

Phil 185.7.5 — Knight, W. Studies in philosophy and literature. London, 1879.

Phil 400.4 — Laas, E. Idealistische und Positivistische. Berlin, 1879-1884. 3v.

Phil 1730.8.3 — Lanfrey, Pierre. L'église et les philosophes au dix-huitième siècle. Paris, 1879.

NEDL — Phil 486.1.5.3 — Lange, F.A. History of materialism. Boston, 1879-81. 3v.

Phil 5374.7 — Lange, K.M. Über Apperception. Plauen, 1879.

Phil 3493.8 — Last, E. Mehr Licht! Berlin, 1879.

Phil 186.3 — Laws, S.S. Metaphysics. Columbia, Mo., 1879.

Phil 811.2 — Lefèvre, A. Philosophy. London, 1879.

Phil 8412.24 — Lemcke, Carl von. Populäre Asthetik. Leipzig, 1879.

Phil 5251.6.4.5 — Lewes, G.H. Problems of life and mind. 3rd series. Boston, 1879-80. 2v.

Phil 5251.6.4 — Lewes, G.H. The study of psychology. London, 1879.

Phil 186.10 — Liard, L. La science positive. Paris, 1879.

Phil 5821.2 — Lindsay, W.L. Mind in the lower animals. London, 1879. 2v.

Phil 3565.45.10 — Lotze, Hermann. Metaphysik. Leipzig, 1879.

Phil 5052.18 — Macfarlane, Alexander. Principles of the algebra of logic. Edinburgh, 1879.

Phil 8887.30 — Mallock, W.H. Is life worth living? N.Y., 1879.

Phil 8667.11 — Medina, Juan J. La cruzada del error. Sevilla, 1879.

Phil 1020.6 — Mehren, A.F. Correspondance philosophique d'Ibn Sab'in. Florence, 1879.

Phil 2490.84.10 — Mill, John Stuart. Auguste Comte et le positivisme. 2. éd. Paris, 1879.

Phil 575.2 — Momerie, A.W. Personality. Edinburgh, 1879.

Phil 4605.1.49 — Monrad, M.J. Denkrichtungen der neueren Zeit. Bonn, 1879.

Phil 293.7 — Montagu, A. Cours de philosophie scientifique. Paris, 1879.

Phil 7054.8.5 — Moses, William S. Spirit identity. London, 1879.

Phil 8592.15.2 — Müller, F.M. Lectures on the origin and growth of religion. London, 1879.

Phil 5252.30 — Müller, G.E. Zur Grundlegung der Psychophysik. 2. Ausg. Berlin, 1879.

Phil 5252.13.2 — Murphy, J.J. Habit and intelligence. 2d. ed. London, 1879.

Phil 5253.4 — Netter, S. De l'intuition. Strasbourg, 1879.

Phil 98.1 — Noack, L. Philosophie-Geschichtliches Lexikon. Leipzig, 1879.

Phil 6123.4 — Nothnagel, H. Topische Diagnostik der Gehirnkrankheiten. Berlin, 1879.

Phil 2490.101 — Nyström, A. Positivism. Stockholm, 1879.

Phil 3808.121.5 — Penzig, Rudolph. Arthur Schopenhauer und die menschliche Willensfreiheit. Halle, 1879.

Phil 4210.129.5 — Petri, Giuseppe. Risposta ad alcuni appunti...sul libro A. Rosmini ed i neoscolastici. Torino 1879.

Phil 260.6 — Pfeifer, X. Die Controverse und der Beharren der Elemente. Dellingen, 1879.

Phil 9245.8.5 — Pfleiderer, E. Zur Ehrenrettung des Eudämonismus. Tübingen, 1879.

Phil 9410.3 — Prantl, Carl. Über die Berechtigung des Optimismus. München, 1879.

Phil 346.1 — Proelss, K.R. Vom Ursprung der Menschlichen Erkenntnis. Leipzig, 1879.

1879 - cont.

Phil 8610.875.27 — Pullen, H.W. Modern Christianity, a civilized heathenism. N.Y., 1879.

NEDL Phil 7080.11 — Radestock, P. Schlaf und Traum. Leipzig, 1879.

Phil 5227.2 — Ribot, T. La psychologie allemande contemporaine. Paris, 1879.

Phil 5628.51.10 — Rohling, August. Louise Lateau: her stigmas and ecstasy. N.Y., 1879.

Phil 4210.40 — Rosmini-Serbati, Antonio. Philosophisches System. Regensburg, 1879.

Phil 6060.8 — Salamanea, F. de. The philosophy of handwriting. London, 1879.

Phil 8615.1.7 — Salter, W.M. On a foundation for religion. Boston, 1879. 17 pam.

Phil 5768.20 — Schellwien, R. Der Wille, die Lebensgrundmacht. Berlin, 1879.

Phil 3808.35.4 — Schopenhauer, Arthur. Die Welt als Wille und Vorstellung. 5. Aufl. Leipzig, 1879. 2v.

Phil 193.85 — Schütz, Ludwig. Einleitung in die Philosophie. Paderborn, 1879.

Phil 5722.2 — Schuster, P.R. Gibtesunbewusste und vererbte Vorstellungen? Leipzig, 1879.

Phil 6945.9 — Seguin, E.C. Lunacy reform. v.1-4. N.Y., 1879-

Phil 2270.74.5 — Spencer, Herbert. Data of ethics. London, 1879.

Phil 2270.74.1.5 — Spencer, Herbert. Data of ethics. N.Y., 1879.

Phil 2270.74 — Spencer, Herbert. Data of ethics. N.Y., 1879.

Phil 2270.31.5 — Spencer, Herbert. System der synthetischen Philosophie: Ethik. Stuttgart, 1879-95. 2v.

Phil 3246.196 — Spir, A. Johann Gottlieb Fichte nach seinen Briefen. Leipzig, 1879.

Phil 5480.2 — Spruijt, C.B. Proeve van eene geschiedenis van de leer der aangeboren begrippen. Leiden, 1879.

Phil 3500.39 — Steckelmacher, M. Die formale Logik Kant's in ihren Beziehungen zur Transcendentalen. Breslau, 1879.

Phil 7039.8 — Stevens, E. Winchester. The Watseka wonder. Chicago, 1879.

Phil 5058.26 — Stinson, J.H. Organon of science. Eureka, Calif., 1879.

Phil 525.4 — Story, T. (pseud.). Substantialism, or Philosophy of knowledge. Boston, 1879.

Phil 5374.5 — Stricker, S. Studien über das Bewusstsein. Wien, 1879.

Phil 4635.3.33 — Sylwan, O.C. Vetenskapens evangelium. Stockholm, 1879.

Phil 720.3 — Tabor, J.A. The supreme law. Colchester, 1879.

Phil 8644.1.5 — Tait, P.G. Paradoxical philosophy. London, 1879.

Phil 8610.831.5 — Taylor, Robert. The devil's pulpit. v.1, no.1-15,17-23; v.2, no.1. London, 1879.

Phil 8644.6.2 — Teichmüller, G. Uber die Ansterblichkeit der Seele. 2. Aufl. Leipzig, 1879.

Phil 5059.4.3 — Thomson, W. Outline of the necessary laws of thought. N.Y., 1879.

Phil 8894.5 — Tiberghien, G. Éléments de morale universelle. Bruxelles, 1879.

Phil 3808.121 — Tschofen, Johann. Die Philosophie Arthur Schopenhauers. München, 1879.

Phil 5768.4 — Tübingen, Germany. Universität. Verzeichnies der Doctoren: Begriff der Wollens...von C. Sigwart. Tübingen, 1879.

Phil 8422.14A — Véron, Eugène. Aesthetics. London, 1879.

Phil 8601.8 — Vignoli, Tito. Mito e scienza saggio. Milano, 1879.

Phil 5831.1 — Vignoli, Tito. Über das Fundamentalgesetz der Intelligenz im Thierreiche. Leipzig, 1879.

Phil 3503.5 — Volkelt, Johannes. Immanuel Kant's Erkenntnisstheorie nach ihren Grundprincipien Analysirt. Leipzig, 1879.

Phil 672.9 — Walter, J.E. Perception of space and matter. Boston, 1879.

Phil 9495.20.2 — Ware, J. Hints to young men. Boston, 1879.

Phil 5772.2.4 — Wiese, L. Die Bildung des Willens. Berlin, 1879.

Phil 5520.28 — Wilson, William D. The influence of language on thought. Albany, 1879.

Phil 1150.9 — Wolf, S. Hypatia, die Philosophin von Alexandria. Vienna, 1879.

Phil 3915.06 — Wundt, Wilhelm. Der Spiritismus. Leipzig, 1879-1913. 7 pam.

Phil 7068.79 — Zöllner, J.K.F. Die transcendentale Physik und die sogenannte Philosophie. Leipzig, 1879.

188-

Phil 6990.33.5 — Brewer, E.C. Dictionary of miracles. Philadelphia, 188-?

Phil 8877.20 — Counsel, E. Maxims. Melbourne, 188-?

Phil 7054.170 — Dawburn, Charles. The science of spirit return. Springfield, Mass., 188-.

Phil 2115.89A — Geil, Georg. Über die Abhängigkeit Locke's von Descartes. Strassburg, 188-.

Phil 3565.70 — Lotze, Hermann. Outline of psychology. Minneapolis, 188-?

Phil 2805.31.5 — Pascal, Blaise. Les première, quatrième et treizième lettres provinciales. 13. éd. Paris, 188-.

Phil 8615.2.7 — Sheldon, Walter L. Ethical culture; its threefold attitude. St. Louis, Mo? 188-?

Phil 2270.45.4.7 — Spencer, Herbert. First principles. N.Y., 188-?

Phil 2270.45.17 — Spencer, Herbert. First principles. N.Y., 188-.

Phil 2270.45.4.10 — Spencer, Herbert. First principles. N.Y., 188-.

Phil 6132.27 — Wilder, Alexander. Mind, thought and cerebration. n.p., 188-?

1880

Phil 3482.1.5 — Adamson, R. Über Kant's Philosophie. Leipzig, 1880.

Phil 5041.27 — Bahnsen, J. Der Widerspruch im Wessen und Wesen der Welt. Berlin, 1880-82. 2v.

Phil 5241.2.5 — Bain, A. Mental science. N.Y., 1880.

Phil 4352.1.50 — Balmes, Jaime. Elements of logic. N.Y., 1880.

Phil 5041.6 — Barnes, William. An outline of Rede-Craft (Logic). London, 1880.

Phil 130.4 — Barni, Jules. Les martyrs de la libre pensée. 2. éd. Paris, 1880.

Phil 6111.10.2 — Bastian, H.C. The brain as an organ of mind. N.Y., 1880.

Phil 6951.12.4 — Beard, G.M. Practical treatise on nervous exhaustion. 2. ed. N.Y., 1880.

Phil 6951.12.3 — Beard, G.M. Practical treatise on nervous exhaustion. 2. ed. N.Y., 1880.

Phil 176.20 — Bergmann, J. Sein und Erkennen. Berlin, 1880.

Phil 5041.38 — Bertini, G.M. La logica. Roma, 1880.

Phil 5374.6 — Bertrand, A. L'aperception du corps humain. Paris, 1880.

Phil 665.43 — Beskow, B. von. Om själens helsa. 4e uppl. Stockholm, 1880.

Phil 3483.2 — Bessel-Hagen, F. Die Grabstätte Immanuel Kants. Königsberg, 1880.

1880 - cont.

Phil 8951.1 — Bestmann, H.J. Geschichte der christlichen Sitte. Nödling, 1880-85. 2v.

Phil 6111.21 — Bischoff, T.L.W. von. Das Hirngewicht des Menschen. Bonn, 1880.

Phil 1880.30 — Bowen, F. Gleanings from a literary life 1830-80. N.Y., 1880.

Phil 1880.46.8 — Bowen, F. Treatise on logic. 8th ed. Boston, 1880.

Phil 600.4.5 — Broglie, Paul. Le postivisme et la science expérimentale. Paris, 1880-81. 2v.

Phil 5811.5 — Büchner, L. Mind in animals. London, 1880.

Htn Phil 5545.4* — Butler, S. Unconscious memory. London, 1880.

Phil 8582.1.2 — Caird, J. An introduction to the philosophy of religion. N.Y., 1880.

Phil 1200.3 — Capes, W.W. Stoicism. London, 1880.

Phil 9430.3.1 — Caro, E.M. Le pessimisme au XIX siècle. 2. éd. Paris, 1880.

Phil 9430.3.10 — Caro, E.M. Pessimisen i nittonde arhundradet. Stockholm, 1880.

Phil 4769.1.65 — Chicherin, Boris N. Mistitsizm v nauke. Moskva, 1880.

Phil 8627.2 — Cobbe, F.P. The hope of the human race. London, 1880.

Phil 5242.7 — Colsenet, E. La vie inconsciente. Paris, 1880.

Phil 3822.5 — Colsnet, Edmond. De mentis essentia Spinoza quid senserit. Thesis. Parisiis, 1880.

X Cg Phil 2490.51.7 — Comte, Auguste. A general view of positivism. 2d ed. London, 1880.

Phil 2490.41.5 — Comte, Auguste. La philosophie positive. Paris, 1880-81. 2v.

Phil 8692.2.5 — Cooke, J.P. Religion and chemistry. N.Y., 1880.

Phil 6112.7.5 — Cornelius, K.S. Zur Theorie der Wechselwirkung zwischen Leib und Seele. Halle, 1880.

Phil 400.39 — Coste, Adolphe. Dieu et l'âme. Paris, 1880.

Phil 5242.12 — Cyples, W. An inquiry into the process of human experience. London, 1880.

Phil 5043.2 — Davis, N.K. The theory of thought. N.Y., 1880.

Phil 6673.7 — Despine, P. Étude scientifique sur le somnambulisme. Paris, 1880.

Phil 8658.12.2 — Doedes, J.I. Inleiding tot de leer van God. Utrecht, 1880.

Phil 5640.24 — Dreher, E. Beiträge zu einer exacten Psycho-Physiologie. Halle, 1880.

Phil 178.34.5 — Dreher, Eugen. Beiträge zu einer exacten Psycho-Physiologie. n.p., 1880-91. 4 pam.

Phil 4004.1 — Espinas, Alfred. La philosophie expérimentale en Italie. Paris, 1880.

Phil 179.3.8 — Eucken, R. Fundamental concepts of modern philosophical thought. N.Y., 1880.

Phil 410.3 — Evellin, F. Infini et quantité. Paris, 1880.

Phil 5815.4 — Falco, Francesco. I fatti psichici della vita animale. Lucca, 1880.

Phil 2405.2.2 — Ferraz, Marin. Traditionalisme et ultramontanisme. 2e éd. Paris, 1880.

Phil 4210.115 — Ferré, Pietro M. Degli universali secondo la teoria rosminiana. Casale, 1880-86. 11v.

Phil 6115.11.2 — Feuchtersleben, E.F.V. Zur Diätetik der Seele. Hamburg, 1880.

Phil 9495.17.15 — Fowler, O.S. Private lectures on perfect men, women and children. N.Y., 1880.

Phil 2115.90 — Fowler, T. Locke. London, 1880.

Phil 2115.90.3 — Fowler, T. Locke. N.Y., 1880?

Phil 5246.27.5 — Glogau, Gustav. Die Form und die Bewegungsgesetze des Geistes. Breslau, 1880. 2 pam.

Phil 1511.4 — Glossner, M. Das Objektivität-Prinzip der aristotelisch-scholastischen Philosophie. Regensburg, 1880.

Phil 181.25.5 — Gonçalvez de Magalhães, J.G. Commentarios e pensamentos. Rio de Janeiro, 1880.

Phil 8696.7 — Gray, Asa. Natural science and religion. N.Y., 1880.

Phil 6956.3 — Guislain, J. Leçons orales phrénopathies. Paris, 1880. 2v.

Phil 8696.6 — Gulliver, John P. Christianity and science. Andover, 1880.

Phil 3310.5.31 — Gutberlet, C. Die Metaphysik. Münster, 1880.

Phil 2035.40.10 — Hamilton, William. Lectures on metaphysics and logic. N.Y., 1880.

Phil 3415.66 — Hartmann, Eduard von. Zur Geschichte und Begründung des Pessimismus. Berlin, 1880.

Phil 7082.58 — Hedenius, Per. Om drömmen. Stockholm, 1880.

Phil 6677.2 — Heidenhain, R.P.H. Animal magnetism. London, 1880.

Phil 182.12.6 — Hellenbach, L.B. Die Vorurtheile des gemeinen Verstandes. Wien, 1880.

Phil 5817.12 — Hement, Felix. De l'instinct et de l'intelligence. Paris, 1880.

Phil 8882.9.5 — Hickok, L.P. A system of moral science. Boston, 1880.

Phil 8957.5 — Hill, Thomas. The hydrostatic paradox in morals. Portland, 1880.

Phil 807.11 — Hodgson, Shadworth H. Philosophy in relation to its history. London, 1880.

Phil 170.5 — Holland, F.M. Facts about Hegel and other essays. Boston, 1880-81.

Phil 6677.19 — Hont, A.E. La lumière sur le magnétisme. Neuchâtel, 1880.

Phil 338.14 — Hoppe, J.I. Die persönliche Denkthätigkeit. Würzburg, 1880.

Phil 9560.2 — Hughes, T. True manliness. Boston, 1880?

Phil 2050.36 — Hume, David. Essays: literary, moral, and political. London, 1880.

Phil 6959.3.2 — Jacobi, M.P. The prevention of insanity. Boston, 1880-82. 3 pam.

Phil 5300.2A — James, W. The feeling of effort. Boston, 1880.

Phil 2668.30 — Janet, Paul A.R. Traité élémentaire de philosophie. Paris, 1880.

Phil 5645.6.5 — Jeffries, B.J. Report of the examination of school children for color blindness. Boston, 1880.

Phil 5049.3.4 — Jevons, W.S. Logic (science primers). N.Y., 1880.

Phil 5049.5.2 — Jevons, W.S. Studies in deductive logic. London, 1880.

Phil 5249.15 — Jochnick, W. Mensklighetens vitigaste frågor. v.1-2. Stockholm, 1880-81.

Phil 600.49 — Kainer, J. Seven lectures on the doctrine of positivism...May, June and July, 1879. London, 1880.

Phil 3480.53.6 — Kant, Immanuel. Traüme eines Geistersehers. Leipzig, 1880?

Phil 185.50 — Kirchner, F. Die Hauptpunkte der Metaphysik. Cöthen, 1880.

Phil 6945.20 — Kirkbride, T.S. On the construction, organization and general arrangements of hospitals for the insane. 2. ed. Philadelphia, 1880.

Phil 8590.17 — Kreiss. Theophilosophie. Berlin, 1880.

1880 - cont.

Phil 185.29   Kühne, B. Die höchste Aufgabe der Philosophie. Einsiedeln, 1880.

Phil 8591.22   La Belle, Alfred. Essai sur l'origine des cults. Paris, 1880.

Phil 486.1.5.9   Lange, F.A. History of materialism and criticism of its present importance. Photoreproduction. Boston, 1880-81. 3v.

NEDL Phil 2050.97   Latimer, J.E. Immediate perception as held by Reid and Hamilton. Leipzig, 1880.

Phil 3493.22   Lehmann, Otto. Über Kant's Principien der Ethik und Schopenhauer's Beurteilung derselben. Greifswald, 1880.

Phil 3425.120   Levi, Giuseppe. La dottrina dello stato di G.F.G. Hegel. Pavia, 1880-84.

X Cg   Phil 9430.8   Lloyd, R.J. Pessimism, a study in contemporary sociology. Liverpool, 1880.

Phil 5251.38   Loomans, Charles. De la connaissance de soi-même. Bruxelles, 1880.

Phil 3565.30.3A   Lotze, Hermann. System der Philosophie. 2e Aufl. Leipzig, 1880-84. 2v.

Phil 186.53.5   Luthardt, C.E. De moderna verldsåsigterna. Lund, 1880.

Phil 2125.55   McCosh, James. The emotions. N.Y., 1880.

Phil 2520.93   Mahaffy, J.P. Descartes. Edinburgh, 1880.

Phil 4170.7.40   Mamiani della Rovere, Terenzio. Della religione positiva e perpetua. Milano, 1880.

Phil 5402.3.5   Mantegazza, P. Fisiologia del dolore. Firenze, 1880.

Phil 8887.2   Marion, H. De la solidarité morale. Paris, 1880.

Phil 6962.2.9A   Maudsley, H. The pathology of mind. N.Y., 1880.

Phil 3625.1.25   Mendelssohn, Moses. Schriften zur Philosophie. Leipzig, 1880.

Phil 3494.24   Meydenbauer, A. Kant oder Laplace? Marburg, 1880.

Phil 6122.10   Möbius, P.J. Das Nervensystem des Menschen. Leipzig, 1880.

Phil 5052.8   Monck, W.H.S. An introduction to logic. Dublin, 1880.

Htn   Phil 7075.5.2*   Moreau, P. Des aberrations du sens génésique. 2. ed. Paris, 1880.

Phil 1812.3   Morris, G.S. British thought and thinkers. Chicago, 1880.

Phil 7054.8   Moses, William S. Higher aspects of spiritualism. London, 1880.

Phil 8592.15   Müller, F.M. Lectures on the origin and growth of religion. London, 1880.

Phil 5252.11   Munsell, O.S. Psychology. N.Y., 1880.

Phil 294.1   Nason, L.H. History of the prehistoric ages. Chicago, 1880.

Phil 6963.1   National association for the protection of the insane, 1880-1882. Boston, 1880. 2v.

Phil 5115.1   Naville, J.E. La logique de l'hypothèse. Paris, 1880.

Phil 3552.242   Neff, L. Abfassungszeit von Leibnizens Unvorgreiflichen Gedanken. Durlach, 1880.

Phil 1350.12   Nemanic, D. De stoicorum romanorum. Görz, 1880.

Phil 3640.37   Nietzsche, Friedrich. Der Wanderer und sein Schatten. Chemnitz, 1880.

Phil 8593.12   Nyström, A. Gyldene ord ur mensklighetens allmänna religion. 2. uppl. Stockholm, 1880.

Phil 8889.1   Ollé-Laprune, L. De la certitude morale. Paris, 1880.

Phil 4210.82   Paoli, F. Della vita di Antonio Rosmini-Serbati. Torino, 1880-84. 2v.

Phil 2805.32.2   Pascal, Blaise. The provincial letters. Cambridge, Eng., 1880.

Phil 1535.9   Pesch, T. Institutiones philosophiae naturalis. Friburgi, 1880.

Phil 9245.8   Pfleiderer, E. Eudämonismus und Egoismus. Leipzig, 1880.

Phil 600.7.86   Poéy, Andrés. M. Littré et Auguste Comte. 2e éd. Paris, 1880.

Phil 8663.3.86.2   Pringle, Allen. Ingersoll in Canada. 2. ed. Toronto, 1880.

Phil 3525.92   Proksch, A. Karl Christian Friedrich Krause. Leipzig, 1880.

Phil 8520.3   Pünjer, G.C.B. Geschichte der christlichen Religionsphilosophie seit der Reformation. Braunschweig, 1880-83. 2v.

Phil 5027.1   Rabus, L. Der neuesten Bestrebung...Logik. Erlangen, 1880.

Phil 348.4.5   Rehmke, J. Die Welt als Wahrnehmung und Begriff. Berlin, 1880.

Phil 5190.4.5   Rethwisch, E. Der Begriff der Definition. Berlin, 1880.

Phil 645.4   Robert, Louis. De la certitude et des formes recontes du scepticisme. Paris, 1880.

Phil 510.132   Rosenthal, L.A. Die monistische Philosophie. Berlin, 1880.

Phil 3499.12.5   Runze, Max. Kant's Kritikan Humes Skepticismus. Berlin, 1880.

Phil 7054.33   Samson, G.W. The physical in spiritualism. Philadelphia, 1880.

Phil 7054.34   Sargent, Epes. The scientific basis of spiritualism. Boston, 1880.

Phil 7060.37.15   Savile, B.W. Apparitions; a narrative of facts. 2. ed. London, 1880.

Phil 5828.3   Schneider, G.H. Der thierische Will. Leipzig, 1880.

Phil 6968.4   Schüle, H. Handbuch der Geisteskrankheiten. Leipzig, 1880.

Phil 5258.16   Siciliani, P. Prolégomènes a la psychogénie moderne. Paris, 1880.

Phil 5228.1   Siebeck, H. Geschichte der Psychologie. Gotha, 1880-84.

Phil 4065.117   Sigwart, C. Die Lebensgeschichte Giordano Bruno's. Tübingen, 1880.

Phil 9035.7   Smiles, S. Character. N.Y., 1880?

Phil 9120.4.3   Smiles, S. Duty. London, 1880.

Phil 2266.30.10   Smith, Adam. Essays; philosophical and literary. London, 1880?

Phil 4769.1.45   Solov'ev, V.S. Kritika otvlechennykh nachal. Moskva, 1880.

Phil 7054.13   Stevenson. William G. Does spiritualism transcend natural law? Poughkeepsie, 1880.

Phil 5258.25.16   Sully, J. Sensation and intuition. 2d ed. London, 1880.

Phil 193.43   Swedenborg, E. Ontology. Photoreproduction. Philadelphia, 1880.

Phil 2885.31.8   Taine, Hippolyte Adolphe. Der Verstand. v.1-2. Bonn, 1880.

Phil 978.48   Theosophy and the higher life. London, 1880.

Phil 8674.10   Thoughts on theism with suggestions towards a public religious service. London, 1880.

Phil 194.38   Traina, G. Saggio dei principali sistemi. Palermo, 1880.

Phil 5769.4   Turner, G.L. Wish and will. London, 1880.

Phil 820.1.6   Ueberweg, F. Grundriss der Geschichte der Philosophie. v.1-2. 6. ed. Berlin, 1880-1914.

1880 - cont.

Phil 820.1.2.5   Ueberweg, F. Grundriss der Geschichte der Philosophie. 5. Aufl. Berlin, 1880.

Phil 4983.8.6   Varona, Enrique. Conferencias filosóficas. Ser.1, 3. Habana, 1880. 2v.

Phil 3841.1.10   Vloten, J. van. Spinoza. 's Gravenhage, 1880.

Phil 1158.6   Wallace, W. Epicureanism. London, 1880.

Phil 8647.1   Weiss, J. The immortal life. Boston, 1880.

Phil 4260.87.5   Werner, K. Emerico Amari in seinern Verhaltniss zu G.B. Vico. Wien, 1880.

Phil 6972.2.15   Wernicke, C. Uber den wessenschaftlichen Standpunkt. Cassel, 1880.

Phil 9530.11   Whipple, E.P. Success and its conditions. Boston, 1880.

Phil 4655.1.50   Wikner, Pontus. Några drag af kulturens offerväsen. Upsala, 1880.

Phil 4655.1.55   Wikner, Pontus. Narkissos-sagan och platonismen. Upsala, 1880.

Phil 4655.1.30   Wikner, Pontus. Om egenskapen och närgränsande tankeföremál. Upsala, 1880.

Phil 3022.3.15   Windlband, Wilhelm. Die Blüthezeit der deutschen Philosophie. Leipzig, 1880.

Phil 8847.4   Winter, F.J. Der Individualismus. Leipzig, 1880.

Phil 5062.23   Wolff, Hermann. Logik und Sprachphilosophie. Berlin, 1880.

NEDL Phil 6132.33   Wood, H. Brain-work. Philadelphia, 1880.

Phil 3915.45.2   Wundt, Wilhelm. Grundzüge der physiologischen Psychologie. v.1-2. Leipzig, 1880.

Phil 3915.40   Wundt, Wilhelm. Logik. Stuttgart, 1880-83. 2v.

Phil 1130.8.3   Zeller, Eduard. The Stoics, Epicureans, and Sceptics. London, 1880.

Phil 8900.4   Ziller, T. Allgemeine philosophische Ethik. Langensalza, 1880.

Phil 7060.97   Zöllner, J.C.F. Transcendental physics. London, 1880.

1881

Phil 3246.80   Adamson, R. Fichte. Philadelphia, 1881.

Phil 3850.5.85   African Spir und die Bedeutung seiner Philosophie. Leipzig, 1881.

Phil 7052.15.2   Aldrete y Soto, Luis de. Aldrete ó Los espiritistas españoles. 2. ed. Barcelona, 1881.

Phil 8875.24   Alger, W.R. The school of life. Boston, 1881.

Phil 175.5   Amersin, F. Gemeinverständliche Weisheitslehre. Triest, 1881.

Phil 175.20   Appleton, J.H. Doctor Charles E.C.B. Appleton: his life and literary relics. London, 1881.

Phil 7108.388   Avé-Lallemant, F.C.B. Der Magnetismus mit seinen mystischen Verirrungen. Leipzig, 1881.

Phil 6111.1.9   Bain, A. Geist und Körper. 2. Aufl. Leipzig, 1881.

Phil 5241.7.2   Bascom, J. The science of mind. N.Y., 1881.

Phil 6951.12.10A   Beard, G.M. American nervousness. N.Y., 1881.

Phil 6945.8   Beard, G.M. The asylums of Europe. Cambridge, 1881.

Phil 5811.7   Beard, G.M. Trance and trancoidal states in the lower animals. N.Y., 1881.

Phil 8610.881.10   Bennett, D.M. An infidel abroad. N.Y., 1881.

Phil 3821.5   Berendt, M. Spinoza's Erkenntnisslehre. Berlin, 1881.

Phil 1870.40.12   Berkeley, G. A treatise concerning the principles of human knowledge. Philadelphia, 1881.

Htn   Phil 4073.81*   Berti, D. Nuovi documenti su T. Campanella. Roma, 1881.

Phil 1701.12   Bertini, G. Maria. Storia della filosofia moderna. pt.1. Torino, 1881.

Phil 5635.33   Besser, L. Was ist Empfindung? Bonn, 1881.

Phil 332.9   Betz, H.J. Ervaringswijsbegeerte. 's-Gravenhage, 1881.

Phil 2270.102   Blanc, Elie. Les nouvelles bases de la morale d'après Herbert Spencer. Lyon, 1881.

Phil 5643.16   Bleuler, E. Zwangsmässige Lichtempfindungen. Leipzig, 1881.

Phil 8402.35   Blümner, Hugo. Laokoon-studien. Freiburg, 1881-82.

Phil 2038.80   Bower, G.S. Hartley and James Mill. London, 1881.

Phil 2038.80.5   Bower, G.S. Hartley and James Mill. N.Y., 1881.

Phil 2270.90.2   Bowne, B.P. The philosophy of Herbert Spencer. N.Y., 1881.

Phil 5811.5.20   Büchner, L. La vie psychique des bêtes. Paris, 1881.

Phil 3483.13   Burger, D. Kants wipbegeerte, kortelijk verklaard. 's Gravenhage, 1881.

Phil 8582.64   Caird, John. An introduction to the philosophy of religion. N.Y., 1881.

Phil 8610.881   Cairns, John. Unbelief in the eighteenth century as contrasted with its earlier and later history. Edinburgh, 1881.

Phil 5938.7.15   Capen, N. Reminiscences of Dr. Spurzheim and George Combe. N.Y., 1881.

Phil 6112.4.2   Carpenter, W.B. Principles of mental psychology. London, 1881.

Htn   Phil 6112.4.3*   Carpenter, W.B. Principles of mental psychology. London, 1881.

Phil 177.30   Caspari, Otto. Zusammenhang der Dinge. Breslau, 1881.

Phil 9342.12.5   Cobbe, F.P. The duties of women. Boston, 1881.

Phil 1900.81.3   Collins, W.L. Butler. Edinburgh, 1881.

Phil 1900.81   Collins, W.L. Butler. Philadelphia, 1881.

Phil 8610.881.30   The conflicts of the age. N.Y., 1881.

Phil 8692.1   Cook, J. Christ and modern thought. Boston, 1881.

Phil 4210.119   Cornoldi, G.M. Il rosminiamismo. Roma, 1881.

Phil 8610.881.35   Correspondance d'un sceptique et d'un croyant. Genève, 1881.

Phil 8658.5   Diman, J.L. The theistic argument as affected by recent theories. Boston, 1881.

Phil 9410.1   Duboc, K.J. Der Optimismus als Weltanschauung. Bonn, 1881.

Phil 8583.7   Dühring, E.K. Der Werth des Lebens. Leipzig, 1881.

Phil 478.1   Duncan, W.S. Conscious matter. London, 1881.

Phil 8663.3.87   Edgett, G.W. The mistakes of R.G. Ingersoll on nature and God. Boston, 1881.

Phil 5520.1   Egger, V. La parole intérieure. Paris, 1881.

Phil 3525.87   Eucken, Rudolf. Zur Erinnerung an K.C.F. Krause. Leipzig, 1881.

Phil 6114.5.16   Evans, W.F. The divine law of cure. Boston, 1881.

Phil 6114.5.4   Evans, W.F. Mental medicine. 6. ed. Boston, 1881.

Phil 6114.12.5   Exner, Sigmund. Untersuchungen über die Localisation der Functionen. Wien, 1881.

Phil 8630.13   Farrar, F.W. Mercy and judgment. London, 1881.

Phil 2266.80.3   Farrer, J.A. Adam Smith. London, 1881.

Phil 2266.80   Farrer, J.A. Adam Smith. London, 1881.

Phil 1990.10.5   Ferrier, J.F. Philosophical works. v.2. Edinburgh, 1881.

X Cg   Phil 3235.72.5   Feuerbach, Ludwig. The essence of Christianity. 2nd ed. London, 1881.

Phil 8585.9   Fowle, T.W. A new analogy. London, 1881.

486

Chronological Listing

1881 - cont.

Phil 1850.83A Fowler, J. Bacon. N.Y., 1881.
Phil 978.21 Fragments of occult truth. no. 1-8. n.p., 1881.
Phil 1870.84.1 Fraser, Alexander Campbell. Berkeley. Edinburgh, 1881.
NEDL Phil 1870.84 Fraser, Alexander Campbell. Berkeley. Philadelphia, 1881.
Phil 8696.3 Gardiner, F. Occasional papers. Middletown, Conn., 1881. 3 pam.
Phil 8956.1A Gass, F.W.H.J. Geschichte der christlichen Ethik. Berlin, 1881-87. 2v.
Phil 2115.117 Getschmann, W. Die Pädagogik des John Locke. Köthen, 1881.
Phil 8610.881.20 Gibson, Ellen E. The godly women of the Bible. N.Y., 1881.
Phil 5440.27 Gjellerup, Karl. Arvelighed og moral. Kjøbenhavn, 1881.
Phil 6116.5 Goltz, F.L. Über die Verrichtungen. Bonn, 1881.
Phil 8586.5 Graham, W. The creed of science, religious, moral and social. London, 1881.
Phil 7080.4 Granville, J.M. Sleep and sleeplessness. Boston, 1881.
Phil 181.36 Grassmann, R. Das Weltleben oder die Metaphysik. Stettin, 1881.
Phil 5046.10 Gregory, D.S. Practical logic. Philadelphia, 1881.
Phil 8696.2 Grote, A.R. The new infidelity. N.Y., 1881.
Phil 3310.5.32 Gutberlet, C. Die Psychologie. Münster, 1881.
Phil 9035.51 Hagemann, C.L.A. Was ist Charakter und wie Kann er durch die Erziehung gebildet? Dorpat, 1881.
Phil 3007.5 Hall, G.S. Aspects of German culture. Boston, 1881.
Phil 6317.1 Hammond, W.A. On certain conditions of nervous derangement. N.Y., 1881.
Phil 9347.14 The harmonium. Chicago, 1881.
Phil 3415.19 Hartmann, Eduard von. Lichtstrahlen aus Eduard von Hartmann's sämmtlichen Werken. Berlin, 1881.
Phil 5645.5 Head, J.F. Color blindness. Boston, 1881.
Phil 3425.37 Hegel, Georg Wilhelm Friedrich. Hegel's doctrine of reflection. N.Y., 1881.
Phil 5585.9.5 Heman, Karl F. Die Erscheinung der Dinge. Leipzig, 1881.
Phil 7054.35 Henke, O. Der Gespensterglaube der Gegenwart. Mülheim, 1881.
Phil 182.18.8 Henton, J. Philosophy and religion. London, 1881.
NEDL Phil 2045.50.2 Hobbes, Thomas. Leviathan. Oxford, 1881.
Phil 4803.454.65F Hoene-Wroński, Józef Maria. Nomothétique messianique. Paris, 1881.
Phil 5817.4 Hoffman, S. Thier-Psychologie. Stuttgart, 1881.
Phil 182.53 Hoffner, Paul. Grundlinien der Philosophie als Aufgabe. Mainz, 1881. 2v.
NEDL Phil 5643.12.5 Hoppe, J.F. Psychologish-physiologische Optik. Leipzig, 1881.
Phil 6119.2 Jaeger, G. Die Neuralanalyse. Leipzig, 1881.
Phil 184.15.3 Jochnick, W. Menniskan. Stockholm, 1881. 5 pam.
Phil 3480.32.9 Kant, Immanuel. Critique of pure reason. Edinburgh, 1881.
Phil 3480.32.8A Kant, Immanuel. Critique of pure reason. London, 1881. 2v.
Htn Phil 3480.32.8.2* Kant, Immanuel. Critique of pure reason. London, 1881. 2v.
Phil 3480.30.7 Kant, Immanuel. Kritik der reinen Vernunft. Kiel, 1881.
Phil 3480.79.7 Kant, Immanuel. Zum ewigen Frieden. Leipzig, 1881?
Phil 185.4 Kirchmann, J. Katechismus der Philosophie. Leipzig, 1881.
Phil 8885.27 Kirckner, F. Ethik. Leipzig, 1881.
Phil 8665.8 Kleutgen, J. Praeter introductionem continens partem primamque est De ipso deo. Ratisbonae, 1881.
Phil 3310.1.125 Knoodt, Peter. Anton Günther. Wien, 1881. 2v.
Phil 2520.110 Koch, Anton. Die Psychologie Descartes. München, 1881.
Phil 3808.89 Koeber, R. von. Schopenhauer's Erlösungslehre. Leipzig, 1881?
Phil 2138.84 Kohn, Benno. Untersuchungen über das Causalproblem. Wien, 1881.
Phil 3492.2.15 Krause, A. Populäre Darstellung von Immanuel Kant's Kritik der reinen Vernunft. Lahr, 1881.
Phil 3492.3 Küpffer, C. Der Schädel Immanuel Kant's. Braunschweig, 1881?
Phil 6681.1 Ladame, P. La névrose hypnotique. Paris, 1881.
Phil 9400.5 Lathrop, S.G. Fifty years and beyond. Chicago, 1881.
Phil 8520.4A Lechler, G.V. Geschichte des Englischen Deismus. Stuttgart, 1881.
Phil 5643.15 Le Conte, J. Sight. N.Y., 1881.
Phil 3552.67 Leibniz, Gottfried Wilhelm. La monadologie. Paris, 1881.
Phil 3585.1.90 Lepsius, J. Johann Heinrich Lambert; eine Darstellung seiner kosmologischen und philosophischen Leistungen. München, 1881.
Phil 2115.51A Locke, J. The conduct of the understanding. Oxford, 1881.
Phil 5051.21 Loeive, J.H. Lehrbuch der Logik. Wien, 1881.
Phil 3565.69 Lotze, Hermann. Grundzüge der Psychologie. Leipzig, 1881.
Phil 4466.1.80 Louzada de Magalhaes, J.J. Silvestre Pinheiro Ferreira. Bonn, 1881.
Phil 6961.5 Luys, J. Traité clinique et pratique des maladies mentales. Paris, 1881.
Phil 5051.15.5 Lyng, Georg V. Laerebog i den objektive logik. Christiania, 1881.
Phil 4080.1.80 Mabilleau, L. Étude historique...Cesare Cremonini. Paris, 1881.
Phil 4065.109 Mariano, R. Giordano Bruno: la vita e l'uomo. Roma, 1881.
Phil 8962.1.5 Martensen, H.L. Christian ethics. Edinburgh, 1881. 2v.
Phil 1350.5.4 Martha, Constant. Les moralistes sous l'Empire romain. 4e éd. Paris, 1881.
Phil 8592.6.20 Martineau, James. The relation between ethics and religion. London, 1881.
Phil 7080.8 Marvaud, J.L.A. Le sommeil et l'insomnie. Paris, 1881.
Phil 6854.6 Masaryk, Tomáš Gottigue. Der Selbstmord als sociale Massenerscheinung des modernen Civilisation. Wien, 1881.
Phil 5643.23 Mauthner, L. Gehirn und Auge. Wiesbaden, 1881.
Phil 1117.2A Mayor, J.B. Sketch of ancient philosophy. Cambridge, 1881.
Phil 8592.39 Medina, Juan J. Cuadros disolventes. Sevilla, 1881.
Phil 3246.80.5 Melzer, Ernst. Die Unsterblichkeitstheorie. Neisse, 1881.
Phil 2138.40.15 Mill, John S. Om friheten. Upsala, 1881.
Phil 2138.35.3.23 Mill, John S. A system of logic. 8th ed. N.Y., 1881.
Phil 6322.11 Mitchell, S.W. Lecture on diseases of the nervous system. Philadelphia, 1881.
Phil 2035.85 Monck, W.H.S. Sir William Hamilton. English philosopher. London, 1881.
Phil 5052.11 Monrad, M.J. Udsigt over den høiere logik. Christiania, 1881.
Phil 293.7.2 Montagu, A. Cours de philosophie scientifiques et ses conséquences sociales. 2. ed. Paris, 1881.
Phil 6122.7.9 Mosso, A. Über den Kreislauf des Blutes. Leipzig, 1881.
Phil 6122.11 Munk, H. Über die Funktionen der Grosshirnrinde. Berlin, 1881.

1881 - cont.

Phil 4210.81.4 Nardi, P. de. La filosofia di Antonio R-S. Pt. 1. Bellinzona, 1881.
Phil 645.3 Owen, J. Evenings with skeptics. N.Y., 1881. 2v.
Phil 2805.44 Pascal, Blaise. Gedanken. Leipzig, 1881.
Phil 3497.3.23 Paulsen, Friedrich. Was uns Kant sein kann? Leipzig, 1881.
Phil 3497.17 Pfleiderer, Edmund. Kantischer Kritizismus und englische Philosophie. Halle, 1881.
Phil 3415.84 Plümacher, O. Der Kampf um's Unbewusste. Berlin, 1881.
Phil 3808.134 Plumacher, G. Zwei Individualisten der Schopenhauer'schen Schule. Wien, 1881.
NEDL Phil 8685.9 Plumptre, C.E. General sketch...history of pantheism. London, 1881. 2v.
Phil 5545.22 Ribot, T. Les maladies de la mémoire. Paris, 1881.
Phil 5545.22.2 Ribot, T. Les maladies de la mémoire. Paris, 1881.
Phil 5257.23 Riche, A. Essai de psychologie; sur le cerveau. Paris, 1881.
NEDL Phil 27.2 Rivista di filosofia scientifica. Milano, 1881-1891. 10v.
Phil 8610.881.25 Rodenhausen, C. Christenthum ist Heidenthum. Hamburg, 1881.
Phil 192.65 Roisel, Godefroy de. La substance; essai de philosophie rationnelle. Paris, 1881.
Phil 8597.34 Romberg, P.A. Filosofi och religion. Karlskrona, 1881.
Phil 5057.8 Royce, J. Primer of logical analysis. San Francisco, 1881.
Htn Phil 2250.35* Royce, Josiah. Primer of logical analysis. San Francisco, 1881.
Phil 8892.23 Royer, Clémence. Le bien et la loi morale; éthique. Paris, 1881.
Phil 192.30 Rümelin, G. Reden und Aufsätze. Freiburg, 1881. 3v.
Phil 192.30.5 Rümelin, G. Reden und aufsätze. Freiburg, 1881. 2v.
Phil 3499.12 Runze, Max. Kant's Bedeutung auf Grund der Entwicklungsgeschichte Seiner Philosophie. Berlin, 1881.
Phil 6128.18 Sapolini, G. Un tredicesimo nervo craniale. Milano, 1881.
Phil 7054.34.10 Sargent, Epes. The proof palpable of immortality. 3. ed. Boston, 1881.
Phil 8673.10 Savage, M.J. Belief in God. 2. ed. Boston, 1881.
Phil 8893.31.5 Savage, M.J. The morals of evolution. Boston, 1881.
Phil 6028.3 Schack, S. Physiognomische Studien. Jena, 1881.
Phil 3808.70.12A Schopenhauer, Arthur. Die beiden Grundprobleme der Ethik. Leipzig, 1881.
Phil 3808.45 Schopenhauer, Arthur. Selected essays. Milwaukee, 1881.
Phil 193.17 Schultze, F. Philosophie der Naturwissenschaft. Leipzig, 1881.
Phil 8893.3 Schuppe, W. Grundzüge der Ethik und Rechtsphilosophie. Breslau, 1881.
Phil 3500.8 Schurman, J.G. Kantian ethics. London, 1881.
Phil 6122.8.5 Se sia l'anima o il cervello che pente e pensa. Firenze, 1881.
Phil 5585.9 Sergi, G. Teoria fisiologica della percezione. Milano, 1881.
Phil 5645.23 Sergi, Giuseppe. Fisiologia e psicologia del colore. Milano, 1881.
Phil 8893.7 Sewall, F. The new ethics. N.Y., 1881.
Phil 9178.8 Sherwood, M.E.W. Amenities of home. N.Y., 1881.
Phil 193.27 Sigwart, Christoph von. Kleine Schriften. Freiburg, 1881. 2v.
Phil 3500.20.15 Simmel, G. Das Wesen der Materie nach Kants physischer Monadologie. Inaug. Diss. Berlin, 1881.
Phil 9120.4 Smiles, S. Duty. N.Y., 1881.
Phil 2270.74.7 Spencer, Herbert. Data of ethics. 3rd ed. London, 1881.
Phil 2270.70.5 Spencer, Herbert. Principles of psychology. London, 1881. 2v.
Phil 3819.41 Spinoza, Benedictus de. Kurzer Tractat von Gott. Freiburg, 1881.
Phil 5780.7 Spitta, H. Die Willensbestimmungen und ihr Verhältniss zu den Impulsiven. Tübingen, 1881.
Phil 299.5 Spitzer, H. Über Ursprung...des Hylozoismus. Graz, 1881.
Phil 8598.37 Storrs, Richard S. The recognition of the supernatural. N.Y., 1881.
Phil 3850.1.35 Strauss, D.F. Der alte und der neue Glaube. 2. Aufl. Bonn, 1881.
Phil 5058.18.5 Strümpell, L. Grundriss der Logik. Leipzig, 1881.
Phil 5058.20 Swinburne, A.J. Picture logic. London, 1881.
Phil 4635.3.31 Sylwan, O.C. Naturvetenskap eller metafysik? Stockholm, 1881.
Phil 2885.34A Taine, Hippolyte Adolphe. Philosophie de l'art. Paris, 1881. 2v.
Phil 1540.47 Talamo, Salvatore. L'aristotelismo della scolastica nella storia. 3. ed. Siena, 1881.
Phil 5640.39 Taylor, C.F. Sensation and pain. N.Y., 1881.
Phil 1524.1 Townsend, W.J. The great schoolmen of the Middle Ages. London, 1881.
Phil 2270.101 Traina, Tommaso. La morale di Herbert Spencer. Torino, 1881.
Phil 3503.1 Vaihinger, H. Commentar zu Kants Kritik der reinen Vernunft. Stuttgart, 1881. 2v.
Phil 3504.3A Watson, J. Kant and his English critics. N.Y., 1881.
Phil 3504.36 Weir, Archibald. The critical philosophy of Kant. London, 1881.
Phil 4260.87 Werner, K. Giambattista Vico als Philosophie und Gelehrterforscher. Wien, 1881.
Phil 1020.4.25 Werner, Karl. Der Averroismus in der christlich-peripatetischen Psychologie des späteren Mittelalters. Wien, 1881.
Phil 3504.21F Werner, Karl. Kant in Italien. Wien, 1881.
Phil 1527.2 Werner, Karl. Die Scholastik des späteren Mittelalters. Wien, 1881. 4v.
Phil 6972.2 Wernicke, C. Lehrbuch der Gehirnkrankheiten. v.1-2. Kassel, 1881.
Phil 4655.1.40 Wikner, Pontus. Öppet sändebref till teologisk tidskrift. Upsala, 1881.
Phil 497.5 Wilder, S.H. Unscientific materialism. N.Y., 1881.
Phil 5640.4.7 Wilson, G. The five gateways of knowledge. 7th ed. London, 1881.
Phil 3025.1 Zart, G. Einfluss der englischen Philosophen...deutschen Philosophen. Berlin, 1881.
Phil 1130.4A Zeller, Eduard. History of Greek philosophy. London, 1881. 2v.
Phil 8850.1 Ziegler, T. Geschichte der Ethik. Bonn, 1881-86. 2v.
Phil 3450.5.80 Zirngiebl, Eberhard. Johannes Huber. Gotha, 1881.
Phil 8715.3 Zöllner, J.F.K. Naturwissenschaft und christliche Offenbarung. Leipzig, 1881.

1881 - cont.

Phil 7060.97.3   Zöllner, J.C.F. Transcendental physics. 2. ed. Boston, 1881.

1882

Phil 4515.91   Åberg, L.H. Den Boströmska verldsåsigten i sina grunddrag framstäld. Stockholm, 1882.

Phil 4655.1.80.2   Åberg, L.H. Granskning af P. Wikners kritik. Stockholm, 1882.

Phil 331.1   Abbot, F.E. Scientific philosophy. London, 1882.

Phil 9160.4   Allen, N. The New England family. New Haven, 1882.

Phil 5240.19   The alternative. London, 1882.

Phil 4073.82   Amabile, L. Fra Tommaso Campanella: la sua congiura. Napoli, 1882-. 3v.

Phil 3245.82   Ambrosius, J.M. Om Immanuel Hermann Fichte's teism och etik. Lund, 1882.

Phil 5040.15   Andreasi, A. Arte logica. Verona, 1882.

EDL Phil 9430.1   Bacmeister, A. Der Pessimismus und die Sittenlehre. Gütersloh, 1882.

Phil 2138.81A   Bain, A. John Stuart Mill. London, 1882.

Phil 2138.81.5   Bain, A. John Stuart Mill. N.Y., 1882.

Phil 9430.7   Barlow, J.W. The ultimatum of pessimism. London, 1882.

Phil 8876.9   Basford, J.L. Sparks from the philosophers stone. London, 1882.

Phil 6111.10.3   Bastian, H.C. Das Gehirn als Organ des Geistes. Leipzig, 1882.

Phil 6951.12   Beard, G.M. Psychology of the Salem witchcraft...1697. Photoreproduction. N.Y., 1882.

Phil 8581.41   Benitez de Lugo, A. El cristianismo y la filosofia. Sevilla, 1882.

Phil 1106.3   Benn, A.W. The Greek philosophers. London, 1882. 2v.

Phil 8876.15   Bersot, D.P.E. Un moraliste. Paris, 1882.

Phil 4363.2.80A   Bigelow, John. Molinos the quietist. N.Y., 1882.

En Phil 4363.2.81*   Bigelow, John. Molinos the quietist. N.Y., 1882.

Phil 282.2   Boase, H.S. Few words on evolution and creation. London, 1882.

Phil 3483.7   Bolliger, A. Anti-Kant oder. Basel, 1882.

Phil 3120.2.3   Bolzano, Bernard. Gesammelte Schriften. 2. Ausg. Wien, 1882.

Phil 5041.36.5   Borelius, J.J. Lärobok i den formella logiken. 4. Uppl. Lund, 1882.

Phil 9075.2   Bouillier, F.C. La vraie conscience. Paris, 1882.

Phil 5643.21   Bowditch, H.P. Optical illusions of motion. Cambridge, 1882.

Phil 176.27.5   Bowne, B.P. Metaphysics. N.Y., 1882.

Phil 176.27   Bowne, B.P. Metaphysics. N.Y., 1882.

Phil 3552.81   Braeutigam, L. Leibniz und Herbart über die Freiheit des menschlichen Willens. Heidelberg, 1882.

Phil 1135.13   Breton, G. Essai sur la poésie philosophique en Grèce. Paris, 1882.

Phil 8581.48   Bridges, J.H. Five discourses on positive religion. London, 1882.

Phil 7054.61.12   Brittan, Samuel B. The battleground of the spiritual reformation. N.Y., 1882.

Phil 8581.68.10   Broglie, Paul. La définition de la religion. Paris, 1882.

Phil 4065.105   Brunnhofer, H. Giordano Bruno's Weltanschauung. Leipzig, 1882.

Phil 4210.116.20   Buroni, Giuseppe. Della nuova dichiarazione quasi ultima della S. Congregazione dell'Indice. Torino, 1882.

Phil 802.8.2   Carbonel, Pierre. Histoire de la philosophie depuis les temps les plus reculés jusqu'à nos jours. 2e éd. Avignon, 1882.

Phil 8692.7   Carpenter, W.B. Doctine of evolution in its relation to theism. London, 1882.

Phil 6952.5   Channing, W. The mental status of guiteau. Cambridge, 1882.

Phil 6112.23   Cleland, J. The relation of brain to mind. Glasgow, 1882.

Phil 8582.35.9   Cobbe, F.P. The peak in Darien...an octave of essays. Boston, 1882.

Phil 8877.18   Compayré, J.G. Éléments d'instruction morale et civique. Paris, 1882.

DL Phil 7068.82.5   Confessions of a medium. London, 1882.

Phil 177.23   Courtney, W.L. Studies in philosophy. London, 1882.

Phil 178.44.5   Delff, Heinrich K.H. Über den Weg, zum Wissen und zur Gewissheit zu Gesangen. Leipzig, 1882.

Phil 2520.53.2   Descartes, René. Unstersuchungen über die Grundlagen der Philosophie. 2e Aufl. Heidelberg, 1882.

Phil 6953.4.2   Descourtis, G. Du fractionnement des opérations cérébrales. Paris, 1882.

Phil 6953.4   Descourtis, G. Du fractionnement des opérations cérébrales. Paris, 1882.

Phil 8878.41   Dessaignes, J.P. Etudes de l'homme moral. Paris, 1882. 3v.

Phil 8610.882   Ellis, John. Skepticism and divine relation. N.Y., 1882.

Phil 3486.1   Erdmann, B. Reflexionen Kants zur kritischen Philosophie. Leipzig, 1882-84. 2v.

Phil 5044.3.4   Everett, C.C. The science of thought. Boston, 1882.

Phil 3210.51   Fechner, G.T. Revision der Hauptpunkte der Psychophysik. Leipzig, 1882.

Phil 3525.95   Fernandez Valbuena, Ramiro. Se opone El Krausismo a la fé católica? Badajoz, 1882[1883]

Phil 5374.4   Fitzgerald, P.F. Essay on the philosophy of self-consciousness. London, 1882.

Phil 270.6   Foster, F.H. The doctrine of the transcendent use of the principle of causality. Leipzig, 1882.

Phil 2262.81A   Fowler, T. Shaftesbury and Hutcheson. London, 1882.

Phil 9145.5   Friends for Pennsylvania, New Jersey and Delaware. Address on some growing evils of the day. Philadelphia, 1882.

Phil 5640.9.2   Genzmer, A.O.H. Untersuchungen über die Sinneswahrnehmungen des neugeborenen Menschen. Halle, 1882.

Phil 8631.2   Gross, J.B. The belief in immortality. Philadelphia, 1882.

Phil 8881.18   Gross, J.B. What makes us unhappy? Philadelphia, 1882.

Phil 3310.1.3   Günther, Anton. Gesammelte Schriften. Bd.1-9. Wien, 1882. 9v.

Phil 3310.5.33   Gutberlet, C. Logik und Erkenntnisstheorie. Münster, 1882.

Phil 672.28   Gutberlet, Constantin. Die neue Raumtheorie. Mainz, 1882.

Phil 2270.84.8   Guthrie, M. On Mr. Spencer's unification of knowledge. London, 1882.

Phil 5545.177   Hartenbach, E. Dr. Ewald Hartenbach's Kunst. 15. Aufl. Quedlinburg, 1882.

Phil 3415.30.9   Hartmann, Eduard von. Philosophie des Unbewussten. 9. Aufl. Berlin, 1882.

1882 - cont.

Phil 3415.60   Hartmann, Eduard von. Die Religion des Geistes. Berlin, 1882.

Phil 3007.2   Heine, H. Religion and philosophy in Germany. London, 1882.

Phil 8957.8   Heppe, H. Christliche Sittenlehre. Elberfeld, 1882.

Phil 3801.451   Heussler, Hans. Schellings Entwicklungslehre dargestellt. Frankfurt, 1882.

Phil 3415.96   Heymons, C. Eduard von Hartmann. Berlin, 1882.

Phil 5247.9.4   Hickok, L.P. Empirical psychology. Boston, 1882.

Phil 8587.16.2   Hill, T. Geometry and faith. Boston, 1882.

Phil 978.20   Hints on esoteric theosophy. no. 1-2. Calcutta, 1882.

Phil 7054.10   Holland, C. Spiritual or magnetic forces. 2. ed. N.Y., 1882.

Phil 6117.5.6   Holmes, O.W. Mechanism in thought and morals. Boston, 1882.

Phil 2050.24   Hume, David. Essay on miracles. London, 1882. 5 pam.

Phil 2050.36.5   Hume, David. Essays: moral, political and literary. London, 1882. 2v.

Phil 3499.1   Immanuel Kant. Königsberg, 1882. 3 pam.

Phil 8663.3.33   Ingersoll, Robert G. The Christian religion. Manchester, 1882.

Phil 8663.3.40   Ingersoll, Robert G. The Christian religion. N.Y., 1882.

Phil 6959.3   Jacobi, M.P. The prevention of insanity. Boston, 1882.

Phil 2070.31   James, William. On some Hegelisms. London, 1882.

Phil 2070.07   James, William. The sense of dizziness in deaf-mutes. n.p., 1882-1911. 11 pam.

Phil 575.25   Jeanmaire, Charles. L'idée de la personnalité. Thèse. Toulouse, 1882.

Phil 5645.6.15   Jeffries, B.J. Color-names, color-blindness. Boston, 1882.

Phil 8834.2   Jodl, Friedrich. Geschichte der Ethik. v.1-2. Stuttgart, 1882-1889.

Phil 7082.52   Jóhannsson, Jón. Draumur. Akureyri, 1882.

Phil 9349.2   Johnson, F. True womanhood. Cambridge, 1882.

Phil 184.9.5   Joly, H. Cours de philosophie. 7. éd. Paris, 1882.

Phil 3480.32.10   Kant, Immanuel. Critique of pure reason. N.Y., 1882.

Phil 3480.45.10   Kant, Immanuel. Kritik der praktischen Vernunft. 3. Aufl. Heidelberg, 1882. 2 pam.

Phil 1710.1.2   Knauer, V. Geschichte der Philosophie mit besonderer Berücksichtung der Neuzeit. 2e Aufl. Wien, 1882.

Phil 3830.2   Knight, E. Spinoza, essays by Land, Fischer, Vloten, and Renan. London, 1882.

Phil 2520.92   Krantz, E. Essai sur l'esthétique de Descartes. Paris, 1882.

Phil 5643.56   Kries, Johannes von. Die Gesichts-Empfindungen und ihre Analyse. Leipzig, 1882.

Phil 3493.1.5   Laas, E. Kants Stellung in der Geschichte des Conflicts zwischen Glauben und Wissen. Berlin, 1882.

Phil 8412.4   Laprade, Victor de. Histoire du sentiment de la nature. Paris, 1882.

Phil 8886.30   Leathes, Stanley. The foundations of morality. London, 1882.

Phil 3552.75   Leibnizens Briefwechsel...Bernstorff. Hannover, 1882.

Phil 6121.17   Lewis, W. Bevan. The human brain. London, 1882.

Phil 186.12.5   Liebmann, O. Gedanken und Thatsachen. Strassburg, 1882-1899. 2v.

Phil 3565.60   Lotze, Hermann. Grundzüge der Naturphilosophie. Leipzig, 1882.

Phil 3565.35.2   Lotze, Hermann. Grundzüge der praktischen Philosophie. Leipzig, 1882.

Phil 3011.1   Lotze, R.H. Geschichte der deutschen Philosophie - Kant. Leipzig, 1882.

Phil 6121.7   Luys, J. The brain and its functions. N.Y., 1882.

Phil 5051.15   Lyng, Georg V. Grundtankernes system. v.1-3. Christiania, 1882-1887.

Phil 6962.1   Magnan, V. Leçons cliniques sur les maladies mentales. Paris, 1882-91.

Phil 3110.85.5   Martensen, Hans L. Jacob Böhme. Leipzig, 1882.

Phil 3832.1A   Martineau, J. A study of Spinoza. London, 1882.

Phil 510.135   Mayer, A. Die monistische Erkenntnislehre. Leipzig, 1882.

Phil 812.8   Mener, J.B. Geschichte der Philosophie zum Gebrauche. Bonn, 1882.

Phil 5643.76   Metz, Bernhard. Über die pseudoskopische Ablenkung paralleler Linien. Marburg, 1882.

Phil 2270.89   Michelet, C.L. Herbert Spencer's System der Philosophie. Halle, 1882.

Phil 187.17   Mivart, St. G. Nature and thought. London, 1882.

Phil 4210.130   Moglia, A. I suareziani e l'abate Rosmini. Piacenza, 1882.

Phil 3494.8   Morris, G.S. Kant's Critique of pure reason. Chicago, 1882.

Phil 7150.9.5   Morsell, H. Suicide. N.Y., 1882.

Phil 7077.4.2   Moses, William S. Psychography. 2d ed. London, 1882.

Phil 187.22   Mühry, A. Kritik und Kurze Darlegung der exacten Natur-Philosophie. Göttingen, 1882.

Phil 5252.10   Müller, F.A. Das Axiom der Psychophysik. Marburg, 1882.

Phil 4210.81   Nardi, P. de. Antonio Rosmini ed i gesuiti. Torino, 1882.

Phil 2520.107   Natorp, P. Descartes' Erkenntnisstheorie. Marburg, 1882.

Phil 5053.6   Neudecker, G. Grundlegung der reinen Logik. Würzburg, 1882.

Phil 8593.4   Nichols, J.R. From whence, what, where? Boston, 1882.

Phil 188.15   Nielsen, F.K. Sjaele-og taenkelaere i almenfattelig. 4e udg. Kjøbenhavn, 1882.

Phil 8888.9   Nobili-Vitelleschi, F. Morale induttiva. Roma, 1882-91. 4v.

Phil 8638.1   Noel, R. Philosophy of immortality. London, 1882.

Phil 3495.5   Noiré, L. Die Lehre Kants...Vermorst. Mainz, 1882.

Phil 575.4   Olssen, W.W. Personality. N.Y., 1882.

Phil 9354.2.5   O'Reilly, B. True men as we need them. 4th ed. N.Y., 1882.

Phil 2050.105   Paoli, Alessandro. Hume e il principio di causa. Napoli, 1882.

Phil 5627.84   Park, M. Remarkable vision and death bed experience of Ada Park. Pulaski, N.Y., 1882.

Phil 2805.40.22   Pascal, Blaise. Pensées choisies. 2. éd. Paris, 1882.

Phil 2805.31   Pascal, Blaise. Première, quatrième et treizième lettres provinciales. Paris, 1882.

Phil 3565.117   Pfleiderer, E. Lotze's philosophische Weltanschauung nach ihren Grundzügen. Berlin, 1882.

Phil 3565.78   Pfleiderer, E. Lotze's philosophische Weltanschauungen nach ihren Grundzugen. Berlin, 1882. 5 pam.

Phil 3280.81   Pfleiderer, E. Verzeichniss der Doctoren. Tübingen, 1882.

Phil 1135.52   Poestion, J.C. Griechische Philosophinnen. Bremen, 1882.

Phil 8595.27   Pontanelli, E. Los dos grandes problemas de la humanidad. N.Y., 1882.

Phil 190.15.5   Porter, N. Science and sentiment. N.Y., 1882.

1882 - cont.

Phil 5440.8	Proctor, R.A. Hereditary traits. N.Y., 1882.
Phil 3235.116	Ran, Albrecht. Ludwig Feuerbach's Philosophie. Leipzig, 1882.
Phil 125.2	Rand, Benjamin. Tables of philosophy. Cambridge, 1882.
Phil 9430.9	Rehmke, J. Der Pessimismus und die Sittenlehre. Leipzig, 1882.
Phil 2262.85	Rehorn, F. Moral sense und Moral-Prinzip bei Shaftesbury. Inaug. Diss. Bonn, 1882.
Phil 5545.22.5	Ribot, T. Diseases of memory. N.Y., 1882.
Phil 5440.4.9	Ribot, T. L'hérédité psychologique. 2. éd. Paris, 1882.
Phil 3552.116	Ritter, P.H. De monadenleer van Leibniz. Leiden, 1882.
Phil 8892.3	Rolph, W.H. Biologische Probleme. Leipzig, 1882.
Phil 3499.6.18	Romundt, H. Antäus. Leipzig, 1882.
Phil 4210.41	Rosmini-Serbati, Antonio. The philosophical system. London, 1882.
Phil 4210.42	Rosmini-Serbati, Antonio. Il razionalismo. Prato, 1882.
Phil 6127.15.5	Rüdinger, N. Ein Beitrag zur Anatomie des Sprach-Centrums. Stuttgart, 1882.
Phil 8672.7	Runze, G. Der ontologische Gottesbeweis. Halle, 1882.
Phil 299.1	Schlesinger, J. Die Entstehung der physischen...Welt. Wien, 1882.
Phil 1145.18	Schmidt, L. Die Ethik der alten Griechen. Berlin, 1882.
Phil 1020.1	Schmölders, A. Essai...Ecoles philosophiques chez les Arabes. Paris, 1882.
Phil 5768.1	Schneider, G.H. Der menschliche Wille. Berlin, 1882.
Phil 7060.101	Schneider, Wilhelm. Der neuere Geisterglaube. Paderborn, 1882.
Phil 2038.81	Schoenlank, B. Hartley und Priestley. Photoreproduction. Halle, 1882.
Phil 3808.50	Schopenhauer, Arthur. De la quadruple racine du principe de la raison suffisante. Paris, 1882.
Phil 6128.28	Schreber, D.G.M. Das Buch der Erziehung an Leib und Seele. 2. ed. Leipzig, 1882.
Phil 193.16	Schubert-Soldern, R. von. Über Transcendenz der Objects und Subjects. Leipzig, 1882.
Phil 818.1.3.3	Schwegler, F.C.A. Geschichte der Philosophie. Stuttgart, 1882.
Phil 8598.7.3	Seeley, R. Natural religion. Boston, 1882.
Phil 8598.7	Seeley, R. Natural religion. London, 1882.
Phil 3018.4	Seth, A. Developmnt from Kant to Hegel. London, 1882.
Phil 978.9.10	Sinnett, A.P. The occult world. Boston, 1882.
Phil 299.8	Soury, Jules. Philosophie naturelle. Paris, 1882.
Phil 2270.55.8	Spencer, Herbert. Social statics. N.Y., 1882.
Phil 2270.31.3	Spencer, Herbert. System der synthetischen Philosophie: Psychologie. Stuttgart, 1882-86. 2v.
Phil 3819.10.8	Spinoza, Benedictus de. Opera quotquot reperta sunt. Hagae, 1882-83. 2v.
Phil 3819.20	Spinoza, Benedictus de. Die Unvollendeten lateinischen Abhandlungen. Heidelberg, 1882.
Phil 7080.15.2	Spitta, H. Die Schlaf- und Traumzustände der menschlichen Seele. 2. Aufl. Tübingen, 1882.
NEDL Phil 299.4.2	Stallo, J.B. Concepts and theories of modern physics. N.Y., 1882.
Phil 672.14.9	The stars and the earth. 5th American ed. Boston, 1882.
Phil 193.55.9	Stein, Ludwig. Die Willensfreiheit...bei den jüdischen philosophen des Mittelalters. n.p., 1882-1908. 9 pam.
NEDL Phil 8893.23.2	Stephen, L. The science of ethics. N.Y., 1882.
Phil 5258.23	Stricker, S. Studien über die Bewegungsvorstellungen. Wien, 1882.
Phil 3500.12A	Stuelsenberg, J. Life of Immanuel Kant. London, 1882.
Phil 6128.7	Swedenborg, E. The brain. London, 1882-87.
Phil 6689.11	Tamburini, A. Anleitung zur experimentellen Untersuchung des Hypnotismus. Wiesbaden, 1882-85.
Phil 8610.831.20	Taylor, Robert. The devil's pulpit. London, 1882. 2v.
Phil 194.18	Teichmüller, G. Die Wirkliche und die scheinbare Welt. Breslau, 1882.
Phil 3501.1.5	Thiele, G. Die Philosophie Immanuel Kant. Halle, 1882.
Phil 5440.6	Thompson, E. Rowell. Heredity. Boston, 1882.
Phil 5769.2	Thomsen, H. Die rechtliche Willens Bestimmung. Kiel, 1882.
Phil 4210.141.5	Trullet, Angelo Parere intorno alle dottrine ed alle opere di Antonio Rosmini-Serbati. Modena, 1882.
Phil 5060.1.6	Ueberweg, F. System der Logik. 5e Aufl. Bonn, 1882.
Phil 3552.116.5	Vallier, Charles A. De possibilibus apud Leibnitium. Thesis. Burdigalae, 1882.
Phil 2035.88	Veitch, J. Hamilton. Philadelphia, 1882.
Phil 5261.2	Vignoli, T. Myth and science. N.Y., 1882.
Phil 3504.1	Wallace, William. Kant. Edinburgh, 1882.
Phil 3504.1.3	Wallace, William. Kant. Philadelphia, 1882.
Htn Phil 3801.874*	Watson, John. Schelling's transcendental idealism. Chicago, 1882.
Phil 3801.874.2A	Watson, John. Schelling's transcendental idealism. Chicago, 1882.
Phil 3415.95	Weber, Alfred. Wille zum Leben oder Wille zum Guten? Strassburg, 1882.
Phil 8897.10	Wells, K.G. Lessons in ethics. pt.1. Boston, 1882.
Phil 1540.9	Werner, Karl. Die nominalisirende Psychologie der Scholastik des späteren Mittelalters. Wien, 1882.
Phil 6972.10.4	Wharton, F. Treatise on mental unsoundness. 4. ed. Philadelphia, 1882.
Phil 8897.45	Witte, J.H. Grundzüge der Sittenlehre. Bonn, 1882.
Phil 5772.7	Witte, J.H. Über Freiheit des Willens. Bonn, 1882.
Phil 9035.33	Wolff, Hermann. Gemüth und Charakter sechs Vorträge. Leipzig, 1882.
Phil 822.5	Wolff, M. Bidrag till filosofiens historia. Stockholm, 1882.
Phil 8712.5.5	Wright, George F. Studies in science and religion. Andover, 1882.
Phil 1130.2.6	Zeller, Eduard. Die Philosophie der Griechen. Register. Leipzig, 1882.
Phil 200.3	Zimmermann, R. Anthroposophie. Wien, 1882.

1883

Phil 6110.12	Aeby, C.T. Schema des Faserverlaufes im menschlichen Gehirn und Rückenmark. Bern, 1883.
Phil 6110.16	Althaus, J. On failure of brain-power. London, 1883.
Phil 282.1	Barratt, A. Physical metempiric. London, 1883.
Phil 2270.87	Beard, G.M. Herbert Spencer on American nervousness. N.Y., 1883.
Phil 6951.12.5	Beard, G.M. Die Nervenschwäche. 2. Aufl. Leipzig, 1883.
Phil 8876.86	Bergmann, J. Über das Richtige. Berlin, 1883.
Phil 9550.10	Bergmann, Julius. Über den Utilitarianismus. Marburg, 1883.
Phil 8610.883.10	Berthet, André. Les débats de la conscience, catéchisme laïque. Paris, 1883.

1883 - cont.

Phil 3821.7.5	Betz, H.J. Spinoza en Kant. 's Gravenhage, 1883.
Phil 4515.31.3	Boström, C.J. Grundlinier till philosophiska civil- och criminalrätten. Upsala, 1883.
Phil 4515.10	Boström, C.J. Skrifter af C.J. Boström utgifna af H. Edfeldt. v.1-3. Upsala, 1883-1901. 2v.
Phil 8610.870.10	Bradlaugh, Charles. Theological essays. London, 1883.
Phil 5041.20	Bradley, F.H. Principles of logic. London, 1883.
Phil 6671.10.20	Braid, James. Neurypnologie. Paris, 1883.
Phil 5241.19	Buccola, G. La legge del tempo. Milano, 1883.
X Cg Phil 3425.80.3A	Caird, Edward. Hegel. Edinburgh, 1883.
X Cg Phil 3425.80	Caird, Edward. Hegel. Philadelphia, 1883.
Phil 410.2	Cantor, Georg. Grundlagen einer allgemeinen Monnichfaltigkeitslehre. Leipzig, 1883.
Phil 600.7.95	Caro, Elme. M. Littré et le positivisme. Paris, 1883.
Phil 177.8.9	Carus, Paul. Ursache Grund und Zweck. Dresden, 1883.
Phil 3565.80	Caspari, O. Hermann Lotze. Breslau, 1883.
Phil 5242.2	Cesca, G. Le teorie nativistiche e genetiche della localizzazione spaziale. Verona, 1883.
Phil 630.14	Cesca, Giovanni. Il nuovo realismo contemporaneo. Verona, 1883.
Phil 5812.1	Chadbourne, P.A. Instinct. 2nd ed. N.Y., 1883.
Phil 6952.23.10	Charcot, J.M. Etude critique et clinique de la doctrine des localisations motrices. Paris, 1883.
Phil 8582.22	Coan, T.M. Topics of the time. Questions of belief. N.Y., 1883.
Phil 3484.2.8	Cohen, H. Kant's Einfluss auf die deutsche Kultur. Berlin, 1883.
Phil 333.3	Cohen, H. Das Princip der Infinitesimal-Methode und seine Geschichte. Berlin, 1883.
Phil 8657.5	Coke, H. Creeds of the day. London, 1883. 2v.
Phil 177.41	Commer, E. System der Philosophie. v.1-4. Münster, 1883.
Phil 8877.18.2	Compayré, J.G. Lectures morales et civiques. Paris, 1883.
Phil 2490.12	Comte, Auguste. Opuscules de philosophie sociale. Paris, 1883.
Phil 177.17	Concord lecturer on philosophy. Cambridge, 1883.
Phil 978.36.5	Constant, L. Unpublished writings. Calcutta, 1883.
Phil 3552.244	Dafert, F.W. Gottfried Wilhelm Leibnitz als Deutscher. Wien, 1883.
Phil 6750.10	Davis, C.H.S. The classification...feeble minded, imbecile and idiotic. N.Y., 1883.
Phil 5243.5	Delboeuf, J.R.L. Examen critique de la loi psychophysique. Paris, 1883.
Phil 2555.4.31	Derepas, Gustave. De necessitate legum naturalium. Thesis. Lutetiae, 1883.
Phil 960.3	Deussen, P. System des Vedânta. Leipzig, 1883.
Phil 178.11	Drious, C.J. Cours de philosophie. Paris, 1883.
Phil 3485.3	Ducros, L. Quando et quomodo Kantium humius. Burgigalae, 1883.
Phil 8583.7.5	Dühring, E.K. Der Ersatz der Religion. Karlsruhe, 1883.
Phil 3808.118	Dueros, Louis. Schopenhauer. Thèse. Paris, 1883.
Phil 3791.31	Eiehl, Alois. Über wissenschaftliche und nichtwissenschaftliche Philosophie. Freiburg, 1883.
Phil 3552.128	Engler, Otto. Darstellung und Kritik des leibnitzischen Optimismus. Inaug.-Diss. Jena, 1883.
Phil 5325.2	Ferri, L. La psychologie de l'association. Paris, 1883.
Phil 6115.4	Ferrière, E. L'âme est la fonction du cerveau. Paris, 1883. 2v.
Phil 6675.8	Fischer, E.L. Der sogenante Lebensmagnetismus oder Hypnotismus. Mainz, 1883.
Phil 8620.31	Fischer, Engelbert Lorenz. Das Problem des Übels und die Theodicee. Mainz, 1883.
Phil 3487.1	Fischer, Kuno. Kritik der Kantischen Philosophie. München, 1883.
Phil 8585.6	Fisher, G.P. The grounds of theistic and Christian belief. N.Y., 1883.
Phil 6115.6	Flechsig, P. Plan des menschlichen Gehirns. Leipzig, 1883.
Phil 5245.18	Ford, Corydon. The synthesis of mind. n.p., 1883-1893.
Phil 8830.3	Fouillée, A. Critique; systèmes de morale contemporaine. Paris, 1883.
Phil 2262.81.5A	Fowler, T. Shaftesbury and Hutcheson. N.Y., 1883.
Phil 5045.2.6	Fowler, Thomas. Inductive logic. Oxford, 1883.
Phil 5246.1.2A	Galton, F. Inquiries into the human faculty. N.Y., 1883.
Phil 7068.83.6	Gay, Susan E. John William Fletcher, clairvoyant. London, 1883.
Phil 3425.206	Geijer, R. Hegelianism och positivism. Lund, 1883.
Phil 5216.1	Gilardin, Alphonse. Considérations sur les divers systèmes de psychologie. Paris, 1883.
Phil 2494.81	Gillet, M. L'Utopie de Condorcet. Paris, 1883.
Phil 8881.9	Gilson, B. Manuel de philosophie morale. Louvain, 1883.
Phil 8881.12A	Gizycki, G. Grundzüge der Moral. Leipzig, 1883.
Phil 3280.82	Göpfert, E. Geulincx' ethisches System. Breslau, 1883.
Phil 8696.8	Goodwin, H. Walks in the regions of science and faith. London, 1883.
Phil 5090.4	Gréard, Mlle. La certitude philosophique. Paris, 1883.
Phil 2020.30A	Green, T.H. Prolegomena to ethics. Oxford, 1883.
Phil 8610.883	Greg, Percy. Without God. London, 1883.
Phil 8881.20	Greg, W.R. Enigmas of life. London, 1883.
Phil 2050.107	Grimthorpe, E.B. A review of Hume and Huxley on miracles. London, 1883.
Phil 2270.82	Ground, W.D. Examination of Herbert Spencer's theory of the will. London, 1883.
Phil 8125.22	Grucker, Emile. Histoire des doctrines litteraires. Paris, 1883.
Phil 3310.5.34	Gutberlet, C. Ethik und Naturrecht. Münster, 1883.
Phil 8881.39	Guyot, Yves. La morale: la moralé théologique. Paris, 1883.
Phil 7054.40	Hall, T.B. Modern spiritualism; or Opening way. Boston, 1883.
Phil 5247.3	Hamilton, E.J. The human mund. N.Y., 1883.
Phil 6317.1.2	Hammond, W.A. On certain conditions of nervous derangement. 3d ed. N.Y., 1883.
Phil 8662.3	Harris, S. The philosophical basis of Theism. N.Y., 1883.
Phil 182.5.9	Harris, W.T. Philosophy in outline. N.Y., 1883.
Phil 3415.67	Hartmann, Eduard von. Religious metaphysics. N.Y., 1883.
Phil 270.7.2	Hazard, R.G. Man a creative first cause. Boston, 1883.
Htn Phil 270.7.3*	Hazard, R.G. Man a creative first cause. Boston, 1883.
Phil 270.7	Hazard, R.G. Man a creative first cause. Boston, 1883.
Phil 1145.77	Heinze, Max. Der Eudämonismus in der griechischen Philosophie. Leipzig, 1883.
Phil 7054.24	Helleberg, C.C. A book written by the spirits of the so-called dead. Cincinnati, 1883.
Phil 3489.33	Herbart, J.F. Haupt-Momente der kritischen Philosophie. Münster, 1883.
Phil 2270.86	Herbert Spencer on the Americans and the Americans on Spencer. N.Y., 1883.

Chronological Listing

1883 - cont.

Phil 8520.1	Hicks, L.E. A critique of design-arguments. N.Y., 1883.
Phil 182.21	Hofmann, A.W. Inaugural address. Boston, 1883.
Phil 5247.11.3	Hopkins, M. An outline study of man. N.Y., 1883.
Phil 978.39	Hume, A.C. No revelation infallible. Calcutta, 1883.
Phil 2050.37.25	Hume, David. Eine Untersuchung über die Principien der Moral. Wien, 1883.
Phil 978.19	Iyer, S.S. Theosophical miscellanies. v.1-2. Calcutta, 1883.
Phil 184.2.9	Jacques, A. Manuel de philosophie. 9. ed. Paris, 1883.
Phil 5249.1	Jahn, M. Psychologie als Grundwissenschaft der Pädagogik. Leipzig, 1883.
Phil 1750.4	Janet, P. Les maîtres de la pensée moderne. Paris, 1883.
Phil 2668.50.4	Janet, Paul A.R. Final causes. 2d ed. N.Y., 1883.
Phil 2668.55.5	Janet, Paul A.R. Theory of morals. N.Y., 1883.
Phil 1135.53	Joannides, A. Pragmateia peri tes par Athenagorai filosofikes geoses. Jena, 1883.
Phil 5465.19	Joly, Henri. L'imagination. 2. éd. Paris, 1883.
Phil 3480.59	Kant, Immanuel. Prolegomena and metaphysical foundations. Photoreproduction. London, 1883.
Phil 630.35	Keferstein, H. Die Realität der Aussenwelt in der Philosophie. Käthen, 1883.
Phil 8589.5.40	Kellogg, J.A. Philosophy of Henry James. N.Y., 1883.
Phil 8590.2.2	Kidd, J. On the adaption of external nature, physical condition, Man. Philadelphia, 1883.
Phil 5250.10.5	Kirchner, F. Katechismus der Psychologie. Leipzig, 1883.
Phil 8635.2	Kirk, H.C. The possibility of not dying. N.Y., 1883.
Phil 5648.15	Klinkenberg, E. Der Raumsinn der Haut. Inaug. Diss. Bonn, 1883.
Phil 341.15	Koch, Julius L. Erkenntnistheoretische Untersuchaungen. Göppingen, 1883.
Phil 2270.141.5	Lacy, William M. An examination of the philosophy of the unknowable as expounded by Herbert Spencer. Philaldelphia, 1883.
Phil 3415.104	Lasson, A. Die Entwickelung der religiösen...nach Eduard von Hartmann. Halle, 1883.
Phil 3493.4	Lasswitz, K. Die Lehre Kants von der Idealität. Berlin, 1883.
Phil 5821.8	Lazarus, M. Über die Reize des Spiels. Berlin, 1883.
Phil 3552.22	Leibniz, Gottfried Wilhelm. Kleinere philosophische Schriften. Leipzig, 1883.
Phil 3552.67.3	Leibniz, Gottfried Wilhelm. La monadologie. Paris, 1883.
Phil 3552.63.15	Leibniz, Gottfried Wilhelm. Die Theodicee. Leipzig, 1883. 2v.
Phil 3831.6	Lesbazeilles, P. De logica Spinozae. Paris, 1883.
Phil 6681.4.15	Liébeault, A.A. Étude sur le zoomagnétisme. Paris, 1883.
Phil 186.12.8	Liebmann, O. Über philosophische Tradition. Strassburg, 1883.
Phil 5251.8	Lipps, T. Seelenlebens. Bonn, 1883.
Phil 2115.51.10	Locke, J. Leitung des Verstandes. Heidelberg, 1883.
Phil 3565.65	Lotze, Hermann. Grundzüge der Logik. Leipzig, 1883.
Phil 3565.45.5A	Lotze, Hermann. Grundzüge der Metaphysik. Leipzig, 1883.
Phil 3565.31.15	Lotze, Hermann. Métaphysique. Paris, 1883.
Phil 4210.83.5	MacWalter, G.S. Life of Antonio Rosmini-Serbati. London, 1883.
Phil 1350.6	Martha, Constant. Etudes morales sur l'antiquité. Paris, 1883.
Phil 2050.104.5	Masaryk, T.G. Počet pravděpodobnosti a Humova skepse. Praha, 1883.
Phil 5762.1	Maudsley, H. Body and will. London, 1883.
Phil 3625.1.48	Mendelssohn, Moses. Moses Mendelssohn. Leipzig, 1883.
Phil 6048.83.2	Metz, V. de. Handbook of modern palmistry. 2. ed. N.Y., 1883.
Phil 3494.29	Michalsky, O. Kant's Kritik der reinen Vernunft und Herder's Metakritik. Diss. Breslau, 1883.
Phil 2138.45.20	Mill, John S. Tre religions-filosofiska afhandlingar. Stockholm, 1883.
Phil 2138.50.17	Mill, John S. L'utilitarisme. Paris, 1883.
Phil 5545.64	Mnemosyne, Organ für Gedächtniskunst. Leipzig, 1883-1885.
Phil 4363.2.37	Molinos, M. de. Golden thoughts from the spiritual guide. N.Y., 1883.
Phil 6963.3	Neumann, H. Über die Knochenbrüche bei Geisteskranken. Berlin, 1883.
Phil 813.2.5	Noire, L. Die Entwickelung der abendländischen Philosophie Critik der reinen Vernunft. Mainz, 1883.
Phil 978.11	Olcott, H.S. Collection of lectures on theosophy and archaic religions. Madras, 1883.
Phil 4225.1.90	Onoranze funebri a Bertrando Spaventa. Napoli, 1883.
Phil 400.43	Ott, Aguste. Critique de l'idéalisme et du criticisme. Paris, 1883.
Phil 2805.30.29	Pascal, Blaise. Quatorzième lettre provinciale. Paris, 1883.
Phil 8890.5	Patterson, J.S. Conflict in nature and life. N.Y., 1883.
Phil 190.35	Perriollat, Charles. Essai de philosophie scientifique. Paris, 1883.
Phil 190.10	Peters, C. Willenswelt und Weltwille. Leipzig, 1883.
Phil 490.5	Pfaff, A.B.I.F. Die Entwickelung der Welt auf atomischer Grundlage. Heidelberg, 1883.
Phil 8595.4.2.2	Pfleiderer, O. Religionsphilosophie. 2. Aufl. Berlin, 1883-84. 2v.
Phil 5525.16	Philbert, Louis. Le rire. Paris, 1883.
Phil 5055.1.5A	Pierce, C.S. Studies in logic. Boston, 1883.
Phil 190.16.5	Pressensé, E. de. Les origines. 3e éd. Paris, 1883.
Phil 5545.22.6	Ribot, T. Diseases of memory. N.Y., 1883.
Phil 5767.1	Ribot, T. Les maladies de la volonté. Paris, 1883.
Phil 5374.28	Richter, Rudolf. Herbart'sch und Bergmann'sche Problem des Bewusstseins. Inaug. Diss. Greifswald, 1883?
Phil 8597.9	Riddle, A.G. Alcastor. n.p., 1883.
Phil 5827.1	Romanes, G.J. Mental evolution in animals. London, 1883.
Phil 4210.50	Rosmini-Serbati, Antonio. The origin of ideas. London, 1883-84. 3v.
Phil 3235.83	Schat Petersen, L.W. Ludwig Feuerbach og kristendommen. København, 1883.
Phil 9420.4	Schneider, G.H. Freud und Leid des Menschengeschlechte. Stuttgart, 1883.
Phil 3500.6	Schneider, O. Die psychologische Entwickelung des Apriori...Kants Kritik der reinen Vernunft. Bonn, 1883.
Phil 3808.36.2	Schopenhauer, Arthur. The world as will and idea. Boston, 1883-86. 3v.
Phil 7054.131	Schultze, F. Die Grundgedanken des Spiritismus und die Kritik derselben. Leipzig, 1883.
Phil 193.19	Scott, J. McD. Theories and criticisms. Halifax, 1883.
Phil 8419.44	Séailles, G. Essai sur le génie dans l'art. Paris, 1883.
Phil 8893.5.5	Secrétan, C. Le principe de la morale. Lausanne, 1883.
Phil 193.23	Seth Pringle-Pattison, A. Essays in philosophical criticism. London, 1883.

1883 - cont.

Phil 7068.83.12	Sociedad de Estudios Espiritistas de Key West. Contestatión a los detractores del espiritismo. Key West, 1883.
Phil 58.2.3	Society for Psychical Research, London. Proceedings. v.1, pt.2-3. London, 1883.
Phil 9430.24.2	Sommer, Hugo. Der Pessimismus und die Sittenlehre. Berlin, 1883.
Phil 2270.74.4	Spencer, Herbert. Data of ethics. N.Y., 1883.
Phil 3819.31	Spinoza, Benedictus de. Ethik demonstrated in geometrical order. London, 1883.
Phil 193.81	Spitzer, Hugo. Ueber das Verhältnis der Philosophie. Leipzig, 1883.
Phil 3500.10.10	Stadler, A. Kants Theorie der Materie. Leipzig, 1883.
Phil 3235.111	Starcke, C.N. L. Feuerbach; en monografi. Kjøbenhavn, 1883.
Phil 3808.136	Stern, I. Arthur Schopenhauer. Zürich, 1883.
Phil 1718.1	Stöckl, A. Geschichte der neueren Philosophie. Mainz, 1883. 2v.
Phil 9560.5	Storrs, R.S. Manliness in the scholar. N.Y., 1883.
Phil 5325.2.10	Stricker, Salomon. Studien über die Association der Vorstellungen. Wien, 1883.
Phil 8419.41	Sully Prudhomme, R.F.A. L'expression dans les beaux-arts. Paris, 1883.
Phil 5190.20	Thiede, J. Über die Negation, den Widerspruch und den Gegensatz. Inaug.-Diss. Berlin, 1883.
Phil 2270.115	Thyren, Johan. Kritik framställning af Herbert Spencer's "Principles of Psychology". Akademisk afhandling. Lund, 1883.
Phil 7054.119	Truesdell, J.W. The bottom facts...science of spiritualism. N.Y., 1883.
Phil 5060.3.10	Uphues, Karl. Grundlagen der Logik. Breslau, 1883.
Phil 8896.7	Vallier, C.A. De l'intention morale. Paris, 1883.
Phil 196.11.9	Varnbüler, Theodore. Die Lehre vom Sein. Leipzig, 1883.
Phil 2035.88.3	Veitch, J. Sir William Hamilton: the man and his philosophy. London, 1883.
Phil 4265.3.39	Vera, A. Saggi filosofici. Napoli, 1883.
Phil 4372.1.39	Vives, Juan Luis. Satellitium animi. Wien, 1883.
Phil 6971.3	Voisin, A. Lecons cliniques...maladies mentales. Paris, 1883.
Phil 4022.1.5	Werner, K. Die cartesische-malebranche'sche Philosophie in Italien. Pt.1-2. Wien, 1883.
Phil 4065.104	Wickström, V.H. Giordano Brunos metafysik. Lund, 1883.
Phil 8602.9	Wilson, W.D. The foundations of religious belief. N.Y., 1883.
Phil 2115.119	Winter, Hermann. Darlegung und Kritik der Lokeschen Lehre vom empirischen Ursprung der sittlichen Grundsätze. Inaug.-Diss. Bonn, 1883.
Phil 9075.29	Wohlrabe, W. Über Gewissen und Gewissensbildung. Gotha, 1883.
Phil 5062.23.5	Wolff, Hermann. Logik und Sprachphilosophie. Leipzig, 1883.
Phil 8714.1	Yorke, J.F. Notes on evolution and Christianity. N.Y., 1883.
Phil 7080.12	Yung, E. Le sommeil normal. Paris, 1883.
Phil 1130.3	Zeller, Eduard. Grundriss der Geschichte der griechischen Philosophie. Leipzig, 1883.
Phil 1135.5	Zeller, Eduard. A history of eclecticism in Greek philosophy. London, 1883.
Phil 1130.9	Zeller, Eduard. History of eclecticism in Greek philosophy. London, 1883.

1884

Phil 8582.3.6	Argyll, G.D.C. The unity of nature. London, 1884.
Phil 8582.3.7	Argyll, G.D.C. The unity of nature. London, 1884.
Phil 3552.262	Auerbach, S. Zur Entwickelungsgeschichte der leibnitzschen Monadenlehre. Diss. Dessau, 1884.
Phil 1855.60	Bain, Alexander. Practical essays. London, 1884.
Phil 8876.62.3	Barbier, Louise. La loi morale fondée sur l'etude comparée des deux natures de l'homme. Paris, 1884.
Phil 3565.128	Bartell, Fr., pastor. Lotze's religionsphilosophische Gedanken im Lichte der göttlichen Offenbarung. Hannover, 1884.
Phil 6111.2	Beaunie, H.E. Recherches...l'activité cérébrale. v.1-2. Paris, 1884-86.
Phil 6671.4	Bérillon, E. Hypnotisme experimental. Paris, 1884.
Phil 1870.20.3	Berkeley, G. Selections (Fraser). 3rd ed. Oxford, 1884.
Phil 6671.5.5	Bernheim, H. De la suggestion. Paris, 1884.
Phil 2520.85	Bierendempfel, G. Descartes als Gegner des Sensualismus und Materialismus. Wolfenbüttel, 1884.
Phil 3483.14	Bilharz, Altons. Erläuterungen zu Kant's Kritik der reinen Vernunft. Wiesbaden, 1884.
Phil 7060.30	Blackburn, D. Thought-reading. London, 1884.
Phil 4515.32.2	Boström, C.J. Grundlinier till philosophiska statslärans propaedeutik. 2. uppl. Upsala, 1884.
Phil 5241.21	Bouillier, F.C. Études familières de psychologie et de morale. Paris, 1884.
Phil 7082.68	Brander, Robert. Der Schlaf und das Traumleben. Leipzig, 1884.
Phil 130.3	Brasch, M. Die Klassiker der Philosophie. Leipzig, 1884-85. 3v.
Phil 6990.33	Brewer, E.C. A dictionary of miracles. Philadelphia, 1884.
Phil 332.3	Brodbick, A. Das Wesen des Wissens. Stuttgart, 1884.
Phil 7054.57.5	Brownson, O.A. The spirit-rapper, an autobiography. Detroit, 1884.
Phil 5650.12	Brücke, Ernst. Über die Wahrnehmung. Wien, 1884.
Phil 2555.2.80	Büchner, A. Un philosophe amateur, essai biographique sur Léon Dumont. Paris, 1884.
Phil 3425.236	Bullinger, A. Hegels Lehre vom Widerspruch. Dillingen, 1884.
Phil 5645.1	Burnett, S.M. Theories of color-perception. Philadelphia, 1884.
Phil 1900.40	Butler, Joseph. Analogy of religion. London, 1884.
Phil 8877.1	Calderwood, H. Handbook of moral philosophy. London, 1884.
Phil 8657.12	Candlish, J.S. The kingdom of God. Edinburgh, 1884.
Phil 6952.2A	Carnochan, J.M. Cerebral localization...insanity. N.Y., 1884.
Phil 177.45	Charles, Émile. Éléments de philosophie. Paris, 1884-85. 2v.
Phil 1850.81	Church, R.W. Bacon. London, 1884.
Phil 1850.81.4	Church, R.W. Bacon. N.Y., 1884.
Phil 8877.75	Clifford, William K. The scientific basis of morals, and other essays. N.Y., 1884.

1884 - cont.

Phil 6952.6A Clouston, T.S. Clinical lectures on mental diseases. Philadelphia, 1884.

Phil 2490.41.4 Comte, Auguste. Die positive Philosophie. v.1-2. Heidelberg, 1884.

Phil 2490.77 Comte, Auguste. Testament. Paris, 1884.

Phil 6112.8 Corning, J.L. Brain exhaustion. N.Y., 1884.

Phil 802.2.5.11 Cousin, V. Histoire générale de la philosophie. 11e éd. Paris, 1884.

Phil 7068.84.15 Crookes, William. Der Spiritualismus und die Urssenschaft. 2. Aufl. Leipzig, 1884.

Phil 8952.2 Croslegh, C. Christianity judged by its fruits. London, 1884.

Phil 8693.9 Dale, T. Nelson. The outskirts of physical science. Boston, 1884.

Phil 5400.19.2 Darwin, Charles. Der Ausdruck der Gemüthsbewegungen bei dem Menschen und den Thieren. 4. Aufl. Stuttgart, 1884.

NEDL Phil 9513.1 Dole, C.F. The citizen and the neighbor. Boston, 1884.

Phil 672.3.5 Dunan, C. Essai sur les formes a priori. Paris, 1884.

Phil 8878.16 Durand Desormeaux, F. Etudes philosophiques. Paris, 1884. 2v.

Phil 178.8 Durand Désormeaux, Fernand. Réflexions et pensées. Paris, 1884.

Phil 4515.83 Edfeldt, Hans. Om Boströms ideelära. Uppsala, 1884.

Phil 9558.3 Ellinger, G. Verhältniss der offentlichen Meinung zu Wahrheit und Lüge. Berlin, 1884.

Phil 9344.6 Ellis, John. Deterioration of the Puritan stock. N.Y., 1884.

Phil 8659.4 Ercole, P. d'. Il teismo filosofico cristiano. pt.1. Torino, 1884.

Phil 6114.5.12 Evans, W.F. A mental-cure illustrated influence of the mind on the body. Boston, 1884.

Phil 3246.81 Everett, C.C. Fichte's Science of knowledge. Chicago, 1884.

Phil 286.1 Faye, H.A.E. L'origine du monde. Paris, 1884.

Phil 3210.53 Fechner, G.T. Über die Frage des Weber'schen Gesetzes. Leipzig, 1884.

Phil 3210.70 Fechner, G.T. Über die Methode der richtigen und falschen Fälle. Leipzig, 1884.

Phil 180.36 Fetzer, K.A. Philosophische Leitbegriffe. Tübingen, 1884.

Phil 8630.3 Fiske, J. The destiny of man. Boston, 1884.

Phil 365.4 Fiske, J. Excursions of an evolutionist. Boston, 1884.

Phil 4260.82 Flint, R. Vico. Philadelphia, 1884.

Phil 6955.9 Folsom, C.F. Abstract of the statutes of the United States, and of the several territories relating to the custody of the insane. Philadelphia, 1884.

Phil 5755.3.2 Fouillée, A. La liberté et le déterminisme. 2. éd. Paris, 1884.

Phil 8880.38 Fowler, Thomas. Progressive morality; an essay in ethics. London, 1884.

Phil 3805.170 Frahne, A. Der Begriff der Eigentümlichkeit oder Individualität bei Schleiermacher. Halle, 1884.

Phil 8955.2 Frank, F.H.R. System du christliche Sittlichkeit. Erlangen, 1884-87. 2v.

Phil 180.12.10 Frohschammer, J. Die Philosophie als Idealwissenschaft und System. München, 1884.

Phil 5440.3 Galton, F. Record of family faculties. London, 1884.

Phil 5465.16 Glogan, Gustav. Die Phantasie. Halle, 1884.

Phil 5246.27 Glogau, Gustav. Grundriss der Psychologie. Breslau, 1884.

Phil 8580.7 Goblet d'Alviella, E. L'évolution religieuse contemporaine chez les anglais, les américains, et les hindous. Paris, 1884.

Phil 2020.30.2A Green, T.H. Prolegomena to ethics. 2d ed. Oxford, 1884.

Phil 6116.14 Grimké, S.S. Personified unthinkables, an argument against physical causation. Ann Arbor, 1884.

Phil 8881.22 Guilly, E.P. La nature et la morale. Paris, 1884.

Phil 2270.84.5A Guthrie, M. On Mr. Spencer's data of ethics. London, 1884.

Phil 8407.3 Guyau, M. Les problèmes de l'esthétique comtemporaine. Paris, 1884.

Phil 8696.5 Guyot, Arnold. Creation. N.Y., 1884.

Phil 8610.884.20 Hardwicke, H.J. Popular faith unveiled. n.p., 1884.

Phil 6957.6 Harrison, G.L. Legisation on insanity. Philadelphia, 1884.

Phil 3415.32.2 Hartmann, Eduard von. Philosophy of the unconscious. London, 1884. 3v.

Phil 3415.32 Hartmann, Eduard von. Philosophy of the unconscious. London, 1884. 3v.

Phil 182.8 Hedge, F.H. Atheism in philosophy. Berlin, 1884.

Phil 8882.11 Hill, W.H. Ethics, or Moral philosophy. Baltimore, 1884.

Phil 5047.5 Hill, Walter H. Elements of philosophy comprising logic, ontology or general metaphysics. Baltimore, 1884.

Phil 182.33 Hinton, C.H. Scientific romances. Nos. 1-5,7-8. London, 1884-1888. 7v.

Phil 182.19.13 Hodgson, S.H. The relation of philosophy to science, physical and psychological. London, 1884.

Phil 5247.23.25 Höfler, Alois. Zur Propädeutik-Frage. Wien, 1884.

Phil 4803.454.70 Hoene-Wroński, Józef Maria. Caméralistique; économie politique et finances. Paris, 1884.

Phil 9359.6.25 Holland, Josiah G. Titcomb's letters to young people. 50th ed. N.Y., 1884.

Phil 5643.12.9 Hoppe, J.F. Die Drehbare Bilderscheibe. Leipzig, 1884.

Phil 2050.81 Howison, G.H. Hume and Kant. San Francisco, 1884. 2 pam.

Phil 9035.3 Hyde, T.A. How to study character. N.Y., 1884.

Phil 8588.1 Ibarreta, R.H. La religion al alcance de todos. 5. ed. Madrid, 1884.

Phil 7060.38 Ingram, J.H. Haunted homes. London, 1884.

Phil 7060.38.2 Ingram, J.H. Haunted homes. London, 1884.

Phil 5759.1.2 James, W. The dilemma of determinism. n.p. 1884.

Phil 5249.3.5 Janes, Elijah. Human psychology. Oakland, 1884.

Phil 8884.21 Janet, Paul. Elements of morals. N.Y., 1884.

Phil 5049.3.6 Jevons, W.S. Logic (science primers). N.Y., 1884.

Phil 1200.27.2 Jordan, T. The stoic moralists, and the Christians in the first two centuries. 2d ed. Dublin, 1884.

Phil 184.10 Jouin, R.P.L. Compendium logicae et metaphysicae. N.Y., 1884.

Phil 3480.50.4 Kant, Immanuel. Critik der Urtheilskraft. Hamburg, 1884.

Phil 3480.30.56 Kant, Immanuel. Kritik der reinen Vernunft. Heldeberg, 1884.

Phil 5620.2 Keller, J. Der Ursprung der Vernunft. Heidelberg, 1884.

Phil 5635.25 Kessler, Jacob. Untersuchungen über den Temperatursinn. Inaug. Diss. Bonn, 1884.

Phil 5050.3 Keynes, J.N. Studies and exercises in formal logic. London, 1884.

Phil 3415.91.5 Koeber, Raphael. Das philosophische System Eduard von Hartmann's. Breslau, 1884.

Phil 4580.31 Køffding, Harald. Formel logik. København, 1884.

Phil 3492.2.5 Krause, A. Immanuel Kant wider Kuno Fischer. Lahr, 1884.

Phil 6978.12 Kraussold, Karl. Melancholie und Schuld. Stuttgart, 1884.

Phil 6990.3 Lasserre, H. Les épisodes miraculeux de Lourdes. Paris, 1884.

Phil 3493.8.5 Last, E. Die realistische und die idealistische Weltanschauung entwickelt an Kants Idealität von Zeit und Raum. Leipzig, 1884.

Phil 315.1 Laurie, S.S. Metaphysica nova et vetusta. London, 1884.

Phil 811.2.5 Lefèvre, A. La Philosophie. 2e éd. Paris, 1884.

Phil 5645.24 Lehmann, A. Farvernes elementaere aestetik. Kjøbenhavn, 1884.

Phil 9470.2 Lévy-Bruhl, L. L'idée de responsabilité. Paris, 1884.

Phil 186.12.11 Liebmann, O. Die Klimax der Theorieen. Strassburg, 1884.

Phil 3801.522 Lisco, Heinrich. Geschichtsphilosophie Schellings, 1792-1809. Inaug. Diss. Jena, 1884.

Phil 8412.27 Little, J.S. What is art? London, 1884.

Phil 8886.9 Lloyd, J. Duty and faith. Manchester, 1884.

Phil 3565.72 Lotze, Hermann. Grundzüge der Religionsphilosophie. 2e Aufl. Leipzig, 1884.

Phil 3565.31 Lotze, Hermann. Logic. Oxford, 1884.

Phil 3565.31.2 Lotze, Hermann. Metaphysic. Oxford, 1884.

Phil 3565.32.1.3 Lotze, Hermann. Outline of Metaphysic. Boston, 1884.

NEDL Phil 1925.80 Lowrey, C.E. Philosophy of Ralph Cudworth. N.Y., 1884.

Phil 2125.45.7 McCosh, James. A criticism of the critical philosophy. N.Y., 1884.

Phil 6682.1 Magnin, P. Étude clinique et expérimentale sur l'hypnotisme. Paris, 1884.

Phil 2520.93.2.5 Mahaffy, J.P. Descartes. Edinburgh, 1884.

Phil 8667.10 Mallock, William H. Atheism and the value of life. London, 1884.

Phil 3494.25 Markull, G. Ueber Glauben und Wissen. Progr. Danzig, 1884.

Phil 8413.23 Martha, C. La délicatesse dans l'art. Paris, 1884.

Phil 2050.104 Masaryk, T.G. David Hume's Skepsis. Wien, 1884.

Phil 8887.62 Masci, F. Coscienza, volontà, libertà. Lanciano, 1884.

NEDL Phil 23.4 Mendel, E. Neurologisches Centralblatt. Leipzig, 1884-93. 10v.

Phil 3552.92A Merz, J.T. Leibniz. Philadelphia, 1884.

Phil 6962.5 Meynert, T. Psychiatrie. Wien, 1884.

Phil 3625.2 Michelet, K.L. Wahrheit aus meinem Leben. Berlin, 1884.

X Cg Phil 2138.45.5 Mill, John S. Three essays on religion. N.Y., 1884.

Phil 5252.53 Mischer, Psychological Fragen. Stendal, 1884.

Phil 6122.12 Mitchell, S.W. Fat and blood. Philadelphia, 1884.

Phil 365.3 Mivart, St. G. A limit to evolution. London? 1884.

Phil 8702.11 Moigno, F.N.M. Un pequeño libro de actualidad. Puerto Rico, 1884.

Phil 4605.1.46 Monrad, M.J. Tankeretninger i den nyere tid. 2 opl. Christiania, 1884.

Phil 5822.1A Morgan, C.L. Introduction to comparative psychology. London, 1884.

Phil 5401.1 Mosso, A. La paura. Milano, 1884.

Phil 9352.8.3 Munger, Theodore T. On the threshold. Boston, 1884.

Phil 5400.13 Nahlowsky, J.W. Das Gefühlsleben. Leipzig, 1884.

Phil 1118.2 Natorp, Paul. Forschungen zur Geschichte der Erkenntnissproblems im Alterthum. Berlin, 1884.

Phil 510.9.6 Noiré, Ludwig. Aphorismen zur monistischen Philosophie. 2. ed. Mainz, 1884.

Phil 510.9.11 Noiré, Ludwig. Einleitung und Begründung einer monistischen Erkenntnis-Theorie. 2e Ausg. Mainz, 1884.

Phil 5255.1 Paine, A.W. The new philosophy. Bangor, 1884.

Phil 3552.296.15 Pfleiderer, Edmund. Leibniz und Geulinx mit besonderer Beziehung auf ihr beiderseitiges Uhrengleichniss. Tübingen, 1884.

Phil 3837.25 Rackwitz, Max. Studien über Causalität und Identität als Grundprincipien des Spinozismus. Halle, 1884.

Phil 5425.9 Radestock, P. Genie und Wahnsinn. Breslau, 1884.

Phil 8672.1 Randles, M. First principles of faith. London, 1884.

Phil 665.37 Reich, E. Die Geschichte der Seele. Minden, 1884.

Phil 3270.3.93 Reich, Edward. Weltanschauung und Menschenleben...Jakob Frohschammer's. Grossenhain, 1884.

Phil 510.4 Reichenau, W. Monistische Philosophie von Spinoza bis auf unserer Tage. Köln, 1884.

Phil 5257.72 Rein, Thiodolf. Sielutieteen oppikirja. Helsingissa, 1884.

Phil 8418.24 Reynolds, J. Discourses. London, 1884.

Phil 3837.14 Ricco, Cesare. Le dottrine giuridiche...di Spinoza e Hobbes. Giovinazzo, 1884.

Phil 5257.6 Richet, Charles. L'homme et l'intelligence. Paris, 1884.

Phil 3499.3 Riedel, O.J. Die monadologischen...Bestimmungen...Kant's. Hamburg, 1884.

Phil 6687.3 Rieger, Dr. Der Hypnotismus. Jena, 1884.

Phil 8892.3.3 Rolph, W.H. Biologische Probleme. 2. Aufl. Leipzig, 1884.

Phil 5827.1.3A Romanes, G.J. Mental evolution in animals. N.Y., 1884.

Phil 193.5 Sanctis, F. de. La scienza e la vita. Philadelphia, 1884.

Phil 3805.12 Schleiermacher, Friedrich. Sämmtliche Werke. 2. Aufl. Berlin, 1884.

Phil 3246.247 Schmidt-Warneck, J. von. Die Sociologie Fichte's. Berlin, 1884.

Phil 1535.16 Schneider, C.M. Das Wissen Gottes. v.1-4. Regensburg, 1884-86. 3v.

Phil 3428.158 Schoel, A. Johann Friedrich Herbart's philosophische Lehre von der Religion. Dresden, 1884.

Phil 349.1 Schubert-Soldern, R. von. Grundlagen einer Erkenntnisstheorie. Leipzig, 1884.

Phil 3415.100 Schüz, A. Philosophie und Christentum. Stuttgart, 1884.

Phil 818.1.16 Schwegler, F.C.A. Handbook of the history of philosophy. 9th ed. Edinburgh, 1884.

Phil 5258.15 Setchénov, J. Etudes psychologiques. Paris, 1884.

Phil 5828.15 Shepherd, James. Instinct. Kirkcaldy, 1884.

Phil 5100.2A Sidgwick, A. Fallacies. N.Y., 1884.

Phil 978.9.3 Sinnett, A.P. Esoteric Buddhism. 3rd ed. London, 1884.

Phil 2270.67.5 Spencer, Herbert. What knowledge is of most worth. N.Y., 1884.

Phil 3819.71 Spinoza, Benedictus. Lettres inédites en français. Paris, 1884.

Phil 3819.61 Spinoza, Benedictus. Stelkonstige reeckening van den regenboog. Leiden, 1884.

Phil 193.31 Spir, A. von. Denken und Wirklichkeit. v.1-4. Leipzig, 1884-1885. 3v.

Phil 8708.4 Stokes, G.G. On the absence of real opposition between science and revelation. London, 1884?

Phil 720.2 Stokes, G.J. Objectivity of truth. London, 1884.

Phil 2725.12.81 Stosz, Wilhelm. Le Sage als Vorkämpfer der Atomistik. Inaug. Diss. Halle, 1884.

1884 - cont.

Phil 200.2.75	Strassburger Abhandlungen zur Philosophie E. Zeller zu 70n Geburtstage. Freiburg, 1884.
Phil 8643.5	Straub, J. The consolations of science. Chicago, 1884.
Phil 5258.22	Strümpell, L. Grundriss der Psychologie. Leipzig, 1884.
Phil 5460.1.5	Sully, J. Die Illusionen. Leipzig, 1884.
Phil 5460.1.3	Sully, J. Illusions: a psychological study. N.Y., 1884.
Phil 5460.1.2	Sully, J. Illusions: a psychological study. pt.1-2. N.Y., 1884.
Phil 8674.1	Tait, J. Mind in matter. London, 1884.
Phil 1200.19	Thamin, Raymond. Un problème moral dans l'antiquité. Paris, 1884.
Phil 5259.3	Thompson, D.G. System of psychology. London, 1884. 2v.
Phil 5640.7	Thomson, W. The six gateways of knowledge. N.Y., 1884.
Phil 5829.3.4	Toussenel, A. L'esprit des bêtes; zoologie passionnelle. Paris, 1884.
Phil 7068.84	Truesdell, J.W. The bottom facts concerning the science of spiritualism. N.Y., 1884.
Phil 6129.3.2	Tuke, D.H. Illustration of the mind upon the body. 2d ed. Philadelphia, 1884.
Phil 1719.2	Tullock, J. Modern theories in philosophy and religion. Edinburgh, 1884.
Phil 196.1.8	Vacherot, E. Le nouveau spiritualisme. Paris, 1884.
Phil 9010.24	Vaes, Lachlan. Amusements and the Christian life. Philadelphia, 1884.
Phil 6131.1	Varigny, H.C. de. Recherches expérimentales sur l'excitabilité électrique. Paris, 1884.
Phil 8896.9	Véron, Eugène. La morale. Paris, 1884.
Phil 9035.20	Vogler, M. Die Verwahrlosung der modernen Charakters. Leipzig, 1884.
Phil 5261.1.3	Volkmann, W. Lehrbuch der Psychologie. Göthen, 1884-8. 2v.
Phil 5261.1.2	Volkmann, W. Lehrbuch der Psychologie. v.1-2. Göthen, 1884-85.
Phil 6132.22	Wahle, R. Gehirn und Bewusstsein. Wien, 1884.
Phil 8677.1	Ward, W.G. Essays on the philosophy of theism. London, 1884. 2v.
Phil 260.3	Welling, J.C. Atomic philosophy. Washington, 1884.
Phil 4022.1	Werner, K. Die italienische Philosophie. v. 1-5. Wien, 1884-86. 2v.
Phil 4210.125.10F	Werner, Karl. A. Rosmini's Stellung in der Geschichte der neueren Philosophie. Wien, 1884.
Phil 4210.125	Werner, Karl. Die italien Philosophie. Wien, 1884.
Phil 197.9A	Windelband, W. Präludien. Freiburg, 1884.
Phil 8712.21	Wittstein, T. Der Streit zwischen glauben. Hannover, 1884.
Phil 8712.4.5	Woodrow, J. Evolution. Columbia, S.C., 1884.
Phil 200.2.8	Zeller, E. Vorträge und Abhandlungen Geschichtlichen Inhalts. 3. Aufl. Leipzig, 1884.
Phil 1535.12	Zigliara, F.T.M. Summa philosophica in usum scholarum. Lyon, 1884. 3v.
Phil 2050.182	Zimmermann, R. Über Hume's empirische Begründung der Moral. Wien, 1884.

1885

Phil 3425.119	Åberg, Lawrence H. Hegel och Boströms rättsfilosofiska grundtankar. Upsala, 1885.
Phil 8655.5	Abbot, F.E. Scientific theism. Boston, 1885.
Phil 1850.80A	Abbott, E.A. Francis Bacon. London, 1885.
Phil 2520.169	Adam, C.E. De methodo apud Cartesium, Spinozam et Leibnitium. Lutetiae, 1885.
Phil 8401.20	Adam, Charles. Essai sur le jugement. Paris, 1885.
Phil 4170.7.90	Angelini, A. Di Terenzio Mamiani filosofo. Roma, 1885. 2v.
Phil 3808.80.2	Asher, D. Das Endergebniss der Arthur Schopenhauer Philosophie. Leipzig, 1885.
Phil 1850.35.2.3	Bacon, Francis. The advancement of learning. 3rd ed. Oxford, 1885.
Phil 5241.2.15	Bain, A. Le émotions et la volonté. 3e éd. Paris, 1885.
Phil 2520.183	Barthel, A. Descartes' Leben und Metaphysik. Inaug.-Diss. Erlangen, 1885.
Phil 3565.87	Bauer, C. Programm der Realschule zu Meerane. n.p., 1885.
Phil 8876.57	Beaussire, Émile. Les principes de la morale. Paris, 1885.
Cg Phil 8691.2	Beecher, H.W. Evolution and religion. pt.1. N.Y., 1885.
Phil 1106.2	Benard, Charles. La philosophie ancienne. Paris, 1885.
Phil 3483.34	Bendixson, A. Kritiska studier till Kants transcendentala ästetik. Upsala, 1885.
Phil 6400.2	Bernard, D. De l'aphasie. Paris, 1885.
Phil 978.6.85	Besant, Annie. Autobiographical sketches. Photoreproduction. London, 1885.
Phil 8876.79	Bizyenos, Georgios. Psychologikai meletai apo tou kalou. Athens, 1885.
Phil 3110.26	Böhme, J. Sein Leben und seine theosophischen Werke. Stuttgart, 1885.
Phil 5041.20.8	Bosanquet, B. Knowledge and reality. London, 1885.
Phil 4515.35	Boström, C.J. Föreläsningar i religionsfilosofi. Stockholm, 1885.
Phil 5402.8.3	Bouillier, F. Du plaisir et de la douleur. 3e ed. Paris, 1885.
Phil 8691.16	Broglie, Paul. La science et la religion. Paris, 1885.
Phil 7059.6	Buchanan, J.R. Manual of psychometry. Boston, 1885.
Phil 2493.80	Burger, K. Ein Beitrag zur Beurteilung Condillacs. Altenburg, 1885.
Phil 6111.40	Butts, Bryan J. Hints on metaphysics. Boston, 1885.
Phil 2490.98.1	Caird, Edward. The social philosophy and religion of Comte. Glasgow, 1885.
Phil 4210.131	Calzi, Carlo. L'antropologia soprannaturale di A. Rosmini. Firenze, 1885.
Phil 5425.13	Candolle, A. de. Histoire des sciences et des savants. Genève, 1885.
Phil 8403.10.3	Carriere, Moriz. Aesthetik. 3. Aufl. Leipzig, 1885. 2v.
Phil 510.6A	Carus, P. Monism and meliorism. N.Y., 1885.
Phil 4265.1.85	Cattaneo, G. Idee di G.C. Vanini sull...evoluzione. Milano, 1885.
Phil 8877.6	Chaney, G.L. Every day life and every day morals. Boston, 1885.
Phil 6112.22	Christiani, A. Zur Physiologie des Gehirnes. Berlin, 1885.
Phil 5812.2	Clevenger, S.V. Comparative physiology and psychology. Chicago, 1885.
Phil 3484.2.2	Cohen, H. Kant's Theorie der Erfahrung. 2. Aufl.
Phil 9230.12.5	Collier, Jeremy. An essay upon gaming. Edinburgh, 1885.

1885 - cont.

Phil 6112.8.5	Corning, J.L. Brain rest. N.Y., 1885.
Phil 974.2	Coulomb, E. Some account of my intercourse with Mme. Blavatsky. London, 1885.
Phil 6060.1	Crepieux-Jamin, J. Traite de graphologie. Paris, 1885.
Phil 8693.8	Dana, J.D. Creation or biblical cosmogony. Oberlin, 1885.
Phil 5043.21	Davidson, William L. The logic of definition. London, 1885.
Phil 7080.27	Delboeuf, Joseph. Le sommeil et les rêves. Paris, 1885.
Phil 365.30	Derr, Ezra Z. Evolution versus involution. N.Y., 1885.
Phil 2805.227	Deschanel, E.A.E.M. Pascal, La Rochefoucauld, Bossuet. Paris, 1885.
Phil 178.50	Dieterich, K. Grundzüge der Metaphysik. Freiburg im Breisgau, 1885.
Phil 5043.245	Drbal, M. Propaedeutische Logik. Wien, 1885.
Phil 3485.8	Drobisch, M.W. Kants Dinge an sich und sein Erfahrungsbegriff. Hamburg, 1885.
Phil 8693.5.10A	Drummond, H. Natural law in the spiritual world. N.Y., 1885.
Phil 8693.5.2	Drummond, H. Natural law in the spiritual world. 17th ed. London, 1885.
Phil 525.1	Du Prel, C.F. Die Philosophie der Mystik. Leipzig, 1885.
Phil 5545.5	Ebbinghaus, H. Über das Gedächtnis. Leipzig, 1885.
Phil 8629.2	English, C.D. The philosophy of a future state. Philadelphia, 1885.
Phil 4815.368.30	Erösdi, Mihály. Kritikus objectiv metaphysîka. Budapest, 1885.
Phil 179.03	Eucken, R. Prolegomena...Einheit des Geisteslebens. Leipzig, 1885.
Phil 6114.5.7	Evans, W.F. Mental medicine. 15th ed. Boston, 1885.
Phil 8630.13.5	Farrar, F.W. Future retribution. N.Y., 1885.
Phil 4110.4.90F	Ferri commemorazione prof. Luigi. Roma, 1885.
Phil 8585.6.6	Fisher, G.P. Faith and rationalism. N.Y., 1885.
Phil 8585.6.3	Fisher, G.P. The grounds of theistic and Christian belief. N.Y., 1885.
Phil 978.10	Five years of theosophy. London, 1885.
Phil 8880.29.5	Flügel, Otto. Das Ich und die sittlichen Ideen im Leben der Völker. Langensalza, 1885.
Phil 180.8.3	Franck, A. Essais de critique philosophique. Paris, 1885.
Phil 3487.11	Fricker, K.V. Zu Kants Rechtsphilosophie. Lipsiae, 1885.
Phil 3850.12.85	Fröhlich, Gustaf. Dr. Karl Volkmar Stoys Leben. Dresden, 1885.
Phil 8615.11	Gannett, W.C. The religion of the "ethical culture societies." Chicago, 1885.
Phil 3488.11	Gerhard, Carl. Kant's Lehre von der Freiheit. Heidelberg, 1885.
Phil 4065.88	Giancola, Francesco. Giordano Bruno. Roma, 1885.
Phil 645.2.5	Glanvill, J. Scepsis scientifica: or, Confest ignorance, the way to science. London, 1885.
Phil 8580.7.15	Goblet d'Alviella, E. The contemporary evolution of religious thought in England. London, 1885.
Phil 8881.38	Godwin, John H. Active principles, or Elements of moral science. London, 1885.
Phil 6956.1	Gowers, W.R. Lectures on the diagnosis of disease of the brain. London, 1885.
Phil 3310.5.35	Gutberlet, C. Naturphilosophie. Münster, 1885.
Phil 4362.1.80	Gutierrez, P.F.M. Fr. Luis de León y la filosofia espanole. Madrid, 1885.
Phil 2270.85	Harrison, F. Nature and reality of religion. A controversy. N.Y., 1885.
Phil 3415.43	Hartmann, Eduard von. Philosophische Fragen. Leipzig, 1885.
Phil 7060.103	Hartmann, K.R.E. von. Der Spiritismus. Leipzig, 1885.
Phil 3489.38	Henrich, Adolf. Kant's Deduktion der reinen Verstandesbegriffe. Emmerich, 1885.
Phil 6048.85.1	Heron-Allen, Edward. A manual of cheirosophy. 10th ed. London, 1885.
Phil 6117.4	Hill, A. The plan of the central nervous system. Chicago, 1885.
NEDL Phil 2055.2.80	Hinton, James. Life and letters. London, 1885.
Phil 182.19	Hodgson, S.H. Philosophy and experience. London, 1885.
Phil 8663.3.93	Homo (pseud.). Analogy, or The theology of nature. New Haven, 1885.
Phil 8882.21.15	Hopkins, M. The law of love and love as a law. N.Y., 1885.
Phil 665.14	ipper, P. Geistesleben und Descendenzlehre. Naumburg, 1885.
Phil 5243.9	Irbal, M. Lehrbuch der empirischen Psychologie. Wien, 1885.
Phil 6958.1	Ireland, W.W. The blot upon the brain. Edinburgh, 1885.
Phil 3491.7	Jahn, Max. Der Einfluss der Kantischen Psychologie auf die Pädagogik als Wissenschaft. Leipzig, 1885.
Phil 8589.5.5A	James, H. Literary remains. Boston, 1885.
Phil 5249.3	Janes, Elijah. Human psychology. Oakland, 1885.
Phil 2496.84	Janet, Paul. Victor Cousin et son oeuvre. Paris, 1885.
Phil 5049.3.7	Jevons, W.S. Logic (science primers). N.Y., 1885.
Phil 809.1.2	Joel, M. Beiträge zur Geschichte der Philosophie. Breslau, 1885.
Phil 5400.73	Jungmann, J. Das Gemüth. 2e Aufl. Freiburg, 1885.
Phil 9550.9	Kaler, Emil. Der Ethik des Utiliarismus. Inaug. Diss. Hamburg, 1885.
Phil 5460.5	Kandinsky, V. Kritische und klinische Betrachtungen im Gebiete der Sinnestäuschungen. Berlin, 1885.
Phil 3480.70.10A	Kant, Immanuel. Introduction to logic. Photoreproduction. London, 1885.
Phil 3480.85.3	Kant, Immanuel. De kracht van den wil in het beheerschen van ziekelijke aandoeningen. 3. druk. Leeuwarden, 1885.
Phil 3425.577.2	Kedney, J.S. Hegel's aesthetics; a critical exposition. Chicago, 1885.
Phil 8885.22	Kittel, Rudolf. Sittliche fragen. Stuttgart, 1885.
Phil 5220.3	Knauer, V. Grundlinien zur Aristotelisch-Thomistischen Psychologie. Wien, 1885.
Phil 185.22.6	Koch, J.L.A. Grundriss der Philosophie. 2e Aufl. Göppingen, 1885.
Phil 185.37	Kreyenbühl, J. Die Bedeutung der Philosophie für die Erfahrungswissenschaften. Heidelberg, 1885.
Phil 8701.7.2	Laing, Samuel. Modern science and modern thought. 2. ed. London, 1885.
Phil 5400.50	Lange, C.G. Om sindsbevaegelser. Kjobenhavn, 1885.
Phil 6321.8	Lanteirès, André. Essai descriptif sur les troubles psychopathiques avec lucidités d'esprit. Paris, 1885.
Phil 5051.11	Lasson, Adolf. Der Satz vom Widerspruch. Halle, 1885.
Phil 2138.96	Lauret, Henri. Philosophie de Stuart Mill. Thèse. Neufchâteau, 1885.
Phil 8886.5.5	Laurie, S.S. Ethica: or The ethics of reason. London, 1885.

1885 - cont.

Phil 4215.1.89   Levi, G. Del carattere meglio determinante la filosofia di Romagnosi. Parma, 1885.

Phil 8591.8.5   Lilly, W.S. Ancient religion and modern thought. 2. ed. London, 1885.

Phil 5251.8.7   Lipps, T. Psychologische Studien. Heidelberg, 1885.

Phil 2138.100   Löchen, Arne. Om J. Stuart Mills logik. Kristiania, 1885.

Phil 3565.10   Lotze, Hermann. Kleine Schriften. Leipzig, 1885-91. 4v.

Phil 3565.51   Lotze, Hermann. Microcosmos. N.Y., 1885. 2v.

Phil 3565.51.2   Lotze, Hermann. Microcosmos. v.1-2. 2. ed. N.Y., 1885.

Phil 3565.50.5   Lotze, Hermann. Mikrokosmus. v.1-3. Leipzig, 1885-1896. 2v.

Phil 3565.32.3   Lotze, Hermann. Outline of practical philosophy. Boston, 1885.

Phil 7080.6   Lyman, H.M. Insomnia and other disorders of sleep. Chicago, 1885.

Phil 187.4   Maguire, T. Lectures on philosophy. London, 1885.

Phil 7068.55.14   Mahan, A. Modern mysteries, explained and exposed. Boston, 1885.

Phil 2115.88   Manly, G.W. Contradictions in Locke's theory of knowledge. Leipzig, 1885.

Phil 6022.1   Mantegazza, P. La physionnomie. Paris, 1885.

Phil 6122.9   Marique, J.M.L. Recherches expérimentales sur le mécanisme de fonctionnement des centres psychomoteurs du Cerveau. Bruxelles, 1885.

Phil 3494.2   Marquardt, A. Kant und Crusius. Kiel, 1885.

Phil 3110.85   Martensen, Hans L. Jacob Böhme. Photoreproduction. London, 1885.

Phil 3525.85   Martin, B.R. Karl Christian Friedrich Krause's Leben, Lehre und Bedeutung. Leipzig, 1885.

Phil 8887.4   Martineau, J. Types of ethical theory. Oxford, 1885.

Htn   Phil 2150.2.30*   Martineau, James. Types of ethical theory. Oxford, 1885. 2v.

Phil 1117.2.5   Mayor, J.B. Sketch of ancient philosophy. Cambridge, 1885.

Phil 6051.3   Metz, V. de. Hand-book of modern palmistry. N.Y., 1885?

Phil 3832.2   Meyer, M. Die Tugendlehre Spinoza's. Fleusburg, 1885.

Phil 6122.4   Mills, C.K. Toner lectures, IX. Mental overwork. Washington, 1885.

Phil 9150.2   Morgan, C.L. The springs of conduct. London, 1885.

Phil 9352.10   Mowry, William A. Talks with my boys. Boston, 1885.

Phil 978.53   Murdoch, J. Theosophy unveiled. Madras, 1885.

Phil 8888.1.3   Nahlowsky, J.W. Allgemeine Ethik. 2. Aufl. Pleizig, 1885.

Phil 5520.32   Noiré, Ludwig. Logos; Ursprung und Wesen der Begriffe. Leipzig, 1885.

Phil 5640.20   Nordvall, A.L. Psykologiska studier. Stockholm, 1885.

Phil 9353.3   Notes for boys...on morals, mind and manners. London, 1885.

Phil 2805.85   Nourrisson, J.F. Pascal physicien et philosophe. Paris, 1885.

Phil 4515.81   Nybläeus, A. Tvänne uppsatser om den Boströmska filosofien. Lund, 1885.

Phil 1200.29   Ogereau, F. Essai sur le système philosophique des stoïciens. Paris, 1885.

Phil 4110.3.83   Onoranze funebri a Francesco Fiorentino. Napoli, 1885.

Phil 8594.3.2   Opzoomer, C.W. Order. n.p., 1885.

Phil 8594.3   Opzoomer, C.W. Order. n.p., 1885.

Phil 5054.3.5   Orti y Lara, J.M. Lógica. Madrid, 1885.

Phil 1190.5   Pappenheim, E. Die Tropen der griechischen Skeptiker. Berlin, 1885.

Phil 2805.30.5   Pascal, Blaise. Lettres écrites à un provincial. Paris, 1885-86. 2v.

Phil 2805.31.2   Pascal, Blaise. Première, quatrième et treizième lettres provinciales. Paris, 1885.

Phil 2805.30.4   Pascal, Blaise. Les provinciales. Paris, 1885. 2v.

Phil 1158.15.2   Pater, Walter. Marius the Epicurean. 2. ed. London, 1885. 2v.

Phil 8595.3   Perrin, R.S. The religion of philosophy. N.Y., 1885.

Phil 8890.20   Porter, N. Elements of moral science. N.Y., 1885.

Phil 8890.20.1   Porter, N. Elements of moral science. N.Y., 1885.

Phil 1870.86   Porter, N. The two-hundredth birthday of Bishop George Berkeley. N.Y., 1885.

Phil 5025.1.2   Prantl, Carl von. Geschichte der Logik. v.2. Leipzig, 1885.

Phil 190.16.2   Pressensé, E. de. Study of origins. 2ed. N.Y., 1885.

Phil 190.16.10   Pressensé, E. de. Variétés morales et politiques. Paris, 1885.

Phil 365.11   Preyer, W. Aus Natur- und Menschenleben. Berlin, 1885.

Phil 9075.16   Rée, Paul. Die Entstehung des Gewissens. Berlin, 1885.

Phil 5767.5   Rée, Paul. Die Illusion der Willensfreiheit. Berlin, 1885.

Phil 2840.30   Renouvier, C.B. Esquisse d'une classification systématique. Paris, 1885-86. 2v.

Phil 5227.2.3   Ribot, T. La psychologie allemande contemporaine. 2. éd. Paris, 1885.

Phil 6327.46   Ribot, Théodule. Les maladies de la personnalité. Paris, 1885.

Phil 6619.4.2   Richer, Paul. Études cliniques sur la grande hystérie ou hystéro-épilepsie. 2. ed. Paris, 1885.

Phil 5767.4   Rieger, Conrad. Experimentelle Untersuchungen. Jena, 1885.

Phil 298.3   Rindell, E. Framställning af teorierna om det kosmiska före Sölger och Hegel. Helsingfors, 1885.

Phil 5827.1.28   Romanes, G.J. Die geistige Entwicklung im Tierreich. Leipzig, 1885.

Phil 3499.6.20   Romundt, H. Grundlegung zur Reform der Philosophie. Berlin, 1885.

Phil 4210.70   Rosmini-Serbati, Antonio. Saggio storico critico sulle categorie e la dialettica. v.1-2. Torino, 1885.

Htn   Phil 192.16.5*   Royce, Josiah. Religious aspect of philosophy. Boston, 1885.

NEDL   Phil 192.16A   Royce, Josiah. Religious aspect of philosophy. Boston, 1885. (Changed to KD 55178)

Phil 8597.43   Rudin, W. Om det personligas betydelse. Upsala, 1885?

Phil 5257.54   Ryland, F. A student's handbook of psychology and ethics. London, 1885.

Phil 8615.1.5   Salter, W.M. Der Religion der Moral. Leipzig, 1885.

Phil 9430.10.4   Saltus, Edgar. The philosophy of disenchantment. N.Y., 1885.

Phil 4570.1.81   Schéele, Frans von. Samuel Grubbe's skönhetslära. Akademisk afhandling. Upsala, 1885.

Phil 5628.52.5   Schmöger, Karl Erhard. Leben der Gottseligen Anna Katharina Emmerich. Freiburg, 1885.

Phil 5768.17   Schwartzkopff, P. Die Freiheit des Willens als Grundlage der Sittlichkeit. Leipzig, 1885.

1885 - cont.

Phil 818.1.4   Schwegler, F.C.A. Geschichte der Philosophie. 13. Aufl. Stuttgart, 1885.

Phil 1818.1   Seth, A. Scottish philosophy. Edinburgh, 1885.

Phil 7054.11   Shelhamer, M.F. Life and labor in the spirit world. Boston, 1885.

Phil 5258.77.5   Sibbern, F.C. Loeren om de menneskelige Folelser. Kjøbenhavn, 1885.

Phil 6328.9   Simonin, A.H. Les sentiments, les passions et la folie explications des phénomènes de la pensée et des sensations. Paris, 1885.

Phil 978.9.8   Sinnett, A.P. Esoteric Buddhism. Boston, 1885.

Phil 978.9.7   Sinnett, A.P. Esoteric Buddhism. 5th ed. London, 1885.

Phil 978.65   Sinnett, Patience E. The purpose of theosophy. London, 1885.

Phil 5768.15   Sommer, H. Uber das Wesen und die Bedeutung. Berlin, 1885.

Phil 9150.4   Sorley, W.R. On the ethics of naturalism. London, 1885.

Phil 8419.26   Spence, Joseph. Crito, or A dialogue on beauty. Edinburgh, 1885.

Phil 8419.26.1   Spence, Joseph. Crito, or A dialogue on beauty. Edinburgh, 1885.

Phil 2270.45.14   Spencer, Herbert. First principles. 4th ed. N.Y., 1885.

Phil 3235.88   Starcke, Carl N. Ludwig Feuerbach. Stuttgart, 1885.

Phil 8893.22   Steinthal, H. Allgemeine Ethik. Berlin, 1885.

Phil 510.26   Stern, M.L. Philosophischer und naturwissenschaftlicher Monismus. Leipzig, 1885.

Phil 5258.25.2   Sully, J. Outlines of psychology. N.Y., 1885.

NEDL   Phil 7054.7   Underhill, A. Leah. The missing link in modern spiritualism. N.Y., 1885.

Phil 5061.3   Veitch, John. Institutes of logic. Edinburgh, 1885.

Phil 1721.2   Vignoli, Tito. L'era nuova del pensiero. Milano, 1885.

Phil 3492.2.55   Vold, John M. Albrecht Krause's Darstellung der Kantischen Raumtheorie und der Kantischen Lehre. Cristiania, 1885.

Phil 7060.22   Vulpius, W. Uber den psychischen Mechanismus der Sinnestäuschungen. Jena, 1885.

Phil 5070.3   Ward, Wilfred. The wish to believe. Photoreproduction. London, 1885.

Phil 8897.6.20   Wayland, F. The elements of moral science. Rangoon, 1885.

Phil 400.6   Webb, J.E. The veil of Isis...essays on idealism. Dublin, 1885.

Phil 3415.91   Weckesser, A. Der empirische Pessimismus. Bonn, 1885.

Phil 3552.280   Wendt, Emil. Die Entwickelung der leibnizschen Monadenlehre bis zum Jahre 1695. Inaug. Diss. Berlin, 1885.

Phil 197.31   Widemann, P.H. Erkennen und Sein, Losung des Problems. Karlsruhe, 1885.

Phil 197.27   Wilson, John. Thoughts on science, theology, and ethics. London, 1885.

Phil 5440.14   Withington, C.F. Consanguineous marriages; their effect upon offspring. Boston, 1885.

Phil 3504.8.5   Witte, J.H. Kantischer Kriticismus Gegenüber unkritischen Dilettantismus. Bonn, 1885.

Phil 6132.2   Wood, H.C. Brain-work and overwork. Philadelphia, 1885.

Phil 8647.4   Wright, T.F. Life eternal. Boston, 1885.

Phil 3915.76.3   Wundt, Wilhelm. Essays. Leipzig, 1885.

Phil 1130.6.8   Zeller, Eduard. Socrates and the Socratic schools. 3rd ed. London, 1885.

Phil 5402.10   Zimmermann, O. Die Wonne des Leids. 2e Aufl. Leipzig, 1885.

1886

Phil 8655.5.5   Abbot, F.E. Scientifc theism. 2. ed. Boston, 1886.

Phil 175.3   Alexander, A. Some problems of philosophy. N.Y., 1886.

Phil 8401.8   Alt, Theodor. Die Grenzen der Kunst und die Buntfarbigkeit der Antike. Berlin, 1886.

Phil 2733.80   André, Y.M. La vie du R.P. Malebranche, Bibliothèque Oratorienne. Paris, 1886.

Phil 8655.10   Armstrong, R.A. Man's knowledge of God. London, 1886.

Phil 6053.2.1   Arpentigny, Casimir Stanislas d'. La science de la main. The science of the hand. London, 1886.

Phil 1200.20   Avenel, J. Le stoïcisme et les stoïciens. Paris, 1886.

Phil 3090.27   Baader, Franz von. Leben und theosophische Werke. v.1-2. Stuttgart, 1886-87.

Phil 5241.2.13   Bain, A. The emotions and the will. N.Y., 1886.

Phil 6400.1   Ballet, G. Le langage intérieur. Paris, 1886.

Phil 176.57.2   Barzellotti, G. Santi, solitari e filosofi. 2nd ed. Bologna, 1886.

Phil 665.54   Bastian, Adolf. Die Seele indischer und hellenischer Philosophie in den Gespenstern moderner Geisterseherei. Berlin, 1886.

Phil 6111.33   Bastide, Jules. La pensée et le cerveau. Paris, 1886.

Phil 8581.38   Baumann, J. Religionsphilosophie auf modernwissenschaftlicher Grundlage. Leipzig, 1886.

Phil 176.81   Bender, Hedwig. Zur Lösung des metaphysischen Problems. Berlin, 1886.

Phil 8581.6   Bender, W. Das Wesen der Religion. Bonn, 1886.

Phil 176.20.5   Bergmann, J. Vorlesungen über Metaphysik. Berlin, 1886.

Phil 6671.4.5   Bérillon, E. De la suggestion. Paris, 1886.

Phil 1535.21.2   Biedermann, G. Philosophie des Geistes. Prag, 1886.

Phil 5011.3   Binde, Robert. Begriff, Urteil und Schluss in ihrer gemeinsamen Wurze. pt.1-2. Glogan, 1886-87.

Phil 5620.1A   Binet, A. La psychologie du raisonnement. Paris, 1886.

Phil 3110.22   Böhme, J. Works. Glasgow, 1886.

Phil 6671.9   Bottey, F. Le magnétisme animal. Paris, 1886.

Phil 801.2   Box, E.B. Handbook...history of philosophy. London, 1886.

Phil 7068.86.40   Brackett, E.A. Materialized apparitions. Boston, 1886.

Phil 176.60   Bruner, J.J. La experiencia y la especulación. Santiago de Chile, 1886.

Phil 745.3   Bunge, Gustav von. Vitalismus und Mechanismus. Leipzig, 1886.

Htn   Phil 1106.5.5*   Burley, W. Liber de vita et moribus philosophorum. Tübingen, 1886.

Phil 8656.18   Burman, E.O. Om teismen. Upsala, 1886.

Phil 176.38   Burnouf, E.L. La vie et la pensée. Paris, 1886.

Phil 8877.62   Carneri, B. Entwicklung und Glückseligkeit. Stuttgart, 1886.

Phil 3160.4.3   Carriere, M. Gesammelte Werke. v.1-14. Leipzig, 1886-94. 12v.

Phil 8403.15   Carus, Paul. The principles of art. Boston, 1886.

Phil 8657.6   Cazenove, J.G. Historic aspects...being attributes of God. London, 1886.

Phil 6672.3   Chazarain, L.T. Découverte de la polarité humaine. Paris, 1886.

Phil 400.63   Chiapelli, A. Dottrina della realtà del mondo esterno. Parte prima. Firenze, 1886.

493
Chronological Listing

1886 - cont.

Phil 802.1 Cicchitti-Suriani, F. Sinossi della storia di filosofia. Torino, 1886.
Phil 8877.52 Class, Gustav. Ideale und Güter; Untersuchungen zur Ethik. Erlangen, 1886.
Phil 3484.8 Classen, August. Über den Einfluss Kants auf die Theorie der Sinneswahrnehmung. Leipzig, 1886.
X Cg Phil 177.14.2 Clifford, W.K. Lectures and essays. 2nd ed. London, 1886.
Phil 8693.5.70 Cockburn, S. The laws of nature...reply to Professor Drummond. London, 1886.
Phil 2493.45.3 Condillac, Etienne Bonnot. Traité des sensations. Premiére partie. Photoreproduction. Paris, 1886.
Phil 978.15.3 Cook, M.C. Light on the path. N.Y., 1886?
Phil 8827.1 Courtney, W.L. Constructive ethics. London, 1886.
Phil 5435.1 Creighton, C. Illustrations of unconscious memory in disease. London, 1886.
Phil 7060.108.5 Crookes, William. Recherches sur les phénomènes du spiritualisme. Paris, 1886.
Phil 6672.12 Cullere, A. Magnétisme et hypnotisme. Paris, 1886.
Phil 6953.11 Dejerine, J. L'hérédité dans les maladies du système nerveux. Paris, 1886.
Phil 178.44.10 Delff, Heinrich K.H. Die Hauptprobleme der Philosophie und Religion. Leipzig, 1886.
Phil 2450.80 Denis, J. Bayle et Jurien. Caen, 1886.
Phil 2520.35.8 Descartes, René. Discours de la méthode pour bien conduire sa raison et chercher la vérité dans les sciences. Paris, 1886.
Phil 3195.5.81 Deubler, Konrad. Tagebücher...Bauernphilosophen. Leipzig, 1886. 2v.
Phil 5043.8 Dodgson, C.L. The game of logic. London, 1886.
Phil 6673.9 Donati, Alberto. I misteri svelati dello ipnotismo. Roma, 1886.
Phil 2805.82 Droz, E. Étude sur le scepticisme de Pascal. Paris, 1886.
Phil 8583.12 Drustowitz, H. Moderne Versuche eines Religionsersatzes. Heidelberg, 1886.
Phil 1703.3 Du Marchie van Voorlhnipen, H. Nagelaten Geschriften. Arheim, 1886. 2v.
Phil 5643.9 Egger, V. L'oeil et l'oreille. Paris, 1886.
Phil 5244.14 Elsas, Adolf. Über die Psychophysik. Marburg, 1886.
Phil 1705.1 Falckenberg, R. Geschichte der neueren Philosophie. Leipzig, 1886.
Phil 7068.86.10F Farmer, John S. Twixt two worlds. London, 1886.
Phil 6675.2 Féré, C. La médecine d'imagination. Paris, 1886.
Phil 6115.3.6 Ferrier, D. The functions of the brain. 2d ed. London, 1886.
Phil 6955.4.5 Folsom, C.F. Mental disease. n.p., 1886.
Phil 6115.7 Folsom, C.F. The relation of our public schools to the disorders of the nervous system. Boston, 1886.
Phil 8880.14 Fowler, T. The principles of moral. v.1-2. Oxford, 1886-87.
Phil 7068.86.11 Franco, P.G. Die Geister der Finsterniss. Ausburg, 1886.
Phil 6116.11F Gavoy, E.A. L'encephale; structure et description inconographique du cerveau. Paris, 1886. 2v.
Phil 3565.111 Geijer, Reinhold. Hermann Lotzes tankar om tid och timlighet i kritisk belysning. Lund, 1886.
Cg Phil 6116.2 Golgi, C. Sulla fina anatomia degli organi centrali. Napoli, 1886.
Phil 806.4.2 Gonzalez y Diaz Turíon, Ceferinto. Historia de la filosofía. Madrid, 1886. 4v.
n Phil 2020.32* Green, T.H. The witness of God and faith. London, 1886.
Phil 2020.10 Green, T.H. Works. v.1,3. London, 1886-88. 2v.
Phil 337.5.5 Grung, Frants. Aandslaenker. Kjøbenhavn, 1886.
Phil 337.5 Grung, Frants. Das Problem der Gewissheit. Heidelberg, 1886.
Phil 7068.86.20A Gurney, Edmund. Phantasms of the living. London, 1886. 2v.
Phil 525.6 Gutiérrez, Marcelino. El misticismo ortodoxo en sus relaciones con la filosofia. Valladolid, 1886.
Phil 5047.19 Harms, Friedrick. Logik. Leipzig, 1886.
Phil 3415.71 Hartmann, Eduard von. Moderne Probleme. Leipzig, 1886.
Phil 3415.63 Hartmann, Eduard von. The religion of the future. London, 1886.
Phil 3425.56.20 Hegel, Georg Wilhelm Friedrich. The introduction to Hegel's Philosophy of fine art. London, 1886.
Phil 3425.56.15 Hegel, Georg Wilhelm Friedrich. The philosophy of art. Edinburgh, 1886.
Phil 6117.1.5 Herzen, A. Les conditions physiques de la conscience. Genève, 1886.
Phil 182.33.2 Hinton, C.H. Scientific romances. London, 1886.
Phil 9520.2.2 Hinton, James. The mystery of pain. Boston, 1886.
Phil 5545.14.2 Holbrook, M.S. How to strengthen the memory. N.Y., 1886.
Phil 4135.1 Iaja, Donato. Saggi filosofici. Napoli, 1886.
Phil 7060.38.3 Ingram, J.H. The haunted homes and family traditions of Great Britain. 3. ed. London, 1886.
Phil 6958.1.3 Ireland, W.W. The blot upon the brain. N.Y., 1886.
Phil 184.11.2 Jacoby, L. Die Idee der Entwicklung. Zürich, 1886.
Phil 5249.3.2 Janes, Elijah. Human psychology. N.Y., 1886.
Phil 5760.1 Kahl, W. Die Lehre von Primat des Willens. Strassburg, 1886.
Phil 3625.1.105 Kahut, Adolf. Moses Mendelssohn und seine Familie. Dresden, 1886.
Phil 8665.7 Kent, G. Det absolute gudshegreb. Kristiania, 1886.
Phil 95.1.3 Kirchner, Friedrich. Wörterbuch der philosophischen Grundbegriffe. Heidelberg, 1886.
Phil 2050.88 Knight, William. Hume. Philadelphia, 1886.
Phil 185.22 Koch, J.L.A. Die Wirchlichkeit und ihre Erkenntnis. Göppingen, 1886.
Phil 3565.124 Kögel, Fritz. Lotzes Aesthetik. Göttingen, 1886.
Phil 6681.2 Lafontaine, C. L'art de magnétiser. Paris, 1886.
Phil 600.13 Lagarrigue, J. Lettres sur le positivisme. Vincennes, 1886.
Phil 672.6 Lange, C.C.L. Die geschichtliche Entwickelung des Bewegungsbegriffes. Leipzig, 1886.
Phil 4515.86 Leander, P.J.H. Boströms lära om guds ideer. Lund, 1886.
Phil 6961.1 Legrain, M. Du délire chez les dégénérés. Paris, 1886.
Phil 3552.41.5 Leibniz, Gottfried Wilhelm. Nouveaux essais sur l'entendement humain. Paris, 1886.
Phil 8886.33 Lessona, Marco. L'utilità e il senso morale. Torino, 1886.
Phil 7054.20 Light on the hidden way. Boston, 1886.
Phil 4210.83 Lockhart, W. Life of Antonio Rosmini-Serbati. 2. ed. London, 1886. 2v.
Phil 3565.58 Lotze, Hermann. Grundtraek af religionsfilosofien. København, 1886.
Phil 3565.51.1 Lotze, Hermann. Microcosmos. v.1-2. N.Y., 1886.
Phil 3565.32.5 Lotze, Hermann. Outline of aesthetics. Boston, 1886.
Phil 3565.32 Lotze, Hermann. Outline of Metaphysic. Boston, 1886.

1886 - cont.

Phil 3565.32.4 Lotze, Hermann. Outline of psychology. Boston, 1886.
Phil 6121.6 Luciani, L. Die Functions-Localisation die Grosshirnrinde. Leipzig, 1886.
Phil 2125.50 McCosh, James. Psychology: the cognitive powers. N.Y., 1886.
Phil 5635.5.4 Mach, Ernst. Beiträge zur Analyse de Empfindungen. Jena, 1886.
Phil 5252.2.5 Mahan, A. System of mental philosophy. 4th ed. Chicago, 1886.
NEDL Phil 2733.30.2 Malebranche, Nicolas. De la recherche de la vérité. v.2. Paris, 1886.
Phil 2733.30 Malebranche, Nicolas. De la recherche de la vérité. v.2. Paris, 1886.
Phil 2128.40A Mandeville, B. Bernard de Mandeville's Bienenfabel. Diss. Halle, 1886. 2v.
Htn Phil 7075.11.5* Mantegazza, P. Gli amori degli uomeni. Milano, 1886.
Phil 5402.3.10 Mantegazza, P. Physiologie du plaisir. Paris, 1886.
Phil 8887.4.2 Martineau, J. Types of ethical theory. 2. ed. Oxford, 1886. 2v.
Phil 8887.4.3 Martineau, J. Types of ethical theory. 2. ed. Oxford, 1886. 2v.
Phil 9150.18 Massebieau, Eugéne. De principe de la morale. Thèse. Alençon, 1886.
Phil 7068.86.50 Maudsley, H. Natural causes and supernatural seemings. London, 1886.
Phil 5762.6 Meyer, W. Die Wahlfreiheit des Willens in ihrer Nichtigkeit. Gotha, 1886.
Phil 1150.11A Meyer, W.A. Hypatia von Alexandria. Heidelberg, 1886.
Phil 2115.133 Milhac, F. Essai sur les idées religieuses de Locke. Thèse. Genève, 1886.
Phil 2138.35.4 Mill, John S. A system of logic. London, 1886.
Phil 5545.20.5 Miller, Adam. Mental gymnastics, or lessons on memory. 4. ed. Chicago, 1886.
Phil 5545.20 Miller, Adam. Mental gymnastics. Chicago, 1886.
Phil 6967.3.25 Mills, Charles K. Benjamin Rush and American psychiatry. n.p., 1886.
Phil 8592.12 Momerie, A.W. The basis of religion. Edinburgh, 1886.
Phil 575.2.2 Momerie, A.W. Personality. 3rd ed. Edinburgh, 1886.
Phil 6682.8 Morselli, E.A. Il magnetismo animale. Torino, 1886.
Phil 5401.1.5 Mosso, A. La peur. Paris, 1886.
Phil 187.89 Muzquiz, J.M. La verdadera legitimidad y el verdadero liberalismo. Habana, 1886.
Phil 8593.4.10 Nichols, J.R. Whence, what, where? Boston, 1886.
Phil 3640.31.2 Nietzsche, Friedrich. Jenseits von Gut und Böse. Leipzig, 1886.
Phil 3640.11.2 Nietzsche, Friedrich. Menschliches, allzumenschliche sein Buch für freie Geister. Leipzig, 1886.
Phil 5635.23 Nitsche, Adolf. Versuch einer einheitlichen Lehre von der Gefühlin. Innsbruck, 1886.
Phil 813.1.7 Nourrisson, J.F. Tableau des progrès de la pensée humaine. 7e éd. Paris, 1886.
Phil 4065.88.12 Paris Zezin, Luis. Fray Giordano Bruno y su tiempo. 2a ed. Madrid, 1886.
Phil 2805.15 Pascal, Blaise. Oeuvres de Blaise Pascal. Paris, 1886-95. 2v.
Phil 8965.10 Peabody, A.P. Christian morals. Boston, 1886.
Phil 8595.4.10 Pfleiderer, O. The philosophy of religion. London, 1886-88. 4v.
Phil 6025.1 Piderit, Leo. Mimik und Physiognomik. Detmold, 1886.
Phil 8416.31 Pierson, A. Schöhiedszon en levenswijsheid. Arnhem, 1886.
Phil 3497.2 Porter, N. Kant's ethics. Chicago, 1886.
Phil 7060.33 Preyer, W. Die Erklärung des Gedankenlesens. Leipzig, 1886.
Phil 7068.86.60A Putman, A. Post-mortem confessions. Boston, 1886.
Phil 192.1 Rabier, E. Leçons de philosophie. Paris, 1886. 2v.
Phil 4285.1.90 Ragnisco, P. Giacomo Zabarella il filosofo Pietro Pompanazzi. Roma, 1886-87.
Phil 1850.93 Reichel, E. Wer Schrieb das "Norum Organon" von Francis Bacon. Stuttgart, 1886.
Phil 4630.2.36 Rein, T. Lärobok i den formella logiken. Helsingfors, 1886.
Phil 525.13 Reischle, Max. Ein Wort...über die Mystik in der Theologie. Freiburg, 1886.
Phil 7068.84.10 Reminiscences and memories of Henry Thomas Butterworth and Nancy Irvin Wales. Lebanon, Ohio, 1886.
Phil 8707.2 Reusch, F.H. Nature and the Bible. Edinburgh, 1886. 2v.
Phil 6682.16 Reymond, Mine. Vve. Cours de magnétisme. Paris, 1886.
Phil 5227.2.5 Ribot, T. German psychology of to-day. N.Y., 1886.
Phil 3625.1.135 Ritter, I.H. Mendelssohn und Lessing. 2e Aufl. Berlin, 1886.
NEDL Phil 2045.81 Roberstson, G.C. Hobbes. Philadelphia, 1886.
Phil 3499.6.9 Romundt, H. Ein neuer Paulus. Berlin, 1886.
Phil 4210.60 Rosmini-Serbati, Antonio. Psychology. London, 1886-88. 3v.
Phil 4630.4.30 Ruin, Waldemar. Kunskap och ideal. Helsingfors, 1886.
Phil 5425.38 Sanborn, K.A. The vanity and insanity of genius. N.Y., 1886.
Phil 3838.4 Santayana, G. The ethical doctrine of Spinoza. Cambridge, 1886.
Phil 6968.1 Saury, H. Étude clinique sur la folie héréditaire. Paris, 1886.
Phil 8708.1 Savage, M.J. Evolution and religion. Philadelphia, 1886.
Phil 8419.4 Schasler, Max. Ästhetik, Grundzüge der Wissenschaft des Schönen und der Kunst. Leipzig, 1886. 2v.
Phil 672.30 Schneid, Mathias. Die philosophische Lehre von Zeit und Raum. Mainz, 1886.
Phil 818.10 Scholten, J.H. Kortfattet fremstilling ad filosofiens historie. 3. Opl. Kjøbenhavn, 1886.
Phil 6968.4.3 Schüle, H. Klinische Psychiatrie. 3. Aufl. Leipzig, 1886.
Phil 1123.1 Schulze, E. Ubersicht über die griechische Philosophie. Leipzig, 1886.
Phil 5058.100 Schulze, Ernst. Grundriss der Logik und Übersicht über die Griechische Philosophie für die prima der Gymnasien. Leipzig, 1886.
Phil 8893.12 Sigwart, C. Vorfragen der Ethik. Freiburg, 1886.
Phil 299.3 Siljeström, P.A. Tretten aftnar hos en spiritist. Stockholm, 1886.
Phil 978.9.8.5 Sinnett, A.P. Esoteric Buddhism. 3d ed. Boston, 1886.
NEDL Phil 978.5.800 Sinnett, A.P. Incidents in the life of Madame Blavatsky. London, 1886.
Phil 3838.3 Smith, H. Spinoza...environment. Cincinnatti, 1886.
Phil 4225.1.52 Spaventa, Bertrando. Prolusione e introduzione alle lezioni di filosofia nella Università di Napoli. 2a ed. Napoli, 1886.
Phil 2270.45.5 Spencer, Herbert. First principles. N.Y., 1886.

1886 - cont.

Phil 2270.20   Spencer, Herbert. Select works. N.Y., 1886.
Phil 2270.55.9   Spencer, Herbert. Social statics. N.Y., 1886.
Phil 5258.45   Spitta, Heinrich. Einleitung in die Psychologie als Wissenschaft. Freiburg, 1886.
Phil 2490.150   Sterzel, Georg Friedrick. A. Comte als Pädagog. Leipzig, 1886.
Phil 193.41   Strümpell, L. Die Einleitung in die Philosophie. Leipzig, 1886.
Phil 5258.25.5   Sully, J. Teacher's handbook of psychology. London, 1886.
Phil 665.17   Svoboda, A.V. Kritische Geschichte der Ideale. Leipzig, 1886.
Phil 2115.135   Tarantino, G. Giovanni Locke. Milano, 1886.
Phil 8599.13   Teichmüller, Gustav. Religionsphilosophie. Breslau, 1886.
Phil 4065.96   Tocco, Felice. Giordano Bruno. Firenze, 1886.
Phil 820.1.2   Ueberweg, F. Grundriss der Geschichte der Philosophie. v.1-2,3. 7. Aufl. Berlin, 1886-88. 2v.
Phil 3502.3   Unold, J. Die ethnologischen und anthropogeographischen...bei I. Kant und J.R. Forster. Leipzig, 1886.
Phil 821.3   Vallet, P. Histoire de la philosophie. 3e ed. Paris, 1886.
Phil 7082.104.4   La vera spiegazione numerica dei sogni. 4a ed. Palermo, 1886.
Phil 352.1   Volkelt, J. Erfahrung und Denken. Hamburg, 1886.
Phil 8846.1   Voltz, H. Die Ethik als Wissenschaft. Strassburg, 1886.
Phil 3504.1.20   Wallace, William. Kant. Edinburgh, 1886.
Phil 8897.38   Wallaschek, R. Ideen zur praktischen Philosophie. Tübingen, 1886.
Phil 6032.1   Warner, F. Physical expression its modes. N.Y., 1886.
Phil 822.1.2   Weber, A. Histoire de la philosophie européenne. Paris, 1886.
Phil 9182.1.2   Weber, M.W. Über die Sozalen-Pflichten der Familie. 2. Aufl. Berlin, 1886.
Phil 3915.46   Wundt, Wilhelm. Eléments de psychologie physiologique. Paris, 1886. 2v.
Phil 3915.65   Wundt, Wilhelm. Ethik. Stuttgart, 1886.
Phil 8715.1.10   Zahm, John Augustine. The Catholic church and modern science. Notre Dame, Ind., 1886.
Phil 1130.5.2   Zeller, Eduard. Outlines of history of Greek philosophy. London, 1886.
Phil 1130.5   Zeller, Eduard. Outlines of history of Greek philosophy. N.Y., 1886.
Phil 1145.76   Ziegler, T. Die Ethik der Griechen und Römer. Bonn, 1886.
Phil 4060.2.82   Zimmels, B. Leo Hebraeus, ein jüdischer Philosoph. Breslau, 1886.

1887

Phil 3482.2.35   Adickes, E. Kants Systematik als Systembilden der Factor. Berlin, 1887.
Phil 7068.87.5   Assier, Adolphe d'. Posthumous humanity. London, 1887.
Phil 9245.9.1   Avebury, John Lubbock. The pleasures of life. N.Y., 1887.
Phil 9035.1   Azam, E. Le caractère. Paris, 1887.
Phil 5041.3.5   Bain, Alexander. Logic deductive and inductive. N.Y., 1887.
Phil 6671.2   Barety, A. Le magnetisme animal. Paris, 1887.
Phil 9510.4   Barrow, I. Sermons on evil-speaking. N.Y., 1887.
Phil 5649.12   Bastian, H.C. The "muscular sense". London, 1887.
Phil 9513.4   Batchelor, George. Social equilibrium. Boston, 1887.
Phil 5241.55.10   Beck, Joseph. Grundriss der empirischen Psychologie und Logik. 7. Aufl. Stuttgart, 1887.
Phil 9341.2.10   Beecher, H.W. Lectures to young men. Edinburgh, 1887.
Phil 8050.47   Begg, W.P. The development of taste, and other studies in aesthetics. Glasgow, 1887.
Phil 9500.4   Benjamin, F.N. (Mrs.). The sunny side of shadow. Boston, 1887.
Phil 8402.6   Bergmann, J. Über das Schöne. Berlin, 1887.
Phil 1535.21   Biedermann, G. Natur-Philosophie. Prag, 1887-89. 3v.
Phil 6671.7   Binet, A. Le magnétisme animal. Paris, 1887.
Phil 8691.13   Borrows, Samuel Jure. Science and immortality. Boston, 1887.
Phil 5241.21.5   Bouillier, F.C. Nouvelles études familières de psychologie et de morale. Paris, 1887.
Phil 6671.8   Bourru, H. La suggestion mentale. Paris, 1887.
Phil 5241.15   Bowne, B.P. Introduction to psychological theory. N.Y., 1887.
Phil 8656.8.5   Bowne, B.P. Philosophy of theism. N.Y., 1887.
Phil 176.72   Braun, Edmond. La logique de l'absolu. Paris, 1887.
Phil 1190.6   Brochard, Victor. Les skeptiques grecs. Paris, 1887.
Phil 4065.60   Bruno, Giordano. The heroic enthusiasts. pt.1-2. London, 1887-1889. 2v.
Phil 6400.5.5   Bulin, René. Eine besondere Art der Wortblindhut, Dyslehre. Wiesbaden, 1887.
Htn   Phil 1980.2.80*   Cabot, J.E. Memoir of Ralph Wlado Emerson. Boston, 1887. 2v.
Phil 6112.4.9   Carpenter, W.B. Principles of mental psychology. 4th ed. N.Y., 1887.
Phil 8520.15.3   Carriere, Moriz. Die philosophische Weltanschauung. 2. Aufl. Leipzig, 1887. 2v.
Phil 3484.14   Cesca, La "cosa in se". Torino, 1887.
Phil 1140.1   Chaignet, A.E. Histoire de la Psychologie des Grecs. Paris, 1887-93. 5v.
Phil 125.1   Chicchitti-Suriani. Nozioni elementari di logica. Torino, 1887.
Phil 9342.4.2   Cobbett, W. Advice to young men. London, 1887.
Phil 5243.7   Dewey, John. Psychology. N.Y., 1887.
Phil 178.14   Dietrich, K. Protest Gegen die moderne Wissenschaft. Hamburg, 1887.
Phil 9343.7   Dodge, Grace H. A bundle of letters to busy girls. N.Y., 1887.
Phil 334.5   Dorner, August. Das menschliche Erkennen. Berlin, 1887.
Phil 8953.5   Dorner, I.A. System of Christian ethics. N.Y., 1887.
Phil 8693.5.11   Drummond, H. Natural law in the spiritual world. N.Y., 1887.
Phil 178.51   Dubuc, Paul. Essai sur la méthode en métaphysique. Paris, 1887.
Phil 6673.4.7   Du Potet, J. de S. Manuel de l'étudiant magnétiseur. 5e éd. Paris, 1887.
Phil 6954.1   Earle, P. The curability of insanity. Philadelphia, 1887.
Phil 3486.6   Elsmann, W. Begriff des höchsten Gutes bei Kant und Schleiermacher. Leipzig, 1887.
Phil 6954.2   Emminghaus, H. Die psychischen Störungen. Tübingen, 1887.
Phil 9145.8   Estienne, Antoine Minim. A charitable remonstrance. Edinburgh, 1887.
Phil 8879.10   Everett, C.C. The ultimate facts of ethics. Boston, 1887.

1887 - cont.

Phil 8880.23   Fairbairn, R.B. Of the doctrine of morality in its relation to grace of redemption. N.Y., 1887.
Phil 180.24   Faug, Balthasar. Les vraies bases de la philosophie. 3e éd. Paris, 1887.
Phil 3210.67.2   Fechner, G.T. Das Büchlein vom Leben nach dem Tode. 3. Aufl. Hamburg, 1887.
Phil 4065.114   Ferrari, Sante. G. Bruno, F. Fiorentino, T. Mamiani. Mantova, 1887.
Phil 2405.2.3   Ferraz, Marin. Spiritualisme et libéralisme. 2e éd. Paris, 1887.
Phil 180.25F   Ferri, Luigi. Della idea del vero e...dell'essere. Roma, 1887.
Phil 336.4   Fischer, Englebert Lorenz. Die Grundfragen der Erkenntnistheorie. Mainz, 1887.
Phil 1705.4.6   Fischer, K. History of modern philosophy. N.Y., 1887.
Htn   Phil 2225.7.32*   Fitzgerald, John J. The new education; three papers. Boston, 1887.
Phil 5160.1   Fitzgerald, Penelope F. A treatise...sufficient reason. London, 1887.
Phil 90.1.4   Fleming, William. Vocabulary of philosophy. 4th ed. N.Y., 1887.
Phil 5755.6   Fonsegrive, G. Essai sur le libre arbitre. Paris, 1887.
Phil 6115.8   François-Franck, C. Leçons sur les fonctions motrices du cerveau et sur l'épilepsie cérébrale. Paris, 1887.
Phil 4065.92.3   Frith, I. Life of Giordano Bruno. Boston, 1887.
Phil 4065.92   Frith, I. Life of Giordano Bruno. London, 1887.
Phil 410.5   Fullerton, G.S. Conception of the infinite. Philadelphia, 1887.
Phil 3488.7.23   Gallovich, J. Kant criticismusa az Isten léteröl. Inaug. Diss. Eger, 1887.
Phil 4570.3.81   Geijer, R. Humanistiska sektioner contra den sakkunniga nämden. Lund, 1887.
Phil 6676.1   Gessman, G. Magnetismus und Hypnotismus. Wien, 1887.
Phil 7054.39   Gibier, P. Le spiritisme. Paris, 1887.
NEDL   Phil 5545.11   Granville, J.M. Secret of a good memory. Boston, 1887.
Phil 1200.5   Haake, A. Die Gesellschaftslehre der Stoiker. Berlin, 1887.
Phil 288.4   Hahn, Otto. Die Philosophie des Bewussten. Tübingen, 1887.
Phil 5440.16   Harris, George. Christ's teaching concerning heredity. n.p., 1887.
Phil 5757.8   Hebler, Karl. Elemente einer philosophischen Freiheitslehre. Berlin, 1887.
Phil 5757.2   Heman, C.F. Zur Geschichte der Lehre von der Freiheit des menschlichen Willens. Leipzig, 1887.
Phil 3428.43.5   Herbart, J.F. Lehrbuch zur Psychologie. 3. Aufl. Leipzig, 1887.
Phil 3428.11   Herbart, J.F. Sämmtliche Werke. v.1-19. Langensalza, 1887-1912. 14v.
Phil 2045.51.3A   Hobbes, Thomas. Leviathan. 3rd ed. London, 1887.
Phil 5247.10.13   Höffding, H. Psychologie in Umrissen auf Grundläge der Erfahrung. Leipzig, 1887.
Phil 8882.31   Huntington, F.D. Good talking and good manners. Syracuse, 1887.
Phil 5374.52   Jaesche, E. Werden, Sein und Erscheinungsweise des Bewusstseins. Heidelberg, 1887.
Phil 19.17   Jahrbuch für Philosophie und spekulative Theologie. Paderborn, 1887. 25v.
Phil 5049.6.6   Jevons, W.S. The principles of science. London, 1887.
Phil 7060.35   Johnson, F. The new psychic studies. N.Y., 1887.
Phil 5049.14   Johnstone, Lawrence. A short introduction to the study of logic. London, 1887.
Phil 3480.32.8.9   Kant, Immanuel. Critique of pure reason. London, 1887.
Phil 3480.67.105   Kant, Immanuel. The philosophy of law. London, 1887.
Phil 5050.3.2   Keynes, J.N. Studies and exercises in formal logic. 2nd ed. London, 1887.
Phil 8835.1   Köstlin, K.R. Geschichte der Ethik. Tübingen, 1887.
Phil 5400.16   Kröner, E. Das körperliche Gefühl. Breslau, 1887.
Phil 5520.27.2   Kussmaul, A. Die Störungen der Sprache. Leipzig, 1887.
Phil 486.6   L, B.L. Matter and energy. London, 1887.
Phil 5251.1.15   Ladd, G.T. Elements of physiological psychology. N.Y., 1887.
Phil 8663.3.90   Lambert, L.A. Tactics of infidels. Buffalo, 1887.
Phil 3280.86   Land, J.P.N. Arnold Geulincx te Leiden. Amsterdam, 1887.
Phil 5400.50.5   Lange, C.G. Über Gemüthsbewegungen. Leipzig, 1887.
Phil 8886.8.2   Letourneau, C. L'évolution de la morale. Paris, 1887.
Phil 4065.100   Levi, David. Giordano Bruno. Torino, 1887.
Phil 7054.21   Lewis, H.C. The alleged physical phenomena of spiritualism. Boston, 1887.
Phil 3565.45.12   Lotze, Hermann. Grundzüge der Metaphysik. 2. Aufl. Leipzig, 1887.
Phil 3565.31.4   Lotze, Hermann. Metaphysic. 2. ed. Oxford, 1887. 2v.
Phil 3565.32.5.5   Lotze, Hermann. Outlines of logic and encyclopaedia of philosophy. Boston, 1887.
Phil 1145.97   Lutharдt, C.E. Die antike Ethik in ihrer geschichtlichen Entwicklung als Einleitung in die Geschichte der christlichen Moral. Leipzig, 1887.
Phil 575.82   Lutosławski, W. El personalismo. Madrid, 1887.
Phil 5400.38   Luys, Jules. Les émotions chez les sujets en état d'hypnotisme. Paris, 1887.
Phil 187.43   McTaggart, William. Absolute relativism. London, 1887.
Phil 2520.93.3   Mahaffy, J.P. Descartes. Philadelphia, 1887.
Phil 2730.30   Maine de Biran, Pierre. Science et psychologie. Paris, 1887.
Phil 3494.22   Manns, Richard. Die Stellung des Substanzbegriffes. Inaug. Diss. Bonn, 1887.
Phil 5402.3   Mantegazza, P. Le estase umane. Milano, 1887. 2v.
Phil 4265.3.80   Mariano, R. Augusto Vera. Napoli, 1887.
Phil 6122.21   Marston, L.M. Essentials of mental healing. Boston, 1887.
Phil 2115.108   Martinak, E. Zur Logik Lockes. Graz, 1887.
Phil 4215.1.100   Martino, R. de. Saggio su G.D. Romagnosi. Napoli, 1887.
Phil 7068.87.20   Massey, C.C. Zöllner. London, 1887.
Phil 8887.9   Maude, J.E. The foundations of ethics. N.Y., 1887.
Phil 5052.20   Mendive, José. Elementos de lógica. 2a ed. Valladolid, 1887.
Phil 3833.6   Menitescu, Joan. Die Affectenlehre Spinoza's. Leipzig, 1887.
Phil 7060.61   La merveilleuse hystorie de l'esprit de Lyon. Paris, 1887.
Phil 2138.79.10.3   Mill, John S. Autobiography. N.Y., 1887.
Phil 2490.84.4   Mill, John Stuart. The positive philosophy of Auguste Comte. N.Y., 1887.
Phil 8637.8   Miller, J. Are souls immortal? 3rd ed. Princeton, N.J., 1887.
Phil 8610.884.10   Momerie, A.W. Agnosticism. 2. ed. Edinburgh, 1887.
Phil 8592.19   Morison, J.C. The service of man. London, 1887.

Chronological Listing

Phil 5374.2   Morrill, J.S. Self-consciousness of noted persons. Boston, 1887.

Phil 3425.102A   Morris, G.S. Hegel's philosophy of the state. Chicago, 1887.

Phil 5520.3   Müller, F.M. Science of thought. London, 1887.

Phil 5520.3.5   Müller, F.M. Science of thought. v.2. N.Y., 1887.

Phil 5643.80   Neiglick, H. Zur Psychophysik des Lichtsinns. Leipzig, 1887.

Phil 3640.33   Nietzsche, Friedrich. Die fröhliche Wissenschaft. Leipzig, 1887.

Phil 6963.5   Nothnagel, H. Über die Localisation der Gehirnkrankheiten. Wiesbaden, 1887.

Phil 294.2   Nourrisson, J.F. Philosophies de la nature. Paris, 1887.

Phil 600.37.5   Nyström, Anton. Positivismen och Herbert Spencer. Stockholm, 1887.

Phil 6684.1   Ochorowicz, J. De la suggestion mentale. Paris, 1887.

Phil 189.10   Olivier, Aimé. De l'absolu. Paris, 1887.

Phil 2805.72   Pascal, Blaise. Opuscules philosophiques. Paris, 1887.

Phil 9035.6   Peabody, A.P. Building a character. Boston, 1887.

Phil 8890.9.2   Peabody, A.P. Moral philosophy. Boston, 1887.

Phil 4210.132   Pederzolli, G. La filosofia di Antonio Rosmini. Rovereto, 1887.

Phil 7060.102.2   Pennsylvania. University. Seybert Commission for Investigating Modern Spiritualism. Preliminary report. Philadelphia, 1887.

Phil 7060.102   Pennsylvania. University. Seybert Commission for Investigating Modern Spiritualism. Preliminary report. Philadelphia, 1887.

Phil 6619.2.5   Pitres, Albert. Des anesthésies hystériques. Bordeaux, 1887.

Phil 5055.13.2   Poetter, F.C. Logik. 2. Aufl. Gütersloh, 1887.

Phil 5255.5.6   Porter, Noah. The human intellect. 4th ed. N.Y., 1887.

Phil 4065.176   Previti, Luigi. Giordano Bruno e i suoi tempi. Prato, 1887.

Phil 8520.32   Pünjer, G.C.B. History of the Christian philosophy of religion. Edinburgh, 1887.

Phil 192.2   Rabus, L. Lehrbuch zur Einleitung in die Philosophie. Erlangen, 1887-1895. 2v.

Phil 1817.7   Raffel, J. Die voraussetzungen Welche den empiresmus Lockis. Inaug.-Diss. Berlin, 1887?

Phil 9530.42   Ranson, J.C. The successful man. Richmond, 1887.

Phil 6327.1   Regnard, P. Sorcellerie, magnètisme, morphinisme. Paris, 1887.

Phil 7040.2.5   Ribot, T. Diseases of personality. Photoreproduction. N.Y., 1887.

Phil 7054.37.35   Rivail, H.L.D. El génesis. San Martin de Provensals, 1887.

Phil 817.10   Roberty, E. de. L'ancienne et la nouvelle philosophie. Paris, 1887.

Phil 6687.6.9   Rochas d'Aiglun, A. de. Les forces non définies. Paris, 1887.

Phil 8597.40   Rogeri, G. Iddio, l'uomo e la religione. Revere, 1887.

Phil 6127.3   Rohon, J.V. Bau und Verrichtungen des Gehirns. Heidelburg, 1887.

Phil 3499.6.5   Romundt, H. Die drei Fragen Kants. Berlin, 1887.

Phil 1075.1.5   Rose, Valentin. Leben des Heiligen David von Thessalonilke. Berlin, 1887.

Phil 192.34   Ryland, F. Questions on psychology, metaphysics, and ethics. London, 1887.

Phil 4073.87   Sante Felici, G. Die religionsphilosophischen Grundanschauungen des Thomas Campanella. Inaug. Diss. Halle, 1887.

Phil 6028.3.10   Schack, S. La physionomie chez l'homme. Paris, 1887.

Phil 1930.18.80   Schilpp, Paul. The philosophy of Rudolf Carnap. La Salle, 1887.

Phil 6328.3   Scholz, F. Die Diätetik des Geistes. Leipzig, 1887.

Phil 8893.42   Schubert-Soldern, R. von. Grundlagen zu einer Ethik. Leipzig, 1887.

Phil 5258.8   Schubert-Soldern, R. von. Reproduction, Gefühl und Wille. Leipzig, 1887.

Phil 9150.3   Schurman, J.G. The ethical import of Darwinism. N.Y., 1887.

Phil 3246.83   Schwabe, G. Fichtes und Schopenhauer's Lehre von Willen. Jena, 1887.

Phil 818.1.4.5   Schwegler, F.C.A. Geschichte der Philosophie. 14. Aufl. Stuttgart, 1887.

Phil 193.20   Scottish metaphysics. Edinburgh, 1887.

Phil 3425.92A   Seth, A. Hegelianism and personality. Edinburgh, 1887.

Phil 2725.1.80   Seyfarth, H. Louis de la Forge. Jena, 1887.

Phil 4225.3.89   Sichirollo, G. La mia conversione dal Rosmini a S. Tommaso. Padova, 1887.

Phil 6028.1   Simms, J. Human faces. N.Y., 1887.

Phil 6028.1.5   Simms, J. Physiognomy illustrated. N.Y., 1887.

Phil 5058.34   Sjoberg, Gustaf. Lärobok i logik af Gustaf Sjöberg och Gustaf Klingberg. Stockholm, 1887.

Phil 8893.14.15   Smiles, Samuel. The art of living. Boston, 1887.

Phil 8893.14   Smiles, Samuel. Life and labour. London, 1887.

Phil 3915.82   Sommer, Hugo. Individualismus oder Evolutionismus? Berlin, 1887.

Phil 2115.136   Sommer, R. Locke's Verhältnis zu Descartes. Diss. Berlin, 1887.

Phil 2270.30.5   Spencer, Herbert. Data of ethics. London, 1887.

Phil 193.31.15   Spir, A. von. Esquisses de philosophie critique. Paris, 1887.

Phil 6968.7   Spitzka, E.C. Insanity, its classification. N.Y., 1887.

Phil 7039.8.2   Stevens, E. Winchester. The Watseka wonder. Chicago, 1887.

Phil 5710.14   Stewart, A. Our temperaments. London, 1887.

Phil 8643.4   Stockwell, C.T. The evolution of immortality. Chicago, 1887.

Phil 978.32.5   Street, J.C. The hidden way across the threshold. Boston, 1887.

Phil 3425.208   Stuhrmann, J. Die Wurzeln der Hegelschen Logik bei Kant. Neustadt, 1887.

Phil 7068.87.10   Theobald, Morell. Spirit workers in the home circle. London, 1887.

Phil 8620.11   Thompson, D.G. The problem of evil. London, 1887.

Phil 9530.10   Tilley, W.J. Masters of the situation. Chicago, 1887.

Phil 978.13   Tukarama Tatya. A guide to theosophy. Bombay, 1887.

Phil 3425.97   Werner, J. Hegels Offenbarungsbegriff. Leipzig, 1887.

Phil 8712.3.3   White, Andrew Dickson. New chapters in the warfare of science. (Meteorology.) N.Y., 1887.

Phil 5643.42   Wilbrand, H. Die Seelenblindheit als Herderscheinung. Wiesbaden, 1887.

Phil 4655.2.30   Wildhagen, A. Vor tids determinisme. Kristiania, 1887.

Phil 6132.14   Wörner, Ernst. Biblische Anthropologie. Stuttgart, 1887.

Phil 5262.24   Wollny, F. Grundriss der Psychologie. Leipzig, 1887.

Phil 3915.45.3   Wundt, Wilhelm. Grundzüge der physiologischen Psychologie. Leipzig, 1887- 2v.

X Cg   Phil 6694.3   Younger, D. Full, concise instructions in mesmerism. 3. ed. London, 1887.

Phil 200.2   Zeller, E. Philosophische Aufsätze. Leipzig, 1887.

Phil 6135.2   Zuckerkandl, E. Über das Riechcentrum. Stuttgart, 1887.

1888

Phil 4060.5.30   Angiulli, A. La filosofia e la scuola. Napoli, 1888.

Phil 3960.10   Antal, Geza von. Die holländische Philosophie im neunzehnten Jahrhundert. Utrecht, 1888.

Phil 5651.1   Aubert, H.R. Physiologische Studien...Orientierung. Tübingen, 1888.

Phil 331.2   Avenarius, R. Kritik der Reinen Erfahrung. Leipzig, 1888.

Phil 600.3   Balfour, A.T. Religion of humanity. Edinburgh, 1888.

Phil 600.3.2   Balfour, A.T. Religion of humanity. London, 1888.

Htn   Phil 7075.10*   Ball, B. La folie erotique. Paris, 1888.

Phil 6951.2   Ball, B. La morphinomanie. Paris, 1888.

Phil 3821.1   Baltzer, A. Spinoza's Entwicklungsgang. Kiel, 1888.

Phil 6111.10.5   Bastian, H.C. Le cerveau organe de la pensée chez l'homme et chez les animaux. 2. ed. Paris, 1888.

Phil 8826.1   Becker, J.H. Ursprung...Sittlichkeit. Leipzig, 1888.

Phil 8691.17   Bell, A.J. Whence comes man; from nature or from God? London, 1888.

Phil 8581.6.4   Bender, W. Das Wesen der Religion. 4. Aufl. Bonn, 1888.

Phil 6671.5.4   Bernheim, H. Die Suggestion und ihre Heilwirkung. Leipzig, 1888.

Phil 6671.7.5   Binet, A. Animal magnetism. N.Y., 1888.

Phil 4520.3.31   Björkman, N.O. Om det absoluta förnuftet. Stockholm, 1888.

Phil 978.5.6   Blavatsky, H.P. The secret doctrine. v.3. London, 1888-97.

Phil 5400.9   Bobtschew, N. Die Gefühlslehre...von Kant bis auf unsere Zeit. Leipzig, 1888.

Phil 3483.36   Böhringer, A. Kant's erkenntnis-theoretischer Idealismus. Freiburg, 1888.

Phil 7054.177   Bonfiglioli, Casimiro. Lo spiritismo nella unianità. Bologna, 1888.

Phil 5041.16   Bosanquet, B. Logic, or The morphology of knowledge. Oxford, 1888. 2v.

Phil 2477.1.06   Boutroux, Émile. Philosophical pamphlets, 1888-1909. Paris, 1888-1909.

Phil 1701.14   Brasch, Moritz. Die Philosophie der Gegenwart. Leipzig, 1888.

Phil 4065.11   Bruno, Giordano. Opere. Gottinga, 1888. 2v.

Phil 4065.40   Bruno, Giordano. Spaccio de la bestia trionfante. Roma, 1888.

Phil 4210.133   Bulgarini, G.B. La storia della questione rosminiana. Milano, 1888.

Phil 5325.16   Burchhardt, F. Die Vorstellungsreihe. Meissen, 1888.

Phil 9530.1   Butler, B.F. How to get rich. Boston, 1888.

Phil 1900.76   Butler, Joseph. Sermons I, II, III upon human nature. Edinburgh, 1888.

Phil 3822.1   Caird, John. Spinoza. Philadelphia, 1888.

Phil 2402.2   Caro, E.M. Philosophie et philosophes. Paris, 1888.

Phil 177.7   Carpenter, W.B. Nature and man. London, 1888.

Phil 1802.1   Carrau, L. La philosophie religieuse en Angleterre. Paris, 1888.

Phil 9075.20   Carrau, Ludovic. La conscience psychologique et morale. Paris, 1888.

Phil 630.14.501   Case, Thomas. Physical realism. London, 1888.

Phil 177.71   Ceballos Dosamantes, J. El perfeccionismo absoluto. México, 1888.

Phil 4080.10.35   Ceretti, Pietro. Saggio circa la ragione logica di tutte le cose (Pasaelogices specimen). v.1-5. Torino, 1888-1905. 7v.

Phil 5242.17   Clark, William. The formation of opinion. Cambridge, 1888?

Phil 9342.5   Collyer, R. Talks to young men. Boston, 1888.

Phil 177.19.15   Conti, Augusto. L'armonia delle cose. Firenze, 1888. 2v.

Phil 8692.2.1   Cooke, J.P. The credentials of science, the warrant of faith. 2. ed. N.Y., 1888.

Phil 6952.10   Cowles, E. Insistent and fixed ideas. Baltimore, 1888.

Phil 8877.27   Craufurd, A.H. Enigmas of the spiritual life. London, 1888.

Phil 7068.88.10   Cumberland, Stuart. A thought-reader's thoughts. London, 1888.

Phil 7054.7.5   Davenport, R.B. The death blow to spiritualism...true story of the Fox sisters. N.Y., 1888.

Phil 7103.2   Dessoir, Max. Bibliographie des modernen Hypnotismus. Berlin, 1888.

Phil 178.17.10   Dessoir, Max. Bibliographie des modernen Hypnotismus. n.p., 1888-1913. 25 pam.

Phil 6113.13.3   Dewey, J.H. The way, the truth and the life...Christian theosophy. 3d ed. N.Y., 1888.

Phil 3552.299   Dieckhoff, A.W. Leibnitz Stellung zur Offenbarung. Rostock, 1888.

Phil 9010.17   Dix, M. The drift of the age. Springfield, 1888.

Phil 8878.26   Döring, A. Philosophische Güterlehre. Berlin, 1888.

Phil 8735.12   Domet de Vorges, E. Cause efficiente et cause finale. Paris, 1888.

Phil 8693.3   Dove, J. A vindication of the divine authority. n.p., 1888.

Phil 8693.5.20   Drummond, H. Naturens lagar och andens verld. Stockholm, 1888.

Phil 5627.70   Dupain, J.M. Etude clinique sur le délire religieux. Thèse. Paris, 1888.

Phil 7060.34   Du Prel, C.F. Die monistische Seelenlehre. Leipzig, 1888.

Phil 6674.7   Edgerley, W.J. Lessons in the mechanics of personal magnetism. Washington, D.C., 1888.

Phil 3486.2   Erhardt, Franz. Kritik der Kantischen Antinomienlehre. Cöthen, 1888.

Phil 179.3   Eucken, R. Die Einheit des Geisteslebens. Leipzig, 1888.

Phil 5545.8   Fauth, P. Das Gedächtnis. Gütersloh, 1888.

Phil 1200.6   Favre, Jules. La morale des stoiciens. Paris, 1888.

Phil 1110.1.7   Ferrier, J.F. Philosophical works. v.2. Edinburgh, 1888.

Phil 5755.2A   Fischer, E.K.B. Über die menschliche Freiheit. Heidelberg, 1888.

Phil 180.18.5   Flügel, D. Die Probleme der Philosophie und ihre Lösungen historisch-critisch Dargestellt. 2.Aufl. Cöthen, 1888.

Phil 6115.9   Fromentel, Henry de. Les synalgies et les synesthésies. Paris, 1888.

Phil 8585.22   Frothingham, E.L. Christian philosophy. / Baltimore, 1888-1890. 2v.

Phil 7150.2   Geiger, K.A. Der Selbstmord. Augsburg, 1888.

Phil 5046.9.5   Gilmore, J.H. Outlines of logic. N.Y., 1888.

Phil 8631.10   Girard, Victor. La transmigration des âmes. Paris, 1888.

Phil 3488.9   Gizycki, G. von. Kant und Schopenhauer. Leipzig, 1888.

Phil 3552.93.5   Glöckner, G. Der Gottesbegriff bei Leibniz. Langensalza, 1888.

Phil 181.27   Gourd, J.J. Le phénomène; esquisse de philosophie générale. Paris, 1888.

Phil 3808.85   Grisebach, E.R. Edita und Inedita Schopenhaueriana. Leipzig, 1888.

Phil 5640.34   Grotenfelt, A. Das Webersche Gesetz und die psychische Relativatät. Helsingfors, 1888.

Phil 3808.86.15   Gwinner, W. Denkrede auf Arthur Schopenhauer. Leipzig, 1888.

Phil 8697.2   Hark, J.M. The unity of truth in Christianity and evolution. N.Y., 1888.

Phil 3415.15   Hartmann, Eduard von. Ausgewählte Werke. Leipzig, 1888. 12v.

Phil 3415.61.3   Hartmann, Eduard von. Die des Christenthums. 3. Aufl. Leipzig, 1888.

Phil 3415.71.2   Hartmann, Eduard von. Moderne Probleme. 2. Aufl. Leipzig, 1888.

Phil 3565.81   Hartmann, K.R.E. Lotze's Philosophie. Leipzig, 1888.

Phil 5247.57   Hill, D.J. Elements of psychology. N.Y., 1888.

Phil 672.15   Hinton, Charles H. A new era of thought. London, 1888.

Phil 8882.16   Höffding, H. Ethik. Leipzig, 1888.

Phil 400.3   Holmes, N. Realistic idealism in philosophy itself. Boston, 1888. 2v.

Phil 7054.45.5   Home, Daniel Dunglas (Mrs.). D.D. Home, his life and mission. London, 1888.

Phil 7060.18   Hoppe, J.F. Erklärung der Sinnestäuschungen. Würzburg, 1888.

Phil 270.8   Houten, S. van. Causalitäs-Gesetz in der Socialwissen. Harlem, 1888.

Phil 2050.75   Hume, David. Letters. Oxford, 1888.

Phil 2050.53   Hume, David. Treatise on human nature. Oxford, 1888.

Phil 184.20   Jacquinet, M. Essai de philosophie pour tous. Paris, 1888.

Phil 4210.91   Jarvis, Stephen E. Rosmini, a Christian philosopher. 2. ed. Market Weighton, 1888.

Phil 5049.4.2.5   Jevons, W.S. Elementary lessons in logic. London, 1888.

Phil 5759.4   Joyau, Emmanuel. Essai sur la liberté morale. Paris, 1888.

Phil 3480.76   Kant, Immanuel. Das nachgelassene Werk. Lahr, 1888.

Phil 3480.25   Kant, Immanuel. Philosophy of Kant as contained in extracts. N.Y., 1888.

Phil 5545.17   Kay, D. Memory. London, 1888.

Phil 5545.17.3   Kay, D. Memory. N.Y., 1888.

Phil 5440.10   Kendall, H. The kinship of men. Boston, 1888.

Phil 5250.10   Kirchner, F. A student's manual of psychology. London, 1888.

Phil 6960.8   Kirehhoff. Beziehungen das Dämonen- und Hexenwesens zur deutschen Irrenpflege. Berlin, 1888.

Phil 4655.1.82   Kjellberg, Elis. Carl Pontus Wikner. Upsala, 1888.

Phil 3830.4   Kniat, Joseph. Spinoza's Ethik gegenüber der Erfahrung. Posen, 1888.

Phil 3808.89.5   Koeber, R. von. Die Philosophie Arthur Schopenhauers. Heidelberg, 1888.

Phil 270.15   Koenig, E. Entwickelung des Casualproblems. Leipzig, 1888.

Phil 6680.2   Krafft-Ebing, R. von. Eine experimentelle Studie. Stuttgart, 1888.

Phil 6960.4.3   Krafft-Ebing, R. von. Lehrbuch der Psychiatrie. 3. Aufl. Stuttgart, 1888.

Phil 1145.22   Kühn, O. Sittlichen Ideen der Griechen. Leipzig, 1888.

Phil 9430.6   Küssner, G. Kritk des Pessimismus. Leipzig, 1888.

Phil 8591.33   Labanca, B. Della religione e della filosofia cristiana. Pt.2. Torino, 1888.

Phil 5585.11.11F   La Rive, Lucien de. Sur la collection des sensations. Genève, 1888.

Phil 5325.22   Lehmann, A. Om gedenkelse. Kjóbenhavn, 1888.

Phil 8961.11   Lehmkuhl, A. Theologia moralis. Freiburg, 1888. 2v.

Phil 8836.4   Lessona, Marco. La storia della filosofia morale; studio. Torino, 1888.

Phil 1135.31   Liebeck, H. Untersuchungen zur Philosophie der Griechen. 2nd ed. Freiburg, 1888.

Phil 186.31   Lightfoot, John. Studies in philosophy. Edinburgh, 1888.

Phil 7068.88.20   Lippitt, F.J. Physical proof of another life. Washington, 1888.

Phil 5251.8.25   Lipps, T. Psychologie der Komik. n.p., 1888-1906. 23 pam.

Phil 3831.10   Lotsij, M.C.L. Spinoza's wijsbegeerte. Utrecht, 1888-?

Phil 8412.19.5   Lotze, Hermann. Grundzüge der Asthetik; Diktate aus den Vorlesungen. 2. Aufl. Leipzig, 1888.

Phil 8612.21   Lovatelli, E. Thanatos. Roma, 1888.

Phil 1850.84.2   Lovejoy, B.G. Francis Bacon. London, 1888.

Phil 3425.228   Lucia, V. de. L'Hegel in Italia. Vasto, 1888.

Phil 8961.3   Luthardt, C.E. Geschichte der christlichen Ethik. Leipzig, 1888-93. 2v.

Phil 400.5   Lyon, G. L'idéalisme en Angleterre. Paris, 1888.

Phil 2125.50.3   McCosh, James. Psychology: the motive powers. N.Y., 1888.

Phil 3625.5.78.10   Maimon, Salomon. Salomon Maimon. Boston, 1888.

Phil 7076.14   Mantegazza, Paolo. Die Ekstasen des Menschen. Jena, 1888.

Phil 3415.98   Marcus, A. Hartmann's inductive Philosophie im Chassidismus. Wien, 1888.

Phil 1517.4   Martigné, P. de. La scolastique et les traditions franciscaines. Paris, 1888.

Phil 8702.5   Martin, J.L. Anti-evolution: Girardeau vs. Woodrow. Memphis, Tenn.? 1888.

Phil 2520.120   Martin, W.A.P. The Cartesian philosophy before Descartes. Peking, 1888.

Phil 8592.6   Martineau, James. Study of religion. Oxford, 1888. 2v.

Phil 8592.6.3   Martineau, James. A study of religion. Oxford, 1888. 2v.

Phil 8592.6.4   Martineau, James. A study of religion. 1. American ed. Oxford, 1888. 2v.

Phil 6122.31   Mercier, Charles A. The nervous system and the mind. London, 1888.

Phil 6122.52   Merriman, H.B. (Mrs.). What shall make us whole? Boston, 1888.

NEDL Phil 5545.50   Middleton, A.E. Memory systems. 1. American ed. N.Y., 1888.

Phil 8637.18   Mifflin, Mildred. Out of darkness into light. Shelbyville, 1888.

Phil 8667.6   Momerie, A.W. Belief in God. Edinburgh, 1888.

Phil 8592.20   Monaco, C. La ragione naturale. Caserta, 1888.

Phil 6750.5   Moreau, P. Fous et Bouffons. Paris, 1888.

Phil 4065.83   Morselli, E. Giordano Bruno. Torino, 1888.

Phil 5252.12   Münsterberg, H. Beiträge zur experimentische Psychologie. Freiberg, 1888-92.

Phil 5762.3   Münsterberg, H. Die Willenshandlung. Freiburg, 1888.

Phil 6122.23.1   Mulford, Prntice. Your forces and how to use them. N.Y., 1888-92. 6v.

Phil 5252.14   Murray, J.C. Handbook of psychology. Boston, 1888.

Phil 4210.81.15   Nardi, P. de. La compagnia di Gesu et la recente condanna di A. Rosmini. Intra, 1888. 5 pam.

Phil 5253.1   Natorp, P. Einleitung in die Psychologie. Freiburg, 1888.

Phil 1850.87   Nichol, J. Bacon. Philadelphia, 1888-89. 2v.

Phil 3640.11.4   Nietzsche, Friedrich. Der Fall Wagner; und die Geburt der Trajödie. Leipzig, 1888.

Phil 2805.85.5   Nourrisson, J.F. Pascal physicien et philosophe. Défense de Pascal. Paris, 1888.

Phil 6963.2   Noyes, W. Paranoia. Baltimore, 1888-89.

Phil 6124.1   Obersteiner, H. Anleitung beim Studium des Baues der nervösen Centratorgane. Leipzig, 1888.

Phil 3552.266   Ohse, Jakob. Untersuchungen über den Substansbegriff bei Leibniz. Inaug.-Diss. Dorpat, 1888.

Phil 8594.5.2   Oliphant, L. Scientific religion. 2. ed. Edinburgh, 1888.

Phil 1850.151   Pamer, C. Bacon von Verulam und seine Stellung in der Geschichte der Philosophie. Triest, 1888.

Phil 8416.30   Parker, H.W. The spirit of beauty; essays, scientific and aesthetic. N.Y., 1888.

Phil 2805.42.2   Pascal, Blaise. The thoughts of Blaise Pascal. London, 1888.

Phil 960.149.5   Paul, N.C. A treatise on the Yoga philosophy. 3d ed. Bombay, 1888.

Phil 8610.888   Pearson, Karl. The ethic of freethought. London, 1888.

Phil 5545.21   Pick, E. Memory and its doctors. London, 1888.

Phil 9430.5   Plümacher, O. Der Pessimismus. Heidelberg, 1888.

Phil 8705.4.2   Powell, E.P. Our heredity from God. 2. ed. N.Y., 1888.

Phil 3808.85.15   Reich, Emil. Schopenhauer als Philosoph der Tragödie. Wien, 1888.

Phil 3499.19   Reichardt, W. Kant's Lehre vom den synthetischen Urtheilen...Mathematik. Leipzig, 1888.

Phil 5257.20   Rémond, A. Recherches expérimentales sur la durée des actes psychiques les plus simples et sur la vitesse des courants. Paris, 1888.

Phil 27.15.5   La revue occidentale. Tables des matières, 1878-1889. Paris, 1888.

Htn   Phil 27.1.5*   Revue philosophique. Tables 1876-1912. Paris, 1888- 4v.

Phil 7060.102.9   Richmond, Almon B. What I saw at Cassadaga lake: Seybert Commission report. Boston, 1888.

Phil 5057.21   Richter, A. Grundlegung der philosophischen Wissenschaften und Elemente der Logik. Halle, 1888.

Phil 3805.159   Ritschl, Otto. Schleiermacher's Stellung zum Christentum. Gotha, 1888.

Phil 1122.3.13   Ritter, Heinrich. Historia philosophiae graecae et romanae. 7.ed. Gotha, 1888.

Phil 3808.140   Rodhe, J. Schopenhauers filosofiska grundtankar i systematisk framställning och Kritisk belysning. Lund, 1888.

Phil 5827.1.13   Romanes, G.J. Animal intelligence. N.Y., 1888.

Phil 5827.1.5   Romanes, G.J. Mental evolution in men. London, 1888.

Phil 3837.4   Rovijen, A.J.L. van. Inventaire de livrés de B. Spinoza. La Haye, 1888.

Phil 5640.23   Rubinstein, S. Aus der Innenwelt. Leipzig, 1888.

Phil 3246.189   Sahlin, Enar. Johann Gottlieb Fichtes idealism. Upsala, 1888.

Phil 8615.1.20   Salter, W.M. Christmas from an ethical standpoint. Chicago, 1888.

Phil 4065.85   Schiattarella, R. La dottrina di Giordano Bruno. Palermo, 1888.

Phil 3425.117   Schmitt, E.H. Das Geheimniss der hegelschen Dialektik. Halle, 1888.

Phil 3808.69.3   Schopenhauer, Arthur. Le fondement de la morale. 3. éd. Paris, 1888.

Phil 6968.2   Schramm, F. Über die Zweifelsucht und Berührungsangst. Berlin, 1888.

Phil 6688.22   Schrenck von Notzing, A. Ein Beitrag zur therapeutischen Verwerthung des Hypnotismus. n.p., 1888-97. 18 pam.

Phil 9150.3.2   Schurman, J.G. The ethical import of Darwinism. N.Y., 1888.

Phil 3552.94   Schwarz, H. Die Leibniz'sche Philosophie. Jena, 1888.

Phil 6968.5   Séglas, J. Paranoia, systematized delusions. N.Y., 1888.

Phil 3120.7.81   Seiling, Max. Mäinlander, ein neuer Messias. München, 1888.

Phil 5258.70   Sergi, G. La psychologie physiologique. Paris, 1888.

Phil 193.24   Sewall, F. The new metaphysics. London, 1888.

Phil 193.25.4   Shields, C.W. Philosophia ultima. N.Y., 1888-1889. 3v.

Phil 3808.167   Siedel, K.G. Die Lehre von der Freiheit bei Kant und Schopenhauer. Inaug. Diss. Erlangen, 1888.

Phil 5058.13.15   Sigwart, H.C.W. Die Impersonalien. Freiburg, 1888.

Phil 7082.152.2   Simon, Paul Max. Le monde des rêves. 2. éd. Paris, 1888.

Phil 8893.14.2   Smiles, Samuel. Life and labour. N.Y., 1888.

Phil 5058.14   Smith, J.C. Culmination of the science of logic. Brooklyn, 1888.

Phil 2270.60.10   Spencer, Herbert. Classification des sciences. Paris, 1888.

Phil 2270.77.10   Spencer, Herbert. The coming slavery and other essays. N.Y., 1888.

Phil 3819.32   Spinoza, Benedictus de. Ethics, demonstrated after the methods of geometers. N.Y., 1888.

Phil 3018.9.5   Stählin, Leonhard. Kant, Lotze, and Ritschl. Leipzig, 1888.

Phil 5545.23   Stokes, W. Memory. London, 1888.

Phil 193.42   Stuckenberg, J.H.W. Introduction to the study of philosophy. N.Y., 1888.

Phil 193.69.8   Stumpf, K. Gustav Engel...Klangfarbe. n.p., 1888-1915. 23 pam.

Phil 5258.25.5.3   Sully, J. Teacher's handbook of psychology. N.Y., 1888.

Phil 2150.8.80   Testimonials in favor of J.S. Mackenzie. Glasgow, 1888. 2 pam.

Phil 3565.123   Thieme, K. Glaube und Wissen bei Lotze. Leipzig, 1888.

Phil 8709.1   Townsend, L.T. The Bible and other ancient literature in the nineteenth century. N.Y., 1888.

Phil 6129.3.3   Tuke, D.H. Geist und Körper. Jena, 1888.

Phil 819.6   Tyler, S. The progress of philosophy. Philadelphia, 1888.

Chronological Listing

Phil 5585.11   Uphues, G.K. Wohrnehmung und Empfindung. Leipzig, 1888.
Phil 8422.6   Valdes Rodriguez, Manuel. Relaciones entre lo bueno, lo bello y lo verdadero. Tesis, 1888.
Phil 5261.5   Varona, Enrique José. Conferencias filosoficas. Havana, 1888.
Phil 3890.1.80   Veeck, O. Darstellung...Trendelenburgs. Gotha, 1888.
Phil 5061.1.11   Venn, J. The logic of chance. London, 1888.

X Cg   Phil 5061.1.11   Venn, J. The logic of chance. London, 1888.
Phil 5545.50.5   Verneuil, Henri. La mémoire au point de vue physiologique. Paris, 1888.
Phil 3841.2   Vold, J.M. Spinozas erkjendelsestheori. Kristiania, 1888.
Phil 5062.27   Wadstein, E.A. "Moralens matematik". Stockholm, 1888.
Phil 978.38   Walker, E.D. Reincarnation. Boston, 1888.
Phil 7060.104.9   Wallace, A.R. If a man die shall he live again? San Francisco, 1888.
Phil 8602.1   Ward, D.J.H. How religion arises. Boston, 1888.
Phil 197.30   Weber, Theodor. Metaphysik. v.1-2. Gotha, 1888-1891.
Phil 8897.7   Wedgwood, J. The moral ideal. London, 1888.
Phil 8972.4   Werner, Karl. System der christlichen Ethik. Regensburg, 1888. 2v.
Phil 8712.3.4   White, Andrew Dickson. New chapters in the warfare of science. (Geology). N.Y., 1888.
Phil 4515.98   Wikner, P. Om den svenske tänkaren Boström. Göteborg, 1888.
Phil 8423.13   Wilkens, Claudius. Aesthetik i ømrids. Kjøbenhavn, 1888.
Phil 2045.82   Wille, B. Der Phänomenalismus der T. Hobbes. Kiel, 1888.
Phil 8602.28.5   Wimmer, Richard. Im Kampf um die Weltanschauung. 3. und 4. Aufl. Freiburg, 1888.
Phil 1127.2.9   Windelband, W. Geschichte der alten Philosophie. Nördlingen, 1888.
Phil 5262.18   Witte, J.H. Das Wesen der Seele und die Natur der geistigen Vorgänge im Lichte. Halle-Saale, 1888.
Phil 3504.17   Wohlrabe, Wilhelm. Kant's Lehre vom Gewissen. Halle, 1888.
Phil 1130.7.5   Zeller, Eduard. Plato and the older academy. London, 1888.

Phil 4655.1.80   Åberg, L.H. Carl Pontus Wikner. Sockholm, 1889.
Phil 475.1   Abendroth, Robert. Das Problem der Materie. v.1. Leipzig, 1889.
Phil 5330.1   Aiken, C. Methods for mind training. N.Y., 1889.
Phil 8875.5   Alexander, S. Moral order and progress. London, 1889.
Phil 8655.3   Anderson, J.H. God or no God. Osceola, Neb., 1889.
Phil 720.1.2   Argyll, G.D.C. What is truth? N.Y., 1889.
Phil 5810.3.2   Avebury, John L. On the senses, instincts, and intelligence of animals. 2nd ed. London, 1889.
Phil 5810.3.3   Avebury, John L. Die Sinne und das geistige Leben der Thiere. Leipzig, 1889.
Phil 9245.9.2.3   Avebury, John Lubbock. The pleasures of life. London, 1889.
Phil 1850.50.4   Bacon, Francis. Novum organum. T. Fowler. 2nd ed. Oxford, 1889.
Phil 5241.3   Baldwin, J.M. Hand book of psychology. Senses and intellect. 1. ed. N.Y., 1889.
Phil 8876.61   Balsillie, David. The ethic of nature and its practical bearings. Edinburgh, 1889.
Phil 3552.80   Barchudarian, J. Inwiefern ist Leibniz in der Psychologie ein Vorgänger Herbarts. Jena, 1889.
Phil 8691.18   Barthélemy-Saint-Hilaire, J. La philosophie dans ses rapports avec les sciences et la religion. Paris, 1889.
Phil 8826.4   Bastian, Adolf. Der ethnischen Ethik. Berlin, 1889.
Phil 4065.116   Battaglini, F. Giordano Bruno e il Vaticano. Roma, 1889.
Phil 6671.16   Beaunis, H. Der künstlich Hervorgerufene Somnambulismus. Leipzig, 1889.
Phil 5635.18   Beaunis, H. Les sensations internes. Paris, 1889.
Phil 672.2   Bellermann, G. Beweis aus der neueren Raumtheorie. Berlin, 1889.
Phil 2475.1.40   Bergson, Henri. Essai sur les données immédiates de la consciènce. Paris, 1889.
Phil 6400.2.2   Bernard, D. De l'aphasie. Paris, 1889.
Phil 4065.82   Berti, D. Giordano Bruno da Nola. Torino, 1889.
Phil 8663.3.85   Bertron, Ottilie. Review of Col. Ingersoll's attacks upon Christianity. Philadelphia, 1889.
Phil 6671.25   Björnström, F.J. Hypnotism. N.Y., 1889.
Phil 1106.9   Blass, F. Ideale und materielle Lebensauschauung. Kiel, 1889.
Phil 978.5.24   Blavatsky, H.P. The key to theosophy. London, 1889.
Phil 978.5.12   Blavatsky, H.P. The voice of the silence. N.Y., 1889.
Phil 978.5.13   Blavatsky, H.P. The voice of the silence. N.Y., 1889.
Phil 4070.1.60   Bonavino, Cristoforo. Ultima critica. Milano, 1889-93. 3v.
Phil 8876.69   Bouillier, F. Questions de morale pratique. Paris, 1889.
Phil 8610.889.5   Bradlaugh, C. Humanity's gain from unbelief. London, 1889.
Phil 978.33   Brailsford-Bright, J. Theosophy and modern socialism. London, 1889.
Phil 3900.1.80   Brasch, M. Welt- und Lebensanschauung Friedrich Ueberweg. Leipzig, 1889.
Phil 5751.7.3   Bray, Charles. The philosophy of necessity. 3. ed. London, 1889.
Phil 8876.41.6   Brentano, Franz. Vom Ursprung sittlicher Erkenntnis. Leipzig, 1889.
Phil 7054.25   Brown, Robert. Demonology and witchcraft. London, 1889.
Phil 600.5   Brütt, M. Der Positivismus. Hamburg, 1889.
Phil 4065.41   Bruno, Giordano. Reformation des Himmels. Leipzig, 1889.
Phil 4065.50.2   Bruno, Giordano. Von der Ursache, dem Princip und dem Einen. 2. Ausg. Heidelberg, 1889.
Phil 978.46   Buck, J.D. The nature and aim of theosophy. Cincinnati, 1889.
Phil 1106.6   Burt, B.C. Brief history of Greek philosophy. Boston, 1889.
Phil 3484.1.3A   Caird, E. A critical account of the philosophy of Kant. Glasgow, 1889. 2v.
Phil 3484.1.5   Caird, E. A critical account of the philosophy of Kant. v.2. N.Y., 1889.
Phil 5003.5   Cambridge. University. Library. Catalog of a collection of books on philosophy. Cambridge, 1889.
Phil 720.1   Campbell, G.D. What is truth? Edinburgh, 1889.
Phil 9430.3   Caro, E.M. Le pessimisme au XIX siècle. 4. éd. Paris, 1889.
Phil 177.8   Carus, Paul. Fundamental problems. Chicago, 1889.
Phil 8610.889   Christianity and agnosticism. N.Y., 1889.
Phil 3484.2.25   Cohen, H. Kant's Begrundung der Aesthetik. Berlin, 1889.

Phil 4065.121   Comandini, A. Per Giordano Bruno dal 1876 al 1889. Roma, 1889.
Phil 2490.78   Comte, Auguste. Lettres à des positivistes anglais. London 1889. 2v.
Phil 2490.78.10   Comte, Auguste. Lettres à Richard Congreve. London, 1889.
Phil 6672.5   Congrès Internationale de L'Hypnotisme. Comptes rendue. Paris, 1889.
Phil 978.15.4   Cook, M.C. Light on the path. Boston, 1889.
Phil 6672.6   Coste, P. Marie Léon. L'inconscient étude sur l'hypnotisme. Paris, 1889.
Phil 2138.82.5   Courtney, W.S. Life of John Stuart Mill. London, 1889.
Phil 2138.82.7A   Courtney, W.S. Life of John Stuart Mill. London, 1889.
Phil 8877.48   Cutler, Carroll. The beginnings of ethics. N.Y., 1889.
Phil 7080.37   Dandolo, G. La coscienza nel sonno. Padova, 1889.
Phil 630.8   Dauriac, L. Croyance et réalité. Paris, 1889.
Phil 5635.26   Deichmann, Ludwig. Erregung secundärer Empfindungen im Gebiete der Sinnesorgane. Inaug. Diss. Greifswald, 1889.
Phil 6673.17.10   Delboeuf, J. Le magnétime animal. Paris, 1889.
Phil 5243.7.2   Dewey, John. Psychology. N.Y., 1889.
Phil 8953.1   Döllinger, J.J.I. von. Geschichte der Moralstreitigheiten. v.1-2. Nordlingen, 1889.
Phil 3195.9.83   Druskowitz, H. Eugen Dühring. Heidelberg, 1889.
Phil 178.15   Duboc, K.J. Hundert jahre Zeitgeist in Deutschland. Leipzig, 1889.
Phil 525.2   Du Prel, Karl. Philosophy of mysticism. London, 1889. 2v.
Phil 5642.19   Ellinger, A. Über Doppelempfindung. Diss. Stuttgart, 1889.
Phil 5545.7   Evans, W.L. Memory training. N.Y., 1889.
Phil 9145.6   Eyre, L.L. Fashionable society. Philadelphia, 1889.
Phil 8660.6   Faber, F.W. The creator and the creature. London, 1889.
Phil 2730.83   Favre, Charles. Essai sur la métaphysique...de Maine de Biran. Antibes, 1889.
Phil 2405.2.5   Ferraz, Marin. Histoire de la philosophie pendant la révolution (1789-1804). Paris, 1889.
Phil 3246.26   Fichte, Johann Gottlieb. Popular works. London, 1889. 2v.

X Cg   Phil 3246.60   Fichte, Johann Gottlieb. Science of rights. London, 1889.
Phil 1705.4.4   Fischer, K. Geschichte der neueren Philosophie. v.1-8. Heidelberg, 1889-1901. 10v.
Phil 180.19.5   Fouillée, Alfred. L'avenir de la metaphysique fondée sur l'experience. Paris, 1889.
Phil 5045.3   Freyer, Paul. Beispiele zur Logik. Berlin, 1889.
Phil 4006.1   Gabotto, F. L'epicureismo italiano. Piemonte, 1889.
Phil 4070.1.85   Galletti, B. Critica dell'Ultima critica di Cristoforo Bonavino. Palermo, 1889.
Phil 6316.3   Gérard, J. La grande névrose. Paris, 1889.
Phil 8881.12.5   Gizycki, G. Students manual of ethical philosophy. London, 1889.
Phil 2138.93   Gomperz, T. John Stuart Mill. Wien, 1889.
Phil 6619.12   Grafé, A. Étude sur quelques paralysies d'origine psychique. Bruxelles, 1889.
Phil 181.17   Greppo, C. The exegesis of life. N.Y., 1889.
Phil 3450.10.80   Groenewegen, H.J. Paulus van Hermert, als godgeleerde en als wijsgeer. Proefschrift. Amsterdam, 1889.
Phil 6615.2   Guinon, Georges. Les agents provocateurs de l'hystérie. Paris, 1889.
Phil 1050.4   Guttmann, J. Die philosophie der Soloman ibn Gabirol. Göttingen, 1889.
Phil 8882.36   Harms, F. Ethik. Leipzig, 1889.
Phil 182.5   Harris, W.T. Introduction to the study of philosophy. N.Y., 1889.
Phil 8610.889.10   Hart, William. The candle from under the bushel. N.Y., 1889.
Phil 338.2   Hartmann, E. von. Das Grundproblem der Erkenntnissth. Leipzig, 1889.
Phil 3415.72   Hartmann, Eduard von. Kritische Wanderungen durch die Philosophie der Gegenwart. Leipzig, 1889.
Phil 182.44.5   Hartmann, F. The life of Jehoshua, the prophet of Nazareth. Boston, 1889.
Phil 270.7.10   Hazard, R.G. Causation and freedom in willing. Boston, 1889.
Phil 5757.1.4   Hazard, R.G. Freedom of mind in willing. Boston, 1889.
Phil 8882.32.5   Hensel, P. Ethisches Wissen und ethisches Handeln. Freiburg, 1889.
Phil 6117.1   Herzen, A. Grundlinien einer allgemeinen Psychophysiologie. Leipzig, 1889.
Phil 1850.112   Heussler, Hans. Francis Bacon. Breslau, 1889.
Phil 9347.15   Hewett, M.E.G. High school lectures. London, 1889.
Phil 3827.2   Hissbach, K. Ist ein Durch...Spinoza und Leibniz Vorchanden? Weimar, 1889.
Phil 5047.24   Hjelmérus, Alfred. Formella logiken baserad på identitetsprincipen. Lund, 1889.
Phil 1807.1   Höffding, H. Einleitung in die englische Philosophie. Leipzig, 1889.
Phil 5247.10.19   Höffding, H. Psykologiske undersogeler. Kjøbenhavn, 1889.
Phil 5247.11.7   Hopkins, M. An outline of man; or, The body and mind in one system. N.Y., 1889.
Phil 4110.3.95F   In memoria di Francesco Fiorentino. Catanzaro, 1889.
Phil 8663.3.35   Ingersoll, Robert G. The limits of toleration. N.Y., 1889.
Phil 6958.1.5   Ireland, W.W. Through the ivory gate. Edinburgh, 1889.
Phil 1850.92   Janet, P. Bacon Verulamius. Angers, 1889.
Phil 6959.1   Janet, Pierre. L'automatisme psychologique. Paris, 1889.
Phil 3480.80.79   Kant, Immanuel. Den evigi fred. Fagerhand, 1889.
Phil 3480.30.5A   Kant, Immanuel. Kritik der reinen Vernunft. Berlin, 1889.
Phil 3480.30.5.5   Kant, Immanuel. Kritik der reinen Vernunft. Hamburg, 1889.
Phil 3499.1.5   Kant, Immanuel. Lose blätter aus Kants nach lass, Mitgetheit von Rudolf Reicke. Königsberg, 1889-98.
Phil 3480.27.5   Kant, Immanuel. Lose Blätter aus Kants Nachloss. Königsberg, 1889-98.
Phil 1020.5   Kayser, C. Das Buch von der Erkenntniss der Wahrheit. Leizig, 1889.
Phil 978.37   Kneisel, R. Die Lehre von der Seelenwanderung. Leipzig, 1889.
Phil 8411.3.5   Köstlin, K. Prolegomena zur Ästhetik. Tübingen, 1889.
Phil 3805.182   Kroker, P. Die Tugendlehre Schleiermachers. Erlangen, 1889.
Phil 5251.1.15.3   Ladd, G.T. Elements of physiological psychology. London, 1889.
Phil 186.66   Laffitte, Pierre. Cours de philosophie première. Paris, 1889-1894. 2v.
Phil 4110.3.86   La Giovine Calabria. Giornale. Catanzaro. Per Francesco Fiorentino nella inaugurazione del monumento in Catanzaro. Catanzaro, 1889.

1889 - cont.

Phil 3808.91   Lehmann, E. Die verschiedenartigen Elemente der Schopenhauer'schen Willenslehre. Strassburg, 1889.

Phil 3552.77   Leibniz, Gottfried Wilhelm. Der Briefwechsel. Hannover, 1889.

Phil 6961.3.2   Letchworth, W.P. The insane in foreign countries. N.Y., 1889.

Phil 3425.106   Lévy-Bruhl, L. La théorie de l'état dans Hegel. Paris, 1889.

Phil 6681.4.5   Liébeault, A.A. Le sommeil provoqué et les etats analogues. Paris, 1889.

Phil 5251.7.3   Lindner, G.A. Lehrbuch der empiriochen Psychologie. 9. Aufl. Wien, 1889.

Phil 5251.7.5   Lindner, G.A. Manual of empirical psychology. Boston, 1889.

Phil 4210.83.3   Lockhart, W. Vie d'Antonio Rosmini-Serbati. Paris, 1889.

Phil 5425.4.5   Lombroso, C. L'homme de génie. Paris, 1889.

Phil 3565.60.2   Lotze, Hermann. Grundzüge der Naturphilosophie. 2. Aufl. Leipzig, 1889.

Phil 3493.12   Ludwich, A. Zur Kantfeier der Albertina. Regimontii, 1889.

Phil 2125.30   McCosh, James. First and fundamental truths. N.Y., 1889.

Phil 2125.50.2   McCosh, James. Psychology: the cognitive powers. N.Y., 1889.

Phil 5411.5.4   Mantegazza, P. Fisiologia dell'odio. 4a ed. Milano, 1889.

Phil 5411.5.10   Mantegazza, P. Die Physiologie des Hasses. Jena, 1889.

Phil 1117.2.7   Mayor, J.B. A sketch of ancient philosophy. Cambridge, Eng., 1889.

Phil 4313.1   Menéndez y Pelayo, M. Discurso leído en la universidad central. Madrid, 1889.

Phil 6962.5.5   Meynert, T. Klinische Vorlesungen über Psychiatrie. v.1-2. Wien, 1889-90.

Phil 2035.80.8   Mill, J.S. Examination...Hamilton's philosophy. 6th ed. London, 1889.

Phil 7039.6A   Mitchell, Silas Weir. Mary Reynolds: a case of double consciousness. Philadelphia, 1889.

Phil 5620.4   Mivart, S.G. Origin of human reason. London, 1889.

Phil 187.17.5   Mivart, St. G. On truth. London, 1889.

Phil 3625.5.91   Moeltzner, A. Salomon Maimons erkenntnistheoretische Verbesserungsveruche der Kantischen Philosophie. Inaug. Diss. Greifswald, 1889.

Phil 575.2.3   Momerie, A.W. Personality. 4th ed. Edinburgh, 1889.

Phil 8413.15   Monrad, M.J. Æsthetik. Christiania, 1889-90. 2v.

Phil 6682.12   Morand, J.S. Le magnétisme animal. Paris, 1889.

Phil 5401.1.12   Mosso, A. Die Furcht. Leipzig, 1889.

Phil 7068.89.3   Müller, Egbert. Enthüllung des Spukes von Resau. 3. Aufl. Berlin, 1889.

Phil 6322.2   Müller, F.C. Psychologie des Bewusstseins. Leipzig, 1889.

Phil 8592.15.5   Müller, F.M. Natural religion. London, 1889.

Phil 8887.36   Münsterberg, H. Der Ursprung der Sittlichkeit. Freiburg, 1889.

Phil 3495.15   Nakashima, R. Kant's doctrine of the "thing-in-itself". New Haven, 1889.

Phil 2115.137   Nardi, Pietro de. Caratteri della filosofia di Giovanni Locke. Firenze, 1889.

Phil 3495.2   Nicolai, G.W. Ist der Begriff des Schönen bei Kant. Kiel, 1889.

Phil 3640.32   Nietzsche, Friedrich. Götzen-Dämmerung. Leipzig, 1889.

Phil 5440.2   Nisbet, J.F. Marriage and heredity. London, 1889.

Phil 3495.8.5   Norelius, G. Om Kants sedelära. Upsala, 1889.

Phil 5465.29   Ölzelt-Newin, A. Über Phantasie-Vorstellungen. Graz, 1889.

Phil 8594.5.5   Oliphant, L. Scientific religion. Buffalo, 1889.

Phil 2520.133   Oprescu, Georg. Descartes' Erkenntnisslehre. Inaug.-Diss. Göttingen, 1889.

Phil 6684.3   Ottolenghi, S. Nuovo studi sull'ipnotismo. Torino, 1889.

Phil 5055.22   Papineau, Arthur B. Philosophy II and III in Harvard College. Cambridge, 1889.

Phil 1190.5.5   Pappenheim, E. Der angebliche Heraklitismus des Skeptikers. Berlin, 1889.

Phil 2805.32.6.20   Pascal, Blaise. The provincial letters. London, 1889.

Phil 5255.2   Paulhan, F. L'activité mentale. Paris, 1889.

Phil 8890.6.5   Paulsen, F. System der Ethik. Berlin, 1889.

Phil 5066.12.15   Peano, G. I principii di geometria logicamente esposti. Torino, 1889.

Phil 2225.14   Pearson, A.N. A search for knowledge. Melbourne, 1889.

Phil 8640.4   Phelps, E.S. The struggle for immortality. Boston, 1889.

Phil 190.41   Pichard, P. Doctrine du réel. Paris, 1889.

Phil 5330.1.15   Pilzecker, A. Die Lehre von der sinnlichen Aufmerksamkeit. Inaug. Diss. München, 1889.

Phil 8890.17   Platt, J. Life. N.Y., 1889.

Phil 8705.4.5   Powell, E.P. Liberty and life. Chicago, 1889.

Phil 410.6   Přihonsky, F. B. Bolzano's Paradoxien des Unendlichen. Berlin, 1889.

Phil 8595.9   Pritchard, C. Occasional thoughts...astronomer, nature, revelation. London, 1889.

Phil 1900.83   Pynchon, T.R. Bishop Butler. N.Y., 1889.

Phil 8892.1   Randolph, R. Sober thoughts on staple themes. Philadelphia, 1889.

Phil 5257.9   Raue, C.G. Psychology as a natural science. Philadelphia, 1889.

Phil 4630.2.43   Rein, T. Anteckningar i filosofi och historia. Helsingfors, 1889.

Phil 8597.33   Reischle, Max. Die Frage nach dem Wesen der Religion. Freiburg, 1889.

Phil 5330.4.6   Ribot, T. Psychologie de l'attention. Paris, 1889.

Phil 5330.4.5   Ribot, T. Psychology of attention. N.Y., 1889.

Phil 4065.89.20   Riehl, A. Giordano Bruno. Leipzig, 1889.

Phil 575.5   Ritchie, E. The problem of personality. Ithaca, N.Y., 1889.

Phil 600.36   Robinet, E. Den positiva filosofien i sammandrag. Stockholm, 1889.

Phil 5827.1.6   Romanes, G.J. Mental evolution in man, origin of human faculty. N.Y., 1889.

Phil 3565.114   Rosenquist, G.G. Lotzes religionsfilosofi. Helsingfors, 1889.

Phil 5500.9   Rosinski, A. Das Urteil und die Lehre vom synthetischen Charakter desselben. Leipzig, 1889.

Phil 4210.65   Rosmini-Werbati, Antonio. Quaranta proposizioni attribute ad A. Rosmini. Milano, 1889.

Phil 6687.11   Rossi-Pagnoni, F. Quelques essais de médiumnité hypnotique. Paris, 1889.

Phil 6053.6   St. Hill, Katharine. Hands of celebrities. Westminster, 1889?

Phil 8615.1   Salter, W.M. Ethical religion. Boston, 1889.

Phil 5649.8.5   Schäfer, Karl. Die Erklärung der Bewegungsempfindungen. Inaug. Diss. Jena, 1889.

1889 - cont.

Phil 3801.777   Schirnhafer, R. von. Vergleich zwischen den Lehren Schelling's und Spinoza's. Zürich, 1889.

Phil 193.153   Schmick, J.H. Geist oder Stoff? Leipzig, 1889.

Phil 9530.8   Schmidt, F.L. An object in life. N.Y., 1889.

Phil 9075.23   Schmidt, W. Das Gewissen. Leipzig, 1889.

Phil 3808.55   Schopenhauer, Arthur. Pensées et fragments. 9. éd. Paris, 1889.

Phil 3808.51.5   Schopenhauer, Arthur. Two essays. London, 1889[1888]

Phil 1730.10   Seredi, P. Lajos. Az ismeret eredetének kérdése a XVII és XVIII szazad filozofiai küzdelmeiben Kantig. Eperjes, 1889.

Phil 4210.134   Sernagiotto, L. Antonio Rosmini all'estero. Venezia, 1889.

Phil 3500.22   Seydel, R. Der Schlüssel zum objektiven Erkennen. Halle, 1889.

Phil 299.19   Sidereal evolution, or A new cosmology. Boston, 1889.

Phil 5058.12.2   Sigwart, H.C.W. Logik. Freiberg, 1889-1893. 2v.

Phil 5649.8   Souriau, Paul. L'esthétique du mouvement. Paris, 1889.

Phil 2270.35   Spencer, Herbert. Epitome of the synthetic philosophy. N.Y., 1889.

Phil 2270.105   Spicker, Gideon. Spencer's Ansicht über das Verhältniss der Religion zur Wissenschaft. Münster, 1889.

Phil 5258.45.5   Spitta, Heinrich. Die psychologische Forschung und ihre Aufgabe in der Gegenwart. Freiburg, 1889.

Phil 3018.9   Stählin, Leonhard. Kant, Lotze, and Ritschl. Edinburgh, 1889.

Phil 4635.2.33   Starke, C.N. Etikens teoretiske grundlag. Kjøbenhavn, 1889.

Phil 5400.17   Steinitzer, M. Die menschlichen und tierischen Gemütsbewegungen. München, 1889.

Phil 5520.52   Stöhr, Adolf. Umriss einer Theorie der Namen. Leipzig, 1889.

Phil 2138.106   Störring, G.W. John Stuart Mill's Theorie über den psychologischen Ursprung des Vulgärglaubens an die Aussenwelt. Inaug. Diss. Berlin, 1889.

Phil 5258.25.3   Sully, J. Outlines of psychology. 6th ed. London, 1889.

Phil 2885.32.5A   Taine, Hippolyte Adolphe. Lectures on art. 2nd series. N.Y., 1889.

Phil 2885.31.6   Taine, Hippolyte Adolphe. On intelligence. N.Y., 1889. 2v.

Phil 194.1   Taylor, B.S. Helps to understanding of nature. Albion, 1889.

Phil 194.18.5   Teichmüller, G. Neue Grundlegung der Psychologie und Logik. Breslau, 1889.

Phil 2610.81   Thomas, P. Felix. Philosophie de Gassendi. Paris, 1889.

Phil 194.14   Thwing, E.P. Windows of character. N.Y., 1889.

Phil 3552.276   Trepte, Adolf. Die metaphysische Unvollkommenheit...bei Augustin und Leibniz. Inaug. Diss. Halle, 1889.

Phil 7060.99   Tuttle, H. Studies in outlying fields of psychic science. N.Y., 1889.

Phil 5545.71   Uphues, Goswin K. Über die Erinnerung. Leipzig, 1889.

Phil 4260.89   Vadalà-Papale, G. Dati psicologici nella dottrina giuridica. Roma, 1889.

Phil 196.12   Veitch, John. Knowing and being. Edinburg, 1889.

Phil 5061.1   Venn, J. Principles of empirical or inductive logic. London, 1889.

Phil 9430.27   Voigt, G. Der moderne Pessimismus. Heilbronn, 1889.

Phil 196.18   Vold, J.M. Verdensbetragtning, Sokrates og fantasi. Kristiania, 1889.

Phil 3503.4.3   Vorländer, K. Die Kantische Begründung der Moralprinzips. Solingen, 1889.

Phil 8897.38.5   Wallaschek, R. Studien zur Rechtsphilosophie. Leipzig, 1889.

Phil 8897.7.2   Wedgwood, J. The moral ideal. London, 1889.

Phil 5262.10   Welch, A.S. The teacher's psychology. N.Y., 1889.

Phil 8610.889.15   Wheeler, Joseph Mazzini. A bibliographical dictionary of freethinkers of all ages and nations. London, 1889.

Phil 6972.8   White, A.D. New chapters in the warfare of science. v.1-2. N.Y., 1889.

Phil 4655.1.72   Wikner, Pontus. I mensklighetens lifsfrågor. Stockholm, 1889. 2v.

Phil 5374.11.3   Wolff, J. Das Bewusstsein und sein Object. Berlin, 1889.

Phil 2115.100.5   Worcester, E.E. The religious opinions of John Locke. Geneva, N.Y., 1889.

Phil 2115.100   Worcester, E.E. The religious opinions of John Locke. Thesis. Geneva, N.Y., 1889.

Phil 3915.30   Wundt, Wilhelm. System der Philosophie. Leipzig, 1889.

Phil 1130.5.4   Zeller, Eduard. Outlines of history of Greek philosophy. N.Y., 1889.

189-

Phil 978.6.61.5   Besant, Annie. The seven principles of man. 15th ed. London, 1889.

Phil 978.6.70   Besant, Annie. The sphinx of theosophy. London, 189-?

Phil 6060.1.4   Crepieux-Jamin, J. L'ecriture et le caractère. 6e ed. Paris, 189-?

Phil 3195.6.79.6   Dilthey, Wilhelm. Biographisch-literarischer Grundriss der allgemeinen Geschichte der Philosophie. 6. Aufl. Trebnitz, 189-.

Phil 8693.5.14   Drummond, H. Natural law in the spiritual world. N.Y., 189-.

Phil 7054.45.50   Gardy, Louis. Le médium D.D. Home. Genève, 189-.

Phil 8663.3.83   The great Ingersoll controversy. Photoreproduction. N.Y., 189-?

Phil 2050.87.5   Huxley, Thomas H. Hume. N.Y., 189-?

Phil 8610.890.20   Kelso, John R. The real blasphemers. N.Y., 189-?

Phil 575.2.5   Momerie, A.W. Personality. Edinburgh, 189-?

Phil 3640.64.5   Nietzsche, Friedrich. Unzeigemässe Betrachtungen. Leipzig, 189-?

Phil 3640.11.5   Nietzsche, Friedrich. Unzeitgemässe Betrachtungen. Leipzig, 189-?

Phil 6968.5.15   Séglas, J. Le délire des négations. Paris, 189-.

Phil 2270.74.12   Spencer, Herbert. Data of ethics. NY., 189-?

Phil 5627.1.5   Starbuck, E.D. A study of conversion. n.p., 189-?

Phil 7068.95   Tindall, A.F. Spiritual Christianity revealed by occultism. London, 189-.

1890

Phil 8580.1   Abbot, F.E. The way out of agnosticism. Boston, 1890.

Phil 1850.103   Adam, Charles. Philosophie de François Bacon. Paris, 1890.

Phil 7060.103.5   Aksakov, Aleksandr N. Animismus und spiritismus...als Entgegnung auf Dr. Ed. V. Hartmann's Werk "Der Spiritismus". Leipzig, 1890.

1890 - cont.

Phil 9160.8 Alcalde Prieto, D. Cuadros de familia. Valladolid, 1890.
Phil 8655.6 Alden, H.M. God in his world. N.Y., 1890.
Phil 8875.4 Alexander, A. A theory of conduct. N.Y., 1890.
Phil 5643.2 Angelucci, A. Untersuchungen über die Sehthätigkeit. Giessen, 1890.
Phil 1135.68 Baeumker, C. Das Probleme der Materie in der griechischen Philosophie. Münster, 1890.
Phil 5241.3.3 Baldwin, J.M. Handbook of psychology. Senses and intellect. N.Y., 1890.
Phil 5241.5.3 Ballauf, L. Die Grundlehren der Psychologie und ihre Anwendung auf die Lehre. Cöthen, 1890.
Phil 6400.1.3 Ballet, G. Die innerliche Sprache und die verschiedenen Formen der Aphasie. Leipzig, 1890.
Phil 8876.96 Barnett, M.J. The five redeemers. Boston, 1890.
Phil 1850.111 Barthélemy-Sainte-Hilaire, Jules. Étude sur François Bacon. Paris, 1890.
Phil 801.16.5 Baumann, J. Geschichte der Philosophie nach Ideengehalt und Beweisen. Gotha, 1890.
Phil 6951.16 Bennett, C. The modern malady. London, 1890.
Phil 9550.15A Bentham, J. Utilitarianism. London, 1890.
Phil 3915.162 Benzoni, R. Esposizione analitica del sistema di filosofia di Guglielmo Wundt. Palermo, 1890.
Phil 5640.2.4 Bernstein, J. Five senses of man. N.Y., 1890.
Phil 978.6.4 Besant, Annie. Why I became a theosophist. N.Y., 1890.
Phil 5203.1 Bibliographie der Psycho-Physiologischen. Hamburg, 1890.
Phil 8402.4 Biese, Alfred. Das Associationsprincip und der Anthropomorphismus in der Ästhetik. Kiel, 1890.
Phil 7042.4 Binet, Alfred. On double consciousness. Chicago, 1890.
Phil 5241.49 Bleibtreu, K. Zur Psychologie der Zukunft. Leipzig, 1890.
Phil 1050.9 Bois, Henri. Essai sur les origines se la philosophie. Paris, 1890.
Phil 8876.74 Bolliger, Adolf. Beiträge zur Dogmatik und Ethik. Aaran, 1890.
Phil 2840.85 Bonnard, Edmond. Le criticisme de M. Renouvier. Thèse. Lausanne, 1890.
Phil 4065.94A Brinton, D.G. Giordano Bruno. Philadelphia, 1890.
Phil 176.33.10 Büchner, L. Fremdes und Eignes. Leipzig, 1890.
Phil 6112.24 Cappie, James. Intra-cranial circulation and its relation to physiology of brain. Edinburgh, 1890.
Phil 5242.20 Cardols, Joseph. Eléments de psychologie. Namur, 1890.
Phil 9530.2 Carnegie, A. How to win fortune. N.Y., 1890.
Phil 22.6.5 Carus, P. Monism: its scope and review of The Monist. Chicago, 1890-1891.
Phil 8877.41 Carus, Paul. The ethical problem. Chicago, 1890.
Phil 4080.10.60 Ceretti, Pietro. Opere postume. Torino, 1890.
Phil 665.38 Coconnier, M.J. L'âme humaine. Paris, 1890.
Phil 5135.4 Coleridge, J.D. Thinking for ourselves. v.1-2. London, 1890.
Phil 5752.2.10 Collins, A. Philosophical inquiry...human liberty. London, 1890.
Phil 6112.19 Colville, W.W.J. Spiritual therapeutics. Chicago, 1890.
Phil 8610.890.10 Contra el altar y el trono; artículos varios, publicados en "El Progreso" de 1884-85 por su director, R. Verea. N.Y., 1890.
Phil 9230.2 Convocation of the Province of York. Report of the committee on betting and gambling. London, 1890.
Phil 4260.102.10 Cotugno, R. Giovambattista Vico. Il suo secolo e le sue opere. Pt.1. Trani, 1890.
Phil 2115.104 Curtis, M.M. An outline of Locke's ethical philosophy. Leipzig, 1890.
Phil 8610.890.35 La dea ragione. Milano, 1890.
Phil 6673.17 Delboeuf, J. Magnétiseurs et médecins. Paris, 1890.
Phil 7103.2.1 Dessoir, Max. Bibliographie des modernen Hypnotismus. Nachtrag. Berlin, 1890.
Phil 7042.2 Dessoir, Max. Das Doppel-Ich. Leipzig, 1890.
Phil 178.5 Deussen, P. Elemente der Metaphysik. 2. Aufl. Leipzig, 1890.
Phil 334.2 Du Bois-Reymond, P. Über die Grundlagen der Erkenntnis in der exacten Wissenschaften. Tübingen, 1890.
Phil 5374.47 Dwelshauvers, G. Psychologie de l'apperception. Bruxelles, 1890.
Phil 804.3.5 Erdmann, J.E. History of philosophy. London, 1890. 3v.
Phil 804.3.7 Erdmann, J.E. History of philosophy. v.1, 2d ed.; v.2, 3d ed. London, 1890-92. 2v.
Phil 8735.13 Erhart, Franz. Mechanismus und Teleologie. Leipzig, 1890.
Phil 8829.2 Eucken, Rudolf. Die Lebensanschauungen der grossen Denker. Leipzig, 1890.
Phil 5044.3.5 Everett, C.C. The science of thought. Rev. ed. Boston, 1890.
Phil 3005.3.7 Falckenberg, Richard. Über die gegenwärtige Lage der deutschen Philosophie. Leipzig, 1890.
Phil 3487.13 Falkenheim, H. Die Entstehung der Kantischen Ästhetik. Diss. Berlin, 1890.
Phil 6955.1.5 Falret, J.P. Études cliniques sur les maladies mentales et nerveuses. Paris, 1890.
Phil 6115.2.2 Farges, A. Le cerveau, l'âme et les facultés. Paris, 1890.
Phil 3210.75 Fechner, G.T. Wissenschaftliche Briefe. Hamburg, 1890.
Phil 5245.19 Feldegg, F. Das Gefühl als Fundament der Weltordnung. Wien, 1890.
Phil 6115.3 Ferrier, D. The Croonian lectures on cerebral localisation. London, 1890.
Phil 180.33 Fischer, Ludwig. Grundriss des Systems der Philosophie als Bestimmungslehre. Wiesbaden, 1890.
Phil 286.2.5 Fiske, J. Outlines of cosmic philosophy. 11. ed. Boston, 1890. 2v.
Phil 8610.890 Fitzgerald, P.F. (Mrs.). A protest against agnosticism. London, 1890.
Phil 5525.9 Fleet, F.R. Theory of wit and humor. London, 1890.
Phil 180.7 Flournoy, T. Métaphysique et psychologie. Genève, 1890.
Phil 5627.78 Foster, R.S. Philosophy of Christian experience. 3d series. N.Y., 1890.
Phil 336.1 Fouillée, A. L'évolutionnisme des idées-forces. Paris, 1890.
Phil 5812.4 Foveau de Courmelles, F.V. Les facultés mentales des animaux. Paris, 1890.
Phil 6675.7 Foveau de Courmelles, F.V. L'hypnotisme. Paris, 1890.
Phil 180.8.5 Franck, A. Nouveaux essais de critique philosophique. Paris, 1890.
Phil 2115.92 Fraser, A.C. Locke. Edinburgh, 1890.
Phil 2115.92.2A Fraser, A.C. Locke. Philadelphia, 1890.
Phil 9220.8 Friendship; Cicero, Bacon, Emerson. Chicago, 1890.
Phil 3487.15 Fröhlich, G. Immanuel Kant. Langensalza, 1890.
Phil 8881.1 G., W.A. The contrast: duty and pleasure, right and wrong. London, 1890.

Phil 8030.4 Gayley, Charles. A guide to the literature of aesthetics. Berkeley, 1890.
Phil 4363.3.110 Gestoso y Pérez, José. Valdes y Mañara. Sevilla, 1890.
Phil 7082.132 Giessler, Carl Max. Aus den Tiefen des Traumlebens. Halle-Saale, 1890.
Phil 3488.10 Gisevius, H. Kant's Lehre von Raum und Zeit. Hannover, 1890.
Phil 665.13 Glanvill, Joseph. A letter on praeexistence to Richard Baxter. Osceola, 1890.
Phil 806.4 Gonzalez, Z. Histoire de la philosophie. Paris, 1890-91. 4v.
Phil 1050.18 Gortein, H. Der Optimismus und Pessimismus in der jüdischen Religionsphilosophie. Berlin, 1890.
Phil 2020.30.3A Green, T.H. Prolegomena to ethics. 3d ed. Oxford, 1890.
Phil 5046.15 Gross, Peter. Vorschule der Logik. Berlin, 1890.
Phil 2270.125 Grosse, Ernst. Herbert Spencer's Lehre von dem Unerkennbaren. Leipzig, 1890.
Phil 5246.19 Gutberlet, C. Die Psychologie. 2. Aufl. Münster, 1890.
Phil 8882.43 Hansen, Hans C. Moral, religion og videnskab. Kjøbenhavn, 1890.
Phil 3425.86 Harris, W.T. Hegel's logic. Chicago, 1890.
Phil 7068.90.10 Haven, Gilbert. Heavenly messenger. Washington, 1890.
Phil 3808.88 Hertslet, M.L. Schopenhauers-Register. Leipzig, 1890.
Phil 338.6.3 Heymans, G. Die Gesetze und Elemente des wissenschaftlichen Denkens. v.1-2. Leiden, 1890-94.
Phil 8632.12 Hirn, G.A. La vie future et la science moderne. Colmar, 1890.
Phil 5047.14.5 Höfler, Alois. Philosophische Propädeutik. Prag, 1890.
Phil 8610.890.30 Holyoake, G.J. What would follow on the effacement of Christianity. Buffalo, 1890.
Phil 7054.45 Home, Daniel Dunglas (Mrs.). The gift of D.D. Home. London, 1890.
Phil 8882.22 Hughes, H. Principles, natural and supernatural morals. London, 1890-91. 2v.
Phil 182.59 Hugueny, Charles. Système de la nature. Nancy, 1890.
Phil 7059.12.13 Hull, Moses. All about devils. Chicago, 1890.
Phil 7059.12.11 Hull, Moses. Jesus and the mediums. Chicago, 1890.
Phil 18.1.5 International journal of ethics. Seventy-five year index. Chicago, 1890. 2v.
Phil 5435.8A James, William. Habit. N.Y., 1890.
Phil 5249.2A James, William. Principles of psychology. N.Y., 1890. 2v.
Htn Phil 5249.2* James, William. Principles of psychology. N.Y., 1890. 2v.
Phil 5249.2.01A James, William. Principles of psychology. N.Y., 1890. 2v.
NEDL Phil 5249.2.01 James, William. Principles of psychology. v.2. N.Y., 1890.
Phil 2668.65 Janet, Paul A.R. Éléments de philosophie scientifique. Paris, 1890.
Phil 2725.2.85 Janet, Paul A.R. La philosophie de Lamennais. Paris, 1890.
Phil 5249.6.10 Jastrow, J. The time-relations of mental phenomena. n.p. 1890-1912. 10 pam.
Phil 5049.8 Jevons, W.S. Pure logic and other minor works. London, 1890.
Phil 5049.12.9 Jones, E.E.C. Elements of logic as a science of propositions. Edinburgh, 1890.
Phil 9035.4 Jordan, F. Character as seen in body and parentage. London, 1890.
Phil 3480.69 Kant, Immanuel. Allgemeine Naturgeschichte. Theorie des Himmels. Leipzig, 1890.
Phil 2240.82 Kappes, M. Der "common sense" als Princip der Gewissheit. München, 1890.
Phil 341.11 Kauffmann, Max. Fundamente der Erkenntnistheorie und urssenschaftslehre. Leipzig, 1890.
Phil 341.1 Kerry, B. System einer Theorie der Grenzbegriffe. Leipzig, 1890.
Phil 5050.13 Kirchner, F. Katechismus der Logik. Leipzig, 1890.
Phil 95.1 Kirchner, Friedrich. Wörterbuch der philosophischen Grundbegriffe. Heidelberg, 1890.
Phil 4769.1.90 Kireev, A.A. Slavianofil'stvo i natsionalizm; otvet k Solov'evy. Petrograd, 1890.
Phil 5760.2 Klippel, T. Determinismus und Strafe. Berlin, 1890.
Phil 6960.1 Knapp, P.C. The insanity of doubt. Baltimore, 1890.
Phil 185.7 Knight, W. Essays in philosophy. Boston, 1890.
Phil 5250.9 Körner, F. Die Seele und ihre Thätigkeiten. 2. Aufl. Leipzig, 1890.
Phil 186.16 Ladd, G.T. Introduction to philosophy. N.Y., 1890.
Phil 186.42 Lasson, Adolf. Zeitliches und Zeitloses. Leipzig, 1890.
Phil 4112.80 Lastrucci, V. Pasquale Galluppi; studio critico. Firenze, 1890.
Phil 6681.3 Lehmann, A. Die Hypnose. Leipzig, 1890.
Phil 3552.25 Leibniz, Gottfried Wilhelm. Philosophical works. New Haven, 1890.
Phil 5545.18 Leland, C.G. Mastery of memorizing. Harrisburg, 1890-91.
Phil 6961.10 Lewis, W.B. A text-book of mental diseases. Philadelphia, 1890.
Phil 2515.2.125 Liebscher, H. Charron und sien Werk, "de la Sagesse". Leipzig, 1890.
Phil 5761.15 Loewe, Johann H. Die speculative Idee der Freiheit. Prag, 1890.
Phil 6681.12 Luys, J. Leçons cliniques sur les principaux phenomènes de l'hypnotisme. Paris, 1890.
Phil 9245.5 Macmillan, M. The promotion of general happiness. London, 1890.
Phil 8702.4 MacQueary, H. The evolution of man and Christianity. N.Y., 1890.
Phil 5360.1 Maennel, B. Über abstraktion. Gütersloh, 1890.
Phil 6022.1.8 Mantegazza, P. Physiognomik und Mimik. v.1-2. Leipzig, 1890.
Phil 8592.26 Marillier, Léon. La liberté de conscience. Paris, 1890.
Phil 3494.35 Massonius, M. Ueber Kant's Transscendentale Aesthetik. Diss. Leipzig, 1890.
NEDL Phil 8145.2 Menendez y Pelayo. Historia de las ideas. Madrid, 1890.
Phil 6962.4 Mercier, C.A. Sanity and insanity. London, 1890.
Phil 6682.6.15 Moll, Albert. Hypnotism. 2. ed. London, 1890.
Phil 9145.7.5 Montegazza, P. The Tartuffian age. Boston, 1890.
Phil 7150.6 Motta, Emilio. Bibliografia del suicidio. Bellinzona, 1890.
Phil 3832.7 Müller, J. Der Begriff die sittlichen Unvollkommenheit bei Descartes und Spinoza. Leipzig, 1890.
Phil 6122.11.2 Munk, H. Uber die Funktionen der Grosshirnrinde. 2. Aufl. Berlin, 1890.
Phil 8637.19 Murphy, R.W. A key to the secret vault. San Francisco, 1890.

Chronological Listing

1890 - cont.

Phil 5125.6   Naden, Constance C.W. Induction and deduction. London, 1890.

Phil 5053.4   Nagy, Albino. Fondamenti del calcolo logico. Napoli, 1890.

Phil 2115.137.5   Nardi, Pietro de. Del rinnovamento delle dottrine di Gall e...di Locke. Firenze, 1890.

Phil 5053.5.2   Nitsche, Adolf. Lehrbuch der Logik. 2e Aufl. Innsbruck, 1890.

Phil 2270.113   Nörregård, Jens. Studier over Spencer, Lotze og Grundtvig. København, 1890.

Phil 6684.2.3   Osgood, H. Therapeutic value of suggestion. Boston, 1890.

Phil 9355.8   Paine, Harriet E. Girls and women. Boston, 1890.

Phil 2266.82   Paszkowski, W. Adam Smith als Moralphilosoph. Halle, 1890.

Phil 6129.1   Phomson, W.H. Medical aspects of mental dicipline. N.Y., 1890.

Phil 5255.14   Piat, Clodius. L'intellect actif. Thèse. Paris, 1890.

Phil 5255.11   Pikler, Gyula. The psychology of belief in objective existence. pt.1. London, 1890.

Phil 3415.84.2   Plümacher, O. Der Kampf um's Unbewusste. Leipzig, 1890.

Phil 6685.5   Preyer, W. Der Hypnotismus. Wien, 1890.

Phil 3837.13   Rauh, F. Quatenus doctrina quam Spinoza de fide. Thesis. Tolosae, 1890.

Phil 5330.4.7   Ribot, T. The psychology of attention. Chicago, 1890.

Phil 5545.22.10   Ribot, T. Viljans sjukdomar. 6. uppl. Stockholm, 1890.

Phil 400.37   Ricardon, A. De l'idéal. Etude philosophique. Paris, 1890.

Phil 3837.6   Ricardou, A. De hrimauae mentis aeternitate apud Spinoza. Lutet., 1890.

Phil 4195.40   Rigg, J.M. Giovanni Pico della Mirandola: his life. London, 1890.

Phil 2730.93   Rostan, E. La religion de Maine de Biran. Thèse. Paris, 1890.

Phil 5425.65   Royse, Noble K. A study of genius. Chicago, 1890.

Phil 6127.4   Rubenstein, S. Zur Natur der Bewegungen. Leipzig, 1890.

Phil 260.1   Sasswitz, K. Geschichte de Atomistik. Hamburg, 1890. 2v.

Phil 6028.3.2   Schack, S. Physiognomische Studien. 2e Aufl. Jena, 1890.

Phil 1535.34   Schneid, Mathias. Spezielle Metaphysik im Geiste des Heil. Paderborn, 1890-92. 2v.

Phil 3808.25.30   Schopenhauer, Arthur. Counsels and maxims. London, 1890.

Phil 3808.2   Schopenhauer, Arthur. Religion: a dialogue. London, 1890.

Phil 2266.81   Schubert, Johannes. Adam Smith's Moralphilosophie. Leipzig, 1890.

Phil 125.3   Schultze, F. Stammbaum der Philosophie. Jena, 1890.

NEDL Phil 5938.10   Sizer, N. Heads and faces. N.Y., 1890.

Phil 9035.7.5   Smiles, S. Character. Chicago, 1890.

Phil 9120.4.5   Smiles, S. Duty. Chicago, 1890.

Phil 8893.14.7   Smiles, Samuel. Self-help. Chicago, 1890.

Phil 8893.14.13   Smiles, Samuel. Thrift. Chicago, 1890.

Phil 665.45   Soul shapes. London, 1890.

Phil 2270.71.10   Spencer, Herbert. Uppfostran i intellektuelt, moraliskt och fysiskt afseende. 2a uppl. Stockholm, 1890.

Phil 1050.3   Spiegler, J.S. Geschichte der Philosophie des Judenthums. Leipzig, 1890.

Phil 6028.2   Stanton, M.O. A system...physiognomy. Philadelphia, 1890. 2v.

Phil 645.27   Starcke, C.N. Skepticismus. Kjøbenhavn, 1890.

Phil 8598.81   Steckelmacher, M. Die Gottesidee der Offenbarung. Mannheim, 1890.

Phil 5258.20   Steele, G.M. Rudimentary psychology. Boston, 1890.

Phil 3552.96   Stein, L. Leibniz und Spinoza. Berlin, 1890.

Phil 3425.308   Sterrett, James M. Studies in Hegel's philosophy of religion. N.Y., 1890.

Phil 5585.21   Stiborius. Die Kategorien der sinnlichen Perception. Leipzig, 1890.

Phil 7082.26   Tissié, Philippe. Les rêves. Paris, 1890.

Phil 1135.125   Trubetskoi, S. Metafizika v drevnei Gretsii. Moskva, 1890.

Phil 6689.3   Tuckey, C.L. Psycho-therapeutics. London, 1890.

Phil 2050.236   Uhl, Josef. Humes Stellung in der englischen Philosophie. v.1-2. Prag, 1890-91.

Phil 5330.5   Uhl, L.L. Attention. Baltimore, 1890.

Phil 4650.1.47   Vannérus, Allen. Om erfarenheten ett kunskapsteoretiskt studieförsök. Akademisk afhandling. Stockholm, 1890.

Phil 978.43   Ver-Planck, J.C. (Mrs.). The wonder-light, true philosophy for children. N.Y., 1890.

Phil 3808.100A   Wallace, W. Life of Arthur Schopenhauer. London, 1890.

Phil 3808.100.5   Wallace, W. Life of Arthur Schopenhauer. N.Y., 1890.

Phil 303.6   Wolff, H. Kosmos die Weltentwickelung. Leipzig, 1890.

Phil 8900.1   Zeigler, T. Sittliches Sein und sittliches Werden. 2. Aufl. Strassburg, 1890.

Phil 1130.5.3   Zeller, Eduard. Outlines of history of Greek philosophy. N.Y., 1890.

1891

Phil 4513.3.33   Åberg, L.N. Fyra föreläsningar. Uppsala, 1891.

Phil 6990.19.5   Abbott, E.A. Philomythus, an antidote against credulity. London, 1891.

Phil 9160.1.5   Abbott, Jacob. A primer of ethics. Boston, 1891.

Phil 8580.10   Abranches, J. dos Santos. Questões fundamentaes. Coimbra, 1891.

Phil 1105.5   Apell, Otto. Beiträge zur Geschichte der griechischen Philosophie. Leipzig, 1891.

Phil 1505.1   Appel, H. Lehre der Scholastiker von der Synteresis. Rostock, 1891.

Phil 175.12   Avenarius, R. Der menschliche Weltbegriff. Leipzig, 1891.

Phil 75.1   Averra, Adolfo. Bibliografia delle Scienze Filosofiche. Torino, 1891.

Phil 1850.35.4   Bacon, Francis. The advancement of learning. 4th ed. Oxford, 1891.

Phil 7060.70   Badaud, P. Coup d'oeil sur la magie au XIXe siècle. Paris, 1891.

Phil 176.82   Baker, Arthur. Outlines of logic, psychology and ethics. London, 1891.

Phil 5241.3.2   Baldwin, J.M. Handbook of psychology...feeling and will. N.Y., 1891.

Phil 7054.43   Bartlett, G.C. The Salem seer. N.Y., 1891.

Phil 176.10.5   Baumann, Julius J. Elemente der Philosophie. Leipzig, 1891.

Phil 8876.58   Bender, Hedwig. Über das Wesen der Sittlichkeit. Halle, 1891.

Phil 3552.115   Beneke, H.F. Leibniz als Ethiker. Erlangen, 1891.

Phil 3745.1.80   Bergemann, P. Ernst Platner als Moralphilosophe. Halle, 1891.

1891 - cont.

Phil 6671.5   Bernheim, H. Hypnotisme. Paris, 1891.

Phil 2805.88   Bertrand, J.L.F. Blaise Pascal. Paris, 1891.

Phil 974.2.25   Besant, A. The theosophical society and H.P.B. Three articles. London, 1891?

Phil 978.6.5   Besant, Annie. Why I became a theosophist. N.Y., 1891.

Phil 2262.80   Bierens de Haan, J.D. De beteekenis van Shaftesbury in de Engelsche ethiek. Proefschrift. Utrecht, 1891.

Phil 9150.9.2   Bixby, James T. The crisis in morals. Boston, 1891.

Phil 8876.22   Bösch, I.M. Das menschliche Mitgefühl. Winterthur, 1891.

Phil 3235.84   Bolin, Wilhelm. Ludwig Feuerbach. Stuttgart, 1891.

Phil 176.56.2A   Bosanquet, B. Essays and addresses. London, 1891.

Phil 6951.15   Bouveret, L. La neurasthénie. 2. éd. Paris, 1891.

Phil 3246.187   Burman, E.O. Die Transscendentalphilosophie Fichte's und Schelling's. Upsala, 1891.

Phil 3425.80.7   Caird, Edward. Hegel. Edinburgh, 1891.

Phil 6112.2.4   Call, A.P. Power through repose. Boston, 1891.

Phil 8735.1   Call, W.M.W. Final causes. London, 1891.

Phil 6112.10   Carus, P. The soul of man. Chicago, 1891.

Phil 177.8.3   Carus, Paul. Fundamental problems. 2nd ed. Chicago, 1891.

Phil 3915.83   Cesca, Giovanni. L'animismo di Guglielmo Wundt. n.p., 1891.

Phil 2515.2.42   Charron, P. A treatise on wisdom. N.Y., 1891.

Phil 672.244   Cheek, John M. The perception of time. Charlotte, N.C.? 1891.

Phil 270.5   Christinnecke, J. Causalität und Entwicklung. Jena, 1891.

Phil 2880.1.83   Claassen, J. Ludwig von Saint-Martin. Stuttgart, 1891.

Phil 177.19.10   Conti, Augusto. Il vero nell'ordine o Ontologia e logica. 2a ed. Firenze, 1891. 2v.

Phil 1504.1   Correns, Paul. Die dem Boethius. v.1, pt.1. Münster, 1891.

Phil 6952.9   Cotard, J. Études sur les maladies cérébrales et mentales. Paris, 1891.

Phil 6112.9   Courmont, F. Le cervelet et ses fonctions. Paris, 1891.

Phil 6952.10.2   Cowles, E. Neurasthenia and its mental symptoms. Boston, 1891.

Phil 2733.82   Cruse, P.J. Malebranche en Zijne Bestrijders. Utrecht, 1891.

Phil 5545.69.15   Dandolo, Giovanni. La dottrina della memoria. Réggio nell'Emilia, 1891.

Htn   Phil 8878.4.5*   Davies, J.L. Order and growth. London, 1891.

Phil 5635.1   Delabarre, E.B. Über Bewegungsempfindungen. Freiburg, 1891.

Phil 6313.1.5   Delbrück, A. Die pathologische Lüge und die psychisch abnormen Schwindler. Stuttgart, 1891.

Phil 7068.91.4   Dénis, Léon. Après la mort. Paris, 1891.

Phil 3485.1   Deussen, Paul. Der kategorische Imperativ. Kiel, 1891.

Phil 3552.107   Dillmann, E. Eine neue Darstellung der leibnizischen Monadenlehre. Leipzig, 1891.

Phil 6673.15   Du Prel, Carl. Experimentalpsychologie und Experimentalmetaphysik. Leipzig, 1891.

Phil 8584.1   Eddy, J. Thoughts on religion and morality. Providence, R.I., 1891.

Phil 3585.9.81   Ellissen, O.A. Friedrich Albert Lange. Leipzig, 1891.

Phil 804.3.6   Erdmann, J.E. History of philosophy. v.1, 2d ed.; v.2-3, 3d ed. London, 1891-92. 3v.

X Cg   Phil 804.3.7   Erdmann, J.E. History of philosophy. 2d ed. v.3. London, 1891.

Phil 5125.5   Erhardt, F. Der Satz von Grunde als Prinzip der Schliessens. Halle, 1891.

Phil 8879.10.8   Everett, C.C. Ethics for young people. Boston, 1891.

Phil 1350.9.5   Farrar, F.W. Seekers after God. London, 1891.

Phil 4110.3.89   Ferrari, G.M. Commemorazione di Francesco Fiorentino. Roma, 1891.

Phil 5245.20   Fischer, E.L. Theorie der Gesichtswahrnehnung. Mainz, 1891.

Phil 8660.2.7   Fiske, J. The idea of God. Boston, 1891.

Phil 270.18   Fonsegrive, G.L. La causalité efficiente. Thèse. Paris, 1891.

Phil 2605.4.31   Fonsegrive, George L. Éléments de philosophie. Paris, 1891-1892. 2v.

Phil 6675.6.7   Forel, A. Der Hypnotismus. 2. Aufl. Stuttgart, 1891.

Phil 281.5   Fourviéro, Savié de. La creacioun dou mounde. Avignoun, 1891. 2v.

Htn   Phil 6400.3*   Freud, S. Zur Auffassung der Aphasien. Leipzig, 1891.

Phil 180.12.15   Frohschammer, J. Über das Mysterium magnum des Daseins. Leipzig, 1891.

Phil 8956.5   Gallwitz, Hans. Das Problem der Ethik...Gegenwart. Göttingen, 1891.

Phil 5425.2.5   Galton, F. Hereditary genius. N.Y., 1891.

Phil 3552.117   Gesche, Paul. Die Ethik Leibnizens. Halle, 1891.

Phil 3280.10   Geulincx, A. Opera philosophica. Hagae, 1891. 3v.

Phil 8881.10   Gilman, N.P. Conduct as a fine art. Boston, 1891.

Phil 6116.16F   Gotch, Francis. On the mammalian nervous system. London, 1891.

Phil 4070.1.96   Gotran, P. Due del 48 - Ernest Renan and Cristoforo Bonavino saggio critico filosofico. Firenze, 1891.

Phil 5246.8   Granger, F.S. Psychology. London, 1891.

Phil 4582.5.30   Halvorson, G. Grundtraek af metafysik. Kristiania, 1891.

Phil 5047.12   Hamilton, E.J. The modalist, or The laws of rational conviction. Boston, 1891.

Phil 5247.3.9   Hamilton, E.J. The perceptionalist. N.Y., 1891.

Phil 6957.2.5   Hammond, W.A. A treatise on insanity in its medical relations. N.Y., 1891.

Phil 8662.10   Harris, T.L. God's breath in man. Santa Rosa, 1891.

Phil 3489.3   Hegler, A. Die Psychologie in Kant's Ethik. Freiburg, 1891.

Phil 3428.36.5   Herbart, J.F. Allgemeine praktische Philosophie. 3. Ausg. Hamburg, 1891.

Phil 3428.45   Herbart, J.F. Text-book in psychology. N.Y., 1891.

Phil 5170.6   Hillebrand, F. Die neuen theorien der Kategorischen Schlüsse. Wien, 1891.

Phil 8408.5   Hirth, Georg. Aufgaben der Kunstphysiologie. München, 1891.

Phil 4580.65   Høffding, Harald. Etiske undersøgelser. København, 1891.

Phil 4803.454.61   Hoene-Wroński, Józef Maria. Reforma absoluta przeto ostateczna wiedzy ludzkiej. Paryz, 1891.

Phil 182.60   Hubbe-Schleiden, Wilhelm. Das Dasein als Lust, Leid, und Liebe. Braunschweig, 1891.

Phil 5249.2.02   James, William. The principles of psychology. London, 1891. 2v.

Phil 5249.2.5.3   James, William. Psychology. N.Y., 1891.

Phil 5545.16   Jastrow, J. Statistical study of memory. N.Y., 1891.

Phil 340.1.2   Jaures, J. De la réalité du monde sensible. Paris, 1891.

Htn   Phil 8589.4*   Johnson, F.H. What is reality? Boston, 1891.

Phil 5249.23.5   Joly, Henri. Psychologie des grands hommes. 2. éd. Paris, 1891.

Chronological Listing

1891 - cont.

	Phil 978.7.5	Judge, W.Z. Letters that have helped me. N.Y., 1891.
	Phil 978.7.9	Judge, W.Z. Letters that have helped me. 4th ed. N.Y., 1891.
	Phil 3480.25.2	Kant, Immanuel. Philosophy of Kant as contained in extracts. N.Y., 1891.
	Phil 3480.58.40	Kant, Immanuel. Prolégomènes a toute métaphysique future. Paris, 1891.
	Phil 8885.15	Ein Katechismus der moral und Politik für das deutsche Volk. 2e Aufl. Leipzig, 1891.
	Phil 5685.5	Kielblock, A. The stage fright. Boston, 1891.
	Phil 8411.7.15	Knight, W. The philosophy of the beautiful. N.Y., 1891-93. 2v.
	Phil 6960.3	Koch, J.L.A. Die psychopathischen Minderwertigkeiten. Ravensburg, 1891-93. 3v.
	Phil 8960.7	Kramer, J.W. The right road. N.Y., 1891.
	Phil 5400.76	Kratz, H. Ästhetik. Gütersloh, 1891.
	Phil 2045.96	Larsen, Eduard. Thomas Hobbes' filosofi. København, 1891.
	Phil 6961.11	Levillain, F. La neurasthénie. Paris, 1891.
	Phil 5251.6.5.2	Lewes, G.H. The physical basis of mind. Boston, 1891.
	Phil 6681.4.10	Liébeault, A.A. Thérapeutique suggestive, son mécanisme, propriétés du sommeil provoqué. Paris, 1891.
	Phil 2115.46	Locke, J. Philosophy of Locke in extracts. N.Y., 1891.
	Phil 7060.31	Lombroso, C. Inchiesta sulla trasmissione del pensiero. Torino., 1891.
EDL	Phil 5425.4.9	Lombroso, C. The man of genius. London, 1891.
	Phil 3565.65.5	Lotze, Hermann. Grundzüge der Logik und Encyklopädie der Philosophie. 3e Aufl. Leipzig, 1891.
	Phil 2125.35	McCosh, James. The tests of the various kinds of truth. N.Y., 1891.
	Phil 7080.39	MacFarlane, A.W. Insomnia and its therapeutics. N.Y., 1891.
	Phil 8702.3	Mackenzie, H. Evolution illuminating the Bible. London, 1891.
	Phil 8413.20	Mantegazza, P. Epikur; Physiologie des Schönen. Jena, 1891.
	Phil 365.22	Marichal, H. Essai de philosophie évolutive. Bruxelles, 1891.
	Phil 5628.50.15	Marin, Paul. Coup d'oeil sur les thaumaturges et les médiums du XIXe siècle. Paris, 1891.
	Phil 1117.1.2	Marshall, John. Short history of Greek philosophy. London, 1891.
	Phil 8887.4.5	Martineau, J. Types of ethical theory. v.1-2. 3. ed. Oxford, 1891.
	Phil 6122.24	Massalongo, Robert. Mielopatia da fulmine. Napoli, 1891.
	Phil 3425.213	Maturi, S. L'idea di Hegel. Napoli, 1891.
	Phil 2412.3	Maumus, Vincent. Les philosophes contemporains. Paris, 1891.
	Phil 293.6	Meyer, E.H. Die eddische Kosmogonie. Freiburg, 1891.
	Phil 2138.37.15	Mill, John S. The student's handbook...of Mill's logic. London, 1891.
	Phil 1117.7	Mitchell, E.M. (Mrs.). A study of Greek philosophy. Chicago, 1891.
ı	Phil 7075.8*	Moll, Albert. Die conträre Sexualempfindung. Berlin, 1891.
	Phil 6682.17	Moreau, P.G. L'hypnotisme. Paris, 1891.
	Phil 3140.80	Müller, H. Johannes Clauberg. Jena, 1891.
	Phil 8887.26	Murray, J.C. An introduction to ethics. Paisley, 1891.
	Phil 5249.2.99	Myers, F.W.H. The principles of psychology. London, 1891.
	Phil 1850.104	Natge, Hans. Über Francis Bacons Formenlehre. Leipzig, 1891.
	Phil 5585.22	Nichols, H. The psychology of time. N.Y., 1891.
	Phil 5425.3	Nisbet, J.F. Insanity of genius. London, 1891.
	Phil 4610.7.31	Norström, V. Om pligt, frihet och förnuft. Upsala, 1891.
	Phil 6684.1.5	Ochorowicz, J. Mental suggestion. v.1-4. N.Y., 1891.
	Phil 8889.4	Ogden, John. Elements of ethical science. Bismarck, N.D., 1891.
	Phil 3890.1.83	Orphal, H. Die religionsphilosophischen Anschauungen Trendelenburg's. Eisleben, 1891.
	Phil 2270.99	Pace, E. Das Relativitätsprincip bei Herbert Spencer. Leipzig, 1891.
	Phil 8890.23	Palmer, G.H. The glory of the imperfect. Boston, 1891.
DL	Phil 1158.15.3	Pater, Walter. Marius the Epicurean. London, 1891.
	Phil 525.17	Paulhan, F. Le nouveau mysticisme. Paris, 1891.
	Phil 8890.6.5.8	Paulsen, F. System der Ethik. 2. Aufl. Berlin, 1891.
	Phil 8640.3	Petavel-Ollief, E. Le problème de l'immortalité. Paris, 1891-92. 2v.
	Phil 2415.4	Picavet, F. Les idealogues. Paris, 1891.
	Phil 7054.43.20	Pioda, Alfredo. Memorabilia. Bellinzona, 1891.
	Phil 6619.2	Pitres, Albert. Leçons cliniques sur l'hystérie et l'hypnotisme faites à l'hôpital Saint André de Bordeaux. Paris, 1891. 2v.
	Phil 9355.11	A present to youth and young men. Birmingham, Eng., 1891. 2v.
	Phil 4015.1	Puglia, F. Il risorgimento filosofico in Italia. Napoli, 1891.
	Phil 8610.891.10	Putnam, S.P. My religious experience. N.Y., 1891.
	Phil 3425.279	Rackwitz, Max. Hegels Ansicht über die Apriorität von Zeit und Raum und die kantischen Kategorien. Halle, 1891.
	Phil 3790.6.31	Rauscher, J.O. Darstellung der Philosophie. Salugan, 1891.
	Phil 6687.10	Regnier, L.R. Hypnotisme et croyances anciennes. Paris, 1891.
	Phil 6687.1.15	Reichenback, C. Le fluide des magnétiseurs. Paris, 1891.
	Phil 7068.91.25	Revelations of a spirit medium. St. Paul, 1891.
	Phil 5440.4.2	Ribot, T. Heredity. N.Y., 1891.
	Phil 5330.4.10	Ribot, T. Uppmärksamhetens psykologi. Stockholm, 1891.
	Phil 6327.46.10	Ribot, Théodule. The diseases of personality. Chicago, 1891.
	Phil 7060.126	Richet, C. Experimentelle Studien. Stuttgart, 1891.
	Phil 1750.5	Roberty, E. de. La philosophie du siècle. Paris, 1891.
	Phil 8842.1	Rod, E. Les idées morales du temps present. Paris, 1891.
	Phil 5170.4	Rodier, G. De vi propria syllogismi. Thesis. v.1-2. Parisiis, 1891.
	Phil 8642.6	Rogers, E.H. National life in the spirit world. Chelsea? 1891.
	Phil 8893.1A	Salter, W.M. What can ethics do for us? Chicago, 1891.
	Phil 7068.91.10	Sargent, Epes. The scientific basis of spiritualism. 6th ed. Boston, 1891.
	Phil 193.109	Schiattarella, R. Note e problemi di filosofia contemporanea. Palermo, 1891.
	Phil 5374.25	Schlegel, Emil. Das Bewusstsein. Stuttgart, 1891.
	Phil 3808.28	Schopenhauer, Arthur. Art of literature. London, 1891.
	Phil 3808.26	Schopenhauer, Arthur. Counsels and maxims. London, 1891.
	Phil 3808.51.6	Schopenhauer, Arthur. On the fourfold root of the principle of sufficient reason and on the will in nature; two essays. London, 1891.

1891 - cont.

	Phil 3808.12	Schopenhauer, Arthur. Sämmtliche Werke. Leipzig, 1891. 6v.
	Phil 3808.29.5	Schopenhauer, Arthur. Studies in pessimism. London, 1891.
	Phil 3808.24.20	Schopenhauer, Arthur. Über den Satz vom Grunde. Leipzig, 1891.
	Phil 3808.24	Schopenhauer, Arthur. Über Urtheil, Kritik, Beifall, Ruhm, Warheit und Irrthum. Leipzig, 1891.
	Phil 3808.35.3	Schopenhauer, Arthur. Die Welt als Wille und Vorstellung. Halle, 1891? 2v.
	Phil 3808.11.2	Schopenhauer, Arthur. Werke. Leipzig, 1891. 2v.
	Phil 3808.11	Schopenhauer, Arthur. Werke. 2. Aufl. Leipzig, 1891. 2v.
	Phil 5058.5.5	Schröder, E. Vorlesungen über der Algebra der Logik. Leipzig, 1891-95. 4v.
NEDL	Phil 1925.81	Scott, William Robert. Introduction to Cudworth's treatise...with life. London, 1891.
	Phil 5425.11	Scripture, E.W. Arithmetical prodigies. Worcester, 1891.
	Phil 5258.13	Scripture, E.W. Problem of psychology. London, 1891.
	Phil 5325.9	Scripture, E.W. Über der associativen Verlauf der Vorstellungen. Leipzig, 1891.
	Phil 5325.9.5	Scripture, E.W. Vorstellung und Gefühl. Leipzig, 1891.
	Phil 9120.2	Seelye, J.H. Duty. Boston, 1891.
	Phil 7054.43.15	Senillosa, Felipe. Concordancia del espiritismo con la ciencia. v.1-2. Buenos Aires, 1891.
	Phil 5768.3	Seth, J. Freedom as an ethical postulate. Edinburgh, 1891.
	Phil 1718.8	Seth, Pringle-Pattison Andrew. The present position of the phisophical sciences. Edinburgh, 1891.
	Phil 2280.8.95	Seth Pringle-Pattison, Andrew. Testimonials in favor of Andrew Seth. Photoreproduction. Edinburgh, 1891.
	Phil 8615.2.3	Sheldon, Walter L. The meaning of the ethical movement, fifth anniversary address. St. Louis, 1891.
	Phil 193.44	Shoup, F.A. Mechanism and personality. Boston, 1891.
	Phil 5228.1.5	Siebeck, H. Beiträge...Psychologie. Giessen, 1891.
	Phil 5938.10.5	Sizer, Nelson. Forty years in phrenology. N.Y., 1891.
	Phil 8893.14.3	Smiles, Samuel. Life and labour. Chicago, 1891.
	Phil 8598.13	Snell, M.M. One hundred theses, foundations of human knowledge. Washington, 1891.
	Phil 6750.8	Sollier, P. Psychologie de l'idiot. Paris, 1891.
	Phil 6128.21	Soury, Jules. Histoire des doctrines...les fonctions du cerveau. Paris, 1891.
	Phil 525.44	Specht, G. Die Mystik im Irrsinn. Wiesbaden, 1891.
	Phil 2270.77	Spencer, Herbert. Data of ethics. Pt. IV. Justice. N.Y., 1891.
	Phil 2270.40.5	Spencer, Herbert. Essays. N.Y., 1891. 3v.
	Phil 6328.19.5	Starr, Moses A. Familiar forms of nervous disease. 2d ed. N.Y., 1891.
	Phil 349.4	Steiner, R. Die Grundfrage der Erkenntnisstheorie. n.p., 1891.
	Phil 193.36.5	Steudel, A. Das goldene ABC der Philosophie. Berlin, 1891.
	Phil 3260.80	Strasosky, H. Jacob Friedrich Fries. Hamburg, 1891.
	Phil 9220.5.5	Streamer, Volney. In friendship's name. Chicago, 1891.
	Phil 9430.12.2	Sully, J. Pessimism. 2. ed. N.Y., 1891.
	Phil 6689.1	Tarkhanof, J.R. Hypnotisme, suggestion. Paris, 1891.
	Phil 6129.6	Taylor, E.W. The mental element in the treatment of disease. Boston, 1891.
	Phil 3552.227	Thilly, Frank. Leibnizens Streit gegen Locke. Heidelberg, 1891.
	Phil 8599.10	Tyler, Charles Mellon. The study of the history and philosophy of religion. Ithica, N.Y., 1891.
	Phil 1535.24	Urráburu, J.J. Institutiones philosophicae. Vallistoleti, 1891-1908. 8v.
	Phil 196.11.5	Varnbüler, Theodore. Der Organismus der Allvernunft und das Leben der Menschheit in Ihm. Prag, 1891.
	Phil 5651.2	Verworn, M. Gleichgewicht und Otolithenorgan. Bonn, 1891.
	Phil 3565.116	Vorbrodt, G. Principien der Ethick und Religionsphilosophie Lotzes. Dessau, 1891.
	Phil 5649.16	Waller, A.D. The sense of effort. n.p., 1891?
	Phil 7068.91.15	Weatherly, L.A. The supernatural? Bristol, 1891.
	Phil 6132.3	Wilson, D. The right hand. Left handedness. London, 1891.
	Phil 197.47	Worms, René. Éléments de philosophie scientifique et...morale. Paris, 1891.
	Phil 5265.1	Ziehen, Theodor. Leitfaden der physiologischen Psychologie. Jena, 1891.

1892

	Phil 7060.12	Ackermann, G. Über die Entwickelung von Wahnideen. Weimar, 1892.
	Phil 3246.80.3	Adamson, R. Fichte. Philadelphia, 1892.
	Phil 5465.4.5	Ambrosi, L. Saggio sulla immaginazione. Roma, 1892.
	Phil 7140.128	Arnold, Hans. Schulmedizin und Wunderkuren. Leipzig, 1892.
	Phil 3805.90	Bachmann, F. Entwickelung der Ethik Schleiermachers. Leipzig, 1892.
	Phil 8876.63	Baets, Maurice de. Les bases de la morale et du droit. Paris, 1892.
	Phil 1504.1.2	Baeumker, C. Avencebrolis fons vitae. v.1, pt.2-3. Münster, 1892. 2v.
NEDL	Phil 1504.1.2	Baeumker, C. Avencebrolis fons vitae. v.1, pt.4. Münster, 1892.
	Phil 2520.84	Bark, F. Descartes' Lehre von den Leidenschaften. Rostock, 1892.
	Phil 7012.2	Bathurst, James. Atomic-consciousness. Exeter, 1892.
	Phil 176.14	Bax, E.B. Problem of reality. London, 1892.
	Phil 801.15	Bergmann, J. Geschichte der Philosophie. Berlin, 1892-93. 2v.
	Phil 86.1	Bertrand, A. Lexique de philosophie. Paris, 1892.
	Phil 978.6.61	Besant, Annie. The seven principles of man. London, 1892.
	Phil 978.6.60	Besant, Annie. The seven principles of man. London, 1892.
	Phil 4710.1	Bezobrazova, M. Handschriftliche...Philosophie in Russland. Leipzig, 1892.
	Phil 6311.18	Binet, Alfred. Les altérations de la personnalité. Paris, 1892.
	Phil 6951.3	Blandford, G.F. Insanity and its treatment. Edinburgh, 1892.
	Phil 978.5.28A	Blavatsky, H.P. The theosophical glossary. London, 1892.
	Phil 4815.223.30	Bodnár, Zsigmond. Szellemi haladásunk törvénye. Budapest, 1892.
	Phil 6990.3.25	Boissarie, P.G. Lourdes und seine Geschichte vom medizinischen Standpunkte. 2. ed. Augsburg, 1892.
	Phil 8691.9	Bonney, T.G. Christian doctrines and modern thought. London, 1892.
	Phil 8050.38	Bosanquet, B. A history of aesthetic. London, 1892.

1891 - cont.

Phil 6671.5 Bernheim, H. Hypnotisme. Paris, 1891.
Phil 2805.88 Bertrand, J.L.F. Blaise Pascal. Paris, 1891.
Phil 974.2.25 Besant, A. The theosophical society and H.P.B. Three articles. London, 1891?
Phil 978.6.5 Besant, Annie. Why I became a theosophist. N.Y., 1891.
Phil 2262.80 Bierens de Haan, J.D. De beteekenis van Shaftesbury in de Engelsche ethiek. Proefschrift. Utrecht, 1891.
Phil 9150.9.2 Bixby, James T. The crisis in morals. Boston, 1891.
Phil 8876.22 Bösch, I.M. Das menschliche Mitgefühl. Winterthur, 1891.
Phil 3235.84 Bolin, Wilhelm. Ludwig Feuerbach. Stuttgart, 1891.
Phil 176.56.2A Bosanquet, B. Essays and addresses. London, 1891.
Phil 6951.15 Bouveret, L. La neurasthénie. 2. éd. Paris, 1891.
Phil 3246.187 Burman, E.O. Die Transscendentalphilosophie Fichte's und Schelling's. Upsala, 1891.
Phil 3425.80.7 Caird, Edward. Hegel. Edinburgh, 1891.
Phil 6112.2.4 Call, A.P. Power through repose. Boston, 1891.
Phil 8735.1 Call, W.M.W. Final causes. London, 1891.
Phil 6112.10 Carus, P. The soul of man. Chicago, 1891.
Phil 177.8.3 Carus, Paul. Fundamental problems. 2nd ed. Chicago, 1891.
Phil 3915.83 Cesca, Giovanni. L'animismo di Guglielmo Wundt. n.p., 1891.
Phil 2515.2.42 Charron, P. A treatise on wisdom. N.Y., 1891.
Phil 672.244 Cheek, John M. The perception of time. Charlotte, N.C.? 1891.
Phil 270.5 Christinnecke, J. Causalität und Entwicklung. Jena, 1891.
Phil 2880.1.83 Claassen, J. Ludwig von Saint-Martin. Stuttgart, 1891.
Phil 177.19.10 Conti, Augusto. Il vero nell'ordine o Ondologia e logica. 2a ed. Firenze, 1891. 3v.
Phil 1504.1 Correns, Paul. Die dem Boethius. v.1, pt.1. Münster, 1891.
Phil 6952.9 Cotard, J. Études sur les maladies cérébrales et mentales. Paris, 1891.
Phil 6112.9 Courmont, F. Le cervelet et ses fonctions. Paris, 1891.
Phil 6952.10.2 Cowles, E. Neurasthenia and its mental symptoms. Boston, 1891.
Phil 2733.82 Cruse, P.J. Malebranche en Zijne Bestrijders. Utrecht, 1891.
Phil 5545.69.15 Dandolo, Giovanni. La dottrina della memoria. Réggio nell'Emilia, 1891.
Htn Phil 8878.4.5* Davies, J.L. Order and growth. London, 1891.
Phil 5635.1 Delabarre, E.B. Uber Bewegungsempfindungen. Freiburg, 1891.
Phil 6313.1.5 Delbrück, A. Die pathologische Lüge und die psychisch abnormen Schwindler. Stuttgart, 1891.
Phil 7068.91.4 Dénis, Léon. Après la mort. Paris, 1891.
Phil 3485.1 Deussen, Paul. Der kategorische Imperativ. Kiel, 1891.
Phil 3552.107 Dillmann, E. Eine neue Darstellung der leibnizischen Monadenlehre. Leipzig, 1891.
Phil 6673.15 Du Prel, Carl. Experimentalpsychologie und Experimentalmetaphysik. Leipzig, 1891.
Phil 8584.1 Eddy, J. Thoughts on religion and morality. Providence, R.I., 1891.
Phil 3585.9.81 Ellissen, O.A. Friedrich Albert Lange. Leipzig, 1891.
Phil 804.3.6 Erdmann, J.E. History of philosophy. v.1, 2d ed.; v.2-3, 3d ed. London, 1891-92. 3v.
X Cg Phil 804.3.7 Erdmann, J.E. History of philosophy. 2d ed. v.3. London, 1891.
Phil 5125.5 Erhardt, F. Der Satz von Grunde als Prinzip der Schliessens. Halle, 1891.
Phil 8879.10.8 Everett, C.C. Ethics for young people. Boston, 1891.
Phil 1350.9.5 Farrar, F.W. Seekers after God. London, 1891.
Phil 4110.3.89 Ferrari, G.M. Commemorazione di Francesco Fiorentino. Roma, 1891.
Phil 5245.20 Fischer, E.L. Theorie der Gesichtswahrnehmung. Mainz, 1891.
Phil 8660.2.7 Fiske, J. The idea of God. Boston, 1891.
Phil 270.18 Fonsegrive, G.L. La causalité efficiente. Thèse. Paris, 1891.
Phil 2605.4.31 Fonsegrive, George L. Éléments de philosophie. Paris, 1891-1892. 2v.
Phil 6675.6.7 Forel, A. Der Hypnotismus. 2. Aufl. Stuttgart, 1891.
Phil 281.5 Fourviéro, Savié de. La creacioun dou mounde. Avignoun, 1891. 2v.
Htn Phil 6890.3* Freud, S. Zur Auffassung der Aphasien. Leipzig, 1891.
Phil 180.12.15 Frohschammer, J. Uber das Mysterium magnum des Daseins. Leipzig, 1891.
Phil 8956.5 Gallwitz, Hans. Das Problem der Ethik...Gegenwart. Göttingen, 1891.
Phil 5425.2.5 Galton, F. Hereditary genius. N.Y., 1891.
Phil 3552.117 Gesche, Paul. Die Ethik Leibnizens. Halle, 1891.
Phil 3280.10 Geulincx, A. Opera philosophica. Hagae, 1891. 3v.
Phil 8881.10 Gilman, N.P. Conduct as a fine art. Boston, 1891.
Phil 6116.16F Gotch, Francis. On the mammalian nervous system. London, 1891.
Phil 4070.1.96 Gotran, P. Due del 48 - Ernest Renan and Cristoforo Bonavino saggio critico filosofico. Firenze, 1891.
Phil 5246.8 Granger, F.S. Psychology. London, 1891.
Phil 4582.5.30 Halvorson, G. Grundtraek af metafysyk. Kristiania, 1891.
Phil 5047.12 Hamilton, E.J. The modalist, or The laws of rational conviction. Boston, 1891.
Phil 5247.3.9 Hamilton, E.J. The perceptionalist. N.Y., 1891.
Phil 6957.2.5 Hammond, W.A. A treatise on insanity in its medical relations. N.Y., 1891.
Phil 8662.10 Harris, T.L. God's breath in man. Santa Rosa, 1891.
Phil 3489.3 Hegler, A. Die Psychologie in Kant's Ethik. Freiburg, 1891.
Phil 3428.36.5 Herbart, J.F. Allgemeine praktische Philosophie. 3. Ausg. Hamburg, 1891.
Phil 3428.45 Herbart, J.F. Text-book in psychology. N.Y., 1891.
Phil 5170.6 Hillebrand, F. Die neuen theorien der Kategorischen Schlüsse. Wien, 1891.
Phil 8408.5 Hirth, Georg. Aufgaben der Kunstphysiologie. München, 1891.
Phil 4580.65 Høffding, Harald. Etiske undersøgelser. København, 1891.
Phil 4803.454.61 Hoene-Wroński, Józef Maria. Reforma absolutna przeto ostateczna wiedzy ludzkiej. Paryz, 1891.
Phil 182.60 Hubbe-Schleiden, Wilhelm. Das Dasein als Lust, Leid, und Liebe. Braunschweig, 1891.
Phil 5249.2.02 James, William. The principles of psychology. London, 1891. 2v.
Phil 5249.2.5.3 James, William. The principles of psychology. N.Y., 1891.
Phil 5545.16 Jastrow, J. Statistical study of memory. N.Y., 1891.
Phil 340.1.2 Jaures, J. De la réalite du monde sensible. Paris, 1891.
Htn Phil 8589.4* Johnson, J. What is reality? Boston, 1891.
Phil 5249.23.5 Joly, Henri. Psychologie des grands hommes. 2. éd. Paris, 1891.

1891 - cont.

Phil 978.7.5 Judge, W.Z. Letters that have helped me. N.Y., 1891.
Phil 978.7.9 Judge, W.Z. Letters that have helped me. 4th ed. N.Y., 1891.
Phil 3480.25.2 Kant, Immanuel. Philosophy of Kant as contained in extracts. N.Y., 1891.
Phil 3480.58.40 Kant, Immanuel. Prolégomènes a toute métaphysique future. Paris, 1891.
Phil 8885.15 Ein Katechismus der moral und Politik für das deutsche Volk. 2e Aufl. Leipzig, 1891.
Phil 5685.5 Kielblock, A. The stage fright. Boston, 1891.
Phil 8411.7.15 Knight, W. The philosophy of the beautiful. N.Y., 1891-93. 2v.
Phil 6960.3 Koch, J.L.A. Die psychopathischen Minderwertigkeiten. Ravensburg, 1891-93. 3v.
Phil 8960.7 Kramer, J.W. The right road. N.Y., 1891.
Phil 5400.76 Kratz, H. Asthetik. Gütersloh, 1891.
Phil 2045.96 Larsen, Eduard. Thomas Hobbes' filosofi. København, 1891.
Phil 6961.11 Levillain, F. La neurasthénie. Paris, 1891.
Phil 5251.6.5.2 Lewes, G.H. The physical basis of mind. Boston, 1891.
Phil 6681.4.10 Liébeault, A.A. Thérapeutique suggestive, son mécanisme, propriétés du sommeil provoqué. Paris, 1891.
Phil 2115.46 Locke, J. Philosophy of Locke in extracts. N.Y., 1891.
Phil 7060.31 Lombroso, C. Inchiesta sulla trasmissione del pensiero. Torino., 1891.
NEDL Phil 5425.4.9 Lombroso, C. The man of genius. London, 1891.
Phil 3565.65.5 Lotze, Hermann. Grundzüge der Logik und Encyklopädie der Philosophie. 3e Aufl. Leipzig, 1891.
Phil 2125.35 McCosh, James. The tests of the various kinds of truth. N.Y., 1891.
Phil 7080.39 MacFarlane, A.W. Insomnia and its therapeutics. N.Y., 1891.
Phil 8702.3 Mackenzie, H. Evolution illuminating the Bible. London, 1891.
Phil 8413.20 Mantegazza, P. Epikur; Physiologie des Schönen. Jena, 1891.
Phil 365.22 Marichal, H. Essai de philosophie évolutive. Bruxelles, 1891.
Phil 5628.50.15 Marin, Paul. Coup d'oeil sur les thaumaturges et les médiums du XIXe siècle. Paris, 1891.
Phil 1117.1.2 Marshall, John. Short history of Greek philosophy. London, 1891.
Phil 8887.4.5 Martineau, J. Types of ethical theory. v.1-2. 3. ed. Oxford, 1891.
Phil 6122.24 Massalongo, Robert. Mielopatia da fulmine. Napoli, 1891.
Phil 3425.213 Maturi, S. L'idea di Hegel. Napoli, 1891.
Phil 2412.3 Maumus, Vincent. Les philosophes contemporains. Paris, 1891.
Phil 293.6 Meyer, E.H. Die eddische Kosmogonie. Freiburg, 1891.
Phil 2138.37.15 Mill, John S. The student's handbook...of Mill's logic. London, 1891.
Phil 1117.7 Mitchell, E.M. (Mrs.). A study of Greek philosophy. Chicago, 1891.
Htn Phil 7075.8* Moll, Albert. Die conträre Sexualempfindung. Berlin, 1891.
Phil 6682.17 Moreau, P.G. L'hypnotisme. Paris, 1891.
Phil 3140.80 Müller, H. Johannes Clauberg. Jena, 1891.
Phil 8887.26 Murray, J.C. An introduction to ethics. Paisley, 1891.
Phil 5249.2.99 Myers, F.W.H. The principles of psychology. London, 1891.
Phil 1850.104 Natge, Hans. Über Francis Bacons Formenlehre. Leipzig, 1891.
Phil 5585.22 Nichols, H. The psychology of time. N.Y., 1891.
Phil 5425.3 Nisbet, J.F. Insanity of genius. London, 1891.
Phil 4610.7.31 Norström, V. Om pligt, frihet och förnuft. Upsala, 1891.
Phil 6684.1.5 Ochorowicz, J. Mental suggestion. v.1-4. N.Y., 1891.
Phil 8889.4 Ogden, John. Elements of ethical science. Bismarck, N.D., 1891.
Phil 3890.1.83 Orphal, H. Die religionsphilosophischen Anschauungen Trendelenburg's. Eisleben, 1891.
Phil 2270.99 Pace, E. Das Relativitätsprincip bei Herbert Spencer. Leipzig, 1891.
Phil 8890.23 Palmer, G.H. The glory of the imperfect. Boston, 1891.
NEDL Phil 1158.15.3 Pater, Walter. Marius the Epicurean. London, 1891.
Phil 525.17 Paulhan, F. Le nouveau mysticisme. Paris, 1891.
Phil 8890.6.5.8 Paulsen, F. System der Ethik. 2. Aufl. Berlin, 1891.
Phil 8640.3 Petavel-Olliet, E. Le problème de l'immortalité. Paris, 1891-92. 2v.
Phil 2415.4 Picavet, F. Les idealogues. Paris, 1891.
Phil 7054.43.20 Pioda, Alfredo. Memorabilia. Bellinzona, 1891.
Phil 6619.2 Pitres, André. Leçons cliniques sur l'hystérie et l'hypnotisme faites à l'hôpital Saint André de Bordeaux. Paris, 1891. 2v.
Phil 9355.11 A present to youth and young men. Birmingham, Eng., 1891. 2v.
Phil 4015.1 Puglia, F. Il risorgimento filosofico in Italia. Napoli, 1891.
Phil 8610.891.10 Putnam, S.P. My religious experience. N.Y., 1891.
Phil 3425.279 Rackwitz, Max. Hegels Ansicht über die Apriorität von Zeit und Raum und die kantischen Kategorien. Halle, 1891.
Phil 3790.6.31 Rauscher, J.O. Darstellung der Philosophie. Salugan, 1891.
Phil 6687.10 Regnier, L.R. Hypnotisme et croyances anciennes. Paris, 1891.
Phil 6687.1.15 Reichenback, C. Le fluide des magnétiseurs. Paris, 1891.
Phil 7068.91.25 Revelations of a spirit medium. St. Paul, 1891.
Phil 5440.4.2 Ribot, T. Heredity. N.Y., 1891.
Phil 5330.4.10 Ribot, T. Uppmärksamhetens psykologi. Stockholm, 1891.
Phil 6327.46.10 Ribot, Théodule. The diseases of personality. Chicago, 1891.
Phil 7060.126 Richet, C. Experimentelle Studien. Stuttgart, 1891.
Phil 1750.5 Roberty, E. de. La philosophie du siècle. Paris, 1891.
Phil 8842.1 Rod, E. Les idées morales du temps present. Paris, 1891.
Phil 5170.4 Rodier, G. De vi propria syllogismi. Thesis. v.1-2. Parisiis, 1891.
Phil 8642.6 Rogers, E.H. National life in the spirit world. Chelsea? 1891.
Phil 8893.1A Salter, W.M. What can ethics do for us? Chicago, 1891.
Phil 7068.91.10 Sargent, Epes. The scientific basis of spiritualism. 6th ed. Boston, 1891.
Phil 193.109 Schiattarella, R. Note e problemi di filosofia contemporanea. Palermo, 1891.
Phil 5374.25 Schlegel, Emil. Das Bewusstsein. Stuttgart, 1891.
Phil 3808.28 Schopenhauer, Arthur. Art of literature. London, 1891.
Phil 3808.26 Schopenhauer, Arthur. Counsels and maxims. London, 1891.
Phil 3808.51.6 Schopenhauer, Arthur. On the fourfold root of the principle of sufficient reason and on the will in nature; two essays. London, 1891.

1891 - cont.

Phil 3808.12   Schopenhauer, Arthur. Sämmtliche Werke. Leipzig, 1891. 6v.

Phil 3808.29.5   Schopenhauer, Arthur. Studies in pessimism. London, 1891.

Phil 3808.24.20   Schopenhauer, Arthur. Über den Satz vom Grunde. Leipzig, 1891.

Phil 3808.24   Schopenhauer, Arthur. Über Urtheil, Kritik, Beifall, Ruhm, Warheit und Irrthum. Leipzig, 1891.

Phil 3808.35.3   Schopenhauer, Arthur. Die Welt als Wille und Vorstellung. Halle, 1891? 2v.

Phil 3808.11.2   Schopenhauer, Arthur. Werke. Leipzig, 1891. 2v.

Phil 3808.11   Schopenhauer, Arthur. Werke. 2. Aufl. Leipzig, 1891. 2v.

Phil 5058.5.5   Schröder, E. Vorlesungen über der Algebra der Logik. Leipzig, 1891-95. 4v.

NEDL Phil 1925.81   Scott, William Robert. Introduction to Cudworth's treatise...with life. London, 1891.

Phil 5425.11   Scripture, E.W. Arithmetical prodigies. Worcester, 1891.

Phil 5258.13   Scripture, E.W. Problem of psychology. London, 1891.

Phil 5325.9   Scripture, E.W. Über der associativen Verlauf der Vorstellungen. Leipzig, 1891.

Phil 5325.9.5   Scripture, E.W. Vorstellung und Gefühl. Leipzig, 1891.

Phil 9120.2   Seelye, J.H. Duty. Boston, 1891.

Phil 7054.43.15   Senillosa, Felipe. Concordancia del espiritismo con la ciencia. v.1-2. Buenos Aires, 1891.

Phil 5768.3   Seth, J. Freedom as an ethical postulate. Edinburgh, 1891.

Phil 1718.8   Seth, Pringle-Pattison Andrew. The present position of the phisophical sciences. Edinburgh, 1891.

Phil 2280.8.95   Seth Pringle-Pattison, Andrew. Testimonials in favor of Andrew Seth. Photoreproduction. Edinburgh, 1891.

Phil 8615.2.3   Sheldon, Walter L. The meaning of the ethical movement, fifth anniversary address. St. Louis, 1891.

Phil 193.44   Shoup, F.A. Mechanism and personality. Boston, 1891.

Phil 5228.1.5   Siebeck, H. Beiträge...Psychologie. Giessen, 1891.

Phil 5938.10.5   Sizer, Nelson. Forty years in phrenology. N.Y., 1891.

Phil 8893.14.3   Smiles, Samuel. Life and labour. Chicago, 1891.

Phil 8598.13   Snell, M.M. One hundred theses, foundations of human knowledge. Washington, 1891.

Phil 6750.8   Sollier, P. Psychologie de l'idiot. Paris, 1891.

Phil 6128.21   Soury, Jules. Histoire des doctrines...les fonctions du cerveau. Paris, 1891.

Phil 525.44   Specht, G. Die Mystik im Irrsinn. Wiesbaden, 1891.

Phil 2270.77   Spencer, Herbert. Data of ethics. Pt. IV. Justice. N.Y., 1891.

Phil 2270.40.5   Spencer, Herbert. Essays. N.Y., 1891. 3v.

Phil 6328.19.5   Starr, Moses A. Familiar forms of nervous disease. 2d ed. N.Y., 1891.

Phil 349.4   Steiner, R. Die Grundfrage der Erkenntnisstheorie. n.p., 1891.

Phil 193.36.5   Steudel, A. Das goldene ABC der Philosophie. Berlin, 1891.

Phil 3260.80   Strasosky, H. Jacob Friedrich Fries. Hamburg, 1891.

Phil 9220.5.5   Streamer, Volney. In friendship's name. Chicago, 1891.

Phil 9430.12.2   Sully, J. Pessimism. 2. ed. N.Y., 1891.

Phil 6689.1   Tarkhanof, J.R. Hypnotisme, suggestion. Paris, 1891.

Phil 6129.6   Taylor, E.W. The mental element in the treatment of disease. Boston, 1891.

Phil 3552.227   Thilly, Frank. Leibnizens Streit gegen Locke. Heidelberg, 1891.

Phil 8599.10   Tyler, Charles Mellon. The study of the history and philosophy of religion. Ithaca, N.Y., 1891.

Phil 1535.24   Urráburu, J.J. Institutiones philosophicae. Vallistoleli, 1891-1908. 8v.

Phil 196.11.5   Varnbüler, Theodore. Der Organismus der Allvernunft und das Leben der Menschheit in Ihm. Prag, 1891.

Phil 5651.2   Verworn, M. Gleichgewicht und Otolithenorgan. Bonn, 1891.

Phil 3565.116   Vorbrodt, G. Principien der Ethick und Religionsphilosophie Lotzes. Dessau, 1891.

Phil 5649.16   Waller, A.D. The sense of effort. n.p., 1891?

Phil 7068.91.15   Weatherly, L.A. The supernatural? Bristol, 1891.

Phil 6132.3   Wilson, D. The right hand. Left handedness. London, 1891.

Phil 197.47   Worms, René. Éléments de philosophie scientifique et...morale. Paris, 1891.

Phil 5265.1   Ziehen, Theodor. Leitfaden der physiologischen Psychologie. Jena, 1891.

1892

Phil 7060.12   Ackermann, A. Über die Entwickelung von Wahnideen. Weimar, 1892.

Phil 3246.80.3   Adamson, R. Fichte. Philadelphia, 1892.

Phil 5465.4.5   Ambrosi, L. Saggio sulla immaginazione. Roma, 1892.

Phil 7140.128   Arnold, Hans. Schulmedizin und Wunderkuren. Leipzig, 1892.

Phil 3805.90   Bachmann, F. Entwickelung der Ethik Schleiermachers. Leipzig, 1892.

Phil 8876.63   Baets, Maurice de. Les bases de la morale et du droit. Paris, 1892.

Phil 1504.1.2   Baeumker, C. Avencebrolis fons vitae. v.1, pt.2-3. Münster, 1892. 2v.

DL Phil 1504.1.2   Baeumker, C. Avencebrolis fons vitae. v.1, pt.4. Münster, 1892.

Phil 2520.84   Bark, F. Descartes' Lehre von den Leidenschaften. Rostock, 1892.

Phil 7012.2   Bathurst, James. Atomic-consciousness. Exeter, 1892.

Phil 176.14   Bax, E.B. Problem of reality. London, 1892.

Phil 801.15   Bergmann, J. Geschichte der Philosophie. Berlin, 1892-93. 2v.

Phil 86.1   Bertrand, A. Lexique de philosophie. Paris, 1892.

Phil 978.6.60   Besant, Annie. The seven principles of man. London, 1892.

Phil 978.6.61   Besant, Annie. The seven principles of man. London, 1892.

Phil 4710.1   Bezobrazova, M. Handschriftliche...Philosophie in Russland. Leipzig, 1892.

Phil 6311.18   Binet, Alfred. Les altérations de la personnalité. Paris, 1892.

Phil 6951.3   Blandford, G.F. Insanity and its treatment. Edinburgh, 1892.

Phil 978.5.28A   Blavatsky, H.P. The theosophical glossary. London, 1892.

Phil 4815.223.30   Bodnár, Zsigmond. Szellemi haladásunk törvénye. Budapest, 1892.

Phil 6990.3.25   Boissarie, P.G. Lourdes und seine Geschichte vom medizinischen Standpunkte. 2. ed. Augsburg, 1892.

Phil 8691.9   Bonney, T.G. Christian doctrines and modern thought. London, 1892.

Phil 8050.38   Bosanquet, B. A history of aesthetic. London, 1892.

1892 - cont.

Phil 9430.2   Bourchenin, D. La trace du pessimisme dans la société. Paris, 1892.

Phil 8876.25   Bowne, B.P. The principles of ethics. N.Y., 1892.

Phil 4065.120   Brambilla, E. Studi letterari. Sugli eroici furori di G. Bruno. Milano, 1892.

Phil 5425.35A   Brentano, F. Das Genie. Leipzig, 1892.

X Cg Phil 1133.1.2   Burnet, John. Early Greek philosophy. London, 1892.

Phil 1701.4   Burt, Bery C. History of modern philosophy. Chicago, 1892. 2v.

Phil 177.1.5   Caird, Edward. Essays on literature and philosophy. Glasgow, 1892. 2v.

Phil 177.1   Caird, Edward. Essays on literature and philosophy. N.Y., 1892. 2v.

Phil 6112.1.3   Calderwood, H. The relations of mind and brain. 3d ed. London, 1892.

Phil 4235.4.81   Catania. R. Scuola Normale Maschile Superiore. Per le solenni onoranze al filosofo Vincenzo Tedeschi Paterno Castello. Catania, 1892.

Phil 802.5   Cesca, Giovanni. I fattori della evoluzione filosofica. Padova, 1892.

Phil 6952.23.20   Charcot, J.M. Clinique des maladies du système nerveaux. Paris, 1892-93. 2v.

Phil 8403.4   Cherbuliez, V. L'art et la nature. Paris, 1892.

Phil 600.61   Chicherin, Boris A. Polozhitel'naia filosofiia i edinstvo nauki. Moskva, 1892.

Phil 978.56   Clark, S.C. Short lessons in theosophy. Boston, 1892.

Phil 978.71   Coulomb, E.J. Le secret de l'absolu. Paris, 1892.

Phil 8877.20.2   Counsel, E. Maxims. 2nd ed. Melbourne, 1892.

Phil 8582.29   Coxe, A. Cleveland. Holy writ and modern thought. N.Y., 1892.

Phil 177.24   Curtis, M.M. Philosophy and physical science. Cleveeland, 1892.

Phil 7068.92.25   Daniels, Cora Linn Morrison. As it is to be. 5. ed. Franklin, Mass., 1892.

Phil 6673.12   Darly, Joseph. Day visions and clairvoyant night dreams. London, 1892.

Phil 5243.27   Davis, N.K. Elements of psychology. N.Y., 1892.

Phil 7059.20   Denis, Léon. Pourquoi la vie! Paris, 1892.

Phil 2520.28A   Descartes, René. Philosophy in extracts from his writings. N.Y., 1892.

Phil 6060.2   Deschamps, L. La philosophie de l'écriture. Paris, 1892.

Phil 2493.81   Dewaule, L. Condillac et la psychologie anglaise contemporaine. Paris, 1892.

Phil 8404.13.5   Diez, Max. Theorie des Gefühls zur Begrundung des Asthetik. Stuttgart, 1892.

Phil 8878.30.2   Dittes, F. Über die sittliche Freiheit. 2e Aufl. Leipzig, 1892.

Phil 9343.7.6   Dodge, Grace H. Thoughts of busy girls. N.Y., 1892.

Phil 8583.9.5   Dole, Charles F. The smoke and the flame. Boston, 1892.

Phil 478.3   Dreher, Eugen. Der Materialismus. Berlin, 1892.

Phil 8693.5.3   Drummond, H. Natural law in the spiritual world. Philadelphia, 1892.

Phil 8878.39   Duboc, Julius. Grundriss einer Einheitlichen. Leipzig, 1892.

Phil 178.16   Dumesni, G. Du role des concepts. Paris, 1892.

Phil 7068.92.55   Du Prel, K.L.A.F.M.A. Das Rätsel des Menschen. Leipzig, 1892.

Phil 400.73   Dwelshauvers, G. Les méthodes de l'idéalisme scientifique. Paris, 1892. 2 pam.

Phil 179.11   Eitle, Johannes. Grundriss der Philosophie. Freiburg, 1892.

Phil 3565.112   Elgström, Albin. Hermann Lotzes uppfattning af människans valfrihet. Lund, 1892.

Phil 5044.1A   Erdmann, B. Logik. Halle, 1892.

Phil 7068.92.65   Ermacora, G.B. I fatti spiritici e le ipotesi affrettate. Padova, 1892.

Phil 1705.1.2   Falckenberg, R. Geschichte der neueren Philosophie. 2e Aufl. Leipzig, 1892.

Phil 3270.1.81   Falken, H.N. Kuno Fischer und der litterarhistorische Methode. Berlin, 1892.

Phil 3160.6.81   Festner, Carl. Christian August Crusius als Metaphysiker. Halle, 1892.

Phil 3487.1.15   Fischer, Kuno. Die hundertjährige Gedächtnissfeier der Kantischen Kritik der reinen Vernunft. 2. Aufl. Heidelberg, 1892.

Phil 3487.1.2   Fischer, Kuno. Kritik der Kantischen Philosophie. 2. Aufl. Heidelberg, 1892.

Phil 180.12.5   Frohschammer, J. System der Philosophie im Umriss. München, 1892.

Phil 5649.13   Fullerton, G.S. On the perception of small differences. Philadelphia, 1892.

Phil 5425.2.2   Galton, F. Hereditary genius. 2. ed. London, 1892.

Phil 9420.8   Gardair, J. Philosophie de Saint Thomas. Les passions et la volonté. Paris, 1892.

Phil 8661.1   Goblet D'Alviella, E. Lectures on the origin and growth of the conception of God. London, 1892.

Phil 7054.26   Golden light angels's visits to my farm in Florida. N.Y., 1892.

Phil 5246.22   Gonzalez Serrano, U. Estudios psicológicos. Madrid, 1892.

Phil 6116.13F   Grashey, H. Experimentelle Beiträge zur Lehre von der Blut-Circulation in der Schädel-Rückgratshöhle. München, 1892.

Phil 8407.10.5   Groos, Karl. Einleitung in die Ästhetik. Giessen, 1892.

Phil 7068.92.35   Gurney, Edmund. Les hallucinations télépathiques. 2. ed. Paris, 1892.

Phil 8881.43   Gutberlet, C. Ethik und Religion. Münster, 1892.

Phil 3255.89   Haggenmacher, O. Über Sebastian Francks Erstlingsschrift. Zürich, 1892.

Phil 3489.12   Hansen, Oscar. Undersøgelser verdrørende grundlaget for Kants erkendelsesteori. København, 1892.

Phil 8125.20   Harnack, Otto. Die klassische Ästhetik der Deutschen. Leipzig, 1892.

Phil 5247.15   Hebberd, S.S. An introduction...science of thought. Madison, 1892.

Phil 807.2   Hegel, G.W.F. Lectures on history of philosophy. London, 1892-96. 3v.

Phil 3425.32.2   Hegel, Georg Wilhelm Friedrich. Logic. 2nd ed. Oxford, 1892.

Phil 3425.71.5   Hegel, Georg Wilhelm Friedrich. Theory of right, duties, and religion. Ann Arbor, 1892.

Phil 3255.80   Hegler, Alfred. Geist und Schrift bei Sebastian Franck. Freiburg, 1892.

Phil 5374.38   Heisler, N. Ein Ausflug in das Gebiet des Bewusstseins. Basel, 1892.

Phil 2115.94   Hertling, G. von. John Locke und die Schule von Cambridge. Freiburg, 1892. 2v.

1892 - cont.

	Phil 5247.10.6	Höffding, H. Outlines of psychology. London, 1892.
	Phil 5247.10.3	Höffding, H. Psykologi i omrids paa grundlag af erfarung. 3. ed. København, 1892.
	Phil 3890.1.105	Hoffmann, Edmund. Die Psychologie Friedrich Adolf Trendelenburgs. Inaug. Diss. Greifswald, 1892?
	Phil 6117.8A	Horsley, V. The brain and spinal cord. London, 1892.
	Phil 3850.5.90	Humanus. African Spir. Leipzig, 1892.
	Phil 8882.31.5	Huntington, F.D. Good talking a fine art. Syracuse, 1892.
	Phil 8697.5	Huxley, T.H. Essays upon some controverted questions. N.Y., 1892.
	Phil 8882.24	Hyde, W. De W. Practical ethics. N.Y., 1892.
	Phil 5047.9	Hyslop, J.H. Elements of logic. N.Y., 1892.
	Phil 5249.2.4A	James, William. Psychology. N.Y., 1892.
	Phil 5049.12.5	Jones, E.E.C. An introduction to general logic. London, 1892.
	Phil 9430.28	Jouvin, Léon. Le pessimisme. Paris, 1892.
	Phil 6960.9	Kaan, Hanns. Der neurasthenische Angstaffect bei Zwangsvorstellungen und der primordiale Grübelzwang. Wien, 1892.
	Phil 3640.187	Kaatz, Hugo. Die Weltanschauung Friedrich Nietzsches. Dresden, 1892.
	Phil 3480.52	Kant, Immanuel. Kritik of judgment. London, 1892.
	Phil 3425.577	Kedney, J.S. Hegel's aesthetics; a critical exposition. 2nd ed. Chicago, 1892.
	Phil 6680.1.4.5	Kerner, J. Die Seherin von Prevorst. 2. Aufl. Stuttgart, 1892.
	Phil 8885.5	Kies, M. The ethical principle. Ann Arbor, 1892.
	Phil 7059.19	King, Maria M. Real life in the spirit land. 5. ed. Hammonton,N.J., 1892.
	Phil 810.3	Knauer, Vincenz. Die haupt Probleme der Philosophie. Wien, 1892.
	Phil 185.56	Kniepf, Albert. Theorie der Geisteswerthe. Leipzig, 1892.
	Phil 3552.89	Koppehl, H. Die Verwandtschaft Leibizens mit Thomas von Aquino. Jena, 1892.
	Phil 5250.18.10	Kraepelin, Emil. Über die Beeinflussung einfacher psychischer Vorgänge durch einige Arzneimittel. Jena, 1892.
Htn	Phil 6100.10*	Kronthal, P. Schnitte durch das centrale Nervensystem des Menschen. Berlin, 1892.
Htn	Phil 9351.2*	Lectures to young men. N.Y., 1892.
	Phil 3808.122	Lehman, Rudolf. Schopenhauer und die Entwickelung der monistischen Weltanschauung. Berlin, 1892.
	Phil 5400.15	Lehmann, A. Die Hauptgesetze des menschlichen Gefühlslebens. Leipzig, 1892.
	Phil 1915.81	Le Rossignol, J.E. Ethical philosophy of Samuel Clarke. Leipzig, 1892.
	Phil 8591.8	Lilly, W.S. The great enigma. N.Y., 1892.
	Phil 8886.18	Lilly, W.S. On right and wrong. London, 1892.
	Phil 2115.14.7	Locke, J. Philosophical works. London, 1892. 2v.
	Phil 3565.32.6	Lotze, Hermann. Outlines of logic and of encyclopaedia of philosophy. Boston, 1892.
	Phil 5585.4	Lukens, H.T. Die Vorstellungsreihen. Gütersloh, 1892.
	Phil 2125.73	McCosh, James. Our moral nature, being a brief system of ethics. N.Y., 1892.
	Phil 5425.6	Macdonald, A. Genius and insanity. Lewes, 1892.
	Phil 8702.3.5	Mackenzie, H. Modern science unlocking the Bible. London, 1892.
	Phil 5052.19	McLachlan, D.B. Reformed logic. London, 1892.
	Phil 6962.1.10	Magnan, V. Le délire chronique à évolution systématique. Paris, 1892.
	Phil 6962.1.3	Magnan, V. Psychiatische Vorlesungen. v.2-6. Leipzig, 1892-93.
	Phil 6962.17	Mathieu, A. Neurasthénie. Paris, 1892.
	Phil 3832.4	Matthes, Ewald. Die Unsterblichkeitslehre des Benedictus Spinoza. Inaug. Diss. Heidelberg, 1892.
	Phil 3625.1.43	Mendelssohn, Moses. Briefe. Berlin, 1892.
	Phil 5252.27	Meynert, T. Sammlung von populär- wissenschaftlichen Vorträgen über den bau und die leistungen des gehirns. Wien, 1892.
	Phil 9352.14	Miller, James R. Girls: faults and ideals. N.Y., 1892.
	Phil 5642.9	Millet, J. Audition colorée. Paris, 1892.
	Phil 8702.14	Mir, Miguel. Harmonia entre a sciencia a fé. v.2. Coimbra, 1892.
	Phil 6682.6.3	Moll, Albert. Hypnotism. London, 1892.
	Phil 4475.1.80	Moniz Barreto, G. Oliveira Martins: estudo de psychologia. Paris, 1892.
	Phil 4605.1.31	Monrad, M.J. Tro og viden. Kristiania, 1892.
	Phil 5252.33.5	Monrad, Marcus. Psychologie; grundrids til brug. Christiania, 1892.
	Phil 293.26	Morelli, C. Lo sviluppo del mondo nelle principali teorie filosofiche. Avellino, 1892.
	Phil 6122.7.4	Mosso, A. Die Ermüdung. Leipzig, 1892.
	Phil 8887.25	Muirhead, J.H. The elements of ethics. N.Y., 1892.
	Phil 5823.2	Nadaillac, J.F.A. Intelligence et instinct. Paris, 1892.
	Phil 3565.126	Nath, Max. Die Psychologie Hermann Lotzes in ihrem Verhältnis zu Herbart. Halle, 1892.
	Phil 4515.81.5	Nyblaeus, A. Bidrag till en karakteristik af den Boströmska filosofien. Lund, 1892.
	Phil 5400.46	Oelzelt-Newin, A. Über sittliche Dispositionen. Graz, 1892.
	Phil 3835.9	Pasig, Walter. Spinozas Rationalismus und Erkenntnislehre im Lichte. Leipzig, 1892.
	Phil 8890.45	Patten, Simon N. Economic causes of moral progress. Philadelphia, 1892.
	Phil 190.3.2	Paulsen, F. Einleitung in die Philosophie. Berlin, 1892.
	Phil 9035.41	Perez, Bernard. Le caractère à l'homme. Paris, 1892.
	Phil 6325.3	Pontoppidan, Knud. Psychiatriske foreläsinger. Kjobenhavn, 1892-95.
	Phil 8505.2	Potter, W.J. The Free Religious Association. Boston, 1892.
	Phil 3565.83	Powers, J.H. Kritische Bemerkungen zu Lotzes Seelenbegriff. Göttingen, 1892.
	Phil 7054.27	Putnam, A. Flashes of light from the spirit land. Boston, 1892.
	Phil 2053.125	Rampendahl, R. Eine Würdigung der ethik Hutchesons. Inaug.-Diss. Leipzig, 1892.
	Phil 8842.3	Rees, D. Contemporary English ethics. Leipzig, 1892.
	Phil 2240.35	Reid, Thomas. The philosophy of Reid...in the "Inquiry into the human mind". N.Y., 1892.
	Phil 5227.1.5	Ribot, T. English psychology. London, 1892.
	Phil 6327.46.18	Ribot, Théodule. Personlighetens sjukdomar. Stockholm, 1892.
	Phil 192.21	Rickert, H. Der Gegenstand der Erkenntniss. Freiburg, 1892.
	Phil 7028.4	Rouxel. Rapports du magnétisme et du spiritisme. Paris, 1892.

1892 - cont.

Phil 1717.3A	Royce, J. Spirit of modern philosophy. Boston, 1892.
Phil 8892.43	Ruiz Gómez, J.E. El nuevo mundo moral ó La nueva vida del hombre. Madrid, 1892.
Phil 193.4	Salter, W.M. First steps in philosophy. Chicago, 1892.
Phil 6128.1	Scervini, P. Anatomia dei centri nervosi. Napoli, 1892.
Phil 8968.10	Scharling, C. Henrik. Christliche Sittenlehre nach evangesischlutherischer Auffassung. Bremen, 1892.
Phil 1200.7	Schmekel, A. Die Philosophie der mittleren Stoa. Berlin, 1892.
Phil 7140.8.5	Schmidkung, Hans. Psychologie der Suggestion. Stuttgart, 1892.
Phil 7140.8	Schrenck-Notzing, Albert. Die Suggestions-Therapie. Stuttgart, 1892.
Phil 5828.8	Schultz, F. Vergleichende Seelenkunde. Leipzig, 1892-97. 2v.
Phil 5585.10	Schwarz, H. Das Wahrnehmungsproblem. Leipzig, 1892.
Phil 6968.5.5	Séglas, J. Des troubles du langage...aliénés. Paris, 1892.
Phil 1195.10	Seitz, K. Die Schule von Gaza. Heidelberg, 1892.
Phil 8893.10	Sharp, F.C. Das aesthetische Element in der Moral. Berlin, 1892.
Phil 8615.17	Sheldon, Walter L. Ethics and the belief in a God. St. Louis, 1892.
Phil 5058.22.9	Sidgwick, A. Distinction and the criticism of beliefs. London, 1892.
Phil 8893.41	Simmel, G. Einleitung in die Moralwissenschaft. Berlin, 1892-93. 2v.
Phil 193.59.30	Simmel, G. Die Probleme der Geschichtsphilosophie. n.p., 1892-1909. 9 pam.
Phil 6688.2	Sinnett, A.P. The relationale of mesmerism. Boston, 1892.
Phil 9035.7.13	Smiles, S. El carácter; version española. Paris, 1892.
Phil 8968.4	Smyth, N. Christian ethics. N.Y., 1892.
Phil 7068.92.45	Some account of the vampires of onset, past and present. Boston, 1892.
Phil 5228.2	Sommer, R. Grundzüge einer Geschichte der deutschen Psychologie. Würzburg, 1892.
Phil 2270.45.15	Spencer, Herbert. First principles. N.Y., 1892.
Phil 2270.73	Spencer, Herbert. Principles of ethics. N.Y., 1892-93. 2v.
Phil 9495.3.2	Sperry, L.B. Confidential talks with young men. N.Y., 1892.
Phil 193.65	Spicker, Gideon. Die Ursachen des Verfalls der Philosophie in alter und neuer Zeit. Leipzig, 1892.
Phil 3819.35.3	Spinoza, Benedictus de. Philosophy of Spinoza. N.Y., 1892.
Phil 5710.9	Stewart, A. Our temperaments; their study and teaching. 2. ed. London, 1892.
Phil 5440.15	Strahan, S.A.K. Marriage and disease. London, 1892.
Phil 4769.8.20	Strakhov, N.N. Mir kak tseloe. 2. izd. Sankt Peterburg, 1892.
Phil 5258.25.11	Sully, J. Human mind. N.Y., 1892. 2v.
Phil 5258.25.5.5	Sully, J. Teacher's handbook of psychology. 3d ed. N.Y., 1892.
Phil 1200.36	Thereianos. Dianeamma Stöikës philesophks. Tergeoië, 1892.
Phil 104.3	Thomson, J.R. A dictionary of philosophy in the words of philosophers. 2nd ed. London, 1892.
Phil 7082.51	Thorleifsdóttir, Elízabet. Draumur. Reykjavík, 1892.
Phil 2138.120	Towers, C.M.D. John Stuart Mill and the London and Westminster review. v.1-2. Boston, 1892.
Phil 8894.21	Traub, Friedrich. Die sittliche Weltordnung. Freiburg, 1892.
Phil 3428.83	Turic, D. Der Entschluss im dem Herbarts Metaphysik. Langensalza, 1892.
Phil 2520.84.5	Twardowski, K. Idee und Perception. Wien, 1892.
Phil 4650.1.40	Vannérus, Allen. Vetenskapernas system. Stockholm, 1892.
Phil 6830.4	Venturi, Silvio. Li digenerazioni psico-sessuali. Torino, 1892.
Phil 1721.1	Volkett, J. Vorträge zur Einführung in die Philosophie der Gegenwart. Photoreproduction. München, 1892.
Phil 197.62	Wade, Joseph M. A few texts. Wise to the wise. Boston, 1892.
Phil 196.5.7	Wake, C.S. Explanation of Van Nostrand's theory of the mental constitution. Chicago, 1892.
Phil 3552.286	Wanke, Georg. Das Stetigkeitsgesetz bei Leibniz. Inaug. -Diss. Kiel, 1892.
Phil 5545.25	Ward, G.W. Dates by name. Baltimore, 1892.
Phil 8897.4	Waters, R. Intellectual pursuits. N.Y., 1892.
Phil 3801.874.5	Watson, John. Schelling's transcendental idealism. 2nd ed. Chicago, 1892.
Phil 2270.138	Weber, Reinhard H. Die Philosophie von Herbert Spencer. Darmstadt, 1892.
Phil 353.6	Weisengrün, P. Das Problem. Leipzig, 1892.
Phil 1200.9	Werzechin, Otto Heinrich Robert. Die Wandlung der stoichen Lehre. Newstrelitz, 1892.
Phil 8610.892	Wheeler, J.M. Bible studies. London, 1892.
Phil 1850.108	Wigston, William F. The Columbus of literature. Chicago, 1892.
Phil 822.2A	Windelband, W. Geschichte der Philosophie. Freiburg, 1892.
Phil 5232.2	Wollny, F. Historisch-psychologischer Tractat. Leipzig, 1892.
Phil 8602.30.3	Wood, Henry. God's image in man. Boston, 1892.
Phil 8897.31	Wood, W. Ideals of life - symposium on the coming man. N.Y., 1892.
Phil 3842.6	Worms, René. La morale de Spinoza. Paris, 1892.
Phil 3915.43	Wundt, Wilhelm. Hypnotismus und Suggestion. Leipzig, 1892.
Phil 3915.55.8	Wundt, Wilhelm. Vorlesungen über die Menschen- und Thierseele. 2. Aufl. Hamburg, 1892. 2v.
Phil 8900.1.5	Zeigler, T. Social ethics. London, 1892.
Phil 1130.2.11	Zeller, Eduard. Die Philosophie der Griechen. v. 1,3-6. Leipzig, 1892. 5v.
Phil 1130.2.9	Zeller, Eduard. Die Philosophie der Griechen. v.2. Leipzig, 1892.
Phil 1130.8.5	Zeller, Eduard. The Stoics, Epicureans, and Sceptics. London, 1892.
Phil 5265.1.5	Ziehen, Theodor. Introduction to physiological psychology. n.p., 1892.

1893

Phil 8875.19	Åberg, L.H. Filosofisk sedelära. v.1-4. Uppsala, 1893-94.
Phil 665.44	Aber, Mary R.A. Souls. Chicago, 1893.
Phil 4065.111	Acanfora-Venturelli, R. Il monismo teosofico di G.B. Palermo, 1893.

1893 - cont.

Phil 3085.2.85   Aders, Fritz. Jacob Friedrich Abel als Philosophie. Inaug. Diss. Berlin, 1893.

Phil 8875.12   Alaux, J.E. Philosophie morale et politique. Paris, 1893.

Phil 9245.9.7   Avebury, John Lubbock. The pleasures of life. London, 1893.

Phil 9245.9.3   Avebury, John Lubbock. The pleasures of life. N.Y., 1893.

Phil 1900.87   Ayer, Joseph Cullen. Versuch einer Darstellung der Ethik Joseph Butlers. Inaug. Diss. Leipzig, 1893.

Phil 1850.35.3   Bacon, Francis. The advancement of learning. v.2. London, 1893-95.

Phil 2270.135   Bager-Sjögren, J. Herbert Spencer och utvecklingsfilosofien. Lund, 1893.

Phil 5241.3.15   Baldwin, J.M. Elements of psychology. N.Y., 1893.

Phil 8581.32   Balmforth, R. The new reformation...moral and social problems. London, 1893.

Phil 6990.3.55   Barbé, Daniel. Lourdes: hier, aujourd'hui, demain. Paris, 1893.

Phil 6990.3.54   Barbé, Daniel. Lourdes: yesterday, today and tomorrow. Baden, 1893.

Phil 801.11   Bascom, John. An historical interpretation of philosophy. N.Y., 1893.

Phil 6111.10.15   Bastian, H.C. On the neural processes underlying attention and volition. London, 1893.

Phil 6615.4   Bastian, Henry Charlton. Various forms of functional paralysis. London, 1893.

Phil 8581.33   Beach, D.N. The newer religious thinking. Boston, 1893.

Phil 5640.2.5   Bernstein, J. Les sens. 5e éd. Paris, 1893.

Phil 176.86   Bertrand, A. Principes de philosophie. Paris, 1893.

Phil 978.6.63.5   Besant, Annie. Death - and after? London, 1893.

Phil 5545.2   Biervliet, J.J. von. La mémoire. Gand, 1893.

Phil 176.152   Biese, Alfred. Die Philosophie des Metaphorischen. Hamburg, 1893.

Phil 176.44   Blackwell, A.B. The philosophy of individuality. N.Y., 1893.

Phil 8876.54   Blondel, Maurice. L'action. Paris, 1893.

Phil 3552.123   Blondel, Maurice. De vinculo substantiali. Thesis. Paris, 1893.

Phil 1135.131   Bois, Henri. Le dogme grec. Paris, 1893.

Phil 8876.25.5   Bowne, B.P. The principles of ethics. N.Y., 1893.

Phil 6111.27.2   Brackett, Anna C. The technique of rest. N.Y., 1893.

Phil 1885.37   Bradley, Francis H. Appearance and reality. London, 1893.

Phil 9045.8   Brinley, C.A. Citizenship. Philadelphia, 1893.

Phil 9245.11.3   Brinton, Daniel G. The pursuit of happiness. Philadelphia, 1893.

Phil 7054.152   Brofferio, Angelo. Per lo spiritismo. 2. ed. Milano, 1893.

Phil 1535.26   Brothers of the Christian Schools. Elementary course of Christian philosophy. N.Y., 1893.

Phil 3483.22   Buchner, E.F. A study of Kant's psychology. N.Y., 1893.

Phil 4983.8.90   Cabrera, Francisco de A. Razón contra razón...de Enrique José de Varona. 3. ed. Habana, 1893.

Phil 2490.98A   Caird, Edward. The social philosophy...of Comte. 2nd ed. Glasgow, 1893.

Phil 6112.2.5   Call, A.P. Power through repose. Boston, 1893.

Phil 510.17   Carneri, Bartolomäus von. Empfindung und Bewusstsein. Bonn, 1893.

Phil 177.8.12A   Carus, Paul. Primer of philosophy. Chicago, 1893.

Phil 8692.10.15   Carus, Paul. The religion of science. Chicago, 1893.

Phil 5212.2   Cattell, J.M. The progress of psychology. N.Y., 1893?

Phil 6535.7   Charity Organization Society, London. The epileptic and crippled child and adult. Photoreproduction. London, 1893.

Phil 2045.92   Chevrillon, André. Qui fuerint saeculo XVII imprimis apud Hobbesium Anglicae solutae orationis progressus. Insulae, 1893.

Phil 8692.2.2   Cooke, J.P. The credentials of science the warrent of faith. N.Y., 1893.

Phil 5752.4   Crombie, A. Essay on philosophical necessity. London, 1893.

Phil 8693.12   Dadson, Arthur J. Evolution and religion. London, 1893.

Phil 5545.69   Dandolo, Giovanni. La dottrina della "memoria", tedesco. Padova, 1893.

Phil 5627.77   Daniels, A.H. The new life. Worcester, 1893.

Phil 8658.8   Davidson, W.L. Theism as grounded in human nature. London, 1893.

Phil 1020.5.5   Dayser, G. Das Buch von der Erkenntniss der Wahrheit. Strassburg, 1893.

Phil 1135.97   Deichmann, C. Das Problem des Raumes in der griechischen Philosophie bis Aristoteles. Halle, 1893.

Phil 3823.6.5   Delblos, Victor. Le problème moral dans la philosophie de Spinoza. Paris, 1893.

Phil 178.44   Delff, Heinrich K.H. Philosophie des Gemüths. Husum, 1893.

Phil 8878.27   DeMotte, J.B. The secret of character building. Chicago, 1893.

Phil 8615.7   Desjardins, P. The present duty. Philadelphia, 1893.

Phil 5257.21   Dessoir, Max. Psychologische Skizzen, von Edmund W. Rells. Leipzig, 1893.

Phil 960.3.2   Deussen, P. On the philosophy of the Vedânta in its relations to occidental metaphysics. Bombay, 1893.

Phil 334.1   Dippe, A. Untersuchungen über die Bedeutung der Denkform. Jena, 1893.

Phil 178.42   Dittes, Friedrich. Gesammelte Schriften. Heft I. Leipzig, 1893.

Phil 3003.1   Drews, A. Die deutsche Spekulation seit Kant. Berlin, 1893. 2v.

Phil 7060.42   Dyer, T.F.T. The ghost world. London, 1893.

Phil 5244.18   Ellefsen, Olaf. Om moralens oprindelse. Kristiania, 1893.

Phil 7054.188   Eriksen, R. Sjaelens gaade. Kristiania, 1893.

Phil 179.3.31   Eucken, R. Die Grundbegriffe der Gegenwart. 2. Aufl. Leipzig, 1893.

Phil 9344.9   Everett, C.C. Ethics for young people. Boston, 1893.

Phil 1705.1.5   Falckenberg, R. History of modern philosophy. N.Y., 1893.

Phil 1535.17   Farges, A. Études philosophiques. Paris, 1893-1902. 8v.

Phil 180.2   Fawcett, E.D. The riddle of the universe. London, 1893.

Phil 6115.11.6   Feuchtersleben, E.F.V. Zur Diätetik der Seele. 2. Aufl. Halle, 1893.

Phil 5642.11   Flournoy, T. Des phénomènes de synopsie. Paris, 1893.

Phil 1850.98   Fonsegrive, G.L. François Bacon. Paris, 1893.

Phil 2520.89   Fouillée, A. Descartes. Paris, 1893.

Phil 336.1.5   Fouillée, A. La psychologie des idées-forces. Paris, 1893. 2v.

Phil 5421.10.3   Friedlaender, Julius. Der Pessimismus im Lichte einer höheren Weltauffassung. Berlin, 1893.

Phil 3488.22   Gartelmann, Henri. Sturz der Metaphysik als Wissenschaft. Berlin, 1893.

1893 - cont.

Phil 181.5   Gerber, G. Das Ich. Berlin, 1893.

Phil 5402.2   Gilman, B.T. Syllabus of...lectures on the psychology of pain. Worcester, Mass., 1893.

Phil 1111.1   Gomperz, T. Griechische Denker. Leipzig, 1893. 3v.

Phil 6116.15   Gorton, D.A. The monism of man. N.Y., 1893.

Phil 8586.4   Gould, George M. The meaning and method of life. N.Y., 1893.

Phil 510.23   Gutberlet, C. Der mechanische Monismus. Paderborn, 1893.

Phil 510.1.1   Haeckel, Ernst. Der Monismus als Band zwischen Religion und Wissenschaft. 6e Aufl. Bonn, 1893.

Phil 6677.1   Hart, E. Hypnotism, mesmerism. N.Y., 1893.

Phil 3415.32.8   Hartmann, Eduard von. Philosophy of the unconcious. 2nd ed. London, 1893. 2v.

Phil 182.70   Heegaard, S. Om opdragelse. 4e Opl. v.1-2. Kjøbenhavn, 1893.

Phil 3425.65A   Hegel, Georg Wilhelm Friedrich. The ethics of Hegel. Boston, 1893.

Phil 3425.68.5   Hegel, Georg Wilhelm Friedrich. System der Sittlichkeit. Osterwiech, 1893.

Phil 8587.15.2   Higginson, T.W. The sympathy of religions. Chicago, 1893.

Phil 182.16   Hill, D.J. Genetic philosophy. N.Y., 1893.

Phil 3489.16   Høffding, H. Kontinuiteten i Kants filosofiske udviklingsgang. Kjøbenhavn, 1893.

Phil 5247.10.14   Høffding, H. Psychologie in Umrissen auf Grundläge der Erfahrung. Leipzig, 1893.

Phil 6677.13   Howard, W.L. Hypnotism as a therapeutic agent. Baltimore, 1893.

Phil 7060.28   Hudson, T.J. Law of psychic phenomena. Chicago, 1893.

Phil 2050.71A   Hume, David. Philosophy of Hume. N.Y., 1893.

Phil 2050.70   Hume, David. Treatise of morals. Photoreproduction. Boston, 1893.

Phil 2050.42   Hume, David. Eine Untersuchung über den menschlichen Verstand. Leipzig, 1893.

Phil 8697.5.3   Huxley, T.H. Essays upon some controverted questions. N.Y., 1893.

NEDL Phil 9150.5   Huxley, T.H. Evolution and ethics. London, 1893.

Htn Phil 2055.3.30*   Huxley, Thomas H. The Romanes lecture 1893. London, 1893.

Phil 9515.3.88   Ischer, R. J.G. Zimmermann's Leben und Werke. Bern, 1893.

Phil 3428.84   Ivanoff, T. Die abweichungen Steinthals von Herbart. Jena, 1893.

Phil 5249.2.11   James, William. Psychology. N.Y., 1893.

Phil 5545.173   Janet, Pierre. L'amnésie continue. Paris, 1893.

Phil 6615.6   Janet, Pierre. État mental des hystériques. Paris, 1893-94. 2v.

Phil 2409.2   Joyau, Emmanuel. La philosophie en France pendant la révolution. Paris, 1893.

Phil 978.7.2   Judge, W.Z. The ocean of theosophy. 2nd ed. N.Y., 1893.

Phil 1850.90   Jung, E. Causa finalis. Eine Bakostudie. Giessen, 1893.

Phil 3480.57.10   Kant, Immanuel. Immanuel Kant's Prolegomena zu einer jeden künftigen Metaphysik. 3. Aufl. Berlin, 1893. 3 pam.

Phil 8885.37   Katô, Hiroyuke. Der Kampf ums recht des Stärkeren und seine Entwickelung. Tokyô, 1893.

Phil 6680.3   Kiesewetter, C. Mesmer's Leben und Lehre. Leipzig, 1893.

Phil 7052.6   Kiesewetter, Karl. Die Entwickelungsgeschichte des Spiritismus. Leipzig, 1893.

Phil 9170.2   Kinney, A. The conquest of death. N.Y., 1893.

Phil 8635.8   Knight, W.A. Aspects of theism. London, 1893.

Phil 5374.33   Kodis, J. Zur Analyse des Apperceptions begriffes. Berlin, 1893.

Phil 5250.14   Königbauer, J. Grundzüge der Psychologie und Logik. 2. Aufl. Regensburg, 1893.

Phil 6960.4   Krafft-Ebing, R. von. Lehrbuch der Psychiatrie. Stuttgart, 1893.

Htn Phil 7075.7.8*   Krafft-Ebing, Richard von. Psychopathia sexualis. Stuttgart, 1893.

Phil 6680.2.3   Kraft-Ebing, R. von. Hypnotische Experimente. Stuttgart, 1893.

Phil 5250.2.5   Külpe, Oswald. Grundriss der Psychologie. Leipzig, 1893.

Phil 5374.7.5   Lange, K.M. Apperception. Boston, 1893.

Phil 5251.3.5   Langer, P. Psychophysische Streitfragen. Ohrdruf, 1893.

Phil 8591.13   LeGallienne, R. The religion of a literary man. N.Y., 1893.

Phil 6121.26   Lenhossék, Mihaly. Der Feinere bau des Nervensystems im Lichte neuester Forschungen. Berlin, 1893.

Phil 3552.98   Leroy, G.V. Die philosophische Probleme...Leibniz und Clarke. Mainz, 1893.

Phil 5251.6.5   Lewes, G.H. The physical basis of mind. London, 1893.

Phil 2520.144   Liedtke, V. De Beweise für das dasein Gottes. Heidelberg, 1893.

Phil 1850.114   Liljeqvist, E. Om Francis Bacon filosofi med särskild hänsyn till det etiska problemet. Uppsala, 1893.

Phil 9351.16.2   Lindsay, A.R.B. What is worth while? N.Y., 1893.

Phil 5051.30   Lipps, T. Grundzüge der Logik. Hamburg, 1893.

Phil 2115.11.2   Locke, J. Works. London, 1893. 10v.

Phil 5545.157   Loewenton, E. Versuche über das Gedächtnis. Inaug. Diss. Dorpat, 1893.

Phil 6121.6.5   Luciani, L. Das Keinhirn. Leipzig, 1893.

Phil 292.2   Lukas, F. Die Grundbegriffe...Kösmogonien. Leipzig, 1893.

Phil 2045.80   Lyon, G. La philosophie de Hobbes. Paris, 1893.

Phil 6322.10   MacDonald, A. Abnormal man. Washington, D.C., 1893.

Phil 6962.1.2   Magnan, V. Leçons cliniques sur les maladies mentales. 2. éd. Paris, 1893.

Phil 6962.1.5   Magnan, V. Recherches sur les centres nerveux. 2. série. Paris, 1893.

Phil 3120.1.80   Maosherr, T. J.A.E. Biedermann. Jena, 1893.

Phil 2115.134   Marion, Henri. J. Locke: sa vie et son oeuvre. 2e éd. Paris, 1893.

Phil 6022.2   Martin, William W. Our noses. London, 1893.

Phil 2045.91   Messer, W.A. Das Verhältnis von Sittengesetz...bei Hobbes. Mainz, 1893.

Phil 2655.1.81   Meyer, E. Der Philosoph Franz Hemsterhuis. Breslau, 1893.

Phil 3808.129   Millioud, Maurice. Étude critique système philosophique de Schopenhauer. Lausanne, 1893.

Phil 52.2   Minnesota. University. Department of Philosophy. Papers. Minneapolis, 1893-

Phil 8592.33   Møller, Otto. Noget om determinisme og frihed. Kjøbenhavn, 1893.

Phil 8520.2   Müller, F.M. Theosophy or psychological religion. London, 1893.

Phil 9352.8.7   Munger, Theodore T. On the threshold. 26th ed. Boston, 1893.

Phil 3552.283   Nithack, J. Darstellung und Kritik der Lehre Leibniz' von der menschlichen Wahlfreiheit. Inaug. Diss. Halle, 1893.

Phil 6750.6   Noir, J. Étude sur les tics. Paris, 1893.

Phil 5425.7.3   Nordau, M. Entartung. 2. Aufl. Berlin, 1893. 2v.

Chronological Listing

1893 - cont.

Phil 3425.222   Norelius, G. Grunddragen af Hegels filosofi och ästetik. Norrköping, 1893.

Phil 2733.88   Novaro, Mario. Die Philosophie des Nicolaus Malebranche. Berlin, 1893.

NEDL Phil 2414.1   Owen, J. The skeptics of the French renaissance. London, 1893.

Phil 4014.1   Owen, J. Skeptics of the Italian Renaissance. Photoreproduction. London, 1893.

Phil 1158.15.5   Pater, Walter. Marius the Epicurean. London, 1893.

Phil 336.1.15   Pawlicki, S. A. Fouillée's Neue Theorie der Ideenloréfts. Wien, 1893.

Phil 7054.163   Petersilea, Carlyle. Mary Anne Carew; wife, mother, spirit. London, 1893.

Phil 5255.22   Pioger, J. La vie et la pensée. Paris, 1893.

Phil 8610.893   Putnam, S.P. Why don't he lend a hand? N.Y., 1893.

Phil 8430.22   Raymond, G.L. The genesis of art form. N.Y., 1893.

Phil 8430.34   Raymond, G.L. The genesis of art form. N.Y., 1893.

Phil 3808.163   Richter, Raoul. Schopenhauer's Verhältnis zu Kant in seinen Grundzügen. Leipzig, 1893.

Phil 192.10A   Ritchie, D.G. Darwin and Hegel. London, 1893.

Phil 7068.93.10   Rivail, H.L.D. Spiritualist philosophy. Boston, 1893.

Phil 645.29   Roberty, E. de. Agnosticisme. 2e éd. Paris, 1893.

Phil 192.31   Roberty, E. de. Recherche de l'unité. Paris, 1893.

Phil 1717.3.5A   Royce, J. Spirit of modern philosophy. Boston, 1893.

Phil 6127.15   Rüdinger, N. Über die Wage und Ziele. München, 1893.

Phil 8892.9   Ryland, F. Ethics. London, 1893.

Phil 5440.5   Sanson, A. L'hérédité. Paris, 1893.

Phil 4210.90   Sarlo, Francesco de. Le basi della psicologia e della biologia secondo il Rosmini. Roma, 1893.

Phil 9150.24   Sarolea, Charles. La liberté et le déterminisme rapports avec la théorie de l'évolution. Thèse. Bruxelles, 1893.

Phil 7068.93.15   Savage, Minot J. Psychics; facts and theories. Boston, 1893.

Phil 7080.47   Scholz, F. Sleep and dreams. N.Y., 1893.

Phil 3808.76.15   Schopenhauer, Arthur. Briefe. Leipzig, 1893.

Phil 3808.37   Schopenhauer, Arthur. De vier hocksteenen der Wereld en harr Bouwmeester. v.1-2. 's-Gravenhage, 1893.

Phil 5500.2.5   Schrader, E. Die bewusste Beziehung. Leipzig, 1893.

Phil 8893.98   Seaverns, A.S. Thoughts for the thoughtful. N.Y., 1893.

Phil 193.136   Segall-Socolin, I. Zur Verjüngung der Philosophie. 1e Reihe. Berlin, 1893.

Phil 3425.92.2   Seth, A. Hegelianism and personality. 2d ed. Edinburgh, 1893.

Phil 8598.39   Seydel, Rudolf. Religionsphilosophie im Umriss. Freiburg, 1893.

Phil 8708.2.7   Shaler, N.S. The interpretation of nature. 2. ed. Boston, 1893.

Phil 8893.10.5   Sharp, F.C. The aesthetic element in morality. N.Y., 1893.

Phil 5058.22.15   Sidgwick, A. The process of argument. London, 1893.

Phil 8598.9   Siebeck, Hermann. Lehrbuch der Religionsphilosophie. Freiburg, 1893.

Phil 349.6   Skrochowski, F. Human knowledge. Cnacow, 1893.

Phil 7140.1   Souriau, P. La suggestion dans l'art. Paris, 1893.

Phil 2270.77.20   Spencer, Herbert. A rejoinder to Professor Weismann. London, 1893?

NEDL Phil 2270.56.5   Spencer, Herbert. Social statics. N.Y., 1893.

Phil 6968.9   Stearns, H.P. Lectures on mental disease. Philadelphia, 1893.

Phil 3640.300   Stein, Ludwig. Friedrich Nietzsches Weltanschauung und ihre Gefahren. Berlin, 1893.

NEDL Phil 193.35   Stephen, L. An agnostic's apology. London, 1893.

NEDL Phil 193.35.1   Stephen, L. An agnostic's apology. London, 1893.

Phil 5325.11   Stern, L.W. Analogie in volkstümlichen Denken. Berlin, 1893.

Phil 2275.70   Stewart, D. Outlines of moral philosophy. Edinburgh, 1893.

Phil 7150.3   Strahan, S.A.K. Suicide and insanity. London, 1893.

Phil 1865.180   Surra, G. Studio sulla morale di Geremia Bentham. Torino, 1893.

Phil 9530.9   Thayer, W.M. Ethics of success. Boston, 1893.

Phil 351.1   Uphues, G.A. Psychologie des Erkennens I. Leipzig, 1893.

Phil 61.1.5   Vienna. Universität. Philosophische Gesellschaft. Veröffentlichung. Leipzig, 1893- 3v.

Phil 6691.1   Vincent, R.H. Elements of hypnotism. London, 1893.

Phil 6750.9   Voisin, J. L'idiotie. Paris, 1893.

Phil 9362.16.6   Wagner, C. Jeunesse. 8e ed. Paris, 1893.

Phil 9362.16.5   Wagner, C. Youth. N.Y., 1893.

Phil 8062.4   Walter, Julius. Die Geschichte der Ästhetik im Altertum. Leipzig, 1893.

Phil 3504.26   Wegner, Gustav. Kantlexikon. Berlin, 1893.

Phil 3640.175   Weigand, Wilhelm. Friedrich Nietzsche. München, 1893.

Phil 8897.50.2   Weiss, Berthold. Die ethische Aufgabe des Menschen. Berlin, 1893.

Phil 3552.97   Wernick, G. Der Begriff der Materie bei Leibniz. Jena, 1893.

Phil 6972.2.5   Wernicke, C. Gesammelte Aufsätze und kritische Riferate. Berlin, 1893.

Phil 7082.28   Weygandt, Wilhelm. Entstehung der Träume. Leipzig, 1893.

Phil 6132.6.5   Whipple, L.E. The philosophy of mental healing. N.Y., 1893.

Phil 4655.1.58   Wikner, Pontus. Tankar och frågor inför menniskones son. 4. uppl. Stockholm, 1893.

Phil 9150.29   Williams, C.M. A review of the systems of ethics founded on the theory of evolution. N.Y., 1893.

Phil 8647.8   Willink, Arthur. The world of the unseen. N.Y., 1893.

Phil 2725.1.81   Wolff, E. De la Forges Psychologie. Jena, 1893.

Phil 3915.45.4   Wundt, Wilhelm. Grundzüge der physiologischen Psychologie. 4. Aufl. Leipzig, 1893. 2v.

Phil 3915.40.2   Wundt, Wilhelm. Logik. Stuttgart, 1893-95. 3v.

Phil 3808.165   Wyczołkowska, A. Schopenhauers Lehre von der menschlichen Freiheit in ihrer Beziehung zu Kant und Schelling. Inaug. Diss. Wien, 1893.

Phil 5400.75   Ziegler, T. Das Gefühl. Stuttgart, 1893.

1894

Phil 4513.2.31   Aars, K.B.R. Tanker og syn En liden studie. Kristiania, 1894.

Phil 2400.2   Adam, C. La philosophie en France. Paris, 1894.

Phil 8615.5.9   Adler, Felix. Creed and deed. N.Y., 1894.

Phil 5040.10   Alfonso, N.R. d'. Principii di logica reale. Torino, 1894.

Phil 8580.12.2   Allen, J.H. Positive religion. Boston, 1894. 5v.

Phil 5400.68   Ambrosi, L. La dottrina del sentimento nella storia della filosofia. Roma, 1894.

1894 - cont.

Phil 8625.3.15   Andresen, Karl. Wir werden wieder geboren. Hamburg, 1894.

Phil 8520.9   Anzoletti, Luisa. La fede nel soprannaturale. Milano, 1894.

Phil 2270.134   Arfvidsson, H.D. Religion och vetenskap...Spencers. Diss. Lund, 1894.

Phil 7054.14   Arnold, H. Wie errichtet und leitet man spiritistische Zirkel in der Familie? Leipzig, 1894.

Phil 3482.3   Arnoldt, Emil. Kritische excurse im Gebiete der Kant-Forschung. Köningsburg, 1894.

Phil 5241.2.27   Bain, A. The senses and the intellect. 4th ed. N.Y., 1894.

Phil 5041.3.10   Bain, Alexander. Logique déductive et inductive. 3e éd. Paris, 1894. 2v.

Phil 176.45.5   Baldwin, J.M. Imitation. n.p., 1894-1904. 8 pam.

Phil 5257.3.25   Baumann, Rehmke, Joh: Lehrbuch der allgemeinen Psychologie. Göttingen, 1894.

Phil 5125.7   Benzoni, Roberto. L'induzione. Pt.1-3. Genova, 1894.

Phil 5241.96   Bergström, J.A. An experimental study of some of the conditions of mental activity. Worcester, 1894.

Phil 978.6.9   Besant, Annie. The building of the kosmos. London, 1894.

Phil 5545.77   Binet, A. Psychologie des grands calculateurs et joueurs d'échecs. Paris, 1894.

Phil 5425.36   Bleibtreu, K. Letzte Wahrheiten. Leipzig, 1894.

Phil 1020.17.5   Boer, Tjitze de. Die Widersprüche der Philosophie nach al Gozzali und ihr Ausgleich durch Ibn Rosd. Strassburg, 1894.

Phil 3821.10   Bohin, Vilhelm. Spinoza. Berlin, 1894.

Phil 3552.255   Boirac, Aemilius. De spatio apud Leibnitium. Thesis. Paris, 1894.

Phil 176.68   Boirac, Émile. L'idée du Phénomène. Thèse. Paris, 1894.

Phil 8581.44   Bois, Henri. De la connaissance religieuse. Paris, 1894.

Htn Phil 6990.3.27*   Boissarie, P.G. Lourdes depuis 1858 jusqu'à nos jours. Paris, 1894.

Phil 8725.1   Bonham, J. Secularism; its progress and morals. N.Y., 1894.

Phil 3001.3   Brasch, M. Leipziger Philosophen. Leipzig, 1894.

Phil 600.4   Broglie, A.T.P. La réaction contre le positivisme. Paris, 1894.

Phil 3821.3   Brunschvicg, L. Spinoza. 2. éd. Paris, 1894.

Phil 9035.44   Bryant, S.W. Short studies in character. London, 1894.

Phil 476.3.9   Büchner, L. Man in the past, present and future. N.Y., 1894.

Phil 6112.2.2   Call, A.P. As a matter of course. Boston, 1894.

Phil 3552.297   Capesius, J. Der Apperceptionsbegriff bei Leipzig und dessen Nachfolgern. Hermannstadt, 1894.

Phil 331.2.8   Carstanjen, F. Richard Avenarius' Biomechanische Grundlegung. München, 1894.

Phil 6619.6   Cattani, Giuseppe. Isterismo e sentimento. 19. ed. Milano, 1894.

Phil 4525.3.30   Cavallin, P. Identiska och syntetiska satser. Lund, 1894.

Phil 8877.61   Christ, Paul. Die sittliche Weltordnung. Leiden, 1894.

Phil 7054.32   Clerk, A.M. Spiritism; the keystone of Christianity. London, 1894.

Phil 5500.8   Cornelius, Hans. Versuch einer Theorie der Existenzialurteile. München, 1894.

Phil 6112.9.4   Courmont, F. Le cervelet et ses fonctions. Paris, 1894.

Phil 178.54.3   Dandolo, G. Appunti di filosofia. 3. ed. Padova, 1894.

Phil 178.54.5   Dandolo, G. L'obbietto della filosofia e la verità. Padova, 1894.

Phil 5400.19.3.5   Darwin, Charles. The expression of the emotions in man and animals. N.Y., 1894.

Phil 8878.35   Davies, William. The pilgrim of the infinite. London, 1894.

Phil 2520.35.4   Descartes, René. Discours de la méthode pour bien conduire sa raison et chercher la vérité dans les sciences. Paris, 1894.

Phil 803.3   Deussen, P. Allgemeine Geschichte der Philosophie. v.1, pts.1-3. v.2, pts.1-3. Leipzig, 1894-1917. 7v.

Phil 803.3.1A   Deussen, P. Allgemeine Geschichte der Philosophie. v.1-2. Leipzig, 1894-1920. 7v.

NEDL Phil 178.5.5   Deussen, P. Elements of metaphysics. London, 1894. (Changed to KD 25702)

Phil 3805.166   Diebow, Paul. Die Pädagogik Schleiermachers im Lichte seiner und unserer Zeit. Halle, 1894.

Phil 3485.4   Drews, A.C.H. Kants Naturphilosophie als Grundlage seines Systems. Berlin, 1894.

Phil 5643.51   Drott, Anton. Die Aussengrenzen des Gesichtsfeldes für weisse und farbige Objecte beim normalen Auge. Inaug. Diss. Breslau, 1894?

Phil 803.2.4   Duehring, Eugen. His Gesammtcursus der Philosophie. Leipzig, 1894-95. 2v.

Phil 1145.51   Dugas, L. L'amité antique d'après les moeurs populaires. Thèse. Paris, 1894.

Phil 6673.4.3   Du Potet, J. de S. Traité complet de magnétisme animal. 5e éd. Paris, 1894.

Phil 665.8A   DuPrel, C. Die Entdeckung der Seele durch die Geheimwissenschaften. v.1-2. Leipzig, 1894-95.

Phil 6953.5   Dupuy, Paul. De l'automatisme psychologique. Bordeaux, 1894.

Phil 6313.2   Durand, J.P. Le merveilleux scientifique. Paris, 1894.

Phil 8879.19   Edfeldt, Hans. Om de etiska grundbegreppen. Upsala, 1894.

Phil 3585.9.80   Ellissen, O.A. Friedrich Albert Lange. Leipzig, 1894.

Phil 179.2   Erhardt, F. Metaphysik. Leipzig, 1894.

Phil 5244.5   Exner, S. Entwurf zu einer physiologischen Erklärung der psychischen Erscheinungen. Leipzig, 1894.

Phil 6114.12   Exner, Sigmund. Entwurf zu einer psychologischen Erklärung der psychischen Erscheinungen. Leipzig, 1894.

Phil 672.32   Fallen angels. London, 1894.

Phil 6400.11   Ferrand, Auguste. Le langage, la parole et les aphasies. Paris, 1894.

Phil 5325.2.5   Ferri, L. La psicologia dell'associazione dall'Hobbes. Roma, 1894.

Phil 180.31   Fischer, Engelbert Lorenz. Das Grundproblem der Metaphysik. Mainz, 1894.

Phil 6115.21.3   Forel, A. Gehirn und Seele. 4. Aufl. Bonn, 1894.

Phil 5400.43   Frey, Max von. Die Gefühle und ihr Verhältnis zu den Empfindungen. Leipzig, 1894.

Phil 6955.12   Friedmann, M. Über den Wahn. v.1-2. Wiesbaden, 1894.

Phil 8406.8   Frothingham, A.L. The philosophy of art. Princeton, 1894.

Phil 960.4   Garbe, R. Die Samkhya - Philosophie. Leipzig, 1894.

Phil 4195.80   Giovanni, V. di. Giovanni Pico. Palermo, 1894.

Phil 7072.6.5   Glendinning, Andrew. The veil lifted; modern developments of spirit photography. London, 1894.

Phil 3826.2   Godfernaux, A. De Spinoza. Paris, 1894.

Phil 5246.7   Godfernaux, A. Le sentiment et la pensée. Paris, 1894.

Chronological Listing

Phil 4757.3.25   Golubinskii, F.A. Premudrost' i blagost' Bozhiia v sud'bakh mira i cheloveka; o konechnych prichinakh. 4. izd. Sankt Peterburg, 1894.

Phil 181.41   González Serrano, U. En pro y en contra. Madrid, 1894.

Phil 6676.7   Grossmann, J. Die Bedeutung der hypnotischen Suggestion als Heilmittel. Berlin, 1894.

Phil 510.1.1.5   Haeckel, Ernst. Monism. London, 1894.

Phil 6048.94.5   Hamon, Louis. Cheiro's language of the hand. N.Y., 1894.

Phil 6048.94.10   Hamon, Louis. Comfort's palmistry guide by Cheiro (pseud.) palmist. Augusta, 1894.

Phil 8697.16   Harrison, A.J. The ascent of faith. N.Y., 1894.

Phil 8610.894   Hartmann, J. God and man in the appetites. N.Y., 1894.

Phil 182.66   Hauptmann, C. Die Metaphysik in der modernen Physiologie. Jena, 1894.

Phil 3425.50   Hegel, Georg Wilhelm Friedrich. Hegel's philosophy of mind. Oxford, 1894.

Phil 3489.10   Heinze, Max. Vorlesungen Kants über Metaphysik aus drei Semestern. Leipzig, 1894.

Phil 3808.143   Herrig, Hans. Gesammelte Aufsätze über Schopenhauer. Leipzig, 1894.

Phil 338.6.2   Heymans, G. Gesetze und Elemente des wissenschaftlichen Denkens. Leipzig, 1894.

Phil 8882.12   Hilty, K. Glück. Frauenfeld, 1894.

Phil 5425.5.6   Hirsch, William. Genie und Entartung. 2. Aufl. Berlin, 1894.

Phil 2045.51.9   Hobbes, Thomas. Leviathan. London, 1894.

Phil 4580.36   Høffding, Harald. Den nyere filosofis historie. København, 1894-95. 2v.

Phil 8882.44   Hoekstra, S. Zedenleer. Amsterdam, 1894. 3v.

Phil 2270.92.90   Hudson, William Henry. An introduction to the philosophy of Herbert Spencer. N.Y., 1894.

Phil 5125.8   Hughes, Henry. The theory of inference. London, 1894.

Phil 2050.40   Hume, David. An enquiry...human understanding. Oxford, 1894.

Phil 2050.87.10   Huxley, Thomas H. Hume. N.Y., 1894.

Phil 5628.50.20   Imbert-Gourbeyre, Antoine. La stigmatisation, l'extase divine, et les miracles de Lourdes. Clermont-Ferrand, 1894. 2v.

Phil 6958.6   International Congress of Charities, Corrections and Philanthropy, Chicago, 1893. Commitment, detention care, and treatment of the insane. Baltimore, 1894.

Phil 340.2   Jaja, Donato. L'intuito nella conoscenza. Napoli, 1894.

Phil 2020.81   James, G.F. Thomas Hill Green und der Utilitarismus. Halle, 1894.

Phil 2668.50.5   Janet, Paul A.R. Final causes. 3d ed. N.Y., 1894.

Phil 6959.1.3   Janet, Pierre. L'automatisme psychologique. 2. ed. Paris, 1894.

Phil 7054.148   Judson, Abby A. The bridge between two worlds. Minneapolis, 1894.

Phil 3480.59.25   Kant, Immanuel. Vorlesungen Kants über Metaphysik aus drei Semestern. Leipzig, 1894.

Phil 5250.5   Kellogg, A.M. Elementary psychology. N.Y., 1894.

Phil 8620.35   Keppler, Paul. Das Problem des Leidens in der Moral. Freiburg im Breisgau, 1894.

Phil 9150.15   Kies, Marietta. Institutional ethics. Boston, 1894.

Phil 8885.26   Kleffler, Henri. Philosophie du sens commun. Paris, 1894-95. 3v.

Phil 5330.2   Kohn, H.E. Zur Theorie der Aufmerksamkeit. Halle, 1894.

Phil 5250.18   Kraepelin, Emil. Om sjalsarbete. Stockholm, 1894.

Phil 3415.97   Kurt, N. Wahrheit und Dichtung in den Hauptlehren Eduard von Hartmann's. Leipzig, 1894.

Phil 5251.1.2   Ladd, G.T. Primer of psychology. N.Y., 1894.

Phil 6390.2   Landmann, S. Die Mehrheit geistiger Persönlichkeiten in einem Individuum. Stuttgart, 1894.

Phil 7068.94.5   Lang, Andrew. Cock Lane and common-sense. London, 1894.

Phil 5374.7.6   Lange, K.M. Apperception. Boston, 1894.

Phil 5545.182   Lasson, Adolf. Das Gedächtnis. Berlin, 1894.

Phil 7060.86.5   Lee, F.G. Lights and shadows. London, 1894.

Phil 8886.20   Lefèvre, G. Obligation morale et idéalisme. Paris, 1894.

Phil 400.36   Lefèvre, Georges. Obligation morale et idéalisme. Thèse. Paris, 1894.

Phil 3808.92   Lehmann, R. Schopenhauer. Berlin, 1894.

Phil 8886.8   Letourneau, C. L'évolution de la morale. Paris, 1894.

Phil 5465.15   Leuchtenberger, G. Die Phantasie ihr Wesen. Erfurt, 1894.

Phil 3460.88   Lévy-Bruhl, L. La philosophie de Jacobi. Paris, 1894.

Phil 9455.5   Lewis, G.C. An essay on the influence of authority in matters of opinion. London, 1894.

Phil 8591.7.10   Liddon, H.P. Some elements of religion. 10. ed. London, 1894.

Phil 7054.50   Lillie, Arthur. Modern mystics and modern magic. N.Y., 1894.

Phil 1516.1.2   Littlejohn, J.M. Political theory of the schoolmen. College Springs, 1894.

Phil 2115.36   Locke, J. Essay concerning human understanding. Oxford, 1894. 3v.

Phil 6321.4   Loewenfeld, L. Pathologie und Therapie de Neurasthenie und Hysterie. Wiesbaden, 1894.

Phil 5425.4.15   Lombroso, C. Entartung und Genie. Leipzig, 1894.

Phil 5425.4   Lombroso, C. L'uomo di genio. Torino, 1894.

Phil 2125.75*   McCosh, James. Philosophy of reality: should it be favored by America? N.Y., 1894.

Phil 9045.14   MacCunn, John. Ethics of citizenship. Glasgow, 1894.

Phil 5762.12.5   Mach, F.J. Die Willensfreiheit des Menschen. Paderborn, 1894.

Phil 4170.7.48   Mamiani della Rovere, Terenzio. Lo Spedalieri. Roma, 1894.

Phil 2885.83   Margerie, Amédée de. H. Taine. Paris, 1894.

Phil 5402.11   Marshall, H.R. Pain, pleasure, and aesthetics. N.Y., 1894.

Phil 187.9   Martin, F. La perception extérieure. Paris, 1894.

Phil 2115.95   Martinak, E. Die Logik John Lockes'. Halle, 1894.

Phil 5627.119   Meige, Henry. Les possédées noires. Paris, 1894.

Phil 6682.4   Mesnet, E. Outrages à la pudeur....Somnambulisme. Paris, 1894.

Phil 7080.32   Michaelis, A.O. Der Schlaf nach seiner Bedeutung. Leipzig, 1894.

Phil 5762.10   Milesi, D. La negazione del libero arbitrio ed il criterio del giusto. Milano, 1894.

Phil 2520.138.5   Milhaud, G.S. Num Cartesii methodus tantum valeat in suo opere illustrando quantum ipse senserit. Thesis. Montpellier, 1894.

Phil 5052.6   Minto, William. Logic. N.Y., 1894.

Phil 6322.1.10   Mobius, P.J. Über den Begriff der Hysterie und andere Vorwürfe vorwegend psychologischen Art. Leipzig, 1894.

Phil 8592.50.5   Molinari, G. de. Religion. 2. ed. London, 1894.

Phil 6962.7   Moreau, P. Les excentriques. Paris, 1894.

Phil 5822.1.3   Morgan, C.L. Introduction to comparative psychology. London, 1894.

Phil 7068.94.45   Moses, W.S. Spirit teachings. London, 1894.

Phil 6122.7   Mosso, A. La fatigue intellectuelle et physique. Paris, 1894.

Phil 9352.11   Moxom, P.S. The aim of life. Boston, 1894.

Phil 3270.3.85   Münz, Bernhard. Jakob Frohschammer. Breslau, 1894.

Phil 960.7.5   Muller, F.M. Three lectures on the Vedânta philosophy. London, 1894.

Phil 4210.81.12F   Nardi, P. de. Di Antonio Rosmini-Serbati reformatore. Forli, 1894.

Phil 188.11.5   Naville, Ernest. La définition de la philosophie. Genève, 1894.

Phil 672.11   Nichols, H. Our notions of number and space. Boston, 1894.

Phil 5425.7.5   Nordau, M. Dégénérescence. Paris, 1894. 2v.

Phil 189.6   Ormond, A.T. Basal concepts in philosophy. N.Y., 1894.

Phil 3428.95.2   Ostermann, W. Die Hauptsächlichstein der Herbartschen Psychologie. 2. Aufl. Oldenburg, 1894.

Phil 7068.94.15   Parish, Edmond. Über die Trugwahrnehmung. Leipzig, 1894.

Phil 2805.40.25   Pascal, Blaise. Thoughts on religion and philosophy. London, 1894.

Phil 8890.39   Pascal, G. de. Philosophie morale et sociale. Paris, 1894.

Phil 8890.6.5.9   Paulsen, F. System der Ethik. 3. Aufl. Berlin, 1894. 2v.

Phil 5066.12.10   Peano, G. Notations de logique mathématique. Turin, 1894.

Phil 5628.12   Perales y Gutiérrez, Arturo. El supernaturalismo de Santa Teresa y la filosofia médica. Madrid, 1894.

Phil 3497.13   Pesch, T. Kant et la science moderne. Paris, 1894.

Phil 7068.94.35   Pettis, O.G. Autobiography by Jesus of Nazareth. Washington, 1894.

Phil 8595.4.11   Pfleiderer, O. Philosophy and development of religion. N.Y., 1894. 2v.

Phil 8640.10   Philipson, J. The natural history of hell. N.Y., 1894.

Phil 5765.6   Piat, Clodius. La liberté. Paris, 1894-95. 2v.

Phil 5055.10   Piola, Giuseppe. Elementi di logica guiridica. Roma, 1894.

Phil 7068.94.10   Podmore, Frank. Apparitions and thought-transference. London, 1894.

Phil 6125.8   Polak, A.J. Gedachten over geest. n.p., 1894.

Phil 8610.894.5   Putnam, S.P. Four hundred years of freethought. N.Y., 1894.

Phil 8597.32.5   Rauwenhoff, D.L.W.E. Religionsphilosophie. 2. Aufl. Braunschweig, 1894.

Phil 8418.5   Raymond, G.L. Art theory; an introduction to the study of comparative aesthetics. N.Y., 1894.

Phil 9357.6   Reclus, Elisée. L'ideal et la jeunesse. Bruxelles, 1894.

Phil 5257.3   Rehmke, J. Lehrbuch der allgemeinen Psychologie. Hamburg, 1894.

Phil 5767.1.12   Ribot, T. The diseases of the will. Chicago, 1894.

Phil 3791.36   Riehl, Alois. Introduction to theory of science and metaphysics. London, 1894.

Phil 192.13.5   Robertson, G.C. Philosophical remains. London, 1894.

Phil 9075.7   Robertson, J.D. Conscience. London, 1894.

Phil 3837.2   Roe, E.D. The probability; a critique of Spinoza's demonstration. Andover, 1894.

Phil 8672.6.5   Royce, J. The conception of God. N.Y., 1894.

Phil 193.48   Sanchez, C.L. Estudios de la filosofia. Buenos Aires, 1894.

Phil 5258.4.3   Sanford, E.C. Course in experimental psychology. Boston, 1894.

Phil 193.9.2   Schiller, F.C.S. Riddles of the Sphinx. London, 1894.

Phil 349.10.5A   Schuppe, W. Grundriss der Erkenntnistheorie und Logik. Berlin, 1894.

Phil 2520.98   Schwarz, H. Die Lehre von den Sinnesqualitäten...Descartes. Halle, 1894.

Phil 630.16   Schwarz, Hermann. Was will der kritische Realismus? Leipzig, 1894.

Phil 5258.21   Schweden, P. Über elementarische psychische Prozesse. Berlin, 1894.

Phil 8893.8   Seth, J. A study of ethical principles. Edinburgh, 1894.

Phil 3565.106   Simon, Theodor. Leib und Seele bei Fechner und Lotze als vertreten Zweier massgebenden Weltanschauungen. Göttingen, 1894.

Phil 1928.80   Spaulding, F.E. Richard Cumberland...englischen Ethik. Leipzig, 1894.

Phil 2270.45.25   Spencer, Herbert. First principles. N.Y., 1894.

Phil 2270.70.10   Spencer, Herbert. Principles of psychology. N.Y., 1894. 2v.

Phil 3819.31.6   Spinoza, Benedictus de. Ethic demonstrated in geometrical order. N.Y., 1894.

Phil 3819.35   Spinoza, Benedictus de. Philosophy of Spinoza. N.Y., 1894.

Phil 4635.2.31   Starcke, C.N. Samvittighedslivet. København, 1894-97.

Phil 5768.9.95   Steiner, Rudolf. Die Philosophie der Freiheit. Berlin, 1894.

Phil 3838.8   Stern, Jakob. Die Philosophie Spinoza's. 2. Aufl. Stuttgart, 1894.

Phil 8843.8   Stieglitz, T. Über den Ursprung des Sittlichen und die Formen seiner Erscheinung. Wien, 1894.

Phil 7140.3   Stoll, O. Suggestions und Hypnotismus...Volkerpsychologie. Leipzig, 1894.

Phil 818.3   Straszewski, M. Dzieje filozofii w zarysie. Krakowie, 1894.

Phil 5258.98   Surbled, Georges. Éléments de psychologie. Paris, 1894.

Phil 5258.98.2   Surbled, Georges. Éléments de psychologie. 2e éd. Paris, 1894.

Phil 5520.9.5   Sutro, Emil. The basic law of vocal utterance. N.Y., 1894.

Phil 5259.16.2   Thoden van Velzen, H. De wetenschap van ons geestelijk wezen. 2. druk. Amsterdam, 1894.

Phil 3890.8.120   Thomasius, Christian. Kleine deutsche Schriften. Halle, 1894.

Phil 630.1   Thouverez, E. Le réalisme métaphysique. Paris, 1894.

Phil 9220.11   Trumbull, H.C. Friendship the master-passion. Philadelphia, 1894.

Phil 3640.99   Türck, Hermann. Friedrich Nietzsche und seine philosophischen Irrewege. München, 1894.

Phil 3235.87   Turban, Theodor. Das Wesen des Christentumes von Ludwig Feuerbach. Inaug. Diss. Karlsruhe, 1894.

Phil 350.1   Twardowski, K. Zur Lehre von Inhalt und Gegenstand. Wien, 1894.

Phil 820.1.1   Ueberweg, F. Grundriss der Geschichte der Philosophie. Berlin, 1894. 3v.

1894 - cont.

Phil 820.1.3   Ueberweg, F. Grundriss der Geschichte der Philosophie. Berlin, 1894-97. 5v.

Phil 3805.95   Uhlhorn, Otto. Schleiermachers Entwurf einer Kritik der bisherigen Sittenlehre dargestellt. Oldenburg, 1894. 2v.

Phil 8600.1   Upton, C.B. Lectures on the bases of religious belief. London, 1894.

Phil 5261.6   Van Norden, Charles. The psychic factor; outline of psychology. N.Y., 1894.

Phil 5061.1.6   Venn, J. Symbolic logic. London, 1894.

Phil 3425.96A   Wallace, W. Prolegomena to Hegel's philosophy. Oxford, 1894.

Phil 7054.48   Weil, Samuel. The religion of the future. Boston, 1894.

Phil 6972.2.10   Wernicke, C. Grundriss der Psychiatrie in klinischen Vorlesungen. v.1-2. Leipzig, 1894.

Phil 4655.1.18   Wikner, Pontus. Vittra skrifter. 3. uppl. Stockholm, 1894.

Phil 197.34   Wille, Bruno. Philosophie der Befreiung. Berlin, 1894.

Phil 5942.2   Williams, N.M. A vindication of phrenology. London, 1894.

Phil 400.11   Willmann, O. Geschichte des Idealismus. Braunschweig, 1894-1897. 3v.

Phil 7068.94.25   Wilmot, T.S. Twenty photographs of the risen dead. Lonon, 1894.

Phil 8602.28   Wimmer, Richard. Hrad är sanning? Stockholm, 1894.

Phil 3842.7   Wrzecionko, R. Der Grundganke der Ethik des Spinoza. Wien, 1894.

Phil 3915.55.5A   Wundt, Wilhelm. Lectures on human and animal psychology. London, 1894.

Phil 6975.1   Ziehen, T. Psychiatrie. Berlin, 1894.

1895

Phil 5645.8   Abney, W. de W. Colour vision. London, 1895.

Phil 3482.2   Adickes, E. Kant - Studien. Kiel, 1895. 2v.

Phil 3482.9   Aguanno, G. d'. La filosofia etico-giuridica de Kant a Spencer. Pt.I. Palermo, 1895.

Phil 7060.103.7   Aksakov, Aleksandr N. Animisme et spiritisme. Paris, 1895.

Phil 3482.8   Albert, Georg. Kant's transcendentale Logik. Wien, 1895.

Phil 8612.5   Alden, Henry M. A study of death. N.Y., 1895.

VPhil 5205.16   The American journal of psychology. Worcester, Mass., 1895-96.

Phil 3482.5.7   Apel, Max. Kants Erkenntnistheorie und seine Stellung zur Metaphysik. Berlin, 1895.

Phil 5545.1   Arréat, L. Mémoire et imagination. Paris, 1895.

Phil 7054.178   Azzi, Gaetano. Idea vera dello spiritismo. Torino, 1895.

Phil 3821.14   Bäck, Leo. Spinozas Erste Einwirkungen auf Deutschland. Berlin, 1895.

Phil 176.5.5   Balfour, A.J. Foundations of belief. N.Y., 1895.

Phil 7068.95.10   Barrett, Harrison D. Life work of Mrs. Cora L.V. Richmond. Chicago, 1895.

Phil 4110.4.98   Barzellotti, G. Commemorazione dell'accademico Luigi Ferri. Roma, 1895.

Phil 2885.80   Barzellotti, G. Hippolito Taine. Roma, 1895.

Phil 4110.4.99   Barzellotti, G. Luigi Ferri. Roma, 1895.

Phil 8581.92   Baumann, J. Die Grundfrage der Religion. Stuttgart, 1895.

Phil 1504.2   Baumgartner, M. Die Erkenntnislehre. v.2, pt.1. Münster, 1895.

Phil 8656.10   Baynes, H. The idea of God...in the light of language. London, 1895.

Phil 5241.37   Benedikt, M. Die Seelenkunde des Menschen als eine Erfahrungswissenschaft. Leipzig, 1895.

Phil 5241.48   Biervliet, Jules Jean van. Éléments de psychologie humaine. Gand, 1895.

Phil 1170.6A   Bigg, C. Neoplatonism. London, 1895.

Phil 3552.110   Bodemann, E. Die Leibniz-Handschriften. Hannover, 1895.

Phil 5041.16.5   Bosanquet, B. The essentials of logic. London, 1895.

Phil 2477.1.40   Boutroux, Émile. De l'idée de loi naturelle dans la science et la philosophie contemporaines. Paris, 1895.

Phil 2477.1.50   Boutroux, Émile. Questions de morale et d'éducation. Paris, 1895?

Phil 5440.1   Bradford, A.H. Heredity and Christian problems. N.Y., 1895.

Phil 2045.83   Brandt, G. Grundlinien der Philosophie von T. Hobbes. Kiel, 1895.

Phil 3483.19   Brennekam, M. Ein Beitrag zur Kritik der Kantschen Ethik. Inaug. Diss. Greefswald, 1895.

Phil 3120.8.31   Brentano, Franz. Meine Letzten wünsche für Oesterreich. Stuttgart, 1895.

Htn   Phil 6720.6*A   Breuer, Josef. Studien über Hysterie. Leipzig, 1895.

Phil 8876.103   Brooklyn Ethical Association. Life and the conditions of survival. Chicago, 1895.

Phil 8430.7   Burckhard, M. Asthetik und Sozialwissenschaft. Stuttgart, 1895.

Phil 8877.1.5   Calderwood, H. Handbook of moral philosophy. London, 1895.

Phil 4110.4.93   Cantoni, Carlo. Luigi Ferri. Roma, 1895.

Phil 1802.3   Carlson, J.S. Om filosofien i Amerika. Upsala, 1895.

Phil 3565.80.5   Caspari, O. Hermann Lotze. 2. Aufl. Breslau, 1895.

Phil 3246.198   Cesca, G. L'idealismo soggetivo di I.G. Fichte. Padova, 1895.

Phil 6952.17   Chaslin, Philippe. La confusion mentale primitive. Paris, 1895.

Phil 177.27   Cochin, D. La monde extérieur. Paris, 1895.

Phil 8877.43   Coppens, Charles. A brief text-book of moral philosophy. N.Y., 1895.

Phil 75.12   Cosentini, F. Bibliotheca philosophica. Sassari, 1895.

Phil 7068.93.26   Coste, A. Les phénomèmes psychiques occultes. 2. ed. Montpellier, 1895.

Phil 3808.95.5   Crämer, Otto. Arthur Schopenhauer's Lehre von der Schuld in ethischer Beziehung. Inaug. Diss. Heidelberg, 1895.

Phil 6312.6   Crichton-Brown, J. The Cavendish lecture on dreamy mental states. London, 1895.

Phil 6953.1   Dallemagne, J. Dégénérés et déséquilibrés. Bruxelles, 1895.

Phil 5043.2.5   Davis, N.K. Elements of inductive logic. N.Y., 1895.

Phil 1504.2.2   Doctor, Max. Die Philosophie. v.2, pt.2. Münster, 1895.

Phil 6113.17   Dorman, Marcus. From matter to mind. London, 1895.

Phil 2138.83   Douglas, C. John Stuart Mill. Edinburgh, 1895.

Phil 2230.5A   Dresser, A.G. The philosophy of P.P. Quimby. Boston, 1895.

Phil 178.12.55   Dresser, H.W. The immanent God. Boston, 1895.

Phil 178.12.8   Dresser, H.W. The power of silence. Boston, 1895.

Phil 178.43   Dreyer, Friedrich. Studien zu Methodenlehre und Erkenntnisskritik. Leipzig, 1895-1903.

Phil 2125.77   Dulles, J.H. McCosh bibliography. Princeton, 1895.

1895 - cont.

Phil 6625.2   Dumas, Georges. Les états intellectuels dans la mélancolie. Paris, 1895.

Phil 672.3   Dunan, C. Théorie psychologique de l'espace. Paris, 1895.

Phil 3486.14.10   Eisler, Rudolf. Die Weiterbildung der Kant'schen Aprioritätslehre bis zur Gegenwart. Inaug. Diss. Leipzig, 1895.

Phil 8659.7   Elliot, George. God is spirit, God is love. London, 1895.

Phil 7068.95.15   Erny, Alfred. Le psychisme expérimental. Paris, 1895.

Phil 5245.13   Faggi, A. Principi di psicologia moderna. Palermo, 1895.

Phil 5045.4   Ferrari, Ambrogio. Introduzione alla logica. Alessandria, 1895.

Phil 5520.4   Ferrero, G. Les lois psychologiques du symbolisme. Paris, 1895.

X Cg   Phil 3246.55.10   Fichte, Johann Gottlieb. Discours a la nation allemande. Paris, 1895.

Htn   Phil 6115.18.5*   Fletcher, Horace. Emancipation. Chicago, 1895.

Phil 3640.88   Förster-Nietzsche, E. Das Leben Friedrich Nietzsche's. Leipzig, 1895. 2v.

Phil 9035.10   Fouillée, A. Tempérament et caractère. Paris, 1895.

Phil 180.26   François Adolphe. Les grands problèmes. Paris, 1895.

Phil 8660.5.2   Fraser, A.C. Philosophy of theism. N.Y., 1895.

Phil 5755.13   Fruit, John P. Determinism from Hobbes to Hume. Inaug. Diss. Leipzig, 1895.

Phil 3890.1.110   Gál, Keleman. Trendelenburg Bölcseleti rendszere tekintettie. Kolozsvárt, 1895.

Phil 337.6   Gardair, M.J. Philosophie de Saint Thomas. La connaissance. Paris, 1895.

Phil 3280.30   Geulincx, A. Van de Hooft-Deuchden. Antwerp, 1895.

Phil 3805.165   Geyer, Otto. Friedrich Schleiermachers Psychologie. Inaug. Diss. Leipzig, 1895.

Phil 8881.7   Giles, A.E. Moral pathology. London, 1895.

Phil 8956.2   Gladden, Washington. Ruling ideas of the present age. Boston, 1895.

Phil 3488.12   Gneisse, Karl. Das sittliche Handeln nach Kants Ethik. Colmar, 1895.

Phil 3488.6   Goldfriedrich, J.A. Kants Ästhetik. Leipzig, 1895.

Phil 5648.9   Griffing, H. On sensations from pressure and impact. N.Y., 1895.

Phil 287.1   Gunkel, H. Schöpfung und Chaos. Göttingen, 1895.

Phil 3489.28   Hacks, Jakob. Über Kant's synthetische Urteile a priori. Pt.1-4. Kattowitz, 1895-99.

Phil 510.1.1.7   Haeckel, Ernst. Monism. London, 1895.

Phil 4582.4.35   Hägerström, Axel. Om den moraliska känslan och driften sasom förnuftiga. Upsala, 1895.

Phil 4582.4.31   Hägerström, Axel. Undersökning af den empiristiska etikens möjlighet. Upsala, 1895.

Phil 5247.1.2   Halleck, R.P. Psychology and psychic culture. N.Y., 1895.

Phil 6048.94.7   Hamon, Louis. Cheiro's language of the hand. N.Y., 1895.

Phil 260.5   Hannequin, A. Essai critique sur l'hypothèse des Atoms. Paris, 1895.

Phil 3552.252   Hannequin, A. Quae fuerit prior Leibnitii philosophia. Thesis. Paris, 1895.

Phil 182.4.10   Harms, F. Metaphilosophie. Leipzig, 1895.

Phil 3425.86.5   Harris, W.T. Hegel's logic. 2d ed. Chicago, 1895.

Phil 3415.45   Hartmann, Eduard von. The sexes compared and other essays. London, 1895.

Phil 3425.60.5   Hegel, Georg Wilhelm Friedrich. Lectures on the philosophy of religion. London, 1895. 3v.

Phil 5330.6.2   Heinrich, W. Die moderne psysiologische Psychologie...Aufmerksamkeit. Leipzig, 1895.

Phil 6048.95   Henderson, Eliza Easter. A guide to palmistry. Boston, 1895.

Phil 8957.5.5   Hill, Thomas. The postulates of revelation and of ethics. Boston, 1895.

Phil 6117.24   Hirth, George. Lokalisations-Psychologie. Die Lokalisationstheorie. 2. Aufl. München, 1895.

Phil 6957.11   Hitzig, E. Über den Quärulantenwahnsinn. Leipzig, 1895.

Phil 3489.14   Hoar, Robert. Der angebliche Mysticismus Kants. Brugg, 1895.

Phil 1707.1A   Höffding, H. Geschichte der Philosophie. Leipzig, 1895. 2v.

Phil 5047.30   Hontheim, J. Der logische Algorithmus. Berlin, 1895.

Phil 7059.12.9   Hull, Moses. The spiritual Alps and how we ascend them. 5th ed. Chicago, 1895.

Phil 7059.12.5   Hull, Moses. Two in one...spiritualism of the Bible settled. Chicago, 1895.

Phil 2050.60.28   Hume, David. Traktat über die menschliche Natur. Hamburg, 1895-1906. 2v.

Phil 8882.25   Hyslop, J.H. The elements of ethics. N.Y., 1895.

Phil 6117.6   Hyslop, T.B. Mental physiology. Philadelphia, 1895.

Phil 2050.191   Jahn, Franz. David Humes Kausalitätstheorie. Inaug. Diss. Leipzig, 1895.

Phil 2070.30.5A   James, William. Is life worth living? Philadelphia, 1895.

Phil 5500.3   Jerusalem, W. Die Urtheilsfunction. Wien, 1895.

Phil 184.15.5   Jochnick, W. Några grundlinjer fill filosofien. Stockholm, 1895.

Phil 3565.82.5   Jones, Henry. A critical account of the philosophy of Lotze. Glasgow, 1895.

Phil 3565.82   Jones, Henry. A critical account of the philosophy of Lotze. N.Y., 1895.

Phil 7068.95.20   Judson, Abby A. Why she became a spiritualist. 3. ed. Cincinnati, 1895.

Phil 9150.1.2   Kelly, E. Evolution and effort. N.Y., 1895.

Phil 8885.4   Kidd, J. Morality and religion. Edinburgh, 1895.

Phil 3808.130   Kiehl, Daniel. Naturlijke historie van den Filistijn. 's Gravenhage, 1895.

Phil 5250.3   Kirkpatrick, E.A. Inductive psychology. N.Y., 1895.

Phil 8590.9   Knowles, E.R. The supremacy of the spiritual. Boston, 1895.

Phil 341.2   Koch, Emil. Das Bewusstsein der Transcendenz. Halle an der Saale, 1895.

Phil 3640.242   Kretzer, Eugen. Friedrich Nietzsche. Leipzig, 1895.

Phil 3492.70.2   Kühnmann, Eugen. Kants und Schillers Begründung der Ästhetik. Marburg, 1895.

Phil 3492.70   Kühnmann, Eugen. Kants und Schillers Begründung der Ästhetik. München, 1895.

Phil 185.12.7   Külpe, O. Einleitung in die Philosophie. Leipzig, 1895.

Phil 5250.2   Külpe, Oswald. Outlines of psychology. London, 1895.

Phil 5251.1.5   Ladd, G.T. Philosophy of mind. N.Y., 1895.

Phil 5251.1.10   Ladd, G.T. Psychology descriptive and explanatory. N.Y., 1895.

Phil 186.71   La Hautière, E. de. Philosophie. Paris, 1895.

Phil 3280.85   Land, J.P.N. Arnold Geulincx und seine Philosophie. Haag, 1895.

Phil 8610.895   Landers, C.M. The skeptics defense against all Christian or other priests. Rochester, 1895.

1895 - cont.

Phil 6021.1 — Landsberg, I. Wahrsagekunst aus der menschlichen Gestalt. Berlin, 1895.
NEDL Phil 5425.37 — Legrain, M. Les dégénérés. Paris, 1895.
Phil 1750.16 — Leschbrand, A. Substanzbegriff in der neueren Philosophie. Rostock, 1895.
Phil 6060.3 — Lombroso, C. Grafologia. Milano, 1895.
Phil 3565.51.5 — Lotze, Hermann. An outline of the Microcosmos. Oberlin, 1895.
Phil 186.29 — Louage, Augustin. A course of philosophy. 4. ed. N.Y., 1895.
Phil 260.2A — Mabilleau, S. Histoire de la philosophie atomistique. Paris, 1895.
Phil 187.97 — McCrossan, J.D. Logic and other nonsense. London, 1895.
Phil 187.45 — Marchesini, G. Saggio sulla naturale unità del pensiero. Firenze, 1895.
Phil 9352.7.15 — Marden, O.S. Architects of fate. Boston, 1895.
Phil 9352.7.3 — Marden, O.S. Pushing to the front. Boston, 1895.
Phil 5401.9 — Marrel, P. Les phobies. Paris, 1895.
Phil 8413.11 — Marshall, Henry. Aesthetic principles. N.Y., 1895.
Phil 6122.1.4 — Maudsley, H. Body and mind. N.Y., 1895.
Phil 6962.2.6 — Maudsley, H. The pathology of mind. London, 1895.
Phil 5650.3 — Mentz, P. Die Wirkung akustischer Sinnesreize auf Puls und Athmung. Leipzig, 1895.
Phil 6400.4 — Meringer, R. Versprechen und Verlesen. Stuttgart, 1895.
Phil 2138.101 — Michel, Henry. De Stuarti Millii individualismo. Thesis. Parisiis, 1895.
Phil 293.15 — Mikos, J. Hypothesen über einige kosmologische und geologische Momente. Leipzig, 1895.
Phil 8702.15 — Mikos, J. Eine wissenschaftliche Wellanschauung auf religiöser Grundlage. Leipzig, 1895.
Phil 2138.40.6 — Mill, John S. On liberty. N.Y., 1895.
Phil 2138.50.6 — Mill, John S. Utilitarianism. 12th ed. London, 1895.
Phil 187.17.9 — Mivart, St. G. The helpful science. N.Y., 1895.
Phil 6122.7.15 — Mosso, A. La température du cerveau, études thermometriques. Turin, 1895.
Phil 8593.11 — A new departure. Boston, 1895.
Phil 3640.10.2 — Nietzsche, Friedrich. Werke. Leipzig, 1895-1926. 19v.
Phil 5425.7.10 — Nordau, M. Degeneration. 2. ed. N.Y., 1895.
Phil 5425.7.12 — Nordau, M. Degeneration. 4. ed. N.Y., 1895.
Phil 5425.7.12.5 — Nordau, M. Degeneration. 5. ed. London, 1895.
NEDL Phil 5425.7.13 — Nordau, M. Degeneration. 6. ed. London, 1895.
Phil 2055.1.81 — Norden, Joseph. Die Ethik Henry Homes. Inaug. Diss. Halle, 1895.
Phil 4610.7.32 — Norström, V. Om natursammanhang och frihet. Göteborg, 1895.
Phil 3833.2 — Nossig, Alfred. Ueber die bestimmende Ursache des Philosophirens. Stuttgart, 1895.
Phil 972.5 — Olcott, H.S. Old diary leaves; Story of theosophy. N.Y., 1895.
Phil 489.1A — Ostwald, W. Überwindung des wissenschaftlichen Materialismus. Leipzig, 1895.
Phil 1119.1 — Otten, Alois. Einleitung in die Geschichte der Philosophie. Paderborn, 1895.
Phil 296.14 — Panizza, O. Der Illusionismus und die Rettung. Leipzig, 1895.
Phil 1158.15.7 — Pater, Walter. Marius the Epicurean. London, 1895.
Phil 5330.21.5 — Patrizi, M.L. La graphique psychométrique de l'attention. Turin, 1895.
Phil 190.3.3 — Paulsen, F. Einleitung in die Philosophie. 3e Aufl. Berlin, 1895.
Phil 7068.87.9.5 — Pennsylvania. University. Seybert Commission for Investigating Modern Spiritualism. Preliminary report. Philadelphia, 1895.
Phil 2050.85 — Petzholtz, E. Die Hauptpunkte der Humeschen Erkenntnislehre. Berlin, 1895.
Phil 585.216 — Plantiko, Otto. Rousseaus, Herders und Kants Theorie vom Zukunftsideal der Menschheitsgeschichte. Inaug. Diss. Greifswald, 1895.
Phil 8840.1.8 — Prévost-Paradol, L.A. Études sur les moralistes français. 8e éd. Paris, 1895.
Phil 6060.6 — Preyer, William. Zur Psychologie des Schreibens. Hamburg, 1895.
Phil 6127.7.10 — Ramón y Cajal, S. Les nouvelles idées sur la structure du système nerveux. Paris, 1895.
Phil 6967.1 — Regis, E. Practical manual of mental medicine. Philadelphia, 1895.
Phil 5440.23 — Retzius, Gustaf. Om förvärfvade egenskapers ärftlighet. Stockholm, 1895.
Phil 735.15 — Ritschel, Otto. Über Wethurtheile. Freiburg, 1895.
Phil 6687.6.2 — Rochas d'Aiglun, A. L'extériorisation de la sensibilité. 2e éd. Paris, 1895.
Phil 510.2 — Romanes, G.J. Mind and motion and monism. N.Y., 1895.
Phil 8597.12.5 — Romanes, G.J. Thoughts on religion. Chicago, 1895.
Phil 8597.12 — Romanes, G.J. Thoughts on religion. London, 1895.
Phil 4080.8.80 — Romano, Pietro. La filosofia di Augusto Conti. Genova, 1895.
Phil 8967.1.10 — Rothe, R. Uebersicht der theologischen Ethik. Bremen, 1895.
Phil 6687.12 — Rouxel. Histoire et philosophie du magnétisme. Paris, 1895. 2v.
Phil 8672.6 — Royce, J. The conception of God. Berkeley, 1895.
Phil 5258.4 — Sanford, E.C. Course in experimental psychology. Boston, 1895.
Phil 8598.38 — Satterlee, Henry Y. A creedless Gospel and the Gospel creed. N.Y., 1895.
Phil 6688.1 — Schaffer, K. Suggestion und Reflex. Jena, 1895.
Phil 1718.2 — Schellwien, R. Der Geist der neueren Philosophie. Leipzig, 1895.
Phil 193.82 — Schmitz-Dumont, A. Natur Philosophie als exakte Wissenschaft. Leipzig, 1895.
Phil 3808.23 — Schopenhauer, Arthur. Handschriftlicher Nachlass. Leipzig, 1895.
Phil 5585.10.5 — Schwarz, H. Umwälzung der Wahrnehmungshypothesen. Leipzig, 1895.
Phil 5258.13.5 — Scripture, E.W. Thinking, feeling, doing. Meadville, 1895.
Phil 6968.5.10 — Séglas, J. Leçons cliniques sur les maladies. Paris, 1895.
Phil 5058.13 — Sigwart, H.C.W. Logic. 2nd ed. London, 1895. 2v.
Phil 3930.1 — Smith, Garnet. The melancholy of Stephen Allard. N.Y., 1895.
Phil 978.14 — Solovef, V.S. Nodern priestess of Isis. London, 1895.
Phil 3808.95 — Sommerlad, F. Darstellung und Kritik. Offenbach, 1895.
Phil 2270.35.2 — Spencer, Herbert. Epitome of the synthetic philosophy. N.Y., 1895.

1895 - cont.

Phil 2270.73.3 — Spencer, Herbert. Principles of ethics. N.Y., 1895. 2v.
Phil 2270.73.4 — Spencer, Herbert. Principles of ethics. N.Y., 1895-96. 2v.
Phil 2270.70.12 — Spencer, Herbert. Principles of psychology. N.Y., 1895. 2v.
Phil 2270.74.25 — Spencer, Herbert. Le rôle moral de la bienfaisance. Paris, 1895.
Phil 3819.36 — Spinoza, Benedictus de. Ethica. 's Gravenhage, 1895.
Phil 3819.10.9 — Spinoza, Benedictus de. Opera quotquot reperta sunt. 2. ed. Hagae, 1895-96. 3v.
Phil 3819.45 — Spinoza, Benedictus de. Tractus De intellectus emendatione. N.Y., 1895.
Phil 3625.1.190 — Stadler, Károly. Mendelssohn Mózes, a zsidó Sokrates. Szekesfehérvárott, 1895.
Phil 5400.11 — Stanley, Hiram Miner. Studies in the evolutionary psychology of feeling. London, 1895.
Phil 9245.40 — Steele, Mary D. A happy life. Dayton, Ohio, 1895.
Phil 3640.214 — Steiner, Rudolf. Friedrich Nietzsche: ein Kämpfer gegen seiner Zeit. Weimar, 1895.
Phil 5360.3 — Stöhr, Adolf. Die Vieldeutigkeit des Urtheiles. Leipzig, 1895.
Phil 4769.8.21 — Strakhov, N.N. Filosofskie ocherki. Sankt Peterbrug, 1895.
Phil 8893.32 — Strümpell, L. Abhandlungen aus dem Gebiete der Ethik, der Staatswissenschaft, der Ästhetik und der Theologie. Leipzig, 1895.
Phil 2885.34.8 — Taine, Hippolyte Adolphe. Philosophie de l'art. 8. éd. Paris, 1895?
Phil 8969.1 — Thamin, R. Saint Ambroise et la morale chrétienne au IV siècle. Paris, 1895.
Phil 3246.85.2 — Thompson, A.B. Unity of Fichte's Doctrine of knowledge. Boston, 1895.
Phil 575.6 — Thompson, H.M. The world and the wrestlers. N.Y., 1895.
Phil 3501.8 — Thon, O. Die Grundprinzipien der Kantischen Moralphilosophie. Berlin, 1895.
Phil 8894.16 — Tille, A. Von Darwin bis Nietzsche. Leipzig, 1895.
Phil 5769.5 — Traeger, L. Wille, Determinismus, Strafe. Berlin, 1895.
Phil 3270.1.83 — Türck, Hermann. Meine Erfahrungen mit Kuno Fischer. Jena, 1895.
Phil 196.12.5 — Veitch, John. Dualism and monism. Edinburg, 1895.
Phil 5261.2.5 — Vignoli, T. Peregrinazioni psicologiche. Milano, 1895.
Phil 8422.15.5 — Volkelt, Johannes. Asthetische Zeitfragen. München, 1895.
Phil 3552.99 — Volz, L. Die Erkenntnisstheorien bei Leibniz und Kant. Rostock, 1895.
Phil 5070.15 — Vorbrodt, Gustav. Psychologie des Glaubens. Göttingen, 1895.
Phil 8676.3 — Voysey, C. Theism as a science of natural theology. London, 1895.
Phil 9182.4.6 — Wagner, Charles. La vie simple. 2. éd. Paris, 1895.
Phil 822.6.5 — Wahle, R. Geschichtlicher Uberblick über die Entwicklung der Philosophie bis zu ihrer letzten Phase. Wien, 1895.
Phil 197.2 — Watson, J. Comte, Mill, and Spencer, an outline of philosophy. Glasgow, 1895.
Phil 9245.14 — Watson, J. Hedonistic theories. Glasgow, 1895.
Phil 8677.11.10 — Weill, Alexandre. Gesetze und Mysterien der Liebe. 1. Aufl. Berlin, 1895.
Phil 1127.1 — Wendland, Paul. Beiträge zur Geschichte der griechischen Philosophie. Berlin, 1895.
Phil 197.19 — Whittaker, T. Essays and notices: philosophical and psychological. London, 1895.
Phil 4655.1.48 — Wikner, Pontus. "Gud är kärleken." 2. uppl. Stockholm, 1895.
Phil 197.10 — Winter, N. Pan-Gnosticism. N.Y., 1895.
Phil 8715.1 — Zahm, John Augustine. Bible, science and faith. Baltimore, 1895.
Phil 1130.5.5 — Zeller, Eduard. Outlines of history of Greek philosophy. London, 1895.
Phil 5265.1.6 — Ziehen, Theodor. Introduction to physiological psychology. London, 1895.

1896

Phil 3482.7 — Aars, Kristian Birch-Reichenwald. Die Autonomie der Moral mit besondere Berucksichtigung der Morallehre Immanuel Kants. Hamburg, 1896.
Phil 3482.2.5 — Adickes, E. German Kantian bibliography. v.1-3. Boston, 1896[1893]
Phil 6110.8 — Alaux, J.E. Théorie de l'âme humaine. Paris, 1896.
Phil 8875.33 — Albert, Henri. Les dangers du moralisme. n.p., 1896?
Phil 9245.9.50 — Avebury, John Lubbock. Duty of happiness. Philadelphia, 1896.
Phil 5041.4 — Ballantine, W.G. Inductive logic. Boston, 1896.
Phil 665.209 — Baraduc, H. L'âme humaine. Paris, 1896.
Phil 3483.6 — Basch, V. Essai critique sur l'esthétique de Kant. Paris, 1896.
Phil 1504.2.4 — Baumgartner, M. Die Philosophie. v.2, pt.4. Münster, 1896.
Phil 9558.2.5 — Beecher, H.W. Industry and idleness. Philadelphia, 1896.
Phil 3483.23 — Bensow, O. Till Kants lära om tinget i och för sig. Lund, 1896.
Phil 6311.18.5 — Binet, Alfred. Alteration of personality. N.Y., 1896.
Phil 6311.18.6 — Binet, Alfred. Alterations of personality. London, 1896.
Phil 7042.4.1 — Binet, Alfred. On double consciousness. Chicago, 1896.
Phil 978.5.25 — Blavatsky, H.P. The key to theosophy. 2nd American ed. N.Y., 1896.
Phil 978.5.15 — Blavatsky, H.P. The voice of the silence. 5th ed. London, 1896.
Phil 8876.40 — Bodnai, Zsigmond. Az orkölcsi törvény alkalmazása. Budapest, 1896.
Phil 4815.223.35 — Bodnár, Zsigmond. Az orkölcsi világ. Budapest, 1896.
Phil 282.16 — Bolland, G.J.P.J. Hat wereldraadsel. Leiden, 1896.
Phil 8676.39.5 — Bon, Fred. Grundzüge der wissenschaftlichen und technischen Ethik. Leipzig, 1896.
Phil 930.34 — Borel, Henri. De chinesche filosofi. 3. druk. Amsterdam, 1896-97. 2v.
Phil 8612.12.2 — Bourdeau, L. Le problème de la mort. 2. éd. Paris, 1896.
Phil 2050.90 — Brede, W. Der Unterschied der lehren Humes. Halle, 1896.
Phil 2050.214 — Brede, Wilhelm. Der Unterschied der Lehren Humes im Treatise und im Inquiry. Halle, 1896.
Phil 9161.5 — Brière, L. de la. La jeune mariée. Paris, 1896.
Phil 3425.348 — Bryant, W. McK. Hegel's educational ideas. N.Y., 1896.
Phil 1900.11 — Butler, Joseph. Works. Oxford, 1896. 2v.
NEDL Phil 3425.80.5 — Caird, Edward. Hegel. Philadelphia, 1896.
Phil 3808.105 — Caldwell, W. Schopenhauer's system...philosophical significance. Edinburgh, 1896.

Phil 1153.5   Caspari, A. De cynicis. Chemnitz, 1896.
Phil 8877.60   Chabot, Charles. Nature et moralité. Paris, 1896.
Phil 1850.81.3   Church, R.W. Bacon. London, 1896.
Phil 8877.51   Cohen, C. An outline of evolutionary ethics. London, 1896.
Phil 410.10   Cohn, Jonas. Geschichte des Unendlichkeitsproblems im abendländischen Denken bis Kant. Leipzig, 1896.
Phil 2490.54.15   Comte, Auguste. Allmän öfversikt af positivismen. Stockholm, 1896.
Phil 2490.41.3   Comte, Auguste. The postive philosophy. London, 1896. 3v.
Phil 2490.77.2   Comte, Auguste. Testament d'Auguste Comte, avec les documents qui s'y rapportent. Paris, 1896.
Phil 4080.8.35   Conti, Augusto. Nuovi discorsi del tempo o famiglia, patria e Dio. Firenze, 1896-97. 2v.
Phil 4210.118   Cornelio, A.M. Antonio Rosmini e il suo monumento in Milano. Torino, 1896.
Phil 6672.7   Crocq, Jean J. L'hypnotisme scientifique. Paris, 1896.
Phil 5465.42   Curry, S.S. Imagination and dramatic instinct. Boston, 1896.
Phil 5400.19.3.10   Darwin, Charles. The expression of the emotions in man and animals. N.Y., 1896.
Phil 7054.127   Davies, Charles M. The great secret, and its unfoldment in occultism. 2. ed. London, 1896.
Phil 4110.4.95   Dejob, Charles. Notice sur Luigi Ferri. Versailles, 1896.
Phil 9171.1.9   De Lambert, A.T. de M. de C. De l'éducation des jeunes gens. Paris, 1896.
Phil 7042.2.2   Dessoir, Max. Das Doppel-Ich. 2e Aufl. Leipzig, 1896.
NEDL   Phil 5243.7.3   Dewey, John. Psychology. 3d ed. N.Y., 1896.
Phil 4803.454.79   Dickstein, Samuel. Katalog dzieł i rekopisów Hoene-Wrońskiego. Kraków, 1896.
Phil 284.3   Dinger, H. Prinzip der Entwickelung. Jena, 1896.
Phil 5520.46   Dodge, Raymond. Die motorischen Wortvorstellungen. Halle, 1896.
Phil 178.12.5   Dresser, H.W. The perfect whole. Boston, 1896.
Phil 178.15.5   Duboc, K.J. Jenseits vom Wirklichen. Dresden, 1896.
Phil 5520.48   Dugas, L. Le psittacisme et la pensée symbolique. Paris, 1896.
Phil 8878.18.5   Dymond, J. Essays...principles of morality. Philadelphia, 1896.
Phil 335.4   Ehrat, P. Die Bedeutung der Logik. Zittau, 1896.
Phil 8879.2.9   Eliot, C.W. The happy life. N.Y., 1896.
Phil 8879.2.3   Eliot, C.W. The happy life. N.Y., 1896.
Phil 8879.2.5   Eliot, C.W. The happy life. N.Y., 1896.
Phil 8879.2A   Eliot, C.W. The happy life. N.Y., 1896.
Phil 804.3.4   Eliot, C.W. The happy life. N.Y., 1896-97.
Phil 804.3.4   Erdmann, J.E. Grundriss der Geschichte der Philosophie. 4. Aufl. Berlin, 1896. 2v.
Phil 5044.5.10   Erdmann, J.E. Outlines of logic and metaphysics. 4th rev. ed. London, 1896.
Phil 179.3.17   Eucken, R. Geistigen Lebensinhalt. Leipzig, 1896.
Phil 8620.4   Evil and evolution. London, 1896.
Phil 665.42   Feilberg, Ludvig. Om ligelob og Kredsning i Sjaelelivet. Kjøbenhavn, 1896.
Phil 5245.22   Ferrari, G.C. Psychological papers. Reggio, 1896-1900.
Phil 5755.4   Fiamingo, G. Individual determinism and social science. Philadelphia, 1896.
Phil 6115.6.7   Flechsig, P. Gehirn und Seele. 2e Ausg. Leipzig, 1896.
Phil 6115.6.5   Flechsig, P. Localisation der geistigen Vorgänge. Leipzig, 1896.
Phil 8660.5.3   Fraser, A.C. Philosophy of theism. 2. series. N.Y., 1896.
Phil 3270.3.88   Friedrich, J. Jakob Frohschammer. Fürth, 1896.
Phil 3825.9   Friedrichs, Max. Der Substanzbegriff Spinozas neu und gegen die herrschenden Ansichten zu Gunsten des Philosophen erläutert. Inaug. Diss. Greifswald, 1896.
Phil 3640.251   Gerhard, H.F. Die künstlerischen Mittel der Darstellung in Nietzsches "Zarathustra". Berlin, 1896.
Phil 1900.84   Gladstone, W.E. Studies subsidiary to works of...Butler. Oxford, 1896.
Phil 8633.1   Gordon, G.A. Immortality and the new theodicy. Boston, 1896.
Phil 5816.3   Groos, K. Die Spiele der Thiere. Jena, 1896.
Phil 5246.34   Güttler, C. Psychologie und Philosophie. München, 1896.
Phil 8881.26   Guyau, M. Esquisse d'une morale. Paris, 1896.
Phil 1750.17   Haas, A. Über den Einfluss der Epicureischen...Philosophie des 16 und 17 Jahrhunderts. Berlin, 1896.
Phil 5757.10   Hansen, H.C. Om begrebet frihed en filosofisk afhandling. Kristiania, 1896.
Phil 8882.4   Harris, G. Moral evolution. Boston, 1896.
Phil 6677.1.5   Hart, E. Hypnotism, mesmerism and the new witchcraft. Hamburg, 1896.
Phil 5047.41   Hawley, Thomas de R. Infallible logic. Lansing, 1896.
Phil 3808.87.5   Hecker, M.F. Metaphysik und Asketik. Bonn, 1896.
Phil 3425.71   Hegel, Georg Wilhelm Friedrich. Philosophy of right. London, 1896.
Phil 5643.8.5   Helmholtz, H. Handbuch der physiologischen Optik. Hamburg, 1896.
Phil 6957.14   Henry, Jules. Du délire des negations (Syndrome de Cotard) dans la paralysie générale. Paris, 1896.
Phil 5247.22.5   Heymans, G. Quantitative Untersuchungen über der öptische Paradoxon. n.p., 1896-1913. 13 pam.
Phil 5047.8   Hibben, J.G. Inductive logic. N.Y., 1896.
Phil 6117.18   Hill, Leonard. Physiology and pathology of cerebral circulation. London, 1896.
Phil 5115.8   Hillebrand, F. Zur Lehre von der Hypothesenbildung. Wien, 1896.
Phil 8408.37   Hirn, Yrjö. Förstudier till en konstfilosofi på psykologisk grundval. Helsingfors, 1896.
Phil 5425.5   Hirsch, William. Genius and degeneration. N.Y., 1896.
Phil 338.1   Hobhouse, L.T. Theory of knowledge. London, 1896.
Phil 8832.2   Hoekstra, S. Geschiedenis van de zedenlier. Amsterdam, 1896. 2v.
Phil 8587.33   Horn, E.F.B. Tolv forebaesninger over tro og taenkning. Kristiania, 1896.
Phil 7068.96.30   Hubbard, H.S. Beyond. Boston, 1896.
Htn   Phil 2070.30*   James, William. Is life worth living? Philadelphia, 1896.
Phil 8884.1A   James, William. Is life worth living? Philadelphia, 1896.
Phil 5249.2.1   James, William. Principles of psychology. N.Y., 1896. 2v.
Phil 8884.19   Jelgersma, D.G. De ontkening der moraal. Amsterdam, 1896.
Phil 5249.5   Jodl, Friedrich. Lehrbuch der Psychologie. Stuttgart, 1896.
Phil 5648.16   Judd, Charles H. Über Reumwahrnehmungen im Gebiet des Tastsinnes. Inaug. Diss. Leipzig, 1896.
Phil 7060.154   Kaarsberg, H.S. Om satanismen. Kjøbenhavn, 1896.

Phil 8590.26.5   Kaftan, Julius. Das Christentum und die Philosophie. 3. Aufl. Leipzig, 1896.
Phil 6060.19   Keene, John H. The mystery of handwriting. Boston, 1896.
Phil 5250.19   Key, Ellen. Krinns-psykologi och krinnlig logik. Stockholm, 1896.
Phil 8411.11   Kirstein, Anton. Entwurf einer Ästhetik der Natur und Kunst. Paderborn, 1896.
Phil 5627.80   Koch, E. Die Psychologie in der Religionswissenschaft. Freiburg, 1896.
Phil 3625.1.139   Kornfeld, H. Moses Mendelssohn und die Aufgabe der Philosophie. Berlin, 1896.
Phil 6960.5   Kraepelin, E. Psychiatrie. Leipzig, 1896.
Phil 185.25   Kralik, R. Weltweisheit. v.1-3. Wien, 1896.
Phil 185.25.5   Kralik, R. Weltwissenschaft. Wien, 1896.
Phil 3425.101   Kredenburch, W.C.A. De staatsleer van Hegel. Utrecht, 1896.
Phil 645.16   Kreibig, J.K. Geschichte und Kritik des ethischen Skepticismus. Wien, 1896.
Phil 5250.13.5   Krueger, Felix. Ist Philosophie ohne Psychologie möglich? Eine Erwiderung. München, 1896.
Phil 3492.32.5   Kügelgen, C.W. von. Immanuel Kant Auffassung von der Bibel und seine Auslegung derselben. Leipzig, 1896.
Phil 3460.84   Kusch, E. C.G.J. Jacobi und Helmholtz auf dem Gymnasium. Potsdam, 1896.
NEDL   Phil 5251.1.15.8   Ladd, G.T. Elements of physiological psychology. N.Y., 1896.
Phil 5251.1.16   Ladd, G.T. Outlines of physiological psychology. N.Y., 1896.
Phil 930.26   Lanessan, J.M. La morale des philosophies chinois. Paris, 1896.
Phil 3565.108   Lange, Paul. Die Lehre vom Instinkte bei Lotze und Darwin. Berlin, 1896.
Phil 3210.81.2   Lasswitz, Kurd. Gustav Theodor Fechner. Stuttgart, 1896.
Phil 5251.10.9   Lazarus, M. Über Tact, Kunst, Freundschaft und Sitten. 3e Aufl. Berlin, 1896.
Phil 8591.23   Lee, Gerald S. The shadow Christ. N.Y., 1896.
Phil 3552.40A   Leibniz, Gottfried Wilhelm. New essays concerning human understanding. N.Y., 1896.
Phil 5648.2   Lemon, J.S. The skin considered as an organ of sensation. Gardner, Mass., 1896.
Phil 5627.20.10   Leuba, J.H. Studies in the psychology of religious phenomena. Worcester, 1896.
Phil 5251.43   Lévy, Albert. Le sens intime en psychologie. Bruxelles, 1896.
Phil 1195.7   Liljeqvist, Efraim. Antik och modern sofistik. Göteborg, 1896.
Phil 7054.50.2   Lillie, Arthur. The worship of Satan in modern France. London, 1896.
Phil 811.5   Loewenthal, E. Geschichte der Philosophie im Umriss. Berlin, 1896.
Phil 5545.38   Loisette, A. Assimilative memory. N.Y., 1896.
Phil 187.61   Maack, F. Naturforschung und Philosophie. Kiel, 1896.
Phil 5252.23.20   MacDougall, R. The physical characteristics of attention. n.p., 1896-1904. 15 pam.
Phil 9495.35.15   Macfadden, B.A. The virile powers of superb manhood. London, 1896.
Phil 52.3   McGill University. Department of philosophy. Papers, 1-4. Montreal, 1896-99.
Phil 187.104   Maltese, F. Il problema morale. Vittoria, 1896.
Phil 1350.6.3   Martha, Constant. Etudes morales sur l'antiquité. Paris, 1896.
Phil 3832.3   Meinsma, K.O. Spinoza en zijn kring. 's Gravenhage, 1896.
Phil 2750.9.30   Merten, O. Des limites de la philosophie. Paris, 1896.
Phil 7068.96.40   Mery, Gaston. La voyante de la rue de Paradis. Paris, 1896.
Phil 1712.2   Merz, J.T. History of European thought, 19th century. Edinburgh, 1896-1914. 4v.
Phil 2138.35.5   Mill, John S. A system of logic. London, 1896.
Phil 6122.20   Mills, A.W. Practical metaphysics. Chicago, 1896.
Phil 6400.9   Mirallie, C. De l'aphasie sensorielle. Paris, 1896.
Phil 4605.1.36   Monrad, M.J. Philosophisk propaedentik. 5. opl. Christiania, 1896.
X Cg   Phil 5822.1.10A   Morgan, C.L. Habit and instinct. London, 1896.
Phil 5401.1.10   Mosso, A. Fear. London, 1896.
Phil 8592.34   Myers, J.H. Philosophy of faith. Syracuse, N.Y., 1896.
Phil 5645.31   Nagel, W.A. Der Lichtsinn augenloser Tiere. n.p., 1896-1908. 7 pam.
Phil 2520.96   Netter, A. Notes sur le vie de Descartes. Nancy, 1896.
Phil 3495.7   Neumark, David. Die Freiheitslehre bei Kant. Hamburg, 1896.
Phil 3640.70   Nietzsche, Friedrich. The case of Wagner. Photoreproduction. Nietzsche, 1896.
Phil 3640.40.5   Nietzsche, Friedrich. Thus spake Zarathustra. N.Y., 1896.
Phil 3640.10A   Nietzsche, Friedrich. Werke. Leipzig, 1896-1926. 20v.
Phil 9490.2   Olney, R. The scholar in politics. Philadelphia, 1896.
Phil 8595.15.18   Paine, Thomas. The age of reason. N.Y., 1896.
Phil 5825.6.4   Pardies, Ignace. Discours de la connaissance des bestes. 4. éd. Paris, 1896.
Phil 2805.40.18   Pascal, Blaise. Pensées. Fribourg, 1896.
Phil 8890.6.6   Paulsen, F. System der Ethik. Berlin, 1896-97. 2v.
Phil 5070.5   Payot, J. De la croyance. Paris, 1896.
Phil 815.7   Penjon, A. Précis d'histoire de la philosophie. Paris, 1896.
Phil 5628.13   Petrus de Dacia. Vita Christinae Stumbelensis edibit Johannes Paukon. Gotoburgi, 1896.
Phil 8595.4.3   Pfleiderer, O. Religionsphilosophie. 3. Aufl. Berlin, 1896.
Phil 7068.96.35   Pribytkov, V nom. Aufrichtige Unterhaltungen über den Spiritismus. Leipzig, 1896?
Phil 349.8   Prudhomme, Sully. Que Sais-je? Paris, 1896.
Phil 6125.10   Pupin, Charles. Le neurone et les hypothèses. Paris, 1896.
Phil 5585.7   Rau, A. Empfinden und Denken. Giessen, 1896.
Phil 5425.8   Regeneration. A reply to Max Nordau. N.Y., 1896.
Phil 817.7   Rehmke, J. Grundriss der Geschichte der Philosophie. Berlin, 1896.
Phil 5400.18.4   Ribot, T. La psychologie des sentiments. Paris, 1896.
Phil 8892.30   Ritter, Eli F. Moral law and civil law; parts of the same thing. N.Y., 1896.
Phil 8892.29.15   Ritter, P.H. Etiske fragmenter. København, 1896.
Phil 192.13   Robertson, G.C. Elements of general philosophy. London, 1896.
Phil 5257.7   Robertson, G.C. Elements of psychology. London, 1896.
Phil 8892.4.10   Roberty, E. de. L'éthique. Le bien et le mal. Paris, 1896.

Chronological Listing

1896 - cont.

Phil 7052.8 — Rochas d'Aiglun, Albert de. L'extériorisation de la motricité. Paris, 1896.

Phil 4070.1.93 — Romano, P. Ausonio Franchi. Savona, 1896.

Phil 8610.896.5 — Roselli, G. Confutazione degli argomenti teologici. Foggia, 1896.

Phil 1717.3.8 — Royce, J. The spirit of modern philosophy. Boston, 1896.

Phil 6619.4.5 — Sanctis, Sante de. I sogni e il sonno nell'isterismo e nella epilessia. Roma, 1896.

Phil 8419.40.6A — Santayana, G. The sense of beauty. N.Y., 1896. 3v.

Phil 4225.2.31 — Sarlo, Francesco de. Saggi di filosofia. Torino, 1896-97. 2v.

Phil 5258.72 — Scheele, Frans von. Det mänskliga själslifvet. Stockholm, 1896.

Phil 2490.87 — Schoff, W.F. A neglected chapter in the life of Comte. Philadelphia, 1896.

Phil 3808.30 — Schopenhauer, Arthur. Art of controversy. London, 1896.

Phil 3808.36.5 — Schopenhauer, Arthur. The world as will and idea. v.2. London, 1896.

Phil 3565.125 — Schröder, Arthur. Geschichtsphilosophie bei Lotze. Diss. Leipzig, 1896.

Phil 8610.896 — Schurman, J.G. Agnosticism and religion. N.Y., 1896.

Phil 8893.39.5 — Schwarz, Hermann. Grundzüge der Ethik. Leipzig, 1896.

Phil 8423.8.25 — Schweizer, V. Ludolf Wienbarg als jungdeutscher Asthetiker und Kunstkritiker. Leipzig, 1896.

Phil 8615.2 — Sheldon, Walter L. An ethical movement. N.Y., 1896.

Phil 299.2 — Silberstein, S.J. Disclosures of the universal mysteries. N.Y., 1896.

Phil 8893.56 — Silva Cordeira, J.A. da. A crise em seus aspectos morals. Coimbra, 1896.

Phil 978.9.9 — Sinnett, A.P. Esoteric Buddhism. 6th ed. Boston, 1896.

Phil 5258.19 — Snider, D.J. Psychology and the psychosis. St.Louis, 1896.

Phil 2270.40.8 — Spencer, Herbert. Essays. N.Y., 1896. 3v.

Phil 2270.45.27 — Spencer, Herbert. First principles. N.Y., 1896.

Phil 2270.74.35 — Spencer, Herbert. La morale des différents peuples et la morale personnelle. Paris, 1896.

Phil 3500.23 — Stehr, H. Über Immanuel Kant. Leipzig, 1896.

Phil 8893.23.5 — Stephen, L. Social rights and duties. London, 1896. 2v.

Phil 8643.26 — Stern-Gwiazdowski, H. von. Leben wir nach unseren Tode weiter? Leipzig, 1896.

Phil 5258.41 — Sterrett, John D. The power of thought. N.Y., 1896.

Phil 5258.27.12 — Stout, G.F. Analytic psychology. N.Y., 1896. 2v.

Phil 3018.10 — Strümpell, Ludwig. Abhandlungen zur Geschichte de Metaphysik, Psychologie. Leipzig, 1896.

Phil 126.3 — Stumpf, C. Tafeln zur Geschichte der Philosophie. Berlin, 1896.

Phil 9495.36* — Symonds, J.A. A problem in modern ethics. London, 1896.

Phil 194.19 — Tarozzi, Giuseppe. Lezioni di filosofia. v.1-3. Torino, 1896-1898.

Phil 4110.4.102 — Tauro, G. Luigi Ferri. Roma, 1896.

Phil 194.22 — Thomas, William C. Cosmic ethics. London, 1896.

Phil 3565.108.5 — Tienes, Alfred. Lotze's Gedanken zur den Principienfragen der Ethik. Heidelberg, 1896.

Phil 2045.85 — Tönnies, F. Hobbes Leben und Lehre. Stuttgart, 1896.

Phil 8894.17.22 — Trine, Ralph W. What all the world's a-seeking. N.Y., 1896.

Phil 5525.8 — Ueberhorst, K. Das Komische. Leipzig, 1896-1900. 2v.

Phil 351.2 — Ulrich, Georg. Grundlegung des Systems aller möglichen Erfahrung. Berlin, 1896.

Phil 5940.1.3 — Uncle Sam's letters on phrenology. N.Y., 1896.

Phil 7068.96.15 — Underwood, Sara A. Automatic or spirit writing, with other psychic experiences. Chicago, 1896.

Phil 8895.2 — Unold, J. Grundlegung für eine moderne praktisch-ethische Lebensanschauung. Leipzig, 1896.

Phil 5261.11 — Vannérus, Allen. Om psykisk energi. Stockholm, 1896.

Phil 3915.105 — Vannérus, Allen. Vid studiet af Wundts psykologi. Stockholm, 1896.

Phil 302.2 — Vial, L.C.E. L'amour dans l'univers. Paris, 1896.

Phil 196.14 — Vogel, August. Die höchsten FragenBeleuchtet von den grössten Denkern der Neuzeit. Berlin, 1896-

Phil 352.3 — Volkmann, P. Erkenntnistheoretische Grundzüge der Naturwissenschaften. Leipzig, 1896.

Phil 3805.101 — Vowinckel, Ernst. Religion und Religionen bei Schleiermacher und Hegel. Erlangen, 1896.

Phil 197.26 — Wahle, R. Das Ganze der Philosophie und ihr Ende. Wien, 1896.

Phil 7068.96.10 — Wallace, Alfred R. Miracles and modern spiritualism. London, 1896.

Phil 3504.29 — Wallenberg, G. Kants Zeitlehre. Berlin, 1896.

Phil 822.1.5 — Weber, A. History of philosophy. N.Y., 1896.

Phil 8677.11.5 — Weill, Alexandre. Lois et mystères de la création. Paris, 1896.

Phil 270.14 — Wentscher, M. Über Physische und Psychische Kausalität. Leipzig, 1896.

Phil 8712.3.5 — White, Andrew Dickson. History of the warfare of science with theology in Christendem. N.Y., 1896. 2v.

Phil 822.7 — Wikner, Pontus. Filosofiens historia efter Pontus Wikner's kollegium. Rock Island, Ill., 1896.

Phil 7068.96.20 — Wilson, Ebenezer V. The truths of spiritualism. Chicago, 1896.

Phil 197.13.3 — Wood, H. Studies in the thought world. Boston, 1896.

Phil 3246.90 — Wotschke, Theodor. Fichte und Erigena. Halle, 1896.

Phil 5062.31 — Wrzecionko, R. Das Wesen des Denkens. Wien, 1896.

Phil 3915.47.7 — Wundt, Wilhelm. Grundriss des Psychologie. Leipzig, 1896.

Phil 3915.55.7 — Wundt, Wilhelm. Lectures on human and animal psychology. London, 1896.

Phil 35.4 — Zeitschrift für Timmanante Philosophie. Berlin, 1896-99. 4v.

Phil 5265.1.2 — Ziehen, Theodor. Leitfaden der physiologischen Psychologie. 3. Aufl. Jena, 1896.

Phil 4210.121F — Zucchi, N. Parole dette da N. Zucchi per l'inaugurazione del monumento ad Antonio Rosmini in Milano. n.p., 1896.

1897

Phil 4515.99 — Åt minnet af C.J. Boström, 1797-1897. Festskrift. Stockholm, 1897.

Phil 9490.1 — Adams, C.K. The present obligations of the scholar. Madison, Wis., 1897.

Phil 5330.1.3 — Aiken, C. Methods for mind training. N.Y., 1897.

Phil 8655.4 — Allen, G. The evolution of the idea of God. N.Y., 1897.

Phil 3425.237.5 — Allievo, G. Esame dell'Hegelianismo. Torino, 1897.

Phil 9500.3 — Anderson, Maggie P. Sick-room thoughts and gleanings. Saint John, N.B., 1897.

Phil 4070.1.80 — Angelini, A. Ausonio Franchi. Roma, 1897.

1897 - cont.

Phil 3910.125 — Arnsperger, W. Christians Wolff's Verhältnis zu Lubniz. Weimar, 1897.

Phil 7059.15 — Atkinson, Lulu Hurst. Lulu Hurst...writes her biography. Rome, Ga., 1897.

Phil 9245.9.55 — Avebury, John Lubbock. Le bonheur de vivre. v.1-2. Paris, 1897-98.

Phil 8951.8 — Babrovnitzki, I. Sushchestvennyia cherty pravoslavnago. Elisavetgrad, 1897.

Phil 8691.15 — Bach, W.H. Big Bible stories. Lilly Dale, N.Y., 1897.

Phil 5241.3.8 — Baldwin, J.M. Mental development. 2. ed. N.Y., 1897.

Phil 5241.3.5A — Baldwin, J.M. Social and ethical interpretations. Mental development. N.Y., 1897.

Phil 3808.166 — Bamberger, Herz. Das Tier in der Philosophie Schopenhauer's. Inaug. Diss. Wirzburg, 1897.

Phil 8876.73 — Bang, N.H. Begrebet moral; analyse og kritik. København, 1897.

Phil 5041.34 — Barker, Johnson. A digest of deductive logic for the use of students. London, 1897.

Phil 8876.9.5 — Basford, J.L. Seven seventy seven sensations. Boston, 1897.

Phil 6400.13 — Bastian, H.C. The Lumleian lectures on some problems in connection with aphasia and new speech defects. n.p., 1897.

X Cg Phil 1182.5 — Bauer, W. Der altere Pythagoreismus. Berlin, 1897.

Phil 176.82.5 — Bender, Hedwig. Philosophie, Metaphysik und Einzelforschung. Leipzig, 1897.

Phil 978.6.15 — Besant, Annie. The ancient wisdom. London, 1897.

Phil 978.6.64 — Besant, Annie. Karma. (Theosophical manual IV). London, 1897.

Phil 978.6.62 — Besant, Annie. Reincarnation (Theosophical manual II). London, 1897.

Phil 5650.2 — Bezold, Friedrich. þer die funktionelle Prüfung des menschlichen Gehörorgans. Wiesbaden, 1897.

Phil 3120.40.50 — Bierens de Haan. J.D. De norm der waarheid is in ons-zelf. Utrecht, 1897.

Phil 176.76 — Bilharz, Alfons. Metaphysik als Lehre vom Vorbewussten. Bd.I. Wiesbaden, 1897.

Phil 3625.1.85 — Biltz, Otto. Der Phädo Platos und Mendelssohns. Inaug. Diss. Berlin, 1897.

Phil 978.5.30 — Blavatsky, H.P. Studies in occultism. 2nd ed. Boston, 1897.

Phil 8876.59 — Böhmer, Gustav. Ein Buch von der deutschen Gesinnung fünf ethische Essays. München, 1897.

Phil 3120.11.96 — Bolland, G.J.P.J. Aanschomving en verstand. Leiden, 1897.

Phil 5426.9.8A — Boole, M.E. The mathematical psychology of Gratry and Boole. London, 1897.

Phil 4515.40 — Boström, C.J. Föreläsningar i etiken. Upsala, 1897.

Phil 3483.4 — Boström, G. Kritisk framställning of Kants frihetslära. Lund, 1897.

Phil 332.2 — Bowne, B.P. Theory of thought and knowledge. N.Y., 1897.

Phil 720.14.2 — Brochard, V. De l'erreur. 2e éd. Paris, 1897.

Phil 7054.149 — Brown, John. Mediumistic experiences of John Brown. 3. ed. San Francisco, 1897.

Phil 5500.7 — Brunschvicg, Léon. La modalité du jugement. Thèse. Paris, 1897.

Phil 7054.169 — Budington, Henry A. Death is birth. Springfield, Mass., 1897.

Phil 1504.2.3 — Bülow, G. Des dominicus gundissalinus. v.2, pt.3. Münster, 1897.

Phil 3552.236 — Bugarski, G.M. Die Natur des Willens bei Leibniz. Leipzig, 1897.

Phil 8692.12 — Ceballos Dosamantes, J. Ciencia y religion del porvenir. México, 1897.

Phil 5722.4.5 — Chabaneix, P. Essai sur le subconscient dans les oeuvres. Bordeaux, 1897.

Phil 6112.5.5 — Charcot, J.M. La foi qui guérit. Paris, 1897.

Phil 9240.4 — Clamageran, J.J. La lutte contre le mal. Paris, 1897.

Phil 9530.3 — Cleveland, G. The self-made man. N.Y., 1897.

Phil 3808.101 — Colvin, S.S. Schopenhauer's doctrine of the Thing-in-itself. Providence, 1897.

Phil 5042.14 — Commer, Ernst. Logik. Paderborn, 1897.

Phil 978.15 — Cook, M.C. Light on the path. Point Loma, California, 1897.

Phil 5425.10 — Cooley, C.H. Genius, fame and the comparison of races. Philadelphia, 1897.

Phil 5242.8 — Cornelius, H. Psychologie. Leipzig, 1897.

Phil 8582.24 — Craufurd, A.H. Christian instincts and modern doubt. London, 1897.

Phil 477.7 — Cros, Antoine. Les nouvelles formules du matérialisme. Paris, 1897.

Phil 802.3 — Crozier, F.B. History of intellectual development. v.1,3. London, 1897. 2v.

Phil 705.4 — Dall, C.H. Transcendentalism in New England. Boston, 1897.

Phil 5400.19.7 — Darwin, Charles. The expression of the emotions in man and animals. N.Y., 1897.

Phil 3485.24 — Daxer, Georg. Über die Anlage. Hamburg, 1897.

Phil 7054.157.5 — Delanne, Gabriel. L'évolution animique. Paris, 1897.

Phil 7054.157 — Delanne, Gabriel. Le phénomène spirite. 5. ed. Paris, 1897.

Phil 6313.1 — Delbrück, A. Gerichtliche psychopathologie. Leipzig, 1897.

Phil 2520.36 — Descartes, René. The method, meditation and selections. Edinburgh, 1897.

Phil 2520.19 — Descartes, René. Oeuvres de Descartes. Paris, 1897. 12v.

Phil 5213.1 — Dessoir, M. Geschichte der neueren deutschen Psychologie. Berlin, 1897.

Phil 8878.11.7 — Dewey, John. The study of ethics, a syllabus. Photoreproduction. Ann Arbor, 1897.

Phil 7068.97.42 — Dippel, Joseph. Der neuere Spiritismus in seinem Wesen dargelegt und nach seinem Werte geprüft. 2. Aufl. München, 1897.

Phil 5043.8.7 — Dodgson, C.L. Symbolic logic. pt.1. 4th ed. London, 1897.

Phil 6113.2.3 — Donaldson, H.H. The growth of the brain. London, 1897.

Phil 4195.82 — Dorez, Léon. Pic de la Mirandole en France, 1485-1488. Paris, 1897.

Phil 8693.4.3.10 — Draper, J.W. History of the conflict between religion and science. N.Y., 1897.

Phil 178.12.2 — Dresser, H.W. In search of a soul. Boston, 1897.

Phil 178.18 — Drews, Arthur. Das Ich als Grundproblem der Metaphysik. Freiburg, 1897.

Phil 5243.17 — Dubot, T. Psychologie. Paris, 1897.

Phil 8828.1 — Dupuy, Paul. La question morale à la fin du XIXe siècle. Paris, 1897.

Phil 1200.37 — Dyroff, Adolf. Die Ethik der alten Stoa. Berlin, 1897.

Phil 5545.27 Edridge-Green, F.W. Memory and its cultivation. N.Y., 1897.

Phil 8879.12 Ehrenfels, C. System der Werttheorie. Leipzig, 1897.

Phil 5244.10.10 Elsenhans, Theodor. Selbstbeobachtung und Experiment in der Psychologie. Freiburg, 1897.

Phil 6114.10 Erhardt, Franz. Die Wechselwirkung zwischen Leib und Seele. Leipzig, 1897.

Phil 3805.84 Esselborn, F.W. Die philosophischen Voraussetzingen von Schleiermachers Determinismus. Ludwigshafen, 1897.

Phil 8829.2.2 Eucken, Rudolf. Die Lebensanschauungen der grossen Denker. Leipzig, 1897.

Phil 1705.1.7 Falckenberg, R. History of modern philosophy. N.Y., 1897.

Phil 3210.69 Fechner, G.T. Kollektivmasslehre. Leipzig, 1897.

Phil 480.1 Ferraris, Ç.F. Il materialismo storico. Palermo, 1897.

Phil 8735.21 Ferrière, Émile. La cause première d'après les données experimentales. Paris, 1897.

Phil 3246.72.5 Fichte, Johann Gottlieb. Science of ethics...based on Science of knowledge. London, 1897.

Phil 8880.6 Fitzgerald, P.F. The rational, or scientific ideal of morality. London, 1897.

Phil 9245.24.3 Fletcher, Horace. Happiness as found in forethought minus fearthought. Chicago, 1897.

Phil 6115.18.6.5 Fletcher, Horace. Menticulture, or The ABC of true living. Chicago, 1897.

Phil 5815.3 Fluegel, Otto. Das Seelenleben der Tiere. 3e Aufl. Langensalza, 1897.

Phil 4210.122F Fogazzaro, A. La figura di Antonio Rosmini. Milano, 1897.

Phil 5925.6 Fowler, J.A. A manual of mental science for teachers and students. London, 1897.

Phil 5245.14 François, A. Leçons élémentaires de psychologie. Paris, 1897.

Phil 8880.28 Frins, Victor. De actibus humanis. Friburgi Brisgoviae, 1897-1911.

Phil 960.4.5 Garbe, Richard. The philosophy of ancient India. Chicago, 1897.

Phil 8881.24 Garrison, W.P. Parables for school and home. N.Y., 1897.

Phil 2270.85.5 Gaupp, Otto. Herbert Spencer. Stuttgart, 1897.

Phil 5816.5 Gentry, Thomas G. Life and immortality. Philadelphia, 1897.

Phil 7054.9 Giles, A.E. English and parental versions of Bible...in the light of modern spiritualism. Boston, 1897.

Phil 8586.29 Giovanni, V. di. Critica religiosa e filosofia lettere e saggi. Palermo, 1897. 2v.

Phil 9346.11 Gizycki, Paul von. Vom Baume der Erkenntnis. Berlin, 1897.

Phil 2050.91 Goebel, H. Das Philosophie in Humes Geschichte von England. Marburg, 1897.

Phil 3625.1.111 Goldstein, L. Die Bedeuterung Moses Mendelssohn. Inaug. Diss. Konigsberg, 1897.

Phil 2630.1.79 Gratry, Auguste. Souvenirs de ma jeunesse. 5e ed. Paris, 1897.

Phil 6420.4 Greenbaum, Ferdinand. Erklärung des Stotterns, dessèn Heilung und Verhütung. Leipzig, 1897.

Phil 3826.4 Grunwald, Max. Spinoza in Deutschland. Gekrönte Preisschrift. Berlin, 1897.

Phil 5400.44 Gurewitsch, Aron. Zur Geschichte des Achtungsbegriffes und zur Theorie der sittlichen Gefühle. Inaug. Diss. Würzburg, 1897.

Phil 8586.8.5 Guyau, M.J. The non-religion of the future. London, 1897.

Phil 5401.2 Hall, G.S. Study of fears. Worcester, 1897.

Phil 6117.36 Hallervorden, E. Arbeit und Wille. pt.1-2. Würzburg, 1897.

Phil 9245.13 Hamerton, P.G. The quest of happiness. Boston, 1897.

Phil 6957.5 Hamon, A. La responsabilité. Lyon, 1897.

X Cg Phil 6048.94.9 Hamon, Louis. Cheiro's language of the hand. 9th ed. N.Y., 1897.

Phil 4502.2 Hansen, Oscar. Filosofien i Danmark i dit 18. og 19. aarhundrede. København, 1897.

Phil 5247.25 Harms, F. Psychologie. Leipzig, 1897.

Phil 3808.87 Hecker, M.F. Schopenhauer. Köln, 1897.

Phil 3425.27A Hegel, Georg Wilhelm Friedrich. The wisdom of religion of a German philosopher. London, 1897.

Phil 5047.31 Heilner, R. System der Logik. Leipzig, 1897.

Phil 5545.37.5 Hering, Ewald. On memory and specific energies of the nervous system. 2. ed. Chicago, 1897.

Phil 3489.17 Hicks, G.D. Die Begriffe Phänomenon und Noumenon. Leipzig, 1897.

Phil 8882.37 Hoffmann, A. Ethik. Freiburg, 1897.

Phil 8663.3.45 Ingersoll, Robert G. The house of death. London, 1897.

Phil 8663.3.37 Ingersoll, Robert G. Ingersoll to the clergy. N.Y., 1897.

Phil 6115.6.8 Jacobi, M.P. (Mrs.). Considerations on Flechsig's "Gehirn und Seele". N.Y., 1897.

Phil 5249.1.2 Jahn, M. Psychologie als Grundwissenschaft der Pädagogik. Leipzig, 1897.

Phil 8633.1.2A James, W. Human immortality. Two supposed objections. Boston, 1897. 2v.

Phil 184.3 James, W. The will to believe and other essays. N.Y., 1897.

Phil 2668.70 Janet, Paul A.R. Principes de la métaphysique et de psychologie. Paris, 1897. 2v.

Phil 5627.74.2 Joly, H. Psychologie des saints. 2. éd. Paris, 1897.

Phil 2225.1.80 Judd, W.B. Noah Porters Erkenntnislehre. Jena, 1897.

Phil 3640.243 Kaftan, Julius. Das Christentum und Nietzsches Herremoral. Berlin, 1897.

Phil 3808.137 Keutel, Otto. Über die Zweck Mässigkeit in der Natur bei Schopenhauer. Leipzig, 1897.

Phil 9075.22 Knowlton, Pitt G. Origin and nature of conscience. Oberlin, 1897.

Phil 187.52.80 Kowalewski, A. Die Philosophie des Bewusstseins von Friedrich Michelis. Berlin, 1897.

Phil 1930.4.81 Kowalewski, Arnold. Kritische Analyse von Arthur Colliers Clavis Universalis. Inaug. Diss. Griefswald, 1897.

Phil 5330.29 Kreibig, Josef C. Die Aufmerksamkeit. Wien, 1897.

Phil 3492.13.3 Kronenberg, M. Kant. München, 1897.

Phil 185.12 Külpe, O. Introduction to philosophy. London, 1897.

Phil 9230.11 Labrousse, Louis. De l'exception de jeu. Paris, 1897.

Phil 8961.10 Lachmann, J.J. Religion og ethik. Kjobenhavn, 1897.

Phil 342.1 Ladd, G.T. Philosophie of knowledge. N.Y., 1897.

Phil 9410.6.2 Landesmann, H. Der grundlose Optimismus. Dresden, 1897.

Phil 7068.97.5 Lang, Andrew. The book of dreams and ghosts. London, 1897.

Phil 5251.21 Langwieser, Karl. Der Bewusstseinsmechanismus. Leipzig, 1897.

Phil 8836.2.6 Lecky, W.E.H. History of European morals. 3. ed. N.Y., 1897. 2v.

Phil 186.76.5 Le Dantec, Félix. Le déterminisme biologique et la personnalité consciente. Paris, 1897.

Phil 8886.44 Leuba, J.H. The psycho-physiology of the moral imperative. n.p., 1897.

Phil 4575.94 Leufren, E.J. Kritisk exposition of Benjamin Höijers. Upsala, 1897.

Phil 4515.85 Liljeqvist, Efraim. Om Boströms äldsta skrifter. Göteborg, 1897.

Phil 4210.123F Lilla, V. Le fonti del sistema filosofico di Antonio Rosmini. Milano, 1897.

Phil 3493.9.5 Lind, Paul von. Immanuel Kant und Alexander von Humboldt. Inaug. Diss. Erlangen, 1897.

Phil 8591.18 Lindsay, James. Recent advances in theistic philosophy of religion. Edinburgh, 1897.

Phil 2115.49.15 Locke, J. Über den menschlichen Verstand. Leipzig, 1897. 2v.

Phil 292.4 Logan, J.D. Three papers reprinted. n.p., 1897-99.

Phil 2050.180 Long, William J. Über Hume's Lehre von den Ideen. Inaug. Diss. Heidelberg, 1897.

Phil 6121.18 Loomis, E. Seven essays on the subject of your practical forces on the subject of practical occultism. Chicago, 1897.

Phil 3565.51.4 Lotze, Hermann. Microcosmos. v.1-2. N.Y., 1897.

NEDL Phil 3425.98 McGilvary, E. Principle and method of the Hegelian dialectic. Berkeley, 1897.

Phil 5635.5.2 Mach, Ernst. Contributions to the analysis of the sensations. Chicago, 1897.

Phil 8887.1.3 Mackenzie, J.S. A manual of ethics. 3rd ed. London, 1897.

Phil 3494.14 Major, David R. The principle of teology. Ithaca, N.Y., 1897.

Phil 3832.6 Malapert, P. De Spinozae politica. Thesis. Paris, 1897.

Phil 7080.13 Manaceïne, M. de. Sleep, its physiology, pathology, hygiene and psychology. London, 1897.

Phil 9530.25.10 Marden, Orison S. Success. Boston, 1897.

Phil 7068.97.30 Mason, R.O. Telepathy and the subliminal self. N.Y., 1897.

Phil 4195.83 Massetani, D.G. La filosofia cabbalistica di Giovanni Pico. Empoli, 1897.

Phil 6122.1.17 Maudsley, H. Natural causes and supernatural seemings. London, 1897.

Phil 8962.2 Maushach, J. Christentum und Weltmoral. Münster, 1897.

Phil 2050.192 Meinardus, H. David Hume als Religionsphilosoph. Inaug. Diss. Coblenz, 1897.

Phil 5222.1 Mercier, D. Les origines de la psychologie contemporaine. Paris, 1897.

Phil 2138.55 Mill, John S. The ethics of John Stuart Mill. Edinburgh, 1897.

Phil 4363.2.35 Molinos, M. de. The spiritual guide of Michael de Molinos. Philadelphia, 1897.

Htn Phil 3625.10.30* Münsterberg, H. Verse; von Hugo Terberg. Grossenhain, 1897.

Phil 3270.3.83 Münz, Bernhard. Briefe von und über Jakob Frohschammer. Leipzig, 1897.

Phil 8413.13 Muller, Josef. Eine Philosophie des Schönen in Natur und Kunst. Mainz, 1897.

Phil 1504.2.5 Nagy, A. Die philosophischen Abhandlungen. v.2, pt.5. Münster, 1897.

Phil 188.7A Nettleship, R.L. Philosophical lectures and remains. London, 1897.

Phil 6123.5 Newcomb, C.B. All's right with the world. Boston, 1897.

Htn Phil 6123.5.2* Newcomb, C.B. All's right with the world. Boston, 1897.

Phil 3425.99 Noël, G. La logique de Hegel. Paris, 1897.

Phil 2520.141 Nordlindh, Arvid. Descates' lära om känslan. Akademisk afhaudling. Upsala, 1897.

Phil 189.9.5 Opitz, H.G. Grundriss einer Seinswissenschaft. v.1-2. Leipzig, 1897-1899.

Phil 4112.82 Pagano, V. Galluppi e la filosofia italiana. Napoli, 1897.

Phil 2270.136 Pagnone, A. Le intuizioni morali e l'eredità nello Spencer. Torino, 1897.

Phil 6125.12.3 Panizza, M. La fisiologia del sistema nervoso. Roma, 1897.

Phil 5460.6 Parish, E. Hallucinations and illusions. London, 1897.

Phil 2805.40.15 Pascal, Blaise. Pensées. Paris, 1897.

Phil 1158.15.10 Pater, Walter. Marius the Epicurean. London, 1897.

Phil 5625.69 Patrizi, M.L. I riflessi vascolari nelle membra e nel cervello dell'uomo. Reggio-Emilia, 1897.

Phil 5330.21 Patrizi, M.L. Il tempo di reazione semplice. Reggio-Emilia, 1897.

Phil 365.5 Pearson, K. Chances of death...studies in evolution. London, 1897. 2v.

Phil 8705.3 Perce, W.R. Geneses and modern science. N.Y., 1897.

Phil 8446.27 Perès, Jean. L'art et le reel; essai de metaphysique fondée sur l'esthétique. Paris, 1897.

Phil 7085.8 Perry, L. de. Les somnambules extra-lucides. Paris, 1897.

Phil 3497.13.6 Pesch, T. Le kantisme et ses erreurs. Paris, 1897.

Phil 575.13 Piat, C. La personne humaine. Paris, 1897.

Phil 490.3 Pictet, Raoul. Étude critique du matérialisme et du spiritualisme. Genève, 1897.

Phil 3850.9.92 Pira, Karl. Framställning och kritik af J.S. Mills, Lotzes och Sigwarts...i logiken. Stockholm, 1897.

Phil 7068.97.10 Podmore, Frank. Studies in psychical research. London, 1897.

Phil 7068.97.11 Podmore, Frank. Studies in psychical research. N.Y., 1897.

Phil 8890.49 Popov I.V. Estestvennyi nravstvennyi zakon. Sergiev, 1897.

Phil 8965.9 Porret, James A. Les philosophies morales du temps présent. Genève, 1897.

Phil 3890.8.95 Pufendoy, Samne. Briefe an Christian Thomasius. München, 1897.

Phil 5520.18 Quantz, J.O. Problems in the psychology of reading. Chicago, 1897.

Phil 6615.14 Ranschburg, Pál. Neue Beiträge zur Psychologie des hysterischen Geisteszustandes. Leipzig, 1897.

Phil 6978.12.5 Raubinovitch, Jacques. La mélancolie. Paris, 1897.

Phil 525.91 Récéjac, Edonard. Essai sur les fondements de la connaissance mystique. Paris, 1897.

Phil 5057.10 Regnaud, P. Précis de logique évolutionniste. Paris, 1897.

Phil 176.5.51 Rey, J. La philosophie de M. Balfour. Paris, 1897.

Phil 5404.4.5 Ribot, T. Die Erblichkeit. Paris, 1897.

Phil 348.3 Ribot, T. L'évolution des idées générales. Paris, 1897.

Phil 5400.18 Ribot, T. The psychology of the emotions. London, 1897.

Phil 6327.46.7 Ribot, Théodule. Les maladies de la personnalité. 7. éd. Paris, 1897.

Chronological Listing

1897 - cont.

Phil 3640.118A — Riehl, Alois. Friedrich Nietzsche der Künstler und der Denker. Stuttgart, 1897.

Phil 3640.178.5 — Ritschl, Otto. Nietzsches Welt und Lebensanschauung. Freiburg, 1897.

Phil 4210.5 — Rosmini-Serbati, Antonio. Per Antonio Rosmini nel 1o centenario dalla sua nascita. Milano, 1897. 2v.

Phil 4210.135 — Rovereto. Comitato Centrale per la Commemorazione di A. Rosmini. Commemorazione del primo centenario dalla nascita di A. Rosmini. Milano, 1897.

Phil 5257.22.3 — Ryland, F. Psychology. 7. ed. London, 1897.

Phil 8598.24.2 — Sabatier, Auguste. Esquisse d'une philosophie de la religion. Paris, 1897.

Phil 5585.45 — Sachs, H. Die Entstehung der Raumvorstellung. Breslau, 1897.

Phil 6688.6 — Sage, X.L. Hypnotism as it is. N.Y., 1897.

Phil 6048.97.13 — Saint-Germain, C. de. Practical palmistry illustrated. Chicago, 1897.

Phil 6048.97.9 — Saint-Germain, C. de. The practice of palmistry. Chicago, 1897. 2v.

Phil 2128.83 — Sakmann, Paul. Bernard de Mandeville und die Bienenfabel. Freiburg, 1897.

Phil 3640.210 — Salis-Marschlins, M. von. Philosoph und Edelmensch. Leipzig, 1897.

Phil 299.11.5 — Scheffler, Hermann. Realität und Ideelität ferner Naturkraft und Schöpfungskraft. Braunschweig, 1897.

Phil 5258.43 — Schmidt, E. Zum Begriff und Sitz der Seele. Freiburg, 1897.

Phil 3808.31.2 — Schopenhauer, Arthur. On human nature. London, 1897.

Phil 5258.50.5 — Schuchter, Josef. Empirische Psychologie. Brixen, 1897.

Phil 8673.5 — Schwab, L.H. The kingdom of God. N.Y., 1897.

Phil 8893.62 — Schwalb, Carl J. Ethische und philosophische Betrachtungen auf empirischer Grundlage. Zürich, 1897.

Phil 5258.13.10 — Scripture, E.W. The new psychology. London, 1897.

Phil 8843.2 — Selby-Bigge, L.A. British moralists. v.1-2. Oxford, 1897.

Phil 8673.17 — Seth, A. Two lectures on theism delivered on the occasion of the sesquicentennial celebration of Princeton University. N.Y., 1897.

Phil 193.23.5 — Seth Pringle-Pattison, A. Man's place in the cosmos. N.Y., 1897.

Phil 8660.2.10 — Shanahan, E.T. John Fiske on the idea of God. Washington, 1897.

Phil 8598.12.15 — Smith, Goldwin. Guesses at the riddle of existence. N.Y., 1897.

Phil 2270.56.6 — Spencer, Herbert. Social statics. N.Y., 1897.

Phil 3819.74 — Spinoza, Benedictus de. Brieven,,,vertoog over het zuivere denken. Amsterdam, 1897.

Phil 8050.59 — Spitzer, Hugo. Kritische studien zur Ästhetik der Gegenwart. Wien, 1897.

Phil 9495.1.8 — Stall, Sylvanus. What a young boy ought to know. Philadelphia, 1897.

Phil 5627.1.10 — Starbuck, E.D. Some aspects of religious growth. n.p., 1897.

Phil 8893.50 — Staudinger, Franz. Das Sittengesetz. 2. Aufl. Berlin, 1897.

Phil 8419.42 — Stein, H. von. Vorlesungen über Ästhetik. Stuttgart, 1897.

Phil 8419.46 — Stone, W.F. Questions on the philosophy of art. London, 1897.

Phil 193.142.5 — Straub, L.W. Aufsatzentürufe. 3e Aufl. Leipzig, 1897.

Phil 6128.9 — Strömberg, J.D. Undersökningar i läran om själ och kropp. Lund, 1897.

Phil 720.7 — Strümpell, L. Die Unterschiede der Wahrneiten und der Irrthümer. Leipzig, 1897.

Phil 5258.25.6 — Sully, J. Teacher's handbook of psychology. N.Y., 1897.

Phil 8610.897 — Taber, H.M. Faith or fact. N.Y., 1897.

Phil 194.43 — Tardé, G. L'opposition universelle. Paris, 1897.

Phil 8844.1 — Thamin, R. Extraits des moralistes. Paris, 1897.

Phil 5627.81 — Thompson, J.B. The other paraclete. n.p., 1897.

Phil 8599.11 — Tiele, C.P. Elements of the science of religion. Edinburgh, 1897-99. 2v.

Phil 5259.5.5 — Titchener, E.B. An outline of psychology. N.Y., 1897.

Phil 3640.249 — Tönnies, Ferdinand. Der Nietzsche-Kultus; eine Kritik. Leipzig, 1897.

Phil 2295.40.5 — Toland, John. Das Pantheistikon. Leipzig, 1897.

Phil 8894.17.3 — Trine, Ralph W. In tune with the infinite. N.Y., 1897.

Phil 8894.17.23* — Trine, Ralph W. What all the world's a-seeking. Boston, 1897.

Phil 8894.20 — Trojano, Paolo R. Ethica. Napoli, 1897.

Phil 3565.129 — Tuch, Ernst. Lotzes Stellung zum Occasionalismus. Berlin, 1897.

Phil 8599.10.6 — Tyler, Charles Mellen. Bases of religious belief. N.Y., 1897.

Phil 8896.18 — Valentine, M. Theoretical ethics. Chicago, 1897.

Phil 4515.84 — Vannérus, Allen. Till Boströms teoretiska filosofi. Stockholm, 1897.

Phil 196.13 — Vaz, F.M. Estudos philosóphicos. Porto, 1897. 2v.

Phil 9495.4.5 — Warren, M.A. Almost fourteen. N.Y., 1897.

Phil 5832.3 — Wasmann, E. Vergleichende Studien über das Seelenleben der Ameisen und der höheren Thiere. Freiburg, 1897.

Phil 7068.97.22 — Watch Tower Bible and Tract Society. What say the scriptures about spiritualism? Brooklyn, 1897.

Phil 7068.97.20 — Watch Tower Bible and Tract Society. What say the scriptures about spiritualism? Allegheny, Pa., 1897.

Phil 400.7.2 — Watson, J. Christianity and idealism. N.Y., 1897.

Phil 400.7 — Watson, J. Christianity and idealism. N.Y., 1897.

Phil 6332.1* — Weir, J. The psychical correlation of religious emotion and sexual desire. 2d ed. Louisville, Ky., 1897.

Phil 6332.1.2 — Weir, J. The psychical correlation of religious emotion and sexual desire. 2d ed. Louisville, Ky., 1897.

Phil 3504.7 — Wenley, R.M. An outline introduction of Kant's Critique of pure reason. N.Y., 1897.

Phil 9430.25 — Wentscher, M. Über den Pessimismus und seine Wurzeln. Bonn, 1897.

Phil 8897.62.3 — Whiting, Lilian. The world beautiful. Boston, 1897.

Phil 5832.11 — Wolff, Gustav. Zur Psychologie des Erkennens. Leipzig, 1897.

Phil 3504.16 — Wolff, Hermann. Neue Kritik der reinen Vernunft. Leipzig, 1897.

Phil 1890.80 — Woods, J.H. Thomas Browns Causationstheorie. Leipzig, 1897.

Phil 3915.65.5 — Wundt, Wilhelm. Ethik. London, 1897-1901. 3v.

Phil 3915.47.4 — Wundt, Wilhelm. Grundriss des Psychologie. 2. Aufl. Leipzig, 1897.

Phil 3915.47 — Wundt, Wilhelm. Outlines of psychology. Leipzig, 1897.

Phil 3915.30.2 — Wundt, Wilhelm. System der Philosophie. 2. Aufl. Leipzig, 1897.

1898

Phil 5240.24 — Aars, K.B.R. Inledning til psychologien. Kristiania, 1898.

Phil 7060.106 — Aksakov, Aleksandr N. Vorläuser des Spiritismus. Leipzig, 1898.

Phil 8875.15 — Allihn, Friedrich H. Grundriss der Ethik. 2e Aufl. Langensalza, 1898.

Phil 5374.32 — Ambrosi, L. I principii della conoscenza. Roma, 1898.

Phil 5465.4 — Ambrosi, L. La psicologia della immaginazione. Roma, 1898.

Phil 8685.14 — Amryc, C. Pantheism. n.p., 1898.

Phil 6111.38 — Babbitt, E.D. Human culture and cure. pt.3-4. Los Angeles, 1898.

Phil 1504.2.6 — Baeumker, C. Die Impossibilia. v.2. pt.6. Münster, 1898.

Phil 5241.3.28 — Baldwin, J.M. The story of the mind. N.Y., 1898.

Phil 3428.85 — Ballauff, F. Entstehung und Bedeutung; Herbarts. Aurich, 1898.

Phil 8951.13 — Ballerini, A. Opus theologicum morale in Busernbaum Medullam. 3.ed. Prati, 1898-1901. 7v.

Phil 6671.13.7 — Barnes, W.A. Psychology, hypnotism, personal magnatism and clairvoyance. Boston, 1898.

Phil 7068.98.5 — Baudidi Vesme, C. Geschichte des Spiritismus. Leipzig, 1898-1900.

Phil 8876.11.10 — Baumann, Julius. Realwissenschaftliche Begründung der Moral. Leipzig, 1898.

Phil 1106.3.5 — Benn, A.W. The philosophy of Greece. London, 1898.

Phil 3246.97 — Bensow, Oscar. Zu Fichtes Lehre von Nicht- ich. Bern, 1898.

NEDL Phil 5374.8.5 — Bergson, H. Essai sur les données immédiates de la conscience. 2. èd. Paris, 1898.

X Cg Phil 5374.8 — Bergson, H. Essai sur les données immédiates de la conscience. 2. èd. Paris, 1898.

Phil 1701.7.5 — Berr, Henri. La synthèse des connaissances et l'histoire. Thèse. Paris, 1898.

Phil 978.6.63 — Besant, Annie. Death - and after? London, 1898.

Phil 5241.39 — Bierens de Haan, P. Hoofdlijnen eener psychologie met metafysischen grondslag. Amsterdam, 1898.

Phil 8876.39 — Bon, Fred. Über das Sollen und das Gute. Leipzig, 1898.

Phil 2477.1.32 — Boutroux, Émile. De la contingence des lois de la nature. 3. éd. Paris, 1898.

Phil 176.27.2 — Bowne, B.P. Metaphysics. N.Y., 1898.

Phil 4065.60.30 — Bruno, Giordano. Eroici furori, Übersetzt von L. Kuhlenbeck. Leipzig, 1898.

Phil 476.3.2.4 — Büchner, L. Kraft und Stoff. Frankfurt, 1898.

Phil 5241.38 — Buell, C.S. Essentials of psychology. Boston, 1898.

Phil 3483.60 — Burckhardt, W. Kant's objectiver Idealismus. Naumburg, 1898.

Htn Phil 6672.9.17* — Cahagnet, L. Magnetic magic. n.p., 1898.

Phil 8430.8 — Carpenter, Edward. Angels' wings. London, 1898.

Phil 8627.14 — Carpenter, Joseph E. The place of immortality in religious belief. London, 1898.

Phil 930.1 — Çarus, P. Chinese philosophy. Chicago, 1898.

Phil 4807.6F — Česká akademie věd a umění. Památník na oslavu padesátiletého panovnického jubilea jeho veličenstva císaře a krále Františka Josefa I. Praha, 1898.

Phil 8582.33.2 — Charbonnel, Victor. La volonté de vivre. 2. éd. Paris, 1898.

Phil 2490.109 — Cirra, Émile. Appréciation générale du positivisme. Paris, 1898.

Phil 177.84.5 — Clark, S.C. Key-notes for daily harmonies. Boston, 1898.

Phil 2490.65 — Comte, Auguste. Auguste Comte méconnu. Extraits de son oeuvre finale (1851-1857). Paris, 1898.

Phil 5042.7 — Creighton, J.E. An introductory logic. N.Y., 1898.

Phil 5753.6 — Dallemagne, Jules. Physiologie de la volonté. Paris, 1898.

Phil 3808.123 — Damm, Oscar. Schopenhauers Ethik im Verhaltnis zu seiner Erkenntnislehre und Metaphysik. Annaberg, 1898.

Phil 5585.41 — Dandolo, G. Le integrazioni psichiche e la percezione. Padova, 1898.

Phil 8610.898 — D'Arusmont, Frances Wright. Six lectures on the nature of knowledge, free enquiry, the more important divisions and essentials of knowledge, religion, morals, opinions. London, 1898.

Phil 1870.85 — Dick, S.M. The principle of synthetic unity in Berkeley and Kant. Lowell, 1898.

Phil 178.12.7 — Dresser, H.W. The perfect whole. 3rd ed. Boston, 1898.

Phil 178.12.9.5 — Dresser, H.W. The power of silence. 7th ed. Boston, 1898.

Phil 178.12.12 — Dresser, H.W. Voices of hope. Boston, 1898.

Phil 5243.10.1 — Drobisch, M.W. Empirische Psychologie. 2e Aufl. Hamburg, 1898.

Phil 6953.9 — Duprat, G.L. L'instabilité mentale. Paris, 1898.

Phil 3824.1 — Elbogen, Ismar. Der Tractatus de Intellectus emendatione. Breslau, 1898.

Phil 3824.1.5 — Elbogen, Ismar. Der Tractatus de Intellectus emendatione. Diss. Breslau, 1898.

Phil 8694.2 — Elder, William. Ideas from nature. Philadelphia, 1898.

Phil 5244.6 — Elsenhaus, T. Psychologie und Logik. Leipzig, 1898.

Phil 7060.44 — Ermacora, G.B. La telepatia. Padova, 1898.

Phil 5814.1 — Evans, E.P. Evolutional ethics and animal psychology. N.Y., 1898.

Phil 7068.98.20 — Falcomer, M.T. Contributo di fatti pella soluzione del problema di psicologia. Selessandria, 1898.

Phil 5245.28F — Farpon y Tuñón, José. Discurso leido...2 de julio de 1898. Manila, 1898.

Phil 2115.118 — Fechtner, Eduard. John Locke, ein Bild aus den geistigen Kämpfen Englands. Stuttgart, 1898.

Phil 5440.7 — Féré, C. La famille névropathique. Paris, 1898.

Phil 6115.25 — Ferrari, G.C. Ricerche ergografiche nella donna. Reggio Emilia, 1898.

Phil 1705.4.3 — Fischer, K. Geschichte der neueren Philosophie. v.2-10. Heidelberg, 1898-1904. 7v.

Phil 7068.98.30 — Fitler, C.H. New thoughts. Philadelphia, 1898.

Phil 9245.24 — Fletcher, Horace. Happiness. N.Y., 1898.

Phil 6115.18.7 — Fletcher, Horace. Menticulture. Chicago, 1898.

Phil 6115.18.7.5 — Fletcher, Horace. Menticulture. Chicago, 1898.

Phil 7068.98.10 — Fontenay, Guillaume de. A propos d'Eusapia Paladino. Paris, 1898.

Phil 2490.104 — Fornelli, N. L'opera di Augusto Comte, in occasione del primo centenario della sua nascita. Milano, 1898.

Phil 2240.81 — Fraser, A.C. Thomas Reid. London, 1898.

Phil 3552.270 — Frenzel, Bernhard. Der Associationsbegriff bei Leibniz. Leipzig, 1898.

Phil 3100.127 — Friedrich, H. Friedrich Edward Beneke. Wiesbaden, 1898.

Phil 5545.29 — Fuller, H.H. The art of memory. St. Paul, Minn., 1898.

Phil 8880.21 — Fulliquet, G. Essai l'obligation morale. Paris, 1898.

Phil 3640.80 — Gallwitz, H. Friedrich Nietzsche. Dresden, 1898.

1898 - cont.

Phil 3640.80.5   Gallwitz, H. Friedrich Nietzsche. Ein Lebensbild. Dresden, 1898.

Phil 4210.117   Gentile, G. Rosmini e Gioberti. Pisa, 1898.

Phil 4115.99   Gentile, G. Rosmini e Gioberti. Pisa, 1898.

Phil 4060.1.95   Ghisleri, Arcangelo. Nel LXX compleanno di Roberto Ardigò. Cremona, 1898.

Phil 2805.90   Giraud, V. Pascal l'homme, l'oeuvre, l'influence. Fribourg, 1898.

Phil 3140.81   Göpfert. Claubergstudien. Meiningen, 1898.

Phil 6316.2   Goldscheider, A. Die Bedeutung der Reize für Pathologie und Therapie. Leipzig, 1898.

Phil 6116.12   Goldscheider, A. Gesammette Abhandlungen. v.1-2. Leipzig, 1898.

Phil 3488.4.5   Goldschmidt, L. Kant und Helmholtz. Hamburg, 1898.

Phil 9245.30   Gomperz, H. Kritik des Hedonismus. Stuttgart, 1898.

Phil 5246.50   Grassi-Bertazzi, G.B. I fenomeni psichici. Catania, 1898.

Phil 4060.1.98   Groppali, A. Nel settantesimo anniversario di Roberto Ardigò. Torino, 1898.

Phil 3826.9   Grzymisch, S. Spinoza's Lehren von der Ewigkeit und Unsterblichkeit. Breslau, 1898.

Phil 8881.26.5   Guyau, M. A sketch of morality. London, 1898.

Phil 3415.106.8   Haacke, Hermann. Neuere Stimmen der Kritik über Eduard von Hartmanns Werke. Leipzig 1898.

Phil 182.71   Hansen, O. Opdragelseslaere. Kjobenhavn, 1898.

Phil 3415.69   Hartmann, Eduard von. Ethische Studien. Leipzig, 1898.

Phil 338.22   Hausdorff, Felix. Das Chaos im kosmischer Auslese. Leipzig, 1898.

Phil 6317.4   Hélat, C. Névroses et possessions diaboliques. 2. éd. Paris, 1898.

Phil 5648.7   Henri, V. Raumwahrnemungen des Tastsinnes. Berlin, 1898.

Phil 5648.7.2   Henri, V. Raumwahrnemungen des Tastsinnes. Berlin, 1898.

Phil 182.28   Hibben, J.G. The problems of philosophy. N.Y., 1898.

Phil 2045.20   Hobbes, Thomas. The ethics of Thomas Hobbes, by E.H. Sneath. Photoreproduction. Boston, 1898.

Phil 8957.6   Hocking, William J. Modern problems and Christian ethics. London, 1898.

Phil 182.19.11   Hodgson, S.H. Metaphysic of experience. London, 1898. 4v.

Phil 5247.23.8   Höfler, Alois. Physiologische oder experimentelle Psychologie am Gymnasium? Wien, 1898.

Phil 5047.10   Hoffman, F.S. Sphere of science. N.Y., 1898.

Phil 2648.31.15   Holbach, Paul Henri T. Sociales System oder Naturliche Principien der Moral und der Politik. Leipzig, 1898.

Phil 1900.175   Hughes, Henry. A critical examination of Butler's analogy London, 1898.

Phil 2050.37   Hume, David. Essays: moral, political and literary. N.Y., 1898. 2v.

Phil 8697.5.15   Huxley, T.H. Science and Christian tradition; essays. N.Y., 1898.

Phil 5330.20   Hylan, J.P. The fluctuation of attention. N.Y., 1898.

Phil 3890.7.81   Jacobskötter, A. Die Psychologie Dieterich Liedemanns. Inaug. Diss. Erlangen, 1898.

Phil 184.3.3.5A   James, W. The will to believe and other essays in popular philosophy. N.Y., 1898.

Phil 5249.2.20   James, William. Sjalslifrets. Uppsala, 1898.

Phil 6959.1.5   Janet, Pierre. Névroses et idées fixes. Paris, 1898. 2v.

Phil 3552.273   Jasper, Joseph. Leibniz und die Scholastik. Inaug. Diss. Münster, 1898-99.

Phil 3640.204   Kalina, P.E. Fundament und Einheit in Friedrich Nietzsches Philosophie. Leipzig, 1898.

Phil 8885.21.2   Kirchner, F. Ethik; Katechismus der Sittenlehre. 2e Aufl. Leipzig, 1898.

Phil 7060.45   Kleinpaul, R. Die Lebendigen und die Toten. Leipzig, 1898.

Htn   Phil 7054.124*   Knaggs, Samuel T. Human fads, foibles, fallacies. Sydney, 1898.

Phil 5760.6   Kneib, Philipp. Die Willensfreiheit und die innere Verantwortlichkeit. Mainz, 1898.

Phil 9550.4   Krueger, F. Der Begriff des Absolut Wertvollen. Leipzig, 1898.

Phil 8885.29   Krueger, Felix. Der Begriff des absolut Wertvollen. Leipzig, 1898.

Phil 3850.1.84   Kuenkler, Heinrich. Zum Gedächtnis an David Friedrich Strauss. Wiesbaden, 1898.

Phil 5251.1.20   Ladd, G.T. Descriptive psychology. N.Y., 1898.

Phil 8663.3.88   Lambert, L.A. Ingersoll's Christmas sermon delivered by Rev. L.A. Lambert. Akron, 1898.

Phil 8591.12   Lang, Albert. Making of religion. London, 1898.

Phil 8510.25   Larsen, H. Martensen. Jesus und die Religionsgeschichte. Freiburg, 1898. 3 pam.

Phil 1135.100   Laudowicz, Felix. Wesen und Ursprung der Lehre von der Präexistenz der Seele und von der Seelenwanderung in der griechischen Philosophie. Berlin, 1898.

Phil 4582.4.83   Leander, P.H.J. Svar på kritik af ett kompêtensutlåtande. Lund, 1898.

Phil 3552.65   Leibniz, Gottfried Wilhelm. The monadology. Oxford, 1898.

Phil 9351.9   Le Roup, Hugues. Nos filles qu'en ferons-nous? 5. ed. Paris, 1898.

Phil 5545.72   Leroy, Eugène B. Étude sur l'illusion de fausse reconnaissance. Paris, 1898.

Phil 3493.9   Lind, Paul von. Eine unsterbliche Entdeckung Kants. Leipzig, 1898.

Phil 5525.13   Lipps, T. Komik und Humor. Hamburg, 1898.

Phil 400.10   Lloyd, A.H. Dynamic idealism. Chicago, 1898.

Phil 6121.18.5   Loomis, E. Occult science library; seven essays. Chicago, 1898.

Phil 575.8   Lutosławski, W. Über die Grundvoraussetzungen und Consequenzen der individualistischen Weltanschauung. Helsingfors, 1898.

Phil 5252.18.30   McDougall, William. A contribution towards an improvement in psychological method. n.p., 1898-1914. 8 pam.

Phil 600.28   Marchesini, G. La crisi del positivismo...filosofico. Torino, 1898.

Phil 8592.17   Marshall, H.K. Instinct and reason. N.Y., 1898.

Phil 1117.1.3   Marshall, John. Short history of Greek philosophy. London, 1898.

Phil 5821.1.15   Marx, Moses. Charles Georges Leroy und seine "Lettres philosophiques." Strassburg, 1898.

Phil 8592.44   Masci, Filippo. L'idealismo indeterminista. Napoli, 1898.

Phil 5252.42.15   Meyer, M.F. Über Tonverschmelzung. n.p., 1898-1913. 20 pam.

Phil 5090.7.5   Milhaud, G. Le rationnel. Paris, 1898.

Phil 2138.35.5.3   Mill, John S. A system of logic. London, 1898.

Phil 8592.11   Mills, B.F. Twentieth century religion. Boston, 1898.

Phil 5822.2   Mills, W. The nature and development of animal intelligence. London, 1898.

Phil 343.2   Mivart, G. The groundwork of science. N.Y., 1898.

Phil 6322.1.5   Mobius, P.J. Vermischte Aufsätze. Leipzig, 1898.

Phil 6682.6.4   Moll, Albert. Hypnotism. 4th ed. London, 1898.

Phil 3428.87   Moosherr, T. Herbarts Metaphysik. Basel, 1898.

Phil 187.117   Morando, G. Corso elementare di filosofia. Milano, 1898-1899. 3v.

Phil 9065.1.5   Morley, J. On compromise. London, 1898.

Phil 187.70   Müller, Josef. System der Philosophie. Mainz, 1898.

Phil 5374.39   Müller, R. Das normale Bewusstsein. Leipzig, 1898.

Phil 6122.29   Müller, Wilhelm. Rede Gehalten zur Feier der akademischen Preisverteilung am 23 Juni 1898. Jena, 1898.

Phil 2266.83   Muir, Ethel. The ethical system of Adam Smith. Thesis. Halifax, N.S., 1898.

Phil 5763.1   Naville, E. Le libre arbitre. Genève, 1898.

Phil 5253.5   Nicati, W.M. La psychologie naturelle. Paris, 1898.

Phil 2920.1.80   Ollé-Laprune, L. Etienne Vacherot. Paris, 1898.

Phil 8595.15.19   Paine, Thomas. Age of reason. N.Y., 1898.

Phil 8890.23.3   Palmer, G.H. The glory of the imperfect. N.Y., 1898.

Phil 5255.13.5   Panizza, Mario. I nuovi elemente della psicofisiologia. Roma, 1898.

Htn   Phil 8890.24*   Pater, W. Conclusion: an essay. N.Y., 1898.

Phil 3497.3A   Paulsen, Friedrich. Immanuel Kant. Stuttgart, 1898.

Phil 1122.4   Payot, E. Les auteurs philosophiques, grecs. Paris, 1898.

Phil 5066.12.5   Peano, G. Arithmétique. Turin, 1898.

Phil 665.39   Pietropaolo, F. L'anima nel mondo greco e romano nel medio evo e nella filosofia moderna. Roma, 1898.

Phil 8416.40   Pilar, Ivo. Secesija. Zagreb, 1898.

Phil 2880.2.82   Pillon, F. La philosophie de Charles Secrétan. Paris, 1898.

Phil 190.39   Poirson, Charles. Le dynamisme absolu. Lyon, 1898.

Phil 190.17   Powell, J.W. Truth and error. Chicago, 1898.

Phil 5057.9   Read, C. Logic; deductive and inductive. London, 1898.

Phil 6127.6   Rehmke, J. Aussenwelt und Innenwelt, Leib und Seele. Griefswald, 1898.

Phil 3837.17   Richter, Raoul. Der Willensbegriff in der Lehre Spinoza's. Leipzig, 1898.

Phil 3640.118.2   Riehl, Alois. Friedrich Nietzsche der Künstler und der Denker. 2e Aufl. Stuttgart, 1898.

Phil 1122.3.17   Ritter, Heinrich. Historia philosophiae graecae. Gotha, 1898.

Phil 7068.98.15   Robinson, William E. Spirit state writing and kindred phenomena. N.Y., 1898.

Phil 8597.12.8   Romanes, G.J. Thoughts on religion. Chicago, 1898.

Phil 8672.6.4A   Royce, J. The conception of God. N.Y., 1898.

Phil 2250.65   Royce, Josiah. Studies of good and evil. Hamden, 1898.

Phil 192.16.7A   Royce, Josiah. Studies of good and evil. N.Y., 1898.

Phil 3500.45   Salits, Peter. Darstellung und Kritik des Kantischen Lehre von der Willensfreiheit. Rostock, 1898.

Phil 8893.74   Sandström, A. Modern; romantik och etik. Stockholm, 1898.

Phil 8419.40.5   Santayana, G. The sense of beauty, being the outlines of aesthetic theory. N.Y., 1898.

Phil 3640.289   Sanz y Escartin, Eduardo. Federico Nietzsche y el anarquismo intelectual. Madrid, 1898.

Phil 8893.43.10   Sarlo, Francisco de. Metafisica, scienza e moralità. Roma, 1898.

Phil 299.11   Scheffler, Hermann. Die Grundlagen des Weltsystems. Braunschweig, 1898.

Phil 3838.5   Scheidemantel, H. Die Grundprobleme der Ethik Spinoza's. Leipzig, 1898.

Phil 3790.1.93   Scherer, C.C. Das Tier in der Philosophie des H.S. Reimarus. Diss. Würzburg, 1898.

Phil 299.12   Schoeler, H. von. Kritik der wissenschaftlichen Erkenntnis. Leipzig, 1898.

Phil 5722.16   Schofield, A.T. The unconscious mind. London, 1898.

Phil 5649.10   Schultze, Ernst. Über die Umwandlung willkürlicher Bewegungen in unwillkürliche. Leipzig, 1898.

Phil 8643.6   Seebach, E. Die Lehre von der bedingten Unsterblichkeit in ihren Entstehung geschichtlichen Entwickelung. Krefeld, 1898.

Phil 3018.5   Seibert, C. Geschichte der neueren deutschen Philosophie. Gottingen, 1898.

Phil 6128.39   Seward, T.F. The Don't Worry movement. N.Y., 1898.

Phil 8615.4   Sidgwick, H. Practical ethics. London, 1898.

Phil 7140.2A   Sidis, B. The psychology of suggestion. N.Y., 1898.

Phil 9120.4.13   Smiles, S. El deber; versión española. Paris, 1898.

Phil 2805.87   Souriau, M. Pascal. Paris, 1898.

Phil 2270.43   Spencer, Herbert. Various fragments. N.Y., 1898.

Phil 193.65.5   Spicker, Gideon. Der Kampf zweier Weltanschauungen. Stuttgart, 1898.

Phil 8598.22   Sprague, F.H. Spiritual consciousness. Wollaston, 1898.

Phil 5350.1   Stern, L.W. Psychologie der Veränderungsauffassung. Breslau, 1898.

X Cg   Phil 9495.124.2   Stockham, A.B. (Mrs.). Karezza, ethics of marriage. Chicago, 1898.

Phil 5258.27   Stout, G.F. A manual of psychology. v.1-2. London, 1898-99.

Phil 8893.28.8   Sullivan, W.R. Morality as a religion. London, 1898.

Phil 7082.32.2   Surbled, Georges. Le rêve. 2e éd. Paris, 1898.

Phil 8843.4   Sutherland, A. The origin and growth of moral instinct. London, 1898. 2v.

Phil 4803.799.80   Świezawski, Leon. Jan Śniadecki, jego zycie i działalność naukowa. Petersburg, 1898.

Phil 8894.28   Thwing, C.F. The best life; an address. N.Y., 1898.

Phil 3552.302   Tirtsch, Gergely. Leibniz erkolcatana. Balassagyarmat, 1898.

Phil 5259.5A   Titchener, E.B. A primer of psychology. N.Y., 1898.

Phil 2520.100   Touchard, G. La morale de Descartes. Paris, 1898.

Phil 8894.17.20   Trine, Ralph W. The greatest thing ever known. N.Y., 1898.

Phil 5831.2   Verworn, M. Die sogenannte Hypnose der Thiere. Jena, 1898.

Phil 8422.7.10   Vischer, F.T. Das Schöne und die Kunst. Stuttgart, 1898.

Phil 4757.3.20   Vvedenskii, Aleksei I. Protoierei Feodor Aleksandrovich Golubinski. Sergiev, 1898.

Phil 9182.4   Wagner, Charles. Auprès du foyer. Paris, 1898.

Phil 8602.14   Wallace, W. Lectures and essays on natural theology and ethics. Oxford, 1898.

Phil 3504.45   Washington, W.M. The formal and material elements of Kant's ethics. N.Y., 1898.

Phil 4075.81   Waters, W.G. Jerome Cardan. London, 1898.

Phil 197.2.2   Watson, J. Outline of philosophy with notes. 2d ed. Glasgow, 1898.

Phil 3110.90   Wernicke, A. Meister Jacob Böhme. Braunschweig, 1898.

Phil 8633.1.3   Wheeler, B.I. Dionysos and immortality. Boston, 1898.

Chronological Listing

1898 - cont.

Phil 7054.4.9 — Whiting, Lilian. After her death. Boston, 1898.
Phil 8897.62.5 — Whiting, Lilian. The world beautiful. 3rd ser. Boston, 1898.
Phil 8887.4.18 — Wilkinson, J.J. James Martineaus Ethik...Kritik. Inaug. Diss. Leipzig, 1898.
Phil 3552.103 — Willareth, O. Die Lehre vom Uebel. Strassburg, 1898.
Phil 3235.85 — Wintzer, Wilhelm. Der natürliche Sittenlehre Ludwig Feuerbachs. Leipzig, 1898.
Phil 8897.26 — Woltmann, L. System der moralischen Bewusstseins. Düsseldorf, 1898.
Phil 8712.5.9 — Wright, George F. Scientific aspects of Christian evidences. N.Y., 1898.
Phil 3915.47.25 — Wundt, Wilhelm. Leerboek der zielkunde. Amsterdam, 1898?
Phil 8677.13 — Wyneken, G.A. Amor dei intellectualis. Greifswald, 1898.
Phil 3504.37 — Wyneken, G.A. Hegels Kritik Kants. Greifswald, 1898.
Phil 3504.37.5 — Wyneken, G.A. Hegels Kritik Kants. Inaug. Diss. Greifswald, 1898.
Phil 356.1 — Ziehen, T. Psychophysiologische Erkenntnistheorie. Jena, 1898.
Phil 3640.123 — Zoccoli, Ettore G. Federico Nietzsche. Modena, 1898.

1899

Phil 7072.2 — Alberg, Albert. Frost flowers on the windows. Chicago, 1899.
Phil 5240.31 — Alrutz, S.G.L.R. Om själslifvets studium på fysiologisk grundval. Stockholm, 1899.
Phil 8690.3 — Anzoletti, Luisa. Per un nuovo patto fra la scienze e la religione. Milano, 1899.
Phil 2270.126 — Ardigò, R. La dottrina Spenceriana dell'inconoscible. Roma, 1899.
Phil 5241.3.9 — Baldwin, J.M. Interpretation sociale et morale des principes du développement mental. Paris, 1899.
Phil 6111.26 — Barker, L.F. The nervous system and its constituent neurones. N.Y., 1899.
Phil 6111.16.5 — Bechterew, W. von. Die Leitungsbahnen im Gehirn und Rückenmark. Leipzig, 1899.
Phil 1106.13 — Bender, W. Mythologie und Metaphysik. Die Entstehung der Weltanschauungen im greichisch Altertums. Stuttgart, 1899.
Phil 5642.17 — Benoist, Emilien. Contribution à l'étude de l'audition colorée. Paris, 1899.
Phil 1870.20.4 — Berkeley, G. Selections annotated. 5th ed. Oxford, 1899.
Cg Phil 1701.7 — Berr, Henri. Avenir de la philosophie. Paris, 1899.
Phil 4462.1.30 — Bevilaqua, Clovis. Esboços e fragmentos. Rio de Janeiro, 1899.
Phil 6400.8 — Bianchi, Leonardo. Licções sobre as localisações cerebraes. Rio de Janeiro, 1899.
Phil 8876.64 — Biedermann, Karl. Zeit- und Lebensfragen aus dem Gebiete der Moral. Breslau, 1899.
Phil 5620.1.5 — Binet, A. The psychology of reasoning. Chicago, 1899.
Phil 4710.16 — Bobrov, E.A. Filosofiia v Rossii; materialy. Kazan, 1899.
Phil 3120.11.95 — Bolland, G.J.P.J. Open brief aan den heer K.J.A.M. Schaepman. Leiden, 1899.
Phil 3821.13 — Bolland, G.J.P.J. Spinoza. Leiden, 1899.
Phil 1885.37.3 — Bradley, Francis H. Appearance and reality. London, 1899.
Cg Phil 6671.10.15 — Braid, James. Neurypnology. London, 1899.
Phil 5585.23 — Braude, M. Die Elemente der Reinen Wahrnehmung. Lemberg, 1899.
Phil 5330.6.5 — Braunschweiger, D. Die Lehre von der Aufmerksamkeit. Leipzig, 1899.
Phil 8656.9.2 — Bruce, A.B. The moral order of the World. N.Y., 1899.
Phil 4065.105.15 — Brunnhofer, H. Giordano Bruno's Lehre vom Kleinsten als die Quelle der prastabilirten Harmonie des Leibnitz. 2. Aufl. Leipzig, 1899.
Phil 8582.1.5 — Caird, J. The fundamental ideas of Christianity. Glasgow, 1899. 2v.
Phil 8692.10 — Carus, Paul. The dawn of a new era. Chicago, 1899.
Phil 3484.5 — Carus, Paul. Kant and Spencer. Chicago, 1899.
Phil 4668.40.30 — Castrén, Zacharias. Uskonnonfilosofian käsitteestä ja metoodista. Helsingissä, 1899.
Phil 8627.3 — Charles, R.H. A critical history of the doctrine of a future life in Israel. London, 1899.
Phil 6112.21 — Christison, J.S. Brain in relation to mind. Chicago, 1899.
Phil 1850.81.6 — Church, R.W. Bacon. N.Y., 1899.
Phil 8657.14.15 — Cieszkowski, August D. Ojcze-nasz. Poznań, 1899-1906. 4v.
Phil 6112.17 — Clark, Susie C. A look upward. Boston, 1899.
Phil 8657.7 — Clarke, W.N. Can I believe in God the Father. N.Y., 1899.
Phil 177.44.5 — Cohn, Jonas. Gefühlston und Sättigung der Farben. n.p., 1899-1915. 16 pam.
Phil 8735.4 — Cossmann, P.N. Elemente der empirischen Teleologie. Stuttgart, 1899.
Phil 6060.1.10* — Crepieux-Jamin, J. La graphologie en exemples. Paris, 1899.
Phil 8877.24.5 — Curtis, G.W. Aves recte vivendi. N.Y., 1899.
Phil 8658.6 — D'Arcy, C.F. Idealism and theology. London, 1899.
Phil 5400.19.4 — Darwin, Charles. The expression of the emotions in man and animals. N.Y., 1899.
Phil 8953.2 — Davidson, William L. Christian ethics. London, 1899.
Phil 5403.1.3 — Dearborn, Gran N. The emotion of joy. N.Y., 1899.
Phil 2520.37 — Descartes, René. Discourse on method. Chicago, 1899.
Phil 3003.2 — Deutschthümler, W. Ueber Schopenhauer zu Kant; ein Kleines Geschichtsbild. Wien, 1899.
Phil 7068.99.4 — Dheur, P. Les hallucinations volontaires. Paris, 1899.
Phil 8878.18.7 — Dix, A. Der Egoismus. Leipzig, 1899.
Phil 8583.9 — Dole, Charles F. Theology of civilization. N.Y., 1899.
Phil 178.12.19 — Dresser, H.W. Methods and problems of spiritual healing. N.Y., 1899.
Phil 178.12.14 — Dresser, H.W. Voices of freedom. N.Y., 1899.
Phil 2230.95 — Dresser, J.A. The true history of mental science. Boston, 1899.
Phil 2270.92 — Dubois, J. Spencer et le principe de la morale. Paris, 1899.
Phil 2885.82 — Dutoit, G. Die Theorie des Milieu. Bern, 1899.
Phil 89.1 — Eisler, R. Wörterbuch der Philosophie Begriffe und aus Drücke. Berlin, 1899.
Phil 8879.17 — Eleutheropoulos, A. Die Sittlichkeit und der philosophische Sittlichkeitswahn. Berlin, 1899.
Phil 6990.3.35 — Estrade, J.B. Les apparitions de Lourdes. Tours, 1899.
Phil 3428.91 — Felsh. Erläuterungen zu Herbarts Ethik. Langensalza, 1899.
Phil 480.6 — Fernandez de Santanna, M. O materialismo em face da sciencia. Lisboa, 1899. 2v.
Phil 180.29 — Ferrari, Giuseppe M. Scritti varj. v.1-3. Roma, 1899-1927. 3v.

1899 - cont.

Phil 3825.3 — Ferriere, E. La doctrine de Spinoza. Paris, 1899.
Phil 9520.3 — Fierens-Gevaert, H. La tristesse contemporaine. Paris, 1899.
Phil 3805.87 — Fischer, M. Schleiermachers. Berlin, 1899.
Phil 8585.17 — Fiske, J. Through nature to God. Boston, 1899.
Phil 8585.26 — Flügel, O. Zur philosophie der Christentums. Langensalza, 1899.
Phil 9150.19 — Folkmar, D. L'anthropologie philosophique. Thèse. Paris, 1899.
Phil 6115.21.4 — Forel, A. Gehirn und Seele. 5. und 6. Aufl. Bonn, 1899.
Phil 6675.6 — Forel, A. Hypnotism and cerebral activity. Worcester, 1899.
Phil 2115.90.7 — Fowler, T. Locke. N.Y., 1899.
Phil 8955.1 — Fox, J.J. Religion and morality. N.Y., 1899.
Phil 5643.25.2 — Franz, Shepherd I. After images. N.Y., 1899.
Phil 8660.5 — Fraser, A.C. Philosophy of theism. 2. ed. Edinburgh, 1899.
Phil 1870.84.2.3 — Fraser, Alexander Campbell. Berkeley. Philadelphia, 1899.
Phil 3825.2 — Fullerton, G.S. On Spinozistic immortality. Philadelphia, 1899.
Phil 600.26 — Gamboa, Ignacio. El positivismo filosófico. Mérida, 1899.
Phil 5374.148.2 — Geley, Gustave. L'être subconscient. Paris, 1899.
Phil 5246.15 — Gerard-Varet, G. L'ignorance et l'irréflexion. Paris, 1899.
Phil 8520.19 — Geyser, Joseph. Das philosophische Gottesproblem in seinen wichtigsten Auffassungen. Bonn, 1899.
Phil 7068.99.33 — Gibier, P. Psychism; analysis of things existing. 3. ed. N.Y., 1899.
Phil 4756.5.30 — Giliarov-Platonov, N.P. Sbornik sochinenii. v.1-2. Moskva, 1899-1900.
Phil 8881.27 — Gleed, J.W. Real life. n.p., 1899.
Phil 5046.7 — Gneisse, K. Deduction und Induction. Strassburg, 1899.
Phil 8956.9 — Göransson, N.J. Utkast till en undersökning af religionen. Sköfde, 1899.
Phil 7060.43.5 — Goodrich-Freer, A. The alleged haunting of B-- house. London, 1899.
Phil 3100.80 — Granzow, O. Friedrich Edward Benekes Leben. Bern, 1899.
Phil 1535.18 — Gredt, Joseph. Elementa philosophiae Aristotelico-Thomisticae. Romae, 1899.
Phil 2020.30.4 — Green, T.H. Prolegomena to ethics. 4th ed. Oxford, 1899.
Phil 7054.182 — Grimard, Edouard. Une échappée sur l'infini. Paris, 1899.
Phil 3640.212 — Grimm, Eduard. Das Problem Friedrich Nietzsches. Berlin, 1899.
Phil 5816.3.5 — Groos, K. Die Spiele der Menschen. Jena, 1899.
Phil 5246.24 — Guérin, Jules. Les différentes manifestations. Paris, 1899.
Phil 510.1.2.5 — Haeckel, Ernst. Die Welträthsel. Stuttgart, 1899.
Phil 3552.101 — Hahn, R. Die Entwickelung der leibnizischen Metaphysik. Halle, 1899.
Phil 7068.99.40 — Hall, T.B. The purity and destiny of modern spiritualism. Boston, 1899.
Phil 6677.17 — Harraden, L.A. Complete illustrated course of twenty lessons in magnetic healing. n.p., 1899.
Phil 6117.9 — Héger, P. La mission de la physiologie expérimentale. Bruxelles, 1899.
Phil 5330.6 — Heinrich, W. Die moderne psysiologische Psychologie...Aufmerksamkeit. Zürich, 1899.
Phil 5247.62 — Heinrich, W. Zur Prinzipienfrage der Psychologie. Zürich, 1899.
Phil 3640.211 — Henne am Rhyn, O. Anti-Zarathustra. Altenburg, 1899.
Phil 6117.23 — Hering, Ewald. Zur Theorie der Nerventhätigkeit. Leipzig, 1899.
Phil 182.28.2 — Hibben, J.G. The problems of philosophy. N.Y., 1899.
Phil 8882.26.5 — Hillis, N.D. Right living as a fine art. N.Y., 1899.
Phil 4580.15 — Høffding, Harald. Mindre arbejder. Räkke 1-2. København, 1899-1905.
Phil 5047.23.5 — Høffding, Harald. Det psykologiske grundlag for logiske domme. København, 1899.
Phil 3552.282 — Hohenemser, E. Die Lehre von den kleinen Vorstellungen bei Leibniz. Heidelberg, 1899.
Phil 9347.2.3 — Hubbard, E. A message to Garcia. East Aurora, 1899.
Phil 8662.14 — Hudson, T.J. Divine pedigree of man. Chicago, 1899.
Phil 8587.27.3 — Huntington, William R. Four key-words of religion. 2. ed. N.Y., 1899.
NEDL Phil 8697.1 — Hutton, R.H. Aspects of religious and scientific thought. London, 1899.
Phil 400.30.5 — Hyde, W. De W. Practical idealism. N.Y., 1899.
Phil 6678.1 — Imbert-Gourbeyre, A. L'hypnotisme et la stigmatisation. Paris, 1899.
Phil 8663.3.2 — Ingersoll, Robert G. Ingersollia. Chicago, 1899.
Phil 3246.88 — Ivanoff, C. Darstellung der Ethik Johann Gottlieb Fichtes. Leipzig, 1899.
Phil 184.3.3.7 — James, W. The will to believe and other essays in popular philosophy. N.Y., 1899.
Phil 184.3.3 — James, W. The will to believe and other essays in popular philosophy. N.Y., 1899.
Phil 184.3.7.25 — James, W. Der Wille zum Glauben. Stuttgart, 1899.
Phil 5249.2.2 — James, William. Principles of psychology. v.2. N.Y., 1899.
Phil 184.12 — Jerusalem, W. Einleitung in die Philosophie. Wien, 1899.
Phil 3270.3.90 — Johann, F. Systematische und kritische Darstellung der Psychologie Jakob Frohschammers. Würzburg, 1899.
Phil 8884.4.2 — Jordan, W.G. Kingship of self-control individual problems. N.Y., 1899.
Phil 3480.40.13 — Kant, Immanuel. Anthropologie in pragmatischer Hinsicht. Leipzig, 1899.
Phil 3480.30.15 — Kant, Immanuel. Kritik der reinen Vernunft. Halle, 1899?
Phil 2050.112 — Keller, Anton. Das Causalitätsproblem bei Malebranche und Hume. Rastatt, 1899.
Phil 5250.12.3 — Kroman, Kristian. Korfattet taenke-og sjaelelaere. 3. udg. København, 1899.
Phil 3010.14 — Kronenberg, Moritz. Moderne Philosophen; Porträts und Charakteristiken. München, 1899.
Phil 1115.1 — Kühnemann, E. Grundlehren der Philosophie. Berlin, 1899.
Phil 4065.99.2 — Kuhlenbeck, L. Bruno. 2e Aufl. Leipzig, 1899.
Phil 186.79.5 — Lacuria, P.F.G. Les harmonies de l'être exprimées par les nombres. v.1-2. Paris, 1899.
Phil 186.16.5 — Ladd, G.T. Theory of reality. N.Y., 1899.
Phil 5051.7A — Lafleur, P.T. Illustrations of logic. Boston, 1899.
Phil 8591.16 — La Grasserie, R. de. De la psychologie des religions. Paris, 1899.
Phil 1850.117 — Lalande, A. Quid de mathematica senserit Baconus. Thesis. Lutetiae, 1899.
Phil 365.31.5 — Lalande, André. La dissolution opposée à l'évolution dans les sciences physiques et morales. Paris, 1899.

1899 - cont.

Phil 3960.12   Land, Jan P.N. De wijsbegeerte in de Nederlanden. 's Gravenhage, 1899.

Phil 5403.5   Lange, C.G. Bidrag til nydelsernes fysiologi som grundlag for en rationel aestetik. Kjobenhavn, 1899.

Phil 4600.2.34   Larsson, Hans. Viljans frihet. Lund, 1899.

Phil 978.8.30   Leadbeater, C.W. Invisible helpers. London, 1899.

Phil 8886.14   Lecky, W.E.H. The map of life. N.Y., 1899.

Phil 8886.60   Lee, James W. The making of a man. St. Louis, 1899.

Phil 3493.3   Lefkovits, M. Die Staatslehre auf Kantischer Grundlage. Bern, 1899.

Phil 5251.20.9   Lehmann, Alfred. Die körperlichen Äusserungen psychischer Zustände. Leipzig, 1899-1905. 4v.

Phil 3552.41   Leibniz, Gottfried Wilhelm. Nouveaux essais sur l'entendement humain. Paris, 1899.

Phil 525.49   Lejeune, Paul. Introduction à la vie mystique. Paris, 1899.

Phil 5761.3   Leland, C.G. Have you a strong will? London, 1899.

Phil 9035.18   Lemmon, G.J. Eternal building, or The making of manhood. N.Y., 1899.

Phil 5251.22   Leuchtenberger, G. Houptbegriffe der Psychologie. Berlin, 1899.

Phil 2411.2   Levy-Bruhl, L. History of modern philosophy in France. London, 1899.

Phil 3640.105.5   Lichtenberger, H. Die Philosophie Friedrich Nietzsches. Dresden, 1899.

Phil 5051.14   Lightfoot, John. Logic and education. London, 1899.

Phil 3246.99.10   Lindau, Hans. Johann Gottlieb Fichtes Lehren von Staat und Gesellschaft in ihrem Verhältnis zum neueren Sozialismus. n.p., 1899.

Phil 9150.22   Lingle, T.W. Die Bedeutung der Entwickelungsgeschichte. Leipzig, 1899.

Phil 8886.15   Lipps, T. Die ethischen Grundfragen. Hamburg, 1899.

Phil 5821.4   Loeb, J. Einleitung...Gehirnphysiologie...Psychologie. Leipzig, 1899.

Phil 186.22   Lorensen, C. Essay on positive theology or a new system of philosophy. Waterbury, 1899.

Phil 3635.90   Lorenz, Heinrich. Dr P.J. Möbius als Philosoph. Inaug. Diss. Wiesbaden, 1899.

Phil 3565.35   Lotze, Hermann. Grundzüge der praktischen Philosophie. 3. Aufl. Leipzig, 1899.

Phil 7060.79   Ludwig, W. Spaziergänge eines Wahrheitssuchers. Leipzig, 1899.

Phil 665.7   Lutosławski, W. Seelenmacht; Abriss einer zeitgemässen Weltanschauung. Leipzig, 1899.

Phil 8610.899.25   Mackenzie, G.L. Brimstone ballads and other verse. London, 1899.

Phil 3494.19.25   Marcus, Ernst. Die exakte Aufdeckung des Fundaments der Sittlichkeit und Religion...Kant. Leipzig, 1899.

Phil 5252.62   Martin, L.J. Zur Analyse der Unterschiedsempfindlichkeit. Leipzig, 1899.

Phil 187.72   Masci, Filippo. Elementi di filosofia per le scuole secondarie. Napoli, 1899-1904. 2v.

Phil 7068.97.34   Mason, R.O. Telepathy and the subliminal self. N.Y., 1899.

Phil 8837.7   Mayer, Gottlob. Die Lehre vom Erlaubten in der Geschichte der Ethic seit Schleier Macher. Leipzig, 1899.

Phil 8887.35   Mercer, A.G. Notes of an outlook on life. London, 1899.

Phil 8592.18   Merriman, H.B. Religio pictoris. Boston, 1899.

Phil 3235.80   Meyer, M. Ludwig Feuerbach's Moralphilosophie. Berlin, 1899.

Phil 6060.7.7   Michon, J.H. Méthode pratique de graphologie. Paris, 1899.

Phil 2138.75   Mill, John S. Lettres inédites. Paris, 1899.

Phil 3808.102   Möbius, P.J. Über Schopenhauer. Leipzig, 1899.

X Cg   Phil 7075.8.3   Moll, Albert. Die conträre Sexualempfindung. Berlin, 1899.

Phil 6122.7.5   Mosso, A. Psychic processes and muscular exercise. n.p., 1899. 2 pam.

Phil 960.7   Muller, F.M. The six systems of Indian philosophy. N.Y., 1899.

Phil 3640.302   Naumann, Gustav. Zarathustra-Commentar. Leipzig, 1899-1901. 4v.

Phil 4225.5   Nel primo centenario della morte di Nicola Spedalieri. Roma, 1899.

Phil 3640.35.5   Nietzsche, Friedrich. Humain, trop humain. Paris, 1899.

Phil 3640.26   Nietzsche, Friedrich. Pages choisies. 5e éd. Paris, 1899.

Phil 6123.6   Nisbet, J.F. The human machine. London, 1899.

Phil 5520.32.5   Noiré, Ludwig. Origin of language and logos theory. 2. ed. Chicago, 1899.

Phil 4610.7.18   Norström, V. Hvad är sanning. Göteborg, 1899.

Phil 2672.80   Ollé-Laprune, L. Théodore Jouffroy. Paris, 1899.

Phil 5635.27   Oppenheimer, Z. Physiologie des Gefühls. Heidelberg, 1899.

Phil 6053.4   Oxenford, Ina. Life studies in palmistry. London, 1899.

Phil 5255.13   Panizza, Mario. Nuova teorica fisiologica della conoscenza. Roma, 1899.

Phil 2605.1.81   Pasmanik, D. Alfred Fouillées psychischen Monismus. Bern, 1899.

Phil 8890.6.9   Paulsen, F. System of ethics. N.Y., 1899.

Phil 8890.6.11   Paulsen, F. System of ethics. N.Y., 1899.

Phil 3497.3.9   Paulsen, Friedrich. Kant der Philosophie des Protestantismus. Berlin, 1899.

Phil 5545.21.5   Pick, E. Lectures on memory culture. N.Y., 1899.

Phil 8685.13   Pike, G.R. The divine drama; the manifestation of God. N.Y., 1899.

Phil 8890.25   Pitcairn, E.H. Unwritten laws of active careers. London, 1899.

Phil 3835.1.2   Pollock, F. Spinoza. 2nd ed. London, 1899.

Phil 5170.1   Poretsky, P. Sept lois fondamentales de la théorie des égalités logiques. Kazan, 1899.

Phil 2725.4.87   Raillard, Célestin. Pierre Leroux et ses oeuvres. Chateauroux, 1899.

Phil 3552.105   Rall, H.F. Der leibnizsche Substanzbegriff. Halle, 1899.

Phil 6127.7   Ramón y Cajal, S. Comparative study of the sensory areas. Human cortex. n.p., 1899?

Phil 6127.7.5   Ramón y Cajal, S. Textura del sistema nervioso del hombre y de los Vertebrados. V.1-2. Madrid, 1899. 3v.

Phil 3808.162   Rappaport, S. Spinoza und Schopenhauer. Berlin, 1899.

Phil 8967.4   Rau, Albrecht. Die Ethik jesu. Giessen, 1899.

Phil 5400.20   Rauh, F. De la méthode dans la psychologie des sentiments. Paris, 1899.

Phil 525.5.5   Récéjac, Edonard. Essays on the bases of mystic knowledge. London, 1899.

Phil 192.33   Reinke, J. Die Welt als That. Berlin, 1899.

Phil 3552.100   Renouvier, Charles. La nouvelle monadologie. Paris, 1899.

Phil 348.3.5   Ribot, T. Evolution of general ideas. Chicago, 1899.

Phil 5227.2.6   Ribot, T. German psychology of to-day. N.Y., 1899.

Phil 3640.178   Ritschl, Otto. Nietzsches Welt und Lebensanschauung. 2. Aufl. Leipzig, 1899.

Phil 8610.899   Robertson, J.M. A short history of freethought, ancient and modern. London, 1899.

Phil 8892.4.5   Roberty, E. de. L'éthique. Les fondements de l'éthique. 2. ed. Paris, 1899.

Phil 1717.4   Rogers, A.K. A brief introduction to modern philosophy. N.Y., 1899.

Phil 6127.8   Rogers, A.K. Parallelism of mind and body. Chicago, 1899.

Phil 6127.8.5   Rogers, A.K. Parallelism of mind and body. Chicago, 1899.

Phil 8967.1.85   Roltzmann, H.J. R. Rothe's speculatives System. Freiburg, 1899.

Phil 510.3   Sack, J. Monistische Gottes und Weltanschuung. Leipzig, 1899.

Phil 6688.6.2   Sage, X.L. Hypnotism as it is. Rochester, 1899.

Phil 7082.86   Sanctis, Sante de. I sogni. Torino, 1899.

Phil 8643.11   Savage, M.J. Life beyond death. N.Y., 1899.

Phil 4635.4.31   Schéele, Frans von. Filosofiens uppgift. Upsala, 1899.

Phil 4635.4.33   Schéele, Frans von. Filosofiska studier. Första samlingen. Stockholm, 1899.

Phil 5258.72.5   Scheele, Frans von. Lärobok i psykologi. Stockholm, 1899.

Phil 5768.20.15   Schellwien, R. Wille und Erkenntnis. Hamburg, 1899.

Phil 3790.1.90   Scherer, C.C. Der biologisch-psychologische Gottesbeweis bei Herman S. Reimarus. Würzburg, 1899.

Phil 5722.16.2   Schofield, A.T. The unconscious mind. 2. ed. London, 1899.

Phil 5190.3   Schultz, Julias. Psychologie der Axiome. Göttingen, 1899.

Phil 3500.34   Schweitzer, Albert. Die Religionsphilosophie Kants. Freiburg, 1899.

Phil 1818.1.5   Seth, A. Scottish philosophy. 3e ed. Edinburgh, 1899.

Phil 8893.8.2   Seth, J. A study of ethical principles. 5th ed. N.Y., 1899.

Phil 1050.4.9   Seyerlen, R. Die gegenseitigen Bezeihungen. Jena, 1899.

Phil 5585.20   Siegel, Carl. Entwickelung der Raumvorstellung. Leipzig, 1899.

Phil 5258.210   Sighele, Scipio. Mentre il secolo muore. Milano, 1899.

Phil 8610.899.30   Sirai and Olympus. N.Y., 1899.

Phil 5627.91   Slocum, Phebe B. Akin. Witnessing. Brattleboro, 1899.

Phil 5545.30   Smith, D.T. The philosophy of memory. Louisville, Ky., 1899.

Phil 665.46   Smith, O.J. A short view of great questions. N.Y., 1899.

Phil 349.11   Smith, Walter. Methods of knowledge. N.Y., 1899.

Phil 5768.16   Snider, Denton J. The will and its world. St. Louis, 1899.

Phil 6968.22   Sommer, Robert. Lehrbuch der psychopathologischen untersuchungs Methoden. Berlin, 1899.

Phil 6128.21.5   Soury, Jules. Le système nerveux centrale. Paris, 1899. 2v.

Phil 2270.73.5   Spencer, Herbert. Principles of ethics. N.Y., 1899.

Htn   Phil 7068.99*   Spoer, Adela Goodrich-Freer. Essays in psychical research. London, 1899.

Phil 7068.99.20   Spoer, Adela Goodrich-Freer. Essays in psychical research. 2. ed. London, 1899.

Phil 5258.99   Stanley, H.M. An outline sketch. Chicago, 1899.

NEDL   Phil 5627.1   Starbuck, E.D. The psychology of religion. London, 1899.

Phil 5627.1   Starbuck, E.D. The psychology of religion. London, 1899.

Phil 5258.27.2   Stout, G.F. A manual of psychology. N.Y., 1899.

Phil 9220.5.6   Streamer, Volney. In friendship's name. 10th ed. N.Y., 1899.

Phil 7082.92   Stumpf, E.J.G. Der Traum und seine Dentung. Leipzig, 1899.

Phil 5642.7   Suarez de Mendoza, Ferdinand. L'audition colorée. 2. éd. Paris, 1899.

Phil 5520.9   Sutro, Emil. Duality of voice. N.Y., 1899.

Phil 978.31   Theosophy Publishing Company. The pitt and marrow of some sacred writings. N.Y., 1899.

Phil 5400.56   Thomas, Félix. L'éducation des sentiments. Paris, 1899.

Phil 8709.3   Topinard, P. Science and faith. Chicago, 1899.

Phil 1870.87   Tower, C.V. The relation of Berkeley's later to his early ideal. Ann Arbor, 1899.

Phil 5255.15   Troilo, E. Il misticismo moderno. Torino, 1899.

Phil 5425.15   Türck, H. Der geniale Mensch. Berlin, 1899.

Phil 8610.899.55   Turner, M.M. (Mrs.). The Bible God, Bible teachings. N.Y., 1899.

Phil 5520.42   Vailati, G. Alcune osservasioni sulle questioni di parole. Torino, 1899.

Phil 960.8   Valentin, O. Shaddarcaneshu en religionsstudie. Stockholm, 1899.

Phil 8971.1   Van Dyke, Henry. The gospel for a world of sin. N.Y., 1899.

Phil 5261.10.2   Verluys, J. Beginselen der Zielkunde. 2e. Druk. Amsterdam, 1899.

Phil 4210.85   Vidari, G. Rosmini e Spencer. Milano, 1899.

Phil 5261.3   Villa, G. La psicologia contemporanea. Torino, 1899

Phil 3842.3   Wahle, R. Kurze Erklarung Ethic von Spinoza. Wien, 1899.

Phil 8972.3   Walker, James. Government of the thoughts. Boston, 1899.

Phil 8610.899.15   Ward, James. Naturalism and agnosticism. London, 1899. 2v.

Phil 8610.899.17   Ward, James. Naturalism and agnosticism. v.1. v.2 lost. N.Y., 1899.

Phil 5832.3.4   Wasmann, E. Instinct und Intelligenz im Thierreich. Freiburg, 1899.

Phil 1900.85   Weeda, W.H. Joseph Butler als zedekundige. Utrecht, 1899.

Phil 8677.6   Weener, J. Scheping en voorzienigheid. Utrecht, 1899.

Phil 5832.6   Weir, J. The dawn of reason. N.Y., 1899.

Phil 3552.102   Werckmeister, Walther. Der leibnizsche Substanzbegriff. Halle, 1899.

Phil 6692.3   Wetterstrand, O.G. Hypnotism and its application to practical medecine. N.Y., 1899.

Phil 8712.3.15   White, Andrew Dickson. Histoire de la lutte entre la science et la théologie. Paris, 1899.

Phil 8602.31   Wienel, H. Die Wirkungen Des Geistes und der Glister. Freiburg, 1899.

Phil 8897.55   Wiggin, F.A. Cubes and spheres in human life. Boston, 1899.

Phil 1127.2   Windelband, W. History of ancient philosophy. N.Y., 1899.

Phil 8602.34   Wobbermin, G. Zwei akademische Vorlesungen über Grundprobleme der systematischen Theologie. Berlin, 1899.

Phil 6132.17.9   Wood, Henry. Ideal suggestion through mental photography. 9. ed. Boston, 1899.

Phil 8602.13   Woods, J.H. The value religious facts. N.Y., 1899.

Phil 5834.1.20   Yerkes, R.M. Reaction of entomostraca to...light. n.p., 1899-1916. 44 pam.

Phil 2138.89F   Zuccante, G. La morale utilitaria dello Stuart Mill. Milano, 1899.

1899 - cont.

Phil 5835.2 — Zürn, Friedrich A. Die intellectuellen Eigenschaften der Pferde. Stuttgart, 1899.
Phil 3845.1 — Zulawski, J. Problem der Kausalität bei Spinoza. Bern, 1899.

19-

Phil 175.41 — Alessio, Roberto de. Ensayos de filosofía prática. Montevideo, 19- .
Phil 6110.9 — Allen, James. As a man thinketh. N.Y., 19- .
Phil 6110.9.5 — Allen, James. As a man thinketh. N.Y., 19- .
Phil 6110.9.3 — Allen, James. As a man thinketh. N.Y., 19- .
Phil 5811.12.10 — Bauke, Leopold. Tierfabeln und andere Irrtümer in der Tierkunde. 19. Aufl. Stuttgart, 19- ?
Phil 2477.9.84 — Bernard, Claude. Philosophie, manuscrit inédit. Paris, 19- . ⁔
Phil 5545.2.6 — Biervliet, J.J. van. Esquisse d'une éducation de la mémoire. 2. éd. Gand, 19- .
Phil 8877.62.12 — Carneri, B. Grundlegung der Ethik. Stuttgart, 19- .
Phil 3822.6.5 — Chartier, Emile A. Spinoza. 5. éd. Paris, 19- .
Phil 7069.00.10 — Cooper, William Earnshaw. Spiritual manifestations. Exeter, 19- .
Phil 2115.148 — Curti, M. The great Mr. Locke, America's philosopher, 1783-1861. n.p., 19- .
Phil 2520.45.5 — Descartes, René. Il discorso del metodo. Milano, 19- .
Phil 2805.217 — Desgrippes, George. Études sur Pascal de l'automatisme a la foi. Paris, 19- .
Phil 9575.10 — Du Lassage, Henri. A moral e o capitalismo. Pôrto, 19- .
Phil 5241.184.80 — Dummer, Ethel Sturges. Mary Everest Boole; a pioneer student of the unconscious. n.p., 19- ?
Phil 9035.14.5 — Foster, John. Decision of character. N.Y., 19- .
Phil 1706.1.6 — Gaultier, Jules de. De Kant à Nietzsche. 6e éd. Paris, 19- .
Phil 600.45 — Halleux, Jean. Les principes du positivisme contemporain. Paris, 19- ?
Phil 5047.15 — Hourticq, R. Leçons de logique et de morale. Paris, 19- ?
Phil 6990.17 — Huelster, A. Miracles in the light, science and history. Chicago, 19- .
Phil 2050.87.5.7A — Huxley, Thomas H. Hume. N.Y., 19- ?
Phil 990.1.3 — Iqbal, S.M. The development of metaphysics in Persia. Lahore, 19- .
Phil 185.30 — Kann, A. Ein philosophischer Gedankengang. Wien, 19- .
Phil 150.5 — Lalande, André. Sur la critique et la fixation du langage philosophique. Paris, 19- . 2 pam.
Phil 6121.25 — Leavitt, C.F. Leavitt-science. Chicago, 19- .
Phil 8701.4.13 — Lodge, Oliver Joseph. Faith and knowledge, April, 1902. London, 19- .
Phil 4803.537.40 — Lutosławski, Wincenty. Eine Bekehrung. Kempten, 19- .
Phil 1850.113.3 — Macaulay, Thomas Babington. Essay on Bacon. Oxford, 19- .
Phil 8615.14.15 — Martin, Alfred W. What human life is for. n.p., 19- .
Phil 2150.17.94A — Mayo, Elton. Excerpts from civilization - the perilous adventure. Cambridge, Mass. 19- .
Phil 2138.40.7 — Mill, John S. On liberty. London, 19- .
Phil 2138.40.8 — Mill, John S. On liberty. London, 19- .
Phil 5374.22 — Montague, W.P. Consciousness a form of energy. N.Y., 19- ? 2 pam.
Phil 8610.877.15 — Monteil, Edgar. The freethinker's catechism. N.Y., 19- ?
Phil 8610.877.17 — Monteil, Edgar. The freethinker's catechism. N.Y., 19- ?
Phil 4872.193.30 — Mukerjea, Jyoti S. Humanism. Nagpur, 19- .
Phil 3640.41* — Nietzsche, Friedrich. Also sprach Zarathustra. Leipzig, 19- .
Phil 3640.42 — Nietzsche, Friedrich. Así hablaba Zarathustra. Valencia, 19- .
Phil 7069.00.37 — Omni Victis (pseud.). Super-physical projection. n.p., 19- ?
Phil 8595.15.4.3 — Paine, Thomas. Theological works. Chicago, 19- ?
Phil 2805.32.7 — Pascal, Blaise. The provincial letters. 1st Canadian ed. Toronto, 19- .
Phil 8890.6.15 — Paulsen, F. Zur Ethik und Politik. Berlin, 19- . 2v.
Phil 8890.6.17 — Paulsen, F. Zur Ethik und Politik. Berlin, 19- ? 2v.
Phil 7069.00.80 — Personal magnetism...by a diplomat. n.p., 19- ?
Phil 9530.44 — Platt, C. The essence of success. London, 19- ?
Phil 4065.113 — Reiner, Julius. Giordano Bruno und seine Weltanschauung. Berlin, 19- ?
Phil 6420.8 — Rosenberg, William L. Stuttering, its cause and remedy. Cleveland, 19- ?
Phil 298.2 — Rosley, Carl. Das Körpergesetz. San Francisco, 19- .
Phil 9177.4 — Rowntree, Constance M. The right relationship between parents and children. Bannisdale, 19- ?
Phil 6048.99.5 — St. Hill, K. The grammar of palmistry. Philadelphia, 19-
Phil 3808.60.10 — Schopenhauer, Arthur. Philosophie et philosophes. 2. éd. Paris, 19- .
Phil 3808.35.6 — Schopenhauer, Arthur. Die Welt als Wille und Vorstellung. Stuttgart, 19- ? 2v.
Phil 3808.36.10 — Schopenhauer, Arthur. The world as will and idea. London, 19- . 3v.
Phil 3808.36.10.5 — Schopenhauer, Arthur. The world as will and idea. 7th ed. London, 19- . 3v.
Phil 5828.12 — Sorel, C.L.F. De l'intelligence chez l'animal. Paris, 19-
Phil 1850.17 — Spedding, James. The collection of books used by James Spedding as his working library in preparing his...works of Sir F. Bacon. London, 19- ?
Phil 3819.33.10 — Spinoza, Benedictus de. Ethica. Amsterdam, 19- .
Phil 7061.15 — Spiritual and Ethical Society, N.Y. Publications. N.Y., 19- .
Phil 5627.72 — Stead, W.T. The revival in the West. 4. ed. London, 19- .
Phil 510.1.35 — Steiner, R. Two essays on Haeckel. London, 19- .
Phil 8599.28 — Tampoe, A.McG. Coomarasamy. Life negation; an Indian study of Christ. London, 19- .
Phil 5259.18 — Tapy, George H. Outline of psychology. Crawfordsville, 19- .
Phil 6692.5 — Wolff, C. Hipnotisms teatral. Barcelona, 19- .
Phil 200.5.5 — Zucca, Antioco. Le veritable role de l'homme dans l'universe. Paris, 19- ?
Phil 3507.9 — Zwingmann, H. Kants Staatstheorie. München, 19- ?

190-

Phil 7012.2.5 — Bathurst, James. Atomic consciousness reviewed. Bristol, 190-?
Phil 187.56.9 — McTaggart, J.M.E. Introduction to the study of philosophy. Cambridge, Eng., 190-.

190- - cont.

Phil 2138.40.47 — Mill, John S. On liberty. London, 190-?
Phil 3640.412 — Zur Erinnerung an Friedrich Nietzsche. Leipzig, 190-?

1900

Phil 175.22 — Aars, K.B.R. Zur psychologischen Analyse der Welt. Leipzig, 1900.
Phil 8875.21.5 — Achelis, J. Ethik. 2nd ed. Leipzig, 1900.
Phil 8886.12.5 — Avebury, John Lubbock. The use of life. N.Y., 1900.
Phil 1850.36 — Bacon, Francis. The advancement of learning. London, 1900.
Phil 1850.35.5 — Bacon, Francis. The advancement of learning. 5th ed. Oxford, 1900.
Phil 9220.7 — Bacon, Francis. For friendship's sake. N.Y., 1900.
Phil 5241.45 — Baratono, Adelchi. I fatti psichici elementari. Torino, 1900.
Phil 6671.13 — Barnes, W.A. Personal magnetism and clairvoyance. 4th ed. Boston, 1900.
Phil 7140.10 — Barrows, C.M. Suggestion instead of medicine. Boston, 1900.
Phil 2885.80.5 — Barzellotti, G. La philosophie de H. Taine. Paris, 1900.
Phil 5590.24 — Baumann, Emilio. Psico-cinesia, ouvero L'arte di formare il carattere. Pte. 1. Roma, 1900.
Phil 510.1.14 — Baumann, J. Häckels Welträthsel nach ihren starken und ihren schwachen Seiten. Leipzig, 1900.
Phil 5241.43 — Benigni, Edvige. Elementi di psicologia sperimentale positiva. Torino, 1900.
X Cg Phil 6111.12 — Bergson, Henri. Matière et mémoire. Paris, 1900.
Phil 7069.00.65 — Berndt, G.H. Das Buch der Wunder und der Geheimwissenschaften. 2. Aufl. v.1-2. Leipzig, 1900.
Phil 978.6.20 — Besant, Annie. Evolution of life and form. 2nd ed. London, 1900.
Phil 5400.39 — Bhagavan, Das. The science of the emotions. London, 1900.
Phil 3821.8 — Bierens de Haan, J.D. Levensleer naar de beginselen van Spinoza. 's Gravenhage, 1900.
Phil 7140.4 — Binet, A. La suggestibilité. Paris, 1900.
Phil 9150.9.3 — Bixby, James T. The ethics of revolution. Boston, 1900.
Phil 3483.26 — Boldt, Georg. Protestantismens idé och Immanuel Kant. Helsingfors, 1900.
Phil 600.29 — Bombard, Emile. La marche de l'humanité et les grands hommes d'après la doctrine positive. Paris, 1900.
Phil 5651.4 — Bomier, Pierre. L'orientation. Paris, 1900.
Phil 2805.92 — Boutroux, E. Pascal. Paris, 1900.
Phil 2520.101 — Boutroux, P. L'imagination et les Math Selon Descartes. Paris, 1900.
Phil 5425.16 — Bovio, G. Il genio. Milano, 1900.
Phil 8876.67 — Bowker, R.R. The arts of life. Boston, 1900.
Phil 3821.17 — Brockdorff, C. Beiträge über die Verhältnis Schopenhauers zu Spinoza. Hildesheim, 1900.
Phil 6311.29 — Buckley, James M. Faith-healing. N.Y., 1900.
Phil 176.33.15 — Büchner, L. Im Dienste der Wahrheit. Giessen, 1900.
Phil 1900.19 — Butler, Joseph. Whole works. London, 1900. 2v.
Phil 600.24 — Calderoni, Giuseppe. Il positivismo. Roma, 1900.
Phil 1020.8 — Carra de Vaux. Avicenne. Paris, 1900.
Phil 8620.13A — Carus, D.P. History of the devil and idea of evil. Chicago, 1900.
Phil 8627.9 — Chambers, A. Man and the spiritual world. Philadelphia, 1900.
Phil 8657.8 — Clarke, J.C.C. Man and his Divine Father. Chicago, 1900.
Phil 5627.26.2 — Coe, George A. The spiritual life; studies in the science of religion. N.Y., 1900.
Phil 9450.8 — Coit, S. Ethical democracy. London, 1900.
Phil 5545.6 — Colegrove, F.W. Memory. N.Y., 1900.
Phil 8610.900 — Cooley, P.J. Evolution; an exposition of Christian dogmas and pagan myths. N.Y., 1900.
Phil 5042.7.2 — Creighton, J.E. An introductory logic. N.Y., 1900.
Phil 4080.3.35 — Croce, Benedetto. La prima forma della estetica e della logica. Messina, 1900.
Phil 349.22 — Czernovitz. Gymnasium. Xenia Czernowiciensia. Czernowitz, 1900.
Phil 5753.10 — Dandolo, G. Le integrazioni psichiche e la volontà. Padova, 1900.
Phil 7069.00.20 — Daniels, Cora L. As it is to be. Exeter, 1900.
Phil 6953.10 — Dantas, J. Pintores e poetas de Rilhafolles. Liboa, 1900.
Phil 8878.21 — Davis, Noals K. Elements of ethics. Boston, 1900.
Phil 5467.5 — Deahl, J.N. Imitation in education. N.Y., 1900.
Phil 525.45.5 — Delacroix, H. Essai sur le mysticisme spéculatif. Paris, 1900.
Phil 8404.12 — Delville, Jean. La mission de l'art. Bruxelles, 1900.
Phil 1504.3 — Domański, B. Die Psychologie des Nemesius. v.3, pt.1. Münster, 1900.
Phil 5643.45 — Dor, Louis. La fatigue oculaire et le surmenage visuel. Paris, 1900.
Phil 178.12.16 — Dresser, H.W. Education and the philosophical ideal. N.Y., 1900.
Phil 5243.22 — Dressler, Max. Vorlesungen über Psychologie. Heidelberg, 1900.
Phil 9245.26 — Dudoc, J. Die Lust als socialethisches Entwicklungsprincip. Leipzig, 1900.
Phil 2490.111 — Dumas, G. Quid Auguste Comte de suae altatis psychologis senserit. Lutetiae, 1900.
Phil 5403.6 — Dumas, G. La tristesse et la joie. Paris, 1900.
Phil 8878.33 — Dupuy, Paul. Les fondements de la morale. Paris, 1900.
Phil 8878.20 — Durand, J.P. Nouvelles recherches sur l'esthetique et la morale. Paris, 1900.
Phil 178.39 — Durand, J.P. Variétés philosophiques. 2e éd. Paris, 1900.
Phil 6673.16.5 — Durville, H. The theory and practice of human magnetism. Chicago, 1900.
Phil 1109.1 — Eleutheropulos, A. Philosophie und der Lebensauffassung der Griechtens. Berlin, 1900-01. 2v.
Phil 3480.30.6.5 — Erdmann, B. Beiträge zur Geschichte...Anhang zur. 5. Aufl. Berlin, 1900.
Phil 5520.7 — Erdmann, Karl O. Die Bedeutung des Wortes. Leipzig, 1900.
Phil 8735.16 — Etrillard, E. Etudes philosophiques sur les causes premières et les causes finales. Paris, 1900.
Phil 2020.80.2A — Fairbrother, W.H. Philosophy of Thomas Hill Green. 2nd ed. London, 1900.
Phil 5245.19.5 — Feldegg, F. Beiträge zur Philosophie des Gefühls. Leipzig, 1900.
Phil 5635.7 — Féré, C. Sensation et mouvement. Paris, 1900.
Phil 8585.18 — Ferguson, G. The religion of democracy. N.Y., 1900.
Phil 2115.122 — Ferrari, G. Il sensismo francese. Modena, 1900.
Phil 8633.1.5 — Fiske, J. Life everlasting. Boston, 1900.
Phil 7060.67.5 — Flammarion, C. L'inconnu et les problèmes psychiques. Paris, 1900.
Phil 7069.00.28 — Flammarion, C. L'inconnu, The unknown. N.Y., 1900.

1900 - cont.

Phil 6115.13.6   Fleury, D.M. de. Introduction à la médicine de l'esprit. 6. éd. Paris, 1900.

Phil 6115.13   Fleury, D.M. de. Medicine and the mind. London, 1900.

Phil 7060.80.9   Flournoy, J. Des Indes à la planète Mars. Paris, 1900.

Phil 7069.00.30   Flournoy, Théodore. From India to the planet Mars. N.Y., 1900.

Phil 8610.888.10   Foote, G.W. The Bible handbook of freethinkers and inquiring Christians. London, 1900.

Phil 8695.6   Frémont, G. Que l'orgueil de l'esprit est le grand écueil de la foi. Paris, 1900.

Phil 3805.88   Fuchs, Emil. Schleiermachers Religionsbegriff und religiöse Stellung zur Zeit der ersten Ausgabe der Reden, 1799-1806. Inaug. Diss. Giessen, 1900.

Phil 7069.00.32   Gaffield, E.C. A series of meditations on the ethical and physical relation of spirit to the human organism. Syracuse,.N.Y., 1900.

Phil 5246.28   Gale, Harlow. Psychological studies. Minneapolis, 1900.

Htn   Phil 2520.148*   Ganguli, S. Descartes. Bombay, 1900.

Phil 1706.1   Gaultier, Jules de. De Kant à Nietzsche. Paris, 1900.

Phil 2270.85.2   Gaupp, Otto. Herbert Spencer. Stuttgart, 1900.

Phil 1020.9   Gauthier, L. La philosophie Musulmane. Paris, 1900.

Phil 6116.10   Gehuchten, Arthur van. Anatomie du système nerveux de l'homme. Louvain, 1900. 2v.

Phil 5816.5.3   Gentry, Thomas G. Intelligence in plants and animals. N.Y., 1900.

Phil 8631.3   Gordon, G.A. The witness to immortality. Boston, 1900.

Phil 2406.1   Gorham, Charles. Ethics of the great French rationalists. London, 1900.

Phil 5046.19   Grassmann, R. Die Logik. Stettin, 1900.

Phil 600.25   Greef, Guillaume. Problémes de philosophie positive. Paris, 1900.

Phil 2030.1.80   Greenslet, F. Joseph Glanvill. N.Y., 1900.

Phil 960.142   Griswold, Hervey De Witt. Brahman: a study in the history of Indian philosophy. N.Y., 1900.

Phil 8407.21   Grosse, Ernst. Kunstwissenschaftliche Studien. Tübingen, 1900.

Phil 5817.6   Hachet-Souplet, P. Examen psychologique des animaux. Paris, 1900.

Phil 510.1.6A   Haeckel, Ernst. The riddle of the universe. N.Y., 1900.

Phil 3425.40.5.6   Hegel, Georg Wilhelm Friedrich. The philosophy of history. N.Y., 1900.

Phil 3428.44   Herbart, J.F. Lehrbuch zur Psychologie. Hamburg, 1900.

Phil 8408.32   Herzog, J.A. Was ist Ästhetisch? Leipzig, 1900.

Phil 8882.26   Hillis, N.D. Great books as life teachers. Edinburgh, 1900.

Phil 8882.12.3   Hilty, K. Glück. Frauenfeld, 1900.

Phil 5643.44   Hinshelwood, J. Letter, word, and mind blindness. London, 1900.

Phil 3428.162   Hintz, R. Herbarts Bedeutung für die Psychologie. Berlin, 1900.

X Cg   Phil 1707.1.5   Höffding, H. History of modern philosophy. London, 1900.

Phil 4582.2.31   Hofstedt, A. Arbetets ära kulturhistorisk undersökning. Stockholm, 1900.

Phil 182.51   Horion, Charles. Testament philosophique...essai de synthése evolutioniste. Bruxelles, 1900.

Phil 9347.2   Hubbard, E. A message to Garcia. N.Y., 1900.

Phil 2270.93   Hudson, William Henry. An introduction to the philosophy of Herbert Spencer. 2nd ed. N.Y., 1900.

Phil 6000.4   Hughes, Henry. Die Mimik des Menschen auf grundvoluntarischer Psychologie. Frankfurt, 1900.

Phil 807.8   Hunter, T. History of philosophy. N.Y., 1900.

Phil 5047.11   Husserl, Edmund. Logische Untersuchungen. Halle, 1900.

Phil 8587.25   Hyndman, F.A. The time of transition. London, 1900.

Phil 8663.3.3   Ingersoll, Robert G. The works. N.Y., 1900-02. 12v.

Phil 8633.1.50   James, William. Human immortality. Boston, 1900.

Phil 5249.2.38   James, William. On some of life's ideals. N.Y., 1900.

Phil 5249.2.6   James, William. Psychology. N.Y., 1900.

Phil 365.42   Jevons, Frank B. Evolution. London, 1900.

Phil 8884.4.17   Jordan, W.G. The majesty of calmness. N.Y., 1900.

Phil 3640.87   Kalthoff, A. Friedrich Nietzsche. Berlin, 1900.

Phil 3565.85   Kalweit, P.F.M. Die praktische Begründung des Gottesbegriffs bei Lotze. Jena, 1900.

Phil 3480.69.5   Kant, Immanuel. Cosmogony. Glasgow, 1900.

Phil 3480.32.7.5   Kant, Immanuel. Critique of pure reason. N.y., 1900.

Phil 3480.53A   Kant, Immanuel. Dreams of a spirit seer. London, 1900.

Phil 3480.14   Kant, Immanuel. Gesammelte Schriften. v.1-24,28. Berlin, 1900-36. 27v.

Phil 3480.30.6   Kant, Immanuel. Kritik der reinen Vernunft. 5. Aufl. Berlin, 1900.

Phil 3480.56A   Kant, Immanuel. Metaphysische Anfangsgründe Naturwissenschaft. Leipzig, 1900.

Phil 3890.8.101   Kayser, R. Christian Thomasius und der Pietismus. Hamburg, 1900.

Phil 8885.9   Kedney, J.S. Problems in ethics. N.Y., 1900.

Phil 9150.1.5   Kelly, E. Evolution and effort. 2. ed. N.Y., 1900.

Phil 176.41.5   Knight, William. Lord Monboddo. London, 1900.

Phil 4803.497.420   Kozlowski, Wladysław M. Szkice filozoficzne. Warszawa, 1900.

Phil 400.14   Kretschmer, E. Die Ideale und die Seele. Leipzig, 1900.

Phil 5250.4.5   Kroell, H. Die Aufbau der menschlichen Seele. Leipzig, 1900.

Phil 5250.13.20   Krueger, Felix. Beobachtungen über zweiklänge. Leipzig, 1900-08. 10 pam.

Phil 5203.2   Laehr, H. Die Literatur der Psychiatrie, Neurologie und Psychologie. v.1-3. Berlin, 1900. 4v.

Phil 8886.19.5   Lagerborg, R. Moralens vasen. Helsingfors, 1900.

VPhil 9590.37   Lagrange, Charles Henri. Mathématique de l'histoire, géométrie et cinématique. Bruxelles, 1900.

Phil 705.13   Landström, Gustaf. Locke och Kant. Uppsala, 1900.

Phil 8591.12.2   Lang, Albert. Meaning of religion. 2. ed. London, 1900.

Phil 8886.27   Laplaigne, H. Morale d'un égoiste; essai de morale sociale. Paris, 1900.

Phil 2050.93   Lechartier, G. David Hume. Paris, 1900.

NEDL   Phil 3552.66   Leibniz, Gottfried Wilhelm. La monadologie, avec étude et notes. Paris, 1900.

Phil 3552.18.5   Leibniz, Gottfried Wilhelm. Oeuvres philosophiques. 2e éd. Paris, 1900. 2v.

Phil 3850.5.95   Lessing, Theodor. African Spir's Erkenntnislehre. Inaug. Diss. Giessen, 1900.

Phil 2490.88   Lévy-Bruhl, L. La philosophie d'Auguste Comte. Paris, 1900.

Phil 3640.106.4   Lichtenberger, H. Friedrich Nietzsche. Dresden, 1900.

Phil 3640.106.5   Lichtenberger, H. Friedrich Nietzsche. 2e Aufl. Dresden, 1900.

Phil 3246.99   Lindau, Hans. Johann Gottlieb Fichte und der neuere Socialismus. Berlin, 1900.

1900 - cont.

Phil 5821.4.5   Loeb, J. Comparative physiology of the brain and comparative psychology. N.Y., 1900.

Phil 510.27   Loewenthal, Eduard. Der Bankrott der Darwin-Haeckel'schen Entwicklungstheories und die Krönung des monistischen Gebäudes. Berlin, 1900.

Phil 4065.86   Louis, G. Giordano Bruno. Berlin, 1900.

Phil 6121.9   Lueddeckens, F. Rechts und Linkshändigkeit. Leipzig, 1900.

Phil 186.34   Lyon, Otto. Das Pathos der Resonanz. Leipzig, 1900.

Phil 9495.2   Lyttelton, E. Training of the young in laws of sex. London, 1900.

Phil 8887.37.90   Mabie, H.W. The life of the spirit. N.Y., 1900.

Phil 293.9   McEwen, J.W. An essay on creation. Philadelphia, 1900.

Phil 5635.5.5   Mach, Ernst. Die Analyse der Empfindungen. Jena, 1900.

Phil 2270.91A   Macpherson, H. Spencer and Spencerism. N.Y., 1900.

Phil 5762.14   Manno, R. Heinrich Hertz - für die Willensfreiheit? Leipzig, 1900.

Phil 9550.12   Marchesini, G. La teoria dell'utile. Milano, 1900.

Phil 8592.6.2   Martineau, James. Study of religion. London, 1900. 2v.

Phil 3494.15.3   Mellin, G.S.A. Marginalien und Register zu Kants Kritik der Erkenntnisvermögen. Pt. 1-2. Gotha, 1900-02.

Phil 187.25.4   Mercier, D. Cours de philosophie. 4e éd. v.4. Louvain, 1900.

Phil 1135.44   Milliaud, G. Les philosophes-geometres de la Gréce. Paris, 1900.

Phil 5932.3   Möbius, P.J. Über die Anlage zur Mathematik. Leipzig, 1900.

Phil 5545.160   Mondolfo, R. Memoria e associazione nella scuola cartesiana. Firenze, 1900.

Phil 5822.1.15   Morgan, C.L. Animal behaviour. London, 1900.

Phil 5052.10   Müller, E. Über die Algebra der Logik. v. 1-2. Leipzig, 1900-01.

Phil 5252.12.9A   Münsterberg, H. Grundzüge der Psychologie. Leipzig, 1900.

Phil 3585.7.86   Münz, Bernhard. Moritz Lazarus. Berlin, 1900.

Phil 188.11.10   Naville, Ernest. Les philosophies négatives. Paris, 1900.

Phil 6123.5.5   Newcomb, C.B. Discovery of a lost trail. Boston, 1900.

Phil 7069.00.35   News from the invisible world. 3. ed. London, 1900.

Phil 960.17.5   Noble, M.E. Kali the mother. London, 1900.

Phil 345.1   Ormond, A.T. Foundations of knowledge. London, 1900.

Phil 3565.115   Otto, Clemens. Hermann Lotze über das Unbewusste. Labes, 1900.

Phil 2805.55   Pascal, Blaise. Discours sur les passions de l'amour. Paris, 1900.

Phil 9430.17   Paulsen, F. Schopenhauer und Naturgeschichte des Pessimismus. Berlin, 1900.

Phil 3497.3.19   Paulsen, Friedrich. Kants Verhaltnis zur Metaphysik. Berlin, 1900.

Phil 5765.2   Payot, Jules. L'éducation de la volonté. Paris, 1900.

Phil 8640.2   Perdelwitz, R. Die Lehre von der Unsterblichkeit der Seele. Leipzig, 1900.

Phil 5825.7.2   Perez, Bernard. Mes deux chats. 2. éd. Paris, 1900.

Phil 190.18.5   Perry, R.B. Studies in theory of knowledge. n.p., 1900-1910.

Phil 5415.3   Petrini, E. Om sympatiska känslor. Upsala, 1900.

Phil 5255.20   Petrini, Edvard. Om känslolagar. Upsala, 1900.

Phil 190.34   Petrone, Igino. I limiti del determinismo scientifico. Modena, 1900.

Phil 346.7   Petronievics, B. Prinzipien der Erkenntnislehre. Berlin, 1900.

Phil 346.2   Petzoldt, J. Einführung in die Philosophie der reinen Erfahrung. v.1-2. Leipzig, 1900.

Phil 5765.3   Pfänder, A. Phänomenologie des Wollens. Leipzig, 1900.

Phil 3850.9.90   Philosophische Abhandlungen Christoph Sigwart zu seine 70. Geburtstage gewidmet. Tübingen, 1900.

Phil 490.6   Pikler, G. Das Grundgesetz alles neuro-psychologischen Lebens. Leipzig, 1900.

Phil 2705.82   Poritzky, J.E. Julien Offray de La Mettrie. Berlin, 1900.

Phil 8891.2   Questions de morale. Paris, 1900.

Phil 5525.21   Raulin, J.M. Le rire et les exhilarants. Paris, 1900.

Phil 8418.4   Raymond, G.L. The representative significance of form. N.Y., 1900.

Phil 7069.00.60   Rayon, M. The mystic self. Chicago, 1900.

Phil 8672.9   Read, E.A. The idea of God in relation to theology. Chicago, 1900.

Phil 3428.163   Regler, Walter. Herbarts Stellung zum Eudämonismus. Leipzig, 1900.

Phil 3499.10   Reininger, Robert. Kants Lehre vom Unneren sinn und seine Theorie der Erfahrung. Wein, 1900.

Phil 5465.5   Ribot, T. Essai sur l'imagination créatrice. Paris, 1900.

Phil 3425.180   Richert, Hans. Hegels Religionsphilosophie. Bromberg, 1900.

Phil 575.7   Richmond, W. Essay on personality as a philosophical principle. London, 1900.

Phil 4065.89.5   Riehl, A. Giordano Bruno. 2e, Aufl. Leipzig, 1900.

Phil 8892.4   Roberty, E. de. Constitution de l'éthique. Paris, 1900.

Phil 192.45   Roure, L. Doctrines et problèmes. Paris, 1900.

Phil 8633.1.4   Royce, J. The conception of immortality. Boston, 1900.

Phil 192.16.10A   Royce, Josiah. The world and the individual. N.Y., 1900-1901. 2v.

Phil 3499.5   Ruyssen, T. Kant. Paris, 1900.

Phil 4630.5.2   Rydberg, V. Filosofiska föreläsningar. Stockholm, 1900-01. 4v.

Phil 5257.22.5   Ryland, F. The story of thought and feeling. London, 1900.

Phil 2880.1.45   Saint-Martin, L.C. Tableau naturel des rapports qui existent entre Dieu, l'homme et l'univers. Paris, 1900.

Phil 665.57   Sarlo, Francesco di. Il concetto dell'anima nella psicologia contemporanea. Firenze, 1900.

Phil 5400.61   Savescu, Michael. Die Gefühlslehre in der neuesten französischen Psychologie. Leipzig, 1900.

Phil 4580.82   Schiodte, C. Bemaerkninger om den Høffdingske filosofi. København, 1900.

Phil 3808.104   Schlüter, R. Schopenhauers Philosophie. Leipzig, 1900.

Phil 3500.16   Schmidt, Karl. Beiträge zur Entwicklung der Kant'schen Ethik. Inaug. Diss. Marburg, 1900.

Phil 3500.16.5   Schmidt, Karl. Beiträge zur Entwicklung der Kant'schen Ethik. Inaug. Diss. Marburg, 1900.

Phil 299.20   Schneidewin, M. Die Unendlichkeit der Welt. Berlin, 1900.

Phil 510.18   Schoeler, von. Probleme. Leipzig, 1900.

Phil 5258.28   Schultze, F. Psychologie der Naturvölker. Leipzig, 1900.

Phil 5768.5   Schwarz, H. Psychologie des Willens. Leipzig, 1900.

Phil 2053.80   Scott, William Robert. Francis Hutcheson, his life, teaching and position in the history of philosophy. Cambridge, 1900.

Phil 3565.120   Seibert, F. Lotze als Anthropologe. Wiesbaden, 1900.

Chronological Listing

1900 - cont.

Phil 2262.35.3A Shaftesbury, A.A.C. Characteristicks. N.Y., 1900. 2v.
Phil 2262.77 Shaftesbury, A.A.C. Life. Unpublished letters. London, 1900.
Phil 8893.14.9 Smiles, Samuel. Ayudate! Self-help. 5. ed. Paris, 1900.
Phil 8615.3 Society of Ethical Propagandists. Ethics and religion. London, 1900.
Phil 5545.31 Sollier, P. La problème de la mémoire. Paris, 1900.
Phil 4225.1 Spaventa, Bertrando. Scritti filosofici. Napoli, 1900.
Phil 2270.45.9 Spencer, Herbert. First principles. N.Y., 1900.
Phil 8893.35 Spínola, R. Moral razonada. Guatemala, 1900.
Phil 8643.7 Spitta, H. Mein Recht auf Leben. Tübingen, 1900.
Phil 5467.1 Steel, R. Imitation or mimetic force. London, 1900.
Phil 4065.84 Stein, H. von. Giordano Bruno, Gedanken über seine Lehre. Leipzig, 1900.
Phil 3160.2.87 Steiner, R. Bartholomäus Carneri, der Ethiker des Darwinismus. Dresden, 1900.
Phil 1818.2.5 Stephen, Leslie. The English Utilitarians. v.2. London, 1900.
Phil 5258.35.12 Stern, W. Über Psychologie der individuellen Differenzen. Leipzig, 1900.
Phil 5258.47 Stirling, James H. What is thought? Edinburgh, 1900.
Phil 6968.16 Storring, Gustav. Vorlesungen über Psychopathologie. Leipzig, 1900.
Phil 126.3.2 Stumpf, C. Tafeln zur Geschichte der Philosophie. Berlin, 1900.
Phil 960.9.5 Sugivra, Sadajiro. Hindu logic as preserved in China and Japan. Philadelphia, 1900.
Phil 5258.25.3.5 Sully, J. Outlines of psychology. N.Y., 1900.
Phil 194.17 Taft, Oren B. Hypothesis for a ceptacle theory. Chicago, 1900.
Phil 7150.19 Tapia, Ambrosios. Los suicidios en Cataluña y en general en toda España. Barcelona, 1900.
Phil 2045.106 Tarantino, G. Saggio sulle idee morali e politiche di T. Hobbes. Napoli, 1900.
Phil 8894.23.5 Tarrozzi, G. La virtù contemporanea. Torino, 1900.
Phil 5259.7.3 Thorndike, E.L. The human nature club. N.Y., 1900.
Phil 6420.6 Thorpe, Eliza Jane Ellery. Speech hesitation. N.Y., 1900.
Phil 8701.3 Troels Lund, Troels Frederik. Himmelsbild und Weltanschauung. Leipzig, 1900.
Phil 1135.81 Trubetskoi, S.N. Uchenie o Logose. Moskva, 1900.
Phil 350.2 Turner, F.S. Knowledge, belief and certitude. London, 1900.
Phil 7069.00.40 Tuttle, Hudson. Arcana of spiritualism. Manchester, 1900.
Phil 7069.00.53 Tuttle, Hudson. Mediumship and its laws. 3. ed. Chicago, 1900.
Phil 8965.2 University of Pennsylvania. The Boardman Lectureship in Christian ethics. Philadelphia, 1900.
Phil 6130.1 Uschakoff, J. Das Lokalisationsgesetz. Helsingfors, 1900.
Phil 6130.1.2 Uschakoff, J. Das Lokalisationsgesetz. Leipzig, 1900.
Phil 9045.9 Varela, Alfredo. Patria! Livro da Mocidade. Rio de Janeiro, 1900.
Phil 3503.4.30 Vorländer, K. Kant und der Sozialismus unter besonderer Verücksichtigung der neuesten theoretischen Bewegung innerhalb des Marxismus. Berlin, 1900.
Phil 197.33 Waldeck, Oscar. Zur Analyse der aesthetischen Substanz. Dresden, 1900.
Phil 3565.131 Wartenberg, Mscislaw. Das problem des Wirkens und die monistische Weltanschauung. Leipzig, 1900.
Phil 8897.29.8 Washington, B.T. Sowing and reaping. Boston, 1900.
Phil 7082.130 What are dreams? N.Y., 1900.
Phil 7054.4.15 Whiting, Lilian. The spiritual significance. Boston, 1900.
Phil 6132.11 Wichmann, R. Die Rückenmarksnewen über ihre Segmentbezüge. Berlin, 1900.
Phil 6132.10 Wilson, A. Brain and body: the nervous system. 2d ed. London, 1900.
Phil 1504.3.3 Wittmann, M. Die Stellung. v.3, pt.3. Münster, 1900.
:DL Phil 497.7 Woltmann, L. Der historische Materialismus. Düsseldorf, 1900.
Phil 1504.3.4 Worms, M. Die Lehre von der Anfangslosigkeit. v.3, pt.4. Münster, 1900.
Phil 1527.1 Wulf, M. de. Histoire de la philosophie médiévale. Louvain, 1900.
Phil 3915.70 Wundt, Wilhelm. Völkerpsychologie. Leipzig, 1900- 5v.
Phil 3640.81 Zeitler, Julius. Nietzsches Asthetik. Leipzig, 1900.
Phil 5465.25 Zeller, E. Über den Einfluss des Gefühls auf die Thätigkeit der Phantasie. Tübingen, 1900.
Phil 8605.4 Zethraeus, A.G. Isätalät-ordens (sanningssökarnes) vishetslära. Stockholm, 1900.
Phil 5525.33 Ziegler, J. Das Komische. Leipzig, 1900.
Phil 3640.89 Ziegler, Theobald. Friedrich Nietzsche. Berlin, 1900.
Phil 5265.1.4 Ziehen, Theodor. Leitfaden der physiologischen Psychologie. 5. Aufl. Jena, 1900.

1901

Phil 5640.19 Abrutz, Sydney. Om sinnesrörelsernas fysiologi och psykologi. Upsala, 1901.
Phil 1135.69 Apelt, O. Ansichten der griechischen Philosophen. Eisen, 1901.
Phil 4060.1.2 Ardigo, Roberto. Opere filosofiche. Padova, 1901-13. 11v.
Phil 8625.5.17 Arnold, Edwin. Death and afterwards. N.Y., 1901.
Phil 1700.4 Arréat, Lucien. Dix années de philosophie. Paris, 1901.
Phil 1020.7 Asin Palacios, M. Algazel. Dogmática, moral, ascética. v. 1-3. Zaragola, 1901. 2v.
Phil 7069.01.10 Atkinson, W.W. Thought-force in business and everyday life. 2. ed. Chicago, 1901.
DL Phil 1850.35.6 Bacon, Francis. The advancement of learning. St. Louis, 1901.
Phil 1850.35.8 Bacon, Francis. The advancement of learning. 1st ed. London, 1901-05. 2v.
Phil 1850.50.12 Bacon, Francis. Novum organum. St. Louis, 1901.
Phil 3425.103 Baillie, J.B. The origin and significance of Hegel's logic. London, 1901.
DL Phil 86.3A Baldwin, J.M. Dictionary of philosophy. v.1. London, 1901-05.
Phil 5241.3.24 Baldwin, J.M. The story of the mind. N.Y., 1901.
Phil 176.5.8 Balfour, A.J. Foundations of belief. London, 1901.
Phil 705.21 Barkman, H. Bidrag till denTransscendentala kategoriläran. Uppsala, 1901.
Phil 3483.25 Barkman, H. Kategorilära enligt Kantiska principer. Akademisk afhandling. Upsala, 1901.

1901 - cont.

Phil 4215.1.83 Bartolomei, A. Del significato e del valore delle dottrine di Romagnosi per il criticismo contemporaneo. Roma, 1901.
Phil 5070.13 Bazaillas, A. La crise de la croyance. Paris, 1901.
Phil 3640.190 Bélart, Hans. Friedrich Nietzsches Ethik. Leipzig, 1901.
Phil 6051.21 Benham, William G. The law of scientific hand reading. N.Y., 1901.
Phil 1870.45.3 Berkeley, G. Three dialogues...Hylas and Philonous. Chicago, 1901.
Phil 1870.13A Berkeley, G. Works. Oxford, 1901.
Phil 8626.10 Bernies, V. Spiritualité et immortalité. Paris, 1901.
Phil 978.6.44A Besant, Annie. Thought power; its control and culture. London, 1901.
Phil 4210.135.10 Bettanini, A. Anniversario della festa secolare per Antonio Rosmini. n.p., 1901.
Phil 3640.223 Biedenkapp, Georg. Friedrich Nietzsche und Friedrich Naumann als Politiker. Göttingen, 1901.
Phil 6111.36 Biervliet, J.J. L'homme droit et l'homme gauche. Gand, 1901.
Phil 8876.47 Black, Hugh. Culture and restraint. N.Y., 1901.
Phil 8581.22 Blamires, W.L. Studies and speculation in natural history. London, 1901.
Phil 1506.2 Blanc, Elie. Manuale philosophiae scholasticae. Lugduni, 1901. 2v.
X Cg Phil 7075.9 Bloch, Iwan. Le Marquis de Sade et son temps. Berlin, 1901.
Phil 5650.11 Bonnier, Pierre. L'audition. Paris, 1901.
Phil 4515.32.3 Boström, C.J. Grundlinier till philosophiska statslärans propaedeutik. 3. uppl. Stockholm, 1901.
Phil 176.64 Bourdeau, L. Problème de la vie, essai de sociologie générale. Paris, 1901.
Phil 41.12 British Psychological Society. The British Psychological Society, 1901-1961. London, 1901-1961.
Phil 4065.32.20 Bruno, Giordano. Le ombre delle idee. Catania, 1901.
Phil 8520.8 Caldecott, Alfred. The philosophy of religion in England and America. N.Y., 1901.
Phil 5242.13 Calkins, M.W. An introduction to psychology. N.Y., 1901.
Phil 8582.18A Campagnac, E.T. The Cambridge Platonists. Oxford, 1901.
Phil 177.4.12 Cantoni, C. Corso elementare di filosofia. Milan, 1901.
Phil 7082.114 Cavallin, Paul. Dröm och vaka. Stockholm, 1901.
Phil 8692.17 Chicherin, Boris N. Nauka i religiia. Moskva, 1901.
Phil 1850.81.5 Church, R.W. Bacon. N.Y., 1901.
Phil 5627.76 Collins, F.P. My religious experience. Kansas City, Mo., 1901.
Phil 8403.24.5 Conti, Auguso. Il bell nel vero o estetic. 4. ed. Firenze, 1901. 2v.
Phil 177.19.20 Conti, Augusto. Ai figli del popolo; consigli. Firenze, 1901.
Phil 978.15.5 Cook, M.C. Through the gates of gold. Boston, 1901.
NEDL Phil 3552.106 Couturat, L. La logique de Leibniz. Paris, 1901.
Phil 4260.146 Croce, B. Giambattista Vico, primo scopritore della scienza estetica. Napoli, 1901.
Phil 8627.5 Curtis, L.Q. Immortal life. N.Y., 1901.
Phil 8693.12.5 Dadson, Arthur J. Evolution, and its bearing on religions. London, 1901.
Phil 284.9 Dandolo, G. La causa e la legge. Padova, 1901.
Phil 2520.37.10 Descartes, René. Discourse on method. London, 1901.
Phil 2520.14.9 Descartes, René. Meditationes de prima philosophia. München, 1901.
Phil 7068.95.27 Desertis, V.C. Psychic philosophy as the foundation of a religion of natural law. 2. ed. London, 1901.
Phil 3640.169 Deussen, Paul. Erinnerungen an Friedrich Nietzsche. Leipzig, 1901.
Phil 178.12.47 Dresser, H.W. The Christ ideal. N.Y., 1901.
Phil 178.12.17 Dresser, H.W. Living by the spirit. N.Y., 1901.
Phil 178.12.11 Dresser, H.W. The power of silence. N.Y., 1901.
Phil 5425.42 Duche, Émile. De la precocité intellectuelle. Paris, 1901.
Phil 8878.29 Dumont, Arsène. La morale basée sur la démographie. Paris, 1901.
Phil 2490.113 Dussauze, W. Essai sur la religion d'apres A. Comte. Thèse. Saint-Amand, 1901.
Phil 3486.16 Eck, Samuel. Aus den grossen Tagen der deutschen Philosophie. Tübingen, 1901.
Phil 335.1.5 Eisler, Rudolf. Das Bewusstsein der Aussenwelt. Leipzig, 1901.
Phil 1704.2.5 Eleutheropulos, A. Die Philosophie und die Lebensauffassung der germanisch-romanischen Völker. Berlin, 1901.
Phil 4115.107 Ercole, Pasquale d'. Commemorazione della personalità e del pensiero filosofico. Torino, 1901.
Phil 1504.3.5 Espenberger, J.N. Die Philosophie des Petrus Lombardus. v.3, pt.5. Münster, 1901.
Phil 8584.5.14 Eucken, Rudolf. Der Wahrheitsgehalt der Religion. Leipzig, 1901.
Phil 8584.5.15 Eucken, Rudolf. Der Wahrheitsgehalt der Religion. Leipzig, 1901.
Phil 8584.5 Eucken, Rudolf. Das Wesen der Religion, philosophisch Betrachtet. Leipzig, 1901.
Phil 3565.113 Falckenberg, R. Hermann Lotze. Stuttgart, 1901.
Phil 7054.3 Farnese, A. A wanderer in the spirit lands. Chicago, 1901.
Phil 3487.7 Feder, Ernst. Von G.E. Schulze zu A. Schopenhauer. Diss. Aarau, 1901.
Phil 8585.24 Fernandes de Santanna, Manuel. Apologetica. Lisboa, 1901.
Phil 8585.19 Fielding-Hall, H. The hearts of men. N.Y., 1901.
Phil 3425.118 Fischer, Kuno. Hegels Leben, Werke und Lehre. v.1-2. Heidelberg, 1901.
Phil 8630.3.6A Fiske, J. Life everlasting. Boston, 1901.
Phil 6955.13 Fleury, M. de. Les grands symptômes neurasthéniques. Paris, 1901.
Phil 7082.120 Foucault, Marcel. De somniis observationes et cogitationes. Thesis. Paris, 1901.
Phil 5245.15 Foucault, Marcel. La psychophysique. Paris, 1901.
Phil 8630.10 Franck, K. Wie wird's sein? Halle, 1901.
Htn Phil 6480.23.7* Freud, Sigmund. Über den Traumdeutung. Wiesbaden, 1901.
Phil 3425.84.10 Gabler, G.A. Kritik des Bewusstseins. Leiden, 1901.
Phil 9560.12 Gardair, J. Philosophie de Saint Thomas. Les passions et la volonté. Paris, 1901.
Phil 181.60 Gener, Pompeyo. Inducciones, ensayos de filosofia y de crítica. Barcelona, 1901.
Phil 4115.60 Gioberti, V. Il pensiero civile. Torino, 1901.
Phil 4115.81 Gioberti, V. Primo centenario di V. Gioberti. Torino, 1901. 2 pam.
Phil 91.3 Goblot, E. Le vocabulaire philosophique. Paris, 1901.
Phil 3488.4.10 Goldschmidt, L. Kant Kritik oder Kantstudium? Gotha, 1901.

1901 - cont.

Phil 1111.1.9 — Gomperz, T. Greek thinkers and history of ancient philosophy. v.4. London, 1901.

Phil 3488.7 — Goujon, H. Kant et Kantistes. Lille, 1901.

Phil 5649.2 — Gourgeon, J. L'exploration physiologique...du sens musculaire. Paris, 1901.

Phil 5651.6 — Grasset, Joseph. Les maladies de l'orientation et de l'equilibre. Paris, 1901.

Phil 8407.7 — Griveau, Maurice. La sphère de beauté, lois d'évolution. Paris, 1901.

Phil 510.1.2.4 — Haeckel, Ernst. Die Welträthsel. 6e Aufl. Bonn, 1901.

Phil 510.1.2 — Haeckel, Ernst. Die Welträthsel. 7e Aufl. Bonn, 1901.

Phil 1807.2 — Halévy, E. La formation du radicalisme philosophique. Paris, 1901-04. 3v.

Phil 5374.9 — Hall, L. The evolution of consciousness. London, 1901.

Phil 2270.103 — Halleux, Jean. L'évolutionnisme en morale. Paris, 1901.

Phil 5247.21 — Hanspaul, F. Die Seelentheorie und die Gesetze. 2. Aufl. Berlin, 1901.

Phil 6049.01.5 — Hargett, Joseph Bryant. New discoveries in palmistry. N.Y., 1901.

Phil 8587.26 — Harnack, Adolf. Das Wesen des Christentums. 4. Aufl. Leipzig, 1901.

Phil 8587.26.12 — Harnack, Adolf. What is Christianity? London, 1901.

Phil 3160.2.85 — Harpf, Adolf. Darwin in der Ethik. Leoben, 1901.

Phil 7060.48 — Harris, J. Inferences from haunted houses. London, 1901.

Phil 5247.17 — Hartmann, E. Die moderne Psychologie. Leipzig, 1901.

Phil 2262.87 — Hatch, Irvin C. Der Einfluss Shaftesburys auf Herder. Diss. Berlin? 1901?

Phil 2805.106 — Hatzfeld, A. Pascal. Paris, 1901.

Phil 8893.11.18 — Hayward, F.H. The ethical philosophy of Sidgwick. Photoreproduction. London, 1901.

Phil 3425.60.15 — Hegel, Georg Wilhelm Friedrich. Vorlesungen über die Philosophie der Religion. Leiden, 1901. 2v.

Phil 3255.80.5 — Hegler, Alfred. Sebastian Francks lateinische Paraphrase der deutschen Theologie und seine hollandische erhaltenen Traktate. Tübingen, 1901.

Phil 3640.211.5 — Henne am Rhyn, O. Anti-Zarathustra. 2e Aufl. Altenburg, 1901?

Phil 6317.12 — Herrlin, Axel. Själslifvets underjordiska verld. Malmo, 1901.

Phil 8882.41 — Herrmann, W. Ethik. Tübingen, 1901.

Phil 9347.3 — Hersey, H.E. To girls. A budget of letters. Boston, 1901.

Phil 8882.26.9 — Hillis, N.D. A man's value to society. Edinburgh, 1901.

Phil 5817.5 — Hobhouse, L.T. Mind in evolution. London, 1901.

Phil 338.3 — Hodder, A. The adversaries of the sceptic. London, 1901.

Phil 4580.38.15 — Høffding, Harald. Regionsphilosophie. Leipzig, 1901.

Phil 4580.32 — Høffding, Harald. Ved aarhundredeskiftet. København, 1901.

Phil 8615.10 — Hoffmann, P. La religion basée sur la morale. 2. éd. Bruxelles, 1901.

Phil 3489.13 — Hofmann, Paul. Kant's Lehre vom Schlusse. Inaug. Diss. Berlin, 1901.

Phil 310.730 — Hollitscher, Jakob J. Das historische Gesetz; zur Kritik der materialistischen Geschichtsauffassung von Jakob Hollitscher. Dresden, 1901.

Phil 4372.1.80 — Hoppe, G. Psychologie des Juan Luis Vives. Berlin, 1901.

Phil 400.12 — Howison, G.H. Limits of evolution. N.Y., 1901.

Phil 1135.60 — Huit, C. Philosophie de la nature chez les anciens. Paris, 1901.

Phil 7082.72 — Hutchinson, Horace Gordon. Dreams and their meanings. London, 1901.

Phil 5627.3A — Hylan, J.P. Public worship. Chicago, 1901.

NEDL Phil 7060.38.5 — Ingram, J.H. The haunted homes and family traditions of Great Britain. 5. ed. London, 1901.

Phil 7060.38.9 — Ingram, J.H. The haunted homes and family traditions of Great Britain. 5th ed. London, 1901.

Phil 2045.101 — Iodice, A. Le teorie di Hobbes e Spinoza. Napoli, 1901.

Phil 8884.5 — Jackson, A. Deafness and cheerfulness. Boston, 1901.

Phil 5249.2.24 — James, William. Principii di psicologia. Milano, 1901.

Phil 7076.20.5 — Janet, Pierre. Une extatique. Paris, 1901.

NEDL Phil 5249.6 — Jastrow, J. Fact and fable in psychology. Boston, 1901.

Phil 3829.1 — Joachim, H.H. A study of the Ethics of Spinoza. Oxford, 1901.

Phil 184.32 — Joël, K. Philosophenwege. Berlin, 1901.

Phil 2733.85 — Joly, H. Malebranche. Paris, 1901.

Phil 8884.23 — Jordan, Furneaux. Moral nerve and the error of literary verdicts. London, 1901.

Phil 8884.4 — Jordan, W.G. Kingship of self-control individual problems. N.Y., 1901.

Phil 2672.75 — Jouffroy, Théodore S. Correspondance. Paris, 1901.

Phil 8884.15.15 — Juvalta, E. Prolegomeni a una morale distinta dalla metafisica. Pavia, 1901.

Phil 3492.5 — Kaftan, J. Rede...Jubiläums...Königreichs Preussen 18 Januar 1901. Berlin, 1901.

Phil 1135.47 — Kalthoff, A. Die Philosophie der Griechen. Berlin, 1901.

Phil 3480.28.40 — Kant, Immanuel. Kant- Aussprüche. Leipzig, 1901.

Phil 3480.74 — Kant, Immanuel. Über Pädagogik. 3. Aufl. Langensalza, 1901.

Phil 8590.10.9 — King, Henry C. Reconstruction in theology. N.Y., 1901.

Phil 185.7.9 — Knight, W. Varia; studies on problems of philosophy and ethics. London, 1901.

Phil 3915.85 — König, Edmund. Wilhelm Wundt. Stuttgart, 1901.

Phil 6960.5.11 — Kraepelin, E. Einfuhrung in die psychiatrische Klenik dreissez Vorlesungen. Leipzig, 1901.

Phil 1865.151A — Kraus, Oskar. Zur Theorie des Wertes. Halle, 1901.

Phil 5374.9.9 — Kries, Johannes. Über die materiellen Grundlagen der Bewusstseins-Erscheinungen. Tübingen, 1901.

Phil 3640.314 — Kronenberg, M. Friedrich Nietzsche und seine Herrenmoral. München, 1901.

Phil 3805.167 — Kügelgen, C. von. Schleiermachers Reden und Kants Predigten. Leipzig, 1901.

Phil 2730.89 — Kühtmann, A. Maine de Biran. Bremen, 1901.

Phil 1850.117.5 — Lalande, A. L'interpretation de la nature dans le Valerius terminus. Mâcon, 1901.

Phil 365.14 — Lambek, C. Udkast til en sjaelelig bevaegelseslaere. København, 1901-1906.

Phil 8412.31 — Lange, K. von. Das Wesen der Kunst. Berlin, 1901. 2v.

Phil 8870.8 — Larned, J.N. A multitude of counselors. Boston, 1901.

Phil 8886.14.2 — Lecky, W.E.H. The map of life. N.Y., 1901.

Phil 342.10 — Leclère, Albert. Essai critique sur le droit d'affirmer. Paris, 1901.

Phil 342.2 — Leder, H. Untersuchungen über Augustins Erkenntnistheorie. Warburg, 1901.

Phil 8666.5 — Leighton, J.A. Typical modern conceptions of God. N.Y., 1901.

1901 - cont.

Phil 5642.13 — Lemaitre, A. Audition colorée et phénomènes connexes. Paris, 1901.

Phil 6681.13 — Leonidas (pseud.). Stage hypnotism. Chicago, 1901.

Phil 6961.6.2 — Lincoln, D.F. Sanity of mind. N.Y., 1901.

Phil 2050.186 — Linke, Paul. David Humes Lehre vom Wissen. Diss. Leipzig, 1901.

Phil 2115.51.6 — Locke, J. The conduct of the understanding. 5th ed. Oxford, 1901.

Phil 3100.125 — Löwenberg, Adolf. Friedrich Edward Beneke. Berlin, 1901.

Phil 2050.108 — Lüers, Adolf. David Humes religionsphilosophische Anschauungen. Berlin, 1901.

Phil 186.73.10 — Lutoslawski, W. Wykłady jagiellońskie. Kraków, 1901-1902. 2v.

Phil 8887.1.4 — Mackenzie, J.S. A manual of ethics. 4th ed. N.Y., 1901.

Phil 3425.100.5A — McTaggart, John McTaggart Ellis. Studies in Hegelian cosmology. Cambridge, 1901.

Phil 6122.54 — Mainini, Carlos. Téorica del sistema nervioso. n.p., 1901.

Phil 4170.6.35 — Marchesini, G. Il simbolismo nella conoscenza. Torino, 1901.

Phil 5520.6 — Martinak, E. Psychologische Untersuchungen zur Bedeutungslehre. Leipzig, 1901.

Phil 8887.4.10 — Martineau, J. Types of ethical theory. 3. ed. Oxford, 1901. 2v.

Phil 8592.6.8 — Martineau, James. Inter Amicos. London, 1901.

Phil 187.114.10 — Masaryk, T.G. Ideály humanitní. Praha, 1901.

Phil 5252.45 — Masci, Filippo. El materialismo psicofisico. Napoli, 1901.

Phil 3565.84 — Matagrin, A. Essai sur l'esthétique de Lotze. Paris, 1901.

Phil 8667.12 — Mayer, P. Der teleologische Gottesbeweis und der Darwinismus. Mainz, 1901.

Phil 510.1.21 — Menzi, Theodor. Ernst Haeckels Welträtsel oder der Neomaterialismus. Zürich, 1901.

Phil 5252.15 — Mercier, C.A. Psychology normal and morbid. London, 1901.

Phil 8887.34 — Mezes, S.E. Ethics descriptive and explanatory. N.Y., 1901.

Phil 5545.56 — Miles, E.H. How to remember without memory systems or with them. London, 1901.

Htn Phil 22.4.8* — Mind; a unique review of ancient philosophy (a parody). London, 1901.

Phil 5252.51 — Mortensen, M. Grundrids af psykologi og paedogogik. 2. utg. København, 1901.

Phil 510.1.31 — Müller, D.A. Scheinchristentum und Haeckels Welträtsel. Inaug. Diss. Gotha, 1901.

Phil 5627.201 — Murisier, Ernest. Les maladies du sentiment religieux. Paris, 1901.

Phil 8620.25 — Nagel, E. Das Problem der Erlösung. Basel, 1901.

Phil 53.2 — National Association for Study of Epilepsy and Care and Treatment of Epileptics. Transactions, 1901. Buffalo, 1901.

Phil 2805.91.3 — Nazelle, R.J. Étude sur Alexandre Vinet critique de Pascal. Alençon, 1901.

Phil 8963.4 — Nepliuev, N.N. Polnoe sobranie sochinenii. Sankt Peterburg, 1901. 2v.

Phil 5090.3.2 — Newman, J.H. An essay in aid of a Grammar of assent. London, 1901.

Phil 8888.5 — Nicoll, W.R. Letters on life. N.Y., 1901.

Phil 3640.25.10 — Nietzsche, Friedrich. Gedichte und Sprüche. Leipzig, 1901.

Phil 3640.28 — Nietzsche, Friedrich. Nietzsche as critic. N.Y., 1901.

Phil 4610.7.35 — Norström, V. Hvad vi behöfva. Stockholm, 1901.

Phil 3640.194 — Norström, Vitalis. Friedrich Nietzsche. Stockholm, 1901.

Phil 7069.01.5 — The occultist's handbook. Chicago, 1901.

Phil 9470.3 — Oliveira Guimarães, José Joaquim d'. De morali responsabilitate. Conimbrigae, 1901.

Phil 5520.33 — Oltuszewski, W. Psychologie und Philosophie der Sprache. Berlin, 1901.

Phil 3496.3 — Orestano, F. Der Tugendbegriff bei Kant. Inaug. Diss. Palermo, 1901.

Phil 5425.33 — Pacheco, Albino Augusto. Degenerescencia. Diss. inaug. Coimbra, 1901.

Phil 8890.23.7A — Palmer, G.H. The field of ethics. Boston, 1901.

Phil 6125.12 — Panizza, M. Le metodo nello studio del fenomeno biopsichio. Roma, 1901.

Phil 3210.84 — Pastor, Willy. Im GeisteFechners. Leipzig, 1901.

Phil 5765.2.5 — Payot, Jules. Die Erziehung des Willens. Leipzig, 1901.

Phil 8610.888.3A — Pearson, Karl. The ethic of freethought. 2. ed. London, 1901.

Phil 190.46 — Peladan, J. Traité des antinomies. Paris, 1901.

Phil 3110.85.50 — Penny, A.J. An introduction to the study of Jacob Boehme's writings. N.Y., 1901.

Phil 4769.1.115 — Piaskovskii, N.Ia. Kak myslil Vladimir Solov'ev o voskresenie. Moskva, 1901.

Phil 5585.12 — Pierce, A.H. Studies in auditory and visual space perception. N.Y., 1901.

Phil 5055.7 — Pokorny, T. Beiträge zur Logik der Urtheile und Schlüsse. Leipzig, 1901.

Phil 8610.875.30 — Pullen, H.W. Modern Christianity, a civilized heathenism. N.Y., 1901.

Phil 5255.9 — Putnam, Daniel. A text book of psychology. N.Y., 1901.

Phil 8892.5 — Ratzenhofer, G. Positive Ethik. Leipzig, 1901.

Phil 5257.37 — Reiff, Paul. Der moderne psychophysische Parallelismus. Inaug. Diss. Heilbronn, 1901.

Phil 2840.55 — Renouvier, C.B. Les dilemmes de la métaphysique pure. Paris, 1901.

Phil 2840.60 — Renouvier, C.B. Histoire et solution des problèmes métaphysiques. Paris, 1901.

Phil 2150.6.82F — Ritschl, Otto. Die Causalbetrachtung in den Geisteswissenschaften. Bonn, 1901.

Phil 817.4 — Rogers, A.K. A student's history of philosophy. N.Y., 1901.

Phil 3499.27 — Rosikat, K.A. Kants Kritik der reinen Vernunft. Königsberg, 1901.

Phil 192.16.11A — Royce, Josiah. The world and the individual. N.Y., 1901. 2v.

Phil 9450.4 — Ruemelin, G. Politics, and the moral law. N.Y., 1901.

Phil 8597.24 — Runze, Georg. Katechismus der Religionsphilosophie. Leipzig, 1901.

Phil 672.16 — Russell, B. Is position in time or space absolute or relative? London, 1901.

Phil 2493.86 — Saltykow, W. Die Philosophie Condillacs. Inaug.-Diss. Bern, 1901.

Phil 5258.4.4 — Sanford, E.C. Course in experimental psychology. Boston, 1901.

Phil 3808.125 — Sannders, T.B. Schopenhauer; a lecture. London, 1901.

Chronological Listing

1901 - cont.

Phil 8598.23 Savage, M.J. Passing and permanent in religion. N.Y., 1901.
Phil 3640.160 Schacht, W. Nietzsche. Bern, 1901.
Phil 3500.15 Schlaff, O. Kant's Lehre vom Genie. Göttingen, 1901.
Phil 1145.18.1 Schmidt, L. Hé éthiké tón archaión Hellénón. Athenas, 1901.
Phil 3552.275 Schmoger, F. Leibniz in seiner Stellung zur tellurischen Physik. München, 1901.
Phil 5400.21 Schutz, L.H. Die Lehre von den Leidenschaften. Hagen, 1901.
Phil 8893.39 Schwarz, Hermann. Das sittliche Leben, eine Ethik auf psychologische Grundlage. Berlin, 1901.
Phil 5258.13.15 Scripture, E.W. The new psychology. London, 1901.
Phil 5058.22 Sidgwick, A. The use of words in reasoning. London, 1901.
Phil 9150.8 Smith, A.W. A new theory of evolution. N.Y., 1901.
Phil 5058.21 Smith, G.H. Logic. N.Y., 1901.
Phil 6049.01 Smith, R.C. Cheirosophy, the hand. London, 1901.
Phil 5545.31.5 Sollier, P. Les troubles de la mémoire. Paris, 1901.
Phil 1050.4.17 Solomon Ibn-Gabirol. La fuente de la vída. Madrid, 1901.
Phil 5465.17 Sourian, Paul. L'imagination de l'artiste. Paris, 1901.
Phil 2270.70.14 Spencer, Herbert. Principles of psychology. N.Y., 1901. 2v.
Phil 3819.39.5 Spinoza, Benedictus de. Improvement of the understanding. N.Y., 1901.
Phil 3819.39 Spinoza, Benedictus de. Improvement of the understanding. Washington, 1901.
Phil 1900.94 Spooner, W.A. Bishop Butler. London, 1901.
Phil 8893.51 Stange, Karl. Einleitung in die Ethik. Leipzig, 1901.
Phil 1718.15 Steiner, Rudolf. Welt- und Lebensanschauungen im neunzehnten Jahrhundert. v.1-2. Berlin, 1901.
Phil 5643.48 Stilling, Jacob. Psychologie der Gesichtsvorstellung. Berlin, 1901.
Phil 3890.6.80 Störring, Gustav. Die Erkenntnistheorie von Tetens. Leipzig, 1901.
Phil 665.32 Stone, M.M. A practical study of the soul. N.Y., 1901.
Phil 5258.27.1 Stout, G.F. A manual of psychology. 2d ed. London, 1901.
Phil 9358.4 Strong, J. The times and young men. N.Y., 1901.
Phil 978.57 Stuart, C. A dialogue. n.p., 1901.
Phil 193.118 Svoboda, A.V. Ideale Lebensziele. Leipzig, 1901. 2v.
Phil 193.43.5 Swedenborg, E. Ontology. Boston, 1901.
n Phil 1145.55* Symonds, John A. A problem in Greek ethics. London, 1901.
Phil 6969.1 Talcott, S.H. Mental diseases...modern treatment. N.Y., 1901.
Phil 8894.18.5 Tarantino, Giuseppe. Il problema della morale di fronte al positivismo ed alla metafisica. Pisa, 1901.
Phil 8894.23.15 Tarrozzi, G. Idea di una scienza del bene. Firenze, 1901.
Phil 8894.12 Taylor, A.E. The problem of conduct. London, 1901.
Phil 5259.7 Thorndike, E.L. The human nature club. N.Y., 1901.
Phil 5259.5.9 Titchener, E.B. Experimental psychology. v.1-2; v.2, pt.1. n.p., 1901-27. 5v.
Phil 3552.246 Urbach, B. Leibnizens Rechtfertigung des Uebels. Prag, 1901.
Phil 196.8.7 Varisco, B. Scienza e opinioni. Roma, 1901.
Phil 5628.10 Vernier, André. L'extase et la personalité. Thèse. Montauban, 1901.
Phil 8896.4.9 Vidari, Giovanni. Problemi generali di etica. Milano, 1901.
Phil 8125.16 Volbehr, Theodor. Das Verlangen nach einer neuen deutschen Kunst. Leipzig, 1901.
Phil 3808.103 Volkelt, J. Arthur Schopenhauer. Stuttgart, 1901.
Phil 7054.156 Von Ravens, Clara I. The scribe of a soul. Seattle, 1901.
Phil 510.1.22 Wagner, Richard. Aether und Wille. Leipzig, 1901.
Phil 2880.1.82 Waite, Arthur E. The life of Louis C. de Saint-Martin. London, 1901.
Phil 353.1 Walter, J.E. The Principles of knowledge. West Newton, Pa., 1901. 2v.
Phil 9420.7 Walters, H.G. The wisdom of passion. Boston, 1901.
Phil 2805.115 Warmuth, K. Das religiös-ethische Ideal Pascals. Leipzig, 1901.
DL Phil 8712.3.9 White, Andrew Dickson. History of the warfare of science with theology in Christendem. N.Y., 1901. 2v.
Phil 6132.24 White, H.P. The philosophy of health. no.1-3. Kalamazoo, Mich., 1901.
DL Phil 1170.5 Whittaker, Thomas. Neo-Platonists::Study in history of Hellenism. Cambridge, 1901.
Phil 4065.97 Wilde, Georg. Giordano Bruno's Philosophie in den Hauptbegriffen Materie und Form. Breslau, 1901.
Phil 197.34.10 Wille, Bruno. Materie nie ohne Geist. Berlin, 1901.
Phil 6132.28 Wilson, Floyd B. Paths to power. N.Y., 1901.
Phil 8612.6 Wilson, J.K. Death; the meaning and result. N.Y., 1901.
Phil 1127.2.5 Windelband, W. History of ancient philosophy. N.Y., 1901.
Phil 822.2.11 Windelband, W. History of philosophy. 2. ed. N.Y., 1901.
Phil 197.13 Wood, H. The symphony of life. Boston, 1901.
Phil 3210.82 Wundt, W. Gustav Theodor Fechner. Leipzig, 1901.
Phil 3915.47.10 Wundt, Wilhelm. Grundriss des Psychologie. 4. Aufl. Leipzig, 1901.
Phil 3915.75 Wundt, Wilhelm. Sprachgeschichte und Sprachpsychologie. Leipzig, 1901.
Phil 353.3 Wyneken, Ernst. Das Ding an Sich und das Naturgesetz der Seele. Heidelberg, 1901.
Phil 2885.110 Zeitler, Julius. Die Kunstphilosophie von H.A. Taine. Leipzig, 1901.

1902

Phil 8875.16 Aall, Anathon. Macht und Pflicht. Leipzig, 1902.
Phil 8580.9 Abbot, F.L. Faith built on reason. Boston, 1902.
Phil 7076.16 Achelis, Thomas. Die Ekstase in ihrer kulturellen Bedeutung. Berlin, 1902.
Phil 8610.902.15 Adams, R.C. Good without God. N.Y., 1902.
Phil 5040.7 Aikins, H.A. The principles of logic. N.Y., 1902.
Phil 9550.5 Albee, Ernest. A history of English utilitarianism. London, 1902.
Phil 175.14 Alexander, H.B. The problem of mataphysics and the meaning of metaphysical explenation. Diss. N.Y., 1902.
Phil 175.14.2 Alexander, H.B. The problem of metaphysics and the meaning of metaphysical explenation. N.Y., 1902.
Phil 5710.13 Alfonso, Nicolo R. La dottrina dei temperamenti nell'antichità e ai nostri giorni. Roma, 1902.
Phil 5645.9 Allen, Frank. Persistence of vision in color blind subjects. n.p., 1902.
Phil 5300.4 Angell, J.R. A preliminary study...partial tones...of sound. Chicago, 1902.
Phil 6110.1 Anton, G. Bau, Leistung und Erkrankung des menschlichen Stirnhirnes. T.1. Graz, 1902.

1902 - cont.

Phil 3585.1.80 Baensch, Otto. Johann Heinrich Lamberts Philosophie und seine Stellung zu Kant. Inaug. Diss. Magdeburg, 1902.
Phil 365.6 Baldwin, J.M. Development and evolution. N.Y., 1902.
Phil 176.45 Baldwin, J.M. Fragments in philosophy and science. N.Y., 1902.
Phil 5241.3.6 Baldwin, J.M. Social and ethical interpretations. Mental development. N.Y., 1902.
Phil 332.8 Bastian, Adolf. Die Lehre von Denken zur Ergänzung. v.1-3. Berlin, 1902-05.
Phil 176.10.11 Baumann, Julius J. Die grundlegenden Thatsachen. 2e Aufl. Stuttgart, 1902.
Phil 5241.23 Bawden, H.H. A syllabus of psychology. Poughkeepsie, N.Y., 1902.
Phil 8876.48 Benedict, W.R. World views and their ethical implications. Cincinnati, 1902.
Phil 5241.59.5 Bentley, I.M. The psychology of mental arrangement. Worcester, 1902.
Phil 6671.4.9 Bérillon, E. Historie de l'hypnotisme expérimental. Paris, 1902.
Phil 978.6.25 Besant, Annie. Esoteric christianity. N.Y., 1902.
Phil 8125.28 Birt, Theodor. Laienurtheil über bildende Kunst bei den Alten. Marburg, 1902.
Phil 7059.11.2 Bland, T.A. In the world celestial. 2. ed. Chicago, 1902.
Phil 3425.214 Bolland, G.J.P.J. Alte Vernunft und neuer Verstand. Leiden, 1902.
Phil 332.4 Bon, F. Die Dogmen der Erkenntnistheorie. Leipzig, 1902.
NEDL Phil 5643.26 Bourdon, B. La perception visuelle de l'espace. Paris, 1902.
Phil 2805.92.7 Boutroux, E. Pascal. Manchester, 1902.
Phil 8656.8.7 Bowne, B.P. Theism. N.Y., 1902.
Phil 665.10 Bradford, A.H. The ascent of the soul. N.Y., 1902.
Phil 1885.37.5A Bradley, Francis H. Appearance and reality. 2d ed. London, 1902.
Phil 8402.47 Bray, Lucien. Du beau. Paris, 1902.
Phil 8876.41 Brentano, Franz. Origin of knowledge of right and wrong. London, 1902.
Phil 9045.3 Brewer, D.J. American citizenship. Yale lectures. N.Y., 1902.
Phil 8610.902 Brooklyn Philosophical Association. Facts worth knowing. N.Y., 1902.
Phil 5241.22 Brooks, H.J. The elements of mind. London, 1902.
Phil 3822.1.10 Caird, John. Spinoza. Edinburgh, 1902.
Phil 1020.7.5 Carra de Vaux, Le Bon. Gazali. Photoreproduction. Paris, 1902.
Phil 930.1.5 Carus, P. Chinese philosophy. 2d ed. Chicago, 1902.
Phil 3552.111 Cassirer, E. Leibniz' System. Marburg, 1902.
Phil 8627.9.3 Chambers, A. Our life after death. Philadelphia, 1902.
Phil 2520.106 Christiansen, B. Das Urteil bei Descartes. Hanau, 1902.
Phil 177.84 Clark, S.C. The melody of life. N.Y., 1902.
Phil 2805.179 Clark, William. Pascal and the Port Royalists. Edinburgh, 1902.
Phil 177.28A Cohen, Hermann. Logik der reinen Erkenntnis. Berlin, 1902. 3v.
Phil 2490.72 Comte, Auguste. Lettres d'Auguste Comte à divers. v.1-2. Paris, 1902-05. 3v.
Phil 3822.3 Couchond, P.L. Benoit de Spinoza. Paris, 1902.
Phil 8582.31 Cremer, Herman. Das Wesen des Christentums. 3. Aufl. Gütersloh, 1902.
Phil 4080.3.31 Croce, Benedetto. Estetica come scienza dell'espressione e linguistica generale. Milano, 1902.
Phil 5242.24 Crüger, J. Grundritz der Psychologie. 2. Aufl. Leipzig, 1902.
Phil 4075.83 Cumston, Charles Greene. Notes on life and writings of Gironimo Cardano. Boston, 1902.
Phil 8952.6 Cunningham, W. The gospel of work. Cambridge, 1902.
Phil 6012.1 Cuyer, E. La mimique. Paris, 1902.
Phil 3801.320 Delbos, Victor. De posteriore Schellingii philosophia. Thesim. Lutetiae, 1902.
Phil 3210.87 Dennert, E. Fechner als Naturphilosoph und Christ. Gütersloh, 1902.
Phil 3552.83.5 Dewey, J. Leibniz's new essays concerning the human understanding. Chicago, 1902.
Phil 3640.111 Dowerg, R. Friedrich Nietzsches "Geburt der Tragödie". Leipzig, 1902.
Phil 178.12.18 Dresser, H.W. A book of secrets. N.Y., 1902.
Phil 3415.89 Drews, A. Eduard von Hartmanns philosophisches System. Heidelberg, 1902.
Phil 8583.7.3 Dühring, E.K. Der Werth des Lebens. 6. Aufl. Leipzig, 1902.
Phil 5525.24 Dugas, L. Psychologie du rire. Paris, 1902.
Phil 178.19 Dunan, Charles. Essais de philosophie générale. 5th ed. Paris, 1902.
Phil 178.40 Dyroff, Adolf. Über den Existenzialbegriff. Freiburg im Breisgau, 1902.
Phil 3120.10.81 Eckstein, Ernst. Der Begriff des Daseins bei Julius Bergmann. Inaug. Diss. Erlangen, 1902.
Phil 8405.6 Eddy, Arthur. Delight, the soul of art. Philadelphia, 1902.
Phil 179.5 Eichbaum-Lange, W. Was heisst Philosophie? Leipzig, 1902.
Phil 735.2A Eisler, R. Studien zur Werttheorie. Leipzig, 1902.
Phil 3640.122.5 Eisler, Rudolf. Nietzsche's Erkenntnistheorie und Metaphysik. Leipzig, 1902.
Phil 3425.455 Erdmann, Johann Eduard. Abhandlung über Leib und Seele. Leiden, 1902.
Phil 179.34 Everett, C.C. Immortality. Boston, 1902.
Phil 5627.5 Everett, C.C. The psychological elements of religious faith. N.Y., 1902.
Phil 850.11 Fabre, Joseph. La pensée antique (de Moise à Marcaurèle). Paris, 1902.
Phil 3825.6 Ferrari, G.M. L'etica di B. Spinoza. Napoli, 1902.
Phil 8880.39 Ferrari, G.M. Il problema etico. Rome, 1902.
Phil 180.41 Ferro, A.A. Concetto della filosofia. Savona, 1902.
Phil 286.2.9 Fiske, J. Outlines of cosmic philosophy. Boston, 1902. 4v.
Phil 8585.17.5 Fiske, J. Studies in religion. Boston, 1902.
Phil 8660.4.4 Flint, R. Theism (Baird lectures for 1876). 10. ed. London, 1902.
Phil 900.2 Fluegel, M. Philosophy, qabbala and vedánta. Baltimore, 1902.
Phil 3428.89 Flügel, Otto. Die Bedeutung der Metaphysik Herbarts. Langensalza, 1902.
Phil 3640.117.5 Fouillée, Alfred E. Nietzsche et l'immoralisme. Paris, 1902.
Phil 9530.12 Fowler, M.C. The boy! How to help him succeed. Boston, 1902.

Chronological Listing

1902 - cont.

Phil 1870.88   Freedman, L.A. Substanz und Causalitat bei Berkeley. Strassburg, 1902.

Phil 5045.7   Freytag, Willy. Der Realismus und Dastransscendenzproblem. Halle, 1902.

Phil 9150.11   Funk, I.K. The next step in evolution. N.Y., 1902.

Phil 7069.02.5   Gaffield, E.C. A celestial message. Boston, 1902.

Phil 3640.712   Garnier, Paul-Louis. Réflexions sur Nietzsche. Paris, 1902.

Phil 1706.1.23   Gaultier, Jules de. Le Bovarysme. 3. éd. Photoreproduction. Paris, 1902.

Phil 410.7   Geissler, Kurt. Die Grundsätze und das Wesen des Unendlichen in der Mathematik und Philosophie. Leipzig, 1902.

Phil 5246.14   Geyser, J. Grundlegung der empirischen Psychologie. Bonn, 1902.

Phil 3585.8.83   Gjurits, D. Erkenntnistheorie des Ernst Laas. Inaug. Diss. Leipzig, 1902.

Phil 8881.41   Goldscheid, Rudolf. Zur Ethik des Gesamtwellens. Leipzig, 1902.

Phil 8881.44   Gomperz, Heinrich. Über den Begriff des sittlichen Ideals. Bern, 1902.

Phil 5246.12.12   Gordy, J.P. New psychology. N.Y., 1902.

Phil 5465.44   Gore, W.C. The imagination in Spinoza and Hume. Chicago, 1902.

Phil 8881.28   Gorton, D.A. Ethics civil and political. N.Y., 1902.

Phil 8407.10   Groos, Karl. Der ästhetische Genuss. Giessen, 1902.

Phil 672.24   Guyau, M.J. La genèse de l'idée de temps. 2e éd. Paris, 1902.

Phil 3489.11   Hägerström, Axel. Kants Ethik...dargestellt. Upsala, 1902.

Phil 8882.27   Hamilton, E.J. The moral law - theory and practice of duty. N.Y., 1902.

Phil 3585.8.85   Hanisch, Rudolf. Der Positivismus von Ernst Laas. Inaug. Diss. Halle, 1902.

Phil 182.81   Hart, Julius. Die neue Welterkenntnis. Leipzig, 1902.

Phil 6957.15   Hartenberg, P. La névrose d'angoisse. Paris, 1902.

Phil 400.75   Hartmann, Alma von. Zurück zum Idealismus. Berlin, 1902.

Phil 5651.3   Hartmann, F. Die Orientierung; die Physiologie. Leipzig, 1902.

Phil 3425.70.15   Hegel, Georg Wilhelm Friedrich. Grundlinien der Philosophie des Rechts. Leiden, 1902.

Phil 338.4   Heim, Karl. Psychologismus oder Antipsychologismus. Berlin, 1902.

Phil 6117.10   Hellpach, W. Die Grenzwissenschaften der Psychologie. Leipzig, 1902.

Phil 3120.1.125   Hennig, M. A.E. Biedermanns Theorie...religiöse Erkenntnis. Leipzig, 1902.

Phil 7054.128   Henry, T.S. "Spookland", a record of research. Chicago, 1902.

Phil 3425.105A   Hibben, J.G. Hegel's logic. N.Y., 1902.

Phil 9245.16.2   Hillis, N.D. Quest of happiness. N.Y., 1902.

Phil 672.15.7   Hinton, Charles H. The recognition of the fourth dimension. Washington, 1902.

Phil 807.5   Hoffding, H. Filosofiske problemer. København, 1902.

Phil 3489.6   Hoffmann, A. Immanuel Kant. Halle, 1902.

Phil 8882.24.9   Hyde, W. De W. The cardinal virtues. N.Y., 1902.

Phil 9349.3   Jacks, William. Singles from life's gathering. Glasgow, 1902.

Phil 5627.6.2.4   James, William. Varieties of religious experience. N.Y., 1902.

Htn   Phil 5627.6.2*   James, William. Varieties of religious experience. N.Y., 1902.

Htn   Phil 5627.6.1*   James, William. Varieties of religious experience. N.Y., 1902.

Phil 5627.6.2.5   James, William. Varieties of religious experience. N.Y., 1902.

Phil 809.2   Janet, P. History of the problems of philosophy. London, 1902. 2v.

Phil 340.1   Jaures, J. De la réalite du monde sensible. Paris, 1902.

Phil 5249.8   Jerusalem, W. Lehrbuch der Psychologie. Wien, 1902.

Phil 3491.2   Johansson, J. Kants eticka asikt. Lund, 1902.

Phil 9430.18   Jordan, D.S. The philosophy of despair. San Francisco, 1902.

Phil 8884.4.9   Jordan, W.G. The power of truth. N.Y., 1902.

Phil 8834.4   Judge, M.H. The ethical movement in England, 1902. London, 1902.

Htn   Phil 6319.1.25*   Jung, C.G. Zur Psychologie und Pathologie sogenannter occulter Phänomene. Inaug. Diss. Leipzig, 1902.

Phil 3246.94   Kabitz, Willy. Studien zur Entwicklungsgeschichte der Fichteschen Wissenschaftslehre. Berlin, 1902.

Phil 3480.46.5   Kant, Immanuel. Critique de la raison pratique. 2. éd. Paris, 1902.

Phil 3480.21.22   Kant, Immanuel. Der einzig mögliche Beweisgrund zu einer Demonstration des Daseyns Gottes. 2. Aufl. Leipzig, 1902.

Phil 3480.50.13A   Kant, Immanuel. Kritik der Urtheilskraft. 3. Aufl. Leipzig, 1902.

Phil 3480.100   Kant, Immanuel. Die letzten Gedanken. Hamburg, 1902.

Htn   Phil 3480.58*   Kant, Immanuel. Prolegomena to any future metaphysics. Chicago, 1902.

Phil 5643.72   Karplus, S. Beitrag zur Lehre von den Geschichtsempfindungen. Inaug. Diss. Berlin, 1902.

Phil 810.4   Karppe, S. Essais de critique et d'histoire de philosophie. Paris, 1902.

Phil 8411.10   Keussler, G. von. Die Grenzen der Ästhetik. Leipzig, 1902.

Phil 4655.1.82.2   Kjellberg, Elis. Carl Pontus Wikner. Stockholm, 1902.

Phil 3915.85.5   König, Edmund. Wilhelm Wundt als Psycholog und als Philosoph. Stuttgart, 1902.

Phil 6960.5.5   Kraepelin, E. Clinical psychiatry. N.Y., 1902.

Phil 3492.2.10   Krause, A. Die letzten Gendanken Immanuel Kants. Hamburg, 1902.

Phil 735.89A   Kreibig, J.C. Psychologische Grundlegung eines Systems der Wert-Theorie. Wien, 1902.

Phil 5250.4   Kroell, H. Die Seele im Lichte des Monismus. Strassburg, 1902.

Phil 3830.3   Kühnemann, E. Über die Grundlagen der Lehre des Spinoza. Halle, 1902.

Phil 5760.3   Kurt, N. Die Willensprobleme. Weimar, 1902.

Phil 8886.17   Ladd, G.T. Philosophy of conduct. N.Y., 1902.

Phil 5761.4.2   Lapie, P. Logique de la volonté. Paris, 1902.

Phil 8870.9   Larned, J.N. A primer of right and wrong. Boston, 1902.

Phil 3640.216.10   Lasserre, Pierre. Les morale de Nietzsche. Paris, 1902.

Phil 3210.28   Lasswitz, K. Gustav Theodor Fechner. Stuttgart, 1902.

Phil 525.47   Latta, R. The old mysticism and the new pluralism. Glasgow, 1902.

Phil 8886.40   Laudatio, Giorgio. La giustizia e la morale. Trani, 1902.

1902 - cont.

Phil 1811.1   Laurie, H. Scottish philosophy. Glasgow, 1902.

Phil 978.8.9   Leadbeater, C.W. Outline of theosophy. London, 1902.

Phil 8412.7   Lechalas, G. Études esthétiques. Paris, 1902.

Phil 5761.3.2   Leland, C.G. Have you a strong will? London, 1902.

Phil 3246.92   Léon, Xavier. La philosophie de Fichte, ses rapports avec la conscience contemporaine. Paris, 1902.

Phil 3525.83   Leonhardi, Hermann. Karl C.F. Krause's Leben und Lehre. Leipzig, 1902.

Phil 3831.8   Leopold, J.H. Ad Spinozae opera posthuma. Hagae, 1902.

Phil 2490.88.10   Lévy-Bruhl, L. Die Philosophie August Comte's. Leipzig, 1902.

Phil 2138.90   Lewels, Max. John Stuart Mill. Münster, 1902.

Phil 6420.10   Lewis, George Andrew. The practical treatment of stammering and stuttering. Detroit, 1902.

Phil 3915.40.2.2   Lindan, Hans. Namenverzeichniss und Sachregister zu Wundt's Logik. 2. Aufl. Stuttgart, 1902.

Phil 5374.10   Lipps, Theodor. Einheiten und Relationen. Leipzig, 1902.

Phil 5761.12   Lipps, Theodor. Vom Fühlen, Wollen und Denken. Leipzig, 1902.

Phil 8412.10.5   Lipps, Theodor. Von der Form des ästhetischen Apperception. Halle, 1902.

Phil 7140.6   Loryea, J.H. Is man a free agent? London, 1902.

Phil 4710.5   Lourié, Osip. La philosophie russe contemporaine. Paris, 1902.

Phil 8887.38.5   Mabie, H.W. Works and days. N.Y., 1902.

Phil 8637.6.5   McConnell, S.D. The evolution of immortality. N.Y., 1902.

Phil 187.27   Mackenzie, J.S. Outlines of metaphysics. London, 1902.

Phil 9035.26   Malapert, P. Le caractère. Paris, 1902.

Phil 8610.902.36   Mangasarian, M.M. A new catechism. 2. ed. Chicago, 1902.

Phil 978.17   Man's place in the universe. London, 1902.

Phil 3494.19.30   Marcus, Ernst. Kants Revolutionsprinzip (Kopernikanisches Prinzip). Herford, 1902.

Phil 187.114   Masaryk, T.G. Die Ideale der Humanität. Wien, 1902.

Phil 187.51   Maudsley, Henry. Life in mind and conduct. London, 1902.

Phil 343.5   Meinong, A. Über Annahmen. Leipzig, 1902.

Phil 6962.10.5   Mendel, Emanuel. Leitfaden der Psychiatrie. Stuttgart, 1902.

Phil 6962.4.4   Mercier, C.A. A text-book of insanity. London, 1902.

Phil 187.25   Mercier, D. Cours de philosophie. 3e éd. v.1. Louvain, 1902.

Phil 187.25.2   Mercier, D. Cours de philosophie. 3e éd. v.2. Louvain, 1902.

Phil 9075.37   Merrington, E.N. The possibility of a science of casuistry. Sydney, 1902.

Phil 2490.97   Milhaud, Gaston. Le positivisme et le progrès de l'esprit. Paris, 1902.

Phil 5374.56   Minot, C.S. The problem of consciousness in its biological aspects. N.Y., 1902.

Phil 8610.902.25   Mortimer, G. The new morality. London, 1902.

Phil 5762.2   Müffelmann, L. Das Problem der Willensfreiheit. London, 1902.

Phil 400.18   Muff, Christian. Idealismus. 3e Aufl. Halle, 1902.

Phil 8887.25.9   Muirhead, J.H. Philosophy and life. London, 1902.

Phil 4210.81.8   Nardi, P. de. Rosmini e Kant. Forli, 1902.

Phil 3195.1.80   Neubert-Drobisch, W. Moritz Wilhelm Drobisch. Leipzig, 1902.

Phil 3640.76A   Nietzsche, Friedrich. Briefe. v.1-5. 3rd ed. Berlin, 1902. 6v.

Phil 295.09   Ostwald, W. Vorlesungen über Naturphilosophie. Leipzig, 1902.

Phil 295.1   Ostwald, W. Vorlesungen über Naturphilosophie. 2. Aufl. Leipzig, 1902.

Phil 6051.7   Oxenford, I. The complete palmist. Chicago, 1902.

Phil 3497.12   Palágyi, Melchiar. Kant und Bolzano. Halle, 1902.

Phil 5055.11   Palágyi, Melchior. Der streit der Psychologisten. Leipzig, 1902.

Phil 8890.23.9   Palmer, G.H. Field of ethics. Boston, 1902.

Phil 6125.17   Patterson, C.B. Dominion and power. 2d ed. N.Y., 1902.

Phil 575.9   Paulham, F. Les caractères. Paris, 1902.

Phil 5255.2.12   Paulhan, F. Analystes et esprits synthétiques. Paris, 1902.

Phil 5066.12   Peano, G. Aritmetica generale e algebra elementare. Torino, 1902.

Phil 8670.10   Pereira de Sampaio, José. A idéa de Deus. Porto, 1902.

Phil 365.16   Petavel-Olliff, E. Le plan de l'évolution. Lausanne, 1902.

Phil 3640.181   Petrone, Igino. F. Nietzsche e L. Tolstoi. Napoli, 1902.

Phil 3552.300   Pflugbell, R. Der Begriff der ewigen Wahrheiten bei Leibniz. Inaug. Diss. Leipzig, 1902.

Phil 3450.8.80   Philosophische Abhandlungen dem Andenken Rudolf Haymns. Halle, 1902.

Phil 900.7   Pizzi, Italo. Pessimismo orientale. Bari, 1902.

Phil 7069.02.11   Podmore, Frank. Modern spiritualism. London, 1902. 2v.

Phil 9045.4   Potte, Henry Codman. Citizen in relation in his relationship to the industrial situation. N.Y., 1902.

Phil 9530.28   Practical wisdom! letters. N.Y., 1902.

Phil 8416.22   Pudor, H. Laokoon; kunstheoretische Essays. Leipzig, 1902.

Phil 6965.11   Putnam, J.J. Studies in neurological diagnosis. Boston, 1902.

Phil 348.6   Ratzenhofer, Gustav. Die Kritik des Intellects. Leipzig, 1902.

Phil 9150.7   Read, M.S. English evolutionary ethics. N.Y., 1902.

Phil 5257.3.5   Rehmke, J. Die Seele des Menschen. Leipzig, 1902.

Phil 9035.15   Ribery, C. Essai de classification naturelle des caracteres. Paris, 1902.

Phil 8587.26.80   Rolffs, Ernst. Harnack's Wesen des Christentums und die religiösen Strömmungen der Gegenwart. Leipzig, 1902.

Phil 3499.6   Romundt, H. Kants philosophische Religionslehre. Gotha, 1902.

Phil 8418.25   Rouart, Eugène. L'artiste et la société. Paris, 1902.

Phil 8672.6.6   Royce, The conception of God. N.Y., 1902.

Phil 8598.24.7   Sabatier, Auguste. Outlines of a philosophy of religion. N.Y., 1902.

Phil 3640.122   Sánchez Torres, E. Nietzsche, Emerson, Tolstoy. Barcelona, 1902.

Phil 7069.02.20   Savage, Minot J. Can telepathy explain? N.Y., 1902.

Phil 510.1.9   Scarrett, W.R. The riddle of the universe; a review. n.p., 1902.

Phil 3800.386.2   Schelling, F.W.J. von. Münchener Vorlesungen. Leipzig, 1902.

Phil 3640.224   Schian, Martin. Friedrich Nietzsche und das Christentum drei Vorträge. Görlitz, 1902.

Phil 5520.38   Schmieder, A. Anregungen zur psychologischen Betrachtung der Sprache. Langensalza, 1902.

Chronological Listing

Phil 3565.86   Schoen, H. La métaphysique de Hermann Lotze. Paris, 1902.

Phil 960.10.5   Schrader, F.O. Über den Stand der indischen Philosophie zur Zeit Mahávíras und Buddhas. Inaug. Diss. Strassburg, 1902.

Phil 5258.50   Schuchter, Josef. Kurzgefaszte empirische Psychologie. Wien, 1902.

Phil 5258.78   Schultz, J. Briefe über genetische Psychologie. Berlin, 1902.

Phil 5058.32   Schultze, Fritz. Grundlinien der Logik in schematischer Darstellung. Leipzig, 1902.

Htn   Phil 9245.15   Schwarz, H. Glück und Sittlichkeit. Halle, 1902.

Htn   Phil 7069.02.30*   Searching the truth. N.Y., 1902.

VPhil 1153.20   Sebestyén, Károly. A einikusok. Budapest, 1902.

Phil 8708.11   Sedgwick, William. Man's position in the universe. London, 1902.

Phil 6128.41   Segno, A.V. The law of mentalism. 26th ed. Los Angeles, 1902.

Phil 400.47   Seidenberger, J.B. Grundlinien idealer Weltanschauung. Braunschweig, 1902.

Phil 193.23.7   Seth Pringle-Pattison, A. Man's place in the cosmos. 2d ed. Edinburgh, 1902.

Phil 5643.28   Seyfert, R. Über die Auffassung einfachster Raumformen. Leipzig, 1902.

Phil 193.47   Sidgwick, H. Philosophy, its scope and relations. Photoreproduction. London, 1902.

Phil 8843.1.5   Sidgwick, Henry. Lectures on the ethics of T.H. Green. London, 1902.

Phil 6968.12   Sidis, Boris. Psychopathological researches. N.Y., 1902.

Phil 5545.34   Siehl, A. Zum Studium der Merkfähigkeit. Berlin, 1902.

Phil 3552.238   Silberstein, Adela. Leibniz' Apriorismus. Weimar, 1902.

NEDL   Phil 2520.119A   Smith, N.K. Studies in the Cartesian philosophy. N.Y., 1902.

Phil 8708.8   Smyth, Newman. Through science to faith. N.Y., 1902.

Phil 3640.711   Solov'ev, Evgenii A. Nitsshe. Sankt Peterburg, 1902.

Phil 8673.8   Specker, Gideon. Versuch eines neuen Gottesbegriffs. Stuttgart, 1902.

Phil 2270.41   Spencer, Herbert. Facts and comments. N.Y., 1902.

Phil 2270.41.5   Spencer, Herbert. Facts and comments. N.Y., 1902.

Phil 2270.41.6   Spencer, Herbert. Facts and comments. N.Y., 1902.

Phil 5258.30.3   Spiller, G. The mind of man. "Ethical series." London, 1902.

Phil 7054.128.5   Lo spiritismo e la scienza di Ateo e Trinacrio. Trecastagne, 1902.

Phil 1818.2.7.5   Stephen, Leslie. History of English thought in the eighteenth century. v.2. 3rd ed. N.Y., 1902.

Phil 1818.2.3   Stephen, Leslie. History of English thought in XVIIIth century. 3rd ed. London, 1902.

Phil 5850.347.5   Stern, Louis W. Zur Psychologie der Aussage. Berlin, 1902.

Phil 5258.27.15   Stout, G.F. Analytic psychology. London, 1902. 2v.

Phil 400.13   Sturt, H. Personal idealism; philosophical essays of members of Oxford University. London, 1902.

Phil 5525.4   Sully, J. An essay on laughter. London, 1902.

Phil 5520.9.2   Sutro, Emil. Das Doppelwesen der Menschlichen Stimme. Berlin, 1902.

Phil 1504.3.6   Switalski, B.W. Des Chalcidius Kommentar zu Platos Timaeus. v.3, pt.6. Münster, 1902.

Phil 8420.11   Tafts, James. On the genesis of the aesthetic categories. Chicago, 1902.

Phil 17.1.5   The Hibbert journal. Index. v.1-10. Boston, 1902-1911.

Phil 978.16   Tingley, K.A. (Mrs.) The mysteries of the heart doctrine. Point Loma, Calif., 1902.

Phil 4112.85   Tranfo, C.T. Saggio sulla filosofia del Galluppi. Napoli, 1902.

Phil 8894.20.10   Trojano, Paolo R. La filosofia morale. Torino, 1902.

Phil 8709.8   Tuttle, Hudson. Religion of man and ethics of science. Chicago, 1902.

Phil 820.1.4   Ueberweg, F. Grundriss der Geschichte der Philosophie. v.1-2,4. 9. Aufl. Berlin, 1902. 3v.

Phil 3640.244   Vaihinger, Hans. Nietzsche als Philosoph. Berlin, 1902.

Phil 4650.1.51   Vannérus, Allen. Filosofiska konturer. Göteborg, 1902.

Phil 4650.1.31   Vannérus, Allen. Till kritiken af den religiösa kunskapen. Stockholm, 1902.

Phil 5061.2   Varona, E.J. Nociones de lógica. Habana, 1902.

Phil 7082.148   Vaschide, Nicolas. La psychologie du rêve au point de une médical. Paris, 1902.

Phil 4769.1.135   Velichko, Vasilii L. Vladimir Solov'ev. Sankt Peterburg, 1902.

Phil 61.1   Vienna. Universität. Philosophische Gesellschaft. WissenschaftlicheBeilage. Leipzig, 1902-1915. 2v.

Phil 5261.3.12   Villa, G. Enleitung in die Psychologie der Gegenwart. Leipzig, 1902.

Phil 5722.38.1   Waldstein, Louis. The subconscious self and its relation to education and health. N.Y., 1902.

Phil 3504.1.10   Wallace, William. Kant. Edinburgh, 1902.

Phil 9035.12   Washington, B.S. Character building. N.Y., 1902.

Phil 8897.27   Watson, John. The homely virtues. N.Y., 1902.

Phil 8897.30   Wentscher, M. Ethik. Leipzig, 1902.

Phil 5640.10   Williams, C.H. Vision: color, sense and hearing. Chicago, 1902.

Phil 5262.17.2   Witmer, L. Analytical psychology. Boston, 1902.

Phil 497.9.2   Wollny, F. Der Materialismus im Verhältnis zu Religion und Moral. 2e Aufl. Leipzig, 1902.

Phil 8647.6   Woodruff, J.L.M. The king's garden. N.Y., 1902.

Phil 5585.14   Wrinch, F.S. Über das Verhältniss der Ebenmerk...Gebiet des Zeitsinns. Leipzig, 1902.

Phil 3915.35   Wundt, Wilhelm. Einleitung in die Philosophie. Leipzig, 1902.

Phil 3915.45.5   Wundt, Wilhelm. Grundzüge der physiologischen Psychologie. 5. Aufl. Leipzig, 1902. 3v.

Phil 3915.47.2   Wundt, Wilhelm. Outlines of psychology. Leipzig, 1902.

Phil 3915.38   Wundt, Wilhelm. Philosophie und Psychologie. Leipzig, 1902.

Phil 5643.31   Zehender, W. Über optische Täuschung. Leipzig, 1902.

Phil 5235.1   Ziehen, T. Über die Beziehungen zwischen Gehirn und Seelenleben. Leipzig, 1902.

Phil 6135.3   Ziehen, Theodore. Über die allgemeinen Beziehungen. Leipzig, 1902.

Phil 3450.6.80   Zimmer, Friedrich. Grundriss der Philosophie nach Friedrich Harms. Tübingen, 1902.

Phil 8900.2   Zini, Zino. Il pentimento e la morale ascentica. Torino, 1902.

Phil 800.3   Adams, C. Études sur les principaux philosophes. Paris, 1903.

Phil 1700.1   Adamson, R. The development of modern philosophy. Photoreproduction. Edinburgh, 1903 2v.

Phil 3549.15.80   Adickes, Erich. Vier Schriften des Herrn Professor Kappes. Pt.1-2. Berlin, 1903.

Phil 3640.85   Albert, H. Frederic Nietzsche. Paris, 1903.

Phil 8875.9   Albertson, Ralph. Little Jeremiads. Lewiston, 1903.

Phil 281.3   Alexejeff, W.G. Mathematik als Grundlage der Weltanschauung. Jurjew, 1903.

Phil 5240.6.15   Angell, J.R. The relations of structural and functional psychology to philosophy. Chicago, 1903.

Phil 5115.5   Ashley, M.L. The nature of hypothesis. Chicago, 1903.

Phil 8626.1.10   Baguenault de Puchesse, F. A immortalidade, a morte e a vida. Porto, 1903.

Phil 1855.30   Bain, Alexander. Dissertaions on leading philosophical topics. London, 1903.

Phil 5645.10   Baker, Emma S. Experiments on tne aesthetics of light and colour. Toronto, 1903.

Phil 6111.51   Barker, L.F. A description of the brains...of two brothers dead of hereditary ataxia. Chicago, 1903.

Phil 1200.10   Barth, P. Die Stoa. Stuttgart, 1903.

Phil 801.16   Baumann, J. Gesamtgeschichte der Philosophie. 2. Aufl. Gotha, 1903.

Phil 1701.10   Baumann, Julius. Deutsche und ausserdeutsche Philosophie. Gotha, 1903.

Phil 3625.3.91   Beer, Theodor. Die Weltanschauung eines modernen Naturforschers. Dresden, 1903.

Phil 6671.17   Belfiore, Giulio. Magnetismo e ipnotismo. 2. ed. Milano, 1903.

Phil 8876.97   Bell, F.O. The minor moralist. London, 1903.

Phil 400.17   Bergmann, J. System des objectiven Idealismus. Marburg, 1903.

Phil 978.6.30   Besant, Annie. Birth and evolution of the soul. 2nd ed. London, 1903.

Phil 7080.16   Bigelow, John. The mystery of sleep. N.Y., 1903.

Phil 5465.9   Biuso, C. La fantasia. Catania, 1903.

Phil 3640.196   Bjerre, Poul. Det geniala vansinnet. Göteborg, 1903.

Phil 978.5.18   Blavatsky, H.P. The voice of the silence. 6th ed. London, 1903.

Phil 8612.20   Block, Oscar. Om døden; en almenfattelig fremstilling. København, 1903. 2v.

Phil 5627.7.5   Bois, Henri. Sentiment religieux et sentiment moral. Paris, 1903.

Phil 8581.49   Bolliger, A. Drei ewige Lichter. Berlin, 1903.

Phil 5751.5   Bolliger, Adolf. Die Willensfreiheit. Berlin, 1903.

Phil 3808.181   Bonanno, S. La "Volanta" in Arturo Schopenhauer. Torino, 1903.

Phil 4372.1.85   Bonilla y San Martin, D.A. Luis Vives y la filosofía del renacimiento. Madrid, 1903.

Phil 4515.31   Boström, C.J. Grundlinier till philosophiska civil- och criminalrätten. Stockholm, 1903.

Phil 2805.92.3   Boutroux, E. Pascal. 3. éd. Paris, 1903.

Phil 8581.21   Bowker, R.R. Of religion. Boston, 1903.

Phil 8581.24.25   Brierley, J. Vi och världsalltet. Stockholm, 1903.

Phil 8951.12   Broglie, L'abbé de. La morale sans Dieu. Paris, 1903.

Phil 5241.63   Brough, J. The study of mental science. London, 1903.

Phil 5241.44.5   Bunge, Carlos O. Principes de psychologie. Paris, 1903.

Phil 6111.13   Busse, L. Geist und Körper, Seele und Leib. Leipzig, 1903.

Phil 400.26   Caird, E. Idealism and theory of knowledge. London, 1903.

Phil 3822.2.5   Camerer, T. Spinoza und Schleiermacher. Stuttgart, 1903.

Phil 177.8.5   Carus, Paul. The surd of metaphysics. Chicago, 1903.

Phil 8877.49   Castellotti, G. de. Saggi di etica e di diritto. Ser. 1-2,3-5. Ascoli Piceno, 1903-06. 2v.

Phil 4369.2.80   Cazac, H.P. Le lieu d'origine, du philosophe Francisco Sanchez. Bordeaux, 1903.

Phil 6053.8   Cerchiari, G. Luigi. Chiromanzia e tatuaggio. Milano, 1903.

Phil 177.46.5   Cesca, Giovanni. La filosofia della vita. Messina, 1903.

Phil 9035.38   Churchill, L.A. The magnet. N.Y., 1903.

Phil 5325.23   Claparède, Édouard. L'association des idées. Paris, 1903.

Phil 9035.35   Colville, N.J. Fate mastered, destiny fulfilled. London, 1903.

Phil 2490.71   Comte, Auguste. Correspondance inédite. Paris, 1903-04. 4v.

Phil 177.29   Cornelius, H. Einleitung in die Philosophie. Leipzig, 1903.

Phil 3552.253   Cresson, André. De liberate apud Leibnitium. Thesis. Paris, 1903.

Phil 8877.29   Cresson, Andre. La morale de la raison theorique. Paris, 1903.

Phil 2050.101.5   Daiches, Sally. Über das Verhältnis der Geschichtsschreibung David Hume's zu seiner praktischen Philosophie. Leipzig, 1903.

Phil 178.54   Dandolo, G. Appunti di filosofia. v.1-3. Messina, 1903-1909.

Phil 5545.69.5   Dandolo, Giovanni. La memoria. Messina, 1903.

Phil 9450.12   Deschamps, Louis. Principes de morale sociale. Paris, 1903.

Phil 178.17   Dessoir, Max. Philosophisches Lesebuch. Stuttgart, 1903.

Phil 3485.1.5   Deussen, Paul. Der kategorische Imperativ. 2. Aufl. Kiel, 1903.

Phil 5043.16A   Dewey, John. Studies in logical theory. Chicago, 1903.

Phil 8878.11.13   Dewey, John. Logical conditions of a scientific treatment of morality. Chicago, 1903.

Phil 1703.1   Dewing, Arthur Stone. Introduction to History of modern philosophy. Philadelphia, 1903.

Phil 7060.66   Diederich, Benno. Von Gespenstergeschichten. Leipzig, 1903.

Phil 3640.386   Diefke, Max. Was Muss man von Nietzsche Wissen? Berlin, 1903.

Phil 3195.3.31   Dietzgen, Joseph. Das Acquisit der Philosophie und Briefe. Stuttgart, 1903.

Phil 3195.3.6   Dietzgen, Joseph. Josef Dietzgens kleinere Philosophie. Stuttgart, 1903.

Phil 178.36   Dilles, Ludwig. Wieg zur Metaphysik als exakten Wissenschaft. Stuttgart, 1903-06. 2v.

Phil 5520.12   Dittrich, O. Grundzüge der Sprachpsychologie. Halle, 1903.

Phil 1108.1   Döring, A. Geschichte der griechischen Philosophie. Leipzig, 1903. 2v.

Phil 8583.11.5   Dorner, A. Grundprobleme der Religionsphilosophie. Berlin, 1903.

Phil 8583.11   Dorner, A. Grundriss der Religionsphilosophie. Leipzig, 1903.

1903 - cont.

Phil 178.34 — Dreher, Eugen. Philosophische Abhandlungen. Berlin, 1903.

Phil 178.12.25 — Dresser, H.W. Man and the divine order. N.Y., 1903.

Phil 3195.9.77 — Dühring, E. Sache, Leben, und Feinde. 2. Aufl. Leipzig, 1903.

Phil 3823.3 — Duff, R.A. Spinoza's political and ethical philosophy. Glasgow, 1903.

Phil 5465.10 — Dugas, L. L'imagination. Paris, 1903.

Phil 8878.22 — Duprat, G.L. Morals: a treatise on the psycho-sociological bases of ethics. London, 1903.

Phil 3200.16.30 — Ebner, Felix. Moe obrashchenie. 2. izd. Moskva, 1903.

Phil 8584.8 — Edfeldt, Hans. Filosofisk religionslära. Uppsala, 1903.

Phil 5244.12.3 — Eisler, Rudolf. Psychologie im Umriss. 3e Aufl. Leipzig, 1903.

Phil 4655.1.81 — Eklund, J.A. Pontus Wikner. Stockholm, 1903.

Phil 1504.4.4 — Engelkemper, W. Die religions-philosophische Lehre. v.4., pt.4. Münster, 1903.

Phil 3235.81.5 — Engels, Friedrich. Ludwig Feuerbach. Chicago, 1903.

Phil 179.3.13 — Eucken, R. Gesammelte Aufsätze zur Philosophie. Leipzig, 1903.

Phil 3640.84 — Ewald, Oscar. Nietzsches Lehre. Berlin, 1903.

Phil 3903.1.91 — Ferro, A.A. La teoria della conoscenza in G. Volkelt. Aosta, 1903.

Phil 3235.15 — Feuerbach, Ludwig. Ludwig Feuerbachs sämmtliche Werke. Stuttgart, 1903-11. 10v.

Phil 3235.45 — Feuerbach, Ludwig. Das Wesen des Christenthums. Stuttgart, 1903.

Phil 6115.18.10 — Fletcher, Horace. The new menticulture. N.Y., 1903.

Phil 8610.903 — Flint, Robert. Agnosticism. Edinburgh, 1903.

Phil 8406.10 — Fontaine, André. Essai sur le principe et les lois de la critique d'art. Paris, 1903.

Phil 8695.4 — Froehlich, J. Das Gesetz von der Erhaltung der Kraft und der Geist des Christentums. Leipzig, 1903.

Phil 705.3.5 — Frothingham, Octavius Brooks. Transcendentalism in New England. Boston, 1903.

Phil 337.3 — Gaillard, Gaston. De l'étude des phénomènes du point de vue de leur probleme particular. Paris, 1903.

Phil 5400.22 — Gent, W. Volumpulscurven bei Gefühlen und Affecten. Leipzig, 1903.

Phil 4006.2.7 — Gentile, G. Dal Genovesi al Galuppi. Napoli, 1903.

Phil 4369.2.84 — Giarratano, C. Il pensiero di Francesco Sanchez. Napoli, 1903.

Phil 8631.4 — Gilbert, L. Side-lights on immortality. London, 1903.

Phil 8586.18 — Girgensohn, Karl. Die religion. Leipzig, 1903.

Phil 6316.1 — Gley, E. Etudes de psychologie. Paris, 1903.

Phil 2050.181 — Goldstein, J. Die empiristische Geschichtsauffassung Humes. Leipzig, 1903.

Phil 1735.6 — Gómez Izquierdo, Alberto. Historia de la filosofía del siglo XIX. Zaragoza, 1903.

Phil 1111.1.5 — Gomperz, T. Griechische Denker. Leipzig, 1903-09. 3v.

Phil 8881.33 — Gorodenskii, N. Nravstvennoe soznanie cheloviechestva. Sergiev, 1903.

Phil 5643.52A — Gould, George M. Biographic clinics. Philadelphia, 1903-05. 6v.

Phil 3260.81 — Grape, Johannes. Die Prinzipien der Ethik bei Fries. Dessau, 1903.

Phil 3552.111.9 — Grassi-Bertazzi, G. L'inconscio nella filosofia di Leibnitz. Catania, 1903.

Phil 510.1.10 — Haeckel, Ernst. Les énigmes de l'univers. Paris, 1903.

Phil 510.1.3 — Haeckel, Ernst. Die Welträthsel. Bonn, 1903.

Phil 510.1.3.5 — Haeckel, Ernst. Die Welträthsel. Stuttgart, 1903.

Phil 8882.35 — Hansen, Søren. Etikens begrundelse. København, 1903.

Phil 8587.26.3 — Harnack, Adolf. Das Wesen des Christentums. Leipzig, 1903.

Phil 8587.26.16 — Harnack, Adolf. What is Christianity? 2d ed. N.Y., 1903.

Phil 7106.6 — Harte, Richard. Hypnotism and the doctors. London, 1903.

Phil 3489.7 — Hauck, P. Urteile und Kategorien; eine Studie zu Kants Logik. Strassburg, 1903.

Phil 8610.903.10 — Hawley, J.S. Tradition versus truth. N.Y., 1903.

Phil 182.34 — Hayward, J.K. A rebuttal of spiritism. N.Y., 1903.

Phil 8832.1 — Hentsch, Alice Adele. De la littérature didactique du Moyen Age. Photoreproduction. Halle, 1903.

Phil 5425.31 — Herrlin, Axel. Snille och själssjukdom. Lund, 1903.

Phil 8882.12.5 — Hilty, K. Happiness. N.Y., 1903.

Phil 5409.5 — Hitchcock, C.M. The psychology of expectation. N.Y., 1903.

Phil 2045.25 — Hobbes, Thomas. Philosophy of Hobbes in extracts and notes from his philosophy. Minneapolis, 1903.

Phil 630.3 — Hodge, W.H. Intuitive perception, presented by a new philosophy of natural realism. Lancaster, 1903.

Phil 182.36 — Höffding, H. Philosophische Probleme. Leipzig, 1903.

Phil 4580.62 — Höffding, Harald. Morale essai sur les principes théoriques. Paris, 1903.

Phil 179.3.105 — Höhlmann, Hans. Rudolf Euckens Theologie. Berlin, 1903.

Phil 3625.3.83 — Hönigswald, R. Zur Kritik der Machschen Philosophie. Berlin, 1903.

Phil 1145.10 — Holstein, R. Bedeutung des 7 Jahrhunderts. Stettin, 1903.

Phil 5635.20 — Holt, Edwin B. An experimental study of sensation. Cambridge, Mass., 1903.

Phil 3640.121.15 — Horneffer, Ernst. Vorträge über Nietzsche. Berlin, 1903.

Phil 6117.12 — Hudson, T.J. The law of mental medicine. Chicago, 1903.

Phil 8685.20 — Hugenholtz, P.H. Ethisch pantheisme. Amsterdam, 1903.

Phil 2050.37.5 — Hume, David. Essays: moral, political and literary. London, 1903.

Phil 6118.1 — Ingalese, R. The history and power of mind. N.Y., 1903.

Phil 183.2 — Ingraham, A. Swain school lectures. Chicago, 1903. 2v.

Phil 8883.2 — Irons, D. Study in psychology of ethics. Edinburgh, 1903.

Phil 6959.5 — Jahrmärker, M. Zur Frage der Dementia Praecox. Halle, 1903.

NEDL Phil 5627.6.5 — James, William. Varieties of religious experience. N.Y., 1903.

Phil 6959.1.9A — Janet, Pierre. Les obsessions et la psychasthénie. Paris, 1903. 2v.

Phil 184.12.2 — Jerusalem, W. Einleitung in die Philosophie. Wien, 1903.

Phil 5249.5.5 — Jodl, Friedrich. Lehrbuch der Psychologie. 2. Aufl. v.1-2. Stuttgart, 1903.

Phil 8615.8.15 — Jodl, Friedrich. Über das Wesen und die Aufgabe der ethischen Gesellschaft. 2. Aufl. Wien, 1903.

Phil 1135.62 — Joël, Kar. Der Ursprung der Naturphilosophie aus dem Geiste der Mystik. Basel, 1903.

Phil 5415.5 — Jones, J.W.L. Sociality and sympathy. N.Y., 1903.

Phil 400.16 — Kassner, R. Der indische Idealismus. München, 1903.

Phil 9410.2 — Keller, Helen. Optimism. N.Y., 1903.

Phil 2100.3.30 — Kemble, Duston. The higher realism. Cincinnati, 1903.

Phil 8590.24A — Keppler, P.W. von. Wahre und falsche Reform. Freiburg, 1903.

Phil 3492.23 — Kessler, A. Kants ansicht von der Grundlage der Empfindung. Darmstadt, 1903.

Phil 8886.8.10 — Key, Ellen. Moralens utveckling: fri bearbetning efter Letourneau. Stockholm, 1903.

Phil 3428.153 — Kinkel, Walter. J.F. Herbart, sein Leben und seine Philosophie. Giessen, 1903.

Phil 8635.6 — Kneib, P. Die Beweise für die Unsterblichkeit der Seele. Freiburg, 1903.

Phil 5643.27 — Kohler, J. Der simultane Farben- und Helligkeitskontrast. Leipzig, 1903.

Phil 5643.29 — König, Arthur. Gesammelte Abhandlungen der physiologischen Optik. Leipzig, 1903.

Phil 8885.18.20 — Köroman, Kristian. Begrebet "det etiske". København, 1903.

Phil 3525.86.5 — Krause, K.C.F. Dei Briefwechsel Karl Christian Friedrich Krauses. Leipzig, 1903.

Phil 8885.24 — Kutna, G. Egoismus und Altruismus als Grundlage des Sittlichen. Berlin, 1903.

Phil 8886.19 — Lagerborg, R. La morale publique. Paris, 1903.

Phil 5520.21.15 — Landauer, Gustav. Skepsis und Mystik. Berlin, 1903.

Phil 4515.94 — Landström, Gustaf. Om tänkaren Kristofer Jakob Boström och hans filosofi. Stockholm, 1903.

Phil 8412.8 — Laurila, K.S. Versuch einer Stellungnahme zu den Hauptfragen der Kunstphilosophie. Helsingfors, 1903.

Phil 6681.14 — Leadbeater, C.W. Clairvoyance. 2d ed. London, 1903.

Phil 978.8.15 — Leadbeater, C.W. Man visible and invisible. N.Y., 1903.

Phil 978.8.10 — Leadbeater, C.W. Outline of theosophy. 2d ed. Chicago, 1903.

Phil 978.8.35 — Leadbeater, C.W. Reincarnation; a lecture. Harrogate, 1903.

Phil 8836.2.15 — Lecky, W.E.H. A survey of English ethics. London, 1903.

Phil 3552.19 — Leibniz, Gottfried Wilhelm. Opuscules et fragments inédits. Paris, 1903.

Phil 5761.3.3 — Leland, C.G. Have you a strong will? London, 1903.

Phil 1145.45 — Levi, A. Delitto e pena nel pensiero dei Greci. Torino, 1903.

NEDL Phil 2490.88.5 — Lévy-Bruhl, L. The philosophy of Auguste Comte. N.Y., 1903.

Phil 3210.83 — Liebe, R. Fechner's Metaphysik. Greifswald, 1903.

Phil 3210.83.2 — Liebe, R. Fechner's Metaphysik. Leipzig, 1903.

Phil 5251.8.5 — Lipps, T. Leitfaden der Psychologie. Leipzig, 1903.

Phil 8412.10 — Lipps, Theodor. Asthetik; Psychologie des Schönen und der Kunst. Hamburg, 1903-06. 2v.

Phil 8591.20.5 — Loisy, Alfred. Autour d'un petit livre. Paris, 1903.

Phil 5251.19 — Lubac, Emile. Esquisse d'un système de psychologie rationnelle. Paris, 1903.

Phil 6536.10 — Lundborg, Herman B. Die progressive myoklonus-epilepsie. Upsala, 1903.

Phil 510.1.17 — McCabe, Joseph. Haeckel's critics answered. London, 1903.

Phil 4065.87 — McIntyre, J.S. Giordano Bruno. London, 1903.

Phil 3425.104A — Mackintosh, R. Hegel and Hegelianism. Edinburgh, 1903.

Phil 8702.7.2 — Mallock, W.H. Religion as a credible doctrine. N.Y., 1903.

Phil 2045.93 — Mandolfo, R. Saggi per la storia della morale utilitaria. Verona, 1903-04.

Phil 812.5 — Mannheimer, A. Geschichte der Philosophie in übersichthcher Darstellung. v.1-3. Frankfurt, 1903-08.

Phil 5653.7 — Marchand, L. Le goût. Paris, 1903.

Phil 5762.8 — Marucci, Achille. La volontà. Roma, 1903.

Phil 187.26 — Marvin, W.T. Introduction to systematic philosophy. N.Y., 1903.

Phil 7069.03.35 — Maxwell, J. Les phénomènes psychiques. Paris, 1903.

Phil 5252.71 — Mead, George H. The definition of the psychical. Chicago, 1903.

Phil 187.28.2 — Mechnikov, I.I. Études sur la nature humaine. Paris, 1903.

Phil 187.28 — Mechnikov, I.I. Études sur la nature humaine. 2. ed. Paris, 1903.

Phil 6631.5 — Meige, Henry. Der Tic. Leipzig, 1903.

Phil 187.25.3 — Mercier, D. Cours de philosophie. 6e éd. v.3. Louvain, 1903.

Phil 5585.47 — Messenger, J. Franklin. Perception of number. Thesis. N.Y., 1903.

Phil 665.7.15 — Messer, Max. Die moderne Seele. 3e Aufl. Leipzig, 1903.

Phil 2138.40.10 — Mill, John S. On liberty. London, 1903.

Phil 187.42 — Mondolfo, Rodolfo. Saggi per la storia della morale utilitaria. Verona, 1903. 2 pam.

Phil 343.3 — Montgomery, G.R. The place of values. Bridgeport, 1903.

Phil 2115.6 — Moore, A.W. Existence, meaning, and reality in Locke's essay. Chicago, 1903.

Phil 8702.8 — Moore, W.U. The cosmos and the creeds. London, 1903.

Phil 3805.97 — Munro, R. Schleiermacher, personal and speculative. Paisley, 1903.

Phil 7069.03.10 — Myers, Frederic William Henry. Human personality and its survival of bodily death. N.Y., 1903. 2v.

Phil 188.12 — Natorp, Paul. Philosophische Propädeutik. Marburg, 1903.

Phil 9528.1 — Not in the curriculum. N.Y., 1903.

Phil 400.122 — Novgorodtsev, P.I. Problemy idealizma. Moskva, 1903.

Phil 5545.33 — Ogden, R.M. Untersuchungen über den Einfluss der Geschwindigkeit des lauten Lesens. Leipzig, 1903.

Phil 189.8 — Olzelt-Newin, A. Kleinere philosophische Schriften. Leipzig, 1903.

Phil 3640.85.5 — Orestano, Francesco. Le idee fondamentali de F. Nietzsche. Palermo, 1903.

Phil 2050.101.3A — Orr, James. David Hume and his influence on philosophy and theology. Edinburgh, 1903.

Phil 2050.101 — Orr, James. David Hume and his influence on philosophy and theology. N.Y., 1903.

Phil 5055.11.5 — Palágyi, Melchior. Die Logik auf dem Scheidewege. Berlin, 1903.

Phil 9240.7 — Palmer, G.H. The nature of goodness. Boston, 1903.

Phil 2520.168 — Parenty, Henri. Les tourbillons de Descartes et la science moderne. Paris, 1903.

Phil 8890.32 — Pascot, Giovanni. Scienze ausiliarie della morale. Udine, 1903.

Phil 8890.6.7 — Paulsen, F. System der Ethik. Stuttgart, 1903. 2v.

Phil 5585.13 — Pearce, H.J. Über den Einfluss von Nebenreizen. Leipzig, 1903.

Phil 5545.165 — Pelman, Christopher L. Memory training, its law and their application to practical life. pts.1-5. Chicago, 1903.

Phil 6051.11 — Phanos (pseud.). Elements of hand-reading. London, 1903.

Phil 5465.12 — Philippe, Jean. L'image mentale; évolution et dissolution. Paris, 1903.

Phil 8595.11 — Phillips, S.L. The testimony of reason. Washington, 1903.

Chronological Listing

1903 - cont.

Phil 575.30 Platzhoff-Lejeune, E. Werk und Persönlichkeit. Minden, 1903.
Phil 5115.4 Poincaré, Henri. La science et l'hypothèse. Paris, 1903.
Phil 9450.6 Post, Louis F. Ethics of democracy. N.Y., 1903.
Phil 8596.1 Quetin, M.A. L'origine de la religion. Montauban, 1903.
Phil 192.39 Rée, Paul. Philosophie. Berlin, 1903.
Phil 4630.2.31 Rein, T. Uppsatser och tal. Helsingfors, 1903.
Phil 192.33.5 Reinke, J. Die Welt als Tat. 3e Aufl. Berlin, 1903.
Phil 575.31 Renouvier, Charles. Le personnalisme suivi d'une étude sur la perception extrême. Paris, 1903.
Phil 5767.1.10 Ribot, T. The diseases of the will. 3. ed. Chicago, 1903.
Phil 5400.18.6 Ribot, T. Psychologie der Gefühle. Altenburg, 1903.
Phil 8707.7 Rice, William N. Christian faith in an age of science. N.Y., 1903.
Phil 365.7 Richard, G. L'idée d'evolution. Paris, 1903.
Phil 192.20 Richards, L.S. New propositions in...philosophy. Plymouth, 1903.
Phil 8892.20 Riego, Julio del. Nociones fundamentales de ética ó filosofía moral. Madrid, 1903.
Phil 3791.50 Riehl, Alois. Zur Einführung in der Philosophie des Gegenwart. Leipzig, 1903.
Phil 3640.270.90 Ritteleyer, F. Friedrich Nietzsche und das Erkenntnisproblem. Leipzig, 1903.
Phil 8892.49 Roberts, G.L. The domain of utilitarian ethics. Philadelphia, 1903.
Phil 2520.159 Rodrigues, G. Quid de mundi externi existentia...Cartesius. Thesis. Lutetiae Parisiorum, 1903.
Phil 5257.11A Royce, Josiah. Outlines of psychology. N.Y., 1903.
Phil 6000.3 Rudolph, H. Der Ausdruck der Gemütsbewegungen. Dresden, 1903. 2v.
Phil 3499.5.5 Ruyssen, T. Quid de natura...senserit Kantius. Nemausi, 1903.
Phil 3552.111.15 Rydberg, Viktor. Leibniz' Theodicee. Leipzig, 1903.
Phil 3500.26 Sänger, E.A. Kants Lehre vom Glauben. Leipzig, 1903.
Phil 2270.104 Salvadori, Guglielmo. L'etica evoluzionista...di Herbert Spencer. Torino, 1903.
Phil 8893.46 Salvadori, Guglielmo. Saggio di uno studio sui sentimenti morali. Firenze, 1903.
Phil 5258.44.5 Sarlo, Francesco de. Idati della esperienza psichica. Firenze, 1903.
Phil 930.39.5 Scherbatskii, F.I. Teoriia poznaniia i logika po ucheniu pozdreishikh buddistov. Sankt Peterburg, 1903-09. 2v.
Phil 193.9.5A Schiller, F.C.S. Humanism philosophical essays. London, 1903.
Phil 3805.22 Schleiermacher, Friedrich. Dialektik. Berlin, 1903.
Phil 6128.15.3 Schofield, A.T. The force of mind. N.Y., 1903.
Phil 3808.71 Schopenhauer, Arthur. The basis of morality. London, 1903.
Phil 3808.51.7 Schopenhauer, Arthur. On the fourfold root of the principle of sufficient reason. London, 1903.
Phil 8843.6 Scotti, Giulio. La metafisica nella morale moderna. Milano, 1903.
Phil 8893.33 Séailles, G. Les affirmations de la conscience moderne. Paris, 1903.
Phil 5258.146 Seliger, Josef. Das sociale Verhalten. Bern, 1903.
Phil 8708.44 Semeria, Giovanni. Scienza e fede e il liro preteso conflitto. Roma, 1903.
Phil 960.39.10 Shcherbatskii, F.I. Teoriia poznaniia i logika po ucheniiu pozdneishikh buddistov. Sankt Peterburg, 1903-09. 2v.
Phil 349.15 Siegel, Carl. Zur Psychologie und Theorie der Erkenntnis. Leipzig, 1903.
Phil 4809.796.36 Smetana, Augustin. Úvahy o budoncnosti lidstva. Praha, 1903.
Phil 1123.4 Snider, D.J. Ancient European philosophy...Greek. St. Louis, Mo., 1903.
Phil 5648.3 Sobeski, M. Über Täuschungen des Tastsinns. Breslau, 1903.
Phil 7069.03.25 Sollier, P. Les phénomènes d'autoscopie. Paris, 1903.
tn Phil 3819.73.10F* Spinoza, Benedictus de. Nachbildung der im Jahre 1902 noch Erhaltenen...Briefe. Haag, 1903.
Phil 3625.8.85 Spitzer, David. Darstellung und Kritik der Thierpsychologie Georg Friedrich Meier's. Inaug. Diss. Györ, 1903.
Phil 7069.03.45 Spivey, T.S. Lavius Egyptus. Cincinnati, 1903. 2v.
Cg Phil 193.35.2 Stephen, L. An agnostic's apology. 2d ed. N.Y., 1903.
Phil 193.35.4 Stephen, L. An agnostic's apology and other essays. 2d. ed. London, 1903.
Phil 5850.347 Stern, Louis W. Angewandte Psychologie. n.p., 1903. 2 pam.
Phil 193.67A Stern, Paul. Grundprobleme der Philosophie. Berlin, 1903.
Phil 8893.49 Stern, Wilhelm. Das Wesen des Mitleids. Berlin, 1903.
Phil 2070.91 Stettheimer, E. Die Urteilsfreiheit als Grundlage der Rechtfertigung des religiösen Glaubens. Inaug. Diss. Wittenburg, 1903.
Phil 2070.91.2 Stettheimer, E. Die Urteilsfreiheit als Grundlage der Rechtfertigung des religiösen Glaubens. Inaug. Diss. Wittenburg, 1903.
Phil 5075.1 Stirling, J.H. The categories. Edinburgh, 1903.
Phil 9495.124 Stockham, A.B. (Mrs.). Karezza, ethics of marriage. Chicago, 1903.
Phil 8893.53.5 Störring, Gustav. Moralphilosophische Streitfragen. Leipzig, 1903.
Phil 5258.27.5 Stout, G.F. Groundwork of psychology. N.Y., 1903.
Phil 8598.66 Strakhov, F.A. Voprosy zhizni. Christchurch, Hants, Eng., 1903.
Phil 6128.11.2 Strong, C.A. Why the mind has a body. N.Y., 1903.
Phil 6128.11 Strong, C.A. Why the mind has a body. N.Y., 1903.
Phil 6128.12 Stumpf, C. Leib und Seele. Der Entwicklungs gedanke. Leipzig, 1903.
Phil 8735.3 Sully-Prudhomme, René F.A. Le problème de causes finales. Paris, 1903.
Phil 665.71 Syme, David. The soul. London, 1903.
Phil 9590.10 Symes, (Mrs.). Character reading. Akron, O., 1903.
Phil 3915.145 Szczurat, Vassil. Wundt's Apperzeptionstheorie. Brody, 1903.
Phil 5407.5.2 Tardieu, E. L'ennui; étude psychologique. Paris, 1903.
Phil 194.11* Taylor, A.E. Elements of metaphysics. London, 1903.
Phil 1900.86 Taylor, W.E. Ethical and religious theories of Bishop Butler. Toronto, 1903.
Phil 5259.9 Thompson, H.B. The mental traits of sex. Chicago, 1903.
Phil 819.5.2 Turner, W. History of philosophy. Boston, 1903.
Phil 5060.3 Uphues, G. Zur Krisis in der Logik. Berlin, 1903.
Phil 4650.1.33 Vannérus, Allen. Ateism contra teism. Stockholm, 1903.
Phil 4650.1.35 Vannérus, Allen. Kulturidealism. Stockholm, 1903.
Phil 196.8.12 Varisco, B. Studi di filosofia naturale. Roma, 1903.
Phil 4260.35.20 Vico, G.B. Principi di una scienza nuova. Milano, 1903.

1903 - cont.

Phil 5261.3.5 Villa, G. Contemporary psychology. London, 1903.
Phil 821.1 Vorländer, K. Geschichte der Philosophie. v.1-2. Leipzig, 1903.
Phil 8601.9 Voysey, C. Religion for all mankind. London, 1903.
Phil 9182.4.15 Wagner, Charles. The better way. N.Y., 1903.
Phil 3100.82 Wandschneider, A. Die Metaphysik Benekes. Berlin, 1903.
Phil 5832.7.5 Watson, John B. Animal education; an experimental study on the psychological development of the white rat. Chicago, 1903.
Phil 400.48 Weber, Louis. Vers le positivisme absolu par l'idéalisme. Paris, 1903.
Phil 3905.30 Weininger, Otto. Geschlecht und Charakter. Wien, 1903.
Phil 8647.9 Weir, J.F. Human destiny in the light of revelation. Boston, 1903.
Phil 3504.28 Weis, Ludwig. Kant: Naturgesetze, Natur- und Gotteserkennen. Berlin, 1903.
Phil 5520.23 Welby, Victoria. What is meaning. London, 1903.
Phil 3565.123 Wentscher, E. Das Kausalproblem in Lotzes Philosophie. Halle, 1903.
Phil 5374.15 Wheeler, C.K. The autobiography of the I or ego. Boston, 1903.
Phil 8897.53 Wijnaendts Francken, C.J. Ethische stundien. Haarlem, 1903.
Phil 1504.4 Willner, H. Des Adelard von Bath Traktat. v.4, pt.1. Münster, 1903.
Phil 822.2.3 Windelband, W. Lehrbuch der Geschichte der Philosophie. 3. Aufl. Tübingen, 1903.
Phil 8897.44 Woffny, F. Leitfaden der Moral. 2. Aufl. Leipzig, 1903.
Phil 197.13.15 Wood, H. The new thought simplified. Boston, 1903.
Phil 5649.6 Woodworth, R.S. Le mouvement. Paris, 1903.
Phil 3915.50 Wundt, Wilhelm. Naturwissenschaft und Psychologie. Leipzig, 1903.
Phil 8423.19F Wyneken, Karl. Der Aufbau der form beim natürlichen Werden und kunstlerischen Schoffen. Atlas. Freiburg, 1903-
Phil 8423.19 Wyneken, Karl. Der Aufbau der Form beim naturlichen Werden und kunstlerischen Schoffen. Freiburg, 1903- 2v.

1904

Phil 5040.7.1 Aikins, H.A. The principles of logic. 2nd ed. N.Y., 1904.
Phil 4080.10.88 Alemanni, V. Pietro Ceretti. Milano, 1904.
Phil 5810.1 Allen, J.B. The associative processes of the guinea pig. Granville, Ohio, 1904.
Phil 8875.10 Altgeld, J.P. The cost of something for nothing. Chicago, 1904.
X Cg Phil 7082.50 Andrésson, Friðik. Draumur Friðiks Andréssonar. Reykjavík, 1904. (Changed to XM 1329)
Phil 3482.5 Apel, Max. Immanuel Kant. Berlin, 1904.
Phil 1700.5 Armani, T. Da G. Bruno e da A. Gentile allo Spencer e all' Ardigò. Camerino, 1904.
Phil 175.15 Armstrong, A.C. Transitional eras in thought. N.Y., 1904.
Phil 6110.6 Arnett, L.D. The soul, a study of past and present beliefs. n.p., 1904.
Phil 175.16 Arnold, R.B. Scientific fact and metaphysical reality. London, 1904.
Phil 175.24 Auerbach, Mathias. Einfälle und Betrachtungen. Dresden, 1904.
Phil 8612.11.2 Aurelj, T. La vita e la morte. 2. ed. Roma, 1904.
Phil 1850.35.7A Bacon, Francis. The advancement of learning. Boston, 1904.
NEDL Phil 1855.80 Bain, Alexander. Autobiography. London, 1904.
Phil 8581.23 Ballard, A. From talk to text. N.Y., 1904.
Phil 3483.52 Bárány, Gerö. Kant Immanuel; halálának századik évfordulójára. Kolozsvár, 1904.
Phil 7060.119 Baring-Gould, S. Book of ghosts. London, 1904.
Phil 2045.110 Battelli, G. Le dottrine politiche dell'Hobbes e dello Spinoza. Firenze, 1904.
Phil 3483.8.5 Bauch, Bruno. Luther und Kant. Berlin, 1904.
Phil 575.72 Bazaillas, Albert. La vie personnelle. Paris, 1904.
Phil 3640.190.30 Bélart, Hans. Nietzsches Metaphysik. Berlin, 1904.
Phil 7069.04.10 Bell, Clark. Spiritism, hypnotism and telepathy. 2. ed. N.Y., 1904.
Phil 8876.81 Bellaigue, A. La science morale. Paris, 1904.
Phil 8876.44.5 Belot, G. Études sur philosophie morale au XIXeme siècle. Paris, 1904.
Phil 8876.75 Bergemann, Paul. Ethik als Kulturphilosophie. Leipzig, 1904.
Phil 5241.27 Berger, H. Über die körperlichen Äusserungen psychologischen Zustände. Jena, 1904. 2v.
Phil 1870.40.13 Berkeley, G. A treatise concerning the principles of human knowledge. Chicago, 1904.
Phil 5520.650 Bervi, Vasilii V. Kritika osnovnykh idei estestvoznaniia. Photoreproduction. Sankt-Peterburg, 1904.
Phil 978.6.35 Besant, Annie. Some problems of life. 2nd ed. London, 1904.
Phil 978.6.45 Besant, Annie. Study in consciousness. London, 1904.
Phil 978.6.40 Besant, Annie. Theosophy and new psychology. London, 1904.
Phil 176.115.8 Bierens de Haan, J.D. Wysgeerige studies. 's-Gravenhage, 1904.
Phil 8951.10 Bindi, Enrico. Religione e morale, scritti varii. Firenze, 1904.
Phil 4520.8.46 Bjarnason, Ágúst. Upphaf kristninnar og...Jesús Kristur. Reykjavík, 1904.
Phil 8656.17.5 Blatchford, R. God and my neighbor. London, 1904.
Phil 3260.82 Bliedner, E. Philosophie der Mathematik. Jena, 1904.
X Cg Phil 7075.9.5 Bloch, Iwan. Neue Forschungen über den Marquis de Sade. Berlin, 1904.
Phil 8612.20.5 Block, Oscar. Döden; populär framställning. Stockholm, 1904. 2v.
Phil 3120.11.92 Bolland, G.J.P.J. Zuivere rede. Leiden, 1904.
Phil 5241.24.2A Bosanquet, B. Psychology of the moral self. London, 1904.
Phil 2477.1.07 Boutroux, Émile. Philosophical pamphlets. Paris, 1904-05. 2 pam.
Phil 8876.42 Brent, C.H. The splendor of the human body. N.Y., 1904.
Phil 8581.24.18 Brierley, J. Själslifvet. Stockholm, 1904.
Phil 4065.15 Bruno, Giordano. Gesammelte Werke. Leipzig, 1904-09. 6v.
Phil 8691.11 Buisson, F. La religion, la morale, et la science...quatre conference. 3. éd. Paris, 1904.
Phil 1135.20 Caird, Edward. Volution of theology in Greek philosophers. Glasgow, 1904. 2v.
Phil 600.21 Cantecor, Georges. Le positivisme. Paris, 1904.
Phil 5242.35.10 Carpenter, Edward. The art of creation. London, 1904.
Phil 5242.2.5 Cesca, G. L'attività psichica. Messina, 1904.
Phil 1535.32 Cherubini, F. Cursus philosophicus. Romae, 1904. 2v.

Chronological Listing

Phil 978.22   Corbett, S. Extracts from the Vâhan. London, 1904.
Phil 177.31   Crane, A. The new philosophy. San Francisco, 1904.
Phil 3484.9   Cresson, André. La morale de Kant. Paris, 1904.
Phil 4260.05   Croce, Benedetto. Bibliografia vichiana. Napoli, 1904-10.
Phil 8877.28   Curbipet. Fragments of the elements and principles of the life of man. Bombay, 1904.
Phil 2270.114   Dallari, Gino. Il pensiero filosofico di Herbert Spencer. Torino, 1904.
Phil 6113.3.5   Dexter, E.G. Weather influences. N.Y., 1904.
Phil 178.49   Dressler, Max. Die Welt als Wille zum Selbst. Seidelberg, 1904.
Phil 3640.83   Drews, Arthur. Nietzsches Philosophie. Heidelberg, 1904.
Phil 284.6   Driesch, Hans. Naturbegriffe und natururteile. Leipzig, 1904.
Phil 2050.95   Elkin, W.B. Hume. Ithaca, 1904.
Phil 5425.18   Ellis, H. Study of British genius. London, 1904.
Phil 179.13   Elsenhans, T. Die Aufgabe einer Psychologie der Deutung als Vorarbeit für die Geisteswissenschaften. Giessen, 1904.
Phil 3486.11   Elsenhans, Theodor. Kants Rassentheorie und ihre bleibende Bedeutung. Leipzig, 1904.
Phil 179.6   Engle, J.S. Analytic interest psychology. Baltimore, 1904.
Phil 5545.39   Ephrussi, P. Experimentalle Beiträge...vom Gedächtnis. Leipzig, 1904.
Phil 3486.1.10   Erdmann, B. Historische Untersuchungen über Kants Prolegomena. Halle, 1904.
Phil 179.3.5   Eucken, R. Geistige Strömungen derGegenwart. Leipzig, 1904.
Phil 6954.4   Evensen, Hans. Dementia praecox. Kristiania, 1904.
Phil 3640.82   Faguet, E. En lesant Nietzsche. Paris, 1904.
Phil 5755.11   Fahrion, Karl. Das Problem der Willensfreiheit. Heidelberg, 1904.
Phil 3487.2   Falckenberg, R. Gedächtnisrede auf Kant. Erlangen, 1904.
Phil 665.36   Falke, R. Gibt es eine Seelenwanderung? Halle, 1904.
Phil 8880.19   Farr, Lorin G. Ideal and real; the students calendar. Portland, Maine, 1904.
Phil 5245.29   Felsch. Die Hauptpunkte der Psychologie. Cöthen, 1904.
Phil 8880.1.7   Feltham, O. Resolves. London, 1904.
Phil 3235.77   Feuerbach, Ludwig. Ausgewahlte Briefe von und an L. Feuerbach. v.1-2. Leipzig, 1904.
Phil 8585.19.3   Fielding-Hall, H. The hearts of men. 3rd ed. London, 1904.
Phil 1140.8   Firniani, S. Le idee psicologiche in Grecia nel periodo presofistico e l'esposizione critica di Aristotele. Napoli, 1904.
Phil 6955.13.10   Fleury, M. de. Manuel pour l'étude des maladies du système nerveaux. Paris, 1904.
Phil 180.20   Flint, Robert. Philosophy as scientia scientarum. N.Y., 1904.
Phil 5627.73   Flournoy, T. Le génie religieux. Neuchâtel, 1904.
Phil 9490.6   Forbes, W.C. Letter to an undergraduate. n.p., 1904.
Phil 5045.2.15   Fowler, Thomas. Logic, deductive and inductive. Oxford, 1904-05.
Phil 3825.4   Freudenthal, J. Spinoza, sein Leben und seine Lehre. Stuttgart, 1904.
Phil 3487.17   Freudenthal, Jacob. Immanuel Kant. Breslau, 1904.
Phil 180.35   Freytag, Willy. Uber den Begriff der Philosophie. Halle, 1904.
Phil 1135.23   Friedländer, M. Griechische Philosophie im alten Testament. Berlin, 1904.
Phil 9075.27   Friedmann, J. Die Lehre vom Gewissen in den Systemen des ethischen Idealismus. Budapest, 1904.
Phil 7060.54   Funk, Isaac Kaufmann. The widow's mite and other psychic phenomena. N.Y., 1904.
Phil 8407.17   Gadmann, E. Subjekt und Objekt des ästischen Aktes. Halle, 1904.
Phil 8586.10   Galloway, G. Studies in the philosophy of religion. Edinburgh, 1904.
Phil 3640.167.2   Gaultier, J. de. Nietzsche et la réforme philosophique. 2. éd. Paris, 1904.
Phil 1350.7   Gentile, G. Studi sullo stoicismo romano. Trani, 1904.
Phil 8881.29   Gibson, W.R.B. A philosophical introduction to ethics. London, 1904.
Phil 3428.96.4   Gleichmann, A. Über Herbarts Lehre der Stufen des Unterrichts. 4. Aufl. Langensalza, 1904.
Phil 3805.99   Goebel, Louis. Herder und Schleiermachers Reden. Gotha, 1904.
Phil 5046.18   Goesch, H. Uber die kritische Logik. Berlin, 1904.
Phil 2270.180   Gol'denveizer, A.S. Gerbert Spencer. Idei svoboda i prava. Sankt Peterburg, 1904.
Phil 3488.4.15   Goldschmidt, L. Kant über Freiheit. Gotha, 1904.
Phil 3625.1.113   Goldstein, L. Moses Mendelssohn. Konigsberg, 1904.
Phil 1145.32   Gomperz, H. Die Lebensauffassung der griechischen Philosophen. Jena, 1904.
Phil 8586.19   Grane, Georg. Selbstbwusstsein und Willensfreiheit. Berlin, 1904.
Phil 7069.04.35   Grasset, J. Le spiritisme devant la science. Montpellier, 1904.
Phil 8586.35   Grohmann, W. Lutherische Metaphysik. Leipzig, 1904.
Phil 8586.26   Güttler, C. Wissen und Glauben. 2e Aufl. München, 1904.
Phil 3415.106.9   Haacke, Hermann. Stimmen der Kritik über Eduard von Hartmanns Werke. Leipzig, 1904.
Phil 4582.4.38   Hägerström, Axel. Stat och rätt. Upsala, 1904.
Phil 8697.10   Hand, J.E. Ideals of science and faith. N.Y., 1904.
Phil 5640.35.5   Handbuch der Physiologie des Menschen. v.3-4. Braunschweig, 1904-09. 3v.
Phil 8587.26.13   Harnack, Adolf. What is Christianity? 2. ed. N.Y., 1904.
Phil 3808.106   Hauff, W. Die Überwindung des Schopenhauerschen Pessimismus durch F. Nietzsche. Halle, 1904.
Phil 8610.904   Hedderwick, J.A. Do we believe? London, 1904.
Phil 338.4.5   Heim, Karl. Das Weltbild der Zukunst. Berlin, 1904.
Phil 6615.8   Hellpach, Willy. Grundlinien einer Psychologie der Hysterie. Leipzig, 1904.
Phil 8587.14   Heydenreichs, K.H. Betrachtungen über die Religion. v.1-2. Leipzig, 1904.
Phil 672.15.5   Hinton, Charles H. The fourth dimension. London, 1904.
Phil 5247.10.8   Höffding, H. Outlines of psychology. London, 1904.
Phil 3640.125   Hollitscher, Jakob. Friedrich Nietzsche. Wein, 1904.
Phil 8957.3   Holt, A.E. The function of Christian ethics. Chicago, 1904.
Phil 8587.28   Hoppe, Edmund. Natur und Offenbarung. 2. Aufl. Hannover, 1904.
Phil 9050.3   Hubert, P.G. Liberty and a living. 2nd ed. N.Y., 1904.
Phil 7060.28.10   Hudson, T.J. The evolution of the soul and other essays. Chicago, 1904.

Phil 2050.41   Hume, David. An enquiry...human understanding. Chicago, 1904.
Phil 575.10   Hyde, W. De W. From Epicurus to Christ...study in...personality. N.Y., 1904.
Phil 2490.95.5   Ingram, John K. Practical morals. London, 1904.
Phil 2520.105A   Iverach, James. Descartes, Spinoza...new philosophy. N.Y., 1904.
Phil 2520.105.2   Iverach, James. Descartes, Spinoza and the new philosophy. Edinburgh, 1904.
Phil 5525.7   Jahn, Franz. Das Problem des Komischen. Potsdam, 1904.
Phil 8884.1.6   James, William. Is life worth living? Philadelphia, 1904.
Phil 8884.1.5   James, William. Is life worth living? Philadelphia, 1904.
Phil 5627.6.5.10   James, William. Varieties of religious experience. N.Y., 1904.
Phil 5643.73   Janet, P. La durée des senstaions visuelles élémentaires. Paris, 1904.
Phil 2840.80   Janssens, B. Le néo-criticisme de Charles Renouvier. Louvain, 1904.
Phil 3480.65.8   Kant, Immanuel. Grundlegung zur Metaphysik der Sitten. Leipzig, 1904.
Phil 3480.30.44   Kant, Immanuel. Kritik der reinen Vernunft. Stuttgart, 1904.
Phil 3492.41   Königsberg Universität. Zur Erinnerung an Immanuel Kant. Halle, 1904.
Phil 8885.12   Koppelmann, W. Kritik des sittlichen Bewusstseins vom philosophische und historische Standpunkt. Berlin, 1904.
Phil 8885.18.5   Koröman, Kristian. Ethik. Leipzig, 1904.
Phil 6960.5.7   Kraepelin, E. Clinical psychiatry. N.Y., 1904.
Phil 3525.75   Krause, K.C.F. Lebenlehre. 2. Aufl. Leipzig, 1904.
Phil 1710.3   Krejčí, F. O filosofii přítomnosti. V Praze, 1904.
Phil 8885.18   Kroman, Kristian. Etik I. København, 1904.
Phil 3492.13.2   Kronenberg, M. Kant. 2. Aufl. München, 1904.
Phil 3492.32   Kügelen, C.W. von. Die Bibel bei Kant. Leipzig, 1904.
Phil 8591.27   Laberthonnière, L. Le réalisme chrétien et l'idealisme grec. Paris, 1904.
Phil 3493.10   Lagerwall, A. Transscendentalfilosofiens problem och metod hos Kant. Göteborg, 1904.
Phil 5251.28   Lambek, C. Psyckologiske studier. Supplementhefte til tidsskrift for aandskultur. København, 1904.
Phil 270.17   Lang, Albert. Das Kausalproblem. Köln, 1904.
Phil 6051.15   La Seer, E.J. Illustrated palmistry. N.Y., 1904.
Phil 6990.3.5   Lasserre, H. Our lady of Lourdes. N.Y., 1904.
Phil 978.8.2   Leadbeater, C.W. The christian creed. 2nd ed. London, 1904.
Phil 3552.24   Leibniz, Gottfried Wilhelm. Hauptschriften zur Grundelung der Philosophie. Leipzig, 1904-06. 2v.
Phil 3585.7.90   Leicht, Alfred. Lazarus, der Begründer der Volkerpsychologie. Leipzig, 1904.
Phil 2411.4   Levi, Adolfo. L'indeterminismo nella filosofia francese contemporanea. Firenze, 1904.
Phil 3235.82   Lévy, Albert. La philosophie de Feuerbach. Thèse. Paris, 1904.
Phil 3640.86   Levy, Albert. Stirner et Nietzsche. Paris, 1904.
Phil 8591.25.2   Lévy, L.G. Une religion rationnelle et laïque. 2. éd. Dijon, 1904.
Phil 3625.11.82   Liljequist, E. Meinongs allmänna värdeteori. Göteborg, 1904.
Phil 510.1.27   Loofs, F. Anti-Haeckel. 3rd ed. London, 1904.
Phil 5251.23   Losskii, N.O. Die Grundlehren der Psychologie. Leipzig, 1904.
Phil 8592.22   Mach, Franz. Das religions- und Weltproblem. 2. Aufl. Dresden, 1904. 2v.
Phil 3832.8   Mänoloff, P. Willensfreiheit und Erziehungsmöglichkeit Spinoza. Diss. Bern, 1904.
Phil 6022.1.7.5   Mantegazza, P. Physiognomy and expression. 3rd ed. London, 1904.
Phil 8887.49   Mauxion, Marcel. Essai sur les éléments et l'évolution. Paris, 1904.
Phil 7054.159   Maxwell, Joseph. Un récent procès spirite. Bordeaux, 1904.
Phil 187.28.4   Mechnikov, I.I. Studien über die Natur des Menschen. Leipzig, 1904.
Phil 5585.15   Meinong, A. Untersuchungen zur Gegenstandstheorie und Psychologie. Leipzig, 1904.
Phil 187.25.5   Mercier, D. Curso de philosophia. v.1. Logica. v.3. Psychologia. Vizeu, 1904. 2v.
Phil 1712.2.4   Merz, J.T. History of European thought, 19th century. Edinburgh, 1904. 2v.
Phil 3494.13   Messer, A. Kant's Ethik. Leipzig, 1904.
Phil 22.4.3   Mind. Index to new series. v. 1-12. London, 1904.
Phil 8667.13   Monod, W. Un athée. Neuchâtel, 1904.
Phil 187.32.5   Montgomery, E. Vitality and organization of protoplasm. Austin, Texas, 1904.
Phil 5649.14   Moore, T.V. A study in reaction time and movement. Diss. Washington, 1904.
Phil 6122.7.3.5   Mosso, A. Fatigue. London, 1904.
Phil 5252.30.5   Müller, G.E. Die Gesichtspunkte und der Tatsachen der psychophysischen Methodik. Wiesbaden, 1904.
Phil 6122.23   Mulford, P. Your forces and how to use them. N.Y., 1904. 2v.
Phil 5252.14.5   Murray, J.C. An introduction to psychology. N.Y., 1904.
Phil 8888.1.6   Nahlowsky, J.W. Die ethischen Ideen als die Waltenden Mächte. Langensalza, 1904.
Phil 2270.131   Nardi, P. de. L'assoluto inconoscible di H. Spencer. Forlì, 1904.
Phil 5253.8   Nelson, Leonard. Die kritische Methode und das Verhaltnis der Psychologie zur Philosophie. Göttingen, 1904.
Phil 294.3   Nichols, H. Treatise on cosmology. Cambridge, 1904.
Phil 5643.30   Nuel, J.P. La vision. Paris, 1904.
Phil 3640.200.9   Oehler, Richard. Friedrich Nietzsche und die Vorsokratiker. Leipzig, 1904.
Phil 5764.3   Offner, Max. Willensfreiheit, Zurechnung, und Verantwortung. Leipzig, 1904.
Phil 3496.2   Ortner, F. Kant in Österreich und Vincenz. Klagenfurt, 1904.
Phil 8633.1.6.5   Osler, W. Science and immortality. Boston, 1904.
Phil 3425.274   Ott, Emil. Die Religionsphilosophie Hegels. Berlin, 1904.
Phil 5520.50   Owen, E.T. Interrogative thought and the means of its expression. Madison, 1904.
Phil 9150.4.9   Pagnone, Annibale. L'eredità organica e la formazione delle idealità morale. Torino, 1904.
Phil 8890.23.16   Palmer, G.H. The nature of goodness. Boston, 1904.
Phil 2805.40.17A   Pascal, Blaise. Pensées. Paris, 1904. 3v.
Phil 2805.42.9   Pascal, Blaise. The thoughts of Blaise Pascal. London, 1904.

1904 - cont.

Phil 1158.15.12 — Pater, Walter. Marius the Epicurean. 4th ed. London, 1904. 2v.

Phil 5545.36 — Paulhan, F. La fonction de la mémoire. Paris, 1904.

Phil 190.3.12 — Paulsen, F. De metaphysiska problemen. Stockholm, 1904.

Phil 3497.3.5 — Paulsen, Friedrich. Immanuel Kant. 4. Aufl. Stuttgart, 1904.

Phil 7069.04.60 — Peebles, J.M. The demonism of the ages. Battle Creek, Mich., 1904.

Phil 5374.12 — Perry, R.B. Conceptions and misconceptions of conciousness. N.Y., 1904.

Phil 5255.8 — Pfänder, A. Einführung in die Psychologie. Leipzig, 1904.

Phil 5765.5 — Pfister, Oskar. Die Willensfreiheit. Berlin, 1904.

Phil 8705.7 — Phillips, S.L. Agreement of evolution and Christianity. Washington, 1904.

Phil 190.33 — Philosophische Gesellschaft zu Berlin. Philosophische Aufsätze. Berlin, 1904.

Phil 8685.11 — Picton, J.A. The religion of the universe. London, 1904.

Phil 296.9 — Portig, Gustav. Die Grundzüge der monistischen und dualistischen Weltanschauung. Stuttgart, 1904.

Phil 3915.159 — Prever, G. La filosofia di Guglielmo Wundt. Cuorgné, 1904.

Phil 8416.25 — Prölss, Robert. Ästhetik; Belehrungen über die Wissenschaft vom Schönen und der Kunst. 3. Aufl. Leipzig, 1904.

Phil 191.2 — Quensel, H. Geht es aufwärts? Cöln, 1904.

Phil 3428.94 — Raaf, H. de. Herbarts' metafyzica, psychologie in ethiek. Groningen, 1904.

Phil 102.8 — Radlov, Ernest L. Filosofskii slovar'. Sankt Peterburg, 1904.

Phil 1870.89 — Raffel, Friedrich. Ist Berkeley ein Freihändler? Kiel, 1904.

Phil 75.13.5 — Rand, Benjamin. Philosophical library for the American continent. Cambridge, 1904.

Phil 2270.116 — Ranzoli, C. La fortuna di Herbert Spencer in Italia. Verona, 1904.

Phil 8418.2 — Ratzal, Friedrich. Uber Naturschilderung. München, 1904.

Phil 978.55 — Rees, J.R. The threefold path to peace. N.Y., 1904.

Phil 2840.70 — Renouvier, C.B. Les derniers entretiens, recueillis par Louis Prat. Paris, 1904.

Phil 5440.30 — Revda, A. Il destino delle dinastie. Torino, 1904.

Phil 6060.24 — Rexford, John. What handwriting indicates. N.Y., 1904.

Phil 7082.124 — Richardson, Phelps. A book on the interpretation of dreams. Worcester, 1904-05.

Phil 645.9 — Richter, Raoul. Der Skeptizismus in der Philosophie. Leipzig, 1904-08.

Phil 192.21.2 — Rickert, H. Der Gegenstand der Erkenntniss. Tübingen, 1904.

Phil 1717.5.2 — Riehl, Alois. Philosophie der Gegenwart. 2e Aufl. Leipzig, 1904.

Phil 3640.271 — Rittelmeyer, F. Friedrich Nietzsche und die Religion. Ulm, 1904.

Phil 600.19 — Rodrigues, Gustave. L'idée de relation. Paris, 1904.

Phil 817.16 — Rothenbücher, A. Geschichte der Philosophie. Berlin, 1904.

Phil 8418.12 — Roussel-Despierres, F. L'idéal esthétique. Paris, 1904.

Phil 2270.94A — Royce, Josiah. Herbert Spencer; an estimate and review. N.Y., 1904.

Phil 5520.11 — Rozwadowski, J. von. Wortbildung und Wortbedeutung. Heidelberg, 1904.

Phil 5500.1 — Ruyssen, T. Essai sur l'évolution psychologique du jugement. Nimes, 1904.

Phil 5520.30 — Saint-Paul, Georges. Le langage intérieur et les paraphasies. Paris, 1904.

Phil 7080.19 — Sawyer, James. Insomnia: its causes and cure. Birmingham, 1904.

Phil 8597.3.18 — Schettler, R. Samuel Reimarus zur Religion. Leipzig, 1904.

Phil 6688.9 — Schrenck von Notzing, A.P. Die Traumtänzerin Magdeleine G. Stuttgart, 1904.

Phil 5258.70.5 — Sergi, G. L'origine dei fenomeni psichici e il loro significato biologico. 2. ed. Torino, 1904.

Phil 9358.6 — Shearer, W.J. Morals and manners. N.Y., 1904.

Phil 6968.12.15 — Sidis, Boris. An inquiry into the nature of hallucination. n.p., 1904-12. 10 pam.

Phil 3500.20.2 — Simmel, G. Kant: sechzehn Vorlesungen. Leipzig, 1904.

Phil 4815.790.30 — Simòn, József Sándor. A spekulativ termeszettudomány alapgondolatai mint az egységes érzet filozofia rendszere. Budapest, 1904.

Phil 8708.17 — Smith, Orlando Jay. Balance the fundamental verity. Boston, 1904.

Phil 1718.5 — Snider, Denton J. Modern European philosophy. Saint Louis, 1904.

Phil 58.4 — Society for Psychical Research, London. Combined index. London, 1904. 3v.

Phil 9150.4.3 — Sorley, W.R. On the ethics of naturalism. 2. ed. London, 1904.

Phil 8843.5 — Sorley, W.R. Recent tendencies in ethics. Edinburgh, 1904.

Phil 4225.1.40 — Spaventa, Bertrando. Principii di etica. Napoli, 1904.

Phil 2270.79A — Spencer, Herbert. An autobiography. N.Y., 1904. 2v.

Phil 2270.40.30 — Spencer, Herbert. Essais de morale, de science et d'esthétique. 5e éd. Paris, 1904.

Phil 2270.41.9 — Spencer, Herbert. Faits et commentaires. 2e éd. Paris, 1904.

Phil 2270.56.7 — Spencer, Herbert. Social statics. N.Y., 1904.

Phil 6968.11 — Stedman, H.R. Case of moral insanity. Boston, 1904.

Phil 193.55.3 — Stein, Ludwig. Der Sinn des Daseins. Tübingen, 1904.

Phil 2045.86.2 — Stephen, Leslie. Hobbes. London, 1904.

Phil 2045.86 — Stephen, Leslie. Hobbes. London, 1904.

Phil 8125.14 — Stöcker, Helene. Zur Kunstanschauung des XVIII. Jahrhunderts. Berlin, 1904.

Phil 5643.82 — Stöhr, Adolf. Grundfragen der psychophysiologischen Optik. Leipzig, 1904.

Phil 5649.5 — Storey, Thomas Andrew. Studies in voluntary muscular contraction. Palo Alto, Calif., 1904.

Phil 9220.5.9 — Streamer, Volney. In friendship's name. 14th ed. N.Y., 1904.

Phil 9220.5 — Streamer, Volney. What makes a friend? 9th ed. N.Y., 1904.

Phil 6128.11.9 — Strong, C.A. Reply to Bakewell. n.p., 1904.

Phil 193.106 — Stuart, H.W. The logic of self-realization. Berkeley, 1904.

Phil 299.6 — Stunz, F. Naturbetrachtung und Naturkenntnis. Leipzig, 1904.

Phil 5520.9.3 — Sutro, Emil. Duality of thought and language. N.Y., 1904.

1904 - cont.

Phil 3915.158 — Svensson, P.I.K. Kunskapsteoretiska studier med särskild hänsyn till Wundts åsikt. Lund, 1904.

Phil 8893.59 — Svensson, P.K. Om autonoma och heteronoma moralprinciper. Lund, 1904.

Phil 8598.48 — Svensson, P.K. Religionsfilosofi. Lund, 1904.

Phil 2520.78 — Swarte, V. de. Descartes, directeur spirituel. Paris, 1904.

Phil 8894.18 — Tarantino, Giuseppe. Il principio dell'ética e la crisi morale contemporanea; memoria. Napoli, 1904.

Phil 5467.6 — Tarde, Gabriel. Les lois de l'imitation; étude sociologique. 4. éd. Paris, 1904.

Phil 5769.7 — Teisen, N. Om viljens frihed. København, 1904.

Phil 3120.10.80 — Theile, Günther. Philosophische Streifzüge an deutschen Hochschulen. Berlin, 1904.

Phil 2725.4.81 — Thomas, P. F. Pierre Leroux. Paris, 1904.

Phil 8599.11.5 — Tiele, C.P. Grundzüge der Religionswissenschaft. Tübingen, 1904.

Phil 3501.11 — Troeltsch, E. Das Historische in Kants Religionsphilosophie. Berlin, 1904.

Phil 4065.91 — Troilo, Erminio. La filosofia di Giordano Bruno. Torino, 1904.

Phil 2730.81 — Truman, N.E. Maine de Biran's philosophy of will. N.Y., 1904.

Phil 8844.3 — Tufts, J.H. The individual and his relation to society. N.Y., 1904.

Phil 8844.2 — Turner, Arthur T. A new morality. London, 1904.

Phil 5374.29 — Uphues, Goswin. Vom Bewusstsein. Osterwieck, 1904.

Phil 3503.1.5 — Vaihinger, H. Zu Kants Gedächtnis. Berlin, 1904.

Phil 1801.2 — Van Becelaere, L. La philosophie en Amérique depuis les origine jusqu'à nos jours, 1607-1900. N.Y., 1904.

Phil 4650.1.37 — Vannérus, Allen. Lära och lif. Stockholm, 1904.

Phil 196.8.3 — Varisco, B. La conoscenza. Pavia, 1904.

Phil 196.4 — Verworn, M. Naturwissenschaft und Weltanschauung. 2e Aufl. Leipzig, 1904.

Phil 821.2 — Vogel, August. Überblick über der Geschichte der Philosophie. Leipzig, 1904-05.

Phil 5627.9 — Vorbrodt, G. Beiträge zur religiösen Psychologie. Leipzig, 1904.

Phil 1127.4 — Waddington, Charles. La philosophie ancienne et la critique historique. Paris, 1904.

Phil 9182.4.5 — Wagner, Charles. By the fireside. N.Y., 1904.

Phil 9182.4.10 — Wagner, Charles. The simple life. N.Y., 1904.

Phil 9182.4.9 — Wagner, Charles. The simple life. N.Y., 1904.

Phil 8677.7 — Walcott, G.D. Kantian and Lutheran elements in Ritschls' conception of God. N.Y., 1904.

Phil 8677.12.2 — Walter von Walthoffen, Hippolyt. Die Gottesidee in religiöser und spekulativer Richtung. Wien, 1904.

Phil 497.8 — Wartenberg, Mzcislaw. Das idealistische Argument in der Kritik des Materialismus. Leipzig, 1904.

Phil 5262.8 — Watt, H.J. Experimentelle...Theorie des Denkens. Leipzig, 1904.

Phil 3504.19 — Weber, Heinrich. Hamann und Kant. München, 1904.

Phil 3905.30.3 — Weininger, Otto. Geschlecht und Charakter. 3. Aufl. Wien, 1904.

Phil 3905.35 — Weininger, Otto. Über die letzten Dinge. Wien, 1904.

Phil 3504.12.5 — Wernieke, A. Theorie des Gegenstandes...bei I. Kant. Braunschweig, 1904.

Phil 2422.2 — Wijnaendts Francken, C.J. Fransche moralisten. Haarlem, 1904.

Phil 9495.5 — Willson, R.N. Social evil in university life. N.Y., 1904.

Phil 3640.82.15 — Willy, Rudolf. Friedrich Nietzsche. Zürich, 1904.

Phil 3504.18 — Windelband, W. Immanuel Kant und seine Weltanschauung. Heidelberg, 1904.

Phil 1722.2.5 — Windelband, W. Die Philosophie im Beginn des Zwanzigsten. Heidelberg, 1904.

Phil 5772.5.2 — Windelband, Wilhelm. Über Willensfreiheit. Tübingen, 1904.

Phil 8423.4 — Witasek, Stephan. Grundzüge der allgemeinen Ästhetik. Leipzig, 1904.

Phil 3915.46.6 — Wundt, Wilhelm. Principles of physiological psychology. London, 1904.

Phil 510.15 — Ziegler, J.H. Die wahre Einheit von Religion und Wissenschaft. Zürich, 1904.

NEDL Phil 177.32 — Zoltowski, A. Graf August Cieszkowski's "Philosophie der Tat". Posen, 1904.

1905

Phil 5750.3.2 — Ach, Narziss. Über die Willenstätigkeit und das Denken. Göttingen, 1905.

Phil 8615.5.10 — Adler, Felix. The essentials of spirituality. N.Y., 1905.

Phil 8615.5.5 — Adler, Felix. Life and destiny. N.Y., 1905.

Phil 8615.5 — Adler, Felix. The religion of duty. N.Y., 1905.

Phil 5240.16 — Alfonso, N.R. I limiti dell'esperimento in psicologia. Roma, 1905.

Phil 5240.29 — Aliotta, A. La misura in psicologia sperimentale. Firenze, 1905.

Phil 5240.5.30 — Angell, J.R. Psychology. 2. ed. N.Y., 1905.

Phil 331.6 — Apel, Paul. Geist und Materie. Berlin, 1905. 2v.

Phil 510.129 — Ashcroft, E.A. The world's desires. London, 1905.

X Cg Phil 1865.82 — Atkinson, Charles M. Jeremy Bentham. London, 1905.

Phil 2400.3 — Avezac-Lavigne, C. Saint-Simonisme-Positivisme. Paris, 1905.

Phil 9530.22 — Babcock, M.D. The success of defeat. N.Y., 1905.

Phil 1850.50.13A — Bacon, Francis. Novum organum. London, 1905.

Phil 3808.10 — Baer, J. Schopenhauer - Bibliothek. Frankfurt, 1905.

Phil 3565.127 — Baerwald, Leo. Die Entwicklung der Lotzeschen Psychologie. Berlin, 1905.

Phil 176.3.5 — Bahnsen, J. Wie ich Wurde was ich Ward. München, 1905.

Phil 5645.11A — Baird, J.W. The color sensitivity of the peripheral retina. Washington, 1905.

Phil 5211.2.5 — Baldwin, J.M. Sketch of the history of psychology. Lancaster, 1905.

Phil 510.1.20 — Ballard, Frank. Haeckel's monism false. London, 1905.

Phil 3483.12 — Baumann, J. Anti-Kant. Gotha, 1905.

Phil 5041.35 — Baumgartner, M. Logik und Erkentnistheorie. Facsimile. n.p., 1905-06.

Phil 7140.105 — Bekhterev, W.M. Die Bedeutung der Suggestion. Wiesbaden, 1905.

Phil 7069.05.30 — Bennett, E.T. Automatic speaking and writing. London, 1905.

Phil 645.15 — Berthelot, M. Science et libre pensée. 2e éd. Paris, 1905.

Phil 6111.14 — Binet, A. L'ame et le corps. Paris, 1905.

Phil 7042.4.2 — Binet, Alfred. On double consciousness. Chicago, 1905.

1905 - cont.

Phil 3195.8.80 — Birkenbihl, M. Georg Friedrich Daumer. Inaug. Diss. Aschaffenburg, 1905.

Phil 4520.8.40 — Bjarnason, Agúst. Andatrúin. Reykjavík, 1905.

Phil 5041.28 — Black, George A. Problem: science (function) analysis. N.Y., 1905.

Phil 3808.116.10 — Bossert, Adolphe. Schopenhauer als Mensch und Philosoph. Dresden, 1905.

Phil 2270.106 — Boutroux, É. La religion selon Herbert Spencer. Paris, 1905.

Phil 5811.17 — Brenes Mesén, Roberto. La voluntad en los microorganismos. Costa Rica, 1905.

Phil 8581.24.5 — Brierley, J. Ourselves and the universe. N.Y., 1905.

Phil 5241.74 — Brockdorff, Cay L.G.C. Die philosophischen Anfangsgründe der Psychologie. Heldesheim, 1905.

Phil 8581.68.15 — Broglie, Paul. Les fondements intellectuels de la foi chrétienne. Paris, 1905.

Phil 3483.32 — Brotherus, K.R. Immanuel Kants Philosophie der Geschichte. Helsingfors, 1905.

Phil 8951.15 — Bruce, William S. Social aspects of Christian morality. London, 1905.

Phil 176.85.13 — Brunschvicg, L. L'idéalisme contemporain. Paris, 1905.

Phil 2055.1.80 — Bühler, K. Studien über Henry Home. Bonn, 1905.

Phil 4302.5 — Bullón y Fernández, E. Los precursores españoles de Bacon y Descartes. Salamanca, 1905.

Phil 331.2.30 — Bush, W.T. Avenarius and the stand point of pure experience. N.Y., 1905.

Phil 5242.13.5 — Calkins, M.W. Der doppelte Standpunkt...Psychologie. Leipzig, 1905.

Phil 6112.2.9 — Call, A.P. Freedom of life. Boston, 1905.

Phil 5402.13 — Castez, G. La douleur physique. Paris, 1905.

Phil 3484.6 — Chamberlain, H.S. Immanuel Kant. Die Persönlichkeit...in das Werke. München, 1905.

Phil 8627.9.5 — Chambers, A. Thoughts of the spiritual. London, 1905.

Phil 8870.5 — Coit, Stanton. The message of man. London, 1905.

Phil 5425.2.7 — Constable, F.C. Poverty and hereditary genius (criticism of Galton's theory). London, 1905.

Phil 2730.82 — Couailhac, M. Maine de Biran. Paris, 1905.

Phil 5042.8 — Couturat, L. L'algèbre de la logique. 1st ed. Paris, 1905.

Phil 5042.8.2 — Couturat, L. L'algèbre de la logique. 2e éd. Paris, 1905.

Phil 3460.85 — Crawford, A.W. The philosophy of F.H. Jacobi. N.Y., 1905.

Phil 8633.1.7 — Crothers, S.M. The endless life. Boston, 1905.

NEDL Phil 5627.7.8 — Davenport, F.M. Primitive traits in religious revivals. N.Y., 1905.

Phil 3485.7 — Delbos, Victor. La philosophie pratique de Kant. Paris, 1905.

Phil 3640.94.9 — Dernoscheck, G.A. Das problem des egoistischen Perfektionismus in der Ethik Spinozas und Nietzsches. Annaberg, 1905.

Phil 6113.23 — De Voe, W. Healing currents from the battery of life. 2. ed. Chicago, 1905.

Phil 8583.10A — Dickinson, G.L. Religion, a criticism and a forecast. N.Y., 1905.

Phil 3425.311 — Dilthey, Wilhelm. Die Jugendgeschichte Hegels. Berlin, 1905.

Htn Phil 5545.93* — Doeblin, Alfred. Gedächtnisstörungen bei der Korsakoffschen Psychose. Berlin, 1905.

Phil 575.32 — Dreyer, Hans. Personalismus und Realismus. Berlin, 1905.

Phil 6953.12.5 — Dubois, Paul. Psychic treatment of nervous disorders. N.Y., 1905.

Phil 5243.13 — Dubray, C.A. The theory of psychical dispositions. Washington, 1905.

Phil 8878.34 — Dugas, L. Cours de morale thérique et pratique. v.1-2. Paris, 1905-06.

Phil 2490.110 — Dumas, G. Psychologie de deux messies positivistes Saint-Simon et Auguste Comte. Paris, 1905.

Phil 6673.16 — Durville, H. Magnétisme personnel ou psychique. Paris, 1905.

Phil 7140.12 — Ebbard, R.J. How to acquire and strengthen will-power. London, 1905.

Phil 179.7 — Eisler, R. Kritische Einführung in die Philosophie. Berlin, 1905.

Phil 8405.5 — Eleutheropoulos, Abroleläs. Das Schöne. Berlin, 1905.

Phil 8879.2.12 — Eliot, C.W. The happy life. N.Y., 1905.

Phil 179.19 — Emmelin, Axel. Enhets- och mangfaldsproblemet inom metfysiken. Lund, 1905.

Phil 3235.81.20 — Engels, Friedrich. Liudvig Feierbakh. 2. izd. Geneva, 1905.

Phil 270.21 — Erdmann, Benno. Über Inhalt und Geltung des Kausalgesetzes. Halle, 1905.

Phil 8829.2.5 — Eucken, Rudolf. Die Lebensanschauungen der grossen Denker. Leipzig, 1905.

Phil 175.12.9 — Ewald, Oskar. Richard Avenarius. Berlin, 1905.

Phil 8585.1.5 — Fairbairn, A.M. The philosophy of the Christian religion. London, 1905.

Phil 3246.79.10 — Fichte, Johann Gottlieb. Über die Einzig mögliche Störung der akademischen Freiheit. Heidelberg, 1905.

Phil 5520.10 — Finck, F.N. Die Aufgabe und Gliederung der Sprachwissenschaft. Halle, 1905.

Phil 6115.18.9 — Fletcher, Horace. The new menticulture. London, 1905.

Phil 3428.89.5 — Flügel, Otto. Der philosophie J.F. Herbart. Leipzig, 1905.

Phil 3195.1.81 — Flügel, Otto. Religionsphilosophie der Schule Herbarts, Drobisch und Hartenstein. Langensalza, 1905.

Phil 7054.18 — Ford, S.L. Interwoven. Letters from a son to his mother. Boston, 1905.

Phil 8880.24 — Fouillée, Alfred. Les elements sociologiques de la morale. Paris, 1905.

Phil 3487.3.2 — Fouillée, Alfred. Le moralisme de Kant et l'amoralisme contemporain. 2. éd. Paris, 1905.

Phil 5545.163 — Fränkl, Ernst. Über Vorstellungs-Elemente und Aufmerksamkeit. Augsburg, 1905.

Phil 3808.152 — Francken, C.J. Wijnaendts. Arthur Schopenhauer, een levensbeeld. Haarlem, 1905.

Phil 2005.2.81 — Fraser, A.C. Biographica philosophica. 2d ed. Edinburgh 1905.

Htn Phil 5525.6* — Freud, Sigmund. Der Witz und seine Beziehung zum Unbewussten. Leipzig, 1905.

Phil 1135.85 — Freytag, W. Die Entwicklung der Grossen Erkenntnistheorie. Hale, 1905.

Phil 3160.7.85 — Friedmann, P. Darstellung und Kritik der naturalistischen Weltanschauung H. Czolbes. Inaug. Diss. Berlin, 1905.

Phil 5755.8 — Froehlich, Joseph Anselm. Der Wille zu höheren Einheit. Heidelberg, 1905.

Phil 5440.12 — Galippe, V. L'hérédité des stigmates de dégénérescence. Paris, 1905.

1905 - cont.

Phil 5520.29 — Garlanda, Fedérico. La filosofia delle parole. 3. ed. Roma, 1905?

Phil 181.61 — Geddes, Patrick. The world without and the world within. Bournville, 1905.

Phil 4570.3.31 — Geijer, R. Samvetet. Stockholm, 1905.

Phil 4756.5.31 — Giliarov-Platonov, N.P. Voprosy very i tserkvi. Moskva, 1905.

Phil 2805.90.3 — Giraud, V. Pascal l'homme, l'oeuvre, l'influence. Paris, 1905.

Phil 1190.7 — Goedeckmeyer, A. Die Geschichte des griechischen Skeptizismus. Leipzig, 1905.

Phil 8407.13 — Göller, Adolf. Das ästhetische Gefühl. Stuttgart, 1905.

Phil 978.18.3 — Goffield, E.C. The past revealed. Boston, 1905.

Phil 5756.3 — Goldscheid, R. Grundlinien zu einer Kritik der Willenskraft. Wien, 1905.

Phil 3488.4.20 — Goldschmidt, L. Kant's "Privatmeinungen" über das Jenseits. Gotha, 1905.

Phil 287.3 — Gomperz, Heinrich. Weltanschauungslehre. Jena, 1905-08. 2v.

Phil 1111.1.11 — Gomperz, T. Greek thinkers; a history of ancient philosophy. London, 1905-13. 4v.

Phil 3808.107.10 — Grisebach, Eduard. Schopenhauer. Berlin, 1905.

Phil 5246.19.10 — Gutberlet, C. Psychophysik. Mainz, 1905.

Phil 182.57 — Haacke, Wilhelm. Vom Strome des Seins. Leipzig, 1905.

Phil 8610.905 — Haeckel, Ernst. A universal monistic alliance. Los Angeles, 1905.

Phil 510.1.4 — Haeckel, Ernst. Världsgåtorna. Stockholm, 1905.

Phil 510.1.15 — Haeckel, Ernst. The wonders of life. N.Y., 1905.

Phil 1504.5.2 — Hahn S. Thomas Bradwardinus. v.5, pt.2. Münster, 1905.

Phil 2520.109A — Haldane, E.S. Descartes, his life and times. London, 1905.

Phil 182.35.2 — Haldane, Richard B. The pathway to reality. London, 1905.

Phil 5640.35 — Handbuch der Physiologie des Menschen. v.3. Braunschweig, 1905.

Phil 2270.95 — Harrison, F. The Herbert Spencer lecture. Oxford, 1905.

Phil 182.47 — Hatch, D.P. Scientific occultism. Los Angeles, 1905.

Phil 3425.60.55 — Hegel, Georg Wilhelm Friedrich. Hegels Religionsphilosophie in gekürzter Form. Jena, 1905.

Phil 3425.56.5 — Hegel, Georg Wilhelm Friedrich. The introduction to Hegel's Philosophy of fine art. London, 1905.

Phil 6957.10.5 — Hellpach, W. Die Hysterie und die moderne Schule. n.p., 1905-1913. 11 pam.

Phil 8882.28 — Henderson, C.H. The children of good fortune. N.Y., 1905.

Phil 7069.05.35 — Hennig, R. Wunder und Wissenschaft. Hamburg, 1905.

Phil 5545.37.10 — Hering, Ewald. On memory and the specific energies of the nervous system. 4. ed. Chicago, 1905.

Phil 5545.37 — Hering, Ewald. Uber das Gedächtnis. Leipzig, 1905.

Phil 4582.1.30 — Herrlin, Axel. Filosofi och facksetenskap. Lund, 1905.

Phil 182.37 — Heymans, G. Einführung in die Metaphysik. Leipzig, 1905.

Phil 338.6 — Heymans, G. Gesetze und Elemente des wissenschaftlichen Denkens. Leipzig, 1905.

Phil 1145.66 — Hirzel, R. Was die Wahrheit war für die Griechen. Jena, 1905.

Phil 2045.27A — Hobbes, Thomas. The metaphysical system of Hobbes. Chicago, 1905.

Phil 338.8 — Hocking, William E. Papers on logic and epistemology. v.1-6. N.Y., 1905.

Phil 1707.1.9 — Höffding, H. Moderne Philosophen. Leipzig, 1905.

Phil 182.36.6 — Höffding, H. The problems of philosophy. N.Y., 1905.

Phil 182.36.5 — Höffding, H. The problems of philosophy. N.Y., 1905.

Phil 2520.108.5 — Hoffmann, A. René Descartes. Stuttgart, 1905.

Phil 182.62 — Holmes, Edmond. What is philosophy? London, 1905.

Phil 8408.35 — Howes, E.D. (Mrs.). The psychology of beauty. Boston, 1905.

Phil 400.12.3 — Howison, G.H. Limits of evolution. 2nd ed. N.Y., 1905.

Phil 7068.96.7.9 — Hudson, Thomson J. The law of psychic phenomena. 30. ed. Chicago, 1905.

Phil 2050.28.15 — Hume, David. Dialoge über natürliche Religion. 3e Aufl. Leipzig, 1905.

Phil 182.38 — Hyslop, J.H. Problems of philosophy. N.Y., 1905.

Phil 7069.05.10 — Hyslop, James Hervey. Science and a future life. Boston, 1905.

Phil 6118.1.3 — Ingalese, R. The history and power of mind. 8th ed. N.Y., 1905.

Phil 184.27 — Jacobsen, O.T. Gennem modsabninger. København, 1905.

Phil 8884.17.3 — Jahn, Max. Ethik als Grundwissenschaft. Leipzig, 1905.

Phil 184.3.3.10 — James, W. The will to believe and other essays in popular philosophy. London, 1905.

Phil 2070.51.5 — James, William. Sentiment of rationality. N.Y., 1905.

Phil 184.12.8 — Jerusalem, W. Gedanken und Denker. Wien, 1905.

Phil 400.20 — Jerusalem, W. Der kritische Idealismus und die reine Logik. Wien, 1905.

Phil 3640.94.5 — Joël, Karl. Nietzsche und die Romantik. Jena, 1905.

Phil 8592.6.80 — Jones, Henry. The philosophy of Martineau in relation to the idealism of the present day. London, 1905.

Phil 8884.4.5 — Jordan, W.G. Self-control, its kingship and majesty. N.Y., 1905.

Phil 5627.67 — Kaltenbaach, J. Étude psychologique des plus anciens reveils religieux aux États-Unis. Thèse. Genève, 1905.

Phil 3480.30.17 — Kant, Immanuel. Critik der reinen Vernunft, 1781. 1. Aufl. Riga, 1905.

Phil 3480.24.2 — Kant, Immanuel. Kleinere Schriften zur Logik und Metaphysik. v.1-4. 2. Aufl. Leipzig, 1905.

Phil 3480.57.13 — Kant, Immanuel. Prolegomena zu einer jeden künftigen Metaphysik. 4. Aufl. Leipzig, 1905.

Phil 3790.8.80 — Keirstead, W.C. Metaphysical presuppositions of Ritschl. Chicago, 1905.

Phil 5627.10.3 — King, Irving. The differentiation of the religious consciousness. N.Y., 1905.

Phil 5627.10 — King, Irving. The differentiation of the religious consciousness. N.Y., 1905.

Phil 341.3 — Kleinseter, H. Erkenntnistheorie der Naturforschung. Leipzig, 1905.

Phil 8590.11.2 — Kneib, Philipp. Wissen und Glauben. 2. Aufl. Mainz, 1905.

Phil 2050.88.15 — Knight, William. Hume. Edinburgh, 1905.

Phil 5648.6 — Kobylecki, S. Wahrnehmbarkeit plötzlicher Drückveranderungen. Leipzig, 1905.

Phil 5643.58 — Kolbenheyer, E.G. Die sensorielle Theorie der optischen Raumempfindung. Leipzig, 1905.

Phil 6960.5.12 — Kraepelin, E. Einführung in die psychiatrische Klinik. Leipzig, 1905.

Phil 3525.65 — Krause, K.C.F. Vorlesung über psychische Anthropologie. Leipzig, 1905.

Phil 2855.2.95 — Krauss, S. Théodule Ribots Psychologie. Jena, 1905.

Phil 8885.31 — Kronenberg, Moritz. Ethische Präludien. München, 1905.

Chronological Listing

1905 - cont.

Phil 3492.6 Kuberka, F. Kant's Lehre von der Sinnlichkeit. Halle, 1905.
Phil 3010.2 Külpe, O. Die Philosophie der Gegenwart in Deutschland. Leipzig, 1905.
Phil 7069.05.12 Kvaran, E.H. Samband vidframlida menn. Reykjavik, 1905.
Phil 5400.74 Lagerborg, R. Das Gefühlsproblem. Leipzig, 1905.
Phil 2725.2.52.5 Lamennais, F.R. de. Das Volksbuch von Félicité de Lamennais. Leipzig, 1905.
Phil 8886.24.5 Lanessan, J.I. de. La morale des religions. Paris, 1905.
X Cg Phil 6049.05 Lawrence, E. The science of palmistry. London, 1905.
Phil 4582.1.81 Leljeqvist, E. Marginalanmärkningar till Docenten Herrlins skrift "Filosofi och fackvetenskap". Göteborg, 1905.
Phil 8961.18 Lemme, Ludwig. Christliche Ethik. Berlin, 1905. 2v.
Phil 5627.68 Léo, A. Étude psychologique sur la prière d'après deux enquêtes américaines. Thèse. Cahors, 1905.
Phil 3525.84 Leonhardi, Hermann. Karl Christian Friedrich Krause als philosophischer Denker Gewürdigt. Leipzig, 1905.
Phil 5520.17 Leroy, E.B. Le langage. Paris, 1905.
Phil 8886.29 Lévy-Bruhl, L. Ethics and moral science. London, 1905.
Phil 186.10.5 Liard, L. La science positive. 5. ed. Paris, 1905.
Phil 8886.15.6 Lipps, T. Die ethischen Grundfragen. 2e Aufl. Hamburg, 1905.
Phil 5251.8.8 Lipps, T. Psychologische Studien. Leipzig, 1905.
Phil 5643.32 Listing, J.B. Beitrag zur physiologischen Optik. Leipzig, 1905.
Phil 5251.16 Louden, D.M. van. Onderzoek naar den duur der eenvoudige psychische processen v.n. bij de Psychosen. Amsterdam, 1905.
Phil 4710.5.2A Lourié, Osip. La philosophie russe contemporaine. 2. ed. Paris, 1905.
Phil 3905.80 Lucka, E. Otto Weininger: sein Werk und Persönlichkeit. Wien, 1905.
Phil 5821.5 Lukas, F. Psychologie der niedersten Tiere. Wien, 1905.
Phil 343.4 Mach, E. Erkenntnis und Irrtum. Leipzig, 1905.
Phil 6682.22 Magnia, E. L'art et hypnose. Genève, 1905?
Phil 1870.90 Malan, D.F. Het idealisme van Berkeley. Utrecht, 1905.
Phil 510.155 Malenovskii, A.A. Empiriomonizm. v.1-3. S'ankt Peterburg, 1905-06.
Phil 8702.7.5 Mallock, W.H. The reconstruction of belief. London, 1905.
Phil 8702.7.7 Mallock, W.H. The reconstruction of religious belief. N.Y., 1905.
Phil 5222.2 Mantorani, Giuseppe. Psicologia fisiologica. 2. ed. Milano, 1905.
Phil 187.83 Marchesini, A. L'imaginazione creatrice nella filosofia. Torino, 1905.
Phil 4170.6.40 Marchesini, G. Le finzioni dell'anima. Bari, 1905.
Phil 2050.221 Martin, John J. Shaftesbury's und Hutcheson's Verhältnis zu Hume. Inaug. Diss. Halle, 1905.
Itn Phil 5252.62.5* Martin, L.J. Psychology of aesthetics. n.p., 1905-1907. 4 pam.
Phil 2138.105 Martinazzoli, A.L. La teorica dell'individualismo secondo J.S. Mill. Milano, 1905.
Phil 8887.4.13 Martineau, J. Tides of the spirit. Boston, 1905.
Phil 5238.2 Martius, Götz. Beiträge zur Psychologie und Philosophie. Leipzig, 1905.
Phil 9352.12 Mather, Persis (pseud.). The counsels of a worldly godmother. Boston, 1905.
Phil 187.28.22 Mechnikov, I.I. Etiudy o prirode cheloveka. Izd. 2. Moskva, 1905.
Phil 3246.93A Medicus, Fritz. Johann Gottlieb Fichte; Dreizehn Vorlesungen gehalten and der Universität Halle. Berlin, 1905.
Phil 3808.107.5 Melli, Giuseppe. La filosofia di Schopenhauer. Firenze, 1905.
Phil 9560.29 Miller, J.R. The beauty of kindness. N.Y., 1905.
Phil 1504.5.4 Minges, Parthenius. Ist duns scotus indeterminist? v.5, pt.4. Münster, 1905.
Phil 3635.6 Möbius, Paul. Ausgewählte Werke. Leipzig, 1905-11. 8v.
Phil 6962.13 Monakow, Constantin von. Gehirnpathologie. 2. Aufl. Wien, 1905. 2v.
Phil 1712.9 Mondolfo, R. Il dubbio metodico e la storia della filosofia. Padova, 1905.
Phil 4210.124 Morando, G. Esame critico delle XL proposizioni rosminiane condaunate dalla S.R.U. inquisizione. Milano, 1905.
Phil 187.29 Morgan, C.L. The interpretation of nature. Bristol, 1905.
Phil 900.9 Motora, Y. An essay on Eastern philosophy. Leipzig, 1905.
Phil 400.35 Mouw, J.A. der. Het absoluut idealisme. Leiden, 1905.
Phil 8637.7 Münsterberg, S. The eternal life. Boston, 1905.
Phil 9495.24 New York. Homeopathic Medical Society. Communication on Public Education. Second communication. Albany? 1905.
Phil 3640.41.4 Nietzsche, Friedrich. Also sprach Zarathustra. Leipzig, 1905?
Phil 4610.7.10 Norström, V. Tankelinier. Stockholm, 1905.
Cg Phil 6965.5 Paton, Stewart. Psychiatry. Philadelphia, 1905.
Phil 9558.9 Paulhan, F. Les mensonges du caractère. Paris, 1905.
Phil 8965.3 Peabody, F.G. Jesus Christ and the Christian character. N.Y., 1905.
Phil 55.1.10 Pennsylvina. University. Laboratory of Neuropathology. Contributions. Philadelphia, 1905. 5v.
Phil 5627.34.5 Perrier, Louis. Les obsessions dans la vie religieuse. Thèse. Montpellier, 1905.
Phil 815.3 Perrin, R. St. J. The evolution of knowledge. N.Y., 1905.
Phil 190.18A Perry, R.B. The approach to philosophy. N.Y., 1905.
Phil 5765.7 Peterson, Julius. Willensfreiheit, moral und strafrecht. München, 1905.
Phil 9355.7 Phillips, John H. Old tales and modern ideals. N.Y., 1905.
Phil 1520.2 Picavet, F. Histoire...des philosophies médiévales. Paris, 1905.
Phil 6965.10 Pick, Arnold. Studien über motorische Apraxie. Leipzig, 1905.
Phil 4195.10 Pico della Mirandola, Giovanni. Ausgewählte Schriften. Jena, 1905.
Phil 8685.11.5 Picton, J.A. Pantheism, its story and significance. London, 1905.
Phil 5115.4.6 Poincaré, Henri. Science and hypothesis. London, 1905.
Phil 5115.4.5 Poincaré, Henri. Science and hypothesis. N.Y., 1905.
Phil 8416.23 Porena, M. Che cos'é il bello? Schema d'un estetica psicologica. Milano, 1905.
Phil 3625.4.81 Post, Karl. Johannes Müllers philosophische Anschauungen. Inaug. Diss. Halle, 1905.
Phil 2280.6.87 Potter, H.C. A sermon, memorial of the Rev. Charles W. Shields. Princeton, N.J., 1905.
Phil 2805.100 Prudhomme, S. La vraie religion selon Pascal. Paris, 1905.

1905 - cont.

Phil 3246.86.5 Raich, Maria. Fichte, seine Ethik...Problem des Individualismus. Tübingen, 1905.
Phil 3246.86 Raich, Maria. Fichte, seine Ethik...Problem des Individualismus. Thesis. Tübingen, 1905.
Phil 6127.13 Randall, F.H. Psychology. London, 1905.
Phil 102.3 Ranzoli, C. Dizionario di scienze filosofiche. Milano, 1905.
Phil 7069.05.15 Rayon, M. Fads or facts. Chicago, 1905.
Phil 192.22 Read, C. The metaphysics of nature. London, 1905.
Phil 5325.20 Renda, A. La dissociazione psicologica. Torino, 1905.
Phil 9030.3 Revel, Camille. Le hasard. Paris, 1905.
Phil 270.57 Revel, Camille. Le hasard sa loi et ses conséquences dans les sciences et en philosophie. Paris, 1905.
Phil 192.24 Richard, A. Souvenirs...d'un penseur moderne. Genève, 1905.
Phil 3499.7 Richter, Otto. Kants Auffassung des Verhaltnisses von Glaüben und Wissen. Lauban, 1905.
Phil 4065.89 Riehl, A. Giordano Bruno. Edinburgh, 1905.
Phil 192.10.5 Ritchie, D.G. Philosophical studies. London, 1905.
Phil 8140.3 Rolla, Alfredo. Storia delle idee estetiche in Italia. Torino, 1905.
Phil 3499.6.13 Romundt, H. Kants Kritik der reinen Vernunft Abgekürzt auf Grund ihrer Entstehungsgeschichte. Gotha, 1905.
Phil 192.53 Rudin, W. Tillvarons problem. Stockholm, 1905.
Phil 192.38 Runze, Georg. Metaphysik. Leipzig, 1905.
Phil 8591.14 Sadd, G.T. The philosophy of religion. N.Y., 1905. 2v.
Phil 8615.1.3 Salter, W.M. Ethical religion. London, 1905.
Phil 8615.1.15 Salter, W.M. Moral aspiration and song. Philadelphia, 1905.
Phil 193.49A Santayana, G. Life of reason. N.Y., 1905. 5v.
Phil 3195.2.79 Sattel, G. Martin Deutingers Gotteslehre. Regensburg, 1905.
Phil 3808.75.5 Schopenhauer, Arthur. Écrivains et style. Paris, 1905.
Phil 5500.2 Schrader, E. Elemente der Psychologie des Urteils. Leipzig, 1905.
Phil 2840.81 Séailles, G. Philosophie de Charles Renouvier. Paris, 1905.
Phil 3018.5.3 Seibert, C. Geschichte der neueren deutschen Philosophie. 2e Aufl. Gottingen, 1905.
Phil 1135.23.15 Sellin, Ernst. Die Spuren griechischer Philosophie. 1e and 2e Aufl. Leipzig, 1905.
Phil 8893.30.3 Senac de Meilhan, G. Considérations sur l'esprit et les moeurs. Paris, 1905.
Phil 3500.21 Sentroul, C. L'objet de la métaphysique selon Kant. Louvain, 1905.
Phil 3850.10.80 Serch, Paul. Friedrich Schlegels Philosophie Anschauungen in ihrer Entwicklung und systematischen Ausgestaltung. Berlin, 1905.
Phil 8893.8.3 Seth, J. A study of ethical principles. 8. ed. N.Y., 1905.
Phil 2262.60.2 Shaftesbury, A.A.C. Religion und Tugend. Leipzig, 1905.
Phil 2262.60 Shaftesbury, A.A.C. Untersuchung über die Tugend. Leipzig, 1905.
Phil 193.134.10 Shestov, L. Apotheoz pespohveiossiti. Sankt Peterburg, 1905.
Phil 3500.19 Sidgwich, H. Lectures on the philosophy of Kant. London, 1905.
Phil 7042.6A Sidis, Boris. Multiple personality: an experimental investigation. N.Y., 1905.
Phil 3500.20 Simmel, G. Kant: sechzehn Vorlesungen. Leipzig, 1905.
Phil 978.9.18 Sinnett, A.P. The growth of the soul. 2nd ed. London, 1905.
Phil 3640.640 Slobodskoi, I. Fridrikh Nitsche. Sankt Peterburg, 1905.
Phil 5258.19.5 Snider, D.J. Feeling psychologically treated. St.Louis, 1905.
Phil 6128.32 Snyder, John Jacob. How to obtain happiness and health. Chicago, 1905.
Phil 5400.23 Sollier, P. Le mécanisme des émotions. Paris, 1905.
Phil 5648.5 Spearman, C. Normaltäuschungen in der Lagewahrnehmung. Leipzig, 1905.
Phil 2270.79.10 Spencer, Herbert. Eine Autobiographie. Stuttgart, 1905. 2v.
Phil 2270.74.20 Spencer, Herbert. Les bases de la morale évolutionniste. 8e éd. Paris, 1905.
Phil 3819.36.31 Spinoza, Benedictus de. Ethica ordine geometrico demonstrata. Hagae, 1905.
Phil 193.34.5 Steffens, H. Henrik Steffens indledning til förelaesninger in Kobenhavn 1803. Kobenhavn, 1905.
Phil 5330.14 Stevens, H.C. Plethysmographic study of attention. n.p., 1905.
Phil 1535.11.8 Stöckl, A. Lehrbuch der Philosophie. Mainz, 1905-12. 2v.
Phil 4210.136 Stopppani, Pietro. Antonio Rosmini. Milano, 1905.
Phil 8592.6.6 Sunderland, J.T. James Martineau and his Great Book. Toronto, 1905.
Phil 5627.83 Swetenham, L. Religious genius. London, 1905.
Phil 5258.33 Swoboda, H. Studien zur Grundlegung der Psychologie. Leipzig, 1905.
Phil 3640.114 Thilly, F. Philosophy of Friedrich Nietzsche. Photoreproduction. N.Y., 1905.
Phil 6689.5 Thomas, Northcote W. Crystal gasping. London, 1905.
Phil 7069.05.20 Thomas, Northcote W. Thought transference. N.Y., 1905.
Phil 3425.126 Thomsen, A. Hegel. København, 1905.
Phil 7082.51.1 Thorleifsdóttir, Elizabet. Draumur. Reykjavík, 1905.
Phil 5259.7.5 Thorndike, E.L. The elements of psychology. N.Y., 1905.
Phil 5259.7.6 Thorndike, E.L. The elements of psychology. 2d ed. N.Y., 1905.
Phil 5829.5 Toenjes, H. Principles of animal understanding. N.Y., 1905.
Phil 3640.94 Tosi, T. F. Nietzsche, R. Wagner e la tragedie Greca. Firenze, 1905.
Phil 8599.19.10 Troeltsch, Ernst. Psychologie und Erkenntnistheorie in der Religionswissenschaft. Tübingen, 1905.
Phil 8592.6.15 Upton, Charles B. Doctor Martineau's philosophy; a survey. London, 1905.
Phil 365.17 Valle, G. La psicogenesi della coscienza. Milano, 1905.
Phil 4650.1.39 Vannérus, Allen. Kunskapslära. Stockholm, 1905.
Phil 5261.4 Vaz Ferreira, C. Ideas y observaciones. Montevideo, 1905.
Phil 3890.2.80 Verweyen, J. Ehrenfried Walther von Tschirnhaus. Bonn, 1905.
Phil 7140.119 Vigouroux, A. Le contagion mentale. Paris, 1905.
Phil 8601.6 Vilenkin, N.M. Religiia budushchago. Sankt Peterburg, 1905.
Phil 400.20.5 Villa, Guido. L'idealismo moderno. Torino, 1905. 2v.

1905 - cont.

Phil 8422.5   Volkelt, J. System der Ästhetik. München, 1905-14. 3v.

Phil 8423.14   Waetzoldt, W. Das Kunstwerk als Organismus. Leipzig, 1905.

Phil 9182.4.12   Wagner, Charles. Why appeal to America. N.Y., 1905.

Phil 9558.40   Walker, James L. The philosophy of egoism. Denver, 1905.

Phil 6972.9   Wallaschek, R. Psychologie und Pathologie der Vorstellung. Leipzig, 1905.

Phil 8602.20   Wallis, Louis. Egoism. Chicago, 1905.

Phil 5262.23   Walsemann, Hermann. Methodisches Lehrbuch der Psychologie. Potsdam, 1905.

Phil 5648.4   Weber, E.H. Tastsinn und Gemeingefühl. Leipzig, 1905.

Phil 9035.68   Whitby, Charles J. The logic of human character. London, 1905.

Phil 303.9.3   Wille, Bruno. Das Lebendige all; idealistische Weltanschauung. Hamburg, 1905.

Phil 197.42.3   Wilson, F.B. Man limitless. 3d. ed. N.Y., 1905.

Phil 9495.5.6   Wilson, Robert N. The American boy and the social evil. Philadelphia, 1905.

Phil 8602.29   Wishart, A.W. Primary facts in religious thought. Chicago, 1905.

Phil 5062.22.5   Wolf, Abraham. The existential import of categorical predication. Cambridge, 1905.

Phil 3504.10   Wolf, Johannes. Verhaltnis des Beiden ersten Auflagen der Kritik der reinen Vernunft Zueinander. Inaug. Diss. Halle, 1905.

Phil 8602.30   Wood, Henry. Life more abundant. Boston, 1905.

Phil 3915.47.5   Wundt, Wilhelm. Grundriss des Psychologie. 7. Aufl. Leipzig, 1905.

Phil 197.52   Wynaendts Franchen, C.J. Inleiding tot de wijsbegeerte. Haarlem, 1905.

Phil 623.15   Ziegler, Leopold. Der abendländische Rationalismus. Jena, 1905.

Phil 9558.10   Zyromski, Ernest. L'orgueil humain. 2. éd. Paris, 1905.

1906

Phil 175.17   Abbott, F.E. The syllogistic philosophy. Boston, 1906. 2v.

Phil 5240.21   Adumkiewicz, A. Die Eigenkraft der Materie. Wien, 1906.

Phil 4215.1.91   Aguanno, Giuseppe d'. Gian Domenico Roamgnosi filosofo e giureconsulto. Pt.2. Parma, 1906.

Phil 4080.8.83   Alfani, Augusto. Della vita e delle opere. Firenze, 1906.

Phil 5040.13   Almquist, S. Vårt tankelif. Stockholm, 1906.

Phil 5810.4   Alsberg, M. Die Grundlagen des Gedächtnisses, der Vererbung und der Instinkte. München, 1906.

Phil 8625.3   Andresen, Karl. Die Unsterblichkeitsfrage. Leipzig, 1906.

Phil 8875.18   Antieh, José. Egoismo y altruismo. Barcelona, 1906.

Phil 5325.5.2   Arnold, Felix. The psychology of association. N.Y., 1906.

Phil 5325.5   Arnold, Felix. The psychology of association. N.Y., 1906.

Phil 5240.4   Arnold, G.F. Psychology applied to legal evidence. Calcutta, 1906.

Phil 3808.231   Arnold, Otto. Schopenhauer pädägogische. Leipzig, 1906.

Phil 8401.6   Arréat, Lucien. Art et psychologie individuelle. Paris, 1906.

Phil 8881.26.18   Aslan, G. La morale selon Guyau. Paris, 1906.

Phil 6311.21   Bailey, Pearce. Diseases of the nervous system resulting from accident and injury. N.Y., 1906.

Phil 332.7   Baillie, T.B. An outline of the idealistic construction of experience. London, 1906.

VPhil 8400.49   Bakalov, Georgi. Izkustvo i kritika. Sofiia, 1906.

Phil 5041.29   Baldwin, J.M. Thought and things. London, 1906-11. 3v.

Phil 5241.45.5   Baratono, Adelchi. Fondamenti di psicologia sperimentale. Torino, 1906.

Phil 6671.13.5   Barnes, W.A. Personal influence. Boston, 1906.

Phil 176.10.10   Baumann, Julius J. Welt- und Lebensansichte in Ihren. Gotha, 1906.

Phil 5241.61   Baumgartner, M. Grundriss der Psychologie. Dillingen, 1906.

Phil 1140.5   Beare, J.G. Greek theorie of elementary cognition. Oxford, 1906.

Phil 7076.18   Beck, Paul. Die Ekstase. Bad Sachsa, 1906.

Phil 623.9   Benn, A.W. The history of English rationalism in the nineteenth century. London, 1906. 2v.

Phil 1870.60.3A   Berkeley, G. A new theory of vision. London, 1906.

Phil 978.6.43   Besant, Annie. Thought power; its control and culture. London, 1906.

Phil 9341.16   Beveridge, Albert J. The young man and the world. N.Y., 1906.

Phil 8581.31   Bierer, E. The evolution of religions. N.Y., 1906.

Phil 6060.10   Binet, Alfred. Les révélations de l'écriture d'après un controle scientifique. Paris, 1906.

Phil 801.27.20   Bjarnason, A. Nitjánda áldin. Reykjavik, 1906.

Phil 4520.8.48   Bjarnason, Agúst. "Andatrúin" krufin. Reykjavík, 1906.

Phil 4520.8.36   Bjarnason, Agúst. Níjtánda öldin. Reykjavík, 1906.

Phil 86.7   Blanc, Elie. Dictionnaire de philosophie ancienne. Paris, 1906.

Phil 6951.11   Bleuler, E. Affektivität, Suggestibilität, Paranoia. Halle, 1906.

Phil 3120.11.94   Bolland, G.J.P.J. Het schoone en de kunst of de naaste en onmiddelijke zelfbevrediging van absolute geestelijkheid in het kort besproken. Amsterdam, 1906.

Phil 3120.11.93   Bolland, G.J.P.J. Verslag van de rede. Leiden, 1906.

Phil 6951.19   Boulenger, Association des idées chez les idiots. Gand, 1906.

Phil 6671.15   Bramwell, J.M. Hypnotism. 2nd ed. London, 1906.

Phil 3801.233.8   Braun, Otto. Schellings geistige Wandlungen in den Jahren 1800-1810. Leipzig, 1906.

Phil 3801.233.5   Braun, Otto. Schellings geistige Wandlungen in den Jahren 1800-1810. Inaug. Diss. Leipzig, 1906.

Phil 8581.24   Brierley, J. Religion and experience. N.Y., 1906.

Phil 801.13   Brockdorff, C. von. Die Geschichte der Philosophie. Hildesheim, 1906.

Phil 8581.68.5   Broglie, Paul. Religion et critique. 3. éd. Paris, 1906.

Phil 3850.20.80   Bruck, Reinhard. Heinrich Steffens. Diss. Borna, 1906.

Phil 7140.107   Brügelmann, W. Die Behandlung und kranken durch Suggestion. Leipzig, 1906.

Phil 1900.43   Butler, Joseph. The analogy of religion, natural and revealed. 1st ed. London, 1906.

Phil 645.19   Calo, Giovanni. Il problema della libertà nel pensiero contemporaneo. Milano, 1906.

Phil 510.17.5   Carneri, Bartolomäus von. Empfindung und Bewusstsein. 2e Aufl. Stuttgart, 1906.

Phil 5643.33.2   Carr, Harvey. A visual illusion of motion during eye closure. Lancaster, 1906.

1906 - cont.

Phil 333.5   Cassirer, Ernst. Das Erkenntnisproblem in der Philosophie. Berlin, 1906-57. 4v.

Phil 510.1.19   Chwolson, O.D. Hegel, Haeckel, Kossuth und das zwölfte Gebot. Braunschweig, 1906.

Phil 8657.14.5   Cieszkowski, August D. Notre Père. Paris, 1906.

Phil 5585.24   Claparède, E. Expériences collectives sur le...confrontation. Genève, 1906.

Phil 9342.4.10   Cobbett, W. Advice to young men. London, 1906.

Phil 8582.41   Crawford-Frost, W.A. The philosophy of integration. Boston, 1906.

Phil 5042.9   Croke, J.L.O. Logic. London, 1906.

Phil 3428.88   Davidson, John. New interpretation of Herbart's psychology. Edinburgh, 1906.

Phil 1955.10.30   Davis, Charles G. The philosophy of live. 2nd ed. Chicago, 1906.

Phil 5650.19   Deenik, Arie. Het onderscheidingsvermogen voor toonintensiteiten. Leiden, 1906.

Phil 8878.42   Del Mar, E. The divinity of desire. N.Y., 1906.

Phil 9075.10   Delvolve, Jean. L'organisation de la conscience morale. Paris, 1906.

Phil 2520.68   Descartes, René. Regln zur des Geistes. Leipzig, 1906.

Phil 960.130   Desia, Shantaram Anant. A study of Indian philosophy. Bombay, 1906.

Phil 8404.15.2   Dessoir, Max. Ästhetik und allgemeine Kunstwissenschaft in den Grundzügen dargestellt. Stuttgart, 1906.

Phil 960.3.4.5   Deussen, P. Outline of the Vedânta system of philosophy. Cambridge, 1906.

Phil 960.3.4A   Deussen, P. Outline of the Vedânta system of philosophy. 2d ed. N.Y., 1906.

Phil 960.3.7   Deussen, P. The philosophy of the Upanishads. Edinburgh, 1906.

Phil 334.7   Dietzgen, J. The positive outcome of philosophy. Chicago, 1906.

Phil 8404.13   Diez, Max. Algemeine ästhetik. Leipzig, 1906.

Phil 8633.1.9   Dole, C.F. The hope of immortality, our reasons. N.Y., 1906.

Phil 284.12   Dole, George Henry. The philosophy of creation. N.Y., 1906.

Phil 8878.38   Dorner, August. Individuelle und sozial Ethik. Berlin, 1906.

Phil 9163.2   Doumer, P. Livre de mes fils. Paris, 1906.

Phil 178.12.27A   Dresser, H.W. Health and the inner life. N.Y., 1906.

Phil 3415.89.2   Drews, A. Eduard von Hartmanns philosophische System. Heidelberg, 1906.

Phil 8693.5.40   Drummond, H. Lowell lectures on the ascent of man. 13th ed. N.Y., 1906.

Phil 6113.8.5   Dubois, Paul. The influence of the mind on the body. N.Y., 1906.

Phil 3640.174   Düringer, Adelbert. Nietzsche's Philosophie. 2. Aufl. Leipzig, 1906.

Phil 284.4   Duhem, P. La theorie physique. Paris, 1906.

Phil 5525.5   Dumas, G. La sourire. Paris, 1906.

Phil 5075.2   Dupréel, Eugène. Essai sur les catégories. Bruxelles, 1906.

Phil 4210.106   Dyroff, Adolf. Rosmini. Mainz, 1906.

Phil 6114.4   Eisler, R. Leib und Seele. Leipzig, 1906.

Phil 1704.2   Eleutheropulos, A. Einführung in eine wissenschaftliche Philosophie. Leipzig, 1906.

Phil 9575.2   Eliot, C.W. Great riches. N.Y., 1906.

Phil 3260.83   Elsenhans, Theodor. Fries und Kant. v.1-2. Giessen, 1906.

Phil 3195.2.120   Endres, Joseph A. Martin Deutinger. Mainz, 1906.

Phil 3235.81.35   Engels, Friedrich. Ludwig Feuerbach. Chicago, 1906.

Phil 2270.128   Ethical review. No. 4, Dec. 1906. Herbert Spencer memorial number. London, 1906.

Phil 8694.1   Eucken, R. Wissenschaft und Religion. München, 1906.

Phil 3004.1.2   Eucken, Rudolf. Beiträge zur Einführung in die Geschichte der Philosophie. 2. Aufl. Leipzig, 1906.

Phil 3005.3.10   Falckenberg, Richard. La filosofía alemana desde Kant. Madrid, 1906.

Phil 8406.22   Fanciulli, G. La coscienza estetica. Torino, 1906.

Phil 3210.67.3   Fechner, G.T. Das Büchlein vom Leben nach dem Tode. 6. Aufl. Hamburg, 1906.

Phil 3210.40   Fechner, G.T. Zend-Avesta. Hamburg, 1906.

Phil 3120.11.82   Fechter, Paul. Die Grundlagen der Realdialektik. Inaug. Diss. München, 1906.

Phil 3246.209   Ferro, A.A. La filosofia di G.A. Fichte. Savona, 1906.

Phil 3246.68.3   Fichte, Johann Gottlieb. Vocation of man. Chicago, 1906.

Phil 3640.188   Fischer, E.L. F. Nietzsche. Regensburg, 1906.

Phil 3487.1.8   Fischer, Kuno. Kant's leben und die Grundlagen seiner Lehre. Heidelberg, 1906.

Phil 8880.18.2   Fite, Warner. An introductory study of ethics. N.Y., 1906.

Phil 3270.4.80   Fleischmann, M. Anselm von Feuerbach der Jurist, als Philosoph. Inaug. Diss. München, 1906.

Phil 3808.132   Flink, Carl G. Schopenhauers Seelenwanderungslehre. Berlin, 1906.

Phil 180.18   Flügel, D. Die Probleme der Philosophie und ihre Losungen. Cöthen, 1906.

Phil 7069.06.5   Flugrit gegn andatrúnni. Reykjavik, 1906.

Phil 336.1.4   Fouillée, A. L'évolutionnisme des idées-forces. Paris, 1906.

Phil 180.45   Fritzsche, A.R. Vorschule der Philosophie. Leipzig, 1906.

Phil 3487.12   Frost, Walter. Der Begriff der Urteilskraft bei Kant. Halle, 1906.

Phil 8880.34   Fuchs, Emil. Gut und Böse. Tübingen, 1906.

Phil 180.17.5   Fullerton, G.S. An introduction to philosophy. N.Y., 1906.

Phil 5425.2.13   Galton, F. Noteworthy families (Modern science). London, 1906.

Phil 400.55   Gaultier, J. de. Les raisons de l'idéalisme. 2e éd. Paris, 1906.

Phil 3488.8   Gerland, G. Immanuel Kant, seine geographischen und anthropologischen Arbeiten. Berlin, 1906.

Phil 5413.13   Gesell, Arnold L. Jealousy. Diss. Worcester, 1906.

Phil 177.28.2   Görland, A. Index zu Hermann Cohens Logik...Erkenntnis. Berlin, 1906.

Phil 3488.4.25   Goldschmidt, L. Kant und Haeckel. Gotha, 1906.

Phil 5816.4   Graeser, Kurt. Die Vorstellungen der Tiere. Berlin, 1906.

Phil 8586.33   Graf, A. Per una fede. Milano, 1906.

Phil 5545.11.5   Granville, J.M. Secret of a good memory. n.p., 1906.

X Cg   Phil 2020.15A   Green, T.H. Works of Thomas H. Green. London, 1906. 3v.

Phil 1135.165   Guyot, Henri. L'infinite divine depuis Philon le Juif jusqu'à Platin. Paris, 1906.

Phil 8587.40   Hallock, C. Luminous bodies here and hereafter (the shining ones). N.Y., 1906.

Chronological Listing

Phil 6990.5 Hamilton, M. Incubation....Pagan...Christian Churches. London, 1906.

Phil 8587.41 Hatch, D.P. The twentieth century Christ. Boston, 1906.

Phil 5400.24 Hayes, Samuel P. Study of the affective qualities. n.p., 1906.

Phil 3425.45.20 Hegel, Georg Wilhelm Friedrich. Encyclopädie der philosophischen Wissenschaften. Leiden, 1906.

Phil 3425.108 Hegel...Gedankenwelt in Auszügen aus seine Werken. Stuttgart, 1906.

Phil 530.20.20 Hegler, A. Beiträge zur Geschichte der Mystik in der Reformationszeit. Berlin, 1906.

Phil 3450.7.80 Heinze, Max. Philosophische Abhandlungen. Berlin, 1906.

Phil 6957.10 Hellpach, W. Grundgedanken zur Wissenschaftslehre der Psychopathologie. Leipzig, 1906.

Phil 5635.22 Henmon, V.A.C. The time of perception as a measure of differences in sensations. N.Y., 1906.

Phil 5640.11 Henmon, V.A.C. Time of perception as a measure of differences in sensations. N.Y., 1906.

Phil 7069.06.7 Hennig, R. Die moderne Spuk- und Geisterglaube. Hamburg, 1906.

Phil 182.73 Hermann, E. Grundriss der Philosophie. Lahr, 1906.

Phil 5757.9 Hight, G.A. The unity of will. London, 1906.

Phil 400.21 Hinman, E.L. The physics of idealism. Lincoln, 1906.

Phil 672.15.10 Hinton, Charles H. A language of space. London, 1906.

Phil 9245.48 Hodge, George. The pursuit of happiness. N.Y., 1906.

Phil 9167.5 Hodges, George. The happy family. N.Y., 1906.

Phil 8632.2 Höffding, H. The philosophy of religion. London, 1906.

Phil 182.36.7 Höffding, H. The problems of philosophy. N.Y., 1906.

Phil 5047.14 Höfler, Alois. Grundlehren der Logik und Psychologie. Leipzig, 1906.

Phil 5047.34 Hönigswald, R. Beiträge zur Erkenntnistheorie uhd Methodenlehre. Leipzig, 1906.

Phil 5047.13 Hooper, C.E. The anatomy of knowledge. London, 1906.

Phil 3640.124 Horneffer, Auguet. Nietzsche als Moralist und Schriftsteller. Jena, 1906.

Phil 3640.121.10 Horneffer, Ernst. Vorträge über Nietzsche. Berlin, 1906.

Phil 1504.5.3 Horten, M. Buch der Ringsteine Alfârâbis. v.5, pt.3. Münster, 1906.

Phil 9347.2.5* Hubbard, E. A message to Garcia. N.Y., 1906.

Phil 1535.27.2 Huber, Sebastian. Grundzüge der Logik und Noëtik. Paderborn, 1906.

Phil 1050.6 Husik, Isaac. Judah Messer Leon's commentary on the Vitus logica. Leiden, 1906.

Phil 6990.3.9 Huysmans, J.K. Les foules de Lourdes. 21. éd. Paris, 1906.

Phil 7069.06.10 Hyslop, James Hervey. Borderland of psychical research. 2. ed. Boston, 1906.

Phil 7069.06.11 Hyslop, James Hervey. Enigmas of psychical research. Boston, 1906.

Phil 8663.3.12 Ingersoll, Robert G. Collection of Robert G. Ingersoll's famous speeches. N.Y., 1906.

Phil 70.5 International Congress of Arts and Sciences, St. Louis, 1904. Proceedings. Philosophy and mathematics. Washington, 1906.

Phil 5759.5 Jäkel, Josef. Die Freiheit des menschlichen Willens. Wien, 1906.

Phil 5627.6.7 James, William. L'expérience religieuse. Paris, 1906.

Phil 5627.6.10 James, William. Den religiösä erfarenheten. Stockholm, 1906.

Phil 5627.6.12A James, William. Religiøse erfaringer. København, 1906.

Phil 2805.109 Janssens, Edgard. La philosophie et l'apologétique de Pascal. Louvain, 1906.

Phil 5722.15 Jastrow, J. The subconscious. Boston, 1906.

Phil 9575.3 Jenks, J.W. Great fortunes: The winning, the using. N.Y., 1906.

Phil 8589.7 Jevons, Frank B. Religion in evolution. London, 1906.

Phil 525.39 Joël, Karl. Der Ursprung der Naturphilosophie aus dem Geiste der Mystik. Jena, 1906.

Phil 1145.35 Jones, W.H.S. Greek morality in relation to institutions. London, 1906.

Phil 575.11 Jones, W.T. Idee der Persönlichkeit bei den englischen Denken. Jena, 1906.

Phil 7069.06.13 Jónsson, G. Ur dularheimum. Reykjavik, 1906.

Phil 9075.38 Kabisch, R. Das Gewissen. Göttingen, 1906.

Phil 3480.28.35 Kant, Immanuel. Ausgewählt und Bearbeitet von L. Weis. Hamburg, 1906.

Phil 3480.65.7 Kant, Immanuel. Grundlegung zur Metaphysik der Sitten. Leipzig, 1906.

Phil 3549.10.5 Kassner, Rudolf. Motive; essays. Berlin, 1906.

Phil 5585.16 Katz, David. Experimentelle Beiträge zur Psychologie...des Zeitsinns. Leipzig, 1906.

Phil 8885.19.7 Kautsky, Karl. Ethics and the materialist conception of history. Chicago, 1906.

Phil 8885.19.9 Kautsky, Karl. Ethik und materialistische Geschichtsauffassung. Stuttgart, 1906.

Phil 8590.16 Key, Ellen. Der Lebensglaube. Berlin, 1906.

Phil 291.1 Keyserling, H. Das Gefüge der Welt. München, 1906.

Phil 8590.10.7 King, Henry C. Letters on the greatness and simplicity of the Christian faith. Boston, 1906.

Phil 810.2 Kinkel, W. Geschichte der Philosophie. v.1-2. Giessen, 1906.

Phil 8960.1 Kirn, Otto. Zur Feier des Reformationsfestes. Leipzig, 1906.

Phil 6120.1 Klein, A. Die modernen Theorien über Verhältnis von Leib und Seele. Breslau, 1906.

Phil 4260.83.2 Klemm, Otto. G.B. Vico als Geschichtsphilosoph. Leipzig, 1906.

Phil 4260.83 Klemm, Otto. G.B. Vico als Geschichtsphilosoph. Inaug. Diss. Leipzig, 1906.

Phil 3552.259 Kolls. Zur Chronologie der leibnizischen Abhandlung "De vera methodo philosphiae et theologiae". Schönberg, 1906.

Phil 665.18 Kostyleff, Nicolas. Les substituts de l'âme. Paris, 1906.

Phil 1504.5.5 Krebs, E. Meister Dietrich. v.5, pt.5-6. Münster, 1906.

Phil 7140.106 Krebs, Stanley le Fevre. The law of suggestion. 1st ed. Chicago, 1906.

Phil 5760.4 Kulew, T. Das Probleme der Willensfreiheit und der Grundbegriffe der Strafrechts. Sofia, 1906.

Phil 8411.19 Kulke, Eduard. Kritik der Philosophie des Schönen. Leipzig, 1906.

Phil 7069.06.15 Kvaran, E.H. Dularfull fyrirbrigð Reykjavik, 1906.

Phil 2885.84.5 Lacombe, Paul. La psychologie des individus et des societés chez Taine. Paris, 1906.

Phil 4600.1.31 Landquist, John. Filosofiska essayer. Stockholm, 1906.

Phil 8886.41 Landry, Adolph. Principes de morale rationnelle. Paris, 1906.

Phil 3425.108A Lasson, G. Hegel...Gedankenwelt in Auszügen aus seine Werken. Stuggart, 1906.

Phil 186.19 Laurie, S.S. Synthetica. London, 1906. 2v.

Phil 525.48 Leclère, A. Le mysticisme catholique et l'âme de Dante. Paris, 1906.

Phil 186.20 Lee, G.S. The voice of the machines. Northampton, 1906.

Phil 2805.93 Lefranc, A. Défense de Pascal...est-il un faussaire? Paris, 1906.

Phil 5251.20.5 Lehmann, Alfred. Lehrbuch der psychologischen Methodik. Leipzig, 1906.

Phil 3808.179 Lessing, Theodor. Schopenhauer, Wagner, Nietzsche. München, 1906.

Phil 5251.11 Liguet, G.H. Idée générales de psychologie. Paris, 1906.

Phil 6121.10.5 Lipps, G.F. Die psychischen Massmethoden. Braunschweig, 1906.

Phil 2115.74.10 Locke, J. Zwei Abhandlungen über Regierung. Halle, 1906.

Phil 510.1.12 Lodge, Oliver. Life and matter. A criticism of Prof. Haeckel's riddle. N.Y., 1906.

Phil 5841.14 Loewenfeld, Leopold. Sexualleben und Nervenleiden. Wiesbaden, 1906.

Phil 8412.19 Lotze, Hermann. Grundzuge der Ästhetik. 3. Aufl. Leipzig, 1906.

Phil 5051.22 Lutoslawski, W. Logika ogolna czyli Teorja poznania i logika formalna. London, 1906.

Phil 5052.12 MacColl, H. Symbolic logic and its applications. London, 1906.

Phil 2125.50.5 McCosh, James. Psychology: the cognitive powers. N.Y., 1906.

Phil 343.4.3 Mach, E. Erkenntnis und Irrtum. 2. Aufl. Leipzig, 1906.

Phil 672.17 Mach, E. Space and geometry. Chicago, 1906.

Phil 5762.4 Mack, Joseph. Kritik der Freiheitstheorien. Leipzig, 1906.

Phil 5052.13 Macleane, D. Reason, thought and language. London, 1906.

Phil 9035.26.2 Malapert, P. Les éléments du caractère. 2e éd. Paris, 1906.

Phil 6122.35 Marden, Orison S. Every man a king. N.Y., 1906.

Phil 6962.14 Marie, A. La demence. Paris, 1906.

Phil 6122.28 Marschik, S. Geist und Seele. Berlin, 1906.

Phil 6122.16 Marsh, H.D. Diurnal course of efficiency. N.Y., 1906.

Phil 6122.16.2 Marsh, H.D. Diurnal course of efficiency. N.Y., 1906.

Phil 5520.25 Mauthner, Fritz. Beiträge zu einer Kritik der Sprache. 2. Aufl. Stuttgart, 1906.

Phil 3832.5 Mauthner, Fritz. Spinoza. Berlin, 1906.

Phil 487.3 Mayer, Adolf. Los vom Materialismus! Heidelberg, 1906.

Phil 187.28.8 Mechnikov, I.I. Studier öfver människans natur. Stockholm, 1906.

Phil 3801.565 Mehlis, Georg. Schellings Geschichtsphilosophie in den Jahren 1799-1804. Heidelberg, 1906.

Phil 343.5.15 Meinong, A. Über die Erfahrungsgrundlagen unseres Wissens. Berlin, 1906.

Phil 2138.50.8 Mill, John S. Utilitarianism. Chicago, 1906.

Phil 6322.1.15 Möbius, P.J. Die Nervosität. 3e Aufl. Leipzig, 1906.

Phil 4363.2.5 Molinos, M. de. Guia espiritual. Barcelona, 1906.

Phil 6122.14 Morat, J.P. Physiology of the nervous system. Chicago, 1906.

Phil 7150.16 Moreau, Jacques. Du suicide chez les enfants. Thèse. Paris, 1906.

Phil 187.29.3 Morgan, C.L. The interpretation of nature. N.Y., 1906.

Phil 5627.11 Moses, J. Pathological aspects of religions. Worcester, 1906.

Phil 400.19 Münsterberg, H. Science and idealism. Boston, 1906.

Htn Phil 3625.10.35* Münsterberg, H. Science and idealism. Boston, 1906.

Phil 188.12.5 Natorp, Paul. Jemand und ich. Stuttgart, 1906.

Phil 5330.8 Nayrac, J.P. Physiologie et psychologie de l'attention. Paris, 1906.

Phil 3640.11.10A Nietzsche, Friedrich. Werke. Leipzig, 1906-09. 11v.

Phil 8668.3 Norlin, C. Étude laique de la notion de Dieu. Paris, 1906.

Phil 4610.7.50 Norström, V. Den nyaste människan. Stockholm, 1906.

Phil 9495.39.5 Northcote, Hugh. Christianity and sex problems. Philadelphia, 1906.

Phil 9035.32 Norton, Carol. Studies in character. Boston, 1906.

Phil 8593.6 Noyes, R.K. Views of religion. Boston, 1906.

Phil 510.11 Olivier, J. von. Monistische Weltanschauung, Leipzig, 1906.

Phil 5620.13.3 Ollé-Laprune, L. La raison et le rationalisme. 3. éd. Paris, 1906.

Phil 960.140 Oltramare, Paul. L'histoire des idées theosophiques dans l'Inde. Paris, 1906-23. 2v.

Phil 189.6.5 Ormond, A.T. Concepts of philosophy. N.Y., 1906.

Phil 1504.6 Ostler, H. Die Psychologie. v.6, pt.1. Münster, 1906.

Phil 8633.1.8 Ostwald, W. Individuality and immortality. Boston, 1906.

Phil 1119.2.21 Ovink, B.J.H. Overzicht der grieksche wijsbegeerte. 2e druk. Zutphen, 1906.

Phil 3270.5.80 Pachaly, E. J.G.H. Feders Erkenntnistheorie und Metaphysik. Inaug. Diss. Leipzig, 1906.

Phil 600.20 Pacheu, Jules. Du positivisme au mysticisme. 2e éd. Paris, 1906.

Phil 1715.2 Papini, Giovanni. Il crepuscolo dei filosofi. Milano, 1906.

Phil 5055.20 Pastore, Annibale. Logica formale...modelli meccanici. Torino, 1906.

Phil 6125.17.5 Patterson, C.B. The will to be well. 5th ed. N.Y., 1906.

Phil 9355.2.5 Peachman, Henry. The compleat gentleman. London, 1906.

Phil 8595.12 Perry, R.B. Religion and mere morality. Boston, 1906.

Phil 600.16 Petzoldt, Joseph. Das Weltproblem vom positivistischen Standpunkte aus. Leipzig, 1906.

Phil 8595.4.12 Pfleiderer, O. Religion und Religionen. München, 1906.

Phil 8595.4.15 Pfleiderer, O. Uber das Verhältnis der Religionsphilosophie. Berlin, 1906.

Phil 5500.4 Pfordten, O.F. von. Versuch einer Theorie von Urteil und Begriff. Heidelberg, 1906.

Phil 8595.32 Philips, Vivian. The churches and modern thought. London, 1906.

Phil 25.18 Philosophische Wochenschrift und Literatur-Zeitung. v.1-7. Leipzig, 1906-07. 7v.

Phil 5545.40 Pohlmann, A. Experimentelle Beiträge zur Lehre vom Gedächtnis. Berlin, 1906.

Phil 1630.30 Poppi, Antonino. Causalità e infinità nella scuola padovana dal 1480 al 1513. Padova, 1906.

Phil 3195.9.80 Posner, S. Abriss der Philosophie Eugen Dührings. Inaug. Diss. Breslau, 1906.

Phil 525.50.5 Poulain, A. Des graces d'oraison. 5e éd. Paris, 1906.

Phil 3835.4.2 Powell, E.E. Spinoza and religion. Chicago, 1906.

Phil 325.2 Prat, Louis. Caractére empirique et la personne. Paris. 1906.

1906 - cont.

Phil 7039.4.1 — Prince, Morton. The dissociation of a personality. N.Y., 1906.

Phil 8595.13 — Pritchett, H.S. What is religion. Boston, 1906.

Phil 960.15A — Rámanáthan, P. The spirit of the East contracted with spirit of the West. N.Y., 1906.

Phil 8597.21 — Rámanthán, P. The culture of the soul. N.Y., 1906.

Phil 75.13.9 — Rand, Benjamin. Selected works on history of philosophy in English language. Boston, 1906.

Phil 7069.06.20 — Raupert, John G. The dangers of spiritualism. 2. ed. London, 1906.

Phil 8892.26.8 — Rayot, E. Précis de morale. 8. ed. Paris, 1906.

Phil 3499.8 — Renouvier, C. Critique de la doctrine de Kant. Paris, 1906.

Phil 8842.5 — Reybekiel, A. Das biologische Prinzip in den moralphilosophischen Anschauungen W. Rolph's, M. Guyau's und Fr. Nietzsches. Krakau, 1906.

Phil 5465.5.5 — Ribot, T. Essay on the creative imagination. Chicago, 1906.

Phil 6327.46.14 — Ribot, Théodule. The diseases of personality. 4th ed. Chicago, 1906.

Phil 5767.2.3A — Rickaby, Joseph. Free will and four English philosophers. London, 1906.

Phil 8892.31 — Ritter, T.H. Lifvets konst. Stockholm, 1906.

Phil 3837.9 — Rivaud, Albert. Les notions d'essence...de Spinoza. Paris, 1906.

Phil 1122.7 — Rivaud, Albert. Le problème du devenir et la notion de la matière dans la philosophie grecque depuis les origines jusqu'à Theophraste. Paris, 1906.

Phil 8610.899.5 — Robertson, J.M. A short history of freethought, ancient and modern. 2. ed. London, 1906. 2v.

Phil 8597.15 — Robinson, E.K. The religion of nature. London, 1906.

Phil 3499.6.15 — Romundt, H. Der Professorenkant. Gotha, 1906.

Phil 645.10 — Rossi, G. Agrippa di Nettesheym e la direzione scettica. Torino, 1906.

Phil 5257.11.5 — Royce, Josiah. Outlines of psychology. N.Y., 1906.

Phil 1817.2 — Rusk, Robert R. Pragmatische und humanistische Strömung. Jena, 1906.

Phil 5057.11 — Russell, J.E. An elementary logic. N.Y., 1906.

Phil 6028.5 — Sanctis, Sante de. Die Mimik des Denkens. Halle, 1906.

Phil 193.49.1 — Santayana, G. Life of reason. N.Y., 1906. 5v.

Phil 2490.119 — Schaefer, Albert. Die Moralphilosophie Auguste Comte's Versuch einer Darstellung und Kritik. Basel, 1906.

Phil 3800.200.30 — Schelling, F.W.J. von. Bruno. Torino, 1906.

Phil 5645.25 — Schenck, F. Über die physiologischen Grundlagen des Farbensinns. Marburg, 1906.

Phil 3890.6.83 — Schinz, Max. Die Moralphilosophie von Tetens. Leipzig, 1906.

Phil 2885.105 — Schlaf, Johannes. Kritik der Taineschen Kunsttheorie. Wien, 1906.

Phil 165.5 — Schmid, Bastian. Philosophisches Lesebuch zum Gebrauch an höheren Schulen und zum Selbststudium. Leipzig, 1906.

Phil 1504.4.5A — Schneider, A. Die Psychologie Alberts des Grossen. v.4, pt.5-6. v.1 rejected 1971. Münster, 1906.

Phil 3808.36.10.3 — Schopenhauer, Arthur. The world as will and idea. London, 1906-09. 3v.

Phil 5258.60 — Schultz, Paul. Gehirn und Seele. Leipzig, 1906.

Phil 349.12.5 — Schwartzkopff, P. Was ist Denken? Wernigerode, 1906.

Phil 5545.161 — Segno, A.V. The secret of memory. Los Angeles, 1906.

Phil 193.51 — Shaler, S.P. The masters of fate...the power of the will. N.Y., 1906.

Phil 6128.13 — Sherrington, C.S. The integrative action of the nervous system. N.Y., 1906.

Phil 2280.1.80 — Sidgwick, A. Henry Sidgwick. London, 1906.

Phil 8550.388 — Siebert, Otto. Die Religionsphilosophie in Deutschland in ihren gegenwärtigen Hauptvertretern. Langensalza, 1906.

Phil 3500.20.5 — Simmel, G. Kant und Goethe. Berlin, 1906.

Phil 8598.33.3 — Simmel, G. Die Religion. Frankfurt, 1906.

Phil 193.89 — Sinibaldi, T. Elementos de philosophia. 3a ed. Coimbra, 1906. 2v.

Phil 8598.12.5 — Smith, Goldwin. Inquest of light. N.Y., 1906.

Phil 193.54 — Sortais, G. Traité de philosophie. Paris, 1906-1907. 3v.

Phil 193.74 — Stapfer, Paul. Questions esthétiques et religeuses. Paris, 1906.

Phil 5650.14 — Starch, D. Perimetry of the localization of sound. Pt.1-2. Thesis. n.p., 1906.

Phil 193.53 — Stern, L.W. Person und Sache. Leipzig, 1906- 2v.

Phil 8893.53 — Störring, Gustav. Ethische Grundfragen. Leipzig, 1906.

Phil 193.50 — Studies in philosophy and psychology. Boston, 1906.

Phil 400.13.5 — Sturt, H. Idola theatri; a criticism of Oxford thought and thinkers. London, 1906.

Phil 3246.87.2 — Talbot, E.B. Fundamental principle of Fichte's philosophy. N.Y., 1906.

Phil 3246.87 — Talbot, E.B. Fundamental principle of Fichte's philosophy. Diss. N.Y., 1906.

Phil 3805.103 — Thilo, C.A. Schleiermachers Religionsphilosophie. Langensalza, 1906.

Phil 8430.40 — Thode, H. Kundt und Sittlichkeit. Heidelberg, 1906.

Phil 8644.7 — Thompson, R.J. The proofs of life after death. Paris, 1906.

Phil 2270.127A — Thomson, J.A. Herbert Spencer. London, 1906.

Phil 6129.1.4 — Thomson, W.H. Brain and personality. N.Y., 1906.

Phil 2218.86A — Thorpe, J.E. Joseph Priestley. London, 1906.

Phil 150.1 — Tönnies, F. Philosophische Terminologie. Leipzig, 1906.

Phil 194.31A — Troilo, Erminis. Filosofia, vita e modernita. Roma, 1906.

Phil 1135.81.5 — Trubetskoi, S.N. Uchenie o Logose. Moskva, 1906.

Phil 8644.3 — Turner, F.H. Beside the new-made grave. Boston, 1906.

Phil 8674.6 — Tuttle, Hudson. Evolution of the God and Christ ideas. Berlin, 1906.

Phil 7069.08.45 — The twice-born. London, 1906.

Phil 2270.160 — Two (pseud.). Home life with Herbert Spencer. Bristol, 1906.

Phil 820.1.5 — Ueberweg, F. Grundriss der Geschichte der Philosophie. 10. ed. Berlin, 1906. 4v.

Phil 3502.1 — Uphues, G.K. Kant und seine Vorgänger. Berlin, 1906.

Phil 4265.5.30 — Vanni, Icilio. Saggi di filosofia sociale e giuridica. Bologna, 1906-11. 2v.

Phil 5261.5.5 — Varona, Enrique José. Curso de psicologia. Fascimile 2. Havana, 1906.

Phil 8422.2 — Volbehr, Theodor. Gibt es Kunstgesetze. Esslingen, 1906.

Phil 352.1.5 — Volkelt, J. Die quellen der menschlichen Gewissheit. München, 1906.

Phil 5262.25 — Wahle, Richard. Über den Mechanismus des geistigen Lebens. Wien, 1906.

Phil 525.19 — Waite, A.E. Studies in mysticism and certain aspects of the secret tradition. London, 1906.

1906 - cont.

Phil 9182.6 — Wallace, Henry. Uncle Henry's letters to the farm boy. 4. ed. N.Y., 1906.

Phil 8897.29A — Washington, B.T. Putting the most into life. N.Y., 1906.

Phil 5832.3.9 — Wasmann, E. Menschen und Tierseele. Köln, 1906.

Phil 9530.24 — Waterman, Nixon. Boy wanted. Chicago., 1906.

Phil 3905.31 — Weininger, Otto. Sex and character. London, 1906.

Phil 5062.16 — Weinstein, B. Die philosophische Grundlagen der Wissenschaften. Leipzig, 1906.

Phil 5650.4 — Wells, F.L. Linguistic lapses. N.Y., 1906.

Phil 8897.28 — Westermarck, E. The origin and development...moral ideas. 2nd ed. London, 1906-17. 2v.

Phil 197.17 — Wheeler, C.K. Hundredth century philosophy. Boston, 1906.

Phil 400.21.5 — Willems, C. Die Erkenntnislehre des modernen Idealismus. Trier, 1906.

Phil 8423.16 — Winckelmann, Johann Joachim. Johann Winckelmann, G. Ephraim Lessing klassische Schönheit. Jena, 1906.

Phil 1504.5 — Wittmann, M. Zur Stellung Avencebrolis. v.5, pt.1. Münster, 1906.

Phil 510.1.25 — Wobbermin, Georg. Ernst Haeckel im Kampf gegen die christliche Weltanschauung. Leipzig, 1906.

Phil 197.13.8 — Wood, H. Studies in the thought world. 8th ed. Boston, 1906.

Phil 5440.9 — Woods, F.A. Mental and moral heredity in royalty. N.Y., 1906.

Phil 8647.2 — Woods, J.H. Practice and science of religion. London, 1906.

Phil 9245.17 — Wright, W.K. Ethical significances of pleasure. Chicago, 1906.

Phil 3915.76 — Wundt, Wilhelm. Essays. Leipzig, 1906.

Phil 3915.40.3 — Wundt, Wilhelm. Logik. 3. Aufl. Stuttgart, 1906-08. 3v.

Phil 3915.55.12 — Wundt, Wilhelm. Vorlesungen über die Menschen- und Thierseele. Hamburg, 1906. 2v.

Phil 8897.42 — Wyneken, Ernst F. Das Naturgestz der Seele und...Freiheit. Heidelberg, 1906.

Phil 5265.1.4.2 — Ziehen, Theodor. Leitfaden der physiologischen Psychologie. 7. Aufl. Jena, 1906.

Phil 200.5 — Zucca, Antioco. L'uomo e l'infinito. Roma, 1906.

1907

Phil 8875.14 — Aars, K.B.R. Gut und Böse. Christiania, 1907.

Phil 4513.2.35 — Aars, K.B.R. Haben die naturgesetze Wirklichkeit? Christiania, 1907.

Phil 7052.7 — Abbott, D.P. Behind the scenes with the mediums. Chicago, 1907.

Phil 8401.24 — Adams, E.K. The aesthetic experience: its meaning in a functional psychology. Chicago, 1907.

Phil 4508.7 — Adelborg, Gustaf Otto. Om det personligt andliga. Stockholm, 1907.

Phil 9035.25 — Adickes, E. Charakter und Weltanschauung. Tübingen, 1907.

Phil 800.2 — Alexander, A.B.D. A short history of philosophy. Glasgow, 1907.

Phil 8875.17 — Allen, James. From poverty to power. N.Y., 1907.

Phil 2840.82 — Arnal, A. La philosophie religieuse de C. Renouvier. Paris, 1907.

Phil 8625.5.15 — Arnold, Edwin. Death and afterwards. London, 1907.

Phil 3425.128 — Aschkenasy, H. Hegels Einfluss auf die Religionsphilosophie in Deutschland. Berlin, 1907.

Phil 331.2.5 — Avenarius, R. Kritik der Reinen Erfahrung. Leipzig, 1907.

Phil 5643.43.5 — Bader, Paul. Augentauschungen. Leipzig, 1907.

Phil 1106.1A — Bakewell, C.M. Source book in ancient philosophy. N.Y., 1907.

Phil 1106.1.5 — Bakewell, C.M. Source book in ancient philosophy. N.Y., 1907.

Phil 8581.39 — Barnes, Earl. Where knowledge fails. N.Y., 1907.

Phil 960.12 — Barnett, L.D. Brahma-knowledge, outline of philosophy of the Vedânta. London, 1907.

Phil 3552.112.5 — Baruzi, Jean. Leibniz et l'organisation religieuse. Paris, 1907.

Phil 176.14.5 — Bax, E.B. The roots of reality. London, 1907.

Phil 8876.51 — Bayet, Albert. La morale scientifique. 2e ed. Paris, 1907.

Phil 3640.190.5 — Bélart, Hans. Friedrich Nietzsche und Richard Wagner. Berlin, 1907.

Phil 8876.44 — Belot, G. Études de morale positive. Paris, 1907.

Phil 8876.55.5 — Bennett, Arnold. The reasonalbe life, being hints for men and women. London, 1907.

Phil 1865.51.10 — Bentham, Jeremy. An introduction to the principles of morals and legislation. Oxford, 1907.

X Cg — Phil 4752.2.30 — Berdiaev, Nikolai Aleksandrovich. Sub specie aeternitatis. Sankt Peterburg, 1907.

Phil 6400.7 — Bernheim, Hippolyte. Doctrine de l'aphasie. Paris, 1907.

Phil 1106.10 — Bertling, Oskar. Geschichte der alten Philosophie. Leipzig, 1907.

Phil 5241.48.5 — Biervliet, Jules Jean van. La psychologie quantitative. Gand, 1907.

Phil 6111.14.6 — Binet, A. The mind and the brain. London, 1907.

Phil 5620.1.7 — Binet, A. The psychology of reasoning. Chicago, 1907.

Phil 5627.22 — Binet-Sangle, Charles. Les lois psychophysiologique du développement des religions. Paris, 1907.

Phil 9400.3 — Bishop, E.M. Seventy years young. N.Y., 1907.

Phil 978.5.11 — Blavatsky, H.P. An abridgement by K. Hilliard of The secret doctrine. N.Y., 1907.

Phil 176.47A — Blewett, G.J. Study of nature...with other essays. Toronto, 1907.

Phil 7069.07.9 — Bois, Jules. Le miracle moderne. 4. ed. Paris, 1907.

Phil 8876.82 — Bonucci, A. L'orientazione psicologica dell'etica e della filosofia del diritto. Perugia, 1907.

Phil 3483.15 — Borowski, L.E. Immanuel Kant. 2. Aufl. Halle, 1907.

Phil 5241.25 — Brackenbury, L. Primer of psychology. London, 1907.

Phil 5635.37 — Brentano, Franz. Untersuchungen zur Sinnespsychologie. Leipzig, 1907.

Phil 600.31.9 — Bridges, J.H. Essays and addresses. London, 1907.

Phil 8581.24.20 — Brierley, J. Vårt gemensamma lif. Stockholm, 1907.

Phil 5465.6 — Brittain, H.L. A study in imagination. n.p., 1907.

Phil 801.14.3 — Brothier, Léon. Histoire populaire de la philosophie. 3. ed. Paris, 1907.

Phil 978.24 — Bruhn, Wilhelm. Theosophie und Theologie. Glückstadt, 1907.

Phil 4065.13 — Bruno, Giordano. Opere italiane. Bari, 1907. 2v.

Phil 3640.645 — Brzozowski, S.L. Fryderyk Nietzsche. Stanisɫawów, 1907.

Phil 2490.98.7 — Caird, Edward. Philosophie sociale et religion d'Auguste Comte. Paris, 1907.

Phil 365.13 — Calderoni, G. L'evoluzione e i suoi limiti. Roma, 1907.

Chronological Listing

1907 - cont.

Phil 333.11	Calderoni, M. La previsione nella teoria della conoscenza. Milano, 1907.
Phil 4112.84	Campari, A. Galluppi e Kant nella dottrina morale. Conegliano, 1907.
Phil 3484.10.2	Cantoni, Carlo. Emanuele Kant. 2. ed. Milano, 1907.
Phil 4210.113	Carabellese, P. La teoria della percezione intellettiva. Bari, 1907.
Phil 7069.07.10	Carrington, Hereward. The physical phenomena of spiritualism. Boston, 1907.
Phil 930.1.2	Carus, P. Chinese thought. Chicago, 1907.
Phil 177.46	Cesca, Giovanni. La filosofia dell'azione. Milano, 1907.
Phil 8627.9.7	Chambers, A. Problems of the spiritual. Philadelphia, 1907.
Phil 8582.33.5	Charbonnel, Victor. The victory of will. Boston, 1907.
Phil 3484.2.15	Cohen, H. Kommentar zu Immanuel Kant's Kritik. Leipzig, 1907.
Phil 177.44	Cohn, Jonas. Führende Denker. Leipzig, 1907.
Phil 4065.112	Cotugno, R. Giordano Bruno e le sue opere. Trani, 1907.
Phil 333.6	Coursault, J.H. The learning process. Theory of knowledge. N.Y., 1907.
Phil 8692.3	Coutts, John. The divine wisdom...nature, man and bible. London, 1907.
Phil 3425.109.4	Croce, B. Ciò che è vivo e ciò che è morto della filosofia di Hegel. Bari, 1907.
Phil 5643.57	Daublebsky, Storneck von. Der Sehraum auf grund der Erfahrung. Leipzig, 1907.
Cg Phil 1200.17	Davidson, W.L. The stoic creed. Edinburgh, 1907.
Phil 1200.17	Davidson, W.L. The stoic creed. Edinburgh, 1907.
Phil 5813.2	Davis, H.B. The raccoon: a study in animal intelligence. London, 1907.
Phil 284.11	Dennert, E. Die Weltanschauung des modernen Naturforschers. Stuttgart, 1907.
Phil 803.3.2	Deussen, P. Allgemeine Geschichte der Philosophie. Leipzig, 1907-020. 3v.
Phil 960.3.9	Deussen, P. Outlines of Indian philosophy. Berlin, 1907.
Phil 8878.23.4	Dickinson, G.L. The meaning of good. 4th ed. N.Y., 1907.
Phil 284.5	Dippe, Alfred. Naturphilosophie. München, 1907.
Phil 1145.37	Dobbs, A.E. Philosophy and popular morals in ancient Greece. Dublin, 1907.
Phil 5643.43	Dodge, Raymond. An experimental study of visual fixation. Lancaster, 1907.
Phil 178.12.60	Dresser, H.W. The greatest truth. N.Y., 1907.
Phil 8878.24	DuBois, P. The culture of justice. N.Y., 1907.
Phil 3640.245	Düringer, Adelbert. Nietzsches Philosophie und das neutige Christentum. Leipzig, 1907.
Phil 5330.10	Dürr, E. Die Lehre von der Aufmerksamkeit. Leipzig, 1907.
Phil 630.20	Dürr, Ernst. Grundzüge einer realistischen Weltanschauung. Leipzig, 1907.
Phil 8878.32	DuRoussaux, L. Ethique; traité de philosophie morale. Bruxelles, 1907.
Phil 3808.147	Ebstein, W. Arthur Schopenhauer seine wirklichen und vermeintlichen Krankheiten. Stuttgart, 1907.
Phil 978.23.3	Edger, L. The elements of theosophy. London, 1907.
Phil 7069.07.35	Edgerly, Webster. Book of the Psychic Society. Washington, 1907.
Phil 5244.11	Eichberg, T. Psychologische Probleme. Stuttgart, 1907.
Phil 525.46	Elkinton, J. The light of mysticism. Philadelphia, 1907.
Phil 8735.11	Elkus, S.A. The concept of control. N.Y., 1907.
Phil 5044.1.2	Erdmann, B. Logik. 2e Aufl. Halle, 1907.
Phil 6114.11.10	Erdmann, B. Wissenschaftliche Hypothesen über Leib und Seele. Köln, 1907.
Phil 8829.2.9	Eucken, Rudolf. Grundlinien einer neuen Lebensanschauung. Leipzig, 1907.
Phil 3486.4	Evellin, F. La raison pure...essai sur la philosophie Kantienne. Paris, 1907.
Phil 3210.25	Fechner, G.T. Ausgewählte Schriften. Berlin, 1907.
Phil 3210.45.10	Fechner, G.T. Über die Seelenfrage. 2. Aufl. Hamburg, 1907.
Phil 7069.07.17	Flammarion, C. Les forces naturelles inconnues. Paris, 1907.
Phil 7069.07.18	Flammarion, C. Mysterious psychic forces. Boston, 1907.
Phil 9165.3	Foerster, F.W. Lebenskunde, ein Buch für Knaben und Mädchen. Berlin, 1907.
Phil 6115.21	Forel, A. Hygiene of nerves and mind in health and disease. London, 1907.
Phil 6675.6.5	Forel, A. Hypnotism or suggestion and psychotherapy. N.Y., 1907.
Phil 6115.23	Frany, Shepherd I. On the functions of the cerebrum. N.Y., 1907.
Phil 575.20	Frew, D.I. Cosmic inquiry pertaining to origin and development of individuality. Salt Lake City, 1907.
Phil 3808.159	Friedlander, Salomo. Schopenhauer, seine Persönlichkeit in seinen Werken. Bd.II. Stuttgart, 1907.
Phil 180.22	Frischeisen-Köhler, M. Moderne Philosophie. Stuttgart, 1907.
Phil 5649.15	Froeberg, Sven. Relation between magnitude of stimulus and the time of reaction. Diss. N.Y., 1907.
Phil 3246.253	Froelich, Franz. Fichtes Reden an die deutsche Nation. Berlin, 1907.
Phil 7069.07.21	Funk, Isaac K. The psychic riddle. N.Y., 1907.
Phil 5246.1.10	Galton, F. Inquiries into human faculty and its development. London, 1907.
Phil 3890.9.90	Gamper, J. Paul Vital Ignoz Troxlers Leben und Philosophie. Diss. Bern, 1907.
Phil 3826.6	Gans, M.E. Spinozismus. Wien, 1907.
Phil 3625.7.90	Gaquoin, Karl. Die transcendentale Harmonie bei Ernst Marcus. Wiesbaden, 1907.
Phil 8520.22	Gardner, P. The growth of Christianity. London, 1907.
Phil 8881.37	Gaultier, Jules de. La dépendance de la morale et l'indépendance des moeurs. Paris, 1907.
Phil 5246.38	Geiger, Moritz. Methodologische und experimentelle Beiträge zur Quantitätslehre. Leipzig, 1907.
Phil 4065.102.8	Gentile, G. Giordano Bruno nella storia della cultura. Milano, 1907.
Phil 665.33	Gibbons, J. Theories of the transmigration of souls. London, 1907.
Phil 179.3.82	Gibson, W.R.B. Rudolf Eucken's philosophy of life. London, 1907.
Phil 5520.14	Ginneken, J. van. Principes de linguistic psychologique. Paris, 1907.
Phil 5756.8	Gjerdsjø, O. Determinismen og dens konsekvenser. Kristiania, 1907.
Phil 5246.7.3	Godfernaux, A. Le sentiment et la pensée. 3. éd. Paris, 1907.
Phil 4353.12	Gomez Izquierdo, A. Un filosofo catalan, Antonio Comellas y Cluet. Madrid, 1907.

1907 - cont.

Phil 5756.4	Gomperz, Heinrich. Das Problem der Willensfreiheit. Jena, 1907.
Phil 8881.40	Gottschick, Johannes. Ethik. Tübingen, 1907.
Phil 3488.19	Grabowsky, N. Kants Grundirrtümer in seiner Kritik der reinen Vernunft, und die Reformation des geistigen Innenlebens der Menschheit. Leipzig, 1907.
Phil 6956.5.5	Grasset, Joseph. The semi-insane and semi-responsible. N.Y., 1907.
Phil 8881.55	Griggs, Edward H. The use of the margin. N.Y., 1907.
Phil 1504.6.3	Grunwald, G. Geschichte der Gottesbewise. v.6, pt.3. Münster, 1907.
Phil 5756.6.2	Gutberlet, C. Die Willensfreiheit und ihre Gegner. 2. Aufl. Fulda, 1907.
Phil 8586.8.10	Guyau, M.J. Framtidens irreligion. Stockholm, 1907.
Phil 9450.7	Hadley, A.T. Standards of public morality. N.Y., 1907.
Phil 6317.13	Halberg, F. Om det abnorme. København, 1907.
Phil 3552.122	Halbwachs, Maurice. Leibniz. Paris, 1907.
Phil 338.5	Hamelin, O. Essai sur les elements principaux de la reprèsentation. Paris, 1907.
Phil 5585.17	Hamilton, F.M. The perceptual factors in reading. N.Y., 1907.
Phil 7060.93	Harper, C.G. Haunted houses. London, 1907.
Phil 182.39	Harriman, F. Philosophy of common sense. N.Y., 1907.
Phil 600.11	Harrison, F. The creed of a layman. London, 1907.
Phil 600.11.2	Harrison, F. The creed of a layman. N.Y. 1907.
Phil 182.39.5	Harrison, F. The philosophy of common sense. London, 1907.
Phil 3415.70	Hartmann, Eduard von. System der Philosophie im Grundriss. Bad Sachsa, 1907-09. 8v.
Phil 5627.33	Hébert, Marcel. Le divin. Paris, 1907.
Phil 3425.73	Hegel, Georg Wilhelm Friedrich. Phänomenologie des Geistes. Leipzig, 1907.
Phil 3425.72.90	Hegel, Georg Wilhelm Friedrich. Phänomenologie des Geistes. Leipzig, 1907.
Phil 3425.61	Hegel, Georg Wilhelm Friedrich. Theologische Judendschriften. Tübingen, 1907.
Phil 3425.40.6	Hegel, Georg Wilhelm Friedrich. Vorlesungen über die Philosophie der Geschichte. Leipzig, 1907.
Phil 5635.5.11	Hell, B. Ernst Mach's Philosophie. Stuttgart, 1907.
Phil 9575.4	Hensel, W.U. Wealth and worth. South Bethlehem, Pa., 1907.
Phil 2880.4.80	Hérnon, Camille. La philosophie de M. Sully Prudhomme. Paris, 1907.
Phil 8408.6	Hildebrand, A. The problem of form in painting and sculpture. N.Y., 1907.
Phil 8882.12.9	Hilty, K. Steps of life, further essays on happiness. N.Y., 1907.
Phil 1707.1.15	Höffding, H. Lehrbuch der Geschichte der neueren Philosophie. Leipzig, 1907.
Phil 5374.14.9	Hoffmann, Alfred. Vom Bewusstsein. Leipzig, 1907.
Phil 9075.11	Huckel, O. Modern study of conscience. Philadelphia, 1907.
Phil 2050.68	Hume, David. Dialogues concerning natural religion. Edinburgh, 1907.
Phil 2050.41.5A	Hume, David. An enquiry...human understanding. Chicago, 1907.
Phil 8610.907	Hunt, E.J. The evolution of faith; an essay. London, 1907.
Phil 5047.9.5	Hyslop, J.H. Logic and argument. N.Y., 1907.
Phil 1020.8.9	Ibn Sina. Die metaphysik Ayicennas. Halle, 1907-09.
Phil 6958.4	Ilberg, Georg. Geisteskrankheiten. Leipzig, 1907.
Phil 530.11.5	Inge, William R. Studies of English mystics. London, 1907.
Phil 6619.10	Ingenieros, José. Le langage musical et ses troubles hystériques. Paris, 1907.
Phil 3808.127	Irvine, David. Philosophy and Christianity; an introduction to the works of Schopenhauer. London, 1907.
Phil 184.3.15	James, W. Pragmatism, a new name. N.Y., 1907.
Phil 5249.2.6.10	James, William. Psychology. N.Y., 1907.
Phil 5627.6.12.25	James, William. Die religiöse Erfahrung. Leipzig, 1907.
Phil 5249.8.10	Jerusalem, W. Lehrbuch der Psychologie. 4. Aufl. Wien, 1907.
Phil 3640.247.5	Jesinghaus, W. Nietzsches Stellung zu Weib. 3e Aufl. Leipzig, 1907.
Phil 6119.4	Jones, E.E. Influence of bodily posture on mental activities. N.Y., 1907.
Phil 8581.18.8	Jones, H.D. John Balguy, an English moralist of the 18th century. Leipzig, 1907.
Phil 7082.48	Jónsson, Brynjólfur. Dulraenar smásögur. Bessastadir, 1907.
Phil 5249.7.5.3	Judd, C.H. Laboratory equipment for psychological experiments. N.Y., 1907.
Phil 5249.7.5.2	Judd, C.H. Laboratory manual of psychology. N.Y., 1907.
Phil 5249.7	Judd, C.H. Psychology. General introduction. N.Y., 1907.
Phil 6959.8	Jung, C.G. Über die Psychologie der Dementia Praecox. Halle, 1907.
Phil 8884.15.5	Juvalta, E. Il metodo dell'economica pura nell'etica. Pavia, 1907.
Phil 3480.51.30	Kant, Immanuel. Critica del giudizio. Bari, 1907.
Phil 3480.65.15	Kant, Immanuel. Fondements de la métaphysique des moeurs. 2. éd. Paris, 1907?
Phil 3480.65.40	Kant, Immanuel. Fundamental principles of the metaphysics of ethics. London, 1907.
Phil 3415.90.5	Kappstein, Theodor. Eduard von Hartmann. Gotha, 1907.
Phil 8885.19.8	Kautsky, Karl. Ethics and the materialist conception of history. Chicago, 1907.
Phil 2636.80	Keim, A. Helvétius sa vie et son oeuvre. Paris, 1907.
Phil 8885.35	Kirkham, S.D. Where dwells the soul serene. 3rd ed. San Francisco, 1907.
Phil 3010.10	Knauer, Rudolf. Der Voluntarismus. Berlin, 1907.
Phil 3492.8	König, E. Kant und die Naturwissenschaft. Braunschweig, 1907.
Phil 2805.94	Köster, Adolph. Die Ethik Pascal. Tübingen, 1907.
Phil 8411.9	Kohnstamm, O. Kunst als Ausdruckstätigkeit; biologische Voraussetzungen der ästhetik. München, 1907.
Phil 3492.9	Koppelmann, W. Die Ethic Kants. Berlin, 1907.
Phil 5627.69	Kriebel, O.S. Conversion and religious experience. Pennsburg, Pa., 1907.
Phil 185.12.4	Külpe, O. Einleitung in die Philosophie. 4. Aufl. Leipzig, 1907.
Phil 3492.7	Külpe, O. Immanuel Kant. Leipzig, 1907.
Phil 2725.11.31	Lachelier, Jules. Études sur le syllogisme. Paris, 1907.
Phil 8412.22	Lange, K. von. Das Wesen der Kunst. Berlin, 1907.
Phil 6681.6.3	Lapponi, Guiseppe. Iypnotismo e spiritismo. 3. ed. Roma, 1907.
Phil 2477.10.90	Latreille, C. Francisque Bouillier. Paris, 1907.

1907 - cont.

Phil 3195.9.81 — Lau, Hamann. Eugen Dühring als Religionsphilosoph. Inaug. Diss. Lübeck, 1907.

Phil 8886.6.10 — Laycock, F.U. Motives of mankind. London, 1907.
Phil 5761.3.7 — Leland, C.G. The mystic will. Chicago, 1907.
Phil 5761.3.5 — Leland, C.G. The mystic will. Chicago, 1907.
Phil 3831.7 — Léon, Albert. Les éléments cartésiens. Paris, 1907.
Phil 5627.75 — Leroy, E.B. Interprétation psychologique des visions intellectuelles. Paris, 1907.
Phil 3493.5 — Levy, Heinrich. Kants Lehre vom Schematismus der reinen Verstandesbegriffe. Teil I. Halle, 1907.
Phil 5821.6 — Lewandowsky, M. Die Funktionen des zentralen Nervensystems. Jena, 1907.
Phil 1811.3.5 — Liard, Louis. Les logiciens anglais contemporains.'57
Phil 1811.3.5 — 44's. Les logiciens anglais contemporains. 5e éd. Paris, 1907.
Phil 9351.11 — Lingard, R. A letter of advice to a young gentleman. N.Y., 1907.
Phil 186.38 — Lipps, Gottlob F. Mythenbildung und Erkenntnis. Leipzig, 1907.
Phil 510.13 — Lipsius, Friedrich R. Die Religion des Monismus. Berlin, 1907.
Phil 645.8 — Lloyd, A.H. The will to doubt. London, 1907.
Phil 8701.4.4 — Lodge, Oliver Joseph. The substance of faith allied with science. N.Y., 1907.
Phil 186.43 — Lublinski, Samuel. Die Humanität als Mysterium. Jena, 1907.
Phil 1812.4 — MacCunn, J. Six radical thinkers. London, 1907.
Phil 8887.60 — McGinley, A.A. The profit of love. N.Y., 1907.
Phil 5640.3.5 — M'Kendrick, J.G. The physiology of the senses. N.Y., 1907.
Phil 187.27.5 — Mackenzie, J.S. Lectures on humanism. London, 1907.
Phil 187.31 — Malapert, P. Leçons de philosophie. Paris, 1907-1908. 2v.
Phil 4060.1.83 — Marchesini, G. La vita e il pensiero di Roberto Ardigo. Milano, 1907.
Phil 8887.58 — Marcus, E. Das Gesetz der Vernunft und die ethischen Strömungen der Gegenwart. Herford, 1907.
Phil 510.21 — Marcus, Hugo. Die Philosophie des Monopluralismus. Berlin, 1907.
Phil 510.1.29 — Marcus, S.P. Monism? London, 1907.
Phil 9352.7.17 — Marden, O.S. The optimistic life. N.Y., 1907.
Phil 5627.123 — Marie, Auguste. Mysticisme et folie. Paris, 1907.
Phil 187.28.11 — Mechnikov, I.I. Essais optimistes. Paris, 1907.
Phil 187.28.15 — Mechnikov, I.I. Etiudy optimizma. Moskva, 1907.
Phil 343.5.9 — Meinong, A. Über die Stellung der Gegenstand Theorie im System der Wissenschaften. Leipzig, 1907.
Phil 5252.17 — Mellone, Sydney Herbert. Elements of psychology. Edinburgh, 1907.
Phil 6962.10 — Mendel, Emanuel. Text-book of psychiatry. Philadelphia, 1907.
Phil 1712.3 — Merten, O. L'état présent de la philosophie. Namur, 1907.
Phil 1712.2.3A — Merz, J.T. History of European thought, 19th century. v.1-3. Edinburgh, 1907-1912. 2v.
Phil 3552.92.5 — Merz, J.T. Leibniz. Edinburgh, 1907.
Phil 5190.10.20 — Miller, Clyde R. The process of persuasion. Firenze, 1907.
Phil 510.14 — Milliet, J. Paul. Remarques sur la monadologie. Paris, 1907.
Phil 4215.1.103 — Mistrali, Dario. G.D. Romagnosi. Borgo San Donnino, 1907.
Phil 5252.16 — Mitchell, W. Structure and growth of the mind. London, 1907.
Phil 5374.14 — Mittenzwey, K. Über abstrahierende Apperception. Leipzig, 1907.
Phil 5252.39.2 — Mobius, P. Die Hoffnungslosigkeit allen Psychologie. Halle, 1907.
Phil 8667.7 — Moisant, Xavier. Dieu. Paris, 1907.
Phil 187.32 — Montgomery, E. Philosophical problems. N.Y., 1907.
Phil 5401.4 — Morse, J. The psychology and neurology of fear. Worcester, 1907.
Phil 6682.21 — Moutin, Lucien. Le magnétisme humain. Paris, 1907.
Phil 7069.07.25 — Myers, F.W.H. Human personality. N.Y., 1907.
Phil 1050.7 — Neumark, D. Geschichte der jüdischen Philosophie der Mittelalters. Berlin, 1907. 3v.
Phil 2494.80 — Niedlich, J.K. Condorcet's "Esquisse d'un tableau historique". Sorai, 1907.
Phil 3640.31A — Nietzsche, Friedrich. Beyond good and evil. N.Y., 1907.
Phil 4610.7.33 — Norström, V. Naturkunskapens själfbesinning. Stockholm, 1907.
Phil 8414.15.2 — Noyes, Carleton E. The gate of appreciation. Boston, Mass., 1907.
Phil 8889.3 — Orestano, F. I valori umani. Milan, 1907.
Phil 8594.15 — Orr, J. The Christian view of God and the world. 8. ed. N.Y., 1907.
Phil 8704.1.5 — Otto, Rudolf. Naturalism and religion. London, 1907.
Phil 2070.86 — Paetz, W. Die erkenntnis-theoretischen Grundlagen von William James "The Varieties of Religious Experience." Eilenburg, 1907.
Phil 4210.107.5 — Pagani, G.B. The life of Antonio Rosmini-Serbati. London, 1907.
Phil 5255.23 — Palágyi, M. Naturphilosophische Vorlesungen über die Grundprobleme des Bewusstseins und des Lebens. Charlottenburg, 1907.
Phil 8595.1.4A — Parker, T. A discourse of matters pertaining to religion. Boston, 1907.
Phil 2805.40.19 — Pascal, Blaise. Pensées. Paris, 1907.
Phil 1158.15.13 — Pater, Walter. Marius the Epicurean. 4th ed. London, 1907. 2v.
Phil 8890.44 — Pauler, Akós. Az ethikai megismerés természete. Budapest, 1907.
Phil 5635.8 — Paulsen, J. Das Problem der Empfindung. Giessen, 1907.
Phil 3415.90 — Paulus, H. Die Gottesbeweise Eduard von Hartmanns. Würzburg, 1907.
Phil 190.21 — Pearson, N. Some problems of existence. London, 1907.
Phil 190.42 — Pelazza, A. La metafisica dell'esperienza. Bergamo, 1907.
Phil 8890.26 — Perry, R.B. Conception of moral goodness. n.p., 1907.
Phil 296.8.3 — Pesch, Tilmann. Die grossen Welträtsel. Freiburg, 1907. 2v.
Phil 530.20.7 — Pfeiffer, Franz. Deutsche Mystiker des vierzehnten Jahrhunderts. 2e Aufl. Göttingen, 1907. 2v.
Phil 8595.4.13 — Pfleiderer, O. Religion and historic faiths. N.Y., 1907.
Phil 190.37 — Pfordten, Otto. Vorfragen der Naturphilosophie. Heidelberg, 1907.
Phil 5825.2 — Pfungst, Oskar. Das Pferd des Herrn von Osten. Leipzig, 1907.
Phil 3835.2 — Picton, Allanson. Spinoza, handbook to the Ethics. London, 1907.

1907 - cont.

Phil 5055.14.5 — Pira, Karl. Om grundformerna i den reella logiken. Stockholm, 1907.
Phil 3095.81 — Poppe, B. Alexander G. Baumgarten. Borna, 1907.
Phil 5627.6.95A — Porret, J.A. Au sujet de la conversion...théorie de Wm. James. Genève, 1907.
Phil 5627.56.4 — Pratt, James B. The psychology of religious belief. N.Y., 1907.
Phil 5190.10.15 — Prezzalini, G. L'arte di persuadere. Firenze, 1907.
Phil 8408.30.15 — Profesor Dr. Otakar Hostinský, 1847-1907. Praha, 1907.
Phil 2520.123 — Prost, Joseph. Essai sur l'atomisme...la philosophie cartesienne. Paris, 1907.
Phil 2270.97 — Quesada, E. Herbert Spencer y sus doctrinas sociológicas. Buenos Aires, 1907.
Phil 5360.4 — Queyrat, F. L'abstraction et son rôle dans l'éducation intellectuelle. 2e éd. Paris, 1907.
Phil 5643.53 — Rachlman, E.Zur vergleichenden Physiologie des Gesichtsinnes. Jena, 1907.
Phil 3525.82 — Ranft, M. Der Philosoph K.C.F. Krause als Erzieher. Halle, 1907.
Phil 8892.13 — Rashdall, Hastings. The theory of good and evil. Oxford, 1907. 2v.
Phil 5057.16 — Re, Alfonso del. Lezioni di algebra della logica. Napoli, 1907.
Phil 1540.15 — Reiners, Josef. Der aristotelische Realismus in der Frühscholastik. Inaug.-Diss. Bonn, 1907.
Phil 298.4 — Reinke, J. Die Natur und Wir. Berlin, 1907.
Phil 5400.26 — Revault d'Allonnes, G. Les inclinations; leur role dans la psychologie des sentiments. Paris, 1907.
Phil 5400.18.15 — Ribot, T. Essai sur les passions. Paris, 1907.
Phil 5400.18.9 — Ribot, T. La logique des sentiments. 2. éd. Paris, 1907.
Phil 4170.7 — Richerche di psichiatria...dedicate al...E. Morselli. Milano, 1907.
Phil 1817.3A — Riley, I.W. American philosophy. N.Y., 1907.
Phil 1817.4 — Robertson, J.M. Pioneer humanists. London, 1907.
Phil 5330.9 — Roehrich, E. L'attention spontanée et volontaire. Paris, 1907.
Phil 1717.9 — Rösener, Karl. Moderne Propheten. München, 1907.
Phil 8418.7 — Rogerio Sanchez, J. Estética general. Madrid, 1907.
Phil 8597.16 — Rogers, A.K. The religious conception of the world. N.Y., 1907.
Phil 3705.3.90 — Rolla, A. La filosofia energetica. Torino, 1907.
Phil 4210.35 — Rosmini-Serbati, Antonio. Compendio di etica e breve storia di essa. Roma, 1907.
Phil 9513.3 — Ross, E.A. Sin and society. Boston, 1907.
Phil 530.40.15 — Rousselot, P. Los místicos españoles. Barcelona, 1907. 2v.
Phil 5520.26 — Rowland, Eleanor H. The psychological experiences connected with the different parts of speech. Lancaster, 1907.
Phil 5643.34 — Ruediger, W.C. The field of distinct vision. n.p., 1907.
Phil 2270.132 — Sacerdote, S. La vita di H. Spencer, ed "I primi principii". Torino, 1907.
Phil 6128.14 — Saleeby, C.W. Worry; the disease of the age. N.Y., 1907.
Phil 8893.43.5 — Sarlo, Francisco de. L'attività pratica e la coscienza morale. Firenze, 1907.
Phil 8893.43 — Sarlo, Francisco de. Principii di scienza etica. Milano, 1907.
Phil 3800.57 — Schelling, F.W.J. von. Schöpferisches Handeln. Herausgegeben und Eingeleitet von Emil Fuchs. Jena, 1907.
Phil 193.9.9 — Schiller, F.C.S. Studies in humanism. London, 1907.
Phil 3640.195 — Schlaf, Johannes. Der "Fall" Nietzsche. Leipzig, 1907.
Phil 3640.195.5 — Schlaf, Johannes. Die Kritik und mein "Fall Nietzsche". Leipzig, 1907.
Phil 3850.25.80 — Schmidt, Hugo. Die Lehre von der psychologischen Kausalität in der Philosophie Ludwig Strümpells. Inaug. Diss. Lejpzig, 1907.
Phil 5627.82 — Schneider, E. Les raisons du coeur. Paris, 1907.
Phil 5768.12 — Schuch, Hermann. Kant, Schopenhauer, Ihering. München, 1907.
Phil 349.14 — Schultz, J. Die drei Welten der Erkenntnistheorie. Göttingen, 1907.
Phil 5610.1 — Scott, W. The psychology of public speaking. Philadelphia, 1907.
Phil 5258.13.6 — Scripture, E.W. Thinking, feeling, doing. N.Y., 1907. 2v.
Phil 8968.5 — Scullard, H.H. Early Christian ethics in the West. London, 1907.
Phil 6750.7.10 — Seguin, E. Idiocy. Albany, 1907.
Phil 8893.63 — Sera, L.G. Sulle tracce della vita. Roma, 1907.
Phil 193.23.9 — Seth Pringle-Pattison, A. The philosophical radicals and other essays. Edinburgh, 1907.
Phil 510.1.45 — Shiltov., A. Ernst Gekkel' pered sudom logiki. Khar'kov, 1907.
Phil 8598.9.5 — Siebeck, Hermann. Zur Religionsphilosophie. Tübingen, 1907.
Phil 3808.108 — Simmel, G. Schopenhauer und Nietzsche. Leipzig, 1907.
Phil 2280.1.86 — Sinclair, A.G. Der Utilitarismus bei Sidgwick...Spencer. Heidelberg, 1907.
Phil 299.7.5 — Snyder, C. The world machine...cosmic mechanism. N.Y., 1907.
Phil 5325.7 — Sollier, Paul. Essai sur l'association. Paris, 1907.
Phil 2050.106 — Sopper, A.J. David Hume's kenleer en ethiek. Leiden, 1907.
Phil 6128.38.2 — Spinney, W.A. Health through self-control in thinking, breathing, eating. Boston, 1907.
Phil 3819.33 — Spinoza, Benedictus de. Ethique. Paris, 1907.
Phil 2270.118.10 — Stadler, August. Herbert Spencer; Zürcher Rathaus-Vortrag gehalten am 6. dezember 1906. Zürich, 1907.
Phil 3270.8.80 — Stamm, E. Konstantin Frantz' Jugendjahre und erste Schriften. Heidelberg, 1907.
Phil 8893.50.5 — Staudinger, Franz. Wirtschaftliche Grundlagen der Moral. Darmstadt, 1907.
NEDL Phil 2070.91.5 — Stettheimer, E. The will to believe as a basis for defense of religious faith. N.Y., 1907.
Phil 3850.1.75 — Strauss, D.F. Der papier-Reisende. Weimar, 1907.
Phil 2805.95 — Strowski, F. Pascal et son temps. Paris, 1907-22. 3v.
Phil 3850.35 — Stumpf, Karl. Zur Einteilung der Wissenschaften. Berlin, 1907.
Phil 8865.660 — Suyematsu, Kencho. The ethics of Japan. Washington, 1907.
Phil 193.52 — Systematische Philosophie. Berlin, 1907.
Phil 365.8 — Thompson, H.C. New reading of evolution. Chicago, 1907.
Phil 9050.5.5 — Thorsch, Berthold. Der Einzelne und die Gesellschaft. Dresden, 1907.
Phil 194.13 — Trojano, P.R. Le basi dell'umanismo. Torino, 1907.
Phil 4770.1 — Trubetskoi, S.N. Sobranie sochinenii. v.1-2,5-6. Moskva, 1907. 4v.

Chronological Listing

1907 - cont.

Phil 8709.12 Trumbull, William. Evolution and religion. N.Y., 1907.
Phil 24.1.5 Twenty Years of The Open Court. An index, 1887-1906. Chicago, 1907.
Phil 8599.20.2 Tyler, W.F. The dimensional idea as an aid to religion. London, 1907.
Phil 672.27 Ulrich, Georg. Der Begriff des Raumes. Berlin, 1907.
Phil 5643.47 Urbantschitsch, V. Über subjektive optische Anschauungsbilder. Leipzig, 1907.
Phil 4021.1 Vailati, Giovanni. De quelques caractères du mouvement philosophique contemporain en Italie. Paris, 1907.
Phil 75.14 Valverde Téllez, E. Bibliografía. México, 1907.
Phil 5261.12 Vannérus, A. De psykologiska vetenskapernas system. Stockholm, 1907.
Phil 4650.1.41 Vannérus, Allen. Vetenskapssystematik. Stockholm, 1907.
Phil 196.5 Van Nostrand, J.J. Prefatory lessons in a mechanical philosophy. Chicago, 1907.
Phil 196.5.3F Van Nostrand, J.J. Prefatory lessons in a mechanical philosophy. Chicago, 1907.
Phil 5061.1.2 Venn, J. Principles of empirical or inductive logic. London, 1907.
Phil 7069.07.32 La vita di Gesù. 2. ed. Roma, 1907.
Phil 3503.4.5 Vorländer, K. Kant, Schiller, Goethe. Leipzig, 1907.
Phil 197.29 Walthoffen, H. Walter von. Lebensphilosophie und Lebenskunst. Wien, 1907.
Phil 8602.15 Watson, J. The philosophical basis of religion. Glasgow, 1907.
Phil 5832.9.5 Watson, John B. Kinaesthetic and organic sensations. Lancaster, 1907.
Phil 3640.91 Weber, Ernst. Die pädogogischen Gedanken...jungen Nietzsche. Leipzig, 1907.
Phil 197.32 Weidenbach, Oswald. Mensch und Wirklichkeit. Giessen, 1907.
Phil 3504.40 Weissfeld, M. Kants Gesellschaftslehre. Bern, 1907.
Phil 6132.18 Wells, D.W. Psychology applied to medicine. Philadelphia, 1907.
Phil 1145.40 Wendt, M. Der Intellektualismus in der griechischen Ethik. Leipzig, 1907.
Phil 3504.7.5 Wenley, R.M. An outline introduction of Kant's Critique of pure reason. N.Y., 1907.
Phil 3842.5 Wenzel, Alfred. Die Weltanschauung Spinozas. Bd.1. Leipzig, 1907.
Phil 8423.3 Wernaer, R.M. Das ästhetische Symbol. Leipzig, 1907.
Phil 3504.12 Wernieke, A. Kant und kein Ende? 2. Aufl. Braunschweig, 1907.
Phil 6132.6 Whipple, L.E. Mental healing. N.Y., 1907.
Phil 6132.6.10 Whipple, L.E. Practical health. N.Y., 1907.
Phil 3805.89 Wickert, R. Die Pädagogik Schleiermachers. Leipzig, 1907.
Phil 2050.179 Wijnaendts Francken, C.J. David Hume. Haarlem, 1907.
Phil 7082.59 Wijnaendtsfrancken, Cornelis Johannes. Die psychologie van het droomen. Haarlem, 1907.
Phil 3270.1.80 Windelband, W. Kuno Fischer Gedächtnisrede. Heidelberg, 1907.
Phil 1722.2.7 Windelband, W. Die Philosophie im Beginn des Zwanzigsten. Jahrhunderts. 2e Aufl. Heidelberg, 1907.
Phil 1722.2.8 Windelband, W. Die Philosophie im Beginn des zwanzigsten Jahrhunderts. Heidelberg, 1907.
Phil 197.9.3A Windelband, W. Präludien. 3. ed. Tübingen, 1907.
Phil 510.130 Worsley, A. Concepts of monism. London, 1907.
Phil 1527.1.9.5 Wulf, M. de. Scholasticism old and new. N.Y., 1907.
Phil 3915.47.3 Wundt, Wilhelm. Outlines of psychology. 3rd ed. Leipzig, 1907.
Phil 3915.30.5 Wundt, Wilhelm. System der Philosophie. 3. Aufl. v.1-2. Leipzig, 1907.
Phil 9495.128 Wylm, Antoine. La morale sexuelle. Paris, 1907.
Phil 5834.1 Yerkes, R.M. The dancing mouse. N.Y., 1907.
Phil 4809.894.1 Zahradmk, Vincenc. Filosofické spisy. Praha, 1907-18. 3v.
Phil 1130.3.8 Zeller, Eduard. Grundriss der Geschichte der griechischen Philosophie. 8th ed. Leipzig, 1907.

1908

Phil 7052.7.5 Abbott, D.P. The history of a strange case. Chicago, 1908.
Phil 5240.5 Abelson, R. Mental fatigue - 1908. Leipzig, 1908.
Phil 1105.4 Adamson, Robert. The development of Greek philosophy. Edinburgh, 1908.
Phil 6310.1.15 Adler, A. Die Theorie der Organminderwertigkeit. Leipzig, 1908.
Phil 3585.10.82 Ahrem, Maximilien. Das Problem des tragischen bei Theodor Lipps und Johannes Volkelt. Inaug. Diss. Nürnberg, 1908.
Phil 2115.99 Alexander, S. Locke. London, 1908.
Phil 5240.6.2 Angell, J.R. Psychology. 4. ed. N.Y., 1908.
Phil 3482.5.3 Apel, Max. Kommentar zu Kants "Prologomena". Schöneberg, 1908.
Phil 281.4.5A Arrhenius, S. World's in the making. London, 1908.
Phil 960.33 Atkinson, W.W. A series of lessons on the inner teachings of the philosophies and religions of India. Chicago, 1908.
Phil 1504.3.2 Baeumker, C. Witelo. v.3, pt.2. Münster, 1908.
Phil 270.30 Baglioni, B. Il principio di causalità. Perugia, 1908.
Phil 8876.14.2 Baldwin, W. The sayings of the wise. London, 1908.
Phil 8626.9 Ball, J.W. Absolute idealism and immortality. Lincoln, 1908.
Phil 281.4 Bamberger, L. Die Vorstellung von Weltebäude im Wandel du Zeit. Leipzig, 1908.
Phil 6951.7 Barrus, C. Nursing the insane. N.Y., 1908.
Phil 4080.8.85 Barzellotti, G. Due filosofi italiani. Roma, 1908.
Phil 5811.12.5 Bauke, Leopold. Unterscheidet das tier Mann und Frau? Berlin, 1908.
Phil 332.6 Baumann, J. Der Wissensbegriff. Heidelberg, 1908.
Phil 8876.51.5 Bayet, Albert. L'ideé de bien. Paris, 1908.
Phil 8876.56 Becher, Erich. Die Grundfrage der Ethik. Köln, 1908.
Phil 6111.16 Bechterew, W. von. Die Funktionen der Nervencentra. Jena, 1908. 3v.
Phil 6111.16.12 Bechterew, W. von. Psyche und Leben. Wiesbaden, 1908.
Phil 6951.5.3 Beers, C.W. A mind that found itself. N.Y., 1908.
Phil 9150.10 Benett, W. Ethical aspects of evolution. Oxford, 1908.
Phil 1106.3.9 Benn, A.W. Early Greek philosophy. London, 1908.
Phil 7069.08.10 Bennett, E.T. The direct phenomena of spirtualism. London, 1908.
Phil 2475.1.50 Bergson, Henri. L'évolution créatrice. 4. éd. Paris, 1908.
L Phil 5525.11.10 Bergson, Henri. Le rire. 5. éd. Paris, 1908.
Phil 735.1 Berguer, G. La notion de valeur. Genève, 1908.
Phil 1870.73.5 Berkeley, G. Le journal philosophique. Commonplace book. Paris, 1908.

1908 - cont.

Phil 1870.10.5 Berkeley, G. Works. London, 1908. 3v.
Phil 3640.90.5 Bernoulli, Carl A. Franz Overbeck und Friedrich Nietzsche. Jena, 1908. 2v.
Phil 176.63 Bertz, Eduard. Weltharmonie monistische Betrachtungen. Dresden, 1908.
X Cg Phil 978.6.86 Besant, Annie. Annie Besant: an autobiography. London, 1908.
Phil 8876.43 Beveridge, A.J. Work and habits. Philadelphia, 1908.
Phil 3483.43 Biéma, Emile van. L'espace et les temps chez Leibnizet chez Kant. Paris, 1908.
Phil 8633.1.11 Bigelow, W.S. Buddhism and immortality. Boston, 1908.
Phil 5241.34 Bilharz, A. Neue Denklehre. Wiesbaden, 1908.
Phil 5170.5 Billia, Lorenzo M. Quatres règles inexactes du syllogisme. Heidelberg, 1908?
Phil 801.27 Bjarnason, A. Austurlönd. Reykjavik, 1908.
Phil 4520.8.30 Bjarnason, Ágúst. Austurlönd. Reykjavík, 1908.
Phil 6100.14 Blackburn, I.W. Illustrations of the gross morbid anatomy of the brain in the insane. Washington, 1908.
Phil 3110.38 Böhme, J. De la signature des choses. Paris, 1908.
Phil 4302.4 Bonilla y San Martin, A. Historia de la filosofía española. Madrid, 1908.
Phil 5648.11 Book, W.F. The psychology of skill. Missoula, Mont., 1908.
Phil 7060.74 Boucher, G. Une séance de spiritisme. Niort, 1908.
Phil 5241.26 Boucher, J. Psychologie. Paris, 1908.
Phil 801.10 Boutroux, E. Études d'histoire de la philosophie. Paris, 1908.
NEDL Phil 8691.6.1 Boutroux, E. Science et religion. Paris, 1908.
Phil 176.27.12 Bowne, B.P. Personalism. Boston, 1908.
Phil 801.2.5 Box, E.B. Handbook...history of philosophy. London, 1908.
Phil 7069.08.12 Brackett, E.A. Materialized apparitions. Boston, 1908.
Phil 1885.37.7 Bradley, Francis H. Appearance and reality. 2d ed. London, 1908.
Phil 3801.233 Braun, Otto. Hinauf zum Idealismus! Schelling-Studien. Leipzig, 1908.
Phil 1200.18 Bréhier, Émile. La théorie des incorporels dans l'ancien stoïcisme. Thèse. Paris, 1908.
Phil 801.13.2 Brockdorff, C. von. Die Geschichte der Philosophie. Osterwieck, 1908.
Phil 575.12.5 Brockdorff, Cay. Die wissenschaftliche Selbsterkenntnis. Stuttgart, 1908.
Phil 575.12 Bruce, H.A. Riddle of personality. N.Y., 1908.
Phil 7060.68 Bruce, Henry Addington Bayley. Historic ghosts and ghost hunters. N.Y., 1908.
Phil 5650.5 Bruner, A.G. The hearing of primitive peoples. N.Y., 1908.
Phil 176.73 Brunner, Constantin. Die Lehre von den Geistigen und vom Volke. Berlin, 1908. 2v.
Phil 5241.33 Buck, J.D. Constructive psychology. Chicago, 1908.
Phil 1135.63 Burle, E. Notion de droit naturel. Trevoux, 1908.
Phil 176.48 Butler, N.M. Philosophy. N.Y., 1908.
Phil 4080.3.305 Cantoni, Carlo. In memoria di Carlo Cantoni. Pavia, 1908.
Phil 7069.08.15 Carrington, Hereward. The coming science. Boston, 1908.
Phil 7069.08.16 Carrington, Hereward. The physical phenomena of spiritualism. Boston, 1908.
Phil 7069.07.12 Carrington, Hereward. The physical phenomena of spiritualism. 2. ed. Boston, 1908.
Phil 8620.15 Carver, T.N. The economic basis of the problem of evil. Cambridge, 1908.
Phil 1750.21 Chide, A. Le mobilisme moderne. Paris, 1908.
Phil 4110.3.92 Chimirri, Bruno. Inaugurazione del monumento a Francesco Fiorentino in Sambiase, 15 novembre 1908. Catanzaro, 1908.
Phil 1850.81.9 Church, R.W. Bacon. London, 1908.
Phil 6952.15 Clark, L.P. Neurological and mental diagnosis. N.Y., 1908.
Phil 8403.22 Clay, Felix. The origin of the sense of beauty. London, 1908.
Phil 9045.5 Cleveland, G. Good citizenship. Philadelphia, 1908.
Phil 8657.20 Cohen, Chapman. Socialism, atheism and Christianity. London, 1908.
Phil 333.8 Cohn, Jonas. Voraussetzungen und Ziele des Erkennens. Leipzig, 1908.
Phil 8610.880.14 Congrès Universel de la Libre Pensée, 14th, Prague, 1907. Světový kongres volné myšlenky v Praze 8,9,10,11 a 12 září 1907. Podrobná Zpráva. Praha, 1908.
Phil 802.6 Conti, Augusto. Storia della filosofía; lezioni. 6a ed. Roma, 1908-09. 2v.
Phil 2115.123 Corti, S. La teoria della conoscenza in Locke e Leibnitz. Siena, 1908.
Phil 525.43 Costa Guimaraes, Francisco da. Contribution à la pathologie des mystiques. Paris, 1908.
Phil 600.12 Cottin, P. Positivisme et anarchie. Paris, 1908.
Phil 4080.3.31.3 Croce, Benedetto. Estetica come scienza dell'espressione e linguistica generale. 3a ed. Bari, 1908.
Phil 5627.16 Cutten, G.B. The psychological phenomenon of Christianity. N.Y., 1908.
Phil 5585.25 Cyon, Elie von. Das Ohrlabyrinth als Organ der mathematischen Sinne fur Raum und Zeit. Berlin, 1908.
Phil 284.10 Dandolo, G. Intorno al valore della scienza. Padova, 1908.
Phil 525.45 Delacroix, H. Études d'histoire et de psychologie du mysticisme. Paris, 1908.
Phil 8583.33.15 Delitzsch, Friedrich. Whose son is Christ? Boston, 1908.
Phil 8583.33 Delitzsch, Friedrich. Zur Weiterbildung der Religion. Stuttgart, 1908.
Phil 2520.11.24 Descartes, René. Die Prinzipien der Philosophie. 3. Aufl. Leipzig, 1908.
Phil 960.3.8 Deussen, P. The philosophy of the Upanishads. Edinburgh, 1908.
Phil 8878.11.9A Dewey, John. Ethics. N.Y., 1908.
Phil 8878.11.8 Dewey, John. Ethics [lecture]. N.Y., 1908.
Phil 3940.1.90 Diels, Hermann. Gedächtnisrede auf Eduard Zeller. Berlin, 1908.
Phil 9163.3 Diggle, J.W. Home life. London, 1908.
Phil 6113.5 Dogiel, A.S. Der Bau der Spinalganglien des Menschen und der Säugetiere. Jena, 1908.
Phil 6113.4 Dorland, W.A.N. The age of mental virility. N.Y., 1908.
Phil 5585.18 Downey, June Etta. Control processes in modified hand-writing. Chicago? 1908?
Phil 178.12.26 Dresser, H.W. Philosophy of the spirit. N.Y., 1908.
Phil 178.12.40 Dresser, H.W. A physician to the soul. N.Y., 1908.
Phil 284.4.7 Duhem, P. Ziel und Struktur der physikalischen Theorien. Leipzig, 1908.
Phil 3823.7 Dumrath, O.H. Spinoza. Stockholm, 1908.
Phil 2270.96 Duncan, D. Life and letters of Herbert Spencer. N.Y., 1908. 2v.

1908 - cont.

Phil 5243.15.20   Dunlap, K. Concerning fluctuating and inaudible sounds. n.p., 1908-1916. 15 pam.

Phil 5243.14   Dwelshauvers, George. La synthèse mentale. Paris, 1908.

Phil 5244.7   Ebbinghaus, H. Abriss der Psychologie. Leipzig, 1908.

Phil 5244.7.5   Ebbinghaus, H. Psychology, an elementary text-book. Boston, 1908.

Phil 3805.102   Eck, Samuel. Über die Herkunft des Individualitäts - Gedankens bei Schleiermacher. Giessen, 1908.

Phil 9035.31   Ekenhans, Theodor. Charakterbildung. Leipzig, 1908.

Phil 1170.7   Elsee, Charles. Neoplatonism in relation to Christianity; an essay. Cambridge, 1908.

Phil 3790.1.95   Engert, Joseph. Herman S. Reimarus als Metaphysiker. Inaug. Diss. Paderborn, 1908.

Phil 5044.1.6   Erdmann, B. Umrisse zur Psychologie des Denkens. 2e Aufl. Tübingen, 1908.

Phil 6114.6   Erdmann, B. Wissenschaftliche Hypothesen über Leib und Seele. Köln, 1908.

Phil 3824.2   Erhardt, Franz. Die Philosophie des Spinoza. Leipzig, 1908.

Phil 2070.108A   Essays philosophical and psychological in honor of William James. N.Y., 1908.

Phil 8879.13   Eucken, R.C. Einführung...Philosophie des Geisteslebens. Leipzig, 1908.

Phil 3486.5   Ewald, O. Kants kritischer Idealismus. Berlin, 1908.

Phil 1705.6   Fabre, Joseph. La pensée moderne. Paris, 1908.

Phil 6951.5.10   Farrar, C.B. The autopathography of C.W. Beers. n.p., 1908.

Phil 8955.3   Fassler, A. A new gospel. N.Y., 1908.

Phil 3210.59   Fechner, G.T. Nanna. Hamburg, 1908.

Phil 8695.5.3   Ferreira da Silva, A.J. A cultura das sciencias e os ensinamentos da igreja. Porto, 1908.

Phil 8695.5   Ferreira da Silva, A.J. O ideal religioso e a cultura scientifica. Porto, 1908.

Phil 3235.55   Feuerbach, Ludwig. Vorlesungen über das Wesen der Religion nebst Zusätzen und Anmerkungen. Stuttgart, 1908.

Phil 3235.55.5   Feuerbach, Ludwig. Das Wesen der Religion. Leipzig, 1908.

Phil 1705.4.9   Fischer, K. Einleitung in die Geschichte der neueren Philosophie. Heidelberg, 1908.

Phil 3850.1.95   Fischer, Kuno. Über David Friedrich Strauss. Heidelberg, 1908.

Phil 3552.319   Fleckenstein, Joachim O. Gottfried Wilhelm Leibniz. München, 1908.

Phil 6115.17   Fletcher, E.A. Law of rhythmic breath. N.Y., 1908.

Phil 6115.18   Fletcher, Horace. Optimism; a real remedy. Chicago, 1908.

Phil 8880.25   Fonsegrive, George. Morale et societé. 4e ed. Paris, 1908.

Phil 9495.43   Forel, Auguste. Sexuelle Ethik. München, 1908.

Phil 336.1.6   Fouillée, A. Morale des idées-forces. Paris, 1908.

Phil 336.1.7   Fouillée, A. Morale des idées-forces. 2. ed. Paris, 1908.

Phil 187.23.7   Frischkopf, B. Die Psychologie der neuen Löwener-Schule. Luzern, 1908.

Phil 5755.7   Froehlich, Joseph Anselm. Freiheit und Notwendigkeit als elemente einer einheitlichen Weltanschauung. Leipzig, 1908.

Phil 336.2   Furry, W.D. The aesthetic experience. Its nature in epistemology. Baltimore, 1908.

Phil 5425.2.18   Galton, F. Memories of my life. London, 1908.

Phil 2733.87   Gaonach, J.M. La théorie des idées dans la philosophie de Malebranche. Brest, 1908.

Phil 6316.9   Gard, W.L. Some neurological and psychological aspects of shock. Thesis. n.p., 1908.

Phil 7069.08.20   Garland, Hamlin. The shadow world. N.Y., 1908.

Phil 2490.89   Georges, A. Le système psychologique d'Auguste Comte. Lyon, 1908.

Phil 5425.29.3   Gerhardi, Karl A. Das Wesen des Genies. Jauer, 1908.

Phil 181.59   Germer, Hugo. Schönheit, Güte, Zweck. 1. Teil: Kant und Schopenhauer. Berlin, 1908.

Phil 5046.8   Gibson, W.R.B. The problem of logic. London, 1908.

Phil 705.5.5A   Goddard, H.C. Studies in New England transcendentalism. N.Y., 1908.

Phil 705.5   Goddard, H.C. Studies in New England transcendentalism. Thesis. N.Y., 1908.

Phil 9430.26   Goldschmidt, Kurt Walter. Der Wert des Lebens. Berlin, 1908.

Phil 6116.6   Gould, G.M. Righthandedness and lefthandedness. Philadelphia, 1908.

Phil 7060.69   Grasset, J. L'occultisme: hier et aujourd'hui. Montpelier, 1908.

Phil 6956.5.2   Grasset, Joseph. Demifous et demiresponsables. 2. éd. Paris, 1908.

Phil 6116.9.5   Grasset, Joseph. Introduction physiologique à l'étude de la philosophie. Paris, 1908.

Phil 2805.107   Griselle, E. Pascal et les Pascalins d'après des documents contemporains. Fribourg, 1908.

Phil 6116.7   Gulick, L.H. Mind and work. N.Y., 1908.

Phil 2270.98   Häberlin, P. Herbert Spencer's Grundlagen der Philosophie. Leipzig, 1908.

Phil 807.10   Hamma, Mattheas. Geschichte der Philosophie. 2. Aufl. Münster, 1908.

Phil 5247.36   Hannahs, E.H. Lessons in psychology. Albany, 1908.

Phil 182.45.5   Hannequin, A. Etudes d'histoire des sciences. Paris, 1908. 2v.

Phil 510.1.24   Hansen, Adolf. Grenzen der Religion und Naturwissenschaft. Giessen, 1908.

Phil 182.40   Hébert, M. Le pragmatisme. Paris, 1908.

Phil 807.2.20   Hegel, G.W.F. Vorlesungen über die Geschichte der Philosophie. Leiden, 1908.

Phil 182.28.3   Hibben, J.G. The problems of philosophy. N.Y., 1908.

Phil 8408.6.5   Hildebrand, A. Das Problem der Form in der Bildendenkunst. 6. Aufl. Strassburg, 1908.

Phil 2490.114   Hillemand, C. La vie et l'oeuvre de A.C. et de Pierre Laffitte. Paris, 1908.

VPhil 182.136   Hit és haladás; mult és jövö tarsadalmi kifejlés fokozatos hitnyilvánulasaként fogvaföl. Torda, 1908.

Phil 8882.30   Hobhouse, L.T. Morals in evolution. London, 1908. 2v.

Phil 735.7   Hocking, William E. Papers on the theory of value. Lancaster, Pa., 1908. 2 pam.

Phil 1707.1.12   Höffding, H. Histoire de la philosophie moderne. 2e éd. Paris, 1908. 2v.

Phil 1707.1.6   Höffding, H. History of modern philosophy. v.2. London, 1908.

Phil 1707.1.11   Höffding, H. Philosophes contemporains. Paris, 1908.

Phil 5247.23.4   Höfler, Alois. Grundlehren der Psychologie. 4. Aufl. Wien, 1908.

1908 - cont.

Phil 1900.45   Holland, H.S. The optimism of Butler's "analogy". Oxford, 1908.

Phil 3210.86   Hollander, K. von. Über die Bedeutung von Fechners "Nanna". Göttingen, 1908.

Phil 6980.355   Holmberg, Gunnar. Modern svensk psykiatri under redaktion av Gunnar Holmberg. Stockholm, 1908.

Phil 8662.9   Hood, John. The beauty of God. Baltimore, 1908.

Phil 9347.2.25   Hubbard, E. Health and wealth. East Aurora, 1908.

Phil 1150.10   Hubbard, E. Hypatia. N.Y., 1908.

Phil 7069.08.22   Hyslop, James Hervey. Psychical research and the resurrection. Boston, 1908.

Phil 990.1.2   Igbal, S.M. The development of metaphysics in Persia. London, 1908.

Phil 7060.76   Jacolliot, Louis. Occult science in India. N.Y., 1908.

Phil 184.3.16   James, W. Pragmatism, a new name. N.Y., 1908.

Phil 184.3.21   James, W. Der Pragmatismus. Leipzig, 1908.

Phil 184.3.7.30   James, W. Viljan till tro och andra essayer. Stockholm, 1908.

Phil 5627.6.6   James, William. L'expérience religieuse. 2. éd. Paris, 1908.

Phil 8634.2.5   James, William. Människans odödlighet. Stockholm, 1908.

Phil 5249.11   Jander, E. Leitfaden der Psychologie. Leipzig, 1908.

Phil 8430.30   Jaszi, Oszhai. Muveszet és erkölcs. Budapest, 1908.

Phil 6119.6   Jewett, F.G. Control of body and mind. Boston, 1908.

Phil 5759.2   Joël, Karl. Der freie Wille, eine Entwicklung in Gesprächen. München, 1908.

Phil 530.35.10   Jørgensenn, J. I det Høje. Kristiania, 1908.

Phil 5049.10   Joyce, G.A. Principles of logic. London, 1908.

Phil 6319.1.65   Jung, C.G. Der Inhalt der Psychose. Leipzig, 1908.

Phil 2520.129   Jungmann, Karl. René Descartes, eine Einführung. Leipzig, 1908.

Phil 185.18   Kaftan, Julius. Drei akademische Reden. Tübingen, 1908.

Phil 3640.87.7   Kalthoff, A. Zarathustra-Predigten. Jena, 1908.

Phil 3480.57.40   Kant, Immanuel. Prolegomena in Sprachlicher Bearbeitung, von Emil Kühn. Gotha, 1908.

Phil 5627.79   Kaplan, J.H. Psychology of prophecy. Philadelphia, 1908.

Phil 291.4   Kassowitz, Max. Welt - Leben - Seele. Wien, 1908.

Phil 3120.12.80   Kegel, Martin. Bruno Bauers Übergang von der hegelschen Rechten zum Radikalismus. Inaug. Diss. Leipzig, 1908.

Phil 179.3.91   Kesseler, K. Die Vertiefung der kantischen Religions-Philosophie. Bunzlau, 1908.

Phil 3915.148   Klenke, Friedrich. Der Mensch. Graz, 1908.

Phil 575.29   König, Karl. Rhythmus, Religion, Persönlichkeit. Jena, 1908.

Phil 2805.94.3   Köster, Adolph. Die Ethik Pascal. Inaug.-Diss. Tübingen, 1908.

X Cg   Phil 3850.1.96   Kohut, Adolph. David Friedrich Strauss als Denker und Erzieher. Leipzig, 1908.

Phil 7069.08.50   Kotik, N. Die Emanation der psychophysischen Energie. Wiesbaden, 1908.

Phil 3808.109A   Kowaleski, A. Arthur Schopenhauer und seine Weltanschaung. Halle, 1908.

Phil 2494.83   Krynska, S. Entwicklung und Fortschritt nach Condorcet und A. Comte. Diss. Bern, 1908.

VPhil 185.99   Kudriavtsev-Platonov, Viktor D. Vvedenie v filosofiiu. Izd. 7. Sergiev Posad, 1908.

Phil 410.9   Kuhns, Levi O. The sense of the infinite. N.Y., 1908.

Phil 3270.6.80   Kurz, August. Über Christian Gabriel Fischers vernünftige Gedanken von der Natur. Inaug. Diss. Halle, 1908.

Phil 186.49   Lambek, C. Indledning til kulturens filosofi. København, 1908.

Phil 8591.21   Landmark, J.D. Erkjendelses-teortisk religionsfilosofi. København, 1908.

Phil 5761.11   Landquist, J. Viljan. Stockholm, 1908.

Phil 8886.24   Lanessan, J.l. de. La morale naturelle. Paris, 1908.

Phil 292.3   Lassivitz, Kurd. Seelen und Ziele. Beiträge zum Weltverständnis. Leipzig, 1908.

Phil 525.40   Latteo, Ernesto. Il misticismo. Torino, 1908.

Phil 978.8.25   Leadbeater, C.W. Dreams; what they are and how they are caused. 4th ed. London, 1908.

Phil 8886.23   Leclère, A. La morale rationnelle. Paris, 1908.

Phil 1133.11   Leclère, Albert. La philosophie grecque avant Socrate. Paris, 1908.

Phil 9575.5   Lee, G.S. Inspired millionaires...America. Northampton, 1908.

Phil 3552.25.2   Leibniz, Gottfried Wilhelm. Philosophical works. 2nd ed. New Haven, 1908.

Phil 705.48   Leighton, Walter Leatherbee. French philosophers and New England transcendentalism. Charlottesville, 1908.

Phil 8886.22   Leith, W.C. Apologia diffidentis. London, 1908.

Phil 4011.1   Levi, A. Saggio di una bibliografia filosofia italiana. Bologna, 1908.

Phil 6961.9.5   Liepmann, Hugo. Drei Aufsätze aus dem Aprariegebut. Berlin, 1908.

Phil 1516.2   Ligeard, H. La théologie scolastique. Paris, 1908.

Phil 5251.12   Lipmann, O. Grundriss der Psychologie für Juristen. Leipzig, 1908.

Phil 186.37   Lipps, Theodor. Philosophie und Wirklichkeit. Heidelberg, 1908.

Phil 5251.13   Lloyd, W.E. Psychology, normal and abnormal. Los Angeles, 1908.

Phil 8636.05   Lodge, Oliver Joseph. The immortality of the soul. Boston, 1908.

Phil 8701.4   Lodge, Oliver Joseph. Science and immortality. N.Y., 1908.

Phil 7054.166   Longley, Mary. Teachings...from the spirit world. Chicago, 1908.

Phil 9410.5.3   Loomis, Charles. The knack of it. 2. ed. N.Y., 1908.

Phil 175.13.9   Lorenz, B. Die Philosophie A.M. Ampères. Berlin, 1908.

Phil 342.3   Losskii, N. Die Grundlegung des Intuitivismus. Halle, 1908.

Phil 5070.12   Lowrie, Ossip. Croyance religieuse et croyance intellectuelle. Paris, 1908.

Phil 5465.13   Lucka, Emil. Die Phantasie. Wien, 1908.

Phil 6122.17   MacDonald, R. Mind, religion and health. N.Y., 1908.

Phil 343.4.5   Mach, E. La connaissance et l'erreur. Paris, 1908.

Phil 8592.22.6   Mach, Franz. Die Krisis im Christentum. 2. Aufl. Dresden, 1908.

Phil 7069.08.24   Macrae, Norman. Highland second-sight. Dingwall, 1908?

Phil 5400.37   Maier, H. Psychologie des emotionalen Denkens. Tübingen, 1908.

Phil 2730.45   Maine de Biran, Pierre. Essai de restitution de l'ecrit...L'apperception immédiate. Thèse. Paris, 1908.

Phil 8413.8   Manzari, A. Principii di estetica. Napoli, 1908.

Phil 5252.20   March, J.L. A theory of mind. N.Y., 1908.

Phil 9530.25   Marden, Orison S. He can who thinks he can. N.Y., 1908.

Chronological Listing

1908 - cont.

Phil 6122.27	Maule, G.E. Life and law. 1st ed. Ogden, 1908.
Phil 187.28.13	Mechnikov, I.I. Beiträge zur einer optimistischen Weltauffassung. München, 1908.
Phil 3640.90	Mencken, Henry. Philosophy of Friedrich Nietzsche. Boston, 1908.
Htn Phil 3640.90*	Mencken, Henry. Philosophy of Friedrich Nietzsche. Boston, 1908.
Phil 3494.9	Merren, R. Über der Bedeutung v. Leibniz...für Kant. Leipzig, 1908.
Phil 5252.28.5	Messer, A. Empfindung und Denken. Leipzig, 1908.
Phil 5545.46	Meumann, E. Ökonomie und Technik des Gedächtnisses. Leipzig, 1908.
Phil 8080.3	Meumann, Ernst. Einführung in die Ästhetik der Gegenwart. Leipzig, 1908.
NEDL Phil 343.16	Meyerson, Émile. Identité et réalité. Paris, 1908.
Phil 2035.80.40	Mill, J.S. Eine Prüfung der Philosophie Sir William Hamiltons. Halle, 1908.
Phil 2490.84.15	Mill, John Stuart. Auguste Comte and positivism. London, 1908?
Phil 5252.21	Milliet, J.P. La dynamis et les trois ames. Paris, 1908.
Phil 1504.7	Minges, P. Der angebliche Exzessive Realismus Dons Scotus. v.7, pt.1. Münster, 1908.
Phil 8592.53	Mitchell, H.B. Talks on religion. N.Y., 1908.
Phil 4060.1.88	Mondolfo, Rodolfo. Il pensiero di Roberto Ardigo. Mantova, 1908.
Phil 510.139	Der Monismus dargestellt in Beiträgen seiner Vertreter. v.1-2. Jena, 1908.
Phil 22.6.3	The monist. Complete index. v.1-17. Chicago, 1908.
Phil 52.4	Montana. University. Psychological series. Missoula, 1908.
Phil 978.25	Morrison, D. The open door of the soul. Boston, 1908.
Phil 7069.08.40	Morselli, E. Psicologia e "spiritismo". Torino, 1908. 2v.
Phil 3640.218.2	Mügge, M.A. Friedrich Nietzsche. London, 1908.
Phil 735.90	Münsterberg, H. Philosophie der Werte. Leipzig, 1908.
Phil 8962.5	Murray, J.C. A handbook of Christian ethics. Edinburgh, 1908.
Phil 5402.15	Nádejde, D.C. Die biologische Theorie der Lust und Unlust. Leipzig, 1908.
Phil 8593.8.2	Natorp, Paul. Religion inneralb der Grenzen. Tübingen, 1908.
Phil 188.9	Nelson, L. Ist metaphysikfreie Naturwissenschaft möglich? Göttingen, 1908.
Phil 344.1	Nelson, L. Über das sogenannte Erkenntnisproblem. Göttigen, 1908.
Phil 1133.16	Nestle, W. Die Vorsokratiker. Auschauungen, 1908.
Phil 1050.16	Neumark, D. Jehuda Hallevi's philosophy in its principles. Cincinnati, 1908.
Phil 2885.81	Nève, P. La philosophie de Taine. Paris, 1908.
Phil 75.32	New York. Public Library. List of books in the New York Public Library relating to philosophy. N.Y., 1908.
Phil 188.8	Newcomb, C.B. Principles of psychic philosophy. Boston, 1908.
Phil 3640.76.15	Nietsche, Friedrich. Briefe an Peter Gast. Leipzig, 1908.
Phil 3640.77.15	Nietzsche, Friedrich. Ecce homo. Leipzig, 1908.
Phil 3640.25	Nietzsche, Friedrich. Gedichte und Sprüche. Leipzig, 1908.
Phil 3640.40.2	Nietzsche, Friedrich. Thus spake Zararhustra. N.Y., 1908.
Phil 813.2.3	Noire, L. A sketch...development of philosophical thought. London, 1908.
Phil 99.1	Odebrecht, Rudolf. Kleines philosophisches Wörterbuch. Berlin, 1908.
Phil 7060.92.29	O'Donnell, Elliot. Bona-fide adventures with ghosts. Bristol, 1908.
Phil 7060.92.5	O'Donnell, Elliot. Some haunted houses. London, 1908.
Phil 1714.2	Ollé-Laprune, L. La philosophie et le temps présent. 5e éd. Paris, 1908
Phil 4210.108	Palhoriès, F. La philosophie de Rosmini. Thèse. Paris, 1908.
Phil 4210.108.5	Palhoriès, F. Rosmini. Paris, 1908.
Phil 2225.7.30*	Palmer, George H. The teacher. Boston, 1908.
Phil 1870.105	Papini, G. Giorgio Berkeley. Milano, 1908.
Phil 2805.26	Pascal, Blaise. Pascal; ein brevier seiner Schriften. Stuttgart, 1908.
Phil 190.3.9	Paulsen, F. Philosophia militans. 3e und 4e Aufl. Berlin, 1908.
Phil 4210.137F	Pedrotti, Pietro. Discorso...per Antonio Rosmini. Rovereto, 1908.
Phil 8640.8	Peters, M.C. After death - what? N.Y., 1908.
Phil 5650.6	Peterson, J. Combination tones and other related auditory phenomena. Chicago, 1908.
Phil 2648.80	Petifils, E. Socialiste-révolution au commencement du XVIII siècle. Paris, 1908.
Phil 2610.115	Pfeiffer, Adalbert. Die Ethik des Peter Gassendi. Inaug.-Diss. Borna, 1908.
Phil 190.28	Piat, Clodius. Insuffisance des philosophies de l'intuition. Paris, 1908.
Phil 2840.84	Picard, Roger. La philosophie sociale de Renouvier. Paris, 1908.
Phil 5255.11.9	Pikler, Gyula. Das Beharren und die Gegensätzlichkeit des Erlebens. Stuttgart, 1908.
Phil 5255.11.5	Pikler, Gyula. Zwei Vorträge über dynamische Psychologie. Leipzig, 1908.
Phil 3585.10.91	Pikler, Julius. Über Theodor Lipps' Versuch einer Theorie des Willens. Leipzig, 1908.
Phil 7069.08.27	Podmore, Frank. The naturalisation of the supernatural. N.Y., 1908.
Phil 7080.21	Powell, S.P. The art of natural sleep. N.Y., 1908.
Phil 1145.70	Programm der koniglichen Bismarck-Gym? Pyritz, 1908.
Phil 3425.122	Purpus, Wilhelm. Zur Dialektik des Bewusstseins nach Hegel. München, 1908.
Phil 6686.1.5	Quackenbos, J.D. Hypnotic therapeutics. N.Y., 1908.
Phil 5257.24	Raaf, H. de. Die Elemente der Psychologie. 3. Aufl. Langensalza, 1908.
Phil 192.23	Rageot, G. Les savants et la philosophie. Paris, 1908.
Phil 1717.6	Rand, Benjamin. Modern classical philosophers. Boston, 1908.
Phil 1717.6.3A	Rand, Benjamin. Modern classical philosophers. Boston, 1908.
Phil 8707.5	Raymond, G.L. The psychology of inspiration. N.Y., 1908.
Phil 5425.28	Reibmayr, Albert. Die Entwicklungsgeschichte des Talentes und Genies. München, 1908. 2v.
Phil 7069.08.30	Reichel, Willy. An occultist's travels. N.Y., 1908.
Phil 8672.8	Reinhard, J. Gott und die Seele. Inaug. Diss. Erlangen, 1908.

1908 - cont.

Phil 3625.3.82	Reinhold, Ferdinand. Machs Erkenntnistheorie. Leipzig, 1908.
Phil 6132.5	Religion and medicine. v.1-2,4,6-7. v.3,5 lost. Boston, 1908. 5 pam.
Phil 27.10	Renaissance und Philosophie. Bonn, 1908. 13v.
Phil 2840.50.5	Renouvier, C.B. Science de la morale. Paris, 1908. 2v.
Phil 5827.6	Reuter, Odo M. Die Seele der Tiere im Lichte der Forschung. Leipzig, 1908.
Phil 5627.12	Revault D'Allonnes, G. Psychologie d'une religion. Paris, 1908.
Phil 192.25	Rey, A. Leçons élémentaire de psychologie et de philosophie. Paris, 1908.
Phil 1717.7	Rey, A. La philosophie moderne. Paris, 1908.
Phil 5330.4.15	Ribot, T. Die Psychologie der Aufmerksamkeit. 9 Aufl. Leipzig, 1908.
Phil 1522.3.3	Rickaby, Joseph. Scholasticism. N.Y., 1908.
Phil 1522.3	Rickaby, Joseph. Scholasticism. London, 1908.
Phil 3791.35.2A	Riehl, Alois. Der philosophische Kritcismus. 2e Aufl. Leipzig, 1908.
Phil 8670.9	Rigou, Arthur C. The problem of theism. London, 1908.
Phil 1504.6.6	Rousselot, P. Pour l'histoire du problème. v.6. pt.6. Münster, 1908.
Phil 8418.19	Roux, J. Le sentiment de la beauté; étude de psychologie. Paris, 1908.
Phil 8892.12.9	Royce, J. The philosophy of loyalty. N.Y., 1908.
Phil 8892.12.4	Royce, J. The philosophy of loyalty. N.Y., 1908.
Phil 8892.12.10	Royce, J. The philosophy of loyalty. N.Y., 1908.
Phil 8892.12.5A	Royce, J. Race questions, provincialism and other American problems. N.Y., 1908.
Phil 5257.11.3	Royce, Josiah. Outlines of psychology. N.Y., 1908.
Phil 3808.117	Rzewuski, S. L'optimisme de Schopenhauer. Paris, 1908.
Phil 8598.24.9	Sabatier, Auguste. Philosophie de l'effort. Paris, 1908.
Phil 6968.15	Sailo, Francesco. La patologia mentale im rapporto. Milano, 1908.
Phil 2885.100	Salomon, Michel. H. Taine. Paris, 1908.
Phil 3195.2.80	Sattel, G. Martin Deutinger als Ethiker. Paderborn, 1908.
Phil 3800.180.15	Schelling, F.W.J. von. Sistema dell'idealismo trancendentale. Bari, 1908.
Phil 3800.36	Schelling. F.W.J. von. Schelling als persönlichkeit Briefe, Reden, Aufsätze. Leipzig, 1908.
Phil 8598.27	Schinz, Max. Wahrheit der Religion nach den neuesten Vertretern der Religionsphilosophie. Zürich, 1908.
Phil 3805.50	Schleiermacher, Friedrich. Die Weihnachtsfeier. Leipzig, 1908.
Phil 3460.86A	Schmid, F.A. Friedrich Heinrich Jacobi. Heidelberg, 1908.
Phil 3246.234	Schmidt, Erich. Fichtes Reden an die deutsche Nation. Berlin, 1908.
Phil 400.22	Schmidt, F.J. Zur Wiedergeburt des Idealismus. Leipzig, 1908.
Phil 193.77	Schmitt, Eugen H. Kritik der Philosophie. Leipzig, 1908.
Phil 299.9	Schnehen, W. Energetische Weltanschauung. Leipzig, 1908.
Phil 3808.70.5	Schopenhauer, Arthur. Die beiden Grundprobleme der Ethik. 5. Aufl. Leipzig, 1908.
Phil 3808.60.8	Schopenhauer, Arthur. Parerga en Paralipomena. Amsterdam, 1908. 2v.
Phil 3808.15.7	Schopenhauer, Arthur. Sämmtliche Werke. 2. Aufl. Leipzig, 1908. 6v.
Phil 5520.13	Sechehaye, C.A. Programme et méthodes de la linguistique théorique. Paris, 1908.
Phil 3425.344	Sehring, L. Hegel. Berlin, 1908.
Phil 9120.8	Sérol, Maurice. Le besoin et le devoir religieux. Paris, 1908.
Phil 6990.3.29	Shanley, W.J. The story of Lourdes. Hartford, 1908.
Phil 9075.12	Sharp, F.C. Study of influence, of custom on world judgment. Madison, 1908.
Phil 8893.10.10	Sharp, F.C. A study of the influence of custom. Madison, Wis., 1908.
Phil 193.97	Sharpe, A.B. The spectrum of truth. London, 1908.
Phil 8598.30	Shaw, Charles G. The precinct of religion in culture of humanity. London, 1908.
Phil 9495.131	Sicard de Plauzales, J. La fonction sexuelle au point de vue de l'éthique et de l'hygiène sociales. Paris, 1908.
Phil 5828.11	Sokolowsky, A. Beobachtungen über die Psyche. Frankfurt, 1908.
Phil 4769.1.85	Solov'ev, V.S. Pis'ma. Sankt Peterburg, 1908-09.
Phil 9245.20	Souriau, Paul. Les conditions du bonheur. Paris, 1908.
Phil 4018.2	Spaventa, Bertrando. La filosofia italiana. Bari, 1908.
Phil 3819.33.3	Spinoza, Benedictus de. Éthique. Paris, 1908.
Phil 3819.33.5	Spinoza, Benedictus de. Éthique. Paris, 1908.
Phil 193.31.7	Spir, A. von. Denken und Wirklichkeit. 4e aufl. Leipzig, 1908.
Phil 3640.219	Spitteler, Carl. Meine Beziehungen zu Nietzsche. München, 1908.
Phil 8893.34	Stanton, S.B. The essential life. N.Y., 1908.
Phil 1718.7	Stein, Ludwig. Philosophische Strömungen der Gegenwart. Stuttgart, 1908.
Phil 6328.2	Stekel, Wilhelm. Nervöse Angstzustände und ihre Behandlung. Berlin, 1908.
Phil 3838.8.5	Stern, Jakob. Die Philosophie Spinoza's. 3. Aufl. Stuttgart, 1908.
Phil 493.2	Stevens, S.E. Philosophy of the great unconscious. Boston, 1908.
Phil 1200.11	Stock, St. George. Stoicism. London, 1908.
Phil 5058.30.10	Störring, Gustav. Experimentelle Untersuchungen über Einfache schlussprozesse. Leipzig, 1908.
Phil 5841.16	Stoll, Otto. Die Geschlechtsleben in der Völkerpsychologie. Leipzig, 1908.
Phil 6990.3.40	Storer, M.L. (Mrs.). The story of a miracle at Lourdes, Aug., 1907. N.Y., 1908.
Phil 665.48.5	Stosch, George. Själen och hennes historia. Stockholm, 1908.
Phil 5828.5	Strassen, O.Z. Die neuere Tierpsychologie. Leipzig, 1908.
Phil 5627.14.2	Strong, A.L. A consideration of prayer. Chicago, 1908.
Phil 1718.4	Stumpf, K. Die Wiedergeburt der Philosophie. Leipzig, 1908.
Phil 8893.67.5	Stumpf, Karl. Vom ethischen Skeptizismus; Rede. Berlin, 1908.
Phil 6128.29	Surbled, Georges. L'âme et le cerveau. 3. éd. Paris, 1908.
Phil 705.8	Tarrida del Mármol, F. Problemas trascendentales. Paris, 1908.
Phil 2045.89	Taylor, A.E. Thomas Hobbes. London, 1908.
Phil 194.24	Thone, Johannes F. System der Metaphysik. Dresden, 1908.
Phil 5400.25	Titchener, E.B. Lectures on the elementary psychology of feeling and attention. N.Y., 1908.

Chronological Listing

1908 - cont.

Phil 720.13 — Tonquédec, J. de. La notion de vérité dans la "philosophie nouvelle". Paris, 1908.

Phil 6750.18 — Tredgold, A.F. Mental deficiency (Amentia). N.Y., 1908.

Phil 8894.17.15 — Trine, Ralph W. On the open road. N.Y., 1908.

Phil 194.21.3 — Troward, Thomas. The Edinburgh lectures on mental science. 3d. ed. London, 1908.

Phil 510.16 — Unold, Johannes. Der Monismus und seine Ideale. Leipzig, 1908.

Phil 5645.22 — Utitz, Emil. Grundzüge der ästhetischen Farbenlehre. Stuttgart, 1908.

Phil 8434.3.5 — Van Dyke, J.C. Nature for its own sake. 5th ed. N.Y., 1908.

Phil 31.1.5 — Vierteljahrsschrift für Wissen Philosophie. Generalregister zu Jahrgang, I-XXX. Leipzig, 1908.

Phil 6990.47.5 — Virchow, R. Über Wunder. 2. Aufl. Frankfurt, 1908.

Phil 9075.25 — Vogt, Fritz. Das Wesen des Gewissens. Inaug. Diss. Greifswald, 1908.

Phil 8712.20 — Wahrmund, L. Katholische Weltanschauung und freie Wissenschaft. München, 1908.

Phil 6132.7 — Walton, G.L. Why worry? Philadelphia, 1908.

Phil 5832.8 — Washburn, M.F. The animal mind. N.Y., 1908.

Phil 3504.3.5 — Watson, J. The philosophy of Kant explained. Glasgow, 1908.

Phil 510.19.2 — Weiss, Bruno. Monismus, Monistenbund, Radikalismus und Christentum. 2e Aufl. Breme, 1908.

Phil 197.16 — Wells, H.G. First and last things. N.Y., 1908.

Phil 510.144 — Wendland, J. Monismus in alter und neuer Zeit. Basel, 1908.

Phil 1145.41 — Wendt, M. Geschichte der griechischen Ethik. Leipzig, 1908. 2v.

Phil 8602.43 — Werner, Max. Das Christentum und die monistische Religion. Berlin, 1908.

Phil 8897.28.3 — Westermarck, E. The origin and development...moral ideas. London, 1908-12. 2v.

Phil 2490.90 — Whittaker, T. Comte and Mill. London, 1908.

Phil 7060.113 — Willson, Beckles. Occultism and common sense. London, 1908.

Phil 7069.09.30 — Willson, Beckles. Occultism and common-sense. N.Y., 1908?

Phil 197.28 — Willy, Rudolf. Die Gesamterfahrung vom Gesichtspunkt des Primörmonismus. Zürich, 1908.

Phil 5374.162 — Wirth, Wilhelm. Die experimentelle analyse der Bewusstseinsphänomenma. Brauschweig, 1908.

Phil 5262.11 — Witasek, S. Grundlinien der Psychologie. Leipzig, 1908.

Phil 5772.6 — Wodehouse, Helen. The logic of will. London, 1908.

Phil 9375.6 — Wood, H.A.W. Money hunger. N.Y., 1908.

Phil 6132.17.15 — Wood, Henry. The new old healing. Boston, 1908.

Phil 197.23 — Woodbridge, F.J.E. Metaphysics. N.Y., 1908.

Phil 5262.9 — Woodworth, R.S. Psychology. N.Y., 1908.

Phil 6132.4 — Worcester, Elwood. Religion and medicine. N.Y., 1908.

Phil 197.37 — Wrench, G.T. The grammar of life. London, 1908.

Phil 3915.70.2 — Wundt, Wilhelm. Völkerpsychologie. 2nd ed. Leipzig, 1908-20. 12v.

Phil 3940.1.85 — Zeller, Eduard. Erinnerungen eines Neunzigjährigen. Stuttgart, 1908.

Phil 306.1 — Ziegler, Johann H. Die Struktur der Materie und das Welträtsel. Bern, 1908.

Phil 3850.1.87 — Ziegler, T. David Friedrich Strauss. Strassburg, 1908. 2v.

Phil 5545.41 — Ziehen, T. Das Gedächtnis. Berlin, 1908.

Phil 5265.1.3 — Ziehen, Theodor. Leitfaden der physiologischen Psychologie. Jena, 1908.

1909

Phil 175.19 — Abauzit, Frank. L'absolutisme intellectuel. Saint-Blaise, 1909.

Phil 4060.7 — Acari, P. Un meccanismo umano. Milano, 1909.

Phil 3805.104 — Alin, Folke. Studier öfver Schleiermachers uppfattning af det evangeliska skapelsebegreppet. Lund, 1909.

Phil 800.1 — Allgemeine Geschichte der Philosophie. Berlin, 1909.

Phil 178.4.100 — The Alpha Union for freedom through truth. 4th ed. Hertfordshire, 1909.

Phil 6110.14 — The Arcane formulas, or Mental alchemy. Chicago, 1909.

Phil 9245.9.75 — Avebury, John Lubbock. Peace and happiness. N.Y., 1909.

Phil 331.2.21 — Avenarius, R. L'empiriocriticismo. Roma, 1909.

Phil 525.28 — Bain, James L.M. The Christ of the Holy Grail. London, 1909.

Phil 6111.59 — Baker, R.S. New ideals in healing. N.Y., 1909.

Phil 3552.112 — Baruzi, Jean. La pensée chretienne...Leibniz. Paris, 1909.

Phil 5811.13 — Baudouin, Charles. Das Lernen des Hundes. Inaug. Diss. Berlin, 1909.

Phil 8876.45 — Beary, H.R. Individual development of man. N.Y., 1909.

Phil 2805.108 — Beerens, J.F. De casuïstiek en Pascal. Utrecht, 1909.

Phil 5627.15 — Begbie, H. Twice-born men, a clinic in regeneration. N.Y., 1909.

Phil 176.102 — Bellomia Barone, F. Il problema fondamentale dell'essere. Ortona a Mare, 1909.

Phil 1106.3.11 — Benn, A.W. Early Greek philosophy. N.Y., 1909?

Phil 176.87 — Benn, Alfred W. Revaluations. London, 1909.

Phil 3120.2.80 — Bergmann, H. Das philosophische Werk Bernard Bolzanos. n.p., 1909.

Phil 2475.1.57 — Bergson, Henri. Einführung in die Metaphysik. Jena, 1909.

Phil 2475.1.50.2A — Bergson, Henri. L'évolution créatrice. 5. éd. Paris, 1909.

Phil 8626.12 — Berry, J.B.N. Some assurances of immortality. N.Y., 1909.

Phil 5465.7 — Betts, G.H. The distribution and functions of mental imagery. N.Y., 1909.

Phil 6111.29 — Bevan, J.O. The genesis and evolution of the individual soul. London, 1909.

Phil 5241.46 — Billia, Lorenzo M. Has the psychological laboratory proved helpful. Chicago, 1909.

Phil 6111.15 — Björnson, B. Wise-Kunst. N.Y., 1909.

Phil 1506.2.5 — Blanc, Elie. Traité de philosophie scolastique. Lyon, 1909. 3v.

Phil 3790.4.87 — Bloch, Ernst. Kritische Erörterungen über Rickert. Diss. Ludwigshafen, 1909.

Phil 3110.36.5 — Böhme, J. High and deep searching out. London, 1909.

Phil 7069.09.2 — Bormann, W. Der Schotte Home. Leipzig, 1909.

Phil 176.49 — Bourdeau, J. Pragmatisme et modernisme. Paris, 1909.

Phil 8691.6.5 — Boutroux, E. Science and religion in contemporary philosophy. London, 1909.

Phil 8581.37.5 — Bowne, Borden P. Studies in Christianity. Boston, 1909.

Phil 8610.891.5 — Bradlaugh, Charles. Doubts in dialogue. London, 1909.

Phil 3640.107 — Brandes, G. Friedrich Nietzsche. N.Y., 1909.

1909 - cont.

Phil 3415.93 — Braun, Otto. Eduard von Hartmann, von Otto Braun. Stuttgart, 1909.

Phil 179.3.109 — Braun, Otto. Rudolf Euckens Philosophie und das Bildungsproblem. Leipzig, 1909.

Phil 8581.34 — Bremond, Henri. L'inquiétude religieuse. 2nd series. Paris, 1909. 2v.

Htn — Phil 6720.6.10* — Breuer, Josef. Studien über Hysterie. Leipzig, 1909.

Phil 3425.116.5 — Brie, S. Der Volksgeist bei Hegel. Berlin, 1909.

Phil 9341.9 — Brown, C.R. The young man's affairs. N.Y., 1909.

Phil 9045.6 — Bryce, J. The hindrances to good citizenship. New Haven, 1909.

Phil 9045.6.2 — Bryce, J. The hindrances to good citizenship. New Haven, 1909[1919]

Phil 575.22 — Buckham, John W. Personality and the Christian ideal. Boston, 1909.

Phil 3790.1.97 — Büttner, Wilhelm. Hermann S. Reimarus als Metaphysiker. Inaug. Diss. Paderborn, 1909.

Phil 8876.49 — Bunge, E.O. Il diritto. 3. ed. Torino, 1909.

Phil 1701.5 — Burns, C. Delisle. The growth of modern philosophy. London, 1909.

Phil 5643.36 — Burrow, N.J. The determination of the position. Baltimore, 1909.

Phil 8620.20 — Burton, Marion LeRoy. The problem of evil. Chicago, 1909.

Htn — Phil 8656.11* — Butler, Samuel. God the known and God the unknown. London, 1909.

Phil 3808.138 — Calas, T. Schopenhauer; pessimisme-athéisme. Thèse. Montauban, 1909.

Phil 5242.35 — Carpenter, Edward. L'arte della creazione. Roma, 1909.

Phil 7069.09.3 — Carrington, Hereward. Eusapia Palladino and her phenomena. N.Y., 1909.

Phil 75.15 — Carus, P. Philosophy as a science. Chicago, 1909.

Phil 2490.125 — Cherfils, C. L'esthétique positiviste. Paris, 1909.

Phil 2465.31 — Claparède, E. La psychologie animale de Charles Bonnet. Genève, 1909.

Phil 5242.9 — Claparède, E. Rapport sur la terminologie psychologique. Genève, 1909.

Phil 6672.13 — Claparède, Édouard. Recherches expérimentales sur guelques processus psychiques simples dans un cas d'hypnose. Genève, 1909.

Phil 6112.14 — Clements, J. Metaphysics of the nature and in the conception of the soul. Boston, 1909.

Phil 8827.6 — Cohn, Frederick. Evolutionism and idealism in ethics. Thesis. Omaha, Nebr., 1909.

Phil 1930.4.35 — Collier, Arthur. Clavis universalis. Chicago, 1909.

Phil 177.34 — Cooley, W.F. The individual. N.Y., 1909.

Phil 8877.47 — Cope, Henry F. The friendly life. N.Y., 1909.

Phil 3805.98 — Cramaussel, E. La philosophie religieuse de Schleiermacher. Genève, 1909.

Phil 5042.7.3 — Creighton, J.E. An introductory logic. 3rd ed. N.Y., 1909.

Phil 3425.109 — Croce, B. Lebendiges und Totes in Hegels Philosophie. Heidelberg, 1909.

Phil 5042.10 — Croce, B. Logica come scienza del concetto puro. Bari, 1909.

Phil 8877.34.4 — Croce, Benedetto. Filosofia della pratica; economica ed etica. Bari, 1909.

Phil 8877.55 — Cronin, Michael. The science of ethics. Dublin, 1909.

Phil 2523.85 — Cruet, Jean. La philosophie morale et sociale de Destutt de Tracy, 1754-1836. Tours, 1909.

Phil 978.40 — Curtiss, F.H. Letters from the teacher. Denver, 1909?

Phil 1504.8 — Daniels, A. Quellenbeitrage und Untersuchungen zur Geschichte. v.8, pt.1-2. Münster, 1909.

Phil 5243.32 — Dattino, Giovanni. La psicologia dei testimoni. Napoli, 1909.

Phil 8878.25 — Davies, A.E. The moral life; a study in genetic ethics. Baltimore, 1909.

Phil 3552.114 — Davillé, L. Leibniz historien. Paris, 1909.

Phil 8583.17 — Delany, Selden P. The ideal of Christian worship. Milwaukee, 1909.

Phil 8583.34 — Dennert, E. Klassiker du religiösen Weltanschauung. Bd.1. Hamburg, 1909.

Phil 2490.100 — Deroisin, Hippolyte P. Notes sur Auguste Comte. Paris, 1909.

Phil 5243.7.16 — Dewey, John. Psychology and social practice. Chicago, 1909.

Phil 6980.224 — Dick, Samuel. Psychotherapy. Minneapolis? 1909.

Phil 8633.1.12 — Dickinson, G.L. Is immortality desirable? Boston, 1909.

Phil 1133.17 — Diès, Auguste. Le cycle mystique. Paris, 1909.

Phil 4464.1.30 — Diniz, Almachio. Questões actuaes de philosophia e direito. Rio de Janeiro, 1909.

Phil 178.12.11.9 — Dresser, H.W. The power of silence. 2nd ed. N.Y., 1909.

Phil 6953.8 — Dromard, Gabriel. La mimique ches les aliénés. Paris, 1909.

Phil 5627.85 — Dryden, S.H. Daisy Dryden. 3. ed. Boston, 1909.

Phil 8878.24.5 — DuBois, P. Self-control and how to secure it. N.Y., 1909.

Phil 6313.3 — Dubois, Paul. Les psychonévroses et leur traitement moral. 3e éd. Paris, 1909.

Phil 8878.37.5 — Dürr, Ernst. Grundzüge der Ethik von Dr. E. Dürr. Heidelberg, 1909.

Phil 178.45 — Durand, Eugène. Cours de philosophie. Paris, 1909-21. 2v.

Phil 5814.3 — Edinger, Ludwig. Über Tierpsychologie. Leipzig, 1909.

Phil 3450.7.81 — Eleutheropulos, A. Max Heinze. Leipzig, 1909.

Phil 8584.7 — Eliot, C.W. The religion of the future. Berlin, 1909.

Phil 3486.7 — Ernst, W. Der Zweckbegriff bei Kant. Halle, 1909.

Phil 179.3.6 — Eucken, R. Geistige Strömungen der Gegenwart. 4e Aufl. Leipzig, 1909.

Phil 179.3.21 — Eucken, R. The life of the spirit. London, 1909.

Phil 179.3.27.15 — Eucken, R. The meaning and value of life. London, 1909.

Phil 8584.5.5 — Eucken, Rudolf. Christianity and the new idealism. London, 1909.

Phil 8829.2.12 — Eucken, Rudolf. The problem of human life. N.Y., 1909.

Phil 8879.10.5 — Everett, C.C. Theism and the Christian faith. N.Y., 1909.

Phil 179.8 — Ewald, O. Gründe und Abgründe. v.1-2. Berlin, 1909.

Phil 8695.8 — Fargues, Paul. Transformisme et christianisme. Paris, 1909.

Phil 180.2.9 — Fawcett, E.D. The individual and reality. London, 1909.

Phil 3235.45.6 — Feuerbach, Ludwig. Das Wesen des Christenthums. Leipzig, 1909.

Phil 3246.55.6A — Fichte, Johann Gottlieb. Reden an die deutsche Nation. Leipzig, 1909.

Phil 180.40 — Finckh, T. Lehrbuch der philosophischen Propädeutik. Heidelberg, 1909.

Phil 5045.6.3 — Fischer, Kuno. Philosophische Schriften. System der Logik und Metaphysik. 3e Aufl. Heidelberg, 1909.

1909 - cont.

Phil 2520.102.2 Foucher de Careil, A. Descartes, la princesse Elizabeth et la reine Christine. Paris, 1909.

Phil 8881.26.21 Fouillée, A. La morale, l'art...d'après Guyau. Paris, 1909.

Phil 8630.7 Frank, Henry. Modern light on immortality. 2. ed. Boston, 1909.

Phil 3428.92 Franke, Friedrich. J.F. Herbart; Grundzüge seiner Lehre. Leipzig, 1909.

Phil 8880.31 Franze, Paul. Idealistische Sittenlehre. Leipzig, 1909.

Phil 6315.2.20* Freud, Sigmund. Sammlung kleiner Schriften zur Neurosenlehre. 2e, 4e, 5e Folge. Leipzig, 1909-22. 3v.

Phil 6480.23* Freud, Sigmund. Die Traumdeutung. Leipzig, 1909.

Phil 9495.12 Friedlander, B. Die liebe Platons. Berlin, 1909.

Phil 5402.7 Fulliquet, G. Le problème de la souffrance. Genève, 1909.

Phil 8586.10.5 Galloway, G. Principles of religious development. London, 1909.

Phil 5425.2.20 Galton, F. Memories of my life. N.Y., 1909.

Phil 5545.166 Gamble, E.A.M. A study in memorising various materials by the reconstruction method. Lancaster, Pa., 1909.

Phil 8586.32 Gardner, P. Modernity and the churches. London, 1909.

Phil 181.35 Garfein-Garski, Stan. Ein neuer Versuch über das Wesen der Philosophie. Heidelberg, 1909.

Phil 806.8 Gasc-Desfosses, E. Études sur les auteurs philosophiques: réponses aux questions. 3e éd. Paris, 1909.

Phil 1020.12 Gauthier, L. La théorie d'Ibn Rochd. Paris, 1909.

Phil 5627.13 Geelkerken, J.G. De empirische godsdienstpsychologie. Amsterdam, 1909.

Phil 5330.12 Geissler, L.R. The measurement of attention. n.p., 1909.

Phil 1504.7.2 Geyer, B. Sententiae divinitatis. Ein Sentanzenbuch der gilbertschen Schule. v.7, pt.2-3. Münster, 1909.

Phil 5046.16 Geyser, J. Grundlagen der Logik und Erkenntnislehre. Munster, 1909.

Phil 4115.53 Gioberti, V. Meditazioni filosofiche inedite. Firenze, 1909.

Phil 5520.22 Gmelin, J.G. Zur Psychologie der Aussage. Hannover, 1909.

Phil 3488.14 Görland, A. Aristoteles und Kant bezüglich der idee der theoretischen Erkenntnis. Giessen, 1909.

Phil 6956.10 Gotewood, Lee C. An experimental study of dermentia preacox. Lancaster, 1909.

Phil 3120.2.84 Gotthardt. J. Bolzano Lehre vom "Satz an Sich". Berlin, 1909.

Phil 1511.1A Grabmann, M. Geschichte der scholastischen Methode. Freiburg, 1909. 2v.

Phil 6049.09 Gratz, Thomas Donelson. Palmistry made easy. Philadelphia, 1909.

Phil 8661.7 Groddeck, G. Hin zu Gottnatur. 2. Aufl. Leipzig, 1909.

Phil 6956.4 Gross, Otto. Über psychopatische Minderwertigkuten. Wien, 1909.

Phil 1504.7.6 Grünfeld, A. Die Lehre vom göttlichen Willen. v.7, pt.6. Münster, 1909.

Phil 5756.5 Günther, Carl. Die Willensfreiheit. Berlin, 1909.

Phil 2630.2.35 Guyau, J.M. Sittlichkeit ohne Pflicht. Leipzig, 1909.

Phil 8882.29 Hall, B. Life and love and peace. N.Y., 1909.

Phil 8408.8 Hart, Julius. Revolution der Asthetik als Einleitung zu einer Revolution der Wissenschaft. Berlin, 1909.

Phil 182.44 Hartmann, F. The life of Jehoshua, the prophet of Nazarette. London, 1909.

Phil 807.9 Hasse, Karl P. Von Plotin zu Goethe. Leipzig, 1909.

Phil 3425.11 Hegel, Georg Wilhelm Friedrich. Werke. Leipzig, 1909.

Phil 1540.18 Heitz, T. Essai historique sur les rapports entre la philosophie et la foi. Thèse. Paris, 1909.

Phil 6677.12.5 Hélot, C. L'hypnotisme franc et l'hypnotisme vrai. Paris, 1909.

Phil 2636.25.5 Helvétius, C.A. De l'esprit, de l'homme. 4e éd. Paris, 1909.

Phil 6117.13 Henry, M. Charles. Psycho-biologie et énergétique. Paris, 1909.

Phil 5247.26 Hering, Ewald. Die Deutungen des psychophysischen Gesetzes. Tübingen, 1909.

Phil 5047.16 Hermant, Paul. Les principales théories de la logique contemporaine. Paris, 1909.

Phil 6117.27 Herz, H. Energie und seelische Rechtkräfte. Leipzig, 1909.

Phil 270.34 Hessen, S. Individuelle Kausalität. Berlin, 1909.

Phil 6677.10 Hilgu, Wilhelm. Die Hypnose und die Suggestion. Jena, 1909.

Phil 5047.17 Hoag, C.G. The logic of argument. Haverford, 1909.

Phil 2045.50.9 Hobbes, Thomas. Leviathan. Oxford, 1909.

Phil 8882.56 Hochfelder, J. The supreme law of the future man. 2nd ed. N.Y., 1909.

Phil 4580.30 Høffding, Harald. Danske filosofer. København, 1909.

Phil 8408.12 Hogarth, William. The analysis of beauty. Pittsfield, 1909.

Phil 5780.2 Hollingworth, H.L. The inaccuracy of movement. N.Y., 1909.

Phil 5780.2.5 Hollingworth, H.L. The inaccuracy of movement. N.Y., 1909.

Phil 8587.31 Horneffer, Ernst. Das klassische Ideal. 2-3. Aufl. Leipzig, 1909.

Phil 8587.30 Horneffer, Ernst. Die künftige Religion. Leipzig, 1909.

Phil 8419.26.5 Howard, W.G. Reiz ist Schönheit in Bewegung; a Rettung of Joseph Spence. n.p., 1909.

Phil 8050.67 Howard, W.G. Ut pictura poesis; a historical investigation. Cambridge, 1909.

Phil 6117.12 Huckel, O. Mental medicine. N.Y., 1909.

Phil 2050.66 Hume, David. Anfänge und Entwicklung der Religion. Leipzig, 1909.

Phil 2050.87.8 Huxley, Thomas H. Hume. London, 1909.

Phil 7069.06.11.5 Hyslop, James Hervey. Problem der Seelenforschung. Stuttgart, 1909.

Phil 5070.6 Inge, William R. Faith. London, 1909.

Phil 5402.6 Ioteyko, I. Psycho-physiologie de la douleur. Paris, 1909.

Phil 184.13 Jacoby, Günther. Der Pragmatismus. Leipzig, 1909.

Phil 5249.12 Jäger, Hermann. Die gemeinsame Wurzel der Kunst, Moral und Wissenschaft. Berlin, 1909.

Phil 184.3.23A James, W. A pluralistic universe. London, 1909.

Phil 184.3.16.2 James, W. Pragmatism, a new name. London, 1909.

Phil 5249.2.21 James, William. Principios de psicología. Madrid, 1909. 2v.

Phil 5249.2.13 James, William. Psychologie. Leipzig, 1909.

Phil 5249.2.13.5 James, William. Psychology. N.Y., 1909.

Phil 7069.09.5A James, William. Report on Mrs. Piper's Hodgson-control. n.p., 1909.

Phil 6959.1.12 Janet, Pierre. Les névroses. Paris, 1909.

Phil 600.14 Jodl, F. L'etica del positivismo. Messina, 1909.

1909 - cont.

Phil 6319.3 Joffroy, A. Fugues et vagabondage. Paris, 1909.

Phil 5049.11.2 Jones, A.L. Logic inductive and deductive. N.Y., 1909.

Phil 2805.99 Jordan, H.R. Blaise Pascal. London, 1909.

Phil 8884.11 Joussain, A. Le fondement psychologique de la morale. Paris, 1909.

Phil 3491.8 Jünemann, Franz. Kantiana. Leipzig, 1909.

Phil 3552.114.5A Kabitz, Willy. Die Philosophie des Jungen Leibnitz. Heidelberg, 1909.

Phil 3480.46.23 Kant, Immanuel. Critica della ragion pratica. Bari, 1909.

Phil 3480.26 Kant, Immanuel. Les grands philosophes. Paris, 1909.

Phil 3480.28.40.3 Kant, Immanuel. Kant- Aussprüche. Leipzig, 1909.

Phil 179.3.84 Kappstein, T. Rudolf Eucken. Berlin, 1909.

Phil 2520.153 Kastil, Alfred. Studien zur neueren Erkenntnistheorie. Halle, 1909.

Phil 1504.7.4 Keicher, O. Raymundus Lullus. v.7, pt.4-5. Münster, 1909.

Phil 3492.12A Kelly, Michael. Kants philosophy as rectified by Schopenhauer. London, 1909.

Phil 3640.101 Kennedy, J.M. The quintessence of Nietzsche. London, 1909.

Phil 185.17 Kern, Berthold P. Das Problem des Lebens in kritischer Bearbeitung. Berlin, 1909.

Phil 3492.15.5 Kesseler, Kurt. Die lösung der widersprüche des Dasiens. Bunzlau, 1909.

X Cg Phil 978.44 Kingsford, Anna. The perfect way, or The finding of Christ. London, 1909.

Phil 400.46 Kingsland, William. Scientific idealism. London, 1909.

Phil 8885.11.5 Kirn, O. Vårtids etiska Lifsåskådningar. Stockholm, 1909.

Phil 3235.109 Kohut, Adolph. Ludwig Feuerbach, sein Leben und seine Werke. Leipzig, 1909.

Phil 6960.5.3 Kraepelin, E. Psychiatrie. Leipzig, 1909-15. 4v.

Phil 185.16.5 Kreibig, J.C. Die intellektuellen Funktionen. Wien, 1909.

Phil 960.42 Krishnachandra, B. Studies in Vedantism. Calcutta, 1909.

Phil 400.49.10 Kröger, Otto. Die Weltanschauung des absoluten Idealismus. Harz, 1909.

Phil 400.23 Kronenberg, M. Geschichte der deutschen Idealismus. München, 1909. 2v.

Phil 2885.84 Lacombe, Paul. Taine historien et sociologue. Paris, 1909.

Phil 8701.15 Ladd, H.O. The trade of scientific thought away from religious beliefs. Boston, 1909.

Phil 8886.37 Lalande, André. Précis raisonné de morale pratique. 2. ed. Paris, 1909.

Phil 5051.18 Lambek, C. Om psychologiske beviser. København, 1909.

Phil 2705.30.55 La Mettrie, Julien Offray de. Der Mensch eine Maschine. Leipzig, 1909.

Phil 187.32.80 Lane, Charles A. Montgomery's philosophy of vital organization. Chicago, 1909.

Phil 270.17.5 Lang, Albert. Aphoristische Betrachtungen über das Kausalproblem. Köln, 1909.

Phil 8701.6 Lang, O. Am Wendepunkt der Ideen. Wien, 1909.

Phil 5821.9 Langfeldt. Tier- und Menschenverstand. München, 1909.

Phil 8666.7 La Paquerie, J. Les arguments de l'athéisme. Paris, 1909.

Phil 4600.2.32 Larsson, Hans. Ideer och makter. 2. uppl. Lund, 1909.

Phil 3640.420 Lauscher, A. Friedrich Nietzsche. Essen, 1909.

Phil 8836.2.18 Lecky, E. A memoir of W.E.H. Lecky. London, 1909.

Phil 8886.23.5 Leclère, A. L'éducation morale rationnelle. Paris, 1909.

Phil 186.21 Leclére, A. Pragmatisme, modernisme, protestantisme. Paris, 1909.

Phil 5627.20.5 Leuba, J.H. The psychological origin and the nature of religion. London, 1909.

Phil 4600.4.35 Lidforss, Bengt. Onda makter och goda. Malmö, 1909.

Phil 811.10 Lindsay, James. Studies in European philosophy. Edinburgh, 1909.

Phil 5635.10 Lippmann, F. Du déterminisme psychologique. Strasbourg, 1909.

Phil 6121.10 Lipps, G.F. Grundriss der psychophysik. Leipzig, 1909.

Phil 7069.10.19 Lodge, Oliver Joseph. The survival of man. N.Y., 1909.

Phil 5390.4 Loewenfeld, Leopold. Über die Dummheit. Wiesbaden, 1909.

Phil 8430.19 Loisel, A. L'expérience esthétique et l'ideal chrétien. Paris, 1909.

Phil 7069.09.7 Lonbroso, Cesare. After death - what? Boston, 1909.

Phil 1135.24 Louis, M. Doctrines religieuses. Paris, 1909.

Phil 8663.3.89 Lucas, H.M. View of Lambert's "Notes on Ingersoll." N.Y., 1909.

Phil 5051.6.5 Luquet, G.H. Eléments de logique formelle. Paris, 1909.

Phil 665.7.5 Lutosławski, W. Nieśmiertelność duszy i wolność woli. Warszawa, 1909.

Phil 1504.6.4 Lutz, E. Die Psychologie bonaventuras. v.6, pt.4-5. Münster, 1909.

Phil 2262.91 Lyons, Alexander. Shaftesbury's ethical principle of adaptation to universal harmony. N.Y., 1909?

Phil 6122.30 McComb, Samuel. The power of self suggestion. N.Y., 1909.

Phil 3425.116 Mackenzie, Millicent Hughes. Hegel's educational theory and practice. Photoreproduction. London, 1909.

Phil 5520.16 MacNamara, N.C. Human speech; its physical basis. N.Y., 1909.

Phil 1535.6.20 Maher, Michael. Psychology. 6th ed. v.5. London, 1909.

Phil 8520.13 Maier, Heinrich. An der Grenze der Philosophie. Photoreproduction. Tübingen, 1909.

Phil 6122.34.3 Marden, Orison S. Peace, power and plenty. N.Y., 1909.

Phil 5374.43 Marshall, H.R. Consciousness. London, 1909.

Phil 8592.67 Marvin, D.E. The church and her prophets. N.Y., 1909.

Phil 5052.21 Matičević, Stephan. Zur Grundlegung der Logik. Wien, 1909.

Phil 6122.42 Matisse, Georges. L'intelligence et le cerveau. Paris, 1909.

Phil 600.15 Maurras, C. L'avenir d'intelligence. Paris, 1909.

Phil 2490.126 Mehlis, G. Die Geschichtsphilosophie Auguste Comtes. Leipzig, 1909.

Phil 3832.3.15 Meinsma, K.O. Spinoza und sein Kreis. Berlin, 1909.

Phil 8887.43 Merrington, E.N. Morales et religions. Paris, 1909.

Phil 5252.52 Meyer, Hans. Zur Psychologie der Gegenwart. Köln, 1909.

Phil 187.53 Michaltschew, Dimitri. Philosophische Studien. Leipzig, 1909.

Phil 5403.3 Mignard, M. La joie passive. Paris, 1909.

Phil 6122.56 Miller, A.G. Train development. N.Y., 1909.

Phil 8592.13 Miller, Andrew. The problem of theology in modern thought. London, 1909.

Phil 5252.22 Miller, T.E. The psychology of thinking. N.Y., 1909.

Phil 6322.20 Mitchell, John K. Self help for nervous women. Philadelphia, 1909.

Phil 6322.1 Möbius, P.J. Stachyologie, weitere vermischte Aufsätze. Leipzig, 1909.

Phil 6682.6.9 Moll, Albert. Hypnotism. London, 1909?

Phil 8887.55 Moore, J.H. The new ethics. London, 1909.

1909 - cont.

Phil 7072.6.10	Morse, James Johnson. Spirit photography. Manchester, 1909.
Phil 2490.115	Mourgue, R. La philosophie biologique d'A.C. Lyon, 1909.
Phil 8615.8	Mourik Broekman, M.C. von. De "Deutsche Gesellschaft für ethische Kultur". n.p., 1909.
Phil 9352.10.5	Mowry, William A. Talks with my boys. 5th ed. N.Y., 1909.
Phil 6990.3.50	Müller, G.A. Nach Lourdes. Luzern, 1909.
Phil 8887.50.12	Müller, Johannes. Hindrances of life. N.Y., 1909.
Phil 735.90.5	Münsterberg, H. The eternal values. Boston, 1909.
Phil 5252.12.13.2	Münsterberg, H. On the witness stand. N.Y., 1909.
Phil 6980.484	Münsterberg, Hugo. Psychotherapy. N.Y., 1909.
Phil 5635.12	Murray, E. Organic sensation. n.p., 1909.
Phil 5252.19	Myers, C.S. Text-book of experimental psychology. N.Y., 1909.
Phil 9290.2	Nagel, O. Die Welt als Arbeit. Stuttgart, 1909.
Phil 5763.2	Natorp, Paul. Sozialpädagogik. Theorie der Willenserziehung. 3. Aufl. Stuttgart, 1909.
Phil 5053.3	Naville, A. Logique de l'identité...contradiction. Genève, 1909.
Phil 188.11	Naville, Ernest. Les systèmes de philosophie. Paris, 1909.
Phil 3495.6	Nelson, Leonard. Untersuchungen...Kantischen Erkenntnistheorie. Göttingen, 1909.
Phil 3640.41.8A	Nietzsche, Friedrich. Also sprach Zarathustra. Leipzig, 1909.
Phil 3640.36	Nietzsche, Friedrich. Humano, demasiado humano. Valencia, 1909?
Phil 3640.76.5	Nietzscher, Friedrich. Friedrich Nietzsches Briefe an Mutter und Schwester. Leipzig, 1909. 2v.
Phil 2630.2.129	Nilsson, A. Guyaus estetik. Lund, 1909.
Phil 5252.15.6	Noel, J. Un philosophie belge, Colins. Mons, 1909.
Phil 99.2	Odebrecht, Rudolf. Kleines philosophiches Wörterbuch. Berlin, 1909.
Phil 7060.92.15	O'Donnell, Elliot. Haunted houses of London. London, 1909.
Phil 5545.63	Offner, Max. Das Gedächtnis. Berlin, 1909.
Phil 814.1	Oldham, A. An introduction to the study of philosophy. Dublin, 1909.
Phil 2115.97	Ollion, H. La philosophie générale de John Locke. Paris, 1909.
Phil 960.13	Oltramare, P. La formule bouddhique des douze causes. Geneve, 1909.
Phil 5425.24	Ostwald, W. Grosse Männer. Leipzig, 1909.
Phil 189.7	O'Sullivan, J.M. Old criticism and new pragmatism. Dublin, 1909.
Phil 3496.1	Otto, R. Kantisch-Fries'sche Religionsphilosophie. Tübingen, 1909.
Phil 7069.09.10	Paget, Walburga v.H. Colloquies with an unseen friend. London, 1909.
Phil 4112.81	Palhoriès, F. La theorie idéologique de Galluppi. Paris, 1909.
Phil 8890.34	Pardines, Maurice. Critique des conditions de l'action. Paris, 1909. 2v.
Phil 2520.01	Paris. Bibliothèque National. Département des Imprimés. Catalogue des ouvrages de Descartes. Paris, 1909.
Phil 9550.6	Parris, M. Total utility and the economic judgment. Philadelphia, 1909.
Phil 3745.5.85	Paulsen, Friedrich. Aus meinen Leben. Jena, 1909.
Phil 5765.2.9	Payot, Jules. The education of the will. N.Y., 1909.
Phil 7054.167.10	Peebles, J.M. Spirit mates, their origin and destiny. Battle Creek, 1909.
Phil 1520.3	Perrier, J.L. Revival of scholastic philosophy, XIX century. N.Y., 1909.
Phil 1520.3.3	Perrier, J.L. Revival of scholastic philosophy, XIX century. N.Y., 1909.
Phil 8890.26.5	Perry, R.B. The moral economy. N.Y., 1909.
Phil 5055.9	Pesloüan, C.L. de. Les systèmes logiques et la logistique. Paris, 1909.
Phil 1135.104	Peter, C.L. von. Problem des Zufalls in der griechischen Philosophie. Berlin, 1909.
Phil 270.16	Petersen, J. Kausalität Determinismus. München, 1909.
Phil 346.4.5	Pichler, H.. Über die Erkennbarkeit. Wien, 1909.
Phil 6400.12	Pick, A. Über das Sprachverständnis. Leipzig, 1909.
VPhil 5255.11.10	Pikler, Gyula. A lelektan alapelvei. Budapest, 1909.
Phil 6685.7	Podmore, F. Mesmerism and christian science...history of mental healing. Philadelphia, 1909.
Phil 6125.11	Powell, Hyman R. The Emmanuel movement in a New England town. N.Y., 1909.
Phil 190.23	Pratt, J.B. What is pragmatism. N.Y., 1909.
Phil 3497.5	Prichard, H. Kant's theory of knowledge. Oxford, 1909.
Phil 7039.4.15	Prince, Morton. My life as a dissociated personality. Boston, 1909.
Phil 5409.6	Pyle, W.H. Experimental study of expectation. n.p., 1909.
Phil 720.15	Ramousse, Gatien. Essai d'une théorie scientifique du concept de vérité. Thèse. Saint-Amand, 1909.
Phil 192.27	Rashdall, H. Philosophy and religion. London, 1909.
Phil 7069.09.17	Raupert, John G. Modern spiritism. 2. ed. St. Louis, 1909.
Phil 192.26	Rausch, Alfred. Elemente der Philosophie. Halle, 1909.
Phil 8707.8	Rawson, F.L. The evolution of the world; or, Science from a religious point of view. Garden City, 1909.
Phil 8418.5.2	Raymond, G.L. Art in theory; an introduction to the study of comparative aesthetics. 2. ed. N.Y., 1909.
Phil 8418.4.2	Raymond, G.L. The representative significance of form. 2. ed. N.Y., 1909.
Phil 8892.14	Read, Carveth. Natural and social morals. London, 1909.
Phil 8672.10	Religion and life;...address by...faculty of Meadville Theological School.
Phil 2120.1.80	Remacle, G. La philosophie de S.S. Laurie. Bruxelles, 1909.
Phil 720.5	Rhodes, D.P. Philosophy of change. N.Y., 1909.
Phil 3808.94.10	Ribot, T. La philosophie de Schopenhauer. 12. éd. Paris, 1909.
Phil 4265.4.85	Ricci, Umberto. Necrologio di Giovanni Vailati. Roma, 1909.
Phil 5827.5	Richardson, F. A study of sensory control in the rat. n.p., 1909.
Phil 7069.09.20	Rider, Fremont. Are the dead alive? N.Y., 1909.
Phil 6127.17	Rieger, Conrad. Über Apparate in dem Hirn. Jena, 1909.
Phil 7069.09.40	Robbins, A. Both sides of the veil. Boston, 1909.
Phil 5827.5.2	Robinson, R. (Mrs.). A study of sensory control in the rat. Lancaster, Pa., 1909.
Phil 6687.6	Rochas, d'Aiglun, A. L'extériorisation de la sensibilité. 6e éd. Paris, 1909.
Phil 8892.17	Rodrigues, G. Le problème de l'action. Paris, 1909.

1909 - cont.

Phil 4363.1.80	Rodriguez, J.I. Vida del Doctor José Manuel Mestre. Habana, 1909.
Phil 2050.195	Rödder, Paul. Über Hume's Erkenntnistheorie. Gollnow, 1909.
Phil 3640.545	Rogachev, B. Fr. Nitsshe. Parizh, 1909.
Phil 510.28	Rosny, J.H. Le pluralisme. Paris, 1909.
Phil 623.14	Roulleaux Dugage, G. Théorie des principes de l'absolu. Paris, 1909.
Phil 8597.17	Rowland, E.H. Right to believe. Boston, 1909.
Phil 8597.20.5	Royce, Josiah. What is vital in Christianity? N.Y., 1909.
Phil 2805.98	St. Cyres, S.H.N. Pascal. London, 1909.
Phil 6990.12.5	Saintyves, P. Le discernement du miracle. Paris, 1909.
Phil 8708.12	Sampson, H.E. Progressive creation. London, 1909. 2v.
Phil 282.4.9	Schenker, M. C. Batteux von seine nachahmungs Theorie in Deutsch. Leipzig, 1909.
Phil 193.9.13	Schiller, F.C.S. Etudes sur l'humanisme. Paris, 1909.
Phil 193.80	Schinz, Albert. Anti-pragmatism. Boston, 1909.
Phil 665.24	Schmidt, Wilhelm. Der Kampf um die Seele. Gütersloh, 1909.
Phil 5828.6	Schneider, K.C. Vorlesungen über Tierpsychologie. Leipzig, 1909.
Phil 8893.47.2	Schneider, Wilhelm. Göttliche Weltordnung und religionslose Sittlichkeit. Paderborn, 1909.
Phil 5058.5.9A	Schröder, E. Abriss der Algebra der Logik. Leipzig, 1909. 2v.
Phil 349.20	Schultz, Julius. Die Maschinen-Theorie des Lebens. Göttingen, 1909.
Phil 8881.26.28	Schwartz, E.J. M. Guyaus Moral. Inaug. Diss. Strassburg, 1909.
Phil 349.12	Schwartzkopff, P. Das Wesen der Erkenntnis. Heidelberg, 1909.
Phil 5258.34.4	Seashore, C.E. Elementary experiments in psychology. N.Y., 1909.
Phil 5545.54.5	Semon, R. Die mnemischen Empfindungen. Leipzig, 1909.
Phil 2262.57	Shaftesbury, A.A.C. Ein Brief über den Enthusiasmus. Die Moralisten, eine philosophische Rhapsodie. Leipzig, 1909.
Phil 5249.2.85	Shargha, I.K. Examination of Prof. W. James' psychology. London, 1909.
Phil 8598.73	Shumaker, E.E. God and man. N.Y., 1909.
Phil 8893.11.22	Sidgwick, H. Die Methoden der Ethick. v.1-2. Leipzig, 1909.
Phil 8968.9	Smart, G.T. Studies in conduct. N.Y., 1909.
Phil 8598.12.9	Smith, Goldwin. No refuge but in truth. N.Y., 1909.
Phil 193.73	Snider, Denton J. Cosmos and diacosmos...nature psychologically treated. St. Louis, 1909.
Phil 8980.801	Sokolov, Andrei V. Filosofiia bor'by. Moskva, 1909.
Phil 5070.8	Sollier, P. Le doute. Paris, 1909.
Phil 8643.8	Sopote, M. Grades of life. Letters on immortality. Oxford, 1909.
Phil 2270.72	Spencer, Herbert. L'evoluzione del pensiero. Milano, 1909. 2v.
Phil 2270.76	Spencer, Herbert. L'evoluzione morale. Milano, 1909.
Phil 2270.74.30	Spencer, Herbert. Qu'est-ce que la morale? Paris, 1909.
Phil 8643.17	Spiegler, Julius. Die Unsterblichkeit der Seele. 3. Aufl. Leipzig, 1909.
Phil 2490.107	Spielfogel, R. Comte's moralphilosophische Methode. Zürich, 1909.
Phil 5440.9.5	Spillman, W.J. "Mental and moral heredity in royalty" - Woods. Lancaster, 1909.
Phil 3819.38	Spinoza, Benedictus de. God, man, and human welfare. Chicago, 1909.
Phil 3819.38.3	Spinoza, Benedictus de. Spinoza's short treatise on God, man and human welfare. Chicago, 1909.
Phil 193.31.8	Spir, A. von. Moralität und Religion. 4e aufl. Leipzig, 1909.
Phil 8673.4	Staab, K. Die Gottesbeweise. Paderborn, 1909.
Phil 8643.21	Stanton, H.C. The starry universe the Christian's future empire. N.Y., 1909.
Phil 315.2	Stein, D. Dualismus oder Monismus. N.Y., 1909.
Phil 193.55	Stein, Ludwig. Le sens de l'existence. Paris, 1909.
Phil 978.49.36	Steiner, R. Initiation and its results. N.Y., 1909.
Phil 6328.2.17	Stekel, Wilhelm. Was im Grund der seele Ruht. 4e. Aufl. Wien, 1909?
Phil 5258.37	Stern, N. Das Denken und sein Gegenstand. München, 1909.
Phil 3500.31	Sternberg, Kurt. Versuch einer Entwicklungsgeschichte des Kantischen...des Kriticismus. Berlin, 1909.
Phil 349.7	Störring, G. Einführung in die Erkenntnistheorie. Leipzig, 1909.
Phil 9220.5.11	Streamer, Volney. In friendship's name. 16th ed. N.Y., 1909.
Phil 3500.30	Strecker, Reinhard. Kants Ethik. Giessen, 1909.
Phil 735.4	Strich, Walter. Das Wertproblem in der Philosophie der Gegenwart. Berlin, 1909.
Phil 5627.14	Strong, A.L. The psychology of prayer. Chicago, 1909.
Phil 8893.67	Stumpf, Karl. Vom ethischen Skeptizismus. Leipzig, 1909.
Phil 3805.184	Süskind, H. Der Einfluss Schellings auf die Entwicklung von Schleiermachers System. Tübingen, 1909.
Phil 5059.14	Taylor, William J. Elementary logic. N.Y., 1909.
Phil 8644.5	Teed, Cyrus R. The immortal manhood. 2. ed. Estero, 1909.
Phil 978.26	Theosophy Society in America. A primer of theosophy. Chicago, 1909.
Phil 2730.85	Tisserand, Pierre. L'anthropologie de Maine de Biran. Paris, 1909.
NEDL Phil 5259.5.10A	Titchener, E.B. Lectures on the experimental psychology of the thought-processes. N.Y., 1909.
Phil 3501.5	Tocco, Felice. Studi Kantiani. Milano, 1909.
Phil 8894.19	Tönnies, Ferdinand. Die Sitte. Frankfurt, 1909.
Phil 6969.2	Town, C.H. The train of thought. Philadelphia, 1909.
Phil 8894.17.5	Trine, Ralph W. Auf dem Wege zur Wahrheit. Stuttgart, 1909.
Phil 8599.15	Troward, T. The Doré lectures. N.Y., 1909.
Phil 194.12	True, H.B. How to obtain our own. N.Y., 1909.
Phil 8644.8	Tucker, C.C. On the doctrine of personal identity. London, 1909.
Phil 7054.116.2	Tuttle, H. Arcana of nature. London, 1909.
Phil 5060.3.5	Uphues, G. Erkenntniskritische Logik. Halle, 1909.
Phil 5260.5	Uphues, G. Erkenntniskritische Psychologie. Halle, 1909.
Phil 351.1.5	Uphues, G.K. Geschichte der Philosophie als Erkenntniskritik. Halle, 1909.
Phil 735.10	Urban, W.M. Valuation: its nature and laws. London, 1909.
Phil 8600.4	Usher, E.P. The Greek gospel; an interpretation of the coming faith. Grafton, Mass., 1909.
Phil 4769.1.86	Usnadse, D. von. Wladimir Ssolowiow. Halle, 1909.
Phil 4600.4.36	Utkast och silhuetter. Malmö, 1909.

Chronological Listing

1909 - cont.

Phil 6053.10 Vaschide, Nicolas. Essai sur la psychologie de la main. Paris, 1909.

Phil 5625.79 Veraguth, Otto. Das psychogalvanische Reflexphänomen. Berlin, 1909.

Phil 9361.3.6 Vertua-Gentile, Anna. Come devo compotarmi? 6. ed. Milano, 1909.

Phil 1540.11 Verweyen, Johannes. Das Problem der Willensfreiheit. Heidelberg, 1909.

Phil 8846.3 Vidari, Giovanni. L'individualismo nelle dottrine morali del secolo XIX. Milano, 1909.

Phil 960.11 Vidyabhusana, Satis Chandra. History...mediaeval school of Indian logic. Calcutta, 1909.

Phil 5261.9 Vogt, P. Studenbilder der philosophischen Propadeutik. Freiburg, 1909. 2v.

Phil 496.1 Volkmann, P. Die materialistische Epoche des neunzehnten Jahrhunderts. Leipzig, 1909.

Phil 510.20 Volkmann, Paul. Fähigkeiten der Naturwissenschaften und Monismus der Gegenwart. Leipzig, 1909.

Phil 2915.75 Voltaire, F.M.A. de. Lettres philosophiques. Paris, 1909. 2v.

Phil 735.9 Vos, H. von de. Werte und Bewertungen in der Denkevolution. Berlin, 1909.

Phil 6990.11 Waddle, C.W. Miracles of healing. n.p., 1909.

Phil 3808.111 Wagner, G.F. Encyclopädisches Register...Schopenhauer. Karlsruhe, 1909.

Phil 6132.7.10 Walton, G.L. Those nerves. Philadelphia, 1909.

Phil 303.13 Warren, W.F. The earliest cosmologies. N.Y., 1909.

Phil 8897.4.2 Waters, R. Culture by self-help in a literary, an academic or an oratorical career. N.Y., 1909.

Phil 5627.135 Wauer, G.A. Studien zur Religionspsychologie. Plauen, 1909.

Phil 822.1.12 Weber, A. History of philosophy. N.Y., 1909.

Phil 8520.16 Wegener, R. Das Problem der Theodicee. Halle, 1909.

Phil 5425.30 Wendel, Georg. Über das Genie. Strassburg, 1909.

Phil 8712.10 Wenley, R.M. Modern thought and crisis in belief. N.Y., 1909.

Phil 5262.12 Wenzlaff, G.G. The mental man. N.Y., 1909.

Phil 3808.110 Whittaker, T. Schopenhauer. London, 1909.

Phil 8897.52.5 Wilkens, C. Livets grundvardier. København, 1909.

Phil 3805.161 Willich, E. von. Aus Schleiermacher's Hause: Jugender'en seiner Stiefsohnes. Berlin, 1909.

Phil 6132.8 Willman, R. Errors of mind healing. St. Joseph, 1909.

Phil 197.18 Willmann, O. Die Wichtigsten philosophischen Fachausdrücke in historischer Anordnung. Kempten, 1909.

Phil 9362.14 Wilson, Calvin D. Making the most of ourselves. Chicago, 1909.

Phil 7069.09.70 Wiltse, May B. Theorem or teleology of spiritualism. New-Rockford, N. Dak., 1909.

Phil 3022.3.2 Windlband, Wilhelm. Die Philosophie im deutschen Geistesleben des 19. Jahrhunderts. Tübingen, 1909.

Phil 3022.3 Windlband, Wilhelm. Die Philosophie im deutschen Geistesleben des 19. Jahrhunderts. 2e Aufl. Tübingen, 1909.

Phil 2138.102 Winslow, Christian. Stuart Mills etik. København, 1909.

Phil 8897.32 Wittman, M. Die Grundfragen der Ethik. Kempten, 1909.

Phil 8423.6 Wize, K.F. Abriss einer Wissenschaftslehre der Asthetik. Berlin, 1909.

Phil 8520.14 Wolff, Karl. Schillers Theodizee bis zum Beginn der Kantischen Studien. Leipzig, 1909.

Phil 5635.9 Woodrow, H. Quantitative study of rhythm. N.Y., 1909.

Phil 1527.1.5A Wulf, M. de. History of medieval philosophy. 3. ed. London, 1909.

Phil 3915.47.9 Wundt, Wilhelm. Grundriss des Psychologie. 9. Aufl. Leipzig, 1909.

Phil 6134.2 Yoakum, C.S. Experimental study of fatique. Chicago, 1909.

Phil 1130.3.9 Zeller, Eduard. Grundriss der Geschichte der griechischen Philosophie. 9th ed. Leipzig, 1909.

Phil 5754.3 Zickendraht, K. Der Streit zwischen Erasmus und Luther über die Willensfreiheit. Leipzig, 1909.

191-

Phil 3821.27 Baer, Joseph. Spinoza. Frankfurt, 191-?

Phil 5811.12 Bauke, Leopold. Ist das tier Unvernünftig? 31. Aufl. Stuttgart, 191-?

Phil 3425.212 Caird, Edward. Hegel. Milano, 191-

Phil 8627.9.9 Chambers, A. Ourself after death. Chicago, 191-.

Phil 8878.36.8 Deshumbert, Marius. Morale fondée sur les lois de la nature. 3e éd. Paris, 191-.

Phil 5045.5 Friedlaender, S. Logik, die Lehre von Denken. Berlin, 191-?

Phil 4970.1.30 Ingenieros, José. La simulación en la lucha por la vida. Valencia, 191-?

Phil 5545.70 Kjerstad, C.L. The form of the learning curves for memory. Private ed. Chicago, 191-?

Phil 6060.16 Kronsbein, W. Die physiologischen und psychologischen Beziehungen zwischen Sprache und Schrift. Weinsberg, 191-?

Phil 3565.74 Lotze, Hermann. Der Zusammenhang der Dinge. Berlin, 191-?

Phil 2515.1.80 Louis Couturat (1868-1914). Coulomniers, 191-?

Phil 4363.2.36 Molinos, M. de. The spiritual guide of Michael de Molinos. London, 191-?

Phil 6750.14 Munro, Caroline S.G. The blight of the feeble-minded. Boston, 191-?

Phil 3640.185.10 Reiner, Julius. Friedrich Nietzsche. 8. Aufl. Berlin, 191-.

Phil 3805.30.10 Schleiermacher, Friedrich. Über die Religion. Berlin, 191-.

Phil 5325.10.2 Sutherland, A.H. Critique of word association reactions. n.p., 191-.

Phil 9245.27 Zerbst, Max. Die Philosophie der Freude. Leipzig, 191-.

1910

Phil 5750.3 Ach, Narziss. Über den Willensakt und das Temperament. Leipzig, 1910.

Phil 8875.21 Achelis, J. Ethik. Leipzig, 1910.

Phil 4751.3.6 Aikhenval'd, G. Iu.I. Otdel'nyia stranitsy. Moskva, 1910.

Phil 6110.3 Alexander, F.M. Man's supreme inheritance. London, 1910.

Phil 7150.18 Altavilla, Enrico. La psicologia del suicidio. Napoli, 1910.

Phil 5627.17 Ames, E.S. Psychology of religious experience. Boston, 1910.

Phil 9340.12 Andreas-Salomé, Lou. Die Erotik. Frankfurt, 1910.

Phil 5810.2 Appleton, L.E. A comparative study of the play activities of adult savages and civilized children. Chicago, 1910.

1910 - cont.

Phil 4060.1.30 Ardigo, Roberto. An inconsistent preliminary objection against positivism. Cambridge, 1910.

Phil 5330.11 Arnold, F. Attention and interest...study in psychology. N.Y., 1910.

Phil 1700.3 Atkinson, William W. The crucible of modern thought. Chicago, 1910.

Phil 8402.28.5 Babbitt, Irving. The new Laocoon. Boston, 1910.

Phil 8402.28 Babbitt, Irving. The new Laocoon. Boston, 1910.

Phil 2493.83 Baguenault de Puchesse, Gustave. Condillac; sa vie, sa philosophie, son influence. Paris, 1910.

Phil 8402.22 Balfour, A.J. Criticism and beauty. Oxford, 1910.

Phil 801.19 Barr, Knut. Världsförklaringar och lifsåskådningar. Stockholm, 1910.

Phil 1135.105 Bauch, B. Das Substanzproblem in der griechischen Philosophie bis zur Blütezeit. Heidelberg, 1910.

Phil 176.136 Bawden, Henry H. The principles of pragmatism. Boston, 1910.

Phil 3640.190.11 Bélart, Hans. Friedrich Nietzsches Leben. 2. Aufl. Berlin, 1910?

Phil 2520.130 Belharz, Alfons. Descartes, Hume and Kant. Wiesbaden, 1910.

Phil 8876.55 Bennett, Arnold. How to live on 24 hours a day. N.Y., 1910.

Phil 3625.8.95 Bergmann, E. Georg Friedrich Meier als mitbegründer der deutschen Athetik unter Benutzung ungedruckter Quellen. Leipzig, 1910.

Phil 2280.1.93 Bernays, Paul. Das Moralprinzip bei Sidgwick und bei Kant. Göttingen, 1910.

Phil 6671.5.3 Bernheim, H. Hypnotisme et suggestion. Paris, 1910.

Phil 978.6.50 Besant, Annie. The changing world. Chicago, 1910.

Phil 801.27.5 Bjarnason, A. Hellas. Reykjavik, 1910.

Phil 4520.8.34 Bjarnason, Agúst. Hellas. Reykjavik, 1910.

Phil 8626.8 Björklund, Gustaf. Death and resurrection. London, 1910.

Phil 8626.8.5 Björklund, Gustaf. Om döden och uppstandeken fran cellärans synpunkt. London, 1910.

Phil 9530.18.4 Bligh, Stanley M. The direction of desire. London, 1910.

Phil 9495.125 Bloch, Iwan. The sexual life of our time. London, 1910?

Phil 2477.5.30 Boberil, Roger. Essais philosophiques. Rennes, 1910. 2 pam.

Phil 5041.30 Bode, B.H. An outline of logic. N.Y., 1910.

Phil 3110.35.5 Böhme, J. Concerning the three principles of divine essence. London, 1910.

Phil 3801.222 Bolland, G.J.P.L. Schelling, Hegel, Fechner en de nieuwere theosophie. Leiden, 1910.

Phil 8691.6.10 Boutroux, E. Wissenschaft und Religion in der Philosophie unserer Zeit. Leipzig, 1910.

Phil 2477.1.25 Boutroux, Emile. Choix de textes. Paris, 1910.

Phil 2070.147.5 Boutroux, Emile. Décès de M. William James. Paris, 1910.

Phil 8581.37 Bowne, Borden P. Essence of religion. Boston, 1910.

Phil 978.27 Bragdon, C. The beautiful necessity. Rochester, N.Y., 1910.

Phil 8581.68.20 Broglie, Paul. Les conditions modernes. Paris, 1910.

Phil 6111.53.2 Brown, Charles R. Faith and health. 2. ed. N.Y., 1910.

Phil 3821.11 Brunner, Constantin. Spinoza Gegen Kant und die Sache der geistigen Wahrheit. Berlin, 1910.

Phil 5357.1 Brunswig, A. Vergleichen und die Relationserkenntnis. Leipzig, 1910.

Phil 4803.241.30 Brzozowski, Stanisław L. Idee. Lwów, 1910.

Phil 5585.19 Büttner, A. Zweierlei Denken. Leipzig, 1910.

Phil 5242.13.9 Calkins, M.W. A first book in psychology. N.Y., 1910.

Phil 720.6 Carus, P. Truth on trial. Chicago, 1910.

Phil 8877.42 Carus, Paul. The ethical problem. 3rd ed. Chicago, 1910.

Phil 333.5.5 Cassirer, Ernst. Substanzbegriff und Funktionsbegriff. Berlin, 1910.

Phil 8627.7 Cheney, William A. Can we be sure of mortality? N.Y., 1910.

Phil 400.24.5 Chiappelli, Alessandro. Dalla critica al nuovo idealismo. Milano, 1910.

Phil 5242.15 Clark University, Worcester, Mass. Lectures and addresses before departments of psychology and pedagogy...20 anniversary. Worcester, 1910.

Phil 8657.7.6 Clarke, W.N. The Christian doctrine of God. N.Y., 1910.

Phil 8403.31 Cohn, Jonas. algemeine Asthetik. Leipzig, 1910.

Phil 5242.19 Cohn, Max. Über das Denken. Berlin, 1910.

Phil 8615.9.2 Coit, Stanton. The spiritual nature of man. Bayswater, 1910.

Phil 5070.11 Coke, Henry J. The domain of belief. London, 1910.

Phil 8877.30 Cole, W.M. The American hope. N.Y., 1910.

Phil 9513.5 Coleman, George William. Searchlights. Boston, 1910.

Phil 6312.5 Collins, J. Letters to a neurologist. 2nd series. N.Y., 1910.

Phil 6112.19.5 Colville, W.W.J. Glints of wisdom. N.Y., 1910.

Phil 5648.10 Cook, H.D. Die taktile Schätzung von Ausgefüllten und leeren Strecken. Leipzig, 1910.

Phil 6312.1.3 Coriat, I.H. Abnormal psychology. N.Y., 1910.

Phil 3808.112.9 Covotti, Aurelio. La vita e il pensiero di Arturo Schopenhauer. Milano, 1910.

Phil 8582.36 Crane, A.M. A search after ultimate truth. Boston, 1910.

Phil 3425.109.5 Croce, B. Ce qui est vivant et ce qui est mort de la philosophie de Hegel. Paris, 1910.

Phil 4080.3.33 Croce, Benedetto. Problemi di estetica e contributi alla storia dell'estetica italiana. Bari, 1910.

Phil 177.35 Croce, Benedetto. Saggi filosofici. Bari, 1910-52. 14v.

Phil 2115.161 Crons, E. Die religions philosophischen lehren Lockes. Halle, 1910.

Phil 3484.6.18 Curtiner, Egon B. Chamberlain gegen Schopenhauer. Düsseldorf, 1910.

Phil 6112.29 Curtis, A.M. Of meditation and health. London, 1910.

Phil 802.4A Cushman, H.E. A beginner's history of philosophy. Boston, 1910-11. 2v.

Phil 978.47 Darlès, Jean. Glossaire raisonné de la théosophie du qnosticisme et de l'ésotérisme. Paris, 1910.

Phil 2490.138 Darp, Jan van. De ethiek van Auguste Comte. Utrecht, 1910.

Phil 623.3 Delvolvé, J. Rationalisme et tradition. Paris, 1910.

Phil 4931.3.80* Dénes, Lajos. Emlékkönyv Alexander Bernat hatvanadík születése napjára. Budapest, 1910.

Phil 178.17.3 Dessoir, Max. Philosophisches Lesebuch. Stuttgart, 1910.

Phil 178.31 Dewing, A.S. Life as reality. N.Y., 1910.

Phil 3195.3.80 Dietzgen, Joseph. Joseph Dietzgens Philosophie. München, 1910.

Phil 88.1 Dorner, A. Encyklopädie der Philosophie. Leipzig, 1910.

Phil 4200.1.80 Douglas, A.H. Philosophy and psychology of...Pomponazzi. Cambridge, 1910.

Phil 178.12.33 Dresser, H.W. A message to the well. N.Y., 1910.

X Cg (Phil 9530.18.4)

Htn (Phil 4931.3.80*)

Chronological Listing

1910 - cont.

Phil 284.6.5 Driesch, Hans. Zwei Vorträge zur Naturphilosophie. Leipzig, 1910.
Phil 6113.8.20 Dubois, Paul. De l'influence de l'esprit sur le corps. 9. éd. Berne, 1910.
Phil 600.17 Dubuisson, A. Positivisme intégral. Paris, 1910.
Phil 7060.141 Duchâtel, Edmond. La vue à distance...des cas de psychomètrie. Paris, 1910.
Phil 334.4 Dürr, Ernst. Erkenntnis-Theorie. Leipzig, 1910.
Phil 5401.3 Dugas, L. La timidité. Paris, 1910.
Phil 3823.5 Dunin-Borkowski, Stanislaus von. Der Junge de Spinoza. Münster, 1910.
Phil 665.8.2 DuPrel, C. Die Entdeckung der Seele durch die Geheimwissenschaften. 2e Aufl. Leipzig, 1910. 2v.
Phil 525.1.2 Du Prel, Karl. Die Philosophie der Mystik. 2e Aufl. Leipzig, 1910.
Phil 5244.7.9 Ebbinghaus, H. Précis de psychologie. Paris, 1910.
Phil 400.27 Ebbinghaus, J. Relativer und absoluter Idealismus. Leipzig, 1910.
Phil 3640.98.15 Eckertz, Erich. Nietzsche als Künstler. München, 1910.
Phil 5244.13 Ehrenberg, Hans. Kritik der Psychologie als Wissenschaft. Tübingen, 1910.
Phil 510.142 Eisler, Rudolf. Geschichte des Monismus. Leipzig, 1910.
Phil 1504.8.3 Endres, J.A. Petrus Damiani. v.8, pt.3. Münster, 1910.
Phil 3235.81.8 Engels, Friedrich. Ludwig Feuerbach und der Ausgang der klassischen deutschen Philosophie. 5. Aufl. Stuttgart, 1910.
Phil 5520.7.2 Erdmann, Karl O. Die Bedeutung des Wortes. 2. Aufl. Leipzig, 1910.
Phil 179.3.25 Eucken, R. Der Sinn und Wert des Lebens. Leipzig, 1910.
Phil 8584.5.7 Eucken, Rudolf. Der religiöse Wahrheitsbegriff in der Philosophie Rudolf Euckens. Göttingen, 1910.
Phil 180.27 Fabbricotti, Carlo A. Appunti critici di filosofia contemporanea. Firenze, 1910.
Phil 2138.110 Fabbricotti, Carlo A. Positivismo? John Stuart Mill. Firenze, 1910.
Phil 8830.4 Faquet, Émile. La démission de la morale. Paris, 1910.
Phil 4520.9.90 Festskrift tillägnad E.O. Burman. Upsala, 1910.
Phil 6115.11.19 Feuchtersleben, E.F.V. Health and suggestion: the dietetics of the mind. N.Y., 1910.
Phil 3246.71 Fichte, Johann Gottlieb. Die philosophischen Schriften zum Atheismusstreit. Leipzig, 1910.
Phil 75.30 Florence. Biblioteca Filosofica. Catalogo della Biblioteca filosofica. Text and supplement. Firenze, 1910.
Phil 5245.30 Foltz, Otto. Grundriss der Psychologie für Lehrer- und Lehrerinen-Bildungs-Anstalten. Österwiech-Harz, 1910.
Phil 5648.4.5 Foucault, Marcel. L'illusion paradoxale et le seuil de Weber. Montpelier, 1910.
Phil 9010.18 Fowler, Montague. The morality of social pleasures. London, 1910.
Phil 4756.1.29 Frank, Semen L. Filosofiia i zhizn', etiudy i nabroski po filosofii kul'tury. Sankt Peterburg, 1910.
Phil 6315.2.75.8 Freud, Sigmund. Drei Abhandlungen zur Sexualtheorie. Leipzig, 1910.
Htn Phil 6315.2.4.5* Freud, Sigmund. Über Psychoanalyse. Leipzig, 1910.
Phil 180.32 Frost, Walter. Naturphilosophie. v.1. Leipzig, 1910.
Phil 3310.2.80 Ganewa, R. Die Erkenntnistheorie von Carl Göring. Inaug. Diss. Heidelberg, 1910.
Phil 8881.46 Garello, Luigi. Levjathan; ricerche sulla natura morale dell'uomo. Torino, 1910.
Phil 2475.1.99 Gillouin, R. Henri Bergson. Paris, 1910.
Phil 4115.42 Gioberti, V. La teorica delle mente umana. Milano, 1910.
Phil 2805.90.5 Giraud, V. Blaise Pascal études d'histoire morale. Paris, 1910.
Phil 6116.8 Giss, A.J. Die menschliche Geistestätigkeit in der Weltentwicklung. Leipzig, 1910.
Phil 1133.18 Goebel, Karl. Die vorsokratische Philosophie. Bonn, 1910.
Phil 3488.4 Goldschmidt, L. Zur Wiedererweckung Kantischer Lehre. Gotha, 1910.
Phil 181.81 Gould, G.M. The infinite presence. N.Y., 1910.
Phil 5640.38 Greenwood, Major. Physiology of the special senses. London, 1910.
Phil 6316.4 Gregor, Adalbert. Leitfaden der experimentellen Psychopathologie. Berlin, 1910.
Phil 337.2 Gross, Felix. Form und Materie des Erkennens. Leipzig, 1910.
Phil 3640.159.15 Grützmacher, R.H. Nietzsche und wir Christen. Berlin, 1910.
Phil 337.8 Gurland-Eljaschoff, E. Erkenntnistheoretische Studien auf antipsychologistischer Grundlage. Bern, 1910.
Phil 2750.1.79 Gusgens, J. Die Naturphilosophie des Joannes...Magnenus. Bonn, 1910.
Phil 3808.86.7 Gwinner, W. Schopenhauer's Leben. Leipzig, 1910.
Phil 6677.5 Haberman, J.V. Hypnosis. N.Y., 1910.
Phil 182.43 Häberlin, Paul. Wissenschaft und Philosophie. Basel, 1910. 2v.
Phil 8957.4 Hall, T.C. History of ethics...Christianity. N.Y., 1910.
Phil 3425.73.5 Hegel, Georg Wilhelm Friedrich. The phenomenology of mind. London, 1910.
Phil 5360.2 Heinrich, E. Untersuchungen zur Lehre vom Begriff. Inaug. Diss. Göttingen, 1910.
Phil 3915.150 Heinzelmann, G. Der Begriff der Seele und die Idei der Unsterblichkeit. Tübingen, 1910.
Phil 5627.37 Henke, Frederick G. A study in the psychology of ritualism. Diss. Chicago, 1910.
Phil 5757.6 Henle, Rudolf. Vorstellungs- und Willentheorie. Leipzig, 1910.
Phil 8662.6 Henri, P.E. Religion d'amour ou Dieu existe. Marseille, 1910.
Phil 3805.178 Herz, Henriette de Lemos. Schleiermacher und seine.Lieben. Magdeburg, 1910.
Phil 5047.8.8 Hibben, J.G. Logic, deductive and inductive. N.Y., 1910[1905].
Phil 3425.105.15 Hibben, J.G. La logica di Hegel. Torino, 1910.
Phil 1707.2A Hibben, J.G. Philosophy of the enlightenment. N.Y., 1910.
Phil 3425.277 Hirā-Lāl, H. Hegelianism and human personality. Calcutta, 1910.
Phil 2045.55 Hobbes, Thomas. Metaphysical system. Chicago, 1910.
Phil 182.36.17 Höffding, H. Den menneskelige tanke. Kjobenhavn, 1910.
Phil 990.26 Horten, Max. Die philosophischen Ansichten von Razi und Tusi. Bonn, 1910.
Phil 2050.45 Hume, David. Ricerche sull'intelletto umano e sui principii della morale. Bari, 1910.
Phil 8632.10 Hunt, Jasper B. Existence after death implied by science. London, 1910.
Phil 7069.10.5 Hyslop, James Hervey. Science and a future life. 5. ed. Boston, 1910.

1910 - cont.

Phil 8633.2 In after days; thoughts on the future life. N.Y., 1910.
Phil 5070.6.5 Inge, William R. Faith and its psychology. N.Y., 1910.
Phil 3625.1.170 Isaacs, Abram Samuel. Step by step. Philadelphia, 1910.
Phil 9035.16 Jastrow, J. The qualities of men. Boston, 1910.
Phil 184.12.5 Jerusalem, W. Introduction to philosophy. N.Y., 1910.
Phil 7069.10.10 Jones, Amanda T. A psychic autobiography. N.Y., 1910.
Phil 400.25.2 Jones, H. Idealism as a practical creed. 2nd ed. Glasgow, 1910.
Phil 8884.4.13 Jordan, W.G. The power of purpose. N.Y., 1910.
Phil 8589.9 Joussain, André. Romantisme et religion. Paris, 1910.
Phil 8960.2 Kachnik, Josef. Ethica catholica. Olomucii, 1910-12. 3v.
Phil 185.36 Kaïres, Theophilos. Philosophiká. Athens, 1910.
Phil 3480.82.6 Kant, Immanuel. Beobachtungen über das Gefühl des Schönen und Erhabenen. Berlin, 1910.
Phil 3480.31.8 Kant, Immanuel. Critica della raigon pura. v.1-2. Bari, 1910.
Phil 3492.16 Katzer, Ernst. Luther und Kant. Giessan, 1910.
Phil 5620.6 Keary, C.F. The pursuit of reason. Cambridge, 1910.
Phil 5050.8 Kells, S.C. Typical methods of thinking. N.Y., 1910.
Phil 3492.12.5 Kelly, Michael. Kant's ethics and Schopenhauer's criticism. London, 1910.
Phil 3640.246 Kerler, D.H. Nietzsche und die Vergeltungsidee. Ulm, 1910.
Phil 343.5.50 Kerler, D.H. Über Annahmen; eine Streitschrift. Ulm, 1910.
Phil 3492.15 Kesseler, Kurt. Kant und Schiller. Bunzlau, 1910.
Phil 3808.196 Keyserling, H. Schopenhauer als Verbilder. Leipzig, 1910.
Phil 8590.7 King, I. The development of religion. N.Y., 1910.
Phil 6060.12 Klages, Ludwig. Die Probleme der Graphologie. Leipzig, 1910.
Phil 3415.101 König, N. Die metaphysische Begründung der Ethik in Eduard von Hartmanns philosophischen System. Leipzig, 1910.
Phil 3492.13.5 Kronenberg, M. Kant. 4. Aufl. München, 1910.
Phil 2490.124 Kühnert, H. August Comtes Verhältnis zur Kunst. Leipzig, 1910.
Phil 185.12.5 Külpe, O. Einleitung in die Philosophie. 5. Aufl. Leipzig, 1910.
Phil 341.5 Külpe, O. Erkenntnistheorie und Naturwissenschaft. Leipzig, 1910.
Phil 8430.31 Kunzle, Magnus. Ethik und Ästhetik. Freiburg, 1910.
Phil 3808.112.15 Kusten, Wallebald. Zürück zu Schopenhauer. Berlin, 1910.
Phil 186.24 Lagos, C.D. La doctrina de los siglos. Santiago, 1910.
Phil 186.25 Laguna, T. de. Dogmatism and evolution. N.Y., 1910.
Phil 5400.50.6 Lange, C.G. Die Gemüthsbewegungen. 2e Aufl. Würzburg, 1910.
Phil 4600.2.45 Larsson, Hans. Intuition. 3e uppl. Stockholm, 1910.
Phil 4600.2.35 Larsson, Hans. Viljans frihet. Lund, 1910.
Phil 1535.33 La Scala, Puis. Cursus philosophicus ad usum seminariorum. Parisiis, 1910. 2v.
Phil 3210.81 Lasswitz, Kurd. Gustav Theodor Fechner. Stuttgart, 1910.
Phil 672.18 Lechalas, G. Étude sur l'espace et le temps. Paris, 1910.
Phil 623.1.20 Lecky, W.E.H. History of the rise and influence of the spirit of rationalism in Europe. v.1-2. London, 1910.
Phil 8666.15 Lederer, Julius. Gott und Teufel im 20. Jahrhundert. 4. Aufl. Berlin, 1910?
Phil 3850.1.98 Lévy, Albert. David Fredéric Strauss, la vie et l'oeuvre. Paris, 1910.
Phil 5500.6 Lewis, T.A. Judgment as belief. Baltimore, 1910.
Phil 186.23 Lindsay, J. The fundamental problems of metaphysics. Edinburgh 1910.
Phil 5070.7 Lindsay, J. The psychology of belief. Edinburgh, 1910.
Phil 5251.13.2 Lloyd, W.E. Psychology, normal and abnormal. N.Y., 1910.
Phil 8701.4.7 Lodge, Oliver Joseph. Reason and belief. N.Y., 1910.
Phil 7069.10.20 Lodge, Oliver Joseph. The survival of man. 3. ed. London, 1910.
Phil 3640.98 Ludovici, Anthony M. Nietzsche, his life and works. London, 1910.
Phil 735.8 Lüdemann, H. Das Erkennen und die Werturteile. Leipzig, 1910.
Phil 8591.32 Lütgert, Wilhelm. Natur und geist Gottes; Vorträge zur Ethik. Leipzig, 1910.
Phil 5761.8.5 Lutosławski, W. Rozwójpotęgi woli przez psychofizyczne ćiviczenia. Warszawa, 1910.
Phil 6121.15 Lyon, I.L.R. The wonders of life. N.Y., 1910.
Phil 5822.6 McCabe, Joseph. The evolution of mind. London, 1910.
Phil 510.1.18 McCabe, Joseph. Haeckel's critics answered. London, 1910.
Phil 8887.37 McConnell, R.M. Duty of altruism. N.Y., 1910.
Phil 1812.4.5 MacCunn, J. Six radical thinkers. London, 1910.
Phil 8663.3.91 McDonald, E.M. Col. Robert G. Ingersoll as he is. N.Y., 1910?
Phil 5252.18.5.4 McDougall, William. An introduction to social psychology. 3d ed. London, 1910.
Phil 187.107 MacEachran, John M. Pragmatismus; eine neue Richtung der Philosophie. Leipzig, 1910.
Phil 5635.5.10 Mach, Ernst. Contributions to the analysis of the sensations. Chicago, 1910.
Phil 8887.59 Mackenzie, J.S. A manual of ethics. 4. ed. London, 1910.
Phil 187.56.4 McTaggart, J.M.E. Dare to be wise. London, 1910.
Phil 3425.100.9 McTaggart, John McTaggart Ellis. A commentary on Hegel's logic. Cambridge, 1910.
Phil 6322.3 Marie, Auguste. Traité international de psychologie pathologique. Paris, 1910-12. 3v.
Phil 97.3 Mauthner, F. Wörterbuch der Philosphie. München, 1910. 2v.
Phil 3425.121 Mayer-Moreau, K. Hegels Socialphilosophie. Tubingen, 1910.
Phil 8887.41.5 Meakin, F. Function, feeling, and conduct. N.Y., 1910.
Phil 343.5.2 Meinong, A. Über Annahmen. 2. Aufl. Leipzig, 1910.
Phil 8637.10 Mellone, S.H. The immortal hope. Edinburgh, 1910.
Phil 6682.10 Melvelle, John. Crystal-gazing and the wonders of clairvoyance. London, 1910.
Phil 6682.10.2 Melvelle, John. Crystal-gazing and the wonders of clairvoyance. London, 1910.
Phil 4352.1.89 Menendez y Pelayo, D.M. Das palabras sobre centenario de Balmes. Vich, 1910.
Phil 5628.53 Merkt, Josef. Die Wundmale des heiligen Franziskus von Assisi. Leipzig, 1910.
Phil 6962.9 Meyerhof, O. Beiträge zur psychologischen Theorie der Geistesstörungen. Göttingen, 1910.
Phil 2138.76A Mill, John S. Letters of John Stuart Mill. London, 1910. 2v.
Phil 3120.15.90 Moebius, A. Constantin Brunners Lehre, das Evangelium. Berlin, 1910.
Phil 8962.6 Montgomery, G.R. The unexplored self. N.Y., 1910.
Phil 187.39A Moore, A.W. Pragmatism and its critics. Chicago, 1910.

Chronological Listing

1910 - cont.

Phil 575.16 Mouchet, E. Examen del concepto de identidad. Buenos Aires, 1910.
Phil 3808.112.20 Mülethaler, J. Die Mystik bei Schopenhauer. Berlin, 1910.
Phil 5252.12.17 Münsterberg, H. American problems. N.Y., 1910.
Phil 5722.12 Münsterberg, Hugo. Subconscious phenomena. Boston, 1910.
Phil 8887.25.6 Muirhead, J.H. The elements of ethics. London, 1910.
Phil 9495.129 Muller, J.P. Kønsmoral og livslykke. 3. opl. København, 1910.
Phil 7069.10.30 Myers, Gustavus. Beyond the borderline of life. Boston 1910.
Phil 5253.1.9 Natorp, P. Allgemeine Psychologie. 2. Aufl. Marburg, 1910.
Phil 735.3 Nicholson, Anne M. The concept standard. N.Y., 1910.
Phil 3640.30.5 Nietzsche, Friedrich. Aurora. Valencia, 1910?
Phil 3640.15 Nietzsche, Friedrich. Complete works. v.1,3,7,9-10,13,18. Edinburgh, 1910-13. 7v.
NEDL Phil 3640.15 Nietzsche, Friedrich. Complete works. v.2,4-6,8,11,14-15,17. Edinburgh, 1910-13. 9v.
Phil 3640.43 Nietzsche, Friedrich. La gaya ciencia. Valencia, 1910?
Phil 4610.7.38 Norström, V. Masskultur. Stockholm, 1910.
Phil 3014.1A Oesterreich, K. Die deutsche Philosophie inder zweiten Halfte des neunzehnten Jahrhund. Tübingen, 1910.
Phil 575.14 Oesterreich, K. Die Phänomenologie des Ich in ihren Grundproblem. Leipzig, 1910.
Phil 189.9 Opitz, H.G. Die Philosophie der Zukunft. Leipzig, 1910.
Phil 295.1.6 Ostwald, W. Natural philosophy. N.Y., 1910.
Phil 9400.2 Paine, Harriet E. Old people. Boston, 1910.
Phil 3640.166 Pallarès, V. de. Le crépuscule d'une idole, Nietzsche, nietzschéisme, nietzscheens. Paris, 1910.
Phil 8640.5 Palmer, Fred. Winning of immortality. London, 1910.
Phil 5170.3 Pastore, A. Sillogismo e proporzione. Milano, 1910.
Phil 1158.15.14A Pater, Walter. Marius the Epicurean. London, 1910. 2v.
Phil 6125.7.5 Paulhan, F. La physiologie de l'esprit. 5. éd. Paris, 1910.
Phil 190.3.8.5 Paulsen, F. Inleiding tot de wijsbegeerte. Amsterdam, 1910.
Phil 5625.75.30 Pavlov, Ivan P. The work of the digestive glands. London, 1910.
Phil 5765.2.9.5 Payot, Jules. The education of the will. N.Y., 1910.
Phil 5545.47 Peillaube, E. Les images. Paris, 1910.
Phil 5545.44 Peiron, Henri. L'évolution de la mémoire. Paris, 1910.
Phil 9450.10 Pensa, Henri. De la morale politique. Paris, 1910.
Phil 2070.129 Perry, R.B. William James. Boston? 1910.
Phil 5411.6 Pfister, Oskar. Analytische Untersuchungen über die Psychologie des Hasses und der Versöhnung. Leipzig, 1910.
Phil 815.4 Pfordten, Otto. Konformismus eine Philosophie der normatwen Werte. Heidelberg, 1910-13.
Phil 705.12 Phalén, Adolf K. Kritik af subjektivismen. Uppsala, 1910.
Phil 9245.32 Piat, Clodius. La morale du bonheur. Paris, 1910.
Phil 5374.17.5 Pikler, Gyula. Die Stelle des Bewusstseins in der Natur. Leipzig, 1910.
Phil 5620.7 Pillsbury, W.B. The psychology of reasoning. N.Y., 1910.
Phil 5467.2 Pistolesi, G. L'imitazione; studio di psicologia. Torino, 1910.
Phil 7069.10.40 Podmore, Frank. The newer spiritualism. London, 1910.
Phil 6115.11.28 Pollak, G. The hygiene of the soul; the memoir of a physician and philosopher. N.Y., 1910.
Phil 346.8 Porten, Max von der. Entstehen von Empfindung und bewisstsein. Leipzig, 1910.
Phil 5415.9 Prandtl, A. Die Einfühlung. Leipzig, 1910.
Phil 190.27 Prat, Louis. Contes pour les métaphysiciens. Paris, 1910.
Phil 7039.4.3 Prince, Morton. The dissociation of a personality. N.Y., 1910.
Phil 8670.8 Prolegomena to theism. N.Y., 1910.
Phil 6125.5 Psychotherapeutics; a symposium. Boston, 1910.
Phil 9495.30 Public Morals Conference, London, 1910. The nation's morals. London, 1910.
Phil 8597.25 Rade, Martin. Die Stellung des Christentums zum Geschlechtsleben. Tübingen, 1910.
Phil 6128.17F Ramström, M. Emannuel Swedenborg's investigations in natural science and the basis for his statements concerning the functions of the brain. Uppsala, 1910.
Phil 5585.7.5 Rau, A. Das Wesen des menschlichen Verstandus und Bewusstseins. München, 1910.
Phil 7060.72.7 Raupert, J.G. The supreme problem. Buffalo, 1910.
Phil 6990.31 Regnault, Félix. La genèse des miracles. Paris, 1910.
Phil 5374.17 Rehmke, J. Das Bewusstsein. Heidelberg, 1910.
Phil 348.4 Rehmke, J. Philosophie als Grundwissenschaft. Leipzig, 1910.
Phil 6687.1.6 Reichenback, C. Der sensitive Mensch. Leipzig, 1910. 2v.
Phil 5257.17 Reichwein, G. Die neueren Untersuchungen über Psychologie des Denkens. Halle, 1910.
Phil 8597.18 Religion of the spiritual evolution of man. Chicago, 1910.
Phil 5545.66 Renda, A. L'oblio; saggio sull'attività selettiva della coscienza. Torino, 1910.
Phil 2840.75 Renouvier, C.B. Correspondance de Renouvier et Secrétan. Paris, 1910.
Phil 4215.3.30 Rensi, Giuseppe. Le antinomie dello spirito. Piacenza, 1910.
Phil 817.6 Reyes Ruiz, Jesús Maria. Historia de la filosofia y terminología filosofica. 2. ed. Granada, 1910.
Phil 5400.18.25 Ribot, T. Problèmes de psychologie affective. Paris, 1910.
Phil 6060.25.10 Rice, L.G. (Mrs.). Practical graphology. Chicago, 1910.
Phil 3910.81 Richler, H. Über Christian Wolffs Ontologie. Leipzig, 1910.
Phil 8892.30.2 Ritter, Eli F. Moral law and civil law; parts of the same thing. Westerville, Ohio, 1910.
Phil 5767.8 Roretz, Karl von. Der Zweckbegriff im psychologischen und erkenntnistheoretischen Denken. Leipzig, 1910.
Phil 4352.1.82 Roure, Narciso. Las ideas de Balmes. Madrid, 1910.
Phil 4352.1.80 Roure, Narciso. La vida y las obras de Balmes. Madrid, 1910.
Phil 5780.3 Rowe, E.C. Voluntary movement. n.p., 1910.
Phil 510.5 Ruckhaber, Erich. Des Daseins und Denkens Mechanik und Metamechanik. Hirschberg, 1910.
Phil 3499.11 Ruge, Arnold. Das Problem der Freiheit in Kants Erkenntnistheorie. Leipzig, 1910.
Phil 5257.13 Ruger, Henry A. Psychology of efficiency. N.Y., 1910.
Phil 192.28.5A Russell, B. Philosophical essays. London, 1910.
Phil 2805.98.10 St. Cyres, S.H.N. Pascal. N.Y., 1910.
Phil 6968.13 Schaefer, H. Allgemeine Gerichtliche Psychiatrie. Berlin, 1910.

1910 - cont.

Phil 5585.44 Schapp, W. Beiträge zur Phänomenologie der Wahrnehmung. Halle, 1910.
Phil 3800.340.20 Schelling, F.W.J. von. Ricerche filosofiche su...libertá umana. Lanciano, 1910.
Phil 193.9.3 Schiller, F.C.S. Riddles of the Sphinx. London, 1910.
Phil 575.27 Schlaf, Johannes. Das absolute Individuum. Berlin, 1910.
Phil 3805.15 Schleiermacher, Friedrich. Werke. Leipzig, 1910-11. 4v.
Phil 3805.33 Schleiermacher Kurze Darstellung des theologischen Studiums. Leipzig, 1910.
Phil 3805.30.15 Schleiermachers Glaubenslehre. Leipzig, 1910.
Phil 8673.7 Schmidt, Wilhelm. L'origine de l'idée de Dieu. pt.1. Paris, 1910.
Phil 193.76 Schneider, Albert. Wirklichkeiten. Strassburg, 1910.
Phil 8417.3.15 Schneider, René. L'esthétique classique chez Quatremère. Paris, 1910.
Phil 8417.3.20 Schneider, René. Quatremère de Quincy et son intervention dans les arts, 1788-1830. Paris, 1910.
Phil 349.10 Schuppe, W. Grundriss der Erkenntnistheorie und Logik. 2. Aufl. Berlin, 1910.
Phil 8598.51 Scudder, D. The passion for reality. N.Y., 1910.
Phil 193.57A Searle, A. Essays I-XXX. Cambridge, 1910.
Phil 2515.4.90 Segond, J. Cournot et la psychologie vitaliste. Thèse. Paris, 1910.
Phil 6128.16 Sermyn, W.C. de. Contribution à l'étude de certaines facultés cérébrales méconnues. Sawsanne, 1910.
Phil 2262.50 Shaftesbury, A.A.C. Die Moralisten, eine philosophische Rhapsodie. Jena, 1910.
Phil 525.51.2 Sharpe, A.B. Mysticism: its true nature and value. London, 1910?
Phil 5058.22.19 Sidgwick, A. The application of logic. London, 1910.
Phil 193.59.2.3A Simmel, G. Hauptprobleme der Philosophie. Leipzig, 1910.
Phil 8893.36 Smith, J.A. Knowing and acting. Oxford, 1910.
Phil 8643.19 Smyth, John P. The gospel of the hereafter. N.Y., 1910.
Phil 8643.30 Smyth, Newman. Modern belief in immortality. N.Y., 1910.
Phil 193.56 Snowden, J.H. The world a spiritual system. N.Y., 1910.
Phil 5828.11.5 Sokolowsky, A. Aus dem Seelenleben höherer Tiere. Leipzig, 1910.
Phil 530.20.35 Spamer, Adolf. Über die Zersetzung und Vererbung in den deutschen Mystikertexten. Diss. Giessen, 1910.
Phil 2270.40.35A Spencer, Herbert. Essays on education and kindred subjects. London, 1910.
Phil 2270.75 Spencer, Herbert. Resumen sintético de los principios de la moral. Paris, 1910.
Phil 978.30.5 Speyer, J.S. De indische theosophie en hare beteekenis voor ons. Leiden, 1910.
Phil 3819.30.25 Spinoza, Benedictus de. Die Ethik. Leipzig, 1910.
Phil 3819.38.5 Spinoza, Benedictus de. Spinoza's short treatise on God, man and his well-being. London, 1910.
Phil 3819.57.5 Spinoza, Benedictus de. Der theologisch-politische Traktat. 2. Aufl. Leipzig, 1910.
Phil 7054.22 Stead, William T. After death or Letters from Julia. 3. ed. Chicago, 1910.
NEDL Phil 1850.101 Steeves, G.W. Francis Bacon, a sketch of his life. London, 1910.
Phil 978.49.7 Steiner, R. Theosophy. 18th ed. N.Y., 1910.
Phil 978.49.35 Steiner, R. The way of initiation. 1st American ed. N.Y., 1910.
Phil 193.37.5 Stöckl, Albert. Grundzüge der philosophie. 2e Aufl. v.1-2. Mainz, 1910.
Phil 5058.31.5 Stöhr, Adolf. Lehrbuch der Logik in psychologisierender Darstellung. Leipzig, 1910.
Phil 720.10 Stoner, J.R. Logic and imagination in the perception of truth. N.Y., 1910.
Phil 126.3.3 Stumpf, C. Tafeln zur Geschichte der Philosophie. Berlin, 1910.
Phil 193.69 Stumpf, K. Philosophische Reden und Vorträge. Leipzig, 1910.
Phil 331.2.25 Suter, Jules. Die Philosophie von Richard Avenarius. Zurich, 1910.
Phil 2070.130 Switalski, B.W. Der Wahrheitsbegriff des Pragmatismus nach William James. Braunsberg, 1910.
Phil 5380.3.3 Tarde, G. L'opinion et la foule. 3rd éd. Paris, 1910.
Phil 4235.1.35 Telesius, B. De rerum natura. Modena, 1910. 3v.
Phil 9359.8 Tenow, Elsa. Kärlek och lycka af Elsa Törne, [Pseud.]. Stockholm, 1910.
Phil 978.42 Theosophical manuals. v.1-18. Point Loma, 1910. 4v.
Phil 3120.11.80 Thodoroff, C. Julius Bahnsen und die Hauptprobleme seiner charakterologie. Erlangen, 1910.
Phil 3801.837 Tillich, Paul. Die religionsgechichtliche Konstruktive in Schellings positiver Philosophie. Breslau, 1910.
Phil 3501.10 Toll, C.H. Die erste Antinomie Kants und der Pantheismus. Berlin, 1910.
Phil 8420.23 Tollemonde, G. de. Du juste milieu; traité général de philosophie et d'art. Paris, 1910.
Phil 8599.14 Torrey, D.C. Protestant modernism. Boston, 1910.
Phil 8599.14.2 Torrey, D.C. Protestant modernism. N.Y., 1910.
Phil 3890.1.75 Trendelenburg, A. Contribution to history of the word person. Chicago, 1910. 2 pam.
Phil 8894.17.4 Trine, Ralph W. Set synliga i samklang med det o synliga. Stockholm, 1910.
Phil 4235.1.90 Troilo, E. Bernardino Telesio. Modena, 1910.
Phil 194.21.5 Troward, Thomas. The creative process in the individual. London, 1910.
Phil 5643.8.30 Tscherning, M. Herman von Helmholtz und der Akkommodationstheorie. Leipzig, 1910.
Phil 9490.5 Tucker, W.J. Personal power counsels to college men. Boston, 1910.
Phil 9045.7 Tucker, W.J. Public mindedness, an aspect of citizenship. Concord, 1910.
Phil 300.2 Tunzelmann, G.W. de. Treatise on electrical theory and problem of universe. London, 1910.
Phil 400.5.5 Turner, J.P. Idealistic beginnings in England. n.p., 1910.
Phil 8599.20 Tyler, W.F. The dimensional idea as an aid to religion. N.Y., 1910.
Phil 400.24 Upward, A. The new world. N.Y., 1910.
Phil 4650.1.45 Vannérus, Allen. Til det andliga lifvets filosofi. Stockholm, 1910.
Phil 5771.1 Van Peyma, P.W. The why of the will. Boston, 1910.
Phil 1504.8.6 Vansteenberghe, E. Le "de Ignota Litteratura." v.8, pt.6-7. Münster, 1910.
Phil 7080.34 Veronese, F. Versuch einer Physiologie des Schlafes und des Traumes. Leipzig, 1910.
Phil 6131.3.5 Verworn, M. Die Entwicklung des menschlichen Geistes. Jena, 1910.

1910 - cont.

Phil 6131.3 Verworn, M. Die Mechanik des Geisteslebens. Leipzig, 1910.

Phil 9430.21 Vögele, Albert. Der Pessimismus und das Tragische in Kunst und Leben. Freiburg, 1910.

Phil 6536.7 Vogt, Heinrich. Die Epilepsie im Kindesalter mit besonderer Berücksichtigung erzieherischer, unterrichtlicher und forensischer Fragen. Berlin, 1910.

Phil 7082.138 Vold, John Mourly. Über den Traum. Leipzig, 1910-1912. 2v.

Phil 352.3.5 Volkmann, P. Erkenntnistheoretische Grundzüge der Naturwissenschaften. Leipzig, 1910.

Phil 510.20.5 Volkmann, Paul. Die Eigenart der Natur und der Eigensinn des Monismus. Leipzig, 1910.

Phil 8601.10 Vrooman, H. Religion rationalized. Philadelphia, 1910.

Phil 8972.5 Walter, Franz. Der Leib und sein Recht im Christentum. Donauwörth, 1910.

Phil 303.8 Warrain, F. La synthèse concrète. Paris, 1910.

Phil 5832.3.13 Wasmann, E. Menschen und Tierseele. 5. Aufl. Köln, 1910.

Phil 510.141 Wasmann, Erich. Entwicklungstheorie und Monismus. Innsbruck, 1910.

Phil 8602.16 Waterhouse, E.S. Modern theories of religion. London, 1910.

Phil 9362.13 Waterman, Nixon. The girl wanted. Chicago, 1910.

Phil 197.43 Wehnert, B. Wissenschaft, Philosophie, Kunst und Religion. Dortmund, 1910.

Phil 3905.30.15 Weininger, Otto. Sex and character. Photoreproduction. London, 1910.

Phil 3504.7.15 Wenley, R.M. Kant and his philosophical revolution. Edinburgh, 1910.

Phil 3504.12.10 Wernieke, A. Die Begründung des deutschen Idealismus durch I. Kant. Braunschweig, 1910.

Phil 5262.13 Whipple, G.M. Manual of mental and physical tests. Baltimore, 1910.

Phil 8712.3.10 White, Andrew Dickson. History of the warfare of science with theology in Christendom. N.Y., 1910. 2v.

Phil 3504.42 Wiegershausen, H. Aenesidem-Schulze, der Gegner Kants. Inaug. Diss. Münster, 1910.

Phil 197.51 Wiensteln, M.B. Welt- und libenanschauungen Hevoorgegangen aus Religion, Philosophie und Naturerkenntnis. Leipzig, 1910.

Phil 8620.19 Willcox, I.L. The psychological aspect of...sin and salvation. Oxford, 1910.

Phil 3425.110 Windelband, W. Die Erneuerung des Hegelianismus. Heidelberg, 1910.

Phil 5643.55 Witasek, Stephan. Psychologie der Raumwahrnehmung des Auges. Heidelberg, 1910.

Phil 353.2 Wodehouse, H. The presentation of reality. Cambridge, 1910.

Phil 3910.25 Wolff, Christian von. Wolffsche Begriffsbestimmungen. Leipzig, 1910.

Phil 1850.102 Wolff, E. Francis Bacon und seine Quellen. Berlin, 1910. 2v.

Phil 197.20 Wright, A.L. Modernism according to the law of sensual impression. Albany, 1910.

Phil 2422.1 Wulf, M. de. Histoire de la philosophie en Belgique. Bruxelles, 1910.

Phil 1527.1.9 Wulf, M. de. Scholasticism old and new. Dublin, 1910.

Phil 1127.3 Wundt, Max. Griechische Weltanschauung. Leipzig, 1910.

Phil 3915.45.6 Wundt, Wilhelm. Grundzüge der physiologischen Psychologie. 6. Aufl. Leipzig, 1910. 3v.

Phil 3915.8 Wundt, Wilhelm. Kleine Schriften. Leipzig, 1910-11. 2v.

Phil 3915.69.5 Wundt, Wilhelm. Die Prinzipien der mechanischen Naturlehre. Stuttgart, 1910.

Phil 306.2.2 Zehnder, Ludwig. Das Leben im Weltall. Tübingen, 1910.

Phil 35.9 Zeitschrift für die gesamte Neurologie und Psychiatrie. Berlin, 1910.

Phil 35.9.5 Zeitschrift für die gesamte Neurologie und Psychiatrie. Berlin, 1910.

Phil 200.2.15 Zeller, E. E. Zellers kleine Schriften, unter Mitwirking. Berlin, 1910. 3v.

Phil 3415.92 Ziegler, Leopold. Das Weltbild Hartmanns. Leipzig, 1910.

Phil 3425.127 Zóltowski, A. Metoda Hegla i zasady filosofii spekulatywej. Krakow, 1910.

Phil 3585.2.80 Zum 70. Geburtstag Otto Liebmanns festschrift Kantstudien. Berlin, 1910.

1911

Phil 5210.1 Aall, A. Psykologiens historie i Norge. Kristiania, 1911.

Phil 331.4 Aars, Kristian B. Die idee zum ursprung des gedankens. Kristiania, 1911.

Phil 5010.1 Adamson, R. A short history of logic. Edinburgh, 1911.

Phil 3482.2.12 Adickes, E. Kants Ansichten über Geschichte und Bau der Erde. Tübingen, 1911.

Phil 3482.2.20 Adickes, E. Untersuchungen zu Kants Physischer Geographie. Tübingen, 1911.

Phil 5240.33 Alexander, S. Foundations and sketch plan of a conational psychology. Cambridge, Eng., 1911.

Phil 2730.86 Amendola, G. Maine de Biran. Firenze, 1911.

Phil 4265.4.81 L'anima; saggi e guidizi. Maggio 1911. G. Vailati. Firenze, 1911.

Phil 4352.1.160 Arboleya y Martinéz, Maximiliane. Balmes politico. Barcelona, 1911.

Phil 4260.84 Arcari, P. Processi...di scienza nuova in G.B. Vico. Friburgo, 1911.

Phil 2840.83A Archambault, P. Renouvier. Paris, 1911.

Phil 1350.8 Arnold, E.V. Roman stoicism. Cambridge, 1911.

Phil 4610.9.80 Asmussen, E. Entwicklungsgang und grundprobleme der philosophie Rasmus Nielsens. Inaug. Diss. Flensburg, 1911.

Phil 5240.22 Atkinson, William W. Your mind and how to use it. Holyoke, Mass., 1911.

Phil 3625.5.78 Atlas, S. Lebensgeschichte. München, 1911.

Phil 3820.1.8 Auerbach, B. Spinoza; ein Denkerleben. Berlin, 1911.

Phil 3483.21 Baake, Wilhelm. Kants Ethik bei den englischen Moralphilosophen des 19. Jahrhunderts. Leipzig, 1911.

Phil 9050.4.5 Bailey, L.H. The outlook to nature. N.Y., 1911.

Phil 86.3.5 Baldwin, J.M. Dictionary of philosophy. v.1,3. N.Y., 1911. 3v.

Phil 5241.3.30A Baldwin, J.M. The individual and society. Boston, 1911.

Phil 5751.8 Ballard, F. Determinism: false and true. London, 1911.

Phil 4352.1.35 Balmes, Jaime. Curso de filosofia elemental. v.1-4. Barcelona, 1911.

Phil 282.6 Baratsch, W. Kosmologische Gedanken. Leipzig, 1911.

Phil 3640.208 Barbat, V.J. Nietzsche, tendances et problèmes. Zürich, 1911.

1911 - cont.

Phil 8951.4 Barbour, G.F. Philosophical study of Chrisian ethics. Edinburgh, 1911.

Phil 7069.11.10 Barrett, William F. Psychical research. N.Y., 1911.

Phil 3483.8 Bauch, Bruno. Geschichte der Philosophie. v.5. Leipzig, 1911.

Phil 1020.13 Bauer, H. Die Psychologie Alhazens. Münster, 1911.

Phil 2730.87 Baumgarten, Franz. Die Erkenntnislehre von Maine de Biran. Krakau, 1911.

Phil 6111.19 Becher, E. Gehirn und Seele. Heidelberg, 1911.

Phil 176.110 Becher, Carl. Die moderne Weltanschauung. Berlin, 1911.

Phil 5627.15.3 Begbie, H. Souls in action. N.Y., 1911.

Phil 6951.17 Belbèze, Raymond. La neurasthénie ruale. Paris, 1911.

Phil 6111.42 Bell, Charles. Idee einer neuen Hirnanatomie (1811). Leipzig, 1911.

Phil 8876.55.13A Bennett, Arnold. The human machine. N.Y., 1911.

Phil 9341.12 Bennett, Arnold. Mental efficiency. N.Y., 1911.

Phil 3270.9.80 Berger, Hermann. Julius Frauenstädt, sein Leben, seine Schriften und seine Philosophie. Inaug. Diss. v.8. Rostock, 1911.

Phil 2475.1.51.2 Bergson, Henri. Creative evolution. N.Y., 1911.

Phil 2475.1.51.6 Bergson, Henri. Creative evolution. N.Y., 1911.

Phil 2475.1.51.8 Bergson, Henri. Creative evolution. N.Y., 1911.

Phil 2475.1.40.2 Bergson, Henri. Essai sur les données immédiates de la conscience. 9. éd. Paris, 1911.

Phil 2475.1.69.6 Bergson, Henri. Laughter. London, 1911.

Phil 2475.1.60 Bergson, Henri. Matière et mémoire. 7. éd. Paris, 1911.

Phil 2475.1.61 Bergson, Henri. Matter and memory. N.Y., 1911.

Phil 2475.1.67 Bergson, Henri. La perception du changement. Oxford, 1911.

Phil 9550.7 Bernard, L.L. Transition to an objective standard of social control. Chicago, 1911.

Phil 176.55 Berthelot, René. Un romantisme utilitaire. Paris, 1911. 3v.

Phil 8125.18 Betgmann, Ernst. Die Begrundung der deutschen Ästhetik durch...Baumgarten und...Meier. Leipzig, 1911.

Phil 332.13 Beysens, J.T. Criteriologie of de leer over waarheid en zekerheid. 2. druk. Leiden, 1911.

Phil 2630.2.131 Bjarnason, Agust. Jean-Marie Guyau. Kobenhavn, 1911.

Phil 176.52 Bjorkman, E. Is there anything new under the sun? N.Y., 1911.

Phil 5041.28.3 Black, George A. Problem; science-analysis. N.Y., 1911.

Phil 8626.11 Blades, Franklin. Is the life of man eternal? N.Y., 1911.

Phil 176.89 Blundell, A. Idealism, possible and impossible. London, 1911.

Phil 4060.1.80 Bluwstein, J. Die Weltauschauung Roberto Ardigo. Leipzig, 1911.

Phil 3483.54 Bodansky, Siegfried. Kants Dissertation vom Jahre 1770 und ihre Beziehung zur Kritik der Reinen Vernunft. Friedele, 1911-13.

Phil 3475.1.80 Börner, W. Friedrich Jodl - eine Studie. Stuttgart, 1911.

Phil 5811.10.10 Bohn, Georges. Die Entstehung des Denkvermögens. Leipzig, 1911?

Phil 5811.10 Bohn, Georges. La nouvelle psychologie animale. Paris, 1911.

Phil 8610.911.4 Bongini, V. Il pregiudizio religioso. Roma, 1911.

Phil 4302.4.5 Bonilla y San Martin, A. Historia de la filosofia española. Madrid, 1911.

Phil 8581.26 Bonnefon, C. Dialogue sur la vie et sur la mort. 3. éd. Paris, 1911.

Phil 8620.14 Bonniot, P.J. de. Le problème du mal. 3. éd. Paris, 1911.

Phil 720.12 Bonucci, A. Verità e realtà. Modena, 1911.

Phil 332.5 Boodin, J.E. Truth and reality. N.Y., 1911.

Phil 3821.6 Borrell, Philippe. Benôit Spinoza. Paris, 1911.

Phil 5041.16.2A Bosanquet, B. Logic, or The morphology of knowledge. Oxford, 1911. 2v.

Phil 2070.111A Boutroux, É. William James. Paris, 1911.

Phil 179.3.81.7 Boutroux, Émile. Rudolf Euckens Kampf um einen neuen Idealismus. Leipzig, 1911.

Phil 5241.17.13A Brentano, Franz. Von der Klassifikation der psychischen Phänomene. Leipzig, 1911.

Phil 8581.36 Brown, Charles R. Modern man's religion. N.Y., 1911.

Phil 5241.28 Brown, W. Essentials of mental measurement. Cambridge, 1911.

Phil 6111.18 Bruce, H.A. Scientific mental healing. Boston, 1911.

Phil 9150.13 Bruneteau, E. La doctrine morale de l'évolution. Paris, 1911.

Phil 8620.21 Bruyssel, Ernest van. Mal et ses origines. Paris, 1911.

Phil 8581.54.5 Bulgakov, C. Dva grada. Moskva, 1911.

Phil 2655.1.82 Bulle, F. Franziskus Hemsterhuis und der deutsche Irrationalismus. Jena, 1911.

Phil 8581.25 Burris, M.A. Creation's way. Smithville, Ohio, 1911.

Phil 5627.6.20A Busch, K.A. William James als Religionsphilosoph. Göttingen, 1911.

Phil 5722.3A Butler, S. Unconscious memory. N.Y., 1911.

Phil 8403.32 Cabat, Walter. The place of beauty in American life. N.Y., 1911.

Phil 1802.5 Cadman, S.P. Charles Darwin and other English thinkers. Boston, 1911.

Phil 5242.13.10 Calkins, M.W. A first book in psychology. 2. ed. N.Y., 1911.

Phil 6112.2.15 Call, A.P. Brain power for business men. Boston, 1911.

Phil 5425.13.15 Candolle, A. de. Zur Geschichte der Wissenschaften und der Gelehrten. Leipzig, 1911.

Phil 4060.1.85 Carelle, Antonio. Naturalismo italiano. Padova, 1911.

Phil 2475.1.90 Carr, H.W. Henri Bergson; the philosophy of change. London, 1911.

Phil 5350.2.8A Carr, H.W. Henry Bergson: philosophy of change. London, 1911.

Phil 575.17 Carus, P. Personality. Chicago, 1911.

Phil 177.8.15 Carus, Paul. Philosophie als Wissenschaft. Chicago, 1911.

Phil 333.5.3 Cassirer, Ernst. Das Erkenntnisproblem in der Philosophie. 2. Aufl. Berlin, 1911. 2v.

Phil 5400.27 Chabrier. Les émotions et les états organiques. Paris, 1911.

Phil 2630.1.86 Chauvin, A. Le père Gratry, 1805-1872. Paris, 1911.

Phil 9450.9.5 Christensen, A. Politik og massemoral. København, 1911.

Phil 3484.16 Christiansen, B. Kritik der Kantischen Erkenntnislehre. Hanau, 1911.

Phil 2475.1.95 Coignet, C. De Kant à Bergson. Paris, 1911.

Phil 2490.155 Comte, Auguste. Early essays on social philosophy. London, 1911.

Phil 2490.32 Comte, Auguste. L'islamisme au point de vue social. Paris, 1911.

Phil 6312.1 Coriat, I.H. Abnormal psychology. London, 1911.

Phil 5627.21 Cornelison, I.A. The natural history of religious feeling. N.Y., 1911.

1911 - cont.

Phil 8692.3.5 Coutts, John. Old lamps and new light of science. London, 1911.
Phil 8877.31 Crane, F. Human confessions. Chicago, 1911.
Phil 177.35.5 Croce, Benedetto. Philosophie de la pratique. Paris, 1911.
Phil 802.7 Cunz, T. Geschichte der Philosophie in gemeinverständlicher Darstellung. Marburg, 1911.
Phil 6112.12 Cutter, G.B. Three thousand years of mental healing. N.Y., 1911.
Phil 8878.31 Dalmau y Gratacós, F. Elementos de filosofia. Barcelona, 1911.
Phil 5753.3 Dearborn, G.V.N. Neurology of Apraxia. Boston, 1911.
Phil 2520.45.12 Descartes, René. Il discorso del metodo. Assisi, 1911.
Phil 2520.61.7 Descartes, René. Uber die Leidenschaften der Seele. 3e Aufl. Leipzig, 1911.
Phil 5213.1.5 Dessoir, M. Abriss einer Geschichte der Psychologie. Heidelberg, 1911.
Phil 1108.2 Deussen, P. Philosophie der Griechen. Leipzig, 1911.
Phil 3110.151 Deussen, Paul. Jakob Böhme. Leipzig, 1911.
Phil 8628.7.5 Dickinson, G.L. Religion and immortality. Boston, 1911.
Phil 8628.7 Dickinson, G.L. Religion and immortality. London, 1911.
Phil 2115.101 Didier, J. John Locke. Paris, 1911.
Phil 1870.99 Didier, Jean. Berkeley. Paris, 1911.
Phil 3195.3 Dietzgen, Joseph. Sämtliche Schriften. Wiesbaden, 1911. 3v.
Phil 2070.89 Dijk, I. van. Het pragmatisme van William James. Groningen, 1911.
Phil 8583.11.15 Dorner, A. Pessimismus...Nietzsche und Naturalismus. Leipzig, 1911.
Phil 745.6.7 Driesch, H. Il vitalismo. Milano, 1911. 2v.
Phil 8878.24.7 DuBois, P. The education of self. N.Y., 1911.
Phil 5080.2 Dubs, Arthur. Das Wesen des Begriffs und des Begreifens. Halle, 1911.
Phil 2403.4 Duclaux, A.M.F.R. The French ideal. N.Y., 1911.
Phil 6113.9 Dudley, L. Egyptian elements in the legend of the body and soul. Baltimore, 1911.
Phil 8878.37 Dürr, Ernst. Das Gute und das Sittliche. Heidelberg, 1911.
Phil 6805.2 Dugas, Laurent. La dépersonnalisation. Paris, 1911.
Phil 178.19.5 Dunan, Charles. Les deux idéalismes. Paris, 1911.
Phil 2490.91 Dupuy, P. Le positivisme. Paris, 1911.
Phil 5400.28 Dussauze, H. Les règles esthétiques et les lois du sentiment. Montauban, 1911.
Phil 8693.6 Dwight, T. Thoughts of a catholic anatomist. London, 1911.
Phil 8878.52 Dyer, W.A. The richer life. Garden City, 1911.
Phil 5244.7.15 Ebbinghaus, H. Grundzüge der Psychologie. Leipzig, 1911. 2v.
Phil 3004.3 Ehrenberg, Hans. Die Parteiung der Philosophie. Leipzig, 1911.
Phil 6114.4.5 Eisler, R. Geist und Körper. Göttingen, 1911.
Phil 179.26 Eleutheropulos, A. Philosophie: allgemeine Weltanschauung. Zürich, 1911.
Phil 7082.160 Ellis, Havelock. The world of dreams. Boston, 1911.
Phil 1509.5 Endres, J.A. Geschichte der mittelalterlichen Philosophie. 2. Aufl. Kemplin, 1911.
Phil 4080.10.80 Ercole, P. d'. Il saggio di panlogica ovvero l'enciclopedia filosofica. Torino, 1911.
Phil 4755.1 Ern, Vladimir F. Bor'ba za Logos. Moskva, 1911.
Phil 179.18 Ettlinger, Max. Philosophische Fragen der Gegenwart. Kempten, 1911.
Phil 179.3.29 Eucken, R. Life's basis and life's ideal. London, 1911.
Phil 8584.5.3 Eucken, Rudolf. The truth of religion. N.Y., 1911.
Phil 8880.27 Faguet, Émile. Les préjugés nécessaires. Paris, 1911.
Phil 8401.2.10 Fedeles, Constantin. Versuch über Alison's Asthetik, Darstellung und Kritik. München, 1911.
Phil 5400.62 Ferrari, G.C. Le emozioni e la vita del subcosciente. Bologna, 1911.
Phil 8695.5.5 Ferreira da Silva, A.J. Duas allocuções; a religiaõ, amparo do homen na vida. Porto, 1911.
Phil 3246.17 Fichte, Johann Gottlieb. Werke. Leipzig, 1911. 6v.
Phil 1504.10.3 Fischer, J. Die Erkenntnislehre Anselms von Canterbury. Münster, 1911.
Phil 3640.97 Fischer, W. Nietzsches Bild. München, 1911.
Phil 8880.26 Fleuriau, A. de. L'activité réflexive. Paris, 1911.
Phil 5249.2.28A Flournoy, T. La philosophie de William James. St. Blaise, 1911.
Phil 7069.11.19 Flournoy, Théodore. Esprits et médiums. Genève, 1911.
Phil 7069.11.20 Flournoy, Theodore. Spiritism and psychology. N.Y., 1911.
Phil 9495.14.2 Foerster, F.W. Marriage and the sex problem. London, 1911.
Phil 180.19 Fouillée, Alfred. La pensée. 2e éd. Paris, 1911.
Phil 8695.3 Frankland, F.W. Thoughts on ultimate problems. 4. ed. London, 1911.
Phil 9150.12 Franklin, C.K. What nature is. Boston, 1911.
Phil 6315.22 Franz, Shepherd I. Collected papers. n.p., 1911-13.
Phil 6315.2.20.5 Freud, Sigmund. Sammlung kleiner Schriften zur Neurosenlehre aus den Jahren 1893-1906. 2. Aufl. 1e, 2e Folge. Leipzig, 1911-21. 2v.
Phil 7082.8.2 Freud, Sigmund. Uber den Traum. 2. Aufl. Wiesbaden, 1911.
Phil 3640.112 Friedlaender, S. Friedrich Nietzsche, intellektuale Biographie. Leipzig, 1911.
Phil 5413.5 Friedmann, Max. Uber die Psychologie der Eifersucht. Wiesbaden, 1911.
Phil 5756.9 Gaede, Udo. Etwas vom Begriff des Willens in der neueren Psychologie. Berlin, 1911.
Phil 5627.25 Garban, Louis. Deviations morbides du sentiment religieux. Paris, 1911.
Phil 8881.51 Gasté, Maurice de. Réalités imaginatives. Paris, 1911.
Phil 1706.2 Gaultier, P. La pensée contemporaine. Paris, 1911.
Phil 8881.42.3 Gaultier, Paul. L'ideal moderne. Paris, 1911.
Phil 8407.14.4 Gaultier, Paul. Le sens de l'art. 4. éd. Paris, 1911.
Phil 2805.102 Gazier, A. Les derniers jours de Blaise Pascal. Paris, 1911.
Phil 4235.1.85 Gentile, Bernardino Telesio. Bari, 1911.
Phil 1135.25 Gilbert, O. Griechische Religionsphilosophie. Leipzig, 1911.
Phil 2475.1.106 Gillouin, R. La philosophie de M. Henri Bergson. Paris, 1911.
Phil 2475.1.105 Gillouin, R. La philosophie de M. Henri Bergson. Paris, 1911.
Phil 5115.6 Görland, Albert. Die Hypothese. Göttingen, 1911.
Phil 1706.3 Goldstein, J. Wandlungen in der Philosophie der Gegenwerk. Leipzig, 1911.
Phil 8881.35 González y Martinez de Pinillos. Ética. Madrid, 1911.
Phil 8586.11 Gourd, J.J. Philosophie de la religion. Paris, 1911.

1911 - cont.

Phil 2490.99 Grasset, Joseph. Un demifou de génie. Montpelier, 1911.
Phil 7069.11.30 Greene, Anvernetta (pseud.). Psychisms through Anvernetta Greene. Newark, 1911.
Phil 1865.81 Greyvenstein, J.H.J.A. Het sociale utilisme van Bentham. Utrecht, 1911.
Phil 1504.10.4 Guttmann, J. Die philosophischen Lehren. v.10, pt.4. Münster, 1911.
Phil 3790.8.85 Hack, Valentin. Die Auffassung vom Wesen der Religion bei A. Ritschl. Diss. Leipzig, 1911.
Phil 4582.4.33 Hägerström, Axel. Om moraliska föreställningars sanning. Stockholm, 1911.
Phil 182.1.8 Hagemann, G. Elemente der Philosophie. Freiburg, 1911-1922. 3v.
Phil 3640.96 Halévy, D. Life of Friedrich Nietzsche. N.Y., 1911.
Phil 3640.103 Hamblen, E.S. Friedrich Nietzsche and his new gospel. Boston, 1911.
Phil 2520.111 Hamelin, O. Le système de Descartes. Paris, 1911.
Phil 5047.12.3 Hamilton, E.J. Perzeptionalismus und Modalismus. N.Y., 1911.
Phil 3425.191 Hammacher, Emil. Die Bedeutung der Philosophie Hegels. Leipzig, 1911.
Phil 6017.1.2 Hartenberg, Paul. Physionomie et caractère. Paris, 1911.
Phil 3425.70.5 Hegel, Georg Wilhelm Friedrich. Grundlinien der Philosophie des Rechts. Leipzig, 1911.
Phil 8587.39 Heiberg, J.L. Religion og moral. 2. oplag. Kjobenhavn, 1911.
Phil 6117.10.3 Hellpach, W. Die geopsychischen Erscheinungen. Leipzig, 1911.
Phil 5545.67 Henry, Charles. Mémoire et habitude. Paris, 1911.
Phil 5635.11 Henry, Charles. Sensation et énergie. Paris, 1911.
Phil 4769.1.89 Herbigny, Michel d'. Un Neuman Russe: Vladimir Soloviev (1853-1900). 2. ed. Paris, 1911.
Phil 182.37.2 Heymans, G. Einführung in die Metaphysik. 2. Aufl. Leipzig, 1911.
Phil 5247.22 Heymans, G. Das Künftige Jahrhundert der Psychologie. Leipzig, 1911.
Phil 182.28.5 Hibben, J.G. A defence of prejudice. N.Y., 1911.
Phil 5757.17 Hilbert, Gerhard. Moderne Willensziele. Leipzig, 1911.
Phil 7069.11.40 Hill, John A. New evidences in psychical research. London, 1911.
Phil 8592.43 Hinrichs, B. Die religionsphilosophischen Elemente in J. David Michaelis' Dogmatik. Diss. Göttingen, 1911.
Phil 2045.53 Hobbes, Thomas. Leviatano. Bari, 1911-12. 2v.
Phil 182.36.15 Höffding, H. Der menschliche Gedanke. Leipzig, 1911.
Phil 5247.10.15 Höffding, H. Pensée humaine. Paris, 1911.
Phil 4580.33.5 Høffding, Harald. Personlighetsprincipen i filosofin. Stockholm, 1911.
Phil 5817.9.5 Holmes, S.J. Evolution of animal intelligence. N.Y., 1911.
Phil 182.42 Huizinga, A.V.C.P. The American philosophic pragmatism. Boston, 1911.
Phil 2050.68.17 Hume, David. Die Naturgeschichte der Religion. Frankfurt, 1911.
Phil 4585.1.31 Ibsen, Sigurd. Menneskelig kvintessens. Kristiania, 1911.
Phil 8610.911 Indiana Rationalist Association. The light of reason. Indianapolis, Ind., 1911.
Phil 2475.1.216 Jacobbson, M. Henri Bergsons intuitionsfilosofi. Lund, 1911.
Phil 184.3.30 James, W. Memories and studies. London, 1911.
Phil 184.3.18 James, W. Le pragmatisme. Paris, 1911.
Phil 184.3.27A James, W. Some problems of philosophy. N.Y., 1911.
Phil 184.3.28 James, W. Some problems of philosophy. N.Y., 1911.
Phil 3246.91 Janson, F. Fichtes Reden an die deutsche Nation. Berlin, 1911.
Phil 8884.14 Jeudon, L. La morale de l'honneur. Paris, 1911.
Phil 184.16 Jodl, F. Aus der Werkstatt der Philosophie. Wien, 1911.
Phil 5049.12 Jones, E.E.C. A new law of thought and its logical bearings. Cambridge, 1911.
Phil 510.133 Jordan, H. Die Lebenserscheinungen. Leipzig, 1911.
Phil 2055.1.82 Joseph, M. Die Psychologie Henry Home's. Inaug.-Diss. Halle, 1911.
Phil 410.8 Jourdain, E.F. On the theory of the infinite in modern thought. London, 1911.
Phil 19.11.5 Journal of psycho-asthetics. Supplements. Fairbault, 1911.
Phil 3480.21.23 Kant, Immanuel. Der einzig mögliche Beweisgrund zu einer Demonstration des Daseyns Gottes. 3. Aufl. Leipzig, 1911.
Phil 3480.93 Kant, Immanuel. Kants Briefe ausgewählt. Leipzig, 1911.
Phil 3480.19.25 Kant, Immanuel. Populäre Schriften. Berlin, 1911.
Phil 3480.105 Kant, Immanuel. Wörte Kants. Minden, 1911.
Phil 9495.21 Karsch-Haach, F. Das gleichgeschlechtliche Leben der Naturvölker. München, 1911.
Phil 3640.113 Keiper, Wilhelm. Nietzsche, poeta. Buenos Aires, 1911.
Phil 3425.195 Kelly, Michael. Hegel's charlatanism exposed. London, 1911.
Phil 6120.6.5 Kenilworth, W.W. Thoughts on things psychic. N.Y., 1911.
Phil 341.9 Kern, Berthold. Das Erkenntnisproblem...kritische Lösung. Berlin, 1911.
Phil 291.3 Kern, Berthold. Weltanschauungen und Welterkenntnis. Berlin, 1911.
Phil 179.3.81 Kessler, K. Rudolf Euckens Werk. Bunzlau, 1911.
Phil 8635.4 Keyserling, Hermann. Unsterblichkeit. 2. Aufl. München, 1911.
Phil 9035.19 King, Henry C. How to make a rational fight for character. N.Y., 1911.
Phil 8590.10.15 King, Henry C. Seeming unreality of the spiritual life. N.Y., 1911.
Phil 400.27.15 Kinkel, Walter. Idealismus und Realismus. Göttingen, 1911.
Phil 810.1.9 Kirchner, F. Geschichte der Philosophie. Leipzig, 1911.
Phil 8885.11 Kirn, O. Sittliche Lebens anschauungen der Gegenwart. 2. Aufl. Leipzig, 1911.
Phil 5220.1 Klemm, O. Geschichte der Psychologie. Leipzig, 1911.
Phil 3910.128 Kohlmeyer, Ernst. Kosmos und Kosmonomie bei Christian Wolff. Göttingen, 1911.
Phil 5250.6 Kostyleff, N. La crise de la psychologie expérimentale. Paris, 1911.
Phil 3492.2.17 Krause, A. Populäre Darstellung von Immanuel Kant's Kritik der reinen Vernunft. 2. Aufl. Hamburg, 1911.
Phil 3525.86 Krause, K.C.F. Pädagogischen Gedanken K.C.F. Krauses in ihrem Zusammenhange mit seiner Philosophie Dargestellt. Inaug. Diss. Leipzig, 1911.
Phil 3415.94 Krüger, Gustav. Der Vitalismus Eduard von Hartmanns und seine philosophischen Grundlagen. Inaug. Diss. Schwerin, 1911.

1911 - cont.

Phil 3010.2.5 — Külpe, O. Die Philosophie der Gegenwart in Deutschland. Leipzig, 1911.

Phil 8961.5 — La Barre, A. La morale d'après St. Thomas. Paris, 1911.

Phil 4065.103.5 — Labriola, Arturo. Giovanni Bovio e Giordano Bruno. Napoli, 1911.

Phil 5251.1.18 — Ladd, G.T. Elements of physiological psychology. N.Y., 1911.

Phil 5251.1.22 — Ladd, G.T. Elements of physiology, psychology. N.Y., 1911.

Phil 8886.57 — Lagresille, Henry. Monde moral, l'ordre des fins et des progrès. Paris, 1911.

Phil 8961.6 — Lahy, J.M. La morale de Jésus. Paris, 1911.

Phil 5590.42 — Larned, Josephus N. A study of greatness in men. Boston, 1911.

Phil 4600.2.50 — Larsson, Hans. Gränsen mellan sensation och emotion. 2e uppl. Lund, 1911.

Phil 4600.2.53 — Larsson, Hans. Reflexioner för dagen. Lund, 1911.

Phil 5051.5 — Lask, E. Die Logik der Philosophie und die Kategorienlehre. Tübingen, 1911.

Phil 8636.4 — Lathbury, C. The great morning. Minneapolis, 1911.

Phil 1145.75 — Lavell, C.F. Evolution of Greek moral education. Kingston, 1911.

Phil 5135.3 — Le Bon, Gustave. Les opinions et les croyances. Paris, 1911.

Phil 8961.7 — Le Bosquet, John E. The war within. Boulder, Col., 1911.

Phil 2020.82 — Leland, A.P. Educational theory...T.H. Green. N.Y., 1911.

Phil 342.7 — Leser, Hermann. Einfuhrung in die Grundprobleme der Erkenntnistheorie. Leipzig, 1911.

Phil 7060.78 — Lewes, M.L. Stranger than fiction. London., 1911.

Phil 2520.122 — Liard, Louis. Descartes. 3e éd. Paris, 1911.

Phil 186.39 — Liard, Louis. Wissenschaft und Metaphysik. Leipzig, 1911.

Phil 4600.4.38 — Lidforss, Bengt. Modärna apologeter. Malmö, 1911.

Phil 8520.25 — Lindau, Hans. Die Theodicee im 18 Jahrhundert. Leipzig, 1911.

Phil 6121.11 — Lindsay, A.A. Mind the transformer, the new psychology. 7. ed. Los Angeles, 1911.

Phil 2475.1.83 — Lindsay, A.D. The philosophy of Bergson. London, 1911.

Phil 8701.4.3 — Lodge, Oliver Joseph. Man and the universe. 9. ed. London, 1911.

Phil 8701.4.9 — Lodge, Oliver Joseph. Reason and belief. 5. ed. London, 1911.

Phil 4762.2.30 — Lopatin, Lev M. Filosofskiia kharakteristiki i rechi. Moskva, 1911.

Phil 3565.51.10 — Lotze, Hermann. Microcosmo. Pavia, 1911-16. 2v.

Phil 3640.98.5 — Ludovici, Anthony M. Nietzsche and art. London, 1911.

Phil 4356.2.81 — Lueben, Robert. Sebastian Fox Morzillo und seine erkenntnistheoretische Stellung zur Naturphilosophie. Inaug. Diss. Bonn, 1911.

NEDL Phil 186.73.20 — Lutosławski, W. Iskierki Warszawskie. Ser. 1. Warszawa, 1911.

Phil 4803.537.30 — Lutosławski, Wincenty. Iskierki warszawskie. Warszawa, 1911.

Phil 8592.3 — Macdonald, L.B. Life in the making. Boston, 1911.

Phil 6122.13.5 — McDougall, William. Body and mind. N.Y., 1911.

Phil 2070.133 — McGilvary, Evander B. The fringe of William James's psychology, the both sides of logic. n.p., 1911.

Phil 5635.5.6 — Mach, Ernst. Die Analyse der Empfindungen. 6. Aufl. Jena, 1911.

Phil 8592.48.10 — Macintosh, D.C. The reaction against metaphysics in theology. Chicago, 1911.

Phil 2733.45 — Malebranche, Nicolas. Pensiere metafisici. Lanciano, 1911.

Phil 3494.19.15 — Marcus, Ernst. Logik. 2. Aufl. Herford, 1911.

Phil 9352.7.7 — Marden, O.S. Pushing to the front. Petersburg, N.Y., 1911.

Phil 187.72.5 — Masci, Filippo. Intelletualismo e pragmatismo. Napoli, 1911.

Phil 6682.11 — Mason, Rufus O. Hypnotism and suggestion in theraputics. N.Y., 1911.

Phil 3260.86 — Mechler, W. Die Erkenntnislehre bei Fries. Inaug. Diss. Berlin, 1911.

Phil 187.28.6.7 — Mechnikov, I.I. Nature of man. N.Y., 1911.

Phil 5249.2.95 — Ménard, A. Analyse et critique des principes de la psychologie. Paris, 1911.

Phil 5249.2.81 — Ménard, A. Analyse et critique des principes de la psychologie de W. James. Paris, 1911.

Phil 3494.18 — Menzer, Paul. Kants Lehre von der Entwicklung in Natur und Geschichte. Berlin, 1911.

Phil 5762.11.2 — Messer, August. Das Problem der Willensfreiheit. Göttingen, 1911.

Phil 3801.566 — Metzger, Wilhelm. Die Epochen der Schellingschen Philosophie von 1795 bis 1802. Heidelberg, 1911.

Phil 2138.35.5.10 — Mill, John S. A system of logic. London, 1911.

Phil 3494.11.5 — Miller, E.M. Moral action and natural law in Kant. Melbourne, 1911.

Phil 52.5 — Missouri. University. Studies. Philosophie and education series. Columbia, 1911.

Htn Phil 7069.11.45* — Moberly, C.A.E. An adventure. London, 1911.

Phil 2840.87 — Montpellier. Université. Inauguration d'un buste de C. Renouvier le 4 mai 1911. Montpellier, 1911.

Phil 7069.11.50 — Moore, William U. Glimpses of the next state (the education of an agnostic). London, 1911.

Phil 400.27.9 — Morselli, Emilio. Il fondamento dell' idealismo etico. Livorno, 1911.

Phil 52.6 — Münchener philosophische Abhandlungen. Leipzig, 1911.

Phil 400.18.5 — Muff, Christian. Idealismus. 5e Aufl. Halle, 1911.

Phil 5252.19.8 — Myers, C.S. An introduction to experimental psychology. Cambridge, 1911.

Phil 5252.19.2.5 — Myers, C.S. A text book of experimental psychology with laboratory exercises. 2nd ed. pt.1. Cambridge, 1911.

Phil 188.12.20 — Natorp, Paul. Philosophie: ihr Problem und ihre Probleme. Göttingen, 1911.

Phil 6123.3 — Neff, S.S. Power through perfected ideas. Philadelphia, 1911.

Phil 3640.40.3 — Nietzsche, Friedrich. Thus spake Zarathustra. 2d ed. N.Y., 1911.

Phil 4757.4 — Nikolai Iakovlevich Grot v ocherkäkh, vospominaniiakh i pis'makh tovarishchei . Sankt Peterburg, 1911.

Phil 188.13 — Nyman, A. Kämpande intelligens. Malmö, 1911.

Phil 7060.92.20 — O'Donnell, Elliot. By ways of ghost-land. London, 1911.

Phil 3640.200.25 — Oehler, Richard. Nietzsche als Bildner der Persönlichkeit. Leipzig, 1911?

Phil 5545.63.2 — Offner, Max. Das Gedächtnis. 2. Aufl. Berlin, 1911.

Phil 8594.7 — Opitz, H.G. Das Christentum im Freilichte. Leipzig, 1911.

Phil 3640.100A — Orage, A.R. Friedrich Nietzsche. Chicago, 1911.

Phil 345.2 — Ostwald, N. Die Wissenschaft. Leipzig, 1911.

1911 - cont.

Phil 510.8.5 — Ostwald, W. Monistische Sonntagspredigten. Series 1-3,4. Leipzig, 1911-13. 2v.

Phil 8633.1.8.5 — Ostwald, W. Personlighet och odödlighet. Stockholm, 1911.

Phil 5627.58 — Pacheu, Jules. L'expérience mystique et l'activité subconciente. Paris, 1911.

Phil 8890.28 — Palhoriès, F. Nouvelles orientations de la morale. Paris, 1911.

Phil 5765.4A — Palmer, G.H. The problem of freedom. Boston, 1911.

Phil 346.6 — Paoli, Giulio C. Considerazioni filosofiche sulla dottrina della conoscenza. Milano, 1911.

Phil 2805.40.40 — Pascal, Blaise. Tankar i religiösa frägor. 2. uppl. Stockholm, 1911.

Phil 5055.8 — Paulhan, F. La logique de la contradiction. Paris, 1911.

Phil 190.3.8 — Paulsen, F. Introduzione alla filosofia. Milano, 1911.

Phil 5643.50 — Pauwels, Friedrich. Beiträge zur Lehre vom optischen Zeitsinn. Inaug. Diss. Frieburg, 1911?

Phil 3246.91.9 — Perego, Luigi. L'idealismo etico di Fichte. Modena, 1911.

Phil 2805.104 — Petitot, H. Pascal sa vie religieuse. Paris, 1911.

Phil 5055.12 — Phalen, A.K. Om det kvantitativa betraktelsesättet i logiken. Uppsala, 1911.

Phil 3415.107 — Pohorilles, N.E. Entwicklung und Kritik der Erkenntnistheorie Eduard von Hartmanns. Wien, 1911.

Phil 296.6 — Poincaré, H. Leçons sur les hypotheses cosmogoniques. Paris, 1911.

Phil 3425.247.5 — Purpus, Wilhelm. Eduard von Hartmanns Kritik der dialektischen Methode Hegels. Ansbach, 1911.

Phil 4060.1.97 — Quadrelli, Ercole. Le problème des origines. Gerace Marina, 1911.

Phil 3837.10 — Rabenort, W.L. Spinoza as educator. N.Y., 1911.

Phil 5257.30 — Radziwillowicz, P. Zagadnienia psychologji. Kraków, 1911?

Phil 5545.169 — Ranachburg, P. Das kranke Gedachtnis. Leipzig, 1911.

Phil 150.15 — Ranzoli, C. Il linguaggio dei filosofi. Padova, 1911.

Phil 8892.18 — Rauh, F. Études de morale. Paris, 1911.

Phil 8418.6 — Raymond, G.L. The essentials of aesthetics in music. N.Y., 1911.

Phil 6687.4 — Recollection of a society clairvoyant. London, 1911.

Phil 9035.17 — Rehmeké, J. Zur Lehre vom Gemüt. Leipzig, 1911.

Phil 5767.3 — Rehmke, Johanes. Die Willessfreiheit. Leipzig, 1911.

Phil 5257.18 — Rehwoldt, F. Uber respiratorische Affektsymptome. Leipzig, 1911.

Phil 348.5 — Reininger, R. Philosophie des Erkennens. Leipzig, 1911.

Phil 8597.30 — The religion of ther future and other essays. London, 1911.

Phil 9575.6 — Remsen, D.S. Post-Mortem use of wealth. N.Y., 1911.

Phil 1504.10 — Renz, O. Die Synteresis nach dem hl. Thomas von Aquin. v.10, pt.1-2. Münster, 1911.

Phil 150.20 — Report of the committee on definitions of the American Philosophical Association. N.Y., 1911.

Phil 5257.15 — Rey, A. Leçons de psychologie et de philosophie. 3. éd. Paris, 1911.

Phil 192.25.5 — Rey, A. Les sciences philosophiques. 2. ed. Paris, 1911.

Phil 7069.06.35 — Richardson, J.E. The great work. 12. ed. Chicago, 1911.

Phil 3640.164 — Richter, Claire. Nietzsche et les théories biologiques contemporaines. 2. éd. Paris, 1911.

Phil 192.37.10 — Richter, Raoul. Dialoge über Religionsphilosophie. Leipzig, 1911.

Phil 7060.91 — Robbins, Anne M. Both sides of the veil. Boston, 1911.

Phil 9558.5 — Rogues de Fursac, J. L'avarice. Paris, 1911.

Phil 4356.1.80 — Ronilla y San Martin, A. Fernando de Córdoba. Madrid, 1911.

Phil 8892.15.2 — Roosevelt, T. Applied ethics being one of the Wm.B. Noble lectures for 1910. Cambridge, 1911.

Phil 8892.15 — Roosevelt, T. Applied ethics being one of the Wm.B. Noble lectures for 1910. Cambridge, 1911.

Phil 2250.51 — Royce, Josiah. La filosofia della fedeltá. Bari, 1911.

Phil 192.16.18A — Royce, Josiah. William James and other essays on the philosophy of life. N.Y., 1911.

Phil 4352.1.95 — Ruano y Corbo, J.M. Balmes apologista. Santiago, 1911.

Phil 510.5.15 — Ruckhaber, Erich. Der Mechanismus des menschlichen Denkens. Brackwede, 1911.

Phil 7069.11.70 — Russel, Fox. Hugsíminn. Reykjavik, 1911.

Phil 3808.112 — Ruyssen, T. Les grands philosophes; Schopenhauer. Paris, 1911.

Phil 8643.20.3 — Sabatier, Armand. Essai sur l'immortalité au point de vue du naturalisme évolutionniste. 3. éd. Paris, 1911.

Phil 58.9 — St. Andrews University. Publications of the departments of philosophy and divinity. Glasgow, 1911.

Phil 1523.6 — Saitta, Giuseppe. La scolastica del secolo XVI e la politica dei Gesuiti. Torino, 1911.

Phil 1818.7 — Santayana, George. The genteel tradition in American philosophy...public address...1911. Berkeley, 1911.

Phil 510.10 — Saulze, J.B. Le monisme matérialiste. Paris, 1911.

Phil 3800.170.10 — Schelling, F.W.J. von. Einleitung zu seinem Entwurf eines Systems der Naturphilosophie. Leipzig, 1911.

Phil 3800.340.5 — Schelling, F.W.J. von. Über das Wesen der menschlichen Freiheit. Leipzig, 1911.

Phil 193.9.15 — Schiller, F.C.S. Humanismus...pragmatische Philosophie. Leipzig, 1911.

Phil 3805.36 — Schleiermacher, Friedrich. Grundriss der philosophischen Ethik. Leipzig, 1911.

Phil 3790.4.81 — Schlunke, Otto. Die Lehre vom Bewusstsein bei Heinrich Rickert. Inaug. Diss. Leipzig, 1911.

Phil 6060.5 — Schneidemühl, Georg. Handschrift und Charakter. Leipzig, 1911.

Phil 3808.76.20 — Schopenhauer, Arthur. Briefwechsel und andere Dokumente; Ausgewählt und Herausgegeben von Mar Brahn. Leipzig, 19

Phil 3808.55.11 — Schopenhauer, Arthur. Pensées et fragments. 25. éd. Paris, 1911.

Phil 3808.13 — Schopenhauer, Arthur. Sämmtliche Werke. v.1-6,9-11,13-16. München, 1911-42. 13v.

Phil 3808.22.15 — Schopenhauer, Arthur. The wisdom of Schopenhauer. London, 1911.

Phil 3850.13.35 — Schulze, G.E. Aenesidemus. Berlin, 1911.

Phil 2880.2.80 — Secrétan, L. Charles Secrétan: sa vie et son oeuvre. Lausanne, 1911.

Phil 3425.198 — Sedlák, F. A holiday with a Hegelian. London, 1911.

Phil 5627.19 — Segond, J. La prière-étude de psychologie religieuse. Paris, 1911.

Phil 3808.113 — Seillière, E. Arthur Schopenhauer. Paris, 1911.

Phil 525.8 — Seillière, E. Les mystiques du néo-romantisme. Paris, 1911.

Phil 5545.54 — Semon, R. Die Mneme als erhaltendes Prinzip im Wechsel des organischen Geshehens. 3. Aufl. Leipzig, 1911.

Phil 3500.21.5 — Sentroul, C. Kant und Aristoteles. n.p., 1911.

Phil 8893.8.5 — Seth, J. A study of ethical principles. 12. ed. N.Y., 1911.

1911 - cont.

Phil 193.64.5 — Shaw, C.G. The value and dignity of human life. Boston, 1911.

Phil 5058.25 — Shearman, A.T. The scope of formal logic. London, 1911.

Phil 6750.11 — Sherlock, E.B. Feeble minded, guide to study. London, 1911.

Phil 6128.25 — Sherman, J.C. The stunted saplings. Boston, 1911.

Phil 179.3.81.5 — Siebert, Otto. Rudolf Euckens Welt- und Lebensanschauung. 2. Aufl. Langensalza, 1911.

Phil 193.59.2A — Simmel, G. Hauptprobleme der Philosophie. Leipzig, 1911.

Phil 193.59.5 — Simmel, G. Philosophische Kultur. Leipzig, 1911.

Phil 5828.10 — Skowronnek, Fritz. Seelenleben der Tiere. Berlin, 1911.

Phil 8893.97 — Smith, F.B. Men wanted. N.Y., 1911.

Phil 193.73.5 — Snider, Denton J. The biocomos...life psychologically ordered. St. Louis, 1911.

Phil 2475.1.81 — Solomon, J. Bergson. London, 1911.

Phil 4769.1.122 — Solov'ev, V.S. Russkaia ideia. Moskva, 1911.

Phil 8598.65.5 — Sorel, G. La religione d'oggi. Lanciani, 1911.

Phil 8893.37 — Sorley, W.R. The moral life and moral worth. Cambridge, Eng., 1911.

Phil 4225.1.32 — Spaventa, Bertrando. Logica e metafisica. Bari, 1911.

Phil 3819.60 — Spinoza, Benedictus de. Dio. Lanciano, 1911.

Phil 525.56.5 — Steiner, R. Mystics of the Renaissance. N.Y., 1911.

Phil 7082.38 — Stekel, Wilhelm. Die Sprache des Traumes. Wiesbaden, 1911.

Phil 8598.41 — Stern, Adolf. Die religiöse Stellung der vornehmsten Denker. Berlin, 1911.

Phil 8968.6 — Stern, M.L. Monistische Ethik. Leipzig, 1911.

Phil 5258.35 — Stern, W. Die differentielle Psychologie. Leipzig, 1911.

Phil 2475.1.82 — Stewart, J.W.K. A critical exposition of Bergson's philosophy. London, 1911.

Phil 818.5A — Stöckl, A. Handbook of the history of philosophy. N.Y., 1911.

Phil 4800.2.2 — Struve, Henryk. Historya logiki jako teoryi pozuania w Polsce. Wyd. 2. Warszawa, 1911.

Phil 1135.102 — Sunne, D.G. Some phases...Post-Aristotelian period. Chicago, 1911.

Phil 8420.18 — Tari, Antonio. Saggi di estetica e metafisica. Bari, 1911.

Phil 2070.112 — Tarozzi, G. Compendio dei principii di psicologia. Milano, 1911.

Phil 8894.23 — Tarrozzi, G. Filosofia morale e nozioni affini. Bologna, 1911.

Phil 1524.2 — Taylor, H.O. The mediaeval mind. London, 1911. 2v.

Phil 2070.87 — Teisen, N. William James' laere om retten til at tro. København, 1911.

Phil 5259.14 — Theone, Alois S. Die Mechanik des Seelenlebens. Bonn, 1911.

Phil 8894.15 — Thouverez, Émile. Eléments de morale théoretique et pratique appliquée a la pédagogie. 2. éd. Paris, 1911.

Phil 2419.2 — Tornezy, Albert. La légende des "philosophes". Paris, 1911.

Phil 5259.10 — Toulouse. Technique de psychologie experiment. Paris, 1911. 2v.

Phil 9490.9 — Trisca, P.C. Die Pflichten der Intelligenten. Jena, 1911.

Phil 3501.4 — Tsanoff, P.A. Schopenhauer's criticism of Kant's Theory of experience. N.Y., 1911.

Phil 9560.9 — Tschubrovitz, P. Die Entwicklung der Moraltugenden. Leipzig, 1911.

Phil 7060.91.5 — Tuckett, I.L. The evidence for the supernatural. London, 1911.

Phil 5059.12 — Turner, W. Lessons in logic. Washington, 1911.

Phil 7060.253 — Turvey, Vincent N. The beginnings of seership. London, 1911.

Phil 3890.6.84 — Uebele, Wilhelm. Johann Nicolaus Tetens. Inaug. Diss. Berlin, 1911.

Phil 525.7.1 — Underhill, Evelyn. Mysticism. 3rd ed. N.Y., 1911.

Phil 3903.3.30 — Vaihinger, Hans. Die Philosophie des Als Ob. Berlin, 1911.

Phil 4265.4.5F — Vailati, G. Scritti (1863-1909). Leipzig, 1911.

Phil 1526.1 — Verweyen, Johannes M. Philosophie und Theologie im Mittelalter. Bonn, 1911.

EDL Phil 4260.35.9 — Vico, G.B. La science nouvelle. Bari, 1911-16. 3v.

Phil 8896.4.3 — Vidari, Giovanni. Elementi di etica. 3. ed. Milano, 1911.

Phil 5261.3.9 — Villa, G. La psicologia contemporanea. Milano, 1911.

Phil 6331.4 — Vittoz, Roger. Treatment of neurasthenia by teaching of brain control. London, 1911.

Phil 4769.1.91 — Vladimire Solov'eve. Moskva, 1911.

Phil 821.1.3 — Vorländer, K. Geschichte der Philosophie. Leipzig, 1911. 2v.

Phil 3503.4 — Vorländer, K. Immanuel Kant's Leben. Leipzig, 1911.

Phil 9400.7 — Vorse, M.H. (Mrs.). Autobiography of an elderly woman. Boston, 1911.

Phil 3504.1.15 — Wallace, William. Kant. Edinburgh, 1911.

Phil 8712.11 — Walsh, J.J. The popes and science. N.Y., 1911.

Phil 3552.109 — Ward, A.W. Leibniz as a politician. Manchester, 1911.

Phil 8677.8 — Ward, James. The realm of ends, or Pluralism and theism. Cambridge, 1911.

Phil 8647.3 — Warren, William F. Religions of the world and the world religion. N.Y., 1911.

Phil 3808.113.5 — Warschauer, Erich. Schopenhauers Rechts- und Staatslehre. Kattowitz, 1911.

Phil 5545.48 — Watt, H.J. Economy and training of memory. N.Y., 1911.

Phil 5520.23.5 — Welby, Victoria. Significs and language. London, 1911.

Phil 303.7 — Weltanschauung. Philosophie und Religion. Berlin, 1911.

Phil 5062.17 — Welton, James. An intermediate logic. London, 1911.

Phil 9430.31 — Weng, Gustav. Schopenhauer-Darwin, Pessimismus oder Optimismus? Berlin, 1911.

Phil 3504.12.15 — Werneke, A. Kants kritischer Werdegang. Braunschweig, 1911.

Phil 3504.11 — Wheeler, C.K. Critique of pure Kant. Boston, 1911.

Phil 9035.68.5 — Whitby, Charles J. Makers of man, a study of human initiative. London, 1911.

Phil 510.24 — Wobbermin, Georg. Monismus und Monotheismus. Tübingen, 1911.

Phil 197.40 — Wordsworth, J.C. Short essays in constructive philosophy. London, 1911.

Phil 3915.48 — Wundt, Wilhelm. Einführung in die Psychologie. Leipzig, 1911.

Phil 3915.6 — Wundt, Wilhelm. Zur Psychologie und Ethik. Leipzig, 1911.

Phil 5264.2.2 — Yerkes, R.M. Introduction to psychology. N.Y., 1911.

Phil 5774.1 — Young, G.P. The ethics of freedom. Toronto, 1911.

Phil 1130.6.9 — Zeller, Eduard. Grundriss der Geschichte der griechischen Philosophie. Leipzig, 1911.

Phil 8605.2 — Zoppola, G. Il pensiero religioso. Lugano, 1911. 2 pam.

1912

Phil 5643.38 — Adams, H.F. Autokinetic sensations. Chicago, 1912.

Phil 400.29 — Aliotta, A. La reazione idealistica contro la scienza. Palermo, 1912.

Phil 3808.149 — Allievo, G. Giobbe e Schopenhauer. Torino, 1912.

Phil 4351.4 — Alvarado, Francisco. Obras escogidas del filosofo rancio. Madrid, 1912.

Phil 3565.88 — Ambrosi, L. Ermanno Lotze e la sua filosofia. Milano, 1912.

Phil 5238.1 — Angell, J.R. Chapters from modern psychology, 1911. London, 1912.

Phil 6110.20 — Arai, T. Mental fatique. N.Y., 1912.

Htn Phil 4112.83* — Arnone, N. Pasquale Galluppi giacobino. Napoli, 1912.

Phil 4761.1.80 — Askoldov, C. Aleksei Aleksandrovich Kozlov. Moskva, 1912.

Phil 5240.8 — Aveling, Francis. On the consciousness of the universal. Thesis. London, 1912.

Phil 2262.78.5 — Bacharach, A. Shaftesburys Optimismus und sein Verhältnis zum Leibnizschen. Inaug. Diss. Thann, 1912.

Phil 1504.10.6 — Baeumker, F. Die Lehre Anselms von Canterbury. v.10, pt.6. Münster, 1912.

Phil 9045.15 — Baldwin, S.E. The relations of education to citizenship. New Haven, 1912.

Phil 2475.1.109A — Balsillie, D. An examination of Professor Bergson's philosophy. London, 1912.

Phil 282.6.2 — Baratsch, W. Kosmologische Gedanken. 2. ed. Leipzig, 1912.

Phil 282.9 — Bardonnet, L. L'universe-organisme. Paris, 1912. 2v.

Phil 7060.116 — Batchel, R. The stoneground ghost tales. Cambridge, Eng., 1912.

Phil 9075.15 — Bauer, Arthur. La conscience collective et la morale. Paris, 1912.

Phil 1504.9 — Baur, L. Die philosophischen Werke des Robert Grosseteste. v.9. Münster, 1912.

Phil 8876.51.9 — Bayet, Albert. Le mirage de la vertu. Paris, 1912.

Phil 3245.85 — Beckedorf, H. Die Ethik Immanuel Hermann Fichtes. Inaug. Diss. Hannover, 1912.

Phil 176.110.5 — Becker, Carl. Vom geistigen Leben und Schaffen. Berlin, 1912.

NEDL Phil 6951.5.2 — Beers, C.W. A mind that found itself. 2. ed. N.Y., 1912.

Phil 3640.190.20 — Bélart, Hans. Friedrich Nietzsches Freundschafts-Tragödie mit Richard Wagner und Cosime Wagner-Liszt. Dresden, 1912.

Phil 3821.12 — Bellangé, C. Spinoza et la philosophie moderne. Paris, 1912.

Phil 6049.00.7 — Benham, W.G. The laws of scientific hand reading. N.Y., 1912.

Phil 1106.3.15 — Benn, A.W. History of ancient philosophy. London, 1912.

Phil 1701.6 — Benn, A.W. History of modern philosophy. London, 1912.

Phil 9341.12.5 — Bennett, Arnold. Mental efficiency and other hints to men and women. London, 1912.

Phil 2630.2.122 — Bergmann, Ernst. Die Philosophie Guyaus. Leipzig, 1912.

Phil 2475.1.50.4 — Bergson, Henri. L'évolution créatrice. 9. éd. Paris, 1912.

Phil 2475.1.50.6 — Bergson, Henri. L'évolution créatrice. 10. éd. Paris, 1912.

Phil 2475.1.56 — Bergson, Henri. An introduction to metaphysics. N.Y., 1912.

Phil 2475.1.60.2 — Bergson, Henri. Matière et mémoire. 8. éd. Paris, 1912.

Phil 2475.1.61.2 — Bergson, Henri. Matter and memory. N.Y., 1912.

Phil 1870.60.15 — Berkeley, G. Versuch einer neuen Theorie der Gesichtswahrnehmung. Leipzig, 1912.

Phil 525.54.5 — Bernhart, J. Bernhardische und Eckhartische Mystik. Kempten, 1912.

Phil 978.6.13 — Besant, Annie. Essays and addresses. v.2-4. London, 1912-13. 3v.

Phil 176.76.5 — Bilharz, Alfons. Philosophie als Universalwissenschaft. Wiesbaden, 1912.

Phil 282.10 — Bixby, J.T. The open secret; a study of life's deeper forces. Boston, 1912.

Phil 2520.170 — Bohatec, Josef. Die cartesianische Scholastik. Leipzig, 1912.

Phil 5811.10.5 — Bohn, Georges. Die neue Tierpsychologie. Leipzig, 1912.

Phil 7060.129.9 — Boirac, Émile. La psychologie inconnue. 2. ed. Paris, 1912.

VPhil 3640.760 — Borský, Lev. Bedřich Nietzsche. Praha, 1912.

Phil 575.18A — Bosanquet, B. The principle of individuality and value.

Phil 3808.116.3 — Bossert, Adolphe. Schopenhauer. 3. éd. Paris, 1912.

Phil 176.58 — Bourdeau, J. La philosophie affective. Paris, 1912.

Phil 176.42.15 — Boutroux, E. The beyond that is within. London, 1912.

Phil 801.10.5 — Boutroux, E. Historical studies in philosophy. London, 1912.

Phil 2805.92.9 — Boutroux, E. Pascal. 5. éd. Paris, 1912.

Phil 2070.111.5 — Boutroux, E. William James. Leipzig, 1912.

Phil 2070.147 — Boutroux, Emile. William James. 2d ed. N.Y., 1912.

Phil 3483.10A — Bowne, B.P. Kant and Spencer. Boston, 1912.

Phil 6111.37 — Boyd, T.P. The voice eternal. 2nd ed. San Francisco, 1912-14.

Phil 5041.20.3 — Bradley, F.H. Principles of logic. N.Y., 1912.

Phil 3801.232 — Bréhier, Émile. Schelling. Paris, 1912.

Phil 5211.1 — Brett, G.S. History of psychology. London, 1912-21. 3v.

Phil 176.54A — Brochard, V. Etudes de philosophie ancienne et de philosophie moderne. Paris, 1912.

Phil 600.18 — Brunetière, F. Sur les chemins de la croyance. Paris, 1912.

Phil 177.33.3 — Calkins, Mary Whiton. The persistent problems of philosophy. 3d ed. N.Y., 1912.

Phil 8877.35 — Carpenter, W.B. Life's tangled thread. London, 1912.

Phil 5400.53 — Cartault, A. Les sentiments généraux. Paris, 1912.

Phil 8582.19 — Carver, T.N. The religion worth having. Boston, 1912.

Phil 8582.19.2A — Carver, T.N. The religion worth having. Boston, 1912.

Phil 4210.112 — Caviglione, C. Il Rosmini vero. Voghera, 1912.

Phil 8582.27 — Chandler, Arthur. Faith and experience. 2. ed. London, 1912.

Phil 3640.104 — Chatterton-Hill, G. Philosophy of Nietzsche. London, 1912.

Phil 9495.40 — Chauvin, A. De la préservation morale de l'enfant. Paris, 1912.

Phil 6112.26.5 — Cheney, A.C.P. (Mrs.). What it is that heals. London, 1912.

Phil 665.25 — Christiansen, Broder. Vom Selbstbewusstsein. Berlin, 1912.

Phil 8657.14.20 — Cieszkowski, August D. Bóg i palingenezya. Poznań, 1912.

Phil 8582.28 — Claraz, Jules. La faillité des religions. Paris, 1912.

Phil 530.11.7 — Cloud of unknowing. A book of contemplation. London, 1912.

Phil 6112.25.6 — Clouston, T.S. Hygiene of mind. 6th ed. London, 1912.

Phil 5042.11 — Coffey, P. The science of logic. London, 1912. 2v.

1912 - cont.

Phil 365.39   Collin, C. Brorskabets religion. Kristiania, 1912.

Phil 8877.38   Cooke, H.P. Maurice, the philosopher. Cambridge, 1912.

Phil 525.77   Cordelier, John. The path of the eternal wisdom. 2d ed. London, 1912.

Phil 8582.20   Cornford, F.M. From religion to philosophy. London, 1912.

Phil 4260.85.5   Croce, B. Le fonti della gnoseologia Vichiana. Napoli, 1912.

Phil 4080.3.31.4   Croce, Benedetto. Estetica come scienza dell'espressione e linguistica generale. 4a ed. Bari, 1912.

Phil 5325.8   Culler, A.J. Interference and adaptability. N.Y., 1912.

Phil 978.28   Curtiss, H.A. The voice of Isis. Los Angeles, 1912.

Phil 8657.9   Cyon, E. von. Gott und Wissenschaft. v.1-2. Leipzig, 1912.

Phil 8692.11   Cyon, Elie de. Dieu et science. 2. éd. Paris, 1912.

Phil 8693.13   Dalin, C.O. Infor de stora varldsproblemen. Stockholm, 1912.

Phil 3905.88   Dallago, Carl. Otto Weiningers und sein Werk. Innsbruck, 1912.

Phil 5243.26   Dam, Axel. Om muligheden af formel opdragelse af de intellektuelle evner. København, 1912.

Phil 3808.145   Damm, O.F. Arthur Schopenhauer. Leipzig, 1912.

Phil 9045.13   Defoy, H. Le citoyen. Paris, 1912.

Phil 5640.16   Dell, J.A. The gateways of knowledge. Cambridge, 1912.

Phil 2475.1.111   Desaymard, J. La pensée de Henri Bergson. Paris, 1912.

Phil 2520.45   Descartes, René. Discorso sul metodo e meditazioni. Bari, 1912. 2v.

Phil 2520.14.2   Descartes, René. Meditationes de prima philosophia. 2e. Aufl. München, 1912.

Phil 5213.1.9A   Dessoir, M. Outline...history of psychology. N.Y., 1912.

Phil 960.3.3   Deussen, P. System of the Vedânta. Chicago, 1912.

Phil 7084.6   Diepgen, Paul. Traum und Traumdeutung als medizinisch-naturwissenschaftliches Problem im Mittelalter. Berlin, 1912.

Phil 5043.17   Döring, A. Grundlinien der Logik. Leipzig, 1912.

Phil 178.12.29   Dresser, H.W. Human efficiency. N.Y., 1912.

Phil 1703.2   Drews, Arthur. Die Philosophie im ersten Drittel des 19. Jahrhunderts. Leipzig, 1912.

Phil 178.22   Driesch, H. Ordnungslehre. Jena, 1912.

Phil 178.21   Dubray, C.A. Introductory philosophy. N.Y., 1912.

Phil 178.16.5   Dumesni, G. La sophistique contemporaine. Paris, 1912.

Phil 5243.15   Dunlap, K. A system of psychology. N.Y., 1912.

Phil 8878.22.2   Duprat, G.L. La morale. Théorie psycho-sociologique d'une conduite rationnelle. 2. ed. Paris, 1912.

Phil 8879.16.2   Eisler, Julius. Lehrbuch der allgemeinen Ethik. 2e Aufl. Wien, 1912.

Phil 89.1.15   Eisler, R. Philosophen - Lexikon. Berlin, 1912.

Phil 2475.1.415   Elliots, Hugh Samuel Roger. Modern science and the illusions of Professor Bergson. London, 1912.

Phil 978.45   Encausse, G. La réincarnation. Paris, 1912.

Phil 179.21   Eriksen, Richard. Tidens kurs. Kristiania, 1912.

Phil 5460.9   Etchart, Carlos R. La ilusion. Buenos Aires, 1912.

Phil 5252.25   Etudes de psychologie. Louvain, 1912.

Phil 179.3.32   Eucken, R. Erkennen und Leben. Leipzig, 1912.

Phil 179.3.7.4   Eucken, R. Main currents of modern thought. London, 1912.

Phil 179.3.55   Eucken, R. Naturalism or idealism? Photoreproduction. Cambridge, 1912.

Phil 179.3.35   Eucken, R. Religion and life. N.Y., 1912.

Phil 8584.5.16   Eucken, Rudolf. Hauptprobleme der Religionsphilosophie der Gegenwart. Berlin, 1912.

Phil 179.9   Eusebietti, Pietro. Corso elementare di filosofia. Milano, 1912. 3v.

Phil 805.4   Faguet, E. Initiation philosophique. Paris, 1912.

Phil 4967.20   Farias Brito, Raymundo de. A base physica do espirito. Rio de Janeiro, 1912.

Phil 3210.67.5   Fechner, G.T. Little book of life after death. Boston, 1912.

Phil 5465.216   Fernald, Mabel Ruth. The diagnosis of mental imagery. Thesis. Princeton, N.J., 1912.

Phil 5635.24   Fernberger, Samuel W. Relation of methods of just perceptible differences and constant stimuli. n.p., 1912.

Phil 8585.23.5   Figgis, J.N. Civilisation at the cross roads. N.Y., 1912.

Phil 9345.8   Fischer, E.L.C. Heart and soul culture. Philadelphia, 1912.

Phil 2520.119.15.5   Fischer, Kuno. Descartes' Leben, Werke und Lehre. 5e Aufl. Heidelberg, 1912.

Phil 7069.12.10   Fish, Eben. Voices from the open door. Cleveland, 1912.

Phil 8893.12.15   Flaig, Josef. Christoph Sigwarts Beiträge zu Grundlegung und Aufbau der Ethik. Stuttgart, 1912.

Phil 8880.29   Flügel, Otto. Das Ich und die sittlichen Ideen im Leben. 5e Aufl. Langensalza, 1912.

Phil 3640.88.3   Förster-Nietzsche, E. Der junge Nietzsche. Leipzig, 1912.

Phil 3640.88.5   Förster-Nietzsche, E. Life of Nietzsche. N.Y., 1912-15. 2v.

Phil 3640.88.6   Förster-Nietzsche, E. The young Nietzsche. London, 1912.

Phil 2800.1.87   Fonsegrive, Georges. Léon Ollé-Laprune, l'homme et le penseur. Paris, 1912.

Phil 7060.152   Fontenay, G. de. La photographie et l'étude des phénomènes psychiques. Paris, 1912.

Phil 9165.5   Forsyth, P.T. Marriage, its ethic and religion. London, 1912.

Phil 8585.20   Forsyth, P.T. Principle of authority in relation to certainty. London, 1912.

Phil 3260.152.5   Fraenkel, Georg. Die kritische Rechtsphilosophie bei Fries. Göttingen, 1912.

Phil 8880.32   Franze, Paul. Das höchste Gut. Berlin, 1912.

Phil 6315.2.8   Freud, Sigmund. Over psychoanalyse. Leiden, 1912.

X Cg   Phil 6315.2.19   Freud, Sigmund. Selected papers on hysteria and other psychoneuroses. N.Y., 1912.

Phil 6315.2.6.10   Freud, Sigmund. Über Psychoanalyse. 2e Aufl. Leipzig, 1912.

Phil 5525.6.3   Freud, Sigmund. Der Witz und seine Beziehung zum Unbewussten. 2. Aufl. Leipzig, 1912.

Phil 1705.7   Freyer, Johannes. Geschichte der Geschichte der Philosophie. Leipzig, 1912.

Phil 336.3   Frischeisen-Köhler, Max. Wissenschaft und Wirklichkeit. Leipzig, 1912.

Phil 6315.9.2   Fuchs, R.F. Phisiologik Praktikum für Mediziner. 2. Aufl. Wiesbaden, 1912.

Phil 286.4   Fullerton, G.S. The world we live in. N.Y., 1912.

Phil 6315.5   Furtmüller, Carl. Psychoanalyse und ethik. München, 1912.

Phil 2725.19.95   Gagnebin, S. La philosophie de l'institutio. St.-Blaise, 1912.

Phil 1706.1.32   Gaultier, Jules de. Entretiens avec ceux d'hier et d'aujourd'hui. 2e éd. Paris, 1912.

Phil 8881.36   Gehring, Albert. Shadows and realities. Cleveland, 1912.

1912 - cont.

Phil 2270.112   Geraskoff, Michael. Die sittliche Erziehung nach Herbert Spencer. Zürich, 1912.

Phil 8881.31   Gerkrath, E. Grundlinien der Ethik. Charlottenburg, 1912.

Phil 5246.14.5   Geyser, J. Lehrbuch der allgemeinen Psychologie. 2. Aufl. Munster, 1912.

Phil 8631.14   Ghyvelde, F. de. Le ciel, séjour des élus. Montréal, 1912.

Phil 5465.14   Giachetti, Apriano. La fantasia. Torino, 1912.

Phil 2520.117   Gilson, E. Index scolastico-cartésien. Paris, 1912.

Phil 4115.25   Gioberti, V. Nuova protologia brani scelti da tutte le sue opere. Bari, 1912. 2v.

Phil 6990.3.42   Grandmaison de Bruno, F. Twenty cures at Lourdes. St. Louis, 1912.

Phil 2835.82   Graves, F.P. Peter Ramus and educational reforms of the 16th century. N.Y., 1912.

Phil 8631.13   Grenfell, W.T. On immortality. Boston, 1912.

Phil 2630.2.10   Guyau, J.M. Philosophische Werke. Leipzig, 1912-1914. 6v.

Phil 8586.8.3   Guyau, J.M. L'irréligion de l'avenir. 18. éd. Paris, 1912.

Phil 5817.6.9   Hachet-Souplet, P. La genèse des instincts. Paris, 1912.

Phil 8697.6   Hall, F.J. Recent work of angelican theologians. Chicago, 1912.

Phil 3007.5.5   Hall, G.S. Founders of modern psychology. N.Y., 1912.

Phil 5047.12.9   Hamilton, E.J. Erkennen und Schlieszen. N.Y., 1912.

Phil 5247.3.7   Hamilton, E.J. The perceptionalist. N.Y., 1912.

Phil 6053.12   Hamon, Louis. Cheiro's memoirs. Philadelphia, 1912.

Phil 182.85   Hartmann, Alma. Zwischen Dichtung und Philosophie. Berlin, 1912.

Phil 807.9.2   Hasse, Karl P. Von Plotin zu Goethe. Jena, 1912.

Phil 5648.12   Hayes, M.H.S. A study of cutaneous after-sensations. Chicago, 1912.

Phil 3425.75   Hegel, Georg Wilhelm Friedrich. Neue Briefe...und Verwandtes. Leipzig, 1912.

Htn   Phil 3425.29*   Hegel, Georg Wilhelm Friedrich. Wissenschaft der Logik. Nürnberg, 1912. 3v.

Phil 2520.113   Heimsoeth, H. Die Methode der Erkenntnis bei Descartes. Giessen, 1912.

Phil 182.14.10   Hemsterhuis, F. Philosophische Schriften. Karlsruhe, 1912. 2v.

Phil 3428.30.55   Herbart, J.F. Lehrbuch zur Einleitung in die philosophie. 4. Aufl. Leipzig, 1912.

Phil 672.130   Herbertz, R. Die Philosophie des Raumes. Stuttgart, 1912.

Phil 75.19   Herbertz, R. Die philosophische Literatur. Stuttgart, 1912.

Phil 182.46   Hermance, W.E. Unorthodox conception of being. N.Y., 1912.

Phil 3808.154   Hochfeld, Sophus. Das künstlerische in der Aprache Schopenhauers. Leipzig, 1912.

Phil 8662.7   Hocking, W.E. The meaning of God in human experience. New Haven, Conn., 1912.

Phil 1707.1.19A   Höffding, H. A brief history of modern philosophy. N.Y., 1912.

Phil 5645.28   Höllner, Hans. Die Störungen des Farbensinnes ihre klinische Bedeutung und ihre Diagnose. Berlin, 1912.

Phil 7060.122   Hoffman, Frank S. Psychology and common life. N.Y., 1912.

Phil 6117.25   Hollingworth, H.L. The influence of caffein on mental and motor efficiency. N.Y., 1912.

Phil 630.5.5A   Holt, E.B. The new realism. N.Y., 1912.

Phil 5757.5   Horne, H.H. Free will and human responsibility. N.Y., 1912.

Phil 2050.20   Hume, David. Oeuvres philosophiques choisies. Paris, 1912. 2v.

Phil 8587.24   Huntington, H. Cué bono? or What shall it profit. London, 1912.

Phil 8882.24.8   Hyde, W. De W. Self-measurement. N.Y., 1912.

Phil 8588.1.5   Ibarreta, R.H. La religion al alcance de todos. 35. ed. Barcelona, 1912.

Phil 525.65   Ihringer, Bernhard. Der Schuldbegriff bei den Mystikern der Reformationszeit. Bern, 1912.

NEDL   Phil 7060.38.15   Ingram, J.H. The haunted homes and family traditions of Great Britain. London, 1912.

Phil 3829.3.25   Jacobi, F.E. Jacobi's Spinoza Büchlein. München, 1912.

Phil 184.24   Jacobsson, M. Pragmatiska uppfostringsprinciper. Lund, 1912.

Phil 6119.5   Jacoby, G.W. Suggestion and psychotherapy. N.Y., 1912.

Phil 184.3.10A   James, W. Essays in radical empiricism. N.Y., 1912.

Phil 184.3.30.5A   James, W. Memories and studies. N.Y., 1912.

Phil 184.3.16.3   James, W. Pragmatism, a new name. N.Y., 1912.

Phil 184.3.3.15   James, W. The will to believe and other essays in popular philosophy. London, 1912.

Phil 5249.2.35   James, William. Précis de psychologie. 3. éd. Paris, 1912.

Phil 5249.2.89   Jastrow, J. Notes in psychology. Madison, 1912.

Phil 9075.17   Jeffs, Harry. Concerning conscience. London, 1912.

Phil 665.30   Joël, Karl. Seele und Welt. Jena, 1912.

Phil 7082.46   Jónasson, Hermann. Draumar. Reykjavík, 1912.

Phil 5440.18   Josefovici, U. Die psychische Vererbung. Leipzig, 1912.

Phil 184.18   Joussain, A. Esquisse d'une philosophie. Paris, 1912.

Phil 6319.1.7.9   Jung, C.G. Wandlungen und Symbole der Libido. Leipzig, 1912.

Phil 179.3.86   Kade, Richard. Rudolf Euckens noologische Methode. Leipzig, 1912.

Phil 3480.40.15   Kant, Immanuel. Anthropologie in pragmatischer Hinsicht. 5. Aufl. Leipzig, 1912.

Phil 3480.91   Kant, Immanuel. Briefwechsel. München, 1912. 3v.

Phil 3480.58.10   Kant, Immanuel. Prolegomena to any future metaphysics. 3d ed. Chicago, 1912.

Phil 3480.18.7   Kant, Immanuel. Vermischte Schriften. Leipzig, 1912.

Phil 3480.15   Kant, Immanuel. Werke. v.1-7,9,11. Berlin, 1912. 9v.

X Cg   Phil 3480.15   Kant, Immanuel. Werke. v.8,10. Berlin, 1912. 2v.

Phil 3260.88   Kastil, Alfred. Jakob F. Fries' Lehre von der unmittelbaren Erkenntnis. Göttingen, 1912.

Phil 8635.3   Kaufmann, H. Die Unsterblichkeitsbeweise. Paderborn, 1912.

Phil 179.3.90   Kesseler, K. Rudolf Euckens Bedeutung für das modern Christentum. Bunzlau, 1912.

Phil 8885.10.5   King, H.C. National living. N.Y., 1912.

Phil 5250.7   Koffka, K. Zur Analyse der Vorstellungen und ihre Gesetze. Leipzig, 1912.

Phil 6320.3   Kollarits, Jenö. Charakter und Nervosität. Berlin, 1912.

Phil 1504.11.3   Krebs, E. Theologie und Wissenschaft nach de Lehre. v.11, pt.3-4. Münster, 1912.

Phil 6315.2.325   Kronfeld, A. Über die psychologischen Theorien Freuds und verwandte Anschauungen. Leipzig, 1912.

Phil 630.7A   Külpe, O. Die Realisierung. Leipzig, 1912. 3v.

Chronological Listing

1912 - cont.

Phil 3625.5.87 Kuntze, Friedrich. Die Philosophie Salomon Maimons. Heidelberg, 1912.
Phil 2270.141 Lacy, William M. Examination of the philosophy of the unknowable as expounded by Herbert Spencer. Philadelphia, 1912.
Phil 6121.30 Larson, Christian I. Your forces and how to use them. N.Y., 1912.
Phil 4600.2.44 Larsson, Hans. Intuitionsproblemet. Stockholm, 1912.
Phil 4600.2.36 Larsson, Hans. Studier och meditationer. 4e uppl. Lund, 1912.
Phil 5500.5 Lask, E. Die Lehre vom Urteil. Tübingen, 1912.
Phil 9035.52 Lasurski, A. Über das Studium der Individualität. Leipzig, 1912.
Phil 5400.29 Latour, Marius. Premiers principes d'une théorie générale des émotions. Paris, 1912.
Phil 8591.75 Laurila, K.S. Vapaamielisyys. Helsingissä, 1912.
Phil 8666.6.5 Le Dantec, Felix. L'athéisme. Paris, 1912.
Phil 186.76 Le Dantec, Félix. Contre la métaphysique; questions de méthode. Paris, 1912.
Phil 5251.20 Lehmann, Alfred. Grundzüge der Psychophysiologie. Leipzig, 1912.
Phil 1516.3 Lehmen, Alfonso. Lehrbuch der Philosophie. 4e Aufl. n.p., 1912-19. 4v.
Phil 3552.26 Leibniz, Gottfried Wilhelm. Opere varie. Bari, 1912.
Phil 3585.7.92 Leicht, Alfred. Lazarusstudien. Meissen, 1912.
Phil 2475.1.113 LeRoy, E. Une philosophie nouvelle Henri Bergson. Paris, 1912.
Phil 5627.20 Leuba, J.H. A psychological study of religion. N.Y., 1912.
Phil 1535.23 Levesque, l'abbé. Précis de philosophie. Paris, 1912.
Phil 3640.106A Lichtenberger, H. The gospel of superman. N.Y., 1912.
Phil 3640.105 Lichtenberger, H. La philosophie de Nietzsche. 3e éd. Paris, 1912.
Phil 4600.4.32 Lidforss, Bengt. Fragment och miniatyrer. 2. uppl. Malmö, 1912.
Phil 3493.6 Liebmann, Otto. Kant und die Epigonen. Berlin, 1912.
Phil 3552.126 Lieder, F.W.C. Friedrich Spie and the théodicée of Leibniz. Urbana, 1912.
Phil 4575.95 Liljekrantz, B. Benjamin Höijer. Lund, 1912.
Phil 3246.99.5 Lindau, Hans. Die Schriften zu Johann Gottlieb Fichte's Atheismusstreit. München, 1912.
Phil 342.5 Linke, Paul F. Die phänomenale Sphäre und das Bewusstsein. Halle an der Saale, 1912.
Phil 5761.5 Lipps, G.F. Das Problem der Willensfreiheit. Leipzig, 1912.
Phil 2115.76 Locke, J. Lettres inédites. La Haye, 1912.
Phil 510.1.13.5 Lodge, Oliver. Life and matter. 2nd ed. London, 1912.
Phil 7069.12.51 Lodge, Oliver Joseph. La survivance humaine. 3. ed. Paris, 1912.
Phil 9171.8 Lofthouse, William F. Ethics and the family. London, 1912.
Phil 3565.30.25 Lotze, Hermann. System der Philosophie. Leipzig, 1912. 2v.
Phil 5520.37 Lourié, Ossip. Le langage et la verbomanie. Paris, 1912.
Phil 3425.78A Lowenberg, Jacob. Hegel's Entwürfe zur Enzyklopädie und Propadentik. Leipzig, 1912.
Phil 5251.18 Lynch, Arthur. Psychology; a new system. London, 1912. 2v.
Phil 1750.20 McClure, M.T. Study of realistic movement in contemporary philosophy. Staunton, 1912.
Phil 5627.30 McComas, Henry Clay. Psychology of religious sects. N.Y., 1912.
Phil 8592.2 McConnell, S. Christianity. N.Y., 1912.
Phil 5252.18.12 McDougall, William. Psychology, the study of behavior. London, 1912.
Phil 5252.18.11A McDougall, William. Psychology, the study of behavior. N.Y., 1912.
Phil 3494.10 Macmillan, R.A.C. Crowning phase of critical philosophy...Kant. London, 1912.
Phil 3425.39 Macran, H.S. Hegel's doctrine of formal logic. Oxford, 1912.
Phil 5822.4A Máday, Stefan. Psychologie des Pferdes und der Dressur. Berlin, 1912.
Phil 3552.130 Mahnke, D. Leibniz als Gegner der Gelehrteneinseitigkeit. Stade, 1912.
Phil 3625.5.35 Maimon, Salomon. Versuch einer neuen Logik, oder Theorie. Berlin, 1912.
Phil 2805.77 Maire, Albert. L'oeuvre scientifique de Blaise Pascal. Paris, 1912.
Phil 5052.38 Mally, Ernst. Gegenstandstheoretische Grundlagen der Logik und Logistik. Leipzig, 1912.
Phil 4803.555.32 Mankowski, Mieczysław. Złoty dar człowieka. Wyd. 2. Kraków, 1912.
Phil 9245.28.10 Marden, Orison S. Arbetsglädje-livsglädje. Stockholm, 1912.
Phil 9450.11 Martin, Félix. La morale républicaine. Paris, 1912.
Phil 2733.86 Martin, J. Malebranche. Paris, 1912.
Phil 187.26.5 Marvin, W.T. A first book in metaphysics. N.Y., 1912.
Phil 3625.1.56 Mendlessohn, Moses. Moses Mendelssohn; eine Auswahl aus seinen Schriften und Briefen. Frankfurt, 1912.
Phil 70.2 Mental Hygiene Conference and Exhibit. Proceedings, 1911. N.Y., 1912.
Phil 5052.14 Mercier, C. A new logic. London, 1912.
Phil 1712.2.5 Merz, J.T. A history of European thought in the nineteenth century. Edinburgh, 1912-27. 4v.
Phil 1712.5.2 Messer, A. Geschichte der Philosophie vom Beginn der Neuzeit zum Ende des 18. Jahrhunderts. Leipzig, 1912.
Phil 343.7 Messer, August. Einführung in die Erkenntnistheorie. Leipzig, 1912.
Phil 3494.37 Metzger, Wilhelm. Untersuchungen zur Sitten - und Rechtslehre Kants und Fichtes. Heidelberg, 1912.
Phil 343.16.5 Meyerson, Émile. Identité et réalité. 2. éd. Paris, 1912.
Phil 8667.9 Michelet, Georges. Dieu et l'agnosticisme contemporaine. 3. éd. Paris, 1912.
Phil 5090.7 Milhaud, G. Essai sur les conditions et les limites. 3e éd. Paris, 1912.
Phil 1135.75 Montagni, G.R. L'evoluzione presocratica. Castello, 1912.
Phil 3494.12 Monzel, Alois. Die historischen Voraussetzungen,...der Kantischen Lehre. Bonn, 1912.
Phil 8520.18.2 Moore, Edward C. An outline of the history of Christian thought since Kant. London, 1912.
Phil 8887.21.7 Moore, George Edward. Ethics. N.Y., 1912.
Phil 3494.16.5 Morente, M.G. La estética de Kant. Thesis. Madrid, 1912.
Phil 5822.1.25 Morgan, C.L. Instinct and experience. N.Y., 1912.
Phil 3640.102 Morr, P.M. Nietzsche. Boston, 1912.
Phil 3640.218 Mügge, M.A. Friedrich Nietzsche. London, 1912.

1912 - cont.

Phil 2050.110 Münster, O. Det Hume'ske problem. København, 1912.
Phil 5850.278.5 Münsterberg, H. Psychologie und Wirtschaftsleben. Leipzig, 1912.
Phil 9035.83 Muñoz, Juan A. El caracter. México, 1912.
Phil 187.35 Murray, D.L. Pragmatism. London, 1912.
Phil 5253.1.5 Natorp, P. Allgemeine Psychologie. Tübingen, 1912.
Phil 3495.10.10 Natorp, Paul. Kant und die Marburger Schule. Berlin, 1912.
Phil 5053.7.4 Nicoli, P. Elementi di logica. Milano, 1912.
Phil 3640.30.9 Nietzsche, Friedrich. Aurore. 7e éd. Paris, 1912.
Phil 4610.7.15 Norström, V. Religion och tanke. Stockholm, 1912.
Htn Phil 7075.6.3* Orsi, Alberto. La donna nuda. 3. ed. Milano, 1912.
Phil 5330.18 Ostermann, W. Das Interesse. 3e Aufl. Oldenburg, 1912.
Phil 345.4 Ostler, H. Die Realität der Aussenwelt. Paderborn, 1912.
Phil 525.52 Oulmont, Charles. Le verger, le temple et la cellule. Paris, 1912.
Phil 190.51 Paget, Violet. Vital lies. London, 1912. 2v.
Phil 8633.1.15 Palmer, George H. Intimations of immortality in the sonnets of Shakespeare. Boston, 1912.
Phil 2805.40.36 Pascal, Blaise. Pensées et opuscules. 6. éd. Paris, 1912.
Phil 3915.152 Passkönig, Oswald. Die Psychologie Wilhelm Wundts. Leipzig, 1912.
Phil 5400.45.9 Paulhan, Frédéric. Les phénomènes affectifs et les lois de leur apparition. 3d éd. Paris, 1912.
Phil 5765.2.3 Payot, Jules. L'éducation de la volonté. Paris, 1912.
Phil 6325.9 Pelman, Carl. Psychische Grenzzustände. 3. Aufl. Bonn, 1912.
Phil 3110.86 Penny, A.J. Jacob Boehme. London, 1912.
Phil 5627.34 Perrier, Louis. Le sentiment religieux. Paris, 1912.
Phil 1715.3.2 Perry, R.B. Present philosophical tendencies. London, 1912.
Phil 296.7.2 Petzoldt, J. Das Weltproblem vom Standpunkte. 2. Aufl. Leipzig, 1912.
Phil 3425.115 Phalén, A. Das Erkenntnisproblem in Hegels Philosophie. Upsala, 1912.
Phil 2999.2 La philosophie allemande au XIXe siècle. Paris, 1912.
Phil 3160.3.80 Philosophische Abhandlungen H. Cohen zum 70sten Geburtstag dargebracht. Berlin, 1912.
Phil 8640.7.2 Piat, A. La destinée de l'homme. 2. éd. Paris, 1912.
Phil 346.4 Pichler, H. Möglichkeit und Widerspruschlosigkeit. Leipzig, 1912.
Phil 8595.14.5 Piercy, B.H. Superstition and common sense. London, 1912.
Phil 7080.25 Pieron, H. Le problème physiologique du sommeil. Paris, 1912.
Phil 5643.37 Poffenberger, A.T. Reaction time to retinal stimulation. N.Y., 1912.
Phil 346.11 Polak, L. Kennisleer contra materíe-realisme. Amsterdam, 1912.
Phil 190.31 Pollack, Walter. Perspektive und Symbol in Philosophie und Rechtswissenschaft. Berlin, 1912.
Phil 25.19 Psiche, rivista di studi psicologici. v.1-4. Firenze, 1912. 4v.
Phil 6125.5.5 Psychotherapeutics. Boston, 1912.
Phil 331.2.9 Raab, F. Philosophie von Avenarius' Biomechanische. Leipzig, 1912.
Phil 192.1.9 Rabier, E. Leçons de philosophie. 9e éd. Paris, 1912.
Phil 5257.31 Radha-Krishnan, S. Essentials of psychology. London, 1912.
Phil 5227.3A Rand, B. The classical psychologists. Boston, 1912.
Phil 575.33 Randall, J.H. The culture of personality. N.Y., 1912.
Phil 1885.80 Rashdall, H. The metaphysic of Mr. F.H. Bradley. London, 1912.
Phil 7059.8 Rebman, F.J. The human aura. Storm Lake, Iowa, 1912.
Phil 25.14.5 Register zum philosophischen Jahrbuch. Fulda, 1912.
Phil 125.4 Reiner, Julius. Philosophisches Wörterbuch. Leipzig, 1912.
Phil 3903.3.99 Reininger, R. Über H. Vaihingers "Philosophie des Als Ob". Leipzig, 1912.
Phil 3499.10.10 Reininger, Robert. Kants kritischer Idealismus. Leipzig, 1912.
Phil 8633.1.14 Reisner, George A. The Egyptian conception of immortality. Boston, 1912.
Phil 2840.42 Renouvier, C.B. Essais de critique générale. Paris, 1912. 2v.
Phil 2840.41 Renouvier, C.B. Essais de critique générale. Premier essai. Paris, 1912. 2v.
Phil 4215.3.38 Rensi, Giuseppe. Il genio etico, ed altri saggi. Bari, 1912.
Phil 7069.02.17 Richardson, J.E. The great psychological crime. 11th ed. Chicago, 1912.
Phil 8597.31 Richter, R. Religionsphilosophie. Leipzig, 1912.
Phil 192.21.5 Rickert, H. Philosophie: ihr Wesen, ihre Probleme. Leipzig, 1912.
Phil 5257.16 Rith, L. L'intelligence. Thèse. Paris, 1912.
Phil 817.5 Robert, A.A. Histoire de la philosophie. Québec, 1912.
Phil 623.4 Robertson, J.M. Rationalism. London, 1912.
Phil 5057.13 Robinson, A.T. The applications of logic. N.Y., 1912.
Phil 3270.7.80 Römer, Alfred. Der Gottesbegriff Franks. Inaug. Diss. Halle, 1912.
Phil 3425.114 Roques, P. Hegel; sa vie et ses oeuvres. Paris, 1912.
Phil 3552.264 Rosenfeld, J. Die doppelte Wahrheit...Leibniz und Hurne. Diss. Bern, 1912.
Phil 192.32 Roustan, D. Leçons de philosophie. Paris, 1912.
Phil 8597.20.10 Royce, Josiah. The sources of religious insight. Edinburgh, 1912.
Phil 8597.19A Royce, Josiah. The sources of religious insight. N.Y., 1912.
Phil 192.16.15A Royce, Josiah. The sources of religious insight. N.Y., 1912.
Phil 5062.18.3 Ruge, Arnold. Encyclopädie der philosophischen Wissenschaften in Verbindung mit W. Windelband. Pt.1. Logik. Photoreproduction. Tübingen, 1912.
Phil 1717.8 Ruggiero, G. de. La filosofia contemporanea. Bari, 1912.
Phil 192.28 Russell, B. The problems of philosophy. London, 1912.
Phil 192.28.2A Russell, B. The problems of philosophy. N.Y., 1912.
Phil 6990.12 Saintyves, P. La simulation du merveilleux. Paris, 1912.
Phil 1523.6.5 Saitta, Giuseppe. Le origine del neo-tomismo. Bari, 1912.
Phil 9150.14 Sanderson, J.R. The relation of evolutionry theory to ethical problem. Toronto, 1912.
Phil 6128.22 Sankey, Dora J. Bible authority for metaphysical healing. Boston, 1912.
Phil 6128.33 Sarjant, L.G. Is the mind a coherer? London, 1912.
Phil 5058.24 Schiller, F.C.S. Formal logic. London, 1912.
Phil 193.9.6 Schiller, F.C.S. Humanism philosophical essays. 2. ed. London, 1912.

Chronological Listing

1912 - cont.

Phil 3805.20 Schleiermacher, Friedrich. Friedrich Schleiermacher. Langensalza, 1912.

Phil 400.42 Schmidt, F.J. Der philosophische Sinn. Göttingen, 1912.

Phil 103.3 Schmidt, Heinrich. Philosophisches Wörterbuch. Leipzig, 1912.

Phil 5258.38 Schmied-Kowarzik, W. Umriss einer neuen analytischen Psychologie. Leipzig, 1912.

Phil 5828.6.5 Schneider, K.C. Tierpsychologisches Praktikum. Leipzig, 1912.

Phil 3808.60.30 Schopenhauer, Arthur. Parerga et Paralipomena: fragments sur l'histoire de la philosophie. Paris, 1912.

Phil 3808.35.5 Schopenhauer, Arthur. Die Welt als Wille und Vorstellung. München, 1912-13. 2v.

Phil 2475.1.213 Schrecker, P. Henri Bergsons Philosophie der Persönlichkeit. München, 1912.

Phil 3915.80 Schumann, H. Wundts Lehre vom Willen. Leipzig, 1912.

Phil 193.68 Schwarz, H. Grundfragen der Weltanschauung. 2e Aufl. Leipzig, 1912.

Phil 8598.49.5 Segerstedt, T.K. Det religiösa sanningsproblemet. Stockholm, 1912.

Phil 4080.3.90 Settimelli, Emilio. La critica di Benedetto Croce. Bologna, 1912.

Phil 8643.15 Shaw, Fred G. Our future existence. London, 1912.

Phil 5520.20 Sheffield, A.D. Grammar and thinking. N.Y., 1912.

Phil 818.7.3 Siebert, Otto. Was jeder Gebildete aus der Geschichte. 3e Aufl. Langensalza, 1912.

Phil 2218.87 Sigsbee, Ray A. Das philosophische System Joseph Priestleys. Heidelberg, 1912.

Phil 349.25 Silfverberg, K.W. Der Wirklichkeitsdualismus. Helsingfors, 1912.

Phil 8598.33 Simmel, G. Die Religion. 2. Aufl. Frankfurt, 1912.

Phil 8708.10 Simpson, James Y. The spiritual interpretation of nature. 2. ed. London, 1912.

Phil 1850.133 Skemp, A.R. Francis Bacon. London, 1912.

Phil 58.10.3 Societá per gliStudi Filosofici, Palermo. Bibliotheca Filosofica. Annuario. Palermo, 1912-

Phil 58.2.5 Society for Psychical Research, London. Presidential addresses, 1882-1911. Glasgow, 1912.

Phil 9075.21 Sollier, Paul. Morale et moralité. Paris, 1912.

Phil 818.14 Sortais, G. Histoire de la philosophie ancienne. Paris, 1912.

Phil 1504.8.4 Soto, P.B. Petri Compostellani. v.8, pt.4. Münster, 1912.

Phil 3195.6.83A Spranger, Eduard. Wilhelm Dilthey. Berlin, 1912.

Phil 3500.10.5 Stadler, A. Kant akademische Vorlesungen. Leipzig, 1912.

Phil 5058.09 Stadler, A. Logik. Leipzig, 1912.

Phil 8598.28 Stapfer, P. L'inquiétude religieuse du temps présent. Paris, 1912.

Phil 1504.11 Steinbüchel, T. Der Zweckgedanke in der Philosophie. v.11, pt.1-2. Münster, 1912.

Phil 1718.11 Steinilber, E. Essais critiques sur les idées philosophiques contemporaines. Paris, 1912.

Phil 8643.18.2 Steinmann, Theophil. Der religiose Unsterblichkeitsglaube. 2. Aufl. Göttingen, 1912.

Phil 7084.46 Stekel, Wilhelm. Die Träume der Dichter. Wiesbaden, 1912.

Phil 1135.33 Stettner, E. Antike Humanität in moderner Beleuchtung. Bieletz, 1912.

Phil 8893.52 Steudel, F. Alte und neue Tafeln. Berlin, 1912?

Phil 193.60 Stewart, H.L. Questions of the day in philosophy and psychology. London, 1912.

Phil 2280.15.80 Stirling, Amelia H. James Hutchinson Stirling, his life and work. London, 1912.

Phil 1818.4 Stock, Saint George. English thought for English thinkers. London, 1912.

Phil 4803.810.30 Straszewski, Maurycy. Dzieje filozoficznej myśli polskiej w okresie porozbiorowym. Kraków, 1912.

Phil 3905.90 Sturm, Bruno. Gegen Weininger. Wien, 1912.

Phil 9530.29 Tapper, Thomas. Youth and opportunity. N.Y., 1912.

Phil 8644.4 Taylor, D. The composition of matter and the evolution of the mind. London, 1912.

Phil 9560.7 Terraillon, E. L'honneur sentiment et principle moral. Paris, 1912.

Phil 3280.83 Terraillon, E. La morale de Geulincx. Paris, 1912.

Phil 5545.51 Test of accuracy of testimony of by-standers. n.p., 1912.

Phil 194.33 Teste, Paulin. Le precurseur. Le Haye, 1912.

Phil 8610.912 Thomas, J.C. The darkness, the dawn and the day. London, 1912.

Phil 2050.98 Thomsen, A. David Hume: sein Leben und seine Philosophie. Berlin, 1912.

Phil 525.73 Thulié, H. La mystique divine. Paris, 1912.

Phil 2045.85.2 Tönnies, F. Thomas Hobbes. 2e Aufl. Osterwieck, 1912.

Phil 8599.19.2 Troeltsch, Ernst. Die Absolutheit des Christentums. 2. Aufl. Tübingen, 1912.

Phil 7080.23 Trömmer, E. Das Problem des Schlafes. Wiesbaden, 1912.

Phil 600.35 Troilo, E. Il positivismo e i diritti dello spirito. Torino, 1912.

Phil 5627.96.5 Trumbull, Charles G. Taking men alive. N.Y., 1912.

Phil 930.5 Tucci, G. Storia della filosofia cinese antica. Bologna, 1912.

Phil 2070.85 Ubbink, J.G. Het pragmatisme van William James. Arnhem, 1912.

Phil 5260.8.5 Ufer, Christian. Systematische Psychologie für Oberlyzeen und Seminare. Leipzig, 1912.

Phil 525.7.2 Underhill, Evelyn. Mysticism. 4th ed. N.Y., 1912.

Phil 5258.22.5 Unger, Rudolf. Die kinderpsychologischen Bestrebungen L. Strümpells. Strassburg, 1912.

Phil 4265.1.18 Vanini, Lucilio, afterwards Giulio Cesare. Opere. Lecce, 1912. 2v.

Phil 8422.9 Vendéen, E. Principes du beau. Paris, 1912.

Phil 4215.2.81 Ventura, L. Tommaso Rossi e la sua filosofia. Genova, 1912.

Phil 8896.5 Vietinghoff, Jeanne de. La liberté intérieure. Paris, 1912.

Phil 5831.3 Vincent, S.B. The function of the vibrissae in the behavior of the white rat. Chicago, 1912.

Phil 8601.7 Vogel, W. La religion de l'évolutionisme. Bruxelles, 1912.

Phil 4772.10 Vvedenskii, A.I. Logika, kak chast' teorii poznaniia. 2. izd. Sankt Peterburg, 1912.

Phil 8110.6 Wallace,H.B. Die Kritik der rationalcn Ästhetik in England im achtzehnten Jahrhundert. Jena, 1912.

Phil 5062.25 Waller, A.D. A contribution to the psychology of logic. London, 1912.

Phil 6132.15 Walsh, J.J. Psychotherapy. London, 1912.

Phil 8677.8.2 Ward, James. The realm of ends, or Pluralism and theism. 2. ed. Cambridge, 1912.

1912 - cont.

Phil 8602.15.9 Watson, J. The interpretation of religious experience. Glasgow, 1912. 2v.

Phil 8602.18.15 Webb, C.C.J. Natural and comparative religion. Oxford, 1912.

Phil 822.1.14 Weber, A. History of philosophy. N.Y., 1912.

Phil 3260.152 Weiss, Georg. Fries' Lehre von Ahndung in Ästhetik. Göttingen, 1912.

Phil 3925.15 Wendel, G. Vermischte Schriften. Berlin, 1912.

Phil 197.39 Whitby, C.J. The open secret. London, 1912.

Phil 5772.11 Wijnaendts Francken, C.J. Het vraagstuk vanden vrijen wil. Haarlem, 1912.

Phil 8897.36 Wilbois, J. Devoir et durée. Paris, 1912.

Phil 197.25.7 Williams, C.L. The passing of evolution. Berkeley, 1912.

Phil 197.18.10 Willmann, O. Aus der Werkstatt der philosophia perennis. Freiburg, 1912.

Phil 197.18.5 Willmann, O. Philosophische Propädeutik. Freiburg, 1912-1914. 3v.

Phil 8602.17 Wilm, Emil Carl. Problem of religion. Boston, 1912.

Phil 365.28 Wilson, J.C. On an evolutionist theory of axioms. Oxford, 1912.

Phil 5262.14 Wirth, W. Psychophysik. Leipzig, 1912.

Phil 8897.20.5 Witherspoon, J. Lectures on moral philosophy. Princeton, 1912.

Phil 1050.12 Wolfson, Harry A. Maimonides and Halevi. Philadelphia, 1912.

Phil 1527.1.6 Wulf, M. de. Histoire de la philosophie médiévale. 4e éd. Louvain, 1912.

Phil 3915.65.10 Wundt, Wilhelm. Ethik. 4. Aufl. Stuttgart, 1912. 3v.

Phil 3915.49A Wundt, Wilhelm. Introduction to psychology. London, 1912.

Phil 5400.75.5 Ziegler, T. Das Gefühl. 5e Aufl. Berlin, 1912.

Phil 1535.12.5 Zigliara, F.T.M. Summa philosophica in usum scholarum. 15. ed. v.3. Paris, 1912.

Phil 7069.12.98 Zingaropoli, F. Telepatia e sogno. Napoli, 1912.

Phil 4803.896.235 Zñaniecki, Florian. Humanizm i poznanie. Warszawa, 1912.

Phil 4803.896.230 Zñaniecki, Florian. Studja nad filozofja wartosci. Warszawa, 1912.

1913

Phil 4513.6.31 Aall, H.H. Interessen som normativ idé. Kristiania, 1913.

Phil 182.76 Abhandlungen aus dem Gebiete der Philosophie und ihrer Geschichte. Freiburg, 1913.

Phil 5645.8.5 Abney, W. de W. Researches in colour vision. London, 1913.

Phil 5893.6 Abraham, Karl. Dreams and myths; a study in race psychology. N.Y., 1913.

Phil 3482.2.21 Adickes, E. Ein neu aufgefundenes Kollegheft nach Kants Vorlesung über Psysischegeographie. Tübingen, 1913.

Phil 5640.17 Aitken, E.H. The five windows of the soul. London, 1913.

Phil 5640.17.5 Aitken, E.H. Le va del l'anima. Torino, 1913.

Phil 672.20 Allan, A. Space and personality. Edinburgh, 1913.

Phil 800.1.5 Allgemeine Geschichte der Philosophie. 2. Aufl. Leipzig, 1913.

Phil 2270.175 Allievo, Giuseppe. La psicologia di Herbert Spencer. 2a ed. Torino, 1913.

Phil 3820.3 Altkircli, Ernst. Spinoza im Porträt. Jena, 1913.

Phil 5400.42 Andrews, Cyril B. Life, emotion, and intellect. London, 1913.

Phil 3585.10.94 Anschütz, G. Theodor Lipps' neuere Urteilslehre. Leipzig, 1913.

Phil 5240.7 Anschütz, Georg. Die Intelligenz, eine Einführung in die Haupttatdachenfet. Harz, 1913.

Phil 5240.7.5 Anschütz, Georg. Über die Erforschung der Denkvorgänge. Osterwieck, 1913.

Phil 4060.1.23 Ardigo, Roberto. Pagine scelte. Genova, 1913.

Phil 331.5 Aster, Ernst von. Prinzipien der Erkenntnislehre. Leipzig, 1913.

Phil 8580.16 Atkins, Gaius G. Pilgrims of the lonely road. N.Y., 1913.

Phil 281.7 Auerbach, Felix. Ektropismen en ny teori om livets bevarande i varldsprocessen. Stockholm, 1913.

NEDL Phil 281.4.9 Auerbach, Felix. Werden der Welten. Leipzig, 1913.

Phil 9245.9.4 Avebury, John Lubbock. The pleasures of life. v.1-2. London, 1913-14.

Phil 331.2.10 Avenarius, R. Zur Terminalfunktion. Berlin, 1913.

Phil 8402.28.10 Babbitt, Irving. The new Laocoon; an essay on the confusion of the arts. Boston, 1913.

Phil 8050.49 Baer, Hans. Grundriss eines Systems. Strassburg, 1913.

Phil 5241.178 Baeumker, Clemens. Anschauung und Denken. Paderborn, 1913.

Phil 7150.15 Baker, W.E. Diary of a suicide. N.Y., 1913.

Phil 5211.2A Baldwin, J.M. History of psychology. N.Y., 1913. 2v.

Phil 5241.3.6.10 Baldwin, J.M. Social and ethical interpretations. Mental development. 5. ed. N.Y., 1913.

Phil 8656.12 Barbour, G.F. Ethical approach to theism. Edinburgh, 1913.

Phil 8876.78 Barry, John D. Intimations. San Francisco, 1913.

Phil 2520.114.11 Barth, Heinrich. Descartes' Begründung der Erkenntnis. Bern, 1913.

Phil 705.6 Barthel, E. Elemente der transzendentalen Logik. Strassburg, 1913.

Phil 1905.11.78 Bascom, John. Things learned by living. N.Y., 1913.

Phil 2515.4.92 Battanelli, E.P. Cournot métaphysicien de la connaissance. Thèse. Paris, 1913.

Phil 9161.7 Beck, Frank O. Marching manward. N.Y., 1913.

Phil 5241.30 Bekhterev, V. La psychologie objective. Paris, 1913.

Phil 2401.1 Belin, J.P. Le mouvement philosophique, 1748-1789. Paris, 1913.

Phil 2475.1.192 Benda, Julien. Une philosophie pathétique. Paris, 1913.

Phil 8581.40 Benett, W. Religion and free will. Oxford, 1913.

Phil 5585.27 Benussi, Vittorio. Psychologie der Zeitauffassung. Heidelberg, 1913.

Phil 8876.52 Berge, Vincent. La vraie morale basée sur l'étude de la nature. 3. ed. Paris, 1913.

Phil 3745.1.153 Bergmann, Ernst. Ernst Platner und die Kunstphilosophie. Leipzig, 1913.

Phil 2705.83 Bergmann, Ernst. Die Satiren des Herrn Maschine. Leipzig, 1913.

Phil 2475.1.56.2 Bergson, Henri. An introduction to metaphysics. London, 1913.

Phil 978.6.88 Besant, Annie. Theosophy and the theosophical society. Adyar, 1913.

Phil 1200.14 Bevan, E.R. Stoics and sceptics. Oxford, 1913.

Phil 8876.72 Beysens, J.T. Ethiek of natuurlijke zedenleer. Leiden, 1913.

Phil 6111.14.3 Binet, A. L'ame et le corps. Paris, 1913.

1913 - cont.

Phil 8581.27   Biroth, H. Tolerance in religion; liberal thoughts of modern thinkers. Rome, 1913.
Phil 4520.8.42   Bjarnason, Agúst. Almenn rökfraeði Reykjavík, 1913.
Phil 2070.82.5   Bloch, Werner. Der Pragmatismus von James und Schiller. Leipzig, 1913.
NEDL Phil 6951.17   Blondel, C. La conscience morbide. Thèse. Paris, 1913.
Phil 5926.1.18   Blondell, Charles. La psycho-physiologie de Gall. Thèse. Paris, 1913.
Phil 6420.12   Bluemel, Charles Sidney. Stammering and cognate defects of speech. N.Y., 1913. 2v.
Phil 332.20A   Bon, F. Von den Begriffen, den Urteilen und der Wahrheit. Leipzig, 1913.
Phil 8876.53   Bonet-Maury, G. L'unité morale des religions. Paris, 1913.
Phil 8626.21   Bonner, H.B. (Mrs.). The Christian hell. London, 1913.
Phil 1135.152   Boreas, Theophilos. Hē archē tēs ōeri metempsykōseōs doxēs tōn Hellēnon philosophōn. Athens, 1913.
Phil 282.13   Boreas, Theophilos. Tis filosofias i ipothesis ke i epitonvion ropi. Athens, 1913.
Phil 630.6   Bosanquet, B. Distinction between mind and its objects. Manchester, 1913.
Phil 575.18.5   Bosanquet, B. Value and destiny of the individual. London, 1913.
Phil 1750.113   Boutroux, E. De l'idée de la loi naturelle. Paris, 1913.
Phil 672.172   Bragdon, C.F. A primer of higher space. Rochester, 1913.
Phil 5241.17.17   Brentano, Franz. La classificazione delle attivitapsichiche. Lanciano, 1913.
Phil 6311.28   Bridger, A.E. Minds in distress. London, 1913.
Phil 5241.71   Britz, Carl August. Eine theoretische und experimentelle Untersuchung über den psychologischen der Klarheit. Diss. Saarlouis, 1913.
Phil 176.77   Brod, Max. Anschauung und Begriff. Leipzig, 1913.
Phil 2070.83   Brugmans, H.J.F.W. Waarheidstheorie van William James. Groningen, 1913.
Phil 3483.18   Buchenau, A. Kants Lehre vom kategorischen Imperativ. Leipzig, 1913.
Phil 315.8   Buckham, J.W. Dualism or duality? n.p., 1913.
Phil 3483.16   Bund, Hugo. Kant als Philosophie des Katholizismus. Berlin, 1913.
Phil 176.80   Burckhardt, Georg E. Was ist Individualismus? Leipzig, 1913.
Phil 8610.913A   Bury, J.B. A history of freedom of thought. N.Y., 1913.
Phil 6111.13.2   Busse, L. Geist und Körper, Seele und Leib. 2. Aufl. Leipzig, 1913.
Phil 9495.138   Cabot, R.C. The Christian approach to social morality. N.Y., 1913.
Phil 177.38   Caldwell, W. Pragmatism and idealism. London, 1913.
Phil 5242.16   Campbell, P.A. The game of mind. N.Y., 1913.
Phil 177.52   Candidus, L. Das Weltstreben. München, 1913.
Phil 8877.32   Carpenter, T.E. The doctrines of life. Boston, 1913.
Phil 7069.13.5   Carrington, Hereward. Death, its causes and phenomena. 2. ed. London, 1913
Phil 2050.178   Casazza, G. Hume, Kant e lo scetticismo filosofico. Roma, 1913.
Phil 8627.3.5   Charles, R.H. A critical history of the doctrine of a future life in Israel. 2. ed. London, 1913.
Phil 8627.11   Chiappelli, A. Amore, morte ed immortalità. Milano, 1913.
Phil 2490.92   Chiappini, T. Les idées politiques d'Auguste Comte. Paris, 1913.
Phil 177.70   Cifarelli, Natale. Abbozzi di filosofia umana. Bari, 1913.
Phil 2520.114   Cochin, D. Descartes. Paris, 1913.
Phil 8877.36   Coffin, J.H. The socialized conscience. Baltimore, 1913.
Phil 8877.63   Cohn, Georg. Etik og sociologi. Kjøbenhavn, 1913.
OL Phil 2475.1.77   Columbia University. Library. A contribution to a bibliography of Henri Bergson. N.Y., 1913.
Phil 2475.1.77   Columbia University. Library. A contribution to a bibliography of Henri Bergson. N.Y., 1913.
Phil 7069.13.10   Colville, William J. Mystic light essays. 1st ed. N.Y., 1913.
Phil 177.19.5   Conti, Augusto. Filosofia elementare. Firenze, 1913.
Phil 665.19   Corey, J.W. The soul; its organ and development. Los Angeles, 1913.
Phil 1702.4   Correnti di filosofia contemporanea, a cura di circolo filosofico di Genova. Genova, 1913.
Phil 177.58   Costa, Alessandro. Filosofia e buddhismo. Torino, 1913.
Phil 4235.3.90   Credaro, L. Alfonso Testa e i primordii del Kantismo in Italia. Catania, 1913.
Phil 4260.85   Croce, B. The philosophy of Giambattista Vico. London, 1913.
Phil 3425.109.10   Croce, B. Saggio sullo Hegel. Bari, 1913.
OL Phil 4080.3.34   Croce, Benedetto. Brevario di estetica. Laterza, 1913.
Phil 177.35.9   Croce, Benedetto. Philosophy of the practical. London, 1913.
Phil 8877.72   Crothers, S.McC. Three lords of destiny. Boston, 1913.
Phil 8582.32   Cunow, Heinrich. Ursprung der Religion und des Gottesglaubens. Berlin, 1913.
Phil 525.15.5   Curtis, Adela M. The new mysticism. 3d ed. London, 1913.
Phil 7069.13.15   Dallas, Helen A. Across the barrier. London, 1913.
Phil 735.5   Dashiell, J.F. Philosophical status of values. N.Y., 1913.
Phil 2520.35.14   Descartes, René. Discours de la méthode. Londres, 1913.
Phil 2520.19.2   Descartes, René. Oeuvres de Descartes. Suppl. Index général. Paris, 1913.
Phil 803.5   Deter, C.J. Abriss der Geschichte der Philosophie. Berlin, 1913.
Phil 8693.7   Deyo, M.L. Spiritual evolution. Binghamton, N.Y., 1913.
Phil 400.32   Dide, Maurice. Les idealistes passionnés. Paris, 1913.
Phil 2050.99   Didier, J. Hume. Paris, 1913.
Phil 178.37   Dingler, Hugo. Die Grundlagen der Naturphilosophie. Leipzig, 1913.
Phil 5520.12.5   Dittrich, O. Die Probleme der Sprachpsychologie. Leipzig, 1913.
Phil 2475.1.119   Dodson, G.R. Bergson and the modern spirit. Boston, 1913.
Phil 1504.11.6   Dreiling, R. Der Konzeptualismus. v.11, pt.6. Münster, 1913.
Phil 1703.2.5   Drews, Arthur. Die Philosophie im zweiten Drittel des 19. Jahrhunderts. Berlin, 1913.
Phil 5043.18A   Driesch, H. Die Logik als Aufgabe. Tübingen, 1913.
Phil 8878.24.10   DuBois, P. L'éducation de soi-même. Paris, 1913.
Phil 3640.171   Duverger, A. Friedrich Nietzsche een levensbeeld. Amsterdam, 1913.
Phil 5545.5.7A   Ebbinghaus, H. Memory. N.Y., 1913.
Phil 7082.54   Einarsson, Guðhundur. Draumvitran Guðhundar Einarssonar. n.p., 1913?
Phil 89.1.5   Eisler, R. Handwörterbuch der Philosophie. Berlin, 1913.

1913 - cont.

Phil 179.16   Erberg, K. Tsel tvorchestva. Moskva, 1913.
Phil 5465.18   Erdmann, Benno. Die Funktionen der Phantasie im wissenschaftlichen Denken. Berlin, 1913.
Phil 179.3.27   Eucken, R. Sinn und Wert des Lebens. 3rd ed. Leipzig, 1913.
Phil 8879.13.10   Eucken, R.C. Ethics and modern thought. N.Y., 1913.
Phil 8879.13.5   Eucken, R.C. Present-day ethics. London, 1913.
Phil 8829.2.10   Eucken, Rudolf. Grundlinien einer neuen Lebensanschauung. 2e Aufl. Leipzig, 1913.
Phil 9495.28   Exner, M.J. The physician's answer. N.Y., 1913.
Phil 180.23.2   Faguet, Emile. Initiation philosophique. Paris, 1913.
Phil 978.29   Farnsworth, E.C. Special teachings from the arcane science. Portland, Maine, 1913.
Phil 8388.114.5   Fauconnet, A. L'esthetique de Schopenhauer. Paris, 1913.
Phil 180.30   Fazio-Allmayer, V. Materia e sensazione. Milano, 1913.
Phil 3210.26.5   Fechner, G.T. Kleine Schriften. 2. Aufl. Leipzig, 1913.
Phil 4756.2.30.5   Fedorov, N.F. Filosofiia obshchago dela. v.2. Vernyi, 1913-
Phil 8500.12   Feigel, F.K. Die französische Neokriticismus. Tübingen, 1913.
Phil 4215.1.80.5   Ferrari, Giuseppe. La mente di G.D. Romagnosi. Milano, 1913.
Phil 6675.10   Feyrer, E.C. Practical psychology. Springfield, Mass., 1913.
Phil 8585.19.5   Fielding-Hall, H. The world soul. N.Y., 1913.
Phil 5245.26   Finnbogason, G. L'intelligence sympathetique. Paris, 1913.
Phil 805.3   Fletcher, O.O. Introduction to philosophy. N.Y., 1913.
Phil 3450.14.80   Flitner, Willy. August Ludwig Hülsen und der Bund der freien Männer. Naumberg, 1913.
Phil 400.28   Fouillée, A. Le mouvement idéaliste et la réaction contre la science positive. 3. ed. Paris, 1913.
Phil 286.5   Fouillée, Alfred. Esquisse d'une interprétation du monde. Paris, 1913.
Phil 3640.117   Fouillée, Alfred E. Nietzsche et l'immoralisme. 3e éd. Paris, 1913.
Phil 6615.10   Fox, Charles Daniel. Psychopathology of hysteria. Boston, 1913.
Phil 8630.5A   Frazer, J.G. Belief in immortality. London, 1913-24. 3v.
Phil 6315.4   Friedländer, A. Der Morphinismus, Kokainismus, Alkoholismus und Saturnismus. Jena, 1913.
Phil 510.146   Friedrich, Gustav. Die Farce des Jahrhunderts oder Des monisten Glück und Ende. Leipzig, 1913.
Phil 3005.5   Friedrichs, A. Klassische Philosophie und Wirtschaftswissenschaft. Gotha, 1913.
Phil 8880.30   Friso, Luigi. Filosofia morale. 3a ed. Milano, 1913.
Phil 5246.21   Gabius, P. Denkökonomie und Energieprinzip. Berlin, 1913.
Phil 960.14.5   Gandhi, V.R. Speeches and writings of the Karma philosophy. Bombay, 1913.
Phil 8595.4.113   Gastrow, Paul. Pfleiderer als Relionsphilosophie. Berlin, 1913.
Phil 9560.7.5   Gay, Antoine. L'honneur, sa place dans la morale. Paris, 1913.
Phil 974.4.35   Gay, S.E. The life works of Mrs. Besant. London, 1913?
Phil 3808.156   Gebhardt, Carl. Schopenhauer-Bilder, Grundlagen einer Ikonographie. Frankfurt, 1913.
Phil 5246.25.3   Gemelli, Agostino. Psicologia e biologia. 3. ed. Firenze, 1913.
Phil 4006.2   Gentile, G. I problemi della scolastica e il pensiero italiano. Bari, 1913.
Phil 3425.209   Gentile, G. La riforma della dialettica Hegeliana. Messina, 1913.
Phil 8696.28   Giesswein, Sándor. Vilagegyetem es a lélek világa. Budapest, 1913.
Phil 9075.19   Gillet, Marie S. L'éducation de la conscience. Paris, 1913.
Phil 2520.116   Gilson, E. La doctrine cartésienne de la liberté et la théologie. Paris, 1913.
Phil 2520.116.5   Gilson, E. La liberté chez Descartes et la théologie. Paris, 1913.
Phil 8407.18   Gleichen-Russwurm, A. Sieg der Freude. Stuttgart, 1913.
Phil 5545.85   Gloy, Hans. Gedächtnis-Ausbildung. Berlin, 1913.
Phil 8881.45   Gomer, A. de. L'obligation morale raisonnée. Paris, 1913.
Phil 181.34   Gourmont, Rémy de. Promenades philosophiques. 3rd series. Paris, 1913. 3v.
Phil 1511.1.5   Grabmann, M. Der Gegenwartswert der geschichtlichen Erforschung der mittelalterlichen Philosophie. Wien, 1913.
Phil 6956.11   Grasset, Joseph. Le psychisme inférieur. 2. éd. Paris, 1913.
Phil 8696.9   Gridley, Albert L. First chapter of Genesis as the rock foundation for science and religion. Boston, 1913.
Phil 8407.24   Griggs, Edward. The philosophy of art. N.Y., 1913.
Phil 3488.5   Gross, Felix. Kant und Wir. Heidelberg, 1913.
Phil 1535.22   Guidi, P.L. Principia philosophica. v.1-2. Florentino, 1913-14.
Phil 2605.1.80   Guyau, Augustin. La philosophie...d'Alfred Fouillée. Paris, 1913.
Phil 5817.6.5   Hachet-Souplet, P. De l'animal a l'enfant. Paris, 1913.
Phil 1707.3   Hadley, A.T. Some influences in modern philosophic thought. New Haven, 1913.
Phil 510.1.8   Haeckel, Ernst. Die wereldraadselen. Baarn, 1913.
X Cg Phil 9495.11   Hall, W.S. Biological, physiological and sociological reproduction, also sexual hygiene. 14. ed. Chicago, 1913.
Phil 6117.14   Harris, D.F. Nerves. London, 1913.
Phil 3808.114.10   Hasse, Heinrich. Schopenhauer Erkenntnislehre. Leipzig, 1913.
Phil 525.15.15   Hasse, Karl P. Das Wesen der Persönlichkeit. Meerane, 1913.
Phil 8632.19   Haynes, E.S.P. The belief in personal immortality. N.Y., 1913.
Phil 3425.41   Hegel, Georg Wilhelm Friedrich. Schriften zur Politik und Rechtsphilosophie. Leipzig, 1913.
Phil 8587.36   Hegenwald, H. Gegenwartsphilosophie und christliche Religion. Leipzig, 1913.
Phil 8587.12   Hehn, Johannes. Wege zum Monotheismus. Würzburg, 1913.
Phil 2038.82   Heider, Maria. Studien über David Hartley. Inaug. Diss. Bergisch Gladbach, 1913.
Phil 5247.40   Heilmann, K. Psychologie und Logik. 15. Aufl. Berlin, 1913.
Phil 270.22   Heim, Gustav. Ursache und Bedingung. Leipzig, 1913.
Phil 1135.23.9   Heinisch, Paul. Griechische Philosophie und altes Testament. Münster, 1913-14. 2v.
Phil 8882.32   Hensel, P. Hauptprobleme der Ethik. 2e aufl. Leipzig, 1913.

Chronological Listing

Phil 1135.115   Herbertz, R. Das Wahreitsproblem in der griechischen Philosophie. Berlin, 1913.

Phil 182.50   Herbertz, Richard. Philosophie und Einzelwissenschaften. Bern, 1913.

Phil 8957.7   Hermanns, W. Über den Begriffs der Mässigung. Inaug. Diss. Aachen, 1913.

Phil 7150.10   Hertog, Mattheus M. De zedelijke waardeering den zelfmoord. 's Gravenhage, 1913.

Phil 482.3   Hessen, Robert. Die Philosophie der Kraft. Stuttgart, 1913.

Phil 3246.160   Hielscher, H. Das Denksystem Fichtes. Berlin, 1913.

Phil 3450.25.10   Hiller, Kurt. Die Weisheit der Langenweile. Leipzig, 1913.

Phil 6315.2.90.2   Hitschmann, Eduard. Freud's Neurosenlehre. 2. Aufl. Leipzig, 1913.

Phil 6315.2.90.5   Hitschmann, Eduard. Freud's theories of the neuroses. N.Y., 1913.

Phil 6315.2.90.6   Hitschmann, Eduard. Freud's theories of the neuroses. N.Y., 1913.

Phil 365.25   Hobhouse, L.T. Development and purpose. London, 1913.

Phil 8882.16.3   Höffding, H. Etik. København, 1913.

Phil 1707.1.8   Höffding, H. Storia della filosofia moderna. Torino, 1913. 2v.

Phil 5047.23   Høffding, Harald. Formel logik, til brug ved forelaesninger. 6. udgave. København, 1913.

Phil 6117.37   Horn, Paul. Über nervöse Erkraukungen nach Eisenbahnunfällen. Bonn, 1913.

Phil 4803.846.80   Horodyski, Władysław. Bronisław Trentowski (1808-1869). Kraków, 1913.

Phil 3827.6   Huan, G. Le Dieu de Spinoza. Arras, 1913.

Phil 7069.13.20   Hude, Fru Anna. The evidence for communication with the dead. London, 1913.

Phil 19.9   Husserl, E. Jahrbuch für Philosophie und phänomenologische Forschung. Halle, 1913. 13v.

Phil 182.67   Husserl, Edmund. Ideen zu einer reinen Phänomenologie und phänomenologischen Philosophie. Halle, 1913.

Phil 5047.11.2   Husserl, Edmund. Logische Untersuchungen. 2. Aufl. v. 1-2, pt. 1-2. Halle, 1913. 3v.

Phil 8697.5.20   Huxley, T.H. Science and Christian tradition; essays. N.Y., 1913.

Phil 9167.4   Hyde, William de W. The quest of the best. N.Y., 1913.

Phil 5248.2   Ingenieros, J. Principios de psicología biológica. Madrid, 1913.

Phil 8400.36   International Congress on Aesthetics, 1st, Berlin, 1913. Bericht. Stuttgart, 1913.

Phil 9495.23   International Congress on School Hygiene, 4th, Buffalo, 1913. Report of sex education sessions. N.Y., 1913.

Phil 3552.272   Jaenicke, Kurt. Das Verhaltnis des Korperlichen zum Geistigen und die Entwicklung des Geistigen bei Leibniz. Cöthen, 1913.

Phil 2070.60   James, William. L'idée de vérité. Paris, 1913.

Phil 6959.4   Jaspers, K. Allgemeine Psychopathologie. Berlin, 1913.

Phil 3640.247   Jesinghaus, W. Nietzsche und Christus. Berlin, 1913.

Phil 575.19   Jevons, F.B. Personality. N.Y., 1913.

Phil 8834.2.10   Jodl, Friedrich. Ethik und Moralpädagogik. Stuttgart, 1913.

Phil 9035.30   Jones, A.J. Character in the making. London, 1913.

Phil 179.3.114   Jones, Abel John. Rudolf Eucken. London, 1913.

Phil 6319.2.6   Jones, Ernest. Papers on psycho-analysis. N.Y., 1913.

Phil 530.15.25   Jovy, Ernest. Une mystique en pays Perthois au XVIIe siècle Marie Darizy de Verget. Vitry-Le-François, 1913.

Phil 400.51   Jünemann, F. Der philosophische Idealismus und das Grundproblem der Erkenntnistheorie. Neisse, 1913. 4v.

Phil 6319.1.70   Jung, C.G. Versuch einer Darstellung der psycho analytischen Theorie. Leipzig, 1913.

Phil 5545.76   Kammel, W. Über die erste Einzelerinnerung. Leipzig, 1913.

Phil 3480.28   Kant, Immanuel. Kleinere Schriften zur Geschichts-Philosophie Ethik und Politik. Leipzig, 1913.

Phil 3480.30.18   Kant, Immanuel. Kritik der reinen Vernunft. 10. Aufl. Leipzig, 1913.

Phil 3480.57.14   Kant, Immanuel. Prolegomena zu einer jeden künftigen Metaphysik. 5. Aufl. Leipzig, 1913.

Phil 3480.71.15   Kant, Immanuel. La religion dans les limites de la raison. Paris, 1913.

Phil 3480.16   Kant, Immanuel. Sämtliche Werke. v.1-9 und Ergänzungsband. 10. Aufl. Leipzig, 1913. 10v.

Phil 3480.26.10   Kant, Immanuel. Theorie und praxis. Leipzig, 1913.

VPhil 8050.92   Kelecsényi, János. Az esztétika alapvet elvei. Budapest, 1913.

Phil 5325.24   Kern, B. Assoziationspsychologie und Erkenntnis. Berlin, 1913.

Phil 3552.127   Kiefl, Franz X. Der europäische Freiheitskampf. Mainz, 1913.

Phil 8590.10   King, Henry C. Religion as life. N.Y., 1913.

Phil 2475.1.85   Kitchin, D.B. Bergson for beginners. London, 1913.

Phil 4655.1.83   Kjellberg, Elis. Mer om och af Pontus Wikner. Upsala, 1913.

Phil 5247.13.25   Klein, Anton. Juan Huarte und der Psychognosis der Renaissance. Inaug. Diss. Bonn, 1913.

Phil 341.6   Kleinpeter, Hans. Der Phänomenalismus. Leipzig, 1913.

Phil 5400.42.5   Koch, Bernhard. Experimentelle Untersuchungen. Leipzig, 1913.

Phil 19.10   Köhler, M.F. Jahrbücher der Philosophie. Berlin, 1913. 3v.

Phil 3552.263   Köhler, Paul. Der Begriff der Repräsentation bei Leibniz. Bern, 1913.

Phil 3492.36   Köhler, W. Kant. Berlin, 1913.

Phil 5050.9   Koppelmann, W. Untersuchungen zur Logik Gegenwart. Berlin, 1913-18. 2v.

Phil 4595.1.31   Krebs, C. Handling og iaggttagelse. København, 1913.

Phil 185.12.8   Külpe, O. Einleitung in die Philosophie. 6. Aufl. Leipzig, 1913.

Phil 3010.2.26   Külpe, O. The philosophy of the present in Germany. N.Y., 1913.

Phil 7150.14   Kürten, O. Statistik des Selbstmordes im Königreich Sachsen. Leipzig, 1913.

Phil 4160.1.40   Labanca, Baldassare. Il mio testamento. Agnone, 1913.

Phil 4160.1.85   Labanca, Baldassare. Ricordi autobiografici. Agnone, 1913.

Phil 4600.1.35   Landquist, John. Essayer. Stockholm, 1913.

Phil 8836.2.11   Lecky, W.E.H. History of European morals. N.Y., 1913. 2v.

Phil 186.76.15   Le Dantec, Félix. Le conflit. 6e ed. Paris, 1913.

Phil 5525.12.5   Leir, Giulio A. Il comico. Genova, 1913.

Phil 530.15.5   Le Jonvello, H. Une mystique bretonne aux XVIIe siècle. Paris, 1913.

Phil 1850.107   Lemaire, Paul. François Bacon. Paris, 1913.

Phil 2475.1.115   LeRoy, E. The new philosophy of Henri Bergson. N.Y., 1913.

Phil 8886.29.5   Lévy-Bruhl, L. La morale et la science des moeurs. 5. ed. Paris, 1913.

Phil 2490.88.3   Lévy-Bruhl, L. La philosophie d'Auguste Comte. 3. éd. Paris, 1913.

Phil 5460.2   Leyendecker, Herbert. Zur Phänomenologie der Täuschungen. Inaug. Diss. Halle, 1913.

Phil 5460.2.3   Leyendecker, Herbert. Zur Phänomenologie der Täuschungen. 1. Teil. Halle, 1913.

Phil 4600.4.40   Lidforss, Bengt. Polemiska inlägg. Malmö, 1913.

Phil 8886.32   Limentani, Ludovico. I presupposti formali...etica. Genova, 1913.

Phil 510.13.5   Lipsius, Friedrich R. Einheit der Erkenntnis und Einheit des Seins. Leipzig, 1913.

Phil 2115.49   Locke, J. Versuch über den menschlichen Verstand. Leipzig, 1913. 2v.

Phil 2475.1.135   Lovejoy, A.O. Bergson and romantic evolutionism. Berkeley, 1913.

Phil 186.50   Ludowici, A. Das genetische Prinzip. München, 1913.

Phil 8412.28   Lundegårdh, H. Ludvig sju dialoger om idé. Stockholm, 1913.

Phil 5051.6   Luquet, G.H. Essai d'une logique systematique et simplifiée. Lille, 1913.

Phil 5761.8   Lutosławski, W. Volenté et liberté! Paris, 1913.

Phil 8667.15   McCabe, J. The existence of God. London, 1913.

Phil 187.80   Maggiore, G. L'unita del mondo nel sistema del pensiero. Palermo, 1913.

Phil 5627.27.5   Mainage, T. Introduction à la psychologie des convertis. Paris, 1913.

Phil 5252.86   Major, David R. The elements of psychology. Columbus, 1913.

Phil 5252.34   Marbe, K. Grundzüge der forensischen Psychologie. München, 1913.

Phil 4170.6.30   Marchesini, G. La dottrina positiva delle idealità. Roma, 1913.

Phil 9245.28   Marden, Orison S. The joys of living. N.Y., 1913.

Phil 525.37   Maréchal, J. Dalla percezione sensible all'intuizione mistica. Firenze, 1913.

Phil 400.28.5   Marischini, G. La dottrina positiva delle idealità. Roma, 1913.

Phil 5762.5   Martin, E. Psychologie de la volonté. Paris, 1913.

Phil 4170.5.30   Maturi, S. Introduzione alla filosofia. Bari, 1913.

Phil 5643.84   Maxfield, F.N. An experiment in linear space perception. Princeton, 1913.

Phil 3246.215   Mayer, Otto. Fichte über das Volk. Leipzig, 1913.

Phil 8592.27   Mead, G.R.S. Quests old and new. London, 1913.

Phil 8887.41   Meakin, J.P. A man worth while. Rahway, N.J., 1913.

Phil 187.28.25   Mechnikov, I.I. Sorok let iskaniia ratsional'nago mirovozzreniia. Moskva, 1913.

Phil 343.5.19   Meinong, A. Gesammelte Abhandlungen. Leipzig, 1913. 2v.

X Cg   Phil 3640.90.3   Mencken, Henry. Philosophy of Friedrich Nietzsche. 3d ed. Boston, 1913.

Phil 3850.6.81   Merkel, Franz R. Der Naturphilosoph Gotthilf Heinrich Schubert und die deutsche Romantik. München, 1913.

Phil 1712.5   Messer, A. Geschichte der Philosophie. Leipzig, 1913.

Phil 1712.5.5   Messer, A. Die Philosophie der Gegenwart. 3e Aufl. Leipzig, 1913.

Phil 5545.49.3A   Meumann, E. The psychology of learning. N.Y., 1913.

Phil 8837.9   Meyer, R.M. Le mouvement moral vers 1840. Paris, 1913.

Phil 3640.127   Meyer, Richard M. Nietzsche. München, 1913.

Phil 5252.26   Meyer, Semi. Probleme der Entwicklung des Geistes. Leipzig, 1913.

Phil 8413.24   Moerth, L. Was ist Schön? Eine ästhetische Studie. München, 1913?

Phil 3494.12.10   Monzel, Alois. Die Lehre vom inneren Sinn bei Kant. Bonn, 1913.

Phil 7069.13.30   Moore, William U. The voices. London, 1913.

Phil 630.6.5   Müller, Aloys. Wahrheit und Wirklichkeit: Untersuchungen zum realistischen Wahrheitsproblem. Bonn, 1913.

Phil 8612.13   Müller, J. Vom Leben und Sterben. 3. Aufl. München, 1913.

Phil 2150.6.30   Münsterberg, H. American patriotism and other social studies. N.Y., 1913.

Phil 5850.278.7   Münsterberg, H. Psychology and industrial efficiency. Boston, 1913.

Phil 5252.12.29   Münsterberg, H. Social studies of today. London, 1913.

Phil 187.38   Muller, J.B. De kennisleer van het Anglo-Amerikanisch pragmatisme. 's-Gravenhage, 1913.

Phil 8887.39   Murdoch, J.G. Economics as the basis of living ethics. Troy, 1913.

Phil 5545.55   Myers, G.C. Study in incidental memory. N.Y., 1913.

Phil 8837.5   Myers, P.V. History as past ethics. Boston, 1913.

Phil 6323.2   Naegeli, Otto. Über den Einfluss von Rechtsansprüchen bei Neurosen. Leipzig, 1913.

Phil 2775.1.80   Naville, E. Ernest Naville, sa vie et sa pensée. Genève, 1913-17. 2v.

Phil 188.10   Neilson, W.A. Lectures on the five-foot shelf of books. 4. Philosophy. N.Y., 1913.

Phil 8610.913.25   The new New England primer. Newport, Vt., 1913.

Phil 7069.13.32   Nielsson, H. Hví slaer pú mig? v.1-2. Reykjavik, 1913.

Phil 3640.15.2   Nietzsche, Friedrich. Complete works. v.11,16. London, 1913. 2v.

Phil 7060.92.19   O'Donnell, Elliot. Animal ghosts. London, 1913.

Phil 5545.63.5   Offner, Max. Das Gedächtnis. Berlin, 1913.

Phil 6964.1.6   Oppenheim, H. Lehrbuch der Nervenkrankheiten. 6. Aufl. Berlin, 1913. 2v.

Phil 5254.6   Orr, T.V. Applied mental efficiency. Chicago, 1913.

Htn   Phil 7075.6.7*   Orsi, Alberto. Lussuria e castità. Milano, 1913.

Phil 510.8   Ostwald, W. Monism as the goal of civilization. Hamburg, 1913.

Phil 735.6   Ostwald, W. Die Philosophie der Werte. Leipzig, 1913.

Phil 7060.131   Osty, Eugène. Lucidité et intuition. Paris, 1913.

Phil 400.50   Ovink, B.J.H. Het kritisch idealisme. Utrecht, 1913.

Phil 190.20.3   Papini, Giovanni. Sul pragmatismo. Milano, 1913.

Phil 5825.3   Parmelee, M. The science of human behavior. N.Y., 1913.

Phil 2805.30.26   Pascal, Blaise. Provinciales. 9. éd. Paris, 1913.

Phil 4200.4.30   Pastore, A. Il pensiero puro. Milano, 1913.

Phil 5255.2.2   Paulhan, F. L'activité mentale. 2. éd. Paris, 1913.

Phil 9075.26   Pauly, Karl. Zur Theorie des Gewissens. Inaug. Diss. Greifswald, 1913.

Chronological Listing

1913 - cont.

Phil 6750.16 — Pennsylvania. Commission on Segregation, Care and Treatment of the Feebleminded and Epileptic Persons. Report of the commission. Harrisburg, 1913.

Phil 8595.18 — Perovsky-Petrovo, Solovovo. Le sentiment religieux, base logique de la morale? Paris, 1913.

Phil 6325.13 — Peters, W. Die Beziehungen der Psychologie zur Medizin. Würzburg, 1913.

Phil 3890.1.85 — Petersen, Peter. Die Philosophie Friedrich Adolf Trendelenburgs. Hamburg, 1913.

Phil 3497.11 — Petras, Otto. Der Begriff des Bösen in Kants Kritizismus. Leipzig, 1913.

Phil 346.12 — Phalén, Adolf. Beiträge zur Klärung des Begriffs. Uppsala, 1913.

Phil 346.3 — Philip, A. The dynamic foundation of knowledge. London, 1913.

Phil 575.13.2 — Piat, C. La personne humaine. 2e éd. Paris, 1913.

Phil 1520.2.5 — Picavet, F. Essais sur l'histoire générale et comparée des theologies et des philosophies médiévales. Paris, 1913.

Phil 8595.14 — Piercy, B.H. Facts and fancies. London, 1913.

Phil 296.6.2 — Poincaré, H. Leçons sur les hypotheses cosmogoniques. 2. ed. Paris, 1913.

Phil 8705.12 — Pollach, Friedrich. Gesetz von der Erhaltung der Energie und der christliche Glaube. Fulda, 1913.

Phil 5325.10.5 — Popp, Walter. Kritische Bemerkungen zur Associationstheorie. Teil 1. Leipzig, 1913.

Phil 978.63 — Powell, F.G.M. Studies in the lesser mysteries. London, 1913.

Phil 4769.1.110 — Radlov, E.L. Vladimir Solov'ev; zhizn' i uchenie. Sankt Peterburg, 1913.

Phil 102.8.2 — Radlov, Ernest L. Filosofskii slovar'. Izd. 2. Moskva, 1913.

Phil 5635.14 — Rahn, Carl. Relation of sensation to other categories in contemporary psychology. Princeton, 1913.

Phil 5645.14 — Rand, G. Factor...sensitivity of retina to color. Princeton, 1913.

Phil 6327.4 — Rank, Otto. Die Bedeutung der Psychoanalyse. Wiesbaden, 1913.

Phil 8892.13.5 — Rashdall, Hastings. Ethics. London, 1913.

Phil 2070.82 — Reverdin, H. La notion d'expérience d'après William James. Genève, 1913.

Phil 2855.2.81 — Ribot, Théodule. Théodule Ribot; choix de textes. Paris, 1913.

Phil 1522.4 — Richard, J. Introduction à l'étude et à l'enseignement de la scolastique. Paris, 1913.

Phil 3837.7 — Richter, G.T. Spinozas philosophische Terminologie. Leipzig, 1913.

Phil 192.37.3 — Richter, Raoul. Einführung in die Philosophie. 3e Aufl. Leipzig, 1913.

Phil 192.37.5 — Richter, Raoul. Essays. Leipzig, 1913.

Phil 1717.5.4 — Riehl, Alois. Zur Einführung in die Philosophie der Gegenwart. 4. Aufl. Leipzig, 1913.

Phil 4368.1.80 — Rigau, P. La obra del filósofo español Diego Ruiz. Paris, 1913.

Phil 1122.3.25 — Ritter, Heinrich. Historia philosophiae graecae. 9th ed. Gotha, 1913.

Phil 3837.11 — Robinson, L. Metafizika Spinozy. Sankt Peterburg, 1913.

Phil 6967.11.15 — Rogues de Fursac, J. Manual of psychiatry. 3. ed. N.Y., 1913.

Phil 1504.11.5 — Rohner, A. Das Schöpfungsproblem bei Moses Maimonides. v.11, pt.5. Münster, 1913.

Phil 2250.43.5 — Royce, Josiah. Il mondo e l'individuo. Bari, 1913-14. 4v.

Phil 8597.20A — Royce, Josiah. The problem of Christianity. N.Y., 1913. 2v.

Phil 2855.1.31 — Royer-Tollard. Les fragments philosophiques. Paris, 1913.

Phil 5062.18 — Ruge, Arnold. Logic. London, 1913.

Phil 3499.9 — Ruisch, Arnold. Freiheit Unstirblichkeit und Gott. Leipzig, 1913.

Phil 5627.27.15 — Runze, George. Essays zur Religionspsychologie. Berlin, 1913.

Phil 192.28.8 — Russell, B. Scientific method in philosophy. Oxford, 1913.

Phil 192.29A — Russell, J.E. A first course in philosophy. N.Y., 1913.

Phil 2515.2.81 — Sabrié, J.B. De l'humanisme au rationalisme. Pierre Charron. Paris, 1913.

Phil 299.10 — Sagaret, Jules. Le système du monde des chaldéens à Newton. 2 éd. Paris, 1913.

Phil 8598.45.5 — Sanders, Frederic W. A reasonable religion (Religio doctoris). Boston, 1913?

Phil 8598.45 — Sanders, Frederic W. Religio doctoris; meditations upon life and thought. Boston, 1913.

Phil 193.49.5 — Santayana, G. Winds of doctrine. London, 1913.

Phil 5415.7.5 — Scheler, Max. Zur Phänomenologie und Theorie der Sympathiegefühle. Halle, 1913.

Phil 3800.722 — Schelling, F.W.J. von. Briefwechsel mit Niethammer von seiner Berufung nach Jena. Leipzig, 1913.

Phil 3800.61A — Schelling, F.W.J. von. Gedichte und poetische Übersetzungen. Leipzig, 1913.

Phil 5258.61.3 — Schilling, Gustav, of Giessen. Lehrbuch der Psychologie. Langensalza, 1913.

Phil 5258.65 — Schindler, Ferdinand. Lehrbuch der Psychologie. Troppau, 1913.

Phil 3808.75 — Schopenhauer, Arthur. Über Schriftstellerei und Stil. Leipzig, 1913.

Phil 4580.113 — Schott, Georg. Harald Høffding, als Religionsphilosoph. München, 1913.

Phil 4580.113.3 — Schott, Georg. Harald Høffding als Religionsphilosoph. Inaug. Diss. München, 1913.

Phil 5627.40 — Schroeder, Theodore. Erotogenesis of religion. St. Louis, 1913.

Phil 5258.42 — Schulz, B. Psychologische Wanderungen auf Seitenwegen. Jena, 1913.

Phil 2630.2.127 — Schumm, Felix. Jean Marie Guyaus Religionsphilosophie. Tübingen, 1913.

Phil 8643.9 — Schwarz, H. Der Gottesgedanke in der Geschichte der Philosophie. Heidelberg, 1913.

Phil 665.49 — Scofield, A. Insights and heresies. Boston, 1913.

Phil 193.75 — Sedgwick, W. Man and his future. Philadelphia, 1913.

Phil 2475.1.89 — Segoud, J. L'intuition Bergsonienne. Paris, 1913.

Phil 525.8.5 — Seillière, E. Mysticisme et domination. Paris, 1913.

Phil 525.15 — Seisdedos Sanz, J. Principios fundamentales de la mistica. v.1-2,3. Madrid, 1913. 2v.

Phil 3805.155 — Selbie, W.B. Schleiermacher. London, 1913.

Phil 5258.59 — Selz, Otto. Über die Gesetze des geordneten Denkverlaufs. Stuttgart, 1913. 2v.

Phil 3500.21.15 — Sentroul, C. Kant et Aristote. 2. éd. Louvain, 1913.

1913 - cont.

Phil 5400.49 — Sergio, Antonio. Da natureza da affecção. Rio de Janeiro, 1913.

Phil 8893.55.2 — Seu, Mohit C. The elements of moral philosophy. 2. ed. London, 1913.

Phil 5228.3 — Sganzini, Carlo. Die Fortschritte der Völkerpsychologie. Bern, 1913.

Phil 193.64 — Shaw, C.G. The ego and its place in the world. N.Y., 1913.

Phil 8598.31 — Shotwell, James T. The religious revolution of to-day. Boston, 1913.

Phil 5525.12 — Sidis, B. The psychology of laughter. N.Y., 1913.

Phil 3018.6 — Siegel, C. Geschichte der deutschen Naturphilosophie. Leipzig, 1913.

Phil 3805.155.5 — Siegmund-Schultze, F. Schleiermachers Psychologie. Tübingen, 1913.

Phil 9045.21 — Sighele, Seipio. Morale privata e morale politica. Milano, 1913.

Phil 3500.20.3 — Simmel, G. Kant: sechzehn Vorlesungen. 3. Aufl. München, 1913.

Phil 6328.1 — Sjobring, H. Den individual psykologiska frage ställungen inom psykistrien. Uppsala, 1913.

Phil 8968.16 — Smith, G.B. Social idealism and the changing theology. N.Y., 1913.

Phil 5828.13 — Söderhjelm, H. Instinkterna och det mänskliga känslolivet. Helsingfors, 1913.

Phil 5645.19 — Souriau, Paul. L'esthétique de la lumière. Paris, 1913.

Phil 3640.180 — Spindler, Josef. Nietzsches Persönlichkeit und Lehre. Stuttgart, 1913.

Phil 3819.36.30 — Spinoza, Benedictus de. L'etica. Milano, 1913.

Phil 3819.10.9.3 — Spinoza, Benedictus de. Opera quotquot reperta sunt. 3. ed. v.1-4. Hagae, 1913-14. 2v.

Phil 349.13.2 — Stadler, A. Die Grundbegriffe der Erkenntnis. Leipzig, 1913.

Phil 2270.118.2 — Stadler, August. Herbert Spencer. Spencers Ethik. Leipzig, 1913.

Phil 3805.155.7 — Stammer, Martin O. Schleiermachers Asthetizismus in Theorie und Praxis wahrend der Jahre 1796 bis 1802. Leipzig, 1913.

Phil 8598.55.2 — Stange, Carl. Christentum und moderne Weltanschauung. Leipzig, 1913-14. 2v.

Phil 7069.13.40 — Station, Horace C. Telepathy of the celestial world. N.Y., 1913.

Phil 3195.6.81 — Stein, Arthur. Der Begriff des Geistes bei Dilthey. Bern, 1913.

Phil 6328.2.35 — Stekel, Wilhelm. Das liebe Ich. Berlin, 1913.

Phil 3500.24 — Stériad, A. L'interprétation de la doctrine de Kant. Paris, 1913.

Phil 193.37.2 — Stevens, Samuel Eugene. Science and superstition. N.Y., 1913.

Phil 5710.6 — Stevenson, J.G. Religion and temperament. London, 1913.

Phil 6060.13 — Stoll, Jakob. Zur Psychologie der Schreibfehler. Zürich, 1913.

Phil 5258.27.9 — Stout, G.F. A manual of psychology. 3. ed. London, 1913.

Phil 5465.20 — Strang, W. Imagination and fancy. London, 1913.

Phil 960.27 — Suali, Luigi. Introduzione allo studio della filosofia indiania. Pavia, 1913.

Phil 5325.10 — Sutherland, A.H. Critique of word association reactions; an experimental study. Menasha, Wisc., 1913.

Phil 3915.156 — Svensson, P.I.K. Wundts etik, framställning och granskning. Lund, 1913.

Phil 9220.3A — Taylor, Jeremy. A discourse of friendship. Cedar Rapids, 1913.

Phil 8709.6 — Temple, William. The faith and modern thought. London, 1913.

Phil 5259.6.8 — Tetens, J.N. Über die allgemeine speculativische Philosophie. Berlin, 1913.

Phil 8894.11.5 — Thilly, F. Introduction to ethics. N.Y., 1913.

Phil 2270.130 — Thouverez, Emile. Herbert Spencer. Paris, 1913.

Phil 5259.5.25 — Titchener, E.B. Elementos de psicología. Paris, 1913.

Phil 2477.6.80 — Tonquedec, J. de. Immanence: essai critique sur la doctrine de M. Maurice Blondel. 2e éd. Paris, 1913.

Phil 7082.34 — Traugott, Richard. Der Traum. Würzburg, 1913.

Phil 1524.3 — Trikál, Josef. Benezetö a közepkori keresztény hölcselet tortenelmehe. Budapest, 1913.

Phil 8701.3.4 — Troels Lund, Troels Frederik. Himmelsbild und Weltanschauung. 4. Aufl. Leipzig, 1913.

Phil 8894.14 — Troufleau, L. Morale pratique. 3e éd. Paris, 1913.

Phil 4769.1.105 — Truhetskoï, E.N. Mirosozertsanie Vl.C. Solov'eva. v.1-2. Moskva, 1913.

Phil 8709.4 — Tucker, G.M. A layman's apology. Boston, 1913.

Phil 6689.3.5 — Tuckey, C.L. Treatment by hypnotism and suggestion. 6. ed. London, 1913.

Phil 4065.93 — Turnbull, C. Life and teachings of Giordano Bruno, 1548-1600. San Diego, 1913.

Phil 525.7.10 — Underhill, Evelyn. The mystic way. London, 1913.

Phil 735.11 — Valli, Luigi. Il valore supremo. Genova, 1913.

Phil 4650.1.70 — Vannérus, Allen. Den empiriska naturuppfattningen. 2. ed. Stockholm, 1913.

Phil 8896.6 — Varona, E.J. Conferencias sobre el fundamento de la moral. N.Y., 1913.

Phil 196.16 — Verweyen, J.M. Philosophie des Möglichen. Leipzig, 1913.

Phil 510.7 — Wakeman, T.B. Addresses...at and in reference to the 1st Monist congress. Cos Cob, 1913.

Phil 8897.34 — Wallace, A.R. Social environment and moral progress. N.Y., 1913.

Phil 6132.7.15 — Walton, G.L. Calm yourself. Boston, 1913.

Phil 1722.4.5 — Wardwell, R.J. Contemporary philosophy. London, 1913.

Phil 5262.8.5 — Watt, H.J. Psychology. A lecture. London, 1913.

Phil 6132.9 — Weaver, E.E. Mind and health. N.Y., 1913.

Phil 5640.15 — Wells, G.R. Influence of stimulus...duration on reaction time. Princeton, 1913.

Phil 8423.18 — Wembridge, Eleanor Harris Rowland. The significance of art. Boston, 1913.

Phil 8897.35 — Wentscher, E. Grundzüge der Ethik. Leipzig, 1913.

Phil 3565.89 — Wentscher, M. Hermann Lotze. Heidelberg, 1913.

Phil 3504.15 — Wesselsky, Anton. Forberg und Kant. Leipzig, 1913.

Phil 8610.913.20 — Whyte, A.G. The religion of the open mind. London, 1913.

Phil 8602.26 — Wilson, D.A. The faith of all sensible people. London, 1913.

Phil 5062.20 — Windelband, W. Die Prinzipien der Logik. Tübingen, 1913.

Phil 3504.13 — Witter, C.E. Pragmatic elements in Kant's philosophy. Chicago, 1913.

Phil 8897.56 — Wright, Henry W. Self realization. N.Y., 1913.

Phil 8660.8.5 — Wüchner, J.G. Frohschammers Stellung zum Theismus. Paderborn, 1913.

1913 - cont.

Phil 1527.1.8   Wulf, M. de. Geschichte der mittelalterlichen Philosophie. Tübingen, 1913.

Phil 3915.59.3   Wundt, Wilhelm. Elemente der Völkerpsychologie. 2. Aufl. Leipzig, 1913.

Phil 3915.60   Wundt, Wilhelm. Die Psychologie im Kampf ums Dasein. Leipzig, 1913.

Phil 356.1.5   Ziehen, T. Erkenntnistheorie...Grundlage. Jena, 1913.

Phil 525.24   Zielinski, C. Der Begriff der Mystik. Jena, 1913.

1914

Phil 5722.5   Abramowski, Édouard. Le subconscient normal. Paris, 1914.

Phil 6310.1.40   Adler, A. Heilen und Bilden. München, 1914.

Phil 7060.147   Alexandre Bisson, J. Les phénomènes dits de matérialisation. Paris, 1914.

Phil 400.29.5   Aliotta, A. The idealistic reaction against science. London, 1914.

Phil 3808.115   Anspach, F.W. Schopenhauer und Chamfort. Göttingen, 1914.

Phil 1020.9.5   Asian Palacios, M. Abenmasarra y su escuela. Madrid, 1914.

Phil 365.9   Auvard, Alfred. L'evoluisme. Paris, 1914.

Phil 1504.13.6   Baeumker, F. Das Inevitable des Honorius Augustodunensis. v.13, pt.6. Münster, 1914.

Phil 282.7   Becher, Erich. Naturphilosophie. Leipzig, 1914.

Phil 1504.17   Beemelmans, F. Zeit und Ewigkeit nach Thomas von Aquino. v.17, pt.1. Münster, 1914.

Phil 3808.153   Beer, Margrieta. Schopenhauer. London, 1914.

Phil 960.30   Belloni-Filippi, F. I maggiori sistemi filosofici indiani. Milano, 1914.

Phil 2475.1.192.5   Benda, Julien. Une philosophie pathétique. Paris, 1914.

Phil 2475.1.191   Benda, Julien. Sur le succès du Bergsonisme. Paris, 1914.

Phil 1106.3.2A   Benn, A.W. The Greek philosophers. London, 1914.

Phil 6990.3.19   Benson, R.H. Lourdes. St. Louis, 1914.

Phil 8050.36   Bergmann, E. Geschichte der Asthetik und Kunstphilosophie. Leipzig, 1914.

NEDL Phil 176.51.20   Bergson, H. Intuition og rerdensanskueke oversat af Knud Terlov. Kobenhavn, 1914.

NEDL Phil 176.51.25   Bergson, H. Den skabende udvikling. Kobenhavn, 1914.

Phil 2475.1.66.5   Bergson, Henri. Dreams. N.Y., 1914.

Htn Phil 1870.95.2*   Berkeley, G. Berkeley and Percival. Cambridge, 1914.

Phil 1870.95   Berkeley, G. Berkeley and Percival. Cambridge, 1914.

Phil 3915.154   Bernstein, Xenja. Die Kunst nach Wilhelm Wundt. Nürnberg, 1914.

Phil 3850.24.90   Beuschlein, K. Die Möglichkeit der Gotteserkenntnis in der Philosophie Gideon Spickers. Diss. Würzburg, 1914.

Phil 5241.60   Bjerre, Poul. Studier i själstäkekonst. Stockholm 1914.

Phil 176.59   Blair, D. The master-key. Wimbledon, 1914.

Phil 179.3.99   Booth, Meyrick. Rudolf Eucken; his philosophy. London, 1914.

Phil 5041.16.9   Bosanquet, B. The essentials of logic. London, 1914.

Phil 4065.101.2   Boulting, William. Giordano Bruno. London, 1914.

Phil 2477.1.44   Boutroux, Émile. Natural law in science and philosophy. London, 1914.

Phil 1885.35   Bradley, Francis H. Essays on truth and reality. Oxford, 1914.

Phil 3640.107.5   Brandes, G. Friedrich Nietzsche. London, 1914.

Phil 2630.1.84   Braun, Ludwig L. Gratrys Theorie der religiosen Erkenntnis. Strassburg, 1914.

Phil 5241.78   Breitwieser, Joseph V. Psychological experiments. Colorado Springs, 1914.

Phil 8581.28   Brent, C.H. Presence. N.Y., 1914.

Phil 6311.1.2   Brill, A.A. Psychanalysis; its theories. Philadelphia, 1914.

Phil 630.12A   Broad, Charles D. Perception, physics and reality. Cambridge, 1914.

Phil 5435.7   Brown, Warner. Habit interference in sorting cards. Berkeley, 1914.

Phil 5640.33   Brown, Warner. The judgment of very weak sensory stimuli. Berkeley, 1914.

Phil 7060.68.5   Bruce, Henry Addington Bayley. Adventurings in the psychical. Boston, 1914.

Phil 5811.11   Brun, Rudolf. Die Raumorientierung der Ameisen. Jena, 1914.

Phil 3483.11   Brunswig, A. Das Grundproblem Kants. Leipzig, 1914.

Phil 3483.18.5   Buchenau, A. Grundprobleme der Kritik der reinen Vernunft. Leipzig, 1914.

Phil 1106.8   Burnet, J. Greek philosophy. pt. 1. London, 1914.

Phil 5627.31   Burr, Anna Robeson. Religious confessions and confessants. Boston, 1914.

Phil 8827.5   Cabot, R.C. What men live by. Boston, 1914.

Phil 8877.65.8   Cabot, Richard C. What men live by. Boston, 1914.

Phil 5242.13.12   Calkins, M.W. A first book in psychology. 4. ed. N.Y., 1914.

Phil 6112.2.11   Call, A.P. How to live quietly. Boston, 1914.

Phil 3822.2.10   Camerer, T. Die Lehre Spinozas. 2. Aufl. Stuttgart, 1914.

Phil 8403.13.5   Canitt, Edgar. The theory of beauty. London, 1914.

Phil 4210.138   Capone-Braga, G. Saggio su Rosmini il mondo delle idee. Milano, 1914.

Phil 8582.34   Carabellese, P. L'essere e il problema religioso. Bari, 1914.

Phil 4075.79.15   Cardano, Girolamo. Des Girolamo Cardano von Mailand (Buergers von Bologna) eigene Lebenbeschreibung. Jena, 1914.

Phil 6834.2   Carpenter, Edward. Intermediate types among primitive folk. N.Y., 1914.

Phil 2475.1.185   Carr, Herbert W. The Philosophy of change. London, 1914.

Phil 7069.14.5   Carrington, Hereward. The problems of psychical research. London, 1914.

Phil 5242.25   Cartault, A. L'intellectuel. Paris, 1914.

Phil 3640.120A   Carus, Paul. Nietzsche. Chicago, 1914.

Phil 1870.94   Cassirer, E. Berkeleys System. Giessen, 1914.

Phil 8877.50.5   Cathrein, Victor. Die Einheit des sittlichen Bewusstseins der Menschheit. Freiburg, 1914. 3v.

Phil 177.47   Cellarier, Felix. La métaphysique et sa méthode. Paris, 1914.

Phil 3484.6.5   Chamberlain, H.S. Immanuel Kant. London, 1914. 2v.

Phil 177.42   Christiansen, H. MeineLösung der Welträtsel. Wiesbaden, 1914.

Phil 5627.26   Coe, George A. The spiritual life; studies in the science of religion. Chicago, 1914.

Phil 177.91   Coffey, Peter. Ontology; or The theory of being. London, 1914.

Phil 177.43   Cohn, Jonas. DerSinn der gegenwärtigen Kultur. Leipzig, 1914.

Phil 7069.14.10   Colville, William J. Light and colors. N.Y., 1914.

1914 - cont.

Phil 7069.14.20   Comstock, William C. Will higher of God and free will of life. Boston, 1914.

Phil 2490.76   Comte, Auguste. Six lettres inédites à Romeo Pouzin. Paris, 1914.

Phil 7069.14.30   Cooper, William E. Where two worlds meet. London, 1914

Phil 177.54   Corbeil, S. La normalienne en philosophie. Montreal, 1914.

Phil 6312.1.5   Coriat, I.H. Abnormal psychology. 2. ed. N.Y., 1914.

Phil 333.9   Cosalini, Alessandro. Studi filosofici sulla cognizione. Roma, 1914.

Phil 4260.102   Cotugno, R. La sorte di G.B. Vico e le polemiche...della fine del XVII alla metà del XVIII secolo. Bari, 1914.

Phil 5042.8.5A   Couturat, L. The algebra of logic. Chicago, 1914.

Phil 5647.5   Cowan, Edwina Abbott. The effect of adaptation on the temperature difference linien. Thesis. Princeton, N.J. 1914.

Phil 5242.14.12   Crane, A.M. Right and wrong thinking. Boston, 1914.

Phil 4080.3.34.5   Croce, Benedetto. Brevario de estetica. Lisboa, 1914.

Phil 8877.34   Croce, Benedetto. Cultura e vita morale. Bari, 1914.

Phil 8877.39   Culp, C.J. The ethical ideal of renunciation. Thesis. N.Y., 1914.

Phil 2648.91   Cushing, M.P. Baron d'Holbach. N.Y., 1914.

Phil 5243.19   Damm, Hermann. Korrelative Beziehungen zwischen Elementarenvergleichsleistungen. Inaug. Diss. Leipzig, 1914.

Phil 7054.118   Danmar, William. Modern nirvanaism. N.Y., 1914.

Phil 7069.14.40   D'Aute-Hooper, T. Spirit-psychometry and trance communications by unseen agencies. London, 1914.

Phil 8583.20   Denkmann, D.K. Metaphysik der Geschichte. Leipzig, 191

Phil 2520.39.20   Descartes, René. I principii della filosofia. Bari, 1914.

Phil 5635.15   Desvaux, Antoine. Introduction à une étude du courant de chaleur. Thèse. Paris, 1914.

Phil 5043.20   Dinwiddie, William. Essentials of logic. N.Y., 1914.

Phil 1135.94   Doerfler, Josef. Vom mythos zum logos. Freistadt, 1914.

Phil 5625.75.80   Dontchef-Dezeuze, M. L'image et les réflexes conditionnels dans les travaux de Pavlov. Paris, 1914.

Phil 178.12.43   Dresser, H.W. The religion of the spirit in modern life. N.Y., 1914.

Phil 745.6A   Driesch, H. The history and theory of vitalism. London, 1914.

Phil 745.7.9A   Driesch, H. The problem of individuality. London, 1914.

Phil 745.7.15   Driesch, H. Über der grundsätzliche Unmöglichkeit einer "Vereinigung" von universeller Teleologie und Mechanism Heidelberg, 1914.

Phil 5243.16   Dromard, Gabriel. Les mensonges de la vie intérieure. 2e éd. Paris, 1914.

Phil 5753.5   Duchatel, Edmond. Les miracles de la volonté. Paris, 1914.

Phil 284.4.2   Duhem, P. La theorie physique, son objet, sa structure. 2. éd. Paris, 1914.

Phil 6113.11   Dunlap, Knight. An outline of psychobiology. Baltimore, 1914.

Phil 179.14F   Eck, Samuel. Gedanke und Persönlichkeit. Giessen, 1914.

Phil 8890.30   Ecole des Hautes Études Sociales. Morale religieuse et morale laïque. Paris, 1914.

Phil 3585.10.97   Ehlen, Nikolaus. Die ErkenntnisDer Aussenwelt nach Theodor Lipps. Inaug. Diss. Münster, 1914.

Phil 5244.8   Eisenmeier, J. Die Psychologie und ihre Zentralestellung in der Philosophie. Halle, 1914.

Phil 8735.8   Eisler, Rudolf. Der Zweck; seine Bedeutung für Natur und Geist. Berlin, 1914.

Phil 510.124   Erdmann, Benno. Über den modernen Monismus. Berlin, 19

Phil 7060.135   Etchart, Carlos R. Psychologie énergétique. Paris, 1914.

Phil 3195.2.125   Ettlinger, Max. Die Asthetik Martin Deutingers. Kempten, 1914.

Phil 179.3.15   Eucken, R. Colleted essays. London, 1914.

Phil 179.3.41   Eucken, R. Knowledge and life. N.Y., 1914.

Phil 179.3.45   Eucken, R. Zur Sammlung der Geistert. Leipzig, 1914.

Phil 180.23   Faguet, Emile. Initiation into philosophy. N.Y., 1914.

X Cg   Phil 2475.1.145   Farges, Albert. Philosophie de M. Bergson. 2e ed. Paris, 1914.

Phil 978.29.5   Farnsworth, E.C. The heart of things. Portland, Maine, 1914.

Phil 3210.67.9   Fechner, G.T. On life after death. Chicago, 1914.

Phil 3791.124   Festschrift für Alois Riehl. Halle, 1914.

Phil 3246.50.9   Fichte, Johann Gottlieb. Första inledningen till vetenshapsläran. Stockholm, 1914.

Phil 3246.36   Fichte, Johann Gottlieb. Ideen über Gott und Unsterblichkeit. Leipzig, 1914.

Phil 3246.54   Fichte, Johann Gottlieb. Johann Gottlieb Fichte über den Begriff des wahrhaften Kraiges. Leipzig, 1914.

Phil 9245.21   Finot, Jean. Progrès et bonheur. Paris, 1914. 2v.

Phil 6115.20   Fitch, Michael H. The physical basis of mind and morals. Chicago, 1914.

Phil 6420.14   Fletcher, John Madison. An experimental study of stuttering. Thesis. Worcester, 1914.

Phil 2475.1.139.5   Florian, M. Der Begriff der Zeit bei Henri Bergson. Greifswald, 1914.

Phil 510.125.4   Flügel, O. Monismus und Theologie. 4e Aufl. Gotha, 1914.

Phil 6115.21.5   Forel, A. Gehirn und Seele. 12. Aufl. Leipzig, 1914.

Phil 6015.1   Fosbroke, Gerald Eltac. Character reading through analysis of the features. N.Y., 1914.

Phil 9495.22   Foster, W.T. The social emergency. Boston, 1914.

Phil 6315.2.33   Freud, Sigmund. Psychopathology of everyday life. London, 1914.

Phil 7082.8.14   Freud, Sigmund. Die Traumdeutung. 4. Aufl. Leipzig, 1914.

Phil 3260.50.5   Fries, J.F. System der Logik. 3e Aufl. Leipzig, 1914.

Phil 3246.171   Fuchs, Emil. Vom Werden dreier Denker. Tübingen, 1914.

Phil 180.17.2   Fullerton, G.S. A system of metaphysics. N.Y., 1914.

Phil 4210.127   Galli, Gallo. Kant e Rosmini. Città de Castello, 1914.

Phil 3488.3   Galli, Gallo. Kant e Rosmini. Citta di Castello, 1914.

Phil 5545.68   Gallinger, A. Zur Grundlegung einer Lehre von der Erinnerung. Halle, 1914.

Phil 181.42   Gans, Max E. Zur Psychologie der Begriffsmetaphysik. Wien, 1914.

Phil 8661.5   Garrigou-Lagrange, R. Dieu, son existence et sa nature. Paris, 1914.

Phil 8407.14.10   Gaultier, Paul. The meaning of art. Philadelphia, 1914.

Phil 3819.75   Gebhardt, Carl. Spinoza, Lebensbeschreibung und Gespräche. Leipzig, 1914.

Phil 6312.15   Geikie Cobb, W.J. Spiritual healing. London, 1914.

Phil 525.16.5   Gem, S. Harvey. The mysticism of William Law. London, 1914.

Phil 5645.18   Geuter, Peter. Der Farbensinn und seine Störungen. Leipzig, 1914.

Chronological Listing

1914 - cont.

Phil 181.33   Geyer, D.L. Pragmatic theory of truth as developed by Peirce, James and Dewey. n.p., 1914?

Phil 5246.14.10   Geyser, J. Die Seele, ihr Verhältnis zum Bewusstsein. Leipzig, 1914.

Phil 8881.34   Görland, Albert. Ethik als Kritik der Weltgeschichte. Leipzig, 1914.

Phil 3246.170   Gogarten, F. Fichte als religiöser Denker. Jena, 1914.

Phil 9070.31   Grenfell, W.T. The prize of life. N.Y., 1914.

Phil 8610.914   Griggs, H.S. The book of truth. Brooklyn, 1914.

Phil 2520.118   Gröber, G. Descartes; Methode des richtigen Vernunftgebrauches 1637. Strassburg, 1914.

Phil 8881.32   Grossmann, L. The real life. N.Y., 1914.

Phil 1135.41   Gundel, Wilhelm. Beiträge zur...Ananke und Heimarmene. Giessen, 1914.

Phil 5374.18   Halt, E.B. The concepts of consciousness. London, 1914.

Phil 6957.7   Hart, Bernard. The psychology of insanity. Cambridge, 1914.

Phil 5247.18   Harvey, N.A. Elementary psychology. Chicago, 1914.

Phil 5400.30   Harvey, N.A. The feelings of man. Baltimore, 1914.

Phil 3790.7.81   Hasse, Heinrich. Die Philosophie Raoul Richters. Leipzig, 1914.

Phil 5850.227   Hayward, C.N. Re-creating human nature. N.Y., 1914.

Phil 7082.116   Henning, Hans. Der Traum. Wiesbaden, 1914.

Phil 8587.13.90   Herrmann, R. Christentum und Geschichte bei W. Herrmann. Leipzig, 1914.

Phil 1504.14.5   Hertling, G. von. Albertus Magnus, Beiträge zu seiner Würdigung. 2. Aufl. v.14, pt.5-6. Münster, 1914.

Phil 1707.7   Hertling, G.F. von. Historische Beiträge zur Philosophie. München, 1914.

Phil 8882.34   Heymans, Gerardus. Einführung in die Ethik auf Grundlage der Erfahrung. Leipzig, 1914.

Phil 3246.169   Hidvall, Karl Z.K. Fichtes filosofi i förhallande till Kants kriticism. Uppsala, 1914.

Phil 5757.7   Hilber, H. (pseud.). Über Willenseinheit bei Arbeitsgehmeinschaft. Leipzig, 1914.

Phil 9520.2.5   Hinton, James. The mystery of pain. N.Y., 1914.

Phil 3246.174   Hirsch, Emanuel. Fichtes Religionsphilosophie. Göttingen, 1914.

Phil 3640.176   Hocks, Erich. Das Verhältnis der Erkenntnis zur Unendlichkeit der Welt bei Nietzsche. Leipzig, 1914.

Phil 645.23   Hönigswald, Richard. Die Skepsis in Philosophie und Wissenschaft. Göttingen, 1914.

Phil 5374.23   Hofmann, Paul. Die antithetische Struktur des Bewusstseins. Berlin, 1914.

Phil 5247.16.5   Hollingworth, H.L. Outlines for applied and abnormal psychology. N.Y., 1914.

Phil 5247.16   Hollingworth, H.L. Outlines for experimental psychology. N.Y., 1914.

Phil 7060.100   Holt, H. On the cosmic relations. Boston, 1914. 2v.

Phil 400.31   Howaleivsky, M. Über die Antinomienlehre als Begründung des transzendentalen idealismus. Inaug. Diss. Göttingen, 1914.

Phil 3829.3.10   Jacobi, F.E. Sulla dottrina dello Spinoza. Bari, 1914.

Phil 290.1   Jacobsson, M. Naturens lag. Stockholm, 1914.

Phil 2225.2.80   Jacoby, Günther. Die "neue Wirklichkeitslehre". Berlin, 1914?

Phil 9558.8   Jakobovits, J. Lüge im Urteil der neuesten deutschen Ethiker. Inaug. Diss. Paderborn, 1914.

Phil 184.3.22.5A   James, W. The meaning of truth. N.Y., 1914.

Phil 5435.8.3A   James, William. Habit. N.Y., 1914.

Phil 2070.33   James, William. Introduction à la philosophie. Paris, 1914.

Phil 2070.28   James, William. The meaning of truth. N.Y., 1914.

Phil 5627.6.13   James, William. Die religiöse Erfahrung. Leipzig, 1914.

Phil 1709.1   Joël, Karl. Die philosophische Krisis der Gegenwart. Leipzig, 1914.

Phil 7082.46.5   Jónasson, Hermann. Dulrímir. Reykjavík, 1914.

Phil 8634.5   Jones, John Daniel. Our life beyond. Boston, 1914.

L Phil 19.2.6   Journal of nervous and mental disease. Index. N.Y., 1914-1925.

Phil 6990.15   Joyce, G.H. The question of miracles. St. Louis, 1914.

Phil 6319.1.67   Jung, C.G. Der Inhalt der Psychose. 2. Aufl. Leipzig, 1914.

Phil 6319.1.72   Jung, C.G. Psychologische Abhandlungen. Leipzig, 1914.

Phil 6319.1.74   Jung, C.G. Psychotherapeutische Zeitfragen. Leipzig, 1914.

Phil 8884.15   Juvalta, E. Il vecchio e il nuovo problema della morale. Bologna, 1914.

Phil 5820.2   Kafka, Gustav. Einführung in die Tierpsychologie auf experimenteller und ethnologischer Grundlage. Leipzig, 1914.

Phil 2070.81A   Kallen, H.M. William James and Henri Bergson. Chicago, 1914.

Phil 3480.52.2   Kant, Immanuel. Critique of judgement. 2d ed. London, 1914.

Phil 3480.33   Kant, Immanuel. Idee zu einer allgemeinen Geschichte in weltbürgerlicher Absicht. Wiesbaden, 1914.

Phil 3480.81.4   Kant, Immanuel. Metaphysische Anfangsgründe der Naturwissenschaft. Leipzig, 1914.

Phil 3480.18.16   Kant, Immanuel. Trois opuscules scientifiques. Mistral, 1914.

Phil 3830.13   Kechek'ian, Stepan F. Eticheskoe mirosezaresanie Spinoza. Moskva, 1914.

Phil 2475.1.152   Keller, Adolf. Eine Philosophie des Lebens. (H. Bergson). Jena, 1914.

Phil 3100.81   Kempen, Aloys. Benekes religions Philosophie im Zusammenhang seines Systems, seine Gottes- und Unsterblickkeitslehre. Münster, 1914.

Phil 6120.6   Kenilworth, W.W. Le contrôle psychique. Paris, 1914.

Phil 3640.101.5   Kennedy, J.M. Nietzsche. London, 1914.

Phil 8885.20   Kerler, Dietrich H. Jenseits von Optimismus und Pessimismus. Ulm, 1914.

Phil 8700.1   Keyser, C.J. Science and religion, rational and superrational. New Haven, 1914.

Phil 185.21.2   Kinkel, Walter. Vom Sein und von der Seele. 2. Aufl. Giessen, 1914.

Phil 7060.45.5   Kleinpaul, R. Volkspsychologie, Berlin, 1914.

Phil 5250.8   Kleinpeter, H. Vorträge zur Einführung in die Psychologie. Leipzig, 1914.

Phil 5220.1.5   Klemm, O. A history of psychology. N.Y., 1914.

Phil 2070.80A   Knox, H.V. The philosophy of William James. London, 1914.

Phil 341.7   Köhler, Watther. Geist und Freiheit. Tübingen, 1914.

Phil 3492.24   Köster, Adolph. Der Junge Kant. Berlin, 1914.

Phil 5050.11   Konig, Julius. Neue Grundlagen der Logik Arithmetic. Leipzig, 1914.

1914 - cont.

Phil 6120.5   Kostyleff, N. Mécanisme cérébral de la pensée. Paris, 1914.

Phil 5250.16   Kramar, W. Neue Grundlagen zur Psychologie des Denkens. Brünn, 1914.

Phil 3625.12.80   Krieg, Max. Fritz Mauthners Kritik der Sprache. München, 1914.

Phil 1504.12.2   Kroll, J. Die Lehren des Hermes Trismegistos. v.12, pt.2-4. Münster, 1914.

Phil 5250.12   Kroman, Kristian. Korfattet taenke-og sjaelelaere. 5. udg. København, 1914.

Phil 3492.18   Kroner, Richard. Kants Weltanschauung. Tübingen, 1914.

Phil 720.9   Ladd, G.T. What can I know? N.Y., 1914.

Phil 8886.25   Laguna, T. de. Introduction to the science of ethics. N.Y., 1914.

Phil 8591.19   Lamanna, E.P. La religione nella vita dello spirito. Firenze, 1914.

Phil 3493.7   Larsson, Hans. Kants deduktion av kategorierna. 2. uppl. Lund, 1914.

Phil 3493.7.5   Larsson, Hans. Kants transsecndentala deduktion af kategorierna. Lund, 1914.

Phil 4600.2.40   Larsson, Hans. Psykologi paa Dansk red Stig Bredstrup. København, 1914.

Phil 3246.172   Lask, Emil. Fichtes Idealismus und die Geschichte. Tübingen, 1914.

Phil 3425.108.5   Lasson, G. Hegel; handschriftliche Zusätze zu seiner Rechtsphilosophie. Leipzig, 1914. 3v.

Phil 6961.7   Lauze, Charles A. La psychose hallucinatoire chronique. Thèse. Paris, 1914.

Phil 2730.84   LaValette, Monbrun A. de. Essai de biographie historique...Maine de Biran. Paris, 1914.

Phil 2805.165   La Vallette-Monbrun, A. de. Maine de Biran, critique et disciple de Pascal. Paris, 1914.

Phil 9171.5   Lawton, R.O. The making of a home. Boston, 1914.

Phil 5374.24.5   Legahn, August F. Entricklungsgeschichte des Bewusstseins. Leipzig, 1914.

Phil 5400.15.2   Lehmann, A. Die Hauptgesetze des menschlichen Gefühlslebens. 2. Aufl. Leipzig, 1914.

Phil 8701.23   Lemonnyer, Antoine. La révélation primitive, et les données actuelles de la science. Paris, 1914.

Phil 186.52   Lessing, T. Philosophie als Tat. Göttingen, 1914.

Phil 735.14   Lessing, Theodor. Studien zur Wertaxiomatik. 2e Ausg. Leipzig, 1914.

Phil 8591.39   Leufvén, E. Det religiösa kunskapsproblemet. Uppsala, 1914.

Phil 7140.5   Lévy, Alfred. La psychose d'influence. Thèse. Paris, 1914.

Phil 342.4   Levy, Heinrich. Über die apriorischen Elemente. Leipzig, 1914.

Phil 8886.28   Lewis, George Edward. Pay your fare. N.Y., 1914.

Phil 186.26   Liddy, Ray Balmer. Relation of science and philosophy. Thesis. Toronto, 1914?

Phil 2266.114   Limentani, L. La morale della simpatia; saggio sopra l'etica di Adamo Smith. Genova, 1914.

Phil 5051.16.6   Lindner, Gustav A. Lehrbuch der allgemeinen Logik. 6e Aufl. Wien, 1914.

Phil 4600.5.31   Ljunglund, L. Livets bejakande. Stockholm, 1914.

Phil 8701.4.2   Lodge, Oliver Joseph. Science and immortality. N.Y., 1914.

Phil 8591.29   Lönborg, Sven. Religion och vetenskap. Stockholm, 1914.

Phil 3801.529   Losacco, Michele. Schelling. Milano, 1914?

Phil 3640.98.9   Ludovici, Anthony M. Who is to be master of the world? Edinburgh, 1914.

Phil 6961.8   Lurié, Aron. Multiple Sklerose mit amnestischer Aphasie. Inaug. Diss. Königsberg, 1914.

Phil 8965.2.5   Mabie, H.W. Ethics and the Garger neighborhood, 1914. Philadelphia, 1914.

Phil 8701.4.50   McCabe, Joseph. The religion of Sir Oliver Lodge. London, 1914.

Phil 40.3   MacCracken, H.M. A propaganda of philosophy; a history of the American Institute of Christian Philosophy, 1881-1914. N.Y., 1914.

Phil 5635.5.9   Mach, Ernst. The analysis of sensations. Chicago, 1914.

Phil 4803.558.20   Mahrburg, Adam. Pisma filozoficzne. Warszawa, 1914. 2v.

Phil 2730.30.20   Malebranche, Nicolas. Erforschung der Wahrheit. München, 1914.

Phil 187.41   Malter, Mrs. M.P. The world process. Fresno, Cal., 1914.

Phil 3850.16.92   Mamelet, A. Le relativisme philosophique chez G. Simmel. Paris, 1914.

Phil 5822.5   Mangold, Ernst. Hypnose und Katalepsie bei Tieren. Jena, 1914.

Phil 3494.19.40   Marcus, Ernst. Die Bewersführung in der Kritik der reinen Vernunft. Essen, 1914.

Phil 2475.1.125   Maritain, Jacques. La philosophie Bergsonienne. Paris, 1914.

Phil 5252.40   Martin, Otto. Zur Psychologie des Verstehens wissenschaftlicher Texte. Inaug. Diss. Freiburg, 1914.

Phil 4080.3.85   Masnovo, Omero. L'estetica di Benedetto Croce. Parma, 1914.

Phil 3246.93.5   Medicus, Fritz. Fichtes Leben. Leipzig, 1914.

Phil 8592.28   Mellor, Stanley. Religion as effected by modern science philosophy. London, 1914.

Phil 6962.4.5   Mercier, C.A. A text-book of insanity. London, 1914.

Phil 5252.28   Messer, A. Psychologie. Stuttgart, 1914.

Phil 1133.10   Meyer, Hans. Geschichte der Lehre von den Keimkräften von der Stoa bis zum Ausgang der Patristik. Bonn, 1914.

Phil 270.19   Meyer-Pforzheim, C.W. Der Kausalitätsbegriff. Hamburg, 1914.

Phil 9245.41   Miltenberger, W.F. De felicitate. Washington, D.C., 1914.

Phil 2475.1.230   Mitchell, A. Studies in Bergson's philosophy. Lawrence, 1914.

Phil 5330.16   Mitchell, David. Influence of distractions on the formation of judgments in lifted weight experiments. Princeton, 1914.

Phil 8887.44   Mitra, Ambika C. The elements of morals. 2. ed. Calcutta, 1914.

Phil 4520.8.50   Mjarnason, Ágúst. Rannsókn dularfullra fyrirbrigd. Reykjavík, 1914.

Phil 8633.1.17   Moore, G.F. Metempsychosis. Cambridge, 1914.

Phil 9590.2   Moore, J.H. The law of biogenesis. Chicago, 1914.

Phil 3640.218.4   Mügge, M.A. Friedrich Nietzsche. 4th ed. London, 1914.

Phil 9415.5   Mueller-Lyer, Franz. Soziologie der Leiden. München, 1914.

Phil 5850.278   Münsterberg, H. Grundzüge der Psychotechnik. Leipzig, 1914.

1914 - cont.

Phil 5850.278.13   Münsterberg, H. Psicologia de la actividad industrial. Madrid, 1914.

Phil 5252.12.35   Münsterberg, H. Psychology and social sanity. Garden City, 1914.

Phil 5252.12.45   Münsterberg, H. Psychology general and applied. N.Y., 1914.

Phil 187.55.3   Muñiz, Narcisse. Problèmes de la vie. Paris, 1914.

Phil 3495.6.5   Nelson, Leonard. Die kritische Ethik bei Kant, Schilles und Fries. Göttingen, 1914.

Phil 8703.1   Netto. F.J. Sociabilidade natural do homem. Povoa de Varzim, 1914.

Phil 1135.29   Neustadt, E. Die religiös-philosophische Bewegung der Hellenismus. Leipzig, 1914.

Phil 3640.39   Nietzsche, Friedrich. Ainsi parlait Zarathustra. 29e éd. Paris, 1914.

Phil 3640.15.3   Nietzsche, Friedrich. Complete works. 3. ed. v.11. N.Y., 1914.

Phil 745.5   Noll, Alfred. Die "Lebenskraft" in der Schriften der Vitalisten und ihrer Gegner. Leipzig, 1914.

Phil 7060.92.25   O'Donnell, Elliot. Haunted highways and byways. London, 1914.

Phil 5254.1   Ogden, R.M. An introduction to general psychology. N.Y., 1914.

Phil 9354.1   Olcott, Gage. Meditations of a young man. Boston, 1914.

Phil 2475.1.149   Olgiati, Francesco. La filosofia di Enrico Bergson. Torino, 1914.

Phil 8594.6   Ollé-Laprune, L. La vitalite chrétienne. Paris, 1914.

Phil 4372.3.85   Ortega, Euselio. Francisco de Valles, el Divino. Madrid, 1914.

Phil 5224.1   Orth, Johannes. Der psychologische Begriff des Unbewutzten in der Schelling'schen Schule. Heidelberg, 1914.

Phil 2490.93   Ostwald, W. Auguste Comte. Leipzig, 1914.

Phil 9430.22   Palante, Georges. Pessimisme et individualisme. Paris, 1914.

Phil 8416.26   Pap, Julius. Kunst und Illusion. Leipzig, 1914.

Phil 8595.20   Pariser, E. Einführung in die Religions-Psychologie. Halle, 1914.

Phil 4316.1   Parpal y Marques, C. Antecedentes de la escuela filosófica Catalana del siglo XIX. Barcelona, 1914.

NEDL Phil 2805.17   Pascal, Blaise. Oeuvres. Paris, 1914-23. 14v.

Phil 5255.2.6   Paulhan, F. Esprits logiques et esprits faux. Paris, 1914.

Phil 9255.5   Paulhan, Frederic. La morale de l'ironie. 2. éd. Paris, 1914.

Phil 3497.3.7   Paulsen, Friedrich. Kant. Milano, 1914.

Phil 8890.29   Payot, Jules. Cours de morale. 9. ed. Paris, 1914.

Phil 8965.11   Peabody, F.G. The Christian life in the modern world. N.Y., 1914.

Phil 5058.7.18   Pelazza, Amelio. Guglielmo Schuppe e la filosofia dell'immanerza. Milano, 1914.

Phil 5545.59   Perrin, F.A.C. An experimental...study of human learning. Princeton, 1914.

Phil 1535.9.5   Pesch, T. Institutiones logicae et ontologicae quas secundum principia S. Thomae Aguinatis. Friburgi, 1914.

Phil 190.30   Petitot, H. Introduction à la philosophie. Paris, 1914.

Phil 5255.12   Petrescu, Nicolaus. Die Denkfunktion der Verneinung. Leipzig, 1914.

Phil 530.20.9   Pfeiffer, Franz. Deutsche Mystiker des vierzehnten Jahrhunderts. v.2. Göttingen, 1914.

Phil 2050.111   Phalén, Adolf. I. Hume's psykologiska härledning av kausalitetsföreställningeII. Hypotesen om det omedvetna i empirisk psykologi. Uppsala, 1914.

Phil 5115.4.7   Poincaré, Henri. Science and hypothesis. London, 1914.

Phil 8640.1.5   Pomponazzi, P. Trattato sull'immortalità dell'anima. Roma, 1914.

Phil 3497.9   Porten, M. von der. Die Grundlagen der Kantschen Philosophie. Leipzig, 1914.

Phil 6990.20   Poulpiquet, E. Le miracle et ses suppléances. Paris, 1914.

Phil 7080.35   Poyer, G.P. Contribution à la pathologie du sommeil. Le sommeil automatique. Thèse. Paris, 1914.

Phil 7069.14.50   Primot, Alphonse. La psychologie d'une conversion du positivisme au spiritualisme. Paris, 1914.

Phil 6325.8.5   Prince, Morton. The unconscious. N.Y., 1914.

Phil 1504.13.2   Probst, J.H. La mystique de Ramon Lull et l'art de contemplació. v.13, pt.2-3. Münster, 1914.

Phil 6965.6   Provost, Maurice. Aliénation mentale, chez les employés de chemins de fer et de transports publics. Thèse. Paris, 1914.

Phil 5255.6   Psychological Laboratory. Bedford College for Women. University of London. Psychological studies. London, 1914.

Phil 3835.6   Pulcini, C. L'etica di Spinoza. Genova, 1914.

Phil 6127.11   Rabbow, Paul. Antik Schriften über Seelenheilung und Seelenleitung. Leipzig, 1914.

Phil 4809.727.30   Rádl, Emanuel. Úvahy vědeché a filosofické. Praha, 1914.

Phil 9075.13   Rashdall, H. Is conscience an emotion? Boston, 1914.

Phil 192.26.3   Rausch, Alfred. Elemente der Philosophie. 3. Aufl. Halle, 1914.

NEDL Phil 6967.1.5   Regis, E. La psychoanalyse des névroses. Paris, 1914.

Phil 4215.3.31   Rensi, Giuseppe. Formalismo e amoralismo giuridico. Verona, 1914.

Phil 705.10   Rensi, Giuseppe. La trascendenza; studio sul problema morale. Torino, 1914.

Phil 5057.15   Restrepo-Hernandez, J. Lecciones de lógica dictadas en el Colegio. 2nd ed. Bogota, 1914.

Phil 27.4.2   Revue philosophique de Louvain. Table, 1894-1913. Louvain, 1914.

Phil 5257.29   Rhodes, G. The mind at work. London, 1914.

Phil 5465.5.4   Ribot, T. Essai sur l'imagination créatrice. 4. éd. Paris, 1914.

Phil 5649.11.3   Ribot, Théodule. La vie inconsciente et les mouvements. 3. éd. Paris, 1914.

Phil 9530.17   Rice, Elwood E. Rice leaders of the world association, its inspiration, realization and objects. N.Y., 1914.

Htn Phil 8892.38F*   Roback, A.A. The status of ethics. n.p., 1914.

Phil 5057.122   Robert, Arthur. Leçons de logique. Québec 1914.

Phil 2530.82   Roretz, Karl. Diderots Weltanschauung. Wien, 1914.

Phil 5425.21   Roscoe, T.G. Mental and physical decadence. London, 1914.

Phil 8597.20.2   Royce, Josiah. The problem of Christianity. N.Y., 1914.

Phil 192.43   Ruge, Arnold. Einführung in die Philosophie. Leipzig, 1914.

Phil 2475.1.132   Ruhe, A. Henri Bergson, an account of his life. London, 1914.

Phil 2475.1.133   Ruhe, A. Henri Bergson. Stockholm, 1914.

1914 - cont.

Phil 192.28.9   Russell, B. Our knowledge of the external world. Chicago, 1914.

Phil 2475.1.129   Russell, B. The philosophy of Bergson. Cambridge, 1914.

Phil 5057.14   Russell, L.J. An introduction to logic. London, 1914.

Phil 5257.33   Ruttmann, W.J. Die Hauptergebnisse der modernen Psychologie. Leipzig, 1914.

Phil 2475.1.139   Sait, Una B. Ethical implications of Bergson's philosophy. N.Y., 1914.

Phil 349.19   Sauerbeck, E. Vom Wesen der Wissenschaft. Leipzig, 1914.

Phil 9245.56   Schauffler, Robert H. The joyful heart. Boston, 1914.

Phil 3800.135   Schelling, F.W.J. von. Briefe über Dogmatismus und Kritizismus. Leipzig, 1914.

Phil 600.27   Schinz, Max. Die Anfänge des französischen Positivismus. Teil I. Strassburg, 1914.

Phil 3805.45   Schleiermacher, Friedrich. Monologen nebst den Vorarbeiten. 2. Aufl. Leipzig, 1914.

Phil 510.1.39   Schmidt, Heinrich. Was wir Ernst Haeckel Verdanken. Leipzig, 1914. 2v.

Phil 3640.855   Schmidt, Otto Ernst. Nietzsche der falsche Prophet. Leipzig, 1914.

Phil 510.152   Schmitz, Oscar A.H. Die Weltanschauung des Halbgebildeten. München, 1914.

Phil 7069.14.58   Schrenck von Notzing, Albert. Die Kampf und die Materialisationsphänomene. München, 1914.

Phil 7069.14.60   Schrenck von Notzing, Albert. Materialisationsphaenomene. München, 1914.

Phil 4210.114   Schwaiger, Georg. Die Lehre vom sentimento fondamentale bei Rosmini nach ihrer Anlage. Inaug. Diss. Fulda, 1914.

Phil 8893.71   Seidel, A. Wegweiser zum moralischen Handeln. Leipzig, 1914.

Phil 7060.110   Seymour, S.J.D. True Irish ghost stories. Dublin, 1914.

Phil 2262.39A   Shaftesbury, A.A.C. Second characters. Cambridge, 1914.

Phil 9035.21   Shand, A.F. The foundations of character. London, 1914.

Phil 960.25   Shastri, Prabhu D. The conception of freedom in Hegel, Berigson and Indian philosophy. Calcutta, 1914.

Phil 7080.24———   Shepard, J.F. The circulation and sleep. Text and atlas. N.Y., 1914. 2v.

Phil 4769.4.15   Shpet, Gustav. Iavlenie i smysl. Moskva, 1914.

Phil 5058.22.5   Sidgwick, A. Elementary logic. Cambridge, 1914.

Phil 6968.12.5   Sidis, Boris. Symptomatology, psychognosis, and diagnosis of psychopathic diseases. Boston, 1914.

Phil 1135.76   Sikes, E.E. The anthropology of the Greeks. London, 1914.

Phil 6328.5.5   Silberer, Herbert. Probleme der Mystik und ihrer Symbolik. Wien, 1914.

Phil 5768.13   Slosson, P.W. Fated or free? Boston, 1914.

Phil 8598.53   Snaith, John. The philosophy of spirit. London, 1914.

Phil 5258.118   Society of Applied Psychology. Psychology and achievement. San Francisco, 1914.

Phil 4769.1.10   Solov'ev, V.S. Ausgewählte Werke. Jena, 1914-16. 2v.

Phil 8598.29   Spencer, F.A.M. The meaning of Christianity. 2. ed. London, 1914.

Phil 978.30   Speyer, J.S. Die indische Theosophie. Leipzig, 1914.

Phil 3819.70.5   Spinoza, Benedictus de. Briefwechsel; Übertragen und mit Einleitung. Leipzig, 1914.

Phil 3819.36.33   Spinoza, Benedictus de. Ethica, ordine geometrico demonstrata. Hagae, 1914.

Phil 3819.36.20   Spinoza, Benedictus de. L'etica. Milano, 1914.

Phil 3819.15   Spinoza, Benedictus de. Oeuvres de Spinoza. Paris, 1914. 2v.

Phil 3819.11.2   Spinoza, Benedictus de. Sämmtliche Werke. Leipzig, 1914-22. 3v.

Phil 5627.28   Stalker, James. Christian psychology. 3. ed. N.Y., 1914.

Phil 7054.22.5   Stead, William T. After death; a personal narrative. N.Y., 1914.

Phil 193.63   Stebbing, L.S. Pragmatism and French voluntarism. Cambridge, 1914.

Phil 5258.29.5   Stratton, G.M. Experimental psychology. N.Y., 1914.

Phil 672.21   Study, E. Die realistische Weltansicht und die Lehre vom Raume. Braunschweig, 1914.

Phil 5330.23   Suter, Jules. Zur Theorie der Aufmerksamkeit. Zürich, 1914.

Phil 930.33   Suzuki, Daisetz T. A brief history of early Chinese philosophy. 2. ed. London, 1914.

Phil 7082.60   Sveinsson, Ingimundur. 2 draumur. Reykjavík, 1914.

Phil 400.31.10   Sydow, Eckhart von. Der Gedanke des Ideal-Reichs in der idealistischen Philosophie von Kant bis Hegel. Leipzig, 1914.

Phil 2885.30.8   Taine, Hippolyte Adolphe. De l'intelligence. 13. éd. Paris, 1914. 2v.

Phil 4060.5.80   Taura, Giacoma. La vita ed il pensiero di Andrea Anguilli. Milano, 1914.

Phil 194.16   Thayer, H.D. Physio-Psychics. Philadelphia, 1914.

Phil 819.7.2A   Thilly, F. A history of philosophy. N.Y., 1914.

Phil 6129.5   Thomas, André. Localisations cérébelleuses. Paris, 1914.

Phil 6129.4   Thompson, J.J. Mirage of the nervous system. n.p., 1914.

Phil 6129.1.8   Thomson, W.H. Brain and personality. N.Y., 1914.

Phil 2020.83   Townsend, H.G. Principle of individuality in the philosophy of T.H. Green. Lancaster, 1914.

Phil 6750.18.5   Tredgold, A.F. Mental deficiency (Amentia). 2d ed. N.Y., 1914.

Phil 9540.5   Trevelyan, G.M. De haeretico comburendo. Cambridge, Eng., 1914.

Phil 2630.3.82   Trial, Louis. Jean-Jacques Gourd 1850-1909. Nimes, 1914.

Phil 3501.7   Trivero, Camillo. Nuova critica della morale Kantiana. Milano, 1914.

Phil 5374.20   Turró, R. Origines de la connaissance. Paris, 1914.

Phil 365.37   Tyler, J.M. The place of the church in evolution. Boston, 1914.

Phil 820.1.7   Ueberweg, F. Grundriss der Geschichte der Philosophie. v.2-4. 11. Aufl. Berlin, 1914-28. 3v.

Phil 4466.2.80   Uedelhofen, M. Die Logik Petrus Fonseca's mit Ausschluss des Sprachlogischen. Inaug. Diss. Bonn, 1914.

Phil 525.7.5   Underhill, Evelyn. Practical mysticism. London, 1914.

Phil 2750.2.80   Van der Elst, Robert. Michelet, naturaliste. Paris, 1914.

Phil 4650.1.53   Vannérus, Allen. Metafysik. Lund, 1914.

Phil 530.20.40   Vansteenberghe, E. Autour de la docte ignorance. Munster en Westphalie, 1914?

Phil 5261.8   Varendonck, J. La psychologie du témoignage. Gand, 1914.

Phil 196.8   Varisco, B. The great problems. London, 1914.

Phil 7080.28   Vaschide, Nicolas. Le sommeil et les rêves. Paris, 1914.

Phil 2480.80   Vermeil de Conchard, P.P. Trois études sur Cabanis. Brive, 1914.

Phil 8896.14   Vesper, Noël. Anticipations à une morale du risque. Paris, 1914.

Phil 4260.17   Vico, G.B. Opere. Bari, 1914. 6v.

1914 - cont.

Phil 1821.5   Vogt, P.B. From John Stuart Mill to William James. Washington, 1914.

Phil 5831.4   Volkelt, Johannes. Über die vorstellungen Deutiere. v.2. Leipzig, 1914.

Phil 3246.236   Vysheslavtsev, B. Etika Fikhte. Moskva, 1914.

Phil 822.3   Wägner, S. Filosofiens historia i sammandrag. Lund, 1914.

Phil 303.10   Wälte, Théodore. Philosophie d'un ignorant. Genève, 1914.

Phil 672.9.5   Walter, J.E. Nature and cognition of space and time. W. Newton, Pa., 1914.

Phil 5832.9   Watson, John B. Behavior. N.Y., 1914.

Phil 5832.9.2A   Watson, John B. Behavior. N.Y., 1914.

Phil 6100.15   Weed, L.H. Reconstruction of the nuclear masses in the lower portion of the human brain-stem. Washington, 1914.

Phil 353.13   Wendel, Georg. Kritik des Erkennens. Bonn, 1914.

Phil 5772.8   Werner, S. Das Problem von der menschlichen Willensfreiheit. Berlin, 1914.

Phil 5262.13.2   Whipple, G.M. Manual of mental and physical tests. Pt. 1-2. Baltimore, 1914-15. 2v.

Phil 3504.14   Whitney, G.J. An introduction to Kant's critical philosophy. N.Y., 1914.

Phil 197.25.5   Williams, C.L. As if; a philosophical phantasy. San Francisco, 1914.

Phil 6332.3   Williams, Edward H. Increasing your mental efficiency. N.Y., 1914.

Phil 2475.1.225   Wilm, E.C. Henri Bergson. N.Y., 1914.

Phil 197.9.13A   Windelband, W. Einleitung in der Philosophie. Tübingen, 1914.

Phil 197.9.7   Windelband, W. Die Hypothese des Unbewussten. Heidelberg, 1914.

Phil 8602.24   Wittels, Fritz. Über den Tod und über den Glauben an Gott. Wien, 1914.

Phil 5330.24   Woodrow, H. The measurement of attention. Princeton, 1914.

Phil 1504.12.5   Würschmidt, J. Theodoricus Teutonicus de Vriberg De iride et radialibus impressionibus. v.12, pt.5-6. Münster, 1914.

Phil 3915.56.2   Wundt, Wilhelm. Reden und Aufsätze. 2. Aufl. Leipzig, 1914.

Phil 3915.67   Wundt, Wilhelm. Sinnliche und übersinnliche Welt. Leipzig, 1914.

Phil 1630.2   Zanta, Léontine. La renaissance du stoicisme au XVIe siècle. Paris, 1914.

Phil 356.1.10   Ziehen, T. Zum gegenwärtigen Stand der Erkenntnistheorie. Wiesbaden, 1914.

Phil 5265.1.4.3   Ziehen, Theodor. Leitfaden der physiologischen Psychologie. 10. Aufl. Jena, 1914.

Phil 672.131   Zini, Zino. La doppa maschera dell'universo. Milano, 1914.

Phil 6520.7.9   Zoepf, L. Die Mystikerin Margaretha Ebner. Leipzig, 1914.

Phil 8605.2.5   Zoppola, G. A vapore. Firenze, 1914.

1915

Phil 5750.4   Ahlberg, Alf. Viljans frihet från transcendental-filosofiens ståndpunkt. Stockholm, 1915.

Phil 8875.11   Alvarez, Agustín. Creación del mundo moral. 2a ed. Buenos Aires, 1915.

Phil 175.25   Ambrosi, Luigi. Il primo passo alla filosofia. v.3. 5a ed. Milano, 1915.

Phil 7082.56   Austmann, S.J. Sögur af ýmsu tagi. Winnipeg, 1915.

Phil 331.3   Avey, Albert E. An analysis of process of conceptual cognition. Cincinnati, 1915.

Phil 5041.29.2   Baldwin, J.M. Genetic theory of reality. N.Y., 1915.

Phil 8656.13   Balfour, A.J.B. Theism and humanism. N.Y., 1915.

Phil 5241.32   Ballard, J.H. Some phases of the psychology of puzzle learning. N.Y., 1915.

Phil 7069.15.10   Barker, Elsa. War letters from the living dead man. N.Y., 1915.

Phil 5751.3   Barrett, Edward Boyd. Strength of will. N.Y., 1915.

Phil 282.7.11   Becher, Erich. Weltgebäude, Weltgesetze, Weltentwicklung. Berlin, 1915.

Phil 1050.16.5   Berger, Emil. Das Problem der Erkenntnis in der Religions-Philosophie Jehuda Hallevis. Inaug-Diss. Berlin, 1915.

Phil 3246.173   Bergmann, Ernst. Fichte, der Erzieher zum Deutschtum. Leipzig, 1915.

Phil 2401.6   Bergson, H. La philosophie. Paris, 1915.

Phil 2475.1.63   Bergson, Henri. The meaning of the war. London, 1915.

Phil 1870.30.15   Berkeley, G. Alciphron. Leipzig, 1915.

Phil 1870.65.15   Berkeley, G. Siris. Leipzig, 1915.

Phil 5751.9   Bessmer, Julius. Das menschliche Wollen. Freiburg, 1915.

Phil 4520.8.32   Bjarnason, Agúst. Drauma-joi, sannar sagnir. Reykjavík, 1915.

Phil 4520.8.38   Bjarnason, Agúst. Vesturlönd. Reykjavík, 1915.

Phil 5241.40   Bocci, Balduino. I primi teoremi di psicologia. Siena, 1915.

Phil 3425.201   Boer, J. de. De beteekenis van de Hegel-studie voor onzen tijd. Baarn, 1915.

Phil 9435.2   Bok, Edward. Why I believe in poverty. Boston, 1915.

Phil 3120.11.97   Bolland, G.J.P.J. De natuur. Leiden, 1915.

Phil 8402.13   Bosanquet, B. Three lectures on aesthetic. London, 1915.

Phil 2477.1.66   Boutroux, Émile. Certitude et vérité. London, 1915.

Phil 3640.128.2   Brahn, Max. Friedrich Nietzsches Meinung über Staaten und Kriege. 2e Aufl. Leipzig, 1915.

Phil 5241.31   Bramshausen, N. Einführung in die experimentelle Psychologie. Leipzig, 1915.

Phil 8581.35   Bridges, H.J. Criticisms of life. Boston, 1915.

Phil 600.31.5   Bridges, J.H. Illustrations of positivism. Chicago, 1915.

Phil 575.12.2   Bruce, H.A. Riddle of personality. N.Y., 1915.

Phil 7080.26   Bruce, H.A. Sleep and sleeplessness. Boston, 1915.

Phil 5640.6.25   Brühl, P.N. Die specifischen Sinnesenergien nach John Müller. Fulda, 1915.

Phil 525.53   Buckham, J.N. Mysticism and modern life. N.Y., 1915.

Phil 6951.9   Burr, Colonel Bell. Handbook of psychology and mental disease. 4. ed. Philadelphia, 1915.

Phil 6111.32.5   Butler, Hiram Erastus. Practical methods to insure success. 31st ed. Applegate, Calif., 1915.

Phil 8877.65.30   Cabot, Richard C. Prescriptions. Boston, 1915.

Phil 7060.94   Capper, Alfred. A rambler's recollections and reflections. London, 1915.

Phil 9220.4.3   Carpenter, Edward. Ioläus; anthology of friendship. 3d ed. London, 1915.

Phil 7060.75.5   Carrington, H. True ghost stories. N.Y., 1915.

Phil 8877.37   Caso, Antonio. Filósofos y doctrinas morales. Mexico, 1915.

Phil 177.37   Caso, Antonio. Problemas filosóficos. México, 1915.

1915 - cont.

Phil 1135.93   Chevalier, Jacques. Notion du Necessaire chez Aristote. Paris, 1915.

Phil 8582.8   Cheyne, G. Philosophical principles of religion. v.1-2. London, 1915-16.

Phil 9450.9   Christensen, A. Politics and crowd-morality. London, 1915.

Phil 283.5   Clay, J. Schets eener kritische geschiedenis van het begrip natuurwet. Leiden, 1915.

Phil 2490.53.15   Comte, Auguste. Abhandlung über den Geist des Positivismus. Leipzig, 1915.

Phil 9450.14   Cook, Silas A. The essence and the ethics of politics. N.Y., 1915.

Phil 7082.72.15   Coriat, Isador Henry. The meaning of dreams. Boston, 1915.

Phil 8610.915   Coughlin, D.R. Review of the Bibles. East Aurora, N.Y., 1915.

Phil 7069.15.20   Crawford, Mary MacDermont. Peeps into the psychic world. Philadelphia, 1915.

Phil 5400.32   Crile, George W. The origin and nature of the emotions. Philadelphia, 1915.

Phil 4170.3.84   Croce, B. Ricerche e documenti Desanctisiani. Dal carteggio inedito di A.C. de Meis. Napoli, 1915.

Phil 3425.109.14A   Croce, B. What is living and what is dead of the philosophy of Hegel. London, 1915.

Phil 8877.34.5   Croce, Benedetto. Filosofia della pratica; economia ed etica. 2a ed. Bari, 1915.

VPhil 9245.125   Curry, Samuel Silas. The smile. Boston, 1915.

VPhil 5627.215.15   Czakó, Ambrosius. A vallás lelektana, irta Czakó Ambró. Pécs, 1915.

Phil 5043.23   Dam, Axel. Logik til brug under laereruddannelsen paa seminarierne. København, 1915.

Phil 5043.19   Davies, A.E. A text-book of logic. Columbus, 1915.

Phil 525.18   Dawkins, M.B. Mysticism, an epistemological problem. New Haven, 1915.

Phil 5545.61   DeCamp, J.E. Study of retroactive inhibition. Thesis. Princeton, 1915.

Phil 3003.4   Delbos, Victor. L'esprit philosophique de l'Allemagne et la pensée française. Paris, 1915.

Phil 5090.8   Dellepiane, A. Les sciences et la méthode reconstructives. Paris, 1915.

Phil 2520.53.4   Descartes, René. Meditationen über die Grundlagen der Philosophie. 4e Aufl. Leipzig, 1915.

Phil 3003.3A   Dewey, John. German philosophy and politics. N.Y., 1915.

Phil 9495.115   Dourães Castro. O racionalismo atrevido do Snr. Frederico de Ancede. Porto, 1915.

Phil 178.27   Driscoll, John T. Pragmatism and the problem of the idea. N.Y., 1915.

Phil 1109.1.5   Eleutheropulos, A. Die Philosophie und der sozialen Zûstanden (materielle und ideele Entwicklung) des Greichentums. 3e Aufl. Zürich, 1915.

Phil 9490.8   Eliot, C.W. The training for an effective life. Boston, 1915.

Phil 6114.14   Ellsworth, P. Health and power. Holyoke, Mass., 1915.

Phil 1504.17.2   Endes, J.A. Forschungen zur Geschichte der frümittelalterlichen Philosophie. v.17, pt.2-3. Münster, 1915.

Phil 5244.17   Eriksen, R. Taenkningens psychologiske utviklingsbetingelser. Kristiania, 1915.

Phil 400.34   Eucken, Rudolf. Die Träger des deutschen Idealismus. Berlin, 1915.

Phil 9495.28.5   Exner, M.J. Problems and principles of sex education. N.Y., 1915.

Phil 3808.155   Eymer, Karl. Arthur Schopenhauer. n.p., 1915.

Phil 176.27.8   Flewelling, R.T. Personalism and the problems of philosophy. N.Y., 1915.

Phil 8585.20.80   Foakes-Jackson, F.J. The faith and the war; a series of essays. London, 1915.

Phil 3640.88.7   Förster-Nietzsche, E. Der einsame Nietzsche. München, 1915.

Phil 3640.88.9   Förster-Nietzsche, E. Wagner und Nietzsche zur zeit Freundschaft. München, 1915.

X Cg   Phil 6480.23.5   Freud, Sigmund. The interpretation of dreams. 4th ed. London, 1915. 2v.

Phil 3005.12   Frischeisen-Köhler, M. Geistige Werte. Berlin, 1915.

Phil 3246.290   Funcke, Eduard. Neues zu den politischen Anschauungen des Jungen Fichte. Hildesheim, 1915.

Phil 4260.94   Gentile, Giovanni. Studi vichiani. Messina, 1915.

Phil 181.39   Geyser, Joseph. Allgemeine Philosophie...der Natur. Münster, 1915.

Phil 5627.24   Gill, E.H.K. Psychological aspects of Christian experience. Boston, 1915.

Phil 5246.17   Givler, Robert C. The conscious cross-section. Seattle, 1915.

Phil 5246.18   Glover, William. Know your own mind...book of practical psychology. Cambridge, 1915.

Phil 6619.14   Godefroy, Jan C.L. Onderzoekingen over de aandachtsbepaling bij gezonden en zielszieken. Groningen, 1915?

Phil 7069.15.28   Gravies, L.C. The natural order of spirit. Boston, 1915.

Phil 2020.135   Günther, Oskar. Das Verhältnis der Ethik T.H. Greens zu Derjenigen Kants. Inaug. Diss. Dresden, 1915.

Phil 1195.5   Gunning, C.P. Dissertatio inauguralis de sophistis Graeciae. Amstelodami, 1915.

Phil 5757.12.6   Haddock, F.C. Power of will. 55th ed. Meriden, 1915.

Phil 510.1.23   Haeckel, Ernst. Ewigkeit. Berlin, 1915.

Phil 182.1.10   Hagemann, G. Logik und Nötik. 9e und 10e Aufl. Freiburg, 1915.

Phil 8632.16   Hall, G.S. Thanataphobia and immortality. n.p., 1915.

Phil 6117.32   Hall, H.J. The untroubled mind. Boston, 1915.

Phil 5247.20   Hamelinck, M. Etude préparatoire à la détermination experimentale de diverses individuel rhythmen. Gand, 1915.

Phil 9150.21   Hanssen, Andreas. Etiken og evolutionslaeren. København, 1915.

Phil 3425.77   Hegel, Georg Wilhelm Friedrich. Hegels erstes System. Heidelberg, 1915.

Phil 8587.35   Heinzelmann, G. Die erkenntnistheoretische Begründung der Religion. Basel, 1915.

Phil 3625.3.80   Henning, Hans. Ernst als Philosoph, Physiker und Psychologie, eine Monographie. Leipzig, 1915.

Phil 2045.65   Hobbes, Thomas. Grundzüge der Philosophie. v.1-3. Leipzig, 1915-18.

Phil 5817.5.2   Hobhouse, L.T. Mind in evolution. London, 1915.

Phil 1512.9   Hochstetter, E. Die subjektiven GrundlagenDer scholastischen Ethik. Halle, 1915.

Phil 1707.1.13   Höffding, H. Modern philosophers. London, 1915.

Chronological Listing

1915 - cont.

Phil 5047.18	Holman, Henry. Questions on logic. 2nd ed. London, 1915.
Phil 8632.5	Holmes, John H. Is death the end? N.Y., 1915.
Phil 5755.5	Holt, E.B. The Freudian wish and its place in ethics. N.Y., 1915.
Phil 5755.5.2	Holt, E.B. The Freudian wish and its place in ethics. N.Y., 1915.
Phil 7069.15.30	Holt, Henry. On the cosmic relations. Boston, 1915. 2v.
Phil 2475.1.211	Hoogveld, J.E.H.J. "De nieuwe wijsbegeerte." Een studie over Henri Bergson. Utrecht, 1915.
Phil 5817.10	Hubbert, Helen B. Effect of age on habit formation in the albino rat. Baltimore, 1915.
Phil 410.75	Isenkrahe, Caspar. Das Endliche und das Unendliche. Münster, 1915.
Phil 5627.6.3	James, William. Varieties of religious experience. London, 1915.
Phil 9035.16.5	Jastrow, J. Character and temperament. N.Y., 1915.
Phil 8884.13	Johnston, George A. An introduction to ethics, for training colleges. London, 1915.
Phil 1830.2	Johnston, George A. Selections from the Scottish philosophy of common sense. Chicago, 1915.
Phil 6319.1.16	Jung, C.G. Diagnostische Assoziationsstudien. v.1-2. Leipzig, 1915.
Phil 6319.1	Jung, C.G. The theory of psychoanalysis. N.Y., 1915.
Phil 5325.15	Jung, Carl G. Über das Verhalten der Reaktionszeit. Leipzig, 1915.
Phil 3903.2.125	Jung, Johannes. Karl Vogts Weltanschauung. Paderborn, 1915.
Phil 3903.2.126	Jung, Johannes. Karl Vogts Weltanschauung. Inaug. Diss. Paderborn, 1915.
Phil 3480.80.80	Kant, Immanuel. Avhandlingar om fred och rätt. Stockholm, 1915.
Phil 5627.36	Kato, Katsuji. The psychology of oriental religious experience. Menaska, Wis., 1915.
Phil 6750.13	Key, Wilhelmine E. Feeble-minded citizens in Pennsylvania. Philadelphia, 1915.
Phil 935.5	Kishinami, T. The development of philosophy in Japan. Princeton, 1915.
Phil 1540.8	Knappe, O.F. The scholastic theory of the species sensibilis. Washington, 1915.
Phil 8590.4	Koenig, Julius. Religion a curse! Why? N.Y., 1915.
Phil 2115.105	Krakowski, E. Les sources médiévales de la philosophie de Locke. Paris, 1915.
Phil 2115.106	Krakowski, E. Les sources médiévales de la philosophie de Locke. Thèse. Paris, 1915.
Phil 5250.13	Krueger, Felix. Über Entwicklungspsychologie. Leipzig, 1915.
Phil 9120.7	Ladd, G.T. What ought I to do? N.Y., 1915.
Phil 5070.9	Ladd, G.T. What should I believe? London, 1915.
Phil 6681.6.5	Lapponi, Guiseppe. Hypnotism and spiritism...travel. 2. ed. N.Y., 1915.
Phil 4600.2.48	Larsson, Hans. Filosofien och politiken. Stockholm, 1915.
Phil 978.8.11	Leadbeater, C.W. Outline of theosophy. London, 1915.
Phil 5643.78	Leeser, Otto. Über Linien- und Flächenvergleichung. Inaug. Diss. Leipzig, 1915.
Phil 3552.39	Leibniz, Gottfried Wilhelm. Neue Abhandlungen über den menschlichen verstand. 3e Aufl. Leipzig, 1915.
Phil 525.49.5	Lejeune, Paul. An introduction to the mystical life. London, 1915.
Phil 186.55.5	Liljekrantz, B. Verklighetsproblemet i den antika filosofien. Göteborg, 1915.
Phil 4515.85.5	Liljeqvist, Efraim. Boströms äldsta latinska dissertationer. Thesis. Lund, 1915.
Phil 8701.4.5	Lodge, Oliver Joseph. The substance of faith allied with science. London, 1915.
Phil 525.234	Lodyzhenskii, M.V. Svet nezrimyi. Izd. 2. Petrograd, 1915.
Phil 2630.2.125	Łuczewski, Kazimierz. Das Problem der Religion in der Philosophie Guyaus. Posen, 1915.
Phil 8413.12	McAlpen, Colin. Hermara, a study in compatative aesthetics. London, 1915.
Phil 343.6	Macintosh, D.C. Problem of knowledge. N.Y., 1915.
Phil 9550.8	Mackaye, J. The happiness of nations. N.Y., 1915.
Phil 5822.10	MacNamara, N.C. Instinct and intelligence. London, 1915.
Phil 5627.27	Mainage, T. La psychologie de la conversion. Paris, 1915.
Phil 5722.6	Martin, L. Ein experimenteller Beitrag zur Erforschung. Leipzig, 1915.
Phil 5545.62	Martin, M.A. Transfer effects of practice in cancellation tests. N.Y., 1915.
Phil 8887.45	Mazumdar, A.K. Outlines of moral philosophy. Culcutta, 1915.
Phil 3832.10.15	Meijer, W. Spinoza, een levensbeeld. Amsterdam, 1915.
Phil 343.5.25	Meinong, A. Über Möglichkeit und Wahrscheinlichkeit. Leipzig, 1915.
Phil 665.26	Melegari, Dora. Il destarsi delle anime. Milano, 1915.
Phil 3832.9	Meozzi, A. Le dottrine politiche e religiose di B. Spinoza. Arezzo, 1915.
Phil 8702.9	Merz, J.T. Religion and science. Edinburgh, 1915.
Phil 343.10	Metzger, Arnold. Untersiechungen zur Frage die Differenz der Phänomenologie und des Kantianismus. Jena, 1915.
Phil 1504.18	Michel, K. Der "liber de consonanci a nature et gracie." v.18, pt.1. Münster, 1915.
Phil 7060.111.19	Middelton, Jessie A. Another grey ghost book. London, 1915.
Phil 7060.111.15	Middleton, Jessie A. The grey ghost book. London, 1915.
Phil 6990.13	Mir y Noguera, Juan. El milagro. 2. ed. Barcelona, 1915. 3v.
Phil 8837.6	Moore, T.V. Historical introduction to ethics. N.Y., 1915.
Phil 5252.31	Morando, G. Psicologia. 2a. ed. Voghera, 1915.
Phil 6122.26	Mott, Frederick Walker. Nature and nurture in mental development. N.Y., 1915.
Phil 3640.218.5	Mügge, M.A. Friedrich Nietzsche. N.Y., 1915?
Phil 5850.278.15	Münsterberg, H. Business psychology. Chicago, 1915.
Phil 8888.6.25	Nelson, Leonard. Ethische Methodenlehre. Leipzig, 1915.
Phil 960.17	Noble, M.E. Religion and dharma. London, 1915.
Phil 4610.7.12	Norström, V. Tankar och forskningar. Stockholm, 1915.
Phil 8889.3.7	Orestano, Francesco. Prolegomeni alla scienza del bene e del mali. Roma, 1915.
Phil 4365.1.5	Ors y Rovira, E. d'. Aprendizaje y heroismo. Madrid, 1915.
Phil 8890.23.5	Palmer, G.H. The glory of the imperfect. Boston, 1915.
Phil 5645.15	Parsons, J.H. Introduction to study of colour vision. Cambridge, 1915.
Phil 5080.4	Pauler, Ákos. A fogalom problémája a teozta logikaban. Budapest, 1915.

1915 - cont.

Phil 3850.7.81	Pelazza, Aurelio. W. Schuppe and the immanent philosophy. London, 1915.
Phil 5765.8	Pelikán, F. Entstehung und Entwicklung der Kontingentismus. Berlin, 1915.
Phil 3425.202	Pen, K.J. Over het onderscheid tusschen de wetenschap van Hegel en de wijsheid van Bolland. Leiden, 1915.
Phil 190.18.9	Perry, R.B. Philosophy. n.p., 1915.
Phil 5440.28.5	Peters, Wilhelm. Über Vererbung psychischer Fähigkeiten. Leipzig, 1915.
Phil 6325.1.3	Pfister, Oskar. The psychoanalytic method. London, 1915.
Phil 55.4.5	Philadelphia Neurological Society. Proceedings of the 30th anniversary, November 27-28, 1914. Philadelphi? 1915.
Phil 346.3.5	Philip, A. Essays towards a theory of knowledge. London, 1915.
Phil 7069.15.40	Philpott, Anthony J. The quest for Dean Bridgman Conner. London, 1915.
Phil 3552.121	Piat, C. Leibniz. Paris, 1915.
Phil 346.5	Piat, Clodius. L'intelligence et la vie. Paris, 1915.
Phil 5255.7.5	Pillsbury, W.B. The essentials of psychology. N.Y., 1915.
Phil 5850.311	Piorkowski, C. Beiträge zur psychologischen Methodologie der wirtschaftlichen Berufseignung. Leipzig, 1915.
Phil 8965.7	Powell, John W. What is a Christian? N.Y., 1915.
Phil 8735.9	Prandtl, Antonin. Über Teleologie des Geistes und über Teleologie überhaupt. Leipzig, 1915.
Phil 190.36	Prather, Charles E. Divine science. Denver, Col., 1915.
Phil 7039.10	Prince, Walter Franklin. The Doris case of multiple personality. York, Pa., 1915-16. 2v.
Phil 3245.87	Rakate, Georg. Immanuel Hermann Fichte. Leipzig, 1915.
Phil 8418.6.10	Raymond, G.L. An art philosopher's cabinet. N.Y., 1915.
Phil 6327.2	Raynier, Julien. Les états dépresifs...chez les militaires. Thèse. Paris, 1915.
Phil 8597.23	Reisner, Edward H. Religious values and intellectual consistency. N.Y., 1915.
Phil 348.3.4	Ribot, T. L'évolution des ideés générales. 4. éd. Paris, 1915.
Phil 7069.15.50	Richmond, Cora L. My experiences while out of my body and my return after many days. Boston, 1915.
Phil 7069.15.53	Richmond, Cora L. Psychosophy. Chicago, 1915.
Phil 192.21.3	Rickert, H. Der Gegenstand der Erkenntniss. 3. Aufl. Tübingen, 1915.
Phil 3925.6.90	Rickert, H. Wilhelm Windelband. Tübingen, 1915.
Phil 5190.4	Rickert, H. Zur Lehre von der Definition. 2e Aufl. Tübingen, 1915.
Phil 1817.3.5	Riley, I.W. American thought. N.Y., 1915.
Phil 8892.21	Robert, A. Leçons de morale. Quebec, 1915.
Phil 5257.19	Robert, Arthur. Leçons de psychologie. Québec, 1915.
Phil 5525.15	Roetschi, Robert. Der ästhetische Wert des Komischen und das Wesen des Humors. Bern, 1915.
Phil 5643.68.5	Rubin, Edgar. Synsoplevedefigurer. København, 1915.
Phil 930.25	Rudd, H.F. Chinese moral sentiments before Confucius. Diss. Chicago? 1915?
Phil 3850.18.15	Scheler, Max. Abhandlungen und Aufsätze. Leipzig, 1915. 2v.
Phil 1504.17.4	Schneider, A. Die abendländische Spekulation. v.17, pt.4. Münster, 1915.
Phil 3120.8.94	Schneider, Karl. Zur Kritik der Urteilslehre Franz Brentanos. Heidelberg, 1915.
Phil 3808.71.2	Schopenhauer, Arthur. The basis of morality. 2nd ed. London, 1915.
Phil 1504.13.5	Schulemann, G. Das Kausalprinzip. v.13, pt.5. Münster, 1915.
Phil 575.28	Schulz, Bernhard. Das Bewusstseinsproblem. Wiesbaden, 1915.
Phil 3500.54	Schwarz, W. Immanuel Kant als Pädagoge. Langensalza, 1915.
Phil 5627.35	Sears, Annie L. The drama of the spiritual life. N.Y., 1915.
Phil 8598.49	Segerstedt, T.K. Gammal och my religiositet. Stockholm, 1915.
Phil 2050.100	Shearer, Edna Aston. Hume's place in ethics. Diss. Bryn Mawr, 1915.
Phil 6750.17	Sheffield, Herman B. The backward baby. N.Y., 1915.
Phil 6128.24	Sheppard, E.E. The thinking universe. Los Angeles, 1915.
Phil 7069.15.60	Sigfússon, S. Dulsýnir. Reykjavik, 1915.
Phil 9035.24	Sisson, E.O. The essentials of character. N.Y., 1915.
Phil 8893.14.8.20	Smiles, Samuel. Self-help. N.Y., 1915.
Phil 5828.7	Smith, E.M. The investigation of mind in animals. Cambridge, 1915.
Phil 2733.89	Spehner, Edmund. Malebranches Lehre von der Erkenntnis in psychologischer Hinsicht. Inaug.-Diss. Borna, 1915.
Phil 3819.36.35	Spinoza, Benedictus de. Etica...testo latino. Bari, 1915.
Phil 3819.59	Spinoza, Benedictus de. Tractatus politicus. Lanciano, 1915.
Phil 6128.30	Starrett, D.W. The last lap. Boston, 1915.
Phil 315.3	Stefanescu, M. Le dualisme logique. Paris, 1915.
Phil 3500.25	Stefanescu, M. Essai sur le rapport entre le dualisme. Paris, 1915.
Phil 6021.2.85	Steinbrucker, C. Lavaters physiognomische...Kunst. Berlin, 1915.
Phil 7080.51	Stekel, W. Der Wille zum Schlaf! Wiesbaden, 1915.
Phil 193.53.5	Stern, L.W. Vorgedanken zur Weltanschauung. Leipzig, 1915.
Phil 672.25	Stevens, E.M. Psychology of space perception. New Orleans, 1915.
Phil 3640.109	Stewart, H.L. Nietzsche and the ideals of modern Germany. London, 1915.
Phil 6128.31.5	Stiles, Percy G. The nervous system and its conservation. Philadelphia, 1915.
Phil 5058.31	Stöhr, Adolf. Leitfaden der Logik in psychologisierender Darstellung. 2e Aufl. Leipzig, 1915.
Phil 5258.39	Sturt, Henry. Principles of understanding. Cambridge, 1915.
Phil 1135.83	Thomas Aquinas, Sister. The pre-Socratic use of [Psyche]. Washington, 1915.
Phil 1819.1	Thormeyer, Paul. Die grossen englischen Philosophen, Locke, Berkeley, Hume. Leipzig, 1915.
Phil 194.30	Tilgher, A. Teoria del pragmatismo trascendentale. Milano, 1915.
Phil 8894.13	Tomkins, D.B. The individual and society. Thesis. Somerville, N.J., 1915.
Phil 194.21.2	Troward, Thomas. The Edinburgh lectures on mental science. N.Y., 1915.
Phil 820.1.6.5	Ueberweg, F. Grundriss der Geschichte der Philosophie. v.2. 10. ed. Berlin, 1915.
Phil 525.7.5.3	Underhill, Evelyn. Practical mysticism; a little book for normal people. N.Y., 1915.

1915 - cont.

Phil 5261.7 — Valdarnini, Angelo. Elementi scientifici di psicologia e logica. 3-4. ed. pt.1-2. Torino, 1915.

Phil 1504.14.2 — Vansteenberghe, E. Autour de la "Docte Ignorance." v.14, pt.2-4. Münster, 1915.

Phil 6750.12 — Virginia. State Board of Charities and Corrections. Mental defectives in Virginia. Richmond, 1915.

X Cg Phil 4952.1.5 — Vvedenskii, A.I. Psikhologiia bez vsiakoi metafiziki. Petrograd, 1915.

Phil 8712.11.2 — Walsh, J.J. The popes and science. N.Y., 1915.

Phil 197.24 — Walter, Johnston E. Subject and object. West Newton, Pa., 1915.

Phil 6132.7.6 — Walton, G.L. Peg along. Philadelphia, 1915.

Phil 5262.19.5 — Ward, J. Naturalism and agnosticism. 4th ed. London, 1915.

Phil 1722.3 — Webb, C.C.J. A history of philosophy. London, 1915.

Phil 8602.18.7 — Webb, C.C.J. Problems in the relations of God and man. London, 1915.

Phil 8602.18.5 — Webb, C.C.J. Studies in the history of natural theology. Oxford, 1915.

Phil 822.12 — Webb, Clement C.J. A history of philosophy. N.Y., 1915.

Phil 8712.16 — Webber, G.P. Tro och vebande. Stockholm, 1915. 3v.

Phil 3805.96 — Wendland, J. Die Religiöse Entwicklung Schleiermachers. Tübingen, 1915.

Phil 8897.63.5 — Wilson, Woodrow. When a man comes to himself. N.Y., 1915.

Phil 197.9.4 — Windelband, W. Präluder. Stockholm, 1915.

Phil 5643.71 — Winkler, F. Studien über Wahrnehmungstauschungen. Leipzig, 1915.

Phil 5643.83 — Wirth, Wilhelm. Zur psychophysischen Analyse der repsoldschen Mikrometerrigistrierung von Sterndurchgängen. Leipzig, 1915.

Phil 3640.108 — Wolf, A. The philosophy of Nietzsche. London, 1915.

Phil 3640.110 — Wright, Willard H. What Nietzsche taught. N.Y., 1915.

Phil 3915.71.2 — Wundt, Wilhelm. Nationen und ihre Philosophie. Leipzig, 1915.

Phil 9430.36 — Zdziechowski, M. Pessymizm romantyzm a podstawy chrześcijaństwa. v.1-2. Krakow, 1915.

Phil 5265.1.9 — Ziehen, Theodor. Die Grundlagen der Psychologie. v.1-2. Leipzig, 1915.

1916

Phil 4351.4.5 — Alvarado, Francisco. Las cartas inéditas del filosofo rancio. Madrid, 1916.

Phil 1506.4 — Baeumker, Clemens. Platonismus in Mittelalter. München, 1916.

Phil 4115.93 — Balbino, G. Il primato d'un popolo; Fichte e Gioberti. Catania, 1916.

Phil 8656.13.3 — Balfour, A.J.B. L'idée de Dieu et l'esprit humain. 4. éd. Paris, 1916.

Phil 5649.7 — Barnes, J.C. Voluntary isolation of control in a natural muscle group. Diss. Princeton, 1916.

Phil 5241.41 — Batson, W.H. Acquisition of skill. Princeton, 1916.

Phil 801.22 — Bensow, Oscar. Grunddragen af filosofiens historia. Stockholm, 1916. 2v.

Phil 282.8 — Berdiaev, N. Smysl tvorchestva. Moskva, 1916.

DL Phil 5525.11.5 — Bergson, Henri. Il riso, saggio sul significato del comico. Bari, 1916.

Phil 801.12 — Bevan, J.O. Handbook of history and development of philosophy. London, 1916.

Phil 6750.216 — Binet, Alfred. The intelligence of the feeble-minded. Baltimore, 1916.

Phil 4520.8.52 — Bjarnason, Ágúst. Almenn sálarfraeđ Reykjavík, 1916.

Phil 8876.104 — Blanchard, Mme. Common sense. N.Y., 1916.

Phil 8876.105 — Blanchard, Mme. Timidity. N.Y., 1916.

Phil 4520.1.31 — Blomquist, G. Lyckovägar. Stockholm, 1916.

Phil 176.71 — Bonaventura, E. Le qualità del mondo fisico. Firenze, 1916.

Phil 332.5.5 — Boodin, J.E. A realistic universe. N.Y., 1916.

Phil 5041.15.2 — Boole, George. The laws of thought. Chicago, 1916.

Phil 5648.17 — Boring, Edwin G. Cutaneous sensation after nerve-division. London, 1916.

Phil 4065.101 — Boulting, William. Giordano Bruno, his life, thought and martyrdom. London, 1916.

Phil 2477.1.34 — Boutroux, Emile. The contingency of the laws of nature. Chicago, 1916.

Phil 2477.1.63 — Boutroux, Émile. Philosophy and war. London, 1916.

Phil 2477.1.64 — Boutroux, Émile. Philosophy and war. N.Y., 1916.

Phil 4001.3 — Braschi, C. I filosofi italiani dal XVIII al XIX secolo. Milano, 1916.

Phil 176.65 — Brass, T. Chapter from story of Pauline Parsons. Ashland, 1916.

Phil 2475.1.158 — Brockdorff, Cary. Die Wahrheit über Bergson. Berlin, 1916.

Phil 8691.10 — Brookshire, E.V. The law of human life; scriptures in the light of science. N.Y., 1916.

Phil 4210.89 — Bruno, J.F. Rosmini's contribution to ethical philosophy. N.Y., 1916.

Phil 4357.1.81 — Carvalho, Joaquim de. Antonio de Gouveia e o Aristotelismo la renascenca. Coimbra, 1916.

Phil 3484.6.3 — Chamberlain, H.S. Immanuel Kant. Die Persönlichkeit...in das Werke. 3. Aufl. München, 1916.

Phil 960.26 — Chamberlain, Houston. Arische Weltanschauung. 3. Aufl. München, 1916.

Phil 7069.16.10 — Churchill, Lida A. The truth about our dead told by those who know. 1st ed. N.Y., 1916.

Phil 8582.26 — Collingwood, Robin George. Religion and philosophy. London, 1916.

Phil 1750.103 — Compagnion, Jean. La philosophie scolastique au XXe siècle. Critique néo-scotiste du Thomisme. Paris, 1916.

Phil 5545.58 — Coover, J.E. Formal discipline...experimental psychology. Thesis. Princeton, 1916.

Phil 5042.13 — Cordier, Paul. Les problèmes de la logique. Paris, 1916.

Phil 333.10 — Cornelius, Hans. Transcendentale Systematik. Teil 1-2. München, 1916.

Phil 9560.10 — Courtenay, Charles. The empire of silence. N.Y., 1916.

Phil 2138.94 — Crawford, J.F. The relation of inference to fact in Mill's logic. Chicago, 1916.

Phil 2138.119 — Crawford, John F. The relation of inference to fact in Mill's logic. Chicago, 1916.

Phil 177.55 — Crowell, Frank. Man - God's masterpiece. N.Y., 1916.

Phil 2475.1.157 — Cunningham, G.W. A study in the philosophy of Bergson. N.Y., 1916.

Phil 575.71 — Daudet, Léon A. L'hérédo; essai sur le drame intérieur. Paris, 1916.

Phil 6113.7 — Dearborn, G.V.N. Influence of joy. Boston, 1916.

Phil 3823.6 — Delblos, Victor. Le spinozisme. Paris, 1916.

1916 - cont.

Phil 5753.7.2 — Demeny, Georges. L'éducation de l'effort psychologie-physiologie. 2. éd. Paris, 1916.

Phil 8583.16.8 — Deussen, Paul. Bibelns filosofi. Stockholm, 1916.

Phil 5043.16.5 — Dewey, J. Essays in experimental logic. Chicago, 1916.

Phil 2530.19 — Diderot, Denis. Dederot's early philosophical works. Chicago, 1916.

Phil 8583.14 — Drake, Durant. Problems of religion. Boston, 1916.

Phil 6113.19 — Driesch, Hans. Leib und Seele. Leipzig, 1916.

Phil 3823.9 — Dunham, J.H. Freedom and purpose; an interpretation of the psychology of Spinoza. Princeton, N.J., 1916.

Phil 5722.8 — Dwelshauvers, G. L'inconscient. Paris, 1916.

Phil 8584.9 — Eberhardt, Paul. Von der Möglichkeit und der Notwendigkeit der reinen Religion. Gotha, 1916.

Phil 9220.9 — Eglinger, Ruth. Der Begriff der Freundschaft in der Philosophie. Inaug. Diss. Basel, 1916.

Phil 285.1 — Ehrenfils, C. Kosmogonie. Jena, 1916.

Phil 179.15 — Einhorn, David. Der Kampf um einen Gegenstand der Philosophie. Wien, 1916.

Phil 8694.3 — Emery, J.A. Quelques lettres au physicien G.L. Le Sage. Paris, 1916.

Phil 5850.188 — Erismann, T. Angewandte Psychologie. Berlin, 1916.

Phil 4115.84 — Ern, V.F. Filosofiia dzhoberti. Moskva, 1916.

Phil 179.10 — Ettinger-Reichmann, Regina. Die Immanenzphilosophie. Göttingen, 1916.

Phil 3004.1.10 — Eucken, Rudolf. Die Träger des deutschen Idealismus. Berlin, 1916.

Phil 5244.21 — Evans, John E. The effect of distraction on reaction time. N.Y., 1916.

Phil 5755.20.2 — Fassbender, Martin. Wollen; eine königliche Kunst. 2. und 3. Aufl. Freiburg, 1916.

Phil 180.2.5 — Fawcett, E.D. World as imagination. Series 1-2. London, 1916-1921. 2v.

Phil 6315.1 — Ferenczi, Sandor. Contributions to psycho-analysis. Boston, 1916.

Phil 4610.7.90 — Festskrift tillägnad Vitalis Norström. Göteborg, 1916.

Phil 7069.16.17 — Finnbogason, Gudmundr. Pörfin á vinnuvísindum. Reykjavik, 1916.

Phil 5360.8 — Fisher, S.C. The process of generalizing abstraction. Thesis. Princeton, N.J., 1916.

Phil 286.2.15 — Fiske, J. Outlines of cosmic philosophy. Boston, 1916. 4v.

Phil 8050.54 — Flaccus, L.W. Artists and thinkers. N.Y., 1916.

Phil 8630.9.10 — Fosdick, H.E. The assurance of immortality. N.Y., 1916.

Phil 8630.7.5 — Frank, Henry. Psychic phenomena; science and immortality. 2. ed. Boston, 1916.

Phil 5525.6.5A — Freud, Sigmund. Wit and its relation to the unconscious. N.Y., 1916.

Phil 7069.16.20 — Fuller, George A. Wisdom of the ages. 2. ed. Boston, 1916.

Phil 6116.17 — Gaskell, Walter H. The involuntary nervous system. London, 1916.

Phil 7140.110 — Gaupp, Robert. Wahn und Irrtum im Leben der Völker. Tübingen, 1916.

Phil 181.49 — Geijer, Reinhold. Filosofiens historiska hufvudformer. Uppsala, 1916.

Phil 5816.6 — Gesellschaft für Tierpsychologie. Die Seele des Tieres. Berlin, 1916.

Phil 5246.23 — Giese, Fritz. Psychologische Beiträge. Langensalza, 1916-

Phil 4357.2.3 — Giner de los Rios, Francisco. Obras completas. v.1-19. Madrid, 1916-27. 15v.

Phil 705.18 — Girard, William. Du transcendentalisme considéré essentiellement dans sa définition et ses origines françaises. Berkeley, 1916.

Phil 400.57 — Giuliano, B. Il valore degl'ideali. Torino, 1916.

Phil 8407.18.5 — Gleichen-Russwurm, A. Die Schönheit. Stuttgart, 1916?

Phil 7069.16.25 — Grabinski, B. Neuere mystik. Hildesheim, 1916.

Phil 1504.17.5 — Grabmann, M. Forschungen über die lateinischen Aristoteles. v.17, pt.5-6. Münster, 1916.

Phil 2475.1.175 — Grandjian, Frank. Une révolution dans la philosophie. 2e ed. Genève, 1916.

Phil 6676.6 — Grásset, J. L'hypnotisme et la suggestion. 4. éd. Paris, 1916.

Phil 8407.16.2 — Grzegorzewska, M. Essai sur le développement du sentiment esthétique. Paris, 1916.

Phil 8407.16 — Grzegorzewska, M. Essai sur le développement du sentiment esthétique. Paris, 1916.

Phil 9347.10 — Hackley, E.A. (Mrs.). The colored girl beautiful. Kansas City, 1916.

Phil 5520.31 — Häberlin, Paul. Symbol in der Psychologie. Bern, 1916.

Phil 182.63 — Hallett, T.G.P. That life is the origin and purpose of the universe. London, 1916.

Phil 8587.58 — Hallimond, J.G. The miracle of answered prayers. N.Y., 1916.

Phil 6957.18 — Hamilton, A.M. Recollections of an alienist. N.Y., 1916.

Phil 525.20 — Hamilton, C.H. A psychological interpretation of mysticism. Diss. Chicago, 1916.

Phil 5817.11 — Hamilton, Gilbert V. A study of perseverance reactions. N.Y., 1916.

Phil 8882.40 — Hamilton, William E. Studies in moral science. Chicago, 1916.

Phil 5465.24 — Hammer, Bertil. Fantasien. Uppsala, 1916.

Phil 8882.45 — Hansen, Osvald. Etikkens grundlag. Kobenhavn, 1916.

Phil 4800.6 — Harassek, Stefan. Kant w Polsce przed rokiem 1830. Kraków, 1916.

Phil 5402.9 — Harbin, R.M. Paradoxical pain. Boston, 1916.

Phil 665.28 — Hein, Joseph. Aktualität oder Substantialität der Seele? Inaug. Diss. Paderborn, 1916.

Phil 5655.5 — Henning, H. Der Geruch. Leipzig, 1916.

Phil 3195.3.82 — Hepner, Adolf. Josef Dietzgens philosophische Lehren. Stuttgart, 1916.

Phil 5047.20 — Herbertz, Richard. Prolegomena zu einer realistischen Logik. Halle, 1916.

Phil 525.30.2 — Herman, E. The meaning and value of mysticism. 2nd ed. London, 1916.

Phil 6117.20 — Herrick, C.J. An introduction to neurology. Philadelphia, 1916.

Phil 1504.19.2 — Hessen, J. Die Begründung der Erkenntnis. v.19, pt.2-3. Münster, 1916.

Phil 510.25 — Heyde, Erich. Grundlegung der Wertlehre. Leipzig, 1916.

Phil 5325.18 — Hintermann, H. Experimentelle Untersuchung der Bewusstseinsvorgänge. Zürich, 1916.

Phil 2475.1.169 — Höffding, Harald. Philosophie de Bergson. Paris, 1916.

Phil 4580.63 — Höffding, Harald. Den store humor. Kjøbenhavn, 1916.

Phil 7060.139.5 — Hubbell, Walter. The great Amherst mystery. 10th ed. N.Y., 1916.

Phil 2270.93.16A — Hudson, William Henry. Herbert Spencer. London, 1916.

Phil 6945.25 Hurd, Henry M. The institutional care of the insane in the United States and Canada. Baltimore, 1916-17. 4v.

Phil 1050.10 Husik, I. History of medieval Jewish philosophy. N.Y., 1916.

Phil 8882.24.15 Hyde, W. De W. Are you human? N.Y., 1916.

Phil 4309.1 Ingenieros, José. La cultura filosófica en España. Madrid, 1916.

Phil 184.3.20 James, W. Pragmatism. Stockholm, 1916.

Phil 2070.65.4 James, William. Gli ideali della vita. 4a ed. Torino, 1916.

Phil 6021.2.87 Janentzky, C.J.C. Lavaters physiognomische Fragmente. Halle, 1916.

NEDL Phil 184.16.5 Jodl, F. Vom Lebenswege. Stuttgart, 1916-1917. 2v.

Phil 7082.52.2 Jóhannsson, Jón. Draumur. 2. Utgáfa. Reykjavík, 1916.

Phil 3425.207 Jong, K.H.E. de. Hegel und Plotin. Leiden, 1916.

Phil 2805.111 Jovy, Ernest. D'où irent l' "Ad tuum, Domine Jesu, de Pascal? Paris, 1916. 2 pam.

Phil 6319.1.6 Jung, C.G. Analytical psychology. N.Y., 1916.

Phil 6319.1.5A Jung, C.G. Collected papers on analytical psychology. London, 1916.

Phil 6319.1.9.5 Jung, C.G. Psychology of the unconscious. London, 1916.

Phil 6319.1.9A Jung, C.G. Psychology of the unconscious. N.Y., 1916.

Phil 3480.131.3 Kant, Immanuel. Kant Laienbrevier. 3. Aufl. München, 1916.

Phil 6320.2 Kaplan, Leo. Psychoanalytische Probleme. Leipzig, 1916.

Phil 341.10 Kastenholz, Joseph. Der Begriff des Dinges in der Philosophie der Gegenwart. Inaug. Diss. Bonn, 1916.

Phil 7069.16.30 Kates, George W. The philosophy of spiritualism. Boston, 1916.

Phil 8665.4 Kawaguchi, U. The bearing of the evolutionary theory on the conception of God. Thesis. Menasha, Wis., 1916.

Phil 341.8 Kehr, Theodor. Das Bewusstseinsproblem. Tübingen, 1916.

Phil 9035.84.10 King, Henry C. How to make a rational fight for character. N.Y., 1916.

Phil 8665.5 Klostermann, E. Späte Vergeltung aus der Geschichte der Theodicee. Strassburg, 1916.

Phil 9350.1 Knott, Laura A. Vesper talks to girls. Boston, 1916.

Phil 8885.33 Koch, Gregor. Das menschliche Leben. Ensiedeln, 1916.

Phil 8590.12 Köhler, Friedrich. Kulturwege und Erkenntnisse. Leipzig, 1916. 2v.

Phil 6320.4 Kortsen, K.K. De psykiske spaltninger. København, 1916.

Phil 5190.2 Kramp, Leo. Das Verhältnis von Urteil und Satz. Bonn, 1916.

Phil 3625.9.80 Kraus, Oskar. Anton Marty; sein Leben und seine Werke. Halle, 1916.

Phil 5050.10 Kries, Johannes von. Logik. Tübingen, 1916.

Phil 3493.13.5 Lamanna, E.P. Il fondamento morale...secondo Kant. Firenze, 1916.

Phil 5251.17 Lanfeld, H.S. Elementry laboratory course in psychology. Boston, 1916.

Phil 665.34 Larkin, E.L. The matchless altar of the soul. Los Angeles, 1916.

Phil 4600.2.37 Larsson, Hans. Hemmabyarna världsbetraklelser i femton kapitel. Stockholm, 1916.

Phil 6321.1 Lattimore, E.L. Some illustrative clinic cases. Thesis. Menasha, 1916.

Phil 3552.56 Leibniz, Gottfried Wilhelm. Abhandlung über die beste philosophische Ausdrucksweise. Berlin, 1916.

Phil 3552.23 Leibniz, Gottfried Wilhelm. Deutsche Schriften. Leipzig, 1916. 2v.

Phil 8735.17 Lesparre, A. de G. L'idée de finalité. Paris, 1916.

Phil 8636.2 Leuba, James H. The belief in God and immortality. Boston, 1916.

Phil 3552.277 Liebniz: zum Gedächtnis seines. 200. Jahrigen Todestages. Hannover, 1916.

Phil 5520.117 Lintsbakh, Ia. Printsipy filosofskogo iazyka. Petrograd, 1916.

Phil 4515.93 Ljunghoff, Johannes. Christopher Jacob Boström Sveriges Platon. Uppsala, 1916.

Phil 7069.16.40 Lodge, Oliver Joseph. Raymond. N.Y., 1916.

Phil 7069.16.41 Lodge, Oliver Joseph. The survival of man. 7. ed. London, 1916.

Phil 575.110 Lucka, E. Grenzen der Seele. Berlin, 1916.

Phil 5645.21 Lucky, Bertha. The specific brightness of colors. Lincoln, 1916.

Phil 3640.98.20 Ludovici, Anthony M. Nietzsche, his life and works. London, 1916.

Phil 6961.15 Lugaro, E. La psichiatria tedesca. Firenze, 1916.

Phil 7069.16.65 McKenzie, J.H. Spirit intercourse. 5th ed. London, 1916.

Phil 7082.154 Maeder, Alphonse. The dream problem. N.Y., 1916.

Phil 187.31.7 Malapert, P. Leçons de philosophie. v.1. 6. ed.; v.2. 7. ed. Paris, 1916-1918. 2v.

Phil 187.50 Marbe, Karl. Die Gleichförmigkeit in der Welt. München, 1916-1919. 2v.

Phil 5252.32 Marchesini, Giovanni. Psicologia elementare, ad uso dei licei. pt.1-3. Firenze, 1916. 2v.

Phil 8637.13 Martin, A.W. Faith in a future life. N.Y., 1916.

Phil 8615.14 Martin, Alfred W. Deity, duty, destiny; selections from addresses. N.Y., 1916.

Phil 187.68 Marty, Anton. Gesammelte Schriften. Halle, 1916-1918. 2v.

Phil 672.124 Marty, Anton. Raum und Zeit. Halle, 1916.

Phil 6122.1.19 Maudsley, H. Organic to human; psychology and sociology. London, 1916.

Phil 270.43 Mercier, Charles A. On causation, with a chapter on belief. London, 1916.

Phil 575.21 Merrington, E.N. The problem of personality. London, 1916.

Phil 343.9 Merton, Adolf. Gedanken über Grundprobleme der Erkenntnistheorie. München, 1916.

Phil 2475.1.165 Miller, L.H. Bergson and religion. N.Y., 1916.

Phil 575.235 Miller, Reinhold. Persönlichkeit und Gemeinschaft zur Kritik der neothomistischen Persönlichkeitsauffassung. Berlin, 1916.

Phil 6122.39 Mills, James P. Illumination; spiritual healing. N.Y., 1916.

Phil 8520.17 Monod, Albert. De Pascal à Chateaubriand. Paris, 1916.

Phil 5330.17 Morgan, H.H.B. The overcoming of distraction and other resistances. N.Y., 1916.

Phil 1504.19 Müller, W. Der Staat in seinen Beziehungen zur sittlichen. v.19, pt.1. Münster, 1916.

Phil 5252.38 Müller-Freienfels, R. Das Denken und die Phantasie. Leipzig, 1916.

Phil 4635.2.90 Naesgaard, S. Starkes psykologi. København, 1916.

Phil 3552.257 Nathan, Bernhard. Uber das Verhältnis der leibnizischen Ethik zu Metaphysik und Theologie. Diss. Jena, 1916.

Phil 53.3F National Committee for Mental Hygiene. Eight annual meeting (typed announcements). n.p., 1916.

Phil 6750.15 National Conference of Charities and Corrections. Feeble-mindedness and insanity. Chicago, 1916?

Phil 3640.77A Nietzsche, Friedrich. Briefwechsel mit Franz Overbeck. Leipzig, 1916.

Phil 3640.25.7 Nietzsche, Friedrich. Gedichte und Sprüche. Leipzig, 1916.

Phil 9495.39 Northcote, Hugh. Christianity and sex problems. 2d ed. Philadelphia, 1916.

Phil 7060.92.41 O'Donnell, Elliot. Twenty years' experience as a ghost hunter. London, 1916.

Phil 179.3.125 Oldendorff, Paul. Von deutscher Philosophie des Lebens. Langensalza, 1916.

Phil 8889.1.10 Ollé-Laprune, L. Les sources de la paix intellectuelle. 7. ed. Paris, 1916.

Phil 8964.1 Ottley, Robert L. Christian ideas and ideals. London, 1916.

Phil 630.31 Padovani, U.A. Il neorealismo anglo-americano. Firenze, 1916.

Phil 2250.80 Papers in honor of Josiah Royce on his sixtieth birthday. Lancaster, Pa., 1916.

Phil 7069.16.50 Parker, Frank E. Christian wisdom. Cambridge, Mass., 1916.

Phil 6125.9 Patrick, G.T.W. The psychology of relaxation. Boston, 1916.

Phil 6125.9.3 Patrick, G.T.W. The psychology of relaxation. Boston, 1916.

Phil 3497.8 Pekelharing, C. Kant's Teleologie. Gröningen, 1916.

Phil 3808.119.5 Pfordten, T. von der. Staat und Recht bei Schopenhauer. München, 1916.

Phil 5255.7 Pillsbury, W.B. Fundamentals of psychology. N.Y., 1916.

Phil 346.10 Piper, H. Prinzipielle Grundlagen. Göttingen, 1916.

Phil 6325.8.6 Prince, Morton. The unconscious. N.Y., 1916.

Phil 3015.2 Przygodda, Paul. Deutsche Philosophie v.2. Berlin, 1916.

Phil 6126.5 Quackenbos, J.D. Body and spirit. N.Y., 1916.

Phil 102.3.2 Ranzoli, C. Dizionario di scienze filosofiche. 2a ed. Milano, 1916.

Phil 192.44.2 Rappoport, A.S. A primer of philosophy. London, 1916.

Phil 8967.3 Rashdall, H. Conscience and Christ; six lectures. London, 1916.

Phil 192.42 Redgrove, H.S. Matter, spirit and the cosmos. London, 1916.

Phil 192.52 Rein, Doris. Hvad er kultur? Kristiania, 1916.

Phil 3640.185 Reiner, Julius. F. Nietzsche. Stuttgart, 1916.

Phil 348.5.5 Reininger, R. Das psycho-physische Problem. Wien, 1916.

Phil 192.25.9 Rey, A. Logique et morale. 4. ed. Paris, 1916.

Phil 8707.7.3 Rice, William N. The return to faith. N.Y., 1916.

Phil 3808.119 Richert, Hans. Schopenhauer; seine Persönlichkeit. 3. Aufl. Leipzig, 1916.

Phil 8610.916 Ricker, M.M. I don't know, do you? East Aurora, N.Y., 1916.

Htn Phil 9495.35* Robie, W.F. Rational sex ethics. Boston, 1916.

Phil 9358.9 Saint-Jacques, F. Lettres à Claude. Québec, 1916.

Phil 525.20.5 Salomon, Gotfried. Beitrag zur Problematik von Mystik und Glaube. Strassburg, 1916.

Phil 3018.7A Santayana, G. Egotism in German philosophy. Photoreproduction. London, 1916?

Phil 4065.160 Saraw, Julie. Der Einfluss Plotins auf Giordano Brunos Degli eroici furori. Borna-Leipzig, 1916.

Phil 1718.6 Sarlo, Francesco de. Filosofi del tempo nostro. Firenze, 1916.

Phil 1504.13 Schedler, M. Die Philosophie des Macrobius. v.13, pt.1. Münster, 1916.

Phil 5828.16 Schmid, Bastian. Das Tier und Wir. Leipzig, 1916.

Phil 978.88 Schmidt, A.N. Iz rukopisei Anny Nikolaevny Shmidt. Moskva, 1916.

Phil 193.79 Schnyder, Otto. Philosophische Reden. Zürich, 1916.

Phil 3625.1.125 Scholz, Heinrich. Die Hauptschriften zum pantheismus Streit. Berlin, 1916.

Phil 3808.29.15 Schopenhauer, Arthur. Uren met Schopenhauer. Baarn, 1916.

Phil 5627.39 Schroeder, Theodore. Erotogenesis of religion. N.Y., 1916.

Phil 630.9 Sellars, R.W. Critical realism. N.Y., 1916.

Phil 1535.30 Shallo, Michael. Lessons in scholastic philosophy. Philadelphia, 1916.

Phil 6968.12.7 Sidis, Boris. The causation and treatment of psychopathic diseases. Boston, 1916.

Phil 525.31 The silent voice. 2d ser. London, 1916.

Phil 7082.45 Símonardottir, Helga. Draumur. Reykjavík, 1916.

Phil 8644.13 Slater, J.R. Living for the future. Boston, 1916.

Phil 8643.12 Slattery, C.L. The gift of immortality. Boston, 1916.

Phil 6968.14 Smith, S. Who is insane? N.Y., 1916.

Phil 5440.20 Sommer, Georg. Geistige Veranlagung und Vererbung. Leipzig, 1916.

Phil 812.9.9 La sophistique étude de philosophie comparée. n.p., 1916.

Phil 3819.72 Spinoza, Benedictus de. Briefwechsel und andere Dokumente. Leipzig, 1916.

Phil 1504.15 Stadler, H.J. Albertus Magnus. v.15,16. Münster, 1916. 2v.

Phil 5258.76.10 Starcke, C.N. Kritiken af min psychologi svar til mine kritikere. Kjøbenhavn, 1916.

Phil 4635.2.34F Starcke, C.N. Den menneskelige tänkning. Kopenhagen, 1916.

Phil 5768.10 Steiner, Rudolf. The philosophy of freedom. London, 1916.

Phil 3018.8 Stockum, T.C. Spinoza, Jacobi, Lessing. Groningen, 1916.

Phil 3838.7 Stockum, T.C. van. Spinoza's beoordeeling en invloed in duitschland van 1677 tob 1750. Groningen, 1916.

Phil 5058.30 Störring, Gustav. Logik. Leipzig, 1916.

Phil 5400.41 Störring, Gustav. Psychologie des menschlichen Gefühlslebens. Bonn, 1916.

Phil 3246.175 Strecker, Reinhard. Die Anfänge von Fichtes Staatsphilosophie. Leipzig, 1916.

Phil 5058.33.4 Subrahmanyam, A. Logic, inductive and deductive. Madras, 1916.

Phil 1135.130 Swain, Joseph W. The Hellenic origins of Christian asceticism. N.Y., 1916.

Phil 8599.18 Thompson, J. Buckland. Exact science of Christianity. Garden City, N.Y., 1916.

Phil 6969.4 Thuillier-Landry, L. Études sur les délires d'évolution démentielle précoce. Thèse. Paris, 1916.

Phil 5255.18 Titchener, E.B. A beginner's psychology. N.Y., 1916.

Phil 5260.6 Ude, Johnson. Einführung in die Psychologie. Graz, 1916.

Phil 3903.3.50 Vaihinger, Hans. Der Atheismusstreit gegen die Philosophie des Als Ob. Berlin, 1916.

1916 - cont.

Phil 3640.126.4 Vaihinger, Hans. Nietzsche als Philosoph. 4e Aufl. Berlin, 1916.
Phil 672.23 VanRiper, B.W. Some views of the time problem. Diss. Menasha, 1916.
Phil 5400.40 Vives, Juan L. Tratado del alma. Madrid, 1916.
Phil 3805.190 Vogelsang, A.A. De preeken von Schleiermacher Praefschrift. Leiden, 1916.
Phil 5780.6 Washburn, M.F. Movement and mental imagery. Boston, 1916.
Phil 8602.18 Webb, C.C.J. Group theories of religion and the individual. London, 1916.
Phil 5635.17 Weidensall, C.J. Studies in rhythm. Cincinnati, 1916.
Phil 2262.84 Weiser, C.F. Shaftesbury und das deutsche Geistesleben. Leipzig, 1916.
Phil 9120.9 Wendt, Hans H. Die sittliche Pflicht. Göttingen, 1916.
Phil 8897.28.5 Westermarck, E. Moralens uppkomst och utveckling. Stockholm, 1916.
Phil 9035.23 White, William A. Mechanisms of character formation. N.Y., 1916.
Phil 8897.37 Whittaker, Thomas. Theory of abstract ethics. Cambridge, 1916.
Phil 8897.52 Wilkens, C. Etisk vurdering. København, 1916.
Phil 197.25 Williams, C.L. Creative involution. N.Y., 1916.
Phil 8897.59 Wilson, M.H. Vocational guidance. Boston, 1916.
Phil 9513.16 Wilson, Matthew Hale. An inductive study of standards of right. Boston, 1916.
Phil 9070.34.5 Wilson, W. On being human. N.Y., 1916.
Phil 1050.14.2 Wolfson, Harry A. Crescas on problem of divine attributes. Philadelphia, 1916.
Phil 7069.16.60 Worth, Patience. Patience Worth; a psychic mystery. N.Y., 1916.
Phil 8712.5.18 Wright, George F. Story of my life and work. Oberlin, 1916.
Phil 8602.19 Wright, H.W. Faith justified by progress. N.Y., 1916.
Phil 8423.5 Wright, W.H. The creative will, studies in the philosophy and syntax of aesthetics. N.Y., 1916.
Phil 3915.59 Wundt, Wilhelm. Elements of folk psychology. London, 1916.
Phil 3552.125.9 Wundt, Wilhelm. Gottfried Wilhelm Leibnitz. Gestorben 1716. Stuttgart, 1916.
Phil 3915.71 Wundt, Wilhelm. Die Nationen und ihre Philosophie. Leipzig, 1916.
Phil 5834.1.9A Yerkes, R.M. Mental life of monkeys and apes. Cambridge, 1916.
Phil 7140.122 Yoritomo-Tashi. Influence; how to exert it. N.Y., 1916.
Phil 199.2 Younghusband, F. The sense of community. London, 1916.
Phil 356.2 Zilsel, Edgar. Das Anwendungsproblem. Leipzig, 1916.

1917

Phil 6110.13 Abrutz, Sydney. Till nervsystems dynamik. Stockholm, 1917.
Phil 6310.1 Adler, A. The neurotic constitution; individualistic psychology. N.Y., 1917.
Phil 175.26 Aliotta, Antonio. La guerra eterna e il dramma dell'esistenza. Napoli, 1917.
Phil 960.18.5 Altekar, A.S. Sources of Hindu dharma in its socio-religious aspects. Chicago, 1917.
Phil 960.16 Ananda Achárya. Brahmadarsanam...introduction to the study of Hindu philosophy. London, 1917.
Phil 8677.9.80 Archer, William. God and Mr. Wells. N.Y., 1917.
Phil 331.2.13 Avenarius, R. Philosophie als Denken der Welt Gemäss dem Prinzip des kleinsten Kraftmasses. 3. Aufl. Berlin, 1917.
Phil 7060.82.4 Barrett, W.F. On the threshold of the unseen. London, 1917.
Phil 8581.58 Barrow, George A. The validity of the religious experience. Boston, 1917.
Phil 9530.43 Barton, Bruce. More power to you. N.Y., 1917.
Phil 7069.17.10 Bates, Emily K. Our living dead. London, 1917.
Phil 6111.50 Batten, L.W. The relief of pain by mental suggestion. N.Y., 1917.
Phil 3483.8.8 Bauch, Bruno. Immanuel Kant. Berlin, 1917.
Phil 8735.15 Becher, Erich. Die fremddienliche Zweckmässigkeit der Pflanzgallen und dieHypothese eines überindividuellen Seelischen. Leipzig, 1917.
Phil 2475.1.197 Benda, Julien. Le bergsonisme. 5e éd. Paris, 1917.
Phil 1865.60 Bentham, Jeremy. Not Paul, but Jesus. Camden, 1917.
Phil 2005.3.80 Beresford, J.D. W.E. Ford: a biography. London, 1917.
Phil 2005.3.81 Beresford, J.D. W.E. Ford: a biography. London, 1917.
Phil 6671.5.9 Bernheim, H. Automatisme et suggestion. Paris, 1917.
Phil 8951.14 Beysens, J.T. Hoofdstukken uit de bijzondere ethiek. v.1-5. Bussum, 1917-19-.
Phil 3640.179 Binder, Elsa. Malwida vom Meysenburg und Friedrich Nietzsche. Berlin, 1917.
Phil 7060.129 Boirac, Émile. L'avenir des sciences psychiques. Paris, 1917.
Phil 7069.17.13 Boirac, Émile. Our hidden forces. N.Y., 1917.
Phil 3120.35.30 Bolland, G.J.P.J. Natuurbegrip en leuen. Leiden, 1917. 2 pam.
Phil 6049.17 Bouchet, G. Cosmogonie humaine. Vichy, 1917.
Phil 4210.140 Bozzetti, Giuseppe. Rosmini nell'ultima critica di Ausonio Franchi. Firenze, 1917.
Phil 6311.1.3 Brill, A.A. Psychanalysis. 2. ed. Philadelphia, 1917.
Phil 5649.9 Browne, George H. The esthetics of motion. New Ulm, 1917.
Phil 3120.30.22A Buber, Martin. Volker, Staaten und Zion. Berlin, 1917.
Phil 974.3.155 Bugaev, Boris N. Rudolf Steiner i gete v mirovozzrenii sovremennosti. Moskva, 1917.
Phil 8581.54 Bulgakov, S. Sviet nevechernii. Moskva, 1917.
Phil 1701.9.5 Busse, Ludwig. Die Weltanschauungen der grossen Philosophie der Neuzeit. 6e Aufl. Leipzig, 1917.
Phil 5751.4 Bussey, Gertrude C. Typical recent conceptions of freedom. Thesis. Greenfield, 1917.
Phil 7069.17.23 Cadwallader, Mary E. Hydesville in history. Chicago, 1917.
Phil 2040.80 Carlini, Armando. Herbert di Cherbury e la scuola di Cambridge. Roma, 1917.
Phil 4080.3.80 Carr, Herbert Wildon. The philosophy of Benedetto Croce. London, 1917.
Phil 6112.20 Carroll, Robert S. The mastery of nervousness based upon self-reeducation. N.Y., 1917.
Phil 7069.17.23 Clodd, Edward. The question: "If a man die, shall he live again?" London, 1917.
Phil 5627.26.5 Coe, George A. The psychology of religion. Chicago, 1917.
Phil 3484.2.16A Cohen, H. Kommentar zu Immanuel Kant's Kritik. 2. Aufl. Leipzig, 1917.
Phil 2490.52 Comte, Auguste. La méthode positive en seize leçons. Paris, 1917.

1917 - cont.

Phil 7069.17.24 Cook, Walter. Reflections on "Raymond". London, 1917.
Phil 51.2 Coover, J.E. Experiments in psychical research at Stanford Junior University. Stanford, 1917.
Phil 7069.17.25 Coover, John Edgar. Experiments in psychical research at Leland Stanford Jr. University. n.p. 1917.
Phil 177.39 Creative intelligence: Essays in pragmatic attitude. N.Y., 1917.
Phil 5042.10.5 Croce, B. Logic as the science of the pure concept. London, 1917.
Phil 1750.123.5 Denkers over zeil en leven. Amsterdam, 1917.
Phil 8878.36 Deshumbert, Marius. An ethical system based on the laws of nature. Chicago, 1917.
Phil 960.3.15 Deussen, P. Vedânta, Platon und Kant. 2. Aufl. Wien, 1917.
Phil 2520.121 Dimier, Louis. Descartes. Paris, 1917.
Phil 575.81 Dittrich, O. Individualismus, Universalismus, Personalismus. Berlin, 1917.
Phil 3485.5 Döring, W.O. Das Lebenswerk Immanuel Kants. 4. Aufl. Lübeck, 1917.
Phil 8658.10 Dotterer, R.H. The argument for a finitist theology. Diss. Lancaster, Pa., 1917.
Phil 178.12.35 Dresser, H.W. Handbook of the new thought. N.Y., 1917.
Phil 178.12.37 Dresser, H.W. The spirit of the new thought. N.Y., 1917.
Phil 178.12.39 Dresser, H.W. The victorious faith, moral ideals in war time. N.Y., 1917.
Phil 5813.3 Drever, James. Instinct in man. Cambridge, Eng., 1917.
Phil 5545.65 Dugas, L. La mémoire et l'oubli. Paris, 1917.
Phil 8583.19 Dunkmann, D.K. Religionsphilosophie. Gütersloh, 1917.
Phil 6113.11.2 Dunlap, Knight. An outline of psychobiology. 2d ed. Baltimore, 1917.
Phil 9530.15 Durant, E.E. How to make your mark in life. Boston, 1917.
Phil 178.30 Durant, William. Philosophy and social problem. N.Y., 1917.
Phil 1504.19.4 Ebner, J. Die Erkenntnislehre Richards von St. Viktor. v.19, pt.4-6. Münster, 1917.
Phil 1050.20 Efros, Israel I. The problem of space in Jewish mediaeval philosophy. N.Y., 1917.
Phil 2270.120 Elliot, Hugh S.R. Herbert Spencer. London, 1917.
Phil 9495.29 Ellis, Havelock. Essays in war-time. 1st series. Boston, 1917.
Phil 179.3.70 Eucken, R. Moral und Lebensanschauung. 2. Aufl. Leipzig, 1917.
Phil 6115.22 Fairburn, W.A. Mentality and freedom. N.Y., 1917.
Phil 3005.3.3 Falckenberg, Richard. Hilfslrich zur Geschichte der Philosophie seit Kant. 3e Aufl. Leipzig, 1917.
Phil 8080.10 Farnsworth, E.C. The ideales and tendencies of modern art. Portland, 1917.
Phil 665.42.5 Feilberg, Ludvig. Nutids själavård; om största utbytet av själens gåvor. Stockholm, 1917.
Phil 3640.115 Figgis, J.N. The will to freedom. N.Y., 1917.
Phil 3640.119.10 Filser, Benno. Die Asthetik Nietzsches. Passau, 1917.
Phil 2070.84A Flournoy, T. Philosophy of William James. N.Y., 1917.
Phil 2405.3 Fonsegrive, G. De Taine à Régny. L'évolution des idées. Paris, 1917.
Phil 5070.10 Forbes, Waldo. Cycles of personal belief. Boston, 1917.
Phil 180.19.9 Fouillée, Alfred. Extraits des grands philosophes. 6e éd. Paris, 1917.
Phil 4756.1.40 Frank, Semen L. Dusha chelovieka. Moskva, 1917.
Phil 6315.2.62.5 Freud, Sigmund. Delusion and dream. N.Y., 1917.
Phil 6315.2.3.5 Freud, Sigmund. History of the psychoanalytic movement. N.Y., 1917.
Phil 6315.2.33.5 Freud, Sigmund. Psychopathology of everyday life. London, 1917.
Phil 6315.2.33.6 Freud, Sigmund. Psychopathology of everyday life. N.Y., 1917.
Phil 5245.21 Fröbes, Joseph. Lehrbuch der experimentellen Psychologie. Freiburg, 1917. 2v.
Phil 3552.125 Ganz, Hans. Das Unbewusste bei Leibniz...Theorien. Zürich, 1917.
Phil 2475.1.267 García Morente, M. La filosofía de Henri Bergson. Madrid, 1917.
Phil 5651.77 Garten, S. Die Bedeutung unserer Sinne für die Orientierung in Luftraume. Leipzig, 1917.
Phil 3826.12 Gelbraus, Samuel. Die Metaphysik der Ethik Spinozas im Quellenlichte der Kabbalah. Wien, 1917.
Phil 4006.2.5A Gentile, G. Le origini della filosofia contemporanea in Italia. v. 1-3. Messina, 1917-21. 4v.
Phil 5046.11 Gentile, G. Sistema di logica come teoria del conscere. Pisa, 1917.
Phil 3925.5.80 Goldstandt, H. Weissenborns Stellung zum Theismus. Inaug. Diss. Würzburg, 1917.
Phil 8586.15 Graham, Bothwell. Philosophy of Christianity. Columbia, 1917.
Phil 9346.8 Gulick, L.H. The dynamic of manhood. N.Y., 1917.
Phil 8697.8 Hamlin, G.S. Human nature. N.Y., 1917.
Phil 8632.6 Harris, J.C. The inevitable future. 4. ed. Sydney, 1917.
Phil 5425.57 Hayward, F.H. Professionalism and originality. Chicago, 1917.
Phil 3425.23 Hegel, Georg Wilhelm Friedrich. Hegels Philosophie. Berlin, 1917.
Phil 6117.10.5 Hellpach, W. Die geopsychischen Erscheinungen. 2. Aufl. Leipzig, 1917.
Phil 8735.6A Henderson, L.J. The order of nature. Cambridge, 1917.
Phil 182.65 Henkel, Tom. Creative psychics, the art of regeneration. Los Angeles, 1917.
Phil 5545.159 Herrlin, Axel. Minuet. Stockholm, 1917.
Phil 7069.17.26 Hill, John Arthur. Psychical investigations. N.Y., 1917.
Phil 665.27 Hirt, Walter. Ein neuer Weg zur Erforschung der Seele. München, 1917.
Phil 4580.50 Høffding, Harald. Der totalitätsbegriff. Leipzig, 1917.
Phil 4580.40 Høffding, Harald. Totalitet som kategori en erkendelseteoretisk undersøgelse. København, 1917.
Phil 1112.3 Hönigwald, R. Die Philosophie des Altertums. München, 1917.
Phil 5653.5 Hollingworth, H.L. The sense of taste. N.Y., 1917.
Phil 3640.119 Huan, Gabriel. La philosophie de Frédéric Nietzsche. Paris, 1917.
Phil 5247.13.3 Huarte de San Juan, J. Examen de ingenios para las sciencias. Barcelona, 1917.
Phil 3489.15 Huch, Lilly. Der Begriff Wissenschaft im Kantischen Sinne. Berlin, 1917.
Phil 6958.3 Imianitoff, Mme. Contribution à l'étude du rôle des emotions. Thèse. Paris, 1917.
Phil 8633.3 Immortality; an essay. N.Y., 1917.
Phil 9035.29.3 Ingenieros, José. El hombre mediocre. 3d ed. Buenos Aires, 1917.

1917 - cont.

Phil 8589.15   Jacobsson, M. Om förhållandet mellan religion och moral. Stockholm, 1917.

Phil 8634.7   Jaeger, Paul. Innseits; zur Verständigung über die Jenseitsfrage. Tübingen, 1917.

Phil 2070.40   James, William. Causeries pédagogiques. 4th ed. Lausanne, 1917.

Phil 5249.2.45 James, William. Energies of men. N.Y., 1917.

Phil 5249.2.40 James, William. Några livsideal samt de store männen och deres omgiming. Stockholm, 1917.

Phil 2070.35   James, William. Philosophie de l'expérience. Paris, 1917.

Phil 2070.49   James, William. La théorie de l'émotion. 5e éd. Paris, 1917.

Phil 1709.3   Jørgensen, J. Brudshjkher ar filosofiens historii. København, 1917.

Phil 7069.17.27 Joire, Paul. Psychical and supernormal phenomena. N.Y., 1917.

Phil 8589.6   Jones, William T. Spiritual ascent of man. N.Y., 1917.

Phil 3491.1   Jonquière, Georg. Die grundsätzliche Unanehmbarkeit. Bern, 1917.

Phil 2475.1.212 Jorgensen, J. Henri Bergson's filosofi i omrids. København, 1917.

Phil 5249.7.2   Judd, C.H. Psychology. General introduction. Boston, 1917.

Phil 3480.80.75 Kant, Immanuel. Ecrits politiques. Paris, 1917.

Phil 3480.83   Kant, Immanuel. Worin besteht der Fortschritt zum bessern im Menschengeschlecht? Wiesbaden, 1917.

Phil 3480.79.10 Kant, Immanuel. Zum ewigen Frieden. Berlin, 1917.

Phil 6680.4   Kaplan, Leo. Hypnotismus, animismus. Leipzig, 1917.

Phil 3246.201   Kerler, D.H. Die Fichte-Schelling'sche Wissenschaftslehre. Ulm, 1917.

Phil 3850.18.82 Kerler, D.H. Max Scheler. Ulm, 1917.

Phil 2475.1.196 Kerler, Dietrich H. Henri Bergson und das Problem des Verhältnisses zwischen Leib und Seele. Ulm, 1917.

Phil 3246.177   Kerler, Dietrich H. Die Philosophie des Absoluten in der Fichteschen Wissenschaftslehre. Inaug. Diss. Ansbach, 1917.

Phil 8665.3   Keyser, L.S. A system of natural theism. Burlington, Ia., 1917.

Phil 185.52   King, Mrs. E.D. The lotus path. Los Angeles, 1917.

Phil 960.18   Kitch, Ethel May. The origin of subjectivity in Hindu thought. Chicago, 1917.

Phil 9350.2   Kittredge, H.C. Ten minute talks to boys. Concord, N.H., 1917.

Phil 5640.125   Kreibig, Josef K. Die Sinne des Menschen. 3. Aufl. Leipzig, 1917.

Phil 7069.17.29 Kvaran, E.H. Líf og daudi. Reykjavik, 1917.

Phil 341.13   Kynast, R. Das Problem der Phänomenologie. Breslau, 1917.

Phil 575.24   Laird, John. Problems of the self. London, 1917.

Phil 2520.136   Landormy, Paul. Descartes. 5e éd. Paris, 1917?

Phil 972.9   Lazenby, C. The work of the masters. London, 1917.

Phil 5070.14   Le Bon, Gustave. La vie des vérités. Paris, 1917.

Phil 8612.7   LeDantec, F. Le problème de la mort et la conscience universelle. Paris, 1917.

Phil 8612.7.5   LeDantec, F. Le problème de la mort et la conscience universelle. Paris, 1917.

Phil 186.36.4   Lehmann, R. Lehrbuch der philosophischen Propädeutik. 4. Aufl. Berlin, 1917.

Phil 75.16   Levi, Alessandro. Bibliografia filosofica italiana, 1914-15. Roma, 1917.

Phil 5761.9   Lévy, Paul Émile. L'éducation rationelle de la volonté. 10e éd. Paris, 1917.

Phil 5051.17.9 Liard, Louis. Logique. 9e éd. Paris, 1917?

Phil 4600.4.30 Lidforss, Bengt. Dagsbilder. Malmö, 1917.

Phil 7069.17.30 Light on the future. London, 1917.

Phil 4610.7.87 Liljedal, E. Vitalis Norström. Stockholm, 1917-18. 2v.

Phil 630.11   Lindsay, James. A philosophical system of theistic idealism. Edinburgh, 1917.

Phil 2115.47.5 Locke, J. Essay concerning human understanding. Chicago, 1917.

Phil 8591.20   Loisy, Alfred. La religion. Paris, 1917.

Phil 6121.14.5 Lucas, Keith. The conduction of the nervous impulse. London, 1917.

Phil 186.50.2   Ludowici, A. Spiel und Widerspiel. 2. Ausg. München, 1917.

Phil 3210.88   Lülmann, C. Monismus und Christentum bei G.T. Fechner. Berlin, 1917.

Phil 187.27.9   Mackenzie, J.S. Elements of constructive philosophy. London, 1917.

Phil 187.62   Mahnke, D. Der Wille zur Ewigkeit. Halle, 1917.

Phil 5052.16   Marchisini, G. Logica elementare. Firenze, 1917.

Phil 3494.13   Marck, S. Kant und Hegel. Tübingen, 1917.

Phil 3494.19.5 Marcus, Ernst. Kants Weltgebäude. München, 1917.

Phil 8887.2.5   Marion, H. Leçons de morale. 17. ed. Paris, 1917.

Phil 812.4   Marvin, W.T. The history of European philosophy. N.Y., 1917.

Phil 2490.96   Maurras, Charles. L'avenir de l'intelligence. 2e éd. Paris, 1917.

Phil 187.28.3   Mechnikov, I.I. Études sur la nature humaine. 5. ed. Paris, 1917.

Phil 2475.1.198 Meckauer, Walter. Der Intuitionismus und seine Elemente bei Henri Bergson. Leipzig, 1917.

Phil 8413.14   Medicus, Fritz. Grundfragen der Asthetik. Jena, 1917.

Phil 8592.23   Mehlis, Goerg. Einfuhrung in ein System...Religions. Tübingen, 1917.

Phil 5052.9.9   Mellone, S.H. An introductory text-book of logic. 9th ed. Edinburgh, 1917.

Phil 7069.17.31 Mercier, Charles A. Spiritualism and Sir Oliver Lodge. London, 1917.

Phil 1517.3   Mercier, Désiré. A manual of modern scholastic philosophy. 2nd ed. London, 1917. 2v.

Phil 187.77   Monaco, Nicolao. Praelectiones metaphysicae specialis. Romae, 1917-1920. 3v.

Phil 525.32   Montague, M.P. Twenty minutes of reality. N.Y., 1917.

Phil 3246.178   Moog, Willy. Fichte über den Krieg. Darmstadt, 1917.

Phil 3494.16   Morente, M.G. La filosofía de Kant. Madrid, 1917.

Phil 3012.2   Muirhead, J.H. German philosophy in relation to the war. London, 1917.

Phil 6122.47   Murray, William J. The Astor lectures. N.Y., 1917.

Phil 4635.2.92 Naesgaard, S. Starckes forsvar, metoder og resultater. København, 1917.

Phil 7082.110   Narayan, Ram. The dream problem. Delhi, 1917?-22. 2v.

Phil 8888.6   Nelson, Leonard. Kritik der praktischen Vernunft. Leipzig, 1917.

Phil 7082.186   Nicoll, Maurice. Dream psychology. London, 1917.

Phil 3640.31.3 Nietzsche, Friedrich. Beyond good and evil. N.Y., 1917.

1917 - cont.

Phil 3640.31.9 Nietzsche, Friedrich. Beyond good and evil. N.Y., 1917.

Phil 3640.76.9 Nietzsche, Friedrich. Nietzsches Briefe. Leipzig, 1917.

Phil 4610.7.40 Norström, V. Om viljans frihet. Stockholm, 1917.

Phil 5627.71   Oesterreich, T.K. Einfürung in die Religionspsychologie. Berlin, 1917.

Phil 9070.43   Onis y Sanchez, F. de. Disciplina y rebeldia. San José, Costa Rica, 1917.

Phil 1519.1   Overbeck, Franz. Vorgeschichte und Jugend der mittelalterlichen Scholastek. Basel, 1917.

Phil 3015.1   Papillault, G. Science française, scolastique allemande. Paris, 1917.

Phil 190.26   Parker, DeWitt H. Self and nature. Cambridge, 1917.

Phil 630.15   Parkhurst, Helen. Recent logical realism. Thesis. Bryn Mawr, 1917.

Phil 9530.26   Parlette, R.A. A book of rejoicing, big business. Chicago, 1917.

Phil 9035.37   Parlette, R.A. The university of hard knocks. Chicago, 1917.

Phil 2475.1.195 Peckham, George W. Logic of Bergson's philosophy. N.Y., 1917.

Phil 5825.4   Peterson, Joseph. The effect of length of blind alleys on maze learning. N.Y., 1917.

Phil 6325.1   Pfister, Oskar. The psychoanalytic method. N.Y., 1917.

Phil 8965.8   Piat, Clodius. Idées directrices de la morale chrétienne. Paris, 1917.

Phil 4115.86.5 Piccoli, Valentino. L'estetica di Vincenzo Gioberti. Milano, 1917.

Phil 5640.125.5 Pikler, Gyula. Sinnesphysiologische Untersuchungen. Leipzig, 1917.

Phil 2630.1.83 Pointud-Guillemot, B. La doctrine sociale de Gratry. Thèse. Paris, 1917.

Phil 2630.1.81 Pointud-Guillemot, B. Essai sur la philosophie de Gratry. Thèse. Paris, 1917.

Phil 5255.50   Pyle, William H. The science of human nature. Boston, 1917.

Phil 9120.157   Radcke, Fritz. Pflicht oder Lust? Langensalza, 1917.

Phil 7069.17.32 Randall, Edward Caleb. The dead have never died. N.Y., 1917.

Phil 192.41   Rawson, F.L. Life understood from a scientific and religious point of view. 4th ed. London, 1917.

Phil 665.23   Révésy, Béla. Geschichte des Seelenbegriffes. Stuttgart, 1917.

Phil 5400.18.19 Ribot, T. Essai sur les passions. 4. éd. Paris, 1917.

Phil 3640.93.2 Richter, R. Friedrich Nietzsche. 3. Aufl. Leipzig, 1917.

Phil 8610.917   Ricker, M.M. I am not afraid, are you? East Aurora, N.Y., 1917.

Phil 5643.46   Ritter, Sarah M. The vertical-horizontal illusion. Princeton, 1917.

Phil 7084.28   Rivers, William Halse Rivers. Dreams and primitive culture. Manchester, 1917-18.

Phil 5850.326   Roback, A.A. The moral issues involved in applied psychology. n.p., 1917.

Phil 5627.29   Roback, A.A. The psychology of confession. Montreal, 1917.

Phil 7069.17.40 Robertson, Helen F. The letters of a woman who wa. Minneapolis, 1917.

Phil 2855.2.82 Robot, Théodule. Théodule Ribot; choix de textes. Paris, 1917?

Phil 5585.49   Rogers, Anna Sophie. An analytic study of visual perceptions. Thesis. Worcester, Mass., 1917.

Phil 6327.3   Rogues de Fursac, J. Manuel de psychiatrie. Paris, 1917.

Phil 2490.94   Rouvre, C. de. L'amoureuse histoire d'Auguste Comte et de C. de Vaux. Paris, 1917.

Phil 3925.6.92 Ruge, Arnold. Wilhelm Windelband. Leipzig, 1917.

Phil 177.40   Sabine, George H. Philosophical essays in honor of J.E. Creighton. N.Y., 1917.

Phil 4115.85   Saitta, Giuseppe. Il pensiero di Vincenzo Gioberti. Messina, 1917.

Phil 3640.116A Salter, William M. Nietzsche the thinker; a study. N.Y., 1917.

Phil 3018.7.9   Santayana, G. L'erreur de la philosophie allemande. Paris, 1917.

Phil 3500.28   Sartiaux, F. Morale Kantienne et morale humaine. Paris, 1917.

Phil 3800.67   Schelling, F.W.J. von. Gedichte. Jena, 1917.

Phil 3805.29   Schleiermacher, Friedrich. Ein poetischer Brief Schleiermachers. Halle, 1917.

Phil 5520.18.5 Schmidt, William A. An experienced study in the psychology of reading. Theses. Chicago, 1917.

Phil 299.13   Schneider, K.C. Die Welt wie sie Jetzt ist und wie sie sein Wird. Wien, 1917.

Phil 193.96   Schneidkunz, H. Philosophische Propädeutik in neuster Literatur. Halle, 1917.

Phil 6315.2.83 Schultze, J.H. Sigmund Freud's Sexualpsychoanalyse. Berlin, 1917.

Phil 3246.176   Schwarz, Hermann. Fichte und Wir. Osterwieck, 1917.

Phil 8610.917.10 Secular Society, Ltd. A fight for right. London, 1917.

Phil 2475.1.179 Seillière, E. L'avenir de la philosophie Bergsonienne. Paris, 1917.

Phil 5058.27   Sellars, R.W. Essentials of logic. Boston, 1917.

Phil 193.66   Sellars, Roy Wood. Essentials of philosophy. N.Y., 1917.

Phil 8893.58   Seta, Ugo della. Filosofia morale. Roma, 1917-19. 2v.

Phil 8595.17   Seth Prugle Pattison, A. The idea of God. Aberdeen, 1917.

Phil 8893.40   Severn, Elizabeth. The psychology of behavior. N.Y., 1917.

Phil 6328.5   Silberer, Herbert. Problems of mysticism and its symbolism. N.Y., 1917.

Phil 3640.225   Simon, Theodor. Richtlinien christlicher Apologetik wider Nietzsche. Berlin, 1917.

Phil 400.33   Sinclair, May. A defence of idealism. N.Y., 1917.

Phil 5058.28   Smith, Henry B. A primer of logic. Pulaski, 1917.

Phil 3500.32   Sornmerlath, Ernst. Kants Lehre vom Intelligiblencharakter. Leipzig, 1917.

Phil 3819.27   Spinoza, Benedictus de. Uren met Spinoza. 2. druk. Baarn, 1917.

Phil 3838.14   Spinoza Redivivus: eine Fibel für Anfanger. Berlin, 1917.

Phil 8610.913.10 Stansbury, H. In quest of truth. London, 1917.

Phil 8893.34.10 Stanton, S.B. The hidden happiness. N.Y., 1917.

Phil 5258.35.5 Stern, W. Die Psychologie und der Personalismus. Leipzig, 1917.

Phil 193.78.5   Sternberg, Kurt. Der Kampf zwischen Pragmatismus und Idealismus in Philosophie und Weltkrieg. Berlin, 1917.

Phil 5258.63   Stöhr, Adolf. Psychologie. Wien, 1917.

Phil 3246.175.2 Strecker, Reinhard. Die Anfänge von Fichtes Staatsphilosophie. Leipzig, 1917.

Phil 5259.5.28 Studies in psychology. Worcester, 1917.

1917 - cont.

Phil 8893.44   Sugimori, K. The principles of the moral empire. London, 1917.

Phil 4065.178   Szemere, Samu. Giordano Bruno. Budapest, 1917.

Phil 7060.143   Taillepied, Noël. Traicté de l'apparition des esprits. Paris, 1917.

Phil 8599.17   Temple, William. Mens creatrix. v.1-2. London, 1917.

Phil 5829.7   Thompson, E.L. An analysis of the learning process in the snail. Cambridge, 1917.

Phil 1200.16   Thompson, J.W. The last pagan. Chicago, 1917.

Phil 8894.22   Trivero, Camillo. Saggi di etica. Milano, 1917.

Phil 7069.17.45   Troland, L.T. A technique for the experimental study of telepathy. Albany, N.Y., 1917.

Phil 3501.13   Trubetskoi, E. Metafizika predpolozheniia poznaniia opyt preodolevaniia Kanta. Moskva, 1917.

Phil 5425.15.10   Türck, H. Der geniale Mensch. 8. Aufl. Berlin, 1917.

Phil 3195.6.86   Unger, Rudolf. Weltanschauung und Dichtung...Dilthey. Zürich, 1917.

Phil 630.10   Vance, John G. Reality and truth. London, 1917.

Phil 8896.10   Vecchia, Paolo. Elementi di morale e cenni di economia politica. 8. ed. Torino, 1917?

Phil 352.5.2   Verworm, Max. Die Frage nach den Grenzen der Erkenntnis. 2. Aufl. Jena, 1917.

Phil 8896.4.4   Vidari, Giovanni. Elementi di etica. 4. ed. Milano, 1917.

Phil 6750.25   Wallin, John E.W. Problems of subnormality. Yonkers-on-Hudson, 1917.

Phil 8602.41   Walsh, Walter. The world rebuilt. London, 1917.

Phil 5832.8.5   Washburn, M.F. The animal mind. 2. ed. N.Y., 1917.

Phil 5650.9A   Watt, Henry J. Psychology of sound. Cambridge, 1917.

Phil 8677.9.5   Wells, H.G. God the invisible king. London, 1917.

Phil 8677.9   Wells, H.G. God the invisible king. N.Y., 1917.

Phil 2150.1.80   Wenley, R.M. Life and work of George Sylvester Morris. N.Y., 1917.

Phil 8423.17   Werner, Alfred. Impressionismus und Expressionismus. Leipzig, 1917.

Phil 8897.39   Werner, Charles. Études de philosophie morale. Genève, 1917.

Phil 7069.17.50   White, Mary Blount. Letters from Harry and Helen. N.Y., 1917.

Phil 6132.19   Wilson, H.B. Does Christ still heal? N.Y., 1917.

Phil 3625.3.89   Wlassak, R. Ernst Mach: Gedächtnisrede. Leipzig, 1917.

Phil 7054.129   Wright, Alfred A. Spiritual science, universal religion. N.Y., 1917.

Phil 3915.66.2   Wundt, Wilhelm. Griechische Weltanschauung. 2. Aufl. Leipzig, 1917.

Phil 3552.125.5   Wundt, Wilhelm. Leibniz, zu seinen Zweihundertzahrigen. Leipzig, 1917.

Phil 8649.1.2   Yeiser, J.O. Evolution proving immortality. Omaha, 1917.

Phil 6694.1   Yeshilian, M.A. Hypnotism and telepathy. N.Y., 1917.

1918

Phil 8580.29   Adam, J.D. Under the highest leadership. N.Y., 1918.

Phil 8615.5.15   Adler, Felix. An ethical philosophy of life. N.Y., 1918.

Phil 3625.3.105   Adler, Friedrich. Ernst Machs Uberwindung des mechanischen Materialismus. Wien, 1918.

Phil 4513.1.31   Ahlberg, A. Filosfiska essayer. Stockholm, 1918.

Phil 6110.3.1   Alexander, F.M. Man's supreme inheritance. N.Y., 1918.

Phil 5240.6.9   Angell, J.R. An introduction to psychology. N.Y., 1918.

Phil 4060.1.35   Ardigo, Roberto. Natura naturans. Ostiglia, 1918.

Phil 3482.6.2   Aster, Ernst. Immanuel Kant. 2. Aufl. Leipzig, 1918.

Phil 2045.94   Balz, Albert G.A. Idea and essence in the philosophies of Hobbes and Spinoza. N.Y., 1918.

Phil 7069.18.10   Barker, Elsa. Letters from a living dead man. N.Y., 1918.

Phil 2805.110   Barrès, Maurice. L'angoisse de Pascal. Paris, 1918.

Phil 7060.82.5   Barrett, W.E. On the threshold of the unseen. 3. ed. London, 1918.

Phil 960.40   Barua, B.M. Prolegomena to a history of Buddhist philosophy. Calcutta, 1918.

Phil 5520.32.7   Berg, Anton. Die Anschauungen Ludwig Noirés über Ursprung und Wesen von Sprache und Vernunft. Diss. Darmstadt, 1918.

Phil 2475.1.103   Bergson, Henri. Choix de texte avec étude du...R. Gillouin. Paris, 1918.

Phil 2475.1.71   Bergson, Henri. Discours de réception. Paris, 1918.

Phil 3640.121.2   Bertram, Ernst. Nietzsche. Berlin, 1918.

Phil 5241.47   Betz, W. Psychologie des Denkens. Leipzig, 1918.

Phil 176.115.2   Bierens de Haan, J.D. De verborgen harmonie. 2e druk. Amsterdam, 1918.

Phil 735.12   Blechman, Nathan. The philosophic function of value. Boston, 1918.

Phil 176.69   Bloch, Ernst. Geist der Utopie. München, 1918.

Phil 3120.22   Blüher, Hans. Empedokles, oder das Sakrament des freien Todes. n.p., 1918.

Phil 7069.18.21   Boirac, Émile. Psychic science. London, 1918.

Phil 7069.18.20   Boirac, Émile. The psychology of the future. N.Y., 1918.

Phil 2401.4   Bondi, P. Études littéraires: essais sur les philosophes. Florence, 1918.

Phil 8876.50   Bosanquet, B. Some suggestions in ethics. London, 1918.

Phil 6111.18.5   Bruce, H.A. Nerve control and how to gain it. N.Y., 1918.

Phil 3483.40   Brückmann, W. Immanuel Kant: sein Leben und sein Lehre. v.1-2. Königsberg, 1918-19.

Phil 7069.18.40   Bryan, William J. The truth about spiritualism. N.Y., 1918.

Phil 8050.48   Burger, Fritz. Weltanschauungsprobleme und Lebenssysteme in der Kunst der Vergangenheit. München, 1918.

Phil 7069.18.50   Cameron, Margaret. The seven purposes. N.Y., 1918.

Phil 9590.26   Carr, H.W. Life and finite individuality. London, 1918.

Phil 400.41   Carr, Herbert Wildon. The new idealist movement in philosophy. London, 1918.

Phil 1535.29   Carrasquilla, R.M. Lecciones de metafísica y ética. 2. ed. Bogotá, 1918.

Phil 6112.20.2   Carroll, Robert S. The mastery of nervousness based upon self-reeducation. 2nd ed. N.Y., 1918.

Phil 8582.25.5   Carson, Capshaw, (pseud.). An appeal to the real leaders of men. Chicago, 1918.

Phil 8582.25   Carson, Capshaw, (pseud.). A witness testifies. Chicago, 1918.

Phil 4060.2.80   Carvalho, Joaquim de. Leão Hebreu, filósofo. Coimbra, 1918.

Phil 3002.3   Cassirer, Ernst. Freitheit und Form. 2e Aufl. Berlin, 1918.

Phil 177.50   Chainey, George. Times garland of grace. San Diego, 1918.

Phil 4525.1.31   Christensen, S. Indad. København, 1918.

Phil 4330.15   Clascar, Federico. Estudi sobre la filosofia a Catalunya en el siglo XVIII. Barcelona, 1918.

Phil 7069.18.60   Clodd, Edward. The question: "If a man die, shall he live again?" N.Y., 1918.

1918 - cont.

Phil 525.33   Cobb, Stanwood. The essential mysticism. Boston, 1918.

Phil 3484.2.3   Cohen, H. Kant's Theorie der Erfahrung. 3. Aufl. Berlin, 1918.

Phil 7069.18.70   Comstock, William C. Thought for help from those who know men's need. Boston, 1918.

Phil 177.73.5   Constable, F.C. Myself and dreams. N.Y., 1918.

Phil 7060.142   Constable, Frank C. Telergy, the communion of souls. London, 1918.

Phil 7082.168   Craig, Katherine Taylor. The fabric of dreams. N.Y., 1918.

Phil 7060.132   Crawford, W. J. The reality of psychic phenomena. N.Y., 1918.

Phil 7069.18.80   Crawford, William J. Hints and observations for those investigating the phenomena of spiritualism. N.Y., 1918.

Phil 3002.2   Crile, G.W. The fallacy of the German state philosophy. Garden City, 1918.

Phil 7069.18.90   Cushman, Emma Crow. Insight. Boston, 1918.

Phil 802.4.3   Cushman, H.E. A beginner's history of philosophy. Boston, 1918-19.

Phil 802.4.2A   Cushman, H.E. A beginner's history of philosophy. Boston, 1918-20. 2v.

Phil 178.32   Delbos, Victor. Figures et doctrines des philosophes. 4e éd. Paris, 1918.

Phil 3805.153   Dentice di Accadia, Cecilia. Schleiermacher. Milano, 1918.

Phil 8878.46   Donati, G. La morale. Forli, 1918.

Phil 7069.18.95   Doyle, Arthur Conan. The new revelation. N.Y., 1918.

Phil 7069.18.95.6   Doyle, Arthur Conan. The new revelation. 6th ed. London, 1918.

Phil 2055.2.81   Ellis, Edith M. James Hinton. London, 1918.

Phil 6314.1   Emerson, L.E. Nervousness; its causes, treatment and prevention. Boston, 1918.

Phil 3552.249   Ernst, Charles. Die Tierseele in der leibnizschen Philosophie. Wiesbaden, 1918.

Phil 179.3.28.5   Eucken, R. Geistesprobleme und Lebensfragen. Leipzig, 1918.

Phil 179.3.50   Eucken, R. Die geistigen Forderungen der Gegenwart. 3e Aufl. Berlin, 1918.

Phil 179.3.19   Eucken, R. Der Kampf um einen Geistigen Lebensinhalt. Leipzig, 1918.

Phil 179.3.27.3   Eucken, R. Der Sinn und Wert des Lebens. 6. Aufl. Leipzig, 1918.

Phil 8829.2.7   Eucken, Rudolf. Die Lebensanschauungen der grossen Denker. 12. Aufl. Leipzig, 1918.

Phil 8879.15   Everett, W.G. Moral values. N.Y., 1918.

Phil 3903.1.81   Festschrift Johannes Volkelt zum 70. Geburtstag. München, 1918.

Phil 3246.28   Fichte, Johann Gottlieb. Predigten. Leipzig, 1918.

Phil 5627.32   Finot, Jean. Saints, initiés et possédés modernes. Paris, 1918.

Phil 6315.2.25   Freud, Sigmund. Reflections on war and death. N.Y., 1918.

Phil 6315.2.9.10   Freud, Sigmund. Vorlesungen zur Einführung. 2. Aufl. Leipzig, 1918.

Phil 180.34   Friedlaender, S. Schöpferische Indifferenz. München, 1918.

Phil 6315.3   Frink, H.W. Morbid fears and compulsions, their psychology. N.Y., 1918.

Phil 3808.135   Frost, Walter. Schopenhauer als erbe Kants in der philosophischen Seelenanalyse. Bonn, 1918.

Phil 181.135   Garcia Calderon, Francisco. Ideologías. Paris, 1918.

Phil 4260.92   Gemmingen, Otto. Vico, Hamann und Herder. Inaug. Diss. Borna, 1918.

Phil 181.45.9   Gentile, Giovanni. Teoria generale dello spirito come atto puro. 2a ed. Pisa, 1918.

Phil 4757.1.35   Gershenzon, M.O. Troistvennyi obraz sovershenstva. Moskva, 1918.

Phil 8586.16   Gese, Paul. Einleitung in die Religionsphilosophie über die verschiedenen Standpunkt und Methoden zur Enforchung des Wesens der Religion. Göttingen, 1918.

Phil 2520.158   Giunchi, O. L'individualismo nel Cartesio e nel Rousseau. Novara, 1918.

Phil 181.40   Gleichen-Russwurm, A. von. Der freie Mensch. Berlin, 1918.

Phil 9220.10.9   Gleichen-Russwurm, Alexander von. Freundschaft. Stuttgart, 1918?

Phil 8881.58   Goddard, H.C. Morale. N.Y., 1918.

Phil 7069.18.97   God's world. Chicago, 1918.

Phil 8881.34.5   Görland, Albert. Neubegründung der Ethik aus ihrem Verhältnis zu den besonderen Gemeinschaftswissenschaften. Berlin, 1918.

Phil 7069.18.98   Gook, Arthur. Andatrúin afhjúpud Akureyri, 1918.

Phil 3120.2.82   Gotthardt, J. Das Wahrheits Problem. Inaug. Diss. Trier, 1918.

Phil 5648.14   Goudge, Mabel E. A qualitative and quantitative study of Weber's illusion. Thesis. Worcester, Mass., 1918.

Phil 8661.9   Gratry, A. De la connaissance de Dieu. 9. éd. Paris, 1918. 2v.

Phil 5046.20   Grau, Kurt J. Grundriss der Logik. Leipzig, 1918.

Phil 1750.123   Groot, J.V. de. Denkers van onzen tijd. Uitgevers, 1918.

Phil 181.38   Güttler, Karl. Gesammelte Abhandlungen. München, 1918.

Phil 7069.18.100   Gurney, Edmund. Phantasms of the living. London, 1918.

Phil 8632.7   Hall, Charles A. They do not die. London, 1918.

Phil 5625.80   Hamel, I.A. A study and analysis of the conditioned reflex. Diss. Washington, 1918.

Phil 6957.7.5   Hart, Bernard. The modern treatment of mental disorders. Manchester, 1918.

Phil 3640.177   Hasse, Heinrich. Das Problem des Sokrates. Leipzig, 1918.

Phil 5627.41   Heavenly bridegrooms...erotogenetic...religion. N.Y., 1918.

Phil 2115.112A   Hefelbower, S.G. The relation of John Locke to English deism. Chicago, 1918.

Phil 3425.77.2   Hegel, Georg Wilhelm Friedrich. Hegels erstes System. Heidelberg, 1918.

Phil 6117.43   Herrick, C.J. Introduction to neurology. Philadelphia, 1918.

Phil 7069.18.110   Hicks, Betsey B. The bugle. N.Y., 1918.

Phil 7069.18.112   Hill, John Arthur. Man is a spirit. N.Y. 1918.

Phil 5640.25   Hillebrand, F. Ewald Hering ein Gedenkwort der Psychophysik. Berlin, 1918.

Phil 5047.24.5   Hjelmérus, Alfred. Den aristoteliska logiken jämförd med modern logik. Umea, 1918.

Phil 9035.27   Hocking, W.E. Human nature and its remaking. New Haven, 1918.

Phil 3827.3.5   Høffding, H. Spinozas ethica, analyse og karakteristik. København, 1918.

Chronological Listing

Phil 4580.37 Høffding, Harald. O plevelse og tydning religionsfilosofiske studier. Kjøbenhavn, 1918.

Phil 5247.23.15 Höfler, Alois. Hundert psychologische Schulversuche. 4. Aufl. Leipzig, 1918.

Phil 1750.118 Hönigswald, R. Philosophische Motive im neuzeitlichen Humanismus. Breslau, 1918.

Phil 5525.18 Hoffding, Harald. Humor als Lebensgefühl. Leipzig, 1918.

Phil 7069.18.120 "I heard a voice."N.Y., 1918.

Phil 8958.1 Ideström, A. Kristendomen och det etiska behovet. Stockholm, 1918.

Phil 6958.4.2 Ilberg, Georg. Geisteskrankheiten. 2. Aufl. Leipzig, 1918.

Phil 3425.238 Il'in, Ivan A. Filosofiia Gegelia. Moskva, 1918.

Phil 808.1 Ingegnieros, José. Proposiciones relativas al porvenir de la filosofía. v.1-2. Buenos Aires, 1918.

Phil 6958.2 Ingenieros, José. Simulación de la locura. 8. ed. Buenos Aires, 1918.

Phil 5048.2 Iversen, H. To essays om vor erkendelse. Kjøbenhavn, 1918.

Phil 184.3.19 James, W. Le pragmatisme. Paris, 1918.

Phil 8634.2.7 James, William. Menneskets udødelighed. Kjøbenhavn, 1918.

Phil 3552.258 Jasinowski, B. Die analytische Urteilslehre Leibnizens. Diss. Wien, 1918.

Phil 5249.6.5 Jastrow, J. The psychology of conviction. Boston, 1918.

Phil 8884.16 Jodl, Friedrich. Allgemeine Ethik. 1. und 2. Aufl. Stuttgart, 1918.

Phil 3665.1.85 Jørgensen, J.F. Paul Natorp som repraesentant for den kritiske idealisme. København, 1918.

Phil 8634.4 Johnston, R.F. Letters to a missionary. London, 1918.

Phil 6319.2.2 Jones, Ernest. Papers on psycho-analysis. London, 1918.

Phil 6119.7 Jones, Wallace Franklin. A study of handedness. Vermillion, S.D., 1918.

Phil 192.28.28 Jourdain, P. The philosophy of Mr. B*rtr*nd R*ss*ll. London, 1918.

Phil 4630.2.80 Juhlajulkaisu omistettu Th. Reinille hänen täyttäessään 80 vuotta. Helsingissä, 1918.

Phil 6319.1.15 Jung, C.G. Studies in word association. London, 1918.

Phil 2520.124 Kahn, Lina. Metaphysics of the supernatural as illustrated by Descartes. N.Y., 1918.

Phil 3480.80.125 Kant, Immanuel. Az örök héke. Budapest, 1918.

Phil 8411.17 Katann, O. Ästhetisch-literarische Arbeiten. Wien, 1918.

Phil 8885.19.5 Kautsky, Karl. Ethics and the materialist conception of history. Chicago, 1918.

Phil 6320.1 Kempf, E.J. The autonomic functions and the personality. N.Y., 1918.

Phil 8885.16 Keyser, Leander S. A system of general ethics. Burlington, 1918.

Phil 185.52.15 King, Mrs. E.D. Aum, the cosmic silence. Los Angeles, 1918. 2 pam.

Phil 185.52.10 King, Mrs. E.D. The flashlights of truth. Los Angeles, 1918.

Phil 185.52.5 King, Mrs. E.D. The higher metaphysics. Los Angeles, 1918.

Phil 5425.26 Knowlson, Thomas S. Originality, a popular study of creative mind. Philadelphia, 1918.

Phil 4803.522.80 Kosmowska, J.W. Karol Libelt jako działacz polityczny i społeczny, ur. 1807 um. 1875. Poznań, 1918.

Phil 6960.7 Kretschmer, E. Der sensitive Beziehungwahn. Berlin, 1918.

Phil 3492.13 Kronenberg, M. Kant; sein Leben und sein Lehre. 5. Aufl. München, 1918.

Phil 186.16.15 Ladd, G.T. Knowledge, life and reality. New Haven, 1918.

Phil 575.23 Ladd, George T. Secret of personality. N.Y., 1918.

Phil 4600.7.30 Lagerborg, Rolf. Invita Minerva. Stockholm, 1918.

X Cg Phil 2115.114 Lamprecht, S.P. The moral and political philosophy of John Locke. N.Y., 1918.

Phil 8886.24.9 Lanessan, J.I. de. L'idéal moral du matérialisme et la guerre. Paris, 1918.

Phil 2805.178 Laros, M. Das Glaubensproblem bei Pascal. Düsseldorf, 1918.

Phil 525.22.2 Lehmann, Edvard. Mystik in Heidentum und Christentum. 2e Aufl. Leipzig, 1918.

Phil 186.28 Leighton, J.A. The field of philosophy. Columbus, Ohio, 1918.

Phil 2530.84 Leo, Werner. Diderot als Kunstphilosophie. Inaug.-Diss. Erlangen, 1918.

Phil 5051.10.2 Lewis, Clarence I. A survey of symbolic logic. Berkeley, 1918.

Phil 7060.144 Liljencrants, Johan. Spiritism and religion. Diss. Lynchburg, Va., 1918.

Phil 5585.29 Linke, Paul F. Grundlagen der Wahrnehmungslehre. München, 1918.

Phil 186.41 Lipsius, Friedrich R. Naturphilosophie und Weltanschauung. Leipzig, 1918.

Phil 2115.115 Lodge, Rupert C. The meaning...of...philosophy of John Locke. Minneapolis, 1918.

Phil 7082.106 Lomer, Georg. Der Traumspiegel. München, 1918.

Phil 5401.5 Lord, H.G. The psychology of courage. Boston, 1918.

Phil 4762.1.30 Losskii, Nikolai Onufrievich. Vvedenie v filosofiiu. Petrograd, 1918.

Phil 5645.16 Luckiesh, M. The language of color. N.Y., 1918.

Phil 6122.13.11 McDougall, William. Body and mind. 4th ed. London, 1918.

Phil 6122.13.3 McDougall, William. Physiological psychology. London, 1918.

Phil 630.18 McDowall, A.S. Realism, a study in art and thought. London, 1918.

Phil 6322.5 Maeder, Alphonse. Heilung und Entwicklung im Seelenleben. Zürich, 1918.

Phil 7069.18.130A Maeterlinck, Maurice. The light beyond. N.Y., 1918.

Phil 5052.28 Maier, H. Logik und Erkenntnistheorie. 2. abd. Tübingen, 1918.

X Cg Phil 187.49 Malkani, G.R. The problem of nothing. Amalner, 1918.

Phil 7069.18.132 Martin, Alfred Wilhelm. Psychic tendencies of to-day. N.Y., 1918.

Phil 8887.52 Mehlis, Georg. Probleme der ethik. Tübingen, 1918.

Phil 270.33 Meinong, A. Zum Erweise des allgischen Kausalgesetzes. Wien, 1918.

Phil 4363.4.30 Menéndez y Pelayo, M. Ensayos de crítica filosófica. Madrid, 1918.

Phil 187.46 Menzer, Paul. Weltanschauungsfragen. Stuttgart, 1918.

Phil 4605.2.31 Menzinger, A. Fra før Kant. København, 1918.

Phil 5222.1.5 Mercier, D. The origins of contemporary psychology. N.Y., 1918.

Phil 8887.53 Messer, A. Ethik. Leipzig, 1918.

Phil 5762.11 Messer, August. Das Problem der Willensfreiheit. 2. Aufl. Göttingen, 1918.

Phil 8633.1.18 Moore, Clifford H. Pagan ideas of immortality. Cambridge, 1918.

Phil 5252.12.10 Münsterberg, H. Grundzüge der Psychologie. 2. Aufl. Leipzig, 1918.

Phil 1200.15.7 Murray, G. The stoic philosophy. London, 1918.

Phil 5850.279 Myers, Charles S. Present-day applications of psychology. 2nd ed. London, 1918.

Phil 22.13 Mysl' i slovo filosofskii ezhegodnik. Moskva, 1918-21.

Phil 3160.3.82 Natorp, Paul. Hermann Cohen. Marburg, 1918.

Phil 270.29 Neef, Fritz. Kausalität und Originalität. Tübingen, 1918.

Phil 294.5 Newlyn, Herbert N. The relationship...mystical and the sensible world. London, 1918.

Phil 3640.34 Nietzsche, Friedrich. The genealogy of morals. N.Y., 1918.

Phil 9490.10 Osler, W. A way of life. London, 1918.

Phil 5645.20 Ostwald, Wilhelm. Die Farbenlehre. v.1-2,4. Leipzig, 1918-22. 3v.

Phil 5645.4.25 Ostwald, Wilhelm. Goethe, Schopenhauer und die Farbenlehre. Leipzig, 1918.

Phil 8705.13 Panin, Ivan. The writings of Ivan Panin. New Haven, 1918.

Phil 6325.16 Paschal, Franklin C. The Witmer cylinder test. Hershey, Pa., 1918.

Phil 2475.1.194 Penido, M.T.L. La méthode intuitive de M. Bergson.

Phil 1715.3.5A Perry, R.B. The present conflict of ideals. N.Y., 1918.

Phil 5850.308 Peters, C.C. Human conduct. N.Y., 1918.

Phil 8890.37.5 Petrone, Igino. Ascetica. Milano, 1918.

Phil 8890.37 Petrone, Igino. Etica. Milano, 1918.

Phil 6325.1.5 Pfister, Oskar. Wahrheit und Schönheit in der Psychoanalyse. Zürich, 1918.

Phil 705.14 Plessner, H. Krisis der transzendentalen Wahrheit im anfang. Heidelberg, 1918.

Phil 3017.6 Rádl, E. Romantická véda. V Praze, 1918.

Phil 5841.18.2 Rank, Otto. Der Künstler; Ansatze zu einer Sexualpsychologie. 2. - 3. Aufl. Wien, 1918.

Phil 3790.2.30.8 Rathenau, W. Zur Mechanik des Geistes. 8e und 9e Aufl. Berlin, 1918.

Phil 400.40 Rauschenberger, W. Der kritische Idealismus. Leipzig, 1918.

Phil 5057.17 Rehmke, Johannes. Logik, oder Philosophie als Wissenslehre. Leipzig, 1918.

Phil 4630.2.45 Rein, T. Lefnadsminnen. Helsingfors, 1918.

Phil 5057.19 Rieber, Charles H. Footnotes to formal logic. Berkeley, 1918.

Phil 1717.5.9 Riehl, Alois. Inleiding tot de hedendaagsche wijsbegeerte. Zutphen, 1918.

Phil 8610.918 Riley, Isaac W. Early free thinking societies in America. N.Y., 1918.

Phil 4580.81.5 Rindom, E. Harald Høffding. Kjøbenhavn, 1918.

Phil 4580.81 Rindom, E. Samtaler med Harald Høffding, 1909-1918. København, 1918.

Phil 5780.8 Roback, Abraham A. The interference of will-impulses. Lancaster, Pa., 1918.

Phil 817.8 Ruggiero, Guido de. Storia della filosofia. v.1-2,4 (pt. 1.) Bari, 1918- 2v.

Phil 5258.49 Sallwürk, Ernst von. Die Seele des Menschen. Karlsruhe, 1918.

Phil 3808.182 Salomaa, J.E. Schopenhauer ja von Hartmann. Turku, 1918.

Phil 8708.12.5 Sampson, H.E. Theou sophia...divine mysteries. London, 1918.

Phil 193.49.9 Santayana, G. Philosophical opinion in America. London, 1918. 2v.

Phil 5258.44 Sarlo, Francesco de. Psicologia e filosophia. Firenze, 1918.

Phil 3800.65 Schelling, F.W.J. von. Philosophie. Berlin, 1918?

Phil 349.9 Schlick, Moritz. Allgemeine Erkenntnislehre. Berlin, 1918.

Phil 6060.5.2 Schneidemühl, Georg. Die Handschriftenbeurtilung. 2e Aufl. Leipzig, 1918.

Phil 3790.4.82 Schneider, Max. Die erkenntnistheoretischen Grundlagen in Rickerts Lehre von der Transzendenz. Inaug. Diss. Dresden, 1918.

Phil 3808.29.25 Schopenhauer, Arthur. La pensée de Schopenhauer. Paris, 1918.

Phil 3850.6.75 Schubert, G.H. Gotthilf Heinrich Schubert in seinen Briefen. Stuttgart, 1918.

Phil 7069.18.140 Sciens, (pseud.). How to speak with the dead. N.Y., 1918.

Phil 6990.21.5 Sebastian, L. Fürst Alexander von Hohenlohe-Schillings. Inaug. Diss. Kempten, 1918.

Phil 193.98 Segal, Hyman. The law of struggle. N.Y., 1918.

Phil 525.8.9 Seillière, E. Le péril mystique dans l'inspiration des démocraties contemporaines. Paris, 1918.

Phil 5440.19 Sériot, Pauline. Effets nocifs du croisement des races sur la formation du caractère. Thèse. Paris, 1918.

Phil 5325.14 Sganzini, Carlo. Neuere Einsichten...Ideenassoziationen. Bern, 1918.

Phil 8598.34 Shebbeare, Charles J. Challenge of the universe. London, 1918.

Phil 193.70 Sheldon, W.H. Strife of systems and productive duality. Cambridge, 1918.

Phil 3500.20.4 Simmel, G. Kant: sechzehn Vorlesungen. 4. Aufl. München, 1918.

Phil 193.59.15 Simmel, G. Lebensanschauung; vier...Kapitel. München, 1918.

Phil 5465.214 Smith, Frederick Madison. The higher powers of man. Thesis. Lamoni, Ia., 1918.

Phil 3500.27 Smith, N.K. Commentary to Kant's Critique of pure reason. London, 1918.

Phil 4769.1.50 Solov'ev, V.S. Det onda. Tre samtal. Stockholm, 1918.

Phil 8893.45 Solov'ev, Vladimir. The justification of the good. N.Y., 1918.

Phil 630.13 Sorley, W.R. Moral values and the idea of God. Cambridge, 1918.

Phil 630.42 Spaulding, E.G. The new rationalism. N.Y., 1918.

Phil 349.13 Stadler, A. Grundbegriffe der Erkenntnis. Leipzig, 1918.

Phil 5258.58 Stadler, August. Einleitung in die Psychologie. Leipzig, 1918.

Phil 2270.118 Stadler, August. Herbert Spencer. Spencers Ethik. Leipzig, 1918.

Phil 2128.84 Stammler, A. Mandevilles Bienenfabel. Berlin, 1918.

Phil 818.2.5 Starcke, C.N. Types af den filosofiske bankings historie. København, 1918.

Phil 1718.7.5 Stein, Ludwig. Philosophical currents of the present day. Calcutta, 1918-19. 2v.

Phil 3018.14 Steiner, R. Vom Menschenrätsel. Berlin, 1918.

1918 - cont.

Phil 960.118   Stephen, D.J. Studies in early Indian thought. Cambridge, 1918.

Phil 6688.10   Stephenson, Charles Y. (Mrs.). Clairvoyance and crystal gazing. London, 1918.

Phil 5374.21   Strong, Charles A. The origin of consciousness. London, 1918.

Phil 735.13   Stuart, H.W. Valuation as a logical process. Thesis. Chicago, 1918.

Phil 2280.2.75   Sully, James. My life and friends. London, 1918.
Phil 3501.6   Tegen, Einar. Studier till uppkomsten av Kants. Uppsala, 1918.

Phil 7069.18.150   Thy son liveth. Boston, 1918.
Phil 5059.13   Tookey, J.J. An elementary handbook of logic. N.Y., 1918.
Phil 819.8   Troilo, E. Figure e studii di storia della filosofia. Roma, 1918.

Phil 4065.91.5   Troilo, Erminio. Giordano Bruno. Roma, 1918.
Phil 350.4   Turró, R. La base trofica de la intelegencia. Madrid, 1918.

Phil 5467.3   Utitz, Emil. Psychologie der Simulation. Stuttgart, 1918.
Phil 3903.3.33   Vaihinger, Hans. Die Philosophie des Als Ob. 3. Aufl. Leipzig, 1918.

Phil 4650.1.43   Vannérus, Allen. Logik och vetenskapslära. Stockholm, 1918.

Phil 270.28   Verworn, Max. Kausale und konditionale Weltanschauung. 2. aufl. Jena, 1918.

Phil 352.1.15   Volkelt, J. Gewissheit und Wahrheit. München, 1918.
Phil 2915.75.2   Voltaire, F.M.A. de. Lettres philosophiques. Paris, 1918.
Phil 5262.19   Ward, James. Psychological principles. Cambridge, 1918.
Phil 8602.22   Watson, A.C. The logic of religion. Diss. Chicago, 1918.
Phil 4372.1.115   Watson, Foster. Les relacions de Juan Luis Vives amb els Anglesos i amb l'Angleterra. Barcelona, 1918.

Phil 197.16.4   Wells, H.G. First and last things. London, 1918.
Phil 7069.18.159   Werner-Hagen. Gedankenlesen und Hellsehen. Berlin, 1918.
Phil 7069.18.160   Whiting, Lilian. After her death. Boston, 1918.
Phil 7084.14.8   Wickwar, John William. Dreams: what they are and what they mean. 3d ed. London, 1918.

Phil 6132.20   Winbigler, C.F. Handbook of instructions for healing and helping others. Los Angeles, 1918.

Phil 5772.5   Windelband, Wilhelm. Über Willensfreiheit. 3. Aufl. Tübingen, 1918.

Phil 8677.10   Wobbermin, George. Christian belief in God. New Haven, 1918.

Phil 6332.5   Wolfram, E. Gegen Psycho-Analyse. Leipzig, 1918.
Phil 8602.23   Wunderle, Georg. Grundzüge der Religionsphilosophie. Paderborn, 1918.

Phil 6335.5   Zander, R. Vom Nervensystem. 3. Aufl. Leipzig, 1918.
Phil 8850.2   Zangenberg, Therese. Asthetische Gesichtspunkte in der englischen Ethik des 18. Jahrhunderts. Langensalza, 1918.

Phil 35.6.2.5   Zeitschrift für Psychologie. Register, 51-150. Leipzig, 1918-1943. 4v.

Phil 575.56   Zilsel, Edgar. Die Geniereligion. Wien, 1918.

1919

Phil 4500.2   Aall, Anathon. Filosofien i Norden. Kristiania, 1919.
Phil 400.38   Adams, George P. Idealism and the modern age. New Haven, 1919.

Phil 3850.16.81   Adler, Max. Georg Simmels Bedeutung für die Geistesgeschichte. Wien, 1919.

Phil 4513.1.35   Ahlberg, A. Filosfi och vetenskap. Stockholm, 1919.
Phil 7069.19.5   Aksakov, A.N. Animus und Spsiritismus. Leipzig 1919. 2v.

Phil 5627.138   Anderson, J.B. Applied religious psychology. Boston, 1919.

Phil 1700.2   Anthologie der neueren Philosophie. Berlin, 1919.
Phil 4060.1.40   Ardigo, Roberto. L'idealismo e la scienza. Roma, 1919.
Phil 8950.6.2   Arregui, Antonio M. Summarium theologiae morales. Bilbao, 1919.

Phil 5240.17.2   Aster, Ernst von. Einführung in die Psychologie. 2. Aufl. Leipzig, 1919.

Phil 7069.19.10   Barker, Elsa. Last letters from the living dead man. N.Y., 1919.

Phil 7069.19.15   Barrett, William F. On the threshold of the unseen. N.Y., 1919.

Phil 1701.8   Bauch, Bruno. Neuere Philosophie bis Kant. 3. Aufl. Berlin, 1919.

Phil 6111.30   Baylor, Courtenay. Remaking a man...mental refitting. N.Y., 1919.

Phil 960.43.2   Belvalkar, S.K. An outline scheme for a history of Indian philosophy. Poona, 1919. 2v.

L Phil 6111.12.15   Bergson, Henri. Materie und Gedächtnis. Jena, 1919.
Phil 2475.1.61.4A   Bergson, Henri. Matter and memory. London, 1919.
Phil 4200.1.81   Betzendörfer, Walter. Die Lehre von der zweifachen Wahrheit bei Petrus Pomponatius. Inaug. Diss. Tübingen, 1919.

Phil 8656.19   Beysens, J.T. Theodicee of natuurlijke godsleer. 2. druk. Bussum, 1919.

Phil 6311.2   Bjerre, P. The history of psychoanalysis. Boston, 1919.
Phil 8656.17   Blatchford, R. God and my neighbor. Chicago, 1919.
Phil 978.5.5   Blavatsky, H.P. Isis unveiled. v.1-2. Point Loma, California, 1919. 4v.

Phil 3120.22.5   Blüher, Hans. Gesammelte Aufsätze. Jena, 1919.
Phil 801.17   Bodrero, E. I limiti della storia della filosofia. Roma, 1919.

Phil 3110.27   Böhme, J. Six theosophic points, and other writings. London, 1919.

Phil 8610.919   Bonner, Hypatia Bradlaugh (Mrs.). Christianity and conduct. London, 1919.

Phil 7069.19.20   Boyce, Adam. The great beyond and its inhabitants. London, 1919.

Phil 8876.76   Braileanu, T. Die Grundlegung zur einer Wissenschaft der Ethik. Wien, 1919.

Phil 6311.3   Bridges, J.W. An outline of abnormal psychology. Columbus, 1919.

Phil 2045.100   Brockdorff, Cay von. Hobbes im Lichte seiner didaktischen und pädagogischen Bedeutung. Kiel, 1919.

Phil 176.109   Brouwer, L.E.J. Wiskunde, waarheid, werkkeijkheid. Gröningen, 1919.

Phil 9341.9.5   Brown, C.R. Yale talks. New Haven, 1919.
Phil 672.29.3   Browne, Robert T. The mystery of space. N.Y., 1919.
Phil 2555.5.90   Brulez, L. Delboeufs Bedeutung für die Logik. Diss. Berlin, 1919.

Phil 4065.43   Bruno, Giordano. L'éthique et le deuxième dialogue du spaccio. Paris, 1919.

Phil 5241.51   Bumke, Oswald. Psychologische Vorlesungen für Hörer aller Fakultälen. Wiesbaden, 1919.

1919 - cont.

Phil 5241.44   Bunge, Carlos O. Estudios filosóficos. Buenos Aires, 1919.

Phil 7069.19.30   Cameron, Margaret. Twelve lessons from the seven purposes. N.Y., 1919.

Phil 2475.1.185.5   Carr, Herbert W. Henri Bergson; the philosophy of change. London, 1919.

Phil 7069.19.40   Carrington, Hereward. Modern psychical phenomena. N.Y., 1919.

Phil 7069.19.45   Carrington, Hereward. Psychical phenomena. N.Y., 1919.
Phil 6112.20.5   Carroll, Robert S. Our nervous friends. N.Y., 1919.
Phil 1135.145   Casel, Otto. De philosophorum graecorum silentis mystics. Giessen, 1919.

Phil 177.37.5   Caso, Antonio. La existencia como economía como desinterés y como caridad. México, 1919.

Phil 4080.3.121.20   Castellano, G. Ragazzate letteraris: appunti...Croce. Napoli, 1919.

Phil 4065.95   Charbonnel, J.R. L'éthique de Giordano Bruno. Paris, 1919.

Phil 4002.1   Charbonnel, J.R. La pensée italienne au XVIe siècle. Paris, 1919.

Phil 7069.19.55   Christ in you. N.Y., 1919.
Phil 5752.7   Cohen, Chapman. Determinism or free-will? London, 1919.
Phil 5627.55.5   Cohen, Chapman. Religion and sex. London, 1919.
Phil 978.60.15   Cooper, I.S. Theosophy simplified. 3d ed. Hollywood, 1919.

Phil 177.29.2   Cornelius, H. Einleitung in die Philosophie. 2e Aufl. Leipzig, 1919.

Phil 7069.19.50   Corson, Hiram. Spirit messages. Boston, 1919.
Phil 8952.3   The cost of living; a personal reflection and its outcome. n.p., 1919.

Phil 6112.33   Courtney, J.W. The conquest of nerves. N.Y., 1919.
Phil 7069.19.60   Crawford, William J. Experiments in psychical science. N.Y., 1919.

Phil 7069.19.65   Crawford, William J. The reality of psychic phenomena, raps, levitations. N.Y., 1919.

Phil 7069.19.70   Curtiss, Harriette A. Realms of the living dead. N.Y., 1919.

Phil 7069.19.80   Dallas, Helen A. Death the gate of life? N.Y., 1919.
Phil 960.121   Dandoy, G. An essay on the doctrine of the unreality of the world in the Advaita. Calcutta, 1919.

Phil 5465.21   Daudet, Léon. Le monde des images; suite de l'hérédo. Paris, 1919.

Phil 178.46.5   Decoster, Paul. La réforme de la conscience. Bruxelles, 1919.

Phil 6953.6   Delgado, Honorio F. La psiquiatría psicológica. Lima, 1919.

Phil 7069.19.90   Denis, Léon. Life and destiny. N.Y., 1919.
Phil 2520.43   Descartes, René. Abhandlung über die Methode. Leipzig, 1919-20. 2 pam.

Phil 6313.6   Deschamps, Albert. Les maladies de l'esprit et les asthénies. Paris, 1919.

Phil 6313.4.3   Dessoir, Max. Vom Jenseits der Seele. 3. Aufl. Stuttgart, 1919.

Phil 178.5.3   Deussen, P. Die Elemente der Metaphysik. 6e Aufl. Leipzig, 1919.

Phil 8583.16   Deussen, Paul. Die Philosophie der Bibel. 2. Aufl. Leipzig, 1919.

Phil 1508.1.2   Deussen, Paul. Die Philosophie des Mittelalters. 2. Aufl. Leipzig, 1919.

Phil 5643.67   Dittler, Rudolf. Stereoskopisches Sehen und Messen. Leipzig, 1919.

Phil 3808.180   Doring, W.O. Schopenhauer. Zürich, 1919.
Phil 6060.15A   Downey, June E. Graphology and the psychology of handwriting. Baltimore, 1919.

Phil 7069.19.93   Doyle, Arthur Conan. The vital message. London, 1919.
Phil 7069.19.92   Doyle, Arthur Conan. The vital message. N.Y., 1919.
Phil 6480.167   Dream dictionary. Cincinnati, 1919.
Phil 178.12.42   Dresser, H.W. A history of the new thought movement. N.Y., 1919.

Phil 178.12.49   Dresser, H.W. On the threshold of the spiritual world. N.Y., 1919.

Phil 8878.40   Dugard, Marie. La culture morale. 8e éd. Paris, 1919.
Htn Phil 178.33*   Duncan, R. Prometheus (les grandes crucifiés). Paris, 1919.

Phil 5243.18.4   Dyroff, Adolf. Einführung in die Psychologie. 4e Aufl. Leipzig, 1919.

Phil 6114.9   Ebbecke, Ulrich. Die kortikalen Erregungen. Leipzig, 1919.

Phil 5244.7.4   Ebbinghaus, H. Abriss der Psychologie. 6e Aufl. Leipzig, 1919.

Phil 804.6   Einhorn, D. Begründung der Geschichte der Philosophie als Wissenschaft. Wien, 1919.

Phil 179.25   Ekelund, V. Attiskt. Stockholm, 1919.
Phil 9495.29.10   Ellis, Havelock. The philosophy of conflict. 2nd series. Boston, 1919.

Phil 9495.29.5   Ellis, Havelock. The philosophy of conflict. 2nd series. London, 1919.

Phil 3235.81.9   Engels, Friedrich. Ludwig Feuerbach und der Ausgang der klassischen deutschen Philosophie. 6. Aufl. Stuttgart, 1919.

Phil 8829.2.8   Eucken, Rudolf. Der Lebensanschauungen der grossen Denker. 13e und 14e Aufl. Berlin, 1919.

Phil 3210.30.5   Fechner, G.T. Tagesansicht gegenüber der Nachtansicht. 3. Aufl. Leipzig, 1919.

Phil 3246.78   Fichte, Johann Gottlieb. Briefe, Ausgewahlt und Herausgegeben von E. Bergmann. Leipzig, 1919.

Phil 3246.76   Fichte, Johann Gottlieb. Neue Fichte-funde, aus der Heimat und Schweiz. Gotha, 1919.

Phil 3246.195   Fichte und deutschlande Not. Berlin, 1919.
Phil 180.33.5   Fischer, Ludwig. Wirklichkeit, Wahrheit und Wissen. Berlin, 1919.

Phil 180.7.2   Flournoy, T. Métaphysique et psychologie. 2. éd. Genève, 1919.

Phil 6315.6   Forel, Auguste. L'activité psychique. Genève, 1919.
Phil 7054.173.10   Forster, David. The vital choice, Endor or Calvary. London, 1919.

Phil 805.5.4   Fouillée, Alfred. Histoire de la philosophie. 14e éd. Paris, 1919.

Phil 8630.7.9   Frank, Henry. The challenge of the war. Boston, 1919.
Phil 6955.11   Franz, S.I. Handbook of mental examining methods. 2. ed. N.Y., 1919.

Phil 665.55   Fringe, J.W. Life everlasting and psychic evolution. London, 1919.

Phil 3850.16.95   Frischeisen-Köhler, Max. Georg Simmel. Berlin, 1919.
Phil 7150.51   Fuellkrug, Gerhard. Der Selbstmord. Schwerin, 1919.

Chronological Listing

1919 - cont.

Phil 8881.48   Galli, E. Alle radici della morale. Milano, 1919.
Phil 5374.37   Galli, Ettore. Nel domonio dell' "io". Milano, 1919.
Phil 5246.33.5   Galli, Ettore. Nel mondo dello spirito. Milano, 1919.
Phil 181.37.2   Geiger, Joseph R. Some religious implications of pragmatism. Chicago, 1919.
Phil 181.43   Geissler, Kurt. Das System der Seinsgebiete als Grundlage einer umfassenden Philosophie. Leipzig, 1919.
Phil 5374.149   Geley, Gustave. De l'inconscient au conscient. Paris, 1919.
Phil 5374.148   Geley, Gustave. L'être subconscient. 4e éd. Paris, 1919.
Phil 5400.134   Ginneken, J. van. Gelaat, gebaar en klankexpressie. Leiden, 1919.
Phil 5246.20   Goddard, H.H. Psychology of the normal and subnormal. N.Y., 1919.
Phil 8610.919.20   Gorham, C.T. A plain man's plea for rationalism. London, 1919.
Phil 3006.3.2   Gramzow, Otto. Geschichte der Philosophie seit Kant. 2. Aufl. Charlottenburg, 1919-28. 2v.
Phil 8610.902.5   Greenwood, Granville George. The faith of an agnostic. 2. ed. London, 1919.
Phil 2115.124   Gregory, Raymond. A study of Locke's theory of knowledge. Wilmington, Ohio, 1919.
Phil 2115.124.5   Gregory, Raymond. A study of Locke's theory of knowledge. Thesis. Wilmington, Ohio, 1919.
Phil 5465.26   Griffitts, Charles H. Individual differences in imagery. Diss. n.p., 1919?
Phil 181.50   Grisebach, E. Wahrheit und Wirklichkeiten. Halle, 1919.
Phil 7069.19.100   Grove, Harriet McC. Gone west, by a soldier doctor. N.Y., 1919.
Phil 3826.5   Gunning, J.H. Spinoza en de idee der personlijkleid. 2. druk. Baarn, 1919.
Phil 6117.40   Haanel, C.F. The master key. St. Louis, 1919.
Phil 482.4   Haering, T.L. Die Materialisierung des Geistes. Tübingen, 1919.
Phil 8408.33   Hamann, R. Asthetik. 2. Aufl. Leipzig, 1919.
Phil 7069.19.110   Hardy, Thomas J. Spiritism in the light of the faith. London, 1919.
Phil 8408.7   Hartman, H.G. Aesthetics: a critical theory of art. Columbus, 1919.
Phil 2050.175   Hasse, Heinrich. Das Problem der Gültigkeit. Leipzig, 1919.
Phil 5247.33.2   Hecke, Gustav. Psychologie. 2. Aufl. Braunschweig, 1919.
Phil 5635.30   Heilig, G. Die sinnlichen Gefühle des Menschen. Jena, 1919.
Phil 4515.82   Hellström, Carl. Om viljefrihetsläran i Boströms definitiva filosofi. Uppsala, 1919.
Phil 807.12   Helms, Poul F. Fra Plato til Bergson. København, 1919.
Phil 7054.180   Henslow, G. Proofs of the truth of spiritualism. London, 1919.
Phil 7069.19.120   Henslow, George. The proofs of the truths of spiritualism. 2. ed. London, 1919.
Phil 7069.19.130   Herbine, Charlotte G. The meeting of the spheres. N.Y., 1919.
Phil 4352.1.99   Hermkes, Maria. Die Fundamental-Philosophie des Jaime Balmes. Inaug. Diss. Krefeld, 1919.
Phil 3007.3   Heussner, Alfred. Die philosophischen Weltanschauungen. 5. Aufl. Göttingen, 1919.
Phil 5655.3F   Heyninx, Albert. Essai d'olfactique physiologique. Bruxelles, 1919.
Phil 7054.132   Hill, J. Arthu. Spiritualism. N.Y., 1919.
Phil 9347.9   Hill, James L. The worst boys in town. Boston, 1919.
Phil 7069.20.162   Hill, John A. Psychical miscellanea. London, 1919.
Phil 8882.33   Hirst, E.W. Self and neighbor. London, 1919.
Phil 4580.35.7   Höffding, Harald. Kort oversigt over den nyere filosofis historie. 7e ed. Kjøbenhavn, 1919
Phil 5247.23.7   Höfler, Alois. Grundlehren der Psychologie. 7. Aufl. Wien, 1919.
Phil 9245.31   Holmes, E. The secret of happiness. London, 1919.
Phil 6117.22   Holmes, F.L. The law of mind in action. N.Y., 1919.
Phil 7069.19.140   Holt, Henry. The cosmic relations and immortality. Boston, 1919. 2v.
Phil 5247.19.2   Hunter, W.S. General psychology. Chicago, 1919.
Phil 8587.29   Hunzinger, A.W. Das Christentum im Weltanschauungskampf. 3. Aufl. Leipzig, 1919.
Phil 8632.8.5   Hyslop, J.H. Life after death. N.Y., 1919.
Phil 7069.19.147   Hyslop, James H. Contact with the other world. N.Y., 1919.
Phil 8883.3.2   Ingenieros, José. Hacia una moral sin dogmas. 2a ed. Buenos Aires, 1919.
Phil 6619.8.5   Ingenieros, José. Histeria y sugestión 5. ed. Buenos Aires, 1919.
Phil 2070.35.10   James, William. Religiøse erfaringer en undersøgelse af den menneskelige natur. 3e udg. Nørregaard, 1919.
Phil 2070.55   James, William. Saggi pragmatisti. Lanciano, 1919.
Phil 6959.1.15   Janet, Pierre. Les médications psychologiques. Paris, 1919. 3v.
Phil 809.3   Jansen, W. Geschiedenis der wijsbegeerte. Zutphen, 1919-21. 2v.
Phil 184.19   Jaspers, K. Psychologie der Weltanschauung. Berlin, 1919.
Phil 5190.15   Joachim, Harold. Immediate experience and meditation. Oxford, 1919.
Phil 1709.1.2   Joël, Karl. Die philosophische Krisis derGegenewart. 2e Aufl. Leipzig, 1919.
Phil 9450.17   Joklík, F. Naše dějinné poslání; čaovas úvaha politicko-ethická. Praha, 1919?
Phil 9349.4   Joly, Henri. Pour les jeunes. Paris, 1919.
Phil 8589.10   Jones, David A. Philosophic thought and religion. London, 1919.
Phil 6319.2.1   Jones, Ernest. Papers on psycho-analysis. N.Y., 1919.
Phil 525.55   Jones, Rufus M. Studies in mystical religion. London, 1919.
Phil 5620.8   Jonsson, K.G. Undersökningar...problemräkningens förutsättningar och förlopp. Uppsala, 1919.
Phil 3640.182   Kämpfer, Hartfried. Zum Nietzsche-Verständnis. Celle, 1919.
Phil 3480.19.13   Kant, Immanuel. Ausgewählte Kleine Schriften. Leipzig, 1919.
Phil 3480.31.9   Kant, Immanuel. Critica della raigon pura. 2. ed. Bari, 1919-21. 2v.
Phil 3480.28.4   Kant, Immanuel. Kants Weltanschanung. Darmstadt, 1919.
Phil 3480.45.18   Kant, Immanuel. Kritik der praktischen Vernunft als Prüfung der tätigen Vernunft. 3. Aufl. Lübeck, 1919.
Phil 3480.82.25   Kant, Immanuel. Opmerkingen over het gevoll van Schoone en Vorheveve. Sneck, 1919.
Phil 3480.71.4   Kant, Immanuel. Die Religion innerhalb der Grenzen der blossen Vernunft. 4. Aufl. Leipzig, 1919.

1919 - cont.

Phil 3480.79.12   Kant, Immanuel. Zum ewigen Frieden. 2. Aufl. Leipzig, 1919.
Phil 5250.11   Kaploun, Albert. Psychologie générale. Lausanne, 1919.
Phil 8885.19   Kautsky, Karl. Ethik und materialistische Geschichtsauffassung. Stuttgart, 1919.
Phil 8885.23   Kellerwessel, Josef. Beitrage zur Theorie der sittlichen Erkenntnis. Münster, 1919.
Phil 9520.4.8   Keppler, Paul W. Das Problem des Leidens. 8. und 9. Aufl. Freiburg, 1919.
Phil 3110.155   Kielholz, A. Jakob Boehme. Leipzig, 1919.
Phil 7069.19.150   King, Basil. The abolishing of death. N.Y., 1919.
Phil 9220.2.20   King, H.C. Laws of friendship human and devine. N.Y., 1919.
Phil 5250.7.10   Koffka, K. Beiträge zur Psychologie der Gestalt. Leipzig, 1919.
Phil 3492.30   Kolb, Victor. Immanuel Kant: der modernen Zeit. 2. Aufl. Wien, 1919.
Phil 3120.8.81   Kraus, Oskar. Franz Brentano. München, 1919.
Phil 7069.19.152   Kvaran, E.H. Trú og sannanir. Reykjavik, 1919.
Phil 2520.147   Labordère, Marcel. Une profession de foi cartésienne. Paris, 1919.
Phil 186.44   Lambeck, G. Philosophische Propädeutik. Leipzig, 1919.
Phil 4600.1.40   Landquist, John. Det levande forflutna. Stockholm, 1919.
Phil 3831.9.3   Lasbax, Émile. La hiérarchie dans l'univers chez Spinoza. Thèse, Paris, 1919.
Phil 8620.32   Lasbax, Émile. Le problème du mal. Paris, 1919.
Phil 186.45   Lasker, E. Die Philosophie des Unvollendbar. Leipzig, 1919.
Phil 3640.216   Lasserre, Pierre. Les idées de Nietzsche sur la musique. Paris, 1919?
Phil 3425.108.7   Lasson, G. Beiträge zur Hegelforschung. Berlin, 1919-21. 2v.
Phil 8412.8.10   Laurila, K.S. Estetiikhan peruskysymyksia. Porvoo, 1919.
Phil 6321.2.3   Lay, Wilfrid. Man's unconcious conflict. N.Y., 1919.
Phil 7069.19.155   Leaf, Horace. What is this spiritualism? N.Y., 1919.
Phil 5850.256   Lehmann, A. Størst unbytte af legemligt og aandeligt arbejde. København, 1919.
Phil 5761.3.10   Leland, C.G. Have you a strong will? N.Y., 1919.
Phil 672.126   Levi, Adolfo. Il concetto del tempo. Milano, 1919.
Phil 6121.12.5   Lickley, J.D. The nervous system. N.Y., 1919.
Phil 186.35.5   Liebert, Arthur. Wie ist kritische Philosophie überhaupt möglich? Leipzig, 1919.
Phil 8886.36   Lilly, William S. An invisible kingdom. London, 1919.
Phil 5761.10   Lindworsky, J. Der Wille, seine Erscheinung und seine Beherrschung. Leipzig, 1919.
Phil 5251.24   Liqueno, Jose M. Compendio de psicologia contemporanea. Córdoba, 1919.
Phil 7069.19.160   Living waters. N.Y., 1919.
Phil 9351.14   Llonu, Lastenia Lurriva de. Cartas a mi hijo. Lima, 1919.
Phil 8701.8   Loisy, Alfred. De la discipline intellectuelle. Paris, 1919.
Phil 5325.155   Loring, Mildred W. Methods of studying controlled word associations. Baltimore, 1919.
Phil 342.3.5   Losskii, N. The intuitive basis of knowledge. London, 1919.
Phil 8610.919.30   Lyttleton, Edward. The parson and the atheist. London, 1919.
Phil 7054.173   McComb, Samuel. The future life in the light of modern inguiry. N.Y., 1919.
Phil 343.4.6   Mach, E. Die Leitgedanken meiner naturwissenschaftlichen Erkenntnislehre und ire Aufnahme durch die Zeitenossen. Leipzig, 1919.
Phil 8592.48.3   Macintosh, D.C. Theology as an empirical science. N.Y., 1919.
Phil 7069.19.163   Mann, Walter. The follies and frauds of spiritualism. London, 1919.
Phil 187.44   Mann, William E. Theories about the truth of things. Franklin, Mass., 1919.
Phil 4060.1.82   Marchesini, G. Lo spirito evangelico di Roberto Ardigo. Bologna, 1919.
Phil 5401.6   Marks, J. Courage today and tomorrow. N.Y., 1919.
Phil 8887.48   Marshall, H.R. Mind and conduct. N.Y., 1919.
Phil 8050.76   Mascello, Leonardo. Aesthetcà di silencio. Rio de Janeiro, 1919.
Phil 5252.36.2   Meerkatz. Einführung in die Psychologie. 2. Aufl. Halle, 1919.
Phil 7140.113   Meijer, A.F. Experimenten omtrent suggestibilteit bij senuw- en zielszieken. Amsterdam, 1919.
Phil 2475.1.203   Mercanti, Pietro. Il pensiero filosofico cotemporaneo e la psicologia del Bergson. Roma, 1919?
Phil 8612.10   Mercer, Edward. Why do we die? London, 1919.
Phil 7069.19.165   Mercier, C.A. Spirit experiences. London, 1919.
Phil 187.47   Merz, John T. A fragment on the human mind. Edinburgh, 1919.
Phil 812.6   Messer, August. Geschichte der Philosophie in Atlertum und Mittelalter. Leipzig, 1919.
Phil 7054.173.15   Meyer, F.B. The modern craze of spiritualism. London, 1919.
Phil 8430.36   Michel, E. Der Weg zum Mythos. Jena, 1919.
Phil 8637.11   Milne, J. Napier. The dream that comes true. London, 1919.
Phil 5052.25   Moog, Willy. Logik, Psychologie und Psychologismus. Halle, 1919.
Phil 187.66   Moog, Willy. Das Verhältnis der Philosophie zu den Einzel-Wissenschaften. Halle, 1919.
Phil 8125.12   Moos, Paul. Die deutsche Ästhetik der Gegenwart. Berlin, 1919.
Phil 575.26   Moroney, Timothy. The idea of personality. Diss. Washington, 1919.
Phil 575.34   Müller-Freienfels, Richard. Persönlichkeit und Weltanschauung. Berlin, 1919.
Phil 5052.23   Mukerji, A.C. A text-book of inductive logic. Allahabad, 1919.
Phil 7069.19.173   Myers, Fred W.H. Human personality and its survival of bodily death. London, 1919.
Phil 7069.19.170   Myers, Fred W.H. Human personality and its survival of bodily death. London, 1919.
Phil 5253.7   Naesgaard, S. Kortfattet sjaelelaere. København, 1919.
Phil 9495.37.15   National Council of Public Morals for Great and Greater Britain. Campaigns of peace. N.Y., 1919.
Phil 8638.2   Nicoll, N.R. Reunion in eternity. N.Y., 1919.
Phil 4610.7.45   Nordström, V. Tal och tankar. Stockholm, 1919.
Phil 7060.92.35   O'Donnell, Elliot. Haunted places in England. London, 1919.
Phil 960.120   Oldenberg, Hermann. Vorwissenschaftliche Wissenschaft die Weltanschauung der Brahamana. Göttingen, 1919.

1919 - cont.

Phil 4365.1.10   Ors y Rovira, E. d'. Grandeza y servidumbre de la intelegencia. Madrid, 1919.

Phil 190.20.7   Papini, Giovanni. L'altra metà. 3a ed. Firenze, 1919.

Phil 2415.5   Parodi, Dominique. La philosophie contemporaine en France. Paris, 1919.

Phil 5765.2.10   Payot, Jules. Le travail intellectuel et la volonté. Paris, 1919.

Phil 525.23   Pedrick, Katharine F. How to make perfection appear. Boston, 1919.

Phil 5627.55   Pennock, Gilbert L. The consciousness of communion with God. New Brunswick, N.J., 1919.

Phil 4620.3   Péturss, Helgi. Nýall. Reykjavík, 1919.

Phil 8890.38   Pfordten, O. Ethik. Berlin, 1919.

Phil 8890.36   Pichler, Hans. Grundzüge einer Ethik. Graz, 1919.

Phil 3552.129   Pichler, Hans. Leibniz. Graz, 1919.

Phil 5640.125.7   Pikler, Gyula. Hypothesenfreie Theorie der Gegenfarben. Leipzig, 1919.

Phil 5640.125.8   Pikler, Gyula. Theorie der Konsonanz und Dissonanz. Leipzig, 1919.

Phil 8890.33   Pitt-Rivers, Goerge. Conscience and fanaticism. London, 1919.

Phil 190.29   Politeo, Giorgio. Scritti filosofici et letterari. Bologna, 1919.

Phil 6060.6.3   Preyer, William. Zur Psychologie des Schreibens. Leipzig, 1919.

Phil 7069.19.180   Private Dowding. N.Y., 1919.

Phil 7069.19.190   Randall, Edward Caleb. The dead have never died. N.Y., 1919.

Phil 192.40   Randall, J.H. The spirit of the new philosophy. London, 1919.

Phil 5827.7   Reeves, Cora Daisy. Discrimination of light of different wave-lengths by fish. N.Y., 1919.

Phil 5627.102   Reik, Theodor. Probleme der Religionspsychologie. 1. Teil. Leipzig, 1919.

Phil 8418.10   Rensi, G. La scepsi estetica. Bologna, 1919.

Phil 645.22   Rensi, Giuseppe. Lineamenti di filosofia scetica. Bologna, 1919.

Phil 8707.7.5   Rice, William N. The poet of science and other addresses. N.Y., 1919.

Phil 192.36   Richardson, C.A. Spiritual pluralism and recent philosophy. Cambridge, 1919.

Phil 192.36.10   Richardson, C.A. Spiritual pluralism and recent philosophy. Cambridge, 1919.

Phil 5257.6.5   Richet, Charles. Essai de psychologie général. 10. éd. Paris, 1919.

Phil 5390.6   Richet, Charles. L'homme stupide. Paris, 1919.

Phil 192.37   Richter, Raoul. Einführung in die Philosophie. 4e Aufl. Leipzig, 1919.

Phil 1535.6.14   Rickaby, Joseph. Moral philosophy. 4th ed. London, 1919.

Phil 1717.5.5   Riehl, Alois. Zur Einführung in die Philosophie der Gegenwart. 5e Aufl. Leipzig, 1919.

Phil 1817.3.9   Riley, I.W. La philosophie française en Amérique. Paris, 1919.

Phil 974.3.50   Rittelmeyer, F. Von der Theosophie Rudolf Steiners. Nürnberg, 1919.

Phil 6952.18.25   Robinson, Victor. The Don Quixote of psychiatry. N.Y., 1919.

Phil 3640.170   Rodriguez Aniceto, N. Maquiarelo y Nietzsche. Madrid, 1919.

Phil 3790.8.82   Rosén, Hugo. Föhållandet mellan moral och religion...den Ritschelska skolan. Lund, 1919.

Phil 2805.175   Roux, Marie. Pascal en Poitou et les Poitevins. Paris, 1919.

Phil 2250.45A   Royce, Josiah. Lectures on modern idealism. New Haven, 1919.

Phil 9455.17   Rühlmann, Paul. Kulturpropaganda. Charlottenburg, 1919.

Phil 5257.43   Rupp, Hans. Probleme und Apparate zur experimentellen Pädagogik und Jugendpsychologie. Leipzig, 1919.

Phil 192.28.17   Russell, B. Mysticism and logic and other essays. London, 1919.

Phil 3160.5.81   Saal, Ernst. Hans Cornelius Erkenntnistheorie im Verhältnis zu der Kants. Diss. Giessen, 1919.

Phil 8673.9   Sacchi, Gaetano. Esistenza di Dio. Roma, 1919.

Phil 735.18.2   Scheler, Max. Vom Umsturz der Werte. 2e Aufl. Leipzig, 1919. 2v.

Phil 530.20.45   Schellenberg, E.L. Die deutsche Mystik. Berlin, 1919.

Phil 5828.16.5   Schmid, Bastian. Das Tier in seinen Spielen. Leipzig, 1919.

Phil 1925.82   Schmitz, Harry J. Cudworth und der Platonismus. Diss. Bonn, 1919.

Phil 193.99   Schneider, H. Metaphysik als exakte Wissenschaft. Pt.1-3. Leipzig, 1919-1921.

Phil 3808.18   Schopenhauer, Arthur. Sämmtliche Werke. Leipzig, 1919. 2v.

Phil 3808.17   Schopenhauer, Arthur. Sämmtliche Werke in fünf Bänden. Leipzig, 1919. 5v.

Phil 4260.85.25   Scrocca, A. Giambattista Vico nella critica di Benedetto Croce. Napoli, 1919.

Phil 5258.64   Segond, J. Intuition et anitié. Paris, 1919.

Phil 3838.6   Severijn, Johannes. Spinoza en de gereformeerde theologie zijner dagen. Utrecht, 1919.

Phil 193.64.9   Shaw, C.G. The ground and goal of human life. N.Y., 1919.

Phil 5525.12.3   Sidis, B. The psychology of laughter. N.Y., 1919.

Phil 7082.88   Siemens, Otto. Wissenschaftliche Traum de Terei. Leipzig, 1919?

Phil 978.9.25   Sinnett, A.P. Collected fruits of occult teaching. London, 1919.

Phil 193.72   Slesser, Henry H. The nature of being...essay in ontology. London, 1919.

Phil 5058.28.9   Smith, Henry B. Non-Aristotelian logic. Philadelphia, 1919.

Phil 7069.19.200   Smith, Hester T. Voices from the void. N.Y., 1919.

Phil 8643.14.5   Snowden, J.F. Can we believed in immortality. N.Y., 1919.

Phil 7069.19.210   "So saith the spirit." London, 1919.

Phil 2225.6.80   Spettmann, P.H. Die Psychologie des Johannes Pecham. Inaug. Diss. Münster, 1919.

Phil 9070.24   Spillman, Harry Collins. Personality. N.Y., 1919.

Phil 3819.73   Spinoza, Benedictus de. Der Briefwechsel Spinozas. Halle, 1919. 2v.

Phil 3819.14.5   Spinoza, Benedictus de. Chief works. v.2. London, 1919.

Phil 3819.36.60   Spinoza, Benedictus de. Ethica. München, 1919.

Phil 7069.19.215   Spiritual reconstruction. N.Y., 1919.

Phil 2636.83   Stanganelli, Irma. La teoria pedagogica di Helvetius. Napoli, 1919.

Phil 8643.16   Stanley, T.P. The gift of immortality. Collingswood, 1919.

1919 - cont.

Phil 2520.156   Starcke, C.N. René Descartes. Kjøbenhavn, 1919.

Phil 193.78   Sternberg, Kurt. Einführung in die Philosophie vom Stand...Kritizismus. Leipzig, 1919.

Phil 2805.112.5   Stewart, Hugh F. La sainteté de Pascal. Paris, 1919.

Phil 8893.53.7   Störring, Gustav. Die sittlichen Forderungen und die Frage ihrer Gultigkeit. Leipzig, 1919.

Phil 8520.23   Straubinger, H. Die Religion und ihre Grundwahrheiten in der deutschen Philosophie seit Leibniz. Freiburg, 1919.

Phil 3120.6.85   Struck, Gustav. Friedrich Bouterwek. Inaug. Diss. Rostock, 1919.

Phil 3838.13   Stumpf, K. Spinozastudien. Berlin, 1919.

Phil 5460.4   Svenson, Frey. Vanföreställningarnas och sinnesvillornas psykologi. Stockholm, 1919.

Phil 6129.9   Tepp, Max. Vom Sinn des Körpers. Hamburg, 1919.

Phil 7069.19.220   Thy son liveth. Boston, 1919.

Phil 6317.5   Tridon, André. Psychoanalysis, its history, theory and practice. N.Y., 1919.

Phil 600.39   Troeltsch, E. Die Dynamik der Geschichte nach der Geschichtsphilosophie des Positivismus. Berlin, 1919. 101v.

Phil 6689.7.3   Trömner, Ernst. Hypnotismus und Suggestion. 3e Aufl. Leipzig, 1919.

Phil 8599.15.5   Troward, T. The Doré lectures. N.Y., 1919.

Phil 194.21.7   Troward, Thomas. The law and the word. N.Y., 1919.

Phil 6329.2.5   Turco, Natale. Il trattamento morale dello scrupole e dell'ossessione morbossa. Torino, 1919-20. 2v.

Phil 6329.12.5.2   Turel, Adrien. Selbsterlösung. 1. und 2. Aufl. Berlin, 1919.

Phil 2070.119   Turner, J.E. An examination of William James's philosophy. Oxford, 1919.

Phil 194.26   Turró, R. Filosofia critica. 1a ed. Madrid, 1919.

Phil 7060.151   Tweedale, V.C. Ghosts I have seen. N.Y., 1919.

NEDL   Phil 525.7.3   Underhill, Evelyn. Mysticism. 8th ed. N.Y., 1919.

Phil 8600.2   Union de Libres Penseurs et de Libres Croyants pour la Culture Morale. Le sentiment religieux à l'heure actuelle. Paris, 1919.

Phil 8685.15   Urquhart, W.S. Pantheism, and the value of life. Thesis. London, 1919.

Phil 194.13.25   Venturini, M. La filosofia dell'umanesimo di P.R. Trojano, 1863-1909. Torino, 1919.

Phil 3805.156   Völter, Hans. Schleiermacher und die Gegenwart. Heilbronn, 1919.

Phil 7069.19.225   Vold, Karl. Andatrú vorra tíma. Reykjavik, 1919.

Phil 6141.4   Von Boeckmann P. Nerve force. N.Y., 1919.

Phil 3503.4.10   Vorländer, K. Kant als Deutscher. Darmstadt, 1919.

Phil 1822.1   Waddington, M. The development of British thought. Toronto, 1919.

Phil 4655.3.30   Waerland, Are. Materie eller ande? 3. uppl. Uppsala, 1919.

Phil 8897.40   Walcott, Gregory. Tsing Hua lectures on ethics. Boston, 1919.

Phil 735.75   Walker, Cyril T.H. The construction of the world. Oxford, 1919.

Phil 400.44   Walker, W. Idealism. London, 1919.

Phil 7069.19.230   Wallace, Mary B. The thinning of the veil. N.Y., 1919.

Phil 9558.11   Walston, C. Truth; an essay in moral reconstruction. Cambridge, 1919.

Phil 6132.7.2   Walton, G.L. Why worry? 2d ed. Philadelphia, 1919.

Phil 3504.20   Warda, Arthur. Die Druckschriften Immanuel Kants. Wiesbaden, 1919.

Phil 5262.20   Warren, H.C. Human psychology. Boston, 1919.

Phil 7069.19.240   Watson, Albert D. The twentieth plane. Philadelphia, 1919.

Phil 575.52   Webb, C.C.J. God and personality. Aberdeen, 1919.

Phil 8897.47   Weigelin, Ernst. Sitte, Recht und Morale. Berlin, 1919.

Phil 1722.5.2   Wenzig, Carl. Die Weltanschuungen der Gegenwart. 2e Aufl. Leipzig, 1919.

Phil 7060.151.20   Wickwar, J.W. The ghost world. London, 1919.

Phil 8423.8   Wienbarg, Ludolf. Asthetische Feldzüge. 2. Aufl. Hamburg, 1919.

Phil 3504.25.5   Willems, C. Kant's Erkenntnislehre. Trier, 1919.

Phil 3504.25   Willems, C. Kant's Sittenlehre. Trier, 1919.

Phil 5832.10   Wiltbank, R.T. Transfer of training in white rats upon various series of mazes. Chicago, 1919.

Phil 197.46   Wirth, William. Zur Orientierung der Philosophie am Bewusstseinsbegriff. München, 1919.

Phil 5062.22   Wolf, Abraham. Exercises in logic and scientific method. London, 1919.

Phil 1050.14   Wolfson, Harry A. Note on Crescas's definition of time. Philadelphia, 1919.

Phil 3915.40.4   Wundt, Wilhelm. Logik. 4. Aufl. Stuttgart, 1919-21. 3v.

Phil 62.2   Wyoming. University. Department of Psychology. Bulletin. 2. ed. no.1-3. Laramie, Wyoming, 1919-

Phil 9495.37   Young Women's Christian Association, United States. National Board. War Council Work. Social Morality Committee. Report...Je. 1917 to Jl. 1919. N.Y.? 1919?

Phil 1130.2.15   Zeller, Eduard. Die Philosophie der Griechen. 6e Aufl. Leipzig, 1919-23. 6v.

Phil 3507.6   Ziegeler, E. Kants Sittenlehre in gemeinverständlicher Darstellung. Leipzig, 1919.

Phil 200.8   Zimmermann, K. Die Gemeinschaft der Einsamen. Jena, 1919.

Phil 3845.25   Zum Charakter Spinozas. 2. Aufl. Halle, 1919.

Phil 70.23   Zur Psychoanalyse der Kriegsneurosen. Leipzig, 1919.

192-

Phil 7069.20   Almasque, Jose A. Memorias de un fraile. Habana, 192-?

Phil 1870.15   Berkeley, G. Philosophische Werke. Leipzig, 192-. 3v.

Phil 5520.78   Beyer, Alfred. Der Sieg des Denkens. Berlin, 192-.

Phil 7140.116.15   Coué, Emile. The world's greatest power. pt.3-6. London, 192-. 2 pam.

Phil 2070.132   Delattre, F. William James Bergsonien. Paris, 192-.

Phil 4359.1.81   Endara, Julio. José Ingenieros y el porvenir de la filosofía. 2a ed. Buenos Aires, 192-.

Phil 6315.2.68   Freud, Sigmund. Group psychology and the analysis of the ego. N.Y., 192-?

Phil 5248.2.25   Gonzalez Velez, J. Resumen sintético y brevisémo del sistema de psicologia. Habana, 192-.

Phil 8586.8.15   Guyau, M.J. Die irreligion der Zukunft. Leipzig, 192-?

Phil 1750.25   Heitzman, M. Mikolaj Hill. Studjum z histoiji filozofji atomistycznej. Krakow, 192-?

Phil 9347.2.13   Hubbard, E. A message to Garcia. n.p., 192-.

Phil 5249.13.5   Jung, Carl G. Psychological types. n.p., 192-.

Chronological Listing

192- - cont.

Phil 978.62 — Juste, Michael. The white brother; an occult autobiography. London, 192-?

Phil 5190.10.1 — MacPherson, William. The psychology persuasion. N.Y., 192-?

Phil 4313.2 — Mendez Bejarano, M. Historia de la filosofía en España hasta el siglo XX. Madrid, 192-.

Phil 2520.180 — Mitrovitch, R. La théorie des sciences chez Descartes d'après sa géométrie. Thèse. Paris, 192-?

Phil 298.6 — Riddell, Newton N. Science of creation. Des Moines, Iowa, 192-.

Phil 9035.45.4 — Roback, A.A. Psicologia del caracter. Traduccion de Santo Rubiano. Madrid, 192-?

Phil 5258.89 — Schjelderup, H. Referat av H. Schjelderups forelaesninger over psykologi. Oslo, 192-.

Phil 2340.6.90 — Sorley, W.R. James Ward, 1843-1925. London, 192-.

Phil 3819.30.30 — Spinoza, Benedictus de. Ethik. 7. Aufl. Leipzig, 192-?

Phil 974.3.5 — Steiner, Rudolf. The story of my life. London, 192-.

1920

Phil 5545.74 — Achilles, E.M. Experimental studies in recall and recognition. N.Y., 1920.

Phil 672.120 — Alexander, S. Space, time and deity. London, 1920. 2v.

Phil 175.26.2 — Aliotta, Antonio. La guerra eterna e il dramma dell'esistenza. 2a ed. Napoli, 1920.

Phil 281.11 — Alt, Theodor. Fundamentum Weltanschauung. Mannheim, 1920.

Phil 672.143 — Alvarez de Toledo, A. Le problème de l'espace. Paris, 1920.

Phil 4170.3.82 — Amante, B. Un santo nel secolo XIX: A.C. de Meis. Lanciano, 1920.

Phil 3640.158 — Andler, Charles. Nietzsche, sa vie et sa pensée. Paris, 1920-31. 6v.

Phil 4060.1.25 — Ardigo, Roberto. Scritti vari. Firenze, 1920.

Phil 1105.7 — Aster, E. Geschichte der antiken Philosophie. Berlin, 1920.

Phil 176.101 — Backer, S. de. Disputationes metaphysicae. Fasc.1-3. Paris, 1920-1923.

Phil 1850.35.12 — Bacon, Francis. Of the advancement of learning. 5th ed. Oxford, 1920.

Phil 176.79 — Badoureau, A. Causeries philosophiques. Paris, 1920.

Phil 7069.20.10 — Balfour, Gerald W. The ear of Dionysius. N.Y., 1920.

Phil 7069.20.20 — Bamber, L. Kelway. Claude's second book. N.Y., 1920.

Phil 3110.163 — Barker, C.J. Pre-requisites for the study of Jakob Böhme. London, 1920.

Phil 176.95 — Bauch, Bruno. Anfangsgründe der Philosophie. Gotha, 1920.

Phil 3483.8.3 — Bauch, Bruno. Immanuel Kant. 3. Aufl. Berlin, 1920.

Phil 7140.115 — Baudouin, C. Suggestion and autosuggestion. London, 1920.

Phil 176.14.10 — Bax, E.B. The real, the rational and the alogical. London, 1920.

Phil 7054.174.5 — Bazett, L.M. After-death communications. London, 1920.

Phil 7069.20.30 — Bazter, Francis K. Does telepathy explain spiritualism? N.Y., 1920.

Phil 6951.5.4.2 — Beers C.W. A mind that found itself. 4. ed. N.Y., 1920.

Phil 8876.60 — Benett, William. Freedom and liberty. London, 1920.

Phil 8876.55.20 — Bennett, Arnold. The human machine. London, 1920.

Phil 2475.1.45 — Bergson, Henri. L'énergie spirituelle. 5. éd. Paris, 1920.

Phil 2475.1.46 — Bergson, Henri. Mind energy. London, 1920.

Phil 2475.1.75 — Bergson, Henri. Zeit und Freiheit. Jena, 1920.

Phil 1870.40.35 — Berkeley, G. Abhandlung über die Prinzipien der menschlichen Erkenntnis. London, 1920.

Phil 1870.40.25 — Berkeley, G. Les principes de la connaissance humaine. Paris, 1920.

Phil 1870.66.5 — Berkeley, G. La siris. Paris, 1920.

Phil 5751.12 — Bermann, G. El determinismo en la ciencia y en la vida. Buenos Aires, 1920.

Phil 4001.1 — Berthé de Besaucèle, Louis. Les Cartériens d'Italie. Thèse. Paris, 1920.

Phil 176.115.9 — Bierens de Haan, J.D. Idee - studies. 3e druk. Amsterdam, 1920.

Phil 176.115.35 — Bierens de Haan, J.D. De weg tot het inzicht. Amsterdam, 1920.

Phil 6311.2.2 — Bjerre, P. The history and practice of psychanalysis. Boston, 1920.

Phil 2520.139 — Blanchet, Léon. Les antécédents historique du "Je pense, donc je suis". Paris, 1920.

Phil 4073.84 — Blanchet, Léon. Campanella. Paris, 1920.

Phil 7060.250 — Bland, Oliver. The adventures of a modern occultist. N.Y., 1920.

Phil 978.5.26 — Blavatsky, H.P. The key to theosophy. Los Angeles, 1920.

Phil 978.5.20 — Blavatsky, H.P. The voice of the silence. 4th ed. Point Loma, 1920.

Phil 176.70 — Blood, B.P. Pluriverse. Boston, 1920.

Phil 3120.22.25F — Blüher, Hans. In medias res. Jena, 1920.

Phil 3120.22.35 — Blüher, Hans. Die Wiedergeburt der platonischen Akademie. Jena, 1920. 4 pam.

Phil 7084.44 — Boehm, Arthur. Rätsel des Traumes und des Zufalls. Leipzig, 1920.

Phil 3110.45 — Böhme, J. The confessions of Jacob Böhme. London, 1920.

Phil 3110.28.2 — Böhme, J. Schriften. Leipzig, 1920.

Phil 3483.37 — Boette, Werner. Kants religion. Langensalza, 1920.

Phil 2805.186 — Bohlin, J. Blaise Pascal. v.1-2. Stockholm, 1920-21.

Phil 5811.10.7 — Bohn, Georges. La naissance de l'intelligence. Paris, 1920.

Phil 410.6.5 — Bolzano, B. Paradoxien des Unendlichen. Leipzig, 1920.

Phil 7069.20.40 — Bond, Frederick B. The gate of remembrance. 3. ed. Boston, 1920.

Phil 176.84 — Bonlnois, Helen. The law of being. London, 1920.

Phil 6990.3.31 — Bonnières, L. de. Dans la lumière de Lourdes. Paris, 1920.

Phil 2805.203 — Bornhausen, K. Pascal. Basel, 1920.

Phil 5041.16.15 — Bosanquet, B. Implication and linear inference. London, 1920.

Phil 8581.62 — Bosanquet, Bernard. What religion is. London, 1920.

Phil 6311.5 — Bousfield, Paul. The elements of practical psychoanalysis. London, 1920.

Phil 7069.19.27 — Bozzano, E. Les phénomènes de hantise. Paris, 1920.

Phil 5722.7 — Bradley, M.K. The logic of the unconscious mind. London, 1920.

Phil 972.12 — Brander-Pracht, K. Der neue Mensch. Berlin, 1920.

Phil 176.90 — Brausewetter, A. Die Weltanschauung als Erlebnis. Heft 3-4. Leipzig, 1920. 2v.

Phil 525.29 — Brenier de Montmorand, Antoine F.J.H.L.M. Psychologie des mystiques catholiques orthodoxes. Paris, 1920.

Phil 8633.1.20 — Brown, Charles R. Living again. Cambridge, 1920.

1920 - cont.

Phil 5751.6 — Brulez, Lucien. Het vrijheidsbegrip. 's Gravenhage, 1920.

Phil 4065.45 — Bruno, Giordano. Spaccio della bestia trionfante. v.1-2. Lanciano, 1920.

NEDL Phil 176.85.3 — Brunschvicg, L. Introduction à la vie de l'esprit. 3e éd. Paris, 1920.

Phil 3120.30.49 — Buber, Martin. Die Rede. 2. Aufl. Leipzig, 1920.

Phil 3425.210 — Bülow, F. Die Entwicklung der Hegelschen Sozialphilosophie. Leipzig, 1920.

Phil 8876.87 — Bullock, Arthur B. The supreme human tragedy and other essays. London, 1920.

Phil 176.80.5 — Burckhardt, Georg E. Individuum und Welt als Werk. München, 1920.

Phil 8581.42 — Burroughs, John. Accepting the universe. Boston, 1920.

Phil 6111.32 — Butler, Hiram Erastus. Practical methods to insure success. 33rd ed. Applegate, Calif., 1920.

Phil 5811.15 — Buytendijk, Frederik Jacobus Johannes. Psychologie der dieren. Haarlem, 1920.

VPhil 8877.96 — Čáda, F. Čádova etika individualní. Praha, 1920.

Phil 177.57 — Calderoni, M. Il pragmatismo a cura di Giovanni Papini. Lanciano, 1920.

Phil 177.86 — Camera, Ugo. Saggio di una sistema di filosofia busato sulla suggestione. Aquila, 1920.

Phil 9495.27 — Cansinos Assens, Rafael. Ética y estética de los sexos. Madrid, 1920.

Phil 7069.20.50 — Carrington, Hereward. The coming science. N.Y., 1920.

Phil 7069.07.13 — Carrington, Hereward. The physical phenomena of spiritualism. 3. ed. N.Y., 1920.

Phil 7069.20.53A — Carrington, Hereward. Your psychic powers and how to develop them. N.Y., 1920.

Phil 7069.20.61 — Carter, Huntly. Spiritualism, its present-day meaning. Philadelphia, 1920.

Phil 4080.3.120 — Castellano, G. Introduzione allo studio...B. Croce. Bari, 1920.

Phil 8877.58 — Challaye, F. Les principes généraux de la science et de la morale. Paris, 1920.

Phil 7069.20.70 — Chevreuil, L. Proofs of the spirit world. N.Y., 1920.

Phil 1702.2.5 — Chiappelli, A. La crisi del pensiero moderno. Citta di Castello, 1920.

Phil 4080.3.122 — Chiocchetti, E. La filosofia di Benedetto Croce. 2a ed. Milano, 1920.

Phil 5242.27 — Choisnard, P. L'éducation psychologique à propos de la grande guerre. Paris, 1920.

Phil 3850.5.93 — Claparède-Spir, H. Un pprécurseur. Lausanne, 1920.

Phil 8627.8 — Clarke, W.N. Immortality. New Haven, 1920.

Phil 8403.19 — Coen, Augusto. L'estetica sperimentale. Roma, 1920.

Phil 3484.2.17 — Cohen, H. Kommentar zu Immanuel Kant's Kritik. 3. Aufl. Leipzig, 1920.

Phil 8610.880.18 — Congrès Universel de la Libre Pensée, 18th, Prague, 1920. XVIII. Světový kongres volné myšlenky v Praze od 5-9 září, 1920. Přípravy. Praha, 1920?

Phil 8520.11 — Cooke, George W. The social evolution of religion. Boston, 1920.

Phil 6312.1.7 — Coriat, I.H. Repressed emotions. N.Y., 1920.

Phil 400.72 — Corti, Settimio. La rivincita dell'idealismo. Rieti, 1920.

Phil 623.17 — Courtney, J.E. Freethinkers of the nineteenth century. London, 1920.

Phil 2515.3.32 — Cresson, A. L'invérifiable; les problèmes de la métaphysique. 2e éd. Paris, 1920.

Phil 5042.10.4 — Croce, B. Logica come scienza del concetto puro. 4a ed. Bari, 1920.

Phil 7069.20.80 — Crockett, Albert Stevens. Revelations of Louise. N.Y., 1920.

Phil 8877.55.2 — Cronin, Michael. The science of ethics. 2nd ed. Dublin, 1920-22. 2v.

Phil 6312.3 — Culpin, Millais. Psychoneuroses of war and peace. Cambridge, Eng., 1920.

Phil 7069.20.82 — Culpin, Millais. Spiritualism and the new psychology. London, 1920.

Phil 177.49 — Cunningham, H.E. An introduction to philosophy. Boston, 1920.

Phil 7069.20.90 — Davis, Andrew J. A stellar key to the summer land. 6th ed. Los Angeles, 1920.

Phil 7069.20.100 — Dearmer, Nancy K. The fellowship of the picture. N.Y., 1920.

Phil 7069.20.110 — De Voras, Anna F. A cloud of witnesses. N.Y., 1920.

Phil 8583.17.5 — Delany, Selden P. Christian practice. N.Y., 1920.

Phil 530.20.50 — Denifle, H. Das geistliche Leben. 7. Aufl. Graz, 1920.

Phil 510.1.33 — Dennert, E. Die Wahrheit über Ernst Haeckel und seine "Welträtsel". Halle, 1920.

Phil 3485.9 — Dentrice di Accadia, C. Il razionalismo religioso di E. Kant. Bari, 1920.

Phil 3640.155 — De Villers, Sireyx. La faillite du surhomme et la physologie de Nietzsche. Paris, 1920.

Phil 8583.9.10 — Dole, Charles F. A religion for the new day. N.Y., 1920.

Phil 5243.20 — Doll, Edgar Arnold. The growth of intelligence. Diss. Princeton, 1920.

Phil 8953.6 — Donat, J. Summa philosophiae christianae. v.7-8. Oeniponte, 1920-21.

Phil 5043.26 — Donati, G. La logica. Forli, 1920.

Phil 7069.20.115 — Doyle, Arthur Conan. Verbatim report of a public debate on "The truth of spiritualism" between A.C. Dolye and Joseph McCabe. London, 1920.

Phil 630.21A — Drake, Durant. Essays in critical realism. London, 1920.

Phil 7069.20.120 — Dresser, Horatio W. The open vision. N.Y., 1920.

Phil 1703.2.3 — Drews, Arthur. Die Philosophie im ersten Drittel des 19. Jahrhunderts. Berlin, 1920.

Phil 5753.8.2 — Driesch, H. Das Problem der Freiheit. 2. Aufl. Darmstadt, 1920.

Phil 6313.5 — Dunlap, K. Mysticism, Freudianism and scientific psychology. St. Louis, 1920. 2v.

Phil 178.41 — Dupont, Paul. Les problèmes de la philosophie et leur enchainement scientifique. Paris, 1920.

Phil 5753.11 — Duprat, G.L. L'éducation de la volonté et des facultés logiques. Paris, 1920.

Phil 5213.2 — Dwelshauvers, Georges. La psychologie française contemporaine. Paris, 1920.

Phil 3486.10.5 — Ehrlich, W. Der Freiheitsbegriff bei Kant und Schopenhauer. Berlin, 1920.

Phil 5545.73 — Eichthal, Eugène d'. Du rôle de la mémoire dans nos conceptions. Paris, 1920.

Phil 3640.197 — Ekman, Karl. Nietzsches estetik. Helsingfors, 1920.

Phil 5244.10.6 — Elsenhans, Theodor. Lehrbuch der Psychologie. Tübingen, 1920.

Phil 5244.10 — Elsenhans, Theodor. Psychologie und Logik. 5e Aufl. Berlin, 1920.

1920 - cont.

Phil 179.20   Endres, J.A. Einleitung in die Philosophie. Kempten, 1920.

Phil 2885.86   Engel, Otto. Der Einfluss Hegels auf die Bildung der Gedankenwelt Hippolyte Taines. Stuttgart, 1920.

Phil 3450.4.80   Engestrom, Sigfrid. Studier till Wilhelm Hermanns etik. Uppsala, 1920.

Phil 179.12   Eno, Henry Lane. Activism. Princeton, N.J., 1920.

Phil 5244.15   Erdmann, B. Grundzüge der Reproduktions Psychologie. Berlin, 1920.

Phil 5244.9.5   Erismann, T. Psychologie. Berlin, 1920.

Phil 525.81   Farges, Albert. Les phénomènes mystiques distingués de leurs contrefaçons humaines et diaboliques. Paris, 1920.

Phil 400.62   Faye, Eugène de. Idéalisme et réalisme. Paris, 1920.

Phil 3425.125   Fazio-Allmayer, C. La teoria della libertà nella filosofia di Hegel. Messina, 1920.

Phil 185.18.50   Festgabe für Julius Kaftan zu seinem 70. Geburtstage, 30 Sept. 1918. Tübingen, 1920.

Phil 3246.59   Fichte, Johann Gottlieb. Rechtslehre vorgetragen von Ostern bis Michaelis 1812. Leipzig, 1920.

Phil 8406.15   Figari, Pedro. Art, esthétique, idéal. Paris, 1920.

Phil 7080.44   Fish, Luther S. Knowledge exchanged; phenomenon of sleep. Cheveland, 1920.

Phil 7069.20.130   Flammarion, Camille. La mort et son mystère. Paris, 1920-1921. 2v.

Phil 2475.1.201   Flewelling, Ralph. Bergson and personal realism. N.Y., 1920.

Phil 4815.558.80   Fraknói, Vilmos. Martinovicsnak istentagadó elveket hirdető, imént fölfedezett francia munkája. Budapest, 1920.

Phil 6315.2.20.7   Freud, Sigmund. Sammlung kleiner Schriften. 3. Aufl. 1e, 2e Folge. Leipzig, 1920-21. 2v.

Phil 6315.2.4A   Freud, Sigmund. Über Psychoanalyse. 5e Aufl. Leipzig, 1920.

Phil 978.58   Frohnmeyer, L.J. Die theosophische Bewegung. Stuttgart, 1920.

Phil 6315.55   Frost, M. Erzieherliebe als Heilmittel. Bern, 1920.

Phil 510.128   Frutiger, P. Volonté er conscience. Genève, 1920.

Phil 5520.30.5   Fruttchey, Frank. Voice, speech, thinking. 2. ed. Detroit, Mich., 1920.

Phil 8881.60   Gabelli, Aristide. L'uomo e le scienze morali. Torino, 1920.

Phil 5246.33   Galli, Ettore. Nel mondo dello spirito. Milano, 1920.

Phil 9495.139   Galloway, T.W. Sex and life. N.Y., 1920.

Phil 1885.87   Gamertsfelder, W.S. Thought, existence and reality as viewed by F.H. Bradley and B. Bosanquet. Columbus, 1920.

Phil 5374.150   Geley, Gustave. From the unconscious to the conscious. Glasgow, 1920.

Phil 8696.10   Gemelli, Agostino. Religione e scienza. Milano, 1920.

Phil 8696.10.5   Gemelli, Agostino. Scienza ed apologetica. Milano, 1920.

Phil 8586.17   Gentile, G. Discorsi di religione. Firenze, 1920.

Phil 4065.102   Gentile, G. Giordano Bruno i el pensiero de rinascimento. Firenze, 1920.

Phil 4225.1.95   Gentile, Giovanni. Bertrando Spaventa. Firenze, 1920.

Phil 181.45.30   Gentile, Giovanni. Scritti vari. Lanciano, 1920-1926. 5v.

Phil 181.45.11   Gentile, Giovanni. Teoria generale dello spirito come atto puro. 3a ed. Bari, 1920.

Phil 4115.76   Gioberti, V. Lettere inedite di V. Gioberti e P. Galluppi. Roma, 1920.

Phil 806.7   Gleich, S. von. Von Thales bis Steiner. Stuttgart, 1920.

Phil 5246.20.5   Goddard, H.H. Human efficiency and levels of intelligence. Princeton, 1920.

Phil 8661.12.5   Godfrey, W.S. Theism found wanting. London, 1920.

Phil 3488.4.30   Goldschmidt, L. Weder Kant noch Goethe. Gotha, 1920.

EDL Phil 735.83   Goldstein, M. Der Wert des Zwecklosen. Dresden, 1920.

Phil 5620.10   Grandjean, F. La raison et la vue. Paris, 1920.

Phil 7069.20.140   Gray, James M. Spiritism and the fallen angels in the light of the Old and New Testaments. N.Y., 1920.

Phil 8620.24   Gree, Peter. The problem of evil. London, 1920.

Phil 3808.141   Groener, M. Schopenhauer und die Juden. München, 1920.

Phil 3006.4   Gronau, Gotthard. Die Philosophie der Gegenwart. Langensalza, 1920-22. 2v.

Phil 7069.20.145   Grunewald, F. Physikalisch-mediumistische Untersuchungen. Pfullingen, 1920.

Phil 3665.1.79   Gschwind, H. Die philosophischen Grundlagen von Natorps Sozialpadagogik. Leipzig, 1920.

Phil 6116.25   Guillain, Georges. Travaux neurologiques de guerre. Paris, 1920.

Phil 2475.1.202   Gunn, John Alex. Bergson and his philosophy. London, 1920.

Phil 181.44.5   Gurnhill, James. Interpretation of the spiritual philosophy. London, 1920.

Phil 182.102   Haesaert, J. Introduction a la philosophie expérimentale. Gand, 1920.

Phil 7069.20.150   Haldeman, Isaac M. Can the dead communicate with the living? N.Y., 1920.

Phil 8882.39   Hall, G. Stanley. Morale. N.Y., 1920.

Phil 6317.6   Hallingworth, H.L. The psychology of functional neuroses. N.Y., 1920.

Phil 8882.38   Handyside, John. The historical method in ethics and other essays. Liverpool, 1920.

Phil 8632.17   Hardenberg, H. Wir sollen nicht sterben. Darmstadt, 1920.

Phil 8697.9   Hardwick, J.C. Religion and science. London, 1920.

Phil 5047.40   Harvard University. Department of Philosophy. Logic cases for philosophy, 1919-1920. Cambridge, Mass., 1920.

Phil 6117.30   Head, Henry. Studies in neurology. London, 1920. 2v.

Phil 8632.11   Heagle, David. Do the dead still live? Philadelphia, 1920

Phil 3425.46   Hegel, Georg Wilhelm Friedrich. Encyclopädie der philosophischen Wissenschaften. 2. Aufl. Leipzig, 1920.

Phil 3425.56.30   Hegel, Georg Wilhelm Friedrich. The philosophy of fine art. London, 1920. 4v.

Cg Phil 3425.40.7   Hegel, Georg Wilhelm Friedrich. Vorlesungen über die Philosophie der Weltgeschichte. v.2-5. Leipzig, 1920. 4v.

Phil 5643.11.9   Hering, E. Grundzüge zur Lehre vom Lichtsinne. Leipzig, 1920.

Phil 575.51.40   Hermann, Oskar. Dr. Klages, Entwurf einer Charakterkunde. Leipzig, 1920.

Phil 3915.160   Heussner, A. Einführung in Wilhelm Wundt's Philosophie und Psychologie. Göttingen, 1920.

Phil 8620.24.5   Heyl, Paul R. The mystery of evil. Chicago, 1920.

Phil 9495.127.6   Hildebrand, Dietrich von. In defence of purity. Chicago, 1920.

Phil 7069.20.160   Hill, John A. Psychical miscellanea. N.Y., 1920.

Phil 3246.197   Hirsch, E. Christentum und Geschichte in Fichtes Philosophie. Tübingen, 1920.

1920 - cont.

Phil 5425.45   Hock, Alfred. Die methodische Entwicklung der Talente und des Genies. Leipzig, 1920.

Phil 1707.1.6.5   Höffding, H. A history of modern philosophy. London, 1920. 2v.

Phil 5247.10.4   Höffding, H. Psykologi i omrids paa grundlag af erfarung. 9. ed. København, 1920.

Phil 182.49   Hoernlé, R.F.A. Studies in contemporary metaphysics. N.Y., 1920.

Phil 75.23   Hoffmans, Jean. La philosophie et les philosophes. Bruxelles, 1920.

Phil 9120.160   Hofmann, Paul. Eigengesetz oder Pflichtgebot? Berlin, 1920.

Phil 5585.50   Hoisington, Louis B. On the non-visual perception of the length of lifted rods. Thesis. Worcester, Mass., 1920.

Phil 6117.31   Hollander, Bernard. In search of the soul and the mechanism of thought, emotion and conduct. London, 1920. 2v.

Phil 182.56.2   Hooper, Charles. Common sense and the rudiments of philosophy. 2d ed. London, 1920.

Phil 3640.121.5   Horneffer, Ernst. Nietzsche-Vorträge. Leipzig, 1920.

Phil 3640.193   Howard, E. Friedirch Nietzsche und die klassische Philologie. Photoreproduction. Gotha, 1920.

Phil 5627.56.7   Howley, John. Psychology and mystical experience. London, 1920.

Phil 2050.42.8   Hume, David. Eine Untersuchung über den menschlichen Verstand. 8e Aufl. Leipzig, 1920.

Phil 7069.20.170   Humphreys, Eliza Margaret J.G. The truth of spiritualism. Philadelphia, 1920.

Phil 5640.127   Hurst, A.F. The Croonian lectures. London, 1920.

Phil 6118.2   Ioteyko, Josefa. La fatigue. Paris, 1920.

Phil 410.75.5   Isenkrahe, Caspar. Untersuchungen über das Endliche und das Unendliche. Bonn, 1920. 3v.

Phil 5357.2   Jaensch, E.R. Einige allgemeiner Fragen der Psychologie und Biologie des Denkens. Leipzig, 1920.

Phil 184.3.35   James, W. Collected essays and reviews. N.Y., 1920.

Phil 184.3.24   James, W. A pluralistic universe. London, 1920.

Phil 184.3.7.15   James, W. La volonté de croire. Paris, 1920.

Phil 2070.75A   James, William. Letters. Boston, 1920. 2v.

Phil 2070.75.3A   James, William. The letters of William James. Boston, 1920. 2v.

Phil 5627.6.8   James, William. Religiøs røynsle i sine ymse former. Øslo, 1920.

Phil 6615.6.7   Janet, Pierre. The major symptoms of hysteria. 2. ed. N.Y., 1920.

Phil 8589.11   Jeanette, Agnes. The seventh seal. Philadelphia, 1920.

Phil 5049.9   Jevons, W.S. Logica. Milano, 1920.

Phil 630.19.2   Joad, Cyril Edwin. Essays in common sense philosophy. N.Y., 1920.

Phil 3475.1.81   Jodl, Margarete. Friedrich Jodl sein Leben und Wirken. Stuttgart, 1920.

Phil 9035.36   Jones, W. Tudor. The training of mind and will. London, 1920.

Phil 1870.98.3   Joussain, André. Exposé critique de la philosophie de Berkeley. Thèse. Paris, 1920.

Phil 8885.25   Kane, Robert. Worth lectures. London, 1920.

Phil 3480.65.6   Kant, Immanuel. Grundlegung zur Metaphysik der Sitten. 5. Aufl. Leipzig, 1920.

Phil 3480.45.15   Kant, Immanuel. Kritik der praktischen Vernunft. 7. Aufl. Leipzig, 1920.

Phil 3480.30.20   Kant, Immanuel. Kritik der reinen Vernunft. Leipzig, 1920.

Phil 3480.30.35   Kant, Immanuel. Kritik der reinen Vernunft. München, 1920.

Phil 3480.70.3   Kant, Immanuel. Logik. 3. Aufl. Leipzig, 1920.

Phil 3480.57.15   Kant, Immanuel. Prolegomena zu einer jeden künftigen Metaphysik. 6. Aufl. Leipzig, 1920.

Phil 3480.110   Kant, Immanuel. Zwei Schriften über die Grundlegenden der Naturwissenschaften. Berlin, 1920.

Phil 3492.20   Kellermann, B. Das Ideal im System der Kantischen Philosophie. Berlin, 1920.

Phil 7069.20.180   Kernahan, Coulson. Spiritualism. N.Y., 1920.

Phil 8590.15   Kesseler, Kurt. Kritik der neukantischen religionsphilosophie der Gegenwart. Leipzig, 1920.

Phil 185.35   Keyserling, H. Philosophie als Kunst. Darmstadt, 1920.

Phil 7084.8   Kimmins, Charles William. Children's dreams. London, 1920.

Phil 7069.20.190   King, John S. Dawn of the awakened mind. N.Y., 1920.

Phil 7069.20.192   Kingsford, S.M. Psychical research for the plain man. London, 1920.

Phil 810.2.5   Kinkel, W. Allgemeine Geschichte der Philosophie. Osterwieck, 1920-27. 4v.

Phil 6060.12.5   Klages, Ludwig. Handschrift und Charakter. 2e Aufl. Leipzig, 1920.

Phil 3549.8.92   Klages, Ludwig. Mensch und Erde. München, 1920.

Phil 3850.16.85   Knevels, Wilhelm. Simmels Religionstheorie. Leipzig, 1920.

Phil 705.11   Knittermeyer, Hinrich. Der Terminus transszendental in seiner historischen Entwickelung bis zu Kant. Inaug. Diss. Marburg, 1920.

Phil 185.19   Knowlson, T.S. A thought book on Socratic method. London, 1920?

Phil 8590.14   Köhler, R. Der Begriff a priori in der modernen Religionsphilosophie. Leipzig, 1920.

Phil 630.23   Kremer, René. Le néo-réalisme américain. Louvain, 1920.

Phil 978.59.65   Krishnamarti, J. Talks in Europe, 1968. Wassenaar, 1920.

Phil 5250.12.15   Kroman, Kristian. Grundtraek af sjælelaeren. 6. udg. København, 1920.

Phil 6960.6   Kronfeld, Arthur. Das Wesen der psychiatrischen Erkenn. Berlin, 1920.

Phil 5250.2.8   Külpe, Oswald. Vorlesungen über Psychologie. Leipzig, 1920.

Phil 9430.34   Lacy, B.F. Pessimism. Philadelphia, 1920.

Phil 2477.1.100   LaFontaine, A.P. La philosophie d'E. Boutroux. Paris, 1920.

Phil 342.8   Lagerborg, R. Vetenskapliga vanföreställningars. Helsingfors, 1920.

Phil 4580.115   La Harpe, J. La réligion comme conservation de la valeur dans ses rapports avec...H. Höffding. Lausanne, 1920.

Phil 2725.10.30   Lahr, Charles. Cours de philosophie. 23e éd. Paris, 1920. 2v.

Phil 630.22   Laird, John. A study in realism. Cambridge, 1920.

Phil 5251.39   Landquist, J. Människokunskap. Stockholm, 1920.

Phil 811.1.3   Landtman, G. Inledning till det filosofiska tänkandet. Helsingfors, 1920.

Phil 7069.20.205   Lane, Anne W. Life in the circles. N.Y., 1920.

Phil 7069.20.200   Lane, Anne W. To walk with God. N.Y., 1920.

Chronological Listing

Phil 8412.23.2	Langfeld, Herbert Sidney. The aesthetic attitude. N.Y., 1920.
Phil 4600.2.52	Larsson, Hans. Den intellektuella askadningens filosofi. Stockholm, 1920.
Phil 4600.2.46	Larsson, Hans. Intuition. 4e uppl. Stockholm, 1920.
Phil 4600.2.39	Larsson, Hans. Kunskapslivet. 3e uppl. Stockholm, 1920.
Phil 4600.2.38	Larsson, Hans. Under världskrisen. Stockholm, 1920.
Phil 3310.1.130	Lauden, V.J.C. Peter Franz Knoodt als Philosoph. Elberfeld, 1920.
Phil 7069.20.210	Lees, Robert James. Through the mists. London, 1920.
Phil 5251.20.15	Lehmann, Alfred. Den individuelle sjaelelige udrikling. København, 1920.
Phil 5251.20.20	Lehmann, Alfred. Uppfostran till arbete. Stockholm, 1920.
Phil 5761.9.5	Lévy, Paul Émile. The rational education of the will. 9. ed. Philadelphia, 1920.
Phil 735.17	Liebert, A. Das Problem der Geltung. 2e Aufl. Leipzig, 1920.
Phil 8412.21	Lippold, F. Bausteine zu einer Ästhetik der inneren Form. München, 1920.
Phil 4362.5	Lloreus y Barba, F.J. Lecciones de filosofia. Barcelona, 1920. 3v.
Phil 2115.70.15	Locke, J. Epistola su la tolleranza. Lanciano, 1920. 2v.
Phil 2115.29	Locke, J. La filosofia di G. Locke. Firenze, 1920-21. 2v.
Phil 8701.4.3.5	Lodge, Oliver Joseph. Man and the universe. N.Y., 1920.
Phil 5051.12	Lodge, Rupert C. An introduction to modern logic. Minneapolis, 1920.
Phil 5520.37.5	Lourié, Ossip. La graphomanie. Paris, 1920.
X Cg Phil 6321.3.2	Low, Barbara. Psycho-analysis. London, 1920.
Phil 400.56	Lugaro, E. Idealismo filosofico e realismo politico. Bologna, 1920.
Phil 1865.170	Lundin, Hilda G. The influence of J. Bentham on English democratic development. Iowa City, 1920.
Phil 7069.20.220	McCabe, J. Spiritualism. N.Y., 1920.
Phil 623.16	McCabe, Joseph. A biographical dictionary of modern rationalists. London, 1920.
Phil 5252.18.8	McDougall, William. The group mind. Cambridge, 1920.
Phil 5252.18.8.3	McDougall, William. The group mind. N.Y., 1920.
Phil 5252.18.8.2	McDougall, William. The group mind. 2d ed. N.Y., 1920.
Phil 8413.21	McDowall, S.A. Beauty and the beast; an essay in evolutionary aesthetic. Cambridge, Mass., 1920.
Phil 7069.20.230	McEvilly, Mary A. Meslom's messages from the life beyond. N.Y., 1920.
Phil 7069.20.232	McEvilly, Mary A. To woman from Meslom. N.Y., 1920.
Phil 5252.41	McKim, William D. A study for the times. N.Y., 1920.
Phil 6750.220	MacMurchy, H. The almosts, a study of the feeble minded. Boston, 1920.
Phil 5190.10	MacPherson, William. The psychology of persuasion. London, 1920.
Phil 5374.35	Mager, Alois. Die Enge des Bewusstseins. Stuttgart, 1920.
Phil 7069.20.240	Magnussen, Julius. God's smile. N.Y., 1920.
Phil 2730.40	Maine de Biran, Pierre. Mémoire sur les perceptions obscures. Paris, 1920.
Phil 2730.15	Maine de Biran, Pierre. Oeurves. Paris, 1920-1939. 12v.
Phil 9070.30	Major, Clare Tree. How to develop your will-power. N.Y., 1920.
Phil 4752.1.32	Malinovskii, Aleksandr A. Filosofiia zhivogo opyta. Moskva, 1920.
Phil 187.49.5	Malkani, G.R. Metaphysics of energy. Amalner, 1920.
Phil 3494.19.6	Marcus, Ernst. Kants Weltgebäude. 2. Aufl. München, 1920.
Phil 5252.37	Marett, R.R. Psychology and folk-lore. N.Y., 1920.
Phil 7069.20.250	Maturin, Edith Money. Rachel comforted. N.Y., 1920.
Phil 8887.51	Mecklin, John M. An introduction to social ethics. N.Y., 1920.
Phil 5252.46	Mentré, F. Espèces et variétés d'intelligences. Thèse. Paris, 1920.
Phil 5252.46.5	Mentré, F. Espèces et variétés d'intelligences. Thèse. Paris, 1920.
Phil 293.12	Merezhkovskii, K.S. Fragments du "Schema d'une nouvelle philosophie de l'univers". Genève, 1920.
Phil 3552.298	Merkel, Franz R. G.W. Leigniz und die China Mission. Leipzig, 1920.
Phil 1712.5.4	Messer, A. Geschichte der Philosophie vom Beginn der Neuzeit zum Ende des 18. Jahrhunderts. Leipzig, 1920.
Phil 5252.28.2	Messer, A. Psychologie. 2. Aufl. Stuttgart, 1920.
Phil 8887.53.10	Messer, A. Sittenlehre. Leipzig, 1920.
Phil 3246.179	Messer, August. Fichte. Leipzig, 1920.
Phil 5762.9	Meumann, Ernst. Intelligenz und Wille. 3. Aufl. Leipzig, 1920.
Phil 343.14	Meurer, W. Ist Wissenschaft überhaupt Möglich? Leipzig, 1920.
Phil 6322.4	Miller, Hugh C. Functional nerve disease. London, 1920.
Phil 187.33.5	Montague, W.P. Introductory course in philosophy. Syllabus. N.Y., 1920.
Phil 8637.12	Moore, Justin H. The world beyond. N.Y., 1920.
Phil 293.14	Moraes Carvalho, A.A. de. Le problème de l'univers. Lisbonne, 1920.
Phil 187.54	Motion, George. Fragments of philosophy: Democracy. Nelson, B.C., 1920.
Phil 8887.50	Müller, Johannes. Neue Wegweiser; Aufsätze und Reden. München, 1920.
Phil 6322.13	Muralt, Alexander von. Ein Pseudoprophet. München, 1920.
Phil 8120.6A	Mustoxidi, T.M. Histoire de l'esthétique française, 1700-1900. Paris, 1920.
Phil 5850.279.7	Myers, Charles S. Mind and work. London, 1920.
Phil 5610.2	Neil, C.E. Sources of effectiveness in public speaking. Philadelphia, 1920.
Phil 293.8.75	Neubert, Fritz. Einleitung in eine kritische Ausgabe von B. de Maillets Telliamed. Berlin, 1920.
Phil 7069.20.259	Occult diary. Chicago, 1920.
Phil 7060.92.47	O'Donnell, Elliot. The Banshee. London, 1920.
Phil 7069.20.260	O'Donnell, Elliot. The menace of spiritualism. Chicago, 1920.
Phil 7069.20.261	O'Donnell, Elliot. The menace of spiritualism. London, 1920.
Phil 7060.92.45	O'Donnell, Elliot. More haunted houses of London. London, 1920.
Phil 189.4.14F	Oersted, H.C. Naturvidenskabeligě skrifter. København, 1920. 3v.
Phil 6324.1	O'Higgins, H. The secret springs. N.Y., 1920.
Phil 7059.22	Our unseen guest. N.Y. 1920.
Phil 5425.40	Palcos, Alberto. El genio; ensayo sobre su génesis. Buenos Aires, 1920.
Phil 8890.23.21	Palmer, George H. Altruism. N.Y., 1920.

Phil 3835.7	Palmodo, Kurt. Der Freiheitsbegriff in der Lehre Spinozas. Weiden, 1920.
Phil 190.20.4	Papini, Giovanni. Pragmatismo, 1903-1911. 2. ed. Firenze, 1920.
Phil 8416.29	Parker, de W.H. The principles of aesthetics. Boston, 1920.
Phil 2415.5.2	Parodi, Dominique. La philosophie contemporaine en France. Paris, 1920.
Phil 2805.32.25	Pascal, Blaise. Les lettres provinciales. Manchester, 1920.
Phil 8673.6.2	Pattison, A. The idea of God. 2. ed. N.Y., 1920.
Phil 5400.45	Paulhan, Frédéric. Les transformations sociales des sentiments. Paris, 1920.
Phil 5255.31	Pauli, R. Psychologisches Praktikum. Jena, 1920.
Phil 5255.31.10	Pauli, R. Über psychische Gesetzmässigkeit. Jena, 1920.
Phil 3497.3.6	Paulsen, Friedrich. Immanuel Kant. 6. Aufl. Stuttgart, 1920.
Phil 5765.2.11	Payot, Jules. Le travail intellectuel et la volonté. Paris, 1920.
Phil 7069.20.270	Pennsylvania. University. Seybert Commission for Investigating Modern Spiritualism. Preliminary report. Philadelphia, 1920.
Phil 2475.1.207	Pentimalli, G.H. Bergson. Torino, 1920.
Phil 2070.01A	Perry, Ralph B. Annotated bibliography of writings of William James. N.Y., 1920.
Phil 5325.19	Pétrovitch, D. L'association des idées obéitelles à des lois? Thèse. Caen, 1920.
Phil 5255.8.2	Pfänder, A. Einführung in die Psychologie. 2. Aufl. Leipzig, 1920.
Phil 6325.1.30	Pfister, Oskar. Zum Kampf um die Psychoanalyse. Wien, 1920.
Phil 735.77	Picard, Maurice. Values immediate and contributory and their interrelation. N.Y., 1920.
Phil 5640.125.9	Pikler, Gyula. Theorie der Empfindungsstärke und Insbesondere des Weberschen Gesetzes. Leipzig, 1920.
Phil 815.6A	Pim, Herbert M. Short history of Celtic philosophy. Dundalk, 1920.
Phil 190.32	Pitt, St. George Lane-Fox. Free will and destiny. London, 1920.
Phil 7069.20.272	Platts, J. The witness. London, 1920.
Phil 190.75	Popper, J. Das Individuum und die Beertung menschlicher Existenzen. 2. Aufl. Photoreproduction. Dresden, 1920.
Phil 5627.56	Pratt, James B. The religious consciousness. N.Y., 1920.
Phil 3640.172	Proost, K.F. Friedrich, Nietzsche, zijn leven en zijn werk. Uitgave, 1920.
Phil 9355.6	Purinton, E.E. The triumph of the man who acts. N.Y., 1920.
Phil 2250.86	Raccuglia, Pietro. Il concetto sintetico del reale e la sua evoluzione nel pensiero di Josiah Royce. Palermo, 1920.
Phil 2280.8.93	Rahder, J. Pringle-Pattison's Gifford lectures. v.1-2. Leipzig, 1920.
Phil 7054.174	Raupert, J.G. The new black magic. N.Y., 1920.
Phil 8892.24	Raymond, George L. Ethics and natural law. N.Y., 1920.
Phil 8892.24.5	Raymond, George L. Ethics and natural law. 2. ed. N.Y., 1920.
Phil 7069.20.280	Raynor, Frank C. Through jewelled windows. London, 1920.
Phil 6967.10.2	Read, C. Stanford. Abnormal mental strain. London, 1920.
Phil 6967.10	Read, C. Stanford. Military psychiatry in peace and war. London, 1920.
Phil 9045.75	Reidenbach, Clarence. A critical analysis of patriotism as an ethical concept. Indianpolis? 1920.
Phil 192.63	Reiser, Beat. System der Philosophie. v.1. Einsiedeln, 1920.
Phil 8892.34	Renauld, J.F. Manuel de morale. Paris, 1920.
Phil 4215.3.33	Rensi, Giuseppe. La filosofia dell'autorita. Palermo, 1920.
Phil 4215.3.32	Rensi, Giuseppe. Polemiche antidogmatiche. Bologna, 1920.
Phil 5400.18.12	Ribot, T. La logique des sentiments. 5. éd. Paris, 1920.
Phil 5545.150	Richards, Lysander. The analysis and cause of existence of memory and The analysis and cause of unconsciousness and sleep. pt.1-2. n.p., 1920.
Phil 3640.118.6	Riehl, Alois. Friedrich Nietzsche. 6e Aufl. Stuttgart, 1920.
Phil 3640.118.7	Riehl, Alois. Friedrich Nietzsche. 7e Aufl. Stuttgart, 1920.
Phil 5620.9	Rignano, Eugenio. Psychologie du raisonnement. Paris, 1920.
Phil 8597.27	Rignano, Eugenio. Religione, materialismo, socialismo. Bologna, 1920.
Phil 6327.5A	Rivers, W.H.R. Instinct and the unconscious. Cambridge, Eng., 1920.
Phil 6127.14	Rivers, W.H.R. Mind and medicine. 2d ed. Manchester, 1920.
Phil 8842.4	Robertson, J.M. A short history of morals. London, 1920.
Phil 7069.20.290	Robertson, Mabel N. "The other side of God's door". London, 1920.
Phil 3425.91.19	Rosenkranz, K. Erläuterungen zu Hegel's Encyklopädie der philosophischen Wissenschaften. Leipzig, 1920.
Phil 348.7.3	Rougier, Louis. Les paralogismes du rationalisme. Thèse. Paris, 1920.
Phil 8892.12.15A	Royce, J. The philosophy of loyalty. N.Y., 1920.
Phil 2250.55	Royce, Josiah. Fugitive essays. Cambridge, 1920.
Phil 4585.9.81	Rubin, E. En ung dansk filosof. København, 1920.
Phil 5257.34	Ruckmick, C.A. The brevity book on psychology. Chicago, 1920.
Phil 1717.8.2	Ruggiero, G. de. La filosofia contemporanea. 2a ed. Bari, 1920. 2v.
Phil 4630.4.40	Ruin, Waldemar. Kulturen och tiden. Helsingfors, 1920.
Phil 5850.331	Sachs, Hildegard. Zur Organisation der Eignungspsychologie. Leipzig, 1920.
Phil 7085.10	Sadger, Isidor. Sleep walking and moon walking. N.Y., 1920.
Phil 525.27	Sageret, Jules. La vague mystique. Paris, 1920.
Phil 8893.70	Sallwürk, E v. Ethik in entwickelnder Darstellung. Langensalza, 1920.
Phil 193.49.15	Santayana, G. Character and opinion in the United States. N.Y., 1920.
Phil 193.49.20	Santayana, G. Little essays drawn from writings of George Santayana. N.Y., 1920.
Phil 3805.76.9	Schleiermacher, Friedrich. Briefwechsel mit seiner Braut. 2. Aufl. Gotha, 1920.
Phil 8893.48	Schneider, H.W. Science and social progress. Lancaster, Pa., 1920.
Phil 7069.20.298	Schofield, A.T. Modern spiritism. London, 1920.

Chronological Listing

Phil 2262.88 Schonfeld, V. Die Ethik Shaftesburys. Diss. Budapest, 1920.

Phil 3808.25.7 Schopenhauer, Arthur. Aphorismen zur Lebensweisheit. Leipzig, 1920.

Phil 3808.38.5 Schopenhauer, Arthur. Il mondo come volontà e rappresentazione. 2. ed. Bari, 1920-21. 2v.

Phil 3808.77 Schopenhauer, Arthur. Schopenhauer et ses disciples. Paris, 1920.

Phil 7069.20.303 Schrenck von Notzing, Albert. Phenomena of materialisation; a contribution to the investigation of mediumistic telepactics. London, 1920.

Phil 7069.20.301 Schrenck von Notzing, Albert. Physikalische Phaenomene des Mediumismus. München, 1920.

Phil 2725.11.81A Séailles, G. La philosophie de Jules Lachelier. Paris, 1920.

Phil 8643.25.4 Seeberg, R. Ewiges Leben. Leipzig, 1920.

Phil 193.92 Seltmann, Otto. Das Urteil der Vernunft. Caliv, 1920.

Phil 5640.22 Semon, R. Bewusstseinsvorgang und Gehirnprozess. Wiesbaden, 1920.

Phil 7069.20.300 Sewell, May Wright. Neither dead nor sleeping. Indianapolis, 1920.

Phil 7069.20.300* Sewell, May Wright. Neither dead nor sleeping. Indianapolis, 1920.

Phil 9035.21.2 Shand, A.F. The foundations of character. London, 1920.

Phil 5850.340 Shaw, Charles G. Short talks on psychology. N.Y., 1920.

Phil 525.25 Shirley, Ralph. Occultists and mystics of all ages. London, 1920.

Phil 7054.186 Simon, Otto J. The message of Anne Simon. Boston, 1920.

Phil 2418.1 Simon, Paul M. Der Pragmatisme in der modernen französischen Philosophie. Paderborn, 1920.

Phil 6060.23 Smith, Albert J. Applied graphology. N.Y., 1920.

Phil 5058.28.15 Smith, Henry B. Letters on logic, to a young man. Philadelphia, 1920.

Phil 672.121 Smith, W.W. A theory of the mechanism of survival; the fourth dimension. London, 1920.

Phil 7069.20.310 Smith, Walter W. The foundations of spiritualism. N.Y., 1920.

Phil 6128.34 Sommer, George. Leib und Seele in ihrem verhältnis Zueinander. Leipzig, 1920.

Phil 1818.5 Sorley, William R. A history of English philosophy. Cambridge, Eng., 1920.

Phil 2270.76.5 Spencer, Herbert. Le basi della morale. 3a ed. Piacenza, 1920.

Phil 1123.5 Stace, W.T. Critical history of Greek philosophy. London, 1920.

Phil 3500.33.6A Stange, Carl. Die Ethik Kants zur Einführung in die Kritik der praktischen Vernunft. Leipzig, 1920.

Phil 3500.33.4 Stange, Carl. Der Gedankengang der Kritik der reinen Vernunft. Leipzig, 1920.

Phil 5585.31 Steinberg, Wilhelm. Die Raumwahrnehmung der Blinden. München, 1920.

Phil 8598.56 Störring, G. Die Frage der Wahrheit der christlichen Religion. Leipzig, 1920.

Phil 193.90 Stuart, (Mrs.) C. The threshold of the new. London, 1920.

Phil 5258.25.4 Sully, J. Outlines of psychology. London, 1920.

Phil 5627.56.5 Swisher, Walter. Religion and the new psychology. Boston, 1920.

Phil 5259.13.2 Tansley, A.G. The new psychology. London, 1920.

Phil 1750.22A Taylor, Henry O. Thought and expression in the 16th century. N.Y., 1920. 2v.

Phil 7069.20.320 Tertium Quid (pseud.). The verdict:-? London, 1920.

Phil 194.23 Thalheimer, A. The meaning of terms 'existence' and 'reality'. Princeton, 1920.

Phil 7069.20.330 Thiébault, Jules. The vanished friend. N.Y., 1920.

Phil 104.2.2 Thornmeyer, P. Philosophisches Wörterbuch. 2. Aufl. Leipzig, 1920.

Phil 194.8.5 Tommaseo, N. Studii filosofici. Lanciano, 1920.

Phil 6329.1.10 Tridon, André. Psychoanalysis; its history, theory and practice. N.Y., 1920.

Phil 6329.1.3 Tridon, André. Psychoanalysis and behavior. N.Y., 1920.

Phil 5425.15.15 Türck, H. Der geniale Mensch. 10. Aufl. Berlin, 1920?

Phil 7060.151.5 Tweedale, C.L. Man's survival after death. 2. ed. London, 1920.

Phil 525.7.7 Underhill, Evelyn. The essentials of mysticism and other essays. London, 1920.

Phil 9495.120 United States. Public Health Service. Fighting venereal diseases. Washington, 1920.

Phil 8661.8.80 Urquhart, James. William Honyman Gillespie. Edinburgh, 1920.

Phil 672.122.7 Uspenskii, P.D. Tertium organum. Rochester, 1920.

Phil 8897.43 Van Wesep, H.B. The control of ideals. N.Y., 1920.

Phil 5061.4.5 Vaz Ferreira, Carlos. Lógica viva. Montevideo, 1920.

Phil 5261.14 Visser, H.L.A. Collectief-psychologische omtrekken. Haarlem, 1920.

Phil 8896.11 Vivante, Lello. Principii di etica. Roma, 1920.

Phil 8422.15 Volkelt, Johannes. Das ästhetische Bewusstsein. Photoreproduction. München, 1920.

Phil 3503.8 Vosters, J. La doctrine du droit de Kant. Bruxelles, 1920.

Phil 2520.137 Wahl, Jean. Du rôle de l'idée de l'instant dans la philosophie de Descartes. Paris, 1920.

Phil 510.126 Wahl, Jean. Les philosophies pluralistes. Paris, 1920.

Phil 510.126.3 Wahl, Jean. Les philosophies pluralistes. Thèse. Paris, 1920.

Phil 6480.125 Walsh, William S. The psychology of dreams. N.Y., 1920.

Phil 5262.19.3A Ward, James. Psychological principles. 2d ed. Cambridge, Eng., 1920.

Phil 8677.8.3 Ward, James. The realm of ends, or Pluralism and theism. 3. ed. Cambridge, 1920.

Phil 8897.41 Ward, Stephen. The ways of life. London, 1920.

Phil 8897.41.3 Ward, Stephen. The ways of life. N.Y., 1920.

Phil 525.26 Watkin, Edward Ingram. The philosophy of mysticism. London, 1920.

Phil 1050.14.5 Waxman, Meyer. The philosophy of Don Hasdai Crescas. N.Y., 1920.

Phil 575.52.7 Webb, C.C.J. Divine personality and human life. London, 1920.

Phil 8602.18.20 Webb, C.C.J. Philosophy and the Christian religion. Oxford, 1920.

Phil 6332.2.7 Wells, F.L. Mental adjustments. N.Y., 1920.

Phil 8712.15 Westaway. Science and theology. London, 1920.

Phil 5642.15 Wheeler, R.H. The synaesthesia of a blind subject. Eugene, 1920.

Phil 8712.3.11 White, Andrew Dickson. History of the warfare of science with theology in Christendom. N.Y., 1920. 2v.

Phil 8620.40 Whyte, A.G. The natural history of evil. London, 1920.

Phil 3504.27 Wichmann, G. Platon und Kant. Berlin, 1920.

Phil 735.80 Wiederhold, K. Wert Begriff und Wertphilosophie. Berlin, 1920.

Phil 5772.10 Wiesner, Johann. Die Freihert des menschlichen Willens. Wien, 1920.

Phil 4655.1.2 Wikner, Pontus. Skrifter. Stockholm, 1920-27. 12v.

Phil 7069.20.340 Williams, Gail. Fear not the crossing. N.Y., 1920.

Phil 197.9.14A Windelband, W. Einleitung in der Philosophie. 2. Aufl. Tübingen, 1920.

Phil 575.54 Wolf, H. De persoonlijkheidsidee bij meisterl Ekhart, Leibniz en Goethe. Amsterdam, 1920.

Phil 8712.14 Woodburne, A.S. The relation between religion and science. Chicago, 1920.

Phil 7069.20.350 Wright, George E. The church and psychical research. London, 1920.

Phil 7069.20.352 Wright, George E. Practical views on psychic phenomena. N.Y., 1920.

Phil 8423.7 Wulf, M. de. L'oeuvre d'art et la beauté. Louvain, 1920.

Phil 3915.77.50 Wundt, Wilhelm. Erlebtes und Erkanntes. Stuttgart, 1920.

Phil 3915.70.10 Wundt, Wilhelm. Die Zukunft der Kultur. Leipzig, 1920.

Phil 3022.4 Wust, Peter. Die Auferstehung Metaphysik. Leipzig, 1920.

Phil 3640.173 Wyck, B.H.C.K. Friedrich Nietzsche. Baarn, 1920.

Phil 3705.1.80 Zehme, Berthold. Jakob Hermann Abereit. Inaug. Diss. Lindau, 1920.

Phil 5835.1.3 Ziegler, H.E. Der Begriff des Instinktes einst und jetzt. 3. Aufl. Jena, 1920.

Phil 400.130 Zschimmer, Eberhard. Technik und Idealismus. Jena, 1920.

Phil 8650.1 Zucca, A. Essere e non essere. Roma, 1920.

Phil 5065.1A Zuhen, Theodor. Lehrbuch der Logik. Bonn, 1920.

Phil 2475.1.200 Zulen, P.S. La filosofía de lo inexpresable. Lima, 1920.

Phil 7069.20.360 Zymonidas, Allessandro. The problems of mediumship. London, 1920.

Phil 7069.21.10 Abbott, Anne. The two worlds of attraction. Boston, 1921.

Phil 6310.2.8 Abraham, Karl. Klinische Beitrage zur Psychoanalyse aus den Jahren 1907-1926. Leipzig, 1921.

Phil 9558.10.10 Aires Ramos da Silva de Eca, M. Reflexões sobre a vaidade dos homens. Facsimile. Rio de Janeiro, 1921.

Phil 3820.4 Alexander, Samuel. Spinoza and time. London, 1921.

Phil 475.2 Apel, Paul. Die Uberwindung des Materialismus. 3e Aufl. Berlin, 1921.

Phil 8401.16 Appin, Adolph. L'oeuvre d'art vivant. Genève, 1921.

Phil 8625.4 Arjuna. The single eye. N.Y., 1921.

Phil 7082.112.1 Arnold-Forster, Mary Story-Maskelyne. Studies in dreams. London, 1921.

Phil 7082.112 Arnold-Forster, Mary Story-Maskelyne. Studies in dreams. N.Y., 1921.

Phil 2520.160 Aster, E. von. Einführung in die Philosophie Descartes. München, 1921.

Phil 331.5.10 Aster, Ernst von. Geschichte der neueren Erkenntnistheorie. Berlin, 1921.

Phil 3090.23 Baader, Franz von. Schriften. Leipzig, 1921.

Phil 176.78 Baillie, J.B. Studies in human nature. London, 1921.

Phil 2630.6.80 Barrenechea, M.A. Un idealismo estético; la filosofia de Jules de Gaultier. Buenos Aires, 1921.

Phil 960.40.4 Barua, B.M. A history of pre-Buddhistic Indian philosophy. Calcutta, 1921.

Phil 3246.204.2 Bauch, Bruno. Fichte und unsere Zeit. 2. Aufl. Erfurt, 1921.

Phil 3483.8.9 Bauch, Bruno. Immanuel Kant. 2. Aufl. Berlin, 1921.

Phil 7140.115.3 Baudouin, C. Suggestion and autosuggestion. London, 1921.

Phil 7140.115.5 Baudouin, C. Suggestion and autosuggestion. N.Y., 1921.

Phil 8876.80 Baumgarten, O. Praktische Sittenlehre. Tübingen, 1921.

Phil 9530.36.5 Beaverbrook, W.M.A. Success. 2. ed. London, 1921.

Phil 6951.5.15 Beers, C.W. The mental hygiene movement. N.Y.? 1921.

Phil 6951.5.5 Beers, C.W. A mind that found itself. 5. ed. N.Y., 1921.

Phil 8876.44.2 Belot, G. Études de morale positive. 2e éd. Paris, 1921. 2v.

Phil 2475.1.73 Bergson, Henri. Schöpferische Entwicklung. Jena, 1921.

Phil 5400.39.3 Bhagavan, Das. La science des émotions. Bruxelles, 1921.

Phil 176.115.15 Bierens de Haan, J.D. Vergezichten. Studies. Amsterdam, 1921.

Phil 5241.84 Bleuler, Eugen. Naturgeschichte der Seele und ihres Bewusst-Werdens. Berlin, 1921.

Phil 8876.54.5 Blondel, Maurice. L'azione. Firenze, 1921. 2v.

Phil 3110.55.35 Böhme, J. Die lochteure Pforte. Berlin, 1921.

Phil 3110.27.10 Böhme, J. Sex puncta theosophica. Leipzig, 1921.

Phil 1020.17 Boer, Tjitze de. De wijsbegeerte in den Islam. Haarlem, 1921.

Phil 974.3.11 Boldt, Ernst. Von Luther bis Steiner. München, 1921.

Phil 176.83 Boll, Marcel. Attardés et précurseurs. Paris, 1921.

Phil 600.33 Boll, Marcel. La science et l'esprit positif chez les penseurs contemporains. Paris, 1921.

Phil 1106.12 Bolland, G.J.P.J. De oorsprong der grieksche wijsbegeerte. 3e uitg. Leiden, 1921.

Phil 7069.20.42 Bond, Frederick B. The gate of remembrance. 4th ed. N.Y., 1921.

Phil 1701.11 Bosanquet, Bernard. The meeting of extremes in contemporary philosophy. London, 1921.

Phil 1020.15 Bouyges, P.M. Notes sur les philosophes arabes. Beyrouth, 1921.

Phil 6111.34 Brandler-Pracht, Karl. Geheime Seelenkräfte. Berlin, 1921.

Phil 2045.108 Brandt, Frithiof. Den mekaniske naturopfattelse hos Thomas Hobbes. København, 1921.

Phil 5241.35.2 Breese, B.B. Psychology. N.Y., 1921.

Phil 3001.5 Bréhier, Émile. Histoire de la philosophie allemande. Paris, 1921.

Phil 525.92 Brenes Mesen, R. El misticismo como instrumento de investigación de la verdad. San José de Costa Rica, 1921.

Phil 8876.41.7A Brentano, Franz. Vom Ursprung sittlicher Erkenntnis. 2e Aufl. Leipzig, 1921.

Phil 6311.3.2 Bridges, J.W. An outline of abnormal psychology. 2d ed. Columbus, 1921.

Phil 5241.52 Brierley, S.S. (Mrs.). An introduction to psychology. London, 1921.

Phil 5241.50 Briffault, Robert. Psyche's lamp. London, 1921.

Phil 6311.1.5 Brill, A.A. Fundamental conceptions of psychoanalysis. N.Y., 1921.

Phil 8581.43.2 Brod, M. Heidentum, Christentum, Judentum. München, 1921. 2v.

Phil 5241.28.2A Brown, W. Essentials of mental measurement. 2. ed. Cambridge, Eng., 1921.

1921 - cont.

Phil 8691.20 Bruhn, Wilhelm. Glauben und Wissen. Leipzig, 1921.

Phil 978.24.5 Bruhn, Wilhelm. Theosophie und Anthroposophie. Leipzig, 1921.

Phil 8581.56 Bruhn, Wilhelm. Der Vernunftcharakter der Religion. Leipzig, 1921.

Phil 176.85.15 Brunschvicg, L. L'idéalisme contemporain. 2e éd. Paris, 1921.

Phil 176.85.10 Brunschvicg, L. Nature et liberté. Paris, 1921.

Phil 2725.11.83 Brunschvicg, L. Notice sur la vie et les travaux de Jules Lachelier. Paris, 1921.

Phil 5241.53 Brunswig, A. Einführung in die Psychologie. München, 1921.

Phil 5628.10.5.1 Buber, Martin. Ekstatische Konfessionen. Leipzig, 1921.

Phil 8581.45.15 Buonaiuti, Ernesto. Escursioni spirituali. Roma, 1921.

Phil 1905.9.6 Burthogge, R. The philosophical writings. Chicago, 1921.

Phil 7054.187 Cadwallader, Mary E. Mary S. Vanderbilt, a twentieth century seer. Chicago, 1921.

Phil 4080.9.33 Carlini, Armando. Avviamento allo studio della filosofia. 3a ed. Firenze, 1921.

Phil 4080.9.35 Carlini, Armando. La vita dello spirito. Firenze, 1921.

Phil 3484.11 Cassirer, Ernst. Kants Leben und Lehre. Berlin, 1921.

Phil 3484.6.4 Chamberlain, H.S. Immanuel Kant. Die Persönlichkeit...in das Werke. 4. Aufl. München, 1921.

Phil 8582.56 Chamberlain, H.S. Mensch und Gott. München, 1921.

Phil 177.68 Chartier, Émile. Quatre-vingt et un chapitres sur l'esprit et les passions. Paris, 1921.

Phil 4753.1.35 Chelpanov, G. Uchebnik logiki. Kharbin, 1921.

Phil 2520.135 Chevalier, J. Descartes. Paris, 1921.

Phil 8582.38 Chiocchetti, E. Religione e filosofia. Milano, 1921.

Phil 3822.7A Chronicon Spinozanum. Hagae, 1921-27. 8v.

Phil 8403.14 Ciaccio, G. Il vera interiore. Sarzana, 1921.

Phil 8610.921 Cohen, Chapman. A grammar of freethought. London, 1921.

Phil 8657.16 Cohen, Chapman. Theism or atheism. London, 1921.

Phil 2840.91 Concato, E. Introduzione alla filosofia del Renouvier. Marostica Vicenza, 1921.

Phil 177.60 Conrad-Martius, Hedwig. Metaphysiche Gespräche. Halle, 1921.

Phil 1170.8 Corbière, C. Le christianisme et la fin de la philosophie antique. Paris, 1921.

Phil 7069.21.20 Cornillier, PE. The survival of the soul and its evolution after death. London, 1921.

Phil 6952.20 Cotton, Henry A. The defective delinquent and insane. Princeton, 1921.

Phil 8692.3.7 Coutts, John. Homely thoughts on the city of God and way to find it. London, 1921.

Phil 7072.20 Crawford, William Jackson. The psychic structures at the Goligher Circle. London, 1921.

Phil 6060.1.17 Crepieux-Jamin, J. Les bases fondamentales de la graphologie. Paris, 1921.

Phil 4080.3.36 Croce, Benedetto. The essence of aesthetic. London, 1921.

Phil 8878.44 Dam, Axel. Livets vardiproblemer. København, 1921.

Phil 7069.21.70 Danils, H. Anden. Stockholm, 1921.

Phil 7054.118.5 Danmar, William. Modern nirvanaism. Jamaica, 1921.

Phil 2490.108 Deherme, G. Aus jeunes gens un maitre: Auguste Comte; une direction: le positivisme. Paris, 1921.

Phil 4073.85 Dentice di Accadia, C. Tommaso Campanella. Firenze, 1921.

Phil 4260.91 Donati, Benvenuto. Autografi e documenti vichiani inediti o dispersi. Bologna, 1921.

Phil 178.55 Donati, G. La metafisica. Savignano, 1921.

Phil 7054.175.10 Doyle, Arthur Conan. The wanderings of a spiritualist. London, 1921.

Phil 7054.175.11 Doyle, Arthur Conan. The wanderings of a spiritualist. N.Y., 1921.

Phil 8878.28.2 Drake, Durant. Problems of conduct. Boston, 1921.

Phil 178.70 Drews, A. Einführung in die Philosophie. Berlin, 1921.

Phil 1703.2.10 Drews, Arthur. Die Philosophie im lekten Drittel des 19. Jahrhunderts. Berlin, 1921.

Phil 178.22.5 Driesch, H. Das Ganze und die Summe. Leipzig, 1921.

Phil 8828.2 Du sage antique au citoyen moderne. Paris, 1921.

Phil 4363.2.84 Dudon, P. Le quiétiste espanol. Paris, 1921.

Phil 5243.23.5 Dumville, B. The fundamentals of psychology. London, 1921.

Phil 5525.20A Eastman, Max. The sense of humor. N.Y., 1921.

Phil 6314.4 Edson, D.O. Getting what we want. N.Y., 1921.

Phil 179.3.75 Eucken, R. Lebenserinnerungen. Leipzig, 1921.

Phil 179.3.75.25 Eucken, R. Lebenserinnerungen. Stockholm, 1921.

Phil 179.3.76 Eucken, R. Rudolf Eucken, his life, work and travels. London, 1921.

Phil 3487.10 Färber, Max. Die Kantische Freiheitslehre. Berlin, 1921.

Phil 1705.1.3 Falckenberg, R. Geschichte der neueren Philosophie. 8e Aufl. Berlin, 1921.

Phil 978.29.10 Farnsworth, E.C. The deeper mysteries. Portland, Maine, 1921.

Phil 6315.1.5 Ferenczi, Sandor. Psycho-analysis and the war neurosis. Photoreproduction. London, 1921.

Phil 805.6.3 Fiorentino, F. Compendio di storia della filosofia. vol. 1-2, pt.1. Firenze, 1921-22. 2v.

Phil 805.6.2 Fiorentino, F. Manuele di storia della filosofia. Torino, 1921. 2v.

Phil 180.33.10 Fischer, Ludwig. Das Vollwirkliche und das Als-ob. Berlin, 1921.

Phil 8880.41 Flake, Otto. Die moralische Idee. München, 1921.

Phil 7069.21.31 Flammarion, C. Imod døden. Kjøbenhavn, 1921.

Phil 7069.21.30 Flammarion, Camille. Death and its mystery. pt.1,3. N.Y., 1921-23. 2v.

Phil 7069.21.33 Flournoy, Theodor. Spiritismus und experimental-psychologie. Leipzig, 1921.

Phil 3640.88.10 Förster-Nietzsche, E. The Nietzsche-Wagner correspondence. N.Y., 1921.

Phil 3487.3.3 Fouillée, Alfred. Le moralisme de Kant et l'amoralisme contemporain. Paris, 1921.

Phil 4815.558.85 Fraknói, Vilmos. Martinovics élete. Budapest, 1921.

Phil 6315.2.44 Freud, Sigmund. Massenpsychologie und Ich-Analyse. Leipzig, 1921.

Htn Phil 5380.77* Freud, Sigmund. Massenpsychologie und Ich-Analyse. Leipzig, 1921.

Phil 805.7 Freudenberg, G. Die philosophiegeschichtliche Wahrheit. Inaug. Diss. Berlin, 1921.

Phil 6315.3.2 Frink, H.W. Morbid fears and compulsions, their psychology. London, 1921.

Phil 180.17.12 Fullerton, G.S. An introduction to philosophy. N.Y., 1921.

Phil 6316.6 Gadelius, Bror. Det mänskliga själslivet i belysning av sinnessjukläkarens erfarenhet. Stockholm, 1921-24. 4v.

Phil 2250.85 Galgano, Maria. Il pensiero filosofico e morale di Josiah Royce. Roma, 1921.

1921 - cont.

Phil 5374.151 Geney, Gustave. From the unconcious to the conscious. N.Y., 1921.

Phil 4120.4.125 Gentile, Giovanni. Il concetlo moderno della scienza e il problema universitario. Roma, 1921.

Phil 181.45 Gentile, Giovanni. Saggi critici. Ser. I. Napoli, 1921.

Phil 8631.8 Genung, John F. The life indeed. Boston, 1921.

Phil 6048.89.7 Gessmann, G.W. Katechismus der Handelskunst. Berlin, 1921.

Phil 5926.2.2 Gessmann, G.W. Katechismus der Kopfformkunde. 2. Aufl. Berlin, 1921.

Phil 91.4 Giese, Fritz. Psychologisches Wörterbuch. Leipzig, 1921.

Phil 1511.3 Gilson, Étienne. Études de philosophie médiévale. Strasbourg, 1921.

Phil 5627.94 Girgensohn, K. Der seelische Aufbau des religiösen Erlebens. Leipzig, 1921.

Phil 7069.21.35 Glenconner, Pamela. The earthen vessel. London, 1921.

Phil 8050.55 Gori, Gino. Studi di estetica dell'irrazionable. Milano, 1921.

Phil 3585.10.80 Gothot, Heinrich. Die Grundbestimmungen über die Psychologie des Gefühls bei Theodor Lipps. Mülheim-Ruhr, 1921.

Phil 1511.1.10 Grabmann, M. Die Philosophie des Mittelalters. Berlin, 1921.

Phil 9346.5.5 Gratry, A.J. Les sources. 16. éd. Paris, 1921.

Phil 7069.21.37 Green, H.L. Think on these things. Pasadena, 1921.

Phil 3640.159.5 Grützmacher, R.H. Nietzsche. Leipzig, 1921.

Phil 4120.2.30 Guastella, Cosmo. Le ragioni del fenomenismo. v. 1-3. Palermo, 1921-23. 2v.

Phil 1706.5.10 Güttler, C. Einführung in die Geschichte der Philosophie seit Hegel. München, 1921.

Phil 181.47 Guillou, Henri. Essai de philosophie générale élémentaire. Paris, 1921.

Phil 181.44 Gurnhill, James. Christian philosophy discussed under the topics of absolute values. London, 1921.

Phil 5247.28 Haas, Wilhelm. Die psychische Dingwelt. Bonn, 1921.

Phil 5247.30 Häberlin, Paul. Der Gegenstand der Psychologie. Berlin, 1921.

Phil 3640.228 Haiser, Franz. Im Anfang war der Streit. München, 1921.

Phil 338.10 Haldane, R.B. The reign of relativity. New Haven, 1921.

Phil 338.10.2 Haldane, R.B. The reign of relativity. 2. ed. London, 1921.

Phil 2520.111.2 Hamelin, O. Le système de Descartes. 2e éd. Paris, 1921.

Phil 2475.1.204 Hamilton, George R. Bergson and future philosophy. London, 1921.

Phil 6957.7.3 Hart, Bernard. The psychology of insanity. Cambridge, 1921.

Phil 338.11 Hartmann, N. Grundzüge einer Metaphysik der Erkenntnis. Berlin, 1921.

Phil 575.45 Heath, Arthur G. The moral and social significance of the conception of personality. Oxford, 1921.

Phil 3425.70.9 Hegel, Georg Wilhelm Friedrich. Grundlinien der Philosophie des Rechts. 2. Aufl. Leipzig, 1921.

Phil 3425.73.1 Hegel, Georg Wilhelm Friedrich. Phänomenologie des Geistes. 2. Aufl. Leipzig, 1921.

Phil 182.78 Heiler, Josef. Das Absolute. München, 1921.

Phil 3425.220 Heller, Hermann. Hegel und der nationale Machtstaatsgedanke in Deutschland. Leipzig, 1921.

Phil 338.12 Helmholtz, H. Schriften zur Erkenntnistheorie. Berlin, 1921.

Phil 182.50.5 Herbertz, Richard. Das philosophische Urerlebnis. Bern, 1921.

Phil 8957.22 Hermanson, Robert Fredrik. Oikeus ja uskonnolliset totuudet. Porvoossa, 1921.

Phil 182.61 Herpe, Hans. Einleitung in die Kategorienlehre. Leipzig, 1921.

Phil 8882.41.5 Herrmann, W. Ethik. 5e Aufl. Tübingen, 1921.

Phil 270.27 Heuer, W. Warum Fragen die menschen Warum? Heidelberg, 1921.

Phil 179.3.106 Heussner, A. Einführung in Rudolf Euckens Lebens- und Weltanschauung. Göttingen, 1921.

Phil 3489.25 Heussner, A. Hilfs-Büchlein für Kant-Leser. v.1-2. Göttingen, 1921-22.

Phil 8882.42 Hill, Owen. Ethics, general and special. London, 1921.

Phil 5247.27 Hill, Owen Aloysuis. Psychology and natural theology. N.Y., 1921.

Phil 6317.7 Hingley, R.H. Psycho-analysis. London, 1921.

Phil 2045.54 Hobbes, Thomas. Leviathan. Paris, 1921.

Phil 6957.9 Hoch, August. Benign stupors. N.Y., 1921.

Phil 4580.36.3 Høffding, Harald. Den nyere filosofis historie. v.1-10. Kjøbenhavn, 1921-22. 2v.

Phil 4803.454.51 Hoene-Wroński, Józef Maria. Prodrom mesjanizmu albo filozofji absolutnej. Lwów, 1921.

Phil 1112.7 Hoffmann, Ernst. Die griechische Philosophie von Thales bis Platon. Leipzig, 1921.

Phil 8408.30.10 Hostinský, Otakar. Otakara Hostinského esthetika. Praha, 1921.

Phil 182.55 Hudson, Jay W. The truths we live by. N.Y., 1921.

Phil 8587.32 Hügel, Friedrich von. Essays and addresses on the philosophy of religion. London, 1921.

Phil 8587.29.10 Hunzinger, A.W. Hunzinger. Hamburg, 1921-22. 2v.

Phil 7069.21.40 Ingalese, Richard. Fragments of truth. N.Y., 1921.

Phil 48.5.10 Institut Général Psychologique. Notes et documents concernant l'oeuvre, 1900-1921. Paris, 1921.

Phil 6319.5 Jackson, Josephine A. Outwitting our nerves. N.Y., 1921.

Phil 6119.11 Jackson, Josephine Agnes. Outwitting our nerves. N.Y., 1921.

Phil 8410.5 Jacques, G.H. A system of aesthetics. Dublin, 1921-

Phil 2070.65.5 James, William. Gli ideali della vita. 5a ed. Torino, 1921.

Phil 9349.5 Jamin, F. Conseils aux jeunes de France après la victoire. 2e éd. Paris, 1921.

Phil 809.2.10 Janet, P. Histoire de la philosophie. Paris, 1921.

Phil 184.28 Janssen, O. Vorstudien zur Metaphysik. Halle, 1921. 2v.

Phil 8884.7 Janssens, E. La morale de l'impératif catégorique et la morale du bonheur. Louvain, 1921.

Phil 8884.18 Joad, Cyril E.M. Common-sense ethics. N.Y., 1921.

Phil 3235.110 Jodl, F. Ludwig Feuerbach. 2. Aufl. Photoreproduction. Stuttgart, 1921.

Phil 1114.1 Joël, Karl. Geschichte der antiken Philosophie. Tübingen, 1921.

Phil 5049.16A Johnson, William Ernest. Logic. pt.1. Cambridge, Eng., 1921-24. 3v.

Phil 6060.20 Joire, Paul. Traité de graphologie scientifique. 2d ed. Paris, 1921.

Phil 1930.6.125   Jones, Henry. The life and philosophy of Edward Caird. Glasgow, 1921.

Phil 5819.3   Josey, Charles C. The role of instinct in social psychology. N.Y., 1921.

Phil 5759.3   Joss, Hermann. Der Wille. Bern, 1921.

Phil 1870.98   Joussain, André. Exposé critique de la philosophie de Berkeley. Paris, 1921.

Phil 978.7.15   Judge, W.Z. Echoes from the Orient. 3rd ed. Point Loma, Calif., 1921.

Phil 5249.13.8   Jung, Carl G. Psychologische Typen. Zürich, 1921.

Phil 1133.19A   Kafka, Gustav. Die Vorsokratiker. München, 1921.

Phil 3830.11   Kaim, J.R. Die Philosophie Spinozas. München, 1921.

Phil 5250.23   Kaim, J.R. Psychologische Probleme in der Philosophie. München, 1921.

Phil 2280.5.95   Kallen, H.M. America and the life of reason. N.Y., 1921.

Phil 3480.77   Kant, Immanuel. En Andeskadares drömmar i ljusetay metafysikens drömmar. Lund, 1921. 10v.

Phil 3480.18.12   Kant, Immanuel. Kleinere philosophische Schriften. Leipzig, 1921.

Phil 3480.16.25   Kant, Immanuel. Werke in acht Büchern. v.1-4,5-8. Berlin, 1921. 2v.

Phil 3480.24   Kant, Immanuel. Zur Logik und Metaphysik. 2. Aufl. Leipzig, 1921. 4v.

Phil 3549.10.60   Kassner, Rudolf. Wer indische Gedanke. 2. Aufl. Leipzig, 1921.

Phil 6320.1.5   Kempf, E.J. Psychopathology. St. Louis, 1921.

Phil 1710.2   Kerler, D.H. Die auferstandene Metaphysik. Ulm, 1921.

Phil 8590.18.3   King, Basil. The conquest of fear. Garden City, 1921.

Phil 7069.21.43   Kirchhoff, P. Der moderne Okkultismus in Lichte des Experiments! Köln, 1921.

Phil 6060.12.10   Klages, Ludwig. Handschrift und Charakter. 3. und 4. Aufl. Leipzig, 1921.

Phil 575.51   Klages, Ludwig. Prinzipien der Charakterologie. 3e Aufl. Leipzig, 1921.

Phil 291.2F   Klyce, Scudder. Universe. Winchester, Mass., 1921.

Phil 5820.4.10   Köhler, Wolfgang. Intelligenzprüfungen an Menschenaffen. 2. Aufl. Berlin, 1921.

Phil 3640.161   Kohler, F.P. Friedrich Nietzsche. Leipzig, 1921.

Phil 8590.13.5   Krarup, F.C. Religionsfilosofi. København, 1921.

Phil 400.49   Kröger, Otto. Die Philosophie des reinen Idealismus. Bonn, 1921.

Phil 3010.3   Kroner, R. Von Kant bis Hegel. Tübingen, 1921-24. 2v.

Phil 8411.13   Külpe, O. Grundlagen der Ästhetik. Leipzig, 1921.

Phil 5250.2.3A   Külpe, Oswald. Outlines of psychology. London, 1921.

Phil 7060.256   Kummerich, M. Gespenster und Spuk. Ludwigshafenam Bodensee, 1921.

Phil 4600.6.2   Lagerwall, A. Skrifter. Göteborg, 1921.

Phil 8430.18.5   Lalo, C. L'arte et la vie sociale. Paris, 1921.

Phil 2705.35   La Mettrie, Julien Offray de. L'homme machine, suivi de l'Art de jouir. Paris, 1921.

Phil 5251.25   Larguier des Bancels, Jean. Introduction à la psychologie. Paris, 1921.

Phil 1116.3   Larsson, Hans. Den grekiska filosofien. Stockholm, 1921.

Phil 5585.32   Lavelle, Louis. La dialectique du monde sensible. Strasbourg, 1921.

Phil 5585.32.3   Lavelle, Louis. La dialectique du monde sensible. Thèse. Strasbourg, 1921. 2 pam.

Phil 5585.33   Lavelle, Louis. La perception visuelle de la profondeur. Strasbourg, 1921.

Phil 6321.5A   Lawrence, David Herbert. Psycho-analysis and its unconscious. N.Y., 1921.

Phil 7054.184   Lawrence, E. Spiritualism among civilised and savage races. London, 1921.

Phil 6321.2.5   Lay, Wilfrid. Man's unconcious conflict. N.Y., 1921.

Phil 3246.185   Leibholz, G. Fichte und der demokratischen Gedanke. Freiburg, 1921.

Phil 720.16   Lelesz, H. La conception de la vérité. Thèse. Paris, 1921.

Phil 5640.26   Lemaire, J. Etude sur la connaissance sensible des objets extérieurs. Liege, 1921.

Phil 8701.10   Leslie, John. Revelation and science. Aberdeen, 1921.

Phil 8412.17   Lesparre, A. de G. Essai sur le sentiment esthétique. Paris, 1921.

Phil 3585.14.5   Lessing, Theodor. Die verfluchte Kultur. München, 1921.

Phil 5627.20.6   Leuba, J.H. The psychological origin and the nature of religion. London, 1921.

Phil 645.28   Levi, Adolfo. Sceptica. Torino, 1921.

Phil 342.9   Liljeckrantz, B. Ur världsförklaringarnas och kunskapsteoriernas urkunder. Stockholm, 1921.

Phil 5761.10.2   Lindworsky, J. Der Wille, seine Erscheinung und seine Beherrschung. 2. Aufl. Leipzig, 1921.

Phil 400.66   Lippa, L. von. Der Aufstieg von Kant zu Goethe. Berlin, 1921.

Phil 6321.6   Long, C.E. Collected papers on the psychology of phantasy. N.Y., 1921.

Phil 4260.90   Longo, Michele. Giambattista Vico. Torino, 1921.

Phil 6961.12   Loosmore, W.C. Nerves and the man. N.Y., 1921.

Phil 292.20   Lugones, Leopoldo. El tamaño del espacio. Buenos Aires, 1921.

Phil 4769.1.92   Luk'ianov, S.M. O Vl. S. Solov'eve v ego molodye gody. Kniga 3. Vyp. I. Petrograd, 1921. 2v.

Phil 187.56   McTaggart, J.M.E. The nature of existence. Cambridge, Eng., 1921-1927. 2v.

Phil 3246.180   Maggiore, G. Fichte. Castello, 1921.

Phil 487.7   Mann, Walter. Modern materialism. London, 1921.

Phil 5402.3.15   Mantegazza, P. L'anima delle cose. Torino, 1921.

Phil 3494.19.2   Marcus, Ernst. Der kategorische Imperativ. München, 1921.

Phil 6122.43   Marguardt, H. Der Mechanismus der Seele. Holstein, 1921.

Phil 2750.11.59   Maritain, Jacques. Eléments de philosophie. Paris, 1921-23. 2v.

Phil 8592.31   Matthews, W.R. Studies in Christian philosophy. London, 1921.

Phil 3832.5.5   Mauthner, Fritz. Spinoza; eine Umriss seine Lebens und Wirkens. Dresden, 1921.

Phil 3246.79.50   Meyer, Friedrich. Eine Fichte-Sammlung. Leipzig, 1921.

Phil 5252.42   Meyer, M.F. Psychology of the other one. Columbia, 1921.

Phil 2520.138   Milhaud, G.S. Descartes savant. Paris, 1921.

Phil 4012.4   Miranda, L. Die Hegel a Croce e da Jellinek a Chiovenda. Bari, 1921.

Phil 6322.6   Mitchell, T.W. The psychology of medicine. London, 1921.

Phil 75.17   Moog, Willy. Philosophie. Gotha, 1921.

Phil 5252.43   Moore, J.S. The foundations of psychology. Princeton, 1921.

Phil 3640.156   Muckle, Friedrich. Friedrich Nietzsche und der Zusammenbruch der Kultur. München, 1921.

Phil 6122.40   Müller, A. Bismarck, Nietzsche, Scheffel, Mörike; der Einfluss nervöser Zustände auf ihr Leben und Schaffen. Bonn, 1921.

Phil 7069.21.57   Mukerji, S. Indian ghost stories. Allahabad, 1921.

Phil 9380.1   Munson, E.L. The management of men. N.Y., 1921.

Phil 575.47   Myerson, Abraham. The foundations of personality. Boston, 1921.

Phil 5253.6   Naccarati, S. The morphologic aspect of intelligence. N.Y., 1921.

Phil 294.6   Neeff, F. Prolegomena zu einer Kosmologie. Tübingen, 1921.

Phil 8888.6.27   Nelson, Leonard. Ethischer Realismus. Leipzig, 1921.

Phil 2805.187   Neri, F. Un ritratto immaginario di Pascal. Torino, 1921.

Phil 294.7   Nernst, Walther. Zum Gültigkeitsbereich der Naturgesetze. Berlin, 1921.

Phil 9035.34   Newfang, Oscar. The development of character. N.Y., 1921.

Phil 3640.78   Nietzsche, Friedrich. Selected letters. London, 1921.

Phil 3246.190   Nindelband, N. Fichte's Idee des deutschen Staates. Tübingen, 1921.

Phil 8593.9   Nygren, A. Religiöst apriori. Lund, 1921.

Phil 3640.221   Oehler, Max. Den Manen Friedrich Nietzsches. München, 1921.

Phil 8889.1.15   Ollé-Laprune, L. Le prix de la vie. 43. ed. Paris, 1921.

Phil 5645.20.2   Ostwald, Wilhelm. Die Farbenlehre. 2. Aufl. Leipzig, 1921.

Phil 8890.41   Parodi, D. Le problème morale et la pensée contemporaine. 2. ed. Paris, 1921.

Phil 270.24   Pastore, Annibale. Il problema della causalità con particolare reguardo alla teoria del metodo sperimentale. Torino, 1921. 2v.

Phil 5255.46   Paton, S. Human behavior. N.Y., 1921.

Phil 5325.21   Paulhan, Fr. Le mensonge du monde. Paris, 1921.

Phil 8890.6.8   Paulsen, F. System der Ethik. 11. und 12. Aufl. Stuttgart, 1921. 2v.

Phil 9245.33   Payot, Jules. La conquête du bonheur. Paris, 1921.

Phil 5765.2.20   Payot, Jules. Will-power and work. 2. ed. N.Y., 1921.

Phil 525.23.5   Pedrick, Katharinn F. Du moyen de manifester la perfection. Paris, 1921.

Phil 3015.3   Petersen, Peter. Geschichte der aristotelischen Philosophie in protestantischen Deutschland. Leipzig, 1921.

Phil 365.15   Petronievics, B. L'évolution universelle. Paris, 1921.

Phil 5374.154.2   Peucesco, M.G. Le mécanisme du courant de la conscience. Thèse. Paris, 1921.

Phil 5055.16   Pfänder, A. Logik. Halle, 1921.

Phil 6325.1.35   Pfister, Oskar. Die Behandlung schwer erziehlbarer und abnormer Kinder. Bern, 1921.

Phil 6325.1.40   Pfister, Oskar. Vermeintliche Nullen und angebliche Musterkinder. Bern, 1921.

Phil 5330.7.7   Pillsbury, W.B. Attention. London, 1921.

Phil 8416.33   Pilo, Mario. Estetica lexioni sur bello. 2. ed. Milano, 1921.

X Cg   Phil 490.4.3   Plekhanov, G.V. Beiträge zur Geschichte des Materialismus. 3. Aufl. Stuttgart, 1921.

Phil 5440.25   Poyer, Georges. Les problèmes généraux de l'hérédité psychologique. Paris, 1921.

Phil 5440.25.3   Poyer, Georges. Les problèmes généraux de l'hérédité psychologique. Thèse. Paris, 1921. 2 pam.

Phil 6325.8.7   Prince, Morton. The unconscious. 2d ed. N.Y., 1921.

Phil 6325.2A   Putnam, J.J. Addresses on psycho-analysis. London, 1921.

Phil 5255.32.5   Putnam, J.J. Human nervous. Boston, 1921.

X Cg   Phil 2230.10.5   Quimby, P.P. The Quimby manuscripts. N.Y., 1921.

Htn   Phil 2230.10*   Quimby, P.P. The Quimby manuscripts. 1st ed. N.Y., 1921.

Phil 7069.21.50   Randall, John H. The new light on immortality. N.Y., 1921.

Phil 672.137   Ranzoli, C. Prime linee di una teoria realistica dello spazio e del tempo. Messina, 1921.

Phil 2035.86.30   Rasmussen, S. Studier over W. Hamiltons filosofi. København, 1921.

Phil 6830.6.4   Rau, Hans. Die Grausamkeit mit besonder Bezugnahme auf sexualle Factoren. 4. Aufl. Berlin, 1921.

Phil 8418.6.3   Raymond, G.L. The essentials of aesthetics in music. 3.ed. N.Y., 1921.

Phil 2030.1.81   Redgrove, H. Stanley. Joseph Glanvill and physical research in the seventeenth century. London, 1921.

Phil 5374.153   Reed, Charles J. The law of vital transfusion and the phenomenon of consciousness. San Francisco, 1921.

Phil 3790.9.80   Rehmke, J. Johannes Rehmke. Leipzig, 1921.

Phil 645.22.2   Rensi, Giuseppe. Lineamenti di filosofia scetica. Bologna, 1921.

Phil 3425.124   Reyburn, Hugh A. The ethical theory of Hegel. Oxford, 1921.

Phil 5465.5.3   Ribot, T. Essai sur l'imagination créatrice. 6. éd. Paris, 1921.

Phil 192.21.15   Rickert, H. Allgemeine Grundlegung der Philosophie. Tübingen, 1921.

Phil 348.9   Rickert, H. Der Gegenstand der Erkenntnistheorie. 4. und 5. Aufl. Tübingen, 1921.

Phil 1817.3.5.5   Riley, I.W. Le génie américain. Paris, 1921.

Phil 6327.6   Rinaldo, Joel. Psychoanalysis of the "reformer". N.Y., 1921.

Phil 5257.19.3   Robert, Arthur. Leçons de psychologie. 3. éd. Québec, 1921.

Phil 2475.1.209   Rodrigues, G. Bergsonisme et moralité. Paris, 1921.

Phil 3640.168   Römer, H. Nietzsche. Leipzig, 1921. 2v.

Phil 5125.14   Rougier, Louis. La structure des théories déductives. Paris, 1921.

Phil 5643.68   Rubin, Edgar. Visuell wahrgenommene figuren. København, 1921.

Phil 3499.28   Rüther, R. Kant und Antikant. Paderborn, 1921.

Phil 1717.8.5A   Ruggiero, G. de. Modern philosophy. London, 1921.

Phil 5227.4   Ruin, Hans. Erlebnis und Wissen. Helsingfors, 1921.

Phil 5257.25   Russell, Bertrand Russell. The analysis of mind. London, 1921.

Phil 193.49.16   Santayana, G. Character and opinion in the United States. N.Y., 1921.

Phil 193.49.2   Santayana, G. The life of reason. v.2-3. N.Y., 1921. 2v.

Phil 8893.86.5   Scheler, Max. Der formalismus in der Ethik und die materiale Wertethik. 2. Aufl. Halle, 1921.

Phil 665.69   Schleich, C.L. Von der Seele. Berlin, 1921.

Phil 8612.24   Schleich, Carl L. Das Problem des Todes. Berlin, 1921.

Phil 818.17   Schlunk, M. Die Weltanschauung von den Griechen bis zu Hegel. Hamburg, 1921.

Phil 3552.260   Schmalenbach, H. Leibniz. München, 1921.

1921 - cont.

Phil 193.111 Schmieder, J. Einführung in System und Geschichte der Philosophie. Leipzig, 1921.

Phil 1523.8 Schneider, Artur. Die Erkenntnislehre bei Beginn der Scholastik. Fulda, 1921.

Phil 8598.50 Scholz, H. Die Religionsphilosophie des Als-Ob. Leipzig, 1921.

Phil 3808.62 Schopenhauer, Arthur. Morale e religione. Torino, 1921.

Phil 5258.96.5 Schulze, Rudolf. Die moderne Seelenlehre; Begabungsforschung und Berufsberatung. 3. Aufl. Leipzig, 1921.

Phil 8598.44 Schwarz, Hermann. Das Ungegebene; eine Religions- und Wertphilosophie. Tübingen, 1921.

Phil 3890.6.85 Schweig, Helmut. Die Psychologie des Enkennens bei Bonnet und Tetens. Trier, 1921.

Phil 5545.54.10 Semon, R. The mneme. Leipzig, 1921.

Phil 4195.84 Semprini, G. Giovanni Pico della Mirandola. Todi, 1921.

Phil 4115.87 Sgroi, Carmelo. L'estetica e la critica letteraria in V. Gioberti. Firenze, 1921.

Phil 5150.1 Sheffer, H.M. General theory of notational relativity. Cambridge, 1921.

Phil 6328.5.10 Silberer, Herbert. Der Zufall und die Kaboldstreiche. Bern, 1921.

Phil 3500.20.6 Simmel, G. Kant: sechzehn Vorlesungen. 5. Aufl. München, 1921.

Phil 193.59.20A Simmel, G. Der Konflikt der modernen Kultur. 2. Aufl. München, 1921.

Phil 8893.91.90 Sinclair, Upton. The book of life. Chicago, 1921.

Phil 8643.24 Smith, O. Tho material, why not immortal? Boston, 1921.

Phil 5258.66.3 Smith, Stevenson. Chapters in general psychology. Seattle, 1921.

Phil 630.13.7 Sorely, W. R. Moral values and the idea of God. 2nd ed. N.Y., 1921.

Phil 1818.5.5 Sorley, William R. A history of English philosophy. N.Y., 1921.

Phil 1718.10 Sortais, Gaston. La philosophie moderne. Paris, 1921-22.

Phil 4065.98 Spampanato, V. Vita di Giordano Bruno. v.1-2. Messina, 1921.

Phil 8598.83 Sperry, Willard L. The disciplines of liberty. New Haven, 1921.

Phil 193.87 Spirito, U. Il pragmatismo nella filosofia contemporanea. Firenze, 1921.

Phil 5258.62 Staak, Hermann. Aufbau der höheren geistigen Entwicklung. Rostock, 1921.

Phil 9358.15.5 Starrett, H.E. (Mrs.). The charm of fine manners. Philadelphia, 1921.

Phil 7060.254 Stead, William T. Real ghost stories. N.Y., 1921.

Phil 3415.99 Steffes, J.P. Eduard von Hartmanns Religionsphilosophie des Unbewuszten. Mergentheim, 1921?

Phil 3805.169 Steinberg, Julius. Liebe und Ehe in Schleiermachers Kreis. Dresden, 1921.

Phil 978.49.40 Steiner, R. Die Aufgabe der Geisteswissenschaft und deren Bau in Dornach. Berlin, 1921.

Phil 978.49.45 Steiner, R. Die Schwelle der geistigen Welt. 10. Aufl. Berlin, 1921.

Phil 978.49.90 Steiner, R. Von Seelenrätseln. Berlin, 1921.

Phil 5768.10.5 Steiner, Rudolf. Die Philosophie der Freiheit. Berlin, 1921.

Phil 6328.2.5 Stekel, Wilhelm. The beloved ego. London, 1921.

Phil 6328.2.15 Stekel, Wilhelm. The depth of the soul. London, 1921.

Phil 193.138 Stern, M.R. von. Weltanschauung; Ergbnnisse freien Denkens. Linz, 1921.

Phil 5258.35.3 Stern, W. Die differentielle Psychologie. Leipzig, 1921.

Phil 5258.84 Strasser, Vera. Psychologie der Zusammenhänge und Beziehungen. Berlin, 1921.

Phil 4802.2 Straszewski, Maurycy. Polska filozofja narodowa, 15 wykładow. Krakow, 1921.

Phil 3640.157 Strecker, Karl. Nietzsche und Strindberg. München, 1921.

Phil 3500.49 Sturm, A. Kant, Schopenhauer, Nietzsche und deren...Gemüt. Langensalza, 1921.

Phil 3110.165 Swainson, W.P. Jacob Boehme, the Teutonic philosopher. London, 1921.

Phil 194.28 Tassy, E. La philosophie constructive. Paris, 1921.

Phil 7140.118 Thamiry, E. De l'influence: étude psychologique. Thèse. Lille, 1921.

Phil 3565.109 Thomas, Evan E. Lotze's theory of reality. London, 1921.

Phil 194.25.5 Thomas, P.F. Cours de philosophie pour les classes de philosophie A et B. 5e éd. Paris, 1921.

Phil 835.4 Thomas, Viktor. Das Erkenntnisproblem; ein historischkritischer Versuch. Stuttgart, 1921.

Phil 850.12 Tilgher, A. Filosofi antichi. Todi, 1921.

Phil 974.2.15 Tingley, K.A. (Mrs.). Helena Petrovna Blavatsky. Point Loma, Calif., 1921.

Phil 5259.11.5 Trabue, M.R. Measure your mind. Garden City, 1921.

Phil 6329.1.8 Tridon, André. Easy lessons in psychoanalysis. N.Y., 1921.

Phil 7084.4.10 Tridon, André. Psychoanalysis, sleep and dreams. N.Y., 1921.

Phil 974.3.85 Tröger, Walter. Grundriss der Anthroposophie in engem Anschluss an die Schriften Dr. Rudolf Steiners. Breslau, 1921.

Phil 7069.21.60 Tweedale, Charles L. Man's survival after death. N.Y., 1921?

Phil 6331.1 Valentine, C.W. Dreams and the unconscious; an introduction to the study of psycho-analysis. London, 1921.

Phil 5261.8.5 Varendonck, J. L'évolution des facultés conscientes. Thèse. Gand, 1921.

Phil 7225.2A Varendonck, Julien. The psychology of day-dreams. London, 1921.

Phil 4170.3.80 Vecchio-Veneziani, Augusta del. La vita e l'opere di A.C. de Meis. Bologna, 1921.

Phil 960.11.5 Vidyabhusana, Satis Chandra. A history of Indian logic. Calcutta, 1921.

Phil 196.29.5 Vincenzi, M. Rionas y byondas. San José, 1921.

Phil 8050.61 Voigtländer, E. Zur Gesetzlichkeit der abendländischen Kunst. Bonn, 1921.

Phil 821.1.6 Vorländer, K. Geschichte der Philosophie. 6. Aufl. Leipzig, 1921.

Phil 3503.4.2 Vorländer, K. Immanuel Kants Leben. 2. Aufl. Leipzig, 1921.

Phil 3504.33 Wagner, Walther. Die Vereinigung von Kant und Marx. Langensalza, 1921.

Phil 7069.21.90 Warcollier, R. La télépathie, recherches experimentales. Paris, 1921.

Phil 5325.17 Warren, Howard C. A history of the association psychology. N.Y., 1921.

1921 - cont.

Phil 5325.17.2 Warren, Howard C. A history of the association psychology. Diss. Baltimore, 1921.

Phil 5942.3F Warren, J.C. The collection of the Boston Phrenological Society, a retrospect. N.Y., 1921.

Phil 6332.4.3 Watts, Frank. Abnormal psychology and its educational applications. London, 1921.

Phil 5627.57 Wells, W.R. The biological foundations of belief. Boston, 1921.

Phil 5062.17.8 Welton, James. Groundwork of logic. London, 1921.

Phil 270.41 Wentscher, E.S. Geschichte des Kausalproblems in der neueren Philosophie. Leipzig, 1921.

Phil 6972.14.20 White, William Alanson. Foundations of psychiatry. N.Y., 1921.

Phil 640.2 Wichmann, Ottomar. Die Scholastiker. München, 1921.

Phil 197.9.15 Windelband, W. Introduction to philosophy. London, 1921.

Phil 8602.36 Winkler, R. Phänomenologie und Religion. Tübingen, 1921.

Phil 960.124 Woodroffe, J.G. The world as power reality. Madras, 1921.

Phil 3915.78 Wundt, Wilhelm. Erlebtes und Erkanntes. 2. Aufl. Stuttgart, 1921.

Phil 3915.59.7 Wundt, Wilhelm. Probleme der Völkerpsychologie. 2. Aufl. Stuttgart, 1921.

Phil 8605.3.5 Zacchi, P.A. L'uomo. Roma, 1921. 2v.

Phil 4060.1.87 Zamboni, G. Il valore scientifico del positivismo di Roberto Ardigò. Verona, 1921.

Phil 306.3.5 Ziegler, Konrat. Weltuntergang in Sage und Wissenschaft. Leipzig, 1921.

1922

Phil 193.21.25 Abauzit, Frank. L'enigme du monde. Paris, 1922.

Phil 6310.1.39 Adler, A. Heilen und Bilden. München, 1922.

Phil 6110.10.10 Adler, Alfred. Über den nervösen Charakter. München, 1922.

Phil 281.8 Adler, Arthur. Das heutige Weltbild. Brieg, 1922.

Phil 175.34 Ahlberg, Alf. De filosofiska grundproblemen. Stockholm, 1922.

Phil 800.2.3 Alexander, A.B.D. A short history of philosophy. 3. ed. Glasgow, 1922.

Phil 400.29.9 Aliotta, A. Relativismo e idealismo. Napoli, 1922.

Phil 175.26.5 Aliotta, Antonio. La teoria di Einstein. Palmero, 1922.

Phil 5710.12 Allendy, R. Les tempéraments. Paris, 1922.

Phil 3640.158.3 Andler, Charles. Nietzsche, sa vie et sa pensée. 3. éd. Paris, 1922.

Phil 5240.40 Anile, Antonio. La salute del pensiero "I libro d'oro". Bari, 1922.

Phil 974.3.110 Apel, Max. Geheimwissenschaft. Charlettenburg, 1922.

Phil 5240.26 Apfelbach, Hans. Das Denkgefühe, eine Untersuchung über den emotionalen Charakter der Denkprozesse. Wien, 1922.

Phil 1105.6 Appleton, R.B. The elements of Greek philosophy from Thales to Aristotle. London, 1922.

Phil 8950.6 Arregui, Antonio M. Summarium theologiae morales. Bilbao, 1922.

Phil 978.74.30 Bailey, A.A. (Mrs.). The consciousness of the atom. 2d ed. N.Y., 1922.

Phil 3001.10 Bauch, Bruno. Jena und die Philosophie des deutschen Idealismus. Jena, 1922.

Phil 6311.6.5 Baudouin, C. Studies in psychoanalysis, N.Y., 1922.

Phil 6311.6 Baudouin, C. Studies in psychoanalysis. London, 1922.

Phil 7150.21.2 Bayet, Albert. Le suicide et la morale. Thèse. Paris, 1922.

Phil 5520.39 Beck, Ernst H.F. Die Impersonalien in sprachpsychologischer, logischer und linguistischer Hinsicht. Leipzig, 1922.

Phil 1735.8 Bergmann, Ernst. Der Geist des XIX. Jahrhunderts. Breslau, 1922.

Phil 6951.14 Bergmann, W. Die Seelenleiden der Nervösen. 2. und 3. Aufl. Freiburg, 1922.

Phil 176.51.29 Bergson, H. La filosofia dell'intuizione. Lanciano, 1922.

Phil 2475.1.39.5 Bergson, Henri. Durée et sumultanéité à propos de la théorie d'Einstein. Paris, 1922.

Phil 525.54 Bernhart, J. Die philosophische Mystik des Mittelalters. München, 1922.

Phil 3640.90.7 Bernoulli, Carl A. Nietzsche und die Schweiz. Leipzig, 1922.

Phil 6111.35 Bianchi, L. The mechanism of the brain. Edinburgh 1922.

Phil 176.115.45 Bierens de Haan, J.D. Wereldorde engeestesleven. 2e Aufl. Amsterdam, 1922.

Phil 5241.54 Binet, Alfred. L'étude expérimentale de l'intelligence. Photoreproduction. Paris, 1922.

Phil 5241.64 Binswanger, L. Einführung in die Probleme der allgemeinen Psychologie. Berlin, 1922.

Phil 3110.11.2 Böhme, J. Sämmtliche Werke. v.1-7. Leipzig, 1922. 6v.

Phil 5627.103 Bohne, G. Die religiöse Entwicklung der Jugend in der Reifezeit. Leipzig, 1922.

Phil 8050.38.5 Bosanquet, B. A history of aesthetic. London, 1922.

Phil 735.16 Bougle, Celestin C. Leçons de sociologie sur l'évolution des valeurs. Paris, 1922.

Phil 1200.28 Boza Masvidal, A.A. El estoicismo. Tesis. Habana, 1922.

Phil 5041.20.5A Bradley, F.H. Principles of logic. 2nd ed. London, 1922. 2v.

Phil 8656.15 Brewster, F.C. God; revelation by Christianity and astronomical science. Newport, 1922.

Phil 8581.43 Brod, M. Heidentum, Christentum, Judentum. München, 1922. 2v.

Phil 7140.116.71 Brooks, C.H. The practice of autosuggestion by the method of Emile Coué. London, 1922.

Phil 7140.116.70 Brooks, C.H. The practice of autosuggestion by the method of Emile Coué. N.Y., 1922.

Phil 7140.116.72 Brooks, C.H. The practice of autosuggestion by the method of Emile Coué. N.Y., 1922.

Phil 7140.116.73A Brooks, C.H. The practice of autosuggestion by the method of Emile Coué. N.Y., 1922.

Phil 5241.28.10 Brown, W. Psychology and psychotherapy. London, 1922.

Phil 5241.73 Brugmans, H.J. Psychologische methoden en begrippen. Haarlem, 1922.

Phil 3425.253 Brunswig, Alfred. Hegel. München, 1922.

Phil 5241.70 Bühler, Karl. Handbuch der Psychologie. Jena, 1922.

Phil 5440.31 Bumke, O. Kultur und Ertartung. Berlin, 1922.

Phil 5722.14 Bumke, O. Das Unterbewusstsein, eine Kritik. Berlin, 1922.

Phil 7074.20 Burke, Jane R. The one way. N.Y., 1922.

Phil 6951.9.5 Burr, Colonel Bell. Practical psychology and psychiatry. 5. ed. Philadelphia, 1922.

Chronological Listing

1922 - cont.

Phil 623.23   Busson, Henri. Les sources et le développement du rationalisme dans la littérature française de la Renaissance. Thèse. Paris, 1922.

Phil 623.23.5   Busson, Henri. Les sources et le développement du rationalisme dans la littérature française de la Renaissance. Paris, 1922.

Phil 525.35   Butler, Cuthbert. Western mysticism. London, 1922.

Phil 1107.3   Capelle, Wilhelm. Die griechische Philosophie. Berlin, 1922-34. 3v.

Phil 3160.2.75   Carneri, B. Bartholomäus von Carneri's Briefwechsel mit E. Häckel und F. Jodl. Leipzig, 1922.

Phil 510.127   Carr, H. Wildon. A theory of monads. London, 1922.

Phil 802.18   Casey, F. Thinking. London, 1922.

Phil 2045.98   Catlin, George E.G. Thomas Hobbes as philosopher, publicist and man of letters. Oxford, 1922.

NEDL Phil 2805.177   Chevalier, J. Pascal. Paris, 1922.

Phil 7069.22.3   Chevreuil, L. Le spiritisme dans l'église. Paris, 1922.

Phil 4120.4.81   Chiocchetti, E. La filosofia di Giovanni Gentile. Milano, 1922.

Phil 8952.4   Christianity and problems of today. N.Y., 1922.

Phil 8657.14.10   Cieszkowski, August D. Ojcze-nasz. v.1-3. Poznań, 1922.

Phil 5520.34   Clark, Ruth S. An experimental study of silent thinking. N.Y., 1922.

Phil 974.2.7   Cleather, A.L. (Mrs.). H.P. Blavatsky, a great betrayal. Calcutta, 1922.

Phil 974.2.5   Cleather, A.L. (Mrs.). H.P. Blavatsky, her life and work for humanity. Calcutta, 1922.

Phil 665.63   Clymer, R.S. The science of the soul. Quakertown, 1922.

Phil 8627.13   Cohen, Chapman. The other side of death. London, 1922.

Phil 8582.44   Colas, Émile. La mystique et la raison. Paris, 1922.

Phil 6312.4   Core, D.E. Functional nervous disorders. Bristol, 1922.

Phil 2840.86   Cornwell, I. Les principes du droit dans la philosophie de C. Renouvier. Thèse. Paris, 1922?

Phil 8610.922   Costa, U. da. Die Schriften. Amsterdam, 1922.

Phil 7140.116   Coué, Emile. Selfmastery through conscious autosuggestion. N.Y., 1922.

Phil 8692.3.9   Coutts, John. The harmony and unity of the kingdom of God. London, 1922.

Phil 8877.54   Cox, George C. The public conscience. N.Y., 1922.

Phil 8877.66   Crane, Anker. Lykkens smil. København, 1922.

Phil 5242.38   Cresson, André. Les réactions intellectuelles élémentaires. Paris, 1922.

Phil 4260.85.2   Croce, B. La filosofia di Giambattista Vico. 2a. ed. Bari, 1922.

Phil 8877.34.9   Croce, Benedetto. Fragmente zur Ethik; Übersetzt von J. Schlosser. Zürich, 1922.

Phil 8877.34.8   Croce, Benedetto. Frammenti di etica. Bari, 1922.

Phil 960.28   Daqupta, S. A history of Indian philosophy. v. 2-5. Cambridge, Eng., 1922-49. 4v.

Phil 310.4.10   Deborin, A.M. Vvedemie v filosofii dialecticheskogo materializma. Moskva, 1922.

Phil 178.46   Decoster, Paul. Le règne de la pensée. Bruxelles, 1922.

Phil 5627.61   Delacroix, H. La religion et la foi. Paris, 1922.

Phil 178.53   Delius, Rudolf von. Urgesetze des Lebens. Darmstadt, 1922.

Phil 3485.11   Deneffe, A. Kant und die catholische Wahrheit. Freiburg, 1922.

Phil 2520.11.25   Descartes, René. Die Prinzipien der Philosophie. 4e Aufl. Leipzig, 1922.

Phil 960.3.19   Deussen, P. Vedânta und Platonismus im Lichte der kantischen Philosophie. Berlin, 1922.

Phil 3195.7.80   Deussen, Paul. Mein Leben. Leipzig, 1922.

Phil 3805.85.2   Dilthey, Wilhelm. Leben Schleiermachers. 2. Aufl. Berlin, 1922.

Phil 6113.22   Dorm, T. G. Heymans' psychischen Monismus. Tübingen, 1922.

Phil 1703.2.15   Drews, Arthur. Die deutsche Philosophie der Gegenwart. Berlin, 1922.

Phil 1703.2.6   Drews, Arthur. Die Philosophie im zweiten Drittel des 19. Jahrhunderts. Berlin, 1922.

Phil 745.7   Driesch, H. Geschichte des Vitalismus. 2e Aufl. Leipzig, 1922.

Phil 5043.18.10   Driesch, H. Wessen und Denken. Leipzig, 1922.

Phil 178.22.4   Driesch, H. Wirklichkeitslehre. Leipzig, 1922.

Phil 2475.1.241   Dryssen, Carl. Bergson und die deutsche Romantik. Marburg, 1922.

Phil 7149.2   Duckworth, J. Herbert. Autosuggestion and its personal application. N.Y., 1922.

Phil 5243.15.5   Dunlap, K. The elements of scientific psychology. St. Louis, 1922.

Phil 5525.20.5   Eastman, Max. The sense of humor. N.Y., 1922.

Phil 89.1.7   Eisler, R. Handwörterbuch der Philosophie. 2. Aufl. Berlin, 1922.

Phil 9035.70   Elliot, H.S.R. Human character. London, 1922.

Phil 8584.6   Ellwood, C.A. The reconstruction of religion. N.Y., 1922.

Phil 5014.1   Enriques, Federigo. Per la storia della logica. Bologna, 1922.

Phil 179.3.67   Eucken, R. Der Kampf um die Religion in der Gegenwart. 1. und 2. Aufl. Langensalza, 1922.

Phil 179.3.52   Eucken, R. Prologomena und Epilog zu einer Philosophie des Geistlebens. Berlin, 1922.

Phil 179.3.61   Eucken, R. The spiritual outlook of Europe today. London, 1922.

Phil 3210.67.4   Fechner, G.T. Das Büchlein vom Leben nach dem Tode. 8. Aufl. Leipzig, 1922.

Phil 3549.2.80   Feldkeller, P. Graf Keyserlings Erkenntnisweg zum Übersinnlichen. Darmstadt, 1922.

OL Phil 5400.52   Feleky, A. Feelings and emotions. N.Y., 1922.

Phil 6315.1.20   Ferenczi, Sandor. Populäre vorträge über Psychoanalyse. Leipzig, 1922.

Phil 4260.81.10   Ferrari, G. Il genio di Vico. Lanciano, 1922.

Phil 3235.60   Feuerbach, Ludwig. Philosophie der Zukunft. Stuttgart, 1922.

Phil 3246.44.5   Fichte, Johann Gottlieb. Darstellung der Wissenschaftslehre aus den Jahre 1801, 1804. v.1-2. Leipzig, 1922.

Phil 3246.47.25   Fichte, Johann Gottlieb. Die Grundzüge des gegenwartigen Zeitalters. 2. Aufl. Leipzig, 1922.

Phil 3246.79.25   Fichte, Johann Gottlieb. Tat und Freiheit, ein Fichtebuch. 3. Aufl. Hamburg, 1922.

Phil 8880.36   Field, G.C. Moral theory. An introduction to ethics. London, 1922.

Phil 6315.13   Fielding, W.J. The caveman within us. N.Y., 1922.

Phil 2805.183   Filleau de la Chaise, J. Discours sur les pensées de M. Pascal. Paris, 1922.

1922 - cont.

Phil 3270.10.31   Flake, Otto. Das neuantike Weltbild. Darmstadt, 1922.

Phil 3903.3.95   Fliess, B. Einführung in die Philosophie des Als Ob. Bielefeld, 1922.

Phil 9165.3.6   Foerster, F.W. Lebensführung. Berlin, 1922.

Phil 4640.2.30   Fórólfsson, S. Dulmaetti og dultrú. Reykjavík, 1922.

Phil 6060.22   French, William L. The psychology of handwriting. N.Y., 1922.

Phil 6315.2.6   Freud, Sigmund. Introductory lecture on psycho-analysis. London, 1922.

Phil 6315.2.6.5   Freud, Sigmund. Über Psychoanalyse. 6e Aufl. Leipzig, 1922.

Phil 6315.2.10A   Freud, Sigmund. Vorlesungen zur Einführung in die Psychoanalyse. 2. Aufl. Leipzig, 1922.

Phil 6315.2.10.5A   Freud, Sigmund. Vorlesungen zur Einführung in die Psychoanalyse. 4. Aufl. Leipzig, 1922.

Phil 8880.37.3   Freyer, Hans. Antäus. Jena, 1922.

Phil 7140.124   Friedrichs, T. Zur Psychologie der Hypnose und der Suggestion. Stuttgart, 1922.

Phil 3160.3.81   Fritzsche, R.A. Hermann Cohen. Berlin, 1922.

Phil 5245.21.2A   Fröbes, Joseph. Lehrbuch der experimentellen Psychologie. 2. und 3. Aufl. Freiburg, 1922-1923. 2v.

Phil 8880.35   Fullerton, G.S. Handbook of ethical theory. N.Y., 1922.

Phil 181.51   Galli, Ettore. Alle soglie della metafisica. Milano, 1922.

Phil 8586.10.9   Galloway, G. Religion and modern thought. Edinburgh, 1922.

Phil 5246.29   Garrett, Henry E. A study of the relation of accuracy to speed. N.Y., 1922.

Phil 5246.30   Gates, G.S. Individual differences as affected by practice. N.Y., 1922.

Phil 1706.1.13   Gaultier, Jules de. La philosophie officielle et la philosophie. Paris, 1922.

Phil 181.45.5   Gentile, Giovanni. The theory of mind as pure act. London, 1922.

Phil 4757.1.30   Gershenzon, M.O. Kliuch very. Peterburg, 1922.

Phil 7069.24.18   Geschichte der okkultischen (metapsychischen) Forschung von der Antike bis zur Gegenwart. Pfullingen, 1922.

Phil 6048.97.4   Gessmann, G.W. Katechismus der Handflächenkunde. 4. Aufl. Berlin, 1922.

Phil 6060.17.3   Gessmann, G.W. Katechismus der Handschriften-Deutung. 3. Aufl. Berlin, 1922.

Phil 8669.3.25   Geyser, Joseph. Intellekt oder Gemüt? Eine philosophische Studie über Rudolf Ottos Buch "Das Heilige". Freiburg, 1922.

Phil 1511.3.5   Gilson, Etienne. La philosophie au moyen âge. v.2. Paris, 1922.

Phil 4115.23   Gioberti, V. Pagine scelte, edite ed inedite. Torino, 1922.

Phil 5246.17.7   Givler, Robert C. Psychology; the science of human behavior. N.Y., 1922.

Phil 181.40.5   Gleichen-Russwurm, A. von. Philosophische Profile. Stuttgart, 1922.

Phil 3425.258.10   Glockner, Hermann. Die ethisch-politische Persönlichkeit des Philosophen. Tübingen, 1922.

Phil 5046.12.4   Goblot, Edmond. Traité de logique. Paris, 1922.

Phil 7069.22.10   Godard, André. Le surnaturel contemporain. Paris, 1922.

Phil 1111.7   Gomperz, T. Griechische Denker. 4. Aufl. Berlin, 1922-31. 3v.

Phil 8407.15   Gordon, Kate. Esthetics. N.Y., 1922.

Phil 3488.13   Goretti, Cesare. Il carattere formale della filosofia giuridica Kantiana. Milano, 1922.

Phil 8407.34   Gornfel'd, A.G. Puti tvorchestva. Peterburg, 1922.

Phil 8586.23   Gould, Gerald. The helping hand. London, 1922.

Phil 7069.22.11   Grabinski, B. Spuk und Geistererscheinungen oder was sonst? 2. Aufl. Hildesheim, 1922.

Phil 6956.6   Grant-Smith, Rachel. The experiences of an asylum patient. London, 1922.

Phil 5722.20   Grau, Kurt Joachim. Bewusstsein, Unbewusstes, Unterbewusstes. München, 1922.

Phil 9346.10A   Gray, Arthur Herbert. Men, women and God. N.Y., 1922.

Phil 5816.10   Griffith, C.R. An historical survey of vestibular equilibration. Urbana, 1922.

Phil 8586.27   Grimm, die zwei Wege im religiösen Denken. Göttingen, 1922.

Phil 8586.25   Grundler, O. Elemente zu einer religionsphilosophie auf Phänomenonlogischer Grundlage. Kempten, 1922.

Phil 2406.2   Gunn, J.A. Modern French philosophy. London, 1922.

Phil 2406.2.2   Gunn, J.A. Modern French philosophy. N.Y., 1922.

Phil 3246.202   Gurwitsch, G. Die Einheit der Fichteschen Philosophie. Berlin, 1922.

Phil 1706.5   Guttler, C. Einführung in die Geschichte der neueren Philosophie des Auslandes. München, 1922.

Phil 3808.86.3   Gwinner, W. Arthur Schopenhauer. Leipzig, 1922.

Phil 338.10.5   Haldane, R.B. The philosophy of humanism. New Haven, 1922.

Phil 338.10.4   Haldane, R.B. Le regne de la relativité. Paris, 1922.

Phil 6117.34   Han, S.J. The problem of mind and body. n.p., 1922.

Phil 2070.92   Hansen, V. William James og hans breve. Stockholm, 1922.

Phil 8587.34.2   Hauter, Charles. Religion et réalité. Thèse. Strasbourg, 1922.

Phil 3640.183   Havenstein, M. Nietzsche als Erzieher. Berlin, 1922.

Phil 3640.213   Heckel, K. Nietzsche: sein Leben und seine Lehre. Leipzig, 1922.

Phil 3640.213.5   Heckel, K. Nietzsche: sein Leben und seine Lehre. Leipzig, 1922.

Phil 288.3   Heermance, E.L. Chaos or cosmos? N.Y., 1922.

Phil 1707.8   Heimsoeth, H. Die sechs grossen Themen der abendländischen Metaphysik. Berlin, 1922.

Phil 7069.22.12   Hein, Rudolf. Der Fluidalkörper des Menschen...okkulten Erscheinungen. Leipzig, 1922.

Phil 7069.22.14   Hellberg, E. Telepathie. Prien, 1922.

Phil 1512.7   Hessen, John. Patristische und scholastische Philosophie. Breslau, 1922.

Phil 9347.11.2   Hicks, S. Difficulties; an attempt to help. London, 1922.

Phil 3640.165   Hildebrandt, K. Nietzsches Weltkampf mit Sokrates und Plato. Dresden, 1922.

Phil 3450.25   Hiller, Kurt. Der Aufbruch zum Paradies; Sätze. München, 1922.

Phil 8882.110   Hirsch, Maximilian. Das Problem der Vernunftherrschaft.

Phil 338.17   Höffding, H. Der Relationsbegriff. Leipzig, 1922.

Phil 5047.14.10   Höfler, Alois. Logik. 2e Aufl. Wien, 1922.

Phil 4803.454.41   Hoene-Wroński, Józef Maria. Prolegomena do mesjanizmu. Lwów, 1922-25. 3v.

Phil 630.5.7   Holt, E.B. The new realism. N.Y., 1922.

Chronological Listing

Phil 8587.28.5   Hoppe, Edmund. Glauben und Wissen. 2. Aufl. Gütersloh, 1922.

Phil 530.20.53   Hornstein, X. de. Les grands mystiques allemands du XIVe siècle. Lucerne, 1922.

Phil 930.28A   Hu, Suh. Development of logical method in China. Shanghai, 1922.

Phil 182.106.5   Huch, Ricarda. Vom Wesen des Menschen; Natur und Geist. 3. Aufl. Prein, 1922.

Phil 8632.1.12   Hudson, T.J. A scientific demonstration...future life. 12th ed. Chicago, 1922.

Phil 3549.2.96   Hupfeld, R. Graf Hermann Keyserling. Bonn, 1922.

Phil 5248.2.5   Ingenieros, J. Prinzipien der biologischen Psychologie. Leipzig, 1922.

Phil 8615.21   Jacobs, Leo. Three types of practical ethical movements. N.Y., 1922.

Phil 2270.133   Jaeger, Max. Herbert Spencer's Prinzipien der Ethik. Hamburg, 1922.

Phil 4710.4.10   Jakovenko, B. Ocherki russkoi filosofii. Berlin, 1922.

Phil 184.3.41   James, W. On the vital reserves. N.Y., 1922.

Phil 184.3.16.5   James, W. Pragmatism, a new name. N.Y., 1922.

Phil 525.58   Janentzky, C. Mystik und Rationalismus. München, 1922.

Phil 6319.6   Jelliffe, S.E. Psychoanalysis and the drama. N.Y., 1922.

Phil 290.2.3   Jellinek, K. Das Weltengeheimnis. Stuttgart, 1922.

Phil 3665.3.80   Jentgens, Gerhard. Der philosophische Entwicklungsgang des Johannes Neeb 1767-1843. Düsseldorf, 1922.

Phil 7069.22.30   Jesus' teachings; by Shakespeare's spirit. N.Y., 1922.

Phil 630.19.7   Joad, Cyril Edwin. Common sense theology. London, 1922.

Phil 5249.14   Johanson, A.M. Influence of incentive and punishment upon reaction-time. N.Y., 1922.

Phil 8589.12   Jones, Henry. A faith that enquires. N.Y., 1922.

Phil 5819.3.5   Josey, Charles C. The social philosophy of instinct. N.Y., 1922.

Phil 6319.1.5.5   Jung, C.G. Collected papers on analytical psychology. London, 1922.

Phil 5820.2.5   Kafka, Gustav. Handbuch der vergleichenden Psychologie. München, 1922. 3v.

Phil 185.23   Kanovitch, A. The will to beauty. N.Y., 1922.

Phil 3480.40.16   Kant, Immanuel. Anthropologie in pragmatischer Hinsicht. 6. Aufl. Leipzig, 1922.

Phil 3480.90   Kant, Immanuel. Briefwechsel. Leipzig, 1922.

Phil 3480.14.5   Kant, Immanuel. Gesammelte Schriften. Bd.X-XII. Berlin, 1922. 3v.

Phil 3480.45.17   Kant, Immanuel. Kritik der praktischen Vernunft als Prüfung der tätigen Vernunft. 3. Aufl. Lübeck, 1922.

Phil 3480.30.25   Kant, Immanuel. Kritik der reinen Vernunft. 12. Aufl. Leipzig, 1922.

Phil 3480.50.15   Kant, Immanuel. Kritik der Urtheilskraft. 5. Aufl. Leipzig, 1922.

Phil 3480.28.17   Kant, Immanuel. Schriften zur Naturphilosophie. 3. Aufl. Leipzig, 1922. 3v.

Phil 3480.86.5   Kant, Immanuel. Der Streit der Fakultäten. Leipzig, 1922.

Phil 3480.18.9   Kant, Immanuel. Vermischte Schriften. Leipzig, 1922.

Phil 6020.4   Kassner, Rudolf. Die Grundlagen der Psysiognomik. Leipzig, 1922.

Phil 974.3.118   Kaufmann, G. Fruits of anthroposophy. London, 1922.

Phil 3830.6   Kellermann, B. Die Ethik Spinozas über Gott und Geist. Berlin, 1922.

Phil 5655.4   Kenneth, J.H. Osmics; the science of smell. Edinburgh, 1922.

Phil 185.35.2   Keyserling, H. Philosophie als Kunst. 2. Aufl. Darmstadt, 1922.

Phil 341.14   Keyserling, H. Graf von. Schöpferische Erkenntnis. Darmstadt, 1922.

Phil 5820.3   Kindermann, H. Lola, or The thought and speech of animals. London, 1922.

Phil 6120.12   King, D.M. Nerves and personal power. N.Y., 1922.

Phil 2340.8.80   Kingston, Ontario. Queen's University. Faculty of Arts. Philosophical essays presented to John Watson. Kingston, 1922.

Phil 1115.3   Kinkel, Walter. Geschichte der Philosophie von Sokrates bis Aristoteles. Berlin, 1922.

Phil 185.26   Koppelmann, W. Weltanschauungsfragen. 2e Aufl. Berlin, 1922.

Phil 2520.161.5   Koyré, A. Essai sur l'idée de Dieu...chez Descartes. Paris, 1922.

Phil 8080.24   Kreis, Friedrich. Die Autonomie des Ästhetischen in der neuren Philosophie. Tübingen, 1922.

Phil 4809.498.30   Krejčí, František. Pozitivní etika jakožto mravanka na základě přirozeném. Praha, 1922.

Phil 6120.8   Kretschmer, E. Körperbau und Charakter. 3. Aufl. Berlin, 1922.

Phil 3492.13.6   Kronenberg, M. Kant; sein Leben und sein Lehre. 6. Aufl. München, 1922.

Phil 5250.2.9   Külpe, Oswald. Vorlesungen über Psychologie. 2. Aufl. Leipzig, 1922.

Phil 8591.27.5   Laberthonniere, Lucien. Il realismo cristiano e l'idealismo greco. Firenze, 1922.

Phil 8886.35   Laing, B.M. A study in moral problems. London, 1922.

Phil 8633.1.22   Lake, Kirsopp. Immortality and the modern mind. Cambridge, 1922.

Phil 8633.1.22.3   Lake, Kirsopp. Immortality and the modern mind. Cambridge, 1922.

Phil 8430.18   Lalo, C. L'art et la morale. Paris, 1922.

Phil 3493.11   Landtman, G. Immanuel Kant. Stockholm, 1922.

Phil 5400.50.20A   Lange, C.G. The emotions. Baltimore, 1922.

Phil 2805.185   Langenskjold, Agnes. Blaise Pascal. Uppsala, 1922.

Phil 3425.231   Leese, Kurt. Die Geschichtsphilosophie Hegels. Berlin, 1922.

Phil 186.36.5   Lehmann, R. Lehrbuch der philosophischen Propädeutik. 5. Aufl. Leipzig, 1922.

Phil 1116.4   Leisegang, H. Griechische Philosophie von Thales bis Platon. Breslau, 1922.

X Cg   Phil 3246.92.5   Léon, Xavier. Fichte et son temps. Paris, 1922-24. 2v.

Phil 1811.2.5   Leroux, E. Bibliographie méthodique du pragmatisme américain. Thèse. n.p., 1922.

Phil 1811.2.2   Leroux, E. Le pragmatisme américain et anglais. Thèse. Paris, 1922.

Phil 1870.97   Levi, Adolfo. La filosofia di Giorgio Berkeley. Torino, 1922.

Phil 9400.4A   Lionberger, I.H. The felicities of sixty. Boston, 1922.

Phil 2475.1.206   Luce, A.A. Bergson's doctrine of intuition. London, 1922.

Phil 8886.34   Lynch, Arthur. Ethics, an exposition of principles. London, 1922.

Phil 187.57   McCarty, R.J. An essay in practical philosophy: relations of wisdom and purpose. Kansas City, Mo., 1922.

Phil 5252.23.5   MacDougall, R. The general problems of psychology. N.Y., 1922.

Phil 8592.32   McGiffert, A.C. The rise of modern religous ideas. N.Y., 1922.

Phil 665.40   Mackenzie, J.N. Landseer. The universal medium; a new interpretation of the soul. London, 1922.

Phil 8837.8   McKenzie, John. Hindu ethics. London, 1922.

Phil 7140.116.50   Macnaghten, H. Emile Coué, the man and his work. N.Y., 1922.

Phil 8887.54   McNair, G.H. Timely lessons on today's living. Newport, Vt., 1922.

Phil 3425.100.2   McTaggart, John McTaggart Ellis. Studies in the Hegelian dialectic. 2. ed. Cambridge, 1922.

Phil 5252.158   Madden, Edward Harry. Philosophical problems of psychology. N.Y., 1922.

Phil 293.10.2   Maillard, Louis. Quand la lumiére fut. Les cosmogonies anciennes...modernes. Paris, 1922-23. 2v.

Phil 2805.176   Maire, Albert. Essai sur la psychologie de Blaise Pascal. Paris, 1922.

Phil 1750.11.15   Maitra, S.K. The neo-romantic movement in contemporary philosophy. Thesis. Calcutta, 1922.

Phil 2733.36.5   Malebranche, Nicolas. Entretiens sur la métaphysique. v.1-2. Paris, 1922.

Phil 2733.65   Malebranche, Nicolas. Traité de l'amour de Dieu. Paris, 1922.

Phil 525.68   Manacarda, A. Verso una nuova mistica. Bologna, 1922.

Phil 187.44.5   Mann, William E. The truth of things. Boston, 1922.

Phil 4060.1.81   Marchesini, G. Roberto Ardigo, l'uomo e l'umanista. Firenze, 1922.

Phil 9530.25.5   Marden, Orison S. Prosperity, how to attract it. N.Y., 1922.

Phil 343.8   Maréchal, J. Le point de départ de la métaphysique. v.1-5. Bruges, 1922-47. 3v.

Phil 2750.11.84   Maritain, Jacques. Antimoderne. Paris, 1922.

Phil 5762.13   Martin, Alfred H. An experimental study of the factors and types of voluntary choice. N.Y., 1922.

Phil 4170.4.31   Masci, F. Pensiero e conoscenza. Torino, 1922.

Phil 8667.25   Mauthner, F. Der Atheismus und seine Geschichte im Abendlande. Stuttgart, 1922-23. 4v.

Phil 3832.5.7   Mauthner, Fritz. Spinoza. 16. Aufl. Dresden, 1922.

Phil 3832.10   Meijer, W. Spinozana 1897-1922. Heidelberg, 1922.

Phil 1117.5   Melli, G. La filosofia greca. Firenze, 1922.

Phil 3494.21   Menzel, A. Kants Kritik der reinen Vernunft. Berlin, 1922.

Phil 3640.162   Messer, August. Erläuterungen zu Nietzsches Zarathustra. Stuttgart, 1922.

Phil 6122.41   Micklem, E.R. Miracles and the new psychology. Oxford, 1922.

Phil 7069.22.17   Milburn, L.M. The classic of spiritism. N.Y., 1922.

Phil 6322.6.5   Mitchell, T.W. Medical psychology and psychological research. London, 1922.

Phil 5052.24.6   Mitra, A.C. The principles of logic deductive and inductive. Calcutta, 1922. 2v.

Phil 270.31   Mokrzycki, G. Relativisierung des Kausalitätsbegriffes. Leipzig, 1922.

Phil 5252.48   Montet, C. de. Les problemes fondamentaux de la psychologie medical. Berne, 1922.

Phil 5252.49   Montet, C. de. Psychologie et development de l'enfance à la vieillesse. Berne, 1922.

Phil 3012.3   Moog, Willy. Die deutsche Philosophie des 20. Jahrhunderts. Stuttgart, 1922.

Phil 187.59   Moore, G.E. Philosophical studies. London, 1922.

NEDL Phil 8887.21.2   Moore, George Edward. Principia ethica. Cambridge, Eng., 1922.

Phil 8887.21.2   Moore, George Edward. Principia ethica. Cambridge, Eng., 1922.

Phil 343.11   Müller-Freienfels, R. Irrationalismus. Leipzig, 1922.

Phil 2150.6.80   Münsterberg, M. Hugo Münsterberg, his life and work. N.Y., 1922.

Phil 400.45   Mukerji, N.C. The ethical and religious philosophy of idealism. Allahabad, 1922.

Phil 735.19   Mutius, Gerhard von. Gedanke und Erlebnis; Umriss einer Philosophie des Wertes. Darmstadt, 1922.

Phil 5374.31.5   Nasgaard, S. Bevidsthedens form. Kóbenhavn, 1922.

Phil 1133.16.5   Nestle, W. Die Sokratiker. Jena, 1922.

Phil 5435.5   Nicolardot, F. Habitude ou train? Paris, 1922.

Phil 5823.1   Nicolaÿ, Fernand. L'âme et l'instinct; l'homme et l'animal. Paris, 1922.

Phil 7069.22.45   Nielsson, H. Kirken og den psykiske Forskning. Kóbenhavn, 1922.

Phil 8888.7   Nordau, Max. Morals and the evolution of man. London, 1922.

Phil 672.123   Nys, Désiré. La notion d'espace. Bruxelles, 1922.

Phil 8415.5A   Ogden, C.K. The foundations of aesthetics. London, 1922. 2v.

Phil 4762.2.90   Ognev, A.I. Lev Mikhailovich Lopatin. Petrograd, 1922.

Phil 1020.14A   O'Leary, DeLacy. Arabic thought and its place in history. London, 1922.

Phil 8594.8   Ormond, A.T. The philosophy of religion. Princeton, N.J., 1922.

Phil 190.20.8   Papini, Giovanni. L'altra metà. 4a ed. Firenze, 1922.

Phil 1715.2.5   Papini, Giovanni. Le crepuscule des philosophes. Paris, 1922.

Phil 2805.32.30   Pascal, Blaise. Les lettres de Blaise Pascal. Paris, 1922.

Phil 6125.14   Paton, Stewart. Signs of sanity and the principles of mental hygiene. N.Y., 1922.

Phil 5374.36   Pavese, R. Il meccanismo della coscienza. Milano, 1922.

Phil 5545.155   Pear, T.H. Remembering and forgetting. London, 1922.

Phil 5645.38   Peddie, William. Colour vision. London, 1922.

Phil 6125.22   Perin, George L. Self healing simplified. N.Y., 1922.

Phil 1715.3.8A   Perry, R.B. The present conflict of ideals. N.Y., 1922.

Phil 4620.1   Péturss, Helgi. Nýall Nokkur íslenzk drög til heimsfraeð og liffraeð Reykjavík, 1922.

Phil 5374.154   Peucesco, M.G. Le mécanisme du courant de la conscience. Paris, 1922.

Phil 6325.1.10   Pfister, Oskar. Psycho-analysis in the service of education. London, 1922.

Phil 672.33   Phalén, Adolf K. Über die Relativität der Raum- und Zeitbestimmungen. Uppsala, 1922.

Phil 5722.9   Pierce, Frederick. Our unconscious mind and how to use it. N.Y., 1922.

Phil 5640.125.10   Pikler, Gyula. Theorie der Empfindungsqualität als Abbildes des Reizes. Leipzig, 1922.

Phil 7069.17.31.15   Piper, Otto. Der Spuk. 2. Aufl. München, 1922.

Chronological Listing

Phil 8416.11.15 Plekhanov, Georgii Valentinovich. Iskusstvo i obshchestvennaia zhizn'. Moskva, 1922.

Phil 672.132 Poppovich, N.M. Die Lehre vom diskreten Raum in der neueren Philosophie. Wien, 1922.

Phil 6750.222 Porteus, S.D. Studies in mental deviations. Vineland, 1922.

Phil 190.38 Prandtl, Antonin. Einführung in die Philosophie. Leipzig, 1922.

Phil 6125.13 Pratt, J.B. Matter and spirit. N.Y., 1922.

Phil 6965.18 Prinzhorn, H. Bildnerei der Geisteskranken. Berlin, 1922.

Phil 5255.17 Le procès de l'intelligence. Paris, 1922.

Phil 5627.133 Pyon, T.W. Psychology of the Christian life. N.Y., 1922.

Phil 817.11 Rauschenberger, W. Das philosophische Genie und seine Rasseabstammung. Frankfurt, 1922.

Phil 5425.32 Rauschenberger, W. Das Talent und das Genie. Frankfurt, 1922.

Phil 270.32 Rauschenberger, W. Über Identität und Kausalität. Leipzig, 1922.

Phil 2115.132 Reininger, R. Locke, Berkeley, Hume. München, 1922.

Phil 3640.186 Reininger, R. Nietzsches Kampf um den Sinn des Lebens. Wien, 1922.

Phil 8892.35 Renard, G. Des sciences physiques aux sciences morales. Paris, 1922.

Phil 192.46 Richard, R.P. Le probabilisme moral et la philosophie. Paris, 1922.

Phil 192.36.5 Richardson, C.A. The supremacy of spirit. London, 1922.

Phil 7069.22.20 Richet, Charles R. Traité de métapsychique. Paris, 1922.

Phil 8597.28 Richmond, W. Philosophy and the Christian experience. Oxford, 1922.

Phil 1750.122.2 Rickert, H. Die Philosophie des Lebens. Tübingen, 1922.

Phil 6127.18.10 Riggs, A.F. Just nerves. Boston, 1922.

Phil 5257.36 Rignano, E. Come funziona la nostra intelligenza. Bologna, 1922.

Phil 4372.1.84 Rivari, Enrico. La sapienza psicologica e pedagogica di Giovanni L. Vives. Bologna, 1922.

Phil 1905.11.80 Robinson, Sanford. John Bascom, prophet. N.Y., 1922.

Phil 8892.25 Rogers, A.K. The theory of ethics. N.Y., 1922.

Phil 5257.32 Rogers, M.C. Adenoids and diseased tonsils; their effect on general intelligence. N.Y., 1922.

Phil 192.54 Rohrbaugh, L.G. The energy concept. Iowa City?, 1922.

Phil 3499.16 Roretz, Karl. Zur Analyse von Kants Philosoph des organischen. Wien, 1922.

Phil 9495.123 Royden, A.M. Sex and common-sense. N.Y., 1922.

Phil 5257.35 Ruddell, G.A.R. Some things that matter. London, 1922.

Phil 8892.28 Rueff, Jacques. Des sciences physiques aux sciences morales. Paris, 1922.

Phil 193.91.2 Saitschick, R. Der Mensch und sein Ziel. 2. Aufl. München, 1922.

Phil 1865.171 Sánchez-Rivera de la Lastra, Juan. El utilitarismo; estudio de las doctrinas de Jeremías Bentham. Madrid, 1922.

Phil 5590.23.2 Sawicki, Franz. Das Ideal der Persönlichkeit. 2. Aufl. Paderborn, 1922.

Phil 6688.19 Schilder, Paul. Über das Wesen der Hypnose. 2. Aufl. Berlin, 1922.

Phil 8643.27 Schleich, Carl L. Bewusstsein und Unsterblichkeit. Berlin, 1922.

Phil 6615.16 Schleich, Carl Ludwig. Gedankenmacht und Hysterie. Berlin, 1922.

Phil 3805.76.5 Schleiermacher, Friedrich. Schleiermacher als Mensch...Briefe. Gotha, 1922. 2v.

Phil 974.3.55 Schmidt, J.W. Recht und Unrecht der Anthroposophie. Göttingen, 1922.

Phil 974.3.75 Schomerus, H.W. Die Anthroposophie Steiners und Indien. Leipzig, 1922.

Phil 3500.46 Schreiber, C. Kant und die Gottesbeweise. Dresden, 1922.

Phil 8598.43 Schrempf, C. Gegen den Strom. Stuttgart, 1922. 5v.

Phil 3640.248 Schrempf, Christof. Friedrich Nietzsche. Göttingen, 1922.

Phil 193.105 Schultz, J. Die Philosophie am Scheidewege. Leipzig, 1922.

Phil 672.138 Schultze, A. Ist die Welt vierdimensional? Leipzig, 1922.

Phil 8968.11 Schwellenbach, R. Die Erneuerung des Abendlandes. Berlin, 1922.

Phil 193.66.5 Sellars, Roy Wood. Evolutionary naturalism. Chicago, 1922.

Phil 8643.22 Seth Pringle-Pattison, A. The idea of immortality. Oxford, 1922.

Phil 349.17 Shann, George. The evolution of knowledge. London, 1922.

Phil 193.86 Shearon, William. The hypothesis of the universality of life. St. Louis, 1922.

Phil 8598.84 Sheldon, Henry Clay. The essentials of Christianity. N.Y., 1922.

Phil 4769.4.5 Shpet, Gustav. Ocherk razvitiia russkoi filosofii. Petrograd, 1922.

Phil 8893.11.15 Sidgwick, H. The methods of ethics. London, 1922.

Phil 8843.1.10 Sidgwick, Henry. Prime livee di una storia della morale. Torino, 1922.

Phil 6968.12.9 Sidis, Boris. Nervous ills; their cause and cure. Boston, 1922.

Phil 8419.23 Simmel, Georg. Zur Philosophie der Kunst. Potsdam, 1922.

Phil 400.33.5 Sinclair, May. The new idealism. N.Y., 1922.

Phil 8419.31 Siunerberg, K.A. Iskusstvo i narod; sbornik. Peterburg, 1922.

Phil 5058.28.5 Smith, Henry B. A first book in logic. N.Y., 1922.

Phil 5058.28.17 Smith, Henry B. Foundations of formal logic. Philadelphia, 1922.

Phil 5768.18 Solly, J.R. Free will and determinism. London, 1922.

Phil 4769.1.108 Solove'ev, V.S. I fondamenti spirituali della vita. Bologna, 1922.

Phil 6968.19 Souhard, E.E. The kingdom of evils. N.Y., 1922.

Phil 193.88 Spalding, K.J. Desire and reason. London, 1922.

Phil 3903.3.92 Spickerbaum, P. Das Vaihingersche Als-Ob und die Methode der Formensprache in Religion und Theologie. München, 1922.

Phil 2520.163.5 Spinoza, B. de. Descartes' Prinzipien der Philosophie. Leipzig, 1922.

Phil 3819.45.9 Spinoza, Benedictus de. Abhandlung über die Verbesserung des Verstandes. 4. Aufl. Leipzig, 1922.

Phil 3819.35.26 Spinoza, Benedictus de. Ethics and De intellectus emendatione. London, 1922.

Phil 3819.30.35 Spinoza, Benedictus de. Ethik. 10. Aufl. Leipzig, 1922.

Phil 3819.41.15 Spinoza, Benedictus de. Kurze Abhandlung von Gott dem Menschen und seinen Glück. Leipzig, 1922.

Phil 3819.57 Spinoza, Benedictus de. Spinoza; theologisch-politischen Traktat. 4. Aufl. Leipzig, 1922.

Phil 5058.36 Starcke, Carl N. Formel logik, grundlag for forelaesninger. 2. udg. Kjøbenhavn, 1922.

Phil 978.49.100 Steiner, R. The East in the light of the West. London, 1922.

Phil 978.49.25 Steiner, R. The gates of knowledge. Chicago, Ill., 1922.

Phil 978.49.50 Steiner, R. Der Hüter der Schwelle, Seelenvorgänge in scenischen Bildern. Berlin, 1922.

Phil 978.49.19 Steiner, R. An outline of occult science. Chicago, Ill., 1922.

Phil 978.49.55 Steiner, R. Der Seelen Erwachen. Berlin, 1922.

Phil 978.49 Steiner, R. Theosophie. Stuttgart, 1922.

Phil 6328.2.10 Stekel, Wilhelm. Impulshandlungen. Berlin, 1922.

Phil 7082.38.2 Stekel, Wilhelm. Die Sprache des Traumes. 2e Aufl. München, 1922.

Phil 8598.67 Stepanov, I. Mysli o religii. Moskva, 1922.

Phil 5258.97.5 Stephen, Henry. Elements of analytical psychology. 5th. ed. Calcutta, 1922.

Phil 2475.1.262 Stephen, Karin. The misuse of mind. N.Y., 1922.

Phil 2475.1.205 Stephen, Karin. The misuse of the mind. London, 1922.

Phil 1718.14 Stolzle, R. Das Problem des Lebens in der heutigen Philosophie. Paderborn, 1922.

Phil 193.83 Strong, C.A. The wisdom of the beasts. Boston, 1922.

Phil 5258.69 Sullivan, E.T. Mood in relation to performance. N.Y., 1922.

Phil 6128.54 Swindle, Percy Ford. Quantum reactions and associations; a theory of physical and physiological units or quanta. Boston, 1922.

Phil 194.27 Tarner, George E. Some remarks on the axioms and postulates of athetic philosophy. Cambridge, 1922.

Phil 7069.22.40 Tenhaeff, W.H.C. Supernormale vermogens. Amsterdam, 1922.

Phil 7140.118.2 Thamiry, E. De l'influence: étude psychologique, métaphysique, pédagogique. Lille, 1922.

Phil 2340.5.80 Thompson, C.G. The ethics of William Wollaston. Diss. Boston, 1922.

Phil 104.2.3 Thornmeyer, P. Philosophisches Wörterbuch. 3e Aufl. Leipzig, 1922.

Phil 575.130 Tietzen, Hermann. Die menschliche Persönlichkeit in Anlehnung an Zinzendorfsche Gedanken. Stuttgart, 1922.

Phil 5374.30 Tilby, A Wyatt. The evolution of consciousness. London, 1922.

Phil 978.16.5 Tingley, K.A. (Mrs.). Theosophy; the path of the mystic. 2d ed. Point Loma, Calif., 1922.

Phil 5259.5.16 Titchener, E.B. Manuel de psychologie. Paris, 1922.

Phil 2419.4 La tradition philosophique et la pensée française. Paris, 1922.

Phil 6750.18.12 Tredgold, A.F. Mental deficiency (Amentia). 4.ed. N.Y., 1922.

Phil 8599.19.15 Troeltsch, Ernst. Zur religiösen Lage. 2. Aufl. Tübingen, 1922.

Phil 5643.69 Troland, L.T. The present status of visual science. Washington, 1922.

Phil 300.4 Trubetskoi, E.N. Smysl' zhizni. Berlin, 1922.

Phil 5627.60.7 Underhill, E. The life of the spirit and the life of today. London, 1922.

Phil 8612.15 Unger, Rudolf. Herder, Novalis und Kleist. Frankfurt, 1922.

Phil 672.122 Uspenskii, P.D. Tertium organum. 2nd American ed. N.Y., 1922.

Phil 3503.1.2 Vaihinger, H. Kommentar zu Kants Kritik der reinen Vernunft. 2. Aufl. Stuttgart, 1922. 2v.

Phil 4650.1.69 Vannérus, Allen. Etiska tankegångar. Stockholm, 1922.

Phil 575.127 Verweyen, J.M. Der Edelmensch und seine Werte. 2e Aufl. München, 1922.

Phil 8896.4.5 Vidari, Giovanni. Elementi di etica. 5. ed. Milano, 1922.

Phil 8422.7.5 Vischer, F.T. Asthetik; oder, Wissenschaft des Schönen. München, 1922-23. 6v.

Phil 196.19 Vivante, L. Della intelligenza nell'espressione. Roma, 1922.

Phil 8601.15 Vogeler, H. Friede. Bremen, 1922.

Phil 3503.4.25 Vorländer, K. Immanuel Kant und sein Einfluss auf der deutsche Denken. 2. Aufl. Bielefeld, 1922.

Phil 5262.26 Wada, Tomi. An experimental study of hunger in its relation to activity. N.Y., 1922.

Phil 2880.1.82.5 Waite, Arthur E. Saint-Martin; the French mystic. London, 1922.

Phil 8430.25 Walston, C. Harmonism and conscious evolution. London, 1922.

Phil 3504.22A Ward, James. A study of Kant. Cambridge, Eng., 1922.

Phil 3504.20.5 Warda, Arthur. Immanuel Kants Bücher. Berlin, 1922.

Phil 5262.20.5 Warren, H.C. Elements of human psychology. Boston, 1922.

Phil 7060.255 Wasielewski, W. Telepathie und Hellsehen. Halle, 1922.

Phil 197.35 Webster, Florence. The nature of life. N.Y., 1922.

Phil 3640.163.2 Weichelt, Hans. Zarathustrakommentar. 2. Aufl. Leipzig, 1922.

Phil 9362.15.5 Weininger, Otto. Gedanken über Geschlechtsprobleme. Berlin, 1922.

Phil 353.10 Weinmann, R. Philosophie, Welt und Wirklichkeit. München, 1922.

Phil 6332.2.9 Wells, F.L. Mental adjustments. N.Y., 1922.

Phil 2138.108 Wentscher, Ela. Das Problem des Empirismus, dargestellt an John Stuart Mill. Bonn, 1922.

Phil 6972.12 White, H.W. Demonism verified and analyzed. Shanghai, 1922.

Phil 8677.16 Whitehead, George. The case against theism. London, 1922.

Phil 5772.9 Wichmann, O. Wille und Freiheit. München, 1922.

Phil 8423.12 Wieckberg, W. Grundwissenschaftliche Unterlage der Kunstwissenschaft. Charlottenburg, 1922.

Phil 6132.21 Winkler, H. Die Monotonie der Arbeit. Leipzig, 1922.

Phil 8897.70 Winternitz, M. Religion und Moral. Prag, 1922.

Phil 8897.57 Wintzer, Wilhelm. Der Sinn und Zweck des Lebens. Stuttgart, 1922.

Phil 3925.16.41 Wittgenstein, Ludwig. Tractatus logico-philosophicus. London, 1922.

Phil 960.125 Woodroffe, J.G. The world as power, power as life. Madras, 1922.

Phil 960.127 Woodroffe, J.G. The world as power; power as mind. Madras, 1922.

Phil 8602.32 Wright, William K. A student's philosophy of religion. London, 1922.

Phil 3640.191 Würzbach, F. Dionysos. 2e Aufl. München, 1922.

Phil 1527.1.17 Wulf, M. de. Mediaeval philosophy illustrated from the system of Thomas Aquinas. Cambridge, 1922.

Phil 1527.1.15 Wulf, M. de. Philosophy and civilization in the Middle Ages. Princeton, 1922.

Phil 1527.1.16 Wulf, M. de. Philosophy and civilization in the Middle Ages. Princeton, 1922-24.

Chronological Listing

1922 - cont.

Phil 7069.22.91   Wulff, E. Okkultismus. Dresden, 1922.
Phil 1130.5.9   Zeller, Eduard. Outlines of history of Greek philosophy. London, 1922.
Phil 3507.3   Zickendraht, K. Kants Gedanken über Krieg und Frieden. Tübingen, 1922.
Phil 200.6.3   Ziegler, L. Gestaltwandel der Götter. 3. Aufl. Darmstadt, 1922. 2v.
Phil 306.4   Ziehen, T. Grundlagen der Naturphilosophie. Leipzig, 1922.
Phil 2138.89.5   Zuccante, G. Giovanni Stuart Mill e l'utilitarismo. Firenze, 1922.

1923

Phil 175.29   Abbagnano, N. Le sorgenti irrazionali del pensiero. Genova, 1923.
Phil 525.34   Addison, C.M. What is mysticism. N.Y., 1923.
Phil 3210.85   Adolph, H. Die Weltanschauung G.T. Fechners. Stuttgart, 1923.
Phil 4513.1.40   Ahlberg, A. Det ondas problem. Stockholm, 1923.
Phil 5240.28   Ahlenstiehl, H. Über die Stellung der Psychologie im Stammbaum der Wissenschaften. Berlin, 1923.
Phil 3820.5   Alexander, B. Spinoza. München, 1923.
Phil 6110.3.2   Alexander, F.M. Constructive conscious control of the individual. N.Y., 1923.
Phil 175.14.5   Alexander, H.B. Nature and human nature. Chicago, 1923.
Phil 8950.4   Anderson, L.D. The business of living. N.Y., 1923.
Phil 3482.5.5   Apel, Max. Kommentar zu Kants Prologomena. Leipzig, 1923.
Phil 4065.106   Atanassievitch, K. Atanasijević, Ksenija, 1894. Belgrade, 1923.
Phil 8580.16.10   Atkins, Gaius G. Modern religious cults. N.Y., 1923.
NEDL Phil 3483.28   Baeumler, Alfred. Kant's Kritik der Urteilskraft. Halle, 1923.
Phil 1900.88   Baker, A.E. Bishop Butler. London, 1923.
Phil 8656.13.5   Balfour, A.J.B. Theism and thought. London, 1923.
Phil 176.91   Bardonnet, L. L'univers-organisme. Paris, 1923. 4v.
Phil 2805.110.5   Barrès, Maurice. L'angoisse de Pascal, suivi d'une étude sur les deux maisons de Pascal à Clermont-Ferrand. Paris, 1923.
Phil 5645.4.27   Barthel, Ernst. Goethes Relativitätstheorie der Farbe. Bonn, 1923.
Phil 720.21   Bauch, Bruno. Wahrheit, Wert und Wirklichkeit. Leipzig, 1923.
Phil 7140.116.51   Baudouin, C. Emile Coué and his life-work. N.Y., 1923.
Phil 5241.57   Baudouin, C. The power within us. N.Y., 1923.
Phil 176.114   Bauer, G.F. Die Welt als Subjekt-Objekt. Berlin, 1923.
Phil 5627.15.9   Begbie, H. More twice-born men. N.Y., 1923.
Phil 2885.111   Begouëm, Henry. Quelques souvenirs sur H. Taine. Toulouse, 1923.
Phil 8876.55.7   Bennett, Arnold. How to make the best of life. N.Y., 1923.
Phil 525.63   Bennett, C.A. A philosophical study of mysticism. New Haven, 1923.
Phil 5241.58   Bennett, H.E. Psychology and self-development. Boston, 1923.
Phil 4710.66   Berdiaev, N.A. Sofiia; problemy dukhovnoi kul'tury i religioznoi filosofii. Berlin, 1923-
Phil 2475.1.39   Bergson, Henri. Durée et simultanéité. 2e éd. Paris, 1923.
Phil 1870.40.45   Berkeley, G. Tratto dei principii della cognoscenza umana e tre dialogui. Bari, 1923.
Phil 5041.44   Beysens, J.T. Logica of Denkleer. 3e druk. Hilversum, 1923?
Phil 5850.135   Bingham, W.V. Psychology applied. n.p., 1923.
Phil 6311.10   Birnbaum, Karl. Der Aufbau der Psychose. Berlin, 1923.
Phil 9070.23   Bisch, Louis Edward. The conquest of self. Garden City, 1923.
Phil 978.5.27   Blavatsky, H.P. The key to theosophy. 4th ed. Point Loma, Calif., 1923.
Phil 176.69.5   Bloch, Ernst. Tübinger Einleitung in die Philosophie. Berlin, 1923.
Phil 2800.1.88   Blondel, M. Léon Ollé-Laprune. Paris, 1923.
Phil 3110.28   Böhme, J. Schriften Jakob Böhme. Leipzig, 1923.
Phil 8876.68   Bohlin, F. Das Grundproblem der Ethik. Uppsala, 1923.
Phil 6311.9   Bohn, W. Ein Fall von doppeltem Bewusstsein. Inaug. Diss. Breslau, 1923.
Phil 974.3.20   Boldt, Ernst. Rudolf Steiner: ein kämpfer Gegen seine Zeit. München, 1923.
Phil 974.3.25   Boldt, Ernst. Rudolf Steiner und das Epigonenturn. München, 1923.
Phil 5041.43   Bolland, G.J.P.J. G.J.P.J. Bolland's colleges uitgegeven door Ester van Hunes. Haarlem, 1923.
Phil 8581.55   Bolland, G.J.P.J. Wijsbegeerte van den godsdienst bewerkt naar dictaten. Amsterdam, 1923.
Phil 6311.7   Bopp, L. Modern Psychoanalyse, katholische, beichte und pädagogik. Kempten, 1923.
Phil 5241.24.5A   Bosanquet, B. Three chapters on the nature of the mind. London, 1923.
Phil 4515.34   Boström, C.J. Grundlinien eines philosophischen Systems. Leipzig, 1923.
Phil 1106.11   Boswell, F.P. A primer of Greek thought. Geneva, 1923.
Phil 6311.5.5   Bousfield, Paul. The omnipotent self. London, 1923.
Phil 3625.3.85   Bouvier, Robert. La pensée d'Ernst Mach. Paris, 1923.
Phil 8656.16   Bouyssonie, A. Batailles d'idées sur les problèmes de Dieu, du bien, du vrai. Paris, 1923.
Phil 2490.102   Boyer de Sainte-Suzanne, Raymond de. Essai sur la pensée religieuse d'Auguste Comte. Paris, 1923.
Phil 672.172.5   Bragdon, C.F. A primer of higher space. 2nd ed. N.Y., 1923.
Phil 7069.23.5   Brandt, J.v.W. The red octopus. London, 1923?
Phil 2805.188   Bremond, H. En prière avec Pascal. Paris, 1923.
Phil 9590.11   Brewster, E.T. The understanding of religion. Boston, 1923.
Phil 7069.23.2   Brid, J. Malcolm. My psychic adventures. London, 1923.
Phil 2520.157   Brockdorff, Cay von. Descartes und die Fortbildung der kartesianischen Lehre. München, 1923.
Phil 6671.19.3   Brown, William. Suggestion and mental analysis. 3. ed. London, 1923.
Phil 6111.41   Brown, William. Talks on psychotherapy. London, 1923.
Phil 176.117   Bruhn, Wilhelm. Einführung in das philosophische Denken für Anfanger und Alleinlermende. Leipzig, 1923.
Phil 3425.192   Bruijn, J.C. Hegel's phaenomenologie I-II, proeve van tekstverklaring. Proefschrift. Amsterdam, 1923.
Phil 4065.50.4   Bruno, Giordano. Giordano Bruno von der Ursache dem Prinzip und dem Einen. 4e aufl. Leipzig, 1923.

1923 - cont.

Phil 3821.3.3   Brunschvicg, L. Spinoza, et ses contemporaines. 3. éd. Paris, 1923.
Phil 3120.30.43   Buber, Martin. Ich und Du. Leipzig, 1923.
Phil 3483.18.2   Buchenau, A. Kants Lehre vom kategorischen Imperativ. 2. Aufl. Leipzig, 1923.
Phil 5241.51.2   Bumke, Oswald. Psychologische Vorlesungen für Hörer aller Fakultälen. 2. Aufl. München, 1923.
Phil 7074.20.1   Burke, Jane R. The one way. N.Y., 1923.
Phil 176.88   Burne, C.D. The contact between minds. London, 1923.
Phil 8615.19   Cabot, P. The conversion of a sinner. Boston, 1923.
Phil 1135.20.5   Caird, Edward. The evolution of theology in the Greek philosophers. Glasgow, 1923.
Phil 4115.87.10   Calcaterra, C. Polemica giobertiana. Torino, 1923.
Phil 177.82   Calvet, Adolphe. Le discontinu dans la philosophie et dans les sciences exactes. Paris, 1923.
Phil 5242.21   Campion, George G. Elements in thought and emotion. London, 1923.
Phil 4120.2.90   Carlo, Eugenio di. Cosmo Guastella. Palermo, 1923.
Phil 3552.131   Carlotti, G. Il sistema die Leibniz. Messina, 1923.
Phil 333.5.9   Cassirer, Ernst. Philosophie der symbolischen Formen. Berlin, 1923-29. 3v.
Phil 7069.23.9   Cavanagh, M.R. A strange manuscript. N.Y., 1923.
Phil 4080.14.2   Celesia, Paolo. Opere. v.1-7. Roma, 1923-30. 8v.
Phil 2805.182   Chamaillard, E. Pascal, mondain et amoureux. Paris, 1923.
Phil 8403.23.10   Chartier, Émile. Propos sur l'esthetique. paris, 1923.
Phil 4753.1.30   Chelpanov, G. Vvedenie v filosofiiu. Riga, 1923.
Phil 8582.37   Cherix, Robert B. L'arche d'alliance. 2. éd. Paris, 1923.
Phil 5627.92   Chevalier, J. Pour une science de l'individuel. Paris, 1923.
Phil 177.75   Choisnard, Paul. La loi de relation et l'erreur séparatiste en science et en philosophie. Paris, 1923.
Phil 177.62   Cicala, F.B. Introduzione alla teoria dell'essere le relazioni ontotetiche. Città di Castello, 1923.
Phil 87.1   Clauberg, K.N. Systematisches Wörterbuch der Philosophie. Leipzig, 1923.
Phil 974.2.9   Cleather, A.L. (Mrs.) H.P. Blavatsky as I knew her. Calcutta, 1923.
Phil 974.2.10   Cleather, A.L. (Mrs.) H.P. Blavatsky as I knew her. N.Y., 1923. 3 pam.
Phil 525.59   Clemen, Carl. Die Mystik nach Wesen, Entwicklung und Bedeutung. Bonn, 1923.
Phil 4260.95   Cochery, M. Les grandes lignes de la philosophie historique et juridique de Vico. Paris, 1923.
Phil 8610.923   Cohen, Chapman. Essays in freethinking. Series 1. London, 1923.
Phil 3002.4   Cohn, Jonas. Der deutsche Idealismus. Leipzig, 1923.
Phil 5042.18   Cohn, Jonas. Theorie der Dialektik. Leipzig, 1923.
Phil 5042.15A   Columbia Association in Philosophy. An introduction to reflective thinking. Boston, 1923.
Phil 8877.64   Coudenhove-Kalergi, R.N. Ethik und Hyperethik. Leipzig, 1923.
Phil 8877.64.5   Coudenhove-Kalergi, R.N. Krise der Weltanschauung. Wien, 1923.
Phil 7140.116.7   Coué, Émile. How to practice suggestion and autosuggestion. N.Y., 1923.
Phil 7140.116.5   Coué, Émile. My method. Garden City, 1923.
Phil 477.6.5   Cournot, A.A. Matérialisme, vitalisme, rationalisme. Paris, 1923.
Phil 8692.3.10   Coutts, John. A prospective view of the new age. London, 1923.
Phil 5042.29.5   Creighton, J.E. An introductory logic. 4th ed. N.Y., 1923.
Phil 6060.1.15   Crepieux-Jamin, J. Les éléments de l'écriture descanailles. Paris, 1923.
Phil 4080.3.37   Croce, Benedetto. Breviaire d'esthétique. Paris, 1923.
Phil 177.56   Cunynghame, H. Short talks upon philosophy. London, 1923.
Phil 5242.22   Cuvillier, Armand. ABC de psychologie. Paris, 1923.
Phil 178.48   Dam, Axel. Opdragelsens hovedopgaver. 3. udg. Kobenhavn, 1923.
Phil 178.47   Danmar, W. World cognition. N.Y., 1923.
Phil 284.7   Dario, J.M. Praelectiones cosmologiae. Paris, 1923.
Phil 6750.223   Davies, S.P. Social control of the feebleminded. N.Y., 1923.
Phil 8953.3   Dawbarn, C.Y.C. Applied philosophy. London, 1923.
Phil 9150.23   Dawson, M. Nineteenth century evolution and after. N.Y., 1923.
Phil 2490.103   DeGrange, McQuilkin. The science of individuality. Thesis. Lyon, 1923.
Phil 600.32   Deherme, G. Le positivisme dans l'action. Paris, 1923.
Phil 8583.22   Descamps, E. Le génie des religions. Paris, 1923.
Phil 2520.35.15   Descartes, René. Discours de la méthode. Cambridge, Eng., 1923.
Phil 8404.15   Dessior, Max. Ästhetik und allgemeine Kunstwissenschaft. Stuttgart, 1923.
Phil 5243.25   Dessoir, Max. Vom Diesseits der Seele. Leipzig, 1923.
Phil 978.61.10   Dhopeshwarkar, A.D. First principles of theosophy. 3d ed. Adyar, Madras, 1923.
Phil 3195.6.33   Dilthey, Wilhelm. Briefwechsel zwischen Wilhelm Dilthey und den Grafen Paul York von Watenburg. Halle, 1923.
Phil 3195.6.30   Dilthey, Wilhelm. Gesammelte Schriften. v.1-9,11-12. Leipzig, 1923-36. 11v.
Phil 8828.3   Dittrich, Ottmar. Systeme der moral. Bd. 1-3. Leipzig, 1923-26. 3v.
Phil 7140.120   Dolonne, A. Self healing by autosuggestion. London, 1923.
Phil 7069.22.5   Doyle, Arthur Connan. Our American adventure. N.Y., 1923.
Phil 178.22.2   Driesch, H. Ordnungslehre. Jena, 1923.
Phil 6113.19.3   Driesch, Hans. Leib und Seele. 3. Aufl. Leipzig, 1923.
Phil 9343.11   Drury, Samuel S. Backbone; the development of character. N.Y., 1923.
Phil 6673.14   Dubor, G. de. The mysteries of hypnosis. N.Y., 1923.
Phil 6113.21   Dulley, William. Body, soul and spirit. London, 1923.
Phil 7069.23.6   Dumanjó, L. Daniel. Habana, 1923.
Phil 5243.29   Dumas, George. Traité de psychologie. Paris, 1923. 2v.
Phil 672.128   Eddington, A.S. Raum, Zeit und Schwere. Braunschweig, 1923.
Phil 6674.7.15   Edgerley, W.J. Cultivation of personal magnetism. 11. ed. Meriden, Conn., 1923.
Phil 3004.4   Ehrenberg, Hans. Disputation: drei Bücher vom Deutschen. München, 1923-25. 3v.
Phil 3486.10   Ehrlich, W. Kant und Husserl. Halle, 1923.
Phil 179.17   Ellis, Havelock. The dance of life. Boston, 1923.
Phil 179.17.4   Ellis, Havelock. The dance of life. N.Y., 1923.
Phil 5044.1.3   Erdmann, B. Logik. 3e Aufl. Berlin, 1923.
Phil 672.125   Eriksen, R. Consciousness, life and the fourth dimension. London, 1923.

1923 - cont.

Phil 2805.180	Études sur Pascal. Paris, 1923.
Phil 179.3.32.5	Eucken, R. Erkennen und Leben. Berlin, 1923.
Phil 179.3.65	Eucken, R. Mensch und Welt. 3e Aufl. Leipzig, 1923.
Phil 630.30	Evans, Daniel L. The status of values in new realism. Columbus, 1923.
Phil 8584.11.2	Evans, Robert C.T. Man. What? Whence? Whither? 2. ed. Chatham, 1923.
Phil 5245.25	Farnsworth, B.B. Practical psychology for men and women. N.Y., 1923.
Phil 978.29.15	Farnsworth, E.C. Glimpses of inner truth. Portland, 1923.
Phil 850.13	Faure, J.A. L'Egypte et les présocratiques. Paris, 1923.
Phil 4110.5.33	Ferrari, G. Filosofia della rivoluzione. 2. ed. Milano, 1923.
Phil 978.50	Ferrier, John T. Life's mysteries unveiled. London, 1923.
NEDL Phil 3450.16.90	Festschrift für Paul Hensel Erlangen. Greiz, 1923.
Phil 6115.19	Feuchtwanger, E. Die Funktionen des Stirnhirns. Berlin, 1923.
Phil 3235.126	Feuerbach, Ludwig. Sockrinemia. Moskva, 1923.
Phil 3246.55.12	Fichte, Johann Gottlieb. Addresses in the German nation. Photoreproduction. Chicago, 1923.
Phil 3246.35.12	Fichte, Johann Gottlieb. Männeskans bestammelse. Stockholm, 1923.
Phil 3246.66	Fichte, Johann Gottlieb. Philosophie der Maurerei. Leipzig, 1923.
Phil 6015.1.5	Fosbroke, Gerald Eltac. Character qualities outlined and related. N.Y., 1923.
Phil 5245.27	Foster, William S. Experiments in psychology. N.Y., 1923.
Phil 5245.27.5	Foster, William S. Experiments in psychology. N.Y., 1923.
Phil 4756.1.30	Frank, Semen L. Vvedenie v filosofiiu. Berlin, 1923.
Phil 4756.1.33	Frank, Semen L. Zhivoe znanie. Berlin, 1923.
Phil 6315.2.9	Freud, Sigmund. Cinq leçons sur la psychoanalyse. Paris, 1923.
Phil 6315.2.37.5	Freud, Sigmund. Das Ich und das Es. Leipzig, 1923.
Phil 6315.2.59.3	Freud, Sigmund. Jenseits des Lustprinzips. 3. Aufl. Leipzig, 1923.
Phil 180.38.10	Freyer, Hans. Prometheus: Ideen zur Philosophie der Kultur. Jena, 1923.
Phil 180.38	Freyer, Hans. Theorie des objektiven Geistes. Leipzig, 1923.
Phil 1133.20A	Fuller, Benjamin A.G. History of Greek philosophy. N.Y., 1923. 3v.
Phil 4073.95	Gardner, E.G. Tommaso Campanella and his poetry. Oxford, 1923.
Phil 1020.9.3	Gauthier, L. Introduction à l'étude de la philosophie musulmane. Paris, 1923.
Phil 6116.18	Gehring, J.G. The hope of the variant. N.Y., 1923.
Phil 5246.25.5	Gemelli, Agostino. Nuovo orizzonti della psicologia sperimentale. 2. ed. Milano, 1923.
Phil 4006.2.2	Gentile, G. I problemi della scolastica e il pensiero italiano. 2a ed. Bari, 1923.
Phil 3425.209.5	Gentile, G. La riforma della dialettica Hegeliana. 2a ed. Messina, 1923.
Phil 4006.2.9	Gentile, G. Studi sul rinascimento. Firenze, 1923.
Phil 8586.30	Gentile, P. Sommario d'un filosofia della religione. Bari, 1923.
Phil 4710.145	Gershenzon, Mikhail O. Istoriia molodoi Rossii. Moskva, 1923.
Phil 181.39.5	Geyser, Joseph. Einige Hauptprobleme der Metaphysik. Freiburg, 1923.
Phil 365.34.5	Ghose, Aurobinclo. Evolution. 2. ed. Calcutta, 1923.
Phil 8881.50	Gibson, R.W. The morality of nature. N.Y., 1923.
Phil 5246.23.9	Giese, Fritz. Psychotechnisches Praktikum. Halle, 1923.
Phil 4115.98	Gioberti, V. Una lettera inedita a Taparelli d'Azeglio. Roma, 1923.
Phil 5246.35	Giran, Paul. Les origines de la pensée. Paris, 1923.
Phil 2805.90.9	Giraud, V. La vie héroique de Blaise Pascal. 15. éd. Paris, 1923.
Phil 337.7	Glondys, Viktor. Einführung in die Erkenntnistheorie. Wien, 1923.
Phil 8831.2	Goedewaagen, T. Die logische rechtvaadiging der zedelijkheid bij Fichte, Schelling en Hegel. Proefschrift. Amsterdam, 1923.
Phil 530.105.5	Govindácárya, Alkondavilli. A metaphysique of mysticism. Mysore, 1923.
Phil 530.20.55	Grabmann, M. Die Kulturwerte der deutschen Mystik des Mittelalters. Augsburg, 1923.
Phil 8661.15	Graham, Bothwell. The self-evolution of God and His creation of nature. Greenville, S.C., 1923.
Phil 2630.1.25	Gratry, Auguste. Gratry, a cura di Angelica Marrucchi. Milano, 1923.
Phil 5246.32.5	Green, G.H. The mind in action. London, 1923.
Phil 5525.22	Grieg, J.Y.J. The psychology of laughter and comedy. London, 1923.
Phil 3640.184	Griesser, Luitpold. Nietzsche und Wagner. Wien, 1923.
Phil 337.11	Grisebach, E. Erkenntnis und Glaube. Halle an der Saale, 1923.
Phil 337.11.5	Grisebach, E. Probleme der wirklichen Bildung. München, 1923.
Phil 900.6	Grousset, René. Histoire de la philosophie orientale; Inde, Chine, Japan. Paris, 1923.
Phil 3640.192	Gundolf, E. E. Gundolf und Kurt Heldebrandt, Nietzsche als Richter unsrer Zeit. Breslau, 1923.
Phil 6317.2	Hadfield, J.A. Psychology and morals. London, 1923.
Phil 6117.33	Hadfield, J.A. The psychology of power. N.Y., 1923.
Phil 5425.59	Hamann, Otto. Biologie deutscher Dichter und Denker. Zürich, 1923.
Phil 4580.116	Hansen, V. Harald Høffding som religionsfilosof. København, 1923.
Phil 2490.105	Harris, M.S. The positive philosophy of Auguste Comte. Thesis. Hartford, 1923.
Phil 3415.57.2	Hartmann, Eduard von. Kategorienlehre. 2. Aufl. v.1-3. Leipzig, 1923.
Phil 3415.30.15	Hartmann, Eduard von. Philosophie des Unbewussten. 2. Aufl. Leipzig, 1923. 3v.
Phil 974.3.95	Hauer, J.W. Werden und Wesen der Anthroposophie. Stuttgart, 1923.
Phil 5247.33	Hautefeuille, F. d'. Le privilege de l'intelligence. Paris, 1923.
Phil 182.126	Havemann, Hans. Der polare Mensch. Hannover, 1923.
Phil 630.25	Hawes, R.P. The logic of contemporary English realism. Thesis. N.Y., 1923.
Phil 5247.31.5	Hayward, J.W. What is psychology? N.Y., 1923.
Phil 5585.35	Hazelhoff, F.F. De waarnemingstijd. Proefschrift. Groningen, 1923.
Phil 807.2.25	Hegel, G.W.F. Hegels Geschichte der Philosophie. München, 1923.

Phil 3425.48.2	Hegel, Georg Wilhelm Friedrich. Enciclopedia delle scienze filosofiche. 2. ed. v.1-3. Bari, 1923. 2v.
Phil 3425.33	Hegel, Georg Wilhelm Friedrich. Jenenser Logik Metaphysik und Naturphilosophie. Leipzig, 1923.
Phil 3425.34	Hegel, Georg Wilhelm Friedrich. Wissenschaft der Logik. Leipzig, 1923. 2v.
Phil 5627.132.3	Heiler, Friedrich. Das Gebet. 5. Aufl. München, 1923.
Phil 3246.208	Heimsoeth, H. Fichte. München, 1923.
Phil 6317.11	Herbert, S. The unconscious mind. London, 1923.
Phil 5247.41	Hertz, Paul. Über das Denken...Auschauung. Berlin, 1923.
Phil 5722.11	Hesnard, A. L'inconscient. Paris, 1923.
Phil 1707.6	Hessen, Johannes. Die philosophischen Stromungen der Gegenwart. München, 1923.
Phil 8662.22	Hills, Ernest. Philosophie et athéisme. Paris, 1923.
Phil 6317.10	Hinkle, Beatrice. The re-creating of the individual. N.Y., 1923.
Phil 665.27.5	Hirt, Walter. Die Entschleierung der Seele: eine neue Theorie. Berlin, 1923.
Phil 9035.27.5	Hocking, W.E. Human nature and its remaking. New Haven, 1923.
Phil 8587.37	Hocking, W.E. Illicit naturalizing of religion. Chicago, 1923.
Phil 8662.7.5	Hocking, W.E. The meaning of God in human experience. New Haven, 1923.
Phil 1707.1.25	Höffding, H. Compendio di storia della filosofia moderna. Torino, 1923.
Phil 4580.37.5	Høffding, Harald. Erlebnis und Deutung; eine vergleichende Studie zur Religionspsychologie. Stuttgart, 1923.
Phil 4803.454.60	Hoene-Wroński, Józef Maria. Kodeks prawodawstwa społecznego absolutnego. Warszawa, 1923.
Phil 4803.454.55	Hoene-Wroński, Józef Maria. Metapolityke. Warszawa, 1923.
Phil 1707.5	Hönigswald, R. Die Philosophie von der Renaissance bis Kant. Berlin, 1923.
Phil 182.49.5	Hoernlé, R.F.A. Matter, life, mind and God. London, 1923.
Phil 2520.108.6	Hoffmann, A. René Descartes. 2. Aufl. Stuttgart, 1923.
Phil 5850.230	Hollingworth, H.L. Applied psychology. N.Y., 1923.
Phil 3805.164	Holstein, Günther. Die Staatsphilosophie Schleiermachers. Bonn, 1923.
Phil 6317.9A	Hoop, J.H. van der. Character and the unconscious. London, 1923.
Phil 2280.5.97	Hoor, M. George Santayana's theory of knowledge. Diss. n.p., 1923.
Phil 8633.1.23	Horr, George E. The Christian faith and eternal life. Cambridge, 1923.
Phil 1020.18.5	Horten, M. Die Philosophie des Islam. München, 1923.
Phil 7069.23.8	How I know that the dead do live. Boston, 1923.
Phil 182.68	Huidobro, E. Programma analitico razonado de metafisica. Lima, 1923.
Phil 2050.60.30	Hume, David. Traktat über die menschliche Natur. v.1-2. Leipzig, 1923.
Phil 5247.29	Humphrey, J. The story of man's mind. Boston, 1923.
Phil 2477.1.130	Ingenieros, José. Emilio Boutroux y la filosofia universitaria en Francia. Buenos Aires, 1923.
Phil 183.3	Ipsen, J.J. Filosofi og filosofer. København, 1923.
Phil 6119.8	Jakob, C. Elementos de neurobiología. Buenos Aires, 1923.
Phil 184.3.4.5	James, W. The will to believe and other essays in popular philosophy. 1st ed. N.Y., 1923.
Phil 5249.2.5.5	James, William. Psychology. N.Y., 1923.
Phil 5627.6.11	James, William. Den religiösa erfarenheten. Stockholm, 1923.
Phil 6959.1.20	Janet, Pierre. La médecine psychologique. Paris, 1923.
Phil 184.12.3	Jerusalem, W. Einleitung in die Philosophie. Wien, 1923.
Phil 978.61	Jinaräjadäsa, C. How we remember our past lives. Chicago, 1923.
Phil 8834.2.5	Jodl, Friedrich. Geschichte der Ethik. 4. Aufl. Stuttgart, 1923-30. 2v.
Phil 3640.94.6	Joël, Karl. Nietzsche und die Romantik. 2. Aufl. Jena, 1923.
Phil 1870.100	Johnston, G.A. The development of Berkeley's philosophy. London, 1923.
Phil 8589.13	Jones, R.M. Religious foundations. N.Y., 1923.
Phil 2805.111.5	Jovy, Ernest. Pascal et Saint Ignace. Paris, 1923.
Phil 2805.111.10	Jovy, Ernest. Pascal n'a pa inventé le haquet, démonstration lexicographique. Paris, 1923.
Phil 5249.13	Jung, Carl G. Psychological types. London, 1923.
Phil 184.22	Jung, E. Le principe constitutif de la nature organique. Paris, 1923.
Phil 185.23.2	Kanovitch, A. The will to beauty. N.Y., 1923.
Phil 3480.66.49	Kant, Immanuel. Fondazione della metafisica dei costumi. Torino, 1923.
Phil 3480.66.51	Kant, Immanuel. La metafisica dei costumi. v.1-2. Torino, 1923-25.
Phil 3480.25.5	Kant, Immanuel. The philosophy of Kant. 2d ed. Glasgow, 1923.
Phil 3480.28.25	Kant, Immanuel. Scritti minori. Bari, 1923.
Phil 6680.5.2	Kauffmann, M. Suggestion und Hypnose. 2. Aufl. Berlin, 1923.
Phil 5440.26	Kellogg, V.L. Mind and heredity. Princeton, 1923.
Phil 3549.2.75.5	Keyserling, Hermann. Das Reisetagebuch eines Philosophen. 7. Aufl. Darmstadt, 1923. 2v.
Phil 8590.10.5	King, Henry C. Seeing life whole; a Christian philosophy of life. N.Y., 1923.
Phil 6020.3	Klages, L. Ausdrucksbewegung von Gestaltungskraft. Leipzig, 1923.
Phil 2520.161	Koyré, A. Descartes und die Scholastik. Bonn, 1923.
Phil 4800.4	Kozłowski, Władysław M. Les idées françaises dans la philosophie nationale et la poésie patriotique de la Bologne. Grenoble, 1923.
Phil 6615.12	Kretschmer, Ernst. Über hysterie. Leipzig, 1923.
Phil 5640.18	Kries, J. von. Allgemeine Sinnesphysiologie. Leipzig, 1923.
Phil 6020.2.3	Krukenberg, H. Der Gesichtsausdruck des Menschen. 3. und 4. Aufl. Stuttgart, 1923.
Phil 3492.19	Kühnemann, E. Kant. München, 1923-24. 2v.
Phil 5050.12	Kulpe, Oswald. Vorlesungen über Logik. Leipzig, 1923.
Phil 2805.189	Lahorque, P.M. Le réalisme de Pascal. Paris, 1923.
Phil 705.16	Landmann, E. Die Transcendenz des erkennens. Berlin, 1923.
Phil 8701.11	Lane, H.H. Evolution and Christian faith. Princeton, 1923.
Phil 4769.1.96	Lange, E.M. Solowjew. Mainz, 1923.
Phil 3585.30	Lask, Emil. Gesammelte Schriften. Tübingen, 1923. 3v.
Phil 2520.165	Launay, Louis de. Descartes. Paris, 1923.
Phil 5590.448.2	Lazurskii, Aleksandr F. Klassifikatsiis lichnosti. 2. izd. Moskva, 1923.

1923 - cont.

Phil 1516.3.5　Lehmen, Alfonso. Lehrbuch der Philosophie.
　　Freiburg, 1923.
Phil 3552.12　Leibniz, Gottfried Wilhelm. Sämtliche Schriften und
　　Briefe. v.1, pt.1-8. Darmstadt, 1923-50. 8v.
Phil 1116.4.5　Leisegang, H. Hellenistische Philosophie von Aristoteles
　　bis Plotin. Breslau, 1923.
Phil 342.6　Lemaire, J. Notes complementaires sur une thèorie de la
　　connaissance sensible. Bruges, 1923.
Phil 1811.2　Leroux, E. Le pragmatisme américain et anglais.
　　Paris, 1923.
Phil 3831.11　Lévêque, Raphail. Le problème de la vérité dans la
　　philosophie de Spinoza. Strasbourg, 1923.
Phil 5722.10　Levine, I. The unconscious. N.Y., 1923.
Phil 7060.78.5　Lewes, M.L. The queer side of things. London, 1923.
Phil 8520.29　Lewkowitz, A. Religiöse Denker der Gegenwart.
　　Berlin, 1923.
Phil 1711.1　Liebert, A. Die geistige Krisis der Gegenwart.
　　Berlin, 1923.
Phil 186.35.7　Liebert, Arthur. Wie ist kritische Philosophie überhaupt
　　möglich? Leipzig, 1923.
Phil 3640.209　Liebmann, W. Nietzsche für und gegen Vaihinger.
　　München, 1923.
Phil 186.60　Litt, Theodor. Erkenntnis und Leben. Leipzig, 1923.
Phil 8886.38　Loisy, Alfred. La morale humaine. Paris, 1923.
Phil 3493.14.5　Lomber, Wilhelm. Immanuel Kants letzte Lebensjahre und
　　Tod. Königsberg, 1923.
Phil 5051.23.4　Losskiĭ, N.O. Logika. Berlin, 1923.
Phil 745.10　Losskii, Nikolai O. Materiia i zhizn'. Berlin, 1923.
Phil 5251.27　Lothian, A.J.D. An outline of psychology for education.
　　London, 1923.
Phil 3565.50.6　Lotze, Hermann. Mikrokosmus. 6e Aufl. Leipzig, 1923.
　　3v.
Phil 525.61.5　Louismet, S. La contemplation chrétienne. Paris, 1923.
Phil 525.38.2　Louismet, S. Miracle et mystique. 2e ed. Paris, 1923.
Phil 9455.4　Lowell, A.L. Public opinion in war and peace.
　　Cambridge, 1923.
Phil 8412.43　Lunacharskii, Anatolii V. Osnovy pozitivnoi estetiki.
　　Moskva, 1923.
Phil 5251.18.5　Lynch, Arthur. Principles of psychology. London, 1923.
Phil 8610.923.10　McCabe, Joseph. The twilight of the gods. London, 1923.
Phil 6322.8　MacCurdy, J.T. Problems in dynamic psychology.
　　Cambridge, 1923.
Phil 6122.13.13　McDougall, William. Body and mind. 6th ed. London, 1923.
Phil 5252.18.3　McDougall, William. An introduction to social psychology.
　　15th ed. Boston, 1923.
Phil 5252.18.15　McDougall, William. Outline of psychology. N.Y., 1923.
Phil 960.29　McGovern, W.M. A manual of Buddhist philosophy.
　　London, 1923.
Phil 5655.6　McKenzie, Dan. Aromatics and the soul. London, 1923.
Phil 5252.47　McKerrow, J.C. The appearance of mind. London, 1923.
Phil 2733.36.10　Malebranche, Nicolas. Dialogues on metaphysics and on
　　religion. London, 1923.
Phil 2805.191　Malvy, A. Pascal et le problème de la croyance.
　　Paris, 1923.
Phil 187.44.7　Mann, William E. A new theory of evolution. Walpole,
　　Mass., 1923.
Phil 1730.12　Marck, Siegfried. Das Jahrhundert der Aufklärung.
　　Leipzig, 1923.
Phil 4369.2　Marcos Coujáles, B. Miguel Sabuco. Madrid, 1923.
Phil 8887.56.5　Martin, A.W. A philosophy of life and its spiritual
　　values. N.Y., 1923.
Phil 4012.5　Masnovo, A. Il neo-tomismo in Italia (origini e prime
　　vicende). Milano, 1923.
Phil 960.31　Masson-Oursel, Paul. Esquisse d'une histoire de la
　　philosophie indienne. Thèse. Paris, 1923.
Phil 960.31.2　Masson-Oursel, Paul. Esquisse d'une histoire de la
　　philosophie indienne. Thèse. Paris, 1923.
Phil 812.9　Masson-Oursel, Paul. La philosophie comparée.
　　Paris, 1923.
Phil 812.9.2　Masson-Oursel, Paul. La philosophie comparée. Thèse.
　　Paris, 1923.
Phil 3808.126.2　Medilch, P. La theorie de l'intelligence chez
　　Schopenhauer. Paris, 1923.
Phil 5090.9　Meinhandl, F. Über Urteilswahrheit. Leipzig, 1923.
Phil 9550.3.5　Meinong, A. Zur Grundlegung der allgemeinen Werth-Theorie.
　　Graz, 1923.
Phil 5710.8.3　Mercier, C.A. Human temperaments; studies in character. 3.
　　ed. London, 1923?
Phil 1712.5.4.10　Messer, A. Geschichte der Philosophie vom Beginn der
　　Neuzeit zum Ende des 18. Jahrhunderts. 6e und 7e Aufl.
　　Leipzig, 1923.
Phil 3494.13.15　Messer, A. Kommentar zu Kants Kritik der reinen Vernunft.
　　Stuttgart, 1923.
Phil 630.33　Messer, August. Der kritische Realismus. Karlsruhe, 1923.
Phil 8413.25　Meyer, T.A. Asthetik. Stuttgart, 1923.
Phil 6322.4.5　Miller, Hugh C. The new psychology and the parent.
　　N.Y., 1923.
Phil 2493.90　Mondolfo, Rodolfo. Un psicologo associazionista: E.B. de
　　Condillac. Bologna, 1923.
Phil 1133.22　More, Paul E. Hellenistic philosophies (From the death of
　　Socrates to A.D. 451). Princeton, 1923.
Phil 365.12　Morgan, Conwy L. Emergent evolution. London, 1923.
Phil 3625.3.84　Moschetti, A. Fenomenismo e relativismo nel pensiero di E.
　　Mach. Genova, 1923.
Phil 2045.111　Moser, H. Thomas Hobbes: seine logische Problematik.
　　Bern, 1923.
Phil 5520.43　Mouchet, Enrique. El lenguaje interior y los trastornos de
　　la palabra. La Plata, 1923.
Phil 1133.21　Moulard, A. Metpon; étude sur l'idée de mesure dans la
　　philosophie antésocratique. Thèse. Angers, 1923.
Phil 5627.63　Mudge, E.L. The God-experience. Cincinnati, 1923.
Phil 5585.34　Müller, Georg E. Komplextheorie und Gestalttheorie.
　　Göttingen, 1923.
Phil 665.51A　Müller, Walter. Das Problem der Seelenschönheit im
　　Mittelalter. Bern, 1923.
Phil 8413.28　Müller-Freienfels, R. Psychologie der Kunst.
　　Leipzig, 1923-33. 3v.
Phil 575.34.2　Müller-Freienfels, Richard. Persönlichkeit und
　　Weltanschauung. 2e Aufl. Leipzig, 1923.
Phil 575.34.5.2　Müller-Freienfels, Richard. Philosophie der
　　Individualität. 2e Aufl. Leipzig, 1923.
Phil 1740.2　Müller-Freienfels, Richard. Die Philosophie des
　　zwanzigsten Jahrhunderts in ihren Hauptströmungen.
　　Berlin, 1923.
Phil 5763.3　Nabert, Jean. L'expérience intérieure de la liberté.
　　Thèse. Paris, 1923.

1923 - cont.

Phil 5374.31　Nasgaard, S. Die Form der Bewusstheit. München, 1923.
Phil 3915.153　Nef, Willi. Die Philosophie Wilhelm Wundts.
　　Leipzig, 1923.
Phil 1133.16.10　Nestle, W. Die Nachsokratiker. Jena, 1923. 2v.
Phil 2475.1.208　Nicolardot, F. Un pseudonyme Bergsonien? Paris, 1923.
Phil 3640.12.10　Nietzsche, Friedrich. Gedichts. Leipzig, 1923.
Phil 3640.21　Nietzsche, Friedrich. Jugendschriften. München, 1923.
Phil 3640.63.5　Nietzsche, Friedrich. Die Philosophie im tragischen
　　Zeitalter der Griechen. München, 1923.
Phil 8593.13　Nikolai, Pavel N. Mozhet-li sovremennyi obrazovannyi,
　　mysliashchii cheloviek vierit' v bozhectvo Iisusa Khrista.
　　3. izd. Praga, 1923.
Phil 8888.8　Nolan, Preston M. Pertinent and impertinent.
　　Chicago, 1923.
Phil 4610.7.85　Norström, V. Brev, 1889-1916. Stockholm, 1923.
Phil 672.123.10　Nys, Désiré. La notion de temps. 2e éd. Louvain, 1923.
Phil 7069.21.47　Oesterreich, T.K. Occultism and modern science.
　　London, 1923.
Phil 7069.21.45　Oesterreich, T.K. Der Okkultismus im modernen Weltbild. 3.
　　Aufl. Dresden, 1923.
Phil 5520.35　Ogden, Charles K. The meaning of meaning. London, 1923.
Phil 295.2　O'Neill, John. Cosmology; an introduction to the
　　philosophy of matter. London, 1923.
Phil 9528.5　Oppermann, W. Schulfeierstunden. Leipzig, 1923.
Phil 8704.2　Osborn, H.F. Evolution and religion. N.Y., 1923.
Phil 7069.23.10　Osty, Eugène. La connaissance supra-normale. Paris, 1923.
Phil 7069.23.11　Osty, Eugène. Supernormal faculties in man. London, 1923.
Phil 8594.10　Otto, Walter F. Der Geist der Antike und die christliche
　　Welt. Bonn, 1923.
Phil 5425.34.3　Padovan, A. Il genio. 3. ed. Milano, 1923.
Phil 2805.40.35　Pascal, Blaise. Pensées et opuscules. 11e éd.
　　Paris, 1923.
Phil 9245.33.10　Payot, Jules. Erörvringen av lyckan. Stockholm, 1923.
Phil 2225.5.30　Peirce, C.S. Chance, love, and logic. N.Y., 1923.
Phil 190.47　Peiser, Fritz. Systematische Philosophie in
　　leichtfasslicher Darstellung. Berlin, 1923.
Phil 8595.36　Pesch, T. Christliche Lebensphilosophie. 20. bis 22. Aufl.
　　Freiburg, 1923.
Phil 5255.19　Pfister, O. Zur Psychologie des philosophischen Denkens.
　　Bern, 1923.
Phil 6325.1.16　Pfister, Oskar. Expressionism in art. N.Y., 1923.
Phil 6325.1.17　Pfister, Oskar. Some applications of psychoanalysis.
　　London, 1923.
Phil 2805.190　Picard, Emile. Pascal mathématicien et physicien.
　　Paris, 1923.
Phil 4115.86　Piccoli, Valentino. Vincenzo Gioberti. Roma, 1923.
Phil 6125.18　Piéron, Henri. Le cerveau et la pensée. Paris, 1923.
Phil 5765.9　Planck, Max. Kansalgesetz und Willensfreiheit.
　　Berlin, 1923.
Phil 8595.19　Plekhanov, G. O religii. Moskva, 1923.
Phil 5640.27　Plessner, H. Die Einheit der Sinne grundlinien einer
　　Asthesiologie. Bonn, 1923.
Phil 8670.11　Pounder, R.M. Some thoughts about God. Toronto, 1923.
Phil 3850.18.109　Przywara, Erich. Religionsbegründung: Max Scheler, J.H.
　　Neuman. Freiburg, 1923.
Phil 960.128　Radhakrishnan, S. Indian philosophy. London, 1923.
　　2v.
Phil 5257.56　Ranschburg, Pál. Az emberi elme. Budapest, 1923.
　　2v.
Phil 7082.166A　Ratcliff, Arthur James John. A history of dreams.
　　Boston, 1923.
Phil 3499.18　Rauschenberger, W. Die Antinomien Kants. Berlin, 1923.
Phil 672.127.2　Rawitz, B. Raum, Zeit und Gott. Leipzig, 1923.
Phil 720.18　Reid, Louis A. Knowledge and truth. London, 1923.
Phil 5627.102.5　Reik, Theodor. Der eigene und der fremde Gott; zur
　　Psychoanalyse der religiösen Entwicklung. Leipzig, 1923.
Phil 3499.10.5　Reininger, Robert. Kant, seine Anhänger und seine Gegner.
　　München, 1923.
Phil 1535.36.12　Reinstadler, S. Elementa philosophiae scholasticae. 11.
　　and 12. ed. Friburgi, 1923. 2v.
Phil 8597.29　Religion and life; the foundations of personal religion.
　　N.Y., 1923.
Phil 4215.3.35　Rensi, Giuseppe. L'irrazionale, il lavoro, l'amore.
　　Milano, 1923.
Phil 8672.18.3　Reusner, M.A. Nuzhna li vera v Boga. 3. izd.
　　Moskva, 1923.
Phil 6327.46.20　Ribot, Théodule. Le malattie della personalità.
　　Milano, 1923.
Phil 8672.12　Richard, Gaston. L'athéisme dogmatique en sociologie
　　religieuse. Strasbourg, 1923.
Phil 7069.23.15　Richet, Charles. Thirty years of psychical research.
　　N.Y., 1923.
Phil 7069.23.16　Richet, Charles. Traité de métaphysique. 2. ed.
　　Paris, 1923.
Phil 1817.3.7　Riley, I.W. American thought. 2nd ed. N.Y., 1923.
Phil 7084.26　Rivers, William Halse Rivers. Conflict and dream.
　　London, 1923.
Phil 5257.28.5　Roback, A.A. Psychology. Rahway, 1923.
Phil 192.77　Robertson, J.M. Explorations. London, 1923.
Phil 5257.27　Robinson, E.S. Readings in general psychology.
　　Chicago, 1923.
Phil 3499.21　Röver, G. Zur Lehre vom Raum...Lehre Kants.
　　Oldenburg, 1923.
Phil 1817.5.3　Rogers, A.K. English and American philosophy since 1800.
　　N.Y., 1923.
Phil 817.4.15　Rogers, A.K. A student's history of philosophy.
　　N.Y., 1923.
Phil 348.8　Rogers, A.K. What is truth? New Haven, 1923.
Phil 978.51　Rogers, L.W. Elementary theosophy. 2d ed. Chicago, 1923.
Phil 7082.82.2　Rogers, Louis William. Dreams and premonitions. 2d ed.
　　Chicago, 1923.
Phil 6967.11.6　Rogues de Fursac, J. Manuel de psychiatrie. 6. éd.
　　Paris, 1923.
Phil 8892.42　Rolffs, Ernst. Politische Ethik und ethische
　　Weltanschauung. Leipzig, 1923.
Phil 4215.1.25　Romagnosi, G.D. Opuscoli filosofici. Lanciano, 1923.
Phil 3640.217　Rosen, Hugo. Livsproblemet hos Nietzsche.
　　Stockholm, 1923.
Phil 6967.7　Ross, T.A. The common neuroses, their treatment by
　　psychotherapy. London, 1923.
Phil 4073.88　Rossi, M.M. T. Campanella metafisico. Firenze, 1923.
Phil 4777.282.10　Roszkowski, Antonio. Poglądy społeczne i ekonomiczne
　　Augusta Cieszkowskiego. Poznań, 1923.
Phil 7069.23.17　Rowe, Lucien. Le spiritisme d'aujourd'hui et d'hier. 2.
　　ed. Paris, 1923.

Chronological Listing

1923 - cont.

Phil 2250.45.5 Royce, Josiah. Lectures on modern idealism. New Haven, 1923.
Phil 192.16.10.5A Royce, Josiah. The world and the individual. N.Y., 1923-1927. 2v.
Phil 192.28.3 Russell, B. Les problèmes de la philosophie. Paris, 1923.
Phil 7069.23.19 Rutot, A. Le mécanisme de la survie. Paris, 1923.
Phil 8892.27 Ryner, J.H. Le subjectivisme. Paris, 1923.
Phil 4110.1.80 Saitta, Giuseppe. La filosofia di Marsilio Ficino. Messina, 1923.
Phil 6328.6 Sando, I.J. Abnormal behavior. N.Y., 1923.
Phil 645.25.2 Santayana, G. Scepticism and animal faith. London, 1923.
Phil 645.25A Santayana, G. Scepticism and animal faith. N.Y., 1923.
Phil 2270.123 Santayana, George. The unknowable; Herbert Spencer lecture. Oxford, 1923.
Phil 6688.17 Satow, Louis. Hypnotism and suggestion. London, 1923.
Phil 193.104 Sauer, W. Philosophie der Zukunft eine Grundlegung der Kultur. Stuttgart, 1923.
Phil 818.9 Sawicki, Franz. Lebensanschauungen Alter und neuer Denker. Paderborn, 1923. 3v.
Phil 8598.46.2 Scheler, Max. Vom Ewigen im Menschen. 2e Aufl. Leipzig, 1923. 2v.
Phil 5415.7 Scheler, Max. Wesen und Formen der Sympathie. Bonn, 1923.
Phil 3800.195.5 Schelling, F.W.J. von. Esposizione del mio sistema filosofico. Bari, 1923.
Phil 6328.10.10 Schilder, Paul. Das Körperschema...Bewusstsein des eigenen Körpers. Berlin, 1923.
Phil 6328.10 Schilder, Paul. Seele und Leben. Berlin, 1923.
Phil 3805.76 Schleiermacher, Friedrich. Briefe. Berlin, 1923.
Phil 6328.12 Schmitz, O.A.H. Psychoanalyse und Yoga. Darmstadt, 1923.
Phil 3808.62.5 Schopenhauer, Arthur. Aforismi sulla saggezza della vita. Torino, 1923.
Phil 3808.78 Schopenhauer, Arthur. Reisetagebücher aus den Jahren 1803-1804. Leipzig, 1923.
Phil 3808.29.10 Schopenhauer, Arthur. Studies in pessimism. London, 1923.
Phil 7069.14.61 Schrenck von Notzing, Albert. Materialisationsphaenomene. 2. ed. München, 1923.
Phil 193.112 Seailles, G. La philosophie du travail. Paris, 1923.
Phil 5258.34.13 Seashore, C.E. Introduction to psychology. N.Y., 1923.
Phil 5545.54.15 Semon, R. Mnemic psychology. N.Y., 1923.
Phil 2475.1.214 Serini, P. Bergson e lo spiritualismo. Genova, 1923.
Phil 1540.13 Serras, Pereira, M. A tese escolastica do composto humano. Diss. Coimbra, 1923.
Phil 8598.34.5 Shebbeare, Charles J. The design argument reconsidered. London, 1923.
Phil 8598.34.6 Shebbeare, Charles J. The design argument reconsidered. London, 1923.
Phil 2270.150 Shepperson, J. A comparative study of St. Thomas Aquinas and Herbert Spencer. Diss. Pittsburgh, 1923.
Phil 2805.207 Shestor, Lev. La nuit de Gethsémani. Paris, 1923.
Phil 4769.4.10 Shpet, Gustav. Esteticheskie fragmenti. Pts.1-3. Peterburg, 1923.
Phil 193.59.25A Simmel, G. Fragmente und Aufsätze. München, 1923.
Phil 3808.108.3 Simmel, G. Schopenhauer und Nietzsche. 3. Aufl. München, 1923.
Phil 7069.23.20 Simon, Gustave. Chez Victor Hugo. Les tables tournantes de Jersey. Paris, 1923.
Phil 8643.23 Simpson, J.Y. Man and the attainment of immortality. 2. ed. London, 1923.
Phil 193.95 Singer, Edgar A. Modern thinkers and present problems. N.Y., 1923.
Phil 6328.7 Slade, T. Kenrick. Our phantastic emotions. London, 1923.
Phil 8599.19.5 Sleigh, R.S. The sufficiency of Christianity and Ernst Troeltsch. London, 1923.
Phil 4809.796.30 Smetana, Augustin. Vznik a zánik ducha. Praha, 1923.
Phil 5828.7.2 Smith, E.M. The investigation of mind in animals. 2. ed. Cambridge, 1923.
Phil 5058.28.21 Smith, Henry B. How the mind falls into error. N.Y., 1923.
Phil 3500.60.5A Smith, Norman K. A commentary to Kant's "Critique of pure reason". 2d ed. London, 1923.
Phil 5258.71 Snow, Adolph J. Problems in psychology. N.Y., 1923.
Phil 530.15.9 Sourian, M. Le mysticisme en Normandie au XVIIe siècle. Paris, 1923.
Phil 5258.68 Spearman, C. The nature of "intelligence" and the principles of cognition. London, 1923.
Phil 8598.83.5A Sperry, Willard L. The disciplines of liberty. New Haven, 1923.
Phil 3819.72.5 Spinoza, Benedictus de. Briefwechsel und andere Dokumente. Leipzig, 1923.
Phil 3819.36.5 Spinoza, Benedictus de. Ethica op meelkundige wijze uiteengezet. 3. druk. Amsterdam, 1923.
Phil 4018.3 Spirito, Ugo. Il nuovo idealismo italiano. Roma, 1923.
Phil 3838.9 Starcke, C.N. Baruch de Spinoza. København, 1923.
Phil 5258.76.3 Starcke, C.N. Psychologi. 3. udg. Kjøbenhavn, 1923.
Phil 9358.14 Stearns, Alfred E. The challenge of youth. Boston, 1923.
Phil 974.3.15 Steiner, Rudolf. From Luther to Steiner. London, 1923.
Phil 6328.2.4A Stekel, Wilhelm. Conditions of nervous anxiety. London, 1923.
Cg Phil 7075.131 Stekel, William. Der Fetischismus dargestellt für Ärzte und Kriminalogen. Berlin, 1923.
Phil 193.53.2 Stern, L.W. Person und Sache. Leipzig, 1923-1924. 3v.
Phil 193.138.5 Stern, M.R. von. Das Welt-Vakuum. Linz, 1923.
Phil 400.59 Sternberg, K. Idealismus und Kultur. Berlin, 1923.
Phil 5258.112 Stoelting, C.H., Co., Chicago. Psychology and physiology apparatus and supplies. Chicago, 1923.
Phil 5258.144 Störring, G. Psychologie. Leipzig, 1923.
Phil 5412.5 Stratton, G.M. Anger; its religious and moral significance. N.Y., 1923.
Phil 3903.3.90 Strauch, W. Die Philosophie des "Als-Ob" und...Rechtswissenschaft. München, 1923.
Phil 349.21 Strong, C.A. A theory of knowledge. N.Y., 1923.
Phil 8893.57 Sturt, Henry. Human value. Cambridge, 1923.
Phil 2805.222 Suarès, André. Puissances de Pascal. Paris, 1923.
Phil 349.23 Switalski, B.N. Probleme der Erkenntnis. v.1-2. Münster in Westfalen, 1923.
Phil 3905.86 Swoboda, H. Otto Weiningers Tod. 2. Aufl. Wien, 1923.
Phil 5525.27 Talhouet, J. de. Le rire et l'origine des idées. Rennes, 1923.
Phil 5627.59 Thouless, Robert H. An introduction to the psychology of religion. N.Y., 1923.
Phil 1750.125 Tilgher, A. Relativisti contemporanei. Roma, 1923.
Phil 6990.34.5 Touquédec, J. de. Introduction a l'étude du merveilleux et du miracle. 3. éd. Paris, 1923.
Phil 6329.1.9 Tridon, André. Psychoanalysis; its history, theory and practice. N.Y., 1923.

1923 - cont.

Phil 8599.19.21 Troeltsch, Ernst. Christian thought, its history and application. London, 1923.
Phil 5259.15 Tumarkin, Anna. Prolegomena zu einer wissenschaftliche Psychologie. Leipzig, 1923.
Phil 5425.15.27 Türck, H. The man of genius. London, 1923.
Phil 8644.12.5 Turk, Morris H. They live and are not far away. N.Y., 1923.
Phil 6329.4 Turner, Julia. The psychology of self-consciousness. London, 1923.
Phil 5627.60 Underhill, E. The life of the spirit and the life of today. 3d ed. London, 1923.
Phil 672.122.3 Uspenskii, P.D. Tertium organum. 2nd American ed. N.Y., 1923.
Phil 8050.77 Utitz, Emil. Aesthetik. Berlin, 1923.
Phil 3903.3.97 Valeton, Matthée. De "Als ob" philosophie en het psychisch monisme. Amsterdam, 1923.
Phil 2475.1.210 Van Paassen, C.R. De antithesen in de philosophie van Henri Bergson. Haarlem, 1923.
Phil 5261.8.8 Varendonck, J. The evolution of the concious faculties. N.Y., 1923.
Phil 735.87 Vetter, A. Kritik des Gefühls. Prien, 1923.
Htn Phil 3110.169* Vetterling, H. The illuminate of Görlitz, or Jakob Böhme's (1575-1624) life and philosophy. Leipzig, 1923.
Phil 2733.90 Vidgrain, Joseph. Le christianisme dans la philosophie de Malebranche. Thèse. Paris, 1923.
Phil 2733.78 Vidgrain, Joseph. Fragments philosophiques inédits et correspondance. Thèse. Caen, 1923.
Phil 315.5 Vierkandt, A. Der Dualismus mi modernen Weltbild. 2. Aufl. Berlin, 1923.
Phil 3503.4.6 Vorländer, K. Kant-Schiller-Goethe. 2. Aufl. Leipzig, 1923.
Phil 821.1.10 Vorländer, K. Volkstümliche Geschichte der Philosophie. 3. Aufl. Berlin, 1923.
Phil 2421.1 Vorländer, Karl. Französische Philosophie. Breslau, 1923.
Phil 5062.26 Waite, Dorothy J. First lessons in logic. London, 1923.
Phil 978.38.5 Walker, E.D. Reincarnation. Point Loma, Calif., 1923.
Phil 3504.22.5 Ward, James. Immanuel Kant. London, 1923.
Phil 5262.20.9 Warren, H.C. Précis de psychologie. Paris, 1923.
Phil 7069.23.25 Wasylewski, S. Pod urokiem zaświatów. Lwów, 1923.
Phil 5627.62 Waterhouse, E.S. The philosophy of religious experience. Thesis. London, 1923.
Phil 197.32.5 Weidenbach, Oswald. Weltanschauung aus der Geiste der Kritizismus. München, 1923.
Phil 353.4 Weinhandl, F. Die Methode der Gestaltanalyse. Leipzig, 1923.
Phil 672.129 Weitzenböck, R. Over de vierde dimensie. Groningen, 1923.
Phil 8897.49 White, A.K. The moral self; its nature and development. London, 1923.
Phil 197.38 Widgery, A.G. Outlines of a philosophy of life. London, 1923.
Phil 8897.46 Wiggam, A.E. The new decalogue of science. Indianapolis, 1923.
Phil 5627.113 Wijnaendts Francken, C.J. Wereldbeschouwing en Godsdienstig bewustzyn. Haarlem, 1923.
Phil 7069.23.21 Wilkins, H.J. A further criticism of the psychical claims concerning Glastonbury Abbey. Bristol, 1923.
Phil 6332.6 Williams, T.A. Dreads and besetting fears. Boston, 1923.
Phil 978.52 Willis, F.M. Theosophy in outline. Girard, 1923.
Phil 8897.48 Wirpel, Aaron. Observations of a progressive religionist. Cleveland, 1923.
Phil 8897.32.5 Wittman, M. Ethik. München, 1923.
Phil 3850.18.80 Wittmann, Michael. Max Scheler als Ethiker. Düsseldorf, 1923.
Phil 6332.7 Wohlgemuth, A. A critical examination of psycho-analysis. N.Y., 1923.
Phil 5585.51 Wooster, Margaret. Certain factors in the development of a new spatial co-ordination. Thesis. Princeton, 1923.
Phil 7069.23.45 Wright A.A. Momentous memoirs. Boston, 1923.
Phil 5627.66 Wunderle, G. Einführung in die moderne Religionspsychologie. Kempten, 1923.
Phil 6334.5 Yellowlees, H. A manuel of psychotherapy. London, 1923.
Phil 6694.2 Young, Paul C. An experimental study of mental and physical functions in the normal and hypnotic states. Thesis. n.p., 1923.
Phil 4235.1.95 Zavattari, E. La visione della vita...Telesio. Torino, 1923.
Phil 3450.9.80 Zbinden, H. Ein Künder neuer Lebenswege...R.M. Holzapfel. Jena, 1923.
Phil 4710.70.10 Zen'kovskii, V.V. Pravoslavie i kul'tura. Berlin, 1923.
Phil 8426.5 Ziehen, T. Vorlesungen über Ästhetik. Halle, 1923-25. 2v.
Phil 5265.1.15 Ziehen, Theodor. Allgemeine Psychologie. Berlin, 1923.
Phil 3808.131 Zini, Zino. Schopenhauer. Milano, 1923.

1924

Phil 4803.108.1 Abramowski, Edward. Pisma. Warszawa, 1924.
Phil 3482.2.7 Adickes, E. Kant als Naturforscher. Berlin, 1924. 2v.
Phil 3482.2.16 Adickes, E. Kant und das Ding an sich. Berlin, 1924.
Phil 6310.1.5 Adler, A. The practice and theory of individual psychology. London, 1924.
Phil 6310.1.9 Adler, A. Praxis und Theorie der Individual-Psychologie. 2. Aufl. München, 1924.
Phil 8615.5.20 Adler, Felix. The reconstruction of the spiritual ideal. N.Y., 1924.
Phil 4513.1.38 Ahlberg, A. Filosofi och dikt. Stockholm, 1924.
Phil 3808.144 Ahlberg, Alf. Arthur Schopenhauer. Stockholm, 1924.
Phil 4610.7.88 Akesson, Elof. Norströmiana. Stockholm, 1924.
Phil 800.4 Albrich, K. Im Kampf um unsere Stellung zu Welt und Leben. Leipzig, 1924.
Phil 510.137.5 Aliotta, A. L'éternité des esprits. Paris, 1924.
Phil 510.137 Aliotta, A. Il problema di Dio e il nuovo pluralismo. Città di Castello, 1924.
Phil 3820.3.5 Altkircli, Ernst. Maledictus und Benedictus: Spinoza. Leipzig, 1924.
Phil 8401.14.5 André Yves. Essai su le beau. Paris, 1924.
Phil 3640.207 Andreas-Salomé, L. Friedrich Nietzsche in seinen Werken. Dresden, 1924?
Phil 9035.40 Apfelbach, H. Der Aufbau des Charakters. Wien, 1924.
Phil 165.180 Aristotelian Society for the Systematic Study of Philosophy. Concepts of continuity. v.4. London, 1924.
Phil 5500.10 Augier, E. De l'action à la connaissance. Paris, 1924.
Phil 175.28.2 Avey, A.E. Readings in philosophy. N.Y., 1924.
Phil 5241.67 Badareu, D. Essai sur la pensée. Thèse. Paris, 1924.

1924 - cont.

Phil 4818.298.80   Badareu, Dan. Un système matérialiste métaphysique au XIXe siècle: la philosophie de Basile Conta. Paris, 1924.

Phil 8656.13.7   Balfour, A.J.B. Theism and thought. N.Y., 1924.

Phil 735.88   Bamberger, F. Untersuchungen zur Entstehung der Wertproblems in der Philosophie des 19. Jahrhunderts. Halle, 1924.

Phil 705.19   Banfi, Antonio. Immanenza e trascendenza. Alessandria, 1924.

Phil 7140.115.15   Baudouin, C. Suggestion und autosuggestion. Dresden, 1924.

Phil 3483.47   Becher, Erich. Immanuel Kant. München, 1924.

Phil 6951.5.17   Beers, C.W. A new project; the first International Congress on Mental Hygiene. N.Y., 1924.

Phil 672.134.5   Benedicks, Carl. Space and time. London, 1924.

Phil 5241.59   Bentley, I.M. The field of psychology. N.Y., 1924.

Phil 1870.73.7   Berkeley, G. Gli appunti (commonplace book). Bologna, 1924.

Phil 5241.65   Bertrand-Barraud, D. Les valeurs affectives et l'exercice discursif de la pensée. Paris, 1924.

Phil 5241.65.5   Bertrand-Barraud, D. Les valeurs affectives et l'exercice discursif de la pensée. Thèse. Paris, 1924.

Phil 7069.24.50   Besterman, T. Crystal-gazing: a study in the history, distribution, theory, and practice of scrying. London, 1924.

Phil 5400.39.9   Bhagavan, Das. The science of the emotions. 3rd ed. Adyar, 1924.

Phil 7080.16.5   Bigelow, John. Mystery of sleep. N.Y., 1924.

Phil 4520.8.44   Bjarnason, Agúst. Sidraed Reykjavík, 1924.

Phil 4520.6.2   Björklund, G. Skrifter. Upsala, 1924.

Phil 6951.11.5   Bleuler, E. Textbook of psychiatry. N.Y., 1924.

Phil 6311.8   Blondel, C. La psychanalyse. Paris, 1924.

Phil 6311.11   Boas, J.M. La défense psychique. Thèse. Paris, 1924.

Phil 6311.11.2   Boas, J.M. La défense psychique. Thèse. Paris, 1924.

Phil 3110.36.30   Böhme, J. Vom dreifachen Leben des Menschen. Hamburg, 1924.

Phil 6315.2.89   Bonsfield, William A. A neglected complex and its relation to Freudian psychology. London, 1924.

Phil 3450.2.80   Boulan, Emile. François Hemsterhuis, le Socrate hollandais. Groningue, 1924.

Phil 5241.17.5   Brentano, Franz. Psychologie vom empirischen Standpunkt. Leipzig, 1924-25. 2v.

Phil 1801.3   Brockdorff, C. Die englische aufklärungs Philosophie. München, 1924.

Phil 510.131   Brooks, H.J. The riddle of the universe scientifically interpreted. n.p., 1924.

Phil 5241.28.7   Brown, W. Psychology and the sciences. London, 1924.

Phil 4115.79   Bruers, A. Gioberti. (Guide bibliografiche). Roma, 1924.

Phil 3120.15.50   Brunner, Constantin. Vom Einsiedler Constantin Brunner. Potsdam, 1924.

Phil 2805.192   Brunschvicg, L. Le génie de Pascal. Paris, 1924.

Phil 5400.72   Brunswick, D. The effects of emotional stimuli on the gastro-intestinal tone. Baltimore, 1924.

Phil 3640.205   Bubnoff, N. von. Friedrich Nietzsches Kulturphilosophie und Umwertungslehre. Leipzig, 1924.

Phil 4769.6.83   Budilova, E.A. Uchenie I.M. Sechenova ob oshchushchenii i myshlenii. Moskva, 1924.

Phil 8402.40   Buermeyer, L. The aesthetic experience. Merion, Pa., 1924.

Phil 8581.45   Buonaiuti, Ernesto. Verso la luce. Foligno, 1924.

Phil 282.11   Busco, Pierre. Les cosmogonies modernes. Paris, 1924.

Phil 282.11.5   Busco, Pierre. Les cosmogonies modernes. Thèse. Paris, 1924.

Phil 8633.1.24   Cabot, Philip. The sense of immortality. Cambridge, 1924.

Phil 177.76   Calò, G. Maestri e problemi di filosofia. Torino, 1924. 2v.

Phil 6952.21A   Campbell, C.M. A present-day conception of mental disorders. Cambridge, 1924.

Phil 4080.5.90   Carlo, E. di. Simone Corleo. Palermo, 1924.

Phil 177.65   Carr, H.W. The scientific approach to philosophy. London, 1924.

Phil 4080.3.121   Castellano, G. Benedetto Croce. Napoli, 1924.

Phil 4080.12.30   Castelli, Enrico. Filosofia della vita. Roma, 1924.

Phil 3640.215A   Castiglioni, M. Il poema eroico di F. Nietzsche. Torino, 1924.

Phil 8877.50.15   Cathrein, Victor. Moralphilosophie. Leipzig, 1924. 2v.

Phil 4080.3.123   Chiocchetti, E. La filosofia di Benedetto Croce. 3a ed. Milano, 1924.

Phil 5812.6   Choisnard, Paul. Introduction à la psychologie comparée. Paris, 1924.

Phil 477.8   Cía y Alvarez, J.M. La función espiritual. Madrid, 1924.

Phil 177.62.5   Cicala, F.B. Filosofia e diritto. v.1-4. Città di Castello, 1924.

Phil 400.58   Cicala, F.B. Punto di partenza e punti di arrivo dell' "idealismo attuale". Firenze, 1924.

Phil 3484.17F   Clasen, Karl H. Kant-Bildnisse. Königsberg, 1924.

Phil 530.11.10   The cloud of unknowing. London, 1924.

Phil 177.69   Coellen, L. Von der Selbstoffenbarung des göttlichen Lebens. Darmstadt, 1924.

Phil 177.85.5   Collingwood, R.G. Speculum mentis. Oxford, 1924.

Phil 2490.63   Comte, Auguste. Pensées et préceptes. Paris, 1924.

Phil 2493.40.3   Condillac, Etienne Bonnot. Essai sur l'origine des connaissances humnaines. Paris, 1924.

Phil 177.64   Conger, G.P. A course in philosophy. N.Y., 1924.

Phil 7140.116.9   Coué, Émile. Ce que j'ai fait. Nancy, 1924.

Phil 7140.116.11   Coué, Émile. Conscious auto-suggestion. London, 1924.

Phil 7140.116.13   Coué, Émile. Conscious auto-suggestion. N.Y., 1924.

Phil 5115.7   Crane, Esther. The place of the hypothesis in logic. Chicago, 1924.

Phil 2477.1.135   Crawford, L.S. The philosophy of Emil Boutroux. Thesis. Charlotteville, 1924.

Phil 1702.3   Cresson, André. La position actuelle des problèmes philosophiques. Paris, 1924.

Phil 177.35.25   Croce, Benedetto. The conduct of life. N.Y., 1924.

Phil 5042.19   Cunningham, H.E. Textbook of logic. N.Y., 1924.

Phil 8877.74   Cushman, H.E. Ten lessons in ethics. Newton, 1924.

Phil 178.63   Dallago, Carl. Der grosse Universume. Innsbruch, 1924.

Phil 2403.7   Dauriac, L. Contingence et nationalisme. Paris, 1924.

Phil 5520.41   Delacroix, H. Le langage et la pensée. Paris, 1924.

Phil 7082.164   Delage, Yves. Le rêve. Paris, 1924.

Phil 284.8   Descoqus, P. Essai critique sur l'hytemorphisme. Paris, 1924.

Phil 3625.3.87   Dingler, Hugo. Die Grundgedanken der Machschen Philosophie. Leipzig, 1924.

Phil 5043.22   Dotterer, Ray H. Beginners' logic. N.Y., 1924.

1924 - cont.

Phil 7069.24.5   Doyle, Arthur Conan. Our second American adventure. Boston, 1924.

Phil 5243.24.5   Dresser, H. Psychology in theory and application. N.Y., 1924.

Phil 5722.80   Drews, Arthur. Psychologie des Unbewussten. Berlin, 1924.

Phil 178.22.7   Driesch, H. Metaphysik. Breslau, 1924.

Phil 178.22.9   Driesch, H. The possibility of metaphysics. London, 1924.

Phil 270.26   Ducasse, Curt J. Causation and the types of necessity. Seattle, 1924.

Phil 334.6   Dürr, Karl. Wesen und Geschichte der Erkenntnistheorie. Zürich, 1924.

Phil 2855.2.97   Dugas, L. Le philosophie Théodule Ribot. Paris, 1924.

Phil 5243.23.7   Dumville, B. The fundamentals of psychology. 2d ed. London, 1924.

Phil 7054.45.55   Dunraven, W.T.W.-Q. Experiences in spiritualism with D.D. Home. Glasgow, 1924.

Phil 5545.156   Edgell, Beatrice. Theories of memory. Oxford, 1924.

Phil 8584.10   Edwards, D.M. The philosophy of religion. N.Y., 1924.

Phil 3200.8.15   Ehrlich, W. Metaphysik im erkenntniskritischen Grundriss. Halle, 1924.

Phil 7069.24.10   Eínar Níelsen, mídíll. Reykjavik, 1924.

Phil 5814.4   Erhard, H. Hypnose bei Tieren. Giessen, 1924.

Phil 3486.2.7   Erhardt, Franz. Die Grundgedanken der Kritik der reinen Vernunft. Leipzig, 1924.

Phil 3004.2   Ettlinger, Max. Geschichte der Philosophie von der Romantik bis zur Gegenwart. München, 1924.

Phil 8829.2.20   Eucken, Rudolf. The problem of human life. N.Y., 1924.

Phil 5710.7   Ewald, G. Temperament und Charakter. Berlin, 1924.

Phil 2404.2   Ewald, Oskar. Die französische Aufklärungsphilosophie. München, 1924.

Phil 3486.9   Ewing, Alfred Cyril. Kant's treatment of causality. London, 1924.

Phil 9070.26   Fairbanks, Douglas. Youth points the way. N.Y., 1924.

Phil 3487.32   Falkenfeld, Hellmuth. Was ist uns Kant? Weimar, 1924.

Phil 6315.1.7   Ferenczi, Sandor. Versuch einer Genitaltheorie. Leipzig, 1924.

Phil 3665.1.80   Festschrift für Paul Natorp zum siebzigsten Geburtstage. Berlin, 1924.

Phil 3246.18.3   Fichte, Johann Gottlieb. Nachgelassene Werke. Leipzig, 1924. 3v.

Phil 3246.18   Fichte, Johann Gottlieb. Sämmtliche Werke. Leipzig, 1924. 8v.

Phil 3246.73   Fichte, Johann Gottlieb. Über den Unterschied des Geistes und des Buchstabens in der Philosophie. Leipzig, 1924.

Phil 1705.4.50   Fischer, K. Geschichte der neueren Philosophie im Urteil der Jahrzehnte 1852-1924. Heidelberg, 1924.

Phil 7069.24.12   Fischer, Oskar. Experimente mit Raphael Schermann. Berlin, 1924.

Phil 7069.24.15   Flammarion, Camille. Haunted houses. London, 1924.

Phil 7069.24.15.2   Flammarion, Camille. Haunted houses. London, 1924.

Phil 6315.11   Flournoy, Henri. La psychanalyse, les médecins et le public. Neuchâtel, 1924.

Phil 5627.65   Flower, John C. Psychological studies of religious questions. London, 1924.

Phil 4756.1.35   Frank, Semen L. Krushenie kumirov. Berlin, 1924.

Phil 3310.7.90   Franzelin, B. Die neueste Lehre Geysers über des Kausali-Tatspriuzip. Innsbruck, 1924.

Htn   Phil 6315.2.74*   Freud, Sigmund. Aus der Geschichte einer infantilen Neurose. Leipzig, 1924.

Phil 6315.2.70   Freud, Sigmund. Beyond the pleasure principle. N.Y., 1924.

Phil 6315.2.35   Freud, Sigmund. Collected papers. N.Y., 1924-5.

Phil 6315.2.2   Freud, Sigmund. Gesammelte Schriften. Leipzig, 1924-34. 12v.

Phil 6480.23.13   Freud, Sigmund. On dreams. London, 1924.

Phil 6315.2.45   Freud, Sigmund. The psychologie collective et analyse du moi. Paris, 1924.

Phil 6315.2.7   Freud, Sigmund. Über Psychoanalyse. 7e Aufl. Leipzig, 1924.

Htn   Phil 6315.2.76*   Freud, Sigmund. Zeitgemässes über Krieg und Tod. Leipzig, 1924.

Phil 3487.8   Freytag, Willy. Über den Kantischen Idealismus. Leipzig, 1924.

NEDL   Phil 5520.15.7   Funke, O. Innere Sprachform. Reichenberg, 1924.

Phil 3925.4.80   Funker, F. Über Wirblichkeit und Logik; eine kritische Darlegung der Lehre Richard Wahles. Cernauti, 1924.

Phil 8585.25   Furman, R.T. What a man told his son. N.Y., 1924.

Phil 8586.22   Gabriel, R.H. Christianity and modern thought. New Haven, 1924.

Phil 3488.16   Garbeis, F.W. Das Problem des Bewusstseins in der Philosophie Kants. Wien, 1924.

Phil 5585.37   Garrison, W.A. The effect of varied instructions on the perception of distance in terms of arm-movement. Ithaca, 1924.

Phil 1706.1.43   Gaultier, Jules de. La sensibilité métaphysique. 3e éd. Paris, 1924.

Phil 1706.1.35   Gaultier, Jules de. La vie mystique de la nature. Paris, 1924.

Phil 7069.24.21   Geley, Gustave. L'ectoplasmie et la clairvoyance. Paris, 1924.

Phil 3488.15   Gemelli, A. Immanuel Kant, 1724-1924. Milano, 1924.

Phil 8586.17.2   Gentile, G. Discorsi di religione. 2. ed. Firenze, 1924.

Phil 3850.18.81   Geyser, Joseph. Max Schelers Phänomenologie der Religion. Freiburg, 1924.

Phil 7069.24.42   Giese, F. Die Lehre von den Gedankenwellen. 2.-3. Aufl. Leipzig, 1924.

Phil 5374.42   Giése, Fritz. Das ausserpersönliche Unbewusste. Braunschweig, 1924.

Phil 5850.214.15   Giese, Fritz. Psychoanalytische Psychotechnik. Leipzig, 1924.

Phil 2477.6.81   Gilbert, K. Maurice Blondel's philosophy of action. Chapel Hill, 1924.

Phil 5756.11   Gille, Paul. Esquisse d'une philosophie de la dignité humaine. Paris, 1924.

Phil 8520.31   Gillett, C.R. The McAlpin collection of British history and theology. N.Y., 1924.

Phil 2520.116.10   Gilson, E. Descartes et la métaphysique scolastique. Bruxelles, 1924.

Phil 4115.40.5   Gioberti, V. Protologia; estratti. Torino, 1924.

Phil 8881.47   Givler, R.C. The ethics of Hercules. N.Y., 1924.

Phil 8696.11   Goldsmith, W.M. Evolution or Christianity, God or Darwin? St. Louis, 1924.

Phil 9075.34   Gorham, C.T. Why we do right. London, 1924.

Phil 287.4   Grave, F. Das Chaos als objektive Weltregion. Berlin, 1924.

Phil 7082.72.5   Graves, Robert. The meaning of dreams. London, 1924.

1924 - cont.

Phil 2020.30.5   Green, T.H. Prolegomena to ethics. 5th ed. Oxford, 1924.
Phil 5525.23A   Gregory, J.C. The nature of laughter. London, 1924.
Phil 5246.31.5   Griffith, C.R. General introduction to psychology. N.Y., 1924.
Phil 9245.38   Grimanelli, P. La morale positive et le bonheur. Paris, 1924.
Phil 181.52   Groos, Karl. Der Aufbau der Systeme. Leipzig, 1924.
Phil 8407.10.10   Groos, Karl. Beiträge zur Ästhetik. Tübingen, 1924.
Phil 9166.8   Guardini, R. Neue Jugend und katholischer Geist. Mainz, 1924.
Phil 3246.202.5   Gurwitsch, G. Fichtes System der konkreten Ethik. Tübingen, 1924.
Phil 181.53   Guyon, René. Essai de métaphysique materialiste. Paris, 1924.
Phil 3488.17   Guzzo, Augusto. Kant precritico. Torino, 1924.
Phil 3826.8   Guzzo, Augusto. Il pensiero di B. Spinoza. Firenze, 1924.
Phil 6317.2.10   Hadfield, J.A. Psychologi och moral. 2a uppl. Stockholm, 1924.
Phil 6117.33.5   Hadfield, J.A. The psychology of power. N.Y., 1924.
Phil 5247.30.5   Häberlin, Paul. Der Geist und die Triebe: eine Elementarpsychologie. Basel, 1924.
Phil 3007.5.10   Hall, G.S. Founders of modern psychology. N.Y., 1924.
Phil 182.77   Hanan, F. A layman to his sons. London, 1924.
Phil 3110.171   Hankamer, P. Jakob Böhme, Gestalt und Gestaltung. Bonn, 1924.
Cg   Phil 4777.433   Harassek, S. Józef Gołuchowski. Kraków, 1924.
Phil 5247.32   Harford, C.F. Mind as a force. London, 1924.
Phil 3489.30   Harnack, Adolf von. Immanuel Kant, 1724-1924. Berlin, 1924.
Phil 65.2   Hartmann, E.V. Phänomenologie des sittlechen Bewusstens. 3 Aufl. Berlin, 1924.
Phil 3415.65.2   Hartmann, Eduard von. Phänomenologie des sittlichen Bewusstseins. 3. Aufl. Berlin, 1924.
Phil 3415.73.5   Hartmann, Eduard von. Philosophie des Schonen. 2. Aufl. Berlin, 1924.
Phil 3808.114.12   Hasse, Heinrich. Schopenhauers Religionsphilosophie und ihre Bedeutung für die Gegenwart. Frankfurt, 1924.
Phil 3425.76   Hegel, Georg Wilhelm Friedrich. Der Staat. Leipzig, 1924.
Phil 8408.15   Heimann, B. Über den Geschmack. Berlin, 1924.
Phil 3195.10.90   Heinichen, Otto. Driesch's Philosophie. Leipzig, 1924.
Phil 3489.19   Heller, Josef. Kants Persönlichkeit und Leben. Berlin, 1924.
Phil 5643.8.12   Helmholtz, H. Treatise on physiological optics. Rochester, N.Y., 1924-25. 3v.
Phil 5655.5.2   Henning, H. Der Geruch. 2e Aufl. Leipzig, 1924.
Phil 6317.27   Hermann, Imre. Psychoanalyse und Logik. Leipzig, 1924.
Phil 6117.20.5   Herrick, J.A. An introduction to neurology. 3. ed. Philadelphia, 1924.
Phil 6315.2.82   Hesmann, Angelo. La psychanalyse; theorie sexuelle de Freud. Paris, 1924.
Phil 5374.41   Hesnard, A. La relativité de la conscience de soi. Paris, 1924.
Phil 3415.105   Hessen, J. Die Kategorienlehre Eduard von Hartmanns. Leipzig, 1924.
Phil 8520.21.2   Hessen, J. Die Religionsphilosophie des Neukantianismus. 2. Aufl. Freiburg, 1924.
Phil 5757.13   Heuer, Wilhelm. Kausalität und Willensfreiheit. Heidelberg, 1924.
Phil 400.60   Heyde, Johannes E. Realismus oder Idealismus. Leipzig, 1924.
Phil 7069.24.24   Hill, J.A. From agnosticism to belief. London, 1924.
Phil 3640.227   Hirsch, Moriz. Friedrich Nietzsche. Stuttgart, 1924.
Phil 8882.52   Hlucka, J.F. Entwurf eines geschlossenen Systems der ethischen Formen. Wien, 1924.
Phil 3489.18   Hochdorf, Max. Das Kantbuch. Berlin, 1924.
Phil 8662.7.6A   Hocking, W.E. The meaning of God in human experience. New Haven, Conn., 1924.
Phil 3489.22   Hocking, William E. Immanuel Kant and international policies. Washington, D.C., 1924.
Phil 1707.1.6.10   Höffding, H. A history of modern philosophy. v.2. London, 1924.
Phil 3827.3.7   Höffding, H. Spinozas ethica, analyse og karakteristik. Heidelberg, 1924.
Phil 4580.66   Höffding, Harald. Der Begriff der Analogie. Leipzig, 1924.
Phil 4580.51   Höffding, Harald. La relativité philosophique. Paris, 1924.
Phil 4580.38.20   Höffding, Harald. Religionsfilosofi. 3e ed. København, 1924.
Phil 2045.99   Hönigswald, R. Hobbes und die Staatsphilosophie. München, 1924.
Phil 400.52   Hoernlé, R.F.A. Idealism as a philosophical doctrine. London, 1924.
Phil 3270.1.84   Hoffmann, E. Kuno Fischer: Rede...seine 100. Geburstages. Heidelberg, 1924.
Phil 3808.142   Hohenemser, Richard. Arthur Schopenhauer als Psychologie. Leipzig, 1924.
Phil 5252.18.50   Hollander, B. McDougall's social psychology anticipated by 100 years. n.p., 1924.
Phil 5643.74   Holsopple, J.Q. Factors involved in the reduction of post-rotation nystagmus time. Baltimore, 1924.
Phil 7069.24.25   Houdini, Harry. A magician among the spirits. N.Y., 1924.
Phil 2055.15.34A   Hulme, Thomas E. Speculations; essays on humanism and the philosophy of art. N.Y., 1924.
Phil 2050.60.5   Hume, David. Trattato della natura humana. Torino, 1924.
Phil 8588.2.5   Inge, W.R. Personal religion and the life of devotion. London, 1924.
Phil 8589.14.5   Jacks, L.P. A living universe (Hibbert lectures, 1923). N.Y., 1924.
Phil 8400.22   Jahn, Johannes. Die Kunstwissenschaft der Gegenwart in Selbstdarstellungen. Leipzig, 1924.
Phil 7069.24.28   James, William. Etudes et réflexions d'un psychiste. Paris, 1924.
Phil 2070.76   James, William. William James: extraits de sa correspondance. Paris, 1924.
Phil 6959.1.25   Janet, Pierre. Principles of psychotherapy. N.Y., 1924.
Phil 3110.179   Jecht, Richard. Jakob Böhme und Gorlitz. Gorlitz, 1924.
Phil 1709.2   Joad, C.E.M. Introduction to modern philosophy. London, 1924.
Phil 184.23   Jones, R.M. Fundamental ends of life. N.Y., 1924.
Phil 3491.3   Jonson, Erik. Det kategoriska imperativet. Akademisk avhandling. Uppsala, 1924.
Phil 2672.40   Jouffroy, Théodore S. Le cahier vert; comment les dogmes finissent. Lettres inédites. Paris, 1924.
Phil 3480.92   Kant, Immanuel. Briefwechsel. Leipzig, 1924. 2v.

1924 - cont.

Phil 3480.46.25   Kant, Immanuel. Critica della ragion pratica. 3. ed. Bari, 1924.
Phil 3480.17   Kant, Immanuel. Die philosophischen Hauptvorlesungen. München, 1924.
Phil 3480.74.15   Kant, Immanuel. Über Pädagogik. Leipzig, 1924.
Phil 3480.85.20   Kant, Immanuel. Von der Macht des Gemüths durch den blossen Vorsatz seiner krankhaften Gefühle Meister zu seyn. Heidelberg, 1924.
Phil 3480.41   Kant, Immanuel. Eine Vorlesung Kants über Ethik. Berlin, 1924.
Phil 3480.59.21   Kant, Immanuel. Vorlesungen über die Metaphysik. 2. Aufl. Rosswein, 1924.
Phil 5250.17   Kantor, J.R. Principles of psychology. N.Y., 1924-26. 2v.
Phil 5500.11   Katona, G. Psychologie der Relationserfassung und des Vergleichens. Leipzig, 1924.
Phil 9550.13   Keim, Albert. L'épicurisme, l'ascétisme et la morale utilitaire. Paris, 1924.
Phil 7069.24.29   Kemmerich, M. Wunderbare Tatsachen aus dem Reich des Übersinnlichen. Kempten im Allgäu, 1924.
Phil 3160.3.83   Kinkel, N. Hermann Cohen. Stuttgart, 1924.
Phil 3492.29   Kinkel, Walter. Kant zum Gedächtnis. Osterwieck, 1924.
Phil 3905.92   Klaren, Georg. Otto Weininger, der Mensch, sein Werk und sein Leben. Wien, 1924.
Phil 8590.28   Knudson, A.C. Present tendencies in religious thought. N.Y., 1924.
Phil 3492.21   Königsberg. Universität. Immanuel Kant. Leipzig, 1924.
Phil 185.45   Korzybski, A. Time-binding; the general theory. N.Y., 1924. 2 pam.
Phil 3120.8.82   Kraus, Oskar. Franz Brentanos Stellung zur Phänomenologie und Gegenstandstheorie. Leipzig, 1924.
Phil 3492.27   Kremer, Josef. Vorwärts zu Kant! Erfurt, 1924.
Phil 3492.26   Kries, J. von. Immanuel Kant und seine Bedeutung für die Naturforschung der Gegenwart. Berlin, 1924.
Phil 6960.6.5   Kronfeld, Arthur. Psychotherapie. Berlin, 1924.
Phil 8835.2.5   Kropotkin, Petr Alekseevich. Ethics; origin and development. N.Y., 1924.
Phil 3492.39.5   Kuhrke, Walter. Kants Wohnhaus. 2. Aufl. Königsberg, 1924.
Phil 3492.28   Kutter, Hermann. Im Anfang war die Tat: Versuch einer Orientierung in der Philosophie Kants. Basel, 1924.
Phil 4065.103   Labriola, Arturo. Giordano Bruno. Roma, 1924?
Phil 8591.26   Lambek, C. Religionen och nutidsmänniskan. Stockholm, 1924.
Phil 5400.92   Landis, Carney. Studies of emotional reactions. n.p., 1924.
Phil 186.46   Lapshin', I. Filosofia izobreteniia. Praga, 1924. 2v.
Phil 8412.16   La Via, Vincenzo. L'umanità dell'arte. Roma, 1924.
Phil 3790.4.83   Leenmans, H.A. De logica der geschiedeniswetenschap's van H. Rickert. 's Gravenhage, 1924.
Htn   Phil 2725.16.30*   Legouis, Émile. Histoire de la littérature anglaise. Paris, 1924.
Phil 8591.24   Leighton, J.A. Religion, and the mind of to-day. N.Y., 1924.
Phil 8400.32   Leningrad. Gosudarstvennyi Institut Istorii Iskusstv. Zadachi i metody izucheniia iskusstv. Peterburg, 1924.
Phil 2493.89   Lenoir, Raymond. Condillac. Paris, 1924.
Phil 2725.13.34   Lequier, Jules. La recherche d'une première vérité. Paris, 1924.
Phil 7140.125   Lestchinski, A. Essai médico-psychologique sur l'autosuggestion. Neuchâtel, 1924.
Phil 2070.114   Leuba, J.H. The immediate apprehension of God according to William James and W.E. Hocking. n.p., 1924?
Phil 8886.47   Levine, Israel. Reasons and morals. Glasgow, 1924.
Phil 8886.43   Liebert, Arthur. Ethik. Berlin, 1924.
Phil 292.5   Lilburne, H.A. The psychology of the atom. London, 1924.
Phil 186.57   Lindsay, Norman. Creative effort. 1. ed. London, 1924.
Phil 5251.29   Lloyd, R.E. Life and word. London, 1924.
Phil 2115.36.25A   Locke, J. Essay concerning human understanding. Oxford, 1924.
Phil 8591.20.2   Loisy, Alfred. La religion. 2. éd. Paris, 1924.
Phil 3493.14   Lomber, Wilhelm. Die Gratisstätte Immanuel Kants auf Grund authentischer Quellen dargestellt. Königsberg, 1924.
Phil 8886.48   Longo, P. Etica umana. Torino, 1924.
Phil 4762.1.35   Losskii, Nikolai Onufrievich. Sbornik zadach po logike. Praga, 1924.
Phil 3110.172   Ludwig, Else. Jakob Böhme, der Görlitzer Mystiker. 2. Aufl. Bad Smiedeberg, 1924.
Phil 665.41   Lutosławski, W. The world of souls. London, 1924.
Phil 9530.27   Lyons, Albert E. The self-starter. Boston, 1924.
Phil 8887.57   McDougall, William. Ethics and some modern world problems. N.Y., 1924.
Phil 5052.26   Mackaye, James. The logic of conduct. N.Y., 1924.
Phil 735.78   Mackenzie, J.S. Ultimate values in the light of contemporary thought. London, 1924.
Phil 3552.130.5   Mahnke, D. Leibniz und Goethe. Erfurt, 1924.
Phil 2128.41A   Mandeville, B. Fable of the bees. Oxford, 1924. 2v.
Phil 187.44.9   Mann, William E. A new theory of evolution. Walpole, Mass., 1924.
Phil 525.37.5   Maréchal, J. Études sur la psychologie des mystiques. v.1-2. Bruges, 1924-37.
Phil 8413.11.5   Marshall, Henry. The beautiful. London, 1924.
Phil 5252.58.2   Martin, E.D. Psychology. N.Y., 1924.
Phil 5252.58   Martin, E.D. Psychology. pt.1-20. N.Y., 1924.
Phil 5627.187   Martin, Everett D. The mystery of religion. N.Y., 1924.
Phil 2477.8.81   Martin, Robert. Alfred Binet. Thèse. Paris, 1924.
Phil 2805.420   Massis, Henri. Le réalisme de Pascal. St.-Felicien-en-Vivarais, 1924.
Phil 600.40   Mathis, René. La loi des trois états. Thèse. Nancy, 1924.
Phil 525.57   Maw, M.B. Buddhist mysticism. Thèse. Bordeaux, 1924.
Phil 3494.31   Meissinger, K.A. Kant und die deutsche Aufgabe. Frankfurt, 1924.
Phil 3625.15.87   Messer, A. Glauben und Wissen. 3. Aufl. München, 1924.
Phil 3494.13.5   Messer, A. Immanuel Kants Leben und Philosophie. Stuttgart, 1924.
Phil 3494.11.10   Miller, E.M. The basis of freedom: a study of Kant's theory. London, 1924.
Phil 6322.4.7   Miller, Hugh C. The new psychology and the preacher. London, 1924.
  A mind that found itself and its author. N.Y., 1924.
Phil 6951.5.50   Montalto, F. L'intuizione e la verità di fatto saggio; psicologico-metafisico. Roma, 1924.
Phil 187.87   Moore, T.V. Dynamic psychology. Philadelphia, 1924.
Phil 5252.50   Morrison, B.M. A study of the major emotions in persons of defective intelligence. Berkeley, 1924.
Phil 6750.224

Chronological Listing

1924 - cont.

Phil 5052.29   Mosso, Pietro. Principii di logica del potenziamento. Torino, 1924.

Phil 5252.30.9   Müller, G.E. Abriss der Psychologie. Göttingen, 1924.

Phil 5252.38.5   Müller-Freienfels, R. Grundzüge einer Lebenspsychologie. Leipzig, 1924-25. 2v.

Phil 187.63   Muirhead, J.H. Contemporary British philosophy. 1st Ser. N.Y., 1924.

Phil 7069.24.31   Murray, O. The spiritual universe. London, 1924.

Phil 5763.3.5   Nabert, Jean. L'expérience intérieure de la liberté. Paris, 1924.

Phil 5253.7.5   Naesgaard, S. Begrebet som psykologisk element. København, 1924.

Phil 3495.10   Natorp, Paul. Kant über Krieg und Frieden. Erlangen, 1924.

Phil 900.14   Negelein, J. Deltanschauung des indogermanischen Asiens. Erlangen, 1924.

Phil 8888.6.3   Nelson, Leonard. System der philosophischen Rechtslehre und Politik. Leipzig, 1924.

Phil 974.4   New India, Madras. Annie Besant, servant of humanity. Madras, 1924.

Phil 5125.9   Nicod, Jean. Le problème logique de l'induction. Paris, 1924.

Phil 2475.1.208.9   Nicolardot, F. À propos de Bergson. Paris, 1924.

Phil 2475.1.208.5   Nicolardot, F. Flore de G'nose, Laggrond, Pellis et Bergson. Paris, 1924.

Phil 3640.31.4   Nietzsche, Friedrich. Beyond good and evil. N.Y., 1924.

Phil 3640.77.7   Nietzsche, Friedrich. Der werdende Nietzsche. München, 1924.

Phil 6536.5   Ninde, F.W. The application of the auditory memory test to two thousand institut'l epileptics. West Chester, 1924?

Phil 8520.20   Nirenstein, S. The problem of the existence of God, in Maimonides, Alanus and Averroes. Philadelphia, 1924.

Phil 672.142   Nordmann, Charles. Notre maître le temps. Paris, 1924.

Phil 5722.13   Nortbridge, W.L. Modern theories of the unconscious. London, 1924.

Phil 3640.425   Obenauer, K.J. Friedrich Nietzsche der erkstatische Nihilist. Jena, 1924.

Phil 5650.13   Ogden, Robert M. Hearing. N.Y., 1924.

Phil 189.25   Oldfield, C.H. The kingdoms of the spirit. London, 1924.

Phil 1714.3   Olgiati, F. L'anima dell'umanesimo e del rinascimento. Milano, 1924.

Phil 189.11   Otto, M.C. Things and ideals. N.Y., 1924.

Phil 189.13   Ouy, A. Cahier d'études philosophiques. v.1-2. Paris, 1924-1925.

Phil 7076.24   Pagenstecher, Gustav. Aussersinnliche Wahrnehmung. Halle, 1924.

Phil 5255.23.2   Palágyi, M. Naturphilosophische Vorlesungen über die Grundprobleme des Bewusstseins und des Lebens. Leipzig, 1924.

Phil 2630.4.90   Palante, Georges. La philosophie du Bovarysme. Paris, 1924.

Phil 6125.15   Parson, B.S. Lefthandedness. N.Y., 1924.

Phil 2805.40.23   Pascal, Blaise. Pensées. Paris, 1924.

Phil 4200.4.35   Pastore, A. Il solipsismo. Torino, 1924.

Phil 190.56   Patrick, G.T.W. Introduction to philosophy. Boston, 1924.

Phil 5825.5   Patten, Charles J. The passing of the phantoms. London, 1924.

Phil 530.40.25   Peers, E.A. Spanish mysticism. London, 1924.

Phil 5545.165.25   Pelman Institute of America. Pelmanism. Lesson 1,3-12. N.Y., 1924.

Phil 5850.306   Pelman Institute of America. Scientific mind training. N.Y., 1924.

Phil 3110.173   Peuckert, W.E. Das Leben Jakob Böhmes. Jena, 1924.

Phil 190.40.2   Piccoli, V. Introduzione alla filosofia. 2a ed. Milano, 1924.

Phil 4015.2   Piccoli, V. Storia della filosofia italiano. Torino, 1924.

Phil 5055.18   Pichler, Hans. Zur Logik der Gemeinschaft. Tübingen, 1924.

Phil 9035.39   Pierce, Edgar. The philosophy of character. Cambridge, 1924.

Phil 7140.132   Pierce, Frederick. Mobilizing the mid-brain. N.Y., 1924.

Phil 8416.32   Pirenne, H.E. Essai sur le beau. Paris, 1924.

NEDL Phil 6125.23.5   Pratt, George K. Your mind and you. N.Y., 1924.

Phil 6125.23   Pratt, George K. Your mind and you. N.Y., 1924.

X Cg Phil 4710.10   Problemy russkago religioznogo soznaniia. Berlin, 1924.

Phil 1717.6.5A   Rand, Benjamin. Modern classical philosophers. 2nd ed. Boston, 1924.

Phil 6327.4.25   Rank, Otto. Die don Juan-Gestalt. Leipzig, 1924.

Phil 6327.4.5A   Rank, Otto. Das Trauma der Geburt. Leipzig, 1924. 2v.

Phil 1155.5   Ranulf, Svend. Der eleatische satz vom widerspruch. Kjøbenhavn, 1924.

Phil 3808.178   Rasche, F. Der Pessimismus Schopenhauers und das Wert Problem. Crimmitschau, 1924.

Phil 8892.13.2   Rashdall, Hastings. The theory of good and evil. 2. ed. Oxford, 1924. 2v.

Phil 400.69   Redanò, Ugo. La crisi dell'idealismo attuale. Roma, 1924.

Phil 3790.9.30   Rehmke, J. Die philosophische Erbsunde; Was in ich? Marburg, 1924.

Phil 8610.924   Reid, W.N. The supremacy of reason. London, 1924.

Phil 3499.2.3   Reinhold, K.L. Briefe über die Kantische Philosophie. Leipzig, 1924.

Phil 27.3.10   Revue de metaphysique et de morale. Table générale, 1893-1923. Paris, 1924.

Phil 5257.38   Reyburn, H.A. An introduction to psychology. Cape Town, 1924.

Phil 3499.14   Rickert, H. Kant als Philosoph der Modernen. Tübingen, 1924.

Phil 3791.35.3   Riehl, Alois. Der philosophische Kritizismus. Leipzig, 1924-1926. 3v.

Phil 5767.6   Riezler, Kurt. Gestalt und Gesetz. München, 1924.

Phil 6127.18.12   Riggs, A.F. Talks to patients. n.p., 1924-27.

Phil 5400.55   Rikimaru, J. Emotion and endocrine activities. n.p., 1924.

Phil 3415.102   Rintelen, F.J. von. Pessimistische Religionsphilosophie der Gegenwart. München, 1924.

Phil 8892.29.7   Ritter, P.H. Ethische fragmenten. 7. druk. Haarlem, 1924.

Phil 6327.5.5   Rivers, W.H.R. Instinct and the unconscious. 2. ed. Cambridge, Eng., 1924.

Phil 5057.20   Robinson, D.S. The principles of reasoning. N.Y., 1924.

Phil 5643.109   Romains, Jules. Eyeless sight, a study of extra-retinal vision and the paroptic sense. N.Y., 1924.

Phil 4210.20.10   Rosmini-Serbati, Antonio. Introduzione alla filosofia. v.1-4. Torino, 1924-25. 2v.

1924 - cont.

Phil 4210.29   Rosmini-Serbati, Antonio. Il principio della morale. Bari, 1924.

Phil 4210.41.20   Rosmini-Serbati, Antonio. Sistema filosofico. Torino, 1924.

Phil 3837.12A   Roth, Leon. Spinoza, Descartes and Maimonides. Oxford, 1924.

Phil 8892.12.20A   Royce, J. The philosophy of loyalty. N.Y., 1924.

Phil 6327.22   Rühle, Alice G. Freud und Adler. Dresden, 1924.

Phil 5257.25.2   Russell, Bertrand Russell. The analysis of mind. London, 1924.

Phil 192.50   Ryan, J.H. An introduction to philosophy. N.Y., 1924.

Phil 6328.25   Sachs, Hanns. Gemeinsame Tagträume. Leipzig, 1924.

Phil 1718.12   Sageret, Jules. La revolution philosophique et la science. Paris, 1924.

Phil 193.49.3   Santayana, G. The life of reason. v.1,3-5. N.Y., 1924-1925. 4v.

Phil 193.49.23   Santayana, G. Little essays drawn from writings of George Santayana. N.Y., 1924.

Phil 299.14   Sapper, Karl. Das Element der Wirklichkeit und die Welt der Erfahrung. München, 1924.

Phil 5374.50.15   Saunders, H.S. The higher consciouness. Toronto, 1924.

Phil 5070.16   Schiller, F.C.S. Problems of belief. London, 1924.

Phil 5070.16.5   Schiller, F.C.S. Problems of belief. N.Y., 1924.

Phil 3500.58   Schilling, Georg. Kants Lebenswerk als Gabe und Aufgabe. Detmold, 1924.

Phil 5258.85   Schleich, Carl Ludwig. Das ich und die Dämonien. Berlin, 1924.

Phil 3805.17   Schleiermacher, Friedrich. Werke. Berlin, 1924.

Phil 3450.11.80   Schmidt Degener, H. Proeve eener ver gelijkende studie over Plato en Husserl. Groningen, 1924.

Phil 3425.224   Schmidt-Japing, J.W. Die Bedeutung der person Jesu...Hegel. Göttingen, 1924.

Phil 3500.40   Schöndorffer, O. Kants Leben und Lehre. Leipzig, 1924.

Phil 270.58   Scholz, W. von. Der Zufall. Stuttgart, 1924.

Phil 3808.25.5   Schopenhauer, Arthur. Aphorismen zur Lebensweisheit. Stuttgart, 1924.

Phil 3808.20.10   Schopenhauer, Arthur. Philosophische Aphorismen. Leipzig, 1924.

Phil 7069.24.44   Schrenck von Notzing, Albert. Experimente der Fernbewegung. Stuttgart, 1924.

Phil 525.66   Schwarz, Hermann. Auf Wegen der Mystik. Erfurt, 1924.

Phil 5258.86   Schweizer, Walter. Erklären und Verstehen in der Psychologie. Bern, 1924.

Phil 5640.31   Schwertschlager, J. Die Sinneserkenntnis. München, 1924.

Phil 2477.1.139   Schyns, M. La philosophie d'Emile Boutroux. Paris, 1924.

Phil 3500.38   Scott, John W. Kant on the moral life. London, 1924.

Phil 5850.337   Seabury, David. Unmasking our minds. N.Y., 1924.

Phil 2490.112   Seillière, E. Auguste Comte. Paris, 1924.

Phil 5627.113.95   Selbie, W.B. Psychology of religion. Oxford, 1924.

Phil 3500.48   Selz, Otto. Kants Stellung in der Geistesgeschichte. Mannheim, 1924.

Phil 5258.59.7   Selz, Otto. Über die Persönlichkeitstypen. Jena, 1924.

Phil 960.39   Shcherbatskii, F.I. Erkenntnistheorie und Logik. München, 1924.

Phil 7069.24.33   Sigurgeirsson, Oddur. Andatrúin. Reykjavik, 1924.

Phil 5058.13.5   Sigwart, H.C.W. Logic. 5e aufl. Tübingen, 1924. 2v.

Phil 5258.91   Singer, Edgar A. Mind as behavior and studies in empirical idealism. Columbus, Ohio, 1924.

Phil 193.108   Smith, H.B. The collective mind. Columbus, 1924.

Phil 349.28A   Smith, Norman K. Prolegomena to idealist theory of knowledge. London, 1924.

Phil 299.16   Society of Universal Science. Belmont, Mass. The system of the universe. Belmont, 1924.

Phil 5075.3   Spann, Othmar. Kategorienlehre. Jena, 1924.

Phil 3819.36.25   Spinoza, Benedictus de. Etica. Pt.1-2. Firenze, 1924.

Phil 5258.74.4   Spranger, Eduard. Lebensformen; geisteswissenschaftliche Psychologie und Ethik der Personlichkeit. 4. Aufl. Halle, 1924.

Phil 3425.199A   Stace, N.J. The philosophy of Hegel. London, 1924.

Phil 8598.47   Stegenga, P. Twijfel als psychologisch verschijnsel in het religieuse leven. Amsterdam, 1924.

Phil 978.49.62   Steiner, R. Die Mystik im Aufgange des neuzeitlichen Geisteslebens und ihr Verhältnis zur modernen Weltanschauung. 3. Aufl. Stuttgart, 1924.

Phil 978.49.60   Steiner, R. Die Mystik im Aufgange des neuzeitlichen Geisteslebens und ihr Verhältnis zur modernen Weltanschauung. 2. Aufl. Stuttgart, 1924.

Phil 5768.10.30   Steiner, Rudolf. Frihedens filosofi. København, 1924.

Phil 1718.15.5   Steiner, Rudolf. Die Rätsel der Philosophie in ihrer Geschichte. Stuttgart, 1924-26. 2v.

Phil 6328.2.20   Stekel, Wilhelm. Peculiarities of behavior. N.Y., 1924. 2v.

Phil 4635.7.9   Stjernhjelm, Georg. Filosofiska fragment. v.1-2. Stockholm, 1924.

Phil 4210.88.5   Stresa, Italy. Istituto della Carità. Cenni biografici di Antonio Rosmini. Firenze, 1924.

Phil 5850.349.50   Swift, Edgar J. Psychology and the day's work. N.Y., 1924.

Phil 6315.2.81   Tannenbaum, S.A. The psychology of accidents and "symtomatic actions". N.Y., 1924.

Phil 5259.13.10   Tansley, A.G. The new psychology. N.Y., 1924.

Phil 6689.9   Tartaruga, U. Aus dem Reiche der Hellsehwunders. Pfullingen, 1924.

Phil 1124.3   Taylor, M.E.J. Zur Greek philosophy. London, 1924.

Phil 1135.64   Theiler, W. Zur Geschichte der teleologischen Naturbetrachtung bis auf Aristoteles. Inaug. Diss. Zürich, 1924.

Phil 4582.7.90   Thomsen, O. F.G. Howitz, 1789-1826. København, 1924.

Phil 5259.17   Thurstone, L.L. The nature of intelligence. London, 1924.

Phil 5259.5.19   Titchener, E.B. A beginner's psychology. N.Y., 1924.

Phil 5400.25.5   Titchener, E.B. Lectures on the elementary psychology of feeling and attention. N.Y., 1924.

Phil 5259.5.35   Titchener, E.B. A text-book of psychology. N.Y., 1924.

Phil 6329.1.12   Tridon, André. Psychoanalysis and man's unconscious motives. N.Y., 1924.

Phil 8599.19.20   Troeltsch, Ernst. Der Historismus und seine Überwindung; fünf Vorträge. Berlin, 1924.

Phil 3501.14   Troilo, E. Emmanuele Kant. Roma, 1924.

Phil 8644.9   Tsanoff, R.A. The problem of immortality. N.Y., 1924.

Phil 8894.24   Turner, J.E. The philosophic basis of moral obligation; a study in ethics. London, 1924.

Phil 3903.3.34   Vaihinger, Hans. Die Philosophie des Als Ob. 2. Aufl. Leipzig, 1924.

Phil 3903.3.40   Vaihinger, Hans. The philosophy of "As if". London, 1924.

Phil 3503.6.5 Vallois, M. La formation de l'influence Kantienne en France. Thèse. Paris, 1924.
Phil 4650.1.48 Vannérus, Allen. Det yttersta tankegångar. Stockholm, 1924.
Phil 4260.37 Vico, G.B. Die neue Wissenschaft über die gemeinschaftliche Natur der Völker. Munchen, 1924.
Phil 6331.2 Vivante, Leone. Note sopra la originalitá del pensiero. Roma, 1924?
Phil 352.1.2 Volkelt, J. Erfahrung und Denken. Aufl. 2. Leipzig, 1924.
Phil 3503.5.10 Volkelt, Johannes. Kant als Philosoph des Unbedingten. Erfurt, 1924.
Phil 4120.4.80 Volpe, Galvano della. L'idealismo dell'atto e il problema delle categorie. Bologna, 1924.
Phil 3503.4.15 Vorländer, K. Immanuel Kant. Leipzig, 1924. 2v.
Phil 196.23 Vowinckel, E. Metaphysik des Ich. Berlin, 1924.
Phil 4772.10.5 Vvedenskii, A.I. Filosofskie ocherki. Praga, 1924.
Phil 4655.3.33 Waerland, Arc. Idealism och materialism. Uppsala, 1924.
Phil 7069.24.35 Walbrook, L. The case of Lester Coltman. London, 1924.
Phil 5401.7 Walsh, W.S. The mastery of fear. N.Y., 1924.
Phil 8602.1.5 Ward, D.J.H. The biography of God as men have told it. Denver, 1924?
Phil 8847.3 Ward, Stephen. Ethics. London, 1924.
Phil 3504.20.9 Warda, Arthur. Immanuel Kants Cetzte Ehrung. Königsberg, 1924.
Phil 5262.21.2 Watson, John B. Psychology from the standpoint of a behaviorist. 2d ed. Philadelphia, 1924.
Phil 3640.163.7 Weichelt, Hans. Nietzsche der Philosoph des Heroismus. Leipzig, 1924.
Phil 197.48 Weinhandl, F. Einführung in das moderne philosophische Denken. Gotha-Stuttgart, 1924.
Phil 5402.12 Wells, Frederic L. Pleasure and behavior. N.Y., 1924.
Phil 1200.23 Wenley, R.M. Stoicism and its influence. Boston, 1924.
Phil 1822.2 Wentscher, E. Englische Philosophie. Leipzig, 1924.
Phil 8897.28.20 Westermarck, E. The origin and development of the moral ideas. 2nd ed. London, 1924-26.
Phil 6132.43 White, William Alanson. An introduction to the study of the mind. Washington, 1924.
Phil 7069.24.40 Wickland, C.A. Thirty years among the dead. Los Angeles, 1924.
Phil 197.50 Wielenga, B. In de school ijer wysbegeerte. Amsterdam, 1924.
Phil 3504.24.2 Wieser, F. Kant-Festschrift zu Kants 200. Geburststag am April 1924. 2. Aufl. Berlin, 1924.
Phil 3504.24 Wieser, F. Kant-Festschrift zu Kants 200. Geburststag am 22 April 1924. Berlin, 1924.
Phil 525.85 Wieser, Max. Der sentimentale Mensch. Gotha, 1924.
Phil 525.85.2 Wieser, Max. Der sentimentale Mensch gesehen aus der Welt. Gotha, 1924.
Phil 735.85 Wilken, F. Grundzüge einer personalistischen Werttheorie. Jena, 1924.
Phil 5650.15 Wilkinson, G. The mechanism of the cochlea. London, 1924.
Phil 5401.8 Williams, E.H. Our fear complexes. London, 1924.
Phil 197.69 Winderlich, R. Das Ding. Karlsruhe, 1924.
Phil 6315.2.87 Wittels, Fritz. Sigmund Freud. N.Y., 1924.
Phil 8520.24 Wobbermin, G. Religions Philosophie. Berlin, 1924.
Phil 8602.27 Wood, Herbert G. Living issues in religious thought. London, 1924.
Phil 5262.9.10 Woodworth, R.S. Psychology. N.Y., 1924.
Phil 1527.1.6.5 Wulf, M. de. Histoire de la philosophie médiévale. 5e éd. Louvain, 1924-25. 2v.
Phil 3504.32 Wundt, Max. Kant als Metaphysiker. Stuttgart, 1924.
Phil 5265.1.4.5 Ziehen, Theodor. Leitfaden der physiologischen Psychologie. 12. Aufl. Jena, 1924.
Phil 1825.1 Zulen, P.S. Del neohegelianismo al neorealismo. Lima, 1924.
Phil 6315.2.3* Zur Geschichte der psychoanalytischen Bewegung. Leipzig, 1924.
Phil 3507.9.5 Zwingmann, H. Kant. Berlin, 1924.

1925

Phil 6670.2 Abrutz, Sydney. Hypnos och suggestion. Stockholm, 1925.
Phil 5240.23 Adams, H.F. The ways of the mind. N.Y., 1925.
Phil 8615.5.4 Adler, Felix. Vågen till målet. Stockholm, 1925.
Phil 8401.10 Alexander, Samuel. Art and the material. London, 1925.
Phil 8709.9.5 Allen, Leslie H. Bryan and Darrow at Dayton. N.Y., 1925.
Phil 5627.97 Allier, Raoul. La psychologie de la conversion chez les peuples noncivilisés. Paris, 1925. 2v.
Phil 5643.87 Ames, Adelbert. Depth in pictorial art. N.Y., 1925.
Phil 5520.44 Ammann, H.J.F. Die menschliche Rede. Lahr, 1925-28. 2v.
Phil 8875.36 Androutsos, Chrèstos. Systèma èthikès. Athènai, 1925.
Phil 5240.27 Anthony, R. Réflexions d'un biologiste sur l'objet...de la psychologie. Paris, 1925.
Phil 2805.194 Arsovitch, R. Pascal et l'expérience du Puy-de-Dome. Thèse. Montpellier, 1925.
Phil 4080.3.155 Ascoli, M. Intorno alla concezione del diritto nel sistema di Benedetto Croce. Roma, 1925.
Phil 5425.67 Austin, Mary Hunter. Everyman's genius. Indianapolis, 1925.
Phil 3090.24 Baader, Franz von. Schriften zur Gesellschaftsphilosophie. Jena, 1925.
Phil 7069.25.3 Baerwald, R. Die intellektuellen Phänomene. Berlin, 1925.
Phil 270.37 Bang, Niels H. Aarsagsforestillingen. København, 1925.
Phil 3425.232 Barth, Paul. Die Geschichtsphilosophie Hegels und der Hegelianer bis auf Marx und Hartman. 2. Aufl. Photoreproduction. Leipzig, 1925.
Phil 3246.275 Bauch, Bruno. Fichte und der deutsche Staatsgedanke. Beyer, 1925.
Phil 5241.57.10 Baudouin, C. Makten i vår själ. Stockholm, 1925.
Phil 8876.51.19 Bayet, Albert. La morale laïque et ses adversaires. 4e éd. Paris, 1925.
Phil 8876.51.13 Bayet, Albert. La science des faits moraux. Paris, 1925.
Phil 3790.4.85 Beck, Friedrich. Heinrich Rickert und der philosophische transzendenta subjektivismus. Inaug. Diss. Erlangen, 1925.
Phil 176.104 Beck, Maximillian. Wesen und Wert. Berlin, 1925. 2v.
Phil 6951.5.5.7 Beers, C.W. A mind that found itself. Garden City, 1925.
Phil 5041.45 Behn, Siegfried. Romantische oder klassische Logik? Münster, 1925.
Phil 1865.30.30 Bentham, Jeremy. Deontologia. Torino, 1925.
Phil 6671.20 Benussi, V. La suggestione e l'ipnosi come mezzi di analisi psichisa reale. Bologna, 1925.
Phil 5643.79 Berger, E. Beiträge zur Psychologie des Sehens. München, 1925.
Phil 1870.45.10 Berkeley, G. Dialogues entre Hylas et Philonous. Paris, 1925.

Phil 1870.40.50 Berkeley, G. Principi della conoscenza umana. Bologna, 1925.
Phil 3640.580 Binder, J. Nietzsches Raatsauffassung. Göttingen, 1925.
Phil 7069.25.5A Bird, J. Malcolm. "Margery" the medium. Boston, 1925.
Phil 8125.10 Bite-Palevitch. Essai sur les tendances critiques. Paris, 1925.
Phil 5311.2.5 Bjerre, P. Von der Psychoanalyse zur Psychosynthese. Halle, 1925.
Phil 6311.2.5 Bjerre, P. Von der Psychoanalyse zur Psychosynthese. Halle, 1925.
Phil 6311.2.10 Bjerre, P. Wie deine Seele geheilt wird. Halle, 1925.
Phil 978.5.9 Blavatsky, H.P. The secret doctrine. v.1-2. Point Loma, Calif., 1925. 4v.
Phil 2401.2 Boas, George. French philosophies of the romantic period. Baltimore, 1925.
Phil 282.12 Boodin, J.E. Cosmic evolution. N.Y., 1925.
Phil 5648.11.5 Book, W.F. The psychology of skill. N.Y., 1925.
Phil 3110.91 Bornkamm, H. Luther und Böhme. Bonn, 1925.
Phil 2880.5.90 Boudeau, J.M.L. Ernest Seillière. Paris, 1925.
Phil 8581.51 Bouquet, A.C. The Christian religion and its competitors today. Cambridge, Eng., 1925.
Phil 510.150 Bräuer, E.W. Überwindung der Materie. Leipzig, 1925.
Phil 978.80 Bragdon, C.F. Old lamps for new. N.Y., 1925.
Phil 332.14 Brentano, Franz. Versuch über die Erkenntnis. Leipzig, 1925.
Phil 6311.3.3 Bridges, J.W. An outline of abnormal psychology. 3rd ed. Columbus, 1925.
Phil 8626.13 Brightman, E.S. Immortality in post-Kantian idealism. Cambridge, 1925.
Phil 176.94 Brightman, E.S. An introduction to philosophy. N.Y., 1925.
Phil 5241.66 Broad, C.D. The mind and its place in nature. London, 1925.
Phil 5241.28.3 Brown, W. Essentials of mental measurement. 3. ed. Cambridge, Eng., 1925.
Phil 3450.2.85 Brummel, L. Frans Hemsterhuis, een philosofenleven. Haarlem, 1925.
Phil 3552.265 Brunswig, A. Leibniz. Wien, 1925.
Phil 5627.217 Bry, Carl Christian. Verkappte Religionen. Gotha, 1925.
Phil 3120.30.39 Buber, Martin. Ereignisse und Begegnungen. Leipzig, 1925.
Phil 176.80.10 Burckhardt, Georg E. Weltanschauungskrisis. v.1-2. Leipzig, 1925-26.
Phil 705.17 Byers, R.P. Transcendental values. Boston, 1925.
Phil 4073.30 Campanella, Tommaso. Del senso delle cose e delle magia. Bari, 1925.
Phil 2475.1.219 Caramella, S. Bergson. Milano, 1925.
Phil 4080.13.30 Caria, G.M. de. Identità o contraddizione? Palermo, 1925.
Phil 510.140 Cassaigneau, M. Monisme vitaliste. Paris, 1925.
Phil 4210.78 Caviglione, C. Bibliografia delle opere di A. Rosmini. Torino, 1925.
Phil 8877.60.10 Chabot, Charles. Morale théorique et notions historiques. 10e éd. Paris, 1925.
Phil 5242.31 Challaye, F. Psychologie et métaphysique. Paris, 1925.
Phil 1930.7.80 Chamberlin, R.V. Life and philosophy. Salt Lake City, 1925.
Phil 8827.7 Chandavarkar, G.A. A manual of Hindu ethics. 3rd ed. Poona, 1925.
Phil 3425.218 Chang, W.S. Hegel's ethical teaching. Shanghai, 1925.
Phil 2725.14.90 Chartier, Émile. Souvenirs concernant Jules Lagneau. 2. éd. Paris, 1925.
Phil 2725.14.93 Chartier, Émile. Souvenirs concernant Jules Lagneau. 5e éd. Paris, 1925.
Phil 3484.12 Clark, Norman. An introduction to Kant's philosophy. London, 1925.
Phil 8692.15 Cohen, Chapman. God and evolution. London, 1925.
Phil 7082.76 Cohen, G. Das Wesen der Träume. Dresden, 1925.
Phil 5645.26 Collins, Mary. Colour-blindness. London, 1925.
Phil 70.14 Conference of Psychologists, Hanover, New Hanpshire, 1925. Conference of Psychologists called by Laura Spelman Rockefellar Memorial. n.p., 1925. 2v.
Phil 70.14.3 Conference of Psychologists, Hanover, New Hanpshire. Another, slightly variant report of the Thursday morning session. n.p., 1925.
Phil 802.10 Cosentini, F. I grandi filosofi e i grandi sistemi filosofici. Torino, 1925.
Phil 5242.34 Cramaussel, E. Psychologie expérimentale. Paris, 1925.
Phil 8952.5 Crawford, F.G. The Christ ideal for world peace. San Francisco, 1925.
Phil 177.40.5 Creighton, J.E. Studies in speculative philosophy. N.Y., 1925.
Phil 4080.3.54 Croce, Benedetto. Der Begriff des Barock. Zürich, 1925.
Phil 2070.113 Cugini, U. L'empirismo radicale di William James. Genova, 1925.
Phil 5242.29 Cunningham, G.W. Five lectures on the problem of mind. Austin, 1925.
Phil 5242.28 Cutten, George. Mind; its origin and goal. New Haven, 1925.
Phil 87.12 Cuvillier, Armand. Petit vocabulaire de la langue philosophique. Paris, 1925.
Phil 7069.25.4 Danmar, William. Geisterkenntnis. Leipzig, 1925.
Phil 8658.13 Davenport, S.F. Immanence and incarnation. Cambridge, 1925.
Phil 6313.7 Delmas, F. Achille. La personalité humaine. Paris, 1925.
Phil 1508.2 Dempf, Alois. Die Hauptform mittelalterlicher Weltanschauung. München, 1925.
Phil 1508.2.5 Dempf, Alois. Das Unendliche in der mittelalterlichen Metaphysik und in der Kantischendialektik. Münster, 1925.
Phil 8125.8 Denk, Ferdinand. Das Kunstschone und chacaktivstische von Winckelmann bis Friedrich Schlegel. Inaug. Diss. München, 1925.
Phil 6113.28.5 Dercum, F.X. The psychology of mind. 2. ed. Philadelphia, 1925.
Phil 2520.35.16 Descartes, René. Discours de la méthode. Paris, 1925.
Phil 178.52 Descoqs, Paul. Institutiones metaphysicae generalis; éléments d'ontologie. Paris, 1925.
Phil 178.38.5A Dewey, John. Experience and nature. Chicago, 1925.
Phil 5243.31.5 Dide, Maurice. Introduction à l'étude de la psychogénèse. Thèse. Paris, 1925. 2 pam.
Phil 3246.233.5 Döring, W.O. Fichte, der Mann und sein Werke. Lübeck, 1925.
Phil 8693.16 Donat, Josef. Die Freiheit der Wissenschaft. 3. Aufl. Innsbruck, 1925.
Phil 5243.30 Drake, Durant. Mind and its place in nature. N.Y., 1925.
Phil 8878.45 Dresser, H.W. Ethics in theory and application. N.Y., 1925.

1925 - cont.

Phil 803.8 — Dressoir, M. Lehrbuch der Philosophie. Berlin, 1925. 2v.

Phil 5243.28 — Driesch, Hans. The crisis in psychology. Princeton, 1925.

Phil 5401.3.5 — Dugas, L. Les timides dans la littérature et l'art. Paris, 1925.

Phil 5243.15.9 — Dunlap, K. Old and new viewpoints in psychology. St. Louis, 1925.

Phil 6313.12 — Dupré, E. Pathologie de l'imagination et de l'émotivité. Paris, 1925.

Phil 8583.18.2 — Durkheim, E. Les formes élémentaires de la vie religieuse. 2. éd. Paris, 1925.

Phil 5722.8.5 — Dwelshauvers, G. Les mécanismes subconscients. Paris, 1925.

Phil 8953.4 — Dyroff, A. Religion und Moral. Berlin, 1925.

Phil 335.2 — Eaton, R.M. Symbolism and truth. Cambridge, 1925.

Phil 335.1.2A — Eisler, Rudolf. Einführung in die Erkenntnis-Theorie. 2. Aufl. Leipzig, 1925.

Phil 2520.154 — Espinas, Alfred. Études sur l'histoire de la philosophie de l'action. Paris, 1925. 2v.

Phil 804.7 — Ettlinger, M. Philosophisches Lesebuch. München, 1925.

Phil 5814.5 — Ettlinger, Max. Beiträge zur Lehre von der Tierseele und ihrer Entwicklung. Münster, 1925.

Phil 179.3.2 — Eucken, R. Die Einheit des Geisteslebens. 2. Aufl. Berlin, 1925.

Phil 5850.191.5 — Ewer, B.C. Applied psychology. N.Y., 1925.

Phil 8660.10 — Farnell, Lewis R. The attributes of God. Oxford, 1925.

Phil 180.37 — Feldmann, J. Schule der Philosophie. Paderborn, 1925.

Phil 6315.1.17 — Ferenczi, Sandor. The development of psychoanalysis. N.Y., 1925.

Phil 3801.386 — Ferri, Ettore de. La filosofia dell'identità di F. Schelling. Torino, 1925.

Phil 3246.78.9A — Fichte, Johann Gottlieb. Briefwechsel. Leipzig, 1925. 2v.

Phil 8880.18.5 — Fite, Warner. Moral philosophy. N.Y., 1925.

Phil 8088.3 — Folkierski, W. Entre le classicisme et le romantisme. Cracovie, 1925.

Phil 6315.12 — Forel, O.L. La psychologie des névroses. Genève, 1925.

Phil 930.7 — Forke, A. The world conception of the Chinese. London, 1925.

Phil 336.6 — Franceschi, A. Ensayo sobre la teoría del conocimiento. La Plata, 1925.

Phil 286.8 — Frank, S.L. Smysl zhizni. Paris, 1925.

Phil 6315.2.75.11 — Freud, Sigmund. Trois essais sur la théorie de le sexualité. 3e éd. Paris, 1925.

Phil 400.61 — Friedmann, H. Die Welt der Formen. Berlin, 1925.

Phil 5520.49 — Fröschels, E. Psychologie der Sprache. Leipzig, 1925.

Phil 5755.10 — Fröschels, E. Wille und Vernunft. Leipzig, 1925.

Phil 6420.18 — Froeschels, Emil. Das Stottern: assoziative Aphasie. Leipzig, 1925.

Phil 8696.12 — Gager, C.S. The relation between science and theology. Chicago, 1925.

Phil 4112.40.6 — Galluppi, Pasquale. Lettere filosofiche. 2a ed. Firenze, 1925.

Phil 4112.40.7 — Galluppi, Pasquale. Lettere filosofiche e lezioni di logica e metafisica. Torino, 1925?

Phil 5425.2.6 — Galton, F. Hereditary genius. London, 1925.

Phil 5246.36 — Gates, Arthur I. Elementary psychology. N.Y., 1925.

Phil 5246.37 — Gault, Robert H. Outline of general psychology. N.Y., 1925.

Phil 8586.31 — Gehring, Albert. The religion of thirty great thinkers. Boston, 1925.

Phil 4065.102.2 — Gentile, G. Giordana Bruno i el pensiero del rinascimento. 2a ed. Firenze, 1925.

Phil 181.45.19 — Gentile, Giovanni. L'esprit, acte pur. Paris, 1925.

Phil 806.9 — Geschichte der Philosophie. Leipzig, 1925.

Phil 5850.214 — Giese, Fritz. Theorie der Psychotechnik: Grundzüge der praktischen Psychologie. Braunschweig, 1925.

Phil 960.44 — Gomperz, Heinrich. Die indische Theosophie. Jena, 1925.

Phil 181.55 — Greca, Carlo. L'esistere quale oggetto di scienza e di storia. Parte 1a. Girgenti, 1925.

Phil 7069.25.15 — Gruber, K. Parapsychologische Erkenntnisse. München, 1925.

Phil 181.56 — Grünbaum, A.A. Herrschen und Leiben als Grundmotive der philosophische Weltanschauungen. Bonn, 1925.

Phil 181.83 — Guardini, R. Der Gegensatz. Mainz, 1925.

Phil 8407.8 — Guastalla, Pierre. Esthétique. Paris, 1925.

Phil 7069.25.14 — Gulat-Wellenburg, W.K.H. Der physikalische Mediumismus. Berlin, 1925.

Phil 7140.121.5 — Gulat-Wellenburg. Das Wunder der Autosuggestion. Kempten im Allgäu, 1925.

Phil 3826.7 — Gunn, J.A. Benedict Spinoza. Melbourne, 1925.

Phil 7069.25.13 — Guyard, J. The door of death wide open. Boston, 1925.

Phil 400.67 — Guzzo, Augusto. Verità e realtà: apologia dell'idealismo. Torino, 1925.

Phil 9035.42 — Häberlin, Paul. Der Charakter. Basel, 1925.

Phil 510.1.7.5 — Haeckel, Ernst. The riddle of the universe. London, 1925.

Phil 3565.118 — Hahn, Gustav. Der Allbeseelungsgedanke bei Lotze. Stuttgart, 1925.

Phil 5545.158 — Halbwachs, Maurice. Les cadres sociaux de la mémoire. Paris, 1925.

Phil 338.5.2 — Hamelin, O. Essai sur les elements principaux de la représentation. 2. ed. Paris, 1925.

Phil 6317.15 — Hamilton, Gilbert V. An introduction to objective psychopathology. St. Louis, 1925.

Phil 5627.98 — Hardman, Oscar. Psychology and the church. London, 1925.

Phil 6957.7.4 — Hart, Bernard. The psychology of insanity. Cambridge, 1925.

Phil 3415.74 — Hartmann, Eduard von. Das Problem des Lebens. 2. Aufl. Berlin, 1925.

Phil 182.83 — Heidrich, E. Die Gegenwartslinie, Wesen und Grenzen des Determinismus. Görlitz, 1925.

Phil 807.17 — Heinrich, W. Zarys historji filozofji. Warszawa, 1925-30.

Phil 5627.110 — Heinsius, Wilhelm. Krisen katholischer Frömmigkeit. Berlin, 1925.

Phil 2050.176A — Hendel, C.W. Studies in the philosophy of David Hume. Princeton, 1925.

Phil 8735.6.5A — Henderson, L.J. The order of nature. Cambridge, 1925.

Phil 5330.22 — Henning, H. Die Aufmerksamkeit. Berlin, 1925.

Phil 5247.44 — Henning, Hans. Psychologie der Gegenwart. Berlin, 1925.

Phil 8587.42 — Hering, Jean. Phénoménologie et philosophie religieuse. Thèse. Strasbourg, 1925.

Phil 3489.25.3 — Heussner, A. Kleines Kant-Wörterbuch. Göttingen, 1925.

Phil 930.9.5 — Hoang, Tsen-Yue. Étude comparative sur les philosophies de Lao Tseu, Khong Tseu, Mo Tseu. Thèse. Lyon, 1925.

Phil 8832.3.5 — Hobhouse, L.T. Morals in evolution. 5th ed. London, 1925.

1925 - cont.

Phil 6317.16 — Hoeberlin, Carl. Grundlinien der Psychoanalyse. München, 1925.

Phil 4580.35.9 — Høffding, Harald. Kort oversigt over den nyere filosofis historie. 9e ed. Kjøbenhavn, 1925.

Phil 4803.454.46 — Hoene-Wroński, Józef Maria. Propedeutyka mesjaniczna. v.2. Warszawa, 1925.

Phil 5247.37.2 — Hönigswald, R. Die Grundlagen der Denkpsychologie. 2. Aufl. Leipzig, 1925.

Phil 6540.2 — Hollós, Stefom. Psychoanalysis and the psychic disorder of general paresis. N.Y., 1925.

Phil 630.5.10 — Holt, E.B. The new realism. N.Y., 1925.

Phil 4363.3.101 — Homenaje al venerable siervo de dios, Don Miguel. Sevilla, 1925.

Phil 338.19 — Honecker, M. Das Denken. Berlin, 1925.

Phil 1135.150 — Hopgner, T. Orient und griechische Philosophie. Leipzig, 1925.

Phil 3246.205 — Horneffer, Martha. Die Identitätslehre Fichtes in den Jahren 1801-1806. Leipzig, 1925.

Phil 1112.5 — Howald, E. Die Anfänge der europäischen Philosophie. München, 1925.

Phil 338.18 — Hubert, René. Le sens du réel. Paris, 1925.

Phil 8587.32.87 — Hügel, Friedrich von. Some letters. London, 1925.

Phil 8610.925 — Hughes, R. Why I quit going to church. N.Y., 1925.

Phil 6957.12.7 — Hyslop, T.B. The borderland, some of the problems of insanity. N.Y., 1925.

Phil 6957.12 — Hyslop, T.B. The great abnormals. London, 1925.

Phil 4759.1.35 — Il'in, I.A. O soprotivlenii zlu siloiu. Berlin, 1925.

Phil 183.1 — Isbyam, I.C. The ego and physical force. London, 1925.

Phil 184.13.7 — Jacoby, Günther. Allgemeine der Wirklichkeit. Halle, 1925.

Phil 8884.17.10 — Jahn, Max. Ethik als Grundwissenschaft. 4. Aufl. Leipzig, 1925. 2v.

Phil 4710.4 — Jakovenko, B. Filosofi Russi: saggio di storia della filosofia. Firenze, 1925.

Phil 2070.50 — James, William. Máttur manna. Reykjavík, 1925.

Phil 2070.26 — James, William. Pragmatism. N.Y., 1925.

Phil 5249.2.16 — James, William. Psykologi. Uppsala, 1925.

Phil 184.30 — Janet, P. Philosophie; questions complémentaires. Paris, 1925.

Phil 6959.1.18 — Janet, Pierre. Psychological healing. N.Y., 1925. 2v.

Phil 3491.5 — Jansen, B. Der Kritizismus Kants. München, 1925.

Phil 184.19.5A — Jaspers, K. Psychologie der Weltanschauung. Berlin, 1925.

Phil 9150.27 — Jensen, J.V. Evolution og moral. Kjøbenhavn, 1925.

Phil 184.12.10 — Jerusalem, W. Gedanken und Denker. 2. Aufl. Wien, 1925.

Phil 8884.18.6 — Joad, Cyril E.M. Thrasymachus; or The future of morals. London, 1925.

Phil 8589.16 — Johnson, J.W. Fundamentalism versus modernism. N.Y., 1925.

Phil 5238.60 — Johnston, D.K. Religion und wissenschaftliches Heilverfahren. Bahn, 1925. 7 pam.

Phil 6319.1.8 — Jung, C.G. Wandlungen und Symbole der Libido. 2. Aufl. Leipzig, 1925.

Phil 5249.13.7 — Jung, Carl G. Psychologische Typen. Zürich, 1925.

Phil 3480.28.30 — Kant, Immanuel. Antologia Kantiana. Torino, 1925.

Phil 3480.66.50 — Kant, Immanuel. Fondazione della metafisica dei costumi. Torino, 1925?

Phil 3480.65.10 — Kant, Immanuel. Grundlegung zur Metaphysik der Sitten. München, 1925.

Phil 3480.45.25 — Kant, Immanuel. Kritik der praktischen Vernunft nebst Grundlegung zur Metaphysik der Sitten. Leipzig, 1925.

Phil 3480.30.27 — Kant, Immanuel. Kritik der reinen Vernunft. Leipzig, 1925.

Phil 3480.50.22 — Kant, Immanuel. Kritik der Urtheilskraft. Stuttgart, 1925.

Phil 3480.41.2 — Kant, Immanuel. Eine Vorlesung Kants über Ethik. 2. Aufl. Berlin, 1925.

Phil 3808.157 — Kaplan, Leo. Schopenhauer und der Animismus. Leipzig, 1925.

Phil 3640.203 — Kappstein, T. Einführung in Friedrich Nietzsches Zarathustradichtung. Bielefeld, 1925.

Phil 4761.2.30 — Karsavin, L.P. O comnenii, nauke i vere. Berlin, 1925.

Phil 4761.2.35 — Karsavin, L.P. O nachalakh. Berlin, 1925.

Phil 8700.7 — Keebler, R.S. The Tennessee evolution case. Memphis, 1925.

Phil 3492.25 — Keeling, S.V. La nature de l'expérience chez Kant et chez Bradley. Thèse. Montpellier, 1925.

Phil 8835.3 — Keller, M. Ethik als Wissenschaft ein methodologischer Versuch. Zürich, 1925.

Phil 8960.3 — Kent, Charles F. Fundamentals of Christianity. Philadelphia, 1925.

Phil 185.34 — Kerler, D.H. Weltwille und Wertwille. Leipzig, 1925.

Phil 3549.2.78 — Keyserling, Hermann. The travel diary of a philosopher. London, 1925. 2v.

Phil 3549.2.78.2 — Keyserling, Hermann. The travel diary of a philosopher. N.Y., 1925. 2v.

Phil 3552.127.5 — Kiefl, Franz X. Leibniz und die religiöse Wiedervereinigung Deutschlands. 2. Aufl. München, 1925.

Phil 5250.3.6 — Kirkpatrick, E.A. Genetic psychology. N.Y., 1925.

Phil 850.14 — Klippel, M. Philosophie et poésie: Les origines. Paris, 1925.

Phil 8700.9 — Klyce, S. Sins of science. Boston, 1925.

Phil 5820.4.5 — Köhler, Wolfgang. The mentality of apes. London, 1925.

Phil 185.40 — Kolbenheyer, E.G. Die Bauhütte. München, 1925.

Phil 8590.25 — Koppelmann, W. Der Erlösungs- und Heilsgedanke von freisinnig protestantischen Standpunkt. Bonn, 1925.

Phil 185.42 — Kortmulder, R.J. Metaphysicia der rede. Amsterdam, 1925.

Phil 3492.27.5 — Kremer, Josef. Kritik der Vernunftkritik. Erfurt, 1925.

Phil 6960.6.7 — Kronfeld, Arthur. Psychotherapie, Charakterlehre, Psychoanalyze, Hynose, Psychogogik. 2. Aufl. Berlin, 1925.

Phil 3492.50 — Küpenberg, Max. Ethische Grundfragen...Ethikvorselung Kants. Innsbruck, 1925.

Phil 5850.253 — Laird, Donald A. Increasing personal efficiency. N.Y., 1925.

Phil 5850.253.5 — Laird, Donald A. Increasing personal efficiency. N.Y., 1925.

Phil 6121.23 — Laird, John. Our minds and their bodies. London, 1925.

Phil 8412.6 — Lalo, Charles. Notions d'esthétique. Paris, 1925.

Phil 342.11 — Lambek, C. Track af vor erkendelses psykologi. København, 1925.

Phil 486.1.5.7A — Lange, F.A. History of materialism and criticism of its importance. v.1-3. 3rd ed. London, 1925.

NEDL Phil 486.1.5.8 — Lange, F.A. The history of materialism and criticism of its present importance. v.1-3. 3rd ed. N.Y., 1925.

Phil 2725.15.30 — Lasbax, E. La dialectique et le rythme de l'univers. Paris, 1925.

Chronological Listing

Phil 6315.2.91 Laumonier, J. Le freudisme; exposé et critique. Paris, 1925.

Phil 4120.4.82 La Via, G. L'idealismo attuale di Giovanni Gentile. Trani, 1925.

Phil 978.8.19 Leadbeater, C.W. Textbook of theosophy. Chicago, 1925.

Phil 292.6 LeBel, J.A. Cosmologie rationnelle. Le Mans, 1925.

Phil 705.20 Leider, Kurt. Das Transzendentale. Diss. Königsberg, 1925.

Phil 2705.86 Lemée, Pierre. Offray de la Mettrie. Saint-Servan, 1925.

Phil 186.56 Le Senne, R. Introduction à la philosophie. Paris, 1925.

Phil 3640.220 Lessing, Theodor. Nietzsche. Berlin, 1925.

Phil 5627.20.7 Leuba, J.H. The psychology of religious mysticism. London, 1925.

Phil 525.62 Levasti, A. I mistici. Firenze, 1925. 2v.

Phil 1850.123 Levi, Adolfo. Il pensiero di Francesco Bacone. Torino, 1925.

Phil 6121.24 Lhermitte, J. Les fondements biologiques de la psychologie. Paris, 1925.

Phil 672.120.50 Liddell, Anna F. Alexander's space, time and deity. Chapel Hill, 1925?

Phil 5251.33 Love, Mary C. Human conduct and the law. Menasha, 1925.

Phil 5251.31 Lungwitz, H. Die Entdeckung der Seele. Leipzig, 1925.

Phil 5051.6.13 Luquet, G.H. Logique formelle. Paris, 1925.

Phil 187.84 Maar, Jean. Le fondement de la philosophie. Paris, 1925.

Phil 3525.90 MacCauley, Clay. Karl Christian Friedrich Krause. Berkeley, Calif., 1925.

Phil 5052.27 McClure, M.T. An introduction to the logic of reflection. N.Y., 1925.

Phil 6322.8.5 MacCurdy, J.T. The psychology of emotion; morbid and normal. London, 1925.

Phil 3552.130.10 Mahnke, D. Leibnizens Synthese von Universalmathematik und Individualmethaphysik. Halle, 1925.

Phil 2805.78 Maire, Albert. Bibliographie générale des oeuvres de Blaise Pascal. Paris, 1925-27. 5v.

Phil 8837.10 Maitra, Sushil Kumar. The ethics of the Hindus. Calcutta, 1925.

Phil 9550.14 Manzoni, A. Del sistema che fonda la morale sull utilità. Firenze, 1925.

Phil 3494.19.35 Marcus, Ernst. Aus den Tiefen der Erkennens...Kants. München, 1925.

Phil 2725.2.67 Maréchal, C. La Mennais. Paris, 1925.

Phil 2725.2.89 Maréchal, C. La Mennais. Paris, 1925.

Phil 8592.38 Mariavé, Henry. Le philosophe suprême. v.2. Montpellier, 1925-26. 2v.

Phil 2750.11.73 Maritain, Jacques. Théonas. 2. éd. Paris, 1925.

Phil 2750.11.71.5 Maritain, Jacques. Trois réformateurs: Luther-Descartes-Rousseau. Paris, 1925. 2v.

Phil 2750.11.71A Maritain, Jacques. Trois réformateurs: Luther-Descartes-Rousseau. Paris, 1925.

Phil 3625.11.80 Martinak, E. Meinong als Mensch und als Lehrer. Graz, 1925.

Phil 150.10 Mateucci, Arturo. Vocabolarietto di termini filosofici. Milano, 1925.

Phil 8592.69 Matthes, H. Christus-Religion oder philosophische Religion? Göttingen, 1925.

Phil 525.64 Mattiesen, Emil. Der jenseitige Mensch. Berlin, 1925.

Phil 1812.5 Merwe, A.J. van der. Het zondebegrip in de engelsche evolutionislische wijsbegeerte. Utrecht, 1925.

Phil 8887.53.4 Messer, A. Ethik. Leipzig, 1925.

Phil 1870.101 Metz, Rudolf. George Berkeley Leben und Lehre. Stuttgart, 1925.

Phil 5762.9.4 Meumann, Ernst. Intelligenz und Wille. 4. Aufl. Leipzig, 1925.

Phil 325.5 Meurer, W. Gegen den Empirismus. Leipzig, 1925.

Phil 1117.6 Meyer, Hans. Geschichte der alten Philosophie. München, 1925.

Phil 5252.26.10 Meyer, Semi. Die geistige Wirklichkeit. Stuttgart, 1925.

Phil 6315.2.93 Michaëlis, Edgar. Die Menschkeitsproblematik der Freudschen Psychoanalyse. Leipzig, 1925.

Phil 8592.35 Milburn, R.G. The theology of the real. London, 1925.

Phil 2138.40.25 Mill, John S. La libertà. Torino, 1925.

Phil 2138.45.10 Mill, John S. Three essays on religion. London, 1925.

Phil 6122.48 Mohr, Fritz. Psychophysische Behandlungs-Methoden. Leipzig, 1925.

Phil 2630.2.133 Molina, Enrique. Dos filosofos contemporaneos; Guyau-Bergson. Santiago de Chile, 1925.

Phil 7069.25.20 Moll, A. Der Spiritismus. Stuttgart, 1925.

Phil 5400.185 Monakow, Constantin. The emotions, morality and the brain. Washington, 1925.

Phil 7109.195 Moniz, Egas. O padre Faria na história do hipnotismo. Lisboa, 1925.

Phil 343.13A Montague, William P. The ways of knowing. London, 1925.

Phil 187.127 Moore, C.F. The challenge of life. N.Y., 1925.

Phil 2145.15 More, Henry. Philosophical writings. N.Y., 1925.

Phil 8702.12.5 Moreux, T. Les confins de la science et de la foi. Paris, 1925. 2v.

Phil 365.12.7 Morgan, Conwy L. Life, mind and spirit. N.Y., 1925.

Phil 410.77 Mozkowski, A. Der Abbau des "Unendlich". Berlin, 1925.

Phil 5585.38 Müller, Günter. Theorie des Vorstellungsverlaufs. Mannheim, 1925.

Phil 5252.38.15 Müller-Freienfels, R. Die Seele des Alltags. 2. Aufl. Berlin, 1925.

Phil 187.63.5 Muirhead, J.H. Contemporary British philosophy. 2nd ser. N.Y., 1925.

Phil 187.69 Muller, Aloys. Einleitung in die Philosophie. Berlin, 1925.

Phil 575.137 Mutius, Gerhard von. Jenseits von Person und Sache. München, 1925.

Phil 5252.19.3 Myers, C.S. Text-book of experimental psychology. 3d ed. Cambridge, 1925.

Phil 75.27 National Research Council. Research Information Service. Union list of foreign serials cited in Psychological index, 1922. Washington, 1925.

Phil 5763.2.5 Natorp, Paul. Sozialpädagogik. Theorie der Willenserziehung. 6. Aufl. Stuttgart, 1925.

Phil 188.12.9 Natorp, Paul. Vorlesungen über praktische Philosophie. Erlangen, 1925.

Phil 2805.193 Nedelkovitch, D. La pensées philosophique créatrice de Pascal. Paris, 1925.

Phil 2805.201 Nolhac, P. de. Pascal en Auvergne. Saint-Felicien-en-Vivarais, 1925.

Phil 672.142.5 Nordmann, Charles. The tyranny of time. London, 1925.

Phil 3495.9 Northwestern University. Evanston, Illinois. Immanuel Kant. Chicago, 1925.

Phil 1145.74 Oakeley, Hilda D. Greek ethical thought. London, 1925.

Phil 6324.2 Odier, Charles. Étude psychoanalytique. Le complex d'Oedipe. Genève, 1925.

Phil 8594.11 Oltramare, P. La religion et la vie de l'esprit. Paris, 1925.

Phil 189.16 Orestano, F. Nuovi principi. Roma, 1925.

Phil 8704.2.5 Osborn, H.F. The earth spaks to Bryan. N.Y., 1925.

Phil 5850.299 Overstreet, H.A. Influencing human behavior. N.Y., 1925.

Phil 5850.299.5 Overstreet, H.A. Influencing human behavior. N.Y., 1925.

Phil 190.45 Pagani, Silvio. Umanismo antivitale. Milano, 1925.

Phil 5255.24 Paget, Violet. Proteus or The future of intelligence. London, 1925.

Phil 5585.42 Palágyi, M. Wahrnehmungslehre. Leipzig, 1925.

Phil 5255.25.5 Paliard, Jacques. Intuition et réflexion. Thèse. Paris, 1925.

Phil 2730.90 Paliard, Jacques. Le raisonnement selon Maine de Biran. Paris, 1925.

Phil 2730.90.5 Paliard, Jacques. Le raisonnement selon Maine de Biran. Thèse. Paris, 1925.

Phil 190.50 Paret, Hans. Der dialektische Ursprung der Glückseligkeit. Berlin, 1925.

Phil 2805.40.20 Pascal, Blaise. Pensées sur la vérité de la religion chrétienne par J. Chevalier. 2. éd. Paris, 1925. 2v.

Phil 190.48 Pauler, A. von. Grundlagen der Philosophie. Berlin, 1925.

Phil 400.68 Pavese, R. L'idea e il mondo. Torino, 1925.

Phil 2475.1.224 Perego, Luigi. La dinamica dello spirito nella conoscenza: saggio...Bergson. Bologna, 1925.

Phil 5440.28 Peters, Wilhelm. Die Vererbung geistiger Eigenschaften und die psychische Constitution. Jena, 1925.

Phil 3915.161 Petersen, Peter. Wilhelm Wundt und seine Zeit. Stuttgart, 1925.

Phil 5400.57 Phelan, G.B. Feeling experience and its modalities. London, 1925.

Phil 5255.7.8 Pillsbury, W.B. The essentials of psychology. N.Y., 1925.

Phil 3745.6.35 Planck, K.C. Testament eines Deutschen; Philosophie der Natur und Menschheit. 3e Ausg. Jena, 1925.

Phil 5255.28.2 Poffenberger, A.T. Experimental psychology; loose leaf laboratory manual. N.Y., 1925?

Phil 190.43 Polakov, W.N. Man and his affairs from an engineering point of view. Baltimore, 1925.

Phil 8640.1.10 Pomponazzi, P. De immortalitate animae. Messina, 1925.

Phil 3497.14 Poppovich, N.M. Die Entwicklungsgeschichte der vorkritischen Raumphilosophie Kants. Wien, 1925.

Phil 8610.925.10 Powers, H.H. The religion of to-morrow...correspondence between H.H. Powers and William Archer. London, 1925.

Phil 7039.4.6 Prince, Morton. The dissociation of a personality. N.Y., 1925.

Phil 5238.14A Problems of personality: studies presented to Dr. Morton Prince. N.Y., 1925.

Phil 525.22 Qu'est-ce que la mystique? Paris, 1925.

Phil 2050.185 Radakovic, K. Die letzten Fundamente der Hume'schen Erkenntnistheorie. Graz, 1925.

Phil 900.25 Rádl, Emanuel. Západ a východ; filosofia úvahy z cest. Praze, 1925.

Phil 4710.20.5 Radloff, E. von. Russische Philosophie. Bredau, 1925.

Phil 6327.10 Raimann, Emil. Zur psychoanalyse. 2. Aufl. Berlin, 1925.

Phil 6327.4.35 Rank, Otto. Der Doppelganger. Zürich, 1925.

Phil 5841.18.4 Rank, Otto. Der Künstler. 4. Aufl. Leipzig, 1925.

Phil 2035.86.35 Rasmussen, S.V. The philosophy of Sir William Hamilton. Copenhagen, 1925.

Phil 192.51 Rattray, R.F. Fundamentals. Leicester, 1925.

Phil 5257.39.2 Raup, R.B. Complacency; the foundation of human behavior. N.Y., 1925.

Phil 3090.84 Reber, M. Franz von Baader und die Möglichkeit unbedinger pädagogischer Zielsetzung. Nürnburg, 1925.

Phil 6990.3.20 Rebsomen, A. Notre-Dame de Lourdes. Paris, 1925.

Phil 348.4.3 Rehmke, J. Anmerkungen zur Grundwissenschaft. 2. Aufl. Leipzig, 1925.

Phil 8892.39 Rehmke, J. Ethik als Wissenschaft. 3. Aufl. Greifswald, 1925.

Phil 8892.39.5 Rehmke, J. Grundlegung der Ethic als Wissenschaft. Leipzig, 1925.

Phil 8412.10.80 Remos, y Rubio, J.J. Las ideas estéticas de Lipps. Habana, 1925.

Phil 8672.13 Rensi, G. Apologia dell'ateismo. Roma, 1925.

Phil 8707.7.9 Rice, William N. Science and religion. Cincinnati, 1925.

Phil 8842.9 Richard, Gaston. L'évolution des moeurs. Paris, 1925.

Phil 7069.25.10 Richardson, Mark Wyman. Margery, Harvard veritas. Boston, 1925.

Phil 7069.25.9A Richardson, Mark Wyman. Margery - Harvard - Veritas; a study in psychics. Boston, 1925.

Phil 5257.40 Richter, Conrad. Human vibrations. Harrisburg, 1925.

Phil 3791.75 Riehl, Alois. Philosophische Studien aus 4 Jahrzehnten. Leipzig, 1925.

Phil 1618.2 Riekel, August. Die Philosophie der Renaissance. München, 1925.

Phil 4260.97 Rivista internationale di filosofia del diritto. Per il secondo centenario della "Scienza nuova" di Vico. Roma, 1925.

Phil 575.57 Roback, A.A. Character and inhibition. n.p., 1925.

Phil 2730.91 Robef, E. Leibniz et Maine de Biran. Thèse. Paris, 1925.

Phil 192.55 Robef, Euthyme. De l'analyse réflexive. Thèse. Paris, 1925.

Phil 630.27 Roberts, George L. Objective reality. London, 1925.

Phil 192.77.5 Robertson, J.M. Spoken essays. London, 1925.

Phil 978.51.5 Rogers, L.W. Reincarnation, and other lectures. Chicago, 1925.

Phil 6327.21 Rohitsek, A. Der Katillon. Zürich, 1925.

Phil 1522.5 Rougier, Louis. La scolastique et le thomisme. Paris, 1925.

Phil 310.1.5.5 Rozanov, Iakov S. Istoricheskii materializm. Kiev, 1925.

Phil 5767.9 Ruesch, Arnold. Die Unfreiheit des Willens. Darmstadt, 1925.

Phil 8892.37 Russell, Bertrand Russell. What I believe. London, 1925.

Phil 8892.37.3 Russell, Bertrand Russell. What I believe. N.Y., 1925.

Phil 6027.2 Rutz, Ottmar. Vom Ausdruck des Menschen. Celle, 1925.

Phil 325.3 Sacheli, C.A. Fenomenismo. Genova, 1925.

Phil 193.101 Sadler, G.T. A new world by a new vision. London, 1925. 2 pam.

Phil 2880.1.35 Saint-Martin, L.C. Irrtümer und Wahrheit. Stuttgart, 1925. 2v.

Phil 9430.10.10 Saltus, Edgar. The anatomy of negation. N.Y., 1925?

Phil 193.49.25 Santayana, G. Dialogues in limbo. N.Y., 1925.

Phil 4120.4.83 Sarlo, F. de. Gentile e Croce. Firenze, 1925.

Phil 6060.18 Saudek, R. The psychology of handwriting. London, 1925.

1925 - cont.

Phil 5585.44.2   Schapp, W. Beiträge zur Phänomenologie der Wahrnehmung. Erlangen, 1925.

Phil 2493.88.2   Schaupp, Zora. The naturalism of Condillac. Diss. n.p., 1925.

Phil 349.24   Scheler, Max. Die Formen des Wissens und die Bildung. Bonn, 1925.

Phil 6328.10.20   Schilder, Paul. Entwurf zu einer Psychiatrie auf psychoanalysischer Grundlage. Leipzig, 1925.

Phil 1718.9.5   Schjelderup, Harald K. Filosofiens historie. Oslo, 1925.

Phil 5258.85.5   Schleich, Carl Ludwig. Jaget och demonierna. Stockholm, 1925.

Phil 3808.68.5   Schopenhauer, Arthur. Essai sur le Libre Arbitre. 13. éd. Paris, 1925.

Phil 3808.69.8   Schopenhauer, Arthur. Le fondement de la morale. 11. éd. Paris, 1925.

Phil 3808.24.15   Schopenhauer, Arthur. Die Persönlichkeit und das Werk. Leipzig, 1925.

Phil 3808.26.50   Schopenhauer, Arthur. Schopenhauer und Schleiermacher über die Lebensalter. Leipzig, 1925?

Phil 8610.925.30   Schott, Walter E. The immaculate deception. Sausahto, Calif., 1925.

Phil 8893.69   Schulze, K.E. Ethik der Dekadenz. Leipzig, 1925.

Phil 8419.15   Schulze-Soelde, W. Das Gesetz der Schönheit. Darmstadt, 1925.

Phil 3246.207   Schwarz, H. Einführung in Fichtes Reden an die deutsche Nation. 2. Aufl. Langensalza, 1925.

Phil 8893.39.10   Schwarz, Hermann. Ethik. Breslau, 1925.

Phil 5058.27.5   Sellars, R.W. The essentials of logic. Boston, 1925.

Phil 8893.58.10   Seta, Ugo della. I valori morali. 3. ed. Roma, 1925.

Phil 1818.3.5   Seth, J. English philosophers and schools of philosophy. London, 1925.

Phil 8673.11   Sheen, F.J. God and intelligence in modern philosophy. London, 1925.

Phil 299.15   Sidis, W.G. The animate and the inanimate. Boston, 1925.

Phil 193.110   Siegel, Carl. Grundprobleme der Philosophie. Wien, 1925.

Phil 9420.10   Siegfried, R. Lettres et discours sur les passions. Paris, 1925.

Phil 8708.10.5   Simpson, James Y. Landmarks in the struggle between science and religion. N.Y., 1925?

Phil 3001.7   Slotemaker de Bruine, N.A.C. Eschatologie en Historie. Wageningen, 1925.

Phil 5058.41   Smart, Harold R. The philosophical presuppositions of mathematical logic. Thesis. N.Y., 1925.

Phil 3903.3.80   Smit, H.W.V.D.V. Hans Vaihinger en de als-ob-philosophie. Baarn, 1925.

Phil 5058.28.18   Smith, Henry B. A system of formal logic. Ann Arbor, 1925.

Phil 6128.55   Social aspects of mental hygiene. New Haven, 1925.

Phil 4769.1.120   Solov'ev, V.S. Tri rechi v pamiat' Dostoevskogo. Berlin, 1925.

Phil 5828.14   Sommer, R. Tierpsychologie. Leipzig, 1925.

Phil 5400.59.2   Sourian, E. L'abstraction sentimentale. Paris, 1925.

Phil 5400.59   Sourian, E. L'abstraction sentimentale. Thèse. Paris, 1925.

Phil 8893.65   Sourian, M. La fonction pratique de la finalité. Paris, 1925.

Phil 8893.65.2   Sourian, M. La fonction pratique de la finalité. Thèse. Paris, 1925.

Phil 5258.88   Souriau, Étienne. Pensée vivante et perfection formelle. Thèse. Paris, 1925.

Phil 4769.3   Spektorskii, E. Khristianstvo i kul'tura. Sankt Peterburg, 1925.

Phil 6328.24   Sperber, Alice. Über die seelischen Ursachen des Alterns, der Jugendlichkeit und der Schönheit. Leipzig, 1925.

Phil 3819.10.10   Spinoza, Benedictus de. Opera, im Auftrag der Heidelberg Akademie der Wissenschaften Herausgegeben. Heidelberg, 1925. 4v.

Phil 3819.28   Spinoza, Benedictus de. Von den festen und ewigen Dingen. Heidelberg, 1925.

Phil 3801.807   Stefansky, Georg. Das hellenisch-deutsche Weltbild. Bonn, 1925.

Phil 8598.52   Steffes, J.P. Religionsphilosophie. München, 1925.

Phil 978.49.30   Steiner, R. Die geistige Führung des Menschen und der Menschheit. Dornach, 1925.

Phil 978.49.65   Steiner, R. Die Pforte der Einweihung (Initiation). Dornach, 1925.

Phil 978.49.70   Steiner, R. Wahrheit und Wissenschaft. Dornach, 1925.

Phil 974.3   Steiner, Rudolf. Mein Lebensgang. Geotheanum, 1925.

Phil 2733.93   Stieler, Georg. Nikolaus Malebranche. Stuttgart, 1925.

Phil 9035.54   Stipriaan Luiscius, J.M. van. Karakter. Haag, 1925.

Phil 9075.28   Stoker, H.G. Das Gewissen, Erscheinungsformen und Theorie. Bonn, 1925.

Phil 7140.123   Straus, Erwin. Wesen und Vorgang der Suggestion. Berlin, 1925.

Phil 960.37   Strauss, Otto. Indische Philosophie. München, 1925.

Phil 8643.35   Streeter, B.H. Immortality. London, 1925.

Phil 3640.222   Stroux, Johannes. Nietzsches Professur in Basel. Jena, 1925.

Phil 672.133   Sturt, Mary. The psychology of time. London, 1925.

Phil 7150.36   Szittya, E. Selbstmörder. Leipzig, 1925.

Phil 5259.22   Tarozzi, G. Nozioni di psicologia. Bologna, 1925.

Phil 5259.20   Tassy, Edme. L'activité psychique. Paris, 1925.

Phil 6990.28   Tennant, F.R. Miracle and its philosophical presuppositions. Cambridge, 1925.

Phil 1135.64.5   Theiler, W. Zur Geschichte der teleologischen Naturbetrachtung bis auf Aristoteles. Zürich, 1925.

Phil 978.73   The theosophical movement, 1875-1925. N.Y., 1925.

Phil 8709.17   Thomson, J.A. Science and religion; being the Morse lecture for 1924. N.Y., 1925.

Phil 8420.12   Thorburn, J.M. Art and the unconscious; a psychological approach to a problem of philosophy. London, 1925.

Phil 7054.45.60   Tischner, R. Das medium D.D. Home. Leipzig, 1925.

Phil 7069.25.25   Tischner, R. Telepathy and clairvoyance. London, 1925.

Phil 2045.85.3   Tönnies, F. Thomas Hobbes. 3e Aufl. Stuttgart, 1925.

Phil 1719.3   Tonelli, L. L'anima moderna, da Lessing a Nietzsche. Milano, 1925.

Phil 8674.7   Trap, William M. Divine personality. Ann Arbor, 1925.

Phil 6945.14   Treadway, Walter L. Mental hygiene with special reference to the migration of the people. Washington, 1925.

Phil 194.31.5   Troilo, Erminis. Lo spirito della filosofia. Citta di Castello, 1925.

Phil 630.29.5   Turner, J.E. A theory of direct realism and the relation of realism to idealism. N.Y., 1925.

Phil 2050.187   Tvrdý, Josef. Problém skutečnosti u Davida Huma. Brno, 1925.

1925 - cont.

Phil 4803.454.95   Ujejski, Józef. O cenę absolutu; rzecz o Hoene-Wrońskim. Warszawa, 1925.

Phil 195.2.5   Unamuno, M. de. Das tragische Lebensgefühl. München, 1925.

Phil 5627.107.5   Underwood, A.C. Conversion: Christian and non-Christian. N.Y., 1925.

Phil 9035.43   Utitz, Emil. Charakterologie. Charlottenburg, 1925.

Phil 196.20   Valensin, A. A travers la métaphysique. Paris, 1925.

Phil 3503.6   Vallois, M. La formation de l'influence Kantienne en France. Paris, 1925?

Phil 9540.1.5   Van Loon, H.W. Tolerance. N.Y., 1925.

Phil 4650.1.59   Vannérus, Allen. Materiens värld. Stockholm, 1925.

Phil 4650.1.56   Vannérus, Allen. Ursprungens filosofi. Stockholm, 1925.

Phil 6331.5   Van Teslaar, J.S. An outline of psychoanalysis. N.Y., 1925.

Htn   Phil 196.21*   Varvaro, Paolo. Introduzione alla filosofia. Palermo, 1925.

Phil 735.79.1   Vaucher, G. Le langage affectif et les jugements de valeur. Paris, 1925.

Phil 735.79   Vaucher, G. Le langage affectif et les jugements de valeur. Thèse. Paris, 1925.

Phil 5525.30   Victor, C.R. Der Humor und seine Begründung. Bremen, 1925.

Phil 196.19.5   Vivante, Leone. Intelligence in expression. London, 1925.

Phil 6331.2.3   Vivante, Leone. Note sopra la originalità del pensiero. Roma, 1925.

Phil 672.135   Volkelt, Johannes. Phänomenologie und Metaphysik der Zeit. München, 1925.

Phil 510.126.9   Wahl, Jean. The pluralist philosophies of England and America. London, 1925.

Phil 822.6.2   Wahle, R. Die Tragikomödie der Weisheit die Ergebnisse und der Geschichte des Philosophierens. Wien, 1925.

Phil 5525.31   Wallerstein, M. Eine Arbeit über das Lachen und des Komische. Wien, 1925.

Phil 5262.21.6   Watson, John B. Behaviorism. N.Y., 1925.

Phil 5262.21.5   Watson, John B. Behaviorism. N.Y., 1925.

Phil 5640.30   Watt, Henry J. The sensory basis and structure of knowledge. London, 1925.

Phil 822.1.3   Weber, A. Histoire de la philosophie européenne. 9e éd. Paris, 1925.

Phil 822.1.15A   Weber, A. History of philosophy. N.Y., 1925.

Phil 5585.46   Weber, Christian. The concept of duration as key to the logical forms of reason. Thesis. Lincoln, 1925.

Phil 8602.44   Weber, H.E. Das Geisteserbe der Gegenwart und die Theologie. Leipzig, 1925.

Phil 5400.64   Wechsler, David. The measurement of emotional reactions. N.Y., 1925.

Phil 5262.30   Weiss, Albert P. A theoretical basis of human behavior. Columbus, 1925.

Phil 3565.89.5   Wentscher, M. Fechner und Lotze. München, 1925.

Phil 5262.31   Wertheimer, M. Drei Abhandlungen zur Gestalttheorie. Erlangen, 1925.

Phil 5262.31.9   Wertheimer, M. Über Gestalttheorie. Erlangen, 1925.

Phil 6972.14.25   White, William Alanson. Essays in psychopathology. N.Y., 1925.

Phil 8897.64   Whitehead, George. What is morality? London, 1925.

Phil 8897.46.5   Wiggam, A.E. The new decalogue of science. Garden City, 1925.

Phil 8740.3   Will, Robert. Le culte. Thèse. Strasbourg, 1925.

Phil 5062.29   Williams, Henry H. The evaluation of logic. Chapel Hill, 1925.

Phil 3504.23A   Wilm, E.C. Immanuel Kant. New Haven, 1925.

Phil 7069.25.30   Wilson, T.S. Thought transference. London, 1925..

Phil 2138.112   Wisniewski, J. Étude historique et critique de la théorie de la perception extérieure chez John Stuart Mill. Thèse. Paris, 1925.

Phil 1050.12.5   Wolfson, Harry A. The classification of sciences on mediaeval Jewish philosophy. Chicago, 1925.

Phil 107.1   Wynaendts Francken, C.J. Kort woordenboek van wijsgeerige kunstlermen. Haarlem 1925.

Phil 5834.1.13   Yerkes, R.M. Chimpanzee intelligence. Baltimore, 1925.

Phil 6694.2.5   Young, Paul C. An experimental study of mental and physical functions in the normal and hypnotic states. Ithaca, 1925.

Phil 2255.3   Young, Robert F. A Bohemian philosopher at Oxford in the 17th century. London, 1925.

Phil 4080.3.127   Zacchi, Angelo. Il nuovo idealismo italiano di Benedetto Croce. 2a ed. Roma, 1925.

Phil 4080.3.129   Zanacchi, G. L'intuizione di Benedetto Croce. Palermo, 1925.

Phil 306.3   Ziegler, Konrat. Weltentstehung in Sage und Wissenschaft. Leipzig, 1925.

Phil 3940.2.40   Ziegler, L. Dienst an der Welt. Darmstadt, 1925.

Phil 356.3   Zocher, Rudolf. Die objektive Geltung Slogik und der Immanenzir Danke. Tübingen, 1925.

Phil 8050.68   Zonta, Giuseppe. Manualetto d'estetica. Torino, 1925.

Phil 3625.5.89   Zubersky, A. Salomon Maimon und der kritischen Idealismus. Leipzig, 1925.

Phil 5655.7   Zwaardemaker, H. L'odorat. Paris, 1925.

1926

Phil 8580.15   Abbetmeyer, Theo. Das Gralsreich als Streiter wider den Untergang des Abendlandes. Heilbronn, 1926.

Phil 3640.291.5   Ackerknecht, E. Friedrich Nietzsche, der Prophet der schenkenden Tugend. 2e Aufl. Stettin, 1926.

Phil 5648.11.25   Ackerson, Luton. A correlational analysis of proficiency in typing. N.Y., 1926.

Phil 4513.1.42   Ahlberg, A. Tidoreflexer; filosofiska uppsatser. Stockholm, 1926.

Phil 75.26   Alcan, Felix. La philosophie française contemporaine. Paris, 1926.

Phil 1050.15.5   Alderblum, N.H.H. A study of Gersonedes in his proper perspective. N.Y., 1926.

Phil 7084.22   Allendy, René Félix. Les rêves et leur interpretation psychanalytique. Paris, 1926.

Phil 3640.158.5   Andler, Charles. Nietzsche und Jakob Burckhardt. Basel, 1926.

Phil 5040.20.5   Aragón, G.A. Lógica elemental. 4a ed. Habana, 1926.

Phil 175.33   Arch, Robert. Whence, whither, and why? London, 1926.

Phil 5210.2   Arnold, V.H. La psychologie de réaction en Amérique. Thèse. Paris, 1926.

Phil 9575.8   Atwood, Albert W. The mind of the millionaire. N.Y., 1926.

Phil 1850.25.5   Bacon, Francis. François Bacon. Paris, 1926.

Phil 7069.26.80   Baerwald, R. Okkultismus und Spiritismus. Berlin, 1926.

1926 - cont.

Phil 978.74.20 — Bailey, A.A. (Mrs.). Initiation, human and solar. 3d. ed. N.Y., 1926.
Phil 978.74.25 — Bailey, A.A. (Mrs.). Letters on occult meditation. 2d ed. N.Y., 1926.
Phil 8581.52 — Baillie, John. The roots of religion in the human soul. London, 1926.
Phil 801.20 — Baker, A.E. How to understand philosophy. N.Y., 1926.
Phil 6311.12 — Baker, A.E. Psychoanalysis explained and criticized. London, 1926.
Phil 7069.26.2 — Barrett, W. Death-bed visions. London, 1926.
Phil 2401.8 — Baruzi, Jean. Philosophes et savants français du XXe siècle. Paris, 1926. 3v.
Phil 332.11 — Bauch, Bruno. Die Idee. Leipzig, 1926.
Phil 7140.116.55 — Baudouin, C. Der Couéismus. Darmstadt, 1926.
Phil 176.107 — Becher, Erich. Einführung in die Philosophie. München, 1926.
Phil 282.7.16 — Becher, Erich. Metaphysik und Naturwissenschaften. München, 1926.
Phil 176.111 — Benda, Julien. Lettres à Mélisande. Paris, 1926.
Phil 8626.16 — Bennett, F.S.M. Expecto, an essay towards a biology of the world to come. Chester, 1926.
Phil 2401.3.5 — Benrubi, Isaac. Contemporary thought of France. London, 1926.
Phil 3640.293 — Beonio-Brocchieri, V. Federico Nietzsche. Roma, 1926.
Phil 801.25 — Bergmann, E. Weltanschauung. Breslau, 1926. 2v.
Phil 3246.173.10 — Bergmann, Ernst. Fichte und Carl Christian Erhard Schmid. Leipzig, 1926?
Phil 1870.45.20 — Berkeley, G. Drei Dialoge zwischen Hylas und Philonous. Leipzig, 1926.
Phil 1870.73.13 — Berkeley, G. Philosophisches Tagebuch (commonplace book). Leipzig, 1926.
Phil 4359.1.83 — Bermann, G. José Ingenieros. Buenos Aires, 1926.
Phil 282.17 — Bernoulli, C. Romantiske Naturphilosophie. Jena, 1926.
Phil 325.4 — Bertrand-Barraud, D. Des bases critique d'un empirisme psychologique. Paris, 1926.
Phil 176.115.50 — Bierens de Haan, J.D. Menschengeest. Amsterdam, 1926.
Phil 2070.126 — Bixler, Julius S. Religion in the philosophy of William James. Boston, 1926.
Phil 6951.11.2 — Bleuler, E. Affektivität, Suggestibilität, Paranoia. 2. Aufl. Halle, 1926.
Phil 6315.2.95 — Bodin, Jean. Contre Freud. Paris, 1926.
Phil 3110.37.4 — Böhme, J. The signature of all things, with other writings. London, 1926.
Phil 6420.16.5 — Bogue, Benjamin N. Stammering; its cause and cure. Indianapolis, 1926.
Phil 9590.19 — Bok, E.W. Dollars only. N.Y., 1926.
Phil 2733.98 — Bonavino, C. Malebranche. Milano, 1926.
Phil 5241.68 — Bourdon, B. L'intelligence. Paris, 1926.
Phil 5402.16 — Bousfield, P. Pleasure and pain. London, 1926.
Phil 2477.1.55 — Boutroux, Émile. La nature et l'esprit. Paris, 1926.
Phil 3483.35 — Boutroux, Émile. La philosophie de Kant. Paris, 1926.
Phil 1506.7 — Brade, W.R.V. From Plotinus to St. Thomas Aquinas. London, 1926.
Phil 575.60 — Braham, Ernest G. Personality and immortality in post Kantian thought. London, 1926.
Phil 3120.45.45 — Brandenstein, Béla. Grundlegung der Philosophie. Halle, 1926[1970] 6v.
Phil 801.21 — Bréhier, É. Histoire de la philosophie. Paris, 1926. 9v.
Phil 3120.8.32 — Brentano, Franz. Die vier Phasen der Philosophie und ihr augenblicklicher Stand. Leipzig, 1926.
Phil 8615.5.50 — Bridges, Horace J. Aspects of ethical religion; essays in honor of Felix Adler...fiftieth anniversary...Ethical movement, 1876. N.Y., 1926.
Phil 1850.118 — Broad, C.D. The philosophy of Francis Bacon. Cambridge, Eng., 1926.
Phil 3001.9 — Brockdorff, C. Die deutsche Auflslärungsphilosophie. München, 1926.
Phil 5850.143 — Bromberg, R. Toegepaste psychologie. Leiden, 1926.
Phil 3140.82 — Brosch, P. Die Ontologie des J. Clauberg. Greifswald, 1926.
Phil 8581.88 — Brown, C.R. A working faith. Chapel Hill, 1926.
Phil 1828.2 — Brown, Florence W. Alcott and the Concord school of philosophy. n.p., 1926.
Phil 8581.83 — Brown, Oswald E. God and the new knowledge. Nashville, 1926.
Phil 5241.28.13 — Brown, W. Mind and personality. London, 1926.
Phil 5627.100 — Bruehn, W. Religionspsychologie. Breslau, 1926.
Phil 3001.8 — Bruleg, Lucien. Holländische Philosophie. Breslau, 1926.
Phil 3960.14 — Brulez, Lucien. Holländische Philosophie. Breslau, 1926.
Phil 5545.164 — Brunswig, Alfred. Das Gedächtnis und seine Erziehung. Berlin, 1926.
Phil 3120.30.55 — Buber, Martin. Rede über das Erzieherische. Berlin, 1926.
Phil 6111.43 — Bürker, Karl. Neueres über die Zentralisation der Funktionen. Giessen, 1926.
Phil 5722.14.2 — Bumke, O. Das Unterbewusstsein, eine Kritik. 2. Aufl.
Phil 8581.45.10 — Buonaiuti, Ernesto. La religione nella vito dello spirito. Roma, 1926.
Phil 8877.65 — Cabot, Richard C. Adventures on the borderlands of ethics. N.Y., 1926.
Phil 8582.42 — Cadman, S.P. Imagination and religion. N.Y., 1926.
Phil 6952.21.5 — Campbell, C.M. Delusion and belief. Cambridge, 1926.
Phil 4115.88 — Caramella, S. La formazione della filosofia giobertiana. Genova, 1926.
Phil 8422.8 — Carmela, S. I problemi del gusto e dell'arte nella mente di Pietro Verri. Napoli, 1926.
Phil 365.18.5 — Cavling, Viggo. The collective spirit; an idealistic theory of evolution. N.Y., 1926.
Phil 3425.218.5 — Chang, W.S. The development, significance and some limitations of Hegel's ethical teaching. Shanghai, 1926.
Phil 8403.23 — Chartier, Émile. Système des beaux-arts. Paris, 1926.
Phil 2475.1.222 — Chevalier, Jacques. Bergson. Paris, 1926.
Phil 177.66 — Chiocchetti, Emilio. Il pragmatismo. Milano, 1926.
Phil 1020.4.15 — Christ, Paul S. The psychology of the active intellect of Averroes. Thesis. Philadelphia, 1926.
Phil 8952.8 — Christianity and the present moral unrest. London, 1926.
Phil 5627.108.15 — Clark, Glenn. The soul's sincere desire. Boston, 1926.
Phil 9342.4.12 — Cobbett, W. Advice to young men. London, 1926.
Phil 5242.39 — Cole, Lawrence W. Factors of human psychology. Boulder, 1926.
Phil 5242.30 — Collins, Mary. Experimental psychology. London, 1926.
Phil 5242.30.5 — Collins, Mary. A first laboratory guide in psychology. London, 1926.
Phil 5242.30.7 — Collins, Mary. A first laboratory guide in psychology. London, 1926.

1926 - cont.

Phil 70.7 — Congrès des Sociétés Philosophiques, 1921. Congrès des société philosophique américaine, anglaises, belge, italienne. Paris, 1926.
Phil 3484.13 — Cornelius, Hans. Kommentar zu Kant's Kritik der reinen Vernunft. Erlangen, 1926.
Phil 7069.26.4 — Cornillier, P.E. La prédiction de l'avenir. Paris, 1926.
Phil 6312.7 — Coster, Geraldine. Psycho-analysis for normal people. London, 1926.
Phil 6060.1.25 — Crepieux-Jamin, J. The psychology of the movements of handwriting. London, 1926.
Phil 4002.3 — Crespi, Angelo. Contemporary thought of Italy. London, 1926.
Phil 8877.34.2 — Croce, Benedetto. Cultura e vita morale. 2a ed. Bari, 1926.
Phil 4080.3.48.2 — Croce, Benedetto. Nuovi saggi di estetica. 2. ed. Bari, 1926.
Phil 5042.20 — Crumley, T. Logic, deductive and inductive. N.Y., 1926.
Phil 4570.1.85 — Cuelberg, John. Samuel Grubbe; en studie i transcendental religionsfilosofi. Upsala, 1926.
Phil 7082.172 — Daudet, Léon. Le rêve éveillé. Paris, 1926.
Phil 5243.33.3 — Dearden, H. Understanding ourselves. N.Y., 1926.
Phil 310.625 — Deborin, Abram M. Filosofiia i marksizm. Moskva, 1926.
Phil 6315.1.14 — De Forest, Izette. The leaven of love. London, 1926.
Phil 5643.77 — Déjean, Renée. Les conditions objectives de la perception visuelle. Thèse. Paris, 1926. 2 pam.
Phil 5643.77.5 — Déjean, Renée. La perception visuelle. Paris, 1926.
Phil 5520.41.5 — Delacroix, H. L'analyse psychologique de la fonction linguistique. Oxford, 1926.
Phil 6315.2.96 — Delgado, H. Sigmund Freud. Lima, 1926.
Phil 5043.5.3 — DeMorgan, Augustus. Formal logic (1847). London, 1926.
Phil 2520.78.25F — Descartes, René. Correspondence of Descartes and Constantyn Huygeno, 1635-1647. Oxford, 1926.
Phil 2520.45.18 — Descartes, René. Il discorso sul metodo. Torino, 1926.
Phil 2520.35.17 — Descartes, René. Discours de la méthode. Paris, 1926.
Phil 8693.14 — Dessauer, F. Leben, Natur, Religion. 2. Aufl. Bonn, 1926.
Phil 178.38.7A — Dewey, John. Experience and nature. Chicago, 1926.
Phil 5243.31 — Dide, Maurice. Introduction à l'étude de la psychogénèse. Paris, 1926.
Phil 2520.121.5 — Dimier, Louis. La vie raisonnable de Descartes. Paris, 1926.
Phil 5627.99 — Dimond, S.G. The psychology of the Methodist revival. London, 1926.
Phil 178.37.5 — Dingler, Hugo. Der Zusammenbruch der Wissenschaft und der Primat derPhilosophie. München, 1926.
Phil 8828.3.5A — Dittrich, Ottmar. Geschichte der Ethik. Leipzig, 1926-32. 4v.
Phil 3246.233 — Döring, W.O. Der Mann der Tat; eine Fichtebiographie. Lübeck, 1926.
Phil 5125.10 — Dorolle, M. Les problèmes de l'induction. Paris, 1926.
Phil 7069.26.5 — Doyle, Arthur Conan. The history of spiritualism. N.Y., 1926. 2v.
Phil 803.7 — Dresser, H.W. A history of ancient and medieval philosophy. N.Y., 1926.
Phil 5243.28.5 — Driesch, Hans. Grundprobleme der Psychologie. Leipzig, 1926.
Phil 284.6.10 — Driesch, Hans. Metaphysik der Natur. München, 1926.
Phil 3260.87 — Dubislav, W. Die Fries'che Lehre von der Begründung. Dömitz, 1926.
Phil 5620.12 — Dunn, Miriam Frances. The psychology of reasoning. Diss. n.p., 1926.
Phil 803.6.5A — Durant, W. The story of philosophy. N.Y., 1926.
Phil 5244.19 — Edgell, B. Mental life. London, 1926.
Phil 179.24 — Edman, Irwin. Richard Kane looks at life. Boston, 1926.
Phil 179.24.2 — Edman, Irwin. Richard Kane looks at life. Boston, 1926.
Phil 5627.93 — Edward, Kenneth. Religious experience; its nature and truth. Edinburgh, 1926.
Phil 3808.146 — Eichler, Oskar. Die Wurzeln des Frauenhasses bei Arthur Schopenhauer. Bonn, 1926.
Phil 285.3 — Eleutheropulos, A. Die exakten Grundlagen der Naturphilosophie. Stuttgart, 1926.
Phil 5425.18.5A — Ellis, H. A study of British genius. Boston, 1926.
Phil 179.17.5 — Ellis, Havelock. The dance of life. Boston, 1926.
Phil 530.55.7 — Emilie, Sister. Une âme mystique au temps présent. v.1-2. Louvain, 1926-27.
Phil 5014.1.20 — Enriques, Federigo. L'évolution de la logique. Paris, 1926.
Phil 3486.2.9 — Erhardt, Franz. Bleibendes und Vergängliches in der Philosophie Kants. Leipzig, 1926.
Phil 5203.9 — Estey, H.G. A bibliography on psychology. Gardner, 1926.
Phil 3850.16.89 — Fabian, W. Kritik der Lebensphilosophie Georg Simmels. Breslau, 1926.
Phil 5245.17 — Falinski, E. Cahiers de psychologie rationnelle. v.1-4. Paris, 1926.
Phil 180.47 — Falkenfeld, H. Einfuhrung in die Philosophie. Berlin, 1926.
Phil 8406.25 — Fariña Nuñez, Eloy.Conceptos estéticos mitos guaraníes. Buenos Aires, 1926.
Phil 7069.26.90 — Feerhow, F. Die menschliche Aura und ihre experimentelle Erforschung. 2.-3. Aufl. Leipzig, 1926.
Phil 4080.11.80F — Ferrari, G.M. Giovanni Caroli e la sua dottrina filosofica. Modena, 1926.
Phil 8615.16 — Fiftieth anniversary of the Ethical movement. N.Y., 1926.
Phil 5245.81 — Fingerman, G. Estudios de psicologia y de estetica. Buenos Aires, 1926.
Phil 8880.18.9 — Fite, Warner. An adventure in moral philosophy. London, 1926.
Phil 8406.20 — Flaccus, L.W. The spirit and substance of art. N.Y., 1926.
Phil 180.39 — Flewelling, R. Creative personality. N.Y., 1926.
Phil 5755.9 — Forti, E. La décision; essai d'analyse psychologique. Thèse. Paris, 1926.
Phil 8585.27A — Fosdick, Harry E. Adventurous religion and other essays. 1st ed. N.Y., 1926.
Phil 5245.15.5 — Foucault, Marcel. Cours de psychologie. Paris, 1926.
Phil 3120.2.87 — Frank, Paul. Die philosophischen Problem in Dr. Bolzano's "Erbauungsreden". Inaug. Diss. Pritzwalk, 1926.
Phil 8610.926 — Freeman, C.R.B. Towards the answer. Derbyshire, 1926.
Phil 6315.2.47 — Freud, Sigmund. Die Frage der Laienanalyse. Wien, 1926.
Htn Phil 6315.2.60* — Freud, Sigmund. Hemmung, Symptom und Angst. Leipzig, 1926.
Phil 6315.2.18 — Freud, Sigmund. Studien zur Psychoanalyse der Neurosen aus den Jahren 1913-25. Wien, 1926.
Phil 5215.1 — Friedländer, A.A. Die neuzeitliche psychologische Strömungen. Lubeck, 1926.
Phil 3640.167.5 — Gaultier, J. de. Nietzsche. Paris, 1926.
Phil 8956.6 — Geismar, E. Etik. København, 1926.

1926 - cont.

Phil 4260.100   Gemelli, A. G.B. Vico: volume commemorativo. Milano, 1926.

Phil 4006.4   Gemelli, A. Il mio contributo alla filosofia neoscolastica. Milano, 1926.

Phil 672.151   Gent, Werner. Die Philosophie des Raumes und der Zeit. Bonn, 1926.

Phil 525.71   Gentilini, B. De la mística. Santiago de Chile, 1926.

Phil 850.17   Georgov, Ivan. Istoriia na filosofiiata. Sofiia, 1926.

Phil 5046.16.5   Geyser, J. Auf dem Kampffelde der Logik. Freiburg, 1926.

Phil 6116.22   Gibson, Van R. The faith that overcomes the world. N.Y., 1926.

Phil 3425.226   Giese, G. Hegels Staatsidee und der Begriff der Staatserziehung. Halle, 1926.

Phil 5525.29   Gilman, Bradley. A clinic on the comic. Nice, 1926.

Phil 4115.34.6   Gioberti, V. Introduzione allo studio della filosofia. Firenze, 1926.

Phil 4115.24   Gioberti, V. L'Italia, la chiesa e la civiltà universale. Torino, 1926.

Phil 2805.90.15   Giraud, V. Soeurs de grands hommes: J. Pascal. Paris, 1926.

Phil 8586.36   Gogarten, Friedrich. Ich Glaube an den dreieinigen Gott. Jena, 1926.

Phil 1980.3.98   Goldberg, I. Havelock Ellis; a biographical and critical survey. N.Y., 1926.

Phil 575.58   Gordon, R.G. Personality. London, 1926.

Phil 8436.5   Gori, Gino. Il grottesco nell'arte e nella letteratura. Roma, 1926.

Phil 2733.94   Gouhier, Henri. La philosophie de Malebranche et son expérience religieuse. Paris, 1926.

Phil 2733.94.5   Gouhier, Henri. La philosophie de Malebranche et son expérience religieuse. Thèse. Paris, 1926. 2 pam.

Phil 2733.94.7   Gouhier, Henri. La vocation de Malebranche. Paris, 1926.

Phil 1511.1.15   Grabmann, M. Mittelalterliches Geistesleben. München, 1926-36. 3v.

Phil 7140.126   Graeter, Karl. Menschenleiden als Lebensgeheimnis...Autosuggestion. Kandern, 1926.

Phil 5401.10   Gratia, L.E. Le "trac" et la timidité. 2e éd. Paris, 1926.

Phil 2630.1.35   Gratry, Auguste. Méditations inédites. Paris, 1926.

Phil 3006.6   Groethuysen, B. Introduction a la pensée philosophie allemande depuis Nietzsche. Paris, 1926.

Phil 2636.82.3   Grossman, Mordecai. The philosophy of Helvetius. N.Y., 1926.

Phil 2636.82   Grossman, Mordecai. Philosophy of Helvetius. Thesis. N.Y., 1926.

Phil 6956.8   Guimares, A. De hygiene mental e sua importancia em mosso meio. San Paulo, 1926.

Phil 807.15   Habert, O. Le primat de l'intelligence dans l'histoire de la pensée. Paris, 1926.

Phil 8882.48   Häberlin, Paul. Das Gute. Basel, 1926.

Phil 575.61   Haering, T.L. Über Individualität in Natur- und Geistesewelt. Leipzig, 1926.

Phil 182.35.9   Haldane, Richard B. Human experience; a study of its structure. N.Y., 1926.

Phil 182.35.3   Haldane, Richard B. The pathway to reality. London, 1926.

Phil 7069.26.10   Halford, J. The voice. London, 1926.

Phil 1707.9   Hammond, A.L. Anti-intellectualism in present philosophy. Diss. Baltimore, 1926.

Phil 8408.14   Hammond, Robert. Lineamenti d'estetica fondati sul problema gnoseologico. Aleppo, 1926.

Phil 5425.41   Hankin, Ernest H. Common sense and its cultivation. London, 1926.

Phil 288.6   Hartmann, L. Sind Naturgesetze Veränderlich? Halle, 1926.

Phil 8882.50   Hartmann, N. Ethik. Berlin, 1926.

Phil 3808.114.15   Hasse, Heinrich. Schopenhauer. München, 1926.

Phil 6400.14   Head, Henry. Aphasia and kindred disorders of speech. Cambridge, Eng., 1926. 2v.

Phil 3160.6.85   Heimsoeth, H. Metaphysik und Kritik bei Christian August Crusius. Berlin, 1926.

Phil 807.16   Heinemann, Fritz. Die Lehre von der Zweckbestimmung der Menschen. Breslau, 1926.

Phil 7069.26.9   Hellwig, A. Okkultismus und Wissenschaft. Stuttgart, 1926.

Phil 1112.6   Helms, Poul. Den graeske naturfilosofi indtil sofisterne. København, 1926.

Phil 5247.38   Helson, Harry. The psychology of Gestalt. Urbana, 1926.

Phil 5817.13   Hempelmann, F. Tierpsychologie vom Standpunkte des Biologen. Leipzig, 1926.

Phil 5757.14.2   Herrick, C.J. Fatalism or freedom. N.Y., 1926.

Phil 182.79A   Herzberg, Alex. Zur Psychologie der Philosophie und der Philosophen. Leipzig, 1926.

Phil 7069.26.60   Heuzé, P. Fakirs, fumistes et Cie. Paris, 1926.

Phil 7069.26.50   Heuzé P. Où en est la métapsychique. Paris, 1926.

Phil 735.84   Heyde, Johannes E. Wert. Erfurt, 1926.

Phil 2045.67   Hobbes, Thomas. Naturrecht und allgemeines Staatsrecht in den Anfangsgründen. Berlin, 1926.

Phil 5817.5.5   Hobhouse, L.T. Mind in evolution. 3d ed. London, 1926.

Phil 338.17.5   Höffding, H. Erkenntnistheorie und Lebensauffassung. Leipzig, 1926.

Phil 8882.16.5   Höffding, H. Etik. 5te udg. København, 1926.

Phil 5247.37.10   Hönigswald, R. Vom Problem des Rhythmus. Leipzig, 1926.

Phil 9035.47   Hoffmann, H. Das Problem des Charakteraufbaus. Berlin, 1926.

Phil 5247.16.15   Hollingworth, H.L. The psychology of thought approached through studies of sleeping and dreaming. N.Y., 1926.

Phil 2477.9.81   Horton, W.M. The philosophy of the Abbé Bantain. N.Y., 1926.

Phil 974.3.70   Hovels, Karl. Beiträge zur Kritik der anthropologischen Welt- und Lebensanschauung. Inaug. Diss. Rheinland, 1926.

Phil 8587.32.5   Hügel, Friedrich von. Essays and addresses on the philosophy of religion. London, 1926.

Phil 1020.8.12   Ibn Sina. Metaphysices compendium...Latinum...N. Carame. Roma, 1926.

Phil 339.1   Ingarden, Roman. Über die Stellung der Erkenntnistheorie im System der Philosophie. Halle an der Saale, 1926.

Phil 8698.1   Inge, W.P. Science and ultimate truth. London, 1926.

Phil 8883.3.7   Ingenieros, José. Las fuerzas morales. Obra póstuma. Buenos Aires, 1926.

Phil 183.1.5   Isbyam, I.C. The ego and the spiritual truth. London, 1926.

Phil 8883.4   Isbyam, I.C. (pseud.). The self-seeker and his search. London, 1926.

Phil 6980.363.20   Isserlin, Max. Psychotherapie. Berlin, 1926.

Phil 3460.21   Jacobi, F.H. Schriften. Berlin, 1926.

Phil 5425.46   Jacobson, A.C. Genius: some revaluations. N.Y., 1926.

1926 - cont.

Phil 6319.7   Jaensch, W. Grundzuge einer Physiologie und Klinik der psychophysischen Persönlichkeit. Berlin, 1926.

Phil 184.37   Jaller, Arthur. Doppeldenken; Grundlagen einer neuen Weltanschauung. Berlin, 1926.

Phil 5249.2.48   James, William. Energies of men. N.Y., 1926.

Phil 2070.75.5   James, William. The letters of William James. v.1-2. Boston, 1926.

Phil 7076.20   Janet, Pierre. De l'angoisse à l'extase. Paris, 1926-28. 2v.

Phil 5249.16   Jascalevich, A.A. Three conceptions of mind. N.Y., 1926.

Phil 5049.24   Jelenský, Simon. Logika. Praha, 1926.

Phil 184.26   Joad, C.E.M. After-dinner philosophy. London, 1926.

Phil 8884.18.7   Joad, Cyril E.M. Thrasymachus. N.Y., 1926.

Phil 184.34.5   Jørgensen, J. Filosofiske forelassninger son indledning tilvidenskabelige studier. København, 1926.

Phil 184.29   Jones, W.T. Nature, thought and personal experience. London, 1926.

Phil 5249.17   Jordan, G.J. The story of psychology. London, 1926.

Phil 5520.56   Jordan, Leo. Die Kunst des begrifflichen Denkens. München, 1926.

Phil 3090.01   Jost, J. Bibliographie der Schriften Franz v. Baaders. Bonn, 1926.

Phil 978.7.3   Judge, W.Z. The ocean of theosophy. Point Loma, Calif., 1926[1923]

Phil 6319.1.11   Jung, C.G. Analytische Psychologie und Erziehung. Heidelberg, 1926.

Phil 6319.1.35   Jung, C.G. Das Unbewusste im normalen und kranken. Zürich, 1926.

Phil 3480.30.29   Kant, Immanuel. Kritik der reinen Vernunft. Leipzig, 1926.

Phil 3480.30.40   Kant, Immanuel. Kritik der reinen Vernunft. Lübeck, 1926.

Phil 3480.25.40   Kant, Immanuel. Il pensiero filosofico di E.K. v.1-2. Firenze, 1926-25.

Phil 3480.58.5   Kant, Immanuel. Prolegomena to any future metaphysics. Chicago, 1926.

Phil 3480.58.60   Kant, Immanuel. Prolegomeni ad ogni metafisica futura. Torino, 1926.

Phil 810.5   Kaunitz, M.M. Philosophy for plain people. N.Y., 1926.

Phil 3160.9.80   Kern, Hans. Die Philosophie des Carl Gustav Carus. Berlin, 1926.

Phil 5250.22   Keyser, C.J. Thinking about thinking. N.Y., 1926.

Phil 3549.2.50   Keyserling, Hermann. Menschen als Sinnbilder. Darmstadt, 1926.

Phil 3549.2.79.5   Keyserling, Hermann. Die neuentstehende Welt. Darmstadt, 1926.

Phil 3830.8   Klaar, Alfred. Spinoza, sein Leben und seine Lehre. Berlin, 1926.

Phil 575.51.4   Klages, Ludwig. Die Grundlagen der Charakterkunde. 4e Aufl. Leipzig, 1926.

Phil 3640.198   Klages, Ludwig. Die psychologischen Errungenschaften Nietzsches. Leipzig, 1926.

Phil 5374.44.2   Klages, Ludwig. Vom Wesen des Bewusstseins. 2e Aufl. Leipzig, 1926.

Phil 8885.30   Klug, J. Die Tiefen der Seele. Paderborn, 1926.

Phil 6120.9   Knapp, Sheldon. Towards a new era in healing. London, 1926.

Phil 5250.21   König, Josef. Der Begriff der Intuition. Halle, 1926.

Phil 3640.202   Kräutlin, Jonathan. Friedrich Nietzsches Morallehre. Leipzig, 1926.

Phil 8885.32   Kramer, Morris. Song of the optimist. N.Y., 1926.

Phil 1850.119   Kraus, Oskar. Der Machtgedanke und der Friedensidee in des Philosophie der Engländer, Bacon und Bentham. Leipzig, 1926.

Phil 3850.18.83   Kreppel, F. Die Religionsphilosophie Max Schelers. Inaug. Diss. München, 1926.

Phil 6320.6.3   Kretschmer, E. Medizinische Psychologie. 3. Aufl. Leipzig, 1926.

Phil 6120.8.7   Kretschmer, E. Physique and character. N.Y., 1926.

Phil 6615.12.5   Kretschmer, Ernst. Hysteria. N.Y., 1926.

Phil 735.82   Kühn, Lenore. Die Autonomie der Werte. Berlin, 1926-31. 2v.

Phil 7084.4.15   Laforgue, René. Le rêve et la psychanalyse. Paris, 1926.

Phil 8886.45   Laird, John. A study in moral theory. N.Y., 1926.

Phil 96.3   Lalande, A. Vocabulaire technique et critique de la philosophie. Paris, 1926. 2v.

Phil 3493.13   Lamanna, E.P. Kant. Milano, 1926. 2v.

Phil 974.3.90   Lauer, Hans E. Rudolf Steiner's Lebenswerk. Basel, 1926.

Phil 5251.32   La Vaissière, J. de. Elements of experimental psychology. St. Louis, 1926.

Phil 8591.28   Lavollée, R. Raison et foi. Paris, 1926.

Phil 8836.2.13   Lecky, W.E.H. History of European morals. N.Y., 1926.

Phil 5465.23   Leeming, B.C. Imagination, mind's dominant power. N.Y., 1926.

Phil 575.69   Lehmann, G. Über Einzigkeit und Individualität. Leipzig, 1926.

Phil 186.58   Lehmann, Gerhard. Über Einzigkeit und Individualität. Leipzig, 1926.

Phil 3552.66.11   Leibniz, Gottfried Wilhelm. La monadologia. Milano, 1926.

Phil 5425.94   Lenk, Emil. Das Liebesleben des Genies. 2. Aufl. Badeburg, 1926.

Phil 1711.2   Lenoir, R. Les historiens de l'esprit humain. Paris, 1926.

Phil 974.3.65   Lévy, Eugène. Rudolf Steiners Weltanschauung und ihre Gegner. 3. Aufl. Berlin, 1926?

Phil 5761.14   Lewin, Kurt. Vorsatz Wille und Bedürfnis. Berlin, 1926.

Phil 3640.106.2   Lichtenberger, H. The gospel of superman. N.Y., 1926.

Phil 3090.85   Lieb, Fritz. Franz Baaders Jugendgeschichte...von Baaders. München, 1926.

Phil 186.48.5   Lighthall, W.D. Superpersonalism, the outer consciousness. Montreal, 1926.

Phil 2477.1.136   Liguori-Barbieri, E. La filosofia di Émile Boutroux. Pisa, 1926.

Phil 3805.160   Lindroth, H. Schleiermachers religionsbegrepp. Thesis. Uppsala, 1926.

Phil 5251.34.3   Lindworsky, J. Theoretische Psychologie im Umriss. 3. Aufl. Leipzig, 1926.

Phil 5251.8.15   Lipps, T. Psychological studies. 2d ed. Baltimore, 1926.

Phil 5761.12.3   Lipps, Theodor. Vom Fühlen, Wollen und Denken. 3. Aufl. Leipzig, 1926.

Phil 75.20   Literarische Berichte aus dem Gebiete der Philosophie. Sonder Druck von Heft 9/10. Erfurt, 1926.

Phil 8591.20.9   Loisy, Alfred. Religion et l'humanité. Paris, 1926.

Phil 7069.26.12   Luther, F. Der Okkultismus. Leipzig, 1926.

Phil 4803.537.37   Lutosławski, Wincenty. Pewniki polityki polskiej. Wyd. 2. W Szamotułach, 1926.

1926 - cont.

Phil 575.59 McBride, Peter. The riddle of personality: mechanism or mystery? London, 1926.
Phil 5762.17 McCarthy, R.C. The measurement of conation. Chicago, 1926.
Phil 6322.14A McDougall, W. Outline of abnormal psychology. N.Y., 1926.
Phil 5252.18.6 McDougall, William. An introduction to social psychology. Boston, 1926.
Phil 5252.18.16 McDougall, William. Outline of psychology. N.Y., 1926.
Phil 5252.18.13 McDougall, William. Psychologi. København, 1926.
Phil 8592.48.7 Macintosh, D.C. The reasonableness of Christianity. N.Y., 1926.
Phil 187.75 Maier, Heinrich. Philsophie der Wirklichkeit. Tübingen, 1926-1935. 3v.
Phil 4752.1.30 Malinovskii, Aleksandr A. Allgemeine Organisationslehre Tektologie. Berlin, 1926-28. 2v.
Phil 5762.15 Mally, Ernst. Grundgesetze des Sollens. Graz, 1926.
Phil 6990.3.43 Martin, Stuart. The secret of Lourdes. London, 1926.
Phil 1535.37 Marxuach, F. Compendium dialecticae, critical et ontologial. Barcinone, 1926.
Phil 5252.45.5 Masci, Filippo. Introduzione generale alla psicologia. Milano, 1926.
Phil 187.71 Mason, J.W.T. Creative freedom. N.Y., 1926.
Phil 812.9.5 Masson-Oursel, Paul. Comparative philosophy. N.Y., 1926.
Phil 4065.108 Maturi, Sebastiano. Bruno e Hegel. Firenze, 1926.
Phil 2805.418 Mauriac, François. La rencontre avec Pascal. Paris, 1926.
Phil 6682.18 Medeiros e Albuquerque, J.J. de C. da C. O hypnotismo. 3. ed. Rio de Janeiro, 1926.
Phil 5762.16 Medicus, Fritz. Die Freiheit des Willens und ihre Grenzen. Tübingen, 1926.
Phil 187.91 Meiklejohn, A. Philosophy. Chicago, 1926.
Phil 5627.95 Mensching, Gustav. Die heilige Schweigen. Giessen, 1926.
Phil 735.81 Messer, August. Deutsche Wertphilosophie der Gegenwart. Leipzig, 1926.
Phil 187.74 Mignosi, Pietro. Critica dell'identita. Palermo, 1926.
Phil 5252.87 Miller, Edmond M. Brain capacity and intelligence. Sydney, 1926.
Phil 2655.2.80 Mirabaud, R. Charles Henry et l'idéalisme scientifique. Paris, 1926.
Phil 812.10 Misch, Georg. Der Weg in die Philosophie. Leipzig, 1926.
Phil 960.129 Mitra, K.N. Pessimism and life's ideal: the Hindu outlook. Madras, 1926.
Phil 6122.49.3 Monrad-Krohn, G. The clinical examination of the nervous system. 3d ed. London, 1926.
Phil 5252.49.5 Montet, C. de. Le relativisme psychologique et la recherche médicale. Paris, 1926.
Phil 5252.50.2 Moore, T.V. Dynamic psychology. 2d ed. Philadelphia, 1926.
Phil 8592.36 Moore, Willis L. Spiritual gravity of the cosmist. Pasadena, 1926.
Phil 2412.5 Müller, Max. Die französische Philosophie der Gegenwart. Karlsruhe, 1926.
Phil 187.76 Musatti, C.L. Analisi del concetto di realtà empirica. Castello, 1926.
Phil 5400.150 Muszynski, Franz. Unsere Leidenschaften. 2. Aufl. Paderborn, 1926.
Phil 5590.18 Myerson, Abraham. The foundations of personality. Boston, 1926.
Phil 3494.26 Myrho, F. Kritizismus: Eine Sammlung...Neu-Kantianismus. Berlin, 1926.
Phil 4065.107.5 Namer, Émile. Les aspects de Dieu dans la philosophie de Giordano Bruno. Paris, 1926.
Phil 4065.107 Namer, Émile. Les aspects de Dieu dans la philosophie de Giordano Bruno. Thèse. Paris, 1926.
Phil 8090.3 Needham, Harold. Le développement de l'esthétique sociologique en France et en Angleterre au XIX siècle. Paris, 1926.
Phil 5627.220 Neeser, Maurice. Du protestantisme au catholicisme. Paris, 1926.
Phil 3640.605 Nejedlý, Zdeněk. Nietzscheova tragedie. Vinohrady, 1926.
Phil 3640.58 Nietzsche, Friedrich. Vorstufen der Geburt der Tragödie aus dem Geiste der Musik. Leipzig, 1926-28. 3v.
Phil 365.20A Noble, Edmund. Purposive evolution. N.Y., 1926.
Phil 6750.26 Nöll, Heinrich. Intentionalität, Reaktivität und Schwachsinn. Halle, 1926.
Phil 3640.201 Odenwald, T. Friedrich Nietzsche und der heutige Christentum. Giessen, 1926.
Phil 3640.79.100 Oehler, Richard. Nietzscheregister. Leipzig, 1926.
Phil 3640.200 Oehler, Richard. Nietzsches philosophisches Werden. München, 1926.
Phil 5254.2 Ogden, C.K. The meaning of psychology. N.Y., 1926.
Phil 1870.107 Olgiati, F. L'idealismo di G. Berkeley. Milano, 1926.
Phil 7069.26.15 Owen, G.V. The life beyond the veil. London, 1926. 2v.
Phil 2475.1.223 Oxenstierna, G. Tids- och intuitionsproblemen i Bergson's filosofi. Thesis. Uppsala, 1926.
Phil 6325.7 Pagès, Louis. Affectivité et intelligence: étude psycho-pathologique. Paris, 1926.
Phil 6325.7.2 Pagès, Louis. Affectivité et intelligence: étude psycho-pathologique. Thèse. Paris, 1926.
Phil 705.22 Pannwitz, R. Kosmos Atheos. München, 1926.
Phil 8670.16 Papini, G. The memoirs of God. Boston, 1926.
Phil 3450.2.87 Paritzky, J.E. Franz Hemsterhuis, seine Philosophie und ihr Einfluss auf dei deutschen Romantiker. Berlin, 1926.
Phil 2805.19 Pascal, Blaise. Oeuvres complètes. Paris, 1926. 2v.
Phil 5125.11 Patterson, C.H. Problems in logic. N.Y., 1926.
Phil 5055.17 Patterson, Charles H. Problems in logic. N.Y., 1926.
Phil 8595.24 Penel, Raymond. Qu'est-ce que la vérité? Paris, 1926.
Phil 5255.26 Perrin, Fleming. Psychology. N.Y., 1926.
Phil 1715.3.9A Perry, R.B. Philosophy of the recent past. N.Y., 1926.
Phil 735.20.5A Perry, Ralph Barton. General theory of value. N.Y., 1926.
Phil 5722.17 Petraschek, K.O. Die Logik des Unbewussten. München, 1926. 2v.
Phil 8595.22 Phelps, William L. Adventures and confessions. N.Y., 1926.
Phil 5400.63 Picard, Ernest. Problème de la vie affective. Paris, 1926.
Phil 974.3.10 Picht, C.S. Das literarische Lebenswerk Rudolf Steiners. Dornach, 1926.
Phil 5640.125.15 Pikler, Gyula. Theorie des Gedächtnisses. Leipzig, 1926.
Phil 5625.1 Podkopaev, N.A. Die Methodik der Enforschung der bedingten Reflexe. München, 1926.
Phil 5255.28 Poffenberger, A.T. Experimental psychology; loose leaf laboratory manual. Chicago, 1926.
Phil 8595.23A Powicke, F.J. The Cambridge Platonists; a study. London, 1926.
Phil 8595.23.5A Powicke, F.J. The Cambridge Platonists. Cambridge, 1926.

1926 - cont.

Phil 190.38.5 Prandtl, Antonin. Das Problem der Wirklichkeit. München, 1926.
Phil 8599.16.80 Presser, Jacob. Das Buch De tribus impostoribus. Amsterdam, 1926.
Phil 6325.6 Pressey, Sidney L. Mental abnormality and deficiency. N.Y., 1926.
Phil 7069.25.11 Prince, Walter Franklin. A review of the Margery case. Ithaca, 1926.
Phil 7069.26.25 Prince, Walter Franklin. The psychic in the house. Boston, 1926.
Phil 25.33 Psychologies of 1925. Worcester, 1926.
Phil 5255.27 Pyne, John K. The mind. N.Y., 1926.
Phil 8967.8 Rademacher, A. Religion und Leben. Freiburg, 1926.
Phil 4809.727.35 Rádl, Emanuel. Moderní věda. Praha, 1926.
Phil 960.35A Ranade, R.D. A constructive survey of Upanishadic philosophy. Poona, 1926.
Phil 5841.18.10 Rank, Otto. Sexualität und Schuldgefühl. Leipzig, 1926.
Phil 6327.4.9 Rank, Otto. Technik der Psychoanalyse. Leipzig, 1926-31. 3v.
Phil 102.3.3 Ranzoli, C. Dizionario di scienze filosofiche. 3a ed. Milano, 1926.
Phil 8597.35 Reese, Curtis W. Humanism. Chicago, 1926.
Phil 817.14.5 Reinach, S. Lettres à Zoé sur l'histoire des philosophies. Paris, 1926. 3v.
Phil 645.22.12 Rensi, Giuseppe. Apologia dello scetticismo. Roma, 1926.
Phil 645.22.7 Rensi, Giuseppe. Lo scetticismo. Milano, 1926.
VPhil 450.8 Retschlag, Max. Von der Urmaterie zum Urkraft-Elixier. Leipzig, 1926.
Phil 583.2 Reyer, Wilhelm. Einführung in der Phänomenologie. Leipzig, 1926.
Phil 8707.11.2 Riley, W.B. Inspiration or evolution. 2. ed. Cleveland, 1926.
Phil 6327.5.15 Rivers, W.H.R. L'instinct et l'inconscient. Paris, 1926.
Phil 6420.20 Robbins, Samuel D. Stammering and its treatment. Boston, 1926.
Phil 1122.5 Rodier, Georges. Etudes de philosophie grecque. Paris, 1926.
Phil 5257.41 Roffenstein, G. Das Problem des psychologischen Verstehens. Stuttgart, 1926.
Phil 575.65 Rohracher, H. Persönlichkeit und Schicksal. Wien, 1926.
Phil 7082.102 Romsche, Heinrich. Unsere Träume und Traumzustände. Stuttgart, 1926.
Phil 2250.88 Rothman, W. Josiah Royces Versuch einer Synthese von Pragmatismus und Objektivität. Inaug. Diss. Jena, 1926.
Phil 2250.88.2 Rothman, W. Josiah Royces Versuch einer Synthese von Pragmatismus und Objektivität. Jena, 1926.
Phil 6536.14 Rows, R.G. Epilepsy, a functional mental illness. N.Y., 1926.
Phil 192.28.4 Russell, B. Die Probleme der Philosophie. Erlangen, 1926.
Phil 192.28.14 Russell, B. Unser Wissen von der Aussenwelt. Leipzig, 1926.
Phil 5257.25.5 Russell, Bertrand Russell. Analyse de l'esprit. Paris, 1926.
Phil 5258.90 Saint-Paul, G. Thèmes psychologiques. Paris, 1926.
Phil 1020.8.15 Saliba, D. Étude sur la métaphysique d'Avicenne. Paris, 1926.
Phil 1020.8.16 Saliba, D. Étude sur la métaphysique d'Avicenne. Thèse. Paris, 1926.
Htn Phil 4065.01* Salvestrini, V. Bibliografia delle opere di Giordano Bruno. Pisa, 1926.
Phil 645.35.5 Sánchez, Francisco. Que nada se sabe. Madrid, 1926.
Phil 193.49.25.15 Santayana, G. Dialogues in limbo. N.Y., 1926.
Phil 193.49.7 Santayana, G. Winds of doctrine. Studies in contemporary opinion. N.Y., 1926.
Phil 193.104.2 Sauer, W. Philosophie der Zukunft. 2e Aufl. Stuttgart, 1926.
Phil 5258.87 Saxby, I.B. The psychology of the thinker. London, 1926.
Phil 2493.88 Schaupp, Zora. The naturalism of Condillac. Lincoln, 1926.
Phil 349.24.5 Scheler, Max. Die Wissensformen und die Gesellschaft. Leipzig, 1926.
Phil 3800.63 Schelling, F.W.J. von. Shellings Schriften zur Gesellschaftsphilosophie. Jena, 1926.
Phil 6688.18 Schilder, Paul. Lehrbuch der Hypnose. Wien, 1926.
Phil 5258.85.15 Schleich, Carl Ludwig. Von Schaltwerk der Gedanken. 47. bis 49. Aufl. Berlin, 1926.
Phil 3805.49 Schleiermacher, Friedrich. Soliloquies. Chicago, 1926.
Phil 3500.41 Schmalenbach, H. Die Kantische Philosophie und die Religion. Göttingen, 1926.
Phil 3808.60.40 Schopenhauer, Arthur. Frammenti di storia della filosofia. Milano, 1926?
Phil 3808.76.30 Schopenhauer, Arthur. Schopenhauer und Brockhaus. Leipzig, 1926.
Phil 3808.45.15 Schopenhauer, Arthur. Selected essays. London, 1926.
Phil 349.27 Schunck, Karl. Verstehen und Einsehen. Halle an der Saale, 1926.
Phil 3903.1.86 Schuster, Willy. Zwischen Philosophie und Kunst, Johannes Volkelt zum 100 Lehrsemester. Leipzig, 1926.
Phil 5610.1.15 Scott, W.D. The psychology of public speaking. N.Y., 1926.
Phil 7140.116.75 Seeling, Otto. Der Couéismus. Diss. Giessen, 1926.
Phil 193.66.9 Sellars, Roy Wood. The principles and problems of philosophy. N.Y., 1926.
Phil 3310.4.80 Semmelink, J.H. Professor Dr. J.H. Gunning. Zeist, 1926.
Phil 8893.8.15 Seth, J. Essays in ethics and religion with other papers. Edinburgh, 1926.
Phil 8893.8.10 Seth, J. A study of ethical principles. 17. ed. N.Y., 1926.
Phil 4756.2.31 Setniskii, N.A. Kapitalisticheskii stroi v izobrazhenii N.F. Fedorova. Kharbin, 1926. 2 pam.
Phil 7069.26.30 Seymour, S.J.D. True Irish ghost stories. 2. ed. Dublin, 1926.
Phil 8708.13 Shafer, Robert. Christianity and naturalism. New Haven, 1926.
Phil 2262.51 Shaftesbury, A.A.C. Moralisterna, en filosofisk rhapsodi. Stockholm, 1926.
Phil 960.39.5 Shcherbatskii, F.I. La théorie de la connaissance. Paris, 1926.
Phil 5150.1.5 Sheffer, H.M. Notational relativity. n.p., 1926?
Phil 6128.13.7A Sherrington, C.S. The integrative action of the nervous system. New Haven, 1926.
Phil 4769.7.32 Shestov, Lev. Potestas clavium. München, 1926.
Phil 3549.2.94 Shilpnagel, U. Graf Edward von Keyserling und seinepisches Werk. Inaug. Diss. Rostock, 1926.
Phil 8893.87 Sibecas, S. Factores morales. Habana, 1926.

Phil 8893.92A Sinclair, Upton. The book of life. 4th ed. v.1-2. Long Beach, 1926.

Phil 5640.32 Skramlik, E. von. Handbuch der Physiologie der niederen Sinne. Leipzig, 1926.

Phil 5645.30 Sloan, Louise L. The effect of intensity of light...eye and size...on the visibility curve. Diss. n.p., 1926?

Phil 2266.42 Smith, Adam. Theorie der ethischen Gefühle. Leipzig, 1926. 2v.

Phil 5058.28.19 Smith, Henry B. A system of formal logic. pt.1. Columbus, 1926.

Phil 365.19A Smuts, J.C. Holism and evolution. N.Y., 1926.

Phil 3500.43 Souviau, M. Le jugement réfléchissant dans la philosophie critique de Kant. Paris, 1926.

Phil 3500.43.2 Souviau, M. Le jugement réfléchissant dans la philosophie critique de Kant. Thèse. Paris, 1926.

Phil 4018.2.5 Spaventa, Bertrando. La filosofia italiana. 3. ed. Bari, 1926.

Phil 3745.5.90 Speck, Johannes. Friedrich Paulsen, sein Leben und sein Werk. Langensalza, 1926.

Phil 2270.70.15 Spencer, Herbert. Principles of psychology. N.Y., 1926.

Phil 5768.19 Stammler, Gerhard. Notwendigkeit in Natur- und Kulturwissenschaft. Halle, 1926.

Phil 8843.10 Stefanini, L. Il problema morale nello stoicismo e nel cristianesimo. Torino, 1926.

Phil 974.3.80 Steffen, Albert. Begegnungen mit Rudolf Steiner. Zürich, 1926.

Phil 3195.6.84 Stein, Arthur. Der Begriff des Verstehens bei Dilthey. 2. Aufl. Tübingen, 1926.

Phil 9430.32 Stein, Ludwig. Evolution and optimism. N.Y., 1926.

Phil 978.49.145 Steiner, R. Sprachgestaltung und dramatische Kunst. Dornach, 1926.

Phil 3640.214.2 Steiner, Rudolf. Friedrich Nietzsche: ein Kämpfer gegen seiner Zeit. 2e Aufl. Dornich, 1926.

Phil 5645.41 Steinfels, W. Farbe und Dasein. Jena, 1926.

Phil 193.116 Stern, Erich. Zufall und Schicksal. Karlsruhe, 1926.

Phil 818.19 Sternberg, Kurt. Was Heisst und zu welchem Ende studiert man Philosophiegeschichte. Berlin, 1926.

Phil 7069.26.35 Stobart, M.A. Torchbearers of spiritualism. N.Y., 1926.

Phil 5125.12 Störring, G. Das urteilende und schliessende Denken in kausaler Behandlung. Leipzig, 1926.

Phil 6328.11 Stollenhoff, H. Kurzes Lehrbuch der Psychoanalyse. Stuttgart, 1926.

Phil 8843.9 Stoops, J.D. Ideals of conduct. N.Y., 1926.

Phil 2138.111 Street, Charles L. Individualism and individuality in the philosophy of John Stuart Mill. Milwaukee, 1926.

Phil 8598.57.8 Streeter, Burnett. Reality; a new correlation of science and religion. N.Y., 1926.

Phil 8598.57 Streeter, Burnett. Reality; a new correlation of science and religion. N.Y., 1926.

Phil 7069.26.40 Sudre, R. Introduction à la métapsychique humaine. Paris, 1926.

Phil 6128.40.6 Sunner, Paul. The brain and the mind. N.Y., 1926.

Phil 5400.60 Szymanski, J.S. Gefühl und Erkennen. Berlin, 1926.

Phil 8894.30 Taeusch, C.F. Professional and business ethics. N.Y., 1926.

Phil 194.17.5 Taft, Oren B. Evolution of idea; a thesis. Chicago, 1926.

Phil 1850.120 Taylor, Alfred. Francis Bacon. London, 1926?

Phil 6129.6.5 Taylor, E.W. Psychotherapy. Cambridge, 1926.

Phil 6329.3 Taylor, W.S. Readings in abnormal psychology. N.Y., 1926.

Phil 7069.26.70 Tenhaeff, W.H.C. Beknopte Handleiding der psychical research. 's Gravenhage, 1926. 3v.

Phil 5259.23 Ten Seldam, W.H. Psychologische hoofdstukken. Amsterdam, 1926.

Phil 2115.131 Tex, Jan den. Locke en Spinoza over de tolerantie. Amsterdam, 1926.

Phil 6969.6 Thalbitzer, S. Emotion and insanity. London, 1926.

Phil 5829.8 Thorlakson, B.C. Le fondement physiologique des instincts des systèmes nutritif. Thèse. Paris, 1926.

Phil 7080.40A Thorláksson, Björg Caritas. Svefn og draumar. Reykjavík, 1926.

Phil 193.107 The three conventions; metaphysical dialogues, principia metaphysica, and commentary. N.Y., 1926.

Phil 7069.25.12 Tillyard, R.J. Some recent personal experiences with Margery. N.Y., 1926.

Phil 978.16.13 Tingley, K.A. (Mrs.). The gods await. Point Loma, California, 1926.

Phil 3640.206 Tissi, Silvio. Nietzsche. Milano, 1926.

Phil 5259.5.10.5 Titchener, E.B. Lectures on the experimental psychology of the thought-processes. N.Y., 1926.

Phil 5259.5.37 Titchener, E.B. A text-book of psychology. N.Y., 1926.

Phil 6969.10 Tramer, Moritz. Technisches Schaffen Geisteskranker. München, 1926.

Phil 8120.8 Traz, Georges de. Diderot à Valéry. Paris, 1926.

Phil 4060.1.91 Troilo, Erminio. Ardigò. Milano, 1926.

Phil 5259.19 Troland, L.T. The mystery of mind. N.Y., 1926.

Phil 8674.8 Turner, J.E. Personality and reality. N.Y., 1926.

Phil 820.1.7.5A Ueberweg, F. Grundriss der Geschichte der Philosophie. 12. Aufl. Berlin, 1926-51. 5v.

Phil 8421.2 Ulricus Engelberti, Argentinensis. Des Ulricus Engelberti von Strassburg O. Pr. (+1277) Abhandlung de Pulchro. München, 1926.

Phil 5627.60.5 Underhill, E. The life of the spirit and the life of today. N.Y., 1926.

Phil 2805.196 Valensin, A. A la suite de Pascal. Saint-Felicien-en-Vivarais, 1926.

Phil 6331.3 Verband der Vereine Katholischer Akademiker, Kevalaer. Religion und Seelenleiden. v. 1,2,3,6. Düsseldorf, 1926. 4v.

Phil 630.28 Verda, Mary. New realism in the light of scholasticism. N.Y., 1926.

Phil 3640.525 Verweyen, J. Wagner und Nietzsche. Stuttgart, 1926.

Phil 1526.2 Verweyen, Johannes M. Die Philosophie der Mittelalters. 2e Aufl. Berlin, 1926.

Phil 3640.199 Vetter, A. Nietzsche. München, 1926.

Phil 4260.27 Vico, G.B. L'estetica di G.B. Vico allraverso la scienza nuova e gli scritti minari. Napoli, 1926.

Phil 3195.6.85 Wach, Joachim. Die Typenlehre Trendelenburgs und ihr Einfluss auf Dilthey. Tübingen, 1926.

Phil 1750.124 Wach, Joachim. Das Verstehen. Tübingen, 1926-33. 3v.

Phil 978.64 Wachsmuth, G. Die ätherischen Bildekräfte in Kosmos, Erde und Mensch. Dornach, 1926.

Phil 5722.38.2 Waldstein, Louis. The subconscious self and its relation to education and health. N.Y., 1926.

Phil 5062.36 Wallas, G. The art of thought. London, 1926.

Phil 5850.385 Wallas, Graham. The art of thought. N.Y., 1926.

Phil 3246.214 Wallner, Nico. Fichte als politischen Denker. Halle, 1926.

Phil 6332.8 Wallon, H. Psychologie pathologique. Paris, 1926.

Phil 6332.34 Wanke, Georg. Psychoanalyse: Geschichte, Wesen. 2. Aufl. Halle, 1926.

Phil 5262.29 Ward, Henshaw. Thobbing; a seat at the circus of the intellect. Indianapolis, 1926.

Phil 5832.8.7 Washburn, M.F. The animal mind. 3. ed. N.Y., 1926.

Phil 197.49 Wattjes, J.G. Practische wijsbegeerte. 2e druk. Delft, 1926.

Phil 3504.30 Webb, Clement C.J. Kant's philosophy of religion. Oxford, 1926.

Phil 2555.6.90 Weber, Georg. Die Philosophie Debrye's. Inaug.-Diss. Augsburg, 1926.

Phil 197.54 Weber, Maximilian. Kritik der Weltanschaungen. Langensalza, 1926.

Phil 2050.199 Wegrich, Arno. Die Geschichtsauffassung David Hume's im Rahmen seines philosophischen Systems. Inaug. Diss. Köln, 1926.

Phil 5850.385.30 Weimer, H. Fehlerbehandlung und Fehlerbewertung. Leipzig, 1926.

Phil 5262.32 Werner, Heinz. Einführung in die Entwicklungspsychologie. Leipzig, 1926.

Phil 6972.15 Wertheimer, F.I. The significance of the physical constitution in mental disease. Baltimore, 1926.

Phil 8602.33.2 Whitehead, A.N. Religion in the making. N.Y., 1926.

Phil 8602.33A Whitehead, A.N. Religion in the making. N.Y., 1926.

Phil 8712.17 Wieman, H.N. Religious experience and scientific method. N.Y., 1926.

Phil 6972.13 Wildermuth, H. Seele und Seelenkrankheit. Berlin, 1926.

Phil 5360.5 Willwoll, A. Begriffsbildung: eine psychologische Untersuchung. Leipzig, 1926.

Phil 197.44 Wilson, George A. The self and its world. N.Y., 1926.

Phil 6332.12 Wittels, Fritz. Die Technik der Psychoanalyse. München, 1926.

Phil 5062.22.9 Wolf, Abraham. Essentials of logic. London, 1926.

Phil 197.23.5 Woodbridge, F.J.E. The realm of mind. N.Y., 1926.

Phil 197.40.5 Wordsworth, J.C. Adventures in philosophy. N.Y., 1926.

Phil 5232.3 Wray, W.J. The new psychology and the gospel. London, 1926.

Phil 1527.1.5.9 Wulf, M. de. History of medieval philosophy. London, 1926. 2v.

Phil 5834.1.15 Yerkes, R.M. The mind of a gorilla. Worcester, Mass., 1926.

Phil 930.27 Zenker, E.V. Geschichte der chinesischen Philosophie. Reichenberg, 1926-27. 2v.

Phil 4710.70 Zen'kovskii, V.V. Russkie mysliteli i Evropa. Paris, 1926.

Phil 5425.39 Zilsel, Edgar. Die Entstehung des Geniebegriffes. Tübingen, 1926.

Phil 6319.8 Zolowicz, E. Die Persönlichkeitsanalyse. Leipzig, 1926.

Phil 1725.1 Zuccante, Giuseppe. Uomini e dottrine. Torino, 1926.

Phil 5265.2 Zwanenburg, S. Inleiding tot de psychologie. Utrecht, 1926.

Phil 1750.104 Zybura, John. S. Present-day thinkers and the new scholasticism. Saint Louis, 1926.

Phil 400.74 Abbagnano, N. Il nuovo idealismo inglese ed americano. Napoli, 1927.

Phil 3482.2.25 Adickes, E. Kant und die als-ob-Philosophie. Stuttgart, 1927.

Phil 9035.53.2A Adler, Alfred. Understanding human nature. Garden City, N.Y., 1927.

Phil 9035.53 Adler, Alfred. Understanding human nature. N.Y., 1927.

Phil 5190.21.5 Adler, M.J. Dialectic. N.Y., 1927.

Phil 3549.2.90 Adolph, H. Die Philosophie des Grafen Keyserling. Stuttgart, 1927.

Phil 4120.2.92 Albeggiani, F. Il sistema filosofico di Cosmo Guastella. Firenze, 1927.

Phil 6310.4.4 Alexander, Franz G. Psychoanalyse der Gesamtpersönlichkeit. Leipzig, 1927.

Phil 8401.22.5 Alexander, Samuel. Art and instinct. Oxford, 1927.

Phil 8401.22 Alexander, Samuel. Artistic creation and cosmic creation. London, 1927.

Phil 5750.6 Allendy, René F. Le problème de la destinée. Paris, 1927.

Phil 9035.45.15 Allport, G.W. The psychology of character by A.A. Roback. Princeton, 1927.

Phil 3801.134 Allwohn, Adolf. Der Mythos bei Schelling. Charlottenburg, 1927.

Phil 4769.1.97 Ambrozaitis, K. Die Staatslehre W. Solowjews. Paderborn, 1927.

Phil 3820.7 Amzalak, M.B. Spinoza. Lisboa, 1927.

Phil 2610.84 Andrieux, L. Pierre Gassendi. Thèse. Paris, 1927.

Phil 5642.20 Anschütz, Georg. Kurze Einführung in die Farbe-Ton-Forschung. Leipzig, 1927.

Phil 8690.4 Anthony, H.D. Relativity and religion. London, 1927.

Phil 3820.6 Appuhn, C. Spinoza. Paris, 1927.

Phil 5642.18 Argelander, A. Das Farbenhören und der synäthetische Faktor der Wahrnehmung. Jena, 1927.

Phil 85.1 Arnaiz y Alcalde, N. Diccionario manual de filosofía. Madrid, 1927.

Phil 2250.87 Aronson, M.J. La philosophie morale de Josiah Royce. Paris, 1927.

Phil 2250.87.2 Aronson, M.J. La philosophie morale de Josiah Royce. Thèse. Paris, 1927.

Phil 960.36 Arunáchalam, P. Light from the East. London, 1927.

Phil 1800.1 Aster, E. Geschichte der englischen Philosophie. Bielefeld, 1927.

Phil 5040.14 Avey, A.E. The function and forms of thought. N.Y., 1927.

Phil 5041.42 Bachelard, G. Essai sur la connaissance approchée. Thèse. Paris, 1927.

Phil 3092.1 Bachofen, J.J. Selbstbiographie undAntrittsrede. Halle, 1927.

Phil 7140.127 Baerwald, Richard. Psychologie der Selbstverteidigung in Klampf-, Not- und Krankheitzeiten. Leipzig, 1927.

Phil 3808.151.2 Baillot, A. Influence de la philosophie de Schopenhauer in France. Thèse. Paris, 1927. 2 pam.

Phil 5465.28 Baïtch, Baïa. La psychologie de la rêverie. Thèse. Paris, 1927.

Phil 2730.94 Barbillion, G. De l'idée de dieu dans la philosophie de Maine de Biran. Thèse. Grenoble, 1927. 2 pam.

Phil 8876.92 Barclay, Thomas. The wisdom of Lang-Sin. N.Y., 1927.

Phil 3483.42 Barth, Heinrich. Philosophie der praktischen Vernunft. Tübingen, 1927.

Chronological Listing

Phil 9150.26   Bartholomew, I.G. The cause of evil. London, 1927.
Phil 3483.6.2   Basch, V. Essai critique sur L'esthétique de Kant. 2. éd. Paris, 1927.
Phil 3425.239   Basch, Victor. Les doctrines politiques des philosophes de l'Allemagne; Leibnitz, Kant, Fichte, Hegel. Paris, 1927.
Phil 7069.27.5   Bateman, A.B. Christianity and spiritualism. London, 1927.
Phil 5241.42.5   Baudin, E. Cours de psychologie. 5e éd. Paris, 1927.
Phil 176.112   Baudin, E. Introduction générale à la philosophie. Paris, 1927.
Phil 3090.83   Baumgardt, D. Franz von Baader und die philosophische Romantik. Halle, 1927.
Phil 332.12   Baumgarten, Arthur. Erkenntnis, Wissenschaft, Philosophie. Tübingen, 1927.
Phil 5710.10   Baxter, M.F. An experimental study of...temperaments. Diss. Ithaca, N.Y., 1927.
Phil 5627.15.11   Begbie, H. Life changers. N.Y., 1927.
Phil 400.64   Beggerow, H. Die Erkenntnis der Wirklichkeiten. Halle, 1927.
Phil 960.43   Belvalkar, S.K. History of Indian philosophy. v.2,7. Poona, 1927-33. 2v.
Phil 2255.1.90   Benjamin, A.C. The logical atomism of Bertrand Russell. Diss. Champaign, Ill., 1927?
Phil 7069.27.10   Bennett, E.N. Appolonius. London, 1927?
Phil 8581.69.3   Berdiaev, N.A. Filosofiia svobodnogo dukha. v.1-2. Parizh, 1927.
Phil 1735.8.2   Bergmann, Ernst. Der Geist des XIX. Jahrhunderts. 2. Aufl. Breslau, 1927.
Phil 5241.72   Berman, Louis. The religion called behaviorism. N.Y., 1927.
Phil 3790.10.91   Bertele, H. Paul Rée's Lehre vom Gewissen. Thesis. München, 1927.
Phil 5241.65.10   Bertrand-Barraud, D. De la nature affective de la conscience. Paris, 1927.
Phil 1200.14.5   Bevan, E.R. Stoïciens et sceptiques. Paris, 1927.
Phil 1701.15   Bierens de Haan, J. Hoofdfiguren der geschiedenis van het urjsgeerig denden. 2e druk. Haarlem, 1927.
Phil 5211.5   Bierviet, J.J. van. La psychologie d'aujourd'hui. Paris, 1927.
Phil 3905.82   Biró, Paul. Die Sittlichkeitsmetaphysik Otto Weiningers. Wien, 1927.
Phil 3905.82.2   Biró, Paul. Die Sittlichkeitsmetaphysik Otto Weiningers. Diss. Wien, 1927.
Phil 978.5.22   Blavatsky, H.P. The voice of the silence. Peking, 1927.
Phil 630.32   Boas, George. The datum as essence in contemporary philosophy. Niort, 1927.
Phil 3110.50.10   Böhme, J. L'aurore naissante. Milan, 1927.
Phil 3120.31.30   Boem, W. Über die Möglichkeit systematischer Kulturphilosophie. Saale, 1927.
Phil 5850.138   Bogen, Helmuth. Psychologische Grundlegung der praktischen Berufsberatung. Langensalza, 1927.
Phil 3826.10   Bolin, Wilhelm. Spinoza. 2. Aufl. Darmstadt, 1927.
Phil 974.7   Bolt, Ernst. Die Philosophie der Liebe. v.1-2. Berlin, 1927.
Phil 282.14   Bommersheim, P. Beiträge zur Lehre von Ding und Gesetz. Leipzig, 1927.
Phil 5241.69   Bonsfield, Paul. The mind and its mechanism. London, 1927.
Phil 2490.116   Borchert, M. Der Begriff des Kulturzeitalters bei Comte. Diss. Halle, 1927.
Phil 176.56.7   Bosanquet, B. Science and philosophy and other essays. London, 1927.
Phil 3549.2.87   Boucher, M. La philosophie de H. Keyserling. 6. éd. Paris, 1927.
Phil 2401.5   Boutroux, E. Nouvelles études d'histoire de la philosophie. Paris, 1927.
Phil 2520.134.5   Boutroux, Émile. Des vérités éternelles chez Descartes. Paris, 1927.
Phil 8876.27.7   Bradley, Francis Herbert. Ethical studies. 2nd ed. Oxford, 1927.
Phil 5041.41   Brandt, F. Formel logik. København, 1927.
Phil 7069.27.11   Bret, Thomas. Précis de métapsychic. Paris, 1927. 2v.
Phil 5241.66.5   Broad, C.D. The mind and its place. N.Y., 1927.
Phil 1506.8   Bruni, Gerardo. Riflessioni sulla scolastica. Roma, 1927.
Phil 176.73.2   Brunner, Constantin. Die Lehre von den Geistigen und vom Volk. 2. Aufl. Potsdam, 1927. 2v.
Phil 4065.25   Bruno, Giordano. Giordano-Bruno-Buch. Bad Oldesloe, 1927.
Phil 801.23   Brunschvicg, L. Le progrès de la conscience dans la philosophie. Paris, 1927. 2v.
Phil 176.106   Buchanan, S.M. Possibility. London, 1927.
Phil 176.106.2   Buchanan, S.M. Possibility. N.Y., 1927.
Phil 176.116   Bulgakov, S.N. Die Tragödie der Philosophie. Darmstadt, 1927.
Phil 5465.32   Bundy, Murray W. The theory of imagination in classical and mediaeval thought. Urbana, 1927.
Phil 5080.3   Burkamp, W. Begriff und Beziehung. Leipzig, 1927.
Phil 5241.75.12   Burloud, Albert. La pensée conceptuelle. Thèse. Paris, 1927.
Phil 5241.75   Burloud, Albert. La pensée d'après les recherches experimentales de H.J. Watt, de Messer et de Bühler. Paris, 1927.
Phil 5241.75.2   Burloud, Albert. La pensée d'après les recherches experimentales de H.J. Watt, de Messer et de Bühler. Thèse. Paris, 1927.
Phil 5374.45.2   Burrow, Trigant. The social basis of consciousness. N.Y., 1927.
Phil 525.35.5   Butler, Cuthbert. Western mysticism. 2d ed. London, 1927.
Phil 4073.75   Campanella, Tommaso. Lettere. Bari, 1927.
Phil 6952.21.6   Campbell, C.M. Delusion and belief. Cambridge, 1927.
Phil 8582.45.3   Capron, F.H. The anatomy of truth. 3. ed. London, 1927.
Phil 8692.13.8   Capron, F.H. The conflict of truth. 8. ed. London, 1927.
Phil 2655.3.90   Carbonara, C. L'idealismo di O. Hamelin. Napoli, 1927?
Phil 8403.30   Carey, Arthur. The majority report on art. Newport, R.I., 1927.
Phil 5242.32   Carlill, H.F. Socrates, or The emancipation of mankind. London, 1927.
Phil 8582.43   Carr, Herbert W. Changing backgrounds in religion and ethics. N.Y., 1927.
Phil 6012.7   Carus, Karl G. Über Grund und Bedeutung der verschiedenen formenen der hand in verschiedenen Personen. Berlin, 1927.
Phil 177.8.25   Carus, Paul. The point of view: an anthology. Chicago, 1927.
Phil 8877.58.15   Challaye, F. Cours de morale, a l'usuge des écoles primaires superieures. Paris, 1927.

Phil 8877.58.5   Challaye, F. Philosophie scientifique et philosophie morale. 3. ed. Paris, 1927.
Phil 5627.109   Chansou, J. Étude de psychologie religieuse sur...la prière. Thèse. Toulouse, 1927. 2 pam.
Phil 5242.36   Chavigny, P. L'esprit de contradiction. Paris, 1927.
Phil 7069.27.12   Chevalier, F. Albert Chevalier comes back. London, 1927.
Phil 8952.7   Christian ethics. Philadelphia, 1927.
Phil 177.83   Coaley, C.H. Life and the student. N.Y., 1927.
Phil 8610.927.20   Cohen, Chapman. Essays in freethinking. 2. series. London, 1927.
Phil 477.9.5   Cohen, Chapman. Materialism re-stated. London, 1927.
Phil 75.22   Cohen, F. Philosphie. Antiquarists-Katalog 159/160. Bonn, 1927.
Phil 5242.33   Coleman, L.R. Psychology; a simplification. N.Y., 1927.
Phil 2493.45.20   Condillac, Étienne Bonnot. Trattato delle sensazioni. Bologna, 1927.
Phil 978.60.2   Cooper, Irving S. Reincarnation, the hope of the world. 2d ed. Chicago, 1927.
Phil 5042.7.10   Creighton, J.E. An introductory logic. 4th ed. N.Y., 1927.
Phil 2402.4   Cresson, A. Les courants de la pensée philosophique française. Paris, 1927. 2v.
Phil 4265.2.90   Cristofoli, A. Il pensiero religioso di P.G. Ventura. Milano, 1927.
Phil 4080.3.78   Croce, Benedetto. An autobiography. Oxford, 1927.
Phil 4080.3.10   Croce, Benedetto. Gesammelte philosophische Schriften in deutscher Übertragung. v.1 (no.1-4), v.2 (no. 1-3). Tübingen, 1927-1930. 7v.
Phil 4080.3.30   Croce, Benedetto. Il presupposto filosofico della concezione liberale Nota. Napoli, 1927.
Phil 5545.162   Cuff, N.B. The relation of over-learning to retention. Nashville, 1927.
Phil 5628.5   Cutten, George Barton. Speaking with tongues, historically and psychologically considered. New Haven, 1927.
Phil 177.72   Cuvillier, Armand. Manuel de philosophie. Paris, 1927. 2v.
Phil 3195.14.34   Dacqué, Edgar. Urwelt, Sage und Menschheit, eine naturhistori-metaphysische Studie. 4. Aufl. München, 1927.
Phil 7069.27.19   Daily News, London. Ghosts in the Great War. London, 1927.
Phil 7069.27.18   Daily News, London. Uncanny stories. London, 1927.
Phil 7069.27.17   Daily News, London. Warnings from beyond. London, 1927.
Phil 7069.27.15   Dallas, H.A. Leaves from a psychic note-book. London, 1927.
Phil 530.105   Dasgupta, S.N. Hindu mysticism. Chicago, 1927.
Phil 6842.2   Dawes, C.R. The marquis de Sade. London, 1927.
Phil 8404.11   Delacroix, Henri. Psychologie de l'art. Paris, 1927.
Phil 8828.4   Dempf, Alois. Ethik des Mittelalters. München, 1927.
Phil 2520.35.21   Descartes, René. Discours de la méthode. Evreux, 1927.
Phil 2520.35.19   Descartes, René. Discours de la méthode. Paris, 1927.
Phil 2520.52.50   Descartes, René. Meditazioni filosofiche. Torino, 1927.
Phil 2520.29A   Descartes, René. Selections. N.Y., 1927.
Phil 7069.27.50   Doyle, Arthur Conan. Phineas speaks. London, 1927.
Phil 8878.47.5   Driesch, Hans. Ethical principles in theory and practice. N.Y., 1927.
Phil 6113.19.9   Driesch, Hans. Mind and body. N.Y., 1927.
Phil 8878.47   Driesch, Hans. Die sittliche Tat. Leipzig, 1927.
Phil 8583.21   Drown, E.S. Religion or God? Cambridge, 1927.
Phil 5190.4.10   Dubislav, W. Über die Definition. 2. Aufl. Berlin, 1927.
Phil 2805.195.5   Duclaux, A.M.F.R. Portrait of Pascal. London, 1927.
Phil 3485.13   Dünnhaupt, Rudolf. Sittlichkeit, Staat und Recht bei Kant. Berlin, 1927.
Phil 672.136A   Dunne, John W. An experiment with time. N.Y., 1927.
Phil 803.6.25   Durant, W. The story of philosophy. Cambridge, 1927.
Phil 1955.4.87   Durant, Will. Transition. N.Y., 1927.
Phil 335.3   Ehrlich, Walter. Das unpersonale Erlebnis. Halle, 1927.
Phil 89.1.4   Eisler, R. Wörterbuch der Philosophie Begriffe und aus Drücke. 4. Aufl. Berlin, 1927-29. 3v.
Phil 89.1.8   Eisler, Rudolf. Wörterbuch der philosophischen Begriffe. 4. Aufl. Berlin, 1927-30. 3v.
Phil 5244.20   Elder, William. Studies in psychology. London, 1927.
Phil 3425.248   Emge, C.A. Hegels Logik und die Gegenwart. Karlsruhe, 1927.
Phil 8584.16   Enckendorff, M.L. Kindschaft zur Welt. Jena, 1927.
Phil 3235.81.12   Engels, Friedrich. Ludwig Feuerbach. Wien, 1927.
Phil 5014.1.5   Enriques, Federigo. Zur Geschichte der Logik. Leipzig, 1927.
Phil 179.3.20   Eucken, R. Rudolf Eucken; ein Geistesbild. Berlin, 1927?
Phil 8584.5.15.4   Eucken, Rudolf. Der Wahrheitsgehalt der Religion. 4. Aufl. Berlin, 1927.
Phil 3808.150   Fahsel, H. Die Überwindung des Pessimismus. Freiburg, 1927.
Phil 1705.1.4   Falckenberg, R. Geschichte der neueren Philosophie. 9. Aufl. Berlin, 1927.
Phil 3790.4.88   Faust, August. Heinrich Rickert und seine Stellung innerhalb der eutschen Philosophie der Gegenwart. Tübingen, 1927.
Phil 5045.13   Fechner, Oskar. Das Verhältnis der Kategorienlehre zur formalen Logik. Rostock, 1927.
Phil 8599.19.95   Fellner, Karl. Das überweltliche Gut und die innerweltlichen Güter. Diss. Leipzig, 1927.
Phil 6315.1.16   Ferenczi, Sandor. Bausteine zur Psychoanalyse. Leipzig, 1927-39. 4v.
Phil 6315.1.13   Ferenczi, Sandor. Further contributions to the theory and technique of psycho-analysis. N.Y., 1927.
Phil 5755.12   Fernkorn, C.M. Willensfreiheit und Verantwortlichkeit. Greifswald, 1927.
Phil 3195.10.100   Festschrift Hans Driesch zum 60. Geburtstag. v.1-2. Leipzig, 1927.
Phil 4600.2.90   Festskrift tillägnad Hans Larsson. Stockholm, 1927.
Phil 180.52.5   Fialko, M. Passivnost'. Paris, 1927.
Phil 6115.6.12   Flechsig, P. Meine myelogenetische Hirnlehre. Berlin, 1927.
Phil 4080.3.132   Flora, F. Croce. Milano, 1927.
Phil 5627.65.5   Flower, John C. An approach to the psychology of religion. London, 1927.
Phil 930.7.5   Forke, A. Geschichte der alten chinesischen Philosophie. Hamburg, 1927.
Phil 8630.9   Fosdick, H.E. Spiritual values and eternal life. Cambridge, 1927.
Phil 2840.88   Foucher, Louis. La jeunesse de Renouvier et sa première philosophie. Paris, 1927.
Phil 2840.88.2   Foucher, Louis. La jeunesse de Renouvier et sa première philosophie. Thèse. Paris, 1927. 2 pam.
Phil 3910.126   Frauendienst, W. Christian Wolff als Staatsdenker. Berlin, 1927.

1927 - cont.

Phil 7150.22 Frenay, A.D. The suicide problem in the United States. Diss. Boston, 1927.

Phil 6315.2.46A Freud, Sigmund. The problem of lay analysis. N.Y., 1927.

Htn Phil 6315.2.61* Freud, Sigmund. Die Zukunft einer Illusion. Wien, 1927.

Phil 8880.46 Freudenberg, G. Grenzen der Ethik. Leipzig, 1927.

Phil 3825.4.2 Freudenthal, J. Spinoza: Leben und Lehre. 2. Aufl. v.1-2. Heidelberg, 1927.

Phil 1850.121 Frost, Walter. Bacon und die Naturphilosophie. München, 1927.

Phil 8406.6F Fry, R.E. Transformations; critical and speculative essays on art. N.Y., 1927.

Phil 8695.7 Fulton, William. Nature and God. Edinburgh, 1927.

Phil 181.57 Galli, Gallo. Spirito e realta. Milano, 1927.

Phil 8586.10.25 Galloway, G. Faith and reason in religion. London, 1927.

Phil 8586.10.17 Galloway, G. The philosophy of religion. N.Y., 1927.

Phil 665.52 Gardeil, A. La structure de l'âme et l'expérience mystique. Paris, 1927. 2v.

Phil 181.58 Gastelum, B.J. Inteligencia y simbolo. Madrid, 1927.

Phil 3826.11 Gebhardt, Carl. Spinoza; vier Reden. Heidelberg, 1927.

Phil 3195.10.105 Gehlen, Arnold. Zur Theorie der Setzung und des setzungshaften Wissens bei Driesch. Leipzig, 1927.

Phil 3195.10.95 Gehlen, Arnold. Zur Theorie der Setzung und des setzungshaften Wissens bei Driesch. Inaug. Diss. Leipzig, 1927.

Phil 7069.24.22 Geley, Gustave. Clairvoyance and materialisation, a record of experiments. London, 1927.

Phil 2805.197 Gentile, F. Pascal: saggio d'interpretazione storica. Bari, 1927.

Phil 4260.94.5 Gentile, Giovanni. Studi vichiani. Firenze, 1927.

Phil 8407.11 Ghyka, M.C. Esthétique des proportions dans la nature et dans les arts. Paris, 1927.

Phil 8092.7 Gilbert, Katherine Everett. Studies in recent aesthetic. Chapel Hill, 1927.

Phil 1020.8.19 Gilson, Etienne. Avicenne et le point de départ de Duns Scot. Paris, 1927.

Phil 4115.75 Gioberti, V. Epistolario. Firenze, 1927-37. 11v.

Phil 735.86 Goblot, E. La logique des jugements de valeur. Paris, 1927.

Phil 672.139 Goldsbrough, G.F. Recent discussions on "Time". London, 1927.

Phil 6316.7 Gordon, R.G. The neurotic personality. London, 1927.

Phil 8407.22 Goudal, Jean. Volontés de l'art moderne. Paris, 1927.

Phil 7084.16 Green, George Henry. The terror-dream. London, 1927.

Phil 9230.14 Green, Peter. Betting and gambling. London, 1927.

Phil 5246.39 Griffith, Percy. A synthetic psychology. London, 1927.

Phil 8407.4 Griveau, Maurice. Histoire esthétique de la nature. Paris, 1927-30. 3v.

Phil 400.65 Groos, H. Der deutsche Idealismus und das Christentum. München, 1927.

Phil 530.50.5 Groult, Pierre. Les mystiques des Pays-Bas. Louvain, 1927.

Phil 3450.11.90 Grunwaldt, H.H. Ueber die Phänomenologie Husserl. Berlin, 1927.

Phil 9558.20 Guyon, René. La cruauté. Paris, 1927.

Phil 930.30 Hackmann, H. Chinesische Philosophie. München, 1927.

Phil 6117.38 Häberlin, Paul. Leib und Seele. Bern, 1927.

Phil 510.1.7.10 Haeckel, Ernst. The substance of the riddle of the universe. N.Y., 1927.

Phil 8587.51 Haecker, T. Christentum und Kultur. München, 1927.

Phil 5190.22 Hänssler, Ernst H. Zur Theorie der Analogie und des sogenannten Analogieschlusses. Diss. Basel, 1927.

Phil 1807.3 Haldar, H. Neo-Hegelianism. London, 1927.

Phil 9167.3.9F Halifax, G.S. The lady's new-years gift, or Advice to a daughter. Kensington, 1927.

Phil 5585.43 Hamburger, R. Neue Theorie der Wahrnehmung und des Denkens. Berlin, 1927.

Phil 2840.98 Hamelin, Octave. Le système de Renouvier. Paris, 1927.

Phil 7069.27.45 Harper, C.G. Haunted houses. 3. ed. London, 1927.

Phil 8632.14 Harris, J. Immortality. London, 1927.

Phil 6317.17.2 Hart, Bernard. Psychopathology. N.Y., 1927.

Phil 182.80 Hart, Joseph K. Inside experience. N.Y., 1927.

Phil 1200.32 Hartmann, H. Gewissheit und Wahrheit; der Streit zwischen Stoa und akademischer Skepsis. Halle (Saale), 1927.

Phil 6317.26 Hartmann, Heinz. Die Grundlagen der Psychoanalyse. Leipzig, 1927.

X Cg Phil 3425.88.2 Haym, Rudolf. Hegel und seine Zeit. 2. Aufl. Leipzig, 1927.

Phil 5247.43 Heath, Archie E. How we behave. London, 1927.

Phil 3425.60.17 Hegel, Georg Wilhelm Friedrich. Die Naturreligion. Leipzig, 1927.

Phil 3425.60.19 Hegel, Georg Wilhelm Friedrich. Die Religionen der geistigen Individualität. Leipzig, 1927.

Phil 3425.12 Hegel, Georg Wilhelm Friedrich. Sämtliche Werke. Stuttgart, 1927-40. 29v.

Phil 3425.19 Hegel, Georg Wilhelm Friedrich. Schriften zur Gesellschaftsphilosophie. Jena, 1927.

Phil 3425.223 Heimann, B. System und Methode in Hegels Philosophie. Leipzig, 1927.

Phil 3425.01 Hellersberg firm, booksellers. Berlin. Hegel und die Hegelianer; eine Bibliothek. Charlottenburg, 1927?

Phil 182.84 Hellmund, H. Das Wesen der Welt. Zürich, 1927.

Phil 3428.31 Herbart, J.F. Introduzione alla filosofia. 2. ed. Bari, 1927.

Phil 3489.23 Herrmann, Karl. Einführung in die neukantische Philosophie. Halle, 1927.

Phil 1540.14 Heuel, Meinolf. Die Lehre vom Human Naturale bei Thomas Aquin, Bonaventura und Duns Scotus. Inaug. Diss. Koblenz, 1927.

Phil 182.37.10 Heymans, G. Gesammelte kleinere Schriften. Den Haag, 1927. 3v.

Phil 3489.21 Heyse, Hans. Der Begriff der Ganzheit und die Kantische Philosophie. München, 1927.

Phil 9495.127.5 Hildebrand, Dietrich von. Reinheit und Jungfräulichkeit. Köln, 1927.

Phil 365.25.2 Hobhouse, L.T. Development and purpose. London, 1927.

Phil 7082.70 Hoche, Alfred. Das Träumende ich. Jena, 1927.

Phil 4580.67 Høffding, Harald. Religiøse tanketyper. København, 1927.

Phil 400.52.5 Hoernlé, R.F.A. Idealism as a philosophy. N.Y., 1927.

Phil 7150.25 Hoffman, F.L. Suicide problems. Newark, 1927.

Phil 5247.16.16 Hollingworth, H.L. The psychology of thought approached through studies of sleeping and dreaming. N.Y., 1927.

Phil 7069.27.40 Holms, A.C. The fundamental facts of spiritualism. London, 1927.

Phil 5047.32 Honecker, M. Logik: eine Systematik der logischen Probleme. Berlin, 1927.

1927 - cont.

Phil 182.82 Hook, Sidney. The metaphysics of pragmatism. Chicago, 1927.

Phil 8882.51 Horne, H.H. Jesus as a philosopher, and other radio talks. N.Y., 1927.

Phil 2490.25 Hubert, René. Les grands philosophes...choix de textes. Paris, 1927.

Phil 3850.18.84 Hügelmann, H. Max Schelers Persönlichkeitsidee. Diss. Leipzig, 1927.

Phil 8662.12 Huhn, Friedrich. Der Beweis vom dasein Gottes. Berlin, 1927.

Phil 2050.41.25 Hume, David. Enquiries concerning the human understanding and concerning the principles of morals. 2nd ed. Oxford, 1927.

Phil 2050.45.5 Hume, David. Ricerche sull'intelletto umano e sui principii della morale. 2a ed. Bari, 1927.

Phil 2050.23 Hume, David. Selections. N.Y., 1927.

Phil 5247.19.7 Hunter, W.S. General psychology. Chicago, 1927.

Phil 8434.4 Hussey, C. The picturesque. London, 1927.

Phil 8587.48 Huxley, J.S. Religion without revelation. N.Y., 1927.

Phil 5465.27.2 Jaensch, Erich. Die Eidetik und typologische Forschungsmethode in ihrer Bedeutung für die Jugendpsychologie. 2e Aufl. Leipzig, 1927.

Phil 5465.27.5 Jaensch, Erich. Die Streitfrage zwischen Assoziation. Berlin, 1927.

Phil 5585.40.2 Jaeusch, Erich. Über den Aufbau der Wahrnehmungswelt. 2. Aufl. Leipzig, 1927-1931. 2v.

Phil 672.141 Jakubisiak, Augustin. Essai sur les limites de l'espace et du temps. Paris, 1927.

Phil 184.3.34A James, W. Selected papers on philosophy. London, 1927.

Phil 184.3.5 James, W. The will to believe and other essays in popular philosophy. N.Y., 1927.

Phil 5249.2.3 James, William. Principles of psychology. N.Y., 1927.

Phil 5249.21.5 Janet, Pierre. La pensée interieure et ses troubles. pts.1-6. Paris, 1927.

Phil 8664.5 Jernegan, P.F. Man and his God. n.p., 1927.

Phil 290.3 Joffe, Isaac L. Expository history of the cosmos. N.Y., 1927.

Phil 8410.9 Joffe, Jeremiia I. Kul'tura i stil'. Leningrad, 1927.

Phil 2240.84 Jones, O.McK. Empiricism and intuitionism in Reid's common sense philosophy. Princeton, 1927.

Phil 184.41 Jordan, David S. The higher foolishness. Indianapolis, 1927.

Phil 5627.105 Jordan, G.J. A short psychology of religion. N.Y., 1927.

Phil 5627.101 Josey, C.C. The psychology of religion. N.Y., 1927.

Phil 3800.10 Jost, J. F.W.J. von Schelling: Bibliographie. Bonn, 1927.

Phil 2805.111.15 Jovy, Ernest. Études pascaliennes. Paris, 1927-36. 9v.

Phil 3480.31.20 Kant, Immanuel. Critique de la raison pure. Paris, 1927.

Phil 3480.32.17 Kant, Immanuel. Critique of pure reason. 2. ed. N.Y., 1927.

Phil 3480.50.18 Kant, Immanuel. Erste Einleitung in die Kritik der Urteilskraft. Leipzig, 1927.

Phil 3480.33.10 Kant, Immanuel. The idea of a universal history on a cosmopolitical plan. Hanover, N.H., 1927.

Phil 3480.25.10 Kant, Immanuel. The philosophy of Kant. Glasgow, 1927.

Phil 4761.2.40 Karsavin, L.P. Tserkov', lichnost' i gosudarstvo. Parizh, 1927.

Phil 6120.10 Keiller, William. Nerve tracts of the brain and cord. N.Y., 1927.

Phil 8590.15.5 Kesseler, Kurt. Religionsphilosophie. Leipzig, 1927.

Phil 3549.2.35 Keyserling, Hermann. Mensch und Erde in Darstellungen. Darmstadt, 1927.

Phil 3549.2.52 Keyserling, Hermann. Wiedergeburt. Darmstadt, 1927.

Phil 3549.2.79.2 Keyserling, Hermann. The world in the making. London, 1927.

Phil 3549.2.79 Keyserling, Hermann. The world in the making. N.Y., 1927.

Phil 974.2.20 Kingsland, W. Was she a charlatan? London, 1927.

Phil 8960.4 Kirk, Kenneth E. Conscience and its problems. London, 1927.

Phil 3549.8.90 Klages, Ludwig. Persönlichkeit. Potsdam, 1927.

Phil 6060.50 Klages, Ludwig. Zur Ausdruckslehre und Charakterkunde. Heidelberg, 1927.

Phil 3450.18.200 Klösters, Joseph. Die "Kritische Ontologie" Nicolai Hartmanns und ihre Bedeutung für das Erkenntnisproblem. Inaug. Diss. Fulda, 1927.

Phil 8590.19 Knittermeyer, Heinrich. Die philosophie und das Christentum. Jena, 1927.

Phil 530.11.15 Knowles, David. The English mystics. London, 1927.

Phil 575.64 Knudson, A.C. The philosophy of personalism. N.Y., 1927.

Phil 5820.4.15 Köhler, Wolfgang. L'intelligence des singes supérieurs. Paris, 1927.

Phil 6320.7 Kohnstamm, O. Erscheinungsformen der Seele. München, 1927.

Phil 5250.29 Kozlowski, W.M. Thought considered as action and the logical axioms. N.Y., 1927.

Phil 978.59.5 Krishnamurti, J. At the feet of the master. Chicago, 1927?

Phil 978.59.14 Krishnamurti, J. The search. N.Y., 1927.

Phil 978.59.15 Krishnamurti, J. The search. N.Y., 1927[1928].

Phil 8633.1.26 Krüger, G. Immortality of man. Cambridge, 1927.

Phil 165.361 Ksiega pamiątkowa ku czci prof. W. Heinricha. Kraków, 1927.

Phil 3492.50.5 Küpenberg, Max. Der Begriff der Pflicht in Kants vorkritischen Schriften. Innsbruck, 1927.

Phil 5760.7 Kuntz, Leo F. Education of the will in the light of modern research. Diss. Washington, D.C., 1927.

Phil 835.6 Kuntze, Friedrich. Erkenntnistheorie. München, 1927.

Phil 185.39 Kynast, R. Im Weg zur Metaphysik. Leipzig, 1927.

Phil 186.61 Lafora, G.R. Don Juan, Los milagros y otros ensayos. Madrid, 1927.

Phil 5520.45 Laguna, Grace A. de. Speech; its function and development. New Haven, 1927.

Phil 2705.37 La Mettrie, Julien Offray de. Man a machine. Chicago, 1927.

Phil 186.54.5 Landino, C. Camaldolensische Gespräche. Jena, 1927.

Phil 3160.9.83 Langewisch, Eva. Das teleologische Prinzip bei Carl Gustav Carus. Inaug. Diss. Würzburg, 1927.

Phil 2295.85 Lantoine, Albert. Un précurseur de la franc-maçonnerie, John Toland, 1670-1722. Paris, 1927.

Phil 8060.3 Lapcević, Draguicha. La philosophie de l'art classique. Paris, 1927.

Phil 3425.250 Larenz, Karl. Hegels Zurechnungslehre und der Begriff der objektiven Zurechnung. Leipzig, 1927.

Phil 3425.240 Lassalle, F. Die hegelsche und rosenkranzsche Logik. Leipzig, 1927.

1927 - cont.

Phil 974.3.91 Lauer, Hans E. Rudolf Steiners Anthroposophie in Weltanschauungskampfe der Gegenwart. 8. Aufsätze. Basel, 1927.

Phil 186.59 Lehmann, Gerhard. Vorschule der Metaphysik. Berlin, 1927.

Phil 3552.51 Leibniz, Gottfried Wilhelm. Discourse on metaphysics. Chicago, 1927.

Phil 3552.53 Leibniz, Gottfried Wilhelm. Den förutbestämda harmonien. Stockholm, 1927.

Phil 8599.19.100 Leidreiter, Erich. Troeltsch und die Absoluheit des Christentums. Inaug. Diss. Mahrungen, 1927.

Phil 8886.68 Leighton, J.A. The individual and the social order. N.Y., 1927.

Phil 365.27 LeRoy, Édouard. L'exigence idéaliste et le fait de l'évolution. Paris, 1927.

Phil 3011.4 Levy, H. Die Hegel-Renaissance in der deutschen Philosophie. Charlottenburg, 1927.

Phil 5761.9.12 Lévy, Paul Émile. Le traitement moral. Paris, 1927.

Phil 1711.1.5 Liehert, A. Zur Kritik der Gegenwart. Langensalza, 1927.

Phil 9558.45 Lipmann, Otto. Die Lüge Sprach- und literaturwissenschaftlicher und entwicklungsgeschichtlicher Betrachtung. Leipzig, 1927.

Phil 342.12 Lipps, Hans. Untersuchungen zur Phänomenologie der Erkenntnis. v.1-2. Bonn, 1927-28.

Phil 2045.109 Lips, Julius. Die Stellung des Thomas Hobbes zu den politischen Parteien der grossen englischen Revolution. Leipzig, 1927.

Phil 5410.5 Litwinski, Léon. La psychologie de l'ingratitude. Bruxelles, 1927.

Phil 2115.75.9 Locke, J. The correspondence of John Locke and Edward Clarke. Cambridge, 1927.

Phil 2115.75.10 Locke, J. The correspondence of John Locke and Edward Clarke. London, 1927.

Phil 2115.51.20 Locke, J. Della guida dell'intelligenza nella ricerca della verità. Lanciano, 1927.

Phil 2115.45.40 Locke, J. I principi dell'illuminismo eclettico, estratti dal "Saggio sull'intelligenza umano". Torino, 1927.

Phil 8701.13 Lorbeer, Floyd Irwing. A message of light, containing scientifc foundation for religion. Los Angeles, 1927.

Phil 5051.37 Losev, Aleksei F. Muzyka kak predmet logiki. Moskva, 1927.

Phil 5051.23.7 Losskii, N.O. Handbuch der Logik, Übersetzung von W. Sesemann. Leipzig, 1927.

Phil 9410.7 Lovejoy, Arthur O. Optimism and romanticism. n.p., 1927.

Phil 3425.245 Lowenstein, Julius. Hegels Staatsidee. Berlin, 1927.

Phil 8701.12 Luckey, L.W.A. Whence comest thou? Whither goest thou? Boston, 1927.

Phil 186.50.10 Ludowici, A. Denkfibel; die Lehre vom organischen Gegensatz. München, 1927.

Phil 5251.35 Lund, F.H. Psychology: the science of mental activity. N.Y., 1927.

Phil 9035.49 McDougall, W. Character and the conduct of life. N.Y., 1927.

Phil 5252.60 McDowall, R.J.S. The mind. N.Y., 1927.

Phil 187.79 MacLeod, A.H.D. Sur diverses questions se présentant dans l'étude du concept de réalité. Paris, 1927.

Phil 187.79.2 MacLeod, A.H.D. Sur diverses questions se présentant dans l'étude du concept de réalité. Paris, 1927.

Phil 2730.60 Maine de Biran, Pierre. Journal intime. 5e éd. Paris, 1927-1931. 2v.

Phil 187.93 Marcel, Gabriel. Journal métaphysique. Paris, 1927.

Phil 3494.19.10 Marcus, Ernst. Die Zeit- und Raumlehre Kants. München, 1927.

Phil 187.106 Masson, T.L. The city of perfection. N.Y., 1927.

Phil 5411.7 Mathis, René. La haine. Thèse. Nancy, 1927.

Phil 4073.89 Mattei, R. de. La politica di Campanella. Roma, 1927.

Phil 525.78 Mehlis, G. Die Mystik. München, 1927.

Phil 2733.101 Mennicken, Peter. Die Philosophie des Nicolas Malebranche. Leipzig, 1927.

Phil 2515.4.97 Mentré, F. Pour qu'on lise Cournot. Paris, 1927.

Phil 8887.61 Mersch, Émile. L'obligation morale, principe de liberté. Louvain, 1927.

Phil 5070.17 Mertens, Paul. Zur Phänomenologie des Glaubens. Inaug. Diss. Fulda, 1927.

Phil 1712.5.10 Messer, A. Die Philosophie der Gegenwart. Leipzig, 1927.

Phil 6322.17 Meyer, Max F. Abnormal psychology. Columbia, 1927.

Phil 400.70 Mignosi, Pietro. L'idealismo. Milano, 1927.

Phil 2840.89 Milhaud, G. La philosophie de Charles Renouvier. Paris, 1927.

Phil 3455.1.01 Miller, Wilhelm A. Isenkrahe-Bibliographie. 3e Aufl. Berlin, 1927.

Phil 8702.13 Millikan, R.A. Evolution in science and religion. New Haven, 1927.

Phil 8110.13 Mirabent, F. La estética inglesa del siglo XVIII. Barcelona, 1927.

Phil 530.15.20 The mirror of simple souls. London, 1927.

Phil 6322.6.10 Mitchell, T.W. Problems in psychopathology. London, 1927.

Phil 343.15 Mochi, Alberto. La connaissance scientifique. Paris, 1927.

Phil 2020.84 Montagné, Paul. Un radical religieux. v.1-2. Thèse. Toulouse, 1927.

Phil 187.82 Moore, J.S. Rifts in the universe. New Haven, 1927.

Phil 5252.67 Morgan, John J.B. An introduction to psychology. N.Y., 1927.

Phil 187.81 Mossig, T. Wirklichkeit. Leipzig, 1927.

Phil 2840.90 Mouy, P. L'idée de progrès dans la philosophie de Renouvier. Paris, 1927.

Phil 2840.90.2 Mouy, P. L'idée de progrès dans la philosophie de Renouvier. Thèse. Paris, 1927.

Phil 2733.100 Mouy, P. Les lois du choc des corps d'après Malebranche. Paris, 1927.

Phil 2733.100.2 Mouy, P. Les lois du choc des corps d'après Malebranche. Thèse. Paris, 1927.

Phil 8637.24.2 Muderspach, L. Bag død og grav. 2. udg. København, 1927.

Phil 187.86.10 Müller-Freienfels, R. Geheimnisse der Seele. München, 1927.

Phil 187.86 Müller-Freienfels, R. Metaphysik des Irrationalen. Leipzig, 1927.

Phil 3805.171 Müsebeck, Ernst. Schleiermacher in der Geschichte der Staatsides. Berlin, 1927.

Phil 6322.15 Mullen, J.J. Psychological factors in the pastoral treatement of scruples. n.p., 1927.

Phil 1050.5.5 Munk, S. Mélanges de philosophie Juive et Arabe. Paris, 1927.

Phil 7069.26.13A Murchison, C. The case for and against psychical belief. Worcester, 1927.

1927 - cont.

Phil 6962.15 Myerson, Abraham. The psychology of mental disorders. N.Y., 1927.

Phil 8668.4.5 Newton, J.F. My idea of God. Boston, 1927.

Phil 5253.9 Noltenius, F. Die Gefühlswerte. Leipzig, 1927.

Phil 188.14 Nordenholz, A. Welt als Individuation. Leipzig, 1927.

Phil 8415.3.5 Odebrecht, R. Grundlegung einer ästhetischen Werttheorie. Berlin, 1927-

Phil 4065.110 Olschki, L. Giordano Bruno. Bari, 1927.

Phil 189.12 Oppenheimer, F.J. The new tyranny; mysticism, scepticism. N.Y., 1927.

Phil 189.20 Osmond, A. My philosophy of life. Salt Lake City, 1927.

Phil 189.17 Où chercher le réel? Paris, 1927.

Phil 5254.3 Overstreet, H. Allen. About ourselves. N.Y., 1927.

Phil 7069.27.30 Owen, G.V. Problems which perplex. London, 1927.

Phil 190.44 Page, Harvey L. Section I. Auto-philosophy founded on the straight and the curve; the 4 and the 9 of Pythagoras. San Antonio, 1927.

Phil 2520.175 Palau, J.Y. Descartes y el idealismo subjetiva moderno. Barcelona, 1927.

Phil 7069.27.33 Palmer, E.C. The riddle of spiritualism. London, 1927.

Phil 525.60 Parke, Jean. The immaculate perception. N.Y., 1927.

Phil 5585.39A Parsons, John H. An introduction to the theory of perception. Cambridge, 1927.

Phil 8890.42 Paton, H.J. The good will. London, 1927.

Phil 5625.75A Pavlov, Ivan P. Conditioned reflexes. Oxford, 1927.

Phil 5625.75.10 Pavlov, Ivan P. Les reflexes conditionelles. Paris, 1927.

Phil 530.40.27 Peers, E.A. Studies of the Spanish mystics. London, 1927-30. 2v.

Phil 5850.306.5 Pelman Institute of America. Scientific mind training. N.Y., 1927.

Phil 5374.154.9 Peucesco, M.G. Mouvement et pensée. Paris, 1927.

Phil 5627.112 Pfennigsdorf, Emil. Der religiöse Wille. 2. Aufl. Leipzig, 1927.

Phil 9245.37.2 Phelps, William L. Happiness. N.Y., 1927.

Htn Phil 9245.37* Phelps, William L. Happiness. N.Y., 1927.

Phil 8595.25A Philips Brooks House Association. Harvard University. Religion and modern life. N.Y., 1927.

Phil 5255.30 Phillips, D.E. An elementary psychology. Boston, 1927.

Phil 5055.18.5 Pichler, Hans. Die Logik der Seele. Erfurt, 1927.

Phil 5255.18.5 Piéron, Henri. Psychologie experimentale. Paris, 1927.

Phil 6125.18.5 Piéron, Henri. Thought and the brain. London, 1927.

Phil 5850.314 Poffenberger, A.T. Applied psychology; its principles and methods. N.Y., 1927.

Phil 190.27.5 Prat, Louis. L'harmonisme. Paris, 1927.

Phil 5627.56.3A Pratt, James B. The religious consciousness. N.Y., 1927.

Phil 8705.14 Prepin, Michael T. The new reformation. N.Y., 1927.

Phil 7069.16.63 Prince, W.F. The case of Patience Worth. Boston, 1927.

Phil 5225.3 Prinzhorn, H. Leib-Seele-Linheit. Potsdam, 1927.

Phil 575.70 Prinzhorn, H. Um die Persönlichkeit. Bd.1. Heidelberg, 1927.

Phil 6325.10.5 Prinzhorn, Hans. Gespräch über Psychoanalyse zwischen Frau, Dichter und Arzt. Heidelberg, 1927.

Phil 5827.8.5 Rabaud, E. L'orientation lointaine et la reconnaissance des lieux. Paris, 1927.

Phil 192.59 Rabeau, Gaston. Réalité et relativité. Paris, 1927.

Phil 575.85 Rădulescu-Motru, C. Personalismul energetic. Bucuresti, 1927.

Phil 6327.4.13 Rank, Otto. Grundzüge einer genetischen Psychologie. v.1-2. Wien, 1927-28.

Phil 4017.1 Rava, Adolfo. Descartes, Spinoza et la pensée italienne. Paris, 1927.

Phil 5435.4.5 Ravaisson-Mollien, Felix. De l'habitude. Paris, 1927.

Phil 8597.36 Raven, Charles E. The creator spirit. Cambridge, 1927.

Phil 3552.01 Ravier, E. Bibliographie de la philosophie de Leibniz. Thèse. Caen, 1927.

Phil 3552.261 Ravier, E. Le système de Leibniz et le problème des rapports de la raison et de la foi. Thèse. Caen, 1927.

Phil 8597.35.10 Reese, Curtis W. Humanist sermons. Chicago, 1927.

Phil 5725.4 Reichner, H. Experimentelle und kritische Beiträge zur Psychologie des Verstehens. Inaug. Diss. Leipzig, 1927.

Phil 5627.102.10 Reik, Theodor. Dogma und Zwangsidee eine psychoanalytische Studie zur Entwicklung der Religion. Leipzig, 1927.

Phil 6327.12.25 Reik, Theodor. Wie man psychologe wird. Leipzig, 1927.

Phil 5767.10.5 Reiner, Hans. Freiheit, Wollen und Aktivität. Leipzig, 1927.

Phil 3499.25 Reinhard, Walter. Über das Verhältnis von Sittlichkeit und Religion bei Kant. Bern, 1927.

Phil 348.10 Reisner, E. Das Selbstopfer der Erkenntnis. München, 1927.

Phil 192.57 Renda, Antonio. Il criticismo: fondamenti etico-religiosi. Palermo, 1927.

Phil 192.64 Revel, Camille. Esquisse d'un essai sur les facultés humaines. Lyons, 1927.

Phil 298.5 Rey, Abel. Le retour éternel et la philosophie de la physique. Paris, 1927.

Phil 192.60.5 Richet, Charles. L'homme impuissant. Paris, 1927.

Phil 5257.6.10 Richet, Charles. L'intelligence et l'homme. Paris, 1927.

Phil 5257.40.5 Richter, Conrad. Principles in bio-physics. Harrisburg, 1927.

Phil 5620.9.7 Rignano, Eugenio. Psychology of reasoning. N.Y., 1927.

Phil 9150.28 Ritter, William E. The natural history of our conduct. N.Y., 1927.

Phil 9035.45.5 Roback, A.A. A bibliography of character. Cambridge, Mass., 1927.

Phil 9035.45 Roback, A.A. The psychology of character. London, 1927.

Phil 9035.45.2 Roback, A.A. The psychology of character. N.Y., 1927.

Phil 5057.20.7 Robinson, D.S. Illustrations of the methods of reasoning. N.Y., 1927.

Phil 5257.27.6 Robinson, E.S. Practical psychology; human nature in everyday life. N.Y., 1927.

Phil 7069.27.20 Robotton. Realms of light and healing. London, 1927.

Phil 8842.6 Rogers, A.K. Morals in review. N.Y., 1927.

Phil 5627.104 Rohrbaugh, L.G. The science of religion: an introduction. N.Y., 1927.

Phil 192.58 Roretz, Karl. Die Metaphysik: eine fiktion. Wien, 1927.

Phil 6980.652.8 Rosanoff, A.J. Manuel of psychiatry. 6. ed. N.Y., 1927.

Phil 3160.3.84 Rosenzweig, L. La restauration de l'a priori kantien par H. Cohen. Paris, 1927.

Phil 192.56 Rossi, M.M. Per una concezione attivistica della filosofia. Bologna, 1927.

Phil 7150.23 Rost, Hans. Bibliographie des Selbstmords. Augsburg, 1927.

Phil 745.8 Rudy, Hirsch. Die Entwicklung der vitalistischen Naturphilosophie im 20. Jahrhundert. Inaug. Diss. Charlottenburg, 1927.

1927 - cont.

Phil 817.8.9 — Ruggiero, Guido de. Sommario di storia della filosofia. Bari, 1927.

Phil 192.28.21A — Russell, B. A free man's worship. 2d ed. Portland, 1927.

Phil 2255.1.30A — Russell, Bertrand Russell. Philosophy. N.Y., 1927.

Phil 2255.1.10A — Russell, Bertrand Russell. Selected papers. N.Y., 1927.

Phil 9245.49 — Russell, Dora. The right to be happy. N.Y., 1927.

Phil 8707.10 — Russell, H.N. Fate and freedom. New Haven, 1927.

Phil 270.52 — Sageret, Jules. Le lasard et la destinée. Paris, 1927.

Phil 5374.46 — Saint Prix, J. de. La conscience comme principe spirituel. Paris, 1927.

Phil 4115.85.2 — Saitta, Giuseppe. Il pensiero di Vincenzo Gioberti. 2a ed. Firenze, 1927.

Phil 3425.246 — Salditt, Maria. Hegels Shakespeare-Interpretation. Berlin, 1927.

Phil 3500.44 — Samsom, A. Kants kennis der grieksche Philosophie. Thesis. Alphen aan den Rijn, 1927.

Phil 5627.107 — Sanctis, S. de. Religious conversion. London, 1927.

Phil 193.49.30 — Santayana, G. Platonism and the spiritual life. N.Y., 1927.

Phil 7069.27.23 — Saunders, R.H. Healing through spirit agency. London, 1927.

Phil 3800.32 — Schelling, F.W.J. von. Schellings Werke. München, 1927-28. 5v.

Phil 8598.77 — Schmidt, H.W. Zeit und Ewigkeit. Gutersloh, 1927.

Phil 5643.90 — Schmülling, Wilhelm. Aufdeckung latenter eidetischer Anlagen und des integrierton Typus mit der Intermittenz-Methode. Inaug. Diss. Marburg, 1927.

Phil 3018.22 — Schneider, P. Deutschen Philosophen des 19. Jahrhunderts. Berlin, 1927.

Phil 530.20.65 — Scholz, W. von. Deutsche Mystiker. Berlin, 1927.

Phil 3808.65.30 — Schopenhauer, Arthur. La volontà nella natura. Milano, 1927.

Phil 3500.55 — Schultz, Martin. Kants Religion innerhalb der Grenzen der blossen Vernunft. Königsberg, 1927.

Phil 6328.13 — Schultz-Hencke, Harald. Enführung in die Psychoanalyse. Jena, 1927.

Phil 193.113 — Schweizer, Robert. Der charakterwolle und der begriffiche Gegenstand. Leipzig, 1927.

Phil 5374.156 — Seidel, A. Bewusstsein als Verhangnis. Bonn, 1927.

Phil 3018.13 — Seillière, E. Morales et religions nouvelles en Allemagne. Paris, 1927.

Phil 8893.68 — Sherman, C.L. The moral self: an introduction to the science of ethics. Boston, 1927.

Phil 7069.27.38 — Sherrill, E.P. The mechanism of death. Boston, 1927.

Phil 6128.47.7 — Shinn, F.S. (Mrs.). The game of life and how to play it. 7th ed. N.Y., 1927.

Phil 8708.14A — Shipley, Maynard. The war on modern science. N.Y., 1927.

Phil 3500.53 — Siehr, Carl. Kant und das freie Wort und Gerechtigkeit und...bei Kant. Königsberg, 1927.

Phil 7069.27.27 — Sinel, J. The sixth sense. London, 1927.

Phil 8893.72 — Skala, Richard. Der Stachel der Ethik. Wien, 1927.

Phil 5058.28.28 — Smith, Henry B. Symbolic logic: method and development. N.Y., 1927.

Phil 5258.66.2 — Smith, Stevenson. General psychology. N.Y., 1927.

Phil 8843.11 — Sneath, E.H. Evolution of ethics...in great religions. New Haven, 1927.

Phil 7069.27.60 — Snipes, Joseph F. Fifty years in psychic research. Boston, 1927.

Phil 7061.5 — Society for Psychical Research, London. Library catalogue of the Society for Psychical Research. Glasgow, 1927.

Phil 6968.21 — Sondén, Tarsten. A study of somatic conditions in manic-depressive psychosis. Inaug. Diss. Uppsala, 1927.

Phil 4260.98 — Sorrentino, A. La retorica et la poetica di G.B. Vico. Torino, 1927.

Phil 5258.92.2 — Spaier, A. La pensée concrète. Thèse. Paris, 1927.

Phil 5258.68.5A — Spearman, C. The abilities of man; their nature and measurement. N.Y., 1927.

Phil 5258.68.2 — Spearman, C. The nature of "intelligence" and the principles of cognition. London, 1927.

Phil 7069.27.25 — Speer, W.H. Companions still. London, 1927?

Phil 5203.7 — Spek, J. van der. Literatuurlijsten en atlas. Groningen, 1927.

Phil 8599.19.90 — Spiess, Emil. Die Religionstheorie von Ernst Troeltsch. Paderborn, 1927.

Phil 3819.31.9 — Spinoza, Benedictus de. Ethic demonstrated in geometrical order. London, 1927.

Phil 3819.29A — Spinoza, Benedictus de. The philosophy of Spinoza. N.Y., 1927.

Phil 720.33 — Stefansson, V. The standardization of error. N.Y., 1927.

Phil 8419.12.5 — Stein, Leo. The ABC of aesthetics. N.Y., 1927.

Phil 978.49.75 — Steiner, R. Das Initiaten-Bewusstsein. Dornach, 1927.

Phil 978.49.80 — Steiner, R. Praktische Ausbildung des Denkens. Stuttgart, 1927.

Phil 978.49.85 — Steiner, R. Wendepunkte des Geisteslebens. Dornach, 1927.

Phil 7082.38.3 — Stekel, Wilhelm. Die Sprache des Traumes. 3e Aufl. München, 1927.

Phil 6328.2.40 — Stekel, Wilhelm. Zwang und Zweifel. Berlin, 1927-28. 2v.

Phil 1818.2.8 — Stephen, Leslie. History of English thought in the eighteenth century. v.2. London, 1927.

Phil 193.115 — Stickers, J. Die Wiedergeburt der systematischen Philosophie. Berlin, 1927.

Phil 7082.98 — Stiles, Percy Goldthwait. Dreams. Cambridge, 1927.

Phil 5258.27.6 — Stout, G.F. Groundwork of psychology. 2d ed. London, 1927.

Phil 3805.163 — Strobel, Anton. Die Pädagogik und Philosophie Schleiermachers in ihren Bezienungen zu J.J. Tousseau. Inaug. Diss. n.p., 1927.

Phil 2070.120 — Stumpf, Carl. William James nach seinen Briefen. Berlin, 1927.

Phil 3425.230 — Sturge, M.C. Opposite things. Bristol, 1927.

Phil 8709.10 — Talamo, S. Il rinnovamento...tomistico e la scienza. Roma, 1927.

Phil 194.19.30 — Tarozzi, Giuseppe. L'idea di esistenza e la pensabilità del reale trascendente. Bologna, 1927.

Phil 179.3.112 — Die Tatwelt, Zeitschrift für Erneuerung des Geiteslebens. Berlin, 1927.

Phil 2050.184 — Taylor, A.E. David Hume and the miraculous. Cambridge, Eng., 1927.

Phil 8420.17 — Teige, Karel. Stavba a báseň; umènídues a zítra. Praha, 1927.

Phil 2115.138 — Tellkamp, A. Das Verhältnis John Locke's zur Scholastik. Münster, 1927.

Phil 5059.17 — Templin, Olin. A guide to thinking; a beginner's book in logic. Garden City, N.Y., 1927.

1927 - cont.

Phil 8709.11 — Thallackson, E. Science, evolution, religion. Boston, 1927.

Phil 194.35 — Thomas, E.E. The ethical basis of reality. London, 1927.

Phil 5259.21 — Thomson, M.K. The springs of human action. N.Y., 1927.

Phil 5259.24.2 — Tickell, Sydney. Psychology really simplified in terms of machinery. Cirencester, 1927.

Phil 5259.5.9.5 — Titchener, E.B. Experimental psychology. v.1-2. N.Y., 1927. 4v.

Phil 5259.28 — Torrey, D.C. The normal person. Jaffrey, New Hampshire, 1927.

Phil 2150.15.107 — Tremmel, William C. The social concepts of George Herbert Mead. Emporia, 1927.

Phil 4890.10 — Tsuchida, Kyoson. Contemporary thought of Japan and China. London, 1927.

Phil 4890.10.2 — Tsuchida, Kyoson. Contemporary thought of Japan and China. N.Y., 1927.

Phil 8674.8.7 — Turner, J.E. The nature of deity; a sequel to Personality and reality. London, 1927.

Phil 194.41 — Twardowski, Kazimierz. Rozprawy i artykuly filozoficzne. Livóv, 1927.

Phil 5722.21.9 — The unconscious: a symposium. N.Y., 1927.

Phil 8600.3.5 — Underhill, E. Man and the supernatural. London, 1927.

Phil 1750.748 — Utitz, Emil. Die Überwindung des Expressionismus. Stuttgart, 1927.

Phil 575.62 — Valentine, P.F. The psychology of personality. N.Y., 1927.

Phil 9035.50 — Vance, J.G. A mirror of personality. London, 1927.

Phil 9540.1.10 — Van Loon, H.W. Tolerance. Garden City, 1927.

Phil 5261.16 — Varvaro, P. L'intelligenza. Palermo, 1927.

Phil 4260.25.5 — Vico, G.B. Vico, d'après la traduction de Michelet. Paris, 1927.

Phil 8422.16 — Vischer, R. Drei Schriften zum ästhetischen Formproblem. Halle, 1927.

Phil 6331.2.5 — Vivante, Leone. Notes on the originality of thought. London, 1927.

Phil 3120.15.95 — Von Constantin Brunner und seinem Werk. Berlin, 1927.

Phil 3549.2.92 — Vondran, Hugo. Kritik der Philosophie des Grafen H. Keyserling. Diss. Erlangen, 1927.

Phil 821.1.7 — Vorländer, K. Geschichte der Philosophie. 7. Aufl. Leipzig, 1927. 2v.

Phil 197.45 — Ward, James. Essays in philosophy. Cambridge, Eng., 1927.

Phil 5832.13 — Warden, C.J. A short outline of comparative psychology. N.Y., 1927.

Phil 5850.385.60 — Weber, Wilhelm. Die praktische Psychologie im Wirtschaftsleben. Leipzig, 1927.

Phil 3805.172 — Wehrung, Georg. Schleiermacher in der Zeit seines Werdens. Gütersloh, 1927.

Phil 5262.40 — Weinhandl, F. Die Gestaltanalyse. Erfurt, 1927.

Phil 7069.27.55 — Wells, H.B. Spiritual America. Boston, 1927.

Phil 3425.271 — Wenke, Hans. Hegels Theorie des objektiven Geistes. Halle, 1927.

Phil 5722.19 — Wenzl, Aloys. Das unbewusste Denken. Karlsruhe, 1927.

Phil 974.4.10 — West, G. Mrs. Annie Besant. London, 1927.

Phil 860.33.5 — Whitehead, A.N. Religion in the making. N.Y., 1927.

Phil 353.9A — Whitehead, A.N. Symbolism: its meaning and effect. N.Y., 1927.

Phil 8602.35 — Wieman, Henry Nelson. The wrestle of religion with truth. N.Y., 1927.

Phil 3120.13.90 — Wigersma, I.B. Bolland. Amsterdam, 1927.

Phil 3022.3.3 — Windlband, Wilhelm. Die Philosophie im deutschen Geistesleben des 19. Jahrhunderts. 3. Aufl. Tübingen, 1927.

Phil 3842.8 — Wolf, Abraham. The oldest biography of Spinoza. London, 1927.

Phil 1050.13 — Wolfson, Harry A. Solomon Pappenheim on time and space ar his relation to Locke and Kant. Vienna, 1927.

Phil 8712.18 — Wood, A. In pursuit of truth. London, 1927.

Phil 6536.6 — Wreschner, A. Psychologische Untersuchungen an Normalen, Schwachbegabten und Epileptikern. Leipzig, 1927.

Phil 3915.01 — Wundt, E.W. Wolff's Werk: ein Verzeichnis seiner sämtlichen Schriften. München, 1927.

Phil 3246.212 — Wundt, Max. Johann Gottlieb Fichte. Stuttgart, 1927.

Phil 960.38 — Yevtic, Paul. Karma and reincarnation in Hindu. Thesis. London, 1927.

Phil 8426.3 — Ziegenfuss, W. Die phänomenologische Ästhetik nach Grundsätzen und bisherigen Ergebnissen kritisch Dargestellt. Borna, 1927.

1928

Phil 5040.19 — Adjukiewicz, Kazimierz. Glówne zasady metodologji nauk i logiki. Warszawa, 1928.

Phil 6310.1.11 — Adler, A. Die Technik der Individual-Psychologie. Teil 1-2. München, 1928-30.

Phil 9035.53.5 — Adler, Alfred. Menschenkenntnis. 2. Aufl. Leipzig, 1928.

Phil 6110.10.11 — Adler, Alfred. Über den nervösen Charakter. 4. Aufl. München, 1928.

Phil 9035.53.4 — Adler, Alfred. Understanding human nature. N.Y., 1928.

Phil 5850.108 — Alexander, James. Thought-control in everyday life. N.Y., 1928.

Phil 623.21 — Aliotta, A. Le origini dell'irrazionalismo contemporaneo. Napoli, 1928.

Phil 2477.6.85 — Archambault, P. Vers un realisme integral...Blondel. Paris, 1928.

Phil 5525.32.5 — Armstrong, M. Laughing: an essay. London, 1928.

Phil 5525.32 — Armstrong, M. Laughing: an essay. N.Y., 1928.

Phil 3450.9.30 — Astrov, V. Rudolf Maria Holzapfel. Jena, 1928.

Phil 5241.77 — Baade, Walter. Allgermeine Einfuhrung in das Gesamtgebiet der Psychologie. Leipzig, 1928.

Phil 3090.65 — Baader, Franz von. Seele und Welt. Berlin, 1928.

Phil 5241.76 — Baar, Jacob. Psychology. N.Y., 1928.

Phil 1850.50.25 — Bacon, Francis. Novum organum. Lanciano, 1928.

Phil 7082.170 — Baege, Max Hermann. Naturgeschichte des Traums. Leipzig, 1928.

Phil 6390.4 — Bagby, English. The psychology of personality. N.Y., 1928.

Phil 1158.25A — Bailey, Cyril. The Greek atomists and Epicurus. Oxford, 1928.

Phil 8581.52.10 — Baillie, John. The interpretation of religion. N.Y., 1928.

Phil 5241.85 — Barbado, M. Introducción a la psicología experimental. Madrid, 1928.

Phil 8691.19 — Barry, W. The triumph of life. London, 1928.

Phil 176.121 — Barthel, Ernst. Die Welt als Spannung und Rhythmus. Leipzig, 1928.

Chronological Listing

597

1928 - cont.

Phil 801.26 — Beccari, Arturo. Storia della filosofia e della scienza. Torino, 1928.

Phil 282.7.19 — Becher, Erich. Grundlagen und Grenzen des Naturerkennens. München, 1928.

Phil 900.10 — Beck, Lily M.A. The story of Oriental philosophy. N.Y., 1928.

Phil 1750.126.3 — Benda, Julien. The great betrayal. London, 1928.

Phil 1750.126.6A — Benda, Julien. The treason of the intellectuals. N.Y., 1928.

Phil 2401.3.12 — Benrubi, Isaac. Philosophische Strömungen der Gegenwart in Frankreich. Leipzig, 1928.

Phil 8876.83 — Bentley, Joseph. How to sleep on a windy night. Philadelphia, 1928.

Phil 3246.173.2 — Bergmann, Ernst. Johann Gottlieb Fichte der Erzieher. 2. Aufl. Leipzig, 1928.

Phil 2475.1.69.5 — Bergson, Henri. Le rire. Paris, 1928.

Phil 7069.28.4 — Bird, J. Malcolm. The Margery mediumship. N.Y., 1928.

Phil 5710.11 — Bloor, Constance. Temperament, a survey of psychological theories. London, 1928.

Phil 3120.22.10 — Blüher, Hans. Philosophie auf Posten, Schriften 1916-21. Heidelberg, 1928.

Phil 3120.22.40 — Blüher, Hans. Traktat über die Heilkunde. Jena, 1928.

Phil 5041.39.2 — Bogoslovsky, B.B. The technique of controversy. London, 1928.

Phil 5041.39 — Bogoslovsky, B.B. The technique of controversy. N.Y., 1928.

Phil 8876.84 — Bonatelli, Paolo. Spunti di dottrina etica. Bologna, 1928.

Phil 282.15 — Bontecou, Daniel J. A chart of nature. Chicago, 1928.

Phil 3483.44 — Borries, Kurt. Kant als Politiker. Leipzig, 1928.

Phil 5545.230 — Bousfield, William Robert. The basis of memory. N.Y., 1928.

Phil 176.108 — Bradford, Gamaliel. Life and I. Boston, 1928.

Phil 978.80.10 — Bragdon, C.F. The new image. N.Y., 1928.

Phil 2045.108.5 — Brandt, Frithiof. Thomas Hobbes' mechanical conception of nature, Copenhagen, 1928.

Phil 1200.18.5 — Bréhier, Emile. La théorie des incorporels dans l'ancien stoïcisme. 2e éd. Paris, 1928.

Phil 5241.17.20 — Brentano, Franz. Vom sinnlichen und noetischen Bewusstsein. Leipzig, 1928.

Phil 400.71 — Brightman, E.S. A philosophy of ideals. N.Y., 1928.

Phil 2150.7.90 — Broad, Charles D. John McTaggart Ellis McTaggart, 1866-1925. London, 1928.

Phil 8581.53 — Brown, William A. Beliefs that matter. N.Y., 1928.

Phil 8402.29 — Bruno, F. Il problema estetica contemporanea. Lanciano, 1928.

Phil 4065.61 — Bruno, Giordano. De gl'heroici furori. Torino, 1928.

Phil 525.67 — Buonaiuti, E. Il misticismo medioevale. Pinerolo, 1928.

Phil 3195.10.99 — Burchard, H. Der entelechiebegriff bei Aristoteles und Driesch. Inaug. Diss. Quakenbrück, 1928.

Phil 1106.8.4 — Burnet, J. Greek philosophy. pt.1. London, 1928.

DL Phil 5041.40 — Burtt, Edwin Arthur. Principles and problems of right thinking. N.Y., 1928.

Phil 5520.54 — Buyssens, T. Langage et pensée, vie et matière. Brasschaat, 1928.

Phil 5811.15.5 — Buytendijk, Frederik Jacobus Johannes. Psychologie des animaux. Paris, 1928.

Phil 8877.44.5 — Calkins, Mary W. The good man and the good. N.Y., 1928.

Phil 802.11 — Capone Braga, G. Il mondo delle idee. pt. 1a, 2a. Città di Cástello, 1928-33. 2v.

Phil 333.12 — Carnap, Rudolf. Der logische Aufbau der Welt. Berlin, 1928.

Phil 333.12.5A — Carnap, Rudolf. Scheinprobleme in der Philosophie. Berlin, 1928.

Phil 177.65.5 — Carr, H.W. The unique status of man. N.Y., 1928.

Phil 5752.6 — Carr, Herbert W. The freewill problem. London, 1928.

Phil 8877.68 — Carritt, Edgar T. Theory of morals. London, 1928.

Phil 9560.14.18 — Cartojan, N. Fiore di virtù in literature româneasca. Bucarsti, 1928.

Phil 7150.24 — Cavan, R.S. Suicide. Chicago, 1928.

Phil 8050.28.5 — Chambers, Frank. Cycles of taste. Cambridge, 1928.

Phil 2520.164 — Chartier, A. Etude sur Descartes. Paris, 1928.

Phil 9245.54.5 — Chartier, E. Propos sur le bonheur. 18e éd. Paris, 1928.

Phil 2475.1.222.5A — Chevalier, Jacques. Henri Bergson. N.Y., 1928.

Phil 2475.1.222.10 — Chevalier, Jacques. Henri Bergson. Paris, 1928.

Phil 177.77 — Chevalier, Jacques. Trois conférences d'Oxford. Paris, 1928.

Phil 4710.50 — Chizhevskii, O. Filosofiia na Ukraïni. Vyd. 2. Praga, 1928.

Phil 5242.37 — Claremont, C.A. Intelligence, and mental growth. N.Y., 1928.

Phil 5627.108 — Clark, Glenn. Fishers of men. Boston, 1928.

Phil 5627.111 — Clemen, Carl. Die Anwendung der Psychoanalyse auf Mythologie und Religionsgeschichte. Leipzig, 1928.

Phil 477.9 — Cohen, Chapman. Materialism: has it been exploded?...debate. London, 1928.

Phil 177.28.10 — Cohens, Hermann. Schriften zur Philosophie und Zeitgeschichte. Berlin, 1928. 2v.

Phil 5780.9 — Conrad, H. Psychologie und Besteuerung. Stuttgart, 1928.

Phil 177.73 — Constable, F.C. I am. London, 1928.

Phil 9528.6 — Cooper, John M. Religion outlines for colleges. Washington, D.C., 1928.

Phil 8877.69 — Copeland, Edwin B. Natural conduct. Stanford, Calif., 1928.

Phil 6420.24 — Coriat, Isador H. Stammering; a psychoanalytic interpretation. N.Y., 1928.

Phil 5042.10.3 — Croce, B. Logica come scienza del concetto puro. 5a ed. Bari, 1928.

Phil 1507.3 — Currie, F.J. Universal scholastic philosophy publicly defended. n.p., 1928.

Phil 4215.1.01 — Cusani Confalonieri, L.G. G.D. Romagnosi. Carate Brianza, 1928.

Phil 7082.66 — Cutting, Mary Stewart. What dreams mean to you. London, 1928.

Phil 3195.14.45 — Dacqué, Edgar. Leben als Symbol. München, 1928.

Phil 5243.36 — Dashiell, J.F. Fundamentals of objective psychology. Boston, 1928.

Phil 178.46.10 — Decoster, Paul. Acte et synthèse. Bruxelles, 1928.

Phil 9495.127.15 — Dennett, M.W. (Mrs.). The sex side of life; an explanation for young people. Astoria, 1928.

Phil 2520.61.19 — Descartes, René. Traité des passions. Paris, 1928.

Phil 178.38.10 — Dewey, John. The philosophy of John Dewey. N.Y., 1928.

Phil 978.61.5 — Dhopeshwarkar, A.D. The divine vision. London, 1928.

Phil 178.57 — Dixon, E.T. The guidance of conduct. London, 1928.

1928 - cont.

Phil 7069.28.16 — Doyle, Arthur Conan. A word of warning. London, 1928.

Phil 8878.28.10 — Drake, Durant. The new morality. N.Y., 1928.

Phil 1703.5 — Dresser, H.W. A history of modern philosophy. N.Y., 1928.

Phil 1050.4.13 — Dreyer, Kare. Die religiöse Gedankenwelt des Salomo ibn Gabirol. Inaug. Diss. Leipzig, 1928.

Phil 178.22.20 — Driesch, H. Der Mensch und die Welt. Leipzig, 1928.

Phil 2805.204 — Droulers, C. La cité de Pascal. Paris, 1928.

Phil 7069.28.20 — Dudley, O.F. The abomination in our midst. London, 1928.

Phil 8583.23 — Dugard, Marie. Sur les frontières de la foi. Paris, 1928.

Phil 672.148.5 — Durand-Doat, J. Essai sur l'étendue. Paris, 1928.

Phil 672.148 — Durand-Doat, J. Essai sur l'étendue. Thèse. Paris, 1928.

Phil 178.56 — Durand-Doat, J. Le sens de la métaphysique. Paris, 1928.

Phil 178.56.2 — Durand-Doat, J. Le sens de la métaphysique. Thèse. Paris, 1928.

Phil 8658.14 — Dyroff, Adolf. Probleme der Gotteserkenntnis. Münster, 1928.

Phil 1540.45 — Egentin, Richard. Gottesfreundschaft. Augsburg, 1928.

Phil 7140.116.80 — Emile Coué: sa méthode, son esprit, son influence. Paris, 1928.

Phil 3425.243 — Ephraim, F. Untersuchungen über den Freiheitsbegriff Hegels in seinen Jugendarbeiten. Berlin, 1928.

Phil 3824.2.5 — Erhardt, Franz. Die Weltanschauung Spinozas. Stuttgart, 1928.

Phil 630.30.5 — Evans, Daniel L. New realism and old reality. Princeton, 1928.

Phil 8659.5 — Evans, Joseph. Theistic monism. London, 1928.

Phil 180.44A — Farber, M. Phenomenology as a method and as a philosophical discipline. n.p., 1928.

Phil 8406.12 — Farnell, Lewis R. Hedonism and art. London, 1928.

Phil 1850.124 — Fazio-Allmayer, V. Saggio su Francesco Bacone. Palermo, 1928.

Phil 8406.9 — Federn, Karl. Das aesthetische Problem. Hannover, 1928.

Phil 4756.2.30 — Fedorov, N.F. Filosofiia obshchago dela. Izd.2. Kharbin, 1928-

Phil 180.43 — Feldkeller, Paul. Verständigung als philosophisches Problem. Erfurt, 1928.

Phil 5750.001 — Fellin, J. Die Willensfreiheit; zur Bibliographie. Graz, 1928.

Phil 575.66 — Fernandez, R. De la personnalité. Paris, 1928.

Phil 4582.4.88 — Festskrift tillägnad Axel Hägerström den 6 september 1928. Upsala, 1928.

Phil 5045.12 — Feys, R. Le raisonnement entermes de faite dans la logique russellienne. Louvain, 1928.

Phil 3246.79.65 — Fichte, Johann Gottlieb. Fichte Schriften zur Gesellschaftsphilosophie. v.1-2. Jena, 1928-29.

Phil 4005.5 — La filosofia contemporanea in Italia dal 1870 al 1920. Napoli, 1928.

Phil 3425.249 — Fischer, Hugo. Hegels Methode in ihrer ideengeschichtlichen Notwendigkeit. Habilitationsschrift. München, 1928.

Phil 8406.7.5 — Fischer, Kuno. Diotima; die Idee des Schönen. Leipzig, 1928.

Phil 180.56 — Fischer-Mampoteng, F.C. Menschsein als Aufgabe. Heidelberg, 1928.

Phil 6315.20 — Fishbein, M. Why men fail. N.Y., 1928.

Phil 6420.14.5 — Fletcher, John Madison. The problem of stuttering. N.Y., 1928.

Phil 5245.31 — Flower, J.C. Psychology simplified. London, 1928.

Phil 8955.4 — Flynn, V.S. The norm of morality. Diss. Washington, 1928.

Phil 5252.18.54 — Fochtman, V.A. Das Lieb-Seele-Problem bei George Trumbull Ladd und William McDougall. Inaug. Diss. München, 1928.

Phil 480.7 — Franck, Otto. Der Weg zur Wirklichkeit. Leipzig, 1928.

Phil 7080.38 — Fraser-Harris, D.F. Morpheus, or The future of sleep. London, 1928.

Phil 8585.28A — Freud, Sigmund. The future of an illusion. London, 1928.

Phil 8585.28.3 — Freud, Sigmund. The future of an illusion. N.Y., 1928.

Phil 3425.256 — Frost, Walter. Hegels Asthetik. München, 1928.

Phil 5241.55.21 — Fürst, Joseph. Grundriss der empirischen Psychologie und Logik. 21e Aufl. Stuttgart, 1928.

Phil 5246.1.9 — Galton, F. Inquiries into the human faculty. London, 1928.

Phil 5816.9 — Garnett, Arthur C. Instinct and personality. London, 1928.

Phil 806.12 — Gasiorowski, W. Historja filozofji. Sandomierz, 1928.

Phil 8881.42.9 — Gaultier, Paul. Les moeurs du temps. 3e éd. Paris, 1928.

Phil 1706.8 — Gause, Hermann. Über die Problematik der neueren Philosophie. Inaug. Diss. Basel, 1928.

Phil 8407.23 — Geiger, Moritz. Zugänge zur Asthetik. Leipzig, 1928.

Phil 3246.213 — Gelpcke, E. Fichte und die Gedankenwelt der Sturm und Drang. Leipzig, 1928.

Phil 8956.8.15 — Genicot, Edouard. Casus conscientiae propositi ac soluti. 6. ed. Louvain, 1928.

Phil 4006.2.15 — Gentile, G. Il pensiero italiano del secolo XIX. Milano, 1928.

Phil 2885.88 — Gibaudan, R. Les idées sociales de Taine. Paris, 1928.

Phil 3270.4.82 — Gielhammer, L. Die politischen Grundlagen. Berlin, 1928.

Phil 5850.214.10 — Giese, Fritz. Arbeits- und Berufspsychologie. Halle, 1928.

Phil 8586.36.5 — Gogarten, Friedrich. Glaube und Wirklichkeit. Jena, 1928.

Phil 575.58.3 — Gordon, R.G. Personality. N.Y., 1928.

Phil 9558.10.15 — Grau, Kurt J. Eitelkeit und Schamgefühl. Leipzig, 1928.

Phil 5246.31.2 — Griffith, C.R. General introduction to psychology. N.Y., 1928.

Phil 181.50.5 — Grisebach, E. Gegenwart. Halle, 1928.

Phil 3425.244 — Grupe, Walter. Mundts und Kühnes Verhältnis zu Hegel und seinen Gegnern. Halle, 1928.

Phil 8407.8.5 — Guastalla, Pierre. L'esthetique et l'art. Paris, 1928.

Phil 5425.86 — Gun, W.T.J. Studies in hereditary ability. London, 1928.

Phil 6317.2.7 — Hadfield, J.A. Psychology and morals. N.Y., 1928.

Phil 8882.55 — Haldane, J.B.S. Science and ethics. London, 1928.

Phil 182.101 — Haldane, J.S. The sciences and philosophy. London, 1928.

Phil 2840.93 — Hansen, Valdemar. Charles Renouvier og frihedsproblemet. København, 1928.

Phil 9035.75 — Hartshore, H. Studies in deceit. N.Y., 1928.

Phil 288.7 — Hartung, J.F. Die physikalische Energie und die Brücke. Obersalzbrunn, 1928.

Phil 630.34 — Hasan, S.Z. Realism: an attempt to trace its origin. Cambridge, 1928.

Phil 3665.5.90 — Hauer, Eugen. Person und Handlung in der Ethik Leonard Nelsons. Inaug. Diss. Bonn, 1928.

Phil 8587.34.5 — Hauter, Charles. Essai sur l'objet religieux. Thèse. Strasbourg, 1928.

Phil 7069.28.12 — Haynes, Frederick H. The book of spiritual wisdom by "Cuno". London, 1928.

Phil 3425.24 — Hegel, Georg Wilhelm Friedrich. Erste Druckschriften. Leipzig, 1928.

1928 - cont.

	Phil 3850.22.90	Heller, Joseph E. Solgers Philosophie der ironischen Dialektik. Berlin, 1928.
	Phil 3850.22.90.2	Heller, Joseph E. Solgers Philosophie der ironischen Dialektik. Diss. Berlin, 1928.
	Phil 3245.84	Herrmann, H.A. Die Philosophie Immanuel Hermann Fichtes. Berlin, 1928.
	Phil 3850.18.88	Herrmann, J. Die Prinzipien der formalen Gesetzes Ethik Kants und der materialen Wertethik Schelers. Diss. Breslau, 1928.
	Phil 510.143	Herzberg, L. Die philosophischen Hauptströmungen im Monistenbund. Inaug. Diss. Leipzig, 1928.
	Phil 1707.12	Hevigel, H. Das neue Denken. Berlin, 1928.
	Phil 8832.4A	Hibino, Yutaka. Nippon shindo ron; or, The national ideals of the Japanese people. Cambridge, Eng., 1928.
	Phil 5047.33A	Hilbert, David. Grundzüge der theoretischen Logik. Berlin, 1928.
	Phil 5817.16	Hingston, R.W.G. Problems of instinct and intelligence. London, 1928.
	Phil 5247.42A	Hocking, W.E. The self: its body and freedom. New Haven, 1928.
	Phil 338.17.9	Höffding, H. Les conceptions de la vie. Paris, 1928.
	Phil 4580.79	Høffding, Harald. Erindringer. København, 1928.
	Phil 4803.454.32	Hoene-Wroński, Józef Maria. Lit do papiezy o maglacej potrzebie obechej spełnienia religli. Warszawa, 1928.
	Phil 9035.47.5	Hoffmann, H. Charakter und Umwelt. Berlin, 1928.
	Phil 974.3.105	Hoffmann, K. Die Anthroposophie Rudolf Steiners und die moderne Geisleswissenschaft. Diss. Giessen, 1928.
	Phil 5247.16.22	Hollingworth, H.L. Mental growth and decline. N.Y., 1928.
	Phil 5247.16.25	Hollingworth, H.L. Psychology: its facts and principles. N.Y., 1928.
	Phil 5047.32.10	Honecker, M. Gegenstandslogik und Denklogik Vorschlag zu einer Neugestaltung der Logik. 2. Aufl. Berlin, 1928.
	Phil 2648.90	Hubert, René. D'Holbach et ses amis. Paris, 1928.
	Phil 8587.32.25	Hügel, Friedrich von. Reading from Friedrich von Hügel. London, 1928.
	Phil 8587.32.85	Hügel, Friedrich von. Selected letters 1896-1924. London, 1928.
	Phil 4580.117	Hürtgen, Robert. Das Gottesproblem bei Harald Høffding. Inaug. Diss. Bonn, 1928.
	Phil 5247.58	Hughes, P. Introduction to psychology. Bethlehem Pa., 1928.
	Phil 1512.11	Hugon, Edward. Cursus philosophiae thomistica. 3. éd. v.1-6. Paris, 1928. 3v.
	Phil 92.1	Hugon, Paul D. Our minds and our motives. N.Y., 1928.
	Phil 2050.68.25	Hume, David. Storia naturale della religione e saggio sul suicidio. Bari, 1928.
	Phil 2050.58	Hume, David. Treatise on human nature. Oxford, 1928.
	Phil 5247.19.25	Hunter, W.S. Human behavior. Chicago, 1928.
	Phil 482.5	Huré, Jules. Les origines judéo-chrétiennes du matérialisme contemporain. Paris, 1928.
	Phil 7069.28.35	Jaeschke, Willy K. Die parapsychologischen Erscheinungen. 2. Aufl. Leipzig, 1928.
	Phil 184.31	Jakowenko, B. Vom Wesen des Pluralismus. Bonn, 1928.
	Phil 184.3.17	James, W. Pragmatism, a new name. N.Y., 1928.
	Phil 2070.46.10	James, William. Principî di psicologia (estratti). Torino, 1928.
	Phil 5627.6.4A	James, William. Varieties of religious experience. N.Y., 1928.
	Phil 5545.170	Janet, Pierre. L'évolution de la mémoire. Paris, 1928.
	Phil 5819.5	Jarmer, Karl. Das Seelenleben der Fische. München, 1928.
	Phil 5850.244	Jastrow, Joseph. Keeping mentally fit, a guide to everyday psychology. N.Y., 1928.
	Phil 5850.244.5	Jastrow, Joseph. Keeping mentally fit. N.Y., 1928.
	Phil 5819.4	Jenkins, Marion. The effect of segregation on the sex behavior of the white rat as measured by the abstruction method. Worcester, Mass., 1928.
	Phil 7082.140	Ježower, Ignaz. Das Buch der Träume. Berlin, 1928.
	Phil 960.131	Jhā, Gangānātha. The philosophical discipline. Calcutta, 1928.
	Phil 365.40	Joad, C.E.N. The meaning of life. London, 1928.
	Phil 184.34	Jørgensen, J. Filosofiens og apdragelsene grundproblemer. København, 1928.
	Phil 7069.28.40	Johnson, G.L. The great problem and the evidence. London, 1928.
	Phil 6119.9	Jones, F. Wood. The matrix of the mind. Honolulu, 1928.
	Phil 340.6	Jordon, Bruno. Die Ideenlehre. Leipzig, 1928.
	Phil 5400.71	Joussain, A. Les passions humaines. Paris, 1928.
	Phil 5722.18	Jung, C.G. Die Beziehungen zwischen dem ich und dem Unbewussten. Darmstadt, 1928.
	Phil 6319.1.13	Jung, C.G. Two essays on analytical psychology. London, 1928.
	Phil 6319.1.14	Jung, C.G. Two essays on analytical psychology. N.Y., 1928.
	Phil 6319.1.7	Jung, C.G. Über die Energetik der Seele und andere psychologische Abhandlungen. Zürich, 1928.
	Phil 5249.13.20	Jung, Carl G. Contributions to analytical psychology. London, 1928.
	Phil 3480.52.9	Kant, Immanuel. Critique of teleological judgment. Oxford, 1928.
	Phil 3480.30.45	Kant, Immanuel. Kritik der reinen Vernunft. Berlin, 1928.
	Phil 5050.3.5	Keynes, J.N. Studies and exercises in formal logic. 4th ed. London, 1928.
	Phil 5525.34	Kimmins, G.W. The springs of laughter. London, 1928.
	Phil 8590.18.20	King, Basil. Faith and success. Garden City, 1928.
	Phil 6060.12.16	Klages, Ludwig. Einführung in die Psychologie der Handschrift. 2. Aufl. Heidelberg, 1928.
Htn	Phil 1955.6.90F*	Klyce, S. Dewey's suppressed psychology. Winchester, Mass., 1928.
	Phil 5760.8	Knox, Howard V. The will to be free. London, 1928.
	Phil 365.19.60	Kolbe, F.C. A Catholic view of holism. N.Y., 1928.
	Phil 3640.252	Kramer, H.G. Nietzsche und Rousseau. Inaug. Diss. Borna, 1928.
	Phil 630.23.10	Kremer, René. La théorie de la connaissance chez les néo-réalistes anglais. Louvain, 1928.
	Phil 978.59.20	Krishnamurti, J. Life in freedom. N.Y., 1928.
	Phil 978.59.10	Krishnamurti, J. The pool of wisdom; Who brings the truth; By what authority and three poems. Eerde, 1928.
	Phil 5250.12.17	Kroman, Kristian. Grundtraek af sjaelelaeren. 7. udg. København, 1928.
	Phil 185.41	Kroner, Richard. Die Selbstverwirklichung des Geistes. Tübingen, 1928.
	Phil 5650.17	Kucharski, P. Recherches sur l'exitabilité auditive. Thèse. Paris, 1928.
	Phil 9558.14	Küppers, L. Psychologische Untersuchungen über die Lüge. Inaug. Diss. Bedburg-Erft, 1928.
	Phil 5627.115	Kupky, Oscar. The religious development of adolescents. N.Y., 1928.
	Phil 3492.31	Kynast, R. Kant: sein System als Theorie des Kulturbewusstseins. München, 1928.
	Phil 8110.2	Ladd, H.A. With eyes of the past. N.Y., 1928.
	Phil 2490.132	Lagarrigue, L. Politique internationale. Paris, 1928.
	Phil 186.69	Laird, John. Modern problems in philosophy. London, 1928.
	Phil 811.6	Lamanna, E. Paolo. Manuale di storia della filosofia ad uso delle scuole. Firenze, 1928. 2v.
	Phil 7069.28.45	Lambert, Helen C.S. A general survey of psychical phenomena. N.Y., 1928.
	Phil 5425.44	Lange, Wilhelm. Genie-Irrsinn und Ruhm. München, 1928.
	Phil 186.68	Larrabee, Harold A. What philosophy is. N.Y., 1928.
	Phil 8583.11.90	Lau, Paul. August Dorners Religionsphilosophie. Inaug. Diss. Königsberg, 1928.
	Phil 2725.35.50	Lavelle, Louis. De l'être. Paris, 1928.
	Phil 5251.36	Leary, Daniel Bell. Modern psychology, normal and abnormal. Philadelphia, 1928.
	Phil 2070.127	Le Breton, M. La personnalité de William James. Paris, 1928.
	Phil 2477.6.87	Lefévre, Frédéric. L'itinéraire philosophique de M. Blondel. Paris, 1928.
	Phil 8591.45	Leh, L.L. Christianity reborn. N.Y., 1928.
	Phil 186.67	Leisegang, H. Denkformen. Berlin, 1928.
	Phil 3120.11.84	Leiste, Heinrich. Die Charakterologie von Julius Bahnsen. Diss. Köln, 1928.
	Phil 365.27.5	LeRoy, Édouard. Les origines humaines et l'évolution de l'intelligence. Paris, 1928.
	Phil 7069.28.50	Leroy, O. La lévitation. Paris, 1928.
	Phil 5627.106	A letter of a friend. Chicago, 1928.
	Phil 8591.30	Lewis, John. The passion for life. New Haven, 1928.
	Phil 672.140	Lewis, Wyndham. Time and Western man. N.Y., 1928.
	Phil 5401.12	Liebeck, O. Das Unbekannte und die Angst. Leipzig, 1928.
	Phil 5585.29.2	Linke, Paul F. Grundlagen der Wahrnehmungslehre. 2. Aufl. München, 1928.
	Phil 186.60.10	Litt, Theodor. Wissenschaft, Bildung, Weltanschauung. Leipzig, 1928.
	Phil 2115.26	Locke, J. Selections. Chicago, 1928.
	Phil 8886.67	Löwith, K. Das Individuum in der Rolle des Mitmenschen. München, 1928.
	Phil 8886.38.5	Loisy, Alfred. La morale humaine. 2. ed. Paris, 1928.
	Phil 5400.69	Loosmore, W.C. Ourselves and our emotions. London, 1928.
	Phil 342.3.10	Losskii, N. L'intuition, la matière et la vie. Paris, 1928.
	Phil 186.64	Losskii, N.O. The world as an organic whole. London, 1928.
	Phil 3565.30.30	Lotze, Hermann. Logik, drei Bücher vom Denken. 2e Aufl. Leipzig, 1928.
	Phil 486.8	Lovecchio, Antonino. Filosofia della prassi e filosofia dello spirito. Palmi, 1928.
	Phil 665.7.7	Lutosławski, W. Pre-existence and reincarnation. London, 1928.
	Phil 8633.1.28	Lyman, E.W. The meaning of selfhood and faith in immortality. Cambridge, 1928.
	Phil 5252.61.2	MacCurdy, J.T. Common principles in psychology and physiology. Cambridge, 1928.
	Phil 5252.61	MacCurdy, J.T. Common principles in psychology and physiology. N.Y., 1928.
	Phil 6322.29.5	MacFadden, B. StrengtheningThe nerves. N.Y., 1928.
	Phil 8887.64	MacKaye, James. Convictionism versus non-convictionism. n.p., 1928.
	Phil 3832.11A	McKeon, R. The philosophy of Spinoza. N.Y., 1928.
	Phil 2475.1.226	MacWilliam, J. Criticism of the philosophy of Bergson. Edinburgh, 1928.
	Phil 2733.41	Malebranche, Nicolas. Méditations chrétiennes. Paris, 1928.
	Phil 5425.43	Marks, Jeannette. Genius and disaster. London, 1928.
	Phil 5400.66	Marston, W.M. Emotions of normal people. London, 1928.
	Phil 8702.16A	Mather, K.F. Science in search of God. N.Y., 1928.
	Phil 8702.16.2	Mather, K.F. Science in search of God. N.Y., 1928.
	Phil 75.28	Meiner, Felix. Philosophischer Handkatalog. 1er Nachtrag über die Jahre 1927/28. Leipzig, 1928.
	Phil 4580.118	Meis, Hans. Darstellung und Würdigung der Ethik Harald Høffdings. Inaug. Diss. Obersassel, 1928.
	Phil 8592.41	Mellone, S.H. Back to realities. London, 1928.
	Phil 5545.167	Memory. By an ignorant student. London, 1928.
	Phil 1517.3.5	Mercier, Désiré. A manual of modern scholastic philosophy. 3rd ed. London, 1928. 2v.
	Phil 2050.01	Metz, Rudolf. Bibliographie der Hume-Literatur. Erfurt, 1928.
	Phil 3832.12	Meurling, H. Fullkomlighetsbegreppet i Spinozas filosofi. Diss. Uppsala, 1928.
	Phil 6962.18	Mignard, Maurice. L'unité psychique et les troubles mentaux. Paris, 1928.
	Phil 2138.40.14	Mill, John S. Die Freiheit. Leipzig, 1928.
	Phil 3494.11.15A	Miller, E.M. Moral law and the highest good; a study of Kant's doctrine. Melbourne, 1928.
	Phil 8667.16	Miller, T.A. The mind behind the universe. N.Y., 1928.
	Phil 8177.5	Mitrovics, Gyula. A magyar esztétikai irodolan történeto. Debrecen, 1928.
	Phil 343.15.5	Mochi, Alberto. De la connaissance à l'action. Paris, 1928.
	Phil 4080.3.145	Molina, G. Saggio su Benedetto Croce. Genova, 1928.
	Phil 6322.21	Monakow, Constantin von. Introduction biologique à l'étude de la neurologie et de la psychopathologie. Paris, 1928.
	Phil 5722.23.2	Montmasson, J.M. Le rôle de l'inconscient dans l'invention scientifique. Thèse. Bourg, 1928.
	Phil 5627.120	Morgan, William Joseph. La psychologie de la religion dans l'Amérique. Thèse. Paris, 1928.
	Phil 5052.30	Morselli, E. Principios de lógica. Buenos Aires, 1928.
	Phil 8413.7	Munro, Thomas. Scientific method in aesthetics. N.Y., 1928.
	Phil 5253.7.2	Naesgaard, S. Kortfattet sjaelelaere. København, 1928.
	Phil 8703.2	Needham, Joseph. Science, religion and reality. N.Y., 1928.
	Phil 3890.8.105	Neisser, Liselotte. Christian Thomasius und seine Beziehungen zum Pietismus. Inaug. Diss. München, 1928.
	Phil 3850.18.87	Neive, Heinrich. Max Schelers Auffassung. Diss. Photoreproduction. Würzburg, 1928.
	Phil 8888.11	Nivard, M. Ethica. Paris, 1928.
	Phil 8414.13	Novak, Mirko. Základy vĭdy o umĕní, se zvláštním zřením k vĕdeckému studiu hudby. Praha, 1928.
	Phil 575.68	Oakeley, Hilda D. A study in the philosophy of personality. London, 1928.
	Phil 7060.92.55	O'Donnell, Elliot. Confessions of a ghost hunter. London, 1928.

1928 - cont.

Phil 4756.2.35	Ostromirov, A. Nikolai Fedorovich Fedorov i sovremennost'. v.1-3. Kharbin, 1928.
Phil 8669.3.5	Otto, Rudolf. The idea of the holy. London, 1928.
Phil 345.3	Overhuber, H.E. Die Geltungsgrundlagen metaphysischer Urteile. München, 1928.
Phil 8415.6	Ozzòla, L. L'arte come conoscenza degli individuali. Roma, 1928.
Phil 815.9	Palhariés, F. Vies et doctrines des grands philosophes à travers les âges. Paris, 1928. 3v.
Phil 5255.40	Palmés, F.M. Psicología. Barcelona, 1928.
Phil 4080.3.139	Pardo, Ferruccio. La filosofia teoretica di Benedetto Croce. Napoli, 1928.
Phil 8890.41.10	Parodi, D. Les bases psychologiques de la vie morale. Paris, 1928.
Phil 2805.21	Pascal, Blaise. Oeuvres. Paris, 1928-29. 6v.
Phil 5360.6	Paulhan, F. Les puissances de l'abstraction. Paris, 1928.
Phil 190.3.7	Paulsen, F. Introduction to philosophy. 2. American ed. N.Y., 1928.
Phil 5625.75.3	Pavlov, Ivan P. Conditioned reflexes. London, 1928.
Phil 2050.200	Pelikán, Ferdinand. Fikcionalism novověké filosofie zvláště u Humea a Kanta. Praha, 1928.
Phil 5225.2	Petermann, Bruno. Die Wertheimer-Koffka-Köhlersche Gestalttheorie und das Gestaltproblem systematisch und kritisch Dargestellt. Leipzig, 1928.
Phil 1980.3.90	Peterson, Houston. Havelock Ellis, philosopher of love. Boston, 1928.
Phil 8615.18	Petrović, E. U znaku preporoda. Odjek Vivodićevoj pokreta. Sarajevo, 1928.
Phil 6325.1.20	Pfister, Oskar. Psychoanalyse und Weltanschauung. Leipzig, 1928.
Phil 6325.1.25	Pfister, Oskar. Religiosität und Hysterie. Leipzig, 1928.
Phil 5648.19	Piéron, Henri. Les sensibilités cutanées. v.1-3. Paris, 1928-32.
Phil 5520.51A	Pillsbury, Walter B. The psychology of language. N.Y., 1928.
Phil 8965.12	Piper, Otto. Die Grundlagen der evangelischen Ethik. Gütersloh, 1928.
Phil 3745.7	Plessner, Helmuth. Die Stufen des Organischen und des Marisch; Einleitung in die philosophische Anthropologie. Berlin, 1928.
Phil 6125.20	Polen, Laura. Körperbau und Charakter. Inaug. Diss. Leipzig, 1928.
Phil 5255.37	Politzer, Georges. Critique des fondements de la psychologie. Paris, 1928.
Phil 1885.82	Pounder, R.M. The one and the many...Bradley's "Appearance and reality". Diss. Cambridge, 1928.
Phil 5635.34	Pradines, M. Philosophie de la sensation. Paris, 1928-34. 3v.
Phil 960.132	Prasad, Jwala. Introduction to Indian philosophy. Allahabad, 1928.
Phil 9120.161	Prichard, H.A. Duty and interest. Oxford, 1928.
Phil 3640.229	Prinzhorn, Hans. Nietzsche und das XX Jahrhundert. Heidelberg, 1928.
Phil 25.33.3	Psychologies of 1925. 3d ed. Worcester, 1928.
Phil 491.2	Quarto di Palo, A. Materia (appunti di critica). Roma, 1928.
Phil 5827.8	Rabaud, E. How animals find their way about. Leipzig, 1928.
Phil 960.128.10	Radhakrishnan, S. The Vedânta according to Samkara and Ramanuja. London, 1928.
Phil 8707.12	Rahn, Carl. Science and the religious life. New Haven, 1928.
Phil 192.68	Ranke, Karl E. Die Kategorien des Lebendigen. München, 1928.
Phil 3450.4.85	Redeker, Martin. Wilhelm Herrmann im kampf Gegen die positivistische Lebensanschauung. Gotha, 1928.
Phil 5400.65A	Regmert, Martin L. Feelings and emotions. Worcester, Mass., 1928.
Phil 3790.9.20	Rehmke, J. Gesammelte philosophische Aufsätze. Erfurt, 1928.
Phil 5257.3.10	Rehmke, J. Der Mensch. Leipzig, 1928.
Phil 672.144	Reichenbach, H. Philosophie der Raum-Zeit-Lehre. Berlin, 1928.
Phil 4635.5.81.3	Rein, T. Juhana Vilhelm Snellman. Helsingissa, 1928.
Phil 8707.13	Reuterdahl, A. The God of science. Minneapolis, 1928.
Phil 3210.89	Rezazadeh-Schafagh, Sadeg. Mystische Motive in Fechners Philosophie. Inaug. Diss. Charlottenburg, 1928.
Phil 7069.28.10	Richardson, Mark Wyman. The thumbprint and cross correspondence experiments made with the medium Margery during 1927-1928. n.p., 1928.
Phil 18.7.11	Richman, John. Development...psycho-analytical theory of psychosis, 1893-1926. London, 1928.
Phil 298.8	Richter, G. Die Philosophie der Eimmaligkeit. Wien, 1928-32. 3v.
Phil 192.21.3.6	Rickert, H. Der Gegenstand der Erkenntniss. 6. Aufl. Tübingen, 1928.
Phil 6327.11	Rickman, J. Index psychoanalyticus, 1893-1926. London, 1928.
Phil 8707.14	Rigdon, Jonathan. Science and religion as they look to a layman. Danville, Ind., 1928.
Phil 8892.45	Rignano, E. Il fine dell'uomo. Bologna, 1928.
Phil 5827.9	Rizzolo, Attilio. Etudes expérimentales sur l'exitabilité de l'écorce cérébrale du chien. Thèse. Paris, 1928.
Phil 5257.28.9	Roback, A.A. Popular psychology. Cambridge, 1928.
Phil 9035.45.3	Roback, A.A. The psychology of character. N.Y., 1928.
Phil 1122.6.5	Robin, Léon. Greek thought. N.Y., 1928.
Phil 1122.6.3	Robin, Léon. La pensée grecque et les origines de l'esprit scientifique. Paris, 1928.
Phil 3837.15	Robinson, Lewis. Kommentar zu Spinozas Ethik. v.1-2. Leipzig, 1928.
Phil 192.62	Roguin, Ernest. Sociologie; partie de philosophie. Lausanne, 1928-1929. 3v.
Phil 4210.30	Rosmini-Serbati, Antonio. Principi della scienza morale. Torino, 1928.
Phil 4210.32	Rosmini-Serbati, Antonio. Storia comparativa e critica dei sistemi intorno al principio della morale, a cura di C. Caviglione. Pt. 1. Torino, 1928.
Phil 5257.42	Rostohar, M. Studie z vyvojové psychologie. Brno, 1928.
Phil 8892.41	Roth, Leon. The science of morals; an essay in method. London, 1928.
Phil 2490.94.10	Rouvre, C. de. Auguste Comte et le catholicisme. Paris, 1928.
Phil 5257.11.15	Royce, Josiah. Lineamenti di psicologia. Bari, 1928.
Phil 310.1.5	Rozanov, Iakov S. Filosofsko-sotsiologicheskaia literatura marksizma za 1917-1927. Moskva, 1928.

1928 - cont.

Phil 102.4	Ruckmick, C.A. German-English dictionary of psychological terms. Iowa City, 1928.
Phil 5257.34.5	Ruckmick, C.A. The mental life. N.Y., 1928.
Phil 930.25.2	Rudd, H.F. Chinese social organs. Chicago, 1928.
Phil 3095.82	Ruman, Albert. Die Aesthetik Alex Gottlieb Baumgartens. Halle, 1928.
Phil 645.30	Russell, B.A.W. Sceptical essays. N.Y., 1928.
Phil 8892.37.10	Russell, Bertrand Russell. What I believe. N.Y., 1928.
Phil 6128.42	Sadler, William S. The truth about mind cure. Chicago, 1928.
Phil 193.124	Sagcret, Emile. Essais de philosophie synthetique. Paris, 1928.
Phil 5258.94	Sahai, Mahajot. A new primer of psychology. London, 1928.
Phil 193.121	Saitta, G. Filosofia italiana e umanesimo. Venezia, 1928.
Phil 193.49.35	Santayana, G. The realm of essence: book first of Realms of being. London, 1928.
Phil 193.122	Sarlo, F. de. Introduzione alla filosofia. Milano, 1928.
Phil 6060.18.10	Saudek, R. Experiments with handwriting. London, 1928.
Phil 6060.18.20	Saudek, R. Schrift und Mensch. Berlin, 1928.
Phil 6128.44	Saunders, R.H. Health; its recovery and maintanance, by Abduhl Latif. London, 1928.
Phil 3090.86	Sauter, J. Baader und Kant. Jena, 1928.
Phil 2880.6	Sauvage-Jousse, P. Le métaverbe. Paris, 1928.
Phil 3800.200.17	Schelling, F.W.J. von. Bruno. Leipzig, 1928.
Phil 7080.41	Schenk, Paul. Versuch einer psychologischen Theorie des Schlafes. Inaug. Diss. Leipzig, 1928.
Phil 299.21	Schilder, Paul. Gedanken zur Naturphilosophie. Wien, 1928.
Phil 6328.10.21	Schilder, Paul. Introduction to a psychoanalytic psychiatry. N.Y., 1928.
Phil 5258.89.5	Schjelderup, H. Psychologie. Berlin, 1928.
Phil 5627.116	Schjelderup, K. von. Die Askese; eine religionspsychologische Untersuchung. Berlin, 1928.
Phil 9495.130	Schmalhausen, S.D. Why we misbehave. Garden City, N.Y., 1928.
Phil 5258.38.5	Schmied-Kowarzik, W. Umriss einer analytischen Psychologie. 2. Aufl. Teil I. Leipzig, 1928.
Phil 193.119	Schnass, F. Einführung in die Philosophie. Osterwieck, 1928.
Phil 5625.106	Schneersohn, Fischel. Der Weg zum Menschen. Berlin, 1928.
Phil 6328.14.2	Schneider, Kurt. Die psychopathischen Personlichkeiten. 2. Aufl. Leipzig, 1928.
Phil 3808.22.3	Schopenhauer, Arthur. The works of Schopenhauer, abridged. Garden City, 1928.
Phil 3808.22	Schopenhauer, Arthur. The works of Schopenhauer, abridged. N.Y., 1928.
Phil 6968.25	Schou, H.J. Religiøsitet og sygelige sindstilstande. 3. udg. København, 1928.
Phil 5402.14	Schwarz, Balduin. Untersuchungen zur Psychologie des Weinens. Inaug. Diss. München, 1928.
Phil 1133.23	Scoon, Robert. Greek philosophy before Plato. Princeton, 1928.
Phil 6128.46.7	Seabury, David. Growing into life. N.Y., 1928.
Phil 5258.34.10	Seashore, C.E. Psychology in daily life. N.Y., 1928.
Phil 8598.35.15	Sellars, Roy W. Religion coming of age. N.Y., 1928.
Phil 672.147	Sevin, Emile. Le temps absolu et l'espace à quatre dimensions. Paris, 1928.
Phil 8893.10.15	Sharp, F.C. Ethics. N.Y., 1928.
Phil 960.41	Shastri, P.D. The essentials of Eastern philosophy. N.Y., 1928.
Phil 5258.95	Shastri, Prabhu D. Elementary psychology. Calcutta, 1928.
Phil 2520.167	Sirven, J. Les années d'apprentissage de Descartes (1596-1628). Albi, 1928.
Phil 2520.167.2	Sirven, J. Les années d'apprentissage de Descartes (1596-1628). v.1-2. Thèse. Albi, 1928.
Phil 5850.340.50	Smith, E.D. Psychology for executives. N.Y., 1928.
Phil 8708.16	Snowden, J.H. Old faith and new knowledge. N.Y., 1928.
Phil 4319.1	Solana, Marcial. Los grandes escolásticos espanoles de los siglos XVI y XVII. Madrid, 1928.
Phil 193.93.2	Sorel, Georges. De l'utilité du pragmatisme. 2e ed. Paris, 1928.
Phil 400.76	Spann, Othmar. Der Schöpfungsgang des Geistes. Theil I. Jena, 1928.
Phil 8708.15	Spaulding, E.G. What am I? N.Y., 1928.
Phil 3819.76	Spinoza, Benedictus de. The correspondence of Spinoza. London, 1928.
Phil 5258.74.9A	Spranger, Eduard. Types of men. Halle, 1928.
Phil 5058.43	Stammler, G. Begriff, Urteil, Schluss. Halle, 1928.
Phil 720.33.5	Stefansson, V. The standardization of error. London, 1928.
Phil 978.82	Stein, W.J. Weltgeschichte im Lichte des heiligen Gral. Stuttgart, 1928.
Phil 978.49.95	Steiner, R. Esquisse d'une cosmogonie psychologique, d'après des conférences faites à Paris en 1906. Paris, 1928.
Phil 978.49.110	Steiner, R. Philosophy and anthroposophy. London, 1928.
Phil 974.3.7	Steiner, Rudolf. The story of my life. London, 1928.
Phil 3585.1.95	Sterkman, P. De plaats van J.H. Lambert...idealisme voor Kant. 's-Gravenhage, 1928.
Phil 349.29	Stern, Günther. Uber das Haben. Bonn, 1928.
Phil 5250.72	Stinchfield, S.M. The psychology of speech. Boston, 1928.
Phil 623.22	Strich, Walter. Der irrationale Mensch. Berlin, 1928.
Phil 126.3.4	Stumpf, C. Tafeln zur Geschichte der Philosophie. 4. Aufl. Berlin, 1928.
Phil 2070.120.2A	Stumpf, Carl. William James nach seinen Briefen. Berlin, 1928.
Phil 8893.57.10	Sturt, Henry. Moral experience, an outline of ethics for class-teaching. London, 1928.
Phil 2490.117	Style, Jane M. Auguste Comte thinker and lover. London, 1928.
Phil 3839.5	Tak, W.G. van der. Bento de Spinoza. 's Gravenhage, 1928.
Phil 4040.1.93	Tarozzi, Giuseppe. Roberto Ardigo. Roma, 1928.
Phil 194.36.2	Taylor, H.O. Human values and verities. London, 1928.
Phil 194.36	Taylor, H.O. Human values and verities. N.Y., 1928.
Phil 6325.8.80	Taylor, William Sentman. Morton Prince and abnormal psychology. N.Y., 1928.
Phil 8599.21	Tennant, F.R. Philosophical theology. Cambridge, 1928-30. 2v.
Phil 2605.3.40	Theodore Flournoy, 1854-1920. Genève, 1928.
Phil 194.37	Thomas, Elyston. What existence means. London, 1928.
Phil 8674.11	Thornton, L.S. The incarnate Lord. London, 1928.
Phil 8650.354.5	Thouless, R.H. The control of the mind. London, 1928.
Phil 5627.59.5	Thouless, Robert H. An introduction to the psychology of religion. 2. ed. Cambridge, Eng., 1928.
Phil 7069.28.75	Thurston, Herbert. Modern spiritualism. St-Louis, 1928.

Chronological Listing

1928 - cont.

Phil 7140.11 — Tietjens, E. Die Desuggestion; ihre Bedeutung und Auswertung. Berlin, 1928.

Phil 6124.4 — Tilney, Frederick. The brain from ape to man. N.Y., 1928. 2v.

Phil 6689.10 — Tischner, Rudolf. Franz Anton Mesmer. München, 1928.

Phil 5259.5.38 — Titchener, E.B. A text-book of psychology. N.Y., 1928.

Phil 960.134 — Tombleson, J.B. As above, so below. London, 1928.

Phil 194.39 — Tourville, Henri. Precis de philosophie fondamentale d'apres la methode d'observation. Paris, 1928.

Phil 5259.19.9 — Troland, L.T. The fundamentals of human motivation. N.Y., 1928.

Phil 6420.22 — Trumper, Max. A hemato-respiratory study of 101 consecutive cases of stammering. Thesis. Philadelphia, 1928.

Phil 5650.18 — Tullio, Pietro. L'orecchio. Bologna, 1928.

Phil 3625.14.90 — Turner, William D. Georg Elias Müller. Cambridge, 1928.

Phil 5722.22 — The unconscious: a symposium. N.Y., 1928.

Phil 8600.3 — Underhill, E. Man and the supernatural. N.Y., 1928.

Phil 7069.28.100 — Underhill, Margaret. Your infinite possibilities. London, 1928.

Phil 6330.1 — Urbantschitsch, R. Psycho-analysis for all. London, 1928.

Phil 5627.121 — Uren, A.R. Recent religious psychology. Edinburgh, 1928.

Phil 2490.118.10 — Uta, Michel. La loi des trois etats dans la philosophie d'Auguste Comte. Bourg, 1928.

Phil 2490.118 — Uta, Michel. La théorie du savoir dans la philosophie d'Auguste Comte. Paris, 1928.

Phil 2490.118.5 — Uta, Michel. La théorie du savoir dans la philosophie d'Auguste Comte. Thèse. Bourg, 1928.

Phil 960.144 — Väth, Alfons. Im Kampfe mit der Zauberwelt des Hinduismus. Berlin, 1928.

Phil 7069.28.90 — Valdry, Luma. Living secrets. London, 1928.

Phil 196.8.15 — Varisco, B. Sommario di filosofia. Roma, 1928.

Phil 5261.15 — Vaughan, W.F. The lure of superiority. N.Y., 1928.

Phil 5261.20 — Vaughn, J. Positive versus negative instruction. N.Y., 1928.

Phil 8601.11 — Veiga, Antonio D.A. Lei das contrastes. Porto, 1928.

Phil 5435.12 — Veldt, Jacobus van der. L'apprentissage du mouvement et l'automatisme. Louvain, 1928.

Phil 196.22 — Vincenzi, Moises. Mi segunda dimension. San José, 1928.

Phil 575.67 — Volkelt, Johannes. Das Problem der Individualität. München, 1928.

Phil 8602.37 — Waggoner, John G. The beautiful sunset of life. Boston, 1928.

Phil 9035.55 — Wahle, Richard. Entstehung der Charakters. München, 1928.

Phil 2050.234 — Wallenfels, Walter. Die Rechtsphilosophie David Humes. Göttingen, 1928.

Phil 3246.224 — Walz, G.A. Die Staatsidee des Rationalismus...und die Staatsphilosophie Fichte's. Berlin, 1928.

Phil 4803.454.91 — Warrain, Francis. Wiązanie metafizyczme sporządzone według prawa stworzenia Hoene-Wrońskiego. Warszawa, 1928.

Phil 5262.21.15 — Watson, John B. The battle of behaviorism. London, 1928.

Phil 5262.21.10A — Watson, John B. The ways of behaviorism. 1st ed. N.Y., 1928.

Phil 6132.25 — Waylen, H. An apostle of healing...Pastor Richard Howton. London, 1928.

Phil 3450.17.90 — Weinzierl, H. Zur Entwicklungsgeschichte der neuern katholischen Philosophie...Hertlings. Inaug. Diss. Reimlingen, 1928.

Phil 5262.34 — Weld, Harry P. Psychology as science, its problems and points of view. London, 1928.

Phil 5262.34.2 — Weld, Harry P. Psychology as science, its problems and points of view. N.Y., 1928.

Phil 197.14.5 — Wentscher, Max. Metaphysik. Berlin, 1928.

Phil 8647.10 — Where are the dead? London, 1928.

Phil 6972.14.30 — White, William Alanson. Lectures in psychiatry. N.Y., 1928.

Phil 353.9.2 — Whitehead, A.N. Symbolism: its meaning and effect. Cambridge, Eng., 1928.

Phil 6332.9.15 — Whitehead, George. Gods, devils, and men. London, 1928.

Phil 5627.140 — Whitehead, George. Religion and woman. London, 1928.

Phil 7069.28.95 — Whitehead, George. Spiritualism explained. London, 1928.

Phil 1170.5.3 — Whittaker, Thomas. Neo-Platonists. Photoreproduction. 2nd ed. Cambridge, 1928.

Phil 5232.4 — Wickham, H. The misbehaviorists. N.Y., 1928.

Phil 3120.2.90 — Wiegand, H. Der Wahrheitsbegriff in der Lehre. Inaug. Diss. Alfeld Leine, 1928.

Phil 5262.42 — Wiggam, Albert E. Exploring your mind with the psychologists. Indianapolis, 1928.

Phil 9495.142 — Wolf, J. Die neue Sexualmoral und das Geburtenproblem unserer Tage. Jena, 1928.

Phil 197.65.5 — Wust, Peter. Die Dialelitik des Geistes. Augsburg, 1928.

Phil 6134.13A — Yogananda, Swami. Descriptive outline. 9th ed. Los Angeles, 1928.

Phil 7080.43 — Zambeccari, G. Il sonne e la vigilia. Firenze, 1928.

Phil 1130.3.13 — Zeller, Eduard. Grundriss der Geschichte der griechischen Philosophie. 13e Aufl. Leipzig, 1928.

Phil 8850.3 — Zucker, Friedrich. Syneidesis-conscientia. Jena, 1928.

Phil 8092.8 — Zum Felde, A. Estetica del novecientos. Buenos Aires, 1928?

1929

Phil 800.5 — Aall, Anothon. Filosofiens historie. Oslo, 1929.

Phil 5810.5 — Adams, Donald K. Experimental studies of adaptive behavior in cats. Diss. Baltimore, 1929.

Phil 5240.41 — Adams, John. Everyman's psychology. 1. ed. Garden City, 1929.

Phil 3482.2.30 — Adickes, E. Kants Lehre von der doppelten Affektion unseres ich als Schlüssel zu seiner Erkenntnis Theorie. Tübingen, 1929.

Phil 6310.1.25A — Adler, A. The case of Miss R. N.Y., 1929.

Phil 6310.1.20 — Adler, A. The science of living. Garden City, N.Y., 1929.

Phil 6310.1.21 — Adler, A. The science of living. N.Y., 1929.

Phil 8580.21 — Alexander, H.B. Truth and the faith. N.Y., 1929.

Phil 8580.20 — Alexander, Mikhailovich. The religion of love. N.Y., 1929.

Phil 2725.8.85 — Alfaric, Prosper. Laromiguière et son école. Paris, 1929.

Phil 6990.32 — Allen, Simeon C. Miracles and medicine. Boston, 1929.

Phil 7069.29.5 — Allison, Lydia W. Leonard and Soule experiments in psychical research. Boston, 1929.

Phil 6302.10 — American Psychiatric Association. Committee on Relations with the Social Science. Proceedings...colloquium on personality investigation. 1st - 2nd, 1928-1929. Baltimore, 1929.

Phil 8580.17 — Ames, Edward S. Religion. N.Y., 1929.

1929 - cont.

Phil 5040.16 — Anderson, Louis. Das logische; seine Gesetze und Kategorien. Leipzig, 1929.

Phil 9075.31 — Anderson, Louis F. Die Seele und das Gewissens. Leipzig, 1929.

Phil 5240.32 — Armstrong-Jones, K. The growth of the mind. Edinburgh, 1929?

Phil 3482.10 — Asmus, V.F. Dialektika Kanta. Moskva, 1929.

Phil 310.1.8 — Asmus, Valentin F. Ocherki istorii dialektiki v novoi filosofii. 2. izd. Moskva, 1929. 2 pam.

Phil 2150.6.83 — Aspelin, G. Utgångspunkterna för Münsterbergs värdelära. Lund, 1929.

Phil 720.23 — Aveling, Francis. The psychological approach to reality. London, 1929.

Phil 9530.41 — Babson, Roger Ward. Storing up triple reserves. N.Y., 1929.

Phil 3625.1.185 — Baeck, Leo. Mendelssohn Gedenkfeier der Jüdischen Gemeinde zu Berlin am 8, Sept. 1929. Berlin, 1929.

Phil 3640.240.5 — Baeumler, Alfred. Bachofen und Nietzsche. Zürich, 1929.

Phil 1535.1.35 — Balmes, Jaime. El criterio. Madrid, 1929.

Phil 5041.47.5 — Balzano, Bernard. Wissenschaftslehre. Leipzig, 1929-31. 4v.

Phil 3483.48 — Barié, G.E. Oltre la critica. Milano, 1929.

Phil 8581.87 — Barnes, H.E. The twilight of Christianity. N.Y., 1929.

Phil 1801.5 — Barron, J.T. The idea of the absolute in modern British philosophy. Thesis. Washington, D.C., 1929.

Phil 5041.48 — Baudry, L. Petit traité de logique formelle. Paris, 1929.

Phil 2805.209 — Bayet, Albert. Les provinciales de Pascal. Paris, 1929.

Phil 7069.29.7 — Beatty, Mabel. Man made perfect. Lonodon, 1929.

Phil 3001.11 — Becher, Erich. Deutsche Philosophen. München, 1929.

Phil 6951.5.6 — Beers, C.W. A mind that found itself. Garden City, 1929.

Phil 5400.77 — Begtrup, Julius. Some prominent characteristics of human nature and a new conception of God. London, 1929.

Phil 801.29.5 — Behn, Siegfried. The eternal magnet, a history of philosophy. N.Y., 1929.

Phil 1750.129 — Belgion, Montgomery. Our present philosophy of life. London, 1929.

Phil 8581.57 — Bell, Bernard I. Beyond agnosticism, a book for tired mechanists. N.Y., 1929.

Phil 8610.929.40 — Berdiaev, N.A. Marksizm i religiia. Paris, 1929.

Phil 3640.121.3 — Bertram, Ernst. Nietzsche; Versuch einer Mythologie. Berlin, 1929.

Phil 3640.230 — Bianquis, G. Nietzsche en France; l'influence de Nietzsche sur la pensée française. Paris, 1929.

Phil 3120.40.40 — Bierens de Haan, J.D. De strijd tusschen idealisme en naturalisme in de 19. eeuw. Haarlem, 1929.

Phil 2070.136 — Biró, B. A tudatalatti világ: William James lélektanában. Szeged, 1929.

Phil 978.5.85 — Blavatsky, H.P. Some unpublished letters. London, 1929.

Phil 801.28 — Boas, George. The adventures of human thought. N.Y., 1929.

Phil 801.28.5 — Boas, George. The major traditions of European philosophy. N.Y., 1929.

Phil 6060.26 — Bobertag, Otto. Ist die Graphologie zuverlässig? Heidelberg, 1929.

Phil 1750.127.2 — Boehm, Benno. Sokrates im achtzehnten Jahrhundert. Leipzig, 1929.

Phil 1750.127 — Boehm, Benno. Sokrates im achtzehnten Jahrhundert. Leipzig, 1929.

Phil 3549.8.80 — Börlin, E. Darstellung und Kritik der Charakterologie von Ludwig Klages. Giessen, 1929.

Phil 6311.34.12 — Bonaparte, Marie. Stratiotikoi kai koinōnikoi polemoi. Manchester, N.H., 1929.

Phil 672.149 — Bonaventura, Enzo. Il problema psicologico del tempo. Milano, 1929.

Phil 2465.82 — Bonnet, Georges. Charles Bonnet (1720-1793). Thèse. Paris, 1929.

Phil 5211.4A — Boring, E.G. A history of experimental psychology. N.Y., 1929.

Phil 3552.287 — Boutroux, Emile. La philosophie allemande au XVII siècle. Paris, 1929.

Phil 8610.889.7 — Bradlaugh, C. Humanity's gain from unbelief. London, 1929.

Phil 575.60.5 — Braham, Ernest G. Ourselves and reality. London, 1929.

Phil 8581.77A — Brémond, H. Introduction à la philosophie de la prière. Paris, 1929.

Phil 3120.8.40 — Brentano, Franz. Über die Zukunft der Philosophie. Leipzig, 1929.

Phil 8656.21 — Brentano, Franz. Vom Dasein Gottes. Leipzig, 1929.

Phil 2733.102 — Bridet, L. La théorie de la connaissance dans la philosophie de Malebranche. Paris, 1929.

Phil 2733.102.5 — Bridet, L. La théorie de la connaissance dans la philosophie de Malebranche. Thèse. Paris, 1929.

Phil 8626.17 — Bromberg, F.G. Man's immortality proved by study of his natural constitution. Mobile, Ala., 1929.

Phil 5241.28.17 — Brown, W. Science and personality. New Haven, 1929.

Phil 2750.8.89 — Brunet, Pierre. Maupertuis. Paris, 1929. 2v.

Phil 2750.8.87 — Brunet, Pierre. Maupertuis. Thèse. Paris, 1929. 2 pam.

Phil 1506.8.10 — Bruni, Gerardo. Progressive scholasticism. Saint Louis, Mo., 1929.

Phil 176.106.10 — Buchanan, S.M. Poetry and mathematics. N.Y., 1929.

Phil 5211.3.2 — Bühler, Karl. Die Kirse der Psychologie. 2. Aufl. Jena, 1929.

Phil 176.124 — Burkamp, Wilhelm. Die Struktur der Ganzheiten. Berlin, 1929.

Phil 6111.58 — Buzzard, E.F. An outline of neurology and its outlook. London, 1929.

Phil 5400.31.9 — Cannon, W.B. Bodily changes in pain, hunger, fear and rage. 2d ed. N.Y., 1929.

Phil 3002.5 — Carabellese, Pantaleo. Il problema della filosofia da Kant a Fichte (1781-1801). Palermo, 1929.

Phil 5042.21A — Carnap, Rudolf. Abriss der Logistik. Wien, 1929.

Phil 3552.279 — Carr, H.W. Leibniz. London, 1929.

Phil 8582.46 — Castelli, Enrico. Filosofia e apologetica. Roma, 1929.

Phil 3484.15 — Cavicchi, G. de. Saggio Culle contraddizioni di Emanuele Kant. Catania, 1929.

Phil 2475.1.375 — Černý, V. Ideové kořeny současného umění. Praha, 1929.

Phil 177.81 — Cesalpino, Andrea. Questions péripatéliciennes. Paris, 1929.

Phil 2475.1.227 — Challaye, F. Bergson. Paris, 1929.

Phil 8403.27 — Challaye, F. Esthétique. Paris, 1929.

Phil 8403.27.5 — Challaye, F. L'art et la beauté. Paris, 1929.

Phil 5435.9 — Chevalier, J. L'habitude, essai de métaphysique scientifique. Paris, 1929.

Phil 5212.5 — Chin, Robert. Psychology in America. N.Y., 1929.

1929 - cont.

Phil 5242.42   Chircoulesco, D. Essai sur les principes d'une psychologie évolutive. Bucarest, 1929.

Phil 5627.164   Clark, E.T. The psychology of religious awakening. N.Y., 1929.

Phil 5242.48   Clarke, Edwin L. The art of straight thinking. N.Y., 1929.

Phil 735.93   Clarke, Mary E. A study in the logic of value. London, 1929.

Phil 177.79A   Clemenceau, G. In the evening of my thought. Boston, 1929. 2v.

Phil 1802.4   Coates, A. Sceptical examination of contemporary British philosophy. London, 1929.

Phil 6952.24   Cobb, Stanley. An outline of neuropathology for students of general medicine. Cambridge, 1929.

Phil 665.53   Coffin, Joseph H. The soul comes back. N.Y., 1929.

Phil 8610.929.25   Cohen, Chapman. Four lectures on freethought and life. London, 1929.

Phil 9035.76   Columbia University. Teachers College. Character Education Inquiry. Studies in the nature of character. v.2. N.Y., 1929.

Phil 5249.13.95   Corrie, Joan. C.G. Jung's Psychologie im Abriss. Zürich, 1929.

Phil 177.80   Cresson, André. Les septèmes philosophiques. Paris, 1929.

ltn   Phil 4080.3.38*   Croce, Benedetto. Aesthetica in nuce. Napoli, 1929.

Phil 178.60   Dakin, John E. Rhythmic affinity, a philosophic hypothesis. N.Y., 1929.

Phil 8610.929.20   Darrow, C. Infidels and heretics. Boston, 1929.

Phil 5813.5   Debblee, George B. Instinct and intuition. London, 1929.

Phil 310.624   Deborin, Abram M. Dialektika i estestvoznanie. Izd. 3. Moskva, 1929.

Phil 8404.15.5   Dessoir, Max. Beiträge zur allgemeinen Kunstwissenschaft. Stuttgart, 1929.

Phil 1845.3.90   Devaux, P. Le système d'Alexander. Paris, 1929.

Phil 8693.15   Dewart, E.H. (Mrs.). The march of life. Boston, 1929.

Phil 178.58   Dewe, Joseph A. Les deux ordres, psychique el material. Paris, 1929.

Phil 178.58.5   Dewe, Joseph A. Les deux ordres, psychique et materiel. Thèse. Paris, 1929.

Phil 178.38.16   Dewey, John. The quest for certainty. N.Y., 1929.

Phil 178.38.15A   Dewey, John. The quest for certainty. N.Y., 1929.

Phil 8878.11.12   Dewey and Tufts. Ethics. N.Y., 1929.

Phil 5243.34.10   Dimnet, E. The art of thinking. London, 1929.

Phil 5243.34.3   Dimnet, E. The art of thinking. N.Y., 1929.

Phil 5243.34.9A   Dimnet, E. The art of thinking. N.Y., 1929.

Phil 5243.34.5A   Dimnet, E. The art of thinking. N.Y., 1929.

Phil 178.37.10   Dingler, Hugo. Metaphysik als Wissenschaft vom Letzten. München, 1929.

Phil 178.59   Dotterer, Ray H. Philosophy by ways of the sciences. N.Y., 1929.

tn   Phil 7069.29.20*   Doyle, Arthur Conan. The Roman Catholic church, a rejoinder to Herbert Thurston). London, 1929.

Phil 3485.12   Drago, Pietro C. La mistica kantiana. Messina, 1929.

Phil 5627.118   Dresser, Horatio W. Outlines of the psychology of religion. N.Y., 1929.

Phil 178.22.25   Driesch, H. Man and the universe. London, 1929.

Phil 8404.8.5   Ducasse, Curt. The philosophy of art. Toronto, 1929.

Phil 8878.49   Dunham, James. Principles of ethics. N.Y., 1929.

Phil 178.30.5   Durant, William. The mansions of philosophy. N.Y., 1929.

Phil 5585.54.7   Duret, René. Les facteurs pratiques de la croyance dans la perception. Paris, 1929?

Phil 5585.54.5   Duret, René. Les facteurs pratiques de la croyance dans la perception. Thèse. Paris, 1929.

Phil 5585.54.2   Duret, René. L'objet de la perception. Thèse. Paris, 1929.

Phil 5585.54   Duret, René. L'objet de la perception. Thèse. Paris, 1929.

Phil 8694.4A   Eddington, Arthur. Science and the unseen world. N.Y., 1929.

Phil 8879.23   Edgell, B. Ethical problems. London, 1929.

Phil 5814.6   Eichler, Walter. Über die Erregbarkeitsmessung. Inaug. Diss. München, 1929.

Phil 179.17.15   Ellis, Havelock. The dance of life. Boston 1929.

Phil 179.17.18   Ellis, Havelock. The dance of life. N.Y., 1929.

Phil 179.17.20   Ellis, Havelock. The dance of life. N.Y., 1929.

Phil 8584.13   Emge, Carl A. Der philosophische Gehalt der religiösen Dogmatik. München, 1929.

Phil 3625.1.153   Encyclopaidia Judaica. Moses Mendelssohn zur 200 jahrigen Wiederkehr seines Gehertstages. Berlin, 1929.

Phil 3486.13   England, Frederick E. Kant's conception of God. London, 1929.

Phil 89.3.10   English, Horace B. A student's dictionary of psychological terms. 3rd ed. Yellow Springs, Ohio, 1929.

Phil 5014.1.30   Enriques, Federigo. The historic development of logic. N.Y., 1929.

Phil 1955.6.91   Essays in honor of John Dewey...seventeenth birthday. N.Y., 1929.

Phil 2725.4.85   Evans, David O. Pierre Leroux and his philosophy in relation to literature. n.p., 1929.

Phil 270.38   Faggiotto, A. La causa trinitaria unica sostanza del cosmo. Padova, 1929.

Phil 3120.2.95   Fels, Heinrich. Bernard Bolzano. Leipzig, 1929.

Phil 3450.11.95   Festschrift Edmund Husserl. Halle an der Saale, 1929.

Phil 735.120   Fiedler, K. Die Stufen der Erkenntnis. München, 1929.

Phil 6315.14   Fisher, Vivian E. An introduction to abnormal psychology. N.Y., 1929.

Phil 3425.261   Foster, Michael B. Die Geschichte als Schicksal des Geistes in der hegelschenPhilosophie. Tübingen, 1929.

Phil 3549.2.99   Franceschi, G.J. Keyserling. 2. ed. Buenos Aires, 1929.

Phil 5645.32.2   Franklin, Christine L. Colour and colour theories. London, 1929.

Phil 6115.23.5   Frany, Shepherd I. The evolution of an idea. 2d ed. Los Angeles, 1929.

Phil 3625.1.121   Freudenthal, M. Zum sweihundertjährigen Geburtstag Moses Mendelssohns; vier Abhandlungen. Berlin, 1929.

Phil 5045.11   Frey, T. Die Theorie der diskursiven Erkenntnis. Dorpat, 1929.

Phil 3270.3.95   Fried, Günther. Phantasie Wahrheit und Erkenntnis. Inaug. Diss. Tübingen, 1929.

Phil 8585.29   Friend, Nellie E. God and you. N.Y., 1929.

Phil 5585.56   Fröhlich, F.W. Die Empfindungszeit. Jena, 1929.

Phil 6955.15   Frostig, Jakób. Das schizophrene Denken. Leipzig, 1929.

Phil 7069.29.40   Fullwood, A.M. The song of Sano Tarot. N.Y., 1929.

Phil 9590.3   García, E.A. Negación de la nueva verdad. Buenos Aires, 1929.

Phil 8696.15   Gaulter, A. The riddle of nature. London, 1929.

1929 - cont.

Phil 5628.55   Gerlich, Fritz. Die Stigmatisierte Therese Neumann von Konnersreuth. München, 1929. 2v.

Phil 3425.258   Glockner, Hermann. Hegel. Stuttgart, 1929.

Phil 5246.40   Gomperz, H. Über Sinn und Sinngebilde. Tübingen, 1929.

Phil 5500.12   Gordin, Jakob. Untersuchungen zur Theorie des unendlichen Urteils. Berlin, 1929.

Phil 2733.94.10   Gouhier, Henri. Malebranche. Paris, 1929.

Phil 5046.21   Govi, Mario. Fondazione della metodalogia. Torino, 1929.

Phil 3488.24   Gračanin, G. La personnalité morale d'après Kant. Thèse. Paris, 1929.

Phil 5046.22   Grebe, Wilhelm. Die Form des Erkennens. München, 1929.

Phil 2020.30.15   Green, T.H. Prolegomena to ethics. 5th ed. Oxford, 1929.

Phil 181.71.5   Guénon, R. Autorité spirituelle et pouvoir temporel. Paris, 1929.

Phil 971.5.5   Guénon, R. Le theosophise; histoire d'une pseudo-religion. 2. ed. Paris, 1929.

Phil 3625.5.93   Gueroult, M. La philosophie transcendantale de Salomon Maimon. Paris, 1929.

Phil 3625.5.94   Gueroult, M. La philosophie transcendantale de Salomon Maimon. Thèse. Paris, 1929.

Phil 672.145   Gunn, J.A. The problem of time. London, 1929.

Phil 7069.29.45   Hack, Gwendolyn Kelley. Modern psychic mysteries. London, 1929.

Phil 8408.16   Häberlin, Paul. Allgemeine Ästhetik. Basel, 1929.

Phil 3425.254   Haering, Theodor L. Hegel, sein Wollen und sein Werke. Leipzig, 1929-1938. 2v.

Phil 3552.122.5   Halbwachs, Maurice. Leibniz. Paris, 1929.

Phil 182.35.10   Haldane, Richard B. Human experience; a study of its structure. London, 1929.

Phil 8832.5   Hall-Quest, A.L. It's not our fault. N.Y., 1929.

Phil 5247.46   Hamilton, Hughbert C. The effect of incentives on accuracy of discrimination measured on the Galton bar. Thesis. N.Y., 1929.

Phil 8587.44   Harkness, George E. Conflicts in religious thought. N.Y., 1929.

Phil 2225.5.90   Hartshorne, Charles. Continuity, the form of forms in Charles Peirce. n.p., 1929.

Phil 1980.3.92   Havelock Ellis, in appreciation. Berkeley Heights, N.J., 1929.

Phil 3425.62   Hegel, Georg Wilhelm Friedrich. Die absolute Religion. Leipzig, 1929.

Phil 3425.39.2   Hegel, Georg Wilhelm Friedrich. Hegel's logic of world and idea. Oxford, 1929.

Phil 3425.34.30   Hegel, Georg Wilhelm Friedrich. Science of logic. N.Y., 1929.

Phil 3425.28   Hegel, Georg Wilhelm Friedrich. Selections. N.Y., 1929.

Phil 3489.27   Heidegger, Martin. Kant und das Problem der Metaphysik. Bonn, 1929.

Phil 3450.19.25   Heidegger, Martin. Was ist Metaphysik? Bonn, 1929.

Phil 1707.10   Heinemann, Fritz. Neue Wege der Philosophie, Geist, Leben, Existenz. Leipzig, 1929.

Phil 3195.11.90   Hermann, C. Max Dessoir Mensch und Werk. Stuttgart, 1929.

Phil 5247.45.2   Herrick, C.J. The thinking machine. 2. ed. Chicago, 1929.

Phil 182.90   Herrigel, E. Die metaphysische Form. Tübingen, 1929.

Phil 182.79.5   Herzberg, Alex. The psychology of philosophers. London, 1929.

Phil 5643.176   Hillebrand, Franz. Lehre von den Gesichtsempfindungen auf Grund hinterlassener Aufzeichnungen. Wien, 1929.

Phil 3489.24   Hirsch, Richard. Kant-Bibliothek. Wien, 1929.

Phil 182.88A   Hocking, W.E. Types of philosophy. N.Y., 1929.

Phil 182.91   Hofmann, P. Metaphysik oder verstehende Sinnwissenschaft? Berlin, 1929.

Phil 8587.56   Hough, Lynn Harold. Whither Christianity. N.Y., 1929.

Phil 8610.929.35   Housman, L. The religious advance toward rationalism, delivered at Conway Hall on Sept. 25, 1929. London, 1929.

Phil 2050.69.30   Hume, David. Untersuchung über diePrinzipien der Moral. Leipzig, 1929.

Phil 2050.77A   Hume, David. Unveröffentlichte Briefe David Humes. Leipzig, 1929.

Phil 5047.11.10   Husserl, Edmund. Formale und transzendentale Logik. Halle, 1929.

Phil 5249.19   Jaensch, Erich. Über Gestaltpsychologie und Gestalttheorie. Langensalza, 1929.

Phil 184.3.34.5   James, W. Selected papers on philosophy. London, 1929.

Phil 9255.15   Jancke, Rudolf. Das Wesen der Ironie. Leipzig, 1929.

Phil 809.2.15   Janet, P. Histoire de la philosophie. Supplement. Paris, 1929.

Phil 184.30.15   Janet, P. Philosophie. 8e éd. Paris, 1929.

Phil 575.83   Janet, P. L'évolution psychologique de la personnalité. Paris, 1929.

Phil 6615.6.8   Janet, Pierre. The major symptoms of hysteria. 2. ed. N.Y., 1929.

Phil 184.26.5A   Joad, C.E.M. Matter, life and value. London, 1929.

Phil 184.35.5   Jolivet, Régis. La notion de substance. Paris, 1929.

Phil 184.35   Jolivet, Régis. La notion de substance. Paris, 1929.

Phil 1870.109A   Joseph, H.W.B. A comparison of Kant's idealism with that of Berkeley. London, 1929.

Phil 8410.4   Julianez Islas, L. El culto di lo bello. La Plata, 1929.

Phil 3480.32.20   Kant, Immanuel. Critique of pure reason. London, 1929.

Phil 3480.39   Kant, Immanuel. Kant's inaugural dissertation and early writings on space. London, 1929

Phil 3480.45.16   Kant, Immanuel. Kritik der praktischen Vernunft. 9. Aufl. Leipzig, 1929.

Phil 3480.25.20A   Kant, Immanuel. Selectiones. N.Y., 1929.

Phil 672.146   Kaschmieder, E. Zeitbezug und Sprache. Berlin, 1929.

Phil 5050.14   Keeling, S.V. Logic and reasoning. London, 1929.

Phil 185.35.10   Keyserling, H. The recovery of truth. N.Y., 1929.

Phil 341.14.5   Keyserling, H. Graf von. Creative understanding. N.Y., 1929.

Phil 3549.2.78.5   Keyserling, Hermann. The travel diary of a philosopher. N.Y., 1929.

Phil 8590.18.25   King, Basil. Adventures in religion. Garden City, 1929.

NEDL   Phil 185.44   Klages, Ludwig. Der Geist als Widersacher der Seele. v.1-3. Leipzig, 1929-1932. 4v.

Phil 575.51.15   Klages, Ludwig. The science of character. London, 1929.

Phil 3801.491   Knittermeyer, H. Schelling und die romantische Schule. München, 1929.

Phil 5250.15.11   Köhler, Wolfgang. Gestalt psychology. N.Y., 1929.

Phil 5250.15.15   Köhler, Wolfgang. Gestalt psychology. N.Y., 1929.

Phil 185.49   Kotarbiński, Tadeusz. Elementy. Lwów, 1929.

Phil 4803.282.80   Kowalski, Kazimierz Józef. Filozofja Augusta Hr. Cieszkowskiego w świetle zasad filozofji. Poznań, 1929.

Phil 3110.92   Koyré, Alexandre. La philosophie de Jacob Boehme. Thèse. Paris, 1929.

Phil 3110.92.5   Koyré, Alexandre. La philosophie de Jakob Boehme. Paris, 1929.

1929 - cont.

Phil 185.60.10   Kraus, O. Selbstdarstellung. Leipzig, 1929.
Phil 3850.27.95   Kraus, Oskar. Albert Schweitzer. 2. Aufl. Berlin, 1929.
Phil 5250.25   Krejčí, F.V. Základy vědeckého systému psychologie. Praha, 1929.
Phil 3492.35   Kress, Rudolf. Die soziologischen Gedanken Kants in Zusammenhang seiner Philosophie. Berlin, 1929.
Phil 6680.1.25   Kretschmar, F. Die Seherin von Prevorst. Weinsberg, 1929.
Phil 3640.286   Kroekel, F. Europas Selbsbesinnung durch Nietzsche. München, 1929.
Phil 1710.4   Kröner, Franz. Die Anarchie der philosophischen Systeme. Leipzig, 1929.
Phil 1710.5.3   Krutch, Joseph W. The modern temper. N.Y., 1929.
Phil 8620.36   Kühler, Hans. Das Problem der Theodizee. Inaug. Diss. Bonn, 1929.
Phil 9035.59.5   Künkel, Fritz. Einfuhrung in die Charakterkunde auf individualpsychologischer Grundlage. 2. Aufl. Leipzig, 1929.
Phil 9035.58   Künkel, Fritz. Let's be normal! N.Y., 1929.
Phil 9035.59.30   Künkel, Fritz. Vitale Dialektik. Leipzig, 1929.
Phil 3850.18.90   Kürth, Herbert. Das Verhältnis von Ethik und Ästhetik bei Max Scheler. Diss. Leipzig, 1929.
Phil 8411.22   Kuhr, Victor. Ästhetisches Erleben und kunstlerisches Schaffen. Stuttgart, 1929.
Phil 530.20.67   Kunisch, H. Das Wort "Grund" in der Sprache der deutschen Mystik des 14. und 15. Jahrhunderts. Inaug.-Diss. Osnabrück, 1929.
Phil 735.92   Laird, John. The idea of value. Cambridge, Eng., 1929.
Phil 5125.13   Lalande, André. Les théories de l'induction et de l'expérimentation. Paris, 1929.
Phil 5628.55.6   Lama, Friedrich. Therese Neumann; a stigmatist of our days. Milwaukee, 1929.
Phil 1540.16   Landry, Bernard. L'idée de chrétienté chez les scolastiques du XIIIe siècle. Paris, 1929.
Phil 3640.233   Langer, Norbert. Das Problem der Romantik bei Nietzsche. Münster, 1929.
Phil 1116.5   Lasacco, Michele. Introduzione alla storia della filosofia greca e appendice di testi tradotti. Bari, 1929.
Phil 7069.29.50   Lascelles, (pseud.). Beyond, a continuation of the seekers. London, 1929.
Phil 5051.24A   Latta, Robert. The elements of logic. London, 1929.
Phil 9530.32   Laurie, Ossip. L'arrivisme. Paris, 1929.
Phil 2475.1.231   Laurila, K.S. La théorie du comique de M.H. Bergson. Helsinki, 1929.
Phil 7060.2.15   Lavater , L. Of ghostes and spirites walking by nyght. London, 1929.
Phil 2070.127.5   Le Breton, M. La personnalité de William James. Paris, 1929.
Phil 400.79   Leese, Kurt. Philosophie und Theologie im Spätidealismus. Berlin, 1929.
Phil 3552.51.10   Leibniz, Gottfried Wilhelm. Discours de métaphysique. Paris, 1929.
Phil 3552.66.16   Leibniz, Gottfried Wilhelm. La monadologia. Torino, 1929.
Phil 3552.29.25   Leibniz, Gottfried Wilhelm. Opere filosofiche; estratti. Bologna, 1929.
Phil 720.27   Lemaitre, C. L'amour du vrai. Louvain, 1929.
Phil 4060.2.40   Leo Hebraeus. Dialoghi d'amore. Bari, 1929.
Phil 4060.2.42   Leo Hebraeus. Dialoghi d'amore. Heidelberg, 1929.
Phil 2050.193.5   Leroy, André. La critique et la religion chez David Hume. Thèse, Paris, 1929.
Phil 186.70   LeRoy, Édouard. La pensée intuitive. Paris, 1929.
Phil 2520.174   Leroy, Maxime. Descartes le philosophie au masque. Paris, 1929. 2v.
Phil 2045.112   Levi, Adolfo. La filosofia di Thommaso Hobbes. Milano, 1929.
Phil 5761.14.10   Lewin, Kurt. Die Entwicklung des experimentellen Willenspsychologie. Leipzig, 1929.
Phil 342.13A   Lewis, Clarence I. Mind and the world-order. N.Y., 1929.
Phil 186.35.15   Liebert, Arthur. Geist und Welt der Dialektik. Berlin, 1929.
Phil 5821.12   Ligon, Ernest M. A comparative study of certain incentives in the learning of the white rat. Diss. Baltimore, 1929.
Phil 5761.10.15   Lindworsky, J. The training of the will. Milwaukee, 1929.
Phil 8886.50.3   Lippmann, W. A preface to morals. N.Y., 1929.
Phil 8886.50   Lippmann, W. A preface to morals. N.Y., 1929.
Phil 5520.53.2   Lorimer, F. The growth of reason. N.Y., 1929.
Phil 3565.51.50   Lotze, Hermann. Das Dasein der Seele. Leipzig, 1929?
Phil 5722.24   Lubac, Emile. Les niveaux de conscience et d'inconscient et leurs intercommunications. Paris, 1929.
Phil 3493.15   Lubnichi, Naum. Critique des eléments fondamentaux de la doctrine Kantienne. Paris, 1929.
Phil 186.77.5   Ludovici, August. Denkfibel; der Gegensatz als Richtmass. 2e Aufl. München, 1929.
Phil 5051.25   Lünemann, Arthur. Logik der Philosophie. Wien, 1929.
Phil 5051.28   Lukasiewicz, Jan. Elementy logiki matematycznej. Warszawa, 1929.
Phil 6060.27.5   Lungspeer, A.S.L. Lehrbuch der wissenschaftlichen Graphologie. Leipzig, 1929.
Phil 8592.47   McCabe, Joseph. Story of religious controversy. Boston, 1929.
Phil 8610.929.15   MacDonald, G.E. Fifty years of freethought. v.1. pt.1-2. N.Y., 1929-31. 2v.
Phil 8637.17   McDonald, N.T. The dawn beyond the sunset. London, 1929.
Phil 9035.57   McDonough, M.R. The empirical study of character. Diss. Washington, 1929.
Phil 487.6.3   McDougall, William. Modern materialism and emergent evolution. N.Y., 1929.
Phil 8633.1.29   Mackenzie, W.D. Man's consciousness of immortality. Cambridge, 1929.
Phil 1560.10   McKeon, Richard P. Selections from medieval philosophers. N.Y., 1929-1930. 2v.
Phil 2730.35.5   Maine de Biran, Pierre. The influence of habit on the faculty of thinking. Baltimore, 1929.
Phil 5240.30.2   Mairet, Philippe. A.B.C. of Adler's psychology. N.Y., 1929.
Phil 2733.61.7   Malebranche, Nicolas. Conversations chrétiennes. Paris, 1929.
Phil 2733.61.5   Malebranche, Nicolas. Conversatiõns chrétiennes dans lesquelles on justifie la vérité de la religion. Thèse. Paris, 1929.
Phil 5022.1   Marck, Siegfried. Die Dialektik in der Philosophie der Gegenwart. v.1-2. Tübingen, 1929-31.
Phil 3120.8.96   Margolius, Hans. Die Ethic Franz Brentanos. Leipzig, 1929.
Phil 2750.11.71.10   Maritain, Jacques. Three reformers: Luther, Descartes, Rousseau. Paris, 1929?

1929 - cont.

Phil 5252.65   Mathaei, Rupprecht. Das Gestaltproblem. München, 1929.
Phil 6315.2.99   Maylan, Charles E. Freuds tragischer Komplex. 2e Aufl. München, 1929.
Phil 187.88   Meek, Charles. The will to function. Bisley, 1929.
Phil 3625.1.15A   Mendelssohn, Moses. Gesammelte Schriften. v.1-3,7,11,16. Berlin, 1929-32. 6v.
Phil 3625.1.49   Mendelssohn, Moses. Moses Mendelssohn. Berlin, 1929.
Phil 3625.1.53   Mendelssohn, Moses. Moses Mendelssohn. Berlin, 1929.
Phil 9560.23   Mensing, C. An activity analysis of the four cardinal virtues. Diss. Washington, 1929.
Phil 3494.13.20   Messer, A. Kommentar zu Kants ethischen und religionsphilosophischen Hauptschriften. Leipzig, 1929.
Phil 2050.188   Metz, Rudolf. David Hume: Leben und Philosophie. Stuttgart, 1929.
Phil 3780.90   Metzke, Erwin. Karl Rosenkranz und Hegel. Leipzig, 1929.
Phil 8592.35.10   Milburn, R.G. The logic of religious thought. London, 1929.
Phil 530.35.5   Misciattelli, Piero. The mystics of Siena. Cambridge, Eng., 1929.
Phil 293.16   Mitchell, William. Nature and feeling. Adelaide, 1929.
Phil 7082.108   Monteith, Mary E. A book of true dreams. London, 1929.
Phil 8887.21.3   Moore, George Edward. Principia ethica. Cambridge, Eng., 1929.
Phil 8413.5   Moore, T.S. Armour for aphrodite. London, 1929.
Phil 187.92   Moreau, J. Perspectives sur les relativités humaines. 2. ed. Paris, 1929.
Phil 5850.277   Moss, F.A. Applications of psychology. Boston, 1929.
Phil 5222.4   Müller-Freienfels, R. Die Hauptrichtungen der gegenwärtigen Psychologie. Leipzig, 1929.
Phil 187.86.15   Müller-Freienfels, R. Mysteries of the soul. London, 1929.
Phil 187.63.12   Muirhead, J.H. The use of philosophy. Cambridge, 1929.
Phil 5252.63A   Murchison, C.A. The foundations of experimental psychology. Worcester, 1929.
Phil 5203.8A   Murchison, C.A. The psychological register. v.2-3. Worcester, 1929.
Phil 6322.18A   Murphy, Gardiner. An outline of abnormal psychology. N.Y., 1929.
Phil 5222.3   Murphy, Gardner. Historical introduction to modern psychology. N.Y., 1929.
Phil 8667.23   Murry, John M. God, being an introduction to the science of metabiology. London, 1929.
Phil 5850.279.13   Myers, Charles S. Psychological conceptions in other sciences. Oxford, 1929.
Phil 6322.23.5   Myerson, A. The nervous housewife. Boston, 1929.
Phil 7061.10   National Laboratory of Psychical Research, London. Short title catalogue of works...from c.1450 to 1929. London, 1929.
Phil 1050.7.9   Neumark, D. Essays in Jewish philosophy. Vienna, 1929.
Phil 3640.10.15   Nietzsche, Friedrich. Gesammelte Werke. München, 1929-29. 23v.
Phil 8415.3   Odebrecht, R. Gefühl und schöpferische Gestaltung. Berlin, 1929.
Phil 5250.13.80   Odebrecht, Rudolf. Gefühl und Ganzheit. Berlin, 1929.
Phil 7069.29.70   O'Donnell, Elliot. Famous curses. London, 1929.
Phil 3552.288   Olgiati, Francesco. Il significato storico di Leibniz. Milano, 1929.
Phil 6060.33   Olyanova, N. What does your handwriting reveal? N.Y., 1929.
Phil 189.19   Ottaviano, C. Metafisica del concreto. Roma, 1929.
Phil 4115.89   Palhories, F. Gioberti. Paris, 1929.
Phil 9355.9   Park, John Edgar. New horizons. Norton, 1929.
Phil 5255.41   Patrick, G.T.W. What is the mind? N.Y., 1929.
Phil 1190.9   Patrick, Mary M. The Greek sceptics. N.Y., 1929.
Phil 5055.21.5   Pauler, Akás. Logik. Berlin, 1929.
Phil 5520.60   Paulhan, F. La double fonction du langage. Paris, 1929.
Phil 5255.33   Petermann, B. Die Wertheimer-Koffka-Köhlersche Gestalttheorie und das Gestaltproblem. Leipzig, 1929.
Phil 4260.103   Peters, Richard. Der Aufbau der Weltgeschichte bei Giambattista Vico. Stuttgart, 1929.
Phil 9430.33   Petraschek, K.O. Die Rechtsphilosophie des Pessimismus. München, 1929.
Phil 5055.16.5   Pfänder, A. Logik. 2. aufl. Halle, 1929.
Phil 5938.12.5   Phrenological Institution, Brighton. The boy - what will he become? Hove, 1929.
Phil 6025.9   Picard, Max. Das Menschengesicht. 2. Aufl. München, 1929.
Phil 6125.19   Pieper, Gustav. Das geistige Heilverfahren. Magdeburg, 1929.
Phil 6125.21   Pierce, S.W. The layman looks at doctors. N.Y., 1929.
Phil 5255.18.15   Piéron, Henri. Le développment mental et l'intelligence. Paris, 1929.
Phil 5255.18.10   Piéron, Henri. Principles of experimental psychology. London, 1929.
Phil 5225.1A   Pillsbury, W.B. The history of psychology. N.Y., 1929.
Phil 7069.30.25   Piper, Alta L. Life and work of Mrs. Piper. London, 1929.
Phil 9245.46.5   Pitkin, W.B. The psychology of happiness. N.Y., 1929.
Phil 5125.15   Planella Guille, J. El razonamiento inductivo. Barcelona, 1929?
Phil 575.75   Plant, Paul. Die Psychologie der produktiven Persönlichkeit. Stuttgart, 1929.
Phil 190.60   Poortman, J.J. Tweeërlej subjectiviteit. Haarlem, 1929.
Phil 7069.29.100   Pórdrdóttir, Théodóra. Arangur reynslu minnar í dulraenum afnum. Akureyri, 1929.
Phil 3549.7.90   Port, Kurt. Das System der Werte. München, 1929.
Phil 3640.255   Pourtalès, Guy de. Nietzsche en stalie. 15. éd. Paris, 1929.
Phil 8416.28   Prall, D.W. Aesthetic judgment. N.Y., 1929.
Phil 9035.60   Priddle, Oamer D. Procedures in developing character controls through instructions. Thesis. Philadelphia, 1929.
Phil 6325.8.15   Prince, Morton. Clinical and experimental studies in personality. Cambridge, Mass., 1929.
Phil 6325.8.8   Prince, Morton. The unconscious. 2d ed. N.Y., 1929.
Phil 6325.10   Prinzhorn, Hans. Psychotherapie. Leipzig, 1929.
Phil 190.54.10   Przywara, Erich. Ringen der Gegenwart. Augsburg, 1929. 2v.
Phil 5255.36   Psychologische Studien. Festschrift gewidmet Paul Ranschburg. Budapest, 1929.
Phil 530.20.87   Quint, J. Deutsche Mystikertexte des Mittelalters. Bonn, 1929.
Phil 6327.4.6A   Rank, Otto. The trauma of birth. London, 1929.
Phil 6327.4.19   Rank, Otto. Wahrheit und Wirklichkeit. Leipzig, 1929.
Phil 3499.23   Ratke, Heinrich. Systematisches Handlexikon zu Kants Kritik der reinen Vernunft. Leipzig, 1929.
Phil 6127.19   Rees, John R. The health of the mind. Cambridge, Eng., 1929.

1929 - cont.

Phil 348.4.2 — Rehmke, J. Philosophie als Grundwissenschaft. 2. Aufl. Leipzig, 1929.

Phil 5525.39 — Reik, Theodor. Lust und Leid im Witz; sechs psychoanalytische Studien. Wien, 1929.

Phil 6327.12.30 — Reik, Theodor. Der Schrecken und andere psychoanalytische Studien. Wien, 1929.

Phil 1535.36.13 — Reinstadler, S. Elementa philosophiae scholasticae. 13. ed. Friburgi , 1929. 2v.

Phil 5257.44 — Rexroad, Carl N. General psychology for college students. N.Y., 1929.

Phil 192.60.10 — Richet, Charles. The impotence of man. Boston, 1929.

Phil 5190.4.2 — Rickert, H. Zur Lehre von der Definition. 3. Aufl. Tübingen, 1929.

Phil 6127.18 — Riggs, A.F. Intelligent living. Garden City, 1929.

Phil 8842.7 — Riley, Isaac. Men and morals. Garden City, 1929.

Phil 4115.94 — Rinaldi, R. Gioberti e il problema religioso del risorgimento. Firenze, 1929.

Phil 974.3.51 — Rittelmeyer, F. Rudolf Steiner enters my life. London, 1929.

Phil 817.2.1 — Ritter, A.H. Geschichte der Philosophie. v.1-4. Hamburg, 1929-53.

Phil 1122.8 — Rivaud, Albert. Les grands couvants de la pensée antique. Paris, 1929.

Phil 9070.15 — Robert, B.R. The glorious game. N.Y., 1929.

Phil 8610.929 — Robertson, J.M. A history of freethought in the nineteenth century. London, 1929.

Phil 1717.11 — Robinson, D.S. Anthology of recent philosophy. N.Y., 1929.

Phil 5257.27.3 — Robinson, E.S. Readings in general psychology. Chicago, 1929.

Phil 978.51.3 — Rogers, L.W. Elementary theosophy. 3rd ed. Chicago, 1929.

Phil 8418.14 — Rogger, K. Essai sur la valeur expressive de l'art. Dijon, 1929.

VPhil 2475.1.470 — Romanowski, Henryk. Nowa filozofja. Lublin, 1929.

Phil 8597.49 — Ross, John Elliot. Truths to live by. N.Y., 1929.

Phil 3837.12.5 — Roth, Leon. Spinoza. London, 1929.

Phil 3625.1.117 — Rothman, W. Mendelssohn's character and philosophy of religion. n.p., 1929.

Phil 1717.8.3 — Ruggiero, G. de. La filosofia contemporanea. 3a ed. Bari, 1929. 2v.

Phil 192.28.8.5 — Russell, B. Méthode scientifique en philosophie. Paris, 1929.

Phil 192.28.19 — Russell, B. Mysticism and logic. N.Y., 1929.

Phil 8610.927.7 — Russell, Bertrand Russell. Why I am not a Christian. Girard, Kansas, 1929.

Phil 1717.12 — Russell, Leonard. An introduction to philosophy. London, 1929.

Phil 5643.85 — Rutten, F.J.T. Psychologie der waarneming. Diss. Nijmegen, 1929.

Phil 4769.1.95 — Sacke, G. W.S. Solowjews Geschichtsphilosophie. Berlin, 1929.

Phil 5722.26 — Sadler, W.S. The mind at mischief. N.Y., 1929.

Phil 7069.29.105 — Sage, Michel. Frú Piper og Ensk-Vestraena Salarransóknarfjelagid Reykjavik, 1929.

Phil 2050.215 — Salmon, C.V. The central problem of David Hume's philosophy. Halle , 1929.

Phil 349.30 — Salomaa, J.E. The category of relation. Helsinki, 1929.

Phil 1818.6 — Salomaa, J.E. Idealismus undRealismus in der englischen Philosophie der Gegenwart. Helsinki, 1929.

Phil 5258.140 — Sanctis, Sante de. Psicologia sperimental. Roma, 1929-30. 2v.

Phil 6060.18.15 — Saudek, R. Experimentelle Graphologie. Berlin, 1929.

Phil 5258.101 — Scheidemann, Norma Valentine. Experiments in general psychology. Chicago, 1929.

Phil 3850.18.5 — Scheler, Max. Mensch und Geschichte. Zürich, 1929.

Phil 193.127 — Scheler, Max. Philosophische Weltanschauung. Bonn, 1929.

Phil 3425.260 — Schelling-Wollny, Kurt. Hegels Wissenschaft von der Wirklichkeit und ihre Quellen. München, 1929.

Phil 6060.76 — Schermann, Rafael. Die Schrift lügt nicht! Berlin, 1929.

Phil 5058.24.10 — Schiller, F.C.S. Logic for use. London, 1929.

Phil 1718.9.10 — Schjelderup, Harald K. Geschichte der philosophischen Ideen von der Renaissance bis zur Gegenwart. Berlin, 1929.

Phil 3500.41.10 — Schmalenbach, H. Kants Religion. Berlin, 1929.

Phil 9495.130.7 — Schmalhausen, S.D. Why we misbehave. N.Y., 1929.

Phil 6315.2.86 — Schmidt, Wilhelm. Der Ödipus-Komplex der Freudschen Psychoanalyse. Berlin, 1929.

Phil 3415.109 — Schnehen, W. von. Eduard von Hartmann. Stuttgart, 1929.

Phil 6328.15 — Schnell, János. Eredmények a magyar kiaérleti gyógypedagógiai és orvosi psychologia. Budapest, 1929.

Phil 349.20.5 — Schultz, Julius. Die Maschinen-Theorie des Lebens. 2. Aufl. Leipzig, 1929.

Phil 5850.337.9 — Seabury, David. Unmasking our minds. N.Y., 1929.

Phil 3850.26.90 — Semewald, L. Carl Christian Ehrhard Schmid und sein Verhältnis zu Fichte. Inaug. Diss. Leipzig, 1929.

Phil 5938.12 — Severn, J.M. Life story and experiences of a phrenologist. Brighton, Eng., 1929.

Phil 193.134 — Shestov, L. Na vesakh Iova. Parizh, 1929.

Phil 8708.10.9 — Simpson, James Y. Nature. New Haven, 1929.

Phil 4809.498.80 — Šimsa, Jaroslav. Sboruiík ku poctĕ Frantiska Krejciho. Praha, 1929.

Phil 8708.18 — Singer, Charles. Religion and science considered in their historical relations. N.Y., 1929.

Phil 4769.1.101 — Skobtsov, E. Mirosozertsanie Vl. Solov'eva. Paris, 1929.

Phil 193.123 — Smith, Thomas V. Essays in philosophy by 17 Ph.D.'s of University of Chicago. Chicago, 1929.

Phil 193.123.5 — Smith, Thomas V. The philosophic way of life. Chicago, 1929.

Phil 3850.20.84 — Smits, J.P. Filosofies opooedkundige sketse. Amsterdam, 1929.

Phil 8419.48 — Souriau, E. L'avenir de l'esthétique essai sur l'objet d'une science naissante. Paris, 1929.

Phil 8598.60 — Speculum religionis, being essays, presented to C.G. Montefiore. Oxford, 1929.

Phil 8598.83.10 — Sperry, Willard L. Signs of these times. Garden City, N.Y., 1929.

Phil 4080.3.135 — Spirito, Ugo. Benedetto Croce. Roma, 1929.

Phil 7069.29.90 — Spiritual and Ethical Society, New York. How do the dead communicate. n.p., 1929.

Phil 8419.28 — Stace, W.T. The meaning of beauty, a theory of aesthetics. London, 1929.

Phil 1523.7 — Stadelmann, R. Vom Geist des ausgehenden Mittelalters. Halle, 1929.

Phil 8893.79 — Stapledon, W.O. A modern theory of ethics. London, 1929.

Phil 2340.9.90 — Stoll, Marion R. Whewell's philosophy of induction. Diss. Lancaster, Pa., 1929.

Phil 5258.27.10 — Stout, G.F. A manual of psychology. 4th ed. London, 1929.

1929 - cont.

Phil 8598.61 — Strachan, Robert H. The authority of Christian experience. London, 1929.

Phil 8893.80 — Strain, J. The postulates of the moral life. Cambridge, 1929.

Phil 8893.78 — Streeter, Burnett. Moral adventure. N.Y., 1929.

Htn Phil 194.36.4* — Taylor, H.O. Human values and verities. Pt.I. N.Y., 1929.

Phil 194.36.3 — Taylor, H.O. Human values and verities. Pt.I. N.Y., 1929.

Phil 5829.9 — Thomas, Maurice. L'instinct: théories - réalité. Paris, 1929.

Phil 1955.6.01 — Thomas, Milton H. A bibliography of John Dewey. N.Y., 1929.

Phil 6329.5 — Tissi, Silvio. La psicanalisi. Milano, 1929.

Phil 5259.5.50 — Titchener, E.B. Systematic psychology; prolegomena. N.Y., 1929.

Phil 6750.18.15 — Tredgold, A.F. Mental deficiency (Amentia). 5th ed. N.Y., 1929.

Phil 5259.25 — Trejos, J. Resumen de psicología. San José, 1929.

Phil 8701.3.6 — Troels Lund, Troels Frederik. Himmelsbild und Weltanschauung. 5. Aufl. Leipzig, 1929.

Phil 819.8.5 — Troilo, E. Sommario di storia della filosofia. Milano, 1929.

Phil 5259.19.15A — Troland, L.T. The principles of psychology. N.Y., 1929. 3v.

Phil 5259.15.10 — Tumarkin, Anna. Die Methoden der psychologischen Forschung. Leipzig, 1929.

Phil 819.5.7 — Turner, W. History of philosophy. Boston, 1929.

Phil 735.10.5 — Urban, W.M. The intelligible world. London, 1929.

Phil 1526.3 — Vaintrob, M. Istoriia srednevekovoi filosofii. Riga, 1929.

Phil 196.27 — Vasconcelos, J. Tratado de metafisica. Mexico, 1929.

Phil 3625.1.163 — Verland der vereine für Jüdische Geschichte und Literatur in Deutschland. Gedenkbuch für Moses Mendelssohn. Berlin, 1929.

Phil 3425.255 — Volpe, Galvano di. Hegel romantico e mistico (1793-1800). Firenze, 1929.

Phil 3425.257 — Wahl, Jean A. La malheur de la conscience dans la philosophie de Hegel. Paris, 1929.

Phil 1822.3 — Warren, Austin. The Concord school of philosophy. n.p., 1929.

Phil 5262.21.3 — Watson, John B. Psychology from the standpoint of a behaviorist. 3d ed. Philadelphia, 1929.

Phil 8602.39 — Webb, c.C.J. Religion and the thought of today. London, 1929.

Phil 6972.16 — Wechsler, Israel S. The neuroses. Philadelphia, 1929.

Phil 5850.385.28 — Weimer, H. Psychologie der Fehler. 2e Aufl. Leipzig, 1929.

Phil 197.48.10 — Weinhandl, F. Über das aufschliessende Symbol. Berlin, 1929.

Phil 5262.30.5 — Weiss, Albert P. A theoretical basis of human behavior. 2d ed. Columbus, 1929.

Phil 8602.38 — Welby-Gregory, Victoria. Echoes of larger life. London, 1929.

Phil 5262.35 — Wexberg, Erwin. Individual psychology. N.Y., 1929.

Phil 5262.36 — Wheeler, R.H. The science of psychology. N.Y., 1929.

Phil 303.12 — Whitehead, Alfred N. Process and reality. Cambridge, Eng., 1929.

Phil 303.12.3 — Whitehead, Alfred N. Process and reality. N.Y., 1929.

Phil 8897.66 — Whitney, R.E. Morality in the making. N.Y., 1929.

Phil 8599.19.105 — Wieneke, Friedrich. Die Entwicklung des philosophischen Gottesbegriffs bei Ernst Troeltsch. Inaug. Diss. Berlin, 1929.

Phil 930.35 — Wilhelm, R. Chinesische Philosophie. Breslau, 1929.

Phil 1540.17A — Winter, E.K. Die Sozialmetaphysik der Scholastik. Leipzig, 1929.

Phil 5262.9.15 — Woodworth, R.S. Psychology. N.Y., 1929.

Phil 8897.58 — Wright, William K. General introduction to ethics. N.Y., 1929.

Phil 3246.212.5 — Wundt, Max. Fichte-Forschungen. Stuttgart, 1929.

Phil 5330.25 — Yeh, Ling. La psychologie de l'intérêt. Thèse. Lyon, 1929.

Phil 199.3 — Yerington, William. Emerson and beyond. Columbus, Ohio, 1929.

Phil 200.11 — Zehnder, M. Universe and reality. Toronto, 1929.

Phil 3808.158 — Zuccante, G. Osservazioni critiche alla filosofia di Arturo Schopenhauer. Milano, 1929.

193-

Phil 6951.5.52 — American Foundation for Mental Hygiene, Inc. A mind that found itself and its author. N.Y., 193-?

Phil 575.142.10 — Berdiaev, N.A. Ia i mir ob"ektov. Paris, 193-?

Htn Phil 332.4.9* — Bon, F. Die Grundlagen der Logik und Mathematik. n.p., 193-. 2v.

Phil 3821.20 — Brakell Buys, W.R. de V. van. Het Godsbegrip bij Spinoza. Utrecht, 193-?

Phil 3120.30.39.5 — Buber, Martin. Ereignisse und Begegnungen. Berlin, 193-?

Phil 978.76 — Cannon, Alex. The power of karma in relation to destiny. London, 193-?

Phil 5242.53 — Carus, K.G. Vorlesungen über Psychologie. Erlerbach, 193-?

Phil 1540.24 — DeMatteis, F. L'occasionalismo e il suo sviluppo nel pensiero de N. Malebranche. Napoli, 193-?

Phil 978.49.800 — Dornach. Goetheanum. Goetheanum. Dornach, 193-?

Phil 8583.36 — Dynamic religion, a personal experience. N.Y., 193-.

Phil 2225.5.97 — Freeman, Eugene. The categories of Charles Peirce. Diss. Chicago, 193-.

Phil 2520.189 — Garin, Pierre. Thèses cartésiennes et thèses thomistes. Thèse. Bruges, 193-?

Phil 182.1.81 — Halasy-Nagy, J. A filozófia kis tükre. 2. kiad. Budapest, 193-?

Phil 2475.1.300 — Iliev, Alhanasso. Le Bergsonisme. Sofia, 193-?

Phil 4972.5.10 — Korn, Alejandro. Ensayos críticos. Buenos Aires, 193-.

Phil 4710.12 — Losskii, N.O. Dialekticheskii materializm v SSSR. Paris, 193-?

Phil 3585.13.30 — Ludendurff, Mathilde. Statt Heiligenschein oder Hexenzeichen mein Leben. v.2- München, 193- 5v.

Phil 8667.17 — Matthews, W.R. God in Christian experience. N.Y., 193-?

Phil 3640.436 — Mette, H.J. Sachlicher Vorbericht zur Gesamtausgabe der Werke Friedrich Nietzsches. n.p., 193-?

Phil 8887.50.10 — Müller, Johannes. Hemmungen des Lebens. München, 193-?

Phil 3640.54 — Nietzsche, Friedrich. Jenseits von Gut und Böse. Leipzig, 193-?

Phil 3640.34.5 — Nietzsche, Friedrich. Zur Genealogie der Moral. Leipzig, 193-?

Phil 9070.32 — Perlaky, Lajos. A ma életmüvészete. Budapest, 193-?

Phil 7082.72.10 — Roback, Abraham Aaron. The meaning of dreams. n.p., 193-

193- - cont.

Phil 9065.2   Sikken, William. Het compromis als zedelijk vraagstuk. Academie proefachaft. Assen, 193-.

Phil 5627.134.35   Slattery, Sarah L. A year with the Oxford Group. Cambridge, 193-?

Phil 978.49.16   Steiner, R. Knowledge of the higher worlds and its attainment. N.Y., 193-?

Phil 3120.22.80   Thies, Heinz. Die Rolle der Erotik in der männlichen Gesellschaft. Baum, 193-.

Phil 106.1.15   Voltaire, Francois Marie Arouet de. Voltaire's philosophical dictionary. N.Y., 193-.

Phil 5070.20   Wagner, Hans. Elements des Glaubens. Inaug. Diss. München, 193-.

Phil 1130.2.17   Zeller, Eduard. La filosofia dei Greci nel suo sviluppo storico. Firenze, 193-. 2v.

Phil 8900.7   Zen'kovskii, V.V. Dar svobody. Paris, 193-?

Phil 3640.303   Zickendraht, Karl. Sieben Thesen wider den Nietzsche-Geist. Basel, 193-.

1930

Phil 331.7   Aaron, R.I. The nature of knowing. London, 1930.

Phil 1800.2   Adams, George P. Contemporary American philosophy. N.Y., 1930. 2v.

Phil 6310.1.3   Adler, A. Problems of neurosis. London, 1930.

Phil 2250.89   Albeggiani, F. Il sistema filosofico di Josiah Royce. Palermo, 1930.

Phil 4960.220.5   Alberini, Coriolano. Die deutsche Philosophie in Argentinien. Berlin, 1930.

Phil 3850.3.81   Alberty, Gerhard. Gotthilf Samuel Steinbart, 1738-1809. Inaug. Diss. Gotha, 1930.

Phil 6310.4.5   Alexander, Franz G. The psychoanalysis of the total personality. N.Y., 1930.

Phil 2045.113   Alloggio, Sabino. Critica della concezione dello stato in Tommaso Hobbes. Napoli, 1930.

Phil 3850.54.80   Andorn, Hans. Salomon Ludwig Steinheims "Offenbarung nach dem Lehrbegriff der Synagoge". Berlin, 1930.

Phil 2805.213   Antoniadis, S. Pascal traducteur de la Bible. Thèse. Leyde, 1930.

Phil 4600.8   Asfelin, G. Studier Aillägnade Efraim Liljequish. Lund, 1930. 2v.

Phil 6310.3   Aster, E. Die Psychoanalyse. Berlin, 1930.

Phil 2225.7.85A   Ayer, Alfred Jules. The autobiography of a philosopher. Boston, 1930.

Phil 2225.7.87   Ayer, Alfred Jules. The autobiography of a philosopher. Boston, 1930.

Phil 2750.10.90   Baas, George. A critical analysis of the philosophy of Emile Meyerson. Baltimore, 1930.

Phil 1701.18   Bagdasar, N. Filosofia contemporana a istorici. Bucureşti, 1930.

Phil 5241.81   Bailey, A.A. (Mrs.). The soul and its mechanism (the problem of psychology). N.Y., 1930.

Phil 978.74.5   Bailey, A.A. (Mrs.). A treatise on cosmic fire. 2d ed. N.Y., 1930[1925]

Phil 672.156   Baker, John Tull. An historical and critical examination of English space and time theories. Thesis. Bronxville, N.Y., 1930.

Phil 5125.17   Ballantine, William G. The basis of belief, proof by inductive reasoning. N.Y., 1930.

Phil 2262.90   Bandini, L. Shaftesbury; etica e religione, la morale del sentimento. Bari, 1930.

Phil 3450.11.99   Bannes, Joachim. Versuch einer Darstellung und Beurteilung der Grundlagen der Philosophie E. Husserls. Breslau, 1930.

Phil 3450.11.100   Bannes, Joachim. Versuch einer Darstellung und Beurteilung der Grundlagen der Philosophie E. Husserls. Inaug. Diss. Breslau, 1930.

Phil 1701.16   Baratono, Adelchi. Filosofia in margine. Milano, 1930.

Phil 2475.1.235   Basu, P.S. Berkeley and le Vedanta. Montpellier, 1930.

Phil 7069.30.2   Battersby, Henry F.P. Psychic certainties. London, 1930.

Phil 8581.59   Bauer, Joachim M. The modern notion of faith. Diss. Washington, 1930.

Phil 8581.61   Bauhofer, O. Das Metareligiöse. Leipzig, 1930.

Phil 8626.18   Bavan, Edwyn R. The hope of a world to come underlying Judaism and Christianity. London, 1930.

Phil 8826.5   Bayet, Albert. La morale des gaulois. Paris, 1930.

Phil 7069.30   Behr, Hermann. Letters from eternity. N.Y., 1930.

Phil 176.149   Benjamin, Harold. Man, the problem-solver. Boston, 1930.

Phil 1701.6.25   Benn, A.W. History of modern philosophy. London, 1930.

Phil 1865.30.35   Bentham, Jeremy. Deontologia. Torino, 1930.

Phil 1870.73   Berkeley, G. Commonplace book. London, 1930.

Phil 5241.80   Bernhard, E.A. Philosophische und naturwissenschaftliche Grundlagen der Psychologie. Berlin, 1930.

Phil 2477.8.83   Bertrand, F.L. Alfred Binet et son oeuvre. Paris, 1930.

Phil 2477.8.84   Bertrand, F.L. Alfred Binet et son oeuvre. Thèse. Paris, 1930.

Phil 7069.30.1   Besterman, T. Some modern mediums. London, 1930.

Phil 6111.45   Bianchi, L. Foundations of mental health. N.Y., 1930.

Phil 3120.40.35   Bierens de Haan, J.D. De zin van het komische. Leiden, 1930.

Phil 4710.15   Billig, Joseph. Der russische Idealismus der 30er Jahre und seine Überwindung. Inaug. Diss. Berlin, 1930.

Phil 6311.10.15   Birnbaum, Karl. Handwörterbuch der medizinischen Psychologie. Leipzig, 1930.

Phil 2805.219   Bishop, M. Pascal. N.Y., 1930.

Phil 176.69.10   Bloch, Ernst. Spuren. Berlin, 1930.

Phil 3552.123.5   Blondel, Maurice. Une énigme historique, le "vinculum substantiali" d'après Leibniz. 1. éd. Paris, 1930.

Phil 1701.17   Boas, George. Our new ways of thinking. N.Y., 1930.

Phil 3110.31   Böhme, J. De electione gratiae and quaestiones theosophicae. London, 1930.

Phil 5627.129   Bolley, Alphons. Gebetsstimmung und Gebet. Düsseldorf, 1930.

Phil 8876.89   Bonar, J. Moral sense. London, 1930.

Phil 2725.17.90   Bonnet, Georges. La morale de Félix Le Dantec (1869-1917). Thèse. Poitiers, 1930.

Phil 5041.49   Bonnot, Lucien. Logique positive; essai d'un théorie nouvelle de la connaissance. Dijon, 1930.

Phil 3745.6.90   Borne, G. von dem. Karl Christian Plancks Anthropologie auf de Grundlage seiner Logik des reinen Denkens. Inaug. Diss. Winnendens, 1930.

Phil 720.24   Borowne, S.S.S. A pragmatist theory of truth and reality. Thesis. Princeton, 1930.

Phil 5374.51   Bostock, John. The neural energy constant. London, 1930.

Phil 6111.52   Boston Mental Hygiene Survey. Report of the Boston mental hygiene survey. Boston, 1930.

Phil 5465.33   Bouthoul, G. L'invention. Paris, 1930.

1930 - cont.

Phil 6111.48   Bowman, A. Mind and brain in thought and reason process. London, 1930.

Phil 7069.30.2.15   Bozzano, Ernesto. Letteratura d'Oltretomba. Città della Pieve, 1930.

Phil 5627.125   Brabant, F.H. Religion and the mysterious. London, 1930.

Phil 1885.37.15   Bradley, Francis H. Appearance and reality. Oxford, 1930.

Phil 5041.41.5   Brandt, F. Formel logik til brug ved filosofikum. 3e udg. København, 1930.

Phil 6980.132   Bratz, Emil. Humor in der Neurologie und Psychiatrie. Berlin, 1930.

Phil 332.14.10   Brentano, Franz. Wahrheit und Evidenz. Leipzig, 1930.

Phil 5811.16   Bretegnier, Louis. L'activité psychique chez les animaux. Paris, 1930.

Phil 5811.16.5   Bretegnier, Louis. L'activité psychique chez les animaux. Thèse. Toulouse, 1930.

Phil 5241.79   Bridges, J.W. Psychology, normal and abnormal. N.Y., 1930.

Phil 8656.22   Brightman, E.S. The problem of God. N.Y., 1930.

Phil 3110.174   Brinton, H. The mystic will. N.Y., 1930.

Phil 8876.88   Broad, C.D. Five types of ethical theory. London, 1930.

Phil 3640.232   Brock, Werner. Nietzsches Idee der Kultur. Bonn, 1930.

Phil 8581.53.5   Brown, William A. Pathways to certainty. N.Y., 1930.

Phil 4065.50.10   Bruno, Giordano. Cause, principe et unité. Paris, 1930.

Phil 8402.30   Bruyne, Edgar. Esquisse d'une philosphie de l'art. Bruxelles, 1930.

Phil 8626.19   Budgett, H.M. The avenue of beeches. London, 1930.

Phil 1540.20   Buonamici, G. La dottrina della conoscenza secondo Aristotele e la scuola. pt.1. Pisa, 1930.

Phil 8400.14A   Burgum, E.B. The new criticism; an anthology of modern aesthetics. N.Y. , 1930.

Phil 8581.60   Burkart, Anna D. The person in religion. Thesis. Philadelphia, 1930.

Phil 5402.17   Burlton Allen, A.H. Pleasure and instinct. London, 1930.

Phil 5425.49   Cabanés, Auguste. Grands Névropathes. Paris, 1930-31. 3v.

Phil 4215.1.85   Caboara, L. La filosofia del diritto di G.D. Romagnosi. Citta, 1930.

Phil 5465.40   Cadman, S. Parkes. Imagination. N.Y., 1930.

Phil 5242.41   Calabresi, R. La determinazione del presente psichico. Firenze, 1930.

Phil 4080.3.141   Calogero, G. Studi crociani. Rieti, 1930.

Phil 4260.104   Caramella, S. Antologia vichiana. Messina, 1930.

Phil 2477.11.90   Carbonara, C. Léon Brunschvicg. Napoli, 1930.

Phil 4075.79.20A   Cardano, Girolamo. The book of my life. N.Y., 1930.

Phil 5042.22A   Carmichäel, R.D. The logic of discovery. Chicago, 1930.

Phil 510.127.10   Carr, H. Wildon. Cogitans cogitata. Los Angeles, 1930.

Phil 2805.210   Chaix-Ruy, Jules. Le jansénisme; Pascal et Port-Royal. Paris, 1930.

Phil 2805.177.5A   Chevalier, J. Pascal. N.Y., 1930.

Phil 4803.799.85   Chrzanowski, Ignacy. Jan Śniadecki jako nauczyciel narodu. Kraków, 1930.

Phil 5242.43   Clergué, G. Essai de psychologie critique sur la nature première. Thèse. Paris, 1930.

Phil 9342.4.15   Cobbett, W. Advice to young men. London, 1930.

Phil 5242.39.4   Cole, Lawrence W. Factors of human psychology. Boulder, 1930[1935]

Phil 7080.45   Collins, Joseph. Insomnia, how to combat it. N.Y., 1930.

Phil 2493.45.30   Condillac, Étienne Bonnot. Condillac's treatise on the sensations. Los Angeles, 1930.

Phil 70.12   Conference on Individual Psychological Differences. Proceedings, Washington, D.C., May 9-10, 1930. Washington, D.C., 1930.

Phil 7069.25.11.5   Crandon, Le R.G. The Margery mediumship. n.p., 1930.

Phil 5242.40   Crawley, Sumner Lee. Syllabus for the first course in experimental psychology. N.Y., 1930.

Phil 177.35.30   Croce, Benedetto. Etermitá storicità della filosofia. Rieti, 1930.

Phil 978.66   Crump, Basil. Evolution as outlined in the Archaic Eastern records. Peking, 1930.

Phil 1925.65   Cudworth, R. A sermon preached before the House of Commons, March 31, 1647. N.Y., 1930.

Phil 7069.30.4   Cummins, G.D. Paul in Athens (the scripts of Cleophas). London, 1930.

Phil 7069.30.5   Dallas, Helen A. Comrades on the homeward way. Lonodon, 1930.

Phil 6750.223.10   Davies, S.P. Social control of the mentally deficient. N.Y., 1930.

Phil 7054.6.50   Davis, A.J. Introduction to the writings of Andrew J. Davis. Boston, 1930.

Phil 9495.146   Dawson, C. Christianity and sex. London, 1930.

Phil 3801.319   Dekker, Gerbrand J. Die Rückwendung zum Mythos. München, 1930.

Phil 5520.41.3   Delacroix, H. Le langage et la pensée. 2. éd. Paris, 1930.

Phil 1540.40   Dempf, Alois. Metaphysik des Mittelalters. München, 1930.

Phil 575.74   Denison, J.H. The enlargement of personality. N.Y., 1930.

Phil 9495.127   Dennett, M.W. (Mrs.). Who's obscene? N.Y., 1930.

Phil 2520.21.5   Descartes, René. Hauptschriften zur Grundlegung seiner Philosophie. Heidelberg, 1930.

Phil 2520.53.10   Descartes, René. Meditações metafísicas. Coimbra, 1930.

Phil 6313.8.5   Deutsch, Helene. Psychoanalyse der Neurosen. Wien, 1930.

Phil 178.38.35   Dewey, John. Construction and criticism. N.Y., 1930.

Phil 5243.34.15   Dimnet, E. L'art de penser. Paris, 1930.

Phil 178.37.15   Dingler, Hugo. Das System. München, 1930.

Phil 7069.30.6   Dingwall, E.J. Ghosts and spirits in the ancient world. London, 1930.

Phil 178.22.30   Driesch, H. Philosophische Forschungswege. Leipzig, 1930.

Phil 178.22.4.5   Driesch, H. Wirklichkeitslehre. 3e Aufl. Leipzig, 1930.

Phil 5043.27   Dubs, Homer. Rational induction. Chicago, 1930.

Phil 5243.29.10   Dumas, George. Nouveau traité de psychologie. v.1-8. Paris, 1930-36. 7v.

Phil 7150.27.5   Durkheim, E. La suicide. Paris, 1930.

Phil 735.94   Eaton, Howard O. The Austrian theory of value. Norman, 1930.

Phil 8694.4.5   Eddington, Arthur. Science and the unseen world. N.Y., 1930.

Phil 575.76   Ehrlich, Walter. Stufen der Personalität. Halle, 1930.

Phil 3486.14   Eisler, Rudolf. Kant-Lexikon. Berlin, 1930.

Phil 335.5   Elbert, J.W. Étude sur la phénoménologie. Thèse. Nancy, 1930.

Phil 5244.22   Ellis, Willis D. Gestalt psychology and meaning. Berkeley, 1930.

Phil 8584.14   Elving, S. Five books of Joses, a catechism of rational religion. Newllano, La., 1930.

Phil 6940.5   Eugenics Society, London. Family council law in Europe. London, 1930.

Chronological Listing

Phil 8633.1.30   Falconer, Robert A. The idea of immortality. Cambridge, 1930.

Phil 5460.10.2   Faure, Henri. Études sur l'hallucination. Thèse. Paris, 1930. 2v.

Phil 5625.83   Fearing, F. Reflex action. Baltimore, 1930.

Phil 8402.42.5   Fiebig, Ernst. Bobriks Ästhetik; Beiträge zur Lehre des ästhetischen Formalismus. Bonn, 1930.

Phil 2475.1.266   Figueroa, E.L. Bergson, exposición de sus ideas fundamentales. La Plata, 1930.

Phil 310.558   Fingert, B.A. Kratkii uchebnik istoricheskogo materializma. Leningrad, 1930.

Phil 336.7.5   Fischer, L. The structure of thought. London, 1930.

Phil 5245.44   Fisher, R.A. The psychology of desire. Saskatoon, 1930.

Phil 5374.48   Fite, Warner. The living mind. N.Y., 1930.

Phil 2070.84.5   Flournoy, T. Die Philosophie von William James. Tübingen, 1930.

Phil 6420.26   Fogerty, Elsie. Stammering. N.Y., 1930.

Phil 5245.15.10   Foucault, Marcel. Premières leçons de psychologie expérimentale a l'usage des candidats au baccalauréat. Paris, 1930.

Phil 6315.2.51   Freud, Sigmund. Civilization and its discontents. N.Y., 1930.

Htn   Phil 6315.2.64.1*   Freud, Sigmund. Das Unbehagen in der Kultur. Wien, 1930.

Phil 180.48   Freund, Ludwig. Am Ende der Philosophie. München, 1930.

Phil 8406.23   Friche, V.M. Problemy iskusstvovedeniia: sbornik statei. Moskva, 1930.

Phil 7069.30.7   Friedländer, A.A. Telepathie und Hellsehen. Stuttgart, 1930.

Phil 400.61.5   Friedmann, H. Die Welt der Formen. 2e Aufl. München, 1930.

Phil 181.64   Gamertsfelder, Walter Sylvester. Fundamentals of philosophy. N.Y., 1930.

Phil 5216.2   Garrett, Henry E. Great experiments in psychology. N.Y., 1930.

Phil 8881.42.15   Gaultier, Paul. La leçon des moeurs contemporaines. 2e éd. Paris, 1930.

Phil 181.75   Geiger, M. Die Wirklichkeit der Wissenschaften und die Metaphysik. Bonn, 1930.

Phil 4006.2.8   Gentile, G. Storia della filosofia italiani dal Genovesi al Galuppi. 2a ed. Milano, 1930. 2v.

Phil 1540.19   Gessner, Jakob. Die Abstraktionslehre in der Scholastik bis Thomas von Aquin. Inaug.-Diss. Tulda, 1930.

Phil 8696.16   Gibbs, Jessie W. Evolution and Christianity. Memphis, 1930.

Phil 5246.41   Gilliland, A.R. General psychology for professional students. Boston, 1930.

Phil 2520.116.15   Gilson, E. Études sur le rôle de la pensée médiévale dans la formation du système cartésien. Paris, 1930.

Phil 1511.3.15   Gilson, Étienne. Les sources gréco-arabes de l'augustinisme avicennisant. Paris, 1930.

Phil 5627.94.5   Girgensohn, K. Der seelische Aufbau des religiösen Erlebens. 2. Aufl. Gütersloh, 1930.

Phil 181.62   Goldberg, Isaac. Fine art of living. Boston, 1930.

Phil 8831.4   Gore, Charles. Philosophy of the good life. London, 1930.

Phil 7069.30.8   Grant, Isabel. Conversations with the other world. London, 1930.

Phil 1750.130   Grattan, Clinton H. The critique of humanism; a symposium. N.Y., 1930.

Phil 1750.130.5A   Grattan, Clinton H. The critique of humanism. N.Y., 1930.

Phil 8586.38   Grensted, L.W. Philosophical implications of Christianity. Oxford, 1930.

Phil 2880.2.85   Grin, Edmond. Les origines et l'évolution de la pensée de Charles Secrétan. Lausanne, 1930.

Phil 6116.21.5   Groves, E.R. Introduction to mental hygiene. N.Y., 1930.

Phil 8407.5   Grudin, Louis. A primer of aesthetics. N.Y., 1930.

Phil 600.42   Grunicke, Lucia. Der Begriff der Tatsache in der positivistischen Philosophie des 19. Jahrhunderts. Halle, 1930.

Phil 7069.30.8.15   Guénon, R. L'erreur spirite. Paris, 1930.

Phil 3246.217   Guerault, Martèal. L'evolution et la structure de la doctrine de la science chez Fichte. Paris, 1930. 2v.

Phil 3246.217.2   Guerault, Martèal. L'evolution et la structure de la doctrine de la science chez Fichte. Thèse. Strasbourg, 1930. 2 pam.

Phil 5203.6   Gunn, John A. Psyche and Minerva. Melbourne, 1930.

Phil 3006.7   Gurvitch, G. Les tendances actuelles de la philosophie allemande. Photoreproduction. Paris, 1930.

Phil 930.30.10   Hackmann, H. Chinesche wijsgeeren. Amsterdam, 1930. 2v.

Phil 6317.2.8   Hadfield, J.A. Psychology and morals. 8th ed. London, 1930.

Phil 3850.18.100   Hafkesbrink, H. Das Problem des religiösen Gegenstandes bei Max Scheler. Diss. Gütersloh, 1930.

Phil 7150.26   Halbwachs, M. Les causes du suicide. Paris, 1930.

Phil 672.150   Hallett, H.F. Alternitas; a Spinozistic study. Oxford, 1930.

Phil 6317.6.10   Hallingworth, H.L. Abnormal psychology. N.Y., 1930.

Phil 8587.45   Hamburger, Leo. Die Religion in ihrer dogmatischen und ihrer reinen Form. München, 1930.

Phil 5217.1   Hart, Charles A. The Thomistic concept of mental faculty. Diss. Washington, 1930.

Phil 9035.77   Hartshore, H. Studies in the organization of character. N.Y., 1930.

Phil 3425.70.50   Hegel, Georg Wilhelm Friedrich. Eigenhändige Raudhemerkungen zu seiner Rechtsphilosophie. Leipzig, 1930.

Phil 3425.70.10   Hegel, Georg Wilhelm Friedrich. Grundlinien der Philosophie des Rechts. 3. Aufl. Leipzig, 1930.

Phil 3425.12.3   Hegel, Georg Wilhelm Friedrich. Hamann. Stuttgart, 1930.

Phil 3425.60.20   Hegel, Georg Wilhelm Friedrich. Vorlesungen über die Beweise vom Dasein Gottes. Leipzig, 1930.

Phil 960.136   Heimann, B. Studien zur Eigenart indischen Denkens. Tübingen, 1930.

Phil 6957.17.5   Henderson, D.K. A text-book of psychiatry for students and practitioners. 2. ed. London, 1930.

Phil 5817.15.3   Herrick, C. Judson. Brains of rats and men. Chicago, 1930.

Phil 3850.18.95   Herzfeld, Hans. Begriff und Theorie vom Geist bei Max Scheler. Diss. Leipzig, 1930.

Phil 3450.16.10   Heusel, Paul. Kleine Schriften und Vorhäge. Tübingen, 1930.

Phil 7069.30.9   Hinchliffe, Emilie. The return of Captain W.G.R. Hinchliffe. London, 1930.

Phil 6957.28   Hinsie, Leland. The treatment of schizophrenia. Baltimore, 1930.

Phil 3640.237   Hirschhorn, S. Vom Sinn des Tragischen bei Nietzsche. Freiburg, 1930.

Phil 2045.53.10   Hobbes, Thomas. Il leviatano. Messina, 1930.

Phil 2045.26   Hobbes, Thomas. Selections. N.Y., 1930.

Phil 4110.1.85   Hobert, Werner. Metaphysik des Marsilius Ficinus. Inaug. Diss. Koblenz, 1930.

Phil 6677.14   Hodson, Geoffrey. The science of seership. Philadelphia, 1930.

Phil 5247.23.20   Höfler, Alois. Psychologie. 2e Aufl. Wien, 1930.

Phil 182.62.10   Holmes, Edmond. Philosophy without metaphysics. London, 1930.

Phil 5757.16   Hooper, Charles E. The fallacies of fatalism. London, 1930.

Phil 4580.120   Horreüs de Hass, G. Harald Høffding en zijne beteekenis voor godsdienstwipbegeerte en zedeleer. Huister Heide, 1930.

Phil 8662.13   Horton, Walter M. Theism and the modern mood. N.Y., 1930.

Phil 5247.13.4   Huarte de San Juan, J. Examen de ingenios para las sciencias. Madrid, 1930. 2v.

Phil 2050.20.5   Hume, David. Oeuvres philosophiques choisies. Paris, 1930.

Phil 5850.231   Huth, Albert. Exakte Persönlichkeitsforschung. Leipzig, 1930.

Phil 4803.537.80   Information about Professor Wincenty Lutosławski for those who wish to organize his lectures. Wilno, 1930.

Phil 4803.462.50   Ingarden, Roman. Psycho-fizjologiuzna teorja poznania i jejkrytyka. Lwów, 1930.

Phil 8958.2   Inge, W.R. Christian ethics and modern problems. London, 1930.

Phil 5374.49   Ishyam, J.C. Infinity and ego. London, 1930.

Phil 5465.27.4   Jaensch, Erich. Eidetic imagery and typological methods of investigation. London, 1930.

Phil 8589.17   Joad, Cyril E.M. Present and future of religion. London, 1930.

Phil 1955.6.92   John Dewey, the man and his philosophy. Cambridge, 1930.

Phil 525.55.10   Jones, Rufus M. Some exponents of mystical religion. N.Y., 1930.

Phil 5249.20   Joussain, A. Les sentiments et l'intelligence. Paris, 1930.

Phil 5249.13.9   Jung, Carl G. Psychologische Typen. Zürich, 1930.

Phil 2475.1.228   Jurěvičs, Pauls. Le problème de la connaissance dans la philosophie de Bergson. Paris, 1930.

Phil 291.5   Kaiser, Wilhelm. Kosmos und Menschenwesen im Spiegel der platonischen Körper. Basel, 1930.

Phil 8411.18   Kallen, H.M. Indecency and the seven arts, and other adventures of a pragmatist in aesthetics. N.Y., 1930.

Phil 3480.67.10   Kant, Immanuel. Che cosa significa orientarsi nel pensare. Lanciano, 1930.

Phil 3480.32.60   Kant, Immanuel. Critica ratiunii pure. Bucuresti, 1930.

Phil 3480.65.12   Kant, Immanuel. Grundlegung zur Metaphysik der Sitten. Gotha, 1930.

Phil 3480.32.50   Kant, Immanuel. Kantova Kritika čistého rozmysla. Praha, 1930.

Phil 3480.67.75   Kant, Immanuel. Lectures on ethics. London, 1930.

Phil 3480.58.45   Kant, Immanuel. Prolégomènes a toute métaphysique future. Paris, 1930.

Phil 3480.58.70   Kant, Immanuel. Prolehomena to kozhnoï maïbutn'oi metafisyky. L'Viv, 1930.

Phil 8411.14   Kaplan, Leo. Versuch einer Psychologie der Kunst. Baden-Baden, 1930.

Phil 3160.3.91   Kaplan, Simon. Das Geschichtsproblem in der Philosophie Hermann Cohen. Berlin, 1930.

Phil 4769.1.99   Kaschewnikoff, A. Die Geschichtsphilosophie Wladimir Solowjews. Bonn, 1930.

Phil 5645.33.5   Katz, David. Der Aufbau der Farbwelt. 2. Aufl. Leipzig, 1930.

Phil 7069.30.10   Kernaham, C. "Black objects". London, 1930.

Phil 5250.26   King, W.P. Behaviourism; a symposium by Josiah Morse. London, 1930.

Phil 6060.12.20   Klages, Ludwig. Graphologisches lesebuch. Bonn, 1930.

Phil 575.51.20   Klages, Ludwig. Les principes de la caractérologie. Paris, 1930.

Phil 3640.198.5   Klages, Ludwig. Die psychologischen Errungenschaften Nietzsches. 2e Aufl. Leipzig, 1930.

Phil 7084.18   Klein, David Ballin. The experimental production of dreams during hypnosis. Austin, 1930.

Phil 185.43   Knox, H.V. The evolution of truth and other essays. London, 1930.

Phil 8120.5   König, René. Die naturalistische Ästhetik in Frankreich und ihre Auflösung. Leipzig, 1930.

Phil 3120.30.85   Kohn, Hans. Martin Buber. Hellerau, 1930.

Phil 9495.130.10   Kolnai, Aurel. Sexualethik. Paderborn, 1930.

Phil 4803.497.230   Kowalski, Kazimierz Józef. Podstawy filozofji. Guiezano, 1930.

Phil 4809.524.80   Král, Josef. Studie o G.A. Lindnerovi. Bratislava, 1930.

Phil 1710.3.5   Krejčí, F. Filosofie posledních let před válkou. 2. vyd. Praha, 1930.

Phil 978.59.2   Krishnamurti, J. The kingdom of happiness. N.Y., 1930.

Phil 1710.5.5   Krutch, Joseph W. The modern temper. N.Y., 1930.

Phil 978.67   Kuhn, Alvin Boyd. Theosophy. N.Y., 1930.

Phil 2050.190   Kuypers, M.S. Studies in the eighteenth-century background of Hume's empiricism. Minneapolis, 1930.

Phil 342.14   Laird, John. Knowledge, belief and opinion. N.Y., 1930.

Phil 365.31.15   Lalande, André. Les illusions évolutionnistes. Paris, 1930.

Phil 8886.37.5   Lalande, André. Précis raisonné de morale pratique. 3. ed. Paris, 1930.

Phil 292.7   Langdon-Davies, John. Man and his universe. N.Y., 1930.

Phil 186.72   Langer, Mrs. S.K. The practice of philosophy. N.Y., 1930.

Phil 6321.7.5   La Rue, D.W. Mental hygiene. N.Y., 1930.

Phil 3425.108.10   Lasson, G. Einführung in Hegels Religionsphilosophie. Leipzig, 1930.

Htn   Phil 9495.126*   Lawrence, D.H. Pornography and obscenity. N.Y., 1930.

Phil 6321.5.10   Lawrence, David Herbert. Fantasia of the unconscious. N.Y., 1930.

Phil 2805.208   Leavenworth, I. The physics of Pascal. N.Y., 1930.

Phil 5761.16   Leenhardt, Henry. Le déterminisme des lois de la nature et la réalité. Thèse. Montpellier, 1930.

Phil 3552.65.10   Leibniz, Gottfried Wilhelm. The monadology of Leibniz. Los Angeles, 1930.

Phil 186.28.5   Leighton, J.A. The field of philosophy. 4.ed. N.Y., 1930.

Phil 5627.124.5   Leitner, Hans. Psychologie jugendlicher Religiosität innerhalb des deutschen Methodismus. Inaug. Diss. München, 1930.

Phil 5627.124   Leitner, Hans. Psychologie jugendlicher Religiosität innerhalb des deutschen Methodismus. München, 1930.

Phil 5051.26   LeLeu, Louis. La logique; l'art de penser. Paris, 1930.
Phil 8666.11   Le Roy, Edouard. Le problème de Dieu. Paris, 1930.
Phil 9120.162   Le Senne, René. Le devoir. Paris, 1930.
Phil 9558.15   Le Senne, René. Le mensonge et la caractère. Paris, 1930.
Phil 9558.15.2   Le Senne, René. Le mensonge et la caractère. Thèse. Paris, 1930.
Phil 3450.11.97   Levinas, Emmanuel. La théorie de l'institution dans la phénoménologie de Husserl. Paris, 1930.
Phil 3450.11.98   Levinas, Emmanuel. La théorie de l'institution dans la phénoménologie de Husserl. Thèse. Paris, 1930.
Phil 3493.18   Lewan, Axel. Kring Kants "Tugendlehre". Lund, 1930.
Phil 186.48.10   Lighthall, W.D. The person of evolution. Montreal, 1930.
Phil 3493.16   Litt, Theodor. Kant und Herder als Deuter der Geistigen Welt. Leipzig, 1930.
Phil 7069.30.11   Livingston, Marjorie. The new Nuctemeron (The twelve hours of Apollonius of Tyana). London, 1930.
Phil 7069.30.12   Lodge, Oliver Joseph. Conviction of survival. London, 1930.
Phil 7069.30.12.5   Lodge, Oliver Joseph. Phantom walls. N.Y., 1930.
Phil 315.6A   Lovejoy, A.O. The revolt against dualism. Chicago, 1930.
Phil 7069.30.13   Lovejoy, H.T. Talks with the invisible. Sunderland, 1930.
Phil 186.75   Lumbreras, Pedro. Estudios filosóficos. Madrid, 1930.
Phil 5400.79   Lund, Frederick H. Emotions of men. N.Y., 1930.
Phil 9245.45   Lush, Samuel Beryl. Six roads to happiness. N.Y., 1930.
Phil 186.73   Lutosławski, W. The knowledge of reality. Cambridge, 1930.
Phil 812.11   Macedo, Newton de. A luta pela liberdade no pensamento europeu. Coimbra, 1930.
Phil 7069.30.17   MacGregor, Helen. The psychic faculties and their development. London, 1930.
Phil 8413.9   McMahon, Amos. The meaning of art. N.Y., 1930.
Phil 8592.21.5   McTaggart, J.M.E. Some dogmas of religion. London, 1930.
Phil 1712.12   Malisoff, William M. A calendar of doubts and faiths. N.Y., 1930.
Phil 5052.32   Manheim, Ernst. Zur Logik des Konkreten Begriffs. München, 1930.
Phil 2750.11.52   Maritain, Jacques. An introduction to philosophy. London, 1930.
Phil 2475.1.126   Maritain, Jacques. La philosophie Bergsonienne. 2. éd. Paris, 1930.
Phil 8837.11   Markum, Leo. Mrs. Grundy. N.Y., 1930.
Phil 1517.5   Masnovo, Amato. Da Guglielmo d'Auvergne a San Tomaso d'Aquino. Milano, 1930. 2v.
Phil 187.90   Masnovo, Amato. Problemi di metafisica e di criteriologia. Milano, 1930.
Phil 7069.30.14   Matla, J.L.W.P. La solution du mystère de la mort. La Haye, 1930.
Phil 6322.22   Mauerhofer, Hugo. Der schizoid-dämonische Charakter. Leipzig, 1930.
Phil 1712.11   Mellone, S.H. The dawn of modern thought. London, 1930.
Phil 9515.3.90   Melzer, Friso. J.G. Zimmermann's "Einsamkeit". Inaug. Diss. Breslau, 1930.
Phil 6322.19.2   Menninger, Karl Augustus. The human mind. N.Y., 1930.
Phil 6322.19   Menninger, Karl Augustus. The human mind. N.Y., 1930.
Phil 3640.234   Mess, Friedrich. Nietzsche der Gesetzgeber. Leipzig, 1930.
Phil 8080.16   Meumann, Ernst. A estética contemporânea. 3. ed. Coimbia, 1930.
Phil 343.16.15   Meyerson, Émile. Identität und Wirklichkeit. Leipzig, 1930.
Phil 343.16.10   Meyerson, Émile. Identity and reality. London, 1930.
Phil 5850.274   Moede, Walther. Lehrbuch der Psychotechnik. Berlin, 1930.
Phil 8592.45   Montague, W.P. Belief unbound. New Haven, 1930.
Phil 187.87.5   Montalto, F. L'intuizione e la verità di fatto saggio; psicologico-metafisico. 2. ed. Roma, 1930.
Phil 3425.262   Moog, Willy. Hegel und die hegelsche Schule. München, 1930.
Phil 2145.55A   More, Henry. Enchiridion ethicum. N.Y., 1930.
Phil 5822.1.20   Morgan, C.L. The animal mind. N.Y., 1930.
Phil 187.29.5   Morgan, C.L. Mind at the crossways. N.Y., 1930.
Phil 6962.19   Morgenthaler, Walter. Die Pflege der Gemüts- und Geisteskranken. Bern, 1930.
Phil 7069.30.15   Mühl, Anita M. Automatic writing. Dresden, 1930.
Phil 343.18.5   Mukerji, A.C. Thought and reality. Allahabad, 1930.
Phil 1750.164   Munson, G.B. The dilemma of the liberated. N.Y., 1930.
Phil 5222.5A   Murchinson, C.A. A history of psychology in autobiography. Worcester, 1930-36. 4v.
Phil 5222.3.5.2   Murphy, Gardner. An historical introduction to modern psychology. 2. ed. N.Y., 1930.
Phil 812.12   Myślicki, Ignacy. Historja filozofji. Warszawa, 1930.
Phil 3280.87   Nagel, Karl. Das Substanzproblem bei Arnold Geulincx. Inaug. Diss. Köln, 1930.
Phil 5643.93   Nahm, E. Über den Vergleich von Komplexen geometrischen Gebilde und tontfreier Farben. Inaug. Diss. Frankfurt, 1930?
Phil 6963.7   Nathan, M. Manuel élémentaire de psychiatrie. Paris, 1930.
Phil 3425.259   Negri, Enrico de. La nascita della dialettica Hegeliana. Firenza, 1930.
Phil 8888.12   Nevins, W.N. The meaning of the moral life. N.Y., 1930.
Phil 5650.23   New York (City). Noise Abatement Commission. City noise. N.Y., 1930.
Phil 3640.20   Nietzsche, Friedrich. Werke. Leipzig, 1930. 2v.
Phil 344.3   Nink, Caspar. Grundlegung der Erkenntnistheorie. Frankfurt am Main, 1930.
Phil 3495.12   Nink, Caspar. Kommentar zu Kants Kritik der reinen Vernunft. Frankfurt, 1930.
Phil 8888.7.10   Nordau, Max. La biologie de l'éthique. Paris, 1930.
Phil 4215.1.87   Norsa, Achille. Il pensiero filosofico di Giandomenico Romagnosi. Milano, 1930.
Phil 3496.5   Odebrecht, Rudolf. Form und Geist. Berlin, 1930.
Phil 5520.35.3   Ogden, Charles K. The meaning of meaning. 3. ed. N.Y., 1930.
Phil 8416.24   Parkhurst, H.H. Beauty; an interpretation of art and the imaginative life. 1st ed. N.Y., 1930.
Phil 2415.5.10   Parodi, Dominique. Du positivisme à l'idéalisme. Paris, 1930. 2v.
Phil 1158.15.15A   Pater, Walter. Marius the Epicurean. N.Y., 1930.
Phil 5255.38   Paterson, D.G. Physique and intellect. N.Y., 1930.
Phil 5400.45.15   Paulhan, Frédéric. Laws of feeling. London, 1930.
Phil 190.3.7.5   Paulsen, F. Introduction to philosophy. 2. American ed. N.Y., 1930.
Phil 735.95   Pell, Orlie A.H. Value theory andCriticism. Thesis. N.Y., 1930.
Phil 1815.1   Perry, C.M. The Saint Louis movement in philosophy. Norman, 1930.

Phil 2520.176   Petit, Henri. Images; Descartes et Pascal. Paris, 1930.
Phil 5400.81   Petrażycki, L. Wstęp do nauki prawa i moralności. Warszawa, 1930.
Phil 3745.8.5   Pfannwitz, Rudolf. Logos eidos, bios. München, 1930.
Phil 9530.31   Pitkin, Walter B. The psychology of achievement. N.Y., 1930.
Phil 490.4.10   Plekhanov, G.V. Le matérialisme militant (materialismus militans). Paris, 1930.
Phil 3640.235   Podach, Erich F. Nietzsches Zusammenbruch. Heidelberg, 1930.
Phil 2672.91   Pommier, J.J.M. Deux études sur Jouffroy et son temps. Paris, 1930.
Phil 4200.1.30   Pomponazzi, Pietro. Les causes des merveilles de la nature, ou Les enchantements. Paris, 1930.
Phil 8595.28   Potter, Charles F. Humanism; a new religion. N.Y., 1930.
Phil 6965.12   Pottier, Claude. Réflexions sur les troubles du langage dans les psychoses paranoïdes. Thèse. Paris, 1930.
Phil 3640.255.5   Pourtalès, Guy de. Amor fati; Nietzsche in Italien. Freiburg, 1930.
Phil 9245.50.10   Powys, J.C. In defense of sensuality. N.Y., 1930.
Phil 5255.34   Prengowski, P. Le concept, le jugement et l'attention. Paris, 1930.
Phil 7069.30.26   Price, Harry. Rudi Schneider; a scientific example of his mediumship. London, 1930.
Phil 8595.29   Prideaux, Sherburne P.T. Man and his religion. London, 1930.
Phil 7069.30.28   Prince, Walter Franklin. The enchanted boundary;...psychical phenomena 1820-1930. Boston, 1930.
Phil 3497.18   Przywara, Erich. Kant Heute. München, 1930.
Phil 25.33.5A   Psychologies of 1930. Worcester, 1930.
Phil 7069.29.80   Purchas, T.A.R. The spiritual adventures of a business man. 2. ed. London, 1930.
Phil 5460.10   Quercy, Pierre. L'hallucination. Paris, 1930. 2v.
Phil 192.75.5   Radulescu-Motin, C. Puterea sufleteasca. Bucuresti, 1930.
Phil 665.60   Rank, Otto. Seelenglaube und Psychologie. Leipzig, 1930.
Phil 8707.17   Ransom, J.C. God without thunder. N.Y., 1930.
Phil 3837.19   Ratner, J. Spinoza on God. N.Y., 1930.
Phil 3640.239   Rauch, Karl. Nietzsches Wirkung und Erbe. Berlin, 1930.
Phil 5057.28   Reajifo, F.M. Elementos de logica. Bogota, 1930.
Phil 6315.2.115.5   Reik, Theodor. Freud als Kulturkritiker. Mit einem Briefe S. Freuds. Wien, 1930.
Phil 8418.17.5   Reimers, N.A. Le concept du beau; essaie d'une théorie. Paris, 1930.
Phil 5057.23   Reiser, Oliver L. Humanistic logic for the mind in action. N.Y., 1930.
Phil 192.57.5   Renda, Antonio. Valori spirituali e realtà. Messina, 1930.
Phil 2840.70.3   Renouvier, C.B. Les derniers entretiens, recueillis par Louis Prat. Paris, 1930.
Phil 2840.70.5   Renouvier, C.B. As ultimas conversações. Coimbra, 1930.
Phil 5330.26   Reynax. L'attention. Paris, 1930.
Phil 6060.25   Rice, L.G. (Mrs.). Who is your mate? N.Y., 1930.
Phil 525.69   Riley, I.W. The meaning of mysticism. N.Y., 1930.
Phil 817.18   Rintelen, F.J. von. Philosophia perennis. Regensburg, 1930. 2v.
Phil 192.67   Rintelen, Fritz J. von. Philosophia perennis. Regensburg, 1930. 2v.
Phil 8672.30   Ritti, Jean Marie Paul. De la notion de Dieu d'après la méthode sentimentale. Paris, 1930.
Phil 8610.929.5   Robertson, J.M. A history of freethought in the nineteenth century. N.Y., 1930. 2v.
Phil 5057.20.2   Robinson, D.S. The principles of reasoning. 2nd ed. N.Y., 1930.
Phil 8642.3   Rogers, C.F. Immortality. London, 1930?
Phil 8892.46   Ross, W.D. The right and the good. Oxford, 1930.
Phil 192.72.5   Rothacker, E. Einleitung in die Geistwissenschaften. 2e Aufl. Tübingen, 1930.
Phil 192.66   Rothschild, R. The destiny of modern thought. N.Y., 1930.
Phil 348.12   Roux, Antoine. Le problème de la connaissance. Paris, 1930.
Phil 3450.9.85   Rudolf Maria Holzapfel. Basel, 1930.
Phil 9245.43.2   Russell, B.A.W. The conquest of happiness. London, 1930.
Phil 9245.43.1   Russell, B.A.W. The conquest of happiness. N.Y., 1930.
Phil 9245.43A   Russell, B.A.W. The conquest of happiness. N.Y., 1930.
Phil 192.69   Ruyer, R. Esquisse d'une philosophie de structure. Paris, 1930.
Phil 192.69.2   Ruyer, R. Esquisse d'une philosophie de structure. Thèse. Paris, 1930.
Phil 2515.4.94   Ruyer, R. L'humanité de l'avenir, d'après Cournot. Paris, 1930.
Phil 2515.4.95   Ruyer, R. L'humanité de l'avenir, d'après Cournot. Thèse secondaire. Paris, 1930.
Phil 3940.3.30   Saager, Q. Der Winterthurer Naturphilosoph J.H. Ziegler. Winterthur, 1930.
Phil 5409.7   Sack, Max. Die Verzweiflung: eine Untersuchung ihres Wesens und ihrer Entstehung. Inaug. Diss. Kallmünz, 1930.
Phil 735.96   Salomaa, J.E. Studien zur Wertphilosophie. Helsinki, 1930.
Phil 8708.19   Sanford, Hugh W. Science and faith, or The spiritual side of science. N.Y., 1930. 2v.
Phil 193.49.37   Santayana, G. The realm of matter. Book second of Realms of being. N.Y., 1930.
Phil 2418.2   Schelle, Meta. Studien zum französischen Pyrrhomismus. Inaug. Diss. Göttingen, 1930.
Phil 8893.84   Schlick, Moritz. Fragen der Ethik. Wien, 1930.
Phil 6968.23   Schneider, Carl. Die Psychologie der Schizophrenen und ihre Bedeutung für die Klinik der Schizophrenie. Leipzig, 1930.
Phil 5258.102A   Schoen, M. Human nature; a first book in psychology. N.Y., 1930.
Phil 3808.35.10   Schopenhauer, Arthur. Die Welt als Wille und Vorstellung. Berlin, 1930.
Phil 3850.44.3   Schrempf, Christof. Gesammelte Werke. Stuttgart, 1930-40.
Phil 5258.110   Schröder, Paul. Stimmungen und Verstimmungen. Leipzig, 1930.
Phil 8050.40   Schulemann, G. Ästhetik. Breslau, 1930.
Phil 8968.12   Scott, Charles A.A. New Testament ethics. Cambridge, Eng., 1930.
Phil 5258.107   Segond, Joseph. Traité de psychologie. Paris, 1930.
Phil 5425.48   Segoud, Joseph. Le problème du génie. Paris, 1930.
Phil 5228.5   Seifert, Friedrich. Die Wissenschaft von Menschen in der Gegenwart. Leipzig, 1930.
Phil 9035.62   Seiterich, Eugen. Die logische Struktur des Typusbegriffes. Inaug. Diss. Freiburg, 1930.
Phil 8598.63   Selbie, W.B. Religion and life. Cambridge, 1930.

Chronological Listing

1930 - cont.

Phil 6310.1.104 — Selbsterziehung der charakters; Alfred Adler zum 60. geburtstage. Leipzig, 1930.

Phil 2020.85 — Selsam, Howard. T.H. Green. N.Y., 1930.

Phil 2520.177 — Serrurier, C. Descartes leer en leven. 's-Gravenhage, 1930.

Phil 3500.59 — Serrus, C. L'esthétique transcendantale et la science moderne. Paris, 1930.

Phil 8598.62 — Seth Pringle-Pattison, Andrew. Studies in the philosophy of religion. Oxford, 1930.

Phil 5525.35 — Seward, Samuel S. The paradox of the ludicrous. Stanford, 1930.

Phil 2262.59A — Shaftesbury, A.A.C. Letter concerning enthusiasm. Paris, 1930.

Phil 8893.11.17 — Sidgwick, H. The methods of ethics. 7. ed. London, 1930.

Phil 8598.68 — Silver, Abba H. Religion in a changing world. N.Y., 1930.

Phil 7069.30.30.2 — Sinclair, Upton B. Mental radio. N.Y., 1930.

Phil 7069.30.30 — Sinclair, Upton B. Mental radio. N.Y., 1930.

Phil 3838.15 — Siwek, Paul. L'ame et le corps d'après Spinoza. Paris, 1930.

Phil 270.46 — Skilvierwski, S.L. Kausalität. Paderborn, 1930.

Phil 8643.19.10 — Smyth, John P. The gospel of the hereafter. N.Y., 1930.

Phil 193.125 — Söhngen, G. Sein und Gegenstand. Münster, 1930.

Phil 4065.115 — Soliani, B. La filosofia di Giordano Bruno. Firenze, 1930.

Phil 5258.106 — Sollier, Paul. La répression mentale. Paris, 1930.

Phil 8120.2 — Soreil, A. Introduction à l'histoire de l'esthétique. Bruxelles, 1930.

Phil 5465.31 — Spearman, Charles. Creative mind. London, 1930.

Phil 5258.100 — Spencer, Willard Wylie. Our knowledge of other minds. New Haven, 1930.

Phil 3819.45.7A — Spinoza, Benedictus de. Ethics and "De intellectus emendatione". London, 1930.

Phil 3819.33.25 — Spinoza, Benedictus de. L'étique. Paris, 1930. 2v.

Phil 193.31.16 — Spir, A. von. Esquisses de philosophie critique. Paris, 1930.

Phil 400.77 — Spirito, Ugo. L'idealismo italiano e i suoi critici. Firenze, 1930.

Phil 7069.30.32 — Stallard, C.L. Beyond our ken. London, 1930.

Phil 3552.289 — Stammler, G. Leibniz. München, 1930.

Phil 5058.46 — Stebbing, Lizzie S. A modern introduction to logic. London, 1930.

Phil 978.49.195 — Steiner, R. Goethes Geistesart in unseren Schicksalsschweren tagen und die deutsche Kultur. Dornach, 1930.

Phil 978.49.205 — Steiner, R. Das volk Schillers und Fichtes. Dornach, 1930.

Phil 978.49.190 — Steiner, R. Das Weltbild des deutschen Idealismus. Dornach, 1930.

Phil 575.77 — Stern, W. Studien zur Personwissenschaft. I. Leipzig, 1930.

Phil 1135.101 — Stettner, Walter. Die Seelenwanderung bei Griechen und Römern. Inaug. Diss. Stuttgart, 1930.

Phil 193.126 — Stone, Charles G. The social contract of the universe. London, 1930.

Phil 5635.32 — Stopford, J.S.B. Sensation and the sensory pathway. London, 1930.

Phil 5258.27.25 — Stout, G.F. Studies in philosophy and psychology. London, 1930.

Phil 3552.293 — Strahm, Hans. Die "Petites Perceptions" im System von Leibniz. Bern, 1930.

Phil 6128.11.15 — Strong, C.A. Essays on the natural origin of the mind. London, 1930.

Phil 2805.95.10A — Strowski, F. Les pensées de Pascal; étude et analyse. Paris, 1930.

Phil 5058.45 — Swabey, Marie. Logic and nature. N.Y., 1930.

Phil 5258.103 — Szymanski, J.S. Psychologie vom Standpunkt der Abhängigkeit des Erkennens von den Lebensbedürfnissen. Leipzig, 1930.

Phil 194.19.35 — Tarozzi, Giuseppe. L'esistenza e l'anima. Bari, 1930.

Phil 8599.22 — Taylor, Alfred E. Faith of a moralist. London, 1930. 2v.

Phil 1750.22.5 — Taylor, Henry O. Thought and expression in the 16th century. 2. ed. N.Y., 1930. 2v.

Phil 194.16.10 — Thayer, H.D. The Herodian me. Atlantic City, 1930.

Phil 7069.30.35 — Thompson, C.J.S. Mystery and love of apparitions. London, 1930.

Phil 194.40 — Thyssen, Johannes. Die philosophische Methode. Halle, 1930.

Phil 4260.105 — Tommaseo, Niccolo. G.B. Vico. Torino, 1930.

Phil 6536.8 — Tracy, Edward A. The basis of epilepsy. Boston, 1930.

Phil 8674.9 — Trattner, Ernest R. The autobiography of God. N.Y., 1930.

Phil 4073.86 — Treves, Paulo. La filosofia politica di Tommaso Campanella. Bari, 1930.

Phil 5059.18 — Tricot, Jules. Traité de logique formelle. Paris, 1930.

Phil 9035.88 — Troth, D.C. Selected readings in character education. Boston, 1930.

Phil 8895.3 — Urban, W.M. Fundamentals of ethics. N.Y., 1930.

Phil 195.3 — Urtin, Henri. Vers une science du réel. Paris, 1930.

Phil 672.122.5 — Uspenskii, P.D. Tertium organum. 2nd American ed. N.Y., 1930.

Phil 4818.410.80 — Vance, Wilson. René Fülöp-Miller's search for reality. London, 1930.

Phil 4582.4.90 — Vannérus, Allen. Hägerströmstudier. Stockholm, 1930.

Phil 575.73 — Vaughan, Richard M. The significance of personality. N.Y., 1930.

Phil 75.24 — Vaunérus, Allen. Svensk filosofi. Stockholm, 1930.

Phil 352.6 — Vialatoux, J. Le discours et l'intuition. Paris, 1930.

Phil 5400.78 — Volkelt, J. Versuch über Fühlen und Wollen. München, 1930.

Phil 8676.6 — Voronitsyn, I.P. Istoriia ateizma. 3. izd. Moskva, 1930.

Phil 5831.5 — Vues sur la psychologie animale. Paris, 1930.

Phil 5850.385.15 — Wallon, Henri. Principes de psychologie appliquée. Paris, 1930.

Phil 3625.1.129 — Walter, Hermann. Moses Mendelssohn, critic and philosopher. N.Y., 1930.

Phil 5400.82 — Wang, Ging Hsi. Galvanic skin reflex and the measurement of emotions. Canton, China, 1930?

Phil 1127.5A — Warbeke, John M. The searching mind of Greece. N.Y., 1930.

Phil 735.91.5 — Ward, Leo Richard. Philosophy of value. Diss. N.Y., 1930.

Phil 5262.20.7 — Warren, H.C. Elements of human psychology. Boston, 1930.

Phil 5627.62.10 — Waterhouse, Eric S. Psychology and religion. London, 1930.

Phil 5262.21.7 — Watson, John B. Behaviorism. N.Y., 1930.

Phil 575.52.15 — Webb, C.C.J. Our knowledge of one another. London, 1930.

Phil 5645.34 — Weidlich, Karl. Farben und Farben-Empfindung. Stettin, 1930.

1930 - cont.

Phil 353.12 — Weinberg, Siegfried. Erkenntnistheorie. Berlin, 1930.

Phil 7069.30.45 — Wells, Helen. The hidden path. Floral Park, N.Y., 1930. 4 pam.

Phil 5625.81 — Wendt, George R. An analytical study of the conditioned knee-jerk. N.Y., 1930.

Phil 5643.88 — Wentworth, H.A. A quantitative study of achromatic and chromatic sensitivity from censes to periphery of the visual field. Diss. Princeton, 1930.

Phil 5850.385.65 — West, P.V. Psychology for religious and social workers. N.Y., 1930.

Phil 5262.36.5 — Wheeler, R.H. Readings in psychology. N.Y., 1930.

Phil 303.12.5 — Whitehead, Alfred N. Process and reality. N.Y., 1930.

Phil 6332.9 — Whitehead, George. Psycho-analysis and art. London, 1930.

Phil 1822.4A — Wickham, H. The unrealists. N.Y., 1930.

Phil 6132.26 — Williams, Frankwood Earl. Some social aspects of mental hygiene. Philadelphia, 1930.

Phil 5262.38 — Witwicki, W. Psychologja. v.1-2. Lwów, 1930.

Phil 5062.22.12 — Wolf, Abraham. Textbook of logic. N.Y., 1930.

Phil 5262.37 — Wyatt, Horace G. Psychology of intelligence and will. London, 1930.

Phil 2840.94 — Yang, Pao-San. La psychologie de l'intelligence chez Renouvier. Thèse. Paris, 1930.

Phil 5627.122 — Yellowlees, David. Psychology's defence of the faith. London, 1930.

Phil 199.4 — Young, E.L. A philosophy of reality. Manchester, 1930.

Phil 4803.454.85 — Zieleńczyk, Adam. Hoene-Wroński. Warszawa, 1930-?

Phil 3507.8 — Zimmermann, Heinz. Der Befreier; eine Begegnung mit Kant. München, 1930.

1931

Phil 1870.113 — Aaron, Richard I. Locke and Berkeley's commonplace book. Aberdeen, 1931. 2 pam.

Phil 5210.3 — Adams, Grace K. Psychology. N.Y., 1931.

Phil 6310.1.36 — Adler, A. What life should mean to you. Boston, 1931.

Phil 6310.1.35 — Adler, A. What life should mean to you. N.Y., 1931.

Phil 175.37 — Adolph, Heinrich. Personalistische Philosophie. Leipzig, 1931.

Phil 5850.108.5 — Alexander, James. Mastering your own mind. N.Y., 1931.

Phil 9035.61.5 — Allers, Rudolf. Psychology of character. München, 1931.

Phil 5810.6 — Allesch, G.J. von. Zur nichteuklidischen Struktur des Phänomenalen Raumes. Jena, 1931.

Phil 5810.8 — Alm, O.W. The effect of habit interference upon performance in maze learning. Worcester, 1931.

Phil 800.6 — Amato, F. d'. Studi di storia della filosofia. Geneva, 1931.

Phil 8580.17.10 — Ames, Edward S. Humanism. Chicago, 1931.

Phil 6315.2.118 — Andreas-Salomé, L. Mein Dank an Freud; offener Brief an S. Freud zu seinem 75. Geburtstag. Wien, 1931.

Phil 525.75 — Anker-Larsen, Johannes. With the door open, my experience. N.Y., 1931.

Phil 2400.4.5 — Anthologie des philosophes français contemporains. 2e éd. Paris, 1931.

Phil 5750.7 — Aveling, Francis. Personality and will. N.Y., 1931.

Phil 5750.10 — Azzalini, Mario. La necessità del volere e la reattività sociale. Padova, 1931.

Phil 5241.82 — Badley, John H. The will to live. London, 1931.

Phil 176.2.10 — Bäggesen, Jen. Aus J. Bäggesen's Briefwechsel mit K.L. Reinhold. Leipzig, 1931. 2v.

Phil 3640.240A — Baeumler, Alfred. Nietzsche der Philosoph und Politiker. Leipzig, 1931.

Phil 176.3.10 — Bahnsen, J. Das tragische als Weltgesetz und der Humor. Leipzig, 1931.

Phil 176.3.7 — Bahnsen, J. Wie ich Wurde was ich Ward. Leipzig, 1931.

Phil 2280.8.90 — Baillie, J.B. Andrew Seth Pringle-Pattison, 1856-1931. London, 1931.

Phil 1135.28.15 — Bandry, J. Le problème de l'origine et de l'eternité du monde. Thèse. Paris, 1931.

Phil 6311.13 — Barbour, C.E. Sin and the new psychology. London, 1931.

Phil 5241.86.5 — Barrett, J.F. Elements of psychology. 2. ed. Milwaukee, 1931.

Phil 332.15 — Barron, J.T. Elements of epistemology. N.Y., 1931.

Phil 5241.83 — Barthel, Ernst. Erkennen und Denken. München, 1931.

Phil 3483.51 — Bartling, Dirk. De structuur van het aesthetisch a priori bij Kant Proef. Assen, 1931.

Phil 525.70 — Bastide, Roger. Les problèmes de la vie mystique. Paris, 1931.

Phil 8826.5.10 — Bayet, Albert. La morale paienne a l'époque gallo-romaine. Paris, 1931.

Phil 3640.253 — Beckenhaupt, D. Nietzsche und das gegenwärtige Geistesleben. Leipzig, 1931.

Phil 5205.32 — Behavior Research Fund, Chicago. A community's adventure. Chicago, 1931? 5 pam.

Phil 1750.129.5 — Belgion, Montgomery. The human parrot and other essays. London, 1931.

Phil 176.111.25 — Benda, Julien. Essai d'un discours cohérent sur les rapports de Dieu et du monde. Paris, 1931.

Phil 525.63.5 — Bennett, C.A. A philosophical study of mysticism. New Haven, 1931.

Phil 8581.63 — Bennett, Charles A. The dilemma of religious knowledge. New Haven, 1931.

Phil 8876.91 — Berdiaev, N.A. O naznachenii cheloveka. Parizh, 1931.

Phil 7150.34 — Berdiaev, N.A. O samoubiistvie. Paris, 1931.

Phil 5850.535.15 — Bertine, Eleanor. How to interview. N.Y., 1931.

Phil 8951.17 — Birchard, Ford G. Out of the rut, a layman's point of view. Boston, 1931.

Phil 8633.1.31 — Bixler, Julius S. Immortality and the present mood. Cambridge, 1931.

Phil 5649.18 — Bogen, H. Gang und Charakter. Leipzig, 1931.

Phil 2705.84.2 — Boissier, Raymond. La Mettrie. Paris, 1931.

Phil 2705.84.2 — Boissier, Raymond. La Mettrie. Thèse. Paris, 1931.

NEDL Phil 3120.11.90 — Bolland, G.J.P.J. Collegium logicum. 2. druk. Amsterdam, 1931. 2v.

Phil 735.98 — Bommersheim, Paul. Wertrecht und Wertmacht. Berlin, 1931.

Phil 8691.21 — Bond, Walter G. Three things that matter; religion, philosophy, science. London, 1931.

Phil 332.5.10 — Boodin, J.E. A realistic universe. N.Y., 1931.

Phil 1750.126.10 — Bourquin, Constant. Itinéraire de Sirius à Jérusalem. Paris, 1931.

Phil 9035.63 — Boven, William. La science du caractère. Neuchâtel, 1931.

Phil 6111.46 — Bowman, Karl M. Personal problems for men and women. N.Y., 1931.

Phil 58.2.25 — Bradley, Herbert Dennis. An indictment of the present administration of the Society for Psychical Research. London, 1931.

Phil 3640.238 — Brann, H.W. Nietzsche und die Frauen. Leipzig, 1931.

1931 - cont.

Phil 3483.49 — Breysig, Kurt. Der Aufbau der Persönlichkeit von Kant. Stuttgart, 1931.

Phil 5400.83 — Britan, H.H. The affective consciousness. N.Y., 1931.

Phil 530.40.40 — Brouwer, Johan. Psychologie der Spaansche mystiek. Amsterdam, 1931.

Phil 9341.9.20 — Brown, C.R. What is your name? New Haven, 1931.

Phil 5374.55 — Brunschvicg, Léon. De la connaissance de soi. Paris, 1931.

Phil 41.4 — Buenos Aires. Universidad Nacional. Facultad de Filosofia y Letras. Archivos del laboratorio de facultad de filosofia y letras psicologicas. Buenos Aires, 1931.

Phil 6311.14 — Bumke, Oswald. Die Psychoanalyse; eine Kritik. Berlin, 1931.

Phil 176.122.10 — Burke, J.B. The emergence of life. London, 1931.

Phil 176.122 — Burke, J.B. The mystery of life. London, 1931.

Phil 7074.20.6 — Burke, Jane R. Let us in. N.Y., 1931.

Phil 7074.20.5 — Burke, Jane R. Let us in. 1st ed. N.Y., 1931.

Phil 5041.40.5 — Burtt, Edwin Arthur. Principles and problems of right thinking. N.Y., 1931.

Phil 3425.264 — Busse, Martin. Phänomenologie des Geistes und der Staat. Berlin, 1931.

Phil 802.12 — Calcagni, Gaetano. Compendio di storia della filosofia. Arce, 1931. 2v.

Phil 283.10 — Calter, A.C. Cosmologia. Boston, 1931.

Phil 177.86.10 — Camera, Ugo. Problemi filosofici. Roma, 1931. 2 pam.

Phil 645.31.5A — Campbell, Charles A. Scepticism and construction. London, 1931.

Phil 802.13 — Caramella, S. Disegno storico della filosofia. Messina, 1931.

Phil 8582.47 — Caramella, S. Religione, teosofia e filosofia. Messina, 1931.

Phil 1702.6 — Carlini, A. Orientamenti della filosofia conteporanea. Roma, 1931.

Phil 4303.1 — Carreras y Artau, T. Introduccio a la història del pensament filosofic a Catalunya. Barcelona, 1931.

Phil 8400.3A — Carritt, E.F. Philosophies of beauty, from Socrates to R. Bridges. N.Y., 1931.

Phil 333.5.10 — Cassirer, Ernst. Philosophie der symbolischen Formen. Index. Berlin, 1931.

Phil 1850.125 — Catalano, E. Il naturalismo e l'individualismo di F. Bacone. Napoli, 1931.

Phil 6952.25 — Cebold, Luis. Psiquiatria social. Lisboa, 1931.

Phil 8956.8 — Cenicot, Edouard. Institutiones theologiae moralis quas in Collegio Lovaniensi Societatis Jesu. 12. ed. Louvain, 1931.

Phil 4710.55 — Chizhevskii, D. Narysy z istorii filosofii na Ukraïni. Praga, 1931.

Phil 177.101 — Christiansen, Broder. Das Gesicht unserer Zeit. München, 1931.

Phil 8615.15 — Chubb, Percival. On the religious frontier. N.Y., 1931.

Phil 2733.103 — Church, Ralph W. A study in the philosophy of Malebranche. London, 1931.

Phil 8877.71 — Clark, Gordon H. Reading in ethics. N.Y., 1931.

Phil 3640.276 — Cohn, Paul. Um Nietzsches Untergang; Beiträge zum Verständnis des Genies. Hannover, 1931.

Phil 6312.5.10 — Collins, J. The doctor looks at life and death. N.Y., 1931.

Phil 4002.5 — Contri, Siro. La filosofia scolastica in Italia nell'ora presente. Bologna, 1931.

Phil 5042.26 — Conze, E. Der Satz vom Widerspruch. Hamburg, 1931.

Phil 7069.31.5 — Cook, Ellen A.P. The voice triumphant, the revelations of a medium. N.Y., 1931.

Phil 1135.157 — Cornford, F.M. The laws of motion in ancient thought. Cambridge, Eng., 1931.

Phil 9590.9 — Cosgrave, J.O. The academy for souls. N.Y., 1931.

Phil 5042.23.5 — Cotter, Anthony C. Logic and epistemology. 2nd ed. Boston, 1931.

Phil 8692.14 — Cotton, Edward. Has science discovered God? N.Y., 1931.

Phil 477.11 — Coudenhove-Kalergi, R.N. Los von Materialismus! Wien, 1931.

Phil 665.70 — Crawshaw, William H. The indispensable soul. N.Y., 1931.

Phil 4080.3.25 — Croce, Benedetto. Etica e politica. Bari, 1931.

Phil 4080.3.20 — Croce, Benedetto. Punti di orientamento della filosofia moderna. Bari, 1931.

Phil 575.78 — Crutcher, Roberta. Personality and reason. London, 1931.

Phil 7069.31.6 — Dahl, Ludwig. We are here. London, 1931.

Phil 5243.36.12 — Dashiell, J.F. An experimental manual in psychology. Boston, 1931.

Phil 5243.36.15 — Dashiell, J.F. Manual to accompany Fundamentals of general psychology. Boston, 1931.

Phil 5585.55 — Dehove, H. La perception exterieure. Lille, 1931.

Phil 2730.95 — Delbos, Victor. Maine de Biran. Paris, 1931.

Phil 2805.215 — Demahis, E. La pensée politique de Pascal. Thèse. St. Amand, 1931.

Phil 5412.7 — Dembo, Tamara. Der Ärger als dynamisches Problem. Inaug. Diss. Berlin, 1931.

Phil 178.38.40 — Dewey, John. Philosophy and civilization. N.Y., 1931.

Phil 2150.7.95 — Dickinson, G.L. John McTaggart Ellis McTaggart. Cambridge, Eng., 1931.

Phil 5043.29 — Dingler, Hugo. Philosophie der Logik und Arithmetik. München, 1931.

Phil 178.37.7 — Dingler, Hugo. Der Zusammenbruch der Wissenschaft und der Primat der Philosophie. 2e Aufl. München, 1931.

Phil 1145.52 — Dirlmeier, Franz. Filos und Filia im vorhellenistischen Griechentum. Inaug. Diss. München, 1931.

Phil 5243.37 — Dodge, Raymond. Conditions and consequences of human variability. New Haven, 1931.

Phil 5243.37.10 — Dodge, Raymond. The craving for superiority. New Haven, 1931.

Phil 575.84 — Donahue, John. Parenthood and civilization. Boston, 1931.

Phil 5190.4.10.3 — Dubislav, W. Über die Definition. 3. Aufl. Leipzig, 1931.

Phil 5545.65.10 — Dugas, L. Les maladies de la mémoire et de l'imagination. Paris, 1931.

Phil 5425.50 — Durant, William. Adventures in genius. N.Y., 1931.

Phil 5044.6 — Eaton, Ralph M. General logic. N.Y., 1931.

Phil 179.24.5 — Edman, Irwin. The contemporary and his soul. N.Y., 1931.

Phil 8584.15A — Einstein, Albert. Cosmic religion. N.Y., 1931.

Phil 9530.33 — Emmel, Paul W. Experience, or A post-graduate course in life. Philadelphia, 1931.

Phil 89.4 — Encyclopaedisch handboek van het moderne denken. Arnhem, 1931. 2v.

Phil 735.99 — Ennismore, R.G. The values of life. London, 1931.

Phil 1865.175 — Everett, Charles W. The education of Jeremy Bentham. N.Y., 1931.

Phil 180.49 — Faust, August. Der Möglichkeitsgedanke. Heidelberg, 1931-1932. 2v.

1931 - cont.

Phil 180.2.15 — Fawcett, E.D. The Zermatt dialogues. London, 1931.

Phil 7069.31.8 — Firth, Violet M. Spiritualism in the light of occult science. London, 1931.

Phil 3246.260 — Fischer, F. Wohin, gehen wir? Langensalza, 1931.

Phil 3640.236 — Fischer, Hugo. Nietzsche apostata, oder die Philosophie des Argernisses. Erfurt, 1931.

Phil 5850.200 — Fisher, V.E. Dissatisfied worker. N.Y., 1931.

Phil 8406.20.5 — Flaccus, L.W. The spirit and substance of art. N.Y., 1931.

Phil 8125.4 — Flemming, Willi. Der Wandel des deutschen Naturgefühls. Halle, 1931.

Phil 8585.30 — Floyd, William. Our gods on trial. N.Y., 1931.

Phil 3640.231A — Foster, George B. Friedrich Nietzsche. N.Y., 1931.

Phil 5627.126 — Fourrier, Maurice. Une expérience religieuse. Paris, 1931.

Phil 5245.33 — Fox, Charles. Mind and its body. London, 1931.

Phil 6315.2.64 — Freud, Sigmund. Das Unbehagen in der Kultur. Wien, 1931.

Phil 6315.19.10 — Fromm, Erich. Die Entwicklung des Christusdogmas. Wien, 1931.

VPhil 337.29 — Gabryl, Franciszek. Noetyka. Vyd. 2. Lublin, 1931.

Phil 5246.42 — Garnett, Arthur C. The mind in action. London, 1931.

Phil 410.78 — Garofalo, Lydia. Il problema dell'infinito dal rinascimento a Kant. Napoli 1931.

Phil 181.77 — Gehlen, A. Wirklicher und unwirklicher Geist. Leipzig, 1931.

Phil 8407.6.5 — Gentile, G. La filosofia dell'arte. Milano, 1931.

Phil 600.44 — Geymonat, L. Il problema della conoscenza nel positivismo. Torino, 1931.

Phil 3640.250 — Giorgianni, E. Nietzsche. Roma, 1931.

Phil 337.4.5 — Glanvill, Joseph. The vanity of dogmatizing. N.Y., 1931.

Phil 3425.336 — Glockner, Hermann. Hegel und seine Philosophie. Heidelberg, 1931.

Phil 181.63 — Goedewaagen, T. Summa contra metaphysicos. Utrecht, 1931.

Phil 1020.4.20 — Grabmann, M. Der lateinische Awerroismus des 13 Jahrhunderts. München, 1931.

Phil 181.65 — Granberry, John C. Students' prolegomena to philosophy. Ann Arbor, 1931.

Phil 5046.22.10 — Grebe, Wilhelm. Erkennen und Zeit. München, 1931.

Phil 8956.7 — Green, Peter. The problem of right conduct. London, 1931.

Phil 2050.196 — Greig, John Y.T. David Hume. London, 1931.

Phil 8661.11 — Griffths, Rees. God in idea and experience. Edinburgh, 1931.

Phil 585.421 — Groethuysen, Bernhard. Philosophische Anthprologie. München, 1931.

Phil 5756.12 — Groos, Helmut. Die Konsequenzen und Inkonsequenzen des Determinismus. München, 1931.

Phil 960.135 — Grousset, René. Les philosophies indiennes, les systèmes. v.1-2. Paris, 1931.

Phil 181.66 — Grünhut, Ladislaus. Das Wesen und der Wert des Seins. Leipzig, 1931.

Phil 5246.43 — Guillaume, Paul. Psychologie. Paris, 1931.

Phil 974.2.35 — H.P.B. in memory of Helena Petrovna Blavatsky. London, 1931.

Phil 1135.136 — Hack, R.K. God in Greek philosophy. Princeton, 1931.

Phil 92.2 — Hamilton, James A. Englisch-Deutsch für Psychologen. Frankfurt, 1931.

Phil 575.79 — Hamilton, O.P. Dreamers and doers. London, 1931.

Phil 6049.31.2 — Hamon, Louis. Fate in the making; revelations of lifetime. N.Y., 1931.

Phil 630.37 — Harlow, V.E. Bibliography and genetic study of American realism. Oklahoma City, 1931.

Phil 9347.13 — Harris, Erdman. Twenty-one. N.Y., 1931.

Phil 3415.32.15 — Hartmann, Eduard von. Philosophy of the unconcious. N.Y., 1931.

Phil 3415.32.16 — Hartmann, Eduard von. Philosophy of the unconcious. N.Y., 1931.

Phil 182.94 — Hartmann, N. Zum Problem der Realitätsgegebenheit. Berlin, 1931.

Phil 8587.47 — Heard, Gerald. Social substance of religion. London, 1931.

Phil 3425.33.10 — Hegel, Georg Wilhelm Friedrich. Jenenser Realphilosophie. Leipzig, 1931-32. 2v.

Phil 182.93.5 — Heidegger, M. Was ist Metaphysik? Bonn, 1931.

Phil 3640.241 — Hellenbrecht, H. Das Problem der freien Rhythmen mit Bezug auf Nietzsche. Berlin, 1931.

Phil 3640.265 — Hellenbrecht, H. Das Problem der freien Rhythmen mit Bezug auf Nietzsche. Inaug. Diss. Bern, 1931.

Phil 3450.26 — Hellpach, Willy. Zwischen Wittenberg und Rom. Berlin, 1931.

Phil 2515.5.90 — Hess, G. Alain (Émile Chartier) in der Reihe der französischen Moralisten. Inaug.-Diss. Berlin, 1931.

Phil 8697.14 — Hill, Mabel. New men worship. 1. ed. N.Y., 1931.

Phil 5425.51 — Hirsch, N.D.M. Genius and creative intelligence. Cambridge, 1931.

Phil 2055.5.90 — Hobson, John A. L.T. Hobhouse; his life and work. London, 1931.

Phil 5627.127 — Hodge, Alexander. Prayer and its psychology. Thesis. London, 1931.

Phil 4580.66.10 — Høffding, Harald. Le concept d'analogie. Paris, 1931.

Phil 4575.25 — Höijer, B.C.H. Filosofiska föreläsningar, 1806-1812. Lund, 1931.

Phil 6117.31.10 — Hollander, Bernard. Brain, mind and the external signs of intelligence. London, 1931.

Phil 6117.39 — Hollen, Aura May. Consciousness and the purpose. Hollywood, 1931.

Phil 5850.230.11 — Hollingworth, H.L. Vocational psychology and character analysis. N.Y., 1931.

Phil 5247.47A — Holt, Edwin B. Animal drive and the learning process. N.Y., 1931.

Phil 8620.38 — Homo (pseud.). Essais. Le don des langues. Paris, 1931.

Phil 1870.110 — Hone, J.M. Bishop Berkeley. London, 1931.

Phil 182.98 — Horn, E. Der Begriff des Begriffes. Inaug. Diss. München, 1931.

Phil 6317.19 — Howden, R.A. The mind in conflict. London, 1931.

Phil 7069.31.10 — Hunt, H. Ernest. Spiritualism for the enquirer. London, 1931.

Phil 182.67.4 — Husserl, Edmund. Ideas: general introduction to pure phenomenology. London, 1931.

Phil 182.67.5 — Husserl, Edmund. Méditations cartésiennes. Paris, 1931.

Phil 8697.13 — Huxley, Julian S. What dare I think? London, 1931.

Phil 8697.13.5 — Huxley, Julian S. What dare I think? N.Y., 1931.

Phil 8587.46 — Hyde, Laurence. The prospects of humanism. London, 1931.

Phil 6119.10 — Jacobson, Edmund. Progressive relaxation. Chicago, 1931.

Phil 7069.31.20 — Jacoby, Samuel A. The immortality of the soul. Los Angeles, 1931.

1931 - cont.

Phil 630.36   Jaensch, Erich. Vorfragen der Wirklichkeitsphilosophie.
Leipzig, 1931.

Phil 672.152   Jaffé, George. Zwei Dialoge über Raum und Zeit.
Leipzig, 1931.

Phil 6319.9   Jahn, Ernst. Machtwille und Minderwertigkeitsgefuhl.
Berlin, 1931.

Phil 2475.1.263 Jankélévitch, V. Bergson. Paris, 1931.
Phil 5249.6.15   Jastrow, J. Effective thinking. N.Y., 1931.
Phil 2725.19.90 Jolivet, R. A la recherche de Dieu. Paris, 1931.
Phil 2475.1.233 Jolivet, Régis. Essai sur la bergsonisme. Lyon, 1931.
Phil 3009.2   Jones, W.T. Contemporary thought of Germany. N.Y., 1931.
2v.

Phil 7069.31.55 Jónsdóttir, J. Bréf frá Íngu. Winnipeg, 1931.
Phil 5049.18   Jorgenson, J. A treatise of formal logic.
Copenhagen, 1931. 3v.

Phil 8884.22   Joseph, H.W.B. Some problems of ethics. Oxford, 1931.
Phil 5049.9.5   Joseph, Horace William Brindley. An introduction to logic.
2nd rev. ed. Oxford, 1931.

Phil 1885.83   Kagey, Rudolf. The growth of F.H. Bradley's logic.
N.Y., 1931.

Phil 6320.8   Kahn, Eugen. Psychopathic personalities. New Haven, 1931.
Phil 3195.6.99   Katsube, Kenzo. Wilhelm Diltheys Methode der
Lebensphilosophie. Hiroshima, 1931.

Phil 400.80   Keller, Erich. Das Problem des Irrationalen im
wertphilosophischen Idealismus der Gegenwart.
Berlin, 1931.

Phil 185.46   Keyser, Cassius Jackson. Humanism and science.
N.Y., 1931.

Phil 1750.131   King, William Peter. Humanism. Nashville, 1931.
Phil 5330.28   Knowlson, T.S. The secret of concentration. 1st. ed.
N.Y., 1931.

Phil 8120.4   König, René. Die naturalitistische Ästhetik in Frankreich
und ihre Auflösung. Borna, 1931.

Phil 2523.90   Kohler, Oskar. Die Logik des Destutt de Tracy.
Inaug.-Diss. Borna, 1931.

Phil 185.47   Kremer, Josef. Einleitung in die Philosophie. Graz, 1931.
Phil 5425.47.5   Kretschmer, Ernst. The psychology of men of genius.
London, 1931.

Phil 978.59.8   Krishnamurti, J. The song of life. Ommen, 1931.
Phil 3492.37   Krüger, Gerhard. Philosophie und Moral in der Kantischen
Kritik. Tübingen, 1931.

Phil 3010.15   Krueger, Gustav. Die Religion der Goethezeit.
Tübingen, 1931.

Phil 1750.140   Krzesinski, André. Une nouvelle philosophie de
l'immanence. Paris, 1931.

Phil 3425.578   Kuhn, Helmut. Die Kulturfunktion der Kunst. Berlin, 1931.
2v.

Phil 2733.104   Labbas, Lucien. La grace et la liberté dans Malebranche.
Paris, 1931.

Phil 2733.104.15 Labbas, Lucien. La grace et la liberté dans Malebranche.
Thèse. Paris, 1931. 2 pam.

Phil 2733.104.10 Labbas, Lucien. L'idée de science dans Malebranche et son
originalité. Paris, 1931.

Phil 665.62   Laborier-Tradens, A. Le bonheur est en nous-mêmes.
Paris, 1931.

Phil 3493.20   Lachièze-Rey, P. L'idéalisme Kantien. Thèse. Paris, 1931.
Phil 6321.10   Laignel-Lavastine, Maxime. Concentric method in the
diagnosis of psychoneurotics. London, 1931.

Phil 8886.45.10 Laird, John. Morals and western religion. London, 1931.
Phil 2705.45   La Mettrie, Julien Offray de. Un pamphlet médical au
XVIIIe siècle. Thèse. Paris, 1931.

Phil 3640.363   Landry, H. Friedrich Nietzsche. Berlin, 1931.
Phil 5627.131   Lang, Wyatt. A study of conversion. London, 1931.
Phil 5425.44.5   Lange, Wilhelm. Das Genie-Problem; eine Einführung.
München, 1931.

Phil 5425.44.10 Lange, Wilhelm. The problem of genius. London, 1931.
Phil 2280.5.90   Larrabee, H.A. George Santayana. pt.1-2. n.p., 1931.
Phil 4515.100   Larsson, Hans. Minnesteckning över Christopher Jacob
Boström. Stockholm, 1931.

Phil 8666.12   Lattey, Cuthbert. God. London, 1931.
Phil 410.79   Latzin, H. Analysis des Unendlichen im Psychischen und
Physischen. Wien, 1931.

Phil 3493.19   Laupichler, Max. Die Grundzüge der materialen Ethik Kants.
Berlin, 1931.

Phil 3011.3   Lehmann, G. Geschichte der nachkantischen Philosophie.
Berlin, 1931.

Phil 2250.90   Leidecker, K.F. Josiah Royce and Indian thought.
N.Y., 1931.

Phil 2050.193   Leroy, André. La critique et la religion chez David Hume.
Paris, 1931.

Phil 2520.174.5 Leroy, Maxime. Descartes social. Paris, 1931.
Phil 3549.8.130 Lewin, James. Geist und Seele. Berlin, 1931.
Phil 2805.212   Lhermet, J. Pascal et la Bible. Thèse. Paris, 1931?
Phil 7080.42   Lhermitte, J.J. Le sommeil. Paris, 1931.
Phil 3493.17   Liebert, Arthur. Kants Ethik. Berlin, 1931.
Phil 7069.31.25 The light and the word. London, 1931.
Phil 186.87   Lindemann, H.A. Weltgeschehen und Welterkenntnis.
Baden, 1931.

Phil 5403.4.10   Lindner, Gustav. Zahada štěsti. Praha, 1931.
Phil 5251.34.15 Lindworsky, J. Experimental psychology. London, 1931.
Phil 7075.140   Linsert, Richard. Kabale und Liebe. Berlin, 1931.
Phil 8886.50.6   Lippmann, W. A preface to morals. London, 1931.
Phil 8886.50.5   Lippmann, W. A preface to morals. N.Y., 1931.
Phil 186.94A   Living philosophies. N.Y., 1931.
Phil 2115.36.30 Locke, J. Essay concerning human understanding.
Cambridge, 1931.

Phil 2115.36.31* Locke, J. Essay concerning human understanding.
Cambridge, 1931.

Phil 5821.14   Loeser, Johann A. Die Psychologie des Emotionalen.
Berlin, 1931.

Phil 811.7   Losacco, Michele. Lineamenti di storia della filosofia.
Napoli, 1931.

Phil 186.99   Losskii, N.O. Tipy mirovozzrenii. Parizh, 1931.
Phil 6961.14   Lundholm, Helge. The manic-depressive pychosis. Durham,
N.C., 1931.

Phil 186.74   Lunn, A.H.M. The flight from reason. N.Y., 1931.
Phil 186.78   Luquet, G.H. Logique, morale, métaphysique. Paris, 1931.
Phil 7069.31.27 Lyttelton, Edith B. Our superconscious mind.
London, 1931.

Phil 7069.31.28 Lyttelton, Edith B. Our superconscious mind. N.Y., 1931.
Phil 187.96   McDonald, M.F. Brief readings in philosophy.
Brooklyn, 1931.

Phil 6322.14.25 McDougall, W. Psychopathologie funktioneller Störungen.
Leipzig, 1931.

Phil 600.43   McGee, John Edwin. A crusade for humanity. London, 1931.

1931 - cont.

Phil 3808.161   McGill, Vivian J. Schopenhauer; pessimist and pagan.
N.Y., 1931.

Phil 8592.48   Macintosh, D.C. Religious realism. N.Y., 1931.
Phil 293.18   McKaye, James. Dynamic universe. N.Y., 1931.
Phil 187.27.13   Mackenzie, J.S. Cosmic problems. London, 1931.
Phil 187.94   McKerrow, J.C. Novius organum. London, 1931.
Phil 1750.132A   McMahon, Francis E. Humanism of Irving Babbitt. Diss.
Washington, D.C., 1931.

Phil 6022.4.5   Märker, Friedrich. Autokraten und Demokraten.
Erlenbach, 1931.

Phil 6022.4.10   Märker, Friedrich. Typen; Grundlagen der Charakterkunde.
Erlenbach, 1931.

Phil 187.95   Manley, R.M. Synthetic philosophy. Cleveland, Ohio, 1931.
Phil 187.102   Mannarino, G. La ragion d'essere della filosofia.
Catanzaro, 1931.

Phil 3494.36   Marchi, Vittore. La filosofia morale di Emmanuel Kant.
Roma, 1931.

Phil 7069.25.12.5 The "Margery" mediumship. N.Y., 1931.
Phil 2750.11.69 Maritain, Jacques. Reflexions sur l'intelligence et sur sa
vie propre. Paris, 1931?

Phil 5252.64   Marston, W.M. Integrative psychology. London, 1931.
Phil 8615.14.5   Martin, Alfred W. Consolations. N.Y., 1931.
Phil 2805.214   Mauriac, F. Blaise Pascal et sa soeur Jacqueline.
Paris, 1931.

Phil 812.16   Mehring, Franz. Zur Geschichte der Philosophie.
Berlin, 1931?

Phil 6060.28   Menard, Pierre. L'écriture et le subsconsient.
Paris, 1931.

Phil 5525.36   Menon, V.K.K. A theory of laughter. London, 1931.
Phil 5627.95.10 Mensching, Gustav. Die Idee der Sünde. Leipzig, 1931.
Phil 5252.120   Messer, August. Einführung in die Psychologie und die
psychologischen Richtungen der Gegenwart. 2. Aufl.
Leipzig, 1931.

Phil 343.14.10   Meurer, O. Selbsterkenntnis. Berlin, 1931.
Phil 343.16.25   Meyerson, Émile. Du cheminement de la pensée.
Paris, 1931. 3v.

Phil 6315.2.94   Michaëlis, Edgar. Die Menschkeitsproblematik der
Freudschen Psychoanalyse. 2. Aufl. Leipzig, 1931.

Phil 7082.44.1   Miller, Gustavus Hindman. Ten thousand dreams interpreted;
or, What's in a dream. Chicago, 1931.

Phil 8962.9   Miltner, C.C. The elements of ethics. N.Y., 1931.
Phil 7069.11.48 Moberly, C.A.E. An adventure. 4th ed. London, 1931.
Phil 5401.11   Mones, L. Why be afraid? Boston, 1931.
Phil 5722.23.10 Montmasson, J.M. Invention and the unconscious.
London, 1931.

Phil 8637.15   Moore, Clifford Herschel. Ancient beliefs in the
immortality of the soul. N.Y., 1931.

Phil 5100.5   Moore, William H. Frequent fallacies. Boston, 1931.
Phil 8125.12.5   Moos, Paul. Die deutsche Asthetik der Gegenwart.
Berlin, 1931.

Phil 5252.38.10 Müller-Freienfels, R. Tagebuch eines Psychologen.
Leipzig, 1931.

Phil 400.78   Muirhead, J.H. The Platonic traditions in Anglo-Saxon
philosophy. London, 1931.

Phil 3425.266   Nadler, Käte. Der dialektische Widerspruch in Hegels
Philosophie und das Paradoxon des Christentums.
Leipzig, 1931.

Phil 315.7   Nahile, Emilia. Il dualismo nella filosofia.
Napoli, 1931.

Phil 6323.3   Nathan, Marcel. Les malades dits imaginaires.
Paris, 1931.

Phil 8703.2.5   Needham, Joseph. The great amphibium; four lectures.
London, 1931.

Phil 9035.67   Neumann, Johannes. Die Entwicklung zur sittlichen
Persönlichkeit. Gütersloh, 1931.

Phil 3808.192   Nietzsche, F.W. Schopenhauer als Erzieher. Leipzig, 1931.
Phil 3640.57A   Nietzsche, Friedrich. L'antéchrist. Paris, 1931.
Phil 3640.77.15.5 Nietzsche, Friedrich. Ecce homo. Leipzig, 1931.
Phil 3640.52.5   Nietzsche, Friedrich. Der Fall Wagner. Leipzig, 1931.
Phil 3640.58.5   Nietzsche, Friedrich. Die Geburt der Tragödie aus dem
Geiste der Musik. Leipzig, 1931.

Phil 3640.22.8   Nietzsche, Friedrich. Nietzsche's Philosophie in
Selbstzeugnissen. Leipzig, 1931. 4v.

Phil 3640.22   Nietzsche, Friedrich. Nietzsche's Werke. v.2-4.
Leipzig, 1931. 3v.

Phil 3640.63   Nietzsche, Friedrich. Die Philosophie im tragischen
Zeitalter der Griechen. Leipzig, 1931.

Phil 3640.17.10 Nietzsche, Friedrich. Die Unschuld des Werdens. v.1-2.
Leipzig, 1931.

Phil 3640.19   Nietzsche, Friedrich. Volks-Nietzsche. Berlin, 1931.
4v.

Phil 3640.63.10 Nietzsche, Friedrich. Vom Nietzen un Nachteil der Historie
für das Leben. Leipzig, 1931.

Phil 3640.17   Nietzsche, Friedrich. Werke. v.1-11. Leipzig, 1931-59.
12v.

Phil 3425.265A   Nink, Caspar. Kommentar zu den grundlegenden Abschnitten
von Hegels Phänomenologie des Geistes. Regensburg, 1931.

Phil 530.20.86   Oehl, W. Deutsche Mystikerbriefe. München, 1931.
Phil 5401.13.10 Oliver, John R. Fear. N.Y., 1931.
Phil 8594.13   Oman, John. The natural and the supernatural. N.Y., 1931.
Phil 2805.211   Orliac, Jehanne d'. Le coeur humain, inhumain, surhumain
de Blaise Pascal. Paris, 1931.

Phil 189.22.5   Ortega y Gasset, José. The modern theme. London, 1931.
Phil 189.21.3   Overstreet, H.A. The enduring guest. N.Y., 1931.
Phil 735.97   Parker, DeWitt H. Human values. N.Y., 1931.
Phil 5627.231.2 Pauls, Theodor. Pietismus. 2. Aufl. Frankfurt, 1931.
Phil 9400.6   Peabody, F.G. The privileges of old age. Cambridge, 1931.
Phil 6325.11   Peck, Martin W. The meaning of psychoanalysis.
N.Y., 1931.

Phil 2225.5.10A Peirce, C.S. Collected papers. Cambridge, 1931. 8v.
Phil 190.18.15A Perry, R.B. A defence of philosophy. Cambridge, 1931.
Phil 5286.15   Petermann, Bruno. Das Gestaltproblem in der Psychologie im
Lichte analytischer Besimmung. Leipzig, 1931.

Phil 5068.92   Petzäll, Ake. Logistischer Positivismus. Göteborg, 1931.
Phil 6025.9.5   Picard, Max. The human face. London, 1931.
Phil 2415.7   Pickman, Edward M. Collapse of the scholastic hierarchy in
17th century France. Boston, 1931.

Phil 7082.64.5   Pierce, Frederick. Dreams and personality. N.Y., 1931.
Phil 5825.8   Pitt, Frances. The intelligence of animals. London, 1931.
Phil 190.53   Planck, Max. Positivismus und reale Aussenwelt.
Leipzig, 1931.

Phil 490.4.10.12 Plekhanov, G.V. Materializmus militans (voinstvuiushchii
materializm). Izd. 2. Moskva, 1931.

Phil 3640.235.10 Podach, Erich F. L'effondrement de Nietzsche. 4e éd.
Photoreproduction. Paris, 1931.

1931 - cont.

Phil 672.154 — Poirier, René. Essai sur quelques caractères des notions d'espace et de temps. Thèse. Paris, 1931.

Phil 5125.16 — Poirier, René. Remarques sur la probabilité de inductions. Thèse. Paris, 1931.

Phil 2725.2.97 — Poisson, Jacques. Le romantisme social de Lamennais. Thèse. Paris, 1931.

Phil 4762.1.90 — Polanowska, Fejga. Losskij's erkenntnistheoretischer Intuitionismus. Inaug. Diss. Berlin, 1931.

Phil 9245.47 — Powys, Llwelyn. Impassioned day. London, 1931.

Phil 190.52 — Pratt, James B. Adventures in philosophy and religion. N.Y., 1931.

Phil 7069.31.31 — Prince, Walter Franklin. Human experiences. Boston, 1931.

Phil 6060.29 — Pulver, Max. Symbolik der Handschrift. Zürich, 1931.

Phil 8596.2 — Quick, O.C. Philosophy and the cross. London, 1931.

Phil 5257.62 — Ramus, Carl. Behind the scenes with ourselves. N.Y., 1931.

Phil 5257.45 — Rattray, Robert F. An outline of genetic psychology according to the theory of inherited mind. London, 1931.

Phil 8597.36.5 — Raven, Charles E. Jesus and the gospel of love. London, 1931.

Phil 3235.112 — Rawidowicz, Simon. Ludwig Feuerbachs Philosophie. Berlin, 1931.

Phil 3850.27.90 — Regester, John D. Albert Schweitzer. N.Y., 1931.

Phil 298.7 — Reichenbach, Hans. Ziele und Wege der heutigen Naturphilosophie. Leipzig, 1931.

Phil 8418.21 — Reid, L.A. A study in aesthetics. London, 1931.

Phil 6327.12.5 — Reik, Theodor. Ritual; psycho-analytical studies. London, 1931.

Phil 192.71 — Reiner, Hans. Phänomenologie und menschliche Existenz. Halle, 1931.

Phil 192.70 — Reininger, Robert. Metaphysik der Wirklichkeit. Wien, 1931.

Phil 3425.304 — Revue de Métaphysique et de Morale. Études sur Hegel. Paris, 1931.

Phil 8520.15 — Richter, Johannes. Die Religionsphilosophie der fichteschen Schule. Berlin, 1931.

Phil 4080.3.137 — Righi, Gaetano. Il Croce interprete del Vico. Bologna, 1931.

Phil 575.57.10 — Roback, A.A. Personality, the crux of social intercourse. Cambridge, Mass., 1931.

Phil 575.57.11 — Roback, A.A. Personality. London, 1931.

Phil 974.2.30 — Robert, C.E.B. The mysterious Madame Helena P. Blavatsky. N.Y., 1931.

Phil 1717.11.5 — Robinson, D.S. Anthology of recent philosophy. N.Y., 1931.

Phil 5062.30.15 — Robinson, Richard. The province of logic; an interpretation of certain parts of Cook Wilson's "Statement and inference". London, 1931.

Phil 8707.15 — Rodger, James George. Passages from the scientist's Bible. Washington, 1931.

Phil 6967.13 — Ruiz Maya, M. Psiquiatria penal y civil. Madrid, 1931.

Phil 193.129.5 — Sainsbury, Geoffrey. The theory of polarity. London, 1931.

Phil 672.153 — Sander, Franz. Die Entwicklung der Raumtheorien in der 2. Hälfte des 17. Jahrhunderts. Inaug.-Diss. Halle, 1931.

Phil 3018.17 — Sannwald, A. Der Begriff der Dialektik und die Anthropologie. München, 1931.

Phil 193.49.40A — Santayana, G. The genteel tradition at bay. N.Y., 1931.

Phil 5258.108 — Scheerer, M. Die Lehre von der Gestalt. Berlin, 1931.

Phil 5258.109 — Schein, Josef. Zentralistische Organisation und Seelenleben. München, 1931. 2v.

Phil 5058.47 — Schingnitz, Werner. Prolegomenon zu einer Logik als Lehre von der Vergegrifflichten Gegenständlichkeit. Leipzig, 1931.

Phil 3805.55 — Schleiermacher, Friedrich. Asthetik. Berlin, 1931.

Phil 5520.55 — Schölkopf, H. Sinn; eine philosophische Untersuchung. Inaug. Diss. Metzingen, 1931.

Phil 5028.2 — Scholz, Heinrich. Geschichte der Logik. Berlin, 1931.

Phil 3808.22.20 — Schopenhauer, Arthur. Works. Abridged. N.Y., 1931.

Phil 3018.15 — Schwarz, H. Deutsche systematische Philosophie nach ihren Gestaltern. Berlin, 1931-34. 2v.

Phil 8708.20 — Science and religion; a symposium. N.Y., 1931.

Phil 8708.24 — Science and religion. London, 1931.

Phil 9358.17 — Seabury, Samuel. Self government and the power of an ideal. n.p., 1931.

Phil 103.4 — Semprini, G. Piccolo dizionario di coltura filosofica e scientifica. Milano, 1931.

Phil 5585.57 — Seward, John P. The effect of practice on the visual perception of form. N.Y., 1931.

Phil 8419.17 — Sewell, Arthur. The physiology of beauty. London, 1931.

Phil 3425.281 — Sfard, D. Du role de l'idée de contradiction chez Hegel. Thèse. Nancy, 1931.

Phil 5828.17 — Shuey, A.M. The limits of learning ability in kittens. Worcester, 1931.

Phil 3425.280 — Siegel, Carl. Georg Wilhelm Friedrich Hegel. Graz, 1931.

Phil 6128.45 — Simmons, D.A. Cosmicology. N.Y., 1931?

Phil 5477.5 — Skaggs, Ernest B. Major forms of inhibition in man. Chicago, 1931.

Phil 525.72 — Smith, Margaret. Studies in early mysticism in the Near and Middle East. London, 1931.

Phil 8673.12 — Smith, N.K. Is divine existence credible? London, 1931.

Phil 8893.81 — Sockman, R.W. Morals of tomorrow. N.Y., 1931.

Phil 193.135 — Somogyi, Jozsef. As ideák problémája. Budapest, 1931.

Phil 193.88.5 — Spalding, K.J. Talks on philosophy. Oxford, 1931.

Phil 5465.31.5 — Spearman, Charles. Creative mind. Cambridge, Eng., 1931.

Phil 400.83 — Stefunini, L. Idealismo cristiano. Padova, 1931?

Phil 978.49.120 — Steiner, R. Eurhythmy as visible speech. London, 1931.

Phil 1123.7 — Stenzel, Julius. Metaphysik des Altertums. München, 1931.

Phil 8893.85 — Stone, M.A. The philosophy of indifference. Providence, 1931.

Phil 193.128 — Stout, G.F. Mind and matter. N.Y., 1931.

Phil 5258.104 — Strecker, Edward A. Discovering ourselves. N.Y., 1931.

Phil 9358.16 — Strickland, C.J. Stray thoughts. Charlotte, N.C., 1931.

Phil 5330.27 — Strong, E.K. Change of interest with age. Palo Alto, 1931.

Phil 349.31 — Stürmann, J.F. Untersuchungen über das Wesen der philosophischen Erkenntnis. Inaug. Diss. Münster in Westfalen, 1931.

Phil 5627.130.10 — Swarts, G. Le banc des pénitents. Paris, 1931.

Phil 5627.130.12 — Swarts, G. Le banc des pénitents. Thèse. Paris, 1931.

Phil 5627.130 — Swarts, G. Salut par la foi et conversion brusque. Paris, 1931.

Phil 5627.130.2 — Swarts, G. Salut par la foi et conversion brusque. Thèse. Paris, 1931.

Phil 5258.105 — Swift, Edgar J. The jungle of the mind. N.Y., 1931.

1931 - cont.

Phil 5850.349 — Symonds, P.M. Diagnosing personality and conduct. N.Y., 1931.

Phil 7069.31.37 — Talks with spirit friends, bench and bar. London, 1931.

Phil 6969.7 — Targowla, René. L'intuition délirante. Paris, 1931.

Phil 819.9 — Tatarkiewiaz, W. Historja filozafji. Lwów, 1931. 2v.

Phil 8709.13 — Taylor, Robert O.P. Universe within us. N.Y., 1931.

Phil 8599.25 — Teichmüller, Gustav. G. Teichmüllers Philosophie des Christentums von E. Tennmann. Tartu, 1931.

Phil 2480.81 — Tencer, Marie. La psychophysiologie de Cabanis. Thèse. Toulouse, 1931.

Phil 7140.11.5 — Tietjens, E. Desuggestion for the attainment of health. London, 1931.

Phil 8420.14.5 — Tilgher, A. Estetica; teoria generale dell'attività artistica. Roma, 1931.

Phil 8420.14 — Tilgher, A. Primi scritti di estetica. Roma, 1931.

Phil 494.1 — Townsend, H.G. Studies in philosophical naturalism. Eugene, 1931.

Phil 6400.33 — Travis, Lee E. Speech pathology. N.Y., 1931.

Phil 7069.31.40 — Trespioli, Gino. "Ultrafamia", esegesi della fenomenologia intellettuale dello spiritismo moderno. Milano, 1931.

Phil 5259.26 — Tripp, Erich. Untersuchungen zur Rechtspsychologie des Individuums. Leipzig, 1931.

Phil 5627.128 — Trout, David McC. Religious behavior. N.Y., 1931.

Phil 8620.37 — Tsanoff, R.A. The nature of evil. N.Y., 1931.

Phil 8674.8.15 — Turner, J.E. The revelation of deity. London, 1931.

Phil 3805.173 — Ungern-Sternberg, Arthur Freiherr von. Freiheit und Wirklichkeit. Gotha, 1931.

Phil 672.122.9 — Uspenskii, P.D. Tertium organum. Berlin, 1931.

Phil 5261.17 — Valentine, Willard Lee. Readings in experimental psychology. 1. ed. N.Y., 1931.

Phil 4120.6.95 — Varano, F.S. Vincenzo de Grazia. Napoli, 1931.

Phil 5115.1.5 — Varano, Francesco S. L'ipotesi nella filosofia di Ernesto Naville. Gubbio, 1931.

Phil 196.8.20 — Varisco, B. Lines de filosofia critica. 2a ed. Roma, 1931.

Phil 2490.120 — Varney, M.M. L'influence des femmes sur Auguste Comte. Thèse. Paris, 1931.

Phil 5401.20F — Vassos, John. Phobia. N.Y., 1931.

Phil 196.24 — Veale, César. Mas espiritu, meuos materia. Buenos Aires, 1931.

Phil 5831.6 — Verlaine, Louis. L'âme des bêtes. Paris, 1931.

Phil 3841.4 — Vloemans, Antoon. Spinoza, de mensch, het leven en het werk. 's Gravenhage, 1931.

Phil 2050.201 — Volpe, Galvano della. La teoria delle passioni di Davide Hume. Bologna, 1931.

Phil 8896.15 — Vysheslavtsev, V. Etika preobrazhennago erosa. Paris, 1931.

Phil 5062.32 — Walcott, G.D. An elementary logic. N.Y., 1931.

Phil 1722.6 — Ward, Charles H. Builders of delusion. Indianapolis, 1931.

Phil 8972.11 — Ward, H.F. Which way religion? N.Y., 1931.

Phil 5832.13.10 — Warden, C.J. Animal motivation. N.Y., 1931.

Phil 2655.2.85 — Warrain, F. L'oeuvre psychobiophysique. Paris, 1931.

Phil 3842.12 — Waton, Harry. The kabbalah and Spinoza's philosophy. N.Y., 1931-32. 2v.

Phil 9495.133.5 — Weatherhead, L.D. Mastery of sex through psychology and religion. 2d ed. London, 1931.

Phil 5850.385.40 — Webb, Ewing T. Strategy in handling people. Chicago, 1931.

Phil 1145.79 — Wehrli, Fritz. Lade biosas. Studien zur ältesten Ethik bei den Griechen. Leipzig, 1931.

Phil 665.59.5 — Weidenbach, H. Die Mechanik der Seele. 3e Aufl. Mannheim, 1931.

Phil 8602.38.10 — Welby-Gregory, Victoria. Other dimensions. London, 1931.

Phil 5504.38A — Wellek, René. Immanuel Kant in England, 1793-1838. Princeton, 1931.

Phil 7069.31.50 — Wells, Helen B. Law governing mediumship. N.Y., 1931.

Phil 6750.231 — Wembridge, Eleanor H.R. Life among the lowbrows. Boston, 1931.

Phil 8847.5 — Wentscher, Max. Geschichte der Ethik. Berlin, 1931.

Phil 5262.35.5 — Wexberg, Erwin. Individualpsychologie. 2. Aufl. Leipzig, 1931.

Phil 9495.132 — Wexberg, Erwin. The psychology of sex. N.Y., 1931.

Phil 197.19.10 — Whittaker, T. Prolegomena to a new metaphysic. Cambridge, Eng., 1931.

Phil 7069.31.32 — Whymant, A.N.J. Psychic adventures in New York. Boston, 1931.

Phil 8897.60 — Wiedling, Hans. Die Wirklichkeit der Ethik. Leipzig, 1931.

Phil 974.4.13 — Williams, Gertrude M. The passionate pilgrim. N.Y., 1931.

Phil 8677.14 — Willink, M.D.R. The holy and the living God. London, 1931.

Phil 3925.7.85 — Wirth, Wilhelm. Wie ich zur Philosophie und Psychologie Ram. Leipzig, 1931.

Phil 6315.2.88.3 — Wittels, Fritz. Freud and his time. N.Y., 1931.

Phil 6315.2.88 — Wittels, Fritz. Freud and his time. N.Y., 1931.

Phil 9070.6 — Wolfe, W.B. How to be happy though human. N.Y., 1931.

Phil 7082.84 — Wood, Clement. Dreams. N.Y., 1931.

Phil 5232.5A — Woodworth, R.S. Contemporary schools of psychology. N.Y., 1931.

Phil 6132.4.13 — Worcester, Elwood. Body, mind and spirit. Boston, 1931.

Phil 5400.80 — Wreschner, Arthur. Das Gefühl. Leipzig, 1931.

Phil 822.9 — Wundt, Max. Geschichte der Metaphysik. Berlin, 1931.

Phil 4815.672.80 — Wurmb, Albert. Darstellung und Kritik der logischen Grundbegriffe der Naturphilosophie Melchior Palagyis. Weisswasser, 1931.

Phil 5832.14 — Wyman, Eva May. On instinct and intelligence. Thesis. Philadelphia, 1931.

Phil 9070.25 — Young, Vashni. A fortune to share. Indianapolis, 1931.

Phil 199.5 — Yura, T. Geisteswissenschaft und Willensgesetz. Berlin, 1931.

Phil 200.9 — Zafiropulo, J. La philosophie effective. Paris, 1931.

Phil 1130.5.15 — Zeller, Eduard. Outlines of history of Greek philosophy. 13th ed. London, 1931.

Phil 1130.5.17 — Zeller, Eduard. Outlines of history of Greek philosophy. 13th ed. London, 1931.

Phil 3425.267 — Zu Georg Wilhelm Friedrich Hegels 100. Todestag (am 14 november 1931). Berlin, 1931.

Phil 9070.39 — Zúñiga, Pallais M. Golpes en cantera reflexiva. San José, 1931.

Chronological Listing

1932

Phil 5850.102 Acilles, P.S. Psychology at work. N.Y., 1932.
Phil 6310.1.6 Adler, A. The practice and theory of individual psychology. N.Y., 1932.
Phil 2515.5.92 Alain professeur par X.X., élève de roi Henri IV. Paris, 1932.
Phil 6110.3.10 Alexander, F.M. The use of the self. N.Y., 1932.
Phil 3110.175 Alleman, G.M. A critique of some philosophical aspects of the mysticism of Jacob Boehme. Thesis. Philadelphia, 1932.
Phil 5850.349.25 Allport, G.W. Review of P.M. Symonds' Diagnosing personality. Cambridge, Mass., 1932.
Phil 5810.7.5 Alverdes, F. The psychology of animals in relation to human psychology. London, 1932.
Phil 9035.65 Aulich, Werner. Untersuchungen über das charakterologische Rhythmusproblem. Inaug. Diss. Halle, 1932.
Phil 672.155 Bachelard, Gaston. L'intuition de l'instant. Paris, 1932.
Phil 525.84 Bailey, A.A. From intellect to intuition. N.Y., 1932.
Phil 400.84 Barrett, Clifford. Contemporary idealism in America. N.Y., 1932.
Phil 6311.15 Barrett, E.B. Absolution. London, 1932.
Phil 5545.174 Bartlett, F.C. Remembering. N.Y., 1932.
Phil 5628.10.10 Baumann, Evert Dirk. De goddelijke waanzin. Assen, 1932.
Phil 5650.20 Beatty, R.T. Hearing in man and animals. London, 1932.
Phil 5402.19 Beebe-Center, J.G. The psychology of pleasantness and unpleasantness. N.Y., 1932.
Phil 5751.14 Benda, Clemens E. Der Wille zum Geist. Berlin, 1932.
Phil 1865.176 Bentham, Jeremy. Bentham's theory of fictions. London, 1932.
Phil 1865.176.2 Bentham, Jeremy. Bentham's theory of fictions. N.Y., 1932.
Phil 2475.1.38.4 Bergson, Henri. Les deux sources. Paris, 1932.
Phil 1870.30.25 Berkeley, G. Alcifrone. Dialoghi. v.1-5. Torino, 1932.
Phil 3640.121.4 Bertram, Ernst. Nietzsche; essai de mythologie. Paris, 1932.
Phil 5041.51 Binder, Frank. Dialectic, or The tactics of thinking. London, 1932.
Phil 5241.87 Bingham, Walter V. Psychology today. Chicago, 1932.
Phil 176.134 Blondeau, Cyrille. Propositions de philosophie. Paris, 1932.
Phil 176.129 Blondel, Maurice. Le problème de la philosophie catholique. Paris, 1932.
Phil 7069.32.20 Breitfield, R. Your psychic self. N.Y., 1932.
Phil 5241.99 Brennan, R.E. General psychology. N.Y., 1932.
Phil 5241.79.10 Bridges, J.W. Personality, many in one. Boston, 1932.
Phil 3821.19 Browne, Lewis. Blessed Spinoza. N.Y., 1932.
Phil 2805.192.10A Brunschvicg, L. Pascal. Paris, 1932.
Phil 282.18 Bürgel, B.H. Die Weltanschauung des modernen Menschen. Berlin, 1932.
Phil 7069.32.10 Bull, Titus. Analysis of unusual experiences in healing relative to diseased minds. N.Y., 1932.
Phil 5041.50 Burkamp, W. Logik. Berlin, 1932.
Phil 176.126 Burnham, James. Introductioon to philosophical analysis. N.Y., 1932.
Phil 6951.20 Burrow, T. The structure of insanity. London, 1932.
Phil 8403.13.10 Canitt, Edger. What is beauty. Oxford, 1932.
Phil 5850.149.5 Capps, Ora L. Controlling your circumstances and affairs of life. Denver, 1932.
Phil 5850.149 Capps, Ora L. Developing and using your inner powers. Denver, 1932.
Phil 4352.1.140 Casanovas, J. Balmes. Barcelona, 1932. 3v.
Phil 1750.141A Cassirer, Ernst. Die Philosophie der Aufklärung. Tübingen, 1932.
Phil 5630.3 Chadwick, Thomas. The influence of rumour on human thought and action. Manchester, 1932.
Phil 8050.28 Chambers, Frank. The history of taste. N.Y., 1932.
Phil 510.149 Chang, T.Ş. Epistemological pluralism. Shanghai? 1932?
Phil 177.68.10 Chartier, Émile. Idées; Platon, Descartes, Hegel. Paris, 1932.
Phil 630.40 Chevalier, Jacques. L'idée et le réel. Grenoble, 1932.
Phil 2885.89 Chevrillon, A. Taine; formation de sa pensée. Paris, 1932.
Phil 7069.32.12 Christie, Anne. The opening of the door. Boston, 1932.
Phil 2115.143 Christophersen, H.O. John Locke, en filosofis forberedelse og grunnleggelse (1632-1689). Oslo, 1932.
Phil 705.23 Christy, Arthur. The Orient in American transcendentalism. N.Y., 1932.
Phil 5242.47 Clarke, Edwin L. The art of straight thinking. N.Y., 1932.
Phil 9530.47 Coffee, John R. Personal achievements. N.Y., 1932.
Phil 735.101 Cohn, Jonas. Wertwissenschaft. Stuttgart, 1932.
Phil 4080.3.143 Colorni, E. L'estetica di Benedetto Croce. Milano, 1932.
Phil 7082.64 Combes, Marguerite. Le rêve et la personnalité. Paris, 1932.
Phil 2490.76.15 Comte, Auguste. Lettres inédites à C. de Blignières. Paris, 1932.
Phil 6012.8 Corman, Louis. Visages et caractères. Paris, 1932.
Phil 1107.4 Cornford, F.M. Before and after Socrates. Cambridge, Eng., 1932.
Phil 8725.2 Coulet. Catholicisme et laïcite. Paris, 1932.
Phil 4260.05.5 Croce, Benedetto. Bibliografia vichiana. Quinto supplemento. Napoli, 1932.
Phil 4080.3.15 Croce, Benedetto. Tre saggi filosofici. Palermo, 1932.
Phil 3195.14.50 Dacqué, Edgar. Vom Sinn der Erkenntnis. München, 1932.
Phil 284.13 D'Arcy, C.F. Providence and the world-order. London, 1932.
Phil 3823.8 De Casseres, B. Spinoza, liberator of God and man, 1632-1932. N.Y., 1932.
Phil 2490.122 Delvolvé, Jean. Réflexions sur la pensée comtienne. Paris, 1932.
Phil 2520.35.26 Descartes, René. Discours de la méthode. Paris, 1932.
Phil 2520.35.25 Descartes, René. Discours de la méthode. Paris, 1932.
Phil 8658.15 Descoqs, Pedro. Praelectiones theologiae naturalis. Paris, 1932. 2v.
Phil 6313.8 Deutsch, Helene. Psycho-analysis of the neuroses. London, 1932.
Phil 8878.11.20A Dewey, John. Ethics. N.Y., 1932.
Phil 6313.22 Dieren, E. van. Professor Freud. Baarn, 1932.
Phil 8878.51.8 Dimnet, Ernest. What we live by. London, 1932.
Phil 8878.51.5 Dimnet, Ernest. What we live by. N.Y., 1932.
Phil 1703.6 Dingler, Hugo. Geschichte der Naturphilosophie. Berlin, 1932.
Phil 3195.15.30 Dingler, Hugo. Der Glaube an die Weltmaschine und seine Überwindung. Stuttgart, 1932.
Phil 5243.38 Dockeray, F.C. General psychology. N.Y., 1932.
Phil 6313.9 Dorer, M. Historische Grundlagen der Psychoanalyse. Leipzig, 1932.
Phil 9070.14 Dowry, S.S. The thoughts of youth. N.Y., 1932.

1932 - cont.

Phil 3640.475 Drain, Henri. Nietzsche et Gide. Paris, 1932.
Phil 7069.32.13 Drouet, Bessie Clarke. Station Astral. N.Y., 1932.
Phil 7069.32.15 Dudley, E.E. Fingerprint demonstrations. Boston, 1932.
Phil 8878.50 Dupréel, Eugène. Traité de morale. Bruxelles, 1932. 2v.
Phil 178.30.10 Durant, William. On the meaning of life. N.Y., 1932.
Phil 5400.85 Dyett, E.G. Une étude des émotions au moyen des tests. Thèse. Paris, 1932.
Phil 1145.53 Eernstman, J.P.A. Oikeios, etairos, epitedeios, filos; bejdtrage tot de kennis van de terminologie. Groningen, 1932.
Phil 3850.18.106 Eklund, H. Evangelisches und Katholisches in Max Schelers Ethik. Inaug. Diss. Uppsala, 1932.
Phil 3850.18.105 Eklund, H. Evangelisches und Katholisches in Max Schelers Ethik. Inaug. Diss. Uppsala, 1932.
Phil 2340.10.90A Emmet, Dorothy M. Whitehead's philosophy of organism. London, 1932.
Phil 1704.1.5 Erdmann, J.E. Versuch...Geschichte der neuern Philosophie. Faksimile. Stuttgart, 1932-33. 10v.
Phil 8954.2 Everett, E.L. Impossible things and other essays. Philadelphia, 1932.
Phil 6955.17 Feber, G.H.A. Beschouwingen over Psychopathenstrafrecht. Zwolle, 1932.
Phil 180.51 Felkin, F.W. A wordbook of metaphysics. London, 1932.
Phil 180.41.10 Ferro, A.A. Scritti filosofici. Milano, 1932.
Phil 2225.5.95 Feuer, L.S. Review: Collected papers of Charles Sanders Peirce. v.6. Scientific metaphysics. Bruges, 1932.
Phil 5245.34 Field, G.C. Prejudice and impartiality. London, 1932.
Phil 5245.32.5 Ford, Adelbert. Group experiments in elementary psychology. N.Y., 1932.
Phil 8585.33 Fornerod, A. Religion et théologie. Lausanne, 1932.
Phil 270.39 Frank, Philipp. Das Kausalgesetz und seine Grenzen. Wien, 1932.
Phil 8585.31 Franken, J.C. Kritische Philosophie und Dialektischen Theologie. Proefschrift. Amsterdam, 1932.
X Cg Phil 6480.23.6 Freud, Sigmund. The interpretation of dreams. London, 1932.
Phil 6315.2.65 Freud, Sigmund. Vier psychoanalytische Krankengeschichten. Wien, 1932.
Phil 337.12 Gätschenberger, R. Zeichen, die Fundamente des Wissens. Stuttgart, 1932.
Phil 1540.21 Garin, Pierre. La théorie de l'idée suivant l'école thomiste. Thèse. Bruges, 1932.
Phil 5246.42.5 Garnett, Arthur C. The mind in action. N.Y., 1932.
Phil 8735.19 Garrigou-Lagrange, Reginaldo. Le réalisme du principe de finalité. Paris, 1932.
Phil 1145.80 Gerlach, Julius. Hanēr hagados. Inaug. Diss. Munchen, 1932.
Phil 2520.179 Gibson, A.B. The philosophy of Descartes. London, 1932.
Phil 1511.3.10 Gilson, Étienne. L'esprit de la philosophie médiévale. Paris, 1932. 2v.
Phil 8430.16 Gleizes, A. Vers une conscience plastique; la forme et l'histoire. Paris, 1932.
Phil 3200.5.90 Glockner, H. Johann Eduard Erdmann. Stuttgart, 1932.
Phil 9450.20 Gogartin, F. Politische Ethik. Jena, 1932.
Phil 9230.13.5F Great Britain. Commission on Lotteries and Betting, 1932-33. Minutes of evidence...first 24 days, Thursday, 30 June, 1932-Thursday, 23 February, 1933. Pt.1-24. London, 1932-33.
Phil 6420.28 Greene, James S. I was a stutterer; stories from life. N.Y., 1932.
Phil 735.104 Groos, Karl. Zur Psychologie und Metaphysik des Wert-Erlebens. Berlin, 1932.
Phil 181.71 Guénon, R. Les états multiples de l'etre. Paris, 1932.
Phil 4065.118 Guzzo, Augusto. I dialoghi del Bruno. Torino, 1932.
Phil 182.111 Haldane, J.S. Materialism. London, 1932.
Phil 8632.18 Halsey, Don Peters. The evidence for immortality. N.Y., 1932.
Phil 4580.119 Harald Høffding in memoriam. København, 1932.
Phil 1512.10 Hart, C.A. Aspects of the new scholastic philosophy. N.Y., 1932.
Phil 8882.50.5 Hartmann, N. Ethics. London, 1932. 3v.
Phil 182.95 Haserot, F.S. Essays on the logic of being. N.Y., 1932.
Phil 5627.132.5 Heiler, Friedrich. Prayer. London, 1932.
Phil 5047.35 Heiss, Robert. Logik des Widerspruchs. Berlin, 1932.
Phil 6317.11.9 Herbert, S. The unconscious in life and art. London, 1932.
Phil 9560.28 Heron, Grace. What word will you choose? Chicago, 1932.
Phil 2515.5.91 Hess, G. Alain (Émile Chartier) in der Reihe der französischen Moralisten. Berlin, 1932.
Phil 5247.22.20 Heymans, G. Einführung in die spezielle Psychologie. Leipzig, 1932.
Phil 1870.112 Hicks, G.D. Berkeley. London, 1932.
Phil 5247.48.2 Higginson, G. Fields of psychology. N.Y., 1932.
Phil 960.137 Hiriyanna, M. Outlines of Indian philosophy. London, 1932.
Phil 9035.27.12 Hocking, W.E. Human nature and its remaking. New Haven, 1932.
Phil 3808.212 Holn, Søren. Schopenhauer ethik. Kjøbenhavn, 1932.
Phil 3489.31 Hoppe, V. Dva základní problémy Kantova kriticismu. Brno, 1932.
Phil 182.98.5 Horn, E. Der Begriff des Begriffes. München, 1932.
Phil 8957.18 Huemmeler, Hans. Jugend an der Maschine. Freiburg, 1932.
Phil 2050.77.15 Hume, David. Letters. Oxford, 1932. 2v.
Phil 5247.29.5 Humphrey, G. The story of man's mind. N.Y., 1932.
Phil 575.10.10 Hyde, W. De W. The five great philosophies of life. N.Y., 1932.
Phil 3450.11.105 Illemann, U. Die Vor- phänomenologische philosophie Edmund Husserls. Inaug. Diss. n.p., 1932.
X Cg Phil 7075.130 Individual psychology and sexual difficulties. pt.1-2. London, 1932-34.
Phil 8958.7 Ioann, Bishop of San Francisco. Beloe inochestvo. Berlin, 1932.
Phil 5651.7 Jaccard, Pierre. Le sens de la direction et l'orientation lointaine chez l'homme. Paris, 1932.
Phil 6119.11.5 Jackson, Josephine Agnes. Outwitting our nerves. 2d ed. N.Y., 1932.
Phil 5819.6 Jackson, T.A. General factors in transfer of training in the white rat. Worcester, 1932.
Phil 5400.91 Janet, Pierre. L'amour et la haine. Paris, 1932.
Phil 6959.1.29 Janet, Pierre. La force et la faiblesse psychologiques. Paris, 1932.
Phil 3801.465 Jankélévitch, V. L'odyssée de la conscience dans la dernière philosophie de Schelling. Thèse. Paris, 1932.
Phil 184.19.10 Jaspers, K. Philosophie. Berlin, 1932. 3v.
Phil 6315.2.101A Jastrow, Joseph. The house that Freud built. N.Y., 1932.

1932 - cont.

Phil 184.12.7   Jerusalem, W.   Introduction to philosophy. N.Y., 1932.
Phil 974.4.20   Jinarajadasa, C.   A short biography of Annie Besant.
                       Adyar, Madras, 1932.
Phil 184.36   Johnson, E.V.   Universal tradition. v.6. Alexandria,
                       Va., 1932.
Phil 8664.4   Jolivet, R.   Études sur la problème de Dieu dans la
                       philosophie contemporaine. Lyon, 1932.
Phil 5520.56.10   Jordan, Leo.   Schule der Abstraktion und der Dialektik.
                       München, 1932.
Phil 3160.3.87   Jospe, Alfred.   Die Unterscheidung von Mythos und Religion
                       hei Hermann Cohen. Inaug. Diss. Oppeln, 1932.
Phil 6319.1.49   Jung, C.G.   Die Beziehungen der Psychotherapie zur
                       Seelsorge. Zürich, 1932.
Phil 6319.1.37   Jung, C.G.   Seelenprobleme der Gegenwart. Zürich, 1932.
Phil 5850.250   Kandhi, S.   The winning of wealth. Boston, 1932.
Phil 4899.162.30   Kaneko, Shōseki.   Über das Wesen und den Ursprung des
                       Menschen. Osaka, 1932.
Phil 3480.80.15   Kant, Immanuel.   Perpetual peace. Los Angeles, 1932.
Phil 8885.34   Kant, Otto.   Zur Biologie der Ethik. Wien, 1932.
Phil 4595.3.31   Karitz, Anders.   Philosophie und Spezialforschung.
                       Lund, 1932.
Phil 6020.4.5   Kassner, Rudolf.   Physiognomik. München, 1932.
Phil 1865.181   Kayser, E.L.   The grand social enterprise; a study of
                       Jeremy Bentham in his relation to liberal nationalism.
                       N.Y., 1932.
Phil 3830.10   Kayser, Rudolf.   Spinoza; Bildnis eines geistigen Helden.
                       Wien, 1932.
Phil 3830.9   Kettner, F.   Spinoza, the biosopher. N.Y., 1932.
Phil 3549.2.30.2   Keyserling, Hermann.   South American meditations. 1st ed.
                       N.Y., 1932.
Phil 3549.2.30   Keyserling, Hermann.   Südamerikanische Meditationen.
                       Stuttgart, 1932.
Phil 5374.53   King, C. Daly.   The psychology of consciousness.
                       London, 1932.
Phil 3549.8.85   Klages, Ludwig.   Die Wissenschaft am Scheidewege von Leben
                       und Geist. Leipzig, 1932.
Phil 6320.11.5   Klein, M.   Die Psychoanalyse des Kindes. Wien, 1932.
Phil 3255.90   Koyré, Alexandre.   Sebastien Franck. Paris, 1932.
Phil 3010.5   Kraft, J.   Von Husserl zu Heidegger. Leipzig, 1932.
Phil 6320.9.5   Kranefeldt, W.M.   Secret ways of the mind. N.Y., 1932.
Phil 9035.64   Kronfeld, Arthur.   Lehrbuch der Charakterkunde.
                       Berlin, 1932.
Phil 185.51   Krueger, F.   Ganzheit und Form. Berlin, 1932.
Phil 2138.114.2   Kubitz, O.A.   Development of John S. Mill's system of
                       logic. Urbana, 1932.
Phil 2138.114   Kubitz, O.A.   Development of John S. Mill's system of
                       logic. Thesis. Urbana, 1932.
Phil 9035.59.20   Künkel, Fritz.   Charakter. Leipzig, 1932.
Phil 3585.13.90   Kurth, Hans.   Die Weltdeutung Mathilde Ludendorffs.
                       München, 1932.
Phil 8411.21   Kuznitzky, G.   Die Seinssymbolik des Schönen und die Kunst.
                       Berlin, 1932.
Phil 3831.15   Lachièze-Rey, P.   Les origines cartésiennes du Dieu de
                       Spinoza. Thèse. Paris, 1932.
Phil 2050.203   Laing, B.M.   David Hume. London, 1932.
Phil 2050.198   Laird, John.   Hume's philosophy of human nature.
                       N.Y., 1932.
Phil 96.4   Lalande, A.   Vocabulaire technique et critique de la
                       philosophie. 4. ed. Paris, 1932. 3v.
Phil 8636.8   Lamont, Corliss.   Issues of immortality. N.Y., 1932.
Phil 292.7.5   Langdon-Davies, John.   Man comes of age. 1st ed.
                       N.Y., 1932.
Phil 5400.84   Lashley, K.S.   Studies in the dynamics of behavior.
                       Chicago, 1932.
Phil 7069.32.50   Lawton, George.   The drama of life after death.
                       N.Y., 1932.
Phil 3552.42   Leibniz, Gottfried Wilhelm.   Nové úvahy o lidské soudnosti
                       od auktora Systému předzjednané harmonie. Praha, 1932.
Phil 3903.3.105   Leidel, A.   Die Philosophie des Als Ob und das Leben
                       Festschrift. Berlin, 1932.
Phil 8886.53   Lemarie, O.   La morale privée. Paris, 1932.
Phil 811.8   Leon, M.   The comedy of human philosophy. Boston, 1932.
Phil 1535.38   LeRohellec, J.   Problèmes philosophiques. Paris, 1932.
Phil 5051.10.10   Lewis, Clarence I.   Symbolic logic. N.Y., 1932.
Phil 5251.34.10   Lindworsky, J.   Theoretical psychology. St. Louis, 1932.
Phil 8591.35   Lion, Aline.   The idealistic conception of religion.
                       Oxford, 1932.
Phil 5203.37   Loattit, Chauncey McKinley.   Handbook of psychological
                       literature. Bloomington, Ind., 1932.
Phil 4260.106   Löhde, Hermann.   Giambattista Vico und das Problem der
                       Bildung. Inaug. Diss. Erlangen, 1932.
Phil 8701.13.5   Lorbeer, Floyd Irwing.   Philosophy of light. Los
                       Angeles, 1932.
Phil 5761.17.5   Lossky, N.O.   Freedom of will. London, 1932.
Phil 8886.52   Lowell, Abbot L.   Conflicts of principle. Cambridge, 1932.
Phil 2045.114   Łubieński, Z.   Die Grundlagen des ethisch-politischen
                       Systems von Hobbes. München, 1932.
Phil 5525.37   Ludovici, A.M.   Secret of laughter. London, 1932.
Phil 6961.13   Lundholm, Helge.   Schizophrenia. Durham, N.C., 1932.
Phil 5251.40.5A   Luria, A.R.   The nature of human conflicts. N.Y., 1932.
Phil 4803.537.45F   Lutosławski, Wincenty.   Jeden łatwy żywot.
                       Dzięgielów? 1932.
Phil 5822.7   McAllister, W.G.   A further study of the delayed reaction
                       in the albino rat. Baltimore, 1932.
Phil 5645.35   MacLeod, R.B.   An experimental investigation of brightness
                       constancy. N.Y., 1932.
Phil 9515.3.95   Maduschka, Leo.   Das Problem des Einsamkeit in 18
                       Jahrhundert. Inaug. Diss. Murnan, 1932.
Phil 5520.64   Mannoury, G.   Les deux pôles de l'esprit. Amsterdam, 1932.
Phil 3494.38   Marc-Wogau, K.   Untersuchungen zur Raumlehre Kants. Inaug.
                       Diss. Lund, 1932.
Phil 343.17   Marcel, Victor.   De l'activité purement immanente. Thèse.
                       Nancy, 1932.
Phil 2520.190   Marcel, Victor.   Étendue et conscience. Thèse.
                       Nancy, 1932.
Phil 9075.32.10   Marchal, Victor.   La coscienza quale dev'essere.
                       Torino, 1932.
Phil 8887.58.10   Marcus, E.   Das Rätsel der Sittlichkeit und seine Lösung.
                       München, 1932.
Phil 2490.121   Marcuse, A.   Die Geschichtsphilosophie Auguste Comtes.
                       Inaug.-Diss. Stuttgart, 1932.
Phil 3425.292   Marcuse, H.   Hegels Ontologie und die Grundlegung einer
                       Theorie der Geschichtlichkeit. Frankfurt, 1932.
Phil 7069.25.12.10   The "Margery" mediumship. N.Y., 1932. 2 pam.

1932 - cont.

Phil 2750.11.48.15   Maritain, Jacques.   Distinguer pour unir. Paris, 1932.
Phil 2750.11.72.5   Maritain, Jacques.   Le songe de Descartes. Paris, 1932.
Phil 5400.89   Marucci, A.   Le passioni nella filosofia e nell'arte.
                       Torino, 1932.
Phil 6990.3.52   Mayer, L.   Lourdes, Konnersreuth oder Gallspach?
                       Schopfheim, 1932.
Phil 97.4   Mayer, M.B.   A primary glossary of psychological and
                       philosophical terms. N.Y., 1932.
Phil 8411.7   Mayoux, J.J.   Richard Payne Knight et le pittoresque essai
                       sur une phase esthétique. Paris, 1932.
Phil 187.100   Mead, George H.   The philosophy of the present.
                       Chicago, 1932.
Phil 365.32   Messenger, E.C.   Evolution and theology. N.Y., 1932.
Phil 3640.435   Mette, H.J.   Der handschriftliche Nachlass Friedrich
                       Nietzsches. Leipzig, 1932.
Phil 343.16.11   Meyerson, Emile.   Identité et réalité. 4. éd. Paris, 1932.
Phil 3425.358   Milan. Universita Cattolica del Sacro Cuare. Hegel nel
                       centenario. Milano, 1932.
Phil 530.35.7   Misciatelli, Piero.   L'Italia mistica. Firenze, 1932.
Phil 960.138   Modi, P.M.   Aksara, a forgotten chapter in the history of
                       Indian philosophy. Inaug. Diss. Baroda, 1932.
X Cg Phil 7075.127   Money-Kyrle, R.E.   The development of the sexual impulses.
                       London, 1932.
Phil 365.36   Monsarrat, K.W.   Desire and creation. Liverpool, 1932.
Phil 812.13   Moog, W.   Das Leben der Philosophen. Berlin, 1932.
Phil 7076.22   Morrison, Paul Guerrant.   The place of the ecstatic trance
                       in the ideal of the good life. Chicago, 1932.
Phil 6962.20   Moss, Fred August.   Foundations of abnormal psychology.
                       N.Y., 1932.
Phil 3790.12.81   Motsch, Karl E.   Matern Reuss. Freiburg, 1932.
Phil 735.103   Müller, Max.   Über Grundbegriffe philosophischer Wertlehre.
                       Inaug. Diss. Freiburg, 1932.
Phil 8837.12 ─────── Muirhead, J.H.   Rule and end in morals. London, 1932.
Phil 187.99   Muller, Maurice.   Individualité, causalité, indeterminisme.
                       Paris, 1932.
Phil 5203.8   Murchison, C.A.   The psychological register. v.3.
                       Worcester, 1932.
Phil 5222.3.10   Murphy, Gardner.   Approaches to personality. N.Y., 1932.
Phil 6122.53   Myers, C.S.   The absurdity of any mind-body relation.
                       London, 1932.
Phil 6980.598   National Committee for Mental Hygiene.   Directory of
                       psychiatric clinics in the United States. 1. ed.
                       N.Y., 1932.
Phil 8888.6.2   Nelson, Leonard.   System der philosophischen Ethik und
                       Pädagogik. Göttingen, 1932.
Phil 4260.124   Nicolini, F.   La giovinezza di Giambattista Vico. 2. ed.
                       Bari, 1932.
Phil 5425.54   Nicolle, Charles.   Biologie de l'invention. Paris, 1932.
Phil 3640.77.20   Nietzsche, Friedrich.   La vie de Friedrich Nietzsche
                       d'après sa correspondance. Paris, 1932.
Phil 5545.193   Nohl, Johanna.   Erinnerung und Gedächtnis.
                       Langensalza, 1932.
Phil 4610.7.25   Norström, V.   Religion und Gedanke. Lund, 1932.
Phil 6323.5   Nunberg, Hermann.   Allgemeine Neurosenlehre auf
                       psychoanalytischer Gundlage. Bern, 1932.
Phil 3640.254   O'Brien, Edward J.   Son of the morning; a portrait of F.
                       Nietzsche. N.Y., 1932.
Phil 365.33   O'Brien, J.A.   Evolution and religion. N.Y., 1932.
Phil 3805.180   Odebrecht, Rudolf.   Schleiermachers System der Asthetik.
                       Berlin, 1932.
Phil 7060.92.57   O'Donnell, Elliot.   Ghosts of London. London, 1932.
Phil 1865.176.5   Ogden, Charles K.   Jeremy Bentham 1832-2032...Bentham
                       centenary lecture...on June 6th, 1930. London, 1932.
Phil 6990.46   Olden, R.   Propheten in deutscher Krise. Berlin, 1932.
Phil 6964.2   Oliver, John R.   Pastoral psychiatry and mental health.
                       N.Y., 1932.
Phil 7069.32.30   Osty, E.   Les pouvoirs inconnus de l'esprit sur la matière.
                       Paris, 1932.
Phil 525.74.5   Otto, Rudolf.   Mysticism East and West. N.Y., 1932.
Phil 400.85.5   Papafava, N.   L'attualismo considerazioni. Milano, 1932.
Phil 5625.75.25   Pavlov, Ivan P.   Vorlesungen über die Arbeit der
                       Grosshirnhemisphären. Lenogiz, 1932.
Phil 4710.25   Pelikán, Ferdinand.   Současná filosofie u Slovanů.
                       Praha, 1932.
Phil 8595.30F   Persons, Lee C.   The religion of the beautiful.
                       Miami, 1932?
Phil 5255.33.10   Petermann, B.   The gestalt theory and the problem of
                       configuration. London, 1932.
Phil 190.55   Philippe, Oscar.   L'inconditionnalité de la philosophie.
                       Paris, 1932.
Phil 190.55.5   Philippe, Oscar.   L'inconditionnalité de la philosophie.
                       Thèse. Nancy, 1932.
Phil 6325.12   Pillsbury, Walter B.   An elementary psychology of the
                       abnormal. 1. ed. N.Y., 1932.
Phil 9530.31.5   Pitkin, Walter B.   Life begins at forty. N.Y., 1932.
Phil 5390.8   Pitkin, Walter B.   A short introduction to the history of
                       human stupidity. N.Y., 1932.
Phil 3640.235.15   Podach, Erich F.   Gestalten um Nietzsche. Weimar, 1932.
Phil 3428.161   Poggi, Alfredo.   La filosofia di G.F. Herbart.
                       Genova, 1932.
Phil 9120.161.10   Prichard, H.A.   Duty and ignorance of fact. London, 1932.
Phil 5255.44   Prinzhorn, H.   Persönlichkeitspsychologie. Leipzig, 1932.
Phil 190.54   Przywara, Erich.   Analogia entis. München, 1932.
Phil 978.68   Purucker, G. de.   Fundamentals of the esoteric philosophy.
                       Philadelphia, 1932.
Phil 1122.25   Ráde, Emanuel.   Dějiny filosofie. Praha, 1932-33.
                       2v.
Phil 8597.38   Radhakrishnan, S.   An idealist view of life. N.Y., 1932.
Phil 5413.10   Raiga, Eugène.   L'envie. Paris, 1932.
Phil 1870.111   Rand, Benjamin.   Berkeley's American sojourn.
                       Cambridge, 1932.
Phil 630.38   Ranzoli, Cesare.   Il realismo puro. Milano, 1932.
Phil 8597.39   Rattray, R.F.   Fundamentals of modern religion.
                       London, 1932.
Phil 1735.12   Rava, Adolfo.   La filosofia Europea nel secolo decimonono.
                       Padova, 1932.
Phil 8892.48   Reiner, Hans.   Der Grund der sittlichen Bindung und das
                       sittlich Gute. Halle, 1932.
Phil 5057.25   Reymond, Arnold.   Les principes de la logique et la
                       critique contemporaine. Paris, 1932.
Phil 2475.1.237   Rideau, Émile.   Le dieu de Bergson. Paris, 1932.
Phil 2475.1.236   Rideau, Émile.   Le dieu de Bergson. Thèse. Paris, 1932.
Phil 2475.1.238   Rideau, Émile.   Les rapports de la matière et de l'esprit
                       dans le bergsonisme. Paris, 1932.

1932 - cont.

Phil 2475.1.238.5   Rideau, Émile. Les rapports de la matière et de l'esprit dans le bergsonisme. Thèse. Paris, 1932.

Phil 735.100   Rintelen, F.J. von. Der Wertgedanke in der europäischen Geistesentwicklung. Halle, 1932.

Phil 7069.20.370   Roberts, W. Adair. A spiritual interpretation of some psychic happenings. London, 1932.

Phil 1717.11.15   Robinson, D.S. An introduction to living philosophy. N.Y., 1932.

Phil 5325.26   Robinson, E.S. Association theory today. N.Y., 1932.

Phil 817.4.20A   Rogers, A.K. A student's history of philosophy. 3d ed. N.Y., 1932.

Phil 298.2.10   Rosley, Carl. Life's reality. Hayward, 1932.

Phil 192.73   Rossignoli, Giovanni. Primi passi nello studio della metafisica. 8a ed. Torino, 1932.

Phil 978.69   Rudolph, Hermann. Theosophischer Kulturbücher. Leipzig, 1932-33.

Phil 5627.134.4   Russell, Arthur J. For sinners only. N.Y., 1932.

Phil 510.147   Russell, C.W. Mind: creative and dynamic. N.Y., 1932.

Phil 193.132   Samuel, Herbert S. Philosophy and the ordinary man. London, 1932.

Phil 5850.332F   Sasha, A.W. Condensed outline of "The laws of life". Oakland, Cal., 1932.

VPhil 6060.78   Saudek, Robert. What your handwriting shows. London, 1932.

Phil 8419.51   Schneiderfranken, J.A. Aus Meiner Malerwerkstatt. Basel, 1932.

VPhil 9070.130   Schneiderfranken, Joseph Anton. Der Weg meiner Schüler. Basel, 1932.

Phil 8673.13   Schock, Adolph. The problem of God's identity in cosmic change. Chicago, 1932.

Phil 8419.45   Schoen, Max. Art and beauty. N.Y., 1932.

Phil 3808.24.17   Schopenhauer, Arthur. Das Bild des Menschen in Schopenhauers Philosophie. Berlin, 1932.

Phil 8586.36.50   Schräter, Fritz. Glaube und Geschichte bei Friedrich Gogarten und Wilhelm Hermann. Inaug. Diss. Kothenanhalt, 1932?

Phil 9470.8   Sears, L. Responsibility. N.Y., 1932.

Phil 2750.10.95   Sée, Henri. Science et philosophie d'après la doctrine de Émile Meyerson. Paris, 1932.

Phil 2520.185   Segond, J. La sagesse cartésienne et la doctrine de la science. Paris, 1932.

Phil 3890.6.86   Seidel, A. Tetens Einfluss auf die kritische Philosophie Kants. Inaug. Diss. Würzburg, 1932.

Phil 630.9.10   Sellars, R.W. The philosophy of physical realism. N.Y., 1932.

Phil 193.133   Seshagiri Row, T.V. New light on fundamental problems. Mylapore, Madras, 1932.

Phil 4769.5   Setnitskii, N.A. O konechnom ideale. Kharbin, 1932.

Phil 8140.2   Sgroi, Carmelo. Gli studi estetici in Italia nel primo trantennio del'900. Firenze, 1932.

Phil 193.143   Shah, R.V. Pourings of a struggling soul. Ahmedabad, 1932.

Phil 193.134.5   Shestov, L. In job's balances. London, 1932.

Phil 5627.134.65   Shoemaker, S.M. The conversion of the church. N.Y., 1932.

Phil 3791.125   Siegel, Carl. Alois Riehl. Graz, 1932.

Phil 193.139   Signpost (pseud.). In tune with the universe. London, 1932.

Phil 193.131   Sills, Milton. Values; a philosophy of human needs. Chicago, 1932.

Phil 1123.8   Smith, T.V. Philosophers in Hades. Chicago, Ill., 1932.

Phil 4803.799.25   Sniadecki, Jan. Korespondencja Jana Sniadeckiego; listy z Krakowa. Krakow, 1932-54. 2v.

EDL Phil 3819.18   Spinoza, Benedictus de. Spisy filosofické. Prag, 1932.

Phil 349.32   Stace, W.T. Theory of knowledge and existence. Oxford, 1932.

Phil 978.49.115   Steiner, R. Eurhythmy as visible song. London, 1932.

Phil 978.49.175   Steiner, R. Mysterienstätten des Mittelalters. Dornach, 1932.

Phil 978.49.225   Steiner, R. Welche Gesichtspunkte liegeni Errichtung der Waldorfschule zu Grunde? Dornach, 1932.

Phil 720.25   Stern, Alfred. Die philosophischen Grundlagen von Wahrheit, Wirklichkeit, Wert. München, 1932.

Phil 193.130   Stocks, J.L. The limits of purpose and other essays. London, 1932.

Phil 9178.9   Stopes, M.C.C. Radiant motherhood. N.Y., 1932.

Phil 1850.127   Sturt, Mary. Francis Bacon; a biography. London, 1932.

Phil 960.139   Syed, M.H. L'optimisme dans la pensée indienne. Thèse. n.p., 1932.

Phil 2340.10.93A   Symposium in honor of the 70th birthday of Alfred North Whitehead. Cambridge, 1932.

Phil 8599.29   Tanquerey, A. The spiritual life. 2. ed. Tournai, 1932.

Phil 194.36.10   Taylor, H.O. Fact: the romance of mind. N.Y., 1932.

Phil 7069.32.40   Taylor, Sarah E.L. Fox - Taylor automatic writing, 1869-1892. Minneapolis, 1932.

Phil 2050.197   Tegen, Einar. Humes uppfattning av jagets identitet. Uppsala, 1932.

Phil 8430.41   Thielicke, H. Das verhältnis zwischen demethischen und dem ästhetischen. Leipzig, 1932.

Phil 575.80   Thompson, Dow. A mind that was different. Wellston, 1932.

Phil 5059.20.2   Thouless, R.H. Straight and crooked thinking. N.Y., 1932.

Phil 1735.10   Tilgher, Adriano. Filosofi e moralisti del novecento. Roma, 1932.

Phil 1150.12   Tollington, R.B. Alexandrine teaching on the universe. London, 1932.

Phil 5829.10   Tolman, Edward C. Purposive behavior in animals and men. N.Y., 1932.

Phil 3425.286   Trott zu Solz, A. v. Hegels Staatsphilosophie. Göttingen, 1932.

Phil 5627.60.10   Underhill, E. The golden sequence. 2. ed. London, 1932.

Phil 8050.300   Utitz, Emil. Geschichte der Asthetik. Berlin, 1932.

Phil 6331.1.5   Valentine, C.W. The new psychology of the unconscious. London, 1932.

Phil 5261.17.10   Valentine, Willard Lee. Psychology laboratory manual. N.Y., 1932.

Phil 4235.1.99   Van Deusen, Neil C. Telesio, the first of the moderns. N.Y., 1932.

Phil 3841.5   Vaz Dias, A.M. Spinoza, mercator en autodidactus. 's Gravenhage, 1932.

Phil 196.30   Vialatoux, J. L'intention philosophique. 1. ed. Paris, 1932.

Phil 5261.19.5   Vialle, L. Le désir du néant. Thèse. Paris, 1932.

Phil 3640.256   Vialle, Louis. Détresses de Nietzsche. Paris, 1932.

Phil 3640.256.5   Vialle, Louis. Détresses de Nietzsche. Thèse. Paris, 1932.

Phil 4260.17.15   Vico, G.B. Autobiografia e scienza nuova. Torino, 1932.

1932 - cont.

Phil 5261.18   Vogel, C.L. Psychology and the Franciscan school. N.Y., 1932.

Phil 5031.1   Vollenhoven, D.H.T. De noodzakelijkheid eener christelijke logica. Amsterdam, 1932.

Phil 8125.6   Vorholz, Gerhard. Der Begriff des Tragischen. Halle, 1932.

Phil 3425.283   Wacker, Herbert. Das Verhältnis des jungen Hegel zu Kant. Berlin, 1932.

Phil 1722.7   Wahl, Jean. Vers le concret; études d'histoire de la philosophie contemporaine. Paris, 1932.

Phil 197.55   Walfenden, J.F. The approach to philosophy. London, 1932.

Phil 8602.42   Walker, Joseph. Humanism as a way of life. N.Y., 1932.

Phil 8712.23   Walker, L.J. Science and revelation. London, 1932.

Phil 8677.15   Walmarans, H.P. Die mens naar die beeld van God. Purmerend, 1932.

Phil 8972.8   Webb, C.J. The contribution of Christianity to ethics. Calcutta, 1932.

Phil 3905.30.10   Weininger, Otto. Geschlecht und Charakter. Berlin, 1932.

Phil 5374.54   Weir, A. Light, a philosophy of consciousness. Oxford, 1932.

Phil 8677.18   Werfel, Franz. Können wir ohne Gottesglauben Leben? Berlin, 1932.

Phil 5520.57   Werner, Heinz. Grundfragen der Sprachphysiognomik. Leipzig, 1932.

Phil 7082.100   Westerfield, Jonathan B. The scientific dream book and dictionary of dream symbols. N.Y., 1932.

Phil 8897.28.15   Westermarck, E. Ethical relativity. N.Y., 1932.

Phil 5262.36.10   Wheeler, R.H. Laws of human nature. N.Y., 1932.

Phil 6972.14.13   White, William Alanson. Outlines of psychiatry. 13. ed. Washington, 1932.

Phil 8602.40   Widney, J.P. The faith that has come to me. Los Angeles, 1932.

Phil 9470.5   Wieschedel, W. Versuch über das Wesen der Verantwortung. Inaug. Diss. Heppenheim, 1932.

Phil 974.4.15   Williams, Gertrude M. The passionate pilgrim. London, 1932.

Phil 6400.24   Winkler, Carl. Abnormal speech. Orange, Conn., 1932.

Phil 8897.61   Winsor, F. The art of behaviour. Boston, 1932.

Phil 3120.2.97   Winter, E. Religion und Offenbarung in der Religionsphilosophie Bernard Bolzanos. Breslau, 1932.

Phil 6420.30   Wolfe, Paul J. A home study course in the correction of stuttering and stammering. n.p., 1932.

Phil 6032.2   Wolff, Werner. Selbstbeurteilung und Fremdbeurteilung im wissentlichen und Unwissentlichen Versuch. Inaug. Diss. Berlin, 1932.

Phil 3842.11   Wolfson, Abraham. Spinoza; a life of reason. N.Y., 1932.

Phil 197.57   Woods, Elizabeth R. Music and meaning. Cambridge, 1932.

Phil 5400.88   Wyatt, H.G. The art of feeling. Boston, 1932.

Phil 5850.391   Yates, Dorothy H. Psychological racketeers. Boston, 1932.

Phil 5265.3F   Zapan, Georg. Ubbarkeit verschiedener Aufgaben. München, 1932.

Phil 3195.10.110   Zilberis, B. Kant und die Philosophie Drieschs. Inaug. Diss. Vilkaviskis, 1932.

Phil 3808.164.5   Zimmern, Helen. Schopenhauer, his life and philosophy. London, 1932.

Phil 3450.11.102   Zocher, Rudolf. Husserls Phänomenologie und Schuppes Logik. München, 1932.

Phil 6135.4.5A   Zweig, Stefan. Mental healers. N.Y., 1932.

1933

Phil 3640.257   Abraham, G.E.H. Nietzsche. London, 1933.

Phil 3640.257.5   Abraham, G.E.H. Nietzsche. N.Y., 1933.

Phil 6310.1.38   Adler, A. Der Sinn des Lebens. Wien, 1933.

Phil 475.3   Aksel'rod, L. I. Protiv idealizma. Moskva, 1933.

Phil 8401.22.10   Alexander, Samuel. Beauty and other forms of value. London, 1933.

Phil 3820.4.5   Alexander, Samuel. Spinoza; an address...tercentenary...birth. Manchester, 1933.

Phil 8655.15   Algermissen Konrad. Die Gottlosenbewegung der Gegenwart. 1. und 2. Aufl. Hannover, 1933.

Phil 5649.19A   Allport, G.W. Studies in expressive movement. N.Y., 1933.

Phil 800.7   Alpern, Henry. The march of philosophy. N.Y., 1933.

Phil 2520.193   Alquié, F. Notes sur la première partie des principes de la philosophie de Descartes. Paris, 1933.

Phil 8875.25   Alquié, F. Notions de morale générale. Paris, 1933.

Phil 8875.25.5   Alquié, F. Le problème moral. Paris, 1933.

Phil 8690.6   Anderson, Paul R. Science in defense of liberal religion. N.Y., 1933.

Phil 8580.24A   Auer, J.A.C.F. Humanism states its case. Boston, 1933.

Phil 6951.28   Babcock, H. Dementia praecox. N.Y., 1933.

Phil 8615.13   Bacon, S.F. An evaluation of the philosophy and pedagogy of ethical culture. Diss. Washington, 1933.

Phil 8626.24   Baillie, John. And the life everlasting. N.Y., 1933.

Phil 3450.19.103   Ballmer, Karl. Aber Herr Heidegger. Basel, 1933.

Phil 8876.115   Barbour, R.R.P. Ethical theory. Adelaide, 1933.

Phil 3552.303   Barié, G.E. La spiritualità dell'essere e Leibniz. Padova, 1933.

Phil 8691.24   Barnes, E.W. Scientific theory and religion. Cambridge, Eng., 1933.

Phil 8876.94   Barrett, C.L. Ethics; an introduction to the philosophy of moral values. N.Y., 1933.

Phil 8656.31   Baskfield, G.T. The idea of God in British and American personal idealism. Thesis. Washington, 1933.

Phil 270.100   Baumann, Evert D. De harmonie der dingen. Leiden, 1933.

Phil 8826.6   Baumgardt, D. Der Kampf um den Lebenssinn den Vorläufern der modernen Ethik. Leipzig, 1933.

Phil 8876.95   Baumgarten, Arthur. Der Weg des Menschen. Tübingen, 1933.

Phil 8691.22   Bavink, B. Science and God. London, 1933.

Phil 8402.8.15   Bayer, Raymond. L'esthétique de la grâce. Paris, 1933. 2v.

Phil 8402.8.10   Bayer, Raymond. L'esthétique de la grâce. Paris, 1933. 2v.

Phil 5252.18.60   Becker, F. Die Instinkt-Psychologie William McDougalls. Reichenberg, 1933.

Phil 6951.5.7   Beers, C.W. A mind that found itself. Garden City, 1933.

Phil 3483.58   Beier, Bruno. Kants Apriorismus. Pfullingen, 1933.

Phil 5241.30.15   Bekhterev, V. General principles of human reflexology. London, 1933.

Phil 8430.6   Benaz, Manuel. Lo bello y la buena a la luz. Buenos Aires, 1933.

Phil 7069.33.10   Benedict, Anna Louise. Continuity of life. Boston, 1933.

Phil 6111.47   Benedict, F.G. Mental effort. Washington, 1933.

Phil 2401.3.15A   Benrubi, Isaac. Les sources et les courants de la philosophie contemporaine en France. Paris, 1933. 2v.

1933 - cont.

Phil 3246.173.5   Bergmann, Ernst. Fichte und der Nationalsozialismus. Breslau, 1933.
Phil 2475.1.38   Bergson, Henri. Les deux sources de la morale et de la religion. 14 éd. Paris, 1933.
Phil 176.128   Bertini, G.M. Idea di una filosofia della vita. Firenze, 1933.
Phil 1050.4.20   Bieler, Majer. Der göttliche Wille (Logosbegriff) bei Gabirol. Breslau, 1933.
Phil 3808.172   Bierens de Haan, J.D. Schopenhauer. 's Gravenhage, 1933.
Phil 3120.40.30   Bierens de Haan, J.D. Het tragische schuld noodlot en bevrijding. Leiden, 1933.
Phil 365.38   Bill, Annie C.B. Questions and answers on conscious evolution. N.Y., 1933.
Phil 8402.12F   Birkhoff, G.D. Aesthetic measure. Cambridge, 1933.
Phil 2070.128   Blau, Théodore. William James. Thèse. Paris, 1933.
Phil 7150.29   Blondel, Charles. Le suicide. Strasbourg, 1933.
Phil 5520.62   Blumenfeld, W. Sinn und Unsinn. München, 1933.
Phil 2401.2.10   Boas, George. The happy beast in French thought of the 17th century. Baltimore, 1933.
Phil 9590.4   Bonnard, L.C. Entufhrön. Paris, 1933.
Phil 8691.23   Boorman, W.R. Independent young thinkers. Boston, 1933.
Phil 5374.57   Boring, E.G. The physical dimensions of consciousness. N.Y., 1933.
Phil 5241.98   Boynton, P.L. Intelligence, its manifestations and measurement. N.Y., 1933.
Phil 5075.4   Brentano, F. Kategorienlehre. Leipzig, 1933.
Phil 8876.93   Brightman, E.S. Moral laws. N.Y., 1933.
Phil 4352.1.101   Briones Ortún, Juan. En torno a Balmes. Bilboa, 1933.
Phil 2150.7.99   Broad, Charles D. Examination of McTaggart's philosophy. Cambridge, Eng., 1933. 3v.
Phil 8581.93   Brownell, B. Earth is enough. N.Y., 1933.
Phil 5041.72   Brunstaed, Friedrich. Logik. München, 1933.
Phil 5241.88   Bühler, Charlotte M. Der menschliche Lebenslauf als psychologisches Problem. Leipzig, 1933.
Phil 6011.5   Bühler, Karl. Ausdruckstheorie. Jena, 1933.
Phil 7069.33.15   Bull, Titus. Nature, man and destiny. N.Y., 1933.
Phil 3160.10.90   Burg, Josef. Konstitution und Gegenstand im logistischen Neupositivismus Rudolf Carnaps. Inaug. Diss. Leipzig, 1933.
Phil 5241.91   Burridge, William. A new physiological psychology. London, 1933.
Phil 9495.135.5   Buschke, A. Sex habits. N.Y., 1933.
Phil 623.24A   Busson, Henri. La pensée religieuse française de Charron à Pascal. Paris, 1933.
Phil 5241.89   Butler, J.R. Human nature. N.Y., 1933.
Phil 5811.15.20   Buytendijk, Frederik Jacobus Johannes. Wesen und Sinn des Spiels. Berlin, 1933.
Phil 8877.65.20A   Cabot, Richard C. The meaning of right and wrong. N.Y., 1933.
Phil 6952.21.10   Campbell, C.M. Towards mental health. Cambridge, 1933.
Phil 5374.58   Campbell, P.A. Consciousness, brain-child. East Cleveland, 1933.
Phil 177.88   Castaner, C. Soul and matter. London, 1933.
Phil 2477.6.89   Castelli, Enrico. Lettres reçues à propos de la communication de M. Blondel. Marseille, 1933.
Phil 5752.8   Cavallo, V. La libertà umana nella filosofia contemporanea. Napoli, 1933.
Phil 8030.2   Chandler, A.R. A bibliography of experimental aesthetics, 1865-1932. Columbus, 1933.
Phil 5042.24   Chapman, Frank M. The fundamentals of logic. N.Y., 1933.
Phil 1885.84   Chappuis, A. Der theoretische Weg Bradley's. Paris, 1933.
Phil 177.77.5   Chevalier, Jacques. Trois conférences d'Oxford. 2. ed. Paris, 1933.
Phil 5242.44   Claparède, Edouard. Causeries psychologiques. Genève, 1933.
Phil 8877.73   Clarke, F. (Mrs.). Give yourself a new deal. Boston, 1933.
Phil 8610.933   Cohen, C. Bradlaugh and Ingersoll. London, 1933.
Phil 177.85   Collingwood, R.G. An essay on philosophical method. Oxford, 1933.
Phil 2494.35   Condorcet, M.J.A.N. Esquisse d'un tableau historique des progrès de l'esprit humain. Paris, 1933.
Phil 333.13   Conger, George P. The horizons of thought. Princeton, 1933.
Phil 2070.134.5   Cornesse, Marie. L'idée de Dieu chez William James. Thèse. Grenoble, 1933.
Phil 2070.134   Cornesse, Marie. Le rôle des images dans la pensée de William James. Thèse. Grenoble, 1933.
Phil 5850.166   Crane, G.W. Psychology applied. Chicago, 1933.
Phil 8827.8   Cresson, André. Le problème moral et les philosophes. Paris, 1933.
Phil 3640.263   Crookshank, F.G. Individual psychology and Nietzsche. London, 1933.
Phil 3195.6.91   Cüppers, Clemens. Die erkenntnistheoretischen Grundgedanken Wilhelm Diltheys. Leipzig, 1933.
Phil 3195.6.92   Cüppers, Clemens. Die erkenntnistheoretischen Grundgedanken Wilhelm Diltheys. Inaug. Diss. Leipzig, 1933.
Phil 400.86   Cunningham, G.W. The idealistic argument in recent British and American philosophy. N.Y., 1933.
Phil 3485.15   Dahl, J. Ernstes und Heiteres über Kant. Cottbus, 1933.
Phil 400.87   Dasgupta, S.N. Indian idealism. Cambridge, Eng., 1933.
Phil 3195.6.89   Degener, Alfons. Dilthey und das Problem der Metaphysik. Bonn, 1933.
Phil 5243.39   Delgadio, H.F. Psicología. Lima, 1933.
Phil 8583.24   Deyo, M.L. A modern conception of religion. Binghamton, 1933.
Phil 3195.6.75   Dilthey, Wilhelm. Der junge Dilthey. Leipzig, 1933.
Phil 3195.6.31   Dilthey, Wilhelm. Von deutscher Dichtung und Musik. Leipzig, 1933.
Phil 2855.3.81   Dopp, Joseph. Félix Ravaisson. Louvain, 1933.
Phil 178.62   Drago, P.C. La genesi del problema fenomenologico. Milano, 1933.
Phil 178.61   Drake, Durant. Invitation to philosophy. Boston, 1933.
Phil 178.22.35   Driesch, H. Philosophische Gegenwartsfragen. Leipzig, 1933.
Phil 7069.33.60   Driesch, Hans. Psychical research. London, 1933.
Phil 3823.5.5   Dunin-Borkowski, Stanislaus von. Spinoza aus den Tagen Spinozas. Münster, 1933. 3v.
Phil 803.6.18   Durant, W. The story of philosophy. N.Y., 1933.
Phil 930.36F   Eberhard, Wolfram. Beiträge zur Kosmologischen Spekulation der Chinesen der Han - Zert. Inaug. Diss. Berlin, 1933.
Phil 6314.5   Egyedi, H. Die Irrtümer der Psychoanalyse. Wien, 1933.
Phil 3640.198.15   Ellermann, H. Nietzsche und Klages. Inaug. Diss. Hamburg, 1933.
Phil 3246.228   Engelbrecht, H.C. Johann Gottlieb Fichte. N.Y., 1933.

1933 - cont.

Phil 4210.155   Esposito, G. Il sistema filosofico di Antonio Rosmini. 2a ed. Milano, 1933.
Phil 179.30   Esser, Gerard. Metaphysica generalis in usum scholarum. Techny, Ill., 1933.
Phil 6951.5.12   Farrar, C.B. Twenty-five years of mental hygiene; a tribute to C.W. Beers. n.p., 1933.
Phil 3528.80   Fiedler, A. Die staatswissenschaftlichen Anschauungen und die politische-publizistische Tätigkeit des Nachkantianers Wilhelm Traugott Krug. Inaug. Diss. Dresden, 1933.
Phil 3625.11.85   Findlay, J.N. Meinong's theory of objects. London, 1933.
Phil 7069.33.56   Fodor, Nandor. Encyclopaedia of psychic science. London, 1933?
Phil 5245.35   Franz, S.I. Psychology. 1. ed. N.Y., 1933.
Phil 3120.2.101   Franzis, Emerich. Bernard Bolzano. Münster, 1933.
Phil 1133.24   Frenkian, A.M. Etudes de philosophie presocratique. Cernăuti, 1933. 2v.
Phil 6315.2.10.10   Freud, Sigmund. Vorlesungen zur Einführung in die Psychoanalyse. Berlin, 1933.
Phil 180.48.10   Freund, Ludwig. Philosophie: ein unlösbares Problem. München, 1933.
Phil 3850.18.108   Frick, Paul. Der weltanschauliche Hintergrund der materialen Wertethik Max Schelers. Diss. Stuttgart, 1933.
Phil 9345.11   Friend, N.E. (Mrs.). Love and you. N.Y., 1933.
Phil 5245.21.7   Fröbes, Joseph. Cursus brevior psychologiae speculativae in usum scholarum. Parisiis, 1933.
Phil 5627.150   Fuglsang-Damgaard, H. Religionspsykologi. København, 1933.
Phil 8673.6.7   Gallagher, Denis Maria. Pringle-Pattison's idea of God. Washington, D.C., 1933.
Phil 181.57.5   Galli, Gallo. Saggio sulla dialettica della realta spirituale. Milano, 1933.
Phil 2840.95   Galli, Gallo. Studi storico-critici sulla filosofia di C. Renouvier. v.1-2. Gubbio, 1933-35.
Phil 5246.45   Galt, William. Phyloanalysis. London, 1933.
Phil 400.96   Gehlen, A. Idealismus und Existentialphilosophie. Leipzig, 1933.
Phil 5756.13   Gehlen, A. Theorie der Willensfreiheit. Berlin, 1933.
Phil 4120.4.45   Gentile, Giovanni. Introduzione alla filosofia. Milano, 1933.
Phil 270.40   Geyser, Joseph. Das Gesetz der Ursache. München, 1933.
Phil 2115.111.15A   Gibson, James. John Locke. London, 1933.
Phil 2725.2.99   Giraud, Victor. La vie tragique de Lamennais. Paris, 1933.
Phil 2520.181   Giuli, Guido de. Cartesio. Firenze, 1933.
Phil 3640.275   Goedewaagen, T. Nietzsche. 's-Gravenhage, 1933.
Phil 181.63.5   Goedewaagen, T. Het spectrum der philosophie in de 20e eeuw. Leiden, 1933.
Phil 181.69   Gorce, M.M. Premiers principes de philosophie. Paris, 1933.
Phil 2490.123   Gouhier, Henri. La jeunesse d'Auguste Comte et la formation du positivisme. Paris, 1933-36. 3v.
Phil 3801.434A   Gray-Smith, R. God in the philosophy of Schelling. Diss. Philadelphia, 1933.
Phil 9230.13   Great Britain. Commission on Lotteries and Betting, 1932-33. Final report. London, 1933.
Phil 6316.8   Groddeck, Georg. Exploring the unconscious. London, 1933.
Phil 5520.58   Groddeck, Georg. Der Mensch als Symbol. Wien, 1933.
Phil 6990.3.60   Groneman, William. Bernadette Soubirous. Leuven, 1933.
Phil 8881.66   Groos, R. Wertethik oder religiöse Sittlichkeit? München, 1933.
Phil 337.9   Günther, E. Die ontologischen Grundlagen der neueren Erkenntnislehre. Halle, 1933.
Phil 3425.291   Günther, G. Grundzüge einer neuen Theorie des Denkens in Hegels Logik. Leipzig, 1933.
Phil 1050.21   Guttmann, J. Die Philosophie des Judentums. München, 1933.
Phil 338.21   Hahn, Hans. Logik, Mathematik und Naturerkennen. Wien, 1933.
Phil 5247.50   Harmon, F.L. The effects of noise upon certain psychological and physical processes. Thesis. N.Y., 1933.
Phil 182.94.10   Hartmann, N. Das Problem des Geistigen Seins. Berlin, 1933.
Phil 630.39   Heacock, Roger. Der monistische Realismus im amerikanischen Denken. Inaug. Diss. Berlin? 1933.
Phil 8408.28   Heller-Heinzelmann, R. L'immaginazione e la vita estetica. Firenze, 1933.
Phil 6957.17.7   Henderson, D.K. A text-book of psychiatry for students and practitioners. 3. ed. London, 1933.
Phil 5627.134   Henson, H.H. The Oxford group movement. N.Y., 1933.
Phil 3827.8   Hessing, Siegfried ed. Spinoza-Festschrift. Heidelberg, 1933.
Phil 623.44   Hobson, John Atkinson. Rationalism and humanism. London, 1933.
Phil 182.99   Höcksmann, F.X. Der Weg zum Sinn des Seins. Wien, 1933.
Phil 4803.454.5   Hoene-Wroński, Józef Maria. L'oeuvre philosophique de Hoené Wronski. Paris, 1933-36. 2v.
Phil 338.20   Hönigswald, R. Geschichte der Erkenntnistheorie. Berlin, 1933.
Phil 182.62.15   Holmes, Edmond. The headquarters of reality. London, 1933.
Phil 3120.8.85   Hoppenstedt, W. von. Franz Brentanos Kantkritik. Inaug. Diss. Kiel, 1933.
Phil 6677.15   Hull, C.L. Hypnosis and suggestibility. N.Y., 1933.
Phil 5247.29.15   Humphrey, G. The nature of learning in its relation to the living system. London, 1933.
Phil 5247.49   Hungerford, H. Bunkless psychology. Washington, 1933.
Phil 8587.57   Hutchinson, Paul. The ordeal of western civilization. Boston, 1933.
Phil 8588.2   Inge, W.R. The eternal values. London, 1933.
Phil 289.1   Inge, W.R. God and the astronomers. London, 1933.
Phil 3552.305.5   Iwanicki, Joseph. Leibniz et les démonstrations mathématiques de l'existence de Dieu. Thèse. Strasbourg, 1933.
Phil 3552.305   Iwanicki, Joseph. Leibniz et les démonstrations mathématiques de l'existence de Dieu. Strasbourg, 1933.
Phil 5627.170   Jahn, Ernst. Religion und Individualpsychologie. Wien, 1933.
Phil 3801.465.5   Jankélévitch, V. L'odyssée de la conscience dans la dernière philosophie de Schelling. Paris, 1933.
Phil 9075.35.5   Jankélévitch, Vladimir. La mauvaise conscience. Paris, 1933.
Phil 9075.35   Jankélévitch, Vladimir. Valeur et signification de la mauvais conscience. Thèse. Paris, 1933.
Phil 6049.33   Jaquin, Noel. The hand of man. London, 1933.
Phil 809.4   Joad, C.E.M. Great philosophies of the world. N.Y., 1933.

1933 - cont.

Phil 8589.17.10 Joad, Cyril E.M. Counter attack from the East. London, 1933.
Phil 5402.22.15 Jones, Eli Stanley. Christ and human suffering. N.Y., 1933.
Phil 5627.134.80 Jones, Olivin Mary. Inspired children. 1. ed. N.Y., 1933.
Phil 8410.6 Jordán de Urríes y Azara, José. Resumen de teoría general del arte. 1. ed. Madrid, 1933.
Phil 1750.143 Juganaru, P. L'apologie de la guerre dans la philosophie contemporaine. Thèse. Paris, 1933.
Phil 5249.13.30 Jung, Carl G. Bericht über das Berliner Seminar. Berlin, 1933.
Phil 810.6 Kafka, G. Geschichtsphilosophie der Philosophiegeschichte. Berlin, 1933.
Phil 575.99 Kamiat, A.H. Social forces in personality stunting. Cambridge, 1933.
Phil 3480.32.21 Kant, Immanuel. Critique of pure reason. London, 1933.
Phil 3480.28.100A Kant, Immanuel. Die drei Kritiken. Leipzig, 1933.
Phil 5250.17.5 Kantor, J.R. A survey of the science of psychology. Bloomington, 1933.
Phil 1870.116 Kaveeshwar, G.W. The metaphysics of Berkeley critically examined in the light of modern philosophy. Mandleshwar, 1933.
Phil 720.26 Kearney, C.M. Two neglected aspects of the truth situation. Thesis. Chicago, 1933.
EDL Phil 185.44.2 Klages, Ludwig. Der Geist als Widersacher der Seele. v.1-3. Gesantverzeichnis. Leipzig, 1933. 4v.
Phil 3160.9.85 Klink, Siegfried. Das Prinzip des Unbewussten bei Carl Gustav Carus. Tübingen, 1933.
Phil 5820.5 Klüver, H. Behavior mechanisms in monkeys. Chicago, 1933.
Phil 3640.260 Knight, A.H.J. Some aspects of the life and work of Nietzsche. Cambridge, 1933.
Phil 5250.30 Krauss, S. Der seelische Konflikt; Psychologie und existentiale Bedeutung. Stuttgart, 1933.
Phil 575.92 Krout, M.H. Major aspects of personality. Chicago, 1933.
Phil 9035.59.15 Künkel, Fritz. Charakter, Einzelmensch und Gruppe. Leipzig, 1933.
Phil 291.6 Künkel, H. Das Gesetz deines Lebens. Jena, 1933.
Phil 2725.11.15 Lachelier, Jules. Oeuvres. Paris, 1933. 2v.
Phil 2475.1.284 Lacombe, R.E. La psychologie bergsonienne; étude critique. Paris, 1933.
Phil 8412.6.5 Lalo, Charles. L'expression de la vie dans l'art. Paris, 1933.
Phil 5251.28.7 Lambek, C. The structure of our apprehension of reality. Copenhagen, 1933.
Phil 6121.27 Lashley, K.S. Integrative functions of the cerebral cortex. Baltimore, 1933.
Phil 2725.35.60 Lavelle, Louis. La conscience de soi. Paris, 1933.
Phil 3552.301 Le Chevallier, L. La morale de Leibniz. Paris, 1933.
Phil 186.86 Leendertz, W. Dogma en existentie. Amsterdam, 1933.
Phil 2411.8 LeFlamanc, Auguste. Les utopies prérévolutionnaires et la philosophie du XVIIIe siècle. Brest, 1933.
Phil 3011.3.10 Lehmann, G. Die Ontologie der Gegenwart in ihren Grundgestalten. Halle, 1933.
Phil 3493.23 Lembke, B. Immanuel Kants Geld-Theorie. Danzig, 1933.
Phil 8587.32.91 Lester-Garland, L.V. The religious philosophy of Baron F. von Hügel. N.Y., 1933.
Phil 186.48.11 Lighthall, W.D. The person of evolution. Toronto, 1933.
Phil 8080.4 Listowel, William Francis Hare. A critical history of modern aesthetics. London, 1933.
Phil 186.60.15 Litt, Theodor. Einleitung in die Philosophie. Leipzig, 1933.
Phil 3640.261 Löwith, Karl. Kierkegaard und Nietzsche. Frankfurt am Main, 1933.
Phil 2475.1.245 Loisy, Alfred. Y a-t-il deux sources de la religion et de la morale? Paris, 1933.
Phil 6321.11 Lorand, Sándor. Psycho-analysis today. London, 1933.
Phil 186.50.20 Ludowici, A. Zugleich. München, 1933.
Phil 5251.35.9 Lund, F.H. Psychology: an empirical study of behavior. N.Y., 1933.
Phil 8591.36 Lyman, E.W. The meaning and truth of religion. N.Y., 1933.
Phil 1517.6 Macdonald, A.J. Authority and reason in the early middle ages. London, 1933.
Phil 5252.18.25 McDougall, William. The energies of men. N.Y., 1933.
Phil 9515.3.96 Maduschka, Leo. Das Problem des Einsamkeit in 18 Jahrhundert. Weimar, 1933.
Phil 6022.4 Märker, Friedrich. Symbolik der Gesichtsformen. Erlenbach, 1933.
Phil 1812.9 Mahony, M.J. History of modern thought, the English, Irish and Scotch schools. N.Y., 1933.
Phil 2070.131 Maire, Gilbert. William James et le pragmatisme religieux. Paris, 1933.
Phil 960.147 Malkani, G.R. Ajñana. London, 1933.
Phil 1712.13 Maréchal, Joseph. Précis d'histoire de la philosophie moderne. Louvain, 1933.
Phil 2750.11.43.5 Maritain, Jacques. De la philosophie chrétienne. Paris, 1933.
Phil 2750.11.51 Maritain, Jacques. Some reflections on culture and literature. Chicago, 1933.
Phil 8633.1.33 Matthews, Shailer. Immortality and the cosmic process. Cambridge, 1933.
Phil 5022.2 Meckies, H. Beiträge zur Geschichte des Induktionsproblems. Münster, 1933.
Phil 3832.13 Melames, S.M. Spinoza and Buddha. Chicago, Ill., 1933.
Phil 1750.133A Mercier, L.J.A. Challenge of humanism. N.Y., 1933.
Phil 343.10.5 Metzger, Arnold. Phänomenologie und Metaphysik. Halle an der Saale, 1933.
Phil 6322.4.15 Miller, Hugh C. Psycho-analysis and its derivations. London, 1933.
Phil 1850.128 Minkowski, Helmut. Einordnung, Wesen und Aufgaben...des Francis Bacon. Leyde, 1933.
Phil 187.110 Mitchell, William. The place of minds in the world. London, 1933.
Phil 6962.22 Mondain, Paul. Les fous satisfaits. Paris, 1933.
Phil 8667.18 Monod, Victor. Dieu dans l'univers. Thèse. Paris, 1933.
Phil 5252.43.5 Moore, J.S. The foundations of psychology. 2d ed. Princeton, 1933.
Phil 6962.21 Moore, T.V. The essential psychoses and their fundamental syndromes. Baltimore, 1933.
Phil 187.29.15A Morgan, C.L. The emergence of novelty. London, 1933.
Phil 9065.1.15 Morley, J. On compromise. London, 1933.
Phil 5052.34 Morris, C.R. Idealistic logic. London, 1933.
Phil 5252.12.18 Münsterberg, H. On the witness stand. N.Y., 1933.
Phil 8887.72 Mukenje, D.G. Daily meditations. N.Y., 1933.
Phil 343.18 Mukerji, A.C. Self, thought and reality. Allahabad, 1933.

1933 - cont.

Phil 5822.8 Munn, Norman L. An introduction to animal psychology. Boston, 1933.
Phil 5252.69A Murphy, Gardner. General psychology. N.Y., 1933.
Phil 5252.19.20 Myers, C.S. A psychologist's point of view. London, 1933.
Phil 5253.10 Neurath, Otto. Einheitswissenschaft und Psychologie. Wien, 1933.
Phil 365.35 Newsholme, H.P. Evolution and redemption. London, 1933.
Phil 9495.134 Newsom, G.E. The new morality. N.Y., 1933.
Phil 3640.38 Nietzsche, Friedrich. Kritik und Zukunft der Kultur. Zürich, 1933.
Phil 3640.58.7 Nietzsche, Friedrich. Socrates und die griechische Tragödie. München, 1933.
Phil 3640.13 Nietzsche, Friedrich. Werke und Briefe. München, 1933-49. 5v.
Phil 930.37 Northern Pacific Railroad Company. The story of the Monad. St. Paul, Minn., 1933.
Phil 189.23 Oakeshott, Michael. Experience and its modes. Cambridge,Eng., 1933.
Phil 8964.2 Oddone, Andrea. Teoria degli atti umani. Milano, 1933.
Phil 1702.6.15 Olgiati, F. Neo-scolastica, idealismo e spiritualismo. Milano, 1933.
Phil 6964.2.6 Oliver, John R. Psychiatry and mental health. N.Y., 1933.
Phil 4365.2.38 Ortega y Gasset, José. The modern theme. N.Y., 1933.
Phil 1540.22 Orth, Albert. Untersuchungen zu Prinzipien Fragen der scholastischen Erkenntnistheorie. Bahenhausen, 1933.
Phil 735.102 Osborne, Harold. Foundations of the philosophy of value. Cambridge, 1933.
Phil 4190.1.90 Ottaviano, Carmelo. Il pensiero di Francesco Orestano. Palermo, 1933.
Phil 5440.29 Outhit, M.C. A study of the resemblance of parents and children in general intelligence. Thesis. N.Y., 1933.
Phil 2475.1.239 Pallière, Aimé. Bergson et le Judaïsme. Paris, 1933.
Phil 2630.1.82 Perraud, A. Le P. Gratry; sa vie et ses oeuvres. 7e ed. Paris, 1933.
Phil 5255.8.15 Pfänder, A. Die Seele des Menschen. Halle, 1933.
Phil 3450.19.95 Pfeiffer, Johannes S. Existenzphilosophie; eine Einführung in Heidegger und Jaspers. Leipzig, 1933.
Phil 5643.94 Physical Society of London. Report of a joint discussion on vision. London, 1933.
Phil 9515.6 Powys, J.C. A philosophy of solitude. N.Y., 1933.
Phil 5520.59 Psychologie du langage. Paris, 1933.
Phil 978.68.5 Purucker, G. de. Occult glossary. London, 1933.
Phil 5257.46 Radecki, Wacław. Tratado de psicología. Buenos Aires, 1933.
Phil 8597.38.10 Radhakrishnan, S. East and West in religion. London, 1933.
Phil 2150.9 Ralston, H.J. Emergent evolution...the philosophy of C. Lloyd Morgan. Boston, 1933.
Phil 3791.126 Ramlow, Lilli. Alois Riehl und H. Spencer. Inaug. Diss. Saalfeld, 1933.
Phil 8430.29A Raphael, Max. Provalon, Marx, Picasso. Paris, 1933.
Phil 2855.3.15 Ravaisson-Mollien, Félix. Testament philosophique et fragments. Paris, 1933.
Phil 5625.82 Razran, G.H.S. Conditioned responses in children. Thesis. N.Y., 1933.
Phil 7069.33.40 Reality. Boston, 1933.
Phil 5525.39.5 Reik, Theodor. Nachdenkliche Heiterkeit. Wien, 1933.
Phil 1817.8 Reiser, O.L. Humanism and new world ideals. Yellow Springs, Colorado, 1933.
Phil 4195.95 Remé, Richard W. Darstellung des Inhalts der Disputationes in astrologiam. Hamburg, 1933.
Phil 4215.3.40 Rensi, Giuseppe. Le ragioni dell'irrazionalismo. 2a ed. Napoli, 1933.
Phil 4372.1.130 Riba y García, Carlos. Luis Vives y el pacifismo. Zaragoza, 1933.
Phil 5420.5 Roback, A.A. Self-consciousness and its treatment. Cambridge, 1933.
Phil 192.74 Robertson, A. Philosophers on holiday. London, 1933.
Phil 6127.20 Rosett, J. Intercortical systems. N.Y., 1933.
Phil 665.61 Rüsche, Franz. Das Seelenpneuma. Paderborn, 1933.
Phil 5627.134.12 Russell, A.J. One thing I know. N.Y., 1933.
Phil 3195.10.113 Sacher, Heinz. Vergleich zwischen Rehmkes und Drieschs Philosophie. Inaug. Diss. Dresden, 1933.
Phil 1718.42 Saffet, Mehmet. Muasir Aurupa felsefesi. Ankara, 1933.
Phil 6100.17 Sager, O. Recherches sur la somatotopie sensitive dans le thalamus des singes. Harlem, 1933.
Phil 8620.39 Samuel, H. The tree of good and evil. London, 1933.
Phil 1750.142 Santayana, George. Some turns of thought in modern philosophy. Cambridge, Eng., 1933.
Phil 1750.142.2 Santayana, George. Some turns of thought in modern philosophy. N.Y., 1933.
Phil 3838.17 Schaub, E.L. Spinoza, the man and his thought. Chicago, 1933.
Phil 3195.12.90 Scheele, Fritz. Hugo Dinglers philosophisches System. Inaug. Diss. Corbach, 1933.
Phil 735.18.5 Scheler, Max. L'homme du ressentiment. Paris, 1933.
Phil 6315.2.103 Schelts van Kloosterhuis, E. Freud als ethnoloog. Proefschrift. Amsterdam, 1933.
Phil 3640.278 Scheuffler, G. Friedrich Nietzsche im Dritten Reich. Erfurt, 1933.
Phil 5190.24 Schilder, Klaas. Zur Begriffsgeschichte des "Paradoxon". Inaug. Diss. Kampen, 1933.
Phil 6328.56 Schläfer-Wolfram, E. Und du wirst Getrieben. Berlin, 1933.
Phil 5465.48 Schmidt, Otto. Zur revision der Eidetek. Marburg, 1933.
Phil 8419.54 Schneiderfranken, J.A. Das Reich der Kunst. Basel, 1933.
Phil 5440.32.5 Schwesinger, G. Heredity and environment. N.Y., 1933.
Phil 5238.6 Scritti di psicologia raccolti in onore di Federico Kiesow. Torino, 1933.
Phil 1158.27 Sedgwick, H.D. Art of happiness. Indianapolis, 1933.
Phil 2295.87 Seeber, Anna. John Toland als politischer Schriftsteller. Inaug. Diss. Schramberg, 1933.
Phil 3838.18 Segond, J. La vie de Benoit de Spinoza. Paris, 1933.
Phil 1718.21 Séronya, Henri. Initiation à la philosophie contemporaine. Paris, 1933.
Phil 3838.19 Sérouya, Henri. Spinoza. Paris, 1933.
Phil 2520.188 Serrus, Charles. La méthode de Descartes et son application à la métaphysique. Paris, 1933.
Phil 2520.188.5 Serrus, Charles. La méthode de Descartes et son application à la métaphysique. Thèse. Paris, 1933.
Phil 5520.61 Serrus, Charles. Le parallélisme logico-grammatical. Thèse. Paris, 1933.
Phil 630.41 Seth Pringle Pattison, Andrew. The Balfour lectures on realism. Edinburgh, 1933.
Phil 8843.12 Sheriff, W.S. Religion and ethics. Thesis. Philadelphia, 1933.

1933 - cont.

Phil 270.42   Silberstein, L. Causality. London, 1933.
Phil 2115.144   Smith, N.K. John Locke, 1632-1704. Manchester, 1933.
Phil 3838.23   Societas Spinoza. Septimana Spinozana. Hagae, 1933.
Phil 9245.53   Somer, Marcelle de. Le rythme de la vie, le bonheur. Gand, 1933.
Phil 8419.13   Spalletti, G. Saggio sopra la bellezza. Firenze, 1933.
Phil 4065.98.5   Spampanato, V. Documenti della vita di Giordano Bruno. Firenze, 1933.
Phil 193.140   Spirito, Ugo. Scienza e filosofia. Firenze, 1933.
Phil 5058.46.10A   Stebbing, Lizzie S. Logical positivism and analysis. London, 1933.
Phil 5058.46.3   Stebbing, Lizzie S. A modern introduction to logic. 2. ed. N.Y., 1933.
Phil 3425.284   Steinbüchel, T. Das Grundproblem der hegelschen Philosophie. Bonn, 1933.
Phil 978.49.155   Steiner, R. Kosmische und menschliche Geschichte. Dornach, 1933-34. 5v.
Phil 6328.2.45   Stekel, Wilhelm. Der Seelenarzt. Leipzig, 1933.
Phil 6328.16   Stephen, Karin. Psychoanalysis and medicine. Cambridge, Eng., 1933.
Phil 3246.245   Stiner, Rudolf. Fichtes Geist mitten unter uns. Dornach, 1933.
Phil 1865.178   Stocks, John L. Jeremy Bentham (1748-1832). Manchester, 1933.
Phil 978.59.97   Suares, Carlo. Krishnamurti. Paris, 1933.
Phil 7069.33.43   Taillepied, N. A treatise of ghosts. London, 1933.
Phil 7069.33.46   Taylor, William G.L. Katie Fox, epochmaking medium. N.Y., 1933.
Phil 2477.6.92   Taymans d'Eypernon, F. Le blondelisme. Louvain, 1933.
Phil 7069.33.45   Tenhaeff, W.H.C. Paragnosie en "Einfuehlen". Proefschrift. Bussum, N.H., 1933.
Phil 3120.17.90   Thöne, Fritz. Erich Becher als Vertreter des Eudämonismus. Diss. Giessen, 1933.
Phil 194.42   Tilby, Aubry W. Right; a study in physical and moral order. London, 1933.
Phil 9035.45.20   Todoranu, D. O conceptie americana despre caracter. Cluj, 1933.
Phil 2805.241.5   Tourneur, Zacharie. Beauté poétique. Muln, 1933.
Phil 3925.8.81   Trefzger, Hermann. Der philosophische Entwicklungsgang von Joseph Weber. Freiburg, 1933.
Phil 6129.7   Trumper, Henry. The message of mysticism in spiritual healing. London, 1933.
Phil 6329.6   Tuinstra, C.L. Het symbool in de psychoanalyse. Amsterdam, 1933.
Phil 8419.39.5   Tumarkin, Anna. Der Ästhetiker Johann G. Sulzer. Frauenfeld, 1933.
Phil 9065.5   Ülken, Hilmi Ziyoi. Telifciilipin tenokurlan. Istanbul, 1933.
Phil 3805.173.5   Ungern-Sternberg, Arthur Freiherr von. Schleiermachers völkische Botschaft. Gotha, 1933.
Phil 5261.23   Valdefievre, P. La psychologie du poéte. Paris, 1933.
Phil 5261.17.12   Valentine, Willard Lee. Psychology laboratory manual. N.Y., 1933.
Phil 4265.1.20   Vanini, Lucilio, afterwards Giulio Cesare. Le opere di Giulio Cesare Vanini e le loro fonti. Milano, 1933-34. 2v.
Phil 5261.19   Vialle, L. Le désir du néant. Paris, 1933.
Phil 7069.34.41   Vilanova, María. El tesoro de la ciencia eterna de Dios. Barcelona, 1933-34. 2v.
Phil 352.7   Vincent, Maxime. La vision interne. Paris, 1933.
Phil 3640.259   Visser, H.L.A. Nietzsche de goede Europeaan. Zutphen, 1933.
Phil 3160.9.87   Wäsche, E. Carl Gustav Carus und die romantische Weltanschauung. Dusseldorf, 1933.
Phil 3640.264   Wahle, Aloys. Der weltanschauliche Gehalt von Nietzsches Dichtungen. Inaug. Diss. Dillingen, 1933.
Phil 8677.17   Walker, L.J. The return to God. London, 1933.
Phil 822.10   Walshe, Thomas J. The quest of reality. London, 1933.
Phil 3549.8.110   Wandrey, Conrad. Ludwig Klages und seine Lebensphilosophie. Leipzig, 1933.
Phil 8602.16.5   Waterhouse, E.S. The philosophical approach to religion. London, 1933.
Phil 8550.342   Webb, Clement C.J. A study of religious thought in England from 1850. Oxford, 1933.
Phil 5645.34.3   Weidlich, Karl. Farben und Farben-Empfindung. Stettin, 1933.
Phil 7069.33.54   Wells, Helen B. Collection mimeographs. N.Y., 1933. 8 pam.
Phil 7069.33.52   Wells, Helen B. Flower-life in ethic. N.Y., 1933. 2 pam.
Phil 7069.33.50   Wells, Helen B. Lessons in etheric and electric vibratory law. N.Y., 1933. 6 pam.
Phil 6132.29   Wenzl, Aloys. Das Leib-Seele-Problem. Leipzig, 1933.
Phil 5627.134.10   What is the Oxford Group? N.Y., 1933.
Phil 822.8A   Whitehead, A.N. Adventures of ideas. N.Y., 1933.
Phil 5850.386.5   Wiggam, A.E. The marks of a clear mind. N.Y., 1933.
Phil 8125.34   Wilhelm, Richard. Friedrich Justus Riedel. Heidelberg, 1933.
Phil 3903.3.109   Willrodt, S. Semifiktionen und Vollfiktionen in der Philosophie des Als Ob von H. Vaihinger. Inaug. Diss. Gräfenhainichen, 1933.
Phil 5590.532   Wimersma Greidanus, H.T. Instinct en karakter proeve eener characterologie op instinct-psychologischen grondalag. Proefschrift. Zeist, 1933.
Phil 3120.2.98   Winter, E. Bernard Bolzano und sein Kreis. Leipzig, 1933.
Phil 8602.34.10   Wobbermin, G. The nature of religion. N.Y., 1933.
Phil 6972.20   Wolfe, Walter Béran. Nervous breakdown; its cause and cure. N.Y., 1933.
Phil 197.58   Wolff, Gustav. Leben und Erkennen. München, 1933.
Phil 6060.12.50   Wollnik, H. Probleme der Graphologie. Inaug. Diss. Leipzig, 1933.
Phil 5640.36   Wolters, A.W.P. The evidence of our senses. London, 1933.
Phil 5262.9.30   Woodworth, R.S. Adjustment and mastery. Baltimore, 1933.
Phil 6132.4.20   Worcester, Elwood. Making life better. N.Y., 1933.
Phil 9455.12   Wright, Quincy. Public opinion and world politics. Chicago, 1933.
Phil 305.1   Younghusband, F.E. The living universe. N.Y., 1933.
Phil 8605.5   Zuver, Dudley. Salvation by laughter. N.Y., 1933.

1934

Phil 6310.1.30   Adler, Gerhard. Entdeckung der Seele. Zürich, 1934.
Phil 5070.19   Ahmet, Nureltin. Conformisme et révolte. Thèse. Paris, 1934.
Phil 9530.37   Alexander, James. Through failure to success. N.Y., 1934.

1934 - cont.

Phil 9035.61.9   Allers, Rudolf. Practical psychology in character development. N.Y., 1934.
Phil 4210.146   Anastasia, M. I principii della politica nella filosofia di Antonio Rosmini. Osimo, 1934.
Phil 960.146   Astreya, B.L. The elements of Indian logic. 2d ed. Benares, 1934.
Phil 8612.26   Baghdigian, B.K. The forgotten purpose. Kansas City, 1934.
Phil 978.74.10   Bailey, A.A. (Mrs.). A treatise on white magic. N.Y., 1934.
Phil 8656.24   Baker, Rannie B. Concept of a limited God. Washington, 1934.
Phil 8402.36   Baratono, A. Il monda sensbile. Milano, 1934.
Phil 8691.24.2   Barnes, E.W. Scientifc theory and religion. N.Y., 1934.
Phil 5650.21   Bartlett, F.C. The problem of noise. Cambridge, 1934.
Phil 176.133   Basch, Victor. Essais d'esthétique, de philosophie et de littérature. Paris, 1934.
Phil 6111.49   Bassett, Clara. Mental hygiene in the community. N.Y., 1934.
Phil 5241.59.15   Bentley, I.M. The new field of psychology. N.Y., 1934.
Phil 2475.1.65   Bergson, Henri. La pensée et le mouvant. 5. éd. Paris, 1934.
Phil 3821.21   Bernard, Walter. The philosophy of Spinoza and Brunner. N.Y., 1934.
Phil 5850.135.20   Bertine, Eleanor. How to interview. 2. ed. N.Y., 1934.
Phil 7069.34.5   Besterman, T. Inquiry into the unknown. London, 1934.
Phil 974.4.25   Besterman, T. Mrs. Annie Besant. London, 1934.
Phil 974.4.30   Bhagavan Das. Annie Besant...and the changing world. Adyar, 1934.
Phil 5241.103   Bills, A.G. General experimental psychology. N.Y., 1934.
Phil 5241.94   Blanché, Robert. La notion de fait psychique. Thèse. Paris, 1934.
Phil 5241.90   Blondel, M. La pensée. Paris, 1934. 2v.
Phil 3552.365   Blumenthal, Erwin. Herders Auseinadersetzung mit der Philosophie Leibnitzens. Diss. Hamburg, 1934.
Phil 3110.37.5   Böhme, J. The signature of all things, with other writings. London, 1934.
Phil 5241.95   Bone, H. Une étude du préjugé au moyen des tests. Thèse. Paris, 1934.
Phil 282.12.10   Boodin, J.E. God and creation. N.Y., 1934. 2v.
Phil 1701.19   Borkenan, Franz. Der Übergang vom Feudalen zum bügerlichen Weltbild. Paris, 1934.
Phil 3850.22.93   Boucher, Maurice K.N.F. Solger; esthétique et philosophie de la présence. Thèse. Paris, 1934.
Phil 6311.16   Boven, William. L'anxiété. Neuchâtel, 1934.
Phil 8656.25   Box, Hubert S. The world and God. Thesis. London, 1934.
Phil 6120.8.25   Braat, J.P. De experimenteele psychologie en Kretschmer's constitutietypen. Amsterdam, 1934.
Phil 6951.24   Braatøy, T. Männer zwischen 15 und 25. Oslo, 1934.
Phil 176.143   Bräuer, Ernst Wasa. Metaphysik als beobachtende Wissenschaft. Berlin, 1934.
Phil 5241.104   Brandt, F. Psykoligi. v.1-2. København, 1934-40.
Phil 176.132   Branford, B. Éros and Psyche. London, 1934.
Phil 1750.144A   Bréhier, Émile. La notion de renaissance dans l'histoire de la philosophie. Oxford, 1934.
Phil 9400.8   Brigham, H. The youth of old age. Boston, 1934.
Phil 8581.67   Brightman, E.S. Personality and religion. N.Y., 1934.
Phil 5751.15   Broad, C.D. Determinism, indeterminism, and libertarianism. Cambridge, Eng., 1934.
Phil 2045.116   Brockdorff, Cay von. Die Urform der "Computatio sive logica" des Hobbes. Kiel, 1934.
Phil 525.89   Brockington, A.A. Mysticism and poetry. London, 1934.
Phil 6480.236   Bruller, Jean. Que tout rêveur doit savoit de la méthode psychanalytique d'interprétation des rêves. Paris, 1934.
Phil 801.23.9   Brunschvicg, L. Les âges de l'intelligence. Paris, 1934.
Phil 801.23.11   Brunschvicg, L. Les âges de l'intelligence. 3. ed. Paris, 1934.
Phil 5585.59   Brunswick, E. Wahrnehmung und Gegenstandswelt. Leipzig, 1934.
Phil 3110.78   Buddecke, W. Verzeichnis von Jakob Böhme-Handschreften. Göttingen, 1934.
Phil 7150.30   Bula, C.A. Analisis estadistico del suicidio. Rosario, 1934.
Phil 7074.20.10   Burke, Jane R. The bundle of life. 1st ed. N.Y., 1934.
Phil 176.88.10   Burne, C.D. The horizon of experience. N.Y., 1934.
Phil 6112.2.8.7   Call, A.P. Power through repose. Boston, 1934.
Phil 575.86   Campbell, C.M. Human personality and the environment. N.Y., 1934.
Phil 7069.34.7   Cannon, Alexander. Powers that be (the Mayfair lectures). London, 1934.
Phil 5042.21.9A   Carnap, Rudolf. Logische Syntax der Sprache. Wien, 1934.
Phil 4080.3.150   Carnevale, Luigi. Il concetto puro della filosofia dello spirito e la storia del secolo XIX di B. Croce. Varese, 1934.
Phil 177.95   Carrasquilla R., Humberto. El hombre. Medellin, 1934.
Phil 8403.42   Chandler, A.R. Beauty and human nature. N.Y., 1934.
Phil 8582.50   Chartier, E. Les dieux. Paris, 1934.
Phil 4210.143   Cheula, Pietro. Rapporti fra Kant e Rosmini. Milano, 1934.
Phil 4070.2.80   Cheula, Pietro. Saggio su la filosofia di Francesco Bonatelli. Milano, 1934.
Phil 8657.19   Christiansen, Broder. Der neue Gott. München, 1934.
Phil 8582.48   Clark, E.H. This world and the next. Boston, 1934.
Phil 7069.34.9   Clark, R. A spiritual spiritualism. London, 1934.
Phil 8633.1.34   Clark, W.E. Indian conceptions of immortality. Cambridge, 1934.
Phil 5042.25   Cohen, Morris R. Introduction to logic and scientific method. N.Y., 1934.
Phil 735.106   Cohn, Aron. Hauptprobleme der Wertphilosophie. Wien, 1934.
Phil 283.13   Collier, K.B. Cosmogonies of our fathers. N.Y., 1934.
Phil 5812.7A   Comparative psychology. N.Y., 1934.
Phil 8190.2   Coomaraswamy, Ananda. The transformation of nature in art. Cambridge, Mass., 1934.
Phil 2120.5   Cooper, B.S. The philosophy of Sir Oliver Lodge. Thesis. Nashville, 1934.
Phil 4352.1.155   Corts Grau, José. Ideario político de Balmes. Madrid, 1934.
Phil 3808.112.13   Covotti, Aurelio. La metafisica del bello e dei costumi di...Schopenhauer. Napoli, 1934.
Phil 1107.5   Covotti, Aurelio. I piesocratici; saggi. Napoli, 1934.
Phil 5649.20   Cox, John William. Manual skill. Cambridge, Eng., 1934.
Phil 8582.49   Creed, J.M. Religious thought in the eighteenth century. Cambridge, Eng., 1934.

Chronological Listing

Phil 8587.32.95   Dakiri, A.H., Jr. Von Hügel and the supernatural. London, 1934.

Phil 6953.13   Damaye, Henri. Psychiatrie et civilisation. Paris, 1934.
Phil 178.46.15   Decoster, Paul. De l'unité métaphysique. Bruxelles, 1934.
Phil 5243.42   Delacroix, Henri. Les grandes formes de la vie mentale. Paris, 1934.

Phil 1135.156   Delatte, A. Les conceptions de l'enthousiasme chez les philosophes presocratiques. Paris, 1934.

Phil 2120.4.90   Devaux, P. Le pragmatisme conceptuel de Clarence Irwing Lewis. Paris, 1934.

Phil 8404.19A   Dewey, J. Art as experience. N.Y., 1934.
Phil 8583.25   Dewey, John. A common faith. New Haven, 1934.
Phil 5213.3   Diehl, Frank. An historical and critical study of radical behaviorism. Baltimore, 1934.

Phil 3195.17.30   Diez, Max. Sprechen. Berlin, 1934.
Phil 3640.258   Dippel, P.G. Nietzsche und Wagner. Bern, 1934.
Phil 6313.10   Dorcus, Roy M. Textbook of abnormal psychology. Baltimore, 1934.

Phil 8583.27   Draghicesco, D. Vérité et révélation. Paris, 1934. 2v.

Phil 3485.14   Dunham, B. A study in Kant's aesthetics. Diss. Lancaster, Pa., 1934.

Phil 5243.14.9   Dwelshauvers, George. L'étude de la pensée. Paris, 1934.
Phil 5244.24   Ehrenstein, Walter. Einführung in die Ganzheitspsychologie. Leipzig, 1934.

Phil 5044.7   Ehrlich, W. Intentionalität und Sinn. Halle, 1934.
Phil 179.32   Elrick, C.F. Tertium quid; ratiocination. St. Louis, 1934.

Phil 9344.10   Elson, F.S. Quiet hints to ministers' wives. Boston, 1934.

Phil 400.89   Etcheverry, A. L'idéalisme français contemporain. Paris, 1934.

Phil 400.89.9   Etcheverry, A. Vers l'immanence intégrale. Thèse. Paris, 1934.

Phil 400.88   Ewing, Alfred E. Idealism. London, 1934.
Phil 6954.6   Ey, Henri. Hallucinations et délire. Paris, 1934.
Phil 3425.295   Fahrenhorst, E. Geist und Freiheit im System Hegels. Leipzig, 1934.

Phil 5245.37   Fauré-Fremiet, P. Pensée et re-création. Paris, 1934.
Phil 8585.32   Feldman, R.V. The domain of selfhood. London, 1934.
Phil 1955.6.96   Feldman, W.T. The philosophy of John Dewey. Baltimore, 1934.

Phil 1955.6.95   Feldman, W.T. The philosophy of John Dewey. Baltimore, 1934.

Phil 5643.92   Ferree, C.E. Studies in physiological optics, Dec. 1928-Oct. 1934. Baltimore, 1934. 2v.

Phil 165.334   Festschrift für Karl Joël zum 70. Geburtstage (27 März 1934). Basel, 1934.

Phil 4762.1.95   Festschrift N.O. Losskij zum 60. Geburtstage. Bonn, 1934.
Phil 3246.17.5   Fichte, Johann Gottlieb. Erganzungsband. Leipzig, 1934.
Phil 3246.15   Fichte, Johann Gottlieb. Nachgelassene Werke. Bonn, 1934-35. 3v.

Phil 7069.31.7   Findlay, J.A. A landmaerum annars heims. Reykjavik, 1934?
Phil 6015.2   Fischer, G.H. Ausdruck und Persönlichkeit. Leipzig, 1934.
Phil 5815.5   Fjeld, Harriett A. The limits of learning ability in rhesus monkeys. Thesis. Worcester, Mass., 1934.

Phil 6315.15   Flügel, G.C. Men and their motives. London, 1934.
Phil 4060.2.85   Fontanesi, Giuseppina. Il problema dell'amore nell'opera di Leone Ebreo. Venezia, 1934.

Phil 930.7.8   Forke, A. Geschichte der mittelalterlichen chinesischen Philosophie. Hamburg, 1934.

Phil 6115.26   Freeman, G.L.V. Introduction to physiological psychology. N.Y., 1934.

Phil 180.38.5   Freyer, Hans. Theorie des objektiven Geistes. 3. Aufl. Leipzig, 1934.

Phil 5046.24   García, David. Introducció a la logística. Barcelona, 1934. 2v.

Phil 6676.9   Garrett, Thomas L. Hypnotism. N.Y., 1934.
Phil 8661.5.5   Garrigou-Lagrange, R. God, His existence and His nature. St. Louis, 1934-36. 2v.

Phil 8407.6   Gentile, G. La filosofia dell'arte in compendio, ad uso delle scuole. Firenze, 1934.

Phil 8407.6.10   Gentile, G. Philosophie der Kunst. Berlin, 1934.
Phil 4120.4.31   Gentile, Giovanni. Discorsi di religione. 3. ed. Firenze, 1934.

Phil 181.72   Gessen, S.I. Weltanschauung Ideologie. Praha, 1934.
Phil 287.7   Geymonat, Ludovico. La nuova filosofia della natura in Germania. Torino, 1934.

Phil 3801.426   Gibelin, Jean. L'esthétique de Schelling d'après la philosophie de l'art. Thèse. Clermont-Ferrand, 1934.

Phil 3640.318   Giese, Fritz. Nietzsche...die Erfüllung. Tübingen, 1934.
Phil 3640.272   Gil Salguero, L. Persona y destino. Buenos Aires, 1934.
Phil 8881.61.5   Glenn, Paul J. Ethics. 4th ed. St. Louis, Mo., 1934.
Phil 6676.10   Goldsmith, M. Franz Anton Mesmer. Photoreproduction. London, 1934.

Phil 5246.46   Goodenough, Florence L. Developmental psychology. N.Y., 1934.

Phil 8586.39   Grant, Malcolm. A new argument for God. London, 1934.
Phil 3310.10   Grebe, W. Geist und Sache. Frankfurt, 1934.
Phil 6116.20   Greene, John G. The emmanuel movement, 1906-1929. n.p., 1934.

Phil 8661.14   Greene, K.C. The evolution of the conception of God. Boston, 1934.

Phil 8631.12   Griffin, N.E. The farther shore; an anthology...on the immortality of the soul. Boston, 1934.

Phil 6945.18   Grines, J.M. Institutional care of mental patients in the United States. Chicago, 1934.

Phil 6316.8.8   Groddeck, Georg. Das Buch vom Es; psychoanalytische Briefe an eine Freuden. 3. Aufl. Leipzig, 1934.

Phil 181.66.5   Gruenwald, Ladislaus. Metafizikai világnézet. Baja? 1934.
Phil 1135.155   Guérin, Pierre. L'idée de justice dans la conception de l'univers les premiers philosophes grecs. Paris, 1934.

Phil 1135.155.5   Guérin, Pierre. L'idée de justice dans la conception de l'univers les premiers philosophes grecs. Thèse. Strasbourg, 1934.

Phil 8586.55.5   Guerin, Pierre. Pensée constructive et réalités spirituelle. Paris, 1934.

Phil 3552.304   Gueroult, M. Dynamique et métaphysique Leibniziennes. Paris, 1934.

Phil 8125.2   Guerrero, Luis. Panorama de la estética clásica-romántica alemana. La Plata, 1934.

Phil 5246.47   Guilford, Joy Paul. Laboratory studies in psychology. N.Y., 1934.

Phil 3450.29.5   Haecker, Theodor. Was ist der Mensch? 2e Aufl. Leipzig, 1934.

Phil 3195.13.90   Hamm, Anton. Die Philosophie Hugo Delffs als Begründung eine theistischen Idealrealismus im Sinne christlicher Weltanschauung. Inaug. Diss. Bottrop, 1934.

Phil 8030.5   Hammond, W.A. A bibliography of aesthetics and of the philosophy of the fine arts from 1900-1932. N.Y., 1934.

Phil 5635.35   Hartshorne, C. The philosophy and psychology of sensation. Chicago, 1934.

Phil 3280.88   Hausmann, P. Das Freiheitsproblem in der Metaphysik und Ethik bei Arnold Geulincx. Inaug. Diss. Würzburg, 1934.

Phil 6317.20   Hendrick, Ives. Facts and theories of psychoanalysis. N.Y., 1934.

Phil 3195.6.95   Hennig, J. Lebensbegriff und Lebenskategorie. Inaug. Diss. Aachen, 1934.

Phil 6117.20.10   Herrick, C.J. An introduction to neurology. 5th ed. Philadelphia, 1934.

Phil 6317.21.5   Heyer, Gustav R. The organism of the mind. N.Y., 1934.
Phil 1527.1.50   Hommage à Monsieur le Professeur Maurice de Wulf. Louvain, 1934.

Phil 8882.57   Howe, E.G. Morality and reality. London, 1934.
Phil 182.100   Howison, G.H. George Holmes Howison, philosopher and teacher. Berkeley, 1934.

Phil 5850.232   Husband, R.W. Applied psychology. N.Y., 1934.
Phil 3425.287.5   Iakovenko, B.-V. Ein Beitrag zur Geschichte des Hegelianismus in Russland. Prag, 1934.

Phil 3425.287   Iakovenko, B.-V. Ein Beitrag zur Geschichte des Hegelianismus in Russland. Prag, 1934.

Phil 8589.14.12   Jacks, L.P. The revolt against mechanism. London, 1934.
Phil 8589.14.9   Jacks, L.P. The revolt against mechanism. N.Y., 1934.
Phil 6119.10.5   Jacobson, Edmund. You must relax. N.Y., 1934.
Phil 290.5   Jaffe, Haym. Natural law as controlled but not determined by experiment. Thesis. Philadelphia, 1934.

Phil 3491.5.15   Jansen, B. La philosophie religieuse de Kant. Paris, 1934.

Phil 6049.34   Jaquin, Noel. Our revealing hands. N.Y., 1934.
Phil 1870.78   Jessop, T.E. A bibliography of George Berkeley. London, 1934.

Phil 5627.137.5   Johnsen, T. Heart and spirit. Oslo, 1934.
Phil 5249.22   Jones, Llewellyn W. An introduction to theory and practice of psychology. London, 1934.

Phil 7069.34.15   Jónsson, J. Framhaldslif og nútímaþekking. Reykjavik, 1934.

Phil 6319.1.45   Jung, C.G. Wirklichkeit des Seele. Zürich, 1934.
Phil 185.58   Kahl-Furthmann, G. Das Problem des Nicht. Berlin, 1934.
Phil 3480.71.7   Kant, Immanuel. Religion within the limits of reason alone. Chicago, 1934.

Phil 2520.187   Keeling, Stanley V. Descartes. London, 1934.
Phil 8590.21   Keller, Aaron. Das Prinzip der Dialektik in der Theologie. Inaug. Diss. Erlangen-Bruck, 1934.

Phil 7150.134   Killeen, M.V. Man in the new humanism. Thesis. Washington, D.C., 1934.

Phil 9513.22   Kirche, Bekenntnis und Sozialethos. Genf, 1934.
Phil 8885.36   Kirk, K.E. Personal ethics. Oxford, 1934.
Phil 6120.13   Kirkpatrick, E.A. Mental hygiene for effective living. N.Y., 1934.

Phil 5627.134.20   Kitchen, V.C. I was a pagan. N.Y., 1934.
Phil 5585.66   Klages, L. Vom Wesen des Rhythmus. Kampen auf Sylt, 1934.
Phil 9530.35   Kleiser, Grenville. How to succeed in life. N.Y., 1934.
Phil 8590.20   Knox, Raymond C. Religion and the American dream. N.Y., 1934.

Phil 310.628   Kommunisticheskaia Akademiia, Moscow. Institut Filosofii. Materialy nauchnoi sessii. Moskva, 1934.

Phil 185.55   Kraft, Julius. Die Unmöglichkeit der Geisteswissenschaft. Leipzig, 1934.

Phil 185.60   Kraus, O. Wege und Abwege der Philosophie. Prag, 1934.
Phil 6320.6.15   Kretschmer, E. A text book of medical psychology. London, 1934.

Phil 8125.36   Krudewig, B. Das Groteske in der Ästhetik seit Kant. Bergisch, 1934.

Phil 165.169   Ksiega pamiątkowa ku uczczeniu piętnastolecia pracy nauczycielskiej w Uniwersytecie Warszawskim profesora Tadeusza Kotarbińskiego. Warszawa, 1934.

Phil 9035.59.9   Künkel, Fritz. Charakter, Wachstum und Erziehung. 2. Aufl. Leipzig, 1934.

Phil 6120.14   Kuntz, A. The autonomic nervous system. Philadelphia, 1934.

Phil 5520.73   Kunz, H. Zur Phänomenologie und Analyse des Ausdrucks. Basel, 1934.

Phil 2045.115   Laird, John. Hobbes. London, 1934.
Phil 2020.86   Lamont, W.D. Introduction to Green's moral philosophy. London, 1934.

Phil 4762.3.80   Laroche, P.G. Ossip-Leurié (L'homme et l'oeuvre). Paris, 1934.

Phil 6321.9.6   Lasswell, H.D. Psychology and politics. Chicago, 1934.
Phil 5520.63   Latif, Israil. The physiological basis of linguistic development. Diss. Lancaster, Pa., 1934.

Phil 8412.8.5   Laurila, K.S. Aesthetische Streitfragen. Helsinki, 1934.
Phil 2725.35.40   Lavelle, Louis. La présence totale. Paris, 1934.
Phil 3552.51.15   Leibniz, Gottfried Wilhelm. Discorso di metafisica "Hortus conclusus". Napoli, 1934.

Phil 3552.78.30   Leibniz, Gottfried Wilhelm. Lettres et fragments inédits sur les problèmes philosophiques. Paris, 1934.

Phil 8886.54   Lenglart, Marcel. Essai sur les conditions du progrès moral. Paris, 1934.

Phil 186.56.10   Le Senne, R. Obstacle et valeur. Paris, 1934.
Phil 9035.69   Lichtenfels, H. Die christliche Religion in ihrer Bedeutung für dieCharaktererziehung. Kallmünz, 1934.

Phil 3493.21   Lindsay, A.D. Kant. London, 1934.
Phil 6681.15   Lloyd, B. Layton. Hypnotism in the treatment of disease. London, 1934.

Phil 186.64.10   Losskii, N.O. Intellectual intuition and ideal being. Praha, 1934.

Phil 5722.24.5   Lubac, Émile. Le cycle de l'inconscient. Paris, 1934.
Phil 1870.115   Luce, Arthur A. Berkeley and Malebranche. London, 1934.
Phil 3805.205   Luetgert, Wilhelm. Schleiermacher. Berlin, 1934.
Phil 8667.19   McAuliffe, A.T. Some modern non-intellectual approaches to God. Washington, D.C., 1934.

Phil 5252.18.37   McDougall, William. The frontiers of psychology. N.Y., 1934.

Phil 487.6.5   McDougall, William. Modern materialism and emergent evolution. 2. ed. London, 1934.

Phil 5252.18.35   McDougall, William. Religion and the sciences of life. London, 1934.

Phil 5649.22   McNeill, H. Motor adaptation and accuracy. Louvain, 1934.
Phil 187.56.5   McTaggart, J.M.E. Philosophical studies. London, 1934.
Phil 2128.43   Mandeville, B. Fable of the bees. London, 1934.

1934 - cont.

Phil 2940.1.90   Manifestation en l'honneur de Monsieur Maurice de Wulf, 7 mars 1934. Louvain, 1934.

Phil 2750.11.74   Maritain, Jacques. Sept leçons sur l'être. Paris, 1934?

Phil 365.41   Mary Frederick, Sister. Religion and evolution since 1859. Diss. Notre Dame, 1934.

Phil 8592.57   Masaryk, T.G. Moderní člověk a náboženství. Praha, 1934.

Phil 4210.144   Massolo, A. Il problema dell'individuo nella filosofia di A. Rosmini. Palermo, 1934.

Phil 4073.90   Mattei, R. de. Studi Campelliani. Firenze, 1934.

Phil 8887.71.10   Maurois, André. Sentiments et coutumes. 56. ed. Paris, 1934.

Phil 3805.200   Meisner, Heinrich. Schleiermachers Lehrjahre. Berlin, 1934.

Phil 3832.14   Meli, Fausto. Spinoza e due antecedenti italiani dello Spinozismo. Firenze, 1934.

Phil 8837.13   Mencken, H.L. Treatise on right and wrong. N.Y., 1934.

Phil 8887.67   Menger, Karl. Moral, Wille und Weltgestaltung. Wien, 1934.

Phil 2520.191   Merrylees, W.A. Descartes. Melbourne, 1934.

Phil 3808.175   Mignosi, P. Schopenhauer. Brescia, 1934.

Phil 3832.16   Milan. Universita Cattolica del Sacro Cuore-Facolta di Filosofia. Spinoza nel terzo centenario della sua nascita. Milano, 1934.

Phil 8837.14   Miloyévitch, Voukossava. La théorie des passions du P. Senault et la morale chrétienne en France au XVIIe siècle. Thèse. Paris, 1934.

Phil 487.8   Mins, H.F. Materialism; the scientific basis. N.Y., 1934.

Phil 1135.154   Mondolfo, R. L'infinito nel pensiero dei Greci. Firenze, 1934.

Phil 8633.1.32   Montague, W.P. The chances of surviving death. Cambridge, 1934.

Phil 4371.5   Montseny y Carret, Juan. La evolución de la filosofía en España. v.1-2. Barcelona, 1934.

Phil 8667.20   Morais, H.M. Deism in eighteenth century America. N.Y., 1934.

Phil 6122.55   Morgan, John J.B. Keeping a sound mind. N.Y., 1934.

Phil 5645.37   Müller, G.E. Kleine Beiträge zur Psychophysik der Farbenempfindungen. Leipzig, 1934.

Phil 5252.72   Munn, Norman L. A laboratory manual in general experimental psychology. Pittsburgh, 1934.

Phil 5252.63.10   Murchison, C.A. Handbook of general experimental psychology. Worcester, 1934.

Phil 187.111   My philosophy, by an unprofessional thinker. Oxford, 1934.

Phil 5627.139   Nagle, Urban. An empirical study of the development of religious thinking in boys from twelve to sixteen years old. Washington, 1934.

Phil 745.9   Neal, Herbert V. Vitalism and mechanism. Lancaster, Pa., 1934.

Phil 4825.10   Nedeljkovič, Dušan. Aperçu de la philosophie contemporaine en Yougoslavie. Beograd, 1934.

Phil 8550.342.5   Nédoncelle, Maurice. La philosophie religieuse en Grand-Bretagne de 1850 à nos jours. Paris, 1934.

Phil 3195.6.97   Nicolai, Heinz. Wilhelm Dilthey und das Problem der dichterischen Phantasie. Inaug. Diss. München, 1934.

Phil 6323.4.5   Nicole, J.E. Psychopathology. 2d ed. Baltimore, 1934.

Phil 2250.91   Norborg, Sven. Josiah Royce. Oslo, 1934.

Phil 188.14.5   Nordenholz, A. Scientologie. München, 1934.

Phil 5850.288.5   O'Connor, Johnson. Psychometrics. Cambridge, Mass., 1934.

Phil 7060.92.60   O'Donnell, Elliot. Family ghosts and ghostly phenomena. 1st ed. N.Y., 1934.

Phil 1870.114   Oertel, Hans. George Berkeley und die englische Literatur. Halle, 1934.

Phil 2520.186   Olgiati, Francesco. Cartesio. Milano, 1934.

Phil 189.16.5   Orestano, F. Verità dimostrate. Napoli, 1934.

Phil 189.24   Oribe, Emilio. Teoría del nous. Buenos Aires, 1934.

Phil 8669.1.5   Orr, John. English deism. Grand Rapids, 1934.

Phil 3805.177   Osborn, A.R. Schleiermacher and religious education. London, 1934.

Phil 9290.9   Overstreet, Harry A. A guide to civilized loafing. N.Y., 1934.

Phil 5627.134.15   The Oxford Group international house party. Oxford, 1934.

Phil 3808.168   Padovani, Umberto A. Arturo Schopenhauer. Milano, 1934.

Phil 2805.40.38   Pascal, Blaise. Pensées. Paris, 1934.

Phil 4710.25.5   Pelikán, Ferdinand. Aus der philosophischen Riffamationsliteratur. Prag, 1934.

Phil 6750.234   Penrose, Lionel S. Mental defect. N.Y., 1934.

Phil 1750.106   Phillips, Richard P. Modern Thomistic philosophy. London, 1934-40. 2v.

Phil 190.62   Die Philosophie; ihre Geschichte und ihre Systematik. Abt. 1,5,7,9,10,12,14,15. Bonn, 1934-1935. 8v.

Phil 5640.37   Phusis, Maurice (pseud.). Classification universelle systématique et coordonnée des connaissances humaines. Paris, 1934.

Phil 2520.192   Picard, Émile. Une édition nouvelle du discours de la méthode de Descartes. Paris, 1934.

Phil 6125.24.4   Pickford, Mary. Why not try God? N.Y., 1934.

Phil 978.70   Pinchin, Edith F. The bridge of the gods in Gaelic mythology. London, 1934.

Phil 197.3.15   Piozzi, H.L.T. (Mrs.). Mrs. Piozzi and Isaac Watts. London, 1934.

Phil 190.58   Pirenne, H.E. Sur l'angoisse métaphysique; essai de philosophie. Bruxelles, 1934.

Phil 490.4.7   Plekhanov, G.V. Essays in the history of materialism. London, 1934.

Phil 9220.12   Price, W.J. Between friends. Norwood, Mass., 1934.

Phil 6060.29.15   Pulver, Max. Trieb und Verbrechen in der Handschrift. 2e Aufl. Zürich, 1934.

Phil 5056.1A   Quine, Willard Van Orman. A system of logistic. Cambridge, 1934.

Phil 6327.15   Rado, Sandor. Die Kastrationsangst des Weibes. Wien, 1934.

Phil 1527.1.6.25   Rand, E.K. Histoire de la philosophie médiévale. v.1-2. Cambridge, Mass., 1934.

Phil 5057.26   Raphael, Max. Zur Erkenntnistheorie der konkreten Dialektik. Paris, 1934.

Phil 2805.216.5   Réguron, Paule. De la théologie à la prière de Pascal. Thèse. Grenoble, 1934.

Phil 2805.216   Réguron, Paule. Les origines du mouvement antijanseniste. Thèse. Grenoble, 1934.

Phil 3120.18.90   Reiser, Joseph. Zur Erkenntnislehre Jakob Sigismund Becko. München, 1934.

Phil 7069.34.25A   Rhine, Joseph B. Extra-sensory perception. Boston, 1934.

Phil 1750.136   Richard, Christian. Le mouvement humaniste en Amerique. Paris, 1934.

1934 - cont.

Phil 1750.136.5   Richard, Christian. Le mouvement humaniste en Amérique et les courants de pensée similaire en France. Thèse. Paris, 1934.

Phil 1750.162   Richards, P.S. Humanism. London, 1934.

Phil 192.21.20   Rickert, H. Grundprobleme der Philosophie. Tübingen, 1934.

Phil 5827.11   Riess, Bernard F. Limits of learning ability in the white rat and the guinea pig. Diss. Worcester, Mass., 1934.

Phil 1122.3.27   Ritter, Heinrich. Historia philosophiae graecae. 10 ed. Gotha, 1934.

Phil 5420.5.5   Roback, A.A. Getting rid of self-consciousness. n.p., 1934.

Phil 5257.27.10   Robinson, E.S. Man as psychology sees him. N.Y., 1934.

Phil 8892.25.15   Rogers, A.K. Ethics and moral tolerance. N.Y., 1934.

Phil 192.54.5   Rohrbaugh, L.G. A natural approach to philosophy. N.Y., 1934.

Phil 3640.262   Rosengarth, W. Nietzsche und George. Leipzig, 1934.

Phil 4210.12   Rosmini-Serbati, Antonio. Opere edite e inedite. Roma, 1934-63. 42v.

Phil 8597.44   Roth, J. Der antichrist. Amsterdam, 1934.

Phil 735.105   Rothschild, R. Reality and illusion. N.Y., 1934.

Phil 5827.10   Rowley, Jean B. Discrimination limens of pattern and size in the goldfish, Carassius auratus. Thesis. Worcester, Mass., 1934.

Phil 1717.8.15   Ruggiero, G. de. Filosofi del novecento. Bari, 1934.

Phil 817.8.5   Ruggiero, Guido de. Storia della filosofia. pt. 1 (v.1-2), pt. 2 (v.1-3), pt. 3 (v.1-2), pt. 4 (v.1-5). Bari, 1934-48. 12v.

Phil 6945.12   Ruggles, A.H. Mental health. Baltimore, 1934.

Phil 2270.139   Rumney, J. Herbert Spencer's sociology. London, 1934.

Phil 5257.47   Russell, J.T. Applicability of the probable error formulae to psychological data. Diss. Chicago, 1934.

Phil 6328.17   Sachs, Wulf. Psychoanalysis. London, 1934.

Phil 1135.85.16   Salzi, Pierre. La genèse de la sensation...chez Protagoras, Platon et Aristote. Thèse. Paris, 1934.

Phil 1135.85.15   Salzi, Pierre. La genèse de la sensation...chez Protagoras. Paris, 1934.

Phil 5635.36.5   Salzi, Pierre. La sensation, étude de sa genèse et de son rôle dans la connaissance. Thèse. Paris, 1934.

Phil 5635.36   Salzi, Pierre. La sensation. Paris, 1934.

Phil 5627.134.70   Sangster, W.E. God does guide us. N.Y., 1934.

Phil 5627.50   Sankey-Jones, N.E. Bibliography of Theodore Schroeder on the psychology of religion. Cos Cob, Conn., 1934.

Phil 193.49.18   Santayana, G. Character and opinion in the United States. N.Y., 1934.

Phil 530.40.45   Santullano, Luis. Místicos españoles. Madrid, 1934.

Phil 310.535   Sarab'ianov, V.N. Dialekticheskii i istoricheskii materializm. Moskva, 1934.

Phil 1718.20   Sassen, F. Geschiedenis van de wijshegeerte der negentiende eeuw. Antwerpen, 1934.

Phil 8843.13   Saunders, K.J. The ideals of East and West. Cambridge, Eng., 1934.

Phil 8843.13.2   Saunders, K.J. The ideals of East and West. N.Y., 1934.

Phil 193.9.25   Schiller, F.C.S. Must philosophers disagree? London, 1934.

Phil 3801.775   Schilling, Kurt. Natur und Wahrheit; Untersuchungen über Entstehung...der Schellingschen Systems. München, 1934.

Phil 103.3.20   Schmidt, Heinrich. Philosophisches Wörterbuch. 9. Aufl. Leipzig, 1934.

Phil 1123.9   Schuhl, Pierre Maxime. Essai sur la formation de la pensée grecque. Paris, 1934.

Phil 8598.90.5   Schulze-Gaevernitz, G. Zur Wiedergeburt des Abendlandes. 2. Aufl. Berlin, 1934.

Phil 349.37   Schwarz, Baldwin. Der Irrtum in der Philosophie. Münster, 1934.

Phil 6328.18   Seabury, David. What makes us seem so queer? N.Y., 1934.

Phil 530.20.75   Seesholtz, A.G. Friends of God. N.Y., 1934.

Phil 1885.85   Segersted, T.K. Value and reality in Bradley's philosophy. Lund, 1934.

Phil 4120.1.81   Semprini, G. Melchiorre Gioia e la sua dottrina politica. Genova, 1934.

Phil 1718.19   Serra, Hunter J. Sentit i valor de la nova filosofía. Barcelona, 1934.

Phil 193.137   Shahani, R.G. The coming of Karuna. London, 1934.

Phil 9530.46   Sherman, Ray W. If you want to get ahead. Boston, 1934.

Phil 5228.6   Sinha, Jadunath. Indian psychology; perception. London, 1934.

Phil 9075.36   Smith, T.V. Beyond conscience. N.Y., 1934.

Phil 645.33   Smith, T.V. Creative sceptics. Chicago, 1934.

Phil 4060.2.83   Sonne, I. Intorno alla vita di Leone Ebreo. Firenze, 1934.

Phil 193.150.10   Spakovski, A. Razreshenie sud'by chelovecheskoi. Novyi Sad, 1934.

Phil 5627.134.60   Spencer, F.A.M. The meaning of the gospels. London, 1934.

Phil 3018.19   Spenlé, J.E. La pensée allemande de Luther à Nietzsche. Paris, 1934.

Phil 8615.12   Spiller, G. The ethical movement in Great Britain. London, 1934.

Phil 7082.90   Spiller, Gustav. A contribution towards a science of dreams. London, 1934.

Phil 8893.90   Staehr, V. von. Logische Struktur des emotionalen Ich. Diss. Saalfeld, 1934.

Phil 2475.1.243   Stallknecht, N.P. Bergson's idea of creation. Princeton, N.J., 1934?

Phil 299.22   Stallknecht, N.P. Studies in the philosophy of creation. Princeton, 1934.

Phil 5058.46.15   Stebbing, Lizzie S. Logic in practice. London, 1934.

Phil 978.49.135   Steiner, R. The problems of our time. London, 1934.

Phil 6328.2.28   Stekel, Wilhelm. Erziehung derEltern. Wien, 1934.

Phil 8598.72   Stocks, J.L. On the nature and grounds of religious belief. London, 1934.

Phil 7069.34.35   Streamline (pseud.). Foretold; stories of modern second-sight. Stirling 1934.

Phil 6028.7   Streble, Hermann. Analyse des Gebarens. Inaug. Diss. Berlin, 1934.

Phil 5228.7   Streeter, B.H. The church and modern psychology. Evanston, Ill., 1934.

Phil 194.11.25   Taylor, A.E. Philosophical studies. London, 1934.

Phil 960.145   Techoueyres, E. A la recherche de l'unité. Reims, 1934.

Phil 2115.145A   Thompson, Samuel M. A study of Locke's theory of ideas. Monmouth, Ill., 1934.

Phil 1900.90   Tomkins, S.S. Conscience, self love and benevolence in the system of Bishop Butler. Thesis. Philadelphia, 1934.

Phil 1819.2   Townsend, H.G. Philosophical ideas in the United States. N.Y., 1934.

Phil 2725.2.101   Treves, P. Lamennais. Milano, 1934.

Chronological Listing

1934 - cont.

Phil 6329.7 — Trog, H. Die Religionstheorie der Psychoanalyse. Diss. Hamburg, 1934.

Phil 8599.23 — Turner, J.E. Essentials in the development of religion. London, 1934.

Phil 7054.116.7 — Tuttle, H. Arcana of spiritualism. Chicago, 1934.

Phil 2805.196.5 — Valensin, A. Balthazar. Paris, 1934.

Phil 2477.6.99 — Valensin, A. Maurice Blondel. 2e éd. Paris, 1934.

Phil 5771.2 — Valla, Lorenzo. De libero arbitrio. Firenze, 1934.

Phil 8676.4 — Vance, J.G. The sovereignty of God. Oxford, 1934.

Phil 8601.12 — Vann, Gerald. On being human; St. Thomas and Mr. Aldous Huxley. N.Y., 1934.

Phil 7069.34.45 — Vilanova, María. Un drama del espacio. Año 1932. Dictado por el espíritu de Blasco Ibáñez. Barcelona, 1934.

Phil 7069.34.47 — Vilanova, María. El regentador del mundo solar os da un radio de luz...julio de 1934. Barcelona, 1934.

Phil 7069.34.47.2 — Vilanova, Maria. La segunda parte que ha dado el regentador del mondo solar, para que los lectores lo leau que va siguiendo su lectura. Barcelona, 1934.

Phil 7069.34.43 — Vilanova, María. Va siguiendo la tercera parte de el radio de luz del regentador del mundo solar. Barcelona, 1934. 8 pam.

Phil 6990.35 — Vilar, Albert. Réflexions sur le miracle et les lois naturelles. Clamecy, 1934.

Phil 3503.9 — Vleeschauwer, H.J. La déduction transcendentale dans l'oeuvre de Kant. v.1-2,3. Antwerp, 1934-36. 2v.

Phil 8896.17.5 — Volney, C.F.C. La loi naturelle. Paris, 1934.

Phil 3841.6 — Vulliaud, P. Spinoza d'après les livres de la bibliothèque. Paris, 1934.

Phil 8612.35 — Wach, Joachim. Das Problem des Todes in der Philosophie unserer Zeit. Tübingen, 1934.

Phil 400.91 — Wagner, G.F. Transcendental-Idealismus. Ulm, 1934.

Phil 1145.81 — Wal, L.G. Het objectiviteitsbeginsel in de oudste Grieksche ethiek. Groningen, 1934.

Phil 2075.6.90A — Warren, Austin. The elder Henry James. N.Y., 1934.

Phil 5207.10 — Warren, Howard Crosby. Dictionary of psychology. N.Y., 1934.

Phil 9495.133.10 — Weatherhead, L.D. Mastery of sex through psychology and religion. N.Y., 1934.

Phil 5545.172 — Weinland, J.D. Improving the memory for faces and names. Boston, 1934.

Phil 197.60 — Weir, Archibald. Shallows and deeps. Oxford, 1934.

Phil 197.59 — Wells, Gabriel. Riddle of being. N.Y., 1934.

Phil 7069.34.62 — Wells, Helen B. As in a mirror. N.Y., 1934. 2 pam.

Phil 7069.30.46F — Wells, Helen B. The hidden path. v.2. N.Y., 1934.

Phil 7069.34.60 — Wells, Helen B. The intelligence of the spaces. N.Y., 1934.

Phil 7069.34.50 — Wells, Helen B. Pythagoras speaks. N.Y., 1934.

Phil 7069.34.63 — Wells, Helen B. Ribbons of the sky. v.1-3. N.Y., 1934-35.

Phil 7069.34.55 — Wells, Helen B. The song of the seven seas. N.Y., 1934.

Phil 6132.36 — Wertham, F. The brain as an organ. N.Y., 1934.

Phil 9362.17 — Weston, S.A. Social and religious problems and young people. N.Y., 1934.

Phil 353.15 — Weyl, H. Mind and nature. Philadelphia, 1934.

Phil 5620.16 — Whittaker, T. Reason. Cambridge, Eng., 1934.

Phil 9070.54 — Wicks, R.R. The reason for living. N.Y., 1934.

Phil 510.148 — Wightman, W.P.D. Science and monism. London, 1934.

Phil 6132.31 — Wile, Ira S. Handedness, right and left. Boston, 1934.

Phil 3022.5 — Wimmershoff, H. Die Lehre von Sündenfall in der Philosophie Schellings. Inaug. Diss. Selingen, 1934.

Phil 5627.134.45 — Winslow, J.C. Why I believe in the Oxford Group. 3. ed. London, 1934.

Phil 193.128.85 — Wisdom, John. Problems of mind and matter. Cambridge, Eng., 1934.

Phil 3842.13A — Wolfson, H.A. The philosophy of Spinoza. Cambridge, 1934. 2v.

Phil 1050.14.3 — Wolfson, Harry A. Studies in Crescas. N.Y., 1934.

Phil 8602.27.10 — Wood, Herbert G. Christianity and the nature of history. Cambridge, Eng., 1934.

Phil 1527.1.6.7A — Wulf, M. de. Histoire de la philosophie médiévale. 6e éd. Louvain, 1934-47. 3v.

Phil 1725.2 — Zema, Demetrius. The thoughtlessness of modern thought. N.Y., 1934.

Phil 200.12 — Zur Philosophie der Gegenwart. Prag, 1934.

1935

Phil 6950.5 — Abby, Carl. Is anyone sane. Boston, 1935.

Phil 5750.3.10 — Ach, Narziss. Analyse des Willens. Berlin, 1935.

Phil 4260.109 — Adams, Henry P. The life and writings of Giambattista Vico. London, 1935.

Phil 6310.4.9 — Alexander, Franz G. Roots of crime. N.Y., 1935.

Phil 5240.34 — Allen, A.H.B. The self in psychology. London, 1935.

Phil 9035.61.12 — Allers, Rudolf. Das Werden der settlichen Person. 4. Aufl. Freiburg, 1935.

Phil 9340.8 — Angell, Frances. Compete Philadelphia, 1935.

Phil 7082.74 — Archer, William. On dreams. London, 1935.

Phil 6110.15 — Arnason, A. Apoplexie und ihre Vererbung. Kopenhagen, 1935.

Phil 1020.7.3 — Asin Palacios, M. La espiritualidad de Algozel y su sentido cristiano. Madrid, 1935-41.

Phil 3000.4 — Aster, E. Von. Die Philosophie der Gegenwart. Leiden, 1935.

Phil 3625.5.60 — Atlas, S. Geschichte des eigenen Lebens. Berlin, 1935.

Phil 8865.342 — Austin, Eugene M. The ethics of the Cambridge Platonists. Philadelphia, 1935.

Phil 4352.1.45 — Balmes, Jaime. Filosofia elemental. Madrid, 1935.

Phil 176.135 — Barrett, Clifford. Philosophy. N.Y., 1935.

Phil 8876.98 — Bauch, Bruno. Grundzüge der Ethik. Stuttgart, 1935.

Phil 176.140.5 — Baur, Ludwig. Metaphysik. 3. Aufl. München, 1935.

Phil 2655.3.93 — Beck, Leslie J. La méthode synthétique d'Hamelin. Paris, 1935.

Phil 3925.9.90 — Becker, J. Die Religionsphilosophie Karl Werners. Inaug. Diss. Bonn, 1935.

Phil 8691.25 — Beckett, Lucile C. The world breath. London, 1935.

Phil 3120.21 — Beerling, Reinier Franciscus. Antithesen. Haarlem, 1935.

Phil 3549.8.100 — Benduk, Hugo. Der Gegensatz vom Seele und Geist bei Ludwig Klages. Werli, 1935.

Phil 5241.93 — Bentley, A.F. Behavior, knowledge, fact. Bloomington, 1935.

Phil 8876.91.15 — Berdiaev, N.A. De la destination de l'homme. Paris, 1935.

Phil 8876.91.5 — Berdiaev, N.A. Von der Bestimmung des Menschen. Bern, 1935.

Phil 8581.69A — Berdyaev, N.A. Freedom and the spirit. N.Y., 1935.

Phil 6311.26 — Bergler, Edmund. Talleyrand, Napoleon, Stendhal, Grabbe, psychoanalytisch-biographishe essays. Wien, 1935.

1935 - cont.

Phil 2475.1.38.6 — Bergson, Henri. The two sources of morality and religion. N.Y., 1935.

Phil 1925.83 — Beyer, Joseph. Ralph Cudworth als Ethiker, Staats-Philosoph und Usthetiker auf Grund des gedruckten Schriften. Inaug. Diss. Bottrop, 1935.

Phil 8520.36 — Bieler, Ludwig. Theios. Wien, 1935-36. 2v.

Phil 5811.18 — Bierens de Haan, J.A. Die tierpsychologische Forschung, ihre Ziele und Wege. Leipzig, 1935.

Phil 365.38.5 — Bill, Annie C.B. The conquest of death; an imminent step in evolution. Boston, 1935.

Phil 2340.9.94 — Blanché, Robert. Le rationalisme de Whewell. Paris, 1935.

Phil 2340.9.93 — Blanché, Robert. Le rationalisme de Whewell. Thèse. Paris, 1935.

Phil 176.129.5 — Blondel, Maurice. L'être et les êtres. Paris, 1935.

Phil 6420.12.5 — Blumel, Charles Sidney. Stammering and allied disorders. N.Y., 1935.

Phil 8876.107 — Börner, W. Politsche Zeitfragen in ethischer Beleuchtung. Wien, 1935.

Phil 5011.4 — Boll, Marcel. La logique. Paris, 1935.

Phil 5241.92A — Boring, E.G. Psychology; a factual textbook. N.Y., 1935.

Phil 5241.92.10 — Boring, E.G. The relation of the attributes of sensation to the dimensions of the stimulus. Baltimore, 1935. 3 pam.

Phil 1905.10.75 — Bosanquet, B. Bernard Bosanquet and his friends. London, 1935.

Phil 5460.11 — Bosch, G. Alucinaciones. Buenos Aires, 1935.

Phil 1885.15 — Bradley, Francis H. Collected essays. Oxford, 1935. 2v.

Phil 3001.12 — Brock, Werner. An introduction to contemporary German philosophy. Cambridge, 1935.

Phil 530.40.42 — Brouwer, Johan. De achtergrond der Spaansche mystiek. Zutphen, 1935.

Phil 5640.42 — Brunswik, Egon. Experimentelle Psychologie in Demonstrationen. Wien, 1935.

Phil 9290.4 — Bryson, Lyman. The use of the radio in leisure time. N.Y., 1935?

Phil 530.15.30 — Buche, Joseph. L'école mystique de Lyon, 1776-1847. Paris, 1935.

Phil 176.137A — Burke, Kenneth. Permanence and change. N.Y., 1935.

Phil 7069.35.7 — Burton, Eva. A natural bridge to cross. N.Y., 1935.

Phil 9245.57 — Cadman, Samuel P. Adventure for happiness. N.Y., 1935.

Phil 6952.21.15 — Campbell, C.M. Destiny and disease in mental disorders. N.Y., 1935.

Phil 7069.34.8 — Cannon, Alexandre. Powers that be (the Mayfair lectures). N.Y., 1935.

Phil 5042.21.15 — Carnap, Rudolf. Philosophy and logical syntax. London, 1935.

Phil 5585.60 — Carr, H.A. An introduction to space perception. N.Y., 1935.

Phil 5042.27 — Castell, Alburey. A college logic; an introduction to the study of argument and proof. N.Y., 1935.

Phil 8430.13 — Castelnuovo, E. El arte y las masas, ensayos sobre una nueva teoría della actividad estética. Buenos Aires, 1935.

Phil 177.68.15 — Chartier, Émile. Sentiments, pasiions et signes. 2e éd. Paris, 1935.

Phil 177.90 — Chávez, E.A. Dios, el universo y la libertad. Barcelona, 1935.

Phil 9035.80 — Cheley, Frank H. After all it's up to you. Boston, 1935.

Phil 4260.108 — Chiocchetti, E. La filosofia di Giambattista Vico. Milano, 1935.

Phil 2050.205 — Church, R.W. Hume's theory of the understanding. London, 1935.

Phil 530.20.105 — Chuzeville, Jean. Les mystiques allemands du XVII au XIX siècle. Paris, 1935.

Phil 5752.9 — Cioffari, Vincenzo. Fortune and fate from Democritus to St. Thomas Aquinas. N.Y., 1935.

Phil 5242.44.5 — Claparède, Édouard. Causeries psychologiques. Ser. 2. Genève, 1935.

Phil 8403.18 — Coculesco, P. Principes d'esthétique. Paris, 1935.

Phil 5752.10 — Compton, Arthur H. The freedom of man. New Haven, 1935.

Phil 4260.110 — Corsano, Antonio. Umanesino e religione in G.B. Vico. Bari, 1935.

Phil 3808.170 — Costa, Alessandro. Il pensiero religioso di Arturo Schopenhauer. Roma, 1935.

Phil 1107.6 — Covotti, Aurelio. Da Aristotele ai Bizantini. Napoli, 1935.

Phil 4215.1.105 — Credali, A. G.D. Romagnosi. Modena, 1935.

Phil 3425.290 — Cross, G.J. Prologue and epilogue to Hegel. Oxford, 1935.

Phil 177.63.5 — Cunningham, G.W. Problem of philosophy. N.Y., 1935.

Phil 8583.35 — D'Arcy, M.C. Mirage and truth. N.Y., 1935.

Phil 8878.54 — Das, Ras-Vihari. The self and the ideal. Calcutta, 1935.

Phil 8583.28.2 — Dawson, Christopher H. Religion and the modern state. London, 1935.

Phil 8583.29 — De Burgh, William George. The relations of morality to religion. London, 1935.

Phil 3450.19.98 — Delp, A. Trogische Existenz; zur Philosophie Martin Heideggers. Freiburg, 1935.

Phil 2520.76.65 — Descartes, René. Lettres sur la morale. Paris, 1935.

Phil 1522.5.15 — Descoqs, P. Thomisme et scolastique à propos de M. Rougier. 2e éd. Paris, 1935.

Phil 8404.17 — De Selincourt, O. Art and morality. London, 1935.

Phil 7082.118 — Dietz, Paul Antoine. Mensch en droom. Leiden, 1935.

Phil 8878.53 — Dingler, Hugo. Das Handeln im Sinne des Höchsten Zieles. (Absolute Ethik). München, 1935.

Phil 349.20.25 — Ditz, Erwin. Der Begriff der Maschine bei Julius Schultz. Inaug. Diss. Leipzig, 1935.

Phil 5243.40 — Dorsey, J.M. The foundations of human nature. N.Y., 1935.

Phil 5243.41.5 — Dreikurs, Rudolf. An introduction to individual psychology. London, 1935.

Phil 478.4 — Driesch, Hans. Die Uberwindung des Materialismus. Zürich, 1935.

Phil 5753.12 — Dwelshauvers, G. L'exercice de la volonté. Paris, 1935.

Phil 3475.2.90 — Eckstein, W. Wilhelm Jerusalem; sein Leben und Werken. Wien, 1935.

Phil 8584.7.5 — Eliot, C.W. The religion of the future. Boston, 1935.

Phil 3235.81.15 — Engels, Friedrich. Ludwig Feuerbach and the outcome of classical German philosophy. N.Y., 1935.

Phil 4363.2.40 — Entrambasaguas y Pena, J. de. Miguel de Molinos, siglo XVII. Madrid, 1935?

VPhil 1750.115 — Faragó, László. A harmadik humanismus és a harmadik birodalom. Budapest, 1935.

Phil 8660.14 — Farmer, H.H. The world and God. London, 1935.

Phil 4582.1.83 — Festskrift till ägnad Axel Herrlin den 30 mars 1935. Lund, 1935.

Phil 180.52 — Fialko, N.M. Passivity and rationalization. N.Y., 1935.

1935 - cont.

Phil 3246.18.5   Fichte, Johann Gottlieb. Eine Teilsammlung mit der Einfuhrung. Stuttgart, 1935.

Phil 180.28.5   Field, G.C. Studies in philosophy. Bristol, 1935.

Phil 5245.39   Finner, P.F. An introduction to experimental psychology. N.Y., 1935.

Phil 3450.19.97   Fischer, Alois. Die Existenzphilosophie Martin Heideggers. Leipzig, 1935.

Phil 8660.13   Fitzpatrick, M.S. Mind and the universal frame. Dublin, 1935.

Phil 180.60   Flechtner, H.J. Freiheit und Bindung. Berlin, 1935.

Phil 5245.40   Focht, Mildred. What is Gestalt-theory. Diss. N.Y., 1935.

Phil 3640.88.15   Förster-Nietzsche, E. Friedrich Nietzsche und die Frauen seiner Zeit. München, 1935.

Phil 5627.134.25   Foot, Stephen. Life began yesterday. N.Y., 1935.

Phil 5627.143   Forsyth, D. Psychology and religion. London, 1935.

Phil 978.59.90   Franceschi, G.J. El Señor Krishnamurti. Buenos Aires, 1935.

Phil 4756.1.45   Frank, Semen L. La connaissance et l'être. Paris, 1935.

Phil 5045.7.5   Fretag, Bruno baron von. Irrational oder Rational? Berlin, 1935.

Phil 6315.2.79   Freud, Sigmund. An autobiographical study. London, 1935.

Phil 6315.2.5.5   Freud, Sigmund. A general introduction to psycho-analysis. N.Y., 1935.

Phil 9450.55   Freyer, Hans. Pallas athene. Jena, 1935.

Phil 3260.35.2   Fries, Jakob Friedrich. Neue oder anthropologische Kritik der Vernunft. 2. Aufl. Berlin, 1935. 3v.

Phil 5627.180.5   Frost, Bede. The art of mental prayer. London, 1935.

Phil 5245.38   Fuller, B. The tyranny of the mind. London, 1935.

Phil 181.57.10   Galli, Gallo. Lineamenti di filosofia. Bologna, 1935.

Phil 4112.60   Galluppi, Pasquale. Sull'analisi e la sintesi. Firenze, 1935.

Phil 6310.1.90   Ganz, M. La psychologie d'Alfred Adler. Neuchâtel, 1935.

Phil 400.90   Gardeil, H.D. Les étapes de la philosophie idéaliste. Paris, 1935.

Phil 3640.301   Gawronsky, Dimitry. Friedrich Nietzsche und das Dritte Reich. Bern, 1935.

Phil 3246.240   Gehlen, Arnold. Deutschtum und Christentum bei Fichte. Berlin, 1935.

Phil 2225.7.90A   George Herbert Palmer, 1842-1933; memorial addressses. Cambridge, 1935.

Phil 4112.87   Giuli, G. de. La filosofia di Pasquale Galluppi. Palermo, 1935.

Phil 5016.1   Göldel, R.W. Die Lehre von der Identität in der deutschen Logik-Wissenschaft seit Lotze. Inaug. Diss. Leipzig, 1935.

Phil 9070.16   Goldmann, R.L. The good fight. N.Y., 1935.

Phil 8612.29   Gómez de la Serna, R. Los muertos, las muertas y otras fantasmagarias. Madrid, 1935.

Phil 8881.62   Govi, Mario. Etica rinnovata su basi scientifiche. Pte.I. Firenze, 1935.

Phil 181.70   Govi, Mario. Preludi filosofici e politici. Milano, 1935.

Phil 1535.18.5   Gredt, Joseph. Die aristotellisch-thomistische Philosophie. Freiburg, 1935. 2v.

Phil 8586.40   Gröbner, Wolfgang. Der Weg Aufwärts. Wien, 1935.

Phil 5046.23   Grote, Albert. Über die Funktion der Copula. Leipzig, 1935.

Phil 5246.48   Groves, Ernest R. Understanding yourself, the mental hygiene of personality. N.Y., 1935.

Phil 2805.220   Guardini, R. Christliches Bewusstsein...Pascal. Leipzig, 1935.

Phil 181.84   Guzzo, Augusto. Idealisti ed empiristi; saggi. Firenze, 1935.

Phil 5247.51   Hadfield, J.A. Psychology and modern problems. London, 1935.

Phil 8587.51.5   Haecker, T. Der Christ und die Geschichte. Leipzig, 1935.

Phil 182.101.7   Haldane, J.S. The philosophy of a biologist. Oxford, 1935.

Phil 182.101.5A   Haldane, J.S. The philosophy of a biologist. Oxford, 1935.

Phil 7069.35.10   Haley, P.S. Modern loaves and fishes. San Francisco, 1935.

Phil 182.94.15   Hartmann, N. Zur Grundlegung der Ontologie. Berlin, 1935.

Phil 4668.121.80   Harva, Uno. Die Philosophie von G.I. Hartman. Turku, 1935.

Phil 978.59.95   Heber, Lilly. Krishnamurti and the world crisis. London, 1935.

Phil 3425.55   Hegel, Georg Wilhelm Friedrich. Die Verfassung des deutschen Reichs. Stuttgart, 1935.

Phil 7069.35.65   Hegy, Reginald. A witness through the centuries. N.Y., 1935.

Phil 8662.15   Heim, Karl. God transcendent. London, 1935.

Phil 3007.8.5   Helbing, Lothar. Der dritte Humanismus. 3. Aufl. Berlin, 1935.

Phil 5850.228   Helke, J.W. Korrelation oder Wertigkeit? Inaug. Diss. Leipzig, 1935.

Phil 5645.36   Henneman, R.H. A photometric study of the perception of object color. N.Y., 1935.

Phil 7069.35.15   Herodius (pseud.). Show me the way; spirit counsels for right living. Boston, 1935.

Phil 182.61.10   Herpe, Hans. Idee und Existenz. Hamburg, 1935.

Phil 8957.9   Hirst, E.W. Jesus and the moralists. London, 1935.

Phil 2045.52.5   Hobbes, Thomas. Leviathan. Cambridge, 1935.

Phil 2115.146   Hofstadter, A. Locke and scepticism. N.Y., 1935.

Phil 5247.55   Hoggland, H. Pacemakers. N.Y., 1935.

Phil 5850.230.15   Hollingworth, H.L. The psychology of the audience. N.Y., 1935.

Phil 8587.49   Houf, Horace T. What religion is and does. N.Y., 1935.

Phil 6317.19.5   Howden, R.A. The man in the street and the new psychology. London, 1935.

Phil 4805.10   Iakovenko, Boris V. La philosophie tchécoslovaque contemporaine. Prague, 1935.

Phil 2520.197   Iriarte, J. Kartesischer oder sanchezischer Zweifel? Inaug.-Diss. Bothrop, 1935.

Phil 5249.21   Janet, Pierre. Les débuts de l'intelligence. Paris, 1935.

Phil 184.19.15   Jaspers, K. Vernunft und Existenz. Groningen, 1935.

Phil 5249.6.20   Jastrow, J. Wish and wisdom. N.Y., 1935.

Phil 184.26.9   Joad, C.E.M. Return to philosophy. London, 1935.

Phil 8589.19.8   Jones, E.S. The Christ of the Mount. N.Y., 1935.

Phil 8699.1   Jones, Richard U. The scientifc eye of faith. Boston, 1935.

Phil 184.38   Joseph, H.W.B. Essays in ancient and modern philosophy. Oxford, 1935.

Phil 5722.18.5   Jung, C.G. Die Beziehungen zwischen dem ich und dem Unbewussten. Zürich, 1935.

Phil 5722.18.15   Jung, C.G. Über die Archetypen. Zürich, 1935.

Phil 5250.32.5   Kaila, Eino. Personlighetens psykologi. Helsingfors, 1935.

1935 - cont.

Phil 1810.2   Kallen, H.M. American philosophy today and tomorrow. N.Y., 1935.

Phil 2475.1.247   Kann, Albert. Henri Bergson und meine Ideen. Wien, 1935.

Phil 3480.86.25   Kant, Immanuel. Le conflit des facultes en trois sections, 1798. Paris, 1935.

Phil 3480.52.15   Kant, Immanuel. On philosophy in general. Calcutta, 1935.

Phil 3480.52.25   Kant, Immanuel. Principie di estetica. Bari, 1935.

Phil 1050.15.9   Karo, Jakob. Kritische Untersuchungen zu Levi hen Gersons (Ralbag) Widerlegung des Aristotelischen Zeitbegriffes. Inaug. Diss. Leipzig, 1935.

Phil 3492.45   Kayser, Rudolf. Kant. Wien, 1935.

Phil 3120.19.90   Keller, E. Die Philosophie Bruno Bauchs, als Ausdruck germanischer Geisteshaltung. Stuttgart, 1935.

Phil 6320.1.9   Kempf, E.J. Physiology of attitude. n.p., 1935.

Phil 185.53   Khristov, M. Filosofskitě printsipi na prirodata. Sofia, 1935.

Phil 978.77.2   King, G.R. The magic presence. Chicago, 1935.

Phil 978.77.1   King, G.R. Unveiled mysteries. 2d ed. Chicago, 1935.

Phil 185.54   Klatzkin, Jakob. Der Erkenntnistrieb als Lebens und Todesprinzip. Zürich, 1935.

Phil 3625.13.90   Kluge, Fritz. Die Philosophie der Mathematik und Naturwissenschaft bei Aloys Müller. Inaug. Diss. Leipzig, 1935.

Phil 3255.81   Körner, Hermann. Studien zur geistesgeschichtlichen Stellung S. Francks. Breslau, 1935.

Phil 5250.7.19   Koffka, K. Principles of Gestalt psychology. London, 1935.

Phil 5250.7.15   Koffka, K. Principles of Gestalt psychology. N.Y., 1935.

Phil 3255.82   Kolbenheyer, Christiane. Die Mystik des Sebastian Franck von Wörd. Inaug-Diss. Würzburg, 1935.

Phil 8960.6   Kramer, H.G. The indirect voluntary, or Voluntarium in causa. Diss. Washington, 1935.

Phil 4352.1.103   Kruse, Paul. Die pädagogischen Elemente in der Philosophie des Jakob Balmes. Inaug. Diss. Neuherberg, 1935.

Phil 8590.23   Kuhlmann, G. Theologische Anthropologie im Abriss. Tübingen, 1935.

Phil 2520.194   Laberthonnière, L. Études sur Descartes. Paris, 1935. 2v.

Phil 5761.18   Lacape, R.S. La notion de liberté et la crise du déterminisme. Paris, 1935.

Phil 8886.45.15   Laird, John. An enquiry into moral nations. London, 1935.

Phil 342.11.5   Lambek, C. Essay on the foundation of cognition. Copenhagen, 1935.

Phil 186.82   Lambert, Henri. Hypothèse sur l'évolution physique et métaphysique de l'énergie. Bruxelles, 1935.

Phil 8636.8.5   Lamont, Corliss. The illusion of immortality. N.Y., 1935.

Phil 575.88   Langan, Hubert E. The philosophy of personalism and its educational applications. Diss. Washington, D.C., 1935.

Phil 4762.4.30   Lapshin, I.I. La synergie spirituelle. Praha, 1935.

Phil 5400.29.5   Latour, Marius. Premiers principes d'une théorie générale des émotions. Paris, 1935.

Phil 3585.14.10   Lessing, Theodor. Gesammelte Schriften in zehn Bäuden. Prag, 1935.

Phil 530.35.15   Levasti, A. Mistici del duecento e del trecento. Milano, 1935.

Phil 3011.5   Lewalter, E. Spanisch-Jesuisitische und Deutsch-Lutherische Metaphysik des 17. Jahrhunderts. Hamburg, 1935.

Phil 5251.41A   Lewin, Kurt. A dynamic theory of personality. N.Y., 1935.

Phil 7084.28.5   Lincoln, Jackson Steward. The dream in primitive cultures. London, 1935.

Phil 8591.38   Lindsay, Eric. Losing religion to find it. London, 1935.

Phil 342.15   Lion, Alene. Anaknisses and the a priori. Oxford, 1935.

Phil 978.72   Ljungström, O. Graded lessons in theosophy. Lund, 1935.

Phil 8701.14   Loewenberg, B.J. The controversy over evolution in New England, 1859-1873. n.p., 1935.

Phil 3640.261.5A   Löwith, Karl. Nietzsches Philosophie der ewigen Wiederkunft des Gleichen. Berlin, 1935.

Phil 186.80   Lombardi, F. L'esperienza e l'uomo. Firenze, 1935.

Phil 8886.56   Lombardi, F. Il mondo degli uomini. Firenze, 1935.

Phil 5251.74   Losskii, N.O. Principles of voluntaristic psychology. n.p., 1935. 2v.

Phil 735.107   Losskii, Nikolai O. Value and existence. London, 1935.

Phil 186.98   Ludendorff, M.S. Ist das Leben sinnlose Schinderei? München, 1935.

Phil 8591.43   Ludendorff, Mathilde S. Aus der Gotterkenntnis meinerwerke. München, 1935.

Phil 8701.16   Lunn, Arnold. Science and the supernatural; a correspondence between Arnold Lunn and J.B.S. Haldane. N.Y., 1935.

Phil 186.81.5   Lupasco, Stéphane. Du devenir logique et de l'affectivité. v.1-2. Paris, 1935-1936. 2v.

Phil 186.81   Lupasco, Stéphane. Du devenir logique et de l'affectivité. v.1-2. Thèse. Paris, 1935.

Phil 1711.5   Luppal, I.K. Istoriko-filosofskie etiudy. Moskva, 1935.

Phil 1750.135   MacCampbell, D. Irving Babbitt. n.p., 1935.

Phil 2280.5.99   MacCampbell, D. Santayana's debt to New England. n.p., 1935.

Phil 1133.28   McClure, Matthew T. The early philosophers of Greece. N.Y., 1935.

Phil 5650.22   McLachlan, Norman W. Noise. London, 1935.

Phil 5620.17   Macmurray, John. Reason and emotion. London, 1935.

Phil 5822.9   Maier, Norman Raymond Frederick. Principles of animal psychology. N.Y., 1935.

Phil 2475.1.249   Maire, Gilbert. Bergson, mon maître. 6e éd. Paris, 1935.

Phil 2733.29.30   Malebranche, Nicolas. De la recherche de la vérité. Paris, 1935.

Phil 5252.74   Malgand, W. De l'action à la pensée. Paris, 1935.

Phil 6962.23   Mallet, Raymond. La démence. Paris, 1935.

Phil 293.24   Mally, E. Erlebnis und Wirklichkeit. Leipzig, 1935.

Phil 8413.34   Malraux, Q. The voices of silence. Garden City, 1935.

Phil 4369.7.5   Manrique, Gervasio. Sanz del Rio. Madrid, 1935.

Phil 187.93.5   Marcel, Gabriel. Être et avoir. Paris, 1935.

Phil 2750.11.85   Maritain, Jacques. Art et scolastique. 3. éd. Paris, 1935.

Phil 2750.11.67   Maritain, Jacques. Freedom in the modern world. London, 1935.

Phil 2750.11.57   Maritain, Jacques. Science et sagesse. Paris, 1935.

Phil 293.21   Mason, F.B. (Mrs.). The great design. N.Y., 1935.

Phil 8413.19   Mather, F.J. Concerning beauty. Princeton, 1935.

Phil 8667.17.7   Matthews, W.R. The purpose of God. London, 1935.

Phil 8413.30   Mauron, C. Aesthetics and psychology. London, 1935.

Phil 1812.6A   Metz, Rudolf. Die philosophischen Strömungen der Gegenwart in Grossbritannien. Leipzig, 1935. 2v.

1935 - cont.

Phil 70.10.8 — Milan. Universita Cattolica del Sacro Cuore. Faculta di Filosofia. Relazione e cumunicazioni presentate al Congresso Nazionale di Filosofia. Milano, 1935. 2v.

Phil 187.110.5 — Mitchell, William. The quality of life. London, 1935?

Phil 293.22 — Mitterer, Albert. Das Rinzen der alten Stoff-Form-Metaphysik mit der heutigen Stoff-Physik. Innsbruck, 1935.

Phil 2475.1.265 — Molina, Enrique. Proyecciones de la intuición. Santiago de Chile, 1935.

Phil 2520.195 — Molitor, Emil. Über die Realitätstheorie Descartes'. Inaug.-Diss. Mayen, 1935.

Phil 3494.48 — Mollowilz, Gerhard. Kants Platosuffassung. Berlin, 1935.

Phil 1117.8 — Mondolfo, Rodolfo. Problemi del pensiero antico. Bologna, 1935.

Phil 960.141 — Mookerjee, S. The Buddhist philosophy of universal flux. Calcutta, 1935.

Phil 575.87 — Morgan, B.S. Individuality in a collective world. N.Y., 1935.

Phil 6322.16.5 — Morgan, John J.B. The psychology of abnormal people with educational applications. N.Y., 1935.

Phil 5520.74 — Müller, H. Experimentelle Beiträge zur Analyse des Verhältnisses von Laut und Sinn. Berlin, 1935.

Phil 5222.4.5 — Müller-Freienfels, R. The evolution of modern psychology. New Haven, 1935.

Phil 3494.41 — Munteano, B. Épisodes Kantiens en Suisse et en France sous le Directoire. Paris, 1935.

Phil 5252.69.10 — Murphy, Gardner. A briefer general psychology. N.Y., 1935.

Phil 530.30.5 — Muschg, Walter. Die Mystik in der Schweiz, 1200-1500. Frauenfeld, 1935.

Phil 8587.32.99 — Nédoncelle, M. La pensée religieuse de F. von Hügel, 1852-1925. Paris, 1935.

Phil 8587.32.101 — Nédoncelle, M. La pensée religieuse de F. von Hügel, 1852-1925. Thèse. Paris, 1935.

Phil 6123.7 — Nicolai, J.F. Psicogenesis. Santiago, 1935.

Phil 8963.3 — Niebuhr, R. Interpretation of Christian ethics. N.Y., 1935.

Phil 3640.24 — Nietzsche, Friedrich. Germans, Jews and France. Newark, 1935.

Phil 188.18 — Nohl, H. Einführung in die Philosophie. Frankfurt, 1935.

Phil 5465.39 — Nussberger, M. Die künstlerische Phantasie. München, 1935.

Phil 6964.3.5 — O'Brien, John D. An outline of psychiatry. 2. ed. St. Louis, Mo., 1935.

Phil 3640.200.15 — Oehler, Richard. Friedrich Nietzsche und die deutsche Zukunft. Leipzig, 1935.

Phil 3246.229 — Oestereich, H. Freiheitsides und Rechtsbegriff in der Philosophie von Johann Gottlieb Fichte. Jena, 1935.

Phil 7069.35.20 — O'Hare, Elizabeth. Universal knowledge; the road home. N.Y., 1935.

Phil 9070.19.2 — Oliver, J.R. The ordinary difficulties of everyday people. N.Y., 1935.

Phil 1850.129 — Ossi, M.M. Saggio su Francesco Bacon. Napoli, 1935.

Phil 5627.134.30F — Oxford Group. The march of events, Oxford, 1935. Oxford, 1935.

Phil 190.59 — Palumbo, A. The mirror of your soul. Boston, 1935.

Phil 623.30 — Paranjpye, Raghunath Purushottam. Rationalism in practice. Calcutta, 1935.

Phil 7069.35.70 — Parkman, Frances. Dedication; being later letters from the writer of "Reality". Boston, 1935.

Phil 190.63 — Parodi, D. En quête d'un philosophie. Paris, 1935.

Phil 190.56.5 — Patrick, G.T.W. Introduction to philosophy. London, 1935.

Phil 9245.51 — Patter, Charles F. Technique of happiness. N.Y., 1935.

Phil 2475.1.255 — Péguy, Charles. Note sur M. Bergson et la philosophie bergsonienne. 6e éd. Paris, 1935.

Phil 9035.71 — Peillaube, E. Caractère et personnalité. Paris, 1935.

Phil 2070.129.5A — Perry, R.B. The thought and character of William James. Boston, 1935. 2v.

Phil 3778.91 — Pfeifer, A. Die Philosophie der Kantperiode Karl Leonhard Reinholds. Inaug. Diss. W. Elberfeld, 1935.

Phil 8670.17 — Picard, Max. Die Flucht vor Gott. 2. Aufl. Erlenbach, 1935.

Phil 8640.12 — Pickford, M. My rendezvous with life. N.Y., 1935.

Phil 5520.66 — Pita, Enrique B. La frase infantil monopalábrica y la intelligencia. Buenos Aires, 1935.

Phil 6125.26 — Pitkin, W.B. Take it easy. N.Y., 1935.

Phil 190.64 — Pohl, Joachim. Philosophie der tragischen Strukturen. Wien, 1935.

Phil 3835.1.15 — Pollock, F. Spinoza. London, 1935.

Phil 3110.176 — Popp, K.R. Jakob Böhme und Issac Newton. Inaug. Diss. Leipzig, 1935.

Phil 5255.42 — Potts, John. Know thyself; a study in mental qualities. Philadelphia, 1935.

Phil 9245.50.5 — Powys, J.C. The art of happiness. N.Y., 1935.

Phil 8595.31 — Przywara, Erich. Plarity; a German Catholic's interpretation of religion. London, 1935.

Phil 5238.8 — Psychologischer Club, Zürich. Die kulturelle Bedeutung der komplexen Psychologie. Berlin, 1935.

Phil 191.3 — Quarto Di Palo, A. Sintesi di un sistema filosofica. Roma, 1935.

Phil 672.157 — Ramige, E.A. Contemporary concepts of time and the idea of God. Boston, 1935.

Phil 3499.29 — Rasker, A.J. De ethick en het probleem van het booze. Proef. Assen, 1935.

Phil 6327.12.13 — Reik, Theodor. Der überraschte Psychologie. Leiden, 1935.

Phil 8892.32.5 — Rensi, Giuseppe. Critica dello morale. Catania, 1935.

Phil 1020.4.31 — Reyes, A. El racionalismo averroísta y el razonamiento luliano. Madrid, 1935.

Phil 7069.34.25.2A — Rhine, Joseph B. Extra-sensory perception. Boston, 1935.

Phil 3195.6.125 — Richey, H.G. Die Überwindung der Subjektivität in der empirischen Philosophie Diltheys und Deweys. Göttingen, 1935.

Phil 3903.3.113 — Richtscheid, H. Das Problem des philosophischen Skeptizismus. Diss. Düsseldorf, 1935.

Phil 3017.4 — Riecke, H. Der Rassegedanke und die neuere Philosophie. Leipzig, 1935.

Phil 8892.50 — Rines, George E. Getting the most out of life. Boston, 1935.

Phil 5257.28 — Roback, A.A. Behaviorism and psychology. Cambridge, 1935.

Phil 3552.306 — Rolland, E. Le déterminisme monadique. Paris, 1935.

Phil 3552.306.5 — Rolland, E. Le déterminisme monadique. Thèse. Paris, 1935.

Phil 9513.6 — Rouger, G. Spécialisation et évolution. Paris, 1935.

Phil 8418.8.5 — Rusu, Liviu. Essai sur la création artistique. Paris, 1935.

Phil 8418.8 — Rusu, Liviu. Essai sur la création artistique comme révélation du sens de l'éxistence. Paris, 1935.

Phil 400.4.15 — Salamonowiez, L. Die Ethik des Positivismus nach Ernst Laas. Inaug. Diss. Dortmund, 1935.

Phil 8893.89 — Samuel, Herbert. Practical ethics. London, 1935.

Phil 349.33 — Sanford, H.W. Concerning knowledge. N.Y., 1935. 2v.

Phil 4065.122 — Saracista, M. La filosofia di Giordano Bruno nei suoi motivi plotiniani. Firenze, 1935.

Phil 8893.91 — Sargent, Porter E. The new immoralities. Boston, 1935.

Phil 5058.47.5 — Schingnitz, Werner. Mensch und Begriff. Leipzig, 1935.

Phil 193.10.15 — Schlegel, Friedrich von. Neve philosophische Schriften. Frankfurt, 1935.

Phil 349.9.10 — Schlick, Moritz. Sur le fondement de la connaissance. Paris, 1935.

Phil 5190.4.20 — Scholz, H. Die sogenannten Dcfinitionen durch Abstraktion. Leipzig, 1935.

Phil 5420.15 — Schouten, Jan. De verlegenheid. Proefschrift. Groningen, 1935.

Phil 705.24 — Schultzer, Bent. Transcendence and the logical difficulties of transcendence; a logical analysis. Copenhagen, 1935.

Phil 2240.85 — Sciacca, M.F. La filosofia di Tomaso Reid. Napoli, 1935.

Phil 818.21 — Sciacca, M.F. Studi sulla filosofia medioevale e moderna. Napoli, 1935.

Phil 1123.10 — Sciacca, Michele F. Studi sulla filosofia antica. Napoli, 1935.

Phil 5258.165.10 — Sechenov, Ivan M. Selected works. Moscow, 1935.

Phil 9255.17 — Sedgewick, Garrett G. Of irony, especially in drama. Toronto, 1935.

Phil 1818.10 — Segerstedt, T.T. The problem of knowledge in Scottish philosophy. Lund, 1935.

Phil 818.22 — Serra Hunter, J. Figures i perspectives de la história del pensament. Barcelona, 1935.

Phil 5058.48 — Shaw, Charles G. Logic in theory and practice. N.Y., 1935.

Phil 960.256 — Sircar, Mahendranath. Eastern lights; a brief account of some phases of life, thought and mysticism in India. Calcutta, 1935.

Phil 5258.113.5 — Skaggs, E.B. A textbook of experimental and theoretical psychology. Boston, 1935.

Phil 6968.24 — Small, Victor R. I knew 3000 lunatics. N.Y., 1935.

Phil 5850.342 — Sollier, Paul. La psychotechnique. Bruxelles, 1935.

Phil 2475.1.253 — Sommer, Erika. Bergson's Einfluss auf die französische Schriftsprache. Inaug. Diss. München, 1935.

Phil 193.93.10 — Sorel, Georges. D'Aristote à Marx. Paris, 1935.

Phil 3850.32.10 — Spann, Othmar. Erkenne dich Selbst. Jena, 1935.

Phil 8643.29 — Spencer, Frederick A.M. The future life. 1. ed. London, 1935.

Phil 735.112 — Spiegelberg, H. Antirelativismus. Zürich, 1935.

Phil 3819.57.25 — Spinoza, Benedictus de. Bogoslovsko-politicheskii traktat. Moskva, 1935.

Phil 5402.20 — Spitz, C. Zur Psychologie des Weinens. Inaug. Diss. Zeulenroda, 1935.

Phil 7069.35.25 — Spivey, T.S. The awakening of the sixth sense; a look into the great unknown. Shawneetown, Ill., 1935.

Phil 3801.806 — Staiger, Emil. Der Geist der Liebe und das Schicksal. Frauenfeld, 1935.

Phil 9358.14.5 — Stearns, Alfred E. To him that overcometh. Boston, 1935.

Phil 193.144 — Steeksma, J. Philosophical inquiry. London, 1935.

Phil 978.49.125 — Steiner, R. Art in the light of mystery wisdom. N.Y., 1935.

Phil 818.20.5 — Steiner, R. Gli enigmi della filosofia. Milano, 1935.

Phil 7082.38.5 — Stekel, Wilhelm. Fortschritte und Technik der Traumdeutung. Wien, 1935.

Phil 5258.35.15 — Stern, W. Allgemeine Psychologie auf personalistischer Grundlage. Haag, 1935.

Phil 1135.28.20 — Sternberg, Kurt. Das Problem des Ursprungs in der Philosophie des Altertums. Breslau, 1935.

Phil 735.108 — Störring, G. Die moderne ethische Wertphilosophie. Leipzig, 1935.

Phil 5258.114 — Straus, Erwin. Vom Sinn der Sinne. Berlin, 1935.

Phil 4769.1.107 — Strémooukhoff, D. Vladimir Soloviev et son oeuvre messianique. Paris, 1935.

Phil 4769.1.107.5 — Strémooukhoff, D. Vladimir Soloviev et son oeuvre messianique. Thèse. Strasbourg, 1935.

Phil 9358.18 — Swan, John N. Four lives. Boston, 1935.

Phil 6328.20 — Szalai, Alexander. Philosophische Grundprobleme der psychoanalytischen Psychlogie. Budapest, 1935.

Phil 720.39 — Tarski, Alfred. De Wahrheitsbegriff in der...Sprachen. Photostat. Leopoli, 1935.

Phil 6316.8.25 — Taylor, H.M. Life's unknown ruler...teaching of George Groddeck. London, 1935. 2v.

Phil 8599.17.10 — Temple, William. Nature, man and God. London, 1935.

Phil 8599.26 — Thielicke, H. Geschichte und Existenz. Gütersloh, 1935.

Phil 8110.4 — Thielke, K.L.F. Literatur- und Kunstkritik in ihren Wechselbeziehungen. Halle, 1935.

Phil 5259.27 — Thomas, Frank C. Ability and knowledge: the London school. London, 1935.

Phil 2340.10.95 — Thompson, J. An analysis of the thought of Alfred N. Whitehead and William E. Hocking concerning good and evil. Diss. Chicago, 1935.

Phil 5259.7.15 — Thorndike, E.L. The psychology of wants, interests and attitudes. N.Y., 1935.

Phil 4370.10 — Torner, F.M. Doña Oliva Sabuco de Nantes. Madrid, 1935.

Phil 8709.18.5 — Tóth, T. God's amazing world. N.Y., 1935.

Phil 5259.25.5 — Trejos, J. Cuestiones de psicología racional. 2. ed. San José de Costa Rica, 1935.

Phil 7069.35 — Tubby, G.O. Psychics and mediums. Boston, 1935.

Phil 195.4 — Utitz, Emil. Die Sendung der Philosophie in unserer Zeit. Leiden, 1935.

Phil 5261.17.19 — Valentine, Willard Lee. Student's guide for beginning the study of psychology. N.Y., 1935.

Phil 5831.6.5 — Verlaine, Louis. Histoire naturelle de la connaissance chez le singe inférieur; le concret. Paris, 1935-36. 3v.

Phil 2045.118 — Vialatoux, J. La cité de Hobbes. Paris, 1935.

Phil 106.1.5 — Voltaire, Francois Marie Arouet de. Dictionnaire philosophique. Paris, 1935-36. 2v.

Phil 6332.10 — Wallin, John E.W. Personality maladjustments and mental hygiene. 1st ed. N.Y., 1935.

Phil 5850.385.19 — Walsh, W.S. Making our minds behave. N.Y., 1935.

Phil 7069.35.75 — Walter Franklin Prince, a tribute to his memory. Boston, 1935.

Phil 2840.96 — Wang, Tsun-Sheng. Le phénoménisme de Charles Renouvier. Thèse. Lyon, 1935.

Phil 735.91.10 — Ward, Leo Richard. Values and reality. N.Y., 1935.

1935 - cont.

Phil 5832.13.15 — Warden, C.J. Comparative psychology. N.Y., 1935-40. 3v.

Phil 197.61 — Watkin, E.I. A philosophy of form. London, 1935.

Phil 353.14 — Weidauer, F. Objektivität, voraussetzungslose Wissenschaft und wissenschaftliche Wahrheit. Leipzig, 1935.

Phil 6400.16 — Weisenburg, T. Aphasia. N.Y., 1935.

Phil 5465.34 — Welch, Livingston. Imagination and human nature. London, 1935.

Phil 7069.35.50 — Wells, Helen B. Key to the spaces...dictated by A.P. Mathewson. N.Y., 1935.

Phil 7069.35.51F — Wells, Helen B. Linking the spaces. N.Y., 1935. 2 pam.

Phil 7069.35.60 — Wells, Helen B. The progressive Pilgrim's progress. N.Y., 1935.

Phil 7069.35.52 — Wells, Helen B. Some laws of materialization. Dictated by John King. N.Y., 1935.

Phil 7069.35.56 — Wells, Helen B. Through the gates of time. v.1. N.Y., 1935.

Phil 7069.35.54 — Wells, Helen B. "Whom the gods love". Dictated by Ernest Wells. N.Y., 1935.

Phil 7080.46 — Weschcke, Charles. Overcoming sleeplessness. St. Paul, 1935.

Phil 8897.65 — Wheelwright, P. A critical introduction to ethics. Garden City, N.Y., 1935.

Phil 2648.92 — Wickwar, William H. Baron d'Holbach; a prelude to the French Revolution. London, 1935.

Phil 822.2.4 — Windelband, W. Lehrbuch der Geschichte der Philosophie. Tübingen, 1935.

Phil 4260.113 — Witzemann, Walter. Politischer Aktivismus und sozialer Mythos. Berlin, 1935.

Phil 5232.6 — Wolfson, H.A. The internal senses in Latin, Arabic, and Hebrew philosophic texts. Cambridge, 1935.

Phil 1050.22 — Wolfson, Harry A. Isaac Israeli on the internal senses. N.Y., 1935.

Phil 5262.9.20 — Woodworth, R.S. Psychology. 3d ed. N.Y., 1935.

Phil 525.87.5 — Younghusband, F.E. Modern mystics. 1st ed. N.Y., 1935.

Phil 8587.32.109 — Zari, A. Frederico von Hügel. Pinerolo, 1935.

Phil 8900.5 — Zinninger, E.D. Ethical philosophy and civilization. Los Angeles, 1935.

Phil 5520.65 — Zipf, G.K. The psycho-biology of language. Boston, 1935.

Phil 530.20.77 — Zippel, W. Die Mystiker und die deutsche Gesellschaft des 13. und 14. Jahrhunderts. Inaug.-Diss. Düren, 1935.

Phil 6035.1 — Zirwes, Ernest. Gesichtsausdruck und Wertraum. Inaug. Diss. Würzburg, 1935.

Phil 6135.5 — Zitex, Edward. A research in report on mental hygiene, brain, exercises, sanitation and foods. New Orleans, La., 1935.

1936

Phil 6310.4.10 — Alexander, Franz G. The medical value of psychoanalysis. N.Y., 1936.

Phil 8580.21.5 — Alexander, H.B. God and man's destiny. 1. ed. N.Y., 1936.

Phil 175.26.9 — Aliotta, Antonio. L'esperimento nella scienza. Napoli, 1936.

Phil 5627.146 — Alm, Ivar. Den religiösa funktionen i människosjälen. Akademisk abhandlung. Stockholm, 1936.

Phil 3850.18.115 — Alpheus, Karl. Kant und Scheler. Diss. Freiburg, 1936.

Phil 1695.22 — Alston, W. Readings in twentieth century philosophy. N.Y., 1936.

Phil 8080.6 — Anceschi, Luciano. Autonomia ed eteronomia dell'arte. Firenze, 1936.

Phil 9245.52 — Andrus, F.N. The evolution of happiness. Boston, 1936.

Phil 400.92 — Astrada, Carlos. Idealismo fenomenológico y metafísica existencial. Buenos Aires, 1936.

Phil 3640.433 — Augustin, G. Nietzsches religiöse Entwicklung. Stuttgart, 1936.

Phil 165.3 — Avey, A.E. Readings in philosophy. N.Y., 1936.

Phil 672.155.10 — Bachelard, Gaston. La dialectique de la durée. Paris, 1936.

Phil 3850.18.113 — Bachus, A. Enzelmensch Familie und Staat in der Philosophie Max Schelers. Inaug. Diss. Düsseldorf, 1936.

Phil 978.74.15 — Bailey, A.A. (Mrs.). A treatise on the seven rays. N.Y., 1936-42. 4v.

Phil 1506.9 — Barbedette, D. Manière d'enseigner la philosophie scolastique. Paris, 1936.

Phil 8876.110 — Barboza, E. Etica. Lima, 1936.

Phil 5241.110 — Barnard, Chester Irving. Mind in everyday affairs. Princeton, 1936.

Phil 8876.100 — Baudin, E. Cours de philosophie morale. Paris, 1936.

Phil 8402.51 — Baumgarten, A. Aesthetica. Bari, 1936.

Phil 1801.4 — Baumgarten, E. Die geistigen Grundlagen des amerikanischen Gemeinwesens. Frankfurt, 1936-8. 2v.

Phil 6111.55 — Beck, L.J. Manual skills and the measurement of handedness. Worcester, 1936.

VPhil 8656.42 — Békassy, Árpád. Az analógia je lentősége a tudomángos es vallásos világismeret kialakulásában. Budapest, 1936.

Phil 4765.1 — Bem, A.L. Zhizn' i smert'; sbornik pamiatniki N.E. Osipova. Praga, 1936.

Phil 2520.198 — Beneš, J. Descartesova metoda ve vědách a ve filosofii. V Praze, 1936.

Phil 705.25 — Bénézé, Georges. Allure du transcendental. Paris, 1936.

Phil 705.25.5 — Bénézé, Georges. Allure du transcendental. Thèse. Paris, 1936.

Phil 735.109 — Bènèzè, Georges. Valeur. Paris, 1936.

Phil 735.109.5 — Bènèzè, Georges. Valeur. Thèse. Paris, 1936.

Phil 5627.134.40 — Benson, C.I. The eight points of the Oxford Group. Melbourne, 1936.

Phil 176.138 — Berdiaev, Nikolai A. Méditations sur l'existence. Paris, 1936.

Phil 5241.106 — Bernal del Riesgo, A. Iniciación en la psicologia. v.1-2. La Habana, 1936.

Phil 6311.20 — Bisch, L.E. Be glad you're neurotic. N.Y., 1936.

Phil 7084.20 — Bjerre, Paul. Das Träumen als Heilungsweg der Seele. Zürich, 1936.

Phil 6420.32 — Blanton, Smiley. For stutterers. N.Y., 1936.

Phil 8876.54.10 — Blondel, Maurice. L'action. Paris, 1936.

Phil 8656.26 — Bocheńske, I.M. De cognitione existential Dei per niam causalitatis relate ad fidem catholicam. Poznań, 1936.

Phil 176.142 — Bolaffio, C. Colui che si chiama "Io sono". Modena, 1936.

Phil 3195.6.101 — Bollnow, O.F. Dilthey, eine Einführung in seine Philosophie. Leipzig, 1936.

Phil 2401.7 — Bonnard, A. Le mouvement antipositiviste contemporain en France. Thèse. Paris, 1936.

Phil 2750.10.105 — Bonnard, A. La notion d'irrationnel chez Emile Meyerson. Thèse. Paris, 1936.

1936 - cont.

Phil 8876.101 — Borle, Charles A. The art of living. Boston, 1936.

Phil 6111.75 — Brickner, Richard Max. The intellectual functions of the frontal lobes. N.Y., 1936.

Phil 6311.19 — Brown, William. Mind, medicine and metaphysics. London, 1936.

Phil 801.23.15 — Brunschvicg, L. La physique du vingtième siècle et la philosophie. Paris, 1936.

Phil 6945.15 — Bryan, William A. Administrative psychiatry. N.Y., 1936.

Phil 3120.30.51 — Buber, Martin. Die Frage an den Einzelnen. Berlin, 1936.

Phil 3120.30.57 — Buber, Martin. Die Stunde und die Erkenntnis. Berlin, 1936.

Phil 575.22.5 — Buckham, John W. Christianity and personality. N.Y., 1936.

Phil 6311.17 — Bull, Titus. The imperative conquest. N.Y., 1936.

Phil 7057.8.15 — Burke, Jane Revere. Messages on healing understood to have been dictated by William James. N.Y., 1936.

Phil 5241.89.10 — Butler, J.R. Human psychology. N.Y., 1936.

Phil 5811.15.10A — Buytendijk, Frederik Jacobus Johannes. The mind of the dog. Boston, 1936.

Phil 176.139 — Byers, R.P. Superuniversity studies. Boston, 1936.

Phil 4215.1.86 — Caboara, L. La filosofia politica di Romagnosi. Roma, 1936.

Phil 8877.65.22 — Cabot, Richard C. The meaning of right and wrong. N.Y., 1936.

Phil 4803.727.80 — Cáceres, Alfredo. La obra psicológica de Radecki, 1910-35. Montevideo, 1936.

Phil 1350.13 — Calderini, A. Virtù romana. Milano, 1936.

Phil 177.33.7 — Calkins, Mary Whiton. The persistent problems of philosophy. N.Y., 1936.

Phil 4073.31 — Campanella, Tommaso. Telogia. Milano, 1936.

Phil 177.97 — Caramella, S. Introduzione alla filosofia e dottrina della practica. Messina, 1936.

Phil 4075.79.25 — Cardano, Girolamo. Ma vie. Paris, 1936.

Phil 177.96 — Cardone, A.D. Il problema del sovraumano. Firenze, 1936.

Phil 4080.9.39 — Carlini, Armando. Il mito del realismo. Firenze, 1936.

Phil 177.93 — Carneades, D. Matter, spirit and living intellect. London, 1936.

Phil 177.92 — Casey, Joseph T. The primacy of metaphysics. Diss. Washington, D.C., 1936.

Phil 2138.115 — Castell, A. Mill's logic of the moral sciences. Diss. Chicago, 1936.

Phil 4080.3.121.5 — Castellano, G. Benedetto Croce. 2a ed. Bari, 1936.

Phil 5242.45 — Chiavacci, G. Saggio sulla natura dell'uomo. Firenze, 1936.

Phil 5066.14.10 — Church, Alonzo. A bibliography of symbolic logic. Monasha, Wisconsin, 1936.

Phil 6992.2 — Cohen, Jacques J. Psychotherapy. London, 1936.

Phil 5042.25.2 — Cohen, Morris R. Introduction to logic and scientific method. N.Y., 1936.

Phil 9513.5.5 — Coleman, George William. This business of living. Boston, 1936.

Phil 9513.5.6 — Coleman, George William. This business of living. Boston, 1936.

Phil 283.12 — Colligan, J.J. Cosmology. N.Y., 1936.

Phil 5850.162 — Collins, Mary. Psychology and practical life. London, 1936.

Phil 70.13 — Congrès International de Philosophie Scientifique, 1st, Paris, 1935. Actes du Congrès International. Paris, 1936. 8v.

Phil 2475.1.251 — Córdoba, Argentina. Universidad Nacional. Instituto de Filosofía. Homenaje a Bergson. Córdoba, 1936.

Phil 2605.1.85 — Costanzi, T.M. Il pensiero di Alfredo Fouillée. Napoli, 1936.

Phil 5649.23 — Covaciu-Ulmeanu. Effort volontaire et chronaxie. Thèse. Paris, 1936.

Phil 974.2.42 — Cox, H.R.W. Who wrote the March-hare attack on the Mahatma letters? Victoria, 1936.

Phil 5585.63 — Cresson, A. La représentation. Paris, 1936.

Phil 6315.2.111 — Dalbiez, R. La méthode psychanalytique et la doctrine freudienne. v.1-2. Thèse. Paris, 1936.

Phil 8693.17 — Davidson, R.F. The heavens and faith. London, 1936.

Phil 6953.14 — Davis, J.E. Principles and practice of recreational therapy for the mentally ill. N.Y., 1936.

Phil 8583.28.4 — Dawson, Christopher H. Religion and the modern state. London, 1936.

Phil 8878.55 — DeBoer, Cecil. The if's and ought's of ethics. Grand Rapids, Mich., 1936.

Phil 2520.78.30 — Descartes, René. Correspondance publiée avec une introduction et des notes par C. Adam et G. Milhaud. 1. éd. Paris, 1936-51. 8v.

Phil 178.17.15 — Dessoir, Max. Einleitung in die Philosophie. Stuttgart, 1936.

Phil 5243.44 — Deut, John Y. Reactions of the human machine. London, 1936.

Phil 8633.1.35 — Dodd, Charles H. The communion of saints. Cambridge, 1936.

Phil 4260.91.5 — Donati, Benvenuto. Nuovi studi sulla filosofia civile di G.B. Vico. Firenze, 1936.

Phil 6313.11 — Drake, R.M. Outline of abnormal psychology. N.Y., 1936.

Phil 5243.43 — Duflo, J. Esquisse d'une énergétique mentale. Paris, 1936.

Phil 5243.15.7 — Dunlap, K. Elements of psychology. St. Louis, 1936.

Phil 5643.96 — Duret, René. Les aspects de l'image visuelle. Paris, 1936.

Phil 2250.92 — Dykhuizen, George. The conception of God in the philosophy of Josiah Royce. Chicago, 1936.

Phil 1108.4 — Dynnik, M.A. Ocherk istorii filosofii klassicheskoi Gretsii. Moskva, 1936.

Phil 5525.20.15 — Eastman, Max. Enjoyment of laughter. N.Y., 1936.

Phil 2805.218A — Eastwood, D.M. The revival of Pascal. Oxford, 1936.

Phil 1050.26 — Ehrich, J. Das Problem der Theodizes in der jüdischen Religionsphilosophie des Mittelalters. Inaug. Diss. Breslau, 1936.

Phil 335.6 — Elie, H. Le complexe significabile. Paris, 1936.

Phil 335.6.2 — Elie, H. Le complexe significabile. Thèse. Paris, 1936.

Phil 179.33 — Emmet, D.M. Philosophy and faith. London, 1936.

Phil 180.61 — La fase attuale della filosofia. Messina, 1936.

Phil 5460.10.5 — Faure, Henri. Les hallucinations. Paris, 1936.

Phil 2477.6.103 — Federici Ajeoldi, G. Interpretazione del problema dell'essere in M. Blondel. Firenze, 1936.

Phil 3120.40.82 — Feestbundel aangeboden aan Dr. J.D. Bierens de Haan. Assen, 1936.

Phil 8120.7 — Feldman, V. L'esthétique française contemporaine. Paris, 1936.

Phil 2475.1.257 — Fénart, Michel. Les assertions bergsoniennes. Paris, 1936.

Chronological Listing

1936 - cont.

Phil 180.63A	Ferm, V. First adventures in philosophy. N.Y., 1936.
Phil 180.54	Fersen, Alessandro. L'universo come guioco. Modena, 1936.
Phil 6955.16	Filho, Roch. Psychiatria e hygiene mental. Maceló, 1936.
Phil 4260.112	Finetti, Giovanni F. Difesa dell'autorità della sacra scrittura contro Giambattista Vico. Bari, 1936.
Phil 180.53	Finley, John H. The mystery of the mind's desire. N.Y., 1936.
Phil 180.55	Fiszer, E. Unité et intelligibilité. Paris, 1936.
Phil 180.55.5	Fiszer, E. Unité et intelligibilité. Thèse. Paris, 1936.
Phil 3425.289	Flechtheim, O.K. Hegels Strafrechtstheorie. Brünn, 1936.
Phil 75.31	Fock, G. Philosophie. Leipzig, 1936.
Phil 3450.19.99	Folwart, H. Kant, Husserl, Heidegger. Breslau, 1936.
Phil 1705.10	Fondane, B. La conscience malheureuse. Paris, 1936.
Phil 180.57	Forest, Aimé. Du consentement à l'être. Paris, 1936.
Phil 990.20	Foroughir, A.H. Civilisation et synthèse. Paris, 1936.
Phil 6315.2.43A	Freud, Sigmund. The problem of anxiety. N.Y., 1936.
Phil 6315.2.72.5	Freud, Sigmund. Selbstdarstellung. 2. Aufl. Wien, 1936.
Phil 8955.6	Frodl, Ferdinand. Gesellschaftslehre. Wien, 1936.
Phil 5625.75.85	Frolov, I.P. I.P. Pavlovs i ego uchenie ob uslovnykh refleksakh. Moskva, 1936.
Phil 5245.41	Fryer, D. An outline of general psychology. N.Y., 1936.
Phil 8407.26	Galli, E. L'estetica e i suoi problemi. Napoli, 1936.
Phil 5374.159	Ganne De Beaucoudrey, E. Perception et courant de conscience. Thèse. Paris, 1936.
Phil 7069.36.5	Garland, Hamlin. Forty years of psychic research; a plain narrative of fact. N.Y., 1936.
Phil 2605.1.83	Gaune de Beaucourdey, E. La psychologie et la métaphysique des idéesforces chez Alfred Fouillée. Thèse. Paris, 1936.
Phil 4006.2.20	Gentile, G. Memorie italiane e problemi della filosofia e della vita. Firenze, 1936.
Phil 4006.2.10	Gentile, G. Studi sul rinascimento. 2a ed. Firenze, 1936.
Phil 8586.41	Gill, Eric. The necessity of belief. London, 1936.
Phil 181.73	Gilson, E. Christianisme et philosophie. Paris, 1936.
Phil 630.43	Gilson, Étienne. Le réalisme méthodique. Paris, 1936?
Phil 7069.36.7	Glardon, R. Le spiritisme en face de l'historie. Lausanne, 1936.
Phil 1050.25	Goldman, S. The Jew and the universe. N.Y., 1936.
Phil 337.10	Goldschmidt, W. Der Linguismus und die Erkenntnistheorie der Verweisungen. Zürich, 1936.
Phil 6400.17	Goldstein, Kurt. The problem of the meaning of words based upon observation of aphasic patients. Worcester, 1936.
Phil 900.11	Grant, Francis. Oriental philosophy. N.Y., 1936.
Phil 2725.13.90	Grenier, Jean. La philosophie de Jules Lequier. Paris, 1936.
Phil 2725.13.91	Grenier, Jean. La philosophie de Jules Lequier. Thèse. Paris, 1936.
Phil 5850.222	Griffith, C.R. An introduction to applied psychology. N.Y., 1936.
Phil 181.50.10	Grisebach, E. Freiheit und Zucht. Zurich, 1936.
Phil 6116.21	Groves, E.R. Readings in mental hygiene. N.Y., 1936.
Phil 5246.47.5A	Guilford, Joy Paul. Psychometric methods. 1. ed. N.Y., 1936.
Phil 2630.11.2	Guitton, Jean. La pensée moderne et le catholicisme. v.6,7,9,10. Aix, 1936. 5v.
Phil 8408.11	Haecker, T. Schönheit; ein Versuch. Leipzig, 1936.
Phil 5545.176	Hajdu, H. Das mnemotechnische Schrifttum. Wien, 1936.
Phil 7069.36.20	Halifax, Charles L.W. Lord Halifax's ghost book. 3. ed. London, 1936.
Phil 2070.92.5	Hansen, V. William James og det religiøse. København, 1936.
Phil 5465.36	Harding, R.E.M. Towards a law of creative thought. London, 1936.
Phil 974.2.40	Hare, H.E. Who wrote the Mahatma letters? London, 1936.
Phil 8587.44.5	Harkness, George E. The resources of religion. N.Y., 1936.
Phil 5047.37	Hartman, S.J. A textbook of logic. N.Y., 1936.
Phil 5247.53	Hartmann, G.W. Gestalt psychology. N.Y., 1936.
Phil 1707.11	Hartmann, Hans. Denkendes Europa; ein Gang durch die Philosophie der Gegenwart. Berlin, 1936.
Phil 5203.11	Harvard University. Psychology Library. Selected reference list. Cambridge, 1936.
Phil 3120.8.87	Hauber, V. Wahrheit und Evidenz bei Franz Brentano. Inaug. Diss. Stuttgart, 1936.
Phil 672.158	Heath, L.R. The concept of time. Photoreproduction. Chicago, 1936.
Phil 1870.118	Hedenius, Ingemar. Sensationalism and theology in Berkeley's philosophy. Inaug. Diss. Uppsala, 1936.
Phil 3425.12.5A	Hegel, Georg Wilhelm Friedrich. Dokumente zu Hegels Entwicklung. Stuttgart, 1936.
Phil 9035.72	Heiss, Robert. Die Lehre vom Charakter. Berlin, 1936.
Phil 8408.17	Heller, R. Das Wesen der Schönheit. Wein, 1936.
Phil 9035.78	Helwig, Paul. Charakterologie. Leipzig, 1936.
Phil 6117.41	Helwig, Paul. Seele als Ausserung. Leipzig, 1936.
Phil 5247.52	Hempel, Carl G. Der Typus Begriff im Lichte der neuen Logik. Leiden, 1936.
Phil 8957.10	Henson, Herbert H. Christian morality; natural, developing, final. Oxford, 1936.
Phil 182.104	Hersch, J. L'illusion philosophique. Paris, 1936.
Phil 3450.24	Hessing, Jacob. Das Selbsthewusstwerden des Geistes. Stuttgart, 1936.
Phil 5247.48.5	Higginson, G. Psychology. N.Y., 1936.
Phil 1865.179	Himes, N.E. Jeremy Bentham and the genesis of English Neo-Malthusianism. London, 1936.
Cg Phil 9495.141	Hitschmann, E. Frigidity in women. Washington, 1936.
Phil 525.16.13	Hobhouse, S.H. Fides et ratio; the book which introduced Jacob Boehme to William Law. n.p., 1936.
Phil 3195.6.115	Hoefer, Josef. Vom Leben zur Wahrheit. Freiburg, 1936.
Phil 3425.288	Hoffmeister, J. Dokumente zu Hegels Entwicklung. Stuttgart, 1936.
Phil 5425.60	Holste, Maria. Das Erlebnis und die Leistung. Inaug. Diss. Düsseldorf, 1936.
Phil 8520.34	Horton, Walter M. Contemporary English theology; an American interpretation. N.Y., 1936.
Phil 974.2.44	Hudson, Irene B. Who wrote the Mahatma letters? Answered. Victoria, 1936.
Phil 6318.1	Israeli, Nathan. Abnormal personality and time. Photoreproduction. N.Y., 1936.
Phil 2750.12.90	Iwanicki, J. Morin et les démonstrations mathématiques de l'existence de Dieu. Paris, 1936.
Phil 5759.6	Jakubisiak, A. La pensée et le libre arbitre. Paris, 1936.
Phil 5627.6.5.15	James, William. Varieties of religious experience. N.Y., 1936.
Phil 184.30.5	Janet, P. Philosophie; questions complémentaires. 5e éd. Paris, 1936.
Phil 5249.21.3	Janet, Pierre. L'intelligence avant le langage. Paris, 1936.
Phil 9255.19	Jankélévitch, Vladimir. L'ironie. Paris, 1936.
Phil 3640.267	Jaspers, Karl. Nietzsche. Berlin, 1936.
Phil 5645.39	Jerrentrup, F. Allgemein Orientierende experimental psychologische Untersuchungen über den zeitlichen Verlauf von Farbwandelspielen. Inaug. Diss. Bochum, 1936.
Phil 184.26.15	Joad, C.E.M. Guide to philosophy. London, 1936.
Phil 184.26.12	Joad, C.E.M. Return to philosophy. N.Y., 1936.
Phil 5100.3	Kamiat, A.H. The critique of poor reason. N.Y., 1936.
Phil 8050.44	Kampanēs, Aristos. Historia tōn aisthētikōn theōriōn. Athēna, 1936.
Phil 3480.32.67	Kant, Immanuel. O pus Postumum. Berlin, 1936.
Phil 3010.6	Kauffmann, H.L. Essai sur l'anti-progressisme et ses origines dans la philosophie allemande moderne. Thèse. Paris, 1936.
Phil 365.43	Kausika, N. The new evolution, being a general solution of all modern life problems, based on truth. Nemmara, 1936.
Phil 8590.22	Keilbach, W. Die Problematik der Religionen. Paderborn, 1936.
Phil 3549.2.47	Keyserling, Hermann. Das Buch vom persönlichen Leben. Stuttgart, 1936.
Phil 365.44	Kingson, B. The moving tent. Wellington, 1936.
Phil 6020.3.5	Klages, L. Grundlegung der Wissenschaft von Ausdruck. Leipzig, 1936.
Phil 575.51.8	Klages, Ludwig. Die Grundlagen der Charakterkunde. 7e und 8e Aufl. Leipzig, 1936.
Phil 3640.266	Klein, Johannes. Die Dichtung Nietzsches. München, 1936.
Phil 185.57A	Klibansky, Raymond. Philosophy and history. Oxford, 1936.
Phil 4762.1.39	Kohanskii, A.S. Lossky's theory of knowledge. Nashville, 1936.
Phil 1810.3	Koitko, D. Iu. Ocherki sovremennoi anglo-amerikanskoi filosofii. Moskva, 1936.
Phil 400.99	Kränzlin, Gerhard. Die Philosophie vom unendlichen Menschen. Leipzig, 1936.
Phil 3195.8.85	Kühne, A. Der Religionsphilosoph Georg F. Daumer. Inaug. Diss. Berlin, 1936.
Phil 6320.10	Künkel, Fritz. Conquer yourself. N.Y., 1936.
Phil 292.9	Laberenne, P. L'origine des mondes. Paris, 1936.
Phil 186.85	Ladet, F. Méditations sur l'omnitude. Paris, 1936.
Phil 186.49.5	Lambek, C. Growth of the mind in relation to culture. Copenhagen, 1936.
Phil 4080.3.147	Lameere, Jean. L'esthétique de Benedetto Croce. Paris, 1936.
Phil 9070.27	Lansing, Florence. The builder. N.Y., 1936.
Phil 2070.135	Lapan, A. The significance of James' essay. Thesis. N.Y., 1936.
Phil 735.119	Larroyo, F. La filosofía de los valores. México, 1936.
Phil 2725.35.30	Lavelle, Louis. Le moi et son destin. Paris, 1936.
Phil 186.86.10	Leendertz, W. Ratio en existentie. Amsterdam, 1936.
Phil 575.89	Lemarié, O. Essai sur la personne. Paris, 1936.
Phil 2733.105	LeMoine, A. Des vérités éternelles selon Malebranche. Paris, 1936.
Phil 2733.105.5	LeMoine, A. Des vérités éternelles selon Malebranche. Thèse. Marseille, 1936.
Phil 2725.13.32.1	Lequier, Jules. La liberté. Paris, 1936.
Phil 2725.13.32	Lequier, Jules. La liberté. Thèse. Paris, 1936.
Phil 5761.19	Leuridan, Charles. L'idée de la liberté morale. Paris, 1936.
Phil 1050.24	Levine, I. Faithful rebels; a study in Jewish speculative thought. London, 1936.
Phil 8423.20	Levy, Hanna. Henri Wölfflin; sa théorie, ses prédécesseurs. Rottweil, 1936.
Phil 5251.42	Levy, Hyman. Thinking. London, 1936.
Phil 5251.41.9	Lewin, Kurt. Principles of topological psychology. 1st ed. N.Y., 1936.
Phil 4265.6.90	Librizzi, C. La filosofia di B. Varisco. Catania, 1936.
Phil 400.93	Liebert, Arthur. Die Krise des Idealismus. Zürich, 1936.
Phil 5627.142	Ligon, E.M. The psychology of Christian personality. N.Y., 1936.
Phil 5627.147.5	Lindworsky, J. The psychology of asceticism. London, 1936.
Phil 575.90	Lochman, M. Inner life of humanity. Pt.1. n.p., 1936.
Phil 2115.36.35	Locke, J. Essay concerning human understanding. An early draft. Oxford, 1936.
Phil 2805.221	Lohde, Richard. Die Anthropologie Pascals. Halle, 1936.
Phil 292.8A	Lovejoy, A.O. The great chain of being. Cambridge, Mass., 1936.
Phil 5722.24.10	Lubac, Émile. Présent conscient et cycles de durée. Paris, 1936.
Phil 5070.21	Lundholm, H. The psychology of belief. Durham, 1936.
Phil 9560.7.9	Maarse, Jan. Een psychologische en zebekundige studie over de hegrippen eer en eergevoel. Proefschrift. Amsterdam, 1936.
Phil 1050.23	Macdonald, D.B. The Hebrew philosophical genius. Princeton, 1936.
Phil 6315.2.109	McDougall, William. Psycho-analysis and social psychology. London, 1936.
Phil 2150.8.79	Mackenzie, J.S. John Stuart Mackenzie. London, 1936.
Phil 1905.12.90	McLarney, James J. The theism of Edgar S. Brightman. Diss. Washington, 1936.
Phil 2115.147	MacLean, K. John Locke and English literature of the eighteenth century. New Haven, 1936.
Phil 2733.60.5	Malebranche, Nicolas. Entretien d'un philosophe chrétien et d'un philosophe chinois. Paris, 1936.
Phil 2733.60.7	Malebranche, Nicolas. Entretien d'un philosophe chrétien et d'un philosophe chinois. Thèse. Marseille, 1936.
Phil 4170.9.30	Mancino, Salvatore. Lettere inedito di S. Mancino a V. Coasin. Palermo, 1936.
Phil 1200.40	Mann, W. Beitrag zur Kenntnis der Sozial- und Staats-philosophischen Anschauungen der Hauptvertreter der neueren Stoa. Inaug. Diss. Halle (Saale), 1936.
Phil 5252.73	Mantell, U. Aktualgenetische Untersuchungen an Situationsdarstellungen. Inaug. Diss. München, 1936.
Phil 8887.69	Margolius, Hans. Grundlegung zur Ethik. Berlin, 1936.
Phil 8702.17	Maria, R. de. Religione e scienza. Palermo, 1936.
Phil 2750.11.54	Maritain, Jacques. Humanisme intégral. Paris, 1936.
Phil 2750.11.66	Maritain, Jacques. La philosophie de la nature. Paris, 1936.
Phil 2490.129	Marvin, F.S. Comte, the founder of sociology. London, 1936.
Phil 1712.14A	Mead, George H. Movements of thought in the nineteenth century. Chicago, 1936.
Phil 343.19	Meisner, E. Erkenntniskritische Weltanschauung. Leipzig, 1936.
Phil 3625.1.42A	Mendelssohn, Moses. Brautbriefe. Berlin, 1936.

Chronological Listing

Phil 2520.196 Mesnard, Pierre. Essai sur la morale de Descartes. Paris, 1936.

Phil 2520.196.5 Mesnard, Pierre. Essai sur la morale de Descartes. Thèse. Paris, 1936.

Phil 5643.97 Metzger, W. Gesetze des Sehens. Frankfurt, 1936.

Phil 187.113 Meyerson, E. Essais. Paris, 1936.

Phil 8887.68 Michel, Virgil. Philosophy of human conduct. Minneapolis, 1936.

Phil 293.23 Minkowski, E. Vers une cosmologie. Paris, 1936.

Phil 8413.31 Mirabent, F. De la bellesa. v.5. Barcelona, 1936.

Phil 293.22.5 Mittere, Albert. Wesensartwandel und Artensystem der physikalischen Körperwelt. Bressanone, 1936. 3v.

Phil 4769.1.103 Mochul'skiĭ, K. Vladimir Solov'ev; zhizn' i uchenie. Paris, 1936.

Phil 187.112 Monteath, K.M. The philosophy of the past. York, 1936.

Phil 8592.55A Moore, Edward C. The nature of religion. N.Y., 1936.

Phil 6322.16.9 Morgan, John J.B. The psychology of abnormal people. 2d ed. N.Y., 1936.

Phil 1900.91 Mossner, E.C. Bishop Butler and the age of reason. N.Y., 1936.

Phil 8413.32 Mottier, G. Le phémomène de l'art. Parisè 1936.

Phil 187.108 Müller, G.E. Philosophy of our uncertainties. Norman, 1936.

Phil 1812.7A Müller, Gustav E. Amerikanische Philosophie. Stuttgart, 1936.

Phil 2150.8.90 Muirhead, J.H. John Stuart Mackenzie, 1860-1935. London, 1936?

Phil 3805.188 Neumann, J. Schleiermacher. Berlin, 1936.

Phil 3640.270 Nicolas, M.P. De Nietzsche à Hitler. Paris, 1936.

Phil 3640.40.30 Nietzsche, Friedrich. Thus spake Zarathustra. N.Y., 1936.

Phil 488.1 Nizan, Paul. Les matérialistes de l'antiquité. Paris, 1936.

Phil 5374.158 Nogué, J. Essai sur l'activité primitive du moi. Paris, 1936.

Phil 5374.158.5 Nogué, J. Essai sur l'activité primitive du moi. Thèse. Paris, 1936.

Phil 5585.64 Nogué, Jean. La signification du sensible. Paris, 1936.

Phil 5585.64.5 Nogué, Jean. La signification du sensible. Thèse. Paris, 1936.

Phil 3495.17 Novák, Mirko. Kanův kriticismus a problém hodnoty. V Bratislave, 1936.

Phil 188.16 Nuñez Requeiro, M. Tratado de metalogica. Rosario, 1936.

Phil 9410.8 Nutrimento, L. La definizione del bene in relazione al problema dell'ottimismo. Padova, 1936.

Phil 5520.35.10 Ogden, Charles K. The meaning of meaning. N.Y., 1936.

Phil 630.45 Olgiati, F. Il realismo. Milano, 1936.

Phil 5254.5 Osborn, John K. A comparison of reactions to personality and achievement test items. Diss. Ann Arbor, 1936.

Phil 400.94 Ottaviano, C. Critica dell'idealismo. Napoli, 1936.

Phil 2805.22 Pascal, Blaise. L'oeuvre de Pascal. Argenteuil, 1936.

Phil 3497.19 Paton, Herbert J. Kant's metaphysic of experience. London, 1936. 2v.

Phil 5055.17.5 Patterson, Charles H. Principles of correct thinking. Minneapolis, 1936.

Phil 2490.127 Peter, J. Auguste Comtes Bild vom Menschen. Inaug.-Diss. Stuttgart, 1936.

Phil 8670.13 Petty, Orville A. Common sense and God. New Haven, 1936.

Phil 1905.10.90 Pfannenstill, Bertil. Bernard Bosanquet's philosophy of the state. Inaug.-Diss. Lund, 1936.

Phil 8595.32.7 Philips, Vivian. Concerning progressive revelation. London, 1936.

Phil 8595.32.5 Philips, Vivian. Concerning progressive revelation. London, 1936.

Phil 190.61A Philosophical essays for A.N. Whitehead. London, 1936.

Phil 5643.98 Piéron, Henri. La connaissance sensorielle et les problèmes de la vision. Paris, 1936.

Phil 1020.19.5 Pines, Salomon. Beiträge zur islamischen Atomenlehre. Berlin, 1936.

Phil 1020.19 Pines, Salomon. Beiträge zur islamischen Atomenlehre. Inaug Diss. Berlin, 1936.

Phil 8416.11.20 Plekhanov, Georgii Valentinovich. Art and society. N.Y., 1936.

Phil 190.65 Pöll, Wilhelm. Wesen und Wesenserkenntnis. München, 1936.

Phil 672.159 Ponsonby, A.P. Life here and now; conclusions derived from an examination of the sense of duration. London, 1936.

Phil 3745.9 Poortman, J.J. De noodzaak. Assen, 1936.

Phil 9530.39.5 Popplestone, C.E. Every man a winner. N.Y., 1936.

Phil 720.29 Price, H.H. Truth and corrigibility. Oxford, 1936.

Phil 7069.36.10 Price, Harry. Confessions of a ghost-hunter. London, 1936.

Phil 7069.36.13 Price, Harry. The haunting of Cashen's Gap. London, 1936.

Phil 8891.3 Quinby, L.J. Natural basis of moral and ethics. Boston, 1936.

Phil 191.4 Quisling, Jörgen. Philosophie, das anthropokosmische System. Berlin, 1936.

Phil 8597.38.15 Radhakrishnan, S. The world's unborn soul. Oxford, 1936.

Phil 4871.5 Radhakrishnan, Sarvepalli. Contemporary Indian philosophy. London, 1936.

Phil 8892.53 Rainsford, F.B. The Isle of Good Intent. Boston, 1936.

Phil 1717.6.6A Rand, Benjamin. Modern classical philosophers. Boston, 1936.

Phil 6327.4.21A Rank, Otto. Truth and reality. N.Y., 1936.

Phil 6327.4.32 Rank, Otto. Will therapy and truth and reality. N.Y., 1936.

Phil 8672.14 Raven, Charles E. Evolution and the Christian concept of God. London, 1936.

Phil 8967.6 Reid, A.C. Christ and the present crisis. Wake Forest, 1936.

Phil 6327.12.15 Reik, Theodor. Surprise and the psycho-analyst. London, 1936.

Phil 6327.12.20 Reik, Theodor. Wir Freud-Schüler. Leiden, 1936.

Phil 817.17 Reitmeister, L.A. The gist of philosophy. N.Y., 1936.

Phil 5257.48 Ritchie, Arthur D. The natural history of mind. London, 1936.

Phil 5420.5.10 Roback, A.A. Self-consciousness self-treated. Cambridge, 1936.

Phil 8610.929.9 Robertson, J.M. A history of freethought in the nineteenth century. 4. ed. London, 1936. 2v.

Phil 5057.27 Romagnosi, G.D. Vedute fondamentali sull'arte logica. Roma, 1936.

Phil 5257.50 Rosling, B. Some aspects of psychology. London, 1936.

Phil 3160.3.89 Rosmarin, T.W. (Mrs.). Religion of reason. N.Y., 1936.

Phil 6327.17.15 Ross, Thomas Arthur. An enquiry into prognosis in the neuroses. Cambridge, Eng., 1936.

Phil 8642.7 Rovighi, S.V. L'immortalità dell'anima nei maestri francescani del secolo XIII. Milano, 1936.

Phil 5400.90 Ruckmick, C.A. The psychology of feeling and emotion. 1st ed. N.Y., 1936.

Phil 665.64 St. Cyr, E. The essay: let us think it over. 12th ed. Chicago, 1936.

Phil 5647.7 Sandovici, Constantin. Les sensations de température. Thèse. Montpellier, 1936.

Phil 193.49.45A Santayana, G. Obiter dicta. N.Y., 1936.

Phil 193.49.50 Santayana, G. The philosophy of Santayana; selections. N.Y., 1936.

Phil 2280.5.7 Santayana, George. The works of George Santayana. N.Y., 1936-40. 14v.

Phil 5465.35 Sartre, Jean P. L'imagination. Paris, 1936.

Phil 3800.340.25 Schelling, F.W.J. von. Of human freedom. Chicago, 1936.

Phil 8968.13 Schilling, Otto. Apologie der katholischen Moral. Paderborn, 1936.

Phil 2885.90 Schmidt, O.A. Hippolyte Taines Theorie. Halle, 1936.

Phil 8893.95.5 Schrempf, C. Die Grundlage der Ethik. Stuttgart, 1936.

Phil 3801.777.25 Schröder, C.M. Das Verhältnis von Heidentum und Christentum in Schellings Philosophie der Mythologie und Offenbarung. München, 1936.

Phil 8673.16 Schütz, A. Gott in der Geschichte. Salzburg, 1936.

Phil 8893.93 Schwarz, O.L. Unconventional ethics. Washington, 1936.

Phil 2477.6.95 Scivittaro, F. L'azione e il pensiero. Roma, 1936.

Phil 6128.46 Seabury, David. How to worry successfully. Boston, 1936.

Phil 2418.3 Segond, J. Art et science dans la philosophie française contemporaine. Paris, 1936.

Phil 8669.3.29 Seifert, P. Die Religionsphilosophie bei Rudolf Otto. Inaug. Diss. Dusseldorf, 1936.

Phil 530.20.80 Seitz, Jasy. Der Traktat des "unbekannten deutschen Mystikers" bei Greith. Leipzig, 1936.

Phil 4195.85 Semprini, G. La filosofia di Pico della Mirandola. Milano, 1936.

Phil 7069.36.15 Sergeant, P.W. Historic British ghosts. London, 1936.

Phil 6128.49 Shaffer, Laurance F. Psychology of adjustment. Boston, 1936.

Phil 5258.121A Sheldon, W.H. Psychology and the promethean will. N.Y., 1936.

Phil 193.147 Silverman, H.L. Random thoughts; liberalism in life and philosophy. N.Y., 1936. 2v.

Phil 4018.4 Simoni, M. Il nuovo spiritualismo in Italia. Napoli, 1936.

Phil 193.145 Singer, E.A. On the contented life. N.Y., 1936.

Phil 2855.7.35 Sitkovskii, E. Filosofiia Zh. B. Robine, ocherk iz istorii frantsuzskogo materializma XVIII v. Moskva, 1936.

Phil 8708.22 Smith, Nathan A. Through science to God. N.Y., 1936.

Phil 5425.58 Somogyi, J. Begabung im Lichte der Eugenik. Leipzig, 1936.

Phil 193.150.5 Spakovski, A. Chelo-vecheskoe "ia" i kul'tura. Novyi Sad, 1936.

Phil 193.152 Spanzini, Carlo. Philosophie und Pädagogik. Bern, 1936.

Phil 630.42.15 Spaulding, E.G. A world of chance. N.Y., 1936.

Phil 5258.115 Starch, Daniel. Controlling human behavior. N.Y., 1936.

Phil 6328.21 Sterba, Richard. Handwörterbuch der Psychoanalyse. Wien, 1936-37.

Phil 9035.21.15 Stout, G.F. Alexander Faulkner Shand, 1858-1936. London, 1936?

Phil 2045.117 Strauss, Leo. The political philosophy of Hobbes. Oxford, 1936.

Phil 8673.15 Streeter, B.H. The God who speaks. N.Y., 1936.

Phil 193.83.5 Strong, C.A. A creed for sceptics. London, 1936.

Phil 5769.8 Tarozzi, G. La libertà umana e la critica del determinismo. Bologna, 1936.

Phil 194.19.25 Tarozzi, Giuseppe. La racerca filosofica. Napoli, 1936.

Phil 270.44 Taube, M. Causation, freedom, and determinism. London, 1936.

Phil 7069.32.45 Taylor, Sarah E.L. Fox - Taylor automatic writing, 1969-1892. Boston, 1936.

Phil 7069.36.50 Thomas, C.D. An amazing experiment. London, 1936.

Phil 194.37.5 Thomas, Elyston. A view of all existence. London, 1936.

Phil 5829.9.5 Thomas, Maurice. La notion de l'instinct et ses bases scientifiques. Paris, 1936.

Phil 8894.26 Titus, H.H. Ethics for today. Boston, 1936.

Phil 2475.1.264 Tonquédec, J. Sur la philosophie Bergsonienne. Paris, 1936.

Phil 2477.6.80.5 Tonquédec, J. de. Deux études sur "La pensée de M. Blondel". Paris, 1936.

Phil 705.28 Troilo, E. La ragioni della trascendenza o del realismo assoluto. Venezia, 1936.

Phil 1200.39 Tsirimbas, Antonios. Die Allgemeinen pädagogischen Gedanken der alten Stoa. Inaug. Diss. München, 1936.

Phil 3450.17.92 Urbanowski, J. Georg von Hertlings Gesellschaftslehre. Inaug. Diss. Battrop, 1936.

Phil 5060.6 Ushenko, A.P. The theory of logic. N.Y., 1936.

Phil 8422.12 Vascoucelos, J. Estética. 2. ed. México, 1936.

Phil 5261.15.10 Vaughan, W.F. General psychology. Garden City, 1936.

Phil 525.79 Vellani, Giovanni E. La mistica dell'avenire. Modena, 1936.

Phil 6691.2 Vinchon, Jean. Mesmer et son secret. Paris, 1936.

Phil 2805.91.2 Vinet, A. Études sur Blaise Pascal. Lausanne, 1936.

Phil 3450.19.90 Vogl, A. Das Problem des Selhstseins bei Heidegger und Kierkegaard. Diss. Giessen, 1936.

Phil 9035.73 Volkmann, E. Über die Formkraft des Vorbildes für die Charakterprägung in der Reifezeit. Inaug. Diss. Würzburg, 1936.

Phil 8422.13 Volpe, G. della. Fondamenti di una filosofia dell'espressione. Bologna, 1936.

Phil 8423.10 Walsh, Dorothy. The objectivity of the judgment of aesthetic value. Lancaster, 1936.

Phil 5241.92.15 Wedell, C.H. Handbook in psychology, to accompany Boring's Psychology. N.Y., 1936.

Phil 9560.7.13 Weidauer, F. Die Wahrung der Ehre und die sittliche Tat. Leipzig, 1936.

Phil 5649.21 Weigand, E. Analyse der Handgeschicklichkeit. Inaug. Diss. Würzburg, 1936.

Phil 600.47 Weinberg, J.R. An examination of logical positivism. London, 1936.

Phil 353.16 Weinschenk, C. Das Wirklichkeitsproblem der Erkenntnistheorie. Leipzig, 1936.

Phil 197.63 Wenzl, Aloys. Wissenschaft und Weltanschaung. Leipzig, 1936.

Phil 3235.114 Weser, H.A. Sigmund Freuds und Ludwig Feuerbachs Religionskritik. Inaug. Diss. Bettrop, 1936.

Phil 5850.385.80 White, Wendell. The psychology of dealing with people. N.Y., 1936.

Phil 8520.28A Wieman, H.N. American philosophies of religion. Chicago, 1936.

1936 - cont.

Phil 1870.117A Wild, John. George Berkeley. Cambridge, 1936.
Phil 3120.8.130 Windischer, Johannes. Franz Brentano und die Scholastik. Innsbruck, 1936.
Phil 5232.5.10 Woodworth, R.S. Contemporary schools of psychology. N.Y., 1936.
Phil 5264.3 Young, P.T. Motivation of behavior. N.Y., 1936.
Phil 3625.1.150 Zarek, O. Moses Mendelssohn. Amsterdam, 1936.
Phil 672.160 Zawirski, Zygmunt. L'évolution de la notion du temps. Cracovie, 1936.
Phil 6335.10 Zweig, S. Die heilung durch den Geist; Mesmer, Mary Baker, Eddy, Freud. Wien, 1936.

1937

Phil 2115.149A Aaron, Richard Ithamar. John Locke. London, 1937.
Phil 175.39 Accambray, Leon. Un testament philosophique. Paris, 1937.
Phil 2520.169.10 Adam, C.E. Descartes; sa vie et son oeuvre. Paris, 1937.
Phil 2520.169.15 Adam, C.E. Descartes; ses amitiés féminines. Paris, 1937.
Phil 5585.62 Akishige, Yoshiharu. Experimentelle Untersuchungen über die Struktur des Wahrnehmungsraumes. Fukuoka, 1937.
Phil 8110.5 Allen, B.S. Tides in English taste (1619-1800); a background for the study of literature. Cambridge, Mass., 1937. 2v.
Phil 575.91A Allport, G.W. Personality; a psychological interpretation. N.Y., 1937.
Phil 5240.35 Anastasi, Anne. Differential psychology. NY., 1937.
Phil 8580.3.25 Anderson, George P. Who wrote "Ethan Allen's Bible"? n.p., 1937.
Phil 4825.12 Atanasijavič, Ksenija. Penseurs yougoslaves. Belgrade, 1937.
Phil 1540.60 Axters, Stephanus. Scholastick Lexicon. Antwerpen, 1937.
Phil 1850.16.15 Bacon, Francis. Francis Bacon. The great instauration. Garden City, 1937.
Phil 3001.13 Baeumler, A. Studien zur dutschen Geistesgeschichte. Berlin, 1937.
Phil 3640.240.3 Baeumler, Alfred. Nietzsche der Philosoph und Politiker. 3e Aufl. Leipzig, 1937.
Phil 3001.16 Balthasar, H.U. Apokalyfse der deutschen Seele. Salzburg, 1937-39. 3v.
Phil 8402.16 Bartlett, E.M. Types of aesthetic judgment. London, 1937.
Phil 6951.5.8 Beers, C.W. A mind that found itself. Garden City, 1937.
Phil 332.17 Bénézé, G. Critique de la mesure. Paris, 1937.
Phil 3110.177 Benz, E. Der Vollkommene Mensch nach Böhme. Stuttgart, 1937.
Phil 8581.69.5 Berdiaev, N.A. God, man and the church. London, 1937.
Phil 8581.69.10 Berdiajew, N.A. Von der Würde des Christentums und der Unwürde der Christen. 4. Aufl. Luzern, 1937.
Cg Phil 7075.132 Bergler, E. Die psychische Importenz des Mannes. Bern, 1937.
Phil 5751.17 Bianca, Giovanni. L'autonomia della volontà. Firenze, 1937.
Phil 6111.54 Bianchini, M.L. La igiene mentale ed it potenziamento della stirpe. Roma, 1937.
Phil 5465.37 Biervliet, J.J. van. La part de l'imagination. Paris, 1937.
Phil 978.5.7 Blavatsky, H.P. Personal memoirs of H.P. Blavatsky. London, 1937.
Phil 8402.52A Boas, George. A primer of cities. Baltimore, 1937.
Phil 8876.107.5 Börner, W. Zur ethischen Lebensgestaltung. Wien, 1937?
Phil 332.18 Boldt, Karl. Die Einheit des Erkenntnisproblems. Leipzig, 1937.
Phil 332.18.5 Boldt, Karl. Die Erkenntnisbeziehung. Tübingen, 1937.
Phil 3120.13.9 Bolland, G.J.P.J. Briefwechsel mit E. von Hartmann. 's Gravenhage, 1937.
Phil 8620.41 Bond, C.J. The nature and meaning of evil. London, 1937.
Phil 1540.23 Bonfarri, G. Lo studio della natura nell'umanesimo. Mantova, 1937.
Phil 1750.147 Brémond, Henri. Autour de l'humanisme d'Erasme à Pascal. Paris, 1937.
Phil 2070.82.8 Brett, George Sidney. William James and American ideals. Toronto? 1937.
Phil 6951.23 Bromberg, W. The mind of man. N.Y., 1937.
Phil 6951.22 Brown, H.C. A mind mislaid. N.Y., 1937.
Phil 5520.67 Bruns, I. Metaphysik des Wortes. Inaug. Diss. Bonn, 1937.
Phil 2520.200A Brunschvicg, L. René Descartes. Paris, 1937.
Phil 1182.10 Brunschvicg, Léon. Le rôle du pythagorisme dans l'évolution des idées. Paris, 1937.
Phil 9070.102 Brunswik, E. Wunsch und Pflicht im Auflau des menschlichen Lebens. Wien, 1937.
Phil 3110.5 Buddecke, W. Die Jakob Böhme-Ausgaben. Göttingen, 1937. 2v.
Phil 2520.201 Buenos Aires. Universidad. Instituto de Filosofía. Descartes. Buenos Aires, 1937. 3v.
Phil 6311.22 Burrow, T. The biology of human conflict. N.Y., 1937.
Phil 5241.97 Burrow, Trigant. Altering frames of reference in the sphere of human behavior. N.Y., 1937.
Phil 5627.153 By the grace of God. London, 1937.
Phil 9495.138.5 Cabot, R.C. Christianity and sex. N.Y., 1937.
Phil 8403.17 Cabrisas y Madero. El sentido del dolor en el arte. La Habana, 1937.
Phil 525.86 Cailliet E. Mysticisme. Cahors, 1937.
Phil 5042.21.14 Carnap, Rudolf. The logical syntax of language. N.Y., 1937.
Phil 5042.21.17 Carnap, Rudolf. Notes for symbolic logic. Chicago, 1937.
Phil 9530.38.15 Carnegie, Dale. How to win friends and influence people. N.Y., 1937.
Phil 9530.38.28 Carnegie, Dale. How to win friends and influence people. 28th ed. N.Y., 1937.
Phil 7069.20.365 Carrington, H. The psychic world. N.Y., 1937.
Phil 8877.68.5 Carritt, Edgar F. An ambignity of the word "good". London, 1937.
Phil 2520.86.3 Cartesio nel terzo centenario nel "Discorso del metodo." Milano, 1937.
Phil 177.103 Cazals de Fabel, Gabriel. Précis de philosophie à l'usage des candidats au baccalaureat. Toulouse, 1937.
Phil 2520.205 Cercle Philosophique, Lorrain. Tricentenaire de la parution du discours de la méthode, 1637-1937. Metz, 1937.
Phil 4210.145 Ceriani, G. L'ideologia rosminiana nei rapporti con la gnoseologia agostiniano-tomistica. Milano, 1937.
Phil 960.167 Chakravarti, A. Humanism and Indian thought. Madras, 1937.
Phil 2725.23.90 Chang Chi Chang. La morale...de M. Lucien Levy-Bruhl. Lyon, 1937.
Phil 8582.51 Chaning-Pearce, Melville. Religion and reality. London, 1937.

1937 - cont.

Phil 6312.10 Chicago. Institute for Psychoanalysis. Five-year report. Chicago, 1937. 2v.
Htn Phil 8657.15* Church, Henry. Miscellanea philo-theologica, or God and man. London, 1937.
Phil 5627.108.25 Clark, Glenn. I will lift up mine eyes. 9. ed. N.Y., 1937.
Phil 2280.5.101 Clemens, C. George Santayana; an American philosopher in exile. Webster Groves, 1937.
Phil 720.30 Cleugh, M.F. Time and its importance to modern thought. London, 1937.
Phil 2477.11.95 Cochet, M.A. Commentaire sur la conversion spirituelle dans la philosophie de L. Branschvicg. Bruxelles, 1937.
Phil 2555.7.90 Cochet, M.A. La métaphysique de Paul Decoster et la science. Bruges, 1937.
Phil 8735.22 Cogni, G. Lo spirito assoluto. Firenze, 1937.
Phil 7069.37 Cole, M.A. Isaiah as read by a clairvoyant. Boston, 1937.
Phil 8877.76 Colesanti, Giulio. Esiste una morale? Catania, 1937.
Phil 4002.7 Corsano, A. Il pensiero religioso italiano dall'umanesimo al giurisdizionalismo. Bari, 1937.
Phil 2750.13 Corte, Marcel de. La philosophie de Gabriel Marcel. Paris, 1937.
Phil 8404.2 Danz, Louis. The psychologist looks at art. London, 1937.
Phil 5243.36.10 Dashiell, J.F. Fundamentals of general psychology. Boston, 1937.
Phil 960.119 Dass, Satya. Self-expression and the Indian social problem. Lahore, 1937.
Phil 8583.29.5 De Burgh, William George. Towards a religious philosophy. London, 1937.
Phil 2520.203 Dem Gedächtnis au René Descartes. Berlin, 1937.
Phil 978.84 Demarquette, Jacques. De la liête á l'auge. Paris, 1937.
Phil 2805.291 Demorest, Jean. Pascal écrivain. Paris, 1937.
Phil 8583.32 De Pauley, W.C. The candle of the Lord. London, 1937.
Phil 2520.35.39 Descarter, René. Discours de la méthode. Paris, 1937.
Phil 2520.45.25 Descartes, René. Discorso sul metodo. Napoli, 1937.
Phil 2520.54 Descartes, René. Entretien avec Burman. Paris, 1937.
Phil 2520.31 Descartes, René. Oeuvres et lettres. Paris, 1937.
Phil 2520.39.30 Descartes, René. Principii di filosofia. Napoli, 1937.
Phil 5243.44.5 Deut, John Y. The human machine. N.Y., 1937.
Phil 178.64 Dixon, W.M. The human situation. N.Y., 1937.
Phil 1153.7 Dudley, D.R. A history of cynicism from Diogenes to the 6th century A.D. London, 1937.
Phil 803.9 Duvall, T.G. Great thinkers; the quest of life for its meaning. N.Y., 1937.
Phil 4829.344.20 Dvorniković, Vladimir. Barba ideja. Beograd, 1937.
Phil 6113.27 Dyer, V.A. You can have it, personality. Long Beach, 1937.
Phil 665.66 Eckhardt, K.E. Irdische Unsterblichkeit. Weimar, 1937.
Phil 1980.4.7 Edman, Irwin. Four ways of philosophy. N.Y., 1937.
Phil 5244.10.9 Elsenhans, Theodor. Lehrbuch der Psychologie. 3e Aufl. Tübingen, 1937-1938.
Phil 6314.7 English, Oliver Spurgeon. Common neuroses of children and adults. N.Y., 1937.
Phil 5244.23 English, V.P. Human mind and its physical machine...human body. San Diego, 1937.
Phil 3450.19.100 Erro, C.A. Dialogo existencial. Buenos Aires, 1937.
Phil 2520.199 Études sur Descartes. Paris, 1937.
Phil 8584.18 Eustace, C.J. Mind and the mystery. N.Y., 1937.
Phil 5044.8 Evans, D.L. Logic, theoretical and applied. Garden City, 1937.
Phil 3850.30.90 Fassbender, Johann. Erkenntnislehre und Metaphysik Jakob Seuglers, 1799-1878. Inaug. Diss. Bonn, 1937.
Phil 5627.149 Ferm, V. Religion in transition. London, 1937.
Phil 5245.42 Fernberger, Samuel W. Elementary general psychology. N.Y., 1937.
Phil 7140.131 Ferri, N.A. The behavior of health. Boston, 1937.
Phil 4513.5.90 Festskrift til Anathon Aall på 70. årsdagen hans, 15 Aug. 1837. Oslo, 1937.
Phil 3245.25 Fichte, Immanuel Hermann. Zeitschrift für Philosophie und speculative Theologie. Bonn, 1937-56. 8v.
Phil 3246.19 Fichte, Johann Gottlieb. Nachgelassene Schriften. Bd.2. Berlin, 1937.
Phil 8880.47.10 Field, Joanna. An experiment in leisure. London, 1937.
Phil 4110.6.30 Filippi, Liutprando. Realtà e idealità. Napoli, 1937.
Phil 1750.161 Fiolle, Jean. La crise de l'humanisme. Paris, 1937.
Phil 336.8 Fondard, L. De la forme a l'idée. Marseille, 1937.
Phil 6675.13 Fox, Alfred J. Mind "magic". N.Y., 1937.
Phil 3825.8.5 Francès, Madeleine. Spinoza. Paris, 1937.
Phil 3825.8 Francès, Madeleine. Spinoza dans les pays Néerlandais. Paris, 1937.
Phil 270.39.5 Frank, P. Le principe de causalité et ses limites. Paris, 1937.
Phil 3005.7 Franz, Erich. Deutsche Klassik und Reformation. Halle, 1937.
Phil 6315.2.5.7 Freud, Sigmund. A general introduction to psycho-analysis. N.Y., 1937.
Phil 6315.2.36 Freud, Sigmund. A general selection from the works of Sigmund Freud. London, 1937.
Phil 5625.75.87 Frolov, I.P. Pavlov and his school. London, 1937.
Phil 930.29.5 Fung, Yu-lan. A history of Chinese philosophy. Peiping, 1937.
Phil 4195.86 Garin, Eugenio. Giovanni Pico della Mirandola. Firenze, 1937.
Phil 735.111 Garnett, Arthur C. Reality and value. New Haven, 1937.
Phil 4357.5 Gastelum, B.J. En el reino de las sombras; Maria de la Luz. Mexico, 1937.
Phil 4195.105 Gautier-Vignal, L. Pic de la Mirandole, 1463-94. Paris, 1937.
Phil 4120.4.35 Gentile, Giovanni. I fondamenti della filosofia del oiritto. 3. ed. Firenze, 1937.
Phil 8620.52 Gillen, Louis Bertrand. La théorie des oppositions et la théologie du péché, au XIIIe siècle. Paris, 1937.
Phil 1511.3.19 Gilson, Etienne. Die Geschichte der christlichen Philosophie. Paderborn, 1937.
Phil 1511.3.23 Gilson, Etienne. Medieval universalism and its present value. N.Y., 1937.
Phil 806.13.1 Gilson, Etienne. The unity of philosophical experience. N.Y., 1937.
Phil 8407.19 Görland, Albert. Ästhetik; kritische Philosophie des Stils. Hamburg, 1937.
Phil 1020.8.20 Goichon, A.M. La distinction de l'essence...d'aprés Ibn Sina. Paris, 1937.
Phil 1020.8.20.2 Goichon, A.M. La distinction de l'essence...d'aprés Ibn Sina. Thèse. Paris, 1937.
Phil 3200.10 Goldmund, M. Die Philosophie Franz Erhardts. Leipzig, 1937.
Phil 181.74 Gotshalk, D.W. Structure and reality. N.Y., 1937.

Chronological Listing

1937 - cont.

Phil 2520.140.3 Gouhier, Henri. Essais sur Descartes. Paris, 1937.
Phil 3805.181 Graeber, Martin. Die Sakramentstheorie Schleiermachers und ihre Weiterbildung innerhalb der kritischen Theologie des 19. Jahrhunderts. Inaug. Diss. Wuppertal, 1937.
Phil 181.90.5 Gredt, Joseph. Elementa philosophiae Aristotelico-Thomisticae. 7. ed. v.2. Friburgi, 1937.
Phil 8407.30 Green, Peter. The problem of art; a text book of aesthetics. London, 1937.
Phil 5816.11 Grindley, G.C. The intelligence of animals. London, 1937.
Phil 3625.16.90 Grohrock, R. Der Kampf der Wesenskultur gegen die Bewusstseinskultur bei Johannes Müller. Inaug. Diss. Speyer, 1937.
Phil 5246.43.5 Guillaume, Paul. La psychologie de la forme. Paris, 1937.
Phil 1511.3.14 Gunn, W.W. A modern social philosophy. Cutting, 1937.
Phil 8586.42 Gunther, G. Christliche Metaphysik und das Schicksal des modernen Bewusstseins. Leipzig, 1937.
Phil 8881.64 Gurvitch, Georges. Morale théorique et science des moeurs. Paris, 1937.
Phil 181.76.5 Guthrie, H. Introduction au problème de l'histoire de la philosophie. Paris, 1937.
Phil 181.76 Guthrie, H. Introduction au problème de l'histoire de la philosophie. Thèse. Paris, 1937.
Phil 181.79 Gutkind, Eric. The absolute collective. London, 1937.
Phil 8080.17 Hannay, Howard. Roger Fry and other essays. London, 1937.
Phil 8587.44.15 Harkness, George E. The recovery of ideals. N.Y., 1937.
Phil 8587.44.10 Harkness, George E. Religious living. N.Y., 1937.
Phil 8587.50 Harper, W.A. Personal religious beliefs. Boston, 1937.
Phil 5247.54 Harrower, M.R. The psychologist at work. London, 1937.
Phil 6957.7.4.7 Hart, Bernard. The psychology of insanity. 4. ed. N.Y., 1937.
Phil 1750.145 Hartshore, Charles. Beyond humanism. Chicago, 1937.
Phil 974.2.50 Hastings, B. (Mrs.). Defence of Madame Blavatsky. Worthing, 1937. 2v.
Phil 92.3 Hauer, E. Philosophen Lexikon. Lief. 1-6. Berlin, 1937.
Phil 270.45 Hawkins, D.J.B. Causality and implication. London, 1937.
Phil 8882.58 Heard, G. The third morality. London, 1937.
Phil 4620.2.90 Hedenius, I. Adolf Phalén in memoriam. Uppsala, 1937.
Phil 8587.53 Heering, H.J. De religienze toekomstverwachting. Amsterdam, 1937.
Phil 3425.40.25 Hegel, Georg Wilhelm Friedrich. Leçons sur la philosophie de l'histoire. Paris, 1937.
Phil 3425.73.2.5 Hegel, Georg Wilhelm Friedrich. Phänomenologie des Geistes. Leipzig, 1937. 2v.
Phil 182.93.8 Heidegger, M. Qu'est-ce que la métaphysique? Paris, 1937.
Phil 960.136.5 Heimann, B. Indian and Western philosophy. London, 1937.
Phil 2040.30.15 Herbert, E. De veritate. Bristol, 1937.
Phil 338.23 Hermann, G. Die Bedeutung der modernen Physik für die Theorie der Erkenntnis. Leipzig, 1937.
Phil 1707.6.5 Hessen, Johannes. Die Geistesstromungen der Gegenwart. Freiburg, 1937.
Phil 8662.16 Hicks, G.D. The philosophical bases of theism. London, 1937.
Phil 3450.18.95 Hirning, H. Nicolai Hartmanns Lehre. Tübingen, 1937.
Phil 3450.19.101 Hoberg, C.A. Das Dasein des Menschen. Zeuleuroda, 1937.
Phil 3450.19.102 Hoberg, C.A. Das Dasein des Menschen. Inaug. Diss. Zeuleuroda, 1937.
Phil 3450.21 Hoche, A. Jahresringe. München, 1937.
Phil 8633.1.36 Hocking, W.E. Thoughts on death and life. N.Y., 1937.
Phil 182.91.5 Hofmann, P. Sinn und Geschichte. München, 1937.
Phil 4120.4.85 Holmes, Roger W. The idealism of Giovanni Gentile. N.Y., 1937.
Phil 6317.9.5 Hoop, J.H. van der. Bewusstseinstypen und ihre Beziehung zur Psychopathologie. Bern, 1937.
Phil 6317.22A Horney, Karen. The neurotic personality of our time. N.Y., 1937.
Phil 5247.56 Hull, C.L. Mind, mechanism and adaptive behavior. Lancaster, 1937.
Phil 8400.36.2 International Congress on Aesthetics, 2nd, Paris, 1937. Deuxième congrès international d'esthétique. Paris, 1937. 2v.
Phil 1715.5 Istoria filosofiei moderne. Bucuresti, 1937.
Phil 3745.8.10 Jäckle, E. Rudolf Pannwitz. Hamburg, 1937.
Phil 184.3.6 James, W. The will to believe. London, 1937.
Phil 2520.202 Jaspers, Karl. Descartes und die Philosophie. Berlin, 1937.
Phil 5066.20 Jørgensen, J. Traek af deduktionsteoriens Udvikling i den nyere Tid. København, 1937.
Phil 5627.152 Jones, W.L. A psychological study of religious conversion. London, 1937.
Phil 1200.42 Jong, K.H.E. De stoa; een wereld-philosophie. Amsterdam, 1937.
Phil 8410.3 Jordan, E. The aesthetic object; an introduction to the philosophy of value. Bloomington, 1937.
Phil 184.40 Josipovici, J. Fragments de vie intérieure. Aix-en-Provence, 1937.
Phil 5249.13.15 Jung, Carl G. Psychological factors determining human behavior. Cambridge, 1937.
Phil 735.110 Jury, G.S. Value and ethical objectivity. London, 1937.
Phil 3480.71.12 Kant, Immanuel. Die Religion innerhalb der Grenzen der blossen Vernunft. 5. Aufl. Leipzig, 1937.
Phil 5250.31 Kastein, G.W. Eine Kritik der Ganzheitstheorien. Leiden, 1937.
Phil 735.115 Katkov, Georg. Untersuchungen zur Werttheorie und Theodizee. Brünn, 1937.
Phil 5220.4 Keller, F.S. The definition of psychology. N.Y., 1937.
Phil 2750.10.99 Kelley, T.R. Explanation and reality in the philosophy of Emile Meyerson. Princeton, 1937.
Phil 400.97 Kellner, Eva. Mann und Frau im deutschen Idealismus. Inaug. Diss. Berlin, 1937.
Phil 5249.13.99 Kellner, Kurt. C.G. Jung's Philosophie auf der Grundlage seiner Tiefenpsychologie. Inaug. Diss. Düren, 1937.
Phil 2630.5.90 Kergomard, Jean. Edmond Goblot, 1858-1935. Paris, 1937.
Phil 3549.2.45 Keyserling, Hermann. The art of life. London, 1937.
Phil 978.77.6 King, G.R. Ascended master discourses. Chicago, 1937.
Phil 8633.1.37 Kittredge, George L. The old Teutonic idea of the future life. Cambridge, 1937.
Phil 575.51.9 Klages, Ludwig. Die Grundlagen der Charakterkunde. 5e Aufl. Jena, 1937.
Phil 575.51.30 Klages, Ludwig. Vorschule der Charakterkunde. 2e Aufl. Leipzig, 1937.
Phil 6320.11 Klein, M. Love, hate and reparation. London, 1937.
Phil 3255.83 Klemm, Karl. Das Paradoxen als Ausdrucksform der spekulativen Mystik Sebastian Francks. Inaug-Diss. Leipzig, 1937.
Phil 5627.148 Knudson, A.C. The vaiidity of religious experience. N.Y., 1937.

1937 - cont.

Phil 185.63 König, J. Sein und Denken. Halle, 1937.
Phil 5425.62 Koller, A.H. The Abbé Du Bos - his advocacy of the theory of climate. Champaign, 1937.
Phil 5760.9 Konczewska, H. Contingence, liberté et la personnalité humaine. Paris, 1937.
Phil 5760.9.5 Konczewska, H. Contingence, liberté et la personnalité humaine. Thèse. Paris, 1937.
Phil 185.62 Konczewska, H. Le probléme de la substance. Paris, 1937.
Phil 70.15 Kongress für Synthetische Lebensforschung. Verhandlungsbericht. Prag, 1937.
Phil 735.114 Kraft, V. Die Grundlagen einer wissenschaftlichen Wertlehre. Wien, 1937.
Phil 4805.5 Král, Josef. Československá filosofie. Praha, 1937.
Phil 735.116 Kraus, O. Die Werttheorien; Geschichte und Kritik. Brünn, 1937.
Phil 9590.17.5 Krol', L.I. Osnovaniia biosofii. v.1-2. Kaunas, 1937.
Phil 9590.17 Krol', L.I. Vvedenie v biosofiia. Kaunas, 1937.
Phil 3549.9.90 Kühnemann, E. Mit unbefangener Stirn. Heilbronn, 1937.
Phil 2725.22 Laberthounière, L. Oeuvres. Paris, 1937.
Phil 8612.31 Landsberg, P.L. Die Erfahrung des Todes. Luzern, 1937.
Phil 5051.27A Langer, S.K. (Mrs.). An introduction to symbolic logic. Boston, 1937.
Phil 6961.17.5 Langfeldt, G. The prognosis in schizophrenia. Copenhagen, 1937.
Phil 5400.29.15 Latour, Marius. Premiers principes d'une théorie générale des émotions. Observations complémentaires. 3me série. Bayonne, 1937.
Phil 5400.29.25 Latour, Marius. Premiers principes d'une théorie générale des émotions. Observations complémentaires. 5me série. Bayonne, 1937.
Phil 5400.29.20 Latour, Marius. Premiers principes d'une théorie générale des émotions. Observations complémentaires. 4me série. Bayonne, 1937.
Phil 2725.35.55 Lavelle, Louis. De l'acte. Paris, 1937.
Phil 1750.146 Leander, F. Humanism and naturalism. Göteborg, 1937.
Phil 6121.34 Lechuga, Z.G. La higiene mental en México. México, 1937.
Phil 4060.2.50 Leo Hebraeus. The philosophy of love. London, 1937.
Phil 2730.96 LeRoy, Georges. L'expérience de l'effort et de la grace chez Maine de Biran. Paris, 1937.
Phil 2730.96.5 LeRoy, Georges. L'expérience de l'effort et de la grace chez Maine de Biran. Thèse. Paris, 1937.
Phil 2493.92 LeRoy, Georges. La psychologie de Condillac. Paris, 1937.
Phil 2493.92.5 LeRoy, Georges. La psychologie de Condillac. Thèse. Paris, 1937.
Phil 811.9 Lewis, John. Introduction to philosophy. London, 1937.
Phil 1050.27 Lichtigfeld, A. Philosophy and revelation in the work of contemporary Jewish thinkers. London, 1937.
Phil 1050.27.5 Lichtigfeld, A. Twenty centuries of Jewish thought. London, 1937.
Phil 3890.10.90 Liehrich, H. Die historische Wahrheit bei Ernst Troeltsch. Diss. Giessen, 1937.
Phil 186.88 Lin, Yu-t'ang. The importance of living. N.Y., 1937.
Phil 5850.258.4 Link, Henry C. The return to religion. N.Y., 1937.
Htn Phil 978.72.10* Ljungström, O. A philosophical overhaul. Lund, 1937.
Phil 186.84 Lodge, R.C. The questioning mind. N.Y., 1937.
Phil 8886.38.8 Loisy, Alfred. La crise morale. Paris, 1937.
Phil 186.89.5 Lolli, E. La conception inductive de la vie. Paris, 1937.
Phil 4973.5.6 Lombardo Toledano, Vicente. Escritos filosóficos. México, 1937.
X Cg Phil 6321.15 London, L.S. Mental therapy. N.Y., 1937. 2v.
Phil 1865.185.2 London. University. University College Library. Catalogue of the manuscripts of Jeremy Bentham in the Library of University College. London, 1937.
Phil 1885.86A Loomba, R.M. Bradley and Bergson. Lucknow, 1937.
Phil 6420.34 McAllister, Anne H. Clinical studies in speech therapy. London, 1937.
Phil 6122.59 McCarthy, R.C. Safeguarding mental health. N.Y., 1937.
Phil 6322.29.3 McFarland, R.A. Psycho-physiological studies at high altitude in the Andes. Baltimore, 1937.
Phil 8637.21 McGavin, E.C. Paradise revisited. Boston, 1937.
Phil 525.82 Mahnke, D. Unendliche Sphäre und Allmittelpunkt. Halle, 1937.
Phil 9352.13 Manchester, R.E. The Saturday letters. Cuyahoga Falls, 1937.
Phil 5052.36 Maritain, J. An introduction to logic. London, 1937.
Phil 187.60.7 Maritain, J. An introduction to philosophy. London, 1937.
Phil 6322.24 Mason, E.C. Why we do it? St. Louis, 1937.
Phil 187.116 Maugé, F. L'esprit et le réel dans les limites du nombre et de la grandeur. Paris, 1937.
Phil 187.116.4 Maugé, F. L'esprit et le réel perçu. Paris, 1937.
Phil 2050.206 Maund, Costance. Hume's theory of knowledge. London, 1937.
Phil 2150.11 Melzer, J.H. An examination of critical monism. Ashland, 1937.
Phil 6322.19.5 Menninger, Karl Augustus. The human mind. 2d ed. N.Y., 1937.
Phil 5627.95.5 Mensching, Gustav. Das heilige Wort. Bonn, 1937.
Phil 4012.6 Miceli di Serradileo, R. Filosofia. Verona, 1937.
Phil 3808.171 Michaelis, G. Arthur Schopenhauer. Leipzig, 1937.
Phil 9515.3.99 Milch, W. Die Einsamkeit. Frauenfeld, 1937.
Phil 187.115 Milville, H.L. Vers une philosophie de l'esprit ou de la totalité. Lausanne, 1937.
Phil 4363.6 Molina, E. De lo espiritual. Concepcion, 1937.
Phil 325.6 Morris, C.W. Logical positivism, pragmatism and scientific empiricism. Paris, 1937.
Phil 525.83 Mukerjee, R. Theory and art of mysticism. London, 1937.
Phil 2340.6.95 Murray, A.H. The philosophy of James Ward. Cambridge, Eng., 1937.
Phil 5390.12 Musil, Robert. Über die Dummheit. Wien, 1937.
Phil 5850.279.17 Myers, Charles S. In the realm of mind. Cambridge, Eng., 1937.
Phil 8593.17 The nature of religious experience. N.Y., 1937.
Phil 665.65 Neuburger, E. Das Verständnis der Seele im Christentum und in der psychologischen Literatur der Gegenwart. Inaug. Diss. Tübingen, 1937.
Phil 6323.6 Neustatter, W.L. Modern psychology in practice. Philadelphia, 1937.
Phil 530.20.85 Neuwinger, R. Die deutsche Mystik unter besonderer Berücksichtigung des "cherubinischen Wandersmannes" Johan Schefflers. Bleicherode am Harz, 1937.
Phil 3640.273 Nietzsche, Frau Franziska O. Der kranke Nietzsche. Wien, 1937.
Phil 188.14.7 Nordenholz, A. Scientologie. München, 1937.
Phil 8668.5 Noyes, A. The unknown god. London, 1937.
Phil 2520.186.10 Olgiati, Francesco. La filosofia di Descartes. Milano, 1937.

1937 - cont.

Phil 189.27 — Oro, A.M. dell'. Protologia; preludio al sapere. Milano, 1937.

Phil 5651.8 — Oster, Wilhelm. Struktur-psychologische Untersuchungen über die Leistung des Zeitsinns. Inaug. Diss. Würzburg, 1937.

Phil 8595.33 — Padovani, U.A. La filosofia della religione e il problema della vita. Milano, 1937.

Phil 5425.61 — Palmer, William J. Genius. Los Angeles, 1937.
Phil 400.94.15 — Parente, A. La morte dell'idealismo. Napoli, 1937.
Phil 2520.227 — Paris. Bibliotheque Nationale. Descartes. Paris, 1937.
Phil 2655.3 — Paris. École Libre des Sciences Politiques. Élie Halévy. Paris, 1937.

Phil 2805.40.28 — Pascal, Blaise. Les pensées et oeuvres choisies. Paris, 1937.

Phil 8840.2 — Paton, H.J. Fashion and philosophy. Oxford, 1937.
Phil 190.66 — Paullier, W. Ciencia, filosofia y laicismo. Buenos Aires, 1937. 2v.

Phil 5627.163 — Pear, T.H. Religion and contemporary psychology. London, 1937.

Phil 672.164 — Pemartin, J. Introducción a una filosofía de lo temporal. Sevilla, 1937.

Phil 9070.13 — Pereira Alves, A. Fe y valor. El Paso, 1937?
Phil 2750.11.90 — Phelan, G.B. Jacques Maritain. N.Y., 1937.
Phil 1750.149 — Philippard, L. Connais-toi toi-même. Paris, 1937.
Phil 5400.96 — Phillips, M. The education of the emotions. London, 1937.
Phil 6025.9.10 — Picard, Max. Die Grenzen der Physiognomik; mit 30 Bildtafeln. Erlenbach, 1937.

Phil 8416.35 — Piccardt, K.L. Het wezen der kunst. Amsterdam, 1937.
Phil 2750.11.230 — Pico, Cesar E. Carta a Jacques Maritain sobre la colaboración de los católicos con los movimientos de tipo fascista. Buenos Aires, 1937.

Phil 2515.2.95 — Piohetta, J.B. Pierre Chanet; une psychologie de l'instinct. Thèse. Paris, 1937.

Phil 630.51 — Pra, Mario dal. Il realismo e il trascendente. Padova, 1937.

Phil 2840.97 — Prat, Louis. Charles Renouvier. Ariège, 1937.
Phil 630.44 — Pratt, James B. Personal realism. N.Y., 1937.
Phil 8416.21 — Purser, J.W.R. Art and truth. Glasgow, 1937.
Phil 3790.13 — Raab, F. Philosophische Gespräche. Berlin, 1937.
Phil 3850.27.99 — Raab, Karl. Albert Schweitzer, Persönlichkeit und Denken. Inaug. Diss. Düsseldorf, 1937.

Phil 192.80 — Rabeau, G. Le jugement d'existence. Wetteren, 1937.
Phil 3850.32 — Räber, H. Othmar Spanns Philosophie. Jena, 1937.
Phil 400.95 — Raju, P.T. Thought and reality; Hegelianism and Advaita. London, 1937.

Phil 5057.26.2 — Raphael, Max. La théorie marxiste de la connaissance. Paris, 1937.

Phil 348.14 — Raretz, Karl von. Au den Quellen unseres Denkens. Wien, 1937.

Phil 3552.02 — Ravier, E. Bibliographie des oeuvres de Leibniz. Paris, 1937.

Phil 8707.18 — Regard, G. Etude biologique. Lausanne, 1937.
Phil 8892.54 — Reid, L.A. Creative morality. London, 1937.
Phil 2240.61 — Reid, Thomas. Philosophical orations of Thomas Reid. Aberdeen, 1937.

Phil 8597.23.5 — Reisner, Edward H. Faith in an age of fact. N.Y., 1937.
Phil 4215.3.45 — Rensi, Giuseppe. La filosofia dell'assurdo. Milano, 1937.
Phil 192.79 — Restrepo, D. Nociones de alta critica. Manziales, 1937.
Phil 7069.37.5A — Rhine, Joseph B. New frontiers of the mind. N.Y., 1937.
Phil 5257.49 — Richmond, W.V. Personality: its development and hygiene. N.Y., 1937.

Phil 2475.1.238.15 — Rideau, Émile. Descartes, Pascal, Bergson. Paris, 1937.

Phil 192.78 — Rivier, W. Le problème de la vie. Paris, 1937.
Phil 5257.28.30 — Roback, A.A. Behaviorism at twenty-five. Cambridge, Mass., 1937.

Phil 5850.326.9 — Roback, A.A. Getting more out of life. n.p., 1937.
Phil 1717.14 — Roberts, Michael. The modern mind. London, 1937.
Phil 735.113 — Rodhe, S.E. Über die Möglichkeit einer Werteinteilung. Lund, 1937.

Phil 2475.1.261 — Rolland, E. Le finalité morale dans le Bergsonisme. Paris, 1937.

Phil 2520.86.5 — Roth, Leon. Descartes' discourse on method. Oxford, 1937.
Phil 4768.1 — Rozental', M.M. Materialisticheskaia dialektika. Moskva, 1937.

Phil 5827.12 — Rubin, E. Mennesker og Høns. København, 1937.
Phil 5257.53 — Ruch, F.L. Psychology and life. Chicago, 1937.
Phil 1750.148 — Rudiger, H. Wesen und Wandlung des Humanismus. Hamburg, 1937.

Phil 5374.60 — Ruyer, Raymond. La conscience et le corps. Paris, 1937.
Phil 978.5.810 — Ryan, C.J. H.P. Blavatsky and the theosophical movement. Point Loma, Calif., 1937.

Phil 8598.24.3 — Sabatier, Auguste. Esquisse d'une philosophie de la religion d'après la psychologie et l'histoire. 10. éd. Paris, 1937.

Phil 365.45 — Salis Goulart, J. O sentido da evolução. Porto Allegre, 1937.

Phil 5258.117 — Schering, W.M. Zuschauen oder Handeln? Leipzig, 1937.
Phil 193.146 — Schmidt, Karl. The creative I and the Divine. N.Y., 1937.
Phil 3808.173 — Schneider, W. Schopenhauer. Vienna, 1937.
Phil 3808.19 — Schopenhauer, Arthur. Sämmtliche Werke. Leipzig, 1937-41. 7v.

Phil 3552.307A — Schrecker, Paul. Leibniz; ses idées sur l'organisation des relations internationales. London, 1937.

Phil 3450.20.10 — Schreiber, H.W. Joseph Hillebraud. Diss. Giessen, 1937.
Phil 3018.21 — Schroeter, R. Geschichte und Geschichtlichkeit in der deutschen Philosophie der Gegenwart. Inaug. Diss. Kölm am Rhein, 1937.

Phil 3425.296 — Schultz, Werner. Die Grundprinzipien der Religionsphilosophie Hegels und der Theologie Schleiermachers. Berlin, 1937.

Phil 3018.24 — Schwarz, Hermann. Grundzüge einer Geschichte der artdeutschen Philosophie. Berlin, 1937.

Phil 6128.46.12 — Seabury, David. Help yourself to happiness. N.Y., 1937.
Phil 2520.214 — Sergio, Antonio. Cartesianismo ideal e cartesianismo real. Lisboa, 1937.

Phil 7084.4.5 — Sharpe, Ella Freeman. Dream analysis: a practical handbook for psycho-analysts. London, 1937.

Phil 8419.47 — Shaw, T.L. Art reconstructed, a new theory of aesthetics. Boston, 1937.

Phil 4752.1.35 — Shcheglov, A.V. Bor'ba Lenina protiv Bogdanovskoi revizii marksizma. Moskva, 1937.

Phil 9513.14 — Sheremetev, Vl.Vl. Dukh vremeni. Shankai, 1937.
Phil 193.185 — Silva Tarouca, Amadeo. Totale Philosophie und Wirklichkeit. Freiburg, 1937.

1937 - cont.

Phil 1523.10 — Simard, G. Les maîtres chrétiens de nos pensées et de nos vies. Ottawa, 1937.
Phil 5058.50 — Sinclair, W.A. The traditional formal logic. London, 1937.
Phil 3838.15.5 — Siwek, Paul. Spinoza et le panthéisme religieux. Paris, 1937.
Phil 3120.8.89 — Skrbensky, L.H. Franz Brentano als Religionsphilosophie. Zürich, 1937.
Phil 8110.12 — Smith, A.C. Theories of the nature and standard of taste in England, 1700-1790. Chicago, 1937.
Phil 4369.3 — Soto, Juan B. La tragedia del pensamiento. Rio Piedras, 1937.
Phil 672.162 — Souriau, Michel. Le temps. Paris, 1937.
Phil 8599.19.107 — Spaleck, G. Religionssoziologische Grundbegriffe bei Troeltsch. Bleichersde, 1937.
Phil 9590.8 — Spallazani, L. The devil laughs. Boston, 1937.
Phil 3850.32.20 — Spann, Othmar. Naturphilosophie. Jena, 1937.
Phil 5228.8 — Spearman, C. Psychology down the ages. London, 1937. 2v.
Phil 6328.27 — Speer, Ernst. Die Liebesfähigkeit. 2e Aufl. München, 1937.
Phil 3819.45.15 — Spinoza, Benedictus de. Traité de la réforme de l'entendement. Paris, 1937.
Phil 5258.116 — Sprott, W.J.H. General psychology. London, 1937.
Phil 5258.116.5 — Sprott, W.J.H. Psychology for everyone. London, 1937.
Phil 575.98 — Stagner, R. Psychology of personality. N.Y., 1937.
Phil 5635.38 — Steige, R. Gefühl und Affekt. Inaug. Diss. Breslau? 1937.
Phil 978.49.165 — Steiner, R. Alte Mythen und ihre Bedeutung. Dornach, 1937.
Phil 978.49.17 — Steiner, R. Knowledge of the higher worlds. 3d English ed. London, 1937.
Phil 3963.2 — Stien, Hendrik. Das Leib-Seele-Problem in der Philosophie Hollands im 19. und 20. Jahrhundert. Lengerich, 1937.
Phil 8893.94 — Stoce, W.J. The concept of morals. N.Y., 1937.
Phil 349.34 — Swabey, William C. Being and being known. N.Y., 1937.
Phil 2475.1.259A — Szathmary, A. The aesthetic theory of Bergson. Cambridge, 1937.
Phil 7069.37.45 — Taylor, William G.L. Immortality. Boston, 1937.
Phil 3450.11.112 — Temuralk, T. Über die Grenzen der Erkennbarkeit. Inaug. Diss. Berlin, 1937.
Phil 3450.11.110 — Temuralk, T. Über die Grenzen der Erkennbarkeit bei Husserl und Scheler. Berlin, 1937.
Phil 7069.28.70 — Thomas, Charles D. Life beyond death, with evidence. 1st ed. London, 1937.
Phil 8599.27 — Thomas, E.E. The political aspects of religious development. London, 1937.
Phil 7069.37.12 — Thomas, J.F. Beyond normal cognition. Boston, 1937.
Phil 4019.1 — Tilgher, A. Antologia dei filosofi italiani del dopoguerra. 2. ed. Modena, 1937.
Phil 8894.27 — Tilgher, A. Filosofia delle morali. Roma, 1937.
Phil 8420.24 — Torossian, A. A guide to aesthetics. Stanford, 1937.
Phil 5627.60.20 — Underhill, E. The spiritual life. N.Y., 1937.
Phil 821.5 — Varsencelos, Jóse. Historia del pensamiento filosofico. Mexico, 1937.
Phil 5585.61 — Vernon, M.D. Visual perception. Cambridge, Eng., 1937.
Phil 7069.37.50 — Vivante, Leone. Studi sulle precognizioni. Firenze, 1937.
Phil 2915.51 — Voltaire, F.M.A. de. Traité de métaphysique, 1734. Manchester, 1937.
Phil 352.8 — Vries, Joseph de. Denken und Sein. Freiburg, 1937.
Phil 3120.2.99 — Waldschmitt, L. Bolzano's Begründung des objektivismus in der theoretischen und praktischen Philosophie. Giessen, 1937.
Phil 197.61.15 — Watkin, E.I. Men and tendencies. London, 1937.
Phil 4515.101 — Wedberg, A. Den logiska strukturen hos Boströms filosofi. Uppsala, 1937.
Phil 3625.3.88 — Weinberg, Carlton Berenda. Mach's empirio-pragmatism in physical science. N.Y., 1937.
Phil 5262.44 — Weiser-Aall, Lily. Volkskunde und Psychologie; eine Einführung. Berlin, 1937.
Phil 4655.1.84 — Werin, A. Pontus Wikner. Lund, 1937.
Phil 6972.17 — Whitwell, James Richard. Historical notes on psychiatry. Photoreproduction. Philadelphia, 1937.
Phil 1200.41 — Wiersma, W. Peri telous. Groningen, 1937.
Phil 9070.28 — Wilkins, Ernest Hatch. Living in crisis. Boston, 1937.
Phil 310.613 — Die Wissenschaft im Lichte des Marxismus. Zürich, 1937.
Phil 3850.4.81 — Wolf, L. John Michael Sailer's Lehre vom Menschen. Diss. Giessen, 1937.
Phil 3842.13.5 — Wolfson, H.A. Some guiding principles in determining Spinoza's mediaeval sources. Philadelphia, 1937.
Phil 197.23.10 — Woodbridge, F.J.E. Nature and mind. N.Y., 1937.
Phil 197.65 — Wust, Peter. Ungewissheit und Wagnis. Salzburg, 1937.
Phil 8612.32 — Ziegler, L. Vom Tod; essay. Leipzig, 1937.
Phil 306.5 — Zirm, E.K. Die Welt als Fühlen. Leipzig, 1937.
Phil 200.5.10 — Zucca, Antioco. I rapporti fra l'individuo e l'universo. Padova, 1937.

1938

Phil 6310.1.22 — Adler, A. Social interest. London, 1938.
Phil 6310.6 — Adler, Alexandra. Guiding human misfits. N.Y., 1938.
Phil 5240.36.5 — Adler, M.J. What man has made of man. N.Y., 1938.
Phil 8580.27 — Aldwinckle, M.R.F. The object of Christian worship. Thesis. Strasbourg, 1938.
Phil 800.8 — Aquilanti, F. Linei fondamentali di storia della filosofia. v.1-3. Milano, 1938-40. 2v.
Phil 8060.4 — Asmus, V.F. Antichnye mysliteli ob iskusstve. 2. izd. Moskva, 1938.
Phil 8875.26 — Astrada, C. La ética formal. La Plata, 1938.
Phil 5750.8 — Auer, Johannes. Die menschliche Willensfreiheit im Lehrsystem des Thomas von Aquin und Johannes Duns Scotus. München, 1938.
Phil 8580.25 — Auvergne, D. Regards catholiques sur le monde. Paris, 1938.
Phil 175.38.4 — Ayer, Alfred J. Language, truth and logic. London, 1938.
Phil 332.19 — Bachelard, Gaston. La formation de l'esprit scientifique. Photoreproduction. Paris, 1938.
Phil 1850.50.26 — Bacon, Francis. Nuovo organo. Firenze, 1938.
Phil 8402.18 — Balet, Leo. Synthetische Kunstwissenschaft. Stuttgart? 1938.
Phil 8581.73 — Ballou, Robert O. The glory of God. N.Y., 1938.
Phil 6111.56 — Barcroft, J. The brain. New Haven, 1938.
Phil 6111.56.10 — Barcroft, Joseph. The dependence of the mind on its physical environment. Newcastle upon Tyne? 1938?
Phil 6315.2.112 — Bartlett, Francis H. Sigmund Freud. Photoreproduction. London, 1938.
Phil 5041.53 — Baudin, E. Précis de logique des sciences. Paris, 1938.

Chronological Listing

Phil 7140.115.20 — Baudouin, C. Suggestion et autosuggestion. 5. ed. Neuchâtel, 1938.
Phil 5241.102 — Beck, M. Psychologie. Leiden, 1938.
Phil 8581.75 — Bell, E.T. Man and his lifebelts. N.Y., 1938.
Phil 5585.65 — Bender, L. A visual motor gestalt test. N.Y., 1938.
Phil 3001.15 — Bense, M. Vom Wesen deutscher Denker. München, 1938.
Phil 3120.64.30 — Bense, Max. Die abendländische Leidenschaft. München, 1938.
Phil 176.138.5 — Berdiaev, Nikolai A. Solitude and society. London, 1938.
Phil 990.25 — Beroukhim, Moussa. La pensée iranienne à travers l'histoire. Thèse. Paris, 1938.
Phil 8656.27 — Bertocci, Peter Anthony. The empirical argument for God in late British thought. Cambridge, 1938.
Phil 2477.12 — Bespaloff, R. Cheninement et carrefours. Paris, 1938.
Phil 8581.72 — Bevan, E.R. Symbolism and belief. London, 1938.
Phil 8581.71 — Bezzant, J.S. Aspects of belief. N.Y., 1938.
Phil 3120.40.45 — Bierens de Haan, J.D. Het rijk van den geest. Zeist, 1938.
Phil 5041.54 — Biser, I. A general scheme for natural systems. Philadelphia, 1938.
Phil 6311.23 — Bluemel, C.S. The troubled mind. Baltimore, 1938.
Phil 5066.10 — Bochénski, I.M. Noue lezioni di logica simbolica. Roma, 1938.
Phil 3552.309 — Boehm, A. Le "vinculum substantiale" chez Leibniz. Paris, 1938.
Phil 3110.12 — Böhme, J. Schriften. Leipzig, 1938.
Phil 3483.53 — Bohatec, J. Die Religionsphilosophie Kants. Hamburg, 1938.
Phil 3001.14 — Bohne, F. Anti-Cartesianismus; deutsche Philosophie im Widerstand. Leipzig, 1938.
Phil 176.141 — Bontadini, G. Saggio di una metafisica dell'esperienza. Milano, 1938.
Phil 9035.81 — Boston. The will to win. Boston, 1938.
Phil 8581.74 — Bowman, Archibald Allan. Studies in the philosophy of religion. London, 1938. 2v.
Phil 7069.38.4 — Bozzano, E. Discarnate influence. London, 1938.
Phil 5590.3 — Brill, A. Individual ascendency. N.Y., 1938.
Phil 8402.49 — Brinkmann, D. Natur und Kunst. Zürich, 1938.
Phil 6311.4.2 — Brown, William. Psychological methods of healing. London, 1938.
Phil 4070.3 — Brunello, B. Lineamenti di filosofia dell'azione. Modena, 1938.
Phil 8878.57 — Burgh, W.G. de. From morality to religion. London, 1938.
Phil 3120.20 — Burkamp, Wilhelm. Wirklichkeit und Sinn. v.1-2. Berlin, 1938.
Phil 5241.75.15 — Burloud, Albert. Principles d'une psychologie des tendances. Paris, 1938.
Phil 5041.40.10 — Burtt, Edwin Arthur. Principles and problems of right thinking. N.Y., 1938.
Phil 176.48.3 — Butler, N.M. Philosophy. N.Y., 1938.
Phil 4080.18 — Calogero, Guido. La conclusione della filosofia del conoscere. Firenze, 1938.
Phil 4080.17 — Carabellese, P. L'idealismo italiano. Napoli, 1938.
Phil 3484.18 — Cassirer, H.W. A commentary on Kant's Critique of judgement. London, 1938.
Phil 2520.207 — Causeries cartésiennes à porpos du troisième centenaire du discours de la méthode. Paris, 1938.
Phil 5465.33.10 — Centre International de Synthèse, Paris. Neuvième semaine internationale de synthèse. L'invention. Paris, 1938.
Phil 5752.11 — Cesari, P. Les déterminismes et les êtres. Thèse. Paris, 1938.
Phil 8030.3 — Chandler, A.R. A bibliography of psychology and experimental aesthetics, 1864-1937. Berkeley, 1938.
Phil 6112.31 — Chappell, M.N. In the name of common sense. N.Y., 1938.
Phil 8582.50.5 — Chartier, E. Propos sur la religion. Paris, 1938.
Phil 5520.68.3 — Chase, Stuart. The tyranny of words. N.Y., 1938.
Phil 8403.12.10 — Chernyshevskii, N.G. Stat'i po estetike. Moskva, 1938.
Phil 8877.79 — Chevalier, J. La vie morale et l'audelà. Paris, 1938.
Phil 8403.20 — Church, Ralph. An essay on critical appreciation. London, 1938.
Phil 177.98 — Coates, Adrian. A basis of opinion. London, 1938.
Phil 2515.7 — Cochet, M.A. Le congrès Descartes...reflexions. Bruges, 1938.
Phil 8403.21 — Collingwood, Robin George. The principles of art. Oxford, 1938.
Phil 2490.58 — Comte, Auguste. La religión universal. Santiago de Chile, 1938.
Phil 525.88 — Concerning mysticism. Guilford, 1938.
Phil 4080.16 — Consentino, A. Temps, espace devenir, moi. Paris, 1938.
Phil 3425.301 — Contri, S. Tetralogia Hegeliana. Bologna, 1938-39. 2v.
Phil 177.100 — Coviello, A. Crítica bibliográfica y análisis cultural. Tucumán, 1938.
Phil 5042.29 — Creighton, J.E. An introductory logic. N.Y., 1938.
Phil 4303.5.5 — Cruz Costa, João. Alguns aspétos da filosofia no Brazil. São Paulo, 1938?
Phil 3640.297 — Daffner, H. Friedrich Nietzsches Randglassen zu Bizets Carmen. Regensburg, 1938.
Phil 9070.29 — Danforth, William Henry. I dare you! Four fold development. 8. ed. St. Louis, Mo., 1938.
Phil 2340.10.97A — Das, Ras-Vihari. The philosophy of Whitehead. London, 1938.
Phil 8953.7 — Davis, H. Moral and pastoral theology. 3. ed. N.Y., 1938. 4v.
Phil 3195.2.85 — Deutinger, Martin. Martin Deutinger. München, 1938.
Phil 5043.16.3A — Dewey, J. Logic; the theory of inquiry. N.Y., 1938.
Phil 5243.45 — Dexter, E.S. Introduction to the fields of psychology. N.Y., 1938.
Phil 2270.140 — Diaconide, Elias. Étude critique sur la sociologie de Herbert Spencer. Paris, 1938.
Phil 178.64.4 — Dixon, W.M. The human situation. London, 1938.
Phil 5043.242.5 — Dotterer, Ray H. Beginners' logic. N.Y., 1938.
Phil 5243.28.8 — Driesch, Hans. Alltagsrätsel des Seelenlebens. Stuttgart, 1938.
Phil 3425.332 — Dürr, Agnes. Zum Problem der hegelschen Dialectik. Berlin, 1938.
Phil 5400.95 — Dunbar, H.F. Emotions and bodily changes. N.Y., 1938.
Phil 672.136.10 — Dunne, John W. An experiment with time. 4th ed. N.Y., 1938.
Phil 672.136.17 — Dunne, John W. The new immortality. London, 1938.
Phil 672.136.15 — Dunne, John W. The serial universe. London, 1938.
Phil 1980.4A — Edman, Irwin. Philosophers holiday. N.Y., 1938.
Phil 5520.70 — Eisenson, J. Psychology of speech. N.Y., 1938.
Phil 1750.151 — Elliott, George R. Humanism and imagination. Chapel Hill, 1938.

Phil 3808.220 — Emge, Carl August. Gedachtnisschrift für Arthur Schopenhauer zur 150. Wiederkehr seines Geburtstages. Berlin, 1938.
Phil 3640.294 — Endres, Hans. Rasse, Ehe, Zucht und Züchtung bei Nietzsche und Heute. Heidelberg, 1938.
Phil 6315.50 — Faithfull, Theodore. The mystery of the androgyne. London, 1938.
Phil 180.2.35 — Farkas, S. Filozófiai értekezések. Aiud-Nagyenyed, 1938.
Phil 3246.230 — Faust, August. Johann Gottlieb Fichte. Breslau, 1938.
Phil 7150.32 — Fedden, Henry R. Suicide, a social and historical study. London, 1938.
Phil 2730.97 — Fessard, G. La méthode de réflexion chez Maine de Biran. Paris, 1938.
Phil 180.58 — Finlayson Elliot, Clarence. Intuicion del ser. Santiago, 1938.
Phil 930.7.10 — Forke, A. Geschichte der neueren chinesischen Philosophie. Hamburg, 1938.
Phil 6315.2.53 — Freud, Sigmund. The basic writings of Sigmund Freud. N.Y., 1938. 3v.
Phil 6315.2.5.6A — Freud, Sigmund. A general introduction to psycho-analysis. Garden City, 1938.
Phil 1135.160 — Fritz, K. von. Philosophie und sprachlicher Ausdruck. N.Y., 1938.
Phil 805.8 — Fuller, B.A.G. A history of philosophy. N.Y., 1938.
Phil 6115.27 — Fulton, J.F. Physiology of the nervous system. London, 1938.
Phil 181.80 — Garcia Morente, Manuel. Lecciones preliminares de filosofia. Tucuman, 1938.
Phil 181.78 — Gattell, B.B. The light of the mind. Philadelphia, 1938.
Phil 8881.65 — Geiger, George R. Towards an objective ethics. Yellow Springs, 1938.
Phil 3450.22 — Gerritsen, T.J.C. La philosophie de Heymass. Paris, 1938.
Phil 3450.22.1 — Gerritsen, T.J.C. La philosophie de Heymass. Thèse. Paris, 1938.
Phil 3488.43 — Gersch, Walter. Der transzendentale Existenzbeweis in Kants Kritischer Metaphysik der ausserbewussten Wirklichkeit. Würzburg, 1938.
Phil 1955.6.25 — Gillio-Tos, M.T. Il pensiero di Giovanni Dewey. Napoli, 1938.
Phil 3310.8 — Glockner, Hermann. Das Abenteuer des Geistes. Stuttgart, 1938.
Phil 1020.8.21 — Goichon, A.M. Lexique de la langue...d'Ibn Sina. Paris, 1938.
Phil 181.82 — Gooch, L.C. Instinct vs. reason; the problem of man. Yazoo City, Miss., 1938.
Phil 1511.5 — Gorce, M.M. Science moderne et philosophie médiévale. Paris, 1938.
Phil 181.69.5 — Gorce, M.M. Traité de philosophie. Paris, 1938.
Phil 5643.100 — Grant, V.W. Psychological optics. Chicago, 1938.
Phil 2825.5 — Grappe, André. La pensée de Maurice Pradines. Paris, 1938.
Phil 5066.1 — Greenwood, T. Les fondements de la logique symbolique. v.1-2. Paris, 1938.
Phil 5246.51 — Gregg, F.M. Psychology of a growing personality. Lincoln, 1938.
Phil 8520.33 — Gross, J. La divinisation du chrétien d'après les pères grecs. Paris, 1938.
Phil 6316.10 — Guthrie, E.R. The psychology of human conflict. N.Y., 1938.
Phil 8408.24 — Hamann, J.G. Scritti e frammenti di estetica. Roma, 1938.
Phil 8957.11 — Handbuch der katholische Sittenlehre. v.1-5. Düsseldorf, 1938. 7v.
Phil 6317.25 — Harrington, M. Biological approach to the problem of abnormal behavior. Lancaster, Pa., 1938.
Phil 182.94.16 — Hartmann, N. Möglichkeit und Wirklichkeit. Berlin, 1938.
Phil 5203.11.10 — Harvard University. Department of Psychology. Books in psychology. v.1-2. Cambridge, 1938.
Phil 575.95 — Harvard University. Harvard Psychological Clinic. Explorations in personality. N.Y., 1938.
Phil 182.105 — Hawkins, D.J.B. Approach to philosophy. London, 1938.
Phil 6317.18.10 — Healy, William. Personality information and action. N.Y., 1938.
Phil 807.2.27 — Hegel, G.W.F. Vorlesungen über die Geschichte der Philosophie. Leipzig, 1938.
Phil 3425.42 — Hegel, Georg Wilhelm Friedrich. Nürnberger Schriften. Leipzig, 1938.
Phil 5066.5 — Hermes, H. Semiotik; eine Theorie der Zeichengestalten als Grundlage für Untersuchungen von formalisierten Sprachen. Leipzig, 1938.
Phil 630.46 — Hicks, G.D. Critical realism. London, 1938.
Phil 5047.33.5 — Hilbert, David. Grundzüge der theoretischen Logik. 2e Aufl. Berlin, 1938.
Phil 4007.1 — Hönigswald, R. Denker der italienischen Renaissance; Gestalten und Probleme. Basel, 1938.
Phil 5627.151 — L'homme et le péché. Paris, 1938.
Phil 5645.42 — Honoré, P. Color light and vision. Detroit, 1938.
Phil 6317.23 — Hopkins, P. The psychology of social movements. London, 1938.
Phil 8520.34.3 — Horton, Walter M. Contemporary continental theology. 2. ed. N.Y., 1938.
Phil 2280.5.102 — Howgate, G.W. George Santayana. Philadelphia, 1938.
Phil 2280.5.102.2 — Howgate, G.W. George Santayana. Thesis. Philadelphia, 1938.
Phil 3808.169 — Hübscher, Arthur. Arthur Schopenhauer. Leipzig, 1938.
Phil 2050.59 — Hume, David. An abstract of a treatise of human nature, 1740. Cambridge, Eng., 1938.
Phil 8612.28 — Husemann, F. Vom Bild und Sinn des Todes. Dresden, 1938.
Phil 5247.13.27 — Iriarte, Mauricio de. Dr. Juan Huarte de San Juan. Münster, 1938.
Phil 7080.49.5 — Jacobson, Edmund. You can sleep well. N.Y., 1938.
Phil 4710.60 — Jakovenko, B.U. Geschichte des Hegelianismus in Russland. Prag, 1938.
Phil 184.39 — Jankélévitch, V. L'alternative. Paris, 1938.
Phil 1750.150 — Jansen, B. Die Pflege der Philosophie. Fulda, 1938.
Phil 184.28.5 — Janssen, O. Dasein und Wirklichkeit. München, 1938.
Phil 184.19.20 — Jaspers, K. Existenzphilosophie. Berlin, 1938.
Phil 5249.6.25 — Jastrow, J. The betrayal of intelligence. N.Y., 1938.
Phil 2050.102 — Jessop, T.E. A bibliography of David Hume. London, 1938.
Phil 9450.16 — Joad, C.E.M. Guide to the philosophy of morals and politics. N.Y., 1938.
Phil 6319.2.4 — Jones, Ernest. Papers on psycho-analysis. 4th ed. Baltimore, 1938.
Phil 6960.10 — Kallmann, F.J. Genetics of schizophrenia. N.Y., 1938.
Phil 3450.23 — Kamm, P. Philosophie und Pädagogik Paul Häberlins in ehren Wandlungen. Diss. Zürich, 1938.
Phil 3549.10 — Kassner, Rudolf. Buch der Erinnerung. Leipzig, 1938.

1938 - cont.

Phil 3549.10.30   Kassner, Rudolf. Der Gottmensch. Leipzig, 1938.
Phil 978.75   Kauga, D.D. Where theosophy and science meet. Adyar, 1938.
Phil 4972.22   Kehl, Renato. Bio-perspectivas. Rio de Janeiro, 1938.
Phil 8635.4.5   Keyserling, Hermann. Immortality. London, 1938.
Phil 978.77.7   King, G.R. Ascended master light. Chicago, 1938.
Phil 3010.7   Klugen, A. von. Die Absage an die Romantik in der Zeit nach den Weltkriege. Berlin, 1938.
Phil 3640.285   Kniggendorf, W. Friedrich Nietzsche - der Deutsche! Erfurt, 1938.
Phil 185.59   Knowledge and society. N.Y., 1938.
Phil 4972.5.15   Korn, Alejandro. Obras. La Plata, 1938-40. 3v.
Phil 4809.497.30   Kozák, Jan Blahoslav. Věda a duch. Praha, 1938.
Phil 2725.21   Lachièze-Rey, P. Le moi, le monde et Dieu. Paris, 1938.
Phil 5400.94.5   Lacroze, R. L'angoisse et l'émotion. Paris, 1938.
Phil 5400.94   Lacroze, R. L'angoisse et l'émotion. Paris, 1938.
Phil 5465.38   Lacroze, René. La fonction de l'imagination. Paris, 1938.
Phil 5465.38.5   Lacroze, René. La fonction de l'imagination. Paris, 1938.
Phil 2725.2.10   Laffitte, Pierre. Moral positiva, sua necessidade atual. Rio de Janeiro, 1938.
Phil 6321.12.5   Laforgue, R. Clinical aspects of psychoanalysis. London, 1938.
Phil 186.91   Lambek, C. Studies in the dynamic coherence. Copenhagen, 1938.
Phil 3450.11.122   Landgrabe, Ludwig. Edmund Husserl zum Gednachtnis. Prag, 1938.
Phil 6961.16   Landis, C. Modern society and mental diseases. N.Y., 1938.
Phil 2520.206   La Plata. Universidad Nacional. Escritos en honor de Descartes. La Plata, 1938.
Phil 6121.28   Lashley, K.S. Experimental analysis of instinctive behavior. Lancaster, Pa., 1938.
Phil 5400.84.6   Lashley, K.S. The thalamus and emotion. Lancaster, 1938.
Phil 6321.13   Leconte, M. Conflits sociaux et psychoses. Paris, 1938.
Phil 8412.20   Lee, H.L. Perception and aesthetic value. N.Y., 1938.
Phil 3425.300   Lenin, V.I. Cahiers sur la dialectique de Hegel. Paris, 1938.
Phil 4362.2   Leret, Carlos. La Trinidad, principio fundamental del universo. Madrid, 1938.
Phil 5590.95   Lersch, Philipp. Der Aufbau des Charakters. Leipzig, 1938.
Phil 5325.27   Lévêque, R. L'éclosion des pensées. Paris, 1938.
Phil 5325.156   Lévêque, R. L'éclosion des pensées. Thèse. Strasbourg, 1938.
Phil 2515.4.99   Lévêque, R. L'élément historique dans...Cournot. Paris, 1938.
Phil 2515.4.100   Lévêque, R. L'élément historique dans la connaissance humaine d'après Cournot. Thèse. Strasbourg, 1938.
Phil 186.93   Liebert, A. Von der Pflicht der Philosophie in unserer Zeit. Zürich, 1938.
Phil 3585.11   Liebert, Arthur. Der Liberalismus als Fordering. Zürich, 1938.
Phil 5645.44   Lindberg, Bengt J. Experimental studies of colour and non-colour attitudes in school children and adults. Copenhagen, 1938.
Phil 3585.12   Litt, Theodor. Die Selbsterkenntnis des Menschen. Leipzig, 1938.
Phil 8591.20.12   Loisy, Alfred. Autres mythes à propos de la religion. Paris, 1938.
Phil 2190.5   Lornay, Stephen Clark. Ockham. LaSalle, Ill., 1938.
Phil 5251.23.5   Losskii, N.O. Chuvstvennaia, intellektual'naia i misticheskaia intuitsiia. Paris, 1938.
Phil 1955.7.90   Luce, A.A. Charles Frederick D'Arcy, 1859-1938. London, 1938.
Phil 5627.166   Lunn, Arnold. Now I see. N.Y., 1938.
Phil 8591.40   Lupton, D. Religion says you can. Boston, 1938.
Phil 5252.18.38   McDougall, William. The riddle of life. London, 1938.
Phil 8592.73   MacLeish, Norman. The nature of religious knowledge. N.Y., 1938.
Phil 2750.14   Madinier, Gabriel. Conscience et amour. Paris, 1938.
Phil 2750.15   Madinier, Gabriel. Conscience et mouvement. Paris, 1938.
Phil 2750.15.1   Madinier, Gabriel. Conscience et mouvement. Thesis. Paris, 1938.
Phil 187.125   Märker, F. Sinn und Gesetze des Lebens. Berlin, 1938.
Phil 410.80   Major, John. Le traité "De l'infini" de Jean Muir. Paris, 1938.
Phil 2733.5.5   Malebranche, Nicolas. Oeuvres complètes. Paris, 1938.
Phil 2733.108   Malebranche nel terzo centenario della nascita. Milano, 1938.
Phil 9352.13.5   Manchester, R.E. The Saturday letters. Cuyahoga Falls, 1938.
Phil 3808.174A   Mann, Thomas. Schopenhauer. Stockholm, 1938.
Phil 5222.6   Manoll, A. La psychologie expérimentale en Italie. Paris, 1938.
Phil 6060.31   Margadant, S.V. Eine tiefenpsychologische Grundlage zur Klages'chen Graphologie. Amsterdam, 1938.
Phil 6322.25   Marin, J. Ensayos freudianos. Santiago de Chile, 1938.
Phil 2750.11.48.10   Maritain, Jacques. The degree of knowledge. N.Y., 1938.
Phil 2750.11.63   Maritain, Jacques. Questions de conscience. Paris, 1938.
Phil 187.114.5   Masaryk, T.G. The ideals of humanity and How to work. London, 1938.
Phil 8592.57.5   Masaryk, T.G. Modern man and religion. London, 1938.
Phil 293.25   Matisse, G. La philosophie de la nature. Paris, 1938. 3v.
Phil 187.100.5   Mead, George H. The philosophy of the act. Chicago, 1938.
Phil 187.28.7   Mechnikov, I.I. Nature of man. London, 1938.
Phil 97.5   Melzer, J.H. Guide to philosophical terminology. Ashland, Ohio, 1938.
Phil 7150.31   Menninger, Karl Augustus. Man against himself. N.Y., 1938.
Phil 1117.12   Menzel, Adolf. Hellenika. Baden, 1938.
Phil 8887.13.5   Meres, F. Palladis tamia. N.Y., 1938.
Phil 2477.11.91   Messaut, J. La philosophie de Léon Brunschvicg. Paris, 1938.
Phil 8702.18   Metzger, H. Atraction universelle et religion naturelle. Paris, 1938. 3v.
Phil 2340.10.99   Miller, D.L. The philosophy of A.N. Whitehead. Minneapolis, 1938.
Phil 5052.37   Miller, James N. The structure of Aristotelian logic. N.Y., 1938.
Phil 3625.3.94   Mises, R. Ernst Mach. 's-Gravenhage, 1938.
Phil 187.118   Monsarrat, K.W. Human powers and their relations. Liverpool, 1938.
Phil 5627.154   Moore, J.M. Theories of religious experience. Thesis. N.Y., 1938.

1938 - cont.

Phil 5822.4.3   Muan, N.L. Psychological development. Boston, 1938.
Phil 187.108.5   Müller, G.E. Der Mensch im Sein. Stuttgart, 1938.
Phil 343.18.9   Mukerji, A.C. The nature of self. Allahabad, 1938.
Phil 7069.38.30   Mulholland, J. Beware familiar spirits. N.Y., 1938.
Phil 6122.57   Murray, J.A.C. An introduction to a Christian psycho-therapy. Edinburgh, 1938.
Phil 8140.5   Napoli, Paolo. Arte e architettura in regime fascista. Roma, 1938.
Phil 6951.5.53   National Committee for Mental Hygiene. The mental hygiene movement. N.Y., 1938.
Phil 3120.8.91   Naturwissenschaft und Metaphysik. Brünn, 1938.
Phil 3120.67.80   Neuwinger, Rudolf. Die Philosophie Ernst Bergmanns. Stuttgart, 1938.
Phil 3640.14   Nietzsche, Friedrich. Werke und Briefe. München, 1938-42. 4v.
Phil 630.47   Noël, L. Le réalisme immédiat. Louvain, 1938.
Phil 9035.79   Nohl, Herman. Charakter und Schicksal. Frankfurt, 1938.
Phil 5627.156   Norborg, S. Varieties of Christian experience. Minneapolis, 1938.
Phil 5520.71   Norris, Tom C. Thought and speech. London, 1938.
Phil 8593.16   Nuñez Regueiro, Manuel. Suma contra una nueva edad media. Rosario, 1938.
Phil 5415.10   Ochanine, D. La sympathie. Paris, 1938.
Phil 3705.4   Odebrecht, R. Welterlebnis. Berlin, 1938.
Phil 5520.35.7   Ogden, Charles K. The meaning of meaning. 5. ed. London, 1938.
Phil 5520.35.5   Ogden, Charles K. The meaning of meaning. 5. ed. N.Y., 1938.
Phil 8415.8A   Ogden, R.M. The psychology of art. N.Y., 1938. 2v.
Phil 5645.40   Olsson, G.F. Experimentelle Untersuchungen. Stockholm, 1938.
Phil 8594.14   Ortegat, Paul. Philosophie de la religion. Bruxelles, 1938.
Phil 2520.210   An outline of Descartes' philosophy. Cambridge, 1938.
Phil 5374.161   Paliard, J. Théorème de la connaissance. Paris, 1938.
Phil 7069.38.65   Parkman, Frances. Vision, being the continuation of "Reality" and "Dedication". Boston, 1938.
Phil 2225.8   Paterson, William R. The passions of life. London, 1938.
Phil 5360.9   Pellet, R. Des premières perceptions du concret à la conception de l'abstrait. Thèse. Lyon, 1938.
Phil 3425.297   Pelloux, L. La logica di Hegel. Milan, 1938.
Phil 3015.4   Pensa, M. Il pensiero tedesco. Bologna, 1938.
Phil 8416.34   Pepper, S.C. Aesthetic quality, a contextualistic theory of beauty. N.Y., 1938.
X Cg   Phil 2070.129.10   Perry, R.B. In the spirit of William James. New Haven, 1938.
Phil 3745.8   Pfannwitz, Rudolf. Lebenshilfe. Zürich, 1938.
Phil 9035.82   Piwowarczyk, W. Charakter. Kielce, 1938.
Phil 190.53.10   Planck, Max. Religion und Naturwissenschaft. Leipzig, 1938.
Phil 3640.235.20   Podach, Erich F. Friedrich Nietzsche und Lou Salomé. Zürich, 1938.
Phil 3552.308   Politella, Joseph. Platonism, Aristoteleanism and Cabelism in the philosophy of Leibniz. Philadelphia, 1938.
Phil 8640.1.12   Pomponazzi, P. Tractatus de immortalitate animae. Haverford, Pa., 1938.
Phil 192.80.2   Rabeau, G. Le jugement d'existence. Paris, 1938.
Phil 5435.4   Ravaisson-Mollien, Felix. De l'habitude. Paris, 1938.
Phil 5640.40   Rawdon-Smith, A.F. Theories of sensation. Cambridge, 1938.
Phil 5125.18   Reade, W.H.F. The problem of inference. Oxford, 1938.
Phil 5227.5   Recent experiments in psychology. 1st ed. N.Y., 1938.
Phil 5465.46   Reeb, Eugène. Les images de Taine à Binet. Thèse complementaire. Nancy, 1938.
Phil 6327.14   Reese, W. L'idée de l'homme dans la neurologie contemporaine. Paris, 1938.
Phil 348.13   Reichenbach, Hans. Experience and prediction. Chicago, 1938.
Phil 735.117   Reid, John R. A theory of value. N.Y., 1938.
Phil 5257.52   Reinbardt, J.M. Social psychology. Chicago, 1938.
Phil 5648.20   Révész, Géza. Die Formenwelt des Tastsinnes. Haag, 1938. 2v.
Phil 5520.145.15   Richards, Ivor Armstrong. Interpretation in teaching. N.Y., 1938.
Phil 5627.134.50F   Rising tide. Chicago, 1938.
Phil 4265.2.96   Rizzo, R. Teocrazia e neo-cattaluisimo nel risorgimento. Palermo, 1938.
Phil 9530.38.50   Roback, A.A. I am winning friends. Cambridge, 1938.
Phil 1145.82   Robin, L. La morale antique. Paris, 1938.
Phil 8597.42   Robinson, D.F. In search of a religion. Chester, 1938.
Phil 8892.55   Roche, J. Le gouvernement de soi. Paris, 1938.
Phil 8842.10.5   Rohmer, J. La finalité morale chez les théologiens de Saint Augustin à Duns Scot. Thèse. Paris, 1938.
Phil 4120.4.87   Romanelli, P. Gentile. N.Y., 1938.
Phil 4080.3.93   Romano Palazzo, F. Influssi del pensiero Kantiano vell Croce. Bari, 1938.
Phil 4972.5.53   Romero, Francisco. Alejandro Korn. La Plata, 1938.
Phil 575.93   Rothacker, E. Die Schichten der Persönlichkeit. Leipzig, 1938.
Phil 4225.4   Sacheli, C.A. Atto e valore. Firenze, 1938.
Phil 8893.99   Sacheli, C.A. Ragion pratica. Firenze, 1938.
Phil 1195.9   Saitta, G. L'illuminismo della sofistica greca. Milano, 1938.
Phil 7069.39.52   Salminen, I. Essence of life in psychic phenomena. Brooklyn, 1938.
Phil 182.101.20   Sampson, A.H. The philosophy of John Scott Haldane. Philadelphia, 1938.
Phil 193.49.38   Santayana, G. The realm of truth. N.Y., 1938.
Phil 3500.63   Schilpp, P.A. Kant's pre-critical ethics. Evanston, 1938.
Phil 193.151   Schjoth, Emil. Gegenstands und verhältenislehre. Oslo, 1938.
Phil 193.141   Schleier, S.T. An analysis of man and his philosophy. St. Louis, 1938.
Phil 3850.29.20   Schlich, M. Gesemmelte Aufsätze, 1926-1936. Wien, 1938.
Phil 1123.11   Schmekel, A. Forschungen. Berlin, 1938.
Phil 349.35   Schmidt, Franz. Kleine Logik der Geisteswissenschaften. München, 1938.
Phil 3838.22   Schmoldt, H. Der Spinozastreit. Inaug. Diss. Würzburg, 1938.
Phil 8598.78   Schneider, H.W. Meditations in season on the elements of Christian philosophy. N.Y., 1938.
Phil 3801.780   Schneider, R. Schellings und Hegels schwäbische Geistesahnen. Würzburg, 1938.
Phil 6990.39   Schreiber, G. Deutsche Mirakelbücher. Dusseldorf, 1938.
Phil 5190.25   Schultzer, B. Observation and protocolstatement. Copenhagen, 1938.

1938 - cont.

Phil 3425.298   Schwarz, Justus. Hegels philosophische Entwicklung. Frankfurt, 1938.

Phil 6328.18.10   Seabury, David. Adventures in self discovery. N.Y., 1938.

Phil 270.55   Segond, J.L.P. Hasard et contingence. Paris, 1938.

Phil 270.56   Segond, J.L.P. Logique du pari. Paris, 1938.

Phil 705.27   Selling, M. Studien zur Geschichte der Transzendantalphilosophie. Inaug. Diss. Lund, 1938.

Phil 193.148   Selsam, H. What is philosophy? N.Y., 1938.

Phil 3838.21   Shauki, Alexander. An introduction to Spinoza's Ethic. London, 1938.

Phil 6805.4   Sherman, Mandel. Mental conflicts and personality. N.Y., 1938.

Phil 8598.79.5   Shestov, L. Athènes et Jerusalem. Paris, 1938.

Phil 8598.85   Shoemaker, S.M. The church can save the world. N.Y., 1938.

Phil 3640.274   Siegel, Carl. Nietzsches Zarathustra; Gehalt und Gestalt. München, 1938.

Phil 8598.80   Silen, S. Den kristna människouppfattningen. Stockholm, 1938.

Phil 960.148   Sinha, Judunath. Indian realism. London, 1938.

Phil 672.163.5   Sivadjian, J. Le temps. Paris, 1938. 6v.

Phil 672.163   Sivadjian, J. Le temps. Paris, 1938.

Phil 5258.120   Skinner, Burrhus F. Behavior of organisms. N.Y., 1938.

Phil 8968.14   Slattery, M. Thy kingdom come...but not now. N.Y., 1938.

Phil 8598.75   Smith, Abbot Edes. Philosophy of life; with an appendix on the Bible. Norwood, 1938.

Phil 2880.7   Sourian, E. Avoir une âme. Paris, 1938.

Phil 4829.803.20   Spakovski, Anatol. Kleinere philosophische Schriften. Velika Kikinda, 1938.

Phil 3819.77   Spinoza, Benedictus de. Lettere. Lanciano, 1938. 2v.

Phil 3850.5.8   Spir, Afrikan. Paroles d'un sage. Paris, 1938.

Phil 193.155   Stefanesco, Marin. Le problème de la méthode. Paris, 1938.

Phil 6328.2.22   Stekel, Wilhelm. Technik der analyschen Psychotherapie. Bern, 1938.

Phil 5258.35.20   Stern, W. General psychology from the personalistic standpoint. N.Y., 1938.

Phil 5650.24   Stevens, Stanley S. Hearing; its psychology and physiology. N.Y., 1938.

Phil 193.130.5   Stocks, J.L. Time; cause and eternity. London, 1938.

Phil 575.97   Stuart, C. Achievement of personality. N.Y., 1938.

Phil 6128.53   Swedenborg, Emanuel. Three transactions on the cerebrum; a posthumous work. V.1-2 and atlas. Philadelphia, 1938-40. 3v.

Phil 4370.5   Tagle, A. La experiencia humana. Buenos Aires, 1938.

Phil 8644.11   Taylor, Alfred E. The Christian hope of immortality. London, 1938.

Phil 5259.29   Taylor, J.G. Popular psychological fallacies. London, 1938.

Phil 8709.15   Teller, Woolsey. The atheism of astronomy. N.Y., 1938.

Phil 7069.38.58   Thomas, Charles D. In the dawn beyond death. London, 1938?

Phil 575.96   Thorpe, L.P. Psychological foundations of personality. N.Y., 1938.

Phil 8420.22   Treves, Marco. Trattato d'estetica. Firenze, 1938.

Phil 310.567   Troise, Emilio. Materialismo dialectico. Buenos Aires, 1938.

Phil 1124.5   Tsatsos, K. He koinonikè filosofia tòn arkhaion Hellènon. Athenai, 1938.

Phil 8894.29   Tuker, M.A.R. Past and future of ethics. London, 1938.

Phil 5625.85   Tullio, P. I riflessi orientative nella studio delle attività mentali. Bologna, 1938.

Phil 7069.38.60   Tyrrell, G.N.M. Science and psychical phenomena. London, 1938.

Phil 3640.299   Umland, Karl. Nietzsches Würdigung des Menschen. Würzburg, 1938.

Phil 5260.9.5   United States. Department of Agriculture. Graduate School. Understanding ourselves. Washington, 1938.

Phil 5261.17.25   Valentine, Willard Lee. Experimental foundations of general psychology. N.Y., 1938.

Phil 4960.260   Varela Dominguez de Ghioldi, Delfina. Filosofía argentina; los ideólogos. Buenos Aires, 1938.

Phil 5261.21   Varnuar, W.C. Psychology in everyday life. N.Y., 1938.

Phil 187.93.30   Vassallo, Angel. Cuatro lecciones sobre metafisica. Buenos Aires, 1938.

Phil 196.29   Vassallo, Angel. Nuevos prolegómenos a la metafisica. Buenos Aires, 1938.

Phil 196.25   Veuthy, L. La pensée contemporaine. Paris, 1938.

Phil 196.26   Vialle, L. Defense de la vie. Paris, 1938.

Phil 1526.4   Vignaux, Paul. Le pensée au moyen âge. Paris, 1938.

Phil 6971.4   Villey, G. La psychiatrie et les sciences de l'homme. Paris, 1938.

Phil 821.4   Visser, S. Zoekers naar wijsheid. Goes, 1938.

Phil 5771.3   Vivanti, L. Il concetto della indeterminazione. Firenze, 1938.

Phil 2422.3   Wade, Ira O. The Clandestine organization and diffusion of philosophic ideas in France from 1700 to 1750. Princeton, 1938.

Phil 3450.16.15   Wahl, Jean A. Sein Leben in seiner Briefen. Frankfurt, 1938.

Phil 5262.41   Wait, W.T. Science of human behavior. N.Y., 1938.

Phil 2655.2.86   Warrain, F. L'oeuvre psychobiophysique. 2 ed. Martins, 1938.

Phil 2340.11   Weiss, Paul. Reality. Princeton, 1938.

Phil 6132.32   Welsh, F.G. (Mrs.). Can we live forever? Chicago, 1938.

Phil 5062.17.5   Welton, James. Intermediate logic. 4th ed. London, 1938.

Phil 1127.5.3   Werner, Charles. La philosophie grecque. Paris, 1938.

Phil 822.11   Westaway, F.W. Obsessions and convictions of the human intellect. London, 1938.

Phil 5232.8   Westerhof, A.C. Representative psychologists. Union Bridge, Md., 1938.

Phil 6972.14.50   White, William Alanson. William Alanson White, the autobiography of a purpose. Garden City, 1938.

Phil 2340.10.98A   Whitehead, Alfred North. Modes of thought. N.Y., 1938.

Phil 6332.11   Wickes, F.G. Inner world of man. N.Y., 1938.

Phil 5170.7   Wilcox, Stanley. The destructive hypothetical syllogism in Greek logic and in Attic oratory. n.p., 1938.

Phil 5262.39A   Wild, K.W. Intuition. Cambridge, Eng., 1938.

Phil 8677.19   Williams, Charles. He came down from heaven. London, 1938.

Phil 3925.10   Wimmer, H.A. Neue Dialoge; zwischen Hylas und Philoneris. Heidelberg, 1938.

Phil 1020.20   Wolfson, H.A. The amphibolous terms in Aristotle. Cambridge, Mass., 1938.

Phil 1050.12.3   Wolfson, Harry A. The amphibolous terms in Aristotle. Cambridge, Mass., 1938.

1938 - cont.

Phil 5262.9.35   Woodworth, R.S. Experimental psychology. N.Y., 1938.

Phil 8602.47.5   Wright, Ronald S. Asking them questions. Second series. London, 1938.

Phil 8090.2   Zabel, M.D. The romantic idealism of art, 1800-1848. Chicago, 1938.

Phil 930.7.50   Zach, E. von. Weitere Verbesserungen zu Forke's Geschichte der chinesischen Philosophie. Batavia, 1938.

Phil 4829.896.30   Zimmermann, Stjepan. Religija i život. Zagreb, 1938.

Phil 5620.18   Zoul, L. On the origin of reason. N.Y., 1938.

1939

Phil 3640.345   Ackermann, O. Kant im Urteil Nietzsches. Tübingen, 1939.

Phil 6310.6.2   Adler, Alexandra. Guiding human misfits. N.Y., 1939.

Phil 1020.21   Affifi, A.E. The mystical philosophy of Muhyid din-ibnul 'Arabi. Cambridge, 1939.

Phil 5240.39   Agramonte y Richardo, R. Compendio de psicología. Habana, 1939.

Phil 1155.10   Albertelli, P. Gli eleati. Bari, 1939.

Phil 1845.3.95   Alexander, Samuel. Philosophical and literary pieces. London, 1939.

Phil 2262.92   Almer, T. Studier i Shaftesburys filosofi. Lund, 1939.

Phil 175.40   Anderson, L.F. God and the cosmic order. N.Y., 1939.

Phil 175.40.5   Anderson, L.F. Logic and the cosmic order. N.Y., 1939.

Phil 5240.37   Anderson, L.F. Psychology and the cosmic order. n.p., 1939.

Phil 1800.3A   Anderson, P.P. Philosophy in America. N.Y., 1939.

Phil 5413.14   Ankles, T.M. A study of jealousy as differentiated from envy. Boston, 1939.

Phil 6110.18   Association for Research in Nervous and Mental Diseases. The interrelationship of mind and body. Baltimore, 1939.

Phil 1750.153   Association Guillaume Budé. L'humanisme en Alsace. Paris, 1939.

Phil 5545.175   Augier, E. La mémoire et la vie. Paris, 1939.

Phil 3425.306   Axmann, Walter. Zur Frage nach dem Ursprung des dialektischen Denkens bei Hegel. Inaug. Diss. Würzburg, 1939.

Phil 3110.180   Baden, Hans J. Das reliqiöse Problem der Gegenwart bei Jakob Böhme. Leipzig, 1939.

Phil 9120.170   Barker, E. The values of life. Glasgow, 1939.

Phil 8876.106   Barrett, J.W. How to overcome your 7 deadly enemies. N.Y., 1939.

Phil 8581.102   Barthel, Ernst. Der Mensch und die ewigen Hintergründe. München, 1939.

Phil 176.146   Bastide, George. De la condition humaine. Thèse. Paris, 1939.

Phil 5041.57   Baumgarten, Arthur. Logik als Erfahrungswissenschaft. Kaunas, 1939.

Phil 9560.31   Baurmann, W. Vertu. Berlin, 1939.

Phil 720.31   Belgodere, F.J.A. La verdad, la ciencia y la filosofía. México, 1939.

Phil 3483.55   Benda, Julien. El pensamiento vivo de Kant. Buenos Aires, 1939.

Phil 5041.55   Bennett, A.A. Formal logic. N.Y., 1939.

Phil 7069.39.4   Bennett, E.N. Apparitions and haunted houses. London, 1939.

Phil 176.145   Bentley, J.E. Visual outline of philosophy. N.Y., 1939.

Phil 2805.228   Benzécri, E. L'esprit humain selon Pascal. Paris, 1939.

Phil 176.150   Benzecri, E. Essai sur la nature et la portee d l'attitude metaphysique. Alcan, 1939.

Phil 1870.45.25   Berkeley, G. Dialoghi tra Hylas e Filonous. Bari, 1939.

Phil 6111.44.5   Berry, Richard J.A. Your brain and its story. London, 1939.

Phil 4965.4   Bibliografia de las obras del Dr. Dn. Alejandro O. Deustua. Lima, 1939.

Phil 6111.57   Bier, A. Die Seele. 3. Aufl. München, 1939.

Phil 5241.100   Billings, E.G. Handbook of elementary psychology. N.Y., 1939.

Phil 8581.78   Bixler, J.S. Religion for free minds. N.Y., 1939.

Phil 6990.44   Blanton, M.G. Bernadette of Lourdes. London, 1939.

Phil 6420.16.9   Bogue, Benjamin N. Stammering; its cause and correction. Indianapolis, 1939.

Phil 6310.8   Bottome, P. Alfred Adler; a biography. N.Y., 1939.

Phil 1905.13   Bowman, A.A. A sacramental universe. Princeton, 1939.

Phil 270.47   Brahma, N.K. Causality and science. London, 1939.

Phil 5520.69   Britton, Karl. Communication. London, 1939.

Phil 5643.102   Brøns, J. The blind sport of Mariotte. Copenhagen, 1939.

Phil 3120.15.31   Brunner, Constantin. Unser Charakter, oder Ich bin der Richtige! Zürich, 1939.

Phil 2225.5.80   Buchler, J. Charles Peirce's empiricism. N.Y., 1939.

Phil 75.34   Buenos Aires. Colegio Máximo. Nuestra bibliográfica de la filosofía católica. Buenos Aires, 1939.

Phil 332.21   Burgh, W.G. Knowledge of the individual. London, 1939.

Phil 3425.305   Burman, E.O. Hegels rättsfilosofi. Uppsala, 1939.

Phil 8581.76   Burtt, Edwin A. Types of religious philosophy. 1. ed. N.Y., 1939.

Phil 4073.32A   Campanella, Tommaso. Epilogo magno (fisiologia italiana). Roma, 1939.

Phil 6672.14A   Cannon, A. Sleeping through space. 1st ed. N.Y., 1939.

Phil 7069.39.9   Carrington, H. Laboratory investigations into psychic phenomena. Philadelphia, 1939.

Phil 3160.9.30   Carus, Karl Gustav. Karl Gustav Carus und Carl Fr. Ph. von Martins. Halle, 1939.

Phil 2750.10.106   Caso, A. Myerson y la fisica moderna. México, 1939.

Phil 6950.6   Cassinelli, B. Histoire de la folie. Paris, 1939.

Phil 2520.208   Cassirer, E. Descartes. Stockholm, 1939.

Phil 5238.7   Centenaire de T. Ribot, jubilé de la psychologie scientifique française, 1839-1939. Agen, 1939.

Phil 5932.1   A challenge to phrenologists. London, 1939.

Phil 8403.23.5   Chartier, Emile. Préliminaires à l'esthétique. Paris, 1939.

Phil 2880.1.88   Chateaution, G. Bibliographie du Martinisme. Lyon, 1939.

Phil 2515.17   Chevalier, J. Cadences. Paris, 1939- 2v.

Phil 3425.303   Chyzhevs'kyi, Dmytro. Gegel' v Rossii. Parizh, 1939.

Phil 3160.3.92   Cohen, Hermann. Briefe. Berlin, 1939.

Phil 2490.70   Comte, Auguste. Nouvelles lettres inédites. Paris, 1939.

Phil 5242.62   Conklin, Edmund Smith. Introductory psychology for students of education. N.Y., 1939.

Phil 5066.9   Cooley, J.C. An outline of formal logic. Pt.1. Cambridge, 1939.

Phil 8583.28.20   Dawson, Christopher H. Beyond politics. London, 1939.

Phil 2555.1.85   Deschamps, L.M. Le vrai système. Paris, 1939.

Phil 1955.6.20   Dewey, John. Freedom and culture. N.Y., 1939.

Phil 1955.6.22   Dewey, John. Intelligence in the modern world. N.Y., 1939.

Chronological Listing

1939 - cont.

Phil 6313.13 — Dicks, H.V. Clinical studies in psychopathology. London, 1939.
Phil 2490.131 — Ducassé, P. Essai sur les origines intuitives du positivisme. Thèse. Paris, 1939.
Phil 2490.130 — Ducassé, P. Méthode et intuition chez Auguste Comte. Thèse. Paris, 1939.
Phil 600.50 — Ducassé, Pierre. La méthode positive et l'intuition comtienne. Paris, 1939.
Phil 1210.10 — Dyroff, A. Der Peripatos über das Greisenalter. Paderborn, 1939.
Phil 1980.4.11 — Edman, Irwin. Candle in the dark. N.Y., 1939.
Phil 335.3.10 — Ehrlich, Walter. Das Verstehen. Zürich, 1939.
Phil 1980.3.95A — Ellis, H. My life; autobiography of Havelock Ellis. Boston, 1939.
Phil 8430.66 — Evans, Joan. Taste and temperament. London, 1939.
Phil 8405.3 — Evans, W.V. Belief and art. Chicago, 1939.
Phil 186.95 — Fadiman, Clifton. I believe. N.Y., 1939.
Phil 2805.223 — Falcucci, C. Le problème de la vérité chez Pascal. Thèse. Toulouse, 1939.
Phil 5215.3 — Fay, J.W. American psychology. New Brunswick, N.J., 1939.
Phil 6315.18 — Federn, Paul. Das psychoanalytische Volksbuch. Bern, 1939.
Phil 8612.30 — Feier, I. Essais sur la mort. Bucarest, 1939.
Phil 5401.15 — Fletcher, P. Life without fear. N.Y., 1939.
Phil 4967.5.10 — Francovich, Guillermo. Supay; diálogos. Sucre, 1939.
Phil 6836.2 — Frederics, Diana. Diana; a strange autobiography. N.Y., 1939.
Phil 5245.43 — Freeman, E. Principles of general psychology. N.Y., 1939.
Phil 6115.27.5 — Fulton, J.F. Physiology of the nervous system. London, 1939.
Phil 9150.30 — Gantz, K.F. The beginnings of Darwinian ethics: 1859-1871. Chicago, 1939.
Phil 6310.1.91 — Ganz, M. Adlers psykologi. Stockholm, 1939.
Phil 7069.39.19 — Garrett, Eileen Jeanette Lyttle. My life as a search for the meaning of mediumship. London, 1939.
Phil 7080.50 — Garvey, Chester R. Activity of young children during sleep. Minneapolis, 1939.
Phil 8696.18 — Gaskell, A. (Mrs.). Whence? Whither? Why? N.Y., 1939.
Phil 3006.8 — Gehl, W. Der germanische Schichsalsglaube. Berlin, 1939.
Phil 1135.158 — Gentile, M. La metafisica presofistica. Padova, 1939.
Phil 8050.78 — Gilbert, Mesk. A history of aesthetics. N.Y., 1939.
Phil 5246.41.4 — Gilliland, A.R. Psychology of individual differences. N.Y., 1939.
Phil 630.43.7 — Gilson, Étienne. Réalisme thomiste. Paris, 1939.
Phil 2045.119A — Gooch, G.P. Hobbes; annual lecture on a master mind. London, 1939.
Phil 5643.101 — Gramont, A. Problèmes de la vision. Paris, 1939.
Phil 8661.19 — Gregoire, A. Immanence et transcendance. Bruxelles, 1939.
Phil 2733.106 — Guéroult, Martial. Etendue et psychologie chez Malebranche. Paris, 1939.
Phil 181.85 — Guglielmini, H. Temas existenciales. Buenos Aires, 1939.
Phil 8882.59 — Habas, R.A. Morals for moderns. N.Y., 1939.
Phil 182.43.10 — Häberlin, Paul. Naturphilosophische Betrachtungen. Zurich, 1939-1940. 2v.
Phil 3640.280 — Härtle, H. Nietzsche und der Nationalsozialismus. 2e Aufl. München, 1939.
Phil 6952.26 — Hanover Bank, New York. The mental hygiene movement from the philanthropic standpoint. N.Y., 1939.
Phil 8587.54 — Hanse, H. "Gott haben." Berlin, 1939.
Phil 5627.162 — Harms, Ernst. Psychologie und Psychiatrie der Conversion. Leiden, 1939.
Phil 6317.17.5 — Hart, Bernard. Psychopathology; its development and place in medicine. Cambridge, 1939.
Phil 3120.8.92 — Hartlich, C. Die ethischen Theorien Franz Brentanos. Wurzburg, 1939.
Phil 3640.325 — Hauff, R. von. Nietzsches Stellung zur christlichen Demut. Inaug. Diss. Tübingen, 1939.
Phil 365.46 — Heard, G. Pain, sex and time. N.Y., 1939.
Phil 3246.242 — Heekman, H. Fichte und das Christentum. Wurzburg, 1939.
Phil 3425.73.20 — Hegel, Georg Wilhelm Friedrich. La phénoménologie de l'esprit. Paris, 1939-41. 2v.
Phil 182.107 — Heinemann, F. Odysseus oder die Zukunft der Philosophie. Stockholm, 1939.
Phil 3640.284 — Heintel, E. Nietzsches "System" in seinen Grundbegriffen. Leipzig, 1939.
Phil 3640.330 — Heinze, Kurt. Verbrechen und Strafe bei Friedrich Nietzsche. Berlin, 1939.
Phil 5627.160 — Hellpach, W. Übersicht der Religionspsychologie. Leipzig, 1939.
Phil 6317.24 — Henderson, D.K. Psychopathic states. N.Y., 1939.
Phil 5325.28 — Herrick, C.J. Awareness. Philadelphia, 1939.
Phil 5047.36 — Hlučka, F. Das Problem der Logik als Entwicklung des Prinzips der Heterothese. Leipzig, 1939.
Phil 182.88.7A — Hocking, W.E. Types of philosophy. N.Y., 1939.
Phil 4580.20 — Høffding, Harald. Correspondence entre H. Høffding et G. Meyerson. Copenhague, 1939.
Phil 5047.38 — Holmes, R.W. The rhyme of reason; a guide to accurate and mature thinking. N.Y., 1939.
Phil 1955.6.103A — Hook, Sidney. John Dewey. N.Y., 1939.
Phil 6317.9.10 — Hoop, J.H. van der. Conscious orientation. London, 1939.
Phil 75.35 — Hope, R. A guide to readings in philosophy. Ann Arbor, 1939.
Phil 6317.22.5A — Horney, Karen. New ways in psychoanalysis. N.Y., 1939.
Phil 9590.6 — Hudson, J.W. The old faiths perish. N.Y., 1939.
Phil 3450.11.114 — Husserl, Edmund. Erfahrung und Urteil. Prag, 1939.
Phil 182.109 — Huxley, A. Unser Glaube. Stockholm, 1939.
Phil 8958.3 — Inge, W.R. Freedom, love and truth. Boston, 1939?
Phil 5645.46 — Ishihara, S. The series of plates designed as tests for colour-blindness. 8. ed. Tokyo, 1939.
Phil 6990.3.100 — Izard, Francis. The meaning of Lourdes. London, 1939.
Phil 6060.30 — Jacoby, Hans. Analysis of handwriting. London, 1939.
Phil 3801.464 — Jäger, G. Schellings politische Anschauungen. Berlin, 1939.
Phil 5819.7 — Janssens, E. Études de psychologie animale. Paris, 1939.
Phil 530.20.32A — Jones, R.M. The flowering of mysticism. N.Y., 1939.
Phil 6319.1.60 — Jung, C.G. Integration of the personality. N.Y., 1939.
Phil 8700.12 — Kettner, F. The synthesis of science and religion. N.Y., 1939.
Phil 6120.18 — Klatt, F. Lebensmächte. Jena, 1939.
Phil 5250.33 — Konczewski, C. La pensée préconsciente. Paris, 1939.
Phil 810.7 — Kratochvil, J. Rukovet filosofie. Brno, 1939.
Phil 2050.208 — Kruse, F.V. Hume's philosophy in his principal work, a treatise of human nature, and in his essays. London, 1939.
Phil 6320.10.5 — Künkel, Fritz. Die Arbeit am Charakter. Schwerin, 1939.

1939 - cont.

Phil 9035.59.7 — Künkel, Fritz. Einfuhrung in die Charakterkunde auf individualpsychologischer Grundlage. 8. Aufl. Leipzig, 1939.
Phil 185.64 — Künkel, H. Die Lebensalter. Jena, 1939.
Phil 7069.39.57 — Labadié, Jean. Aux frontières de l'au-dela. Paris, 1939.
Phil 6961.17 — Langfeldt, G. The schizophreniform states. Copenhagen, 1939.
Phil 3640.281 — Lefebvre, H. Nietzsche. Paris, 1939.
Phil 3552.9 — Leibniz, Gottfried Wilhelm. Oeuvres choisies. Paris, 1939.
Phil 3552.30.10 — Leibniz, Gottfried Wilhelm. Opuscula philosophica selecta. Paris, 1939.
Phil 4011.2 — Lenoir, E. Trois novateurs. Paris, 1939.
Phil 186.56.5 — Le Senne, R. Introduction à la philosophie. Paris, 1939.
Phil 6321.14 — L'hermitte, J.J. L'image de notre corps. Paris, 1939.
Phil 5251.44.7 — Link, Henry C. The rediscovery of man. N.Y., 1939.
Phil 186.92 — Lins, I.M.de B. Escolas filosoficas. Rio, 1939.
Phil 303.12.25 — Lintz, E.J. The unity of the universe. Fribourg, 1939.
Phil 8591.41 — Litt, Theodor. Protestantisches Geschichtswussteins. Leipzig, 1939.
Phil 3640.279 — Lonsbach, R.M. Friedrich Nietzsche und die Juden. Stockholm, 1939.
Phil 5400.79.5 — Lund, Frederick H. Emotions of men. N.Y., 1939.
Phil 5401.14 — Lunn, H.K. Courage; an anthology. London, 1939.
X Cg Phil 4777.536.100 — Lutosławski, W. Postannictwo polskiego narodu. Warszawa, 1939. (Changed to XP 5137, 3/20/72)
Phil 3494.42 — Maier, J. On Hegel's critique of Kant. N.Y., 1939.
Phil 5822.9.10 — Maier, Norman Raymond Frederick. Studies of abnormal behavior in the rat. N.Y., 1939.
Phil 5252.75 — Mander, A.E. Psychology for everyman. London, 1939.
Phil 2750.11.65 — Maritain, Jacques. Quatre essais sur l'esprit dans sa condition charnelle. Paris, 1939.
Phil 2412.4.7 — Maritain, Jacques. Trois réformateurs; Luther, Descartes, Rousseau. Paris, 1939.
Phil 8592.68 — Mathews, B. Through tragedy to triumph. N.Y., 1939.
Phil 8887.71.5 — Maurois, André. Un art de vivre. Paris, 1939.
Phil 7082.94 — Mégroz, Rodolphe Louis. The dream world. N.Y., 1939.
Phil 6122.61 — Meng, H. Seelischer Gesundheitschutz. Basel, 1939.
Phil 1750.155 — Mercati, G. Ultimi contributi alla storia degli umanisti. pt.1-2. Città del Vaticano, 1939.
Phil 4012.6.5 — Miceli di Serradileo, R. La philosophie contemporaine en Italie. Paris, 1939.
Phil 3640.287 — Michel, W. Nietzsche in unserern Jahrhundert. Berlin, 1939.
Phil 6122.58 — Mikesell, W.H. Mental hygiene. N.Y., 1939.
Phil 343.20 — Miller, H. History and science. Berkeley, 1939.
Phil 5068.5 — Mises, R.E. von. Kleines Lehrbuch des Positivismus. The Hague, 1939.
Phil 6322.26 — Money-Kyrle, R.E. Superstition and society. London, 1939.
Phil 343.21A — Moore, George E. Proof of an external world. London, 1939.
Phil 5252.50.10 — Moore, T.V. Cognitive psychology. Chicago, 1939.
Phil 1135.159 — Moreau, J. L'âme du monde de Platon aux Stoiciens. Thèse. Paris, 1939.
Phil 5252.88 — Mourad, Youssef. L'eveil de l'intelligence. Paris, 1939.
Phil 3425.299 — Müller, G.R. Hegel über Offenbarung. München, 1939.
Phil 6022.5 — Muhammad ibn Umar, Fakhr al-Din. La physiognomonie arabe. Thèse. Paris, 1939.
Phil 2280.5.105 — Munitz, M.K. Moral philosophy of Santayana. N.Y., 1939.
Phil 5252.76 — Munzinger, K.F. Psychology. Denver, 1939.
Phil 188.19 — Nicholson, J.A. Introductory course in philosophy. N.Y., 1939.
Phil 3640.277A — Nietzsche, Friedrich. The living thoughts of Nietzsche. N.Y., 1939.
Phil 6323.7.2 — Noyes, Arthur P. Modern clinical psychiatry. 2d ed. Philadelphia, 1939.
Phil 189.28 — O'Connor, E.M. Potentiality and energy. Diss. Washington, 1939.
Phil 1020.14.5 — O'Leary, DeLacy. Arabic thought and its place in history. London, 1939.
Phil 4190.1.35 — Orestano, Francesco. Idee econcetti. Milano, 1939.
Phil 4190.1.45 — Orestano, Francesco. Nuove vedute logiche. Milano, 1939.
Phil 4190.1.30 — Orestano, Francesco. Nuovi principi. Milano, 1939.
Phil 4190.1.40 — Orestano, Francesco. Il nuovo realismo. Milano, 1939.
Phil 6310.1.93 — Orgler, Hertha. Alfred Adler, the man and his work. London, 1939.
Phil 3834.2 — An outline of the philosophy of Spinoza. Boston, 1939.
Phil 2415.8 — Palmer, R.R. Catholics and unbelievers in eighteenth century France. Princeton, 1939.
Phil 3640.398 — Pannwitz, Rudolf. Nietzsche und die Verwandlung des Menschen. Amsterdam, 1939.
Phil 190.63.7 — Parodi, D. En quête d'une philosophie; la conduite humaine et les valeurs idéales. Paris, 1939.
Phil 2225.9 — Perry, C.M. Toward a dimensional realism. Norman, Okla., 1939.
Phil 5590.9.3 — Plant, James S. Personality and the cultural pattern. N.Y., 1939.
Phil 7069.39.45 — Poortman, Johannes J. Drei Forträge über Philosophie und Parapsychologie. Leiden, 1939.
Phil 5255.43A — Pratt, Carroll C. The logic of modern psychology. N.Y., 1939.
Phil 531.2 — Pratt, James B. Naturalism. New Haven, 1939.
Phil 5255.47A — Pressey, Sidney Leavitt. Life; a psychological survey. 1st ed. N.Y., 1939.
Phil 6965.15 — Preu, P.W. Outline of psychiatric case-study. N.Y., 1939.
Phil 6325.8.16 — Prince, Morton. Clinical and experimental studies in personality. Cambridge, Mass., 1939.
Phil 1020.23.5 — Quadri, G. La filosofia degli arabi nel suo fiore. v.1-2. Firenze, 1939.
Phil 6127.21 — Rasmussen, A.T. The principal nervous pathways. N.Y., 1939.
Phil 8892.56 — Reininger, Robert. Wertphilosophie und Ethik. Leipzig, 1939.
Phil 8707.19 — Riba Elichabe, R. La ciencia confirma a Cristo. Rosario, 1939.
Phil 5400.18.5 — Ribot, T. La psychologie des sentiments. 16. éd. Paris, 1939.
Phil 7069.39.50 — Richmond, K. Evidence of identity. London, 1939.
Phil 7069.38.50 — Richmond, Z. Evidence of purpose. London, 1939.
Phil 348.15 — Riveline, M. Essai sur le problème le plus général, action et logique. Thèse. Paris, 1939.
Phil 5257.28.10 — Roback, A.A. The psychology of common sense. Cambridge, 1939.
Phil 5420.5.11 — Roback, A.A. Varför hämmar jag mig själö? Stockholm, 1939.
Phil 6327.13 — Roberts, Harry. The troubled mind. N.Y., 1939.

1939 - cont.

Phil 8842.10   Rohmer, J. La finalité morale. Paris, 1939.
Phil 192.81   Rolbiecki, J.J. Prospects of philosophy. N.Y., 1939.
Phil 5057.30   Romero, Francisco Argentine. Lógica y nóciones de teoria del concimiento. 2. ed. Buenos Aires, 1939.
Phil 5257.51   Rosett, Joshua. The mechanism of thought. N.Y., 1939.
Phil 8707.20   Ross, W.D. Foundations of ethics. Oxford, 1939.
Phil 102.5   Rozental, Mark Moiseevich. Kratkii filosofskii slovar'. Moskva, 1939.
Phil 1522.6   Ryan, J.K. Basic principles and problems of philosophy. Washington, 1939.
Phil 6327.23   Rylander, G. Personality changes after operations on the frontal lobes. Copenhagen, 1939.
Phil 3500.67   Sander, J. Die Begründung der Notwehr in der Philosophie von Kant und Hegel. Bleicherode, 1939.
Phil 6328.23   Sandström, T. Ist die aggressivität ein übel? Stockholm, 1939.
Phil 193.49.19   Santayana, G. Il pensiero americano e altri saggi. Milano, 1939.
Phil 2880.8.44   Sartre, Jean Paul. Esquisse d'une théorie des émotions. Paris, 1939.
Phil 5258.122   Scheidemann, N.V. Lecture demonstrations for general psychology. Chicago, 1939.
Phil 2280.7.30   Schiller, F.C.S. Our human truths. N.Y., 1939.
Phil 1955.6.101   Schilpp, P.A. The philosophy of John Dewey. Evanston, 1939.
Phil 3850.31   Schmalenbach, H. Geist und Sein. Basel, 1939.
Phil 8419.11   Schneider, E. Aesthetic motive. N.Y., 1939.
Phil 3808.176   Schopenhauer, Arthur. Living thoughts presented by Thomas Mann. N.Y., 1939.
Phil 4065.123   Schwartz, M. Giordano Bruno. Erfurt, 1939.
Phil 185.59.5   Selected writings in philosophy. N.Y., 1939.
Phil 5058.51   Serrus, Charles. Essai sur la signification de la logique. Paris, 1939.
Phil 8520.37   Sertillanges, R.P. Le christianisme et les philosophies. Paris, 1939-41. 2v.
Phil 9070.9   Shurtleft, A.D.K. Lighted candles. Boston, 1939.
Phil 9240.3   Skinner, Clarence R. Human nature, or The nature of evil. Boston, 1939.
Phil 6328.22   Smith, J.C. Psykiatriske forelaesninger. København, 1939.
Phil 3450.27.80   Smits, Everard J.F. Herders humaniteitsphilosophie. Assen, 1939.
Phil 193.150   Spakovski, A. Das menschliche Ich und die Kultur; der psychische Dynamismus und seine Gestaltung der Welt. Novi Sad, 1939.
Phil 3819.36.40   Spinoza, Benedictus de. Etica. Milano, 1939.
Phil 3819.29.30   Spinoza, Benedictus de. The living thoughts of Spinoza. N.Y., 1939.
Phil 3850.5.9   Spir, Afrikan. Saggi di filosofia critica. Firenze, 1939.
Phil 193.157   Stapledon, Olaf. Philosophy and living. v.1-2. Harmondsworth, Eng., 1939.
Phil 5058.46.20   Stebbing, Lizzie S. Thinking to some purpose. Harmondsworth, 1939.
Phil 3246.231   Steinbeck, W. Das Bild des Menschen in der Philosophie Fichtes. München, 1939.
Phil 978.49.170   Steiner, R. Bedeutsames aus dem äusseren Geistesleben um die Mitte des XIX Jahrhunderts. Dornach, 1939.
Phil 978.49.180   Steiner, R. Charakteristisches zur Kennzeichnung der gegenwart Wirklichkeits-Entfremdung. Dornach, 1939.
Phil 978.49.160   Steiner, R. Geschichtliche Notwendigkeit und Freiheit. Dornach, 1939.
Phil 978.49.220   Steiner, R. Rudolf Steiner über Schauspielkunst (eine Fragenbeantwortung). Dornach, 1939.
Phil 978.49.150   Steiner, R. Veröffentlichungen aus dem literarischen Frühwerk. Dornach, 1939-41. 4v.
Phil 8620.42   Steinhausen, H. Die Rolle des Bösen. Stockholm, 1939.
Phil 6328.2.25   Stekel, Wilhelm. Technique of analytical psychotherapy. London, 1939.
Phil 193.130.10   Stocks, J.L. Reason and intuition and other essays. London, 1939.
Phil 349.36   Stumpf, Karl. Erkenntnislehre. Bd. I-II. Leipzig, 1939-1940.
Phil 6328.57   Szumowski, W. Névroses et psychoses au moyen age et au début des temps modernes. Paris, 1939.
Phil 400.98   Tallon, H.J. Concept of self in British and American idealism. Washington, 1939.
Phil 2730.102   Thibaud, Marguerite. L'effort chez Maine de Biran et Bergson. Thèse. Grenoble, 1939.
Phil 1955.6.05A   Thomas, Milton H. Bibliography of John Dewey. 2d ed. N.Y., 1939.
Phil 7069.39.55   Thompson, L.S. Geometric telepathy. Los Angeles, 1939.
Phil 5059.20.5   Thouless, R.H. How to think straight. N.Y., 1939.
Phil 2270.151   Tillet, A.W. Herbert Spencer betrayed. London, 1939.
Phil 1850.131   Tinivella, G. Baconee Locke. Milano, 1939.
Phil 9070.4   Tomlison, W.W. Time out to live. N.Y., 1939.
Phil 6750.235   Town, C.H. Familial feeblemindedness. Buffalo, 1939.
Phil 8674.12   Trueblood, D.E. Knowledge of God. N.Y., 1939.
Phil 5627.155   Trueblood, D.E. The trustworthiness of religious experience. London, 1939.
Phil 6329.12   Turel, Adrien. Bachofen-Freud. Bern, 1939.
Phil 5260.9   United States. Department of Agriculture. Graduate School. The adjustment of personality. Washington, 1939.
Phil 5404.1   Urban, J. L'epithymologie. Paris, 1939.
Phil 4829.860.2   Ušeničnik, Aleš. Izbrani spisi. Ljubljana, 1939-41. 10v.
Phil 9540.1   Van Loon, H.W. Tolerance. N.Y., 1939.
Phil 8896.19   Vasconcelos, J. Etica. 2. ed. Mexico, 1939.
Phil 196.29.3   Vassallo, Angel. Elogio de la vigilia. Buenos Aires, 1939.
Phil 5261.15.25   Vaughan, W.F. General psychology. 1st ed. N.Y., 1939.
Phil 4772.1   Veideman, A. Opravdanie zla. Riga, 1939.
Phil 4260.38   Vico, G.B. Sabiduría primitiva de los italianos. Buenos Aires, 1939.
Phil 4260.35.32   Vico, G.B. Scienza nuova...a cura di G. Flores d'Arcais. 2. ed. Padova, 1939.
Phil 5400.97   Vleugel, E.S. De samenhang tussen psycho-galvanische reflex en grondeigenschappen van het temperament. Proefschrift. Groningen, 1939.
Phil 8601.13A   Voegelin, Eric. Die politischen religionen. Stockholm, 1939.
Phil 2050.216   Volpe, Galvano della. Hume, o Il genio dell'empirismo. Firenze, 1939.
Phil 3450.19.91   Wagner de Peyna, A. de. La ontologia fundamental de Heidegger. Buenos Aires, 1939.
Phil 3450.19.104   Wagner de Reyna, A. La ontologia fundamental de Heidegger. Buenos Aires, 1939.

1939 - cont.

Phil 930.38   Waley, Arthur. Three ways of thought in ancient China. London, 1939.
Phil 6132.34   Wallin, J.E.W. Minor mental maladjustments in normal people. Durham, N.C., 1939.
Phil 7069.38.5A   Warcollur, R. Experimental telepathy. Boston, 1939.
Phil 3246.232   Weischedel, W. Der Aufbruch der Freiheit. Leipzig, 1939.
Phil 6315.2.385   Weiss-Rosmarin, Trude. The Hebrew Moses; an answer to Sigmund Freud. N.Y., 1939.
Phil 3450.11.101   Welch, E.P. Edmund Husserl's phenomenology. Los Angeles, 1939.
Phil 197.63.5   Wenzl, Aloys. Philosophie als Weg von den Grenzen der Wissenschaft au die Grenzen der Religion. Leipzig, 1939.
Phil 8897.69   Westermarck, E. Christianity and morals. N.Y., 1939.
VPhil 5850.386.10   Wheeler, Elmer. Word magic; tested answers to 100 everyday situations. N.Y., 1939.
Phil 5850.385.85   White, Wendell. The psychology of making life interesting. N.Y., 1939.
Phil 3504.43   Whitney, G.T. The heritage of Kant. Princeton, 1939.
Phil 9182.7   Wicks, Robert R. One operation and another. N.Y., 1939.
Phil 3640.694   Wilhelm, J. Friedrich Nietzsche und der französische Geist. Hamburg, 1939.
Phil 6132.35   Winkler, J.K. Mind explorers. N.Y., 1939.
Phil 5627.174   Witwicki, Władisław. La foi des éclairés. Paris, 1939.
Phil 9590.7   Wood, F.H. This Egyptian miracle. Philadelphia, 1939.
Phil 8602.47.10   Wright, Ronald S. Asking why. London, 1939.
Phil 930.7.55   Zach, E. von. Einige Verbesserungen zu Forke's Geschichte der chinesischen Philosophie. Batavia, 1939.
Phil 4326.1   Zambrano, M. Pensamiento y poesía en la vida española. México, 1939.
Phil 4825.14   Zeremski, Sava D. Essays aus der südslawischen Philosophie. Novisad, 1939.
Phil 200.13   Zocher, R. Die philosophische Grundlehre. Tübingen, 1939.

194-

Phil 3450.42   Ball, Thomas. Paul Leopold Hoffner als Philosophie. Mainz? 194-?
Phil 4710.135   Bashilov, B. Pravye i levye, blizkie i dal'nie. Buenos Aires, 194-?
Phil 8581.94   Berdiaev, N.A. Khristianstvo i aktivnaia uslovnost'. Parizh, 194-?
Phil 575.142   Berdiaev, N.A. O rabstve i svobode cheloveka. Paris, 194-.
Phil 3246.45.20   Fichte, Johann Gottlieb. Grundriss des Eigenthümlichen der Wissenschaftslehre in Rücksicht. Leipzig, 194-.
Phil 182.94.18   Hartmann, N. Neue Wege der Ontologie. Stuttgart, 194-.
Phil 2070.25.5   James, William. The philosophy of William James, selected from his chief works. N.Y., 194-.
Phil 575.145   Kern, Hans. Die Masken der Siecle. Leipzig, 194-.
Phil 4752.2.80   Lampert, Evengu. Nicolas Berdyaev and the new middle ages. London, 194-.
Phil 5585.82A   Mayo, Elton. Achieving sanity in the modern world. Cambridge, Mass., 194-?
Phil 187.129   Morrish, Furze. Outline of metaphysics. London, 194-.
Phil 6053.12.10   Nelson, Edith Halforel. Out of the silence. London, 194-?
Phil 8595.15.23   Paine, Thomas. Age of reason. N.Y., 194-?
Phil 3808.73   Schopenhauer, Arthur. Die wahren Güter des Lebens. München, 194-?
Phil 7069.38.59   Thomas, Charles D. Beyond life's sunset. London, 194-.
Phil 7069.38.58.5   Thomas, Charles D. In the dawn beyond death. London, 194-.

1940

Phil 6315.2.116   Seguin, C.A. Freud, un gran explorador del alma. Buenos Aires, 1940.
Phil 5590.1   Abaunza, A. Los valores psicologicos de la personalidad. Mexico, 1940.
Phil 3808.177   Adams, J.S. The aesthetics of pessimism. Philadelphia, 1940.
Phil 5240.39.15   Agramonte y Richardo, R. Tratado de psicología general. v.1-2, pt.1. 4a ed. Habana, 1940.
Phil 800.10   Akademiia Nauk SSSR. Institut Filosofii. Istoriia filosofii. Moskva, 1940-1941. 2v.
Phil 8655.11   Albright, W.F. From the stone age to Christianity. Baltimore, 1940.
Phil 9590.1   Alder, V.S. The fifth dimension. London, 1940.
Phil 8580.3.2   Allen, E. Reason, the only oracle of man. N.Y., 1940.
Phil 6315.2.114   Allers, R. The successful error; a critical study of Freudian psychoanalysis. N.Y., 1940.
Phil 6110.17   Association for Research in Nervous and Mental Diseases. The hypothalamus and central levels of autonomic function. Baltimore, 1940.
Phil 5068.6   Ayer, A.J. Foundations of empirical knowledge. London, 1940.
Phil 8581.80   Baillie, James. Spiritual religion. London, 1940.
Phil 5241.101   Baker, H.J. The art of understanding. Boston, 1940.
Phil 1106.1.7   Bakewell, C.M. Source book in ancient philosphy. N.Y., 1940.
Phil 86.3.10   Baldwin, J.M. Dictionary of philosophy. v.2. N.Y., 1940.
Phil 5241.107   Barboza, Enrique. Psicologia. Lima, 1940.
Phil 6311.24   Barker, L.F. Psychotherapy. N.Y., 1940.
Phil 9070.7   Bartlett, A.C. Find your own frontier. Boston, 1940.
Phil 4352.1.60   Baucells Serra, Ramón. Balmes y el nacionalismo espanol. Vich, 1940.
Phil 575.139   Baudouin, Charles. Découverte de la personne, esquisse d'un personnalisme analytique. Paris, 1940.
Phil 6480.160   Baynes, H.G. Mythology of the soul. Baltimore, 1940.
Phil 8581.81A   Bellamy, E. The religion of solidarity. Yellow Springs, 1940.
Phil 2475.1.50.8   Bergson, Henri. L'évolution créatrice. 52. éd. Paris, 1940.
Phil 8581.79   Bewkes, E.G. Experience, reason and faith. N.Y., 1940.
Phil 3821.23   Bidney, David. Psychology and ethics of Spinoza. New Haven, 1940.
Phil 1905.15   Blanshard, B. The nature of thought. N.Y., 1940. 2v.
Phil 5041.15.3   Boole, George. The laws of thought. Chicago, 1940.
Phil 6951.25   Boss, M. Körperliches Kranksein als Folge seelischer Gleichgewichtsstörungen. Bern, 1940.
Phil 6990.45   Boyle, J.L. A pictorial history of Lourdes. Philadelphia, 1940.
Phil 3890.10.100   Brachmann, W. Ernst Troeltschs historische Weltanschauung. Halle, 1940.
Phil 4065.124   Brandt, C. Giordano Bruno. Buenos Aires, 1940.
Phil 801.33   Bréhier, É. La philosophie et son passé. Paris, 1940.
Phil 6625.6   Bright, Timothy. A treatise of melancholie. N.Y., 1940.

1940 - cont.

Phil 8581.67.5   Brightman, E.S. A philosophy of religion. N.Y., 1940.
Phil 5241.28.4   Brown, W. Essentials of mental measurement. 4. ed. Cambridge, Eng., 1940.
Phil 3120.15.30   Brunner, Constantin. Kunst, Philosophie, Mystik, Gesammelte Anfsätze. Zürich, 1940.
Phil 9590.5   Bryan, G.B. Psychic dictatorship in America. Los Angeles, 1940.
Phil 176.147   Bryan, W.L. Wars of families of minds. New Haven, 1940.
Phil 6615.18   Buess, Heinrich. Die Wandlungen des Psychogenie- Begriffs. Inaug. Diss. Hölstein, 1940.
Phil 5274.8   Burt, Cyril. The factors of the mind. London, 1940.
Phil 5811.15.15   Buytendijk, Frederik Jacobus Johannes. Wege zum Verständnis der Tiere. Zürich, 1940?
Phil 8403.36   Camón, Aznar J. El arte desde su esencia. Zaragoza, 1940.
Phil 5425.90   Carroll, H.A. Genius in the making. N.Y., 1940.
Phil 8582.19.5   Carver, T.N. The religion worth having. Los Angeles, 1940.
Phil 6805.6   Cattell, Raymond Bernard. Crooked personalities in childhood and after. N.Y., 1940.
Phil 8582.51.10   Chaning-Pearce, Melville. The terrible crystal; studies in Kierkegaard and modern Christianity. London, 1940.
Phil 4353.5   Chavarri B., Misael. Diez y siete divagaciones. Santiago de Chile, 1940. 2v.
Phil 8582.53   Churchill, W. The uncharted way. Philadelphia, 1940.
Phil 5042.30   Churchman, C.W. Elements of logic. Phildelphia, 1940.
Phil 5812.8   Claremont, C.A. The innumerable instincts of man. London, 1940.
Phil 165.4   Clark, G.H. Selections from Hellenistic philosophy. N.Y., 1940.
Phil 8610.940.1   Cohen, Morris. Almost an autobiography. London, 1940.
Phil 8877.76.5   Colesanti, Giulio. La morale supérieure. Paris, 1940.
Phil 177.85.2   Collingwood, R.G. An essay on metaphysics. Oxford, 1940.
Phil 525.90   Collins, J.B. Christian mysticism. Baltimore, 1940.
Phil 177.99   Compton, A.H. Human meaning of science. Chapel Hill, 1940.
Phil 5042.23.8   Cotter, Anthony C. Logic and epistemology. Boston, 1940.
Phil 1507.4   Coulton, G.G. Studies in medieval thought. London, 1940.
Phil 3822.10   Cresson, André. Spinoza. Paris, 1940.
Phil 333.14PF   Custard, Harry L. The unity of knowledge and the organization of thought. Washington, D.C., 1940.
Phil 3160.11.5   Cysarz, Herbert. Das Unsterbliche. Halle, 1940.
Phil 178.67   Donat, Joseph. Ontologia. 9. ed. Oeniponte, 1940.
Phil 8430.11A   Dudley, Louise. The humanities. 1. ed. N.Y., 1940. 2v.
Phil 672.136.25   Dunne, John W. Nothing dies. London, 1940.
Phil 5780.10   Dupuis, Léon. Les aboulies sociales, le scrupule, la timidité, la susceptibilité, l'autoritarisme. Paris, 1940.
Phil 7069.40.12   Eaton, A.K. A message to a troubled world. Clarmont, Calif., 1940.
Phil 3200.8.20   Ehrlich, W. Ontologie des Bewusstseins. Zürich, 1940.
Phil 665.67   Ellis, W. The idea of the soul. London, 1940.
Phil 8584.19   Espinosa, G. La mascarada cristiana. Santiago de Chile, 1940.
Phil 7069.40.6A   Extra-sensory perception after 60 years. N.Y., 1940.
Phil 186.95.5   Fadiman, Clifton. I believe. London, 1940.
Phil 3450.11.115A   Farber, Marvin. Philosophical essays in memory of Edmund Husserl. Cambridge, 1940.
Phil 5520.82   Fauré-Frémiet, P. La recréation du réel et l'équivoque. Paris, 1940.
Phil 2805.224   Finch, D. La critique philosophique de Pascal au XVIIIe siècle. Diss. Philadelphia, 1940.
Phil 4073.97   Firpo, Luigi. Bibliografia degli scritti di Tommaso Campanella. Torino, 1940.
Phil 990.23   Foroughi, A.H. Systeme de philosophie dynamo synthetique. Paris, 1940. 2v.
Phil 5815.6   Fraenkel, G.S. The orientation of animals. Oxford, Eng., 1940.
Phil 6315.2   Freud, Sigmund. Gesammelte Werke. v. 1-14,16-18. London, 1940-46. 16v.
Phil 1182.15   Fritz, K. Pythagorean politics in southern Italy. N.Y., 1940.
Phil 3640.290   Furstenthal, Achim. Maske und Scham bei Nietzsche. Diss. Basel, 1940.
Phil 4115.105   Fusco, Maria. Vincenzo Gioberti, critico letterario. Catania, 1940.
Phil 1111.7   Gaos, José. Antologia filosofica; la filosofia griega. México, 1940.
Phil 6990.48   García Aceituno, José Luis. Esquípulas. 1. ed. Jalapa, 1940.
Phil 4357.3.32   Garcia Bacca, J.D. Inoitacion a filosofar. v.1-2. Mexico, 1940-42.
Phil 7084.4   Garma, Angel. Psicoanálisis de los sueños. Buenos Aires, 1940.
Phil 8881.69   Garnett, C.B. Wisdom in conduct. N.Y., 1940.
Phil 4006.2.18   Gentile, G. Il pensiero italiano del rinascimento. 3. ed. Firenze, 1940.
Phil 6420.36.1   Gifford, Mabel F. Correcting nervous speech disorders. N.Y., 1940.
Phil 6420.36.5   Gifford, Mabel F. How to overcome stammering. N.Y., 1940.
Phil 181.74.5   Gilson, E. Metaphysics in modern times. Chicago, 1940.
Phil 1511.3.13.5A   Gilson, Étienne. The spirit of mediaeval philosophy. N.Y., 1940.
Phil 1158.35   Giuffrida, Pasquale. L'epicureismo nella letteratura latina nel I secolo a.c. Torino, 1940. 2v.
Phil 9380.2A   Glover, E. The psychology of fear and courage. Harmondsworth, Eng., 1940.
Phil 6316.12   Glover, Edward. An investigation of the technique of psycho-analysis. Baltimore, 1940.
Phil 3640.283   Goday, V. Bersanelli. Humanidad. Buenos Aires, 1940.
Phil 5246.52A   Goldstein, K. Human nature. Cambridge, 1940.
Phil 6316.11A   Gontard, G.V. In defense of love; a protest against "soul surgery" N.Y., 1940.
Phil 287.5   Grant Watson, E.L. Man and his universe. London, 1940.
Phil 9590.12   Greene, Alice. The philosophy of silence. N.Y., 1940.
Phil 8696.17   Gregory, R.A. Religion in science and civilization. London, 1940.
Phil 3110.95   Grunsky, H.A. Jakob Böhme als Schöpfer einer germanischen Philosophie des Willens. Hamburg, 1940.
Phil 5246.47.8   Guilford, Joy Paul. Fields of psychology. N.Y., 1940.
Phil 5816.13   Guillaume, P. La psychologie animale. Paris, 1940.
Phil 4467.1.30   Guimarães, M. A grand concepção de Deus. Rio, 1940.
Phil 4372.1.87   Gutiérrez, Alberto. El pensamiento filosófico de Juan Luis Vives. Buenos Aires, 1940.
Phil 2515.8.80   Guy, Alain. Métaphysique et intuition; le message de Jacques Chevalier. Paris, 1940.

1940 - cont.

Phil 5850.235   Harwood, Sumner. How to work with people. Cambridge, 1940.
Phil 2050.217   Heinemann, Fritz. David Hume. Paris, 1940.
Phil 7069.40.19   Hendrickson, R.J. Divine science and metaphysics. N.Y., 1940.
Phil 3850.27.105   Henrich, R. They thought he was mad; Albert Schweitzer.
Phil 7069.40.4   Hettinger, John. The ultra-perceptive faculty. London, 1940.
Phil 5204.20   Hinsée, Leland Earl. Psychiatric dictionary, with encyclopedic treatment of modern terms. N.Y., 1940.
Phil 8587.62   Hirschmann, Eva. Phänomenologie der Religion. Proefschrift. Würzburg, 1940.
Phil 2045.52.15   Hobbes, Thomas. Leviathan. London, 1940.
Phil 7069.40.16   Hole, C. Haunted England. London, 1940.
Phil 5047.39   Holmes, R.W. Exercises in reasoning, with an outline of logic. N.Y., 1940.
Phil 5247.59   Hook, A. The human mind. London, 1940.
Phil 7069.40.14   Hort, Gertrude M. Three famous occultists: Dr. John Dee. Photoreproducton. Philadelphia, 1940.
Phil 9070.11   Hostel, G. Out of the wilderness. N.Y., 1940.
Phil 182.108   Howells, T.H. Hunger for wholiness. Denver, 1940.
Phil 978.5.9.25   Hyat, T.P. A check list of some books and authors. Stanford, 1940.
Phil 5247.13.28   Iriarte, Mauricio de. El Doctor Huarte de San Juan y su examen de ingenios. Madrid, 1940.
Phil 9425.5   Ironside, Henry A. The way of peace. N.Y., 1940.
Phil 8589.18   James, E.O. Social functions of religion. Nashville, 1940.
Phil 8959.4   Jessof, T.E. Law and love. London, 1940.
Phil 3829.1.7   Joachim, H.H. Spinoza's Tractus. Oxford, 1940.
Phil 184.26.20   Joad, C.E.M. Philosophy for our time. London, 1940.
Phil 3491.10   Jones, W.T. Morality and freedom in...Kant. London, 1940.
Phil 75.47   Joó, Tibor. Magyar nyelvu filozófiai kézúratók a Széchenyi Könyitárban. Budapest, 1940.
Phil 291.15   Kafka, Gustav. Naturgesetz, Freiheit und Wunder. Paderborn, 1940.
Phil 6320.12   Kahn, S. Psychological and neurological definitions and the unconcious. Boston, 1940.
Phil 3480.25.55   Kant, Immanuel. The living thoughts of Kant. N.Y., 1940.
Phil 9070.8   Kern, J.H. Do something about it! N.Y., 1940.
Phil 6990.41   Keyes, F.P.W. (Mrs.). The sublime shepherdess; the life of St. Bernadette of Lourdes. N.Y., 1940.
Phil 978.77.3   King, G.R. The "I am" discourses. 2d ed. Chicago, 1940.
Phil 3640.520   Klein, Werner. Nietzsches Kampf gegen den göttlichen Zwang. Stuttgart, 1940.
Phil 5250.15.16   Köhler, Wolfgang. Dynamics in psychology. N.Y., 1940.
Phil 978.59.7   Krishnamurti, J. Authentic notes of discussions and talks given by Kris at Ojai and Sarabia. Hollywood, 1940.
Phil 8701.18   Laffey, C. Religion and science. London, 1940.
Phil 2490.134   Lagarrigue, L. La paz del mundo y la alianza universal de las doctrinas. Santiago de Chile, 1940.
Phil 186.96   Laird, J. The limits of speculative humanism. London, 1940.
Phil 8666.13   Laird, John. Theism and cosmology. London, 1940.
Phil 8591.42   Lamm, H. The relation of concept and demonstration in the ontological argument. Chicago, 1940.
Phil 2520.211   Landerry, P.C.R. Descartes y su vida, su obra, su pensamiento. México, 1940.
Phil 8412.9   Landmann, E. Grundzüge einer Lehre vom Schönen. Basel, 1940.
Phil 5360.10   Laporte, J.M.F. Le problème de l'abstraction. Paris, 1940.
Phil 9070.1   Lappin, M.M. Let us talk about you. N.Y., 1940.
Phil 292.11   Lavrov, A.S. V poiskakh istiny. Paris, 1940.
Phil 3640.281.5   Lefebvre, H. Nietzsche. Mexico, 1940.
Phil 3552.78.40   Leibniz, Gottfried Wilhelm. Leibniz korrespondiert mit Paris. Hamburg, 1940.
Phil 5221.1   Levine, A.J. Current psychologies. Cambridge, 1940.
Phil 6121.29   Liber, B. Your mental health. N.Y., 1940.
Phil 8961.12   Lindsay, A.D. The two moralities: our duty to God and society. London, 1940.
Phil 5110.1   MacDougall, C.D. Hoaxes. N.Y., 1940.
Phil 8592.48.5   Macintosh, D.C. The problem of religious knowledge. N.Y., 1940.
Phil 5627.161   McKenzie, J.G. Psychology, psychotherapy and evangelicalism. London, 1940.
Phil 575.100   McMorrow, G.J. A metaphysical study on the individual and the person. Diss. Notre Dame, 1940.
Phil 187.122   MacTaggart, M. Man, mind and psychology. London, 1940.
Phil 1117.10   Maddalena, Antonio. Sulla cosmologia ionica da talete a eraclita. Padova, 1940.
Phil 6990.43   Major, R.H. Faiths that healed. N.Y., 1940.
Phil 187.143.5   Mallik, B.K. The real and the negative. London, 1940.
Phil 4972.5.50   Malmurca Sánchez, Ernesto. Para una posición argentina. La Plata, 1940.
Phil 1200.43   Mancini, Guido. L'etica stoica da Zenone a Crisippo. Padova, 1940.
Phil 2750.11.53   Maritain, Jacques. A preface to metaphysics. N.Y., 1940.
Phil 2750.11.76   Maritain, Jacques. Scholasticism and politics. N.Y., 1940.
Phil 2750.11.57.5   Maritain, Jacques. Science and wisdom. N.Y., 1940.
Phil 187.120   Markakis, A. A new philosophy and the philosophical sciences. N.Y., 1940. 2v.
Phil 8592.60   Martin, Cecil Percy. The decline of religion. London, 1940.
Phil 5253.11   Mason, Phillips. The X of psychology. Cambridge, 1940.
Phil 4372.1.90   Mateu y Llopez, F. Catálogo de la exposición bibliográfica celebrada con motivo del IV centenario de la muerte de Luis Vives. Barcelona, 1940.
Phil 5066.7   Mathematics-deductive theory of rate learning. New Haven, 1940.
Phil 2520.216   Mattei, André. L'homme de Descartes. Paris, 1940.
Phil 8887.71   Maurois, André. The art of living. 5. ed. N.Y., 1940.
Phil 2855.6.80   Mélanges de théologie et de philosophie offerts à Arnold Reymond. Lausanne, 1940.
Phil 1955.6.107   Mendoza de Montero, A. Líneas fundamentales de la filosofia de John Dewey. Buenos Aires, 1940.
Phil 9590.13   Menendez Samara, A. Fanatismo y misticismo. México, 1940.
Phil 525.145   Merkel, Rudolph Franz. Die Mystik im Kulturleben der Völker. Hamburg, 1940.
Phil 4012.6.10   Miceli di Serradileo, R. La filosofia italiana actual. Buenos Aires, 1940.
Phil 9380.8   Miller, D.C. The morale of adults. Thesis. Menasha, Wis., 1940.
Phil 6962.25   Miller, E. The neurosis in war. N.Y, 1940.

1940 - cont.

Phil 5252.80   Mira y Lopez E. Problemas psicologicos actuales. Buenos Aires, 1940.

Phil 2555.7.93   Molle, Germaine van. La philosophie de Paul Decoster. Bruxelles, 1940.

Phil 187.33.10   Montague, W.P. The ways of things: a philosophy of knowledge, nature, and value. N.Y., 1940.

Phil 2520.212   Monteiro de Barros Lius, Ivan. Descartes. Rio de Janeiro, 1940.

Phil 187.121   Moore, E.C. The essence of the matter. Berkeley, 1940.

Phil 165.2A   Muelder, Walter G. The development of American philosophy. Boston, 1940.

Phil 5425.72   Müller, Willy. Genie und Talent. München, 1940.

Phil 2295.90   Muff, Margrit. Leibnizenz kritik der Reliogionsphilosophie von John Toland. Abhandlung. Affoltern, 1940.

Phil 3425.302   Mure, G.R.G. Introduction to Hegel. Oxford, 1940.

Phil 187.119   Murray, G. Stoic, Christian and humanist. London, 1940.

Phil 3245.86   Najdanović, D. Die Geschichtsphilosophie Immanuel Hermann Fichtes. Berlin, 1940.

Phil 3245.86.2   Najdanović, D. Die Geschichtsphilosophie Immanuel Hermann Fichtes. Berlin, 1940.

Phil 3640.53.5   Nietzsche, Friedrich. Der Antichrist. 2. Aufl. Berlin, 1940.

Phil 3640.27   Nietzsche, Friedrich. Das Vermächtnis Friedrich Nietzsches. Salzburg, 1940.

Phil 3640.440   Noll, Baldwin. Das Wesen von Friedrich Nietzsches Idealismus. Köln, 1940.

Phil 1900.92   Norton, William J. Bishop Butler, moralist and divine. New Brunswick, 1940.

Phil 4073.99   Orestano, F. Tommaso Campanella. Roma, 1940.

Phil 4365.2.42   Ortega y Gasset, José. Ideas y creencias. Buenos Aires, 1940.

Phil 8964.3   Osborne, A.R. Christian ethics. London, 1940.

Phil 2200.1   Otto, Max Carl. The human enterprise. N.Y., 1940.

Phil 7069.40.15   Palmstierna, E.K. Widening horizons. London, 1940.

Phil 2805.25.50A   Pascal, Blaise. The living thoughts of Pascal. N.Y., 1940.

Phil 2225.5.25   Peirce, C.S. The philosophy of Peirce; selected writings. London, 1940.

Phil 9070.2   Perley, R.N. Today you are a man. Omaha, 1940.

Phil 1955.6.106   The philosopher of the common man; essays in honor of John Dewey to celebrate his 80th birthday. N.Y., 1940.

Phil 8640.13   Pilcher, C.V. The hereafter in Jewish and Christian thought. London, 1940.

Phil 978.78   Plummer, L.G. From atom to kosmos. Point Loma, 1940.

Phil 346.13   Pos, Hendrik J. Filosofie der Wetenschappen. Arnhem, 1940.

Phil 6965.16   Preston, G.H. Psychiatry for the curious. N.Y., 1940.

Phil 2050.209   Price, H.H. Hume's theory of the external world. Oxford, 1940.

Phil 4372.1.120   Puigdollers Oliver, Mariano. La filosofía española de Luis Vives. Barcelona, 1940.

Phil 165.9   Les quarante années scientifique de Theophile Boreas. Athénes, 1940. 2v.

Phil 126.5   Quiles, Ismael. Gráficos de historia de la filosofía. Buenos Aires, 1940.

Phil 5066.11   Quine, Willard van Orman. Mathematical logic. N.Y., 1940.

Phil 4979.5.30   Ramos, Samuel. Hacia un nuevo humanismo. 1. ed. México, 1940.

Phil 6327.12.9   Reik, Theodor. Aus Leiden Freuden. London, 1940.

Phil 6315.2.115A   Reik, Theodor. From thirty years with Freud. N.Y., 1940.

Phil 5257.55   Rexroad, Carl N. Psychology and personality development. Boston, 1940.

Phil 1020.4.30   Reyes, A. Averroes y Lulio. Caracas, 1940.

Phil 8597.46   Richardson, Robert D. Christian belief and practice. London, 1940.

Phil 8610.940.5   Richberg, Donald. G. Hovah explains. Washington, 1940.

Phil 75.33   Riedl, J.O. A catalogue of Renaissance philosophers. Milwaukee, 1940.

Phil 4372.1.93   Ríos Sarmiento, Juan. Juan Luis Vives. 1. ed. Madrid, 1940.

Phil 4972.5.55   Romero, Francisco. Alejandro Korn. Buenos Aires, 1940.

Phil 3640.307   Roos, Carl Nissen. Nietzsche und das Labyrinth. Copenhagen, 1940.

Phil 348.16   Roque Pascual, R. Logical analysis of fictionalism with respect to the theory of truth. Chicago, Ill., 1940.

Phil 1885.88   Ross, R.G. Scepticism and dogma; a study in philosophy of F.H. Bradley. N.Y., 1940.

Phil 2150.12.80   Ross, W.D. John Henry Muirhead. London, 1940?

Phil 102.5.2   Rozental, Mark Moiseevich. Kratkii filosofskii slovar'. Moskva, 1940.

Phil 8597.45   Rüssel, H.W. Gestalt eines christlichen Humanismus. Amsterdam, 1940.

Phil 720.32   Ruja, H. A critique of the postulational theory of the a priori. Diss. Princeton, 1940.

Phil 3018.7.7   Santayana, G. Egotism in German philosophy. N.Y., 1940.

Phil 193.49.39.8A   Santayana, G. The realm of spirit. N.Y., 1940.

Phil 5465.35.10   Sartre, Jean P. L'imaginaire. Paris, 1940.

Phil 5465.35.5   Sartre, Jean P. L'imagination; psychologie. Paris, 1940.

Phil 6990.42   Saunders, E. Lourdes. N.Y., 1940.

Phil 3890.11   Schabad, M. Die Wiederenteleskung des ich in der Metaphysik Teichmüllers. Basel, 1940.

Phil 5590.4   Schettler, C.H. Problems of personality traits. Chicago, 1940.

Phil 2280.5.106   Schilpp, P.A. The philosophy of Santayana. Evanston, 1940.

Phil 665.69.5   Schleich, C.L. Die Wunder der Seele. Berlin, 1940.

Phil 3850.33   Schramm, A. Philosophische Studien zum Begriff der Entscheidung. Inaug. Diss. Berlin, 1940.

Phil 193.156   Schubart, W. Geistige Wandlung. Luzern, 1940.

Phil 3850.27.30   Schweitzer, A. Waffen des Lichts. 1. Aufl. Heilbronn, 1940.

Phil 4225.7   Severgnini, D. L'interiorità teologica dello storicismo. Roma, 1940. 3v.

Phil 7069.40.10   Seymour, C.J. This spiritualism. London, 1940.

Phil 4809.779.80   Shaw, Nellie. A Czech philosopher on the Cotswolds...Francis Sedlák. London, 1940.

Phil 6128.13.9A   Sherrington, C.S. Man on his nature. Cambridge, 1940.

Phil 6049.40   Sigurðson, J.S. Hördin min og höndin in. Reykjavík, 1940.

Phil 7069.40.7   Sitwell, S. Poltergeists. London, 1940.

Phil 9070.3   Smith, G.W. Constructive human relationship. Kutztown, Pa., 1940.

Phil 165.1   Smith, T.V. From Descartes to Kant. Chicago, 1940.

Phil 4319.1.5   Solana, Marcial. Historia de la filosofía española. Madrid, 1940-41. 3v.

Phil 5258.125.5   Soria, T.D. Psicología. 4. ed. México, 1940.

1940 - cont.

Phil 3819.36.70   Spinoza, Benedictus de. Etica. Madrid, 1940.

Phil 193.154   Stace, W.T. The nature of the world; an essay in phenomenalist metaphysics. Princeton, 1940.

Phil 6128.50   Strecker, E.A. Beyond the clinical frontiers. N.Y., 1940.

Phil 299.24   Strömberg, G. The soul of the universe. Philadelphia, 1940.

Phil 2475.1.298   Sundén, Hjalmar. La théorie bergsonienne de la religion. Thèse. Uppsala, 1940.

Phil 5628.55.11   Teodorowicz, Józef. Mystical phenomena in the life of Theresa Neumann. St. Louis, Mo., 1940.

Phil 5259.7.20   Thorndike, E.L. Human nature and the social order. N.Y., 1940.

Phil 2045.120   Thorpe, C.D. The aesthetic theory of Thomas Hobbes. Ann Arbor, 1940.

Phil 5259.30   Tiffin, J. The psychology of normal people. Boston, 1940.

Phil 8894.31   Törngren, P.H. Moralsjukdomen. Stockholm, 1940.

Phil 9245.55A   Trinkhaus, C.E. Adversity's noblemen. N.Y., 1940.

Phil 7069.40.8   Tweedale, C.L. News from the next world. London, 1940.

Phil 196.28   Varela, F. Lecciones de filosofia. Havana, 1940.

Phil 196.27.5   Vasconcelos, J. Manual de filosofia. Mexico, 1940.

Phil 4983.1.30   Vaz Ferreira, Carlos. Fermentario. Buenos Aires, 1940.

Phil 2520.209   Versfeld, M. An essay on the metaphysics of Descartes. London, 1940.

Phil 4260.23   Vico, G.B. Scritti vari e pagine sparse. Bari, 1940.

Phil 5401.16   Watkins, D.E. Stage fright and what to do about it. Boston, 1940.

Phil 5262.45.10   Weatherhead, L.D. Psychology and life. N.Y., 1940.

Phil 5062.35   Weil, R. The art of practical thinking. N.Y., 1940.

Phil 3850.8.85   Weindel, Phil. Das Verhältnis von Glauben und Wissen in der Theologie Franr Anton Staudenmaiers. Düsseldorf, 1940.

Phil 5832.15A   Werner, Heinz. Comparative psychology of mental development. N.Y., 1940.

Phil 5262.36.2   Wheeler, R.H. The science of psychology. N.Y., 1940.

Phil 7069.40.13   White, S.E. The unobstructed universe. N.Y., 1940.

Phil 1955.6.109   White, Stephen, S. A comparison of the philosophies of F.C.S. Schiller and John Dewey. Thesis. Chicago, 1940.

Phil 8972.9   Widgery, A.G. Christian ethics in history and modern life. N.Y., 1940.

Phil 8602.45   Wiley, H.O. Christian theology. Kansas City, 1940-41. 2v.

Phil 9070.5   Wilson, F.T. These three alone. N.Y., 1940.

Phil 9070.10   Wilson, M. Make up your mind. N.Y., 1940.

Phil 735.243   Wittmann, M. Die moderne Wertethik. Münster, 1940.

Phil 8423.23   Woelfflin, H. Das Erklären von Kunstwerken. Köln, 1940.

Phil 197.70   Woltereck, Richard. Ontologie des Lebendigen. Stuttgart, 1940.

Phil 7069.40.17   Wood, E.C. The "how" of divine revelation. Camden, N.J., 1940.

Phil 353.17   Wood, L. The analysis of knowledge. London, 1940.

Phil 197.23.15   Woodbridge, F.J.E. An essay on nature. N.Y., 1940.

Phil 5262.9.25   Woodworth, R.S. Psychology. 4th ed. N.Y., 1940.

Phil 8604.2   Younghusband, F.E. Vital religion. London, 1940.

1941

Phil 4235.1.97   Abbagnano, Nicola. Bernardino Telesio. Milano, 1941.

Phil 5066.28   Ackermann, W. Ein System der typenfreien Logik. Pt.1. Leipzig, 1941-

Phil 8875.27   Adler, Mortimer Jerome. A dialectic of morals. Notre Dame, 1941.

Phil 6110.3.15   Alexander, F.M. The universal constant in living. N.Y., 1941.

Phil 10.47.3   The American journal of orthopsychiatry. Index. Menasha, Wis., 1941-1952. 2v.

Phil 6980.38.10   American Psychiatric Association. Biographical directory of fellows and members of the American Psychiatric Association. N.Y., 1941.

Phil 5590.6   Angyal, Andras. Foundations for a science of personality. N.Y., 1941.

Phil 281.12   Antieke en moderne kosmologie. Arnhem, 1941.

Phil 4351.2.5   Arias, Alejandro C. Estudios literarios y filosóficos. Montevideo, 1941.

Phil 4301.1   Avelino, Andres. Prolegomenos a la unica metafisica posible. Ciudad Trujillo, 1941.

Phil 1200.10.6   Barth, P. Die Stoa. 5. Aufl. Stuttgart, 1941.

Phil 5643.103   Bartley, S. Howard. Vision. N.Y., 1941.

Phil 332.27   Bechert, R. Eine Semiphilosophie im Grundriss Dargestellt. München, 1941.

Phil 2475.1.269   Béguin, Albert. Henri Bergson. Essais et témoignages inédits recueilles. Neuchâtel, 1941.

Phil 176.160.5   Bense, Max. Einleitung in die Philosophie. München, 1941.

Phil 665.72   Berdiaev, N.A. Dukh i real'nost'. Paris, 1941-.

Phil 3450.11.119   Berger, Gaston. Le cogito dans la philosophie de Husserl. Paris, 1941.

Phil 332.23   Berger, Gaston. Recherches sur les conditions de la connaissance. Paris, 1941.

Phil 2475.1.60.4   Bergson, Henri. Matière et mémoire. 36. éd. Paris, 1941.

Phil 2475.1.65.2   Bergson, Henri. La pensée et le mouvant. 12. éd. Paris, 1941.

Phil 2475.1.69   Bergson, Henri. La rire. 57. éd. Paris, 1941.

Phil 5850.135.30   Bingham, Walter van Dyke. How to interview. 3. ed. N.Y., 1941.

Phil 6311.20.5   Bisch, L.E. Why be shy? N.Y., 1941.

Phil 2340.10.100   Blyth, J.W. Whitehead's theory of knowledge. Providence, R.I., 1941.

Phil 3808.188   Borch, Rudolf. Schopenhauer. Boston, 1941.

Phil 5241.105   Boris, J.S. Anselme. Le bonheur s'apprend. 2. éd. Montreal, 1941.

Phil 332.22   Bowers, David F. Atomism, empiricism, and scepticism. Abstract of thesis. Princeton, 1941.

Phil 8581.84   Bradshaw, M.J. Philosophical foundations of faith. N.Y., 1941.

Phil 8691.26   Bragg, W. Science and faith. London, 1941.

Phil 3821.24   Brandt, C. Spinoza y el panteismo. Buenos Aires, 1941.

Phil 3805.183   Brandt, R.B. The philosophy of Schleiermacher. N.Y., 1941.

Phil 3805.187   Bredow, G. Wertanalysen zu Schleiermachers. Diss. Würzburg, 1941.

Phil 4200.2.15   Brickman, Benjamin. An introduction to Francesco Patrizi's Nova de universis philosophia. Thesis. N.Y., 1941.

Phil 176.148   Brownell, B. The philosopher in chaos. N.Y., 1941.

Phil 3549.8.125   Bruhers, E.M.J. De bijdrage von Ludwig Klages tot de algemene psychologie. Roermond, 1941.

Phil 4065.52   Bruno, Giordano. De la causa. Padova, 1941.

Phil 8581.82   Buckham, J.W. The inner world...philosophy of Christianity. N.Y., 1941.

Chronological Listing

1941 - cont.

Phil 5649.24   Bujeau, L.V. Le schematisme, psychologie de l'action. Paris, 1941.

Phil 365.48   Bulford, S. Man's unknown journey. London, 1941.

Phil 3850.27.101   Buri, Fritz. Christentum und Kultur bei Albert Schweitzer. Beru, 1941.

Phil 4482.1.95   Cabral de Moncada, L. Um iluminista portugues do século XVIII; Luiz Antonio Verney. Coimbra, 1941.

Phil 4060.8.30   Calderaro, Francesco. Francesco Arri e il suo spiritualismo. Roma, 1941.

Phil 6312.11.5   Cameron, Donald E. Objective and experimental psychiatry. 2. ed. N.Y., 1941.

Phil 8877.70   Carlos, M. Moral e economia politica. Rio de Janeiro, 1941.

Phil 600.48   Caso, A. Positivismo, neopositivismo y fenomenologia. México, 1941.

Phil 6315.2.120   Castellano, Filemón. El psicoanalisis de Freud. Buenos Aires, 1941.

Phil 5242.46   Cattell, R.B. General psychology. Cambridge, Mass., 1941.

Phil 3235.115   Chamberlain, W.B. Heaven wasn't his destination; the philosophy of Ludwig Feuerbach. London, 1941.

Phil 8582.54   Chauvet-Dusoul, F. Philosophie et religion. Paris, 1941-42. 5v.

Phil 5850.157.5   Cheatham, T.A. I believe in life. Pinehurst, N.C., 1941.

Phil 6952.24.15   Cobb, Stanley. Foundations of neuropsychiatry. 2. ed. Baltimore, 1941.

Phil 2475.1.277   Coviello, A. El proceso filosófico de Bergson y su bibliografía. 2. ed. Tucumán, 1941.

Phil 2490.136A   Cresson, André. Auguste Comte; sa vie, son oeuvre, avec un exposé de sa philosophie. Paris, 1941.

Phil 2475.1.286A   Cresson, André. Bergson; sa vie, son oeuvre, avec un exposé de sa philosophie. Paris, 1941.

Phil 3484.9.5   Cresson, André. Kant; sa vie, son oeuvre, avec un exposé de sa philosophie. Paris, 1941.

Phil 2115.154   Czajkowski, C.J. The theory of private property in John Locke's political philosophy. Notre Dame, 1941.

Phil 6315.2.111.5   Dalbiez, R. Psychoanalytical method and the doctrine of Freud. v.1. v.2 lost. N.Y., 1941.

Phil 530.15.28   Daniel-Rops, Henry. Mystiques de France. Paris, 1941.

Phil 960.28.5   Daqupta, S. Philosophical essays. Calcutta, 1941.

Phil 5243.46   Dearborn, W.F. Predicting the child's development. Cambridge, Mass., 1941.

Phil 1750.24   Derisi, Octavio N. Filosofía moderna y filosofía tomista. Buenos Aires, 1941.

Phil 2805.225   Desbruyères, P. Face à l'épreuve avec Pascal. Lyon, 1941.

Phil 2520.35.37   Descartes, René. Discours de la méthode. (Ouvrages de l'esprit). Manchester, 1941.

Phil 2255.1.35   Dewey, John. The Bertrand Russell case. N.Y., 1941.

Phil 2530.80.10   Dieckmann, Herbert. Diderot's conception of genius. n.p., 1941?

Phil 178.64.6   Dixon, W.M. Thoughts for the times. Glasgow, 1941.

Phil 178.64.5   Dixon, W.M. Thoughts for the times. N.Y., 1941.

Phil 978.79   Dominguez Acosta, F. La exondida senda. Caracas, 1941.

Phil 4210.153.5   Donati, B. Antonio Rosmini. Modena, 1941.

Phil 5545.179   Drees, V.J. The effects of practice on memory performance. Thesis. Washington, 1941.

Phil 178.65   Ducasse, C.J. Philosophy as a science. N.Y., 1941.

Phil 5627.241   Duguid, Julian. I am persuaded. N.Y., 1941.

Phil 3823.11   Dujovne, Leon. Spinoza. Buenos Aires, 1941-45. 4v.

Phil 4195.87   Dulles, A. Princeps concordiae: Pico della Mirandola. Cambridge, 1941.

Phil 6953.15   Dunlap, K. Research in methods of adjustment. Berkeley, 1941.

Phil 178.30.7   Durant, William. The mansions of philosophy. Garden City, 1941.

Phil 8954.3   Eddy, S. Maker of men. N.Y., 1941.

Phil 7069.41.4   Edwards, Harry. The mediumship of Jack Webber. N.Y., 1941.

Phil 6954.7   Ellery, Reginald S. Schizophrenia, the Cinderella of psychiatry. Sidney, 1941.

Phil 3235.81.17   Engels, Friedrich. Ludwig Feuerbach and the outcome of classical German philosophy. N.Y., 1941.

Phil 335.7A   Ewing, A.C. Reason and intuition. London, 1941.

Phil 90.4   Ferrater Mora, José. Diccionario de filosofía. México, 1941.

Phil 180.62   Fischer, E. Zum Geisteskampf der Gegenwart. Basel, 1941.

Phil 8406.20.8   Flaccus, L.W. The spirit and substance of art. N.Y., 1941.

Phil 2515.4.101   Floss, S.W. An outline of the philosophy of Antoine-Augustin Cournot. Philadelphia, 1941.

Phil 8610.941   Floyd, W. Christianity cross-examined. N.Y., 1941.

Phil 5593.41   Fosberg, I.A. An experimental study of the rehability of the Rorschach psychodiagnostic technique. N.Y., 1941.

Phil 5068.8   Frank, P. Between physics and philosophy. Cambridge, 1941.

Phil 5250.15.80   Franquiz Ventura, José A. La filosofía de las ciencias de Wolfgang Köhler. México, 1941.

Phil 6315.2.52   Freud, Sigmund. The living thoughts of Freud. N.Y., 1941.

Phil 6315.2.58   Freud, Sigmund. Schriften aus dem Nachlass 1892-1938. London, 1941.

Phil 6315.19   Fromm, Erich. Escape from freedom. N.Y., 1941.

Phil 5045.14A   Frye, A.M. Rational belief. N.Y., 1941.

Phil 930.29.10   Fung, Yu-lan. The spirit of Chinese philosophy. London, 1941.

Phil 287.6   Garcia Bacca, Juan D. Tipos historicos del filosofar físico. Tucuman, 1941.

Phil 7069.41.7   Garrett, Eileen Jeanette Lyttle. Telepathy in search of a lost faculty. N.Y., 1941.

Phil 5216.2.5   Garrett, Henry E. Great experiments in psychology. N.Y., 1941.

Phil 4372.1.145   Gayano, Lluch Rafael. El folklore en las obras de Luis Vives. Valencia, 1941.

Phil 8400.24A   Genteno, A. The intent of the artist. Princeton, 1941.

Phil 4006.2.30   Gentile, G. La filosofia italiana contemporanea. Firenze, 1941.

Phil 6125.29   Germany. Heer Inspection des Personalprüfwesens. Menschen Formen. Berlin, 1941.

Phil 5440.35   Geurts, P.M.M. De erfelijkheid in de oudere Grieksche wetenschap. Nijmegen, 1941.

Phil 2190.15   Giacon, C. Guglielmo di Occam. Milano, 1941. 2v.

Phil 6116.24PF   Gibbs, F.A. Atlas of electroencephalography. Cambridge, Mass., 1941.

Phil 8586.45   Gilson, Étienne. God and philosophy. New Haven, 1941.

Phil 5246.56   Glaser, E.M. An experiment in the development of critical thinking. N.Y., 1941.

Phil 3488.36   Goessl, Max. Untersuchungen zum Verhältnis von Recht und Sittlichkeit. München, 1941.

1941 - cont.

Phil 337.13   Gondin, W.R. Prefaces to inquiry; a study in the origins and relevance of modern theories of knowledge. N.Y., 1941.

Phil 5465.52A   Gordon, Kate. Studies in the theory of imagination. Los Angeles, 1941.

Phil 3425.307A   Gray, J.G. Hegel's Hellenic ideal. N.Y., 1941.

Phil 5850.221   Gray, John S. Psychology in use. N.Y., 1941.

Phil 735.121   Grenier, Jean. Le choix. Paris, 1941.

Phil 720.35   Grisebach, Eberhard. Was ist Wahrheit in Wirklichkeit? Bern, 1941.

Phil 181.87   Guitton, Jean. Justification du temps. Paris, 1941.

Phil 8661.30   Gutiérrez, Antonio José. La providencia y España. San Sebastián, 1941.

Phil 510.1.16   Haeckel, Ernst. Haeckel und Allmers. Bremen, 1941.

Phil 6957.19   Hanes, E.L. The minds and nerves of soldiers. Pasadena, Calif., 1941.

Phil 1900.93   Harris, W.G. Teleology in the philosophy of Joseph Butler and Abraham Tucker. Thesis. Philadelphia, 1941.

Phil 8662.17   Hartshorne, Charles. Man's vision of God, and the logic of theism. Chicago, 1941.

Phil 5520.75.2   Hayakawa, S.I. Language in action. N.Y., 1941.

Phil 5520.75   Hayakawa, S.I. Language in action. N.Y., 1941.

Phil 5247.75   Hellpach, W. Das Wellengesetz unseres Lebens. Hamburg, 1941.

Phil 5247.13.29   Herrero Pouas, Antolin. Juan Huarte de San Juan. Madrid, 1941.

Phil 3450.24.10   Hessing, Jacob. Logica als leer van zuivere rede. Deel. 1. Bussum, 1941.

Phil 960.137.5   Hiriyanna, M. The quest after perfection. Madras, 1941.

Phil 1807.4   Hocking, William E. Lectures on recent trends in American philosophy. Claremont, 1941.

Phil 7054.190   Holmes, W.H.G. Memories of the supernatural in east and west. London,, 1941.

Phil 9120.165   Hopmann, W. Essai d'une nouvelle explication utilitariste du sentiment d'obligation. Genève, 1941.

Phil 5627.134.55.5   Howard, Peter. Innocent men. London, 1941.

Phil 5627.134.55   Howard, Peter. Innocent men. London, 1941.

Phil 8080.12   Hurtado, L. Espacio y tiempo en el arte actual. Buenos Aires, 1941.

Phil 8882.64   Huxley, Thomas H. Touchstone for ethics. 1st ed. N.Y., 1941.

Phil 70.60   Istituto di Studi Filosofici Serione di Torino. La ricerca filodofica. Roma, 1941.

Phil 2138.117   Jackson, Reginald. An examination of the deductive logic of John S.Mill. London, 1941.

VPhil 6060.30.5   Jacoby, Hans. Self-knowledge through handwriting. London, 1941.

Phil 5325.15.7   Jung, Carl G. Die psychologische Diagnose des Tatbestandes. Zurich, 1941.

Phil 3480.94   Kant, Immanuel. Filosofía de la historia. México, 1941.

Phil 3640.298   Kassler, K. Nietzsche und das Recht. München, 1941.

Phil 5590.13.5   Kehl, R. Psicología da personalidade. 2. ed. Rio de Janeiro, 1941.

Phil 6120.15   Kenyon, F. The myth of the mind. London, 1941.

Phil 3425.320   Knoop, Bernhard. Hegel und die Franzosen. Stuttgart, 1941.

Phil 8599.19.109   Köhler, Walther. Ernst Troeltsch. Tübingen, 1941.

Phil 5250.35   Kornilov, K.N. Psikhologiia. Moskva, 1941.

Phil 1540.82   Krings, Hermann. Ordo. Halle, 1941.

Phil 3549.11   Kroner, Richard. The religious function of imagination. New Haven, 1941.

Phil 6321.16   Laburu, J.A. de. Anormalidades del caracter. Montevideo, 1941.

Phil 8666.14   Laird, John. Mind and deity. London, 1941.

Phil 5425.44.10   Lange, Wilhelm. Das Genie-Problem. 3. Aufl. München, 1941.

Phil 5425.44.23   Lange, Wilhelm. Genies als Problem. 2. Aufl. München, 1941.

Phil 8886.62   Lanz, H. In quest of morals. Stanford, 1941.

Phil 270.50   Laporte, Jean. L'idee de necessité. Paris, 1941.

Phil 4374.5.80   Larroya, Francisco. El romanticismo filosófico observaciones a la weltanschauung de Joaquin Xirau. Mexico, 1941.

Phil 8886.63   Larroyo, F. Los principios de la ética social. 4. ed. Mexico, 1941.

Phil 575.105   Larroyo, Francisco. Exposición y crítica del personalismo espiritualista de nuestro tiempo. México, 1941.

Phil 365.47.10   Lecomte du Noüy, Pierre. L'avenir de l'esprit. Gallimard, 1941.

Phil 5520.76A   Lee, Irving J. Language habits in human affairs. N.Y., 1941.

Phil 978.81   Lee, Pi-cheng. An outline of Karma. n.p., 1941?

Phil 6536.9   Lennox, W.G. Science and seizures. N.Y., 1941.

Phil 535.5   Levin-Goldschmidt, Hermann. Der Nihilismus im Licht einer kritischen Philosophie. Thayngen, 1941.

Phil 6980.419   Lewis, Nolan don Carpentier. A short history of psychiatric achievement. N.Y., 1941.

Phil 8886.61   Leys, W.A.R. Ethics and social policy. N.Y., 1941.

Phil 5590.145   Lipps, Hans. Die menschliche Natur. Frankfurt, 1941.

Phil 9240.1   Lloyd, R.B. The mastery of evil. London, 1941.

Phil 3011.8A   Loewith, Karl. Von Hegel bis Nietzsche. Zürich, 1941.

Phil 4762.1.42   Losskii, Nikolai Onufrievich. Philosophical essays. n.p., 1941.

Phil 8412.14   Lundholm, H. The aesthetic sentiment. Cambridge, 1941.

Phil 5252.77   Mackenzie, M. The human mind. Philadelphia, 1941.

Phil 2020.87   McKirachan, John C. The temporal and eternal in the philosophy of Thomas H. Green. Ann Arbor, 1941.

Phil 8592.62   Magre, M. Le livre des certitudes admirables. Avignon, 1941.

Phil 9070.12   Manchester, R.E. The Saturday letters. Cuyahoga Falls, 1941.

Phil 3425.292.5   Marcuse, H. Reason and revolution; Hegel and the use of social theory. London, 1941.

Phil 2750.11.49A   Maritain, Jacques. Confession de foi. N.Y., 1941.

Phil 2750.11.45A   Maritain, Jacques. Le crépuscule de la civilisation. Montreal, 1941.

Phil 2750.11.33   Maritain, Jacques. Ransoming the time. N.Y., 1941.

Phil 8962.12   Masaryk, J.G. The immortal soul in danger. London, 1941.

Phil 6322.27A   Maslow, A.H. Principles of abnormal psychology. N.Y., 1941.

Phil 187.131   Masson-Oursel, Paul. Le fait métaphysique. Paris, 1941.

Phil 3494.43   Mattern, C.D. Personal freedom within the third antimony. Thesis. Philadelphia, 1941.

Phil 5627.95.15   Mensching, Gustav. Gut und Böse im Glauben der Völker. Leipzig, 1941.

Phil 2805.237   Merezhkovskii, Dimitrii S. Pascal. Paris, 1941.

1941 - cont.

Phil 1812.6.5   Metz, Rudolf. England und die deutsche Philosophie. Stuttgart, 1941.

Phil 2475.1.270   Mexico City. Universidad Nacional. Facultad de Filosofía y Estudios Superiores. Centro de Estudios Filosóficos. Homenaje a Bergson. México, 1941.

Phil 9075.39   Meyer, Rudolf. Der Protest der Gewissens in der Philosophie. Zürich, 1941.

Phil 8887.73   Michaud, Félix. Science et morale. Paris, 1941.

Phil 2138.41   Mill, John S. On social freedom. N.Y., 1941.

Phil 8592.66   Miller, Hugh. Christian truth in history. N.Y., 1941.

Phil 5252.78A   Miller, N.E. Social learning and imitation. New Haven, 1941.

Phil 3450.11.120   Miro Quesada, F. Sentido del movimiento. Lima, 1941.

Phil 1145.83   Mondolfo, Rodolfo. Moralistas griegos. Buenos Aires, 1941.

Phil 6962.19.5   Morgenthaler, Walter. Die Pflege der Gemüts- und Geisteskranken. 4. Aufl. Bern, 1941.

NEDL Phil 5252.79   Mouchet, E. Percepción instinto y razon. Buenos Aires, 1941.

Phil 4012.8   Mueller, F.L. La pensée contemporaine en Italie et l'influence de Hegel. Genève, 1941.

Phil 5253.12   Nicol, Eduardo. Psicología de las situaciones vitales. Mexico, 1941.

Phil 3640.45   Nietzsche, Friedrich. Schwert des Geistes. Stuttgart, 1941.

Phil 8176.2   Novák, Mirko. Česká estetika. Praha, 1941.

Phil 4364.1.70   Núñez Regueiro, M. On the knowledge and progress of oneself. Rosario, 1941.

Phil 188.16.10   Nuñez Requeiro, M. Metafisica y ciencia. Buenos Aires, 1941.

Phil 5850.291   Oldfield, R.C. The psychology of the interview. London, 1941.

Phil 3496.6   Olivier, Paul. Zum Willinsproblem bei Kant und Reinhold. Berlin, 1941.

Phil 3640.445   Olzien, Otto H. Nietzsche und das Problem der dichterischen Sprache. Berlin, 1941.

Phil 8594.13.10   Oman, John. Honest religion. Cambridge, Eng., 1941.

Phil 8416.13   Pagano, José L. Motivos de estética. 2. ed. Buenos Aires, 1941.

Phil 2225.10   Parker, D.H. Experience and substance. Ann Arbor, 1941.

Phil 190.68   Parkes, Henry B. The pragmatic test; essays on the history of ideas. San Francisco, 1941.

Phil 2805.25.52   Pascal, Blaise. Les pages immortelles de Pascal, choisies et expliquées par F. Mauriac. N.Y., 1941.

Phil 5765.2.4   Payot, Jules. L'éducation de la volonté. Paris, 1941.

Phil 6536.11   Penfield, W. Epilepsy and cerebral localization. 1st ed. Springfield, 1941.

Phil 5255.45   Pennsylvania. University. Bicentennial Conference. Modern psychology. Philadelphia, 1941.

Phil 8595.34A   Pennsylvania. University. Bicentennial Conference. Religion and the modern world. Philadelphia, 1941.

Phil 6325.15   Pennsylvania. University. Bicentennial Conference. Therapeutic advances in psychiatry. Philadelphia, 1941.

Phil 5590.5   Periot, M. Hippocrate avait raison. Marseille, 1941.

Phil 6325.14   Porteus, S.D. The practice of clinical psychology. N.Y., 1941.

Phil 3850.18.120F   Povina, Alfredo. La obra sociologica de Max Scheler. Cordoba, 1941.

Phil 8840.3   Prell, H.H. Das Unmittelbare in der Philosophie der Moral. Amsterdam, 1941.

Phil 7069.41.5   Price, Harry. The most haunted house in England. London, 1941.

Phil 5255.48   Pulver, Max. Selbsterfahrung. Zürich, 1941.

Phil 5066.11.10A   Quine, Willard van Orman. Elementary logic. Boston, 1941.

Phil 4352.2   Rabello, Sylvio. Farias Brito. Rio de Janeiro, 1941.

Phil 6127.7.20   Ramón y Cajal, S. El pensamiento vivo de Cajal. Buenos Aires, 1941.

Phil 6327.4.23A   Rank, Otto. Beyond psychology. Camden, 1941.

Phil 2240.60.30   Reid, Thomas. Essays on the intellectual powers of man. London, 1941.

Phil 4368.2.33   Romero, Francisco. Filosofía contemporanea estudios y notas. Buenos Aires, 1941.

Phil 2417.4A   Rosenfield, Leonora D.C. From beast-machine to man-machine. N.Y., 1941.

Phil 6327.17.10   Ross, Thomas Arthur. Lectures on war neuroses. London, 1941.

Phil 1750.159   Rossi, Edmundo. Retorno à vida (ensaios). São Paulo, 1941.

Phil 3850.27.103   Russell, L.M. The path to reconstruction...Albert Schweitzer's philosophy of civilization. London, 1941.

Phil 665.68   Sadler, W.S. The evolution of the soul. Chicago? 1941.

Phil 299.25   Samtonge, F. Sumina cosmologiae. Montreal, 1941.

Phil 193.49.25.5   Santayana, G. Diálogos en el limbo. Buenos Aires, 1941.

Phil 8598.82   Sayers, Dorothy L. The mind of the maker. London, 1941.

Phil 8598.82.5   Sayers, Dorothy L. The mind of the maker. N.Y., 1941.

Phil 5710.15   Schaer, K.F. Charakter, Blutgruppe und Konstitution. Zürich, 1941.

Phil 2340.10.101A   Schilpp, Paul A. The philosophy of Alfred North Whitehead. Evanston, 1941.

Phil 818.27   Schnittkind, H.T. Living biographies of great philosophers. Garden City, 1941.

Phil 5066.16   Schröber, Karl. Ein allgemeiner Kalkülbegriff. Leipzig, 1941.

Phil 3640.540   Schulze, Friedrich. Der junge Nietzsche in den Jahren. Leipzig, 1941.

Phil 5850.338   Selling, L.S. Studies on the problem driver. Detroit, 1941.

Phil 5440.33   Sen Gupta, N. Heredity in mental traits. 1. ed. London, 1941.

Phil 5520.61.10   Serrus, Charles. La langue, le sens, la pensée. Paris, 1941.

Phil 2475.1.272   Sertillanges, A.G. Henri Bergson et le catholicisme. Paris, 1941.

Phil 5258.123   Sherman, M. Basic problems of behavior. N.Y., 1941.

Phil 6128.13.11   Sherrington, C.S. Man on his nature. N.Y., 1941.

Phil 9240.2.5   Simard, Georges. Maux présents et foi chrétienne. 2. éd. Montréal, 1941.

Phil 1750.157   Simond, D. Antipolitique. Lausanne, 1941.

Phil 2050.210   Smith, N.K. The philosophy of David Hume. London, 1941.

Phil 4369.5   Sondereguér, Pedro. El enigma de la realidad. Buenos Aires, 1941.

Phil 9070.45   Spezzafumo de Faucamberge, S. Se suffire à soi-même. Paris, 1941.

Phil 4225.15.30   Spirito, Ugo. La vita come arte. Firenze, 1941.

Phil 8893.101   Stebbing, L.S. Ideals and illusions. London, 1941.

1941 - cont.

Phil 978.49.210   Steiner, R. Geschichte des Hypnotismus und des Somnambulismus. Basel, 1941.

Phil 978.49.215   Steiner, R. Die Geschichte des Spiritismus. Basel, 1941.

Phil 2805.112.7   Stewart, Hugh F. The secret of Pascal. Cambridge, Eng., 1941.

Phil 7069.41.6   Temple, Laurence. The shining brother. London, 1941.

Phil 1524.4   Thomas, Elliott C. History of the schoolmen. London, 1941.

Phil 5059.20.10   Thouless, R.H. How to think straight. N.Y., 1941.

Phil 6129.8   Travis, L.E. Personal problems of everyday life. N.Y., 1941.

Phil 5380.5.15   Trotter, Wilfred. Instincts of the herd in peace and war. 3. ed. N.Y., 1941.

Phil 5060.6.7   Ushenko, A.P. The problems. Princeton, 1941.

Phil 5060.6.5   Ushenko, A.P. The problems of logic. London, 1941.

Phil 5525.40   Victoria, Marcos. Ensayo preliminar sobre lo cómico. Buenos Aires, 1941.

Phil 1721.9   Vieteck, George S. The seven against man. Scotch Plains, N.J., 1941.

Phil 5425.63   Voronoff, Serge. Du crétin au génie. N.Y., 1941.

Phil 974.3.115   Wachsmuth, G. Die Geburt der Geisteswissenschaft. Dornach, 1941.

Phil 3450.11.116   Welch, E.P. Philosophy of Edmund Husserl...development of his phenomenology. N.Y., 1941.

Phil 5850.385.82   White, Wendell. The psychology of dealing with people. N.Y., 1941.

Phil 303.12.6   Whitehead, Alfred N. Process and reality; an essay in cosmology. N.Y., 1941.

Phil 3120.8.100   Winter, E. Fanz Brentanos Ringen um eine neue Gottessicht. Brünn, 1941.

Phil 197.67   World Wide Revival Prayer Movement. Preparing the way. Atlantic City, 1941.

Phil 1722.8   Wright, W.K. A history of modern philosophy. N.Y., 1941.

Phil 3450.11.113   Xirau, J. La filosofía de Husserl. Buenos Aires, 1941.

Phil 5590.2   Young, Kimball. Personality and problems of adjustment. N.Y., 1941.

Phil 5590.2.1   Young, Kimball. Personality and problems of adjustment. N.Y., 1941.

Phil 6695.1   Zilboorg, G. A history of medical psychology. N.Y., 1941.

Phil 5265.4   Zürcher, W. Über die Intelligenz und ihren Ort im Gefüge des Verhalttens. Bern, 1941.

1942

Phil 9558.10.12   Aires Ramos da Silva de Eca, M. Reflexões sobre a vaidade dos homens. São Paulo, 1942.

Phil 8610.832   Aldred, G.A. The devil's chaplain. (Robert Taylor, 1784-1844). Glasgow, 1942.

Phil 6310.9   Allen, Frederick H. Psychotherapy with children. N.Y., 1942.

Phil 4000.17   Alliney, G. I pensatori della seconda metà del secolo XIX. Milano, 1942.

VPhil 9070.124   Almásy, József. A tizparancsalat a közéletben. Budapest, 1942.

Phil 9380.3   American Psychiatric Association. Military Mobilization Committee. Psychiatric aspects of civilian morale. N.Y., 1942.

Phil 585.125   Aolliet, Joseph. L'homme social. Paris, 1942.

Phil 9070.59   Ashley Montagu, M.F. How to find happiness and keep it. 1st ed. Garden City, 1942.

Phil 4112.88   Auria, Renata d'. Il Galluppi. Roma, 1942.

Phil 3090.62   Baader, Franz von. Lettres inédites. Paris, 1942-51. 4v.

Phil 3090.61   Baader, Franz von. Lettres inédites de Franz von Baader. Thèse. Paris, 1942.

Phil 5465.56   Bachelard, G. L'eau et les rêves. Paris, 1942.

Phil 8581.52   Baillie, John. Invitation to pilgrimage. London, 1942.

Phil 8656.30   Bandeira de Mello, L.M. Próva matemático da existencia de Deus. Leopoldina, 1942.

Phil 575.135   Bañuelos García, M. Personalidad y caracter. Madrid, 1942.

Phil 8400.23   Bases of artistic creation essays by Maxwell Anderson, Rhys Carpenter and Roy Harris. New Brunswick, 1942.

Phil 2475.1.290   Benrubi, Isaak. Bergson. Buenos Aires, 1942.

Phil 2475.1.280   Benrubi, Isaak. Souvenirs sur Henri Bergson. Neuchâtel, 1942.

Phil 1870.40.22   Berkeley. The principles of human knowledge. London, 1942.

Phil 4070.4.30   Bertini, Giovanni M. Scritti filosofici. Milano, 1942.

Phil 5041.58   Beth, Evert Willem. Summulae logicales. Groningen, 1942.

Phil 3110.13   Böhme, J. Sämtliche Schriften. Stuttgart, 1942. 10v.

Phil 3120.23.81   Bogdanski, A.A. The significance of Clemens Baeumker in neo-scholastic philosophy. Milwaukee, 1942.

Phil 1750.179   Bollnow, O.F. Existenzphilosophie. 2e Aufl. Stuttgart, 1942?

Phil 5211.4.20   Boring, E.G. Sensation and perception in the history of experimental psychology. N.Y., 1942.

Phil 1750.166.12   Bottai, Giuseppe. Verteidigung des Humanismus. 2. Aufl. Berlin, 1942.

Phil 5360.12   Bouisson, R. Essai sur l'abstraction. Gap, 1942.

Phil 6311.27   Bowlby, John. Personality and mental illness, psychiatric diagnosis. N.Y., 1942.

Phil 8581.86   Brightman, E.S. The spiritual life. N.Y., 1942.

Phil 1870.120A   Broad, C.D. Berkeley's argument about material substance. London, 1942.

Phil 75.38   Brugger, Ilse. Filosofía alemana traducida al español. Buenos Aires, 1942.

Phil 75.38.5   Brugger, Ilse. Filosofía alemana traducida al español. Supplement. Pt.1. Buenos Aires, 1942.

Phil 2805.242   Buchholz, E. Blaise Pascal. 2. Aufl. Göttingen, 1942.

Phil 8612.33   Bürgel, B.H. Saat und Ernte. Berlin, 1942.

Phil 4210.147   Bulferetti, Luigi. Antonio Rosmini nella restaurazione. Firenze, 1942.

Phil 9035.86   Burloud, Albert. Le caractère. Paris, 1942.

Phil 4963.1   Buzzi, E. De donde venimos. Lima, 1942.

Phil 8582.55   Cailliet, Émile. The life of the mind. N.Y., 1942.

Phil 5374.61   Campbell, Percy A. Body and self, one and inseparable. San Francisco, 1942.

Phil 2520.215   Cannabrava, E. Descartes e Bergson. São Paulo, 1942?

Phil 5066.8   Carnap, Rudolf. Introduction to semantics. Cambridge, 1942.

Phil 2520.208.5   Cassirer, E. Descartes, Corheille, Christine de Suede. Paris, 1942.

Phil 802.14   Challaye, F. Petite histoire des grandes philosophies. Paris, 1942.

1942 - cont.

Phil 1885.89   Church, Ralph Withington. Bradley's dialectic. London, 1942.

Phil 5066.18   Churchman, C.W. Towards a general logic of propositions. Thesis. Philadelphia, 1942.

Phil 530.35.20   Chuzeville, Jean. Les mystiques italiens. Paris, 1942.

Phil 4080.3.160   Cione, Edmondo. L'opera filosofica...di Benedetto Croce. Bari, 1942.

Phil 6112.32   Clarke, Eric K. Mental hygiene for community nursing. Minneapolis, 1942.

Phil 6312.14   Clerambault, G.G. Oeuvre psychiatrique. v.1-2. Paris, 1942. 2v.

Phil 177.102   Cobb, Henry V.Z. Man's way, a first book in philosophy. 1st ed. London, 1942.

Phil 177.85.10   Collingwood, R.G. The new leviathan, or Man, society, civilization and barbarism. Oxford, 1942.

Phil 5066.9.5A   Cooley, J.C. A primer of formal logic. N.Y., 1942.

Phil 8877.84   Coornhert, D.V. Zedekunst. Leiden, 1942.

Phil 3640.292   Copleston, F. Friedrich Nietzsche. London, 1942.

Phil 3195.10.117   Coviello, A. El filósofo Hans Driesch. Tucumán, 1942.

Phil 4964.67   Coviello, Alfredo. Una página de historía en la naciente filosofía argentina y otros ensayos críticos. Tucumán, 1942.

Phil 2520.217   Cresson, André. Descartes; sa vie, son oeuvre, avec un exposé de sa philosophie. 1e éd. Paris, 1942.

Phil 3640.306   Cresson, André. Nietzsche; sa vie, son oeuvre, avec un exposé de sa philosophie. 1e éd. Paris, 1942.

Phil 2805.229.5   Cresson, André. Pascal; sa vie, son oeuvre, avec un exposé de sa philosophie. 2e éd. Paris, 1942.

Phil 8050.22   Croce, Benedetto. Storia dell'estetica per saggi. Bari, 1942.

Phil 4369.2.82   Cruz Costa, João. Ensaio sobre a vida e a obra do filósofo Francisco Sanchez. São Paulo, 1942.

Phil 4352.2.5   Cruz Costa, Joao. Farias Brito on uma adventura do esprito. Sao Paulo, 1942.

Phil 6112.34   Cuny, Louis. Contribution à l'étude de l'action vasomotrice. Thèse. Paris, 1942.

Phil 5190.70   Das, Adhar Chandra. Negative fact, negation and truth. Calcutta, 1942.

Phil 5753.13   Davidson, M. The free will controversy. London, 1942.

Phil 8583.28.5   Dawson, Christopher H. The judgment of the nations. N.Y., 1942.

Phil 5243.48   Delay, Jean P.L. Les ondes cérébrales et la psychologie. Paris, 1942.

Phil 5545.90   Delay, Jean Paul Louis. Les dissolutions de la mémoire. Paris, 1942.

Phil 2520.218   Descartes, René. Les pages immortelles de Descartes. Paris, 1942.

Phil 8628.8   Desmond, Shaw. How you live when you die. London, 1942.

Phil 3003.3.5   Dewey, John. German philosophy and politics. N.Y., 1942.

Phil 4003.5   Dezza, Paolo. I neotomisti italiani del XIX secolo. Milano, 1942-44. 2v.

Phil 178.26.5   Dilthey, Wilhelm. Introduction à l'étude des sciences humaines (Einleitung in die Geisteswissenschaften). 1re éd. Paris, 1942.

Phil 5401.16.5   Dollard, John. Victory over fear. N.Y., 1942.

Phil 2733.107   Ducassé, Pierre. Malebranche; sa vie, son oeuvre, avec un exposé de sa philosophie. 1e éd. Paris, 1942.

Phil 8740.4   Dun, Angus. Not by bread alone. 2. ed. N.Y., 1942.

Phil 6314.6   Ebaugh, Franklin Gessford. Psychiatry in medical education. N.Y., 1942.

Phil 3585.1.105   Eisenring, Max F.E. Johann Heinrich Lambert und die wissenschaftliche Philosophie der Gegenwart. Zürich, 1942.

Phil 8629.3   Elliott, W.H. Rendezvous; the life that some call death. London, 1942.

Phil 2340.10.102   Ely, Stephen Lee. The religious availability of Whitehead's God. Madison, 1942.

Phil 4966.2   Estable, C. Psicología de la vocación. Montevideo, 1942.

Phil 2475.1.282   Études Bergsoniennes, hommage à Henri Bergson (1859-1941). Paris, 1942.

Phil 5627.176   Festugière, André M.J. La sainteté. 1. éd. Paris, 1942.

Phil 3450.11.124   Fisch, Isidor. Husserl's Internationalitäts und Urteilslehre. Inaug. Diss. Basel, 1942.

Phil 5400.99   Foster, George S. Our hunches; the effect of emotions on our lives and habits. N.Y., 1942.

Phil 1915.83   Fránquiz Ventura, José Antonio. Borden Parker Browne's treatment of the problem of change and identity. Rio Piedras, 1942.

Phil 6996.5   Freeman, Walter. Psychosurgery. Springfield, 1942.

Phil 8406.14   Friedländer, Max J. On art and connoisseurship. London, 1942.

Phil 4006.5.33   Garin, Eugenio. Filosofi italiani del quattro cento. Firenze, 1942.

Phil 8586.47   Garnett, A.C. A realistic philosophy of religion. Chicago, 1942.

Phil 5850.211   Garrett, A.M. Interviewing, its principles and methods. N.Y., 1942.

Phil 4120.4.11   Gentile, Giovanni. Opere. v. 1-28,30-38,42. Firenze, 1942. 36v.

Phil 5246.70   Gibb, Andrew. In search of sanity. N.Y., 1942.

Phil 6956.12   Graves, Alonzo. The eclipse of a mind. N.Y., 1942.

Phil 182.94.82   Guggenberger, Alois. Der Menschengeist und das Sein. Krailling bei München, 1942.

Phil 5246.47.10A   Guilford, Joy Paul. Fundamental statistics in psychology and education. N.Y., 1942.

Phil 3640.310   Guisso, Lorenzo. Nietzsche. Milano, 1942.

Phil 3007.10.5   Haering, Theodor Lorenz. Das deutsche in der deutschen Philosophie. 2. Aufl. Stuttgart, 1942.

Phil 7069.42.5   Hamilton, T. Glen. Intention and survival. Toronto, 1942.

Phil 6957.20   Hanfmann, E. Conceptual thinking in schizophrenia. N.Y., 1942.

Phil 6117.44   Hathaway, S.R. Physiological psychology. N.Y., 1942.

Phil 5203.10   Hawes, M. What to read on psychology. Chicago, 1942.

Phil 3425.38   Hegel, Georg Wilhelm Friedrich. Hegel; Volk, Staat. Stuttgart, 1942.

Phil 6400.25   Hein, Leopold. Speech and voice. London, 1942.

Phil 5850.228.15   Hepner, Harry W. Psychology applied to life and work. N.Y., 1942.

Phil 575.101   Hertel, François. Pour un ordre personnaliste. Montréal, 1942.

Phil 8662.18   Heydon, J.K. The God of reason. N.Y., 1942.

Phil 2055.7.5   Hocking, William E. What man can make of man. N.Y., 1942.

Phil 1807.6   Holmes, E.C. Social philosophy and the social mind. N.Y., 1942.

Phil 1807.5A   Holmes, E.C. Social philosophy and the social mind. Thesis. N.Y., 1942.

Phil 6117.45   Holmes, Ernest R. New thought terms and their meanings. N.Y., 1942.

Phil 6317.22.10A   Horney, Karen. Self-analysis. N.Y., 1942.

Phil 8587.55   Hughes, T.H. Psychology and religious truth. London, 1942.

Phil 182.110   Humphreys, H.S. The cylindriad. Evansville, 1942.

Phil 2070.138A   In commemoration of William James, 1842-1942. N.Y., 1942.

Phil 6119.12   Jackson, A.S. The answer is...your nerves. Madison, Wis., 1942.

Phil 6319.1.180   Jacobi, Jolan. The psychology of C.G. Jung. London, 1942.

Phil 340.5   Jacoby, P.J. "Common sense" in eEpistemology. Thesis. NOtre Dame, 1942.

Phil 2070.76.5A   James, William. As William James said: extracts from the published writings. N.Y., 1942.

Phil 6049.42   Jennings, Alice D. Your hand tells all; a manual of simplified palmistry. N.Y., 1942.

Phil 8050.70   Kallen, H.M. Art and freedom; a historical and biographical interpretation. N.Y., 1942. 2v.

Phil 8960.8   Kenmare, D. (pseud.). The philosophy of love. London, 1942.

Phil 5650.26   Kennedy, Helen. A study of children's hearing as it relates to reading. Thesis. n.p., 1942.

Phil 3549.2.60   Keyserling, Hermann. Betractungen der Stille und Besinnlichkeit. Jena, 1942.

Phil 5593.42.5   Klopfer, Bruno. The Rorschach technique; a manual for a projective method of personality diagnosis. Yonkers-on-Hudson, 1942.

Phil 5643.105   Kluver, H. Visual mechanisms. Lancaster, 1942.

Phil 8411.16   Kornfeld, M. L'énigme du beau. Paris, 1942.

Phil 6120.16   Krieg, Wendell J.S. Functional neuroanatomy. Philadelphia, 1942.

Phil 5590.11   Landis, Carney. Personality and sexuality of the handicapped woman. N.Y., 1942.

Phil 5425.44.3   Lange, Wilhelm. Genie, Irrsinn und Ruhm. 3. Aufl. München, 1942.

Phil 186.97   Langer, Mrs. S.K. Philosophy in a new key. Cambridge, Mass., 1942.

Phil 400.104   La Via, Vincenzo. Idealismo e filosofia. Messina, 1942.

Phil 3493.24   Lazzarini, Renato. Dalla religione naturale prekantiani alla religione morale di Kant. Roma, 1942.

Phil 5467.4   Lejins, Peter P. The concept of imitation. Part of thesis. Chicago, 1942.

Phil 8886.64   Le Senne, René. Traité de morale générale. 1. ed. Paris, 1942.

Phil 9070.18   A letter to my son. By a solider's mother. 1st ed. N.Y., 1942.

Phil 6321.18   Levine, M. Psychotherapy in medical practice. N.Y., 1942.

Phil 6060.32   Lewinson, T.S. Handwriting analysis. N.Y., 1942.

Phil 4265.6.80   Librizzi, C. Il pensiero di B. Varisco. Padova, 1942.

Phil 930.39   Lin, Mou-Sheng. Men and ideas; an informal history of Chinese political thought. N.Y., 1942.

Phil 5221.5   Lottin, Odon. Psychologie et morale aux XIIe et XIIIe siècles. v.1-6. Louvain, 1942. 8v.

Phil 5643.104A   McFarland, R.A. Studies of visual fatigue. Boston, 1942.

Phil 4372.1.97   Marañon, G. Luis Vives. Madrid, 1942.

Phil 8430.39   Meier, N.C. Art in human affairs. N.Y., 1942.

Phil 6322.19.10   Menninger, Karl Augustus. Love against hate. 1st ed. N.Y., 1942.

Phil 5252.85   Merleau-Ponty, M. La structure du comportement. 1. ed. Paris, 1942.

Phil 2805.230   Michaut, Gustave. Pascal, Molière, Musset; essais de critique et de psychologie. Paris, 1942.

Phil 2138.25   Mill, John S. The spirit of the age. Chicago, 1942.

Phil 5722.25   Miller, James G. Unconsciousness. N.Y., 1942.

Phil 1182.20   Minar, Edwin L. Early Pythagorean politics and theory. Baltimore, 1942.

Phil 3552.311   Mönnich, Conrad Willem. De natuurlijke kennis gods bij Leibniz. Rotterdam, 1942.

Phil 4363.6.10   Molina, E. Confesión filosófica y llamado de superación a la América Hispana. Santiago, 1942.

Phil 4012.7   Mondolfo, Rodolfo. La filosofia politica di Italia en el siglo XIX. Buenos Aires, 1942.

Phil 1117.8.10   Mondolfo, Rodolfo. El pensamiento antiguo. Buenos Aires, 1942. 2v.

Phil 8592.63   Morris, Charles W. Paths of life, preface to a world religion. N.Y., 1942.

Phil 5590.10   Motivation and visual factors; individual studies of college students. Hanover, 1942.

Phil 2150.12   Muirhead, J.H. Reflections by a journeyman in philosophy. London, 1942.

Phil 5252.76.5   Munzinger, K.F. Psychology. N.Y., 1942.

Phil 8592.65   Murray, R. Time and the timeless. London, 1942.

Phil 9380.4   Nash, Jay Bryan. Building morale. N.Y., 1942.

Phil 575.140   Nédoncelle, Maurice. La réciprocité des consciences; essai sur la nature de la personné. Thèse. Paris, 1942.

Phil 344.4   Negley, Glenn. The organization of knowledge...philosophical analysis. N.Y., 1942.

Phil 8593.20   Nigg, Walter. Religiöse Denker. Bern, 1942.

Phil 8414.7   Nolte, Fred O. Art and reality. Lancaster, 1942.

Phil 1955.6.112   Okun, Sid. John Dewey; a Marxian critique. Chicago, 1942.

Phil 9450.18   Oppler, A.C. Ethics in public administration. Cambridge, 1942.

Phil 8595.35   Palmstierna, E.K. The world's crisis and faiths. London, 1942.

Phil 1715.2.10   Papini, Giovanni. Gli amanti de Sofia, 1902-1918. Firenze, 1942.

Phil 4372.1.95   Paris. Bibliotheque Nationale. Vives. Paris, 1942.

Phil 2805.40.45   Pascal, Blaise. Pascal's apology for religion. Cambridge, Eng., 1942.

Phil 2805.42.35   Pascal, Blaise. Pensées. Paris, 1942.

Phil 9355.2.10   Peacham, Henry. The truth of our times. N.Y., 1942.

Phil 190.69   Pepper, Stephen C. World hypotheses; a study of evidence. Berkeley, 1942.

Phil 9070.13.5   Pereira Alves, A. La utilidad de la honradez. Buenos Aires, 1942.

Phil 9400.10   Perry, Ralph B. Plea for an age movement. N.Y., 1942.

Phil 5643.106   Peskin, James Charles. The regeneration of visual purple in the living animal. Thesis. N.Y., 1942.

Phil 2280.14.80   Philosophical essays in honor of Edgar Arthur Singer, Jr. Philadelphia, 1942.

Phil 5066.36.20   Piaget, Jean. Classes, relations et nombres. Paris, 1942.

Phil 5255.7.15   Pillsbury, W.B. Handbook of general psychology.

Phil 5850.314.5   Poffenberger, A.T. Principles of applied psychology. N.Y., 1942.

1942 - cont.

Phil 8416.10   Portnoy, Julius. A psychology of art creation. Philadelphia, 1942.

Phil 735.282   Preti, Giulio. Fenomenologia del valore. Milano, 1942.
Phil 8416.17   Pro, Diezo F. Tres aspectos de la cultura. Mendoza, 1942.
Phil 365.49   Przyluski, Jean. L'évolution humaine. Paris, 1942.
Phil 6060.29.5   Pulver, Max. Auf Spuren des Menschen. Zürich, 1942.
Phil 8670.14   Pythian-Adams, W.J. The people and the presence. London, 1942.

Phil 2070.137   Raback, A.A. William James. Cambridge, 1942.
Phil 5400.100   Rapaport, David. Emotions and memory. Baltimore, 1942.
Phil 5590.30   Raushenbush, E. Psychology for individual education. N.Y., 1942.
Phil 6327.16   Ray, Marie B. Doctors of the mind; the story of the psychiatry. Boston, 1942.
Phil 9530.40   Reilly, William J. How to improve your human relations, by straight thinking. N.Y., 1942.
Phil 2255.4   Reiser, Oliver L. A new earth and a new humanity. N.Y., 1942.
Phil 8597.52   Religion, humanism. Stockholm, 1942.
Phil 2855.6.25   Reymond, A. Philosophie spiritualiste. Lausanne, 1942. 2v.
Phil 2520.285   Richter, L. René Descartes. Hamburg, 1942.
Phil 5257.28.15   Roback, A.A. Psychorama; a mental outlook and analysis. Cambridge, 1942.
Phil 1122.6.10   Robin, Léon. La pensee hellenique des origines a epicule questions de methode. 1.ed. Paris, 1942.
Phil 6127.22   Rogers, Carl R. Counseling and psychotherapy; newer concepts in practice. Boston, 1942.
Phil 5057.30.5   Romer, Francisco Argentine. Lógica y nóciones de teoria del concimiento. 5. ed. Buenos Aires, 1942.
Phil 6327.17.5   Ross, Thomas Arthur. The common neuroses. 2. ed. London, 1942.
Phil 2050.213.5   Ross, William G. Human nature and utility in Hume's social philosophy. Thesis. Garden City, N.Y., 1942.
Phil 2050.213   Ross, William W.G. Human nature and utility in Hume's social philosophy. Garden City, N.Y., 1942.
Phil 492.10   Rossi, M.M. Alle fonti del deismo e del materialismo moderno. Firenze, 1942.
Phil 8620.43   Rougemont, Denis de. La part du diable. N.Y., 1942.
Phil 9415.10   Rowley, Harold H. Submission in suffering. Cardiff, 1942.
Phil 102.6A   Runes, D.D. The dictionary of philosophy. N.Y., 1942.
Phil 8892.57   Ruvo, Vincenzo de. I valori morali. Bari, 1942.
Phil 6328.25.5   Sachs, Hanns. The creative unconscious. Cambridge, 1942.
Phil 2477.6.110   Salvo, Franco. La logica della vita moralie in Maurice Blondel. Palermo, 1942.
Phil 4980.41   Sánchez Reulet, Aníbal. Raíz y destino de la filosofía. Tucumán, 1942.
Phil 6315.19.5   Schaar, John H. The fear of freedom. London, 1942.
Phil 3800.387.5   Schelling, F.W.J. von. The ages of the world. N.Y., 1942.
Phil 3800.387   Schelling, F.W.J. von. The ages of the world. N.Y., 1942.
Phil 6328.10.30   Schilder, Paul. Goals and desires of man, a psychological survey of life. N.Y., 1942.
Phil 5258.124   Schilder, Paul. Mind: perception and thought in their constructive aspects. N.Y., 1942.
Phil 187.59.80   Schilpp, P.A. The philosophy of G.E. Moore. Evanston, 1942.
Phil 3808.43   Schopenhauer, Arthur. Complete essays. v.1-7. N.Y., 1942.
Phil 3500.52.5   Schultz, John. Ensayo de una clara exposición del contenido de la critica de la razón pura. Cordoba, 1942.
Phil 8419.29   Schumacher, F. Die Sprache der Kunst. Stuttgart, 1942.
Phil 6315.2.122   Sears, R.R. Survey of objective studies of psychoanalytic concepts. N.Y., 1942.
Phil 5258.143   Seashore, R.H. Fields of psychology. N.Y., 1942.
Phil 193.70.5   Sheldon, W.H. America's progressive philosophy. New Haven, 1942.
Phil 5590.8   Sheldon, William H. The varieties of temperament; a psychology of constitutional differences. N.Y., 1942.
Phil 9380.5A   Society for the Psychological Study of Social Issues. Civilian morale. N.Y., 1942.
Phil 4065.125   Il sommario del processo di Giordano Bruno. Citta del Vaticano, 1942.
Phil 735.122   Sreenivasa Iyengar, K.R. The metaphysics of value. Mysore, 1942.
Phil 8633.1.42   Steere, Douglas. V. Death's illumination of life. Cambridge, 1942.
Phil 974.3.83   Steffen, Albert. Auf Geisteswegen. Dornach, 1942.
Phil 978.49.185   Steiner, R. Die not Nach dem Christus. Dornach, 1942.
Phil 4225.23.30   Stellini, J. Scritti filosofica. Milano, 1942.
Phil 6968.26   Stern, Edith M. Mental illness. N.Y., 1942.
Phil 2805.112.10   Stewart, Hugh F. Blaise Pascal. London, 1942.
Phil 5258.142   Streletski, C. Clavier psychologigue. Paris, 1942.
Phil 5590.7   Studies in personality. Contributions in honor of Lewis M. Terman. 1. ed. N.Y., 1942.
Phil 3090.87   Susini, Eugene. Franz von Baader et le romantisme mystique. Thesis. Paris, 1942. 2v.
Phil 3090.87.5   Susini, Eugene. Franz von Baader et le romantisme mystique. v.2-3. Paris, 1942. 2v.
Phil 5258.149   Suter, Jules. Psychologie; Grundlagen und Aufbau. Frauenfeld, 1942.
Phil 8599.31   Taft, Charles Phelps. Do we still need religion? N.Y., 1942.
Phil 5259.32   Tilquin, A. Le behaviorisme. Thèse. Paris, 1942-45.
Phil 8969.3   Traherne, Thomas. Of magnanimity and charity. N.Y., 1942.
Phil 8599.33   Trueblood, D.E. The logic of belief. 1. ed. N.Y., 1942.
Phil 8844.4   Tsanoff, R.A. The moral ideals of our civilization. N.Y., 1942.
Phil 8599.32   Tsanoff, R.A. Religious corssroads. N.Y., 1942.
Phil 7069.42.10   Tyrrell, George N.M. Apparitions. London, 1942?
Phil 3246.239   Unruh, F.F. von. Johann Gottlieb Fichte. Stuttgart, 1942.
Phil 8422.3   Vieira de Almeida, F. Filosofia da arte; ensaio. Coimbra, 1942.
Phil 974.3.116   Wachsmuth, G. Bibliographie der Werke Rudolf Steiners in die Geburt. Dornach, 1942.
Phil 9590.18   Waddington, C.H. Science and ethics. London, 1942.
Phil 5262.43.5   Walker, Kenneth M. The circle of life. London, 1942.
Phil 5262.43   Walker, Kenneth M. Diagnosis of man. London, 1942.
Phil 1750.156   Walsh, Gerald G. Medieval humanism. N.Y., 1942.
Phil 5645.43   Weaver, H.B. A study of discriminative serial action. Thesis. Philadelphia, 1942.
Phil 5066.17   Wernick, William. Complete sets of logical functions. Thesis. N.Y., 1942.
Phil 5850.385.70   Weston, Sidney A. Finding your way in life. N.Y., 1942.
Phil 197.44.5   Wilson, George A. Reckoning with life. New Haven, 1942.
Phil 8712.25   Wilson, Robert M. The witness of science. 1. ed. London, 1942.

Phil 2070.139   Wisconsin. University. William James, the man and the thinker. Madison, 1942.
Phil 8602.46   Wolfson, H.A. The double faith theory in Clement, Saadia, Averroes and St. Thomas. Philadelphia, 1942.
Phil 3640.388   Würzbach, F. Nietzsche. Berlin, 1942.
Phil 4374.5.30   Xirau, Joaquín. Lo fugaz y lo eterno. Mexico, 1942.
Phil 1825.2   Zazzo, René. Psychologues et psychologies et psychologies d'Amérique. Paris, 1942.

1943

Phil 182.94.80   Alarco, L.F. Nicolai Hartmann y la idea de la metafisica. Lima, 1943.
Phil 6110.19   Alexander, R. The doctor alone can't cure you. Overton, 1943.
Phil 7069.43.5   Allen, Maurice. Our invisible friends. N.Y., 1943.
Phil 175.43   Alquié, Ferdinand. Le désir d'éternité. 1. ed. Paris, 1943.
Phil 5520.77   American Congress on General Semantics. Papers from the second American congress on general semantics, August, 1941. Chicago, 1943.
Phil 4351.1.25   Amoroso Lima, A. Las edades del hombre. Buenos Aires, 1943.
Phil 3640.295   Arevalo Martinez, R. Nietzsche el conquistador. Guatemala, 1943.
Phil 75.36   Argentine Republic. Comisión Nacional de Cooperación Intelectual. Bibliografía argentina de publicaciones filosóficas, años 1937 a 1943. Buenos Aires, 1943.
Phil 4351.2   Arias, Alejandro C. Sobre la cultura. Montevideo, 1943.
Phil 525.97.5   Arsen'ev, N.S. Ostkirche und Mystik. 2. Aufl. München, 1943.
Phil 4351.1.33   Arteaga, E. La belleza ideal. Madrid, 1943.
Phil 1505.3   Association Guiellaume Bodé. Quelques aspects de l'humanisme médiéval. Paris, 1943.
Phil 1540.26   Association Guillaume Bude, Paris. Quelques aspects de l'humanisme médiéval. Paris, 1943.
Phil 5465.56.20   Bachelard, G. L'air et les songes. Paris, 1943.
Phil 8691.27   Baker, Albert E. Science, Christianity and truth. London, 1943.
Phil 176.138.15   Berdiaev, Nikolai A. Slavery and freedom. London, 1943.
Phil 6111.60   Bills, A.G. The psychology of efficiency. N.Y., 1943.
Phil 3120.25   Bohnenblust, Gottfried. Vom Adel des Geistes; gesammelte Reden. Zürich, 1943.
Phil 8581.85   Boodin, J.E. Religion of tomorrow. N.Y., 1943.
Phil 4515.50   Boström, C.J. Om religion, vishet och dygd. Stockholm, 1943.
Phil 5722.27   Brinkmann, Donald. Probleme des Unbewussten. Zürich, 1943.
Phil 4822.4   Bunkov, Angel Iliev. Prinos kum istoriiata na bulgarskata filosofska misul'. Sofiia, 1943.
Phil 6952.28   Caravedo, B. Tratamiento social de los enfermos de la mente. Lima, 1943.
Phil 4002.8   Carbonara, Cleto. Il secolo XV. Milano, 1943.
Phil 2402.6   Caso, A. Filósofos y moralistas franceses. México, 1943.
Phil 1702.7   Castell, Alburey. An introduction to modern philosophy. N.Y., 1943.
Phil 8627.20   Cerný, Ladislav. The day of Yahweh and some relevant problems. Praha, 1943.
Phil 4260.120   Chaix-Ruy, Jules. La formation de la pensée philosophique de G.B. Vico. Gap, 1943.
Phil 4260.116   Chaix-Ruy, Jules. Vie de J.B. Vico. Gap, 1943.
Phil 802.16   Chartier, Emile. Abreges pour les aveugles. Paris, 1943.
Phil 4753.2.30   Chernyshevskii, N.G. Antropologicheskii printsip v filosofii. Moskva, 1943.
Phil 1135.195   Chicoteau, Marcel. Les attributs de l'ephectisme grec et leur survivance dans une cosmologie racinienne. Cardiff, 1943?
Phil 8877.71.15   Clark, Gordon H. Reading in ethics. 2nd ed. N.Y., 1943.
Phil 6312.12   Cobb, S. Borderlands of psychiatry. Cambridge, 1943.
Phil 9070.22   Cole, Walton E. Standing up to life. Boston, 1943.
Phil 5627.107.10   Collins, Joyce. The sparrow hath found herself a house. Dublin, 1943.
Phil 2490.29   Comte, Auguste. Oeuvres choisis. Paris, 1943.
Phil 333.15   Coninces, A. L'unité de la connaissance humaine. Bruges, 1943.
Phil 8877.78.3   Conwell, Russell H. Acres of diamonds. N.Y., 1943.
Phil 1920.1.30   Craik, Kenneth James Williams. The nature of explanation. Cambridge, 1943.
Phil 8582.57   Crawford, Benjamin F. The political faith of our fathers. Carnegie, Pa., 1943.
Phil 177.104   Cysarz, Herbert. Das Schöpferische. Halle, 1943.
Phil 5590.14   Davidson, Helen H. Personality and economic background. N.Y., 1943.
Phil 6953.14.5   Davis, J.E. Principles and practice of rehabilatation. N.Y., 1943.
Phil 5590.20   Delgado, Honoria. La personalidad y el carácter. Lima, 1943.
Phil 2520.55   Descartes, René. Regulae ad directionem ingenii. Torino, 1943.
Phil 7069.43.10   Dowding, H.C.T. Many mansions. London, 1943.
Phil 7069.43.20   Driesch, Hans. Parapsychologie. Zürich, 1943.
Phil 3485.20   Drossbach, P. Kant und die Gegenwärtige Naturwissenschaft. Berlin, 1943.
Phil 5400.95.5   Dunbar, H.F. Psychosomatic diagnosis. N.Y., 1943.
Phil 3485.16   Durante, Gaetano. Gli epigoni di Kant. Firenze, 1943.
Phil 4824.4   Espinosa, G. Un pretendido interprete suramericano de Spinoza. Caracas, 1943.
Phil 6674.8   Estabrooks, G.H. Hypnotism. N.Y., 1943.
Phil 3450.11.118A   Farber, Marvin. The foundation of phenomenology; Edmund Husserl. Cambridge, 1943.
Phil 3210.67.12   Fechner, G.T. On life after death. N.Y., 1943.
Phil 3246.74   Fichte, Johann Gottlieb. Rufe an die deutsche Nation. Berlin, 1943.
Phil 6115.29   Fink, David H. Release from nervous tension. N.Y., 1943.
Phil 4960.655   Francovich, Guillermo. Filósofos brasileños. Buenos Aires, 1943.
Phil 9530.48   Friedländer, Max. Wie Rationalisiert man sein Leben. Zürich, 1943?
Phil 5478.5   Frustration and aggression. New Haven, 1943.
VPhil 6115.27.7   Fulton, J.F. Physiology of the nervous system. 2. ed. London, 1943.
Phil 9575.9   Gallegas Rocafull, J.M. Un aspecto del orden cristiano. México, 1943.
Phil 2520.221   Galli, Gallo. Studi cartesiani. Torino, 1943.
Phil 1111.5   Garcia Bacca, J.D. Sobre estetica griega. Mexico, 1943.
Phil 3640.296   Garcia Barcena, R. Responso heroico. La Habana, 1943.

Chronological Listing

Phil 7069.43 Garrett, Eileen Jeanette Lyttle. Awareness. N.Y., 1943.
Phil 5625.86 Gellhorn, Ernst. Autonomic regulations. N.Y., 1943.
Phil 8740.10 Gilson, Étienne. Théologie et histoire de la spiritualité. Paris, 1943.
Phil 4260.119 Giusso, Lorenzo. La filosofia di G.B. Vico e l'età barocca. Roma, 1943.
Phil 9220.13 Gonçalves Viana, M. Psicolgia da Amizade. Porto, 1943.
Phil 3850.18.125 Gongora Perea, C. El espiritu y la vida en la filosofía de Max Scheler. Lima, 1943.
Phil 9070.20 Greenbie, M.L.B. The art of living in wartime. N.Y., 1943.
Phil 5246.31.10 Griffith, C.R. Principles of systematic psychology. Urbana, 1943.
Phil 8586.48 Griffith, G.O. Interpreters of man. London, 1943.
Phil 6956.13 Grinker, Roy. War neuroses in North Africa. N.Y., 1943.
Phil 5246.54 Guerrero, L.J. Psicología. 4. ed. Buenos Aires, 1943.
Phil 3310.12 Gulden, P.H. Albert Görlands systematische Philosophie. Assen, 1943.
Phil 182.43.5 Häberlin, Paul. Anthropologie philosophique. Paris, 1943.
Phil 3007.10 Haering, Theodor Lorenz. Die deutsche und die europäische Philosophie. Stuttgart, 1943.
Phil 9380.7 Harvard University. Department of Psychology. Worksheets on morale. Cambridge, 1943.
Phil 3450.19.10 Heidegger, Martin. Was ist Metaphysik? 4e Aufl. Frankfort, 1943.
Phil 6420.38 Heltman, Harry J. First aide for stutterers. Boston, 1943.
Phil 3007.9 Hessen, Johannes. Die Ewigkeitswerte der deutschen Philosophie. Hamburg, 1943.
Phil 8882.60 Hires, H. For my children. N.Y., 1943.
Phil 6317.28 Howe, Eric Graham. The triumphant spirit. London, 1943.
Phil 4809.727.80 Hromádka, Josef Lukl. Don Quijote české filosofie, Emanuel Rádl, 1873-1942. V New Yorku, 1943.
Phil 5247.56.5 Hull, C.L. Principles of behavior. N.Y., 1943.
Phil 978.83 Humphreys, Christmas. Karma and rebirth. London, 1943.
Phil 9070.103 Il'in, Ivan A. Die ewigen Grundlagen des Lebens. Zürich, 1943.
Phil 184.3.12 James, W. Essays in radical empiricism. N.Y., 1943.
Phil 184.3.45 James, W. Essays on faith and morals. N.Y., 1943.
Phil 184.3.17.5 James, W. Pragmatism. N.Y., 1943.
Phil 5590.16 Jennings, Helen H. Leadership and isolation. N.Y., 1943.
Phil 8620.44 Joad, C.E.M. God and evil. London, 1943.
Phil 3640.342 Johnsson, Milker. Nietzsche och tredje riket. Stockholm, 1943.
Phil 6319.1.36 Jung, C.G. Uber die Psychologie des Unbewussten. 5. Aufl. Zürich, 1943.
Phil 4769.6.82 Kaganov, V. Mirovozzrenie I.M. Sechenova. Moskva, 1943.
Phil 3549.8.40 Klages, Ludwig. Vom Sinn des Lebens. Jena, 1943.
Phil 185.54.5 Klatzkin, Jakob. In praise of wisdom. N.Y., 1943.
Phil 3450.15.90 Klitzner, Julius. Hieronymus Hiruhaim: zum deutschen Geist im Barock Böhmens. Prag, 1943.
Phil 6120.19 Kraines, S.H. Managing your mind. N.Y., 1943.
Phil 6980.398 Krapf, E. Eduardo. Tomas de Aquino y la psicopatología. Buenos Aires, 1943.
Phil 3850.27.97 Kraus, Oskar. Albert Schweitzer. London, 1943.
Phil 8622.2 Kroner, Richard. The primacy of faith. N.Y., 1943.
Phil 9070.21 Landau, Rom. Letter to Andrew. London, 1943.
Phil 5850.255 Langer, W.C. Psychology and human living. N.Y., 1943.
Phil 365.47.15 Lecomte du Noüy, Pierre. L'avenir de l'esprit. N.Y., 1943.
Phil 3011.3.15 Lehmann, G. Die deutschen Philosophie der Gegenwart. Stuttgart, 1943.
Phil 8961.13 Lewis, Clive Staples. Christian behaviour. London, 1943.
Phil 5402.21.10 Lewis, Clive Staples. The problem of pain. London, 1943.
Phil 8591.44.5A Lewis, Clive Staples. The screwtape letters. N.Y., 1943.
Phil 2280.5.107 Lida, R. Belleza, arte y poesía en la estética de Santayana. Tucumán, 1943.
Phil 3640.495 Liebmann, K. Friedrich Nietzsche. München, 1943.
Phil 8701.19 Lindsay, A.D. Religion, science, and society in the modern world. New Haven, 1943.
Phil 3585.1.100F Loewenhaupt, Friedrich. Johann Heinrich Lambert. Mülhausen, 1943?
Phil 6321.17 Low, A.A. Secret of self-help in psychiatric aftercare. v.1-3. Chicago, 1943.
Phil 8591.36.10 Lyman, E.W. Religion and the issues of life. N.Y., 1943.
Phil 1930.8.90 McCallum, R.B. Robin George Collingwood, 1889-1943. London, 1943.
Phil 9380.6 MacCurdy, J.T. The structure of morale. Cambridge, Eng., 1943.
Phil 8592.64 Mackay, J.A. Heritage and destiny. N.Y., 1943.
Phil 5590.17 Magoun, F.A. Balanced personality. N.Y., 1943.
Phil 5252.83 Marf, Gustav. Grundriss der Psychologie. Bern, 1943.
Phil 187.139 Marias Aquilera, J. El tema del hombre. Madrid, 1943.
Phil 2750.11.89 Maritain, Jacques. Art and poetry. N.Y., 1943.
Phil 2750.11.58 Maritain, Jacques. Christianisme et démocratie. N.Y., 1943.
Phil 2750.11.35 Maritain, Jacques. Redeeming the time. London, 1943.
Phil 2750.11.45.5 Maritain, Jacques. The twilight of civilization. N.Y., 1943.
Phil 8667.22 Mascall, E.L. He who is; a study in traditional theism. London, 1943.
Phil 8887.6.15 Mason, J. A treatise on self-knowledge. N.Y., 1943.
Phil 5252.81A Masserman, J.H. Behavior and neurosis. Chicago, 1943.
Phil 8962.13 Massimi, Massimo. Catholic morality. Paterson, 1943.
Phil 1812.8 Matthews, K. British philosophers. London, 1943.
Phil 97.6 Means, B.W. Selected glossary of philosophical terms. Hartford, Connecticut, 1943.
Phil 6122.61.5 Meng, H. Praxis der seelischen Hygiene. Basel, 1943.
Phil 6322.28 Mira y López, E. Psychiatry in war. 1st ed. N.Y., 1943.
Phil 4710.75 Mitin, M.B. Filosofskaia nauka v SSSR za 25 let. Moskva, 1943.
Phil 4012.9 Montanari, Fausto. Riserve su l'umanesimo. Milano, 1943.
Phil 8413.26 Morris, B. The aesthetic process. Evanston, 1943.
Phil 2050.212 Mossner, E.C. The forgotten Hume, le bon David. N.Y., 1943.
Phil 3120.8.110 Mueller, Richard. Franz Brentanos Lehre von den Gemütsbewegungen. Brünn, 1943.
Phil 187.123 Muller, H.J. Science and criticism. New Haven, 1943.
Phil 2412.6 Muller, Maurice. De Descartes à Marcel Proust. Neuchâtel, 1943.
Phil 343.22 Murphy, A.E. The uses of reason. N.Y., 1943.
Phil 5590.15 Murray, Henry A. Thematic apperception test. Cambridge, Mass., 1943. 2v.
Phil 530.30.10A Muschg, Walter. Mystische Texte aus dem Mittelalter. Basel, 1943.
Phil 8615.20 Muzzey, David S. Ethical religion. N.Y., 1943.

Phil 8888.13 Nabert, Jean. Éléments pour une éthique. 1st ed. Paris, 1943.
Phil 9070.42 Nash, R.S.J. Label your luggage. Dublin, 1943.
Phil 8593.19 Nass, R.B. Two popular philosophic-scientific essays in the spirit of faith and religion. Brooklyn, N.Y., 1943.
Phil 2648.94 Naville, Pierre. Paul Thiry d'Holbach et la philosophie scientifique au XVIIIe siècle. 2. éd. Paris, 1943.
Phil 5590.28 Nédoncelle, M. La personne humaine et la nature. 1. éd. Paris, 1943.
Phil 8703.2.10 Needham, Joseph. Time: the refreshing river; essays and addresses, 1932-1942. London, 1943.
Phil 3425.328 Negri, Enrico de. Interpretazione di Hegel. Firenze, 1943.
Phil 575.120 Newcomb, Theodore Mead. Personality and social change. N.Y., 1943.
Phil 8593.18 Nicodemus (pseud.). Renaissence; an essay in faith. London, 1943.
Phil 3640.41.15 Nietzsche, Friedrich. Also sprach Zarathustra. Stuttgart, 1943.
Phil 3640.16 Nietzsche, Friedrich. Fünf Vorreden in fünf ungeschriebenen Büchern. Berlin, 1943.
Phil 3640.50 Nietzsche, Friedrich. Von neuen Freiheiten des Geistes. 1. Aufl. München, 1943.
Phil 5640.41 Nogué, Jean. Esquisse d'un système des qualités sensibles. Paris, 1943.
Phil 3640.17.11 Oehler, R. Nietzsche. Register. Stuttgart, 1943.
Phil 3640.79.105 Oehler, Richard. Nietzscheregister. Stuttgart, 1943.
Phil 3640.505 Pannwitz, Rudolf. Nietzsche und die Verwandlung des Menschen. Amsterdam, 1943.
Phil 9530.45.5 Panzer, Martin. It's your future. N.Y., 1943.
Phil 2805.42.37 Pascal, Blaise. Pensées. London, 1943.
Phil 4620.3.5 Péturss, Helgi. Sannyall. Reykjavík, 1943.
Phil 3255.92 Peuckert, W.C. Sebastian Franck. München, 1943.
Phil 2070.140 Piane, A.L. delle. William James. Montevideo, 1943.
Phil 4195.36.2 Pico della Mirandola, Giovanni. Dignità dell'uomo. 2. ed. Firenze, 1943.
Phil 182.67.80 Pierola, Raul A. Apuntes dispersos sobre fenomenologia. Santa Fe, 1943.
Phil 2415.12A Pintard, René. La libertinage érudit dans la première mortié du XVII siècle. v.1-2. Paris, 1943.
Phil 4170.5.80 Pra, Mario dal. Il pensiero di Sebastiano Maturi. Milano, 1943.
Phil 5255.49 Pradines, Maurice. Traité de psychologie générale. 1st éd. v.1-2, pt.1-2. Paris, 1943-46. 3v.
Phil 6125.25 Preston, G.H. The substance of mental health. N.Y., 1943.
Phil 5465.133 Przyluski, J. Créer. Paris, 1943.
Phil 5247.13.32 Ramis Alonso, M. A propósito de examen de ingenios del Dr. Huarte. Palma de Mallorca, 1943.
Phil 102.3.4 Ranzoli, C. Dizionario di scienze filosofiche. 4. ed. Milano, 1943.
Phil 6127.23 Rathbone, J.L. Relaxation. N.Y., 1943.
Phil 8707.21 Raven, C.E. Science, religion, and the future. Cambridge, Eng., 1943.
Phil 3425.221 Reichlin-Meldegg, Karl A. Die Autolatrie oder Selbstanbetung. Pforzheim, 1943.
Phil 192.83 Rice, Cale Y. A new approach to philosophy. Lebanon, Tennessee, 1943.
Phil 5252.18.65 Robinson, A.L. William McDougall, M.B., D.S.C., F.R.S.: a bibliography. Durham, 1943.
Phil 9070.41 Roche, A. Knots and crosses. Dublin, 1943.
Phil 8597.50 Roetschi, R. Humanität und Idealismus. Bern, 1943.
Phil 6327.18 Roheim, Geza. The origin and function of culture. N.Y., 1943.
Phil 4210.140.5 Rosmini. Roma, 1943.
Phil 4215.8.32 Ruggiero, Guido de. L'esistenzialismo. 1. ed. Bari, 1943.
Phil 5465.41 Rumpf-Thevenot, Theodor Richard. Phantasie - ewiger Born. Zürich, 1943.
Phil 1740.4 Runes, Dagobert D. Twentieth century philosophy; living schools of thought. N.Y., 1943.
Phil 3850.27.103.5 Russell, L.M. The path to reconstruction. London, 1943.
Phil 2880.8.55 Sartre, Jean Paul. L'être et le néant. Paris, 1943[1946].
Phil 2475.1.274 Scharfstein, B.A. Roots of Bergson's philosophy. N.Y., 1943.
Phil 8419.8 Scheffler, Karl. Form als Schicksa. 2. Aufl. Erlenbach, 1943.
Phil 3800.32.3 Schelling, F.W.J. von. Schellings Werke. München, 1943. 6v.
Phil 818.24A Schilling, Kurt. Geschichte der Philosophie. München, 1943-44. 2v.
Phil 103.3.25 Schmidt, Heinrich. Philosophisches Wörterbuch. Stuttgart, 1943.
Phil 3808.75.10 Schopenhauer, Arthur. Gedanken über Schriftstellerei und ahnliche Gegenslande. Dortmund, 1943.
Phil 3808.72 Schopenhauer, Arthur. Lebensweisheit. Berlin, 1943.
Phil 3808.35.28 Schopenhauer, Arthur. Le monde comme volonté et comme représentation. 8. éd. v.3. Paris, 1943.
Phil 4170.10.80 Sciacca, Michele F. Martinetti. Brescia, 1943.
Phil 5585.67 Sechenov, I.M. Elementy mysli. Moskva, 1943.
Phil 525.99 Serrano Plaja, A. Los místicos. Buenos Aires, 1943.
Phil 6328.28 Sladen, F.J. Psychiatry and the war. 1st ed. Baltimore, 1943.
Phil 7140.140 Slavson, S.R. An introduction to group therapy. N.Y., 1943.
Phil 193.72.5 Slesser, Henry H. The judicial office and other matters. London, 1943.
Phil 3640.311 Smelik, Evert Louis. Vergelden en wergeven. Thesis. 's-Gravenhage, 1943.
Phil 349.38 Smith, A.H. A treatise on knowledge. Oxford, 1943.
Phil 5850.341 Smith, May. An introduction to industrial psychology. London, 1943.
Phil 193.123.8 Smith, Thomas V. The philosophic way of life in America. 2d. ed. N.Y., 1943.
Phil 960.152 Sommerfeld, S. Indienschau und Indiendeutung romantischer Philosophen. Zürich, 1943.
Phil 193.159A Souriau, Étienne. Les différents modes d'éxistence. Paris, 1943.
Phil 978.49.140 Spring, P.J. Essays on human science. Winter Park, 1943.
Phil 5058.46.25 Stebbing, Lizzie S. A modern elementary logic. London, 1943.
Phil 3585.1.45F Steck, Max. Bibliographia Lambertiana. Berlin, 1943.
Phil 7082.38.6 Stekel, Wilhelm. The interpretation of dreams. N.Y., 1943. 2v.
Phil 575.138 Stiefel, Kurt. Persönlichkeit und Form. Zürich, 1943.
Phil 5135.6 Stoetzel, Jean. Théorie des opinions. 1. éd. Paris, 1943.
Phil 6328.26 Stolz, Karl R. The church and psychotherapy. N.Y., 1943.

1943 - cont.

Phil 6328.30 — Strachey, Alix. A new German-English psycho-analytical vocabulary. Baltimore, 1943.
Phil 5258.104.5 — Strecker, Edward A. Discovering ourselves. 2d ed. N.Y., 1943.
Phil 8599.21.5 — Tennant, F.R. The nature of belief. London, 1943.
Phil 5259.7.30 — Thorndike, E.L. Man and his works. Cambridge, 1943.
Phil 5627.165 — Thornhill, Alan. One fight more. London, 1943.
Phil 8894.26.5 — Titus, H.H. What is mature morality. N.Y., 1943.
Phil 6329.8 — Tomkins, S.S. Contemporary psychopathology. Cambridge, 1943.
Phil 4960.610 — Torres, João Camillo de Oliveira. O positivismo no Brasil. Petropolis, 1943.
Phil 2805.241 — Tourneur, Zacharie. Une vie avec Blaise Pascal. Paris, 1943.
Phil 2840.99.5 — Verneaux, Roger. L'idealisme de Renouvier. Thèse. Paris, 1943.
Phil 4260.35.33 — Vico, G.B. Scienza nuova...a cura di G. Flores d'Arcais. 3. ed. Padova, 1943.
Phil 7069.43.15 — Wade, A.M. Evidences of immortality. N.Y., 1943.
Phil 9495.143 — Walton, A.H. New vistas...religion, sex and morals. London, 1943.
Phil 5520.94 — Wasmuth, E. Sophie, oder Über die Sprache. Berlin, 1943.
Phil 3925.12 — Weber, Alfred. Das Tragische und die Geschichte. Hamburg, 1943.
Phil 705.29 — Wells, R.V. Three Christian transcendentalists. N.Y., 1943.
Phil 197.68 — White, S.E. Anchors to windward. N.Y., 1943.
Phil 6049.42.8A — Wolff, C. The human hand. N.Y., 1943.
Phil 3504.46 — Wolff, E.M. Étude du role de l'imagination dans la conaissance chez Kant. Thèse. Carcassonne, 1943.
Phil 5635.39 — Wolff, E.M. La senation et l'image. Thèse. Carcassonne, 1943.
Phil 575.115 — Wolff, W. The expression of personality. N.Y., 1943.
Phil 8972.10 — Wyse, Alexander. Moral and social questions arranged for high school religious discussion groups and study clubs. Paterson, 1943.
Phil 34.3 — Year book of neurology, psychiatry and endocrinology. Chicago, 1943.
Phil 5834.1.25 — Yerkes, R.M. Chimpanzees; a laboratory colony. New Haven, 1943.
Phil 5400.101 — Young, Paul T. Emotion in man and animal. N.Y., 1943.
Phil 6335.15 — Zilboorg, Gregory. Mind, medicine and man. N.Y., 1943.

1944

Phil 7069.44.45 — Abhedânanda. Life beyond death. Calcutta, 1944.
Phil 4301.1.5 — Avelino, Andres. Une lettre à Jacques Maritain. Ciudad Trujillo, 1944.
Phil 7069.44.35 — Baird, A.T. One hundred cases for survival after death. N.Y., 1944.
Phil 8581.89 — Baker, A.E. Prophets for a day of judgment. London, 1944.
Phil 5850.127 — Band, Francis. La science des caractères. Paris, 1944.
Phil 8581.90 — Bandeira de Mello, L.M. Teoria do destino. Gazeta de Leopoldina, 1944.
Phil 9070.33 — Banning, M.C. Conduct yourself accordingly. N.Y., 1944.
Phil 2050.219 — Baratono, A. Hume e l'illuminismo inglese. 2a ed. Milano, 1944.
Phil 400.100 — Bartolomeis, F. de. Idealismo ed esistenzialismo. Napoli, 1944.
Phil 3450.32.80 — Bártschi, Lina. Der Berner Philosoph Carl Hebler. Bern, 1944.
Phil 8876.108.7 — Beauvoir, Simone de. Pour une morale de l'ambiguité suivi de Pyraus et Cinéas. Paris, 1944.
Phil 7069.44.17 — Bendit, L.J. Paranormal cognition in human psychology. London, 1944.
Phil 176.138.16 — Berdiaev, Nikolai A. Slavery and freedom. N.Y., 1944.
Phil 2475.1.51 — Bergson, Henri. Creative evolution. N.Y., 1944.
Phil 2475.1.40.4 — Bergson, Henri. Essai sur les données immédiates de la conscience. 43. éd. Paris, 1944.
Phil 1870.73.18 — Berkeley, G. Philosophical commentaries generally called the commonplace book. London, 1944.
Phil 525.113 — Bertin, G. I mistice medievali. Milano, 1944.
Phil 3640.304 — Blanco, Julio E. Homenaje a Friedrich Nietzsche en el primer centenario de su nacimiento. Baranquilla, 1944.
Phil 8581.95 — Blondel, Maurice. La philosophie et l'esprit chrétien. Paris, 1944.
Phil 3195.6.107 — Bork, A. Diltheys Auffassung des griechischen Geistes. Berlin, 1944.
Phil 8581.91 — Bosley, Harold A. The philosophical heritage of the Christian faith. Chicago, 1944.
Phil 3120.40.80 — Brahell Brujs, W.R. van. Ter herdenling van Dr. J.D. Bierens de Haan. Naarden, 1944.
Phil 5241.17.23 — Brentano, Franz. Psychologie du point de vue empirique. Paris, 1944.
Phil 6315.2.124 — Brill, A.A. Freud's contribution to psychiatry. N.Y., 1944.
Phil 6951.26 — Brown, Carlton. Brainstorm. N.Y., 1944.
Phil 8951.20 — Brown, Charles R. Dreams come true. N.Y., 1944.
Phil 4065.27 — Bruno, Giordano. Giordano Bruno. 2. ed. Milano, 1944.
Phil 7069.44 — Burton, Jean. Heyday of a wizard. 1. ed. N.Y., 1944.
Phil 7069.44.20 — Butterworth, G.W. Spiritualism and religion. London, 1944.
Phil 2805.226 — Cailliet, E. The clue to Pascal. London, 1944.
Phil 9035.85 — Carr, Wells. Know thyself. N.Y., 1944.
Phil 333.5.15 — Cassirer, Ernst. An essay on man. New Haven, 1944.
Phil 8582.58 — Cave, S. The Christian estimate of man. London, 1944.
Phil 8582.59 — Christlieb, M.L. How can I bear suffering? London, 1944.
Phil 3850.5.94 — Claparède-Spir, H. Evocation. Genève, 1944.
Phil 5042.25.5A — Cohen, Morris R. A preface to logic. N.Y., 1944.
Phil 8627.15 — Cojazzi, Antonio. L'anima umana non muore. Torino, 1944.
Phil 2490.58.5 — Comte, Auguste. Religión universal, el amor por principio. Santiago de Chile, 1944.
Phil 8400.2 — Concinnitas. Basel, 1944.
Phil 8952.11 — Constantino, S.A. Amen, amen. N.Y., 1944.
Phil 4080.3.45 — Croce, Benedetto. Pensieri vari (ristampa). Bari, 1944.
Phil 4080.3.40 — Croce, Benedetto. Perche non possiamo non derci cristiani. Bari, 1944.
Phil 6952.27 — Crutcher, H.B. Foster home care for mental patients. N.Y., 1944.
Phil 7069.44.5 — Cummins, G.D. After Pentecost; the Alexandrian chronicle of Cleophas. London, 1944.
Phil 87.12.5 — Cuvillier, Armand. Kücük felsefesözlügü. Ankara, 1944.
Phil 2042.5 — DeBurgh, William George. George Dawes Hicks. London, 1944.
Phil 5243.5.50 — Delgrado, Honario. El tiempo y la vida animica normal. Lima, 1944.

1944 - cont.

Phil 8583.37 — Dent, Phyllis. The growth of the spiritual life. London, 1944.
Phil 2520.52.32 — Descartes, René. Meditationes de prima philosophia. Paris, 1944.
Phil 2520.27.5 — Descartes, René. Pensées, choisies. Paris, 1944.
Phil 7069.44.25 — Desmond, S. Love after death. London, 1944.
Phil 6313.10.2 — Dorcus, Roy M. Textbook of abnormal psychology. 2d ed. Baltimore, 1944.
Phil 196.8.80 — Drago, Pietro C. La filosofia di Bernardino Varisco. Firenze, 1944.
Phil 8404.8 — Ducasse, Curt. Art, the critics and you. N.Y., 1944.
Phil 8879.24 — Eby, L.S. The quest for moral law. N.Y., 1944.
Phil 6954.7.5 — Ellery, Reginald S. Schizophrenia, the Cinderella of psychiatry. Sydney, 1944.
Phil 8954.4 — Elliot, W.H. As I was saying. London, 1944?
Phil 286.7 — Faria Gersão Ventura, Augusta. A maquina do mundo. Porto, 1944.
Phil 9590.22.3 — Fearon, Arthur D. How to think. San Francisco, 1944.
Phil 4110.8.30 — Fedi, Remo. Il bene e la libertà. Milano, 1944.
Phil 90.4.10 — Ferrater Mora, José. Diccionario de filosofía. 2. ed. México, 1944.
Phil 5066.24 — Feys, Robert. Logistiek geformaliseerde logica. Antwerpen, 1944.
Phil 3246.35.8 — Fichte, Johann Gottlieb. Die Bestimmung des Menschen. Leipzig, 1944.
Phil 3246.35.8.5 — Fichte, Johann Gottlieb. Die Bestimmung des Menschen. 2. Aufl. Leipzig, 1944.
Phil 3246.79.60 — Fichte, Johann Gottlieb. Fichte für Heute. Bremen, 1944?
Phil 3246.55.7 — Fichte, Johann Gottlieb. Reden an die deutsche Nation. Leipzig, 1944.
Phil 9050.9 — Fitch, R.E. A certain blind man. N.Y., 1944.
Phil 9400.11 — Flake, A. Life at eighty as I see it. Nashville, 1944.
Phil 510.1.37 — Franz, Victor. Ernst Haeckel. v.1-2. Jena, 1944.
Phil 978.49.200 — Freeman, Arnold. Who was Rudolf Steiner? Sheffield, 1944.
Phil 5545.180 — Furst, Bruno. How to remember. N.Y., 1944.
Phil 9455.20 — Gallup, G.H. A guide to public opinion polls. Princeton, 1944.
Phil 9070.36 — Garcia, Garia. Modelando el porvenir. Lima, 1944.
Phil 8881.70 — García Máynez, E. Etica: etica empirica; etica de bienes; etica formal; etica valorativa. México, 1944.
Phil 5046.6.1 — Gatry, A.J.A. Logic. LaSalle, Ill., 1944.
Phil 181.45.15 — Gentile, Giovanni. Teoria generale dello spirito come atto puro. 6a ed. Firenze, 1944.
Phil 1511.3.12 — Gilson, Étienne. L'esprit de la philosophie médiévale. 2e éd. Paris, 1944.
Phil 1511.3.7 — Gilson, Etienne. La philosophie au moyen âge. 2e éd. Paris, 1944.
Phil 8831.5 — Ginsberg, M. Moral progess; being the Frazer lecture delivered within the University of Glasgow on 18th April 1944. Glasgow, 1944.
Phil 181.89 — Glockner, Hermann. Einführung in das Philosophieren. Berlin, 1944.
Phil 1020.8.23 — Goichon, A.M. La philosophie d'Avicenne et son influence in Europe médiévale. Paris, 1944.
Phil 9166.7 — Grossman, J.S. Do you know your daughter? N.Y., 1944.
Phil 5246.43.10 — Guillaume, Paul. Manuel de psychologie. Paris, 1944.
Phil 3640.96.5A — Halévy, D. Nietzsche. Paris, 1944.
Phil 8620.44.5 — Headlam, A.C. Why I am satisfied; an open letter to Prof. C.E.M. Joad. Oxford, 1944.
Phil 5627.132.10 — Heard, Gerald. A preface to prayer. 1. ed. N.Y., 1944.
Phil 8587.47.5 — Heard, Gerald. The recollection. Palo Alto, 1944.
Phil 3425.40.5.9A — Hegel, Georg Wilhelm Friedrich. The philosophy of history. N.Y., 1944.
Phil 3425.60.16 — Hegel, Georg Wilhelm Friedrich. Vorlesungen über die Philosophie der Religion. Leipzig, 1944-
Phil 3425.40.11 — Hegel, Georg Wilhelm Friedrich. Vorlesungen über die Philosophie der Weltgeschichte. Leipzig, 1944. 4v.
Phil 6317.20.5A — Hendrick, Ives. Facts and theories of psychoanalysis. 2d ed. N.Y., 1944.
Phil 8957.9.5 — Hirst, E.W. Studies in Christian love. London, 1944.
Phil 8697.17 — Hocking, W.E. Science and the idea of God. Chapel Hill, 1944.
Phil 3195.6.94 — Hodges, Herbert A. Wilhelm Dilthey. London, 1944.
Phil 8697.7 — Hodgson, Leonard. Theology in an age of science. Oxford, 1944.
Phil 9070.38 — Hopkinson, A.W. Pastor's psychology. London, 1944.
Phil 6317.29 — Howe, Eric Graham. Invisible anatomy. London, 1944.
Phil 7040.22A — Hunt, Joseph M. Personality and the behavior disorders. N.Y., 1944. 2v.
Phil 6418.4 — Ingraham, F.D. Spina bifida and cranium bifidum. Boston, 1944.
Phil 8958.5 — Izu Loiteque, Gofronia. Libertad. Venezuela, 1944.
Phil 960.150 — Jast, Louis S. Reincarnation and karma. N.Y., 1944.
Phil 184.26.25 — Joad, C.E.M. Philosophy. London, 1944.
Phil 9470.6 — Jordan, Rudolf. Homo sapiens socialis, principles of the philosophy of responsibility. Johannesburg, 1944.
Phil 3480.97 — Kant, Immanuel. Von der Würde des Menschen. Leipzig, 1944.
Phil 6960.12 — Kasanin, J.S. Language and thought in schizophrenia. Berkeley, 1944.
Phil 9070.40 — Katterhenry, E.A. Can you take it? St. Louis, Mo., 1944.
Phil 5286.10 — Katz, David. Gestaltpsychologie. Basel, 1944.
Phil 95.1.5 — Kirchner, Friedrich. Wörterbuch der philosophischen Begriffe. Leipzig, 1944.
Phil 3549.8.30 — Klages, Ludwig. Rhymen und Runen aus dem Nachlass. Leipzig, 1944.
Phil 6120.20 — Klein, David B. Mental hygiene. N.Y., 1944.
Phil 2520.161.10 — Koyré, A. Entretiens sur Descartes. N.Y., 1944.
Phil 6615.12.3 — Kretschmer, Ernst. Hysterie, reflex und instikt. 3. Aufl. Leipzig, 1944.
Phil 5250.39 — Künkel, Fritz. In search of maturity. N.Y., 1944.
Phil 6321.12.10 — Laforgue, R. Psychopathologie de l'échec. Paris, 1944.
Phil 3640.384.5 — Landmann, M. Zum Stil des Zarathustra. n.p., 1944.
Phil 4600.2.30 — Larsson, Hans. Postscriptum. Stockholm, 1944.
Phil 186.101 — Lasaga y Travieso, J.I. Manual de introducción a la filosofia de acuerdo. 2. ed. Facs. 1-8. La Habana, 1944-1946.
Phil 7084.24 — Layard, John Willoughby. The lady of the hare, being a study in the healing power of dreams. London, 1944.
Phil 365.47.17 — Lecomte du Noüy, Pierre. La dignité humaine. N.Y., 1944.
Phil 8591.44.10 — Lewis, Clive Staples. The case for Christianity. N.Y., 1944.
Phil 8961.13.10 — Lewis, Clive Staples. Christian behaviour. N.Y., 1944.
Phil 2120.6.30 — Lewis, John. Marxism and modern idealism. London, 1944.
Phil 5520.92 — Lipps, Hans. Die Verbindlichkeit der Sprache. Frankfurt, 1944.

Chronological Listing

Phil 5401.18   Litwinski, Léon de. La timidité constitutionnelle et ses formes passive et active. Lisbonne, 1944.

Phil 4973.41   Lizarte Martínez, Angel. Dios, espíritu y materia; esencia. 2. ed. Montevideo, 1944.

Phil 6321.11.10   Lorand, Sándor. Psycho-analysis today. N.Y., 1944.

Phil 935.11   Lüth, Paul. Die japanische Philosophie. Tübingen, 1944.

Phil 8591.50   Lunn, Arnold. Good gorilla. London, 1944.

Phil 5252.60.12   McDowall, R.J.S. Sane psychology. 2d ed. London, 1944.

Phil 2150.13A   McKeon, Richard P. The philosophic bases of art and criticism. Chicago? 1944.

Phil 2733.43   Malebranche, Nicolas. Méditations pour se disposer à l'humilité et à la pénitence. Paris, 1944.

Phil 812.19   Marias Aguilera, J. San Anselmo y el insensato. Madrid, 1944.

Phil 2750.11.58.5   Maritain, Jacques. Christianity and democracy. N.Y., 1944.

Phil 2750.11.37.5   Maritain, Jacques. De Bergson à Thomas d'Aquin. N.Y., 1944.

Phil 2750.11.37   Maritain, Jacques. De Bergson à Thomas d'Aquin. Paris, 1944.

Phil 2750.11.72   Maritain, Jacques. The dream of Descartes. N.Y., 1944.

Phil 6322.40   Matthew, A.V. Depth psychology and education. Kolhapur, 1944.

Phil 3625.17.30   Medicus, Fritz. Das mythologische in der Religion. Erlenbach, 1944.

Phil 2475.1.288   Meyer, François. La pensée de Bergson. Grenoble, 1944.

Phil 2138.79.8.4   Mill, John S. Autobiography. N.Y., 1944.

Phil 6122.63   Miller, W.H. How to relax. N.Y., 1944.

Phil 8592.70   Moffatt, J. The thrill of tradition. London, 1944.

Phil 3640.312   Molina, Enrique. Nietzsche, dionisíaco y asceta. Santiago, 1944.

Phil 187.118.5   Monsarrat, K.W. Thoughts, deeds and human happiness. London, 1944.

Phil 812.23   Moore, Charles A. Philosophy - East and West. Princeton, 1944.

Phil 7069.44.10   Moore, M.G. Things I can't explain. London, 1944.

Phil 812.17   Moreira da Sá, A. Os precursores de Desartes. Lisboa, 1944.

Phil 2150.1.130   Mott, F.J. The crisis of opinion. Boston, 1944.

Phil 5440.40   Mottram, Vernon Henry. The physical basis of personality. Harmondsworth, 1944.

Phil 8413.29   Mueller, A.E. The world as spectacle, an aesthetic view of philosophy. N.Y., 1944.

Phil 6122.64   Muhlbery, W. Mental adjustments. Cincinnati, O., 1944.

Phil 3425.310   Myers, Henry Alonzo. The Spinoza-Hegel paradox. Ithaca, 1944.

Phil 4080.3.170   Nicolini, Fausto. Benedetto Croce. Napoli, 1944.

Phil 3640.62   Nietzsche, Friedrich. Federico Nietzsche. 3. ed. Milano, 1944.

Phil 5254.2.15   Ogden, C.K. The ABC of psychology. Harmondsworth, 1944.

Phil 7069.44.40   O'Neill, Herbert V. Spiritualism as spiritualists have written of it. London, 1944.

Phil 189.24.5   Oribe, Emilio. Teoría del nous. Buenos Aires, 1944.

Phil 530.15.40   Paillard, Etienne. Lumière éternelle. Paris, 1944.

Phil 4080.3.175   Parente, Alfredo. Il pensiero politico di Benedetto Croce e u nuovo liberalismo. 2. ed. Napoli, 1944.

Phil 8670.15   Parkes, J.W. God and human progress. Harmondsworth, Eng., 1944.

Phil 190.76   Pegis, Anton C. Essays in modern scholasticism in honor of John F. McCormick. Westminster, Md., 1944.

Phil 5627.168   Pfister, Oskar. Das Christentum und die Angst; eine religions-psychologische, historische und religionshygienische Untersuchung. Zürich, 1944.

Phil 5360.18   Pikas, Anatol. Abstraction and concept formation. Cambridge, 1944.

Phil 978.78.5   Plummer, L.G. Star habits and orbits. Covina, Calif., 1944.

Phil 4752.2.100   Porret, Eugene. La philosophie chrétienne en Russie. Neuchâtel, 1944.

Phil 9400.9   Poweys, J.C. The art of growing old. London, 1944.

Phil 6125.25.5   Preston, G.H. The substance of mental health. London, 1944.

Phil 6965.17   Psychoanalytic orientation in case work. N.Y., 1944.

Phil 3195.6.105   Pucciarelli, E. Introduccion a la filosofía de Dilthey. Buenos Aires, 1944.

Phil 6327.20   Radzinowicz, Leon. Mental abnormality and crime. London, 1944.

Phil 6127.24   Ray, Marie B. Lyons. How never to be tired, or Two lifetimes in one. Indianapolis, Ind., 1944.

Phil 9590.20   Reinhardt, K.F. A realistic philosophy. Milwaukee, 1944.

Phil 525.93   Reinhold, Hans. The soul afire. N.Y., 1944.

Phil 396.3   Reiser, Oliver Leslie. Planetary democracy. N.Y., 1944.

Phil 3499.30   Renda, A. Conoscenza e moralita in Kant. Palermo, 1944.

Phil 3837.20.5   Rensi, Giuseppe. Spinoza. 2. ed. Milano, 1944.

Phil 1190.15   Robin, Léon. Pyrrkon et le scepticisme grec. 1. éd. Paris, 1944.

Phil 2610.86   Rochot, Bernard. Les travaux de Gassendi sur Épicure. Paris, 1944.

Phil 2610.87   Rochot, Bernard. Les travaux de Gassendi sur Épicure et sur l'atomisme. Thèse. Paris, 1944.

Phil 6687.14   Rodriquez, Rafael E. Psicoterapia por medio de la hipnosis. Montevideo, 1944.

Phil 575.136   Romero, F.A. Filosofía de la persona y otros ensayos de filosofía. Buenos Aires, 1944.

Phil 4368.2.35   Romero, Francisco. Filosofía contemporanea estudios y notas. 2. ed. Buenos Aires, 1944.

Phil 8620.43.3   Rougemont, Denis de. La part du diable. N.Y., 1944.

Phil 6315.2.127A   Sacho, H. Freud, master and friend. Cambridge, Mass., 1944.

Phil 6688.29   Salter, Andrew. What is hypnosis. N.Y., 1944.

Phil 645.35   Sánchez, Francisco. Que nada se sabe. Buenos Aires, 1944.

Phil 2280.5.87   Santayana, George. Persons and places. London, 1944.

Phil 2280.5.85A   Santayana, George. Persons and places. v.1,3. N.Y., 1944-53. 2v.

Phil 3960.16   Sassen, Ferdinand. De wijsbegeerte der middeleuvren in de Nederlanden. Lochen, 1944.

Phil 2255.1.100   Schilpp, Paul A. The philosophy of Bertrand Russell. Evanston, Ill., 1944.

Phil 8598.86   Schmidt, K. From science to God. 1. ed. N.Y., 1944.

Phil 3425.318   Schmidt, Werner. Hegel und die Idee der Volksordnung. Leipzig, 1944.

Phil 3018.30   Scifert, F. Schäpferische deutsche Philosophie. Köhn, 1944.

Phil 3850.27.108   Seaver, George. Albert Schweitzer: revolutionary christian. N.Y., 1944.

Phil 818.23   Serrano, J. História de filosofia; ou Pensamento filosófico através dos séculos. Rio de Janeiro, 1944.

Phil 2477.9.85   Sertillanges, A.G. La philosophie de Claude Bernard. Paris, 1944.

Phil 7069.44.30   Seymour, C.J. Curiosities of psychical research. London, 1944.

Phil 6968.28   Sharp, A.A. Dynamic era of court psychiatry, 1914-44. Chicago, 1944.

Phil 1750.158   Sheldon, W.H. Process and polarity. N.Y., 1944.

Phil 5258.132   Simon, M. Tratado de psicología. Lima, 1944. 2v.

Phil 193.158   Sinclair, W.A. An introduction to philosophy. London, 1944.

Phil 6328.66   Small, Saul Mouchly. Symptoms of personality disorder. N.Y., 1944.

Phil 1020.7.10   Smith, Margaret. Al-Ghazáli, the mystic. London, 1944.

Phil 5850.341.5   Smith, May. Handbook of industrial psychology. N.Y., 1944.

Phil 9590.40   Spalding, Baird Thomas. Life and teaching of the masters of the Far East. Los Angeles, California, 1944. 5v.

Phil 8893.102   Stevenson, Charles Leslie. Ethics and language. New Haven, 1944.

Phil 6328.29   Strecker, E.A. Fundamentals of psychiatry. London, 1944.

Phil 7084.10   Teillard, Ania. Traumsymbolik. Zürich, 1944.

Phil 5259.31   Thomae, Hans. Das Wesen der menschlichen Antriebsstruktur. Leipzig, 1944.

Phil 8599.34   Thomas, George Finger. The vitality of the Christian tradition. N.Y., 1944.

Phil 5585.68   Thurstone, L.L. A factorial study of perception. Chicago, 1944.

Phil 8420.13   Torres-García, J. Universalismo constructivo. Buenos Aires, 1944.

Phil 6060.36   Trillat, Raymond. Éléments de graphologie pratique. Paris, 1944.

Phil 2730.99.5   Vancourt, Raymond. La théorie de la connaissance chez Maine de Biran. 2e éd. Paris, 1944.

Phil 4983.5.85   Varela, Félix. Cartas a Elpidio sobre la impiedad. v.1-2. Habana, 1944.

Phil 4983.5.6   Varela, Félix. Miscelanea filosófica. Habana, 1944.

Phil 5425.70   Veiga Azvedo, A.V. O problema do génio; ensaio para uma tesse de redução. Lisboa, 1944.

Phil 2840.99   Verneaux, Roger. Renouvier. Thèse. Paris, 1944.

Phil 4260.17.7   Vico, G.B. The autobiography of Giambattista Vico. Ithaca, 1944.

Phil 705.33   Wahl, J. Existence humaine et transcendance. Neuchâtel, 1944.

Phil 8602.50   Walker, K.M. Meaning and purpose. London, 1944.

Phil 8972.12   Warner, F.E. Future of man. London, 1944.

Phil 7081.2   Weiss, Harry Bischoff. Oneirocritica Americana. N.Y., 1944.

Phil 5262.31.15   Wertheimer, M. Gestalt theory. N.Y., 1944.

Phil 8602.49   Wheeler, F. What do Christians believe? London, 1944.

Phil 9415.12   Wilds, Louis T. Why good people suffer. Richmond, Va., 1944.

Phil 8712.26   Williston, A.L. Beyond the horizon of science. Boston, 1944.

Phil 3120.2.98.5   Winter, E. Der Bolzanoprozess. Brünn, 1944.

Phil 3022.6   Wundt, Max. Die Wurzeln der deutschen Philosophie in Staam und Vasse. Berlin, 1944.

Phil 974.5   Zimmer, Heinrich. Der Weg zum Selbst. Zürich, 1944.

1945

Phil 5080.5   Aaron, Richard I. Our knowledge of universals. London, 1945.

Phil 960.155   Abegg, Emil. Indische Psychologie. Zürich, 1945.

Phil 4340.15   Academia...Madrid. Academia Española. Discursos leídos en las recepciones públicas de la Real Academia Española. Ser. 2. Madrid, 1945- 6v.

Phil 1190.20   Amand de Merdito, Emmanuel. Fatalisme et liberté dans l'antique grecque. Louvain, 1945.

Phil 6980.38.2   American Psychiatric Association. One hundred years of American psychiatric Association, 1844-1944. N.Y., 1945.

Phil 735.136   Archivio di Filosofia. La crisi dei valori. Roma, 1945.

Phil 4961.805   Ardao, Arturo. Filosofía pre-universitaria en el Uruguay. Montevideo, 1945.

Phil 8836.2.80   Auchmuty, J.J. Lecky. London, 1945.

Phil 1870.121   Baladi, Naguit. La pensée religieuse de Berkeley. La Caire, 1945.

Phil 5811.19   Bally, Gustav. Vom Ursprung und von den Grenzen der Freiheit. Basel, 1945.

Phil 7069.45   Barnes, M.S. Long distance calling. N.Y., 1945.

Phil 176.151   Barth, Hans. Wahrheit und Ideologie. Zürich, 1945.

Phil 3640.320   Bataille, Georges. Sur Nietzsche. Paris, 1945.

Phil 7082.80   Baudouin, Charles. Introduction à l'analyse des rêves. Genève, 1945.

Phil 801.32   Baumgarten, A. Die Geschichte der abendländischen Philosophie eine Geschichte des geistigen Fortschritts der Menscheit. Genève, 1945.

Phil 1865.22   Bentham, Jeremy. The limits of jurisprudence defined. N.Y., 1945.

Phil 2475.1.38.2   Bergson, Henri. Les deux sources de la morale et de la religion. Genève, 1945.

Phil 2475.1.35   Bergson, Henri. Discours sur la politesse. Paris, 1945.

Phil 2475.1.40.6   Bergson, Henri. Essai sur les données immédiates de la conscience. Genève, 1945.

Phil 2475.1.50.10   Bergson, Henri. L'évolution créatrice. Genève, 1945.

Phil 2475.1.69.7   Bergson, Henri. Le rire. Genève, 1945.

Phil 960.157   Bernard, Theos. Philosophical foundations of India. London, 1945.

Phil 6659.2   Binger, Carl A.L. Personality in arterial hypertension. N.Y., 1945.

Phil 8402.12.5   Birkhoff, G.D. Medida estetica. Rosario, 1945.

Phil 5400.103   Bisch, L.E. Your nerves. N.Y., 1945.

Phil 5241.108   Bittle, Alestine N.C. The whole man. Milwaukee, 1945.

Phil 5241.109   Blackburn, J.M. Psychology and the social pattern. London, 1945.

Phil 5643.107   Brandt, Herman F. The psychology of seeing. N.Y., 1945.

Phil 5211.6   Brennan, R.E. History of psychology. N.Y., 1945.

Phil 8581.67.10   Brightman, E.S. Nature and values. N.Y., 1945.

Phil 4210.151   Brunello, Bruno. Antonio Rosmini. Milano, 1945.

Phil 8951.21A   Brunner, Heinrich E. Justice and the social order. London, 1945.

Phil 4215.3.80   Buonaiui, E. Giuseppe Rensi. Roma, 1945.

Phil 672.165   Burgelin, Pierre. L'homme et le temps. Photoreproduction. Paris, 1945.

Phil 5520.80   Burke, Kenneth. A grammar of motives. N.Y., 1945.

Chronological Listing

Phil 2805.226.5   Cailliet, E. Pascal; genius in the light of scripture. Philadelphia, 1945.

Phil 4073.37   Campanella, Tommaso. Artiveneti. Firenze, 1945.

Phil 6980.157   Campbell, John D. Everyday psychiatry. Philadelphia, 1945.

Phil 2880.8.80   Campbell, Robert. Jean Paul Sartre; ou une littérature philosophique. Paris, 1945.

Phil 4060.8.81   Cancarini, Itala. Acri. Brescia, 1945.

Phil 2520.224   Carbonara, Cleto. Renato Cartesio e la tradizione ontologica. Torino, 1945.

Phil 7069.45.45   Carington, Whately. Telepathy. 2. ed. London, 1945.

Phil 5722.29   Casey, D.M. La théorie du subconscient de Morton Prince. Paris, 1945.

Phil 6312.13   Cebola, Luiz. As grandes crises do homen ensaio de psicopatologia individual e colectiva. Lisboa, 1945.

Phil 9070.44   Chamberlain, F.E. The lighted pathway. Los Angeles, Calif., 1945.

Phil 525.95   Cheney, Sheldon. Men who have walked with God. N.Y., 1945.

Phil 8403.12   Chernyshevskii, N.G. Esteticheskie otnosheniia iskusstva k deistvitel'nosti. Moskva, 1945.

Phil 7069.45.5   Clark, Ida C.G. Men who wouldn't stay dead. N.Y., 1945.

Phil 9560.33   Cleghorn, S.N. The seamless robe; the religion of loving kindness. N.Y., 1945.

Phil 9070.22.5   Cole, Walton E. The three R's of religion. Boston, 1945.

Phil 2515.9.30   Corte, Marcel de. Philosophis des moeurs contemporaines. Bruxelles, 1945.

Phil 6315.2.129   Cové, M. L'oeuvre paradoxale de Freud. 1. éd. Paris, 1945.

Phil 4080.3.75   Croce, Benedetto. La Borghesia. Bari, 1945.

Phil 4080.3.50   Croce, Benedetto. Considerazioni sul problema morale del tempo nostro. Bari, 1945.

Phil 4080.3.28   Croce, Benedetto. Etica e politica. 3. ed. Bari, 1945.

Phil 4960.605.10   Cruz Costa, João. A filosofia no Brasil. Pôrto Alegre, 1945.

Phil 8953.8   D'Arcy, Martin Cyrile. The mind and heart of love. London, 1945.

Phil 5066.22   Daval, R. Le raisonnement mathématique. Paris, 1945.

Phil 2520.55.10   Descartes, René. Règles pour la direction de l'esprit. Paris, 1945.

Phil 8583.38   Dimond, S.G. Heart and mind. London, 1945.

Phil 5520.86   Dobrogaev, S.M. Charl'z Darvin o proiskhozhdenii rechi. Leningrad, 1945.

Phil 334.8.5   Donat, J. Critica. 9. ed. Monachü, 1945.

Phil 7069.45.30   Dowden, Hester. The book of Johannes, by Peter Fripp. London, 1945.

Phil 7069.45.25   Dowding, H.C.T. Lychgate. London, 1945.

Phil 9590.21   Drummond, D.D. Today we think of our tomorrows. Richmond, Va., 1945.

Phil 6980.241   Dumas, A.G. A psychiatric primer for the veteran's family and friends. Minneapolis, 1945.

Phil 7069.45.50   Duncan, V.H.M. The trial of Mrs. Duncan. London, 1945.

Phil 5435.10.5   Dunlap, Knight. Habits, their making and unmaking. N.Y., 1945.

Phil 7069.45.20   Edwards, H.J. The science of spirit healing. London, 1945.

Phil 6980.259   Ellery, R.S. Psychiatric aspects of modern warfare. Melbourne, 1945.

Phil 179.33.5   Emmet, D.M. The nature of metaphysical thinking. London, 1945.

Phil 3235.81.24   Engels, Friedrich. Ludwig Feuerbach et la fin de la philosophie classique allemande. Paris, 1945.

Phil 6314.7.4   English, Oliver Spurgeon. Emotional problems of living. N.Y., 1945.

Phil 5593.45   Erickson, Mary R. Large scale Rorschach techniques. 1. ed. Springfield, Ill., 1945.

Phil 1750.190   L'existence. Paris, 1945.

Phil 705.31   Ezilasi, Wilhelm. Wissenschaft als Philosophie. Zürich, 1945.

Phil 4110.9.30   Fabro, Cornelio. Problemi dell'esistenzialismo. Roma, 1945.

Phil 90.5   Fachwörterbuch der Philosophie. Zürich, 1945.

Phil 3210.67.10   Fechner, G.T. On life after death. Chicago, 1945.

Phil 3475.3.80   Feith, R.C. Psychologismus und Transzendentalismus bei K. Jaspers. Bern, 1945.

Phil 6315.16.10   Fenichel, Otto. The psychoanalytic theory of neurosis. N.Y., 1945.

Phil 4356.3.10   Ferrater Mora, José. Variaciones sobre el espíritu. Buenos Aires, 1945.

Phil 3246.66.5   Fichte, Johann Gottlieb. Philosophy of masonry. Seattle, 1945.

Phil 5245.45.2   Flügel, John Carl. Man, morals and society. London, 1945.

Phil 8406.18   Focillon, Henri. Vita delle forme, di Henri Focillon. Padova, 1945.

Phil 1750.160   Fondy, John T. The educational principles of American humanism. Diss. Washington, D.C., 1945.

Phil 4960.405   Francovich, Guillermo. La filosofía en Bolivía. Buenos Aires, 1945.

Phil 8585.35A   Frank, Erich. Philosophical understanding and religious truth. 1st ed. London, 1945.

Phil 2005.12   Frankel, Charles. The love of anxiety, and other essays. 1st ed. N.Y., 1945.

Phil 8400.35   Gallatin, A.E. Of art: Plato to Picasso. N.Y., 1945.

Phil 530.40.60   Gallegos Rocafull, J.M. La experiencia de Dios en los místicos españoles. México, 1945.

Phil 4957.10   Gaos, José. Pensamiento de lengua española. México, 1945.

Phil 4307.1   Gaos, José. Pensamiento español. México, 1945.

Phil 181.80.5   Garcia Morente, Manuel. Ensayos. Madrid, 1945.

Phil 4600.4.80   Geijerstam, G.L. af. Så minns Bengt Lidforss. Stockholm, 1945.

Phil 178.46.80   Gerard, Jacques. La metaphysique de Paul Decoster. Paris, 1945.

Phil 1111.9   Gigon, Olof. Der Ursprung der griechischen Philosophie von Hesiod bis Parmenides. Berlin, 1945.

Phil 3488.26   Goldmann, L. Mensch, Gemeinschaft und Welt in der Philosophie Immanuel Kants. Zürich, 1945.

Phil 8661.18   Gonzalez Alvarez, Angel. El tema de Dios en la filosofía existencial. Madrid, 1945.

Phil 5246.46.5   Goodenough, Florence L. Developmental psychology. 2. ed. N.Y., 1945.

Phil 6060.34   Graphologia. v.1-2,3-4. Bern, 1945. 2v.

Phil 4635.9.30   Grieg, Harald V. Torgny Segershedt. Oslo, 1945.

Phil 6980.336.5   Grinker, Roy R. Men under stress. Philadelphia, 1945.

Phil 181.71.10   Guénon, R. La métaphysique orientale. 2. ed. Paris, 1945.

Phil 8407.31.5   Guggenheimer, R.H. Sight and insight, a prediction of new perceptions in art. N.Y., 1945.

Phil 337.14   Guia, Michele. Storia delle science ed epistemologia. Torino, 1945.

Phil 8661.17   Gururmurti, D. God and progress. Madras, 1945.

Phil 3640.90.12A   Gutersohn, U. Friedrich Nietzsche und der moderne Mensch. 2. Aufl. St. Gallen, 1945.

Phil 338.24   Hawkins, D.J.B. The criticism of experience. London, 1945.

Phil 5590.21A   Heath, C.W. What people are. Cambridge, Mass., 1945.

Phil 1145.85   Heinimann, Felix. Nomos und physis. Basel, 1945.

Phil 585.179   Hidalgo, Alberto. El universo está cerca. Buenos Aires, 1945.

Phil 5400.105   Hinsie, L.E. The person in the body. N.Y., 1945.

Phil 6314.8   Hobman, J.B. David Eder; memoirs of a modern pioneer. London, 1945.

Phil 6317.22.20   Horney, Karen. Our inner conflict. N.Y., 1945.

Phil 5627.134.75   Howard, Peter. Ideas have legs. London, 1945.

Phil 8587.60   Huxley, Aldous. The perennial philosophy. 1. ed. N.Y., 1945.

Phil 8587.60.5   Huxley, Aldous. The perennial philosophy. 5. ed. N.Y., 1945.

Phil 6319.1.182   Jacobi, Jolan. Die Psychologie von C.G. Jung. Zürich, 1945.

Phil 6959.7   Jong, Herman H. de. Experimental catatonia, a general reaction form of the central nervous system. Baltimore, 1945.

Phil 7069.45.65   Jordan, Alfred McKay, (Mrs.). Science from the unseen. N.Y., 1945.

Phil 4710.65   Jovchuk, M.T. Osnovnye cherty russkoi klassicheskoi filosofii XIX v. Moskva, 1945.

Phil 5249.13.25   Jung, Carl G. Psychologische Betrachtungen; eine Auslese aus den Schriften. Zürich, 1945.

Phil 270.51   Junkersfeld, M.J. The Aristotelian-Thomistic concept of chance. Indiana, 1945.

Phil 6680.7A   Kahn, S. Suggestion and hypnosis made practical. Boston, 1945.

Phil 5250.17.10   Kantor, J.R. Psychology and logic. Bloomington, 1945. 2v.

Phil 6320.14   Kaplan, Oscar J. Mental disorders in later life. Stanford, Calif., 1945.

Phil 5250.36A   Kardiner, Abram. The psychological frontiers of society. N.Y., 1945.

Phil 5250.37.5   Katz, David. Psychologischer Atlas. Basel, 1945.

Phil 7069.45.55   Keith, Cassius C. The dawn of a new day, a revelation. Kansas City, Mo., 1945.

Phil 3092.1.5   Kerényi, Karoly. Bach ofen und die Zukunft des Humanismus. Zürich, 1945.

Phil 8960.9   Knight, F.H. The economic order and religion. N.Y., 1945.

Phil 2045.126   Konijnenburg, Willem van. Thomas Hobbes' Leviathan. Proefschrift. Assen, 1945.

Phil 4710.30   Kruzhkov, U.S. O russkoi klassicheskoi filosofii XIX v. Moskva, 1945.

Phil 6120.21   Kupper, H.I. Back to life. N.Y., 1945.

Phil 2805.2089A   Lafuma, Louis. Trois pensées inédites de Pascal. Paris, 1945.

Phil 2725.35.20   Lavelle, Louis. Du temps et de l'eternité. Paris, 1945.

Phil 5590.22   Lecky, Prescott. Self-consistency; a theory of personality. N.Y., 1945.

Phil 2150.15.80   Lee, G.C. George Herbert Mead. N.Y., 1945.

Phil 8701.20   Lee, John H. Are science and religion at strife? Evanston, 1945.

Phil 8666.16.5   Lewis, Clive Staples. Beyond personality; the Christian idea of God. London, 1945.

Phil 8591.44.11   Lewis, Clive Staples. The case for Christianity. N.Y., 1945.

Phil 9240.5   Lindsay, A.D. The good and the clever. Cambridge, 1945.

Phil 5251.46   Loux, Samuel. Man and his fellowmen. London, 1945.

Phil 6321.20   Lowy, Samuel. New directions in psychology toward individual happiness and social progress. N.Y., 1945.

Phil 8666.17.10   Lubac, Henri de. Le drame de l'humanisme athée. 3. éd. Paris, 1945.

Phil 1870.115.10   Luce, Arthur A. Berkeley's immaterialism. London, 1945.

Phil 5850.260   Lurton, D.E. Make the most of your life. London, 1945.

Phil 343.23   Mack, R.D. The appeal to immediate experience. N.Y., 1945.

Phil 8050.72   McMahon, Amos. Preface to an American philosophy of art. Chicago, 1945.

Phil 2150.14.30   McMahon, T.E. A Catholic looks at the world. N.Y., 1945.

Phil 2733.30.4   Malebranche, Nicolas. De la recherche de la vérité. Paris, 1945. 2v.

Phil 2250.94   Marcel, Gabriel. La métaphysique de Royce. Paris, 1945.

Phil 3640.305.10   Martin, A.W.O. von. Nietzsche und Burckhardt; zwei geistige Welten im Dialog. 3e Aufl. Basel, 1945.

Phil 5593.45.5   Maslow, Paul. Rorschach psychology. Brooklyn, 1945.

Phil 2520.220   Mateu y Llopis, Felipe. Descartes. Barcelona, 1945.

Phil 4959.205   Mayagoitia, David. Ambiente filosófico de la Nueva España. México, 1945.

Phil 6322.19.7   Menninger, Karl Augustus. The human mind. 3d ed. N.Y., 1945.

Phil 1750.115.25   Merleau-Ponty, Maurice. Phénoménologie de la perception. Paris, 1945.

Phil 1750.115.26   Merleau-Ponty, Maurice. Phénoménologie de la perception. Paris, 1945.

Phil 2138.02A   Mill, John S. Bibliography of the published writings of J.S. Mill. Evanston, Ill., 1945.

Phil 1050.4.25   Millás y Vallicrosa, José María. Sêlomó Ibn Gabirol como poeta y filósofo. Madrid, 1945.

Phil 9590.24   Milum, John P. Man and his meaning. London, 1945.

Phil 270.49   Miró Quesada, Oscar. El problema de la libertad y la ciencia. Lima, 1945.

Phil 2750.16.30   Molle, G. van. La connaissance dialectique et l'expérience existentielle. Liège, 1945.

Phil 6322.30   Moncrieff, A.A. Psychology in general practice. London, 1945.

Phil 4210.149   Morando, Dante. Rosmini. 2a ed. Brescia, 1945.

Phil 8581.81.80   Morgan, A.E. The philosophy of Edward Bellamy. N.Y., 1945.

Phil 1712.25   Mueller, Max. Das christliche Menschenbild und die Weltanschauungen der Neuzeit im Breiszau. Freiburg, 1945.

Phil 5593.45.10   Munroe, R.L. Prediction of the adjustment and academic performance of college students. Stanford, 1945.

Phil 5252.84   Murphy, L.B. Emotional factors in learning. N.Y., 1945.

Phil 6123.8   National Committee for Mental Hygiene, Inc. Division on Rehabilition. Bibliography. Mental hygiene in industry. N.Y., 1945.

Phil 5850.281   National Research Council. Psychology for the returning serviceman. 1st ed. Washington, 1945.

1945 - cont.

Phil 4357.2.80	Navarro, Martin. Vida y obras de Don Francisco Giner de los Rios. 1. ed. Mexico, 1945.
Phil 3425.312	Niel, Henri. De la médiation dans la philosophie de Hegel. Paris, 1945.
Phil 3425.316	Niel, Henri. De la médiation dans la philosophie de Hegel. Thèse. Paris, 1945.
Phil 3640.308	Nietzsche; conférences prononcées à Genève sous les auspices de la fondation Marie Gretler. Erlenbach, 1945.
Phil 3640.79.20	Nietzsche, Friedrich. Van vornehmen Menschen. Klosterberg, 1945.
Phil 4600.2.80	Nyman, Alf. Hans Larsson. Stockholm, 1945.
Phil 5520.35.8	Ogden, Charles K. The meaning of meaning. 7. ed. N.Y., 1945.
Phil 6310.1.95	Oliver Brachfield, F. Les sentiments d'infériorité. Genève, 1945.
Phil 5590.34	Pastori, Giuseppina. Il substrato biologico della personalità. Brescia, 1945.
Phil 5465.160	Patron Miranda, Joaquin R. La tecnica divina: el movimiento. Campeche, 1945.
Phil 8416.34.5	Pepper, S.C. The basis of criticism in the arts. Cambridge, 1945.
Phil 190.18.25A	Perry, R.B. One world in the making. 1st ed. N.Y., 1945.
Phil 2415.10	Pervicax (pseud.). Les infiltrations germaniques dans la pensée française. Paris, 1945.
Phil 9230.15	Peterson, V.W. Gambling, should it be legalized? Chicago, Ill., 1945.
Phil 4195.36	Pico della Mirandola, Giovanni. Dignità dell'uomo. 3. ed. Firenze, 1945.
Phil 5640.43	Piéron, Henri. Aux sources de la connaissance la sensation. 3. éd. Paris, 1945.
Phil 5890.3.1	Pintner, Rudolf. The psychology of the physically handicapped. N.Y., 1945.
Phil 735.123	Polin, Raymond. Essai sur la compréhension des valeurs. Thèse. Paris, 1945.
Phil 978.85	Poppelbaum, H. Man's eternal biography; three essays on life and death. N.Y., 1945.
Phil 7069.45.15	Price, Harry. Poltergeist over England; three centuries of mischievous ghosts. London, 1945.
Phil 978.68.10	Purucker, G. de. Studies in occult philosophy. Covina, California, 1945.
Phil 6536.13	Putnam, T.J. Convulsive seizures; how to deal with them. 2d. ed. Philadelphia, 1945.
Phil 8891.4	Quillian, W.F. The moral theory of evolutionary naturalism. New Haven, 1945.
Phil 6327.4.30	Rank, Otto. Will therapy and truth and reality. N.Y., 1945.
Phil 6980.631	Rapaport, David. Diagnostic psychological testing. Chicago, 1945. 2v.
Phil 6980.635.5	Rees, J.R. The shaping of psychiatry by war. London, 1945.
Phil 2255.5	Reid, James K. Whither humanity; the philosophy of a doctor. London, 1945.
Cg Phil 7075.137	Reik, T. Psychology of sex relations. N.Y., 1945.
Phil 8842.11	Robertson, Archibald M.A. Morals in world history. London, 1945.
Phil 3850.27.93	Robock, A.A. The Albert Schweitzer jubilee book. Cambridge, 1945.
Phil 298.14	Roth, Samuel. The peep-hole of the present. N.Y., 1945.
Phil 8620.43.7	Rougemont, Denis de. The devil's share. 2. ed. N.Y., 1945.
Phil 817.19A	Russell, B.R. A history of Western philosophy. N.Y., 1945.
Phil 6980.668	San Francisco, Department of Public Health. An experiment in the psychiatric treatment of promiscuous girls. San Francisco, 1945.
VPhil 310.708.2	Sándor, Pál. A történelmi materializmus története. 2. kiad. Budapest, 1945.
Phil 103.3.30	Schmidt, Heinrich. Philosophisches Wörterbuch. N.Y., 1945.
Phil 5058.27.7	Sellars, R.W. The essentials of logic. Boston, 1945.
Phil 5258.134	Sherman, Mandel. Intelligence and its deviations. N.Y., 1945.
Phil 7069.45.10	Sherwood, Jane. The country beyond; a study of survival and rebirth. London, 1945.
Phil 1523.11	Slesser, Henry H. Order and disorder; a study of mediaeval principles. London, 1945.
Phil 4769.1.70	Solov'ev, V.S. The meaning of love. London, 1945.
Phil 4570.4.81	Spongberg, V.H. The philosophy of Erik Gustaf Geijer. Rock Island, 1945.
Phil 9590.23	Steiner, L.R. (Mrs.). Where do people take their troubles? Boston, 1945.
Phil 7069.45.35	Stevens, William O. Unbidden guests, a book of real ghosts. N.Y., 1945.
Phil 2805.112.15	Stewart, Hugh F. The heart of Pascal. Cambridge, 1945.
Phil 3246.237	Stine, R.W. The doctrine of God in the philosophy of Fichte. Philadelphia, 1945.
Phil 6328.29.10	Strecker, E.A. Psychiatry in modern warfare. N.Y., 1945.
Phil 7069.45.60	Swaffer, Hannen. My greatest story. London, 1945.
Phil 8709.15.5	Teller, Woolsey. Essays of an atheist. N.Y., 1945.
Phil 2225.5.98	Thompson, M.H. The pragmatic philosophy of C.S. Pierce. Part of thesis. Chicago, 1945.
Phil 184.19.18	Tonquédec, J. de. L'existence d'après Karl Jaspers. Paris, 1945.
Phil 5627.245.1	Tournier, Paul. Technik und Glaube. Basel, 1945.
Phil 6329.10	Tramer, Moritz. Lehrbuch der allgemeinen Kinderpsychiatrie. Basel, 1945.
Phil 2880.8.82	Troisfontaines, Roger. Le choix de Jean Paul Sartre. Paris, 1945.
Phil 8709.19	Tute, Richard C. After materialism - what? 1. ed. N.Y., 1945.
Phil 351.3	Uexküll, T. von. Wirklichkeit als Geheimmis und Auftrag. Bern, 1945.
Phil 2475.1.292	Valery, Paul. Henri Bergson. Paris, 1945.
Phil 2805.231.5	Valot, Stephen. Regardons vivre Blaise Pascal. 2. éd. Paris, 1945.
Phil 3450.19.106	Vanni Rovighi, S. Heidegger. Brescia, 1945.
Phil 3503.10	Vanni Rovighi, Sofia. Introduzione allo studio di Kant. Como, 1945.
Phil 5061.4.15	Vaz Ferreira, Carlos. Lógica viva (adaptación prática y didáctica). Buenos Aires, 1945.
Phil 850.19	Verbeke, G. L'évolution de la doctriné du pneuma. Paris, 1945.
Phil 2840.99.10	Verneaux, Roger. L'idéalisme de Renouvier. Paris, 1945.
Phil 2840.99.15	Verneaux, Roger. Renouvier, disciple et critique de Kant. Paris, 1945.

1945 - cont.

Phil 3450.19.96	Waelhens, A. de. La filosofía de Martin Heidegger. Madrid, 1945.
Phil 3504.31.10	Wasianski, E.A.C. Immanuel Kant in seinen letzen Lebensjahren. Zürich, 1945.
Phil 5627.172	Webb, Clement C.J. Religious experience; a public lecture. London, 1945.
Phil 1822.5	Weber, Conrad G. Studies in the English outlook in the period between the world wars. Bern, 1945.
Phil 6980.775	Wechsler, Israel S. The neurologist's point of view. N.Y., 1945.
Phil 3504.44	Weldon, Thomas D. Introduction to Kant's Critique of pure reason. Oxford, 1945.
Phil 6972.19.5	Wells, Frederick L. Mental examiners handbook. 2. ed. N.Y., 1945.
Phil 8419.39	Wili, Hans. Johann G. Sulzer; Personlichkeit und Kunstphilosophie. St. Gallen, 1945.
Phil 822.2.4.5	Windelband, W. Lehrbuch der Geschichte der Philosophie. Genf, 1945?
Phil 6332.13	Wolberg, Lewis R. Hypoanalysis. N.Y., 1945.

1946

Phil 3905.84	Abrahamsen, David. The mind and death of a genius. N.Y., 1946.
Phil 9035.53.10	Adler, Alfred. Understanding human nature. N.Y., 1946.
Phil 8615.5.23	Adler, Felix. Our part in this world. N.Y., 1946.
Phil 2475.1.294	Adolphe, Lydie. La philosophie religieuse de Bergson. Paris, 1946.
Phil 800.12	Aleksandrov, G.F. Istoriia zapnoevropliskoi filosofii. Izd. 2. Moskva, 1946.
Phil 6310.4.20	Alexander, Franz G. Psychoanalytic threapy. N.Y., 1946.
Phil 525.101	Allen, Warner. The timeless moment. London, 1946.
Phil 2880.1.85	Amadou, R. Louis C. de Saint-Martin et le Martinisme. Paris, 1946.
Phil 4482.1.90	Andrade, Antonio Alberto de. Vernei a filosofia portuguesa. Braga, 1946.
Phil 2805.245	Andreas, Peter. Pascal. Strasbourg, 1946.
Phil 3425.317	Antoni, Carlo. Considerazioni su Hegel e Marx. Napoli, 1946.
Phil 5258.140.5	Appecciafuoco, Romolo. La psicologia sperimentale di Sante de Panctis. Roma, 1946.
Phil 8624.100	Archivio di Filosofia. Il problema dell'immortalità. Roma, 1946.
Phil 9070.47.5	Ashton, M.O. To whom it may concern. 2. ed. Salt Lake City, 1946.
Phil 1020.7.2	Asin Palacios, M. Obras escogidas. Madrid, 1946.
Phil 6953.16.3	The autobiography of David. London, 1946.
Phil 2520.81.15	Baillet, A. Vie de Monsieur Descartes. Paris, 1946.
Phil 176.227	Balthasar, Nicolas J.J. Mon moi dans l'être. Louvain, 1946.
Phil 3640.316	Baranger, William. La pensée de Nietzsche. Paris, 1946.
Phil 332.24	Barlow, K.E. The state of public knowledge. London, 1946.
Phil 1200.10.7	Barth, P. De Stoa. 6. Aufl. Stuttgart, 1946.
Phil 2805.247A	Baudin, Émile. Etudes historiques et critiques sur la philosophie de Pascal. v.1-3. Neuchâtel, 1946-47. 4v.
Phil 2805.209.5	Bayet, Albert. Les provinciales de Pascal. Paris, 1946.
Phil 1870.123	Bender, Frans. George Berkeley's philosophy re-examined. Amsterdam, 1946.
Phil 8951.23	Bennett, J. Christian ethics and social policy. N.Y., 1946.
Phil 176.138.20	Berdiaev, Nikolai A. Essai de metaphysique eschatologique. Paris, 1946.
Phil 4752.2.60	Berdiaev, Nikolai Aleksandrovich. Khristianstvo i antisimitizm. Parizh, 1946.
Phil 4752.2.35	Berdiaev, Nikolai Aleksandrovich. Russkaia ideia. Parizh, 1946.
Phil 2475.1.30	Bergson, Henri. The creative mind. N.Y., 1946.
Phil 2475.1.60.6	Bergson, Henri. Matière et mémoire. Genève, 1946.
Phil 2475.1.65.4	Bergson, Henri. La pensée et le mouvant. Genève, 1946.
Phil 8581.66.15	Bergson, Henri. The two sources of morality and religion. N.Y., 1946.
Phil 5627.178	Berguer, Georges. Traité de psychologie de la religion. Lausanne, 1946.
Phil 8402.20	Bernard, Charles. Esthétique et critique. Paris, 1946.
Phil 3552.313	Berse, Max. Über Leibniz: Leibniz und seine Ideology. Jena, 1946.
Phil 400.102	Bianca, Giovanni. Essenza ed esistenza, idealità e realtà. Catania, 1946.
Phil 8581.78.5	Bixler, J.S. Conversations with an unrepentant liberal. New Haven, 1946.
Phil 1830.5A	Blau, Joseph L. American philosophic addresses. N.Y., 1946.
Phil 5850.140	Bonnardel, Raymond. L'adaption de l'homme à son métier. 1. éd. Paris, 1946.
Phil 410.11	Borel, Émile. Les paradoxes de l'infini. Paris, 1946.
Phil 2805.233	Boulan, Émile. De Pascal à Victor Hugo. Groningue, 1946.
Phil 1870.122	Brayton, Alice. George Berkeley in Apulia. Boston, 1946.
Phil 6980.135	Brill, Abraham A. Lectures on psychoanalytic psychiatry. N.Y., 1946.
Phil 5241.28.20	Brown, W. Personality and religion. London, 1946.
Phil 8070.2	Bruyne, Edgar de. Etudes d'esthétique médiévale. Brugge, 1946. 3v.
Phil 5041.40.20	Burtt, Edwin Arthur. Right thinking. 3rd ed. N.Y., 1946.
Phil 8402.2	Buzin, Germain. Le crépuscule des images. Paris, 1946.
Phil 177.105	Calogero, G. Lezioni di filosofia. v.2-3. Roma, 1946. 2v.
Phil 2880.8.81	Campbell, Robert. Jean Paul Sartre. Paris, 1946.
Phil 1702.9	Campo, M. Variazioni sulla storia della filosofia moderna. Brescia, 1946.
Phil 87.3	Candou, José M. Diccionario manual de filosofia. Madrid, 1946.
Phil 5850.148.5	Caner, George C. It's how you take it. N.Y., 1946.
Phil 7069.46.5	Cannon, A. The shadow of destiny. London, 1946?
Phil 1930.11.30	Cargill, S.T. The philosophy of analogy and symbolism. London, 1946?
Phil 7069.46.25	Carington, Whately. Thought transference. N.Y., 1946.
Phil 630.48	Carre, Meyrick H. Realists and nominalists. London, 1946.
Phil 5590.120	Case, V.S. Your personality. N.Y., 1946.
Phil 5590.32	Cattell, Raymond B. Description and measurement of personality. Yonkers-on-Hudson, 1946.
Phil 3484.19	Chartier, Emile. Lettres à Sergio Solmi sur la philosophie de Kant. Paris, 1946.
Phil 5242.51	Clawson, J. Psychology in action. N.Y., 1946.
Phil 530.11.9	Cloud of unknowing. A book of contemplation. 4. ed. London, 1946.

1946 - cont.

Phil 1930.10.30	Cohen Morris, R. The faith of a liberal. Selected essays. N.Y., 1946.
Phil 2490.31.5	Comte, Auguste. Cours de philosophie positive. 8. éd. Paris, 1946.
Phil 2490.27	Comte, Auguste. Le prolétariat dans la societe moderne. Paris, 1946.
Phil 6980.198	Cooke, Elliot D. All but me and thee. Washington, 1946.
Phil 8403.41	Coomaraswamy, A.K. Figures of speech or figures of thought. London, 1946.
Phil 802.15	Copleston, F. A history of philosophy. v.1,4-8. London, 1946-50. 6v.
Phil 3808.186	Copleston, Frederick. Arthur Schopenhauer. London, 1946.
Phil 3552.253.5	Cresson, André. Leibniz, sa vie, son oeuvre. Paris, 1946.
Phil 3808.184	Cresson, André. Schopenhauers a vie, son oeuvre. Paris, 1946.
Phil 8582.60	Cullmann, Oscar. Christus und die Zeit. Zollikon-Zürich, 1946.
Phil 4803.313.35	Czezowski, Tadeusz. O naukach humanistycznych. Toruń, 1946.
Phil 4803.313.30	Czezowski, Tadeusz. O uniwersytecie i studiach uniwersyteckjck. Toruń, 1946.
Phil 3823.10	Darbon, A. Etudes Spinozistes. Paris, 1946.
Phil 9400.12	De Gruchy, C. Creative old age. San Francisco, 1946.
Phil 1980.3.94	Delisle, Françoise Roussel. Friendship's odyssey. London, 1946.
Phil 8404.7	Deren, Maya. An anagram of ideas on art. N.Y., 1946.
Phil 2520.219A	Descartes, René. Descartes, 1596-1650. Genève, 1946.
Phil 7069.46.15	Desmond, Shaw. Spiritualism. London, 1946?
Phil 178.17.17	Dessoir, Max. Einleitung in die Philosophie. 2. Aufl. Stuttgart, 1946.
Phil 1955.6.30	Dewey, John. Problems of men. N.Y., 1946.
Phil 3195.6.35	Dilthey, Wilhelm. Die Philosophie des Lebens. Frankfurt, 1946.
Phil 3640.690	Doisy, M. Nietzsche, homme et surhomme. Bruxelles, 1946.
Phil 3552.314	Drago del Boca, S. Leibniz. Milano, 1946.
Phil 1750.163	Drewinc, H. VierGestalten aus den Zeitalter des Humanismus. Saint Gallen, 1946.
Phil 5627.169	Dumas, Georges. Le surnaturel et les dieux d'après les maladies mentales. Paris, 1946.
Phil 5850.176	Dunlap, Knight. Personal adjustment. 1. ed. N.Y., 1946.
Phil 8583.39	Dunlap, Knight. Religion. N.Y., 1946.
Phil 9558.23	Dunn, Ellen Catherine. The concept of ingratitude in renaissance English moral philosophy. These. Washington, D.C., 1946.
Phil 5244.25	Edwards, Allen L. Statistical analysis for students in psychology and education. N.Y., 1946.
Phil 8954.4.5	Elliot, W.H. Bring me my bow. London, 1946.
Phil 179.35	Esser, Pieter H. Levensaspecten. Zutphen, 1946.
Phil 735.276	Europaeisches Forum, Alpbach, Austria, 1946. Erkenntnis und Wert. Salzburg, 1946.
Phil 525.109	Eustace, C.J. An infinity of questions. London, 1946.
Phil 5245.46	Fales, Walter. Wisdom and responsibility. Princeton, 1946.
Phil 4080.3.185	Fano, Giorgio. La filosofia del Croce. 1a ed. Milano, 1946.
Phil 3210.77	Fechner, G.T. Religion of a scientist. N.Y., 1946.
Phil 2225.5.100	Feibleman, James. An introduction to Peirce's philosophy. 1st ed. N.Y., 1946.
Phil 2005.9.30	Feibleman, James. The revival of realism. Chapel Hill, 1946.
Phil 8870.11	Felseneer, Jean. Morale de savants d'Hippocrate à Einstein. Bruxelles, 1946.
Phil 8406.11	Feltkamp, W.C. Zien en verstaan. Amsterdam, 1946.
Phil 2520.231	Finance, J. de. Cogito cartésien et réflexion thomiste. Thèse. Paris, 1946[1945].
Phil 3825.7.2A	Fischer, Kuno. Baruch Spinoza's Leben und Charakter. Heidelberg, 1946.
Phil 5593.46	Ford, Mary E.N. The application of the Rorschach test to young children. Minneapolis, 1946.
Phil 805.9	Foss, Martin. The idea of perfection in the western world. Princeton, 1946.
Phil 4756.1.45.5	Frank, Semen L. God with us; three meditations. London, 1946.
Phil 1133.26	Freeman, Kathleen. The pre-Socratic philosophers. Cambridge, Mass., 1946[1947]
Phil 1133.26.2	Freeman, Kathleen. The pre-Socratic philosophers. Oxford, 1946.
Phil 6980.308	Freud, Anna. The pyscho-analytical treatment of children. London, 1946.
Phil 6315.2.79.5	Freud, Sigmund. An autobiographical study. 2d ed. London, 1946.
Phil 6315.2.75.10	Freud, Sigmund. Drei Abhandlungen zur Sexualtheorie. 7. Aufl. Wien, 1946.
Phil 6315.2.72	Freud, Sigmund. Şelbstdarstellung. London, 1946.
Phil 6315.2.7.5	Freud, Sigmund. Über Psychoanalyse. 9e Aufl. Wien, 1946.
Phil 8406.13	Frey, Dagobert. Kunstwissenchaftliche Grundfragen. Wien, 1946.
Phil 8406.14.5	Friedländer, Max J. Von Kunst und Kennerschaft. Zürich, 1946.
Phil 3552.312	Friedmann, G. Leibniz et Spinoza. Paris, 1946.
Phil 4260.118	Fubini, Mario. Stile i umanità di Giambattista Vico. Bari, 1946.
Phil 3487.20	Fuentes Mares, J. Kant y la evolución de la conciencia socio-política moderna. México, 1946.
Phil 5756.14	Gardet, Louis. La mesure de notre liberté. Tunis, 1946.
Phil 5246.58	Gibson, A.B. Thinkers at work. London, 1946.
Phil 806.13.2	Gilson, Etienne. The unity of philosophical experience. N.Y., 1946.
Phil 575.141	Giordani, Roberto. Dalla dialettica alla apodittica. Roma, 1946.
Phil 481.2	Glagolev, B. Materializm v svete sovremennoi nauki. Frankfurt, 1946.
Phil 8407.29	Goffin, Peter (pseud.). The realm of art. London, 1946.
Phil 4960.635	Gómez Robledo, Antonio. La filosofía en el Brasil. México, 1946.
Phil 4372.1.82	Gomis, J.B. Criterio social de Luis Vives. Madrid, 1946.
Phil 6980.335	Graber, Gustav. Seelenspiegel des Kindes. Zürich, 1946.
Phil 1750.166	Les grands appels de l'homme contemporain. Paris, 1946.
Phil 1850.135	Gundry, W.G.C. Francis Bacon, a map of days. London, 1946.
Phil 4582.4.40	Hägerström, Axel. De socialistiska idéernas historia. Stockholm, 1946.
Phil 3552.318	Hamburger Akademische Rundschau. Gottfried Wilhelm Leibniz. Hamburg, 1946.
Phil 5247.61	Harriman, P.L. Twentieth century psychology. N.Y., 1946.

1946 - cont.

Phil 8408.36.2	Haspers, John. Meaning and truth in the art. Hamden, Connecticut, 1946.
Phil 3489.34	Havet, Jacques. Kant et le problème du temps. Paris, 1946.
Phil 1512.12	Hawkins, D.J.B. A sketch of mediaeval philosophy. London, 1946.
Phil 5247.63	Hayek, F.A. von. Individualism: true and false. Dublin, 1946.
Phil 6980.351.5	Herzberg, Alexander. Active psychotherapy. N.Y., 1946.
Phil 6315.2.82.10	Hesnard, Angelo. Freud dans la société d'après guerre. Genève, 1946.
Phil 5205.34	Hildebrant, R. Zur Kritik der Psychologie. Marburg, 1946. 4 pam.
Phil 2045.52.20	Hobbes, Thomas. Leviathan. Oxford, 1946.
Phil 2477.6.105	Hommage à Maurice Blondel. Paris, 1946.
Phil 6957.22	Hoskins, Roy G. The biology of schizophrenia. 1. ed. N.Y., 1946.
Phil 5170.8	Howard, D.T. Analytical syllogistics. Evanston, 1946.
Phil 5627.134.76	Howard, Peter. Ideas have legs. N.Y., 1946.
Phil 2055.8.30	Hyde, Lawrence. Isis and Osiris. London, 1946.
Phil 3425.319.5A	Hyppolite, Jean. Genèse et structure de la phénoménologie de l'esprit de Hegel. Paris, 1946.
Phil 3425.319	Hyppolite, Jean. Genèse et structure de la phénoménologie de l'esprit de Hegel. Thèse. Paris, 1946.
Phil 3425.315	Il'in, Ivan A. Die Philosophie Hegels als kontemplative Gotteslehre. Bern, 1946.
Phil 1750.285	Jaspers, Karl. L'esistenzialismo. Roma, 1946.
Phil 3640.267.5	Jaspers, Karl. Nietzsche und das Christentum. Hameln, 1946.
Phil 3475.3.35	Jaspers, Karl. Die Schuldfrage. 2. Aufl. Zürich, 1946.
Phil 5520.85	Johnson, Wendel. People in guandaries. N.Y., 1946.
Phil 2075.4.30	Jones, G.V. Democracy and civilization. London, 1946.
Phil 2880.8.90	Juin, Hubert. Jean-Paul Sartre. Photoreproduction. Bruxelles, 1946.
Phil 6319.1.10.5	Jung, C.G. Die Psychologie der Übertragung. Zürich, 1946.
Phil 5850.247	Jung, Carl G. Aufsätze zur Zeitgeschichte. Zürich, 1946.
Phil 5249.13.10	Jung, Carl G. Psychologische Typen. Zürich, 1946.
Phil 5520.90	Kainz, Friedrich. Einführung in dei Sprachpsychologie. Wien, 1946.
Phil 3480.75.20	Kant, Immanuel. Über den Gemeinspruch: Das mag in Theorie richtig sein taugt, aber nicht für die Praxis. Frankfurt, 1946.
Phil 3552.316	Kanthack, K.H. Leibniz. Berlin, 1946.
Phil 3549.10.35	Kassner, Rudolf. Transfiguration. Erlenbach, 1946.
Phil 3549.10.40	Kassner, Rudolf. Wandlung. Zürich, 1946.
Phil 3830.10.5	Kayser, Rudolf. Spinoza. N.Y., 1946.
Phil 4710.80	Khaskhachikh, F.I. O poznavaemosti mira. Moskva, 1946.
Phil 291.14	Kiss, Elek. A világ fejlödése az atom szemléletében. Kolozsvár, 1946.
Phil 6320.15	Klapman, J.W. Group psychotherapy; theory and practice. N.Y., 1946.
Phil 1845.3.100	Konvitz, Milton R. On the nature of value; the philosophy of Samuel Alexander. N.Y., 1946.
Phil 5250.35.2	Kornilov, K.N. Psikhologiia. Moskva, 1946.
Phil 810.8	Krakowski, Edouard. La philosophie gardienne de la cité de Plotin à Bergson. Paris, 1946.
Phil 2050.113	Kydd, Rachel M. Reason and conduct in Hume's treatise. London, 1946.
Phil 8412.6.10	Lalo, Charles. L'art et la vie. Paris, 1946-47. 3v.
Phil 8886.65	Lamont, William D. The principles of moral judgement. Oxford, 1946.
Phil 6321.25	Landis, Carney. Text book of abnormal psychology. N.Y., 1946.
Phil 4655.1.85	Lange, Dagmar M. Pontus Wikner som vitter författare. Nora, 1946.
Phil 835.2	Lauer, Hans Erhard. Die Wiedergeburt der Erkenntnis in der Entwicklungsgeschichte. Freiburg, 1946.
Phil 850.22	LaVia, V. Il problema della fondazione della filosofia e l'oggettivismo antico. 2. ed. Roma, 1946.
Phil 9400.13	Lawton, George. Aging successfully. N.Y., 1946.
Phil 8591.55	Lee, Atkinson. Groundwork of the philosophy of religion. London, 1946.
Phil 1750.181	Lefebvre, Henri. L'existentialisme. Paris, 1946.
Phil 2880.8.86	Lefevre, Luc J. L'existentialiste est-il un philosophe? Paris, 1946. 2v.
Phil 3552.79.20	Leibniz zu seinem 300. Geburtstag. 1-7. Berlin, 1946-52.
Phil 3160.3.95	Levin-Goldschmidt, Hermann. Hermann Cohen und Martin Buber. Genève, 1946.
Phil 186.113	Levitskii, S.A. Osnovy organicheskogo mirovozzreniia. n.p., 1946.
Phil 342.13.5A	Lewis, Clarence I. An analysis of knowledge and value. La Salle, Ill., 1946.
Phil 8591.44.15A	Lewis, Clive Staples. The great divorce. N.Y., 1946.
Phil 3585.11.30	Liebert, Arthur. Der universale Humanismus. Zürich, 1946.
Phil 5590.26A	Liebman, Joshua Loth. Peace of mind. N.Y., 1946.
Phil 3552.317	Litt, Theodore. Leibniz und die deutsche Gegenwart. Wiesbaden, 1946.
Phil 4080.3.195	Lombardi, A. La filosofia di Benedetto Croce. Roma, 1946.
Phil 6321.11.15	Lorand, Sándor. Technique of psychoanalytic therapy. N.Y., 1946.
Phil 6980.433	Lowrey, Lawson G. Psychiatry for social workers. N.Y., 1946.
Phil 7082.188.1	Lowy, Samuel. Psychological and biological foundations of dream-interpretation. London, 1946.
Phil 6315.2.131	Ludwig, Emil. Der entzauberte Freud. 9. Aufl. Zürich, 1946.
Phil 4260.117	Luginbühl, Johannes. Die Axiomatik bei Giambattista Vico. Bern, 1946.
Phil 1712.15	Magnino, Bianca. Alle origini della crisi contemporanea. Roma, 1946.
Phil 5850.264	Maier, Norman Raymond Frederick. Psychology in industry. Boston, 1946.
Phil 2630.7.90	Marcireau, J. René Guenon et son oeuvre. Poitiers, 1946.
Phil 2750.11.48.20	
	Maritain, Jacques. Distinguer pour unir. 4. éd. Paris, 1946.
Phil 4080.3.425	Marone, Gherardo. Ensayo sobre el pensamiento de Benedetto Croce. Buenos Aires, 1946.
Phil 1517.5.5	Masnovo, Amato. Da Guglielmo d'Auvergne. 2. ed. Milano, 1946. 3v.
Phil 6980.459	Masserman, Jules Hymen. Principles of dynamic psychiatry. London, 1946.
Phil 3494.44	Massolo, Arturo. Introduzione alla analitica Kantiaña. Serie 2. Firenze, 1946.
Phil 2150.17.95A	Mayo, Elton. Notes on a lecture on equilibrium. Cambridge, 1946?

1946 - cont.

Phil 187.133   Mead, Hunter. Types and problems of philosophy.
                N.Y., 1946.
Phil 187.135   Medicus, Fritz. Natur und Geist. Erlenback-Zurich, 1946.
Phil 270.62.5   Michotte, A.E. La perception de la causalité.
                Louvain, 1946.
Phil 2138.40.42 Mill, John S. On liberty. Considerations on representative
                government. Oxford, 1946.
Phil 3832.17   Millner, Simond. The face of Benedictus Spinoza.
                N.Y., 1946.
Phil 2733.109   Montcheuil, Y. de. Malebranche et la quiétisme.
                Paris, 1946.
Phil 5520.84A   Morris, Charles W. Signs, language and behavior.
                N.Y., 1946.
Phil 8702.19.5 Morrison, Abraham C. Man does not stand alone.
                N.Y., 1946.
Phil 5252.89   Munn, Norman Leslie. Psychology. Boston, 1946.
Phil 6322.13.5 Muralt, Alexander von. Wahnsinniger oder Prophet?
                Zürich, 1946.
Phil 5252.84.2 Murphy, L.B. Emotional factors in learning. N.Y., 1946.
Phil 1020.22.5 Nadvi, Muzaffar Uddir. Muslim thought and its source.
                Lahore, 1946.
Phil 8703.2.15 Needham, Joseph. History is on our side. London, 1946.
Phil 2520.222   Néel, Marguerite. Descartes et la princesse Elisabeth.
                Paris, 1946.
Phil 1118.3   Nestle, W. Griechische Weltanschauung in ihrer Bedeutung
                für die Gegenwart. Stuttgart, 1946.
Phil 6980.504   New York Academy of Medicine. Modern attitudes in
                psychiatry. N.Y., 1946.
Phil 3640.52   Nietzsche, Friedrich. Der Fall Wagner. Frankfurt, 1946.
Phil 3640.73   Nietzsche, Friedrich. The living thoughts of Nietzsche.
                London, 1946.
Phil 4365.2.33A Ortega y Gasset, José. Concord and liberty. 1st. ed.
                N.Y., 1946.
Phil 1750.166.117 Paparelli, Gioacchino. Tra umanesimo e reforma.
                Napoli, 1946.
Phil 2805.74.10 Pascal, Blaise. Entretien avec M. de Saci. 2. éd.
                Aix, 1946.
Phil 2805.45   Pascal, Blaise. Pascal. Paris, 1946.
Phil 2805.42.25 Pascal, Blaise. Pascal's Pensées. Mt. Vernon, 1946?
Phil 2515.5.93 Pascal, Georges. La pensée d'Alain. Paris, 1946.
Phil 3497.19.5 Paton, Herbert J. The categorical imperative.
                London, 1946.
Phil 5625.75.2 Pavlov, Ivan P. Polnoe sobranie trudov. v.2-5.
                Moskva, 1946. 4v.
Phil 4803.680.30 Pełka-Peliński, Stanisław. Na drogach współczesnej
                kultury. Lódz, 1946.
Phil 1750.173   Pesch, Edgar. L'existentialisme. Paris, 1946.
Phil 6315.2.140 Pesch, Edgar. La pensée de Freud et la psychanalyse.
                Paris, 1946.
Phil 2805.253   Peters, F.E. Blaise Pascal. Hamburg, 1946.
Phil 2980.10   Philosophie in der Schweiz. Erlenbach, 1946.
Phil 4195.34   Pico della Mirandola, Giovanni. Disputationes adversus
                astrologiam divinatricem. Firenze, 1946-52. 2v.
Phil 4805.20   Popelová, Jiřina. Studie o současné české filosofii.
                Praha, 1946.
Phil 346.14   Price, Henry H. Thinking and representation.
                London, 1946.
Phil 5056.1.10A Quine, Willard Van Orman. A short course in logic.
                Cambridge, 1946.
Phil 4080.18.80 Raggiunti, Renzo. Tre brevi studi: La conclusione della
                filosofia del conoscere di Guido Calogero. Firenze, 1946.
Phil 6327.16.7 Ray, Marie B. Doctors of the mind, what psychiatry can do.
                Boston, 1946.
Phil 3552.328   Richter, L. Leibniz und sein Russland. Berlin, 1946.
Phil 348.17   Riet, G. van. L'épistémologie thomiste. Louvain, 1946.
Phil 6127.22.10A Rogers, Carl R. Counseling with returned servicemen. 1.
                ed. N.Y., 1946.
Phil 4080.3.165 Romarell, Patrick. Croce versus Gentile. N.Y., 1946.
Phil 1540.25   Rüegg, Walter. Cicero und der Humanismus; formale
                Untersuchungen über Petrarca und Erasmus. Zürich, 1946.
Phil 6967.15   Ruesch, Jurgen. Chronic disease and psychological
                individualism. N.Y., 1946.
Phil 1717.8.20 Ruggiero, G. de. Filosofi del novecento. 3e ed.
                Bari, 1946.
Phil 4215.8.30 Ruggiero, Guido de. Existentialism. London, 1946.
Phil 4215.8.35 Ruggiero, Guido de. Myths and ideals. London, 1946.
Phil 817.20   Ryan, Arthur H. Perennial philosophers. Dublin, 1946.
Phil 2880.1.47 Saint-Martin, L.C. Tableau naturel des rapports qui
                existent entre Dieu, l'homme et l'univers.
                Rochefort-sur-Mer, 1946.
Phil 1818.9   Sakmann, Paul. Die Denker und Kämpfer der englischen
                Aufklärung. Stuttgart, 1946.
Phil 4479.2.30 Santos, Delfin. Meditação sobre a cultura. Lisboa, 1946.
Phil 2880.8.40A Sartre, Jean Paul. L'existentialisme est un humanisme. 5.
                ed. Paris, 1946.
Phil 3890.10.110 Schaaf, J.J. Geschichte und Begriff. Tübingen, 1946.
Phil 6319.1.184 Schär, Hans. Religion und Seele in der Psychologie C.G.
                Jung. Zürich, 1946.
Phil 3800.387.10 Schelling, F.W.J. von. Die Weltalter; Fragmente.
                München, 1946.
Phil 2255.1.102 Schilpp, Paul A. The philosophy of Bertrand Russell.
                Evanston, Ill., 1946.
Phil 1818.8   Schneider, H.W. A history of American philosophy.
                N.Y., 1946.
Phil 1980.4.30 Schneider, R.E. Positivism in the United States.
                Rosario, 1946.
Phil 5520.390   Segerstedt, T. Torgnysson. Die Macht des Wortes.
                Zürich, 1946.
Phil 6128.13.10 Sherrington, C.S. Man on his nature. Cambridge,
                Eng., 1946.
Phil 3640.430   Siegmund, G. Nietzsche der Atheist und Anti-christ. 4e
                Aufl. Paderborn, 1946.
Phil 3838.26   Sikkes, J.W.T.E. Spinoza. Den Haag, 1946.
Phil 193.147.5 Silverman, H.L. Philosophy and its significance in
                contemporary civilization. Boston, 1946.
Phil 9290.10   Simnett, William E. Leisure, how to enjoy it.
                London, 1946.
Phil 5528.2   Sperisen, Walter. Arbeitsschen, eine
                psychologischpädagogische Studie. Bern, 1946.
Phil 5722.28   Spiess, Emil Jakob. Rätsel der Seele. Olten, 1946.
Phil 1523.12   Steenberghen, F. Atistote en Occident. Louvain, 1946.
Phil 193.162   Steenberghen, F. Ontologie. Louvain, 1946.
Phil 3640.815   Steinbuechel, Theodor. Nietzsche; eine christliche
                Besinnung. Photoreproduction. Stuttgart, 1946.
Phil 8893.102.2 Stevenson, Charles Leslie. Ethics and language. New
                Haven, 1946.

1946 - cont.

Phil 5258.136A Symonds, P.M. The dynamics of human adjustment.
                N.Y., 1946.
Phil 193.160   Szilasi, Wilhelm. Macht und Ohnmacht des Geistes.
                Bern, 1946.
Phil 8709.21   Thomas, W. On the resolution of science and faith.
                N.Y., 1946.
Phil 5780.12   Trey, M. de. Der Wille in der Handschrift. Bern, 1946.
Phil 2880.8.82.2 Troisfontaines, Roger. Le choix de Jean Paul Sartre. 2.
                éd. Paris, 1946.
Phil 1750.165   Truc, G. De J.P. Sartre à L. Lavelle. Paris, 1946.
Phil 1750.166.25 Ulmann, Andre. L'humanisme du 20e siècle. Paris, 1946.
Phil 525.7.15   Underhill, Evelyn. Collected papers of Evelyn Underhill.
                London, 1946.
Phil 2420.1   Urwin, Kenneth. A century for freedom; a survey of the
                French philosophers. London, 1946.
Phil 2310.1.30 Ushenko, A.P. Power and events. Princeton, 1946.
Phil 5261.17.26 Valentine, Willard Lee. Experimental foundations of
                general psychology. N.Y., 1946.
Phil 8711.2   Vignon, Paul. Au sauffle de l'esprit créatur.
                Paris, 1946.
Phil 2422.5   Wahl, Jean A. Tableau de la philosophie française.
                Paris, 1946.
Phil 5645.45   Wellmer, E.N. Retinal structure and colour vision.
                Cambridge, Eng., 1946.
Phil 8602.51   Werfel, Franz. Zwischen Oben und Unten. Stockholm, 1946.
Phil 7069.46   White, Stewart E. The stars are still there. 1. ed.
                N.Y., 1946.
Phil 303.14   Whittaker, E. Space and spirit. London, 1946.
Phil 8897.72   Wijnaendts Francken, C.J. Vier moralisten.
                Amsterdam, 1946.
Phil 974.2.55A Williams, G.M. Priestess of the occult, Madame Blavatsky.
                N.Y., 1946.
Phil 6132.37   Williams, Roger J. The human frontier. N.Y., 1946.
Phil 5832.16   Wimersama Greidanus, H.T. van. De hormische psychologie
                van den mensch. Leiden, 1946.
Phil 6980.779   Witmer, Helen L. Psychiatric interviews with children.
                N.Y., 1946.
Phil 930.40   Wong, Gung-Hsing. The Chinese mind. N.Y., 1946.
Phil 497.10.5   Worrall, R. L. The outlook of science. 2nd ed.
                N.Y., 1946.
Phil 1530.10   Zaragüeta Bengoechea, Juan. Una introducción moderna a la
                filosofía escolástica. Granada, 1946.
Phil 5400.107   Zazzo, Revné. Le devenir de l'intelligence. Paris, 1946.
Phil 5068.11   Zuurdeeg, Willem Frederik. A research for the consequences
                of the Vienna circle philosophy for ethics. Proefschrift.
                Utrecht, 1946.

1947

Phil 1750.270.5 Abbagnano, Nicola. Introduzione all'esistenzialismo.
                Torino, 1947.
Phil 5040.21.5 Abbott, F.K. The elements of logic. London, 1947.
Phil 9035.53.6 Adler, Alfred. Menschenkenntnis. 5. Aufl. Zürich, 1947.
Phil 3482.2.100 Aebi, Magdalena. Kant's Begründung der "Deutschen
                Philosophie". Basel, 1947.
Phil 5240.44   Aeppli, E. Psychologie des Bewussten und Unbewussten.
                Zürich, 1947.
Phil 4060.4.2   Aliotta, Antonio. Opere complete. Roma, 1947. 7v.
Phil 672.166   Allen, Chalinder. The tyranny of time. N.Y., 1947.
Phil 5630.5A   Allport, G.W. The psychology of rumor. N.Y., 1947.
Phil 4260.121   Amerio, Franco. Introduzione allo studio di G.B. Vico.
                Torino, 1947.
Phil 4073.100   Amerio, Romano. Campanella. Brescia, 1947.
Phil 5210.5   Anan'ev, B.G. Ocherki po istorii russkoi psikhologii XVII
                i XIX v. Moskva, 1947.
Phil 7069.47.35 Anspacher, L.K. Challenge of the unknown. N.Y., 1947.
Phil 3552.350   Archivio di Filosofia. Leibniz. Il congresso
                internazionale di filosofia, Roma, 1946. Roma, 1947.
Phil 850.21A   Armstrong, A.H. An introduction to ancient philosophy.
                London, 1947.
Phil 9560.35   Ashley, Robert. Of honour. San Marino, 1947.
Phil 5040.22   Asmus, V.F. Logika. Moskva, 1947.
Phil 8580.30A   Attwater, D. Modern Christian revolutionaries.
                N.Y., 1947.
Phil 1905.20A   Baker, H.C. The dignity of man. Cambridge, 1947.
Phil 3001.16.5 Balthasar, H.U. Prometheus. Heidelburg, 1947.
Phil 720.37   Balthaser, Hans. Wahrheit. Einsiedeln, 1947.
Phil 8402.24   Banfi, Antonio. Vita dell'arte. Milano, 1947.
Phil 6111.62   Bankoff, G.A. The conquest of brain mysteries.
                London, 1947.
Phil 5011.5   Barbu, Z. Le développement de la pensée dialectique.
                Paris, 1947.
Phil 1750.167.2 Barrett, William. What is existentialism? N.Y., 1947.
Phil 1750.167   Barrett, William. What is existentialism? N.Y., 1947.
Phil 332.25   Barth, Heinrich. Philosophie Erscheinung. Basel, 1947.
                2v.
Phil 6111.61.1 Bartley, Samuel Howard. Fatigue and impairment in man. 1.
                ed. N.Y., 1947.
Phil 8876.108.5A Beauvoir, Simone de. Pour une morale de l'ambiguité.
                Paris, 1947.
Phil 5590.40   Becker, Josef. Einfuhrung in die Charakterkunde.
                Nurnberg, 1947.
Phil 1750.169   Beerling, Reimer. Het existentialisme. 's
                Gravenhage, 1947.
Phil 4075.84   Bellini, Angelo. Girolamo Cardano e il suo tempo.
                Milano, 1947.
Phil 1750.235   Benda, J. Tradition de l'existentialisme. Paris, 1947.
Phil 176.138.8 Berdiaev, Nikolai A. Solitude and society. London, 1947.
Phil 4752.2.40 Berdiaev, Nikolai Aleksandrovich. Dialectique
                existentielle du divin et de l'humain. Paris, 1947.
Phil 6311.30.5 Berg, Charles. Deep analysis. 1st American ed.
                N.Y., 1947.
Phil 2475.1.37 Bergson, Henri. Le bon sens et études classiques.
                Clermont, 1947.
Phil 6980.105   Berne, Eric. The mind in action. N.Y., 1947.
Phil 3120.27.30 Binswanger, L. Ausgewählte Vorträge und Aufsätze.
                Bern, 1947. 2v.
Phil 5041.59.2 Black, Max. Critical thinking. N.Y., 1947.
Phil 2880.8.96 Blanzat, Marc. L'homme Sartre. Paris? 1947?
Phil 1701.20   Bochénski, J.M. Europäische Philosophie der Gegenwart.
                Bern, 1947.
Phil 3110.55.5 Böhme, J. The way to Christ. 1st ed. N.Y., 1947.
Phil 3120.2.61 Bolzano, Bernard. Bolzano-Brevier. Wien, 1947.
Phil 1750.166.10 Boucher, Maurice. Goethescher Geist und zwanzigstes
                Jahrhundert. Mainz, 1947.
Phil 2880.8.88 Boutang, P. Sartre, est-il un possédé? Paris, 1947.

646

1947 - cont.

Phil 5425.74 Bowerman, Walter. Studies in genius. N.Y., 1947.
Phil 2477.13 Bréhier, Émile. Science et humanisme. Paris, 1947.
Phil 575.51.42 Breukers, Eugenio Marie Josephine. Levensvormen. Roermond, 1947.
Phil 3120.26.30 Brod, Max. Diesseits und Jenseits. Winterthur, 1947. 2v.
Phil 165.6 Bronstein, D.J. Basic problems of philosophy. N.Y., 1947.
Phil 52.9A Brown, A.W. The metaphysical society. N.Y., 1947.
Phil 1701.21 Brunner, Auguste. La personne incarnée, étude sur la phénoménologie et la philosophie existentialiste. Paris, 1947.
Phil 3640.380 Brunngraber, Rudolf. Was zu Kommen hat. Wien, 1947.
Phil 3120.30.72 Buber, Martin. Between man and man. London, 1947.
Phil 3120.30.63 Buber, Martin. Dialogisches Leben. Zürich, 1947.
Phil 8612.33.5 Bürgel, B.H. Anfang und Ende. Berlin, 1947.
Phil 176.153 Burgmüller, H. Zur Klärüng der Begriffe. 1. Aufl. München, 1947.
Phil 3850.27.200 Buri, Fritz. Albert Schweitzer und unsere Zeit. Zürich, 1947.
Phil 5241.111 Burt, Cyril. Intelligence and fertility. London, 1947.
Phil 6980.148 Burton, A. Case histories in clinical and abnormal psychology. v.2. N.Y., 1947.
Phil 6312.16 Cameron, N. The psychology of behavior disorders. Boston, 1947.
Phil 5380.90.5 Cantril, H. The invasion from Mars. Princeton, 1947.
Phil 2402.5 Capone Braga, G. La filosofia francese e italiana del settecenta. 3a ed. v.1-2. Padova, 1947.
Phil 5643.108 Carmichael, Leonard. Reacting and visual fatigue. Boston, 1947.
Phil 8877.68.10 Carritt, Edgar F. Ethical and political thinking. Oxford, 1947.
Phil 1750.141.7A Cassirer, Ernst. Rousseau, Kant, Goethe; two essays. Princeton, 1947.
Phil 1930.13.30 Cattell, James M. James McKeen Cattell. Lancaster, Pa., 1947. 2v.
Phil 2475.1.302.5 Challaye, F. Bergson. Paris, 1947.
Phil 4080.19 Chiavacci, G. La ragione poetica. Firenze, 1947.
Phil 5465.50 Chicago. University. Committee on Social Thought. The works of the mind. Chicago, 1947.
Phil 3450.19.108 Chiodi, Pietro. L'esistenzialismo di Heidegger. Torino, 1947.
Phil 1750.255 Le choix, le monde, l'existence. Grenoble, 1947.
Phil 1702.8 Ciardo, Manlio. Le quattro epoche dello storicismo. Bari, 1947.
Phil 9450.23 Claparède, Edouard. Morale et politique. Neuchâtel, 1947.
Phil 8582.62 Cleobury, F.H. God, man and the absolute. London, 1947?
Phil 8877.75.5 Clifford, William K. The ethics of belief. London, 1947.
Phil 2493.22 Condillac, Étienne Bonnot. Oeuvres philosophiques. Paris, 1947-51. 3v.
Phil 672.168 Coomaraswamy, A. Time and eternity. Ascona, 1947.
Phil 600.51 Cornforth, M. Science and idealism. N.Y., 1947.
Phil 6312.7.5 Coster, Geraldine. Psycho-analysis for normal people. 3. ed. N.Y., 1947.
Phil 5042.10.6 Croce, B. Logica come scienza del concetto puro. 7. ed. Bari, 1947.
Phil 4260.07 Croce, Benedetto. Bibliografia vichiana. Napoli, 1947-48. 2v.
Phil 4080.3.55 Croce, Benedetto. Il concetto moderno della storia. Bari, 1947.
Phil 5238.10A Current trends in psychology. Pittsburgh, 1947.
Phil 1750.55 Damur, Carl. Das Test der Seele. Bern, 1947.
Phil 8953.8.2 D'Arcy, Martin Cyrile. The mind and heart of love, lion and unicorn. N.Y., 1947.
Phil 2880.8.94 Dauphin, E.J. Ekecrate; dialogue sur l'existentialisme. Montpellier, 1947.
Phil 178.68 Dempf, Alois. Selbstkritik der Philosophie und vergleichende Philosophiegeschichte im Umriss. Wien, 1947.
Phil 3485.17 Denckmann, G. Kants Philosophie des Ästhetischen. Heidelberg, 1947.
Phil 4080.3.200 Derisi, Octavio N. La filosofía del espíritu. Madrid, 1947.
Phil 2520.69 Descartes, René. Descartes. Paris, 1947.
Phil 2520.52.70 Descartes, René. The living thoughts of Descartes. Philadelphia, 1947.
Phil 3195.11.35 Dessoir, Max. Buch der Erinnerung. 2. Aufl. Stuttgart, 1947.
Phil 5520.86.10 Dobrogaev, S.M. Rechevye refleksy. Moskva, 1947.
Phil 3475.3.95 Dufrenne, M. Karl Jaspers et la philosophie de l'existence. Paris, 1947.
Phil 3425.435 Dulckeit, Gerhard. Die Idee Gottes im Geiste der Philosophie Hegels. München, 1947.
Phil 8583.40 Dunham, J.H. The religion of philosophers. Philadelphia, 1947.
Phil 1980.4.15 Edman, Irwin. Philosopher's quest. N.Y., 1947.
Phil 8405.10 Edwards, A.T. The things which are seen. London, 1947.
Phil 7069.47.20 Ehrenwald, Jan. Telepathy and medical psychology. London, 1947.
Phil 8405.2.5 Ehrlich, Walter. Ästhetik. Chur, 1947.
Phil 5545.183 Ellenberger, F. Le mystère de la mémoire. Genève, 1947.
Phil 9380.9 English, Raymond. The pursuit of purpose. London, 1947.
Phil 7069.47.40 Estabrooks, George Hoben. Spiritism. 1. ed. N.Y., 1947.
Phil 9240.6 Ewing, Alfred C. The definition of good. N.Y., 1947.
Phil 3640.376 Farré, R. De l'influence de Nietzsche sur la pensée politique allemande. Thèse. Baden-Baden, 1947.
Phil 8050.52 Fasola, Guista Nicco. Della critica. Firenze, 1947.
Phil 525.175 Felice, Philippe de. Foules en délire. Paris, 1947.
Phil 336.10 Fireman, Peter. Sound thinking. N.Y., 1947.
Phil 4073.97.5 Firpo, Luigi. Ricerche Campanelliane. Firenze, 1947.
Phil 336.12 Fischer, Anton. Die philosophischen Grundlagen der wissenschaftlichen Erkenntnis. Wien, 1947.
Phil 440.4 Fischer, Ernst. Freiheit und Persönlichkeit. Wien, 1947.
Phil 8406.20.9 Flaccus, L.W. The spirit and substance of art. N.Y., 1947.
Phil 3640.334 Flake, Otto. Nietzsche. 2e Aufl. Baden-Baden, 1947.
Phil 3805.186 Flückiger, Felix. Philosophie und Theologie bei Schleiermacher. Basel, 1947?
Phil 8406.18.5 Focillon, Henri. Vie des formes. 3. ed. Paris, 1947.
Phil 6315.2.20.15 Freud, Sigmund. On war, sex and neurosis. N.Y., 1947.
Phil 8880.48A Fromm, Erich. Man for himself. N.Y., 1947.
Phil 336.11.5 Froschels, Emil. The human race, a study in the nature of knowledge. N.Y., 1947.
Phil 336.11 Froschels, Emil. The human race. N.Y., 1947.
Phil 5478.5.6 Frustration and aggression. New Haven, 1947.
Phil 2730.104 Funke, Gerhard. Maine der Biran. Bonn, 1947.
Phil 181.104 Gaos, José. Filosofia de la filosofia e historia de la filosofia. México, 1947.

1947 - cont.

Phil 4006.5.40 Garin, Eugenio. La filosofia. v.1-2. Milano, 1947.
Phil 4006.5.35 Garin, Eugenio. Der italienische Humanismus. Bern, 1947.
Phil 181.102 Geiger, G.R. Philosophy and the social order. Boston, 1947.
Phil 5246.25.10 Gemelli, Agostino. Introducione alla psicologia. Milano, 1947.
Phil 4115.31 Gioberti, V. Cours de philosophie, 1841-1842. Milano, 1947.
Phil 5246.53 Goldstein, K. Human nature in the light of psychopathology. Cambridge, Mass., 1947.
Phil 8696.19 Gordon, Ronald G. The philosophy of a scientist. London, 1947.
Phil 8430.32 Gotshalk, D.W. Art and the social order. Chicago, 1947.
Phil 2730.100 Gouhier, Henri. Les conversions de Maine de Biran. Paris, 1947.
Phil 6400.18 Granich, L. Aphasia: a guide to retraining. N.Y., 1947.
Phil 8407.37 Greenough, H. Form and function; remarks on art. Berkeley, 1947.
Phil 2128.85 Grégoire, F. Bernard de Mandeville et la "Fable des Abeilles". Thèse. Nancy, 1947.
Phil 3552.315 Guggenberger, Alois. Leibniz. Stuttgart, 1947.
Phil 181.110 Gunther, H.R.G. Personlichkeit und Geschichte. Augsburg, 1947.
Phil 3450.29.70 Haecker, Theodor. Tag- und Nachtbücher. München, 1947.
Phil 3850.27.111 Hagedorn, Hermann. Prophet in the wilderness. N.Y., 1947.
Phil 6117.46 Halstood, W.C. Brain and intelligence. Chicago, 1947.
Phil 182.112 Hardie, C.D. Background to modern thought. London, 1947.
Phil 6317.31 Harding, M.E. Psychic energy, its source and goal. N.Y., 1947.
Phil 8408.36 Haspers, John. Meaning and truth in the arts. Chapel Hill, 1947.
Phil 3705.5 Hauck, W.A. Das Geheimnis des Lebens. Heidelburg, 1947.
Phil 6957.17.20 Henderson, D.K. A text-book of psychiatry for students and practitioners. Oxford, 1947.
Phil 720.94 Hennemann, Gerhard. Zum Problem der Voraussetzungslosigkeit und Objektivtät in der Wissenschaft. Photoreproduction. Bonn, 1947.
Phil 2880.8.92 Henri-Hoyen, E. Sartre contre l'homme. Genève, 1947.
Phil 1750.177 Hessen, J. Existenzphilosophie. Essen, 1947.
Phil 3450.30 Hessen, Johannes. Lehrbuch der Philosophie. München, 1947-50. 3v.
Phil 182.146 Hessen, Johannes. Von der Aufgabe der Philosophie und dem Wesen des Philosophen; zwei Vorlesungen. Heidelberg, 1947.
Phil 2045.52.25 Hobbes, Thomas. Leviathan. London, 1947.
Phil 8882.30.10 Hobhouse, L.T. The rational good. London, 1947.
Phil 3455.3.80 Hof, Ulrich im. Isaak Iselin. Basel, 1947. 2v.
Phil 3640.338A Hofmiller, Josef. Friedrich Nietzsche. Hamburg, 1947.
Phil 6315.2.136 Hollitscher, W. Sigmund Freud; an introduction. London, 1947.
Phil 6315.2.138 Hollitscher, W. Sigmund Freud; an introduction. N.Y., 1947.
Phil 1830.10 Hook, Sidney. Freedom and experience. Ithaca, 1947.
Phil 3450.28.10 Horkheimer, Max. Dialektik der Aufklärung. Amsterdam, 1947.
Phil 3450.28 Horkheimer, Max. Eclipse of reason. N.Y., 1947.
Phil 8587.32.112 Hügel, Friedrich. Baron von Hügel, man of God. London, 1947.
Phil 2805.243 Humbert, Pierre. Cet effrayant génie...l'oeuvre scientifique de Pascal. Paris, 1947.
Phil 2050.68.7 Hume, David. Hume's dialogues concerning natural religion. London, 1947.
Phil 2475.1.296 Husson, León A. L'intellectualisme de Bergson. Paris, 1947.
Phil 2475.1.297 Husson, León A. L'intellectualisme de Bergson. Thèse. Paris, 1947.
Phil 4803.462.1 Ingarden, Roman. Spór o istnienie świata. Kraków, 1947-48. 2v.
Phil 4803.462.20 Ingarden, Roman. Szkice z filozofii literatury. Lódź, 1947.
Phil 70.16 Inter-American Congress of Philosophy, 1st, Port-au-Prince, 1944. Travaux du congrès international de philosophie. Port-au-Prince, 1947.
Phil 4309.5 Iriarte, Joaquin S.J. Menendez Pelayo y la filosofia española. Madrid, 1947.
Phil 1114.5 Jaeger, Werner W. The theology of the early Greek philosophers. Oxford, 1947.
Phil 3640.267.3 Jaspers, Karl. Nietzsche. 2e Aufl. Berlin, 1947.
Phil 3475.3.40 Jaspers, Karl. Die ontwort on Sigrid Undset. Konstang, 1947.
Phil 5049.20 Jaspers, Karl. Von der Wahrheit. München, 1947.
Phil 2880.8.98 Jeanson, Francis. Le problème moral et la pensée de Sartre. Paris, 1947.
Phil 5049.15.15 Joannes XXI, Pope. Petri hispani summulae logicales. Torino, 1947.
Phil 6319.1.43 Jung, C.G. Modern man in search of a soul. N.Y., 1947.
Phil 5850.247.5 Jung, Carl G. Essays on contemporary events. London, 1947.
Phil 1750.275 Kanapa, J. L'existentialisme n'est pas un humanisme. Paris, 1947.
Phil 3480.67.80A Kant, Immanuel. The moral law, or Kant's Groundwork of the metaphysic of morals. London, 1947?
Phil 5250.17.2A Kantor, J.R. Problems of physiological psychology. Bloomington, 1947.
Phil 3549.10.45 Kassner, Rudolf. Das neunzehnte Jahrhundert; Ausdruck und Grösse. Erlenbach, 1947.
Phil 9150.31 Keith, Arthur. Evolution and ethics. N.Y., 1947.
Phil 3549.2.40 Keyserling, Hermann. Das Buch vom Ursprung. Baden-Baden, 1947.
Phil 5066.30 Kiss, Stephen A. Transformations on lattices and structures of logic. N.Y., 1947.
Phil 3549.8.95 Klages, Ludwig. Erforscher und Künder des Lebens. Linz, 1947.
Phil 5250.15.15.5 Köhler, Wolfgang. Gestalt psychology. N.Y., 1947.
Phil 5250.15.15.10 Köhler, Wolfgang. Gestalt psychology. N.Y., 1947.
Phil 5760.13 Kohnstamm, Philipp A. Vrije wil of determinisme. Haarlem, 1947.
Phil 3425.321 Kojève, Alexandre. Introduction à la lecture de Hegel. Paris, 1947.
Phil 8050.64 Krestovskaia, L.A. La laideur dans l'art à travers les âges. Paris, 1947.
Phil 3552.370 Krueger, G. Leibniz als Friedensstifter. Wiesbaden, 1947.
Phil 5761.21 Laird, John. On human freedom. London, 1947.
Phil 2725.35.65 Lavelle, Louis. Introduction à l'ontologie. 1. éd. Paris, 1947.

Chronological Listing

Phil 4080.3.190   LaVia, Pietro. Mente e realtà; il pensiero di Benedetto Croce. Firenze, 1947. 2v.

Phil 8836.2.20   Lecky, W.E.H. A Victorian historian. London, 1947.

Phil 365.47.18   Lecomte du Noüy, Pierre. La dignité humaine. N.Y., 1947.

Phil 8701.21   Lecomte du Nouy, Pierre. Human destiny. N.Y., 1947.

Phil 2520.228   Lefebvre, H. Descartes. Paris, 1947.

Phil 3552.31   Leibniz, Gottfried Wilhelm. Gottfried Wilhelm Leibniz; Gott, Geist, Güte. Gütersloh, 1947.

Phil 3552.63.40   Leibniz, Gottfried Wilhelm. Plädoyer fur Gottes Gottheit. 1. Aufl. Berlin, 1947.

Phil 1750.280   Lepp, Ignoce. Existence et existentialismes. Paris, 1947.

Phil 5520.88   Lewis, Morris M. Language in society. London, 1947.

Phil 5051.29   Lieber, Lillian R. Mits, wits and logic. 1st ed. N.Y., 1947.

Phil 2115.36.31.10   Locke, J. Essay concerning human understanding. London, 1947.

Phil 2115.67   Locke, J. On politics and education. N.Y., 1947.

Phil 2750.18.80   Louvain. Université Catholique. Jubilé Albert Michotte. Louvain, 1947.

Phil 5238.12   Louvain. Université Catholique. Institute Supérieur de Philosophie. Miscellanea psychologica Albert Michotte. Louvain, 1947.

Phil 6315.2.132   Ludwig, Emil. Doctor Freud. N.Y., 1947.

Phil 3850.18.86   Lützeler, Heinrich. Der Philosoph Max Scheler. Bonn, 1947.

Phil 186.103   Luporini, C. Filosofi vecchi e nuovi. Firenze, 1947.

Phil 525.125   Mager, Alois. Mystik als seelische Wirklichkeit. Graz, 1947.

Phil 5052.39   Mander, Alfred E. Logic for the millions. N.Y., 1947.

Phil 325.8   Maravall, Jose Antonio. Las origenes del empirismo en el pensamiento político español del siglo XVII. Granada, 1947.

Phil 9070.114.5   Margolius, Hans. Notes on ethics. Miami, 1947.

Phil 2750.11.42A   Maritain, Jacques. Court traité de l'existence et de l'existent. Paris, 1947.

Phil 2750.11.56   Maritain, Jacques. De la vie d'oraison. Paris, 1947.

Phil 2750.11.47.5   Maritain, Jacques. The person and the common good. N.Y., 1947.

Phil 2750.11.47   Maritain, Jacques. La personne et le bien commun. Paris, 1947.

Phil 2750.11.50   Maritain, Jacques. Raison et raisons. 10. éd. Paris, 1947.

Phil 7106.5   Marks, Robert. The story of hypnotism. N.Y., 1947.

Phil 812.22   Martin, S.G. A history of philosophy. N.Y., 1947.

Phil 3640.692   Martinez Estrada, E. Nietzsche. Buenos Aires, 1947.

Phil 5850.267   Maryland. Conference on Military Contributions to Methology. New methods in applied psychology. College Park, 1947.

Phil 1540.27   Mélanges Auguste Pelzer. Louvain, 1947.

Phil 6060.368   Mendel, A.O. Personality in handwriting. N.Y., 1947.

Phil 2150.24.30   Mika, Lumir Victor. Thinker's handbook. Columbia, Mo., 1947.

Phil 2138.40.35   Mill, John S. On liberty. N.Y., 1947.

Phil 8702.20   Miller, C.W. A scientist's approach to religion. N.Y., 1947.

Phil 812.18   Miller, Hugh. An historical introduction to modern philosophy. N.Y., 1947.

Phil 3195.6.109   Misch, Georg. Vom Lebens- und Gedankenkreis Wilhelm Diltheys. Frankfurt, 1947.

Phil 5593.47   Mons, Walter E. Principles and practise of the Rorschach personality test. London, 1947.

Phil 5252.97   Morgan, J.J.B. Psychology. N.Y., 1947.

Phil 343.24   Morot, E. La pensée negative. Thèse. Paris, 1947.

Phil 5627.185   Morrish, Furze. The ritual of higher magic. London, 1947?

Phil 1750.382   Mougin, Henri. La sainte famille existentialiste. Paris, 1947.

Phil 1750.225   Mounier, Emman. Introduction aux existentialismes. Paris, 1947.

Phil 5590.36   Murphy, Gardner. Personality. N.Y., 1947.

Phil 4112.89   Napoli, G. di. La filosofia di Pasquale Galluppi. Padova, 1947.

Phil 1750.600   Naville, Pierre. Les conditions de la liberté. Paris, 1947.

Phil 2175.3.30   Neilson, Francis. The roots of our learning. N.Y., 1947.

Phil 8593.21   Nestle, Wilhelm. Die Krisis des Cristentums. Stuttgart, 1947.

Phil 6323.4.6   Nicole, J.E. Psychopathology. 4. ed. Baltimore, 1947.

Phil 3640.422   Noll, B. Zeitalter der Feste. Bonn, 1947.

Phil 2175.4.30   Northrop, F.S.C. The logic of the sciences and the humanities. N.Y., 1947.

Phil 3850.18.92   Nota, J. Max Scheler. Utrecht, 1947.

Phil 9070.49.5   Odier, Charles. Les deux sources consciente et inconsciente de la vie morale. 2d éd. Neuchâtel, 1947.

Phil 6964.4   Ogdon, J.A.H. The kingdom of the lost. London, 1947.

Phil 5850.291.3   Oldfield, R.C. The psychology of the interview. 3rd ed. London, 1947.

Phil 814.3   Oyen, Hendrik van. Philosophia. v.1-2. Utrecht, 1947-49. 2v.

Phil 2218.89   Park, Mary Cathryne. Joseph Priestley and the problem of pantiscocracy. Philadelphia, 1947.

Phil 2218.88   Park, Mary Cathryne. Joseph Priestley and the problem of pantiscocracy. Diss. Philadelphia, 1947.

Phil 2805.65   Pascal, Blaise. Deux pièces imparfaites sur la grâce et le concile de trente. Paris, 1947.

Phil 2805.46   Pascal, Blaise. Pascal. Paris, 1947.

Phil 2805.42.27   Pascal, Blaise. Pensées. London, 1947.

Phil 665.90   Pastuszka, J. Dusza ludzka, jej istnienie i natura. Lublin, 1947.

Phil 2805.239   Patrick, D.G.M. Pascal and Kierkegaard. London, 1947. 2v.

Phil 6420.40   Pellman, Charles. Overcoming stammering. N.Y., 1947.

Phil 2225.11   Pepper, Stephen Coburn. A digest of purposive values. Berkeley, 1947.

Phil 8595.37   Persons, Stow. Free religion. New Haven, 1947.

Phil 315.10   Pétrement, Simone. Le dualisme chez Platon. Paris, 1947.

Phil 1520.5   Pieper, Josef. Wahrheit der Dinge. München, 1947.

Phil 3745.21   Polak, Leo. Verzamelde werken. Amsterdam, 1947.

Phil 2475.1.299   Politzer, Georges. Le Bergsonisme. Paris, 1947.

Phil 7069.47.10   Pond, Mariam B. Time is kind. N.Y., 1947.

Phil 3015.5   Prang, Helmut. Der Humanismus. Bamburg, 1947.

Phil 190.77   Preface to philosophy. N.Y., 1947.

Phil 1750.175   Pruche, B. Existentialisme et acte d'être. Paris, 1947.

Phil 6315.2.134   Pruner, Helen W. Freud, his life and his mind. N.Y., 1947.

Phil 6980.614   Psychiatric research papers read at the dedication of the laboratory. Cambridge, 1947.

Phil 6685.13   Purtscher, Nora. Doctor Mesmer. London, 1947.

Phil 1020.23   Quadri, G. La philosophie arabe dans l'Europe médiévale. Paris, 1947.

Phil 192.85.5.2   Raeymaeker, Louis de. Philosophie de l'être. 2. ed. Louvain, 1947.

Phil 6060.46   Rand, H.A. Graphology. Cambridge, Mass., 1947.

Phil 8892.58   Raphael, D. Daiches. The moral sense. London, 1947.

Phil 298.9   Rawson, F. Life understood from a scientific and religious point of view. 7. ed. London, 1947.

Phil 4870.10   Ray, Benoy Gopal. Contemporary Indian philosophers. Allahabad, 1947.

Phil 5066.26   Reichenbach, H. Elements of symbolic logic. N.Y., 1947.

Phil 192.70.5   Reininger, Robert. Metaphysik der Wirklichkeit. 2. Aufl. Wien, 1947. 2v.

Phil 8892.56.5   Reininger, Robert. Wertphilosophie und Ethik. 3. Aufl. Wien, 1947.

Phil 5257.57   Révész, Géza. Die Bedeutung der Psychologie für die Wissenschaft. Bern, 1947.

Phil 7069.47.5A   Rhine, Joseph B. The reach of the mind. N.Y., 1947.

Phil 8430.23   Robertson, A. Contrasts: the arts and religion. London, 1947.

Phil 8892.59   Rodriguez, G.H. Etica y jurisprudencia. Mexico, 1947.

Phil 705.30   Rogers, W.C. Transcendentalism truly remarkable. Boston, 1947.

Phil 5257.58.5   Rohracher, Hubert. Einführung in die Psychologie. 2. Aufl. Wien, 1947.

Phil 1122.9.5   Rüfner, Vinzenz. Grundbegriffe griechischer Wissenschaftslehre. 2. Aufl. Bamberg, 1947.

Phil 817.19.5   Russell, B.R. History of Western philosophy. London, 1947.

Phil 2255.1.40   Russell, Bertrand Russell. Philosophy and politics. London, 1947.

Phil 193.132.10   Samuel, Herbert S. Creative man. Oxford, 1947.

Phil 5028.3   Sándor, Pál. Histoire de la dialectique. Paris, 1947.

Phil 2880.8.42   Sartre, Jean Paul. Existentialism. N.Y., 1947.

Phil 2880.8.43   Sartre, Jean Paul. Ist der Existentialismus ein Humanismus? Zürich, 1947.

Phil 349.18   Schaaf, Juius Jakob. Über Wissen und Selbstbewisstsein. Stuttgart, 1947.

Phil 3850.18.10   Scheler, Max. Bildung und Wissen. Frankfurt, 1947.

Phil 193.190   Schneider, Erich. Auch ein Weg zur Philosophie. Berlin, 1947.

Phil 6328.31   Schwarz, Theodor. Zur Kritik der Psychoanalyse. Zürich, 1947.

Phil 3850.27.21   Schweitzer, A. An anthology. N.Y., 1947.

Phil 3850.27.23   Schweitzer, A. Vom Lich in Uns. Stuttgart, 1947.

Phil 4018.6   Sciacca, M.F. Il secolo XX. Milano, 1947. 2v.

Phil 3850.27.109   Seaver, George. Albert Schweitzer. London, 1947.

Phil 5585.67.5   Sechenov, I.M. Izbrannye filosofskie i psikhologicheskie proizvedeniia. Moskva, 1947.

Phil 818.40   Selbmann, Fritz. Wahrheit und Wirklichkeit. Dresden, 1947.

Phil 4080.3.180   Sgoi, Carmelo. Benedetto Croce. Messina, 1947.

Phil 9450.22   Simon, Yves. Community of the free. N.Y., 1947.

Phil 3500.65A   Smith, A.H. Kantian studies. Oxford, 1947.

Phil 7069.47.15   Soal, Samuel G. The experimental situation in psychical research. London, 1947.

Phil 4769.1.75   Solov'ev, V.S. Crise de la philosophie occidentale. Paris, 1947.

Phil 8430.42   Souriau, Étienne. La correspondance des arts. Paris, 1947.

Phil 8598.92   Spann, Othmar. Religions-Philosophie auf geschichtlicher Grundlage. Wien, 1947.

Phil 3819.43   Spinoza, Benedictus de. Das Endliche und Unendliche. Wiesbaden, 1947.

Phil 349.39.5   Steenberghen, Fernand van. Épistémologie. 2e éd. Louvain, 1947.

Phil 8419.12   Stein, Leo. Appreciation: painting, poetry and prose. N.Y., 1947.

Phil 974.3.120   Strakosch, A. Lebenswege mit Rudolf Steiner. Strasbourg, 1947.

Phil 2475.1.298.5   Sundén, Jalmar. La théorie bergsonienne de la religion. Paris, 1947.

Phil 8633.1.47   Thurman, Howard. The negro spiritual speaks of life and death. N.Y., 1947.

Phil 350.8.2   Thyssen, Johannes. Der philosophische Relativismus. 2. Aufl. Bonn, 1947.

Phil 5590.38   Tomkins, Silvan S. The thematic apperception test. N.Y., 1947.

Phil 194.45   Tomlin, E.W.F. The approach to metaphysics. London, 1947.

Phil 494.3   Tromp, Salco U. The religion of the modern scientist. Leiden, 1947.

Phil 8894.32   Tsanoff, Radoslov A. Ethics. N.Y., 1947.

Phil 5259.34   Tyler, Leona E. The psychology of human differences. N.Y., 1947.

Phil 525.7.20   Underhill, Evelyn. Concerning the inner life, with The house of the soul. London, 1947.

Phil 8951.24.5   Valken, L. Der Glaube bei Emil Brunner. Freiburg, 1947.

Phil 196.26.5   Vialle, L. Introduction a la vie imparfaite. 1. ed. Paris, 1947.

Phil 4260.39   Vico, G.B. Vom Wesen und Weg der geistigen Bildung. Godesberg, 1947.

Phil 4372.1.1A   Vives, Juan Luis. Obras completas. Madrid, 1947-48. 2v.

Phil 1750.185   Wahl, Jean André. Petite histoire de "l'existentialisme". Paris, 1947.

Phil 510.158   Waton, Harry. A true monistic philosophy. N.Y., 1947-1955. 2v.

Phil 8423.15   Weisbach, W. Von Geschmack und seinen Wandlungen. Basel, 1947.

Phil 2340.11.30   Weiss, Paul. Nature and man. N.Y., 1947.

Phil 5262.48.5   Weizäcker, Viktor. Der Gestaltkreis. 3. Aufl. Stuttgart, 1947.

Phil 530.20.93   Wentzlaff-Eggebert, F.W. Deutsche Mystik zwischen Mittelalter und Neuzeit. 2. Aufl. Tübingen, 1947.

Phil 7069.49.5   Westwood, Horace. There is a psychic world. N.Y., 1947.

Phil 7069.47   White, S.E. With folded wings. 1. ed. N.Y., 1947.

Phil 2340.10.96A   Whitehead, Alfred North. Essays in science and philosophy. N.Y., 1947.

Phil 2340.10.30A   Whitehead, Alfred North. Wit and wisdom. Boston, 1947.

Phil 9513.7   Wiese, Leopold von. Ethik in der Schauweise der Wissenschaften. Bern, 1947.

Phil 5262.47   Wolff, W. What is psychology? N.Y., 1947.

Phil 7082.156   Woods, Ralph Louis. The world of dreams. N.Y., 1947.

1947 - cont.

Phil 197.65.10   Wust, Peter. Der Mensch und die Philosophie. 2. Aufl. Münster, 1947.
Phil 2340.13.30   Wylie, Philip. An essay on morals. N.Y., 1947.
Phil 800.12.10   Zhdanov, A.A. Vystuplenie na diskussii po knige G.F. Aleksandrova. "Istoriia zapnoevropeiskoi filosofii". Moskva, 1947.

1948

Phil 1750.270   Abbagnano, Nicola. Esistenzialismo positivo; due saggi. 1. ed. Torino, 1948.
Phil 1750.270.8   Abbagnano, Nicola. Introduzione all'esistenzialismo. 3. ed. Torino, 1948.
Phil 175.44   Adams, George P. Man and metaphysics. N.Y., 1948.
Phil 6310.1.37   Adler, Gerhard. Studies in analytical psychology. London, 1948.
Phil 5585.74   Akademiia Nauk, SSSR. Institut Filosofii. Sektsiia Psikhologii. Issledovaniia po psikhologii vospriiatiia; sbornik. Moskva, 1948.
Phil 525.101.10   Allen, Warner. The happy issue. London, 1948.
Phil 5630.5.2   Allport, G.W. The psychology of rumor. N.Y., 1948.
Phil 5066.32   Ambrose, Alice. Fundamentals of symbolic logic. N.Y., 1948.
Phil 1850.139   Anderson, Fulton H. The philosophy of Francis Bacon. Chicago, 1948.
Phil 5240.43   Andrews, T.G. Methods of psychology. N.Y., 1948.
Phil 1195.12   Antonelli, M. Figures di sofisti in Platon. Torino, 1948.
Phil 4983.1.80   Arias, Alejandro. Vaz Ferreira. 1. ed. México, 1948.
Phil 2280.16.80   Aristotelian Society for the Systematic Study of Philosophy. London. Philosophical studies; essays in memory of L. Susan Stebbing. London, 1948.
Phil 4751.1.32   Arsen'ev, N.S. Pravoslavie, katolichestvo, protestantizm. Parizh, 1948.
Phil 530.50.10   Arters, Stephanus. La spiritualité des Pays-Bas. Louvain, 1948.
Phil 5525.42   Aubouin, Elie. Les genres du risible. Marseille, 1948.
Phil 5525.42.2   Aubouin, Elie. Les genres du risible. Thèse. Marseille, 1948.
Phil 5525.42.10   Aubouin, Elie. Technique et psychologie du comique. Thèse. Marseille, 1948.
Phil 5465.56.10   Bachelard, G. La terre et les rêveries de la volonté. Paris, 1948.
Phil 5465.56.30   Bachelard, G. La terre et les rêveries du repos. Paris, 1948.
Phil 4352.1.55   Balmes, Jaime. Obras completas. Madrid, 1948- 8v.
Phil 4352.1.125   Barcelona. Biblioteca Central. Catálogo de la exposicion bibliográfica. Barcelona, 1948.
Phil 1750.240   Beauvoir, S. de. L'existentialisme et la sagesse des nations. Paris, 1948.
Phil 8910.2   Behn, Siegfried. Ethik; ein Repetitorium. Bonn, 1948.
Phil 1701.22   Benda, J. Trois idoles romantique. Genève, 1948.
Phil 5241.113   Benda, Julien. Du style d'idées. Paris, 1948.
Phil 3425.324   Bense, Max. Hegel und Kierkegaard. Köln, 1948.
Phil 1865.51A   Bentham, Jeremy. An introduction to the principles of morals and legislation. N.Y., 1948.
Phil 2340.10.105   Bera, M.A. A.N. Whitehead; un philosophe de l'expérience. Paris, 1948.
Phil 1750.245   Berger, G. Existentialism and literature in action. Buffalo, 1948.
Phil 9075.40   Bergler, Edmund. The battle of the conscience. Washington, D.C., 1948.
Phil 1870.17   Berkeley, G. Works. London, 1948-53. 9v.
Phil 5011.7   Beth, Evert Willem. Geschiedenis der logica. Den Haag, 1948.
Phil 176.205   Bhattacharya, H.M. The principles of philosophy. Calcutta, 1948.
Phil 5401.30   Bitter, Wilhelm. Die Angstneurose. Bern, 1948.
Phil 3549.2.20   Blätter der Schule der Weisheit; eine Chronik der Weiterentwicklung der Schule der Weisheit für die Mitglieder des Vereins der Freunde des Keyserling-Archivs. v.1-2. Innsbruck, 1948-49.
Phil 5241.90.5   Blondel, M. La pensée. 4. éd. Paris, 1948.
Phil 6311.23.5   Bluemel, C.S. War, politics, and insanity. Denver, 1948.
Phil 1750.205   Bobbio, Norberto. The philosophy of decadentism; a study in existentialism. Oxford, 1948.
Phil 5066.10.5   Bochénski, I.M. Précis de logique mathématique. Bussum, 1948.
Phil 2465.85   Bonnet, Charles. Mèmoires autobiographiques de Charles Bonnet de Genève. Thèse. Paris, 1948.
Phil 5066.34   Boole, George. The mathematical analysis of logic. Oxford, 1948.
Phil 1801.6   Boorstin, D.J. The lost world of Thomas Jefferson. N.Y., 1948.
Phil 5241.112   Boring, E.G. Foundations of psychology. N.Y., 1948.
Phil 3120.45.40   Brandenstein, Béla. Das Bild des Menschen und die Idee des Humanismus. Bregenz, 1948.
Phil 3450.19.94A   Brecht, F.J. Heidegger und Jaspers. Wuppertal, 1948.
Phil 1750.75   Brecht, Franz Josef. Bewusstsein und Existenz. Bremen, 1948.
Phil 3640.340   Brin, Slata G.R. Kollektivistisches in der Philosophie Nietzsches. Basel, 1948.
Phil 5850.145   Brown, William. Oxford essays on psychology. London, 1948.
Phil 3120.30.41   Buber, Martin. Das Problem des Menschen. Heidelberg, 1948.
Phil 4260.122   Buenos Aires. Universidad Nacional. Vico y Herder. Buenos Aires, 1948.
Phil 5850.145.50   Burtt, H.E. Applied psychology. N.Y., 1948.
Phil 1135.161   Callahan, John F. Four views of time in ancient philosophy. Cambridge, 1948.
Phil 2520.225   Carlini, Armando. Il problema di Cartesio. Bari, 1948.
Phil 333.5.17   Cassirer, Ernst. An essay on man. New Haven, 1948.
Phil 4002.9   Cassirer, Ernst. The Renaissance philosophy of man. Chicago, 1948.
Phil 1750.372   Castelli, Enrico. Existentialisme théologique. Paris, 1948.
Phil 1750.685   Černý, Václav. Proní sešit o existencialismii. Phraha, 1948.
Phil 930.41   Chen, Li-Fu. Philosophy of life. N.Y., 1948.
Phil 2805.432   Chinard, Gilbert. En lisant Pascal. Lille, 1948.
Phil 5042.35   Chwistek, Leon. The limits of science. London, 1948.
Phil 400.136   Ciardo, Manlio. Un fallito tentativo di riforma dello hegelismo. Bari, 1948.
Phil 9510.6   Colonéri, L.J. La dénonciation et les dénonciateurs. 4. éd. Paris, 1948.
Phil 9495.148   Comfort, A. Barbarism and sexual freedom. London, 1948.

1948 - cont.

Phil 4080.3.47   Croce, Benedetto. Nuove pagini sparse. Napoli, 1948-49. 2v.
Phil 4080.3.22   Croce, Benedetto. Saggi filosofici. v. 1,3-5,11. Bari, 1948-54. 5v.
Phil 177.35.40   Croce, Benedetto. Ultimi saggi. 2. ed. Bari, 1948.
Phil 3160.11.10   Cysarz, Herbert. Das seiende Sein. Wien, 1948.
Phil 8953.8.6   D'Arcy, Martin Cyrile. La double nature de l'amour. Paris, 1948.
Phil 1750.195   Delfgaauw, B.M.I. Wat is existentialisme? Amsterdam, 1948.
Phil 2520.70   Descartes, René. Descartes, 1596-1650. Genève, 1948.
Phil 5243.25.5   Dessoir, Max. Psychologische Briefe. Berlin, 1948.
Phil 6945.30   Deutsch, Albert. The shame of the States. 1. ed. N.Y., 1948.
Phil 178.38.4   Dewey, John. Reconstruction in philosophy. Boston, 1948.
Phil 5043.30   Dialectica. Neuchâtel. Pouvoir de l'esprit sur le réel. Neuchâtel, 1948.
Phil 3640.418   Dournes, P. Nietzsche vivant. n.p., 1948.
Phil 5400.109   Dumas, G. La vie affective. 1. éd. Paris, 1948.
Phil 8404.20   Dyroff, Adolf. Ästhetik des tätigen Geistes. Bonn, 1948.
Phil 178.40.5   Dyroff, Adolf. Einleitung in die Philosophie. Bonn, 1948.
Phil 165.27   Edman, Irwin. Landmarks for beginners in philosophy. N.Y., 1948?
Phil 285.5   Ehrenfels, C.F. Cosmogony. N.Y., 1948.
Phil 6314.9   Eidelberg, L. Take off your mask. N.Y., 1948.
Phil 2725.4.89   Evans, David O. Le socialisme romantique. Paris, 1948.
Phil 1750.200   L'existentialisme. Paris, 1948.
Phil 5590.45   Eysenck, Hans Jurgen. Dimensions of personality. London, 1948.
Phil 2880.8.100   Fatone, V. El existencialismo y la libertad readoro. 1. ed. Buenos Aires, 1948.
Phil 805.11   Fischl, Johann. Geschichte der Philosophie. Graz, 1948-53. 5v.
Phil 4120.4.95   Fondazione Giovanni Gentile per gli Studi Filosofici. Giovanni Gentile. Firenze, 1948-6. 13v.
Phil 1750.220   Foulquié, Paul. Existentialism. London, 1948.
Phil 2405.4   Frankel, Charles. The faith of reason. N.Y., 1948.
Phil 6315.2.29   Freud, Sigmund. Essais de psychanalyse. Paris, 1948.
Phil 6315.2.79.10   Freud, Sigmund. Moïse et la monothéisme. 8 éd. Paris, 1948.
Phil 6315.2.75.14   Freud, Sigmund. Three contributions to the theory of sex. 4th ed. N.Y., 1948.
Phil 3280.55   Geulincx, A. Ethik, oder über die Kardinaltugenden. Hamburg, 1948.
Phil 2630.9   Gex, Maurice. Variétés philosophiques. Lausanne, 1948.
Phil 1511.3.11   Gilson, Étienne. L'esprit de la philosophie. Paris, 1948.
Phil 2630.8.30   Gilson, Étienne. L'être et l'essence. Paris, 1948.
Phil 3488.26.5   Goldmann, L. La communauté humaine et l'univers chez Kant. Paris, 1948.
Phil 6400.20.2   Goldstein, Kurt. Language and language disturbances. N.Y., 1948.
Phil 1750.726   Gonzalez Casanova, Pablo. El misoneismo y la modernidad cristiana en el siglo XVIII. México, 1948.
Phil 2733.94.6   Gouhier, Henri. La philosophie de Malebranche. Paris, 1948.
Phil 3850.27.119   Grabs, R. Albert Schweitzer. Berlin, 1948.
Phil 1850.137   Green, Adwin W. Sir Francis Bacon. Syracuse, N.Y., 1948.
Phil 1750.171   Grene, M. Dreadful freedom. Chicago, 1948.
Phil 181.131   Grenier, J. Entretiens sur le bon usage de la liberté. Paris, 1948.
Phil 1706.9   Grevillot, J.M. Les grands courants de la pensée contemporaine. Paris, 1948.
Phil 8407.20   Guillou, R. L'art invincible. Paris, 1948.
Phil 8881.64.2   Gurvitch, Georges. Morale théorique et science des moeurs. 2. éd. Paris, 1948.
Phil 5374.63   Gusdorf, G. La découverte de soi. Thèse. 1. éd. Paris, 1948.
Phil 6317.30   Halliday, James. Psychosocial medicine. N.Y., 1948.
Phil 1750.183   Harper, Ralph. Existentialism. Cambridge, 1948.
Phil 1750.305   Hartwig, T. Der Existentialismus. Wien, 1948.
Phil 3425.63   Hegel, Georg Wilhelm Friedrich. Early theological writings. Chicago, 1948.
Phil 3425.29.10   Hegel, Georg Wilhelm Friedrich. Wissenschaft der Logik. Leipzig, 1948.
Phil 1707.13   Heiss, R. Der Gang des Geistes. Bern, 1948.
Phil 3450.26.10   Hellpach, Willy. Universitas litterarum. Stuttgart, 1948.
Phil 8587.67   Hermans, F. Histoire doctrinale de l'humanisme chrétien. Tournai, 1948. 4v.
Phil 3850.18.130   Hessen, J. Max Scheler. Essen, 1948.
Phil 1750.177.1   Hessen, Johannes. Existenzphilosophie. Basel, 1948.
Phil 8587.65   Hessen, Johannes. Religionsphilosophie. v.1-2. Essen, 1948.
Phil 1153.10   Höistad, R. Cynic hero and cynic king. Uppsala, 1948.
Phil 6117.45.5   Holmes, E.S. This thing called life. N.Y., 1948.
Phil 2750.17.90   Hommage à Henri Mieville. Lausanne, 1948.
Phil 165.23   L'homme, le monde. Grenoble, 1948.
Phil 2050.68.3   Hume, David. Dialogues concerning natural religion. N.Y., 1948.
Phil 2050.59.25   Hume, David. Moral and political philosophy. N.Y., 1948.
Phil 5247.29.20   Humphrey, G. Directed thinking. N.Y., 1948.
Phil 3425.319.15   Hyppolite, Jean. Introduction à la philosophie de l'historie de Hegel. Paris, 1948.
Phil 9070.48.5   Iranschähr, H.K. Der Meister und sein Jünger. Olten, 1948-1950. 2v.
Phil 2520.223   Jacob, S.M. Notes on Descartes' règles pour la direction de l'esprit. London, 1948.
Phil 5630.10   Jacobson, David J. The affairs of Dame Rumor. N.Y., 1948.
Phil 4809.465.30   Jahn, Jiljí. Pozmání a život. Praha, 1948.
Phil 2070.27A   James, William. Essays in pragmatism. N.Y., 1948.
Phil 2070.46.20A   James, William. Psychology. Cleveland, 1948.
Phil 184.19.25   Jaspers, K. Der philosophische Glaube. München, 1948.
Phil 2520.202.5   Jaspers, Karl. Descartes und die Philosophie. 2. Aufl. Berlin, 1948.
Phil 5049.25   Jepson, R.W. Clear thinking. 4th ed. London, 1948.
Phil 5049.19   Joachim, Harold H. Logical studies. Oxford, 1948.
Phil 2075.5.30   Joad, Cyril E.W. Decadence. London, 1948.
Phil 1750.210   Jolivet, Régis. Les doctrines existentialistes de Kierkegaard à J.P. Sartre. Paris, 1948.
Phil 2150.1.85   Jones, Marc Edmund. George Sylvester Morris; his philosophical career and theistic idealism. Philadelphia, 1948.
Phil 8411.20   Kainz, F. Vorlesungen über Ästhetik. Wien, 1948.
Phil 5286.10.2   Katz, David. Gestaltpsychologie. 2. Aufl. Basel, 1948.
Phil 5250.37.6   Katz, David. Psychological atlas. n.p., 1948.
Phil 1865.182   Keeton, G.W. Jeremy Bentham and the law. London, 1948.
Phil 7069.48.5   Keith, C.C. Worlds beyond. Hastings, Neb., 1948.

Chronological Listing

Phil 3549.2.70 — Keyserling, Hermann. Graf Hermann Kyserling. Innsbruck, 1948.

Phil 3549.2.79.15 — Keyserling, Hermann. Kritik des Denkens. Innsbruck, 1948.
Phil 3549.2.79.10 — Keyserling, Hermann. Reise durch die Zeit. Innsbruck, 1948.

Phil 4809.489.2 — Klíma, Ladislav. Dílo. v.2- Praha, 1948-
Phil 5590.330 — Kluckhohn, Clyde. Personality in nature, society, and culture. 1. ed. N.Y., 1948.

Phil 3640.347 — Knight, George W. Christ and Nietzsche. London, 1948.
Phil 3850.18.135 — Konthock, K. Max Scheler. Berlin, 1948.
Phil 5170.13 — Korcik, Antoni. Teoriia sylogizmu zdań asertorycznych u azystotelesa. Lublin, 1948.

Phil 5250.35.3 — Kornilov, K.N. Psikhologiia. Izd. 8. Moskva, 1948.
Phil 5620.24 — Lalande, A. La raison et les normes. Paris, 1948.
Phil 9070.21.10 — Landau, Rom. Human relations. London, 1948.
Phil 3640.353 — Lange, Wilhelm. Nietzsche, Krankheit und Wirking. Hamburg, 1948.

Phil 3640.349 — Lavrin, Janko. Nietzsche; an approach. London, 1948.
Phil 5170.10 — Lebzeltern, G. Der Syllogismus. Graz, 1948.
Phil 3552.72 — Leibniz, Gottfried Wilhelm. Textes inédits d'après les manuscrits de la Bibliothèque provinciale. Paris, 1948. 2v.

Phil 5590.95.3 — Lersch, Philipp. Der Aufbau des Charakters. 3. Aufl. Leipzig, 1948.

Phil 5251.41.15A — Lewin, Kurt. Resolving social conflicts. 1st ed. N.Y., 1948.

Phil 3850.27.113 — Lind, Emil. Albert Schweitzer. Bern, 1948.
Phil 342.17 — Litt, Theodor. Denken und Sein. Stuttgart, 1948.
Phil 186.60.20 — Litt, Theodor. Mensch und Welt. München, 1948.
Phil 3585.12.5 — Litt, Theodor. Die Selbsterkenntnis des Menschen. 2. Aufl. Hamburg, 1948.

Phil 8643.31 — Litwell, Constance. Seek paradise. London, 1948.
Phil 1865.183 — London. University. University College Library. Jeremy Bentham, bicentenary celebrations. London, 1948.

Phil 1135.162 — Long, Herbert S. A study of the doctrine of metempsychocis in Greece. Thesis. Princeton, 1948.

Phil 811.11A — Lovejoy, Arthur O. Essays in the history of ideas. Baltimore, 1948.

Phil 3425.322 — Lukács, G. Der junge Hegel. Zürich, 1948.
Phil 623.16.5 — McCabe, Joseph. A rationalist encyclopaedia. London, 1948.

Phil 8887.1.15 — Mackenzie, J.S. A manual of ethics. 6th ed. London, 1948.
Phil 5252.91 — MacKinnon, D.W. Experimental studies in psychodynamics. Cambridge, 1948. 2v.

Phil 3640.836 — Mann, Thomas. Nietzsches Philosophie im Lichte unserer Erfahrung. Berlin, 1948.

Phil 1750.215 — Marcel, Gabriel. The philosophy of existence. London, 1948.

Phil 2630.1.85 — Marias Aguilera, J. La filosofia del Padre Gratry. 2. ed. Buenos Aires, 1948.

Phil 2750.11.40 — Maritain, Jacques. Existence and the existent. N.Y., 1948.

Phil 5052.40 — Marriott, J.W.O.E.D. Some hints on arguing. London, 1948.
Phil 8887.74 — Martínez de Trujillo, Maria. Meditaciones morales. México, 1948.

Phil 3246.243 — Massalo, A. Fichte e la filosofia. Firenze, 1948.
Phil 3552.326 — Matzat, H.L. Gesetz und Freiheit. Köln, 1948.
Phil 2675.2.80 — Mayo, Elton. Some notes on the psychology of Pierre Janet. Cambridge, 1948.

Phil 9070.48 — Meehan, Francis Joseph D. The temple of the spirit. N.Y., 1948.

Phil 5252.93 — Meinertz, Josef. Moderne Seinsprobleme in ihrer Bedeutung für die Psychologie. Heidelberg, 1948.

Phil 1750.166.5 — Mercier, Louis J.A. American humanism and the new age. Milwaukee, 1948.

Phil 2750.20.20 — Merleau-Ponty, Maurice. Sens et non-sens. Paris, 1948.
Phil 3552.355 — Merz, J.T. Leibniz. N.Y., 1948.
Phil 6682.3.2 — Mesmer, F.A. Mesmerism. London, 1948.
Phil 97.12 — Metzke, Erwin. Handlexikon der Philosophie. Heidelberg, 1948.

Phil 3552.322 — Meyer, R.W. Leibniz und die europäische Ordnungskrise. Hamburg, 1948.

Phil 5252.166 — Meyerson, Ignace. Les fonctions psychologiques et les oeuvres. Thèse. Paris, 1948.

Phil 8612.59 — Montanden, Raoul. La mort, cette in connue. Neuchâtel, 1948.

Phil 525.107 — Morot-Sir, E. Philosophie et mystique. Thèse. Paris, 1948.

Phil 8592.63.10 — Morris, Charles W. The open self. N.Y., 1948.
Phil 1750.230 — Mounier, Emman. Existentialist philosophies. London, 1948.

Phil 293.34 — Mueller, Aloys. Die Stellung des Menschen im Kosmos. Bonn, 1948.

Phil 6322.31 — Mullahy, Patrick. Oedipus. 1st ed. N.Y., 1948.
Phil 6322.31.1 — Mullahy, Patrick. Oedipus myth and complex. 1st ed. N.Y., 1948.

Phil 6323.8 — Nacht, Sacha. Le masochisme. 2. éd. Paris, 1948.
Phil 1133.25 — Nassauer, Kurt. Denker der hellenischen Frühzeit. Frankfurt, 1948.

Phil 4959.210 — Navarro, Bernabé. La introducción de la filosofía moderna en México. México, 1948.

Phil 3640.61 — Nietzsche, Friedrich. La lirica di Nietzsche. Messina, 1948.

Phil 3640.60 — Nietzsche, Friedrich. Póesies complètes. Paris, 1948.
Phil 8668.6 — Nink, Gaspar. Philosophische Gotteslehre. München, 1948.
Phil 2138.160 — Nyman, Alf. Leviathan och folkviljan. Stockholm, 1948.
Phil 8669.5 — O'Connor, William R. The natural desire for God. Milwaukee, 1948.

Phil 8964.4 — O'Rahilly, Alfred. Moral principles. Cork, 1948.
Phil 8594.14.5 — Ortegat, Paul. Philosophie de la religion. Gembloux, 1948. 2v.

Phil 2805.40.39 — Pascal, Blaise. Pensées sur la religion. v.1-2. Paris, 1948[1947]

Phil 2070.129.7A — Perry, R.B. The thought and character of William James. Cambridge, 1948.

Phil 346.15 — Pétrin, Jean. Connaissance spéculative et connaissance pratique. Ottawa, 1948.

Phil 1750.250 — Peursen, C.A. van. Riskante philosophie. Amsterdam, 1948.
Phil 190.79 — Pfänder, A. Philosophie der Lebensziele. Göttingen, 1948.
Phil 3640.372 — Pfeie, H. Friedrich Nietzsche und die Religion. Regensburg, 1948.

Phil 2825.10 — Le philosophe. St. Louis, 1948.
Phil 9560.10.20 — Picard, Max. The world of silence. London, 1948.
Phil 8416.11 — Plekhanov, Georgii Valentinovich. Iskusstvo i literatura. Moskva, 1948.

Phil 1815.2 — Pochmann, Henry A. New England transcendentalism and Saint Louis Hegelianism. Philadelphia, 1948.

Phil 5125.27A — Quine, Willard van Orman. Theory of deduction. Pts.1-4. Cambridge, 1948.

Phil 192.85 — Raeymaeker, Louis de. Introduction to philosophy. N.Y., 1948.

Phil 3475.3.85 — Ramming, G. Karl Jaspers und Heinrich Richert Existenzialismus und Wertphilosophie. Bern, 1948.

Phil 8892.13.4 — Rashdall, Hastings. The theory of good and evil. 2. ed. London, 1948. 2v.

Phil 1182.25 — Raven, John E. Pythagoreans and Eleatics. Cambridge, 1948.

Phil 6327.21.30 — Reich, Wilhelm. Listen little man. N.Y., 1948.
Phil 2255.4.5 — Reiser, Oliver L. World philosophy. Pittsburgh, 1948.
Phil 6127.25 — Rennie, T.A.C. Mental health in modern society. N.Y., 1948.

Phil 3960.1 — Repertorium der Nederlanden wijsbegeerte. Amsterdam, 1948-3v.

Phil 3640.336 — Reyburn, Hugh A. Nietzsche. London, 1948.
Phil 3625.1.165 — Richter, Liselotte. Philosophie der Dicht Kunst. Berlin, 1948.

Phil 2750.13.85 — Ricoeur, Paul. Gabriel Marcel et Karl Jaspers. Paris, 1948.

Phil 2255.6 — Ritchie, Arthur D. Essays in philosophy and other pieces. London, 1948.

Phil 817.21 — Rivaud, Albert. Histoire de la philosophie. Paris, 1948-3v.

Phil 1122.6.4 — Robin, Léon. La pensée grecque et les origines de l'esprit scientifique. Paris, 1948.

Phil 1717.16 — Roig Gironella, J. Filosofía y razón. Madrid, 1948.
Phil 4210.22.10 — Rosmini-Serbati, Antonio. Nuovo saggio sull'origine delle idee. 3. ed. Bari, 1948.

Phil 575.93.15 — Rothacker, E. Die Schichten der Persönlichkeit. 4e Aufl. Bonn, 1948.

Phil 3195.6.111 — Roura-Parella, J. El mundo histórico social. México, 1948.

Phil 960.255 — Roy, Ellen (Gottschalk). In man's own image. 1. ed. Calcutta, 1948.

Phil 4215.8.34 — Ruggiero, Guido de. Existentialism: disintegration of man's soul. N.Y., 1948.

Phil 8586.36.60 — Runte, H. Glaube und Geschichte. Festschrift für Friedrich Gogarten. Giessen, 1948.

Phil 2255.1.45 — Russell, Bertrand Russell. Human knowledge; its scope and limits. London, 1948.

Phil 8419.52 — Saarinen, E. Search for form. N.Y., 1948.
Phil 193.49.25.10A — Santayana, G. Dialogues in limbo. N.Y., 1948.

Phil 2880.8.46 — Sartre, Jean Paul. The emotions, outline of a theory. N.Y., 1948.

Phil 2880.8.30 — Sartre, Jean Paul. The psychology of imagination. N.Y., 1948.

Phil 2465.90 — Savioz, R. La philosophie de Charles Bonnet de Genève. Thèse. 1e éd. Paris, 1948. 4v.

Phil 1153.15 — Sayre, Farrand. The Greek cynics. Baltimore, 1948.
Phil 310.280 — Schaff, Adam. Wstp do teorii marksizmu. Warszawa, 1948.
Phil 5425.78 — Scheffler, K. Lebensbild des Talents. Berlin, 1948.
Phil 3800.390.10 — Schelling, F.W.J. von. Clara. München, 1948.
Phil 2520.380 — Schiavo, Mario. Il problema etico in Cartesio. Rome, 1948?

Phil 193.169 — Schilfgaarde, P. von. Over de wijsgeerige verwondering. Assen, 1948.

Phil 5228.12 — Schiller, P. von. Aufgabe der Psychologie. Wien, 1948.
Phil 8419.53 — Schillinger, J. The mathematical basis of the arts. N.Y., 1948.

Phil 3850.29.30 — Schlick, M. Gesetz, Kausalität und Wahrscheinlichkeit. Wien, 1948[1938]

Phil 3640.374 — Schoeck, H. Nietzsches Philosophie. Tübingen, 1948.
Phil 5058.53A — Searles, Herbert L. Logic and scientific methods. N.Y., 1948.

Phil 9255.17.5 — Sedgewick, Garrett G. Of irony, especially in drama. Toronto, 1948.

Phil 8598.96.5 — Sellmair, Josef. Der Mensch in der Fragik. München, 1948.
Phil 9240.8 — Sertellanges, A.G. Le problème du mal. Paris, 1948-1951. 2v.

Phil 6128.13.8 — Sherrington, C.S. The integrative action of the nervous system. Cambridge, Eng., 1948.

Phil 193.161 — Siger de Brabant. Question sur la metaphysique. Louvain, 1948.

Phil 2266.20 — Smith, Adam. Moral and political philosophy. N.Y., 1948.
Phil 8598.88.2 — Solov'ev, Vladimir Sergeevich. Lectures on Godmanhood. London, 1948.

Phil 4319.3 — Spain. Filosofía española y portuguesa de 1500 a 1650. Madrid, 1948.

Phil 3850.5.100 — Spir, Afrikan. Lettres inédites au professeur. Neuchâtel, 1948.

Phil 1750.33 — Stackelberg, J. von. Schuld ist Schicksal. München, 1948.
Phil 8060.6 — Standinger, J. Das schöne als Weltanschauung. Wien, 1948.
Phil 193.183 — Stefanini, Luigi. Metafisica dell'arte e altri saggi. Padova, 1948.

Phil 1750.265 — Steinbüchel, T. Existenzialismus und christliche Ethos. Heidelberg, 1948.

Phil 8893.102.5 — Stevenson, Charles Leslie. Ethics and language. New Haven, 1948.

Phil 6968.30 — Straus, Erwin. On obsession, a clinical and methodological study. N.Y., 1948.

Phil 8708.25 — Strömberg, G. The searchers. Philadelphia, 1948.
Phil 299.24.2 — Strömberg, G. The soul of the universe. 2. ed. Philadelphia, 1948.

Phil 3195.16.80 — Szylkarski, W. Jugendgeschichte Adolf Dyroffs. 2. Aufl. Bonn, 1948.

Phil 2750.13.80 — Tavares, M. de la Salette. Aproximaçoa do pensamento concerto de Gabriel Marcel. Lisboa, 1948.

NEDL Phil 5259.36 — Teplov, B.M. Psikhologiia. Moskva, 1948.
Phil 3640.351 — Thibon, G. Nietzsche; ou Le declin de l'espirit. 13e éd. Lyon, 1948.

Phil 5259.38 — Thirring, H. Homo sapiens. 2. Aufl. Wien, 1948.
Phil 530.11.18 — Thune, Nils. The Behmenists and the Philadelphians. Inaug.-Diss. Uppsala, 1948.

Phil 1750.263 — Troisfontaines, R. Existentialisme et pensée chrétienne. 2e éd. Louvain, 1948.

Phil 2980.5 — Tumarkin, Anna. Wesen und Werden der schweizerischen Philosophie. Frauenfeld, 1948.

Phil 7069.47.30 — Tyrrell, George N.M. The personality of man. W. Drayton, 1948.

Phil 2805.251 — Tytgat, J. Pascal. Gand, 1948.

Phil 5520.374   Upton, Albert. Design for thinking. Whittier, Calif, 1948.

Phil 8895.4   Urwick, Edward. The values of life. Toronto, 1948.

Phil 1750.290   Vedaldi, A. Essere gli altri. 1. ed. Torino, 1948.

Phil 4260.34   Vico, G.B. The new science of Giambattista Vico. Ithaca, 1948.

NEDL Phil 4372.1.35   Vives, Juan Luis. Causas de la decadencia de las artes. Buenos Aires, 1948.

Phil 3246.241   Vlachos, G. Fédéralisme et raison d'état dans la pensée internationale de Fichte. Paris, 1948.

Phil 3246.241.5   Vlachos, G. Fédéralisme et raison d'état dans la pensée internationale de Fichte. Thèse. Paris, 1948.

Phil 3450.19.96.10   Waelhens, A. de. La philosophie de Martin Heidegger. 3e éd. Louvain, 1948.

Phil 2422.5.5   Wahl, Jean A. Französische Philosophie. 1e Aufl. Säkingen, 1948.

Phil 822.13   Wahl, Jean A. The philosopher's way. N.Y., 1948.

Phil 7069.48   Warcollier, R. Mind to mind. N.Y., 1948.

Phil 8735.30   Wasmuth, E. Sokrates und der Engel. Olten, 1948.

Phil 2340.14.30   Wauchope, Oswald S. Deviation into sense. London, 1948.

Phil 5772.12   Weidenbach, Oswald. Ethos contra Logos. München, 1948.

Phil 5062.37   Werkmeister, W.H. An introduction to critical thinking. Lincoln, Neb., 1948.

Phil 5832.15.5   Werner, Heinz. Comparative psychology of mental development. N.Y., 1948.

Phil 9240.9   Whale, J.S. The Christian answers to the problem of evil. 2. ed. London, 1948.

Phil 2340.10.96.2   Whitehead, Alfred North. Essays in science and philosophy. N.Y., 1948.

Phil 630.49   Wild, John. Introduction to realistic philosophy. N.Y., 1948.

Phil 6669.11   Wolfe, Bernard. Hypnotism comes of age. 1st ed. Indianapolis, 1948.

Phil 6060.44   Wolff, Wermer. Diagrams of the unconscious. N.Y., 1948.

Phil 5232.5.15A   Woodworth, R.S. Contemporary schools of psychology. N.Y., 1948.

Phil 825.5   Zea, Leopoldo. Ensayos sobre filosofía en la historia. Mexico, 1948.

Phil 5204.22.2   Zeddies, Adolf. Worterbuch der Psychologie. 2. Aufl. Dortmund, 1948.

Phil 4987.89.30   Zubiri, Xavier. Naturaleza, historia, Dios. Buenos Aires, 1948.

Phil 8975.1   Zwicker, Heinz. Reich Gottes. Bern, 1948.

1949

Phil 2475.1.390   Ades, Albert. Ades chez Bergson. Paris, 1949.

Phil 4803.130.30   Ajdukiewicz, Kazimierz. Zagadnienia i Kierunki filozofii. W Krakowie, 1949.

Phil 5625.75.7   Akademiia Nauk SSSR. Arkhiv. Rukopisnye materialy I.P. Pavlova. Moskva, 1949.

Phil 5068.14   Albrecht, Erhard. Darstellung und Kritik der erkenntnistheoretischen Grundlagen der Kausalitätsauffassung und der Ethik des Neopositivismus. Rostock, 1949.

Phil 800.13.2   Aleksandrov, G.F. A history of western European philosophy. 2d ed. New Haven, 1949.

Phil 1750.335   Alonso-Fueyo, S. Existencialismo y existencialistas. Valencia, 1949.

Phil 5240.35.2   Anastasi, Anne. Differential psychology. N.Y., 1949.

Phil 331.9   Anderson, J.F. The bond of being. St. Louis, 1949.

Phil 4843.6   Apostolopoulos, Ntimês. Syntomê historia tês neoellenikês philosophias. Athena? 1949.

Phil 1750.371   Archivio di Filosofia. Esistenzialismo cristiano. Padova, 1949.

Phil 40.1.3   Aristotelian Society. Synoptic index, 1900-49. Oxford, 1949. 2v.

Phil 850.21.5   Armstrong, A.H. An introduction to ancient philosophy. 2d ed. London, 1949.

Phil 623.25   Bachelard, G. Le rationalisme appliqué. Paris, 1949.

Phil 978.74.35   Bailey, A.A. (Mrs.). The destiny of the nations. N.Y., 1949.

Phil 165.8   Ballauff, T. Das gnoseologische Problem. Göttingen, 1949.

Phil 8951.4.5   Barbour, G.F. Essays and addresses. Edinburgh, 1949.

Phil 5238.16   Baumgarten, F. Progress de la psycotechnique. Bern, 1949-

Phil 8876.108   Beauvoir, Simone de. The ethics of ambiguity. N.Y., 1949.

Phil 176.177.5   Becher, Erich. Einführung in die Philosophie. 2. Aufl. Berlin, 1949.

Phil 1905.21   Beer, Samuel. The city of reason. Cambridge, 1949. 2v.

Phil 176.162   Beerling, R.F. Onsocratische gesprekken. Amsterdam, 1949.

Phil 1750.295   Bence, Max. Technische Existenz, Essays. Stuttgart, 1949.

Phil 623.26   Benda, J. La crise du rationalisme. Paris, 1949.

Phil 7069.49.15   Bendit, Phoebe Daphne Payne. The psychic sense. N.Y., 1949.

Phil 8581.69.7   Berdiaev, N.A. Samopoznanie: opyt filosofskoi avtobiografii. Parizh, 1949.

Phil 4752.2.68   Berdiaev, Nikolai Aleksandrovich. De l'esprit bourgeois. Neuchâtel, 1949.

Phil 4752.2.45   Berdiaev, Nikolai Aleksandrovich. The divine and the human. London, 1949.

Phil 5204.24   Berka, M. Kleines psychologisches Lexicon. Wien, 1949.

Phil 4260.125   Berry, Thomas. The historical theory of Giambattista Vico. Washington, 1949.

Phil 6980.112.10   Binger, C.A.L. More about psychiatry. Chicago, 1949.

Phil 5520.97A   Black, M. Language and philosophy. Ithaca, 1949.

Phil 400.106   Blanchi, R. Les attitudes idéalistes. Paris, 1949.

Phil 3120.22.15   Blüher, Hans. Die Achse der Natur. Hamburg, 1949.

Phil 9245.134   Boelen, Bernard J. Eduaimonie en het wezen der ethiek. Leuven, 1949.

Phil 332.26   Bollnou, Atto. Das Verstehen. Mainz, 1949.

Phil 1750.179.5A   Bollnow, O.F. Existenzphilosophie. 3. Aufl. Stuttgart, 1949.

Phil 176.154   Botelho, Pero de. Da filosofia. 1. ed. Candeia, 1949.

Phil 176.155   Bouchet, Henri. Introduction à la philosophie de l'individu. Paris, 1949.

Phil 2477.1.41   Boutroux, Émile. De l'idée de loi naturelle dans la science et la philosophie contemporaines. Paris, 1949.

Phil 1506.10   Brehser, Emile. La philosophie du moyen âge. Paris, 1949.

Phil 8581.96   Brunner, Heinrich Emil. Christianity and civilisation. N.Y., 1949. 2v.

Phil 8581.96.2   Brunner, Heinrich Emil. Christianity and civilization. N.Y., 1949.

Phil 2520.226   Bruno, A. Cartesio e l'illuminismo. Bari, 1949.

Phil 176.85.20   Brunschvicg, L. La philosophie de l'esprit. 1. éd. Paris, 1949.

Phil 5627.134.33   Buchman, Frank. Remaking the world. N.Y., 1949.

Phil 5241.97.10   Burrow, Trigant. The neurosis of man. London, 1949.

Phil 665.73   Bury, R.G. The devil's puzzle. Dublin, 1949.

Phil 4073.60   Campanella, Tommaso. Dio e la predestinazione. Firenze, 1949-51. 2v.

Phil 8403.13   Canitt, Edgar. An introduction to aesthetics. London, 1949.

Phil 6315.2.144   Carlemans, A. Development of Freud's conception of anxiety. Amsterdam, 1949.

Phil 5242.50   Carlsson, N.G. Dimensions of behaviour. Lund, 1949.

Phil 1802.6   Carré, M.H. Phrases of thought in English. Oxford, 1949.

Phil 802.17   Casserley, J.V.L. The Christian in philosophy. London, 1949.

Phil 4080.12.35   Castelli, Enrico. Introduction à une phenomenologie de notre epoque. Paris, 1949.

Phil 9400.23   Cavan, R.S. Personal adjustments in old age. Chicago, 1949.

Phil 2475.1.303   Cavarnos, C.P. A dialogue between Bergson. Cambridge, 1949.

Phil 177.68.20   Chartier, Émile. Elements de philosophie. Paris, 1949.

Phil 5242.54   Château, J. Psychologie et métaphysique. Paris, 1949.

Phil 177.106   Chatterjee, S. The problems of philosophy. Calcutta, 1949.

Phil 5066.262   Ciger, Juraj. Základy infinitezimálnej logiky a jej axiómy. Bratislava, 1949.

Phil 530.20.90   Clark, J.M. The great German mystics. Oxford, 1949.

Phil 270.60   Coculeseo, P. Hasard et probabilités. Paris, 1949.

Phil 1930.10.10   Cohen, M.R. A dreamer's journey. (Autobiography). Boston, 1949.

Phil 1930.10.35   Cohen, Morris R. Studies in philosophy and science. N.Y., 1949.

Phil 70.19   Congreso Internacional de Filosofia, Barcelona. Actas. Madrid, 1949. 3v.

Phil 177.60.5   Conrad-Martius, Hedwig. Bios und Psyche. Hamburg, 1949.

Phil 75.40   Costa, M.G. Ineditos de filosofia em Portgal. Porto, 1949.

Phil 4080.3.65   Croce, Benedetto. Filosofia e storiografia. Bari, 1949.

Phil 4080.3.60   Croce, Benedetto. My philosophy. London, 1949.

Phil 2805.257   Daniel-Rops, Henry. Pascal et notre coeur. 6. éd. Strasbourg, 1949.

Phil 3485.18   Das, Ras-Vihari. A handbook to Kant's Critique of pure reason. Bombay, 1949.

Phil 1955.8.30   DeBurgh, William G. The life of reason. London, 1949.

Phil 1750.315   Deledalle, G. L'existentiel, philosophies et littératures de l'existence. Paris, 1949.

Phil 5590.60   Deschoux, M. Essai sur la personnalité. 1. éd. Paris, 1949.

Phil 2477.11.93   Deschoux, Marcel. La philosophie de Léon Brunschvicg. Paris, 1949.

Phil 2477.11.98   Deschoux, Marcel. La philosophie de Léon Brunschvicg. Thèse. Paris, 1949.

Phil 6313.14.5   Deutsch, Felix. Applied psychoanalysis. N.Y., 1949.

Phil 1955.6.32A   Dewey, John. Knowing and the known. Boston, 1949.

Phil 1955.6.40A   Dewey, John. The wit and wisdom of J. Dewey. Boston, 1949.

Phil 3195.6.40   Dilthey, Wilhelm. Grundriss der allgemeinen Geschichte der Philosophie. Frankfurt, 1949.

Phil 4210.153   Donati, B. Rosmini e Gioia. Firenze, 1949.

Phil 165.10   Donum lustrale. Noviomagi, 1949.

Phil 5043.33   Dopp, Joseph. Leçons de logique formelle. v.1-3. Louvain, 1949-50. 2v.

Phil 5425.76A   Dovski, Lee van. Genie und Eros. Olten-Bern, 1949. 3v.

Phil 672.136.5   Dunne, John W. An experiment with time. 3rd ed. N.Y., 1949.

Phil 1195.11   Dupréel, E. Les sophistes. Neuchâtel, 1949.

Phil 900.13   Eaton, Gai. The richest vein. London, 1949.

Phil 3235.81.25   Engels, Friedrich. Ludwig Feuerbach and the end of classical German philosophy. Moscow, 1949.

Phil 5421.5   Ernst, F. Vom Heimweh. Zürich, 1949.

Phil 2630.8.80   Etienne Gilson. Paris, 1949.

Phil 632.5   Europaeisches Forum, Alpach, Austria, 1948. Gesetz und Wirklichkeit. Innsbruck, 1949.

Phil 165.15   Falkenhahn, W. Veritati. München, 1949.

Phil 1850.141   Farrington, B. Francis Bacon. N.Y., 1949.

Phil 2880.8.100.2   Fatone, V. El existencialismo y la libertad readoro. 2. ed. Buenos Aires, 1949.

Phil 3210.58   Fechner, G.T. Der Mensch im Kosmos. Berlin, 1949.

Phil 8406.19   Feibleman, J. Aesthetics. N.Y., 1949.

Phil 165.402   Feigl, Herbert. Readings in philosophical analysis. N.Y., 1949.

Phil 4540.5   Feilberg, Ludvig. Samlede skrifter. 3. udg. København, 1949- 2v.

Phil 6115.30   Feldenkrais, M. Body and mature behavior. N.Y., 1949.

Phil 5245.49   Feldkeller, P. Das unpersönliche Denken. Berlin, 1949.

Phil 3270.14.30   Feuling, Daniel. Hauptfragen der Metaphysik. 2. Aufl. Heidelberg, 1949.

Phil 5015.3   Feys, Robert. De onturkkeling van het logisch denken. Antwerpen, 1949.

Phil 4065.145   Firpo, Luigi. Il processo di Giordano Bruno. Napoli, 1949.

Phil 1510.10   Fleckenskein, J.O. Scholastik, Barock exakte Wissenschaften. Einsiedeln, 1949.

Phil 180.64   Foss, Martin. Symbol and metaphor in human experience. Princeton, N.J., 1949.

Phil 4756.1.37   Frank, Semen L. Svet vo t'me; opyt khristianskoi etikhi i sotsial'noi filosofii. Parizh, 1949

Phil 6315.2.8.30A   Freud, Sigmund. Collected papers. London, 1949. 5v.

Phil 6315.2.62.10   Freud, Sigmund. Délire et rêves dans la "gradiva" de Jenson. 8. éd. Paris, 1949.

Phil 8585.28.2   Freud, Sigmund. The future of an illusion. London, 1949.

Phil 6315.2.70   Freud, Sigmund. Ma vie et la psychanalyse. 23. éd. Paris, 1949.

Phil 6315.2.8.20   Freud, Sigmund. An outline of psychoanalysis. 1st. ed. N.Y., 1949.

Phil 6315.2.75.15   Freud, Sigmund. Three essays on the theory of sexuality. 1st English ed. London, 1949.

Phil 6315.2.75.12   Freud, Sigmund. Trois essais sur la théorie de la sexualité. 51. éd. Paris, 1949.

Phil 8050.53   Frey, Dagobert. Grundlegung zu einer vergleichenden Kunstwissenschaft. Innsbruck, 1949.

Phil 3270.11   Friedmann, H. Wissenschaft und Symbol. München, 1949.

Phil 8585.36   Fries, Heinrich. Die Katholische religions philosophie der Gegenwart. Heidelberg, 1949.

1949 - cont.

Phil 6115.27.15   Fulton, J.F. Physiology of the nervous system. 3. ed. N.Y., 1949.

Phil 5046.25   Gabriel, Leo. Logik der Weltanschauung. 1. Aufl. Graz, 1949.

Phil 5258.68.30   Garcia de Onrubia, Luis Felipe. Ensayo sobre la teoria. Buenos Aires, 1949.

Phil 7069.49   Garrett, Eileen Jeanette Lyttle. Adventures in the supernormal. N.Y., 1949.

Phil 4872.109.2   Ghose, Aurobindo. The life divine. N.Y., 1949.
Phil 8881.71   Gilbert, Headley B. Temptation. Dallas, Texas, 1949.
Phil 181.73.5   Gilson, E. Being and some philosophers. Toronto, 1949.
Phil 4357.2.31   Giner de los Rios, Francisco. El pensamiento vivo de Giner de los Rios. Buenos Aires, 1949.
Phil 2475.1.430   Giusso, Lorenzo. Bergson. Milano, 1949.
Phil 960.161   Glasenapp, H. von. Die philosophie der Inder. Stuttgart, 1949.
Phil 9495.149   Glasgow, M. Problems of sex. Boston, 1949.
Phil 165.14   Glockner, H. Philosophisches lesebuch. Stuttgart, 1949-50. 2v.
Phil 6316.12.20   Glover, Edward. Psycho-analysis; a handbook for medical practitioners and students of comparitive psychology. 2d ed. London, 1949.
Phil 672.174   Goeje, C.H. de. Space, time and life; and, What is time? v.1-2. Leiden, 1949.
Phil 3640.357   Götz, K.A. Nietzsche als Ausnahme. Freiburg, 1949.
Phil 2520.140.5   Gouhier, Henri. Essais sur Descartes. 2. éd. Paris, 1949.
Phil 3850.27.106   Grabs, R. Albert Schweitzer. Berlin, 1949.
Phil 4080.3.205   Gramsci, Antonio. Il materialismo storico e la filosofia di Benedetto Croce. 2. ed. Torino, 1949.
Phil 181.88   Guitton, Jean. L'existence temporelle. Paris, 1949.
Phil 3006.7.5   Gurvitch, G. Les tendances actuelles de la philosophie allemande. Paris, 1949.
Phil 8881.72A   Gusdorf, Georges. Traité de l'existence morale. Paris, 1949.
Phil 8587.51.10   Haecker, T. Opuscula. Olten, 1949.
Phil 1750.363   Haefliger, O. Wider den Existentialismus. Bern, 1949.
Phil 8587.66   Hägerström, A.A.T. Religionsfilosofi. Stockholm, 1949.
Phil 1807.2.15   Halévy, E. The growth of philosophic radicalism. London, 1949.
Phil 5590.190   Haring, D.G. Personal character and cultural milieu. N.Y., 1949.
Phil 1750.183.2   Harper, Ralph. Existentialism. Cambridge, 1949.
Phil 1807.7   Harris, Victor I. All coherence gone. Chicago, 1949.
Phil 182.94.19   Hartmann, N. Der Aufbau der realen Welt. 2. Aufl. Meisenheim, 1949.
Phil 8882.50.7   Hartmann, N. Ethik. 3. Aufl. Berlin, 1949.
Phil 182.94.10.5   Hartmann, N. Das Problem des geistigen Seins. 2. Aufl. Berlin, 1949.
Phil 182.94.18.3   Hartmann, Nicolai. Neue Wege der Ontologie. 3.Aufl. Stuttgart, 1949.
Phil 5203.11.15   Harvard University. The Harvard list of books in psychology. Cambridge, 1949.
Phil 8662.19   Hawkins, D.J. The essentials of theism. London, 1949.
Phil 1750.31   Hazard, P. Die Herrschaft der Vermunft. Hamburg, 1949.
Phil 8587.72   Hedenius, Ingemar. Tor och roetande. Stockholm, 1949.
Phil 3450.19.110   Heidegger, Martin. Martin Heideggers Einfluss auf die Wissenschaften aus Anlass seines Sechzig sun Geburtstages verfasst Carlos Astrada. Bern, 1949.
Phil 1750.166.30   Heidegger, Martin. Über den Humanismus. Frankfurt, 1949.
Phil 3450.19.59.1   Heidegger, Martin. Vom Wesen der Wahrheit. Frankfurt, 1949.
Phil 5066.70   Hilbert, D. Grundzüge der theorelischen Logik. 2. Aufl. Berlin, 1949.
Phil 960.137.10   Hiriyanna, M. The essentials of Indian philosophy. London, 1949.
Phil 807.18   Hirschberger, Johannes. Geschichte der Philosophie. Freiburg, 1949-51. 2v.
Phil 2045.61.35   Hobbes, Thomas. De cive; or, The citizen. N.Y., 1949.
Phil 2045.54.5   Hobbes, Thomas. Leviathan. Part I. Chicago, 1949.
Phil 9120.175   Hollingworth, H.L. Psychology and ethics. N.Y., 1949.
Phil 130.6   Hubscher, Arthur. Philosophen der Gegenwart. München, 1949.
Phil 5465.54   Hutchinson, E.D. How to think creatively. N.Y., 1949.
Phil 4352.1.115   Instituto de España. Centenario de Jaime Balmes. Madrid, 1949.
Phil 70.24   International Council for Philosophy and Humanistic Studies. International council for philosophy and humanistic studies. Paris, 1949.
Phil 70.17   International Institute of Philosophy. Nature des problemes en philosophie. Paris, 1949.
Phil 5066.175   Iwanicki, J. Dedukcja naturalna i logistyczna. Warszawa, 1949.
Phil 2070.27.10   James, William. Pragmatism. N.Y., 1949.
Phil 6679.3   Janis, I.L. Are the cominform countries using hypnotic techniques to elicit confessions. Santa Monica, Calif., 1949.
Phil 3475.3.47A   Jaspers, Karl. The perennial scope of philosophy. N.Y., 1949.
Phil 3475.3.58   Jaspers, Karl. Philosophie und Wissenschaft. Zürich, 1949.
Phil 3475.3.55   Jaspers, Karl. Vernunft und Existenz. Bremen, 1949.
Phil 270.59   Joachim, J. Das Problem der Gesetzlichkeit. Hamburg, 1949-2v.
Phil 2075.5.31   Joad, Cyril E.W. Decadence. N.Y., 1949.
Phil 8884.24   Jordan, E. The good life. Chicago, 1949.
Phil 3552.320   Joseph, H.W.B. Lectures on the philosophy of Leibniz. Oxford, 1949.
Phil 3640.355   Jungen, F. Nietzsche. Frankfurt, 1949.
Phil 2475.1.304   Jurévics, Pauls. Henri Bergson. Freiburg, 1949.
Phil 5330.32   Käellén, Elov. Uppmärksamhetsforloppens psykologi. Akademisk avhandling. Göttesburg, 1949.
Phil 5250.38   Kahn, T.C. The Kahn test of symbol arrangement. n.p., 1949.
Phil 3480.56.20   Kant, Immanuel. Essai pour introduire en philosophie le concept de grandeur négative. Paris, 1949.
Phil 3480.25.50A   Kant, Immanuel. The philosophy of Kant. N.Y., 1949.
Phil 3549.10.50   Kassner, Rudolf. Umgang der Jahre. Erlenbach, 1949.
Phil 5250.34.5   Katona, George. Organizing and memorizing. N.Y., 1949.
Phil 5590.55   Kenmare, D. World invisible. London, 1949.
Phil 9220.14   Kennell, Earl. This is friendship. N.Y., 1949.
Phil 6060.12.25   Klages, Ludwig. Graphologie. 4. Aufl. Heidelberg, 1949.
Phil 6060.12.5.20   Klages, Ludwig. Handschrift und Charakter. 23. Aufl. Bonn, 1949.
Phil 6060.12.30   Klages, Ludwig. Was die Graphologie nicht kann. Zürich, 1949.

1949 - cont.

Phil 5125.20   Kneale, William Calvert. Probability and induction. Oxford, 1949.
Phil 4972.5.5   Korn, Alejandro. Obras completas. Buenos Aires, 1949.
Phil 400.99.5   Kränzlin, Gerhard. Das System des Panhumanismus. Zürich, 1949.
Phil 341.16   Kruse, F.V. The foundation of human thought. London, 1949.
Phil 2725.2.41.5   Lamennais, F.R. de. Paroles d'un croyant. Paris, 1949.
Phil 2725.2.41   Lamennais, F.R. de. Les Paroles d'un croyant. Thèse. Paris, 1949.
Phil 1750.166.20   Lamont, Corliss. Humanism as a philosophy. N.Y., 1949.
Phil 1750.166.21   Lamont, Corliss. Humanism as a philosophy. 2nd ed. N.Y., 1949.
Phil 3450.11.128   Landgrabe, Ludwig. Phänomenologie und Metaphysik. Hamburg, 1949.
Phil 5374.65   Latour, M. Autour des fondements de l'être et du connaître selon l'analyse psychologique. Paris, 1949. 2v.
Phil 5251.50   Lawrence, Merle. Studies in human behavior. Princeton, 1949.
Phil 1711.10   Lee, Otis. Existence and inquiry, a study of thought in the modern world. Chicago, 1949.
Phil 2805.259   Lefebvre, H. Pascal. Paris, 1949. 2v.
Phil 2255.1.110   Leggett, H.W. Bertrand Russell. London, 1949.
Phil 3552.57A   Leibniz, Gottfried Wilhelm. Die Hauptwerke. 3. Aufl. Stuttgart, 1949.
Phil 3552.40.5   Leibniz, Gottfried Wilhelm. New essays concerning human understanding. 3rd ed. La Salle, 1949.
Phil 3552.38   Leibniz, Gottfried Wilhelm. Welträtsel und Lebensharmonie. Wiesbaden, 1949.
Phil 3552.24.20   Leibniz, Gottfried Wilhelm. Werke. Stuttgart, 1949.
Phil 4060.2.55   Leo Hebraeus. Dialogos de amor. Madrid, 1949. 2v.
Phil 2411.7   León, Ferdinand. Lebensquellen französischer Metaphysik. Hamburg, 1949.
Phil 735.124A   Lepley, Ray. Value; a cooperative inquiry. N.Y., 1949-50.
Phil 1300.20   Levi, Adolfo. Storia della filosofia romana. Firenze, 1949.
Phil 3450.11.98.5   Levinas, Emmanuel. En découvrant l'existence avec Husserl et Heidegger. Paris, 1949.
Phil 186.105   Lévy-Bruhe, L. Les carnets. 1. ed. Paris, 1949.
Phil 8591.44.20   Lewis, Clive Staples. Transposition, and other addresses. London, 1949.
Phil 8591.44.25   Lewis, Clive Staples. The weight of glory. N.Y., 1949.
Phil 3493.16.5   Litt, Theodor. Kant und Herder als Deuter der Geistigen Welt. 2. Aufl. Heidelberg, 1949.
Phil 8412.11   Loewenberg, J. Dialogues from Delphi. Berkeley, 1949.
Phil 1885.90   Lofthouse, W.F. F.H. Bradley. London, 1949. 2v.
Phil 8886.69   Losskii, N.O. Usloviia absoliutnogo dobra. Parizh, 1949.
Phil 1870.124   Luce, Arthur A. The life of George Berkeley. London, 1949.
Phil 5645.48   Lüscher, Max. Die Farbe als psychologisches Untersuchungsmittel. St. Gallen, 1949.
Phil 5251.51   Lundholm, H. God's failure or man's folly? Cambridge, 1949.
Phil 6122.65   Mabille, P. Initiation à la connaissance de l'homme. Paris, 1949.
Phil 6122.60.5   McKinney, Fred. Psychology of personal adjustment. 2d ed. N.Y., 1949.
Phil 187.93.10   Marcel, Gabriel. Being and having. Westminster, 1949.
Phil 187.93.15   Marcel, Gabriel. Position et approches concrètes du mystére ontologique. Louvain, 1949.
Phil 3450.19.112   Marcia, Renè. Martin Heidegger und die Existenzialphilosophie. Bad Ischl, 1949.
Phil 9245.58   Marcuse, L. Die Philosophie des Glücks. Zürich, 1949.
Phil 2750.11.68   Maritain, Jacques. La signification de l'athéisme contemporain. Paris, 1949.
Phil 2750.11.140   Maritain, Jacques. Son oeuvre philosophique. Paris, 1949?
Phil 525.105   Marquette, Jacques de. Introduction to comparative mysticism. N.Y., 1949.
Phil 3110.85.10   Martensen, Hans L. Jacob Boehme. London, 1949.
Phil 2190.10   Martin, G. Wilhelm von Ockham. Berlin, 1949.
Phil 8667.22.10   Mascall, E.L. Existence and analogy. London, 1949.
Phil 960.166   Masui, J. Approaches de l'Inde. Tours? 1949.
Phil 187.137   Matchette, F.J. Outline of a metaphysics. N.Y., 1949.
Phil 8702.16.5   Mather, K.F. Crusade for life. Chapel Hill, N.C., 1949.
Phil 487.5   Mayer, Charles L. L'homme, esprit ou matière?. Paris, 1949.
Phil 3195.6.114   Mayz Vallenilla, Ernesto. La idea de estructura psiquica in Dilthey. Caracas, 1949.
Phil 8887.75   Messner, J. Social ethics; natural law in the modern world. St. Louis, 1949.
Phil 44.2   Miller, W. The "philosophical". A short history of the Edinburgh Philosophical Institution. Edinburgh, 1949.
Phil 8870.14   Miscellanea moralia in honorem eximii domini Arthur Janssen. v.1-2. Leuven, 1949.
Phil 4351.3   Morreale deCastro, M. Pedro Simon Abril. Madrid, 1949.
Phil 4710.7   Moscow. Universitet. Filosofskii Fakul'tet. Iz istorii russkoi filosofii, sbornik. Leningrad, 1949.
Phil 1750.352   Müller, Max. Existenzphilosophie im geistigen Leben der Gegenwart. Heidelberg, 1949.
Phil 5222.3.5A   Murphy, Gardner. Historical introduction to modern psychology. N.Y., 1949.
Phil 8414.9   Nadiani, A. Fra kaos til form. Oslo, 1949.
Phil 2805.276   Nasmuth, E. Die Philosophie Pascals. Heidelberg, 1949.
Phil 188.9.10   Nelson, L. Socratic method and critical philosophy. New Haven, 1949.
Phil 8888.14   Neumann, Erich. Tiefenpsychologie und neue Ethik. Zürich, 1949.
Phil 5374.163   Neumann, E. Ursprungsgeschichte des Bewusstseins. 1. Aufl. Zürich, 1949.
Phil 4260.123   Nicolini, F. Commento storico alla seconda Scienza nuova. Roma, 1949. 2v.
Phil 4260.124.10   Nicolini, F. La religiosità di Giambattista Vico. Bari, 1949.
Phil 3640.31.5A   Nietzsche, Friedrich. Beyond good and evil. Chicago, 1949.
Phil 3450.11.125A   Osborn, A. Edmund Husserl. 2d ed. Cambridge, 1949.
VPhil 5203.26   Ostvold, Harald. Manual of reference sources in psychology. St. Louis? 1949.
Phil 2200.5A   Otto, Max Carl. Science and the moral life. N.Y., 1949.
Phil 6124.5   Overstreet, H.A. The mature mind. N.Y., 1949.
Phil 4260.126   Paci, Enzo. Ingens sylva. 1. ed. Milano, 1949.
Phil 5585.71   Paliard, J. Pensée implicite et perception visuelle. Paris, 1949.
Phil 1955.6.117   Pan American Union. Division of Philosophy, Letters and Sciences. John Dewey en sus noventa años. Washington, 1949.

1949 - cont.

Phil 190.78 — Pap, Arthur. Elements of analytic philosophy. N.Y., 1949.
Phil 3552.324 — Pape, Ingetrud. Leibniz. Stuttgart, 1949.
Phil 8595.38 — Paul, Leslie A. The meaning of human existence. London, 1949.
Phil 2725.25.90 — Paumen, Jean. Le spiritualisme existentiel de René LeSenne. Paris, 1949.
Phil 8170.5.9 — Pavlov, T.D. Osnovni vuprosi na estetikata. 2. izd. Sofiia, 1949-
Phil 2225.5.35 — Peirce, C.S. Chance, love, and logic. N.Y., 1949.
Phil 165.11 — Philosophie der Wirklichkeitsmäke. Wien, 1949.
Phil 5066.36 — Piaget, Jean. Traité de logique. Paris, 1949.
Phil 190.80 — Pieper, Josef. Musse und Kult. München, 1949.
Phil 5850.310 — Piéron, Henri. Traité de psychologie appliquée. Paris, 1949- 7v.
Phil 9550.16 — Plamenatz, J.P. Mills' utilitarianism. Oxford, 1949.
Phil 2050.257 — Pra, Mario dal. Hume. Milano, 1949.
Phil 5520.104 — Prasod, Kali. The psychology of meaning. Lucknon, 1949.
Phil 8890.47 — Pratt, James B. Reason in the art of living. N.Y., 1949.
Phil 9120.161.20 — Prichard, H.A. Moral obligations. Oxford, 1949.
Phil 8890.48 — Prior, A.N. Logic and the bases of ethics. Oxford, 1949.
Phil 8595.39 — Le problème de la philosophie chrétienne. Paris, 1949.
Phil 5055.23 — Prot, Marcel. Language et logique. Paris, 1949.
Phil 2880.8.106 — Prucke, B. L'homme de Sartre. Grenoble, 1949.
Phil 5066.11.30 — Quine, Willard van Orman. Commutative Boolean functions. Santa Monica, 1949.
Phil 5066.11.25 — Quine, Willard van Orman. On functions of relations. Santa Monica, 1949.
Phil 5066.11.35 — Quine, Willard van Orman. A theorem on parametric Boolean functions. Santa Monica, 1949.
Phil 4317.5 — Quiroz-Martinez, Olga Victoria. La introducción de la filosofía moderna en España. 1. ed. Mexico, 1949.
Phil 8350.2 — Rankin, D.H. The development and philosophy of Australian aestheticism. Melbourne, 1949.
Phil 1750.325 — Reding, M. Die Existenzphilosophie. 1e Aufl. Düsseldorf, 1949.
Phil 8892.60 — Reding, Marcel. Metaphysik der sittlichen Werte. 1. Aufl. Düsseldorf, 1949.
Phil 348.18 — Regnéll, Hans. Symbolization and fictional reference. Lund, 1949.
Phil 6327.21.10 — Reich, Wilhelm. Character analysis. 3. ed. N.Y., 1949.
Phil 1135.163 — Reidemeister, Kurt. Das Exakte denken der Griechen. Hamburg, 1949.
Phil 6327.12.40 — Reik, Theodor. Fragment of a great confession. N.Y., 1949.
Phil 1750.345 — Rencontres Internationales. Pour un nouvel humanisme. Neuchâtel, 1949.
Phil 2630.3.84 — Reymond, M. La philosophie de Jean-Jacques Gourd. Chambéry, 1949.
Phil 5057.20.5 — Robinson, D.S. The principles of reasoning. 3rd ed. N.Y., 1949.
Phil 6117.47 — Roon, K. The new way to relax. N.Y., 1949.
Phil 6980.653 — Rotthaus, Erich. Das sittliche, eine Kraft des menschlichen Unbewussten. Stuttgart, 1949.
Phil 5645.47 — Rouwer, B. Colors and their characters. The Hague, 1949.
Phil 102.5.1 — Rozental, Mark Moiseevich. Handbook of philosophy. N.Y., 1949.
Phil 1717.8.10 — Ruggiero, G. de. Philosophische Strömungen des zivanzigsten Jahrhunderts. Köln, 1949.
Phil 2255.7 — Runes, Dagobert D. Letters to my son. N.Y., 1949.
Phil 2805.255 — Russier, Jeanne. La foi selon Pascal. v.1-2. Thèse. Paris, 1949.
Phil 6127.26 — Ryle, Gilbert. The concept of mind. London, 1949.
Phil 4018.5 — Saitta, G. Il pensiero italiano nell'umanesimo e nel Rinascimento. Bologna, 1949. 3v.
Phil 4957.20 — Sánchez Reulet, Aníbal. La filosofía latinoamericana contemporanea. Washington, 1949.
Phil 8598.94 — Sanders, B.G. Christianity after Freud. London, 1949.
Phil 6328.35 — Sarason, S.B. Psychological problems in mental deficiency. N.Y., 1949.
Phil 1718.24 — Sawicki, F. Lebensanschauungen moderner Denker. Paderborn, 1949-1952. 2v.
Phil 818.24.10 — Schilling, Kurt. Einfuhrung in die Geschichte der Philosophie. Heidelberg, 1949.
Phil 8583.28 — Schlesinger, Bruno P. Christopher Dawson and the modern political crisis. Notre Dame, 1949.
Phil 525.103 — Schnur, H.C. Mystic rebels. N.Y., 1949.
Phil 525.111 — Schreyer, L. Die Vallendeten. Heidelberg, 1949.
Phil 1850.143 — Schuhl, P. La pensée de Lord Bacon. Paris, 1949.
Phil 1123.9.10 — Schuhl, Pierre Maxime. Essai sur la formation de la pensée grecque. 2. ed. Paris, 1949.
Phil 3850.27.40 — Schweitzer, A. Albert Schweitzers Leben und Denken. N.Y., 1949.
Phil 3850.27.45 — Schweitzer, A. Das Christentum und die Welterligionen. München, 1949.
Phil 3850.27.35 — Schweitzer, A. Memoirs of childhood and youth. 1st American ed. N.Y., 1949.
Phil 1718.29 — Sciacca, Michele Federico. Il pensiero moderno. Brescia, 1949.
Phil 6328.46 — Sechehaye, Marguerte Albert. Diagnosties psychologiques. Berne, 1949.
Phil 493.5 — Sellars, R.W. Philosophy for the future. N.Y., 1949.
Phil 1750.310 — Siebers, G. Die Krisis des Existentialismus. Hamburg, 1949.
Phil 4235.10.80 — Silvestro da Valsanzibio. Vita e dottrina di Laetano di Thiene. 2. ed. Padova, 1949.
Phil 315.12 — Singer, Kent. The idea of conflict. Melbourne, 1949.
Phil 8968.8.20 — Soe, N.H.Christliche Ethik. München, 1949.
Phil 3819.35.25A — Spinoza, Benedictus de. Ethics. N.Y., 1949.
Phil 3500.69 — Stavenhagen, F. Kant und Königsberg. Gottingen, 1949.
Phil 4225.9 — Stefanini, Luigi. Metafisica della forma. Padova, 1949.
Phil 2880.8.104 — Stefoni, M. La libertà esistenziale in Jean Paul Sartre. Milano, 1949.
Phil 5520.98 — Stein, Leopold. The infancy of speech and the speech of infancy. London, 1949.
Phil 974.3.119 — Steiner, M. Erinnerungen. v.1-2. Dornach, 1949.
Phil 6968.17 — Stekel, Wilhelm. Compulsion and doubt. N.Y., 1949.
Phil 1818.2.4 — Stephen, Leslie. History of English thought in the eighteenth century. 3rd ed. N.Y., 1949. 2v.
Phil 8598.102 — Straubinger, H. Religionsphilosophie mit Theodizee. 2. Aufl. Freiburg, 1949.
Phil 5058.55 — Strogovich, M.S. Logika. Moskva, 1949.
Phil 2280.13.30 — Swenson, D. Kierkegaardian philosophy in the faith of a scholar. Philadelphia, 1949.
Phil 1524.2.15A — Taylor, H.O. The mediaeval mind. 4th ed. Cambridge, Mass., 1949. 2v.
Phil 8434.5 — Tea, Eva. Il corpo umano. Brescia, 1949.

1949 - cont.

Phil 2651.83 — Tolmer, L. Pierre-Daniel Huet, 1630-1721. Bayeux, 1949.
Phil 130.5 — Tomlin, E.W.F. The great philosophers. London, 1949?
Phil 5722.30 — Tucci, Giuseppe. Teoria e practica del Mandala. Roma, 1949.
Phil 1750.166.75 — Umanesimo e machiavellismo. Padova, 1949.
Phil 1195.13 — Untersteiner, M. Sofisti. Firenze, 1949-62. 2v.
Phil 630.50 — Urban, W.M. Beyond realism and idealism. London, 1949.
Phil 4803.570.80 — Usovicz, Aleksandr. Ksiądz Konstanty Michalski, 1879-1947. Wyd. 1. Kraków, 1949.
Phil 4771.1A — Uspenskii, P.D. In search of the miraculous. 1. ed. N.Y., 1949.
Phil 8735.23 — Van Nuys, K. Science and cosmic purpose. 1. ed. Thesis. N.Y., 1949.
Phil 8422.12 — Vedel, V. Liv og kunst. København, 1949. 2v.
Phil 1750.300 — Verneaux, R. Leçons sur l'existentialisme et ses formes principales. Paris, 1949.
Phil 821.1.9 — Vorländer, K. Geschichte der Philosophie. 9. Aufl. Hamburg, 1949-55. 2v.
Phil 974.3.117 — Wachsmuth, G. Goethe in unserer Zeit. Dornach, 1949.
Phil 1750.188 — Wahl, Jean André. Esquisse pour une histoire de l'existentialisme. Paris, 1949.
Phil 1750.187 — Wahl, Jean André. A short history of existentialism. N.Y., 1949.
Phil 2340.15.30 — Watmough, J.R. Cambridge conversations. Cambridge, 1949.
Phil 8897.76 — Weil, Simone. L'enracinement. 3. éd. Paris, 1949.
Phil 197.63.3 — Wenzl, Aloys. Wissenschaft und Weltanschauung. 2. Aufl. Hamburg, 1949.
Phil 1822.6 — Werkmeister, W.H. A history of philosophical ideas in America. N.Y., 1949.
Phil 8897.65.5 — Wheelwright, P. A critical introduction to ethics. N.Y., 1949.
Phil 705.35 — Whicher, G.F. The transcendentalist revolt against materialism. Boston, 1949.
Phil 8847.10 — Wieman, H.N. The directive in history. Boston, 1949.
Phil 365.50A — Wiener, P.P. Evolution and the founders of pragmatism. Cambridge, 1949.
Phil 3549.10.80 — Wieser, T. Die Einbildungskraft bei Rudolf Kassner. Zürich, 1949.
Phil 3120.2.96 — Winter, E. Leben und Geistige. Halle, 1949.
Phil 1955.6.115 — Wolstein, B. Experience and valuation. Thesis. N.Y., 1949.
Phil 5520.99 — Woodworth, Hugh. The nature and technique of understanding. Vancouver, B.C., 1949.
Phil 353.19 — Woozley, A. Theory of knowledge. London, 1949.
Phil 5170.9 — Wright, G.H. Form and content in logic. Cambridge, 1949.
Phil 3425.330 — Wundt, M. Hegels Logik. Köln, 1949.
Phil 4710.85 — Zen'kovskii, V.V. Istoriia russkoi filosofii. Paris, 1949. 2v.

195

Phil 3850.14.30 — Hasenfuss, Josef. Herman Schell als existentieller Denker und Theologie. 1. Aufl. Würzburg, 1951.

195-

Phil 8580.31 — Amorim de Carvalho. Deus e o homem na poesia e na filosofia. Porto, 195-.
Phil 4752.2.65 — Berdiaev, Nikolai Aleksandrovich. Das Ich und die Welt der Objekte. Darmstadt, 195-?
Phil 3640.400 — Gerbes, Hans E. Zum 50. Todestag Friedrich Nietzsches. n.p., 195-.
Phil 4972.6.30 — Kelly, Celso. Valores do espirito; ensaios. Rio de Janeiro, 195-?
Phil 5822.12 — Miatto, A. Istinto e società animale. Firenze, 195-?
Phil 343.25 — Mouloud, N. Formes structurées et modes productifs. Paris, 195-?
Phil 3640.22.15 — Nietzsche, Friedrich. Philosophy of Nietzsche. N.Y., 195-?
Phil 7082.128 — Otaola, J.R. de. El análisis de los sueños. Barcelona, 195-?
Phil 4872.242.1030 — Radhas Vamidayal. The Sär Bachan; an abstract of the teachings of Swamiji Maharaj. 4th ed. Beas, 195-?
Phil 8708.32 — Schumann, F.K. Uberwindung des Säkularismus in der Wissenschaft. Gladbeck, 195-.
Phil 1750.490 — Universidad Nacional del Litoral. Santa Fé, Argentina. Instituto de Filosofía. Symposium sobre existencialismo. pts.1-7. Rosario, 195-?
Phil 1750.495 — Virasoro, Rafael. Introducción al estudio de la fenomenologia de Husserl. Rosario, 195-?
Phil 8605.8 — Zen'kovskii, V.V. Apologetika. 2. izd. Parizhe, 195-? 3 pam.

1950

Phil 5590.65 — Abt, L.E. Projective psychology. 1.ed. N.Y., 1950.
Phil 1200.50 — Agostino, V. Studi sul reostoicismo. Torino, 1950.
Phil 1105.8 — Alfieri, V.E. Studi di filosofia greca. Bari, 1950.
Phil 2750.11.95 — Allen, E. Christian humanism...Jacques Maritain. London, 1950.
Phil 8951.24 — Allen, E. Creation and grace...Ernie Brunner. London, 1950.
Phil 4752.2.105 — Allen, E. Freedom in God...on Berdyaev. London, 1950. 4 pam.
Phil 8662.15.80 — Allen, E. Jesus, our leader...Karl Heim. London, 1950.
Phil 3475.3.105 — Allen, L. The self and its hazards...K. Jaspers. London, 1950.
Phil 5590.70 — Allport, G.W. The nature of personality. Cambridge, Mass., 1950.
Phil 5627.189 — Allport, Gordon W. The individual and his religion. N.Y., 1950.
Phil 5590.71 — Allport, Gordon Willard. The nature of personality. Cambridge, 1950.
Phil 2520.229.2 — Alquié, F. La découverte métaphysique de l'homme chez Descartes. Thèse. Paris, 1950.
Phil 2520.229 — Alquié, F. La découverte métaphysique de l'homme chez Descartes. 1. éd. Paris, 1950.
Phil 175.43.10 — Alquié, Ferdinand. La nostalgie de l'être. Paris, 1950.
Phil 175.43.11 — Alquié, Ferdinand. La nostalgie de l'être. Thèse. Paris, 1950.
Phil 165.16 — Anteile. Frankfurt am Main, 1950.
Phil 400.115 — Archivio di Filosofia. Il solipsismo. Padova, 1950.
Phil 4961.805.5 — Ardao, Arturo. Espiritualismo y positivismo en el Uruguay. México, 1950.
Phil 1700.6 — Ardley, Gavin. Aquinas and Kant. London, 1950.

Chronological Listing

Phil 672.180   Aspecten van de tijd. Assen, 1950.

Phil 1850.35.20   Bacon, Francis. The advancement of learning. London, 1950.

Phil 165.7   Baldwin, R.C. An introduction to philosophy through literature. N.Y., 1950.

Phil 176.156   Barnes, W. The philosophical predicament. London, 1950.

Phil 7082.80.1   Baudouin, Charles. Introduction à l'analyse des rêves. Paris, 1950.

Phil 5751.18   Baudry, L. La querelle des futurs contingents. Paris, 1950.

Phil 6311.31   Baynes, H. Analytical psychology and the English mind. London, 1950.

Phil 5041.60   Beardsley, M.C. Pratical logic. N.Y., 1950.

Phil 2401.9   Benda, J. De quelques constantes de l'esprit humain. Paris, 1950.

Phil 176.160   Bense, Max. Literaturmetaphysik. 1. Aufl. Stuttgart, 1950.

Phil 4752.2.55   Berdiaev, Nikolai Aleksandrovich. Dream and reality. London, 1950.

Phil 2520.240   Berlin. Freie Universität. Gedenkfeier anlässlich des drei hundertjährigen Todestagen des Philosophen René Descartes. Berlin, 1950.

Phil 2115.165   Bianca, Giuseppe G. La credenza come fondamento. Padova, 1950.

Phil 3450.19.107A   Biemel, W. Le concept de inonde chez Heidegger. Louvain, 1950.

Phil 165.13   Black, M. Philosophical analysis. Ithaca, 1950.

Phil 978.5.1   Blavatsky, H.P. Collected writings. 1st American ed. v.5-8. Los Angeles, 1950. 4v.

Phil 8581.95.10   Blondel, Maurice. Exigences philosophiques du christianisme. 1. éd. Paris, 1950.

Phil 410.6.10.2   Bolzano, B. Paradoxes of the infinite. London, 1950.

Phil 410.6.10   Bolzano, B. Paradoxes of the infinite. New Haven, 1950.

Phil 6311.34.6   Bonaparte, Marie. Treis dialexeis eisagōgēs eis tēn psychanalasē. Athenai, 1950.

Phil 6311.32   Bonaventura, E. La psicoanalisi. 4. ed. Milano, 1950.

Phil 2477.6.120   Bonicelli, B.M. La logica morale in Maurice Blondel. Torino, 1950.

Phil 5211.4.5   Boring, E.G. A history of experimental psychology. 2. ed. N.Y., 1950.

Phil 8581.91.10   Bosley, Harold A. A firm faith for today. 1. ed. N.Y., 1950.

Phil 2880.8.88.5   Boutang, P. Sartre, est-il un possédé? Paris, 1950.

Phil 3120.45.50   Brandenstein, Béla. Der Aufbau des Seins; System der Philosophie. Tübingen, 1950.

Phil 8951.22   Braun, K. Justice and the law of love. London, 1950.

Phil 2401.10   Bréhier, E. Transformation de la philosophie française. Paris, 1950.

Phil 75.43   Bril, G.A. de. Bibliographia philosophica. Rhenum, 1950. 2v.

Phil 5593.50   Broek, P. van den. De Behn-Rorschach-test. 's Gravenhauge, 1950.

Phil 5241.28.25   Brown, W. College psychology. N.Y., 1950.

Phil 176.158   Brunner, August. Der Stufenbau der Welt. 1. Aufl. München, 1950.

Phil 3552.340   Brunner, F. Études sur la signification historique de la philosophie de Leibniz. Thèse. Paris, 1950[1951]

Phil 3120.30.47   Buber, Martin. Zwei Glaubensweisen. Zürich, 1950.

Phil 530.11.6   Bullett, G.W. The English mystics. London, 1950.

Phil 3850.27.101.5   Buri, Fritz. Albert Schweitzer und Karl Jaspers. Zürich, 1950.

Phil 3808.190   Busch, Hugo. Das Testament Arthur Schopenhauer. Wiesbaden, 1950.

Phil 1900.62   Butler, Joseph. Five sermons preached at the Rolls Chapel. N.Y., 1950.

Phil 5520.108   California. University. Philosophical Union. Meaning and interpretation. Berkeley, 1950.

Phil 4265.6.95   Calogero, G. La filosofia di Bernardino Varisco. Messina, 1950.

Phil 5242.52   Cantrie, H. The "why" of man's experience. N.Y., 1950.

Phil 5520.120   Carnap, Rudolf. Testability and meaning. New Haven, 1950.

Phil 6990.3.65   Carrel, A. The voyage to Lourdes. 1. ed. N.Y., 1950.

Phil 9070.52   Carrel, Alexis. Réflexions sur la conduite de la vie. Paris, 1950.

Phil 333.5.20   Cassirer, Ernst. The problem of knowledge. New Haven, 1950.

Phil 8403.25   Castelfranco, G. Lineamenti di estetica. 1. ed. Firenze, 1950.

Phil 5590.100   Cattell, R.B. An introduction to personality study. London, 1950.

Phil 2340.10.126   Cesselin, Felix. La philosophie organique de Whitehead. Thèse. 1e éd. Paris, 1950.

Phil 2340.10.125   Cesselin, Felix. La philosophie organique de Whitehead. 1e éd. Paris, 1950.

Phil 8403.33   Cevallos García, G. Del arte actual y de su existencia. Cuenca, 1950.

Phil 3640.366   Challaye, F. Nietzsche. Paris, 1950.

Phil 960.165.5   Chatterjee, S. The fundamentals of Hinduism. Calcutta, 1950.

Phil 960.165   Chatterjee, S. An introduction to Indian philosophy. 4th ed. Calcutta, 1950.

Phil 6112.35   Chauchard, P. L'influx nerveux et la psychologie. Paris, 1950.

Phil 8403.12.5   Chernyshevskii, N.G. N.G. Chernyshevskii ob iskusstve. Moskva, 1950.

Phil 4065.128   Cicuttini, L. Giordano Bruno. Milano, 1950.

Phil 4752.2.90   Clarke, O.G. Introduction to Berdyaev. London, 1950.

Phil 6825.2.2   Cleckley, Hervey Milton. The mask of sanity. 2. ed. St. Louis, 1950.

Phil 1930.14.31   Cornforth, Maurice Campbell. In defence of philosophy against positivism and pragmatism. N.Y., 1950.

Phil 1930.14.30   Cornforth, Maurice Campbell. In defence of philosophy against positivism and pragmatism. London, 1950.

Phil 3425.109.15   Croce, B. Una pagina sconosciuta degli ultimi mesi della vita di Hegel. Bari, 1950.

Phil 8877.34.6   Croce, Benedetto. Filosofia della pratica; economia ed etica. 6. ed. Bari, 1950.

Phil 6112.36   Culbertson, J.T. Consciousness and behavior. Dubugue, 1950.

Phil 1507.5   Curtis, S.J. A short history of western philosophy in middle ages. London, 1950.

Phil 6313.20   Dallard, John. Personality and psychotherapy. 1st. ed. N.Y., 1950.

Phil 1703.12   Datta, D.M. The chief currents of contemporary philosophy. Calcutta, 1950.

Phil 5753.14   Daudin, H. La liberté de la volonté. 1. éd. Paris, 1950.

Phil 3485.19.2   Daval, Roger. La métaphysique de Kant. Thèse. Paris, 1950.

Phil 3485.19   Daval, Roger. La métaphysique de Kant. 1. éd. Paris, 1950.

Phil 2520.35.45   Descartes, René. Discours de la méthode. Paris, 1950.

Phil 2520.39.16   Descartes, René. Les principes de la philosophie. Paris, 1950.

Phil 2520.234A   Descartes et le cartésianisme hollandais. Paris, 1950[1951].

Phil 960.163   Devanandan, P.D. The concept of Maya. London, 1950.

Phil 6313.17   Dignwall, E.J. Very peculiar people. London, 1950.

Phil 1750.580   Douglas, Kenneth. A critical bibliography of existentialism (the Paris School). New Haven, 1950.

Phil 5590.75   Dürr, Otto. Probleme der Gesinnungsbildung. Heidelberg, 1950.

Phil 2280.5.108   Duron, J. La pensée de George Santayana. Paris, 1950.

Phil 2280.5.108.2   Duron, J. La pensée de George Santayana. Thèse. Paris, 1950.

Phil 5627.134.85A   Eester, Allen W. Drawing-room conversion; Oxford Group movement. Durham, 1950.

Phil 5244.22.5   Ellis, Willis D. A source book of Gestalt. London, 1950.

Phil 3235.81.27   Engels, Friedrich. Ludwig Feuerbach and the end of classical German philosophy. Moscow, 1950.

Phil 720.41   Erismann, T. Denken und Sein. v.1. Wien, 1950.

Phil 8829.2.8.2   Eucken, Rudolf. Die Lebensanschauungen der grossen Denker. 20. Aufl. Berlin, 1950.

Phil 510.154   Eyken, A. Reality and monads. Apeldoorn, 1950.

Phil 2405.5.5   Farber, Marvin. L'activité philosophique contemporaine en France. 1. éd. Paris, 1950. 2v.

Phil 6315.1.10   Ferenczi, Sandor. Sex in psychoanalysis. N.Y., 1950.

Phil 805.10   Ferm, V. A history of philosophical systems. N.Y., 1950.

Phil 3235.78   Feuerbach, Ludwig. Kleine philosophische Schriften. Leipzig, 1950.

Phil 5520.116   Filosofia e linguaggio. Padova, 1950.

Phil 6315.28   Fischer, S. Principles of general psychopathology. N.Y., 1950.

Phil 6980.293   Fisher, Vivian Ezra. The meaning and practice of psychotherapy. N.Y., 1950.

Phil 6315.24   Fliess, R. The psycho-analytic reader. London, 1950.

Phil 1750.166.50   France. Centre National de la Recherche Scientifique. Pensée humaniste et tradition chrétienne aux XVe et XVIe siècle. Paris, 1950.

Phil 6315.17.10   Freud, Anna. The ego and the mechanisms of defence. N.Y., 1950.

Phil 6315.2.8.40A   Freud, Sigmund. Aus den Anfänger der Psychoanalyse. London, 1950.

Phil 6315.2.59.10   Freud, Sigmund. Beyond the pleasure principle. N.Y., 1950.

Phil 6315.2.78   Freud, Sigmund. Dictionary of psychoanalysis. N.Y., 1950.

Phil 6315.2.37.3   Freud, Sigmund. The ego and the id. London, 1950.

Phil 6480.23.18   Freud, Sigmund. The interpretation of dreams. N.Y., 1950.

Phil 6315.2.46.10   Freud, Sigmund. The question of lay analysis. 1. ed. N.Y., 1950.

Phil 3270.11.31   Friedmann, H. Sinnvolle Odyssee. München, 1950.

Phil 3450.19.116   Fritz, E. Die Seinsfrage bei Martin Heidegger. Stuttgart, 1950.

Phil 6315.26A   Fromm-Reichmann, F. Principles of intensive psychotherapy. Chicago, 1950.

Phil 1511.6   Garin, E. Dal medioeno al rinascimento. Firenze, 1950.

Phil 7069.50   Garrett, Eileen Jeanette Lyttle. The sense and nonsense of prophecy. N.Y., 1950.

Phil 5246.29.5   Garrett, Henry E. Psychology. N.Y., 1950.

Phil 8831.6   Gent, W. Der sittliche Mensch. Meisenheim, 1950.

Phil 5585.70   Gibson, J. The perception of the visual world. Boston, 1950.

Phil 5204.6.2   Giese, Fritz. Psychologische Wörterbuch. Tübingen, 1950.

Phil 3640.359   Giesz, Ludwig. Nietzsche. Stuttgart, 1950.

Phil 181.112   Gignoux, Victor. Cours de philosophie. v.3. Paris, 1950.

Phil 181.106   Gilby, Thomas. Phoenix and turtle. London, 1950.

Phil 6315.2.142   Glover, E. Freud or Jung. London, 1950.

Phil 6315.2.141A   Glover, E. Freud or Jung. N.Y., 1950.

Phil 5722.45   Gonseth, J.P. Théâtre de veille et théâtre de songe. Neuchâtel, 1950.

Phil 2225.5.102   Goudge, T.A. The thought of C.S. Peirce. Toronto, 1950.

Phil 2115.159   Gough, J.W. John Locke's political philosophy. Oxford, 1950.

Phil 3850.27.106.10   Grabs, R. Sinngeburg des Lebens. Hamburg, 1950.

Phil 5628.55.15   Graef, Hilda Charlotte. The case of Therese Neumann. Cork, 1950.

Phil 1750.29   Grassi, E. Von Ursprung und Grenzen der Geistewissenschaften und Naturwissenschaften. Bern, 1950.

Phil 4065.126   Greenberg, S. The infinite in Giordano Bruno. N.Y., 1950.

Phil 181.108   Grenier, H. Thomistic philosophy. Charlotte-town, Canada, 1950. 4v.

Phil 2630.7.32   Guénon, René. La règne de la quantité et les signes des temps. 4. éd. Paris, 1950.

Phil 8407.31   Guggenheimer, R.H. Creative vision in artist and audience. N.Y., 1950.

Phil 4757.2.30A   Gurdjieff, Georges Ivanovitch. All and everything. v.1-2. 1st ed. N.Y., 1950. 2v.

Phil 1111.12   Guthrie, William. The Greek philosophers from Thales to Aristotle. N.Y., 1950.

Phil 4120.8.35   Guzzo, Augusto. La moralitá. Torino, 1950.

Phil 5400.112   Haecker, T. Metaphysik des Fühlens. 4. Aufl. München, 1950.

Phil 3450.29   Haecker, Theodor. Journal in the night. London, 1950.

Phil 5545.158.5   Halbwachs, Maurice. La mémoire collective. 1. éd. Paris, 1950.

Phil 9530.50   Halle, L.J. On facing the world. N.Y., 1950.

Phil 165.24   Hanslmeier, J. Natur, Geist, Geschichte. München, 1950.

Phil 5247.67   Hartley, Eugene Leonard. Outside readings in psychology. N.Y., 1950.

Phil 182.94.17   Hartmann, N. Philosophie der Natur. Berlin, 1950.

Phil 325.7   Hartnack, J. Analysis of the problem of perception in British empiricism. Thesis. Cambridge, 1950.

Phil 5650.30   Harvard University. Psycho-Acoustic Laboratory. A bibliography in audition. v.1-2. Cambridge, 1950.

Phil 8832.6   Heard, Gerald. Morals since 1900. London, 1950.

Phil 3450.19.20   Heidegger, Martin. Holzwege. Frankfurt, 1950.

Phil 8632.21   Heiler, Friedrich. Unsterblichkeitsglaube und Jenseitshoffnung in der Geschichte der Religionen. München, 1950.

Phil 165.12   Heinrich, Walter. Die Ganzheit in Philosophie und Wissenschaft. Wien, 1950.

Chronological Listing

Phil 9035.90   Hellek, A. Die Polarität im Aufbau des Charakters. Bern, 1950.

Phil 705.37   Hengstenberg, H.E. Autonomismus und Transzendenzphilosophie. Heidelberg, 1950.

Phil 3450.30.10   Hessen, Johannes. Lehrbuch der Philosophie. 2e Aufl. v.3. München, 1950-

Phil 5047.33.10   Hilbert, David. Principles of mathematical logic. N.Y., 1950.

Phil 8882.66A   Hill, Thomas E. Contemporary ethical theories. N.Y., 1950.

Phil 735.125   Hilliard, A.L. The forms of value. N.Y., 1950.

Phil 1955.6.104   Hook, Sidney. John Dewey. N.Y., 1950.

Phil 6317.32   Hubbard, L. Ron. Dianetics. N.Y., 1950.

Phil 1750.369   Huebner, F.M. Umgang mit Gätterbilden. Frankfurt, 1950.

Phil 575.190   Huibregtse, Kornelis. Anthropologisch-historische benadering van het moderne subjectgevoel. Haarlem, 1950.

Phil 3450.11.30   Husserl, Edmund. Gesammelte Werke. Haag, 1950-52. 12v.

Phil 70.8.5F   Indian Philosophical Congress. Silver jubilee commemoration volume. Madras, 1950. 2v.

Phil 9400.14   Industrial Relations Research Association. The aged and society. Champaign, 1950.

Phil 75.42   Instituto di Studi Filosofici. Bibliografia filosofica italiana dal 1900 al 1950. Roma, 1950. 4v.

Phil 6118.5   International Conference on the Development of the Nervous System. Genetic neurology. Chicago, 1950.

Phil 8664.6   James, E.O. The concept of deity. London, 1950.

Phil 2070.54   James, William. William James. Harmondsworth, 1950.

Phil 400.108   Janssen, O. Seinsordnung und Gehalt der Idealitäten. Meisenheim/Glan, 1950.

Phil 3475.3.71   Jaspers, Karl. Existenzphilosophie. 2. Aufl. Berlin, 1950.

Phil 3475.3.60   Jaspers, Karl. Vernunft und Windervernunft. München, 1950.

Phil 5068.12   Joad, C.E.M. A critique of logical positivism. London, 1950.

Phil 8612.34   Jolivet, Régis. Le problème de la mort chez M. Heidegger et J.P. Sartre. Paris, 1950.

Phil 6319.1.69   Jung, C.G. Gestaltungen des Unbewussten. Zürich, 1950.

Phil 2805.261   Jungo, Michel. Le vocabulaire de Pascal. Paris, 1950.

Phil 3480.47.15   Kant, Immanuel. Critique of practical reason. Chicago, 1950.

Phil 3480.67.85   Kant, Immanuel. Foundations of the metaphysics of morals. Chicago, 1950.

Phil 3480.67.90   Kant, Immanuel. The moral law. N.Y., 1950.

Phil 187.32.85   Keeton, Morris. The philosophy of Edmund Montgomery. Dallas, 1950.

Phil 5250.55   Keller, F. Principles of psychology. N.Y., 1950.

Phil 1810.4   Kennedy, Gail. Pragmatism and American culture. Boston, 1950.

Phil 1182.35   Kerenyi, K. Pythagoras und Orpheus. 3. Aufl. Zürich, 1950.

Phil 6320.11.17A   Klein, M. Contributions to psycho-analysis. London, 1950.

Phil 5650.32   Kostelijk, P.J. Theories of hearing. Leiden, 1950.

Phil 4710.2   Koyré, A. Études sur l'histoire de la pensée philosophique en Russie. Paris, 1950.

Phil 185.65   Kraft, Viktor. Einführung in die Philosophie. Wien, 1950.

Phil 5068.16A   Kraft, Viktor. Der Wiener Kreis. Wien, 1950.

Phil 8885.38   Kresge, E.E. The search for a way of life. N.Y., 1950.

Phil 978.59.30   Krishnamurti, J. Talks, Ojai, California. Ojai, California, 1950.

Phil 1750.350.2   Kuhn, H. Begegnung mit dem Nichts. Tübingen, 1950.

Phil 3493.20.5   Lachièze-Rey, P. L'idéalisme Kantien. Thèse. 2. éd. Paris, 1950.

Phil 2725.24   Lacroix, Jean. Marxisme, existentialisme, personnalisme. Paris, 1950.

Phil 5051.31   LaHarpe, J. de. La logique de l'assertion pure. Paris, 1950.

Phil 8636.8.7   Lamont, Corliss. The illusion of immortality. 2. ed. N.Y., 1950.

Phil 4200.2.20   Lamprecht, F. Zur Theorie der humanistischen Geschichtsschreibung. Zürich, 1950.

Phil 186.109   Lamprecht, S.P. Nature and history. N.Y., 1950.

Phil 2520.344   Laporte, Jean. Le rationalisme de Descartes. Paris, 1950.

Phil 978.49.805   Lauer, H.E. Klassik. Basel, 1950.

Phil 8886.66   Leake, C.D. Can we agree? Austin, 1950.

Phil 2255.1.111   Leggett, H.W. Bertrand Russell. N.Y., 1950.

Phil 2530.88   Lerel, A.C. Diderots Naturphilosophie. Wien, 1950.

Phil 2530.88.2   Lerel, A.C. Diderots Naturphilosophie. Wien, 1950.

Phil 2520.230   Lewis, G. L'individualité selon Descartes. Paris, 1950.

Phil 2520.230.2   Lewis, G. L'individualité selon Descartes. Thèse. Paris, 1950.

Phil 2520.230.10   Lewis, G. Le problème de l'inconscient et le cartesianisme. 1. éd. Paris, 1950.

Phil 8412.15   Lindholm, C. Konsten och tiden. Stockholm, 1950.

Phil 2115.68   Locke, J. Of civil government and toleration. London, 1950.

Phil 3450.19.130   Logstrup, K.E.C. Kierkegaards und Heideggers Existenzanalyse und ihr Verhaltnis. 1-3. Aufl. Berlin, 1950.

Phil 186.107   Loos, A. The nature of man, his world. N.Y., 1950.

Phil 2340.10.120A   Lowe, Victor A. Whitehead and the modern world. Boston, 1950.

Phil 3493.38   Lugarini, Leo. La logica trascendentale Kantiana. Milano, 1950.

Phil 735.128   McCracken, D.J. Thinking and valuing. London, 1950.

Phil 1712.16   McElroy, H.C. Modern philosophers. N.Y., 1950.

Phil 2805.310   Maggioni, Mary J. The pensées of Pascal. Washington, 1950.

Phil 812.21   Mantague, W. Great visions of philosophy. La Salle, Ill., 1950.

Phil 2750.19.5   Marcel, Gabriel. The mystery of being. Chicago, 1950-51. 2v.

Phil 2750.19   Marcel, Gabriel. The mystery of being. London, 1950. 2v.

Phil 2750.23   Maréchal, Joseph. Mélanges Joseph Maréchal. Bruxelles, 1950. 2v.

Phil 7069.50.10   Marion, Frederick. In my mind's eye. 1. ed. N.Y., 1950.

Phil 8550.420   Martins, Mário. Correntes da filosofia religiosa em Braga dos séculos IV-VII. Porto, 1950.

Phil 2515.5.95   Maurois, André. Alain. Paris, 1950.

Phil 5401.26A   May, Rollo. The meaning of anxiety. N.Y., 1950.

Phil 812.20   Mayer, F. A history of ancient and medieval philosophy. N.Y., 1950.

Phil 2150.16.30   Mayer, Frederick. Essentialism. London, 1950.

Phil 1750.166.45   Mennesket i tiden. København, 1950.

Phil 1750.166.115   Mensch und Menschlichkeit. Stuttgart, 1950.

Phil 5627.95.17   Mensching, Gustav. Gut und Böse im Glauben des Völker. 2. Aufl. Stuttgart, 1950.

Phil 8887.76   Messner, J. Das Naturrecht. Innsbruck, 1950.

Phil 2138.48   Mill, John S. Philosophy of scientific method. N.Y., 1950.

Phil 850.23   Misch, G. The dawn of philosophy. London, 1950.

Phil 812.10.5   Misch, Georg. Der Weg in die Philosophie. 2. Aufl. München, 1950.

Phil 187.118.10   Monsarrat, K.W. Human desires and their fulfilment. Liverpool, 1950.

Phil 5252.82.2A   Morgan, Clifford Thomas. Physiological psychology. 2. ed. N.Y., 1950.

Phil 2070.141   Morris, Lloyd R. William James; the message of a modern mind. N.Y., 1950.

Phil 7060.156   Moser, F. Spuk. Baden bei Zürich, 1950.

Phil 575.146   Mounier, E. Le personnalisme. Paris, 1950.

Phil 1812.7.5   Müller, Gustav E. Amerikanische Philosophie. 2. Aufl. Stuttgart, 1950[1936]

Phil 735.126   Mukerjee, Radhakamal. The social structure of values. London, 1950.

Phil 187.141A   Mumford, L. Man as interpreter. 1st ed. N.Y., 1950.

Phil 3425.326A   Mure, G.R.G. A study of Hegel's logic. Oxford, 1950.

Phil 1614.5   Nardi, Bruno. La crisi del Rinascimento e il dubbio cortesiano. Roma, 1950-51.

Phil 8593.22   Nilsson, M.P. Fondamenti di scienza delle religioni. 1. ed. Firenze, 1950.

Phil 8669.4   Oursler, F. Why I know there is a God. 1. ed. Garden City, N.Y., 1950.

Phil 1750.480   Paci, Enzo. Esistenzialismo e storicismo. 1. ed. Milano, 1950.

Phil 1750.330   Paci, Enzo. Il mella e il problema dell'uomo. 1st ed. Torino, 1950.

Phil 2880.8.102   Paissac, H. Le dieu de Sartre. Grenoble, 1950.

Phil 400.117   Pareyson, L. L'estetica dell'idealismo tedesco. Torino, 1950.

Phil 3246.255   Pareyson, L. Fichte. Torino, 1950.

Phil 1750.340   Pareyson, Luigi. Studi sull'esistenzialismo. 2. ed. Firenze, 1950.

Phil 2805.42.30   Pascal, Blaise. Pensées. London, 1950.

Phil 5625.75.5   Pavlov, Ivan P. Izbrannye trudy. Moskva, 1950.

Phil 1815.3   Persons, S. Evolutionary thought in America. New Haven, 1950.

Phil 346.17   Piaget, Jean. Introduction à l'épistémologie génétique. 1. éd. Paris, 1950. 3v.

Phil 5255.51   Piaget, Jean. The psychology of intelligence. N.Y., 1950.

Phil 2725.25.5   Pirlot, J. Destinée et valeur. Namur, 1950?

Phil 3745.6.95   Planck, M. Karl Christian Planck. Stuttgart, 1950.

Phil 8416.11.25   Plekhanov, Georgii Valentinovich. L'art et de vie sociale (quatorze études). Paris, 1950.

Phil 672.170   Plumbe, C.C. Release from time. London, 1950.

Phil 1200.44.5   Pohlenz, Max. Stoa und Staiker. Zürich, 1950.

Phil 365.51   Porter, C. Creative personality. N.Y., 1950.

Phil 1190.22   Pra, Mario dal. Lo scetticismo greco. Milano, 1950.

Phil 1120.5   Pra, Mario dal. La storiografia filosofica antica. 1.ed. Milano, 1950.

Phil 960.195   Prabhavananda, Swami. Vedic religion and philosophy. Madras, 1950.

Phil 346.16   Prichard, H.A. Knowledge and perception. Oxford, 1950.

Phil 5056.1.15   Quine, Willard Van Orman. Methods of logic. N.Y., 1950.

Phil 5257.59   Ram, T. Psycho-astrologische Encyclopedie. Lochem, 1950-51. 2v.

Phil 8967.7   Ramsey, Paul. Basic Christian ethics. N.Y., 1950.

Phil 6327.4.40A   Rank, Otto. Psychology and the soul. Philadelphia, 1950.

Phil 6327.4.33   Rank, Otto. Will therapy and truth and reality. N.Y., 1950.

Phil 3850.27.117   Ratter, Magnus C. Albert Schweitzer, life and message. Boston, 1950.

Phil 960.163.5   Ray Chaudhuri, A.K. The doctrine of Maya. 2nd ed. Calcutta, 1950.

Phil 2805.274   Rennes, J. Pascal et le libertin. Paris, 1950.

Phil 8642.8   Richmond, I. Archaeology. London, 1950.

Phil 5767.11A   Ricoeur, Paul. Philosophie de la volonté. Photoreproduction. Paris, 1950. 2v.

Phil 3790.15.30   Riezler, K. Man, mutable and immutable. Chicago, 1950.

Phil 1817.10   Ritchie, A.D. British philosophers. London, 1950.

Phil 5590.50   Roback, A.A. Personality in theory and practice. Cambridge, Mass., 1950.

Phil 5190.4.25   Robinson, R. Definition. Oxford, 1950.

Phil 4959.240   Robles, Oswaldo. Filósofos mexicanos del siglo XVI. Mexico, 1950.

Phil 192.90   Roche, Jean. Discussions metaphysiques. Paris, 1950.

Phil 4979.10.30   Rodríguez Delgado, Rafael. Introducción a una filosofía de la era atómica. Habana, 1950.

Phil 192.92   Rogge, E. Axiomatik alles möglichen Philosophierens. Meisenheim, 1950.

Phil 5066.42   Rosenbloom, P.C. The elements of mathematical logic. 1st ed. N.Y., 1950.

Phil 9070.50   Ross, William. It's up to you A way to a better life. N.Y., 1950.

Phil 2250.60   Royce, Josiah. The social philosophy of Josiah Royce. Syracuse, 1950.

Phil 2255.1.50   Russell, Bertrand Russell. Unpopular essays. London, 1950.

Phil 2255.1.51   Russell, Bertrand Russell. Unpopular essays. N.Y., 1950.

Phil 193.164   Sadoleto, J. Elogia della sapienza. Napoli, 1950.

Phil 6319.1.57   Schär, Hans. Religion and the cure of souls in Jung's psychology. N.Y., 1950.

Phil 3800.340.1   Schelling, F.W.J. von. Das Wesen der menschlichen Freiheit. 1. Aufl. Düsseldorf, 1950.

Phil 6328.10.40   Schilder, Paul. The image and appearance of the human body. N.Y., 1950.

Phil 4710.6   Schultze, B. Russische Denker. Wien, 1950.

Phil 3850.27.55   Schweitzer, A. The animal world of Albert Schweitzer. Boston, 1950.

Phil 3850.27.50   Schweitzer, A. Denken und Fat. Hamburg, 1950.

Phil 4752.2.95   Seaver, George. Nicolas Berdyaev. London, 1950.

Phil 8598.96   Sellmair, Josef. Humanitas Christiana. München, 1950.

Phil 5525.46   Senise, T. Il riso in psicologia. Napoli, 1950.

Phil 5058.57   Sesmat, A. Logique. Paris, 1950.

Phil 2340.10.115   Shahan, E.P. Whitehead's theory of experience. N.Y., 1950.

Phil 5500.13   Sharp, F.C. Goodwill and ill will. Chicago, 1950.

Phil 6328.32   Sharpe, E.F. Collected papers on psycho-analysis. London, 1950.

1950 - cont.

Phil 5068.20   Simàn, B. Der logische Positivismus und das Existenzproblem der höheren Ideen. Tel-Aviv, 1950.

Phil 193.59.3   Simmel, G. Hauptprobleme der Philosophie. 7. Aufl. Berlin, 1950.

Phil 4065.127   Singer, D. (Waley). Giordano Bruno. N.Y., 1950.

Phil 3838.15.7 Siwek, Paul. Spinoza et le panthéisme religieux. Paris, 1950.

Phil 2250.96   Smith, J.E. Royce's social infinite. N.Y., 1950.

Phil 1718.23   Smith, V.E. Idea man of today. Milwaukee, 1950.

Phil 3640.394A Société Française d'Études Nietzschéennes. Nietzsche. Paris, 1950.

Phil 1750.166.70   Sodalitas Erasmiana. Il valore universale dell'umanesimo. Napoli, 1950.

Phil 4769.1.60 Solov'ev, V.S. A Solovyov anthology. London, 1950.

Phil 1718.22A   Sorokin, P. Social philosophies of an age of crisis. Boston, 1950.

Phil 8893.103A Sorokin, Pitirim Aleksandrovich. Altruistic love. Boston, 1950.

Phil 8893.104   Sorokin, Pitirim Aleksandrovich. Explorations in altruistic love and behavior. Boston, 1950.

Phil 193.163   Spann, O. Philosophenspiegel. 2. Aufl. Wien, 1950.

Phil 3850.37   Spann, Othmar. Das philosophische Gesamtinerk im Auszug. Wien, 1950.

Phil 5258.68.10 Spearman, C. Human ability. London, 1950.

Phil 4752.2.85 Spinka, M. Nicholas Berdyaev. Philadelphia, 1950.

Phil 818.25   Stallknecht, N.P. The spirit of Western philosophy. 1st ed. N.Y., 1950.

Phil 1523.12.5 Steenberghen, F. Philosophie des Mittelalters. Bern, 1950.

Phil 5590.160   Stefanini, L. Metafisica della persona. Padova, 1950.

Phil 978.49.230 Steiner, R. Geisteswissenschaft und die Lebensforderungen der Gegenwart. pt.1-8. Dornach, 1950. 2v.

Phil 6328.2.31 Stekel, Wilhelm. Autobiography. N.Y., 1950.

Phil 1818.2.10A Stephen, Leslie. The English Utilitarians. London, 1950. 3v.

Phil 7082.96   Stevens, William Oliver. The mystery of dreams. London, 1950.

Phil 3552.330   Stieler, Georg. Gottfried Wilhelm Leibniz. Paderborn, 1950.

Phil 349.75   Stillwater Conference on the Nature of Concepts, their Structure and Social Inter-relation, Oklahoma Agricultural and Mechanical College, 1950. The nature of concepts, their inter-relation and role in social structure. Stillwater, Oklahoma, 1950.

Phil 665.80.10 Strasser, Stephan. Het zielsbegrip in de metaphysische en in de empirische psychologie. Leuven, 1950.

Phil 525.115   Summers, M. The physical phenomena of mysticism. N.Y., 1950.

Phil 194.46   Thiel, M. Versuch einer Ontologie der Persönlichkeit. Berlin, 1950.

Phil 535.15   Thielicke, H. Der Nihilismus. Tübingen, 1950.

Phil 8894.33   Toulmin, S. An examination of the place of reason in ethics. Cambridge, England, 1950.

Phil 8599.35   Trautmann, O. Die wiederkehr Göttes. Stuttgart, 1950.

Phil 1750.263.5 Troisfontaines, R. Existentialism and Christian thought. London, 1950.

Phil 819.10   Truc, Gonzague. Histoire de la philosophie. Paris, 1950.

Phil 8601.16   Varadachari, K. Idea of God. Tirupati, 1950.

Phil 4260.152   Varela Domínguez de Ghiolai, Delfina. Filosofía argentina: Vico en los escritos de Sarmiento. Buenos Aires, 1950.

Phil 310.4   Velikaia sila idei lenimizma; sbornik statei. Moskva, 1950.

Phil 1955.6.135 Verra, Valerio. Naturalismo umanistico e sperimentale di John Dewey. Torino, 1950.

Phil 1200.52   Virieux, A. La logique et l'épistémalogie des stoïciens. Lausanne, 1950.

Phil 8896.20   Vivas, E. The moral life and the ethical life. Chicago, 1950.

Phil 1126.2   Vogel, C. Greek philosophy. Leiden, 1950. 3v.

Phil 5585.73   Volkov, N.N. Vospriiatie predmeta i risunka. Moskva, 1950.

Phil 5061.5   Volpe, G. della. Logica come scienza positiva. Messina, 1950.

Phil 5401.22   Wandruszka von Wanstetten, M.W. Angst und Mut. Stuttgart, 1950.

Phil 6332.14   Wartis, Joseph. Soviet psychiatry. Baltimore, 1950.

Phil 197.61.10 Watkin, E.I. A philosophy of form. London, 1950.

Phil 8677.20   Watts, A.W. The supreme identity. London, 1950.

Phil 3425.340.1 Weil, Eric. Hegel et l'état. Paris, 1950.

Phil 3425.340   Weil, Eric. Hegel et l'état. Thèse. Paris, 1950.

Phil 197.71   Weil, Eric. Logique de la philosophie. Paris, 1950.

Phil 353.20   Wein, Hermann. Das Problem des Relativismus. Berlin, 1950.

Phil 2340.11.40 Weiss, Paul. Man's freedom. New Haven, 1950.

Phil 8897.74   Weiss, Richard. World without frontiers. Sydney, 1950.

Phil 8423.22   Weitz, M. Philosophy of the arts. Cambridge, 1950.

Phil 5250.13.85 Wellek, Albert. Die Wiederherstellung der Seelenwissenschaft im Lebenswerk Felix Kruegers. Hamburg, 1950.

Phil 2340.10.110   Wells, Harry K. Process and unreality. N.Y., 1950.

Phil 9400.35   Wijngaarden, H.M. Hoofdproblemen der volwassenheid. Utrecht, 1950.

Phil 5520.103   Winkler, R. Kritik der Wissenschaft. Wien, 1950.

Phil 3842.8.5   Wolf, Abraham. Spinoza, 1632-1677. Amsterdam, 1950.

Phil 3842.13.10 Wolfson, H.A. Spinoza and religion. N.Y., 1950.

Phil 3842.13.12 Wolfson, H.A. Spinoza and religion. N.Y., 1950.

Phil 5262.9.40 Woodworth, R.S. Experimental psychology. N.Y., 1950.

Phil 822.18.9   Wulf, M. Précis d'histoire de la philosophie. 9. ed. Louvain, 1950.

Phil 3925.11.30 Wust, Peter. Gestalten und Gedanken. 4. Aufl. München, 1950.

Phil 5264.3.5   Young, P.T. Motivation of behavior. N.Y., 1950.

Phil 3640.370   Zahn, L. Friedrich Nietzsche. Düsseldorf, 1950.

Phil 4987.53.30 Zambrano, María. Hacia un saber sobre el alma. Buenos Aires, 1950.

1951

Phil 2475.1.294.4   Adolphe, Lydie. La dialectique des images chez Bergson. Thèse. Paris, 1951.

Phil 2475.1.294.5   Adolphe, Lydie. La dialectique des images chez Bergson. 1. éd. Paris, 1951.

Phil 3085.4.31 Adorno, F.W. Minima Moralia. Berlin, 1951.

Phil 525.121   Albrecht, C. Psychologie des mystischen Bewusstseins. Bremen, 1951.

1951 - cont.

Phil 8875.31   Aleksandrov, R.N. Pis'ma k neizvestnomu drugu. Frankfurt, 1951.

Phil 6310.4.15.5A   Alexander, Franz G. Our age of unreason. Philadelphia, 1951.

Phil 5627.189.3 Allport, Gordon W. The individual and his religion. N.Y., 1951.

Phil 3850.27.114   Amadou, Robert. Albert Schweitzer. Bruxelles, 1951.

Phil 1750.512.3 Amoroso Lima, Alceu. El existencialismo, filosofía de nuestro tiempo. 3. ed. Buenos Aires, 1951.

Phil 4120.4.100 Andreola, A. Giovanni Gentile a la sua scuola. Milano, 1951.

Phil 1750.115.20   Archivio di Filosofia. Fenomenologia e sociologia. Padova, 1951.

Phil 4030.5   Archivio di Filosofia. Testi umanistici inediti sul De anima. Padova, 1951.

Phil 4963.3   Ardao, Arturo. Battle y Ordoñez y el positivismo filosófico. Montevideo, 1951.

Phil 7069.51.10 Aron, Robert. Mors et vita. Paris, 1951.

Phil 1540.75   Auer, J. Die Entwicklung der Grandenlehre in der Hochscholastik. v.2. Freiburg, 1951.

Phil 978.74.40 Bailey, A.A. (Mrs.). Unfinished autobiography. N.Y., 1951.

Phil 2520.232   Balz, A.G.A. Cartesian studies. N.Y., 1951.

Phil 476.8   Banfi, A. Storia del materialismo nei secoli XVI e XVII. v.1-2. Milano, 1951-53.

Phil 1930.10.80 Baron, S.W. Freedom and reason. Glencoe, Ill., 1951.

Phil 1955.6.128 Battle, J.J. The metaphysical presuppositions of the philosophy of John Dewey. Thesis. Fribourg, 1951.

Phil 5041.61   Becker, O. Einführung in die Logistik. Meisenheim, 1951.

Phil 8587.32.115   Bedoyere, M. de la. The life of Baron von Hügel. London, 1951.

Phil 3625.11.90 Benndorf, H. Persönliche Erinnerungen an Alexius Meinong. Graz, 1951.

Phil 1701.24   Bense, Max. Die Philosophie. Frankfurt a.M., 1951.

Phil 4752.2.75 Berdiaev, Nikolai Aleksandrovich. Royaume de l'esprit et royaume de César. Neuchâtel, 1951.

Phil 4752.2.50 Berdiaev, Nikolai Aleksandrovich. Tsarstvo dukha i tsarstvo kesaria. Parizh, 1951.

Phil 6951.27   Bergler, E. Money and emotional conflicts. 1. ed. Garden City, 1951.

Phil 1506.11   Bertala, E. Saggi e studi di filosofia medievale. Padova, 1951.

Phil 1801.7.2A Bethell, S.L. The cultural revolution of the seventeenth century. N.Y., 1951.

Phil 5585.72   Blake, R.R. Perception. N.Y., 1951.

Phil 3425.334   Bloch, Ernst. Subjekt-Objekt; Erläuterungen zu Hegel. Berlin, 1951.

Phil 86.5   Boccalaro, M.A. Dizionario filosofico. Bologna, 1951.

Phil 1135.164   Bochenski, I.M. Ancient formal logic. Amsterdam, 1951.

Phil 1701.20.5 Bochénski, J.M. Europäische Philosophie der Gegenwart. 2. Aufl. München, 1951.

Phil 1701.20.7 Bochénski, J.M. La philosophie contemporaine en Europe. 2. éd. Paris, 1951.

Phil 1750.166.55   Bohlin, T.B. Debatt med profanhumanisien. Stockholm, 1951.

Phil 3120.2.30 Bolzano, Bernard. O pokroku a dobročinnosti. Praha, 1951.

Phil 1506.12   Bonafede, Giulio. Saggi sulla filosofia medievale. Torino, 1951.

Phil 6311.34   Bonaparte, Marie. Introduction à la théorie des instincts. 1. éd. Paris, 1951.

Phil 5041.15.6 Boole, George. An investigation of the laws of thought. N.Y., 1951.

Phil 7082.18   Bossard, Robert. Psychologie des Traumbewustseins. Zürich, 1951.

Phil 7076.5   Boyer, Onesimas Alfred. She wears a crown of thorns; Marie Rose Perron, 1902-1936. N.Y., 1951.

Phil 8876.27.12 Bradley, Francis Herbert. Ethical studies. N.Y., 1951.

Phil 5585.75   Brain, W.R. Mind, perception and science. Oxford, 1951.

Phil 1701.23   Bréhier, Émile. Les thèmes actuels de la philosophie. 1. éd. Paris, 1951.

Phil 2262.94   Brett, R.L. The third earl of Shaftesbury. London, 1951.

Phil 6311.33   Brierley, Marjorie Ellis. Trends in psycho-analysis. London, 1951.

Phil 8876.88.5 Broad, C.D. Five types of ethical theory. London, 1951.

Phil 3120.15.33 Brunner, Constantin. Der entlarvte Mensch. Haag, 1951.

Phil 8581.98   Brunschvicg, Léon. De la vraie et de la fausse conversion. 1. éd. Paris, 1951.

Phil 2477.11.30 Brunschvicg, Léon. Écrits philosphiques. 1. éd. Paris, 1951- 3v.

Phil 8050.58   Bruyne, E. de. Geschiedenis van de aesthetica. Antwerpen, 1951. 5v.

Phil 3120.30.70 Buber, Martin. Pointing the way. London, 1951.

Phil 3120.30.68A   Buber, Martin. Two types of faith. London, 1951.

Phil 3120.30.30 Buber, Martin. Urdistanz und Beziehung. Heidelberg, 1951.

Phil 5500.14   Buchler, J. Toward a general theory of human judgment. N.Y., 1951.

Phil 5400.110   Bull, Nina. The attitude theory of emotion. N.Y., 1951.

Phil 6060.42   Bunker, M.N. What handwriting tells about yourself. Cleveland, 1951.

Phil 1506.14   Burch, G.B. Early medieval philosophy. N.Y., 1951.

Phil 176.157   Butler, J. Four philosophers. London, 1951.

Phil 4073.39   Campanella, Tommaso. Opuscali inediti. Firenze, 1951.

Phil 1107.7   Carbonara, Cleto. La filosofia greca. Napoli, 1951. 2v.

Phil 4080.9.40 Carlini, Armando. Alla ricerca di me stesso. Firenze, 1951.

Phil 7069.51   Carrington, H. Haunted people. 1. ed. N.Y., 1951.

Phil 8952.12   Cary-Elwes, C.F. Law, liberty and love. N.Y., 1951.

Phil 2138.122   Casellato, S. Giovanni Stuart Mill e l'utilitarismo inglese. Padova, 1951.

Phil 8877.80   Casserley, J.V.L. Morals and man in the social sciences. London, 1951.

Phil 1750.141.3A   Cassirer, Ernst. The philosophy of the enlightenment. Princeton, N.J., 1951.

Phil 8403.35   Caudwell, C. The creative impulse in writing and painting. London, 1951.

Phil 70.25   Centre International de Synthése, Paris. Valeur philosophique de la psychologie. Paris, 1951.

X Cg   Phil 7075.135   Cleugh, James. The marquis and the chevalier. London, 1951.

Phil 6842.2.5   Cleugh, James. The Marquis and the Chevalier. London, 1951.

Phil 1930.8.87 Collingwood, Robin George. An autotbiography. London, 1951.

Phil 5812.7.10 Comparative psychology. 3rd ed. N.Y., 1951.

1951 - cont.

Phil 70.13.10 — Congrès International de Philosophie des Science, Paris, 1949. Actes. Paris, 1951. 9v.
Phil 1507.6 — Congresso Internationale di Studi Umanistici, Rome. Umanesimo e scienza politica. Milano, 1951.
Phil 1507.8 — Congressus Scholasticus Internationalis, Rome. Scholastico ratione historico-critica instaurada. Romae, 1951.
Phil 4080.3.215 — Corsi, Mario. Le origini del pensiero di Benedetto Croce. 1. ed. Firenze, 1951.
Phil 5592.15 — Cotte, S. Utilisation du dessin comme test psychologique chez les enfants. 3. éd. Marseille, 1951.
Phil 2555.8.30 — Darbon, André. Philosophie de la volonté. 1. éd. Paris, 1951.
Phil 8878.59 — Delvolvé, J. La fonchion morale. Paris, 1951.
Phil 530.20.51 — Denifle, H. Die deutschen Mystiker des 14. Jahrhunderts. Freiburg in der Schweiz, 1951.
Phil 2520.35.40 — Descartes, René. Discours de la méthode. Paris, 1951.
Phil 178.69 — Deschoux, M. Initiation à la philosophie. 1. éd. Paris, 1951.
Phil 6980.222 — Devereaux, G. Reality and dream. N.Y., 1951.
Phil 1955.6.35 — Dewey, John. The influence of Darwin on philosophy. N.Y., 1951.
Phil 8953.9 — Dodd, C.H. Gospel and law. Cambridge, Eng., 1951.
Phil 2255.1.112 — Dorward, Alan. Bertrand Russell. London, 1951.
Phil 3195.10.30 — Driesch, H. Lebenserinnerungen. Basel, 1951.
Phil 6113.29 — Ducasse, C.J. Nature, mind and death. La Salle, Ill., 1951.
Phil 8430.11.2 — Dudley, Louise. The humanities. 2. ed. N.Y., 1951.
Phil 1980.4.20A — Edman, Irwin. Under whatever sky. N.Y., 1951.
Phil 5272.20 — Edwards, Allen Louis. Experimental design in psychological research. N.Y., 1951.
Phil 285.4 — Embry, J. The Namic philosophy. N.Y., 1951.
Phil 165.18 — Essays in psychology. Uppsala, 1951.
Phil 179.36 — Ewing, A.C. The fundamental questions of philosophy. N.Y., 1951.
Phil 1158.30 — Fallat, Jean. Le plaisir et la mort dans la philosophie d'Epicure. Paris, 1951.
Phil 4967.20.5 — Farias Brito, Raymundo de. O mundo interior. Rio de Janeiro, 1951.
Phil 180.76 — Feibleman, James. Ontology. Baltimore, 1951.
Phil 90.4.15 — Ferrater Mora, José. Diccionario de filosofía. 3. ed. Buenos Aires, 1951.
Phil 1805.5 — Fisch, M.H. Classic American philosophers. N.Y., 1951.
Phil 5520.102 — Flesch, R.F. The art of clear thinking. 1. ed. N.Y., 1951.
Phil 5520.100 — Flew, A.G.N. Essays on logic and language. Oxford, 1951.
Phil 5215.2.5 — Flügel, J.C. A hundred years of psychology, 1833-1933. 2nd ed. London, 1951.
Phil 5215.5 — Foulquié, Paul. La psychologie contemporaine. Paris, 1951.
Phil 4065.129 — Fraccari, G. G. Bruno. 1. ed. Milano, 1951.
Phil 1750.359 — Frankl, V.C. Logos und Existenz. Wien, 1951.
Phil 6315.30 — Freeman, L. Fight against fears. N.Y., 1951.
Phil 7082.174A — Fromm, Erich. The forgotten language. N.Y., 1951.
Phil 5545.184 — Furlong, E.J. A study in memory. London, 1951.
Phil 1750.351 — Gabriel, Leo. Existenzphilosophie von Kierkegaard bis Sartre. Wien, 1951.
Phil 4959.220 — Gallegos Rocafull, José Manuel. El pensamiento mexicano en los siglos XVI y XVII. México, 1951.
Phil 1020.28 — Gardet, Louis. La pensée religieus d'Avicenne. Paris, 1951.
Phil 575.148 — Gent, Werner. Person und Psychotherapie. Göttingen, 1951.
Phil 4215.4.80 — Gentiluomo, D. L'ontognoseologia di Cesare Ranzoli. Padova, 1951.
Phil 8696.20A — Gillispie, C.C. Genesis and geology. Cambridge, Mass., 1951.
Phil 2055.7.80A — Gilman, R.C. The bibliography of William E. Hocking. Waterville, Me., 1951.
Phil 5465.58 — Gilson, E. L'école des muses. Paris, 1951.
Phil 2520.116.15.5 — Gilson, E. Études sur le rôle de la pensée médiévale dans la formation du système cartésien. Paris, 1951.
Phil 1750.115.3A — Goodman, Nelson. The structure of appearance. Cambridge, 1951.
Phil 3450.19.114 — Graaff, F. de. Het schuldprableem ein de existentiephilosophie van Martin Heidegger. 's Gravenhage, 1951.
Phil 337.15 — Grassi, E. Die Einheit unseres Wirklichkeitsbildes und die Grenzen der Einzelwissenschaftes. Bern, 1951.
Phil 806.14 — Greca, Carlo. Storia della filosofia. Palermo, 1951.
Phil 1750.132.10 — Grosselin, O. The intuitive voluntarism of Irving Babbitt. Latrohe, Pa., 1951.
Phil 3488.27 — Groyeff, F. Deutung und Darstellung der theoretischen Philosophie Kants. Hamburg, 1951.
Phil 3425.338 — Guccione Monroy, Nino. Hegel ed il problema della moralità. Trapani, 1951.
Phil 2805.270 — Guitton, Jean. Pascal et Leibniz. Paris, 1951.
Phil 9245.59 — Gumpert, M. The anatomy of happiness. N.Y., 1951.
Phil 7082.16 — Gutheil, Emil Arthur. The handbook of dream analysis. N.Y., 1951.
Phil 4120.8.45 — Guzzo, Augusto. Discorsi, 1938-50. Torino, 1951.
Phil 3827.9 — Hamphire, S. Spinoza. Harmondsworth, 1951.
Phil 182.94.12 — Hartmann, N. Teleologisches Denken. Berlin, 1951.
X Cg Phil 7075.139 — Hartwell, S.W. A citizen's handbook of sexual abnormalities and the mental hygiene approach to their prevention. Washington, 1951.
Phil 2138.121.1 — Hayek, Friedrich August von. John Stuart Mill and Harriet Taylor; their correspondence and subsequent marriage. London, 1951.
Phil 2138.121 — Hayek, Friedrich August von. John Stuart Mill and Harriet Taylor; their friendship and subsequent marriage. London, 1951.
Phil 3425.75.5 — Hegel, Georg Wilhelm Friedrich. Hegel Brevier. Zürich, 1951.
Phil 3425.34.31A — Hegel, Georg Wilhelm Friedrich. Science of logic. London, 1951. 2v.
Phil 3489.27.2 — Heidegger, Martin. Kant und das Problem der Metaphysik. 2. Aufl. Frankfurt, 1951.
Phil 8587.68 — Heins, Karl. Die Wandlung im naturwissenschaftlicher Weltbild. 2. Aufl. Hamburg, 1951.
Phil 5627.194 — Hellpach, Willy. Grundriss der Religionspsychologie. Stuttgart, 1951.
Phil 9035.78.5 — Helwig, Paul. Charakterlogie. 2. Aufl. Stuttgart, 1951.
Phil 5066.38A — Henle, Paul. Structure, method, and meaning. N.Y., 1951.
Phil 182.113 — Henle, R.J. Method in metaphysics. Milwaukee, 1951.
Phil 1740.6 — Hessen, Johannes. Die Philosophie des 20. Jahrhunderts. Rottenburg, 1951.

1951 - cont.

Phil 5628.50.25 — Höcht, Johannes Maria. Träger der Wundmale Christi. Wiesbaden, 1951-52. 2v.
Phil 1112.7.5 — Hoffmann, Ernst. Die griechische Philosophie von Thales bis Platon. Heidelberg, 1951.
Phil 2805.267 — Holden, P.G. Pascal. London, 1951.
Phil 5520.101 — Holloway, J. Language and intelligence. London, 1951.
Phil 2880.8.110 — Holz, H.H. Jean Paul Sartre. Meisenheim, 1951.
Phil 9070.53 — Holzamer, Karl. Grundriss einer praktischen Philosophie. Frankfurt am Main, 1951.
Phil 5625.87 — Householder, A.S. Some notes for simple Pavlovian learning. Santa Monica, 1951.
Phil 5627.134.56 — Howard, Peter. The world rebuilt...Frank Buchman. London, 1951.
Phil 3552.332 — Huber, Kurt. Leibniz. München, 1951.
Phil 2050.59.30 — Hume, David. Theory of knowledge. Edinburgh, 1951.
Phil 2050.59.35 — Hume, David. Theory of politics. Edinburgh, 1951.
Phil 8663.3.75 — Ingersoll, Robert G. Letters. N.Y., 1951.
Phil 6980.363.5 — Iudin, Tikhon I. Ocherki istorii otechestvennoi psikhiatrii. Moskva, 1951.
Phil 2805.265 — Jaccard, L.F. Blaise Pascal. Neuchâtel, 1951.
Phil 6319.1.185 — Jacobi, Jolan. The psychology of C.G. Jung. 5th ed. London, 1951.
Phil 3475.3.75 — Jaspers, Karl. Rechenschaft und Ausbuik. München, 1951.
Phil 3475.3.65 — Jaspers, Karl. Way of wisdom. New Haven, 1951.
Phil 1750.115.30A — Jeanson, F. La phénoménologie. Paris, 1951.
Phil 5640.45 — Jeffress, Lloyd A. Cerebral mechanisms in behavior. N.Y., 1951.
Phil 8589.17.15A — Joad, Cyril E.M. Counter attack from the East. 1. Indian ed. Bombay, 1951.
Phil 6319.2.5.5 — Jones, Ernest. Essays in applied psycho-analysis. London, 1951. 2v.
Phil 4926.160.30 — Jordan, Rudolf. The new perspective, an essay. Chicago, 1951.
Phil 2805.256 — Journet, C. Vérité de Pascal. St. Maurice, 1951.
Phil 3850.27.102 — Joy, C.R. Music in the life of Albert Schweitzer. 1st ed. N.Y., 1951.
Phil 5627.190 — Jung, C.G. Arin. Zürich, 1951.
Phil 3552.334 — Kanitz, H.J. Das übergegensätzliche Gezeigt am Kontinuitätsprinzip bei Leibniz. Hamburg, 1951.
Phil 3480.52.10 — Kant, Immanuel. Critique of judgment. N.Y., 1951.
Phil 3480.22 — Kant, Immanuel. Deines Lebens Sinn. Wien, 1951.
Phil 6020.4.6 — Kassner, Rudolf. Physiognomik. Wiesbaden, 1951.
Phil 3120.8.98 — Kastil, A. Die Philosophie Franz Brentanos. München, 1951.
Phil 5250.37.10 — Katz, David. Handbuch der Psychologie. Basel, 1951.
Phil 5425.80 — Kenmare, D. Stolen fire. London, 1951.
Phil 4710.11 — Khaskhachikh, F.I. Materiia i soznanie. Moskva, 1951.
Phil 5593.51 — Kijm, J.M. De varianten der intentionaliteit bij de Rorschachtest. Nijmegen, 1951.
Phil 4843.8 — Kissabou, Maria I. Hē philosophia en Helladi apo tēs Anostaseōs tou ethnous. Athena, 1951.
Phil 575.51.12 — Klages, Ludwig. Die Grundlagen der Charakterkunde. 11e Aufl. Bonn, 1951.
Phil 5820.7 — Klee, James Butt. Problems of selective behavior. Lincoln, 1951.
Phil 5620.22 — Kogan, Zuce. Essentials in problem solving. Chicago, 1951.
Phil 735.114.5 — Kraft, V. Die Grundlagen einer wissenschaftlichen Wertlehre. 2. Aufl. Wien, 1951.
Phil 9070.65 — Kraines, S.H. Live and help live. N.Y., 1951.
Phil 5645.49 — Kravkou, S.V. Tsvetovoe zrenie. Moskva, 1951.
Phil 5710.16 — Kretschmer, Ernst. Körperbau und Charakter. 20. Aufl. Berlin, 1951.
Phil 1750.350 — Kuhn, H. Encounter with nothingness. London, 1951.
Phil 186.125 — Lalande, André. Vocabulaire technique et critique de la philosophie. 6. ed. Paris, 1951.
Phil 96.5 — Lamanna, E.P. Dizionario di termini filosofia. Firenze, 1951.
Phil 2120.8.30 — Lamont, Corliss. The independent mind. N.Y., 1951.
Phil 3640.384 — Landmann, M. Geist und Leben. Bonn, 1951.
Phil 186.97.2 — Langer, Mrs. S.K. Philosophy in a new key. 2d ed. Cambridge,Mass., 1951.
Phil 978.86 — Lehrs, Ernst. Man or matter. London, 1951.
Phil 3552.27 — Leibniz, Gottfried Wilhelm. Schäpferische Vernunft. Marbrug, 1951.
Phil 3552.36 — Leibniz, Gottfried Wilhelm. Selections. N.Y., 1951.
Phil 186.67.3 — Leisegang, H. Denkformen. 2. Aufl. Berlin, 1951.
Phil 186.67.5 — Leisegang, H. Einführung in die Philosophie. Berlin, 1951.
Phil 3585.15 — Leisegang, H. Meine Weltanschaunng. Berlin, 1951.
Phil 1750.354 — Lenz, Joseph. Der moderne deutsche und französische Existentialismus. 2e Aufl. Trier, 1951.
Phil 1811.2.10 — Leroux, E. La philosophie anglaise classique. Paris, 1951.
Phil 5251.41.25 — Lewin, Kurt. Field theory in social science. 1st ed. N.Y., 1951.
Phil 7140.134 — Liebetrau, H. Macht und Geheimnis der Suggestion. Basel, 1951.
Phil 4120.4.120 — Liguori, Ersilia. La pedagogia come scienza filosofica di Giovanni Gentile. Padova, 1951.
Phil 5850.258.5 — Link, Henry C. The way to security. Garden City, 1951.
Phil 186.111 — Lodge, R.C. Applied philosophy. London, 1951.
Phil 6321.30.10 — Loewenstein, R. Christians and Jews. N.Y., 1951.
Phil 6315.2.245 — Loewenstein, Rudolph Maurice. Freud. N.Y., 1951.
Phil 4710.35A — Losskii, N.O. History of Russian philosophy. N.Y., 1951.
Phil 3850.27.120 — Lotar, Peter. Von Sinn des Lebens. Strasbourg, 1951.
Phil 1750.405 — Lukacs, G.S. Existentialismus oder Marxismus? Berlin, 1951.
Phil 5590.80 — McClelland, D.C. Personality. N.Y., 1951.
Phil 8622.10 — MacGregor, G. Doubt and faith. London, 1951.
Phil 2050.223 — MacNabb, Donald George Cecil. David Hume. London, 1951.
Phil 3625.18.30 — Maier, A. Zwei Grundprobleme der scholastischen Naturphilosophie. 2. Aufl. Roma, 1951.
Phil 2750.19.25 — Marcel, Gabriel. Les hommes contre l'humain. Paris, 1951.
Phil 187.8.5 — Marcel, Gabriel. Homo viator. London, 1951.
Phil 2750.19.10 — Marcel, Gabriel. Le mystère de l'être. Paris, 1951. 2v.
Phil 1712.13.2 — Maréchal, Joseph. Précis d'histoire de la philosophie moderne. 2e éd. Bruxelles, 1951.
Phil 8612.45 — Marin, Edgar. L'homme et la mort dans l'histoire. Paris, 1951.
Phil 2750.11.55 — Maritain, Jacques. Neuf leçons sur les notions premières de la philosophie morale. Paris, 1951.
Phil 3494.46 — Maritz, M. Studien zum pflichtbegriff in Kants Kritischer Ethhik. Lund, 1951.
Phil 3494.45 — Martin, Gottfried. Immanuel Kant. Köln, 1951.

Chronological Listing

Phil 4170.10.30   Martinetti, P. Il compito della filosofia e altri saggi inediti ed editi. 1. ed. Torino, 1951.

Phil 487.5.10   Mayer, Charles L. Man: mind or matter? Boston, 1951.

Phil 1712.17A   Mayer, Frederick. A history of modern philosophy. N.Y., 1951.

Phil 187.144   Mayor, R.J.G. Reason and common sense. London, 1951.

Phil 720.40   Medicus, F. Menschlichkeit. Zürich, 1951.

Phil 187.146   Meimberg, R. Über die Einseitigkeit. Berlin, 1951.

Phil 6322.32   Menninger, W.C. Social change and scientific progress. Portland, 1951.

Phil 2805.263A   Mesnard, Jean. Pascal, l'homme et l'oeuvre. Paris, 1951.

Phil 343.16.12   Meyerson, Émile. Identité et réalité. 5. éd. Paris, 1951.

Phil 5520.113   Miller, G.A. Language and communication. 1. ed. N.Y., 1951.

Phil 850.23.2   Misch, G. The dawn of philosophy. Cambridge, 1951.

Phil 5068.5.5A   Mises, R.E. von. Positivism. Cambridge, 1951.

Phil 4769.1.104   Mochul'skiĭ, K. Vladimir Solov'ev. 2. izd. Parizh, 1951.

Phil 3425.342   Möller, Joseph. Der Geist und das Absolute. Paderborn, 1951.

Phil 9450.24   Money-Kyrle, R.E. Psychoanalysis and politics. N.Y., 1951.

Phil 6122.66   Monnier, Marcel. L'organisation des fonctions psychiques. Neuchâtel, 1951.

Phil 5525.44   Monro, David Hector. Argument of laughter. Carlton, Victoria, 1951.

Phil 4080.3.285   Montano, Rocco. Arte. 1. ed. Napoli, 1951.

Phil 165.17   Moore, C.A. Essays in East-West philosophy. Honolulu, 1951.

Phil 4710.7.5   Moscow. Universitet. Filosofskii Fakul'tet. Iz istorii russkoi filosofii, sbornik. Moskva, 1951.

Phil 3625.13.34   Müller, Aloys. Welt und Mensch in ihrem irrealen Aufbau. 4. Aufl. Leiden, 1951.

Phil 4769.1.102   Müller, Ludolf. Solovjev und der Protestantismus. Freiburg, 1951.

Phil 5252.38.20   Müller-Freienfels, R. Menschenkenntnis und Menschenbehandlung. Berlin, 1951.

Phil 9070.51.5A   Mumford, Lewis. The conduct of life. 1st ed. N.Y., 1951.

Phil 5252.89.2   Munn, Norman Leslie. Psychology. 2. ed. Boston, 1951.

Phil 5252.69.15   Murphy, Gardner. An introduction to psychology. N.Y., 1951.

Phil 8615.20.10   Muzzey, David S. Ethics as a religion. N.Y., 1951.

Phil 8592.71   Myers, E.D. Christianity and reason. N.Y., 1951.

Phil 2880.8.122   Natanson, M. A critique of Jean Paul Sartre's ontology. Lincoln, 1951.

Phil 1955.6.119   Nathanson, J. John Dewey. N.Y., 1951.

Phil 3640.77.10   Nietzsche, Friedrich. Brevier. 2. Aufl. Wien, 1951.

Phil 3640.77.15.10   Nietzsche, Friedrich. My sister and I. N.Y., 1951.

Phil 3640.31.15   Nietzsche, Friedrich. Par delà le bien et le mal. Paris, 1951.

Phil 4080.17.5   Nobile Ventura, O.M. Filosofia e religione in un metafisico laico. 1. ed. Milano, 1951.

Phil 5223.1   Nuttin, Jozef. Tendences nouvelles dans la psychologie contemporaine. Louvain, 1951.

Phil 3549.2.100   Ocampo, Victoria. El viajero y una de sus sombras; Keyserling en mis memorias. Buenos Aires, 1951.

Phil 7069.51.5   O'Donnell, Elliot. Ghosts with a purpose. London, 1951.

Phil 189.30   Oliver, W.D. Theory of order. Yellow Springs, Ohio, 1951.

Phil 189.29A   Onians, R.B. The origins of European thought about the body, the mind, the soul. Cambridge, Eng., 1951.

Phil 5465.57   Osborn, A.F. Your creative power. N.Y., 1951.

Phil 8595.15.24   Paine, Thomas. The age of reason. N.Y., 1951.

Phil 960.172   Pal, B.C. An introduction to the study of Hinduism. 2. ed. Calcutta, 1951.

Phil 535.10   Pannwitz, R. Der Nihilismus und die Welt. Nürnberg, 1951.

Phil 2805.40.31   Pascal, Blaise. Pensées sur la religion. Paris, 1951. 3v.

Phil 1925.84   Passmore, J.A. Ralph Cudworth. Cambridge, Eng., 1951.

Phil 2225.12   Paton, H.J. In defence of reason. London, 1951.

Phil 5590.85   Pauli, R. Der Pauli-Test. 2. Aufl. München, 1951.

Phil 9558.10.20   Payne, R. The wanton nymph. London, 1951.

Phil 530.40.47   Peers, E.A. The mystics of Spain. London, 1951.

Phil 530.40.27.5   Peers, E.A. Studies of the Spanish mystics. 2nd ed. London, 1951-60. 3v.

Phil 75.45   Pelzer, A. Répertoires d'incipit pour la littérature latine philosophique. Roma, 1951.

Phil 8670.17.2   Picard, Max. The flight from God. London, 1951.

Phil 5255.18.20   Piéron, Henri. Les problémes fondamentaux de la psychophysique dans la science actuelle. Paris, 1951.

Phil 7140.133   Pöll, Wilhelm. Die Suggestion. München, 1951.

Phil 4752.2.115   Porret, Eugene. Berdiaeff. Neuchâtel, 1951.

Phil 8416.18   Propris, A. de. Brevario della nuova estetica. Roma, 1951.

Phil 5066.11.7   Quine, Willard van Orman. Mathematical logic. Cambridge, Mass., 1951.

Phil 165.20   Radhakrishnan. London, 1951.

Phil 5238.20   Rapaport, D. Organization and pathology of thought. N.Y., 1951.

Phil 8597.51   Reade, W.H.V. The Christian challenge and philosophy. London, 1951.

Phil 6327.21.35   Reich, Wilhelm. Cosmic superimposition. Rangeley, Me., 1951.

Phil 1717.17   Reichenbach, H. The rise of scientific philosophy. Berkeley, 1951.

Phil 3450.11.130   Reinach, Adolf. Was ist Phanomenologie. 1. Aufl. München, 1951.

Phil 6980.635.25   Reitman, F. Psychotic art. N.Y., 1951.

Phil 9070.51   Rencontres Internationales. Les droits de l'esprit et les exigences sociales. Neuchâtel, 1951.

Phil 1750.166.60   Rey, Gabriel. Humanisme et surhumanisme. Paris, 1951.

Phil 298.22   Rice, Laban Lucy. The universe, its origin, nature and destiny. N.Y., 1951.

Phil 5590.90   Richard, G. La psychanalyse de l'homme normal. Lausanne, 1951.

Phil 978.49.810   Rihonët-Coroze, S. Rudolf Steiner. Paris, 1951.

Phil 192.67.5   Rintelen, Fritz J. von. Philosophie der Endlichkeit. Meisenheim, 1951.

Phil 192.78.5   Rivier, W. Les deux chemins. Bruxelles, 1951.

Phil 5227.6   Roback, A.A. History of American psychology. N.Y., 1951.

Phil 6327.28   Rogers, Carl Ransom. Client-centered therapy. Boston, 1951.

Phil 4210.41.30   Rosmini-Serbati, Antonio. Il sistema filosofico. Torino, 1951.

Phil 4210.154   Rovea, G. Filosofia e religione in Antonio Rosmini. Domodossola, 1951.

Phil 492.5   Roy, M.N. Materialism. 2nd ed. Calcutta, 1951.

Phil 2250.10   Royce, Josiah. Logical essays. Dubuque, Iowa, 1951.

Phil 102.5.3   Rozental', Mark Moiseevich. Kratkii filosofskii slovar'. Izd. 3. Moskva, 1951.

Phil 5068.7.4   Russell, Bertrand Russell. An inquiry into meaning and truth. London, 1951.

Phil 2255.1.60   Russell, Bertrand Russell. New hopes for a changing world. London, 1951.

Phil 2255.1.61   Russell, Bertrand Russell. New hopes for a changing world. N.Y., 1951.

Phil 2255.1.55   Russell, Bertrand Russell. The wit and wisdom. Boston, 1951.

Phil 5850.330   Russell, W.L. Peace and power within. Houston, Texas, 1951.

Phil 4980.1.30   Sabato, Ernesto R. Hombres y engranajes. Buenos Aires, 1951.

Phil 7069.51.15   Sabine, Waldo. Second sight in daily life. London, 1951.

Phil 8598.104   Sagesse. Bruges, 1951.

Phil 103.5   Sandström, C.I. Psykologisk ordbak. 2. uppl. Stockholm, 1951.

Phil 193.168   Scarlata, G.P. Lineamenti di metalogica. Padova, 1951.

Phil 6980.674   Schelder, Paul. Psychotherapy. N.Y., 1951.

Phil 4110.11.30   Schiavone, Michelle. Problemi filosofia in Marsilio Ficino. Milano, 1951.

Phil 818.24.5   Schilling, Kurt. Geschichte der Philosophie. München, 1951. 2v.

Phil 2280.5.106.2   Schilpp, P.A. The philosophy of George Santayana. 2nd ed. N.Y., 1951.

Phil 1955.6.102   Schilpp, P.A. The philosophy of John Dewey. 2d ed. N.Y., 1951.

Phil 2340.10.127   Schilpp, Paul A. The philosophy of Alfred North Whitehead. 2nd ed. N.Y., 1951.

Phil 2255.1.103   Schilpp, Paul A. The philosophy of Bertrand Russell. N.Y., 1951.

Phil 103.3.30.5   Schmidt, Heinrich. Philosophisches Wörterbuch. 11. Aufl. Stuttgart, 1951.

Phil 2520.233   Scholz, H. Descartes. Münster, 1951.

Phil 3808.61   Schopenhauer, Arthur. Essays from the Parerga and Paralipomena. London, 1951?

Phil 1145.87   Schwartz, E. Ethik der Griechen. Stuttgart, 1951.
Phil 3850.27.110.2

Phil 3850.27.110   Seaver, George. Albert Schweitzer. Boston, 1951.

Phil 2520.79.10   Seaver, George. Albert Schweitzer. 4th ed. London, 1951.

Phil 193.152.5   Serrurier, C. Descartes. Paris, 1951.

Phil 8980.785   Sganzini, Carlo. Ursprung und Wirklichkeit. Bern, 1951.

Phil 8598.79.5.10   Shariia, P.A. O nekotorykh voprosakh kommunisticheskoi morali. Moskva, 1951.

Phil 9590.25   Shestov, L. Afiny i Ierusalim. Parizh, 1951.

Phil 6128.56   Shishkin, A.F. Burzhuaznaia moral' - oruzhie imperialisticheskoi reaktsii. Moskva, 1951.

Phil 8419.30   Siddall, R.B. Towards understanding our minds. N.Y., 1951.

Phil 349.40   Silcock, Arnold. A background for beauty. London, 1951.

Phil 5258.120.8   Sinclair, W.A. The conditions of knowing. London, 1951.

Phil 5258.185   Skinner, Burrhus F. Science and human behavior. Cambridge, Mass.? 1951.

Phil 5400.59.5   Smith, Frederick Viggers. The explanation of human behavior. London, 1951.

Phil 1750.353   Sourian, E. L'abstraction sentimentale. 2. ed. Paris, 1951.

Phil 3819.29.40   Spier, J.M. Calvinisme en existentie-philosophie. Kampen, 1951.

Phil 8050.60   Spinoza, Benedictus de. Spinoza dictionary. N.Y., 1951.

Phil 3475.3.110   Spoerri, T. Die Struktur der Existenz. Zürich, 1951.

Phil 8968.15   Springer, J.L. Existentiele metaphysica. Assen, 1951.

Phil 187.32.90   Steinbüchel, T. Zerfall des christlichen Ethos im XIX. Jahrhundert. Frankfurt, 1951.

Phil 5238.18   Stephens, I.K. The hermit philosopher of Liendo. Dallas, 1951.

Phil 6805.8   Stevens, S.S. Handbook of experimental psychology. N.Y., 1951.

Phil 103.6   Strecker, Edward Adam. Their mother's sons. Philadelphia, 1951.

Phil 2520.236   Sury, Kurt F. von. Wörterbuch der Psychologie und ihrer Grenzgebiete. Basel, 1951.

Phil 5258.136.5A   Sykes, L.C. A philosopher for the modern university. Leicester, 1951.

Phil 4235.5.30   Symonds, P.M. The ego and the self. N.Y., 1951.

Phil 8420.21   Taddeo da Parma. Le quaestiones de anima de Taddeo da Parma. Milano, 1951.

Phil 3501.15   Tatarkiewicz, W. Skupienie i marzenie. Kraków, 1951.

Phil 7082.190   Teale, A.E. Kantian ethics. London, 1951.

Phil 8969.4   Teillard, Ania. Le rêve, une porte sur le réel. Paris, 1951.

Phil 8599.36   Thielicke, Helmut. Theologische Ethik. v.1-3. Tübingen, 1951. 4v.

Phil 3640.378   Thomas, George Finger. Poetry, religion, and the spiritual life. Houston, 1951.

Phil 5259.40A   Thompson, R.M. Nietzsche and Christian ethics. London, 1951.

Phil 5829.10.2   Tolman, Edward C. Collected papers in psychology. Berkeley, 1951.

Phil 1750.115.35   Tolman, Edward C. Purposive behavior in animals and men. Berkeley, 1951.

Phil 6329.14   Trân-Dúc-Thao. Phénoménologie et materialisme dialectique. Paris, 1951.

Phil 8600.5   Trüb, Hans. Heilung aus der Begegnung. Stuttgart, 1951.

Phil 4021.2   Urban, W.M. Humanity and deity. London, 1951.

Phil 9035.92   Vanni Ronighi, S. Il problema morale nella filosofia italiana della prima metà de secolo XIX. Milano, 1951.

Phil 672.176   Vbbink, G. Karakterkundig woordenbock des Nederlands taal. Baarn, 1951.

Phil 3640.392   Venturini, Saul. Chiacchierata sul concetto di spazio. Milano, 1951.

Phil 4372.1.100   Vitens, Siegfried. Die Sprachkunst Friedrich Nietzsches in Also sprach Zarathustra. Bremen, 1951.

Phil 2750.20   Vivés. Paris, 1951.

Phil 6319.1.186   Waelhens, A. de. Un philosophie de l'ambiguité. Louvain, 1951.

Phil 4757.2.90   Walder, P. Mensch und Welt bei C.G. Jung. Zürich, 1951.

Phil 5545.91   Walker, K.M. Venture with ideas. London, 1951.

Phil 8622.4   Wallon, H. Les mécanismes de la mémoire en rapport avec ses objects. Paris, 1951.

Phil 3195.10.120   Waylen, B. Creators of the modern spirit. N.Y., 1951.

Phil 8647.12   Wenzl, Aloys. Hans Driesch. Basel, 1951.

Phil 6400.19   Wenzl, Aloys. Unsterblichkeit. Berlin, 1951.

   Wepman, J.M. Recovery from aphasia. N.Y., 1951.

1951 - cont.

Phil 380.2.10   Whyte, Lancelot L. Aspects of form. London, 1951.
Phil 5238.22   Wilbur, G.B. Psychoanalysis and culture. N.Y., 1951.
Phil 575.205   Wilde, Arie de. De persoon. Assen, 1951.
Phil 8897.78   Williams, G. Humanistic ethics. N.Y., 1951.
Phil 5062.29.5   Williams, Henry H. Logic for living. N.Y., 1951.
Phil 5066.44   Wright, G.H. van. An essay in modal logic. Amsterdam, 1951.
Phil 5125.21   Wright, G.H. von. A treatise on induction and probability. London, 1951.
Phil 3925.11.20   Wust, Peter. Wege einer Freundschaft. Heidelberg, 1951.
Phil 1527.3   Wyser, Paul. Der Thomismus. Bern, 1951.
Phil 4325.2   Yamuni, Tabush. Concepts e imágenes en pensadores. México, 1951.
Phil 8589.5.30   Young, F.H. The philosophy of Henry James, Sr. N.Y., 1951.
Phil 6134.4A   Young, J.Z. Doubt and certainty in science. Oxford, 1951.
Phil 6315.2.146   Zilboorg, G. Sigmund Freud. N.Y., 1951.
Phil 960.164   Zimmer, H.R. Philosophies of India. N.Y., 1951.
Phil 3903.4.80   Zuidema, Sytse Uebe. Wetenschappelijke bijdragen door leerigen van D.H.M. Vollenhoveu. Franeker, 1951.

1952

Phil 730.5   Aaron, Richard Ithamar. The theory of universals. Oxford, 1952.
Phil 2270.107   Absi, Marcelle. La théorie de la religion chez Spencer et ses sources. Thèse. Beyrouth, 1952.
Phil 525.117   Aegerter, E. Le mysticisme. Paris, 1952.
Phil 2725.11.85   Agosti, Vittorio. La filosofia di Jules Lachelier. Torino, 1952.
Phil 4964.5   Agramonte y Pichardo, R. José Augustin Caballero y las origines de la conciencia cubana. La Habana, 1952.
Phil 5655.9   Airkem, Inc. Odors and the sense of smell. N.Y., 1952.
Phil 6980.33   Alexander, F. Dynamic psychiatry. Chicago, 1952.
Phil 4285.1.100   Aliotta, S. Un precursore della neoscolastica. Noto, 1952.
Phil 9230.20   Allen, David D. The nature of gambling. N.Y., 1952.
Phil 960.17.40   Altekar, A.S. Sources of Hindu dharma in its socio-religious aspects. Shalapur, 1952?
Phil 3850.27.114.5   Amadou, Robert. Albert Schweitzer. Paris, 1952.
Phil 9400.15   American Academy of Political and Social Science, Philadelphia. Social contribution by the aging. Philadelphia, 1952.
Phil 5240.42.5   Ananiew, B.G. Hamptaufgaben der sowjetischen psychologischen Wissenschaft. Berlin, 1952.
Phil 8870.13   Anshen, R.N. Moral principles of action. 1st ed. N.Y., 1952.
Phil 8401.27   Antonio de la Virgen del Carmen. Al arte por el dolor. Burgos, 1952.
Phil 165.19   Archivio di Filosofia. Il compito della Metafisica. Milano, 1952.
Phil 4962.20   Arroyave Calle, J.C. El ser del hombre. Medellín, 1952.
Phil 6110.22   Ashby, William R. Design for a brain. N.Y., 1952.
Phil 1750.373   Astrada, C. La revolución existencialista. n.p., 1952.
Phil 1800.5   Ayer, A.J. British empirical philosophers. London, 1952.
Phil 175.38.15A   Ayer, Alfred J. Language, truth and logic. N.Y., 1952.
Phil 1905.23   Baillie, J.B. Reflections on life and religion. London, 1952.
Phil 1801.8A   Baker, H.C. The wars of truth. Cambridge, 1952.
Phil 630.56   Bakoš, Mik. O socialistickom realizme. Bratislava, 1952.
Phil 6311.36   Balint, Michael. Primary love, and psycho-analytic technique. London, 1952.
Phil 2520.235   Balz, A.G.A. Descartes and the modern mind. New Haven, 1952.
Phil 5211.7   Bamborough, J.B. The little world of man. London, 1952.
Phil 5241.115   Barakin, E.W. Quantitative theory on human behavior. Santa Monica, 1952.
Phil 6311.35   Baruk, Henri. La désorganisation de la personnalité. Paris, 1952.
Phil 5241.114   Bauer, R.A. The new man in Soviet psychology. Cambridge, Mass., 1952.
Phil 1865.184   Baumgardt, David. Bentham and the ethics of today. Princeton, 1952.
Phil 2520.238   Beck, L.J. The method of Descartes. Oxford, 1952.
Phil 5066.48   Becker, O. Untersuchungen über den Modalkalkül. Meinsenheim/Glan, 1952.
Phil 1135.168   Beckmann, F. Humanitas. Münster, 1952.
Phil 176.172   Bedetti, A. Filosofia della vita. Cremons, 1952.
Phil 5238.24   Beiträge aus der Sowjetpsychologie. Berlin, 1952.
Phil 150.25   Belaval, Y. Les philosophes et leur langage. Paris, 1952.
Phil 3552.336   Belaval, Yvor. Pour connaître la pensée de Leibniz. Paris, 1952.
Phil 5425.82   Belt, W.R. The infirmities of genius. London, 1952.
Phil 705.40   Belzer, G. Das Problem der Transzendenz in der Geschichte der neueren Philosophie. Amsterdam, 1952.
Phil 3821.25   Benincá, A. La libertà umana. Caravate, 1952.
Phil 4752.2.33A   Berdiaev, Nikolai Aleksandrovich. The beginning and the end. London, 1952.
Phil 4752.2.78   Berdiaev, Nikolai Aleksandrovich. Christianity and anti Semitism. Aldington, 1952.
Phil 4752.2.43   Berdiaev, Nikolai Aleksandrovich. Ekzistentsial'naia dialektika bozhestvennogo i chelovecheskogo. Parizh, 1952.
Phil 4752.2.70   Berdiaev, Nikolai Aleksandrovich. The realm of spirit and the realm of Caesar. London, 1952.
Phil 6311.26.5   Bergler, Edmund. The superego. N.Y., 1952.
Phil 1870.30.30   Berkeley, G. Alciphron. Paris, 1952.
Phil 1870.22   Berkeley, G. Philosophical writings. Edinburgh, 1952.
Phil 2750.13.90   Bernard, M. La philosophie religieuse de Gabriel Marcel. Le Puy, 1952.
Phil 8620.46   Billicsich, F. Das Problem des Übels in der Philosophie. Wien, 1952. 3v.
Phil 5850.136   Binois, René. La psychologie appliquée. 3. éd. Paris, 1952.
Phil 1750.362   Blackham, H.J. Six existentialist thinkers. London, 1952.
Phil 1540.30   Böhner, P. Medieval logic. Chicago, 1952.
Phil 1540.30.2   Böhner, P. Medieval logic. Manchester, 1952.
Phil 3120.2.35   Bolzano, Bernard. O nejlepším státě. Praha, 1952.
Phil 6311.34.10   Bonaparte, M. Psychanalyse et biologie. 1. éd. Paris, 1952.
Phil 6311.34.5   Bonaparte, Marie. Psychanalyse et anthropologie. Paris, 1952.
Phil 5041.15.4   Boole, George. Studies in logic and probability. London, 1952.
Phil 176.175   Bounet, G. Introduction à tous les cours de philosophie. Paris, 1952.

1952 - cont.

Phil 1750.115.40   Breda, H.L. Problémes actuels de la phénoménologie. Paris, 1952.
Phil 8876.112   Brentano, F. Grundlegung und Anfban der Ethik. Bern, 1952.
Phil 1905.22A   Broad, C.D. Ethics and the history of philosophy. London, 1952.
Phil 6951.29   Brody, E.B. Psychotheraphy with schizophrenia. N.Y., 1952.
Phil 8110.10   Brunius, Teddy. Pionjärer och fullföjare. Stockholm, 1952.
Phil 3120.30.45   Buber, Martin. Bilder von Gut und Böse. Köln, 1952.
Phil 3120.30.74   Buber, Martin. Images of good and evil. London, 1952.
Phil 3120.30.77   Buber, Martin. Zwischen Gesellschaft und Staat. Heidelberg, 1952.
Phil 2200.5.80   Burkhardt, F. The cleavage in our culture. Boston, 1952.
Phil 1133.1.12A   Burnet, John. Early Greek philosophers. 4th ed. London, 1952.
Phil 8610.913.5A   Bury, J.B. A history of freedom of thought. 2. ed. London, 1952.
Phil 9240.10.5   Camus, Albert. L'homme révolté. 94. éd. Paris, 1952.
Phil 4260.128   Cantone, Carlo. Il concetto filosofico di diritto in Giambattista Vico. Mazara, 1952.
Phil 5042.21.20   Carnap, Rudolf. The continuum of inductive methods. Chicago, 1952.
Phil 4303.1.5   Carreras y Artau, T. Estudios sobre médicos-filosófos españoles del siglo XIX. Barcelona, 1952.
Phil 4080.12.50   Castelli, Enrico. Le temps Larcelant. Paris, 1952.
Phil 5403.9   Cazeneuve, Jean. Psychologie de la joie. Paris, 1952.
Phil 2725.25   Centineo, E. René LeSenne. Palermo, 1952.
Phil 3450.19.109   Chiodi, Pietro. L'ultimo. 1e ed. Torino, 1952.
Phil 5012.2A   Clark, Joseph. Conventional logic and modern logic. Woodstock, 1952.
Phil 3822.4.25   Colerus, Johannes. Das Leben des Benedict von Spinoza. Heidelberg, 1952.
Phil 1750.355A   Collins, J.D. The existentialists. Chicago, 1952.
Phil 525.270   Congrès international de psychologie religieuse, 7th, Avon, 1950. Mystique et continence. Bruges, 1952.
Phil 1507.7   Copleston, F.C. Medieval philosophy. London, 1952.
Phil 1507.7.2   Copleston, F.C. Medieval philosophy. N.Y., 1952.
Phil 3425.350   Coreth, Emerich. Das dialektische Sein in Hegel's Logik. Wien, 1952.
Phil 1107.4.5   Cornford, F.M. Principium sapientiae. Cambridge, Eng., 1952.
Phil 310.2   Cornforth, M.C. Dialectical materialism. London, 1952. 3v.
Phil 3552.344   Corsano, A. G.W. Leibniz. Napoli, 1952.
Phil 1920.1.32   Craik, Kenneth James Williams. The nature of explanation. Cambridge, Eng., 1952.
Phil 8663.3.96   Cramer, C.H. Royal Bob. 1. ed. Indianapolis, 1952.
Phil 2050.225   Cresson, A. David Hume. 1. éd. Paris, 1952.
Phil 2477.6.115   Crippà, Romeo. Rassegna di bibliografia blondeliana. Torino, 1952.
Phil 4080.3.70   Croce, Benedetto. Intorno alla dialettica. v.1-2. Bari, 1952.
Phil 5238.26   Current trends. Pittsburgh, 1952.
Phil 6952.29   Custance, J. Wisdom, madness, and folly. N.Y., 1952.
Phil 3450.18.100   Daehler, J. Zur Freiheitslehre von Nicolai Hartmann. Inaug. Diss. Freiburg, 1952.
Phil 4683.55.31   Dāle, Pauls. Vērojumi un pārdomas par cilvēku un gara kultūru. Chicago, 1952.
Phil 4872.55.20   D'Andrade, Joseph C.P. Philosophy and life and other papers. Bombay, 1952.
Phil 5247.13.80   Dantin Gallego, J. La filosofia natural de Huarte de San Juan. Madrid, 1952.
Phil 8735.25   D'Arcy, M.C. The pain of this world and the providence of God. London, 1952.
Phil 130.7   Decurtins, C. Kleines Philosophenlexikon. Affoltern, 1952.
Phil 1508.2.12   Dempf, Alois. Christliche Philosophie. 2. Aufl. Bonn, 1952.
Phil 2520.35.50   Descartes, René. Choix commenté du Discours de la méthode. Geneve, 1952.
Phil 2520.52.75   Descartes, René. Méditations. 4. éd. Paris, 1952.
Phil 8693.20   Dessauer, F. Am Rande der Dinge. 2. Aufl. Frankfurt, 1952.
Phil 8693.20.5   Dessauer, F. Religion im Lichte der heutigen Naturwissenschaft. 3. Aufl. Frankfurt, 1952.
Phil 8404.3   Dorfles, Gillo. Discorso tecnico delle arti. Pisa, 1952.
Phil 5465.132   Dracoulidès, N.N. Psychanalyse de l'artiste et de son oeuvre. Genève, 1952.
Phil 7069.43.22   Driesch, Hans. Parapsychologie. 3. Aufl. Zürich, 1952.
Phil 1900.95   Duncan-Jones, A. Butler's moral philosophy. Harmondsworth, 1952.
Phil 672.136.7   Dunne, John W. An experiment with time. London, 1952.
Phil 3200.14.5   Ebner, Ferdinand. Gesammelte Werke. 2. Aufl. Wien, 1952.
Phil 3235.81.30   Engels, Friedrich. Ludwig Feuerbach. 3. Aufl. Berlin, 1952.
Phil 4110.10.30   Fabi, Bruno. Il tutto e il nulla. 1. ed. Milano, 1952.
Phil 5245.48   Falorni, M.L. Lo studio psicologica dell'intelligenza e della matricità. Firenze, 1952.
Phil 2005.9.32   Feibleman, J. Philosophers lead sheltered lives. London, 1952.
Phil 4352.1.150   Feliu Egidio, Vicente. Sistematizacion del pensamiento de Balmes en orden a la filosofia de la historia. Madrid, 1952.
Phil 6315.1.18A   Ferenczi, Sandor. First contributions to psychoanalysis. London, 1952.
Phil 8406.16   Ferrant, Angel. La esencia humana de las formos. Santander, 1952.
Phil 8585.37   Ferrière, A. L'essentiel. Lausanne, 1952.
Phil 3850.27.122   Feschotte, Jacques. Albert Schweitzer. Paris, 1952.
Phil 5015.2   Filipor, R.P. Logic and dialecta in the Soviet Union. N.Y., 1952.
Phil 5045.15   Fischl, J. Logik; ein Lehrbuch. 2. Aufl. Graz, 1952[1946].
Phil 5066.46   Fitch, F.B. Symbolic logic. N.Y., 1952.
Phil 310.25   Fogarasi, Bela. Filozófiai elöadasok es tanulmányok. Budapest, 1952.
Phil 5400.114   Forti, E. L'émotion. 1. éd. Paris, 1952.
Phil 3270.12.33   Frege, Gottlob. Translations from the philosophical writings of Gottlob Frege. Oxford, 1952.
Phil 5245.47   French, T.M. The integration of behavior. Chicago, 1952-58. 3v.
Phil 7082.8.5   Freud, Sigmund. On dreams. N.Y., 1952.
Phil 2255.1.115   Fritz, C.A. Bertrand Russell's construction of the external world. London, 1952.

1952 - cont.

Phil 4960.230   Fúrlong Cárdiff, Guillermo. Nacimiento y desarollo de la filosofía en el Rio de la Plata, 1536-1810. Buenos Aires, 1952.

Phil 2225.5.93   Gallie, W.B. Peirce and pragmatism. Harmondsworth, 1952.

Phil 8407.28   Gargiulo, A. Scritti di estetica. Firenze, 1952.

Phil 4006.5.37   Garin, Eugenio. L'umanesemio italiano. Bari, 1952.

Phil 4120.4.90   Gentile, Giovanni. Introduzione alla filosofia. 2. ed. Firenze, 1952.

Phil 2880.8.112   Gentiloni Silverj, F. Jean Paul Sartre contro la speranza. Roma, 1952.

Phil 1182.30   Ghyks, M.C. Le nombre d'or. v.1-2. Paris, 1952.

Phil 8407.25   Gilbert, K. Aesthetic studies: architecture and poetry. Durham, 1952.

Phil 8586.49   Gillett, H.T. The spiritual basis of democracy. Oxford, 1952.

Phil 181.73.7   Gilson, E. Being and some philosophers. 2. ed. Toronto, 1952.

Phil 2630.8.35   Gilson, Etienne. Breakdown of morals and Christian education. n.p., 1952?

Phil 2255.1.113   Götlind, E. Bertrand Russell's theories of causation. Inaug. Diss. Uppsala, 1952.

Phil 3120.30.87   Goldstein, Walter Benjamin. Die Botschaft Martin Bubers. Jerusalem, 1952-56. 3v.

Phil 3488.30   González Vicén, J. La filosofía del estado en Kant. Laguna, 1952.

Phil 8062.3   Grand, Y. Recherche des principes d'une philosophie des arts, dits d'imitation chez Platon, Aristote et Plotin. Lausanne, 1952.

Phil 5627.192   Grensted, L.W. The psychology of religion. N.Y., 1952.

Phil 182.43.15   Häberlin, Paul. Philosophin perennis. Berlin, 1952.

Phil 5520.112   Haerber, W.L. A scientific foundation of philosophy. Los Angeles, 1952.

Phil 1807.2.20   Halévy, E. The growth of philosophic radicalism. London, 1952.

Phil 735.130A   Hall, Everett W. What is value? London, 1952.

Phil 2407.5   Hansen, V. Gennembrudsmaend i nyere fransk filosofi. København, 1952.

Phil 8882.68   Hare, Richard Mervyn. The language of morals. Oxford, 1952.

Phil 5590.110   Harrower, M.R. Appraising personality. 1. ed. N.Y., 1952.

Phil 8408.25   Hartford, H. Has God been insulted here? Chicago, 1952.

Phil 3425.14   Hegel, Georg Wilhelm Friedrich. Briefe von und an Hegel. Hamburg, 1952-53. 4v.

Phil 3425.73.2.10   Hegel, Georg Wilhelm Friedrich. Phänomenologie des Geistes. 6. Aufl. Hamburg, 1952.

Phil 3425.40.50   Hegel, Georg Wilhelm Friedrich. Premières publications. Thèse. Paris, 1952.

Phil 3450.18.105   Heimsoeth, H. Nicolai Hartmann, der Denker und sein Werk. Göttingen, 1952.

Phil 5047.35.5   Heiss, Robert. Wesen und Formen der Dialektik. Köln, 1952.

Phil 7069.52   Hettinger, John. Telepathy and spiritualism. N.Y., 1952.

Phil 3120.11.85   Heydorn, H.J. Julius Bahnsen. Göttingen, 1952.

Phil 960.137.15   Hiriyanna, M. Popular essays in Indian philosophy. Mysore, 1952.

Phil 960.137.8   Hiriyanna, M. The quest after perfection. Mysore, 1952.

Phil 5650.42   Hirsh, Ira Jean. The measurement of hearing. N.Y., 1952.

Phil 2045.02   Hobbes, Thomas. A bibliography by H. MacDonald and M. Hargreaves. London, 1952.

Phil 2055.7.10   Hocking, William E. Varieties of educational experience. Madison, N.H., 1952. 2v.

Phil 3195.6.94.5   Hodges, Herbert A. The philosophy of Wilhelm Dilthey. London, 1952.

Phil 182.49.10.2   Hoernlé, R.F.A. Studies in philosophy. Cambridge, Mass., 1952.

Phil 182.49.10   Hoernlé, R.F.A. Studies in philosophy. London, 1952.

Phil 4065.130A   Horowitz, I.L. The Renaissance philosophy of Giordano Bruno. N.Y., 1952.

Phil 5627.134.56.5   Howard, Peter. The world rebuilt. N.Y., 1952.

Phil 1707.14   Hubben, William. Four prophets of our destiny. N.Y., 1952.

Phil 2805.268   Hubert, M.L., Sister. Pascal's unfinished Apology. New Haven, 1952.

Phil 3808.169.5   Hübscher, Arthur. Schopenhauer. Stuttgart, 1952.

Phil 1050.10.10   Husik, I. Philosophical essays. Oxford, 1952.

Phil 182.67.4.2   Husserl, Edmund. Ideas: general introduction to pure phenomenology. London, 1952.

Phil 6117.48   Hutschnecker, A.A. The will to line. London, 1952.

Phil 5465.60   Industrial Research Institute, New York. The nature of creative thinking. N.Y., 1952?

Phil 310.6   Institut Filosofii. Akadamiia Nauk SSSR. O dialekticheskii materializme; sbornik statei. Moskva, 1952.

Phil 8870.12   Institute for Religious Studies, Jewish Theological Seminary of America. Conflict of loyalties. N.Y., 1952.

Phil 8622.12   Jakob, J. Der Konflikt. Basel, 1952.

Phil 3475.3.70   Jaspers, Karl. Existentialism and humanism. N.Y., 1952.

Phil 3475.3.62   Jaspers, Karl. Reason and anti-reason in our time. New Haven, 1952.

Phil 3475.3.61   Jaspers, Karl. Reason and anti-reason in our time. 1st British ed. London, 1952.

Phil 5049.20.10   Jaspers, Karl. Über das tragische. München, 1952.

Phil 184.26.30   Joad, C.E.M. A first encounter with philosophy. London, 1952.

Phil 8699.5   Joad, Cyril E.M. The recovery of belief. London, 1952.

Phil 2340.10.130   Johnson, A.H. Whitehead's theory of reality. Boston, 1952.

Phil 6319.11   Jones, Maxwell. Social psychiatry. London, 1952.

Phil 809.5   Jones, W.T. A history of Western philosophy. N.Y., 1952.

Phil 2075.7.30   Jordan, Elijah. Essays in criticism. Chicago, 1952.

Phil 6319.1.8.2   Jung, C.G. Symbole der Wandlung. Zürich, 1952.

Phil 8589.20   Jung, Carl Gustav. Antwort auf Hiob. Zürich, 1952.

Phil 8622.8   Kimpel, B.F. Religious faith, language, and knowledge. N.Y., 1952.

Phil 7082.176   Klages, Ludwig. Vom Traumbewusstsein. Hamburg, 1952.

Phil 3830.12   Kline, G.L. Spinoza in Soviet philosophy. London, 1952.

Phil 1750.370   Knittermeyer, H. Dit Philosophie der Existenz von der Renaissance bis zur Gegenwart. Wien, 1952.

Phil 5592.5   Koch, Charles. The tree test. Bern, 1952.

Phil 185.40.5   Kolbenheyer, E.G. Die Philosophie de Bauhütte. Wien, 1952.

Phil 810.11   Kroner, Richard. Speculation and revelation in the history of philosophy. London, 1952.

Phil 5238.140   Kuhlen, Raymond. Psychological studies of human development. N.Y., 1952.

Phil 3808.194   Kurth, K.O. Arthur Schopenhauer. Kitzingen, 1952.

1952 - cont.

Phil 735.134   Kurtz, Paul W. The problems of value theory. Thesis. N.Y., 1952.

Phil 2805.249.5   Lafuma, Louis. Controverses pascaliennes. Paris, 1952.

Phil 1711.6   Landgrebe, Ludwig. Philosophie der Gegenwart. Bonn, 1952.

Phil 8412.9.5   Landmann, E. Die Lehre vom Schönen. Wien, 1952.

Phil 3640.414A   Lannoy, Joris C. Nietzsche, ou L'histoire d'un égocentrisme athée. Paris, 1952.

Phil 5520.109   Lee, I.J. How to talk with people. N.Y., 1952.

Phil 3552.78.50   Leibniz, Gottfried Wilhelm. Lettres de Leibniz à Arnauld. 1. éd. Paris, 1952.

Phil 3552.63.30   Leibniz, Gottfried Wilhelm. La monadologie. Paris, 1952.

Phil 3552.63.10   Leibniz, Gottfried Wilhelm. Theodicy. New Haven, 1952.

Phil 900.15   Le Renard, A. L'Orient et sa tradition. Paris, 1952.

Phil 5590.441   Levitov, Nikolai D. Voprosy psikhologii kharaktera. Moskva, 1952.

Phil 8886.61.5   Leys, W.A.R. Ethics and policy decisions. N.Y., 1952.

Phil 75.92   Library of Congress. General Reference and Bibliography Division. Philosophical periodicals. Washington, 1952.

Phil 4011.3   Librizzi, C. Il risorgimento filosofica in Italia. Padova, 1952. 2v.

Phil 5520.135A   Linsky, Leonard. Semantics and the philosophy of language. Urbana, Ill., 1952.

Phil 6321.30   Loewenstein, R. Psychoanalyse de l'antisémitisme. 1. éd. Paris, 1952.

Phil 6980.433.2   Lowrey, Lawson G. Psychiatry for social workers. 2. ed. N.Y., 1952.

Phil 811.12   Ludat-Deniselle, A. Von Thales bis Heidegger. Ratingen, 1952.

Phil 8887.78   MacBeath, A. Experiments in living. London, 1952.

Phil 5252.18.12.10

Phil 8887.80   McDougall, William. Psychology. 2d ed. London, 1952.

   MacGregor, G. Les frontières de la morale et de la religion. Thèse. Paris, 1952.

Phil 5627.225   Magie des extremes. Bruges, 1952.

Phil 1540.28   Maier, A. An der Grenze von Scholastik und Naturwissenschaft. 2. Aufl. Roma, 1952.

Phil 2730.55   Maine de Biran, Pierre. Mémoire sur la décomposition de la pensée. v.1-2. Paris, 1952.

Phil 187.143   Mallik, B.K. Related multiplicity. Oxford, 1952.

Phil 5873.2   Malrieu, Philippe. Les émotions et la personnalité de l'enfant. Thèse. Paris, 1952.

Phil 2750.21   Marc, André. Dialectique de l'affirmation. Paris, 1952.

Phil 187.8.7   Marcel, Gabriel. Homo viator. Paris, 1952.

Phil 2750.19.20   Marcel, Gabriel. Men against humanity. London, 1952.

Phil 187.93.3   Marcel, Gabriel. Metaphysical journal. London, 1952.

Phil 4080.3.220   Marra, Dara. Conversazioni con Benedetto Croce su alcuni libri della sua biblioteca. Milano, 1952.

Phil 5590.135   Mayo, B. The logic of personality. London, 1952.

Phil 5520.106   Meerloo, A.M. Conversation and communication. N.Y., 1952.

Phil 2840.100   Méry, Marcel. La critique du christianisme chez Renouvier. Thèse. Paris, 1952. 2v.

Phil 2805.263.2   Mesnard, Jean. Pascal. London, 1952.

Phil 5822.4.10   Messner, J. Widersprüche in der menschlichen Existenz. Innsbruck, 1952.

Phil 3552.322.5   Meyer, R.W. Leibnitz and the seventeenth century revolution. Cambridge, Eng., 1952.

Phil 3640.402   Mittasch, A. Friedrich Nietzsche als Naturphilosoph. Stuttgart, 1952.

Phil 1750.356   Möller, J. Existenzialphilosophie und katholische Theologie. Baden-Baden, 1952.

NEDL Phil 1135.154.5   Mondolfo, R. El infinitio en el pensamiento de la antiguedad clasica. Buenos Aires, 1952.

Phil 812.25   Mondolfo, R. Problemi e metodi di ricerca nella storia della filosofia. Firenze, 1952.

Phil 8702.21   Morris, D.L. Possibilities unlimited. 1. ed. N.Y., 1952.

Phil 5075.5   Moschetti, A.M. L'unità come categoria. Milano, 1952. 2v.

Phil 4710.7.5.2   Moscow. Universitet. Filosofskii Fakul'tet. Iz istorii russkoi filosofii, sbornik. Moskva, 1952.

Phil 4710.7.7   Moscow. Universitet. Filosofskii Fakul'tet. Iz istorii russkoi filosofii, XVIII-XIX vv. Moskva, 1952.

Phil 4710.7.10A   Moscow. Universitet. Filosofskii Fakul'tet. Izbrannye proizvedeniia russkikh myslitelei vtoroi poloviny XVIII v. Leningrad, 1952. 2v.

Phil 575.146.5   Mounier, E. Personalism. London, 1952.

Phil 8592.80   Mouroux, Jean. The meaning of man. N.Y., 1952.

Phil 2805.278   Moussalli, U. Le vrai visage de Blaise Pascal. Paris, 1952.

Phil 8413.16   Mundt, Ernest. Art, form, and civilization. Berkeley, 1952.

Phil 9070.55   Murrow, E.R. This I believe. N.Y., 1952. 2v.

Phil 2520.241   Nardi, Bruno. Le meditizioni di Cartesio. Roma, 1952.

Phil 8593.23   Neill, T.P. Religion and culture. Milwaukee, 1952.

Phil 6023.1   Nicefaro, A. La fisonomia nell'arte e nella scienza. Firenze, 1952.

Phil 3640.17.4   Nietzsche, Friedrich. Morgenröte. Stuttgart, 1952. 2v.

Phil 3640.14.10   Nietzsche, Friedrich. Werke. Salzburg, 1952. 2v.

Phil 3640.51   Nietzsche, Friedrich. Der Wille zur Macht. Stuttgart, 1952.

Phil 8593.20.2   Nigg, Walter. Religiöse Denker. Berlin, 1952.

Phil 8583.28.10   O'Connor, D.A. The relation between religion and culture according to C. Dawson. Montreal, 1952.

Phil 165.25   Ordre, désordre, lumière. Paris, 1952.

Phil 5465.57.10   Osborn, A.F. Wake up your mind. N.Y., 1952.

Phil 3552.342   Ottaviano, C. Le basi fisico-metafische della filosofia di Leibniz. Padova, 1952.

Phil 5254.3.5   Overstreet, H. Allen. The great enterprise. 1st. ed. N.Y., 1952.

Phil 8964.5   Oyen, Hendrik van. Evangelische Ethik. Basel, 1952. 2v.

Phil 6325.17   Palmer, H.A. The philosophy of psychiatry. N.Y., 1952.

Phil 5401.50   Panse, Friedrich. Angst und Schreck in klinisch psychologischer und sozialmedizinischer Sicht. Stuttgart, 1952.

Phil 2805.272   Pascal, Blaise. Pascal par lui-même. Paris, 1952.

Phil 5620.26   Perelman, Chaim. Rhétorique et philosophie pour une théorie de l'argumentation en philosophie. 1. éd. Paris, 1952.

Phil 5593.52   Pergola, Elio de. Il metodo psicodiagnostico de Rorschach. Roma, 1952.

Phil 8416.16   Petruzzellis, N. Filosofia dell'arte. 2. ed. Mazara, 1952.

Phil 3450.19.95.3   Pfeiffer, Johannes S. Existenzphilosophie. 3e Aufl. Hamburg, 1952.

1952 - cont.

Phil 5255.51.8   Piaget, J. La psychologie de l'intelligence. 3. ed. Paris, 1952.

Phil 5066.36.10   Piaget, Jean. Essai sur les transformations des óperations logiques. 1. ed. Paris, 1952.

Phil 8416.6   Piemonteal, Filippo. Problemi di filosofia dell'arte. Torino, 1952.

Phil 190.80.10   Pieper, Josef. Was heisst akademisch? München, 1952.

Phil 5625.1.5.3   Podkopaev, N.A. Metodika izucheniia uslovnykn refleksov. 3. izd. Moskva, 1952.

Phil 6980.606   Pollak, Otto. Social science and psychotherapy for children. N.Y., 1952.

Phil 5592.35   Porteus, Stanley David. The Porteus maze test manual. London, 1952.

Phil 1955.6.122   Pra, Mario dal. Il pensiero di John Dewey. Milano, 1952.

Phil 1750.368   Prini, P. Esistenzialismo. Roma, 1952.

Phil 5255.54   Pronko, N.H. Empirical foundations of psychology. N.Y., 1952.

Phil 1750.166.65 Przymara, E. Humanitus. Nuinberg, 1952.

Phil 2880.8.124   Quiles, Ismael. Sartre y su existencialismo. 2. ed. Buenos Aires, 1952.

Phil 530.20.95   Quint, Josef. Textbuch zur Mystik des deutschen Mittelalters. Halle, 1952.

Phil 817.22   Radhakrishnan, S. History of philosophy. London, 1952. 2v.

Phil 4871.5.2   Radhakrishnan, Sarvepalli. Contemporary Indian philosophy. 2nd ed. London, 1952.

Phil 4872.242.20 Radhakrishnan, Sarvépalli. Radhakrishnan; an anthology. London, 1952.

Phil 3255.94   Raeber, Kuno. Studien zur Geschichtsbibel Sebastian Francks. Basel, 1952.

Phil 3255.95   Raeber, Kuno. Studien zur Geschichtsbibel Sebastian Francks. Inaug. Diss. Basel, 1952.

Phil 6327.4.7   Rank, Otto. The trauma of birth. N.Y., 1952.

Phil 102.3.5   Ranzoli, C. Dizionario de scienze filosofiche. Milano, 1952.

Phil 5585.77   Rausch, E. Struktur und Metrik figuraloptischer Wahrnehmung. Frankfurt, 1952.

Phil 1750.360A   Reinhardt, Kurt Frank. The existentialist revolt. Milwaukee, 1952.

Phil 5227.7   Reinle, Rico. Das Problems der Entwicklung in der neueren Psychologie. Basel, 1952.

Phil 1750.346   Rencontres Internationales. La connaissance de l'homme on XVe siècle. Neuchâtel, 1952.

Phil 5425.84   Révész, Géza. Talent und Genie. Bern, 1952.

Phil 6327.25   Reviere, Joan. Developments in psycho-analysis. London, 1952.

Phil 9035.45.10   Roback, A.A. The psychology of character. 3. ed. Cambridge, Mass., 1952.

Phil 575.200   Roem, H.A.C. Structuurphenomenologische systematisering van het menszijn door centraalstelling van de vrijheidsbeleving. 's-Gravenhage, 1952.

Phil 6480.194   Roheim, Geza. The gates of the dream. N.Y., 1952.

Phil 4957.35   Romero, Francisco. Sobre la filosofía en América. Buenos Aires, 1952.

Phil 4368.2.45   Romero, Francisco. Teoría del hombre. Buenos Aires, 1952.

Phil 1717.18   Rosmini Serbati, Antonio. Breve schizzo dei sistemi di filosofia moderna e del proprio sistema. Napoli, 1952.

Phil 4210.38   Rosmini-Serbati, Antonio. Esposizione del sistema morale dell'autore e compendio di etica. Mozara, 1952.

Phil 5066.50   Rosser, J.B. Many-valued logics. Amsterdam, 1952.

Phil 5257.60   Roubiczek, Paul. Thinking in opposites. London, 1952.

Phil 8707.22   Rowland, J. One man's mind. London, 1952.

Phil 4872.247.30 Roy, Manendra Nath. Reason, romanticism and revolution. Calcutta, 1952-55. 2v.

Phil 2250.62   Royce, Josiah. The religious philosophy of Josiah Royce. Syracuse, 1952.

Phil 4357.14.80   Rubert Candau, José María. El conocimiento de Dios en la filosofía de Guillermo Rubió. Madrid, 1952?

Phil 4357.9   Rubert Candau, José Maria. El siglo XIV. Madrid, 1952.

Phil 5627.205   Ruemke, H.C. The psychology of unbelief. London, 1952.

Phil 2255.7.5   Runes, Dagobert D. Of God, the devil and the Jews. N.Y., 1952.

Phil 2255.1.65   Russell, Bertrand Russell. Dictionary of mind, matter and morals. N.Y., 1952.

Phil 8735.24   Ruyer, R. Néo-finalisme. 1. éd. Paris, 1952.

Phil 735.132   Ruyer, R. Philosophie dè la valeur. Paris, 1952.

Phil 165.21   Ryan, J.K. Philosophical studies in honor of the very Reverend Ignatius Smith. Westminster, Maryland, 1952.

Phil 1718.26   Sahm, August. Jaspers als Blickpunkt für neue Einsichten. Worms am Rhein, 1952.

Phil 672.202   Samuells, Roberto. La dialéctica del espacio. Madrid, 1952.

Phil 2880.8.62   Sartre, Jean Paul. Das Sein und das Nichts. Hamburg, 1952.

Phil 6328.33A   Scheidlinger, S. Psychoanalysis and group behavior. 1st ed. N.Y., 1952.

Phil 187.59.82   Schilpp, P.A. The philosophy of G.E. Moore. 2. ed. N.Y., 1952.

Phil 4872.242.80 Schilpp, Paul A. The philosophy of Sarvepalli Radhakrishnan. N.Y., 1952.

Phil 3425.360   Schmidt, E. Hegels Lehre von Gott. Gütersloh, 1952.

Phil 3500.71   Schneiberger, Guido. Kants Konzeption der Modalbegriffe. Basel, 1952.

Phil 4225.8.2   Sciacca, Michele Federico. Opere complete. Milano, 1952-56. 7v.

Phil 70.30   Science, language and human rights. Philadelphia, 1952.

Phil 2520.237   Scott, J.F. The scientific work of René Descartes. London, 1952.

Phil 8419.36   Sébag, Henri. Anatomie de l'âme; essai de psych-esthétique. Paris, 1952. 3v.

Phil 8870.38   Sellars, Wilfrid. Readings in ethical theory. N.Y., 1952.

Phil 3838.28   Semerari, G. Il problemi dello Spinozismo. Trani, 1952.

Phil 103.4.5   Semprini, G. Nuovo dizionario di coltura filosofica e scientifica. Torino, 1952.

Phil 960.175   Sharma, C. Indian philosophy. Banaras, 1952.

Phil 8598.98   Sheen, Fulton John. Philosophy of religion. Dublin, 1952.

Phil 3838.32   Shepo, Elias. The strange death of Barukh Spinoza. Cambridge, 1952.

Phil 9590.25.5   Shishkin, A.F. Die bürgerliche Moralinwaffe der imperialistischen Reaktion. Berlin, 1952.

Phil 8419.14   Shishkov, G. Erschopfte Kunst oder Kunstformalismus? Schlehdorf, 1952.

Phil 3018.25   Siebecke, H. Ernte deutscher Humanitat. 2. Aufl. Bad Nauheim, 1952.

Phil 6128.57A   Silverberg, W.V. Childhood experience and personal destiny. N.Y., 1952.

1952 - cont.

Phil 3838.15.10   Siwek, Paul. An coeur du Spinozisme. Paris, 1952.

Phil 8643.32   Siwek, Paul. The enigma of the hereafter. N.Y., 1952.

Phil 2520.119.5   Smith, N.K. New studies in the philosophy of Descartes. London, 1952.

Phil 193.166   Società Italiana di Metapsichica. Oltre i cinque sensi. Torino? 1952.

Phil 5258.88.5   Souriau, A. Elemente der Philosophie und der Mathematik. Basel, 1952.

Phil 193.165   Speiser, A. Elemente der Philosophie und der Mathematik. Basel, 1952.

Phil 1718.28   Spenlé, J.E. Les grands maîtres de l'humanisme européen. Paris, 1952.

Phil 4080.3.210   Sprigge, Cecil Jackson Squire. Benedetto Croce. Cambridge, Eng., 1952.

Phil 4080.3.211   Sprigge, Cecil Jackson Squire. Benedetto Croce. New Haven, 1952.

Phil 8598.100   Stace, W.T. Religion and the modern mind. 1. ed. Philadelphia, 1952.

Phil 5258.145.2   Stager, Ross. Psychology. Instructor's manual. 1st ed. N.Y., 1952.

Phil 5258.145   Stagner, Ross. Psychology. 1st ed. N.Y., 1952.

Phil 8419.9   Stange, Alfred. Die Welt als Gestalt. Köln, 1952.

Phil 1750.357   Stefanini, L. Esistenzialismo ateo e esistenzialismo teistro. Padova, 1952.

Phil 1718.25   Stegmüller, W. Hauptströmungen der Gegenwartphilosophie. Wien, 1952.

Phil 5590.245   Stern, Erich. Experimentelle Persönlichkeitsanalyse nach dem Murray-Test. 1. Aufl. Zürich, 1952.

Phil 193.128.10   Stout, G.F. God and nature. Cambridge, Eng., 1952.

Phil 1750.361   Straelen, H. van. Man the lonely. Tokyo, 1952.

Phil 1540.29   Strauss, Leo. Persecution and the art of writing. Glencoe, Ill., 1952. 2v.

Phil 5058.60   Strawson, P.F. Introduction to logic theory. London, 1952.

Phil 2880.8.114   Streller, Justus. Zur Freiheit verurteilt. Hamburg, 1952.

Phil 5259.13.15   Tansley, A.G. Mind and life. London, 1952.

Phil 1400.5   Tatakès, B.N. Themata christianikès kai buzantinès philosophias. Athens, 1952.

Phil 1955.6.120   Thayer, H.S. The logic of pragmatism. N.Y., 1952.

Phil 8969.5   Thibon, G. What God has joined together. Chicago, 1952.

Phil 130.8   Thieme, Karl. Philosophenbilden. Basel, 1952.

Phil 525.119   Thurston, H. The physical phenomena of mysticism. Chicago, 1952.

Phil 672.260   Tollenaere, M. de. Een philosophie van de tijd. Leuven, 1952.

Phil 5259.42   Tyrrell, G.N.M. Homo faber. London, 1952.

Phil 3900.2   Unger, E. The imagination of reason. London, 1952.

Phil 9400.17   United States. Federal Security Agency. Committee on Aging and Geriatrics. Fact book on aging. Washington, D.C., 1952.

Phil 4352.1.105   Urmeneta, F. de. Principios de filosofia de la historia. Madrid, 1952.

Phil 5627.196   Van Buskirk, J.D. Religion, healing and health. N.Y., 1952.

Phil 6331.6   Van der Veldt, J.H. Psychiatry and Catholicism. 1st ed. N.Y., 1952.

Phil 4983.9.30   Vasconcelos, J. Todología. México, 1952.

Phil 4960.272   Vazela Dominiguez de Ghioldi, Delfina. Para la historia de las ideas argentinas. 1. ed. Buenos Aires, 1952.

Phil 5780.14   Vedenov, A.V. Vospitanie voli u rebenka v sem'e. Moskva, 1952.

Phil 4080.3.225   Vettori, V. Benedetto Croce e gli studi contemporanei d'estetica e storia. Firenze, 1952.

Phil 4260.28   Vico, G.B. La scienza nuova e opere scelte di Giambattista Vico. Torino, 1952.

Phil 5520.107   Vinacke, W.E. The psychology of thinking. 1. ed. N.Y., 1952.

Phil 8050.69   Vlaanderen, Andre. Het zien van kunst en de kunst van het zien. Amsterdam, 1952.

Phil 5061.8   Vries, Joseph de. Logica, cui praemittitur. Friburgi, 1952.

Phil 197.73   Wasmuth, E. Von der Wahrheit der Philosophie. Köln, 1952.

Phil 8847.12   Wedar, S. Duty and utility. Lund, 1952.

Phil 8897.76.5   Weil, Simone. The need for roots. N.Y., 1952.

Phil 8712.27   White, E.A. Science and religion in American thought. Stanford, 1952.

Phil 5535.18   Wictorin, Mauritz. Bidrag till zäknefärdighetens psykologi akademisk. Göteborg, 1952.

Phil 2225.5.85   Wiener, P.P. Studies in the philosophy of Charles Sanders Peirce. Cambridge, Mass., 1952.

Phil 193.30.80   Wildbair, A. Der philosophische Dialog als literarisches Kunstwerk. Bern, 1952.

Phil 5722.78   Williams, John K. The knack of using your subconscious mind. Scarsdale, N.Y., 1952.

Phil 3640.396   Williams, W.D. Nietzsche and the French. Oxford, 1952.

Phil 5262.60   Willwoll, Alexander. Psychologia metaphysica, in Usum scholarum. Friburgi, 1952.

Phil 353.21   Wisdom, John. Other minds. Oxford, 1952

Phil 1527.1.5.20 Wulf, M. de. History of mediaeval philosophy. N.Y., 1952.

Phil 3024.5   Young, William. Toward a reformed philosophy. Grand Rapids, Mich., 1952.

Phil 6135.8   Zaniewski, R. Les théories des milieux et la pédagogie mesologique. Tournai, 1952.

Phil 4959.230.10 Zea, Leopoldo. La filosofía como compromiso, y otros ensayos. 1. ed. México, 1952.

Phil 310.642   Ziherl, Boris. Dijalektički i istoriski materijalizam. 2. Izd. Beograd, 1952.

1953

Phil 585.150   Ahlman, Erik. Ihmisen probleemi. Helsinki, 1953.

Phil 310.3   Akademiia Nauk SSSR. Institut Filosofii. Dialekticheskii materializm. Moskva, 1953.

Phil 260.11   Alfieri, Vittorio Enpo. Atomos idea. Firenzo, 1953.

Phil 1750.364   Allen, E.L. Existentialism from within. London, 1953.

Phil 4060.9.30   Amendala, G. Etica e biografia. Milano, 1953.

Phil 6110.21   American Academy of Political and Social Science. Mental health in the United States. Philadelphia, 1953.

Phil 5240.7.10   Anschütz, Georg. Psychologie. Hamburg, 1953.

Phil 2138.123   Anschutz, R.P. The philosophy of J.S. Mill. Oxford, 1953.

Phil 85.5   Apel, Max. Philosophisches Wörterbuch. 4. Aufl. Berlin, 1953.

Phil 4365.1.15   Aranguren, José. La filosofia di Eugenio d'Ors. Milano, 1953.

Phil 8400.4   Archivio di Filosofia. Filosofia dell'arte. Roma, 1953.

Chronological Listing

1953 - cont.

Phil 3425.356   Asveld, Paul. La pensée, religieuse du jeune Hegel. Louvain, 1953.

Phil 4080.3.265   Attisani, A. Interpretazioni crociane. Messina, 1953.

Phil 3090.28   Baader, Franz von. Über Liebe. München, 1953.

Phil 3850.27.125   Babel, Henry. Que pense Albert Schweitzer? Genève, 1953.

Phil 2477.15   Bachelard, Gaston. Le matérialisme rationnel. Paris, 1953.

Phil 5125.22   Bagchi, S. Inductive reasoning. Calcutta, 1953.

Phil 3925.16.80   Barone, Francesco. Wittgenstein inedito. Torino, 1953.

Phil 8951.25   Barrett, E.B. Life begins with love. Dublin, 1953.

Phil 3549.8.105   Bartels, Enno. Ludwig Klages seine Lebenslehre und das Vitalismusproblem. Meisenheim, 1953.

Phil 3850.27.98   Barthelemy, Guy. Chez le Docteur Schweitzer. Laussame, 1953.

Phil 5066.58   Basson, A.H. Introduction to symbolic logic. London, 1953.

Phil 9075.50   Bastide, G. Meditations pour une éthique de la personne. 1st éd. Paris, 1953.

Phil 8402.8.20   Bayer, Raymond. Essais sur la méthode en esthétique. Paris, 1953.

Phil 176.168   Beck, Lewis White. Philosophic inquiry. N.Y., 1953.

Phil 7150.46   Berdiaev, N.A. Le suicide. Paris, 1953?

Phil 4752.2.77A   Berdiaev, Nikolai Aleksandrovich. Truth and revelation. London, 1953.

Phil 3120.15.97   Bickel, Lothar. Wirklichkeit und Wahrheit des Denkens. Zürich, 1953.

Phil 6980.112   Bingham, J. The inside story. 1. ed. N.Y., 1953.

Phil 3120.27.32   Binswanger, L. Grundformen und Erkenntnis menschlichen Daseins. 2. Aufl. Zürich, 1953.

Phil 1750.166.35.5   Blackham, H.J. The human tradition. Boston, 1953.

Phil 6980.712.100   Blisten, D.R. The social theories of Harry Stack Sullivan. N.Y., 1953.

Phil 3890.8.110   Bloch, E. Christian Thomasius. Berlin, 1953.

Phil 3120.22.20   Blüher, Hans. Werke und Tage. München, 1953.

Phil 3640.404   Blunck, R. Friedrich Nietzsche. München, 1953.

Phil 3110.43   Böhme, J. Über die Umkehr und die Einsicht. Wien, 1953.

Phil 1750.179.10   Bollnow, O.F. Deutsche Existenzphilosophie. Bern, 1953.

Phil 4070.5.30   Boni, Guido. L'essere nella spontaneità creativa e nella riffessione razionale. Roma, 1953.

Phil 176.180   Bosco, Giovanni. Ricerche filosofiche. Napoli, 1953.

Phil 7082.196   Boss, Medard. Des Traum und seine Auslegung. Bern, 1953.

Phil 5635.40   Boulogne, C.D. My friends. N.Y., 1953.

Phil 5211.1.5   Brett, G.S. History of psychology. London, 1953.

Phil 1905.22.10.2A   Broad, C.D. Religion, philosophy and physical research. London, 1953.

Phil 1905.22.10   Broad, C.D. Religion, philosophy and physical research. N.Y., 1953.

Phil 86.6   Brugger, Walter. Philosophisches Wörterbuch. 5. Aufl. Freiburg 1953.

Phil 2805.192.15   Brunschvicg, L. Blaise Pascal. Paris, 1953.

Phil 5425.92   Bryant, J.E. Genius and epilepsy. Concord, Mass., 1953.

Phil 3120.30.75   Buber, Martin. Good and evil. N.Y., 1953.

Phil 3120.30.35   Buber, Martin. Gottesfinsterrns. Zürich, 1953.

Phil 3120.30.62   Buber, Martin. Hin Weise. Zürich, 1953.

Phil 3120.30.53   Buber, Martin. Reden über Erziehung. Heidelberg, 1953.

Phil 9400.16   Buckley, J.C. The retirement handbook. 1st ed. N.Y., 1953.

Phil 3450.19.120   Buddeberg, Else R. Heidegger und die Dichtting. Stuttgart, 1953.

Phil 8656.35   Bulgakov, S.N. Filosofiia imeni. Parizh, 1953.

Phil 5241.97.5   Burrow, Trigant. Science and man's behavior. N.Y., 1953.

Phil 4210.152   Callovini, C. Antonio Rosmini come uomo del risorgimento italiano. Roma, 1953.

Phil 4073.42   Campanella, Tommaso. Della necessita di una filosofia cristiana. Roma, 1953.

Phil 3484.24   Campo, M. La genesi del criticismo kantiano. v.1-2. Varese, 1953-

Phil 4260.129   Caponigri, A.R. Time and idea. London, 1953.

Phil 3484.20   Caracciolo, A. Arti e pensiero nelle laro istanze metafisiche. Roma, 1953.

Phil 8403.37.5   Carbonara, C. Del bello e dell'arte. 2. ed. Napoli, 1953

Phil 5203.12   Carron, René. Guide de l'étudiant en psychologie. Paris, 1953.

Phil 2050.230   Carsi, M. Natura e societá in David Hume. 1. ed. Firenze, 1953.

Phil 2750.11.115   Cassata, M.L. La pedagogia di Jacques Maritain. Palermo, 1953.

Phil 1802.10   Cassirer, E. The platonic renaissance in England. Edinburgh, 1953.

Phil 333.5.12A   Cassirer, Ernst. The philosophy of symbolic forms. New Haven, 1953- 3v.

Phil 333.5.8A   Cassirer, Ernst. Substance and function and Einstein's theory of relativity. N.Y., 1953.

Phil 4340.5   Castro y Rossi, Adolf de. Obras escogidas de filosófos. Madrid, 1953.

Phil 177.112   Chaix-Reys, Jules. Les dimensions de l'être et du temps. Paris, 1953.

Phil 75.44   Chan, Wing-Tsit. An outline and a bibliography of Chinese philosophy. Hanover, N.H., 1953.

Phil 8403.39   Chaudhury, P.J. Studies in comparative aesthetics. Santiniketan, 1953.

Phil 400.110   Cherkashin, P.P. O reaktsionnoi sushchnosti idealizma. Moskva, 1953.

Phil 3850.27.116   Christolles, H. Albert Schweitzer. Stuttgart, 1953.

Phil 802.19   Ciardo, M. Filosofia dell'arte e filosofia come totalità. Bari, 1953.

Phil 4080.3.160.2   Cione, Edmondo. Benedetto Croce. 2. ed. Milano, 1953.

Phil 8430.9   Coculesco, P. Esthétique. Paris, 1953.

Phil 531.4   Cogny, Pierre. Le naturalisme. Paris, 1953.

Phil 930.42   Creel, H.G. Chinese thought from Confucuis to Mao Tse-tung. Chicago, 1953.

Phil 4080.3.42   Croce, Benedetto. Aesthetic as science of expression and general linguistic. N.Y., 1953.

Phil 2475.1.306   Cuisa, Niso. Inchiesta sul Bergsonismo. Sassari, 1953.

Phil 3195.14.40   Dacqué, Edgar. Das verlorene Paradies. 4. Aufl. München, 1953.

Phil 310.13   Danilenko, D.I. Marksistskii filosofskii materializm. Moskva, 1953.

Phil 2045.124   Davy, G. Thomas Hobbes et Jean-Jacques Rousseau. Oxford, 1953.

Phil 6313.15   De Mille, A. Introduction to scientology. 2d ed. Los Angeles, 1953.

Phil 2805.290   Demorest, Jean. Dans Pascal. Paris, 1953.

1953 - cont.

Phil 2520.78.35   Descartes, René. Correspondance avec Armaud et Marus. Paris, 1953.

Phil 1955.6.45   Dewey, John. Essays in experimental logic. N.Y., 1953.

Phil 2530.20   Diderot, Denis. Selected philosophical writings. Cambridge, Eng., 1953.

Phil 3640.500   Diem, Gudrun. Das Wesen der Kunst im Denken Nietzsches. Schorndorf, 1953.

Phil 334.14   Dooyeweerd, Herman. A new critique of theoretical thought. Amsterdam, 1953-58. 4v.

Phil 6113.30   Doran, F.S.A. Mind, a social phenomenon. N.Y., 1953.

Phil 8693.25   Dubarle, D. Humanisme scientifique et raison chrétienne. Paris, 1953.

Phil 1870.134   Dublin. University. Trinity College. Library. Catalogue of manuscripts. Dublin, 1953.

Phil 2805.282   Ducas, A. Discours sur les passions de l'amour de Pascal. Alger, 1953.

Phil 8404.4   Dufrenne, Michel. Phénoménologie de l'expérience esthétique. Paris, 1953.

Phil 1955.9.30   Dunham, B. Giant in chains. 1st ed. Boston, 1953.

Phil 1750.510   Dutt, K. Guru. Existentialism. Basavagundi, 1953.

Phil 6114.15   Eccles, J.C. The neurophysiological basis of mind. Oxford, 1953.

Phil 6114.23   Edwards, Henry James. The evidence for spirit healing. London, 1953.

Phil 5585.130   Ehrenzweig, Anton. The psycho-analysis of artistic vision and hearing. London, 1953.

Phil 4967.10   Elias de Tejada, Francisco. Las doctrinas políticas de Raimundo de Farias Brito. Sevilla, 1953.

Phil 8879.27   Erismann, T. Sein und Wollen. Wien, 1953.

Phil 5204.8.2   Essen, Jac van. Beschrijvend en verklarend woordenboek der psychologie. 2. Druk. Haarlem, 1953.

Phil 2070.35.15   Études Théologiques et Religieuses. Cinquantenaire de la psychologie religieuse de William James. Montpellier, 1953.

Phil 1750.505   Existentialism. London, 1953. 2 pam.

Phil 5590.45.10   Eysenck, Hans Jurgen. The structure of human personality. London, 1953.

Phil 8880.49   Fagathey, Austin. Right and reason. St. Louis, 1953.

Phil 5215.4   Farbstein, Wolf. Romantische Einflüsse in der Geschichte der Psychologie. Zürich, 1953.

Phil 193.49.80   Farré, Luis. Vida y pensamiento de Jorge Santayana. Madrid, 1953.

Phil 4796.96.20   Fath 'Ali Ahmd-zda. Izbrannye filosofskie proizvedeniia. Baku, 1953.

Phil 8430.15   Fazio-Allmayer, V. Moralità dell'arte. Firenze, 1953.

Phil 2750.11.100A   Fecher, C.A. The philosophy of Jacques Maritain. Westminster, 1953.

Phil 4812.196.80   Felber, Stanislav. Ján Bayer, slovenský baconista XVII storočia. Bratislava, 1953.

Phil 6315.16.8   Fenichel, Otto. Collected papers. N.Y., 1953-54. 2v.

Phil 9560.14.10   Fiore di Virtù. The Florentine Fior di virtù of 1491. Philadelphia, 1953.

Phil 5520.100.10   Flew, A.G.N. Logic and language. 2. ser. Oxford, 1953.

Phil 7084.2   Fliess, Robert. The revival of interest in the dream. N.Y., 1953.

Phil 3425.362   Flügge, J. Die sittlichen Grundlagen des Denkens. Hamburg, 1953.

Phil 5045.16.2   Fogarasi, Béla. Logika. 2. kiadás. Budapest, 1953.

Phil 6319.1.188   Fordham, F. An introduction to Jung's psychology. London, 1953.

Phil 8406.4.5   Formaggio, Dino. L'arte come comunicazione. Milano, 1953.

Phil 4080.3.235   Franchini, R. Note biografiche di Benedetto Croce. Torino, 1953.

Phil 960.169   Frauwallner, E. Geschichte der indischen Philosophie. Salzburg, 1953. 2v.

Phil 6315.2.113.2   Freud, Sigmund. Civilisation. London, 1953.

Phil 6315.2.79.15   Freud, Sigmund. On aphasia. London, 1953.

Phil 6315.2.3.10A   Freud, Sigmund. The standard edition of the complete psychological works. v.1-20,22-23. London, 1953-64. 22v.

Phil 5625.75.95   Frolov, I.P. Ivan Petrovich Pavlov. 2. izd. Moskva, 1953.

Phil 575.151A   Frondizi, R. The nature of the self. New Haven, 1953.

Phil 930.29.8   Fung, Yu-lan. A history of Chinese philosophy. Princeton, 1953. 2v.

Phil 5592.20   Furrer, Walter. Die Farbe in des Persönlichkeitsdiagnostik. Basel, 1953.

Phil 3425.364   Fusch, Carl-Ludwig. Der Bildungsbegriff des Jungen Hegel. Weinheim, 1953.

Phil 1750.378   Galamini, L. Esistenza e coesistenza. Milano, 1953.

Phil 337.16   Garaudy, R. La théorie matérialiste de la connaissance. 1. ed. Paris, 1953.

Phil 4006.6.30   Garilli, G. La crisi dell'immanentismo. Palermo, 1953.

Phil 8881.75   Garvin, Lucius. A modern introduction to ethics. Boston, 1953.

Phil 3488.28   Giorgiantonio, M. Kant e la critica del nostro tiempo. Napoli, 1953.

Phil 4688.110.32   Girnius, Juozas. Laisve ir būtist. Brooklyn, 1953.

Phil 1200.55   Goldschmidt, V.E. Le système stoïcien et l'idée de temps. Paris, 1953.

Phil 3310.14   Gomperz, H. Philosophical studies. Boston, 1953.

Phil 5590.115A   Greenacre, P. Trauma, growth and personality. London, 1953.

Phil 3425.734   Grégoire, Franz. L'attitude Hégélienne devant l'existence. Louvain, 1953.

Phil 1135.167   Grilli, A. Il problema della vita contemplativa nel mondo greco-romano. 1. ed. Milano, 1953.

Phil 1111.6   Groningen, B.A. In the grip of the past. Leiden, 1953.

Phil 3552.346.2   Grua, Gaston. Jurisprudence universelle et théodicée selon Leibniz. Thèse. Paris, 1953.

Phil 5246.60   Gruhle, H.W. Verstehen und Einfühlen. Berlin, 1953.

Phil 3475.3.120   Grunert, P.L. Objektive Norm. Inaug. Diss. Bonn, 1953.

Phil 2630.7.30   Guénon, René. The reign of quantity and the signs of the times. London, 1953.

Phil 2520.242   Gueroult, Martial. Descartes, selon l'ordre des raisons. Paris, 1953. 2v.

Phil 181.114   Gusdorf, G. Mythe et métaphysique. Paris, 1953.

Phil 1111.12.5   Guthrie, William. Greek philosophy. Cambridge, Eng., 1953.

Phil 4080.3.250   Guzzo, A. Croce e Gentile. Lugano, 1953.

Phil 4006.7.30A   Guzzo, D. Gli hegeliani d'Italia. Torino, 1953.

Phil 8408.10   Haecker, T. Schönheit; ein Versuch. 3. Aufl. München, 1953.

Phil 4582.4.45   Hägerström, Axel. Inquiries into the nature of law and morals. Stockholm, 1953.

Phil 7082.72.20   Hall, Calvin Springer. The meaning of dreams. N.Y., 1953.

Phil 8408.18   Hartmann, N. Asthetik. Berlin, 1953.

662

Chronological Listing

1953 - cont.

Phil 2055.9.30 Hartshorne, Charles. Reality as social process. Glencoe, Ill., 1953.

Phil 2477.6.108 Hayen, A. Bibliographie blondelienne. Bruxelles, 1953.

Phil 6317.18.2 Healy, William. The structure and meaning of psychoanalysis as related to personality and behavior. N.Y., 1953.

Phil 3425.20 Hegel, Georg Wilhelm Friedrich. The philosophy of Hegel. N.Y., 1953.

Phil 3425.40.30 Hegel, Georg Wilhelm Friedrich. Reason in history. N.Y., 1953.

Phil 182.93.10 Heidegger, M. Einführung in die Metaphysik. Tübingen, 1953.

Phil 3450.19.50 Heidegger, Martin. Der Feldweg. Frankfurt, 1953.

Phil 3450.19.30 Heidegger, Martin. Sein und Zeit. 7e Aufl. Tübingen, 1953.

Phil 8697.18 Heim, Karl. The transformation of the scientific world view. N.Y., 1953.

Phil 1750.365 Heinemann, Fritz. Existentialism and the modern predicament. London, 1953.

Phil 1870.128 Hermathena. Homage to George Berkeley. Dublin, 1953.

Phil 1750.41 Herzberg, Günther. Die grosse Kontroverse. Meisenheim, 1953.

Phil 8957.12 Hildebrand, D. von. Christian ethics. N.Y., 1953.

Phil 3450.33 Hildebrand, D. von. The new tower of Babel. N.Y., 1953.

Phil 3552.338 Hildebrandt, Kurt. Leibniz und das Reich der Gnade. Haag, 1953.

Phil 8587.69 Hodges, H.A. Languages, standpoints, attitudes. London, 1953.

Phil 4987.89.80 Homenaje a Xavier Zubiri. Madrid, 1953.

Phil 1750.367 Hommes, Jakob. Zwiespältiges Dosein. Freiburg, 1953.

Phil 1750.166.95 Hulst, H.C von. Phänomenologie en natuurwetenschap. Utrecht, 1953.

Phil 807.19 Humbert, Pierre. Philosophes et savantes. Paris, 1953.

Phil 2050.59.40 Hume, David. Political essays. N.Y., 1953.

Phil 3425.319.10 Hyppolite, Jean. Logique et existence. 1. ed. Paris, 1953.

Phil 4759.1.40 Il'in, I.A. Aksiomy religioznago opyta. Paris, 1953.

Phil 4073.102 Jacabelli Isaldi, A.M. Tomaso Campanella. Milano, 1953.

Phil 340.7 Jacques, E. Introduction au problème de la connaissance. Louvain, 1953.

Phil 1114.10 Jaeger, Werner W. Die Theologie der Frühen griechischen Denker. Stuttgart, 1953.

Phil 2070.25.7 James, William. The philosophy of William James, selected from his chief works. N.Y., 1953.

Phil 5249.26 Jeffrey, Melville. Beyond sense perception. 1. ed. Los Angeles, 1953.

Phil 184.42 Johnson, R.C. The imprisoned splendour. London, 1953.

Phil 2725.11.90 Jolivet, Régis. De Rosmini à Lachelier. Paris, 1953.

Phil 6315.2.150A Jones, Ernest. The life and work of Sigmund Freud. 1st ed. N.Y., 1953. 3v.

Phil 6319.1.5.7A Jung, C.G. Collected works. v.1,3-5,7-9,11-17. N.Y., 1953-63. 14v.

Phil 6319.1.5.8 Jung, C.G. Collected works. v.1,3-17. London, 1953-63. 15v.

Phil 5249.13.27 Jung, Carl G. Psychological reflections. N.Y., 1953.

Phil 5525.43 Kalina, J. Bojové poslanie humoru a satiry. Bratislava, 1953.

Phil 8411.24 Kaloshin, F.I. Soderzhanie odforma v proizvedeniiakh iskusstva. Leningrad, 1953.

Phil 3480.22.2 Kant, Immanuel. Deines Lebens Sinn. 2. Aufl. Wien, 1953.

Phil 3480.58.22 Kant, Immanuel. Prolegomena to any future metaphysics. Manchester, Eng., 1953.

Phil 3475.3.115 Karl Jaspers zum siebzigsten Geburtslag. Bern, 1953.

Phil 6327.4.80 Karpf, Jay B. The psychology and psychotherapy of Otto Rank. N.Y., 1953.

Phil 9070.56 Kates, J.W. The use of life. 1st ed. N.Y., 1953.

Phil 185.68 Kattsoff, L.O. Elements of philosophy. N.Y., 1953.

Phil 5250.37.20 Katz, David. Studien zur experimentellen Psychologie. Basel, 1953.

Phil 185.67 Klubertanz, G.P. The philosophy of human nature. N.Y., 1953.

Phil 5590.105 Kluckhohn, Clyde. Personality in nature. 2. ed. N.Y., 1953.

Phil 310.495 Kolianskii, N.N. Mir i dusha. Frankfurt am Main? 1953.

Phil 8672.19 Kostenne, P. La foi des athées. Paris, 1953.

Phil 8411.29A Kris, Ernst. Psychoanalytic exploration in art. London, 1953.

Phil 978.59.55 Krishnamurti, J. Education and the significance of life. N.Y., 1953.

Phil 810.9 Kropp, Gerhard. Von Lao-Tse zu Sartre. Berlin, 1953.

Phil 5643.89.80 Krudewig, M. Die Lehren von der visuelfen Wahrnehmung und Vorstellung. Meisenheim, 1953.

Phil 5250.13.25 Krueger, Felix. Zur Philosophie und Psychologie der Ganzheit. Berlin, 1953.

Phil 1750.166.80 Krueger, Gerhard. Abendländische Humanität. Stuttgart, 1953.

Phil 185.66 Krueger, H. Zwischen Dekadenz und Erneuerung. Frankfurt, 1953.

Phil 341.18 Kurth, R. Vonden Grenzen des Wissens. München, 1953.

Phil 1750.166.85 Laloup, Jean. Hommes et machines. Tournai, 1953.

Phil 270.61A Landau, M.A. Ul'mskaia noch': filosofi slucnaia. N'iu Iork, 1953.

Phil 5066.52.2 Langer, S.K.K. An introduction to symbolic logic. 2nd ed. N.Y., 1953.

Phil 8412.40 Langer, Susanne Katherina Knauth. Feeling and form; a theory of art developed from philosophy in a new key. N.Y., 1953.

Phil 2120.9.30 Laucks, I.F. A speculation in reality. N.Y., 1953.

Phil 978.49.805.5 Lauer, H.E. Die zwölf Sumie des Menschen. Basel, 1953.

Phil 1905.22.80 Lean, Martin. Sense - perception and matter. London, 1953.

Phil 8412.32 Lechner, R. The aesthetic experience. Chicago, 1953.

Phil 5465.180 Lehman, Harvey Christian. Age and achievement. Princeton, 1953.

Phil 3552.51.7 Leibniz, Gottfried Wilhelm. Discourse on metaphysics. Manchester, 1953.

Phil 3493.25 Leni di Spadafora, F. Kant nel realismo. Paris, 1953.

Phil 4060.2.38 Leo Hebraeus. Diálogos de amor. 1. ed. Romano, 1953.

Phil 1750.375 Lepp, Ignace. La philosophie Chrêtiennie de l'existance. Paris, 1953.

Phil 2050.229 Leroy, A.L. David Hume. 1. éd. Paris, 1953.

Phil 4080.3.255 Letterature Moderne. Benedetto Croce. Milano, 1953.

Phil 2520.230.20 Lewis, G. René Descartes. Paris, 1953.

Phil 6321.35 Lindner, R.M. Prescription for rebellion. London, 1953.

Phil 3425.346 Litt, Theodor. Hegel. Heidelberg, 1953.

Phil 2115.69 Locke, J. Locke's travels in France. Cambridge, 1953.

1953 - cont.

Phil 7084.40 Loehrich, Rolf Rudolf. Oneirics and psychosomatics. McHenry, Ill., 1953.

Phil 6321.30.5 Loewenstein, R. Drives, affects, behavior. N.Y., 1953.

Phil 3640.410 Lotz, J.B. Zwischen Seligkeit und Verdamnis. Frankfurt, 1953.

Phil 3450.19.118A Lowith, Carl. Heidegger. Frankfurt, 1953.

Phil 8080.14 Ludács, G. Adalékok az estétika történetehez. Budapest, 1953.

Phil 187.145 MacCallum, Reid. Initiation and design, and other essays. Toronto, 1953.

Phil 5548.5A McClelland, D.C. The achievement nature. N.Y., 1953.

Phil 5222.7 Mace, C.A. Current trends in British psychology. London, 1953.

Phil 5520.114 Madinier, G. Conscience et signification. 1. éd. Paris, 1953.

Phil 7072.10 Mahony, Patrick. Unsought visitors; a book of visitations. v.1-2. N.Y., 1953. 2v.

Phil 5252.74.5 Malgand, W. Devant la réalité. 1. éd. Paris, 1953.

Phil 4872.187.30 Mallik, Basanta Kumar. The towering wave. London, 1953.

Phil 4070.6.80 Marchello, G. Felice Battaglia. Torino, 1953.

Phil 9430.35 Marcuse, L. Pessimismus. Hamburg, 1953.

Phil 2475.1.305 Marietti, A. Les formes du mouvement chez Bergson. Le Puy, 1953.

Phil 2750.11.70 Maritain, Jacques. The range of reason. London, 1953.

Phil 1200.53 Martinozzoli, F. Parataxeis. 1st ed. Firenze, 1953.

Phil 3801.560 Massolo, Arturo. Il primo Schelling. Firenze, 1953.

Phil 293.25.5 Matisse, G. L'incohérence universelle. 1. éd. Paris, 1953.

Phil 7054.23.3 Mattison, H. Spirit rapping unveiled. N.Y., 1953.

Phil 5252.95A May, Rollo. Man's search for himself. N.Y., 1953.

Phil 8887.90 Mayer, Charles L. La morale de l'avenir. Paris, 1953.

Phil 6322.33 Mayer, Felix. Dynamische Tiefenspsychologie. Bern, 1953.

Phil 1712.18 Mehl, Roger. Images de l'homme. Genève, 1953.

Phil 22.42.5 Mekarski, S. Myśl filozoficzna Romunristow w Polsce. Londyn, 1953.

Phil 8050.74 Melchers, H. Von Kunst und Künstlern. München, 1953.

Phil 293.27 Melsen, A.G.M. van. The philosophy of nature. Pittsburg, 1953.

Phil 1170.11 Merlan, Philip. From Platonism to Neoplatonism. The Hague, 1953.

Phil 2750.20.10 Merleau-Ponty, Maurice. Eloge de la philosophie. Paris, 1953.

Phil 3450.19.125 Meulen, J.A. van der. Heidegger und Hegel. Groningen, 1953.

Phil 2138.50.20 Mill, John S. Utilitarianism. N.Y., 1953.

Phil 5252.78.5 Miller, N.E. Social learning and imitation. New Haven, 1953.

Phil 4974.50.2 Molina, Enrique. Tragedia y realización del espíritu. 2. ed. Santiago, 1953.

Phil 2150.18.30 Moore, George Edward. Some main problems of philosophy. London, 1953.

Phil 293.28 Morin, J.A. The serpent and the satellite. N.Y., 1953.

Phil 6122.68 Moser, Ulrich. Psychologie der Arbeitswahl und der Arheitsstörungen. Bern, 1953.

Phil 8592.81 Mouroux, Jean. Sens chrétien de l'homme. Paris, 1953.

Phil 6990.50 Mousset, Albert. L'étrange histoire des convulsionnaires de Saint-Medard. Paris, 1953.

Phil 187.149.5 Mueller, G.E. Dialectic; a way into and within philosophy. N.Y., 1953.

Phil 3625.4.30 Müller, J. Vom Gebeimnis des Lebens. Stuttgart, 1953. 3v.

Phil 293.29 Mugler, Charles. Deux thèmes de la cosmologie grecque. Paris, 1953.

Phil 4080.3.385 Murray, G. Benedetto Croce. London, 1953.

Phil 5520.170 Naess, Arne. Interpretation and preciseness. Oslo, 1953.

Phil 1135.177 Napoli, G. La concezione dell'essere nella filosofia. Milano, 1953.

Phil 8430.38 Nebel, G. Das Eregignis es Schönen. Stuttgart, 1953.

Phil 8414.10 Nédoncelle, M. Introduction à l'esthétique. Paris, 1953.

Phil 1713.2 Nicholl, Donald. Recent thought in focus. N.Y., 1953.

Phil 2175.5.30 Nicoll, Maurice. Living time and the integration of the life. London, 1953.

Phil 3640.77.15.12 Nietzsche, Friedrich. My sister and I. N.Y., 1953.

Phil 188.18.5 Nohl, H. Einführung in die Philosophie. 5. Aufl. Frankfurt, 1953.

Phil 3665.6.30 Noll, Baldwin. Philosophie und Politik. Bonn, 1953.

Phil 5535.28 Nuttin, Jozef. Tâche réussite et échec. Louvain, 1953.

Phil 5223.5 Nuttin, Jozef. Tôche relussité et échec. Bruxelles, 1953.

Phil 8963.5 Nygren, A. Agape and Eros. London, 1953.

Phil 6324.4 Oberndorf, Clarence. A history of psychoanalysis in America. N.Y., 1953.

Phil 2496.79.10 Ody, Hermann. Victor Cousin. Saarbrücken, 1953.

Phil 5520.35.9 Ogden, Charles K. The meaning of meaning. 8. ed. N.Y., 1953.

Phil 165.75 Ohio State University, Columbus. Department of Philosophy. Perspectives in philosophy. Columbus, 1953.

Phil 260.14 Okál, M. Grécki atomisti a epikuros. Bratislava, 1953.

Phil 4080.3.240 Olgiati, F. Benedetto Croce e lo storicismo. Milano, 1953.

Phil 1119.5 Olgiati, F. I fondamenti della filosofia classica. 2. ed. Milano, 1953.

Phil 4080.3.330 Omaggio a Benedetto Croce. Torino, 1953.

Phil 4075.85 Ore, Oystein. Cardano, the gambling scholar. Princeton, 1953.

Phil 5465.59 Osborn, A.F. Applied imagination. N.Y., 1953.

Phil 8415.4 Osborne, H. Theory of beauty; an introduction to aesthetics. N.Y., 1953.

Phil 4060.8.83 Paggiaro, L. La filosofia di Francesco Acri. Padova, 1953.

Phil 7150.35 Palazzo, D. Il suicidio sotto l'aspetto fisiopatologico. Napoli, 1953.

Phil 2880.8.120 Palumbo, Giovanni. La filosofia esistenziale di Jean Paul Sartre. Palermo, 1953.

Phil 4845.227.32 Papanoutsos, Euangelos. Ho kosmos toū pneumatos. 2. ed. Athēna, 1953-56. 3v.

Phil 1815.5 Paul, L.A. The English philosophers. London, 1953.

Phil 310.5 Pavlov, T. Ravnosmetka na edna idealistko reaktsionii filosofiia. Sofiia, 1953.

Phil 4824.676.30 Pavlov, Todor Dimitrov. Izkustvoiživot. Sofiia, 1953.

Phil 2225.5.27 Peirce, C.S. Letters to Lady Welby. Photoreproduction. New Haven, 1953.

Phil 8705.16 Pensée scientifique et foi chrétienne. Paris, 1953.

Phil 1195.15 Periphanakes, K. Les sophistes et le droit. Athènes, 1953.

Phil 5593.53 Phillips, L. Rorschach interpretation. N.Y., 1953.

Chronological Listing

1953 - cont.

Phil 5066.36.15	Piaget, Jean. Logic and psychology. Manchester, Eng., 1953.
Phil 9450.26	Pieper, J. Über del Gerechtigkeit. München, 1953.
Phil 8965.13.5	Pieper, Josef. Über die Gerechtigkeit. 1. Aufl. München, 1953.
Phil 5414.15A	Piers, Gerhart. Shame and guilt. Springfield, Ill., 1953.
Phil 4120.4.50	Piglianu, A. Giovanni Gentile. Sassari, 1953.
Phil 165.22	Piper, K. Olfener Horizont. München, 1953.
Phil 8416.11.22	Plekhanov, Georgii Valentinovich. Art and social life. London, 1953.
Phil 190.82A	Plessner, H. Zwischen Philosophie und Gesellschaft. Bern, 1953.
Phil 2750.11.105	Podellaro, N. Maritain. Brescia, 1953.
Phil 6325.25	Podolsky, Edward. Encyclopedia of aberrations. N.Y., 1953.
Phil 2045.122	Polin, Raymond. Politique et philosophie chez Thomas Hobbes. 1. éd. Paris, 1953.
Phil 190.81	Pontifex, Mark. The meaning of existence. London, 1953.
Phil 6985.20A	Powdermaker, Florence. Group psychotherapy. Cambridge, 1953.
Phil 3552.348	Preti, G. Il cristianesimo universale di G.W. Leibniz. 1. ed. Roma, 1953.
Phil 5520.122	Preti, Giulio. Linguaggia comune e linguaggi scientifici. Roma, 1953.
Phil 645.37	Preyre, A.E. The freedom of doubt. London, 1953.
Phil 5520.111A	Price, H.H. Thinking and experience. Cambridge, Mass., 1953.
Phil 6319.1.197	Progoff, Ira. Jung's psychology and its social meaning. London, 1953.
Phil 8050.63	Propris, A de. Storia degli orientamenti artistici. Roma, 1953.
Phil 8670.18	Przywara, Erich. Was ist Gott; cinc Summula. Nürnberg, 1953.
Phil 5255.53	Psychologie moderne et réflexion chrétienne. Paris, 1953.
Phil 3425.354	Puglisi, F. L'estetica di Hegel e i suoi presupposti teoretici. Padova, 1953.
Phil 4120.4.47	Puglisi, F. La pedagogia di G. Gentile. v.1-2. Catania, 1953-54.
Phil 4080.3.405	Puppo, Mario. Croce critico e prosatore. Torino, 1953.
Phil 8966.2	Quacquarelli, Antonio. Il triplice frutto della vita cristiana. Roma, 1953.
Phil 8417.2	Quadri, G. La vita estetica, e lo sviluppo della coscienza. Firenze, 1953.
Phil 8146.2	Querolgavaldá, M. La escuela estetica catalana contemporanea. Madrid, 1953.
Phil 5066.11.20	Quine, Willard van Orman. From a logical point of view. Cambridge, Mass., 1953.
Phil 5056.1.22	Quine, Willard Van Orman. Methods of logic. N.Y., 1953.
Phil 2475.1.370	Quintanilla, Louis. Bergonismo y política. 1. ed. México, 1953.
Phil 960.168.2A	Raju, P.T. Idealistic thought of India. Cambridge, Mass., 1953.
Phil 960.168	Raju, P.T. Idealistic thought of India. London, 1953.
Phil 5520.115	Rapoport, A. Operational philosophy. 1. ed. N.Y., 1953.
Phil 1830.12	Ratner, Sidney. Vision and action. New Brunswick, N.J., 1953.
Phil 8707.21.5A	Raven, C.E. Natural religion and Christian theology. Cambridge, Eng., 1953. 2v.
Phil 6327.21.20	Reich, Wilhelm. The murder of Christ: the emotional plague of mankind. N.Y., 1953.
Phil 6327.21.26	Reich, Wilhelm. Wilhelm Reich, biographical material. v.1. Rangeley, Me., 1953-
Phil 6327.21.25	Reich, Wilhelm. Wilhelm Reich, biographical material. v.2. Rangeley, Me., 1953-
Phil 3790.16.30	Reidemeister, Kurt. Geist und Wirklichkeit. Berlin, 1953.
Phil 6327.12.45	Reik, Theodor. The secret self. N.Y., 1953.
Phil 1540.32	Renucci, P. L'aventure de l'humanisme européen au moyen-âge. Clermont-Ferrand, 1953.
Phil 7069.53	Rhine, Joseph B. New world of the mind. N.Y., 1953.
Phil 192.94	Rideau, E. Paganisme ou christianisme. Tournai, 1953.
Phil 5425.88	Roe, Anne. The making of a scientist. N.Y., 1953.
Phil 1750.366	Rognoni, L. L'espressionismo. Torino, 1953.
Phil 4210.57	Rosmini-Serbati, Antonio. Gnoseologia. Messina, 1953.
Phil 5066.50.5	Rosser, J.B. Logic for mathematicians. N.Y., 1953.
Phil 1850.147	Rossi, Paolo. L'interpretazione baconiana delle janole antiche. Roma, 1953.
Phil 2150.17.90	Rossi-Landi, Ferruccio. Charles Morris. 1st ed. Roma, 1953.
Phil 2255.1.76	Russell, Bertrand Russell. The good citizen's alphabet. London, 1953.
Phil 8708.27	Sabine, P.E. Atoms, men and God. N.Y., 1953.
Phil 4080.3.230	Sainati, V. L'estetica di Benedetto Croce. Firenze, 1953.
Phil 8673.18	Saitta, G. Il problema di Dio e la filosofia della immanenza. Bologna, 1953.
Phil 9240.12	Salmon, E.G. The good in existential metaphysics. Milwaukee, 1953.
Phil 3450.18.110	Samuel, O. A foundation of ontology. N.Y., 1953.
Phil 2280.5.25	Santayana, George. The philosophy of Santayana. N.Y., 1953.
Phil 2880.8.60	Sartre, Jean Paul. Existential psychoanalysis. N.Y., 1953.
Phil 5258.124.5	Schilder, Paul. Medical psychology. N.Y., 1953.
Phil 3425.366	Schlawin, H. Die Dialektik im System Hegels. Inaug. Diss. Bern, 1953.
Phil 3475.3.125	Schmidhauser, N. Allgemeine Wahrheit und existentielle Wahrheit. Bonn, 1953.
Phil 1718.27	Schneider, F. Philosophie der Gegenwart. München, 1953.
Phil 6328.34	Schnetze-Niemann, M. Schöpferische Gestaltung aus dem Unbewussten. München, 1953.
Phil 3850.40	Schnitzler, Otto. Von der Feststellung. Bonn, 1953.
Phil 8598.110.25	Schuon, Frithjof. Transcendent unity of religions. N.Y., 1953.
Phil 4018.7	Sciacca, M.F. La philosophie italienne contemporaine. Lyon, 1953.
Phil 493.6	Seely, Charles Sherlock. Philosophy and the ideological conflict. N.Y., 1953.
Phil 4080.17.15	Semerari, G. Storia e storicismo. Trani, 1953.
Phil 2630.7.95	Sérant, Paul. René Guenon. Paris, 1953.
Phil 4710.84	Shchipanov, I.Ia. Russkaia materialisticheskaia filosofiia XVIII-IX vekov i ee istoricheskoe znachenie. Moskva, 1953.
Phil 7082.150	Siebenthal, Walter von. Die Wissenschaft vom Traum, Ergebnisse und Probleme. Berlin, 1953.
Phil 585.5	Siegmund, Georg. Der Mensch in seinem Dasein. Freiburg, 1953.
Phil 5421.10.10	Silva-Tarouca, Amadeo. Die Logik der Angst. Innsbrucke, 1953.

1953 - cont.

Phil 8708.26	Sinnott, Edmund Ware. Two roads to truth. N.Y., 1953.
Phil 5258.120.10	Skinner, Burrhus F. Science and human behavior. N.Y., 1953.
Phil 3450.19.170	Soler Grimma, Francisco. El origen de la obra de arte y la verdad en Heidegger. Bogota, 1953.
Phil 4769.1.81	Solov'ev, V.S. La grande controverse et la politique chrétienne. Paris, 1953.
Phil 4769.1.40	Solov'ev, V.S. Werke. v.2,3,6,7. Freiburg, 1953. 4v.
Phil 6060.40.5	Sonnemann, Ulrich. Handwriting analysis. N.Y., 1953.
Phil 6680.1.30	Sopp, Erich. Auf den Spuren der Seheim. Sersheim, 1953.
Phil 3665.5.95	Specht, Minna. Leonard Nelson zum Gedächtnis. Frankfurt, 1953.
Phil 6315.2.148	Spehlmann, Rainer. Sigmund Freuds neurologische Schriften. Berlin, 1953.
Phil 1750.353.5	Spier, J.M. Christianity and existentialism. Philadelphia, 1953.
Phil 3819.33.15	Spinoza, Benedictus de. Éthique démontrée suivant l'ordre géométrique et divisée en cinq parties. v.1-2. Paris, 1953.
Phil 818.28	Staerig, H.J. Kleine Weltgeschichte der Philosophie. 3. Aufl. Stuttgart, 1953.
Phil 1750.385	Staritz, Ekkehart. Vom Schein zum Sein. Bonn, 1953.
Phil 1123.12	Stefanini, L. Il preimoginisimo dei Greci. Padova, 1953.
Phil 193.167	Steinberg, W. Grundfragen des menschlichen Seins. München, 1953.
Phil 1540.34	Steinbueckel, T. Vom Menschenbild des christlichen Mittelalters. Basel, 1953.
Phil 978.49.245	Steiner, R. Der materialistische Erkenntnisimpuls und seine Bedeutung für die ganze Menscheitsentwicklung. Basel, 1953.
Phil 3500.73	Stemberger, R. Immanuel Kant als Philosoph und Soziologe. Wien, 1953.
Phil 2880.8.116	Stern, Alfred. Sartre. N.Y., 1953.
Phil 5627.210	Strauss, H.A. Psychologie und astrologische Symbolis. Zürich, 1953.
Phil 8419.25	Streignart, Joseph. Trente-trois oeuvres d'art. v.1-2. Gembloux, 1953?
Phil 3450.33.15	Stroeker, E. Zahl und Raum. Bonn, 1953.
Phil 6980.712	Sullivan, Harry Stack. The interpersonal theory of psychiatry. 1. ed. N.Y., 1953. 4v.
Phil 5274.14	Symposium on Psychological Factor Analysis, Uppsala University, 1953. Uppsala symposium on psychological factor analysis, 17-19 March 1953. Copenhagen, 1953.
Phil 5059.21	Tavanets, P.V. Suzhdenie i ego vidy. Moskva, 1953.
Phil 8709.20	Taylor, F.S. Man and matter. N.Y., 1953?
Phil 2225.5.98.5	Thompson, M.H. The pragmatic philosophy of C.S. Peirce. Chicago, 1953.
Phil 1930.8.95	Tomlin, E.W.F. Robin George Collingwood, 1889-1943. London, 1953.
Phil 4019.10	Tozzi, Antonio. L'eredità del neo-idealismo italiana. Firenze, 1953.
Phil 2750.13.95	Troisfontaines, R. De l'existence à l'être. Namur, 1953. 2v.
Phil 6990.3.70	Trouch, F. Sainte Bernadette Soubirous. Lyon, 1953.
Phil 3890.9.85	Troxler, I.P.V. Der Briefwechsel zwischen Ignoz Paul Vital Troxler. Aran, 1953.
Phil 7069.42.12	Tyrrell, George N.M. Apparitions. London, 1953.
Phil 8980.5	Über Kommunistische Moral. Berlin, 1953.
Phil 301.5	Uexkuell, T. von. Der Mensch und die Natur. Bern, 1953.
Phil 6980.760	United States. Children's Bureau. Residential treatment centers for emotional disturbed children. Washington, 1953.
Phil 5545.186	United States Research and Development Board. Symposium on psychology of learning basic to military training problems. Washington, 1953.
Phil 5548.15	United States Research and Development Board. Committee on Human Resources. Symposium on motivation. Washington, 1953.
Phil 195.5	Urmeneta, F. de. Nuevos ensayos de critica filosofica. Barcelona, 1953.
Phil 8421.4	Ushenko, A.P. Dynamics of art. Indiana, 1953.
Phil 1750.35	Vancourt, R. La phénoménologie et la foi. Tournai, 1953.
Phil 196.32	Vancourt, R. La philosophie et sa structure. v.1,3. Paris, 1953. 2v.
Phil 8971.2	Vann, Gerald. The water and the fire. London, 1953.
Phil 352.9	Varga, A. von. Einführung in die Erkenntnislehre. München, 1953.
Phil 2520.239	Vartanian, A. Diderot and Descartes. Princeton, 1953.
Phil 4983.1.32	Vaz Ferreira, Carlos. Fermentario. Montevideo, 1953.
Phil 6331.7	Viard, Marcel. Le noeu suprême de Socrate. Paris, 1953.
Phil 4260.16	Vico, G.B. Opere. Milano, 1953.
Phil 5525.52	Victoroff, D. Le rire et le risible. 1. éd. Paris, 1953.
Phil 2150.15.90	Victoroff, David. G.H. Mead, sociologue et philosophe. 1. ed. Paris, 1953.
Phil 4265.1.40	Vivante, Leone. Elementi di una filosofia della potenzialità. Firenze, 1953.
Phil 8400.30A	Vivas, Eliseo. The problems of aesthetics. N.Y., 1953.
Phil 978.64.5	Wachsmuth, G. Werdegang der Menschheit. Dornach, 1953.
Phil 3450.19.96.12	Waelhens, A. de. Chemins et impusses de l'ontologie Heideggerienne. Louvain, 1953.
Phil 3450.11.145	Waelhens, A. de. Phénoménologie et vérité. Paris, 1953.
Phil 8870.16	Wagner, J. Was soll ich tun? Braunschweig, 1953.
Phil 197.72	Wahl, J.A. Traité de métaphysique. Paris, 1953.
Phil 3450.18.123	Wahl, Jean André. La structure du monde réel d'apres Nicolai Hartmann. Paris, 1953.
Phil 930.38.5	Waley, Arthur. Three ways of thought in ancient China. London, 1953.
Phil 1870.126	Warmock, G.J. Berkeley. London, 1953.
Phil 1127.6	Weil, S. La source grecque. Paris, 1953.
Phil 845.2	Weinstock, Heinrich. Die Trajödie des Humanismus. Heidelberg, 1953.
Phil 6692.10	Weitzenhoffer, André M. Hypnotism. N.Y., 1953.
Phil 5250.13.87	Wellek, Albert. Das Problem des seeleschen Seins. 2. Aufl. Meisenheim, 1953.
Phil 5262.32.5	Werner, Heinz. Einführung in die Entwicklungspsychologie. 3. Aufl. München, 1953.
Phil 822.1.30	West, H.F. Rebel thought. Boston, 1953.
Phil 3640.442	Weyland, M. Una nueva imagen del hombre a través de Nietzsche y Freud. Buenos Aires, 1953.
Phil 2340.10.25	Whitehead, Alfred North. Alfred North Whitehead; an anthology. N.Y., 1953.
Phil 7080.53	Wiedemann, Fritz. Müde Menschen. Heidenheim, 1953.
Phil 1870.125A	Wisdom, J.O. The unconscious origin of Berkeley's philosophy. London, 1953.
Phil 9540.2	Wise, J.W. From bigotry to brotherhood. N.Y., 1953?

1953 - cont.

Phil 3640.406 | Wiser, Edwin. Nietzsche als Prophet und das Geheimnis des Übermenschen. Affaltern, 1953.

Phil 3925.16.2 | Wittgenstein, Ludwig. Philosophical investigations. N.Y., 1953.

Phil 3925.16 | Wittgenstein, Ludwig. Philosophical investigations. Oxford, 1953.

Phil 600.52 | Wojénski, T. Publicystyka okvesu pozytywizmu. Wrocław, 1953.

Phil 4957.50 | Zea, Leopoldo. América como conciencia. México, 1953.

Phil 4959.230.2 | Zea, Leopoldo. El positivismo en México. 2. ed. México, 1953.

Phil 4710.85.5 | Zen'kovskii, V.V. A history of Russian philosophy. N.Y., 1953. 2v.

Phil 4710.70.15 | Zen'kovskii, V.V. Russian thinkers and Europe. Ann Arbor, 1953.

Phil 4025.1 | Zerella, F. L'eclettisma francese e la cultura filosofica meridionale. 1. ed. Roma, 1953.

Phil 3940.2.30 | Ziegler, L. Spätlese eigener Hand. München, 1953.

1954

Phil 165.60 | A.R. Wadia. Bangalore, 1954.

Phil 5066.28.5 | Ackermann, W. Soluable cases of the decision problem. Amsterdam, 1954.

Phil 5240.45 | Adcock, C.J. Factorial analysis for non-mathematicians. Carlton, 1954.

Phil 4120.4.84 | Aebischer, Max. Der Einzelne und der Staat nachtreibung Giovanni Gentile. Schweiz, 1954.

Phil 310.7 | Akadamiia Nauk SSSR. Institut Filosofii. Dialekticheskii materializm. Moskva, 1954.

Phil 8400.8 | Akademiia Nauk SSSR. Institut Filosofii. Nekotorye voprosy marksistsko-leninskoi estetiki. Moskva, 1954.

Phil 5240.47 | Aktuelle Probleme der Gestalttheorie. Bern, 1954.

Phil 7069.54.20 | Alexander, Rolf. Creative realism. 1. ed. N.Y., 1954.

Phil 7069.54.15 | Amadou, Robert. La parapsychologie. Paris, 1954.

Phil 5593.54.10 | Ames, Louise Bates. Rorschach responses in old age. 1. ed. N.Y., 1954.

Phil 5627.200 | Amstutz, J. Stuxen des Gebets. Bern, 1954.

Phil 165.30 | Analysis. Oxford, England. Philosophy and analysis. N.Y., 1954.

Phil 310.30 | Andreas, Theodor. Zur Widerlegung des dialektische und historische Materialismus. 5. Aufl. n.p., 1954.

Phil 331.10 | Anglès D'Auriac. Essai de philosophie générale. 1. ed. Paris, 1954. 2v.

Phil 8401.12 | Aranio, Ruiz. Umanità dell'arte. Firenze, 1954.

Phil 5590.130 | Arnold, M.B. Human person. N.Y., 1954.

Phil 5040.22.5 | Asmus, V.F. Uchenie logiki o dokazatel'stvi oprovrrzheniia. Moskva, 1954.

Phil 85.10 | Austeda, F. Kleines Worterbuch der Philosophie. Frankfurt, 1954.

Phil 1845.10 | Ayer, Alfred Jules. Philosophical essays. London, 1954.

Phil 6985.25 | Bach, George Robert. Intensive group psychotherapy. N.Y., 1954.

Phil 978.74.45 | Bailey, A.A. (Mrs.). Education in the new age. 1st ed. N.Y., 1954.

Phil 801.34 | Baillot, A.F. La notion d'existence. Paris, 1954.

Phil 3160.9.90 | Bakker, Reinout. Het wijsgerig en psychologisch denken van Carl Gustav Carus in het licht van zijn Godsbeschouwing. Assen, 1954.

Phil 5241.116 | Barrell, Joseph. A philosophical study of the human mind. N.Y., 1954.

Phil 9560.38 | Barrett, E.B. The guest of honour. Dublin, 1954.

Phil 525.241 | Bataille, Georges. L'expérience intérieure. 4. ed. Paris, 1954.

Phil 3095.51.10 | Baumgarten, A.G. Reflections on poetry. Berkeley, 1954.

Phil 332.28 | Bayer, R. Epistémalogie et logique depuis Kant jusqu'a nos jours. 1. ed. Paris, 1954.

Phil 4974.65 | Bazán, Armando. Vida y obra del maestro Enrique Molina. Santiago, 1954.

Phil 4260.130 | Bellofiore, L. La dottrina del diritto naturale in G.B. Vico. Milan, 1954.

Phil 8402.56 | Bense, Max. Asthetica. v.1,2-4. Stuttgart, 1954-2v.

Phil 4752.2.78.2 | Berdiaev, Nikolai Aleksandrovich. Christianity and anti-Semitism. N.Y., 1954.

Phil 2475.1.51.4 | Bergson, Henri. Creative evolution. London, 1954.

Phil 1870.45.6 | Berkeley, G. The dialogues between Hylas and Philonous. N.Y., 1954.

Phil 8612.37 | Berlinger, R. Das Nichts und der Tod. Frankfurt, 1954.

Phil 2477.9.84.2 | Bernard, Claude. Philosophie. Paris, 1954.

Phil 3640.416 | Bindschedler, M.B. Nietzsche und die poetische Lüge. Basel, 1954.

Phil 3195.6.157 | Birand, Kâmiran. Dilthey ve Rickert'te manevi ilimlerin temellendirilmesi. Ankara, 1954.

Phil 8402.58 | Bizzarri, R. Il problema estetico. Brescia, 1954.

Phil 5041.59.5 | Black, Max. Critical thinking. 2nd ed. N.Y., 1954.

Phil 165.13.5A | Black, Max. Problems of analysis. Ithaca, 1954.

Phil 1750.166.35.7 | Blackham, H.J. The human tradition. Boston, 1954.

Phil 176.170 | Blanshard, B. On philosophical style. Bloomington, 1954.

Phil 176.166 | Bloskhurst, J.B. Body, mind and creativity. N.Y., 1954.

Phil 5041.63 | Bochenski, I. Mario. Die zeitgenossischen Denkmethoden. München, 1954.

Phil 3110.45.10 | Böhme, J. Confessions. N.Y., 1954.

Phil 3110.55.25 | Böhme, J. Vom übersinylichen Leben. Hamburg, 1954.

Phil 1511.3.20 | Boehner, Philotheus. Christliche Philosophie von ihren Anfängen bis Nikol von Cues. 3e Aufl. Paderborn, 1954.

Phil 8402.38 | Boldrini, M. Alla ricerca del tempo nell'arte. 1. ed. Milano, 1954.

Phil 978.49.815 | Boos-Hamburger, H. Aus Gesprächen mit Rudolf Steiner. Basel, 1954.

Phil 8120.9 | Bopp, Léon. Philosophie de l'art; ou, Alchimie contre histoire. Paris, 1954.

Phil 5590.165 | Brand, Howard. The study of personality. N.Y., 1954.

Phil 1870.122.5 | Brayton, Alice. George Berkeley in Newport. Newport, R.I., 1954.

Phil 3001.5.3 | Bréhier, Emile. Histoire de la philosophie allemande. 3. ed. Paris, 1954.

Phil 1701.23.3 | Bréhier, Emile. Les thèmes actuels de la philosophie. Paris, 1954.

Phil 3120.8.35 | Brentano, Franz. Religion und Philosophie. Bern, 1954.

Phil 4065.62 | Bruno, Giordano. Des fureurs héroiques. Paris, 1954.

Phil 3120.30.60 | Buber, Martin. Die Schriften über das dialogische Prinzip. Heidelberg, 1954.

Phil 4683.37.30 | Buduls, Hermanis. Cilvēks dzives spoguli. Stockholm, 1954.

1954 - cont.

Phil 4080.3.290 | Buenos Aires. Universidad Nacional. Benedetto Croce. Buenos Aires, 1954.

Phil 176.137.2 | Burke, Kenneth. Permanence and change. 2nd ed. Los Altos, Calif., 1954.

Phil 5400.118 | Burloud, A. Psychologie de la sensibilité. Paris, 1954.

Phil 4080.20.30 | Cairola, G. Scritti. Torino, 1954.

Phil 5066.8.5 | Carnap, Rudolf. Einführung in die symbolische Logik. Wien, 1954.

Phil 5042.21.14.5A | Carnap, Rudolf. The logical syntax of language. London, 1954.

Phil 3484.18.5 | Cassirer, H.W. Kant's first critique. London, 1954.

Phil 4080.12.62 | Castelli, Enrico. Il tempo esaurito. 2. ed. Milano, 1954.

Phil 2250.100A | Catton, J.B. Royce on the human self. Cambridge, 1954.

Phil 5520.68.7 | Chase, Stuart. Power of words. 1. ed. N.Y., 1954.

Phil 8877.82 | Childs, M.W. Ethics in a business society. 1st ed. N.Y., 1954.

Phil 8951.26 | Christian values and economic life. 1st ed. N.Y., 1954.

Phil 1802.10 | Cohen, M.R. American thought. Glencoe, Ill., 1954.

Phil 283.15 | Collin, R. The theory of celestial influence. London, 1954.

Phil 3484.21 | Composto, R. La quarta critica kantiana. Palermo, 1954.

Phil 70.92 | Conference on Science, Philosophy and Religion. Symbols and values; an initial study. N.Y., 1954.

Phil 70.38 | Congresso di Studi Metodologici, Turin, 1952. Atti del congresso di studi metodologici promosso dal centro di studi metodologici. Torino, 1954.

Phil 672.178 | Conrad-Martius, H. Die Zeit. 1. Aufl. München, 1954.

Phil 3425.370 | Contri, Siro. Punti di trascendenza nell'immanentismo hegeliano alla luce della momentalita storiosofica. Milano, 1954.

Phil 310.2.5 | Cornforth, M.C. Historical materialism. N.Y., 1954.

Phil 177.107 | Costello, H.T. A philosophy of the real and the possible. N.Y., 1954.

Phil 8403.45 | Coutinho, Afrânio. Por uma crítica estética. Rio de Janeiro, 1954.

Phil 510.153 | Cramer, Wolfgang. Die Monade. Stuttgart, 1954.

Phil 5465.147 | Crawford, Robert Platt. The techniques of creative thinking. 1. ed. N.Y., 1954.

Phil 1930.15.30 | Creegon, R.F. The shocky existence. Cambridge, 1954.

Phil 2477.6.118 | Crippà, Romeo. Il realismo integrale di M. Blondel. Milano, 1954.

Phil 4080.3.38.3 | Croce, Benedetto. Aesthetica in nuce. 3. ed. Laterza, 1954.

Phil 4080.3.34.12 | Croce, Benedetto. Breviario di estetica; quattro lezioni. 12. ed. Bari, 1954.

Phil 2733.110 | Cuvillier, A. Essai sur la mystique de Malebranche. Paris, 1954.

Phil 177.110 | Cuvillier, Armand. Précis de philosophie: classe de philosophie. Paris, 1954. 2v.

Phil 4872.55.220 | Damle, Prabhakar R. Philosophical essays. Bombay, 1954.

Phil 8953.8.3 | D'Arcy, Martin Cyrile. The mind and heart of love, lion and unicorn. London, 1954.

Phil 6315.1.80 | De Forest, Izette. The leaven of love. Hamden, Conn., 1954.

Phil 1803.10 | Deledalle, G. Histoire de la philosophie américaine. 1e éd. Paris, 1954.

Phil 803.14 | Delfgaauw, B.M.O. Beknopte geschiedenis der wijshegeerte. Baarn, 1954. 2v.

Phil 2475.1.307 | Delhomme, J. Vie et conscience de la vie. Thèse. Paris, 1954.

Phil 5413.15 | Delpierre, Guy. De la jalousie. Paris, 1954.

Phil 1703.10 | Denkers van deze fijd. 2. druk. Francker, 1954-55. 3v.

Phil 2880.8.118 | Desan, Wilfred. The tragic finale. Cambridge, Mass., 1954.

Phil 2520.44 | Descartes, René. Philosophical writings. Edinburgh, 1954.

Phil 8693.20.10 | Dessauer, F. Auf den Spuren der Unendlichkeit. Frankfurt, 1954.

Phil 3960.18 | Dibon, Paul. La philosophie néerlandaise au siècle d'ov. Paris, 1954.

Phil 3195.3.10 | Dietzgen, Joseph. Ausgewählte Schriften. 1. Aufl. Berlin, 1954.

Phil 3195.6.38 | Dilthey, Wilhelm. The essence of philosophy. Chapel Hill, 1954.

Phil 178.64.4.5 | Dixon, W.M. The human situation. London, 1954.

Phil 8735.35 | Dolch, Heimo. Kausalität im Verständnis des Theologen und der Begründer neuzeitlicher Physik. Freiburg, 1954.

Phil 5066.56 | Dürr, K. Lehrbuch der Logistik. Basel, 1954.

Phil 284.4.10 | Duhem, P. The aim and structure of physical theory. Princeton, 1954.

Phil 803.6.19 | Durant, W. The story of philosophy. N.Y., 1954.

Phil 1750.510.2 | Dutt, K. Guru. Existentialism. Basavangudi, 1954.

Phil 2805.288 | Ehrenberg, H. In der Schule Pascals. Heidelberg, 1954.

Phil 3850.27.60 | Ehrfurcht vor dem Leben. Bern, 1954?

Phil 8405.8 | Ekman, Rolf. Estetiska problem. Lund, 1954.

Phil 285.6 | Eliade, Mircea. The myth of the eternal return. N.Y., 1954.

Phil 705.42 | Ellis, Charles Mayo. An essay on transcendentalism, 1842. Gainesville, 1954.

Phil 8400.18 | Elton, William. Aesthetics and language. Oxford, 1954.

Phil 179.38A | Eranos-Jahrbuch. Spirit and nature. N.Y., 1954.

Phil 3004.5 | Erdmann, J.E. Preussen und die Philosophie. Halle, 1954.

Phil 5525.50 | Esar, Evan. The humor of humor. London, 1954.

Phil 5520.75.5A | ETC., a Review of General Semantics. Language, meaning and maturity. 1. ed. N.Y., 1954.

Phil 6314.10 | Evans, Jean. Three men. 1st ed. N.Y., 1954.

Phil 8879.25 | Everett, M.S. Ideals of life. N.Y., 1954.

Phil 3005.10 | Faber, W. Wijsgeren in Nederland. Nijkerk, 1954.

Phil 3960.20 | Faber, W. Wijsgerin in Nederland. Nijkork, 1954.

Phil 815.15 | Fabro, C. Storia della filosofia. Roma, 1954.

Phil 1020.30 | Farrukh, O.A. The Arab genius in science and philosophy. 2d ed. Washington, 1954.

Phil 2605.7.31 | Fauré-Fremiet, P. Esquisse d'une philosophie concrète. 1. ed. Paris, 1954.

Phil 310.10 | Fedoseev, P.N. Usloviia materialicheskoi zhizni obshchestva. Moskva, 1954.

Phil 3246.49.5 | Fichte, Johann Gottlieb. Die Anweisung zum seeligen Leben. Hamburg, 1954.

Phil 3246.32.5 | Fichte, Johann Gottlieb. Eimige Vorlesungen über die Bestimmung des Gelehrten. Jena, 1954.

Phil 3246.79.20 | Fichte, Johann Gottlieb. Erste und zweite Einleitung in die Wissenschaftslehre und Versuch einer neuen Darstellung der Wissenschaftslehre. Hamburg, 1954.

Phil 802.20 | La filosofia della storia della filosofia. Milano, 1954.

Phil 4005.10 | La filosofia italiana fra Ottocento e Novecento. Torino, 1954.

1954 - cont.

Phil 336.14   Fireman, Peter. Perceptualistic theory of knowledge. N.Y., 1954.

Phil 8612.36   Fischer, J.A. Studien zum Todesgedanken in der Alten Kirche. München, 1954.

Phil 3450.18.115F   Fleischer, Helmut. Nicolai Hartmanns Ontologie des idealen Seins. Thesis. Erlangen? 1954.

Phil 2805.280   Fletcher, F.T.H. Pascal and the mystical tradition. Oxford, 1954.

Phil 978.59.100   Fouéré, René. Krishnamurti. 2d ed. Bombay, 1954.

Phil 4967.5   Francovich, Guillermo. Hijos de la roca. México, 1954.

Phil 6315.17.12   Freud, Anna. The ego and the mechanisms of defence. London, 1954.

Phil 7082.8.20   Freud, Sigmund. The interpretation of dreams. London, 1954.

Phil 6315.2.79.20A   Freud, Sigmund. The origins of psycho-analysis. 1st ed. N.Y., 1954.

Phil 180.89   Friedberg, Felix. Thoughts about life. N.Y., 1954.

Phil 3270.11.35   Friedmann, H. Epilegomena. München, 1954.

Phil 5548.10   Fuchs, R. Gewissheit. Meisenheim am Glan, 1954.

Phil 3801.410   Fuhrmans, H. Schelling's Philosophie der Weltalter. Düsseldorf, 1954.

Phil 806.15   Gabriel, Leo. Vom Brahma zur Existenz. 2. Aufl. Wien, 1954.

Phil 5465.65   Galimberti, A. L'imaginazione. Torino, 1954.

Phil 1111.13   Galli, Dario. Il pensiero greco. Padova, 1954.

Phil 1111.14   Galli, Gallo. Corso di storia della filosofia; I sofisti. Socrate, Alcuni dialoghi platonici. Torino, 1954.

Phil 4959.215   Gaos, José. Filosofía mexicana de nuestros días. México, 1954.

Phil 6990.48.2   García Aceituno, José Luis. Esquípulas. 2. ed. Guatemala? 1954.

Phil 4961.915   García Bacca, Juan David. Antología del pensamiento filosófico venezolano. Caracas, 1954.

Phil 2630.10   Gerard, Jacques. L'être et la pensée. Paris, 1954.

Phil 806.16   Geschichte der Philosophie. 2. Aufl. v.1-4,6,8-11. Berlin, 1954. 6v.

Phil 5046.26   Gesellschaft für Deutsch-Ravjetische Freundschaft. Über formale Logik und Dialektik. Berlin, 1954.

Phil 5246.62   Geyer, Horst. Über die Dummheit. Göttingen, 1954.

Phil 270.63   Giacon, Carlo. La causalità nel razionalismo moderno. Milano, 1954.

Phil 4115.20   Gioberti, V. Scritti scelti. Torino, 1954.

Phil 735.150   Glansdorff, Maxime. Théorie générale de la valeur et ses applications en esthétique et en économie. Bruxelles, 1954.

Phil 3488.32   Glasenapp, H. von. Kant und die Religionen des Ostens. Kitzmingen, 1954.

Phil 9245.10   Grasset, B. Sur le plaisir. Paris, 1954.

Phil 4073.104   Grillo, F. Tommaso Campanella in America. N.Y., 1954.

Phil 8631.15   Guardini, R. The last things. London, 1954.

Phil 2030.5A   Guérard, A.L. Battle in the sea. Cambridge, 1954.

Phil 5246.47.6   Guilford, Joy Paul. Psychometric methods. N.Y., 1954.

Phil 3801.445.50   Habermas, J. Das Absolute und die Geschichte. Bonn, 1954.

Phil 3801.445   Habluetzel, Rudolf. Dialektik und Einbildungskraft. Basel, 1954.

Phil 735.165   Halldén, Sören. Emotive propositions. Stockholm, 1954.

Phil 338.26   Harris, E.E. Nature, mind of modern science. London, 1954.

Phil 182.94.20   Hartmann, N. Einführung in die Philosophie. 3. Aufl. Osnabrück, 1954.

Phil 3450.33.10   Hartmann, N. Philosophische Gespräche. Göttingen, 1954.

Phil 5594.154   Hector, H. Der 7-Quadrate-Test. Paderborn, 1954.

Phil 3425.60.3   Hegel, Georg Wilhelm Friedrich. Leçons sur la philosophie de la religion. pt.1-5. Paris, 1954-59. 3v.

Phil 3450.19.40A   Heidegger, Martin. Aus der Erfahrung des Denkens. Pfullingen, 1954.

Phil 3450.19.60   Heidegger, Martin. Vom Wesen der Wahrheit. 3e Aufl. Frankfurt, 1954.

Phil 3450.19.70   Heidegger, Martin. Vorträge und Anpätze. Pfullingen, 1954.

Phil 3450.19.35A   Heidegger, Martin. Was heisst Denken? Tübingen, 1954.

Phil 1707.8.3   Heimsoeth, H. Die sechs grossen Themen der abendländischen Metaphysik. 3e Aufl. Stuttgart, 1954.

Phil 1750.365.5   Heinemann, Fritz. Existentialism and the modern predicament. 2nd ed. London, 1954.

Phil 1750.365.15   Heinemann, Fritz. Existenzphilosophie Lebendig oder Tat? 2e Aufl. Stuttgart, 1954.

Phil 3450.34   Heske, Franz. Organik. Berlin, 1954.

Phil 8882.69   Hesnard, Angelo. Morale sans péché. Paris, 1954.

Phil 8882.71   Hessen, J. Ethik. Leiden, 1954.

Phil 6117.49   Highet, G. Man's unconquerable mind. N.Y., 1954.

Phil 8957.12.5   Hildebrand, D. von. Sittliche Grundhaltungen. Mainz, 1954.

Phil 8408.19   Hiriyanna, M. Art experience. Mysore, 1954.

Phil 2055.7.15A   Hocking, William E. Experiment in education. Chicago, 1954.

Phil 1707.15   Hollenbach, J.M. Sein und Gewissen. Baden-Baden, 1954.

Phil 3800.725   Horn, F. Schelling und Swedenborg. Zürich, 1954.

Phil 2636.85   Horowitz, I.L. Claude Helvetius. N.Y., 1954.

Phil 6319.1.190   Hostie, Raymond. Analytische Psychologie en Godsdienst. Utrecht, 1954.

Phil 1905.10.80.5   Huang, Chia-cheng. De l'humanisme à l'absolutisme. Paris, 1954.

Phil 1905.10.80   Huang, Chia-cheng. Le néo-hegelianisme en Angleterre. Paris, 1954.

Phil 1905.10.80.2   Huang, Chia-cheng. Le néo-hegelianisme en Angleterre. Paris, 1954..

Phil 8408.27   Huber, Kurt. Ästhetik. Ettal, 1954.

Phil 3415.110   Huber, Max. Eduard von Hartmanns Metaphysik und Religionsphilosophie. Winterthur, 1954.

Phil 2050.77.20   Hume, David. New letters. Oxford, 1954.

Phil 1112.8   Huonder, Quirin. Gott und Seele bin Lichte der griechischen Philosophie. München, 1954.

Phil 8612.28.5   Husemann, F. Vom Bild und Sinn des Todes. 2. Aufl. Stuttgart, 1954.

Phil 3450.11.45   Husserl, Edmund. La philosophie comme science rigoureuse. Thèse. Paris, 1954.

Phil 1750.166.90   Huxley, J.S. Evolutionary humanism. Melbourne, 1954.

Phil 3850.27.141   Hygen, J.B. Albert Schweitzers tanker om kulturen. Oslo, 1954.

Phil 8622.25   Interiorité et vie spirituelle. Paris, 1954.

Phil 8958.6   Ioann, Bishop of San Francisco. Vremia very. N'iu-Iork, 1954.

Phil 672.152.5   Jaffé, George. Über Raum. Berlin, 1954.

Phil 1850.145A   Jameson, T.H. Francis Bacon. N.Y., 1954.

1954 - cont.

Phil 184.39.5   Jankélévitch, V. Philosophie première. 1. ed. Paris, 1954.

Phil 2805.286   Jansen, Paule. De Blaise Pascal à Henry Hammond. Paris, 1954.

Phil 8589.21   Jaspers, Karl. Die Frage der Entmychologisierung. München, 1954.

Phil 184.45   Jeandidier, A. Le panpsychisme vital. Paris, 1954.

Phil 2675.3.30   Jeanson, Francis. La vraie vérité, alibi. Paris, 1954.

Phil 5066.60   Juhos, B. van. Elemente der neuen Logik. Frankfurt, 1954.

Phil 2805.315   Julien Eymard d'Angers. Pascal et ses précurseurs. Paris, 1954.

Phil 6319.1.76   Jung, C.G. Von den Wurzeln des Bewusstsens. Zürich, 1954.

Phil 6319.1.78   Jung, C.G. Welt der Psyche. Zürich, 1954.

Phil 8885.41   Kaelin, Bernard. Einführung in die Ethik. 2. Aufl. Sarnen, 1954.

Phil 6816.5   Kahn, Samuel. Make inferiorities and superiorities work for you. Ossining, N.Y., 1954.

Phil 8885.39   Kamiat, A.H. The ethics of civilization. Washington, 1954.

Phil 8590.44   Kamlah, Wilhelm. Der Ruf des Steuermanns. Stuttgart, 1954.

Phil 9495.154   Kardiner, A. Sex and morality. 1st ed. Indianapolis, Ind., 1954.

Phil 3549.10.2   Kassner, Rudolf. Buch der Erinnerung. 2. Aufl. Erlenbach, 1954.

Phil 4796.96.80   Kasumov, Mekhbaly Mamedovich. M.F. Akhundov i russkaia revoliutsionno-demokraticheskaia estetika. Baku, 1954.

Phil 5760.10   Keller, W. Psychologie und Philosophie des Wollens. München, 1954.

Phil 2475.1.315   Kelley, J.J. Bergson's mysticism. Thesis. Fribourg, 1954.

Phil 5545.200   Kendall, Patricia L. Conflict and mood. Glencoe, Ill., 1954.

Phil 3640.393   Kesselring, M. Nietzsche und sein Zarathustra in psychiatrischer Beleuchtung. Aehren Verlag, 1954.

Phil 8885.40   Kettner, F. Biosophy and spiritual democracy. N.Y., 1954.

Phil 8590.29   Kimpel, B.F. The symbols of religious faith. N.Y., 1954.

Phil 6960.13   King, H.E. Psychomotor aspects of mental disease. Cambridge, Mass., 1954.

Phil 185.44.5   Klages, L. Der Geist als Widersacher der Seele. 3. Aufl. München, 1954. 2v.

Phil 5593.54   Klapfer, Bruno. Developments in the Rorschach technique. Yonkers-on-Hudson, 1954. 2v.

Phil 5050.16   Knauss, G. Gegenstand und Umgreifendes. Basel, 1954.

Phil 5592.10   Koch, Karl. Der Baumtest. 2. Aufl. Bern, 1954.

Phil 3492.43   Koenig, Ernst. Arzt und Arztliches bei Kant. Kitzingen, 1954.

Phil 310.9A   Konstantinov, F.V. Istoricheskii materializm. Izd. 2. Moskva, 1954.

Phil 185.69   Krings, H. Fragen und Aufgaben der Ontologie. Tübingen, 1954.

Phil 978.59.35   Krishnamurti, J. The first and last freedom. London, 1954.

Phil 1710.5.10   Krutch, Joseph W. The measure of man. 1. ed. Indianapolis, 1954.

Phil 9070.58   Kuehne, O. Lebenskunst und Lebensgemeinschaft in Gesellschaft und Wirtschaft. Berlin, 1954[1958] 2v.

Phil 9450.25   Künneth, W. Politik zwischen Dämon und Gott. 1. Aufl. Berlin, 1954.

Phil 6980.403   Kugelmass, I.N. The management of mental deficiency in children. N.Y., 1954.

Phil 5593.54.5   Kuhn, Roland. Maskendeutungen im Rorschachschen Versuch. 2. Aufl. Basel, 1954.

Phil 2805.249.10   Lafuma, Louis. Histoire des Pensées de Pascal. Paris, 1954.

Phil 575.251   Lahbabi, Mohamed Aziz. De l'être à la personne. 1. éd. Paris, 1954.

Phil 2725.2.77   Lamennais, F.R. Essai d'un système de philosophie catholique. Rennes, 1954.

Phil 2725.2.76   Lamennais, F.R. de. Une voix de prison. Paris, 1954.

Phil 2705.20   La Mettrie, Julien Offray de. Textes choisis. Paris, 1954.

Phil 310.15   Landesverband Nordshein-West-Tälischer Geschichte. Historie Materialismus und europäisches Geschichtsdenken. 1. Aufl. Düsseldorf, 1954.

Phil 1020.36   Lane-Poole, Stanley. Essay on the brotherhood of purity. Lahore, 1954.

Phil 9495.155   Langdon Davies, J. Sex, sin and sanity. London, 1954.

Phil 3450.11.135   Lauer, Quentin. La genèse de l'intentionalité dans la philosophie de Husserl. Paris, 1954.

Phil 6681.16.5   Le Cron, L.M. Experimental hypnosis. N.Y., 1954.

Phil 4363.3.85   Lede, Luis Perez de Guzman y Sanjuan. Discurso de la verdad. Bilboa, 1954.

Phil 3552.66.13   Leibniz, Gottfried Wilhelm. Monadologie. 2. Ausg. Stuttgart, 1954.

Phil 3552.30.15   Leibniz, Gottfried Wilhelm. Opuscules philosophiques choisis. Paris, 1954.

Phil 3552.78.35   Leibniz, Gottfried Wilhelm. Principes de la nature et de la grace fondés en raison. Paris, 1954.

Phil 2520.245   Leisegang, G. Descartes Dioptrik. Meisenheim am Glan, 1954.

Phil 8520.5.2   Leland, J. A view of the principal deistical writers. London, 1954.

Phil 3801.516   Lendi-Wolff, Christian. Friedrich Wilhelm Joseph von Schelling. Bad Ragaz, 1954.

Phil 5401.28   Leroy, E. Angst und Lachen. Wien, 1954.

Phil 5590.95.6   Lersch, Philipp. Aufbau der Person. 6. Aufl. München, 1954.

Phil 3493.26   Letocart, M. La morale Kantienne. Bruxelles, 1954.

Phil 6980.419.5   Lewis, Nolan don Carpentier. Wartime psychiatry; a compendium. N.Y., 1954.

Phil 3850.27.113.5   Lind, Emil. Ein Meister der Menscheit Albert Schweitzer. Bühl, 1954.

Phil 3585.17   Lipps, Hans. Die Wirklichkeit des Menschen. Frankfurt, 1954.

Phil 2115.72   Locke, J. Essays on the law of nature. Oxford, 1954.

Phil 4075.86   Lucas Dubreton, D. Le monde enchanté de la Renaissance. Paris, 1954.

Phil 486.9   Luce, A.A. Sense without matter, or Direct perception. Edinburgh, 1954.

Phil 8080.14.5   Ludács, G. Beitrage zur Geschichte der Ästhetik. Berlin, 1954.

NEDL Phil 1750.45   Lukács, G. Az ész troufasztása. Budapest, 1954.

Phil 3011.6   Lukács, G. Die Zerstörung der Vernunft. Berlin, 1954.

Phil 6962.28   McAuley, W.F. The concept of schizophrenia. N.Y., 1954.

Phil 5400.116   McGill, V.J. Emotions and reason. Springfield, 1954.

1954 - cont.

Phil 8592.75   McMurrin, S.M. The patterns of our religious faiths. Salt Lake City, 1954.

Phil 1182.40   Maddalena, A. I Pitagorici. Bari, 1954.

Phil 9075.45   Madinier, G. La conscience morale. Paris, 1954.

Phil 3625.5.79   Maimon, Salomon. Autobiography. London, 1954.

Phil 2730.35.3   Maine de Biran, Pierre. Influence de l'habitude sur la faculté de penser. 1e éd. Paris, 1954.

Phil 2730.60.2   Maine de Biran, Pierre. Journal. Neuchâtel, 1954. 3v.

Phil 2128.61   Mandeville, B. A letter to Dion. Liverpool, 1954.

Phil 8592.72   Marain, L. Humanism as the next step. Boston, 1954.

Phil 2750.19.30   Marcel, Gabriel. Le declin de la sagesse. Paris, 1954.

Phil 2750.19.31   Marcel, Gabriel. The decline of wisdom. London, 1954.

Phil 3425.292.10A   Marcuse, H. Reason and revolution; Hegel and the use of social theory. 2nd ed. N.Y., 1954.

Phil 4363.7.5   Marias Aguilera, Julián. Idea de la metafísica. Buenos Aires, 1954.

Phil 2750.11.75   Maritain, Jacques. Approaches to God. 1st ed. N.Y., 1954.

Phil 8887.74.5   Martínez de Trujillo, Maria. Moral meditations. N.Y., 1954.

Phil 575.150   Massa, Eugenio. I fondamenti metafisici "dignitas hominis". Torino, 1954.

Phil 4974.5   Massera, José P. Estudios filosóficos. v.12. Montevideo, 1954.

Phil 2475.1.350   Mathieu, Vittorio. Bergson. Torino, 1954.

Phil 5252.102   Matte Blanco, Ignacio. La psiquica y la naturaleza humana. Santiago, 1954.

Phil 8887.91   Mayer, Charles L. In quest of a new ethics. Boston, 1954.

Phil 525.233   Mediaeval mystique tradition and S. John of the Cross. London, 1954.

Phil 187.135.5   Medicus, Fritz. Vom überzeitlichen in der Zeit. Zürich, 1954.

Phil 575.149   Mel'vil', Iu.K. Amerikanskii personalizm-filosofiia imperialisticheskoi reaktsii. Moskva, 1954.

Phil 5066.65   Menne, Albert. Logik und Existenz. Meisenheim/Glan, 1954.

Phil 8887.75.5   Messner, J. Kulturethik. Innsbruck, 1954.

Phil 5252.100   Metzger, W. Psychologie. 2. Aufl. Darmstadt, 1954.

Phil 5400.132   Michaud, H. La sensibilité. Lyon, 1954?

Phil 270.62A   Michotte, A.E. La perception de la causalité. 2. ed. Louvain, 1954.

Phil 2805.30.800   Mignone, C. Rensi, Leopardi e Pascal. Milano, 1954.

Phil 5222.13   Misiak, Henryk. Catholics in psychology. N.Y., 1954.

Phil 8962.21   Mohr, R. Die christliche Ethik im Lichte der Ethnologie. München, 1954.

Phil 8887.21.4   Moore, George Edward. Principia ethica. Cambridge, Eng., 1954.

Phil 8413.17   Mormone, R. Avviamento alla critica d'arte. Napoli, 1954.

Phil 5203.15   Moscow. Gosudarstvennaia Biblioteka SSSR. Imeni V.I. Lenina. Kak nauka ob"iasniaet psikhologicheskoi deiatel'nosti cheloveka. Moskva, 1954.

Phil 6962.35.1   Moses, Paul Joseph. The voice of neurosis. N.Y., 1954.

Phil 2050.212.5   Mossner, E.C. The life of David Hume. Austin, 1954.

Phil 6480.192   Mozzuchelli, M. I sogni. Milano, 1954.

Phil 5590.180   Mucchielli, R. Caractères et visages. 1. éd. Paris, 1954.

Phil 735.145   Müller, A. Die Grundkategorien des Lebendigen. Meisenheim, 1954.

Phil 3494.50   Mueller, Johannes. Kantisches Staatsdenken und der Preussische Staat. Kitzingen, 1954.

Phil 4810.2.5   Muenz, Teodor. Náhľady filozofov malohontstkej spoločnosti. Bratislava, 1954.

Phil 5585.145   Murloo, Abraham. The two faces of man. N.Y., 1954.

Phil 188.21   Natzmer, G. von. Weisheit der Welt. Berlin, 1954.

Phil 188.20   Neal, H.H. The universe and you. Laguna Beach, Calif., 1954.

Phil 6323.15   Nelson, John. Look before you leap. Washington, D.C., 1954.

Phil 8414.11   Neumann, E. Kunst und schöpferisches Unbewusstes. Zürich, 1954.

Phil 5374.165   Nevratil, Michel. Introduction critique à une découverte de la pensée. Paris, 1954.

Phil 4080.3.410   Nicolini, F. Benedetto Croce. Roma, 1954.

Phil 3640.17.8   Nietzsche, Friedrich. Götzendämmerung. Stuttgart, 1954. 2v.

Phil 3640.47   Nietzsche, Friedrich. Menschliches, Allzumenschliches; ein Buch für freie Geister. v.1-2. Stuttgart, 1954.

Phil 3640.14.15A   Nietzsche, Friedrich. Werke. München, 1954-56. 3v.

Phil 8980.610F   Nivison, A. S. Communist ethics and Chinese tradition. Cambridge, Mass., 1954.

Phil 8050.75   Nohl, H. Die ästhetische Wirklichkeit; eine Einfuhrung. 2. Aufl. Frankfurt, 1954.

Phil 5520.310   Nordisk Sommeruniversitet. Betydningsproblemer. Oslo, 1954.

Phil 8888.15   Nowell-Smith, P.H. Ethics. Melbourne, 1954.

Phil 3705.6.20   Oesterreich, Trangott K. Trangott Konstanin Österreich. Stuttgart, 1954.

Phil 189.29.2   Onians, R.B. The origins of European thought about the body, the mind, the soul. 2. ed. Cambridge, Eng., 1954.

Phil 9530.52   Orage, A.R. The active mind. N.Y., 1954.

Phil 4080.3.245   Osterwalder, T. Die Philosophie Benedetto Croces als moderne Ideenlehre. Berne, 1954.

Phil 5590.125   Overstreet, H.A. The mind alive. N.Y., 1954.

Phil 2138.124   Packe, M. The life of John Stuart Mill. London, 1954.

Phil 165.28   Padovani, U.A. Grande antologia filosofica. Milano, 1954. 16v.

Phil 2825.15   Paliard, J. Profondeur de l'âme. Paris, 1954.

Phil 348.4.80   Palmoe, E. Indledning til filosofi som grundvidenskab efter Johs. København, 1954.

Phil 8407.38   Panofsky, E. Galileo as a critic of the arts. The Hague, 1954.

Phil 346.18   Pardo, R. Del origen a la escencia del conocimiento. Buenos Aires, 1954.

Phil 8416.12   Pareyson, Luigi. Estética. Torino, 1954.

Phil 4757.2.80   Pauwels, L. Monsieur Gurdjieff. Paris, 1954.

Phil 5055.27   Pavese, Roberto. Compendio di logica sintetica. Padova, 1954.

Phil 2225.2.30A   Perry, R.B. Realms of value. Cambridge, Mass., 1954.

Phil 735.20.12   Perry, Ralph Barton. General theory of value. Cambridge, Mass., 1954.

Phil 5590.140   Pfahler, G. Der Mensch und sein Lebenswerkzeug. Stuttgart, 1954.

Phil 4196.30   Pico, G.F. Le epistole de imitatione di G. Pico. Firenze, 1954.

Phil 5520.140   Pike, Kenneth Lee. Language in relation to a unified theory of the structure of human behavior. Glendale, Calif., 1954.

1954 - cont.

Phil 5025.2   Platzeck, E.W. Von der Analogie zum Syllogismus. Paderborn, 1954.

Phil 490.8   Poortman, J.J. Achêma. v.1-2,6. Assen, 1954. 5v.

Phil 7069.54.25   Porten, Harry. The miracle on the wall. Eastbourne, Eng., 1954.

Phil 4352.1.110   Prados y Lopez, M. Balmes, el buen amigo de la verdad. Madrid, 1954?

Phil 978.6.97   Prakasa, Sri. Annie Besant. 2d ed. Bombay, 1954.

Phil 5585.58.5   Price, Henry H. Perception. London, 1954.

Phil 8416.18.5   Propris, A. de. Problemi di estetica e critica. Roma, 1954.

Phil 3475.3.135   Räber, T. Das Dasein in der Philosophie von Karl Jaspers. Diss. Freiburg, 1954.

Phil 6060.48   Ras, M. Los artistas escriben. 1. ed. Madrid, 1954.

Phil 6319.1.192   Rath, Paul. Anima und Animus in der Psychologie C.G. Jung. Winterthur, 1954.

Phil 2750.19.80   Rebollo Peña, A. Critica de la objetividad en el existencialism de Gabriel Marcel. Burgos, 1954.

Phil 5066.26.5   Reichenbach, H. Nomalogical statements and admissable operations. Amsterdam, 1954.

Phil 5057.32   Reichenbach, Hans. Nomological statements and admissible operations. Amsterdam, 1954.

Phil 1750.395   Reidemeister, Kurt. Die Unsachlichkeit der Existenzphilosophie. Berlin, 1954.

Phil 5590.150   Remplein, Heinz. Psychologie der Persönlichkeit. München, 1954.

Phil 8170.2   Reve, K. van het. Sovjet-annexatie der klassieken. Amsterdam, 1954.

Phil 5520.126   Révész, G. Thinking and speaking. Amsterdam, 1954.

Phil 8672.20   Ricciotti, G. Dio nella ricerca umana. 3. ed. Roma, 1954.

Phil 5628.55.25   Rinser, Luise. Die Wahrheit über Konnersreuth. Einsiedeln, 1954.

Phil 623.28   Robertson, A. Rationalism in theory and practice. London, 1954.

Phil 4368.2.90   Rodríguez Acala, Hugo. Francisco Romero, 1891: vija y obra. N.Y., 1954.

Phil 5850.328   Roethlisberger, F.J. Training for human relations. Boston, 1954.

Phil 4961.45.3   Romanell, P. La formación de la mentalidad mexicana. México, 1954.

Phil 4959.225   Romanell, Patrick. La formación de la mentalidad mexicana. 1. ed. México, 1954.

Phil 4210.11   Rosmini-Serbati, Antonio. Anthologie philosophique. Lyon, 1954.

Phil 3499.32   Ross, H.D. Kant's ethical theory. Oxford, 1954.

Phil 102.5.5   Rozental', Mark Moiseevich. Kratkii filosofskii slovar'. Izd. 4. Leningrad, 1954.

Phil 960.170   Ruben, Walter. Geschichte der indischen Philosophie. Berlin, 1954.

Phil 8892.62   Russell, Bertrand Russell. Human society in ethics and politics. London, 1954.

RRC   Phil 5850.330.5   Russell, W.L. Peace and power within. N.Y., 1954.

Phil 310.12   Russia (1917-). Upravlenie Prepodavatel'skogo Obshchestvennogo Nauk. Programma kursa dialekticheskogo i istoricheskogo materializma dlia vyshego uchebrogo zaved. Moskva, 1954.

Phil 4260.131   Sabarini, Raniero. Il tempo in G.B. Vico. Milano, 1954.

Phil 6990.3.38   Saint-Pierre, M. de. Bernadette and Lourdes. N.Y., 1954.

Phil 4957.20.5   Sanchez Reulet, Aníbal. Contemporary Latin-American philosophy. New Mexico, 1954.

Phil 5520.119   Sandman, M. Subject and predicate. Edinburgh, 1954.

Phil 2280.5.88   Santayana, George. The life of reason. N.Y., 1954.

Phil 5593.54.15   Sarason, S.B. The clinical interaction (with specific reference to Rorschach). N.Y., 1954.

Phil 3552.352   Saw, R.L. Leibniz. Harmondsworth, Eng., 1954.

Phil 310.14A   Schaff, Adam. Zu einigen Fragen der marxistischen Theorie der Wahrheit. 1. Aufl. Berlin, 1954.

Phil 3850.18.20A   Scheler, Max. Philosophische Weltanschauung. Bern, 1954.

Phil 3800.200.7   Schelling, F.W.J. von. Bruno. Hamburg, 1954.

Phil 3800.210.15   Schelling, F.W.J. von. Studium generale. Stuttgart, 1954.

Phil 3800.250.20   Schelling, F.W.J. von. Über das Verhältniss der bildenden Künste zu der Natur. Marbach, 1954.

Phil 3640.408   Schlechta, Karl. Nietzsches grosser Mittag. Frankfurt, 1954.

Phil 3805.50.15   Schleiermacher, Friedrich. Die Weihnachtsfeier. Basel, 1954.

Phil 3925.11.50   Schmidt, R.H. Peter Wust. Saarbrüchen, 1954.

Phil 3800.12   Schneeberger, G. Friederich Wilhelm Joseph von Schelling. Bern, 1954.

Phil 299.26   Schöndorfer, Ulrich A. Philosophie des Materie. 1. Aufl. Graz, 1954.

Phil 5593.54.20   Schofer, Roy. Psychoanalytic interpretation in Rorschach testing. N.Y., 1954.

Phil 1135.166   Schroedinger, E. Nature and the Greeks. Cambridge, Eng., 1954.

Phil 8598.110.10   Schuon, Frithjof. Spiritual perspectives and human facts. London, 1954.

Phil 5401.24   Schwartz, C. Neurotic anxiety. N.Y., 1954.

Phil 3450.19.140   Sepich, Juan R. La filosofía de Ser y tiempo de M. Heidegger. Buenos Aires, 1954.

Phil 4260.137   Severgnini, Dante. Studi vichiani. Milano, 1954-56. 2v.

Phil 818.29   Sheldon, W.H. God and polarity; a synthesis of philosophies. New Haven, 1954.

Phil 5722.32.2   Simon, C.W. Considerations for research in a sleep-learning program. Santa Monica, 1954.

Phil 5722.32   Simon, C.W. Considerations for research in a sleep-learning program. Santa Monica, 1954.

Phil 5722.32.5   Simon, C.W. Responses to material presented during various levels of sleep. Santa Monica, 1954.

Phil 5828.18   Sire, Marcel. L'intelligence des animaux. Paris, 1954.

Phil 5628.55.21   Siwek, Paul. The riddle of Konnersreuth; a psychological and religious study. Dublin, 1954.

Phil 7140.140.6   Slavson, S.R. An introduction to group therapy. N.Y., 1954.

Phil 4803.799.21   Śniadecki, Jan. Wybor pism naukowych. Warszawa, 1954.

Phil 7069.54.20   Soal, Samuel G. Modern experiments in telepathy. New Haven, 1954.

Phil 4769.1.78   Solov'ev, V.S. Tri razgovora. N'iu-Iork, 1954.

Phil 1750.610   Sonnemann, Ulrich. Existence and therapy. N.Y., 1954.

Phil 8893.104.5   Sorokin, Pitirim Aleksandrovich. Forms and techniques of altruistic and spiritual growth. Boston, 1954.

Phil 8598.106   Spalding, K.J. Essays on the evolution of religion. Oxford, 1954.

Phil 2270.56.10   Spencer, Herbert. Social statics. N.Y., 1954.

Phil 3819.12.4   Spinoza, Benedictus de. Oeuvres complètes. Paris, 1954.

Chronological Listing

1954 - cont.

Phil 3850.5.15   Spir, Afrikan. Right and wrong. Edinburgh, 1954.
Phil 4120.4.110   Spirito, Ugo. Note sur pensiero di Giovanni Gentile. Firenze, 1954.
Phil 1750.380   Spoerri, Theophil F. Die Herausforderung des Existenzialismus. Hamburg, 1954.
Phil 5258.74.5   Spranger, Eduard. Gedanken zur Daseinsgestaltung. München, 1954.
Phil 6945.45   Stanton, Alfred Hodgin. The mental hospital. N.Y., 1954.
Phil 5058.46.30   Stebbing, Lizzie S. Logic in practice. 4. ed. London, 1954.
Phil 978.49.86   Steiner, R. Wendepunkte des Geisteslebens. 3. Aufl. Freiburg, 1954.
Phil 2805.284   Steinmann, Jean. Pascal. Paris, 1954.
Phil 6328.36   Stern, Erich. Handbuch der klinischen Psychologie. v.1-2. Zürich, 1954. 3v.
Phil 1845.3.110A   Stiernotte, A.P.N.F. God and space time. N.Y., 1954.
Phil 6980.712.5   Sullivan, Harry Stack. The psychiatric interview. N.Y., 1954.
Phil 7069.54   Thurston, Herbert. Ghosts and poltergeists. Chicago, 1954.
Phil 1195.13.3   Untersteiner, M. The sophists. Oxford, 1954.
Phil 2805.196.7   Valensin, A. Balthazar. Paris, 1954.
Phil 2805.305   Vansina, Dirk. Pascal. Bussum, 1954.
Phil 630.53   Veatch, Henry B. Realism and nominalism revisited. Milwaukee, 1954.
Phil 2840.99.20   Verneaux, Roger. Esquisse d'une théorie de la connaissance. Paris, 1954.
Phil 3841.7   Vernière, P. Spinoza et la pensée française avant la révolution. Paris, 1954. 2v.
Phil 3841.7.2   Vernière, P. Spinoza et la pensée française avant la révolution. Thèse. Paris, 1954. 2v.
Phil 4120.4.105   Vettori, V. Giovanni Gentile. Firenze, 1954.
Phil 4260.41   Vico, G.B. L'ideale educativo. Napoli, 1954.
Phil 2053.90   Vigone, L. L'etica del senso morale in Francis Hutcheson. Milano, 1954.
Phil 106.1.10   Voltaire, Francois Marie Arouet de. Dictionnaire philosophique. Paris, 1954.
Phil 310.7.5   Vostrikov, A.V. Marksistskii filosofskii materializm. Moskva, 1954.
Phil 70.34   Vsesoiuznoe Soveshchanie po Voprosam Psikhologii, 2nd, Moskva, 1953. Doklady na soveshchanii po voprosam psikhologii 3-8 iiulia 1953 g. Moskva, 1954.
Phil 705.39   Vuillemin, Jules. L'héritage Kantien et la révolution copernicienne. Paris, 1954.
Phil 165.35.5   Wagner, Johannes. Vom Ursprung und Sinn des philosophischen Fragens. Braunschweig, 1954.
Phil 165.35   Wagner, Johannes. Was ist der Mensch? 2. Aufl. Braunschweig, 1954.
Phil 1750.189   Wahl, Jean André. Les philosophies de l'existence. Paris, 1954.
Phil 3450.18.120   Wahl, Jean André. La théorie des catégories fondamentales dans Nicolai Hartmann. Paris, 1954.
Phil 5645.50   Wal, T.O. Proeve ener practische kleurenpsychologie. Amsterdam, 1954.
Phil 303.18   Wein, Hermann. Zugang zu philosophischen Kosmologie. München, 1954.
Phil 5465.75   Weinberg, J.R. Die Dynamik des schoepferischen Akts. Göttingen, 1954.
Phil 197.74   Wells, H.K. Pragmatism. N.Y., 1954.
Phil 1722.10   Werner, Charles. La philosophie moderne. Paris, 1954.
Phil 7069.54.10   West, D.J. Psychical research today. London, 1954.
Phil 5520.124A   Wheelwright, Phillip Ellis. The burning fountain. Bloomington, 1954.
Phil 2340.10.35A   Whitehead, Alfred North. Dialogues of Alfred North Whitehead. 1st ed. Boston, 1954.
Phil 380.2.5A   Whyte, Lancelot L. Accent on form. N.Y., 1954.
Phil 5627.124.20   Williamson, G. Inside Buchmanism. London, 1954.
Phil 3925.16.60   Wittgenstein, Ludwig. Tractatus logico-philosophicus. Milano, 1954.
Phil 5525.48   Wolfenstein, M. Children's humor. Glencoe, Ill., 1954.
Phil 5262.9.42   Woodworth, R.S. Experimental psychology. N.Y., 1954.
Phil 6315.2.152   Wortis, J. Fragments of an analysis with Freud. N.Y., 1954.
Phil 3925.11.40   Wust, Peter. Im Sinnkreis des Ewigen. 1. Aufl. Graz, 1954.
Phil 2262.95   Zani, Lucio. L'etica di Lord Shaftesbury. Milano, 1954.
Phil 4829.867.80   Zečević, Seraphinus. Francisci Veber theoria de persona; internum drama philosophi sloveni. Montréal, 1954.
Phil 3801.895A   Zeltner, Hermann. Schelling. Stuttgart, 1954.
Phil 4756.1.49   Zen'kovskii, V.V. Sbornik pamiati Semena L. Franka. Miunkhen, 1954.
Phil 974.5.6   Zimmer, Heinrich. Der Weg zum Selbst. Zürich, 1954.
Phil 3808.200   Zint, Hans. Schopenhauer als Erlebnis. München, 1954.
Phil 5599.98   Zulliger, Hans. Der Tafeln-Z-Test für individuelle psychologische Prüfungen, ein abgekürztes Rorschach-Verfahren. Bern, 1954.
Phil 5465.70   Zwicker, Heinz. Seelisches Leben und schöpferische Leistung. Bern, 1954.

1955

Phil 2115.149.5   Aaron, R.I. John Locke. 2nd ed. Oxford, 1955.
Phil 720.43   Aaron, Richard Ithamar. The true and the valid. London, 1955.
Phil 4080.3.280   Abbate, Michele. La filosofia di Benedetto Croce e la crisi della società italiano. Torino, 1955.
Phil 5240.25.15   Abel, Jakob Friedrich von. Rede über das Genie. Marbach, 1955.
Phil 2280.7.80   Abel, Reuben. The pragmatic humanism of F.C.S. Schiller. N.Y., 1955.
Phil 6310.2.14   Abraham, Karl. Clinical papers and essays on psychoanalysis. London, 1955.
Phil 2475.1.294.6   Adolphe, Lydie. L'univers bergsonien. Paris, 1955.
Phil 1885.92   Ahmed, M. The theory of judgment in the philosophies of F.H. Bradley and John Cook Wilson. Dacca, 1955.
Phil 4710.17A   Akademiia Nauk SSSR. Institut Filosofii. Ocherki po istorii filosoficheskoi i obshchestvenno-politicheskoi mysli narodov SSSR. Moskva, 1955. 2v.
Phil 5040.23   Akademiia Nauk SSSR. Institut Filosofii. Vaprosy logiki. Moskva, 1955.
Phil 5585.78   Allport, F.H. Theories of perception and the concept of structure. N.Y., 1955.
Phil 5240.46A   Allport, Gordon Willard. Becoming. New Haven, 1955.
Phil 4630.3.80   Almquist, Karl Gustaf. Andreas Rydelius etiska åkådning. Lund, 1955.

1955 - cont.

Phil 8875.28   American Academy of Political and Social Science, Philadelphia. Ethical standards and professional conduct. Philadelphia, 1955.
Phil 3482.11   Anceschi, T. I presupposti storici e teorici. n.p., 1955.
Phil 3850.27.128   Anderson, E. The world of Albert Schweitzer. N.Y., 1955.
Phil 3085.5.31   Andre, H. Wunderbare Wirklichkeit. Salzburg, 1955.
Phil 4080.3.260   Antoni, Carlo. Commento a Croce. 1. ed. Venezia, 1955.
Phil 5750.9   Antweiler, A. Das Problem der Willensfreiheit. Freiburg, 1955.
Phil 2475.1.320   Arbour, Romeo. Henri Bergson et les lettres françaises. Paris, 1955.
Phil 1630.5   Archivio di Filosofia. Testi umanistici su l'ermetismo. Roma, 1955.
Phil 5520.150   Archivo di Filosofia. Semantica. Roma, 1955.
Phil 6950.7   Arieti, S. Interpretation of schizophrenia. N.Y., 1955.
Phil 6950.7.6   Arieti, S. Interpretation of schizophrenia. N.Y., 1955.
Phil 2280.5.109   Arnett, W.E. Santayana and the sense of beauty. Bloomington, Ind., 1955.
Phil 3808.215   Arthur Schopenhauer. Berlin, 1955.
Phil 5585.80   Association de Psychologie Scientifique de Langue Française. La perception. Paris, 1955.
Phil 4065.140   Badaloni, Nicola. La filosofia di Giordano Bruno. Firenze, 1955.
Phil 9560.40   Baden, H.J. Ende und Anfang der Humanität. Gütersloh, 1955.
Phil 5068.30   Baknadze, K.S. Sub"ektivnyi idealizm. Tbilisi, 1955.
Phil 4065.135   Baldi, E. Giordano Bruno. Firenze, 1955.
Phil 5870.95   Baldwin, Alfred Lee. Behavior and development in childhood. N.Y., 1955.
Phil 2401.15   Barber, W.H. Leibniz in France. Oxford, 1955.
Phil 165.80   Bari (City). Università. Istituto di Storia della Filosofia. Contributi di A. Corsana. Trani, 1955.
Phil 8626.25   Barnes, C.T. The duration of mind. Salt Lake City, 1955.
Phil 1905.24   Barnhart, F.J.C. Principles of the infinite philosophy. N.Y., 1955.
Phil 3552.360   Barone, F. Leibniz e la logica formale. Torino, 1955.
Phil 1801.10   Baskin, M.P. Filosofiia amerikanskogo prosveshcheniia. Moskva, 1955.
Phil 310.17   Baskin, M.P. Materializm i religiia. Moskva, 1955.
Phil 5238.32   Behavior theory and social science. New Haven, 1955.
Phil 5520.200   Beiträge zur Psychologie der Sprache und des Denkens. Berlin, 1955.
Phil 3801.203   Benz, Ernst. Schelling. Zürich, 1955.
Phil 4752.2.72   Berdiaev, Nikolai Aleksandrovich. The meaning of the creative act. N.Y., 1955.
Phil 4752.2.73   Berdiaev, Nikolai Aleksandrovich. Le sens de la création. Paris, 1955.
Phil 1750.50   Berg, J.H. van der. The phenomenological approach to psychiatry. Springfield, Ill., 1955.
Phil 5066.80   Berkeley, E.C. Symbolic logic. N.Y., 1955.
Phil 1870.45.21   Berkeley, G. Drei Dialoge zwischen Hylas und Philonous. Berlin, 1955.
Phil 3425.380   Beyer, W.R. Zwischen Phänomenologie und Logik. Frankfurt, 1955.
Phil 3808.210   Biscardo, R. Il pessimismo romantico nel mondo di Schopenhauer. 1. ed. Bolzano, 1955.
Phil 165.40.5   Bloch, Ernest. Wissen und Hoffen. Berlin, 1955.
Phil 7069.55.25   Bodin, Edward Longstreet. Super purgatory. Daytona Beach, Fla., 1955.
Phil 850.29   Bogliolo, Luigi. La filosofia antica. Torino, 1955.
Phil 3195.6.102   Bollnow, O.F. Dilthey. 2. Aufl. Stuttgart, 1955.
Phil 1750.179.20   Bollnow, O.F. Existenzphilosophie. 4e Aufl. Stuttgart, 1955.
Phil 1750.179.15   Bollnow, O.F. Neue Geborgenheit. Stuttgart, 1955.
Phil 310.11   Bol'shukhin, A.A. Oroli narodnogo max i lichnosti v istorii. Gor'kii, 1955.
Phil 1801.9A   Boman, Lars. Criticism and construction in the philosophy of the America new realism. Stockholm, 1955.
Phil 5590.185   Bourjade, Jean. Principes de caractérologie. Neuchâtel, 1955.
Phil 1701.25   Bousquet, J. Les capitals; ou De Jean Duns Scot à Jean Paulhan. Paris, 1955.
Phil 9560.32   Braithwaite, R.B. Theory of games as a tool for the moral philosopher. Cambridge, Eng., 1955.
Phil 3450.11.150   Brand, Gerd. Welt. Den Haag, 1955.
Phil 176.190   Brates, Georg. Du und die Philosophie. Berlin, 1955.
Phil 5241.120   Brecht, F.J. Vom menschlichen Denken. Heidelberg, 1955.
Phil 1106.16   Bréhier, Émile. Etudes de philosophie antique. Paris, 1955.
Phil 5241.17.25A   Brentano, Franz. Psychologie vom empirischen Standpunkt. Hamburg, 1955.
Phil 8876.41.9   Brentano, Franz. Vom Ursprung sittlicher Erkenntnis. Hamburg, 1955.
Phil 5241.117   Brill, Albert. Fundamental fundamentals. N.Y., 1955.
Phil 8120.10   Brincourt, A. Les oeuvres et les lumières. Paris, 1955.
Phil 9010.30   Brooke, Iris. Pleasures of the past. London, 1955.
Phil 5270.22   Brown, Clarence William. Scientific method in psychology. N.Y., 1955.
Phil 4065.65   Bruno, Giordano. La cena de le cenerè. Torino, 1955.
Phil 3120.30.37   Buber, Martin. Der Mensch und sein Gebild. Heidelberg, 1955.
Phil 5500.14.5   Buchler, J. Nature and judgment. N.Y., 1955.
Phil 2280.5.110A   Butler, Richard. The mind of Santayana. Chicago, 1955.
Phil 5590.170   Cailliet, E. The dawn of personality. 1. ed. Indianapolis, 1955.
Phil 4073.45   Campanella, Tommaso. La prima e la seconda resurrezione. Roma, 1955.
Phil 1750.470   Campbell, Robert. L'esistenzialismo. Napoli, 1955.
Phil 5625.90   Canguilhem, G. La formation du concept de reflexe aux XVII et XVIII siècles. Paris, 1955.
Phil 4963.2   Cannabrava, Euryalo. A cultura brasileira e seus equivocos. Rio de Janeiro, 1955.
Phil 87.4   Cantoro, Umberto. Vocabulario filosofico. Bologna, 1955.
Phil 1182.50   Capparelli, Vincenzo. Il contributo pilagorico alla scienza. Padova, 1955.
Phil 4080.21   Caracciolo, A. La persona e il tempo. 1. ed. pt. 1. Arona, 1955.
Phil 177.120   Carré, Jean Raoul. Le point d'appui pris sur le néant. 1. éd. Paris, 1955.
Phil 2477.6.130   Cartier, Albert. Existence et vérité. Paris, 1955.
Phil 3450.33.13   Caspar, Caspar Toni. Grundlagen der Ontologie Nicolai Hartmanns. Tübingen, 1955.
Phil 8877.86   Castell, Alhurey. An elementary ethics. Englewood Cliffs, 1955.
Phil 2750.23.80   Casula, Mario. Maréchal e Kant. Roma, 1955.

1955 - cont.

Phil 930.44 Chan, Wing-tsit. An outline and a bibliography of Chinese philosophy. Hanover, 1955.
Phil 2515.5.97 Chartier, Émile. Lettres sur la philosophie première. 1. éd. Paris, 1955.
Phil 802.22 Chevalier, Jacques. Histoire de la pensée. v.1-3. Paris, 1955- 2v.
Phil 5520.130 Clark University, Worcester, Massachusetts. Conference on Expressive Language Behavior. On expressive language. Worcester, Mass., 1955.
Phil 3160.13 Cohn, Jonas. Wirklichkeit als Aufgabe. Stuttgart, 1955.
Phil 9495.155.15 Cole, William G. Sex in Christianity and psychoanalysis. N.Y., 1955.
Phil 4080.3.275 Comoth, René. Introduction à la philosophie politique de Benedetto Croce. Liège, 1955.
Phil 3484.27 Coninck, Antoine de. L'analytique transcendentale de Kant. Louvain, 1955-
Phil 310.2.2 Cornforth, M.C. Dialectical materialism. London, 1955-56. 3v.
Phil 333.26 Cornforth, Maurice Campbell. The theory of knowledge. N.Y., 1955.
Phil 4510.35 Corpus philosophorum danicorum medii aevi. Hauniae, 1955-1963. 4v.
Phil 8692.20A Coulson, C.A. Science and Christian belief. Chapel Hill, 1955.
Phil 3425.400 Cresson, André. Hegel. Paris, 1955.
Phil 1955.6.125 Crosser, P.K. The nihilism of John Dewey. N.Y., 1955.
Phil 2750.11.110 Croteau, Jacques. Les fondements thornistes du personnalisme de Maritain. Ottawa, 1955.
Phil 2636.90 Cumming, Ian. Helvetius. London, 1955.
Phil 5923.3 Davies, John D. Phrenology. New Haven, 1955.
Phil 3801.320.10 Dempf, Alois. Schelling; zwei Reden. München, 1955.
Phil 8740.5 De Pierrefeu, Elsa (Tudor). Unity in the spirit. Rindge, N.H., 1955.
Phil 2520.61.16 Descartes, René. Les passions de l'âme. Paris, 1955.
Phil 2520.22 Descartes, René. Philosophical works. N.Y., 1955. 2v.
Phil 6313.14 Deutsch, Felix. The clinical interview. v.1-2. N.Y., 1955. 2v.
Phil 803.10 Devaux, P. De Thales à Bergson. Liége, 1955.
Phil 1955.6.24 Dewey, John. John Dewey. 1st ed. Indianapolis, 1955.
Phil 3195.3.33 Dietzgen, Joseph. Das Wesen der menschlichen Kopfarbeit. Berlin, 1955.
Phil 3195.15.35 Dingler, Hugo. Die Ergreifung des Wirklichen. München, 1955.
Phil 5243.50 Dobbelstein, Herman. Der normale Mensch im Urteil der Psychiatrie. Einsiedeln, 1955.
Phil 178.59.5 Dotterer, Ray H. Postulates and implications. N.Y., 1955.
Phil 3246.250 Drechsler, J. Fichtes Lehre vom Bild. Stuttgart, 1955.
Phil 5592.30 DuMas, F.M. Manifest structure analysis. Missoula, Montana, 1955.
Phil 5238.70 Dunlap and Associates, Stanford, Conn. Mathematical models of human behavior. Stanford, 1955.
Phil 672.136.30 Dunne, John W. Intrusions? London, 1955.
Phil 3823.12 Dunner, J. Baruch Spinoza and western democracy. N.Y., 1955.
Phil 178.71 Durkheim, E. Pragmatisme et socilologie. Paris, 1955.
Phil 335.8 Earle, William A. Objectivity. N.Y., 1955.
Phil 8879.29 Easton, L.D. Ethics. Dubuque, Iowa, 1955.
Phil 1109.2 Eckstein, F. Abriss der griechischen Philosophie. Frankfurt, 1955.
Phil 8879.26 Edel, A. Ethical judgement. Glencoe, 1955.
Phil 1980.4.25 Edman, Irwin. The uses of philosophy. N.Y., 1955.
Phil 8879.28 Edwards, Paul. The logic of moral discourse. Glencoe, Ill., 1955.
Phil 7069.55.15 Ehrenwald, Jan. New dimensions of deep analysis. N.Y., 1955.
Phil 3200.8 Ehrlich, W. Metaphysik. Tübingen, 1955.
Phil 1750.420 Ell, Johannes. Der Existenzialismus in seinem Wesen und Werden. Bonn, 1955.
Phil 6314.7.5 English, Oliver Spurgeon. Emotional problems of living. N.Y., 1955.
Phil 1750.166.100 Etcheverry, A. Le conflit actuel des humanismes. Paris, 1955.
Phil 5238.35 Farrell, B.A. Experimental psychology. N.Y., 1955.
Phil 6315.18.10 Federn, Paul. Ego psychology and the psychoses. N.Y., 1955.
Phil 8585.45 Fedorov, N.I. U tserkovnoi ogrady. Buenos Aires, 1955.
Phil 6315.1.15 Ferenczi, Sandor. Final contributions to the problems and methods of psychoanalysis. London, 1955.
Phil 672.208 Fernández Suárez, Alvaro. El tiempo y el "hay". Madrid, 1955.
Phil 5066.110 Ferrater Mora, José. Lógica matemática. México, 1955.
Phil 1350.14 Ferrero, L. Storia del pitagorismo nel mondo romano. Torino, 1955.
Phil 6315.38 Feuer, L.S. Psychoanalysis and ethics. Springfield, 1955.
Phil 504.2 Février, Paulette. Déterminisme et indéterminisme. 1. éd. Paris, 1955.
Phil 3640.450 Flam, Leopold. Nietzsche. Bussum, 1955.
Phil 5245.45.5 Flügel, John Carl. Man, morals and society. N.Y., 1955.
Phil 5400.120 Flugel, J.C. Studies in feeling and desire. London, 1955.
Phil 8735.40 Fondazione Giorgio Cini, Venice. Centro de Cultura e Civiltà. Il valore del fine nel mondo. Firenze, 1955.
Phil 2405.10 Foucher, Louis. La philosopie catholique en France au XIX siècle avant la renaissance Thomiste et dans son rapporrt avecelle. Paris, 1955.
Phil 1750.220.5 Foulquié, Paul. L'existentialisme. 9e éd. Paris, 1955.
Phil 180.68.5 Foulquié, Paul. Nouveau précis de philosophie a l'usage des candidats au baccalauréat. Paris, 1955. 3v.
Phil 180.68 Foulquié, Paul. Précis de philosophie. 2. ed. v.2-3. Paris, 1955.
Phil 3270.13.21 Frank, Erich. Knowledge. Chicago, 1955.
Phil 3487.25 Frankfurt Universität. Kant und die Wissenchaften. Frankfurt, 1955.
Phil 1510.5 Fremantle, A.J. The age of belief. Boston, 1955.
Phil 6315.2.12 Freud, Sigmund. The origin and development of psychoanalysis. Chicago, 1955.
Phil 9450.27 Freund, Ludwig. Politik und Ethik. Frankfurt, 1955.
Phil 5045.7.3 Freytag, Bruno baron von. Logik. Stuttgart, 1955-67. 2v.
Phil 180.66 Friederichs, K. Die Selbstgestaltung des Lebendigen. München, 1955.
Phil 3120.30.80 Friedman, M.S. Martin Buber. Chicago, 1955.
Phil 5592.25 Frieling, H. Der Farbenspiegel. Göttingen, 1955.
Phil 525.130 Froebe-Kapteyn, Olga. Mensch und Wandlung. Zürich, 1955.
Phil 3235.81.29 Gabaraev, S.S. Materializm Feierbakha. Tbilisi, 1955.
Phil 181.120 Gaigneron, L. de. Le secret de l'être. Paris, 1955.

1955 - cont.

Phil 4210.161 Gambaro, Angiolo. Antonio Rosmini nella cultura del sus tempo. Torino, 1955?
Phil 4961.65 García Bacca, J.D. Antologia del pensamiento filosófico en Colombia. Bogotá, 1955.
Phil 4006.5.45 Garin, Eugenio. Cronache di filosofia italiana. Bari, 1955.
Phil 6319.1.195 Gemelli, A. Psicologia e religione nella concezione analitica di C.G. Jung. Milano, 1955.
Phil 4210.117.2 Gentile, G. Rosmini e Gioberti. 2. ed. Firenze, 1955.
Phil 8831.7 Gentile, Marino. I grandi moralisti. Torino, 1955.
Phil 4060.4.80 Gentiluomo, Domenico. Il relativismo sperimentale di Antonio Aliotta nel suo svolgimento storico. Roma, 1955.
Phil 806.18 Geymonat, Ludoviro. Storia del pensiero filosofico. Milano, 1955-56.
Phil 5465.192.1 Ghiselin, Brewster. The creative process; a symposium. N.Y., 1955.
Phil 1511.3.13.15 Gilson, Étienne. History of Christian philosophy in the Middle Ages. London, 1955.
Phil 1511.3.13.10A Gilson, Étienne. History of Christian philosophy in the Middle Ages. N.Y., 1955.
Phil 3120.8.115 Gilson, Lucie. Méthode et métaphysique selon Franz Brentano. Paris, 1955.
Phil 3120.8.120 Gilson, Lucie. La psychologie descriptive selon Franz Brentano. Paris, 1955.
Phil 665.77 Gindl, I. Seele und Geist. Wien, 1955.
Phil 4065.150 Giusso, Lorenzo. Scienza e filosofia in Giordano Bruno. Napoli, 1955.
Phil 4006.8.30 Giusso, Lorenzo. La tradizione ermetica nella filosofia italiana. Roma, 1955?
Phil 6316.12.5 Glover, Edward. The technique of psycho-analysis. London, 1955.
Phil 6319.1.196 Goldbrunner, Josef. Individuation. London, 1955.
Phil 310.7.10 Golovakha, I.P. Marksistskaia filosofiia v poznavalmosti mira. Kiev, 1955.
Phil 2030.6A Goodman, Nelson. Fact, fiction and forecast. Cambridge, 1955.
Phil 6316.13 Gratton, Henri. Psychoanalyses d'hier et d'aujourd'hui comme thérapeutiques. Paris, 1955.
Phil 6956.15 Green, Sidney L. A manual of first aid for mental health. N.Y., 1955.
Phil 972.15 Greenwalt, E.A. The Point Loma community in California, 1897-1942. Berkeley, 1955.
Phil 1750.390 Gregoire, Franz. Questions concernant l'existentialisme. 2. ed. Louvain, 1955.
Phil 1750.410 Grimsley, Ronald. Existentialist thought. Cardiff, 1955.
Phil 165.40 Gropp, R.O. Festschrift. Berlin, 1955.
Phil 8407.27 Guardo, V. L'estetica e i suoi problemi. Siracusa, 1955.
Phil 2733.106.5 Guéroult, Martial. Malebranche. Paris, 1955. 3v.
Phil 2520.242.5 Gueroult, Martial. Nouvelles réflexions sur la preuve ontologique de Descartes. Paris, 1955.
Phil 5520.180 Guiraud, P. La sémantique. 1. éd. Paris, 1955.
Phil 5520.110 Gusdorf, George. La parole. 1. éd. Paris, 1955.
Phil 4120.8.30 Guzzo, Augusto. La scienza. Torino, 1955.
Phil 5068.24 Haeberli, Hans. Der Begriff der Wissenschaft im logischen Positivismus. Bern, 1955.
Phil 2520.250 Hagmann, Moritz. Descartes. Winterthur, 1955.
Phil 2520.250.2 Hagmann, Moritz. Descartes in der Auffassung durch die Historiker der Philosophie. Winterthur, 1955.
Phil 4595.4.30 Hansen, Valdemar. K. Kroman. København, 1955.
Phil 8832.7 Harkness, G.E. The sources of western culture. London, 1955.
Phil 5274.12 Harmon, Harry Horace. Some observations on factor analysis. Santa Monica, 1955.
Phil 338.39 Harris, E.E. Objectivity and reason. Johannesburg, 1955.
Phil 3640.465 Hartmann, H. Nietzsche, critique d'art. Manosque, 1955.
Phil 3450.18.80 Hartmann, N. Kleinere Schriften. Berlin, 1955. 3v.
Phil 5203.11.20 Harvard University. The Harvard list of books in psychology. Cambridge, 1955.
Phil 5650.25 Harvard University. Psycho-Acoustic Laboratory. Bibliography on hearing. Cambridge, 1955.
Phil 5590.175 Hawthorn, H.B. Sociology of personality functioning. Sioux City, Iowa, 1955.
Phil 182.115 Hedenius, I. Fyra dygder. Stockholm, 1955.
Phil 3425.56.10 Hegel, Georg Wilhelm Friedrich. Ästhetik. Berlin, 1955.
Phil 3425.70.18 Hegel, Georg Wilhelm Friedrich. Grundlinien der Philosophie des Rechts. 4. Aufl. Hamburg, 1955.
Phil 3425.28.12 Hegel, Georg Wilhelm Friedrich. Hegel. Frankfurt, 1955.
Phil 3425.73.8A Hegel, Georg Wilhelm Friedrich. The phenomenology of mind. 2nd ed. London, 1955.
Phil 3425.40.10 Hegel, Georg Wilhelm Friedrich. Die Vernunft in der Geschichte. Hamburg, 1955.
Phil 3450.19.55A Heidegger, Martin. Vom Wesen des Grundes. 4e Aufl. Frankfurt, 1955.
Phil 3450.19.10.2 Heidegger, Martin. Was ist Metaphysik? 7e Aufl. Frankfort, 1955.
Phil 3850.18.170 Heidemann, I. Untersuchungen zur Kantkritik Max Schelers. Köln? 1955.
Phil 3801.448 Heinrich, W. Schellings Lehre von den Letzten Dingen. Salzburg, 1955.
Phil 8697.23 Hennemann, Gerhard. Philosophie, Religion, moderne Naturwissenschaft. Witten, 1955.
Phil 8587.65.3 Hessen, Johannes. Platonismus und Prophetismus. 2. Aufl. München, 1955.
Phil 8587.65.5 Hessen, Johannes. Religionsphilosophie. 2. Aufl. v.1-2. München, 1955.
Phil 3450.33.5 Hildebrand, D. von. Die Menschkeit am Scheideweg. Regensburg, 1955.
Phil 3450.33.7 Hildebrand, D. von. Metaphysik der Gemeinscheaft. Regensburg, 1955.
Phil 8957.12.7 Hildebrand, D. von. True morality and its counterfeits. N.Y., 1955.
Phil 288.15.5 Hoenen, Peter. The philosophical nature of physical bodies. West Baden Springs, Ind., 1955.
Phil 288.15.2 Hoenen, Peter. Quaestiones noeticae de extensione corporea. Romae, 1955.
Phil 92.4 Hoffmeister, J. Wörterbuch der philosophischen Begriffe. Hamburg, 1955.
Phil 8408.12.5 Hogarth, William. The analysis of beauty. Oxford, 1955.
Phil 5850.230.100 Holzschuher, L. von. Praktische Psychologie. 2. Aufl. Seebruck am Chiemsee, 1955.
Phil 3850.27.130 Hommage a Albert Schweitzer. Paris, 1955.
Phil 310.18 Hommes, Jakob. Der technische Eros. Freiburg, 1955.
Phil 6319.1.190.5 Hostie, Raymond. Du mythe à la religion. Bruges, 1955.
Phil 5247.64 Huber, Kurt. Grundbegriffe der Seelenkunde. Ettal, 1955.
Phil 2055.15.30 Hulme, Thomas E. Further speculations. Minnesota, 1955.

Chronological Listing

Phil 2050.41.11A Hume, David. An inquiry concerning human understanding. N.Y., 1955.

Phil 2050.23.2 Hume, David. Selections. N.Y., 1955.

Phil 2050.78.5 Hume, David. Writings on economics. Madison, 1955.

Phil 2055.8.35 Hyde, Lawrence. An introduction to organic philosophy. Reigate, 1955.

Phil 3850.27.140 Hygen, J.B. Albert Schweitzers Kulturkritik. Göttingen, 1955.

Phil 3425.390 Hyppolite, Jean. Études sur Marx et Hegel. Paris, 1955.

Phil 4210.157 Incontro Internazionale Rosminiano, Bolzana. La problematica politico-sociale nel pensiero di Antonio Rosmini. Roma, 1955.

Phil 2070.27.5 James, William. Pragmatism. Chicago, 1955.

Phil 3801.465.10 Jaspers, Karl. Schelling. München, 1955.

Phil 5520.128 Johnson, D.McE. The psychology of thought and judgment. N.Y., 1955.

Phil 6319.1.56 Jung, C.G. Psychology and religion. New Haven, 1955.

Phil 6319.1.80 Jung-Institut, Zürich, Studien zur analytischen Psychologie. Zürich, 1955. 2v.

Phil 7069.55.2A Jung Institute, Zürich. The interpretation of nature and the psyche. London, 1955.

Phil 7069.55 Jung Institute, Zürich. The interpretation of nature and the psyche. N.Y., 1955.

Phil 3480.69.6 Kant, Immanuel. Allgemeine Naturgeschichte und Theorie des Himmels. Berlin, 1955.

Phil 5250.40 Karn, H.W. An introduction to psychology. N.Y., 1955.

Phil 8590.34 Kerényi, Karoly. Umgang mit Göttlichem. Göttingen, 1955.

Phil 5374.44.5 Klages, Ludwig. Vom Wesen des Bewusstseins. 4. Aufl. München, 1955.

Phil 6320.11.10 Klein, M. New directions in psycho-analysis. London, 1955.

Phil 185.67.5 Klubertanz, G.P. Introduction to the philosophy of being. N.Y., 1955.

Phil 8700.14 Kocher, Paul Harold. Science and religion in Elizabethan England. San Marino, Calif., 1955.

Phil 5080.6 Koerner, S. Conceptual thinking. Cambridge, Eng., 1955.

Phil 3492.44 Körner, Stephan. Kant. Harmondsworth, 1955.

Phil 8980.495.5 Kolbanovskii, Viktor N. Kommunisticheskaia moral' i byt. Moskva, 1955.

Phil 4803.495.220 Kollątaj, Hugo. Porządek fizyczno-moralny oraz Pomysty do dzieła Porządek fizyczno-moralny. Warszawa, 1955.

Phil 3120.2.110 Kolman, E. Bernard Bol'tsano. Moskva, 1955.

Phil 2100.4.30 Koren, H.J. An introduction to the philosophy of animate nature. St. Louis, 1955.

Phil 3010.8 Koyré, Alexandre. Mystiques. Paris, 1955.

Phil 3195.15.80 Krampf, W. Die Philosophie Hugo Dinglers. München, 1955.

Phil 185.70 Krishna, Daya. The nature of philosophy. Calcutta, 1955.

Phil 3801.499 Kunz, Hans. Schellings Gedichte und dichtische Pläne. Zürich, 1955.

Phil 2725.11.20 Lachelier, Jules. La nature. 1e éd. Paris, 1955.

Phil 2515.22.20 LaHarpe, Jacqueline Ellen Violette de. Jean-Pierre de Crousaz et le conflit des idées au siècle des lumières. Genève, 1955.

Phil 3425.375 Lakebrink, Bernhard. Hegels dialektische Ontologie und die thomistische Analektik. Köln, 1955.

Phil 735.140 Lamont, W.D. The value judgement. Edinburgh, 1955.

Phil 811.15 Lamprecht, S.P. Our philosophical traditions. N.Y., 1955.

Phil 6321.45 Langstroth, Lovell. Structure of the ego. Stanford, Calif., 1955.

Phil 4080.8.87 Lantrua, A. La filosofia di Augusto Conti. Padova, 1955.

Phil 3450.11.140 Lauer, Quentin. Phénoménologie, existence. Paris, 1955.

Phil 3450.11.142 Lauer, Quentin. Phénoménologie de Husserl. 1st ed. Paris, 1955.

Phil 2725.35 Lavelle, Louis. De l'intimité spirituelle. Paris, 1955.

Phil 186.120 Lazerowitz, M. The structure of metaphysics. London, 1955.

Phil 186.120.2 Lazerowitz, M. The structure of metaphysics. N.Y., 1955.

Phil 342.20 Leary, Lewis. The unity of knowledge. Garden City, N.Y., 1955.

Phil 5051.32 Leblanc, H. An introduction to deductive logic. N.Y., 1955.

Phil 5251.52 Leithauser, J.C. Das unbekannte Ich. Berlin, 1955.

Phil 525.135 Lemaître, S. Textes mystiques d'Orient et d'Occident. Paris, 1955.

Phil 310.8 Lewis, John. Marxism and the irrationalists. London, 1955.

Phil 186.115 Liat, W.S. Methods of comparative philosophy. Leiden, 1955.

Phil 4011.3.5 Librizzi, C. Lo spiritualismo religioso nell'età del Risorgimento italiano. Catania, 1955.

Phil 6321.40 Lindner, R.M. The fifty minute hour. N.Y., 1955.

Phil 8412.29 Lion, Ferdinand. Die Geburt der Aphrodite. Heidelberg, 1955.

Phil 5051.33 Little, W.W. Applied logic. Boston, 1955.

Phil 2250.105A Loewenberg, j. Royce's synoptic vision. n.p., 1955.

Phil 5850.259 Lombard, G.F.F. Behavior in a selling group. Boston, 1955.

Phil 3493.27 Lotz, J.B. Kant und die Scholastik Heute. Pullach, 1955.

Phil 315.6.3 Lovejoy, A.O. The revolt against dualism. La Salle, Ill., 1955.

Phil 3850.16.100 Luongo, M.R. Il relativismo di G. Simmel e di Pirandello. Napoli, 1955?

Phil 9245.60A MacIver, R.M. The pursuit of happiness. N.Y., 1955.

Phil 1517.7 Maier, A. Metaphysische Hintergrunde der spatscholastischen Naturphilosophie. Roma, 1955.

Phil 2733.64 Malebranche, Nicolas. Malebranche et Leibniz. Thèse. Paris, 1955.

Phil 8887.85 Mandelbaum, M.H. The phenomenology of moral experience. Glencoe, Ill., 1955.

Phil 2750.19.26 Marcel, Gabriel. L'homme problematique. Paris, 1955.

Phil 165.250 Marcus, Aage. Livsanskuelse gennem tiderne. København, 1955-58. 10v.

Phil 6315.32 Marcuse, Herbert. Eros and civilization. Boston, 1955.

Phil 6990.60 Marert, Léonce. Nouvelle histoire de Lourdes. Paris, 1955.

Phil 4363.7.10 Marias Aguilera, Julián. Ensayos de convivencia. Buenos Aires, 1955.

Phil 4313.5.10 Marias Aguilera, Julian. Filosofía actual, y Existencialismo en España. Madrid, 1955.

Phil 2475.1.128 Maritain, Jacques. Bergsonian philosophy and Thomism. N.Y., 1955.

Phil 2750.11.43 Maritain, Jacques. An essay on Christian philosophy. N.Y., 1955.

Phil 2750.11.78 Maritain, Jacques. The social and political philosophy of Jacques Maritain. N.Y., 1955.

Phil 3494.45.5A Martin, Gottfried. Kant's metaphysics and theory of science. Manchester, Eng., 1955.

Phil 5722.35 Martin, P.W. Experiment in depth. London, 1955.

Phil 8413.27 Martini, Miro. La deformazione estetica. Milano, 1955.

Phil 1750.695 Martins, Diamantino. Existencialismo. Braga, 1955.

Phil 8837.15 Masson-Ourel, Paul. La morale et l'histoire. 1. éd. Paris, 1955.

Phil 6980.460 Matte Blanco, Ignacio. Estudios de psicología dinámica. Santiago de Chile, 1955.

Phil 2150.16.35 Mayer, Frederick. Patterns of a new philosophy. Washington, 1955.

Phil 8870.15.2 Melden, A.I. Ethical theories. 2nd ed. N.Y., 1955.

Phil 5252.85.5 Merleau-Ponty, M. La structure du comportement. 3. ed. Paris, 1955.

Phil 5252.105 Mertsalov, V.S. K issledovaniiu problem psikhologicheskoi voiny; sbornik statei. Miunkhen, 1955.

Phil 8887.75.10 Messner, J. Ethik. Innsbruck, 1955.

Phil 8620.47 Metzger, A. Freiheit und Tod. Tübingen, 1955.

Phil 3625.20.30 Meyer, Hans. Systematische Philosophie. Paderborn, 1955. 4v.

Phil 4818.571.20 Michăilescce, Ştefan C. Pagini filozofice alese. Bucureşti, 1955.

Phil 2750.11.120 Michener, N.W. Maritain on the nature of man in a Christian democracy. Hull, 1955.

Phil 5066.105 Miller, J.W. Exercises in introductory symbolic logic. Montreal? 1955.

Phil 3790.4.90 Miller-Rostoska, A. Das Individuelle als Gegenstand der Erkenntnis. Winterthur, 1955.

Phil 5252.110 Monsarrat, K.W. On human thinking. London, 1955.

Phil 6962.37 Moore, W.L. The mind in chains. N.Y., 1955.

Phil 8962.15 Morale sans péché? Paris, 1955.

Phil 8980.580 Moscow. Gosudavstvennaia Bibiblioteka SSSR. Imeni V.I. Lenina. Chto chitat' o kommunisticheskoi morali. Moskva, 1955.

Phil 4710.78 Moskalenko, F.Ia. Uchenie ob induktivnykh vyrodakh v istorii russkoi logiki. Kiev, 1955.

Phil 2475.1.310 Mossé-Bastide, R.M. Bergson. Paris, 1955.

Phil 187.154 Mucchielli, Roger. Logique et morale. Paris, 1955.

Phil 974.3.123 Muecke, Johanna. Erinnerungen an Rudolf Steiner. Basel, 1955.

Phil 6322.31.2 Mullahy, Patrick. Oedipus. N.Y., 1955.

Phil 6322.35 Munroe, R.L. Schools of psychoanalytic thought. N.Y., 1955.

Phil 6315.2.155 Natenberg, M. The case history of Sigmund Freud. 1. ed. Chicago, 1955.

Phil 5520.155 Nesbit, F.L. Language meaning. 1. ed. N.Y., 1955.

Phil 1713.3 Newman, J. A time for truth. Dublin, 1955.

Phil 3425.385 Nicolin, F. Gründlinien einer geisteswissenschaftlichen Pädagogik bei G.W.F. Hegel. Bonn, 1955.

Phil 3425.385.2 Nicolin, F. Hegels Bildungstheorie. Bonn, 1955.

Phil 4260.124.5 Nicolini, F. Saggi vichiani. Napoli, 1955.

Phil 4757.2.100 Nicoll, Maurice. Psychological commentaries on the teaching of G.I. Gurdjieff and P.D. Ouspensky. London, 1955-57. 5v.

Phil 9070.57 Nicolson, Harold Georg. Good behavior. London, 1955.

Phil 3640.17.2 Nietzsche, Friedrich. Un zeitgemässe Betrachtungen. Stuttgart, 1955.

Phil 8125.37.5 Nivelle, A. Les théories esthétiques en Allemagne de Baumgarten à Kant. Paris, 1955.

Phil 3013.2 Noack, H. Deutsche Geisteswelt. Darmstadt, 1955. 2v.

Phil 6323.10 Nuttin, Jozef. Psychanalyse et conception spiritualiste de l'homme. 2. ed. Louvain, 1955.

Phil 3450.19.135 Oberti, Elisa. L'estetica nel pensiero di Heidegger. Milano, 1955.

Phil 1560.12 O'Donnell, J. Reginald. Nine medieval thinkers. Toronto, 1955.

Phil 8110.8 Ogden, Henry. English taste in landscape. Washington, 1955.

Phil 1714.4 Oggioni, Emilio. Filosofia e psicologia nel pensiero postromantico. Bologna, 1955.

Phil 2340.10.140 Orsi, Concetta. La filosofia dell'organismo di A.N. Whitehead. Napoli, 1955.

Phil 2200.10 Osborn, Arthur W. The expansion of awareness. Reigate, 1955.

Phil 165.45 Palmeró, J. La philosophie par les textes. Paris, 1955.

Phil 346.19 Pap, Arthur. Analytische Erkenntnistheorie. Wien, 1955.

Phil 815.32 Paris. Institut Catholique. Faculte de Philosophie. Histoire de la philosophie et metaphysique. Paris, 1955.

Phil 190.83 Parpert, F. Philosophie der Einsamkeit. München, 1955.

Phil 2805.73 Pascal, Blaise. Opuscules et lettres. Paris, 1955.

Phil 8595.40 Paton, H.J. The modern predicament. London, 1955.

Phil 5625.75.15 Pavlov, Ivan P. Selected works. Moscow, 1955.

Phil 310.20 Pavlov, Todor D. Osnovnoto v Michurinskoto uchenie v svetlinata na dialekticheskii materializm. Sofia, 1955.

Phil 5850.305A Peale, N.V. The power of positive thinking. N.Y., 1955.

Phil 978.49.830 Peoppig, Fred. Schicksalswege zu Rudolf Steiner. 2. Aufl. Stuttgart, 1955.

Phil 8416.9 Pepper, Stephen. The work of art. Indiana, 1955.

Phil 4620.1.5 Pétursson, Helgi. Erlendar Greiner. Reykjavík, 1955.

Phil 5590.200 Phillipson, H. The object relations technique. London, 1955. 2v.

Phil 8595.45 Philosophies chrétiennes. Paris, 1955.

Phil 8416.19 Piemontese, A. L'intelligenza nell'arte. Milano, 1955.

Phil 8416.11.10 Plekhanov, Georgii Valentinovich. Kunst und Literatur. Berlin, 1955.

Phil 75.46 Polska Akademia Nauk. Komitet Filozoficzny. Bibliografia filozofii polskiej [1750-1830]. v.1,3. Warszawa, 1955. 2v.

Phil 5374.185 Port, Kurt. Die Enge des Bewusstseins. Esslingen, 1955.

Phil 2825.20 Pradines, M. L'aventure de l'esprit dans les espèces. Paris, 1955.

Phil 5025.1.3 Prantl, Carl von. Geschichte der Logik im Abendlande. v.1-4. Graz, 1955. 3v.

Phil 5003.10 Primakovskii, A.P. Bibliografiia po logike. Moskva, 1955.

Phil 5055.25A Prior, Arthur N. Formal logic. Oxford, 1955.

Phil 1750.445 Prohaska, L. Existentialismus und Padagogik. Freiburg, 1955.

Phil 1750.60 Przywara, Erich. In und Gegen. Nürnberg, 1955.

Phil 1815.8 Pucelle, Jean. L'idéalisme en Angleterre. Neuchâtel, 1955.

Phil 4120.4.115 Puglisi, Filippo. La concezione estetico-filosofica di Giovanni Gentile. Catania, 1955.

Phil 4200.5.30 Pusci, F. Lettere. Firenze, 1955. 2v.

Phil 5256.5 Quastler, H. Information theory in psychology. Glencoe, 1955.

Phil 8622.14 Radhakrishnan, S. Recovery of faith. 1. ed. N.Y., 1955.

1955 - cont.

Phil 3475.3.130 Räber, T. Das Glasein in der "Philosophie" von K. Jaspers. Bern, 1955.

Phil 4080.3.270 Raggiunti, R. La conoscenza storica. Firenze, 1955.

Phil 2750.19.90 Rainho, Antonio Angelo Leite. L'existencialisme de M. Gabriel Marcel. Lisbonne, 1955.

Phil 8892.65 Raphael, D. Daiches. Moral judgement. London, 1955.

Phil 960.163.10 Ray Chaudhuri, A.K. Self and falsity in Advaita Vedanta. 1st ed. Calcutta, 1955.

Phil 8418.20.5 Read, Herbert. Icon and idea. Harvard, 1955.

Phil 5421.10 Remits, Ernest L. The feeling of superiority and anxiety-superior. Ottawa, 1955.

Phil 9240.13 Rice, P.B. On the knowledge of good and evil. N.Y., 1955.

Phil 5520.145 Richards, Ivor Armstrong. Speculative instruments. Chicago, 1955.

Phil 5257.28.35 Roback, A.A. Present day psychology. N.Y., 1955.

Phil 1717.11.20 Robinson, D.S. Crucial issues in philosophy. Boston, 1955.

Phil 192.96 Rosenberg, Max. Introduction to philosophy. N.Y., 1955.

Phil 1750.166.105 Roshwald, M. Humanism in practice. London, 1955.

Phil 4210.14 Rosmini-Serbati, Antonio. Antologia pedagogica. 1. ed. Brescia, 1955.

Phil 348.7.5 Rougier, Louis A.P. Traité de la connaissance. Paris, 1955.

Phil 1717.3.20 Royce, J. The spirit of modern philosophy. N.Y., 1955.

Phil 4768.1.5 Rozental', M.M. Chto takoe marksistskaia teoriia poznaniia. Moskva, 1955.

Phil 102.5.12 Rozental, Mark Moiseevich. Petit dictionnaire philosophique. Moscow, 1955.

Phil 817.8.15 Ruggiero, Guido de. Breve storia della filosofia ad uso delle scuole. Bari, 1955. 3v.

Phil 165.26 Runes, D.D. Treasury of philosophy. N.Y., 1955.

Phil 8892.62.5 Russell, Bertrand Russell. Human society in ethics and politics. N.Y., 1955.

Phil 7069.55.20 Saint-Clair, Simone. The heart aflame. London, 1955.

Phil 4961.605 Salazar Bondy, Augusto. La filosofía en el Perú. Wáshington, 1955.

Phil 4369.2.86 Sanches, Francisco. Opera philosophica. Coimbra, 1955.

Phil 8419.40 Santayana, G. The sense of beauty, being the outlines of aesthetic theory. N.Y., 1955.

Phil 3850.18.30A Scheler, Max. Liebe und Erkenntnis. Bern, 1955.

Phil 3850.18.25 Scheler, Max. Vom Umsturz der Werte. 4. Aufl. v.2,3,5,6,8,10. Bern, 1955. 7v.

Phil 3800.386.5 Schelling, F.W.J. von. Zur Geschichte der neueren Philosophie; Münchener Vorlesungen. Stuttgart, 1955.

Phil 3805.31.6 Schleiermacher, Friedrich. On religion. N.Y., 1955.

Phil 103.3.30.10 Schmidt, Heinrich. Philosophisches Wörterbuch. 13. Aufl. Stuttgart, 1955.

Phil 3808.76.40 Schopenhauer, Arthur. Schopenhauer-Brevier. Wiesbaden, 1955.

Phil 6968.32 Schreben, Daniel P. Memoirs of my nervous illness. London, 1955.

Phil 3801.775.20 Schulz, Walter. Die Vollendung des deutschen Idealismus in der Spätphilosophie Schellings. Stuttgart, 1955.

Phil 5722.40 Seifert, F. Tiefenpsychologie. Düsseldorf, 1955.

Phil 2655.3.100 Sesmat, A. Dialectique. Paris, 1955.

Phil 8980.787 Shishkin, Aleksandr F. Osnovy kommunisticheskoi morali. Moskva, 1955.

Phil 960.180 Silburn, Lilian. Instant et cause. Paris, 1955.

Phil 5722.32.10 Simon, C.W. The EEG. Santa Monica, 1955.

Phil 5545.189 Smedslund, Jan. Multiple-probability learning. Oslo, 1955.

Phil 165.135 Sociedad Cubana de Filosofía. Conversaciones filosóficas interamericanas. Habana, 1955.

Phil 193.125.5 Söhngen, G. Philosophische Einübung in die Theologie. Freiburg, 1955.

Phil 3640.460 Sonns, Stefan. Das Gewissen in der Philosophie Nietzsches. Winterthur, 1955.

Phil 8120.3 Soreil, A. Introduction à l'histoire de l'esthétique française. Bruxelles, 1955.

Phil 1750.435 Sourian, E. L'ombre de Dieum. 1e éd. Paris, 1955.

Phil 3850.42 Speiser, Andreas. Die geistige Arbeit. Basel, 1955.

Phil 3819.14.10 Spinoza, Benedictus de. Chief works. N.Y, 1955[1951] 2v.

Phil 3819.30.55 Spinoza, Benedictus de. Die Ethik nach geometrischer Methode dargestellt. Hamburg, 1955.

Phil 2805.300 Spoerri, T. Der verborgene Pascal. Hamburg, 1955.

Phil 8643.40 Staudinger, Josef. Die letzte Zeit. Innsbruck, 1955.

Phil 1523.12.10 Steenberghen, F. Aristotle in the West. Louvain, 1955.

Phil 8419.18 Stefanini, Luigi. Trattato di estetica. Brescia, 1955-

Phil 978.49.820 Steffen, A. Begegnungen mit Rudolf Steiner. Dornach, 1955.

Phil 978.49.76 Steiner, R. Das Initiaten-Bewusstsein. Freiburg, 1955.

Phil 978.49.275 Steiner, R. Das Johannes-Evangelium. 7. Aufl. Dornach, 1955.

Phil 978.49.255 Steiner, R. Die materialistische Weltanschauung des neunzehnten Jahrhunderts. Basel, 1955.

Phil 978.49.145.5 Steiner, R. Methodik und Wesen der Sprachgestaltung. Dornach, 1955.

Phil 3850.27.132 Steinitz, Benno. Albert Schweitzer. Wien, 1955.

Phil 9065.3 Steubing, Hans. Der Kompromiss als ethisches Problem. Gütersloh, 1955.

Phil 974.3.121 Stieglitz, K. von. Die Christosophie Rudolf Steiners. Witten, 1955.

Phil 665.80 Strasser, Stephan. Seele und Beseeltes. Wien, 1955.

Phil 8598.108 Studi di filosofia della religione. Roma, 1955.

Phil 5058.65 Swabey, M. Logic and nature. 2nd ed. N.Y., 1955.

Phil 3120.8.126 Taljaard, J.A.L. Franz Brentano as wysgeer. Franeker, 1955.

Phil 3850.27.135 Tau, Max. Albert Schweitzer und der Friede. Hamburg, 1955.

Phil 5190.27 Tavanets, P.V. Voprosy teorii suzhdeniia. Moskva, 1955.

Phil 4170.7.98 Tavianini, U. Una polemica filosofica dell'1800. Padova, 1955.

Phil 4080.17.10 Tebaldeschi, I. Il problema della natura nel pensiero di Pantaleo Carabellese. Roma, 1955.

Phil 3808.205 Terzi, Carlo. Schopenhauer. Romae, 1955.

Phil 819.7.5 Thilly, F. A history of philosophy. N.Y., 1955.

Phil 819.11 Thonnard, F.J. A short history of philosophy. Paris, 1955.

Phil 3425.395 Tinivella, Giovanni. Critica dell'idea di progresso. Milano, 1955.

Phil 8599.37 Todoli, José. Filosofía de la religion. Madrid, 1955.

Phil 194.45.5 Tomlin, E.W.F. Living and knowing. London, 1955.

Phil 2805.485F Tricentenaire du mémorial de Blaise Pascal, 23 Novembre 1654-1954. Paris, 1955.

Phil 5627.198 Trillhaas, W. Die innere Welt. 2. Aufl. München, 1955.

1955 - cont.

Phil 6315.2.157A Trilling, L. Freud and the crisis of our culture. Boston, 1955.

Phil 8894.32.5 Tsanoff, Radoslov A. Ethics. N.Y., 1955.

Phil 1750.26 Ussher, A. Journey through dread. N.Y., 1955.

Phil 2920.3.32 Valensin, Auguste. Regards. Paris, 1955-56. 3v.

Phil 6322.41 Vandendriessche, Gaston. The parapraxis in the Haizmann case of Sigmund Freud. Louvain, 1955.

Phil 2905.1.255 Viallet, François A. L'univers personnel de Teilhard. Paris, 1955-61. 2v.

Phil 5374.170 Vincent, M. L'image dynamique. Paris, 1955.

Phil 4265.1.41 Vivante, Leone. A philosophy of potentiality. London, 1955.

Phil 2050.232 Vlachos, Georges. Essai sur la politique de Hume. Athènes, 1955.

Phil 8430.35 Vogel, Heinrich. Der Christ und das Schöne. 1. Aufl. Berlin, 1955.

Phil 3585.12.80 Vogel, Paul. Theodor Litt. Berlin, 1955.

Phil 3903.3.110 Vossius, G.J. Universalis philosophiae. Leiden, 1955.

Phil 3503.11 Vuillemin, Jules. Physique et métaphysique Kantiennes. 1. éd. Paris, 1955.

Phil 4710.18 Vysheslavtser, B.P. Vechnoe v russkoi filosofii. N.Y., 1955.

Phil 3890.10.120 Waismann, A. Ernst Troeltsch o el drama del historicismo. Cordoba, 1955.

Phil 525.123.2 Walther, G. Phänomenologie der Mystik. 2. Aufl. Olten, 1955.

Phil 2340.16.30 Weems, B.F. Challenge eternal. N.Y., 1955.

Phil 845.2.5 Weinstock, Heinrich. Realer Humanismus. Heidelberg, 1955.

Phil 3110.190 Weiss, Victor. Die Gnosis Jakob Böhmes. Zürich, 1955.

Phil 5262.49 Wellek, A. Ganzheitspsychologie und Strukturtheorie. Bern, 1955.

Phil 1722.9 White, M.G. The age of analysis. Boston, 1955.

Phil 5850.385.86 White, Wendell. Psychology in living. 3rd ed. N.Y., 1955.

Phil 5545.185 Wieck, H.H. Zur Psychologie und Psychopathologie der Erinnerungen. Stuttgart, 1955.

Phil 1750.400A Wild, John. The challenge of existentialism. Bloomington, 1955.

Phil 630.49.10 Wild, John. The return to reason. Chicago, 1955.

Phil 9495.155.10 Williamson, Geoffrey. Morality fair. London, 1955.

Phil 5850.387.5 Wilner, D.M. Human relations in interracial housing. Minneapolis, 1955.

Phil 1830.15 Winn, R.B. American philosophy. N.Y., 1955.

Phil 5066.85 Wiskundig Genootschap. Amsterdam. Mathematical interpretation of formal systems. Amsterdam, 1955.

Phil 5520.165 Wolfard, M.R. Thinking about thinking. N.Y., 1955.

Phil 9035.98 Wolff, Edgar Maurice. Le individualisme radical fondé sur la caractérologie. Paris, 1955.

Phil 8610.955 Wood, Herbert. Belief and unbelief since 1850. Cambridge, 1955.

Phil 3925.11.25 Wust, Peter. Briefe an Freunde. Münster, 1955.

Phil 110.5 Zaragueta Bengoechea, Juan. Vocabulario filosófico. Madrid, 1955.

Phil 575.147.80 Zaza, N. Étude critique de la notion d'engagement chez E. Mounier. Genève, 1955.

Phil 4959.230.5 Zea, Leopoldo. La filosofía en México. v.1-2. Mexico, 1955.

Phil 5066.75 Zeisler, E.B. Foundations of logic and math. 1. ed. Chicago, 1955- 3v.

Phil 9495.155.5 Zenkovskii, V.V. Na poroge zrelosti. 2. izd. Parizh, 1955.

Phil 4710.70.2 Zen'kovskii, V.V. Russkie mysliteli i Evropa. Izd. 2. Paris, 1955.

Phil 8715.4 Zocher, Rudolf. Philosophie in Begegnung mit Religion und Wissenschaft. München, 1955.

Phil 5592.50 Zulliger, Hans. Der Diapositiv-Z-Test. Bern, 1955?

1956

Phil 175.54 Abraches, Cassiano. Metafísica. Braga, 1956.

Phil 6310.1.27A Adler, A. The individual psychology of Alfred Adler. 1st ed. N.Y., 1956.

Phil 3450.11.160 Adorno, T.W. Zur Metakritik der Erkenntnistheorie. Stuttgart, 1956.

Phil 5414.25 Airas, Erkki. Syyllisyydentuntoon vaikuttavista tekijöistä. Helsinki, 1956.

Phil 8400.13 Akademiia Khudozhestv SSSR. Institut Teorii i Istorii Iskusstva. Ocherki marksistsko-leninskoi estetiki. Moskva, 1956.

Phil 8400.10 Akademiia Nauk SSSR. Institut Filosofii. Voprosy marksistsko-leninskoi estetiki. Moskva, 1956.

Phil 5040.32 Albrecht, Erhard. Die Beziehungen von Erkenntnistheorie, Logik und Sprache. Halle, 1956.

Phil 6315.2.165 Aldington, H.D. Tribute to Freud. N.Y., 1956.

Phil 2445.4.20 Alexandre, M. En souvenir de Michel Alexandre. Paris, 1956.

Phil 2005.10.80 Allan, Donald James. Guy Cromwell Field. London, 1956.

Phil 978.49.825 Allen, P.M. The writings and lectures of Rudolf Steiner. N.Y., 1956.

Phil 2520.193.5 Alquié, F. Descartes, l'homme et l'oeuvre. Paris, 1956.

Phil 6980.40 American Psychiatric Association. Approaches to the study of human personality. Washington, 1956.

Phil 5240.35.3 Anastasi, Anne. Differential psychology. N.Y., 1956.

Phil 8080.9 Anceschi, Luciano. D. Hume e i presupposti empiristici della estetica kantiana. Milano, 1956.

Phil 1750.460 Anders, Günther. Die Antiquiertheit des Menschen. München, 1956.

Phil 930.46 Antica filosofia cinese. v.1-2. Milano, 1956.

Phil 2610.95 Aquirre, Francisco Solano de. El atomismo de Gassendi. Barcelona, 1956.

Phil 165.65 Archivio di Filosofia. Filosofia e simbolismo. Roma, 1956.

Phil 165.67 Archivio di Filosofia. Metafisica ed esperienza religiosa. Roma, 1956.

Phil 4961.805.10 Ardao, Arturo. La filosofía en el Uruguay en el siglo XX. México, 1956.

Phil 6315.2.305 Arlow, J.A. The legacy of Sigmund Freud. N.Y., 1956.

Phil 1845.12 Armstrong, A.E. In the last analysis. N.Y., 1956.

Phil 2855.6.82 Arnold Reymond. Torino, 1956.

Phil 5190.17 Aspects de la dialectique. Paris, 1956.

Phil 5625.95 Association de Psychologie Scientifique de Langue Française. Le conditionnement et l'apprentissage. Strasbourg, 1956.

Phil 8655.12 L'athéisme contemporain. Genève, 1956.

Phil 331.11 Ayer, A.J. The problem of knowledge. London, 1956.

Phil 525.220 Baloković, J.B. Towards the center. N.Y., 1956.

Chronological Listing

Phil 3425.420   Banfi, Antonio. La filosofia di G.G.F. Hegel. Milano, 1956.

Phil 176.207   Barraud, Jean. Philosophie de la qualité. Paris, 1956.

Phil 176.185   Barth, Heinrich. Das Sein der Dinge. Wien, 1956.

Phil 8581.112   Basilius, Harold Albert. Contemporary problems in religion. Detroit, 1956.

Phil 9390.12   Bauernfeind, O. Eid und Frieden. Stuttgart, 1956.

Phil 8402.8   Bayer, Raymond. Traité d'esthétique. Paris, 1956.

Phil 9530.36.8   Beaverbrook, W.M.A. The three keys to success. N.Y., 1956.

Phil 8125.32   Begennu, Siegfried. Zur Theorie des Schönen. Berlin, 1956.

Phil 4961.905   Beltrán Guerrero, Luis. Introducción al positivismo venezolano. Caracas, 1956?

Phil 176.212   Bennett, J.G. The dramatic universe. London, 1956-61. 2v.

Phil 1750.295.5   Bense, Max. Rationalismus und Sensibilität. Krefeld, 1956.

Phil 3640.485   Benz, Ernst. Nietzsches Ideen zur Geschichte des Christentum wider der Kirche. Leiden, 1956.

Phil 5525.54   Bergler, Edmund. Laughter and the sense of humor. N.Y., 1956.

Phil 6671.28   Bernstein, Morey. The search for Bridey Murphy. London, 1956.

Phil 6671.28.5   Bernstein, Morey. The search for Bridey Murphy. 1. ed. Garden City, N.Y., 1956.

Phil 8951.28   Berthélemy, Jean. Structure et dimensions de la liberté. Paris, 1956.

Phil 1750.425   Bertrand, Jean. L'énergie spirituelle et la destinée humaine. Nice, 1956.

Phil 9035.96   Betzendahl, Walter. Der menschliche Charakter in Wertung und Forschung. Paderborn, 1956.

Phil 8980.208   Bezuglov, A.A. Eto kasaetsia usekh. Moskva, 1956.

Phil 3120.15.97.5   Bickel, Lothar. Kultur. Zürich, 1956.

Phil 2520.270   Bievre, C. de. Descartes und Pascal. Brasschaet, 1956.

Phil 5041.65   Bilsky, Manuel. Logic and effective argument. N.Y., 1956.

Phil 6867.30   Binswanger, Ludwig. Drei Formen missglückten : Verstiegenheit, Verschrobenheit, Manieriertheit. Tübingen, 1956.

Phil 6976.30   Binswanger, Ludwig. Drei Formen missglückten Daseins: Verstiegenheit, Verschrobenheit, Manieriertheit. Tübingen, 1956.

Phil 6315.2.226   Binswanger, Ludwig. Erinnerungen an Sigmund Freud. Bern, 1956.

Phil 2733.112   Blanchard, Pierre. L'attention à Dieu selon Malebranche. Paris, 1956.

Phil 282.22   Bleksley, A.E. The problems of cosmology. Johannesburg, 1956.

Phil 2477.6.30   Blondel, Maurice. Les premiers écrits de Maurice Blondel. 1. éd. Paris, 1956.

Phil 8140.4   Blunt, A. Artistic theory in Italy, 1450-1600. Oxford, 1956.

Phil 5011.6   Bocheński, I.M. Formale Logik. Freiburg, 1956.

Phil 730.10A   Bocheński, Innocentius M. The problem of universals. Notre Dame, 1956.

Phil 1701.20.10   Bocheński, J.M. Contemporary European philosophy. 2d ed. Berkeley, 1956.

Phil 3246.225   Boettger, Fritz. Ruf zur Tat; Johann Gottlieb Fichte. 1. Aufl. Berlin, 1956.

Phil 8980.10   Boldyrev, N.I. Vospitanie kommunistecheskoi morali u shkol nikov. Izd. 2. Moskva, 1956.

Phil 5400.128   Bollnow, O.F. Das Wesen der Stimmungen. 3. Aufl. Frankfurt, 1956.

Phil 8626.28   Borgia, Anthony V. Life in the world unseen. London, 1956.

Phil 1750.415   Borrello, Oreste. L'estetica dell'esistenzialismo. Messina, 1956.

Phil 282.19   Boulding, K.E. The image. Ann Arbor, 1956.

Phil 6671.15.6   Bramwell, J.M. Hypnotism: its history, practice, and theory. N.Y., 1956.

Phil 9220.15   Brelting, Rudolf. Die Freundschaft. Düsseldorf, 1956.

Phil 3120.8.45   Brentano, Franz. Die Lehre vom Nrichtigen Urteil. Bern, 1956.

Phil 3450.11.170   Breton, Stanislas. Conscience et intentionalité. Paris, 1956.

Phil 6615.20.5   Breuer, Josef. Studies on hysteria. London, 1956.

Phil 5545.192   Bridoux, André. Le souvenir. 2. éd. Paris, 1956.

Phil 4891.10   Brière, O. Fifty years of Chinese philosophy, 1898-1950. London, 1956.

Phil 270.70   Brill, John. The chance character of human existence. N.Y., 1956.

Phil 5241.118   Bruner, J.S. A study of thinking. N.Y., 1956.

Phil 2805.370.5   Brunet, Georges. Le Pari de Pascal. Paris, 1956.

Phil 176.158.5   Brunner, August. Die Grundragen der Philosophie. 4. Aufl. Freiburg, 1956.

Phil 8581.100   Brunner, August. Die Religion. Freiburg, 1956.

Phil 4065.28   Bruno, Giordano. Opere di G. Bruno e di T. Campanella. Milano, 1956.

Phil 4710.37   Bubnov, Nikolai M. Russische Religionsphilosophen. Heidelberg, 1956.

Phil 3450.19.121   Buddeberg, Else R. Denken und Dichten des Seins. Stuttgart, 1956.

Phil 5590.223   Burckhardt, Georg. Charakter und Umwelt. München, 1956.

Phil 8402.26   Burov, A.I. Esteticheskaia sushchnost' iskusstva. Moskva, 1956.

Phil 1750.772   Bustos, Ismael. El sentido existencial de la política. Santiago de Chile, 1956.

Phil 2480.15   Cabanis, P.J.G. Oeuvres philosophiques. 1. éd. Paris, 1956. 2v.

Phil 7082.22.5   Caillois, Roger. L'incertitude qui vient des rêves. Paris, 1956.

Phil 2520.85.30   Callot, Émile. Problèms du Cartesianisme. Annecy, 1956.

Phil 3925.16.82   Campanale, Domenico. Studi su Wittgenstein. Bari, 1956.

Phil 3484.22   Caramella, Santino. Commentarii alla ragion pura. Palermo, 1956-57.

Phil 585.35   Cardone, Domenico Antonio. Il divenire e l'uomo. v.1-3. 2. ed. Palmi, 1956-57.

Phil 5242.55   Carmichael, L. The making of modern mind. Houston, 1956.

Phil 6315.2.200   Casa de la Cultura Ecuatoriana. Sigmund Freud; homenaje. Cuenca, 1956.

Phil 3450.11.155   Casaubon, Juan A. Germenes de idealismo en las investigaciones logicas de Husserl. Buenos Aires? 1956?

Phil 4002.9.5   Cassirer, Ernst. The Renaissance philosophy of man. Chicago, 1956.

Phil 3160.12.30   Cassirer, Ernst. Wesen und Wirkung des Symbolbegriffs. Oxford, 1956.

Phil 960.200   Challaye, Felicien. Les philosophes de l'Inde. 1. ed. Paris, 1956.

Phil 930.50   Chang, Carsun. China and Gandhian India. Calcutta, 1956.

Phil 5042.40   Chase, Stuart. Guides to straight thinking. 1st ed. N.Y., 1956.

Phil 9075.55   Chauchord, Paul. Les mécanismes cerebraux de la prise de conscience. Paris, 1956.

Phil 4753.2.35   Chernyshevskii, N.G. Das anthropologische Prinzip. Berlin, 1956.

Phil 333.16   Childe, Vere G. Society and knowledge. 1st ed. N.Y., 1956.

Phil 5066.14.5A   Church, Alonzo. Introduction to mathematical logic. Princeton, 1956.

Phil 7069.56.10   Ciba Foundation. Symposium on extrasensory perception. London, 1956.

Phil 4080.3.160.5   Cione, Edmondo. Bibliografia crociana. 1. ed. Roma, 1956.

Phil 2515.10   Cioran, Émile M. La tentation d'exister. 2. éd. Paris, 1956.

Phil 1750.680   Civera, Marin. El hombre. México, 1956.

Phil 1750.80   Civilization du travail? Paris, 1956.

Phil 1300.15   Clarke, M.L. The Roman mind. Cambridge, Mass., 1956.

Phil 1300.10A   Clarke, M.L. The Roman mind. London, 1956.

Phil 3552.375A   Clarke, Samuel. The Leibniz-Clarke correspondence. Manchester, 1956.

Phil 6112.37   Clausen, John A. Sociology and the field of mental health. N.Y., 1956.

Phil 270.75   Cohen, John. Risk and gambling. London, 1956.

Phil 2490.53.20   Comte, Auguste. Rede über den Geist des Positivismus. Hamburg, 1956.

Phil 70.45   Congresso Internacional de Filosofia. Congresso Internacional de Filosofia. São Paulo, 1956.

Phil 2030.1.85   Cope, Jackson I. Joseph Glanvill. St. Louis, 1956.

Phil 2475.1.330   Copleston, F.C. Bergson on morality. London, 1956.

Phil 5068.22   Copleston, F.C. Contemporary philosophy. London, 1956.

Phil 4260.110.5   Corsano, Antonio. Giambattista Vico. Bari, 1956.

Phil 8080.8   Cossio del Pomar, F. Critica de arte de Baudelaire à Malraux. México, 1956.

Phil 177.22.10   Cournot, A.A. An essay on the foundations of our knowledge. N.Y., 1956.

Phil 6312.17   Crow, Lester D. Understanding our behavior. 1st ed. N.Y., 1956.

Phil 4960.605   Cruz Costa, João. Contribuição à história das idéias no Brasil. Rio de Janeiro, 1956.

Phil 4960.605.15   Cruz Costa, João. O positivismo na república. São Paulo, 1956.

Phil 177.72.5   Cuvillier, Armand. Partis pris sur l'art. Paris, 1956.

Phil 2725.30   Daniel-Rops, Henry. Edouard LeRoy et son fauteuil. Paris, 1956.

Phil 2555.8.35   Darbon, André. Les categories de la modalité. 1. éd. Paris, 1956.

Phil 2403.8   Daval, Roger. Histoire des idées en France. 2e éd. Paris, 1956.

Phil 5243.52   Daval, Simone. Psychologie. Paris, 1956. 2v.

Phil 7069.56.20   Davis, S.E. Man being revealed. 1. ed. N.Y., 1956.

Phil 6313.16   Dempsey, P.J.R. Freud. Cork, 1956.

Phil 1660.5   De Santillana, Giorgio. The age of adventure; the Renaissance philosophers. N.Y., 1956.

Phil 2520.78.40   Descartes, René. Descartes par lui-meme. Paris, 1956.

Phil 2520.52.80   Descartes, René. Meditationen über die erste Philosophie. Hamburg, 1956.

Phil 978.59.115   Dhopeshwarkar, A.D. Krishnamurti and the experience. Bombay, 1956.

Phil 8404.6   Diano, Carlo. Linee per una fenomenologia dell'arte. Venezia, 1956.

Phil 2530.15.5   Diderot, Denis. Oeuvres philosophiques. Paris, 1956.

Phil 7069.56.15   Dietz, Paul A. Parapsychologische woordentolk. Den Haag, 1956.

Phil 5500.15   Drozdov, A.V. Voprosy klassifikatsii suzhdenii. Leningrad, 1956.

Phil 6980.254   Ehrenwald, Jan. From medicine man to Freud. N.Y., 1956.

Phil 8879.30   Ehrlich, Walter. Ethik. Tübingen, 1956.

Phil 6115.11.20   Eltz-Hoffmann, L. Feuchtersleben. Salzburg, 1956.

Phil 3235.122   Esin, Ivan M. Die materialistishe Philosophie Ludwig Feuerbachs. 1. Aufl. Berlin, 1956.

Phil 365.52   Ewing, Upton Clary. Thresholds of existence. N.Y., 1956.

Phil 8406.21   Fasola, Giusta Nicco. L'arte nella vita dell'uomo. Pisa, 1956.

Phil 6315.18.5   Federn, Paul. Ich-psychologie und die Psychosen. Bern, 1956.

Phil 3246.79.15A   Fichte, Johann Gottlieb. Fichtes Freiheitslehre. 1. Aufl. Düsseldorf, 1956.

Phil 3246.45.6   Fichte, Johann Gottlieb. Grundlage der gesammten Wissenschaftslehre. Hamburg, 1956.

Phil 3246.47.26   Fichte, Johann Gottlieb. Die Grundzüge des gegenwartigen Zeitalters. Hamburg, 1956.

Phil 3246.53.10   Fichte, Johann Gottlieb. Über den Gelehrten. Berlin, 1956.

Phil 3246.68.15   Fichte, Johann Gottlieb. The vocation of man. N.Y., 1956.

Phil 8585.40   Filosofia. Palmi, 1956.

Phil 1750.65   Flam, Leopold. De krisis van de burgerlijke moraal. Antwerpen, 1956.

Phil 5080.7   Flew, A. Essays in conceptual analysis. London, 1956.

Phil 5045.16   Fogarasi, Béla. Logik. Berlin, 1956.

Phil 180.68.10   Foulquié, Paul. Quelques conseils pour la dissertation. 3. ed. Paris, 1956.

Phil 5245.50   Fraisse, Paul. Manuel pratique de psychologie experimentale. 1. éd. Paris, 1956.

Phil 5585.140.5   Fraisse, Paul. Les structures rythmiques. Thèse. Bruxelles, 1956.

Phil 4756.1.42   Frank, Semen L. Real'nost' i chelovek; metafizika chelovecheskogo bytiia. Parizh, 1956.

Phil 665.75A   Frankel, Charles. The case for modern man. 1st ed. N.Y., 1956.

Phil 5245.55   Fraser, John Munro. Psychology. N.Y., 1956.

Phil 5400.130   Frijda, N.H. De betekenis van de gelaatsexpressie. Amsterdam, 1956.

Phil 6980.309   Fromm-Reichmann, Frieda. Progress in psychotherapy. N.Y., 1956.

Phil 5075.6   Fuerstenberg, Hans. Dialectique du XX siècle. Paris, 1956.

Phil 3488.34   Gablentz, Otto Heinrich von der. Kants politische Philosophie und die Weltpolitik unserer Tage. Berlin, 1956.

Phil 181.57.15   Galli, Gallo. Studi di filosofia. Torino, 1956.

Phil 3450.19.215   Garcia Bacca, Juan David. Comentarios a la esencia de la poesia de Heidegger. Caracas, 1956.

1956 - cont.

Phil 4803.454.80 — Gennadii, abbot. Zakon tvoreniia. Buenos Aires, 1956.
Phil 1750.450 — Giannini, G. L'esistenzialismo positivo di Nicola Abbagnano. Brescia, 1956.
Phil 7069.56.5 — Gibt es Geister? Bern, 1956.
Phil 530.20.100 — Gieraths, Gundolf Maria. Reichtum des Lebens. Düsseldorf, 1956.
Phil 1515.2.5 — Gilen, Leonhard. Kleutgen und die Theorie des Erkenntnisbildes. Meisenheim, 1956.
Phil 1806.2 — Ginestier, Paul. La pensée anglo-saxonne depuis 1900. 1e éd. Paris, 1956.
Phil 8881.73 — Ginsberg, Morris. Reason and experience in ethics. London, 1956.
Phil 5068.26 — Giorgianni, Virgilio. Neopositivismo e scienza de diritto. Roma, 1956.
Phil 6316.12.10 — Glover, Edward. Selected papers on psycho-analysis. London, 1956- 2v.
Phil 8881.74 — Gobry, Ivan. Les niveause de la vie morale. 1. éd. Paris, 1956.
Phil 5046.27 — Gorskii, D.D. Logika. Moskva, 1956.
Phil 535.20 — Graaff, Frank de. Het Europese nihilisme. Amsterdam, 1956.
Phil 2494.87 — Granger, Gilles Gaston. La mathématique sociale du marquis de Condorcet. 1. éd. Paris, 1956.
Phil 806.14.2 — Greca, Carlo. Storia della filosofia. 2. ed. Firenze, 1956.
Phil 8586.50 — Gregg, R.B. Self-transcendence. London, 1956.
Phil 5238.38A — Grinker, R.R. Toward a unified theory of human behavior. 1. ed. N.Y., 1956.
Phil 6327.11.10 — Grinstein, A. The index of psychoanalytic writings. N.Y., 1956-60. 10v.
Phil 3552.346.5 — Grua, Gaston. La justice humaine selon Leibniz. Thèse. Paris, 1956.
Phil 5627.215 — Gruehn, W. Die Frommigkeit der Gegenwart. Münster, 1956.
Phil 6319.1.200 — Gruesen, J.J. The philosophical implication of C.G. Jung's individuation process. Washington, 1956.
Phil 5246.60.5 — Gruhle, H.W. Verstehende Psychologie. 2. Aufl. Stuttgart, 1956.
Phil 3110.185 — Grunsky, H.A. Jacob Böhme. Stuttgart, 1956.
Phil 6315.2.195 — Guatemala (city). Universidad Nacional. Primer centenario del racimiento. Guatemala, 1956.
Phil 1870.130 — Guéroult, Martial. Berkeley. Paris, 1956.
Phil 8407.46 — Guerrero, Luis Juan. Estética operativa en sus tres direcciones. Buenos Aires, 1956-67. 3v.
Phil 2630.11 — Guitton, Jean. Invitation a la pensée et à la vie. Paris, 1956.
Phil 181.114.5 — Gusdorf, G. Traité de métaphysique. Paris, 1956.
Phil 1955.6.130 — Gutzke, M.G. John Dewey's thought and its implications for Christian education. N.Y., 1956.
Phil 4307.2 — Guy, Alain. Les philosophes espagnols d'hier et d'aujourd'hui. Toulouse, 1956. 2v.
Phil 4120.8.40 — Guzzo, Augusto. Parerga. Torino, 1956.
Phil 1750.40 — Haas, William S. The destiny of the mind. N.Y., 1956.
Phil 1750.560.35 — Habachi, René. Vers une pensée méditerranéenne. v.1-4. Beyrouth, 1956- 2v.
Phil 8957.13 — Haering, Bernhard. Macht und Ohnmacht der Religion. Salzburg, 1956.
Phil 8408.20 — Haezrahi, P. The contemplative activity; a study in aesthetics. N.Y., 1956.
Phil 6315.2.450 — Hall, Calvin S. A primer of Freudian psychology. London, 1956.
Phil 3160.12.10 — Hamburg, C.H. Symbol and reality. The Hague, 1956.
Phil 3827.9.3 — Hamphire, S. Spinoza. London, 1956.
Phil 8957.15 — Harding, A.L. Religion, morality, and law. Dallas, 1956.
Phil 5125.23 — Harrod, R.F. Foundations of inductive logic. London, 1956.
Phil 3850.18.140 — Hartmann, Wilfried. Die Philosophie Max Schelers in ihren Beziehungen zu Eduard von Hartmann. Düsseldorf, 1956.
Phil 3425.28.5 — Hegel, Georg Wilhelm Friedrich. Berliner Schriften. Hamburg, 1956.
Phil 3425.70.19 — Hegel, Georg Wilhelm Friedrich. Grundlinien der Philosophie des Rechts. 4. Aufl. Berlin, 1956.
Phil 3425.40.5.10A — Hegel, Georg Wilhelm Friedrich. The philosophy of history. N.Y., 1956.
Phil 3450.19.65 — Heidegger, Martin. Was ist das - die Philosophie? Pfullingen, 1956.
Phil 3450.19.45 — Heidegger, Martin. Zur Seinsfrage. Frankfurt, 1956.
Phil 6317.34 — Heiss, Robert. Allgemeine, Tiefenpsychologie. Bern, 1956.
Phil 9400.18 — Heller, Edward. Spiegel des Altes. Affoltern, 1956.
Phil 5465.85 — Henry, W.E. The analysis of fantasy. N.Y., 1956.
Phil 5047.42 — Hepp, M.H. Thinking things through. N.Y., 1956.
Phil 6017.3 — Herland, Leo. Gesicht und Charakter. 2. Aufl. Zürich, 1956.
Phil 4979.5.80 — Hernández Luna, Juan. Samuel Ramos. México, 1956.
Phil 5247.65 — Herrick, C.J. The evolution of human nature. Austin, 1956.
Phil 6317.35 — Hilgard, E.R. Psychoanalysis as science. N.Y., 1956.
Phil 8882.66.5 — Hill, Thomas E. Ethics in theory and practice. N.Y., 1956.
Phil 6317.33 — Hitschmann, E. Great men. N.Y., 1956.
Phil 1707.24 — Hoenderdaal, G.J. De mens in tweeotrijd. Arnhem, 1956.
Phil 288.15 — Hoenen, Peter. Cosmologia. 5. ed. Romae, 1956.
Phil 6317.36 — Hoff, Hans. Die Zeit und ihre Neurose.ien, 1956.
Phil 5400.140 — Holzkamp, Klaus. Ausdrucksverstehen im Erlebnisaspekt. Inaug. Diss. Berlin, 1956.
Phil 1830.11 — Hook, Sidney. American philosophers at work. N.Y., 1956.
Phil 182.114 — Hospers, John. An introduction to philosophical analysis. London, 1956.
Phil 8408.30 — Hostinsky, Otakar. O umění. Praha, 1956.
Phil 8882.70 — Hourani, G.F. Ethical value. London, 1956.
Phil 5017.5 — Howell, W.S. Logic and rhetoric in England. Princeton, 1956.
Phil 482.6 — Hoyle, Fred. Man and materialism. 1st ed. N.Y., 1956.
Phil 6317.32.5 — Hubbard, L. Ron. Scientology. London, 1956.
Phil 130.6.5 — Hubscher, Arthur. Denker unserer Zeit. München, 1956-57. 2v.
Phil 2050.41.30 — Hume, David. An enquiry concerning human understanding. Chicago, 1956.
Phil 5780.15 — Hunter, Edward. Brainwashing. N.Y., 1956.
Phil 5047.43 — Huppé, B.J. Logic and language. 1st ed. N.Y., 1956.
Phil 8587.70 — Hutchison, J.A. Faith. N.Y., 1956.
Phil 5838.256 — L'instinct dans le comportement des animaux et de l'homme. Paris, 1956.
Phil 5238.210 — Interamerican Congress of Psychology. 3rd, Austin, Texas, 1955. Psychological approaches to intergroup and international understanding. Austin, 1956.

Phil 808.2 — Istituto di Studi Filosofici, Rome. La philosophie de l'histoire de la philosophie. Roma, 1956.
Phil 310.21 — Ivanov, A.I. Vozniknoveniie marksizma, revoliutsionnyi perevorst v filosofii. Moskva, 1956.
Phil 5520.406 — Izutsu, T. Language and magic. Tokyo, 1956.
Phil 6980.365 — Jakab, Irene. Zeichnungen und Gemälde der Geisteskranken. Budapest, 1956.
Phil 8589.25 — Jankélévetch, V. Láusterité et la vie morale. Paris, 1956.
Phil 3475.3.56.1 — Jaspers, Karl. Reason and existenz; five lectures. London, 1956.
Phil 2805.320 — Jerphagnon, L. Pascal et la souffrance. Paris, 1956.
Phil 184.26.18 — Joad, C.E.M. Guide to philosophy. N.Y., 1956.
Phil 7069.56 — Johnson, R.C. Psychical research. N.Y., 1956.
Phil 2075.7.35 — Jordan, Elijah. Metaphysics. Evanston, Ill., 1956.
Phil 8960.10 — Kalmeyer, P. En bog om religion og moral. København, 1956.
Phil 3480.47.20 — Kant, Immanuel. Critique of practical reason. N.Y., 1956.
Phil 3480.32.65 — Kant, Immanuel. Kritik der reinen Vernunft. Wiesbaden, 1956-64. 6v.
Phil 3549.10.55 — Kassner, Rudolf. Zahl und Gesichte. Wiesbaden, 1956.
Phil 185.68.5 — Kattsoff, L.O. Logic and the nature of reality. The Hague, 1956.
Phil 1750.455 — Kaufmann, W.A. Existentialism from Dostoevsky to Sartre. N.Y., 1956.
Phil 3549.2.75.7 — Keyserling, Hermann. Das Reisetagebuch eines Philosophen. Darmstadt, 1956. 3v.
Phil 5643.115 — Kiefer, Theodor. Der visuelle Mensch. München, 1956.
Phil 3549.8.35 — Klages, Ludwig. Mensch und Erde. Stuttgart, 1956.
Phil 6671.27 — Kline, M.V. A scientific report on the search for Bridey Murphy. N.Y., 1956.
Phil 3195.6.113 — Kluback, William. Philosophy of history. N.Y., 1956.
Phil 185.71 — Knox, Crawford. The idiom of contemporary thought. London, 1956.
Phil 5649.25 — Kohl, Kurt. Zum Problem der Sensumotorik. Frankfurt, 1956.
Phil 720.42 — Kohn, David. More than truth. N.Y., 1956.
Phil 5190.35 — Korchyns'ka, H. Try abo chotyry zakony diialektyky. Miunkhen, 1956.
Phil 4803.497.35 — Kotarbiński, Tabeusz. Sprawność i bład. Warszawa, 1956.
Phil 3195.15.81 — Krampf, W. Hugo Dingler. München, 1956.
Phil 978.59.41 — Krishnamurti, J. Commentaries on living. N.Y., 1956.
Phil 3492.18.5 — Kroner, Richard. Kant's Weltanschauung. Chicago, 1956.
Phil 6980.400 — Krout, M.H. Psychology. Minneapolis, 1956.
Phil 8411.23 — Kublanov, B.G. Esteticheskoe chuvstvo i iskusstvo. L'vov, 1956.
Phil 4710.40 — Kulchitskii, Aleksandr. Die marxistisch-sowjetische Konzeption des Menschen. München, 1956.
Phil 2490.140 — Lacroix, Jean. La sociologie d'Auguste Comte. Paris, 1956.
Phil 2475.1.345 — Lahbabi, Mohamed Aziz. Liberté ou libération? Aubier, 1956.
Phil 5400.126 — Lakobson,P.M. Psikhologiia chuvstv. Moskva, 1956.
Phil 5425.44.25 — Lange, Wilhelm. Genie, Irrsinn und Ruhm. 4. Aufl. München, 1956.
Phil 1830.17 — Laslett, Peter. Philosophy. Oxford, 1956.
Phil 5525.56 — Latour, Marius. Le problème du rire et du réel. Paris, 1956.
Phil 2340.10.135 — Lawrence, N.M. Whitehead's philosophical development. Berkeley, 1956.
Phil 8591.60 — Leese, Kurt. Ethische und religiöse Grundfragen im Denken der Gegenwart. Stuttgart, 1956.
Phil 2520.255 — Lefèvre, Roger. La vocation de Descartes. v.1-3. Paris, 1956-1957. 2v.
Phil 3552.32 — Leibniz, Gottfried Wilhelm. Philosophical papers and letters. Chicago, 1956. 2v.
Phil 3552.34 — Leibniz, Gottfried Wilhelm. Philosophical writings. London, 1956.
Phil 3552.67.20 — Leibniz, Gottfried Wilhelm. Vernunftprinzipien der Natur und der Gnade. Hamburg, 1956.
Phil 186.67.8 — Leisegang, H. Einführung in die Philosophie. 3. Aufl. Berlin, 1956.
Phil 2725.30.30 — LeRoy, Edouard. Essai d'une philosophie première. Paris, 1956- 2v.
Phil 5590.95.7 — Lersch, Philipp. Aufbau der Person. 7. Aufl. München, 1956.
Phil 342.13.10A — Lewis, Clarence I. Mind and the world-order. N.Y., 1956.
Phil 5594.156A — Lindquist, Everet F. Design and analysis of experiments in psychology and education. Boston, 1956.
Phil 5585.100 — Linschoten, J. Strukturanalyse der binokularen Tiefenwahrnehmung. Groningen, 1956.
Phil 6980.424 — Lippman, Hyman. Treatment of the child in emotional conflict. N.Y., 1956.
Phil 2115.36.31.12 — Locke, J. Essay concerning human understanding. Chicago, 1956.
Phil 186.135 — Loehrich, R.R. Modus operandi. McHenry, Ill., 1956.
Phil 3640.261.10 — Löwith, Karl. Nietzsches Philosophie der ewigen Wieder kehr des Gleichen. Stuttgart, 1956.
Phil 8591.65 — Loewith, Karl. Wissen, Glaube und Skepsis. Göttingen, 1956.
Phil 4312.5A — Lopez Morillas, Juan. El krausismo español. 1. ed. México, 1956.
Phil 4762.1.38 — Losskii, Nikolai Onufrievich. Obshchedostupnoe vvedenie v filosofiiu. Frankfurt, 1956.
Phil 3585.19 — Lugmayer, Karl. Philosophie der Person. Salzburg, 1956.
Phil 6322.42A — Macalpine, Ida. Schizophrenia, 1677. London, 1956.
Phil 5590.325 — McCary, James Leslie. Psychology of personality. N.Y., 1956.
Phil 1750.23 — McCutcheon, Roger Philip. The present-day relevance of eighteenth-century thought. Washington, 1956.
Phil 2150.19.30 — McGilvary, E.B. Toward a perspective realism. LaSalle, Ill., 1956.
Phil 187.147 — Maisels, Misha. Thought and truth. N.Y., 1956.
Phil 6962.30 — Malzberg, Benjamin. Migration and mental disease. N.Y., 1956.
Phil 3640.470 — Manthey-Zorn, Otto. Dionysus. Amherst, 1956.
Phil 2750.13.30 — Marcel, Gabriel. Du refus à l'invocation. 11. éd. Paris, 1956.
Phil 2250.94.5 — Marcel, Gabriel. Royce's metaphysics. Chicago, 1956.
Phil 6315.2.180 — Marcuse, L. Sigmund Freud. Hamburg, 1956.
Phil 4363.7 — Marias Aguilera, Julián. Reason and life. New Haven, 1956.
Phil 2750.11.65.3 — Maritain, Jacques. Quatre essais sur l'esprit dans sa condition charnelle. Paris, 1956.

1956 - cont.

Phil 9575.15 — Masani, Rustom Pestonji. The role of wealth in society. Bombay, 1956.

Phil 2150.15.95 — Mead, G.H. The social psychology of George Herbert Meal. Chicago, 1956.

Phil 5780.16 — Meerloo, A.M. The rape of the mind. 1. ed. Cleveland, 1956.

Phil 735.175 — Meimberg, Rudolf. Alternativen der Ordnung. Berlin, 1956.

Phil 2725.2.103 — Meinvielle, Jules. De Lamennais à Maritain. Paris, 1956.

Phil 165.95 — Mélanges de philosophie grecque. Paris, 1956.

Phil 1750.465 — Mende, Georg. Studien über die Existenzphilosophie. Berlin, 1956.

Phil 812.35 — Merleau-Ponty, Maurice. Les philosophes célébres. Paris, 1956.

Phil 5850.271 — Merton, R.K. The focused interview. Glencoe, Ill., 1956.

Phil 310.19 — Mesaventures de l'anti-Marxisme. Paris, 1956.

Phil 7082.122 — Meseguer, Pedro. El secreto de los sueños. Madrid, 1956.

Phil 6315.2.170 — Mette, Alexander. Sigmund Freud. Berlin, 1956.

Phil 5052.42 — Meyer, H. Le rôle médiateur de la logique. Assen, 1956.

Phil 8592.85 — Meyer, Hans. Weltanschauungsprobleme der Gegenwart. 1. Aufl. Recklinghausen, 1956.

Phil 1750.430 — Michalson, Carl. Christianity and the existentialists. N.Y., 1956.

Phil 2138.40.46 — Mill, John S. On liberty. N.Y., 1956.

Phil 7159.152 — Millard, Joseph. Edgar Cayce, mystery man of miracles. N.Y., 1956.

Phil 3494.53A — Miller, Oscar W. The Kantian thing-in-itself. N.Y., 1956.

Phil 1504.32 — Minio-Palvello, Lorenzo. Twelfth century logic. Roma, 1956- 2v.

Phil 6322.38 — Mitscherlich, A. Entfaltung des Psychoanalyse. Stuttgart, 1956.

Phil 5238.45 — Moderne Entwicklungsychologie. Berlin, 1956.

Phil 8092.9 — Moholy-Nagy, L. Vision in motion. Chicago, 1956.

Phil 1135.154.10 — Mondolfo, R. L'infinito nel pensiero dell'antichita classica. Firenze, 1956.

Phil 3552.358 — Moreau, Joseph. L'univers leibnizien. Paris, 1956.

Phil 735.160 — Morris, C.W. Varieties of human value. Chicago, 1956.

Phil 596.2 — Morris, Louis W. Polarity; a philosophy of tensions among values. Chicago, 1956.

Phil 310.12.10 — Moscow. Kafedra. Akademiia Obshchestvennogo Nauk. Programma kursa dialekticheskogo i istori cheskogo materializma. Moskva, 1956.

Phil 4802.4 — Moscow. Universitet. Filosofskii fakultet. Izbrannye proizvedeniia progressivnykh pol'skikh myslitelei. Moskva, 1956-58. 3v.

Phil 6962.35 — Moses, Paul Joseph. Die Stimme der Neurose. Stuttgart, 1956.

Phil 575.146.10 — Mounier, E. The character of man. London, 1956.

Phil 2750.22 — Mounier, E. Mounier et sa generation. Paris, 1956.

Phil 5590.320 — Moustakas, Clark E. The self. N.Y., 1956.

Phil 187.149 — Mueller, G.E. The interplay of opposites. N.Y., 1956.

Phil 3850.27.175 — Mueller, Herbert. Albert Schweitzer. Duisburg, 1956.

Phil 2138.125 — Mueller, I.W. John Stuart Mill and French thought. Urbana, 1956.

Phil 8887.50.11 — Müller, Johannes. Hemmungen des Lebens. München, 1956.

Phil 4769.1.102.5 — Müller, Ludolf. Das religionsphilosophische System Vladimir Solowjews. Berlin, 1956.

Phil 3450.11.180 — Mueller, W.H. Die Philosophie Edmund Husserl den Grandzügen ihrer Entstefung. Bonn, 1956.

Phil 187.63.8A — Muirhead, J.H. Contemporary British philosophy. 3rd ser. London, 1956.

Phil 1712.20 — Muller, Philippe. Itineraire philosophique. Neuchâtel, 1956.

Phil 8962.14 — Munby, D.L. Christianity and economic problems. London, 1956.

Phil 8413.7.5 — Munro, Thomas. Toward science in aesthetics. N.Y., 1956.

Phil 4769.1.112 — Munzer, Egbert. Solovyev. London, 1956.

Phil 1712.19 — Myers, Francis M. The warfare of democratic ideals. Yellow Springs, Ohio, 1956.

Phil 5068.40 — Naese, Arne. Wie fördert man heute die empirische Bewegung? Oslo, 1956.

Phil 8414.8 — Nahm, Milton Charles. The artist as creator; an essay of human freedom. Baltimore, 1956.

Phil 5520.185 — Narskii, I.S. Kritika semanticheskogo idealizma. Moskva, 1956.

Phil 2150.15.100 — Natanson, M. The social dynamics of George H. Mead. Washington, 1956.

Phil 2880.8.126 — Naville, Pierre. L'intellectual communiste. Paris, 1956.

Phil 8888.6.30 — Nelson, Leonard. System of ethics. New Haven, 1956.

Phil 9400.22 — New York (State). Legislature. Joint Committee on Problems for the Aging. New channels for the golden years. Albany? 1956.

Phil 9070.50.5 — Nicolson, Harold Georg. Good behaviour; being a study of certain types of activity. Garden City, 1956.

Phil 3640.17.6 — Nietzsche, Friedrich. Also Sprach Zarathustra. Stuttgart, 1956.

Phil 3640.79.10 — Nietzsche, Friedrich. The birth of tragedy and The genealogy of morals. 1. ed. Garden City, N.Y., 1956.

Phil 3640.17.5 — Nietzsche, Friedrich. Die fröhliche Wissenschaft. Stuttgart, 1956.

Phil 3640.65 — Nietzsche, Friedrich. Zeitgemässes und Unzeitgemässes. Frankfurt, 1956.

Phil 5590.195 — Ninck, M. Schicksal und Charakter. Wien, 1956.

Phil 4180.1 — Nizzoli, Mario. De veris principiis et vera ratione philosophandi contra pseudophilosophos. Roma, 1956. 2v.

Phil 6980.516 — Noveck, Simon. Judaism and psychiatry. N.Y., 1956.

Phil 6323.12 — Nuttin, Jozef. Psychoanalyse und Personlichkeit. Freiburg, 1956.

Phil 5401.44 — Odier, Charles. Anxiety and magic thinking. N.Y., 1956.

Phil 7060.92.61 — O'Donnell, Elliot. Phantoms of the night. London, 1956.

Phil 5520.35.12 — Ogden, Charles K. The meaning of meaning. 8. ed. N.Y., 1956.

Phil 1750.535 — Oggioni, Emilio. L'esistenzialismo. Bologna, 1956.

Phil 5548.20 — Olds, James. The growth and structure of motives. Glencoe, Ill., 1956.

Phil 7069.56.25 — Omez, Réginald. Supranormal ou surnaturel. Paris, 1956.

Phil 165.55 — Organ, F.W. The examined life. Boston, 1956.

Phil 6310.1.100 — Orgler, Hertha. Alfred Adler. Wien, 1956.

Phil 5254.7A — Osgood, C.E. Method and theory in experimental psychology. N.Y., 1956.

Phil 5254.3.7 — Overstreet, H. Allen. The mind goes forth. 1st. ed. N.Y., 1956.

Phil 1750.330.5 — Paci, Enzo. Ancora sull'esistenzialismo. Torino, 1956.

Phil 4845.227.44 — Papanoutsos, Euangelos. Neollēnikè philosophia. 2. ed. v.1-2. Athena, 1956-59.

Phil 2805.325 — Paris. Musée National des Granges de Port-Royal. Pascal et les provinciales. Paris, 1956.

1956 - cont.

Phil 2805.50 — Pascal, Blaise. L'homme et l'oeuvre. Paris, 1956.

Phil 2805.30.30 — Pascal, Blaise. Pascal et les provinciales. Paris, 1956.

Phil 3497.19.10 — Paton, Herbert J. Kant on friendship. London, 1956.

Phil 8595.41 — Pavelkin, P.A. Chto takoe religiia; besedy. Moskva, 1956.

Phil 4170.10.85 — Pellegrino, U. Religione ed educazione nell'idealismo trascendente di Piero Martinetti. Brescia, 1956.

Phil 2805.350 — Perdomo, Garcia José. La teoría del conocimiento en Pascal. Madrid, 1956.

Phil 2805.360 — Perdomo, Garcia José. La teoría del conocimiento en Pascal. Madrid, 1956.

Phil 672.185 — Pereira, I.R. The nature of space. 1st ed. N.Y., 1956.

Phil 2225.2.35 — Perry, R.B. The humanity of man. N.Y., 1956.

Phil 1955.6.133 — Pesce, Domenico. Il concetto dell'arte in Dewey e in Berensoni. 1. ed. Firenze, 1956.

Phil 2045.128 — Peters, Richard. Hobbes. Harmondsworth, 1956.

Phil 8640.14 — Petry, Ray C. Christian eschatology and social thought. N.Y., 1956.

Phil 3745.12 — Pfeil, Hans. Überwindung des Massenmenschen durch echte Philosophie. 1. Aufl. Graz, 1956.

Phil 6980.587 — Phillips, Ewing. Psychotherapy. Englewood Cliffs, 1956.

Phil 6315.2.175 — Philp, Howard Littleton. Freud and religious belief. London, 1956.

Phil 4195.38 — Pico della Mirandola, Giovanni. Oration on the dignity of man. Chicago, 1956.

Phil 190.80.15 — Pieper, Josef. Was heisst philosophieren? 3. Aufl. München, 1956.

Phil 190.80.20 — Pieper, Josef. Die Wirklichkeit und das Gute. 6. Aufl. München, 1956.

Phil 3425.450 — Piérola, R.A. Hegel y la estatica. Tucumán, 1956.

Phil 310.24 — Plekhanov, G.V. The development of the monist view of history. Moscow, 1956.

Phil 3425.410 — Poeggeler, Otto. Hegels Kritik der Romantik. Bonn, 1956.

Phil 6980.606.5 — Pollak, Otto. Integrating sociological and psychoanalytic concepts. N.Y., 1956.

Phil 3903.1.95 — Ponnér, Jarl W. Johannes Volkelts lära am det tragiska. Lund, 1956.

Phil 8416.15 — Ponze, Francis. Le murmure condition et destin de l'artiste. Lyon, 1956.

Phil 9290.5 — Prevet, François. La moralité professionnelle des origines à nos jours. Paris, 1956. 2v.

Phil 6306.5 — Progoff, Ira. The death and rebirth of psychology. N.Y., 1956.

Phil 5204.10.2.1 — Psykologisk-pedagogisk uppslagsbok. Supplement. Stockholm, 1956.

Phil 5204.10.2 — Psykologisk-pedagogisk uppslagsbok. 2. uppl. Stockholm, 1956. 3v.

Phil 4210.170 — Pusineri, Giovanni. Antonio Rosmini, uomo di pensiero, di azione, di virtu. Milano, 1956.

Phil 3640.480 — Quinot, Armand. Nietzsche, philosophe de la valeur. Manosque, 1956.

Phil 165.50 — Rader, M.M. The enduring questions. N.Y., 1956.

Phil 4872.242.30 — Radhakrishnan, Sarvépalli. My search for truth. 2nd ed. Agra, 1956.

Phil 6327.15.5 — Rado, Sandor. Psychoanalysis of behavior; collected papers. N.Y., 1956.

Phil 3450.19.145 — Raessingh, Karel Hendrik. Martín Heidegger als godsdienstwijsgeer. Assen, 1956.

Phil 192.85.3 — Raeymaeker, Louis de. Introduction à la philosophie. 4. ed. Louvain, 1956.

Phil 1020.64.2 — Rafi-ud-din, Muhammad. Ideology of the future. 2nd ed. Karachi, 1956.

Phil 1750.440 — Redeker, Hans. Existentialisme. 2. druk. Amsterdam 1956.

Phil 2138.126 — Rees, John C. Mill and his early critics. Leicester, 1956.

Phil 672.182 — Reichenbach, Hans. The direction of time. Berkeley, 1956.

Phil 6327.12.35 — Reik, Theodor. The search within. N.Y., 1956.

Phil 5227.10 — Reith, Herman. An introduction to philosophical psychology. Englewood Cliffs, N.J., 1956.

Phil 6315.2.215 — Relgis, Eugen. Freud, Freudismo y las verdades sociales [a las cieñanos de su nacimiento, 6 de mayo, 1856-1956]. Montevideo, 1956.

Phil 1750.166.110 — Relgis, Eugen. El humanitarismo. Buenos Aires, 1956.

Phil 1717.19A — The revolution in philosophy. London, 1956.

Phil 6315.2.250 — Revue Francaise de Psychanalyse. Hommage à Sigmund Freud. Paris, 1956.

Phil 193.181 — Riconda, Guiseppe. Ugo Spirito. Torino, 1956.

Phil 817.23 — Riel, Hans. Urwissen. 2. Aufl. Wien, 1956.

Phil 6315.2.190 — Riemann, Fritz. Lebendige Psychoanalyse. München, 1956.

Phil 3246.258 — Ritzel, W.W. Fichtes Religionsphilosophie. Stuttgart, 1956.

Phil 5520.397 — Riverso, Emmanuele. La costruzione interpretativa del mondo analizzata dall'epistenrologia genetica. Napoli, 1956.

Phil 5066.90 — Robinson, A. Complete theories. Amsterdam, 1956.

Phil 4972.5.56 — Romero, Francisco. Alejandro Korn. Buenos Aires, 1956.

Phil 310.3.19 — Rozental', M.M. Kategorii materialisti cheskoi dialektiki. Moskva, 1956.

Phil 8892.72 — Rubert y Candau, José M. Fundamento constitutivo de la moral. Madrid, 1956.

Phil 4630.6.30 — Rubin, E. Af efterladte papirer. København, 1956.

Phil 5057.36 — Ruby, Lionel. The art of making sense. London, 1956.

Phil 2255.7.10 — Runes, Dagobert D. On the nature of man. N.Y., 1956.

Phil 192.28.20.2 — Russell, B. An outline of philosophy. London, 1956.

Phil 2255.1.75 — Russell, Bertrand Russell. Logic and knowledge. London, 1956.

Phil 2255.1.78 — Russell, Bertrand Russell. Portraits from memory. London, 1956.

Phil 8408.30.5 — Sádecký, Z. O některých otázkách estetiky Otakara Hostinskéko. Praha, 1956.

Phil 193.170 — Samuel, Otto. Die Ontologie der Kultur. Berlin, 1956.

Phil 4958.505 — Sánchez, Juan Francisco. El pensamiento filosófico en Santo Domingo. Ciudad Trujillo, 1956?

Phil 5870.20 — Sandels, Stina. Utvecklingsykologiska beteendestudier hos barn i aldern 1 1/2 - 8 1/2 år. Thesis. Uppsala, 1956.

Phil 8419.27 — Santangelo, P.E. Discorso sull'arte. Milano, 1956.

Phil 193.49.18.5 — Santayana, G. Character and opinion in the United States. Garden City, 1956.

Phil 8980.770 — Sarich, A.L. Obshchie metody nravstvennogo vospitaniia. Moskva, 1956.

Phil 4080.3.295 — Sartori, G. Croce etico-politico e filosofo. Firenze, 1956.

Phil 2880.8.56.3A — Sartre, Jean Paul. Being and nothingness. N.Y., 1956.

Phil 5412.10 — Saul, Leon Joseph. The hostile mind. N.Y., 1956.

Phil 5058.75 — Schipper, Edith Watson. Principles of applied logic. Dubuque, 1956.

Phil 2262.97 — Schlegel, D.B. Shaftesbury and the French deists. Chapel Hill, 1956.

1956 - cont.

Phil 193.175 Schmidt, Franz. Ordnungslehre. München, 1956.
Phil 9450.28 Schneider, H.W. Three dimensions of public morality. Bloomington, Ind., 1956.
Phil 6315.2.160 Schoenwald, R.L. Freud. 1st ed. N.Y., 1956.
Phil 3808.60.50 Schopenhauer, Arthur. The philosophy of Schopenhauer. N.Y., 1956.
Phil 3808.45.20 Schopenhauer, Arthur. Selections. N.Y., 1956.
Phil 3805.195 Schuffenhauer, Heinz. Der fortschrittliche Gehalt der Pädagogik Schleiermachers. Berlin, 1956.
Phil 5058.53.5 Searles, Herbert L. Logic and scientific methods. 2. ed. N.Y., 1956.
Phil 9450.35 Selekman, Sylvia Kopald. Power and morality in a business society. N.Y., 1956.
Phil 6128.58A Seyle, Hans. The stress of life. N.Y., 1956.
Phil 6128.49.2 Shaffer, Laurance F. The psychology of adjustment. 2d ed. Boston, 1956.
Phil 4980.3 Silva Mello, Antonio da. Man; his life, his education, his happiness. N.Y., 1956.
Phil 1200.56 Simon, Heinrich. Die alte Stoa und ihr Naturbegriff. Berlin, 1956.
Phil 2750.11.130 Simonson, V.L. L'esthétique de Jacques Maritain. Copenhagen, 1956.
Phil 5585.85 Smirnov, M.T. Protsess poznaniia v obuchenii. Moskva, 1956.
Phil 2268.3.100 Smith, Charles. Sensism, the philosophy of the West. N.Y., 1956. 2v.
Phil 9400.20 Smith, E.S. The dynamics of aging. 1st ed. N.Y., 1956.
Phil 720.45 Smith, Gerard. The truth that frees. Milwaukee, 1956.
Phil 9540.8 Smith, Thomas Vernor. The ethics of compromise and the art of containment. Boston, 1956.
Phil 8843.14 Smith, Wilson. Professors and public ethics. Ithaca, N.Y., 1956.
Phil 5585.81 Smythies, J.R. Analysis of perception. London, 1956.
Phil 9495.156A Sorokin, P.A. The American sex revolution. Boston, 1956.
Phil 5625.92 Spence, K.W. Behavior theory and conditioning. New Haven, 1956.
Phil 3819.39.10 Spinoza, Benedictus de. How to improve your mind. N.Y., 1956.
Phil 5066.155 Stahl, Gerold. Introduccion a la logica simbolica. Santiago, Chile, 1956.
Phil 3850.52.35 Stallaert, L. Peilingen. Rotterdam, 1956. 3v.
Phil 349.39.6 Steenberghen, Fernand van. Épistémologie. 3e éd. Louvain, 1956.
Phil 978.49.240 Steiner, R. Drama und Dichtung im Bewusstseins-Umschwung der Neuzeit. Dornach, 1956.
Phil 978.49.117 Steiner, R. Eurythmie als sichtbarer Gesang. 1. Aufl. Dornach, 1956.
Phil 978.49.265 Steiner, R. Vier Mysteriendramen. 2. Aufl. Dornach, 1956.
Phil 978.49.250 Steiner, R. Welt, Erde und Mensch. 2. Aufl. Freiburg, 1956.
Phil 5590.310 Stern, George G. Methods in personality assessment. Glencoe, Ill., 1956.
Phil 5421.15 Stewart, David A. Preface to empathy. N.Y., 1956.
Phil 5400.122 Strasser, S. Das Gemüt. Antwerpen, 1956.
Phil 6328.38 Stuttgart. Institut für Psychotherapie und Tiefenpsychologie. Wiedergeburt des Einzelnen. Stuttgart, 1956.
Phil 9070.90 Sullivan, Aloysius Michael. The three-dimensional man. N.Y., 1956.
Phil 672.195 Sviderskii, V.I. Filosofskoe znachenie prostranstvenno-vremennykh predstavlenii v fizike. Leningrad, 1956.
Phil 6980.717 Szondi, Lipot. Heilwege der Tiefenpsychologie. Bern, 1956.
Phil 6328.40 Szondi, Lipot. Triebpathologie. Bern, 1956. 2v.
Phil 5059.21.6A Tavanets, P.V. Izbrannye trudy russkikh XIX v. Moskva, 1956.
Phil 2905.1.5 Teilhard de Chardin, Pierre. Oeuvres. Paris, 1956-10v.
Phil 194.47 Thévenaz, P. L'homme et sa raison. Neuchâtel, 1956. 2v.
Phil 5829.11 Thorpe, W.H. Learning and instinct in animals. London, 1956.
Phil 8894.34 Timur, Mohammed. The theory of morals. London, 1956.
Phil 2905.2.30 Tonguèdec, J. La philosophie de la nature. v. 1-2. Paris, 1956. 4v.
Phil 2648.93 Topazio, V.W. D'Holbach's moral philosophy. Geneva, 1956.
Phil 494.4 Trakhtenberg, I.V. Razvetie materiazma i ego bor'ba protiv idealizma. Moskva, 1956.
Phil 3890.9.88 Troxler, I.P.V. Philosophische Enzyklopädie und Methodologie der Wissenschaften. Beromünster, 1956.
Phil 2419.5 Tsebenko, M.D. Der Atheismus der französischen Materialisten des 18. Jarhunderts. 1. Aufl. Berlin, 1956.
Phil 310.23 Tuzarinov, V.P. Sootnoshenii kategorii dialekticheskoi marksizma. Leningrad, 1956.
Phil 1720.5 Urmson, J.O. Philosophical analysis. Oxford, 1956.
Phil 4260.148 Uscatescu, George. Juan Batista Vico y el mundo histórico. 1. ed. Madrid, 1956.
Phil 4771.5.2 Uspenskii, P.D. A new model of the universe. 2d ed. N.Y., 1956.
Phil 8422.4.5 Vanslov, V.V. Soderzhanie i forma v iskusstve. Moskva, 1956.
Phil 3425.465 Vecchi, Giovanni. L'estetica di Hegel. Milano, 1956.
Phil 1721.3 Veloso, A. Nos encruzilhadas do pensamento. Porto, 1956.
Phil 3903.5.45 Verhoeven, Cornelius W.M. Symboliek van de voet. Assen, 1956.
Phil 8896.22 Vernet, Maurice. L'homme, maître de sa destinée. Paris, 1956.
Phil 3503.12 Vialatoux, J. La morale de Kant. 1. éd. Paris, 1956.
Phil 6980.772 Volmat, R. L'art pyschopathologique. Paris, 1956.
Phil 5061.5.2 Volpe, G. della. Logica come scienza positiva. 2. ed. Messina, 1956.
Phil 3450.19.155 Wahl, Jean A. Vers la fin de l'ontologie. Paris, 1956.
Phil 6310.1.98 Way, Lewis M. Alfred Adler. Harmondsworth, 1956.
Phil 2340.11.50 Weiss, Paul. Modes of being. New Haven, 1956. 2v.
Phil 5232.9 Wells, H.K. Pavlov and Freud. N.Y., 1956. 2v.
Phil 197.63.7 Wenzl, Aloys. Metaphysik als Weg von den Grenzen der Wissenschaft au die Grenzen der Religion. 2. Aufl. Graz, 1956.
Phil 1722.9.5 White, M.G. Toward reunion in philosophy. Cambridge, 1956.
Phil 6332.19 White, Robert. The abnormal personality. 2. ed. N.Y., 1956.
Phil 2340.10.98.5 Whitehead, Alfred North. Modes of thought. N.Y., 1956.
Phil 3801.879 Wieland, W. Schellings Lehre von der Zeit. Heidelberg, 1956.

1956 - cont.

Phil 974.3.119.5 Wiesberger, Halla. Aus dem Leben von Marie Steiner von Silvers. Dornach, 1956.
Phil 9513.8 Wiese, Leopold von. Das Soziale im Leben und im Denken. Köln, 1956.
Phil 5032.5 Wilson, Curtis. William Heytesbury. Madison, 1956.
Phil 5520.160 Wilson, John. Language and the pursuit of truth. Cambridge, Eng., 1956.
Phil 1127.2.7 Windelband, W. History of ancient philosophy. N.Y., 1956.
Phil 3925.16.4 Wittgenstein, Ludwig. Remarks on the foundations of mathematics. Oxford, 1956.
Phil 3640.455A Wolff, H.M. Friedrich Nietzsche. Bern, 1956.
Phil 8677.21 Wolfson, H.A. The Muslim attributes and the Christian trinity. Cambridge, Mass., 1956.
Phil 1527.1.10 Wulf, M. de. An introduction to scholastic philosophy. N.Y., 1956.
Phil 3925.11.26 Wust, Peter. Briefe an Freunde. 2. Aufl. Münster, 1956.
Phil 3925.11.60 Wust, Peter. Unterwegs zur Heimat. Münster, 1956.
Phil 2115.163 Yolton, John W. John Locke and the way of ideas. London, 1956.
Phil 3935.1.30 Yorck von Wartenburg, Paul. Bewusstseinsstellung und Geschichte. Tübingen, 1956.
Phil 4777.894 Z dziejów polskiej myśli filozoficznej i społecznej. Warszawa, 1956- 3v.
Phil 4710.36 Zen'kovskii, V.V. O mnimom materializme russkoi nauki i filosofii. Miunkhen, 1956.
Phil 4805.15 Zich, Otakar. Lidová přísloví s logického hlediska. Praha, 1956.
Phil 3940.2.35 Ziegler, L. Das Lehrgespräch vom Allgemeinen Menschen in Lieben Abenden. Hamburg, 1956.
Phil 6315.2.146.5 Zilboorg, G. Freud - 1956. N.Y., 1956.
Phil 825.10 Zucchi, Hernan. Estudios de filosofía antiqua y moderna. Tucumán, 1956[1957]

1957

Phil 4962.5 Abad Carretero, Luis. Niñez y filosofía. México, 1957.
Phil 1750.270.10 Abbagnano, Nicola. Philosophie des menschlichen Konflikts. Hamburg, 1957.
Phil 6980.14.100 Ackerknecht, E.H. Kurge Geschichte der Psychiatrie. Stuttgart, 1957.
Phil 3425.405 Adorno, Theodor W. Aspekte der Hegelschen Philosophie. Berlin, 1957.
Phil 1700.7 Aiken, H.D. The age of ideology. Boston, 1957.
Phil 800.10.5 Akademiia Nauk SSSR. Institut Filosofii. Istoriia filosofii. Moskva, 1957. 7v.
Phil 1020.34 Akademiia Nauk Uzbekskoi SSR, Tashkend. Otdel Filosofii i Prava. Materialy poistorii progressivnoi obshchestvennoi filosofskoi mysl v Uzbekistane. Tashkent, 1957.
Phil 9550.5.2 Albee, Ernest. A history of English utilitarianism. London, 1957.
Phil 2475.1.340 Alexander, I.W. Bergson. London, 1957.
Phil 8088.2 Alfieri, V. L'estetica dall'illuminismo. Milano, 1957.
Phil 4060.4.35 Aliotta, Antonio. Critica dell'esistenzialismo. 2. ed. v.2,5. Roma, 1957. 2v.
Phil 331.12 Alquié, Ferdinand. L'expérience. Paris, 1957.
Phil 6980.36 Altschule, Mark David. Roots of modern psychiatry. N.Y., 1957.
Phil 8401.4 Alvard, Julien. L'art moral. Paris, 1957.
Phil 6980.38.5 American Psychiatric Association. Application of basic science techniques to psychiatric research. Washington, 1957.
Phil 4450.6 Andrade, A.A. de. Filósofos portugueses do séc. XVIII. v.1-3. Lisboa, 1957-
Phil 3085.5.35 Andre, H. Annäherung durch Abstand. Salzburg, 1957.
Phil 418.10 Anscombe, Gertrude Elizabeth Margaret. Intention. Oxford, 1957.
Phil 6310.10 Anthony, Joseph. The invisible curtain. N.Y., 1957.
Phil 2490.142 Arbouss-Bastide, Paul. La doctrine de l'éducation universelle dans la philosophie d'Auguste Comte. v.1-2. Paris, 1957.
Phil 2490.142.2 Arbousse-Bastide, Paul. La doctrine de l'éducation universelle dans la philosophie d'Auguste Comte. Paris, 1957. 2v.
Phil 175.45 Archivio di Filosofia. Il compito della fenomenologia. Padova, 1957.
Phil 310.685 Arkhiptsev, Fedor T. V.I. Lenin o nauchnom poniatii materii. Moskva, 1957.
Phil 3475.3.145 Armbruster, Ludwig. Objekt und Transzendenz bei Jaspers. Innsbruck, 1957.
Phil 850.21.10 Armstrong, A.H. An introduction to ancient philosophy. 3d ed. London, 1957.
Phil 5590.230 Arnold, Wilhelm. Person, Charakter, Persönlichkeit. Göttingen, 1957.
Phil 9070.60 Arnoux, André. La voie du bonheur. Paris, 1957.
Phil 3235.118 Arvon, Henri. Ludwig Feuerbach. 1. éd. Paris, 1957.
Phil 4770.5 Avaliani, S.Sh. Filosofskie vzgliady I.R. Tarkhnishvili. Tbilisi, 1957.
Phil 3090.24.5 Baader, Franz von. Gesellschaftslehre. München, 1957.
Phil 140.50 Baan, P.A.H. Psychiatrie in de maatschappij. Groningen, 1957. 8 pam.
Phil 5203.18 Baatz, Walter. Geistes und naturwissenschaftliche Abhandlungen der Mitglieder des Wiener Arbeitskreises. Wien, 1957.
Phil 2477.15.5 Bachelard, Gaston. La poétique de l'espace. 1. éd. Paris, 1957.
Phil 3450.11.190 Bachelard, Suzanne. La logique de Husserl. Paris, 1957.
Phil 5041.75 Bachhuber, A.H. Introduction to logic. N.Y., 1957.
Phil 2477.1.140 Baillot, A. Émile Boutroux et la pensée religieuse. Paris, 1957.
Phil 5241.119 Balint, Michael. Problems of human pleasure and behavior. London, 1957.
Phil 1905.25 Ball, Frank N. Intellectual calculus. Ipswich, 1957.
Phil 8402.32 Ballard, Edward. Art and analysis. The Hague, 1957.
Phil 3483.65 Ballauff, Theodor. Vernünftiger Wille und gläubige Liebe. Meisenheim, 1957.
Phil 4260.132 Banchetti, Silvestro. Il significato morale dell'estetica vichiana. Milano, 1957.
Phil 1740.8 Banfi, Antonio. La filosofia degli ultimi cinquanta anni. Milano, 1957.
Phil 6990.44.20 Barbet, Jean. La dame plus belle que tout. Paris, 1957.
Phil 3450.18.170 Barone, Francisco. Nicolai Hartmann nella filosofia del novecento. Torino, 1957.
Phil 3235.125 Baskin, M.P. Filosofiia Ludviga Feierbakha. Moskva, 1957.
Phil 400.120 Baskin, M.P. Sovremennyi sub"ektivnyi idealizm. Moskva, 1957.

Chronological Listing

Phil 5066.58.2 — Basson, A.H. Introduction to symbolic logic. 2nd ed. London, 1957.

Phil 5627.257.5 — Baudouin, Charles. Psychanalyse du symbole religieux. Paris, 1957.

Phil 176.200 — Bauernfeind, Otto. Die Suingebung des Daseins. Meisenheim, 1957.

Phil 310.40 — Baumgarten, A. Bemerkungen zur Erkenntnistheorie des dialektischen und historischen Materialismus. Berlin, 1957.

Phil 5585.95 — Becker, Egon. Mengenvergleich und Übung. Frankfurt, 1957.

Phil 5068.32 — Beckwith, B.P. Religion. N.Y., 1957.

Phil 5627.107.20 — Behanna, Gertrude Florence. The late Liz. N.Y., 1957.

Phil 2520.280 — Behn, Irene. Der Philosoph und die Königin. Freiburg, 1957.

Phil 530.40.50 — Behn, Irene. Spanische Mystik. Düsseldorf, 1957.

Phil 5470.5 — Bergler, Edmund. The psychology of gambling. N.Y., 1957.

Phil 3246.265 — Bergner, Dieter. Neue Bemerkungen zu Johann Gottlieb Fichte. Berlin, 1957.

Phil 2475.1.78 — Bergson, Henri. Ecrits et paroles. Paris, 1957. 3v.

Phil 2475.1.76 — Bergson, Henri. Memoire et vie. 1e éd. Paris, 1957.

Phil 8980.15 — Berlin. Institut für Gesellschaftswissenschaften. Neues Leben. 1. Aufl. Berlin, 1957.

Phil 6311.38 — Bertine, Eleanor. Menschliche Beziehungen. Zürich, 1957.

Phil 282.20 — Bertrand, René. Le mystère de vivre. Monaco, 1957.

Phil 6980.112.20 — Binswanger, L. Der Mensch in der Psychiatrie. Pfullingen, 1957.

Phil 6951.30 — Binswanger, Ludwig. Schizophrenie. Pfullingen, 1957.

Phil 6315.2.225A — Binswanger, Ludwig. Sigmund Freud. N.Y., 1957.

Phil 585.50 — Biot, René. Poussière vivante. Paris, 1957.

Phil 1701.26 — Birro, Cela. The ways of enjoyment. N.Y., 1957.

Phil 1750.166.35 — Blackham, H.J. Living as a humanist. London, 1957.

Phil 5041.78 — Blanché, Robert. Introduction à la logique contemporaine. Paris, 1957.

Phil 2477.6.20 — Blondel, Maurice. Correspondance, 1899-1912. Paris, 1957. 3v.

Phil 5041.70 — Blyth, J.W. A modern introduction to logic. Boston, 1957.

Phil 1701.17.5 — Boas, George. Dominant themes of modern philosophy. N.Y., 1957.

Phil 3483.70 — Bobbio, Norberto. Diritto e stato nel pensiero di Emanuele Kant. Torino, 1957.

Phil 5211.10 — Bochorishvili, A.t. Prints'pial'nye voprosy psikhologii. Tbilisi, 1957- 2v.

Phil 3110.55.30 — Böhme, J. Glaube und Tat. Berlin, 1957.

Phil 5593.57 — Bohm, E.B. Lehrbuch der Rorschach-Psychodiagnostik. 2. Aufl. Bern, 1957.

Phil 5520.175 — Bois, Joseph S. Explorations in awareness. N.Y., 1957.

Phil 5041.85 — Boll, Marcel. Les étapes de la logique. 4. éd. Paris, 1957.

Phil 8876.118.2 — Bollnow, Otto Friedrich. Einfache Sittlichkeit. 2. Aufl. Göttingen, 1957.

Phil 332.29 — Bologna, Italo. Il pensiero filosofico ed il suo fondamento. Milano, 1957.

Phil 1506.12.5 — Bonafede, Giulio. Storia della filosofia medievale. 2. ed. Roma, 1957.

Phil 1905.26 — Boodin, J.E. Studies in philosophy. Los Angeles, 1957.

Phil 2138.127 — Borchard, Ruth. John Stuart Mill. London, 1957.

Phil 5211.4.7A — Boring, Edwin Garrigues. A history of experimental psychology. 2. ed. N.Y., 1957.

Phil 6311.37 — Boss, Medard. Psychoanalyse und Daseinsanalytik. Bern, 1957.

Phil 5465.140 — Boston Institute. Conference on creativity as a process. Boston, 1957-58.

Phil 6310.8.5 — Bottome, P. Alfred Adler. 3rd ed. London, 1957.

Phil 5374.180 — Brach, Jacques. Conscience et connaissance. Paris, 1957.

Phil 3120.45.30 — Brandenstein, Béla. Vom Sinn der Philosophie und ihrer Geschichte. Bonn, 1957.

Phil 188.12.80 — Brelage, Manfred. Fundamentalanalyse und Regionalanalyse. Köln, 1957.

Phil 5041.80 — Brennan, Joseph Gerard. A handbook of logic. N.Y., 1957.

Phil 6615.20.6 — Breuer, Josef. Studies on hysteria. N.Y., 1957.

Phil 2480.85 — Brive, France. Mussée Ernest Rupin. Cabanis, médecin, philosophe et l'époque révolutionaire. Brive, 1957.

Phil 8691.28 — Broekman, R.W. Het vraagteken achter de horizon van ons Leven. Assen, 1957.

Phil 4065.70 — Bruno, Giordano. Due dialoghi sconosciuti e due dialoghi noti. Roma, 1957.

Phil 4065.75 — Bruno, Giordano. Heroische Leidenschaften und individuelles Leben. Hamburg, 1957.

Phil 3120.30.73 — Buber, Martin. Eclipse of God. N.Y., 1957.

Phil 801.35 — Bueno, Miguel. Las grandes direcciones de la filosofia. México, 1957.

Phil 8402.55 — Bullough, E. Aesthetics; lectures and essays. London, 1957.

Phil 165.70
Phil 5850.145.50.5 — Burnett, Whit. This is my philosophy. 1st ed. N.Y., 1957.

Phil 623.23.10A — Burtt, H.E. Applied psychology. 2. ed. Englewood Cliffs, 1957.

Phil 8505.8.5 — Busson, Henri. De Petrarque á Descartes. Paris, 1957.

Phil 5649.26 — Butinova, M.S. Estestvoznanie i religiia. Moskva, 1957.

Phil 4073.39.5 — Buyteuddigk, Frederik J.J. Attitudes et mouvements. Paris, 1957.

Phil 4073.20 — Campanella, Tommaso. Magia e grazia. Roma, 1957.

Phil 1702.10 — Campanella, Tommaso. Tommaso Campanella, poeta. Salerno, 1957.

Phil 8403.26 — Cannabrava, Euryalo. Ensaios filosóficos. Rio de Janeiro, 1957.

Phil 802.25 — Capasso, Aldo. Arte e sentimento. Firenze, 1957.

Phil 5242.55.5 — Carlini, Armando. Breve storia della filosofia. Firenze, 1957.

Phil 6312.20 — Carmichael, L. Basic psychology. N.Y., 1957.

Phil 177.126 — Caruso, Igor A. Bios, Psyche, Person. Freiburg, 1957.

Phil 8952.13 — Caso, Antonio. Antología filosófica. México, 1957.

Phil 5548.35 — Cattani de Menasce, Giovanni. Saggi di analisi dell'atto morale. Roma, 1957.

Phil 2855.3.83 — Cattell, R.B. Personality and motivation structure and measurement. Yonkers-on-Hudson, N.Y., 1957.

Phil 735.185 — Cazeneuve, Jean. Ravaisson et les médecins animistes et vitalistes. Paris, 1957.

Phil 8692.22 — Césari, Paul. La valeur. 1. ed. Paris, 1957.

Phil 5042.55 — Chauchard, Paul. La création évolutive. Paris, 1957.

Phil 1750.560 — Chauveneau, Jean. La logique moderne. 1. éd. Paris, 1957.

Phil 5585.90 — Chiodi, Pietro. L'esistenzialismo. Torino, 1957.

Phil 5780.17 — Chisholm, R.M. Perceiving. Ithaca, 1957.

Phil 802.21 — Christoff, Daniel. Recherche de la liberté. 1. éd. Paris, 1957.

— Clark, Gordon Haddon. Thales to Dewey. Boston, 1957.

Phil 5212.10 — Clark, Kenneth. America's psychologists. Washington, 1957.

X Cg — Phil 7075.146 — Cleckley, H.M. The caricature of love. N.Y., 1957.

Phil 3120.30.82 — Cohen, A.A. Martin Buber. London, 1957.

Phil 3120.30.82.1 — Cohen, A.A. Martin Buber. N.Y., 1957.

Phil 802.23 — Coleburt, Russell. An introduction to Western philosophy. N.Y., 1957.

Phil 1802.14 — Colie, Rosalie L. Light and enlightenment. Cambridge, 1957.

Phil 4260.135 — Columbu, Mario. Giambattista Vico. Trani, 1957.

Phil 2610.100 — Comité du Tricentenaire de Gassendi. Actes du Congrès du Tricentenaire de Pierre Gassendi. Paris, 1957.

Phil 2070.142 — Compton, C.H. William James. N.Y., 1957.

Phil 2490.51.15 — Comte, Auguste. A general view of positivism. N.Y., 1957.

Phil 4195.90 — Condier, Pierre Marie. Jean Pic de la Mirandole. Paris, 1957.

Phil 4210.160 — Congresso Internazionale di Filosofia Antonio Rosmini, Stresa and Rovereto, 1955. Atti del congresso internazionale di filosofia Antonio Rosmini. Firenze, 1957. 2v.

Phil 177.115 — Connally, F.G. Science versus philosophy. N.Y., 1957.

Phil 3160.15 — Conrad-Martius, Hedwig. Das Sein. München, 1957.

Phil 4960.205 — Copelli y Marroni, Francisco. Esencialismo. 1. ed. Buenos Aires, 1957.

Phil 1133.30 — Cornford, F.M. From religion to philosophy. N.Y., 1957.

Phil 6312.18 — Corsini, R.J. Methods of group psychotherapy. N.Y., 1957.

Phil 5066.130 — Crahay, Franz. Le formalisme logic-mathématique et le problème du non-sens. Paris, 1957.

Phil 2115.168 — Cranston, M.W. John Locke. London, 1957.

Phil 5042.50 — Crawshay-Williams, Rupert. Methods and criteria of reasoning. London, 1957.

Phil 1107.8 — Cresson, André. La philosophie antique. 4e éd. Paris, 1957.

Phil 3808.184.3 — Cresson, André. Schopenhauer. Paris, 1957.

Phil 2905.1.80 — Cristiani, Léon. La vie et l'âme de Teilhard de Chardin. Paris, 1957.

Phil 4080.3.58 — Croce, Benedetto. Liberismo e liberalismo. Milano, 1957.

Phil 4960.605.20 — Cruz Costa, João. Esbozo de una história de las ideas en el Brasil. México, 1957.

Phil 1020.32 — Cruz Hernández, Miguel. Historia de la filosofía española. Madrid, 1957. 2v.

Phil 6112.38 — Cumming, Elaine. Clased ranks. Cambridge, 1957.

Phil 87.13 — Cuvillier, Armand. Nouveau vocabulaire philosophique. 2. éd. Paris, 1957.

Phil 310.415.5 — Cvekl, Jiří. O zákonech dějin. Praha, 1957.

Phil 5620.30 — Dar, B.A. Studies in reason and faith. Lahore, 1957.

Phil 8583.35.5 — D'Arcy, M.C. The meeting of love and knowledge. 1. ed. N.Y., 1957.

Phil 1740.8 — Delfgaauw, Bernardus M.I. De wijsbegeerts va di 20. eeuw. Baarn, 1957.

Phil 4114.85 — Demarco, Domenico. Quello che è vivo del pensiero economico di Antonio Genovesi. Napoli, 1957.

Phil 803.12 — Dempf, Alois. Kritik der historischen Vernunft. Wien, 1957.

Phil 1540.43 — Dempf, Alois. Metafísica de la Edad Media. Madrid, 1957.

Phil 1660.5.2 — De Santillana, Giorgio. The age of adventure; the Renaissance philosophers. Boston, 1957.

Phil 2520.78.5 — Descartes. Paris, 1957.

Phil 8878.11.2 — Dewey, John. Outlines of a critical theory of ethics. N.Y., 1957.

Phil 310.5.5 — Dialekticheskii materializm i sovremennoe estestvozznanie. Moskva, 1957.

Phil 3195.6.30.5 — Dilthey, Wilhelm. Gesammelte Schriften. Stuttgart, 1957- 12v.

Phil 3195.6.45 — Dilthey, Wilhelm. Philosophy of existence. N.Y., 1957.

Phil 3195.6.31.2 — Dilthey, Wilhelm. Von deutscher Dichtung und Musik. 2. Aufl. Stuttgart, 1957.

Phil 88.5 — Dizionario di filosofia. Milano, 1957.

RRC — Phil 8980.330 — Dodon, Larisa L. Kul'tura povedeniia sovetskogo molodogo cheloveka. Izd. 3. Leningrad, 1957.

Phil 8599.19.120 — Drescher, H.G. Glaube und Vernuft bei Ernst Troeltsch. Marburg, 1957.

Phil 8583.41 — Duméry, Henry. Critique et religion. Paris, 1957.

Phil 8658.17 — Duméry, Henry. Le problème de Dieu en philosophie de la religion. Bruges, 1957.

Phil 1703.16 — Duméry, Henry. Regards sur la philosophie contemporaine. Tournai, 1957.

Phil 8622.20 — Duméry, Henry. La tentation de faire du bien. Paris, 1957.

Phil 3485.21 — Duncan, A.R.C. Practical reason and morality. London, 1957.

Phil 8612.38 — Echeverria, José. Réflexions métaphysiques sur la mort et la problème du sujet. Paris, 1957.

Phil 2725.35.80 — Ecole, Jean. La metaphysique de l'être dans la philosophie de Louis Lavelle. Louvain, 1957.

Phil 5592.70 — Edwards, A.L. The social desirability variable in personality assessment and research. N.Y., 1957.

Phil 165.105 — Edwards, Paul. A modern introduction to philosophy. Glencoe, Illinois, 1957.

Phil 585.30 — Ehrlich, Walter. Philosophische Anthropologie. Tübingen, 1957.

Phil 3200.12 — Einsiedel, August von. Ideen. Berlin, 1957.

Phil 6114.16 — Ellis, Albert. How to line with a neurotic. N.Y., 1957.

Phil 4210.185 — Emery, Cuthbert Joseph. Rosmini on human rights. London, 1957.

Phil 89.6 — Enciclopedia filosofica. Venezia, 1957-58. 4v.

Phil 1750.95 — Engelhardt, Wolf von. Der Mensch in der technischen Welt. Köln, 1957.

Phil 5592.40 — Engels, Helma. Der Scenotest. Münster, 1957.

Phil 672.190 — Eranos-Jahrbuch. Man and time. N.Y., 1957.

Phil 6114.17 — Espenschied, Richard. Der Leistungs kräftige Mensch. Hamburg, 1957.

Phil 165.115 — Estudios de historia de la filosofía. Tucumán, 1957. 2v.

Phil 400.88.5 — Ewing, Alfred C. The idealist tradition. Glencoe, Illinois, 1957.

Phil 5421.10.5 — Eysenck, H.J. The dynamics of anxiety and hysteria. London, 1957.

Phil 5244.30 — Eysenck, H.J. Sense and nonsense in psychology. Harmondsworth, Middlesex, 1957.

Phil 5585.110 — Eysenck, Hans Jurgen. Perceptual processes and mental illness. N.Y., 1957.

Phil 1750.525 — Fabro, Cornelio. Dall'essere all'esistente. Brescia, 1957.

Phil 3487.26 — Fang, Joong. Das Antinomenproblem im Entstehungsgang der Transzendentalphilosophie. Münster, 1957.

1957 - cont.

Phil 4967.20.10   Farias Brito, Raymundo de. Finalidade do mundo. 2. ed. Rio de Janeiro, 1957. 3v.

Phil 6315.18.4   Federn, Paul. Das psychoanalytische Volksbuch. 5. Aufl. Bern, 1957.

Phil 6980.286   Fedotov, D.D. Ocherki po istorii otechestvennoi psikhiatrii, vtoria polovina XVIII. Moskva, 1957.

Phil 9150.32   Ferabino, Aldo. Storia dell'uomo avantie dopo Cristo. Assisi, 1957.

Phil 805.13   Ferrater Mora, José. Man at the crossroads. Boston, 1957.

Phil 1750.515   Ferrier, Jean Louis. L'homme dans le monde. Neuchâtel, 1957.

Phil 5625.97   Ferster, Charles B. Schedules of reinforcement. N.Y., 1957.

Phil 5325.30A   Festinger, Leon. A theory of cognitive dissonance. Evanston, Ill., 1957.

Phil 3235.72.7   Feuerbach, Ludwig. The essence of Christianity. N.Y., 1957.

Phil 3450.18.130   Feuerstein, R. Die Modallehre Nicolai Hartmanns. Köln? 1957.

Phil 5068.44   Filiasi Carcano, Paolo. La metodologia nel rinnovarsi del pensiero. Napoli, 1957.

Phil 180.70.5   Fink, Eugen. Oase des Glücks. Freiburg, 1957.

Phil 180.70   Fink, Eugen. Zur ontologischen Frühgeschichte von Raum, Zeit, Bewegung. Den Haag, 1957.

Phil 5245.65   Finkelstein, Ben A. Psychologische skizzen. Amsterdam, 1957.

Phil 8880.18.10   Fite, Warner. The examined life. Bloomington, Ind., 1957.

Phil 180.72   Flam, Leopold. Profielen. Antwerpen, 1957.

Phil 5838.257   Fletcher, Ronald. Instinct in man in the light of recent work in comparative psychology. N.Y., 1957.

X Cg   Phil 7075.144   Fliess, Robert. Erogeneity and libido. N.Y., 1957.

Phil 6315.46   Fordham, M.S.M. New developments in analytical psychology. London, 1957.

Phil 4260.111   Fornaca, Remo. Il pensiero educativo di Giambattista Vico. Torino, 1957.

Phil 6400.21   Forsboom, Bernhard. Das Buch Emanuel. München, 1957.

Phil 8660.15   Fox, Adam. God is an artist. London, 1957.

Phil 5585.140   Fraisse, Paul. Psychologie du temps. 1. éd. Paris, 1957.

Phil 5627.257   Frankl, V.E. The doctor and the soul. N.Y., 1957.

Phil 645.39   Frenkian, Aram M. Scepticismul grec și filosofia indiană. Bucuresti, 1957.

Phil 6315.2.210   Freud, Martin. Glory reflected. London, 1957.

Phil 6315.2.34   Freud, Sigmund. Collected papers. London, 1957-69. 4v.

Phil 6315.2.37.4   Freud, Sigmund. The ego and the id. London, 1957.

Phil 6315.2.38   Freud, Sigmund. A general selection from the works of Sigmund Freud. N.Y., 1957.

Phil 6315.2.205   Freud in der Gegenwart. Frankfurt, 1957.

Phil 1750.500   Funke, Gerhard. Zur transzendentalen Phänomenologie. Bonn, 1957.

Phil 6115.31   Funkenstein, D.H. Mastery of stress. Cambridge, Mass., 1957.

Phil 5245.60   Furtado, Diogo. Vultos e problemas. Coimbra, 1957.

Phil 4080.3.300   Galati, Vito Giuseppe. Colloqui con Benedetto Croce. Brescia, 1957.

Phil 4210.180   Galli, Dario. Studi rosminiani. Padova, 1957.

Phil 4112.75   Galluppi, Pasquale. Una memoria. Padova, 1957.

Phil 3549.8.115   Ganzoni, Werner. Die neue Schau der Seele. Wien, 1957.

Phil 181.3   Garcia Tuduri, Mercedes. Introducción a la filosofía. 4. ed. Habana, 1957.

Phil 4210.159   Garioni Bertolatti, G. Antonio Rosmini. Torino, 1957.

Phil 5360.13   Geach, P.T. Mental acts. N.Y., 1957.

Phil 5500.33   Geer, J.P. van de. A psychological study of problem solving. Amsterdam, 1957.

Phil 5625.86.5   Gellhorn, Ernst. Autonomic imbalance and the hypothalamus. Minneapolis, 1957.

Phil 193.195   Gemeinschaft des Gustes. Wien, 1957.

Phil 310.45   Genevès, F. L'imposture scientifique du matérialisme historique allemand. Bordeaux, 1957.

Phil 2115.170   Giganti, Maria A. John Locke e i limiti della scienza. Padova, 1957.

Phil 2630.8.21   Gilson, Étienne. A Gilson reader. Garden City, 1957.

Phil 978.90   Gleich, Sigismund. Die Wahrheit als Gesamtanfang aller Weltansichten. Stuttgart, 1957.

Phil 5066.125   Goodstein, R.L. Mathematical logic. Leicester, 1957.

Phil 8831.8   Graaf, Johannes de. De bezinning over goed en kwaad in de geschiedenis van het menselijk denken. Utrecht, 1957- 3v.

Phil 5246.65   Graber, Gustav Hans. Psychologie des Mannes. Bern, 1957.

Phil 165.125   Grateloup, León. Expérience - connaissance. Paris, 1957.

Phil 5520.195   Greenwood, David. Truth and meaning. N.Y., 1957.

Phil 337.17   Greeve, T.M. Moral aesthetic and religious insight. New Brunswick, N.J., 1957.

Phil 337.18   Gregoire, F. La nature du psychique. 1. ed. Paris, 1957.

Phil 3450.19.150   Grene, Marjorie. Martin Heidegger. London, 1957.

Phil 9240.14   Grenier, Jean. L'existence malheureuse. Paris, 1957.

Phil 4073.104.2   Grillo, F. A supplement to the critical bibliography. N.Y., 1957. 2v.

Phil 4822.2   Grozev, Groziu. Istoriia na bŭlgarskata filosofiia. Sofiia, 1957- 2v.

Phil 2030.5.5   Guérard, A.L. Fossils and presences. Standord, Calif., 1957.

Phil 2630.11.5   Guitton, Jean. Apprendre à vivre et à penser. Paris, 1957.

Phil 3425.520   Gulian, C.I. Metoda si sistem la Hegel. Bucuresti, 1957. 2v.

Phil 5357.3   Gulliksen, Harold. Reliability for the law of comparative judgment. n.p., 1957. 2 pam.

Phil 2490.160   Gurvitch, Georges. Les fondateurs de la sociologie. Paris, 1957.

Phil 1750.70   Gurwitsch, Aron. Théorie du champ de la conscience. Paris, 1957.

Phil 8881.72.5   Gusdorf, Georges. La vertu de force. 1. éd. Paris, 1957.

Phil 288.8   Häberlin, Paul. Leben und Lebensform. Basel, 1957.

Phil 1707.17   Haensel, Ludwig. Begegnungen und Auseinandersetzungen mit Denkern und Dichtern der Neuzeit. Wien, 1957.

Phil 8957.13.5   Haering, Bernhard. Das Gesetz Christi. 4. Aufl. Freiburg, 1957.

Phil 3549.8.120   Hager, Wilhelm. Ludwig Klages im Memoriam. München, 1957.

Phil 5590.215   Hall, Calvin S. Theories of personality. N.Y., 1957.

Phil 5066.115   Halldén, Sören. On the logic of 'better'. Lund, 1957.

Phil 3827.12   Hallett, H.F. Benedict de Spinoza. London, 1957.

Phil 6677.20   Hammerschlag, Heinz F. Hypnotism and crime. Hollywood, Calif., 1957.

Phil 8697.20   Hanaghan, J. Society, evolution and revelation. Dublin, 1957.

1957 - cont.

Phil 5238.125   Harris, Dale B. The concept of development. Minneapolis, 1957.

Phil 1850.149   Haukart, Robert. François Bacon. Paris, 1957.

Phil 1707.16   Hawkins, D.J.B. Crucial problems of modern philosophy. London, 1957.

Phil 3925.16.88   Hawkins, Dennis John Bernard. Wittgenstein and the cult of language. London, 1957.

Phil 9200.2.5   Heer, Friedrich. Sieben Kapitel aus der Geschichte des Schreckens. Zürich, 1957.

Phil 3425.28.10   Hegel, Georg Wilhelm Friedrich. Hegel. Frankfurt, 1957.

Phil 3450.19.23A   Heidegger, Martin. Holzwege. 3e Aufl. Frankfurt, 1957.

Phil 3450.19.77   Heidegger, Martin. Identität und Differenz. 2e Aufl. Pfullingen, 1957.

Phil 1750.166.30.5   Heidegger, Martin. Lettre sur l'humanisme. Paris, 1957.

Phil 3450.19.75   Heidegger, Martin. Der Satz vom Grund. Pfullingen, 1957.

Phil 2475.1.335   Heidsieck, F. Henri Bergson et la notion d'espace. Paris, 1957.

Phil 1750.365.10   Heinemann, Fritz. Jenseits des Existentialismus. Zürich, 1957.

Phil 5722.50   Helsdingen, R.J. van. Beelden uit het onbewuste. Arnhem, 1957.

Phil 3489.36   Hendel, C.W. The philosophy of Kant and our modern world. N.Y., 1957.

Phil 1750.110   Hengslenberg, Hans Eduard. Philosophische Anthropologie. Stuttgart, 1957.

Phil 5247.72   Henrysson, Sten. Applicability of factor analysis in the behavioral science. Stockholm, 1957.

Phil 600.54   Heyde, Johannes Erich. Entwertung der Kausalität. Zürich, 1957.

Phil 8408.4   Heyl, Bernard. New bearings in esthetics and art criticism. New Haven, 1957.

Phil 8110.11   Hipple, W.J. The beautiful, the sublime, and the picturesque in eighteenth-century British aesthetic theory. Carbondale, 1957.

Phil 960.137.20   Hiriyanna, M. Indian philosophical studies. Mysore, 1957.

Phil 8408.13   Hirsch, W. Die Gültigkeit der Kunst. Köln, 1957.

Phil 182.116   Hirschfeld, G. An essay on mankind. N.Y., 1957.

Phil 2045.52.27   Hobbes, Thomas. Leviathan. Oxford, 1957.

Phil 8633.1.36.5   Hocking, W.E. The meaning of immortality in human experience. N.Y., 1957.

Phil 288.17   Hoenigswald, Richard. Schriften aus dem Nachlass. Stuttgart, 1957- 8v.

Phil 9390.14   Hoffman, H.B. Loyalty by oath. Wallingford, 1957.

Phil 2648.20   Holbach, Paul Henri T. Textes choisis. Paris, 1957.

Phil 165.100   Hommage á Gaston Bachelard. Paris, 1957.

Phil 2050.39.5   Hume, David. An inquiry concerning the principles of morals. N.Y., 1957.

Phil 2050.67.5   Hume, David. The natural history of religion. Stanford, 1957.

Phil 5545.190   Hunter, I.M.L. Memory. Harmondsworth, 1957.

Phil 5047.11.15   Husserl, Edmund. Logique formelle et logique transcendantale. Paris, 1957.

Phil 8587.48.2   Huxley, J.S. Religion without revelation. N.Y., 1957.

Phil 4759.1.50   Il'in, I.A. Put' k ochevidnosti. Miunkhen, 1957.

Phil 808.3   Inciarte, Fernando. Die Reflexionsbestimmungen un dialektischen Denken. Köln, 1957.

Phil 4803.462.5   Ingarden, Roman. Studia z estetyki. Warszawa, 1957-70. 3v.

Phil 8400.36.3   International Congress on Aesthetics, 3rd, Venice, 1956. Proceedings of the third international congress on aesthetics. v. 1-2. Torino, 1957.

Phil 6310.1.102   Internationale Vereinegung für Individualpsychologie, Vienna. Alfred Adler zum Gedenken. Wien, 1957.

Phil 7069.11.49   Iremonger, L. The ghosts of Versailles. London, 1957.

Phil 6319.1.181   Jacobi, Jolan. Komplex. Zürich, 1957.

Phil 2750.11.142   Jacques Maritain. Paris, 1957.

Phil 2675.4   Jankélévitch, Vladimir. Le je-ne-sais-quoi et le presque-Dieu. 1. éd. Paris, 1957.

Phil 574.2   Janssens, Louis. Personalisme en democratisering. Brussel, 1957.

Phil 8410.2   Jarett, J.L. The quest for beauty. Englewood Cliffs, 1957.

Phil 809.6   Jasinowski, Bogumil. Saber y dialectia. Santiago, 1957.

Phil 184.19.30   Jaspers, K. Die grossen Philosophen. München, 1957.

Phil 585.25   Jeffreys, M.V.C. Mystery of man. London, 1957.

Phil 2520.260   Joachim, H.H. Descartes's Rules for the direction of the mind. London, 1957.

Phil 1620.5   Joffanin, Giuseppe. L'uomo antico nel pensiero del Rinascimento. Bologna, 1957.

Phil 94.2   Jolivet, Régis. Vocabulaire de la philosophie. 4. ed. Lyon, 1957.

Phil 6319.1.30   Jung, C.G. Bewusstes und Unbewusstes. Frankfurt, 1957.

Phil 6319.1.73   Jung, C.G. Gegenwart und Zukunft. Zürich, 1957.

Phil 5841.20.8   Jung, Emma. Animus and Anima. N.Y., 1957.

Phil 6049.57   Jursch, Hanna. Hände als Symbol und Gestalt. 7. Aufl. Stuttgart, 1957.

Phil 185.75   Kaelin, Bernard. Einführung in die Logik, Ontologie, Kosmologie, Psychologie. 5. Aufl. Sarnen, 1957.

Phil 8080.11   Kayser, Wolfgang. Das Groteske, seine Gestaltung in Malerei und Dichtung. Oldenburg, 1957.

Phil 4710.11.5   Khaskhachikh, F.I. Materie und Bewusstsein. 5. Aufl. Berlin, 1957.

Phil 5760.12   Kircher, Veronica. Die Freiheit des körpergebundenen Willens. Freiburg, 1957.

Phil 6020.5   Kirchhoff, Robert. Allgemeine Ausdruckslehre. Göttingen, 1957.

Phil 1133.35A   Kirk, G.S. The presocratic philosophers. Cambridge, Eng., 1957.

Phil 5625.75.90   Kiselinchev, A. Die marxistisch-leninistische Widerspiegelungstheorie und die Lehre Pawlows. Berlin, 1957.

Phil 5413.20   Klein, Melanie. Envy and gratitude. London, 1957.

Phil 1750.485.4   Knight, E.W. Literature considered as philosophy. London, 1957.

Phil 5250.42   Knight, Rex. A modern introduction to psychology. 5. ed. London, 1957.

Phil 5592.10.3   Koch, Karl. Der Baumtest. 3. Aufl. Bern, 1957.

Phil 8411.26   Koebner, R. Vom Schönen und seiner Wahrheit. Berlin, 1957.

Phil 176.69.80   Konferenz über Fragen der Blochschen Philosophie. Ernst Blochs Revision des Marxismus. Berlin, 1957.

Phil 4803.497.25   Kotarbiński, Tadeusz. Wybór pism. Warszawa, 1957-58. 2v.

Phil 4803.497.40   Kotarbiński, Tadeusz. Wykłady z dziejów logiki. Łódź, 1957.

677

Chronological Listing

1957 - cont.

Phil 291.7 Koyré, Alexandre. From the closed world to the infinite universe. Baltimore, 1957.

Phil 3010.5.2 Kraft, J. Von Husserl zur Heidegger. 2. Aufl. Frankfurt, 1957.

Phil 185.55.2 Kraft, Julius. Die Unmöglichkeit der Geisteswissenschaft. Frankfurt, 1957.

Phil 3425.445 Kremer-Garietti, Angèle. La pensée de Hegel. Paris, 1957.

Phil 3640.510 Kremer-Marietti, Angèle. Thèmes et structures dans l'oeuvre de Nietzsche. Paris, 1957.

Phil 978.59.42 Krishnamurti, J. Commentaries on living. London, 1957.

Phil 974.3.122.2 Krueck, M.J. Wir Erlebten Rudolf Steiner. 2. Aufl. Stuttgart, 1957.

Phil 1930.10.82 Kuhn, M. Arno. Morris Raphael Cohen. N.Y., 1957.

Phil 5250.50 Kunz, Hans. Über den Sinn und die Grenzen des psychologischen Erkennens. Stuttgart, 1957.

Phil 75.55 Kwee, Swan Liat. Bibliography of humanism. Utrecht, 1957.

Phil 5050.17 Kyle, William M. The elements of deductive logic. 4th ed. Brisbane, 1957.

Phil 5251.54 Lafitte, Paul. The person in psychology. N.Y., 1957.

Phil 5421.10.15 Lain Entraglo, Pedro. La espera y la esperanza. Madrid, 1957.

Phil 1750.166.85.5 Laloup, Jean. Communauté des hommes. 4e éd. Tournai, 1957.

Phil 1750.166.24 Lamont, Corliss. The philosophy of humanism. 4th ed. N.Y., 1957.

Phil 5251.62 Lamouche, André. Psychologie. Paris, 1957.

Phil 8591.12.5 Lang, Albert. Wesen und Wahrheit der Religion. München, 1957.

Phil 8412.33 Lange, A.K. Problems of art. N.Y., 1957.

Phil 186.97.5 Langer, Mrs. S.K. Philosophy in a new key. 3d ed. Cambridge, Mass., 1957.

Phil 5520.240 Language. N.Y., 1957.

Phil 4472.1.30 Lapas de Gusmão. Virtudes e defeitas dos homens. Lisboa, 1957.

Phil 2725.36.30 LaRochefoucauld, Edmée. Pluralité de l'être. Paris, 1957.

Phil 6990.3.92 Laurentin, René. Lourdes. 2. ed. Paris, 1957. 7v.

Phil 3640.490 Lea, F.A. The tragic philosopher. London, 1957.

Phil 5590.220 Leary, Timothy. Interpersonal diagnosis of personality. N.Y., 1957.

Phil 4210.165 Leetham, C.R. Rosmini. London, 1957.

Phil 2520.255.5 Lefèvre, Roger. L'humanisme de Descartes. Paris, 1957.

Phil 3552.445 Leibniz, G.W. The preface to Leibniz' Novissima Sinica. Honolulu, 1957.

Phil 3552.78.15 Leibniz, Gottfried Wilhelm. Correspondance Leibnitz-Clarke présentée d'après les manuscrits originaux des bibliothèques de Hanovre et de Londres. 1. éd. Paris, 1957.

Phil 3552.51.12 Leibniz, Gottfried Wilhelm. Discours de métaphysique et Correspondance aves Arnauld. Paris, 1957.

Phil 176.69.80.5 Leipzig. Universität. Ernst Blochs Revision des Marxismus. Berlin, 1957.

Phil 735.124.5 Lepley, Ray. The language of value. N.Y., 1957.

Phil 2805.330 LeRoy, Georges. Pascal. 1. éd. Paris, 1957.

Phil 8599.40 Le Trocquer, René. Homme, qui suis-je? Paris, 1957.

Phil 165.90 Levi, A.W. Varieties of experience. N.Y., 1957.

Phil 8663.3.95 Lewis, Joseph. Ingersoll the magnificent. N.Y., 1957.

Phil 486.10 Ley, Hermann. Studie zur Geschichte des Materialismus im Mittelalter. Berlin, 1957.

Phil 8886.72 Lillie, William. An introduction to ethics. 3. ed. London, 1957.

Phil 2120.10.20 Lindsay, A.D.L. Selected addresses. Cumberland, 1957.

Phil 2115.70.7 Locke, J. Ein Brief über Toleranz. Hamburg, 1957.

Phil 3475.3.160 Lohff, Wenzel. Glaube und Freiheit. Gütersloh, 1957.

Phil 5520.255 Longebaugh, T. General semantics. 1. ed. N.Y., 1957.

Phil 96.6 Lopes de Mattos, Carlos. Vocabulario filosófico. Sao Paulo, 1957.

Phil 3850.18.145 Lorschield, Bernhard. Max Schelers Phänomenologie des Psychischen. Bonn, 1957.

Phil 3585.28.10 Lotz, Johannes Baptist. Das Urteil und das Sein. München, 1957.

Phil 292.8.5 Lovejoy, A.O. The great chain of being. Cambridge, Mass., 1957.

Phil 3450.19.160 Lüble, Hermann. Bibliographie der Heidegger. Literatur, 1917-1955. Meisenheim am Glan, 1957.

Phil 5251.53 Lückert, Heinz Rolf. Konflikt-Psychologie. München, 1957.

Phil 8412.18 Lukács, György. A különösség mintesztétikai kategória. Budapest, 1957.

Phil 5401.32 Lyon, Josette. L'angoisse. Paris, 1957.

Phil 1830.20 Mace, Cecil Alec. British philosophy in the mid-century. London, 1957.

Phil 5465.80 McKellar, Peter. Imagination and thinking. London, 1957.

Phil 8887.95 Mackinnon, D.M. A study in ethical theory. London, 1957.

Phil 8962.16 McLaughlin, P.J. The church and modern science. N.Y., 1957.

Phil 575.165 Macmurray, John. The self as agent. London, 1957. 2v.

Phil 6980.447 Maeder, Alphonse. Der Psychotherapeut als Paktnei. Zürich, 1957.

Phil 5400.136 Maisonneuve, Jean. Les sentiments. 4. ed. Paris, 1957.

Phil 187.160 Maitra, Sushil. The main problems of philosophy. Calcutta, 1957. 2v.

Phil 165.85 Mandelbaum, Maurice H. Philosophic problems. N.Y., 1957.

Phil 8612.40 Mangoldt, Ursula von. Der Tod als Antwort auf das Leben. München, 1957.

Phil 850.26 Marcer, S.A.B. Earliest intellectual man's idea of the cosmos. London, 1957.

Phil 8592.122.20 Marchal, Jean. L'étrange figure du curé Meslier, 1664-1729. Charleville, 1957.

Phil 9070.114 Margolius, Hans. Aphorismen zur Ethik. Heidelberg, 1957.

Phil 2750.11.79 Maritain, Jacques. On the philosophy of history. N.Y., 1957.

Phil 2750.11.77 Maritain, Jacques. Truth and human fellowship. Princeton, 1957.

Phil 187.156 Martin, Gottfried. Einleitung in die allgemeine Metaphysik. Köln, 1957.

Phil 187.148 Martin, W.O. The order and integration of knowledge. Ann Arbor, 1957.

Phil 8592.100 Martin-Deslias, N. L'invention divine. Paris, 1957.

Phil 8667.26 Martins, Diamantino. O problema de Deus. Braga, 1957.

Phil 343.40 Martins, Diamantino. Teoria do conhecimento. Braga, 1957.

Phil 812.30 Mascia, Carmin. A history of philosophy. Paterson, N.J., 1957.

Phil 5252.115 Maslow, Paul. Intuition versus intellect. N.Y., 1957.

Phil 2750.26.30 Mathieu, Guy. Science du bonheur. Paris, 1957.

Phil 978.59.105 Matwani, Kewal. Krishnamurti. Madras, 1957.

1957 - cont.

Phil 260.12 Mau, Jergen. Zum Problem des Infinitesimalen bei den antiken Atomisten. Berlin, 1957.

Phil 2150.16.40 Mayer, Frederick. Education and the good life. Washington, 1957.

Phil 3640.515 Mehring, Franz. Friedrich Nietzsche. Berlin, 1957.

Phil 1812.5.10 Mel'vil, Iu.K. Amerikanskii pragmatizm. Moskva, 1957.

Phil 6980.489 Meyer, Adolf. Psychobiology. Springfield, 1957.

Phil 8887.105 Meyer, Arthur E. Mind, matter, and morals. 1st. ed. N.Y., 1957.

Phil 400.124 Meynier, Philippe. Essai sur l'idéalisme moderne. Paris, 1957.

Phil 187.151 Miceli di Serradileo, Riccardo. Introduzione alla filosofia. Roma, 1957.

Phil 7084.4.20 Micheloud, Pierrette. Dictionnaire psychanalytique des rêves. Paris, 1957.

Phil 2138.79.8.5 Mill, John S. Autobiography. N.Y., 1957.

Phil 4363.8 Mirabeut Vilaplana, Francisco. Estudios estéticos. Barcelona, 1957. 2v.

Phil 2725.30.80 Miranda, Maria do Carmo Tavares de. Théorie de la vérité chez Edouard LeRoy. Paris, 1957.

Phil 3450.18.125 Mohanty, J.N. Nicolai Hartmann and Alfred North Whitehead. Calcutta, 1957.

Phil 2475.1.325 Montiani, Oddino. Bergson e il suo umanismo integrale. Padova, 1957.

Phil 8962.18 Morale cristiana ed esigenre contemporanee. Milano, 1957.

Phil 8125.26 Morawski, Stefan. Rozwáj myśli. Warszawa, 1957.

Phil 665.84 Morreale de Castro, Margherita. Versiones españolas de animus y anima. Granada? 1957.

Phil 575.147 Mounier, E. Be not afraid. London, 1957.

Phil 6980.485 Mullahy, Patrick. A study of interpersonal relations. N.Y., 1957.

Phil 1020.38 Muminov, I.M. Iz istorii razvitiia...musli v uzbekistane. Tashkent, 1957.

Phil 293.31 Munitz, Milton Karl. Space, time, and creation. Glencoe, 1957.

Phil 575.140.5 Nédoncelle, Maurice. Vers une philosophie de l'amour et de la personne. Aubier, 1957.

Phil 6315.44 New York. Academy of Medicine. Freud and contemporary culture. N.Y., 1957.

Phil 575.120.2.2 Newcomb, Theodore Mead. Personality and social change. N.Y., 1957.

Phil 5500.16 Newell, Allen. Elements of a theory of human problem solving. Santa Monica, 1957.

Phil 3640.72 Nietzsche, Friedrich. Fragments sur l'énergie et la puissance. Paris, 1957.

Phil 3640.40.12 Nietzsche, Friedrich. Thus spake Zarathustra. Chicago, 1957.

Phil 8593.20.5 Nigg, Walter. Prophetische Denker. Zürich, 1957.

Phil 4215.3.83 Nonis, Piero. La scepsi etica di Giuseppe Rensi. Roma, 1957.

Phil 5237.516 Ocherki po istorii russkoi psikhologii. Moskva, 1957.

Phil 7069.57.5 O'Donnell, Elliot. Haunted waters. London, 1957.

Phil 8889.5 Oesterle, J.A. Ethics. Englewood Cliffs, N.J., 1957.

Phil 814.4 Oizerman, T.I. Osnovnye etapy razvitiia domarksistskoi filosofii. Moskva, 1957.

Phil 5274.18 Oléron, Pierre. Les composantes de l'intelligence d'après les recherches factorielles. Paris, 1957.

Phil 181.45.80 Orsi, Domenico d'. Lo spirito come atto puro in Giovanni Gentile. Padova, 1957.

Phil 5520.190 Osgood, C.E. The measurement of meaning. Urbana, 1957.

Phil 1750.330.10 Paci, Enzo. Dall'esistenzialismo al relazionismo. Messina, 1957.

Phil 1715.7 Paci, Enzo. La filosofia contemporanea. 1. ed. Milano, 1957.

Phil 1133.32 Paci, Enzo. Storia del pensiero presocratico. Torino, 1957.

Phil 7069.57 Parapsychology, F. Proceedings of four conferences. N.Y., 1957.

Phil 346.26 París, Carlos. Ciencia. Santiago, 1957.

Phil 5645.53 Paris. Ecole Pratique des Hautes Études. Problèmes. Paris, 1957.

Phil 735.170 Parker, D.H. The philosophy of value. Ann Arbor, 1957.

Phil 3497.22 Pascol, Georges. La pensée de Kant. 2. éd. Paris, 1957.

Phil 5066.140 Pasquinelli, Alberto. Introduzione alla logica simbolica. Torino, 1957.

Phil 8400.26 Pastore, A. Introduzione alla metafisica della poesia. Padova, 1957. 2 pam.

Phil 5055.20.5 Pastore, Annibale. Logicalia. Padova, 1957.

Phil 8890.5.50 Patterson, C.H. Moral standards. 2. ed. N.Y., 1957.

Phil 5255.3.5 Pauli, Richard. Psychologisches Praktikum. 6. Aufl. Stuttgart, 1957.

Phil 5625.75.20 Pavlov, Ivan P. Experimental psychology. N.Y., 1957.

Phil 3850.27.150 Payne, Robert. The three worlds of Albert Schweitzer. N.Y., 1957.

Phil 5520.235 Pear, T.H. Personality, appearance and speech. London, 1957.

Phil 190.84 Pears, D.F. The nature of metaphysics. London, 1957.

Phil 2225.5.20 Peirce, C.S. Essays in the philosophy of science. N.Y., 1957.

Phil 2225.11.5 Pepper, Stephen Coburn. World hypotheses. Berkeley, 1957.

Phil 190.90 Peters, Johannes Arnold Josef. Metaphysica. Utrecht, 1957.

Phil 530.35.25 Petrocchi, Giorgio. Ascesi e mistica trecentesca. Firenze, 1957.

Phil 3850.27.235 Phillips, Herbert M. Albert Schweitzer, prophet of freedom. Evanston, Ill., 1957.

Phil 3745.14.5 Pieper, Josef. Glück und Kontemplation. 1. Aufl. München, 1957.

Phil 8965.13.10 Pieper, Josef. Justice. London, 1957.

Phil 3745.14 Pieper, Josef. Kleines Lesebuch von den Tugenden des menschlichen Herzens. 5. Aufl. München, 1957.

Phil 3850.27.145 Pierhal, Jean. Albert Schweitzer. N.Y., 1957.

Phil 5640.130.2 Piéron, Henri. La sensation. 2. éd. Paris, 1957.

Phil 5204.12.2 Piéron, Henri. Vocabulaire de la psychologie. 2. éd. Paris, 1957.

Phil 5593.57.5 Piotrowski, Z. Perceptanalysis. N.Y., 1957.

Phil 4210.175 Piovani, Pietro. La teodicea sociale di Rosmini. Padova, 1957.

Phil 4710.90 Pokrovskii, S.A. Fal'sifkatsiia istorii russkoi politicheskoi mysli v sovremennoi reaktsionnoi burzhuaznoi literature. Moskva, 1957.

Phil 6965.26 Poljak, Leo. Graphologische Untersuchungen an den Handelschriften von Schizophren-Paranoiden und Epileptikern. Abhandlung. Tübingen, 1957.

Phil 4200.1.15 Pomponazzi, Pietro. De fato. Lucani, 1957.

1957 - cont.

Phil 6125.27 — Portman, Adolf. Don Quijote und Sancho Pansa vom gegenwartigen Stand der Typenlehre. Basel, 1957.

Phil 5025.1.4 — Prantl, Carl von. Geschichte der Logik im Abendlande. v.1-4. Berlin, 1957. 3v.

Phil 575.180 — La présence d'autrui. Paris, 1957.

Phil 2266.157 — Preti, Giulio. Alle origini dell'etica contemporanea Adamo Smith. Bari, 1957.

Phil 7039.4.8 — Prince, Morton. The dissociation of a personality. N.Y., 1957.

Phil 5066.100 — Prior, Arthur Norman. Time and modality. Oxford, 1957.

Phil 6325.18 — Problèmes de psychanalyse. Paris, 1957.

Phil 310.4.5 — Protasenko, Z.M. Printsipy periodizatsii istorii marksistsko-leninskoi filosofii. Leningrad, 1957.

Phil 735.190 — Pucelle, Jean. La source des valeurs. Lyon, 1957. 3v.

Phil 5435.4.2 — Ravaisson-Mollien, Felix. De l'habitude. 2. éd. Paris, 1957.

Phil 5238.75 — Rencontre. Utrecht, 1957.

Phil 5257.64 — Reuchlin, Maurice. Histoire de la psychologie. Paris, 1957.

Phil 192.98 — Revel, Jean Francois. Pourquoi des philosophes? Paris, 1957. 2v.

Phil 5057.25.2 — Reymond, Arnold. Les principes de la logique et la critique contemporaine. Paris, 1957.

Phil 7069.57.15 — Rhine, Joseph B. Parapsychology. Springfield, Ill., 1957.

Phil 1717.20 — La ricerca filosofia nella coscienza delle nuove generazioni. Bologna, 1957.

Phil 6327.11.5 — Rickman, J. Selected contributions to psychoanalysis. London, 1957.

Phil 192.100 — Rinerso, Emmanuele. Metafisica e scientismo. Napoli, 1957.

Phil 192.67.10 — Rintelen, Fritz J. von. Der europäische Mensch. Wien, 1957.

Phil 192.102 — Rivier, William. Le pouvoir de l'esprit. Neuchâtel, 1957.

Phil 6315.2.185 — Roback, A.A. Freudiana. Cambridge, Mass., 1957.

Phil 5590.458 — Robaye, Francine. Niveaux d'aspiration et d'expectation. Paris, 1957.

Phil 2520.275 — Rodis-Lewis, Geneviève. La morale de Descartes. 1. ed. Paris, 1957.

Phil 5592.150 — Rohde, Amanda R. The sentence completion method. N.Y., 1957.

Phil 4215.1.30 — Romagnosi, G.D. Opere di Romagnosi. Milano, 1957.

Phil 4368.2.60 — Romero, Francisco. Filósofos y problemas. 2. ed. Buenos Aires, 1957.

Phil 3790.20 — Rosenstock, Eugen. Zurück in das Wagnis der Sprache. Berlin, 1957.

Phil 4017.5 — Rossi, Mario. Sviluppi dello hegelismo in Italia. Torino, 1957.

Phil 1850.147.5 — Rossi, Paolo. Francesco Bacone, dalla magia alla scienza. Bari, 1957.

Phil 5057.34 — Roure, Marie Louise. Logique et métalogique. Paris, 1957.

Phil 310.3.10 — Rozhin, V.P. Marksistsko-leninskaia dialektika. Leningrad, 1957.

Phil 4768.2.5 — Rubinshtein, Sergei L. Bytie i soznanie o meste psikhologii. Moskva, 1957.

Phil 4769.6.83.5 — Rubinshtein, Sergei L. I.M. Sechenov. Moskva, 1957.

Phil 8430.27 — Ruefenacht, E. Mächte der Gestaltung; vom künstlerischen, philosophischen und religiösen Sein. Zürich, 1957.

Phil 2255.7.15 — Runes, Dagobert D. A book of contemplation. N.Y., 1957.

Phil 2255.1.79 — Russell, Bertrand Russell. Understanding history. N.Y., 1957.

Phil 8610.927.8 — Russell, Bertrand Russell. Why I am not a Christian. N.Y., 1957.

Phil 310.12.15 — Russia (1917-   ). Upravlenie Prepodavatel'skogo Obshchestvennogo Nauk. Programma kursa dialekticheskogo i istoricheskogo materializma. Moskva, 1957.

Phil 5520.220 — Rutt, Theodor. Vom Wesen der Sprache. Ratingen, 1957.

Phil 5058.90 — Saarnio, Uuno. Logikens Uppkomst och Väsen. Helsingfors, 1957.

Phil 5710.20 — Sacherl, Karl. Die Pedanterie. Göttingen, 1957.

Phil 6328.42 — Sachs, Hanns. Masks of love and life. London, 1957.

Phil 4352.1.107 — Sagarra y de Castellarnau, Fernando. Encrucijada. Barcelona, 1957.

Phil 8419.33 — Saitschick, R. Kunstschöpfer und Kunstschaffen. Marburg, 1957.

Phil 3500.75 — Salvucci, Pasquale. La dottrina Kantiana dello schematismo transcendentale. Urbino, 1957.

Phil 2493.94 — Salvucci, Pasquale. Linguaggio e mondo umano in Condillac. Urbino, 1957.

Phil 193.132.15 — Samuel, Herbert S. In search of reality. Oxford, 1957.

Phil 5627.257.10 — Sanson, Henri. Spiritualité de la vie active. Le Puy, 1957.

Phil 193.49.8 — Santayana, G. Winds of doctrine. N.Y., 1957.

Phil 2280.5.84 — Santayana, George. The idler and his works. N.Y., 1957.

Phil 5627.107.15 — Sargant, W.W. Battle for the mind. Melbourne, 1957.

Phil 2725.35.85 — Sargi, Bechara. La participation à l'être. Paris, 1957.

Phil 2880.8.65 — Sartre, Jean Paul. Existentialism and human emotions. N.Y., 1957.

Phil 2880.8.64A — Sartre, Jean Paul. The transcendence of the ego. N.Y., 1957.

Phil 3800.280 — Schelling, F.W.J. von. Philosophie der Mythologie. Darmstadt, 1957. 2v.

Phil 3800.180.7 — Schelling, F.W.J. von. System des transscendentalen Idealismus. Hamburg, 1957.

Phil 5828.19 — Schiller, C.H. Instinctive behavior. N.Y., 1957.

Phil 3235.117 — Schilling, Werner. Feuerbach und die Religion. München, 1957.

Phil 3475.3.140 — Schilpp, P.A. Karl Jaspers. Stuttgart, 1957.

Phil 3475.3.140.5 — Schilpp, P.A. The philosophy of Karl Jaspers. 1st ed. N.Y., 1957.

Phil 3425.475 — Schmandt, Jürgen. Hegel Ethik aus dem Geist der Religion. Bonn, 1957.

Phil 103.3.31 — Schmidt, Heinrich. Philosophisches Wörterbuch. 14. Aufl. Stuttgart, 1957.

Phil 3808.31.5 — Schopenhauer, Arthur. On human nature; essays. London, 1957.

Phil 3808.53 — Schopenhauer, Arthur. Philosophische Meschenkunde. Stuttgart, 1957.

Phil 3808.49.10 — Schopenhauer, Arthur. Über die vierfache Wurzel des Satzes vom zureichen den Grunde. Hamburg, 1957.

Phil 9560.42 — Schottlaender, Rudolf. Theorie des Vertrauens. Berlin, 1957.

Phil 5548.25 — Schreier, F.T. Human motivation. Glencoe, Ill., 1957.

Phil 193.177 — Schulz, Walter. Der Gott der neuzeitlichen Metaphysik. Pfullingen, 1957.

Phil 8598.110 — Schuon, Frithjof. Sentien de gnose. Paris, 1957.

1957 - cont.

Phil 4225.8.38 — Sciacca, Michele Federico. Come si vince a Waterloo. Milano, 1957.

Phil 5258.165 — Sechenov, Ivan M. Oeuvres philosophiques et psychologiques choisies. Moscou, 1957.

Phil 193.148.5 — Selsam, H. Philosophy in revolution. N.Y., 1957.

Phil 1750.530 — Sérouya, Henri. Les philosophies de l'existence. Paris, 1957.

Phil 7150.38 — Shneidman, Edwin S. Clues to suicide. N.Y., 1957.

Phil 193.205 — Shul'gyn, O. L'histoire el la vie. Paris, 1957.

Phil 5058.85 — Sichirollo, Livio. Logica e dialettica. Milano, 1957.

Phil 3090.89 — Siegl, Josef. Franz von Baader. München, 1957.

Phil 1870.132 — Sillem, E.A. George Berkeley and the proofs for the existence of God. London, 1957.

Phil 1718.30 — Silva-Tarouca, Amadeo. Philosophie im Mittelpunkt. Graz, 1957.

Phil 3850.16.31 — Simmel, Georg. Brücke und Tür. Stuttgart, 1957.

Phil 5238.40 — Simon, Brian. Psychology in the Soviet Union. Stanford, Calif., 1957.

Phil 2805.340 — Simonetti, Maria. Studi Pascaliani. Roma, 1957?

Phil 2280.5.130A — Singer, Irving. Santayana's aesthetics; a critical introduction. Cambridge, 1957.

Phil 193.179 — Sinha, Jadunath. Introduction to philosophy. 2d ed. Calcutta, 1957.

Phil 8708.28 — Sinnott, Edmund Ware. Matter. 1. ed. N.Y., 1957.

Phil 1750.85 — Siu, Ralph G.H. The Tao of science. Cambridge, Mass., 1957.

Phil 5258.120.15 — Skinner, Burrhus F. Verbal behavior. N.Y., 1957.

Phil 4195.89 — Sloek, Johannes. Tradition og nybrud. København, 1957.

Phil 193.172 — Smith, J.W. Theme for reason. Princeton, 1957.

Phil 6976.5 — Society of Medical Psychoanalysts. Schizophrenia in psychoanalytic office practice. N.Y., 1957.

Phil 4210.198 — Solari, Gioele. Studi rosminiani. Milano, 1957.

Phil 5058.80 — Spann, Othmar. Gangheitliche Logik. v.1-2. Salzburg, 1957.

Phil 3819.35.30A — Spinoza, Benedictus de. The road to inner freedom. N.Y., 1957.

Phil 575.155 — Stauenhagen, K. Person und Persönlichkeit. Göttingen, 1957.

Phil 3110.195 — Staurt, J.J. Sunrise to eternity. Philadelphia, 1957.

Phil 5520.210 — Stegmüller, W. Das Wahrheitsproblem und die Idee der Semantik. Wien, 1957.

Phil 978.49.260 — Steiner, R. Die Bedeutung der Anthroposophie im Geistesleben der Gegenwart. Dornach, 1957.

Phil 1123.7.5 — Stenzel, Julius. Kleine Schriften zur griechischen Philosophie. 2. Aufl. Darmstadt, 1957.

Phil 7069.57.10 — Stirling, A.M.W.P. Ghosts vivisected. London, 1957.

Phil 6980.710.63 — Stocker, Arnold. De la psychanalyse à la psychosynthese. Paris, 1957.

Phil 665.80.5 — Strasser, Stephan. The soul in metaphysical and empirical psychology. Pittsburgh, 1957.

Phil 818.30 — Strobach, W. Liebe zum Wissen. Wien, 1957.

Phil 4285.2.80 — Studi sul pensiero di Giuseppe Zamboni. Milano, 1957.

Phil 5850.348 — Super, D.E. The psychology of careers. 1st ed. N.Y., 1957.

Phil 525.140 — Suzuki, D.T. Mysticism. N.Y., 1957.

Phil 5402.23 — Szasz, T.S. Pain and pleasure. N.Y., 1957.

Phil 6329.15 — Tashman, H.F. Today's neurotic family. N.Y., 1957.

Phil 194.49 — Taulmin, St. E. Metaphysical beliefs. London, 1957.

Phil 575.160 — Terlecki, Tymon. Krytyka personalistyczna. Londyn, 1957.

Phil 7040.29 — Thigpen, C.H. The three faces of Eve. N.Y., 1957.

Phil 819.7.7 — Thilly, F. A history of philosophy. 3. ed. N.Y., 1957.

Phil 4960.610.2 — Torres, João Camillo de Oliveira. O positivismo no Brasil. 2. ed. Rio de Janeiro, 1957.

Phil 5590.548 — Tournier, Paul. The meaning of persons. N.Y., 1957.

Phil 1524.5 — Traktenberg, O.V. Ocherki po istorii zapadno-evropeiskoi Srednevekovoi filosofii. Moskva, 1957.

Phil 300.6 — Tramer, Moritz. Philosophie des schöpferischen. Bern, 1957.

Phil 6400.33.5 — Travis, Lee E. Handbook speech pathology. N.Y., 1957.

Phil 2150.15.105 — Tremmel, William C. The social concepts of George Herbert Mead. Emporia, 1957.

Phil 960.205 — Tucci, Giuseppe. Storia della filosofia Indiana. Bari, 1957.

Phil 5170.11 — Ţuţugan, F. Silogistica judecaţilor de predicaţie. Bucuresti, 1957.

Phil 4803.462.80 — Tymieniecka, Anna Teresa. Essence et existence. Paris, 1957.

Phil 195.13 — Ulken, Hilmi Zuja. Felsejeye gini. Ankara, 1957. 2 pam.

Phil 960.190A — Umesha, Mishra. History of Indian philosophy. Allahabad, 1957.

Phil 9450.32 — Union Internationale d'Études Sociales. Code de morale politique. Bruxelles, 1957.

Phil 4771.3A — Uspenskii, P.D. The fourth way. 1st American ed. N.Y., 1957.

Phil 4265.4.10 — Vailati, G. Il metodo della filosofia. Bari, 1957.

Phil 8601.17 — Vancourt, Raymond. Pensée moderne et philosophie chrétienne. Paris, 1957.

Phil 6331.6.2 — Van der Veldt, J.H. Psychiatry and Catholicism. 2nd ed. N.Y., 1957.

Phil 8422.4 — Vanslov, V.V. Problema prekrasnogo. Moskva, 1957.

Phil 4810.6 — Várossová, Elena. Kapitoly z dejín slovenskej filozofie. Bratislava, 1957.

Phil 623.50 — Vasa, Andrea. Ricerche sul razionalismo della prassi. Firenze, 1957.

Phil 9490.15 — Vaz Ferreira, C. Moral para intelectuales. La Plata, 1957.

Phil 5771.4 — Vaz Ferreira, C. Los problemas de la libertad y los del determinismo. Buenos Aires, 1957.

Phil 4983.1.5 — Vaz Ferreira, Carlos. Obras. v.1-25. Montevideo, 1957. 20v.

Phil 1721.4 — Veit, Otto. Soziologie der Freiheit. Frankfurt a.M., 1957.

Phil 4260.17.5 — Vico, G.B. Tutte le opere di Giambattista Vico. Milano, 1957.

Phil 4080.3.315 — Vinceguerra, Mario. Croce. Napoli, 1957.

Phil 2750.11.150 — Viotto, Piero. Jacques Maritain. Brescia, 1957.

Phil 1750.494 — Virasoro, Rafael. Existencialismo y moral. Argentina, 1957.

Phil 1721.5 — Vloemans, Antoon. Europa in de spiegel. Den Haag, 1957.

Phil 3450.11.205 — Wahle, Jean A. L'ouvrage posthume de Husserl. Paris, 1957.

Phil 4757.2.95 — Walker, K.M. A study of Gurdjieff's teaching. London, 1957.

Phil 6332.15 — Walker, Nigel. A short history of psychotherapy in theory and practice. London, 1957.

Chronological Listing

1957 - cont.

Phil 530.70.5 — Walter, R. von. Russische Mystik. Düsseldorf, 1957.
Phil 5585.160 — Wapner, Seymour. Perceptual development. Worcester, Mass., 1957.
Phil 5460.12 — Ward, R.H. A drug-taker's notes. London, 1957.
Phil 2045.130 — Warrender, H. The political philosophy of Hobbes. Oxford, 1957.
Phil 822.1.4 — Weber, A. Histoire de la philosophie européenne. Paris, 1957. 3v.
Phil 1722.11 — Weber, Alfred. Histoire de la philosophie européenne. Paris, 1957.
Phil 3425.415 — Wein, Hermann. Realdialektik. München, 1957.
Phil 8050.32 — Weisbach, Werner. Stilbegriffe und Stilphänomene. Wien, 1957.
Phil 5262.51 — Wenzl, Aloys. Theorie der Begabung. 2. Aufl. Heidelberg, 1957.
Phil 5832.15.10 — Werner, Heinz. Comparative psychology of mental development. N.Y., 1957.
Phil 5650.40 — Wever, Ernest. Theory of hearing. N.Y., 1957.
Phil 8602.52 — Wilson, Colin. Religion and the rebel. London, 1957.
Phil 822.2.4.7 — Windelband, W. Lehrbuch der Geschichte der Philosophie. Tübingen, 1957.
Phil 8847.14 — Winkler, Paul. Les sources mystiques des concepts moraux de l'occident. Paris, 1957.
Phil 1830.25 — Winny, James. The frame of order. London, 1957.
Phil 197.72.5 — Wohl, J.A. Un renouvellement de la métaphysique. Est-il possible? Paris, 1957.
Phil 5262.50 — Wolfenstein, M. Disaster, a psychological essay. Glencoe, Ill., 1957.
Phil 2255.1.118 — Wood, Alan. Bertrand Russell. London, 1957.
Phil 5125.21.5 — Wright, G.H. von. The logical problem of induction. 2nd ed. N.Y., 1957.
Phil 5125.21.7 — Wright, G.H. von. The logical problem of induction. 2nd ed. Oxford, 1957.
Phil 5062.38 — Wright, G.H. von. Logical studies. London, 1957.
Phil 930.52 — Yang, Jung-kuo. Istoriia drevnekitaiskoi ideologii. Moskva, 1957.
Phil 6980.794 — Zander, A.F. Role relations in the mental health professions. Ann Arbor, 1957.
Phil 5090.3.80 — Zeno, Father. John Henry Newman. Leiden, 1957.
Phil 200.15.5 — Zerle, Herbert. Die Kunst des Kritisieren. Berlin, 1957.
Phil 165.120 — Ziegler, Klaus. Wesen und Wirklichkeit des Menschen. Göttingen, 1957.
Phil 356.5 — Zinkernagel, Peter. Omverdens problemet. København, 1957.
Phil 4803.896.20 — Znamierowski, Czesław Stanisław. Oceny i normy. Warszawa, 1957.
Phil 7003.5 — Zorab, George. Bibliography of parapsychology. N.Y., 1957.
Phil 630.54 — Zykmund, V. Co je realismus? Praha, 1957.
Phil 8426.9 — Zykmund, Václav. K základní otázce estetiky. Praha, 1957.

1958

Phil 4817.5 — Academia Republicii Socialiste România, Bucharest. Philosophes roumains contemporains. București, 1958.
Phil 440.2 — Adler, Mortimer J. The idea of freedom. Garden City, N.Y., 1958-61. 2v.
Phil 310.6.5 — Akadamiia Nauk SSSR. Institut Filosofii. Osnovy marksistskoi filosofii. Moskva, 1958.
Phil 3425.490 — Albrecht, Wolfgang. Hegels Gottesbeweis. Berlin, 1958.
Phil 5592.55 — Allen, Robert M. Personality assessment procedures. N.Y., 1958.
Phil 6310.14 — Allwohn, Adolf. Das heilende Wort. Göttingen, 1958.
Phil 1750.575 — Alonso-Fueyo, Sabino. El drama del hombre actual. Valencia, 1958.
Phil 7069.58.5 — Amadou, Robert. La télépathie. Paris, 1958.
Phil 6310.20 — American Psychopathological Association. Psychopathology of communication. N.Y., 1958.
Phil 6310.18 — Amidieu du Clos-Vinarie-Paule. Les interréactions des facteurs religieux et psychologiques en hygiène mentale. Thèse. Québec, 1958.
Phil 4851.10A — Amin, Osman. Lights on contemporary Moslem philosophy. Cairo, 1958.
Phil 310.738 — Anders, Georg. Wider die Fälscher der Geschichte. München, 1958.
Phil 6310.12 — Anderson, C.M. Beyond Freud. London, 1958.
Phil 3640.158.4 — Andler, Charles. Nietzsche, sa vie et sa pensée. Paris, 1958. 3v.
Phil 7082.144 — Andreas-Friedrich, Ruth. Ursprung und Sinn der Träume. Zürich, 1958.
Phil 9513.9 — Angell, Robert Cooley. Free society and moral crisis. Ann Arbor, 1958.
Phil 6980.45 — Annell, A.L. Elementär barrpsykiatri. Stockholm, 1958.
Phil 1845.14.2 — Anscombe, G.E.M. Intention. Oxford, 1958.
Phil 3482.12 — Antonopoulos, Georg. Der Menschen als Bürger zweier Welten. Bonn, 1958.
Phil 600.7.100 — Aquarone, Stanislas. The life and works of Émile Littré. Leyden, 1958.
Phil 672.197 — Archivio di Filosofia. Il tempo. Padova, 1958.
Phil 5627.258 — Argyle, Michael. Religious behavior. London, 1958.
Phil 2490.145 — Aron, Raymond. War and industrial society. London, 1958.
Phil 5548.85A — Atkinson, John W. Motives in fantasy, action, and society. Princeton, 1958.
Phil 2477.15.5.2 — Bachelard, Gaston. La poétique de l'espace. 2. éd. Paris, 1958.
Phil 8876.117 — Baier, Kurt. The moral point of view. Ithaca, 1958.
Phil 6315.2.230 — Bakan, David. Sigmund Freud and the Jewish mystical tradition. Princeton, N.J., 1958.
Phil 3425.505 — Bakradze, K.S. Sistema i metod filosofii Gegelia. Tbilisi, 1958.
Phil 1535.1.40 — Balmes, Jaime. Habla Balmes. Barcelona, 1958.
Phil 3120.30.90 — Balthasar, Hans von. Einsame Zinesprache; Martin Buber und das Christentum. Köln, 1958.
Phil 176.195 — Banerjee, N.V. Concerning human understanding. London, 1958.
Phil 8626.20 — Barbarin, Georges. L'après-mort. Paris, 1958.
Phil 4225.15.80 — Barrello, O. L'estetica di M. Spirito. Lugano, 1958.
Phil 1750.167.5 — Barrett, William. Irrational man. London, 1958.
Phil 9400.27 — Bartholody, E Mendelssohn. Der Lebensabend. 1. Aufl. Gütersloh, 1958.
Phil 5520.205 — Bartlett, F.C. Thinking. London, 1958.
Phil 5585.120 — Bartley, S.H. Principles of perception. N.Y., 1958.
Phil 2050.78.80 — Basson, A.H. David Hume. Harmondsworth, 1958.
Phil 1701.35 — Baudry, Bernard. Point de vue sur l'Occident. Paris, 1958.
Phil 8876.119 — Baylis, C.A. Ethics. N.Y., 1958.
Phil 5585.115 — Beardslee, D.C. Readings in perception. Princeton, 1958.

1958 - cont.

Phil 8402.57 — Beardsley, Monroe Curtis. Aesthetics; problems in the philosophy of criticism. N.Y., 1958.
Phil 176.168.5 — Beck, Lewis White. Philosophic inquiry. Englewood Cliffs, N.J., 1958.
Phil 7082.178 — Becker, Raymond de. Les songes. Paris, 1958.
Phil 5400.138 — Bellingroth, Friedhelm. Triebwirkung des Films auf Jugendliche. Bern, 1958.
Phil 1750.126.8 — Benda, Julien. La trahison des clercs. Paris, 1958.
Phil 5811.20 — Beniest-Noirot, Eliane. Analyse du comportement dit maternel chez la souris. Paris, 1958.
Phil 4752.2.63 — Berdiaev, Nikolai Aleksandrovich. Essai d'autobiographie spirituelle. Paris, 1958.
Phil 8402.48 — Berestnev, V.F. Problemy estetiki. Moskva, 1958.
Phil 3900.1.85 — Berger, Herbert. Begründung des Realismus. Bonn, 1958.
Phil 2475.1.66 — Bergson, Henri. The world of dreams. N.Y., 1958.
Phil 8876.123 — Berlin, Isaiah. Two concepts of liberty. Oxford, 1958.
Phil 5850.131 — Bertine, Eleanor. Human relationships. 1. ed. N.Y., 1958.
Phil 5850.130 — Beuesch, H. Wissenschaft der Menschenbehandlung. Heidelberg, 1958.
Phil 850.40 — Birand, Kâmiran. Ilk caǧ felsefesi torihi. Ankara, 1958.
Phil 5590.250 — Boll, Marcel. La personnalité; sa structure. Paris, 1958.
Phil 9560.50 — Bollnow, O.F. Wasen und Wandel der Tugenden. Frankfurt, 1958.
Phil 745.12 — Bollnow, Otto F. Die Lebensphilosophie. Berlin, 1958.
Phil 8591.70 — Bonafede, Giulio. Luciano Laberthomière. Palermo, 1958.
Phil 6980.127 — Bond, Earl Clanford. One mind. N.Y., 1958.
Phil 332.35 — Bonilla, Abelardo. Conocimiento, verdad y belleza. San Salvador, 1958.
Phil 8626.28.5 — Borgia, Anthony V. More about life in the world unseen. London, 1958.
Phil 8620.48 — Borne, Étienne. Le problème du mal. 1. éd. Paris, 1958.
Phil 7082.196.5 — Boss, Medard. The analysis of dreams. N.Y., 1958.
Phil 8691.30 — Boveri, Walter. Ethik und Atomzeitalter. Zürich, 1958.
Phil 5645.55 — Brandt, Frithiof. Form kolarisme. København, 1958.
Phil 176.94.5 — Brigtman, E.S. Person and reality. N.Y., 1958.
Phil 575.185 — Broad, Charlie P. Personal identity and survival. London, 1958.
Phil 5650.34 — Broadbent, D.E. Perception and communication. N.Y., 1958.
Phil 8876.120 — Brock, Erich. Befreiung und Erfüllung. Zürich, 1958.
Phil 600.53 — Broecker, Walter. Dialektik, Positivismus, Mythologie. Frankfurt, 1958.
Phil 5520.225 — Brown, Roger William. Words and things. Glencoe, Ill., 1958.
Phil 5520.225.2 — Brown, Roger William. Words and things. N.Y., 1958.
Phil 5241.122 — Brrermann, Ernst. Allgemeine Psychologie. Paderborn, 1958.
Phil 1200.60 — Brun, Jean. Le stoïcisme. Paris, 1958.
Phil 165.265 — Brunhold, C. De Montaigne à Luis de Broglie. 8. ed. Paris, 1958?
Phil 4080.3.325 — Bruno, Antonino. Economia ed etica nello svolgimento. Siracusa, 1958.
Phil 4065.14A — Bruno, Giordano. Dialoghi italiani. Firenze, 1958.
Phil 3120.30.44 — Buber, Martin. I and thou. Edinburg, 1958.
Phil 3120.30.44.5 — Buber, Martin. I and thou. 2. ed. N.Y., 1958.
Phil 3120.30.42 — Buber, Martin. Ich und Du. Heidelberg, 1958.
Phil 3120.30.64 — Buber, Martin. Schuld und Schuldgefühle. Heidelberg, 1958.
Phil 3120.30.7 — Buber, Martin. Writings. N.Y., 1958.
Phil 1905.27.30 — Bugbee, H.G. The inward morning. State College, Pa., 1958.
Phil 8402.14.20 — Burke, E. A philosophical inquiry into the origin of our ideas of the sublime and beautiful. London, 1958.
Phil 585.10 — Burnett, Whit. The spirit of man. 1st ed. N.Y., 1958.
Phil 8402.26.5A — Burov, A.I. Das ästhetische Wesen. Berlin, 1958.
Phil 5241.97.15 — Burrow, Trigant. A search for man's sanity. N.Y., 1958.
Phil 585.45 — Buytendijk, F.J.J. Das Menschliche. Stuttgart, 1958.
Phil 5811.15.25 — Buytendijk, Frederik Jacobus Johannes. Mensch und Tier. Hamburg, 1958.
Phil 1135.34 — Caiazzo, D. L'idea di giustizia nel pensiero greco. Roma, 1958.
Phil 8403.2 — Camón Aznar, J. El tiempo en el arte. Madrid, 1958.
Phil 4073.50 — Campanella, Tommaso. Cristologia. Roma, 1958. 2v.
Phil 4073.40 — Campanella, Tommaso. De sancta mono triade. Roma, 1958.
Phil 585.70 — Cantoni, Remo. Umano e disumano. 1. ed. Milano, 1958.
Phil 3475.3.170 — Caracciolo, Alberto. Studi Jaspersiani. Milano, 1958.
Phil 4476.2.30 — Cardoso Rangel de Souza Coelho, Maria Luiza. A filosofia de Silvestre Penheiro Ferreira. Braga, 1958.
Phil 4440.2 — Carmen Rovira, María del. Eclécticos portugueses del siglo XVIII y algunas de sus. Mexico, 1958.
Phil 5066.8.10 — Carnap, Rudolf. Introduction to symbolic logic and its applications. N.Y., 1958.
Phil 5242.53.2 — Carus, K.G. Vorlesungen über Psychologie. Darmstadt, 1958.
Phil 720.44 — Casellato, Sante. Di alcune considerazioni intorno alla verità e all'errore. Padova, 1958.
Phil 6990.3.114 — Cassagnard, Jean Marie. Carrel et Zola devant le miracle à Lourdes. Lourdes, 1958.
Phil 5722.65 — Cazaux, Jean. Surréalisme et psychologie. Paris, 1958.
Phil 2630.7.98 — Chacornac, Paul. La vie simple de René Guenon. Paris, 1958.
Phil 9075.60 — Chaperd, Marc. La révolution originelle. Paris, 1958.
Phil 4964.10 — Chaves, Osvaldo. Historia y filosofía. Buenos Aires, 1958.
Phil 4753.2.40 — Chernyshevskii, N.G. Estetika. Moskva, 1958.
Phil 5593.58 — Chiari, Silvano. Bibliografica italiana. Firenze, 1958.
Phil 5593.58.5 — Chiari, Silvano. Introduzione alla psicodiagnosi di Rorschach. Firenze, 1958.
Phil 5238.110 — Ciba Foundation. Ciba Foundation symposium on the neurological basis of behaviour. Boston, 1958.
Phil 2490.165 — Clavel, Marcel. Le centenaire d'Auguste Comte et la nouvelle constitution française. Fontenay-sous-Bois, 1958.
Phil 8403.34 — Cochofel, J.J. Iniciação estética. Lisboa, 1958.
Phil 333.7.2 — Coffey, Peter. Epistemology. Gloucester, Mass., 1958. 2v.
Phil 530.15.45 — Cognet, Louis. Crépuscule des mystiques. Tournai, 1958.
Phil 5242.56 — Cohen, John. Humanistic psychology. London, 1958.
Phil 4002.6 — La collaboration philosophique. Bologna, 1958.
Phil 270.95 — Cordoba, Martín de. Compendio de la fortuna. Madrid, 1958.
Phil 2515.14 — Cordonnier, V. Le sacre de la liberté. Paris, 1958.
Phil 2496.87 — Cornelius, Alfred. Die Geschichtslehre Victor Cousins. Genève, 1958.
Phil 9070.80 — Corts Grau, José. El hombre en vilo. Madrid, 1958.
Phil 177.22.15 — Cournot, A.A. Critique philosophique. 1. ed. Paris, 1958.
Phil 2138.132 — Cranston, M.W. John Stuart Mill. London, 1958.

1958 - cont.

Phil 3552.253.8   Cresson, André. Leibniz, sa vie, son oeuvre. 3. éd. Paris, 1958.

Phil 4080.3.31.10   Croce, Benedetto. Estetica come scienza dell'espressione e linguista generale. 10. ed. Bari, 1958.

Phil 5520.280   Cuatrecasas, Juan. Psicobiologia del lenguage. 2. ed. Buenos Aires, 1958.

Phil 5238.80   Current trends in the description and analysis of behavior. Pittsburgh, 1958.

Phil 5066.120   Curry, Haskell Brooks. Combinatory logic. Amsterdam, 1958.

Phil 177.110.5   Cuvillier, Armand. La dissertation philosophique. Paris, 1958-62. 2v.

Phil 8877.90   Cysarz, Herbert. Individuelle und collektive Ethik. Tübingen, 1958.

Phil 5238.95   Däumling, Adolf. Seelenleben und Menschenbild. München, 1958.

Phil 730.26   Dar, B.A. Studies in the nature of universals. Lahore, 1958.

Phil 8622.30   d'Arcy, M.C. The nature of belief. Dublin, 1958.

Phil 8654.100   De la connaissance de Dieu. Paris, 1958.

Phil 6990.3.75   Deery, Joseph. Our Lady of Lourdes. Dublin, 1958.

Phil 1703.7   Dempf, Alois. Weltordnung und Heilsgeschichte. Einsiedeln, 1958.

Phil 165.130   Derathé, Robert. La justice et la violence. Paris, 1958.

Phil 2520.23A   Descartes, René. Philosophical writings. N.Y., 1958.

Phil 130.10   De Selincourt, Audrey. Six great thinkers. London, 1958.

Phil 284.15   Dessauer, Friedrich. Naturwissenschaftliches Erkennen. Frankfurt, 1958.

Phil 2530.80.5   Dieckmann, Herbert. Diderot: sur Terence. n.p., 1958?

Phil 88.10   Diemer, Alwin. Philosophie. Frankfurt, 1958.

Phil 178.64.4.7   Dixon, W.M. The human situation. Harmondsworth, 1958.

Phil 3850.18.155   Doerry, Gerd. Der Begriff des Wertpersontypus bis Scheler und Spranger. Berlin, 1958.

Phil 803.16   Dolci, Alfredo. Da talete all'esistenzialismo. Milano, 1958.

Phil 1740.14   Dondeyne, Albert. Contemporary European thought and Christian faith. Pittsburgh, 1958.

Phil 8404.3.5   Dorfles, Gillo. Le ascillazioni del gusto. Milano, 1958.

Phil 2733.115   Drefus, Ginette. La volonté selon Malebranche. Paris, 1958.

Phil 310.65   Dudel, S.P. Zakony materialisticheskoi dialektiki. Moskva, 1958.

Phil 8583.41.5   Duméry, Henry. Phénoménologie et religion. 1. éd. Paris, 1958.

Phil 165.165   Edel, Reiner F. Ein Weiser lebt unter uns. Marburg, 1958.

Phil 5244.25.2   Edwards, Allen L. Statistical analysis. N.Y., 1958.

Phil 5238.150   Ehrhardt, H. Psychiatrie und Gesellschaft. Bern, 1958.

Phil 6420.42   Eisenson, John. Stuttering; a symposium. N.Y., 1958.

Phil 585.15   Emmet, D.M. Function. London, 1958.

Phil 8879.31   Endres, Josef. Menschliche Grundhaltungen. Salzubrg, 1958.

Phil 1020.4.35   Fakhry, Majid. Islamic occasionalism and its critique by Averroës and Aquinas. London, 1958.

Phil 4960.225   Farré, Luis. Cincuenta años de filosofía en Argentina. Buenos Aires, 1958.

Phil 5755.14A   Farrer, A.M. The freedom of the will. London, 1958.

Phil 310.60   Fataliev, K.M. Dialecticheskii materializm i voprosy estestvoznaniia. Moskva, 1958.

Phil 960.210   Fausset, H.I. Anson. The flame and the light. London, 1958.

Phil 8980.386   Fedorenko, I.H. Kommunisticheskaia nravntvennost'. Kiev, 1958.

Phil 180.75   Feibleman, James. Inside the great mirror. The Hague, 1958.

Phil 8695.11   Feibleman, James. The pious scientist. N.Y., 1958.

Phil 6955.20   Fein, Rashi. Economics of mental illness. N.Y., 1958.

Phil 90.4.16   Ferrater Mora, José. Diccionario de filosofía. 4. ed. Buenos Aires, 1958.

Phil 3850.27.122.4   Feschotte, Jacques. Albert Schweitzer. 4. éd. Paris, 1958.

Phil 6115.11.14   Feuchtersleben, E.F.V. Ein Dienst zur Nacht ist unser Leben. Graz, 1958.

Phil 3825.10   Feuer, L.S. Spinoza and The use of liberalism. Boston, 1958.

Phil 4110.14.30   Fichera, G. Crisi e valori, ed altri saggi. Padova, 1958.

Phil 705.46   Fieschi, Andrea. Saggio sul trascendente e sul trascendentale. Padova, 1958.

Phil 4005.11   La filosofia contemporanea in Italia. 1. ed. Roma, 1958. 2v.

Phil 3425.460   Findlay, John Niemayer. Hegel. London, 1958.

Phil 180.70.10   Fink, Eugen. Sein. Den Haag, 1958.

Phil 6115.32   Fisher, Seymour. Body image and personality. Princeton, N.J., 1958.

Phil 8660.16   Fishler, Max. What the great philosophers thought about God. Los Angeles, 1958.

Phil 8630.14   Foerst-Crato, Ilse. Ausblicke ins Paradies. München, 1958.

Phil 7069.58.10   Ford, Arthur. Nothing so strange. 1. ed. N.Y., 1958.

Phil 8955.5   Ford, J.C. Contemporary moral theology. Westminster, Md., 1958-63. 2v.

Phil 6319.1.204   Fordham, M.S.M. The objective psyche. London, 1958.

Phil 585.20   Frank, W.D. The rediscovery of man. N.Y., 1958.

Phil 5627.134.34   Frank Buchman. London, 1958.

Phil 5850.205   Frankard, Paul. Analyse critique de la notion de validité. Louvain, 1958.

Phil 5592.75   Frederiksen, Norman Oliver. Response set as a measure of personality. Princeton, 1958.

Phil 6955.18   Freeman, Thomas. Chronic schizophrenia. London, 1958.

Phil 6315.2.62.15A   Freud, Sigmund. Dreams in folklore. N.Y., 1958.

Phil 6315.2.21   Freud, Sigmund. On creativity and the unconscious. N.Y., 1958.

Phil 5400.130.5   Frijda, N.H. Gelaat en karakter. Haarlem, 1958.

Phil 8955.7   Fuchs, Emil. Christliche und marxistische Ethik. Leipzig, 1958. 2v.

Phil 4006.9.30   Galli, Gallo. Filosofi italiani d'oggi e altri scritti. Torino, 1958.

Phil 4080.4.350   Gandolfo, Antonio. Benedetto Croce, critico dei contemporanei. Padova, 1958.

Phil 525.165   Gardet, Louis. Thèmes et textes mystiques. Paris, 1958.

Phil 5195.2   Gardner, Martin. Logic machines and diagrams. N.Y., 1958.

Phil 1540.50A   Garin, Eugenio. Studi sul platonismo medievale. Firenze, 1958.

Phil 3826.14   Garulli, Enrico. Saggi su Spinoza. Urbino, 1958.

Phil 3850.16.105   Gassen, Kurt. Zuch des Dankes an G. Simmel. Berlin, 1958.

1958 - cont.

Phil 4803.454.79.5   Gawecki, Bolesław J. Wroński i o Wrońskim; katalog. Warszawa, 1958.

Phil 1955.6.140   Geiger, George R. John Dewey in perspective. N.Y., 1958.

Phil 5590.315   Gelbmann, Frederich J. Authoritarianism and temperament. Washington, 1958.

Phil 270.85   Gennaro, Giuseppe de. Saggio sui rapporti fra ubertá e causalità. Padova, 1958.

Phil 8407.33   Ghelli, Nino. Problematica dell'arte. Roma, 1958.

Phil 8708.29   Ginger, Ray. Six days or forever? Boston, 1958.

Phil 806.17   Glockuer, H. Die europäische Philosophie. Stuttgart, 1958.

Phil 5850.221.10   Goersdorf, Kurt. Arbeitsfreude - Leistungsanstrengungen. München, 1958.

Phil 5875.115   Gondolatsch, Karl Heinz. Untersuchung der Sympathieäbhangigkeit von Aussageleiustungen bei Kindern und Jugendlichen. Köln, 1958.

Phil 8407.35   Goranov, Krusto. Sudurzhanie i forma v izkustvoto. Sofiia, 1958.

Phil 2030.7   Gotshalk, Dilman Walter. The promise of modern life. Yellow Springs, Ohio, 1958.

Phil 2520.140.8   Gouhier, Henri. Les premières pensées de Descartes. Paris, 1958.

Phil 5160.5.2   Granger, Giles. La raison. 2. éd. Paris, 1958.

Phil 3640.530   Grau, Gerd Günther. Christlicher Glaube und intellektuelle Redlichkeit. Frankfurt, 1958.

Phil 1535.18.3   Gredt, Joseph. Elementa philosophiae Aristotelico-Thomisticae. 12. ed. Barcinone, 1958.

Phil 8831.12   Grégoire, François. Leo grandes doctrines morales. Paris, 1958.

Phil 3425.430A   Grégoire, Franz. Études Hegeliennes. Louvain, 1958.

Phil 1540.55   Gregory, Tullio. Platonismo medievale. Roma, 1958.

Phil 4260.133   Grimaldi, A.A. The universal humanity of Giambattista Vico. N.Y., 1958.

Phil 91.5   Grooten, J. Filosofisch lexicon. Antwerpen, 1958.

Phil 310.50   Gropp, Rugard Otto. Der dialektische Materialismus. Leipzig, 1958.

Phil 181.118   Gruber, F.C. The emergence of the modern mind. Philadelphia, 1958.

Phil 585.85F   Grünsteidl, Edmund. Der Mensch zwischen Atom und Universum. Wien, 1958?

Phil 8586.54   Guardini, Romano. Religion und Offenbarung. Würzburg, 1958.

Phil 817.8.20   Guggiero, Guido de. Storia della filosofia. v.1 (pt. 1-2), v.2 (pt. 1-3), v.3-10. Bari, 1958. 13v.

Phil 2630.11.8   Guitton, Jean. Make your mind work for you. N.Y., 1958.

Phil 5272.8   Gulliksen, Harold. Mathematical solutions for psychological problems. n.p., 1958.

Phil 4795.2.2   Guseinov, Geidar. Iz istorii obshechestvennoi i filosofskoi mysli v Azerbaidzhane. Izd. 2. Baku, 1958.

Phil 5247.68   Hadley, John M. Clinical and counseling psychology. 1. ed. N.Y., 1958.

Phil 8408.41   Hadživasilev, Mito. Odraz, izraz. Skopje, 1958.

Phil 3450.29.10   Haecker, Theodor. Essays. Munchen, 1958.

Phil 3246.292   Hammacher, Vlans. Die ethische Teleologie in Fichtes System als Grundlage seiner Geschichtsphilosophie. Hadien, 1958.

Phil 3120.30.92   Hammerstein, Franz von. Das Messiasproblem bei Martin Buber. Stuttgart, 1958.

Phil 8697.21   Harris, Errol E. Revelation through reason. New Haven, 1958.

Phil 5047.46   Hartkopf, Werner. Die Strukturformen der Probleme. Berlin, 1958.

Phil 338.27   Hartland-Swann, John. An analysis of knowing. London, 1958.

Phil 8662.20   Heer, Freidrich. Alle Moglichkeit liegt bei uns. Nürnberg, 1958.

Phil 182.93.10.2   Heidegger, M. Einführung in die Metaphysik. Tübingen, 1958.

Phil 182.93.13   Heidegger, M. Introduction à la métaphysique. Paris, 1958.

Phil 3450.19.70.5   Heidegger, Martin. Essais et conférences. 2e éd. Paris, 1958.

Phil 3450.19.73   Heidegger, Martin. The question of being. N.Y., 1958.

Phil 3450.19.65.2   Heidegger, Martin. What is philosophy? N.Y., 1958.

Phil 5850.228.20   Heider, Fritz. The psychology of interpersonal relations. N.Y., 1958.

Phil 5627.132.7   Heiler, Friedrich. Prayer. N.Y., 1958.

Phil 1750.365.7   Heinemann, Fritz. Existentialism and the modern predicament. N.Y., 1958.

Phil 3425.442   Heintel, Erich. Hegel und die Analogia Entis. Bonn, 1958.

Phil 6317.20.8   Hendrick, Ives. Facts and theories of psychoanalysis. 3rd ed. N.Y., 1958.

Phil 8697.19   Hengstenberg, Hans E. Sein und Ursprünglichkeit. München, 1958.

Phil 3425.440   Henrici, Peter. Hegel und Blondel. Pullach, 1958.

Phil 8587.71   Herberg, Will. Four existentialist theologians. Garden City, N.Y., 1958.

Phil 3552.385   Herrmann, Karl. Das Staatsdenken bei Leibniz. Bonn, 1958.

Phil 288.1   Hickok, S.P. Rational cosmology. N.Y., 1958.

Phil 8957.14   Hoermann, Karl. Handbuch der christlichen Moral. Innsbruck, 1958.

Phil 6957.25   Hollingshead, A. de B. Social class and mental illness. N.Y., 1958.

Phil 3552.380   Holz, Hans H. Leibniz. Stuttgart, 1958.

Phil 5247.69   Holzner, Burket. Amerikanische und deutsche Psychologie. Würzburg, 1958?

Phil 3007.12   Hommes, Jakob. Krise der Freiheit. Regensburg, 1958.

Phil 70.40   Hook, Sidney. Determinism and freedom in the age of modern science. N.Y., 1958.

Phil 2835.86   Hooykaas, Reijer. Humanisme, science et réforme. Leyde, 1958.

Phil 5047.44   Horn, Heinz. Widerspiegelung und Begriff. Berlin, 1958.

Phil 3640.575   Hotter, Karl. Das Bildungsproblem in der Philosophie Nietzsches. München, 1958.

Phil 5039.2   Houde, Roland. Readings in logic. Dubuque, 1958.

Phil 8408.26   Howell, A.R. Gems of wisdom from the writings of A.R. Howell. Sussex, 1958.

Phil 6317.32.2   Hubbard, L. Ron. Dianetics. Johhannesburg, 1958.

Phil 2055.15.35   Hulme, Thomas E. Speculations. 2nd ed. London, 1958.

Phil 1807.8   Hutin, Serge. La philosophie anglaise et américaine. Paris, 1958.

Phil 6834.6   Hutton, Robert. Of those alone. London, 1958.

Phil 5590.285   Hylander, Ernst. Vom Umgang mit sich Selbst. München, 1958.

Phil 4759.1.45   Il'in, I.A. Poiushchee serdtse. Miunkhen, 1958.

Chronological Listing

Phil 165.140   Im Dienste der Wahrheit. Bern, 1958.
Phil 70.45.5   International Institute of Philosophy. Entretiens philosophiques de Varsovie. Wrocław, 1958.
Phil 5249.24   Jaeger, Marc A. Relativitätstheorie des Menschengeistes. Zürich, 1958.
Phil 7069.58   Jaffe, Aniela. Geistererscheinungen und Vorzeichen. Zürich, 1958.
Phil 3475.3.73   Jaspers, Karl. La bombe atomique et l'avenir de l'homme. Paris, 1958.
Phil 3475.3.52   Jaspers, Karl. Einführung in die Philosophie. Zürich, 1958.
Phil 8589.21.2   Jaspers, Karl. Myth and Christianity. N.Y., 1958.
Phil 3475.3.42   Jaspers, Karl. Philosophie und Welt. München, 1958.
Phil 5049.20.5   Jaspers, Karl. Philosophische Logik. München, 1958.
Phil 3475.3.74   Jaspers, Karl. Wahrheit, Freiheit und Friede. München, 1958.
Phil 270.110   Jaworski, M. Arystolelesowska i tomistyczna teoria przyczyry sprawczej na tle pojęcia bytu. Lublin, 1958.
Phil 8410.8   Jenkins, I. Art and the human enterprise. Cambridge, 1958.
Phil 5049.6.18   Jevons, W.S. The principles of science. N.Y., 1958.
Phil 165.326   Joaquim de Carvalho no Brazil. Coimbra, 1958.
Phil 9065.4   Joehr, W.A. Der Kompromiss als Problem der Gesellschaft. Tübingen, 1958.
Phil 2340.10.130.5   Johnson, A.H. Whitehead's philosophy of civilization. Boston, 1958.
Phil 8870.17   Johnson, Oliver A. Ethics. N.Y., 1958.
Phil 184.47   Jolivet, Régis. L'homme métaphysique. Paris, 1958.
Phil 340.8   Jonckheere, A. La lecture de l'expérience. Paris, 1958.
Phil 5374.190   Joussain, André. Les systèmes de la vie. Paris, 1958.
Phil 9558.25   Jullian, T. Dictionnaire du snobisme. Paris, 1958.
Phil 6319.1.5.9   Jung, C.G. Praxis der Psychotherapie. v.1,3-4,6-8,11,14-16. Zürich, 1958.
Phil 6319.1.68   Jung, C.G. Psyche and symbol. Garden City, 1958.
Phil 6319.1.62.1   Jung, C.G. The undiscovered self. N.Y., 1958.
Phil 5850.250.10   Kahn, Robert L. The dynamics of interviewing. N.Y., 1958.
Phil 3480.115   Kant, Immanuel. Die mundi sensibilis at que intelligibilis forma. Hamburg, 1958.
Phil 3480.22.5   Kant, Immanuel. Über die Form und die Prinzipien der Sinnen - und Geisteswelt. Hamburg, 1958.
Phil 3480.80.50   Kant, Immanuel. Vens la paix perpetuele. 1. éd. Paris, 1958.
Phil 3549.17   Kanthack, Katharina. Vom Sinn der Selbsterkenntnis. Berlin, 1958.
Phil 5850.250.15   Kantor, J.R. Interbehavioral psychology. Bloomington, 1958.
Phil 3492.55   Karapetian, H.A. Kriticheskii analiz filosofii Kanta. Erevan, 1958.
Phil 5592.65A   Karon, Bertram P. The Negro personality. N.Y., 1958.
Phil 185.72   Kaufmann, Walter Arnold. Critique of religion and philosophy. 1. ed. N.Y., 1958.
Phil 1135.82   Kelber, Wilhelm. Die Logoslehre von Heraklit bis Origenes. Stuttgart, 1958.
Phil 4957.45   Kempff Mercado, Manfredo. Historia de la filosofía en Latinoamérica. Santiago de Chile, 1958.
Phil 3850.27.155   Kirschner, Carol F. A selection of writings of and about Albert Schweitzer. Boston, 1958.
Phil 3778.92   Klemmt, Alfred. Karl Leonard Reinholds Elementarphilosophie. Hamburg, 1958.
Phil 1710.7   Klibasky, Raymond. La philosophie au milieu du 20e siècle. Firenze, 1958. 4v.
Phil 3492.40.2   Knox, Israel. The aesthetic theories of Kant. N.Y., 1958.
Phil 5250.15.17   Köhler, Wolfgang. Dynamische Zusammenhänge in der Psychologie. Bern, 1958.
Phil 4761.4.80   Kogan, Iu.Ia. Prosvetitel' XVIII veka Ia.P. Kozel'skii. Moskva, 1958.
Phil 3425.321.10   Kojève, Alexandre. Hegel; eine Vergegenwäitigung. Stuttgart, 1958.
Phil 3830.7   Kołakowski, L. Jednostka i mieskończoność. Warszawa, 1958.
Phil 4807.4   Konference o dějinách české filosofie, Liblice, 1958. Filosofie v dějinách českého národa. Vyd. 1. Praha, 1958.
Phil 291.8   Koren, Henry. Readings in the philosophy of nature. Westminster, Md., 1958.
Phil 5520.96.10   Korzybski, Alfred. Science and sanity. Lakeville, Conn., 1958.
Phil 310.4.3   Kovalgin, V.M. Dialekticheskii materializm o zakonakh nauki. Minsk, 1958.
Phil 6980.398.20   Kramer, Edith. Art therapy in a children's community. Springfield, 1958.
Phil 5425.47.3   Kretschmer, Ernst. Geniale Menschen. 5. Aufl. Berlin, 1958.
Phil 8635.9   Kretzenbacher, Leopold. Die Seelenwaage. Klagenfurt, 1958.
Phil 4941.9   Kriezes, T.A. To Ellinikon ethnos ke i sighxroni epoxi. Athena, 1958.
Phil 810.10   Krueger, Gerhard. Grundfragen der Philosophie. Frankfurt, 1958.
Phil 6320.17A   Kubie, L.S. Neurotic distortion of the creative process. Lawrence, 1958.
Phil 8411.23.5   Kulvanov, B.G. Gnoseologicheskaia priroda literatury i iskusstva. L'vov, 1958.
Phil 310.140   Kurella, Alfred. Der Mensch als Schöpfer seiner Selbst. Berlin, 1958.
Phil 1810.5   Kursanov, G.A. Gnoseologiia sovremennaia pragmatizma. Moskva, 1958.
Phil 3010.11   Kurucz, J. Die Opposition der Jugendbrücken. Saar, 1958.
Phil 310.55   Kutasov, D.A. V chem sostoit osnovnoi vopros filosofii. Moskva, 1958.
Phil 3010.9   Kvochow, Christian C. von. Die Entscheidung. Stuttgart, 1958.
Phil 2805.335   Lacombe, R.E. L'apologétique de Pascal. Paris, 1958.
Phil 5421.10.16   Lain Entralgo, Pedro. La espera y la esperanza. 2. ed. Madrid, 1958.
Phil 7039.12   Lancaster, Evelyn. The final face of Eve. N.Y., 1958.
Phil 8961.15   Łapicki, B. Etyczna kultura starożytnego Rzymu. Łódź, 1958.
Phil 4957.5   Larroyo, Francisco. La filosofía americana, su razón y su sinrazón de ser. Mexico, 1958.
Phil 2730.110   Lassaigne, Jean. Maine de Biran, homme politique. Paris, 1958.
Phil 3450.11.142.5A   Lauer, Quentin. The triumph of subjectivity. N.Y., 1958.
Phil 9530.54   Lebhar, G.M. The use of time. 3. ed. N.Y., 1958.
Phil 2340.10.145   Leclerc, Ivor. Whitehead's metaphysics. London, 1958.

Phil 2725.37.35A   Lefebvre, Henri. Critique de la vie quotidienne. 2e éd. Paris, 1958-68. 2v.
Phil 2520.255.10   Lefèvre, Roger. Le criticisme de Descartes. 1. éd. Paris, 1958.
Phil 1516.4   Leff, Gordon. Medieval thought. Harmondsworth, 1958.
Phil 978.86.2   Lehrs, Ernst. Man or matter. 2d ed. London, 1958.
Phil 3552.79.25   Leibniz, Gottfried Wilhelm. Metaphysische Abhandlung. Hamburg, 1958.
Phil 5592.60   Lennep, Johanna Elisabeth van. Beleving en verbeelding in het tekenen. Amsterdam, 1958.
Phil 2905.1.90   Leroy, Pierre. Pierre Teilhard de Chardin tel que je l'ai connu. Paris, 1958.
Phil 5761.22   Levitskii, S.H. Tragediia svobody. Frankfurt, 1958.
Phil 7084.34   Lewin, Bertram David. Dreams and the uses of regression. N.Y., 1958.
Phil 8636.10   Lindhardt, P.G. Helvedes strategi. n.p., 1958.
Phil 5548.50   Lindzey, Gardner. Assessment of human motives. N.Y., 1958.
Phil 3450.19.180   Llambías de Azevedo, Juan. El antiguo y el nuevo Heidegger y un dialogo con el. Montevideo, 1958.
Phil 5585.135   Logique et Perception. Logique et perception. Paris, 1958.
Phil 4011.4   Lombardi, Franco. La filosofia italiana negli ultimi cento anni. Asti, 1958?
Phil 8886.73   López Aranguren, José Luis. Etica. Madrid, 1958.
Phil 3011.6.5   Lukács, G. La destruction de la raison. Paris, 1958-59. 2v.
Phil 4780.2   Lushchytski, I.N. Narysy pa historyi hramadska-palitychnai i filosofskai dumki u Belarusi u drukoi palavine XIX veku. Minsk, 1958.
X Cg   Phil 7075.152   Luvandowski, Herbert. Ferne Lände, fremde Sitten. 1. Aufl. Stuttgart, 1958.
Phil 5414.20.2   Lynd, Helen Merrell. On shame and the search for identity. N.Y., 1958.
Phil 9240.16   Macht und Wirklichkeit des Bösen. München, 1958.
Phil 665.93   Maeztu, Ramiro de. Defensa del espíritu. Madrid, 1958.
Phil 293.30   Maier, Anneliese. Zwischen Philosophie und Mechanik. Roma, 1958.
Phil 3925.16.84   Malcolmi, Norman. Ludwig Wittgenstein. London, 1958.
Phil 2733.5.10   Malebranche, Nicolas. Oeuvres complètes. v.1-20. Paris, 1958-63. 21v.
Phil 2733.67   Malebranche, Nicolas. Traité de la nature et de la grâce. Paris, 1958. 2v.
Phil 8658.17.80   Malevez, Léopold. Transcendence de Dieu et création des valeurs. Paris, 1958.
Phil 4763.1.30   Malinovskii, V.F. Izbrannye obshchestvenno-politicheskie sochineniia. Moskva, 1958.
Phil 2128.55   Mandeville, B. Il paradosso Mandeville. Firenze, 1958.
Phil 2750.25   Marc, André. L'être et l'esprit. Paris, 1958.
Phil 1750.615   Marck, Siegfried. Die Aufhebung des Irrationalismus. Wilhelmshaven, 1958.
Phil 3494.55   Marguard, Odo. Skeptische Methode im Blick auf Kant. Freiburg, 1958.
Phil 4363.7.2   Marias Aguilera, Julián. Obras. Madrid, 1958-60. 8v.
Phil 4313.5.5   Marias Aguilera, Julian. El oficio del pensamiento. Madrid, 1958.
Phil 2750.11.80A   Maritain, Jacques. Reflections on America. N.Y., 1958.
Phil 2750.11.82   Maritain, Jacques. Reflexions sur l'Amérique. Paris, 1958.
Phil 5068.34   Martin, R.M. Truth and denotation. London, 1958.
Phil 5628.11.6   Mary Minima, Sister. Seraph among angels; the life of St. Mary Magadalene de' Pazzi. Chicago, 1958.
Phil 8592.90   Mascall, E.L. The importance of being human. N.Y., 1958.
Phil 8702.26   Masi, R. Religione. Brescia, 1958.
Phil 3494.61   Mathieu, V. La filosofia trascendentale. Torino, 1958.
Phil 5841.2   Maxey, Wallace de Ortega. Man is a sexual being. Fresno, Calif., 1958.
Phil 5594.158   Maxwell, A.E. Experimental design in psychology and the medical sciences. London, 1958.
Phil 5238.85   May, Rollo. Existence. N.Y., 1958.
Phil 535.25   Mayer, Ernst. Kritik des Nihilismus. München, 1958.
Phil 8887.100   Mayo, Bernard. Ethics and the moral life. London, 1958.
Phil 187.150   Meinertz, Josef. Philosophie. München, 1958.
Phil 6990.52   Meist, Paul. Les cinquant-quatre miracles de Lourdes au jugement du drait canon. Paris, 1958.
Phil 8887.77.5   Melden, A.I. Essays in moral philosophy. Seattle, 1958.
Phil 8887.77   Melden, A.I. Essays in moral philosophy. Seattle, 1958.
Phil 8980.566   Mende, Georg. Treiheit und Verantwortung. Berlin, 1958.
Phil 4974.24   Menezes, O. Raízes pré-socráticas do pensamento atual. Ceará, 1958.
Phil 6322.32.5   Menninger, Karl Augustus. Theory of psychoanalytic technique. N.Y., 1958.
Phil 5590.270   Metelli, Fabio. Le dottrine caratterologiche di Ernest Kretschmer e Gerarhd Pfahler. Padova, 1958.
Phil 6315.2.170.3   Mette, Alexandre. Sigmund Freud. 3. Aufl. Berlin, 1958.
Phil 3425.470   Meulen, Jan van der. Hegel. Hamburg, 1958.
Phil 7150.40   Meyuard, L. Le suicide. Paris, 1958.
Phil 2138.53   Mill, John S. Considerations on representative government. N.Y., 1958.
Phil 8430.3   Moles, Abraham A. Théorie de l'information et perception esthétique. Paris, 1958.
Phil 1117.8.5   Mondolfo, Rodolfo. La camprensione del soggeho. 1. ed. Firenze, 1958.
Phil 8702.22   Monsma, John C. The evidence of God in an expanding universe. N.Y., 1958.
Phil 4210.149.3   Morando, Dante. Antonio Rosmini. Brescia, 1958.
Phil 3640.615   Morawa, Hans. Sprache und Stil von Nietzsches Zarathustra. München, 1958.
Phil 582.4   Moreau, Joseph. La conscience et l'être. Paris, 1958.
Phil 575.170   Morley, Felix. Essays on individuality. Philadelphia, 1958.
Phil 4215.3.85   Morra, Gianfranco. Scetticismo e misticismo nel pensiero di Giuseppe Rensi. Siracuse, 1958.
Phil 1695.10   La morte della filosofia dopo Hegel e le correnti del pensiero contemporaneo. Roma, 1958.
Phil 310.12.12   Moscow. Akademiia Obshchestvennogo Nauk. Programmy po istorii filosofii. Moskva, 1958.
Phil 310.70   Moscow. Gosudarstvennaia Biblioteka SSSR imeni V.I. Lenina. Chto chitat' po filosofii. Moskva, 1958.
Phil 187.152   Moser, Simon. Metaphysik einst und jetzt. Berlin, 1958.
Phil 1750.520   Muehlethaler, Jakob. Existenz und Transzendenz in der gegenwärtegen Philosophie. Basel, 1958.
Phil 5520.340   Mueller, Heinz A. Die Psychologie des Lesens. Lörrach, 1958.

1958 - cont.

Phil 8430.37 — Mumford, L. The role of the creative arts in comtemporary society. Durham, 1958.

Phil 3494.58 — Muralt, André. La conscience transcendentale. Paris, 1958.

Phil 3450.11.195 — Muralt, André de. L'idée de la phénoménologie. Paris, 1958.

Phil 1812.10 — Mure, G.R.G. Retreat from truth. Oxford, 1958.

Phil 5590.260A — Murphy, Gardner. Human potentialities. N.Y., 1958.

Phil 5253.13 — Nahoum, Charles. L'entretien psychologique. Paris, 1958.

Phil 5465.115 — Naksianowicz-Gołaszewska, M. Twórczość a osobowość twórcy. Lublin, 1958.

Phil 5053.10 — Narbutt, Olgierd. O pierwszym polskim podręczniku logiki. Łódź, 1958.

Phil 4013.2 — Nardi, Bruno. Saggi sull'aristotelismo padovana dal secolo XIV al XVI. Firenze, 1958.

Phil 3665.1.30 — Natorp, Paul. Philosophische Systematik. Hamburg, 1958.

Phil 130.9 — Neill, T.P. Makers of the modern mind. 2nd ed. Milwaukee, 1958.

Phil 6315.2.220A — Nelson, B.N. Freud and the 20th century. N.Y., 1958.

Phil 4065.155 — Nelson, J.C. Renaissance theory of love. N.Y., 1958.

Phil 3850.46 — Neu, Theodor. Bibliographie Eduard Spranger. Tübingen, 1958.

Phil 188.22 — Nicolas, M.P. Regards sur l'humain. Paris, 1958.

Phil 3640.76.16 — Nietzsche, Friedrich. Lettres à Peter Gast. Monaco, 1958. 2v.

Phil 3640.40.10 — Nietzsche, Friedrich. Thus spake Zarathustra. London, 1958.

Phil 4225.8.80 — Nobile-Ventura, Attilio. Crisi dell'uomo e conquista. Milano, 1958.

Phil 1813.5 — Noble, D.W. The paradox of progressive thought. Minneapolis, 1958.

Phil 8668.7 — Noto, Antonio di. L'evidenza di Dio nella filosofia del secolo XIII. Padova, 1958.

Phil 6323.7.5 — Noyes, Arthur P. Modern clinical psychiatry. 5th ed. Philadelphia, 1958.

Phil 6964.6 — O'Brien, Barbara (pseud.). Operators and things: the inner life of a schizophrenic. Cambridge, Mass., 1958.

Phil 310.95 — Ogiermann, H.A. Materialistische Dialektik. München, 1958.

Phil 2835.84 — Ong, Walter J. Ramus, method and the decay of dialogue. Cambridge, 1958. 2v.

Phil 2835.84.5 — Ong, Walter J. Ramus and Talon inventory. Cambridge, 1958.

Htn — Phil 2835.84.5*A — Ong, Walter J. Ramus and Talon inventory. Cambridge, 1958.

Phil 8080.2 — Oribe, Emilia. Tres ideales esteticos. Montevideo, 1958.

VPhil 310.5.10 — Oshakov, Zhivko. Istoricheskiiat materializum. Sofiia, 1958.

Phil 4752.2.120 — Osipov, N. Kleveta druzei. Miunkhen, 1958.

Phil 5548.55 — Ossowska, M. Motywy postępowania. Warszawa, 1958.

Phil 8415.2 — Ossowski, S. U podstaw estetyki. Wyd. 3. Warszawa, 1958.

Phil 8965.17 — Palazzini, Pietro. Casus conscientiae. Torino, 1958. 2v.

Phil 5592.95 — Palmés, F.M. Como informar sobre la personalidad propria. Barcelona, 1958.

Phil 5401.34 — Palou, Jean. La peur dans l'histoire. Paris, 1958.

Phil 8595.50 — Panese, Roberto. Necessità e sufficienza del principio cristiano. Padova, 1958.

Phil 310.75 — Pantskhava, I.D. Dialekticheskii materializm. Moskva, 1958.

Phil 346.19.5 — Pap, Athur. Semantics and necessary truth. New Haven, 1958.

Phil 4845.227.36 — Papanoutsos, Euangelos. Philosophia kai paideia. Athena, 1958.

Phil 2805.42.40 — Pascal, Blaise. Pensées. Paris, 1958. 2v.

Phil 346.22 — Pasck, Alan. Experience and the analytic. Chicago, 1958.

Phil 3475.3.155 — Paumen, Jean. Raison et existence chez Karl Jaspers. Bruxelles, 1958.

Phil 8170.6 — Pavlov, T.D. Osnovni vuprosi na marksistko-leninskata estetika. 3. izd. Sofiia, 1958.

Phil 9400.25 — Pax, Schweyerische Lebensmensecherungsgesellschaft, Basel. Der Weg, ins Altern. Basel, 1958.

Phil 5878.10 — Pearson, Gerald Hamilton Jeffrey. Adolescence and the conflict of generations. N.Y., 1958.

Phil 3450.11.101.50 — Pedroli, Guido. La fenomenologia di Husserl. Torino, 1958.

Phil 2225.5.40 — Peirce, C.S. Values in a universe of chance. Stanford, 1958.

Phil 5055.30 — Penev, Mikho. Kritika na logicheskite vuzgledi na burzhoaznite filosofi v Bulgariia. Sofiia, 1958.

Phil 530.11.20 — Pepler, Conrad. The English religious heritage. Saint Louis, 1958.

Phil 735.180 — Pepper, Stephen C. The sources of value. Berkeley, 1958.

Phil 8705.17 — Perego, Angelo S.J. La creazione. Brescia, 1958.

Phil 5055.29 — Perelman, Chaim. Traité de l'argumentation. v.1-2. Paris, 1958.

Phil 1815.3.5 — Persons, S. American minds. N.Y., 1958.

Phil 5548.30 — Peters, R.S. The concept of motivation. London, 1958.

Phil 8620.49 — Petit, François. Le problème du mal. Paris, 1958.

Phil 310.190 — Pfoh, Werner. Philosophie und Gesellschaft. Berlin, 1958.

Phil 6319.1.202 — Philip, Howard Littleton. Jung and the problem of evil. London, 1958.

Phil 3850.27.160 — Phillips, Herbert M. Safari of discovery. N.Y., 1958.

Phil 5825.9 — Piéron, Henri. De l'actinie à l'homme. Paris, 1958. 2v.

Phil 3475.3.150 — Piper, R.C. Karl Jaspers. München, 1958.

Phil 1200.58 — Pire, Georges. Stoïcisme et pedagogie. Liege, 1958.

Phil 9550.16.5 — Plamenatz, J.P. The English utilitarians. 2. ed. Oxford, 1958.

Phil 8416.11.5 — Plekhanov, Georgii Valentinovich. Literatura i estetika. Moskva, 1958.

Phil 346.20 — Polanyi, Michael. Personal knowledge. London, 1958.

Phil 3925.16.86 — Pole, David. The later philosophy of Wittgenstein. London, 1958.

Phil 5627.258.5 — Potempa, Rudolf. Persönlichkeit und Religiosität. Göttingen, 1958.

Phil 960.215 — Prasad, Jwala. History of Indian epistemology. 2d ed. Delhi, 1958.

Phil 5255.44.2 — Prinzhorn, H. Persönlichkeits-Psychologie. 2. Aufl. Heidelberg, 1958.

Phil 310.35 — Probleme des historische Materialismus und der marxistische Sozialismus. Berlin, 1958.

Phil 5826.5 — Quarelli, Elena. Socrate e le bestie. Cuneo, 1958.

Phil 5766.5 — Qu'est-ce que vouloir? Paris, 1958.

Phil 5520.230 — Raevskii, A.N. Psikhologiia rechi v sovetskoi psikhologicheskoi nauke za 40 let. Kiev, 1958.

Phil 192.85.10 — Raeymaeker, Louis de. Riflessioni su temi filosofici fondamentali. Milano, 1958.

Phil 8967.15 — Rahner, Karl. Das Dynamische in der Kirche. Freiburg, 1958.

Phil 8612.54.5 — Rahnez, Karl. Zur Theologie des Todes. 5. Aufl. Freiburg, 1958.

Phil 6990.55 — Rairer, A. Essai sur la spiritualité de Bernadette. Nevers, 1958.

Phil 5421.5.5 — Ramming-Thoen, Fortunata. Das Heimweh. Thesis. Zürich, 1958.

Phil 8707.24 — Randall, John Herman. The role of knowledge in western religion. Boston, 1958.

Phil 5645.70 — Rattleff, Anker. Form, farve og emotioner. København, 1958.

Phil 3837.30 — Rava, Adolfo. Studi su Spinoza e Fichte. Milano, 1958.

Phil 8080.13 — Redeker, Horst. Die Klassische Kulturkritik und das Dilemma der Dekadenz. Berlin, 1958.

Phil 6327.26 — Reed, C.F. Psychopathology. Cambridge, Mass., 1958.

Phil 5227.8 — Reeves, Joan Wynn. Body and mind in Western thought. Harmondsworth, 1958.

Phil 672.144.3 — Reichenbach, H. The philosophy of space and time. N.Y., 1958.

Phil 6327.12.7 — Reik, Theodor. Ritual, psycho-analytical studies. N.Y., 1958.

Phil 298.10 — Reinl, Kurt. Grundriss des Seins. München, 1958.

Phil 1750.166.120 — Renaudet, Augustin. Humanisme et Renaissance. Genève, 1958.

Phil 5592.80 — Rey, André. L'examen clinique en psychologie. Paris, 1958.

Phil 5520.285 — Reznikov, Lazar' O. Poniatie i slovo. Leningrad, 1958.

Phil 1618.5 — Rice, Eugene Franklin. The Renaissance idea of wisdom. Cambridge, 1958.

Phil 2477.6.122 — Ritz, Maria. Le problème de l'être dans l'ontologie de Maurice Blondel. Fribourg, 1958.

Phil 4210.166 — Riva, Clemente. Antonio Rosmini nel primo centenario della morte. Firenze, 1958.

Phil 2255.1.120 — Riverro, Emmanuele. Il pensiero di Bertrand Russell. Napoli, 1958.

Phil 8430.28 — Riverso, M. L'esperienza estetica e la vita del fanciullo. Napoli, 1958.

Phil 348.19 — Rizzi, Erminio. L'esperienza e la sua possibilita. Padova, 1958.

Phil 5238.90 — Roe, Anne. Behavior and evolution. New Haven, 1958.

Phil 3640.570 — Roeschl, Herbert. Nietzsche et la solitude. Manosque, 1958.

Phil 5257.58.6 — Rohracher, Hubert. Einführung in die Psychologie. 6. Aufl. Wien, 1958.

Phil 1817.12 — Romanell, Patrick. Toward a critical naturalism. N.Y., 1958.

Phil 4368.2.40 — Romero, Francisco. Ideas y figuras. 2. ed. Buenos Aires, 1958.

Phil 4368.2.55 — Romero, Francisco. Relaciones de la filosofía: la filosofía y el filósofo. Buenos Aires, 1958.

Phil 1817.15 — Rossi Landi, Ferruccio. Il pensiero americano contemporaneo. Milano, 1958. 2v.

Phil 5850.328.10 — Rotter, Julian. Social learning and clinical psychology. Englewood Cliffs, N.J., 1958.

Phil 310.3.12 — Rozhin, V.P. Predmet i struktura marksistsko-leninskoi filosofii. Leningrad, 1958.

Phil 5257.68 — Rubinshtein, Sergei L. Grundlagen der allgemeinen Psychologie. Berlin, 1958.

Phil 4768.2.7 — Rubinshtein, Sergei L. O myshlenii i putiakh ego issledovania. Moskva, 1958.

Phil 2255.7.20 — Runes, Dagobert D. Letters to my God. N.Y., 1958.

Phil 2255.1.72 — Russell, Bertrand Russell. The will to doubt. N.Y., 1958.

Phil 2520.290 — Russier, Jeanne. Sagesse cartésienne et religion. Paris, 1958.

Phil 5257.70 — Ryle, Gilbert. A puzzling element in the notion of thinking. London, 1958.

Phil 193.258 — Salazar Bondy, Augusto. Irrealidad e idealidad. 1. ed. Lima, 1958.

Phil 4065.02 — Salvestrini, V. Bibliografia di Giordano Bruno. 2. ed. Firenze, 1958.

Phil 3500.80 — Salvucci, Pasquale. Grandi interpreti di Kant. Urbino, 1958.

Phil 4372.1.110 — Sancipriano, M. Il pensiero ssicologico e morale di G.L. Vives. Firenze, 1958.

Phil 165.110 — Satin, J.H. Ideas in context. Boston, 1958.

Phil 665.82 — Sausgruber, Kurt. Atom und Seele. Freiburg, 1958.

Phil 1123.13.10 — Schaerer, René. L'homme antique et la structure du monde interieur d'Homère à Socrate. Paris, 1958.

Phil 8980.792 — Schaff, Adam. Spór o zagadnienie moralności. Warszawa, 1958.

Phil 3850.18.40 — Scheler, Max. Philosophical perspectives. Boston, 1958.

Phil 3160.12.7 — Schilpp, Paul. The philosophy of Ernst Cassirer. N.Y., 1958.

Phil 3640.409 — Schlechta, Karl. Der Fall Nietzsche. München, 1958.

Phil 3805.31.5 — Schleiermacher, Friedrich. On religion. N.Y., 1958.

Phil 3805.30.12 — Schleiermacher, Friedrich. Über die Religion. Hamburg, 1958.

Phil 525.155 — Schloetermann, Heinz. Mystik in den Religionen der Völker. München, 1958.

Phil 5585.105 — Schmeidler, G. ESP and personality patterns. New Haven, 1958.

Phil 730.15 — Schobinger, J.P. Vom Sein der Universalien. Winterthur, 1958.

Phil 3500.77 — Schoeler, Wilhelm. Die transzendentale Einheit der Apperzeption von Immanuel Kant. Bern, 1958.

Phil 8612.42 — Schoepf, Bernhard. Das Tötungsrecht bei den frühchristlichen Schriftstellern. Regensburg, 1958.

Phil 2805.355 — Scholtens, M. Études médico-psychologiques sur Pascal. Haarlem, 1958.

Phil 3808.36.10.10 — Schopenhauer, Arthur. The world as will and representation. Indian Hills, Colo., 1958. 2v.

Phil 6128.59 — Schroedinger, Erwin. Mind and matter. Cambridge, Eng., 1958.

Phil 3425.480 — Schulin, Ernst. Die weltgeschichtliche Erfassung des Orients bei Hegel und Ranke. Göttingen, 1958.

Phil 8598.120 — Schulz-Angern, Karl Friedrich. Ewiges-Vergängliches. Berlin, 1958.

Phil 4210.190 — Sciacca, M.F. La filosofia morale di Antonio Rosmini. 3a ed. Milano, 1958.

Phil 4210.190.5 — Sciacca, M.F. Interpretarioni rosminiane. Milano, 1958.

Chronological Listing

1958 - cont.

Phil 4225.8.36   Sciacca, Michele Federico. Atto ed essere. 2. ed. Milano, 1958.

Phil 4225.8.32   Sciacca, Michele Federico. La filosofia oggi. 3. ed. Milano, 1958. 2v.

Phil 1718.29.5   Sciacca, Michele Federico. Les grands courants de la pensée mondiale contemporaine. v.1-3. Milan, 1958- 6v.

Phil 4225.8.30   Sciacca, Michele Federico. L'interiorità oggettiva. Milano, 1958.

Phil 4225.8.40   Sciacca, Michele Federico. L'uomo. 2. ed. Milano, 1958.

Phil 5421.20   Scott, John Paul. Aggression. Chicago, 1958.

Phil 3850.47   Seifert, Hans. Heinrich Scholz. Münster, 1958.

Phil 3801.781   Semerari, Giuseppe. Interpretazione di Schelling. Napoli, 1958.

Phil 5520.441   Sendel, Bess Selher. The humanity of words. Cleveland, 1958.

Phil 4462.3   Serrão, Joel. Sampaio Bruno. Lisboa, 1958.

Phil 310.3.15   Shakhparonov, M.I. Dialekticheskii materializm i nekotorye problemy fiziki i khimii. Moskva, 1958.

Phil 299.27   Shapley, Harlow. Of stars and men. Boston, 1958.

Phil 8980.787.5   Shishkin, Aleksandr F. Die Grundlagen der kommunistischen Moral. Berlin, 1958.

Phil 5592.45   Shuey, Audrey Mary. The testing of Negro intelligence. Lynchburg, 1958.

Phil 193.220   Siewerth, Gustav. Ontologie du langage. Bruges, 1958.

Phil 6128.62   Simonian, G.A. Soderzhanie i sushchnost' antagonizma mezhdu fizicheskim i umstvennym trudom. Baku, 1958.

Phil 8708.30   Simonsson, Tord. Face to face with Darwinism. Lund, 1958.

Phil 5228.6.5   Sinha, Jadunath. Indian psychology. Calcutta, 1958.

Phil 310.125   Siusiukalov, B.I. Osnovnye zotkony materialisticheskoi dialektiki. Moskva, 1958.

Phil 5258.160   Sjöbring, Henrik. Struktur och utveckling. Lund, 1958.

Phil 5258.120.12   Skinner, Burrhus F. Science and human behavior. N.Y., 1958.

Phil 8893.14.8.25   Şmiles, Samuel. Self-help. London, 1958.

Phil 4803.799.23   Śniadecki, Jan. Pisma filozoficzne. Warszawa, 1958. 2v.

Phil 1830.45   Societá Filosofica Romana. La filosofia contemporanea in U.S.A. Roma, 1958.

Phil 5374.195   Sodan, Guenter. Über den Gebrauch des Ausdrücke "Intention". Berlin, 1958.

Phil 5592.125   Sormani, Jacques. Contribution à l'étude pratique. Marseille, 1958.

Phil 8843.15   Sparshott, F.E. An enquiry into goodness. Chicago, 1958.

Phil 2270.45.30   Spencer, Herbert. First principles. N.Y., 1958.

Phil 5548.45   Spiegel, Berut. Werbepsychologische Untersuchungsmethoden. Berlin, 1958.

Phil 3819.39.7   Spinoza, Benedictus de. On the improvement of the understanding. N.Y., 1958.

Phil 3819.57.15A   Spinoza, Benedictus de. The political works. Oxford, 1958.

Phil 3819.59.5   Spinoza, Benedictus de. Trattato politico. Torino, 1958.

Phil 5520.250   Spirkin, A.G. Myshlenie i iazyk. Moskva, 1958.

Phil 5590.255   Spreither, Franz. Verwirklichen. Konstanz, 1958.

Phil 5548.40   Stacey, Chalmers L. Understanding human motivation. Cleveland, 1958.

Phil 3850.52.40   Stallaert, L. Onze nonger naar oprechtheid. Brugge, 1958.

Phil 3850.52.30   Stallaert, L. Voor alleenstaanden. Rotterdam, 1958.

Phil 8430.49   Stardelov, Georgi. Esci. Skopje, 1958.

Phil 349.41.2   Stark, Werner. The sociology of knowledge. Glencoe, 1958.

Phil 349.41   Stark, Werner. The sociology of knowledge. London, 1958.

Phil 6128.60   Steenberghen, F. van. Psychology, morality and education. London, 1958.

Phil 3808.198   Stefano Escher di, Anna. La filosofia di Arturo Schopenhauer. Padova, 1958.

Phil 978.49.285   Steiner, R. Die Erneuerung der pödagogisch-didaktischen Kunst. Dornach, 1958.

Phil 978.49.270   Steiner, R. Rudolf Steiner in der Waldorfschule. 1. Aufl. Stuttgart, 1958.

Phil 6060.88   Stern, Martin. Entwicklungshemmungen und Graphologie. Thesis. Zürich, 1958.

Phil 6980.710   Strauss, E.B. Psychiatry in the modern world. London, 1958.

Phil 103.6.2   Sury, Ku t F. von. Wörterbuch der Psychologie und ihrer Grenzgebiete. 2. Aufl. Basel, 1958.

Phil 6328.44   Sutherland, John D. Psycho-analysis and contemporary thought. London, 1958.

Phil 6118.8   Symposium on Interdisciplinary Research, University of Wisconsin. Biological and biochemical basis of behavior. Madison, Wis., 1958.

Phil 8610.958   Szczesny, Gerhard. Die Zukunft des Unglaubens. München, 1958.

Phil 5585.125   Tagiuri, Renato. Person perception and interpersonal behavior. Stanford, 1958.

Phil 5425.96   Talent and society. Princeton, 1958.

Phil 4370.15   Tallet, Jorge. The absolute being. N.Y., 1958.

Phil 9035.100   Taulemonde, Jean. Les extériorises. Lyon, 1958[1959]

Phil 3425.425   Teyssèdre, Bernard. L'asthétique de Hegel. Paris, 1958.

Phil 2905.1.145   Thérines, Jacques de. Quodlibets. Paris, 1958.

Phil 8969.10   Thielicke, Helmut. Die Atomwaffe als Frage an die christliche Ethik. Tübingen, 1958.

Phil 5590.240   Thorpe, Louis Peter. Personality. Princeton, 1958.

Phil 5259.40.5   Tolman, Edward C. Behavior and psychological man. Berkeley, 1958.

Phil 4210.93.15   Tommaseo, N. Antonio Rosmini. Domodossola, 1958.

Phil 194.48   Topitsch, Ernst. Vom Ursprung und Ende der Metaphysik. Wien, 1958.

Phil 5850.356   Torgerson, Warren S. Theory and methods of scaling. N.Y., 1958.

Phil 5190.30   Toulmin, S.E. The uses of argument. Cambridge, Eng., 1958.

Phil 3085.6.80   Traaf, B. Alardus Amstelredamus. Amsterdam, 1958.

Phil 3640.585   Troenle, Ludwig. Elitebildung durch agonale Auslese. Wien, 1958.

Phil 6990.3.80   Trois écrivains devant Lourdes. Paris, 1958.

Phil 310.85   Tugarinov, V.P. Sootnoshenie kategorii istoricheskögo materializma. Leningrad, 1958.

Phil 5780.15.10   United States. Congress. House. Communist psychological warfare. Washington, 1958.

Phil 5520.215   Ushenko, A.P. The field theory of meaning. Ann Arbor, 1958.

Phil 2421.7   Valentini, Francesco. La filosofia francese contemporanea. 1a ed. Milano, 1958.

Phil 2920.2.35   Vallin, Georges. La perspective métaphysique. Paris, 1958.

Phil 1721.6   Verneaux, Roger. Histoire de la philosophie moderne. Paris, 1958.

1958 - cont.

Phil 4260.30   Vico, G.B. La difesa dell'umanesimo. Firenze, 1958.

Phil 1526.4.5   Vignaux, Paul. Philosophie au moyen-âge. Paris, 1958.

Phil 3503.13   Vitier, M. Kant. La Habana, 1958.

Phil 2421.5   Volgin, V.P. Razvitie obshchestvennoi mysli vo Frantsii v XVIII veke. Moskva, 1958.

Phil 8400.6   Voprosy estetiki. Moscow, 1958- 8v.

Phil 310.5.3   Vorob'ev, M.F. Zakon otritsaniia otritsaniia. Moskva, 1958.

Phil 5231.5   Voutsinas, Dimitri. Documentation sur la psychologie française. v.1-6. Paris, 1958- 5v.

Phil 310.160   Vranicki, Predrag. Dijalektički i historijski materijalizam i odabrani tekstovi. Zagred, 1958.

Phil 310.80   Vries, Joseph de. Die Erkenntnistheorie des dialektischen Materialismus. München, 1958.

Phil 2421.2   Vyverberg, H.S. Historical pessimism in the French enlightenment. Cambridge, 1958.

Phil 8423.9   Waelhem, M. de. Quelques réflexions sur la conception du beau. Paris, 1958.

Phil 1722.12   Waelkens, Alphonse de. Existence et signification. Louvain, 1958.

Phil 3450.11.200   Wahle, Jean A. Husserl. v.1-2. Paris, 1958.

Phil 1822.7   Warnock, G.J. English philosophy since 1900. London, 1958.

Phil 4800.18   Wasik, Wiktor. Historia filozofii polskiej. Warszawa, 1958-66. 2v.

Phil 5500.18   Wasserman, Paul. Decision-making. Ithaca, 1958.

Phil 9362.19   Watts, Alan W. Nature, man and woman. N.Y., 1958.

Phil 8602.53   Watts, Alan W. The wisdom of insecurity. N.Y., 1958.

Phil 197.85   Wedberg, Anders. Filosofins historia. Stockholm, 1958. 3v.

Phil 6132.38   Wedge, Bryant M. Psychosocial problems of college men. New Haven, 1958.

Phil 3504.44.5   Weldon, Thomas D. Critique of pure reason. 2nd ed. Oxford, 1958.

Phil 3640.560   Welke, Bernhard. Nietzsches Atheismus und das Christentum. Darmstadt, 1958.

Phil 3475.3.165   Welte, Bernard. La foi philosophique chez Jaspers et Saint Thomas d'Aquin. Bruges, 1958.

Phil 5520.345   Weyers, Gertrud. Das Sichbeswien auf Wörber. Köln, 1958.

Phil 9035.94   Wheelis, Allen. The quest for identity. 1st ed. N.Y., 1958.

Phil 187.59.85   White, Alan R. G.E. Moore. Oxford, 1958.

Phil 8088.4   Will, F. Intelligible beauty in aesthetic thought. Tübingen, 1958.

Phil 6060.52   Wintermantel, F. Bibliographia graphologica. Stuttgart, 1958.

Phil 8602.55   Witcutt, W.P. The rise and fall of the individual. N.Y., 1958.

Phil 3925.16.10   Wittgenstein, Ludwig. Preliminary studies for the "Philosophical investigations" generally known as the Blue and Brown books. Oxford, 1958.

Phil 197.72.10   Wohl, J.A. Essence et phénomènes. Paris, 1958.

Phil 3842.14   Wolff, Hans M. Spinozas Ethik. München, 1958.

Phil 6332.16   Wolff, Konrad. Psychologie und Sittlichkeit. Stuttgart, 1958.

Phil 3842.13.2   Wolfson, H.A. The philosophy of Spinoza. v.1-2. N.Y., 1958.

Phil 6980.780   Wolpe, Joseph. Psychotherapy by reciprocal inhibition. Stanford, 1958.

Phil 8602.75   Woods, George. Theological explanation. Welwyn, 1958.

Phil 5401.36   Woodworth, H.M. Sanity. 1st ed. Victoria, B.C., 1958.

Phil 2340.18.30   Wright, Chauncey. Philosophical writings. N.Y., 1958.

Phil 3925.11.28   Wust, Peter. Brief und Aufsätze. Münster, 1958.

Phil 200.17   Zafiropulo, Jean. Vox Zenanias. Paris, 1958.

Phil 200.19   Zaragüela Bengoechea, J. Los veinte lemas que el cultivado en los cincuenta. Madrid, 1958.

Phil 5265.5   Zippert, Erwin. Vom Gleichgewicht der Seele. Ulm, 1958.

Phil 8605.7   Zuurdeeg, Willem. An analytical philosophy of religion. N.Y., 1958.

1959

Phil 5190.85   Abelson, Herbert Irving. Persuasion; how opinions and attitudes are changed. N.Y., 1959.

Phil 5520.305   Achkov, P.A. Myshlenie i iazyk. Moskva, 1959.

Phil 6980.14.102   Ackerknecht, E.H. A short history of psychiatry. N.Y., 1959.

Phil 8520.39   Adam, Antoine. Sur le problème religieux dans la première moitié du XVIIe siècle. Oxford, 1959.

Phil 6310.16   Adler, Kurt. Essays in individual psychology. N.Y., 1959.

Phil 8580.32   Aggebo, Anker. Jeg er nemlig ikke religiös. København, 1959.

Phil 4754.1.30   Ahlberg, René. A.M. Deborin. Berlin, 1959.

Phil 310.120   Ai, Ssu-ch'i. Lektsii po dialekticheskom materializme. Moskva, 1959.

Phil 800.10.10   Akademiia Nauk SSSR. Geschichte der Philosophie. Berlin, 1959- 6v.

Phil 8050.15   Akademiia Nauk SSSR. Institut Filosofii. Iz istorii esteticheskoi mysli novogo vremeni. Moskva, 1959.

Phil 5066.135   Akademiia Nauk SSSR. Institut Filosofii. Logicheskie issledovaniia. Moskva, 1959.

Phil 5210.8   Akademiia Pedagogicheskikh Nauk RSFSR, Moscow. Institut Psikhologii. Psikhologicheskaia nauk a v SSSR. Moskva, 1959.

Phil 6980.32   Albee, George. Mental health manpower trends. N.Y., 1959.

Phil 3850.27.185   Albert Schweitzer, Mensch und Werk. Bern, 1959.

Phil 331.25   Albrecht, E. Beiträge zur Erkenntnistheorie und das Verhältnis von Sprache und Denken. Halle, 1959.

Phil 5040.24   Alekseev, M.N. Dialektika farm myshlemiia. Moskva, 1959.

Phil 2805.375   Alfieri, Vittorio Enzo. Il problema Pascal. Milano, 1959.

Phil 4357.6.80   Alonso, Manuel. Temas filosoficos medievales. Comillas, 1959.

Phil 4962.10   Alvarez, González. Introducción a una metafisica de la contingencia. Cuenca, 1959.

Phil 8725.8   Alvarez, Lili. El seglarismo y su integridad. Madrid, 1959.

Phil 5465.4.10   Ambrosi, L. La psicologia dell'immaginazione nella storia della filosofia. Padova, 1959.

Phil 8110.9   Anceschi, L. L'estetica dell'empirismo inglese. Bologna, 1959.

Phil 8401.30   Anceschi, Luciano. Autonomia ed eteronomia dell'arte. 2. ed. Firenze, 1959.

Phil 3085.5.40   Andre, G.H. Natur und Mysterium. Einsiedeln, 1959.

Phil 310.180   Andreev, I.D. Osnovnye zakony i kategorii materialisticheskoi dialektiki. Moskva, 1959.

Phil 331.20   Andreev, Ivan D. Osnovy teorii poznaniia. Moskva, 1959.

Phil 3925.16.265   Anscombe, Gertrude Elizabeth Margaret. An introduction to Wittgenstein's Tractatus. London, 1959.

Phil 4225.8.85   Antonelli, M.T. Studi in onore di M.F. Sciacca. Milano, 1959.

Phil 6315.2.260   Anzieu, Didier. L'auto-analyse. Paris, 1959.

Phil 331.15   Apostel, Léo. Logique apprentissage et probabilité. Paris, 1959.

Phil 165.66   Archivio di Filosofia. La diaristica filosofica. Padova, 1959.

Phil 672.198   Archivio di Filosofia. Tempo e eternità. Padova, 1959.

Phil 6980.58   Arieti, Silvano. American handbook of psychiatry. N.Y., 1959. 3v.

Phil 850.21.11   Armstrong, A.H. An introduction to ancient philosophy. 3d ed. Westminster, Md., 1959.

Phil 4967.15   Asociación de Egresados de la Facultad de Derecho y Ciencias Sociales de la Universidad de Buenos Aires. La acusación de plagio contra el rector Frondizi. Buenos Aires? 1959.

Phil 1505.4   Aspelin, Gunnar. Ur medeltidens tankevärld. Stockholm, 1959.

Phil 5548.65   Association de Psychologie Scientifique de Langue Française. La motivation. 1. éd. Paris, 1959.

Phil 8401.29   Assunto, Rosario. L'integrazione estetica, studi e ricerche. Milano, 1959.

Phil 4352.1.130   Auhofer, H.J. La sociologia de Jaime Balmes. Madrid, 1959.

Phil 3160.15.5   Avé-Lallemant, E. Der kategoriale Ort des Seelischen in der Naturwirklichkeit. München, 1959.

Phil 6311.40   Balint, Michael. Thrills and regressions. London, 1959.

Phil 8080.7   Ballo, Guido. I miti delle Poetiche. Milano, 1959.

Phil 4070.7.30   Banfi, Antonio. La ricerca della realta. Firenze, 1959. 2v.

Phil 5241.126   Banterwek, Heinrich. Charakter als Naturgesetz. Ulm, 1959.

Phil 2750.11.145   Bars, Henry. Maritain en notre temps. Paris, 1959.

Phil 9070.62   Bartek, Edward. A treasury of parables. N.Y., 1959.

Phil 1106.17   Bartolone, Félippi. L'origine dell'intellettualismo. Palermo, 1959.

Phil 4352.1.112   Batelari, Miguel. Balmes i Casanovas. Barcelona, 1959.

Phil 8402.33   Baudauin, Paul. La beauté et la vie. Paris, 1959.

Phil 8610.959   Bayet, Albert. Histoire de la libre-pensée. Paris, 1959.

Phil 5850.128   Beck, Samuel. Reflexes to intelligence. Glencoe, 1959.

Phil 3805.215   Beckmann, Klaus. Der Begriff der Häresie bei Schleiermacher. München, 1959.

Phil 3425.495   Beerling, R.F. De list de rede in de geschiedenisfilosofie van Hegel. Arnhem, 1959.

Phil 5590.360   Beiträge zur Psychologie der Persönlichkeit. Berlin, 1959.

Phil 8876.91.12A   Berdiaev, N.A. The destiny of man. London, 1959.

Phil 9513.19   Berg, Ludwig. Sozialethik. München, 1959.

Phil 2475.1.5   Bergson, Henri. Oeuvres. 1e éd. Paris, 1959.

Phil 2475.1.42   Bergson, Henri. Time and free will; an essay on the immediate data of consciousness. London, 1959.

Phil 1905.30.30   Berlin, Isaiah. Two concepts of liberty. Oxford, 1959.

Phil 1701.30   Berlinger, Rudolph. Das Werk der Freiheit. Frankfurt, 1959.

Phil 7112.5   Bernstien, Abraham Emmanuel. Explorations of a hypnotist. London, 1959.

Phil 3640.555   Bianquis, Genevieve. Nietzsche devant ses contemporains. Monaco, 1959.

Phil 2475.1.365   Bibliothèque Nationale, Paris. Henri Bergson; exposition. Paris, 1959.

Phil 3120.15.97.10   Bickel, Lothar. Das Leben - eine Aufgabe. Zürich, 1959.

Phil 5592.115   Biedma, Carlos. Die Sprache der Zeichnung. Bern, 1959.

Phil 5548.60   Bindra, Dalbir. Motivation. N.Y., 1959.

Phil 6980.114   Bitter, Wilhelm. Magie und Wunder in der Heilkunde. Stuttgart, 1959.

Phil 9400.30   Blanton, S. Now or never. Englewood Cliffs, N.J., 1959.

Phil 8876.130   Blegvad, Mogeus. Den naturalistiske sejlslutning. København, 1959.

Phil 3450.29.80   Blessing, Eugen. Theodor Haecker. Nürnberg, 1959.

Phil 5011.6.5   Bochénski, I.M. Logisch-philosophische Studien. Freiburg, 1959.

Phil 5066.10.7   Bochénski, I.M. A precis of mathematical logic. Dordrecht, 1959.

Phil 5041.87   Bochenski, Innocentius M. Die zeitgenossischen Denkmethoden. 2. Aufl. Bern, 1959.

Phil 8599.19.115   Bodenstein, Walter. Neige des Historismus. Gütersloh, 1959.

Phil 310.6.10   Bodrenski, J.M. Die dogmatischen Grundlagen der sowjetischen Philosophie. Dordrecht, Holland, 1959.

Phil 5241.130   Boehme, Edwin. Das Gedankenleben und seine Beherrschung. Cöln, 1959.

Phil 1506.13   Bogliolo, Luigi. Il problema della filosofia cristiana. Brescia, 1959.

Phil 1870.150   Bogomolov, A.S. Kritika subektivno-idealisticheskoi filosofii D. Berkli. Moskva, 1959.

Phil 525.170   Bordet, Louis. Religion et mysticisme. Paris, 1959.

Phil 8656.37   Borne, Étienne. Dieu n'est pas mort. Paris, 1959.

Phil 5412.15   Borra, Edoardo. Quando gli uomini perdono le staffe. Roma, 1959.

Phil 8951.27   Bourke, V.J. Ethics. N.Y., 1959.

Phil 6834.5   Bovet, Théodore. Sinnerfülltes Anders-sein. Tübingen, 1959.

Phil 8876.121   Bowes, Pratima. The concept of morality. London, 1959.

Phil 1870.136   Bracken, Harry M. The early reception of Berkeley's immaterialism. The Hague, 1959.

Phil 850.32   Brady, Ignatius. A history of ancient philosophy. Milwaukee, 1959.

Phil 332.30   Brain, W.R. The nature of experience. London, 1959.

Phil 8876.125   Brandt, Richard. Ethical theory. Englewood Cliffs, N.J., 1959.

Phil 3120.8.50   Brentano, Franz. Grundzüge der Ästhetik. Bern, 1959.

Phil 3120.8.60F   Brentano, Franz. Index. Highland Park, Illinois, 1959.

Phil 1750.99   Breton, Stanislas. Approches phénoménologiques de l'idée d'être. Paris, 1959.

Phil 5241.117.5   Brill, Albert. Ascendant psychology. Guilford, Conn., 1959.

Phil 1190.6.5   Brochard, Victor. Les sceptiques grecs. Paris, 1959.

Phil 6311.39   Brown, Norman Oliver. Life against death. 1st ed. Middletown, Conn., 1959.

Phil 1158.37   Brun, Jean. L'épicurisme. Paris, 1959.

Phil 2805.370   Brunet, Georges. Un prétendu traité de Pascal. Paris, 1959.

Phil 3120.15.35   Brunner, Constantin. Materialismus und Idealismus. Köln, 1959.

Phil 5520.315   Brutian, G.A. Teoriia poznaniia obshchei semantiki. Erevan, 1959.

Phil 3120.60.30   Buchheim, Karl. Logik der Tatsachen. München, 1959.

Phil 5241.88.5   Bühler, Charlotte M. Der menschliche Lebenslauf als psychologisches Problem. 2. Aufl. Göttingen, 1959.

Phil 176.225   Bueno, Miguel. Conferencias. 1. ed. México, 1959.

Phil 270.90   Bunge, Mario. Causality. Cambridge, 1959.

Phil 3552.440   Burgelin, Pierre. Commentaire du Discourse de métaphysique de Leibniz. Paris, 1959.

Phil 6311.45   Burton, Arthur. Case studies in counseling and psychotherapy. Englewood Cliffs, N.J., 1959.

Phil 6750.259   Busemann, Adolf. Psychologie der intelligenz defekte. München, 1959.

Phil 5535.2.5   Bush, Robert Ray. Studies in mathematical learning theory. Stanford, 1959.

Phil 4353.15   Caba, Pedro. Sintesis de su obra filosofica: antroposofica y metafisica de la presencia. Mexico, 1959.

Phil 6312.22   Cain, Jacques. Le problème des névroses experimentales. Paris, 1959.

Phil 1980.3.100   Calde-Marshall, A. Havelock Ellis. London, 1959.

Phil 4073.55   Campanella, Tommaso. Della grazia gratificante. Roma, 1959.

Phil 4983.1.85   Campo, Aníbal del. El problema de la creencia y el intelectualismo de Vaz Ferreira. Montevideo, 1959.

Phil 3484.24.10   Campo, M. Schizzo storico della esegesi e critica kantiana. Varese, 1959.

Phil 177.124   Cappellani, G. Dalla materia allo spirito. Mazara, 1959.

Phil 4357.8   Caragorri, P. La paradoja del filósofo. Madrid, 1959.

Phil 4112.90   Cardone, Elsa. La teologia razionale di P. Galluppi. Palmi, 1959.

Phil 4080.9.45   Carlini, Armando. Dalla vita dello spirito al mito del realismo. Firenze, 1959.

Phil 5042.60   Carnap, Rudolf. Induktive Logik und Wahrscheinlichkeit. Wien, 1959.

Phil 5066.8.2   Carnap, Rudolf. Introduction to semantics and formalization of logic. Cambridge, 1959.

Phil 4957.40   Carrillo Narváez, Alfredo. La tragectoria del pensamiento filosófico en Latinoamérica. Quito, 1959.

Phil 7069.59.35   Castellan, Yvonne. Le spiritisme. 2. ed. Paris, 1959.

Phil 4080.12.45   Castelli, Enrico. L'enquête quotidienne. Paris, 1959.

Phil 8952.14   Cathrein, Victor. Philosophia moralis in usum scholarum. Friburgi, 1959.

Phil 4957.30   Caturla Brú, Victoria de. Cuáles son las grandes temas de la filosofia latinoamericana? México, 1959.

Phil 4353.10   Cencillo, J.L. Experiencia profunda del ser. Madrid, 1959.

Phil 1600.15   Céntre d'Études Supérieure. Courants religieux et humanisme à la fin de XVième et au début du XVIième siècle. Paris, 1959.

Phil 1075.5   Chaloian, V.K. Istoriia armians boi filosofii. Erevan, 1959.

Phil 2880.8.128   Champigny, Robert. Stages on Sartre's way. Bloomington, 1959.

Phil 1750.95.10   Charlesworth, Maxwell John. Philosophy and linguistic analysis. Pittsburgh, 1959.

Phil 600.55   Charlton, D.G. Positivist thought in France. Oxford, 1959.

Phil 5374.200   Chauchard, P. Physiologie de la conscience. 4. éd. Paris, 1959.

Phil 2905.1.95   Chauchard, Paul. L'être humain selon Teilhard de Chardin. Paris, 1959.

Phil 8980.276   Chelovek budushchego rozhdaetsia segodnia. Moskva, 1959.

Phil 2475.1.222.15   Chevalier, Jacques. Entretiens avec Bergson. Paris, 1959.

Phil 1750.560.5   Chiodi, Pietro. Il pensiero esistenzialista. Milano, 1959.

Phil 2340.10.150   Christian, William A. An interpretation of Whitehead's metaphysics. New haven, 1959.

Phil 4605.1.80   Christophersen, Halfdan. Marcus Jacob Monrad. Oslo, 1959.

Phil 4080.23   Cicinato, Dante. Verso il trascendimento. Palmi, 1959.

Phil 4080.25   Cini, Giovanni. Senso e natura. Firenze, 1959?

Phil 8622.35   Cirne-Lima, Carlos. Der personale Glaube. Innsbruck, 1959.

Phil 8870.20   Clair, F.F. The ultimate defense. 1st ed. Rutland, 1959.

Phil 5627.259.20   Clark, W.H. The psychology of religion. N.Y., 1959.

Phil 530.11.12   Cloud of Unknowing. The cloud of unknowing. London, 1959.

Phil 525.185   Cognet, Louis. Post-Reformation spirituality. London, 1959.

Phil 8657.21   Collins, J.D. God in modern philosophy. Chicago, 1959.

Phil 177.122   Collins, William B. Metaphysics and man. Dubuque, 1959.

Phil 3450.11.215   Colloque International de Phénoménologie. Husserl et la pensée moderne. La Haye, 1959.

Phil 6990.3.85   Combes, André. Pilerinage spirituel à Lourdes. Paris, 1959.

Phil 2493.30.20   Condillac, Étienne Bonnot. La lógica, o Los primeros elementos del arte de pensar. Caracas, 1959.

Phil 4080.22.31   Coresi, Vincenzo. Assoluto e relativo. 1. ed. Bergamo, 1959.

Phil 333.19   Cortesi, Luigi. Le vie del sapere. Milano, 1959.

Phil 1750.97   Cotereau, Jean. Que l'homme soit! Paris, 1959.

Phil 5627.259   Cox, David. Jung and St. Paul. N.Y., 1959.

Phil 3484.9.10   Cresson, André. Kant; sa vie, son oeuvre, avec un exposé de sa philosophie. 5. éd. Paris, 1959.

Phil 3822.10.4   Cresson, André. Spinoza. 4. éd. Paris, 1959.

Phil 2402.7   Crocker, Lester G. An age of crisis. Baltimore, 1959.

Phil 1721.8   Dalori, Paolo. Il pensiero filosofico odierno. Roma, 1959.

Phil 6750.223.15   Davies, S.P. The mentally retarded in society. N.Y., 1959.

Phil 1508.3   Delhaye, Philippe. La philosophie chrétienne au Moyen Âge. Paris, 1959.

Phil 7082.180   De Martino, Manfred F. Dreams and personality dynamics. Springfield, 1959.

Phil 6313.18   Deshaies, Gabriel. Psychopathologie générale. Paris, 1959.

Phil 9240.18   Dessauer, F.J. Prometheus und die Weltübel. Frankfurt, 1959.

Phil 6113.32   Deutsch, Felix. On the mysterious leap from the mind to the body. N.Y., 1959.

Phil 5243.49   Devoto, Andrea. Saggio sulla psicologia contemporanea. Firenze, 1959.

Phil 3195.6.130   Diaz de Cerio Ruiz, Franco. W. Dilthey y el problema del mundo historico. Barcelona, 1959.

Phil 2450.81.5A   Dibon, Paul. Pierre Bayle. Amsterdam, 1959.

Phil 2530.80A   Dieckmann, Herbert. Cinq leçons sur Diderot. Genève, 1959.

1959 - cont.

Phil 5592.110	Doebeli, Peter. Beiträge zur Psychodiagnostik. Zürich, 1959.
Phil 3485.22	Doerpinghaus, Wilhelm. Der Begriff der Gesellschaft bei Kant. Köln? 1959?
Phil 5548.70	Dollard, John. Scoring human motives. New Haven, 1959.
Phil 9290.6	Donohue, John W. Work and education. Chicago, 1959.
Phil 8404.3.10	Dorfles, Gillo. Il divinire delle arti. Torino, 1959.
Phil 2555.9.30	Dufrenne, Mikel. La notion d'a priori. 1. éd. Paris, 1959.
Phil 735.220	Dujoune, L. Teoría de los valores y filosofía de la historia. Buenos Aires, 1959.
Phil 310.105	Duncher, Hermann. Einführungen in den Marxismus. Berlin, 1959. 2v.
Phil 3850.18.150	Dupuy, Maurice. La philosophie de la religion. Paris, 1959.
Phil 3850.18.151	Dupuy, Maurice. La philosophie de la religion chez Max Scheler. Paris, 1959.
Phil 3850.18.153	Dupuy, Maurice. La philosophie de Max Scheler. Paris, 1959. 2v.
Phil 3850.18.152	Dupuy, Maurice. La philosophie de Max Scheler. 1. éd. Paris, 1959.
Phil 7069.59.45	Durand, M. Technique et panthéon des mediums viêtnamiens. Paris, 1959.
Phil 5592.160	Dureman, I. Psykometriska och experimentalpsykologiska metoder för klinisk tillämpning. Stockholm, 1959.
Phil 4355.5	Echarri, Jaime. Philosophia entis sensibilis. Romae, 1959.
Phil 2477.6.125	École, Jean. La metaphysique de l'être dans la philosophie de Maurice Blondel. Louvains, 1959.
Phil 2805.380	Écrits sur Pascal. Paris, 1959.
Phil 3450.11.210	Edmund Husserl, 1859-1959. La Haye, 1959.
Phil 735.210	Ehrlich, Walter. Hauptprobleme der Wertphilosophie. Tübingen, 1959.
Phil 5203.20	Emanuilova, E. Suvremenna materialisticheska psikhologiia. Sofiia, 1959.
Phil 75.54	Emunds, Heinz. Zugange zur Philosophie. Köln, 1959.
Phil 1704.1.10	Ermolenko, D.V. Kritika sovremennoi burzruaznoi filosofii. Moskva, 1959.
Phil 8419.19.5	Esteticheskoe v deistvitel'nosti i v iskusstve. Moskva, 1959.
Phil 5520.245	ETC., a Review of General Semantics. Our language and our world. 1. ed. N.Y., 1959.
Phil 9240.6.5	Ewing, Alfred C. Second thoughts in moral philosophy. London, 1959.
Phil 8880.49.2	Fagathey, Austin. Right and reason. 2nd ed. St. Louis, 1959.
Phil 4005.12	Faggiotto, Pietro. Esperienza e metafisica. Padova, 1959.
Phil 1750.96	Farber, Marvin. Naturalism and subjectivism. Springfield, Ill., 1959.
Phil 3425.530	Fazio Allmayer, Vito. Ricerche hegeliane. Firenze, 1959.
Phil 1170.15	Feibleman, James. Religious Platonism. London, 1959.
Phil 5520.260	Feldman, Sandor S. Mannerisms of speech and gestures in everyday life. N.Y., 1959.
Phil 4351.4.80	Fernández Largo, Jacinto. Introduccion al estudio del filósofo rancio. Madrid, 1959.
Phil 5245.75	Ferrière, A. L'orthogenèse lumaine. Neuchâtel, 1959.
Phil 6060.54	Fervers, Hans. Wie man Menschen beurteilt. Neuwied, 1959.
Phil 5815.8	Filloux, Jean Claude. Le psychisme animal. Paris, 1959.
Phil 336.16	Fink, Eugen. Alles und Nichts. Den Haag, 1959.
Phil 8050.56	Fischer, Ernest. Von der Notwendigkeit der Kunst. Dresden, 1959.
Phil 5045.17	Flach, W. Negation und Andersheit. München, 1959.
Phil 1750.734	Flam, L. De onverzoenlijken. St. Niklaas, 1959.
Phil 1750.540	Flam, Leopold. Ontbinding en protest. Antwerpen, 1959.
Phil 8735.40.5	Fondazione Giorgio Cini, Venice. Centro de Cultura e Civiltà. Causalità e finalità. Firenze, 1959.
Phil 7150.48	Fondazione Piero Varenna, Milan. Assistenza medico sociale ai tenfati suicide. Milano, 1959.
Phil 165.173	For Roman Ingarden. 's Gravenhage, 1959.
Phil 1540.36	Fortin, E.L. Christianisme et culture phillosophique au cinquième siècle. Paris, 1959.
Phil 3450.11.280	Fragata, Júlio. A fenomenologia de Husserl como fundamento. Braga, 1959.
Phil 2805.365	Francis, Raymond. Les pensées de Pascal en France de 1842 à 1942. Paris, 1959.
Phil 4756.1.48	Frank, Semen L. Religiia i nauka. Posev, 1959.
Phil 6315.66	Frankenstein, Carl. Die Ausserlichkeit des Lebensstils. Amsterdam, 1959.
Phil 3808.225	Franz-Schneider, Lucia. Erinnerungen an das Schopenhauers Schöne Aussicht. Frankfurt, 1959.
Phil 2520.305	Frédérix, Pierre. Monsieur Réné Descartes en son temps. Paris, 1959.
Phil 1980.3.102	Freeman-Ishill, Rose. Havelock Ellis. Berkeley Heights, N.J., 1959.
Phil 6315.2.8.31	Freud, Sigmund. Collected papers. N.Y., 1959. 5v.
Phil 5245.70	From, Franz. Menneshe kundskab. København, 1959. 2v.
Phil 6315.2.235A	Fromm, Erich. Sigmund Freud's mission. 1st ed. N.Y., 1959.
Phil 6980.309.5	Fromm-Reichmann, Frieda. Psychoanalysis and psychotherapy. Chicago, 1959.
Phil 806.25	Galli, Dario. Sensei e soluzzi della filosofia europea. Bologna, 1959.
Phil 5046.32	Garcia Tuduri, R. Lógica. 7. ed. Habana, 1959.
Phil 4006.5.50	Garin, Eugenio. Cronache di filosofia italiana. 2. ed. Bari, 1959.
Phil 181.125	Garin, Eugenio. La filosofia come sapere storico. Bari, 1959.
Phil 5592.105	Gauchet, F. La caracterologie d'Heymans. Paris, 1959.
Phil 5068.42	Gellner, Ernest. Words and things. London, 1959.
Phil 6990.3.112	Gerloff, Hans. Die Heilungen von Lourdes im Lichte der Parapsychologie. Büdingen-Gettenbach, 1959.
Phil 181.130	Giannini, Giorgio. I presupposti della trascendenza. Milano, 1959.
Phil 1111.9.5	Gigon, Olof. Grundprobleme der antiken Philosophie. Bern, 1959.
Phil 8956.10	Gilleman, Gérard. The primacy of charity in moral theology. Westminster, 1959.
Phil 1511.3.22	Gilson, Étienne. Reason and revelation in the Middle Ages. N.Y., 1959.
Phil 3850.27.205	Gittleman, D. Albert Schweitzer. n.p., 1959.
Phil 8622.45	Glaube und Unglaube. Zürich, 1959.
Phil 310.155	Goldmann, Lucien. Recherches dialectiques. 2. éd. Paris, 1959.
Phil 5046.48.2	Gortari, Eli de. Introducción a la lógica dialéctica. 2. ed. México, 1959.

1959 - cont.

Phil 8740.8	Graef, Hilda C. The light and the rainbow. London, 1959.
Phil 525.160	Graef, Hilda Charlotte. Der siebenfarbige Bogen auf den Spuren der grossen Mystiker. Frankfurt, 1959.
Phil 1750.166.15	Granell Muñiz, M. El humanismo como responsabilidad. Madrid, 1959.
Phil 5046.34	Greenwood, David. The nature of science. N.Y., 1959.
Phil 8661.20	Grison, M. Théologie naturelle, ou théodicée. Paris, 1959.
Phil 310.50.5	Gropp, Rugard Otto. Zu Fragen der Geschichte der Philosophie und des dialektischen Materialismus. Berlin, 1959.
Phil 1706.10	Grose. Grote filosofieën en de huidige mens. Amsterdam, 1959.
Phil 735.200	Gruber, Frederick C. Aspects of value. Philadelphia, 1959.
Phil 5046.30	Guenther, Gotthard. Idee und Grundriss einer nicht-aristotalischen Logik. Hamburg, 1959.
Phil 5590.265	Guilford, J.P. Personality. N.Y., 1959.
Phil 6952.23.80	Guillain, Georges. J.M. Charcot, 1825-1893. N.Y., 1959.
Phil 8586.52	Guirdham, A. Christ and Freud. London, 1959.
Phil 2630.11.10	Guitton, Jean. Journal. Paris, 1959. 2v.
Phil 195.6	Gulmer, Karl. Von der Sache der Philosophie. Freiburg, 1959.
Phil 1750.550	Gurr, John E. The principle of sufficient reason in some scholastic systems. Milwaukee, 1959.
Phil 6990.3.88	Guynot, Ernest. Sainte Bernadette. Paris, 1959.
Phil 288.10	Haber, Francis. The age of the world. Baltimore, 1959.
Phil 3450.29.73	Haecker, Theodor. Tag- und Nachtbücher, 1939-1945. 3e Aufl. München, 1959.
Phil 310.165	Hager, Kurt. Der dialektische Materialismus die theoretische Grundlage der Politik der SED. 3. Aufl. Berlin, 1959.
Phil 2730.108	Hallie, P.P. Maine de Biran, reformer. Cambridge, 1959.
Phil 5238.105	Halmos, Paul. Readings in general psychology. London, 1959.
Phil 5590.295	Halsman, Phillipe. Jump book. N.Y., 1959.
Phil 2055.10.30	Hampshire, Stuart. Thought and action. London, 1959.
Phil 1955.6.150	Handlin, Oscar. John Dewey's challenge to education. N.Y., 1959.
Phil 978.92	Hartmann, F. Ausgewählte theasophische Werke. Calw-Wimberg, Württ, 1959.
Phil 2280.1.95	Havard, William C. Henry Sidgwick and later utilitarian political philosophy. Gainesville, 1959.
Phil 288.20	Hawley, Don. The nature of things. N.Y., 1959.
Phil 1707.18	Heer, Friedrich. Die dritte Kraft. Frankfurt, 1959.
Phil 8622.40	Heer, Friedrich. Glaube und Unglaube. München, 1959.
Phil 3425.70.75A	Hegel, Georg Wilhelm Friedrich. Einleitung in die Geschichte der Philosophie. 3. Aufl. Hamburg, 1959.
Phil 3425.46.6	Hegel, Georg Wilhelm Friedrich. Enzyklopädie der philosophischen Wissenschaften. 6. Aufl. Hamburg, 1959.
Phil 182.93.12	Heidegger, M. An introduction to metaphysics. New Haven, 1959.
Phil 3450.19.57	Heidegger, Martin. Unterwegs zur Sprache. Pfullingen, 1959.
Phil 3007.2.5	Heine, H. Religion and philosophy in Germany. Boston, 1959.
Phil 807.16.5	Heinemann, Fritz. Die Philosophie im XX Jahrhundert. Stuttgart, 1959.
Phil 2636.25.6	Helvétius, C.A. De l'esprit. Paris, 1959.
Phil 1955.6.155	Hendel, Charles W. John Dewey and the experimental spirit in philosophy. N.Y., 1959.
Phil 288.12	Hennemann, Gerhard. Naturphilosophie in 19. Jahrhundert. Freiburg, 1959.
Phil 4979.5.85	Hernández Luna, Juan. Dos ideas sobre la filosofía en la Nueva España. México, 1959.
Phil 3120.50.30	Hertz-Eichenrode, Dieter. Der jünghegelianer Bruno Bauer im Vormärz. Berlin, 1959.
Phil 3450.36	Hessen, Johannes. Gustige Kämpf der Zeit im Spiegel und Lebens. Nürnberg, 1959.
Phil 3450.30.5	Hessen, Johannes. Im Ringen um eine zeitnahe Philosophie. Nürnberg, 1959.
Phil 6317.21.104	Heyer, Gustav R. Der Organism der Seele. 4. Aufl. München, 1959.
Phil 7069.59.5	Heywood, Rosalind. The sixth sense. London, 1959.
Phil 3450.33.2	Hildebrand, Christa. Die Wertethik bei Dietrick von Hildebrand. Düsseldorf, 1959.
Phil 5592.130	Hills, J.R. The influence of instructions of repeated measurement on personality inventory scores. Princeton, 1959.
Phil 3450.39.30	Hirsch, Wolfgang. Die Normen des Seins. Amsterdam, 1959?
Phil 338.28	Hirst, R.J. The problems of perception. London, 1959.
Phil 182.88.3	Hocking, W.E. Types of philosophy. 3d ed. N.Y., 1959.
Phil 5247.70	Hoejgaard, Mogens. Mennesker og andre dyr. København, 1959.
Phil 3450.38	Hoffmann, Gustov. Genius der Menscheit. Delmenhorst, 1959.
Phil 3640.590	Hohn, Hans. Die metaphysischen und anthropologischen Voraussetzungen der Politik bei Friedrich Nietzsche. Bonn, 1959.
Phil 8615.23	Hohoff, Tay. A ministry to man. 1. ed. N.Y., 1959.
Phil 2648.62	Holbach, Paul Henri T. Ausgewählte Texte. Berlin, 1959.
Phil 1750.565	Hollenbach, Johannes. Der Mensch der Zukunft. Frankfurt, 1959.
Phil 1707.22	Holm, Søren. O plysningstiden. Kjøbenhavn, 1959.
Phil 8587.73	L'homme au regard de la foi. Paris, 1959.
Phil 6317.38	Hook, Sidney. Psychoanalysis. N.Y., 1959.
Phil 8980.456	Hott, V.S. Dva sviti, dvi morali. Kyiv, 1959.
Phil 930.54	Hou, Wai-lu. A short history of Chinese philosophy. Peking, 1959.
Phil 310.588	Hrušovský, I. Tri iniciatívy v dejinách filozofie. Bratislava, 1959.
Phil 5247.13.18	Huarte de San Juan, J. Examen de ingenios. Gainesville, 1959.
Phil 7069.59.20	Huber, Guido. Übersinnliche Gaben. 1. Aufl. Zürich, 1959.
Phil 3450.19.165	Hühnerfeld, Paul. In Sachen Heidegger. Hamburg, 1959.
Phil 3450.18.135	Hülsmann, Heinz. Die Methode in der Philosophie Nicolai Hartmanns. 1e Aufl. Düsseldorf, 1959.
Phil 8408.23	Huisman, Denis. L'esthétique. 3. éd. Paris, 1959.
Phil 7075.154	Hunt, Morton M. The natural history of love. N.Y., 1959.
Phil 5047.11.20	Husserl, Edmund. Recherches logiques. Paris, 1959. 3v.
Phil 3450.11.235	Husserl. Paris, 1959.
Phil 8882.75	Hytten, E. The concept of morality. Stockholm, 1959.
Phil 7069.59.30	Imbert-Nergal, R. Les sciences occultes ne sont pas des sciences. Paris, 1959.

Chronological Listing

1959 - cont.

Phil 75.58 — Inter-American Congress of Philosophy. Exposición del libro americano. Buenos Aires, 1959?

Phil 5465.90 — Interdisciplinary Symposium on Creativity, Michigan State University of Agriculture. Creativity and its cultivation. N.Y., 1959.

Phil 6118.6 — International Conference on Student Mental Health. The student and mental health. London, 1959.

Phil 70.86 — International Institute of Philosophy. Traditional cultural values. Mysore, 1959.

Phil 4080.3.320 — Iofrida, Vincenzo. La liberta come fondamento dello stato. Milano, 1959.

Phil 6319.1.181.2 — Jacobi, Jolan. Complex, archetype. N.Y., 1959.
Phil 6319.1.181.3 — Jacobi, Jolan. Complex, archtype. London, 1959.
Phil 6319.1.183 — Jacobi, Jolan. Die Psychologie von C.G. Jung. 4. Aufl. Zürich, 1959.

Phil 6119.14 — Jahoda, Marie. Current concepts of positive mental health. N.Y., 1959.

Phil 5590.275 — Janis, Irving L. Personality and persuasibility. New Haven, 1959.

Phil 2475.1.263.5 — Jankélévitch, V. Henri Bergson. Paris, 1959.
Phil 5049.20.3 — Jaspers, Karl. Truth and symbol. N.Y., 1959.
Phil 1870.140 — Jessop, T.E. George Berkeley. London, 1959.
Phil 5585.155 — Johansen, Martin. Voluminalfigurale faenomener. København, 1959.

Phil 9560.44 — Johnson, Oliver A. Rightness and goodness. The Hague, 1959.

Phil 184.49 — Johnstone, Henry Webb. Philosophy and argument. State College, Pa., 1959.

Phil 3805.210 — Jorgensen, Paul. Die Ethik Schleiermachers. München, 1959.

Phil 6319.1.5.10 — Jung, C.G. Basic writings. N.Y., 1959.
Phil 1710.10 — Kaegi, Werner. Humanismus der Gegenwart. Zürich, 1959.
Phil 3801.472 — Kahr-Wallerstein, C. Schellings Frauen: Caroline und Pauline. Bern, 1959.

Phil 4803.472.20 — Kamieński, Henryk. Filozofia ekonomii materialnej ludzkiego społeczństwa. Warszawa, 1959.

Phil 6320.13 — Kaminski, Gerhard. Das Bild vom Ander. Berlin, 1959.
Phil 5722.60 — Kankeleit, Otto. Des Unbewusste als Keimstätte des Schöpferischen. München, 1959.

Phil 3480.47.7A — Kant, Immanuel. Critique of practical reason. 6th ed. London, 1959.

Phil 3480.67.20 — Kant, Immanuel. Qu'est-ceque s'orienter dans la pensée. Paris, 1959.

Phil 3480.120 — Kant, Immanuel. Réponse á Eberhard. Paris, 1959.
Phil 3480.86.10 — Kant, Immanuel. Der Streit der Fakultäten. Hamburg, 1959.
Phil 310.170 — Karavaev, G.G. Istoricheskii materializm. Leningrad, 1959.

Phil 810.12 — Kasm, Badi. L'ideé de preuve in imétaphysique. Paris, 1959.

Phil 4795.6 — Kasumov, Mekhbaly Mamedovich. Ocherki po istorii peredovoi filosofskoi i obshchestvenno-politicheskoi mysli azerbaidzhanskogo naroda v XIX veke. Baku, 1959.

Phil 1750.455.10 — Kaufmann, W.A. The owl and the nightingale. London, 1959.
Phil 5050.20F — Kauger, F. Handbok i logik. Stockholm, 1959.
Phil 3450.19.205 — Kauthack, Katherina. Das Denken des Martin Heideggers. Berlin, 1959.

Phil 310.110 — Kelle, V.Z. Formy obshchestvennogo soznaniia. Moskva, 1959.

Phil 291.9 — Kemeny, John G. A philosopher looks at science. Princeton, N.J., 1959.

Phil 8700.18 — Klotz, John William. Genes. Saint Louis, 1959.
Phil 1710.6 — Knight, Everett. The objective society. London, 1959.
Phil 1710.6.2 — Knight, Everett. The objective society. N.Y., 1959.
Phil 341.35 — Knowledge of other minds. Lahore, 1959.
Phil 165.150 — Koch, Adrienne. Philosophy for a time of crisis. N.Y., 1959.

Phil 5238.100 — Koch, Sigmund. Psychology. v.2-6. v.1 lost. N.Y., 1959. 5v.

Phil 735.118.2 — Köhler, Wolfgang. The place of value in a world of facts. N.Y., 1959.

Phil 5627.230 — Koerner, Margot. Religionspsychopathologische Untersuchungen. Mainz, 1959.

Phil 3450.18.190 — Koerschgen, Hans. Über die Raumlehre Nicolai Hartmanns und ihre Bezlehungen zur modernen Mathematik und Physik. Köln, 1959?

Phil 3801.493 — Koktanek, A.M. Schellings erste münchner Vorlesung. Inaug. Diss. München, 1959.

Phil 8980.496 — Kononenko, E.V. O krasote dushevnoi. Moskva, 1959.
Phil 4972.5.20 — Korn, Alejandro. De San Agustín a Bergson. Buenos Aires, 1959.

Phil 310.255 — Kosanović, I. Dijalektički materijalizam. 4. vyd. Sarajevo, 1959.

Phil 8141.2 — Kőszegi, L. Präparation zu einer Rom-zentrischen Ästhetik. Detmold, 1959.

Phil 5425.100 — Kotsovsky, D. Tragödie des Genius. München, 1959.
Phil 5635.45 — Kovalgin, V.M. Problema oshchushchenii i reflektornaia teoriia. Minsk, 1959.

Phil 6320.19 — Kramer, Charles. La frustration. Neuchâtel, 1959.
Phil 341.20 — Krąpiec, M.A. Realizm ludzkiego poznania. Poznań, 1959.
Phil 185.85 — Krąpiec, M.A. Teoria analogii bytu. Lublin, 1959.
Phil 341.25 — Krausser, Peter. Untersuchuugen über den grundsatzlichen Auspruch der Wahrnehmung. Meisenheim am Glan, 1959.

Phil 1760.10 — Krikorien, Yervant H. Contemporary philosophic problems, selected readings. N.Y., 1959.

Phil 978.59.40 — Krishnamurti, J. Commentaries on living. London, 1959.
Phil 8835.5 — Krook, Dorothea. Three traditions of moral thought. Cambridge, Eng., 1959.

Phil 3425.515 — Kruithof, J. Het uitgangspunt van Hegel's ontologie. Brugge, 1959.

Phil 8700.16 — Kryvelev, I.A. Sovremennoe bogoslov'e i nauka. Moskva, 1959.

Phil 165.170 — Ksiega pamiątkowa ku uczczeniu czterdziestolecia pracy nauczycielskiej. Warszawa, 1959.

Phil 930.56 — Kuo, Mo-jo. Bronzovij vek. Moskva, 1959.
Phil 585.66 — Kwant, Remy C. Wijsbegeerte van de ontmoeting. Utrecht, 1959.

Phil 3425.485 — Lacorte, Carmelo. Il primo Hegel. Firenze, 1959.
Phil 2280.5.115 — Lamont, Corliss. Dialogue on George Santayana. N.Y., 1959.

Phil 1955.6.145 — Lamont, Corliss. Dialogue on John Dewey. N.Y., 1959.
Phil 8636.8.10 — Lamont, Corliss. The illusion of immortality. 3. ed. N.Y., 1959.

Phil 5021.5 — Lamouche, André. Logique de la simplicité. Paris, 1959.
Phil 3450.19.175 — Langan, Thomas. The meaning of Heidegger. N.Y., 1959.
Phil 315.16 — Lavergne, Bernard. Individualisme contre autoritarisme. Paris, 1959.

1959 - cont.

Phil 8886.74 — Leclercq, Francois. Propos sur la morale et la science. Paris, 1959.

Phil 5590.300 — Leeper, Robert. Toward understanding human personalities. N.Y., 1959.

Phil 2725.37.30 — Lefebvre, Henri. La somme et le reste. Paris, 1959. 2v.

Phil 2520.255.15 — Lefèvre, Roger. La métaphysique de Descartes. 1. éd. Paris, 1959.

Phil 310.395 — Lehév, Iwere. Iyöväenluohan maailmankatsomus. Helsinki, 1959.

Phil 3552.24.25 — Leibniz, Gottfried Wilhelm. Opera philosophica. Aalen, 1959.

Phil 8505.8.10 — Leningrad. Muzei Istorii Religii i Ateizma. Istoriia papstva i inkvizitsii. Moskva, 1959.

Phil 3850.18.160 — Lenk, Kurt. Von der Ohnmacht des Geistes. Tübingen, 1959.
Phil 5251.68 — Leont'ev, Aleksei N. Problemy razvitiia psikhiki. Moskva, 1959.

Phil 1870.138 — Leroy, André Louis. George Berkeley. Paris, 1959.
Phil 2750.13.100 — Lê Thanh Tri. L'idée de la participation chez Gabriel Marcel. Fribourg? 1959.

Phil 1711.7 — Levi, Albert. Philosophy and the modern world. Bloomington, 1959.

Phil 5051.10.12 — Lewis, Clarence I. Symbolic logic. 2nd ed. N.Y., 1959.
Phil 8666.18 — Lewis, Hymel D. Our experience of God. London, 1959.
Phil 1135.172 — Lieberg, Godo. Geist und Lust. Tübingen, 1959.
Phil 9500.5 — Lindenberg, Wladimir. Gespräche am Krankenbett. München, 1959.

Phil 5627.259.10 — Lindenberg, Wladimir. Mysterium der Begegnung. München, 1959.

Phil 4973.7 — Lins, Mario. Foundations of social determinism. Rio de Janeiro, 1959.

Phil 2070.145 — Linschoten, Johannes. Op weg naar een fenomenologische psychologie. Utrecht, 1959.

Phil 210.20 — Lipps, Hans. Untersuchungen zu einer Hermeneutischen Logik. 2. Aufl. Frankfurt, 1959.

Phil 4710.3 — Lobkowicz, Nikolaus. Das Widerspruchsprinzie in der neueren sowjetischen Philosophie. Reidel, 1959.

Phil 486.15 — Lodetti, Milka. La matière imaginaire. Paris, 1959.
Phil 165.155 — Logica. Neuchâtel, 1959.
Phil 7069.59.40 — Long, Max Freedom. Psychometric analysis. Vista, Calif., 1959.

Phil 8886.73.2 — López Aranguren, José Luis. Etica. 2. ed. Madrid, 1959.
Phil 342.19 — Lowenberg, Jacob. Reason and the nature of things. La Salle, Ill., 1959.

Phil 8666.17.6 — Lubac, Henri de. Le drame de l'humanisme athée. 6. éd. Paris, 1959.

Phil 5352.5 — Luce, Robert. Individual choice behavior. N.Y., 1959. 2v.

Phil 8591.43.5 — Ludendorff, Mathilde S. In den Gegilden der Gottoffenbarung. Pähl, 1959.

Phil 3585.20 — Luijpen, Wilhelmus Antonius Maria. Existentiële fenomenologie. Utrecht, 1959.

Phil 1750.38 — Lyotard, Jean François. La phénoménologie. 3e éd. Paris, 1959.

Phil 5635.5.8 — Mach, Ernst. The analysis of sensations on the relation of the physical to the psychical. N.Y., 1959.

Phil 5548.95 — Madsen, Kaj Berg. Theories of motivation. Copenhagen, 1959.

Phil 5850.264.25 — Magoun, F.A. The teaching of human relations. Boston, 1959.

Phil 5592.85 — Maistriaux, Robert. L'intelligence et le caractère. Paris, 1959.

Phil 7082.142 — Malcolm, Norman. Dreaming. London, 1959.
Phil 310.150 — Mal'tsev, V.I. Bor'ba v SSSR protiv mekhanitsizma. Moskva, 1959.

Phil 310.100 — Mal'tsev, V.I. Problemy dialekticheskoi logikii. Moskva, 1959.

Phil 1955.6.205 — Mañach, Jorge. Dewey y el pensamiento americano. Madrid, 1959.

Phil 5520.265 — Mandler, George. The language of psychology. N.Y., 1959.
Phil 2750.19.35 — Marcel, Gabriel. El misterio ontologico. Tucumán, 1959.
Phil 1750.590 — Marchello, Giuseppe. La crisi del concetto filosofico. Milano, 1959.

Phil 4012.12 — Marciano, Francesco. Storia della filosofia italiana. Roma, 1959.

Phil 1812.11A — Marcuse, Ludwig. Amerikanisches Philosophieren. Hamburg, 1959.

Phil 4313.5 — Marias Aguilera, Julian. La escuela de Madrid. Buenos Aires, 1959.

Phil 2750.11.48.5 — Maritain, Jacques. Distinguish to unite. London, 1959.
Phil 2750.11.48 — Maritain, Jacques. Distinguish to unite. N.Y., 1959.
Phil 2750.11.88 — Maritain, Jacques. Liturgie et contemplation. Bruges, 1959.

Phil 2750.11.60 — Maritain, Jacques. Pour une philosophie de l'éducation. Paris, 1959.

Phil 8592.110 — Martin, C.B. Religious belief. Ithaca, N.Y., 1959.
Phil 5066.145 — Martin, Richard M. The motion of analytic truth. Philadelphia, 1959.

Phil 187.158 — Martin, William O. Metaphysics and ideology. Milwaukee, 1959.

Phil 3450.19.340 — Martin Heidegger, 26 September 1959. Messkirch, 1959.
Phil 5590.345 — Marzi, Alberto. La personalitá nell'età evolutiva. Firenze, 1959.

Phil 5525.58 — Mason, Michael. The centre of hilarity. London, 1959.
Phil 2825.15.80 — Masset, Pierre. La dialectique de la conscience chez Jacques Paliard. Paris, 1959.

Phil 3425.510 — Massolo, Arturo. Prime ricerche di Hegel. Urbino, 1959.
Phil 8170.4 — Matsa, Ivan. Khudozhestvennoe nasledie i estetickeskoe vospitanie. Moskva, 1959.

Phil 2750.28.30 — Maudoussat, G. La liberté spirituelle. Paris, 1959.
Phil 5520.275 — Mayer, Felix. Schöpferische Sprache und Rhythmus. Berlin, 1959.

Phil 2340.10.155 — Mays, Wolfe. The philosophy of Whitehead. London, 1959.
Phil 8837.16 — Méautis, Georges. Mes pélerinages de l'âme. Paris, 1959.
Phil 5643.120 — Meer, H.C. von der. Die Links-Rechts-Polarisation des phaenomenalen Raumes. Groningen, 1959.

Phil 6319.1.208 — Meier, Carl A. Jung and analytical psychology. Newton, Mass., 1959.

Phil 165.145.5 — Mélanges offerts à Étienne Gilson de l'Académie Française. Toronto, 1959.

Phil 9070.70 — Melden, Abraham. Rights and right conduct. Oxford, 1959.
Phil 5190.24.5 — Melhwish, George. The paradoxical universe. Bristol, Eng., 1959.

Phil 187.170 — Mel'nykov, V.M. O pytannia pro pryrodu filosofs'kykh kategorii. Kyïv, 1959.

Phil 2750.24.30 — Menetrier, Jacques. L'homme quelconque. Paris, 1959.

1959 - cont.

VPhil 978.114   Merchant, Francis. The golden hoard. Houston, 1959.
Phil 310.200   Meurers, Joseph. Wissenschaft im Kollektiv. München, 1959.
Phil 6962.32   Meyer, Henry F. An experiment in mental patient rehabilitation. N.Y., 1959.
Phil 575.210   Michel, Ernst. Der Prozess "Gesellschaft contra Person". Stuttgart, 1959.
Phil 2750.17.30   Mieville, Henri L. Condition de l'homme. Genève, 1959.
Phil 6122.80   Mikhailov, S. Likvidiraneto na protivopolozhnostta mezhdu umstveniia i fizicheokiia trud. Sofiia, 1959.
Phil 5068.38   Miles, Thomas R. Religion and the scientific outlook. London, 1959.
Phil 2138.40.45   Mill, John S. Prefaces to liberty. Boston, 1959.
Phil 5762.19   Miller, David L. Modern science and human freedom. Austin, 1959.
Phil 2725.11.95   Millet, Louis. Le symbolisme dans la philosophie. Paris, 1959.
Phil 2880.8.130   Moeller, Joseph. Absurdes sein? Stuttgart, 1959.
Phil 2636.88   Momdzhian, Khashik. Helvitius, ein streitbarer Atheist das 18. Jahrhunderts. Berlin, 1959.
Phil 2636.88.5   Momdzhian, Khashik. La philosophie d'Helvétius. Moscow, 1959.
Phil 8887.110.5   Montefiore, Alan. A modern introduction to moral philosophy. N.Y., 1959.
Phil 2150.18.35   Moore, George Edward. Philosophical papers. London, 1959.
Phil 8887.21.6   Moore, George Edward. Principia ethica. Cambridge, Eng., 1959.
Phil 5252.68.5   Morris, Charles W. Six theories of mind. Chicago, 1959.
Phil 2805.345   Mortimer, Ernest. Blaise Pascal. London, 1959.
Phil 1750.545   Moscow. Akademiia Obshchestvennykh Nauk. Kritika sovremennoi burzhuaznoi filosofii. Moskva, 1959.
Phil 2475.1.360   Mossé-Bastide, Rose Marie. Bergson et Plotin. 1. éd. Paris, 1959.
Phil 2475.1.360.5   Mossé-Bastide, Rose Marie. Bergson et Plotin. 1. éd. Thèse. Paris, 1959.
Phil 6122.70   Mott, Francis. The nature of the self. London, 1959.
Phil 2750.22.30   Mounier, E. La petite peur du XXe siècle. Neuchâtel, 1959.
Phil 3425.525   Mueller, Gustav E. Hegel. Bern, 1959.
Phil 9070.75   Mueller-Eckhard, Hans. Weltbewältigung. Stuttgart, 1959.
Phil 187.99.5   Muller, Maurice. Idées et archetypes de Platon à Elie Cartan. Neuchâtel, 1959.
Phil 6962.34   Myers, Jerome K. Family and class dynamics in mental illness. N.Y., 1959.
Phil 3552.390   Naert, Emilienne. Leibniz et la querelle du pur amour. Paris, 1959.
Phil 310.210   Narskii, I.S. Marksistskoe ponimanie predmeta filosofii i pozitivizm. Moskva, 1959.
Phil 3195.6.120   Negri, Antonio. Saggi sullo storicismo tedesco. Milano, 1959.
Phil 5238.175   Nelson, Harry. Theoretical foundations of psychology. Princeton, 1959.
Phil 5066.220   Nelson, Leonard. Beiträge zur Philosophie. Frankfurt, 1959.
Phil 5421.25   Nesbitt, Michael. Friendship, love, and values. Princeton, 1959.
Phil 3450.19.190   Neshe, Günther. Martin Heidegger zum siebzigsten Geburtstag. Pfullingen, 1959.
Phil 310.145   Nesterenko, G.I. Obshchestvennoe soznanie i ego formy. Moskva, 1959. 2 pam.
Phil 5590.305   Neumann, Erich. Der schöpferische Mensch. Zürich, 1959.
Phil 3640.33.5   Nietzsche, Friedrich. Die fröhliche Wissenschaft. München, 1959.
Phil 3640.17.7   Nietzsche, Friedrich. Jenseits von Gut und Böse. Stuttgart, 1959.
Phil 3640.77.5   Nietzsche, Friedrich. Unpublished letters. N.Y., 1959.
Phil 3640.17.9   Nietzsche, Friedrich. Der Wille zur Macht. Stuttgart, 1959.
Phil 9450.30   Northrop Filmer, Stuart C. The complexity of legal and ethical experience. 1. ed. Boston, 1959.
Phil 310.215   Novikov, A.I. Bor'ba marksizma-leninizma protiv sovremennogo filosofskogo revizionizma. Leningrad, 1959.
Phil 6323.5.3   Nunberg, Hermann. Allgemeine Neurosenlehre. Bern, 1959.
Phil 3705.7   Oberth, Hermann. Stoff und Leben. Remagen, 1959.
Phil 54.5   Obshchestvo Psikhologov, Moscow, 1. S"ezd, 1959. Tezisy dokladov, 29 iiunia -4 iiulia 1959 g. v.1-3. Moskva, 1959.
Phil 3640.595   Oduev, S.F. Reaktsionnaia sushchnost' nitssheanstva. Moskva, 1959.
Phil 8422.7.30   Oelmueller, W. Friedrich T. Vischer und das Problem der nachhegelschen Asthetik. Stuttgart, 1959.
Phil 2520.320   Oggione, Emilio. Cartesio. Bologna, 1959.
Phil 3425.535   Oiserman, Teodor. Die Philosophie Hegels. 1. Aufl. Berlin, 1959.
Phil 1750.635   Oizerman, T.I. Neotmoizm - filosofiia sovremennoi reaktsionoi burzhuazii. Moskva, 1959.
Phil 165.145   O'Neil, Charles J. An Etienne Gilson tribute presented by his North American students. Milwaukee, 1959.
Phil 8889.7   Osbert, Reuben. Humanism and moral theory. London, 1959.
Phil 3450.19.220   Ott, Heinrich. Denken und Sein. Zollikon, 1959.
Phil 3425.500   Ovsiannikov, M.F. Filosofiia Gegelia. Moskva, 1959.
Phil 1119.6   Owens, Joseph. A history of ancient Western philosophy. N.Y., 1959.
Phil 4210.107   Pagani, G.B. Vita di Antonio Rosmini scritta da un sacerdote dell'istituto della carità. Rovereto, 1959. 2v.
Phil 55.10   Parapsychology Foundation. Report on five years of activities. N.Y., 1959.
Phil 5850.304   Pascal, Gerald. Behavorial change in the clinic. N.Y., 1959.
Phil 5255.58   Pastuszka, J. Charakter cztowieka. Lublin, 1959.
Phil 6980.575   Patterson, Charles H. Counseling and psychotherapy. N.Y., 1959.
Phil 2750.19.95   Peccorini Letona, Francisco. Gabriel Marcel. Barcelona, 1959.
Phil 6125.28   Penfield, Wilder. Speech and brain-mechanisms. N.J., 1959.
Phil 4225.8.95   El pensamiento de Michele Federico Sciacca; homenaje, 1908-1958. Buenos Aires, 1959.
Phil 8416.14   Perls, Hugo. Das Geheimnis der Kunst. Zürich, 1959.
Phil 5520.320   Pfeil, Alfred. Lesen und Benennen in Reaktionsversuch. Frankfurt, 1959.
Phil 1750.605   Pfleger, Karl. Kundschafter der Existenztiefe. Frankfurt, 1959.
Phil 2475.1.355   Pflug, Günther. Henri Bergson. Berlin, 1959.
Phil 6685.14   Philippe, Anthelme Philippe. Vie et paroles du maitre. Lyon, 1959.

1959 - cont.

Phil 165.160   Philosophie der Toleranz. Graz, 1959.
Phil 1750.585   Piccardt, Karel. Wijsgeerte in verval. Amsterdam, 1959.
Phil 5255.60   Piela, Franz. Die Psychologie. Köln, 1959.
Phil 8965.13   Pieper, Josef. Prudence. N.Y., 1959.
Phil 2725.35.90   Piersol, Wesley. La valeur dans la philosophie de Louis Lavelle. Paris, 1959.
Phil 2825.25   Piguet, Jean Claude. De l'esthétique à la métaphysique. La Haye, 1959.
Phil 8965.15   Pike, James A. The next day. 1st ed. Garden City, 1959.
Phil 1715.10   Pinilla, Antonio. El filófofo en la sociedad actual. Lima, 1959.
Phil 8670.19   Pinto, Raphael de Souza. Deus, pensamento e universo. Curitiba, 1959.
Phil 6325.22   Platonov, K.I. The word as a physiological and therapeutic factor. Moscow, 1959.
Phil 8080.15   Plebe, Armando. Processo all'estetica. Firenze, 1959.
Phil 346.20.5A   Polanyi, Michael. The study of man. London, 1959.
Phil 2725.30.90   Polato, Franco. Il pragmatismo epistemológico e religioso di Edouard LeRoy. 1. ed. Padova, 1959.
Phil 5066.150   Popov, A.I. Vredenie v matematicheskuiu logiku. Leningrad, 1959.
Phil 310.130   Presniakov, P.V. Teoriia poznaniia dialekticheskogo materializma. Alma-Ata, 1959.
Phil 5425.104   Princeton Meeting on the Recognition of Excellence, Princeton, 1959. The recognition of excellence. Washington, 1959.
Phil 5255.56   Progoff, Ira. Depth psychology and modern man. N.Y., 1959.
Phil 5374.210   Protasenia, P.F. Proiskhozhdenie soznaniia i ego osobennosti. Minsk, 1959.
Phil 70.1.12.10   Prudian, Georg. Ital'ianskaia vstrecha filosov; o XII Mezhdunarodnom filosofskom Kongresse. Erevan, 1959.
Phil 3745.15   Przywara, Erich. Mensch. Nürnberg, 1959.
Phil 7069.59   Puharich, A. The sacred mushroom. Garden City, 1959.
Phil 5056.1.20   Quine, Willard Van Orman. Methods of logic. N.Y., 1959.
Phil 720.46   Raab, Elmar F.X. Die Wahrheit als metaphysisches Problem. Dillingen, 1959.
Phil 960.220   Rajadhyaksha, N.D. The six systems of Indian philosophy. Bombay, 1959.
Phil 8967.10   Ranwez, E. Morale et perfection. Tournai, 1959.
Phil 5238.142   Rasey, Marie I. The nature of being human. Detroit, 1959.
Phil 165.346   Rasheed, A. The notion of existence. Lahore, 1959.
Phil 1870.145   Rauschenberger, J.P. Über das Problem der Kenntnis und des Sinnes von Erscheinung bei Berkeley. Gernsbach, 1959.
Phil 817.7.5   Rehmke, J. Grundriss der Geschichte der Philosophie. Bonn, 1959.
Phil 5780.18   Reik, Theodor. The compulsion to confess. N.Y., 1959.
Phil 3160.12.80   Rein, Mercedes. Ernst Cassirer. Montevideo, 1959.
Phil 6980.635.26   Reitman, F. Insanity, art and culture. N.Y., 1959.
Phil 3837.35   Révah, J.S. Spinoza et le Dr. Juan de Prado. Paris, 1959.
Phil 8642.9   Rey Altuna, Luis. La inmortalidad del alma a la luz de los filósofos. Madrid, 1959.
Phil 9590.27   Riazantsev, N.I. Sushchestvovet li sud'ba? Moskva, 1959.
Phil 298.12   Rieder, Albert. Die Pole der Gesamtnatur. Pfaffenhofen an der Ilm, 1959.
Phil 6315.2.240   Rieff, Philip. Freud; the mind of the moralist. N.Y., 1959.
Phil 1817.3.8   Riley, I.W. American thought. Gloucester, 1959.
Phil 6967.16   Ringel, Erwin. Einführung in die Grundprobleme der Neurose. Wien, 1959.
Phil 5257.82   Ringness, Thomas A. Psychology in theory and practice. Boston, 1959.
Phil 1135.170   Robbers, Joannes Henricus. Antieke wijsgerige opvattingen in het christelijk denkleven. Roermond, 1959.
Phil 1750.475   Roberts, D.C. Existentialism and religious belief. N.Y., 1959.
Phil 3850.27.180   Rode, Ebbe. Møde med Albert Schweitzer. København, 1959.
Phil 4368.2.85   Rodriguez Acala, Hugo. Mision y pensamiento de Francisco Romero. 1. ed. Mexico, 1959.
Phil 5780.20   Rogge, Oetje G. Why men confess. N.Y., 1959.
Phil 5257.66   Rohrbach, A. La pensée vivante; réales et techniques de la pensée créatrice. Paris, 1959.
Phil 192.104   Roig Gironella, J. Estudios de metafisica. Barcelona, 1959.
Phil 4170.10.90   Romano, F. Il pensiero filosofico di Piero Martinetti. Padova, 1959.
Phil 1182.45   Rongier, Louis. La religion astrale des pythagoriciens. Paris, 1959.
Phil 8892.70   Rosmini-Serbati, Antonio. Principi della scienza morale. Roma, 1959.
Phil 5645.54   Rosseau, René L. Les couleurs. Paris, 1959.
Phil 310.3.8   Rozental', M.M. Kategorien der materialistischen Dialektik. Moskva, 1959.
Phil 4768.2.9   Rubinshtein, Sergei L. Printsipy i puti razvitiia psikhologii. Moskva, 1959.
Phil 817.25   Rudmanśki, S. Z dziejów filozofii. Warzawa, 1959.
Phil 102.6.5   Runes, D.D. Dictionary of thought. N.Y., 1959.
Phil 817.19.4   Russell, B.R. Wisdom of the West. Garden City, 1959.
Phil 2255.1.63   Russell, Bertrand Russell. Common sense and nuclear warfare. London, 1959.
Phil 2255.1.77   Russell, Bertrand Russell. The future of science. N.Y., 1959.
Phil 2255.1.32   Russell, Bertrand Russell. My philosophical development. London, 1959.
Phil 4265.1.35   Rutenburg, V.I. Velikii ital'ianskii ateist Vanini. Moskva, 1959.
Phil 310.175   Rutkevich, M.N. Dialekticheskii materializm. Moskva, 1959.
Phil 4508.10   Ryding, Erik. Den svenska filosofins historia. Stockholm, 1959.
Phil 3450.19.210   Sacristán Luzón, Manuel. Las ideas gnoseologicas de Heidegger. Barcelona, 1959.
Phil 2880.1.60   Saint-Martin, L.C. Ecce homo. Lyon, 1959.
Phil 5258.152   Salber, Wilhelm. Der psychische Gegenstand. Bonn, 1959.
Phil 3640.550   Salin, Edgar. Vom deutschen Verhängnis. Hamburg, 1959.
Phil 8893.105   Sambarino, Mario. Investigaciones sobre la estructura aporético-dialéctica. Montevideo, 1959-60.
Phil 4018.8   Santucci, Antonio. Esistenzialismo e filosofia italiana. Bologna, 1959.
Phil 6328.35.5   Sarason, S.B. Psychological problems in mental deficiency. 3d ed. N.Y., 1959.
Phil 4225.77.30   Sarti, Sergio. L'azione creatice di Sergio Sarti. Brescia, 1959.
Phil 3960.16.5   Sassen, Ferdinand. Geschiedenis van de wijsbegerte in Nederland tot het einde der negentiende eeuw. Amsterdam, 1959.

1959 - cont.

Phil 193.237   Satyananda, Swami. World philosophy. Calcutta, 1959-1963. 3v.

Phil 5590.280   Schachtel, Ernest G. Metamorphosis. N.Y., 1959.

Phil 310.135   Schaff, Adam. Z zagadnień marksistowskiej teorii prawdy. Warszawa, 1959.

Phil 193.215   Schapp, Wilhelm. Philosophie der Geschichten. Leer, 1959.

Phil 1905.22.79   Schilpp, Paul. The philosophy of C.D. Broad. N.Y., 1959.

Phil 3640.409.2   Schlechta, Karl. Der Fall Nietzsche. München, 1959.

Phil 8598.115   Schlesinger, Ruth. Probleme seines religiösen Apriori. Berlin, 1959.

Phil 2070.143   Schmidt, Hermann. Der Begriff der Erfahrungskontinuität bei William James. Heidelberg, 1959.

Phil 9070.67   Schmidt, Karl Otto. Wunder der Lebenskunst. Büdingen, 1959.

Phil 8893.145   Schmoebz, Franz Martin. Das Naturgesetz und seine dynamische Kraft. Freiburg, 1959.

Phil 349.42   Schneider, Friedrich. Die haupt Probleme der Erkenntnistheorie. München, 1959.

Phil 6128.65   Schottlaender, Felix. Das ich und seine Welt. Stuttgart, 1959.

Phil 6128.59.5   Schroedinger, Erwin. Geist und Materie. Braunschweig, 1959.

Phil 7084.42   Schumann, Hans Joachim von. Träume der Blinden vom Standpunkt der Phänomenologie. Basel, 1959.

Phil 8598.110.5   Schuon, Frithjof. Gnosis. London, 1959.

Phil 8598.110.20   Schuon, Frithjof. Language of the self. Madras, 1959.

Phil 5850.335   Schweizerische Stiftung für Angewandte Psychologie. Angewandte Psychologie in der Schweiz. Bern, 1959.

Phil 4225.8.34   Sciacca, Michele Federico. Morte ed immortalità. Milano, 1959.

Phil 735.195   Scientific Conference on New Knowledge...1st. New knowledge in human values. N.Y., 1959.

Phil 3450.11.245   Scrimieri, G. Problemi di logica. Bari, 1959.

Phil 2520.300   Sebba, Gregor. Descartes and his philosophy. Athens, Ga., 1959.

Phil 310.672   Sedlák, Jaromír. Marxisticko-leninská teorie tžíd a třídního boje. Vyd. 1. Praha, 1959.

Phil 6980.679   Seidmann, Peter. Der Weg der Tiefenpsychologie in geistesgeschichtlicher Perspektive. Zürich, 1959.

Phil 70.50   Semana Española de Filosofía, 4th, Madrid, 1957. La forma. Madrid, 1959.

Phil 3245.88   Serwe, Arthur. Die Raum- und Zeitlehre Immanuel Hermann Fichtes. Saarbrücken, 1959.

Phil 8843.16   Shishkin, A.F. Iz istorii eticheskikh uchenii. Moskva, 1959.

Phil 3085.5.80   Sieverth, Gustav. Andre's Philosophie des Lebens. Salzburg, 1959.

Phil 818.32   Sieverth, G. Das Schicksal der Metaphysik von Thomas zu Heidegger. Einsiedeln, 1959.

Phil 9240.15   Sieverth, Gustav. Die Freiheit und das Gute. Freiburg, 1959.

Phil 8419.21   Simat, Zarko. Sotto il velame; aspetti psicologici dell'arte. 1.ed. Roma, 1959.

Phil 3850.16.21   Simmel, Georg. Georg Simmel, 1858-1918. Columbus, 1959.

Phil 1630.22   Simone, F. La reductio artium ad Sacram scripturam. Torino, 1959?

Phil 5520.330   Simonis, Hans. Die Sprachphilosophie O.F. Guppe's und G. Gerber's. Bonn, 1959.

Phil 2280.17.80   Singer, Edgar. Experience and reflection. Philadelphia, 1959.

Phil 5228.14   Skard, Ase Gruda. Psykologi og psykologar i Norge. Oslo, 1959.

Phil 5258.155A   Skinner, Burrhus F. Cumulative record. N.Y., 1959.

Phil 531.8   Skjeroheim, Hans. Objectivism and the study of man. Oslo, 1959.

Phil 8598.67.5   Skvortsov-Stepanov, I.I. Izbra mye ateisticheskie proizve - deniia. Moskva, 1959.

Phil 7069.59.10   Soal, Samuel G. The mind readers. London, 1959.

Phil 8419.34   Sobeski, M. Myśl a marmur, i inne szkice estetyczne. Wyd. 1. Warszawa, 1959.

Phil 600.60   Soler, Ricaurte. El positivismo argentino. Panamá, 1959.

Phil 5590.335   Solger, Friedrich. Das überpersönliche Leben. Berlin, 1959.

Phil 5850.343   Sonnet, André. Lerne menschen Kennen und Behandeln. Freiburg, 1959.

Phil 7069.59.25   Sonnet, Andre. Der Mensch ist voller Geheimnisse. Berlin, 1959.

Phil 7150.47   Spain. Instituto Nacional de Estadística. El suicidio en España durante medio siglo. Madrid, 1959.

Phil 193.210   Spier, Johannes. Van Thales tot sartre. Kampen, 1959.

Phil 6328.48   Spitz, René. A genetic field theory of ego formation. N.Y., 1959.

Phil 299.28   Spoerri, Walter. Spathellenistische Berichte über Welt. Basel, 1959.

Phil 5590.255.2   Spreither, Franz. Verwirklichende Vern-Zentrierung. 2. Aufl. Konstanz, 1959.

Phil 3640.600   Stambaugh, Joan. Untersuchungen zum Problem der Zeit bei Nietzsche. Den Haag, 1959.

Phil 978.49.300   Steiner, R. Aus Schicksals fragender Zeit. Dornach, 1959.

Phil 978.49.305   Steiner, R. Geisteswissenschaft als Lebensgut. Dornach, 1959.

Phil 978.49.295   Steiner, R. Major writings. 1. ed. Englewood, 1959- 6v.

Phil 978.49.280   Steiner, R. Von der Initiation. 3. Aufl. Dornach, 1959.

Phil 7069.59.50   Steinour, Harold Heiges. Exploring the unseen world. 1. ed. N.Y., 1959.

Phil 349.43   Stempkovskaia, V.I. O roli abstraktsnii v poznanii. Moskva, 1959.

Phil 6315.2.255   Stoodley, Bartlett. The concepts of Sigmund Freud. Glencoe, 1959.

Phil 193.200   Strawson, P.F. Individuals. London, 1959.

Phil 632.8   Streatfeild, D. Persephone: a study of two worlds. London, 1959.

Phil 1718.35   Strolz, Walter. Der vergessene Ursprung. Freiburg, 1959.

Phil 6128.66   Stuttgart. Institut für Psychotherapie und Tiefenpsychologie. Felix Schottlaender zum Gedächnis. Stuttgart, 1959.

Phil 4800.12   Suchodolski, Bogdan. Studia z dziejów polskiej myśli filozoficznej i naukowej. Wyd. 1. Wrocław, 1959.

Phil 6112.40   Sugrue, Thomas. There is a river; the story of Edgar Cayce. N.Y., 1959.

Phil 5627.259.15   Sundén, Hjalmar. Religionen och rollerna. Stockholm, 1959.

Phil 310.115   Sviderskii, Vladimir Io. Protivorechivost' dvizheniia i ee proiavleniia. Leningrad, 1959.

Phil 165.190   Le symbole. Paris, 1959.

1959 - cont.

Phil 974.2.60   Symonds, John. Madame Blavatsky. London, 1959.

Phil 6950.10   Symposium on Schizophrenia. Schizophrenia. N.Y., 1959.

Phil 3450.11.220   Szilasi, Wilhelm. Einführung in die Phänomenologie Edmund Husserls. Tübingen, 1959.

Phil 5390.10   Tabori, Paul. The natural science of stupidity. 1. ed. Philadelphia, 1959.

Phil 2905.1.100   Talhonët, Jean de. Le lyrisme et la mystique dans les oeuvres du Pierre Teilhard de Chardin. Paris, 1959.

Phil 4080.3.335   Tanga, Igino. L'estetica di Benedetto Croce nella storia del pensiero e della letteratura. Roma, 1959.

Phil 8599.38   Tarasov, A.A. Sotsial'naia religiia. Miunkhen, 1959.

Phil 4363.3.95   Tassara y Sangian, Luz. Mañara. Sevilla, 1959.

Phil 5722.55   Tauber, Edward. Prelogical experience. N.Y., 1959.

Phil 3425.34.32   Tavadze, I.K.V.I. Lenin o nauke logiki Gegelia. Tbilisi, 1959.

Phil 1750.22.10   Taylor, Henry O. Thought and expression in the 16th century. 2. ed. N.Y., 1959. 2v.

Phil 2905.1.10   Teilhard de Chardin, Pierre. The phenomenon of man. N.Y., 1959.

Phil 2905.1.85   Teldy-Naim, Robert. Faut-il brûler Teilhard de Chardin? Paris, 1959.

Phil 8420.19   Testa, Aldo. Filosofia dell'arte. Bologna, 1959.

Phil 5520.295   Thomsen, Robert. The psychology of thinking. Harmondsworth, 1959.

Phil 1719.5   Thyssen, Johannes. Realismus und moderne Philosophie. Bonn, 1959.

Phil 8420.9   Todd, John. The arts, artists and thinkers. London, 1959.

Phil 75.52   Totok, Wilhelm. Bibliographischer Wegweiser der philosophischen Literatur. Frankfurt, 1959.

Phil 1819.5   Trakhtenberg, O.V. Ocherki po istorii filosofii i sotsiologii Anglii XIX v. Moskva, 1959.

Phil 8674.13   Tresmoutant, Claude. Essai sur la connaissance de Dieu. Paris, 1959.

Phil 8674.14   Tugov, Iu.M. Osnovy nauchnogo ateizma. Moskva, 1959.

Phil 310.265   Tulenov, Z. Zakon kak filosofskaia kategoriia. Alma-Ata, 1959.

Phil 1020.60.5   Ulken, H.Z. Islam duzancesi ve tarihteki yeri. Ankara, 1959.

Phil 5409.8   Union des Religieuses Enseignantes. L'éducation de l'espérance. Paris, 1959?

Phil 8062.6   Utitz, Emil. Bemerkungen zur altgriechischen Kunsttheorie. Berlin, 1959.

Phil 8980.866   Vagovič, Stefano. Etica comunista. Roma, 1959.

Phil 2920.2.30   Vallin, Georges. Être et individualite. Paris, 1959.

Phil 1750.670   Valori, Paolo. Il metodo fenomenologico e la fondazione della filosofia. Roma, 1959.

Phil 4710.82   Vasetskii, G.S. Russkaia progressivnaia filosficheskaia mysl' XIX veka. Moskva, 1959.

Phil 3460.90   Vecchiotti, Icilio. Premessa a Jacobi. 1. ed. Roma, 1959.

Phil 1721.7   Vélez Correa, Jaime. Historia de la filosofia moderna y contemporánea. Bogotá, 1959.

Phil 5627.259.5   Vetter, George. Magic and religion. London, 1959.

Phil 5838.259   Viaud, Gaston. Les instincts. Paris, 1959.

Phil 4260.17.10   Vico, G.B. Opere. Milano, 1959.

Phil 4260.31   Vico, G.B. Il pensiero di Giambattista Vico. Torino, 1959.

Phil 5520.270   Vieira de Almeida, F. Aspectos de filosofia da linguagen. Coimbra, 1959.

Phil 1526.4.10   Vignaux, Paul. Philosophy in the Middle Ages. N.Y., 1959.

Phil 6980.770   Vinchon, Jean. La magie du dession. Paris, 1959.

Phil 4983.74.31   Virasoro, M.A. Desesperación y rebeldía en la conciencia contemporánea. Bahia Blanca, 1959.

Phil 7069.59.15   Visser, B.J.J. Parapsychologie, paragnosie. Roermond, 1959.

Phil 3552.450   Vitale, Ignazio. L'armonia prestabilita in Leibniz. Padova, 1959.

Phil 4372.1.40   Vives, Juan Luis. De anima et vita. Torino, 1959.

Phil 196.34   Vogel, Arthur A. Reality. London, 1959.

Phil 3195.6.140   Waesimann, A. Dilthey o la lírica del historicismo. Tucumán, 1959.

Phil 197.80   Wagner, Hans. Philosophie und Reflexion. München, 1959.

Phil 3640.610   Wahl, J.A. La pensée philosophique de Nietzsche. Paris, 1959.

Phil 3425.257.10   Wahl, Jean A. Commentaires de la logique de Hegel. Paris, 1959.

Phil 5592.100   Wallis, Ingeborg. Formen und Ausprägung der seelischen Nachreifung. Berlin, 1959.

Phil 8612.49   Wasmuth, E. Vom Sinn des Todes. Heidelberg, 1959.

Phil 9070.85   Way, Joseph. Happiness for you now. 2d ed. Adyar, 1959.

Phil 4363.9   Weber, Wilhelm. Wirtschaftethik am Vorabend des Liberalismus. Münster, 1959.

Phil 5520.300   Weinberg, Harry. Levels of knowing and existence. N.Y., 1959.

Phil 8400.31   Weitz, M. Problems in aesthetics. N.Y., 1959.

Phil 6692.10.5   Weitzenhoffer, André M. Stanford hypnotic suseptibility scale. Palo Alto, 1959.

Phil 5262.4.50   Wellek, Albert. Der Kückfall in die Methodenkrise der Psychologie. Göttingen, 1959.

Phil 9240.20   Welte, Bernhard. Über das Böse. Basel, 1959.

Phil 2050.270   Wenzel, Leonhard. David Humes politische Philosophie in ihrem Zusammenhang mit seiner gesamten Lehre. Inaug. Diss. Koln? 1959.

Phil 5262.32.6   Werner, Heinz. Einführung in die Entwicklungspsychologie. 4. Aufl. München, 1959.

Phil 5262.31.25A   Wertheimer, M. Productive thinking. N.Y., 1959. 2v.

Phil 525.180   Weyergans, Franz. Mystiques parmi nous. Paris, 1959.

Phil 2340.17.30   White, Morton Gabriel. Religion, politics, and the higher learning. Cambridge, 1959.

Phil 2340.10.28   Whitehead, Alfred North. American essays in social philosophy. N.Y., 1959.

Phil 3925.17.25   Wigeroma, Baltus. Wordende waarheid. 's Gravenhage, 1959.

Phil 8602.60   Wild, John. Human freedom and social order. Darban, N.C., 1959.

Phil 5068.46   Wilson, Max. Über das Kriterium der Verifizierbarkeit. Berlin, 1959.

Phil 5520.290   Wilson, Neil. The concept of language. Toronto, Canada, 1959.

Phil 6319.1.210   Winckel, Erna van de. De l'inconscient à Dieu. Paris, 1959.

Phil 3850.18.165   Wojtyta, B. Ocena mózliwości zbudowania etybi chresc. Lublin, 1959.

Phil 6319.1.206   Wolff, Toni. Studien zu C.G. Jungs Psychologie. Zürich, 1959.

Phil 2520.295   Wolzogen, J.L. Urvagi do medytacji metafizycznych René Descartés. Warszawa, 1959.

Phil 8423.21   Worringer, W. Abstraktion und Einfühlung. München, 1959.

Chronological Listing

1959 - cont.

Phil 3845.3 Zac, Sylvain. La morale de Spinoza. Paris, 1959.
Phil 1750.774 Zea, Leopoldo. La cultura y el hombre de nuestros días. México, 1959.
Phil 8689.100 Zimmerman, Paul A. Darwin, evolution, and creation. Saint Louis, 1959.
Phil 3507.10 Zocher, Rudolf. Kants Grundlehre. Erlangen, 1959.
Phil 1750.166.125 Zuidema, S.U. Baanbrekers van het humanisme. Franeker, 1959.
Phil 8715.5 Zum Felde, Alberto. Croisto y nosotros. Montevideo, 1959.
Phil 8680.5 Zuver, Dudley. Retreat to reality. N.Y., 1959.
Phil 5835.3.5 Zweig, Adam. Tierpsychologische Beiträge zur Psylogenese der ich-über-ich-instanzen. Bern, 1959.
Phil 5835.3 Zweig, Adam. Tierpsychologische Beiträge zur Psylogenese der ich-über-ich-instanzen. Bern, 1959.

196-

Phil 8673.20.5 The atheist's handbook. n.p., 196-.
Phil 3483.84 Besse, Guy. La morale selon Kant et selon Marx. Paris, 196-.
VPhil 9590.30 De Condé, Minerva E. Forever into the past and future. Boston, 196-.
Phil 3425.612 Garauly, Roger. Le problème Hégélien. Paris, 196-.
Phil 310.225.5 Glezerman, G.E. The laws of social development. Moscow, 196-?
Phil 9400.26 Gonçalves Viana, Mário. Psicologia da maturidade e da velhice. Porto, 196-.
Phil 5411.8 Gonçalves Viana, Mário. Psicologia do ódio. Porto, 196-.
Phil 5590.19.1 Linton, Ralph. The cultural background of personality. N.Y., 196-?
Phil 1523.16 Sprengard, Karl Anton. Systematisch-historische Untersuchungen zur Philosophie des XIV. Jahrhunderts. Bonn, 196-.

1960

Phil 4962.5.5 Abad Carretero, Luis. Vida y sentido. México, 1960.
Phil 8690.12 Abelé, Jean. Le christianisme se désintéressé-t-il de la science? Paris, 1960.
Phil 7069.60.25 Abreu Filho, Julio. Rosa dos ventos; artigos e palestras. São Paulo, 1960.
Phil 7084.36 Abu Schirin. Das goldene ägyptisch-arabische Traumbuch. Heidenheim, 1960.
Phil 310.185 Academia Republicci Populare Romîne. Bucuresti, 1960.
Phil 175.50 Adamczyk, S. Matafzika ogólna czyli ontologia. Lublin, 1960.
Phil 1145.90 Adkins, Arthur. Merit and responsibility. Oxford, 1960.
Phil 1145.90.1 Adkins, Arthur. Merit and responsibility. Oxford, 1960[1970]
Phil 5240.49 Adrian, E.D.A. Factors in mental evolution. Oxford, 1960.
Phil 310.245 Afanas'ev, V.G. Osnovy marksistskoi filosofii. Moskva, 1960.
Phil 310.385 Ahlberg, René. Dialektische Philosophie und Gesellschaft in der Sowiet-Union. Berlin, 1960.
Phil 4803.130.35 Ajdukiewicz, Kazimierz. Jezyk i poznanie. Wyd. 1. Warszawa, 1960-
Phil 310.6.15 Akademiia Nauk SSSR. Institut Filosofii. Grundlagen der marxistischen Philosophie. Berlin, 1960.
Phil 310.198 Akademiia Nauk SSSR. Institut Filosofii. Problemy istorii filosofskoi i sotsiologicreskoi mysli XIX veka. Moskva, 1960.
Phil 310.195 Akademiia Nauk SSSR. Institut Filosofii. Voprosy dialekticheskogo materializma. Moskva, 1960.
Phil 331.21 Akademiia Nauk SSSR. Kafedra Filosofii. Voprosy teorii poznaniia i logiki. Moskva, 1960.
Phil 8400.15 Akademiia Khudozhestv SSSR. Institut Teorii i Istorii Iskusstva. Ocherki marksistsko-leninskoi estetiki. Moskva, 1960.
Phil 5650.36 Akademiia Nauk SSSR. Biblioteka. Fiziologicheskaia akustika. Moskva, 1960.
Phil 5257.69 Akademiia Nauk SSSR. Institut Filosofii, Sektor Psikologii. Protsess myshleniia i zakonomernosti analiza, Sinteza i obobshcheniia. Moskva, 1960.
Phil 270.105.5 Akademiia Nauk SSSR. Institute Filosofii. Problema prichinnost v sovremeni fizike. Moskva, 1960.
Phil 8690.14 Akademiia Nauk SSSR. Institutii Filosofii. Dostizheniia estestvoznaniia i religiia. Moskva, 1960.
Phil 8655.18 Akademiia Nauk SSSR. Muzei Istorii Religii i Ateizma. Istoriia pravoslaviia i russkogo ateizma. Leningrad, 1960.
Phil 310.250 Akhmedli, D. Svoboda i neobkhodimost'. Baku, 1960.
Phil 4080.3.365 Albeggiani, Ferdinando. Inizio e svolgimento della filosofia dello spirito di Benedetto Croce. Palermo, 1960?
Phil 4000.15 Alberghi, Sante. Metafisica e spiritualisti italiani contemporanei. Milano, 1960.
Phil 310.230 Alekseev, M.N. Dialekticheskaia logika. Moskva, 1960.
Phil 6310.4.25 Alexander, Franz G. The western mind in transition. N.Y., 1960.
Phil 575.215A Allport, G.W. Personality and social encounter. Boston, 1960.
Phil 4060.9.35 Amendola, Evakühn. Vita can Giovanni Amendola. Firenze, 1960.
Phil 5585.175 Ames, Adelbert. The morning notes of Adelbert Ames, Jr. New Brunswick, N.J., 1960.
Phil 6947.1854 Amsterdam. Valerius-Kliniek. Een halve eeuw arbeid op psychiatrisch-neurologischgen, terrein 1910-1960. Wagenin, 1960.
Phil 5585.170 Anan'ev, B.G. Psikhologiia chuvstvennogo poznaniia. Moskva, 1960.
Phil 525.215 Andrae, Tor. Islamische Mystiker. Stuttgart, 1960.
Phil 310.305 Andreev, I.D. Dialekticheskii materializm. Moskva, 1960.
Phil 8401.25 Antoni, Carlo. Chiose all'estetica, con un profile dell'autore a cura di G. Calogero. Roma, 1960.
Phil 5592.145 Anzieu, D. Les méthodes projectives. Paris, 1960.
Phil 8400.12 Arata, Rodolfo. I fondamenti del giudizio estetico. Bologna, 1960.
Phil 672.199 Archivio di Filosofia. Tempo e intenzionalità. Padova, 1960.
Phil 1630.10 Archivio di Filosofia. Umanesimo e esoterismo. Padova, 1960.
Phil 1870.142 Armstrong, D.M. Berkeley's theory of vision. Victoria, 1960.
Phil 5465.95 Armstrong, Frank A. Idea-tracking. N.Y., 1960.
Phil 5400.145 Arnold, Magda B. Emotion and personality. N.Y., 1960. 2v.
Phil 6110.22.2 Ashby, William R. Design for a brain. 2. ed. N.Y., 1960.

1960 - cont.

Phil 3482.13 Asmus, V.F. Die Philosophie Kants. Berlin, 1960.
Phil 8092.4 Assunto, Rosario. Teoremi e problemi di estetica contemporanea. Milano, 1960.
Phil 1845.11 Ayer, Alfred Jules. Philosophy and language. Oxford, 1960.
Phil 2477.15.10 Bachelard, Gaston. La poétique de la rêverie. Paris, 1960.
Phil 420.2 Bahm, Archie J. Types of intuition. Albuquerque, 1960[1961]
Phil 5593.60 Bahm, Ewald B. Psychodiagnostisches Vademecum. Bern, 1960.
Phil 2905.1.150 Bailly, Thomas de. Quodlibets. Paris, 1960.
Phil 5241.128 Baker, Lawrence. General experimental psychology. N.Y., 1960.
Phil 1701.45 Bakradze, K.S. Ocherki po istorii noveishei i sovremennoi burzhuaznoi filosofii. Tbilisi, 1960.
Phil 4070.7.5 Banfi, Antonio. Principi di una teoria della ragione. Milano, 1960.
Phil 1955.6.170 Bansola, Adriano. L'etica di John Dewey. Milano, 1960.
Phil 5520.360 Barbara, Dominick A. Psychological and psychiatric aspects of speech and hearing. Springfield, 1960.
Phil 645.45 Baumer, Franklin. Religion and the rise of scepticism. 1st ed. N.Y., 1960.
Phil 8402.8.5 Bayer, Raymond. Von der Methode der Ästhetik. Darmstadt, 1960.
Phil 8581.105 Beck, Lewis W. Six secular philosophers. 1. ed. N.Y., 1960.
Phil 3483.75 Beck, Lewis White. A commentary on Kant's Critique of practical reason. Chicago, 1960.
Phil 1750.640 Begiashvili, A.F. Metod analiza v sovremennoi burzhuaznoi filosofii. Tbilisi, 1960.
Phil 5650.38 Békésy, Georg von. Experiments in hearing. N.Y., 1960.
Phil 3552.400 Belaval, Yvon. Leibniz critique de Descartes. Paris, 1960.
Phil 4807.2 Bělka, František. Kapitaly z dějin českého revolučního myšlení. Vyd. 1. Havlíčkův Brod, 1960.
Phil 8876.91.11 Berdiaev, N.A. The destiny of man. N.Y., 1960.
Phil 8400.17 Berestnev, V.F. Osnovy marksistsko-leninskoi estetiki. Moskva, 1960.
Phil 75.68 Berg, Jan. Selektiv bibliografi i teoretisk filosofi. Stockholm, 1960.
Phil 8876.145 Berge, André. Les maladies de la vertu. Paris, 1960.
Phil 165.240 Bergman, S. Studies in philosophy. Jerusalem, 1960.
Phil 5068.18.5 Bergman, Gustav. Meaning and existence. Madison, 1960.
Phil 2475.1.41 Bergson, Henri. Time and free will; an essay on the immediate data of consciousness. N.Y., 1960.
Phil 2138.145 Berlin, Isaiah. John Stuart Mill and the ends of life. London, 1960?
Phil 3483.82 Berni, M. Il criticismo kantiano. Verona, 1960.
Phil 5649.28 Berning, A. Experimentelle Untersuchungen von Bewegungsstilen. Inaug. Diss. Bonn, 1960.
Phil 2610.105 Berr, Henri. Du scepticisme de Gassendi. Paris, 1960.
Phil 1106.18 Bertozzi, A. Saggi sul pensiero antico. Padova, 1960.
Phil 282.23 Bianchi, Ugo. Teogonie e cosmogonie. Roma, 1960.
Phil 3120.15.97.15 Bickel, Lothar. Aussen und Innen. Zürich, 1960.
Phil 6978.12.15 Binswanger, Ludwig. Melancholie und Manie. Pfullingen, 1960.
Phil 5241.140 Birnbaum, W. Organisches Denken. Tübingen, 1960.
Phil 8876.157 Biroud, K. Manevi limler metadu olorok anlama. Ankara, 1960.
Phil 5886.15 Birren, James Emmett. Handbook of aging and the individual. Chicago, 1960.
Phil 1955.6.160 Blewett, John. John Dewey. N.Y., 1960.
Phil 3120.55.30 Bloch, Ernst. Das Morgen im Heute; eine Auswahl. Frankfurt, 1960.
Phil 176.69.12 Bloch, Ernst. Spuren. Berlin, 1960.
Phil 3110.42 Böhme, J. Vom Lebendigen Glauben. Gütersloh, 1960.
Phil 282.21 Bondi, Hermann. Cosmology. 2. ed. Cambridge, Eng., 1960.
Phil 282.21.5 Bondi, Hermann. The universe at large. Garden City, 1960.
Phil 2255.1.125 Bonifacino, V. Ensayos beligerantes: Bertrand Russell, James Joyce. Montevideo, 1960.
Phil 8951.29 Borowski, A. Teologia moralna. Wyd. 2. Lublin, 1960.
Phil 1750.595 Bos, Julius G. Existentiële zin en onzim. Den Haag, 1960.
Phil 182.94.85 Brandenstein, Béla. Teleologisches Denken. Bonn, 1960.
Phil 3425.576 Braum, Hermann. Realität und Reflexion. Heidelberg, 1960.
Phil 1701.40 Bronowski, Jacob. The Western intellectual tradition. N.Y., 1960.
Phil 585.75 Bruning, Walther. Philosophische Anthropologie. Stuttgart, 1960.
Phil 1701.47 Brytninger i tidens tankelin. Oslo, 1960.
Phil 3120.30.39.10 Buber, Martin. Begegnung. Stuttgart, 1960.
Phil 4710.83 Budilova, E.A. Bor'ba materializma i idealizma v russkoi psikhologicheskoi nauke. Moskva, 1960.
Phil 5241.70.5 Bühler, Karl. Das Gestaltprinzip im Leben des Menschen und der Tiere. Bern, 1960.
Phil 575.240 Bui-Kim-Duong, J.B. L'épanouissement de la personnalité humaine par la conformité au Christ. Fribourg/Suisse, 1960.
Phil 5241.135 Bulyne, D.E. Conflict. N.Y., 1960.
Phil 5520.370 Bunge, Mario. Antologia semantica. Buenos Aires, 1960.
Phil 8610.958.5 Buri, Fritz. Die Substanz des christlichen Glaubens, ihr Verlust und ihre Neugewinnung. Tübingen, 1960.
Phil 8980.252.2 Bychkova, N.V. Moral'kak ee ponimaiut kommunisty. 2. izd. Moskva, 1960.
Phil 8430.10 Caillais, Roger. Meduse et cie. Paris, 1960.
Phil 177.105.2 Calogero, G. Lezioni di filosofia. Torino, 1960. 3v.
Phil 4080.18.5 Calogero, Guido. Scritti. Firenze, 1960. 2v.
Phil 4073.65 Campanella, Tommaso. De homine. Roma, 1960.
Phil 4073.34 Campanella, Tommaso. Legazioni ai Maomettani. Firenze, 1960.
Phil 4073.36 Campanella, Tommaso. Monarchia Messiae. Torino, 1960.
Phil 4073.43 Campanella, Tommaso. Il peccato originale. Roma, 1960.
Phil 1930.16.30 Canger, Georg P. Synoptic naturalism. Minneapolis, 1960.
Phil 5238.115 Cantril, Hadley. Reflections on the human venture. N.Y., 1960.
Phil 4215.9.80 Caracciolo, C. L'idealismo e i suoi limiti nel pensiero di Antonio Renda. Palermo, 1960.
Phil 8403.37 Carbonara, C. Ricerche per un'estetica del contenuto. Napoli, 1960.
Phil 5066.8.6 Carnap, Rudolf. Einfuhrung in die symbolische Logik mit besonderer Berucksichtigung. Wien, 1960.
Phil 4303.10 Cartezon Alvarez, Daniel. De la saudade y sus formas. Nueva York, 1960.
Phil 2475.1.385 Chanyshev, A.N. Filosfiia Anri Bergsona. Moskva, 1960.

Chronological Listing

Phil 165.285   Charisteria; rozprawy filozoficzne, złozone w darze Władysławowi Tatarkiewiczowi. Warszawa, 1960.

Phil 8692.19   Chauvin, Rémy. God of the scientists. Baltimore, 1960.

Phil 960.225   Chennahesavan, Sarasvate. The concept of mind in Indian philosophy. London, 1960.

Phil 575.220   Chevalier, Charles. La confidence et la personne humaine. Paris, 1960.

Phil 8403.38   Chiari, Joseph. Realism and imagination. London, 1960.

Phil 3450.19.109.2   Chiodi, Pietro. L'ultimo Heidegger. 2e ed. Torino, 1960.

Phil 4065.165   Ciardo, Manlio. Giordano Bruno tra l'umanesimo e lo stoicismo. Bologna, 1960.

Phil 8827.10   Ciarletta, Nicola. Eticità e cultura. 1. ed. Milano, 1960.

Phil 1955.6.165   Clark, Gordon H. Dewey. Philadelphia, 1960.

Phil 165.205   Clark, John A. The student seeks an answer. Waterville, Me., 1960.

Phil 165.195   Classics in philosophy and ethics. N.Y., 1960.

Phil 1750.166.130   Cobban, Alfred. In search of humanity. London, 1960.

Phil 1750.166.132   Cobban, Alfred. In search of humanity. N.Y., 1960.

Phil 270.75.5   Cohen, John. Chance, skill, and luck. Baltimore, 1960.

Phil 735.205   Coleburt, Russell. The search for values. London, 1960.

Phil 5242.58   Coleman, J.C. Personality dynamics and effective behavior. Chicago, 1960.

Phil 165.200   Collins, James. Readings in ancient and medieval philosophy. Westminster, 1960.

Phil 2520.325   Cómbès, J. Le dessein de la sagesse cartésienne. Lyon, 1960.

Phil 165.235   Comoth, R. Philosophes du dix neuvième siècle. Bruxelles, 1960.

Phil 70.77   Conference on Psychological Scaling, Princeton, New Jersey. Psychological scaling: theory and applications. N.Y., 1960.

Phil 665.88   Conrad-Martius, H. Die Geistseele des Menschen. München, 1960.

Phil 802.15.5   Copleston, F. A history of philosophy. Westminster, 1960. 8v.

Phil 1107.4.3   Cornford, F.M. Before and after Socrates. Cambridge, Eng., 1960.

Phil 3552.395   Costabel, Pierre. Leibniz et la dynamique. Paris, 1960.

Phil 3850.27.170   Cousins, Norman. Dr. Schweitzer of Lambaréné. N.Y., 1960.

Phil 2115.172   Cox, Richard H. Locke on war and peace. Oxford, 1960.

Phil 177.130   Craig, Hardin. New lamps for old. Oxford, 1960.

Phil 4115.106   Crescenzo, G. de. Pietro Luciani e il giobertismo. Napoli, 1960.

Phil 9075.65   Crippa, Romeo. Studi nella coscienza etica e religiosa del seicento. Brescia, 1960. 3v.

Phil 1750.754   La crise de la raison dans la pensée contemporaine. Bruges, 1960.

Phil 2905.1.82   Cristiani, Léon. Pierre Teilhard de Chardin. London, 1960.

Phil 8952.15   Crofts, Ambrose M. Moral philosophy. Dublin, 1960.

Phil 5592.155   Dahlstrom, W.G. An MMPI handbook. Minneapolis, 1960.

Phil 730.20   Dalos, Patrick M. The critical value of concepts and universal ideas. 2. ed. Rome, 1960.

Phil 5590.340.5   David, Henry Philip. Perspectives in personality research. N.Y., 1960.

Phil 8658.22   Delanglade, Jean. Le probleme de Dieu. Paris, 1960.

Phil 531.6   Dennes, William R. Some dilemmas of naturalism. N.Y., 1960.

Phil 165.225   Derbolav, Josef. Erkenntnis und Verantwortung. Düsseldorf, 1960.

Phil 1930.10.90   Deregibus, A. Il razionalismo di Morris R. Cohen. Torino, 1960.

Phil 8599.16.10   De Tribus Impostoribus. De tribus impostoribus. Berlin, 1960.

Phil 6945.17.2   Deutsch, Albert. The mentally ill in America. 2. ed. N.Y., 1960.

Phil 5243.55   Deutsch, Jaroslav A. The structural basis of behavior. Chicago, 1960.

Phil 1955.6.33   Dewey, John. Knowing and the known. Boston, 1960.

Phil 3120.30.83   Diamand, Malcolm L. Martin Buber, Jewish existentialist. N.Y., 1960.

Phil 5500.20   Dijkhuis, J.H.M. Het beoordelen in de psychologie. Utrecht, 1960.

Phil 1750.166.135   Dijkhuis, P. Polariteitsbesef als een der fundamenten van het humanisme. Assen, 1960.

Phil 3195.6.76   Dilthey, Wilhelm. Der junge Dilthey. 2. Aufl. Stuttgart, 1960.

Phil 5243.65   Dirks, Heinz. Psychologie. Gütersloh, 1960.

Phil 8980.329   Dmitrenko, A.P. Kommunisticheskaia moral' i voinskii dolg. Moskva, 1960.

Phil 6111.16.20   Dmitriev, V.D. Vydaiushchiisia russkii uchenyi V.M. Bekhterev. Cheboksary, 1960.

Phil 5043.33.5   Dopp, Joseph. Formal logic. N.Y., 1960.

Phil 7055.251   Drage, Charles. William King's profession. London, 1960.

Phil 2725.40   Drochner, Karl Heinz. Darstellung einiger Grundzüge des literarischen Werks von Pierre de la Primaudaye. Berlin, 1960.

Phil 6060.56   Dubouchet, Jeanne. L'analogie des phenomenes physiques et psychiques et l'écriture. Bruxelles, 1960.

Phil 310.285   Dubská, Irena. K problematice stranickosti a vědeckosti marksistsko-leninskaia filosofii. Praha, 1960.

Phil 8404.22   Dunham, Barrows. The artist in society. N.Y., 1960.

Phil 5465.105   Durand, G. Les structures anthropologiques de l'imaginajre. Grenoble, 1960.

Phil 7150.27.15   Durkheim, E. Le suicide. Paris, 1960.

Phil 7069.60.10   East, John. Man the immortal. London, 1960.

Phil 6114.15.3   Eccles, J.C. The neurophysiological basis of mind. Oxford, 1960.

Phil 5044.10   Efiroo, S.A. Ot Gegelia k Dzhennago. Moskva, 1960.

Phil 8405.8.2   Ekman, Rolf. Estetiska problem. 2. uppl. Lund, 1960.

Phil 8405.8.5   Ekman, Rolf. Problems and theories in modern aesthetics. Lund, 1960.

Phil 4210.185.5   Emery, Cuthbert Joseph. The Rosminians. London, 1960.

Phil 179.42   Engel, S. Morris. The problem of tragedy. Frederiction, N.B., 1960.

Phil 8879.33   Engst, Jaroslav. Nekotorye problemy nauchnoi etiki. Moskva, 1960.

Phil 8879.32   Ewing, Alfred. Ethics. London, 1960.

Phil 165.275   Experiencia de la vida. Madrid, 1960.

Phil 6314.11   Eysenck, Hans J. Behaviour therapy and the neuroses. Oxford, 1960.

Phil 5590.45.5   Eysenck, Hans Jurgen. Experiments in personality. London, 1960. 2v.

Phil 4110.12.30   Fancelli, M. Discorso sulla speranza. Messina, 1960.

Phil 310.60.5   Fataliev, K.M. Marksistko-leninskaia filosofii i estestroznaniia. Moskva, 1960.

Phil 6980.289   Fenichel, Otto. Problemas de ténica psicoanalitica. México, 1960.

Phil 3235.20   Feuerbach, Ludwig. Manifestes philosophiques; textes choisis. Paris, 1960.

Phil 5815.8.3   Filloux, Jean Claude. Psychologie des animaux. 3. éd. Paris, 1960.

Phil 90.6   Filosofskaia entsiklopediia. Moskva, 1960-70. 5v.

Phil 6980.292   Findl, Fritz. Die psychiatriochen Theorien Rudolf Arndt's. München, 1960.

Phil 3640.452   Flam, Leopold. Wie was Nietzsche? Antwerpen, 1960.

Phil 180.78   Forest, Aimé. Orientazioni metafisiche. Milano, 1960.

Phil 2605.8.30   Fouéré, René. Du temporel à l'intemporel. Paris, 1960. 2v.

Phil 180.80   Fougeyrollas, Pierre. La philosophie en question. Paris, 1960.

Phil 1830.30   Frankel, Charles. The golden age of American philosophy. N.Y., 1960.

Phil 3808.234   Frankfurt am Main. Stadt- und Universitätsbibliothek. Arthur Schopenhauer. Frankfurt, 1960.

Phil 310.300   Frantsev, I.P. Istoricheskii materializm i sotsial'naia filosofiia sovremennoi burzhazii. Moskva, 1960.

Phil 3270.12.35   Frege, Gottlob. Translations from the philosophical writings of Gottlob Frege. Oxford, 1960.

Phil 9540.9   Freie Akademie Nüremberg. Toleranz eine Grundforderung geschichtlichen Existenz. Nürnberg, 1960.

Phil 1750.166.140   Frerichs, J.G. Waarde van de mens en menselijke waardigheid. Zaandam, 1960.

Phil 6315.17.8   Freud, Anna. Psychoanalysis for teachers and parents. Boston, 1960.

Phil 6315.2.66   Freud, Sigmund. Briefe 1873-1939. Frankfurt, 1960.

Phil 5525.6.10   Freud, Sigmund. Jokes and their relation to the unconscious. London, 1960.

Phil 6315.2.67   Freud, Sigmund. Letters. 1st. ed. N.Y., 1960.

Phil 6315.2.14   Freud, Sigmund. Die Unbewusste. Frankfurt, 1960.

Phil 5500.24   Friedrich-Ebert-Stiftung. Überwindung von Vorurteilen. 2. Aufl. Hannover, 1960.

Phil 9513.12   Fröhlich, C.W. Über den Menschen und seine Verhältnisse. Berlin, 1960.

Phil 9495.159.2   Fuchs, Josef Jesuit. De castitate et ordine sexuali. 2nd ed. Roma, 1960.

Phil 8660.20   Fuerstenberg, E. Der Selbstwiderspruch des philosophischen Atheismus. Regensburg, 1960.

Phil 210.31   Gadamer, Hans Georg. Wahrheit und Methode. Tübingen, 1960.

Phil 310.330   Gak, G.M. Formy obshchestvennogo soznaniia. Moskva, 1960.

Phil 310.275   Gak, G.M. Uchenie ob obshchestvennom soznanii v svete teorii poznaniia. Moskva, 1960.

Phil 585.110   Gal'perin, S.I. Kritika teorii biologizatsii cheloveka. Leningrad, 1960.

Phil 3450.11.240   Gaos, J. Introducción a la fenomenología. México, 1960.

Phil 1750.776   Gaos, José. Museo de filosófos. 1. ed. México, 1960.

Phil 337.16.5   Garaudy, Roger. Die materialistische Erkenntnistheorie. Berlin, 1960.

Phil 2406.3   Garaudy, Roger. Perspectives de l'homme. 2e éd. Paris, 1960.

Phil 2880.8.142   Garaudy, Roger. Questions à Jean Paul Sartre. Paris, 1960.

Phil 1750.625   Garin, Eugenio. Bilancio della fenomenologia. Padova, 1960.

Phil 8831.10   Garnett, Arthur. Ethics. N.Y., 1960.

Phil 310.240   Georgiev, F.I. Kategorii materialisticheskoi dialektiki. Moskva, 1960.

Phil 4210.191   Giacon, Carlo. L'oggettivita in Antonio Rosmini. Milano, 1960.

Phil 6315.2.265   Gicklhorn, Josef. Sigmund Freuds akademische Laufbahn im. Wien, 1960.

Phil 8407.32   Giesz, L. Phänomenologie des Kitsches. Heidelberg, 1960.

Phil 1607.5A   Gilbert, Neal. Renaissance concepts of method. N.Y., 1960.

Phil 181.73.10   Gilson, E. Le philosophe et la théologie. Paris, 1960.

Phil 1511.3.17   Gilson, Étienne. Introduction à la philosophie chrétienne. Paris, 1960.

Phil 6980.328   Glasser, William. Mental health or mental illness? N.Y., 1960.

Phil 310.225   Glezerman, G.E. Ozakonakh obskchestvennogo razvitiia. Moskva, 1960.

Phil 31.5.5   Goerdt, Wilhelm. Fragen der Philosophie ein Materialbeitrag...im Spiegel der Zeitschrift "Voprosy Filosofii", 1947-1956. Köln, 1960.

Phil 70.90   Gonseth, Ferdinand. La metaphysique et l'ouverture. Paris, 1960.

Phil 806.36   Gonzalez Cominero, N. Historia philosophiae. v.1. Romae, 1960. 2v.

Phil 181.122   Gonzalo Cosar, M. Introducción a la filosofia. Madrid, 1960.

Phil 3195.15.83   Gorn, Erhard. Die Philosophie Hugo Dinglers. Dusseldorf, 1960.

Phil 535.40   Goudsblom, Johan. Nihilisme en cultuur. Amsterdam, 1960.

Phil 525.190   Grandjean, Louis E. Alt anden gang. København, 1960.

Phil 5627.260.5   Graneris, Giuseppe. La vita della religion e nella storia delle religioni. Torino, 1960.

Phil 337.22   Granger, Gilles Gaston. Pensée formelle et sciences de l'homme. Paris, 1960.

Phil 1806.5   Grant, George. Philosophy in the mass age. N.Y., 1960.

Phil 5585.224   Grauman, C.F. Grundlagen einer Phänomenologie und Psychologie der Perspektivität. Berlin, 1960.

Phil 1806.10   Grave, Selwyn A. The Scottish philosophy of common sense. Oxford, 1960.

Phil 5465.110   Greenacre, P. Estudios psicoanalíticos sobre la actividad creadora. 1. ed. México, 1960.

Phil 2880.8.132   Greene, Norman. Jean Paul Sartre. Ann Arbor, 1960.

Phil 1111.2   Grenet, P.B. Histoire de la philosophie ancienne. Paris, 1960.

Phil 1020.40   Grigorian, S.N. Iz istorii filosofii Srednei Azii i Irana VII-XII vv. Moskva, 1960.

Phil 1750.410.2   Grimsley, Ronald. Existentialist thought. 2nd ed. Cardiff, 1960.

Phil 310.405   Gropp, R.O. Was ist der dialektische Materialismus? München, 1960.

Phil 8419.43.80   Grunert, B. Solgers Lehre vom Schönen in ihrem Verhältnis zur Kunstlehre. Marburg, 1960.

Phil 5246.68   Guirdham, Arthur. Man: divine or social. London, 1960.

Phil 2475.1.380   Guitton, Jean. La vocation de Bergson. Paris, 1960.

Chronological Listing

1960 - cont.

Phil 6116.28 Gurin, Gerald. Americans view their mental health. N.Y., 1960.
Phil 4065.118.5 Guzzo, Augusto. Giordano Bruno. Torino, 1960.
Phil 1750.98 Haag, Karl Hanz. Kritik der neueren Ontologie. Stuttgart, 1960.
Phil 1750.100 Haag, Karl Hanz. Kritik der neueren Ontololgie. Stuttgart, 1960.
Phil 3007.14 Haan, A.A.M. de. Het wijsgerig onderwijs aan het gymnasium illustre. Harderwijk, 1960.
Phil 1707.20 Hadas, Mases. Humanism: the Greek ideal. 1. ed. N.Y., 1960.
Phil 8620.50 Häberlin, P. Das Böse. Bern, 1960.
Phil 5520.112.1 Haerber, W.L. A scientific foundation of philosophy. Los Angeles, 1960.
Phil 182.117 Hall, E.W. Philosophical systems. Chicago, 1960.
Phil 3827.14 Hampshire, Stuart. Spinoza and the idea of freedom. London, 1960.
Phil 4120.4.89 Harris, Henry S. The social philosophy of Giovanni Gentile. Urbana, 1960.
Phil 4368.2.80 Harris, Marjorie. Francisco Romero on problems of philosophy. N.Y., 1960.
Phil 6980.348.10 Hartmann, Heinz. Psychoanalysis and moral values. N.Y., 1960.
Phil 3007.7.2A Hartmann, N. Die Philosophie des deutschen Idealismus. 2. Aufl. Berlin, 1960.
Phil 8882.73 Hawkins, Denis J.B. Man and morals. London, 1960.
Phil 325.10 Hayden Colloquium on Scientific Concept and Method, M.I.T. Evidence and inference. Chicago, 1960.
Phil 3460.91 Hebeisen, A. Friedrich Heinrich Jacobi. Bern, 1960.
Phil 3450.19.78 Heidegger, Martin. Essays in metaphysics. N.Y., 1960.
Phil 3450.19.85.2 Heidegger, Martin. Gelassenheit. 2e Aufl. Pfullingen, 1960.
Phil 3450.19.63 Heidegger, Martin. Der Ursprung des Kunstwerkes. Stuttgart, 1960.
Phil 3450.19.67 Heidegger, Martin. Was ist das- die Philosophie? 2. Aufl. Pfullingen, 1960.
Phil 7069.60.15 Heine, Hilda G. The vital sense. London, 1960.
Phil 165.175 Henrich, Dieter. Die Gegenwart der Griechen im neueren Denken. Tübingen, 1960.
Phil 8662.24 Henrich, Dieter. Der ontologische Gottesbeweis. Tübingen, 1960.
Phil 182.118 Herk, Konrad. Das leuchten des dunckels. Antwerpen, 1960.
Phil 6317.48 Hernfeld, Fred Farau. La psychologie des profondeurs, des origines à nos jours. Paris, 1960.
Phil 1707.26 Herzberg, G. Der Zeitgeist. Meisenheim, 1960.
Phil 6315.2.455 Hesnard, Angelo. L'oeuvre de Freud et son importance pour le monde moderne. Paris, 1960.
Phil 182.120 Heyde, Johannes. Wege zur Klarheit. Berlin, 1960.
Phil 9560.68 Heyst, Jacques. Hypothèse de la vérité. Versailles, 1960.
Phil 8957.12.10 Hildebrand, D. von. Transformation in Christ. Baltimore, 1960.
Phil 5400.155 Hillman, J. Emotion. London, 1960.
Phil 960.137.25 Hiriyanna, M. The mission of philosophy. Mysore, 1960.
Phil 165.210 Höfling, Helmut. Beiträge zer Philosphie und Wissenschaft. München, 1960.
Phil 288.15.10 Hoenen, Peter. The philosophy of inorganic compounds. West Baden Springs, Ind., 1960.
Phil 5477.14 Hövmann, H. Konflikt und Entscheidung. Göttingen, 1960.
Phil 2055.12.30 Hoor, Marten ten. Education for privacy. n.p., 1960.
Phil 165.185 Huber, Gerhard. Philosophie und deristliche Existenz. Basel, 1960.
Phil 3450.19.200 Huebener, Wolfgang. Untersuchungen zur Denhart Martin Heideggers. Berlin, 1960.
Phil 8870.27 Hume, Rolando. Ética inspirado o exterminio. Santa Fe, Argentina, 1960.
Phil 5780.15.2 Hunter, Edward. Brainwashing. N.Y., 1960.
Phil 338.32 Husser, Friedrich F. Zu einem Prinzip der Messung. Meisenhem am Glan, 1960.
Phil 3450.40 Husserl, Edmund. Cartesian meditations. The Hague, 1960.
Phil 3450.11.40A Husserl, Edmund. Cartesian meditations. The Hague, 1960.
Phil 530.10 Hutin, Serge. Les disciples anglais de Jacob Boehme. Paris, 1960.
Phil 8408.22 Huyghe, René. L'art et l'âme. Paris, 1960.
Phil 5590.385 Ignat'ev, E.I. Voprosy psikhologii lichnosti. Moskva, 1960.
Phil 4803.462.21 Ingarden, Roman. O dziele literackim. Warszawa, 1960.
Phil 4803.462.2 Ingarden, Roman. Spór o istnienie świata. Wyd. 2. Warszawa, 1960-61. 2v.
Phil 5238.210.6 Interamerican Congress of Psychology. 6th, Rio de Janeiro, 1959. Promovido pela Sociedade Interamericana de Psicologia com a cooperação de Associação Brasileira de Psicologia Aplicada. Rio de Janeiro, 1960.
Phil 8958.9 Iorio, Tommaso Angelo. Theologia moralis. 5. ed. Neapolis, 1960-64. 3v.
Phil 5585.190.5 Ittelson, William H. Visual space perception. N.Y., 1960.
Phil 6959.10 Jackson, Donald. The etiology of schizophrenia. N.Y., 1960.
Phil 6959.9 Jaco, E.G. The social epidemiology of mental disorders. N.Y., 1960.
Phil 4260.145 Jacobelli Isoldi, Angela Maria. G.B. Vico. Bologna, 1960.
Phil 3552.468 Jalabert, Jacques. Le Dieu de Leibniz. 1. éd. Paris, 1960.
Phil 5627.6.5.16 James, William. Varieties of religious experience. London, 1960.
Phil 2070.20 James, William. William James on psychical research. N.Y., 1960.
Phil 2675.4.5 Jankélévitch, Vladimir. Le pur et l'impur. Paris, 1960.
Phil 3475.3.76 Jaspers, Karl. Die Atombombe und die Zükunft des Menschen. München, 1960.
Phil 3475.3.55.5 Jaspers, Karl. Vernunft und Existenz. München, 1960.
Phil 3475.3.37 Jaspers, Karl. Wahrheit und Wissenschaft. München, 1960.
Phil 974.3.109 Jellinek, Karl. Das Mysterium des Menschen. Zürich, 1960. 2v.
Phil 2045.125 Jessop, T.E. Thomas Hobbes. London, 1960.
Phil 5019.5 Joja, A. Studii de logica. Bucuresti, 1960. 3v.
Phil 6959.6 Jones, Kathleen. Mental health and social policy. London, 1960.
Phil 5500.28 Jordan, Nehemiah. Decision-making under uncertainty and problem solving. Santa Monica, 1960.
Phil 6319.1.36.2 Jung, C.G. Über die Psychologie des Unbewussten. 7 Aufl. Zürich, 1960.
Phil 2750.11.147 Jung, Hava Yol. The foundation of Jacques Maritain's political philosophy. Gainesville, Florida, 1960.
Phil 5477.10 Junker, Erika. Über unterschiedliches Behalten eigener Leistungen. Frankfurt, 1960.
Phil 2905.1.110 Kahane, E. Teilhard de Chardin. Paris, 1960.

Phil 6960.15 Kahn, Theodore. Psychological techniques in diagnosis and evaluation. N.Y., 1960.
Phil 341.30 Kalinowski, J. Teoria poznania praktycznego. Lublin, 1960.
Phil 974.3.132 Kallert, Bernhard. Die Erkenntnistheorie Rudolf Steiners. Stuttgart, 1960.
Phil 8400.21 Kaloshen, F.I. Protiv revizionizma v estetike. Moskva, 1960.
Phil 720.55 Kamlah, Wilhelm. Wissenschaft, Wahrheit, Existenz. Stuttgart, 1960.
Phil 3480.67.95 Kant, Immanuel. An Immanuel Kant reader. N.Y., 1960.
Phil 3480.82.8 Kant, Immanuel. Observations on the feeling of the beautifull and sublime. Berkeley, 1960.
Phil 3480.71.8 Kant, Immanuel. Religion within the limits of reason alone. 2sd ed. La Salle, 1960.
Phil 1830.35 Kanvitz, Milton R. The American pragmatists. N.Y., 1960.
Phil 5238.120 Kaplan, Bernard. Perspectives in psychological theory. N.Y., 1960.
Phil 291.10 Kapp, Reginald O. Towards a unified cosmology. London, 1960.
Phil 5250.37.11 Katz, David. Handbuch der Psychologie. Basel, 1960.
Phil 341.22 Kaufman, G.D. Relativism, knowledge and faith. Chicago, 1960.
Phil 8411.27 Kaufmann, F. Das Reich des Schönen. Stuttgart, 1960.
Phil 1750.455.11 Kaufmann, W.A. From Shakespeare to existentialism. Garden City, 1960.
Phil 8080.11.1 Kayser, Wolfgang. Das Groteske in Malerei und Dichtung. Reinbek, 1960.
Phil 185.95 Keilbach, Wilhelm. Einübung ins philosophische Denken. München, 1960.
Phil 185.90 Kemp, Peter. Person og tänkning. København, 1960.
Phil 8980.481 Khmara, V.V. Cheloveku nado verit. Moskva, 1960.
Phil 5435.13 Khodzhava, Z.I. Problema navyka v psikhologii. Tbilisi, 1960.
Phil 8885.42 Kimpel, B.F. Principles of moral philosophy. N.Y., 1960.
Phil 720.50 King, Peter D. The principle of truth. N.Y., 1960.
Phil 5500.26 Klein, Burton Harold. The decision-making problem in development. Santa Monica, 1960.
Phil 185.80 Koelbel, Gerhard. Über die Einsamkeit. München, 1960.
Phil 3492.44.5 Koerner, Stephan. Kant. Harmondsworth, 1960.
Phil 8980.495 Kon, I.S. Moral kommunisticheskaia i moral' burzhvaznaia. Moskva, 1960. 2 pam.
Phil 291.8.5 Koren, Henry. An introduction to the philosophy of nature. Pittsburg, 1960.
Phil 310.256 Kosanović, I. Istoriski materijalizam. 3. izd. Sarajevo, 1960.
Phil 4803.496.30 Kossak, Jerzy. Bunt na kolanach. Warszawa, 1960.
Phil 8610.960 Kotarbiński, Tad. Przykład indywidualny kształtowania sie postawy wolnomys'licielskiej. Warszawa, 1960.
Phil 1170.17 Koytsogiannopoyloy, D.I. Hellēnikē philosophia kai christianikon dogma. Athens, 1960.
Phil 6980.398.40 Kraft, Thomas. De jeudgpsychiatriche diensten in Nederland. Utrecht, 1960.
Phil 341.32 Kraft, Victor. Erkenntnislehre. Wien, 1960.
Phil 2515.16 Krauss, W. Cartaud de la Villate. Berlin, 1960. 2v.
Phil 5250.60 Kremers, Johan. Scientific psychology and naive psychology. Nijmegen, 1960.
Phil 978.59.44 Krishnamurti, J. Commentaries on living. 1st ed. N.Y., 1960.
Phil 8590.30 Kristensen, William. The meaning of religion. The Hague, 1960.
Phil 8885.45 Kron, Helmut. Ethos und Ethik. Frankfurt, 1960.
Phil 4803.500.20 Kroński, Tadeusz. Rozwazania wokół Hegla. Warszawa, 1960.
Phil 7150.42 Kruijt, Cornuijtus Simon. Zilfmoord. Assen, 1960.
Phil 341.16.5 Kruse, F.V. Erkendelseslaeren og naturvidenskabens grundbegreber. København, 1960.
Phil 341.16.10 Kruse, F.V. Erkenntnis und Wertung; das Grundproblem. Berlin, 1960.
Phil 8665.25 Kryvelev, A.I. O dokazatel'stvakh bytiia Bozhiia. Moskva, 1960.
Phil 8411.28 Kuhn, Helmut. WesenUnd Wirken des Kunstwerks. München, 1960.
Phil 341.34 Kurazhkovskaia, E.A. Dialektika protsessa poznaniia. Moskva, 1960.
Phil 400.121 Kursanov, Georgii A. Sovremennyi ob"ektivnyi idealizm. Moskva, 1960.
Phil 3450.11.230 Kutschera, Franz. Über das Problem des Angangs der Philosophie im Spätwerk Edmund Husserl. München, 1960.
Phil 585.65 Kwant, Remy C. Encounter. Pittsburgh, 1960.
Phil 2725.11.75 Lachelier, Jules. The philosophy of Jules Lachelier. The Hague, 1960.
Phil 6961.19.5 Laing, Ronald David. The divided self; a study. Chicago, 1960.
Phil 5545.220 Laird, Donald. Techniques for efficient remembering. N.Y., 1960.
Phil 96.4.8 Lalande, A. Vocabulaire technique et critique de la philosophie. Paris, 1960.
Phil 2705.35.5A La Mettrie, Julien Offray de. L'homme machine. Princeton, 1960.
Phil 5374.67 Lang, Ernst Hildegard. Das wahre Wesen und Wirken des Bewusstseins in seiner normalen und anormalen Erscheinungen. München, 1960.
Phil 6121.36 Langdon-Davies, I. Man: the known and unknown. London, 1960.
Phil 3850.27.165 Langfeldt, Gabriel. Albert Schweitzer. London, 1960.
Phil 3850.27.166 Langfeldt, Gabriel. Albert Schweitzer. N.Y., 1960.
Phil 665.92 LaNoë, François de. L'appel de l'esprit. Paris, 1960.
Phil 9558.30 Larrañaga, T. De materia gravi in furto apud theologos saeculorum XVI et XVII. Romae, 1960.
Phil 5251.58A Lashley, K.S. The neuropsychology of Lashley. N.Y., 1960.
Phil 6321.9.8 Lasswell, H.D. Psychopathology and politics. N.Y., 1960.
Phil 2725.35.5 Lavelle, Louis. Morale et religion. Paris, 1960.
Phil 5535.56 Lawson, Philippe Reed. Learning and behavior. N.Y., 1960.
Phil 5761.23 Lebacqz, Joseph. Libre arbitre et jugement. Paris, 1960.
Phil 2515.12 LeChevalier, Charles. La confidence et la personne humaine. Aubier, 1960.
Phil 6965.3.90 Lechler, Walther Helmut. Neue Ergebnisse in der Forschung über Philippe Pinel. München, 1960.
Phil 2520.255.20 Lefèvre, Roger. La bataille du "cogito". 1. éd. Paris, 1960.
Phil 3552.405.5 Leibniz, G.W. Fragmente zur Logik. Berlin, 1960.
Phil 3552.405 Leibniz, G.W. Polemika G. Leibnitsa i S. Klarka po voprosam filosofii i estesvoznaniia, 1715-1716 gg. Leningrad, 1960.
Phil 6980.416 Lennard, H.L. The anatomy of psychotherapy. N.Y., 1960.

1960 - cont.

Phil 2725.35.100 — Levert, Paul. L'être et le réel selon Louis Lavelle. Paris, 1960.
Phil 9420.12 — Lewis, C.S. The four loves. London, 1960.
Phil 5051.10.14 — Lewis, Clarence I. A survey of symbolic logic. N.Y., 1960.
Phil 8591.44.12 — Lewis, Clive Staples. More Christianity. N.Y., 1960.
Phil 8591.44.30 — Lewis, Clive Staples. The world's last night. 1. ed. N.Y., 1960.
Phil 5251.56 — Lewis, Don. Quantitative methods in psychology. N.Y., 1960.
Phil 5251.57 — Leyden. Universiteit. De toekomst der psychologie. Leiden, 1960.
Phil 2725.38 — Leyvraz, Jean Pierre. Le temple et le Dieu. Paris, 1960.
Phil 5051.29.3 — Lieber, Lillian R. Mits, wits and logic. 3d ed. N.Y., 1960.
Phil 3552.425 — Lion, Ferdinand. Lebensquellen der deutschen Metaphysik. Frankfurt, 1960.
Phil 2520.315 — Llanos, Alfredo. El problema del voluntarismo en Descartes. Bahia Blanca, 1960.
Phil 8701.22 — Lubac, H. de. The discovery of God. N.Y., 1960.
Phil 5251.60 — Luce, Robert D. Development in mathematical psychology. Glencoe, 1960.
Phil 3585.20.5 — Luijpen, Wilhelmus Antonius Maria. Existential phenomenology. Pittsburgh, 1960.
Phil 3493.29 — Lumia, Giuseppe. La dottrina Kantiana del diritto e dello stato. Milano, 1960.
Phil 2115.167 — Maag, Urs. Die psychologischen Ansichten John Lockes. Aarau, 1960.
Phil 6122.75 — MacConaill, Michael A. Bodily structure and the will. London, 1960.
Phil 8592.105 — MacGregor, Geddes. Introduction to religious philosophy. London, 1960.
Phil 187.165 — MacIver, R.M. Life; its dimensions. N.Y., 1960.
Phil 2725.14.95 — Madinier, G. Vers une philosophie réflexive. Neuchâtel, 1960.
Phil 8592.112 — Magnino, B. Illuminismo e cristianesimo. Brescia, 1960. 3v.
Phil 5762.20 — Maillant, Claude. Cultivez votre volonté. Paris, 1960.
Phil 5400.136.5 — Maisonneuve, Jean. Les sentiments. 5. ed. Paris, 1960.
Phil 310.205 — Makarov, A.D. Dialekticheskii materializm. Moskva, 1960.
Phil 4372.1.105 — Manzoni, Bruno. Vives. Lugano, 1960.
Phil 5401.40 — March, Hans. Verfolgung und Angst in ihren leib-seelischen Auswirkungen. Stuttgart, 1960.
Phil 9495.160.5 — Marchi, L. de. Sesso e cività. 2. ed. Bari, 1960.
Phil 3425.292.12 — Marcuse, H. Reason and revolution; Hegel and the use of social theory. 2nd ed. Boston, 1960.
Phil 2750.11.81 — Maritain, Jacques. Le philosophe dans la cité. Paris, 1960.
Phil 2750.11.149 — Maritain, Jacques. La philosophie morale. Paris, 1960.
Phil 2750.11.86 — Maritain, Jacques. The responsibility of the artist. N.Y., 1960.
Phil 8413.4 — Martano, Guiseppe. La conoscenza sensibile nel razionalismo moderno. Napoli, 1960.
Phil 5415.11 — Maucorps, P.H. Empathies et connaissance d'autrui. Paris, 1960.
Phil 5592.165 — Max Luescher-Institut für Medizinsche Psychologie. Der Lüscher Test. Hergiswil, 1960.
Phil 343.26 — Mayz Vallenilla, E. Ontologia del conocimiento. Caracas, 1960.
Phil 812.42 — Mazzantini, Carlo. Filosofia e storia della filosofia, 1933-1959. Torino, 1960.
Phil 3450.11.255 — Melandri, Enzo. Logica e esperienza in Husserl. Bologna, 1960.
Phil 2750.22.85 — Melchione, Vuceolio. Il metodo di Mounier altri saggi. Milano, 1960.
Phil 3494.60 — Meleschenko, Z.N. Neokantianstvo kak filosofskaia osnova revizionizma. Leningrad, 1960.
Phil 310.260 — Meliukhin, S.I. O dialektike razvitiia neorganicheskoi prirody. Moskva, 1960.
Phil 5252.140 — Menert, Evžen. Fysiologický základ logického myšlení. Praha, 1960.
Phil 585.115 — Mercier, R. La réhabilitation de la nature humaine. Villemomble, 1960.
Phil 1170.11.2 — Merlan, Philip. From Platonism to Neoplatonism. 2nd ed. The Hague, 1960.
Phil 2750.20.30 — Merleau-Ponty, Maurice. Signes. Paris, 1960.
Phil 6322.44 — Miasishchev, V.N. Lichnost' i nevrozy. Leningrad, 1960.
Phil 1560.15 — Michelet, Marcel. Le Rhin Mystique de Maitre Eckert à Thomas à Kempis. Paris, 1960.
Phil 1750.82 — Mihalich, J.C. Existentialism and Thomism. N.Y., 1960.
Phil 2138.79.12 — Mill, John S. John Mill's boyhood visit to France. Toronto, 1960.
Phil 5252.125A — Miller, George. Plans and the structure of behavior. N.Y., 1960.
Phil 575.225 — Minkus, P.A. Philosophy of the person. Oxford, 1960.
Phil 310.310 — Mitin, M.B. Filosofiia i sovremennost'. Moskva, 1960.
Phil 2750.22.80 — Moix, Candide. Emmanuel Mounier. Paris, 1960.
Phil 8887.115 — Molitor, Arnulf. Zum Formalismus in der neueren Ethik. Wien, 1960.
Phil 8400.25 — Mon, Franz. Movens; Dokumente und Analysen zur Dichtung. Wiesbaden, 1960.
Phil 812.41.2 — Mondolfo, Rodolfo. En los origenes de la filosofia. 2. ed. Buenos Aires, 1960.
Phil 8110.3 — Monk, S.H. The sublime; a study of critical theories in 18th century England. Ann Arbor, 1960.
Phil 4195.100 — Monnerjahn, E. Giovanni Pico della Mirandola. Wiesbaden, 1960.
Phil 8667.20.5 — Morais, H.M. Deism in eighteenth century America. N.Y., 1960.
Phil 8962.17 — Morale chrétienne et morale marxiste. Paris, 1960.
Phil 5585.185 — Moreau, J. L'horizon des esprits. Paris, 1960.
Phil 310.235 — Moroz, K.V. Dialekticheskii materializm, ideinoe oruzoiie bor'by za Kommunizm. Moskva, 1960.
Phil 8092.10 — Morpurgo Taghabue, G. L'esthétique contemporaine. Milan, 1960.
Phil 187.152.5 — Moser, Simon. Philosophie und Gegenwart. Meisenheim am Glan, 1960.
Phil 4710.79 — Moskalenko, F.Ia. Gnoseologicheskoe soderzhanie logicheskikh form i metodov. Kiev, 1960.
Phil 165.2.5 — Muelder, Walter G. The development of American philosophy. 2. ed. Boston, 1960.
Phil 3850.16.96 — Mueller, H. Lebensphilosophie und Religion bei Georg Simmel. Berlin, 1960.
Phil 5222.8 — Müller, T.L. Histoire de la psychologie. Paris, 1960.
Phil 3450.19.225 — Mueller-Lauter, W. Möglichkeit und Wirklichkeit bei M. Heidegger. Berlin, 1960.

1960 - cont.

Phil 978.49.835 — Muellner, L. Rudolf Steiner und Brunn am Gebirge bei Wien. Wien, 1960.
Phil 4330.5 — El mundo clasico en el pensamiento español contemporaneo. Madrid, 1960.
Phil 5762.22 — Munn, Allan M. Free will and determinism. Toronto, 1960.
Phil 1020.22.7 — Nadvi, Muzaffar Uddir. Muslim thought and its source. 4th ed. Lahore, 1960.
Phil 5253.8.50 — Naess, Arne. Notes on the foundation of psychology as a science. Oslo, 1960.
Phil 7069.60 — Nagel, E.W. Mind power. 1. ed. N.Y., 1960.
Phil 1518.2 — Nardi, Bruno. Studi di filosofia medievale. Roma, 1960.
Phil 2115.175 — Narshii, I.S. Fislosofiia Dzhona Lokka. Moskva, 1960.
Phil 5068.48 — Narskii, I.S. Sovremennyi pozitivizm. Moskva, 1960.
Phil 600.57 — Narskii, Igor Sergeevich. Ocherki po istorii pozitivizma. Moskva, 1960.
Phil 4800.14 — Narskii, Igor' Sergeevich. Pol'skie mysliteli epokhi Vozrozhdeniia. Moskva, 1960.
Phil 8414.5 — Natev, A. Tsel ili samotselnost na izkustvoto. Sofiia, 1960.
Phil 8050.73 — Nauwelaerts, M.A.M.E. Uren van schoonheid. Antwerpen, 1960.
Phil 188.23 — Nedeljković, Duš. Pragmatizam i djalektika. Beograd, 1960.
Phil 971.6 — Negner, Helena. Beiträge zur Geschichte der Weisheitsreligion. Pforzheim, 1960.
Phil 978.6.90 — Nethercot, A.H. The first five lives of Annie Besant. Chicago, 1960.
Phil 6123.10 — New York (City). University. Institution of Philosophy. Dimensions of mind. N.Y., 1960.
Phil 310.490 — Nichyk, V.M. Dialektychnyi materializm pro katenoriiu prychynnosti. Kyiv, 1960.
Phil 3640.77.27 — Nietzsche, Friedrich. Joyful wisdom. N.Y., 1960.
Phil 3640.17.3 — Nietzsche, Friedrich. Menschliches, Allzumenschliches; ein Buch für freie Geister. Stuttgart, 1960.
Phil 9450.45 — Nitze, P.H. The recovery of ethics. N.Y., 1960.
Phil 8125.37 — Nivelle, A. Kunst- und Dichtungstheorien zwischen Aufklärung und Klassik. Berlin, 1960.
Phil 2775.2.30 — Nizan, Paul. Les chiens de garde. Paris, 1960.
Phil 8593.24 — Noack, H. Sprache und Offenbarung. Gütersloh, 1960.
Phil 4013.5 — Noventa, Giacomo. Nulla di nuova. 1. ed. Milano, 1960.
Phil 4791.2 — Nutsubidze, Shalva Isakovich. Istoriia gruzinskoi filosofii. Tbilisi, 1960.
Phil 8669.6 — O'Brien, Thomas C. Metaphysics and the existence of God. Washington, 1960.
Phil 8060.5 — O'Callaghan, J. Las tres categorías estétecas de la cultura clásica. Madrid, 1960.
Phil 8964.6 — Oesterreichisches Seelsorge-Institut. Weihnachts-Seelsorgertagung, 1959. Der Christ und die Weltwirklichkeit. Wien, 1960.
Phil 1714.6 — Oizerman, Teodor I. Zur Geschichte der vormarxschen Philosophie. Berlin, 1960.
Phil 345.5 — O'Neill, Reginald. Theories of knowledge. Englewood Cliffs, N.J., 1960.
Phil 310.295 — Orlov, V.V. Dialekticheskii materializm i psikhofiziologicheskaia problema. Perm, 1960.
Phil 190.100 — Oromi, Miguel. Métodos y principios filosóficos. Madrid, 1960.
Phil 4365.2.35 — Ortega y Gasset, José. Origen y epílogo de la filosofía. Mexico, 1960.
Phil 5251.41.80 — Ossicuri, Adriano. L'opera di Kurt Lewin nella psicologia contemporanea. Messina, 1960.
Phil 8704.3 — Ostwald, Wilhelm. Wissenschaft contra Gottesglauben. Leipzig, 1960.
Phil 400.94.3 — Ottaviano, C. Critica dell'idealismo. 3. ed. Padova, 1960.
Phil 3450.11.85 — Paci, Enzo. Omaggio a Husserl. Milano, 1960.
Phil 3450.11.86 — Paci, Enzo. Il problema del tempo nella fenomenologia di Husserl. Milano, 1960.
Phil 3450.19.235 — Padellaro De Angelis, Rosa. Heidegger e il problema Kantiano. Torino, 1960.
Phil 8890.56 — Padovani, U.A. Filosofia e morale. Padova, 1960.
Phil 270.129 — Pakistan. Philosophical Congress, 7th, Dacca, Pakistan, 1960. Symposia on basic human values and causality. Lahore, 1960?
Phil 2340.10.165 — Palter, Robert M. Whitehead's philosophy of science. Chicago, 1960.
Phil 8980.673 — Panferov, F.I. O moral'nom oblike sovetskogo cheloveka. Moskva, 1960.
Phil 8050.79 — Panofsky, E. Idea. 2. Aufl. Berlin, 1960.
Phil 2138.135 — Pappe, H. O. John Stuart Mill and the Harriet Taylor myth. Melbourne, 1960.
Phil 2805.74.20 — Pascal, Blaise. L'entretien de Pascal et Sacy. Paris, 1960.
Phil 2805.42.45 — Pascal, Blaise. Pensées. Paris, 1960. 2v.
Phil 8505.9 — Pax Romana, International Catholic Movement for Intellectual and Cultural Affairs. Foi et technique. Paris, 1960.
Phil 9558.10.5 — Payne, Robert. Hubris. N.Y., 1960.
Phil 5238.130 — Peatman, J.G. Festschrift for Gardner Murphy. N.Y., 1960.
Phil 8595.55 — Pegis, Anton C. Christian philosophy and intellectual freedom. Milwaukee, 1960.
Phil 2225.5.50A — Peirce, C.S. Collected papers. v.1-6. Cambridge, 1960. 3v.
Phil 9400.40 — Pennsylvania. Governor's White House Conference Committee on Aging. Subcommittee reports. Harrisburg, 1960.
Phil 3425.550 — Peperzak, Adrien. La jeune Hegel et la vision morale du monde. La Haye, 1960.
Phil 8890.52 — Pepper, Stephen Coburn. Ethics. N.Y., 1960.
Phil 6315.2.140.5 — Pesch, Edgar. La pensée de Freud. Paris, 1960.
Phil 4200.6.30 — Petruzzellis, Nicola. Meditazione critiche. Napoli, 1960.
Phil 4751.2.80 — Peunova, M.N. Mirovozzrenie M.A. Antonovicha. Moskva, 1960.
Phil 165.220 — La philosophie et ses problèmes. Lyon, 1960.
Phil 3850.27.195 — Picht, Werner. Albert Schweitzer. Hamburg, 1960.
Phil 1520.5.10 — Pieper, Josef. Scholasticism. N.Y., 1960.
Phil 1520.5.5 — Pieper, Josef. Scholastik. München, 1960.
Phil 190.85 — Piguet, Jean C. L'oeuvre de philosophie. Neuchâtel, 1960.
Phil 4958.205 — Piñera Llera, Humberto. Panorama de la filosofía cubana. Washington, 1960.
Phil 3425.554 — Piontkovskii, A.A. Hegels Lehre über Staat und Recht und seine Strafrechtstheorie. Berlin, 1960.
Phil 100.2 — Piquet, Jean Claude. Vocabulaire de philosophie. Paris, 1960.
Phil 5592.135 — Pittenger, R.E. The first five minutes. Ithaca, 1960.
Phil 585.135 — Plattel, Martinus Gulielmus. Sociale wijsbegeerte. v.1-2. Utrecht, 1960-64.

Chronological Listing

Phil 6965.20 Plunkett, Richard. Epidemiology and mental illness. N.Y., 1960.

Phil 974.3.112 Poepping, Fred. Rudolf Steiner, der grosse Unbekannte. Wien, 1960.

Phil 600.56 Poey, Andrés. El positivismo. Habana, 1960.

Phil 346.20.3 Polanyi, Michael. Personal knowledge. Chicago, 1960.

Phil 7069.60.20 Pole, W.T. The silent road in the light of personal experience. London, 1960.

Phil 2115.190 Polin, Raymond. La politique morale de John Locke. 1e éd. Paris, 1960.

Phil 5255.62 Ponomarev, Ia.A. Psikhologiia tvorcheskogo myshleniia. Moskva, 1960.

Phil 8890.54 Pons, Walter. Steht uns der Himmel offen. Wiesbaden, 1960.

Phil 8890.54.2 Pons, Walter. Steht uns der Himmel offen. 2. Aufl. Wiesbaden, 1960.

Phil 645.50 Popkin, Richard H. The history of scepticism from Erasmus to Descartes. Assen, 1960.

Phil 5025.3 Popov, P.S. Istoriia logiki novogo vremeni. Moskva, 1960.

Phil 2415.14 Popovych, M.V. Pokhid proty rozumu. Kyiv, 1960.

Phil 346.27 Popper, Karl Raimund. On the sources of knowledge and of ignorance. London, 1960.

Phil 8599.13.80 Posselt, H. Die Religionsphilosophie Gustav Teichmüllers. Marburg, 1960.

Phil 9355.13 Postovoitov, V.K. O kul'ture molodogo rabochego. Moskva, 1960.

Phil 2520.340 Pousa, Narciso. Moral y libertad en Descartes. La Plata, 1960.

Phil 310.345 Praktika, kriterii istiny v nauke. Moskva, 1960.

Phil 165.436 Probleme der Wissenschaftstheorie; Festschrift für Victor Kroft. Wien, 1960.

Phil 4816.6 Problemy filosofii. Moskva, 1960.

Phil 3050.4 Protiv sovremennoi burzhuaznoi ideologii. Moskva, 1960.

Phil 6325.20 Psykoanalytisk diskussionsklub. Psykoanalyse er to ting. København, 1960.

Phil 2020.90 Pucelle, Jean. La nature et l'esprit dans la philosophie de T.H. Green. Louvain, 1960-65. 2v.

Phil 665.86 Quarelli, Elena. Socrates and the animals. London, 1960.

Phil 5066.11.40A Quine, Willard van Orman. Word and object. Cambridge, 1960.

Phil 585.80 Radhakrishnan, Sarvepalli. The concept of man. London, 1960.

Phil 585.80.2 Radhakrishnan, Sarvepalli. The concept of man. London, 1960.

Phil 5767.12 Ramm, T. Die Freiheit der Willensbildung. Stuttgart, 1960.

Phil 6327.30 Rapoport, Robert N. Community as doctor. London, 1960.

Phil 623.35 Het rationalisme. Den Haag, 1960.

Phil 8418.20 Read, Herbert. The forms of things unknown. London, 1960.

Phil 6319.1.85 Read, Herbert. Zum 85. Geburtstag von Professor Dr. Carl Gustav Jung. Zürich, 1960.

Phil 8418.18 Redeker, Horst. Geschichte und Gesetze des Ästhetischen. Berlin, 1960.

Phil 3640.79.60 Reichert, Herbert William. International Nietzsche bibliography. Chapel Hill, N.C., 1960.

Phil 1750.360.2 Reinhardt, Kurt Frank. The existentialist revolt. 2nd ed. N.Y., 1960.

Phil 525.93.5 Reinhold, Hans. The soul afire. N.Y., 1960.

Phil 298.16 Reitzer, Alfons. Das Problem des Materiebegiffes. München, 1960.

Phil 672.210 Restrepo, F. Entre el tiempo y la eternidad. Bogotá, 1960.

Phil 5593.60.5 Rickers-Ovsiankiua, Maria A. Rorschach psychology. N.Y., 1960.

Phil 348.17.5 Riet, G. van. Problèmes d'épistémologie. Louvain, 1960.

Phil 1830.40 Rigobello, Armando. La filosofia americana contemporanea. Torino, 1960.

Phil 817.21.2 Rivaud, Albert. Histoire de la philosophie. 2. ed. Paris, 1960.

Phil 3640.570.5 Roeschel, Herbert. Nietzsche. Paris, 1960.

Phil 5335.6 Rokeach, Milton. The open and closed mind. N.Y., 1960.

Phil 4368.2.50 Romero, Francisco. Ortega y Gasset y el problema de la jefatura espiritual. Buenos Aires, 1960.

Phil 5585.200 Rommetveit, R. Selectivity, intuition and halo effects in social perception. Oslo, 1960.

Phil 192.108 Rosset, Clément. La philosophie tragique. Paris, 1960.

Phil 5545.210 Rossi, Paolo. Clavis universalis. Milano, 1960.

Phil 8707.25 Roth, A. Stiinta si religie. Bucaresti, 1960.

Phil 3450.11.250 Roth, Alois. Edmund Husserls ethische Untersuchungen. Den Haag, 1960.

Phil 2725.35.95 Rothkopf, Wolfgang. Der Einfluss Kants auf die Erkenntnismetaphysik. München, 1960.

Phil 4368.3.5 Rouges, Alberto. Obras completas. Tucumán, 1960.

Phil 192.106 Rougier, Louis. La metaphysique et le langage. Paris, 1960.

Phil 5057.38 Rozental', M.M. Prenlsipy dialekticheskoi logiki. Moskva, 1960.

Phil 310.290 Rozental', Mark M. Kniga dlia chteniia po marksistko filosofii. Moskva, 1960.

Phil 5257.71 Rudolph, Rigmor. Er jeg nig? Traek of Jeg'ets psykologi. Kjøbenhavn, 1960.

Phil 8418.22 Ruefenacht, E. Lebensstufe und Kunstwerk, ihre Symbolik und ihre Foringesetze. 1. Aufl. Zürich, 1960.

Phil 2255.1.58A Russell, Bertrand Russell. Bertrand Russell speaks his mind. 1st ed. Cleveland, 1960.

Phil 8418.16 Russi, Antonio. L'arte et le arti. Pisa, 1960.

Phil 8418.15 Russo, S. Arte e libertá e altri saggi. Padova, 1960.

Phil 5058.92 Saarnio, Uuno. Ord och Mängd. Helsingfors, 1960.

Phil 8430.26 Salicrú Puigvert, C. Moray y arte. Barcelona, 1960.

Phil 8419.35A Salinger, H. Über das Schöne als Sinnbild und Wegweisung. Köln, 1960.

Phil 5258.175 Sarbin, Theodore. Clinical inference and cognitive theory. N.Y., 1960.

Phil 2880.8.57A Sartre, Jean Paul. Critique de la raison dialectique. Paris, 1960.

Phil 2880.8.41.2 Sartre, Jean Paul. Existentialism and humanism. London, 1960.

Phil 3960.16.13 Sassen, Ferdinand. Wijsgerig leven in Nederland in de twintigste eeuw. 3. druk. Amsterdam, 1960.

Phil 5590.420 Saul, Leon J. Emotional maturity. Philadelphia, 1960.

Phil 3640.630 Savounet, Marie. Nietzsche et DuBos. Paris, 1960.

Phil 2050.240 Schaefer, Alfred. Erkenntnis. Berlin, 1960?

Phil 5520.325 Schaff, Adam. Wstęp do semantyki. Warszawa, 1960.

Phil 3850.18.45 Scheler, Max. On the eternal in man. N.Y., 1960.

Phil 3500.63.2 Schilpp, P.A. Kant's pre-critical ethics. 2d ed. Evanstown, 1960.

Phil 3805.32.15 Schleiermacher, Friedrich. Der christliche Glaube; nach den Grundsätzen. Berlin, 1960. 2v.

Phil 3425.562 Schmidt, G. Hegel in Nürnberg. Tübingen, 1960.

Phil 5066.160 Schmidt, H.A. Mathematische Gesetze der Logik. Berlin, 1960.

Phil 8419.16 Schmied, W. Das Poetische in der Kunst. Nürnburg, 1960.

Phil 8735.50 Schmitz, Josef. Disput über das teleologische Denken. Mainz, 1960.

Phil 6906.5 Schneck, Jerome M. A history of psychiatry. Springfield, Ill., 1960.

Phil 8893.110 Schneider, Herbert W. Morals for mankind. Columbia, 1960.

Phil 3018.35 Schoch, Otto D. Der Völherbundsgedanke zur Zeit. Zürich, 1960.

Phil 585.90 Schoeps, H.J. Was ist der Mensch? Göttingen, 1960.

Phil 3808.76.50 Schopenhauer, Arthur. Arthur Schopenhauer; Mensch und Philosoph in seinen Briefen. Wiesbaden, 1960.

Phil 5650.43 Schouteu, Jan F. Five articles on the perception of sound, 1938-1940. Eindhoven, 1960.

Phil 6060.12.55 Schuerer, Wilhelm. Hestia, 1960-61...Ludwig Klages. Bonn, 1960.

Phil 5170.12 Schuhl, Pierre M. Le dominateur el les possibles. 1. éd. Paris, 1960.

Phil 3450.33.8 Schwarz, Baldwin. The human person and the world of values. N.Y., 1960.

Phil 4225.8.42 Sciacca, Michele Federico. La clessidra. 3. ed. Milano, 1960.

Phil 4225.8.44 Sciacca, Michele Federico. In spirito e verità. 4. ed. Milano, 1960.

Phil 493.6.5 Seely, Charles Sherlock. Modern materialism. N.Y., 1960.

Phil 4319.2 Segovia Canosa, R. Tres salvaciones del siglo XVIII español. Xalapa, 1960.

Phil 9470.10 Semerari, Giuseppe. Responsabilitá e comunitá umana. Manduria, 1960.

Phil 8419.38 Severgnini, D. La inevitabile illusione; rilievi modali dell'estetica. Torino, 1960.

Phil 5258.170 Shands, Harley. Thinking and psychotherapy. Cambridge, 1960.

Phil 960.175.5 Sharma, C. A critical survey of Indian philosophy. London, 1960.

Phil 3500.85 Shashkevich, P.D. Teoriia poznaniia I. Kanta. Moskva, 1960.

Phil 4710.100 Shchipanov, I.Ia. Protiv sovremennykh fal'sifikatorov istorii russkoi filosofii. Moskva, 1960.

Phil 310.350 Shirokanov, D.I. Dialektika neobkhodimosti i sluchainosti. Minsk, 1960.

Phil 8843.1.7 Sidgwick, Henry. Outlines of history of ethics for English readers. Boston, 1960.

Phil 5590.400 Sigl-Kiener, I. Über die individuelle Konfiguration des Leitbildes. München, 1960.

Phil 8612.47 Sikken, Willem. Midden in het leven. Kampen, 1960.

Phil 7069.50.6 Silva Mello, Antonio da. Mysteries and realities of this world and the next. London, 1960.

Phil 9560.56 Sinko, Tadeuz. Od filantropii do human i humanizmu. 2. wyd. Warszawa, 1960.

Phil 4809.796.1 Smetana, Augustin. Sebrané spisy. Praha, 1960- 2v.

Phil 70.72 Societá Filosofica Italiana. Veritá e libertá di Guzzo. Palumbo, 1960.

Phil 5585.150 Solley, Charles. Development of the perceptual world. N.Y., 1960.

Phil 3110.192 Solms-Rödelheim, Günther. Die Grundvorstellungen Jacob Böhme. München, 1960.

Phil 8980.802 Sorokin, K.F. Za leninskii stil' v rabote. Kiev, 1960.

Phil 4960.620 Souza, Remy de. Vocação filosófica do Brasil. Salvador, 1960.

Phil 8980.787.10 Soveshchanie po Voprosam Marksistko-Leninskoi Etiki, Leningrad, 1959. Voprosy marksistsko-leninskoi etiki. Moskva, 1960.

Phil 9450.40 Speer, James. For what purpose? Washington, 1960.

Phil 5258.195 Spence, Kenneth Wartenbee. Behavior theory and learning; selected papers. Englewood Cliffs, 1960.

Phil 1750.115.50 Spiegelberg, Herbert. The phenomenological movement. Hague, 1960. 2v.

Phil 2418.7 Spink, John Stephenson. French free-thought from Gassendi to Voltaire. London, 1960.

Phil 3850.27.190 Spinosa, Antonio. Dottor Schweitzer e dintorni. Roma, 1960.

Phil 5374.205 Spirkin, A.G. Proiskhozhdenie soznaniia. Moskva, 1960.

Phil 525.205 Stace, Walter T. Mysticism and philosophy. 1st ed. Philadelphia, 1960.

Phil 349.41.3 Stark, Werner. The sociology of knowledge. London, 1960.

Phil 1718.25.2 Stegmüller, W. Hauptströmungen der Gegenwartphilosophie. 2. Aufl. Stuttgart, 1960.

Phil 5401.38 Stein, Maurice R. Identity and anxiety. Glencoe, 1960.

Phil 5465.100 Stein, Morris. Creativity and the individual. Glencoe, 1960.

Phil 978.49.320 Steiner, R. Christus und die menschliche Seele. Dornach, 1960.

Phil 978.49.330 Steiner, R. Ergebnisse der Geistesforschung. Dornach, 1960.

Phil 978.49.310 Steiner, R. Luzifer-Gnosis, 1903-1908. Dornach, 1960.

Phil 978.49.325 Steiner, R. Das Markus-Evanqelium. Dornach, 1960.

Phil 978.49.315 Steiner, R. Menschenschichsale und Völkerschicksale. Dornach, 1960.

Phil 3925.16.90 Stenius, Erik. Wittgenstein's Tractatus. Ithaca, 1960.

Phil 3425.545 Stiehler, Gottfried. Hegel und der Marxismus über den Widerspruch. Berlin, 1960.

Phil 8419.22 Stolnitz, Jerome. Aesthetics and philosophy of art criticism. Boston, 1960.

Phil 2880.8.115 Streller, Justus. Jean Paul Sartre. N.Y., 1960.

Phil 8419.20 Stubbe, Achilles. Het zien en genieten van schilderkunst. 4. druk. Hasselt, 1960.

Phil 6128.70 Stuttgart. Institut für Psychotherapie und Tiefenpsychologie. Nervose. Stuttgart, 1960.

Phil 7069.60.5 Sudre, René. Treatise on parapsychology. London, 1960.

Phil 1930.8.100 Suranyi-Unger, Nora. Die politische Philosophie von R.G. Collingwood. München, 1960.

Phil 3195.6.135 Suter, Jean F. Philosophie et histoire chez W. Dilthey. Bale, 1960.

Phil 3850.48 Sydow, W. Das Geheimnis des ewigen Lebens und des jüngsten Tages. Berlin, 1960?

Phil 5520.355 Szewczuk, W. Badania eksperymentalne nad rozumieniem zdán. Kraków, 1960.

Phil 8050.26 Tatarkiewicz, Władysław. Historia estetyki. Wrocław, 1960. 2v.

Phil 5066.165 Tavanets, P.V. Primenie logiki v nauke i tekhnika. Moskva, 1960.

1960 - cont.

Phil 8430.24   Taylor, Harold. Art and the intellect. N.Y., 1960.
Phil 2905.1.15   Teilhard de Chardin, Pierre. The divine milieu. 1st ed. N.Y., 1960.
Phil 165.320   Temi e problemi di filosofia classica. Milano, 1960.
Phil 2805.390   Terzi, Carlo. Pascal. Bergamo, 1960.
Phil 3195.10.130   Teufel, Herbert. Der Begriff des Werdens und der Entwicklung bei Driesch. München, 1960.
Phil 2305.5.30   Thalheimer, Alvin. Existential metaphysics. N.Y., 1960.
Phil 8599.42   Thévenaz, Pierre. La condition de la raison philosophique. Neuchâtel, 1960.
Phil 300.10   Third Programme. Rival theories of cosmology. London, 1960.
Phil 6329.17   This, Bernard. La psychanalyse. Paris, 1960.
Phil 5352.10   Thomae, Hans. Der Mensch in der Entscheidung. München, 1960.
Phil 5520.435   Thurman, Kelly. Semantics. Boston, 1960.
Phil 3475.3.175   Tilliette, Xavier. Karl Jaspers. Paris, 1960.
Phil 5548.75   Toman, Walter. An introduction to psychoanalytic theory of motivation. N.Y., 1960.
Phil 350.5   Tomov, Kiril. Poznanie i praktika. Sofiia, 1960.
Phil 6315.19.25   Torres, M. El irracionalismo en Erich Fromm. México, 1960.
Phil 2430.3   Torrey, Norman L. Les philosophes. N.Y., 1960.
Phil 7150.44   Touraine, Yves. Le suicide ascétique. Paris, 1960.
Phil 4235.11.30   Tradu, L. Saggi filosofici vari. Padova, 1960.
Phil 8120.11   Traz, Georges. De Diderot à Valéy. Paris, 1960.
Phil 2905.1.263   Tresmoutant, Claude. Introduccion al pensamiento de Teilhard de Chardin. 2. ed. Madrid, 1960.
Phil 8980.851   Tugarinov, Vasilii P. O tsennostiakh zhizni i kul'tury. Leningrad, 1960.
Phil 2115.180   Tuveson, E.L. The imagination as a means of grace. Berkeley, 1960.
Phil 820.1.7.7   Ueberweg, F. Grundriss der Geschichte der Philosophie. Basel, 1960.
Phil 105.5   Urmson, J.O. The concise encyclopaedia of Western philosophy and philosophers. London, 1960.
Phil 165.368   Vaira. Budapest, 1960.
Phil 4752.2.110   Vallon, Michell A. An apostle of freedom. N.Y., 1960.
Phil 8971.2.5   Vann, Gerald. Morals and man. N.Y., 1960.
Phil 1821.10   Van Wesep, Hendrikus. Seven sages. 1st ed. N.Y., 1960.
Phil 4983.5.22   Varela, Félix. Cartas a Elpidio (Selección). Habana, 1960.
Phil 6315.2.275   Vennes, Gaston. Inconscient freudien et problèmes de liberté. Trois Rivières, 1960.
Phil 5261.22   Vetter, A. Wirklichkeit des Menschlichen. Freiburg, 1960.
Phil 2115.185   Viano, Carlo A. John Locke. Torino, 1960.
Phil 2115.195   Viano, Carlo A. John Locke. Torino, 1960.
Phil 4983.41   Villegas, Abelardo. La filosofía de lo mexicano. México, 1960.
Phil 4080.3.355   Viola, Italo. Problemi di critica crociana. Milano, 1960.
Phil 585.105   Virasoro, M.A. Filosofía de la existencia y antropología filosófica. 1. ed. Bahía Blanca, 1960.
Phil 4372.1.36   Vives, Juan Luis. Obras sociales y políticas. Madrid, 1960.
Phil 5061.6   Voishvillo, Evgenii K. Predmet i znachenie logiki. Moskva, 1960.
Phil 2520.310   Vuillemin, Jules. Mathématiques et métaphysique de Descartes. Paris, 1960.
Phil 9150.33   Waddington, C.H. The ethical animal. London, 1960.
Phil 6332.18   Waelder, Robert. Basic theory of psychoanalysis. N.Y., 1960.
Phil 6032.5   Waldemar, Charles. Lavater, der Menschenkenner. 1. Aufl. Zürich, 1960.
Phil 5460.13   Walter, W.G. The neurophysiological aspects of hallucinations and illusory experience. London, 1960.
Phil 2520.335   Waltheunis, O. De mens Descartes. Brussel, 1960.
Phil 8847.15   Warnock, Mary. Ethics since 1900. London, 1960.
Phil 1722.13   Warsaw. Universytet. Główne zagadnienia i kierunki filozofii. v.1-2. 2. Wyd. Warszawa, 1960.
Phil 5590.355   Waszhewitz, B. Fundamente der Persönlichkeitspsychologie. München, 1960.
Phil 5832.20   Waters, Rolland. Principles of comparative psychology. N.Y., 1960.
Phil 525.200   Watts, Alan W. This is it. N.Y., 1960.
Phil 960.230   Wei-uri-wei (pseud.). Why Lazarus laughed. London, 1960.
Phil 3140.85   Weier, Winfred. Die Stellung des Johannes Clauberg in der Philosophie. Diss. Mainz, 1960.
Phil 5238.145   Weinhandl, Ferdinand. Gestalthaftes Sehen...zum hundertjahrigen Geburtstag von Christian von Ehrenfels. Darmstadt, 1960.
Phil 3925.2.90   Weishedel, Wilhelm. Wirklichkeit und Wirklichkeiten. Berlin, 1960.
Phil 3890.1.84   Weiss, Antonia R. Friedrich Adolf Trendelenburg. Kallmünz, 1960.
Phil 6980.775.50   Weiss, Edward. The structure and dynamics of the human mind. N.Y., 1960.
Phil 5262.48.20   Weizäcker, Viktor. Gestalt und Zeit. 2. Aufl. Göttingen, 1960.
Phil 353.23   Wemme, G. Das Geheimnis der Gegensätze. Krailling, 1960.
Phil 197.75   Wheelwright, Philip. The way of philosophy. N.Y., 1960.
Phil 5627.260   White, Victor. Soul and psyche. London, 1960.
Phil 8602.33.10   Whitehead, A.N. Religion in the making. N.Y., 1960[1954]
Phil 8712.30   Whitehouse, Walter. Order, goodness, glory. London, 1960.
Phil 5722.42   Whyte, Lancelot. The unconscious before Freud. N.Y., 1960.
Phil 9513.7.2   Wiese, Leopold von. Ethik in der Schauweise der Wissenschaften. 2. Aufl. Bern, 1960.
Phil 2270.165   Wiese, Leopold von. Herbert Spencers Einführung in die Soziologie. Köln, 1960.
Phil 3552.410   Wildermuth, A. Wahrheit und Schöpfung. Winterthur, 1960.
Phil 2905.1.105   Wildiers, N.M. Het wereldbeeld van Pierre Teilhard de Chardin. 2. druk. Antwerpen, 1960.
Phil 353.25   Willam, Franz. Aristotelische Erkenntnislehre bei Whately und Newman. Freiburg, 1960.
Phil 5832.25   Winkelstraeter, K.H. Das Betteln der Zoo-Tiere. Bern, 1960.
Phil 585.55   Winkler, Franz E. Man: the bridge. N.Y., 1960.
Phil 107.5   Winn, R.B. A concise dictionary of existentialism. N.Y., 1960.
Phil 3890.2.85   Winter, Eduard. E.W. von Tschirnhaus. Berlin, 1960.
Phil 165.215   Wisser, Richard. Sinn und Sein. Tubingen, 1960.
Phil 310.325   Witt-Hansen, J. Historical materialism. Copenhagen, 1960.
Phil 3925.16.52   Wittgenstein, Ludwig. Schriften...Beiheft. Frankfurt, 1960.
Phil 3925.16.50A   Wittgenstein, Ludwig. Schriften. Frankfurt, 1960-64. 2v.

1960 - cont.

Phil 3925.16.45   Wittgenstein, Ludwig. Tractatus logico-philosophicus. London, 1960.
Phil 8897.82   Witwicki, W. Pogadanki obczajowe. Warszawa, 1960.
Phil 8602.77   Woelber, Hans I. Religion ohne Entscheidung. 2. Aufl. Göttingen, 1960.
Phil 9495.160   Wojtyka, Karol. Miłość i odpowiedzialność. Lublin, 1960.
Phil 3425.540   Wolf, Kurt. Die Religionsphilosophie des Jüngen Hegel. München, 1960.
Phil 2262.99   Wolff, Erwin. Shaftesbury und seine Bedeutung für die englische Literatur des 18. Jhs. Tübingen, 1960.
Phil 3808.230   Wolff, H.M. Arthur Schopenhauer. Bern, 1960.
Phil 1885.93   Wollheim, Richard. F.H. Bradley. Harmondsworth, 1960[1959]
Phil 5262.53   Wolman, Benjamin B. Contemporary theories and systems in psychology. N.Y., 1960.
Phil 6132.40   Wright, B.A. Physical disability; a psychological approach. N.Y., 1960.
Phil 6332.20   Wyrsch, J. Gesellschaft, Kultur und psychische Störung. Stuttgart, 1960.
Phil 2050.238   Zabeeh, F. Hume, precursor of modern empiricism. The Hague, 1960.
Phil 525.210   Zaehner, R.C. Hindu and Muslim mysticism. London, 1960.
Phil 5592.140   Zazzo, René. Manuel pour l'examen psychologique de l'enfant. Neuchâtel, 1960.
Phil 310.670   Zelený, Jindřich. O historickén materialismu. Vyd. 1. V Praze, 1960.
Phil 8605.10   Zen'kovskii, V.V. Osnovy khristianskoi filosofii. Frankfurt, 1960.
Phil 4025.5   Zeppi, Stelio. Il problema del dialogo nel pensiero italiano contemporaneo. Firenze, 1960.
Phil 974.3.124   Zeylmans von Emmichoven, F.W. Rudolf Steiner. Zeist, 1960.
Phil 5066.170   Zinov'ev, Aleksandr A. Filosofskie problemy mnogoznachnoi logiki. Moskva, 1960.

1961

Phil 7150.49   Aarberon, Norman. The cry for help. N.Y., 1961.
Phil 8580.35   Abbagnano, N. La religione. Torino, 1961.
Phil 85.15   Abbagnano, Nicola. Dizionario di filosofia. Torino, 1961.
Phil 5240.51   Abella Gibert, D. El nostre caracter. Barcelona, 1961.
Phil 5625.107   Abramian, Lev. Signal i uslovnyi refleks. Erevan, 1961.
Phil 8401.23   Adamian, Arshag. Stat'i ob iskusstve. Moskva, 1961.
Phil 6310.1.106   Adler, Gerhard. The living symbol. N.Y., 1961.
Phil 8980.126   Agapov, B.N. My ne odin na svete. Moskva, 1961.
Phil 5190.36   Agazzi, Evandro. Introduzione ai problemi dell'assiomatica. Milano, 1961.
Phil 310.380   Akadamiia Nauk SSSR. Kafedra Filosofii. Russkie uchenye v bor'be protiv idealizma i metafiziki vozzrenii v estestvoznanii. Moskva, 1961.
Phil 3003.8   Akademiia Nauk SSSR. Institut Filosofii. Die deutsche Philosophie. Berlin, 1961.
Phil 3003.10   Akademiia Nauk SSSR. Institut Filosofii. Die deutsche Philosophie nach 1945. Berlin, 1961.
Phil 8050.10   Akademiia Nauk SSSR. Institut Filosofii. Iz istorii esteticheskoi mysli drevnosti i srednevekov'ia. Moskva, 1961.
Phil 930.66   Akademiia Nauk SSSR. Institut Filosofii. Izbrannye proizuedeniia progeniia kitaiskikh myslitelei novogo vremeni, 1840-1898. Moskva, 1961.
Phil 8709.23   Akademiia Nauk SSSR. Institut Filosofii. Uspekhi sovremennoi nauki i religiia. Moskva, 1961.
Phil 270.105   Akademiia Nauk SSSR. Institute Filosofii. Problema prichinnosti v sovremennoi biologic. Moskva, 1961.
Phil 6110.24   Akademiia Pedagogicheskikh Nauk RSFSR, Moscow. Institut Psikhologii. Pogranichnye problemy psikhologii i fiziologii. Moskva, 1961.
Phil 331.27   Alejandro, J.M. Estudios gnoseológicos. Barcelona, 1961.
Phil 1505.7   Alessio, Franco Paolo. Studi e ricerche di filosofia medievale. Pavia, 1961.
Phil 6310.4.30   Alexander, Franz G. The scope of psychoanalysis. N.Y., 1961.
Phil 3482.14   Alexandre, Michel. Lecture de Kant. Paris, 1961.
Phil 6980.34   Allers, Rudolf. Existentialism and psychiatry. Springfield, 1961.
Phil 5590.380   Allport, G.W. Pattern and growth in personality. N.Y., 1961.
Phil 6950.12   Alvarez, W.C. Minds that came back. Philadelphia, 1961.
Phil 281.13   Ambacher, Michel. Méthode de la philosophie de la nature. Paris, 1961.
Phil 5040.25   Ambrose, A. Logic. N.Y., 1961.
Phil 6950.14   American Psychiatric Association. Comparative psycholinguistic analysis of two psychotherapeutic interviews. N.Y., 1961.
Phil 5640.135   Anan'ev, B.G. Teoriia oshchushchenii. Leningrad, 1961.
Phil 165.290   Anscombe, G.E.M. Three philosophers. Ithaca, N.Y., 1961.
Phil 8950.7   Antnenko, V.H. Sotsialistychnyi humanizm i khrystianskyi bubov do blyzhiv'oho. Kyïv, 1961.
Phil 5545.215   Antsyferova, L.I. O zakonomernostiakh elementarnoi poznavatel'noi deiatel'nosti. Moskva, 1961.
Phil 8401.28   Apollonio, M. Ontologia dell'arte. Brescia, 1961.
Phil 5238.165   Archivio di Filosofia. Filosofia della alienazione e analisi esistenziale. Padova, 1961.
Phil 8580.33   Archivio di Filosofia. Il problema della demitizzazione. Padova, 1961.
Phil 4983.1.90   Ardao, Arturo. Introducción a Vaz Ferreira. Montevideo, 1961.
Phil 3805.220   Ariebel, Horst. Die Bedeutung des Bösen für die Entwiklung. Ratingen, 1961.
Phil 573.2   Armstrong, David M. Perception and the physical world. London, 1961.
Phil 9290.8   Arvon, Henri. La philosophie du travail. Paris, 1961.
Phil 1700.8   Aseev, I.A. Osnovnye napravleniia burzhuaznoi filosofii i sotsiologii XX veka. Leningrad, 1961.
Phil 5238.188   Association de Psychologie Scientifique de la Langue Française. Les attitudes; symposium, Bordeaux. Paris, 1961.
Phil 5068.52   Astrada, C. Dialéctica y positivismo lógico. Tucumán, 1961.
Phil 175.52   Austin, John L. Philosophical papers. Oxford, 1961.
Phil 4260.140   Badaloni, Nicola. Introduzione a G.B. Vico. Milano, 1961.
Phil 6315.2.270   Bally, Gustav. Einführung in die Psychanalyse Sigmund Freuds. Hamburg, 1961.
Phil 3120.30.91   Balthasar, Hans von. Martin Buber and Christianity. London, 1961.

Chronological Listing

Phil 974.3.128 Baltz, Karl von. Rudolf Steiners musikalische Inpulse. Dornach, 1961.

Phil 1955.6.225 Banerjee, Gour Moham. The theory of democratic education; a critical exposition of John Dewey's philosophy of education. Calcutta, 1961.

Phil 4070.7.35 Banfi, Antonio. Filosofi contemporanei. v.1-2. Milano, 1961.

Phil 4070.7.50 Banfi, Antonio. I problemi di una estetica filosofica. Milano, 1961.

Phil 3640.650 Baroni, C. Nietzsche éducateur. Paris, 1961.

Phil 2750.11.146 Bars, Henry. La politique selon Jacques Maritain. Paris, 1961.

Phil 3270.12.80 Bartelett, J.M. Funktion und Gegenstand. München, 1961.

Phil 176.151.2 Barth, Hans. Wahrheit und Ideologie. 2. Aufl. Erlenbach, 1961.

Phil 960.235 Basanta Kumar Mallik. London, 1961.

Phil 4963.4 Basave Fernandez del Valle, A. Ideario filosófico, 1953-1961. Monterrey, 1961.

Phil 801.37 Baskin, M.P. Filosofiia i zhizn'. Moskva, 1961.

Phil 8876.155 Bastide, Georges. Traite de l'action morale. Paris, 1961. 2v.

Phil 3850.16.110 Bauer, Isidora. Die Tragik in der Existenz des modernen Menschen bei Georg Simmel. München, 1961.

Phil 3850.16.112 Bauer, Isidora. Die Tragik in der Existenz des modernen Menschen bei Georg Simmel. Berlin, 1961.

Phil 8092.6 Bayer, R. L'esthétique mondiale au XXe siècle. Paris, 1961.

Phil 3450.18.150 Beck, Heinrich. Möglichkeit und Notwendigkeit. Pullach, 1961.

Phil 4883.2 Beisembiev, Kasym Beisembievich. Ideino-politicheskie techeniia v Kazakhstane Kontsa XIX-nachala XX veka. Alma-Ata, 1961.

Phil 6980.102 Bellak, L. Contemporary European psychiatry. N.Y., 1961.

Phil 5421.25.5 Benda, Clemen Ernst. The image of love. N.Y., 1961.

Phil 1750.570 Benitez, Claros. Une philosophie pour notre temps. Beirut? 1961.

Phil 3475.3.185F Bentz, Hans Wille. Karl Jaspers in Übersetzungen. Frankfurt, 1961.

Phil 6315.2.290F Bentz, Hans Willi. Sigmund Freud in Übersetzungen. Frankfurt, 1961.

Phil 5241.145 Berg, Jan Hendrik van den. The changing nature of man. 1. ed. N.Y., 1961.

Phil 9558.35 Berg, Robert Frederik. Liegen met en zonder opzet. Utrecht, 1961.

Phil 2475.1.40.10 Bergson, Henri. Essai sur les données immédiates de la conscience. Paris, 1961.

Phil 4791.4 Beritashvili, Ivan Solomonovich. Uchenie o prirode cheloveka v drevnei Gruzii. Tbilisi, 1961.

Phil 6980.105.5 Berne, Eric. Transactional analysis in psychotherapy. N.Y., 1961.

Phil 8402.54 Bernheimer, Richard. The nature of representation. N.Y., 1961.

Phil 5421.15.30 Bezembinder, Thomas G.G. Een experimentele methode om de juistheid van interpersonale perceptie zuiver te bepalen. Proefschrift. Groningen, 1961.

Phil 8876.140 Binkley, Luther J. Contemporary ethical theories. N.Y., 1961.

Phil 3120.27.25 Binswanger, L. Ausgewählte Vorträge und Aufsätze. Bern, 1961. 2v.

Phil 6980.112.50 Bion, Wilfrid R. Experiences in groups. London, 1961.

Phil 6978.12.20 Biran, Sigmund. Melancholie und Todestriebe. München, 1961.

Phil 5838.261 Birney, Robert C. Instinct, an enduring problem in psychology. Princeton, 1961.

Phil 5627.261 Bitter, W. Zur Rettung des Menschlichen in unserer Zeit. Stuttgart, 1961.

Phil 4710.110 Blakeley, Thomas J. Soviet scholasticism. Dordrecht, 1961.

Phil 2905.1.160 Blanchard, Julien P. Méthode et principes du père Teilhard de Chardin. Paris, 1961.

Phil 8876.135A Blanshard, Brand. Reason and goodness. London, 1961.

Phil 3120.55.20 Bloch, Ernst. Gesamtausgabe. Frankfurt, 1961. 15v.

Phil 176.69.15 Bloch, Ernst. Philosophische Grundfragen. Frankfurt, 1961.

Phil 5594.161 Block, J. The Q-sort method in personality assessment. Springfield, Ill., 1961.

Phil 2477.6.32 Blondel, Maurice. Carnets intimes, 1883-1894. Paris, 1961.

Phil 2477.6.34 Blondel, Maurice. Correspondance philosophique. Paris, 1961.

Phil 2477.6.40 Blondel, Maurice. Lettres philosophiques. Paris, 1961.

Phil 6111.63 Blum, Gerald S. A model of the mind. N.Y., 1961.

Phil 176.210 Boas, George. The limits of reason. London, 1961.

Phil 1135.173 Boas, Georje. Rationalism in Greek philosophy. Baltimore, 1961.

Phil 5011.6.6 Bochénski, I.M. A history of formal logic. Notre Dame, Ind., 1961.

Phil 3235.124 Bochmuell, Klaus. Leiblichkeit und Gesellschaft. Göttingen, 1961.

Phil 5722.70 Bochorishvili, A.T. Problema bessoznatel'nogo v psikhologii. Tbilisi, 1961.

Phil 974.3.126 Bock, Emil. Rudolf Steiner. Stuttgart, 1961.

Phil 8402.53 Bodensohn, A. Über das Wesen des Asthetischen. Frankfurt, 1961.

Phil 1020.3.6 Boer, T.J. de. The history of philosophy in Islam. London, 1961.

Phil 1020.49 Bogoutdinov, Alautin M. Ocherki po istorii tadzhikskoi filosofii. Stalinabad, 1961.

Phil 6111.65 Boiko, E. Studies in higher neurodynamics as related to problems of psychology. Jerusalem, 1961.

Phil 5590.423 Bonner, Hubert. Psychology of personality. N.Y., 1961.

Phil 1905.14.100 Boring, E.G. Psychologist at large. N.Y., 1961.

Phil 2477.6.135 Bouillard, Henri. Blondel et le christianisme. Paris, 1961.

Phil 2725.2.105 Bovard, René. Drame de conscience. Paris, 1961.

Phil 5421.20.15 Bovet, Pierre. L'instinct combatif; problèmes de psychologie et d'éducation. 3. éd. Neuchâtel, 1961.

Phil 2070.150 Brennan, Bernard P. The ethics of William James. N.Y., 1961.

Phil 5041.80.2 Brennan, Joseph Gerard. A handbook of logic. 2nd ed. N.Y., 1961.

Phil 6615.20.7 Breuer, Josef. Studies in hysteria. Boston, 1961.

Phil 5627.261.10 Brezzi, Paolo. L'experienza della prehiera. Firenze, 1961.

Phil 165.230 Brinton, Crane. The fate of man. N.Y., 1961.

Phil 2050.245 Broad, C. D. Hume's doctrine of space. London, 1961.

Phil 5241.150 Broadlunt, Donald Eric. Behaviour. 1. ed. N.Y., 1961.

Phil 6315.2.285 Brown, J.A.C. Freud and the post-Freudians. Baltimore, 1961.

Phil 5548.80 Brown, J.S. The motivation of behavior. N.Y., 1961.

Phil 334.14.10 Bruemmer, Vincent. Transcendental criticism and Christian philosophy. Franeker, 1961.

Phil 840.2 Brun, Jean. Les conquêtes de l'homme et la séparation ontologique. Thèse. Paris, 1961.

Phil 8402.39 Brunius, Teddy. Estetik. Stockholm, 1961.

Phil 176.217 Buchler, J. The concept of method. N.Y., 1961.

Phil 5627.134.32 Buchman, Frank. Remaking the world. London, 1961.

Phil 165.295 Bulgarska Akademiia na Naukite, Sofia. Vuprosi na dialekticheskiia materializum i na chastnite kauki. Sofiia, 1961.

Phil 2730.111 Buol, J. Die Anthropologie Maine de Birans. Winterthur, 1961.

Phil 8581.106A Burke, K. The rhetoric of religion. Boston, 1961.

Phil 5421.20.95 Buss, Arnold H. The psychology of aggression. N.Y., 1961.

Phil 8050.24 Buyer, Raymond. Histoire de l'esthétique. Paris, 1961.

Phil 5241.160 Buytendijk, F.J.J. Academische redeväringen. Utrecht, 1961.

Phil 2805.226.6 Cailliet, E. Pascal. N.Y., 1961.

Phil 8430.14 Calcara, A. Discorsi di letteratura e d'arte. Marcianise, 1961.

Phil 8403.40 Calderaro, José. La dimensión estetica del hombre. Buenos Aires, 1961.

Phil 6112.42 California. University Medical Center. Man and civilization: control of the mind. N.Y., 1961.

Phil 4073.65.2 Campanella, Tommaso. De homine. Roma, 1961.

Phil 4073.62F Campanella, Tommaso. Metaphysica. Torino, 1961.

Phil 5242.60 Candland, D.K. Exploring behavior. 1. ed. N.Y., 1961.

Phil 6112.43 Caplan, Gerald. An approach to community mental health. N.Y., 1961.

Phil 848.2 Carbonare, Cleto. La filosofia dell' espirenza e la fondazione dell' umanesims. 2. restampa. Napoli, 1961.

Phil 4075.55 Cardano, Girolamo. The book on games of chance. N.Y., 1961.

Phil 8952.20 Carpenter, Edward. Common sense about Christian ethics. London, 1961.

Phil 3160.12.40 Cassirer, Ernst. The logic of the humanities. New Haven, 1961.

Phil 3160.12.42 Cassirer, Ernst. Zur Logik der Kulturwissenschaften. 2. Aufl. Darmstadt, 1961.

Phil 6312.24 Cattell, Raymond. The meaning and measurement of neuroticism and anxiety. N.Y., 1961.

Phil 6990.58 Celma, Bernal. Curaciones milagrosas. Zaragoza, 1961.

Phil 573.4 Chambers, Frank P. Perception, understanding and society. London, 1961.

Phil 930.44.2 Chan, Wing-tsit. An outline and annotated bibliography of Chinese philosophy. New Haven, 1961.

Phil 5242.66 Charakchiev, Asen. Deistvenostta na misleneto. Sofiia, 1961.

Phil 177.68.25 Chartier, Émile. Propos sur des philosophes. Paris, 1961.

Phil 5812.10 Chauchard, Paul. Des animaux a l'homme. Paris, 1961.

Phil 5812.10.5 Chauchard, Paul. Psychisme humain et psychisme animal. 2e ed. Paris, 1961.

Phil 5812.9 Chauvin, R. Le comportement social chez les animaux. Paris, 1961.

Phil 400.123 Cherkasin, P.P. Gnoseologicheskie korni idealizma. Moskva, 1961.

Phil 5042.70 Chesnokov, P.V. Logicheskaia fraza i predlozhenie. Rostov-na-Donu, 1961.

Phil 3425.560 Chiereghin, F. L'influenza dello Spinozismo nella formazione. Padova, 1961.

Phil 630.55 Chisholm, R.M. Realism and the background of phenomenology. Glencoe, 1961.

Phil 930.60 Chow, Yih-ching. La philosophie chinoise. 2. ed. Paris, 1961.

Phil 4710.115 Chupakhin, I.Ia. Voprosy teorii poniatiia. Leningrad, 1961.

Phil 5520.351 Church, Joseph. Language and the discovery of reality; a developmental psychology of cognition. N.Y., 1961.

Phil 5500.48 Churchman, Charles West. Prediction and optimal decision. Englewood Cliffs, 1961.

Phil 4803.281.20 Chwistek, Leon. Pisma filozoficzne i logiczne. Warszawa, 1961-63. 2v.

Phil 3425.303.5 Chyzhevs'kyi, Dmytro. Hegel bei den Slaven. 2. Aufl. Darmstadt, 1961.

Phil 3425.303.2 Chyzhevs'kyi, Dmytro. Hegel bei den Slaven 2. Aufl. Bad Homburg, 1961.

Phil 1540.72 Cilento, V. La forma Aristotelica in una "Quaestio" medievale. Napoli, 1961.

Phil 1507.9 Cilento, Vincenzo. Medioevo monastico e scolastico. Milano, 1961.

Phil 8692.26 Čížek, D. Od víry k vědě. Praha, 1961.

Phil 5590.375 Cohen, Yehudi A. Social structure and personality. N.Y., 1961.

Phil 530.11.22 Colledge, Eric. The mediaeval mystics of England. N.Y., 1961.

Phil 283.20 Collingwood, Francis. Philosophy of nature. Englewood Cliffs, N.J., 1961.

Phil 1702.11 Collins, James Daniel. A history of modern European philosophy. Milwaukee, 1961.

Phil 2905.1.315 Colomer, Eusebi. Pierre Teilhard de Chardin. Barcelona, 1961.

Phil 5592.178 Conference on Contemporary Issues in Thematic Apperceptive Methods. Contemporary issues in thematic apperceptive methods. Springfield, Ill., 1961.

Phil 177.128 Coreth, Emerich. Metaphysik. Innsbruck, 1961.

Phil 310.2.3 Cornforth, M.C. Dialectical materialism. v.1-3. 3d ed. London, 1961.

Phil 4073.112 Corpano, Antonio. Tommaso Campanella. Bari, 1961.

Phil 3450.19.260 Corvez, Maurice. La philosophie de Heidegger. Paris, 1961.

Phil 2115.168.5 Cranston, M.W. Locke. London, 1961.

Phil 2905.1.175 Crespy, Georges. La pensée théologique de Teilhard de Chardin. Paris, 1961.

Phil 5238.10.2 Current trends in psychological theory. Pittsburgh, 1961.

Phil 165.341 Cuvillier, A. Textes choisis des auteurs philosophiques. v.2. Paris, 1961.

Phil 310.415 Cvekl, Jiři. Lid a osobnost v dějrhách. Praha, 1961.

Phil 5590.370 Dalton, R.H. Personality and social interaction. Boston, 1961.

Phil 310.360 Danilenko, D.I. Dialekticheskii materializm. Moskva, 1961.

1961 - cont.

Phil 9075.70   D'Arcy, Eric. Conscience and its right to freedom. N.Y., 1961.

Phil 1703.12.2   Datta, D.M. The chief currents of contemporary philosophy. 2nd ed. Calcutta, 1961.

Phil 5066.180.5   Day, John P. Inductive probability. London, 1961.

Phil 5066.180   Day, John P. Inductive probability. N.Y., 1961.

Phil 310.320   Deborin, A.M. Filosofiia i politika. Moskva, 1961.

Phil 4080.3.360   DeGennaro, Angelo A. The philosophy of Benedetto Croce. 1st ed. N.Y., 1961.

Phil 5545.181.5   Delay, Jean Paul Louis. Les maladies de la mémoire. 3. éd. Paris, 1961.

Phil 2905.1.115   Delfgaauw, B.M.I. Teilhard de Chardin. Baarn, 1961.

Phil 4351.6.80   Delgado Varela, José M. La gracia divina en el correlativismo. Madrid, 1961.

Phil 5585.205   Dember, William Norton. The psychology of perception. N.Y., 1961.

Phil 6013.3   Denis, Robert. Le visage de l'homme. Paris, 1961.

Phil 585.130   Desan, Wilfrid. The planetary man. Washington, 1961.

Phil 2520.35.47   Descarter, René. Discours de la méthode. 2. ed. Manchester, 1961.

Phil 2520.35.48   Descartes, René. Discours de la méthode. Paris, 1961.

Phil 2520.218.5   Descartes, René. Les pages immortelles de Descartes. Paris, 1961.

Phil 3195.18.30   Dessauer, Friedrich. Durch die Tore der neuen Zeit. Göttingen, 1961.

Phil 8583.43   Dessauer, Philipp. Die naturale Meditation. München, 1961.

Phil 8870.23   Dewey, Robert E. Problems of ethics. N.Y., 1961.

Phil 3195.6.50   Dilthey, Wilhelm. Meanings in history. London, 1961.

Phil 4352.1.79   Dios Mendoza, J. de. Bibliografia balmesiana. Barcelona, 1961.

Phil 5350.3   Dobler, u. Die Lebenswende als Reifungskrisis. München, 1961.

Phil 5243.60   Donceel, Joseph. Philosophical psychology. 2d ed. N.Y., 1961.

Phil 978.49.845   Dornach, Switzerland. Goetheanum. Goetheanum. Dornach, 1961.

Phil 6319.1.214   Dry, Avis Mary. The psychology of Jung. London, 1961.

Phil 2905.1.245   Duroux, P.E. La prévie, la réconciliation de la science et la foi. Lyon, 1961.

Phil 6114.18   Ebertin, B. Gehirn und Seele. Aalen, 1961.

Phil 8405.7   Egorov, A.G. O reaktsionnoi sushchnosti. Moskva, 1961.

Phil 310.270   Ehlen, Peter. Der Acheismus im dialektischen Materialismus. München, 1961.

Phil 3200.8.5   Ehrlich, W. Kulturgeschichtliche Autobiographie. Tübingen, 1961.

Phil 7150.59   Ellis, E.R. Traitor within: our suicide problem. 1st ed. Garden City, N.Y., 1961.

Phil 6114.20   Estabrooks, George Hoben. The future of the human mind. 1st ed. N.Y., 1961.

Phil 8870.25   Ethische verkenningen. Nijkerk, 1961. 10v.

Phil 5645.58   Evans, Ralph. Introduction to color. N.Y., 1961.

Phil 400.88.3   Ewing, Alfred C. Idealism. 3. ed. London, 1961.

Phil 6314.11.5   Eysenck, Hans J. Handbook of abnormal psychology. N.Y., 1961.

Phil 9240.22   Farrer, Austin. Love almighty and ills unlimited. 1st ed. Garden City, N.Y., 1961.

Phil 3270.16.31   Fechner, O. Das System der ontischen Kategorien. Hildesheim, 1961.

Phil 3450.19.255   Feick, Hildegard. Index zu Heideggers Sein und Zeit. Tübingen, 1961.

Phil 978.49.855   Fels, Alice. Studien zur Einführung in die Mysteriendramen Rudolf Steiners. 2. Aufl. Dornach, 1961.

Phil 8880.50   Findlay, John Niemayer. Values and intentions. London, 1961.

Phil 8630.15   Findlay, Stephen. Immortal longings. London, 1961.

Phil 3005.9   Finger, Otto. Von der Materialität des Seele. Berlin, 1961.

Phil 1706.11   Flam, Leopold. La philosophie au tournant de notre temps. Bruxelles, 1961.

Phil 2050.242   Flew, A. Hume's philosophy of belief. London, 1961.

Phil 3425.574   Focht, I. Mogućnost, nužnost, slučajnost, stvarnost. Sarajevo, 1961.

Phil 5421.20.5   Folkard, M.S. A sociological contribution to the understanding of aggression and its treatment. Coulsdon, 1961.

Phil 8980.403   Formirovanie moral'nogo oblika sovetskogo rabochego. Moskva, 1961.

Phil 6955.22   Foucault, Michel. Folie et déraison. Paris, 1961.

Phil 180.68.15   Foulquié, Paul. Cours de philosophie. Paris, 1961.

Phil 3270.15.31   Frackenheim, Emil L. Metaphysics and historicity. Milwaukee, 1961.

Phil 848.4   Franchini, Raffaello. Le origini della dialettica. Napoli, 1961.

Phil 2905.1.205   Francoeur, Robert. The world of Teilhard. Baltimore, 1961.

Phil 6315.52   Frank, J.D. Persuasion and healing. London, 1961.

Phil 6315.2.37.1   Freud, Sigmund. The ego and the id. N.Y., 1961.

Phil 6315.2.42.5A   Freud, Sigmund. Inhibitions, symptoms and anxiety. London, 1961.

Phil 5066.190   Freudenthal, Hans. Exacte logica. Haarlem, 1961.

Phil 9450.27.2   Freund, Ludwig. Politik und Ethik. 2. Aufl. Gütersloh, 1961.

Phil 8735.55   Frolov, I.T. O prichinnosti i tselesoobraznosti v zhivoi prirode. Moskva, 1961.

Phil 5465.120   Furlong, E.J. Imagination. London, 1961.

Phil 4710.130   Galaktionov, A.A. Istoriia russkoi filosofii. Moskva, 1961.

Phil 4120.9.30   Galli, Gallo. Linee fondamentali d'une filosofia dello spirito. Torino, 1961.

Phil 806.30   Gambra Ciudad, R. Historia sencilla de la filosofia. Madrid, 1961.

Phil 181.128   Garcia Bacca, J.D. Elementos de filosofia. 2. ed. Caracas, 1961.

Phil 4357.10   García Lahiguera, Fernando. La libertad. Valencia, 1961.

Phil 181.80.10   Garcia Morente, Manuel. Ejercicios espirituales. Madrid, 1961.

Phil 6316.20   Garfield, Sol. Introductory clinical psychology. N.Y., 1961.

Phil 5246.29.6   Garrett, Henry E. General psychology. 2. ed. N.Y., 1961.

Phil 1706.1.10   Gaultier, Jules de. From Kant to Nietzsche. London, 1961.

Phil 4803.497.480   Gawecki, Bolesław J. Władysław Mieczysław Kozłowski, 1858-1935. Wrocław, 1961.

Phil 1607.10   Gelder, Herman Arend Enno van. The two reformations in the 16th century. The Hague, 1961.

1961 - cont.

Phil 5425.102   Gemant, Andrew. The nature of the genius. Springfield, Ill., 1961.

Phil 3425.568   Georgiav, F.I. Protivopolozhnost' Marksistskogo i Gegelevskogo ucheniia o soznanii. Moskva, 1961.

Phil 3280.31   Geulincx, A. De virtute et primis ejuis proprietatilius. Pretoria, 1961.

Phil 6998.4.5   Ginott, Haim G. Group psychotherapy with children. N.Y., 1961.

Phil 4080.3.340   Giordano-Orsini, Gian Napoleon. Benedetto Croce. Carbondale, 1961.

Phil 4688.110.36   Girnius, Juozas. Tauta ir tautine ištikimybé. Chicago, 1961.

Phil 6946.1.15   Goffman, E. Asylums. Garden City, 1961.

Phil 6956.16   Goldfarb, W. Childhood schizophrenia. Cambridge, 1961.

Phil 365.55   Gondge, Thomas A. The ascent of life. Toronto, 1961.

Phil 9450.50   Gordis, R. Politics and ethics. Santa Barbara, Calif., 1961.

Phil 5360.14   Gorskii, D.P. Vopsosy abstraktsii i obrazovanie poniatiia. Moskva, 1961.

Phil 2475.1.400   Gouhier, Henri. Bergson et le Christ des évangiles. Paris, 1961.

Phil 735.235   Graham, Angus C. The problem of value. London, 1961.

Phil 1535.18.4   Gredt, Joseph. Elementa philosophia. Barcinone, 1961. 2v.

Phil 6625.10   Greenacre, Phyllis. Affective disorders. N.Y., 1961.

Phil 8696.21   Greene, J.C. Darwin and the modern world view. Baton Rouge, 1961.

Phil 2610.110   Gregory, Tullio. Scetticismo ed empirismo. Bari, 1961.

Phil 5374.220   Greidanus, J.H. Fundamental physical theory and the concept of consciousness. Oxford, 1961.

Phil 2905.1.165   Grenet, Paul. Teilhard de Chardin. Paris, 1961.

Phil 1020.41   Grigorian, S.N. Izbrannye proizredenii myshtelei stran Blizhnego Srednego Vostoka. Moskva, 1961.

Phil 4073.104.10   Grillo, F. Questioni Campanelliane. Cosenza, 1961.

Phil 6316.8.12   Groddeck, Georg. Das Buch vom Es. Wiesbaden, 1961.

Phil 6316.8.13   Groddeck, Georg. The look of it. N.Y., 1961.

Phil 8407.1   Gromov, Evgenii S. Esteticheskii ideal. Moskva, 1961.

Phil 5400.157   Grossart, Friedrich. Gefühl und Strebung. München, 1961.

Phil 310.340   Grushin, B.H. Ocherki logiki istoricheskogo issledovaniia. Moskva, 1961.

Phil 3195.6.145   Grzesik, Juergen. Die Geschichtlichkeit als Wesensverfassung des Menschen. Bonn, 1961.

Phil 2630.11.15   Guitton, Jean. Une mère dans sa vallée. Paris, 1961.

Phil 4816.8   Gulian, C.I. Peredovye rumynskie mysliteli XVIII-XIXVV. Moskva, 1961.

Phil 6316.14   Guntrip, H.J.S. Personality structure and human interaction. London, 1961.

Phil 6316.14.5   Guntrip, H.J.S. Personality structure and human interaction. N.Y., 1961.

Phil 1750.560.25   Habachi, René. Une philosophie pour notre temps. Beirut? 1961.

Phil 510.1.2.6   Haeckel, Ernst. Die Welträtsel; gemeinverständliche Studien über monistische Philosophie. Berlin, 1961.

Phil 3450.29.20   Haecker, Theodor. Satire und Polemik. München, 1961.

Phil 4582.4.46   Hägerström, Axel. Ratten och Viljan. Lund, 1961.

Phil 978.49.850   Haeusler, Friedrich. Weltenville und Menschenziele in der Geschichte. Dornach, 1961.

Phil 8882.85   Haezrahi, P. The price of morality. London, 1961.

Phil 974.3.130   Hahn, Herbert. Rudolf Steiner wie ich ihn Sah und Erlebte. Stuttgart, 1961.

Phil 8622.50   Hailsham, Quinten McG. The need for faith in a scientifc age. Glasgow, 1961.

Phil 338.38   Halt, Everett W. Our knowledge of fact and value. Chapel Hill, 1961.

Phil 5585.242   Hamlyn, David Walter. The psychology of perception. London, 1961.

Phil 5585.180   Hamlyn, David Walter. Sensation and perception. N.Y., 1961.

Phil 182.122   Hammond, A.L. Proprieties and vagaries. Baltimore, 1961.

Phil 338.36   Hampshire, S. Feeling and expression. London, 1961.

Phil 7069.61.30   Harlow, Samuel R. A life after death. 1. ed. Garden City, 1961.

Phil 974.3.145   Hartmann, Georg. Erziehung aus Menschenerkenntnis. Dornach, 1961.

Phil 6980.348   Hartmann, Heinz. La psicología del yo y el problema de la adaptación. México, 1961.

Phil 3270.4.84   Hartmann, Richard. P.J.A. Feuerbachs politisches. Berlin, 1961.

Phil 974.3.108   Harwood, A.C. The faithful thinker. London, 1961.

Phil 7069.61.40   Haynes, Renée. The hidden springs. London, 1961.

Phil 8632.20   Head, Joseph. Reincarnation. N.Y., 1961.

Phil 3425.73.9   Hegel, Georg Wilhelm Friedrich. The phenomenology of mind. 2nd ed. London, 1961.

Phil 3425.34.29   Hegel, Georg Wilhelm Friedrich. Science of logic. London, 1961. 2v.

Phil 5217.5   Heidbreder, Edna. Seven psychologies. N.Y., 1961.

Phil 3640.620   Heidegger, M. Nietzsche. Pfullingen, 1961. 2v.

Phil 8432.2   Heidsieck, F. L'inspiration. 1. éd. Paris, 1961.

Phil 5645.57   Heimendahl, E. Licht und Farbe. Berlin, 1961.

Phil 6317.20.15   Hendrick, Ives. The birth of institute. Freeport, 1961.

Phil 182.124   Hengstenberg, Hans Edward. Freiheit und Seinsordnung. Stuttgart, 1961.

Phil 5238.192   Henle, Mary. Documents of Gestalt psychology. Berkeley, 1961.

Phil 3489.40   Hermann, Horst. Das Problem der objektiven Realität bei Kant. Mainz, 1961.

Phil 4070.8.80   Heuser, H. Ludwig Buzorinis. München, 1961.

Phil 338.34   Hill, T.E. Contemporary theories of knowledge. N.Y., 1961.

Phil 8408.21   Hirsch, W. Substanz und Thema in der Kunst. Amsterdam, 1961.

Phil 807.18.5   Hirschberger, Johannes. Geschichte der Philosophie. 5. Aufl. Freiburg, 1961-60. 2v.

Phil 2045.10.5   Hobbes, Thomas. Opera philosophica. Aalen, 1961. 5v.

Phil 2520.330   Hoeven, Pieter van der. Metafysica en fysica bij Descartes. Gorinchem, 1961.

Phil 3489.42   Hofman, Franz. Kants erst Antinomie in ihrer Stellung als Indirekter. Mainz? 1961.

Phil 6117.50   Hofmann, H. Religion and mental health. N.Y., 1961.

Phil 2648.52.6   Holbach, Paul Henri T. Le christianisme dévoilé. Herblay, 1961.

Phil 5247.73   Holland, James G. The analysis of behavior. N.Y., 1961.

Phil 5238.182   Hommage à Georges Henyer. Paris, 1961.

Phil 2055.13.30   Hook, Sidney. The quest for being. N.Y., 1961.

Phil 3475.3.190   Horn, H. Philosophischer und christlicher Glaube. Essen, 1961.

1961 - cont.

Phil 8882.80   Hospers, John. Human conduct. N.Y., 1961.
Phil 5017.6   Howell, W.S. Logic and rhetoric in England. N.Y., 1961.
Phil 310.440   Hrušovský, I. Z minulosti a sučasnosti filozofi. Bratislava, 1961.
Phil 310.410   Hrzal, L. Predmet a metoda historického materialismu. Praha, 1961.
Phil 1707.28   Huebscher, Arthur. Van Hegel zu Heidegger. Stuttgart, 1961.
Phil 1750.90.2   Hughes, Henry Stuart. Consciousness and society. N.Y., 1961.
Phil 1750.725   Humanismus heute. Berlin, 1961.
Phil 5247.74   Hunt, J. Intelligence and experience. N.Y., 1961.
Phil 1750.166.91   Huxley, J.S. The humanist frame. London, 1961.
Phil 183.6   Iadov, V.A. Ideologiia kak forma dukhovnoi deiatel'nosti obshchestva. London, 1961.
Phil 339.5   Iakushevskii, I.T. Praktika i ee rol' v protsese poznaniia. Moskva, 1961.
Phil 8663.4   In search of God and immortality. Boston, 1961.
Phil 4970.1.20   Ingenieros, José. Antología; su pensamiento en sus mejores páginas. Buenos Aires, 1961.
Phil 165.353   Institutiones philosophiae. Torino, 1961-63. 7v.
Phil 70.4   International Congress for Analytical Psychology, 1st, Zurich, 1958. Current trends in analytical psychology. London, 1961.
Phil 8698.5   Irkolin, N.E. Vera i znanie; o Boge, religii. Muinkhen, 1961.
Phil 5585.190   Ittelson, William H. Perceptual changes in psychopathology. New Brunswick, N.J., 1961.
Phil 310.420   Iz istorii marksistsko-leninskoi filosofii posle vtoroi mirovoi voeny. Moskva, 1961.
Phil 6319.12   Jacob, Hans. Western psychotherapy and Hindu-Sãdhanã. London, 1961.
Phil 5249.2.5.10   James, William. Psychology. N.Y., 1961.
Phil 2070.75.10   James, William. Selected letters. N.Y., 1961.
Phil 1750.635.5   Jaroszewski, T.M. Renesans scholastyki. Warszawa, 1961.
Phil 3475.3.77   Jaspers, Karl. The future of mankind. Chicago, 1961.
Phil 3475.3.72   Jaspers, Karl. Wo stehen wir heute. Olten, 1961.
Phil 720.61   Jenny, Guido. Auf der Suche nach Wahrheit. Zürich, 1961.
Phil 585.176   Jeuscher, Ernest. L'homme et son destin. Paris, 1961.
Phil 4360.2   Joannes XXI. Obras filosoficas. 2. ed. Barcelona, 1961.
Phil 6946.1.5   Joint Commission on Mental Illness and Health. Action for mental health. N.Y., 1961.
Phil 6315.2.151   Jones, Ernest. The life and work of Sigmund Freud. London, 1961.
Phil 6319.2.4.5   Jones, Ernest. Papers on psycho-analysis. 5th ed. Boston, 1961.
Phil 5585.214   Jordan, Nehemiah. Perception. Santa Monica, 1961.
Phil 9240.26   Journet, Charles. Le mal. Bruges? 1961.
Phil 5640.132   Juritsch, M. Sinn und Geist. Freiburg, 1961.
Phil 3492.65   Kaczmaeck, S. Początki Kantyzmu. Poznań, 1961.
Phil 3549.19   Kaiser, Josef. Summe der Filosofie. München, 1961.
Phil 310.365   Kalatskii, V.P. Dialekticheskogo materializm. Moskva, 1961.
Phil 8980.472   Kánský, Jiří. Čo je zmyslom našho života? Bratislava, 1961.
Phil 3480.52.12   Kant, Immanuel. The critique of judgement. Oxford, 1961.
Phil 3480.32.26A   Kant, Immanuel. Critique of pure reason. N.Y., 1961.
Phil 3480.28.38   Kant, Immanuel. Frühschriften. Berlin, 1961. 2v.
Phil 3480.35.5   Kant, Immanuel. Lo disertatio de 1770, sobre la forma y los principios del mundo sensible y del inteligible. Madrid, 1961.
Phil 3480.67.100   Kant, Immanuel. The moral law. London, 1961.
Phil 3480.41.10   Kant, Immanuel. Vorlesungen. Berlin, 1961.
Phil 1710.12   Kaplan, A. The new world of philosophy. N.Y., 1961.
Phil 5590.437   Kaplan, Bert. Studying personality cross-culturally. N.Y., 1961.
Phil 575.230   Kaplan, Bert. Studying personality crossculturally. Evanston, Illinois, 1961.
Phil 5653.8   Kare, M.R. Physiological and behavioral aspects of taste. Chicago, 1961.
Phil 8665.20   Karliak, A.S. Ocherki po nauchnomu ateizmu. Minsk, 1961.
Phil 8590.31   Die katholische Glaubenswelt. v.3. Freiburg, 1961.
Phil 5250.65   Kelly, William L. Die neuscholastische und die empirische Psychologie. Meisenheim, 1961.
Phil 8590.34.2   Kerényi, Karoly. Umgang mit Göttlichem. 2. Aufl. Göttingen, 1961.
Phil 810.14   Ketoren, Oliva. Eurooppalaisen ihmisen maailmansatsomus. Helsingissa, 1961.
Phil 720.59   Khachaturian, Haig. The coherence theory of truth. Beirut, 1961.
Phil 310.315   Khrestomatiia po marksistsko-leninskoi filosofii. Moskva, 1961. 3v.
Phil 1135.174   Kienle, W. Die Berichte über die Sukressionen der Philosophen. Berlin, 1961.
Phil 5585.165   Kilpatrick, F.P. Explorations in transactional psychology. N.Y., 1961.
Phil 5238.194   King, R.A. Readings for an introduction to psychology. N.Y., 1961.
Phil 2428.5   Kingston, Frederick Temple. French existentialism; a Christian critique. Toronto, 1961.
Phil 5590.390   Kleiner, Fritz. Das Problem der Persönlichkeit in der amerikanischen Psychologie. München, 1961.
Phil 530.11.15.5   Knowles, David. The English mystical tradition. London, 1961.
Phil 8665.9   Koch, H.G. Abschaffung Tottes? Stuttgart, 1961.
Phil 3120.30.85.2   Kohn, Hans. Martin Buber: sein Werk und seine Zeit. Köln, 1961.
Phil 310.335   Kopnin, P.V. Dialektika kak logika. Kiev, 1961.
Phil 2905.1.140   Kopp, Josef Vital. Entstehung und Zukunft des Menschen. Luzern, 1961.
Phil 4960.250   Korn, Alejandro. El pensamiento argentino. Buenos Aires, 1961.
Phil 8980.496.5   Kosolapov, S.M. Voprosy vospitaniia trudiashchikhsia v dukhe kommunisticheskoi nravstvennosti. Moskva, 1961.
Phil 185.49.2   Kotarbiński, Tadeusz. Elementy teorii poznania. Wyd. 2. Wrocław, 1961.
Phil 5250.70   Kotarbiński, Tadeusz. Osnova primena prakseologije. Beograd, 1961.
Phil 8980.497   Kotov, L.I. Razuitie nravstvennykh ubezhdenii i privychek v protsesse kommunisticheskogo vospitaniia. Moskva, 1961.
Phil 5585.217   Kottenhoff, H. Was ist richtiges Sehen mit Umkehrbillen. Meisenheim am Glan, 1961.
Phil 8980.497.20   Kovalev, S.M. Rabotat' i zhit' po kommunisticheski. Moskva, 1961.
Phil 310.400   Kovalgin, V.M. Marksistskaia filosofiia protiv idealizma i metafiziki. Minsk, 1961.

1961 - cont.

Phil 185.96   Koyré, Alexandre. Etudes d'histoire de la pensée philosophique. Paris, 1961.
Phil 3549.18   Kraus, Annie. Vom Wesen und Ursprung der Dummheit. Köln, 1961.
Phil 5710.18   Kretschmer, Ernst. Körperbau und Charakter. Berlin, 1961.
Phil 3010.3.2   Kroner, R. Von Kant bis Hegel. v.1-2. Tübingen, 1961.
Phil 930.62   Kuo, Mo-jo. Filosofy drevnego kitaia. Moskva, 1961.
Phil 2490.140.5   Lacroix, Jean. La sociologie d'Auguste Comte. 2. éd. Paris, 1961.
Phil 1711.9   Laín Entralgo, Pedro. Teoría y realidad del otro. Madrid, 1961. 2v.
Phil 6961.19   Laing, Ronald David. The self and others. London, 1961.
Phil 5850.253.10   Laird, Donald A. The dynamics of personal efficiency. 1. ed. N.Y., 1961.
Phil 811.16   Lamanna, E. Paolo. Storia della filosofia. Firenze, 1961. 6v.
Phil 8412.30   Lamouche, A. Esthétique. Paris, 1961.
Phil 3585.25   Landmann, M. Der Mensch als Schöpfer und Geschäpf der Kultur. München, 1961.
Phil 585.95   Langdon-Davies, J. On the nature of man. N.Y., 1961.
Phil 5548.101   Langkjaer, Asger. Contributions to a general normalogy, or Theory of purpose-setting. København, 1961.
Phil 735.244   Langweg, R. Das Phänomen der Wertblindheit. Lingen-Ems, 1961?
Phil 4260.147   Lanza, Franco. Saggi di poetica vichiana. Varese, 1961.
Phil 6121.38   La Rivière, A. L'homme et le complexe normal. Paris, 1961.
Phil 6990.3.90   Laurentin, René. Lourdes. Paris, 1961. 6v.
Phil 5590.422   Lazarus, Richard. Adjustment and personality. N.Y., 1961.
Phil 2340.10.148   Leclerc, Ivor. The relevance of Whitehead. London, 1961.
Phil 5066.200   Lee, Harold Newton. Symbolic logic. N.Y., 1961.
Phil 8412.3   Lefrancq, J. Oser penser. Neuchâtel, 1961.
Phil 6961.18   Leibbrand, Werner. Der Wahnsinn. Freiburg, 1961.
Phil 3552.430   Leibniz, G.W. Confessio philosophi. Paris, 1961.
Phil 3552.52   Leibniz, Gottfried Wilhelm. Confessio philosophi. Paris, 1961.
Phil 3552.39.5   Leibniz, Gottfried Wilhelm. Neue Abhandlungen über den menschlichen verstand. Frankfurt, 1961. 2v.
Phil 5221.8   Leigh, D. The historical development of British psychiatry. Oxford, 1961.
Phil 1750.630   Leist, Fritz. Existenz im Nichts. München, 1961.
Phil 8505.8.15   Leningrad. Muzei Istorii Religii i Ateizma. Nauka i religiia. Moskva, 1961.
Phil 5625.101   Le Ny, Jean François. Le conditionnement. Paris, 1961.
Phil 8666.22   Lepp, Ignace. Psychoanalyse de l'atéisme moderne. Paris, 1961.
Phil 2725.44   Levert, Paule. L'idée de commencement. Paris, 1961.
Phil 2725.42   Levinas, Emmanuel. Totalité et l'infini. La Haye, 1961.
Phil 8591.44.6   Lewis, Clive Staples. The screwtape letters and Screwtape proposes a toast. London, 1961.
Phil 186.146   Librizzi, Carmelo. Morale e conoscenza; saggi critici. Padova, 1961.
Phil 165.280   Lieb, Irwin C. Experience, existence and good. Carbondale, 1961.
Phil 3120.4.80   Liebing, H. Zurschen Orthodoxie und Aufklärung. Tubingen, 1961.
Phil 5780.22A   Lifton, Robert. Thought reform and the psychology of totalism. N.Y., 1961.
Phil 8620.54   Ling, Trevor. The significance of Satan. London, 1961.
Phil 3011.7   Linke, Paul F. Niedergangserscheinungen in der Philosophie der Gegenwart. München, 1961.
Phil 930.58   Liou, Kia-hway. L'ésprit synthétique de la Chine. Paris, 1961.
Phil 2115.70.16   Locke, J. Lettera sulla tolleranza. Firenze, 1961.
Phil 2115.61   Locke, J. Scritti editi e inediti sulla tolleranza. Torino, 1961.
Phil 8886.76   Loegstrup, K.E.C. Kunst og etik. Kobenhavn, 1961.
Phil 6980.429   Loewnan, H.W. Reifungskrisen im Kindes- und Jugendalter. Göttingen, 1961.
Phil 6980.431   López Ibor, Juan. La agonía del psicoanalisis. 3. ed. Madrid, 1961.
Phil 8961.16   Lottin, O. Etudes de morale histoire et doctrine. Gembloux, 1961.
Phil 6953.18   Louisiana. Southeast Louisiana Hospital, Mandeville. Psychotherapy with schizophrenics. Baton Rouge, 1961.
Phil 1711.8A   Lovejoy, A.D. Reflections on human nature. Baltimore, 1961.
Phil 292.8.6   Lovejoy, A.O. The great chain of being. Cambridge, Mass., 1961.
Phil 186.140   Lovejoy, A.O. The reason, the understanding and time. Baltimore, 1961.
Phil 1750.115.55   Luijpen, Wilhelmus Antonius Maria. De fenomenologie is een humorisme. Amsterdam, 1961.
Phil 1750.405.5   Lukacs, G.S. Existentialisme ou Marxisme. 2e éd. Paris, 1961.
Phil 4803.536.20   Lukasiewicz, Jan. L zagadnień logiki i filozofii; pisma wybrane. Warszawa, 1961.
Phil 3493.30   Luperini, Cesuce. Spazio e materia in Kant. Firenze, 1961.
Phil 8592.108   MacKinnon, D.M. The borderlands of theology. Cambridge, Eng., 1961.
Phil 8962.20   Maclagan, W.G. The theological frontier of ethics. N.Y., 1961.
Phil 8702.28   MacMurray, John. Religion, art, and science. Liverpool, 1961.
Phil 4769.9.21   Maday, J. Wladimir Sergejewitsch Solowjew. Düsseldorf, 1961.
Phil 6315.2.280   Madison, P. Freud's concept of repression and defense, its theoretical and observational language. Minneapolis, 1961.
Phil 165.270   Magill, F.N. Masterpieces of world philosophy in summary form. 1st ed. N.Y., 1961.
Phil 2905.1.155   Magloire, George. Présence de Pierre Teilhard de Chardin. Paris, 1961.
Phil 310.390   Makarov, Aleksei D. Istoriko-filosofskoe vvedenie k kursu dialektiki istoricheskogo materializma. Moskva, 1961.
Phil 8980.552   Makarova, N.F. Pogovorim o zhizni i sehe. Moskva, 1961.
Phil 2725.11.100   Manchausser, Gaston. L'idéalisme de Lachelier. Paris, 1961.
Phil 165.86   Mandelbaum, Maurice H. Philosophic problems. N.Y., 1961.
Phil 6049.61   Mangoldt, Ursula von. Zeichen des Schicksals im Bild der Hand. Olten, 1961.
Phil 720.60   Manzana Martinez de Marañon, José. Objektivität und Wahrheit. Vitoria, 1961.
Phil 720.63   Manzana Martinez de Marañon, José. Objektivität und Wahrheit. Vitoria, 1961.

1961 - cont.

Phil 2750.30.30   Marc, André. Raison et conversion chrétienne. Paris, 1961.

Phil 5238.199   Margarete Eberhardt, zum 18. August, 1961. Hamburg, 1961.

Phil 4473.1.30   Marinho, José. Teoria do ser e da verdade. Lisboa, 1961.

Phil 2750.11.83   Maritain, Jacques. On the use of philosophy. Princeton, N.J., 1961.

Phil 2750.11.70.5   Maritain, Jacques. The range of reason. N.Y., 1961.

Phil 2750.11.87   Maritain, Jacques. La responsibilité de l'artiste. Paris, 1961.

Phil 2520.345   Marshall, D.J. Physik und Metaphysik bei Descartes. München? 1961.

Phil 343.28   Martel, K. Podstawowe zagadnienia marksistowskiej teorii poznania. Warszawa, 1961.

Phil 187.156.5   Martin, Gottfried. An introduction to general metaphysics. London, 1961.

Phil 75.62   Martínez Gómez, Luis. Bibliografía filosófica. Barcelona, 1961.

Phil 585.145   Martins, D. Mistério do homen. Braga, 1961.

Phil 5238.170   Marx, Melvin Herman. Psychological theory. N.Y., 1961.

Phil 3450.19.230   Marx, Werner. Heidegger und die Tradition. Stuttgart, 1961.

Phil 3925.16.275   Maslow, Alexander. A study in Wittgenstein's Tractatus. Berkeley, 1961.

Phil 270.115   Mazierski, S. Determinizm i indet w aspekcie fizykalrym i filozoficznym. Lublin, 1961.

Phil 4190.2.80   Mazzarella, Pasquale. Ira finito e infinito; saggio sul pensiero di Carmelo Ottaviano. Padova, 1961.

Phil 3801.563   Meier, F. Die Idee der Transzendentalphilosophie. Winterthur, 1961.

Phil 3640.635   Melo, R. de. Considerações sobre Frederico Nietzsche. Coimbra, 1961.

Phil 2490.171   Mendieta y Núñez, L. Homenajes: Augusto Comte. 1. ed. México, 1961.

Phil 5545.205   Meredith, Patrick. Learning, remembering and knowing. N.Y., 1961.

Phil 3425.602   Merker, Nicolas. Le origini della logica hegeliana. Milano, 1961.

Phil 310.16.5   Merleau-Ponty, Maurice. Les aventures de la dialectique. Paris, 1961.

Phil 978.59.110   Methorst-Kuiper, A. Krishnamurti. Amsterdam, 1961.

Phil 812.40   Metzke, Erwin. Coincidentia oppositorum. Witten, 1961.

Phil 1750.660   Meyer, H.J. Die Technisierung der Welt. Tübingen, 1961.

Phil 735.230   Mezing, Otto O. A grammar of human values. Pittsburgh, 1961.

Phil 1117.14   Michaelides, Konstantinos. Mensch und Kosmos im ihrer Zusammengehörigkeit bei den frühen griechischen Denkern. München? 1961?

Phil 6315.2.295   Mikhailov, Feliks T. Za porogom soznaniia; kriticheskii ocherk freidizma. Moskva, 1961.

Phil 2138.79.10.5   Mill, John S. Autobiography. Early draft. Urbana, 1961.

Phil 2138.20   Mill, John S. The philosophy of John Stuart Mill. N.Y., 1961.

Phil 343.31   Millán Puellas, A. La función social de los saberes liberales. Madrid, 1961.

Phil 3494.62   Milmed, Bella Kussy. Kant and current philosophical issues. N.Y., 1961.

Phil 5252.135   Misiak, H. The philosophical roots of scientific psychology. N.Y., 1961.

Phil 1117.8.18   Mondolfo, Rodolfo. Il pensiero antico. 3. ed. Firenze, 1961.

Phil 6322.26.5   Money-Kyrle, R.E. Man's picture of his world. London, 1961.

Phil 4372.1.140   Montegú, Bernardo. Filosofía del humanismo de Juan Luis Vives. Madrid, 1961.

Phil 1812.12   Moore, E.C. American pragmatism. N.Y., 1961.

Phil 8088.8   Morawski, Stefan. Studia z historii myśli estetycznej XVII:i XIX wieku. Warszawa, 1961.

Phil 9560.52   Morisset, B. Le syllogisme prudentiel. Laval, 1961.

Phil 8887.120   Morris, B. Philosophical aspects of culture. Yellow Springs, Ohio, 1961

Phil 6322.48   Moscovici, Serge. La psychanalyse, son image et son public. Paris, 1961.

Phil 1750.645   Moscow. Akademiia Obshchestvennykh Nauk. Kritika sovremennoi burzhuaznoi filosofii i sotsiologii. Moskva, 1961.

Phil 8702.24   Mouiren, Trophine. La création. Paris, 1961.

Phil 2750.22.5   Mounier, E. Ouevres. Paris, 1961. 5v.

Phil 6980.482   Mowrer, O.H. The crisis in psychiatry and religion. Princeton, N.J., 1961.

Phil 5068.50   Mshvenieradze, V.V. Filosofiia reopozitivizma i semantiki. Moskva, 1961.

Phil 1712.21   Mshvenieradze, V.V. Osnovnye fecheniia sovremennoi burzhuaznoi filosofii. Kiev, 1961.

Phil 5590.350   Mucchielli, R. La caractérologie à l'âge scientifique. Neuchâtel, 1961.

Phil 1750.750   Mueller-Schwefe, Hans Rudolf. Existenzphilosophie. Zürich, 1961.

Phil 3120.30.130   München ehrt Martin Buber. München, 1961.

Phil 4810.2   Muenz, Teodor. Filosofia slovenského osvietenstva. Vyd. 1. Bratislava, 1961.

Phil 7069.29.61   Muldoon, Sylvan J. The projection of the astral body. London, 1961.

Phil 2225.5.106   Mullin, Albert A. Philosophical comments on the philosophies of Charles S. Peirce and Ludwig Wittgenstein. Urbana, Ill., 1961.

Phil 5252.89.4A   Munn, Norman Leslie. Psychology. 2. ed. Boston, 1961.

Phil 5627.261.15   Muñoz, Jesu. Psychologia philosophica. Santander, 1961.

Phil 585.152   Muñoz Espinalt, Carlos. Saber-se entendre. Barcelona, 1961.

Phil 2225.5.104   Murphey, M.G. The development of Peirce's philosophy. Cambridge, 1961.

Phil 7069.61A   Murphy, Gardner. Challenge of psychical research. 1. ed. N.Y., 1961.

Phil 165.255   Myers, G.E. Self, religion and metaphysics. N.Y., 1961.

Phil 187.175   Myers, Henry. Systematic pluralism. Ithaca, 1961.

Phil 3552.435   Naert, Emilienne. Mémoire et conscience de soi selon Leibniz. Paris, 1961.

Phil 1955.6.180   Nassif, F.R. En el centenario de John Dewey. La Plata, 1961.

Phil 6816.10.2   Natale, Nicola G. Vita segreta del complesso d'inferiorita. 2. ed. Bologna, 1961.

Phil 6963.8   National Conference on Social Welfare. Mental health and social welfare. N.Y., 1961.

Phil 188.25   Nédoncelle, Maurice. Conscience et logos. Paris, 1961.

Phil 585.100   Nef, John U. Religion and the study of man. Houston, 1961.

1961 - cont.

Phil 5385.5   Nemberg, Herman. Curiosity. N.Y., 1961.

Phil 6323.18   Nemiah, J.C. Foundations of psychopathology. N.Y., 1961.

Phil 8980.602   Nemtsov, V.I. Volneniia, radosti, nadezoidy. Moskva, 1961.

Phil 8505.10   New York University. Institute of Philosophy. Religious experience and truth. N.Y., 1961.

Phil 4314.2   Nicol, Eduardo. El problema de la filosofía hispanica. Madrid, 1961.

Phil 4757.2.105   Nott, C.S. Teachings of Gurdjieff. London, 1961.

Phil 310.470   Novinskii, I.I. Poniatie sviazi v marksistskoi filosofii. Moskva, 1961.

Phil 6323.5.6   Nunberg, Hermann. Practice and theory of psychoanalysis. N.Y., 1961. 2v.

Phil 5223.10   Nuttin, Jozef. Psychology in Belgium. Louvain, 1961.

Phil 5238.160   O'Connor, N. Recent Soviet psychology. N.Y., 1961.

Phil 6100.18   Odette, Laffoneriere. L'ame et le corps. Paris, 1961.

Phil 5764.4   Ofstad, H. An inquiry into the freedom of decision. Oslo, 1961.

Phil 1750.675   Oromi, Miguel. Introducción a la filosofía esencialista. Madrid, 1961.

Phil 189.31   Ortuzar Arriaga, M. El ser y la accion en la dimension humana. Madrid, 1961.

Phil 310.5.15   Oshakov, Zhivko. Niakoi aktualni problemina nauchnogo. komunizum. Sofiia, 1961.

Phil 4800.16   Osipova, Elena Vladimirovna. Filosofiia pol'skogo Prosveshcheniia. Moskva, 1961.

Phil 2880.8.134   Otto, Maria. Rene und Freiheit. Freiburg, 1961.

Phil 190.104   Padovani, U.A. Metafisica classica e pensiero moderno. Milano, 1961.

Phil 8890.58   Palazzini, Pietro. Morale generale. Brescia, 1961.

Phil 5255.66   Palmade, G. L'unité des science humaines. Paris, 1961.

Phil 490.9   Pantin, Igor' K. Materialisticheskoe mirovozrenie i teoriia poznaniia russkikh revoliutsionnikh demokratov. Moskva, 1961.

Phil 8416.5   Papennyi, Z.S. O khudozhestvennom obraze. Moskva, 1961.

Phil 4070.7.80   Papi, Fulveo. Il pensiero di Antonio Banfi. Firenze, 1961.

Phil 8416.8   Pareyson, Luigi. L'estetica e i suoi problemi. Milano, 1961.

Phil 2805.42.11   Pascal, Blaise. The pensées. Harmondsworth, 1961.

Phil 4366.79.30   Pascual Ferránde, Antonio. Ensayos. Barcelona, 1961. 20v.

Phil 4803.281.80   Pasenkiewicz, Kazimierz. Pierwsze systemy semantyki Leona Chwistka. Krakow, 1961.

Phil 190.95   Passmore, John Arthur. Philosophical reasoning. London, 1961.

Phil 1850.153   Patrick, J.M. Francis Bacon. London, 1961.

Phil 310.20.5   Pavlov, Todor D. Teoriiata na otrazhenieto i nashata suvremennost. Sofia, 1961.

Phil 5360.15   Pavlov, V.T. Otnosheniia mezhdu poniatiiami. Kiev, 1961.

Phil 6965.22   Perceval, J. Perceval's narrative. Stanford, 1961.

Phil 4200.7.06   Pergulensis, Paulus. Logica and tractatus de sensu composito et diviso. St. Bonaventure, 1961.

Phil 5255.68   Perlenghini, A. Psicologia degli animali e filosofia del sentimento. Genova, 1961.

Phil 8062.7   Perpeet, Wilhelm. Antike Ästhetik. Freiburg, 1961.

Phil 6125.30   Perron, Roger. Niveaux de tension et contrôle de l'activité. Paris, 1961.

Phil 165.315   Perspectief; feestbundel. Kampen, 1961.

Phil 1135.185   Pesce, Domenico. Idea, numero e anima. Padova, 1961.

Phil 3585.1.85   Peters, Wilhelm S. Johann Heinrich Lamberts Konzeption einer Geometrie auf einer imaginären Kugel. Bonn, 1961.

Phil 2150.15.86   Pfuetze, P.E. Self, society, existence. N.Y., 1961.

Phil 8400.16   Philipson, Morris. Aesthetics today. Cleveland, 1961.

Phil 5585.195   Piaget, Jean. Les mécanismes perceptifs. Paris, 1961.

Phil 5643.123   Piéron, Henri. La vision en lumière intermittente. Paris, 1961.

Phil 5255.64   Pikunas, J. Psychology of human development. N.Y., 1961.

Phil 8705.18   Pilkington, Roger. World without end. London, 1961.

Phil 310.450   Platonov, G.V. Dialekticheskii materializm i voprosy genetike. Moskva, 1961.

Phil 3640.235.25   Podach, Erich F. Friedrich Nietzsches Werke des Zusammenbruchs. Heidelberg, 1961.

Phil 310.370   Podosetnik, V.M. Chto takoe dialekticheskii i istoricheskii materializm. Moskva, 1961.

Phil 2175.5.80   Pogson, Beryl. Maurice Nicoll. London, 1961.

Phil 735.225   Pole, David. Conditions of rational inquiry. London, 1961.

Phil 310.597   Polikarov, A. Materiia i poznanie. Sofiia, 1961.

Phil 190.60.5   Poortman, J.J. De grandparadox. Assen, 1961.

Phil 3497.21   Popov, Sergei I. Kant i Kantianstvo. Moskva, 1961.

Phil 978.49.840   Poppelbaum, H. Entwicklung, Vererbung und Abstammungs. Dornach, 1961.

Phil 1135.175   Precope, J. Iatrophilosophers of the Hellenic states. London, 1961.

Phil 6325.18.5   Problems in psychoanalysis. London, 1961.

Phil 8980.712   Prokof'ev, V.I. Dve morali; moral' religioznaia i moral' kommunisticheskaia. Moskva, 1961.

Phil 8951.11.80   Prupard, Paul. L'abbé Louis Bautain. Tournai, 1961.

Phil 2905.1.120   Rabut, Oliver A. Dialogue with Teilhard de Chardin. London, 1961.

Phil 2905.1.125   Rabut, Oliver A. Teilhard de Chardin. N.Y., 1961.

Phil 4899.255.80   Radul'-Zatulovskii, Iakov B. Ando Sëëki, filosof, materialist XVIII veka. Moskva, 1961.

Phil 192.85.5.5   Raeymaeker, Louis de. The philosophy of being. St. Louis, 1961.

Phil 192.116   Rahman, F. Philosophy, science, and other essays. 1st. ed. Lahore, 1961.

Phil 3425.564   Rahrmoser, Günter. Subjektivität und verden Glichung. Gütersloh, 1961.

Phil 165.245   Ramsey, J.T. Prospect for metaphysics. London, 1961.

Phil 2255.10.34   Rand, Ayn. For the new intellectual; the philosophy of Ayn Rand. N.Y., 1961.

Phil 5767.14   Rankin, K. Choice and chance. Oxford, 1961.

Phil 4210.192   Raschini, Maria M. Il principio dialettico nella filosofia di Antonio Rosmini. Milano, 1961.

Phil 348.20   Reid, L.A. Ways of knowledge and experience. London, 1961.

Phil 9245.62   Rencontres Internationales, Genève, 1961. Les conditions du bonheur. Neuchâtel, 1961.

Phil 5352.15   Restle, Frank. Psychology of judgment and choice. N.Y., 1961.

Phil 70.81   Reunion de Aproximacion Filosofica Cuntifica. La materia. v.2. Zaragoza, 1961.

Phil 7069.61.10   Rhine, Louisa E. Hidden channels of the mind. N.Y., 1961.

Phil 8672.24   Riazantsev, N.I. Chto takoe ateizm. Moskva, 1961.

Chronological Listing

1961 - cont.

Phil 192.99   Ribeiro, Alvaro. Estudos gerais. Lisboa, 1961.
Phil 2115.164   Ricci Garotti, Loris. Locke e i suoi problemi. Urbino, 1961.
Phil 6946.1.10   Ridenour, Nina. Mental health in the United States. Cambridge, 1961.
Phil 5401.47   Riemann, Fritz. Grundformen der Angst und die Antinomien des Lebens. München, 1961.
Phil 2490.172   Riezu, J. Sozialmoral. München, 1961.
Phil 7150.50   Ringel, Erwin. Neue Untersuchungen zum Selbstmordproblem. Wien, 1961.
Phil 192.67.15   Rintelen, Fritz J. von. Beyond existentialism. London, 1961.
Phil 4979.41.30   Rio, Manuel. La liberté; choix, amour, création. Paris, 1961.
Phil 1145.94   Riondato, E. Ethos. Padova, 1961.
Phil 720.62   Rivetti Barbo, Francesca. L'antinomia del mentitore nel pensiero contemporaneo da Peirce a Tarski. Milano, 1961.
Phil 5227.6.10   Roback, A.A. History of psychology and psychiatry. N.Y., 1961.
Phil 7069.61.15   Roberts, D.O. Elizabethan episode. London, 1961.
Phil 1830.51   Robinson, D.S. The story of Scottish philosophy. 1st ed. N.Y., 1961.
Phil 4478.1.30   Rocha, Germano da Costa. Nova filosofia cristã. Lisboa, 1961?
Phil 6980.650.35   Rogers, Carl Ransom. On becoming a person. Boston, 1961.
Phil 8672.22   Rohde, Hubert. Mensch ohne Gott. Freiburg, 1961.
Phil 5520.427   Rossi-Landi, Ferruccio. Significato comunicazioni e parlare comune. Padova, 1961.
Phil 192.110   Rubert Condan, José Marin. Fenomenologia de la accion del hombre. Madrid, 1961.
Phil 974.3.135   Rudolf Steiner-Nachlassverwaltung. Rudolf Steiner, das literarische und künstlerische Werk. Dornach, 1961.
Phil 2255.7.3   Runes, Dagobert D. Letters to my teacher. N.Y., 1961.
Phil 2255.1.52   Russell, Bertrand Russell. Basic writings, 1903-1959. N.Y., 1961.
Phil 2255.1.73   Russell, Bertrand Russell. Fact and fiction. London, 1961.
Phil 2255.1.68   Russell, Bertrand Russell. Has man a future? London, 1961.
Phil 2255.1.36   Russell, Bertrand Russell. Let the people think. 2nd ed. London, 1961.
Phil 8980.787.20   Russia (1917-). Upravlenie Prepodavaniia Obshchestvennykh Nauk. Marksistskaia etika; khrestomatiia. Moskva, 1961.
Phil 3552.420   Saame, Otto. Der Satz vom Gound bei Leibniz. Mainz, 1961.
Phil 8419.2   Sacchetti, E. Che cos è l'arte. Firenze, 1961.
Phil 1850.155   Saint Albans, England. City Council. Catalogue of exhibition organized by the St. Albans City Council in the Council Chamber. St. Albans, 1961.
Phil 2880.1.65   Saint-Martin, L.C. Mon portrait historique et philosophique. Paris, 1961.
Phil 530.40.55   Sainz Rodriguez, P. Espiritualidad española. Madrid, 1961.
Phil 4018.5.2   Saitta, G. Il pensiero italiano nell'umanesimo e nel Rinascimento. 2. ed. Firenze, 1961. 3v.
Phil 8170.3   Sakharova, E.M. Osnovy marksistsko-leninskoi estetiki. Moskva, 1961.
Phil 7069.61.20   Salter, William Henry. Zoar, or The evidence of psychical research concerning survival. London, 1961.
Phil 8708.34   Samuel, Herbert S. A threefold cord. London, 1961.
Phil 4482.2.80   Sant'Anna, Dionisio. Teólogo laico. Seara Nova, 1961.
Phil 5250.365   Saporta, Sol. Psycholinguistics. N.Y., 1961.
Phil 5590.445   Sappenfield, Bert Reese. Personality dynamics. N.Y., 1961.
Phil 6328.52   Sarbin, T.R. Studies in behavior pathology. N.Y., 1961.
Phil 6128.75   Sartakov, S.V. Krasota truda. Moskva, 1961.
Phil 2880.8.33   Sartre, Jean Paul. The psychology of imagination. N.Y., 1961.
Phil 3120.8.135   Satue, A.A. La doctrina de la intencionalidad en Franz Brentano. Barcelona, 1961.
Phil 5402.26.2   Sauerbruch, F. Wesen und Bedeutung des Schmerzes. 2. Aufl. Frankfurt, 1961.
Phil 6315.19.20   Schaar, John H. Escape from authority. N.Y., 1961.
Phil 310.445   Schaff, Adam. Marksizm i egzystencjalizm. Warszawa, 1961.
Phil 3850.18.35   Scheler, Max. Ressentiment. N.Y., 1961.
Phil 672.218   Schlegel, R. Time and the physical world. East Lansing? 1961.
Phil 3890.8.115   Schneiders, Werner. Recht. Münster, 1961.
Phil 8893.120   Schoellgen, W. Konkrete Ethik. Düsseldorf, 1961.
Phil 5066.185   Scholz, H. Grundrüge der mathematische Logik. Berlin, 1961.
Phil 193.225   Scholz, H. Mathesis Universalis. Stuttgart, 1961.
Phil 5028.2.10   Scholz, Heinrch. Concise history of logic. N.Y., 1961.
Phil 3808.47   Schopenhauer, Arthur. Das Erwacher aus dem Leben- Fraum. Pfullingen, 1961.
Phil 3808.63.20   Schopenhauer, Arthur. Parapsychologische Schriften. Basel, 1961.
Phil 1750.665   Schrag, C.O. Existence and freedom. Evanston, Ill., 1961.
Phil 193.230   Schroedinger, Erwin. Meine Weltansicht. Hamburg, 1961.
Phil 5627.261.5   Schulz, Johannes Josef. Bionome Geschlechtsentfaltung. München, 1961.
Phil 8598.110.15A   Schuon, Frithjof. Stations of wisdom. London, 1961.
Phil 972.16   Schwarz, W. Hoffnung in Wichts. München, 1961.
Phil 4225.8.50   Sciacca, Michele Federico. Dull'attualismo. Milano, 1961.
Phil 3425.570   Seeberger, W. Hegel, oder die Entwicklung. Stuttgart, 1961.
Phil 3450.11.300   Seebohm, W.T. Die Bedingungen der Möglichkeit der Transzendentalphilosophie. Bonn, 1961.
Phil 8893.130   Selivanov, F.A. Etika. Tomsk, 1961.
Phil 1900.100   Sharma, Sukhde. Ethics of Butler and the philosophy of action in Bhogavadgita according to Madhusudana Sarasvati. Varanasi, 1961.
Phil 8980.785.20   Shcherbak, F.N. Nravstvennyi oblik razvedchikov budushchego. Leningrad, 1961.
Phil 2340.10.160   Sherburne, Donald W. A Whiteheadian aesthetic. New Haven, 1961.
Phil 5500.22   Sherif, Muzafer. Social judgment. New Haven, 1961.
Phil 5238.155   Shipley, T. Classics in psychology. N.Y., 1961.
Phil 8980.787.15   Shishkin, Aleksandr F. Osnovy marksistskoi etiki. Moskva, 1961.
Phil 5374.215   Shorokhova, E.V. Problema soznaniia v filosofii i estestvoznanii. Moskva, 1961.
Phil 8893.125   Shvartsman, Klara Aronovna. Kritika sovremennykh burzhuaznykh filosofsko-esteticheskikh system. Moskva, 1961.

1961 - cont.

Phil 5228.1.2   Siebeck, H. Geschichte der psychologie. v.1-2. Amsterdam, 1961.
Phil 7150.52   Siegmund, Georg. Sein oder Nichtsein. Trier, 1961.
Phil 5258.190   Simões, M.B. Pora uma psicologia na premeira pessoa. Lisboa, 1961.
Phil 8419.50.5   Šindelář, Dušan. Estetické vnémáné. Praha, 1961.
Phil 8893.115A   Singer, M.G. Generalization in ethics. 1. ed. N.Y., 1961.
Phil 5258.155.5A   Skinner, Burrhus F. Cumulative record. N.Y., 1961.
Phil 5520.380   Slama-Cazacu, T. Langage et contexte. 's-Gravenhage, 1961.
Phil 4873.10   Smet, Richard V. de. Philosophical activity in Pakistan. Lahore, 1961.
Phil 8598.130   Şmith, J.E. Reason and God. New Haven, 1961.
Phil 4803.799.22   Sniadecki, Jan. Pisma pedagogiczne. Wrocław, 1961.
Phil 6980.699   Snyder, William U. The psychotherapy relationship. N.Y., 1961.
Phil 6105.233   Soddy, Kenneth. Identity. Mental health and value systems. London, 1961.
Phil 2490.170   Sokoloff, Boris. The "mad" philosopher. 1st ed. N.Y., 1961.
Phil 5237.516.10   Sokolov, Mikhail V. Iz istorii russkoi psikhologii. Moskva, 1961.
Phil 4352.1.135   Solaguren, Celestino. Metodalogía filosófica de Balmes. Madrid, 1961.
Phil 5238.24.5   Soviet psychology. N.Y., 1961.
Phil 8643.38   Spazier, Wilhelm. Antiphädon. Berlin, 1961.
Phil 3778.94   Spickhoff, K. Die Vorstellung in der Polemik zwischen Reinhold. München, 1961.
Phil 3819.33.20   Spinoza, Benedictus de. Éthique. Paris, 1961.
Phil 6980.704   Spotnitz, Hyman. The couch and the circle. N.Y., 1961.
Phil 8673.20   Sputnik ateista. 2. izd. Moskva, 1961.
Phil 5058.46.7   Stebbing, Lizzie S. A modern introduction to logic. 7. ed. London, 1961.
Phil 1523.12.15   Steenberghen, F. Directives pour la confection d'une monographie. Louvain, 1961.
Phil 8673.19   Steenberghen, Fernand van. Dieu caché. Louvain, 1961.
Phil 3195.6.150   Stefanovies, T. Dilthey; una filosofía de la vida. Montevideo, 1961.
Phil 2418.5   Stein, Jay W. The mind and the sword. N.Y., 1961.
Phil 6980.707   Stein, Morris. Contemporary psychotherapies. N.Y., 1961.
Phil 3778.94   Steiner, R. Geist und Stoff, Leben und Tod. Dornach, 1961.
Phil 978.49.370   Steiner, R. Der goetheanumgedanke Insnitten der Kulturkreis der Gegenwart. Dornach, 1961.
Phil 978.49.335   Steiner, R. Kunst und Kunsterkuntniss. Dornach, 1961.
Phil 978.49.340   Steiner, R. Methodische Grundlagen der Anthroposophie. Dornach, 1961.
Phil 978.49.360   Steiner, Rudolf. Das Künstlerische in seiner Weltmission. Dornach, 1961.
Phil 974.3.3   Stiehler, G. Beiträge zur Geschichte des vormarxistischen Materialismus. 1. Aufl. Berlin, 1961.
Phil 493.10   Stoikhammer, Morris. Kants Zurechnungsidee und Freiheitsantinomie. Köln, 1961.
Phil 3500.90   Stolarek, Z. Gorod chudes svoimi i chuzhimi glazami. Moskva, 1961.
Phil 6990.3.95   Stolovich, L.N. Predmet estetiki. Moskva, 1961.
Phil 8419.19   Stone, Leo. The psychoanalytic situation. N.Y., 1961.
Phil 6328.50   Storr, Anthony. The integrity of the personality. N.Y., 1961.
Phil 6980.709   Strohm, Theodor. Konservative politische Romantik. Berlin, 1961.
Phil 8586.36.65   Sukhov, Andrei D. Sotsial'nye i gnoseologicheskie korni religii. Moskva, 1961.
Phil 8598.125   Sullivan, L.H. Democracy: a man-search. Detroit, 1961.
Phil 585.155   Sulzberger, Cyrus. My brother death. N.Y., 1961.
Phil 2280.20.30   Suvorov, L.M. Bor'ba marksistsko-leninskoi filosofii v SSSR. Moskva, 1961.
Phil 310.435   Svenaeus, G. Methodologie et spéculation esthétique. Lund, 1961.
Phil 4080.3.370   Swabey, W.C. Ethical theory. N.Y., 1961.
Phil 8843.17   Symposium Iberoamericano de Filosofía. Primer Symposium Iberoamericano de Filosofia. Guatemala, 1961.
Phil 70.85   Symposium on Sensory Deprivation. Sensory deprivation. Cambridge, 1961.
Phil 5640.136   Szazs, Thomas Stephen. The myth of mental illness. N.Y., 1961.
Phil 6980.717.25   Szilasi, Wilhelm. Philosophie und Naturwissenschaft. Bern, 1961.
Phil 193.160.5   Taylor, F.K. The analysis of therapeutic groups. London, 1961.
Phil 5850.251   Taylor, Paul. Normative discourse. Englewood, 1961.
Phil 735.240   Tedeschi, Paul. Paradoxe de la pensée anglaise au XVIIe siècle. Paris, 1961.
Phil 1819.7   Teevan, R.C. Color vision. Princeton, 1961.
Phil 5645.56   Teilhard de Chardin, Pierre. Genèse d'une pensée. Paris, 1961.
Phil 2905.1.35   Teilhard de Chardin, Pierre. Hymne de l'univers. Paris, 1961.
Phil 2905.1.40   Teillard, A. Spiritual dimensions. London, 1961.
Phil 7069.61.5   Temperley, H.N.V. A scientist who believes in God. London, 1961.
Phil 8709.22   Teplov, B.M. Problemy individual'nykh razlichii. Moskva, 1961.
Phil 5259.50   Thielicke, H. Nihilism, its origin and nature, with a Christian answer. 1st ed. N.Y., 1961.
Phil 535.16   Thomsen, Henrik. Hvem taenkfe mal; filosofiens hvem-hvad-hvor. København, 1961.
Phil 130.13   Thorpe, Louis P. The psychology of abnormal behavior. N.Y., 1961.
Phil 6329.16   Thurner, Franz K. Kurzzeitige nacheffekte unserer Wahrnehmungen. Berlin, 1961.
Phil 5259.45   Titarenko, Aleksandr I. Protiv fal'sifikatsii filosofii marksizma pragmatistami SShA. Moskva, 1961.
Phil 310.455   Tönnies, Ferdinand. Custom. N.Y., 1961.
Phil 8894.19.5   Toman, Walter. Family constellation. N.Y., 1961.
Phil 5259.55   Torchia Estrada, Juan Carlos. La filosofía en la Argentina. Washington, 1961.
Phil 4960.235   Toro, Antonio del. La crisis del pensamiento cristiano en el siglo XVI. Madrid, 1961.
Phil 8599.46   Touron del Pie, Eliseo. El mundo. Madrid, 1961.
Phil 2750.20.5   Tresmontant, Claude. La métaphysique du christianisme. Paris, 1961.
Phil 8599.44
Phil 9450.57   Tri-ennial Congress of the International Union for the Protection of Public Morality, 3rd, London, 1961. International public morals. Rushden, 1961?

Phil 5722.30.5   Tucci, Giuseppe. The theory and practice of the Mandala. London, 1961.

Phil 194.51   Tucuman, Argentina. Tornadas de filosofia, 21 al 26 de mayo de 1961. Tucuman, 1961.

Phil 6969.12   Tweedie, D.F. Logotherapy and the Christian faith. Grands Rapids, 1961.

Phil 4810.4   Uher, Ján. Filozofia v boji o dnešok. Vyd. 1. Bratislava, 1961.

Phil 195.9   Ulrich, Ferdinand. Homo Abyssus. Johannes, 1961.

Phil 6980.759   Ungersma, Aaron J. The search for meaning. Philadelphia, 1961.

Phil 5520.376   Upton, Albert. Creative analysis. Whittier, Calif., 1961.

Phil 5520.375   Upton, Albert. Design for thinking. Stanford, 1961.

Phil 1865.192   The Utilitarians. Garden City, 1961.

Phil 195.8   Utrecht. Rijks Universiteit. Utrechts Universiteits fonds. Leven en dood. Haarlem, 1961.

Phil 5260.10   Uznadze, Dmitrii N. Eksperimental'nye osnovy psikhologii ustanovki. Tbilisi, 1961.

Phil 8725.5   Vahanian, G. The death of God. N.Y., 1961.

Phil 2920.3.30   Valensin, Auguste. Auguste Valensin. Paris, 1961.

Phil 7069.61.35   Van der Huok, P. Psychic. Indianapolis, 1961.

Phil 4983.5.20   Varela, Félix. Lecciones de filosofía. 5. ed. Habana, 1961. 2v.

Phil 3705.2.85   Veer, Hendrik. Mr. C.W. Opzoomer als wijsgeer. Assen, 1961.

Phil 3705.2.86   Veer, Hendrik. Mr. C.W. Opzoomer als wijsgeer. Assen, 1961.

Phil 9240.30   Veloso, Agostinho. O homem em face da dor. Lisboa, 1961.

Phil 6947.1940   Venray, Netherlands. Psychiatrisch Ziekenhuis Sint Anna. Een halve eeuw. Venray, 1961?

Phil 8676.5   Verret, Michel. Les marxistes et la religion. Paris, 1961.

Phil 4482.1.97   Vieira de Almeida, Francisco. Pontos de referência. Lisboa, 1961.

Phil 1133.39   Vlolmans, A. De voorsokratici. Den Haag, 1961.

Phil 1135.176   Voelke, Andre J. Les rapports avec Autrui dans la philosophie grecque d'Aristole à Panetius. Paris, 1961.

Phil 8980.872   Vokrug tebia, khoroshie liudi. Moskva, 1961.

Phil 106.1.13   Volataire, Francois Marie Arouet de. Dictionnaire philosophique. Paris, 1961.

Phil 3195.3.84   Volkova, V.V. Iosif Ditsgen. Moskva, 1961.

Phil 352.10   Voprosy teorii poznaniia. Perm, 1961.

Phil 3450.19.74.1   Vycinas, V. Earth and gods. The Hague, 1961.

Phil 1722.12.5   Waelkens, Alphonse de. La philosophie et les experiences naturelles. La Haye, 1961.

Phil 5262.56   Waffenschmidt, Walter. Denkformen und Denktechnik. Meisenheim, 1961.

Phil 3640.611   Wahl, J.A. L'avant dernière pensée de Nietzsche. Paris, 1961.

Phil 3450.19.305   Wahl, J.A. Mots, mythes et réalité dans la philosophie de Heidegger. Paris, 1961.

Phil 3450.11.202   Wahle, Jean A. Husserl. Paris, 1961.

Phil 4710.125   Walicki, Andrzej. Filozofia i myśl społeczna rosyjska, 1825-1861. Warzawa, 1961.

Phil 5590.395   Wallace, Anthony F.C. Culture and personality. N.Y., 1961.

Phil 353.29   Wallraff, C.F. Philosophical theory and psychological fact. Tucson, 1961.

Phil 9240.24   Walsh, V.C. Scarcity and evil. Englewood Cliffs, N.J., 1961.

Phil 1145.96   Wankel, H. Kalos Kai Agaltos. Frankfurt, 1961.

Phil 8735.52   Ward, L.R. God and world order. Saint Louis, 1961.

Phil 197.90   Watts, A.W. Psychotherapy. N.Y., 1961.

Phil 8423.2   Weber, J. Paul. La psychologie de l'art. Paris, 1961.

Phil 5850.385.87   Wehowski, D. Ein allgemeines Modell für die Skalierung von Meinungen. Münster? 1961.

Phil 353.27   Weigel, Gustave. Knowledge. Englewood Cliffs, N.J., 1961.

Phil 8897.83   Weil, Eric. Philosophie morale. Paris, 1961.

Phil 8423.11   Weiss, Paul. Nine basic arts. Carbondale, 1961.

Phil 3640.625   Weiss, Tomasz. Fryderyk Nietzsche w piśmiennictwie polskim lat 1890-1914. Wrocław, 1961.

Phil 8897.73   Wellman, Carl. The language of ethics. Cambridge, 1961.

Phil 3310.1.135   Wenzel, Paul. Das wissenschaftliche Anliger des Güntherianismus. Essen, 1961.

Phil 3450.19.56   Weplinger, F. Wahrheit und Geschichtlichkeit. Freiburg, 1961.

Phil 5262.31.26   Wertheimer, M. Productive thinking. London, 1961.

Phil 6980.776   Westman, H. The springs of creativity. N.Y., 1961.

Phil 2340.10.26   Whitehead, Alfred North. Alfred North Whitehead. N.Y., 1961.

Phil 2340.10.40   Whitehead, Alfred North. Alfred North Whitehead. 1st ed. N.Y., 1961.

Phil 672.212   Whitrow, G.J. The natural philosophy of time. London, 1961.

Phil 1170.5.5   Whittaker, Thomas. The Neo-Platonists. 4th ed. Olm, 1961.

Phil 260.13   Whyte, Laucelot Law. Essay on atomism. 1st ed. Middletown, Conn., 1961.

Phil 197.38.5   Widgery, A.G. A philosopher's pilgrimage. N.Y., 1961.

Phil 3246.296   Widmann, J. Analyse der formalen Strukturen des transzendentalen Wissens in Johann Gottlieb Fichtes. München? 1961.

Phil 5625.99   Wieser, S. Das Schreckverhalten des Menschen. Bern, 1961.

Phil 2905.1.130   Wildiers, N.M. Teilhard de Chardin. Paris, 1961.

Phil 8602.65   Wilson, J. Philosophy and religion. London, 1961.

Phil 8897.80   Wilson, John. Reason and morals. Cambridge, Eng., 1961.

Phil 5062.20.10   Windelband, W. Theories in logic. N.Y., 1961.

Phil 70.80   Winn, R.B. Psychotherapy in the Soviet Union. N.Y., 1961.

Phil 2340.19.30   Wisdom, John. The metamorphosis of metaphysics. London, 1961?

Phil 3450.11.260   Witschel, Guenter. Edmund Husserls Lehre von den sekundären Qualitäten. Bonn, 1961.

Phil 3925.16.15A   Wittgenstein, Ludwig. Notebooks. Oxford, 1961. 2v.

Phil 3925.16.47A   Wittgenstein, Ludwig. Tractatus logico-philosophicus. London, 1961.

Phil 197.36.12A   Wittgenstein, Ludwig. Tractatus logico-philosophicus. London, 1961.

Phil 3925.16.46   Wittgenstein, Ludwig. Tractatus logico-philosophicus. Paris, 1961.

Phil 5062.22.16   Wolf, Abraham. Textbook of logic. 2nd ed. London, 1961.

Phil 8602.46.5A   Wolfson, H.A. Religious philosophy. Cambridge, 1961.

Phil 2138.140   Woods, Thomas. Poetry and philosophy. London, 1961.

Phil 5590.365   Wylie, R.C. The self concept. Lincoln, 1961.

Phil 6332.22   Wyss, Dieter. Die tiefenpsychologischen Schulen von der Anfanger bis zur Gegenwart. Göttingen, 1961.

Phil 5190.10.26   Yale University. Institute of Human Relations. The order of presentation in persuasion. New Haven, 1961.

Phil 5548.90   Young, Paul Thomas. Motivation and emotion. N.Y., 1961.

Phil 1195.16   Zadro, Attilio. Ricerche sul linguaggio e sulla logica del sofista. Padova, 1961.

Phil 200.17.5   Zafiropulo, Jean. Appollon et Dionysos. Paris, 1961.

Phil 310.355   Zakharov, F.I. Dialekticheskii materializm i nekotorye voprosy darvinizma. Moskva, 1961.

Phil 3120.8.140   Zawischa, E. Das Rätsel und sein Meister Franz Brentano. n.p., 1961.

Phil 1540.38   Zilli, José B. Introducción a la psicología de los conimbricenses. Bonn, 1961.

Phil 960.164.5   Zimmer, H.R. Philosophie und Religion Indiens. Zürich, 1961.

Phil 5265.6   Zimny, George. Method in experimental psychology. N.Y., 1961.

Phil 8605.15   Žrvotić, Milad. Aktuelni problemi odnosa prema religiji. Beograd, 1961.

1962

Phil 8610.890.42   Abbot, Francis Ellingwood. The way out of agnosticism, or The philosophy of free religion. 2. ed. Ann Arbor, 1962.

Phil 2805.425   Académie des sciences, belles lettres et arts de Clermont-Ferrand. Cinq études sur Blaise Pascal. Clermont-Ferrand, 1962.

Phil 331.31   Adamczyk, S. Krytyka ludzkiego poznania. Wyd.1. Lublin, 1962.

Phil 1800.2.5   Adams, George P. Contemporary American philosophy. N.Y., 1962. 2v.

Phil 1750.705   Adams, Robert. Better part of valor; More, Erasmus, Colet and Vives, on humanism, war, and peace. Seattle, 1962.

Phil 310.505   Afanas'ev, Viktor G. Osnovy filosofskikh znanii. 2. izd. Moskva, 1962.

Phil 4080.3.375   Agazzi, E. Il Giovane Croce e il Marxismo. Torino, 1962.

Phil 8875.30   Aichen, Henry D. Reason and conduct. N.Y., 1962.

Phil 9558.10.14   Aires Ramos da Silva de Eca, M. Reflexões sobre a vaidade dos homens. Rio de Janeiro, 1962.

Phil 8050.20   Akademiia Khudozhestv SSSR. Institut Teorii i Istorii Iskusstva. Istoriia estetiki. Moskva, 1962- 5v.

Phil 4780.4   Akademiia nauk BSSR, Minsk. Instytut filosofii. Iz istorii filosofskoi i obshchestvenno-politicheskoi mysli Belorussii. Minsk, 1962.

Phil 1695.20   Akademiia Nauk SSR. Institut Filosofii. Sovremennye religioznye filosofskie techeniia kapitalisticheskikh stran. Moskva, 1962.

Phil 5040.26   Akademiia Nauk SSSR. Institut Filosofii. Filosofskie voprosy sovremennoi formal'noi logiki. Moskva, 1962.

Phil 310.511   Akademiia Nauk SSSR. Institut Filosofii. Formy myshleniia. Moskva, 1962.

Phil 310.510   Akademiia Nauk SSSR. Institut Filosofii. Zakony myshleniia. Moskva, 1962.

Phil 1700.9   Akademiia Nauk SSSR. Institut Filosofii. Sektor Sovremennoi Burzhuaznoi Filosofii i Sotisiologii Stran Zapada. Noveishie priemy zashchity starogo mira. Moskva, 1962.

Phil 960.245   Akademiia Nauk SSSR. Institut Narodov Azii. Obshchestvenno-politicheskaia i filosofskaia mysl' Indii. Moskva, 1962.

Phil 310.515   Akademiia Nauk SSSR. Nauchnyi Sovet po Filosofskim Voprosam Estestvoznaniia. Dialekticheskii materializm i sovremennoe estestvoznanie. Moskva, 1962.

Phil 4710.50.5   Akademiia Nauk URSR, Kiev. Instytut Filosofii. Z istorii filosofs'koi dumki na Ukraini. Kyïv, 1962.

Phil 4000.16   Alorpio, F. de. Storia e dialogo. Bologna, 1962.

Phil 2520.193.10   Alquié, F. Descartes. Stuttgart, 1962.

Phil 8401.26   Alvarez, Villar A. Filosofia del arte. Madrid, 1962.

Phil 175.59   Amado Levy-Valensi, E. Les niveaux de l'être la connaissance et le mal. Paris, 1962.

Phil 2880.1.95   Amadou, R. De l'agent inconnu au philosophe inconnu. Paris, 1962.

Phil 1800.6   Ames, Van Meter. Zen and American thought. Honolulu, 1962.

Phil 8401.30.5   Anceschi, Luciano. Progetto di una sistematica dell'arte. Milano, 1962.

Phil 4635.9.80   Ancker, E. Torgny Segerstedt, 1876-1945. Stockholm, 1962.

Phil 1850.140   Anderson, Fulton H. Francis Bacon. Los Angeles, 1962.

Phil 1845.15   Anderson, John. Studies in empirical philosophy. Sydney, 1962.

Phil 5210.11   Anzieu, Didier. Esquisse de la psychologie française. Paris, 1962?

Phil 5460.15   APA-AAAS Symposium on Hallucinations. Hallucinations. N.Y., 1962.

Phil 8580.33.5   Archivio di Filosofia. Demitizzazione e immagine. Padova, 1962.

Phil 4961.805.15   Ardao, Arturo. Racionalismo y liberalismo en el Uruguay. Montevideo, 1962.

Phil 175.56   Armour, Leslie. The rational and the real. The Hague, 1962.

Phil 5635.46   Armstrong, David Malet. Bodily sensations. London, 1962.

Phil 5374.69   Arnold, Magda. Story sequence analysis. N.Y., 1962.

Phil 8125.40   Asmus, V.F. Nemetskaia estetika XVIII veka. Moskva, 1962.

Phil 3585.26   Asser-Kramer, G. Neue nege zu Frieden und Freiheit. Pähl/Oberbayern, 1962.

Phil 5238.67   Association de Psychologie Scientifique de Langue Française. Les problèmes de la mesure en psychologie. Paris, 1962.

Phil 3801.168   Assunto, Rosario. Estetica dell'identita. Urbino, 1962.

Phil 331.29   Austin, J.L. Sense and sensibilia. Oxford, 1962.

Phil 175.52.5   Austin, John L. How to do things with words. Cambridge, 1962.

Phil 5041.89   Babaiants, M.S. Zakon iskheichennogo tret'ego. Moskva, 1962.

Phil 5465.56.42   Bachelard, G. La flamme d'une chandelle. 2. éd. Paris, 1962.

Phil 5241.165   Bachrach, Arthur. Experimental foundations of clinical psychology. N.Y., 1962.

Phil 3850.27.215   Baehr, Hans N. Albert Schweitzer, sein Denken und sein Weg. Tübingen, 1962.

Phil 8581.52.30   Baillie, John. The sense of the presence of God. London, 1962.

Phil 4070.7.45   Banfi, Antonio. Filosofia dell'arte; scelta. Roma, 1962.

Phil 7069.62   Banks, Frances. Frontiers of revelation. London, 1962.

Phil 2075.7.80   Barnett, George. Corporate society and education. Ann Arbor, 1962.

Phil 190.102   Barraud, Jean. Le message d'Amédée Ponceau. Paris, 1962.

Phil 1695.15   Barrett, William. Philosophy in the twentieth century. N.Y., 1962. 4v.

Chronological Listing

Phil 623.40 — Bartley, William W. The retreat to commitment. 1st ed. N.Y., 1962.

Phil 8581.114 — Başgil, Ali Fuad. Din ve Lâiklik. Istanbul, 1962.

Phil 176.13 — Baskin, M.P. Krizis burzhuaznogo soznaniia. Moskva, 1962.

Phil 6951.31 — Battie, William. A treatise on madness. London, 1962.

Phil 2805.385 — Baudouin, Charles. Blaise Pascal. Paris, 1962.

Phil 5238.177 — Bauer, Raymond A. Some views on Soviet psychology. Washington, 1962.

Phil 5590.405 — Baughman, E.E. Personality. Englewood Cliffs, N.J., 1962.

Phil 3450.18.140 — Baumgartner, Hans Michael. Die Unbedingtheit des Sittlichen. München, 1962.

Phil 585.140 — Becker, Ernest. The birth and death of meaning. N.Y., 1962.

Phil 3120.21.5 — Beerling, Reinier Franciscus. Heden en verleden. Arnhem, 1962.

Phil 3552.336.5 — Belaval, Yvor. Leibniz; initiation à sa philosophie. Paris, 1962.

Phil 4260.130.5 — Bellofiore, L. La dottrina providenza in G.B. Vico. Padova, 1962.

Phil 6111.64 — Beloff, John. The existence of mind. London, 1962.

Phil 623.9.5 — Benn, A.W. The history of English rationalism in the nineteenth century. N.Y., 1962. 2v.

Phil 6319.1.212 — Bennet, E.A. C.G. Jung. N.Y., 1962.

Phil 525.225 — Bennett, John G. Witness. London, 1962.

Phil 1865.12 — Bentham, Jeremy. The works of Jeremy Bentham. N.Y., 1962. 11v.

Phil 5241.155 — Berg, Charles. Mankind. London, 1962.

Phil 9070.104F — Bergstroem, L. Imperatives and ethics. Stockholm, 1962.

Phil 5421.20.10 — Berkourt, L. Aggression; a social psychological analysis. N.Y., 1962.

Phil 3120.30.105 — Berkovits, Eliezer. A Jewish critique of the philosophy. N.Y., 1962.

Phil 3246.299 — Berlin. Deutsche Staats Bibliothek. Johann Gottlieb Fichte, 1762-1962. Berlin, 1962.

Phil 176.221 — Berlin. Freie Universität. Freiheit als Problem der Wissenschaft. Berlin, 1962.

Phil 5066.195 — Beth, Evert W. Formal methods. Dordrecht, 1962.

Phil 2805.397 — Bibliothèque Nationale, Paris. Blaise Pascal, 1623-1662. Paris, 1962

Phil 3821.23.2 — Bidney, David. The psychology and ethics of Spinoza. 2nd ed. N.Y., 1962.

Phil 5241.166 — Bijkerk, R.J. Psycho-logica. Amsterdam, 1962.

Phil 3483.80 — Bird, G. Kant's theory of knowledge. London, 1962.

Phil 3640.681 — Biser, Eugen. Gott ist tot. München, 1962.

Phil 1905.32.30 — Black, Max. Models and metaphores. N.Y., 1962.

Phil 623.42 — Blanshard, Brand. Reason and analysis. La Salle, Ill., 1962.

Phil 3120.55.35 — Bloch, Ernst. Verfremdungen. Frankfurt, 1962. 2v.

Phil 8402.52.5 — Boas, George. The heaven of invention. Baltimore, 1962.

Phil 5011.6.10 — Bochénski, I.M. Logico-philosophical studies. Dordrecht, 1962.

Phil 3483.83 — Boeversen, F. Die Idee der Freiheit in der Philosophie Kants. Heidelberg, 1962.

Phil 310.500 — Bogdanov, I.A. Sushchnost' i iavlenie. Kiev, 1962.

Phil 365.56 — Bogomolov, A.S. Ideia razvitiia v burzhuaznoifilas, XIX i XV vekov. Moskva, 1962.

Phil 3120.11.98 — Bolland, G.J.P.J. Spreuken. 's Gravenhage, 1962.

Phil 3120.62.30 — Bollnow, Otto Fredrich. Mass und Vermesserheit des Menschen. Göttingen, 1962.

Phil 720.64 — Borne, Etienne. Passion de la vérité. Paris, 1962.

Phil 8612.52 — Boros, Ladislaus. Mysterium mortis. Olten, 1962.

Phil 4515.36 — Boström, C.J. Philosophy of religion. New Haven, 1962.

Phil 3640.710 — Brassard, Werner à. Untersuchungen zum Problem des Übermenschen bei Friedrich Nietzsche. Freiburg, 1962.

Phil 1133.37 — Breden, Heribert. Grund und Gegenwart als Frageziel der frühgriechischen Philosophie. Den Haag, 1962.

Phil 5325.35 — Brehm, Jack W. Explorations in cognitive dissonance. N.Y., 1962.

Phil 1750.700 — Breisach, Ernst. Introduction to modern existentialism. N.Y., 1962.

Phil 332.14.11 — Brentano, Franz. Wahrheit und Evidenz. Hamburg, 1962.

Phil 3450.18.155 — Breton, S. L'être spirituel recherches sur la philosophie de N. Hartmann. Lyon, 1962.

Phil 2477.17.30 — Breton, Stanislas. Essence et existence. Paris, 1962.

Phil 5590.415 — Brim, Orville Gilbert. Personality and decision processes. Stanford, 1962.

Phil 176.220 — Brito, Antonio J. Estudos de filosofia. Lisboa, 1962.

Phil 7069.62.15 — Broad, Charlie. Lectures on physical research. London, 1962.

Phil 623.37 — Brophy, B. Black ship to hell. 1. American ed. N.Y., 1962.

Phil 735.260 — Bruederlin, Kurt. Zur Phänomenologie des Werterlebens. Winterthur, 1962.

Phil 332.36 — Bruner, J.S. On knowing. Cambridge, 1962.

Phil 2477.16.30 — Brunet, Christian. Prolégomenes a une esthétique intégrale. Paris, 1962.

Phil 176.73.3 — Brunner, Constantin. Die Lehre von den Geistigen und vom Volk. 3. Aufl. Stuttgart, 1962. 2v.

Phil 3120.30.76 — Buber, Martin. Logos. Heidelberg, 1962.

Phil 3120.30.15 — Buber, Martin. Werke. München, 1962. 3v.

Phil 5241.88.3 — Bühler, Charlotte M. Psychologie im Leben unserer Zeit. München, 1962.

Phil 978.49.870 — Buehler, W. Meditation als Erkenntnisweg. Stuttgart, 1962.

Phil 801.35.10 — Bueno, Miquel. Ensayos liminares. México, 1962.

Phil 3246.298 — Buhr, Manfred. Akademie...Berlin. Berlin, 1962.

Phil 1182.52 — Burkert, Walter. Weisheit und Wissenschaft. Nürnberg, 1962.

Phil 1865.188 — Burns, J.H. Jeremy Bentham and University College. London, 1962.

Phil 585.143 — Burr, Harold S. The nature of man and the meaning of existence. Springfield, 1962.

Phil 165.332 — Butler, R.J. Analytical philosophy. Oxford, 1962.

Phil 8980.252 — Bychkova, N.V. Moral'kak ee ponimaiut kommunisty. Moskva, 1962.

Phil 4752.2.125 — Caïn, Lucienne. Berdiaev en Russie. Paris, 1962.

Phil 2725.13.95 — Callot, Emile. Propos sur Jules Lequier. Paris, 1962.

Phil 177.105.10 — Calogero, G. Filosofia del dialogo. Milano, 1962.

Phil 2150.18.80 — Campanale, D. Filosofia ed etica scientifica. Bari, 1962.

Phil 4073.68 — Campanella, Tommaso. Vita Christi. Roma, 1962. 2v.

Phil 5400.167 — Canolland, D.K. Emotion::bodily change, an enduring problem in psychology. Princeton, 1962.

Phil 5125.24.6 — Carnap, Rudolf. Logical foundations of probability. 2nd ed. Chicago, 1962.

Phil 4303.6 — Carreras y Artau, J. Apports hispaniques à la philosophie chrétienne. Louvain, 1962.

Phil 8877.68.15 — Carritt, Edgar F. The theory of beauty. London, 1962.

Phil 2150.21.80 — Carver, Vida. C.A. Mace: a symposium. London, 1962.

Phil 333.5.18 — Cassirer, Ernst. An essay on man. New Haven, 1962.

Phil 6315.19.35 — Catemario, A. La società malata. Napoli, 1962.

Phil 3484.25 — Cavagna, G.B. La soluzione kantiana. Bologna, 1962.

Phil 177.136 — Cernuschi, Alberto. Teoría del autodeísmo. Buenos Aires, 1962.

Phil 2805.395 — Chaigne, Louis. Pascal. Paris, 1962.

Phil 1750.730 — Chalin, M.L. Filosofiia otohaianiia i strakha. Moskva, 1962.

Phil 3450.19.265 — Chapelle, Albert. L'ontologie phénoménologique de Heidegger. Paris, 1962.

Phil 333.20 — Chappell, Vere C. The philosophy of mind. Englewood Cliffs, 1962.

Phil 8952.21 — Chauchard, P. Morale du cerveau. Paris, 1962.

Phil 8980.275 — Chelovek budushchego rozhdaetsia segodnia. Novosibirsk, 1962.

Phil 310.430 — Cherkesov, V.I. Materialisticheskaia dialektika kak logika i teoria poznaniia. Moskva, 1962.

Phil 1200.61 — Christensen, J. An essay of the unity of Stoic philosophy. Copenhagen, 1962.

Phil 3450.11.320 — Claesges, Ulrich. Edmund Husserls Theorie. Köln, 1962.

Phil 3850.27.210 — Clark, Henry. The ethical mysticism of Albert Schweitzer. Boston, 1962.

Phil 5042.65 — Clark, Romane. Introduction to logic. Princeton, N.J., 1962.

Phil 2805.409 — Clermont-Ferrand. Musée du Ranquet. Pascal, sa ville et son temps. Clermont-Ferrand, 1962.

Phil 8692.24 — Coggin, Philip. Art, science, and religion. London, 1962.

Phil 5520.385 — Cohen, Laurence Jonathan. The diversity of meaning. London, 1962.

Phil 177.129 — Collins, J.D. The lure of wisdom. Milwaukee, 1962.

Phil 165.338 — Congrès des Sociétés de Philosophie de Langue Française, 11th, Montpellier, 1961. Existence et nature. Paris, 1962.

Phil 5242.64 — Cooley, William. Multivariate procedures for the behavorial sciences. N.Y., 1962.

Phil 4958.510 — Cordero, Armando. Panorama de la filosofía en Santo Domingo. Santo Domingo, 1962.

Phil 1930.12.32 — Cornforth, Maurice Campbell. Science versus idealism. N.Y., 1962.

Phil 2805.229.8 — Cresson, André. Pascal; sa vie, son oeuvre, avec un exposé de sa philosophie. 5. éd. Paris, 1962.

Phil 8876.54.25 — Crippa, R. Profilo della critica blondeliana. Milano, 1962.

Phil 4960.605.25 — Cruz Costa, João. Panorama of the history of philosophy in Brazil. Washington, 1962.

Phil 177.132 — Cruz Malpique, M. Una filosofía da cultura. Porto, 1962.

Phil 2905.1.170 — Cuénot, Claude. Teilhard de Chardin. Paris, 1962.

Phil 6980.210 — Cumming, John. Ego and milieu. N.Y., 1962.

Phil 2430.2 — Cuvillier, Armand. Anthologie des philosophes français. Paris, 1962.

Phil 5627.262.15 — Cvekl, Jiří. Člověk a světový názor. Praha, 1962.

Phil 8980.316 — Danielian, Mal'feda. Nekotorye voprosy marksistisko-leninskoi etiki. Erevan, 1962.

Phil 5243.66 — Daujat, J. Psychologie contemporaine et pensée chrétienne. Tournai, 1962.

Phil 4260.205 — Daus, Hans-Jürgen. Selbstverständnis und Menschenbild in den Selbstdarstellungen Giambattista Vicos und Pietro Giannones. Thesis. Genève, 1962.

Phil 178.74 — Daval, Simone. Classe de philosophie. Paris, 1962. 2v.

Phil 930.64 — Day, A.B. The philosophers of China. N.Y., 1962.

Phil 3640.670 — Deleuze, Gilles. Nietzsche et la Philosophie. Paris, 1962.

Phil 2725.2.110 — Derre, Jean R. Lamennais, ses amis et le mouvement des idées à l'époque romantique, 1824-1834. Paris, 1962.

Phil 2520.35.52 — Descartes, René. Discorso sul metodo. Firenze, 1962.

Phil 6945.17.3 — Deutsch, Albert. The mentally ill in America. 2. ed. N.Y., 1962.

Phil 7082.14 — Diamond, Edwin. The science of dreams. 1st ed. Garden City, 1962.

Phil 2403.9 — Diaz, F. Filosofia e politica nel Settecento francese. Torino, 1962.

Phil 3195.3.35 — Dietzgen, Joseph. Schriften. Berlin, 1962.

Phil 3195.6.30.10 — Dilthey, Wilhelm. Gesammelte Schriften. v.1-17. Stuttgart, 1962- 16v.

Phil 8404.18 — Dmitrieva, N.A. Izobrazhenie i slovo. Moskva, 1962.

Phil 1930.8.105 — Donagan, Alan. The later philosophy of R.G. Collingwood. Oxford, 1962.

Phil 3195.19.30 — Dooyeweerd, H. Verkenningen in de wijsbegeerte. Amsterdam, 1962.

Phil 5066.227 — Dopp, J. Logiques construites par une methode de déduction naturelle. Louvain, 1962.

Phil 8404.3.15 — Dorfles, Gillo. Simbolo. Torino, 1962.

Phil 5590.443 — Dorsey, John Morris. The growth of self-insight. Detroit, 1962.

Phil 165.324 — Drennen, D. A modern introduction to metaphysics. N.Y., 1962.

Phil 585.141 — Dubos, René Jules. The torch of life. N.Y., 1962.

Phil 284.4.12 — Duhem, P. The aim and structure of physical theory. N.Y., 1962.

Phil 7150.27.20 — Durkheim, E. Suicide; a study in sociology. Glencoe, 1962.

Phil 70.88 — East-West Philosopher Conference. Philosophy and culture. 1. ed. Honolulu, 1962.

Phil 978.49.860 — Edmunds, L.F. Rudolf Steiner education. London, 1962.

Phil 8405.2 — Ehrlich, Walter. Aphorismen zur Philosophie der Kunst. Tübingen, 1962.

Phil 5465.126 — Eiseley, Loren. The mind as nature. 1. ed. N.Y., 1962.

Phil 1850.159 — Eiseley, Loren Corey. Francis Bacon and the modern dilemma. Lincoln, 1962.

Phil 165.300 — Emge, Carl August. Kreise um Schopenhauer. Wiesbaden, 1962.

Phil 5044.9 — Emmet, Eric Revell. Thinking clearly. N.Y., 1962.

Phil 5374.225 — Eriksen, Charles. Behavior and awareness. Durham, 1962.

Phil 5244.9.23 — Erismann, Theodor. Allgemeine Psychologie. 3. Aufl. Berlin, 1962-1965. 4v.

Phil 8584.21 — Eryshev, A.A. Religiia, vrag ravnopraviia i druzhby narodov. Kiev, 1962.

Phil 165.330 — Essays in philosophy presented to Dr. T.M.P. Mahadevan. Madras, 1962.

Phil 1704.4 — Estiú, Emilio. Del arte a la historia en la filosofia moderna. La Plata, 1962?

Phil 8430.5 — Eversople, Finley. Christian faith and the contemporary arts. N.Y., 1962.

1962 - cont.

Phil 179.36.3   Ewing, Alfred Cyril. The fundamental questions of philosophy. N.Y., 1962.

Phil 8406.24   Fallico, A.B. Art and existentialism. Englewood Cliffs, 1962.

Phil 5190.37   Faris, John A. Truth-functional logic. London, 1962.

Phil 4796.96.21   Fath 'Ali Ahud-zda. Izbrannye filosfskie proizvedeniia. Moskva, 1962.

Phil 180.77   Feibleman, James. Foundations of empiricism. The Hague, 1962.

Phil 5850.196   Fenlason, Anne. Essentials in interviewing. N.Y., 1962.

Phil 8612.56.5   Ferrater Mora, José. El ser la muerte. Madrid, 1962.

Phil 4466.4.30   Ferreira, A. Ensaios de filosofia para a história. Coimbra, 1962.

Phil 3246.18.4   Fichte, Johann Gottlieb. Gesamtausgabe der Bauerischen Akademie der Wissenschaften. Stuttgart, 1962. 9v.

Phil 3246.18.3.5   Fichte, Johann Gottlieb. Nachgelassene Werke. Bonn, 1962. 3v.

Phil 5585.215   Fisandt, Kai von. Havaitsemisen maailma. Helsinki, 1962.

Phil 5245.80   Fischel, Werner. Struktur und Dynamik. Bern, 1962.

Phil 805.14   Flam, Leopold. Verleden en toehomst van de filosofie. Amsterdam, 1962.

Phil 5245.45.6   Flügel, John Carl. Man, morals and society. Harmondsworth, 1962.

Phil 3195.6.170   Foejo, W. Introducción a Dilthey. Xalapa, 1962.

Phil 8406.4   Formaggio, Dino. L'idea di artisticita. Milano, 1962.

Phil 8110.14   Formigari, Lia. L'estetica del gusto nel settecento inglesa. 1. ed. Firenze, 1962.

Phil 90.8   Foulquié, Paul. Dictionnaire de la langue philosophique. Paris, 1962.

Phil 180.82   Foxe, Arthur N. The common sense from Heraclitus to Pierce. N.Y., 1962.

Phil 3450.11.270   Fragata, Júlio. Problemas da fenomenologia de Husserl. Braga, 1962.

Phil 5585.223   Francès, R. Quelques aspects du développement perceptif. Paris, 1962.

Phil 180.84   Franchini, Raffaello. L'oggetto della filosofia. Napoli, 1962.

Phil 1705.11   Freeman, David. Recent studies in philosophy and theology. Philadelphia, 1962.

Phil 3270.12.40   Frege, Gottlob. Funktion, Begriff, Bedeutung. Göttingen, 1962.

Phil 6315.2.51.5A   Freud, Sigmund. Civilization and its discontents. N.Y., 1962.

Phil 6315.2.37.6   Freud, Sigmund. The ego and the id. N.Y., 1962.

Phil 6315.2.75.17   Freud, Sigmund. Three essays on the theory of sexuality. London, 1962.

Phil 8430.43   Freyre, G. Arte, ciências e trópico. São Paulo, 1962.

Phil 3552.312.2   Friedmann, G. Leibniz et Spinoza. Paris, 1962.

Phil 8406.2   Fuerstenberg, Hans. Les sources de la création artistique. Monaco, 1962.

Phil 1695.23   Gaboriau, F. Novelle initiation philosophique. Tournai, 1962. 6v.

Phil 585.205   Gabriel, Mesmin. Le mal de la culture. Port-au-Prince, 1962.

Phil 1075.6   Gabriel'ian, Genri. Ocherk istorii armianskoi mysli. Erevan, 1962.

Phil 3640.686   Gaède, E. Nietzsche et Valéry. Paris, 1962.

Phil 8980.416   Galdiaev, P.K. Eto ukrashaet cheloveka. Moskva, 1962.

Phil 8586.56   Galitskaia, I.A. Mysli o religii. Moskva, 1962.

Phil 2750.11.152   Gallagher, Donald. The achievement of Jacques and Raïssa Maritain. 1st ed. N.Y., 1962.

Phil 3488.40   Gaos, José. Las críticas de Kant. Caracas, 1962.

Phil 181.132   Gaos, José. De la filosofia. Mexico, 1962.

Phil 1706.12   Gaos, José. Filosofia contemporanea. Caracas, 1962.

Phil 3425.572   Garaudy, Roger. Dieu est mort; étude sur Hegel. Paris, 1962.

Phil 8407.42   Garcia Prado, Carlos, Teorías estéticas. Madrid, 1962.

Phil 5246.76A   Garner, W.R. Uncertainty and structure as psychological concepts. N.Y., 1962.

Phil 4080.3.390   Garosci, A. Il pensiero politico di Benedetto Croce. Torino, 1962.

Phil 8407.39   Gatecki, L. Problematyka estetiki. Kraków, 1962.

Phil 5046.36   Geach, Peter. Reference and generality. Ithaca, N.Y., 1962.

Phil 5246.72   Geldard, F.A. Fundamentals of psychology. N.Y., 1962.

Phil 5640.50   Geldard, Frank A. The human senses. N.Y., 1962.

Phil 5246.74   Gendlin, Eugene. Experiencing and the creation of meaning. N.Y., 1962.

Phil 4114.20   Genovesi, Antonio. Autobiografia, lettere e altri scritti. Milano, 1962.

Phil 672.151.2   Gent, Werner. Die Philosophie des Raumes und der Zeit. 2. Aufl. v.1-2. Hildesheim, 1962.

Phil 3488.41   Gerresheim, E. Die Bedeutung des Terminus transzendental in Immanuel Kants Kritik der reinen Vernunft. Inaug. Diss. Köln, 1962.

Phil 8050.5   Geschichte der Ästhetik. Köln, 1962.

Phil 2050.244   Giarrizzo, G. David Hume politico e storico. Torino, 1962.

Phil 181.73.15   Gilson, E. The philosopher and theology. N.Y., 1962.

Phil 2630.8.32   Gilson, Etienne. L'être et l'essence. Paris, 1962.

Phil 337.26   Giovanni, Biagio de. L'esperienza come oggettivazione. Napoli, 1962.

Phil 8881.77   Gobry, Ivan. Le modèle en morale. Paris, 1962.

Phil 6316.15   Goerres, Albert. The methods and experience of psychoanalysis. London, 1962.

Phil 8980.432   Golovan, I.P. Po dolgu grazhdanina. Moskva, 1962.

Phil 2520.342   Gonhier, Henri. La pensée métaphysique de Descartes. Paris, 1962.

Phil 760.2   González Asenjo, Florencio. El todo y las partes; estudios de ontología formal. Madrid, 1962.

Phil 5850.221.15   Goude, G. On fundamental measurement in psychology. Stockholm, 1962.

Phil 2477.19.80   Gouhier, Henri. Notice sur la vie et les travaux de Gaston Berger, 1896-1960. Paris, 1962.

Phil 3450.18.160   Grabes, H. Der Begriff des a priori in Nicolai Hartmanns Erkenntnismetaphysik und Ontologie. Köln, 1962.

Phil 4080.3.395   Grandi, M. Benedetto Croce e il seicento. Milano, 1962.

Phil 5477.16   Greeff, Etienne de. L'homme et son juge. Paris, 1962.

Phil 1195.17   Grieder, H. Die Bedeutung der Sophistik. Basel, 1962.

Phil 2050.243   Grieve, C.M. The man of (almost) independent mind. Edinburgh, 1962.

Phil 3488.38   Grigor'ian, B.T. Neokantianstvo. Moskva, 1962.

Phil 978.98   Grohmann, Gerbert. Die Pflanze als Lichtsinnesorgan der Erde. Stuttgart, 1962.

Phil 5592.170   Gross, Martin L. The brain watchers. N.Y., 1962.

Phil 4829.491.80   Grubačić, Kosta. Božidar Knežević. Sarajevo, 1962.

1962 - cont.

Phil 5465.124   Gruber, Howard E. Contemporary approaches to creative thinking. N.Y., 1962.

Phil 2630.7.39   Guénon, René. Symboles fondament aux de la science sacrée. Paris, 1962.

Phil 8586.55   Guerin, Pierre. Vérité et religion; essai le problème. Paris, 1962.

Phil 5520.437   Guilhot, Jean. La dynamique de l'expression et de la communication. Paris, 1962.

Phil 806.35   Guiliano, Balbino. Il cammino del pensiero. Firenze, 1962.

Phil 2750.22.90   Guissard, L. Emmanuel Mounier. Paris, 1962.

Phil 2805.404   Guitton, J. Génie de Pascal. Paris, 1962.

Phil 2630.11.25   Guitton, Jean. Le clair et l'obscur. Paris, 1962.

Phil 2630.11.20   Guitton, Jean. Dialogue avec les précurseurs. Aubier, 1962.

Phil 3006.9   Gulyga, A.V. Iz istorii nemetskogo materializma. Moskva, 1962.

Phil 8092.5   Gunzenhaeuser, R. Ästhetisches Mass und Ästhetische Information. Hamburg, 1962.

Phil 5016.2   Gurvitch, Georges. Dialectique et sociologie. Paris, 1962.

Phil 1111.12.10   Guthrie, William. A history of Greek philosophy. Cambridge, 1962. 3v.

Phil 1925.85   Gysi, Lydia. Platonism and Cartesianism. Bern, 1962.

Phil 7069.62.5   Hall, Trevor. The spiritualists; story of F. Cook and Wm. Crookes. London, 1962.

Phil 182.128   Halle, L.J. Men and nations. Princeton, 1962.

Phil 3827.12.5   Hallett, H.F. Creation, emanation and salvation, a Spinozistic study. The Hague, 1962.

Phil 9513.18   Hanis, Robert T. Social ethics. Philadelphia, 1962.

Phil 2475.1.395   Hanna, T. The Bergsonian heritage. N.Y., 1962.

Phil 1750.655   Hanna, Thomas. The lyrical existentialists. 1. ed. N.Y., 1962.

Phil 2840.93.5   Hansen, Valdemar. Charles Renouvier; hans liv og hans tanker. København, 1962.

Phil 3450.18.145   Hanthack, K. Nicolai Hartmann und das Ende der Ontologie. Berlin, 1962.

Phil 6957.7.4.10   Hart, Bernard. The psychology of insanity. Cambridge, 1962.

Phil 1865.190   Hart, H.L.A. Bentham. London, 1962?

Phil 165.328   Hartmann, Klaus. Lebendiger Realismus. Bonn, 1962.

Phil 182.131   Hartnack, J. Philosophical problems. Copenhagen, 1962.

Phil 3925.16.92   Hartnack, Justus. Wittgenstein und die Moderne Philosophie. Stuttgart, 1962.

Phil 2055.9.35   Hartshorne, Charles. The logic of perfection. LaSalle, Ill., 1962.

Phil 1707.16.5   Hawkins, D.J.B. Crucial problems of modern philosophy. Notre Dame, 1962.

Phil 8408.3   Hawkins, Denis John B. The concepts of aesthetics. London, 1962.

Phil 2805.399   Hay, Malcolm. The prejudices of Pascal. London, 1962.

Phil 8587.74   Hayward, John. Existentialism and religious liberalism. Boston, 1962.

Phil 3640.682   Heftrich, Eckhard. Nietzsches Philosophie. Frankfurt, 1962.

Phil 3425.40.55   Hegel, Georg Wilhelm Friedrich. Differenz des Fichte'schen und Schelling'schen Systems der Philosophie. Hamburg, 1962.

Phil 3425.30   Hegel, Georg Wilhelm Friedrich. Glauben und Wissen. Hamburg, 1962.

Phil 3425.76.50   Hegel, Georg Wilhelm Friedrich. Hegel on tragedy. 1st ed. Garden City, N.Y., 1962.

Phil 3425.60.6   Hegel, Georg Wilhelm Friedrich. Lectures on the philosophy of religion. N.Y., 1962. 3v.

Phil 3450.19.32   Heidegger, Martin. Being and time. London, 1962.

Phil 3489.27.15   Heidegger, Martin. Die Frage nach dem Ding. Tübingen, 1962.

Phil 3489.27.10   Heidegger, Martin. Kant and the problem of metaphysics. Bloomington, 1962.

Phil 3450.19.82   Heidegger, Martin. Die Technik und die Kehre. Pfullingen, 1962.

Phil 5402.24   Heidsieck, François. Plaisir et tempérance. Paris, 1962.

Phil 2530.90   Heitmann, K. Ethos des Künstlers und Ethos der Kunst. Münster, 1962.

Phil 8832.8   Held, Virginia. The bewildered age. N.Y., 1962.

Phil 8882.87   Henningsen, N. Moral-hvad er det? København, 1962.

Phil 8587.65.10   Hessen, Johannes. Griechische oder biblische Theologie. München, 1962.

Phil 3827.8.5   Hessing, Siegfried. Spinoza dreihundert Jahre Ewigkeit. Den Haag, 1962.

Phil 1200.76   Hicks, Robert Drew. Stoic and Epicurean. N.Y., 1962.

Phil 182.129   Hildebrandt, K. Ein Weg zur Philosophie. Bonn, 1962.

Phil 5247.66.3   Hilgard, Ernest R. Introduction to psychology. 3. ed. N.Y., 1962.

Phil 338.40   Hintikka, K.J.J. Knowledge and belief. Ithaca, 1962.

Phil 5593.62   Hirt, Michael. Rorschach science; readings in theory and method. N.Y., 1962.

Phil 807.20   A history of philosophy. N.Y., 1962. 4v.

Phil 2045.14   Hobbes, Thomas. The English works of Thomas Hobbes of Malmesbury. Aalen, 1962. 11v.

Phil 6980.354   Hoffer, Abram. Niacin therapy in psychiatry. Springfield, Ill., 1962.

Phil 3450.11.265   Hohl, Hubert. Lebenswelt und Geschichte. Areiburg, 1962.

Phil 5627.262.5   Hopkins, Pryns. The social psychology of religious experience. N.Y., 1962.

Phil 5627.134.77   Howard, Peter. Frank Buchman's secret. Garden City, N.Y., 1962.

Phil 3850.50   Huenermann, Peter. Trinitorische Anthropologie bei Franz Anton Staudenmaiet. Freiburg, 1962.

Phil 2250.110   Humbach, K.T. Das Verhältnis von Einzelperson und Gemeinschaft nach Josiah Royce. Heidelberg, 1962.

Phil 978.91   Husemann, F. Wege und Irrwege in die geistige Welt. Stuttgart, 1962.

Phil 338.41   Hutten, Ernest. The origins of science. London, 1962.

Phil 1750.166.92   Huxley, J.S. The humanist frame. N.Y., 1962.

Phil 182.130   Hva er metafysikk? Aristoteles, Bergson, Heidegger. Oslo, 1962.

Phil 5548.83   Iff, Werner. La motivation à l'avancement professionnel. Paris, 1962.

Phil 9070.103.5   Iliadi, A.N. Prakticheskaia priroda chelovecheskogo poznaniia. Moskva, 1962.

Phil 339.10   Il'in, Ivan A. Put' dukhovnago obnovleniia. Miunkhen, 1962.

Phil 8409.2   Ingarden, R. Untersuchungen zur Ontologie der Kunst. Tübingen, 1962.

Phil 4803.462.30   Ingarden, Roman. Issledovaniia po estetike. Moskva, 1962.

Chronological Listing

Phil 4970.1.11   Ingenieros, José. Obras completas. Buenos Aires, 1962. 8v.

Phil 70.83   International Congress of Applied Psychology, 14th, Copenhagen, 1961. Proceedings. Copenhagen, 1962. 5v.

Phil 310.480   Iurova, I.L. Dialekticheskii materializm i chastnye nauki. Moskva, 1962.

Phil 6319.1.183.6   Jacobi, Jolan. The psychology of C.G. Jung. New Haven, 1962.

Phil 5049.26   Jacoby, G. Die Ansprüche der Logistiker. Stuttgart, 1962.

Phil 5520.422   Jánoska, G. Die sprachlichen Grundlagen der Philosophie. Graz, 1962.

Phil 184.19.35   Jaspers, K. The great philosophers. 1. American ed. N.Y., 1962. 2v.

Phil 3475.3.78   Jaspers, Karl. Der philosophische Glaube Angesichts der Offenbarung. München, 1962.

Phil 310.565   Javůrek, Zdenck. Dialektika oleccného a zuláštního. Praha, 1962.

Phil 2805.321   Jerphagnon, L. Le caractère de Pascal. Paris, 1962.

Phil 7082.12   Jones, Richard Matthew. Ego synthesis in dreams. Cambridge, 1962.

Phil 184.50   Jorn, A. Naturens orden; de divisione naturae. 2. Opl. København, 1962.

Phil 19.6.10   Journal of philosophy, psychology and scientific methods. Fifty year index, 1904-53; and ten year supplement, 1954-63. N.Y., 1962-64. 2v.

Phil 6319.1.47   Jung, C.G. Die Bedeutung des Vaters für das Schicksal des Einzelnen. 4. Aufl. Zürich, 1962.

Phil 6319.1.32   Jung, C.G. Erinneringen. Zürich, 1962.

Phil 2880.8.138   Kaelin, Eugene. An existentialist aesthetic. Madison, 1962.

Phil 5250.72   Kagan, J. Birth to maturity. N.Y., 1962.

Phil 8411.20.5   Kainz, F. Vorlesungen über Ästhetik. Detroit, 1962.

Phil 185.97   Kalsbeek, L. Geloof en wetenschap. Baarn, 1962.

VPhil 185.108   Kamiński, Stanisław. Z teorii i metodologii metafizyki. Wyd. 1. Lublin, 1962.

Phil 3480.14.1   Kant, Immanuel. Gesammelte Schriften. Personenindex. v.1-23. Bonn, 1962-

Phil 5125.29   Katz, Jerrold J. The problem of induction and its solution. Chicago, 1962.

Phil 8590.32   Kazhdan, Al.P. Proiskhozhdenie khristianstva i ego sushchnost'. Moskva, 1962.

Phil 310.554   Kelle, Vladislav Zh. Istoricheskii materializm; kurs lektsii. Moskva, 1962.

Phil 6120.22   Kent, Caron. Man's hidden resources. Melbourne, Arkansas, 1962?

Phil 4791.6   Khidasheli, Shalva Vasil'evich. Osnovnye mirovozzrencheskie napravleniia v feodal'noi Gruzii. Tbilisi, 1962.

Phil 6049.62   Kiener, Franz. Hans, Gebärde und Charakter. München, 1962.

Phil 1133.35.4   Kirk, G.S. The presocratic philosophers. Cambridge, Eng., 1962.

Phil 6120.23   Klier, Sol. Effects of induced stress on learning and performance. n.p., 1962.

Phil 3492.42.5   Klinke, Willibald. Kant for everyman. N.y., 1962.

Phil 310.589.8   Klofáč, Jaroslav. Materialistické pojetí dějin. Vyd. 3. Praha, 1962.

Phil 310.589   Klofáč, Jaroslav. O rozporech ve společnostii. Praha, 1962.

Phil 5020.5   Kneale, William Calvert. The development of logic. Oxford, 1962.

Phil 705.11.5   Knittermeyer, Hinrich. Der Mensch der Erkenntnis. Hamburg, 1962.

Phil 1515.3   Knowles, David. The evolution of medieval thought. Baltimore, 1962.

Phil 8092.2   Koch, Hans. Marxismus und Ästhetik. Berlin, 1962.

Phil 3450.19.250   Kockelmans, A. Martin Heidegger. Teilt, 1962.

Phil 9495.160.15   Koehn-Behrens, Charlotte. Eros at bay; the illusion of modern love. London, 1962.

Phil 5643.121   Koenig, E. Experimentelle Beiträge zur Theorie des binokularen Einfach- und Tefensehens. Meisenheim, 1962.

Phil 6315.2.315   Koenig, K. Die Schicksale Sigmund Freuds und J. Breners. Stuttgart, 1962.

Phil 7069.62.25   Koernev, E.M. Wege Zum Licht; Erlebnisse und Gespräche mit mystikern. Garmisch-Partenkirchen, 1962.

Phil 4710.140   Kogan, Iu.Ia. Ocherki po istorii russkoi ateisticheskoi mysli XVIII v. Moskva, 1962.

Phil 3801.496   Koktanek, A.M. Schellings Seinslehre und Kierkegaard. München, 1962.

Phil 5425.106   Konferentsiia po Problemam Sposobnostei, Leningrad, 1960. Problemy sposobnostei. Moskva, 1962.

Phil 810.15   Kopper, J. Reflexion und Raisonnement im ontologischen Gottesbeweis. Köln, 1962.

Phil 5068.28   Korneeva, Anna I. Kritika neopoz, vzgliadov na prizodu poznaniia. Moskva, 1962.

Phil 8411.30   Kornienko, V.S. O sushchnosti esteticheskogo poznaniia. Novosibirsk, 1962.

Phil 8980.496.10   Kosolapov, S.M. Nravstvennye printsipy stroitelia kommunizma. Moskva, 1962.

Phil 575.248   Kováły, Pavel. Americký personalismus; příspěvek k rozboru krize současného buržoazního myšlení. Praha, 1962.

Phil 6960.5.15   Kraepelin, E. One hundred years of psychiatry. N.Y., 1962.

Phil 8980.498   Krasnor, Iu. M. O kul'ture povedeniia molodogo cheloveka. Moskva, 1962.

Phil 1630.15   Kristeller, P.O. La tradizione aristotelica nel Rinascimento. Padova, 1962.

Phil 8411.2   Kubler, George. The shape of time; remarks on the history of things. New Haven, 1962.

Phil 3425.586   Kuderowicz, Z. Doktryna moralna młodego Hegla. Warszawa, 1962.

Phil 672.216   Kuemmel, F. Über den Begriff der Zeit. Tübingen, 1962.

Phil 3549.21   Kuhn, H. Das Sein und das Gute. München, 1962.

Phil 3549.20   Kwant, R.C. Mens en kritiek. Utrecht, 1962.

Phil 2750.20.80   Kwant, Remigius Cornelius. De fenomenologie van Merleau-Ponty. Utrecht, 1962.

Phil 1750.760   Lacroix, Jean. Histoire et mystère. Tournai, 1962.

Phil 2115.114.5   Lamprecht, S.P. The moral and political philosophy of John Locke. N.Y., 1962.

Phil 585.120   Landmann, Michael. De homine. Freiburg, 1962.

Phil 2120.11.30   Langer, Susanne Katherina (Knauth). Philosophical sketches. Baltimore, 1962.

Phil 8663.3.97   Larson, O.P. American infidel. N.Y., 1962.

Phil 3425.588   Lauener, H. Die Sprache in der Philosophie Hegels. Berlin, 1962.

Phil 2725.35.70   Lavelle, Louis. Manuel de méthodologie dialectique. Paris, 1962.

Phil 186.145   Lea, Frank A. A defence of philosophy. London, 1962.

Phil 5070.23   Lebacqz, Joseph. Certitude et volonté. Bruges, 1962.

Phil 5145.2   Leblanc, Hugues. Statistical and inductive probabilities. Englewood Cliffs, 1962.

Phil 186.143   Lechat, Jean. Analyse et synthèse. Paris, 1962.

Phil 850.31   Legowiiz, J. Filozofia okresu sosarstwa rzymekiego. Warszawa, 1962.

Phil 3552.51.8   Leibniz, Gottfried Wilhelm. Discourse on metaphysics. La Salle, 1962.

Phil 3552.60.10   Leibniz, Gottfried Wilhelm. Essais de Theodicée. Paris, 1962.

Phil 3552.67.30   Leibniz, Gottfried Wilhelm. Grundwahrheiten der Philosophie. Frankfurt, 1962.

Phil 3552.29.35   Leibniz, Gottfried Wilhelm. Leibniz et la racine de l'existence. Par+s, 1962.

Phil 1540.74   Lemny, Richard. Abu Ma'shar and Lah'n Aristoteliaram. Beirut, 1962.

Phil 8505.8.20   Leningrad. Muzei Istorii Religii i Ateizma. Proiskhozhdenie religii. Moskva, 1962.

Phil 310.485   Leningrad. Universitet. Filosofskie voprosy sovremennogo ucheniia o dvizhenii v prirode. Leningrad, 1962.

Phil 310.475   Leningrad. Universitet. Nekotorye voprosy dialekticheskii materializma. Leningrad, 1962.

Phil 310.465   Leningrad. Universitet. Filosofskii Fakultet. Voprosy marksistskoi sotsiologii. Leningrad, 1962.

Phil 5251.64   Leonhard, Karl. Biologische Psychologie. Leipzig, 1962.

Phil 6321.43   Lévy-Valensi, E. Le dialogue psychanalytique. Paris, 1962.

Phil 6321.47   Lévy-Valensi, E. Les rapports intersubjectifs en psychanalyse. Paris, 1962.

Phil 8591.44.35   Lewis, Clive Staples. They asked for a paper. London, 1962.

Phil 8412.37   Librizzi, Carmelo. Conoscenza e arte. Padova, 1962.

Phil 4160.41.30   Librizzi, Carmelo. Morale e religione. Padova, 1962.

Phil 4351.5.80   Llanos, Alfredo. Carlos Astrada. Buenos Aires, 1962.

Phil 2115.49.30   Locke, J. Über den menschlichen Verstand. Berlin, 1962. 2v.

Phil 3050.6   Loewith, Karl. Die Hegelsche Linke; Texte aus den Werken. Stuttgart, 1962.

Phil 165.305   Logic and language. Holland, 1962.

Phil 8412.35   Logroscimo, G. Teoria dell'arte e della critica. Padova, 1962.

Phil 1865.185   London. University. University College Library. Catalogue of the manuscripts of Jeremy Bentham in the Library of University College. 2nd ed. London, 1962.

Phil 4967.20.85   Lopes de Maltos, C. O pensamento de Farias Brito. São Paulo, 1962.

Phil 3850.18.175   Lorscheid, B. Das Leibphänomen. Bonn, 1962.

Phil 2340.10.170   Lowe, Victor A. Understanding Whitehead. Baltimore, 1962.

Phil 2905.1.180   Lubac, Henri de. La pensée religieuse du père Teilhard de Chardin. Paris, 1962.

Phil 165.310   Lucas, Eric. What is a man. London, 1962.

Phil 3425.598   Luebbe, Hermann. Die Hegelsche Rechte. Stuttgart, 1962.

Phil 8400.33   Lukin, Iu.B. Prekrasnoe i zhizn'. Moskva, 1962.

Phil 8622.57   Lutzenberger, H. Das Glaubensproblem in der Religionsphilosophie. München? 1962.

Phil 186.142   Lynch, W.F. The integrating mind. N.Y., 1962.

Phil 1865.186   Mack, Mary P. Jeremy Bentham; an odyssey of ideas. London, 1962.

Phil 9560.54   Mackenzie, C. On moral courage. London, 1962.

Phil 5414.35   McKenzie, John. Guilt. London, 1962.

Phil 2115.147.2   MacLean, K. John Locke and English literature of the eighteenth century. N.Y., 1962.

Phil 5620.28   Macmurray, John. Reason and emotion. 2. ed. N.Y., 1962.

Phil 5465.130   Maire, Gilbert. Les instants privilégiés. Aubier, 1962.

Phil 2733.29.35   Malebranche, Nicolas. De la recherche de la verité. Paris, 1962. 2v.

Phil 2733.38   Malebranche, Nicolas. Lumière et mouvement de l'esprit. Paris, 1962.

Phil 2905.1.450   Mallemann, René de. Notice sur la vie et les travaux de Pierre Teilhard de Chardin. Paris, 1962.

Phil 310.151   Mal'tsev, V.I. Marksistskaia dialektika i sovremennyi mekhanitsizm. Moskva, 1962.

Phil 2128.45   Mandeville, B. Fable of the bees. N.Y., 1962.

Phil 3450.19.370   Manno, Mario. Heidegger e la filosofia. Roma, 1962.

Phil 5222.10   Manswrov, N.S. Sovremennaia curzhuazhaia psikhologiia. Moskva, 1962.

Phil 2412.12A   Manuel, F.E. The prophets of Paris. Cambridge, 1962.

Phil 2750.19.42   Marcel, Gabriel. Fragments philosophiques 1909-1914. Louvain, 1962.

Phil 585.151   Marcel, Gabriel. Man against mass society. Chicago, 1962.

Phil 2750.19.37   Marcel, Gabriel. The philosophy of existentialism. 2nd ed. N.Y., 1962.

Phil 2750.10.110   Marcucci, Silvestro. Emile Meyerson. Torino, 1962.

Phil 6315.2.310.3   Marcuse, Herbert. Eros and civilization. N.Y., 1962.

Phil 6122.97   Mardersptein, I.G. Otrazhenie v khudozhestvennoi literature ucheniia o fiziologii golovnogo mozga. Tashkent, 1962.

Phil 8400.29   Margolis, J. Philosophy looks at the arts. N.Y., 1962.

Phil 8413.33   Maritain, J. Art and scholasticism. N.Y., 1962.

Phil 2750.11.61   Maritain, Jacques. The education of man. Garden City, 1962.

Phil 6980.458   Marlet, J.J.C. De psychiater en zijn pratkijk. Utrecht, 1962.

Phil 6945.35   Martin, Denis V. Adventure in psychiatry. Oxford, 1962.

Phil 5762.32   Marx, Otto. Leben ist Willkür. Hamburg, 1962.

Phil 5548.100   Maslow, Abraham Harold. Toward a psychology of being. Princeton, 1962.

Phil 2805.415   Massis, Henri. Troisième centenaire de la mort de Pascal. Paris, 1962.

Phil 672.214   Matoré, Georges. L'espace humain. Paris, 1962.

Phil 2150.16.45   Mayer, Frederick. New perspectives for education. Washington, 1962.

Phil 5421.30   Mechanu, David. Students under stress. N.Y., 1962.

Phil 5520.106.5   Meerloo, A.M. Het web van menselijke en sociale relaties. Den Haag, 1962.

Phil 1812.15   Mehta, Ved P. Fly and the fly-bottle. 1. ed. Boston, 1962.

Phil 4170.12   Mei, F. Storia e significato del superuomo. Milano, 1962.

Phil 8413.2   Merle, Pierre. Pour une clinique d'art. Paris, 1962.

Phil 2750.20.11   Merleau-Ponty, Maurice. Eloge de la philosophie. Paris, 1962.

Phil 2630.7.105   Meroz, Lucien. René Guénon, ou La sagesse initiatique. Paris, 1962.

Phil 5592.171 — Messick, S. Measurement in personality and cognition. N.Y., 1962.

Phil 5465.121 — Metzger, Wolfgang. Schöpferische Freiheit. 2. Aufl. Frankfurt, 1962.

Phil 4752.2.170 — Meusel, Joachim. Geschichtlichkeit und Mystik im Denken Nikolaj Berdjayews. Berlin? 1962?

Phil 343.16.16 — Meyerson, Emile. Identity and reality. N.Y., 1962.

Phil 4065.170 — Michel, Paul. La caemologie de Giordano Bruno. Paris, 1962.

Phil 5585.211 — Michotte, Albert. Causalité, permanence et réalité phénoménales. Louvain, 1962.

Phil 6122.95 — The Midtown Manhattan study. N.Y., 1962. 2v.

Phil 5592.173 — Mields, J. Diagnostische Möglichkeiten der Intelligenz-Beurteilung. Heidelberg, 1962.

Phil 2050.250 — Mikhalenko, Iu.P. Filosofiia D. Iuma. Moskva, 1962.

Phil 2138.54 — Mill, John S. Essays on politics and culture. Garden City, 1962.

Phil 2138.77.5 — Mill, John S. On Bentham and Coleridge. N.Y., 1962.

Phil 5252.141A — Miller, George A. Psychology, the science of mental life. N.Y., 1962.

Phil 6962.36 — Mills, Enid. Living with mental illness. London, 1962.

Phil 1812.14 — Milne, A.J.M. The social philosophy of English idealism. London, 1962.

Phil 5640.144 — Milne, Lorus J. The senses of animals and men. N.Y., 1962.

Phil 5420.16 — Milsen, G. Studies in self-confrontation. Copenhagen, 1962.

Phil 2045.132A — Mintz, Samuel. The hunting of Leviathan. Cambridge, 1962.

Phil 9070.100 — Moeller, Orla. At vaere ung. København, 1962.

Phil 1750.715 — Molina, Fernando. Existentialism as philosophy. N.Y., 1962.

Phil 4012.7.5 — Mondolfo, Rodolfo. Da Ardigò a Gramsci. Milano, 1962.

Phil 1712.24 — Moniuszko, Antoni. Aczyístość i synteza. Warszawa, 1962.

Phil 4983.1.79 — Montevideo. Universidad. Facultad de Humanidades y Ciencias. Bibliografía de Carlos Vaz Ferreira. Montevideo, 1962.

Phil 2150.18.40 — Moore, George Edward. Commonplace book, 1919-1953. London, 1962.

Phil 3552.470 — Morawietz, Kurt. Gottfried Wilhelm Leibniz. Hannover, 1962.

Phil 293.32 — Morin, Gérard. Vie et cosmos. Paris, 1962.

Phil 5822.14 — Morris, Desmond. The biology of art. London, 1962.

Phil 5822.14.5 — Morris, Desmond. The biology of art. N.Y., 1962.

Phil 343.65 — Moscato, Alberto. Ricerche sulla struttura della conoscenza formale. Milano, 1962.

Phil 8980.581 — Moscow. Akademiia Obshchestvennykh Nauk. Voprosy marksistko-leninskoi etiki. Moskva, 1962.

Phil 310.545 — Moscow. Moskovskii Institut Inzhenerov Zheleznogo Transporta. Nekotorye voprosy teorii poznaniia dialekticheskogo materializma. Moskva, 1962.

Phil 5022.4 — Moscow. Universitet. Filosofskii Fakul'tet. Ocherki po istorii logiki v Rossii. Moskva, 1962.

Phil 330.18 — Mourelos, G. L'épistémologie positive et la critique. Paris, 1962.

Phil 330.18.2 — Mourelos, G. L'épistémologie positive et la critique meyersonienne. Thèse. Paris, 1962.

Phil 7069.51.25 — Muldoon, Sylvan Joseph. The phenomena of astral projection. London, 1962.

Phil 8702.30 — Muller, C. Science et faith, co-existence or synthesis? Louvain, 1962.

Phil 2280.5.79 — Munson, T.N. The essential wisdom of George Santayana. N.Y., 1962.

Phil 5870.110 — Murphy, Lois Barclay. The widening world of childhood. N.Y., 1962.

Phil 270.107 — Musabaeva, N.A. Problemy prichinnosti v filosofii i giologii. Alma-Ata, 1962.

Phil 2255.1.114 — Narskii, I.S. Filosfiia Bertrana Rassela. Moskva, 1962.

Phil 2805.277 — Nasmuth, E. Der unbekannte Pascal. Regensburg, 1962.

Phil 188.24 — Natanson, M. Literature, philosophy and the social sciences; essays in existentialism and phenomenology. The Hague, 1962.

Phil 8400.39 — The nature of beauty. Lahore, 1962.

Phil 813.5 — Natzner, Gert von. Das Weltbild des Menschen. Berlin, 1962.

Phil 5627.262.10 — Nédoncelle, M. Prière humaine, prière divine. Bruges, 1962.

Phil 188.26 — Negri, Antimo. Spirito del tempo e costume speculativo. Firenze, 1962.

Phil 3665.5.30 — Nelson, Leonard. Fortschritte und Rückschritte der Philosophie. Frankfurt, 1962.

Phil 5520.404 — Neubert, Q. Semantischer Positivismus in den USA. Halle, 1962.

Phil 5238.176 — New directions in psychology. N.Y., 1962.

Phil 4080.3.172 — Nicolini, Fausto. Benedetto Croce. Torino, 1962.

Phil 5023.1 — Nidditch, Peter. The development of mathematical logic. London, 1962.

Phil 3495.16 — Nierkaus, F. Das Problem des psychophysischen Kommersiums in der Entwicklung der Kantischen Philosophie. Köln, 1962.

Phil 1750.732 — Noack, Hermann. Die Philosophie Westeuropus. Basel, 1962.

Phil 4967.20.80 — Nogueira, A. Farias Brito e a filosofia do espirito. Rio de Janeiro, 1962.

Phil 3450.19.240 — Noller, Gerhard. Sein und Existenz. München, 1962.

Phil 2175.4.35 — Northrop, F.S.C. Man, nature and God. N.Y., 1962.

Phil 4065.172 — Nowicki, A. Centralne Kategorie filozofii Giordana Bruna. Warszawa, 1962.

Phil 8415.9 — Oberti, Elisa. Contributi all'analisi estetica. Milano, 1962.

Phil 8415.9.5 — Oberti, Elisa. Estetica teoria dell'oggetto artistico come presenz evidenziata. Milano, 1962.

Phil 8980.630 — Obshchestvo pro Rasprostran. O kommunisticheskoi etike. London, 1962.

Phil 165.339 — Oehler, K. Einsichten. Frankfurt a.M., 1962.

Phil 9550.17 — Ofstad, Harald. Upartiskhet og utilitarisme. Stockholm, 1962.

Phil 310.460 — Oizerman, T.I. Formirovanie filosofii marksizma. Moskva, 1962.

Phil 295.4 — Oliveira, I. de. Introduction du sens cosmique en philosophie. Paris, 1962.

Phil 9230.25 — Olmsted, Charlotte. Heads, I win; tails, you lose. N.Y., 1962.

Phil 1750.710 — Olson, Robert. An introduction to existentialism. N.Y., 1962.

Phil 5254.8 — O'Neil, William Matthew. An introduction to method in psychology. 2d. ed. Parkville, 1962.

Phil 4080.3.380 — Onufrio, Salvatore. La politica nel pensiero di Benedetto Croce. Milano, 1962.

Phil 814.5 — Orientamenti filosofici e pedagogico. Milano, 1962. 4v.

Phil 345.6 — Orlov, V.V. Osobennosti chuvstvennogo poznaniia. Perm, 1962.

Phil 1714.5 — Orsi, Domenico d'. Saggi varii di filosofia moderna e contemporanea. Padova, 1962.

Phil 1714.5.5 — Orsi, Domenico d'. Il tramonto della filosofia moderna. Padova, 1962.

Phil 5520.401 — Ortigues, E. Le discours et le symbole. Paris, 1962.

Phil 8980.659 — Osnovy marksysts'ko-leninśkoi etyky. Chernivtsi, 1962.

Phil 6324.6 — Oston, Mortimer. Drugs in psychoanalysis and psychopathology. N.Y., 1962.

Phil 1135.180 — Padellaro De Angelis, Rosa. Il problema cosmologica e l'antivomia unomalteplice. Milano, 1962.

Phil 190.103 — Palacios, L.E. Filosofia del saber. Madrid, 1962.

Phil 6980.573 — Pan-African Psychiatric Conference, 1st, Abeokuta, 1961. First Pan-African psychiatric conference. Ibadan, 1962?

Phil 585.260 — Pannenberg, Wolfhart. Was ist der Mensch? Die Anthropologie der Gegenwart im Lichte der Theologie. Göttingen, 1962.

Phil 8670.20.5 — Pantskhawa, I.D. Istoriia i teoriia ateizma. Moskva, 1962.

Phil 8670.20 — Pantskhawa, I.D. Osnovnye voprosy nauchnogo ateizma. Moskva, 1962.

Phil 3552.444 — Panzer, Ursula. Die Phänomenalität der Res Extensa bei Leibniz. Köln, 1962.

Phil 4845.227.34 — Papanoutsos, Euangelos. Epikaira kai anepikaira. Athena, 1962.

Phil 4845.227.38 — Papanoutsos, Euangelos. Hē ēthikē syneidēsē kai tä problēmatä tes. Athena, 1962.

Phil 4845.227.32.2 — Papanoutsos, Euangelos. Gnosiologia. 2. ed. Athena, 1962.

Phil 6325.23 — Parker, B. My language is me. N.Y., 1962.

Phil 2805.42.50 — Pascal, Blaise. Pensées. N.Y., 1962.

Phil 2805.42.55 — Pascal, Blaise. Pensées. Paris, 1962.

Phil 2805.40.50 — Pascal, Blaise. Pensées sur la religion et sur quelques autres sujets. Monaco, 1962.

Phil 2805.32.26 — Pascal, Blaise. Les provinciales écrits des curés de Paris. Paris, 1962. 2v.

Phil 2805.27 — Pascal, Blaise. Textes inédits. Bruges, 1962.

Phil 2805.393 — Pascal e Nietzsche. Padova, 1962.

Phil 2805.386F — Pascal et Port Royal. Paris, 1962.

Phil 2805.40.55 — Pascal présent, 1662-1962. Clermont, 1962.

Phil 1715.6.5 — Passmore, John Arthur. A hundred years of philosophy. London, 1962.

Phil 5255.58.5 — Pastuszka, J. Charakter cztowieka. Lublin, 1962.

Phil 1750.733 — Patha, Frederick. Existentialist thinkers and thought. N.Y., 1962.

Phil 5625.75.40 — Pavlov, Ivan P. Essays in psychology and psychiatry. N.Y., 1962.

Phil 5625.75.35 — Pavlov, Ivan P. Psychopathology and psychiatry. Moscow, 1962?

Phil 3450.11.295 — Pazanin, A. Das Problem der Philosophie als strenger Wissenschaft. Köln, 1962.

Phil 9355.2.7 — Peacham, Henry. The complete gentleman. N.Y., 1962.

Phil 1145.92 — Pearson, L.I.C. Popular ethics in ancient Greece. Stanford, Calif., 1962.

Phil 1830.50 — Pennsylvania. State University. Philosophy Department. Essays in philosophy. University Park, Penn., 1962.

Phil 8416.36 — Pereira, M.A. Vida e morte das formas. Lisboa, 1962.

Phil 8140.7 — Pesce, Domenico. L'estetica dopo Croce. Firenze, 1962.

Phil 5850.309 — Petersohn, F. Projektive Tests und Fahrtüchtigkeit. Hamburg, 1962.

Phil 6980.687 — Phillips, J.H. Psychoanalyse und Symbolik. Bern, 1962.

Phil 70.91 — La philosophie analytique. Paris, 1962.

Phil 960.240 — Piatigorskii, A.M. Materialy po istorii indiiskoi filosofii. Moskva, 1962.

Phil 4170.11.80 — Pietrangeli, Alfonso. Filippo Maxi e il suo neocriticismo. Padova, 1962.

Phil 5520.443 — Pittau, Massimo. Filosofia e linguaggio. Pisa, 1962.

Phil 9420.13 — Plack, A. Die Stellung der Liebe. Landshut, 1962.

Phil 6965.24 — Plokker, J.H. Geschonden feeld. 's-Gravenhage, 1962.

Phil 8416.37 — Poggioli, Renato. Teoria dell'arte d'avanguardia. Bologna, 1962.

Phil 1750.745 — Pollak, Oscar. Der neue Humanismus. Wien, 1962.

Phil 3925.16.270 — Polochmann, George Kimball. Terms in their proportional contexts in Wittgenstein's Tractatus; an index. Carbondale, 1962.

Phil 8980.707 — Popelová, J. Etika. Praha, 1962.

Phil 346.27.5 — Popper, Karl Raimund. Conjectures and refutations. N.Y., 1962.

Phil 2905.1.215 — Pour comprendre Teilhard. Paris, 1962.

Phil 2218.55 — Priestley, Joseph. Selections from his writings. University Park, 1962.

Phil 5055.25.2 — Prior, Arthur N. Formal logic. 2nd ed. Oxford, 1962.

Phil 8084.2F — Prodi, Paolo. Ricerche sulla teorica delle arti figurative nella riforma cattalica. Roma, 1962.

Phil 8980.712.20 — Protopopova, A.N. V sem'e; vzaimnoe uvazhenie, zabota o detiakh. Moskva, 1962.

Phil 5238.207 — Psychológia a nicktoré otázky súčasnosti. Bratislava, 1962.

Phil 3015.6 — Pupi, A. Alla soglia dell'età romantica. Milano, 1962.

Phil 8706.3 — Queffélec, H. La technique contre la foi? Paris, 1962.

Phil 8400.28.3 — Rader, M.M. A modern book of esthetics. 3. ed. N.Y., 1962.

Phil 192.114 — Raju, P. Introduction to comparative philosophy. Lincoln, 1962.

Phil 5525.62 — Ramondt, Marie. Studien über des Lachen. Groningen, 1962.

Phil 8967.7.5 — Ramsey, Paul. Nine modern moralists. Englewood, 1962.

Phil 1717.21 — Randall, John. The career of philosophy. N.Y., 1962. 2v.

Phil 8170.5 — Rappoport, S.Kh. Tvorit' mir po zakonam krasoty. Moskva, 1962.

Phil 2905.1.185 — Raven, Charles. Teilhard de Chardin. London, 1962.

Phil 6967.5.10 — Ray, Isaac. A treatise on the medical jurisprudence of insanity. Cambridge, 1962.

Phil 4960.650 — Reale, Miguel. Filosofia em São Paulo. São Paulo, 1962.

Phil 1750.166.165 — Rede en religie in het humanisme. Amsterdam, 1962.

Phil 6327.38 — Reich-Dörr, Marta. Zur Psychologie der falschen Anschuldigung und falschen Selbstbezichtigung. Hamburg, 1962.

Phil 6060.58 — Reichert, G. Männlichkeit und Weiblichkeit im Spiegel. Heidelberg, 1962.

Phil 192.112 — Reinhardt, Kent F. A realistic philosophy. 2d. ed. N.Y., 1962.

Phil 3425.584 — Reining, Richard. Das Problem des polytechnischen Orbeitserziehung. Marburg, 1962.

Chronological Listing

Phil 298.18   Remits, E. The law in nature and anxiety-superior. Ottawa, 1962.

Phil 2805.408   Rennes, A. Procès de Pascal. Paris, 1962.

Phil 5257.64.5   Reuchlin, Maurice. Les méthodes quantitatives en psychologie. Paris, 1962.

Phil 7069.57.16   Rhine, Joseph B. Parapsychology, frontier science of the mind. 2. ed. Springfield, 1962.

Phil 2070.144   Riconda, G. La filosofia di William James. Torino, 1962.

Phil 6980.644   Riese, Hertha. Heal the hurt child. Chicago, 1962.

Phil 3790.22   Riessen, Hendrick van. Mens en werk. Amsterdam, 1962.

Phil 5027.2   Rijh, Lambertus. Logica modernorum. Assen, 1962. 3v.

Phil 8707.27   Robert, M.D. Approche contemporaine d'une affirmation de Dieu. Bruges, 1962.

Phil 3850.27.94   Robock, A.A. In Albert Schweitzer's realms. Cambridge, 1962.

Phil 5627.262   Rochedieu, Edmond. Personnalité et vie religieuse chez l'adolescent. Neuchâtel, 1962.

Phil 8082.2   Rocio, Montano. L'estetica del rinascimento e del Barocco. Napoli, 1962.

Phil 4318.2   Rodriguez Aranda, Luis. El desarrollo de la razón en la cultura española. Madrid, 1962.

Phil 6980.650.40   Rogers, Carl Ransom. Psychothérapie et relations humaines. Louvain, 1962. 2v.

Phil 192.115   Rombach, Heinrich. Die Gegenwart der Philosophie. Freiburg, 1962.

Phil 8870.30   Rosenberg, Stuart E. A humane society. Toronto, 1962.

Phil 1930.10.85   Rosenfield, Leonora. Portrait of a philosopher. N.Y., 1962.

Phil 3425.241   Rosenzweig, Franz. Hegel und der Staat. v.1-2. Aalen, 1962.

Phil 4210.68   Rosmini-Serbati, Antonio. Il pensiero giuridico e politico di Antonio Rosmini. Firenze, 1962.

Phil 4017.5.5   Rossi, Mario. Svilluppi dello hegelismo in Italia. Torino, 1962.

Phil 1630.23   Rossi, P. I filosofi e le macchine, 1400-1700. Milano, 1962.

Phil 2417.5   Rossi, Pietro. Gli illuministi francesi. Torino, 1962.

Phil 310.616   Rostov on the Don, Russia. Universitet. Kafedra Dialektichnskogo i Estoricheskogo Materializma. Nekotorye voprosy istoricheskogo materializma. Rostov-na-Donn, 1962.

Phil 8707.29   Rotureau, G. Conscience religieuse et mentalité technique. Paris, 1962.

Phil 348.22   Rozental, M.M. Qué es la teoria Marxista del conocimiento. Santiago, 1962.

Phil 6327.34   Ruitenbeek, H.M. Psychoanalysis and existential philosophy. N.Y., 1962.

Phil 6327.32   Ruitenbeek, H.M. Psychoanalysis and social science. N.Y., 1962.

Phil 3640.680   Rukser, Udo. Nietzsche in der Hispania; ein Beitrag zur hispanischen Kultur- und Geistesgeschichte. Bern, 1962.

Phil 5068.54   Ruml, Vladimir. Základné otázky filosofie logického pozitivismu. Praha, 1962.

Phil 5039.4   Runes, Dagobert D. Classics in logic. N.Y., 1962.

Phil 2255.1.48   Russell, Bertrand Russell. Essays in skepticism. N.Y., 1962.

Phil 2255.1.20   Russell, Bertrand Russell. La filosofia en el siglo XX y otros ensayos. Montevideo, 1962.

Phil 2905.1.220   Russo, F. Essais sur Teilhard de Chardin. Paris, 1962.

Phil 493.7   Russo, F. Science et matérialisme. Paris, 1962.

Phil 5190.28.2   Ryle, G. Dilemmas. Cambridge, Eng., 1962.

Phil 5257.70.5   Ryle, Gilbert. A rational animal. London, 1962.

Phil 310.594   Sabetti, Alfredo. Sulla fondazione del materialismo storico. Firenze, 1962.

Phil 5500.30   Sadacca, Robert. Dimensions of response consistency in paired comparisons. Princeton, 1962.

Phil 6128.79   Sadhu, Mouni. Ways to self-realization. N.Y., 1962.

Phil 3500.93   Salmony, H.A. Kants Schrift. Zürich, 1962.

Phil 2880.8.136   Salvan, Jacques I. To be and not to be. Detroit, 1962.

Phil 6328.54   Salzman, Leon. Modern concepts of psychoanalysis. N.Y., 1962.

Phil 3450.11.335   Sancipriano, Mario. Il logos di Husserl. Torino, 1962.

Phil 5258.192   Sander, F. Ganzheitspsychologie::Grundlagen. München, 1962.

Phil 3200.13   Sandmann, P. Das Weltproblem bei Ferdinand Ebner. München, 1962.

Phil 504.4   Sansgruber, Kurt. Einflüsse der Naturwissenschaften auf unser Weltbild. Brigenz, 1962.

Phil 193.49.60   Santayana, G. Vagabond scholar. N.Y., 1962.

Phil 3500.94   Santeler, J. Die Grundlegung der Menschenwürde bei I. Kant. Innsbruck, 1962.

Phil 8419.61   Santinello, Giovanni. Estetica della forma. Padova, 1962.

Phil 5590.410   Sarason, Irwin G. Contemporary research in personality. Princeton, 1962.

Phil 5590.418   Sarnoff, Irving. Personality, dynamics and development. N.Y., 1962.

Phil 349.70   Sarti, Sergio. Io cogitante ed io problematico. Brescia, 1962.

Phil 5465.35.15   Sartre, Jean P. Imagination. Ann Arbor, 1962[1960]

Phil 5400.202   Sartre, Jean-Paul. Sketch for a theory of the emotions. London, 1962.

Phil 194.30.80   Scalero, L. Adriano Tilgher. Padova, 1962.

Phil 8612.51   Schachtel, H.J. The shadowed valley. N.Y., 1962.

Phil 310.445.5   Schaff, Adam. Filozofiia człowiekas. 2. Wyd. Warszawa, 1962.

Phil 5520.325.2   Schaff, Adam. Introduction to semantics. N.Y., 1962.

Phil 310.447   Schaff, Adam. Marxisme et existentialisme. Paris, 1962.

Phil 3800.730   Schelling, F.W.J. von. Briefe und Dokumente. Bonn, 1962.

Phil 6128.76   Scher, Jordan. Theories of the mind. N.Y., 1962.

Phil 8708.36   Schilling, Harold K. Science and religion. N.Y., 1962.

Phil 3246.300   Schindler, I.M.T. Reflexion und Bildung in Fichte Wissenschaftslehre. Bonn, 1962.

Phil 7069.62.30   Schjelderup, Harald Krabbe. Det skjulte menneske. Köbenhavn, 1962.

Phil 8893.84.8A   Schlick, Moritz. Problems of ethics. N.Y., 1962.

Phil 3450.29.85   Schnarwiler, W. Theodor Haeckers christliches Menschenbild. Frankfurt, 1962.

Phil 3450.19.245   Schneeberger, Guido. Nachlese zu Heidegger. Bern, 1962.

Phil 193.236   Schneider, Herbert Wallace. Ways of being. N.Y., 1962.

Phil 3552.442   Schnelle, H. Zeichensysteme zur wissenschaftlichen Darstellung. Stuttgart, 1962.

Phil 8598.134   Schoell, F. Heimkehr Gottes in seine Wirklichkeit. Erbstetten, 1962.

Phil 3500.92   Schulz, H. Innerer Sinn und Erkenntnis in der Kantischen Philosophie. Düsseldorf, 1962.

Phil 3246.301   Schulz, W. Johann Gottlieb Fichte. Pfullingen, 1962.

Phil 2280.21.5   Schutz, Alfred. Collected papers. The Hague, 1962. 3v.

Phil 2477.6.145   Sciacca, M.E. Dialogo con M. Blondel. Milano, 1962.

Phil 2805.400   Sciacca, M.F. Pascal. 3. ed. Milan, 1962.

Phil 4225.8.52   Sciacca, Michele Federico. Cosi mi parlano le cose muti. Milano, 1962.

Phil 4225.8.46   Sciacca, Michele Federico. Filosofia e metafisica. v.1-2. 2. ed. Milano, 1962.

Phil 4225.8.34.2   Sciacca, Michele Federico. Morte e immortalità. 2. ed. Milano, 1962.

Phil 5258.187   Scott, William. Introduction to psychological research. N.Y., 1962.

Phil 193.235   Seijas, Rodolfo. Carta a Sartre, y otros ensayos. Buenos Aires, 1962.

Phil 193.148.3   Selsam, H. What is philosophy? N.Y., 1962.

Phil 349.52   Selvaggi, Filippo. Scienza e methologia; saggi de epistemologia. Roma, 1962.

Phil 9358.19   Semaines Sociales de France. 48th, Reims, 1961. La montée des jeunes dans la communauté des générations. Lyon, 1962.

Phil 1718.37   Semerarí, Giuseppe. Da Schelling a Merkau-Ponty. Bologna, 1962.

Phil 8708.37   Semmelroth, O. Die Welt als Schöpfung. Frankfurt, 1962.

Phil 3425.587   Serreau, R. Hegel et l'hégélianisme. Paris, 1962.

Phil 2418.4   Sève, L. La philosophie françise contemporaine et sa genèse de 1789 à nos jours. Paris, 1962.

Phil 4225.90.30   Severino, Emanuele. Studi di filosofia della prassi. Milano, 1962.

Phil 1020.50   Sheikh, M. Saeed. Studies in Muslim philosophy. 1st ed. Lahore, 1962.

Phil 7069.62.10   Sidgwick, Eleanor Mildred. Phantasms of the living. N.Y., 1962.

Phil 8968.20   Sidorov, D.I. Khristianstvo i pravstvennost'. Moskva, 1962.

Phil 6060.45   Sievers, A. Gestaltwandel und Gestaltzerfall. Bonn, 1962.

Phil 5520.403   Siewerth, Gustav. Philosophie der Sprache. Einsiedeln, 1962.

Phil 310.603   Silipo, Luigi. Il materialismo dialettico e storico. Padova, 1962.

Phil 1750.450.5   Simona, Maria. La notion de liberte dans l'existentialisme positif de Nicola Abbagnano. Fribourg, 1962.

Phil 5400.162   Simonov, P.V. Metod K.S. Stanislavskogo i fiziologiia emotsii. Moskva, 1962.

Phil 8708.28.2   Sinott, Edmund Ware. Matter, mind and man. N.Y., 1962.

Phil 600.7.105   Six, J.F. Littré devant Dieu. Paris, 1962.

Phil 818.34   Smart, Hawed. Philosophy and its history. La Salle, 1962.

Phil 8598.131   Smart, Ninian. Historical selections in the philosophy of religion. London, 1962.

Phil 5585.212   Smith, Karl. Perception and motion; analysis of space-structured behavior. Philadelphia, 1962.

Phil 2520.119.2   Smith, N.K. Studies in the Cartesian philosophy. N.Y., 1962.

Phil 2905.1.265   Smulders, P.F. Het visioen van Teilhard de Chardin. Brugge, 1962.

Phil 5520.461   Soehingen, Gottlieb. Analogie und Metapher. Freiburg, 1962.

Phil 3819.57.20   Spinoza, Benedictus de. Spinoza on freedom of thought. Montreal, 1962.

Phil 574.4   Stefanini, Luigi. Personalismo filosofico. Brescia, 1962.

Phil 5401.38.2   Stein, Maurice R. Identity and anxiety. Glencoe, 1962.

Phil 978.49.410   Steiner, R. Aus dem mitteleuropäischen Geisteleben. Dornach, 1962.

Phil 978.49.400   Steiner, R. Das Ewige in der Menschenseele. Dornach, 1962.

Phil 978.49.350   Steiner, R. Makrokosmos uund Mikrokosmos. Dornach, 1962.

Phil 978.49.390   Steiner, R. Menschengeschichte im Lichte der Geistesforschung. Berlin, 1962.

Phil 974.3.6   Steiner, Rudolf. Mein Legebensgang. Dornach, 1962.

Phil 974.3.8   Steiner, Rudolf. Die okkulten Grundlagen der Bhagavad Gita. 3. Aufl. Dornach, 1962.

Phil 974.3.2   Steiner, Rudolf. Die Wirklichkeit der höheren Welten. Dornach, 1962.

Phil 8587.32.117   Steinmann, J. Friedrich von Hügel. Paris, 1962.

Phil 2805.284.2   Steinmann, Jean. Pascal. Paris, 1962.

Phil 1818.2.15   Stephen, Leslie. History of English thought in the 18th century. N.Y., 1962. 2v.

Phil 5028.4   Stiazhkin, N.I. Kratkii ochesk istorii obshchei i matemaficheskoi logiki v Rossii. Moskva, 1962.

Phil 1750.690   Strasser, S. Fenomenologie en emperiche Menskunde. Arnhem, 1962.

Phil 5465.134   Štraus, T. Umelecké myslenie. Bratislava, 1962.

Phil 4805.25   Strohs, Slavomil. Marxisticko-leninská filosofie v Ceskoslovensku mezi dvěma světovými válkami. Vyd. 1. Praha, 1962.

Phil 165.322   Studi di filosofia e di storia della filosofia in onore di Francesco Olgiati. Milano, 1962.

Phil 6968.34   Sullivan, Harry Stack. Schizophrenia as human process. N.Y., 1962.

Phil 6328.55   Sundberg, N.D. Clinical psychology. N.Y., 1962.

Phil 974.3.140   Sunden, Hjalmar. Rudolf Steiner. Stockholm, 1962.

Phil 310.117   Sviderskii, Vladimir Io. O dialektike elementov i struktury v obʺektivnom mire i v poznanii. Moskva, 1962.

Phil 5258.180.5   Sykes, G. The hidden remnant. London, 1962.

Phil 5258.180   Sykes, G. The hidden remnant. 1. ed. N.Y., 1962.

Phil 5640.133   Symposium on Principles of Sensory Communication. Sensory communication...Symposium...July 19-Aug. 1, 1959, M.I.T. Cambridge, 1962.

Phil 9245.115   Tatarkiewicz, W. A szczęsciu. Wyd. 3. Warszawa, 1962.

Phil 5585.210   Taylor, James. The behavioral basis of perception. New Haven, 1962.

Phil 2905.1.30   Teilhard de Chardin, Pierre. Letters from a traveler. London, 1962.

Phil 2905.1.45   Teilhard de Chardin, Pierre. La place de l'homme dans la nature. Paris, 1962.

Phil 310.146   Teriaev, G.V. Due fazy kommunisticheskogo obshchestva i zakonomernosti pererastatelnogo sotsializma i kommunizm. Moskva, 1962.

Phil 3450.18.180   Theisen, Hans. Determination und Freiheit bei Nicolai Hartmanns. Köln, 1962.

Phil 5585.216   Thinès, G. Contribution à la théorie de la causalité perceptive. Louvain, 1962.

Phil 194.50   Thomas, H. Understanding the great philosophers. 1st ed. Garden City, N.Y., 1962.

Phil 1955.6.2   Thomas, Milton H. John Dewey. Chicago, 1962.

Phil 4370.7   Tierno, G. E. Tradicíon y modernismo. Madrid, 1962.

Phil 2750.19.105   Tilliette, X. Philosophes contemporains. Paris, 1962.

Chronological Listing

1962 - cont.

Phil 310.586   Tlustý, V. Dialektické rozpory a jejich zakonitosti. Praha, 1962.

Phil 8420.5   Tolstykh, V. Iskusstvo i moral'. Moskva, 1962.

Phil 5590.416   Tomkins, S.S. Affect, imagery, consciousness. N.Y., 1962. 2v.

Phil 5059.22   Toms, Eric. Being, negation, and logic. Oxford, 1962.

Phil 3450.11.285   Toulemont, Rene L'essence de la société selon Husserl. Paris, 1962.

Phil 5590.455.6   Tournier, Paul. Escape from loneliness. Philadelphia, 1962.

Phil 5414.30   Tournier, Paul. Guilt and grace. London, 1962.

Phil 3425.580   Travis, Don Carlos. A Hegel symposium. Austin, 1962.

Phil 3890.14   Treher, W. Das Oknosprinzip. München, 1962.

Phil 8520.40   Tresmontant, C. Les origines de la philosophie chrétienne. Paris, 1962.

Phil 8599.44.2   Tresmontant, Claude. Les idées maîtresses de la métaphysique chrétienne. Paris, 1962.

Phil 2905.1.260   Tresmoutant, Claude. Introduction à la pensée de Teilhard de Chardin. Paris, 1962.

Phil 8050.23   Trudu,, Luciano. Soggettività e oggettività del bello. Padova, 1962.

Phil 8420.7   Trudu, Luciano. La legge del bello. Padova, 1962.

Phil 585.147   Tsanoff, Radoslav. Worlds to know. N.Y., 1962.

Phil 5520.395   Turbayne, C.M. The myth of metaphor. New Haven, 1962.

Phil 1750.101   Tymieniecka, Anna Teresa. Phenomenology and science in contemporary European thought. N.Y., 1962.

Phil 6750.262   United States. President's Panel on Mental Retardation. Report of the mission to Denmark and Sweden. Washington, D.C., 1962.

Phil 4972.5.60   Universidad Nacional del Litoral. Alejandro Korn. Rosario, 1962.

Phil 8980.861   Utkin, S.S. Ocherki po marksistsko-leninskoi etike. Moskva, 1962.

Phil 1540.70   Vallese, Giulia. Da Dante ad Erasmo. Napoli, 1962.

Phil 310.527   Vasil'ev, Iu. Al. V.I. Lenin i nekotorye voprosy nauchnogo predvideniia v obshchestvennom zhizni. Minsk, 1962.

Phil 7069.62.20   Vasil'ev, L.L. Vnushenie na rasstoianii. Moskva, 1962.

Phil 8896.21   Veatch, Henry B. Rational man; a modern interpretation. Bloomington, 1962.

Phil 5585.213   Vernon, Magdalen. The psychology of perception. Harmondsworth, 1962.

Phil 196.35   Villoro, Luis. Paginas filosofias. Mexico, 1962.

Phil 3503.14   Vlachos, G. La pensée politique de Kant. Paris, 1962.

Phil 3503.9.10   Vleeschauwer, H.J. Development of Kantian thought. London, 1962.

Phil 2805.391   Vloemans, A. Pascal. Den Haag, 1962.

Phil 310.520   Voitko, V.I. Dialekticheskii i istoricheskii materializm. Kiev, 1962.

Phil 310.425   Vorob'ev, L.V. Osnovnye kategorii i zakony materialisticheskoi dialektiki. Moskva, 1962.

Phil 2750.22.125   Vu Duy Tu. Individualisme, collectivisme, personnalisme dans l'oeuvre d'Emmanuel Mounier. Bonn, 1962.

Phil 8430.45   Vučković, Vojislav. Umetnost i umetničko delo. Beograd, 1962.

Phil 353.30   Wagner, J. Was Kann ich Wissen? 2. Aufl. Braunschweig, 1962.

Phil 2422.5.2   Wahl, Jean A. Tableau de la philosophie française. Paris, 1962.

Phil 1020.44   Walzer, Richard. Greek into Arabic. Cambridge, 1962. 2v.

Phil 1020.44.2   Walzer, Richard. Greek into Arabic. Oxford, 1962.

Phil 5066.214   Wang, Hao. A survey of mathematical logic. Peking, 1962.

Phil 53.5   Wangh, Martin. Fruition of an eden...in honor of the fiftieth anniversary of the New York Psychoanalytics Society. N.Y., 1962.

Phil 8062.2   Warry, John Gibson. Greek aesthetic theory...in...Plato and Aristotle. London, 1962.

Phil 5262.54   Webb, W.B. The profession of psychology. N.Y., 1962.

Phil 3850.16.115   Weingartner, R.H. Experience and culture; the philosophy of G. Simmel. Middletown, 1962.

Phil 6332.24   Weinschenk, Curt. Die erbliche Lese- rechtssch Reiheschwäche. Bern, 1962.

Phil 6980.775.20   Weinstein, E.A. Cultural aspects of delusion. N.Y., 1962.

Phil 1135.178   Welskopf, E.C. Probleme der Musse im alten Hellas. Berlin, 1962.

Phil 6332.26   Wenar, Charks. Origins of psychosomatic and emotional disturbances. N.Y., 1962.

Phil 5062.39   Wheelwright, P.E. Valid thinking. 1st ed. N.Y., 1962.

Phil 1850.157   Whitaker, Virgil Keeble. Francis Bacon's intellectual milieu. Los Angeles, 1962.

Phil 3552.438   Wiedeburg, P.H. Der junge Leibniz das Keich und Europa. Wiesbaden, 1962. 3v.

Phil 3640.655   Wien, Hermann. Positives antichristentum. Den Haag, 1962.

Phil 62.5   Wiener, P.V. Minutes of the Vienna Psychoanalytic Society. N.Y., 1962- 2v.

Phil 5374.232   Wildangel, G. Beiträge zur Grundlegung der Elementaranalytik des Bewusstseins. Köln, 1962.

Phil 1750.720   Wilde, Jean T. The search for being. N.Y., 1962.

Phil 6332.28   Winch, R.F. Identification and its familial determinants. Indianapolis, 1962.

Phil 5520.458   Wit, Gerard Antonius de. A psychological study of symbolism in word association and symbolic meaning of words. Eindhoven, 1962.

Phil 5262.55   Within, Herman A. Psychological differentiation. N.Y., 1962.

Phil 3910.12   Wolff, Christian von. Gesammlete Werke. Hildesheim, 1962-22v.

Phil 6332.23   Wolstein, B. Irrational despair. N.Y., 1962.

Phil 8712.32   Wood, John Karl. The nature of conflicts between science and religion. Logan, 1962.

Phil 9070.95   Wright, L.B. Advise to a son. Ithaca, N.Y., 1962.

Phil 8602.70   Wynne-Tyson, Esmé. The philosophy of compassion. London, 1962.

Phil 5264.4   Yolton, J.W. Thinking and perceiving. Lasalle, Ill., 1962.

Phil 8520.42   Zampetti, Pier L. Il problema della giustizia nel protestantesimo tedesco contemporaneo. Milano, 1962.

Phil 200.20   Zanstra, H. The construction of reality; lectures on the philosophy on science. N.Y., 1962.

Phil 6335.20   Zeigarnik, B.V. Patologiia myshleniia. Moskva, 1962.

Phil 8220.5   Zemlianova, L.M. Sovremennaia estetika v SShA. Moskva, 1962.

Phil 8980.895   Zemlianskii, D.S. U istokov zhiznennogo puti. Moskva, 1962.

Phil 5520.335.2A   Ziff, Paul. Semantic analysis. Ithaca, 1962.

1962 - cont.

Phil 6335.15.5   Zilboorg, Gregory. Psychoanalysis and religion. N.Y., 1962.

Phil 8900.8   Zink, Sidney. The concepts of ethics. N.Y., 1962.

Phil 356.5.3   Zinkernagel, Peter. Conditions for description. London, 1962.

Phil 5066.210   Zinov'ev, Aleksandr A. Logika vyskazyvanii i teoriia vyvoda. Moskva, 1962.

Phil 4987.60.61   Zunino Dubois, J.C. Entre robles y tilos. La Plata, 1962.

1963

Phil 1505.5   Abbagmano, N. La filosofia medievale. Bari, 1963.

Phil 800.16   Abbagnano, N. Storia della filosofia. 2. ed. Torino, 1963. 3v.

Phil 310.580   Academia Republicii Populare Romine. Biblioteca. Materialismus dialectic si stiintele contemporane ale naturii. Bucuresti, 1963.

Phil 310.581   Academia Republicii Populare Romine. Institut de Filosofie. Dialectica materialista. Bucuresti, 1963.

Phil 281.14   Adamczyk, S. Filozofia przyrody. Lublin, 1963.

Phil 2340.10.210   Adhin, Herman S. Whitehead en de wereld. Proefschrift. Delft, 1963.

Phil 6310.1.42   Adler, A. The problem child. N.Y., 1963.

Phil 3425.589   Adorno, T.W. Drei Studien zu Hegel. Frankfurt, 1963.

Phil 3085.7.30   Adorno, Theodor W. Eingriffe. Frankfurt, 1963.

Phil 2255.1.126   Aiken, L.W. Bertrand Russell's philosophy of morals. N.Y., 1963.

Phil 5040.27   Akademiia Nauk Kazakhskoi SSSR, Alma-Ata. Institut Literatury i Prava. Problemy logiki dialektiki poznaniia. Alma-Ata, 1963.

Phil 75.66   Akademiia Nauk SSSR. Fundamental'naia Biblioteka Obshchestvennykh Nauk. Istoriia zarubezhnoi domarksistskoi filosofii, za 1917-1962 gody. Moskva, 1963.

Phil 8655.19   Akademiia Nauk SSSR. Institut Filosofii. Filosofskie problemy ateizma. Moskva, 1963.

Phil 6110.26   Akademiia Nauk SSSR. Institut Filosofii. Filosofskie voprosy fiziologii vysshei nervnoi deiatel'nosti. Moskva, 1963.

Phil 5066.225   Akademiia Nauk SSSR. Institut Filosofii. Problemy logiki. Moskva, 1963.

Phil 5210.10   Akademiia Nauk SSSR. Institut Filosofii. Sovremennaia psikhologiia v kapitalisticheskikh stranakh. Moskva, 1963.

Phil 175.60   Akademiia Nauk URSR, Kiev. Institut Filosofii. Liudyna i svitohliad. Kyiv, 1963.

Phil 8968.15.80   Alcalá, M. La etica de situación y T. Steinbüchel. Barcelona, 1963.

Phil 331.30   Alexander, Peter. Sensationalism and scientific explanation. London, 1963.

Phil 2520.346   Allard, J.L. Le mathématisme de Descartes. Ottawa, 1963.

Phil 175.43.4   Alquié, Ferdinand. Le désir d'éternité. 4th ed. Paris, 1963.

Phil 8580.38   Alston, William P. Religious belief and philosophical thought. N.Y., 1963.

Phil 5240.52   American Psychological Association. Project on Scientific Information. Exchange in Psychology. Reports. Washington, 1963- 3v.

Phil 5585.170.5   Anan'ev, B.G. Psychologie der sinnlichen Erkenntnis. Berlin, 1963.

Phil 1800.3.5   Anderson, P.P. Platonism in the Midwest. Philadelphia, 1963.

Phil 175.58   Ando, Takatuna. Metaphysics. Hague, 1963.

Phil 5240.53   Anrich, Ernst. Moderne Physik und Tiefenpsychologie. Stuttgart, 1963.

Phil 5520.399   Antal, Laszló. Questions of meaning. The Hague, 1963.

Phil 8030.6   Apresian, Z.G. Estetika; bibliografiia, 1956-60. Moskva, 1963.

Phil 8580.34   Arata, C. Persona ed evidenza nella prospettiva classica. Milano, 1963.

Phil 5628.10.15   Arbman, Ernst. Ecstasy or religious trance. Stockholm, 1963-70. 3v.

Phil 3235.89   Ardab'ev, A.I. Ateizm Ludviga Feierbakha. Moskva, 1963.

Phil 8980.159   Arkhangel'skii, Leonid M. Kategorii marksistskoi etiki. Moskva, 1963.

Phil 331.32   Asmus, V.F. Problema intuitsii v filosofii i matematike. Moskva, 1963.

Phil 5520.409   Association de Psychologie Scientifique de Langue Française. Problèmes de psycholinguistique. Paris, 1963.

Phil 8401.33   Assunto, Rosario. Guidizio estetico critica e censura. Firenze, 1963.

Phil 8401.31   Astakhov, I.B. Iskusstvo i problema prekrasnogo. Moskva, 1963.

Phil 800.14.14   Aster, Ernst von. Geschichte der Philosophie. 14. Aufl. Stuttgart, 1963.

Phil 1750.749   Astrada, C. Existencialismo y crisis de la filosofia. 2. ed. Buenos Aires, 1963.

Phil 4351.5   Astrada, Carlos. Ensayos filosoficos. Bahia Blanca, 1963.

Phil 8980.180   Avraamov, D. Kommunist nravstvennost'. Moskva, 1963.

Phil 1845.11.5   Ayer, Alfred Jules. The concept of a person. N.Y., 1963.

Phil 310.560   Babosov, E.M. Dialektika analiza i sinteza v nauchnom poznanii. Minsk, 1963.

Phil 6990.61   Bach, H. Mirakelbücker bayerischer Wallfahrtsorte. Möhrendorf, 1963.

Phil 1850.15.3   Bacon, Francis. Works. Faksimile-Neudruck. Stuttgart, 1963. 14v.

Phil 5041.47.7   Balzano, Bernard. Grundlegung der Logik. Ausgewählte Paragraphen aus der Wissenschaftslehre. Hamburg, 1963. 2v.

Phil 2733.118   Banchetti, A. Il pensiero e l'opera di Nicola Malebranche. Milano, 1963.

Phil 5590.427   Bandura, A. Social learning and personality development. N.Y., 1963.

Phil 8980.191.5   Bandzeladze, Gela. Opyt izlozheniia sistemy marksistskoi etiki. Tbilisi, 1963.

Phil 1905.33.30   Banerje, N.V. Language. London, 1963.

Phil 2520.348   Barjonet-Huraux, Marcelle. Descartes. Paris, 1963.

Phil 1145.95   Barr, S. The three worlds of man. Columbia, 1963.

Phil 2905.1.200   Barthélemy-Madaule, Madeleine. Bergson et Teilhard de Chardin. Paris, 1963.

Phil 8402.59   Battaglia, F. Il valore estetico. Brescia, 1963.

Phil 6319.1.220   Baudouin, C. L'oeuvre de Jung. Paris, 1963.

Phil 3050.2   Bauer, Edgar. Bibliothek der deutschen Aufklärer des achtzehnten Jahrhunderts. Darmstadt, 1963. 2v.

Phil 8691.31   Bayne, Stephen. Space age to Christianity. N.Y., 1963.

Phil 176.219   Becker, O. Dasein und Dawesen. Pfullingen, 1963.

Phil 8402.60   Belik, Aleksandr P. Estetika i sovremennost'. Moskva, 1963.

Phil 4769.6.81   Belov, P.T. Materializm I.M. Sechenova. Moskva, 1963.

Chronological Listing

Phil 5041.96.3 Berg, Innocentius Jozefus Marie van den. Beginselen der logica. 3. druk. Bilthaven, 1963.

Phil 7042.8.2 Berg, Jan Hendrik van den. Leven in meervoud. 2. druk. Nijkerk, 1963.

Phil 8876.156 Bertocci, Peter. Personality and the good. N.Y., 1963.

Phil 165.340A Besch, L. Menschenbild und Lebensführung. München, 1963.

Phil 3120.27.40 Binswanger, L. Being in the world. N.Y., 1963.

Phil 5066.264 Biriukov, Boris Vl. Krushenie metafizicheskoi kontseptsii univeral'nosti predmetnoi oblasti v logike. Moskva, 1963.

Phil 6158.35 Bishop, Malden Grange. The discovery of love; a psychedelic experience with LSD-25. N.Y., 1963.

Phil 1750.166.145 Blackham, H.J. Objections to humanism. London, 1963.

Phil 3120.55.55 Bloch, Ernst. Tübinger Einleitung in die Philosophie I. Frankfurt, 1963.

Phil 176.129.6 Blondel, Maurice. L'être et les êtres. Paris, 1963.

Phil 176.214 Bochénski, I.M. Philosophy; an introduction. Dordrecht, 1963.

Phil 310.6.12 Bodrenski, J.M. The dogmatic principles of Soviet philosophy. Dordrecht, Holland, 1963.

Phil 5590.428 Boer, J. de. A system of characterology. Assen, 1963.

Phil 6980.124 Bogdanovich, L.A. Carnets d'une psychiatre soviétique. Paris, 1963.

Phil 2225.5.88 Boler, J.F. Charles Peirce and scholastic realism. Seattle, 1963.

Phil 5241.92.20 Boring, E.G. History, psychology and science. N.Y., 1963.

Phil 2805.414 Borne, Etienne. De Pascal à Teilhard de Chardin. Clermont-Ferrand, 1963.

Phil 1750.766 Bošnjak, Branko. Humanizam i socijalizam. Zagreb, 1963.

Phil 6311.37.5 Boss, Medard. Psychoanalysis and daseinsanalysis. N.Y., 1963.

Phil 5520.411 Bottotini, Gianfranco. Il segno dalla fino al cinema. Milano, 1963.

Phil 1850.158 Bowen, Catherine. Francis Bacon. 1st ed. Boston, 1963.

Phil 5627.263 Bowers, M.K. Conflicts of the clergy. Edinburgh, 1963.

Phil 6111.66 Braden, C.S. Spirits in rebellion. Dallas, 1963.

Phil 9560.32.5 Braithwaite, R.B. Theory of games. Cambridge, Eng., 1963.

Phil 1750.756 Brancatisano, F. Per un umanesimo scientifico. Firenze, 1963.

Phil 2045.140 Braun, Dietrich. Der sterbliche Gott oder Leviathan gegen Behemoth. Thesis. Zürich, 1963.

Phil 801.21.6 Bréhier, É. Histoire de la philosophie. Paris, 1963. 3v.

Phil 801.21.5A Bréhier, É. The history of philosophy. v.1-3,5-7. Chicago, 1963. 7v.

Phil 3640.696 Broecker, W. Das was kommt gesehen von Nietzsche und Hölderlin. Pfullingen, 1963.

Phil 3450.11.305 Broekman, J.M. Phänomenologie und Egologie. Den Haag, 1963.

Phil 9161.10 Broendum, L.E. Familielivets etik. København, 1963.

Phil 8622.59 Broglic, Guy de. Pour une théorie rationnelle de l'acte de foi. Paris, 1963. 2v.

Phil 5190.38 Brown, J.A.C. Techniques of persuasion. Baltimore, 1963.

Phil 5593.63.5 Brückner, Peter. Konflikt und Konfliktschicksal. Bern, 1963.

Phil 6111.67 Brun, J. La main et l'esprit. Paris, 1963.

Phil 4210.193 Brunello, B. Rosmini. Bologna, 1963.

Phil 3120.30.78 Buber, Martin. Israel and the world. 2. ed. N.Y., 1963.

Phil 5330.31 Buckner, D. Vigilance. Los Angeles, 1963.

Phil 801.35.5 Bueno, Miguel. Prolegómenos filosóficos. México, 1963.

Phil 3120.55.80 Buetow, H.G. Philosophie und Gesellschaft im Denken Ernst Blochs. Berlin, 1963.

Phil 8622.56 Buhr, H. Der Glaube - was ist das? Pfullingen, 1963.

Phil 176.218 Bunge, Mario. The myth of simplicity. Englewood Cliff, N.J., 1963.

Phil 5645.59 Burnham, R.W. Color. N.Y., 1963.

Phil 6750.259.2 Busemann, Adolf. Psychologie der intelligenz Defekte. München, 1963.

Phil 5274.10 Butler, John M. Quantitative naturalistic research. Englewood Cliffs, 1963.

Phil 2750.19.100 Cain, Seymour. Gabriel Marcel. London, 1963.

Phil 2402.9 Callot, E. Six philosophes français du XVIIIe siècle. Annecy, 1963.

Phil 1630.24 Callot, Emile. Doctrines et figures humanistes. Paris, 1963.

Phil 6312.16.5 Cameron, N. Personality development and psychopathology. Boston, 1963.

Phil 4963.2.5 Cannabrava, Euryalo. Estética da crítica. Rio de Janeiro, 1963.

Phil 585.70.5 Cantoni, Remo. Il problema antropologico nella Filosofia Contemporanea. Milano, 1963.

Phil 4080.26 Cantoni, Remo. Tragico e senso comune. Cremona, 1963.

Phil 5752.14 Capizzi, Antonio. La difesa del libero arbitrio da Erasmo a Kant. 1. ed. Firenze, 1963.

Phil 4080.3.430 Caprariis, Vittorio de. Benedetto Croce. Milano, 1963.

Phil 2515.18 Caraco, Albert. Huit essais sur le mal. Neuchâtel, 1963.

Phil 5042.75 Carbonard, Cleto. Psicologia, logica, dialettica. Napoli, 1963.

Phil 1603.2 Cassier, E. The indivudual and the cosmos in Renaissance philosophy. N.Y., 1963.

Phil 8870.24 Castaneda, H. Morality and the language of conduct. Detroit, 1963.

Phil 3484.23 Casula, Mario. Studi kantiani sul trascendente. Milano, 1963.

Phil 5520.311 Caton, Charles. Philosophy and ordinary language. Urbana, Ill., 1963.

Phil 4960.245 Caturelli, Alberto. La filosofía en Argentina actual. Córdoba, 1963.

Phil 2725.46 Cazeneuve, J. Lucien Lévy-Bruhl, sa vie, son oeuvre. Paris, 1963.

Phil 5039.30 Centro di Studi Filosofici di Gallarate. Teoria della demostrazione. Padova, 1963.

Phil 3450.19.300 Cerezo Galan, Pedro. Arte, verdad y ser en Heidegger. Madrid, 1963.

Phil 3235.127 Çesa, C. Il giovane Feuerbach. Bari, 1963.

Phil 4806.2 Ceskoslovenská akademie věd. Antologie z dějin československé filosofie. Praha, 1963.

Phil 4803.799.90 Chamcówna, Mirosława. Jan Śniadecki. Kraków, 1963.

Phil 2905.1.235 Charbonneau, B. Teilhard de Chardin, prophète d'un âge totalitaire. Paris, 1963.

Phil 8627.3.10 Charles, R.H. Eschatology. N.Y., 1963.

Phil 2402.8 Charlton, D.G. Secular religions in France, 1815-1870. London, 1963.

Phil 582.6 Chatterjee, Margaret. Our knowledge of other selves. Bombay, 1963.

Phil 1750.115.65 Chatteyee, Margaret. Our knowledge of other selves. Bombay, 1963.

Phil 585.157 Chauchard, P. L'homme normal. Paris, 1963.

Phil 8582.65 Chédel, André. Pour un humanisme laïc. Neuchâtel, 1963.

Phil 3425.641 Chiereghin, Franco. L'unità del sapere in Hegel. Padova, 1963.

Phil 1750.560.10 Chiodi, Pietro. Esistenzialismo e fenomenologia. Milano, 1963.

Phil 3484.26 Chiodí, Pietro. Il pensiero di Immanuel Kant. Torino, 1963.

Phil 6315.2.300 Choisy, Maryse. Sigmund Freud. N.Y., 1963.

Phil 1750.744 Christianity and existentialism; essays. Evanston, Ill., 1963.

Phil 705.23.2 Christy, Arthur. The Orient in American transcendentalism. N.Y., 1963.

Phil 850.34 Cilento, Vincenzo. Primessa storica al pensiero antico. Bari, 1963.

Phil 2475.1.465 Colletti, Giovanni. I fondamenti logico-metafisici del bergsonismo e altri scritti. Padova, 1963.

Phil 585.156 Collingwood, F.J. Man's physical and spiritual nature. N.Y., 1963.

Phil 525.232 Colloque de Strasbourg, 1961. La mystique rhénane, Colloque de Strasbourg, 16-19 mai, 1961. Paris, 1963.

Phil 4210.200 Colonna, Salvatore. L'educazione religiosa nella pedagogia di A. Rosmini. Lecce, 1963.

Phil 2494.36 Condorcet, M.J.A.N. Entwurf einer historischen Darstellung. Frankfurt a.M., 1963.

Phil 8657.22 Congar, M.J. Le mystère du temple. 2. éd. Paris, 1963.

Phil 3160.15.10 Conrad-Martius, Hedwig. Schriften zur Philosophie. München, 1963-64. 3v.

Phil 4225.15.85 Conti, O. Polemica sull'immanenza in Ugo Spirito. Milano, 1963.

Phil 7054.175.15 Cooke, I. The return of Arthur Conan Doyle. 2. ed. Liss, 1963.

Phil 2280.5.125 Cory, D. Santayana: the later years. N.Y., 1963.

Phil 672.223 Costa de Beauregard, Olivier. Le second principe de la science du temps. Paris, 1963.

Phil 672.232 Costa de Beauregard, Olivier. La théorie physique et la notion de temps. Bordeaux, 1963.

Phil 2250.106 Costello, Harry. Josiah Royce's seminar, 1913-1914. New Brunswick, 1963.

Phil 2138.146 Cowling, M. Mill and liberalism. Cambridge, Eng., 1963.

Phil 4080.27 Crescini, Angelo. Per una metafisica concreta. Padova, 1963.

Phil 8827.9 Crocker, L. Nature and culture. Baltimore, 1963.

Phil 1020.32.10 Cruz Hernández, Miguel. La filosofía arabe. Madrid, 1963.

Phil 5407.6 Cruz Malpique, Manuel da. Psicologia do tédio. Porto, 1963.

Phil 2905.1.195 Cuénot, Claude. Lexique Teilhard de Chardin. Paris, 1963.

Phil 5066.122 Curry, Haskell Brooks. Foundations of mathematical logic. N.Y., 1963.

Phil 5066.250 Daigneault, Aubert. Théorie des modèles en logique mathématique. Montréal, 1963.

Phil 8878.60 D'Arcy, E. Human acts. Oxford, 1963.

Phil 2475.1.420 Darkaoui, Assad Arabi. Essai sur l'idée de pureté chez Bergson. Damas, 1963.

Phil 70.93 Darmtaedter, Gespräch. Die Herausforderung. München, 1963.

Phil 960.28.2 Dasgupta, Surendra Nath. A history of Indian philosophy. Cambridge, 1963.

Phil 5243.46.2 Dearborn, W.F. Predicting the child's development. 2d rev. ed. Cambridge, Mass., 1963.

Phil 334.9 Decker, H.C. Das Denken in Begriffen als Kriterium (der Menschwerdung). Oosterhout, 1963.

Phil 5850.171 Defares, Peter Bernard. Grondvormen van menselijke relaties. Assen, 1963.

Phil 3485.23 Delekat, Friedrich. Immanuel Kant. Heidelberg, 1963.

Phil 5520.505 Delius, Harald. Untersuchungen zur Problematik der sogenannten synthetischen Sätze apriori. Göttingen, 1963.

Phil 8953.10 Demoulin, Jérôme. Critiques; á la bona consciència dels christians. Barcelona, 1963.

Phil 3450.19.295 Demske, James M. Sein, Mensch und Tod. Freiburg, 1963.

Phil 3823.14 Deregilris, Arturo. La filosofía etico-politica di Spinoza. Torino, 1963.

Phil 2520.32.10 Descartes, René. Oeuvres philosophiques. Paris, 1963- 2v.

Phil 2555.1.86 Deschamps, L.M. Le vrai système. Genève, 1963.

Phil 1182.53 Detienne, M. La notion de daimôn dans le pythagorisme ancien. Paris, 1963.

Phil 1955.6.50 Dewey, John. Philosophy, psychology and social practice. N.Y., 1963.

Phil 5477.12 Diamond, Solomon. Inhibition and choice. N.Y., 1963.

Phil 4965.2 Diaz de Gamarra y Dávalos, J.B. Elementos de filosofía moderna. México, 1963.

Phil 3195.6.155 Diwald, Hellmut. Wilhelm Dilthey. Göttingen, 1963.

Phil 3195.19.35 Dooyeweerd, H. Vernieuwing en bezinning. 2. druk. Zutphen, 1963.

Phil 3450.11.290 Druce, H. Edmund Husserls System der phänomenologischen Psychologie. Berlin, 1963.

Phil 7150.53 Dublin, L.I. Suicide. N.Y., 1963.

Phil 2240.87 Dür, Seweryn. Reid a Kant. Opole, 1963.

Phil 8658.17.10 Duméry, Henry. Raison et religion dans la philosophie de l'actin. Paris, 1963.

Phil 8092.11 Duplessis, V. Surrealism. N.Y., 1963.

Phil 5465.105.2 Durand, G. Les structures anthropologiques de l'imaginaire. 2. éd. Paris, 1963.

Phil 3003.9 Dussort, H. L'ecole de Marbourg. Paris, 1963.

Phil 3195.20.30 Duynstee, Willem Jacob A.J. Verspreide opstellen. Roermond, 1963.

Phil 3200.14 Ebner, Ferdinand. Notizen, Tagebücher, Lebenserinnerungen. v.1-2,3. München, 1963. 2v.

Phil 8879.34 Edel, A. Method in ethical theory. London, 1963.

Phil 2404.3 Ehrard, J. L'idée de nature en France. Paris, 1963. 2v.

Phil 5520.70.5 Eisenson, J. The psychology of communication. N.Y., 1963.

Phil 8050.81 Ekman, Rolf. Estetikens historia från sjuttonhundratalets början till och med Goethe. Lund, 1963.

Phil 8584.22 Eley, A.S. God's own image. Luton, Eng., 1963.

Phil 8879.35 Elken, Robert. Konsequenzen der Naturwissenschaft. Kassel, 1963.

Phil 4803.360.30 Elzenberg, Henryk. Kłopot z istnieniem. Kraków, 1963.

Phil 9164.2 Encontro Latino Americano, 3d, Rio de Janeiro, 1963. Tercero encontro Latino-Americano. Rio de Janeiro, 1963.

Phil 5204.14 The encyclopedia of mental health. N.Y., 1963. 6v.

Phil 8829.3 Engelhardt, Paulus. Sein und Ethos. Mainz, 1963.

Phil 165.350 Ensayos filosóficos. Buenos Aires, 1963.

Phil 165.344 Essays in ontology. Iowa City, 1963.

Phil 335.9 Etcheverry, Auguste. L'homme dans le monde. Paris, 1963.

1963 - cont.

Phil 2750.11.153   Evans, J.W. Jacques Maritain. N.Y., 1963.
Phil 9495.163   Exner, Adam. The amplexus reservatus seen in the history of Catholic doctrine on the use of marriage. Ottawa, 1963.
Phil 5585.220   Ey, Henri. La conscience. Paris, 1963.
Phil 3310.17.80   Faber, Heije. Het christelijk humanisme. Assen, 1963.
Phil 2905.1.230   Face au prophétisme de Teilhard de Chardin. Bruxelles, 1963.
Phil 6115.33   Fair, Charles. The physical foundations of the psyche. Middletown, 1963.
Phil 8406.26   Fanizza, Franco. Estetica problematica. Manduria, 1963.
Phil 5238.191   Farberow, N.L. Taboo topics. N.Y., 1963.
Phil 5755.14.2   Farrer, A.M. The freedom of the will. 2. ed. London, 1963.
Phil 8585.47   Fatone, Vicente. Temas de mistica y religion. Bahía Blance, 1963.
Phil 5585.222   Fauville, A. Perception tachistoscopique et communication. Louvain, 1963.
Phil 7069.63.10   Feilding, Everard. Sittings with Eussapia Palladino and other studies. New Hyde Park, 1963.
Phil 8880.54   Ferraro, L. Dell'egoismo. Novara, 1963.
Phil 3246.72.2   Fichte, Johann Gottlieb. Das System der Sittenlehre nach Prinzipien der Wissenschaftslehre. Neuausgabe, 1963.
Phil 5015.4   Filkorn, V. Pre-dialectical logic. Bratislava, 1963.
Phil 8980.392   Filonovich, Pavel G. O kommunisticheskoi morali. Moskva, 1963.
Phil 585.183   La filosofia dell'uomo di M.T. Antonelli. Roma, 1963.
Phil 310.530   Filosofiia marksizma i neopozitivizma. Moskva, 1963.
Phil 310.629   Filová, Elena. Materializmus proti holizmu. Bratislava, 1963.
Phil 3450.19.320   Finazzo, Giancarlo. L'umo e il mondo nella filosofia di M. Heidegger. Roma, 1963.
Phil 2138.152   Findikoğlu, Z.F. Stuart Mill ve Türkiyedeki tesirleri. Istanbul, 1963.
Phil 180.86   Findlay, J.N. Language, mind and value. London, 1963.
Phil 3625.11.86   Findlay, J.N. Meinong's theory of objects and values. 2. ed. Oxford, 1963.
Phil 6315.54   Fingrette, H. The self in transformation. N.Y., 1963.
Phil 336.17   Flach, W. Zur Prinzipienlehre der Auschauung. Hamburg, 1963.
Phil 3270.17.35   Flam, Leopold. Proeven over het tragisch bewiestzijn en de geschiedenis. Antwerpen, 1963.
Phil 4080.3.420   Focher, Ferruccio. Profilo dell'opera di Benedetto Croce. Cremona, 1963.
Phil 310.556   Fomina, V.A. Aktual'nye problemy istoricheskogo materializma. Moskva, 1963.
Phil 6319.1.205   Fordham, M.S.M. Contact with Jung. London, 1963.
Phil 1750.220.12   Foulquié, Paul. L'existentialisme. 12e éd. Paris, 1963.
Phil 5585.140.3   Fraisse, Paul. The psychology of time. N.Y., 1963.
Phil 5238.196   Fraisse, Paul. Traité de psychologie expérimentale. Paris, 1963. 9v.
Phil 4967.5.5   Francovich, Guillermo. El cinismo. Puebla, 1963.
Phil 165.336   Frank, J. Horizons of a philosopher. Leiden, 1963.
Phil 8880.54   Frankena, W. Ethics. Englewood, 1963.
Phil 5520.408   Fredriksson, G. Det politiska språket. 2. uppl. Uppsala, 1963.
Phil 6315.2.66.5   Freud, Sigmund. Briefe 1909-39. Frankfurt, 1963.
Phil 6315.2.350   Freud, Sigmund. The collected papers of Sigmund Freud. (Studies in parapsychology, v.10). N.Y., 1963.
Phil 6315.2.57   Freud, Sigmund. Psychoanalysis and faith. London, 1963.
Phil 6315.19.30   Fromm, Erich. The dogma of Christ. 1. ed. N.Y., 1963.
Phil 735.242   Frondizi, R. What is value? La Salle, 1963.
Phil 8880.53   Fruchon, Pierre. Création ou consentement. Paris, 1963.
Phil 5525.61   Fry, W.F. Sweet madness. Palo Alto, 1963.
Phil 1760.15A   Funke, Gerhard. Die Aufklärung, in ausgewählten Texten Dargestellt. Stuttgart, 1963.
Phil 1845.16   Furberg, M. Locutionary and illocutionary acts. Göteborg, 1963.
Phil 310.540   Gabriel'ian, G.G. Marksistskaia logika kak dialektika i teoriia poznaniia. Erevan, 1963.
Phil 210.30   Gadamer, Hans Georg. Le problème de la conscience historique. Louvain, 1963.
Phil 5585.218   Galindez, J. El papel del cuerpo en la percepción. Tucuman, 1963.
Phil 4112.30.6   Galluppi, Pasquale. Elementi di filosofia. v.2. Roma, 1963-
Phil 5068.67   Ganguli, Hermanta Kumar. Philosophy of logical construction. 1st ed. Calcutta, 1963.
Phil 5246.77   Garan, D.G. The paradox of pleasure and relativity. N.Y., 1963.
Phil 8980.417   Garaudy, R. Qu'est-ce que la morale marxiste. Paris, 1963.
Phil 181.128.10   Garcia Bacca, J.D. Metafisica natural estabilizada y problematica. Mexico, 1963.
Phil 806.37   García Bacca, Juan David. Siete modelos de filosofar. Venezuela, 1963.
Phil 4195.88   Garin, Eugenio. Giovanni Pico della Mirandola. Parma? 1963.
Phil 181.145   Garulli, Enrico. Esperienza e metafisica nella filosofia moderna. Urbino, 1963.
Phil 5238.195   Gaskill, H.S. Counterpoint. N.Y., 1963.
Phil 1750.166.160   Gastão, Manuel M. Humanismos e suas diversas interpretações. Lisboa, 1963.
Phil 5620.29   Gauthier, Daniel Peter. Practical reasoning. Oxford, 1963.
Phil 2406.4A   Gay, P. The party of humanity. 1st ed. N.Y., 1963.
Phil 2630.12   Geiger, Louis Bertrand. Philosophie et spiritualité. Paris, 1963. 2v.
Phil 7060.10.80   Geiger, M. Aufklärung und Erweckung. Zürich, 1963.
Phil 5400.160   Gellhorn, Ernest. Emotions and emotional disorders. N.Y., 1963.
Phil 8407.2   Gerard, Alexander. An essay on taste (1759). Facsimile. Gainesville, Fla., 1963.
Phil 2630.8.38   Gilson, Étienne. Introduction aux arts du beau. Paris, 1963.
Phil 6980.326   Ginsburg, S.W. A psychiatrist's views on social issues. N.Y., 1963.
Phil 8140.6   Giraldi, Giovanni. L'estetica italiana nella prima metà del secolo XX. Pisa, 1963.
Phil 3310.8.21   Glockner, Hermann. Gesammelte Schriften. Berlin, 1963-66.
Phil 6316.22   Goldstein, M. The experience of anxiety. N.Y., 1963.
Phil 3160.3.100   Goldstein, Walter. Hermann Cohen. Jerusalem, 1963.
Phil 5246.75   Gómez Ibars, J. En el món del invidents. Barcelona, 1963.
Phil 5545.222   Gorczyński, S. Sztuka pamietania. Warszawa, 1963.
Phil 5590.429   Gordon, J.E. Personality and behavior. N.Y., 1963.
Phil 9240.32   Gotshalk, D.W. Patterns of good and evil. Urbana, 1963.
Phil 4363.3.105   Granero, Jesus Maria. Don Miguel Mañara. Sevilla, 1963.

1963 - cont.

Phil 3488.39   Gregor, Mary J. Laws of freedom. N.Y., 1963.
Phil 8080.18   Grenier, Jean. L'imitation et les principes de l'esthétique classique. Paris, 1963.
Phil 6316.8.15   Groddeck, Georg. Au fond de l'homme cela. Paris, 1963.
Phil 672.219   Gruenbaum, A. Philosophical problems of space and time. 1st ed. N.Y., 1963.
Phil 4803.435.30   Grzegorczyk, Andrzej. Schemaly i człowiek. Kraków, 1963.
Phil 4007.5   Guerra, Augusto. Il mondo della sicurezza; Ardigo, Labriola, Croce. Firenze, 1963.
Phil 2630.11.12   Guitton, Jean. The Guitton journals, 1952-1955. London, 1963.
Phil 3425.590   Guzzoni, Ute. Werden zu Sich. Freiburg, 1963.
Phil 1707.29   Haag, Karl Heinz. Die Lehre vom Sein in der modernen Philosophie. Frankfurt, 1963.
Phil 338.45   Haering, Theodor Lorenz. Philosophie des Verstehens. Tübingen, 1963.
Phil 4960.805   Hanisch Espíndola, Walter. En torno a la filosofía en Chile, 1594-1810. Santiago, 1963.
Phil 7069.63   Hankey, M. James Hewat McKenzie, pioneer of psychical research. Londnon, 1963.
Phil 6317.31.2   Harding, M.E. Psychic energy. 2. ed. N.Y., 1963.
Phil 8882.68.5   Hare, Richard Mervyn. Freedom and reason. Oxford, 1963.
Phil 5247.77   Harris, Chester. Problems in measuring change. Madison, 1963.
Phil 2880.8.140   Hartmann, Klaus. Grundzüge der Ontologie Sartres in ihrem Verhältnis zu Hegels Logik. Berlin, 1963.
Phil 3850.18.142   Hartmann, Wilfried. Max Scheler; Bibliographie. Stuttgart, 1963.
Phil 585.181   Hartung, Henri. Unité de l'homme. Paris, 1963.
Phil 5548.102   Harvey, O.J. Motivation and social interaction. N.Y., 1963.
Phil 672.234   Hatano, Seiichi. Time and eternity. Tokyo? 1963.
Phil 8408.39   Havryliuk, P.J. Spetsyfichni osoblynosti zmistu i formy v mystetstvi. Kyïv, 1963.
Phil 5520.75.10   Hayakawa, S.I. Symbol, status. 1. ed. N.Y., 1963.
Phil 70.89   Hayden Colloquium on Scientific Concept and Method, M.I.T. Parts and wholes. N.Y., 1963.
Phil 5247.76   Hays, W. Statistics for psychologists. N.Y., 1963.
Phil 6117.52   Hécaen, Henry. Les gauchers. Paris, 1963.
Phil 5548.103   Heckhausen, H. Hoffnung und Furcht in der Leistungsmotivation. Meisenheim, 1963.
Phil 6400.35   Heese, Gerhard. Sprachpflege kurs für Schwerhörige und Ertaubte. Berlin, 1963.
Phil 3425.74.2   Hegel, Georg Wilhelm Friedrich. Propédiutique philosophique. Paris, 1963.
Phil 3450.19.30.10   Heidegger, Martin. Sein und Zeit. 10e Aufl. Tübingen, 1963.
Phil 807.17.2   Heinrich, W. Zarys historii filozofii średniowiecznej. Warszawa, 1963.
Phil 1750.740   Heiss, R. Die grossen Dialektiker des 19. Jahrhunderts. Köln, 1963.
Phil 3450.11.310   Held, Klaus. Lebendige Gegenwart. Köln, 1963.
Phil 3425.220.5   Heller, Hermann. Hegel und der nationale Machtstaatsgedanke in Deutschland. Aalen, 1963.
Phil 3090.90   Hemmerle, Klaus. Franz von Baaders philosophischer Gedanke der Schöpfung. Freiburg, 1963.
Phil 2905.1.250   Hengstenberg, H.E. Evolution und Schöffung. München, 1963.
Phil 2655.7.30   Henry, Michel. L'essence de la manifestation. Paris, 1963. 2v.
Phil 5238.190   Herlrich, E. Der Mens als Persönlichkeit und Problem. München, 1963.
Phil 5066.247   Hermes, Hans. Einführung in die Mathematische Logik: klassische Prädikatenlogik. Stuttgart, 1963.
Phil 3640.695   Hess, K. Von Nietzsche zu Pannwitz. Lagnau, 1963.
Phil 5238.189   Hiltmann, H. Dialektik und Dynamik der Person. Köln, 1963.
Phil 5401.46   Hiltner, S. Constructive aspects of anxiety. N.Y., 1963.
Phil 5525.63   Hirsch, Wolfgang. Worüber lachen wir? Heidelberg, 1963.
Phil 1750.115.155   Hoeven, Johannes van der. Kritische ondervraging van de fenomenologische rede. Amsterdam, 1963.
Phil 8957.16   Hofmann, Rudolf. Moraltheologisch Erkenntniss- und Methodenlehre. München, 1963.
Phil 8170.7   Honcharenko, M.V. Mystetstvo i estetichne vychovannia. Kyïv, 1963.
Phil 8662.25   Hubbeling, H.G. Is the Christian God-conception philosophically inferior? Assen, 1963.
Phil 2050.37.10   Hume, David. Essays: moral, political and literary. London, 1963.
Phil 6949.363   Hunter, Richard A. Three hundred years of psychiatry, 1535-1860; a history presented in selected English texts. London, 1963.
Phil 182.133   Hurtado, Manuel. The positive absolutes. Mexico, 1963.
Phil 5590.570.2   Huth, Albert. Diagnose der Person. 2. Aufl. Bern, 1963.
Phil 9075.71   Hylkema, G.W. Homo duplex. Haarlem, 1963.
Phil 2750.27.30   Hyppolite, J. Sens et existence dans la philosophie de Maurice Merleau-Ponty. Oxford, 1963.
Phil 5590.436   L'inadaptation, phénomèn social. Paris, 1963.
Phil 8663.5   Information Catholiques Internationales. L'athéisme. Paris, 1963.
Phil 4803.462.60   Ingarden, Roman. Z badań nad folozofią współczesną. Warszawa, 1963.
Phil 4960.215   Ingenieros, José. Las direcciones filosóficas de la cultura argentina. Buenos Aires, 1963.
Phil 1930.17.80   Irvine, E.F. A pioneer of the new psychology. Chatham, 1963.
Phil 75.42.5   Istituto di Studi Filosofici. Bibliografia ragionata delle riviste filosofiche italiane dal 1900 al 1955. Roma, 1963.
Phil 8980.463   Ivanov, Vladimir G. Ocherki marksistsko-leninskoi etiki. Leningrad, 1963.
Phil 2805.407   Jacques, E. Le troisième centenaire de la mort de la Blaise Pascal. Bruxelles, 1963.
Phil 7069.58.2   Jaffe, Aniela. Apparitions and precognition. New Hyde Park, N.Y., 1963.
Phil 184.53   Jancke, Rudolf. Ursprung und Arten des realen Seins. Bern, 1963.
Phil 5407.7   Jankélévitch, Vladimir. L'aventure, l'ennui, le sérieux. Paris, 1963.
Phil 6060.74   Jansen, Abraham. Toetsing van grafologische uitspraken. Amsterdam, 1963.
Phil 184.52   Janssen, O. Gesammelte Abhandlungen zur Frage des Seins. München, 1963.
Phil 6959.4.17   Jaspers, K. General psychopathology. Manchester, 1963.
Phil 3475.3.67   Jaspers, Karl. Lebensfragen der deutschen Politik. München, 1963.

Chronological Listing

Phil 3475.3.66 — Jaspers, Karl. Philosophie und Offenbarungsglaube. Hamburg, 1963.

Phil 3475.3.23 — Jaspers, Karl. Werk und Wirkung. München, 1963.

Phil 2630.11.35 — Jean Guitton, vu par Jacques André. Troyes, 1963.

Phil 1514.2 — Jeanneau, E. La philosophie médiévale. Paris, 1963.

Phil 5249.25 — Joereskog, K.G. Statistical estimation in factor analysis. Stockholm, 1963.

Phil 6980.367A — Johnson, James A. Group therapy. N.Y., 1963.

Phil 4800.20 — Jordan, Zbigniew A. Philosophy and ideology. Dordrecht, 1963.

Phil 5590.235.2A — Jourard, Sidney Marshall. Personal adjustment. 2. ed. N.Y., 1963.

Phil 8620.51 — Journet, C. The meaning of evil. N.Y., 1963.

Phil 6319.1.34 — Jung, C.G. Neurosis, dreams, reflections. N.Y., 1963.

Phil 4803.334.80 — Kaczmarek, Stefan. Anioł Dowgird, filozof nieznany. Poznań, 1963.

Phil 8400.41 — Kagan, Moisei S. Lektsii po marksistsko-leninskoi estetike. Leningrad, 1963- 3v.

Phil 8411.32 — Kahnweiller, D. Confessions esthétiques. Paris, 1963.

Phil 1020.55 — Kamali, Sabin Ahmad. Types of Islamic thought in criticism and reconstruction. Aligarh, 1963.

Phil 8980.472.5 — Kánský, Jiří. Morálka dnes a zajtra. Bratislava, 1963.

Phil 3480.25.30 — Kant, Immanuel. Kant. Oxford, 1963.

Phil 3480.70.21 — Kant, Immanuel. Kant's introduction to logic and his essay on the mistaken subtilty of the four figures. N.Y., 1963.

Phil 3480.125 — Kant, Immanuel. Sochineniia. Moskva, 1963. 6v.

Phil 5220.5 — Kantor, J.R. The scientific evolution of psychology. Chicago, 1963. 2v.

Phil 3890.10.130 — Kasch, W.F. Die Sozialphilosophie von Ernst Troeltsch. Tübingen, 1963.

Phil 5421.15.5 — Katz, R.L. Empathy, its nature and uses. N.Y., 1963.

Phil 8050.65.5 — Kayser, W. The grotesque in art and literature. Bloomington, 1963.

Phil 310.552 — Kedrov, B.M. Edinstvo dialektiki, logiki i teorii poznaniia. Moskva, 1963.

Phil 5400.159 — Kenny, A. Action, emotion and will. London, 1963.

Phil 5066.230 — Kharin, N.N. Matematicheskaia logika i teoriia mnozhestv. Moskva, 1963.

Phil 1750.166.150 — Kiley, W. Human possibilities. N.Y., 1963.

Phil 4752.2.135 — Klamroth, E. Der Gedanke der ewigen Schoepfung. Hamburg, 1963.

Phil 6320.11.25 — Klein, M. Our adult world. N.Y., 1963.

Phil 2340.10.175 — Kline, George Louis. Alfred North Whitehead. Englewood Cliffs, 1963.

Phil 8960.12 — Klomps, Heinrich. Tradition und Fortschritt in der Moraltheologie: die grundsätzliche Bedeutung der Kontroverse zwischen Jansenismus und Probabilismus. Köln, 1963.

Phil 8665.9.5 — Koch, H.G. The abolition of God. Philadelphia, 1963.

Phil 3085.6.85 — Koelker, A. Alardus Amstelredamus en Cornelius Crocus. Nijmegen, 1963.

Phil 3120.2.112 — Kolman, E. Bernard Bolzano. Berlin, 1963.

Phil 291.11 — Komarov, V.N. Kosmos, log i vechnost' mira. Moskva, 1963.

Phil 1710.16 — Korn, Alejandro. Estudios de filosofía contemporánea. 1st ed. Buenos Aires, 1963.

Phil 5635.45.5 — Kovalgin, V.M. Reflektornaia teoriia oskchushchenii. Minsk, 1963.

Phil 4803.498.20 — Krajewski, Władysław. Szkice filozofczne. Wyd. 1. Warszawa, 1963.

Phil 341.42 — Kraus, Hermann. Der Geist als Materie in Gehirnphysiologie und Kausalitätstheorie. Nürnberg, 1963.

Phil 978.59.45 — Krishnamurti, J. Life ahead. London, 1963.

Phil 5068.53 — Küng, Gaide. Ontologie und logistische Analyse der Sprache. Wien, 1963.

Phil 5593.63 — Künsler, W. Über Blutdeutungen im Rorschachschen Formdeutversuch. Bern, 1963.

Phil 6634.5 — Kuijper, Siem. Einge especten vom vrij en dwangmatig herhalen. Hilversum, 1963.

Phil 310.525 — Kursanov, G.A. Dialekticheskii materializm o poniatii. Moskva, 1963.

Phil 3831.16 — Lacharrière, R. Études sur la théorie démocratique. Paris, 1963.

Phil 2477.6.150 — Lacroix, Jean. Maurice Blondel. Paris, 1963.

Phil 6321.12.15 — Laforgue, R. Au dela du scientisme. Genève, 1963.

Phil 8610.963 — Lahoz Lainez, Bienvenido. El destino humano en el realismo introspectivo. Madrid, 1963.

Phil 8886.78 — Lamouche, André. D'une morale de l'amour à une sociologie de la raison. Paris, 1963. 2v.

Phil 3450.11.129 — Landgrabe, Ludwig. Der Weg der Phäramenologie. Gütersloh, 1963.

Phil 3120.30.100 — Lang, Bernhard. Martin Buber und das dialogische Leben. Bern, 1963.

Phil 665.96 — Langre, Michel de. Ame humaine et science moderne. Paris, 1963.

Phil 1750.755 — Lanteri-Laura, G. La psychiatrie phénoménologique. Paris, 1963.

Phil 4972.5.80 — La Plata. Universidad Nacional. Estudios sobre Alejandro Korn. La Plata, 1963.

Phil 5066.241 — Laserna, Mario. Klassenlogik und formale Einteilung der Wissenschaft. Berlin, 1963?

Phil 6121.39A — Lashley, Karl S. Brain mechanisms and intelligence. N.Y., 1963.

Phil 2120.13.5 — Laszlo, Ervin. Essential society; an ontological reconstruction. The Hague, 1963.

Phil 1905.10.95 — LeChevalier, C. Ethique et idéalisme. Paris, 1963.

Phil 5041.16.80 — LeChevalier, Charles. La pensée morale de Bernard Bosanquet. Paris, 1963.

Phil 585.153 — Leclerq, J. La révolution de l'homme au XXe siècle. Tournai, 1963.

Phil 8430.44 — Leeuw, G. van der. Sacred and profane beauty. N.Y., 1963. 10v.

Phil 8961.17 — Lehmann, P.L. Ethics in a Christian context. 1. ed. N.Y., 1963.

Phil 3552.79.30 — Leibniz, Gottfried Wilhelm. Saggi filosofici e lettere. Bari, 1963.

Phil 3640.701 — Leider, Kurt. Friedrich Nietzsche. Lübeck, 1963.

Phil 8886.79 — Lepp, Ignance. La morale nouvelle. Paris, 1963.

Phil 6321.46 — Lertora, A.C. Re-fundamentacion de la psiquiatria. Buenos Aires, 1963.

Phil 2725.45 — Lévêque, R. Unité et diversité. Paris, 1963.

Phil 8400.34 — Levich, M. Aesthetics and the philosophy of criticism. N.Y., 1963.

Phil 5590.424 — Levine, Louis. Personal and social development. N.Y., 1963.

Phil 5520.402 — Lewis, Hywel D. Clarity is not enough. London, 1963.

Phil 5520.402.2 — Lewis, Hywel D. Clarity is not enough. N.Y., 1963.

Phil 8412.36 — Lier, Henri. Les arts de l'espace. 3. éd. Tournai, 1963.

Phil 2115.70.20 — Locke, J. A letter concerning toleration. The Hague, 1963.

Phil 4160.66.14 — Lombardi, Franco. Scritti. Opere. Firenze, 1963- 6v.

Phil 4960.210.2 — Lombardo Toledano, Vicente. Las corrientes filosóficas en la vida de México. 2. ed. México, 1963.

Phil 9450.56 — López Aranguren, J.L. Etica y política. Madrid, 1963.

Phil 3585.28.20 — Lotz, Johannes Baptist. Ontologia. Barcinone, 1963.

Phil 3640.684 — Love, F.R. Young Nietzsche and the Wagnerian experience. Chapel Hill, 1963.

Phil 2120.12.30 — Lovejoy, A.O. The thirteen pragmatisms. Baltimore, 1963.

Phil 8666.17.7 — Lubac, Henri de. Le drame de l'humanisme athée. Paris, 1963.

Phil 1870.115.15 — Luce, Arthur A. The dialectic of immaterialism. London, 1963.

Phil 5251.60.10 — Luce, Robert D. Handbook of mathematical psychology. N.Y., 1963. 2v.

Phil 5272.3 — Luce, Robert D. Readings in mathematical psychology. N.Y., 1963-65. 2v.

Phil 2138.147 — Ludwig, M. Die Sozialethik des John Stuart Mill. Zürich, 1963.

Phil 3585.20.10 — Luijpen, Wilhelmus Antonius Maria. Fenomenologie en atheisme. Utrecht, 1963.

Phil 402.4 — Lund, Erik. De europäiske ideers historie. 2. opl. Gyldendal, 1963.

Phil 6321.48 — Lyons, Joseph. Psychology and the measure of man. N.Y., 1963.

Phil 5590.82.2 — McClelland, D.C. Personality. N.Y., 1963.

Phil 8592.106 — MacGregor, Geddes. The hemlock and the cross. Philadelphia, 1963.

Phil 1865.186.2 — Mack, Mary P. Jeremy Bentham. N.Y., 1963.

Phil 5402.25 — McKenna, A.G. Les réactions psycho-physiologiques à la douleur. Louvain, 1963.

Phil 165.337 — McMullin, Ethan. The concept of matter. Notre Dame, Indiana, 1963.

Phil 8520.44 — Macquarrie, J. Twentieth century religious thought. London, 1963.

Phil 2905.1.275 — Madaule, J. Initiation à Teilhard de Chardin. Paris, 1963.

Phil 1133.49 — Maddalena, Antonio. Ionici; testimonianze e frammenti. Introduzione. 1. ed. Firenze, 1963.

Phil 2340.18.80 — Madden, E. Chauncey Wright and the foundations of pragmatism. Seattle, 1963.

Phil 6122.96.2 — Magnun, Horace. The waking brain. 2. ed. Springfield, Ill., 1963.

Phil 343.30 — Malcolm, N. Knowledge and certainty. Englewood Cliffs, 1963.

Phil 4710.141 — Malinin, V.A. Osnovnye problemy kritiki idealisticheskoi istorii russkoi filosofii. Moskva, 1963.

Phil 2050.254 — Mall, Rom Adhar. Humes Bild vom Menschen. Köln, 1963.

Phil 1712.23 — Mañero Mañero, Salvador. El humanismo. Madrid, 1963.

Phil 5252.151 — Mann, J.H. Frontiers of psychology. N.Y., 1963.

Phil 2750.19.39 — Marcel, Gabriel. The existential background of human dignity. Cambridge, 1963.

Phil 6315.2.310.10 — Marcuse, Herbert. Eros et civilization. Paris, 1963.

Phil 5068.70 — Maros dell'Oro, Angiolo. Il pensiero scientifico in Italia negli anni 1930-1960. Cremona, 1963.

Phil 3120.55.82 — Marsch, Wolf. Hoffen worauf? Hamburg, 1963.

Phil 8637.22 — Martin, E. Reincarnation, the ring of return. New Hyde Park, N.Y., 1963.

Phil 5520.413 — Martin, R.M. Intension and decision. Englewood Cliffs, N.J., 1963.

Phil 2905.1.108 — Martin-Deslias, Noël. Un aventurier de l'esprit, Pierre Teilhard de Chardin. Paris, 1963.

Phil 2070.151 — Martland, T. The metaphysics of William James and John Dewey. N.Y., 1963.

Phil 5252.152 — Marx, M.H. Systems and theories in psychology. N.Y., 1963.

Phil 9590.28 — Masferrer, A. Ensayo sobre el destino. San Salvador, 1963.

Phil 8685.22 — Masferrer, A. Helios. San Salvador, 1963.

Phil 5222.12 — Massucco Costa, Angiola. Psicologia sovietica. Torino, 1963.

Phil 343.50 — Mathieu, Vittorio. Il problema dell'esperienza. Trieste, 1963.

Phil 4170.14 — Mazzilli, Stefano. I sommi problemi. Padova, 1963. 2v.

Phil 5625.103 — Medvedev, N.M. Teoriia otrazheniia i ee estestvenno-nauchnoe obosnovanie. Moskva, 1963.

Phil 8592.113 — Mehl, R. The condition of the Christian philosopher. London, 1963.

Phil 4961.615 — Mejia Valera, Manuel. Fuentes para la historía de la filosofía en el Perú. Lima, 1963.

Phil 6322.19.15 — Menninger, Karl Augustus. The vital balance. N.Y., 1963.

Phil 525.231 — Merlan, P. Monopsychism, mysticism. The Hague, 1963.

Phil 5252.85.10A — Merleau-Ponty, M. The structure of behavior. Boston, 1963.

Phil 2750.20.15 — Merleau-Ponty, Maurice. In praise of philosophy. Evanston, 1963.

Phil 4959.245 — México (City). Universidad Nacional. Consejo Técnico de Humanidades. Estudios de historía de la filosofía en México. 1. ed. México, 1963.

Phil 8735.56 — Meyers, A.M. Die Ursachen aller geschaffenen Dinge. Limburg, 1963?

Phil 97.7 — Miano, V. Dizionario filosofico. Torino, 1963.

Phil 4809.796.80 — Michňáková, Irena. Augustin Smetana. Praha, 1963.

Phil 270.62.10 — Michotte, A.E. The perception of causality. London, 1963.

Phil 2138.11 — Mill, John S. Collected works. v.2,3, 4(2), 5(2), 10,12,13. Toronto, 1963. 9v.

Phil 6322.28.5 — Mira y López, E. Doctrinas psicoanaliticas. Buenos Aires, 1963.

Phil 1630.21 — Mondolfo, R. Figure e idee della filosofia del Rinascimento. Firenze, 1963.

Phil 5525.44.5 — Monro, David Hector. Argument of laughter. Notre Dame, 1963.

Phil 343.45.5 — Morandini, Francesco. Critica. 5. ed. Romae, 1963.

Phil 2115.195 — Morris, C.R. Locke, Berkeley, Hume. London, 1963.

Phil 2805.417 — Moscato, Alberto. Pascal. Milano, 1963.

Phil 1750.646 — Moscow. Akademiia Obshchestvennykh Nauk. Kritika sovremennoi burzhuaznoi filosofii i sotsiologii. Moskva, 1963.

Phil 1712.22 — Moscow. Universitet Filosofeskii Fakul'tet. Protiv sovremennoi burzhuaznoi filosofii. Moskva, 1963.

Phil 3625.4.35 — Müller, J. Ja zur Wirklichkeit. Weilheim, 1963.

Chronological Listing

Phil 5585.226   Mueller, Kurt. Der Aufbau figural-optischer Phänomene bei sukzessiver Reizung. Frankfurt, 1963.

Phil 5465.128   Mueller, Robert E. Inventivity. N.Y., 1963.

Phil 3195.6.160   Mueller-Vollmer, K. Towards a phenomenological theory of literature. The Hague, 1963.

Phil 585.173   Mukerjee, Radhakamal. The dimensions of human evolution. London, 1963.

Phil 187.176   Murphy, Arthur E. Reason and the common good. Englewood Cliffs, 1963.

Phil 8962.34   Murray, Michael V. Problems in conduct. N.Y., 1963.

Phil 2150.20.30   Murty, K. Satchidanda. Metaphysics, man and freedom. N.Y., 1963.

Phil 6323.20   Nacht, Sacha. La présence du psychanalyste. Paris, 1963.

Phil 5253.14   Nassefat, Mortega. Etude quantitative sur l'évolution des opérations inteslectuelles. Neuchâtel, 1963.

Phil 2775.3.30   Naulin, Paul. L'itinéraire de la conscience. Paris, 1963.

Phil 575.247   Nédoncelle, Maurice. Personne humaine et nature. Paris, 1963.

Phil 978.6.91   Nethercot, A.H. The last four lives of Annie Besant. London, 1963.

Phil 98.2   Neuhaeusler, Anton Otto. Grundbegriffe der philosophischen Sprache. München, 1963.

Phil 294.8   Nickel, E.J. Zugang zur Wicklichkeit. Freiburg, 1963.

Phil 4080.3.400   Nicolini, F. Il Croce minore. Milano, 1963.

Phil 2733.119   Nicolosi, Salvatore. Causalità divina e libertà umana nel pensiero di Malebranche. Padova, 1963.

Phil 8586.36.80   Nievergelt, Hans-Ulrich. Hutorität und Begegnung. Zürich, 1963.

Phil 1540.78   Nothdurft, Kalus Dieter. Studien zum Einfluss Senecas auf die Philosophie und Theologie des 12. Jahrhunderts. Leiden, 1963.

Phil 8050.83   Novák, Mirko. Otázky estetiky v přítainnosti i minulosti. Praha, 1963.

Phil 8669.7   O religii; khrestomatiia. Moskva, 1963.

Phil 3450.11.435   Oggioni, Emilio. La fenomenologia di Husserl e il pensiero contemporaneo. Bologna, 1963.

Phil 4170.16.10   Omaggio a Rodolfo Mondolfo. Urbino, 1963.

Phil 5585.227   Oñativia, O.V. Dimensiones de la percepcion. Tucuman, 1963.

Phil 2905.1.210   Onimus, J. Pierre Teilhard de Chardin. Paris, 1963.

Phil 5254.9   Oraison, Mark. Illusion and anxiety. N.Y., 1963.

Phil 6310.1.103   Orgler, Hertha. Alfred Adler, the man and his work. 3d ed. London, 1963.

Phil 8669.9   Ortuzar Arriaga, Martin. Los prenotandos del conocimiento natural de Dios. Madrid, 1963.

Phil 6400.22   Osgood, Charles E. Approaches to the study of aphasia. Urbana, 1963.

Phil 8889.8   Ossowska, Maria. Socjologia moralności. Warszawa, 1963.

Phil 8050.21   Ovsiannikov, M.F. Ocherki istorii esteticheskikh uchenii. Moskva, 1963.

Phil 189.32   Owens, Joseph. An elementary Christian metaphysics. Milwaukee, 1963.

Phil 1750.765   Paci, Enzo. Funzione delle scienze e significato dell'uomo. Milano, 1963.

Phil 1750.752   Paci, Enzo. I problemi dell'economic e la fenomenologia. Milano, 1963.

Phil 960.250   Pandeya, R.C. The problem of meaning in Indian philosophy. 1. ed. Delhi, 1963.

Phil 1750.166.180   Panikkar, Raimundo. Humanismo y cruz. Madrid, 1963.

Phil 2255.1.127   Park, J. Bertrand Russell on education. Columbus, 1963.

Phil 2805.413A   Pascal; testes du tricentenaire. Paris, 1963.

Phil 6980.575.5   Paterson, A.S. Electrical and drug treatment in psychiatry. Amsterdam, 1963.

Phil 4200.2.30   Patrizzi, F. L'amorosa filosofia di F. Patrizzi. Firenze, 1963.

Phil 6325.21   Paul, Louis. Psychoanalytic clinical interpretation. N.Y., 1963.

Phil 3497.3.4.5   Paulsen, Friedrich. Immanuel Kant; his life and doctrine. N.Y., 1963.

Phil 5055.27.3   Pavese, Roberto. Commento alla logica sintetica. Padova, 1963.

Phil 8705.22   Pégand, Georges. Ascèse et science. Paris, 1963.

Phil 1715.12   Pepi, Sergio. Umanismo logico. Roma, 1963.

Phil 8890.60   Perelman, Chaim. The idea of justice and the problem of argument. London, 1963.

Phil 8890.60.1   Perelman, Chaim. Justice et raison. Bruxelles, 1963.

Phil 190.90.5   Peters, Johannes Arnold Josef. Metaphysics; a systematic survey. Pittsburgh, 1963.

Phil 5055.16.6   Pfänder, A. Logik. 3. Aufl. Tübingen, 1963.

Phil 3745.10.15   Pfaender, Alexander. Phänomenologie des Wollens; eine psychologische Analuse. 3. Aufl. München, 1963.

Phil 8520.65   Philipp, Wolfgang. Das Zeitalter der Ausklärung. Bremen, 1963.

Phil 6319.1.216   Philipson, M.H. Outline of a Jungian aesthetics. Evanton, 1963.

Phil 165.400   Philosophical essays, dedicated to Gunnar Aspelin on the occasion of his sixty-fifth birthday, the 23rd of September 1963. Lund, 1963.

Phil 4195.36.5   Pico della Mirandola, Giovanni. La dignità dell'uomo. Matera, 1963.

Phil 4195.40.5   Pico della Mirandola, Giovanni. Ioannis Pici Mirandulae...vita. Modena, 1963.

Phil 5525.38.2   Piddington, Ralph. The psychology of laughter. 2. ed. N.Y., 1963.

Phil 3745.14.15   Pieper, Josef. Belief and faith. N.Y., 1963.

Phil 5204.12.3   Piéron, Henri. Vocabulaire de la psychologie. 3. éd. Paris, 1963.

Phil 3425.554.5   Piontkovskii, A.A. Uchenie Gegelia o prave i gosudarstve i ego ugolovno-pravovaia teoriia. Moskva, 1963.

Phil 4897.10   Piovesana, Gino K. Recent Japanese philosophical thought, 1862-1962. Tokyo, 1963.

Phil 3640.235.30   Podach, Erich F. Ein Blick in Notizbücher Nietzsches. Heidelberg, 1963.

Phil 7069.02.12   Podmore, Frank. Mediums of the 19th century. N.Y., 1963. 2v.

Phil 3450.19.290   Poeggeler, Otto. Der Denkweg Martin Heideggers. Pfullingen, 1963.

Phil 2225.15   Pols, E. The recognition of reason. Carbondale, 1963.

Phil 7082.182   Pongracz, Marion. Das Königreich der Träume. Wien, 1963.

Phil 3745.16   Popma, Klaas. Wijsbegeerte en anthropologie. Amsterdam, 1963.

Phil 1540.84   Prezioso, Faustino Antonio. La species medievale e i prodromi del fenomenismo moderno. Padova, 1963.

Phil 7069.28.85   Prince, Walter Franklin. Noted witnesses for psychic occurrences. N.Y., 1963.

Phil 5275.20   Psychologie et sous-développement. Paris, 1963.

Phil 4200.9.30   Pucci, Raffaele. La fenomenologia contemporanea e il problema dell'uomo. Napoli, 1963.

Phil 3640.688   Puetz, Heinz Peter. Kunst und Künstlerexistenz bei Nietzsche und Thomas Mann. Bonn, 1963.

Phil 5066.11.21   Quine, Willard van Orman. From a logical point of view. 2nd ed. N.Y., 1963.

Phil 8597.53   Rabut, Olivier A. Valeur spirituelle du profane. Paris, 1963.

Phil 4080.18.85   Raggiunti, Renzo. Logica e linguistica nel pensiero di Guido Calogero. Firenze, 1963.

Phil 960.278   Ramaswami Aiyas C.P. Research Endowment Committee. A bibliography of Indian philosophy. 1. ed. Madras, 1963-2v.

Phil 8050.80   Ramos, S. Estudios de estética. México, 1963.

Phil 192.40.10   Randall, J.H. How philosophy uses its past. N.Y., 1963.

Phil 102.3.6   Ranzoli, C. Dizionario de scienze filosofiche. 6. ed. Milano, 1963.

Phil 6310.1.99   Rattner, J. Individualpsychologie. München, 1963.

Phil 6967.20   Rattner, Josef. Das Wesen der schizophrenen Reaktion. München, 1963.

Phil 4215.10.30   Raya, Gino. La fame. 2. ed. Roma, 1963.

Phil 3017.7   Razzug, Aśad. Die Ansätze zu einer Kulturantropologie in der Gegewärtigen deutschen Philosophie. Tübingen, 1963.

Phil 5401.48   Réal, Pierre. Triomphez de l'angoisse. Verviers, 1963.

Phil 3425.599   Rehm, Margarete. Hegels spekulative Deutung der Infinitesimalrechnung. Köln, 1963.

Phil 6980.635.40   Reik, T. The need to be loved. N.Y., 1963.

Phil 585.186   Rendel, David. Earthling and Hellene; a psychological mechanism of evolution and its effect on the human race. Wimbledon, 1963.

Phil 5027.3   Rescher, N. Studies in the history of Arabic logic. Pittsburgh, 1963.

Phil 8892.86   Reyer, Wilhelm. Anthropologische Ethik. Köln, 1963.

Phil 3450.19.280   Richardson, W.J. Heidegger: through phenomenology. The Hague, 1963.

Phil 3790.22.5   Riessen, Hendrick van. Op wijsgerige wegen. Wageningen, 1963.

Phil 348.24   Riet, G. van. Thomistic epistemology. St. Louis, 1963. 2v.

Phil 3499.31   Rigobello, A. I limiti del trascendentale in Kant. Milano, 1963.

Phil 1540.41   Ritter, Gerhard. Via Antigue und via Moderna auf den deutschen Universitaeten des XV Jahrhunderts. Darmstadt, 1963.

Phil 8597.54   Riva, C. Pensiero e coerenza cristiana. Brescia, 1963.

Phil 3450.19.270A   Robinson, J.M.C. The later Heidegger and theology. N.Y., 1963.

Phil 817.24   Rochedieu, Edmond. La pensée occidentale face à la sagesse de l'orient. Paris, 1963.

Phil 6327.35   Rochman, S. Critical essays on psychoanalysis. N.Y., 1963.

Phil 2733.117   Rodis-Lewis, G. Nicolas Malebranche. Paris, 1963.

Phil 1750.742   Roesch, E.J. The totalitarian threat. N.Y., 1963.

Phil 5628.55.30   Roessler, Max. Therese Neumann von Konnersreuth. Wurzburg, 1963.

Phil 2750.20.90   Rofinet, A. Merleau-Ponty. Paris, 1963.

Phil 4365.1.80   Rojo Perez, E. La ciencia de la cultura, teoría históriologica de Eugenio d'Ors. Barcelona, 1963.

Phil 2733.116   Rome, B.K. The philosophy of Malebranche. Chicago, 1963.

Phil 2805.410   Ronnet, G. Pascal et l'homme moderne. Paris, 1963.

Phil 2750.20.85   Roosfen, S. De idee der zelfvervramding. Delft, 1963.

Phil 8892.77   Roschacher, E. Das Recht und die Rechtssätze. Winterthur, 1963.

Phil 5421.25.65   Rosenberg, Stuart E. More loves than one. N.Y., 1963.

Phil 3790.20.5   Rosenstock, Eugen. Die Sprache des Menschengeschlechts. Heidelberg, 1963-64. 2v.

Phil 6967.22   Rosenthal, David. The Genain quadruplets. N.Y., 1963.

Phil 4210.72   Rosmini-Serbati, Antonio. Il giovane Rosmini. Urbino, 1963.

Phil 4210.67   Rosmini-Serbati, Antonio. La societa teocratico. Brescia, 1963.

Phil 1750.751   Rotenstreich, N. Humanism in the contemporary era. The Hague, 1963.

Phil 2255.9   Rotenstreich, N. Spirit and man. The Hague, 1963.

Phil 3837.12.7   Roth, Leon. Spinoza, Descartes and Maimonides. N.Y., 1963.

Phil 3790.24   Rothacker, E. Heitere Erinnerungen. Frankfurt, 1963.

Phil 420.4   Rothacker, Erich. Intuition und Begriff. Bonn, 1963.

Phil 1717.24   Rouche, Gerhard Albin. The philosophy of actuality. Fort Hare, 1963.

Phil 102.5.7   Rozental, Mark Moiseevich. Filosofskii slovar'. Moskva, 1963.

Phil 102.5.8   Rozental, Mark Moiseevich. Filosofskii slovar'. Izd. 2. Moskva, 1963.

Phil 4215.8.21   Ruggiero, Guido de. Scritti politici, 1912-26. Bologna, 1963.

Phil 2255.1.43   Russell, Bertrand Russell. Political ideals. N.Y., 1963.

Phil 1717.22   Russia, 1917. Ministerstvo vysshego Obrazovaniia. Kritika sovremennoi burzhuaznoi ideologii. Petrozavodsk, 1963.

Phil 5272.14   Rydberg, Sven. Bias in prediction; on correction methods. Uppsala, 1963.

Phil 6127.26.5   Ryle, Gilbert. The concept of mind. London, 1963.

Phil 3450.19.275   Sadzik, J. Esthétique de Martin Heidegger. Paris, 1963.

Phil 8843.18   Sahakian, W. Systems of ethics and value theory. N.Y., 1963.

Phil 5058.94   Salmon, W. Logic. Englewood, 1963.

Phil 193.232   Salvucci, P. Saggi. Urbino, 1963.

Phil 310.606   Samek, Antonín. Filosofie a politika. Praha, 1963.

Phil 2750.11.160   Sampaio, L.F.A. L'intuition dans la philosophie de Jacques Maritain. Paris, 1963.

Phil 5643.168   Sanders, Andries Frans. The selective process in the functional visual field. Assen, 1963.

Phil 4018.8.5   Santucci, Antonio. Il pragmatismo in Italia. Bologna, 1963.

Phil 2880.8.45   Sartre, Jean Paul. Esquisse d'une théorie des émotions. Paris, 1963.

Phil 2880.8.35   Sartre, Jean Paul. Essays in aesthetics. N.Y., 1963.

Phil 2880.8.52   Sartre, Jean Paul. Search for a method. 1st American ed. N.Y., 1963.

Phil 3425.604   Sass, H.M. Untersuchungen zur Religionsphilosophie. Münster, 1963.

Phil 2520.343   Sassen, F. Descartes. Den Haag, 1963.

Phil 8893.135   Sathaye, S.G. A philosophy of living. N.Y., 1963.

Phil 5590.280.5   Schachtel, Ernest G. Metamorphosis. London, 1963.

Phil 310.445.4   Schaff, Adam. A philosophy of man. London, 1963.

Phil 193.233   Schazmann, P.E. Siegende Geduld. Bern, 1963.

1963 - cont.

Phil 3640.709 Schieder, Theodor. Nietzsche und Bismarck. Krefeld, 1963.
Phil 8598.135 Schlette, Heinz Robert. Die Religionen als Thema der Theologie. Freiburg, 1963.
Phil 1818.8.2 Schneider, H.W. A history of American philosophy. 2nd ed. N.Y., 1963.
Phil 5400.164 Schneiders, A.A. The anarchy of feeling. N.Y., 1963.
Phil 2045.133 Schnur, R. Individualismus und Absolutismus. Berlin, 1963.
Phil 5645.65 Schoenborn-Buchheim, Elisabeth. Experimentelle Untersuchüngen den Eindruckscharakter von Einzelfarben. Freiburg, 1963?
Phil 5360.24 Schon, Donald A. Displacement of concepts. London, 1963.
Phil 3808.25.25 Schopenhauer, Arthur. The wisdom of life. London, 1963.
Phil 3246.302 Schuffenhauer, H. Die Padagogik Johann Gottlieb Fichtes. Berlin, 1963.
Phil 5465.138 Schuhl, P.M. Imaginer et réaliser. Paris, 1963.
Phil 3500.95 Sciacca, Guiseppe M. L'idea della libertà. Palermo, 1963.
Phil 2240.85.3 Sciacca, M.F. La filosofia di Tommaso Reid. 3a ed. Milano, 1963.
Phil 4018.6.5 Sciacca, M.F. Il pensiero italiano nell'età del Risorgimento. 2. ed. Milano, 1963.
Phil 5620.34 Scivoletto, Angelo. Il segno della ragione. Padova, 1963.
Phil 5828.20 Scott, J.P. Animal behavior. Garden City, 1963.
Phil 4752.2.130 Segundo, J.L. Berdiaeff. Paris, 1963.
Phil 3120.2.120 Seidlerová, I. Politické a pociálné názory Bernard Bolzano. Praha, 1963.
Phil 349.44 Sellars, W. Science, perception, and reality. London, 1963.
Phil 8893.147 Sen Gupta, Santosh Chandra. Good, freewill and God. Calcutta, 1963.
Phil 1695.25 Şervadio, E. La psicoanalisi. Torino, 1963. 3v.
Phil 270.130 Šešić, Bogdan. Nužnost i sloboda. Beograd, 1963.
Phil 8419.55 Sesti, Luigi. Quattro dialoghi sull'arte. Milano, 1963.
Phil 9495.163.5 Sexualité et limitation des naissances. Paris, 1963.
Phil 530.20.120 Seyppel, Joachim Hans. Texte deutscher Mystik des 16. Jahrhunderts. Göttingen, 1963.
Phil 2262.35.4 Shaftesbury, A.A.C. Characteristics of men, manners, opinions, times. Gloucester, Mass., 1963. 2v.
Phil 1020.46 Sharif, M.M. A history of Muslim philosophy. Wiesbaden, 1963. 2v.
Phil 310.570 Sheputo, L.L. Voprosy dialekticheskogo materializma i meditsina. v.2. Moskva, 1963.
Phil 4791.8 Sheroziia, Apollon Epifonovich. Filosofskaia mysl' v Gruzii v pervoi chetverti XX veka. Tbilisi, 1963.
Phil 575.245 Shoemaker, S. Self-knowledge and self-identity. Ithaca, 1963.
Phil 349.45 Shtoff, V.A. Rol' modelei v poznanii. Leningrad, 1963.
Phil 818.32.5 Siewerth, G. Grunfragen der Philosophie in Horizont der Seinsdifferenq. Düsseldorf, 1963.
Phil 310.536 Şimard, É. Communisme et science. Québec, 1963.
Phil 8419.50 Šindelář, Dušan. Smysl věcí. Praha, 1963.
Phil 5039.16 Sju filosofiska studier, tillägnade Anders Wedberg. Stockholm, 1963.
Phil 185.41.5 Skinner, J.E. Self and world; the religious philosophy of Richard Kroner. Philadelphia, 1963.
Phil 193.231.2 Smart, J. Philosophy and and scientific realism. N.Y., 1963.
Phil 193.231 Smart, J. Philosophy and scientific realism. London, 1963.
Phil 5590.426 Smelser, Neil Joseph. Personality and social systems. N.Y., 1963.
Phil 1818.11 Smith, J.E. The spirit of American philosophy. N.Y., 1963.
Phil 8598.133 Smith, W.C. The meaning and end of religion. N.Y., 1963.
Phil 2905.1.267 Smulders, P.F. Theologie und Evolution. Essen, 1963.
Phil 2050.251 Snethlage, J.L. David Hume. Den Haag, 1963.
Phil 818.35 Soares, L.R. Quatro meditacões sobre o filósofo. Porto, 1963.
Phil 3640.697 Sørensen, V. Friedrich Nietzsche. København, 1963.
Phil 5585.225 Sokolov, E.N. Perception and the conditioned reflex. Oxford, 1963.
Phil 5237.516.5 Sokolov, Mikhail V. Ocherki istorii psikhologicheskikh vozznenii v Rossii v XI-XVIII vekakh. Moskva, 1963.
Phil 384.5 Spakovski, Anatol. Freedom, determinism, indeterminism. The Hague, 1963.
Phil 3850.32.22 Spann, Othmar. Naturphilosophie. 2. Aufl. Graz, 1963.
Phil 8419.56 Sparshott, F.E. The structure of aesthetics. Toronto, 1963.
Phil 3745.10.5 Spiegelberg, H. Alexander Pfänders phänomenologie. Den Haag, 1963.
Phil 3819.38.6 Spinoza, Benedictus de. Short treatise on God, man and his well-being. N.Y., 1963.
Phil 310.575 Spizkin, A.G. Kurs marksistskoi filosofii. Moskva, 1963.
Phil 193.243 Staal, J.F. Euclides en Panini. Amsterdam, 1963.
Phil 9255.25 Staecker, Karlheinz. Ironie und Ironiker. Diss. Mainz? 1963.
Phil 7069.63.5 Stearn, J. The door to the future. Garden City, 1963.
Phil 5628.55.35 Steiner, Johannes. Therese Neumann von Konnersreuth. München, 1963.
Phil 978.49.694 Steiner, R. Aus der Akasha-Forschung: Das Fünfte Evangelium. Dornach, 1963.
Phil 978.49.700 Steiner, R. Christ and the spiritual world. London, 1963.
Phil 978.49.383 Steiner, R. Exkurse in das Gebiet des Markus-Evangeliums. Dornach, 1963.
Phil 978.49.625 Steiner, R. Geisteswissenschaftliche Grundlage zum Gedeihen der Landwirtschaft; landwirtschaftlicher Kursus. 4. Aufl. Dornach, 1963.
Phil 978.49.430 Steiner, R. Neugestaltung, des sozialen Organismus. Dornach, 1963.
Phil 978.49.415 Steiner, R. Die soziale Grundforderung unserer Zeit in gländerter Zeitlage. Dornach, 1963.
Phil 3640.675 Steiner, Rudolf. Friedrich Nietzsche, ein Kampfer gegen seine Zeit. Dornach, 1963.
Phil 974.3.16 Steiner, Rudolf. Die Weihnachtstagung zur Begründung. 3. Aufl. Dornach, 1963.
Phil 2805.406 Steinmann, J. Les trois nuits de Pascal. Paris, 1963.
Phil 8968.17 Stelzenberger, J. Synerdesis. Paderborn, 1963.
Phil 8893.102.15 Stevenson, Charles Leslie. Facts and values. New Haven, 1963.
Phil 2050.252 Stewart, J.B. The moral and political philosophy of David Hume. N.Y., 1963.
Phil 1750.736 Straser, S. Phenomenology and the human scientific ideal. Pittsburg, 1963.
Phil 5258.114.5 Straus, Erwin. The primary world of senses. N.Y., 1963.
Phil 3018.36 Stuke, H. Philosophie der Tat. Stuttgart, 1963.
Phil 8419.3 Sturmfels, W. Grundprobleme der Ästhetik. München, 1963.

1963 - cont.

VPhil 585.191 Suchodolski, Bogdan. Narodziny nowożytnej filozofii człowieka. Warszawa, 1963.
Phil 4479.1.30 Sylvan, F. Filosofia e politica no destino de Portugal. Lisboa, 1963.
Phil 5400.165 Symposium on Expression. Expression of the emotions in man. N.Y., 1963.
Phil 5258.193 Szasz, Thomas Stephen. Law, liberty and psychiatry. N.Y., 1963.
Phil 6129.10 Taniguchi, Masaham. Recovery from all diseases. Tokyo, 1963.
Phil 6980.721 Tarachow, S. An introduction to psychotherapy. N.Y., 1963.
Phil 5465.136 Taylor, C.W. Scientific creativity. N.Y., 1963.
Phil 2905.1.55 Teilhard de Chardin, Pierre. Lettres d'Egypte, 1905-1908. Aubier, 1963.
Phil 2905.1.240 Teilhard de Chardin. Paris, 1963?
Phil 6060.57.2 Teillard, Ania. Handschriftendeutung auf tiefenpsychologischen Grundlage. 2. Aufl. Bern, 1963.
Phil 7150.54 Thakur, Upendra. The history of suicide in India. 1st ed. Delhi, 1963.
Phil 5590.430 Thomas, Alexander. Behavioral individuality in early childhood. N.Y., 1963.
Phil 8969.11 Tillich, Paul. Morality and beyond. N.Y., 1963.
Phil 672.224 Tlustý, Vojtěch. Prostor a čas. 2. vyd. Praha, 1963.
Phil 5590.39 Tomkins, Silvan S. Computer simulation of personality. N.Y., 1963.
Phil 5590.455 Tournier, Paul. Le secret d'après une conférence donnée à Athènes en la Salle de la Société d'Archéologie le 12 mai 1963. Genève, 1963.
Phil 5627.248.1 Tournier, Paul. The strong and weak. Philadelphia, 1963.
Phil 2477.6.140 Tresmontant, C. Introduction à la metaphysique de Maurice Blondel. Paris, 1963.
Phil 2475.1.405 Trevisan, A. Essai sur le problèmes. Fribourg, 1963.
Phil 8090.4 Trofimov, P.S. Ocherki istorii marksistskoi estetiki. Moskva, 1963.
Phil 585.148 Tsanoff, Radoslav. Science and human perspectives. London, 1963.
Phil 310.551 Tsaregorodtsev, Gennadi I. Dialekticheskii materializm i meditsina. Moskva, 1963.
Phil 8622.55 Tülilä, Osmo. Epäilyksistä uskoon. Helsinki, 1963.
Phil 195.10 Uemov, A.I. Veshchi, svoistva i otnosheniia. Moskva, 1963.
Phil 210.45 Umanesimo e ermeneutica. Padova, 1963.
Phil 6750.263 United States. Presdent's Panel on Mental Retardation. Report of the task force education and rehabilitation. Washington, D.C., 1963.
Phil 310.590 Uvarov, A.I. Leninskii printsip ob"ektivnosti v poznanii. Tomsk, 1963.
Phil 353.32 Vakhtomin, N.K. O roli kategorii sushchnost' i iavlenie v poznanii. Moskov, 1963.
Phil 1811.5 Van Leeuwen, H.G. The problem of certainty in English thought. The Hague, 1963.
Phil 352.11 Vardapetian, K. O nekotorykh osnovnykh voprosakh marks - leninskoi gnoseologii. Erevan, 1963.
Phil 6131.6 Vasil'ev, Leonid L. Tainstvennye iavleniia chelov psikhiki. Moskva, 1963.
Phil 5520.507 Verhaar, John W.M. Some relations between perception, speech and thought. Proefschrift. Assen, 1963.
Phil 2905.1.257 Viallet, François A. Teilhard de Chardin. Nurnberg, 1963. 2v.
Phil 6331.8 Viane, Andre. Psychologie van het onheilsvoorspellen. Gent, 1963.
Phil 2905.1.280 Vigorelli, G. Il gesuita proibito. Milano, 1963.
Phil 5520.407 Vildomec, V. Multilingualism. Leyden, 1963.
Phil 4957.55 Villegas, Abelardo. Panorama de la filosofía iberoamericana actual. Buenos Aires, 1963.
Phil 3640.702 Vincenzi, M. El caso Nietzsche. San Juan, 1963.
Phil 585.159 Virasoro, M.A. Para una nueva idea del hombre y de la antropología filosófica. Tucuman, 1963.
Phil 8422.17 Volek, Jaroslav. O předmětu a metodě estetáky a obecne teorie umění. Praha, 1963.
Phil 8090.8 Volpe, Galvo della. Crisi dell'estetica romantica. Roma, 1963.
Phil 1126.3 Vos, Harmen de. Inleiding tot de wijsbegeerte van de Grieken en de Romeinen. Nijkerk, 1963.
Phil 4825.1 Vrtăciă, Ludvík. Einführung in den Jugoslawischen Marxismus-Leninismus; Organisation und Bibliographie. Dordrecht, 1963.
Phil 5643.136 Vurpillot, Eliane. L'organisation perceptive: son rôle dans l'évolution des illusion optico-géométrique. Paris, 1963.
Phil 4757.2.97 Walker, K.M. The making of man. London, 1963.
Phil 3504.52 Walsh, William Henry. Kant's moral theology. London, 1963.
Phil 353.18.5 Walsh, William Henry. Reason and experience. Oxford, 1963.
Phil 5066.215 Wang, Hao. A survey of mathematical logic. Peking, 1963.
Phil 5232.10 Watson, Robert Irving. The great psychologists. Philadelphia, 1963.
Phil 8897.6.15 Wayland, F. The elements of moral science. Cambridge, Mass., 1963.
Phil 9182.8 Weber, L.M. Mysterium magnum. Freiburg, 1963.
Phil 5643.133 Weber, Renate. Experimentelle Untersuchung über die anschauliche Grösse. Inaug. Diss. Tübingen? 1963?
Phil 3504.50 Weil, Eric. Problems kantiens. Paris, 1963.
Phil 5520.405 Wein, Hermann. Sprachphilosophie der Gegenwart. Den Haag, 1963.
Phil 2138.151 Weinberg, Adelaide. Theodor Gomperz and John Stuart Mill. Genève, 1963.
Phil 2340.11.60 Weiss, Paul. Philosophy in process. Carbondale, 1963-64. 5v.
Phil 2340.11.55 Weiss, Paul. Religion and art. Milwaukee, 1963.
Phil 6332.30 Wells, Harry K. The failure of psychoanalysis. N.Y., 1963.
Phil 5520.414 Werner, H. Symbol formation. N.Y., 1963.
Phil 5125.30 Wesleyan Conference on Induction. Induction: some current issues. 1st ed. Middleton, 1963.
Phil 4710.9 Wetter, G.A. Die Umkehrung Hegels. Köln, 1963.
Phil 5238.186 White, R.W. The study of lives; essays on personality in honour of Henry A. Murray. N.Y., 1963.
Phil 6980.777 Whittington, H.G. Psychiatry on the college campus. N.Y., 1963.
Phil 6332.11.5 Wickes, F.G. The inner world of choice. N.Y., 1963.
Phil 1750.738 Wild, John. Existence and the world of freedom. Englewood, 1963.

Chronological Listing

1963 - cont.

Phil 2422.6 — Willard, Nedd. Le génie et la folie au dix-huitième siècle. Paris, 1963.

Phil 5125.19.5A — Williams, Donald C. The ground of induction. N.Y., 1963.

Phil 9400.41 — Williams, R.H. Processes of aging. N.Y., 1963. 2v.

Phil 5360.17 — Wilson, J. Thinking with concepts. Cambridge, 1963.

Phil 8423.24 — Wind, Edgar. Art and anarchy, and other essays. London, 1963.

Phil 3504.53 — Wolff, Robert Paul. Kant's theory of mental activity. Cambridge, 1963. 2v.

Phil 6132.41 — Wooldridge, Dean E. The machinery of the brain. N.Y., 1963.

Phil 5421.25.70 — Worms, Jeannine. D'une malédiction. Paris, 1963.

Phil 8897.84 — Wright, G.H. von. The logic of preference, an essay. Edinburgh, 1963.

Phil 8897.85 — Wright, G.H. von. Norm and action. London, 1963.

Phil 9240.31 — Wright, Georg. The varieties of goodness. London, 1963.

Phil 9240.31.5 — Wright, Georg. The varieties of goodness. N.Y., 1963.

Phil 3022.4.5 — Wust, Peter. Gesammelte Werke. Münster, 1963. 10v.

Phil 4374.5.20 — Xirau, Joaquín. Obras. 1. ed. Mexico, 1963.

Phil 8669.8 — Yaroslavl', Russia (City). Gosudarstvennyi Pedagogicheskii Institut. Kafedra Filosofii. Osnovy nauchnogo ateizma. Iaroslavl', 1963.

Phil 3845.3.5 — Zac, Sylvain. L'idée de vie dans la philosophie de Spinoza. Paris, 1963.

Phil 8980.873 — Zapovedi tvoei zhizni. Moskva, 1963.

Phil 5520.416 — Zhinkin, N.I. Myshlenie i rech'. Moskva, 1963.

Phil 3940.2.45 — Ziegler, L. Briefe, 1901-1958. München, 1963.

Phil 5066.171 — Zinov'ev, Aleksandr A. Philosophical problems. Dordrecht, 1963.

Phil 1750.747 — Zinzen, A. Die ontologische Betrachtungsweise. Meisenheim, 1963.

Phil 8612.58 — Zoepfl, Helmut. Der Tod im Phänomen der Bildung und Erziehung. Thesis. München, 1963.

Phil 4210.197 — Zolo, Danilo. Il personalismo rosminiano. Brescia, 1963.

Phil 4987.89.20 — Zubiri, Xavier. Estudios filosóficos. Madrid, 1963.

Phil 5592.172 — Zuest, R. Das Dorfspiel. Bern, 1963.

1964

Phil 5590.502 — Aarts, Josephus Franciscus Maria Carolus. Zelfbeoordelingen. Tilburg, 1964.

Phil 5238.201 — Abrams, A. Unfinished tasks in the behavioral sciences. Baltimore, 1964.

Phil 4816.10 — Academia Republicii Socialiste România, Bucharest. Institutul de Filozofie. Istoria gîradirii sociale şi filozofice în România. Bucureşti, 1964.

Phil 281.20 — Adams, George. Von dem ätherischen Raume. Stuttgart, 1964.

Phil 6310.1.45 — Adler, A. Superiority and social interest. Evanston, Ill., 1964.

Phil 730.25 — Afanas'ev, V.C. Problema tselostnosti v filosofii i biologii. Moskva, 1964.

Phil 150.26 — Afnan, Soheil. Philosophical terminology in Arabic and Persian. Leiden, 1964.

Phil 5066.273 — Agazzi, Evandro. La logica simbolica. Brescia, 1964.

Phil 310.6.6 — Akademiia Nauk SSSR. Institut Filosofii. Osnovy marksistskoi filosofii. Izd. 2. Moskva, 1964.

Phil 331.33 — Akademiia Nauk SSSR. Institut Filosofii. Dialektika teoriia poznaniia. Moskva, 1964- 3v.

Phil 5066.225.5 — Akademiia Nauk SSSR. Institut Filosofii. Formal'naia logika i metodologiia nauki. Moskva, 1964.

Phil 8980.131 — Akademiia Nauk SSSR. Institut Filosofii. Nravstvennost' i religiia. Moskva, 1964.

Phil 8655.20 — Akademiia Nauk SSSR. Institut Filosofii. Osnovy nauchnogo ateizma. 3. izd. Moskva, 1964.

Phil 8980.131.10 — Akademiia Nauk SSSR. Institut Filosofii. Problemy etiki. Moskva, 1964.

Phil 5066.224 — Akademiia Nauk SSSR. Institut Filosofii. Problemy logiki nauchnogo poznaniia. Moskva, 1964.

Phil 310.607 — Akademiia Nauk SSSR. Institut Filosofii. Protiv sovremennykh burzhuaznykh fal'sifikatorov marksistsko-leninskoi filosofii. Moskva, 1964.

Phil 1700.10 — Akademiia Nauk SSSR. Institut Filosofii. Sovremennaia filosofiia i sotsiologiia v stranakh Zapadnoi Evropy i Ameriki. Moskva, 1964.

Phil 8400.40 — Akademiia Nauk SSSR. Institut Istorii Iskusstv. Sovremennoe iskusstvoznanie za rubezhom; ocherki. Moskva, 1964.

Phil 5190.40 — Akademiia Nauk SSSR. Kafedra Filosofii, Leningrad. Problema vozmozhnosti i deistvitel'nosti. Leningrad, 1964.

Phil 8980.8 — Akademiia nauk SSSR. Kafedra Filosofii. Moral'nye oblik stroitelia kommunizma. Moskva, 1964.

Phil 175.61 — Akademiia Nauk SSSR. Nauchnyi Sovet po Filosofskim Voprosam Estestvoznaniia. O sushchnosti zhizni. Moskva, 1964.

Phil 4710.50.10 — Akademiia Nauk URSR, Kiev. Instytut Filosofii. Borot'ba mizh materializmom ta idealizmom na Ukraini. Kyïv, 1964.

Phil 5593.45.20 — Alcock, T. The Rorschach in practice. Philadelphia, 1964[1963]

Phil 8401.32 — Alexander, C.W.J. Notes on the synthesis of form. Cambridge, 1964.

Phil 3085.9.30 — Alff, Wilhelm. Überlegungen; Vierzehn Essays. Heidelberg, 1964.

Phil 8655.13 — Allen, D.C. Doubt's boundless sea. Baltimore, 1964.

Phil 5240.46.2 — Allport, Gordon Willard. Becoming. New Haven, 1964.

Phil 5520.418 — Alston, W. Philosophy of language. Englewood Cliffs, N.J., 1964.

VPhil 5401.51 — Alvarez, Martins d'. O medo no seculo XX. Rio de Janeiro, 1964.

Phil 1830.52 — Amend, V.E. Ten contemporary thinkers. N.Y., 1964.

Phil 8655.22 — Amor Ruibal, Angel Maria. Cuatro manuscritos inéditos: Los principios de donde recibe el ente la existencia. Madrid, 1964.

Phil 5850.111 — Anastasi, A. Fields of applied psychology. N.Y., 1964.

Phil 3850.27.225 — Anderson, E. Albert Schweitzer's of friendship. 1st ed. N.Y., 1964.

Phil 310.638 — Andreev, Kosta. Doktor Petur Genov za marksistkata filosofiia i bolshevizma. Sofiia, 1964.

Phil 8401.36 — Angelov, Valentin. Groznoto. Sofiia, 1964.

Phil 2138.149 — Arata, Fidia. La logica di J. Stuart Mill e la problematica eticosociale. Milano, 1964.

Phil 70.96 — Archivio di Filosofia. Tecnica e casistica. Padova, 1964.

Phil 1540.77 — Armstrong, O.H. Christian faith and Greek philosophy. N.Y., 1964.

Phil 5040.3.20 — Arnauld, Antoine. The art of thinking. Indianapolis, 1964.

1964 - cont.

Phil 5040.3.18 — Arnauld, Antoine. Logique de Port-Royal. Facsimile. Lille, 1964.

Phil 2438.17 — Arnauld, Antoine. Oeuvres de Messire Antoine Arnauld. v.1-43. Paris, 1964. 38v.

Phil 8980.165 — Ash, William F. Marxism and moral concepts. N.Y., 1964.

Phil 5876.5.5 — Asklund, Lis. Brytningstid, en bok om ungdom och samlernad. 5. uppl. Stockholm, 1964.

Phil 5548.85.5 — Atkinson, John W. An introduction to motivation. Princeton, 1964.

Phil 5238.197 — Atkinson, R.C. Studies in mathematical psychology. Stanford, 1964.

Phil 3625.5.45 — Atlas, S. From critical to speculative idealism. The Hague, 1964.

Phil 8580.36 — Augereau, Joseph. La chance suprême de l'homme. Paris, 1964.

Phil 8950.10 — Aula, Olari. Kristikunnan kouluss. Porvoo, 1964.

Phil 800.15 — Axelos, Kostas. Vers la pensée planétaire. Paris, 1964.

Phil 4710.151 — Aznaurov, Artem A. Ocherki po etike velikikh russikh revoliutsionnykh demokratov. Baku, 1964.

Phil 2477.15.6 — Bachelard, Gaston. The poetics of space. N.Y., 1964.

Phil 1850.160 — Bacon, F.V. The philosophy of Francis Bacon. Liverpool, 1964.

Phil 8612.70 — Badawi, Abdurrahmān. Le problème de la mort dans la philosophie existentielle. Le Claire, 1964.

Phil 1158.25.2 — Bailey, Cyril. The Greek atomists and Epicurus. N.Y., 1964.

Phil 1750.115.120 — Bakker, Reinout. De geschiedenis van het fenomenologisch denken. Antwerp, 1964.

Phil 4710.142 — Ballestrem, Karl G. Russian philosophical terminology. Dordrecht, 1964.

Phil 5625.104 — Ban, Thomas A. Conditioning and psychiatry. Chicago, 1964.

Phil 5585.270 — Bánfeti Fuchs, Károly Miklás. Problemen der subliminale perceptie. Assen, 1964.

Phil 1857.2 — Barfield, Owen. Worlds apart; a dialogue of the 1960's. 1st American ed. Middletown, Conn., 1964.

Phil 8092.12 — Barilli, Renato. Per un'estetica mondana. Bologna, 1964.

Phil 2905.1.305 — Barjon, L. La carrière scientifique de Pierre Teilhard de Chardin. Monaco, 1964.

Phil 2905.1.330 — Barral, Louis Marie. Éléments du bâti scientifique Teilhardien. Monaco, 1964.

Phil 1750.167.3A — Barrett, William. What is existentialism? N.Y., 1964.

Phil 5545.174.5 — Bartlett, F.C. Remembering. Cambridge, Eng., 1964.

Phil 176.226 — Bartolone, Filippo. Struttura e significato nella storia della filosofia. Bologna, 1964.

Phil 3640.707 — Bartuschat, Wolfgang. Nietzsche. Heidelberg? 1964.

Phil 8400.42 — Baskin, Mark P. Protiv sovremennogo abstraktsionizma i formalizma. Moskva, 1964.

Phil 4340.10 — Batlori, Miguel. Il pensiero delea rinascenza in Spagna e Portogallo. Milano, 1964.

Phil 6315.2.345 — Bayen, Jeanne Françoise. Sigmund Freud. Paris, 1964.

Phil 4769.1.94 — Bayer, J.J.M. Solowiew. Den Haag, 1964.

Phil 3120.30.95 — Beek, Martinus Adrianus. Martin Buber. Baarn, 1964.

Phil 3821.26 — Belen'kii, M.S. Spinoza. Moskva, 1964.

Phil 410.81 — Benardete, José A. Infinity. Oxford, 1964.

Phil 75.84 — Bendfeldt Rojas, Lourdes. Bibliografía filosófica de publicaciones de las Universidades de Costa Rica y San Carlos de Guatemala y de autores guatemalteos que exhibió la Biblioteca Nacional. Guatemala, 1964.

Phil 525.239 — Bendiscioli, Mario. Der Quietismus zwischen Häresie und Orthodoxie. Wiesbaden, 1964.

Phil 5520.410 — Bennett, J.F. Rationality. London, 1964.

Phil 6311.46 — Benoit, Hubert. Métaphysique et psychanalyse. 2. éd. Paris, 1964.

Phil 5627.264 — Berg, J.H. Psychologie en theologische antropologie. Nijkerk, 1964.

Phil 2477.19.30 — Berger, G. Phénoménologie du temps et prospective. Paris, 1964.

Phil 5068.18.10 — Bergmann, Gustav. Logic and reality. Madison, 1964.

Phil 3850.51 — Berning, V. Das Denken Herman Schells. Essen, 1964.

Phil 8402.61 — Bertheleny, J. Traité d'esthétique. Paris, 1964.

Phil 1540.85 — Bérubé, Camille. La connaissance de l'individuel au Moyen Âge. Montréal, 1964.

Phil 4210.194 — Beschin, G. La comunicazione delle persone nella filosofia. Milano, 1964.

Phil 2725.35.87 — Beschin, Giuseppe. Il tempo e la libertà in L. Lavelle. Milano, 1964.

Phil 3120.32.30 — Beth, Evert Willem. Door wetenschap tot wijsheid. Assen, 1964.

Phil 5648.22 — Betz, Dieter. Untersuchungen im haptischen Raum. Diss. Hamburg, 1964.

Phil 3425.595 — Beyer, W.R. Hegel-Bilder. Berlin, 1964.

Phil 8092.14 — Bianco, Giovanni A. Il rifiuto del mondo nell'arte comtemporanea. Bari, 1964.

Phil 5041.90 — Bierman, Arthur Kalmer. Logic: a dialogue. San Francisco, 1964.

Phil 310.583 — Biriukov, B.V. Dialekticheskii materializm. Moskva, 1964.

Phil 3805.221 — Birkner, Hans J. Schleiermachers christliche Sittenlehre, im Zusammenhang seines philosophisch-theologischen Systems. Berlin, 1964.

Phil 5350.5A — Birren, James E. The psychology of aging. Englewood Cliffs, N.J., 1964.

Phil 5590.438 — Bischof, Ledford J. Interpreting personality theories. N.Y., 1964.

Phil 3925.16.110 — Black, Max. A companion to Wittgenstein's Tractatus. Ithaca, 1964.

Phil 4710.110.5 — Blakeley, Thomas J. Soviet philosophy; a general introduction to contemporary Soviet thought. Dordrecht, 1964.

Phil 4710.110.10 — Blakeley, Thomas J. Soviet theory of knowledge. Dordrecht, 1964.

Phil 3450.19.375 — Bock, Irmgard. Heideggers Sprachdenken. München, 1964.

Phil 978.105 — Bockemnehl, Jochen. Naturwissensehaftliche Grundfragen. Dornach, 1964.

Phil 8870.29 — Boeckle, Franz. Moral zwischen Anspruch und Verantwortung. Düsseldorf, 1964.

Phil 978.94 — Boernsen, Hans. Naturwissenschaft an der Schwelle. Stuttgart, 1964.

Phil 1801.11 — Bogomolov, A.S. Angle-amerikanskaia burzhuaznaia filosofiia epokhi imperializmo. Moskva, 1964.

Phil 2401.16 — Boguslavskii, Veniamin M. U istokov frantsuzskogo ateizma i materializma. Moskva, 1964.

Phil 2477.11.105 — Boirel, R. Brunschvicg; sa vie, son oeuvre avec un exposé de la philosophie. Paris, 1964.

Phil 8691.32 — Booth, E.P. Religion ponders science. 1. ed. N.Y., 1964.

Phil 2880.8.200 — Borrello, Oreste. Studi su Sartre. Bologna, 1964.

Chronological Listing

Phil 4080.3.445   Borsari, Silvano. L'opera di Benedetto Croce. Napoli, 1964.

Phil 5751.19   Bourke, Vernon. Will in Western thought. N.Y., 1964.

Phil 5520.499   Brandt, Elmar. Der theoretische Bedeutungbegriff. Inaug. Diss. München, 1964.

Phil 2905.1.290   Braybrook, N. Teilhard de Chardin. N.Y., 1964.

Phil 1845.3.105   Brettschneider, B.D. The philosophy of Samuel Alexander. N.Y., 1964.

Phil 8581.109   British Broadcasting Corporation. Religion and humanism. London, 1964.

Phil 6060.60   Broeren, Wilhelm. Über die Zuverlässigkeit der Beschreibung von Sprechstimme und Handschrift. Inaug. Diss. n.p., 1964.

Phil 8581.108   Broglie, Guy de. Les signes de crédibilité de la révélation chrétienne. Paris, 1964.

Phil 2050.262   Broiles, R. David. The moral philosophy of David Hume. The Hague, 1964.

Phil 585.161   Browning, Douglas. Act and agent. Coral Gables, Fla., 1964.

Phil 2477.89.30   Bruaire, Claude. L'affirmation de Dieu. Paris, 1964.

Phil 3425.606   Bruaire, Claude. Logique et religion chrétienne dans la philosophie de Hegel. Paris, 1964.

Phil 3246.303   Brueggen, Michael. Der Gang des Denkens in der Philosophie Johann Gottlieb Fichtes. München, 1964.

Phil 1106.19   Brumbaugh, Robert S. The philosophers of Greece. N.Y., 1964.

Phil 2150.18.85   Brunius, Teddy. G.E. Moore's analyses of beauty. Uppsala, 1964[1965].

Phil 4065.50.12   Bruno, Giordano. Cause, principle, and unity. N.Y., 1964.

Phil 4065.45.5   Bruno, Giordano. The expulsion of the triumphant beast. New Brunswick, 1964.

Phil 5500.7.3   Brunschvicg, Léon. La modalité du jugement. 3.éd. Paris, 1964.

Phil 8581.98.5   Brunschvicg, Léon. La raison et la religion. Paris, 1964.

Phil 165.343   Bunge, M. The critical approach to sciences and philosophy. N.Y., 1964.

Phil 8581.45.20   Buonaiuti, Ernesto. Pellegrino di Roma. Bari, 1964.

Phil 2250.112   Buranelli, V. Josiah Royce. N.Y., 1964.

Phil 6311.22.5   Burrow, T. Preconcious foundations of human experience. N.Y., 1964.

Phil 5535.2   Bush, Robert Ray. Stochastic models for learning. N.Y., 1964.

Phil 5649.36   Buytendijk, Frederik Jacobus Johannes. Algemene theorie der menselijke houding en beweging als verbinding en tegenstelling van de fysiologische en de psychologische beschouwig. 3. Druk. Utrecht, 1964.

Phil 5190.41   Cackowski, Zdzisław. Problemy i pseudoproblemy. Warszawa, 1964.

Phil 5400.166   Callwood, J. Love, hate, fear, anger and the other lively emotions. Garden City, 1964.

Phil 4073.67   Campanella, Tommaso. Cosmologia, inediti; theologicorum liber III. Roma, 1964.

Phil 333.21   Canfield, J.V. Readings in the theory of knowledge. N.Y., 1964.

Phil 585.174   Cantoni, Remo. Società e cultura. Milano, 1964.

Phil 4080.3.440   Capanna, Francesco. La religione in Benedetto Croce. Bari, 1964.

Phil 9513.25   Carbonara, Cleto. L'esperienza e la prassi. Napoli, 1964.

Phil 1695.48   Cardiel Reyes, Raul. Los filósofos modernos en la independencia latino-americana. 1. ed. México, 1964.

Phil 2905.1.300   Carles, Jules. Teilhard de Chardin. Paris, 1964.

Phil 1900.96   Carlsson, P.A. Butler's ethics. The Hague, 1964.

Phil 5520.121.2   Carnap, Rudolf. Meaning and necessity. Chicago, 1964.

Phil 6312.28   Carp, Eugène Antoine Desiré Émile. De dubbelganger. Utrecht, 1964.

Phil 5520.423   Carroll, John B. Language and thought. Englewood Cliffs, N.J., 1964.

Phil 5421.20.25   Carthy, John D. The natural history of aggression. London, 1964.

Phil 6312.20.5   Caruso, Igor A. Existential psychology. N.Y., 1964.

Phil 510.156   Carvalho, Rubens di Souza. Filosofia universitária. Rio de Janeiro, 1964.

Phil 8877.91   Casamayor, Louis. La justice, l'homme et la liberté. Paris, 1964.

Phil 2050.260   Castignone, Silvana. Giustizia e bene comune in David Hume. Milano, 1964.

Phil 5242.46.5   Cattell, R.B. Personality and social psychology. San Diego, 1964.

Phil 7069.64.35   Cayce, Hugh Lynn. Venture inward. N.Y., 1964.

Phil 177.138   Ceccato, Silvio. Un tecnico fra i filosofi. Padova, 1964-2v.

Phil 310.602   Černík, Václav. Dialektický vedecký zákon. Bratislava, 1964.

Phil 3425.603.1   Chapelle, A. Hegel et la religion. Paris, 1964. 2v.

Phil 3425.603   Chapelle, A. Hegel et la religion. Paris, 1964.

Phil 5520.555   Chappell, Vere Claiborne. Ordinary language; essays in philosophical method. Englewood Cliffs, N.J., 1964.

Phil 2905.1.96   Chauchard, Paul. Teilhard de Chardin. Paris, 1964?

Phil 8403.39.5   Chaudhury, P.J. Studies in aesthetics. Calcutta, 1964.

Phil 310.555   Chesnokov, Dimitrii I. Istoricheskii materializm. Moskva, 1964.

Phil 9450.59   Chiavacci, Enrico. Etica politica. Roma, 1964.

Phil 5520.412   Christian, W.A. Meaning and truth in religion. Princeton, 1964.

Phil 3552.449   Cione, Edmondo. Leibniz. Napoli, 1964.

Phil 2515.10.15   Cioran, Emile M. La chute dans le temps. Paris, 1964.

Phil 3450.11.322   Claesges, Ulrich. Edmund Husserls Theorie der Raumkonstitution. Den Haag, 1964.

Phil 1135.183   Cogniot, Georges. Le materialisme gréco-romain. Paris, 1964.

Phil 5500.35   Cohen, J. Behavior in uncertainty and its social implications. London, 1964.

Phil 5238.200   Cohen, J. Readings in psychology. London, 1964.

Phil 5643.170   Cohen, Ronald L. Problems in motion perception. Uppsala, 1964.

Phil 5350.6   Coleman, James Samuel. Models of change and response uncertainty. Englewood Cliffs, N.J., 1964.

Phil 1930.8.88A   Collingwood, Robin George. An autobiography. London, 1964.

Phil 283.14.5   Collingwood, Robin George. The idea of nature. Oxford, 1964.

Phil 3450.19.365   Colombo, Arrigo. Martin Heidegger. Bologna, 1964.

Phil 5520.415   Conference on Paralinguistics and Kinesics. Approaches to semiotics. The Hague, 1964.

Phil 720.72   Congrès des Sociétés de Philosophie de Langue Française, 12th, Brussels et Louvain, 1964. La vérité. Louvain, 1964-65. 2v.

Phil 6952.7.5   Conolly, John. An inquiry concerning the indications of insanity. London, 1964.

Phil 5242.65   Construction of a simulation process for initial psychiatric interviewing. Santa Monica, 1964.

Phil 1020.48   Corbin, H. Histoire de la philosophie islamique. Paris, 1964.

Phil 2905.1.360   Corvez, Maurice. De la science à la foi. Tours, 1964.

Phil 6045.19   Corvi, Andreas. Ein schönes Büchlin der kunst Chiromantia dess Wolgelrten Magistri Andree Corvi von Mivandula. Strassburg, 1964.

Phil 1802.8   Cragg, G.R. Reason and authority in the 18th century. Cambridge, Eng., 1964.

Phil 8610.964.5   Crekshut, A.O.J. The unbelievers. London, 1964.

Phil 2475.1.410   Cresson, André. Bergson: sa vie, son oeuvre, avec un exposé de sa philosophie. Paris, 1964.

Phil 4260.85.8   Croce, B. The philosophy of Giambattista Vico. N.Y., 1964.

Phil 3160.6.30   Crusius, Christian August. Die philosophischen Hauptwerke. v.1-3. Hildesheim, 1964- 3v.

Phil 4960.605.5   Cruz Costa, João. A history of ideas in Brazil. Berkeley, 1964.

Phil 6953.19   Dain, Norman. Concepts of insanity in the United States, 1789-1865. New Brunswick, N.J., 1964.

Phil 8583.44   Dallago, Carl. Der Begriff des Absoluten. Innsbruck, 1964.

Phil 6313.23   David, H.P. International resources in clinical psychology. N.Y., 1964.

Phil 165.345   Davies, H.S. The English mind. Cambridge, Eng., 1964.

Phil 5400.170   Davitz, Joel Robert. The communication of emotional meaning. N.Y., 1964.

Phil 4752.2.140   Davy, M.M. Nicolas Berdiaev, l'homme du huitième jour. Paris, 1964.

Phil 75.77   Dawe, Harold G.A. Philosophy in South Africa, 1950-1962. Cape Town, 1964.

Phil 1730.14   DeAngelis, Eurico. Il metodo geometrico nella filosofia del Seicento. Pisa, 1964.

Phil 193.134.15   Déchet, Ferruccio. L'itinerario filosofico di Leone Sestov. Milano, 1964.

Phil 2905.1.415   Decoux, René. L'énergie dans la cosmogenèse de Pierre Teilhard de Chardin. Cran-Annecy, 1964?

Phil 1750.810   DeFeo, Nicola Massimo. Kierkegaard, Nietzsche, Heidegger. Milano, 1964.

Phil 2403.10   Deledalle, Gérard. Les philosophes français d'aujourd'hui par eux-mêmes. Paris, 1964?

Phil 165.360   Delius, Harald. Argumentationen. Göttingen, 1964.

Phil 5585.205.5   Dember, William Norton. Visual perception: the nineteenth century. N.Y., 1964.

Phil 2520.32.15   Descartes, René. Oeuvres. v.1,2,6,8 (pt.1-2), 9 (pt.1-2), 10-11. Paris, 1964. 11v.

Phil 178.69.5   Deschoux, M. Itinéraire philosophique. Paris, 1964-1971. 5v.

Phil 1135.179   Des Places, E. Syngeneia. Paris, 1964.

Phil 1955.6.200   Dewey, John. John Dewey and Arthur F. Bentley. New Brunswick, 1964.

Phil 310.780   Das dialektische Gesetz. 1. vyd. Bratislava, 1964.

Phil 4003.6   Il dialogo prospettive filosofiche. Bologna, 1964.

Phil 5548.104   Dichter, E. Handbook of consumer motivations. N.Y., 1964.

Phil 1703.17   Dictionnaire des idées contemporaines. Paris, 1964.

Phil 623.45   Dictionnaire rationaliste. Paris, 1964.

Phil 6327.28.85   Dijkhuis, Johannes Josephus. De procestheorie van C.R. Rogers. Hilversum, 1964.

Phil 178.76   Dilley, Frank B. Metaphysics and religious language. N.Y., 1964.

Phil 178.75   Doeblin, Alfred. Unser Dasein. Olten, 1964.

Phil 5275.7   Domin, Georg. Psychologie, philosophie, Menschenbild. Halle, 1964.

Phil 5352.16   Downs, A. The value of unchosen alternatives. Santa Monica, 1964.

Phil 165.374   Dr. S. Radhakrishnan souvenir volume. Moradabad, 1964.

Phil 5627.134.90   Driberg, Tom. The mystery of moral re-armament. N.Y., 1964.

Phil 5425.1.3   Duff, W. An essay on original genius. Gainesville, Fla., 1964.

Phil 8658.17.3   Duméry, Henry. The problem of God in philosophy of religion. Evanston, Ill., 1964.

Phil 803.17   Dunham, B. Heroes and heretics. 1st ed. N.Y., 1964.

Phil 9558.27   DuPuy de Clinchamps, Philippe. Le snobisme. Paris, 1964.

Phil 672.236   Durandeaux, Jacques. L'éternité dans la vie quotidienne. Paris, 1964.

Phil 5545.5.9   Ebbinghaus, H. Memory. N.Y., 1964.

Phil 3450.19.315   Echauri, Raúl. El ser en la filosofía de Heidegger. Rosario, 1964.

Phil 5590.444   Edelweiss, Malomar Lund. Personalisation. Wien, 1964.

Phil 5244.25.5   Edwards, Allen L. Statistical methods for the behavioral sciences. N.Y., 1964.

Phil 179.40   Einführung in die Philosophie. Greifswald, 1964. 2v.

Phil 8610.964   Ekmalian, A. Agnostitsizm i problema znaniia i very v burzhuaznoi filosofii. Erevan, 1964.

Phil 1885.94.2   Eliot, T.S. Knowledge and experience in the philosophy of F.H. Bradley. London, 1964.

Phil 1885.94   Eliot, T.S. Knowledge and experience in the philosophy of F.H. Bradley. N.Y., 1964.

Phil 2138.148   Ellery, J.B. John Stuart Mill. N.Y., 1964.

Phil 525.131   Eranos-Jahrbuch. Man and transformation. N.Y., 1964.

Phil 3425.624   Erdei, László. Der Anfang der Erkenntnis. Kritische Analyse des ersten Kapitels der Hegelschen Logik. Budapest, 1964.

Phil 6314.12   Erikson, Eric H. Insight and responsibility. N.Y., 1964.

Phil 3004.6   Esliu, Emilio. De la vida a la existencia en la filosofía contemporanea. La Plata, 1964.

Phil 5214.2   Esper, E.A. A history of psychology. Philadelphia, 1964.

Phil 1750.166.101   Etcheverry, A. Le conflit actuel des humanismes. Roma, 1964.

Phil 6319.1.230   Evans, Richard Isadore. Conversation with Carl Jung and reactions from Ernest Jones. Princeton, 1964.

Phil 8660.21   Fabro, Conelio. Introduzione all'ateismo moderno. Roma, 1964.

Phil 5460.14   Faure, Henri. Hallucinations et réalité. Paris, 1964.

Phil 3925.16.105   Favrholdt, D. An interpretation and critique of Wittgenstein's Tractatus. Copenhagen, 1964.

Phil 9245.116   Fernández, Julio F. Proyecciones espirituales del sufrimiento radiografia del dolor. San Salvador, 1964.

Phil 6315.56   Fernandez, M. The horizons of the mind. N.Y., 1964.

1964 - cont.

Phil 5500.31   Festinger, L. Conflict, decision and dissonance. Stanford, 1964.

Phil 3235.74   Feuerbach, Ludwig. Sämmtliche Werke. v.1-13. Stuttgart, 1964. 12v.

Phil 3850.18.180   Filippone, Vincenzo. Societá e cultura nel pensiero di Max Scheler. Milano, 1964. 2v.

Phil 4235.9.80   Fiorensoli, Dario. Il pensiero filosofico di Guiseppe Tarozzi. Padova, 1964.

Phil 4073.113   Firpo, Luigi. L'iconografia di Tommaso Campanella. Firenze, 1964.

Phil 3270.17.30   Flam, Leopold. Denken en existeren. Amsterdam, 1964.

VPhil 5015.5   Flam, Leopold. De geschiedenis van de dialektiek. St. Niklaas, 1964.

VPhil 8660.22   Flam, Leopold. Geschiedenis van het atheisme. 1. uitg. Brussel, 1964. 4v.

Phil 805.15   Flam, Leopold. L'homme et la conscience tragique. Bruxelles, 1964.

Phil 665.95   Flew, Antony. Body, mind and death. N.Y., 1964.

Phil 5215.2.10   Flügel, J.C. A hundred years of psychology, 1833-1933. London, 1964.

Phil 5215.2.12   Flügel, J.C. A hundred years of psychology, 1833-1933. N.Y., 1964.

Phil 5520.420   Fodor, J.A. The structure of language. Englewood Cliffs, N.J., 1964.

Phil 7069.64.15   Fornell, Earl W. The unhappy medium. Austin, 1964.

Phil 5627.264.25   Fortmann, Henricus Martinus Maria. Als zienda onzienlijke. v.1-3. Hilversum, 1964- 4v.

Phil 5045.18   Fougeyrollas, Pierre. Contradiction et totalité. Paris, 1964.

Phil 1750.220.13   Foulquié, Paul. L'existentialisme. 13e éd. Paris, 1964.

Phil 4080.3.460   Franchini, Raffaello. Croce interprete di Hegel e altri saggi filosofici. Napoli, 1964.

Phil 4756.1.41   Frank, Semen L. Dusha cheloveka. Izd.2. Paris, 1964.

Phil 4756.1.46   Frank, Semen L. S nami Bog; tri razmyshleniia. Paris, 1964.

Phil 6980.305   Frankenstein, C. Persönlichkeitswandel. München, 1964.

Phil 525.249   Fremantle, Anne Jackson. The Protestant mystics. 1st ed. Boston, 1964.

Phil 7082.184   French, Thomas Morton. Dream interpretation, a new approach. N.Y., 1964.

Phil 6315.2.22   Freud, Sigmund. New introductory lectures on psycho-analysis. N.Y., 1964.

Phil 6315.2.57.1   Freud, Sigmund. Psychoanalysis and faith. N.Y., 1964.

Phil 5465.145   Fried, Edrita. Artistic productivity and mental health. Springfield, Ill., 1964.

Phil 165.375   Friedman, Maurice Stanley. The worlds of existentialism. N.Y., 1964.

Phil 3850.27.240   Friends of Albert Schweitzer. A tribute on the ninetieth birthday of Albert Schweitzer. Boston, 1964.

Phil 8660.25   Frontistès, Mario. Il est un Dieu. Padova, 1964.

Phil 8661.25   Gaboriau, Florent. Dieu dans le débat des hommes. Paris, 1964.

Phil 8407.40   Gacher, Dmitrii I. Studii, statii, pisma i spomeni. Sofiia, 1964.

Phil 337.24   Gallagher, K.T. The philosophy of knowledge. N.Y., 1964.

Phil 181.128.5   Garcia Bacca, J.D. Introduccion literaria a la filosofia. 2. ed. Caracas, 1964.

Phil 6980.319   Gebsattel, V.E.F. von. Imago Hominis. Schweinfurt, 1964.

Phil 8050.90   Gehrig, Hans. Wesen und Bestand ästhetischer Bildung in Geschichte und Begenwart. Zürich, 1964.

Phil 8661.22   Gent, Werner. Untersuchungen zum Problem des Atheismus. Hildesheim, 1964.

Phil 365.60   George, Nicolas. D'Einstein à Teilhard. Paris, 1964.

Phil 165.347   Gerner-Beuerle, M. Schäpferisches Leben. München, 1964.

Phil 181.134   Giacon, Carlo. Interiorita e metafisica. Bologna, 1964.

Phil 705.52   Giannini, Giorgio. La tematica della trascendenza. Roma, 1964.

Phil 7150.55   Gibbs, J.P. Status integration and suicide. Eugene, Oreg., 1964.

Phil 8407.41   Gilson, Étienne. Matiéres et formes. Paris, 1964.

Phil 9530.56   Ginzberg, Eli. Talent and performance. N.Y., 1964.

Phil 4080.17.20   Giornate di Studi Carabellesiani, Bologna, 1960. Giornate di studi carabellesiani. Genoa, 1964.

Phil 4688.110.34   Girnius, Juozas. Zmogus de Dievo. Chicago? 1964.

Phil 525.236   Gobry, Ivan. L'expérience mystique. Paris, 1964.

Phil 337.23   Goidukov, I.G. Rot' praktiki v protsesse poznaniia. Moskva, 1964.

Phil 8661.21   Goldstein, Walter Benjamin. Glaube oder Unglaube. Jerusalem, 1964.

Phil 672.220   Gonseth, F. Le problème du temps. Neuchâtel, 1964.

Phil 806.38   Gonzalez Alvarez, Angel. Manual de historia de la filosofia. 3. ed. Madrid, 1964.

Phil 1845.11.10   Gozzelino, Giorgio M. La filosofia di Alfred Jules Ayer. Zürich, 1964.

Phil 5625.75.100   Gray, Jeffrey Alan. Pavlov's typology. N.Y., 1964.

Phil 3925.16.100   Griffin, J.P. Wittgenstein's logical atomism. Oxford, 1964.

Phil 6316.8.20   Groddeck, Georg. Psychoanalytische Schriften zur Literatur und Kunst. Wiesbaden, 1964.

Phil 5520.424   Grodziński, Eugeniusz. Znaczenie słowa w języku naturalnym. Warszawa, 1964.

Phil 9530.60.2   Grossmann, Gustav. Meine Daktor-Dissertation...die Revolution der Begabten. 2. Aufl. München, 1964.

Phil 8956.12   Guitton, Jean. Rapport de Jean Guitton sur les prix de vertu. Paris, 1964.

Phil 310.605   Guntau, Martin. Naturforschung und Weltbild. Berlin, 1964.

Phil 310.582   Gurvich, S.S. Voprosy dialektich materializma; k lektsiiam. Kiev, 1964.

Phil 1750.70.5   Gurwitsch, Aron. The field of consciousness. Pittsburgh, 1964.

Phil 3826.8.2   Guzzo, Augusto. Il pensiero di B. Spinoza. 2. ed. Torino, 1964.

Phil 2225.5.110   Haas, W.P. The conception of law. Fribourg, 1964.

Phil 8697.25   Habgood, J.S. Religion and science. London, 1964.

Phil 8587.76   Haegerstroem, Axel. Philosophy and religion. London, 1964.

Phil 8957.13.10   Haering, Bernhard. Die Gegenwärtige Heilsstunde. Freiburg, 1964.

Phil 8408.38   Halder, A. Kunst und Kult. Freiburg, 1964.

Phil 2055.16.30   Hall, E.W. Categorical analysis. Chapel Hill, 1964.

Phil 5238.203   Harper, Robert J.C. The cognitive processes. Englewood Cliffs, N.J., 1964.

Phil 5871.30   Harris, Irving D. The promised seed; a comparative study of eminent first and later sons. N.Y., 1964.

Phil 6317.26.9   Hartmann, Heinz. Essays on ego psychology. London, 1964.

1964 - cont.

Phil 6317.26.10   Hartmann, Heinz. Essays on ego psychology. N.Y., 1964.

Phil 630.58   Hartnach, Justice. Den ydre verdens eksistens. København, 1964.

Phil 5203.11.22A   Harvard University. The Harvard list of books in psychology. 3. ed. Cambridge, 1964.

Phil 8882.88   Hazlitt, H. The foundations of morality. Princeton, N.J., 1964.

Phil 5247.78   Heard, G. The five ages of man. N.Y., 1964[1963]

Phil 5217.7   Hearnshaw, L.S. A short history of British psychology, 1840-1940. London, 1964.

Phil 5402.27   Heath, R.G. The role of pleasure in behavior. N.Y., 1964.

Phil 3425.611   Hegel, G.W. Propédeutique philosophique. Génève, 1964.

Phil 3425.73.4   Hegel, Georg Wilhelm Friedrich. Einleitung in die Phänomenologie des Geistes. Frankfurt, 1964.

Phil 3425.29.20   Hegel, Georg Wilhelm Friedrich. Hegel's political writings. Oxford, 1964.

Phil 3007.16   Heise, Wolfgang. Aufbruch in die Illusion. 1. Aufl. Berlin, 1964.

Phil 6317.34.5   Heiss, Robert. Allgemeine Tiefenpsychologie. Bern, 1964.

Phil 3640.699   Heller, E. Nietzsche. Frankfurt am Main, 1964.

Phil 3625.3.100   Heller, K. Ernst Mach. Wien, 1964.

Phil 6319.1.221   Helsdingen, R.J. van. Jung. Den Haag, 1964.

Phil 5421.25.10   Helwig, Paul. Liebe und Feindschaft. München, 1964.

Phil 3450.12.100   Hemsterhuis, F. Lettre sur l'homme et ses rapports. New Haven, 1964.

Phil 7150.57   Hendin, H. Suicide and Scandinavia. N.Y., 1964.

Phil 5643.11.10   Hering, E. Outline of a theory of the light sense. Cambridge, 1964.

Phil 6315.2.85   Hermann, István. Sigmund Freud. Budapest, 1964.

Phil 182.104.2   Hersch, J. L'illusion philosophique. Paris, 1964.

Phil 7069.64.5   Heywood, R. ESP: a personal memoir. 1. ed. N.Y., 1964.

Phil 5627.264.10   Hick, John. Faith and the philosophers. N.Y., 1964.

Phil 3585.14.20   Hieronimus, E. Theodor Lessing. Hannover, 1964.

Phil 5066.235   Hilton, Alice Mary. Logic, computing machines, and automation. Cleveland, 1964.

Phil 4802.6   Hinz, Henryk. Polska mysl filosoficzna. Warszawa, 1964.

Phil 165.395   L'histoire de la philosophie; ses problèmes, ses méthodes. Paris, 1964.

Phil 5585.229   Hochberg, Julian E. Perception. Englewood Cliffs, N.J., 1964.

Phil 5525.64.10   Holm, Søren. Humor; en aesthetisk studie. København, 1964.

Phil 5247.80   Holzkamp, Klaus. Theorie und Experiment in der Psychologie. Berlin, 1964.

Phil 6117.45.50   Homaday, William H.D. The inner light. N.Y., 1964.

Phil 2045.134   Hood, F.C. The divine politics of Thomas Hobbes. Oxford, 1964.

Phil 310.610   Horbach, U.I. O vidakh protivorechii. Minsk, 1964.

Phil 2880.8.145   Houbart, Jacques. Un père déuaturé. Paris, 1964.

Phil 2805.435   Hoven, Pieter van der. Blaise Pascal. Baarn, 1964.

Phil 5627.134.54   Howard, Peter. Design for dedication. Chicago, 1964.

Phil 5217.6   Hoyos, C.G. Denkschrift zur Lage der Psychologie. Wiesbaden, 1964.

Phil 3827.15   Hubbeling, H.G. Spinoza's methodology. Assen, 1964.

Phil 3450.11.330   Huelsmann, H. Zur Theorie der Sprache bei E. Husserl. München, 1964.

Phil 2050.67.10   Hume, David. Dialogues sur la religion naturelle. Paris, 1964.

Phil 2050.59.3   Hume, David. A treatise of human nature. Oxford, 1964.

Phil 2150.18.95   Hund, William Byrne. The theory of goodness in the writings of George Edward Moore, 1873-1958. Notre Dame, Ind., 1964.

Phil 5247.81   Hunt, Morton M. The thinking animal. Boston, 1964.

Phil 3450.11.50   Husserl, Edmund. The idea of phenomenology. The Hague, 1964.

Phil 3450.11.75   Husserl, Edmund. The Paris lectures. The Hague, 1964.

Phil 3450.11.35   Husserl, Edmund. The phenomenology of internal time-consciousness. Bloomington, 1964.

Phil 8587.60.7   Huxley, Aldous. The perennial philosophy. N.Y., 1964.

Phil 5247.79   Hyman, R. The nature of psychological inquiry. Englewood Cliffs, N.J., 1964.

Phil 2655.6.30   Hyppolite, J. Leçon inaugurale faite le jeudi 19 déc. 1963. Nougent-le-Rotrou, 1964.

Phil 8409.3   Iastrebova, Nataliia. Konflikti v estetichnogo. Sofiia, 1964.

Phil 3450.19.330   Ijsseling, Samuel. Heidegger. Antwerpen, 1964.

Phil 4803.462.35   Ingarden, Roman. Der Streit um die Existenz der Welt. v.1-2. Tübingen, 1964-65. 3v.

Phil 585.166   International Congress of Philosophy, 13th, Mexico, 1963. Delegation from the USSR. Chelovek i epokha. Moskva, 1964.

Phil 6118.9   Isaacson, R.L. Basic readings in neuropsychology. N.Y., 1964.

Phil 3450.11.415   Janssen, Paul. Geschichte und Lebenswelt. Inaug. Diss. Köln, 1964.

Phil 3780.91   Japtok, E. Karl Rosenkranz als Literaturkritiker. Freiburg, 1964.

Phil 4961.116   Jaramillo Uribe, Jaime. El pensamiento colombiano en el siglo XIX. Bogotá, 1964.

Phil 6959.4.25   Jaspers, K. The nature of psychotherapy. Manchester, 1964.

Phil 3475.3.20   Jaspers, Karl. Three essays. 1st ed. N.Y., 1964.

Phil 3829.1.10   Joachim, H.H. A study of the Ethics of Spinoza. N.Y., 1964.

Phil 9070.106   Jørgensen, T.G. Livsforståelse moralloven livets ophør. København, 1964.

Phil 525.235   Johnson, R.C. The light and the gate. London, 1964.

Phil 5049.16.1   Johnson, William Ernest. Logic. N.Y., 1964. 3v.

Phil 5643.124   Jolansky, Samuel. Optical illusion. N.Y., 1964.

Phil 6319.2.5.7   Jones, Ernest. Essays in applied psycho-analysis. N.Y., 1964. 2v.

Phil 340.9   Jones, P. Chopin. The nature of knowledge. N.Y., 1964.

Phil 5500.32   Jones, William. On decision-making in large organizations. Santa Monica, 1964.

Phil 5325.40F   Jordan, Nehemiah. The theory of cognitive dissonance. Washington, 1964.

Phil 7069.64   Juegensen, F. Rosterna från rymden. Stockholm, 1964.

Phil 5203.27   Jugoslovenska psihološka bibliografija, period od 1952-1964 god. Beograd, 1964.

Phil 3491.12   Julia, Didier. La question de l'homne et la fondement de la philosophie. Aubier, 1964.

Phil 5780.24   Julius, Fritz Hendrik. Tierkreis. v.1-2. Freiburg, 1964-

Phil 6319.1.71A   Jung, C.G. Man and his symbols. London, 1964.

Phil 8589.20.3   Jung, Carl Gustav. Answer to Job. Cleveland, 1964.

VPhil 2520.390   Kalocsai, Dezso. Descartes etikája. Budapest, 1964.

Chronological Listing

Phil 5066.234   Kaluzhnin, Lev A. Chto takoe matematicheskala logika. Moskva, 1964.

Phil 5520.512   Kamrath, Gerhard. Vernunft und Sprache. Heidelberg, 1964.

Phil 3480.52.13A   Kant, Immanuel. The critique of judgement. Oxford, 1964.

Phil 3480.14.2   Kant, Immanuel. Gesammelte Schriften. Personenindex. v.A-L. Bonn, 1964- 6v.

Phil 5066.229   Karp, Carol R. Languages with expressions of infinite length. Amsterdam, 1964.

Phil 8590.33   Kasch, Wilhelm. Atheistischer Humanismus und christliche Existenz in der Gegenwart. Tübingen, 1964.

Phil 8411.36.2   Kassil', Lev A. "Delo vkusa". Izd. 2. Moskva, 1964.

Phil 5545.244   Katzenberger, Lothar Friedrich. Dimensionen des Gedächtnisses. Wurzburg, 1964.

Phil 3640.368.3   Kaufmann, Walter Arnold. Nietzsche: philosopher, psychologist, antichrist. Cleveland, 1964.

Phil 8430.55.2   Kayser, Hans. Akróasis, die Lehre von der Harmonik der Welt. 2. Aufl. Basel, 1964.

Phil 3450.11.350   Keekell, Lothar. Husserl, sa vie, son oeuvre. Paris, 1964.

Phil 5066.228   Keene, G.B. First-order functional calculus. London, 1964.

Phil 8885.46   Kemp, J. Reason, action and morality. London, 1964.

Phil 5592.181   Kempf, H.E. Der Bild-Test. Inaug. Diss. Marburg, 1964?

Phil 810.16   Kempski, Jürgen von. Brechungen. Reinbek, 1964.

Phil 3492.75   Kern, Iso. Husserl und Kant. Den Haag, 1964.

Phil 3450.19.285   King, M. Heidegger's philosophy. N.Y., 1964.

Phil 4809.486.20   Kiselimchev, Asen. Izbrani proizvedeniia. Sofiia, 1964.

Phil 3549.8.2   Klages, Ludwig. Sämtliche Werke. v.1,2,6-8. Bonn, 1964. 5v.

Phil 5710.22   Klibansky, R. Saturn and melancholy. London, 1964.

Phil 9495.164.5   Klomps, H. Ehemoral und Jansenismus. Köln, 1964.

Phil 7150.58   Kobler, Arthur. The end of hope. N.Y., 1964.

Phil 5465.137   Koestler, Arthur. The act of creation. London, 1964.

Phil 5620.32   Kolenda, K. The freedom of reason. San Antonio, 1964.

Phil 8980.495.10   Kommunizm i lichnost! Moskva, 1964.

Phil 70.98   Kongres Psihologa Jugolsavije, 2d, Zagerb, 1964. Materijali. Zagreb, 1964.

Phil 8960.15   Kongress der Deutschsprachigen Moraltheologen, Freiburg, Germany, 1963. Moraltheologie und Bibel. Paderborn, 1964.

Phil 5250.75   Kopnin, P.V. Problemy myshleniia v sovremennoi nauke. Moskva, 1964.

Phil 5520.96.15   Korzybski, Alfred. General semantics seminar, 1937. 2. ed. Lakeville, Conn., 1964.

Phil 310.585   Kosichev, A.D. Bor'ba marksizma-leninizma s ideologiei anarkhizma i sovremennost'. Moskva, 1964.

Phil 6159.10   Kreppel, Gisela Richters. Die psychischen Phänomene im Schwellenbereich des Meshalin. Inaug. Diss. Bonn, 1964.

Phil 8980.498.25   Krešić, Ljubinka. Etičko-humanisticki problemi socijalizma. Beograd, 1964.

Phil 705.50   Krings, Hermann. Transzendentale Logik. München, 1964.

Phil 4010.2   Kristeller, P.O. Eight philosophers of the Italian Renaissance. Stanford, 1964.

Phil 4110.1.89   Kristeller, Paul Oskar. The philosophy of Marsilio Ficino. Gloucester, Mass., 1964.

Phil 8060.8   Krueger, J. Asthetik der Antike. Berlin, 1964.

Phil 3425.605   Kudrna, J. Studie k Hegel om pojetí historie. Praha, 1964.

Phil 8411.33   Kupareo, Raimundo. Tratado de estetica. v.1- Santiago de Chile, 1964-

Phil 5050.24   Kutschera, Franz von. Die Antinomien der Logik. Freiburg, 1964.

Phil 5145.3   Kyburg, Henry E. Studies in subjective probability. N.Y., 1964.

Phil 6159.16.1   La Barre, Weston. The peyote cult. Hamden, 1964.

Phil 8430.47   Ladyhina, Aryadna B. Iskusstvo i sovremennost'. Minsk, 1964.

Phil 2725.14.100   Lagneau, Jules. Célèbres leçons et fragments. 2. éd. Paris, 1964.

Phil 2880.8.143   Laing, R.D. Reason and violence. London, 1964.

Phil 2280.5.140   Lamont, C. The enduring impact of G. Santayana. N.Y., 1964.

Phil 9530.55   Lamprecht, H. Erfolg und Gesellschaft. München, 1964.

Phil 5643.122   Lamy, P. Le mystere de la vision. Paris, 1964.

Phil 8412.38   L'Andelyn, Charles de. Esthétique. Neuchâtel, 1964.

Phil 2835.35   La Ramée, P. de. Dialectique (1555). Genève, 1964.

Phil 5620.31   Larrabee, H.A. Reliable knowledge. Boston, 1964.

Phil 4959.405   Láscaris Comneno, Constantino. Desarrollo de las ideas filosóficas en Costa Rica. Costa Rica, 1964.

Phil 5251.76   Lauer, Hans Erhard. Die Rätsel der Seele: Tiefenpsychologie und Anthroposophie. 2. Aufl. Freiburg, 1964.

Phil 5628.54.4   Lauer, Nikolaus. Barbara Pfister, eine pfälzische Stigmatisierte. 4. Aufl. Speyer, 1964.

Phil 1955.6.190   Lawson, D.E. John Dewey and the world view. Carbondale, 1964.

Phil 186.120.5   Lazerowitz, M. Studies in metaphilosophy. London, 1964.

Phil 6155.4.10   Leary, Timothy Francis. The psychedelic experience. New Hyde Park, 1964.

Phil 3925.11.70   Leenhouwen, Albuinus. Ungesichertheit und Wagnis. Essen, 1964.

Phil 811.17   Legowicz, J. Zarys historii filozofii. Warszawa, 1964.

Phil 6121.40   Leiderman, P.H. Psychological approaches to social behavior. N.Y., 1964.

Phil 310.595   Leningrad. Universitet. Rasprostranenie idei marksistskoi filosofii v Evrope. Leningrad, 1964.

Phil 5520.421   Lenneberg, E.H. New directions in the study of language. Cambridge, 1964.

Phil 2115.197   Leroy, A.L. Locke, sa vie. Paris, 1964.

Phil 5590.95.9   Lersch, Philipp. Aufbau der Person. 9. Aufl. München, 1964.

Phil 8865.372   Levi, Anthony. French moralists; the theory of the passions, 1585-1649. Oxford, 1964.

Phil 811.20   Levin-Goldschmidt, Hermann. Dialogik; Philosophie auf dem Boden der Neuzeit. Frankfurt, 1964.

Phil 6961.20   Levinson, Daniel Jacob. Patienthood in the mental hospital. Boston, 1964.

Phil 5251.65   Levitov, N.D. O psikhicheskikh sostoianiiakh cheloveka. Moskva, 1964.

Phil 5875.15   Lévy-Schoen, Ariane. L'image d'autrui chez l'enfant. Paris, 1964.

Phil 5875.20   Lévy-Schoen, Ariane. Sur le développe de la connaissance d'autrui. Thèse. Paris, 1964.

Phil 2150.18.90   Lewy, C. G.E. Moore on the naturalistic fallacy. London, 1964.

Phil 5520.425   Liebrucks, Bruno. Sprache und Bewusstsein. Frankfurt, 1964. 5v.

Phil 3493.35   Liedtke, Max. Der Begriff der reflektierenden Urteilskraft in Kants Kritik der reinen Vernunft. Hamburg, 1964.

Phil 5485.2   Lienert, Gustav Adolf. Belastung und Regression. Meisenheim am Glan, 1964.

Phil 3850.27.112   Lind, Emil. Die Universalmenschen Goethe und Schweitzer. Neustadt, 1964.

Phil 5548.50.2   Lindzey, Gardner. Assessment of human motives. N.Y., 1964.

Phil 8591.81   Lings, Martin. Ancient beliefs and modern superstitions. London, 1964.

Phil 600.58   Lins, Ivan Monteiro de Barros. História do positivismo no Brasil. São Paulo, 1964.

Phil 5251.66   Linschoten, Johannes. Idolen van de psycholoog. Utrecht, 1964.

Phil 2115.70.25   Locke, J. Lettre sur la tolérance. 1. éd. Montréal, 1964.

Phil 3850.27.220   Loennebo, M. Albert Schweitzers etisk-religiösa iderl. Stockholm, 1964.

Phil 3493.32   Löwisch, Dieter-Jürgen. Immanuel Kant und David Hume's, dialogues concerning natural religion. Bonn, 1964.

Phil 3011.8.2   Loewith, Karl. From Hegel to Nietzsche: the revolution in nineteenth century thought. 1st ed. N.Y., 1964.

Phil 342.18.2   Lonergan, Bernard J.F. Insight. N.Y., 1964.

Phil 5421.20.20   Lorenz, Konrad Zacharias. Das sogenannte Böse. 2. Aufl. Wien, 1964.

Phil 2905.1.180.5   Lubac, Henri de. La prière du père Teilhard de Chardin. Paris, 1964.

Phil 186.154   Lugarini, Leo. Filosofia e metafisica. Urbino, 1964.

Phil 8583.41.20   Luijk, Henk van. Philosophie du fait chrétien. Paris, 1964.

Phil 3585.20.15   Luijpen, Wilhelmus Antonius Maria. Phenomenology and atheism. Pittsburgh, 1964.

Phil 5051.28.5   Lukasiewicz, Jan. Elements of mathematical logic. 2nd ed. Oxford, 1964.

Phil 8182.2   Lukić, Sveta. Umetnost i kriterijumi. Beograd, 1964.

Phil 5545.250   al-Ma'ayirji, Muhammad Ismat. Die postmentalen Erregungen als struktureller Faktor beim Lernen. Thesis. St. Margrethen, 1964.

Phil 5548.5.5   McClelland, D.C. The roots of consciousness. Princeton, N.J., 1964.

Phil 1812.4.10   MacCunn, J. Six radical thinkers. N.Y., 1964.

Phil 6155.16   McGlothlin, William Herschel. Hallucinogenic drugs: a perspective with special reference to peyote and cannalis. Santa Monica, 1964.

Phil 5627.264.20   McLaughlin, Barry. Nature, grace and religious development. N.Y., 1964.

Phil 343.37F   MacLeod, Andries Hugo Donald. De psykiska företeelsernas förhallande till rum och tid. Stockholm, 1964.

Phil 3425.100.2.1   McTaggart, John McTaggart Ellis. Studies in the Hegelian . dialectic. 2. ed. N.Y., 1964.

Phil 2905.1.310   Magloire, G. Teilhard de Chardin. Paris, 1964.

Phil 1517.8   Maier, A. Ausgehedes Mittelalter. Roma, 1964. 2v.

Phil 5822.9.2   Maier, Norman Raymond Frederick. Principles of animal psychology. N.Y., 1964.

Phil 2750.20.135   Maier, Willi. Das Problem der Leiblichkeit bei Jean Paul Sartre und Maurice Merleau-Ponty. Tübingen, 1964.

Phil 735.250   Makiguchi, Tsunesaburo. Philosophy of value. Tokyo, 1964.

Phil 1750.560.20   Mancini, Italo. Filosofi esistenzialisti. Urbino, 1964.

Phil 5520.434   Mancini, Italo. Linguaggio e salvezza. Milano, 1964.

Phil 343.33   Mandelbaum, M.H. Philosophy, science, and sense perception. Baltimore, 1964.

Phil 5238.202   Mandler, J.M. Thinking. N.Y., 1964.

Phil 5052.43   Maneev, A.K. Predmet formal'noi logiki i dialektika. Minsk, 1964.

Phil 5871.20   Mannoni, Maud. L'enfant arriéré et sa mère. Paris, 1964.

Phil 8637.23   Manthey, Franz. Das Problem der Erlösung in den Religionen der Menschheit. Hildesheim, 1964.

Phil 2750.19.32   Marcel, Gabriel. Creative fidelity. N.Y., 1964.

Phil 1750.758   Marcel, Gabriel. La dignité humaine et ses assises existentielles. Paris, 1964.

Phil 6682.24   Marcuse, F.L. Hypnosis through the world. Springfield, Ill., 1964.

Phil 3625.21   Marcuse, L. Aus den Papieren eines bejahrten Philosophie-Studenten. München, 1964.

Phil 8887.121   Margenau, H. Ethics and science. Princeton, 1964.

Phil 4363.7.15   Marias Aguilera, Julián. El tiempo que ni vuelve ni tropieza. Barcelona, 1964.

Phil 530.20.110   Marienwerder, Johannes. Vita Dorotheae Montoviensis. Graz, 1964.

Phil 2750.11.64   Maritain, Jacques. Dieu et la permission du mal. Paris, 1964.

Phil 2750.11.148   Maritain, Jacques. Moral philosophy. N.Y., 1964.

Phil 6322.46   Marmorston, Jessie. Psychoanalysis and the human situation. 1st ed. N.Y., 1964.

Phil 310.587   Marsistsko-leninskaia filosofiia; uchebnoe posobie. Moskva, 1964.

Phil 5066.240   Martin, Roger. Logique contemporaine et formalisation. Paris, 1964.

Phil 3850.18.185   Martin-Izquierdo, Honorio. Das religiöse Apriori bei Max Scheler. Bonn, 1964.

Phil 343.32   Martin Scheerer Memorial Meetings on Cognitive Psychology. University of Kansas, 1962. Cognition: theory, research, promise. N.Y., 1964.

Phil 5722.71   Martins, D. Do inconsciente. Braga, 1964.

Phil 5585.228   Mashhour, M. Psychophysical relations in the perception of velocity. Stockholm, 1964.

Phil 1865.193   Maślinska, Halina. Bentham i jcgo system ctyczny. Warszawa, 1964.

Phil 5627.264.5   Maslow, Abraham Harold. Religions, values and peak-experiences. Columbus, Ohio, 1964.

Phil 8610.964.10   Mason, Gabriel Richard. What I believe. v.1-2. N.Y., 1964?

Phil 5252.81.2   Masserman, J.H. Behavior and neurosis. N.Y., 1964.

Phil 1135.181   Maw, Jürgen. Ionomia. Berlin, 1964.

Phil 2750.32.30   Mayer, Charles Leopold. L'homme face à son destin. Paris, 1964.

Phil 2045.137   Mayer-Tasch, Peter Cornelius. Thomas Hobbes und das Widerstandsrecht. Mainz? 1964.

Phil 2150.15.20   Mead, George Herbert. Selected writings. Indianapolis, 1964.

Phil 8980.564   Medynskii, Grigorii A. Trudnaia kniga. Moskva, 1964.

Phil 7150.63F   Meer, Fatima. Suicide in Durban. Durban, 1964.

Phil 4170.12.5   Mei, Flavio. La missione del filosofo. Milano, 1964.

Phil 5762.24   Melden, Abraham Irving. Free action. London, 1964.

Phil 2150.15.96   Meltzer, Bernard. The social psychology of George Herbert Mead. Kalamazoo, Michigan, 1964.

1964 - cont.

Phil 2750.20.35   Merleau-Ponty, Maurice. The primacy of perception. Evanston, 1964.

Phil 2750.20.24   Merleau-Ponty, Maurice. Sense and non-sense. Evanston, 1964.

Phil 2750.20.32   Merleau-Ponty, Maurice. Signs. Evanston, 1964.

Phil 2750.20.40A   Merleau-Ponty, Maurice. Le visible et l'invisible. Paris, 1964.

Phil 5710.21   Merlin, V.S. Ocherk teori temperamenta. Moskva, 1964.

Phil 5252.154   Merlin, Vol'f S. Tipologicheskie issledovaniia po psikhologii lichnosti i po psikhologii truda. Perm', 1964.

Phil 343.34   Mesthene, Emmanuel G. How language makes us know. The Hague, 1964.

Phil 5402.40   Metz, Willem. Het verschijnsel pijn. Proefschrift. Haarlem, 1964.

Phil 705.49   Metzger, Arnold. Dämonie und Transzendenz. Pfullingen, 1964.

Phil 5401.49   Mexico (City). Universidad Nacional. Facultad de Filosofía y Letras. La esencia del valor. México, 1964.

Phil 3450.19.355   Meyer, Hans. Martin Heidegger und Thomas von Aquin. München, 1964.

Phil 5252.153   Michotte, A.E. Les compléments amodaux des structures perceptives. Louvain, 1964.

Phil 5585.234   Mikhailov, Feliks T. Zagadka chelovecheskogo Ia. Moskva, 1964.

Phil 8980.572   Mikhalevich, Aleksandr Vl. Izmeniat'sia. Moskva, 1964.

Phil 1812.16   Mills, Charles W. Sociology and pragmatism. N.Y., 1964.

Phil 3450.18.175   Moeslang, Alois. Finalität. Freiburg, 1964.

Phil 3450.11.315   Mohanty, J.N. Edmund Husserl's theory of meaning. The Hague, 1964.

Phil 2050.267   Molinari, Ernesto. L'utopia controllata. Milano, 1964.

Phil 1117.16   Mondolfo, Rodolfo. Momenti del pensiero greco e cristiano. Napoli, 1964.

Phil 8887.110.10   Montefiore, Alan. A modern introduction to moral philosophy. London, 1964.

Phil 4957.15   Montevideo. Universidad. Facultad de Humanidades y Ciencias. Aportes a una bibliografía anotada de historía de las ideas en América. Montevideo, 1964.

Phil 2225.5.120A   Moore, Edward C. Studies in the philosophy of Charles Sanders Peirce. 2nd series. Amherst, 1964.

Phil 9540.12   Moore, Katharine. The spirit of tolerance. London, 1964.

Phil 8980.579   Moral'nyi rodeks stroitelia kommunizma. Moskva, 1964.

Phil 8170.8   Morawski, Stefan. Miedzy tradycja a wizja przyszłości. Warszawa, 1964.

Phil 5762.23   Moreau, J. Problèmes et pseudo-problèmes du déterminisme physique, biologique, psychologique. Paris, 1964.

Phil 8622.60   Morgan, E.K. The ordeal of wonder. London, 1964.

Phil 585.169   Morra, Gianfranco. La riscoperta del sacro. Bologna, 1964.

Phil 5520.417   Morric, C.W. Signification and significance. Cambridge, 1964.

Phil 310.591   Moscow. Institut Povyshennoi Kvalifikatsii Prepodovatelei Obshchestvennykh Nauk. Kafedra Dialekticheskogo i Istoricheskogo Materializma. Voprosy istoricheskogo materializma i nauchnogo kommunizma. Moskva, 1964.

Phil 2475.1.425   Mourélos, Giorgos. Bergson et les niveaux de réalité. Paris, 1964.

Phil 2750.11.175   Mrówczyński, Tadeusz. Personalizm Maritaina i współczesna myśl Katolicka. Warszawa, 1964.

Phil 8592.115   Muck, Otto. Christliche Philosophie. Kevelaer, 1964.

Phil 1750.107   Muck, Otto. Die transzendentale Methode in der scholastischen Philosophie der Gegenwart. Innsbruck, 1964.

Phil 2905.1.270   Mueller, Armin. Das naturphilosophische Werk Teilhard de Chardins. Freiburg, 1964.

Phil 1750.352.3   Müller, Max. Existenzphilosophie im geistigen Leben der Gegenwart. 3e Aufl. Heidelberg, 1964.

Phil 5627.264.15   Müller-Eckhard, Hans. Das Unzerstörbare. Stuttgart, 1964.

Phil 735.245   Mukerjee, Radhakamal. The dimensions of values. London, 1964.

Phil 5222.9   Muller, Philippe. La psychologie dans le monde moderne. Bruxelles, 1964.

Phil 5790.2.10   Munnichs, Jozef M.A. Ouderdom en eindigheid. Assen, 1964.

Phil 343.35   Murphy, Arthur Edward. The theory of practical reason. La Salle, Ill., 1964[1965]

Phil 8667.27   Murray, J.C. The problem of God. New Haven, 1964.

Phil 5585.255   Musatti, Cesare L. Condizioni dell'esperienza e fondazione della psicologia. Firenze, 1964.

Phil 310.604   Mužík, Josef. Subjekt a objekt. Praha, 1964.

Phil 585.310   Nabhani, Koribaa. Essai d'une détermination esthétique de l'humain. Thèse. Alger, 1964.

Phil 3552.446   Naert, Emilienne. La pensée politique de Leibniz. Paris, 1964.

Phil 4870.12   Naravane, Vishwanath S. Modern Indian thought; a philosophical survey. Bombay, 1964.

Phil 1020.47   Naso, S.H. An introduction to Islamic cosmological doctrines. Cambridge, 1964.

Phil 4959.210.5   Navarro, Bernabé. Cultura mexicana moderna en el siglo XVIII. 1. ed. México, 1964.

Phil 1158.40   Neck, Gisela. Das Problem der Zeit im Epikureismus. Inaug. Diss. Köln, 1964.

Phil 2490.173   Negt, Oskar. Strukturbeziehungen Zwischen den Gesellschafteslehren Comtes und Heges. Frankfurt a.M., 1964.

Phil 310.651   Nekotorye voprosy marksistsko-leninskoi filosofii. Khar'kov, 1964.

Phil 5365.2   Nesswetha, Wilhelm. Formen der Reaktion auf Konflikte. Diss. Bonn, 1964.

Phil 5590.435   Neugarten, B.L. Personality in middle and late life. N.Y., 1964.

Phil 5374.163.7   Neumann, E. The origins and history of consciousness. N.Y., 1964.

Phil 70.97   New York. Institute of Philosophy. Law and philosophy. N.Y., 1964.

Phil 3805.222   Niebuhr, Richard R. Schleiermacher on Christ and religion. N.Y., 1964.

Phil 3640.15.5   Nietzsche, Friedrich. Complete works. N.Y., 1964. 18v.

Phil 3640.17.12   Nietzsche, Friedrich. Sämtliche Werke. Stuttgart, 1964-65. 12v.

Phil 8668.8   Noce, Augusto del. Il problema dell'ateismo. 2. ed. Bologna, 1964.

Phil 5066.226   Novikov, P.S. Elements of mathematical logic. Edinburgh, 1964.

Phil 525.237   O'Brien, E. Varieties of mystic experience, an anthology and interpretation. 1st ed. N.Y., 1964.

Phil 814.6   O'Connor, Daniel J. A critical history of Western philosophy. N.Y., 1964.

1964 - cont.

Phil 2805.416   L'oeuvre scientifique de Pascal. Paris, 1964.

Phil 8889.9F   Ofstad, Harald. Innføring i moralfilosofi. Stockholm, 1964.

Phil 6805.10   Ohm, August. Persönlichkeitswandlung unter Freiheitsentzug. Berlin, 1964.

Phil 3834.3   Oko, Adolph S. The Spinoza bibliography. Boston, 1964.

Phil 3425.635   Oldrini, Guido. Gli Hegeliani di Napoli. Milano, 1964.

Phil 5520.419   Oleron, P. Les activités intellectuelles. Paris, 1964.

Phil 310.592   Omel'ianovskyi, M.E. Dialektika v naukakh o nezhivoi prirode. Moskva, 1964.

Phil 9070.110   Oraison, Marc. Une morale pour notre temps. Paris, 1964.

Phil 960.246   Organ, T.W. The self in Indian philosophy. London, 1964.

Phil 2905.1.335   Ormea, Ferdinando. Pierre Teilhard de Chardin. 2. ed. Torino, 1964.

Phil 1195.18   Osipova, Valentina. O prirode sofistiki. Erevan, 1964.

Phil 4190.2.30   Ottaviano, Carmelo. La tragicita del reale. Padova, 1964.

Phil 8595.33.5   Padovani, U.A. Cultura e critianesimo. Milano, 1964.

Phil 8595.57   Paggiaro, Luigi. L'esperienza religiosa. Padova, 1964.

Phil 8965.17.2   Palazzini, Pietro. Casus conscientiae. 2. ed. Torino, 1964. 2v.

Phil 100.5   Pallares, Eduardo. Diccionario de filosofía. 1. ed. México, 1964.

Phil 4845.227.40   Papanoutsos, Euangelos. Philosophika problemata. Athena, 1964.

Phil 672.222   Parsons, E. Time devoured. London, 1964.

Phil 575.246   Parsons, Talcott. Social structure and personality. N.Y., 1964.

Phil 2805.13   Pascal, Blaise. Oeuvres complètes. Bruges, 1964-

Phil 2805.32.28   Pascal, Blaise. Provinciales. Paris, 1964.

Phil 2805.412   Pascal. Barcelona, 1964.

Phil 5520.440   Pasquinelli, Alberto. Linguaggio, scienza e filosofia. 2. ed. Bologna, 1964.

Phil 346.28   Pasquinelli, Alberto. Nuevi principi di epistemología. Milano, 1964.

Phil 585.165   Patka, Frederick. Value and existence. N.Y., 1964.

Phil 296.15   Pavese, Roberto. Fisica e metafisica. Padova, 1964[1965]

Phil 5500.45   Pears, David Francis. Predicting and deciding. London, 1964.

Phil 1520.6   Pelzer, Auguste. Études d'histoire littéraire sur la scolastique médiévale. Louvain, 1964.

Phil 4822.6   Penev, Mikho. Za religiozno-idealisticheskata sŭshtnost na bŭlgarskata burzhoazno filosofiia. Sofiia, 1964.

Phil 3801.674   Pereyson, Luigi. L'estetica di Schelling. Torino, 1964.

Phil 8705.20   Perlman, Robert Odehyah. Science and religion for modern man. Jerusalem, 1964.

Phil 4757.2.110   Peters, Arthur A. Boyhood with Gurdjieff. N.Y., 1964.

Phil 3450.11.360   Petersen, Uwe. Das Verhältnis von Theorie und Praxis...Husserls. Heidelburg, 1964.

Phil 1750.166.155   Petrosian, M.J. Gumanizm; opyt filosofskoetich i potsial issled problemy. Moskva, 1964.

Phil 1715.13   Petrović, Gajo. Od Lockea do Ayera. Beograd, 1964.

Phil 8416.16.2   Petruzzellis, N. Filosofia dell'arte. 3. ed. Napoli, 1964.

Phil 1715.14   Pfeiffer, Johannes. Gegen den Strom. Itzehoe, 1964.

Phil 585.163   Phenix, Philip H. Man and his becoming. New Brunswick, N.J., 1964.

Phil 2905.1.345   Philippe de la Trinité, Father. Rome et Teilhard de Chardin. Paris, 1964.

Phil 1815.9   Philosophy. Englewood Cliffs, N.J., 1964.

Phil 5865.5.6   Piaget, Jean. Six études de psychologie. Genève, 1964.

Phil 3850.27.197   Picht, Werner. The life and thought of Albert Schweitzer. N.Y., 1964.

Phil 190.80.6   Pieper, Josef. Leisure, the basis of culture. N.Y., 1964.

Phil 8965.13.15.5   Pieper, Josef. Das Viergespann; Klugheit, Gerechtigkeit, Tapferkeit, Mass. München, 1964.

Phil 4225.8.90   Pignoloni, Emilio. Genesi e sviluppo del rosminianesimo nel pensiero di Michele F. Sciacca. Milano, 1964. 2v.

Phil 8965.18   Pinckaers, Servais. Le renouveau de la morale. Tournai, 1964.

Phil 3925.16.95   Pitcher, George Willard. The philosophy of Wittgenstein. Englewood Cliffs, 1964.

Phil 720.76   Pitcher, George Willard. Truth. Englewood Cliffs, N.J., 1964.

Phil 8575.5   Plantinga, Alvin. Faith and philosophy; philosophical studies in religion and ethics. Grand Rapids, 1964.

Phil 4756.6.50   Platonov, G.V. Kh.M. Fataliev. Makhachkala, 1964.

Phil 585.158   Plessner, H. Conditio humana. Pfullingen, 1964.

Phil 6685.7.5   Podmore, F. From Mesmer to Christian Science. N.Y., 1964.

Phil 5875.25   Pongratz, Josa Maria. Zur Ontogenese des sittlichen Urteils in besonderer Antinüpfung and die einschlägie Theorie Piaget's. Inaug. Diss. Heidelberg? 1964.

Phil 645.50.5   Popkin, Richard H. The history of scepticism. Assen, 1964.

Phil 645.50.7   Popkin, Richard H. The history of scepticism from Erasmus to Descartes. N.Y., 1964.

Phil 270.133   Popov, Stoiko. Prichinnostta v obshtestvoto. Sofiia, 1964.

Phil 8592.122.30   Porshnev, Boris F. Mel'e. Moskva, 1964.

Phil 8595.56.5   Pozov, A. Logos-meditatsiia drevnei tserkvi. Miunkhen, 1964.

Phil 5585.58.7   Price, Henry H. Perception. London, 1964.

Phil 672.221   Priestley, J.B. Man and time. London, 1964.

Phil 1715.11   Prosch, H. The genesis of twentieth century philosophy. 1. ed. Garden City, N.Y., 1964.

Phil 4080.3.405.10   Puppo, Mario. Croce e d'annunzio, e altri saggi. Firenze, 1964.

Phil 4080.3.405.5   Puppo, Mario. Il metodo e la critica di Benedetto Croce. Milano, 1964.

Phil 1695.33   Qüestions de filosofí, Camus, Sartre, Ortega. v.21. Barcelona, 1964.

Phil 2477.15.80   Quillet, Pierre. Bachelard. Paris, 1964.

Phil 5056.1.23   Quine, Willard Van Orman. Methods of logic. N.Y., 1964.

Phil 8892.75   Rader, M.M. Ethics and the human community. N.Y., 1964.

Phil 5875.65   Raffler Engel, Walburga von. Il prelinguaggio infantile. Paideia, 1964.

Phil 8967.15.5   Rahner, Karl. The dynamic element in the church. Freiburg, 1964.

Phil 8612.54   Rahner, Karl. On the theology of death. Freiburg, 1964.

Phil 5467.7   Ramsey, I.T. Models and mystery. London, 1964.

Phil 8707.28   Ramsey, I.T. Religion and science: conflict and synthesis. London, 1964.

Phil 8892.79   Rašovský, Adolf. Ethos und Naturrecht. Wien, 1964.

Phil 3235.112.2   Rawidowicz, Simon. Ludwig Feuerbachs Philosophie. 2. Aufl. Berlin, 1964.

Chronological Listing

Phil 8400.37   Razumnyi, V.A. Esteticheskoe sbornik statei. Moskva, 1964.

Phil 1817.16   Reck, A.J. Recent American philosophy. N.Y., 1964.

Phil 3425.600   Redlich, A. Die Hegelsche Logik als Selbsterfassung der Persönlichkeit. Brinkum, 1964.

Phil 165.348   Reese, William L. Process and divinity. LaSalle, Illinois, 1964.

Phil 6327.12.50   Reik, Theodor. Voices from the inaudible. N.Y., 1964.

Phil 8892.76   Reiner, Hans. Die philosophische Ethik. Heidelberg, 1964.

Phil 3499.33   Reinig, Richard. Zur Kritik des Sowjetismus am Kritizismus Kants. Ratingen, 1964.

Phil 5027.3.5   Rescher, N. The development of Arabic logic. Pittsburgh, 1964.

Phil 5057.41   Rescher, N. Introduction to logic. N.Y., 1964.

Phil 5115.10   Rescher, Nicholas. Hypothetical reasoning. Amsterdam, 1964.

Phil 192.98.2   Revel, Jean Francois. Pourquoi des philosophes? Paris, 1964.

Phil 5520.286   Reznikov, Lazar' O. Gnoseologicheskie voprosy semiotiki. Leningrad, 1964.

Phil 6819.6   Rheingold, Joseph Cyrus. The fear of being a woman; a theory of maternal destructiveness. N.Y., 1964.

Phil 7069.34.26   Rhine, Joseph B. Extra-sensory perception. Boston, 1964.

Phil 9495.164.10   Rhymes, D.A. No new morality. Indianapolis, Ind., 1964.

Phil 2020.88   Richter, M. The politics of conscience. Cambridge, 1964.

Phil 2020.89   Richter, M. The politics of conscience. London, 1964.

Phil 6327.336A   Riessman, Frank. Mental health of the poor. London, 1964.

Phil 5027.4   Risse, Wilhelm. Die Logik der Neuzeit. Stuttgart, 1964-2v.

Phil 1170.18   Rist, John M. Eros and Psyche. Toronto, 1964.

Phil 817.26   Riverso, E. Il pensiero occidentale. v.1-3. Napoli, 1964.

Phil 5850.326.12   Roback, A.A. Aspects of applied psychology and crime. Cambridge, 1964.

Phil 5227.6.2   Roback, A.A. History of American psychology. N.Y., 1964.

Phil 3450.11.340   Robberechts, L. Husserl. Paris, 1964.

Phil 6315.2.380   Robert, Marthe. La révolution psychanalytique. Paris, 1964. 2v.

Phil 7069.48.12   Roberts, Ursula. Mary Baker Eddy, her communications from beyond the grave to Harold Horwood. London, 1964.

Phil 8672.25   Robinson, R. An atheist's values. Oxford, 1964.

Phil 2520.347   Roed, Wolfgang. Descartes. München, 1964.

Phil 5767.15   Rohner, Peter. Das Phänomen des Wollens. Bern, 1964.

Phil 6967.19   Rokeach, M. The three Christs of Ypsilanti. N.Y., 1964.

Phil 1760.20   Rome, Sydney C. Philosophical interrogations. 1. ed. N.Y., 1964.

Phil 4368.2.47   Romero, Francisco. Theory of man. Berkeley, 1964.

Phil 817.27   Roncuzzi, Alfredo. Origini del pensiero europeo. Milano, 1964.

Phil 3890.1.115   Rosensbock, G.G. F.A. Trendelenburg. Carbondale, 1964.

Phil 1717.18.4   Rosmini Serbati, Antonio. Breve schizzo dei sistemi di filosofia moderna e del proprio sistema. 4e ed. Firenze, 1964.

Phil 4210.74   Rosmini-Serbati, Antonio. Leitsätze für Christen von Antonio Rosmini. Einsiedeln, 1964.

Phil 4210.73   Rosmini-Serbati, Antonio. Saggio sui divertimenti publici. Roma, 1964.

Phil 4210.69   Rosmini-Serbati, Antonio. Saggio sul comunismo e socialismo. Pescara, 1964.

Phil 2855.9.30   Rosset, Clément. Le monde et ses remèdes. Paris, 1964.

Phil 585.160   Rothacker, Erich. Philosophische Anthropologie. Bonn, 1964.

Phil 1750.753   Roubiczek, P. Existentialism; for and against. Cambridge, 1964.

Phil 3017.5   Royce, J. Lectures on modern idealism. New Haven, 1964.

Phil 165.349   Rozprawy logiczne. Warszawa, 1964.

Phil 2520.351   Rozsnyai, Ervin. Études sur Descartes. Budapest, 1964.

Phil 5530.20.115   Ruh, Kurt. Altdeutsche und altniederländische Mystik. Darmstadt, 1964.

Phil 5590.432   Ruitenbeek, H.M. The individual and the crowd. N.Y., 1964.

Phil 8610.927.10   Russell, Bertrand Russell. Pourquoi je ne suis pas chrétien. Paris, 1964.

Phil 5330.34   Rutten, Josephus W.H.M. Attentiviteit als psychodiagnosticum. Proefschrift. Maastricht, 1964.

Phil 630.60   Ruvo, Vincenzo de. Introduzione al realismo critico. Padova, 1964.

Phil 4352.1.145   Sainz de Robles, Federico Carlos. Jaime Balmes; estudio y antologia. Madrid, 1964.

Phil 193.238   Salazar Bondy, Augusto. Iniciación filosofia. Lima, 1964.

Phil 193.49.65   Santayana, G. The wisdom of George Santayana. 2d. ed. N.Y., 1964.

Phil 6980.668.10   Santer-Weststrate, Henrietta Cornelia. Gedragstherapie in het bijzonder de methode van wedenkerige remming. Assen, 1964.

Phil 2880.8.58   Sartre, Jean Paul. Marxismus und Existentialismus. Reinbeck, 1964.

Phil 1818.12   Savelle, Max. The colonial origins of American thought. Princeton, 1964.

Phil 8980.770.5   Savez Komunista Srbije. Univerzitetski Komitet. O socijalistickom moralu. Beograd, 1964.

Phil 2905.1.440   Scaltriti, Giacinto. Teilhard de Chardin tra il mito e l'eresia. Roma, 1964.

Phil 193.240   Schaeffler, Richard. Wege zu einer Ersten Philosophie. Frankfurt, 1964.

Phil 1123.13   Schaerer, René. Le heros, le sage et l'événement dans l'humanisme grec. Paris, 1964.

Phil 5520.325.3   Schaff, Adam. Język a poznanie. Warszawa, 1964.

Phil 310.445.10   Schaff, Adam. Marx oder Sartre? Wien, 1964.

Phil 818.37   Schilling, Kurt. Weltgeschichte der Philosophie. Berlin, 1964.

Phil 3585.12.85   Schlemper, Hans Otto. Reflexion und Geseteltungswille. Ratingen, 1964.

Phil 3425.601   Schmidt, H. Verheissung und Schrecken der Freiheit. Stuttgart, 1964.

Phil 193.247   Schmitz, Hermann. System der Philosophie. v.1-3. Pt.1-2. Bonn, 1964. 5v.

Phil 3428.164   Schmitz, Josef Nikolaus. Herbart Bibliographie, 1842-1963. Weinheim, 1964.

Phil 630.57   Schneider, H.W. Sources of contemporary philosophical realism in America. Indianapolis, 1964.

Phil 8598.136   Schneider, Louis. Religion, culture and society. N.Y., 1964.

Phil 6980.674.10   Schneider, Ulment Victor. Music and medicine; inaugural lecture. Johannesburg, 1964. 2v.

Phil 6980.674.25   Schofield, William. Psychotherapy. Englewood Cliffs, N.J., 1964.

Phil 193.230.3   Schroedinger, Erwin. My view of the world. Cambridge, 1964.

Phil 6329.18   Schulze, H. Der progressiv, domesticierte Mensch und seine Neurosen. München, 1964.

Phil 5525.64.5   Schweizer, Werner R. Der Witz. Bern, 1964.

Phil 4225.8.37   Sciacca, Michele Federico. Akt und Sein. 4. Aufl. Freiburg, 1964.

Phil 1718.29.10   Sciacca, Michele Federico. Philosophical trends in the contemporary world. Notre Dame, 1964.

Phil 4225.8.60   Sciacca, Michele Federico. Il problema di Dio e della religione nella filosofia attuale. 4. ed. Milano, 1964.

Phil 4225.8.55   Sciacca, Michele Federico. Studi sulla filosofia moderna. 3. ed. Milano, 1964.

Phil 2520.2   Sebba, G. Bibliographia cartesiana. The Hague, 1964.

Phil 493.6.10   Seely, Charles Sherlock. The philosophy of science. N.Y., 1964.

Phil 6320.11.80   Segal, H. Introduction to the work of M. Klein. N.Y., 1964.

Phil 3450.19.310   Seidel, G.J. Martin Heidegger and the pre-Socratics. Lincoln, 1964.

Phil 8843.2.2   Selby-Bigge, L.A. British moralists. v.1-2. Indianapolis, 1964.

Phil 270.140   Selvaggi, Filippo. Causalità e indeterminismo. Roma, 1964.

Phil 5400.196   Senault, Jean Francois. De l'usage des passions. Paris, 1964.

Phil 2262.35.5   Shaftesbury, A.A.C. Characteristics of men. v.1-2. Indianapolis, 1964.

Phil 1523.14   Shapiro, Herman. Medieval philosophy. N.Y., 1964.

Phil 299.27.5   Shapley, Harlow. Of stars and men. Boston, 1964.

Phil 3425.597   Shinkaruk, V.I. Logika dialektika i teoriia poznaniia Gegelia. Kiev, 1964.

Phil 8893.127   Shvartsman, Klara Aronovna. Etika...bez morali. Moskva, 1964.

Phil 5500.34   Siegel, S. Decision and choice. N.Y., 1964.

Phil 5352.18   Siegel, Sidney. Choice, strategy and utility. N.Y., 1964.

Phil 3640.713   Siegmund, Georg. Nietzsches Kunde vom Tode Gottes. Berlin, 1964.

Phil 4980.52.30   Silva, Vicente Ferreira da. Obras completas. São Paulo, 1964. 2v.

Phil 585.226   Silvestre, Georges. L'harmonie vitale; à temps nouveau, philosophie nouvelle. Paris, 1964.

Phil 8120.12   Simches, S.O. Le romantisme et le goût esthétique du XVIIIe siècle. Paris, 1964.

Phil 408.2   Simondon, Gilbert. L'individuation à la lumière des notions de forme et d'information. Thèse. Paris, 1964.

Phil 4800.22   Skarga, Barbara. Narodziny pozytywizmu polskiego, 1831-1864. Warszawa, 1964.

Phil 5258.120.13   Skinner, Burrhus F. Science and human behavior. N.Y., 1964.

Phil 4635.10.30   Skjervheim, Hans. Vitskapen om mennesket ogden filosofiske refleksjon. Oslo, 1964.

Phil 672.229   Smart, John Jamieson Carswell. Problems of space and time. N.Y., 1964.

Phil 960.249   Smart, Ninian. Doctrine and argument in Indian philosophy. London, 1964.

Phil 2418.6   Smith, C. Contemporary French philosophy. N.Y., 1964.

Phil 5585.230   Smith, Ian Macfarlane. Spatial ability. 1. ed. San Diego, Calif., 1964.

Phil 5590.210.2   Smith, M.B. Opinions and personality. N.Y., 1964.

Phil 7055.256   Smith, Susy. The mediumship of Mrs. Leonard. New Hyde Park, N.Y., 1964.

Phil 5592.175   Smits, Willem C.M. Onderzoek naar de kleurintentionaliteit. Nijmegen, 1964.

Phil 2905.1.266   Smulders, P.F. La vision de Teilhard de Chardin. Paris, 1964.

Phil 3838.30   Sokolov, V.V. Filosofiia Spinozy i sovremennost'. Moskva, 1964.

Phil 3450.11.345   Sokolowski, Robert. The formation of Husserl's concept of constitution. The Hague, 1964.

Phil 6158.5   Solomon, David. LSD: the consciousness-expanding drug. N.Y., 1964.

Phil 6060.40.10   Sonnemann, Ulrich. Handwriting analysis as a psychodiagnostic tool. N.Y., 1964.

Phil 4018.2.10   Spaventa, Bertrando. La Circolarità del pensiero europeo. Palermo, 1964.

Phil 6315.2.330   Spengler, Ernst. Das Gewissen bei Freud und Jung. Zürich, 1964.

Phil 8419.57   Spirito, Ugo. Critica dell'estetica. Firenze, 1964.

Phil 1750.166.195   Spirito, Ugo. Nuovo umanesimo. Roma, 1964.

Phil 5520.459   Spoerri, Theodor. Sprachphänomene und Psychose. Basel, 1964.

Phil 1750.166.153   Spongano, Raffaele. Due saggi sull'umanesimo. Firenze, 1964.

Phil 5258.194   Staats, A.W. Complex human behavior. N.Y., 1964.

Phil 6128.81   Stalpers, Jacobus Antonius. Zelfbehoud, aanpassing en cultuur. Arnhem, 1964.

Phil 2305.6.30   Stark, Franz. Das Problem der moralischen Rechtfertigung bei S.E. Toulmin. München, 1964.

Phil 3640.700A   Stavrou, C.N. Whitman and Nietzsche. Chapel Hill, 1964.

Phil 818.36   Steenberghen, Ferdinand van. Histoire de la philosophie. Louvain, 1964.

Phil 5465.100.2   Stein, Morris. Creativity and the individual. Glencoe, 1964.

Phil 978.49.420   Steiner, R. Geistige Wirkenskräfte. Dornach, 1964.

Phil 978.49.440   Steiner, R. Gesteswissenschaftliche Behandlung. Dornach, 1964.

Phil 978.49.445   Steiner, R. Initiationswissenschaft und Sternenerkenntnis. Dornach, 1964.

Phil 978.49.157   Steiner, R. Kosmische und menschliche Geschichte. Dornach, 1964. 4v.

Phil 978.49.450   Steiner, R. Menschliche und menschheitliche Entwicklungswahrheiten. Dornach, 1964.

Phil 978.49.455   Steiner, R. Vorstufen zum Mysterium von Golgatha. Dornach, 1964.

Phil 5768.10.3   Steiner, Rudolf. The philosophy of freedom. London, 1964.

Phil 5594.153.2   Stephenson, William. The study of behavior. Chicago, 1964.

Phil 5066.242   Stiazhkin, Nikolai Ivanovich. Stanovlenie idei matematischeskoi logiki. Moskva, 1964.

Phil 3425.596   Stiehler, G. Die Dialektik in Hegels Phänomenologie des Geistes. Berlin, 1964.

Phil 3640.725   Stobbe, Erhard. Nietzsches Lehre vom Verbrecher. Inaug. Diss. Marburg, 1964.

Phil 632.10   Stommel, Joannes Antonius. L'unification du réel. Utrecht, 1964?

Chronological Listing

Phil 7069.64.10   Stone, W.C. The other side of the mind. Englewood Cliffs, 1964.

Phil 5066.223   Stonert, H. Język i nauka. Warszawa, 1964.

Phil 6978.5   Straub, Richard Ralph. A view of the levels of perceptual development in autistic syndromes. Academisch proefschrift. n.p., 1964.

Phil 5545.92   Suellwold, F. Das umittelbare Behalten. Göttingen, 1964.

Phil 3805.223   Suenkel, Wolfgang. Friedrich Schleiermachers Begründung der Pädagogik als Wissenschaft. Düsseldorf, 1964.

Phil 6980.712.10   Sullivan, Harry Stack. The fusion of psychiatry and social science. N.Y., 1964.

Phil 2750.11.170   Sullivan, S.M. Maritain's theory of poetic intuition. Fribourg, 1964.

Phil 5590.431A   Symposium on Personality Change, University of Texas. Personality change. N.Y., 1964.

Phil 165.342   Szkice filozoficzne; Romanowi Ingardinowi w darze. Warszawa, 1964.

Phil 672.225   Szumilewicz, Irena. O kierunku upływu czasu. Warszawa, 1964.

Phil 5190.4.30   Tamás, György. Die wissenschaftliche Definition. Budapest, 1964.

Phil 5465.139   Taylor, C.W. Creativity, progress and potential. N.Y., 1964.

Phil 5259.56   Taylor, Charles. The explanation of behavior. London, 1964.

Phil 5548.110   Teevan, Richard Collier. Theories of motivation in learning. Princeton, 1964.

Phil 2905.1.50   Teilhard de Chardin, Pierre. The future of man. London, 1964.

Phil 2905.1.48   Teilhard de Chardin, Pierre. The future of man. 1st American ed. N.Y., 1964.

Phil 2905.1.550   Teilhard de Chardin e a convergência das civilizações e das ciências. Lisboa, 1964?

Phil 5204.16   Telberg, Ina. Russian-English glossary of psychiatric terms. N.Y., 1964.

Phil 8980.827   Terekhov, S.S. Za kommunisticheskuiu nravstvennost'. Leningrad, 1964.

Phil 2905.1.295   Terra, Helmut de. Memories of Teilhard de Chardin. London, 1964.

Phil 5867.15   Thetmark, J.C. Barnesprog. København, 1964.

Phil 9495.164   Thielicke, H. The ethics of sex. 1st ed. N.Y., 1964.

Phil 7150.62   Thomas, Klaus. Handbuch der Selbstmordverhütung. Stuttgart, 1964.

Phil 6329.19   Thompson, Clara M. Interpersonal psychoanalysis. N.Y., 1964.

Phil 1750.796   Tierno Galván, Enrique. Humanismo y sociedad. 1. ed. Barcelona, 1964.

Phil 2725.13.98   Tilliette, Xavier. Jules Lequier. Paris, 1964.

Phil 310.456   Titarenko, Aleksandr I. Pragmatistskii lzhemarksizm filosofiia antikommunizme. Moskva, 1964.

Phil 5520.426   Titone, Renzo. La psicolinguistica oggi. Zürich, 1964.

Phil 270.144   Titze, Hans. Der Kausalbegriff in Philosophie und Physik. Meisenheima, 1964.

Phil 8865.636   Tiwari, Brij Gopal. Secularism and materialism in modern India. Delhi, 1964?

Phil 5066.243   Toernelohm, Håkan. Information and confirmation. Göteborg, 1964.

Phil 2295.36   Toland, John. Christianity not mysterious. Stuttgart, 1964.

Phil 75.65   Totok, Wilhelm. Handbuch der Geschichte der Philosophie. v.2, pt.1. Frankfurt, 1964. 2v.

Phil 5627.247.1   Tournier, Paul. The whole person in a broken world. N.Y., 1964.

Phil 8599.44.10   Tresmontant, Claude. La métaphysique du christianisme. Paris, 1964.

Phil 8420.25   Trofimov, Pavel S. Estetika marksizma-leninizma. Moskva, 1964.

Phil 8181.2   Tsenkov, Boris. Iz istoriiata na esteticheskata misul v Bulgariia. Sofiia, 1964.

Phil 8693.20.15   Tuchel, K. Die Philosophie der Technik. Frankfurt, 1964.

Phil 3552.447   Tymierniecka, A.T. Leibniz' cosmological synthesis. Assen, 1964.

Phil 5520.502   Ulshoefer-Heinloth, Elisabeth. Studien zur sprachkommunikativen Orientierung. Inaug. Diss. Passau, 1964.

Phil 7082.40   Uslar, Detlev von. Der Traum als Welt. Pfullingen, 1964.

Phil 8422.18   Vaiman, Semen T. Marksistskaia estetika i problemy realizma. Moskva, 1964.

Phil 9558.41   Van der Schaar, P.J. Dynamik der Pseudologie. München, 1964.

Phil 6131.6.3   Vasil'ev, Leonid L. Tainstvennye iavleniia chelovecheskoi psikhiki. Izd. 3. Moskva, 1964.

Phil 196.42   Vazquez, Juan Adolfo. Que es la ontologia. Buenos Aires, 1964.

Phil 5585.232   Vekker, Lev M. Vospriiatie i osnovy ego modelirovaniia. Leningrad, 1964.

Phil 5425.107   Venzmer, Gerhard. Genius und Wahn. Stuttgart, 1964.

Phil 2733.121   Verga, Leonardo. La filosofia morale di Malebranche. Milano, 1964.

Phil 1750.301   Verneaux, R. Leçons sur l'existentialisme. 4e éd. Paris, 1964.

Phil 2905.1.285   Vernet, M. La grande illusion de Teilhard de Chardin. Paris, 1964.

Phil 5400.169   Vieira, Manuel. Emoções e felicidade. Lisboa, 1964.

Phil 196.36.10   Vita, Luis Washington. Introdução à filosofia. São Paulo, 1964.

Phil 821.6   Vita, Luís Washington. Monólogos e diálogos. São Paulo, 1964.

Phil 4372.1.5   Vives, Juan Luis. Opera omnia. London, 1964. 8v.

Phil 821.1.15   Vorländer, K. Geschichte der Philosophie. Leipzig, 1964. 4v.

Phil 2730.112   Voutsinas, Dimitri. La psychologie de Maine de Biran, 1766-1824. Paris, 1964.

Phil 352.8.5.3   Vries, Joseph de. Critica. 3. ed. recognita et aucto. Barcinone, 1964.

Phil 310.584   Vserossiiskii Seminar pre Poda Vatelei po Voprosam Sovet Estestvoznaniia. Dialekticheskii materializm i sovremennoe estestvoznanie. Moskva, 1964.

Phil 8423.25   Wahl, Marcelle. Création picturale et ordre cérébral. Paris, 1964.

Phil 8647.13   Walker, Daniel P. The decline of hell. London, 1964.

Phil 5238.198   Wann, T.W. Behaviorism and phenomenology. Chicago, 1964.

Phil 5585.235   Weber, Klaus. Wahrnehmung und mnemische Verarbeitung wertbetonter Reihen. Stuttgart, 1964?

Phil 972.22   Wehr, Gerhard. Der Urmensch und der Mensch der Zukunft. Freiburg, 1964.

Phil 6332.31   Weinberg, Henry. Case book in abnormal psychology. N.Y., 1964.

Phil 1527.4   Weinberg, J.R. A short history of medieval philosophy. Princeton, 1964.

Phil 8602.78   Weiss, P. The God we seek. Carbondale, 1964.

Phil 6834.3   Welter, Ernst Günther. Bibliographie Freundschaftseros; einschliesslich Homoerotik, Homosexualität und der verwandten und vergleichenden Gebiete. Frankfurt, 1964.

Phil 5590.434   Wepman, J.M. The concepts of personality. London, 1964.

Phil 5520.124.2   Wheelwright, Phillip Ellis. The burning fountain. Bloomington, 1964.

Phil 6332.19.3   White, Robert. The abnormal personality. 3d ed. N.Y., 1964.

Phil 8847.17   Whiteley, Charles Henry. The permissive morality. London, 1964.

Phil 8423.8.2   Wienbarg, Ludolf. Ästhetische Feldzüge. Berlin, 1964.

Phil 8865.342.5   Willey, Basil. The English moralists. London, 1964.

Phil 197.93   Wisdom, John. Philosophy and psychoanalysis. Oxford, 1964.

Phil 3925.16.20   Wittgenstein, Ludwig. Philosophische Bemerkungen; aus dem Nachlass. Oxford, 1964.

Phil 3925.16.5   Wittgenstein, Ludwig. Remarks on the foundations of mathematics. Oxford, 1964.

Phil 5545.223   Włodarski, Z. Pamięc jako właściwość poszczególnych analizatorów. Warszawa, 1964.

Phil 6980.780.5   Wolpe, Joseph. The conditioning therapies. N.Y., 1964.

Phil 8647.14   Wood, Frederic Herbert. Through the psychic door. Houston, 1964?

Phil 6105.314   World Federation for Mental Health. Population and mental health. Berne, 1964.

Phil 5262.68   Wulf, Berthold. Idee und Denken. Stuttgart, 1964.

Phil 9362.20   Wylie, Max. Career girl, watch your step. N.Y., 1964.

Phil 4065.173   Yates, F.A. Giordano Bruno. London, 1964.

Phil 1750.102   Zaner, R.M. The problem of embodiment. The Hague, 1964.

Phil 2880.8.185   Zehm, Günter Albrecht. Historische Vernunft und direkte Aktion. Stuttgart, 1964.

1965

Phil 585.178   Aaberg, Thorsten. Livsåskådningar. Stockholm, 1965.

Phil 1750.115.37   Abellio, Raymond. La structure absolue; essai de phénoménologie génétique. Paris, 1965.

Phil 331.35   Abrahamian, Lev. Gnoseologicheskie problemy teorii znakov. Erevan, 1965.

Phil 4803.108.25   Abramowski, Edward. Filozofia społeczna. Warszawa, 1965.

Phil 4817.6   Academia Republicii Socialiste România, Bucharest. Institutu I de Filozofie. Antologia iz istoriiata na rumunskata progresivna misul. Sofiia, 1965.

Phil 331.34   Ackermann, Robert John. Theories of knowledge. N.Y., 1965.

Phil 9495.165   Acland, Richard. Sexual morality. London, 1965.

Phil 310.596   Adajnyk, Walter. Marxism and existentialism. 1. ed. Garden City, N.Y., 1965.

Phil 2150.18.45   Addis, Laird. Moore and Ryle: two ontologists. Iowa City, 1965.

Phil 5040.19.5   Adjukiewicz, Kazimierz. Logika pragmatyczna. Warszawa, 1965.

Phil 175.62   Adler, Mortimer Jerome. The conditions of philosophy. 1st ed. N.Y., 1965.

Phil 8430.46   Adler, Mortimer Jerome. Poetry and politics. Pittsburgh, 1965.

Phil 310.506   Afanas'ev, Viktor G. Osnovy filosofskikh znanii. 3. izd. Moskva, 1965.

Phil 8400.47   Akademiia Nauk SSSR. Institut Filosofii. Estetika: kategorii i iskusstvo. Moskva, 1965.

Phil 5590.456   Akademiia Nauk SSSR. Institut Filosofii. Garmonicheskii chelovek. Moskva, 1965.

Phil 310.601   Akademiia Nauk SSSR. Institut Filosofii. Marksistsko-leninskaia filosofiia i sotsiologiia v SSSR i evropeiskikh sotsialisticheskikh stranakh. Moskva, 1965.

Phil 8875.32   Akademiia Nauk SSSR. Institut Filosofii. Protiv sovremennoi burzhuaznoi etiki. Moskva, 1965.

Phil 4710.50.25   Akademiia Nauk URSR, Kiev. Pobudova naukovoï teorii. Kyïv, 1965.

Phil 8825.5   Akarsu, Bedia. Ahlâk öprelileri. Istanbul, 1965.

Phil 3925.11.80   Aleorta, José Ignacio. Peter Wust, filosofo espiritualista de nuestro tiempo. Bilbao, 1965.

Phil 7072.4   Alexander, Rolf. The power of the mind. London, 1965.

Phil 2520.229.5   Alquié, F. Science et métaphysique chez Descartes. Paris, 1965.

Phil 3482.15   Alquié, Ferdinand. La morale de Kant. Paris, 1965.

Phil 3820.8   Alquié, Ferdinand. Nature et vérité dans la philosophie de Spinoza. Paris, 1965.

Phil 6980.36.2   Altschule, Mark David. Roots of modern psychiatry. 2. ed. N.Y., 1965.

Phil 165.355   American Academy for Jewish Research. Harry Austryn Wolfson. Jerusalem, 1965.

Phil 1750.166.170   Amoroso Lima, Alcew. Pelo humanismo ameaçado. Rio de Janeiro, 1965.

Phil 2070.156   Anderson, Luke. The concept of truth in the philosophy of William James. Rome, 1965.

Phil 5520.480.5   Anderson, Richard Chase. Readings in the psychology of cognition. N.Y., 1965.

Phil 5066.245   Andrews, Peter Bruce. A transfinite type theory with type variables. Amsterdam, 1965.

Phil 5875.100   Andriessen, H. De groei van het geweten. Zeist, 1965.

Phil 6310.21   Angyal, András. Neurosis and treatment. N.Y., 1965.

Phil 960.252   Anikeev, Nikolai P. O materialisticheskikh traditsiiakh v indiiskoi filosofii. Moskva, 1965.

Phil 8980.131.5   Anisimov, Sergei F. Nravstvennyi progressi religiia. Moskva, 1965.

Phil 4060.9.40   Antoni, Giuseppe. Pensiero ed esistenza. Padova, 1965.

Phil 3120.30.110   Anzenbacher, Arno. Die Philosophie Martin Bubers. Wien, 1965.

Phil 8401.35   Apresian, Grant Z. Cheloveku byt' khudozhnikom. Moskva, 1965.

Phil 8401.34   Apresian, Zorii Grantovich. Svoboda khudozhestvennogo tvorchestva. Moskva, 1965.

Phil 5590.460   Arasteh, A. Reza. Final integration in the adult personality. Leiden, 1965.

Phil 8400.4.5   Archivio di Filosofia. Surrealismo e simbolismo. Padova, 1965.

Phil 5040.3.25   Arnauld, Antoine. L'art de penser; la logique de Port Royal. v.1-3. Stuttgart, 1965- 2v.

Phil 5040.4.4.7   Arnauld, Antoine. La logique, ou L'art de penser. Paris, 1965.

Chronological Listing

Phil 8401.40.5 — Arnheim, Rudolf. Art and visual perception. Berkeley, 1965.

Phil 1105.10 — Asmus, Valentin F. Istoriia antichnoi filosofii. Moskva, 1965.

Phil 5590.463 — Association de Psychologie Scientifique de Langue Française. Les modèles de la personnalité en psychologie. 9e symposium de l'association de psychologie scientifique de langue française. Paris, 1965.

Phil 8400.44 — Astakhov, Ivan B. Estetika i sovremennost'. Moskva, 1965.

Phil 5535.1 — Atkinson, Richard G. An introduction to mathematical learning theory. N.Y., 1965.

Phil 8580.37 — Aubert, Jean-Marie. Philosophie de la nature. Paris, 1965.

Phil 9513.48 — Aukrust, Tor. Mennesket i samfunnet. En sosialetikk. Oslo, 1965-

Phil 6310.22 — Axline, Virginia Mae. Dibs: in search of self. Boston, 1965.

Phil 3120.30.120 — Babolin, Albino. Essere e alterità in Martin Buber. Padova, 1965.

Phil 5520.495 — Bacchin, Giovanni Romano. I fondamenti della filosofia del linguaggio. Assisi, 1965.

Phil 2477.15.13 — Bachelard, Gaston. La poétique de la rêverie. 3. éd. Paris, 1965.

Phil 6311.48 — Bachelard, Gaston. La psychanalyse du feu. Paris, 1965.

Phil 4803.186.30 — Baczko, Bronisław. Człowiek i światopoglady. Warszawa, 1965.

Phil 4073.117 — Badaloni, Nicola. Tommaso Campanella. 1. ed. Milano, 1965.

Phil 6315.2.355 — Bailey, Percival. Sigmund the unserene. Springfield, Ill., 1965.

Phil 2750.20.95 — Bakker, Reinout. Merleau-Ponty. Bearn, 1965.

Phil 1135.182 — Baldry, Harold Capame. The unity of mankind in Greek thought. Cambridge, Eng., 1965.

Phil 6311.36.2 — Balint, Michael. Primary love, and psycho-analytic technique. N.Y., 1965.

Phil 978.49.885 — Ballmer, Karl. Ernst Haeckel und Rudolf Steiner. Besazio, 1965.

Phil 7150.61 — Balluseck, Lothar von. Selbstmord. Bad Godesberg, 1965.

Phil 176.228 — Balmes, Raymond. Leçons de philosophie. Paris, 1965-66. 2v.

Phil 3425.422 — Banfi, Antonio. Inconfro con Hegel. Urbino, 1965.

Phil 4070.7.40 — Banfi, Antonio. Studi sulla filosofia del novecento. Roma, 1965.

Phil 4070.7.60 — Banfi, Antonio. L'uomo copernicano. Milano, 1965.

Phil 5238.208 — Banks, Charlotte. Stephanos. London, 1965.

Phil 8826.7 — Banning, Willem. Typen van zedelee. Haarlem, 1965.

Phil 2905.1.325 — Barbour, George Brown. In the field with Teilhard de Chardin. N.Y., 1965.

Phil 1857.1 — Barfield, Owen. Unancestral voice. London, 1965.

Phil 5041.91 — Barker, Stephen Francis. The elements of logic. N.Y., 1965.

Phil 2750.20.100 — Barral, Mary Rose. Merleau-Ponty. Pittsburgh, 1965.

Phil 3120.66.30 — Barth, Heinrich. Erkenntnis der Existenz. Basel, 1965.

Phil 9030.7 — Bartoš, Jaromír. Kategorie nahodilého v dějinách filosofického myšlení. Praha, 1965.

Phil 6951.32 — Bastide, Roger. Soziologie des maladies mentales. Paris, 1965.

Phil 1701.48 — Baumer, Franklin Le van. Intellectual movements in modern European history. N.Y., 1965.

Phil 4080.3.455 — Bausola, Adriano. Filosofia e storia nel pensiero crociano. Milano, 1965.

Phil 3801.194 — Bausola, Adriano. Metafiscia e rivelazione nella filosofia positiva di Schelling. Milano, 1965.

Phil 176.223 — Beardsley, Monroe Curtis. Philosophical thinking. N.Y., 1965.

Phil 1750.166.220 — Beaujon, Edmond. Némésis; ou, La limite. Paris, 1965.

Phil 2520.350 — Beck, Leslie John. The metaphysics of Descartes. Oxford, 1965.

Phil 3483.85 — Beck, Lewis White. Studies in the philosophy of Kant. 1st ed. Indianapolis, 1965.

Phil 6480.200.5 — Becker, Raymond de. Les machinations de la nuit. Paris, 1965.

Phil 7084.48 — Becker, Raymond de. Rêve et sexualité. Paris, 1965.

Phil 3450.11.430 — Beerling, Reiner F. De transcendentale vreemdeling. Hilversum, 1965.

Phil 5520.444 — Begiashvili, Archil. Sovremennaia angliiskaia lingvisticheskaia filosofiia. Tbilisi, 1965.

Phil 1540.90 — Behler, Ernst. Die Ewigkeit der Welt. München, 1965.

Phil 4883.2.5 — Beisembiev, Kasym Beisembievich. Progressivno-demokraticheskaia i marksistskaia mysl' v Kazakhstane nachala XX veka. Alma-Ata, 1965.

Phil 2050.255 — Belgion, Montgomery. David Hume. London, 1965.

Phil 1750.126.8.2 — Benda, Julien. La trahison des clercs. Paris, 1965.

Phil 8402.62A — Bense, Max. Aesthetica. Baden-Baden, 1965.

Phil 8402.56.5 — Bense, Max. Ungehorsam der Ideen. Köln, 1965.

Phil 365.58 — Benz, Ernst. Schöpfungsglaube und Endzeiterwartung. München, 1965.

Phil 4752.2.79 — Berdiaev, Nikolai Aleksandrovich. Christian existentialism. London, 1965.

Phil 2475.1.39.10 — Bergson, Henri. Duration and simultaneity. Indianapolis, 1965.

Phil 5625.112 — Beritashvili, Ivan S. Neural mechanisms of higher vertebrate behavior. 1st English ed. Boston, 1965.

Phil 5520.429 — Berlyne, Daniel E. Structure and direction in thinking. N.Y., 1965.

Phil 6671.28.6 — Bernstein, Morey. The search for Bridey Murphy. Garden City, N.Y., 1965.

Phil 2225.5.125 — Bernstein, Richard J. Perspectives on Peirce. New Haven, 1965.

Phil 2725.50 — Bertoni, Italo. Il neoilluminismo etico di André Lalande. Milano, 1965.

Phil 3640.121.3.5 — Bertram, Ernst. Nietzsche. Bonn, 1965.

Phil 8402.64 — Bianca, Giovanni A. Discussioni sull'arte e sulla condizione dell'uomo. Messina, 1965.

Phil 5627.265 — Bindl, Maria Frieda. Das religiöse Erleben im Spiegel der Bildgestaltung. Freiburg, 1965.

Phil 6951.30.5 — Binswanger, Ludwig. Wahn; Beiträge zu seiner phanomenologischen und daseinsanalytischen Erforschung. Pfullingen, 1965.

Phil 8980.213.5 — Bittighoefer, Bernd. Die Rind dir andere neben Dir. Berlin, 1965.

Phil 3450.48.80 — Bittner, Günther. Sachlichkeit und Bildung; kritische Studie...Hans-Eduard Hengstenberg. München? 1965?

Phil 1830.53 — Black, Max. Philosophy in America. London, 1965.

Phil 2053.92 — Blackstone, William T. Francis Hutcheson and contemporary ethical theory. Athens, Ga., 1965.

Phil 5592.155.5 — Block, Jack. The challenge of response sets. N.Y., 1965.

Phil 2477.6.45 — Blondel, Maurice. Blondel et Teilhard de Chardin. Paris, 1965.

Phil 1701.52 — Bobbio, Norberto. Da Hobbes a Marx; saggi di storia della filosofia. Napoli, 1965.

Phil 5520.446 — Bocheński, Innocentius M. The logic of religion. N.Y., 1965.

Phil 5041.92 — Bocheński, Innocentius M. The methods of contemporary thought. Dordrecht, 1965.

Phil 525.258 — Bodmershof, Wilhelm. Geistige Versenkung. Zürich, 1965.

Phil 1750.560.15 — Bollnow, Otto Friedrich. Franzoischer Existentialismus. Stuttgart, 1965.

Phil 3120.2.40 — Bolzano, Bernard. Wissenschaft und Religion in Vormärz. Berlin, 1965.

Phil 1701.58 — Bonafede, Giulio. Interpretazioni della filosofia moderna. Palermo, 1965.

Phil 5592.177 — Bonner, Hubert. On being mindful of man, essay toward a proactive psychology. Boston, 1965.

Phil 8402.63 — Borev, Iurii B. Vvedenie v estetiku. Moskva, 1965.

Phil 176.25.10 — Borland, Hal Glen. Countryman: a summary of belief. 1st ed. Philadelphia, 1965.

Phil 8612.57 — Boros, Ladislaus. The moment of truth. London, 1965.

Phil 1750.757 — Borowitz, Eugene B. A layman's introduction to religious existentialism. Philadelphia, 1965.

Phil 176.222 — Bouwsma, O.K. Philosophical essays. Lincoln, Nebraska, 1965.

Phil 1870.136.5 — Bracken, Harry M. The early reception of Berkeley's immaterialism, 1710-1733. The Hague, 1965.

Phil 9245.117 — Bradburn, Norman Marshall. Reports on happiness. Chicago, 1965.

Phil 6400.30.2 — Brain, Walter Russell. Speech disorders; aphasia, apraxia and agnosia. 2d ed. London, 1965.

Phil 3120.45.35 — Brandenstein, Béla. Wahrheit und Wirklichkeit. Meisenheim, 1965.

Phil 672.226 — Brandon, Samuel George Frederick. History, time and deity. Manchester, 1965.

Phil 5545.97 — Breer, Paul E. Task experience as a source of attitudes. Homewood, 1965.

Phil 801.33.5 — Bréhier, É. La filosofia e il suo passato. Napoli, 1965.

Phil 1701.23.5 — Bréhier, Émile. Etudes de philosophie moderne. Paris, 1965.

Phil 705.57 — Brelage, Manfred. Studien zur Transzendentalphilosophie. Berlin, 1965.

Phil 4891.10.2 — Brière, O. Fifty years of Chinese philosophy, 1898-1848. N.Y., 1965.

Phil 3640.282.1 — Brinton, Clarence Crane. Nietzsche. 1. ed. N.Y., 1965.

Phil 1133.46 — Broecker, Walter. Die Geschichte der Philosophie vor Sokrates. Frankfurt, 1965.

Phil 2045.136 — Brown, Keith C. Hobbes. Cambridge, 1965.

Phil 5640.138 — Brownfield, Charles A. Isolation; clinical and experimental approaches. N.Y., 1965.

Phil 165.384 — Browning, Douglas. Philosophers of process. N.Y., 1965.

Phil 2050.264 — Brunet, Oliver. Philosophie et esthétique chez David Hume. Paris, 1965.

Phil 2050.258 — Brunetto, Filippo. La questione della vera causa in David Hume. Bologna, 1965.

Phil 3120.30.79 — Buber, Martin. The knowledge of man. N.Y., 1965.

Phil 3120.30.56 — Buber, Martin. Nachlese. Heidelberg, 1965.

Phil 2225.5.130 — Buczyńska, Hanna. Peirce. Warszawa, 1965.

Phil 3001.24 — Buggenhagen, Erich Arnold von. Contribuições à historia da filosofia alemã. São José, 1965.

Phil 3246.298.5 — Buhr, Manfred. Revolution und Philosophie. Berlin, 1965.

Phil 310.600 — Bulgarska Akademiia na Naukite, Sofia. Institut po Filosofiia. Sektsiia po Dialekticheski Materializum i Logika. Problemi na zakonite i kategoriite na dialektikata i logikata. Sofiia, 1965.

Phil 5520.96.80 — Bulla de Villaret, H. Une nouvelle orientation. Paris, 1965.

Phil 2340.10.180 — Burgers, Johannes Martinus. Experience and conceptual activity. Cambridge, Mass., 1965.

Phil 585.190 — Burkhardt, Hans. Dimensionen menschlicher Wirklichkeit. Schweinfurt, 1965.

Phil 3925.16.115 — Burkhardt, Jörg R. Die Bildtheorie der Sprache. München, 1965.

Phil 8691.8.15 — Burnet, Thomas. The sacred theory of the earth. London, 1965.

Phil 5585.245 — Business Research Limited, Bangkok. Esthetic perception of villagers in Northeast Thailand, a pilot study. Bangkok? 1965.

Phil 165.332.2 — Butler, R.J. Analytical philosophy. 2nd series. Oxford, 1965.

Phil 6111.80 — Buytendijk, Frederik Jacobus Johannes. Prolegomena van een antropologische fysiologie. Utrecht, 1965.

Phil 5135.7 — Bzhalava, Iosif T. Vospriiatie i ustanovka. Tbilisi, 1965.

Phil 4752.2.145 — Calian, Carnegie Samuel. The significance of eschatology in the thoughts of Nicolas Berdiaev. Leiden, 1965.

Phil 2402.9.5 — Callot, E. La philosophie de la vie au XVIIIe siècle. Paris, 1965.

Phil 4073.33 — Campanella, Tommaso. De antichristo. Roma, 1965.

Phil 4073.66 — Campanella, Tommaso. I sacri segni, inediti. Roma, 1965. 6v.

Phil 2725.14.92 — Canivez, André. Jules Lagneau. Paris, 1965. 2v.

Phil 4365.1.82 — Capdevila, José Maria. Eugeni d'Ors. Barcelona, 1965.

Phil 8582.72 — Caracciolo, Alberto. La religione come struttura e come modo autonomo della coscienza. Milano, 1965.

Phil 2520.224.5 — Carbonara, Cleto. Renato Cartesio. Napoli, 1965.

Phil 1135.193 — Carbonara Naddei, Mirella. Note sul realismo nel pensiero dei Greci. Napoli, 1965.

Phil 8582.66 — Carrier, Hervé. The sociology of religious belonging. N.Y., 1965.

Phil 585.164 — Castell, Alburey. The self in philosophy. N.Y., 1965.

Phil 2475.1.450 — Cavagna, Giovanni Bruno. La dottrina della conoscenza in Enrico Bergson. Napoli, 1965.

Phil 5520.453 — Centro di Studi Filosofici di Gallarate. 9. Convegno Annuale. Il problema filosofico del linguaggio. Padova, 1965.

Phil 3450.19.79.5 — Chandra, Subhash. Das Phänomen des Todes im Denken Heideggers und in der Lehre Buddhas. Köln, 1965.

Phil 5585.233 — Chateau, Jean. Attitudes intellectuelles et spatiales dans le dessin. Paris, 1965.

Phil 2905.1.340 — Chauchard, Paul. Man and cosmos. N.Y., 1965.

Phil 2905.1.97 — Chauchard, Paul. La pensée scientifique de Teilhard. Paris, 1965.

Phil 310.555.2 — Chesnokov, Dimitrii I. Istoricheskii materializm. izd. 2. Moskva, 1965.

1965 - cont.

Phil 3450.19.108.3 — Chiodi, Pietro. L'esistenzialismo di Heidegger. 3e ed. Torino, 1965.

Phil 2880.8.210 — Chiodi, Pietro. Sartre il marxismo. 1. ed. Milano, 1965.

Phil 525.245 — Choisy, Maryse. L'être et le silence. Genève, 1965.

Phil 333.22 — Chuvstvennoe poznanie. Moskva, 1965.

Phil 4080.28 — Ciardo, Manlio. Esteticità della dialettica nella vita dello spirito. Pisa, 1965.

Phil 6980.182 — Ciba Foundation. Ciba foundation symposium [on] transcultural psychiatry. Boston, 1965.

Phil 1133.40 — Cleve, Felix M. The giants of pre-sophistic Greek philosophy. The Hague, 1965.

Phil 5850.161 — Coetsier, Leo. Toegepaste psychologie. Gent, 1965.

Phil 8657.23 — Coffy, Robert. Dieu des athées: Marx, Sartre, Camus. Lyon, 1965.

Phil 6158.10 — Cohen, Sidney. The beyond within; the LSD story. N.Y., 1965.

Phil 165.352 — Collegium Philosophicum; Studien Joachim Ritter zum 60. Geburtstag. Basel, 1965.

Phil 8610.713.5 — Collins, Anthony. A discourse of free-thinking. Stuttgart, 1965.

Phil 6312.25 — Columbia. University. Psychoanalytic Clinic for Training and Reaserch. New perspectives in psychoanalysis. N.Y., 1965.

Phil 5545.94 — Conference on Learning, Remembering and Forgetting. Learning, remembering, and forgetting. Palo Alto, 1965-

Phil 9530.57 — Conklin, Bob. The power of a magnetic personality. West Ryack, N.Y., 1965.

Phil 4080.3.470 — Convegno Crociano, Bari. Interpretazioni crociane di R. Assunto. Bari, 1965.

Phil 4195.110 — Convegno di Studi Pichiani per il V Centenario della Nascita di Giovanni Pico della Mirandola. Studi pichiani; atti e memorie del Convegno di studi pichiani per il V centenario della nascita di Giovanni Pico della Mirandola, Mondena, Mirandola, 25-26 maggio, 1963. Modena, 1965.

Phil 4195.106A — Convegno Internazionale per il V Centenario della Nascita di Giovanni Pico della Mirandola, Mirandola, 1963. L'opera e il pensiero di Giovanni Pico della Mirandola nella storia dell'umanesimo. Firenze, 1965.

Phil 5039.6 — Copi, Irving M. Readings on logic. N.Y., 1965.

Phil 5066.54.2 — Copi, Irving M. Symbolic logic. 2nd ed. N.Y., 1965.

Phil 5520.436.5 — Cornforth, Maurice Campbell. Marxism and the linguistic philosophy. London, 1965.

Phil 5520.436 — Cornforth, Maurice Campbell. Marxism and the linguistic philosophy. N.Y., 1965.

Phil 8657.30 — Coseglia, Raffaele. L'ateismo contemporaneo [l'aberrante avventura dello spirito] relazioni, studi, esperienze. Napoli, 1965.

Phil 3850.16.118 — Coser, Lewis A. Georg Simmel. Englewood, 1965.

Phil 2725.55 — Cossu, Maria. Il pensiero estetico di Charles Lalo. Cagliari, 1965.

Phil 6315.2.335 — Costigan, Giovanni. Sigmund Freud, a short biography. N.Y., 1965.

Phil 7040.39 — Craft, Michael. Ten studies into psychopathic personality. Bristol, 1965.

Phil 5068.56.15 — Crescini, Angelo. Le origini del metodo analitico. Udine, 1965.

Phil 2905.1.176 — Crespy, Georges. De la science à la théologie. Neuchâtel, 1965.

Phil 4080.30 — Cristaldi, Giuseppe. Filosofia e verità; saggi e note. Milano, 1965.

Phil 4210.205 — Cristaldi, Giuseppe. Prospettive rosminiane. Milano, 1965.

Phil 7069.65.25 — Crouzet, Jean-Philippe. Les merveilles du spiritualisme. Paris, 1965.

Phil 5242.67 — Cruchon, Georges E. Dynamic psychology. N.Y., 1965.

Phil 2905.1.172 — Cuénot, Claude. Teilhard de Chardin. London, 1965.

Phil 2905.1.196 — Cuénot, Claude. Teilhard de Chardin et la pensée catholique: colloque de Venise sous les auspices de Pax Romana. Paris, 1965.

Phil 4803.313.20 — Czezowski, Tadeusz. Filozofia na rozdrożu. Wyd. 1. Warszawa, 1965.

Phil 2477.15.85 — Dagognet, François. Gaston Bachelard. Paris, 1965.

Phil 3640.706 — Danto, Arthur Coleman. Nietzsche as philosopher. N.Y., 1965.

Phil 1750.769 — Darmstaedter Gespräch, 8th, Darmstadt. Angst und Hoffnung in unserer Zeit. Darmstadt, 1965.

Phil 960.248.2 — Dasgupta, Surama. Development of moral philosophy in India. N.Y., 1965.

Phil 6113.33 — Davis, James Allen. Education for positive mental health. Chicago, 1965.

Phil 3640.723 — DeFeo, Nicola M. Analitica e dialettica in Nietzsche. Bari, 1965.

Phil 3640.708 — Deleuze, Gilles. Nietzsche; sa vie, son oeuvre. Paris, 1965.

Phil 2750.20.120 — Derossi, Giorgio. Maurice Merleau-Ponty. Torino, 1965.

Phil 2520.61.20 — Descartes, René. Traité des passions suivi de la correspondance avec la princess Elisabeth. Paris, 1965.

Phil 2430.6 — Desné, Roland. Les materialistes français de 1750 à 1800. Paris, 1965.

Phil 6313.8.10 — Deutsch, Helene. Neuroses and character types. London, 1965.

Phil 8878.61 — Devlin, Patrick. The enforcement of morals. London, 1965.

Phil 5066.233 — Dickoff, James. Symbolic logic and language. N.Y., 1965.

Phil 3640.770 — Dickopp, Karl-Heinz. Nietzsches Kritik des Ich-denke. Bonn, 1965.

Phil 5520.451 — Dienes, Zoltau Paul. Thinking in structures. London, 1965.

Phil 2270.185 — Di Nola, Mario. Il presupposto biologico e individualista della sociologia spenceriana. Colombo, 1965.

Phil 2750.23.85 — Dirven, Edouard. De la forme à l'acte...Joseph Maréchal. Paris, 1965.

Phil 8592.122.15 — Dommanget, Maurice. Le curé Meslier, athée. Paris, 1965.

Phil 1803.15 — Donnell, Franklin H. Aspects of contemporary American philosophy. Würzburg, 1965.

Phil 3425.609 — Dooren, Willem van. Het totaliteitsbegrip bij Hegel en zijn voorgangers. Assen, 1965.

Phil 5043.33.10 — Dopp, Joseph. Notions de logique formelle. Louvain, 1965.

Phil 6313.24 — Dorsey, John Morris. Illness or allness; conversations of a psychiatrist. Detroit, 1965.

Phil 6903.5 — Driver, Edwin D. The sociology and anthropology of mental illness, a reference guide. Amherst, 1965.

NEDL Phil 8980.2 — Drobnitskii, Oleg G. Kratkii slovar' po etike. Moskva, 1965.

Phil 5272.2 — Du Bois, Philip Hunter. An introduction to psychological statistics. N.Y., 1965.

Phil 5243.70 — Dubouchet-Buffet, Jeanne. Essai de formalisation de la psychologie fondé sur l'analogie des phénomènes psychiques et des phénomènes physiques. Thèse. Paris, 1965.

Phil 6953.20 — Dunham, Henry Warren. Community and schizophrenia. Detroit, 1965.

Phil 2340.10.190 — Dunkel, Harold Baker. Whitehead on education. Columbus, 1965.

Phil 8828.8 — Du Plessis, Pieter Gert Wessel. Opskorting van die etiese? Thesis. Potchefstroom, 1965.

Phil 1695.31 — Edie, James M. An invitation to phenomenology. Chicago, 1965.

Phil 4710.144 — Edie, James M. Russian philosophy. 1. ed. Chicago, 1965. 3v.

Phil 165.105.2 — Edwards, Paul. A modern introduction to philosophy. N.Y., 1965.

Phil 972.17 — Eek, Sven. Damodar and the pioneers of the theosophical movement. Adyar, 1965.

Phil 8879.36 — Egemen, Bedi Ziya. Terkiye ilminin problemlen. Ankara, 1965.

Phil 1750.115.185 — Ehel, Gerhard. Untersuchungen zu einer realistischen Grundlegung der phänomenologischen Wesensschau. München, 1965.

Phil 5244.24.5 — Ehrenstein, Walter. Probleme des höheren Seelenlebens. München, 1965.

Phil 5585.130.2 — Ehrenzweig, Anton. The psycho-analysis of artistic vision and hearing. 2d ed. N.Y., 1965.

Phil 804.15 — Ehrlich, Walter. Philosophie der Geschichte der Philosophie. Bad Ragaz, 1965.

Phil 8879.38 — Eichhorn, Wolfgang. Wie ist Ethik als Wissenschaft möglich? Berlin, 1965.

Phil 2404.4 — Emery, Leon. De Montaigne à Teilhard de Chardin via Pascal et Rousseau. Lyon, 1965.

Phil 585.171 — Endres, Josef. Man, as the ontological mean. N.Y., 1965.

Phil 8430.48 — Eremeev, Arkadii F. Vek nauki i iskusstvo. Moskva, 1965.

Phil 1804.5 — Ermolenko, Dimitrii V. Sovremennaia burzhuaznaia filosofiia SShA. Moskva, 1965.

Phil 5871.10 — Erni, Margrit. Das Vaterbild den Tocher. Diss. n.p., 1965.

Phil 530.70.12 — Espiritualidad rusa por San Serafin de Sarov. Madrid, 1965.

Phil 325.14 — Evans, John Llewelyn. The foundations of empiricism. Cardiff, 1965.

Phil 6314.11.10 — Eysenck, Hans J. The causes and cures of neurosis. London, 1965.

Phil 180.88 — Faggiotto, Pietro. Saggio sulla struttura della metafisica. Padova, 1965.

Phil 3487.28 — Falaturi, Abdal-Jawad. Zur Interpretation der Kantischen Ethik im Lichte der Achtung. Inaug. Diss. Bonn, 1965.

Phil 5460.14.10 — Faure, Henri. Les appartenances du délirant. Paris, 1965.

Phil 5460.14.5 — Faure, Henri. Les objets dans la folie. Paris, 1965. 2v.

Phil 8980.386.5 — Fedorenko, I.H. Osnovy marksistsko-leninskoi etiki. Kiev, 1965.

Phil 8520.55 — Feiereis, Konrad. Die Umprägung der natürlichen Theologie in Religionsphilosophie. Leipzig, 1965.

Phil 8585.48 — Feiner, Johannes. Mysterium salutis. Einsiedeln, 1965. 4v.

Phil 2880.8.150 — Fell, Joseph P. Emotion in thought of Sartre. N.Y., 1965.

Phil 4073.120 — Femiano, Salvatore Beniamino. Lo spiritualismo di Tommasco Campanella. Napoli, 1965. 2v.

Phil 805.13.5.2 — Ferrater Mora, José. El hombre en la encrucijada. 2. ed. Buenos Aires, 1965.

Phil 8612.56 — Ferrater Mora, José. Being and death. Berkeley, Calif., 1965.

Phil 90.4.17 — Ferrater Mora, José. Diccionario de filosofía. 5. ed. Buenos Aires, 1965.

Phil 848.6 — Fertig, Hermann. Die Auflösung der klassischen Substanzkonzeption und ein Versuch Rehabilitierung. Inaug. Diss. München, 1965.

Phil 5066.24.5 — Feys, Robert. Modal logics. Louvain, 1965.

Phil 3640.704 — Fink, Eugen. La philosophie de Nietzsche. Paris, 1965.

Phil 3450.4.90 — Fischer-Appelt, Peter. Metaphysik im Horizent der Theologie Wilhelm Herrmanns. München, 1965.

Phil 3270.17.40 — Flam, Leopold. Gestalten van de Westerse subjectiviteit. Amsterdam, 1965.

Phil 6976.20 — Flegel, Horst. Schizophasie in linguistischer Deutung. Berlin, 1965.

Phil 5722.76 — Flottes, Pierre. L'histoire et l'inconscient humain. Genève, 1965.

Phil 9345.12 — Folliet, Joseph. Adam et Eve. Lyon, 1965.

Phil 2605.10.30 — Fontan, Pierre. L'intention réaliste. Paris, 1965.

Phil 5535.4 — Foppa, Klaus. Lernen, Gedächtnis, Verhalten. Köln, 1965.

Phil 2750.11.195 — Forni, Guglielmo. La filosofia della storia nel pensiero politico di Jacques Maritain. Bologna, 1965.

Phil 6955.23 — Foucault, Michel. Madness and civilization. N.Y., 1965.

Phil 5385.6 — Fowler, Harry. Curiosity and exploratory behavior. N.Y., 1965.

Phil 3450.19.335 — Fraga, Gustavo de. Sobre Heidegger. Coimbra, 1965.

Phil 848.4.2 — Franchini, Raffaello. Le origini della dialettica. 2. ed. Napoli, 1965.

Phil 4710.143 — Frank, Semen L. Iz istorii russkoi filosofskoi mysli kontsa XIX i nachala XX v. Washington, 1965.

Phil 4754.163.1 — Frank, Semen L. Reality and man. London, 1965.

Phil 5247.13.33 — Franzbach, Martin. Lessings Huarte-Übersetzung, 1752. Hamburg, 1965.

Phil 3450.43F — Freed, Louis Franklin. R.F.A. Hoernle. Johannesburg, 1965.

Phil 2905.1.400 — Frenaud, Georges. Pensée philosophique et religieuse du père Teilhard de Chardin. Le Chesnay, 1965.

Phil 6315.2.69 — Freud, Sigmund. Briefe 1907-1926. Sigmund Freud and Karl Abraham. Frankfurt, 1965.

Phil 6315.2.79.25 — Freud, Sigmund. Psychanalyse. 2. éd. Paris, 1965.

Phil 6315.2.28 — Freud, Sigmund. A psycho-analytic dialogue. London, 1965.

Phil 5238.206 — Frey-Wehrlin, Caspar J. Spectrum Psychologiae, ein Freundesgabe. Zürich, 1965.

Phil 3850.18.190 — Frings, Manfred S. Max Scheler. Pittsburgh, 1965.

Phil 1695.29 — Fromm, Erich. Socialist humanism. 1st ed. Garden City, N.Y., 1965.

Phil 705.3.7A — Frothingham, Octavius Brooks. Transcendentalism in New England, a history. Gloucester, Mass., 1965.

Phil 4260.118.5.2 — Fubini, Mario. Stile e umanità di Giambattista Vico. 2. ed. Milano, 1965.

Phil 5500.36 — Fulcher, Gordon Scott. Common sense decision-making. Evanston, Ill., 1965.

Phil 8612.55 — Fulton, Robert Lester. Death and identity. N.Y., 1965.

1965 - cont.

Phil 8955.9 Furger, Franz. Gewissen und Klugheit in der katholischen Moraltheologie der letzten Jahrzehnte. Luzern, 1965.

Phil 2250.113 Fuss, Peter Lawrence. The moral philosophy of Josiah Royce. Cambridge, 1965.

Phil 5046.25.5 Gabriel, Leo. Integrale Logik. Wien, 1965.

Phil 165.440 Gadamer, Hans Georg. Philosophisches Lesebuch. Frankfurt a.M., 1965- 3v.

Phil 623.46 Galifret, Yves. Le crépuscule des magiciens. 2. éd. Paris, 1965.

Phil 4120.9.35 Galli, Gallo. L'uomo nell'assoluto. Torino, 1965.

Phil 5590.480 Galli, Norberto. La caratterologia di G. Heymans e di R. LeSenne. Zürich, 1965.

Phil 70.99 Gandillac, Maurice Patronnier de. Entretiens sur les notions de genése et de structure. Paris, 1965.

Phil 3160.12.85 Gaona, Francisco. Das Raumproblem in Cassirers Philosophie der Mythologie. Tübingen, 1965.

Phil 720.65 García López, Jesús. El valor de la verdad y otros estudios. Madrid, 1965.

Phil 3808.233 Garewicz, Jan. Rozdroza pesymizmu. Wyd. 1. Wroctaw, 1965.

Phil 4006.5.38 Garin, Eugenio. Italian humanism. Oxford, 1965.

Phil 5585.231 Garnett, Arthur Campbell. The perceptual process. London, 1965.

Phil 3488.42 Garnett, Christopher Broune. The Kantian philosophy of space. Port Washington, N.Y., 1965.

Phil 3310.15 Gehlen, Arnold. Theorie der Willensfeiheit und frühe philosophische Schriften. Neuvied, 1965.

Phil 181.133 Gellner, Ernest. Thought and change. Chicago, 1965.

Phil 8696.23 Geloof en natuurwetenschap; studies over de verhouding van christelijk geloof en moderne natuurwetenschap. 's-Gravenhage, 1965-67. 2v.

Phil 672.151.10 Gent, Werner. Das Problem der Zeit. Hildesheim, 1965.

Phil 4120.4.126 Gentile, Giovanni. La religione: il modernismo e i rapporti tra religione e filosofia. Firenze, 1965.

Phil 181.164.2 Gentile, Marino. Come si pone il problema meta fisico. 2. ed. Padova, 1965.

Phil 7069.65.5 Gerloff, Hans. The crisis in parapsychology. Tittmoning, 1965.

Phil 6049.65 Gettings, Fred. The book of the hand. London, 1965.

Phil 4872.109.3 Ghose, Aurobindo. The life divine. 3rd ed. N.Y., 1965.

Phil 8050.82 Giacchelti, Vincenzo. Il giardino della mala biscia. Firenze, 1965.

Phil 1135.77 Giannini, Giorgio. Il problema antropologico. Roma, 1965.

Phil 5592.179 Gilberstadt, Harold. A handbook for clinical and actuarial MMPI interpretation. Philadelphia, 1965.

Phil 5867.20 Gilles, Brigitte. Untersuchungen zur Periodik im Spielverhalten 6-10 jähriger Kinder. Bonn, 1965.

Phil 3640.705 Gillner, Helmut. Fryderyk Nietzsche. Warszawa, 1965.

Phil 8407.41.5 Gilson, Étienne. The arts of the beautiful. N.Y., 1965.

Phil 4357.2.30 Giner de los Rios, Francisco. Ensayos y cartas. Mexico, 1965.

Phil 8696.25 Giret, André. L'astronomie et le sentiment religieux. Paris, 1965.

Phil 3246.305 Girndt, Helmut. Die Differenz des Fichtesche und Hegelschen Systems in der Hegelschen Differenzschrift. Bonn, 1965.

Phil 3450.11.79.5 Giulietti, Giovanni. La filosofia del profondo in Husserl e in Zamboni. Treviso, 1965.

Phil 6980.328.5 Glasser, William. Reality therapy, a new approach to psychiatry. N.Y., 1965.

Phil 8980.428 Glebova, Tamara G. Pis'ma k tebe. Moskva, 1965.

Phil 310.612 Goerlich, J. Zur Problematik der materialistische Dialektischen. Berlin, 1965.

Phil 5046.38 Gokieli, Levan P. Logika. v.1- Tbilisi, 1965. 2v.

Phil 623.43 Gol'dberg, N.M. Svobodomyslie i ateizm v SShA, XVII-XIX vv. Leningrad, 1965.

Phil 2880.8.175 Goldstein, Walter. Jean Paul Sartre und Martin Buber. Jerusalem, 1965.

Phil 310.631 González Duran, Guillermo. La dialéctica comunista a la luz de la ciencia. La Paz, 1965.

Phil 2030.6.2 Goodman, Nelson. Fact, fiction and forecast. 2d ed. Indianapolis, 1965.

Phil 4065.174 Gorfunkel', Aleksandr K. Dzhordano Bruno. Moskva, 1965.

Phil 5535.6 Goss, Albert E. Paired-associates learning; the role of meaningfulness, similarity. N.Y., 1965.

Phil 2255.1.128 Gottschalk, Herbert. Bertrand Russell: a life. London, 1965.

Phil 5592.180 Gough, Harrison Gould. The adjective checklist manual. Palo Alto, 1965.

Phil 4467.2.30 Govies, Pinharanda. Peregrinação do absoluto. Lisboa, 1965.

Phil 1540.79 Grabmann, Martin. Interpretazioni medievale del voüsnointinós. Padova, 1965.

Phil 525.240 Graef, Hilda Charlotte. The story of mysticism. 1st ed. Garden City, N.Y., 1965.

Phil 5520.438 Graumann, Carl F. Denken. Köln, 1965.

Phil 6316.23 Greenfield, Norman S. Psychoanalysis and current biological thought. Madison, 1965.

Phil 310.611 Gregor, A. James. A survey of Marxism. N.Y., 1965.

Phil 2855.8.80 Griffiths, David Albert. Jean Reynaud, encyclopédciste de l'époque romantique d'après sa correspondance inédite. Paris, 1965.

Phil 5046.42 Grize, Jean Blaise. Logique et connaissance. Genève, 1965.

Phil 6315.2.360 Grollman, Earl Alan. Judaism in Sigmund Freud's world. N.Y., 1965.

Phil 3006.10 Gropp, Rugard Otto. Von Cusanus bis Marx. Leipzig, 1965.

Phil 6316.8.30 Grossman, Carl M. The wild analyst. N.Y., 1965.

Phil 337.25 Grossmann, Reinhardt Siegbert. The structure of mind. Madison, 1965.

Phil 3120.30.140 Grünfeld, Werner. Der begegnungscharakter der Wirklichkeit...Martin Bubers. Ratingen, 1965.

Phil 3450.19.360 Guilead, Reuben. Etre et liberté. Louvain, 1965.

Phil 5246.47.12 Guilford, Joy Paul. Fundamental statistics in psychology and education. 4. ed. N.Y., 1965.

Phil 672.230 Guillaumaud, Jacques. Du temps physique au temps romanesque. Paris, 1965.

Phil 5592.184 Guillaumin, Jean. La dynamique de l'examen psychologique. Paris, 1965.

Phil 8696.22 Gurev, Grigorii. Velikii konflikt. Moskva, 1965.

Phil 481.4 Gurst, Guenter. Grosse Materialisten. Leipzig, 1965.

Phil 5520.110.5 Gusdorf, George. Speaking (La parole). Evanston, Ill., 1965.

Phil 8697.25.2 Habgood, J.S. Truths in tension. 1. ed. N.Y., 1965.

Phil 3450.29.7 Haecker, Theodor. Was ist der Mensch? München, 1965.

Phil 720.67 Haensel, Carl. Über den Irrtum. Heidelberg, 1965.

Phil 5590.215.2 Hall, Calvin S. Theories of personality. N.Y., 1965.

Phil 7069.65.30 Hall, Trevor H. New light on old ghosts. London, 1965.

Phil 5757.18 Hampshire, Stuart. Freedom of the individual. N.Y., 1965.

Phil 2880.8.156 Hana, Ghenam Georges. Freiheit und Person. München, 1965.

Phil 1020.80 Hanafi, Hasan. Les méthodes d'exegese. Le Caire, 1965.

Phil 5238.244 Hardesty, Francis P. Forderungen an die Psychologie. Bern, 1965.

Phil 6317.42 Harding, Mary Esther. The "I" and the "not-I"; a study in the development of consciousness. N.Y., 1965.

Phil 8882.68.10 Hare, Richard Mervyn. Descriptivism. London, 1965?

Phil 182.132 Harris, Errol E. The foundations of metaphysics in science. London, 1965.

Phil 3925.16.93 Hartnack, Justus. Wittgenstein and modern philosophy. Garden City, 1965.

Phil 5465.142 Hatterer, Lawrence J. The artist in society. N.Y., 1965.

Phil 5520.432 Hayden, Donald E. Classics in semantics. N.Y., 1965.

Phil 270.131 Hayden Colloquium on Scientific Method and Concept. Massachusetts Institute of Technology. Cause and effect. N.Y., 1965.

Phil 5247.86 Hector, Heinz. Gedankengänge in Psychologie. Paderborn, 1965.

Phil 3450.19.28 Heidegger, Martin. German existentialism. N.Y., 1965.

Phil 6400.23 Hekaen, Henry. Pathologie du langage. Paris, 1965.

Phil 6317.45 Hendin, Herbert. Psychoanalysis and social research; the psychoanalytic study of the non-patient. Garden City, 1965.

Phil 2730.113 Henry, Michel. Philosophie et phénoménologie du corps. Paris, 1965.

Phil 8581.110 Hermans, Francis. L'humanisme religieux de l'abbé Henri Bremond, 1865-1933. Paris, 1965.

Phil 5238.204 Hernnstein, Richard J. A source book in history of psychology. Cambridge, 1965.

Phil 585.182 Heschel, Abraham Joshua. Who is man? Stanford, Calif., 1965.

Phil 8662.26 Hidding, Klaas Albert Hendrik. De evolutie van het godsdienstig bewustzijn. Utrecht, 1965.

Phil 974.3.150 Hiebel, Friedrich. Rudolf Steiner im Geistesgang des Abendlandes. Bern, 1965.

Phil 5590.450 Hiese, Manfred. Übertragungsphänomene bei verwahrlosten männlichen Jugendlichen. Erlangen, 1965.

Phil 75.70 Higgins, Charles L. The bibliography of philosophy. Ann Arbor, 1965.

Phil 1750.552.10 Hijmans, Benjamin Lodwijk. Classics and the philosophy of existence. Winnipeg, 1965.

Phil 310.641 Historický materialismus. Praha, 1965.

Phil 3450.44 Hochgesang, Michael. Mythos und Logik im 20. Jahrhundert. München, 1965.

Phil 672.235 Hoelling, Joachim. Ontologische Beiträge zum Raum-Zeit-Problem. Freiburg? 1965.

Phil 8408.40 Hofstsdter, Albert. Truth and art. N.Y., 1965.

Phil 5643.127 Holland, Harry C. The spiral after-effect. Oxford, 1965.

Phil 3640.703 Hollingsdale, Reginald J. Nietzsche: the man and his philosophy. London, 1965.

Phil 525.252 L'homme et la connaissance. Paris, 1965.

Phil 182.134 Horn, Joachim Christian. Monade und Begriff. Der Weg von Leibniz zu Hegel. Wien, 1965.

Phil 5520.430 Hotopf, W.H.N. Language, thought and comprehension. London, 1965.

Phil 3827.16 Hoyack, Louis. Spinoza als uitgangspant. Deventer, 1965.

Phil 4812.457.35 Hrušovsky, Igor. Problémy, portréty, retrospektívy. Vyd. 1. Bratislava, 1965.

Phil 3925.16.125 Hubbeling, Hubertus Gerinus. Inleiding tot het denken van Wittgenstein. Assen, 1965.

Phil 4065.182 Huber, Karl. Einheit und Vielheit in Denken und Sprache Giordano Brunos. Winterthur, 1965.

Phil 5047.47 Hughes, G.E. The elements of formal logic. N.Y., 1965.

Phil 2055.15.37 Hulme, Thomas E. Speculations; essays on humanism and the philosophy of art. London, 1965.

Phil 2050.59.2 Hume, David. An abstract of a treatise of human nature, 1740. Hamden, Conn., 1965.

Phil 2050.72 Hume, David. David Hume: philosophical historian. Indianapolis, 1965.

Phil 8735.57 Hurlbutt, Robert H. Hume, Newton, and the design argument. Lincoln, 1965.

Phil 3450.11.55 Husserl, Edmund. Phenomenology and the crisis of philosophy. N.Y., 1965.

Phil 3450.11.48 Husserl, Edmund. Philosophie als strenge Wissenschaft. Frankfurt am Main, 1965.

Phil 9070.107 Huxley, Julian. You are not the target. N.Y., 1965.

Phil 3425.390.2 Hyppolite, Jean. Etudes sur Marx et Hegel. 2. éd. Paris, 1965.

Phil 7084.38 Hyppolite, Michelson Paul. La mentalité haitienne et le domaine du rêve. Port-au-Prince, 1965.

Phil 165.388 Iadir, C.A. The world of philosophy. Lahore, 1965.

Phil 4710.50.15 Ievdokymenko, V.I. Z istorii filosofs'koi dumky na Ukraini. Kyïv, 1965.

Phil 8698.10 Ikeda, Daisaku. Science and religion. Tokyo, 1965.

Phil 3425.647 Incardona, Nunzio. L'assunzione hegeliana. Palermo, 1965.

VPhil 585.167 International Congress of Philosophy, 13th, Mexico, 1963. Clověk, kto si? Bratislava, 1965.

Phil 310.421 Iovchuk, Mikhail T. Problemy marksistsko-leninskoi filosofii. Moskva, 1965.

Phil 5248.3 Isaacson, Robert Lee. Psychology, the science of behavior. N.Y., 1965.

Phil 730.27 Iugai, Geragim A. Dialektika chasti i tselogo. Alma-Ata, 1965.

Phil 6319.1.183.10 Jacobi, Jolan. Der Weg zur Individuation. Zürich, 1965.

Phil 6319.13 Jacobson, Edith. The self and the object world. London, 1965.

Phil 310.445.25 Jaroszewski, Tadeusz M. Alienacja? Warszawa, 1965.

Phil 575.254 Jaroszewski, Tadeusz M. Osobowość i własność. Warszawa, 1965.

Phil 3475.3.195 Jaspers, Karl. Hoffnung und Sorge. München, 1965.

Phil 3640.267.4 Jaspers, Karl. Nietzsche: an introduction to the understanding of his philosophical activity. Tucson, 1965.

Phil 2880.8.99 Jeanson, Francis. Le problème moral et la pensée de Sartre. Paris, 1965.

Phil 5655.10 Jellinek, Paul. Die psychologischen Grundlagen der Parfümerie. 2. Aufl. Heidelberg, 1965.

Phil 6959.11 Jensen, Susanne. Ein Versuch zur quantitativen Analyse des gruppenpsychotherapeutischen Prozesses mit schizophrenen Patienten. Bonn, 1965.

Phil 5790.5 Jerphagnon, Lucien. De la banalité. Paris, 1965.

Phil 6315.2.340 Johnston, Thomas E. Freud and political thought. 1st. ed. N.Y., 1965.

1965 - cont.

Phil 2880.8.155   Jolivet, Régis. Sartre, ou La théologie de l'absurde. Paris, 1965.

Phil 4683.161.30   Jurevičs, Pauls. Idejas un isteniba; esejas. 2. izd. Stockholm, 1965.

Phil 8959.8   Juva, Mikko. Tästa on kysymys. Söderström, 1965.

Phil 4803.334.81   Kaczmarek, Stefan. Aniol Dowgird, filozof nieznany. Warszawa, 1965.

Phil 5250.76   Kahn, Jack Harold. Human growth and the development of personality. 1. ed. N.Y., 1965.

Phil 8590.42   Kahraman, Ahmet. Dinber tarihi. Istanbul, 1965.

Phil 3480.126   Kant, Immanuel. Ausgewählte Kleine Schriften. Hamburg, 1965.

Phil 3480.50.18.3   Kant, Immanuel. Erste Einleitung in die Kritik der Urteilskraft. Stuttgart, 1965.

Phil 3480.52.20   Kant, Immanuel. First introduction to the Critique of judgment. Indianapolis, 1965.

Phil 3480.67.110   Kant, Immanuel. The metaphysical elements of justice. Indianapolis, 1965.

Phil 8665.23   Karpushin, Vladimir A. Populiarnye lektsii po ateizmu. 2. izd. Moskva, 1965.

Phil 3801.474   Kasper, Walter. Das Absolute in der Geschichte. Mainz, 1965.

Phil 8885.47   Kattsoff, Louis Osgood. Making moral decisions. The Hague, 1965.

Phil 3425.608   Kaufmann, W.A. Hegel. 1st ed. Garden City, N.Y., 1965.

Phil 6750.265   Keblon, Lars. The structure of abilities at lower levels of intelligence. Stockholm, 1965.

Phil 185.98   Keleher, James Francis. Disputed questions in philosophy. N.Y., 1965.

Phil 5520.439   Keller, Benjamin. Toward an informal and creative conference method. Santa Monica, 1965.

Phil 6320.20   Kelman, Harold. New perspectives in psychoanalysis. N.Y., 1965.

Phil 735.254   Kempff Mercado, Manfredo. Cuando valen los valores? Maracaibo, 1965.

Phil 8400.54.5   Keper, Gyorgy. The nature and art of motion. N.Y., 1965.

Phil 8400.54   Kepes, Gyorgy. Structure in art and in science. N.Y., 1965.

Phil 5270.1   Kerlinger, Frederick, N. Foundations of behavioral research. N.Y., 1965.

Phil 2005.11   Kettler, David. The social and political thought of Adam Ferguson. Columbus, 1965.

Phil 341.38   Kevorkian, Hamlet. Veroiatnoe i dostovernoe znanie. Erevan, 1965.

Phil 8030.8   Kiell, Norman. Psychiatry and psychology in the visual arts and aesthetics. Madison, 1965.

Phil 3801.485   Kile, Frederick O. Die theologischen Grundlagen von Schellings Philosophie der Freiheit. Leiden, 1965.

Phil 3090.88   Klamroth, Erich. Die Weltanschauung Franz von Baaders in ihrem Gegensatz zu Kant. Berlin, 1965.

Phil 5780.23   Klausner, Samuel Z. The quest for self-control. N.Y., 1965.

Phil 5066.261.5   Kleene, Stephen Cole. The foundations of intuitionistic mathematics. Amsterdam, 1965.

Phil 3235.130   Klimkeit, Hans-Joachim. Das Wunderverstaendnis Ludwig Feuerbaches in religionsphanomenologischer Sicht. Bonn, 1965.

Phil 1710.13   Kline, George. European philosophy today. Chicago, 1965.

Phil 9560.57   Klubertanz, George Peter. Habits and virtues. N.Y., 1965.

Phil 4769.1.125   Klum, Edith. Natur, Kunst und Liebe in der Philosophie Vladimir Solov'evs. München, 1965.

Phil 2225.5.115   Knight, Thomas Stanley. Charles Peirce. N.Y., 1965.

Phil 3801.496.5   Ko Ktanck, Anton Mirko. Schelling-Studien. München, 1965.

Phil 3450.19.253   Kockelmans, Joseph John. Martin Heidegger. Pittsburgh, 1965.

Phil 2880.8.157   Kohut, Karl. Was ist Literatur? Marburg, 1965.

Phil 165.365   Koktanek, Anton Mirko. Philosophischer Eros im Wandel der Zeit. München, 1965.

Phil 960.253   Komarov, N. Ideologicheskie techeniia sovremennoi Indii. Moskva, 1965.

Phil 310.608   Kommunisticheskaia Partiia. Sovetskogo Soiuza. Zaochnaia Vysshaia Partiinaia Shkola. Katedra Marksistsko-Leninskoi Filosofii. Marksistsko-leninskaia filosofiia. Moskva, 1965.

Phil 8980.616   Kommunisticheskaia Partiia Sovetskogo Soiuza. Novosibirskaia Vysshaia Partiinaia Shkola. Kategorii marksistsko-leninskoi etiki. Moskva, 1965.

Phil 310.599.2   Kosík, Karel. Dialektika konkrétního. 2. Vyd. Praha, 1965.

Phil 5020.10   Kotarbiński, Tadeusz. Leçons sur l'histoire de la logique. Warszawa, 1965.

Phil 5250.78   Kotarbiński, Tadeusz. Praxiology; an introduction to the sciences of efficient action. 1. English ed. Oxford, 1965.

Phil 5590.447.2   Kovalev, Aleksandr G. Psikhologiia lichnosti. 2. izd. Moskva, 1965.

Phil 4803.108.90   Krawczyk, Zbigniew. Socjologia Edwarda Abramowskiego. Warszawa, 1965.

Phil 5250.45.2   Krech, David. Elements of psychology. N.Y., 1965.

Phil 6960.16   Kreitler, Hans. Die wellanscharlie Orienterung der Schizophrenen. München, 1965.

Phil 5865.10   Kriekemans, Albert. Genetische Psychologie, systematischen historisch. v.1,7,9,12. Tielt, 1965- 4v.

Phil 900.27   Krikorian, Sergei. Sovremennaia filosofskaia i sotsiologicheskaia mysl' stran vostoka. Moskva, 1965.

Phil 8411.34   Krivskovskii, Nikolai I. Logika krasoty. Minsk, 1965.

Phil 9070.109   Kuczyński, Janusz. Filozofia życia. Wyd. 1. Warszawa, 1965.

Phil 978.93   Kuhn, Hans. Es Ist an der Zeit. Nürnberg, 1965.

Phil 1020.4.40   Kuksewicz, Zdzislaw. Averroïsme bolonais au XIVe siècle. Wroclaw, 1965.

Phil 4800.24   Kuksewicz, Zdzisław. Z dziejów filosofii na Uniwersytecie Krakowskim w XV wieku. Wrocław, 1965.

Phil 5270.2   Kurtz, Kenneth Hassett. Foundations of psychological research. Boston, 1965.

Phil 5760.14   Kurtz, Paul W. Decision and the condition of man. Seattle, 1965.

Phil 5068.65   Kyserling, Arnold. Der Wiener Denkstil: Mach, Carnap. Graz, 1965.

Phil 5520.433   Laffal, Julius. Pathological and normal language. N.Y., 1965.

Phil 3585.1.35   Lambert, Johann Heinrich. Philosophische Schriften. Reprografischer Nachdruck. v.1-4,6-7,9. Hildesheim, 1965-7v.

Phil 1750.166.23   Lamont, Corliss. The philosophy of humanism. 5th ed. N.Y., 1965.

1965 - cont.

Phil 6321.49   Lampl de Groot, Jeanne. The development of the mind. N.Y., 1965.

Phil 165.370   Landgrebe, Ludwig. Beispiela. Den Haag, 1965.

Phil 176.213   La Rochefoucauld, Edmée de Fels. La nature et l'esprit. Paris, 1965.

Phil 705.54   Lauth, Reinhard. Zur Idee der Transzendentalphilosophie. München, 1965.

Phil 4160.5.230   Lazzarini, Renato. Valore e religione nell'orizzonte esistenziale. Padova, 1965.

Phil 4160.5.30   Lazzerini, Virgilio. Annotaziori per un nuovo criticismo. Milano, 1965.

Phil 5465.148   Lefebve, Maurice Jean. L'image fascinante et le surréel. Paris, 1965.

Phil 2725.37.40   Lefebvre, Henri. Métaphilosophie; prolégomènes. Paris, 1965.

Phil 2520.353   Lefèvre, Roger. La pensée existentielle de Descartes. Paris, 1965.

Phil 3552.21.5   Leibniz, Gottfried Wilhelm. Kleine Schriften zur Metaphysik. Frankfurt, 1965.

Phil 3552.67.40   Leibniz, Gottfried Wilhelm. Monadology, and other philosophical essays. Indianapolis, 1965.

Phil 8666.19   Lelong, Michel. Pour un dialogue avec les athées. Paris, 1965.

Phil 8505.8.25   Leningrad. Muzei Istorii Religii i Ateizma. Muzei istorii religii i ateizma. Leningrad, 1965.

Phil 535.35   Leon, Philip. Beyond belief and unbelief. London, 1965.

Phil 5374.239   Leont'ev, Aleksei N. Problemy razvitiia psikhiki. 2. izd. Moskva, 1965.

Phil 7055.173   Leroy, Roger. Un voyant au XXe siècle: Dieudonné. Paris, 1965.

Phil 7162.265   Lethbridge, Thomas C. E.S.P.; beyond time and distance. London, 1965.

Phil 5590.442   Levita, David Joël de. The concept of identity. Paris, 1965.

Phil 6321.50   Levitas, G.B. The world of psychoanalysis. N.Y., 1965.

Phil 1182.54   Lévy, Isidore. Recherches esséniennes et pythagoriciennes. Genève, 1965.

Phil 5585.141   Lévy-Valensi, Elaine Amado. Le temps dans la vie psychologique. Paris, 1965.

Phil 8591.80   Lewis, Hywel David. Philosophy of religion. London, 1965.

Phil 4600.4.45   Lidforss, Bengt. Bengt Lidforss i urral. Stockholm, 1965.

Phil 8701.24   Lindroth, Hjalmer. Filosofiska och teologiska essayer. Stockholm, 1965.

Phil 8591.83   Lings, Martin. Ancient beliefs and modern superstitions. 1. ed. London, 1965.

Phil 3493.33   Loegstrup, Kocud Ejler Christian. Kants aestetik. København, 1965.

Phil 5066.232   Logic Colloquiam, 8th, Oxford, 1963. Formal systems and recursive functions. Amsterdam, 1965.

Phil 4160.66.12   Lombardi, Franco. Scritti; saggi. v.10-13. Firenze, 1965-4v.

Phil 9513.20   Lopez, Aranguren, José Luis. Moral y sociedad. Madrid, 1965.

Phil 5251.67   Lorenz, Konrad Zacharias. Evolution and modification of behavior. Chicago, 1965.

Phil 8412.39   Losev, Aleksei F. Istoriia esteticheskikh kategorii. Moskva, 1965.

Phil 1750.552.15   Lotz, Johannes Baptist. Sein und Existenz. Freiburg, 1965.

Phil 3425.78.10   Lowenberg, Jacob. Hegel's phenomenology. La Salle, Ill., 1965.

Phil 2905.1.180.6   Lubac, Henri de. The faith of Teilhard de Chardin. London, 1965.

Phil 9558.42   Ludwig, Arnold M. The importance of lying. Springfield, Ill, 1965.

Phil 8725.6   Luebbe, Hermann. Säkularisierung. Freiburg, 1965.

Phil 5590.452   Lückert, Heinz Rolf. Die Problematik der Persönlichkeitsdiagnostik. München, 1965.

Phil 3585.20.20   Luijpen, Wilhelmus Anonius Maria. Phenomenology and metaphysics. Pittsburgh, 1965.

Phil 8666.23   Lunacharskii, Anatolii V. Pochemu nel'zia verit' v boga. Moskva, 1965.

Phil 8980.537   Lushchytski, I.N. Osnovy marksistko-leninskoi etiki. Minsk, 1965.

Phil 2905.1.385   Luyten, Norbert Alfons. Teilhard de Chardin. Fribourg, 1965.

Phil 5421.35.5   Lynch, William F. Images of hope. Baltimore, 1965.

Phil 9550.18   Lyons, David. Forms and limits of utilitarianism. Oxford, 1965.

Phil 1750.767   MacColl, Sylvia. Structure and development of phenomenal reality. N.Y., 1965.

Phil 8980.546   Machovec, Milan. Smysl lidského života. Praha, 1965.

Phil 7082.194   Mackenzie, Norman Jan. Dreams and dreaming. N.Y., 1965.

Phil 165.337.5   McMullin, Ethan. The concept of matter in Greek and medieval philosophy. Notre Dame, 1965.

Phil 8592.116   McPherson, Thomas. The philosophy of religion. London, 1965.

Phil 5055.21.10   Madarászné Zsigmond Anna. A tiszta logika alapkérdesei. Budapest, 1965.

Phil 4080.3.435   Mager, Wolfgand. Benedetto Croces literarisches und politisches Interesse an der Geschichte. Koln, 1965.

Phil 3625.5.2   Maimon, Salomon. Gesammelte Werke. Hildesheim, 1965. 6v.

Phil 4795.8   Mamedov, Sheidabek Faradzhievich. Razvitie filosofskoi mysli v Azerbaidzhane. Moskva, 1965.

Phil 8030.7   Mandel'shtam, Roza S. Marksistskoe iskusstvovedenie. Moskva, 1929. Ann Arbor, 1965.

Phil 3850.18.215   Mandrioni, Héctor Delfor. Max Scheler; un estudio sobre el concepto de espíritu en el formalismo de Max Scheler. Buenos Aires, 1965.

Phil 5350.8   Mann, John Harvey. Changing human behavior. N.Y., 1965.

Phil 4260.153   Manno, Ambrogio G. Lo storicismo di G.B. Vico. Napoli, 1965.

Phil 2750.19.42.5   Marcel, Gabriel. Philosophical fragments, 1904. Notre Dame, Ind., 1965.

Phil 2150.22.30   Marcuse, Herbert. Kultur und Gesellschaft. Frankfurt, 1965. 2v.

Phil 8413.36   Margolis, Joseph. The language of art and art criticism. Detroit, 1965.

Phil 3195.6.185   Marini, Giuliano. Dilthey e la comprensione del mondo umano. Milano, 1965.

Phil 2750.11.85.4   Maritain, Jacques. Art et scolastique. 4. éd. Paris, 1965.

Phil 2750.11.62   Maritain, Jacques. Carnet de notes. Paris, 1965.

Phil 2750.11.91   Maritain, Jacques. Le songe de Descartes. Paris, 1965.

Phil 310.626   Marksizm-leninizm, teoreticheskaia osnova stroitel'stva kommunizma. Moskva, 1965.

Phil 2340.1.80   Maron, M.E. Norbert Wiener. Santa Monica, Calif., 1965.

Phil 525.105.5   Marquette, Jacques de. Confessions d'un mystique contemporain. Paris, 1965.

Phil 4987.89.85   Marquinez Argote, Germán. En torno a Zubiri. Madrid, 1965.

Phil 3425.625   Marsch, Wolf Dieter. Gegenwart Christi in der Gesellschaft; eine Studie zu Hegels Dialektik. München, 1965.

Phil 4080.32   Martano, Giuseppe. La filosofia dell'esperienza di Cleto Carbonara. Napoli, 1965.

Phil 2905.1.355   Martinazzo, Eusebio. Teilhard de Chardin. Romae, 1965.

Phil 5762.34   Martinetti, Piero. La libertà. Torino, 1965.

Phil 5252.155   Marx, Melvin Herman. Theories in contemporary psychology. N.Y., 1965.

Phil 6322.45   Masterson, Jenny Gove. Letters from Jenny. N.Y., 1965.

Phil 3246.304   Masullo, Aldo. La comunitá come fondamento. Napoli, 1965.

Phil 5850.356.10   Matalon, Benjamin. L'analyse hiérarchique. Paris, 1965.

Phil 5066.231   Mates, Benson. Elementary logic. N.Y., 1965.

Phil 7055.108   Mathias, Julio. Don Luis de Alderete y Soto. Málaga, 1965.

Phil 75.69   Matica Slovenská, Turčiansky sv. Martin. Bibliografický Odbor. Bibliografia filozofíckéj Knižnej tvorby na Slovensku. Martin, 1965.

Phil 7069.65.20   Maudiut, Jacques A. Aux fontières de l'irrationnel. Paris, 1965.

Phil 3425.617   Maurer, R.K. Hegel und das Ende der Geschichte. Stuttgart, 1965.

Phil 2412.10.2   Mauzi, Robert. L'idée du bonheur dans la littérature et la pensée françaises. 2e éd. Paris, 1965.

Phil 3494.64   Mayz Vallenilla, Ernesto. El problema de la nada en Kant. Madrid, 1965.

Phil 5762.26   Mazzantini, Carlo. Il problema filosofico del "libero arbitrio" nelle controversie teologiche del secolo XIII. Torino, 1965.

Phil 8413.35   Medlöe, Jon. Kunst og idé. Oslo, 1965.

Phil 1712.18.2   Mehl, Roger. Images of man. Richmond, 1965.

Phil 3625.8.52   Meier, Georg Friedrich. Versuch einer Allegemeinen Auslegungskunst. Dusseldorf, 1965.

Phil 3625.22   Meinong, Alexius. Philosophenbriefe aus den wissenschaftlichen Korrespondez mit Franz Brentano. Graz, 1965.

Phil 3475.3.240   Mekkes, Johan Peter Albertus. Teken en motief der creatuur. Amsterdam, 1965.

Phil 3012.5   Meleshchenko, Zoia N. Nemctskaia filosofia XIX - nachala XX vv. Leningrad, 1965.

Phil 585.198   Melo, Roneu de. O homem contemporâneo. Lisboa, 1965.

Phil 187.177   Melsen, Andreas Gerardus Maria van. Evolution and philosophy. Pittsburgh, 1965.

Phil 5590.440   Menaker, Esther. Ego in evolution. N.Y., 1965.

Phil 75.82   Menchaca, José. Diccionario bio-bibliográfico de filósofos. Bilbao, 1965.

Phil 293.33   Merleau-Ponty, Jacques. Cosmologie du XXe siècle. Paris, 1965.

Phil 1750.115.125   Merleau-Ponty, Maurice. Les sciences de l'homme et la phénoménologie. Paris, 1965.

Phil 1712.2.6   Merz, J.T. A history of European thought in the nineteenth century. N.Y., 1965. 4v.

Phil 2805.421   Mesnard, Jean. Pascal. Bruges, 1965.

Phil 2805.422   Mesnard, Jean. Pascal et les Roannez. Bruges, 1965. 2v.

Phil 4974.27.20   Mestre, Jose Manuel. Obras. Habana, 1965.

Phil 5222.11   Meyer, Donald Burton. The positive thinkers. 1. ed. Garden City, N.Y., 1965.

Phil 4369.2.90   Miccolis, Salvatore. Francesco Sanchez. Bari, 1965.

Phil 6322.47   Michel, André. L'école freudienne devant la musique. Paris, 1965.

Phil 8050.84   Miele, Franco. Teoria e storia dell'estetica. Milano, 1965.

Phil 1200.67   Mignueci, Mario. Il sigiuficato della logica stoica. Bologna, 1965.

Phil 2138.35.20   Mill, John S. A system of logic. London, 1965.

Phil 2490.84.20   Mill, John Stuart. Auguste Comte and positivism. Ann Arbor, 1965.

Phil 1750.166.175   Mollenauer, Robert. Introduction to modernity. Austin, 1965.

Phil 310.562   Molnár, Erik. Les antécédents idéologiques du matérialisme historique. Budapest, 1965.

Phil 2905.1.395   Monestier, André. Teilhard ou Marx? Paris, 1965.

Phil 2885.114   Mongardini, Carlo. Storia e sociologia nell'opera di H. Taine. Milano, 1965.

Phil 7159.173   Montgomery, Ruth S. A gift of prophecy: the phenomenal Jeane Dixon. N.Y., 1965.

Phil 8887.21.10   Moore, George Edward. Ethics. N.Y., 1965.

Phil 5252.156   Morávek, Milan. Otázky vzniku a povahy psychiky. Praha, 1965.

Phil 5252.82.3   Morgan, Clifford Thomas. Physiological psychology. 3. ed. N.Y., 1965.

Phil 8980.581.10   Moscow. Vsesoiuznyi Zaochnyi Politekhunicheskii Institut. Marksistko-leninskaia filosofiia. Moskva, 1965.

Phil 6055.2.2   Mueller, Alfred Eugen. Weltgeschichte graphologisch Gesehen. Köln, 1965.

Phil 735.126.2   Mukerjee, Radhakamal. The social structure of values. 2nd ed. New Delhi, 1965.

Phil 293.31.5   Munitz, Milton Karl. The mystery of existence. N.Y., 1965.

Phil 5350.7   Munn, Norman Leslie. The evolution and growth of human behavior . 2d ed. Boston, 1965.

Phil 8887.122   Munz, Peter. Relationship and solitude. 1st. American ed. Middletown, Conn., 1965.

Phil 3425.610   Mure, G.R.G. The philosophy of Hegel. London, 1965.

Phil 7080.58   Murray, Edward. Sleep, dreams, and arousal. N.Y., 1965.

Phil 5592.176   Murstein, Bernard. Theory and research in projective techniques, emphasizing the TAT. N.Y., 1965.

Phil 270.108   Musabaeva, N.A. Kibernetika i kategoriia prichinnosti. Alma-Ata, 1965.

Phil 6405.2   Myklebust, Helmer R. Development and disorders of written language. N.Y., 1965.

Phil 6323.21   Nacht, Sacha. Traité de psychanalyse. Paris, 1965.

Phil 4610.10.30   Naess, Arne. Hva er filosofi? Oslo, 1965.

Phil 1713.4   Naess, Arne. Moderne filosofer. Stockholm, 1965.

Phil 344.5   Nagel, Ernest. Meaning and knowledge. N.Y., 1965.

Phil 4195.107   Napoli, Giovanni di. Giovanni Pico della Mirandola. Roma, 1965.

Phil 4200.1.84   Nardi, Bruno. Studi su Pietro Pomponazzi. Firenze, 1965.

Phil 672.227   Nebel, Gerhard. Zeit und Zeiten. Stuttgart, 1965.

Phil 3552.460   Nedergaard-Hansen, Leif. Bayle's og Leibniz' drøftelse af theodicé-problemet; en idéhistorisk redegørelse. v.1-2. København, 1965.

Phil 672.233   Needham, Joseph. Time and Eastern man. London, 1965.

VPhil 8400.58   Nēkteré otázky kulturní politiky a marxistické estetiky. 1. vyd. Praha, 1965.

Phil 3495.18   Nieschmidt, Gerd Peter. Praktische Vernunft und Ewiger Friede. München, 1965.

Phil 3640.14.16   Nietzsche, Friedrich. Nietzsche. Index. München, 1965.

Phil 1750.115.75   Nikolov, Elit I. Fenomenologiia i estetika. Sofiia, 1965.

Phil 488.1.5   Nizan, Paul. Les matérialistes de l'antiquité. Paris, 1965.

Phil 4180.2   Nobile-Ventura, Attilio. La maschera e il volto della nostra società. Milano, 1965.

Phil 2520.352   Nocce, Augusto del. Riforma cattolica e filosofia moderna. Bologna, 1965.

Phil 5525.65   Nohain, Jean. Histoire du rure à travers le monde. Paris, 1965.

Phil 5625.108   Notterman, Joseph M. Dynamics of response. N.Y., 1965.

Phil 488.2   Novack, George Edward. The origins of materialism. 1st ed. N.Y., 1965.

Phil 8414.14   Novák, Mirko. Od skutečnosti ku umĕni. Praha, 1965.

Phil 4710.147   Novikov, Avraam I. Leninizm i progressivnye traditsii russkoi obshchestvennoi mysli. Leningrad, 1965.

Phil 9245.118   Novikov, Mikhail I. O schast'e. Moskva, 1965.

Phil 5238.178   Novosibirsk. Gosudartvennyi Pedagogicheskii Institut. Voprosy psikhologii. Omsk, 1965.

Phil 310.621   Nový, Lubomír. Filosofie v neklidné dobĕ. Praha, 1965.

Phil 1750.778   Nuño Montes, Juan Antonio. Sentido de la filosofía contemporánea. Caracas, 1965.

Phil 5590.454   Nuttin, Jozef. La structure de la personnalité. Paris, 1965.

Phil 6124.6   Ochs, Sidney. Elements of neurophysiology. N.Y., 1965.

Phil 3640.79.107   Oehler, Richard. Nietzscheregister. Stuttgart, 1965.

Phil 3801.637   Oeser, Erhard. Die antike Dialektik in der Spätphilosophie Schellings. Wein, 1965.

Phil 1750.768   Oizerman, Teodor Il'ich. Die Entfremdung als historische Kategorie. Berlin, 1965.

Phil 8889.10   Olson, Robert Goodwin. The morality of self-interest. N.Y., 1965.

Phil 5024.1   Öner, Necoti. Fromsy sosydojiokuluna göre mokhyinmensei. Ankara, 1965.

Phil 5592.174   Ong, Jin. The opposite form procedure in inventory construction and research. 1. ed. N.Y., 1965.

Phil 9070.119   Onimus, Jean. Lettres à mes fils. 5. éd. Paris, 1965.

Phil 3850.10.85   Oppenberg, Ursula. Quellenstudien zu Friedrich Schlegels Übersetzungen aus dem Sanskrit. Diss. Narburg, 1965.

Phil 6324.7   Osbert, Reuben. Marxism and psycho-analysis. London, 1965.

Phil 7080.55   Othmer, Ekkehard. Persönlichkeit und Schlafverhalten. Meisenheim, 1965.

Phil 2340.10.215   Paci, Enzo. La filosofia di Whitehead e i problemi del tempo e della struttura. Milano, 1965.

Phil 4200.8.30   Paci, Enzo. Relazioni e significati. v.1-2. Milano, 1965. 3v.

Phil 1750.820   Paci, Enzo. Tempo e relazione. Milano, 1965.

Phil 7069.65.10   Parapsychology Foundation. Ten years of activities. N.Y., 1965.

Phil 5875.150   Pareek, Udai Narain. Developmental patterns in reactions to frustration. N.Y., 1965.

Phil 8416.8.5   Pareyson, Luigi. Theoria dell'arte; saggi di estetica. Milano, 1965.

Phil 3552.448   Parkinson, George H.R. Logic and reality in Leibniz's metaphysics. Oxford, 1965.

Phil 2805.32.27   Pascal, Blaise. Les provinciales. Paris, 1965.

Phil 5190.60   Patel, Peter. Logische und methodologische Probleme der wissenschaftlichen Erklärung. München, 1965.

Phil 2880.8.180   Patte, Daniel. L'athéisme d'un chrétien; ou Un chrétien à l'écoute de Sartre. Paris, 1965.

Phil 5255.72   Paulus, Jean. Les fondements théoriques et méthodologiques de la psychologie. Bruxelles, 1965.

Phil 9070.108   Peale, Norman Vincent. Sin, sex and self control. 1st ed. Garden City, 1965.

Phil 4829.680.30   Pejović, Danilo. Protiv struje. Zagreb, 1965.

Phil 3450.19.400   Penzo, Giorgio. L'unità del pensiero in Martin Heidegger; una ontologia estetica. Padova, 1965.

VPhil 815.25   Perelman, C. An historical introduction to philosophical thinking. N.Y., 1965.

Phil 2905.1.320   Périgord, Monique. L'esthétique de Teilhard. Paris, 1965.

Phil 4757.2.115   Peters, Arthur A. Gurdjieff remembered. London, 1965.

Phil 3925.16.98   Peursen, Cornelis Anthonie van. Ludwig Wittgenstein. Baarn, 1965.

Phil 190.110   Peursen, Cornetis A. van. Feiten, waarden, geburtenissen. Een deiktische ontologie. Hilversum, 1965[1966].

Phil 5825.2.5   Pfungst, Oskar. Clever Hans; the horse of Mr. von Osten. N.Y., 1965.

Phil 1750.770   Philosophes d'aujourd'hui en présence du droit. Paris, 1965.

Phil 165.354   Philosophy and Christianity. Kampen, 1965.

Phil 190.106   Piaget, Jean. Sagesse et illusions de la philosophie. Paris, 1965.

Phil 3450.11.355   Piana, G. Esistenza e storia negli inediti di Husserl. Milano, 1965.

Phil 4195.39   Pico della Mirandola, Giovanni. On the dignity of man. Indianapolis, 1965.

Phil 8965.13.15   Pieper, Josef. The four cardinal virtues. N.Y., 1965.

Phil 270.132   Pilipenko, Nikolai V. Neobkhodimost' i sluchainost'. Moskva, 1965.

Phil 3120.30.170   Pilosof, Nelson. Martin Buber, profeta del diálogo. Montevideo, 1965.

Phil 8416.39   Pimenta, Gustave. Évidences. Paris, 1965.

Phil 6319.1.250   Pintacuda, Luigi. La psicologia religiosa di Karl Jung. Roma, 1965.

Phil 5255.75   Piret, Roger. Psychologie différentielle des sexes. Paris, 1965.

Phil 3497.23   Plaass, Peter. Kants Theorie der Naturwissenschaft. Göttingen, 1965.

Phil 8670.21   Plantinga, Alvin. The ontological argument. Garden City, N.Y., 1965.

Phil 310.598   Planty-Bonjour, Guy. Les categories du materialisme dialectique. Dordrecht, 1965.

Phil 575.253   Platonov, Konstantin K. Lichnost' i trud. Moskva, 1965.

Phil 5255.70   Platonov, Konstantin Konstantinovich. Psychology as you may like it. Moscow, 1965.

1965 - cont.

Phil 585.180 — Platt, John Rader. New views of the nature of man. Chicago, 1965.

Phil 585.135.2 — Plattel, Martinus Gulielmus. Social philosophy. Pittsburgh, 1965.

Phil 310.370.5 — Podosetnik, V.M. A glance at historical materialism. Moscow, 1965.

Phil 5627.265.5 — Pöll, Wilhelm. Religionspsychologie. München, 1965.

Phil 2905.1.370 — Polgár, Ladislaus. Internationale Teilhard-Bibliographie. Freiburg, 1965.

Phil 9245.64 — Polin, Raymond. Le bonheur considéré comme l'un des beaux-arts. Paris, 1965.

Phil 6155.14 — Polland, John C. Drugs and phantasy: the effects of LSD, psilocykin and Sernyl on college students. 1st ed. Boston, 1965.

Phil 346.32 — Pondey, Rajendra Prasad. The problem of fact. Santiniketan, 1965.

Phil 6325.24 — Pontalis, J.B. Après Freud. Paris, 1965.

Phil 5068.55 — Ponte Orvieto, Marina da. L'unità del sapere nel neopositivismo. Padova, 1965.

Phil 978.112 — Poortman, Johannes Jocobus. Philosophy, theosophy, parapsychology, some essays. Leyaen, 1965[1964]

Phil 6060.80 — Pophal, Rudolf. Graphologie in Vorlesungen. Stuttgart, 1965- 3v.

Phil 672.254 — Popma, Klaas Johan. Nadenken over de tijd. Amsterdam, 1965.

Phil 7150.60 — Porterfield, Austin Larimore. Cultures of violence; a study of the tragic man in society. Fort Worth, Texas, 1965.

Phil 8416.38 — Pospelov, Gennadii N. Esteticheskoe i khudozhestvennoe. Moskva, 1965.

Phil 8965.25 — Potterie, I. de. La vie selon l'Esprit, condition du chrétien. Paris, 1965.

Phil 8595.56 — Pozov, A. Osnovy drevne-tserkovnoi antropologii. Madrid, 1965. 2v.

Phil 5402.29 — Prescott, Frederick. The control of pain. N.Y., 1965.

Phil 2050.256 — Price, John Valdimir. The ironic Hume. Austin, 1965.

Phil 2218.60 — Priestley, Joseph. Writings on philosophy, science and politics. 1st ed. N.Y., 1965.

Phil 8980.712.50 — Problemy razvitiia kommunisticheskogo soznaniia. Moskva, 1965.

Phil 5625.105 — Prokasy, William Frederick. Classical conditioning, a symposium. N.Y., 1965.

Phil 5592.37 — Proteus, Stanley David. Porteus maze test. Palo Alto, 1965.

Phil 585.195 — Průcha, Milan. La recontre du cogito et du marxisme. Nancy, 1965.

Phil 5374.236 — Psychedelic Review. The psychedelic reader. New Hyde Park, N.Y., 1965.

Phil 3450.19.380 — Pugliese, Orlando. Vermittlung und Kehre. Freiburg, 1965.

Phil 5055.31 — Puzikov, Petr D. Analiticheskaia sposobnost' myshleniia. Minsk, 1965.

Phil 8706.4 — Quevremont, Pierre. Dieu et l'homme créateur. Paris, 1965.

Phil 5066.11.11 — Quine, Willard van Orman. Elementary logic. N.Y., 1965.

Phil 298.20 — Rademaker, Hans. Die Welt in der Sicht der wissenschaftlichen Vernunft. Bonn, 1965.

Phil 2266.165A — Rae, John. Life of Adam Smith. N.Y., 1965.

Phil 8597.58 — Rahner, Karl. Offenarung und Uberlieferung. Freiburg, 1965.

Phil 2255.10.30 — Rand, Ayn. The virtue of selfishness; a new concept of egoism. N.Y., 1965.

Phil 6327.45 — Rattner, Josef. Der nervöse Mensch und seine Heilung. Zürich, 1965.

Phil 525.243 — Ravier, André. La mystique et les mystiques. Bruges, 1965.

Phil 5465.144 — Razik, Jaher A. Bibliography of creativity; studies and related areas. Buffalo, 1965.

Phil 5227.8.10 — Reeves, Joan Wynn. Thinking about thinking. London, 1965.

Phil 817.7.7 — Rehmke, J. Grundriss der Geschichte der Philosophie. 5. Aufl. Frankfurt, 1965.

Phil 6327.12.55 — Reik, Theodor. Curiosities of the self. N.Y., 1965.

Phil 8892.76.5 — Reiner, Hans. Gut und Böse. Freiburg, 1965.

Phil 5257.75 — Reitman, Walter Ralph. Cognition and thought. N.Y., 1965.

Phil 298.18.5 — Remits, E. The law in nature and the dynamics of openness. Ottawa, 1965.

Phil 5590.150.5 — Remplein, Heinz. Psychologie der Persönlichkeit. 5. Aufl. München, 1965.

Phil 192.98.3 — Revel, Jean Francois. Pourquoi des philosophes? Utrecht, 1965. 2v.

Phil 2450.82 — Rex, Walter. Essays on Pierre Bayle and religious controversy. The Hague, 1965.

Phil 5870.120.5 — Reymond-Rivier, Berthe. Le développement social de l'enfant et de l'adolescent. 5. ed. Bruxelles, 1965.

Phil 672.228 — Reyner, John Hereward. God beyond time. London, 1965.

Phil 7069.65.15 — Rhine, Joseph B. Parapsychology from Duke to FRNM. Durham, 1965.

Phil 2475.1.460 — Ribeiro, Alvaro. Escritores doutrinados. Lisboa, 1965.

Phil 7069.65.40 — Richard, Hermann. La tradition ésotérique et la science. Paris, 1965.

Phil 5066.257 — Richter, Vladimir. Untersuchungen zur operativen Logik der Gegenwart. Freiburg, 1965.

Phil 3790.30 — Richtscheid, Hans. Existenz in dieser Zeit. München, 1965.

Phil 6315.2.365 — Ricoeur, Paul. De l'interprétation. Paris, 1965.

Phil 5767.11.5 — Ricoeur, Paul. Philosophy of the will. v.2, pt. 1. Chicago, 1965-

Phil 2905.1.365 — Rideau, Emile. La pensée du Père Teilhard de Chardin. Paris, 1965.

Phil 3425.618 — Riedel, Manfred. Theorie und Praxis im Denken Hegels. Stuttgart, 1965.

Phil 5400.174 — Riese, Walther. La théorie des passions à la lumière de la pensée médicale du XVIIe siècle. N.Y., 1965.

Phil 3450.19.385 — Rifga, Fuad. Studien zur Asthetik Martin Heideggers und Oskar Beckers. Inaug. Diss. Tübingen, 1965.

Phil 5003.12 — Risse, Wilhelm. Bibliographia logica. Hildesheim, 1965.

Phil 3925.16.180 — Riverso, Emanuele. Il pensiero di Ludovico Wittgenstein. Napoli, 1965?

Phil 2905.1.540 — Rizzo, Enrico. La problematica di Teilhard de Chardin. Bologna, 1965.

Phil 1865.194 — Robbins, Lionel. Bentham in the twentieth century. London, 1965.

Phil 9470.12 — Roberts, Moira. Responsibility and practical freedom. Cambridge, Eng., 1965.

Phil 2733.120 — Robinet, Andre. Système et existence dans l'oeuvre de Malebranche. Paris, 1965.

1965 - cont.

Phil 8597.55 — Robinson, John Arthur Thomas. The new reformation? London, 1965.

Phil 4318.4 — Robledo, Maria N. El mundo clásico en el pensamiento español contemporáneo. Madrid, 1965.

Phil 5403.10 — Rochlin, Gregory. Griefs and discontents. London, 1965.

Phil 5400.172 — Rochlin, Gregory. Griefs and discontents. 1. ed. Boston, 1965.

Phil 5875.10 — Roecker, Doris. Sprachfreie Kategorisierung bei Kleinkindern. Diss. Tübingen, 1965.

Phil 6967.18.2 — Rogers, C.R. Psychothérapie et relations humaines. Louvain, 1965. 2v.

Phil 6967.21 — Rogler, Lloyd H. Trapped: families and schizophrenia. N.Y., 1965.

Phil 585.162 — Román, Julián. El hombre como síntesis del universo. 1. ed. Rosario, 1965.

Phil 3499.40 — Romano, Vincenzo. Kant; il problema della conoscenza. Napoli, 1965.

Phil 8672.26 — Romanov, Aleksandr A. Dorogami zemli. Moskva, 1965.

Phil 192.115.5 — Rombach, Heinrich. Substanz, System, Struktur. Freiburg, 1965. 2v.

Phil 3425.626 — Rondet, Henri. Hegelianisme et christianisme. Paris, 1965.

Phil 5593.10 — Rorschach, Hermann. Gesammelte Aufsätze. Bern, 1965.

Phil 2115.200 — Rosa, Pasquale. Il pensiero filosofico e pedagogico di G. Locke. Napoli, 1965.

Phil 5520.431 — Rosenberg, Sheldon. Directions in psycholinguistics. N.Y., 1965.

Phil 7069.49.12 — Rosenthal, Eric. They walk by night; true South African ghost stories and tales of the supernormal. Cape Town, 1965.

Phil 3499.34 — Rotenstreich, Nathan. Experience and its systematization; studies in Kant. The Hague, 1965.

Phil 2750.11.180 — Rover, Thomas Dominic. The poetics of Maritain. Washington, 1965.

Phil 102.5.10 — Rozental, Mark Moiseevich. Filozoficky slovnik. Bratislava, 1965.

Phil 5360.19 — Rozov, Mikhail A. Nauchnaia abstraktsiia i ee vidy. Novosibirsk, 1965.

Phil 9200.3 — Rudin, Josef. Fanaticismus. Olten, 1965.

Phil 5465.143 — Ruitenbeek, Hendrik M. The creative imagination. Chicago, 1965.

Phil 5068.54.5 — Ruml, Vladimir. Der logische Positivismus. (Übersetzung aus den Techechischen). Berlin, 1965.

Phil 817.28F — Runes, Dagobert. Pictorial history of philosophy. N.Y., 1965.

Phil 8418.30.2 — Ruvo, Vincenzo de. Il bello. 2. ed. Napoli, 1965.

Phil 5525.65.5 — Ruvo, Vincenzo de. Il riso e l'arte del ridere. Bari, 1965.

Phil 2050.272 — Sabetti, Alfredo. David Hume, filosofo della religione. Napoli, 1965.

Phil 8598.140 — Sahakian, William S. Philosophies of religion. Cambridge, 1965.

Phil 8598.138 — Saher, Purvezji Jamshedji. Indische Weisheit und das Abendland. Meisenheim, 1965.

Phil 2477.6.165 — Saint-Jean, Raymond. Genèse de l'action; Blondel, 1882-1893. Bruges, 1965.

Phil 8120.13 — Saisselin, Rémy Gilbert. Taste in eighteenth century France. Syracuse, 1965.

Phil 4961.605.5 — Salazar Bondy, Augusto. Historía de las ideas en el Perú contemporáneo. Lima, 1965.

Phil 5258.152.10 — Salber, Wilhelm. Morphologie des seelischen Geschehens. Ratingen, 1965.

Phil 4363.2.85 — Sanchez-Castañer, Francisco. Miguel de Molinos en Valencia y Roma, nuevos datas biográficos. Valencia, 1965.

Phil 9590.29 — Sanders, Willy. Glück. Köln, 1965.

Phil 8419.60 — Sandstroem, Sven. Konstforskning. Stockholm, 1965.

Phil 3500.96 — Santinello, Giovanni. Metafisica e critica in Kant. Bologna, 1965.

Phil 5402.28 — Sarano, Jacques. La douleur. Paris, 1965.

Phil 2880.8.56.2 — Sartre, Jean Paul. Being and nothingness. N.Y., 1965.

Phil 2880.8.41.3 — Sartre, Jean Paul. Existentialism and humanism. London, 1965.

Phil 2880.8.20A — Sartre, Jean Paul. The philosophy of Jean Paul Sartre. N.Y., 1965.

Phil 2880.8.64.5 — Sartre, Jean Paul. La transcendance de l'égo. Paris, 1965.

Phil 1523.20 — Sassen, Ferdinand. Wijsgerig denken in de middeleeuwen. Haarlem, 1965.

Phil 705.51 — Saur, Karl. Transzendenz als Wirklichkeit. Hamburg, 1965.

Phil 974.3.160 — Savitch, Marie. Marie Steiner von Sivers, Mitarbeiterin von Rudolf Steiner. Dornach, 1965.

Phil 1123.13.5 — Schaerer, René. L'homme devant ses choix dans la tradition grecque. Louvain, 1965.

Phil 310.445.15 — Schaff, Adam. Filozofia człowieka. 3. Wyd. Warszawa, 1965.

Phil 9178.10 — Schapp, Wilhelm. Zur Metaphysik des Muttertums. Den Haag, 1965.

Phil 3800.735 — Schelling, F.W.J. von. Schelling und Cotta. Stuttgart, 1965.

Phil 5520.515 — Schérer, René. Structure et fondement de la communication humaine, essai critique sur les théories contemporaines de la communication. Thèse. Paris, 1965.

Phil 8583.28.15 — Schlagberger, Frans Xavier. Die Geschichts- und Kulturphilosophie Christopher Dawson. München, 1965?

Phil 2520.355 — Schmidt, Gerhart. Aufklärung und Metaphysik. Die Neubegründung des Wissens durch Descartes. Tübingen, 196?

Phil 5520.580 — Schmidt, Siegfried J. Die Beschreibung des Zusammenhangs von Sprache und Denken in der Sprachphilosophie von Locke bis Wittgenstein. n.p., 1965.

Phil 6128.82 — Schmidtke, Heinz. Die Ermüdung; Symptome, Theorien, Messversache. Bern, 1965.

Phil 5258.196 — Schmitt, Friedrich. ABC des Helfens. Stuttgart, 1965.

Phil 525.238 — Schnapper, Edith B. The inward Odyssey. London, 1965.

Phil 705.62 — Schneider, Peter K. Die Wissenschaftsbegrundende Funktion der Transzendent alphilosophie. Freiburg, 1965.

Phil 6128.77 — Schneiders, Alexander A. Personality dynamics and mental health. N.Y., 1965.

Phil 3475.3.210 — Schneiders, Werner. Karl Jaspers in der Kritik. Bonn, 1965.

Phil 5593.65.5 — Scholtz, Walter. Zur Frage der Persönlichkeitsveränderung nach stereotaktischen Operationen. Inaug. Diss. Freiburg, 1965?

Phil 193.225.7 — Scholz, H. Metaphysik als strenge Wissenschaft. 2. Aufl. Darmstadt, 1965.

Phil 5258.199 — Schroeder, Theodore. An evolutionary psychologist. Berkeley Heights, N.J., 1965.

1965 - cont.

Phil 5640.137 — Schultz, Duane P. Sensory restriction. N.Y., 1965.
Phil 3450.19.345 — Schwan, Alexander. Politische Philosophie im Denken Heideggers. Köln, 1965.
Phil 5850.335.10 — Schwartz, David J. The magic of psychic power. West Nyack, N.Y., 1965.
Phil 4225.8.70 — Sciacca, Michele Federico. Dallo spiritualismo critico allo spiritualismo cristiano, 1939-1951. Milano, 1965. 2v.
Phil 4225.8.65 — Sciacca, Michele Federico. La libertà e il tempo. Milano, 1965.
Phil 6968.35 — Searles, Harold F. Collected papers on schizophrenia and related subjects. London, 1965.
Phil 6328.59 — Seifert, Friedrich. Bilder und Urbilder; Erscheinungsformen des Arrhetypus. München, 1965.
Phil 8893.139 — Selsam, Howard. Ethics and progress. N.Y., 1965.
Phil 349.54 — Semerari, Giuseppe. La lotta per la scienza. 1. ed. Milano, 1965.
Phil 8980.780 — Semov, Mois I. Prichini za ostatutsite ot burzhoazniia moral v nasheto obshchestvo. Sofiia, 1965.
Phil 8598.139 — Serrand, A.Z. Evolution technique et théologies. Paris, 1965.
Phil 8673.21 — Sertillanges, Antonio Gilbert. Dieu ou rien? Paris, 1965.
Phil 2050.259 — Sesonske, Alexander. Human understanding: studies in the philosophy of David Hume. Belmont, Calif., 1965.
Phil 8400.43 — Sesonske, Alexander. What is art? N.Y., 1965.
Phil 525.242 — Shakhnovich, Mikhail. Sovremennaia mistika v svete nauki. Leningrad, 1965.
Phil 6968.37 — Shapiro, David. Neurotic styles. N.Y., 1965.
Phil 8865.636.5 — Sharma, Ishwar Chandra. Ethical philosophies of India. London, 1965.
Phil 310.617 — Sheptulin, Aleksandr P. Dialekticheskii materializm. Moskva, 1965.
Phil 8893.137 — Shirk, Evelyn Urban. The ethical dimension. N.Y., 1965.
Phil 7072.3 — Shirley, Ralph. The mystery of the human double. N.Y., 1965.
Phil 6688.30 — Shor, Ronald E. The nature of hypnosis. N.Y., 1965.
Phil 5270.3.1 — Shwayder, David S. The stratification of behaviour. London, 1965.
Phil 5270.3 — Shwayder, David S. The stratification of behaviour. N.Y., 1965.
Phil 5627.236.2 — Siegmend, Georg. Psychologie des Gottesglaubens auf Grund literarischer Selbstzeugnisse. 2. Aufl. Münster, 1965.
Phil 193.248 — Siegwalt, Gérard. Nature et histoire; leur réalité et leur vérité. Leiden, 1965.
Phil 2750.22.105 — Siena, Primo. Il profeta della chiesa proletaria. Torino, 1965.
Phil 2280.18.5 — Sikora, Joseph John. Inquiry into being. Chicago, 1965.
Phil 585.175 — Silva Mello, Antonio da. A superioridade do homen tropical. Rio de Janeiro, 1965.
Phil 8893.136 — Simon, Yves. The tradition of natural law. N.Y., 1965.
VPhil 3552.476 — Simonovits, Istvánné. A dialektika Leibniz filozófiá. Budapest, 1965.
Phil 1750.115.165 — Sini, Carlo. La fenomenologia. 1. ed. Milano, 1965.
Phil 1750.115.140 — Sini, Carlo. Introduzione alla fenomenologia come scienza. Milano, 1965.
Phil 2340.10.220 — Sini, Carlo. Whitehead e la funzione della filosofia. Vicenza, 1965.
Phil 5828.21 — Sluchin, Wladyslaw. Imprinting and early learning. Chicago, 1965.
Phil 5535.3 — Smith, David D. Mammalian learning and behavior. Philadelphia, 1965.
Phil 2636.91 — Smith, David Warner. Helvetius; a study in persecution. Oxford, 1965.
Phil 5520.452 — Smith, Huston. Condemned to meaning. 1. ed. N.Y., 1965.
Phil 8598.137 — Smith, John E. Philosophy of religion. N.Y., 1965.
Phil 5090.62 — Smith, Robert D. Comparative miracles. St. Louis, 1965.
Phil 7072.5 — Smith, Susy. The enigma of out-of-body travel. N.Y., 1965.
Phil 6128.78 — Smythies, John Raymond. Brain and mind. London, 1965.
Phil 3425.613 — Sobotka, Milan. Die idealistische Dialektik der Praxis bei Hegel. Praha, 1965.
Phil 5520.428A — Social Science Research Committee on Linguistics and Psychology. Psycholinguistics; a survey of theory and research problems. Bloomington, 1965.
Phil 6159.5 — Solier, René de. Curandera; les champignons hallucinogènes. Paris, 1965.
Phil 3585.30.5 — Sommerhäuser, Hanspeter. Emil Lask in der Auseinander-Setzung mit Heinrich Rickert. Berlin, 1965.
Phil 630.62 — Sosa López, Emilio. Fronteras de lo real. Córdoba, Argentina, 1965.
Phil 2880.8.170 — Sotelo, Ignacio. Das Problem der dialektischen Vernunft bei Jean Paul Sartre. Köln, 1965.
Phil 1750.785 — Soveral, Eduardo S. O método fenomenológico; estudo para a determinação do seu valor filosófico. Porto, 1965.
Phil 3850.32.24 — Spann, Othmar. Gespräch über Unsterblichkeit; Betrachtungen zweier Krieger im Felde. Graz, 1965.
Phil 3850.53 — Spengler, Oswald. Urfragen. München, 1965.
Phil 5643.125 — Spigel, Irwin Myron. Readings in the study of visually perceived movement. N.Y., 1965.
Phil 165.362 — Spirito, Ugo. Storia antologica dei problemi filosofici. Firenze, 1965. 7v.
Phil 3425.623 — Splett, Jörg. Die Trinitätslehre G.W.F. Hegels. Freiburg, 1965.
Phil 4870.14 — Srivastava, Rama Shanker. Contemporary Indian philosophy. Delhi, 1965.
Phil 3120.8.150 — Srzednicki, Jan. Franz Brentano's analysis of truth. The Hague, 1965.
Phil 349.46 — Stachowiak, Herbert. Denken und Erkennen im kybernetischen Modell. Wien, 1965.
Phil 5401.58 — Starnberger Gespräche. Aspekte der Angst. Stuttgart, 1965.
Phil 349.39.4 — Steenberghen, Fernand van. Épistémologie. 4e éd. Paris, 1965.
Phil 978.49.465 — Steiner, R. Anthroposophie, Psychosophie, Pneumatosophie. Dornach, 1965.
Phil 978.49.650 — Steiner, R. Anthroposophische Gemeinschaftsbildung. Dornach, 1965.
Phil 978.49.490 — Steiner, R. Des Prinzip der spirituellen Ökonomie im Zusammenhang mit Wiederverkörperungsfragen; 22 Vorträge. Dornach, 1965.
Phil 978.49.715 — Steiner, R. Durch den Geist zur Wirklichkeits-Erkenntnis der Menschenrätsel. Dornach, 1965- 6v.
Phil 978.49.470 — Steiner, R. Das Ereignis der Christuserscheinung in der ätherischen Welt. Dornach, 1965.
Phil 978.49.460 — Steiner, R. Die Erkenntnis der Seele und des Geistes. Dornach, 1965.

Phil 978.49.665 — Steiner, R. Die Grundimpulse des weltgeschichtlichen Werdens der Menschheit. 2. Aufl. Dornach, 1965.
Phil 978.49.578 — Steiner, R. Heilpädagogischer Kursus. 3. Aufl. Dornach, 1965.
Phil 978.49.660 — Steiner, R. Nationalökonomischer Kurs. 4. Aufl. Dornach, 1965.
Phil 978.49.560 — Steiner, R. Physiologisch-therapeutisches auf Grundlage der Geisteswissenschaft und zur Therapie und Hygiene. Dornach, 1965.
Phil 2805.284.5 — Steinmann, Jean. Pascal. London, 1965.
Phil 8643.39 — Stendahl, Krister. Immortality and resurrection. N.Y., 1965.
Phil 310.622 — Stepanov, V.I. Dialekticheskii materializm kak metodologiia estestvennonauchnogo poznaniia. Minsk, 1965.
Phil 5841.26 — Stern, Karl. The flight from woman. N.Y., 1965.
Phil 5421.15.20 — Stewart, David A. Money, power, and sex. N.Y., 1965.
Phil 5520.592 — Stoep, F. van der. Taalanalise en taalevaluering as pedagogies-didaktiese diagnostiseungsmetode. Pretoria, 1965.
Phil 3838.31 — Stranso, Leo. Spinoza's critique of religion. N.Y., 1965.
Phil 585.230 — Strasser, Stephan. Bouwstenen voor een filosofische anthropologie. Hilversum, 1965.
Phil 193.242 — Strolz, Walter. Widerspruch und Hoffnung des Daseins. Frankfurt, 1965.
Phil 5066.306 — Die Struktur formalisierter Sprachen. Darmstadt, 1965.
Phil 5170.14 — Subbotin, Aleksandr L. Teoriia sillogistiki v sovremennoi formal'noi logike. Moskva, 1965.
Phil 6980.712.1 — Sullivan, Harry Stack. Collected works. N.Y., 1965. 2v.
Phil 310.630 — Sverdlin, Matvei A. Nekotorye voprosy istoricheskogo materializma i nauchnogo kommunizma. Volgograd, 1965.
Phil 310.627 — Sviderskii, Vladimir I. Nekotorye voprosy dialektiki izmeneniia i razvitiia. Moskva, 1965.
Phil 349.47 — Swartz, Robert Jason. Perceiving, sensing, and knowing. 1. ed. Garden City, N.Y., 1965.
Phil 193.234 — Sweeney, Leo. A metaphysics of authentic existentialism. Englewood Cliffs, N.J., 1965.
Phil 310.620 — Szabó, András. Man and law. Budapest, 1965.
Phil 6328.62.5 — Szasz, Thomas Stephen. The ethics of psychoanalysis; the theory and method of autonomous psychotherapy. N.Y., 1965.
Phil 5585.125.3 — Tagiuri, Renato. Person perception and interpersonal behavior. Stanford, 1965.
Phil 165.366 — Tamás, György. Selected studies. Budapest, 1965.
Phil 5066.252 — Tavanets, P.V. Logicheskaia struktura nauchnogo znaniia. Moskva, 1965.
Phil 2905.1.67 — Teilhard de Chardin, Pierre. Building the earth. London, 1965.
Phil 2905.1.65 — Teilhard de Chardin, Pierre. Building the earth. 1st American ed. Wilkes-Barre, Pa., 1965.
Phil 2905.1.350 — Teilhard de Chardin, Pierre. Écrits du temps de la guerre, 1916-1919. Paris, 1965.
Phil 2905.1.42 — Teilhard de Chardin, Pierre. Hymn of the universe. London, 1965.
Phil 2905.1.60 — Teilhard de Chardin, Pierre. Letters from Egypt. N.Y., 1965.
Phil 2905.1.29 — Teilhard de Chardin, Pierre. Lettres à Léontine Zanta. Bruges, 1965.
Phil 2905.1.73 — Teilhard de Chardin, Pierre. Lettres d'Hastings et de Paris, 1908-1914. Paris, 1965.
Phil 2905.1.36 — Teilhard de Chardin, Pierre. The making of a mind. London, 1965.
Phil 2905.1.70 — Teilhard de Chardin, Pierre. La messe sur le monde. Paris, 1965.
Phil 2905.1.12 — Teilhard de Chardin, Pierre. The phenomonon of man. N.Y., 1965.
Phil 2905.1.445 — Teilhard de Chardin et l'unité du genre humain. Lisboa, 1965.
Phil 1870.165 — Testa, Aldo. Meditazioni su Berkeley. Bologna, 1965.
Phil 4073.116 — Testa, Aldo. Meditazioni su Campanella. Bologna, 1965.
Phil 5548.105 — Thomae, Hans. Die Motivation menschlichen Handelns. Köln, 1965.
Phil 8980.839 — Tkachenko, Vera M. Vernost'. 2. izd. Moskva, 1965.
Phil 1750.166.215 — Toesca, Pietro M. Verità e rivoluzione. Roma, 1965.
Phil 8599.48 — Toinet, Paul. Existence chrétienne et philosophie. Paris, 1965.
Phil 5400.168 — Tomkins, Silvan Solomon. Affect, cognition, and personality. N.Y., 1965.
Phil 8708.29.5 — Tompkins, Jerry R. D-days at Dayton. Baton Rouge, La., 1965.
Phil 8420.13.5 — Torres-García, J. La recuperacion del objeto. v.1-2. Montevideo, 1965.
Phil 672.258.1 — Toulmin, Stephen Edelston. The discovery of time. London, 1965.
Phil 672.258 — Toulmin, Stephen Edelston. The discovery of time. N.Y., 1965.
Phil 5590.455.11 — Tournier, Paul. The adventure of living. N.Y., 1965.
Phil 5590.464 — Tramer, Moritz. Reifung und Formung von Persönlichkeiten. Erlenbach, 1965.
Phil 9495.162.1 — Trobisch, Walter. I loved a girl (including I loved a young man); young Africans speak. N.Y., 1965.
Phil 3450.19.350 — Trotignon, Pierre. Heidegger. Paris, 1965.
Phil 585.300 — Tsatsos, Kōnstantinos. Aphorismoí kaí dialogismoí. v.1-2. Athens, 1965-68.
Phil 8980.851.5 — Tugarinov, Vasilii P. Lichnost' i obshchestvo. Moskva, 1965.
Phil 300.13 — Tuzet, Hélène. Le cosmos et l'imagination. Paris, 1965.
Phil 4803.854.20 — Twardowski, Kazimierz. Wybrane pisma filozoficzne. Warszawa, 1965.
Phil 165.351 — Tymieniecka, Anna Teresa. Contributions to logic and methodology in honor of J.M. Bochenski. Amsterdam, 1965.
Phil 8600.6 — Ugrinovich, Dimitrii M. Filosofskie problemy Kritiki religii. Moskva, 1965.
Phil 351.7 — Ülken, Hilmi Ziya. Bilgi ve değer. Ankara, 1965.
Phil 5590.439 — Ullman, Albert Daniel. Sociocultural foundations of personality. Boston, 1965.
Phil 351.5 — L'unificazione del sapere. Firenze, 1965.
Phil 3120.55.85 — Unseld, Siegfried. Ernst Bloch zu ehren. Frankfurt, 1965.
Phil 5545.262 — Urach, Elisabeth Furstin von. Über die strukturelle Eigenart und personate Bedeutsamkeit der Erinnerung. Inaug. Diss. Bamburg, 1965.
Phil 2775.5.80 — Valenziano, Crispino. Introduzione alla filosofia dell' amore di Maurice Nédoncelle. Roma, 1965.
Phil 978.49.890 — Vallmer, Georg. Die Begegnung Max Heindel mit Rudolf Steiner. Darmstadt, 1965.
Phil 3425.607 — Vancourt, Raymond. La pensée religieuse de Hegel. Paris, 1965.

1965 - cont.

Phil 6331.10 Vandendriessche, Gaston. The parapraxis in the Haizmann case of Sigmund Freud. Louvain, 1965.

Phil 4810.6.5 Várossová, Elena. Prehl'ad dejín slovenskej filozofie. Bratislava, 1965.

Phil 6131.6.5 Vasil'ev, Leonid L. Mysterious phenomena of the human psyche. New Hyde Park, N.Y., 1965.

Phil 4960.240 Vázquez, Juan Adolfo. Antología filosófica argentina del siglo XX. Buenos Aires, 1965.

Phil 5238.213 Vdruženje Psihologa Jugoslavije. Stanje i perspektive jugoslovenske psihologije. Beograd, 1965.

Phil 7067.04 Der Veilfoermige Hintzelmann. Göttingen, 1965.

Phil 6615.22 Veith, Ilza. Hysteria; the history of a disease. Chicago, 1965.

Phil 1721.7.5 Vélez Correa, Jaime. Filosofía moderna y contemporanea. Madrid, 1965.

Phil 310.609 Verbin, Andrei. Mesto istoricheskogo materializma v sisteme nauk. Moskva, 1965.

Phil 2905.1.425 Vernet, Maurice. Vernet contre Teilhard de Chardin. Paris, 1965.

Phil 3450.19.325 Versényi, Laszlo. Heidegger, being and truth. New Haven, 1965.

Phil 6131.10 Vesey, Godfrey Norman A. The embodied mind. London, 1965.

Phil 4260.17.16 Vico, G.B. Autobiografia. 1. ed. Torino, 1965.

Phil 2750.11.150.3 Viotto, Piero. Jacques Maritain. 3. ed. Brescia, 1965.

Phil 310.615 Vislobokov, Aleksei Dmitrievich. O dialektike protsessa poznaniia prirody i kibernetika. Moskva, 1965.

Phil 196.36 Vita, Luis Washington. Que é filosofia. São Paulo, 1965.

Phil 6331.4.5 Vittoz, Roger. Le docteur Roger Vittoz et l'angoisse de l'homme moderne. Paris, 1965.

Phil 310.614 Volovik, L.A. Istina v marksistskoi i domarksovoi filosofii. Moskva, 1965.

Phil 3450.11.375 Voltaggio, Franco. Fondamenti della logica di Husserl. Milano, 1965.

Phil 5420.20 Vom menschlichen Selbst. Stuttgart, 1965.

Phil 310.7.7 Vostrikov, A.V. Teoriia poznaniia dialekticheskogo materializma. Moskva, 1965.

Phil 5780.15.15 Waechter, Michael. Hjärntvätt. Stockholm, 1965.

Phil 2475.1.445 Wahl, Jean André. Bergson. Paris, 1965.

Phil 2940.2.30 Wahl, Jean André. L'expérience métaphysique. Paris, 1965.

Phil 197.92 Wainwright, Donald S. Existentialist essays. N.Y., 1965.

Phil 5068.56 Waismann, Friedrich. The principles of linguistic philosophy. London, 1965.

Phil 3270.12.85 Walker, J.P.B. A study of Frege. Oxford, 1965.

Phil 7162.261.1 Walker, Kenneth M. The extra-sensory mind. N.Y., 1965.

Phil 5520.460 Walters, Theodore W. The Georgetown bibliography of studies contributing to the psycholinguistics of language learning. Washington, 1965.

Phil 2045.135 Watkins, J.W.N. Hobbes' system of ideas; a study in the political significance of philosophical theories. London, 1965.

Phil 585.170 Wein, Hermann. Philosophie als Erfahrungswissenschaft. Den Haag, 1965.

Phil 5032.1 Weinberg, Julius Rudolph. Abstraction, relation, and induction. Madison, 1965.

Phil 6332.32 Weisman, A.D. The existential core of psychoanalysis. Boston, 1965.

Phil 353.34 Weissman, David J. Dispositional properties. Carbondale, 1965.

Phil 5203.25 Wellek, Albert. Gesamtverzeichnis der deutschsparchigen psychologischen Literature der Jahre 1942 bis 1960. Göttingen, 1965.

Phil 575.270 Werff, Jacobus Johannes van der. Zelbeelden zelfideaal. Assen, 1965.

Phil 8712.3.12 White, Andrew Dickson. A history of the warfare of science with theology in Christendem. N.Y., 1965.

Phil 2496.88 Will, Frederic. Flumen historicum: Victor Cousin's aesthetic and its sources. Chapel Hill, 1965.

Phil 1750.759 Williams, John Rodman. Contemporary existentialism and Christian faith. Englewood Cliffs, N.J., 1965.

Phil 5886.10 Williams, Richard Hays. Lives through the years. 1st ed. N.Y., 1965.

Phil 5262.57 Williamson, George Scott. Science, synthesis and sanity. London, 1965.

Phil 6332.40 Winnicott, Donald Woods. The maturational processes and the facilitating environment. London, 1965.

Phil 1750.787 Wintrebert, Paul Marie Joseph. L'existense délivrée de l'existentialisme. Paris, 1965.

Phil 3450.18.185 Wirth, I. Realismus und Apriorismus in Nicolai Hartmanns Erkenntnistheorie. Berlin, 1965.

Phil 353.31 Wisdom, John. Paradox and discovery. N.Y., 1965.

Phil 9540.10 Wolff, Robert Paul. A critique of pure tolerance. Boston, 1965.

Phil 5238.205 Wolman, Benjamin B. Scientific psychology: principles and approaches. N.Y., 1965.

Phil 5262.9.43 Woodworth, R.S. Experimental psychology. N.Y., 1965.

Phil 6132.42 Worrall, Ambrose A. The gift of healing. 1st ed. N.Y., 1965.

Phil 978.100 Wulf, Berthold. Athen und Ephesus. Freiburg, 1965.

Phil 3845.3.10 Zac, Sylvain. Spinoza et l'interpretation de l'écriture. Paris, 1965.

Phil 4376.2 Zambrano, Maria. España, sueño y verdad. Barcelona, 1965.

Phil 3120.24.80 Zee, Teartse van der. Eat oer it libben fan Prof. Dr. Tj. de Boer, 1866-1942. Ljouwert, 1965.

Phil 8980.895.10 Zhuravkov, M.G. Nravstvennye printsipy stroitelia kommunizma. Moskva, 1965.

Phil 1540.87 Zimmermann, Albert. Ontologie oder Metaphysik? Die Diskussion über den Gegenstand der Metaphysik im 13. und 14. Jahrhundert. Habilitationeschrift. Leiden, 1965[1966].

Phil 5871.25 Ziv, Avner. La vie des enfants en collectivité. Paris, 1965.

Phil 5585.138 Zoltobrocki, Josefa. Über systematische Fehler bei wiederholter Schätzung von Zeitintervallen. Frankfurt, 1965.

Phil 4710.149 Zonal'naia Nauchnaia Konferentsiia po Filosofskim Naukam, 2d, Perm', 1965. Materialy. Perm', 1965.

Phil 8426.6 Zotov, Ivan A. Priroda prekrasnogo. Moskva, 1965.

Phil 260.15 Zubor, Vasilii P. Razvitie atomisticheskikh predstavlenii do nachala XIX veka. Moskva, 1965.

Phil 5585.285 Zwaan, Evert Joost. Links en rechts in waarneming en beleving. Proefschrift. Utrecht, 1965.

Phil 5649.38 Zweig, Adam. Grundzüge einer tensor-algebraischen Psycho-Dynamik. v.1-2. Zürich, 1965.

1966

Phil 7055.101 Aakerblom, Lilly. Bortom mänsklig horisont. Stockholm, 1966.

Phil 4080.3.281 Abbate, Michele. La filosofia di Benedetto Croce e la crisi della società italiana. Torino, 1966.

Phil 7011.2.2 Abhedānanda, Swami. The science of psychic phenomena. 2. ed. Calcutta, 1966.

Phil 6310.23 Abraham, Karl. On character and libido development. N.Y., 1966.

Phil 5374.243 Accademia...Vatican City. Pontificia Accademia delle Scienze, Vatican City. Brain and conscious experience. Study Week, September 28 to October 4, 1964. N.Y., 1966.

Phil 5125.32 Ackermann, Robert John. Nondeductive inference. London, 1966.

Phil 165.392 Adelmann, Frederick. The quest for the absolute. Chestnut Hill, 1966.

VPhil 730.31 Admec, Josef. Holismus. Praha, 1966.

Phil 1105.12 Adorno, Francesco. Studi sul pensiero greco. Firenze, 1966.

Phil 3085.7.31 Adorno, Theodor W. Negative Dialektik. Frankfurt, 1966.

Phil 8400.69 Aesthetische Aufsätze. Budapest, 1966.

Phil 310.507 Afanas'ev, Viktor G. Nauchnyi kommunizm. Moskva, 1966.

Phil 800.20 Ahlberg, A. Fran antikens och medeltidens tankevärd. Stockholm, 1966.

Phil 4795.10 Akademiia nauk Azerbaidzhanskoi SSR, Baku. Sektor filosofii. Ocherki po istorii Azerbaidzhanskoi filosofii. Baku, 1966.

Phil 331.33.10 Akademiia nauk SSSR. Institut Filosofii. Erkenntnistheoretische und methodologische Probleme der Wissenschaft. Berlin, 1966.

Phil 5240.54 Akademiia Nauk SSSR. Institut Filosofii. Osnovnye napravleniia issledovanii psikhologii myshleniia v kapitalisticheskikh stranakh. Moskva, 1966.

Phil 735.257 Akademiia Nauk SSSR. Kafedra Filosofii, Leningrad. Problema tsennosti v filosofii. Leningrad, 1966.

Phil 4710.50.20 Akademiia Nauk URSR, Kiev. Instytut Filosofii. Narys istorii filosofii na Ukraini. Kyïv, 1966.

Phil 5643.132 Ákos, Károly. The critical flicker frequency series effect. Budapest, 1966.

Phil 4960.220 Alberini, Coriolano. Problemas de la história de las ideas filosóficas en la Argentina. La Plata, 1966.

Phil 4215.1.110 Alecci, Romolo. La dottrina di G.D. Romognosi intorno alla civiltá. Padova, 1966.

Phil 6980.133 Alexander, Franz G. The history of psychiatry. N.Y., 1966.

Phil 6310.4.35 Alexander, Franz G. Psychoanalytic pioneers. N.Y., 1966.

Phil 5360.25 Alexander, Hubert Griggs. Language and thinking; a philosophical introduction. Princeton, N.J., 1966.

Phil 5066.260 Algebra i matematicheskaia logika. Kiev, 1966.

Phil 2445.5.30 Alguié, Ferdinand. Solitude de la raison. Paris, 1966.

Phil 8875.34 Alisjahbana, Sutan Takdir. Values as integrating forces in personality society and culture. Kuala Lumpur, 1966.

Phil 6158.45 Alpert, Richard. LSD. N.Y., 1966.

Phil 2825.30 Amédée Ponceau, études et témoignages. Bruges, 1966.

Phil 8401.30.7 Anceschi, Luciano. Progetto di una sistematica dell'arte. 2. ed. Milano, 1966.

Phil 2050.261 Anderson, Robert Fendel. Hume's first principles. Lincoln, 1966.

Phil 4482.1.100 Andrade, António Alberto de. Vernei e a cultura do seu tempo. Coimbra, 1966.

Phil 4225.66.80 Antonaci, Antonio. Francesco Storella. Galatina, 1966.

Phil 8171.5 Apresian, Grant Z. Krasota i dobro. Moskva, 1966.

Phil 9495.166.5 Aquinas Institute of Philosophy and Theology. Institute of Spiritual Theology. Sex, love and the life of the spirit. Chicago, 1966.

Phil 4872.242.85 Arapura, John G. Radhakrishnan and integral experience. London, 1966.

Phil 2050.263 Ardal, Páll S. Passion and value in Hume's Treatise. Edinburgh, 1966.

Phil 2280.5.145 Ashmore, Jerome. Santayana, art, and aesthetics. Cleveland, 1966.

Phil 672.237 Askin, Iakov F. Problema vremeni. Moskva, 1966.

Phil 5548.108 Atkinson, John W. A theory of achievement motivation. N.Y., 1966.

Phil 6980.43 Aucelin Schoetzenberger, Anne. Précis de psychodrame, introduction. 1. éd. Paris, 1966.

Phil 2880.8.165 Audry, Colette. Sartre et la réalité humaine. Paris, 1966.

Phil 585.188.2 Auger, Pierre. L'homme microscopique. 2e éd. Paris, 1966.

Phil 3090.22 Baader, Franz von. Sätze ans der erotischen Philosophie und andere Schriften. Frankfurt, 1966.

Phil 3090.24.10 Baader, Franz von. Vom Sinn der Gesellschaft. Köln, 1966.

Phil 3850.27.127 Babel, Henry. Schweitzer tel qu'il fut. Boudry-Neuchâtel, 1966.

Phil 5585.236 Bach, Marcus. The power of perception. Garden City, 1966.

Phil 672.239 Bachelard, Gaston. L'intuition de l'instant. Paris, 1966.

Phil 1850.41.7 Bacon, Francis. Über die Würde und den Fortgang der Wissenschaften. Darmstadt, 1966.

Phil 5627.266.10 Bakan, David. The duality of human existence. Chicago, 1966.

Phil 978.110 Ballmer, Karl. Deutschtum und Christentum in der Theosophie des Goetheanismus. Besazio, 1966.

Phil 5811.19.12 Bally, Gustav. Vom Spielraum der Freiheit. 2. Aufl. Basel, 1966.

Phil 1145.100 Banchetti, Silvestro. La persona umana nella morale dei Greci. Milano, 1966.

Phil 6980.93 Barahona Fernandes, Henrique João de. Filosofia e psiquiatria. Coimbra, 1966.

Phil 8691.33 Barbour, Ian G. Issues in science and religion. Englewood Cliffs, N.J., 1966.

Phil 310.634 Barion, Jakob. Ideologie, Wissenschatt, Philosophie. Bonn, 1966.

Phil 2475.1.440 Barlow, Michel. Henri Bergson. Paris, 1966.

Phil 8400.45 Barrett, Cyril. Collected papers on aesthetics. N.Y., 1966.

Phil 332.25.2 Barth, Heinrich. Philosophie der Erscheinung. 2. Aufl. Basel, 1966.

Phil 2475.1.435 Barthélemy-Madaule, Madeleine. Bergson, adversaire de Kant. Paris, 1966.

Phil 8980.193 Barton, William Ernest. The moral challenge of Communism. London, 1966.

Phil 3425.56.36 Bartsch, Heinrich. Register zu Hegel's Vorlesungen über die Asthetik. Stuttgart, 1966.

Phil 332.37 Battro, Antonio M. Dictionnaire d'epistémologie génétique. Dordrecht, 1966.

Phil 1865.184.2 Baumgardt, David. Bentham and the ethics of today. N.Y., 1966.

Chronological Listing

Phil 4080.3.456 Bausola, Adriano. Etica e politica. Milano, 1966.

Phil 7069.66.30 Beard, Paul. Survival of death: for and against. London, 1966.

Phil 5593.66.15 Beizmann, Cécile. Livret de cotation des formes dans le Rorschach d'après une compilation des cotations de H. Rorschach. Paris, 1966.

Phil 6980.102.5 Bellman, Richard. A simulation of the initial psychiatric interview. Santa Monica, Calif., 1966.

Phil 3120.30.155 Ben-Chorin, Schalom. Zwiesprache mit Martin Buber. München, 1966.

Phil 1870.123.5 Bender, Frans. George Berkeley. Baarn, 1966.

Phil 7010.5 Bender, Hans. Parapsychologie. Entwicklung, Ergebnisse, Probleme. Darmstadt, 1966.

Phil 3425.622 Benner, Dietrich. Theorie und Praxis. System theoretische Betrachtungen zu Hegel und Marx. Wien, 1966.

Phil 3483.86 Bennett, Jonathan Francis. Kant's analytic. Cambridge, 1966.

Phil 5241.145.5.2 Berg, Jan Hendrik van den. De dingen. 2. druk. Nijkerk, 1966.

Phil 9500.8 Berg, Jan Hendrik van den. The psychology of the sickbed. Pittsburgh, 1966.

VPhil 9590.34 Bergel, Bernard. Von der Krankheit und Genesung des Seienden, oder Der zweite Sündenfall. Tel-Aviv, 1966.

Phil 5690.2 Bergler, Reinhold. Psycologie stereotyper Systeme. Bern, 1966.

Phil 6985.40 Berne, Eric. Principles of group treatment. N.Y., 1966.

Phil 1955.6.210 Bernstein, Richard. John Dewey. N.Y., 1966.

Phil 5751.20 Berofsky, Bernard. Free will and determinism. N.Y., 1966.

Phil 3425.595.7 Beyer, W.R. Georg Wilhelm Friedrich Hegel in Nürnberg 1808-1816. Nürnberg, 1966.

Phil 75.76 Bibliography of philosophy. Paris, 1966? 2 pam.

Phil 3120.40.55 Bierens de Haan, J.D. Innerlijk perspectief. Assen, 1966.

Phil 5241.188 Biran, Sigmund. Die ausserpsychologische Voraussetzungen der Tiefenpsychologie. München, 1966.

Phil 5627.266.25 Bjoerkhen, John. Människan och makterna. Stockholm, 1966.

Phil 5041.93 Blanché, Robert. Structures intellectuelles. Paris, 1966.

Phil 1750.552 Blankart, Franz André. Zweiheit, Bezug und Vermittlung. Zürich, 1966.

Phil 5853.8 Blocher, Donald H. Developmental counseling. N.Y., 1966.

Phil 176.129.10 Blondel, Maurice. Dialogues avec les philosophes, Descartes, Spinoza. Paris, 1966.

Phil 5590.578.1 Bloom, Benjamin Samuel. Stability and change in human characteristics. N.Y., 1966.

Phil 6158.40 Blum, Richard H. Utopiates; the use and users of LSD-25. N.Y., 1966.

Phil 5722.72 Blyznychenko, Leonid A. Vvod i zakreplenre informatsii v pamiati cheloveka vo vremia estestvennogo sna. Kiev, 1966.

Phil 5274.3 Bobneva, Margarita I. Tekhnicheskaia psikhologiia. Moskva, 1966.

Phil 585.213 Boehler, Walther. Der mensch zwischen Übernatur und Unternatur. Nürnberg, 1966.

Phil 3450.11.225 Boer, Theodorus de. De ontwikkelingsgang in het denken van Husserl. Assem, 1966.

Phil 974.2.65 Borborka, Geoffrey A. H.P. Blavatsky, Tibet and Tulka. Madras, 1966.

Phil 3483.87 Borodai, I.M. Voobrazhenie i teoriia poznaniia. Moskva, 1966.

Phil 8612.52.5 Boros, Ladislaus. L'homme et son ultime option, Mysterium mortis. Paris, 1966.

Phil 1701.50 Borzaga, Reynold. Contemporary philosophy; phenomenological and existential currents. Milwaukee, 1966.

Phil 310.644 Bosenko, Valerii A. Dialektika kak teoriia razvitiia. Kiev, 1966.

Phil 3450.11.440 Bosio, Franco. Fondazione della logica in Husserl. Milano, 1966.

Phil 8581.113 Bošnjak, Branko. Filozofija i kršćanstvo. Zagreb, 1966.

Phil 4843.1 Boumblinopoulos, Georgios E. Bibliographie critique de la philosophie grecque...1453-1953. Athènes, 1966.

Phil 5011.8 Bowne, G.D. The philosophy of logic, 1880-1908. The Hague, 1966.

Phil 4070.9.1 Bozzetti, Giuseppe. Opere complete: saggi, scritti inediti, opere minori, recensioni. Milano, 1966. 3v.

Phil 5465.194 Braeuer, Gottfried. Das Finden als Moment des Schöpferischen. Tübingen, 1966.

Phil 310.646 Braga, Joaquim. Crítica do materialismo dialéctico. Lisboa, 1966.

Phil 5241.167 Brain, Walter. Science and man. London, 1966.

Phil 165.390 Braun, Cornelis Gerardus Franciscus. Filia. Wijsgerige opstellen in vriendschap aangeboden aan Prof. Dr. J.H. Robbers. Nijmegen, 1966.

Phil 5751.21 Brehm, Jack Williams. A theory of psychological reactance. N.Y., 1966.

Phil 3120.8.20 Brentano, Franz. Die Abkehr von Nichtrealen. Bern, 1966.

Phil 332.14.12 Brentano, Franz. The true and the evident. London, 1966.

Phil 5649.29 Brichcín, Milan. Teoretické a metodologické problémy výzkumů průběhu volních pohybu. Praha, 1966.

Phil 1200.64 Bridoux, André. Le stoïcisme et son influence. Paris, 1966.

Phil 9070.113 Brihat, Denise. Risque et prudence. Paris, 1966.

Phil 2905.1.435 Briones Toledo, Hernán. Pierre Teilhard de Chardin y otros ensayos. Santiago de Chile, 1966.

Phil 9495.166 British Council of Churches. Sex and morality: a report to the British Council of Churches. London, 1966.

Phil 2805.419 Brooms, Jack Howard. Pascal. N.Y., 1966.

Phil 4080.3.450 Brown, Merle Elliott. Neo-idealistic aesthetics. Detroit, 1966.

Phil 6311.47 Brown, Norman Oliver. Love's body. N.Y., 1966.

Phil 3120.30.43.5 Buber, Martin. Ich und Du. Köln, 1966.

Phil 3120.30.20 Buber, Martin. The way of response. N.Y., 1966.

Phil 1905.34 Buchler, Justus. Metaphysics of natural complexes. N.Y., 1966.

Phil 4710.50.30 Buchvarov, Mikhail D. Ukraïns'ko-bolgars'ki filosofs'ki zv'iazki. Kyïv, 1966.

Phil 4822.4.5 Bunkov, Angel Iliev. Razvitie na filosofskata misul v Bulgariia. Sofiia, 1966.

Phil 8622.68 Buri, Fritz. Denkender Glaube. Bern, 1966.

Phil 1750.788 Burnier, Michel Antoine. Les existentialistes et la politique. Paris, 1966.

Phil 3910.130 Burns, John V. Dynamism in the cosmology of Christian Wolf. 1st ed. N.Y., 1966.

Phil 5500.37 Buron, Robert. Decision-making in the development field. Paris, 1966.

Phil 176.224 Burth, Edwin Arthur. In search of philosophic understanding. N.Y., 1966.

Phil 730.30 Butchvarov, Panayot. Resemblance and identity. Bloomington, 1966.

Phil 8980.252.3 Bychkova, N.V. Moral' kak ee ponimaiut kommunisty. Izd. 3. Moskva, 1966.

Phil 930.67 Bykov, Fedor S. Zarozhdenie obshchestvenno-politicheskoi i filosofskoi mysli v kitae. Moskva, 1966.

Phil 5590.453 Byrne, Donn Erwin. Personality research; a book of readings. Englewood Cliffs, N.J., 1966.

Phil 5135.7.5 Bzhalava, Iosif T. Psikhologiia ustanovki i kibernetika. Moskva, 1966.

Phil 5465.149 Caillois, Roger. Images, images, essais sur le rôle et les pouvoirs de l'imagination. Paris, 1966.

Phil 2905.1.405 Calvet, Jean. Réflexions sur le "Phénomène humain" de Pierre Teilhard de Chardin. Paris, 1966.

Phil 8735.58 Canfield, John V. Purpose in nature. Englewood Cliffs, N.J., 1966.

Phil 585.70.10 Cantoni, Remo. Scienze umane e antropologia filosofica. Milano, 1966.

Phil 4080.26.10 Cantoni, Remo. La vita quotidiana. Milano, 1966.

Phil 4070.7.85 Carbonare, Cleto. L'estetica filosofica di Antonio Banfi. Napoli, 1966.

Phil 4080.40.5 Cardone, Domenico Antonio. La filosofia nella storia civile del mondo. Roma, 1966.

Phil 1930.19.30 Carlo, William E. The ultimate reductibility of essence to existence in existential metaphysics. The Hague, 1966.

Phil 4303.7 Carreras y Artau, J. Estudios filosóficos. v.1-2. Barcelona, 1966-1968.

Phil 5627.260.13 Carrier, Hervé. Psycho-sociologie de l'appartenance religieuse. 3. ed. Rome, 1966.

Phil 3160.9 Carus, Karl Gustav. Lebens Erinnerungen und Denkwürdigkeiten. Weimar, 1966. 2v.

Phil 310.758 Cassa, Mario. Ragione dialettica prassi marxista e profezia cristiana. Milano, 1966.

Phil 1750.166.205 Castanos, Stelios. Réponse à Heidegger sur l'humanisme. Paris, 1966.

Phil 1750.372.5 Castelli, Enrico. Esistenzialismo teologico. Roma, 1966.

Phil 1750.372.2 Castelli, Enrico. Existentialisme théologique. 2e éd. Paris, 1966.

Phil 8520.50 Catholic University of America. Workshop on Christian Philosophy and Religious Renewal, 1964. Christian philosophy in the college and seminary. Washington, 1966.

Phil 5590.446 Cattell, Raymond. The scientific analysis of personality. Chicago, 1966.

Phil 2477.15.90 Caws, Mary Ann. Surrealism and the literary imagination; a study of Breton and Bachelard. The Hague, 1966.

Phil 5403.11 Cazeneuve, Jean. Bonheur et civilisation. Paris, 1966.

Phil 70.22.10 Centro di Studi Filosofici di Gallarate. Senso e valore del discorso metafisico. Padova, 1966.

Phil 585.188 Chambliss, Rollin. Meaning for man. N.Y., 1966.

Phil 4891.1 Chan, Wing-tsit. Chinese philosophy, 1949-1963; an annotated bibliography of mainland China publications. Honolulu, 1966-67.

Phil 2050.266 Chappell, Vere Claiborne. Hume. 1st ed. Garden City, N.Y., 1966.

Phil 2750.22.100 Charpentreau, Jacques. L'esthétique personnaliste d'Emmanuel Mounier. Paris, 1966.

Phil 2520.354 Chauvois, Louis. Descartes, sa "Méthode" et ses erreurs en physiologie. Paris, 1966.

Phil 5520.622 Chernokov, Petr V. Osnovnye edinitsy iazyka i myshleniia. Rostov-na-Donu, 1966.

Phil 4753.3 Chernov, Vladimir I. Analiz filosofskikh poniatii. Moskva, 1966.

Phil 6672.16 Chertok, Léon. Hypnosis. 1st ed. Oxford, 1966.

Phil 3425.640 Chiereghin, Franco. Hegel e la metafisica classica. Padova, 1966.

Phil 5520.449A Chomsky, Noam. Cartesian linguistics. N.Y., 1966.

Phil 940.5 Chŏng, Chin-sŏk. Istoriia koreiskoi filosofii. Moskva, 1966.

Phil 3450.11.425 Christoff, Daniel. Husserl; ou, Le retour aux choses. Paris, 1966.

Phil 8692.28 Clark, Cecil Henry Douglas. The scientist and the supernatural: a systematic examination of the relation between Christianity and humanism. London, 1966.

Phil 5520.477 Clarke, Bowman L. Language and natural theology. The Hague, 1966.

Phil 5520.466 Clauss, Karl. General semantics. pt.1. Berlin, 1966. 2v.

Phil 7113.5 Clements, John. Hypnotism; masterpiece of myths. Manchester, 1966.

Phil 5500.44 Clinical and social judgment: the discrimination of behavioral information. N.Y., 1966.

Phil 8575.12 Cockshut, Anthony Oliver John. Religious controversies of the nineteenth century: selected documents. London, 1966.

Phil 2905.1.430 Coffy, Robert. Teilhard de Chardin et le socialisme. Lyon, 1966.

Phil 5520.385.2 Cohen, Laurence Jonathan. The diversity of meaning. 2. ed. London, 1966.

Phil 8622.64 Colloque International sur Mythe et Foi, Rome, 1966. Mythe et foi. Paris, 1966.

Phil 2494.37 Condorcet, M.J.A.N. Esquisse d'un tableau historique des progrès de l'esprit humain. Paris, 1966.

Phil 5535.8 Conference on Acquisition of Skill, New Orleans. Acquisition of skill. N.Y., 1966.

Phil 2750.22.95 Conilh, Jean. Emmanuel Mounier, sa vie, son oeuvre, avec un exposé de sa philosophie. Paris, 1966.

Phil 477.14 Connell, Richard J. Matter and becoming. Chicago, 1966.

Phil 3925.16.96 Copi, Irving Marmer. Essays on Wittgenstein's Tractatus. London, 1966.

Phil 402.2 Corbett, Patrick. Ideologies. N.Y., 1966.

Phil 5068.56.5 Cornman, James W. Metaphysics, reference, and language. New Haven, 1966.

Phil 4114.90 Corpaci, Francesco. Antonio Genovesi. Milano, 1966.

Phil 177.133 Corradi, Gemma. Philosophy and co-existence. Leyden, 1966.

Phil 5272.24 Courts, Frederick A. Psychological statistics. Homewood, Ill., 1966.

Phil 6112.44 Coval, Samuel Charles. Scepticism and the first person. London, 1966.

Phil 1920.1.35 Craik, Kenneth James Williams. The nature of psychology. Cambridge, Eng., 1966.

Phil 3160.20 Cramer, Wolfgang. Die absolute Reflexion. Frankfurt, 1966- 2v.

Phil 5520.445 Creelman, Marjorico Broer. The experimental investigation of meaning. N.Y., 1966.

Phil 1828.6.20 Crescenzo, Giovanni de. Patrick Romanelli e l'odierno naturalismo statunitense. 1. ed. Firenze, 1966.

1966 - cont.

Phil 4080.3.47.2   Croce, Benedetto. Nuove pagini sparse. 2. ed. Bari, 1966. 2v.

Phil 2218.90   Crook, Ronald E. A bibliography of Joseph Priestley, 1733-1804. London, 1966.

Phil 2215.80   Cua, Antonio S. Reason and virtue; a study in the ethics of Richard Price. Athens, 1966.

Phil 2905.1.196.5   Cuénot, Claude. Teilhard de Chardin e il pensiero cattolico. Firenze, 1966.

Phil 5812.12   Cuny, Hilaire. Sur la psychologie animale. Paris, 1966.

Phil 8550.342.10   Curtis, Lewis P. Anglican moods of the eighteenth century. Hamden, Conn., 1966.

Phil 2750.11.185   Daly, Mary F. Natural knowledge of God in the philosophy of Jacques Maritain. Rome, 1966.

Phil 8092.15   Damnjanović, Milan. Strujanja u savremenoj estetici. Zagreb, 1966.

Phil 9530.58   Darvas, Nicolas. The anatomy of success. Indianapolis, 1966.

Phil 165.367   Daues, Vincent F. Wisdom in depth. Milwaukee, 1966.

Phil 6307.408   David, Michel. La psicoanalisi nella cultura italiana. Torino, 1966.

Phil 8404.23   Davydov, Iurii N. Iskusstvo i elita. Moskva, 1966.

Phil 3805.224   Dawson, Jerry F. Friedrich Schleiermacher: the evolution of a nationalist. Austin, 1966.

Phil 1955.6.220   Debdalle, Gerald. L'idée d'expérience dans la philosophie de John Dewey. Thèse. Paris, 1966.

Phil 5325.42   Deese, James. The structure of association in language and thought. Baltimore, 1966.

Phil 8870.28   De George, Richard T. Ethics and society. Garden City, 1966.

Phil 310.636   DeGeorge, Richard T. Patterns of Soviet thought. Ann Arbor, 1966.

Phil 3485.23.2   Delekat, Friedrich. Immanuel Kant. 2. Aufl. Heidelberg, 1966.

Phil 8628.15   Delgado Varela, J.M. Supervivencia del hombre. Madrid, 1966.

Phil 5170.15   DeMorgan, Augustus. On the syllogism, and other logical writings. London, 1966.

Phil 5421.20.35   Denker, Rolf. Aufklärung über Aggression: Kant, Darwin, Freud, Lorenz. Stuttgart, 1966.

Phil 4225.8.105   Dentone, Adriana. La problematica morale nella filosofia della integralita. 2. ed. Milano, 1966.

Phil 2520.55.12   Descartes, René. Regulae ad directionem ingenii. La Haye, 1966.

Phil 8628.10   Des Georges, A. La réincarnation des âmes selon les traditions orientales et occidentales. Paris, 1966.

Phil 3823.16   Deugd, Cornelis de. The significance of Spinoza's first kind of knowledge. Assen, 1966.

Phil 960.3.8.5   Deussen, P. The philosophy of the Upanishads. N.Y., 1966.

Phil 8658.25   Dewart, Leslie. The future of belief; theism in a world come of age. N.Y., 1966.

Phil 5590.465   Diggory, James C. Self-evaluation. N.Y., 1966.

Phil 3120.8.155   Dix, Petrus Gerandus. De verhouting van de psycologie tot de wijsbegeerte in der leer van Brentano. n.p., 1966.

Phil 5190.10.10   Dolce, Danilo. Conversazioni contedine. Milano, 1966.

Phil 165.378   Dommeyer, Frederick C. Current philosophical issues; essays in honor of Curt John Ducasse. Springfield, Illinois, 1966.

Phil 5500.40   Downs, Anthony. Bureaucratic structure and decision-making. Santa Monica, 1966.

Phil 5520.448   Drange, Theodore. Type crossings. The Hague, 1966.

Phil 5043.35   Drieschner, Rudolf. Untersuchungen zur dialogischen Deutung der Logik. Diss. Hambirg, 1966.

Phil 3485.26   Dryer, D.P. Kant's solution for verification in metaphysics. London, 1966.

Phil 9320.7   Duerckheim-Montmartin, Karlfried. Der Alltag als Übung vom Weg zur Verwandlung. 2. Aufl. Bern, 1966.

Phil 178.77   Dufrenne, Mikel. Jalons. La Haye, 1966.

Phil 2555.9.31A   Dufrenne, Mikel. The notion of the a priori. Evanston, Ill., 1966.

Phil 3450.19.415   Duintjer, Otto D. De vraag naar her transcendentale. Leiden, 1966.

Phil 3120.30.175   Dujoune, León. Martin Buber. Buenos Aires, 1966[1965]

Phil 1190.25   Dumont, Jean-Paul. Les sceptiques grecs. Paris, 1966.

Phil 5243.68.2   Duncker, Karl. Zur Psychologie des Produktiven Denkens. 2e Neudruck. Berlin, 1966.

Phil 7069.66.20   Du Plessis, Izak David. Poltergeists of the south. Cape Town, 1966.

Phil 3425.630   Easton, Loyd David. Hegel's first American followers. Athens, 1966.

Phil 5214.4   Ebert, Manfred. Die Bedeutung der Philosophie für die Entwicklung der Psychologie zur Einzelwissenschaft. Inaug. Diss. München, 1966.

Phil 1200.62   Edelstein, Ludwig. The meaning of stoicism. Cambridge, 1966.

Phil 5520.462   Edinburgh. University. Faculty of Social Sciences. Research Board. Conference on Psycholinguistics, 1966. Psycholinguistics papers. Edinburgh, 1966.

Phil 7069.66.35   Edmunds, Simeon. Spiritualism: a critical survey. London, 1966.

Phil 3200.8.10   Ehrlich, W. System der Philosophie. Bad Ragaz, 1966.

Phil 6315.2.383   Eissler, Kurt Robert. Sigmund Freud und die Wiener Universität. Bern, 1966.

Phil 5856.5.2   Ekman, Gösta. Differentiell psykologi. Stockholm, 1966.

Phil 285.6.5   Eliade, Mircea. Kosmos und Geschichte. Hamburg, 1966[1953]

Phil 5238.238   El'kin, David G. Konspekt lektsii po psikhologii. v.3. Odessa, 1966.

Phil 89.5.3   Elseviers filosofische en psychologische encyclopedie. 3. Druk. Amsterdam, 1966.

Phil 4803.360.20   Elzenberg, Henryk. Proby kontaktu; eseje i studia krytyczne. Kraków, 1966.

Phil 8879.40   Emmet, Dorothy Mary. Rules, roles, and relations. N.Y., 1966.

Phil 8400.48   Estetika. Moskva, 1966.

Phil 6315.19.45   Evans, Richard Isadore. Dialogue with Erich Fromm. 1. ed. N.Y., 1966.

Phil 1865.198   Everett, Charles Warren. Jeremy Bentham. London, 1966.

Phil 8694.5   Ewald, Günter. Naturgestez und Schöpfung. Wuppertal, 1966.

Phil 5722.74   Ey, Henri. L'inconscient, 6e Colloque de Bonneval [1960] sous la direction de Henri Ey. Paris, 1966.

Phil 5755.15.1   Farber, Leslie H. The ways of the will. N.Y., 1966.

Phil 3450.11.117   Farber, Marvin. The aims of phenomenology; the motives, methods, and impact of Husserl's thought. 1st ed. N.Y., 1966.

1966 - cont.

Phil 4967.20.15   Farias Brito, Raymundo de. Ineditos e dispersos, notas e variaçoes sôbre assuntos diversos. São Paulo, 1966.

Phil 5421.6   Faulkner, Edwin Jerome. Man's quest for security; a symposium. Lincoln, 1966.

Phil 525.246   Fausset, Hugh I'Anson. The lost dimension. London, 1966.

Phil 5520.442   Fay, Warren H. Temporal sequence in the perception of speed. The Hague, 1966.

Phil 310.618   Fedoseev, Petr. Dialektika sovremennoi epokhi. Moskva, 1966.

Phil 2005.9.20   Feibleman, James. The two story world. 1st ed. N.Y., 1966.

Phil 9220.18   Fentener van Vlissingen, Johannes. Een psychologische theorie van de vriendschap. Proefschrift. Arnhem, 1966.

Phil 4080.3.458   Feo, Italo de. Benedetto Croce e il suo mondo. Torino, 1966.

Phil 9070.112   Feofanov, Iurii V. Lichnoe dostoianie i lichnoe destoinstvo. Moskva, 1966.

Phil 6315.60   Ferdinand, Theodore N. Typologies of delinquency. N.Y., 1966.

Phil 5585.246   Ferenczi, Victor. La perception de l'espace projectif. (Étude réalisée auprès des travailleurs africains analphabètes en France. Montréal, 1966.

Phil 165.376   Feyerabend, Paul. Mind, matter, and method. Minneapolis, 1966.

Phil 3246.35.10   Fichte, Johann Gottlieb. Die Bestimmung des Menschen. Stuttgart, 1966.

Phil 3246.44.10   Fichte, Johann Gottlieb. Wissenschaftslehre 1804. Frankfurt, 1966.

VPhil 585.167.5   Filipec, Jindřich. Člověk a moderní doba. Praha, 1966.

Phil 4826.2   Filozofi. Novi Sad, 1966.

Phil 2605.12.30   Finance, Joseph de. Connaissance de l'être, traité d'ontologie. Paris, 1966.

Phil 5190.65   Finazzo, Giancarlo. Sulla dialettica dell'apriori. Roma, 1966.

Phil 2005.13   Findlay, John N. The discipline of the cave. London, 1966.

Phil 165.386   Findlay, John N. Studies in philosophy: British Academy lectures. London, 1966.

Phil 1750.115.70   Fink, Eugen. Studien zur Phänomenologie, 1930-1939. Den Haag, 1966.

Phil 1110.4   Finley, John Huston. Four stages of Greek thought. Stanford, 1966.

Phil 8092.13   Fischer, Ernst. Kunst und Koexistenz. Reinbek, 1966.

Phil 2225.5.135   Fitzgerald, John J. Peirce's theory of signs as foundation for pragmatism. The Hague, 1966.

Phil 3425.619   Flam, Leopold. De bewustwording; beschouwingen bij de fenomenologie van de geest van Hegel. Bruxelles, 1966.

Phil 180.72.5   Flam, Leopold. Le crépuscule des dieux et l'avenir de l'homme. Paris, 1966.

Phil 3270.17.45   Flam, Leopold. Zelfvervreemding en zelfzijn. Amsterdam, 1966.

Phil 8955.8   Fletcher, Joseph Francis. Situation ethics. Philadelphia, 1966.

Phil 2490.180   Fletcher, Ronald. Auguste Comte and the making of sociology: delivered on November 4, 1965 at the London School of Economics. London, 1966.

Phil 8660.23   Flew, Antony. God and philosophy. 1st American ed. N.Y., 1966.

Phil 7069.64.20   Fodor, Nandor. Between two worlds. West Nyack, 1966.

Phil 7069.33.57   Fodor, Nandor. Encyclopaedia of psychic science. New Hyde Park, N.Y., 1966.

Phil 5755.16   Földesi, Tamás. The problem of free will. Budapest, 1966.

Phil 4967.32   Fontes, Gloria Marly Duarte. Alexandre Rodrigues Ferreira: aspectos de sua vida e obra. Manaus, 1966.

Phil 5585.240   Forgus, Ronald H. Perception. N.Y., 1966.

Phil 8612.62   Foss, Martin. Death, sacrifice, and tragedy. Lincoln, 1966.

Phil 5039.18   Foster, Marguerite H. Probability, confirmation, and simplicity; readings in the philosophy of inductive logic. N.Y., 1966.

Phil 5190.43   Fotheringam, Wallace C. Perspectives on persuasion. Boston, 1966.

Phil 7080.54   Foulkes, David. The psychology of sleep. N.Y., 1966.

Phil 4080.3.461   Franchini, Raffaello. La teoria della storia di Benedetto Croce. Napoli, 1966.

Phil 672.231   Fraser, Julius Thomas. The voices of time. N.Y., 1966.

Phil 3270.12.45   Frege, Gottlob. Logische Untersuchungen. Göttingen, 1966.

Phil 3270.12.37   Frege, Gottlob. Translations from the philosophical writings. 2nd ed. Oxford, 1966.

Phil 6315.2.400   Freijo Balsebre, Enrique. El problema religioso en la historia de la psicologia médica contemporánea. Vitoria, 1966.

Phil 6315.2.56   Freud, Sigmund. On the history of the psychoanalytic movement. N.Y., 1966.

Phil 6315.2.33.8   Freud, Sigmund. The psychopathology of everyday life. N.Y., 1966.

Phil 5066.253   Freudenthal, Hans. The language of logic. Amsterdam, 1966.

Phil 1750.115.100   Funke, Gerhard. Phänomenologie- Metaphysik oder Methode? Bonn, 1966.

Phil 5650.45   Furth, Hans G. Thinking without language. N.Y., 1966.

Phil 5870.10   Gästrin, Jan Emanuel. Teoretisk barnpsykologi. Stockholm, 1966.

Phil 2880.8.225   Gallo, Blas Raúl. Jean Paul Sartre y el marxismo. Buenos Aires, 1966.

Phil 310.643   Garaudy, Roger. Marxisme du XXe siècle. Paris, 1966.

Phil 3925.16.170   Gargani, Aldo Giorgio. Linguaggio di esperienza in Ludwig Wittgenstein. Firenze, 1966.

Phil 4006.5.55   Garin, Eugenio. Cronache di filosofia italiana, 1900-1943. Bari, 1966.

Phil 4006.5.60   Garin, Eugenio. Storia della filosofia italiana. Torino, 1966. 3v.

Phil 365.57   Gatewood, Willard B. Preachers, pedagogues, and politicians. Chapel Hill, 1966.

Phil 3488.47   Gattulo, Mario. Categoria e oggetto in Kant. 1. ed. Firenze, 1966.

Phil 5620.29.2   Gauthier, Daniel Peter. Practical reasoning. Oxford, 1966.

Phil 806.39   Gay, Peter. The enlightenment, an interpretation. 1st ed. N.Y., 1966-69. 2v.

Phil 4120.4.55   Gentile, Giovanni. Gentile. Roma, 1966.

Phil 5046.44   Georgius, Trapezuntius. De re dialectica libellus. Frankfurt, 1966.

Phil 5425.17.5   Gerard, Alexander. An essay on genius, 1774. München, 1966.

1966 - cont.

Phil 7069.65.6 — Gerloff, Hans. The crisis in parapsychology. 2. supplement. Tittmoning, 1966.

Phil 5585.243 — Gibson, James Jerome. The senses considered as perceptual systems. Boston, 1966.

Phil 8696.24 — Gilch, Gerhard. Gebrochemes Weltbild. 1. Aufl. Stuttgart, 1966.

Phil 2477.19.82 — Ginisty, Bernard. Conversion spirituelle et engagement prospectif, essai pour une lecture de Gaston Berger. Paris, 1966.

Phil 4688.110.30 — Girnius, Juozas. Idealas ir laikas. Chicago, 1966.

Phil 735.150.2 — Glansdorff, Maxime. Les déterminants de la théorie générale de la valeur et ses applications en esthétique, en religion, en morale, en économie et en politique. 2e éd. Bruxelles, 1966.

Phil 5590.451 — Glaser, Eric Michael. The psysiological basis of habituation. London, 1966.

Phil 6319.1.196.3 — Goldbrunner, Josef. Individuation. 3. Aufl. Freiburg, 1966.

Phil 5627.266 — Goldbrunner, Josef. Realisation; Anthropologie in Seelsorge und Erziehung. Greiburg, 1966.

Phil 8407.43 — Gol'dentrikht, Semen S. O prirode esteticheskogo tvorchestva. Moskva, 1966.

Phil 310.155.1 — Goldmann, Lucien. Dialektische Untersuchungen. Neuwied, 1966.

Phil 181.136 — Goldmann, Lucien. Sciences humaines et philosophie. Paris, 1966.

Phil 2045.139 — Goldsmith, M.M. Hobbes's science of politics. N.Y., 1966.

Phil 1750.115.2 — Goodman, Nelson. The structure of appearance. Indianapolis, 1966.

Phil 960.260 — Gopinatha, Kaviraja. Aspects of Indian thought. Burdwan, 1966.

Phil 6316.25 — Goraber, Gustav Hans. Die Not des Lebens und ihre Uberwindung. Bern, 1966.

Phil 5374.245.10 — Gorsen, Peter. Zur Phänomenologie des Bewusstseinsstroms. Bonn, 1966.

Phil 2030.7.5 — Gotshalk, Dilman Walter. Human aims in modern perspective. Yellow Springs, Ohio, 1966.

Phil 3475.3.200 — Gottschalk, Herbert. Karl Jaspers. Berlin, 1966.
Phil 2805.430 — Gouhier, Henri. Blaise Pascal. Paris, 1966.
Phil 1955.6.230 — Granese, Alberto. Il Giovane Dewey. 1. ed. Firenze, 1966.
Phil 3640.715 — Granier, Jean. Le problème de la vérité dans la philosophie de Nietzsche. Paris, 1966.

Phil 1850.137.5 — Green, Adwin W. Sir Francis Bacon. N.Y., 1966.
Phil 5585.250 — Green, David Marvin. Signal detection theory and psychophysics. N.Y., 1966.

Phil 5643.126 — Gregory, Richard Langton. Eye and brain. N.Y., 1966.
Phil 337.27 — Grene, Marjorie. The knower and the known. N.Y., 1966.
Phil 8407.44 — Grenier, Jean. Vicissitudes de l'esthétique et révolutions du gout. Paris, 1966.

Phil 5627.266.15 — Griesl, Gottfried. Pastoralpsychologische Studien. Innsbruck, 1966.

Phil 365.62 — Grillo, Ugo. Ultimo umanesimo. Bari, 1966.
Phil 6316.8.10 — Groddeck, Georg. Psychoanalytische Schriften zur Psychsomatik. Wiesbaden, 1966.

Phil 3805.250 — Groell, Johannes. Rezeptivität und Spontaneität. Inaug. Diss. Münster? 1966?

Phil 7082.21 — Grunebaum, Gustave Edmund von. The dream and human societies. Berkeley, 1966.

Phil 8661.45 — Guérard des Lauriers, Michel L. La preuve de Dieu et les cinq voies. Roma, 1966.

Phil 5190.50 — Guha Mozumdar, Roby. Possibilism. Calcutta, 1966.
Phil 337.28 — Guilhot, Jean. Introduction à la psychiatrie de la connaissance. Paris, 1966.

Phil 287.10 — Guitton, Jean. De la signification du cosmos. Paris, 1966.

Phil 181.87.5 — Guitton, Jean. Man in time. Notre Dame, Ind., 1966.
Phil 2630.11.30 — Guitton, Jean. Oeuvres complètes. v.1-2. Paris, 1966.
Phil 3006.9.5 — Gulyga, A.V. Der deutsche Materialismus am Ausgang des 18. Jahrhunderts. Berlin, 1966.

Phil 4757.2.32 — Gurdjieff, Georges Ivanovitch. The herald of coming good. Chicago, 1966.

Phil 1750.773 — Gurwitsch, Aron. Studies in phenomenology and psychology. Evanston, 1966.

Phil 8092.16 — Gus, Mikhail S. Modernizm bez maski. Moskva, 1966.
Phil 5548.106 — Haber, Ralph Norman. Current research in motivation. N.Y., 1966.

Phil 5066.258 — Hackstaff, L.H. Systems of formal logic. Dordrecht, 1966.
Phil 4582.4.49 — Hägerström, Axel. Socialfilosofiska uppsatser. Stockholm, 1966.

Phil 8957.13.15 — Haering, Bernhard. Toward a Christian moral theology. Notre Dame, 1966.

Phil 5850.227.14 — Haernqvist, Kjell. Tillämpad psykologi. 4. uppl. Stockholm, 1966.

Phil 7150.80 — Haffter, Carl. Selbstmordversuche bei Kindern und Jugendlichen. Basel, 1966.

Phil 6957.35 — Hagnell, Olle. A prospective study of the incidences of mental disorder. Stockholm, 1966.

Phil 6480.213 — Hall, Calvin Springer. The content analysis of dreams. N.Y., 1966.

Phil 5585.237 — Hall, Edward Twitchell. The hidden dimension. 1. ed. Garden City, N.Y., 1966.

Phil 3120.65.30 — Hammond, Kenneth R. The psychology of Egon Brunswik. N.Y., 1966.

Phil 5590.552 — Hançerlioğlu, Orhan. Başlangicindan bugüne erdem düşünce. Istanbul, 1966.

Phil 5520.552 — Hançerlioglu, Oshan. Başlan-gicindan bugüne erdem açisindan düsünce. 2. b. Istanbul, 1966.

Phil 7162.266 — Hansel, C.E.M. E.S.P.; a scientific evaluation. N.Y., 1966.

Phil 8430.68 — Hanslick, Eduard. Vom Musikalisch-Schönen. 16. Aufl. Wiesbaden, 1966.

Phil 5627.266.30 — Hartler, Josef. Religiös roll och Kristusliv. Lund, 1966.
Phil 2038.34 — Hartley, D. Observations on man. v.1-2. Gainesville, Fla., 1966.

Phil 2880.8.160 — Hartmann, Klaus. Sartres Sozialphilosophie. Berlin, 1966.
Phil 3850.18.200 — Haskamp, Reinhold J. Spekulativer und Phänomenologischer. Freiburg, 1966.

Phil 735.256 — Hatcher, Harlan Henthorne. The persistent quest for values: what are we seeking? Columbia, 1966.

Phil 5640.136.10 — Hatwell, Yvette. Privation sensorielle et intelligence. Paris, 1966.

Phil 3425.73.10A — Hegel, Georg Wilhelm Friedrich. The phenomenology of mind. 2nd ed. London, 1966.

Phil 3425.15 — Hegel, Georg Wilhelm Friedrich. Politische Schriften. Frankfurt am Main, 1966.

1966 - cont.

Phil 3425.60.12 — Hegel, Georg Wilhelm Friedrich. Vorlesungen über die Philosophie der Religion. Hamburg, 1966. 2v.

Phil 3425.29.12 — Hegel, Georg Wilhelm Friedrich. Wissenschaft der Logik. Göttingen, 1966-

Phil 3450.19.85.5 — Heidegger, Martin. Discourse on thinking. N.Y., 1966.
Phil 665.104 — Heimann, Hans. Die Seele-Grenzbegriff der Naturwissenschaft und Theologie. Bern, 1966.

Phil 288.22 — Heimendahl, Eckart. Dialog des Abendlandes. München, 1966.

Phil 5841.24 — Heimler, Adolf. Reifung und Geschlecht. München, 1966.
Phil 3489.43 — Heimsoeth, Heinz. Transzendentale Dialektik. Ein Kommentar zu Kants Kritik der reinen Vernunft. Berlin, 1966- 4v.

Phil 3489.44 — Heinz, Rudolf. Französische Kantinterpreten im 20. Jahrhundert. Bonn, 1966.

Phil 6980.350 — Held, Fritz. Jugendpsychiatrische Studien. Berlin, 1966.
Phil 3450.11.311 — Held, Klaus. Lebendige Gegenwart. Thesis. Den Haag, 1966.
Phil 5500.41 — Helmer, Olaf. A use of sumulation for the study of future values. Santa Monica, 1966.

Phil 2905.1.575 — Hemkben, Johannes. Pierre Teilhard de Chardin in Selbstzeugnissen und Bilddokumenten. Reinbek, 1966.

Phil 3195.2.90 — Henckmann, Wolfhart. Das Wesen der Kunst in der$Ästhetik Martin Deutingers. München, 1966.

Phil 165.175.5 — Henrich, Dieter. Subjektivität und Metaphysik. Frankfurt, 1966.

Phil 978.118 — Heuser, Annie. Bewisstseinsfragen des Erziehers. Dornach, 1966.

Phil 5535.10.3 — Hilgard, Ernest Ropiequet. Theories of learning. 3. ed. N.Y., 1966.

Phil 5039.20 — Hintikka, Kaarlo Jaakko J. Aspects of inductive logic. Amsterdam, 1966.

Phil 2045.14.2 — Hobbes, Thomas. The English works of Thomas Hobbes of Malmesburg. Aalen, 1966. 11v.

Phil 2055.5.95 — Hobhouse, Leonard Trelawney. Sociology and philosophy. Cambridge, 1966.

Phil 5520.498 — Hoeffe, Wilhelm Laziar. Sprachlicher Ausdrucksgehalt und akustische Struktur. Ratingen bei Düsseldorf, 1966.

Phil 5643.163 — Hoeth, Friedrich. Gesetzlichkeit bei stroboskopischen Alternattivbewegungen. Frankfurt, 1966.

Phil 7118.5 — Hollander, Bernard. Methods and uses of hypnosis and self-hypnosis. Hollywood, Calif. 1966.

Phil 705.64 — Holz, Harald. Transzendentalphilosophie und Metaphysik. Mainz, 1966.

Phil 3425.628 — Hondt, Jacques d'. Hegel; philosophe de l'histoire vivante. Thèse. Paris, 1966.

Phil 8408.42 — Hordiienko, Anatolii. Mystetstvo, diisnist' i svoboda khudozhn'oï tvorchosti. Kyïv, 1966.

Phil 5628.5.5 — Horton, Wade H. The glossolalia phenomenon. 1st ed. Cleveland, 1966.

Phil 288.21 — Hoyle, Fred. Man in the universe. N.Y., 1966.
Phil 4812.457.31 — Hrušovský, Igor. Strukturation und Apperzeption des Konkreten. Bratislava, 1966.

Phil 3827.15.5 — Hubbeling, H.G. Spinoza. Baarn, 1966.
Phil 310.661 — Huber, Eduard. Um eine "dialektische Logik". München, 1966.

Phil 3808.169.10 — Hübscher, Arthur. Leben mit Schopenhauer. Frankfurt, 1966.

Phil 2905.1.420 — Hugedé, Norbert. Le cas Teilhard de Chardin. Paris, 1966.
Phil 8662.27 — Humanism, atheism; principles and practice. Moscow, 1966?
Phil 2963.5 — L'Humanisme belge. Etat de la question, vecherches, perspectives. Anvers, 1966.

Phil 5360.16.1 — Hunt, Earl Busby. Concept learning. N.Y., 1966.
Phil 5643.128 — Hurvich, Leo Maurice. The perception of brightness and darkness. Boston, 1966.

Phil 5247.84.4 — Husén, Torsten. Psykologi. 4. uppl. Stockholm, 1966.
Phil 2145.80 — Hutin, Serge. Henry More. Essai sur les doctrines théosophiques chez les platoniciens de Cambridge. Hildesheim, 1966.

Phil 5218.5 — Iaroshevskii, Mikhail G. Istoriia psikhologii. Moskva, 1966.

Phil 289.2 — Idée de monde et philosophie de la nature. Paris, 1966.
Phil 8403.462.40 — Ingarden, Roman. Przezijni, dzieło, wartość. Kraków, 1966.

Phil 8400.50 — Internationale Hegelkongress, 5th, Salzburg, 1964. Bor'ba idei v estetike. Moskva, 1966.

Phil 8400.51 — Iskusstvo i narod. Moskva, 1966.
Phil 1135.215 — Isnardi Parente, Margherita. Techne. 1. ed. Firenze, 1966.

Phil 3801.465.15 — Jaehnig, Dieter. Schelling. v.2. Pfullingen, 1966.
Phil 2070.75.15 — James, William. The letters of William James and Théodore Flournoy. Madison, 1966.

Phil 8612.61 — Jankélévitch, Valdimir. La mort. Paris, 1966.
Phil 9075.74 — Jankélévitch, Vladimir. La mauvaise conscience. Paris, 1966.

Phil 5585.315 — Jaspars, Joseph Maria Franciscus. On social perception. Leiden, 1966.

Phil 2880.8.195 — Jeason, Francis. Textes de Jean Paul Sartre. Paris, 1966.
Phil 1900.98 — Jeffner, Anders. Butler and Hume on religion. Stockholm, 1966.

Phil 8664.7 — Johann, Robert O. The pragmatic meaning of God. Milwaukee, 1966.

Phil 1750.782 — John, Helen James. The Thomist spectrum. N.Y., 1966.
Phil 8884.25 — Johnson, Oliver Adolph. Moral knowledge. Hague, 1966.
Phil 3310.15.20 — Jonas, Friedrich. Die Institutionenlehre Arnold Gehlens. Tübingen, 1966.

Phil 2075.8 — Jonas, Hans. The phenomenon of life. 1st ed. N.Y., 1966.
Phil 5249.27 — Jones, Harold Ellis. Studies in human development. N.Y., 1966.

Phil 6319.1.5.6 — Jung, C.G. Collected works. v.7. 2nd ed. N.Y., 1966. 2v.

Phil 5592.176.5 — Kahn, Samuel. T.A.T. and understanding people. N.Y., 1966.

Phil 3450.11.365 — Kakabadze, Zurab. Problema ekzistentsial'nogo krizisa i transtsendental'naia fenomenologiia Edmunda Gusserlia. Tbilisi, 1966.

Phil 310.635 — Kalandarishvili, Grigori. Problema otrazheniia dvizheniia v logike poniatii. Tbilisi, 1966.

Phil 6980.372 — Kalff, Dora M. Sandspiel. Zürich, 1966.
Phil 8622.72 — Kanellopoulos, Panagiótēs. Ascent to faith. 1st ed. N.Y., 1966.

VPhil 8885.49 — Kangrga, Milan. Etika i ploboda. Zagreb, 1966.
Phil 3480.14.4 — Kant, Immanuel. Gesammelte Schriften. Allgemeiner Kantindex. Bonn, 1966. 3v.

Phil 3480.14.2.2 — Kant, Immanuel. Gesammelte Schriften. Personenindex. Nachträge. Bonn, 1966.

Phil 3480.71.13 — Kant, Immanuel. Die Religion innerhalb der Grenzen der blossen Vernunft. Hamburg, 1966.

1966 - cont.

Phil 260.16 — Kargon, Robert. Atomism in England from Hariot to Newton. Oxford, 1966.

Phil 5520.455 — Kastein, Shulamith. The birth of language; the case history of a non-verbal child. Springfield, 1966.

Phil 5520.447 — Katz, Jerrold J. The philosophy of language. N.Y., 1966.

Phil 165.382 — Kaulbach, Friedrich. Kritik und Metaphysik; Studien. Berlin, 1966.

Phil 165.364 — Kennick, William E. Metaphysics; readings and reappraisals. Englewood Cliffs, N.J., 1966.

Phil 8835.6 — Kerner, George. The revolution in ethical theory. N.Y., 1966.

Phil 291.12 — Khudushin, Fedor S. Chelovck i priroda. Moskva, 1966.

Phil 5585.244 — Kidd, Aline Halstead. Perceptual development in children. N.Y., 1966.

Phil 5590.449 — Kinsella, Noël A. Toward a theory of personality development. Fredericton, N.B., 1966.

Phil 3425.614 — Kissel, M.A. Etika Gegelia i Krizis sovremennoi burzhuaznoi etiki. Leningrad, 1966.

Phil 3549.8.5 — Klages, Ludwig. Sämmtliche Werke. Supplement. Bonn, 1966.

Phil 5520.542 — Klaus, Georg. Spezielle Erkenntnistheorie. 2. Aufl. Berlin, 1966.

Phil 5643.155 — Kleinhans, Walter H. Stufen der ganzheitlichen Auffassung bei 2- bis 7 järigen Kindern. Thesis. Weinheim, 1966.

Phil 4582.4.95 — Klingberg, Wilhelm. Den intellektuella spärren; trous svärigheter i belysning av Axel Hägerströms filosofi. Stockholm, 1966.

Phil 2905.1.580 — Klohr, Olof. Beiträge zur Deutung von Teilhard de Chardin. Berlin, 1966.

Phil 5125.20.1 — Kneale, William Calvert. Probability and induction. Reprint. Oxford, 1966.

VPhil 2255.1.140 — Knjazeva-Adamović, Svetlana. Filozofija Bertranda Russella: strasno traženje izvesnosti. Zagreb, 1966.

Phil 583.8 — Kockelmans, Joseph John. Phenomenology and physical science. Pittsburgh, 1966.

Phil 4710.148 — Kogan, Leonid A. Krepostnye vol'nodumtsy, XIX vek. Moskva, 1966.

Phil 8411.38 — Kogan, Lev Naumovich. Khudozhestvennyi vkus. Moskva, 1966.

Phil 600.59 — Kołakowski, Leszek. Filozofia pozytywistyczna. Warszawa, 1966.

Phil 1810.6 — Kopnin, Pavel V. Sovremennaia burzhuaznaia filosofiia SShA. Kiev, 1966.

Phil 310.639 — Kopnin, Pavel V. Vvedenie v marksistskuiu gnoseologiiu. Kiev, 1966.

Phil 9560.60 — Korff, Wilhelm. Ehre, Prestige, Gewissen. Köln, 1966.

Phil 185.49.5 — Kotarbiński, Tadeusz. Gnosiology; the scientific approach to the theory of knowledge. 1. English ed. Oxford, 1966.

Phil 4803.497.45 — Kotarbiński, Tadeusz. Medytacje o życiu godziwym. Warszawa, 1966.

VPhil 5250.81 — Kozielecki, Józef. Zagadnienia psychologii myślenia. Wyd. 1. Warszawa, 1966.

Phil 3120.30.125 — Kraft, Werner. Gespräche mit Martin Buber. München, 1966.

Phil 310.640 — Krasnoiarsk, Siberia (City). Gosudarstvennyi Pedagogicheskii Institut. Kafedra Filosofii. Voprosy teoreticheskogo nasledstva V.I. Lenina. Krasnoiarsk, 1966.

VPhil 95.4 — Kratki slovar' po filosofii. Moskva, 1966.

Phil 9558.48 — Kraus, Annie. Über den Hochmut. Frankfurt, 1966.

Phil 6945.50 — Krause, Elliott Arthur. Factors related to length of mental hospital stay. Boston, 1966?

Phil 1170.20 — Kremer, Klaus. Die neuplatonische Seinsphilosophie und ihre Wirkung auf Thomas von Aquin. Leiden, 1966.

Phil 6320.6.20 — Kretschmer, E. Mensch und Lebensgrund. Tübingen, 1966.

Phil 8590.35 — Krieger, Evelina. Abgrund und Gründe. Versuch einer Philosophie christlicher Positivität. Graz, 1966.

Phil 1020.39 — Krikorian, Sergei. Srednevekovaia filosofiia narodov Blizhnego i Srednego Vostoka. Moskva, 1966.

Phil 978.59.22 — Krishnamurti, J. Discussions with Krishnamurti in Europe, 1965. London, 1966.

Phil 1135.188 — Kroeber, Günter. Wissenschaft und Weltansehauung in der Antike. Berlin, 1966.

Phil 8622.2.5 — Kroner, Richard. Between faith and thought: reflections and suggestions. N.Y., 1966.

VPhil 3425.620 — Kroński, Tadeusz. Hegel. wyd. 2. Warszawa, 1966.

Phil 3425.615 — Krueger, H.J. Theologie und Aufklärung. Stuttgart, 1966.

Phil 2885.112 — Krzemień-Ojak, Sław. Taine. Wyd. 1. Warszawa, 1966.

Phil 8411.37 — Kucherenko, Georgii A. Esteticheskoe mnogoobrazie iskusstva sotsialisticheskogo realizma. Moskva, 1966.

VPhil 3195.6.175 — Kuderowicz, Zbigniew. Swiatopogląd a zycie u Dilhteya. Warszawa, 1966.

Phil 8411.28.5 — Kuhn, Helmut. Schriften zur Ästhetik. München, 1966.

Phil 185.100 — Kuhn, Helmut. Traktat über die Methode der Philosophie. München, 1966.

Phil 5203.30 — Kullman, Siv-Aino. Törster Husén. Tryckataskrifter 1940-1965. Stockholm, 1966.

Phil 1830.54 — Kurtz, Paul W. American thought before 1900. 1st ed. N.Y., 1966.

Phil 3492.76 — Kuypers, Karel. Immanuel Kant. Baarn, 1966.

Phil 310.637 — Kuz'min, Vsevolod P. Kategoriia mery v marksistskoi dialektike. Moskva, 1966.

Phil 2750.20.110 — Kwant, Remigius Cornelius. From phenomenology to metaphysics. Pittsburgh, 1966.

Phil 8591.27.6 — Laberthonniere, Lucien. Le réalisme chrétien, précédé de essais de philosophie religieuse. Paris, 1966.

Phil 6321.51 — Lacan, Jacques. Ecrits. Paris, 1966.

Phil 8666.21.5 — Lacroix, Jean. The meaning of modern atheism. N.Y., 1966.

Phil 2411.9 — Lacroix, Jean. Panorama de la philosophie française contemporaine. Paris, 1966.

Phil 5251.70 — Lacroze, René. Eléments d'anthropologie. Paris, 1966.

Phil 1133.48 — Lahaye, Robert. La philosophie ionienne, l'Ecole de Mileti Thales, Anaxemandre, Anaximène, Héraclite d'Ep'hèse. Paris, 1966.

Phil 5850.254 — Lainz, Ronald David. Interpersonal perception. London, 1966.

Phil 2750.10.111 — LaLumia, Joseph. The ways of reason; a critical study of the ideas of Emile Meyerson. London, 1966.

Phil 5875.5 — Lambert, Wallace E. Children's views of foreign peoples. N.Y., 1966.

Phil 2705.35.6 — La Mettrie, Julien Offray de. L'homme machine. Paris, 1966.

Phil 186.147 — Lamouche, André. Rythmologie universelle et metaphysique de l'harmonie. Paris, 1966. 2v.

Phil 6321.49.2 — Lampl de Groot, Jeanne. The development of the mind. London, 1966.

Phil 8701.9.9 — Lamy, Bernard. Entretiens sur les sciences dans lesquels on apprend comment l'on doit étudier les sciences. Paris, 1966.

1966 - cont.

Phil 7069.66.15 — Lance, Pierre. Le spiritualisme athée. Paris, 1966.

Phil 1711.6.5 — Landgrebe, Ludwig. Major problems in contemporary European philosophy. N.Y., 1966.

Phil 1135.194 — Landmann, Michael. Ursprongsbild und Schöpfertat. München, 1966.

Phil 5593.66.5 — Lang, Alfred. Rorschach-Bibliographie, 1921-1964. Bern, 1966.

Phil 2750.20.105 — Langan, Thomas. Merleau-Ponty's critique of reason. New Haven, 1966.

Phil 8961.21 — Langfeldt, Gabriel. Den gylne regel og andre humanistiche moralnormer. Oslo, 1966.

Phil 1711.15 — Láscaris Comneno, Constantino. Estudios de filosofía moderna. 1. ed. San Salvador, 1966.

Phil 2120.13 — Laszlo, Ervin. Beyond scepticism and realism. The Hague, 1966.

Phil 978.96 — Lauer, Hans Erhard. Die Anthroposophie und die Zukunft des Christentums. Stuttgart, 1966.

Phil 6990.3.110 — Laurentin, René. Les apparitions de Lourdes. Paris, 1966.

Phil 3493.48 — Lauter, Josef. Untersuchungen zur Sprache von Kants Kritik der reinen Vernunft. Köln, 1966.

Phil 720.70 — Lauth, Reinhard. Die absolute Ungeschichtlichkeit der Warhrheit. Stuttgart, 1966.

Phil 6121.41 — Lazarus, Richards. Psychological stress and the coping process. N.Y., 1966.

Phil 6155.4 — Leary, Timothy Francis. Psychedelic prayers after the tao te ching. Kerhonkson, 1966.

Phil 5066.251 — Leblanc, Hugues. Techniques of deductive inference. Englewood Cliffs, 1966.

Phil 5465.175 — Lehmann, Günther Kurt. Phantasie und Künstlerische Arbeit. Berlin, 1966.

Phil 5761.25 — Lehrer, Keith. Freedom and determinism. N.Y., 1966.

Phil 978.86.7 — Lehrs, Ernst. Mensch und Materie. 2. Aufl. Frankfurt, 1966.

Phil 3552.33 — Leibniz, Gottfried. Politische Schriften. v.1-2. Wien, 1966-67.

Phil 3552.24.5.3 — Leibniz, Gottfried Wilhelm. Hauptschriften zur Grundelung der Philosophie. 3. Aufl. Hamburg, 1966. 2v.

Phil 3552.73.5 — Leibniz, Gottfried Wilhelm. Logical papers. Oxford, 1966.

Phil 3552.41.10 — Leibniz, Gottfried Wilhelm. Nouveaux essais sur l'entendement humain. Paris, 1966.

Phil 186.152 — Leist, Fritz. Über Leben, Lüge and Liebe. Freiburg, 1966.

Phil 5251.72 — Leite, Dante M. Psicologia diferencial. São Paulo, 1966.

Phil 5465.170 — Le Men, Jean. L'espace figuratif et les structures de la personnalité, une épreuve clinique originale. Paris, 1966. 2v.

Phil 402.18 — Leonardi, Franco. Sociologia dell'ideologia. Catania, 1966.

Phil 8612.52.10 — Lepp, Ignace. La mort et ses mystères. Paris, 1966.

Phil 1195.20 — Levi, Adolfo. Storia della sofistica. Napoli, 1966.

Phil 3120.30.115 — Levin-Goldschmidt, Hermann. Abschied von Martin Buber. Köln, 1966.

Phil 3120.30.165 — Levinson, Nathan P. Martin Buber. Frankfurt, 1966. 2v.

Phil 811.24 — Ley, Hermann. Geschichte der Aufklärung und des Atheismus. Berlin, 1966- 3v.

Phil 8591.86 — Libizzi, Carmelo. Religione e vita. Padova, 1966.

Phil 8666.24.2 — Librizzi, Carmelo. Immanenza e trascendenza. 2. ed. Padova, 1966.

Phil 5590.26.5 — Liebman, Joshua Loth. Hope for man. N.Y., 1966.

Phil 3011.10 — Liedman, Sven Eric. Det organiska livet i tysk debatt, 1795-1845. Thesis. Land, 1966.

Phil 3425.664.2 — Lim, Sok-Zin. Der Begriff der Arbeit bei Hegel. 2. Aufl. Bonn, 1966.

Phil 811.22 — Lindner, Herbert. Der Entwicklungsgang des philosophischen Denkens. Berlin, 1966.

Phil 5070.24 — Lindner, Herbert. Der Zweifel und seine Grenzen. Berlin, 1966.

Phil 8591.84 — Ling, Trevor Oswald. Buddha, Marx, and God: some aspects of religion in the modern world. N.Y., 1966.

Phil 486.25 — Linssen, Robert. Spiritualité de la matière. Paris, 1966.

Phil 960.244 — Litman, Aleksei D. Filosofskaia mysl' nezavisimoi Indii. Moskva, 1966.

Phil 1730.16 — Lively, Jack. The enlightenment. London, 1966.

Phil 1135.184 — Lloyd, Geoffrey Ernest Richard. Polarity and analogy. Cambridge, Eng., 1966.

Phil 2115.51.7 — Locke, J. The conduct of the understanding. N.Y., 1966.

Phil 8980.529 — Loeser, Franz. Deontik, Planung und Leitung der moralischen Entwicklung. Berlin, 1966.

Phil 8591.65.5 — Loewith, Karl. Zur Kritik der Christlichen Überlieferung. Stuttgart, 1966.

VPhil 165.409 — Łówne zagadnienia filozofii. v.3. Warszawa, 1966.

Phil 8591.82 — Lofland, John. Doomsday Cult; a study of conversion proselytization, and maintenance of faith. Englewood Cliffs, 1966.

Phil 5066.269 — The logic of decision and action. Pittsburgh, 1966.

Phil 5068.58 — Logica e analisi. Scritti di P. Filiasi Carcano (et al.). Padova, 1966.

Phil 5421.20.21 — Lorenz, Konrad Zacharias. On aggression. N.Y., 1966.

Phil 735.252 — Loring, L.M. Two kinds of values. London, 1966.

Phil 2905.1.410 — Lubac, Henri de. Teilhard, missionnaire et apologiste. Toulouse, 1966.

Phil 7080.56 — Luce, Gay Gaer. Sleep. N.Y., 1966.

Phil 3585.20.22 — Luijpen, Wilhelmus Antonius Maria. Fenomenologie en metafysica. Utrecht, 1966.

Phil 1750.115.56 — Luijpen, Wilhelmus Antonius Maria. Phenomenology and humanism. Pittsburg, 1966.

Phil 6121.45.2 — Luria, Aleksandr Romanovich. Higher cortical functions in man. N.Y., 1966.

Phil 6121.45.5 — Luria, Aleksandr Romanovich. Human brain and psychological processes. N.Y., 1966.

Phil 5066.255 — Lyndon, Roger C. Notes on logic. Princeton, N.J., 1966.

Phil 5651.9 — Lynn, Richard. Attention, arousal, and the orientation reaction. 1. ed. Oxford, 1966.

Phil 8887.124 — Mabbott, John David. An introduction to ethics. London, 1966.

Phil 2030.8 — MacDonald, Lauchlin D. John Grote. The Hague, 1966.

Phil 1830.20.2 — Mace, Cecil Alec. British philosophy in the mid-century. 2nd ed. London, 1966.

Phil 9070.111 — McGee, Charles Douglas. The recovery of meaning; an essay on the good life. N.Y., 1966.

Phil 187.178 — McGlynn, James. A metaphysics of being and God. Englewood Cliffs, 1966.

Phil 8837.17 — MacIntyre, Alasdair C. A short history of ethics. N.Y., 1966.

Phil 7069.66.25 — Mackenzie, Andrew. The unexplained; some strange cases in psychical research. London, 1966.

1966 - cont.

Phil 6962.38 — Macnab, Francis A. Estrangement and relationship. Bloomington, 1966.

Phil 2050.223.2 — MacNabb, Donald George Cecil. David Hume. 2nd ed. Oxford, 1966.

Phil 2477.6.160 — McNeill, John J. The Blondelian synthesis; a study of the influence of German philosophical sources on the formation of Blondel's method and thought. Leiden, 1966.

Phil 972.18 — Maendl, Hans. Vom Geist des Nordens. Stuttgart, 1966.

Phil 7084.14 — Mahoney, Maria F. The meaning in dreams and dreaming. 1st ed. N.Y., 1966.

Phil 2730.21 — Maine de Biran, Pierre. De l'existence, textes inédits. Paris, 1966.

Phil 3450.33.12 — Maliandi, Ricardo G. Wertobjektivität und Realitätserfahrung. Bonn, 1966.

Phil 8413.39 — Malygin, Vladimir A. O vozvyshennom v mire estetiki. Leningrad, 1966.

Phil 165.86.2 — Mandelbaum, Maurice H. Philosophic problems. N.Y., 1966.

Phil 4060.5.85 — Mandolfo, Santo. I positivisti italiani. Anuilli, 1966.

Phil 165.372 — Mann, Jesse Aloysius. Perspectives on reality; readings in metaphysics. N.Y., 1966.

Phil 5418.4 — Mannin, Ethel Edith. Loneliness; a study of the human condition. London, 1966.

Phil 2880.8.101 — Manser, Anthony Richards. Sartre: a philosophic study. London, 1966.

Phil 6315.2.310.5 — Marcuse, Herbert. Eros and civilization; a philosophical inquiry into Freud. Boston, 1966.

Phil 6980.458.5 — Margolis, Joseph. Psychotherapy and morality. N.Y., 1966.

Phil 4363.7.33 — Marias Aguilera, Julián. Ensayos de teoria. 3. ed. Madrid, 1966.

Phil 4363.7.25 — Marías Aguilera, Julián. Historia de la filosofía. 19. ed. Madrid, 1966.

Phil 2750.11.20 — Maritain, Jacques. Challenges and renewals. Notre Dame, 1966.

Phil 2750.11.44 — Maritain, Jacques. Le paysan de la Garonne. Paris, 1966.

Phil 310.587.2 — Marksistsko-leninskaia filosofiia. 2. Izd. Moskva, 1966.

Phil 1712.26 — Marnell, William Henry. Man-made morals. 1st ed. Garden City, N.Y., 1966.

Phil 3850.27.230 — Marshall, George. An understanding of Albert Schweitzer. N.Y., 1966.

Phil 3552.464 — Martin, Gottfried. Leibniz: logique et métaphysique. Paris, 1966.

Phil 2750.11.190 — Martinez Paz, Fernando. Maritain, politica e ideologia; revolución cristiana en la Argentina. Buenos Aires, 1966.

Phil 4473.78.30 — Martins, Diamantino. Filosofia da plenitude. Braga, 1966.

Phil 5520.288 — Martynov, Viktor V. Kibernetika, semiotika, lingvistika. Minsk, 1966.

VPhil 6400.31 — Maruszewski, Mariusz. Afazja. Wyd. 1. Warszawa, 1966.

Phil 2490.174 — Massing, Otwin. Fortschritt und Gegenrevolution. Die Gesellschaftslehre Comtes in ihrer sozialen Funktion. Stuttgart, 1966.

Phil 6155.6 — Masters, Robert E.L. The varieties of psychedelic experience. 1st ed. N.Y., 1966.

Phil 8092.17 — Matsa, Ivan L. Problemy khudozhestvennoi kul'tury XX veka. Moskva, 1966.

Phil 4080.3.500 — Mattioli, Raffaele. Fedeltà a Croce. Milano, 1966.

Phil 5520.480.2 — Mauro, Tullio de. Introduzione alla semantica. 2. ed. Bari, 1966.

Phil 812.43 — Mayr, Franz Karl. Geschichte der Philosophie. Kevelaer, 1966.

Phil 5590.457 — Megargee, Edwin I. Research in clinical assessment. N.Y., 1966.

Phil 1750.105 — Meglio, Gaetano. Prospettive filosofiche. Padova, 1966.

Phil 3808.235 — Mei, Flavio. Etica e politica nel pensiero di Schopenhauer. Milano, 1966.

Phil 5052.45 — Menne, Albert. Einführung in die Logik. Bern, 1966.

Phil 1750.115.28 — Merleau-Ponty, Maurice. Phenomenology of perception. London, 1966.

Phil 2520.196.10 — Mesnard, Pierre. Descartes, ou Le combat pour la vérité. Paris, 1966.

Phil 4959.245.5 — México (City). Universidad Nacional. Consejo Técnico de Humanidades. Major trends in Mexican philosophy. Notre Dame, 1966.

Phil 343.38 — Miani, Vincenzo. Problemi di gnoseologia e metafisica. Zürich, 1966.

Phil 97.10 — Micraelius, Johann. Lexicon philosophicum terminorum philosophis usitatorum. Düsseldorf, 1966.

VPhil 4012.13 — Mikecin, Vjekoslav. Suvremena talijanska filozofija. Zagreb, 1966.

Phil 1133.41 — Mikhailova, Engelina N. Ioniiskaia filosofiia. Moskva, 1966.

Phil 2138.23 — Mill, John S. John Stuart Mill; a selection of his works. N.Y., 1966.

Phil 530.35F — Misciattelli, Piero. Misticismo senese. Firenze, 1966.

Phil 3832.20 — Misrahi, Robert. Spinoza; présentation, choix et traduction des textes. 2. éd. Paris, 1966.

Phil 8413.38 — Molchanova, Albina S. Na vkus, na tsvet. Moskva, 1966.

Phil 8430.3.5 — Moles, Abraham A. Information theory and esthetic perception. Urbana, 1966.

Phil 2905.1.380 — Mooney, Christopher F. Teilhard de Chardin and the mystery of Christ. London, 1966.

Phil 2905.1.377 — Mooney, Christopher F. Teilhard de Chardin et le mystère du Christ. Paris, 1966.

Phil 6304.2 — Moor, Lise. Glossaire de psychiatrie. Paris, 1966.

Phil 2070.152 — Moore, Edward Carter. William James. N.Y., 1966.

Phil 2150.18.50 — Moore, George Edward. Lectures on philosophy. London, 1966.

Phil 4463.5 — Moraes, Manuel. Cartesianismo em Portugal: Antonio Cordeiro. Braga, 1966.

Phil 5627.215.10 — Moretti-Costanzi, Teodorice. L'estetica pia. Bologna, 1966.

Phil 5252.82.13 — Morgan, Clifford Thomas. Introduction to psychology. 3d ed. N.Y., 1966.

Phil 8413.41 — Morkrejs, Antonín. Umění, skutečnost, poznání. Praha, 1966.

Phil 8667.29 — Moscow. Gosudarstvennaia Biblioteka SSSR Imeni V.I. Lenina. Osnovy nauchnogo ateizma. Moskva, 1966.

Phil 5520.457 — Moscow. Pervyi Moskovskii Gosudarstvennyi Pedagogicheskii Institut Inostrannykh iazykov. Materialy kollokviuma po eksperimental'noi fonetike i psikhologii rechi. Moskva, 1966.

Phil 8670.20.2 — Moscow. Universitet. Kafedra Istorii i Teorii Ateizma. Osnovnye voprosy nauchnogo ateizma. 2. izd. Moskva, 1966.

Phil 5066.254 — Mostowski, Andrzej. Thirty years of foundational studies. Oxford, 1966.

Phil 585.184 — Mukerjee, Radhakamal. The community of communities. Bombay, 1966.

1966 - cont.

Phil 8413.40 — Mundt, Theodor. Ästhetik. Göttingen, 1966.

Phil 5252.89.5 — Munn, Norman Leslie. Psychology. 5. ed. Boston, 1966.

Phil 2980.8 — Muralt, André de. Philosophes en Suisse française. Neuchâtel, 1966.

Phil 8413.37 — Murian, Vasim M. Esteticheskii ideal. Moskva, 1966.

Phil 2905.1.375 — Murray, Michael Hunt. The thought of Teilhard de Chardin. N.Y., 1966.

Phil 4610.12.80 — Mustelin, Olof. Hjalmar Neiglick. Helsingfors, 1966.

Phil 5640.139 — Mykytenko, Danylo A. Vidchuttia i diisnist'. Kyïv, 1966.

Phil 8668.9 — Nabert, Jean. Le désir de Dieu. Paris, 1966.

Phil 4065.107.10 — Namer, Émile. Giordano Bruno, ou L'univers infini comme fondement de la philosophie moderne. Paris, 1966.

Phil 1750.780 — Natanson, Maurice Alexander. Essays in phenomenology. The Hague, 1966.

Phil 5655.15 — NATO Advanced Study Institute on Theories of Odor and Odor Measurement, Istanbul, 1966. Theories of odor and odor measurement. Bebek, Istanbul, 1966.

Phil 2880.8.190 — Nauta, Lolle Wibe. Jean Paul Sartre. Door, 1966.

Phil 440.14 — Nauta, Lolle Wibe. Vrijheid, Horizon der Geschiedenis. Nijkerk, 1966.

Phil 1750.115.170 — Neri, Guido Davide. Prassi e conoscenza. 1. ed. Milano, 1966.

Phil 8400.46 — New York University. Institute of Philosophy, 7th, 1964. Art and philosophy. N.Y., 1966.

Phil 3552.451 — Newman, L.M. Leibniz, 1646-1716. London, 1966.

Phil 1750.166.185 — Niel, André. Les grands appels de l'humanisme contemporain, christianisme, marxisme. Paris, 1966.

Phil 2880.8.162 — Niel, André. Jean-Paul Sartre. Paris, 1966.

Phil 1955.6.215 — Nissen, Lowell. John Dewey's theory of inquiry and truth. The Hague, 1966.

Phil 4225.8.102 — Nobile-Ventura, Attilo. Colloquio con Michele Federico Sciacca. Milano, 1966.

Phil 9035.101 — Norakidze, Vladimir. Tipy kharaktera i fiksirovannaia ustanovka. Tbilisi, 1966.

Phil 1750.777 — Novak, George Edward. Existentialism versus Marxism. N.Y., 1966.

Phil 189.33 — Østerberg, Dag. Forståelsesformer. Et filosofisk bidrag. Oslo, 1966.

Phil 1750.560.30 — Oizerman, Teodor I. Sovremennyi ekzistensialism. Moskva, 1966.

Phil 2750.19.110 — O'Malley, John B. The fellowship of being; an essay on the concept of person in the philosophy of Gabriel Marcel. The Hague, 1966.

Phil 5545.96 — Oppenheim, Abraham Naftali. Questionnaire design and attitude measurement. N.Y., 1966.

Phil 5625.75.105 — Orbeli, Leon A. Vospominaniia o I.P. Pavlove. Leningrad, 1966.

Phil 1750.166.190 — Orrego, Antenor. Hacia un humanismo americano. Lima, 1966.

Phil 4365.2.40 — Ortega y Gasset, José. Unas lecciones de metafísica. Madrid, 1966.

Phil 6980.557 — Ortigues, Marie. Oedipe africain. Paris, 1966.

Phil 7069.66.5 — Osborn, Arthur Walter. The meaning of personal existence. London, 1966.

Phil 8525.15 — Ot Erazma Potterdamskogo do Bertrana Rassela. Moskva, 1966.

Phil 8050.21.2 — Ovsiannikov, M.F. Kurze Geschichte der Ästhetik. Berlin, 1966.

Phil 8400.61 — Ovsiannikov, Mkikhail F. Marksistsko-leninskaia estetika. Moskva, 1966.

Phil 5421.10.30 — Özcan, Mehmed Tevfik. Angoisse (sikinti). Ankara, 1966.

Phil 4960.640 — Paim, Antônio. A filosofia da escola do Recife. Rio de Janeiro, 1966.

Phil 5838.266 — Palmeri, R. The sources of instinctive life, and A theory of mental functioning. N.Y., 1966.

Phil 346.30 — Pape, Ingetrud. Tradition und Transformation der Modalitat Habilitationschrift. Hamburg, 1966-

Phil 8416.8.15 — Pareyson, Luigi. Conversazioni di estetica. Milano, 1966.

Phil 1750.340.8 — Pareyson, Luigi. Esistenza e persona. 3. ed. Torino, 1966.

Phil 2805.445 — Pareyson, Luigi. L'etica di Pascal; corso di filiosfia morale dell'anno accademico 1965-1966. Torino, 1966.

Phil 8416.8.12 — Pareyson, Luigi. I problemi dell'estetica. 2. ed. Milano, 1966.

Phil 6946.40 — Parker, Seymour. Mental illness in the urban Negro community. N.Y., 1966.

Phil 2805.42.58 — Pascal, Blaise. Pensées. Paris, 1966.

Phil 1715.6.7 — Passmore, John Arthur. A hundred years of philosophy. 2nd ed. London, 1966.

Phil 8595.58 — Paus, Ansgar. Religiöser Erkenntnisgrund. Leiden, 1966.

Phil 672.238 — Pavlov, Vasilii T. Logicheskie funktsii kategorii prostranstva i vremeni. Kiev, 1966.

Phil 2050.253.5 — Pears, D.F. David Hume. London, 1966.

Phil 5765.11 — Pears, D.F. Freedom and the will. London, 1966.

Phil 4476.1.30 — Pecegueiro, Jose. Problemas da ciencia e da filosofia contemporanea. Coimbra, 1966.

Phil 3745.20 — Peprzak, Adrien T.B. Gronden en Grenzen. Haarlem, 1966.

Phil 5643.145 — Perception; a seminar conducted by the Philosophy Department of Sri Venkateswara University, 1964. Bombay, 1966.

Phil 6325.26 — Perry, Stewart Edmond. The human nature of science; researchers at work in psychiatry. N.Y., 1966.

VPhil 575.255 — Pešić-Golubović, Zagorka. Problemi savremene teorije ličnosti. Beograd, 1966.

Phil 5374.255 — Petrilowitsch, Nikolaus. Das Gewissen als Problem. Darmstadt, 1966.

Phil 6125.31 — Peursen, Cornelis Anthonie van. Body, soul, spirit; a survey of the body-mind problem. London, 1966.

Phil 3552.478 — Peursen, Cornelis Anthonie van. Leibniz. Baarn, 1966.

Phil 3450.19.95.5 — Pfeiffer, Johannes S. Existenz und Offenbarung. Berlin, 1966.

Phil 8890.66 — Phillips, Dewi Zephaniah. Moral practices. London, 1966[1970]

Phil 3246.306 — Philonenko, Alexis. La liberté humaine dans la philosophie de Fichte. Paris, 1966.

Phil 100.10.4 — Philosophisches Wörterbuch. 4. Aufl. Leipzig, 1966.

Phil 5465.150 — Piaget, Jean. L'image mentale chez l'enfant, étude sur le développement. Paris, 1966.

Phil 5865.5.4 — Piaget, Jean. La psychologie de l'enfant. Paris, 1966.

Phil 1750.783 — Piana, Giovanni. I problemi della fenomenologia. 1. ed. Milano, 1966.

Phil 4210.220 — Piemontese, Filippo. La dottrina del sentimento fondamentale nella filosofia di A. Rosmini. Milano, 1966.

Phil 190.80.25 — Pieper, Josef. Verteidigungsrede für die Philosophie. München, 1966.

Chronological Listing

Phil 1715.16 Piovani, Pietro. Conoscenza storica e coscienza morale. Napoli, 1966.

Phil 7055.205.7 Pires, José. Arigó: vida, mediunidade e martírio. 2. ed. São Paulo, 1966.

Phil 3925.16.120 Pitcher, George Willard. Wittgenstein: the philosophical investigation. 1st ed. Garden City, N.Y., 1966.

Phil 1701.56 Podnár, Ján. Od realizmu k iracionalizmu; zo súčasnej západnej filozofie. 1. vyd. Bratislava, 1966.

Phil 8890.61 Pohl, Hermann Paul Albert. Das Gesetz. Der Morgen der Menschheit. Berlin, 1966.

Phil 346.20.10 Polanyi, Michael. The tacet dimension. 1. ed. Garden City, N.Y., 1966.

Phil 5520.450 Pollio, Howard R. The structural basis of word association behavior. Paris, 1966.

Phil 3835.1.16.2 Pollock, F. Spinoza; his life and philosophy. 2nd ed. N.Y., 1966.

Phil 5039.8 Poloka Akademia Nauk. Instytut Filozofii i Socjologii. Teoria i doświadczenie. Warszawa, 1966.

Phil 3425.616 Polska Akademia Nauk. Zakład Historii Filozofii Nowożytnej i Myśli Społecznej. Polskie spory o Hegla, 1830-1860. Warszawa, 1966.

Phil 4200.1.32 Pomponazzi, Pietro. Corsi inediti dell'insegnamento padovano. Padova, 1966.

Phil 5765.12 Popper, Karl R. Of clouds and clocks. St. Louis, 1966.

Phil 7026.2 Pratt, Joseph G. Parapsychology. N.Y., 1966.

Phil 3805.245 Preuss, Eckhardt. Die Stellung und Bedeutung der Familie in der Pädagogik Schleiermachers. Münster? 1966?

Phil 2218.47 Priestley, Joseph. A scientific autobiography of Joseph Priestley, 1733-1804. Cambridge, 1966.

Phil 5238.211.5 Psikhologicheskie issledovaniia. Tbilisi, 1966.

Phil 5238.211 Psychological research in the U.S.S.R. Moscow, 1966.

Phil 5865.5 Psycologie et épistémologie génétiques, thèmes piagétiens. Paris, 1966.

Phil 4200.9.35 Pucci, Raffaele. Linguaggio e interpetrazione. Napoli, 1966.

Phil 3778.96 Pupi, Angelo. La formazione della filosofia di K.L. Reinhold, 1784-1794. Milano, 1966.

Phil 4330.10 Puy, Francisco. El pensamiento tradicional en la España del siglo XVIII, 1700-1760. Madrid, 1966.

Phil 4316.3 Puy Munãoz, Francisco. El pensamiento tradicional en la España del siglo XVIII, 1700-1760. Madrid, 1966.

Phil 5066.11.12 Quine, Willard van Orman. Elementary logic. Cambridge, 1966.

Phil 5066.276 Quine, Willard van Orman. Selected logic papers. N.Y., 1966.

Phil 5066.11.45 Quine, Willard van Orman. The ways of paradox. N.Y., 1966.

Phil 4761.5.80 Rabinovich, Valerii I. Revoliutsionnyi prosvetitel' F.V. Karzhaviv. Moskva, 1966.

Phil 8622.62 Rahner, Karl. Intellektuelle Redlichkeit und christlicher Glaube. Wien, 1966.

Phil 3850.18.195 Ranly, Ernest W. Scheler's phenomenology of community. The Hague, 1966.

Phil 3310.16.80 Rauche, G.A. The problem of truth and reality in Grisebach's thought. Pretoria, 1966.

Phil 1122.15 Rauche, Gerhard Albin. A student's key to ancient Greek thought. Fort Hare, 1966.

Phil 6844.2 Raynor, Darrell G. A year among the girls. N.Y., 1966.

Phil 8575.14 Reardon, Bernard M.G. Religious thought in the nineteenth century. Cambridge, Eng., 1966.

Phil 6980.734 Redlich, Fredrick. The theory and practice of psychiatry. N.Y., 1966.

Phil 1122.10 Redlow, Götz. Theoria. Theoretische und praktische Lebensauffassung im philosophischen Denken der Antike. Berlin, 1966.

Phil 5257.78 Reese, Ellen P. The analysis of human operant behavior. Dubuque, Iowa, 1966.

Phil 5057.42 Regnier, André. Les infortunes de la raison. Paris, 1966.

Phil 6327.12:60 Reik, Theodor. The many faces of sex. N.Y., 1966.

Phil 8967.20 Reiners, Hermann. Grundintention und sittliches Tun. Freiburg, 1966.

Phil 2905.1.570 Reinhard, Edmond. Teilhard de Chardin. Pähl, 1966.

Phil 8597.56 Reischauer, August K. The nature and truth of the great religions. Tokyo, 1966.

Phil 298.23 Reiser, Oliver Leslie. Cosmic humanism. Cambridge, 1966.

Phil 9550.24 Rescher, Nicholas. Distributive justice; a constructive critique of the utilitarian theory of distribution. Indianapolis, 1966.

Phil 5190.42 Rescher, Nicholas. The logic of commands. London, 1966.

Phil 5360.32 Reumann, Kurt. Das antithetische Kampfbild. Inaug. Diss. Berlin, 1966.

Phil 5590.490 Reuter, Jürgen Paul. Die Persönlichkeitsveränderung im Sinne der Deformierung noch schwerer Hungerdystrophie. Bonn, 1966.

Phil 3450.33.20 Reuter, Otfried. Sittichkert und ethische Werterkenntnis nach D. von Hildebrand. Münster? 1966.

Phil 2855.10.30 Revertin, Henri. Les exigences de la vie de l'esprit. Neuchâtel, 1966.

Phil 5545.238 Rey, André. Les troubles de la mémoire et leur examen psychométrique. Bruxelles, 1966.

Phil 4080.3.485 Ricci, Angelo. Benedetto Croce. Pôrto Alegre, 1966.

Phil 5545.227 Richter, Derek. Aspects of learning and memory. N.Y., 1966.

Phil 5767.11.10 Ricoeur, Paul. Freedom and nature. Evanston, Ill., 1966.

Phil 585.172 Rieff, Philip. The triumph of the therapeutic. 1st ed. N.Y., 1966.

Phil 5593.66.20 Riemsdijk, Jan van. Geschiedenis en perspectieven van de Rorschach. Proefschrift. Utrecht, 1966.

Phil 5871.65 Rifbjerg, Sofie. Psykologisk iagttagelse af børn. København, 1966.

Phil 165.380 Ritzel, Wolfgang. Rationalität, Phänomenalität, Individualität. Bonn, 1966.

Phil 1750.840 Riu, Federico. Ontología del siglo XX: Husserl. Caracas, 1966.

Phil 6315.2.382 Robert, Marthe. The psychoanalytic revolution. London, 1966.

Phil 5643.138 Rock, Irvin. The nature of perceptual adaptation. N.Y., 1966.

Phil 2520.275.10 Rodis-Lewis, Geneviève. Descartes et le rationalisme. Paris, 1966.

Phil 815.20 Rodovani, Umberto Antonio. Sommario di storia della filosofia, con particolare riguardo ai problemi morali e religiosi. Roma, 1966. 3v.

Phil 2725.2.115 Roe, William. Lamennais and England. Oxford, 1966.

Phil 4080.3.472 Roggerone, Giuseppe A. Benedetto Croce e la fondazione del concetto di libertà. Milano, 1966.

Phil 5545.228 Rogovin, Mikhail S. Filosofskie problemy teorii pamiati. Moskva, 1966.

Phil 585.185 Rombach, Heinrich. Die Frage nach dem Menschen. Freiburg, 1966.

Phil 817.27.5 Roncuzzi, Alfredo. Umane certezze; il libro della verità ragionata. Roma, 1966.

Phil 6159.15 Roseman, Bernard. The peyote story. Hollywood, Calif., 1966.

Phil 6327.37.1 Rosenfeld, Herbert A. Psychotic states. N.Y., 1966.

Phil 5841.22 Rosenfels, Paul. Love and power. N.Y., 1966.

Phil 5279.10 Rosenthal, Robert. Experimenter effects in behavioral research. N.Y., 1966.

Phil 2855.9.35 Rosset, Clément. Lettre sur les chimpanzés. Paris, 1966.

VPhil 5257.76 Rostohar, Mihajlo. Psihologija. Ljubljana, 1966.

Phil 310.633 Rostov on the Don, Russia. Gosudarstvennyi Pedagogicheskii. Institut Kafedra Filosofii. Voprosy dialekticheskogo i istoricheskogo materializma. Rostov-na-Donn, 1966.

Phil 585.160.5 Rothacker, Erich. Zur Genealogie des menschlichen Bewusstseins. Bonn, 1966.

Phil 1522.5.5 Rougier, Louis. Histoire d'une faillite philosophique: la scolastique. Paris, 1966.

Phil 165.373 Rouner, Leroy S. Philosophy, religion, and the coming world civilization. The Hague, 1966.

Phil 4768.2.6 Rubinshtein, Sergei L. Sein und Bewusstsein. 4. Aufl. Berlin, 1966.

Phil 6315.2.375 Ruitenbeek, Hendrik Marinus. Freud and America. N.Y., 1966.

Phil 6315.2.370 Ruitenbeek, Hendrik Marinus. Heirs to Freud. N.Y., 1966.

Phil 8418.35 Ruschioni, Ada. Lineamenti di una storia della poetica e dell'estetica. Milano, 1966.

Phil 6127.28 Russel, Roger. Frontiers in physiological psychology. N.Y., 1966.

Phil 5068.7.6 Russell, Bertrand Russell. An inquiry into meaning and truth. London, 1966.

Phil 6328.60 Saada, Denise. L'héritage de Freud. Paris, 1966.

Phil 5650.22.10 Sader, Manfred. Lautheit und Lärn. Göttingen, 1966.

Phil 2477.6.155 Saint-Jean, Raymond. L'apologétique philosophique. Paris, 1966.

Phil 3640.716 Sandvoss, E. Sokrates und Nietzsche. Leiden, 1966.

Phil 575.250 Sanford, Nevitt. Self and society. 1st ed. n.p., 1966.

Phil 5590.468 Sarason, Irwin G. Personality. N.Y., 1966.

Phil 4080.3.525 Sartori, Giovanni. Stato e politica nel pensiero di Benedetto Croce. Napoli, 1966.

Phil 193.241 Sauvage, Micheline. L'aventure philosophique. Paris, 1966.

Phil 5593.66 Schachtel, Ernest G. Experiential foundations of Rorschach's test. N.Y., 1966.

Phil 3120.30.135 Schaeder, Grete. Martin Buber, nebräischer Humanismus. Gottingen, 1966.

Phil 3500.100 Schäfer, Lothar. Kants Metaphysik der Natur. Berlin, 1966.

Phil 3552.474 Schering, Ernst. Leibniz und die Versöhnung der Konfessionen. Stuttgart, 1966.

Phil 2880.13.100 Scheurer, Pierre. An interior metaphysics. Weston, Mass., 1966.

Phil 2280.7.35 Schiller, F.C.S. Humanistic pragmatism. N.Y., 1966.

Phil 3246.300.1 Schindler, I.M.T. Reflexion und Bildung in Fichtes Wissenschaftslehre von 1794. 1. Aufl. Düsseldorf, 1966.

Phil 3801.775.10 Schlanger, Judith E. Schelling et la réalité finie. Paris, 1966.

Phil 8598.135.5 Schlette, Heinz Robert. Towards a theology of religions. Freiburg, 1966.

Phil 5520.465 Schmidt, Franz. Zeichen und Wirklichkeit. Stuttgart, 1966.

Phil 2905.1.495 Schmitz-Moormann, Karl. Das Weltbild Teilhard de Chardins. Köln, 1966.

Phil 9450.60 Schmölz, Franz Martin. Chance und Dilemma der politischen Ethik. Köln, 1966.

Phil 2675.6.80 Schmugge, Ludwig. Johannes von Jandun. Stuttgart, 1966.

Phil 193.244 Schneider, Peter K. Die Begründung der Wissenschaften durch Philosophie und Kybernetik. Stuttgart, 1966.

Phil 3850.14.85 Schneider, Theodor. Teleologie als theologische Kategorie bei Herman Schell. Essen, 1966.

Phil 5413.16 Schoeck, Helmut. Der Neid. Freiburg, 1966.

Phil 5893.2 Schoene, Wolfgang. Über die Psychoanalyse in der Ethnologie. Dortmund, 1966.

Phil 3808.23.5 Schopenhauer, Arthur. Der handschriftliche Nachlass. v.1-3,5. Frankfurt, 1966. 4v.

Phil 7069.66.40 Schult, Arthur. Vom übersinnlichen Wesen des Menschen. Bietigheim, 1966.

Phil 3850.27.75 Schweitzer, A. Die Lehre von der Ehrfurcht von dem Leben. München, 1966.

Phil 3850.27.65 Schweitzer, A. Strassburger Predigten. München, 1966.

Phil 5251.41.85 Schwermer, Josef. Die experimentelle Willenspsychologie Kurt Lewin. Meisenheim, 1966.

Phil 4225.8.68 Sciacca, Michele Federico. Lettere dalla campagna, e scritti affini. 2. ed. Milano, 1966.

Phil 165.369 Science, folklore, and philosophy. N.Y., 1966.

Phil 2053.80.2 Scott, William Robert. Francis Hutcheson, his life, teaching and position in the history of philosophy. N.Y., 1966.

Phil 665.98 Seele, Entwicklung, Leben. Bern, 1966.

Phil 5643.134 Segall, Marshall H. The influence of culture on visual perception. Indianapolis, 1966.

Phil 5465.146 Seidel, George Joseph. The crisis of creativity. Notre Dame, 1966.

Phil 8968.18 Sellers, James. Theological ethics. N.Y., 1966.

Phil 2805.440 Sellier, Philippe. Pascal et la liturgie. Paris, 1966.

Phil 8968.22 Semaine des Intellectuels Catholiques, 1966. Morale humaine, morale chrétienne. Paris, 1966.

Phil 9590.32 Sendy, Jean. Les Dieux nous sont nées. Paris, 1966-

Phil 5258.197 Serebriakoff, Victor. I.Q.: a Mensa analysis and history. London, 1966.

Phil 6319.1.225 Serreano, Miguel. C.G. Jung and Hermann Hesse. London, 1966.

Phil 8419.62 Shamota, Mykola. O svobode tvorchestva. Moskva, 1966.

Phil 4710.146 Shchipanov, I.Ia. Russkie prosvetiteli, ot Radishcheva do dekabristov. Moskva, 1966. 2v.

Phil 310.617.5 Sheptulin, Aleksandr P. Osnovnye zakony dialektiki. Moskva, 1966.

Phil 2340.10.185 Sherburne, Donald W. A key to Whitehead's Process and realty. N.Y., 1966.

Phil 6328.58 Sherman, Murray Herbert. Psychoanalysis in America. Springfield, 1966.

Phil 8598.79.5.15 Shestov, L. Athens and Jerusalem. Athens, 1966.

Chronological Listing

Phil 5058.96   Shirwood, William. William of Sherwood's introduction to logic. Minneapolis, 1966.

Phil 5258.198   Shorokhova, Ekaterina V. Issledovaniia myshleniia v sovetskoi psikhologii. Moskva, 1966.

Phil 4073.115   Shtekli, Al'fred E. Kampanella. Izd. 3. Moskva, 1966.

Phil 5592.45.2   Shuey, Audrey Mary. The testing of Negro intelligence. 2. ed. N.Y., 1966.

Phil 5620.33   Shurter, Robert. Critical thinking. N.Y., 1966.

Phil 5068.57   Shvyrev, Vladimir S. Neopozitivizm i problemy empiricheskogo oboshovaniia nauki. Moskva, 1966.

Phil 310.645   Sichirollo, Livio. Dialejesta-Dialektik voy Homer bis Aristoteles. Hildesheim, 1966.

Phil 5270.4   Sidowski, Joseph B. Experimental methods and instrumentation in psychology. N.Y., 1966.

Phil 4120.4.135   Signorini, Alberto. Il giovane Gentile e Marx. Milano, 1966.

Phil 349.48   Sikora, Joseph John. The Christian intellect and the mystery of being. The Hague, 1966.

Phil 585.224   Silva, Antonio da. Filosofia social. Evora, 1966.

Phil 705.55   Simon, Myron. Transcendentalism and its legacy. Ann Arbor, 1966.

Phil 8893.140   Simonsen, Andreas. Erkendelse og lidenskab. København, 1966.

VPhil 585.192   Šindelář, Jan. Co řeší filosofická antropologie. Vyd. 1. Praha, 1966.

Phil 5871.2   Skasa-Weiss, Eugen. Mütter-Schicksal grosser Söhne. Oldenburg, 1966.

Phil 3450.19.390   Skirbekk, Gunnar. Dei filosofiske vilkår for sanning. Oslo, 1966.

Phil 1135.200   Skovgaard Jensen, Søren. Dualism and demonology. Thesis. København, 1966.

Phil 4769.10   Skvortsov, Lev V. Obretaet li metafizika vtoroe dykhanie. Moskva, 1966.

Phil 5237.512   Slobin, Dan Isaac. Handbook of Soviet psychology. White Plains, N.Y., 1966.

Phil 130.11F   Słownik filozofów. Warszawa, 1966.

Phil 5870.30   Smirnoff, Victor. La psychanalyse de l'enfant. Paris, 1966.

Phil 5545.225   Smirnov, Anatolii A. Problemy psikhologii pamiati. Moskva, 1966.

Phil 2266.41.5   Smith, Adam. The theory of moral sentiments. N.Y., 1966.

Phil 5545.224   Smith, Brian. Memory. London, 1966.

Phil 5421.15.25   Smith, Henry Clay. Sensitivity to people. N.Y., 1966.

Phil 8592.122.10   Société des Études Robespierristes. Études sur le curé Meslier. Paris, 1966.

Phil 6949.366   Society of Medical Psycho-Analysts. The etiology of neuroses. Palo Alto, Calif., 1966.

Phil 7082.198   Il sogno e le civiltà umane. Bari, 1966.

Phil 8525.20   Sokolov, Nikolai P. Istoriia svobodo mysliia i ateizma v Evrope. Moskva, 1966.

Phil 310.632   Soldatov, Vasyl' I. Problema vzaiemovidnoshennia svitohliadu i metodu v dialektychnomu materializmi. Kyiv, 1966.

Phil 4362.10   Soler Puigoriol, Pedro. El hombre, ser indigente: el pensamiento antropológico de Pedro Lain Entralgo. Madrid, 1966.

Phil 1750.784   Solov'ev, Erikh I. Ekzistentsializm i naunchnoe poznanie. Moskva, 1966.

Phil 5643.130   Soltis, Jonas Francis. Seeing, knowing, and believing. Reading, Mass., 1966.

Phil 2750.19.85   Sonsbeeck, Dawiet van. Het zijn als mysterie in de ervaring en het denken van Gabriel Marcel. Bilthoven, 1966.

Phil 310.623   Soveshchanie po Sovremennym Problemam Materialisticheskoi Dialektiki. Materialy. Moskva, 1966. 4v.

Phil 5246.25.80   Spaltro, Enzo. Agostino Gemelli e la psicologia del lavoro in Italia. Milano, 1966.

Phil 4225.1.21   Spaventa, Bertrando. Scritti inediti e rari, 1840-1880. Padova, 1966.

Phil 2520.360   Specht, Rainer. Commercium mentis et corporis. Stuttgart, 1966.

Phil 3819.63   Spinoza, Benedictus de. Letters to friend and foe. N.Y., 1966.

Phil 4225.15.40   Spirito, Ugo. Dal mito alla scienza. Firenze, 1966.

Phil 177.105.30   Spirito, Ugo. Ideale del dialogo o ideale della scienza? Roma, 1966.

Phil 5585.238   Staniland, Alan Charles. Patterns of redundancy. Cambridge, Eng., 1966.

Phil 8673.23   Steenberghen, Fernand van. Hidden God; how do we know that God exists? Saint Louis, 1966.

Phil 1540.35.5   Steenberghen, Fernand van. La philosophie au XIIE siècle. Louvain, 1966.

Phil 6968.36   Stefan, Gregory. In search of sanity. New Hyde Park, 1966.

Phil 978.49.880   Steffen, Albert. Gegenwartsaufgaben der Menschheit. Schweiz, 1966.

Phil 3200.14.80   Steinbuechel, Theodor. Der Umbruch des Denkens. Darmstadt, 1966.

Phil 978.49.670   Steiner, R. Erdenwissen und Himmelserkenntnis. Dornach, 1966.

Phil 978.49.679   Steiner, R. Erziehungskunst; Methodisch-Didaktisches. 4. Aufl. Dornach, 1966. 2v.

Phil 978.49.655   Steiner, R. Geistige und soziale Wandlungen in der Menschheitsentwickelung; achtzehn Vorträge. Dornach, 1966.

Phil 978.49.152   Steiner, R. Gesammelte Aufsätze zur Kultur- und Zeitgeschichte, 1887-1901. Dornach, 1966.

Phil 978.49.162   Steiner, R. Geschichtliche Notwendigkeit und Freiheit. 2. Aufl. Dornach, 1966.

Phil 978.49.483   Steiner, R. Heileurythmie; acht Vorträge. 3. Aufl. Dornach, 1966.

Phil 978.49.502   Steiner, R. Die Impulsierung des weltgeschichtlichen Gescheheus durch geistige Mächte; sieben Vorträge. 2. Aufl. Dornach, 1966.

Phil 978.49.580   Steiner, R. Individuelle Geistwesen und ihr Wirken in der Seele des Menschen. Dornach, 1966.

Phil 978.49.590   Steiner, R. Der Jahres kreislauf als Atmungsvorgang der Erde und die vier grossen Festeszeiten. Dornach, 1966.

Phil 978.49.615   Steiner, R. Die Konstitution der Allgemeinen anthroposophischen Gesellschaft und der freien Hochschule. Dornach, 1966.

Phil 978.49.610   Steiner, R. Kunst im Lichte der Mysterienweisheit. Dornach, 1966.

Phil 978.49.640   Steiner, R. Lebendiges Naturerkennen. Dornach, 1966.

Phil 978.49.408   Steiner, R. Menschenwesen, Menschenschicksal und Weltentwicklunz. 3. Aufl. Dornach, 1966.

Phil 978.49.600   Steiner, R. Die menschliche Seele in ihrem Zusammenhang mit göttlich-geistigen Individualitäten. Dornach, 1966.

Phil 978.49.635   Steiner, R. Mysterienwahrheiten und Weihnachtsimpulse. Dornach, 1966.

Phil 978.49.620   Steiner, R. Die spirituellen Hintergründe der äusseren Welt. Dornach, 1966.

Phil 978.49.515   Steiner, R. Die tieferen Geheimnisse des Menschheitswerdens im Lichte der Evangelien. Dornach, 1966.

Phil 978.49.523   Steiner, R. Das Verhältnis der Sternenwelt zum Menschen und des Menschen zur Steinenwelt. 3. Aufl. Dornach, 1966.

Phil 978.49.630   Steiner, R. Die Welträtsel und die Anthroposophie. 1. Aufl. Dornach, 1966.

Phil 5768.10.35   Steiner, Rudolf. Rudolf Steiner über seine "Philosophie der Freiheit". Stuttgart, 1966.

Phil 2490.175   Steinhauer, Margarete. Die politische Soziologie Auguste Comtes und ihre Differenz zur liberalen Gesellschaftstheorie Condorcets. Meisenheim, 1966.

Phil 3850.54   Steinheim, Salomon Ludwig. Salomon Ludwig Steinheim zum Gedenken. Leiden, 1966.

Phil 1870.155   Steinkraus, Warren Edward. New studies in Berkeley's philosophy. N.Y., 1966.

Phil 1750.552.20   Stenström, Thure. Existentialismen. Stockholm, 1966.

Phil 3270.12.90   Sternfeld, Robert. Frege's logical theory. Carbondale, 1966.

Phil 5258.114.10   Straus, Erwin. Phenomenological psychology. N.Y., 1966.

Phil 3500.98   Strawson, Peter Frederick. The bounds of sense: an essay on Kant's 'Critique of pure reason'. London, 1966.

Phil 5275.5   Strízenec, Michal. Psychológia a kybernetika. Bratislava, 1966.

Phil 1718.38   Stromberg, Roland N. An intellectual history of modern Europe. N.Y., 1966.

Phil 1730.20   Studi sull'illuminismo di G. Solinas. Firenze, 1966.

Phil 193.254   Stuettgen, Albert. Offenheit und Perspektive. Warendorf, 1966.

Phil 525.250   Sunar, Cavit. Mistiszimin ana hatlari. Ankara, 1966.

Phil 5058.70.9   Suppes, Patrick. Introduction to logic. Princeton, N.J., 1966.

Phil 5421.25.76   Suttie, Ian Dishart. The origins of love. N.Y., 1966.

Phil 5640.136.5   Sváb, L. Bibliography of sensory deprivation and social isolation. Prague, 1966.

Phil 818.38   Swieżawski, Stefan. Zagadnienie historii filozofii. Warszawa, 1966.

Phil 5500.42   Symposium on Cognition, 1st, Pittsburgh, 1965. Problem solving: research, method and theory. N.Y., 1966.

Phil 2419.1.2.5   Taine, Hippolyte Adolphe. Les philosophes français du XIXe siècle. Paris, 1966.

Phil 8709.24   Talafous, Camillus D. Readings in science and spirit. Englewood Cliffs, N.J., 1966.

Phil 6329.20   Taylor, Frederick K. Psychopathology. London, 1966.

Phil 585.177   Taylor, Richard. Action and purpose. Englewood Cliffs, N.J., 1966.

Phil 585.168   Taylor, Thomas. A vindication of the rights of brutes (1792). Gainesville, Fla., 1966.

Phil 2905.1.33   Teilhard de Chardin, Pierre. Album. London, 1966.

Phil 2905.1.69   Teilhard de Chardin, Pierre. Je m'explique. Paris, 1966.

Phil 2905.1.25   Teilhard de Chardin, Pierre. Sur le bonheur. Paris, 1966.

Phil 5360.34   Tenzer, Oliver. Abstrakcia. 1. vyd. Bratislava, 1966.

Phil 2905.1.296   Terra, Helmut de. Perspektiven Teilhard de Chardins. München, 1966.

Phil 1170.24   Theiler, Willy. Forschungen zum Neuplatonismus. Berlin, 1966.

Phil 1750.115.62   Thevenaz, Pierre. De Husserl à Merleau-Ponty. Neuchâtel, 1966.

Phil 8430.79   Thiele, Joachim. Verfahren der statistischen Ästhetik. Hamburg, 1966.

Phil 5829.14   Thinès, Georges. Psychologie des animaux. Bruxelles, 1966.

Phil 1719.6   Thyssen, Johannes. Grundlinien eines realistischen Systems der Philosophie. Bonn, 1966. 2v.

Phil 4981.41.100   Tierno Galvan, Enrique. La realidad como resultado. Rio Piedras, 1966.

Phil 3475.3.180   Tollhoetter, Bernhard. Erziehung und Selbstsein. Rätingen, 1966.

Phil 5066.256   Tondl, Ladislav. Problémy sémantiky. Praha, 1966.

Phil 2805.428   Topliss, Patricia. The rhetoric of Pascal. Leicester, 1966.

Phil 3552.452   Totok, Wilhelm. Leibniz. Hannover, 1966.

Phil 5850.356.5   Touraine, Alain. La conscience ouvrière. Thèse. Paris, 1966.

Phil 5627.266.20   Tournier, Paul. L'homme et son lieu. Psychologie et foi. Neuchâtel, 1966.

Phil 5627.245.2   Tournier, Paul. The person reborn. N.Y., 1966.

Phil 4210.235   Traniello, Francesco. Società religiosa e società civile in Rosmini. Bologna, 1966.

Phil 5238.212   Transzendenz als Erfahrung: Beitrag und Widerhall. Weilheim, 1966.

Phil 8610.759.5F   Trinius, Johann Anton. Freydenker-Lexicon. Torino, 1966.

Phil 8050.86   Trofimov, Pavel S. Estetika i iskusstvo. Moskva, 1966.

Phil 5421.15.35   Trost, Jan. Om bildandet av dyader. Uppsala, 1966.

Phil 2905.1.390   Truhlar, Karel Vladimir. Teilhard und Solowjew. Freiburg, 1966.

Phil 4757.5   Tsallaev, Khariton K. Filosofskie i obshchestvenno-politicheskie vozzreniia Afanasiia Gassieva. Ordzhonikidze, 1966.

Phil 310.551.2   Tsaregorodtsev, Gennadi I. Dialekticheskii materializm i meditsina. 2. Izd. Moskva, 1966.

Phil 4773.5   Tutundzhian, Ovsep. Psikhologicheskaja kontseptsiia Anri Vallona. Erevan, 1966.

Phil 5875.110.5   Tuvo, Fulvio. Il disegno nella psicopatologia dell'età evolutiva. Trieste, 1966.

Phil 1750.101.5   Tymieniecka, Anna Teresa. Why is there something rather than nothing? Assen, 1966.

Phil 3850.18.210   Uchiyam, Mivoru. Das Wertwidrige in der Ethik Max Schelers. Bonn, 1966.

Phil 720.86   Ulmer, Karl. Die Wissenschaften und die Wahrheit. Stuttgart, 1966.

Phil 3900.2.5   Unger, Erich. Das Lebendige und das Goettliche. Jerusalem, 1966.

Phil 195.12   Unurn, George. What I believe. London, 1966.

Phil 5260.10.5   Uznadze, Dmitrii N. Psikhologicheskie issledovaniia. Moskva, 1966.

Phil 8980.866.5   Vagovič, Stefano. L'etica comunista. Roma, 1966.

Phil 352.12   Vakhtomin, Nikolai K. Zakony dialektiki, zakony poznaniia. Moskva, 1966.

Chronological Listing

1966 - cont.

Phil 7069.66.45   Vallberg, Viktor. Den kära okunnigheten, eller, Den fördolda kunskapen. Stockholm, 1966.

Phil 8971.4   Vandenbroucke, Francois. La morale monastique du XIe au XVIe siècle. Louvain, 1966.

Phil 6131.7   Van Kaam, Adrian. Existential foundations and psychology. Pittsburgh, 1966.

Phil 196.40   Van Nuys, Kevin. Is reality meaningful? Static contradictions and dynamic resolutions between facts and value. N.Y., 1966.

Phil 3552.472   Vennelusch, Joachim. Gottfried Wilhelm Leibniz; philosopher and politician in the service of a universal culture. Bad Godesberg, 1966.

Phil 75.72   Verbinc, Franc. Filozofski tokovi na Slovenskem. Ljubljana, 1966.

Phil 2835.87   Verdonk, Johannes Jacobus. Petrus Ramus en de wiskunde. Assen, 1966.

Phil 5627.266.5   Vergote, Antoine. Psychologie religieuse. Bruxelles, 1966.

Phil 3903.5.35   Verhoeven, Cornelius W.M. Het grote gebeuren. Utrecht, 1966.

Phil 3503.15   Verondini, Enrico. La filosofia morale di Emanuele Kant. Bologna, 1966.

Phil 4210.230   Verondini, Enrico. Leffere sulla spiritualitá rosminiana. Milano, 1966.

Phil 8676.5.3   Verret, Michel. Les marxistes et la religion. 3. éd. Paris, 1966.

Phil 672.262   Versfeld, Marthinus. Wat is kontemporêr? Johannesburg, 1966.

Phil 8430.57   Vian, Boris. En avant la zizique...et par ici les gros sous. Paris, 1966.

Phil 4260.37.1   Vico, G.B. Die neue Wissenschaft über die gemeinschaftliche Natur der Völker. Hamburg, 1966.

Phil 410.82   Viderskii, Vladimir I. Konechnoe i beskonechnoe. Moskva, 1966.

Phil 2905.1.555   Vidoni, Egidio. L'individuo e il collettivo nella durata secondo Pierre Teilhard de Chardin. Milano, 1966[1965].

Phil 4959.235   Villegas, Abelardo. La filosofía en la historía política de México. 1. ed. México, 1966.

Phil 3640.720   Vogel, Martin. Apollinisch und Dionysisch; Geschichte eines genialen Irrtums. Regensburg, 1966.

Phil 3450.19.420   Vottimo, Gianni. Arte e verità nel pensiero di Martin Heidegger. Torino, 1966.

VPhil 310.163   Vranicki, Predrag. Covjek i historija. Sarajevo, 1966.

Phil 821.1.20   Vycinas, Vincent. Greatness and philosophy. The Hague, 1966.

Phil 672.240   Wallis, Robert. Le temps, quatrième dimension de l'esprit. Paris, 1966.

Phil 974.3.165   Walther, Kurt. Über die neu Mysteriendramen Rudolf Steiners. Freiburg, 1966-67. 3v.

Phil 8847.15.2   Warnock, Mary. Ethics since 1900. 2nd ed. London, 1966.

Phil 315.17   Waterston, G.C. Order and counter-order. N.Y., 1966.

Phil 1200.63   Watson, Gerard. The Stoic theory of knowledge. Belfast, 1966.

Phil 2520.349   Watson, Richard A. The downfall of Cartesianism, 1673-1712. The Hague, 1966.

Phil 575.278   Watts, Alan Wilson. The book; on the taboo against knowing who you are. N.Y., 1966.

Phil 640.4   Watzlaurk, Joseph. Leo XIII and the new scholasticism. Cebu City, 1966.

Phil 2520.385   Wegelingh, William. Cartesiaanse uitzichten. Lochem, 1966.

Phil 5068.56.10   Weingartner, Paul. Deskription, Analytizität und Existenz. Salzburg, 1966.

Phil 822.20   Weishedel, Wilhelm. Die philosophische Hintertreppe. München, 1966.

Phil 8423.26.2   Weisse, Christian H. System der Ästhetik als Wissenschaft von der Idee der Schönheit, reprografischer Nachdruck von 1830. Hildesheim, 1966.

Phil 3925.3.52   Weisse, Christian Hermann. Kleine Schriften zur Ästhetik und ästhetischen Kritik. Hildesheim, 1966.

Phil 9075.73.2   Wermlund, Sven. Samvetets uppkomst. 2. Uppl. Stockholm, 1966.

Phil 5832.15.12   Werner, Heinz. Comparative psychology of mental development. N.Y., 1966.

Phil 8870.36   Wetenschappelijke moraalstudie. Ledeberg, 1966.

Phil 5590.292   White, Robert Winthrop. Lives in progress. 2. ed. N.Y., 1966.

Phil 353.33   Wiedmann, Franz. Das Problem der Gewissheit. Eine erkenntnismetaphsische Studie. München, 1966.

Phil 8897.92   William, Bernard Arthur Owen. Morality and the emotions: an inaugural lecture. London, 1966.

Phil 1822.8   Williams, Bernard. British analytical philosophy. London, 1966.

Phil 325.12   Williams, Donald Cary. Principles of empirical realism. Springfield, Ill., 1966.

Phil 5262.57.5   Williamson, George Scott. Science, synthesis and sanity. Chicago, 1966.

VPhil 978.116   Wilmar, F.H.J. Kinderkrankheinten im Lichte der Anthroposphie. Zeist, 1966.

Phil 1750.775   Wilson, Colin. Introduction to the new existentialism. London, 1966.

Phil 1730.18   Winter, Eduard. Frühaufklärung; der Kampf Gegen den Konfessionalismus in Mittel- und Osteuropa und die deutsch-slawische Begegnung. Berlin, 1966.

Phil 1195.19   Wiśniewski, Bohdan. L'influence des sophistes sur Aristote, Epicur, stoiciens et sceptiques. Wrocław, 1966.

Phil 3925.16.25   Wittgenstein, Ludwig. Lectures and conversations on asthetics. Berkeley, 1966.

Phil 5262.66   Witvrouw, Marcel. Le comportement humain. Bruxelles, 1966.

Phil 6332.33   Wolberg, Lewis Robert. Psychotherapy and the behavoral sciences. N.Y., 1966.

Phil 6332.22.2   Wyss, Dieter. Depth psychology, a critical history. N.Y., 1966.

Phil 5545.95   Yates, Frances Amelia. The art of memory. London, 1966.

Phil 5545.232   Young, John Zachary. The memory system of the brain. Berkeley, 1966.

Phil 5374.244   Young, Warren R. L.S.D. on campus. N.Y., 1966.

Phil 730.28   Zabeeh, Farhang. Universals; a new look at an old problem. The Hague, 1966.

Phil 3845.3.2   Zac, Sylvain. La morale de Spinoza. 2. éd. Paris, 1966.

Phil 6975.5.2   Zaglul, Antonio. Mis quinientos locos; memorias del director de un manicomio. 2. ed. Santo Domingo, 1966.

Phil 310.655   Zaječaranović, Gligorije. Analiza i sinteza u okviru dijalektike Hegela i Marksa. Beograd, 1966.

1966 - cont.

Phil 4967.5.80   Zelada C., Alberto. El pensamiento de Guillermo Francovich. Sucre, 1966.

Phil 930.68   Zempliner, Artur. Cínská filosofie v novověké evropské filosofii. Praha, 1966.

Phil 5599.39   Zeppelin, Ilka Sigried von. Die Variablen der Holtzman Inkblot Technique in ihrer Beziehung zur Introversion und Extraversion. Bern, 1966.

Phil 8980.895.5   Zhuravkov, M.G. Moral'nyi oblik sovetskogo rabochego. Moskva, 1966.

Phil 8426.7   Ziff, Paul. Philosophic turnings. Ithaca, N.Y., 1966.

Phil 4710.150   Zimin, Petr P. Voprosy psikhologii myshleniia v trudakh klassikov russkoi filosofii XIX v. Tashkent, 1966.

Phil 8612.60   Zinker, Joseph Chaim. Rosa Lee; motivation and the crisis of dying. Painesville, Ohio, 1966.

VPhil 1750.797   Životić, Miladin. Pragmatizam i savremena filozofija. Beograd, 1966.

Phil 4752.2.180   Zoppo, Franco. La rivelazione della libertà. Firenze, 1966.

Phil 5593.66.10   Zulliger, Hans. Praxis des Zulliger-Tafeln- und Diapositiv-Tests und ausgewählte Aufsätze. Bern, 1966.

1967

Phil 730.5.2   Aaron, Richard Ithamar. The Theory of universals. 2nd ed. London, 1967.

Phil 4060.10.30   Abbagnano, Nicola. Scritti scelti. Torino, 1967.

Phil 331.41   Abdil'din, Zhabaikhan M. Problema nachala v teoreticheskom poznanii. Alma-Ata, 1967.

Phil 4301.2   Abellán, José Luis. Filosofía española en America, 1936-1966. Madrid, 1967.

Phil 3808.237   Abendroth, Walter. Arthur Schopenhauer in Selbstzeugnissen und Bilddokumenten. Reinbek, 1967.

Phil 7106.10   Abnormal hypnotic phenomena, a survey of nineteenth century cases. London, 1967[1968]. 4v.

Phil 1700.12   Adam, Antoine. Le mouvement philosophique dan la première moitie du XVIIIe siècle. Paris, 1967.

Phil 6110.28   Adám, György. Interoception and behaviour. Budapest, 1967.

Phil 8401.23.5   Adamian, Arshag. Stat'i ob estetike. Erevan, 1967.

Phil 3000.5   Adorno, Theodor W. Jargon der Eigentlichkeit; zur deutschen Ideologie. Frankfurt, 1967.

Phil 8401.37   Adorno, Theodor W. Ohne Leitbild. Frankfurt, 1967.

Phil 2725.35.105   Ainval, Christiane d'. Une doctrine de la présence spirituelle; la philosophie de Louis Lavelle. Louvain, 1967.

Phil 75.75   Akademiia Nauk SSSR. Fundamental'naia Biblioteka Obshchestvennykh Nauk. Kritika burzhuaznoi i reformistskoi filosofii i sotsiologii epokhi imperializma. Moskva, 1967.

Phil 5210.8.5   Akademiia Pedagogicheskikh Nauk RSFSR, Moscow. Institut Psikhologii. Ergebnisse der sowjetischen Psychologie. Berlin, 1967.

Phil 800.18   Alfieri, Vittorio Enzo. Filosofia e filologia. Napoli, 1967.

Phil 4080.3.495   Alfieri, Vittorio Enzo. Pedagogia crociana. Napoli, 1967.

Phil 2070.155A   Allen, Gay Wilson. William James; a biography. N.Y., 1967.

Phil 5240.46.5.2   Allport, Gordon Willard. Becoming. New Haven, 1967.

Phil 175.65   Almeida, Fernando Pinho de. A essência da matéria e o sentido da vida. Coimbra, 1967.

Phil 3565.130   An, Ho-Sang. Hermann Lotzes Bedeutung für das Problem der Beziehung. Bonn, 1967.

Phil 331.9.5   Anderson, J.F. Reflections on the analogy of being. The Hague, 1967.

Phil 7069.67.50   Andreas, Peter. Between heaven and earth, adventures in the search of the nature of man. Toronto, 1967.

Phil 7069.67.50.2   Andreas, Peter. Was niemand glauben will. Berlin, 1967.

Phil 585.245   Andriessen, J.H. Naar omega. Conceptie van nieuw denken. Den Haag, 1967.

Phil 3270.12.95   Angehelli, Ignacio. Studies on Gottlob Frege and Traditional philosophy. Dordrecht, 1967.

Phil 5401.56   Angst; psychische und somatische Aspekte. Bern, 1967.

Phil 3925.16.245   Antiseri, Dario. Dopo Wittgenstein. Roma, 1967.

Phil 165.426   Anton, John Peter. Naturalism and historical understanding. Albany, 1967.

Phil 735.261   Antonovich, Ivan I. Amerikanskaia burzhuaznaia aksiologiia na sluzh e imperializma. Minsk, 1967.

Phil 5210.15   Appley, Mortimertt. Psychology in Canada. Ottawa, 1967.

VPhil 5125.34   Arandjelović, Jovan T. Uloga indukcije u naučnom istraživanju. Beograd, 1967.

Phil 5590.462   Argyle, Michael. The psychology of interpersonal behavior. Harmondsworth, 1967.

Phil 5240.55   Ariete, Silvano. The intrapsycic self. N.Y., 1967.

Phil 8580.40   Armaner, Neda. Inanç ve hareket bütünlüğü bakimindan din terbiyesi. Istanbul, 1967.

Phil 1133.43   Armstrong, Arthur Hilary. The Cambridge history of later Greek and early medieval philosophy. London, 1967.

Phil 8401.40   Arnheim, Rudolf. Toward a psychology of art. Berkeley, 1967.

Phil 7082.6   Arthurs, André. Répertoire des images et symboles oniriques rencontrés au cours des analyses psychotherapiques. Genève, 1967.

Phil 5435.16   Association de Psychologie Scientifique de Langue Française. Les processus d'adaptation; Xe symposium, Marseille, 1965. 1. éd. Paris, 1967.

Phil 8088.6   Assunto, Rosario. Stagionie ragioni nell'estetica del settecento. Milano, 1967.

Phil 8655.14   L'ateismo contemporaneo. Torino, 1967- 4v.

Phil 331.40   Aune, Bruce. Knowledge, mind and nature. N.Y., 1967.

Phil 1750.166.275   Azevedo, Fernando de. Na batalho do humanismo. 2. ed. São Paulo, 1967.

Phil 176.234   Bacchin, Giovanni Romano. L'immediato e la sua negazione. Perugia, 1967.

Phil 3483.28.5   Baeumler, Alfred. Das Irrationalitätsproblem in der Ästhetik und Logik. 2. Aufl. Darmstadt, 1967.

Phil 8876.117.2   Baier, Kurt. The moral point of view. N.Y., 1967.

Phil 5270.6   Bakan, David. On method: toward a reconstruction of psychological investigation. 1st ed. San Francisco, 1967.

Phil 6327.21.80   Baker, Elsworth. Man in the trap. N.Y., 1967.

Phil 8968.15.85   Balle, Theo. Dialogische Existenz. Bamberg, 1967.

Phil 978.108   Ballmer, Karl. Der Macher bim Ich. Besazio, 1967.

Phil 8980.191   Bandzeladze, Gela. Aktual'nye problemy marksistkoi etiki. Tbilisi, 1967.

Phil 4070.7.55   Banfi, Antonio. La crisi. Milano, 1967.

Phil 5627.267.15   Banfi, Antonio. Esperienza religiosa e coscienza religiosa e coscienza filosofica. Urbino, 1967.

1967 - cont.

Phil 4070.7.10   Banfi, Antonio. La filosofia e la vita spirituale. Roma, 1967.

Phil 4803.879.90   Bańku, Józef. Poglądy filozoficzno-społeczne Michała Wiszniewskiego. Wyd. 1. Warszawa, 1967.

Phil 2750.11.210   Barbiellini Amidei, Gaspare. Dopo Maritain. Torino, 1967.

Phil 978.95   Barfield, Owen. Romanticism comes of age. 1st American ed. Middletown, Conn., 1967[1966]

Phil 5520.486   Barfield, Owen. Speaker's meaning. 1. ed. Middletown, 1967.

Phil 1750.790   Barnes, Hazel Estella. An existentialist ethics. 1st ed. N.Y., 1967.

Phil 1750.555.6   Barnes, Hazel Estella. Humanistic existentialism; the literature of possibility. Lincoln, 1967.

Phil 4963.6   Barreto, Luís Pereira. Obras filosóficas. São Paulo, 1967.

Phil 4963.5   Barros, Roque Spencer Maciel de. A evolução do pensamento de Pereira Barreta. São Paulo, 1967.

Phil 6111.70   Barsley, Michael. The other hand; an investigation into the sinister history of left-handedness. 1st ed. N.Y., 1967.

Phil 3425.232.5   Barth, Paul. Die Geschichtsphilosophie Hegels und der Hegelianer bis auf Marx und Hartman. Darmstadt, 1967.

Phil 2475.1.437   Barthélemy-Madaule, Madeleine. Bergson. Paris, 1967.

Phil 2905.1.200.5   Barthélemy-Madaule, Madeleine. La personne et le drame humain chez Teilhard de Chardin. Paris, 1967.

Phil 2115.198   Bartolomeis, Francesco de. John Locke. Il pensiero filosofico e pedagogico. Firenze, 1967.

Phil 930.74   Basic writings of Mo Tzu, Hsün Tzu and Han Fei Tzu. N.Y., 1967.

Phil 3450.19.410   Battaglia, Felice. Heidegger e la filosofia di valori. Bologna, 1967.

Phil 5850.127.5   Battegay, Raymond. Der Mensch in der Gruppe. Bern, 1967-3v.

Phil 7069.67.5   Bayless, Raymond. The enigma of the poltergeist. West Nyack, 1967.

Phil 8402.57.5A   Beardsley, Monroe Curtis. Aesthetic inquiry: essays on art criticism and the philosophy of art. Belmont, Calif., 1967.

Phil 6625.8   Beck, Aaron T. Depression: clinical, experimental, and theoretical aspects. N.Y., 1967.

Phil 5640.140   Békésy, Georg von. Sensory inhibition. Princeton, 1967.

Phil 8402.60.2   Belik, Aleksandr P. Estetika i sovremennost'. Izd. 2. Moskva, 1967.

Phil 5203.14   Benedek, László. Magyar pszichológiai irodalom 1945-66. Budapest, 1967.

Phil 4080.3.505   Benedetti, Ulisse. Benedetto Croce e il fascismo. Roma, 1967.

Phil 4080.3.515   Benedetto Croce. Napoli, 1967.

Phil 5520.551   Bense, Max. Semiotik. Baden-Baden, 1967.

Phil 5041.95   Bentham, Edward. An introduction to logick, 1773. Menston, 1967.

Phil 4752.2.38   Berdiaev, Nikolai Aleksandrovich. Nicolas Berdiaeff ou la Révolte contre l'objectivation. Paris, 1967.

Phil 4210.79.10   Bergamaschi, Cirillo. Bibliografia rosminiana. Milano, 1967. 2v.

Phil 5649.30   Bergès, Jean. Les gestes et la personnalité. Paris, 1967.

Phil 5068.18.2   Bergmann, Gustav. The metaphysics of logical positivism; papers. 2. ed. Madison, 1967.

Phil 3120.8.145   Bergmann, Gustav. Realism; a critique of Brentano and Meinong. Madison, 1967.

Phil 3625.5.95   Bergmann, Hugo. The philosophy of Salomon Maimon. Jerusalem, 1967.

Phil 5241.170   Bertalanffy, Ludwig von. Robots, men, and minds; psychology in the modern world. N.Y., 1967.

Phil 5041.58.7   Beth, Evert Willem. Moderne logica. 2. druk. Assen, 1967.

Phil 6980.106   Bettelheim, Bruno. The empty fortress. N.Y., 1967.

Phil 6990.3.116   Bettez, Norbert Marie. Lourdes et Fatima. Montréal, 1967.

Phil 3425.595.2   Beyer, W.R. Hegel-Bilder; Kritik der Hegel-Deutungen. 2. Aufl. Berlin, 1967.

Phil 4260.157   Bianca, Giovanni A. Il concetto di poesia in Giambattista Vico. Messina, 1967.

Phil 3450.11.420   Biral, Alessandro. L'unità del sapere in Husserl. Padova, 1967.

Phil 6990.68   Bishop, George Victor. Faith healing; God or fraud? Los Angeles, 1967.

Phil 6980.113   Bittner, Günther. Psychoanalyse und soziale Erziehung. München, 1967.

Phil 9495.167.5   Bjerg, Kresten. Moralpsykologi og sexualmoral. København, 1967.

Phil 3483.88   Blaha, Ottokar. Die Ontologie Kants. Ihr Grundriss in der Transzendentalphilosophie. Habilitationsschrift. Salzburg, 1967.

Phil 5041.93.10   Blanché, Robert. Raison et discours, dépense de la logique réflexive. Paris, 1967.

Phil 3120.55.45   Bloch, Ernst. Auswahl aus seinen Schriften. Frankfurt, 1967.

Phil 176.69.12.5   Bloch, Ernst. Spuren. 5. Aufl. Frankfurt, 1967.
Phil 3120.55.40   Bloch, Ernst. Wegzeichen der Hoffnung. Frankfurt, 1967.
Phil 5041.52.6   Blundeville, Thomas. The art of logike. Facsimile. Menston, 1967.

Phil 1200.65   Bodson, Arthur. La Morale sociale des derniers stoïciens, Sénèque, Epictète et Marc Aurèle. Paris, 1967.

Phil 1695.34   Bogomdov, Aleksei S. Iz istorii zarubezhno filosofii XIX-XX vehov. Moskva, 1967.

Phil 5865.4   Bollinger, Heinz. Das Werden der Person. München, 1967.
Phil 5545.98   Bongard, Mikhail M. Problema uznavaniia. Moskva, 1967.
Phil 2750.20.125   Bonomi, Andrea. Esistenza e struttura. Milano, 1967.
Phil 5360.27   Borisov, Vadim N. Urovni logicheskogo protsessa i osnovnye napravleniia ikh issledovaniia. Novosibirsk, 1967.

Phil 5649.34   Both, Frans Jacob. Manuele varrdigheid; cen oriëntatie. Proefschrift. Groningen, 1967.

Phil 6311.52   Bouvet, Maurice. Oeuvres psychanalytiques. Paris, 1967-68. 2v.

Phil 6327.28.80   Braaten, Leif Johan. Klient-sentrert rådgivning og terapi...Carl R. Rogers' psykologi. Oslo, 1967.

Phil 6158.15   Braden, William. The private sea; LSD and the search for God. Chicago, 1967.

Phil 7069.67.30   Bradley, Dorothy Bomar. Psychic phenomena, revelations and experiences. West Nyack, 1967.

Phil 8876.27.16A   Bradley, Francis Herbert. Ethical studies. 2nd ed. Oxford, 1967.

Phil 5170.18   Bradley, Raymond. Logic, physics and metaphysics. Auckland, 1967.

Phil 6315.2.420   Brandell, Gunnar. Freud; enfant de son siècle. Paris, 1967.

Phil 5865.5.16   Brearley, Molly. A guide to reading Piaget. N.Y., 1967.

1967 - cont.

Phil 176.215   Brent, Duncan. Of the seer and the vision. Amsterdam, 1967.

Phil 4829.203.80   Brida, Marija. Benedikt Benković. Beograd, 1967.
Phil 9240.36   Brod, Viktor. Die Ich-du-Beziehung als Erfahrungsgrundlage der Ethik. München, 1967.

Phil 960.258   Brodov, Vasilii V. Indiiskaia filosofiia novogo vremeni. Moskva, 1967.

Phil 6315.2.405   Brome, Vincent. Freud and his early circle; the struggles of psychoanalysis. London, 1967.

VPhil 8951.31   Brumen, Vinko. Iskanja. Buenos Aires, 1967.
Phil 8951.30   Brungs, Robert A. Building the city. N.Y., 1967.
Phil 3120.15.47   Brunner, Constantin. Aus meinem Tagebuch. 2. Aufl. Stuttgart, 1967.

Phil 3120.30.56.40   Buber, Martin. A believing humanism: my testament 1902-1965. N.Y., 1967.

Phil 3120.30.32   Buber, Martin. On Judaism. N.Y., 1967.
Phil 5535.64   Buck, Günther. Lernen und Erfahrung. Stuttgart, 1967.
Phil 3120.68.79   Buhr, Manfred. Wilhelm Raimund Beyer, eine Bibliographie. Wien, 1967.

Phil 5592.192   Busemann, Adolf. Weltanschauung in psychologischer Sicht. München, 1967.

Phil 525.35.8   Butler, Cuthbert. Western mysticism: the teaching of Augustine, Gregory and Bernard. 3rd ed. London, 1967.

Phil 6111.80.5   Buytendijk, Frederik Jacobus Johannes. Prolegomena einer antropologischen Physiologie. Salzburg, 1967.

Phil 3235.128   Bykhovskii, Bernard E. Liudvig Feierbakh. Moskva, 1967.
Phil 5752.12   Cahn, Steven. Fate, logic, and time. New Haven, 1967.
Phil 7082.22   Caillois, Roger. Le rêve et les sociétés humaines. Paris, 1967.

Phil 1135.184.5   Calogero, Giudo. Storia della logica antica. Bari, 1967-
Phil 4080.18.10   Calogero, Guido. Quaderno laico. Bari, 1967.
Phil 8877.94   Campbell, Charles Arthur. In defense of free will. London, 1967.

Phil 585.70.15   Cantoni, Remo. Storicismo e scienze dell'uomo. Milano, 1967.

Phil 8657.32   Capizzi, Antonio. Dall'ateismo all'umanismo. Roma, 1967.
Phil 4340.20   Caponigri, Aloysius Robert. Contemporary Spanish philosophy; an anthology. Notre Dame, 1967.

Phil 1107.7.2   Carbonara, Cleto. La filosofia greca: Aristotele. 2. ed. Napoli, 1967.

Phil 3425.760   Carbonara, Cleto. Hegel e Marx nella polemica del diritto pubblico. Napoli, 1967.

Phil 333.12.2   Carnap, Rudolf. The logical structure of the world. Berkeley, 1967.

Phil 5042.21.14.10   Carnap, Rudolf. The logical syntax of language. London, 1967.

Phil 5400.180   Carstens, Erik. HAD. Kóbenhavn, 1967.
Phil 3002.7   Casper, Bernhard. Das dialogische Denken. Freiburg, 1967.
Phil 3484.23.5   Casula, Mario. L'illuminismo critico. Milano, 1967.
Phil 665.106   Cavarnos, Constantine. Modern Greek philosophers on the human soul. Belmont, 1967.

Phil 440.6   Centro di Studi Filosofici di Gallarate. Libertá e responsabilitá. Padova, 1967.

Phil 7150.65   Centro Nazionale di Prevenzione e Difesa Sociale. Suicidio e tentato suicidio. Milano, 1967.

Phil 2905.3.80   Chabanis, Christian. Gustave Thibon, témoin de la lumière. Paris, 1967.

Phil 3425.603.2   Chapelle, A. Hegel et la religion. Annexes. Nanur, 1967.
Phil 87.15   Chauvin, Étienne. Lexicon philosophicum. 2. Aufl. Dusseldorf, 1967.

Phil 960.272   Chethimattam, John B. Consciousness and reality. Bangalore, 1967.

Phil 3549.8.135   Chidani, Shichiro. Mein Weg zu Ludwig Klages. Hamburg, 1967.

Phil 2255.1.135   Chisholm, John Edward. The theory of knowledge of Bertrand Russell. Rome, 1967.

Phil 1702.12   Ciardo, Manlio. Il dramma della metafisica nell'età contemporanea. Bologna, 1967.

Phil 7040.40   Claridge, Gordon S. Personality and arousal; a psychophysiological study of psychiatric disorder. Oxford, 1967.

Phil 7069.67.20   Cohen, Daniel. Myths of the space age. N.Y., 1967.
Phil 8403.21.7   Collingwood, Robin George. The principles of art. Oxford, 1967.

Phil 2050.265   Collins, James Daniel. The emergence of philosophy of religion. New Haven, 1967.

Phil 5274.2   Colloque International sur les Modèles et la Formalisation du Comportement, Paris, 1965. Les modèles et la formalisation du comportement. Paris, 1967.

Phil 3640.717   Colloque Philosophique International de Royaumont, 7th, 1964. Nietzsche. Paris, 1967.

Phil 283.18   Colmoyer, Ciro. Due contributi di filosofia scientifica. Roma, 1967.

Phil 1750.115.150   Conci, Domenico. La conclusione della filosofia categoriale. Roma, 1967.

Phil 505.5.1   Conger, George Perrigo. Theories of macrocosms and microcosms in the history of philosophy. N.Y., 1967.

Phil 333.24   Connolly, William. Political science and ideology. st ed. N.Y., 1967.

Phil 3963.4   Constandse, Anton Levien. Geschiedenis van het humanisme in Nederland. Den Haag, 1967.

Phil 210.25   Consultation on Hermeneutics. Interpretation: the poetry of meaning. 1st ed. N.Y., 1967.

Phil 4818.298.15   Conta, Vasile. Opera filozofice. Bucureşti, 1967.
Phil 1135.220   Conti, Rosario. Cosmogonie oriĕntali e filosofia presocratiča. Roma, 1967.

Phil 4080.3.510   Contini, Bian Franco. L'influenza culturale di Benedetto Croce. Napoli, 1967.

Phil 5272.4   Coombs, Clyde. A theory of data. N.Y., 1967.
Phil 5875.50   Coopersmith, Stanley. The antecedents of self-esteem. San Francisco, 1967.

Phil 5039.6.5   Copi, Irving M. Contemporary readings in logical theory. N.Y., 1967.

Phil 3850.27.245   Corah, Hakki. Aborra oganga. Istanbul, 1967.
Phil 4968.4.80   Cordiel Reyes, Raúl. Del modernismo al liberalismo. México, 1967.

Phil 5640.142   Corso, John F. The experimental psychology sensory behavior. N.Y., 1967.

Phil 1750.166.210   Corts Grau, José. Los humanismos y el hombre. Madrid, 1967.

Phil 5649.42   Cratty, Bryant J. Social dimensions of physical activity. Englewood Cliffs, 1967.

Phil 8877.95   Creasey, John. Good, God and man; an outline of the philosophy of self-ism. London, 1967.

1967 - cont.

Phil 4210.240	Cristaldi, Mariano. Rosmini antiromantico. Catania, 1967.
Phil 4080.3.23	Croce, Benedetto. Epistolario. v.2. Napoli, 1967.
Phil 4960.605.2	Cruz Costa, João. Contribuição à história das idéias no Brasil. 2. ed. Rio de Janeiro, 1967.
Phil 1020.70	Çubukçu, I.A. Islâm felsefesinde Allah'in varliğinin delilleri. Ankara, 1967.
Phil 4210.202	Cuciuffo, Michele. Morale e politica in Rosmini. Milano, 1967.
Phil 2905.1.173	Cuénot, Claude. Science and faith in Teilhard de Chardin. London, 1967.
Phil 5242.70	Curi, Umberto. Il problema dell'unità del sapere nel comportamentismo. Padova, 1967.
Phil 2775.4.80	Curtis, D.E. Progress and eternal recurrence in the work of Gabriel Naudé, 1600-1650. Hull, 1967.
Phil 5421.20.50	Czapiewski, Winfried. Der Aggression trieb und das Böse. Essen, 1967.
VPhil 178.79	Dambska, Izydora. O narzedziach i przedmiotach poznamia. Wyd. 1. Warszawa, 1967.
Phil 960.257	Damodaran, K. Indian thought; a critical survey. Bombay, 1967.
Phil 5753.16	Danner, Manfred. Gibt es einen freein Willen? Hamburg, 1967.
Phil 3808.238	Dauer, Dorothoa W. Schopenhauer as transmitter of buddhist ideas. Berne, 1967.
Phil 5753.15	Davidovich, Vsevolod E. Problemy chelovechskoi svobody. L'vov, 1967.
Phil 8735.60	De Angelis, Enrico. La critica del finalismo nella cultura cartesiana. Firenze, 1967.
Phil 5592.182	Debaty, Pol. La mésure des attitudes. Paris, 1967.
Phil 5500.50	De Bono, Edward. The five-day course in thinking. N.Y., 1967.
Phil 5871.15	Dechêne, Hans C. Geschwisterkonstellation und psychische Fehlentwicklung. München, 1967.
Phil 8404.25	Defrenza, Giuseppe. Il problema della bellezza e dell'arte. Roma, 1967.
Phil 585.228	Deho, Ambrogio. Alla scoperta della persona umana. Padova, 1967.
Phil 6313.26	Dejung, Beat. Regressionen im Verhalten des Menschen. Zürich, 1967.
Phil 178.78	Delhomme, Yeanne. La pensée et le réel, antique de l'ontologie. Paris, 1967.
Phil 9343.14	Dentico, Salvatore. Gioventu atea? Palermo, 1967.
Phil 8583.45.2	Denzinger, Heinrich. Vier Bücher von der religiösen Erkenntniss. Frankfurt, 1967. 2v.
Phil 5520.520	Derrida, Jacques. De la gammatologie. Paris, 1967.
Phil 3450.11.400	Derride, Jacques. La voix et le phénomène, introduction au problème du signe dans la phénomenologie de Husserl. Paris, 1967.
Phil 8657.25	Des chrétiens interrogent l'athéisme. Paris, 1967-2v.
Phil 2520.22.5	Descartes, René. The philosophical works of Descartes. London, 1967. 2v.
Phil 1108.6	Detienne, Marcel. Les maîtres de vérité dans le Grèce archaique. Paris, 1967.
Phil 5876.10.10	Deutsch, Thelene. Selected problems of adolescence; with special emphasis on group formation. N.Y., 1967.
Phil 1955.6.55	Dewey, John. The early works, 1882-1898. v.2,4. Carbondale, 1967- 2v.
Phil 978.59.120	Dhopeshwarkar, A.D. J. Kishnamurti and awareness in action. Bombay, 1967.
VPhil 310.656	Dialekticheskii i istoricheskii materializm. Moskva, 1967.
Phil 8654.120	Dibattito sull'ateismo. Brescia, 1967.
Phil 6313.25	Dienelt, Karl. Von Freud zu Frankel. Wien, 1967.
VPhil 8404.24	Dimitrov, D.N. Zivotot i umetnosta. Skopje, 1967.
VPhil 2225.5.145	Dobrosielski, Marian. Filozoficzny pragmatyzm C.S. Peirce'a. Warszawa, 1967.
Phil 8980.330.5	Dobrovol'skii, Eugenii N. Osoboe mnenie. Moskva, 1967.
Phil 7069.67.80	Dollo, Corrado. Momenti e problemi dello spiritualismo. Padova, 1967.
Phil 4190.1.80	Dollo, Corrado. Il pensiero filosofico di Francesco Orestano. Padova, 1967.
Phil 1750.800	Domenach, Jean Marie. Le retour de tragique, essai. Paris, 1967.
Phil 8430.64	Dorfles, Gillo. L'estetica del mito. Milano, 1967.
Phil 4803.334.85	Doroshevich, Engel's Konstantinovich. Aniol Dovgird - myslitel' epokhi Prosveshcheniia. Minsk, 1967.
Phil 6158.25	Dossier LSD. Paris, 1967.
Phil 8404.21	Doucher, Hans. Künstlerisches und rationalisiertes Sehen. München, 1967.
Phil 7150.64	Douglas, Jack D. The social meanings of suicide. Princeton, 1967.
Phil 8828.5	Drobnitskii, Oleg G. Kritika sovremennykh burzhuaznykh eticheskikh kontseptsii. Moskva, 1967.
Phil 735.264	Drobnitskii, Oleg G. Mir ozhivshikh predmetov. Moskva, 1967.
Phil 8828.6	Dubois, Pierre. Le problème moral dans la philosophie anglaise de 1900 à 1950. Paris, 1967.
Phil 6060.56.5	Dubouchet, Jeanne. L'écriture des adolescentes, étude psycho-pédagogique. Paris, 1967.
Phil 310.662	Dudel', Savva P. Zakon edinstva i bor'by protivopolozhnostei. Moskva, 1967.
Phil 8404.4.5	Dufrenne, Michel. Esthétique et philosophie. Paris, 1967.
Phil 8953.15	Dunphy, William. The new morality. N.Y., 1967.
Phil 8878.50.1	Dupréel, Eugène. Traité de morale. Bruxelles, 1967. 2v.
Phil 8658.24	Durandeaux, Jacques. Question vivante a un Dieu mort. Paris, 1967.
Phil 2905.1.485	Dussault, Gabriel. Panthéisme, action, oméga chez Teilhard de Chardin. Bruges, 1967.
Phil 270.141	Dzhioev, Otar. Priroda istoricheskoi neobkhodimosti. Tbilisi, 1967.
Phil 930.70	East-West Philosophers Conference. The Chinese mind. Honolulu, 1967.
Phil 960.265	East-west philosophers' conference. The Indian mind; essentials of Indian philosophy and culture. Honolulu, 1967.
Phil 935.13	East-West Philosophers' Conference. The Japanese mind. Honolulu, 1967.
Phil 930.36.5	Eberhard, Wolfram. Guilt and sin in traditional China. Berkeley, 1967.
Phil 3200.15	Eberz, Otfried. Sophia und Logos oder die Philosophie der Wiederherstellung. München, 1967.
Phil 7069.67.75	Ebon, Martin. Beyond space and time. N.Y., 1967.
Phil 1109.5	Edelstein, Ludwig. The idea of progress in classical antiquity. Baltimore, 1967.

1967 - cont.

Phil 6750.267	Edgerton, Robert B. The look of competence; stigma in the lives of the mentally retarded. Berkeley, 1967.
Phil 5465.171	Egen, Horst. Kinderzeichnungen und Umwelt. Bonn, 1967.
Phil 5465.168	Ehrenzweig, Anton. The hidden order of art; a study in the psychology of artistic imagination. Berkeley, 1967.
Phil 804.10	Ehrhardt, Walter E. Philosophiegeschichte und geschichtlicher Septizismus. Bern, 1967.
Phil 489.3	Eisenberg, Rafael. The East-West conflict. N.Y., 1967.
Phil 7055.338	Eisenbud, Jule. The world of Ted Serios. N.Y., 1967.
Phil 6980.263.5	Enfance aliénée. Paris, 1967.
Phil 3925.16.135	Engelmann, Paul. Letters from Ludwig Wittgenstein with a memoir. Oxford, 1967.
Phil 6980.263	Enoch, M. David. Some uncommon psychiatric syndromes. Bristol, 1967.
Phil 672.256	Entretiens sur le temps, sous la direction de Jeanne Hersch et René Poirier. Paris, 1967.
Phil 1170.22	Esser, Hans Peter. Untersuchungen zu Gebet und Gottesverehrung der Neuplatoniker. Köln, 1967.
Phil 8400.65	Estetika i chelovek. Moskva, 1967.
Phil 5790.15	Evrim, Selmin. Psikoloji açisindan şahsiyette bir buud olarak içedönükluk-Dişadönüklük. Istanbul, 1967.
Phil 5465.178	Ewert, Otto Maximilian. Phantasie und Intelligenz bei Jugendlichen. Weinheim, 1967.
VPhil 1750.816	Existencializmus a fenomenológia. Bratislava, 1967.
Phil 5590.45.15	Eysenck, Hans Jurgen. The biological basis of personality. Springfield, 1967.
Phil 8612.72	Fagerberg, Holsten. Om rätten att dö. Stockholm, 1967.
Phil 8585.55	Faggiotto, Agostino. La religione nell'esperienza umana. Padova, 1967.
Phil 5590.471	Fahrenberg, Jochen. Psychophysiologische Persönlichkeitsforschung. Göttingen, 1967.
Phil 8880.70	Fallot, Jean. Pouvoir et morale. Thèse. Saverne, 1967.
Phil 3487.27	Fang, Joong. Kant - Interpretationen. Münster, 1967-
Phil 3450.11.118.3	
Phil 4967.20.20	Farber, Marvin. The foundation of phenomenology. 3d ed. n.p., 1967[1943]
	Farias Brito, Raymundo de. Trechos escolhidos. Rio de Janeiro, 1967.
Phil 2905.1.465	Faricy, Robert L. Teilhard de Chardin's theology of the Christian in the world. N.Y., 1967.
Phil 1705.12	Farré, Luis. Unamuno, William James y Kirkegaard y otros ensayos. Buenos Aires, 1967.
Phil 8955.14	al Faruqi, Ismàil Ragi A. Christian ethics: a historical and systematic analysis of its dominant ideas. Montreal, 1967.
Phil 8585.50	Feaver, J. Clayton. Religion in philosophical and cultural perspective. Princeton, 1967.
Phil 8880.55	Feibleman, James. Moral strategy. The Hague, 1967.
Phil 4466.5.30	Feijó, Diogo Antonio. Cadernos de filosofia. São Paulo, 1967.
Phil 6946.1.20	Felix, Robert Hanna. Mental illness; progress and prospects. N.Y., 1967.
Phil 6980.289.5	Fenichel, Otto. Perversionen, Psychosen, Charakterstörungen. Darmstadt, 1967.
Phil 8880.60	Fernand-Laurent, Camille J. Morâle et tyrannies. Paris, 1967.
Phil 4356.3	Ferrater Mora, José. Obras selectas. Madrid, 1967. 2v.
Phil 4356.3.5	Ferrater Mora, José. El ser y el sentido. Madrid, 1967.
Phil 165.408	Festschrift für Joseph Klien zum 70. Geburtstag. Göttingen, 1967.
Phil 3235.11	Feuerbach, Ludwig. Gesammelte Werke. v.2-4,6-9. Berlin, 1967- 8v.
Phil 3235.25.5	Feuerbach, Ludwig. Grundsätze der Philosophie der Zukunft. Frankfurt, 1967.
Phil 3235.126.5	Feuerbach, Ludwig. Istoriia filosofii. Moskva, 1967. 3v.
Phil 3246.77.2	Fichte, Johann Gottlieb. Grundlage des Naturrechts nach Prinzipien der Wissenschaftslehre. 2. Aufl. Hamburg, 1967.
Phil 3246.46	Fichte, Johann Gottlieb. La theorie de la science expose de 1804. Thèse. Paris, 1967.
Phil 165.427	Filosofskie nauki. Stavropol', 1967.
Phil 4800.26	Filozofia polska. Warszawa, 1967.
Phil 2005.14	Findlay, John N. The transcendence of the cave. London, 1967.
Phil 9470.14	Fingarette, Herbert. On responsibility. N.Y., 1967.
Phil 4200.6.80	Firrito, Giovanni. Ontologia e assiologia critica nel pensiero di Nicola Petruzzellis. Napoli, 1967.
Phil 5815.10.2	Fischel, Werner. Vom Leben zum Erleben. 2. Aufl. München, 1967.
Phil 336.12.2	Fischer, Anton. Die philosophischen Grundlagen der wissenschaftlichen Erkenntnis. 2. Aufl. Wien, 1967.
Phil 4809.393.330	Fišer, zbyněk. Utěcha z ontologie. Vyd. 1. Praha, 1967.
Phil 9075.84	Flither, Andreas. Wirklichkeit und Mass des Menschen. München, 1967.
Phil 5068.60	Fogelin, Robert J. Evidence and meaning: studies in analytic philosophy. London, 1967.
Phil 1750.115.135	Forni, Guglielmo. Il sogno finito. Bologna, 1967.
Phil 8880.58	Forrest, John K. Reality or preachment; the moral crisis of our time. Boston, 1967.
Phil 8880.56	Fourastié, Jean. Essais de morale prospective. Paris, 1967.
Phil 165.171	Fragmenty filozoficzne, seria trzecia. Warszawa, 1967.
Phil 5585.140.2	Fraisse, Paul. Psychologie du temps. 2. éd. Paris, 1967.
Phil 805.20	Franca, Leonel. Noções de história da filosofia. Rio de Janeiro, 1967.
Phil 180.84.5	Franchini, Raffaello. La logica della filosofia. Napoli, 1967.
Phil 4710.158	Frank, Semen L. Die russiche Weltanschauung. 1. Aufl. Darmstadt, 1967.
Phil 5400.192	Franke, Joachim. Ausdruck und Konvention. Habilitationsschrift. Göttingen, 1967.
Phil 3270.12.50	Frege, Gottlob. Kleine Schriften. Hildesheim, 1967.
Phil 3640.735	Frenzel, Ivo. Friedrich Nietzsche; an illustrated biography. N.Y., 1967.
Phil 2475.1.455	Fressin, Augustin. La perception chez Bergson et chez Merleau-Ponty. Paris, 1967.
Phil 6315.17.14	Freud, Anna. Writings of Anna Freud. v.2,4-6. N.Y., 1967. 4v.
Phil 6315.2.68.5A	Freud, Sigmund. Group psychology and the analysis of the ego. N.Y., 1967.
Phil 5066.190.2	Freudenthal, Hans. Exacte logica. 2. druk. Haarlem, 1967.
Phil 6315.58	Friedemann, Adolf. Die Begegnung mit dem kranken Menschen. Bern, 1967.
Phil 585.187	Friedman, Maurice Stanley. To deny our nothingness. N.Y., 1967.

Chronological Listing

1967 - cont.

Phil 5245.82   Friedman, Neil. The social nature of psychological research. N.Y., 1967.
Phil 6115.34   Fritsch, Vilma. La gauche et la droite. Paris, 1967.
Phil 5245.84   Fromme, Allan. Our troubled selves. N.Y., 1967.
Phil 9490.20   Frye, Northrop. The morality of scholarship. Ithaca, 1967.
Phil 1158.38   Furley, David J. Two studies in the Greek atomists. Princeton, N.J., 1967.
Phil 978.49.900   Gabert, Erich. Die Weltgeschichte und das Menschen-Ish. Stuttgart, 1967.
Phil 8612.65   Gaboriau, Florent. Interview sur la mort avec Karl Rabner. Paris, 1967.
Phil 3310.18   Gadamer, H.G. Kleine Schriften. Tübingen, 1967. 3v.
Phil 2880.8.235   Gahamanyi, Célestin. La conception de la liberté chez Jean-Paul Sartre et chez Maurice Merleau-Ponty. Fribourg? 1967.
Phil 585.240   Gattgno, Caleb. Conscience de le conscience. Neuchâtel, 1967.
Phil 2555.10.81   Geissler, Rolf. Boureau-Deslandes, ein Materialist der Frühaufklärung. 1. Aufl. Berlin, 1967.
Phil 130.14   Geldsetzer, L. Philosophengalerie. Düsseldorf, 1967.
Phil 7069.65.7   Gerloff, Hans. The crisis in parapsychology. 3. supplement. Bayerisch Gmain, 1967.
Phil 8831.14   Geschichte der Ethik. v.2. Gütersloh, 1967.
Phil 6980.321   Gesellschaft zur Orderung Tiefenpsychologischer und Psychotherapeutischer Forschung und Weiterbildung in München. Möglichkeiten moderner Psychotherapien. Göttingen, 1967.
Phil 165.430   Gestalt und Wirklichkeit. Berlin, 1967.
Phil 7150.75   Ghysbrecht, Paul. Der Doppelselbstmord. München, 1967.
Phil 8586.45.5   Gilson, Étienne. Les tribulations de Sophie. Paris, 1967.
Phil 4215.3.90   Giornata Rensiana, Genova. Giuseppe Rensi. Milano, 1967.
Phil 5046.46   Goclenius, Rudolph. Problemata logica. v.1-5. Frankfurt, 1967.
Phil 8586.57   Goedt, Michel de. Foi au Christ et dialogues du Chrétien. Bruges, 1967.
Phil 4710.152   Goerdt, Wilhelm. Die Sowjetphilosophie. Basel, 1967.
Phil 672.246   Gold, Thomas. The nature of time. Ithaca, 1967.
Phil 2805.450   Goldmann, Lucien. Weltflucht und Politik. Neuwied, 1967.
Phil 3120.30.88   Goldstein, Walter Benjamin. Martin Buber. Jerusalem, 1967.
Phil 2733.130   Gonnell, Desmond. The vision in God; Malebranche's scholastic sources. Louvain, 1967.
Phil 5046.40   Good, Thomas. A brief English tract of logick, 1677. Facsimile. Leeds, 1967.
Phil 181.69.10   Gorce, M.M. L'escalade des siécles. Saint-Imier, 1967.
Phil 5627.107.25   Gordon, Albert. The nature of conversion. Boston, 1967.
Phil 181.140.2   Gorovitz, Samuel. Philosophical analysis. N.Y., 1967.
Phil 8980.435   Graaf, Johannes de. Moraal, marxisme en ethiek in de sowietunie. Hilversum, 1967.
Phil 270.137   Grabbé, Geneviéve. Les conditions d'une perception de la causalité. Paris, 1967.
Phil 6307.332   Graham, Thomas F. Medieval minds; mental health in the Middle Ages. London, 1967.
Phil 3488.44   Gram, Moltke S. Kant: disputed questions. Chicago, 1967.
Phil 4961.910   Granell Muñiz, Manuel. Del pensar venezolano. Caracas, 1967.
Phil 6316.27   Greenson, Ralph R. The technique and practice of psychoanalysis. London, 1967.
Phil 181.150.5   Gregg, Richard B. What's it all about and what am I? 1. Indian ed. Ahmedabad, 1967.
Phil 181.131.5   Grenier, J. Conversations on the good uses of freedom. 1. American ed. Cambridge, 1967.
Phil 1706.15   Grenier, Jean. Essai sur l'esprit d'orthodoxie. Paris, 1967.
Phil 8881.78   Grice, Geoffry R. The grounds of moral judgement. Cambridge, 1967.
Phil 337.35   Griffiths, A. Phillips. Knowledge and belief. London, 1967.
Phil 5865.2   Grinder, Robert Eugene. A history of genetic psychology. N.Y., 1967.
Phil 181.154   Grundfragen der Wissenschaften und ihre Wurzeln in der Metaphysik. Salzburg, 1967.
Phil 2905.1.460   Guerini, Edmund W. Evolution in the afterlife. 1st ed. N.Y., 1967.
Phil 5425.54.5   Guerster, Eugen. Macht und Geheimnis der Dummheit. Zürich, 1967.
Phil 5246.47.15   Guilford, Joy Paul. The nature of human intelligence. N.Y., 1967.
Phil 8661.28.2   Guilhot, Jean. La psychiatrie morale et le problème de Dieu. Paris, 1967.
Phil 8661.28   Guilhot, Jean. La psychiatrie morale et le problème de Dieu. Thesis. La Haye, 1967.
Phil 8612.74   Guiomar, Michel. Principes d'une esthétique de la mort. Paris, 1967.
Phil 8881.80   Gupta, Rajender Kumas. Studien zur Ethik. Bonn, 1967.
Phil 3425.654   Haag, Karl Heinz. Philosophischer Idealismus. Frankfurt, 1967.
Phil 1750.166.200   Hadas, Moses. The living tradition. N.Y., 1967.
Phil 3450.29.75   Haecker, Theodor. Vergil. Schönheit Metaphysik des Fühlens. München, 1967.
Phil 8612.67   Halldén, Sören. Universum, döden och den logiska analysen. Lund, 1967.
Phil 3925.16.130   Hallett, Garth. Wittgenstein's definition of meaning as use. N.Y., 1967.
Phil 5047.48   Hampel, Hans-Jürgen. Variabilität und Disziplinierung des Denkens. München, 1967.
Phil 8587.78   Hançerlioğlu, Orhan. Fel sefe sölüğü. Istanbul, 1967.
Phil 525.230   Happold, F.C. Mysticism. Baltimore, 1967.
Phil 6980.348.50   Harms, Ernest. Origins of modern psychiatry. Springfield, 1967.
Phil 735.262   Hartman, Robert S. The structure of value; foundations of scientific axiology. Carbondale, 1967.
Phil 3489.45   Hartnack, Justus. Kant's theory of knowledge. N.Y., 1967.
Phil 5520.508   Hartogs, Renatas. Four-letter word games. N.Y., 1967.
Phil 5066.270   Hausman, Alan. Carnap and Goodman: two formalists. Iowa City, 1967.
Phil 3801.448.5   Hayner, Paul Collins. Reason and existence; Schelling's philosophy of history. Leiden, 1967.
Phil 5421.25.15   Hazo, Robert G. The idea of love. N.Y., 1967.
Phil 5548.103.5   Heckhausen, H. The anatomy of achievement motivation. N.Y., 1967.
Phil 3425.69   Hegel, Georg Wilhelm Friedrich. Einleitung in die Asthetik. München, 1967.

1967 - cont.

Phil 3425.71.11   Hegel, Georg Wilhelm Friedrich. Philosophy of right. Oxford, 1967.
Phil 5217.8.2   Hehlmann, Wilhelm. Geschichte der Psychologie. 2. Aufl. Stuttgart, 1967.
Phil 3450.19.74   Heidegger, Martin. Wegmarken. Frankfurt, 1967.
Phil 5850.228.20.5
Phil 1707.8.6   Heider, Fritz. The psychology of interpersonal relations. N.Y., 1967.
  Heimsoeth, H. Metaphysik der Neuzeit. München, 1967.
Phil 6317.50   Henderson, Joseph. Thresholds of initiation. 1. ed. Middletown, 1967.
Phil 9120.180   Henriot, Jacques. Existence et obligation. Paris, 1967.
Phil 8080.20   Hermann, Rolf-Dieter. Künstler und Interpret; zur Modernen Asthetik. Bern, 1967.
Phil 3925.16.175.2   Hermans, Willem Frederich. Wittgenstein in de mode en karze mier niet. 2. druk. Amsterdam, 1967.
Phil 5876.10.5   Hertzman-Ericson, Merit. Svåra unga år. Stockholm, 1967.
Phil 5850.22.95   Herzog, Reinhart. Die Bewahrung der Vernunft. Inaug. Diss. München, 1967.
Phil 5870.25   Hetzer, Hildegard. Zur Psychologie des Kindes. Darmstadt, 1967.
Phil 3925.16.145   High, Dallas. Language, persons, and belief studies in Wittgenstein's Philosophical investigations. N.Y., 1967.
Phil 2045.52.28   Hobbes, Thomas. Leviathan. Oxford, 1967.
Phil 5421.25.30   Hodge, Marshall B. Your fear of love. Garden City, 1967.
Phil 9550.22   Hodgson, D.H. Consequences of utilitarianism. Oxford, 1967.
Phil 4308.1   Höllhuber, I. Geschichte der Philosophie im spanischen Kulturbereich. München, 1967.
Phil 5520.492   Hoermann, Hans. Psychologie der Sprache. Berlin, 1967.
Phil 3455.3.85   Hof, Ulrich im. Isaak Iselin und die Spätaufklärung. Bern, 1967.
Phil 5272.10.3   Hofstaetter, Peter Robert. Quantitative Methoden der Psychologie. 3. Aufl. München, 1967.
Phil 5500.65   Hofstee, Willem Karel Bernard. Method effects in absolute and comparative judgment. Proefschrift. Groningen, 1967.
Phil 2648.25   Holbach, Paul Henri T. D'Holbach portatif. Paris, 1967.
Phil 4500.4.5   Holm, Søren. Filosofien i Norden efter 1900. København, 1967.
Phil 4500.4   Holm, Søren. Filosofien i Norden før 1900. København, 1967.
Phil 2055.13.35   Hook, Sidney. Religion in a free society. Lincoln, 1967.
Phil 5520.481   Horálek, Karel. Filosofie jazyku. Praha, 1967.
Phil 6317.22.25   Horney, Karen. Feminine psychology. N.Y., 1967.
Phil 1020.18.10   Horten, M. Die spekulative und positive Theologie des Islam. Hildesheim, 1967.
Phil 182.114.7   Hospers, John. An introduction to philosophical analysis. Englewood Cliffs, 1967.
Phil 9513.35   Huant, Ernest. Masses, morale et machines. Paris, 1967.
Phil 3450.19.425   Huch, Kurt Jürgen. Philosophiegeschichtliche Voraussetzungen der Heideggerschen Ontologie. Frankfurt, 1967.
Phil 8905.25   Hudon, Louis-Nazaire. Le corps humain dans la pensée de Dieu. Alma, 1967.
Phil 2050.77.25   Hume, David. A letter from a gentleman to his friend in Edinburgh (1745). Facsimile. Edinburgh, 1967.
Phil 7069.64.27   Hunt, Douglas. A handbook on the occult. London, 1967.
Phil 5238.248   Husén, Torsten. Psykologisk bredvielläsning. v. 1-2. Stockholm, 1967.
Phil 1512.14   Hyman, Arthur. Philosophy in the Middle Ages. N.Y., 1967.
Phil 5625.75.110   I.P. Pavlov v vospominaniiakh sovremennikov. Leningrad, 1967.
Phil 5520.482   Iazyk i myshlenie. Moskva, 1967.
Phil 4961.126.5   Ibarguengoitía, Antonio. Filosofía mexicana. 1. ed. Mexico, 1967.
Phil 2905.1.615   Imbrighi, Gastone. La paleogeografia in Teilhard de Chardin. L'Aguila, 1967.
Phil 70.104   Interamerican Congress of Philosophy, 7th, Laval University, 1967. Proceedings of the congress. Quebec, 1967-68. 2v.
Phil 5593.65   International Congress of Rorschach and Projective Methods. Comptes rendus. Paris, 1967-68. 4v.
Phil 5545.254.2   International Interdisciplinary Conference on Learning, Remembering and Forgetting. The organization of recall; proceedings. N.Y., 1967.
Phil 7076.10   Isou, Isidore. Histoire et rénovation de l'automatismé spirituel. Paris, 1967.
Phil 70.103   Iubileinaia Nauchnaia Sessiia Vuzov Ural'skoi zony, Sverdlovsk. Materialy. Sverdlovsk, 1967?
Phil 8409.4   Ivanov, Pavel L. O sushchnosti krasoty. Moskva, 1967.
Phil 8170.9   Iz istorii sovetskoi esteticheskoi mysli. Moskva, 1967.
Phil 672.250   Jacob, André. Temps et langage. Paris, 1967.
Phil 3491.14   Jacobs, Wilhelm Gustav. Trieb als sittliches Phänomen. Bonn, 1967.
Phil 6319.20   Jacobson, Edith. Psychotic conflict and reality. N.Y., 1967.
Phil 5400.175   Jacobson, Edmund. Biology of emotions::new understanding derived from biological multidisciplinary investigation. Springfield, 1967.
Phil 5249.29   Jaeger, Adolf Otto. Dimensionen der Intelligenz. Göttingen, 1967.
Phil 6319.1.235   Jaffé, Aniela. Der Mythus vom Sinn in Werk von C.G. Jung. Zürich, 1967.
Phil 2070.23   James, William. The writings of William James; a comprehensive edition. N.Y., 1967.
Phil 2675.4.30   Jankélévitch, Vladimir. Le pardon. Paris, 1967.
Phil 5325.37   Jaspars, Joseph Maria Franciscus. De vrienden van mijn vrienden. Leiden, 1967.
Phil 6959.4.18   Jaspers, K. General psychopathology. Chicago, 1967.
Phil 3475.3.230   Jaspers, Karl. Kleine Schule des philosophischen Denkens. München, 1967.
Phil 3475.3.205   Jaspers, Karl. Philosophical faith and revelation. N.Y., 1967.
Phil 3475.3.225   Jaspers, Karl. Philosophische Aufsätze. Frankfurt, 1967.
Phil 3475.3.25   Jaspers, Karl. Schicksal und Wille. München, 1967.
Phil 5066.266   Jdel'son, A.V. Matematicheskaia teoriia logicheskogo vyvoda. Moskva, 1967.
VPhil 2750.22.110   Jędrzejczak, Klara. Problemy rewolucji i socjalizmu we współczesnej katolickiej myśli filozoficznej). Poznań, 1967.
Phil 5049.22   Jeffrey, Richard C. Formal logic: its scope and limits. N.Y., 1967.
Phil 6682.3.80   Jensen, Ann. Franz Anton Mesmer. N.Y., 1967.
Phil 3640.722   Jette, Celine. The philosophy of Nietzsche in the light of Thomistic principles. 1st ed. N.Y., 1967.

1967 - cont.

Phil 5548.107   Johannesson, Ingvar. Effects of praise and blame. Stockholm, 1967.

Phil 5545.246   John, Erwin Roy. Mechanisms of memory. N.Y., 1967.

Phil 5853.6.5   Johnson, Paul Emanuel. Person and counselor. Nashville, 1967.

Phil 1930.8.110   Johnston, William Murray. The formative years of R.G. Collingwood. The Hague, 1967[1968]

Phil 585.220   Jolif, Jean Y. Comprendre l'homme. Paris, 1967-

Phil 2880.8.154   Jolivet, Régis. Sartre: the theology of the absurd. Westminster, 1967.

Phil 585.212.2   Jones, Arthur. Menschsein als Auftrag. 2. Aufl. Bern, 1967.

Phil 6319.2.4.6   Jones, Ernest. Papers on psycho-analysis. 5th ed. Boston, 1967.

Phil 310.652A   Jordan, Zbigniew A. The evolution of dialectical materialism. London, 1967.

Phil 5049.9.2.1   Joseph, Horace William Brindley. An introduction to logic. 2nd rev. ed. Oxford, 1967.

Phil 2733.125   Journées Malebranche, Paris, 1965. Malebranche l'homme et l'oeuvre, 1638-1715. Paris, 1967.

Phil 8520.80   Joussain, André. Temps présent et religion. Toulouse, 1967.

Phil 5841.20.5   Jung, Emma. Animus and Anima. Zürich, 1967.

Phil 5465.155   Kagan, Jerome. Creativity and learning. Boston, 1967.

Phil 5548.112   Kages, Wolfgang. Der menschliche Antrieb. Psychologie und Psychopathologie. Stuttgart, 1967.

Phil 720.82   Kalinowski, Jerzy. Le problème de la vérité en morale et en droit. Thèse. Lyon, 1967.

Phil 6320.25   Kalmar, Jacques M. Anti-pensée et monde des conflits. Neuchâtel, 1967.

Phil 3480.65.13   Kant, Immanuel. Grundlegung zur Metaphysik der Sitten. Stuttgart, 1967.

Phil 3480.127   Kant, Immanuel. Philosophical correspondence. Chicago, 1967.

Phil 1750.799   Kanz, Heinrich. Der Sinn heutigen Philosophierens. Ratingen, 1967.

Phil 5545.233   Katzenberger, Lothar Friedrich. Auffassung und Gedächtnis. München, 1967.

Phil 5545.244.1   Katzenberger, Lothar Friedrich. Gedächtnis oder Gedächtnisse? München, 1967.

Phil 5400.190   Kaufmann, Pierre. L'expérience émotionnelle de l'espace. Thèse. Paris, 1967.

Phil 6319.1.245   Kaune, Fritz Jürgen. Selbstverwirklichung. München, 1967.

Phil 8171.200   Kazykhanova, Batish R. Rol' khudozhestvennogo naslediia v esteticheskom vospitanii. Alma-ata, 1967.

Phil 8960.14   Keeling, Michael. Morals in free society. London, 1967.

Phil 2490.182   Kellermann, Paul. Kritik liner Soziologie der Ordnung: Organismus und System bei Comte, Spencer und Parsons. 1. Aufl. Freiburg, 1967.

Phil 8635.12   Kelsey, Denys. Many lifetimes. 1. ed. Garden City, N.Y., 1967.

Phil 5068.68   Khachaturian, Haig. A critical study in method. The Hague, 1967.

Phil 341.36   Khaskhachikh, Fedor I. Voprosy teorii poznaniia dialekticheskogo materializma. Moskva, 1967.

Phil 5625.110   Kimble, Gregory A. Foundations of conditioning and learning. N.Y., 1967.

Phil 1750.78   Kittaka, Rin'ichi. New method of philosophy: an introduction to radiciology. Tokyo, 1967.

Phil 720.68   Kittinger, Kenneth C. A cranium shake-up and a new philosophy to alter the war spirit in man. Los Angeles, 1967.

Phil 5066.261   Kleene, Stephen Cole. Mathematical logic. N.Y., 1967.

Phil 341.37   Klein, Martin. Der zerstückelte Gott. München, 1967.

Phil 5203.31   Klingelhofer, Edward L. A bibliography of psychological research and writings on Africa. Uppsala, 1967.

Phil 5590.105.2   Kluckhohn, Clyde. Personality in nature, society and culture. 2. ed. N.Y., 1967.

Phil 8620.60   Kluger, Rivkah Schärf. Satan in the Old Testament. Evanston, 1967.

Phil 5250.84   Knapp, Franz. Das geistige Leben der Person in den persönlichkeitspsychologischen Schichttheorien. Inaug. Diss. Heidelberg? 1967?

Phil 525.247   Knowles, David. What is mysticism? London, 1967.

Phil 3425.621   Koch, Traugott. Differenz und Versöhnung; eine Interpretation der Theologie G.W.F. Hegels nach seiner "Wissenschaft der Logik." 1. Aufl. Gütersloh, 1967.

Phil 3450.11.380   Kockelmans, Joseph John. Edmund Husserl's phenomenological psychology. Pittsburgh, 1967.

Phil 3450.11.395   Kockelmans, Joseph John. A first introduction to Husserl's phenomenology. Pittsburgh, 1967.

Phil 8590.37   Koehler, Hans. Theologische Anthropologie; die biblische Sicht des Menschen und der Mensch der Gegenwart. München, 1967.

Phil 5250.80   Koestler, Arthur. The ghost in the machine. London, 1967.

Phil 310.654   Kompaneets, Aleksei I. Leninskaia filosofiia i progress fizicheskikh nauk. Moskva, 1967.

Phil 5050.26   Kondakov, Nikolai I. Vvedenie v logiku. Moskva, 1967.

Phil 6120.24   Konorski, Jerzy. Integrative activity of the brain; an interdisciplinary approach. Chicago, 1967.

Phil 4803.495.20   Kotakowski, Leszek. Kultura i fetysze; zbiór rozpraw. Wyd. 1. Warszawa, 1967.

Phil 4803.495.21   Kotakowski, Leszek. Traktat über die Sterblichkeit der Vernunft. München, 1967.

Phil 575.261   Koy, Igor' S. Sotsiologiia lichnosti. Moskva, 1967.

Phil 3450.19.405   Koza, Ingeborg. Das Problem des Grundes in Heideggers Auseinandersetzung mit Kant. Ratingen, 1967.

Phil 5066.268   Kreisel, Georg. Elements of mathematical logic. Amsterdam, 1967.

Phil 185.102   Kreiser, Lothar. Untersuchungen zur Möglichkeit Habilitationsschrift. Leipzig?, 1967?

Phil 5875.30   Kreitler, Hans. Die kognitive Orientierung des Kindes. München, 1967.

Phil 8665.10   Krejčí, Jaroslav. Teleologický, kosmologický, a etický dúkaz existence Boha v neotomismu. Vyd. 1. Praha, 1967.

Phil 735.265   Krohn, Sven. Totuus, arvo ja ihminen. Porvoo, 1967.

Phil 5400.200   Krueger, Felix. Über das Gefühl. Darmstadt, 1967.

Phil 3640.714   Kuczyński, Janusz. Zmierzch mies zczaństwa. Warszawa, 1967.

VPhil 3195.6.180   Kuderowicz, Zbigniew. Dilthey. Warszawa, 1967.

Phil 5068.53.1   Küng, Gaide. Ontology and the logistic analysis of language. Dordrecht, 1967.

Phil 6315.2.425   Kushner, Martin D. Freud, a man obsessed. Philadelphia, 1967.

Phil 70.3.75   Kussmann, Thomas. Achtzehnte Internationale Kongress für Psychologie in Moskau, 1966. Göttingen, 1967.

1967 - cont.

Phil 5050.25   Kutschera, Franz von. Elementare Logik. Wien, 1967.

Phil 5220.6   Kvasov, Dmitrii G. Fiziologicheskaia shkola I.P. Pavlova. Leningrad, 1967.

Phil 3549.22   Kwant, R.C. Critique; its nature and function. Pittsburgh, 1967.

Phil 2880.8.215   Lafarge, René. La philosophie de Jean Paul Sartre. Toulouse, 1967.

Phil 6321.53   Laing, Roland David. The politics of experience. N.Y., 1967.

Phil 1750.552.5   Lakebrink, Bernhard. Klassische Metaphysik. Freiburg, 1967.

Phil 5761.24   Lamont, Corliss. Freedom of choise affirmed. N.Y., 1967.

Phil 5425.44.4   Lange, Wilhelm. Genie, Irrsinn und Ruhm. München, 1967.

Phil 6121.42   Langer, Susanne K. Mind; an essay on human feeling. Baltimore, 1967-

Phil 8412.23.3   Langfeld, Herbert Sidney. The aesthetic attitude. Port Washington, N.Y., 1967.

Phil 585.394   Larson, Victor E. Man: who-whence; a layman's attempt at a logical synthesis. N.Y., 1967.

Phil 1830.17.5   Laslett, Peter. Philosophy, politics, and society, third series. N.Y., 1967.

Phil 4710.19   Laszlo, Ervin. Philosophy in the Soviet Union. Dordrecht, 1967.

Phil 3280.91   Lattre, Alain de. L'Occasionalisme d'Arnold Geulincx. Paris, 1967.

Phil 705.54.5   Lauth, Reinhard. Begriff. München, 1967.

Phil 186.65.35   Lavelle, Louis. Panorama des doctrines philosophiques. Paris, 1967.

Phil 2725.35.10   Lavelle, Louis. Psychologie et spiritualité. Paris, 1967.

Phil 186.65.30   Lavelle, Louis. Science, esthétique, métaphysique. Paris, 1967.

Phil 2725.2.35.5   Le Guillou, Louis. Les discussions critiques. Paris, 1967.

Phil 2880.2.90   Lehner, Felix. Freiheit in Wirtschaft, Staat und Religion: die Philosophie der Gesellschaft von Charles Secrétan. Zürich, 1967.

Phil 3552.431   Leibniz, G.W. Confessio philosophi. Ein Dialog. Frankfurt, 1967.

Phil 3552.23.10   Leibniz, Gottfried Wilhelm. Ermahnung anu die Deutschen. Darmstadt, 1967.

Phil 3552.78.80   Leibniz, Gottfried Wilhelm. The Leibniz-Arnauld correspondence. Manchester, 1967.

Phil 5066.232.20   Leicester, England. University. Summer School in Mathematical Logic. Sets, models and recursion theory. Amsterdam, 1967.

Phil 8412.42   Leijonhiel, Christer. Colours, forms and art. Studies in differential aesthetic psychology. Akademisk avhandling. Stockholm, 1967.

Phil 6360.6   Lempp, Reinhart. Eine Pathologie der psychischen Entwicklung. Bern, 1967.

Phil 4710.154   Leningrad. Universitet. Filosofskii Fakul'tet. Materialy k nauchnoi sessii, posviashchennoi 50-letiiu Velikoi Oktiabr'skoi sotsialisticheskoi revoliutsii. Leningrad, 1967.

Phil 4080.3.480   Lentini, Giacinto. Croce e Gramsci. Palermo, 1967.

Phil 5625.101.5   Le Ny, Jean François. Apprentissage et activités psychologiques. Paris, 1967.

Phil 6854.2   Leonard, Calista V. Understanding and preventing suicide. Springfield, Ill., 1967.

Phil 5520.510   Leont'ev, Aleksei A. Psikholingvistika. Leningrad, 1967.

Phil 7069.67.10   Lethbridge, Thomas. A step in the dark. London, 1967.

VPhil 6980.518   Levi, Vladimir L'. Okhota za mysl'iu. Moskva, 1967.

Phil 3450.11.98.6   Levinas, Emmanuel. En découvrant l'existence avec Husserl et Heidegger. Paris, 1967.

Phil 5421.10.20   Levitt, Eugene Elmer. The psychology of anxiety. Indianapolis, 1967.

Phil 5520.578   Lévy-Valensi, Éliane Amado. La communication. 1.éd. Paris, 1967.

Phil 8591.44.45   Lewis, Clive Staples. Christian reflections. London, 1967.

Phil 1750.115.95   Lexington. Conference on Pure and Applied Phenomenology. Phenomenology of will and action. Chicago, 1967.

Phil 4803.522.35   Libelt, Karol. Samowładztwo rozumu i objawy filozofii słowiańskiej. Warszawa, 1967.

Phil 8886.82   Libnizzi, Carmelo. Il pro e il contro: considerazioni morali. Padova, 1967.

Phil 5520.137   Linsky, Leonard. Refering. London, 1967.

Phil 8080.4.5   Listowel, William Francis Hare. Modern aesthetics. N.Y., 1967.

VPhil 2725.2.120   Litwin, Jakub. Eseje o dialogach wewnętrznych: Diderot, Lamennais. Warszawa, 1967.

Phil 573.6   Locke, Don. Perception and our knowledge of the external world. London, 1967.

Phil 2115.21   Locke, J. Two tracts on government. Cambridge, Eng., 1967.

Phil 6980.429.5   Loebsacu, T. Die unheimlichen Moglichkeiten oder die Manipulierte Seele. Düsseldorf, 1967.

Phil 4080.3.465   Lönne, Karl-Egon. Benedetto Croce als Kritiker seiner Zeit. Tübingen, 1967.

Phil 585.235   Loewith, Karl. Gott, Mensch und Welt in der Metaphysik von Descartes bis zu Nietzsche. Göttingen, 1967.

Phil 5520.513   Logicheskaia semantika i modal'naia logika. Moskva, 1967.

Phil 8886.73.5   López Aranguren, José Luis. Lo que sabemos de moral. Madrid, 1967.

Phil 5272.5   Lord, Frederick M. Estimating true-score distributions in psychological testing. Princeton, 1967.

Phil 8961.19   Lorenz, Willy. Der Gentleman und der Christ. Wien, 1967.

Phil 5876.20   Lorimier, Jacques de. Le projet de vie de l'adolescent, identité psychosociale et vocation. Paris, 1967.

Phil 7069.67.60   Lots-Poole, Marietta. Strange dreams and their portents and other reflections Brentwood, 1967.

Phil 3585.28   Lotz, Johannes Baptist. Der Mensch im Sein. Freiburg, 1967.

Phil 4472.89.30   Lourencao, Eduardo. Heterodoxia. Coimbra, 1967. 2v.

Phil 6158.20   LSD, man and society. 1st ed. Middletown, 1967.

Phil 7069.67.55   Ludlam, Harry. The restless ghosts of Ladye Place, and other true hauntings. London, 1967.

Phil 3585.20.25   Luijpen, Wilhelmus Antonius Maria. Phenomenology of natural law. Pittsburgh, 1967.

Phil 8412.18.5   Lukács, Georg. Über die (Beson derheit) als Kategorie der Asthetik. Neuwied, 1967.

Phil 8886.80.2   Lunn, Arnold. The new morality. London, 1967.

Phil 186.81.10   Lupasco, Stéphane. Qu'est-ce qu'une structure? Paris, 1967.

Phil 1750.38.6   Lyotard, Jean François. La phénoménologie. 6e éd. Paris, 1967.

Chronological Listing

Phil 585.214 Maaz, Wilhelm. Selbstschöpfung oder Selbstintegration des Menschen. Münster, 1967.

Phil 5066.265 McCall, Storrs. Polish logic, 1920-1939 papers. Oxford, 1967.

Phil 7069.67.40 McCreery, Charles. Science, philosophy and E.S.P. London, 1967.

Phil 7069.67.65 McDougall, William. William McDougall: explorer of the mind. N.Y., 1967.

Phil 9245.120 McGill, Vivian Jerauld. The idea of happiness. N.Y., 1967.

Phil 8887.125 McGrath, Patrick. The nature of moral judgement: a study in contemporary moral philosophy. London, 1967.

Phil 75.74 McLean, George F. An annotated bibliography of philosophy in Catholic thought, 1900-1964. N.Y., 1967.

Phil 75.74.5 McLean, George F. A bibliography of Christian philosophy and contemporary issue. N.Y., 1967.

Phil 3450.19.395 Macomber, William B. The anatomy of disillusion; Martin Heideggers notion of truth. Evanston, 1967.

Phil 5222.20 McPherson, Marion White. Problems and procedures in oral histories of the Archives of the History of American Psychology. Akron, 1967.

Phil 70.110 Madrid. Universidad. Seminario de Metafísica. Anales del Seminario de Metafisica. Madrid, 1967.

Phil 9245.128 Maggal, Moshe M. Acres of happiness. 1st ed. N.Y., 1967.

Phil 2520.365 Mahnke, Detlef. Des Aufbau des philosophischen Wissens nach René Descartes. München, 1967.

Phil 8592.118 Mainberger, G. Widerspruch und Zuversicht. Olten, 1967.

Phil 6750.267.5 Maire, Luce. Les enfants de nulle part. Paris, 1967.

Phil 310.390.2 Makarov, Aleksei D. Istoriko-filosofskoe vvedenie k kursu marksistsko-leninskoi filosofii. 2. Izd. Moskva, 1967.

Phil 5022.5 Makovel'skii, Aleksandr O. Istoriia logiki. Moskva, 1967.

Phil 5279.5 Malewski, Andrzej. Verhalten und Interaktion. Tübingen, 1967.

Phil 2050.280 Mall, Rom Adhar. Hume's concept of man. Bombay, 1967.

Phil 5873.2.2 Malrieu, Philippe. Les émotions et la personnalité de l'enfant. 2. éd. Paris, 1967.

Phil 4363.3.38 Manara Vicentelo de Leca, M. de. Discurso de la verdad dedicado á la Imperial Majestad de Dios. Zaragoza, 1967.

Phil 5643.160 Mandy-van Moerbeke, Marie Paule. Movement apparent et préparation perceptive. Louvain, 1967.

Phil 4210.210 Manganelli, Maria. Persona e personalità nell'antropologia di Antonio Rosmini. Milano, 1967.

Phil 6049.67 Mangoldt, Ursula von. Das grosse Buch der Hand. Weilheim, 1967.

Phil 7069.67 Manning, A.G. Helping yourself with E.S.P. West Nyack, 1967.

Phil 3450.19.440 Manno, Ambrogio Giacomo. Esistenza de essere in Heidegger. Napoli, 1967.

Phil 2477.15.95 Mansuy, Michel. Gaston Bachelard et les élements. Paris, 1967.

Phil 7069.64.30 Maple, Eric. The realm of ghost. London, 1967.

Phil 4605.74.31 Marc-Wogan, Konrad. Filosofiska dis Kussioner. Stockholm, 1967.

Phil 6315.2.415 Marc-Wogan, Konrad. Freuds psykoanalys, presentation och kritik. Stockholm, 1967.

Phil 5052.44.2 Marc-Wogau, Konrad. Logik för nybörjare. 2. uppl. Stockholm, 1967.

Phil 8962.22.5 Marck, Wilhelm Henricus Marie van der. Grundzüge einer christlichen Ethik. Düsseldorf, 1967.

Phil 8962.22 Marck, Wilhelm Henricus Marie van der. Toward a Christian ethic. Westminster, 1967.

Phil 8667.52 Maréchal, Pierre. Culte et loix d'une societé d'hommes sans Dieu. Paris, 1967.

Phil 8887.129 Margolius, Hans. System der Ethik. Freiburg, 1967.

Phil 2750.11.41 Maritain, Jacques. De la grâce et de l'humanité de Jèsus. Bruges, 1967.

VPhil 310.659 Markovic, Mihajlo. Humanizam i dijalektika. Beograd, 1967.

VPhil 310.608.5 Marksistsko-leninskaia filosofiia. Moskva, 1967. 2v.

Phil 6155.8 Marshall, William. The art of ecstasy. Don Mills, 1967.

VPhil 3450.11.385 Martel, Karol. U podstaw fenomenologii Husserla. Warszawa, 1967.

Phil 3552.464.5.2 Martin, Gottfried. Leibniz. Logik und Metaphysik. 2. Aufl. Berlin, 1967.

Phil 3494.45.10 Martin, Gottfried. Sachindex zu Kants Kritik der reinen Vernunft. Berlin, 1967.

Phil 310.668 Marxistische Philosophie. Berlin, 1967.

Phil 8667.35 Masi, Giorgio. Dalla religione degli dei alla religione dell'uomo. Milano, 1967.

Phil 3425.668 Massolo, Arturo. Logica hegeliana e filosofia contemporanea. Firenze, 1967.

Phil 585.265 Masullo, Aldo. Il senso del fondamento. Napoli, 1967.

Phil 5520.509 Materialy k konferentsii "Iazyk kak znakovaia sistema osobogo roda. Moskva, 1967.

Phil 5238.215 Matson, Floyd W. Being, seeing and behavior; the psychological sciences. N.Y., 1967.

Phil 5252.96 May, Rollo. Psychology and the human dilemma. Princeton, 1967.

Phil 5465.172 Meerloo, Joost Abraham Maurits. Creativity and eternization. Assen, 1967.

Phil 3450.19.475 Mehta, Jarava Lal. The philosophy of Martin Heidegger. Varanasi, 1967.

Phil 3640.740 Mei, Flavio. Tramonto della ragione. Milano, 1967.

Phil 8592.120 Meinvielle, Julio. Un progresismo vergonzante. Buenos Aires? 1967.

Phil 8887.132 Melsen, Andreas Gerardus Maria van. Physical science and ethics. Pittsburgh, 1967.

Phil 575.260 Merchant, Francis. A search for identity. Salem, 1967.

Phil 2905.1.510 Mermod, Denis. La morale chez Teilhard. Paris, 1967.

Phil 705.49.5 Metzger, Arnold. De Einzelne und der Einsame. Pfullingen, 1967.

Phil 5252.159 Meza, César. Mimo, dependencia, depresión, alcoholismo. 1. ed. Guatemala, 1967.

Phil 8413.42 Michelés, Panagiótés Andreau. Études d'esthétique. Paris, 1967.

Phil 5585.248 Michon, John Albertus. Timing in temporal tracking. Proefschrift. Essen, 1967.

Phil 1200.67.2 Mignucci, Mario. Il significato della logica stoica. 2. edizione riveduta. Bologna, 1967.

Phil 2475.1.475 Milhand, Jean. A Bergson, la patrie reconnaissante. Paris, 1967.

Phil 2138.77.6 Mill, John S. Mill on Bentham and Coleridge. London, 1967.

Phil 6834.1 Millett, Antony P.U. Homosexuality; a bibliography of literature published since 1959 and available in New Zealand. Wellington, 1967.

Phil 5643.140 Models for the perception of speech and visual form; proceedings of a symposium. Cambridge, 1967.

Phil 4160.5.280 Modenato, Francesca. Intenzionalità e storia in Renato Lazzarini. Bologna, 1967.

Phil 9075.77 Mönks, Franz. Gewetens groei en gewetens functie. Nijmegen, 1967.

Phil 8887.123 Monro, David Hector. Empiricism and ethics. Cambridge, Eng., 1967.

Phil 5465.158 Mooney, Ron Lawler. Explorations in creativity. 1. ed. N.Y., 1967.

Phil 8702.32 Moretti, Jean. Biologie et réflexion chrétienne. Paris, 1967.

Phil 5790.2.5 Moriarty, David M. The loss of loved ones. Springfield, 1967.

Phil 3925.16.150 Morick, Harold. Wittgenstein and the problem of other minds. N.Y., 1967.

Phil 5252.157A Morris, Desmond. The naked ape; a zoologist's study of the human animal. 1. ed. N.Y., 1967.

Phil 2905.1.515 Mortier, Jeanne M. Avec Teilhard de Chardin, vues ardentes. Paris, 1967.

Phil 5465.196 Moustakas, Clark E. Creativity and conformity. N.Y., 1967.

Phil 3625.24 Müller, Adam H. Schriften. Neuwield, 1967. 2v.

Phil 3625.13.19 Müller, Aloys. Schriften zur Philosophie. Bonn, 1967. 2v.

Phil 3925.16.185 Mueller, Anselm. Ontologie in Wittgensteins "Tractatus". Bonn, 1967.

Phil 5762.28 Mueller, Heinz Alfred. Spontaneität und Gesetzlichkeit. Bonn, 1967.

Phil 3552.462 Mueller, Kurt. Leibniz-Bibliographie; die Literatur über Leibniz. Frankfurt, 1967.

Phil 3625.26 Müller, Max. Symbolos. München, 1967.

Phil 1750.166.260 Mueller-Schwefe, Hans Rudolf. Humanismus ohne Gott. Stuttgart, 1967.

Phil 2020.140 Mukhopadhyay, Amal Kumar. The ethics of obedience; a study of the philosophy of T.H. Green. Calcutta, 1967.

Phil 8620.62 Murdoch, Iris. The sovereignty of good over other concepts. London, 1967.

Phil 370.2 Musu, Aldo M. Educazione ed esistenza. Padova, 1967.

Phil 8615.20.12 Muzzey, David S. Ethics as a religion. N.Y., 1967.

Phil 585.196 Mynarek, Hubertus. Der Mensch: Sinnziel der Weltentwicklung. Inaug. Diss. München, 1967.

Phil 4803.592.30 Mysłakowski, Zygmunt. Zatracone ścieżki, zagubione słady. Wyd. 1. Warszawa, 1967.

Phil 4897.15 Nakamura, Hajime. A history of the development of Japanese thought from 592 to 1868. v.1-2. Tokyo, 1967.

Phil 8430.51 Naksianowicz-Golaszewska, Maria. Odbiorca sztuki jako krytyk. Wyd.1. Kraków, 1967.

Phil 2050.268 Narskii, Igor' S. Filosofiia Davida Iuma. Moskva, 1967.

Phil 600.57.10 Narskii, Igor Sergeevich. Positivizmus in Vergangenheit und Gegenwart. Berlin, 1967.

Phil 9550.20 Narveson, Jan. Morality and utility. Baltimore, 1967.

Phil 9070.146 Natesan, B. The sympathy of life. Madras, 1967.

Phil 165.410 Natur und Geschichte. Stuttgart, 1967.

Phil 5238.221 Nauchnaia Sessiia Posviashchennaia 50-Letiiu Velikoi Oktiabr'skoi Sotsialisticheskoi Revoliutsii, Sverdlovsk, 1967. Voprosy psikhologii. Sverdlovsk, 1967.

Phil 8703.4 Nauka protiv religii. v.1- Moskva, 1967. 2v.

Phil 2648.94.3 Naville, Pierre. Paul Thiry d'Holbach et la philosophie scientifique au XVIIIe siécle. Paris, 1967.

Phil 1133.45 Nebel, Gerhard. Die Geburt der Philosophie. Stuttgart, 1967.

Phil 5253.15 Neimark, Edith. Stimulus sampling theory. San Francisco, 1967.

Phil 5374.252 Neisser, Ulric. Cognitive psychology. N.Y., 1967.

Phil 310.669 Nekotorye voprosy dialekticheskogo materializma i marksistskoi sotsiologii. Rostov-na-Donn, 1967.

Phil 9560.18.6 Nenna, Giovanni B. Nennio, or A treatise of nobility. Facsimile. Jerusalem, 1967.

Phil 188.28 Newell, Robert. The concept of philosophy. London, 1967.

Phil 4260.155 Nicolini, F. Vico storico. Napoli, 1967.

Phil 3640.56 Nietzsche, Friedrich. L'antéchrist. Paris, 1967.

Phil 3640.58.20 Nietzsche, Friedrich. The birth of tragedy. N.Y., 1967.

Phil 3640.10.5 Nietzsche, Friedrich. Werke. Kritische Gesamtausgabe. Berlin, 1967. 9v.

Phil 3640.51.10 Nietzsche, Friedrich. The will to power. N.Y., 1967.

Phil 1518.5 Nitsche, August. Naturer Kenntnis und politisches Handeln im Mittelalter. Körpen, 1967.

Phil 5258.202 Nobel Conference, 3d, Gustavus Adolphus College, 1967. The human mind. Amsterdam, 1967.

Phil 3450.19.242 Noller, Gerhard. Heidegger und die Theologie. München, 1967.

Phil 5875.90 Nooteboom, Wilhelmina E. Some psychological aspects of the chorcatiform syndrome: development of the intelligence. Assen, 1967.

Phil 4829.616.30 Novaković, Staniša. Problem metafizike u savremenoj analitickoj filozofiji. Beograd, 1967.

Phil 4013.7 Nowicki, Andrzej. Filozofia włoskiego odrodzenia. Warszawa, 1967.

Phil 5068.56.20 Nuchelmans, Gabriël. Proeven van analytisch filosopesen. Hilversum, 1967.

Phil 4752.2.150 Nucho, Fuad. Berdyaev's philosoophy. London, 1967.

Phil 5272.6 Nunnally, Jum Clarence. Psychometric theory. N.Y., 1967.

Phil 384.30 Ofstad, Harald. Two new studies in moral philosophy. Stockholm, 1967.

Phil 5520.35.15.5 Ogden, Charles K. Opposition; a linguistic and psychological analysis. Bloomington, 1967.

Phil 1750.786 Olafson, Frederick. Principles and persons. Baltimore, 1967.

Phil 5520.489 Ong, Walter Jackson. The presence of the word. New Haven, 1967.

Phil 1350.13.5 Oppormann, Hans. Römische Wertbegriffe. Darmstadt, 1967.

Phil 4365.2.36 Ortega y Gasset, José. The origin of philosophy. 1st. ed. N.Y., 1967.

Phil 3450.11.410 Orth, Ernst Wolfgang. Bedeutung, Sim, Gegenstand. Thesis. Bonn, 1967.

Phil 75.79 Ortloff, Johann Andreas. Handbuch der Literatur der Geschichte der Philosophie. Düsseldorf, 1967.

Phil 4190.3.30 Ottonello, Pier Paolo. Dialogo e silenzio. Milano, 1967.

Phil 4210.225 Ottonello, Pier Paolo. L'essere iniziale nell'ontologia di Rosmini. Milano, 1967.

Phil 3450.11.87 Paci, Enzo. La formazione del pensiero di Husserl e il problema della costituzione della natura materiale e della natura animale. Milano, 1967.

Phil 190.114 Pacini, Dante. Sinteses e hipóteses de ser-humano. Rio de Janeiro, 1967.

Phil 4080.3.475   Pagliano Ungari, Graziella. Croce in Francia; ricerche sulla fortuna dell'opera crociana. Napoli, 1967.

Phil 4960.640.5   Paim, Antônio. História das idéias filosóficas no Brasil. São Paulo, 1967.

Phil 4961.140   Pan American Union. Fuentes de la filosofía latinoamericana. Washington, 1967.

Phil 3497.26   Pantaleo, Pasquale. La direzione coscienza-intenzione nella filosofia di Kant e Husserl. Bari, 1967.

Phil 190.107   Pantskhava, Il'ia D. Chelovek, ego zhizn' i bessmertie. Moskva, 1967.

Phil 4070.10.30   Papuli, Giovanni. Girdamo Balduino. Manduzia, 1967.

Phil 310.658   Parniuk, Mikhail A. Determinizm dialekticheskogo materializma. Kiev, 1967.

Phil 2750.11.225   Pavan, Antonio. La formazione del pensiero di J. Maritain. Padova, 1967.

Phil 190.112   Pavese, Roberto. Metafisica e pensiero. Padova, 1967.

Phil 2255.1.130A   Pears, David Francis. Bertrand Russell and the British tradition in philosophy. London, 1967.

Phil 5275.10   Pelikán, Pavel. Homo informationicus, réflexions sur l'homme et l'informatique. Nancy, 1967.

Phil 2225.11.10   Pepper, Stephen Coburn. Concept and quality; a world hypothesis. La Salle, 1967.

Phil 8840.4   Perelman, Chaim. Philosophie morale. Bruxelles, 1967.

Phil 3745.18   Perls, Hugo. Die Komödie der Wahrheit. 10 essays. Bern, 1967.

Phil 5350.10   Persistence and change: Bennington College and its students after twenty-five years. N.Y., 1967.

Phil 8965.20   Peschke, Karlheinz. Naturrecht in der Kontroverse. Salzburg, 1967.

Phil 1120.4   Peters, Francis E. Greek philosophical terms; a historical lexicon. N.Y., 1967.

Phil 5548.30.2   Peters, R.S. The concept of motivation. 2. ed. London, 1967.

Phil 5402.35   Petrie, Asenath. Individuality in pain and suffering. Chicago, 1967.

Phil 5590.472   Petrilowitsch, Nikolaus. Zur Psychologie der Persönlichkeit. Darmstadt, 1967.

Phil 410.85   Petron, Iurii A. Logicheskie problemy abstraktsii beskonechnosti i osushchestvimosti. Moskva, 1967.

Phil 5225.5   Petrovskii, Artur V. Istoriia sovetskoi psikhologii. Moskva, 1967.

Phil 5625.115   Petrushevskii, Stefan A. Dialektika reflektornykh protsessov. Moskva, 1967.

Phil 3745.10.10   Pfaender, Alexendar. Phenomenology of willing and motivation and other phaenomenologica. Evanston, 1967.

Phil 5870.40   Pfahler, Gerhard. Die zwölf wichtigsten Jahre des Lebens. München, 1967.

Phil 1750.115.85   Phenomenology and existentialism. Baltimore, 1967.

Phil 1750.115.90   Phenomenology in America. Chicago, 1967.

Phil 5421.25.35   Philipp, Wolfgang. Die Dreigestalt der Liebe. 1. Aufl. Konstanz, 1967.

Phil 165.405   Die Philosophie und die Wissenschaften. Simon Moser zum 65. Geburtstag. Meisenheim am Glan, 1967.

Phil 346.17.5   Piaget, Jean. Biologie et connaissance, essai sur les relations entre les régulations organiques et les processus cognitifs. Paris, 1967.

Phil 5865.5.7   Piaget, Jean. Six psychological studies. N.Y., 1967.

Phil 730.34   Pichler, Hans. Ganzheit und Gemeinschaft. Wiesbaden, 1967.

Phil 8890.62   Pieper, Josef. Reality and the good. Chicago, 1967.

Phil 8965.16   Piergiovanni, Enzo. La metamorfosi dell'etica medioevale. Bologna, 1967.

Phil 5520.140.2   Pike, Kenneth Lee. Language in relation to a unified theory of the structure of human behavior. 2. ed. The Hague, 1967.

Phil 2477.15.100   Pire, François. De l'imagination poétique dans l'oeuvre de Gaston Bachelard. Paris, 1967.

Phil 5520.443.5   Pittau, Massimo. Problemi di filosofia del linguaggio. Cagliari, 1967.

Phil 9495.167.10   Plack, Arno. Die Gesellschaft und das Böse. München, 1967.

Phil 8670.21.5   Plantinga, Alvin. God and other minds. Ithaca, 1967.

Phil 310.598.2   Planty-Bonjour, Guy. The categories of dialectical materialism. Dordrecht, 1967.

Phil 5627.267   Platonev, Konstantin K. Psikhologiia religii. Moskva, 1967.

Phil 346.34   Podhorytov, Gennadii A. Istorizm kak metod nauchnogo poznaniia. Leningrad, 1967.

Phil 5627.267.5   Pohier, Jacques Marie. Psychologie et théologie. Paris, 1967.

Phil 2475.1.299.5   Politzer, Georges. La fin d'une parade philosophique, le Bergsonisme. Paris, 1967.

Phil 2340.10.205   Pols, Edward. Whitehead's metaphysics. Carbondale, 1967.

Phil 3425.645   Polsko-Czechoslowacka Sesja Naukowa, Poświęcona Recepcji Filozofii Hegle w Krajach Słowiańskich, Warsaw. Der Streit um Hegel bei den Slawen; Symposium. Prag, 1967.

Phil 4752.2.155   Poltoratskii, Nikolai P. Berdiaev i Rossia. N.Y., 1967.

Phil 5225.10   Pongratz, Ludwig Jakob. Problemgeschichte der Psychologie. Bern, 1967.

Phil 346.31   Ponomarev, Iakov A. Psikhika i intuitsiia. Moskva, 1967.

Phil 5535.12   Ponomarev, Iakov A. Znaniia, myshlenie i umstvennoe razvitie. Moskva, 1967.

Phil 8890.68   Pontara, Giuliano. Does the end justify the means? Stockholm, 1967.

Phil 575.266   Ponzio, Augusto. La relazione interpersonale. Bari, 1967.

Phil 2225.5.150   Potter, Vincent G. Charles S. Peirce on norms and ideals. Amherst, 1967.

Phil 346.29   Powell, Betty. Knowledge of actions. London, 1967[1966]

Phil 600.65   Pozzo, Gianni M. Il problema della storia nel positivismo Pozzo. Padova, 1967.

Phil 5255.76   Prangishvili, Aleksandr S. Issledovaniia po psikhologii ustanovki. Tbilisi, 1967.

Phil 4770.2   Praxl, Franz. Die Rechtfertigung Gottes nach Eugen H. Trubetskoj. Inaug. Diss. München, 1967.

Phil 3835.3   Préposiet, Jean. Spinoza et la liberté des hommes. Paris, 1967.

Phil 8416.42   Prestipino, Giuseppe. Lavovo e conoscenza nell'arte. Napoli, 1967.

Phil 5066.102   Prior, Arthur Norman. Past, present and future. Oxford, 1967.

Phil 4170.16   Pró Diego F. Rodolfo Mondolfo. v.1-2. Buenos Aires, 1967-68.

VPhil 310.660   Problemi filozofije marksizma. Beograd, 1967.

Phil 5039.10   Problemi na logikata. Sofiia, 1967- 2v.

Phil 8430.87   Problemy estetiki i esteticheskogo vospitaniia. Moskva, 1967.

Phil 6945.40   Programmation, architecture et psychiatrie. Paris, 1967.

Phil 310.657   Protiv fal'sifikatorov marksistsko-leninskoi filosofii (sbornik statei). Moskva, 1967.

Phil 3640.745   Puetz, Heinz Peter. Friedrich Nietzsche. Stuttgart, 1967.

Phil 5068.71   Pushkin, Veniamin N. Evristika-nauka o tvorcheskom myshlenii. Moskva, 1967.

Phil 4352.2.2   Rabello, Sylvio. Farias Brito. Rio de Janeiro, 1967.

Phil 2750.20.115   Rabil, Albert. Merleau-Ponty, existentialist of the social world. N.Y., 1967.

Phil 4210.215   Radice, Gianfranco. Annali di Antonio Rosmini Serbati. Milano, 1967. 2v.

Phil 3450.11.445   Raggiunti, Renzo. Husserl, dalla logica alla fenomenologia. Firenze, 1967.

Phil 4196.85   Raith, Werner. Die Macht des Bildes. München, 1967.

Phil 2255.10.32   Rand, Ayn. Introduction to objectivist epistemology. N.Y., 1967.

Phil 8610.967.5   Ratnathicam, Daniel S. Honest to man. Colombo, 1967.

Phil 6980.632   Rattner, Josef. Tiefenpsychologie und Humanismus. Zürich, 1967.

Phil 8418.20.10   Read, Herbert. Art and alienation: the role of the artist in society. London, 1967.

Phil 2070.157   Reck, Andrew J. Introduction to William James. Bloomington, 1967.

Phil 5360.26   Reenpää, Yrjö. Wahrnehmen, Beobachten, Konstituieren. Frankfurt, 1967.

Phil 6315.2.395   Reich, Wilhelm. Reich speaks of Freud. N.Y., 1967.

Phil 6127.30   Reimann, Helga. Die Mental Health Bewegung. Tübingen, 1967.

Phil 3425.584.5   Reining, Richard. Zur Grundlegung der polytechnischen Bildung durch Hegel und Marx. Braunschweig, 1967.

Phil 2750.11.200   Reiter, Josef. Intuition und Transzendenz. München, 1967.

Phil 9010.32   Renard, Hubert. L'automobiliste et la morale chrétienne. Paris, 1967.

Phil 3552.454   Rescher, Nicholas. The philosophy of Leibniz. Englewood Cliffs, N.J., 1967.

Phil 1020.62   Rescher, Nicholas. Studies in Arabic philosophy. Pittsburgh, 1967[1968]

Phil 5520.490   Research in verbal behavior and some neurophysiological implications. Papers presented at a conference in New York, 1965. N.Y., 1967.

Phil 4710.50.35   Respublikans'ka Naukova Konferentsiia za Aktual'nykh Pytan' Istorii Filosofii na Ukraïni, Kiev, 1965. Z istorii filosofii na Ukraïni. Kyïv, 1967.

Phil 5272.16   Rey, André. Techniques inédites pour l'examen psychologique. Neuchâtel, 1967.

Phil 5790.2   Rheingold, Joseph Cyrus. The mother, anxiety, and death: the catastrophic death complex. London, 1967.

Phil 7162.267.5   Rhine, Louisa E. ESP in life and lab. N.Y., 1967.

Phil 5871.72   Richter, Horst Eberhard. Eltern, Kind und Neurose. 2. Aufl. Stuttgart, 1967.

Phil 3450.11.370   Ricoeur, Paul. Husserl; an analysis of his phenomenology. Evanston, 1967.

Phil 2905.1.500   Rideau, Émile. Teilhard, oui ou non? Paris, 1967.

Phil 2905.1.366   Rideau, Émile. Teilhard de Chardin; a guide to his thought. London, 1967.

Phil 3640.775   Ries, Wiebrecht. Grundzüge des Nietzsche-Verständnisses in der Deutung seiner Philosophie. Maulburg, 1967?

Phil 1870.160   Ritchie, Arthur David. George Berkeley, a reappraisal. Manchester, 1967.

Phil 348.19.10   Rizzi, Erminio. Il progresso delle conoscenze umane. Padova, 1967.

Phil 6947.1.10   Robb, Barbara. Sans everything; a case to answer. London, 1967.

Phil 3552.461   Robinet, André. Leibniz und Wir. Göttingen, 1967.

Phil 8418.43   Rochlitz, Manfred. Einige philosophische und informationstheoretische Aspekte der moralisch-ästhetischen Verhaltensdetermination der Persönlichkeit. Diss. Leipzig? 1967?

VPhil 5057.43   Rodin, Davor. Aspekti odnosa izmedju Hegelove i Marxove dijalektike. Beograd, 1967.

Phil 3120.55.90   Roeder von Diersburg, Egenolf. Zur Ontologie und Logik offener Systeme. Hamburg, 1967.

Phil 5421.20.30   Rof Carballo, Juan. Violincía y ternura. Madrid, 1967.

Phil 310.663   Rogachev, Petr M. Natsii - narod - chelovechestvo. Moskva, 1967.

Phil 9035.105   Rogers, Raymond. Coming into existence. Cleveland, 1967.

Phil 2070.162   Roggerone, Giuseppe Agostino. James e la crisi della coscienza contemporanea. 2. ed. Milano, 1967.

Phil 8707.34   Rohrbach, Hans. Naturwissenschaft, Weltbild, Glaube. Wuppertal, 1967.

Phil 1750.115.115   Rollin, France. La phénoménologie au départ, Husserl, Heidegger, Gaboriau. Paris, 1967.

Phil 4979.15.30   Romero, Francisco. La estructura de la historia de la filosofía y otros ensayos. Buenos Aires, 1967.

Phil 5520.463   Rorty, Richard. The linguistic turn; recent essays in philosophical method. Chicago, 1967.

Phil 5599.39.10   Rosenstiel, Lutz von. Zur Validität von Formdeutverfahren. München, 1967.

Phil 5190.45   Rosnow, Ralph L. Experiments in persuasion. N.Y., 1967.

Phil 5590.474   Roth, Erwin. Einstellung als Determination individuellen Verhaltens. Habilitationsschrift. Göttingen, 1967.

Phil 3499.36   Rousset, Bernard. La doctrine Kantienne de l'objectivité, l'autonomie comme devoir et devenir. Paris, 1967.

Phil 102.5.14   Rozental, Mark Moiseevich. A dictionary of philosophy. Moscow, 1967.

Phil 8707.32   Rueff, Jacques. Les Dieux et les rois, regards sur le pouvoir créateur. Paris, 1967.

Phil 310.647   Rus, Vojan. Dialektika človcka, misli in sveta. Ljubljana, 1967.

Phil 192.28.6   Russell, B. Philosophical essays. N.Y., 1967.

Phil 2255.1.15   Russell, Bertrand Russell. The autobiography of Bertrand Russell, 1872-1914. 1st American ed. Boston, 1967. 3v.

Phil 3552.104.2   Russell, Bertrand Russell. A critical exposition of the philosophy of Leibniz. 2d ed. London, 1967.

Phil 2255.1.131   Russell, Bertrand Russell. A detailed catalogue of the archives of Bertrand Russell. London, 1967.

Phil 8707.30   Rust, Eric C. Science and faith. N.Y., 1967.

Phil 9495.167   Ryan, Mary Perkins. Love and sexuality. 1st ed. N.Y., 1967.

Phil 4795.4   Rzaev, Agababa. Peredovaia politicheskaia mysl' Rossii i Azerbaidzhana XIX vekai ikh vzaimosviazi. Baku, 1967.

Phil 3425.708   Sabetti, Alfredo. Hegel e il problema della filosofia come storia. Napoli, 1967.

Phil 299.30   Sachsse, Hans. Naturerkenntnis und Wirklichkeit. Braunschweig, 1967.

Chronological Listing

Phil 8598.138.5   Saher, Purvezji Jamshedji. Evolution und Gottesidee. Ratigen, 1967.

Phil 4352.1.165   Sáiz Barberá, Juan. Pensamiento histórico cristiano. 1. ed. Madrid, 1967.

Phil 6060.72   Salberg, Renée de. Nouvelle graphologie pratique. Paris, 1967?

Phil 1750.795   Salvan, Jacques León. The scandalous ghost; Sartre's existentialism as related to vitalism, humanism, mysticism, Marxism. Detroit, 1967.

Phil 3450.11.336   Sancipriano, Mario. L'ethos di Husserl. Torino, 1967.

Phil 193.49.41   Santayana, G. The genteel tradition; nine essays. Cambridge, 1967.

Phil 2280.5.30   Santayana, George. Animal faith and spiritual life. N.Y., 1967.

Phil 4372.1.125   Sanz, Victor. Vigencia actual de Luis Vives. Montevideo, 1967.

Phil 8893.142   Satyananda, Swami. World ethics. Calcutta, 1967.

Phil 5520.491   Saunders, John Turk. The private language problem. N.Y., 1967.

Phil 1885.95   Saxena, Sushil Kumar. Studies in the metaphysics of Bradley. N.Y., 1967.

Phil 5520.325.5   Schaff, Adam. Szkice z filozofii języka. Warszawa, 1967.

Phil 185.40.10   Schaumann, Otto. Die Triebrichtungen des Gewissens. Frankfurt, 1967.

Phil 720.84   Scheffler, Israel. Science and subjectivity. Indianapolis, 1967.

Phil 5871.5   Scheinfeld, Amram. Twins and supertwins. Philadelphia, 1967.

Phil 3450.11.390   Schérer, René. La phénoménologie des "Recherches logiques" de Husserl. Paris, 1967.

Phil 3120.30.150   Schilpp, Paul Arthur. The philosophy of Martin Buber. 1st ed. La Salle, 1967.

Phil 3805.30.12.6   Schleiermacher, Friedrich. Über die Religion. 6. Aufl. Göttingen, 1967.

Phil 2340.10.200   Schmidt, Paul Frederic. Perception and cosmology in Whitehead's philosophy. New Brunswick, 1967.

Phil 4196.80   Schmitt, Charles B. Gianfrancesco Pico della Mirandola, 1469-1533. The Hague, 1967.

Phil 8673.30   Schmucker, Josef. Die primären Quellen des Gottesglaubens. Freiburg, 1967.

Phil 349.42.5   Schneider, Friedrich. Kennen und Erkennen. 2. Aufl. Bonn, 1967.

Phil 165.393   Schoenman, Ralph. Bertrand Russell, philosopher of the century. London, 1967.

Phil 8673.26   Schoonbrood, C.A. Wijsgerige teksten over het absolute. Arnhem, 1967.

Phil 1750.172   Schrader, George Alfred. Existential philosophers. N.Y., 1967.

Phil 5360.20   Schroder, Harold M. Human information processing. N.Y., 1967.

Phil 5203.34   Schueling, H. Bibliographie der psychologischen Literatur des 16. Jahrhunderts. Hildesheim, 1967.

Phil 5374.245.2   Schueling, Hermann. Denkstil. Beschreibung und Deutung der Denkformen. 2. Aufl. Düsseldorf, 1967.

Phil 9530.62   Schuller, Robert. Move ahead with possibility thinking. 1. ed. Garden City, 1967.

Phil 5258.200   Schultz, Hans Jürgen. Was weiss man von der Seele? Stuttgart, 1967.

Phil 3925.16.165   Schulz, Walter. Wittgenstein; die Negation der Philosophie. Pfullingen, 1967.

Phil 6128.80   Schur, Max. The id and the regulatory principles of mental functioning. London, 1967.

Phil 1750.115.80   Schutz, Alfred. The phenomenology of the social world. Evanston, Ill., 1967.

Phil 585.255   Schwarz, Richard. Menschliche Existenz und moderne Welt. Ein internationales Symposion zum Selbstverständnis des heutigen Menschen. Berlin, 1967. 2v.

Phil 2880.8.290   Schwarz, Theodor. Jean-Paul Sartres "Kritik der dialektischen Vernunft". Berlin, 1967.

Phil 8708.31   Scopes, John Thomas. Center of the storm. N.Y., 1967.

Phil 193.252   Sellars, Wilfrid. Philosophical perspectives. Springfield, 1967.

Phil 8980.780.5   Semenov, Mikhail N. O moral'nom avtoritete. Alma-Ata, 1967.

Phil 960.270   Seneviratne, M.J. On the nature of man and society, and other essays. 1st ed. Colombo, 1967.

Phil 8673.32   Il senso dell'ateismo contemporaneo. Bologna, 1967.

Phil 7055.205   Serrano, Geraldo. Arigó, desafio à ciência. Rio de Janeiro, 1967.

VPhil 310.648   Šešić, Bogdan. Dijalektički materijalizam. 2. Izd. Beograd, 1967.

Phil 2520.358.4   Sesonske, Alexander. Meta-meditations; studies in Descartes. Belmont, Calif., 1967[1965].

Phil 1930.8.115   Shalom, Albert. R.G. Collingwood, philosophie et historien. Paris, 1967.

Phil 2138.153   Sharpless, F. Parvin. The literary criticism of J.S. Mill. The Hague, 1967.

Phil 5545.99   Shekhter, Mark S. Psikhologicheskie problemy uznavaniia. Moskva, 1967.

Phil 8673.27   Shekhterman, Efim I. Vera ili zhanie. Alme-Ata, 1967.

Phil 8434.6   Shepard, Paul. Man in the landescape. N.Y., 1967.

Phil 310.617.10   Sheptulin, Aleksandr P. Sistema kategorii dialektiki. Moskva, 1967.

Phil 6990.65   Sherman, Harold Morrow. Wonder healers of the Philippines. London, 1967.

Phil 7150.38.5   Shneidman, Edwin S. Essays in self-destruction. N.Y., 1967.

Phil 5066.263   Shoenfield, Joseph R. Mathematical logic. Reading, Mass., 1967.

Phil 8419.63   Shudria, Kateyna P. Estetychnyi ideal myttsia. Kyiv, 1967.

Phil 8893.127.5   Shvartsman, Klara Aronovna. Ethik ohme Moral. Berlin, 1967.

Phil 9070.116   Simon, Pierre Henri. Pour un garçon de vingt ans, essai. Paris, 1967.

Phil 9240.34   Simon, Ulrich Ernest. A theology of Auschwitz. London, 1967.

Phil 5520.504   Sinclair-de Zwart, Hermina. Acquisition du langage et développement de la pensée, sous-systèmes, et opérations concrètes. Paris, 1967.

Phil 5272.11   Sixtl, Friedrich. Messmethoden der Psychologie. Weinheim, 1967.

VPhil 2490.176   Skarga, Barbara. Ortodoksja i rewizja w pozytywizmie francuskim. Warszawa, 1967.

Phil 978.97   Skerst, Herman von. Der unbekannte Gott. Stuttgart, 1967.

Phil 4800.28   Skolimowski, Henryk. Polish analytical philosophy. London, 1967.

Phil 5867.5   Slovenko, Ralph. Motivations in play, games and sports. Springfield, 1967.

Phil 2266.50   Smith, Adam. The early writings of Adam Smith. N.Y., 1967.

Phil 8598.141   Smith, John Edwin. Religion and empiricism. Milwaukee, 1967.

Phil 3120.30.145   Smith, Ronald Gregor. Martin Buber. Richmond, 1967.

Phil 5645.60   Smits, Willem Canisius Maria. Symboliek van de kleut. Amsterdam, 1967.

Phil 7069.67.25   Smythies, John Raymond. Science and the E.S.P. London, 1967.

Phil 3640.730   Sobejano, Gónzalo. Nietzsche en España. Madrid, 1967.

Phil 5870.17   Söderling, Bertil. Barn av samma stam. Stockholm, 1967.

Phil 2905.1.480   Solages, Bruno de. Teilhard de Chardin, témoignage et étude sur le développement de la pensée. Toulouse, 1967.

Phil 4769.1.130   Solov'ev, V.S. O khristianskom edinstve. Briussell, 1967.

Phil 2905.1.470   Soucy, Claude. Pensée logique et pensée politique chez Teilhard de Chardin. Paris, 1967.

Phil 2905.1.455   Speaight, Robert. Teilhard de Chardin: a biography. London, 1967.

Phil 193.246   Specht, Ernst K. Sprache und Sein. Berlin, 1967.

Phil 3890.9.95   Spiess, Emil Jakob. Ignoz Paul Vital Troxler. Bern, 1967.

Phil 5069.2   Spisoni, Franco. Logica ed esperienz. Milano, 1967.

Phil 7069.67.15   Spraggett, Allen. The unexplained. N.Y., 1967.

Phil 4073.122   Squillace, Mario. La vita eroica di Tommaso Campanella. Roma, 1967.

Phil 6990.3.105   Stafford, Ann (pseud.). Bernadette and Lourdes. London, 1967.

Phil 5068.84   Statera, Gianni. Logica, linguaggio e sociologia. Torino, 1967.

Phil 3850.18.205   Staude, John Raphael. Max Scheler, 1874-1928; an intellectual portrait. N.Y., 1967.

Phil 6112.40.5   Stearn, Jess. Edgar Cayce, the sleeping prophet. Garden City, 1967.

Phil 978.49.895   Steiner, Marie von Sivers. Gesammelte Schriften. Dornach, 1967.

Phil 978.49.375   Steiner, R. Alte und neue Einweihungsmethoden. Dornach, 1967.

Phil 978.49.690   Steiner, R. Biographien und biographische Skizzen, 1894-1905. 1. Aufl. Dornach, 1967.

Phil 978.49.645   Steiner, R. Briefwechel und Dokumente, 1901-1925. 1. Aufl. Dornach, 1967.

Phil 978.49.572   Steiner, R. Erdensterben und Weltenleben und anthroposophisdie Lebensgaben. 2. Aufl. Dornach, 1967.

Phil 978.49.510   Steiner, R. Gegensätze in der Menschheitsentwickelung; 11 Vorträge. Dornach, 1967.

Phil 978.49.540   Steiner, R. Das Geheimnis des Todes; Wesen und Bedeutung Mitteleuropas und die europäischen Volksgeister. Dornach, 1967.

Phil 978.49.530   Steiner, R. Geisteswissenschaft als Erkenntuis der Grundimpulse sozialer Gestaltung. Dornach, 1967.

Phil 978.49.198   Steiner, R. Der Goetheanismus ein Umwandlungsimpuls und Auferstehungsgedanke: Menschenwissenschaft und Sozialwissenschaft. Dornach, 1967.

Phil 978.49.143   Steiner, R. Die Kunst der Rezitation und Deklamation. 2. Aufl. Dornach, 1967.

Phil 978.49.545   Steiner, R. Meditative Betrachtungen und Anleitungen zur Vertiefung der Heilkunst. Dornach, 1967.

Phil 978.49.605   Steiner, R. Der Mensch in seinem Zusammenhange mit dem Kosmos. v.5-6,9. Dornach, 1967- 3v.

Phil 978.49.278   Steiner, R. Menschheitsentwicklung und Christus-Erkenntnis. Dornach, 1967.

Phil 978.49.552   Steiner, R. Natur und Menschin geisteswissenchaftlicher Betrachtung. 2. Aufl. Dornach, 1967.

Phil 978.49.585   Steiner, R. Okkultes Lesen und okkultes Hören. 4. Aufl. Dornach, 1967.

Phil 978.49.680   Steiner, R. Die Philosophie des Thomas von Aquino. 3. Aufl. Dornach, 1967.

Phil 978.49.385   Steiner, R. Die Wissenschaft vom Werden des Menschen. Dornach, 1967.

Phil 310.766.2   Steininger, Herbert. Dialektik, Wissenschaft und Waffe. 2. Aufl. Berlin, 1967.

Phil 4873.5   Stepovniants, Marietta Tigranovna. Filosofiia i sotsiologiia v Pakistane. Moskva, 1967.

Phil 2880.8.116.2   Stern, Alfred. Sartre, his philosophy and existential psychoanalysis. 2.ed. N.Y., 1967.

Phil 6315.2.410   Stewart, Walter A. Psychoanalysis; the first ten years. N.Y., 1967.

Phil 5066.242.5   Stiazhkin, Nikolai Ivanovich. Formirovanre matematicheskoi logiki. Moskva, 1967.

Phil 310.665.2   Stiehler, Gottfried. Der dialektische Widusprud. 2. Aufl. Berlin, 1967.

Phil 103.7   Stockhammer, Morris. Philosophisches Wörterbuch. Köln, 1967.

Phil 8893.53.10   Störring, Gustav. Grundfragen der philosophischen Ethik. Meisenheim, 1967.

Phil 3310.6.80   Stolleis, Michael. Die Moral in der Politik bei Christian Grane. Inaug. Diss. München, 1967.

Phil 3120.19.95   Strasser, Johano. Die Bedeutung des hypothetischen Imperativs in der Ethik Bruno Bauchs. Bonn, 1967.

Phil 349.80   Stroll, Avrum. Epistemology; new essays in the theory of knowledge. N.Y., 1967.

Phil 5374.270   Structuur en sanctie van het bewustzijn. Wassenaar, 1967.

Phil 2880.8.240   Struyker Boudier, C.E.M. Jean Paul Sartre. Tielt, 1967.

Phil 1123.16   Strycker, Emile de. Beknopte geschiedenis van de antieke filosofie. Antwerpen, 1967.

Phil 3500.105   Studien zu Kants philosophischer Entwicklung. Hildesheim, 1967.

Phil 5418.2   Stuttgarter Gemeinschaft "Arzt und Seelsorger". Einsamkeit in medizinisch-psychologischer, theologischer und soziologischer Sicht. Stuttgart, 1967.

Phil 5228.16   Suarez Soto, Vicente. Psicología abismal del mexicano. 2. ed. Puebla de Zaragoza, 1967.

Phil 585.191.5   Suchodolski, Bogdan. Rozwój nowożytnej filozofii człowieka. Warszawa, 1967.

VPhil 585.191.5   Suchodolski, Bogdan. Rozwój nowożytnej filozofii człowieka. Warszawa, 1967.

Phil 8598.125.5   Sukhov, Andrei D. Filosofskie problemy proiskhozhdeniia religii. Moskva, 1967.

Phil 1020.75   Sunar, Cavit. Islam felsefesi der'sleri. Ankara, 1967.

Phil 193.245   Suner, Soffet. Düsuncenin Tarihteki evrimi. Istanbul, 1967.

Phil 5204.18.3   Sury, Kurt F. von. Wörterbuch der Psychologie und ihrer Gunzgebiete. 3. Aufl. Basel, 1967.

Chronological Listing

Phil 310.653 Sutlič, Vanja. Bit i suvremenost. Sarajevo, 1967.
Phil 5360.22 Symposium on Cognition, 2d, Pittsburgh, 1966. Concepts and the structure of memory. N.Y., 1967.
Phil 5870.15 Talbot, Toby. The world of the child. Garden City, 1967.
Phil 3501.20 Taminiaux, Jacques. La nostalgie de la Grèce à l'aube de l'idéalisme allemand. La Haye, 1967.
Phil 194.54 Tanasescu, Horia. Existencialismo; pensamiento oriental y psicoanalisis. México, 1967.
Phil 2905.1.545 Tanner, Henri. Le grain de sénevé. De la science à la religion avec Teilhard de Chardin. Saint-Maurice, 1967.
Phil 350.6 Teoriia poznaniia i sovremennaia nauka. Moskva, 1967.
Phil 5520.660 Testa, Aldo. La struttura dialogica del linguaggio. Bologna, 1967.
Phil 5520.478 Thass-Thienemann, Théodore. The subconscious language. N.Y., 1967.
Phil 2475.1.515 Theau, Jean. La critique bergsonienne du concept. Thèse. Toulouse, 1967.
Phil 1750.115.60 Thevenaz, Pierre. What is phenomenology? Chicago, 1967.
Phil 3019.5 Thijssen-Schoute, Caroline Louise. Uit de Republiek der Letteren. 's-Gravenhage, 1967[1968]
Phil 8980.838 Titarenko, Aleksandr I. Kriterii nravstvennogo progressa. Moskva, 1967.
Phil 575.258 To be or not to be...existential psychological perspectives on the self. Gainesville, 1967.
Phil 8228.2 Tobias, José Antônio. História das idéias estéticas no Brasil. São Paulo, 1967.
Phil 6980.744 Török, Stephan. Thymotherapie. Göttingen, 1967.
Phil 585.210 Toesca, Maurice. Voyage autour de l'homme et au-delà. Paris, 1967.
Phil 5535.32 Toğrol, Beğlan. Duygusal anlam sistemlesi. Istanbul, 1967.
Phil 300.15.5 Tollenaere, M. de. Le corps et le monde. Bruges, 1967.
Phil 300.15 Tollenaere, M. de. Lichaam en wereld. Brugge, 1967.
Phil 310.698 Tomášek, Ladislav. Marxisticka' dialektika a neotomizmus. Vyd. 1. Bratislava, 1967.
Phil 3425.690 Topitsch, Ernst. Die Sozialphilosophie Hegels als Heilslehre und Herrschaftsideologie. Neuwied, 1967.
Phil 4080.3.490 Topuridze, Elena I. Estetika Benedetto Kroche. Tbilisi, 1967.
Phil 2880.8.205 Tordai, Záder. Existance et realité polémique avec certaines thèses fondamentales dé "L'être et le néant" de Sartre. Budapest, 1967.
Phil 165.418 Tradition und Kritik. Stuttgart 1967.
Phil 5870.28 Tran-Thong. Stades et concept de stade de développement de l'enfant dans la psychologie contemporaine. Paris, 1967.
Phil 1819.10 Trawick, Leonard Moses. Backgrounds of romanticism. Bloomington, 1967.
Phil 8525.10 Tribe, David H. One hundred years of freethought. London, 1967.
Phil 4080.3.498 Trieste. Università Facoltà di Lettere e Filosofia. Lezioni crociane. Trieste, 1967.
Phil 3270.12.100 Trinchero, Mario. La filosofia dell'aritmetica di Gottlob Frege. Giappichelli, 1967.
Phil 3450.11.405 Tugendhat, Ernst. Der Wahrheitsbegriff bei Husserl und Heidegger. Berlin, 1967.
Phil 5259.58 Turner, Merle. Philosophy and the science of behavior. N.Y., 1967.
Phil 3502.6 Ueber Theorie und Praxis. Frankfurt, 1967.
Phil 1020.60 Ulken, H.Z. Islam felsefesi kouynoklou ve teni. Ankara, 1967.
Phil 8855.2 Ussel, Jozef Maria Willem van. Sociogenese en evolutie van het probleem der seksuele propaedeuse tussen de 16 de en 18 de eeuw. Gent, 1967. 2v.
Phil 820.2 Ussher, Arland. Sages and schoolmen. Dublin, 1967.
Phil 4225.1.85 Vacca, Giuseppe. Politica e filosofia in Bertrando Spaventa. Bari, 1967.
Phil 3640.726 Vaglia, Anna Teresa. Nietzsche e la letteratura francese. Brescia, 1967.
Phil 4680.312 Valeskalns, Peteris. Ocherk razvitiia progressivnoi filosofskoi iobshchestvenno-politicheskoi mysli v Latvii. Riga, 1967.
Phil 5066.259 Van Heijenoort, Jean. From Frege to Gödel; a source book in mathematical logic, 1879-1931. Cambridge, 1967.
Phil 3503.20 Varga, Alexander von. Macht und Ohnmacht der Vernunft. Zur Einführung in die Philosophie Kants. München, 1967.
Phil 3640.750 Vattimo, Gianni. Ipostesi su Nietzsche. Torino, 1967.
Phil 8601.20 Vattimo, Gianni. Poesia e ontologia. Milano, 1967.
Phil 4065.180 Védrine, Hélène. La conception de la nature chez Giordano Bruno. Paris, 1967.
Phil 5520.487 Ventler, Zeno. Linguistics in philosophy. Ithaca, 1967.
Phil 2421.10 Vereker, Charles. Eighteenth-century optimism. Liverpool, 1967.
Phil 3903.5.30 Verhoeven, Cornelius W.M. Inleiding tot de verwondering. Utrecht, 1967.
Phil 3903.5.40 Verhoeven, Cornelius W.M. Rondom de leegte. Utrecht, 1967.
Phil 6980.768 Verster, Justus. Psychische bijwerkings verschijnselen van moltergan. Assen, 1967.
Phil 8422.7.15 Vischer, F.T. Über das Erhabene und konische Einleitung. Frankfurt, 1967.
Phil 4960.625 Vita, Luís Washington. Tendências do pensamento estético contemporâneo no Brasil. Rio de Janeiro, 1967.
Phil 196.36.5 Vita, Luis Washington. Tríptico de idéias. São Paulo, 1967.
Phil 5061.6.5 Voishvillo, Evgenii K. Poniatie. Moskva, 1967.
Phil 2477.15.110 Voisin, Marcel. Bachelard. Bruxelles, 1967.
Phil 402.10 Volpe, Galvano della. Critica dell'ideologia contemporanea. Roma, 1967.
Phil 106.1.25 Voltaire, Francois Marie Arouet de. Aus dem philosophischen Wörterbuch. Frankfurt, 1967.
Phil 106.1.30 Voltaire, Francois Marie Arouet de. Dictionnaire philosophique. Paris, 1967.
Phil 310.666 Voprosy marksistsko-leninskoi istorii filosofii. Deroslavl', 1967.
Phil 8400.53 Voprosy zarubezhnoi literatury i estetiki. Moskva, 1967.
Phil 8980.872.5 Vstupaia v zhizn'. Moskva, 1967.
Phil 3925.16.140 Waismann, Friedrich. Wittgenstein und der Wiener Kreis. Oxford, 1967.
Phil 3425.658 Waldemar, George. Présence de l'esthetique de Hegel. Paris, 1967.
Phil 5520.488 Waldron, R.A. Sense and sense development. London, 1967.
Phil 1850.162 Wallace, Karl Richards. Francis Bacon on the nature of man. Urbana, 1967.
Phil 8897.90 Warnock, Geoffrey James. Contemporary moral philosophy. N.Y., 1967.
Phil 2880.8.220 Warnock, Mary. Existentialist ethics. London, 1967.

Phil 70.102 Wayne State University. Symposium in the Philosophy of Mind, 1962. Intentionality, minds, and pereception. Detroit, 1967.
Phil 3925.2.95 Weischedel, Wilhelm. Philosophische Grunzgänge. Stuttgart, 1967.
Phil 3460.94 Weischedel, Wilhelm. Streit um die göttlichen Dinge. Darmstadt, 1967.
Phil 8897.88 Weiss, Paul. Right and wrong; a philosophical dialogue between father and son. N.Y., 1967.
Phil 2225.16.80 Wellmer, Albrecht. Methodologie als Erkenntnistheorie. Frankfurt, 1967.
Phil 410.84 Welte, Bernhard. Im Spielfeld von Endlichkeit und Unendlichkeit. Frankfurt, 1967.
Phil 5535.52 Wendeler, Jürgen. Elementare Lernprinzipien; Darstellung und Modifikation von Postulaten der Hull'schen Theorie. Weinheim, 1967.
Phil 9558.12 Wenzel, Siegfried. The sin of sloth. Chapel Hill, 1967.
Phil 735.263 Werkmeister, William H. Man and his values. Lincoln, 1967.
Phil 585.290 Werner, Karl. Speculative Anthropologie. Frankfurt, 1967.
Phil 6980.776.10 Werner, Reiner. Das verhaltensgestörte Kind. 1. Aufl. Berlin, 1967.
Phil 5722.42.2 Whyte, Lancelot. The unconscious before Freud. London, 1967.
Phil 5465.166 Wiart, Claude. Expression picturale et psychopathologie. Paris, 1967.
Phil 5232.11 Wickert, F.R. Readings in African psychology. East Lansing, 1967.
Phil 8423.28 Wiegand, Anke. Die Schönheit und das Böse. München, 1967.
Phil 274.2 Wiggins, David. Identity and spatio-temporal continuity. Oxford, 1967.
Phil 5590.488 Williams, Roger J. You are extraordinary. N.Y., 1967.
Phil 3246.345 Willms, Bernhard. Die totale Freiheit. Köln, 1967.
Phil 575.256 Winckelmans de Cléty, Charles. The world of persons. Thesis. London, 1967.
Phil 9070.117 Windisch, Konrad. Revolution der Satten. Wolfsburg, 1967.
Phil 2280.7.85 Winetrout, Kenneth. F.C.S. Schiller and the dimensions of pragmatism. Columbus, 1967.
Phil 3805.240 Wintsch, Hans Ulrich. Religiosität und Bildung. Thesis. Zürich, 1967.
Phil 5262.70 Wiseman, Stephen. Intelligence and ability. Baltimore, 1967.
Phil 1750.815 Wisser, Richard. Verantwortung im Wondel der Zeit. Mainz, 1967.
Phil 3925.16.30 Wittgenstein, Ludwig. Zettel. Oxford, 1967.
Phil 6980.780.15.2
Phil 3485.28 Wolberg, Lewis Robert. The technique of psychotherapy. 2. ed. N.Y., 1967. 2v.
Phil 6980.780.10 Wolff, Robert. Kant; a collection of critical essays. 1st ed. Notre Dame, 1967.
Phil 5232.5.17 Wolpe, Joseph. Behavior therapy techniques. Oxford, 1967.
Phil 5520.506 Woodworth, R.S. Contemporary schools of psychology. 3. ed. N.Y., 1967.
Phil 3120.2.125 Yolton, John W. Metaphysical analysis. Toronto, 1967.
Phil 5066.211 Zeil, Wilhelm. Bolzano und die Sorben. Bautzen, 1967.
Phil 8426.8 Zinov'ev, Aleksandr A. Osnovy logicheskoi teorii nauchnykh znanii. Moskva, 1967.
Phil 6135.9 Zis', Avner Ia. Iskusstvo i estetika. Moskva, 1967.
Phil 8612.58.1 Ziskind, Robert. Viewpoint on mental health; transcripts, 1963-1965. N.Y., 1967.
Phil 5590.476 Zoepfl, Helmut. Bildung und Erziehung angesichts der Endlichkeit des Menschen. Donauwörth, 1967.
Phil 270.146 Zurabashvili, Avlipii. Problemy psikhologii i patopsikholozii lichnosti. Tbilisi, 1967.
Zwart, P.J. Causaliteit. Assen, 1967[1968]

1968

Phil 4630.7.80 Aaberg, Bengt. Individualitet och universalitet hos Waldemar Rudin. Lund, 1968.
Phil 175.68 Abbagnano, Nieda. Per o contro l'uomo. Milano, 1968.
Phil 4710.160 Abdullaev, Magomed A. Iz istorii filosofskoi i obshchestvenno-politicheskoi mysli narodov Dagestana v XIX v. Moskva, 1968.
Phil 4960.630 Acerboni, Lidia. La filosofia contemporanea in Brasile. Milano, 1968.
Phil 585.208 Adler, Mortimer Jerome. The difference of man and the difference it makes. N.Y., 1968.
Phil 3085.7.80 Adorno, Theodor W. Mit Beiträgen von Kurt Oppens. Frankfurt, 1968.
Phil 530.35.30 Adriani, Maurilio. Italia mistica. Roma, 1968.
Phil 5875.120 Aebli, Hans. Uber den Egozentrismus des Kindes. Stuttgart, 1968.
Phil 310.682 Aktual'nye voprosy istorii marksistsko-leninskoi filosofii. Moskva, 1968.
Phil 5210.20 Alarcón, Reynaldo. Panorama de la psicología en el Perú. Lima, 1968.
Phil 5592.186 Albou, Paul. Les questionnaires psychologiques. Paris, 1968.
Phil 5592.190 Allison, Joel. The interpretation of psychological tests. N.Y., 1968.
Phil 2905.1.2 Almago, Romano S. A basic Teilhard-bibliography, 1955 - Apr. 1968. N.Y., 1968.
Phil 3482.15.5 Alquié, Ferdinand. La critique kantienne de la metaphysique. Paris, 1968.
Phil 8622.74 Amb o sense fe; mots de conversa. Barcelona, 1968.
VPhil 1830.55 Amerikanskie prosveteli. Moskva, 1968-69. 2v.
Phil 5240.60 Analysis of behavioral change. N.Y., 1968.
Phil 585.305 Anan'ev, Boris G. Chelovek kak predmet poznaniia. Leningrad, 1968.
Phil 5585.266 Anan'ev, Boris G. Individual'noe razvitie cheloveka i konstantnost' vospriiatiia. Moskva, 1968.
Phil 8950.12 Anciaux, Paul. Le dynamisme de la morale chrétienne. Gembloux, 1968-69.
Phil 331.20.5 Andreev, Ivan D. Puti i trudnosti poznaniia. Moskva, 1968.
Phil 4822.8 Andreev, Kosta. Kritikata na Dimitur Blagoev na neokantianstvoto v Bulgariia po vuprosite na filosofiiata. Sofiia, 1968.
Phil 8401.25.5 Antoni, Carlo. Scritti di estetica. Napoli, 1968.
Phil 2150.22.80 Antworten auf Herbert Marcuse. Frankfurt, 1968.
Phil 7069.68.15 Appleman, John A. Your psychic powers and immortality. N.Y., 1968.
Phil 8171.5.5 Apresian, Grant Z. Esteticheskaia mysl' narodov Zakavkaz'ia. Moskva, 1968.

1968 - cont.

Phil 8401.34.5   Apresian, Zorii Grantovich. Freedom and the artist. Moscow, 1968.

Phil 5465.173   Arasteh, A. Reza. Creativity in the life-cycle. Leiden, 1968.

Phil 1870.170   Ardley, Gavin W.R. Berkeley's renovation of philosophy. The Hague, 1968[1969]

Phil 1845.17   Armstrong, David M. A materialist theory of the mind. London, 1968.

Phil 8170.10   Asmus, Valenti F. Voprosy teorii i istorii esteiki. Moskva, 1968.

Phil 6360.14   Aspects of autism. London, 1968.

Phil 4513.8.31   Aspelin, Gunnar. Lek och allvar. Lund, 1968.

Phil 402.6   Aspelin, Gunnar. Världsbilder och livsidal. Lund, 1968.

Phil 5238.188.10   Association de Psychologie Scientifique de Langue Française. Le comportement, symposium de l'association de psychologie...(Rome, 1967). Paris, 1968.

Phil 8401.29.10   Assunto, Rosario. L'automobile di Mallarmé e altri ragionamenti intorno, alla vocazione odierna delle arti. Roma, 1968. 10v.

Phil 5040.28   Astat'ev, Vsevdod K. Zakony myshleniia v formal'noi i dialketicheskoi logike. L'vov, 1968.

VPhil 175.66   Atanasijević, Ksenija. Smisao i vrednost eqzistencije. Beograd, 1968.

Phil 308.2   Atbert, Hans. Traktat über kritische Vernunft. Tübingen, 1968.

Phil 5548.85.2   Atkinson, John W. Motives in fantasy, action, and society. Princeton, 1968.

Phil 8655.24   Aubry, Joseph. L'ateismo oggi. 1. ed. Torino, 1968.

Phil 396.5   Ayer, Alfred Jules. The humanist outlook. London, 1968.

Phil 2225.5.155   Ayer, Alfred Jules. The origins of pragmatism: studies in the philosophy of Charles Sanders Peirce and William James. London, 1968.

Phil 5750.12   Ayres, Michel Richard. The refutation of determinism. London, 1968.

Phil 3450.11.191   Bachelard, Suzanne. A study of Husserl's formal and transcendental logic. Evanston, 1968.

Phil 1020.85   Badawi, Abdurrahman. Le transmission de la philosophie grecque au monde arabe. Paris, 1968.

Phil 5402.36   Bakan, David. Disease, pain and suffering. Chicago, 1968.

Phil 5041.97   Bakanialze, Mamiie I. Problema subordinatsii logicheskikh form. Alma-Ata, 1968.

Phil 4368.4   Baliñas, Carlos A. El pensamiento de Amor Ruibal. Madrid, 1968.

Phil 4710.155   Ballestrem, Karl G. Die sowjetische Erkenntnismetaphysik und ihr Verhältnis zu Hegel. Dordrecht, 1968.

Phil 8402.65   Banach, Andrzej. O kiczu. Wyd. 6. Kraków, 1968.

Phil 8876.160   Banner, William Augustus. Ethics: an introduction to moral philosophy. N.Y., 1968.

Phil 5590.514   Bannister, Donald. The evaluation of personal constructs. London, 1968.

Phil 7055.388   Barbosa, Elia. No mundo de Chico Xavier. São Paulo, 1968.

Phil 5401.52   Barker, John Charles. Scared to death; an examination of fear. London, 1968.

Phil 5440.34   Barker, Roger Garlock. Ecological psychology. Stanford, Calif., 1968.

Phil 9495.168.30   Barra, Giovanni. Castità: problema o liberazione? Torino, 1968.

Phil 8661.8.35   Barrett, R.H. A refutation of Mr. U.H. Gillespie's argument a priori for the existence of a great first cause. London, 1968.

Phil 8622.66   Barruffo, Antonio. Dinamismo e maturità della fede. Roma, 1968.

Phil 282.26   Barth, Aron. The creation in the light of modern science. Jerusalem, 1968.

Phil 1750.744.5   Bartolone, Filippo. Valenze esistenziali del cristianesimo. Messina, 1968.

Phil 4170.16.5   Bassi, Enrico. Rodolfo Mondolfo nella vita e nel pensiero socialista. Bologna, 1968.

RRC   Phil 5722.81   Bassin, Filipp. Problema bessoznatel'nogo. Moskva, 1968.

Phil 2750.11.235   Bauer, Hans Ludwig. Schopferische Erkenntnis. München, 1968.

Phil 3246.310   Baumgartner, Hans Michael. Johann Gottlieb Fichte; Bibliographie. Stuttgart, 1968.

Phil 6980.130   Baur, Pierre. Le psychodrame et la vie. Paris, 1968.

Phil 3120.8.165   Bausola, Adriano. Conoscenza e moralità in Franz Brentano. Milano, 1968.

Phil 1750.152.10   Becker, Carl Lotus. The heavenly city of the eighteenth-century philosophers. New Haven, 1968.

Phil 585.140.5   Becker, Ernest. The structure of evil. N.Y., 1968.

Phil 6311.54   Becker, Raymond de. Bilan de la psychologie des profondeurs. Paris, 1968.

Phil 6420.2   Beech, H.R. Research and experiment in Stuttering. Oxford, 1968.

Phil 3120.30.95.5   Beek, Martinus Adrianus. Martin Buber: personalist and prophet. Westminster, 1968.

Phil 3120.21.10   Beerling, Reinier Franciscus. Ideeën en idolen. Arnhem, 1968.

Phil 5627.107.20.5   Behanna, Gertrude Florence. The late Liz. N.Y., 1968.

Phil 8581.115   Bellet, Maurice. Essai d'une critique de la foi. Paris, 1968.

Phil 1865.195   Bentham, Jeremy. The correspondence of Jeremy Bentham. London, 1968. 3v.

Phil 3001.19   Benz, Ernst. Las sources mystiques de la phlosophie romantique allemande. Paris, 1968.

Phil 7082.24.5   Beradt, Charlotte. The third Reich of dreams. Chicago, 1968.

Phil 3120.69.30   Berg, Jan Hendrik van den. Metabletica van de materie. Nijkerk, 1968-

Phil 6980.105.10   Berge, André. Les psychothérapies. 1. éd. Paris, 1968.

Phil 282.24   Berger, Herman. Op zoek naar identiteit. Nijmegen, 1968.

Phil 3483.90   Bergk, Johann Adam. Reflexionen über I. Kant's Metaphysische Anfangsgründe der Tugendlehre. Bruxelles, 1968.

Phil 5545.248   Bergon, Annie van. Task interruption. Amsterdam, 1968.

Phil 6319.1.240   Bertine, Eleanor. Jung's contribution to our time. N.Y., 1968.

Phil 3120.32.21   Beth, Evert Willem. Science a road to wisdom: collected philosophical studies. Dordrecht, 1968.

Phil 4600.4.85   Beyer, Nils. Bengt Lidforss. Stockholm, 1968.

Phil 960.276   Bhagavad Datta. The story of creation as seen by the seers. Delhi, 1968.

Phil 5241.186   Biasutti, Bruno. Critica della società competitiva. Roma, 1968.

Phil 5535.26   Biggs, John Burville. Information and human learning. Melbourne, 1968.

Phil 4080.3.520   Biscione, Michele. Interpreti do Croce. Napoli, 1968.

Phil 8980.213   Bittighoefer, Bernd. Moral und Gesellschaft. Berlin, 1968.

Phil 5520.514   Black, Max. The labyrinth of language. N.Y., 1968.

Phil 5421.25.25   Blais, Gerard. L'amour humain. Sherbrooke, 1968.

Phil 8980.220   Bludov, Iakov S. Prostota i skromnost'. Kiev, 1968.

Phil 8876.162   Blumenfeld, Walter. Vom sittlichen Bewusstsein. Bonn, 1968.

Phil 5039.26   Bober, Juraj. Problémy dialektiky. 1. vyd. Bratislava, 1968.

Phil 5272.12   Bock, R. Darrell. The measurement and prediction of judgment and choice. San Francisco, 1968.

Phil 6311.56   Bodamer, Joachim. Der gefährdete Mensch. Freiburg, 1968.

Phil 3450.11.460   Boehm, Rudolf. Vom Gesichtspunkt des Phänomenologie. Den Haag, 1968[1969]

Phil 176.238   Boehme, Guenther. Der pädagogische Beruf der Philosophie. München, 1968.

Phil 1750.798   Boelen, Bernard Jacques Marie. Existential thinking. Pittsburgh, 1968.

Phil 5590.498   Borgatta, Edgar. Handbook of personality theory and research. Chicago, 1968.

Phil 3925.16.215   Borgis, Ilona. Index zu Ludwig Wittgensteins "Tractatus logico-philosophicus" und Wittgenstein - Bibliographie. Frieburg, 1968.

Phil 8612.86   Bornscheuer, Lothar. Miseriae regum. Diss. Berlin, 1968.

Phil 585.412   Borsodi, Ralph. Seventeen problems of man and society. 1. ed. Anand, 1968.

Phil 4225.1.100   Bortot, Renato. L'hegelismo di Bertrando Spaventa. Firenze, 1968.

Phil 585.355   Bosio, Franco. Antropologia filosfica e occultamento ideologico. Urbino, 1968.

Phil 5590.504   Bouman, Jan C. Psykologi för Erl. Stockholm, 1968.

Phil 8826.8   Bourke, Vernon Joseph. History of ethics. Garden City, 1968.

Phil 176.26.15   Bouterwek, Friedrich. Angangsgründe der speculaterien Philosophie. Bruxelles, 1968.

Phil 176.26.10   Bouterwek, Friedrich. Die Epochen der Vernunft nach der Idee einer Apoditik. Bruxelles, 1968.

Phil 5585.300   Bowman, Jan C. The figure-ground phenomenon in experimental and phenomenological psychology. Thesis. Stockholm, 1968.

Phil 1885.37.20   Bradley, Francis H. Appearance and reality. Oxford, 1968.

Phil 4210.245   Brancaforte, Antonio. Discussioni rosminiane. Catania, 1968.

Phil 2070.150.5A   Brennan, Bernard P. William James. N.Y., 1968.

Phil 6060.82   Bresard, Suzanne. Empreintes. Neuchâtel, 1968.

Phil 8402.68   Brissoni, Armando. Pagine di estetica. Padova, 1968.

Phil 3425.714   Brissoni, Armando. Ricerche sull'estetica di Hegel. Padova, 1968.

Phil 6112.40.10   Bro, Harmon Hartzell. Edgar Cayce on dreams. N.Y., 1968.

Phil 585.177.5   Brown, Donald George. Action. Toronto, 1968.

Phil 6111.85   Bruaire, Claude. Philosophie du corps. Paris, 1968.

Phil 3483.96   Bruch, Jean Louis. La philosophie religieuse de Kant. Thèse. Paris, 1968.

Phil 3120.15.40   Brunner, Constantin. Science, spirit, superstition; a new enquiry into human thought. Toronto, 1968.

Phil 5870.35   Bruun, Ulla-Britta. Förskoleålderns psykologi. Göteborg, 1968.

Phil 3120.30.71   Buber, Martin. Martin Buber, philosophe de la relation. Paris, 1968.

Phil 3120.30.38   Buber, Martin. On the Bible; eighteen studies. N.Y., 1968.

Phil 1630.40   Buck, August. Die humanistische Tradition in der Romania. Hamburg, 1968.

Phil 7230.7   Bucke (R.M.) Memorial Society for the Study of Religious Experience. Trance and possession states. Montreal? 1968.

Phil 5241.88.10   Bühler, Charlotte M. Psychologische Probleme unserer Zeit. Stuttgart, 1968.

Phil 5590.486   Bueva, Liudmila P. Sotsial'naia sreda i soznanie lichnosti. Moskva, 1968.

Phil 4960.660   Buggenhagen, Erich Arnold von. Pensamento filosófico brasileiro na atualidade. São Paulo, 1968.

Phil 3030.4   Buhr, Manfred. Der Anspruch der Vernunft. Berlin, 1968.

Phil 7069.68.50   Bunge, H. Meesters van het verborgene. Amsterdam, 1968.

Phil 1750.788.2   Burnier, Michel Antoine. Choice of action; the French existentialists on the political front line. 1st American ed. N.Y., 1968.

Phil 5650.50   Burns, William. Noise and man. London, 1968.

Phil 5875.60   Burton, Lindy. Vulnerable children; three studies of children in conflict. London, 1968.

Phil 5145.4   Byrne, Edmund F. Probability and opinion. The Hague, 1968.

Phil 7069.65.37   Byrne, Patrick. Irish ghost stories. Cork, 1968.

Phil 5871.110   Cacciagierra, Francesco. I sentimenti del fanciullo nell'ambito familiare. Milano, 1968.

Phil 3195.6.195   Calabrò, Gaetano. Dilthey e il diritto naturale. Napoli, 1968.

Phil 6983.2   Caldwell, William Vernon. LSD psychotherapy; an explosion of psychedelic and psycholytic therapy. N.Y., 1968.

Phil 9495.168   Callahan, Sidney Cornelia. Beyond birth control; the Christian experience of sex. N.Y., 1968.

Phil 4080.38   Campanale, Domenico. Fondamento e problemi della metafisica. Bari, 1968-

Phil 4073.52   Campanella, Tommaso. Apologia di Galileo. Torino, 1968.

Phil 2750.22.115   Campanini, Giorgio. La rivoluzione cristiana. Brescia, 1968.

Phil 7069.68.40   Campbell, John Lorne. Strange things: the story of Fr. Allan McDonald, Ada Goodrich Freer, and the Society for Psychical Research's enquiry into Highland second sight. London, 1968.

Phil 4260.220   Candela, Mercurio. Diritto e umanità in G.B. Vico. Empoli, 1968.

Phil 2515.18.5   Caraco, Albert. La luxure et la mort. Lausanne, 1968.

Phil 4080.40   Cardone, Domenico Antonio. L'ozio, la contemplazione, il giuoco, la tecnica. Roma, 1968.

Phil 585.295   Care, Norman S. Readings in the theory of action. Bloomington, 1968.

Phil 645.65   Cariddi, Walter. Filosofi della scepsi. Lecce, 1968.

Phil 5421.20.65   Carp, Eugène Antoine. Agressie en agressiviteit. Utrecht, 1968.

Phil 9070.134   Carus, Karl Gustav. Die Lebenskunst nach den Inschriften des Tempels zu Delphi. Stuttgart, 1968.

Phil 5790.2.20   Caruso, Igor A. Die Trennung der Liebenden. Bern, 1968.

Phil 5374.235.5   Castaneda, Carlos. The teachings of Don Juan; a yaqui way of knowledge. Berkeley, 1968.

Chronological Listing

Phil 6312.30   Centro di Studi Filosofici di Gallarate. Psicanalisi e filosofia. Padova, 1968.

Phil 4365.2.45   Cepeda Calzada, Pablo. La doctrina de la sociedad en Ortega y Gasset. Valladolid, 1968.

Phil 310.687   Chagin, Boris A. Sub"ektivnyi faktor. Moskva, 1968.

Phil 4260.116.5   Chaix-Ruy, Jules. J.B. Vico et l'illuminisme athée. Paris, 1968.

Phil 585.275   Changing perspectives on man. Chicago, 1968.

Phil 410.90   Chany, Robert de. Sur les confins du fini, métaphysique, physique, mathématiques et religion. Paris, 1968.

Phil 5212.20.2   Chaplin, James Patrik. Systems and theories of psychology. 2. ed. N.Y., 1968.

Phil 5590.494   Chapman, Arthur Harry. Put-offs and come-ons. London, 1968.

Phil 3425.662   Chatelet, François. Hegel. Paris, 1968.

Phil 6312.32   Choisy, Maryse. Mais la terre est sacrée. Genève, 1968.

Phil 3552.471   Chuchmarev, Vladimir I. G.W. Leibnits i russkaia kul'tura. Moskva, 1968.

Phil 2515.10.5   Cioran, Émile M. The temptation to exist. Chicago, 1968.

Phil 177.140   Claeys, R.H. Inleiding tot de metafysica. Gent, 1968.

Phil 3140.1   Clauberg, Johann. Opera omnia philosophica. Reprint. Hildesheim, 1968. 2v.

Phil 450.2   Clements, Tad S. Science and man; the philoosophy of scientific humanism. Springfield, Illinois, 1968.

Phil 6316.32   Coeppert, Hans. Das Ich. München, 1968.

Phil 402.12   Cofrancesco, Dino. Appunti sull'ideologia. Milano, 1968.

Phil 1540.94   Cognet, Louis. Introduction aux mystiques rhéno-flamands. Paris, 1968.

Phil 8582.75   Colish, Marcia L. The mirror of language. New Haven, 1968.

Phil 8582.26.5   Collingwood, Robin George. Faith and reason. Chicago, 1968.

Phil 583.10   Colombo, Arrigo. Sulla fenomenologie e la rivelazione delle cose. Bologna, 1968.

Phil 333.17.1   Colorado. University. Psychology Department. Contemporary approaches to cognition. Cambridge, 1968.

Phil 568.2   The concept of order. Seattle, 1968.

Phil 575.272   Conference on Comparative Philosophy and Culture. East-West studies on the problem of the self. The Hague, 1968.

Phil 6946.1.25   Conolly, John. The construction and government of lunatic asylums. London, 1968.

Phil 5585.320   Conrad, Theodor. Zur Wesenlehre des psychischen Lebens und Erlebens. Den Haag, 1968.

Phil 1695.45   Contemporary philosophy. A survey. Firenze, 1968- 4v.

Phil 7150.65.10   Convegno di Studio su Suicidio eTentato Suicidio in Italia, Milan, 1967. Suicidio e tentato suicidio in Italia. Milano, 1968.

Phil 2515.20   Cordemoy, Géraud de. Oeuvres philosophiques, avec une étude bio-bibliographique. Paris, 1968.

Phil 177.128.2   Coreth, Emerich. Metaphysics. N.Y., 1968.

Phil 8582.78   Corvez, Maurice. L'être et la conscience morale. Louvain, 1968.

Phil 5402.37   Cowan, Joseph Lloyd. Pleasure and pain: a study in philosophical psychology. London, 1968.

Phil 325.16   Cowley, Fraser. A critique of British empiricism. London, 1968.

Phil 8955.8.80   Cox, Harvey G. The situation ethics debate. Philadelphia, 1968.

Phil 5325.44   Cramer, Phede. Word association. N.Y., 1968.

Phil 5649.40   Cratty, Bryant J. Psychology and physical activity. Englewood Cliffs, 1968.

Phil 2905.1.177   Crespy, Georges. From science to theology. Nashville, 1968.

Phil 4080.7.80   Cristallini, Alessandro. Ottario Colecchi, un filosofo da riscoprire. Padova, 1968.

Phil 4080.3.42.10   Croce, Benedetto. Aesthetic as science of expression and general linguistic. N.Y., 1968.

Phil 2905.1.195.5   Cuénot, Claude. Nouveau lexique Teilhard de Chardin. Paris, 1968.

Phil 8952.22   Curran, Charles E. A new look at Christian morality. Notre Dame, 1968.

Phil 5599.93   Dahl, Gerhard. Übereinstimmungsvalidität des HAWE und Entwicklung einer reduzierten Testform. Meisenheim am Glan, 1968.

Phil 5753.17   D'Angelo, Edward. The problem of freedom and determinism. Columbia, 1968.

Phil 365.64   Daniels, George H. Darwinism comes to America. Waltham, Mass., 1968.

Phil 335.10   Danto, Arthur Coleman. Analytic philosophy of knowledge. Cambridge, Eng., 1968.

Phil 3415.115   Darnoi, D.N.K. The unconcious and Eduard von Hartmann; a historico-critical monograph. The Hague, 1968.

Phil 7108.372   Darnton, Robert. Mesmerism and the end of the Enlightenment in France. Cambridge, 1968.

Phil 2555.12.30   Dartan, Jacques. Franchir le Rubicon. Paris, 1968.

Phil 3485.30   Daub, Carl. Predigten nach Kantischen Grundsätzen. Bruxelles, 1968.

Phil 7069.68.60   Daurado, Alzira Guanaes. Igrejas reunidas, plano divino. 1. ed. Rio de Janeiro, 1968.

Phil 5875.110   Debienne, Marie Claire. Le dessin chez l'enfant. Paris, 1968.

Phil 5520.493   De Bono, Edward. The use of lateral thinking. London, 1968.

Phil 8708.29.10   De Camp, Lyon Sprague. The great monkey trial. 1. ed. Garden City, 1968.

Phil 5548.115   DeCharms, Richard. Personal causation. N.Y., 1968.

Phil 2905.1.680   Deckers, Marie Christine. Le vocabulaire de Teilhard de Chardin. Gembloux, 1968.

Phil 5272.6.5   Delbeke, L. Construction of preference spaces. Louvain, 1968.

Phil 274.4   Deleuze, Gilles. Différence et répétition. Thèse. Paris, 1968.

Phil 3823.18   Deleuze, Gilles. L'idée de expression dans la philosophie de Spinoza. Thèse. Paris, 1968.

Phil 3823.18.1   Deleuze, Gilles. Spinoza et le problème de l'expression. Paris, 1968.

Phil 1980.3.104   Delisle, Françoise Roussel. The return of Havelock Ellis, or Limbo or the dove? London, 1968.

Phil 4080.1.85   Del Torre, Maria A. Studi su Cesare Cremonini. Padova, 1968.

Phil 5650.52   Denes, Peter B. The speech chain; the physics and biology of spoken language. Baltimore? 1968.

Phil 5421.20.37   Denker, Rolf. Aufklärung über Aggression: Kant, Darwin, Freud, Lorenz. 2. Aufl. Stuttgart, 1968.

Phil 1730.22   Denker, Rolf. Grenzen liberaler Aufklärung bei Kant und Anderen. Stuttgart, 1968.

Phil 4215.1.115   Dentone, Adriana. Il problema morale in Romagnosi e Cattaneo. Milano, 1968.

Phil 2655.3.105   Deregibus, Arturo. La metafisica critica di Octave Hamelin. Torino, 1968.

Phil 5465.162   De Ropp, Robert S. The master game; pathways to higher consciousness beyond the drug experience. N.Y., 1968.

Phil 193.250   De Santillana, Giorgio. Reflections on men and ideas. Cambridge, 1968.

Phil 5865.5.10   Desbiens, Jean Paul. Introduction à un examen philosophique de la psychologie de l'intelligence chez Jean Piaget. Québec, 1968.

Phil 2520.50.5   Descartes, René. The meditations, and selections from the Principles of René Descartes. n.p., 1968.

Phil 5845.2   Descloitres, Claudine. La psychologie applique en Afrique; bibliographie. Aix-en-Provence, 1968.

Phil 8583.43.5   Dessauer, Philipp. Meditation im christlichen Dasein. München, 1968.

Phil 3485.32   Destutt de Tracy, Antoine Louis Claude. La métaphysique de Kant. Bruxelles, 1968.

Phil 5270.10   Devereux, George. From anxiety to method in the behavioral sciences. The Hague, 1968.

Phil 310.582.5   Dialektiko-materialisticheskii analiz osnovnykh poniatii biologii i meditsiny. Kiev, 1968.

Phil 5238.222   Dialog über den Menschen. Stuttgart, 1968.

Phil 5401.53.2   Diel, Paul. La peur et l'angoisse, phénomène central de la vie et de son évolution. 2e éd. Paris, 1968.

Phil 2905.1.525   Dimensions of the future; the spirituality of Teilhard de Chardin. Washington, 1968.

Phil 8654.114   Dio é morto? 4. ed. Milano, 1968.

Phil 334.10   Dobriianov, Velichko S. Metodologicheskie problemy teoreticheskogo i istoricheskogo poznaniia. Moskva, 1968.

Phil 2520.370   Doney, Willis. Descartes; a collection of critical essays. 1st ed. Notre Dame, 1968.

Phil 8404.3.20   Dorfles, Gillo. Artificio e natura. Torino, 1968.

Phil 1750.166.225   Dresden, Samuel. Het humanistische denken. Italië-Frankrijk 1450-1600. Amsterdam, 1968.

Phil 270.26.5   Ducasse, Curt J. Truth, knowledge and causation. London, 1968.

Phil 705.66   Dürckheim-Montmartin, Karlfried. Überweltliches Leben in der Welt. Weilheim, 1968.

Phil 4080.3.530   Dujovne, León. El pensamiento histórico de Benedetto Croce. Buenos Aires, 1968.

Phil 2555.11.71   Dupréel, Eugène. Similitude et dépassement. Paris, 1968.

Phil 5403.14   Durand, Leo. The psychology of happiness. Blackstone, 1968.

Phil 8583.18.5   Durkheim, E. Les formes élementaires de la vie religieuse. 5e éd. Paris, 1968.

Phil 8980.346   Dzhafarli, Teimuraz M. Byt' chelovekom na zemle. Moskva, 1968.

Phil 5066.195.5   E.W. Beth Memorial Colloquium, Institut Henri Poincaré, 1964. Logic and foundations of science. Dordrecht, 1968.

Phil 2475.1.490   Ebacher, Roger. La philosophie dans la cité technique. Québec, 1968.

Phil 3486.18.2   Eberhard, John. Philosophisches Archiv. Bruxelles, 1968. 2v.

Phil 3004.8   Ebhinghaus, J. Gesammelte Aufsätze, Verträge und Reden. Hildesheim, 1968.

Phil 8405.12   Eco, Umberto. La definizione dell'arte. Milano, 1968.

Phil 5520.565   Eco, Umberto. La strutture assente. Milano, 1968.

Phil 5421.35.10   Edmaier, Alois. Horizonte der Hoffnung. Regensburg, 1968.

Phil 5272.20.3   Edwards, Allen Louis. Experimental design in psychological research. 3d ed. N.Y., 1968.

Phil 4004.2   Efirov, Svetozar A. Ital'ianskaia burzhuaznaia filosofiia XX veka. Moskva, 1968.

Phil 285.8   Ehrhardt, Arnold. The begining. N.Y., 1968.

Phil 5520.610   Ehrlich, Stéphane. Les mécanismes du comportement verbal. Paris, 1968.

Phil 3450.29.90   Eid, Volker. Die Kunst in christlicher Daseinsverantwortung nach Theodor Haecker. Thesis. Würzburg, 1968.

Phil 8954.5   Eisenstadt, Shmuel Noah. The Protestant ethic and modernization. N.Y., 1968.

Phil 5520.560   Eisler, Frieda Goldman. Psycholinguistics: experiments in spontaneous speech. London, 1968.

Phil 4757.2.120   Ekkev, Martin H. Gurdjieff, de mens en zijn werk. Amsterdam, 1968.

Phil 179.44   Elders, Fons. Filosofie als science-fiction. Amsterdam, 1968.

Phil 8879.35.5   Elken, Rober. Ethik naturwissenschaftlich Fundiert und Kirche. Kassel, 1968.

Phil 2255.10.80   Ellis, Albert. Is objectivism a religion? N.Y., 1968.

Phil 2280.5.155   Endovitskii, V.D. Kritika filosofii amerikanskogo kriticheskogo realizma. Moskva, 1968.

Phil 165.422   L'endurance de la pensée; pour saluer Jean Beaufret. Paris, 1968.

Phil 210.50   Esbroeck, Michel van. Herméneutique. Paris, 1968.

Phil 5871.60   Escalona, Sibylle Korsch. The roots of individuality. Chicago, 1968.

Phil 6954.3.10   Esquirol, Etienne. Von den Geisteskrankheiten. Bern, 1968.

Phil 8400.56   Estetika segodnia. Moskva, 1968- 2v.

Phil 9495.168.20   Evely, Louis. Lovers in marriage. N.Y., 1968.

Phil 5421.25.45   Evory, John J. The man and the woman; psychology of human love. N.Y., 1968.

Phil 1980.6   Ewing, Alfred Cyril. Non-linguistic philosophy. London, 1968.

Phil 2805.475   Eydoux, Emmanuel. Dialogue avec Blaise Pascal. Théâtre. Basel, 1968.

Phil 3425.650   Fackenheim, Emil L. The religious dimension in Hegel's thought. Bloomington, Ind., 1968[1967]

Phil 8660.26   Faith in the face of doubt. N.Y., 1968.

Phil 310.746   Fajkus, Brětislaw. Existence, realita, masérie. Vyd. 1. Praha, 1968.

Phil 4260.185   Falco, Enrico de. La biografia di G.B. Vico. Roma, 1968.

Phil 3270.17.50   Falm, Leopold. De bezinning. Amsterdam, 1968.

Phil 5068.88   Fano, Giorgio. Neopositivismo, analisi del linguaggio e cibernetica. Torino, 1968.

Phil 2405.5.2   Farber, Marvin. Philosophic thought in France and the United States. 2. ed. Albany, 1968.

Phil 7150.70   Farber, Maurice. Theory of suicide. N.Y., 1968.

Phil 585.222   Farré, Luis. Antropología filosófica. Madrid, 1968.

Phil 4540.10   Favrhold, David. Filosofi og samfund. København, 1968.

Phil 4110.15.80   Fazio-Allmayer, Bruna. Esistenza e realtà nella fenomenologia di Vito Fazio-Allmayer. Bologna, 1968.

1968 - cont.

Phil 8050.91   Fazio-Allmayer, Bruna. Richerche di estetica e il guidizio stoico. Bologna, 1968.

Phil 3487.29   Fazio-Allmayer, Bruna. L'uomo nella storia in Kant. Bologna, 1968.

Phil 7069.68.35   Federmann, Reinhard. Botschaft aus dem Jenseits. Tübingen, 1968.

Phil 3450.19.1.2   Feick, Hildegard. Index zu Heideggers "Sein und Zeit". 2e Aufl. Tübingen, 1968.

Phil 5585.252   Fellows, Brian S. The discrimination process and development. 1. ed. Oxford, 1968.

Phil 4073.120.5   Femiano, Salvatore Beniamino. La metafisica di Tommaso Campanella. Milano, 1968.

Phil 5625.114   Ferster, Charles B. Behavior principles. N.Y., 1968.
VPhil 1705.13   Filipović, Vladimir. Novija filozofija Zapada i odabrani telestovi. Zagreb, 1968.

Phil 1955.6.235   Filograsso, Nando. Meditazioni deweyane. Urbino, 1968.
Phil 310.720   Filosofiia i nauchnyi kommunizm. Moskva, 1968.
Phil 8880.63   Finance, Joseph de. Grundlegung der Ethik. Freiburg, 1968.

Phil 3640.785   Fink, Eugen. Nietzsches Philosophie. 2e Aufl. Köln, 1968.
Phil 530.20.125   Firtel, Hilde. Dorothea von Montau. Freiburg in der Schweiz, 1968.

Phil 8092.13.10   Fischer, Ernst. Auf den Spuren der Wirklichkeit. Reinbek, 1968.
Phil 4809.393   Fischer, Josef L. Filosofické studie. Praha, 1968.
Phil 5585.312   Fisher, Gerald H. The frameworks for perceptual localization. Newcastle-upon-Tyne, 1968.

Phil 3425.656   Fleishmann, Eugène. La science universelle ou la logique de Hegel. Paris, 1968.

Phil 3450.19.435   Floestad, Guttorm. Heidegger. En innføring i hans filosofi. Oslo, 1968.

Phil 4976.5.80   Flores Caballero, Luis. Humanismo y revolución en América Latina; bosquejo de interpretación del pensamiento materialista de Antenor Orrego. Lima, 1968.

Phil 5627.268   Fobry, Joseph B. The pursuit of meaning. Boston, 1968.
Phil 5245.86   Fodor, Jerry A. Psychological explanation. N.Y., 1968.
Phil 8870.42   La fondazione del giudizio morale. Padova, 1968.
Phil 5875.62   Fonzi, Ada. Disegno e linguaggio al bambino. Torino, 1968.

Phil 8955.10   Fotion, Nicholas G. Moral situation. Yellow Springs, 1968.

Phil 5238.196.1   Fraisse, Paul. Experimental psychology. N.Y., 1968.
Phil 8430.60   Frances, Robert. Psychologie de l'esthétique. Paris, 1968.

Phil 4967.35   Franceschi, Alfredo. Escritos filosóficos. La Plata, 1968.

Phil 3487.30   Francke, Georg Samuel. Über die Eigenschaft der Analysis und der analytischen Methode in der Philosophie. Bruxelles, 1968.

Phil 5755.18   Franklin, Richard Langdon. Freewill and determinism: a study of rival conceptions of man. London, 1968.

Phil 3640.736   Frenzel, Ivo. Friedrich Nietzsche in Selbstzeugnissen und Bilddokumenten. Reinbek, 1968.

Phil 6992.4   Frétigny, Roger. L'imagerie mentale; introduction à l'onirothérapie. Genève, 1968.

Phil 6315.2.79.30   Freud, Sigmund. Brautbriefe. Frankfurt, 1968.
Phil 6315.2.66.10   Freud, Sigmund. Briefe 1873-1939. 2. Aufl. Frankfurt, 1968.

Phil 6315.2.26   Freud, Sigmund. Briefwechsel. Frankfurt, 1968.
Phil 6315.2.62.7   Freud, Sigmund. Delusion and dream, and other essays. Boston, 1968.

Phil 6315.19.41   Fromm, Erich. The heart of man. 1st ed. N.Y., 1968.
Phil 6978.5.5   Fryes, F.B.M. Fremdes unter uns. Meppel, 1968.
Phil 8955.13   Fuchs, Josef. Le renouveau de la théologie morale selon Vatican II. Paris, 1968.

Phil 805.25   Fuelleborn, Georg Gustav. Beträge zur Geschichte der Philosophie. pt.1-12. Bruxelles, 1968. 5v.

Phil 8955.11   Furfey, Paul Hanly. The morality gap. N.Y., 1968.
Phil 8624.105   The future as the presence of shared hope. N.Y., 1968.
Phil 8956.18   Gaboury, Placide. Un monde ambigu. Montréal, 1968.
Phil 1750.351.2   Gabriel, Leo. Existenzphilosophie. 2e Aufl. Wien, 1968.
Phil 1133.47   Gadamer, Hans G. Um die Begriffswelt der Vorsokratiker. Darmstadt, 1968.

Phil 5592.202   Gaestrin, Jan Emanuel. Den svårfångade intelligensen. 2. uppl. Stockholm, 1968.

Phil 9495.168.25   Gagey, Roland. La révolution sexuelle. Paris, 1968.
Phil 4752.2.190   Gaith, Jérome. Nicolas Berdiaeff. Beyrouth, 1968.
Phil 672.242   Gale, Richard. The language of time. London, 1968.
Phil 3826.15   Gallicet Calvetti, Carla. Spinoza. Milano, 1968.
Phil 4120.9.82   Gallo Galli. 2. ed. Torino, 1968.
Phil 623.48   Gambra Ciudad, Rafael. El silencio de Dios. Madrid, 1968.
Phil 5421.20.90   Gamm, Hans-Jochen. Aggression und Friedensfähigkeit in Deutschland. München, 1968.

Phil 3925.16.190   Ganguly, Sachindranath. Wittgenstein's Tractatus, a preliminary. Santiniketan, 1968.

Phil 181.160   Gans, Abraham. Pathologie en therapie der filosofie. Wassenaar, 1968.

Phil 5246.77.5   Garan, D.G. Relativity for psychology. N.Y., 1968.
Phil 7055.211   Garrett, Eileen Jeanette Lyttle. Many voices; the autobiography of a medium. N.Y., 1968.

Phil 7069.68.5   Gauld, Alan. The founders of psychical research. London, 1968.

Phil 8661.23   Gay, Peter. Deism, an anthology. Princeton, 1968.
Phil 7040.43   Gaylin, Willard. The meaning of despair. N.Y., 1968.
Phil 5016.4   Geach, Peter Thomas. A history of the corruptions of logic: an inaugural lecture. Leeds, 1968.

Phil 5279.25.2   Geer, Johannes Petrus van de. De mening van de psycholoog. 2. druk. Haarlem, 1968.

Phil 5350.5.5   Geist, Harold. The psychological aspects of the aging process with sociological implications. St. Louis, 1968.

Phil 8865.534   Geiushev, Ziiaddin B. Eticheskaia mysl' v Azerbaidzhane. Baku, 1968.

Phil 5246.78   Gernhammer, Vilhelm. Ånd og sjael; symboler og symbolik. v.1-2. Silkeborg, 1968.

Phil 9530.65   Getty, Jay Paul. The golden age. N.Y., 1968.
Phil 3280.60   Geulincx, A. Arnold Geulincs collegium oratorium i. e. nova methodus omnis generis orationes. Amsterdam, 1968.

Phil 9075.82   Geweten en vrijheid. Utrecht, 1968.
Phil 525.254   Ghose, Sisirkumar. Mystics and society; a point of view. N.Y., 1968.

Phil 4225.8.110   Giannuzzi, Eugenio. L'uomo e il suo destino. Cosenza, 1968.

Phil 4260.08   Gianturco, Elio. A selective bibliography of Vico scholarship, 1948-68. Firenze, 1968.

Phil 181.158   Giorda, Renato. Psicologia dell'avere. Roma, 1968.
Phil 8407.48   Giorgi, Rubina. Simbolo e schema. Padova, 1968.

1968 - cont.

Phil 6316.12.15   Glover, Edward. The birth of the ego; a nuclear hypothesis. N.Y., 1968.

Phil 6316.15.5   Goerres, Albert. An den Grenzen der Psychoanalyse. München, 1968.

Phil 8586.36.10   Gogarten, Friedrich. Die Frage nach Gott. Tübingen, 1968.
Phil 1730.24   Goldmann, Lucien. Der christliche Bürger und die Aufklärung. Neuwied, 1968.

Phil 525.256.2   González Arintero, Juan. La evolución mística en el desenvolvimiento y vitalidad de la Iglesia. 2. ed. Madrid, 1968.

Phil 2030.6.5A   Goodman, Nelson. Languages of art. Indianapolis, 1968.
Phil 2905.1.565   Gosztonyi, Alexander. Der Mensch und die Evolution; Teilhard de Chardins philosophische Anthropologie. München, 1968.

Phil 3085.10.81   Graaf, Bob de. Petrus Apherdianus, ludimagister ca. 1510-1580. Nieuwkoop, 1968.

Phil 7082.192   Graevenitz, Jutta von. Bedeutung und Deutung des Traumes in der Psychotherapie. Darmstadt, 1968.

Phil 3450.11.455   Granel, Gérard. Le sens du temps et de la perception chez E. Husserl. Paris, 1968.

Phil 181.156   Granger, Gilles Gaston. Essai d'une philosophie du style. Paris, 1968.

Phil 5425.108   Grant, Vernon W. Great abnormals; the pathological genius of Kafka, Van Gogh, Strindenberg and Poe. N.Y., 1968.

Phil 6980.335.20   Greenberg, Ira A. Psychodrama and audience attitude change. Beverly Hills, 1968.

NEDL Phil 181.150   Gregg, Richard B. What's it all about and what am I? N.Y., 1968.

Phil 8586.60   Grillo, Friedrich. Aphoristische Darstellung der Religion. Bruxelles, 1968.

Phil 7082.10   Grinstein, Alexander. On Sigmund Freud's dreams. Detroit, 1968.

Phil 181.152   Grlić, Danko. Zašto. Zagreb, 1968.
Phil 978.49.905   Grosse, Rudolf. Erlebte Pädagogik. Dornach, 1968.
Phil 5066.320   Grünberg, Teo. Sembolik mantik. Istanbul, 1968.
Phil 5216.5   Gučas, Alfonsas. Psichologijos raidci Lietuvoje. Vilnius, 1968.

Phil 5435.14   Guillaume, Paul. La formation des habitudes. Paris, 1968.
Phil 2406.6   Guittoy, Jean. Regards sur la pensée française, 1870-1940. Paris, 1968.

Phil 6956.17   Guntrip, Henry James Samuel. Schizoid phenomena, object relations and the self. London, 1968.

Phil 6980.346   Haakanson, Kaj. Psykisk sjukdom: illusioner och realiteter; en teoretisk studie. Uppsala, 1968.

Phil 8411.43.80   Haase, Rudolf. Hans Kayser. Basel, 1968.
Phil 5325.46   Håseth, Kjell Johan. Norske ord-assosiasjonsnormer. Oslo, 1968.

Phil 5643.150   Haber, Ralph Norman. Contemporary theory and research in visual perception. N.Y., 1968.

Phil 338.44   Habermas, Jürgen. Erkenntnis und Interesse. Frankfurt am Main, 1968.

Phil 574.6   Haering, Bernhard. The Christian existentialist. N.Y., 1968.

Phil 574.6.5   Haering, Bernhard. Personalismus in Philosophie und Theologie. München, 1968.

Phil 978.122   Hagmann, Diego. Antwort auf Lebensrätsel. Zürich, 1968.
Phil 5790.2.25   Hahn, Alois. Einstellungen zum Tod und ihre soziale Bedingtheit. Stuttgart, 1968.

Phil 182.101.10   Haldane, John Burdon Sanderson. Science and life. London, 1968.

Phil 9070.120   Halldén, Söken. Handbok för Tveksamma. Solna, 1968.
Phil 3552.484   Halz, Hans Heinz. Herr und Knecht bei Leibniz und Hegel. Berlin, 1968.

Phil 9500.10.5   Hárdi, István. Psychologie am Krankenbett. Budapest, 1968.

Phil 2725.35.110   Hardy, Gilbert G. La vocation de la liberté chez Louis Lavelle. Paris, 1968.

Phil 9245.130   Harper, Ralph. The path of darkness. Cleveland, 1968.
Phil 8408.45   Harries, Karsten. The meaning of modern art. Evanston, 1968.

Phil 5047.49   Hartnack, Justus. Logik. Klassik og moderne. København, 1968.

Phil 9450.62   Hauser, Richard. Was des Kaisers ist. 1. Aufl. Frankfurt, 1968.

Phil 5465.163   Havelka, Jaroslav. The nature of the creative process in art. The Hague, 1968.

Phil 8882.90   Hedenius, Ingemar. Sjn studier i praktish filosof. Uppsala, 1968.

Phil 8587.80   Heering, Herman Johan. Dogmatische verkenningen. 's-Gravenhage, 1968.

Phil 3425.13A   Hegel, Georg Wilhelm Friedrich. Gesammelte Werke. v.4,7. Hamburg, 1968. 2v.

Phil 3425.20.5   Hegel, Georg Wilhelm Friedrich. Hegel; highlights, an annotated selection. N.Y., 1968.

Phil 3425.52   Hegel, Georg Wilhelm Friedrich. Studienausgabe. Ausgewählt. Frankfurt, 1968. 3v.

Phil 3489.27.20   Heidegger, Martin. What is a thing? Chicago, 1968.
Phil 3450.19.36   Heidegger, Martin. What is called thinking? N.Y., 1968.
Phil 3450.19.430   Heidegger and the quest for truth. Chicago, 1968.
Phil 5867.10   Heidemann, Ingeborg. Der Begriff des Spieles und das ästhetische Weltbild in der Philosphie der Gegenwart [play]. Berlin, 1968.

Phil 8957.20   Heinen, Wilhelm. Liebe als sittliche Grundkraft und ihre Fehlformen. 3. Aufl. Basel, 1968.

Phil 3450.46   Heintel, Erich. Die beiden Labyrinthe der Philosophie. Wien, 1968.

Phil 5585.3.5A   Helmholtz, Hermann van. Helmholtz on perception; its physiology and development. N.Y., 1968.

Phil 3801.450.5   Hemmerle, Klaus. Gott und das Denken nach Schellings Spätphilosophie. Freiburg, 1968.

Phil 210.10   Henrichs, Norbert. Bibliographie der Hermeneutik und ihrer Anwendungs Gereiche seit Schleiermacher. Düsseldorf, 1968.

Phil 5066.282   Herbrand, Jacques. Écrits logiques. Paris, 1968.
Phil 3489.418   Hermann, István. Kant teleológiája. Budapest, 1968.
Phil 2880.8.230   Herra, Rafael Angel. Sartre y los prolegómenos a la antropología. Ciudad Universitaria, 1968.

Phil 1112.12   Hildebrandt, Kurt. Frühe griechische Denker. Bonn, 1968.
Phil 7082.20   Hill, Brian. Gates of horn and ivory. N.Y., 1968.
Phil 5635.17.5   Hiriartborde, Edmond. Les aptitudes rythmiques. Paris, 1968.

Phil 3805.235   Hirsch, Emanuel. Schleiermachers Christusglaube drei Studien. 1. Aufl. Gütalosh, 1968.

Phil 310.696.2   Historical materialism: basic problems. Moscow, 1968.
Phil 1112.10   Hoelscher, Vvo. Anfanchisches Fragen; Studien zur Frühen griechischen Philosophie. Göttingen, 1968.

1968 - cont.

Phil 5068.90   Hoffbauer, Johann Christoph. Versuch über die sicherste und leichteste Anwendung der Analysis in den philosophischen Wissenschaften (Leipzig). Bruxelles, 1968.

Phil 6317.52   Holmes, David S. Reviews of research in behavior pathology. N.Y., 1968.

Phil 3489.52   Holst, Johann Ludolf. Über das Fundament der gesammten Philosophie des Herrn Kant. Halle, 1791. Bruxelles, 1968.

Phil 2150.22.85   Holz, Hans Heinz. Utopie und Anarchismus; zur Kritik der kritischen Theorie H. Marcuses. Köln, 1968.

Phil 7162.267.1   Holzer, Hans W. ESP and you. 1st ed. N.Y., 1968.
Phil 7069.68.10   Holzer, Hans W. Ghosts of the Golden West. Indianapolis, 1968.

Phil 7069.68.30   Holzer, Hans W. The lively ghosts of Ireland. London, 1968.

Phil 7069.68.20   Holzer, Hans W. Psychic investigator. 1st ed. N.Y., 1968.
Phil 338.42   Holzkamp, Klaus. Wissenschaft als Handlung. Berlin, 1968.
Phil 3475.3.235   Hommel, Claus Uwe. Chiffer und Dogma. Zürich, 1968.
Phil 1750.367.5   Hommes, Jakob. Dialektik und Politik. 1e Aufl. Köln, 1968.

Phil 3425.660   Hondt, Jacques d'. Hegel en son temps, Berlin, 1818-1831. Paris, 1968.

Phil 3425.652   Hondt, Jacques d'. Hegel secret, recherches sur les sources cachées de la pensée de Hegel. Paris, 1968.

Phil 8408.54   Hopf, Andreas. Die Struktur des östhetischen Urteils. München, 1968.

Phil 3450.28.15   Horkheimer, Max. Kritische Theorie. Frankfurt, 1968. 2v.

Phil 5592.194   Horst, Paul. Personality; measurement of dimensions. 1. ed. San Francisco, 1968.

Phil 3808.236   Hoyack, Louis. Schopenhauer, waarheid en dwaling. Deventer, 1968.

Phil 4812.457.20   Hrušovský, Igor. Kapitoly z téorie vedy. Bratislava, 1968.

Phil 338.43   Hubenko, Volodymer I. Znannia i peretvorennia diistnosti. Kyiv, 1968.

Phil 5876.22   Hudson, Liam. Frames of mind. London, 1968.
Phil 3808.242   Hübscher, Arthur. Schopenhauer-Bildnisse. Frankfurt, 1968.

Phil 8662.30   Humanism, atheism; principles and practice. Moscow, 1968?
Phil 2050.275   Hume and present day problems; the symposia read at the joint session of the Aristotelian Society, the Scots Philosophical Club and the Mind Association at Edinburgh, July 7th-10th, 1939. N.Y., 1968.

Phil 9070.126   Husén, Torsten. Livsåskådning och religion. Stockholm, 1968.

Phil 8408.48   Hussain, Fakhir. Le jugement esthétique. Paris, 1968.
Phil 3450.11.60   Husserl, Edmund. Briefe an roman ingarden. Den Haag, 1968.

Phil 5047.11.3   Husserl, Edmund. Logische Untersuchungen. v. 1-2, pt. 1-2. Tübingen, 1968[1913]. 3v.

Phil 310.677   Iakhot, Ovshii O. Ocherk marksistskoi filosofii. Moskva, 1968.

Phil 4260.215   Iannizzotto, Matteo. L'empirismo nella gnoseologia di Giambattista Vico. Padova, 1968.

Phil 4769.6.84   Iaroshevskii, Mikhail G. Ivan Mikhailovich Sechenov 1825-1905. Leningrad, 1968.

VPhil 8430.58   Iastrebova, Nataliia A. Esteticheski paraleli. Sofiia, 1968.

Phil 585.266   Il'enkov, Eval'd V. Ob idolakh i idealakh. Moskva, 1968.
Phil 8588.4   Immanuel, ein Buch für Christum und Juden. Bruxelles, 1968.

Phil 183.8   Incardona, Nunzio. Radicalità e filosofía. Palermo, 1968.
Phil 4803.462.55   Ingarden, Roman. Vom Erkennen des literarischen Kunstwerks. Tübingen, 1968.

Phil 6949.368   International Colloquium of Psychopathology of Expression, 4th, Washington, 1966. Psychiatry and art. Basel, 1968.

Phil 70.120   International Congress of Philosophy. Beiträge der bulgarischen Teilnehmer an dem XIV. Wien, 1968.

Phil 70.86.10   International Institute of Philosophy. Démonstration, vérification, justification. Liège, 1968.

Phil 5545.254.4   International Interdisciplinary Conference on Learning, Remembering and Forgetting. Experience and capacity; proceedings. N.Y., 1968.

Phil 3552.7   Internationaler Leibniz-Kongress. Der Internationale Leibniz-Kongress in Hannover. Hannover, 1968.

Phil 5870.60   Isaacs, Susan (Fairhurst). The nursery years. N.Y., 1968.
Phil 4710.153   Istoriia filosofii v SSSR. v.1- Moskva, 1968- 4v.
Phil 672.264   Jacobelli Isoldi, Angela Maria. Tempo e significato. Roma, 1968.

Phil 1020.65   Jad'an, Fahme. L'influence du stoicisme sur la pensée musulmane. Beyrauth, 1968.

Phil 5249.32   Jaeger, Marc A. Geist und Seele im technischen Zeitalter. Zürich, 1968.

Phil 1114.5.2   Jaeger, Werner W. The theology of the early Greek philosophers. London, 1968.

Phil 680.5   Jaeggi, Urs. Ordnung und Chaos. Frankfurt, 1968.
Phil 6319.1.270   Jaffé, Aniela. Aus Leben und Werkstatt von C.G. Jung. Zürich, 1968.

Phil 184.3.30.10   James, W. Memories and studies. N.Y., 1968.
Phil 6319.15   Janse de Jonge, Adriaan Leendert. Psychopathologie en mensbeschouwing. Kampen, 1968.

Phil 809.10   Jaspers, Karl. Aneignung und Polemik. München, 1968.
Phil 8664.9   Javaux, J. Prouver Dieu? Paris, 1968.
Phil 8612.80   Johann, Horst Theodor. Trauer und Trost. München, 1968.
Phil 2075.10   Johann, Robert O. Building the human. N.Y., 1968.
Phil 8430.62   John, Erhard. Probleme der marxistisch-leninistischen Asthetik. Halle, 1968.

Phil 5500.60   Johnsen, Erik. Studies in multiobjective decision models. Lund, 1968.

Phil 5049.28   Johnston, Frederick S. The logic of relationship. N.Y., 1968.

Phil 8959.6   Jonsen, Albert R. Responsibility in modern religious ethics. Washington, 1968.

Phil 2340.10.230   Jordan, Martin. New shapes of reality: aspects of A.N. Whitehead's philosophy. London, 1968.

Phil 5249.31   Jordan, Nehemiah. Themes in speculative psychology. London, 1968.

Phil 5249.30   Jourard, Sidney Marshall. Disclosing man to himself. Princeton, 1968.

Phil 3552.480   Journées, Leibniz. Leibniz, 1646-1716, aspects de l'homme et de l'oeuvre. Paris, 1968.

Phil 8664.10   Jüchen, Aurel von. Atheismus in West und Ost. 1. Aufl. Berlin, 1968.

Phil 6319.1.255   Jung, C.G. Analytical psychology: its theory and practice. London, 1968.

Phil 5066.284   Kac, Mark. Mathematics and logic. N.Y., 1968.

1968 - cont.

Phil 5374.265   Kalmar, Jacques M. Frontières de l'homme. Neuchâtel, 1968.

Phil 3480.34.5   Kant, Immanuel. Gedanken von der wahren Schätzung des lebendigen Kräfte...Mechäniker. Amsterdam, 1968.

Phil 3480.69.5.10   Kant, Immanuel. Kant's cosmogony, as in his essay on The retardation of the rotation of the earth and his national history and theory of the heavens. N.Y., 1968.

Phil 3480.130   Kant, Immanuel. Selected pre-critical writings and correspondence. Manchester, 1968.

Phil 3480.75.30   Kant, Immanuel. Über den Gemeinspruch: Das mag in der Theorie richtig sein taugt. Frankfurt, 1968.

Phil 310.543   Kaprielian, Henri. Osnovy marksistskoi logiki. Erevan, 1968.

Phil 5251.41.90   Kaufmann, Pierre. Kurt Lewin, une théorie du change dans les sciences de l'homme. Paris, 1968.

Phil 3640.368.4   Kaufmann, Walter Arnold. Nietzsche: philosopher, psychologist, antichrist. 3. ed. Princeton, N.J., 1968.

Phil 210.65   Kaulbach, Friedrich. Philosophie der Beschreibung. Köln, 1968.

Phil 5875.70   Kay, William. Moral development: a psychological study of moral growth from childhood to adolescence. London, 1968.

Phil 2520.187.2   Keeling, Stanley V. Descartes. 2d ed. London, 1968.
Phil 2520.375   Kenny, Anthony. Descartes; a study of his philosophy. N.Y., 1968.

Phil 1750.805   Ketcham, Charles Brown. The search for meaningful existence. N.Y., 1968.

Phil 810.17   Keyserling, Arnold. Geschichte der Denkstile. Wien, 1968.
RRC   Phil 6980.383   Kiev, Ari. Psychiatry in the Communist world. N.Y., 1968.
Phil 8980.485   Kiknadze, Dmitrii A. Potrebnosti, povedenie, vospitanie. Moskva, 1968.

Phil 310.671   Kim, Makvim P. Istoriia i kommunizm. Moskva, 1968.
Phil 6140.20   Klein, Donald Charles. Community dynamics and mental health. N.Y., 1968.

Phil 6320.11.19   Klein, M. Contributions to psycho-analysis, 1921-1945. London, 1968.

Phil 3270.12.105   Klemke, E.D. Essays on Frege. Urbana, 1968.
Phil 5360.30   Klerk, Lein Friedrich Wolfgang de. Probabilistic concept learning. Proefschrift. Leiden? 1968.

Phil 4803.755.80   Kliauchenia, Aliaksandr S. Stefan Rudnianskii. Minsk, 1968.

Phil 5020.5.10   Kneale, William Calvert. The development of logic. Oxford, 1968.

Phil 2493.100   Knight, Isabel F. The geometric spirit; the Abbe de Condillac and the French Enlightenment. New Haven, 1968.

Phil 5790.10   Knight, James Allen. For the love of money. Philadelphia, 1968.

Phil 8885.52   Knox, Malcolm. Action. London, 1968.
Phil 1540.92   Koelner Mediaevistentagung. Universalismus und Partikularismus in Mittelalter. Berlin, 1968.

Phil 396.22   Kofler, Leo. Perspektiven des revolutionären Humanismus. Reinbek, 1968.

Phil 850.45   Koje've, Alexandre. Essai d'une histoire raisonnée de la philosophie païenne. Paris, 1968.

Phil 600.59.5   Kolakowski, Leszek. The alienation of reason; a history of positivist thought. Garden City, N.Y., 1968.

Phil 5585.260   Kolers, Paul A. Recognizing patterns; studies in living and automatic systems. Cambridge, 1968.

Phil 8411.40   Kollen, Horace Meyer. Liberty, laughter, and tears. De Kalb, 1968.

Phil 8171.100   Konan, Uladzimir M. Razvitstsio estetychnai dumki u Belarusi. Minsk, 1968.

VPhil 1135.191   Kornatowski, Wiktor. Zarys driejów mysli politycznej starożytnosii. Wyd. 1. Warsawa, 1968.

Phil 730.35   Korotkova, Galina P. Printsipy tselostnosti. Leningrad, 1968.

Phil 4803.497.30   Kotarbiński, Tadeusz. Hasło dobrej roboty. Wyd. 1. Warszawa, 1968.

Phil 5875.75   Koupernir, Cyrille. Développement neuro-psychique du nourrisson. 1. ed. Paris, 1968.

Phil 2905.1.560   Kraft, Ralph Wayne. The relevance of Teilhard. Notre Dame, 1968.

Phil 5068.16.2   Kraft, Viktor. Der Wiener Kreis. Der Ursprung des Neopositivismus. Ein Kapitel der jüngsten Philosophiegeschichte. 2. Aufl. Wien, 1968.

Phil 9245.132   Kramp, Willy. Uber die Freude; zwei Betrachtungen. Hamburg, 1968.

Phil 3195.6.190   Krausser, Peter. Kritik der endlichen Vernunft. Frankfurt, 1968.

Phil 8520.60   Krieger, Evelina. Grenzwege. Freiburg, 1968.
Phil 8400.55   Kritika sovremennoi burzhuaznoi estetiki. Moskva, 1968.
Phil 291.18   Kroeber, Günter. Der Gesetzesbegriff in der Philosophie und den Einzelwissenschaften. Berlin, 1968.

Phil 6060.86   Kroeber-Keneth, Ludwig. L. Kroeber-Keneth's Buch der Graphologie. 1. Aufl. Düsseldorf, 1968.

Phil 8590.40   Kroeger, Athanasius. Mensch und Person. Recklinghausen, 1968.

Phil 8835.2.6   Kropotkin, Petr Alekseevich. Ethics; origin and development. N.Y., 1968.

Phil 665.108   Krueger, Walter. Metaphysische Praxis als Schlüssel zur geistigen Welt. Freiburg, 1968.

Phil 3528.58   Krug, Wilhelm Traugott. Briefe über die Wissenschaftslehre. Bruxelles, 1968.

Phil 3528.55.2   Krug, Wilhelm Traugott. Der Widerstreit der Vernunft mit sich Selbst in der Versöhnungslehre. Bruxelles, 1968.

Phil 8520.70   Kryvelev, Iosif A. Religioznaia kartina mira i ee bogoslovskaia modernizatsiia. Moskva, 1968.

Phil 310.650.3   Kubeš, Miloslav. Clovek, svět a filosofie. Vyd. 3. Praha, 1968.

Phil 8592.122.25   Kucherenko, Gennadii S. Sud'ba "Zaveshchaniia" zhana mel'e v XVIII veke. Moskva, 1968.

Phil 341.39   Kuemmel, Friedrich. Platon und Hegel zur ontologischen Begründung des Zirkels in der Erkenntnis. Tübingen, 1968.

Phil 5425.112   Kuhn-Foelix, August. Vom Wesen des genialen Menschen. Zürich, 1968.

Phil 1020.4.41   Kuksewicz, Zdzislaw. De siger de Bredant à Jacques de Plaisance. Wroclaw, 1968.

Phil 8400.57   Kul'tura chuvstv. Moskva, 1968.
Phil 8411.39   Kuncheva, L.I. Esteticheskoe i eticheskoe v zhizni i v iskusstve. Moskva, 1968.

Phil 400.121.5   Kursanov, Georgii A. Sovremennia idealisticheskaia gnoseologiia. Moskva, 1968.

Phil 3549.24   Kuypers, Karel. Verspreide Geschriften. Assen, 1968. 2v.

Phil 5066.277   Kuzichev, Aleksandr S. Diagrammy Venna. Moskva, 1968.
Phil 2750.20.82   Kwant, Remigius Cornelius. Mens en expressie, in het licht van de wijsbegeerte van Merleau-Ponty. Utrecht, 1968.

Chronological Listing

Phil 5520.656   Kybernetische Analysen geistigen Prozesse. Berlin, 1968.

Phil 3425.675   Labarriere, Pierre Jean. Structures et mouvement dialectique dans la phenoménologie de l'esprit de Hegel. Paris, 1968.

Phil 5520.525   Lacan, Jacques. The language of the self. Baltimore, 1968.

Phil 3450.19.450   Laffoucrière, Odette. Le destin de la pensée et la mort de Dieu selon Heidegger. La Haye, 1968.

Phil 1750.115.130   Landgrebe, Ludwig. Phänomenologie und Geschichte. 1. Aufl. Gütersloh, 1968.

Phil 5871.50   Landolf, Peter. Kind ohne Vater. Bern, 1968.

Phil 5790.30   Langenheder, Werner. Ansatz zu einer allgemeinen Verhaltenstheorie in der Sozialwissenschaften. Köln, 1968.

Phil 2225.18   Langford, Thomas A. Intellect and hope; essays in the thought of Michael Polanyi. Durham, 1968.

Phil 7072.15   Langley, Noel. Edgar Cayce on reincarnation. N.Y., 1968.

Phil 3640.765   Lannoy, Joris C. Dionysos of God. Brugge, 1968.

Phil 720.90   Lanteri-Laura, Georges. Structures subjectives du champ transcendantal. Thèse. Paris, 1968.

Phil 4957.25   Larrayo, Francisco. Historía de las doctrinas filosóficas en Latinoamérica. 1. ed. México, 1968.

Phil 525.264.1   Laski, Marghanita. Ecstasy; a study of some secular and religious experiences. N.Y., 1968.

Phil 3585.12.90   Lassahn, Rudolf. Das Selbsterständnis der Pädagogik Theodor Litts. Wuppertal, 1968.

Phil 978.96.5   Lauer, Hans Erhard. Der Mensch in den Entscheidungen unseres Jahrhunderts. Freiburg, 1968.

Phil 5585.290   Laurondeau, Monique. La premières notions spatiales de l'enfant. Neuchâtel, 1968.

Phil 6021.2.18   Lavater, Johann Caspar. Physiognomische Fragmente zur Beförderung der Menschenkenntnis und Menschenliebe. Zürich, 1968- 4v.

Phil 5590.422.5   Lazarus, Richard. Patterns of adjustment and human effectiveness. N.Y., 1968.

Phil 186.120.4   Lazerowitz, M. Philosophy and illusion. London, 1968.

Phil 5374.234.30   Leary, Timothy Francis. High priest. N.Y., 1968.

Phil 6155.4.5   Leary, Timothy Francis. The politics of ecstasy. N.Y., 1968.

Phil 2475.1.480   Lebacqz, Joseph. De l'identique au multiple. Québec, 1968.

Phil 623.1.7   Lecky, W.E.H. History of the rise and influence of the spirit of rationalism in Europe. N.Y., 1968. 2v.

Phil 6321.55   Leclaire, Serge. Psychanalyser, un essai sur l'ordre de l'inconscient et la pratique de la lettre. Paris, 1968.

Phil 5643.165   Leeuwerberg, Emanuel Laurens Jan. Structural information of visual pattern. The Hague, 1968.

Phil 6155.26   Legewie, Heiner. Persönlichkeitstheorie und Psychopharmaka. Meisenheim, 1968.

Phil 1750.166.280   Legitimo, Gianfranco. Nuovo umanesimo sociale. Torino, 1968.

Phil 3552.35   Leibniz, Gottfried Wilhelm. General investigations concerning the analysis of concepts and truths. Athens, 1968.

Phil 5421.25.50   Lemaire, Ton. De tederheid. Gedachten over de liefde. Utrecht, 1968.

Phil 5130.2   Lenk, Hans. Kritik der logischen Konstanten. Berlin, 1968.

Phil 6021.15   Leonhard, Karl. Der menschliche Ausdruck. Leipzig, 1968.

Phil 5330.36   Leplat, Jacques. Attention et incertitude dans les travaux de surveillance et d'inspection. Paris, 1968.

Phil 2725.25.20   LeSenne, René. LeSenne ou le Combat pour la spiritualisation. Paris, 1968.

Phil 5520.550   Levin, Poul. Semantik. København, 1968.

Phil 4710.159   Levitskii, Sergei A. Ocherki po istorii russkoi filosofskoi i obshchestvennoi mysli. Frankfurt, 1968.

Phil 8886.84   Lévy-Valensi, Eliane Amado. Le temps dans la vie morale. Paris, 1968.

Phil 7082.142.5   Lewis, Hywel David. Dreaming and experience. London, 1968.

Phil 2255.1.95   Lewis, John. Bertrand Russell: philosopher and humanist. London, 1968.

Phil 1730.36   Leyden, Wolfgang von. Seventeenth-century metaphysics. N.Y., 1968.

Phil 9513.42   Lichnost i sotsial'no-nravstvennye otnosheniia vobshchestve. Photoreproduction. Pskov, 1968.

Phil 5590.475   Lichnost' pri sotsializme. Moskva, 1968.

Phil 5590.485   Lidz, Theodore. The person: his development throughout the life cycle. N.Y., 1968.

Phil 7069.68.65   Lietaert, Peerbolte, Maarten. Psychocybernetica. Amsterdam, 1968.

Phil 2070.145.5   Linschoten, Johannes. On the way toward a phenomenological psychology; the psychology of William James. Pittsburgh, 1968.

Phil 4803.468.80   Lipkowski, Otton. Józefa Joteyko. Wyd. 1. Warszawa, 1968.

Phil 5548.120   Litwin, George Henry. Motivation and organizational climate. Boston, 1968.

Phil 4225.15.90   Lizzio, Maria. Marxismo e metafisica. Catania, 1968.

Phil 6121.50   Locke, Don. Myself and others; a study in our knowledge of minds. Oxford, 1968.

Phil 2120.15   Loewenberg, Jacob. Thrice-born. N.Y., 1968.

Phil 7159.260   Logan, Daniel. The reluctant prophet. 1st ed. Garden City, N.Y., 1968.

Phil 5066.280   Logic Colloquium, 11th, Hannover, 1966. Contributions to mathematical logic; proceedings of the logic colloquium, Hannover, 1966. Amsterdam, 1968.

Phil 310.700   Lojacono, Giorgio. L'ideología marxista. Roma, 1968. 3v.

Phil 3475.3.215   Long, Eugene Thomas. Jaspers and Bultmann. Durham, 1968.

Phil 1740.28   López Quintás, Alfonso. Pensadores cristianos contemporáneos. v.1- Madrid, 1968-

Phil 4762.1.36   Losskii, Nikolai Onufrievich. Vospominaniia. München, 1968.

Phil 3585.28.5   Lotz, Johannes Baptist. Ich, du, wir. 1. Aufl. Frankfurt, 1968.

Phil 8591.87   Lotz, Johannes Baptist. Neue Erkenntnisprobleme in Philosophie und Theologie. Freiburg, 1968.

Phil 5535.30   Lovejoy, Elijah. Attention in discrimination learning; a point of view and a theory. San Francisco, 1968.

Phil 5821.16   Lovenz, Konrad Zacharias. Antriebe tierischen und menschlichen Verhaltens. München, 1968.

Phil 2905.1.180.7   Lubac, Henri de. L'éternel féminin, étude sur un texte du père Teilhard de Chardin. Paris, 1968.

Phil 2905.1.180.5.2   Lubac, Henri de. La prière du père Teilhard de Chardin. Paris, 1968.

Phil 3246.340   Ludwig, Karl Friedrich Ernst. Freymüthige Gedanken über Fichte's Appellation gegen die Anklage des Atheismus und deren Veranlassung. Bruxelles, 1968.

Phil 5525.68   Luk, Oleksandr N. O chuvstve iumora i ostroumii. Moskva, 1968.

Phil 5535.20   Lunzer, Eric Anthony. Development in learning. London, 1968- 3v.

Phil 5545.235   Luriiâ, Aleksandr R. The mind of a mnemonist. N.Y., 1968.

Phil 2055.7.90   Luther, A.R. Existence as dialectical tension. The Hague, 1968[1969]

Phil 310.803   MacIntyre, Alasdair C. Marxism and Christianity. N.Y., 1968.

Phil 7069.68.25   MacKenzie, Andrew. Frontiers of the unknown: the insights of psychical research. London, 1968.

Phil 2150.13.6   McKeon, Richard P. Thought, action and passion. Chicago, 1968.

Phil 2045.142   McNeilly, F.S. The anatomy of Leviathan. London, 1968.

Phil 3832.19   McShea, Robert J. The political philosophy of Spinoza. N.Y., 1968.

Phil 4363.12   Madariaga, Salvador de. Portrait of a man standing. London, 1968.

Phil 1812.20   Madden, Edward Harry. Civil disobedience and moral law in nineteenth century American philosophy. Seattle, 1968.

Phil 3246.330   Mader, Johann Karl. Fichte, Feierbach, Marx. Wien, 1968.

Phil 5252.175   Madsen, K.B. Almen psykologi. 3. opl. v.1-2. København, 1968.

Phil 5548.95.4   Madsen, Kaj Berg. Theories of motivation; a comparative study. 4. ed. Kent, Ohio, 1968.

Phil 1712.27   Maier, Anneliese. Zwei Untersuchungen zur nachscholastischen Philosophie. 2e Aufl. Roma, 1968.

Phil 293.8.8   Maillet, Benoît de. Telliamed. Urbana, 1968.

Phil 8702.36   Mairlot, Édouard. Science et foi chrétienne. Bruxelles, 1968.

Phil 3850.56   Malan, Daniel Johannes. 'n Kritiese studie van die wysbegeerte van H.G. Stoker vanuit die standpunt van H. Dooye weerd. Amsterdam, 1968.

Phil 343.56   Mamardashvili, M.K. Formy i soderzhanie mephleniia. Moskva, 1968.

Phil 9070.118   Mandelbaum, Bernard. Choose life. N.Y., 1968.

Phil 1865.196   Manning, David John. The mind of Jeremy Bentham. London, 1968.

Phil 8612.64   Man's concern with death. London, 1968.

Phil 4582.4.100   Marc-Wogan, Konrad. Studier till Axel Hägerströms filosofi. Stockholm, 1968.

Phil 3120.30.185   Marcel, Gabriel. Martin Buber. L'homme et le philosophe. Bruxelles, 1968.

Phil 2750.19.43   Marcel, Gabriel. Pour une sagesse tragique et son au-delà. Paris, 1968.

Phil 5421.10.25   Marchisa, Ernestina. Ansietà e carenze affettive. Napoli, 1968.

Phil 2150.22.38   Marcuse, Herbert. Negations; essays in critical theory. Boston, 1968.

Phil 6322.55   Marcuse, Herbert. Psychoanalyse und Politik. Frankfurt, 1968.

Phil 5762.36   Margenau, Henry. Scientific indeterminism and human freedom. Latrobe, Pa., 1968.

Phil 4363.7.20   Marias Aguilera, Julián. Nuevos ensayos de filosofía. 2. ed. Madrid, 1968.

Phil 2750.11.54.5   Maritain, Jacques. Integral humanism. N.Y., 1968.

Phil 2750.11.44.2   Maritain, Jacques. The peasant of the Garonne. 1. éd. N.Y., 1968.

Phil 310.587.3   Marksistsko-leninskaia filosofiia. 3. Izd. Moskva, 1968.

Phil 5535.24   Marnet, Otto. Soziales Lernen; das Problem der Lertheorien in der Sozialpsychologie. Zürich, 1968.

Phil 2115.215   Martin, Charles Burton. Locke and Berkeley: a collection of ciritical essays. London, 1968.

Phil 5548.100.2   Maslow, Abraham Harold. Toward a psychology of being. 2. ed. Princeton, 1968.

Phil 5593.68   Matejek, Georg. Zur Frage quantitativer und qualitativer Änderungen einiger Rorschach-Kategorien im Schulalter. Weinheim, 1968.

Phil 310.517   Matetialisticheskaia dialektika i metody estestvennykh nauk. Moskva, 1968.

Phil 2750.32.35   Mayer, Charles Leopold. Man faces his destiny. London, 1968.

Phil 2045.160   Mayer-Tasch, Peter Cornelius. Autonomie und Autorität; Rousseau in den Spuren von Hobbes? Neuwied, 1968.

Phil 2150.15.30   Mead, George Herbert. George Herbert Mead. N.Y., 1968.

Phil 5590.483   Mehrabian, Albert. An analysis of personality theories. Englewood Cliffs, N.J., 1968.

Phil 4170.12.10   Mei, Flavio. Eroicità ed ereticalità della filosofia. Milano, 1968.

Phil 6319.1.209   Meier, Carl A. Lehrbuch der komplexen Psychologie C.G. Jungs. Zürich, 1968.

Phil 3625.11   Meinong, Alexius. Gesamtausgabe. Herausgeber: Rudolf Haller und R. Kindinger. Graz, 1968- 3v.

Phil 165.434A   Mélanges à la mémoire de Charles de Koninck. Québec, 1968.

Phil 2280.22.80   Melchert, Norman P. Realism, materialism, and the mind: the philosophy of Roy Wood Sellars. Springfield, Ill., 1968.

Phil 3160.3.98   Melher, Jehuda. Hermann Cohen's philosophy of Judaism. N.Y., 1968.

Phil 2225.5.160   Mel'vil', Iurii K. Charlz Pirs i pragmatizm. Moskva, 1968.

Phil 343.60   Mercier, André. Erkenntnis und Wirklichkeit. Bern, 1968.

Phil 1730.26   Merker, Nicolao. L'illuminismo tedesco. Bari, 1968.

Phil 2750.20.50   Merleau-Ponty, Maurice. Résumés de cours, Collège de France, 1952-1960. Paris, 1968.

Phil 2750.20.55   Merleau-Ponty, Maurice. L'union de l'âme et du corps chez Malebranche, Biran et Bergson. Paris, 1968.

Phil 2750.20.45   Merleau-Ponty, Maurice. The visible and the invisible. Evanston, 1968.

Phil 4363.14   Mestre, Antonio. Ilustración y reforma de la Iglesia. Valencia, 1968.

Phil 5649.32   Metheny, Eleanor. Movement and meaning. N.Y., 1968.

Phil 310.674.2   Metodicheskoe posobre po filosofii. Izd. 2. Moskva, 1968.

Phil 585.285   Metzger, Arnold. Existentialismus und Sozialismus. Pfulingen, 1968.

Phil 5467.8   Miami. University. Symposium on Social Behavior, 1st, 1967. Social facilitation and imitative behavior. Boston, 1968.

Phil 5625.124   Miami Symposium on the Prediction of Behavior. Aversive stimulation. Coral Gables, Fla., 1968.

Phil 2750.29.30   Michaud, Humbert. Analyse de la révolution moderne. Paris, 1968.

Phil 4225.8.75   Michele F. Sciacca in occasione del trenta anno di cattedra universitaria, 1938-1968. Milano, 1968.

Chronological Listing

Phil 3625.2.6   Michelet, K.L. Naturrecht oder Rechts-Philosophie als die praktische Philosophie. Berlin, 1866. Bruxelles, 1968. 2v.

Phil 5725.5   Międzynarodowego Sympozjum Poświęcone Psychologia Rozumienia, Krakow, 1965. Psychologia rozumienia. Warszawa, 1968.

Phil 308.6   Migliorini, Ermanno. Critica, oggetto e logica. Firenze, 1968.

Phil 8980.572.5   Mikhalevich, Aleksandr Vl. Sporiu. Moskva, 1968.

Phil 5875.80   Millar, Susanna. The psychology of play. Harmondsworth, 1968.

Phil 1750.166.255   Millas, Orlando. El humanismo científico de los comunistas. Santiago de Chile, 1968.

Phil 8702.34   Miller, Samuel Howard. Religion in a technical age. Cambridge, 1968.

Phil 6322.60   Minkowski, Eugène. Le temps vécu. Neuchâtel, 1968.

Phil 3494.66.2   Miotti, Peter. Uber die Nichtigkeit der Kantische Grundsätze in der Philosophie...Logik von Professor Kreil. Facsimile. Bruxelles, 1968.

Phil 5590.457.5   Mischel, Walter. Personality and assessment. N.Y., 1968.

Phil 8592.119   Mitchell, Basil. Neutrality and commitment: an inaugural lecture delivered before the University of Oxford on 13 May, 1968. Oxford, 1968.

Phil 6322.50   Modell, Arnold H. Object love and reality. N.Y., 1968.

Phil 8667.45   Moderner Atheismus und Moral. Freiburg, 1968.

Phil 402.8   Mongardini, Carlo. Storia del concetto di ideologia. Roma, 1968.

Phil 5421.20.45   Montagn, Ashley. Man and aggression. London, 1968.

Phil 4371.10   Montseny y Carret, Juan. La evolución de la filosofía en España. Barcelona 1968.

Phil 8667.40   Morel, Georges. Problèmes actuels de religion. Paris, 1968.

Phil 187.182   Moretti-Costanzi, Teodorico. L'ora della filosofia. Bologna, 1968.

Phil 2150.23   Morgan, Arthur Ernest. Observations. Yellow Springs, 1968.

Phil 575.268   Morgan, George W. The human predicament and dissolution and wholeness. Providence, 1968.

Phil 735.272   Moritz, Manfred. Inledning i värdeteori. 2. uppl. Lund, 1968.

Phil 3925.16.160   Morrison, James. Meaning and truth in Wittgenstein's Tractatus. The Hague, 1968.

Phil 8887.127   Moser, Shia. Absolutism and relativism in ethics. Springfield, 1968.

Phil 5374.275   Moutada, Leo. Über die Funktion der Mobilität in der geistigen Entwicklung. Stuttgart, 1968.

Phil 1140.10   Movia, Giancarlo. Anima e intelletto. Padova, 1968.

Phil 5252.162   Mucchielli, Roger. Introduction à la psychologie structurale. 2. ed. Bruxelles, 1968.

Phil 1750.107.2   Muck, Otto. The transcendental method. N.Y., 1968.

Phil 5875.64   Muehling, Ursel. Erstellung eines Projektiven Verfahrens zur psychologischen Untersuchung nichtsprechender und hochgradig sprechbehinderter Kinder. Köln, 1968.

Phil 3850.1.105   Müller, Gotthold. Identität und Immanenz; zur Genese der Theologie von David Friedrich Strauss, eine theologie- und philosophiegeschichtliche Studie. Zürich, 1968.

Phil 9495.168.15   Müller, Michael. Grundlagen der Katholischen Sexualethik. Regensburg, 1968.

Phil 5875.140   Mueller, Rudolf. Entwicklung des sozialen Wertbewusstseins; eine empirische Untersuchung des sittlichen Beuresstseins bei Kindern und Jugendlichen. Thesis. Weinheim, 1968.

Phil 1750.166.235   Mukerjee, Radhakamal. The way of humanism, East and West. Bombay, 1968.

Phil 8592.117   Munson, Thomas N. Reflective theology; philosophical orientations in religion. New Haven, 1968.

Phil 5222.16   Murphy, Gardner. Asian psychology. N.Y., 1968.

Phil 5252.69.20   Murphy, Gardner. Encounter with reality. Boston, 1968.

Phil 5252.69.25   Murphy, Gardner. Psychological thought from Pythagoras to Freud. 1st. ed. N.Y., 1968.

Phil 6957.30   Myers, Jerome Keeley. A decade later: a follow-up of social class and mental illness. N.Y., 1968.

Phil 5070.26   Mynarek, Hubertus. Der Mensch, das Wesen der Zukunft. München, 1968.

Phil 1713.4.2   Naess, Arne. Four modern philosophers. Chicago, 1968.

Phil 645.55   Naess, Arne. Scepticism. London, 1968[1969]

Phil 8414.8.11   Nahm, Milton Charles. Aesthetic experience and its presuppositions. N.Y., 1968.

Phil 8703.5   Nasr, Segyed Hossein. The encounter of man and nature; the spiritual crisis of modern man. London, 1968.

Phil 8888.20   Nassent, Georges. Joie, souffrance et vie morale. Paris, 1968.

Phil 8668.10   Nastol'naia Kniga ateista. Moskva, 1968.

Phil 510.157   Naumenko, Lev K. Monizm kak printsip dialekticheskoi logiki. Alma-Ata, 1968.

Phil 6990.3.106   Neame, Alan. The happening at Lourdes. London, 1968.

Phil 310.676   Nedeljković, Dušan. Humanizam Marksove dijalektike i dijalektike humanizma danas. Beograd, 1968.

Phil 3665.8.30   Neeb, Johann. System der kritischen Philosophie auf den Satz des Bewustseyns gegründet. Bruxelles, 1968. 2v.

Phil 5790.25   Neff, Walter Scott. Work and human behavior. 1. ed. N.Y., 1968.

Phil 4170.3.86   Negrelli, Giorgio. Storicismo e moderatismo nel pensiero politico di Angelo Camillo de Meis. Milano, 1968.

Phil 3495.20.2   Negri, Antimo. La comunità estetica in Kant. 2. ed. Bari, 1968.

Phil 310.722   Nekotorye aktual'nye problemy marksistsko-leninskoi filosofii. Perm', 1968.

Phil 5590.566   Nekotorye problemy sormirovaniia lichnosti. Krasnoiarsk, 1968.

Phil 3665.9.30   Neuhaeusler, Anton Otto. Fragmente keines Vorsokratikers. München, 1968.

Phil 23.11.5   The new scholasticism. Index. v.1-40. Washington, 1968.

Phil 8575.7   New themes in Christian philosophy. Notre Dame, 1968.

Phil 8400.52   Die nicht mehr schönen Künste; Grenzphänomene des Ästhetischen. München, 1968.

Phil 3665.7.30   Nicolai, Friedrich. Philosophische Abhandlungen. Bruxelles, 1968. 2v.

Phil 5253.20   Nicoletti, Ivan. Analisi quantitativa e programmi di ricerca in psicologia epsichiatria. Torino, 1968.

Phil 9513.30   Niebuhr, Reinhold. Faith and politics. N.Y., 1968.

Phil 3640.46   Nietzsche, Friedrich. Basic writings of Nietzsche. N.Y., 1968.

Phil 3640.79.15   Nietzsche, Friedrich. Erkenntnistheoretische Schriften. Frankfurt, 1968.

Phil 3640.23   Nietzsche, Friedrich. Studienausgabe in 4 Bänden. Frankfurt, 1968. 4v.

Phil 3640.51.11   Nietzsche, Friedrich. The will to power. N.Y., 1968.

Phil 5870.117   Nitschke, Alfred. Das verwaiste Kind der Natur. 2. Aufl. Tübingen, 1968.

Phil 1813.10   Norak, Michael. American philosophy and the future. N.Y., 1968.

Phil 5545.240   Norman, Donald A. Memory and attention. N.Y., 1968[1969]

Phil 6323.24   Novey, Samuel. The second look: the reconstruction of personal history in psychiatry and psychoanalysis. Baltimore, 1968.

Phil 8430.85   Novozhilova, Larisa I. Sotsiologiia iskusstva. Leningrad, 1968.

Phil 5535.28.5   Nuttin, Jozef. Reward and punishment in human learning: elements of a behavior theory. N.Y., 1968.

Phil 8654.116   O bogu i o człowieku. Warszawa, 1968.

Phil 8415.9.10   Oberti, Elisa. Per una fondazione fenomenologica della conoscitivitá dell'arte. Milano, 1968.

Phil 310.683   Ocherki istorii marksistsko-leninskoi filosofii v Belorussii, 1919-1968. Minsk, 1968.

Phil 8905.22   Odier, Charles. Les deux sources, consciente et inconsciente, de la vie morale. 2. éd. Neuchâtel, 1968.

Phil 5865.6.2   Oerter, Rolf. Moderne Entwicklungspsychologie. 2. Aufl. Donawörth, 1968.

Phil 5520.620   Oldfield, Richard Charles. Language: selected readings. Harmondsworth, 1968.

Phil 3120.30.160   Oliver, Roy. The wanderer and the way. Ithaca, N.Y., 1968.

Phil 2150.18.100   Olthuis, James H. Facts, values and ethics. Assen, 1968.

Phil 4260.42   Omaggio a Vico di A. Corsano, Paolo Romi, A.M. Jacobelli Inoldi. Napoli, 1968.

Phil 9495.168.10   O'Neil, Robert P. Sexuality and moral responsibility. Washington, 1968.

Phil 3805.252   Oranje, Leendert. God en wereld. Kampen, 1968.

Phil 5520.652   Osnovnye podkhody k modelirovaniia psikhiki i evristicheskomu programmirovaniiu. Moskva, 1968.

Phil 5374.260   Otto, Herbert Arthur. Ways of growth. N.Y., 1968.

Phil 4060.4.85   Pallavicini, Gian Luigi. Il pensiero di Antonio Aliotta. Napoli, 1968.

Phil 3450.19.490   Palmier, Jean Michel. Les écrits politiques de Heidegger. Paris, 1968.

Phil 6980.573.5   Pankow, Gisela. Gesprengte Fesseln der Psychose. München, 1968.

Phil 585.260.3   Pannenberg, Wolfhart. Was ist der Mensch? Die Anthropologie der Gegenwart in Lichte der Theologie. 3e Aufl. Göttingen, 1968.

Phil 4845.227.32.3   Papanoutsos, Euangelos. The foundations of knowledge. Albany, 1968.

Phil 5643.148   Parmenter, Ross. The awakened eye. 1. ed. Middletown, Conn., 1968.

Phil 2340.10.225   Parmentier, Alix. La philosophie de Whitehead. Paris, 1968.

Phil 2477.6.175   Parys, Jean M. van. La vocation de la liberté. Paris, 1968.

Phil 2050.227.1   Passmore, John A. Hume's intentions. N.Y., 1968.

Phil 5274.16   Pawlik, Kurt. Dimensionen des Verhaltens. Bern, 1968.

Phil 2225.5.55.5   Peirce, C.S. Über die Klarheit unserer Gedanken. Frankfurt, 1968.

Phil 815.30   The Pelican history of European thought. v.1,4. Harmondsworth, Middlesex, 1968. 2v.

Phil 1750.835   Penati, Giancarlo. Introduzione alla filosofia come metocultura. Milano, 1968.

Phil 5066.308   Penzov, Inrii E. Elementy matematicheskoi logiki i teorii mnozhestva. Saratov, 1968.

Phil 5055.29.20   Perelman, Chaim. Éléments d'une théorie de l'argumentation. Bruxelles, 1968.

Phil 5055.29.10   Perelman, Chaim. Logique et argumentation. Bruxelles, 1968.

Phil 2150.22.90   Perlini, Tito. Che cosa ha veramente detto Marcuse. Roma, 1968.

Phil 5238.228   Person als Prozess. Bern, 1968.

Phil 8430.53   Pesce, Domenico. Apollineo e dionisiaco nella storia del classicismo. Napoli, 1968.

Phil 4977.5   Pessoa, Fernando. Textos filosóficos. Lisboa, 1968. 2v.

Phil 974.3.175   Petersen, Klaus. Rudolf Steiner. Berlin, 1968.

Phil 6325.30   Peterson, Donald Robert. The clinical study of social behavior. N.Y., 1968.

Phil 6980.583.2   Petrilowitsch, Nikolaus. Probleme der Psychotherapie alternder Menschen. 2. Aufl. Basel, 1968.

Phil 6309.4   Petrilowitsch, Nikolaus. Psychologie der abnormen Persönnlichkeiten. Darmstadt, 1968.

Phil 5272.18   Pfanzogl, Johann. Theory of measurement. Würzburg, 1968.

Phil 585.380   Philibert, Michel André Jean. Les échelles d'âge dans la philosophie. These. Paris, 1968.

Phil 3497.24   Philonenko, Alexis. Théorie et praxis dans la pensée morale et politique de Kant et de Fichte en 1793. Paris, 1968.

Phil 8575.10   Philosophy and contemporary man. Washington, 1968.

Phil 5545.242   Piaget, Jean. Mémoire et intelligence. Paris, 1968.

Phil 5865.5.9   Piaget, Jean. On the development of memory and identity. Worcester, 1968.

Phil 1750.830.8   Piaget, Jean. Le structuralisme. 3e éd. Paris, 1968.

Phil 7069.68.55   Piccardt, Karel. De bovenzinnelijke wereld. Amsterdam, 1968.

Phil 4195.37   Pico della Mirandola, Giovanni. De dignitate hominis. Bad Homburg, 1968.

Phil 5876.10   Piel, Jacques. Analyse des formes prises par la socialité des adolescent dans le cadre de leurs loisis. Bruxelles, 1968.

Phil 8612.68   Pieper, Josef. Tod und Vusterblichkeit. München, 1968.

Phil 258.5   Pieretti, Antonio. Analisi linguistica e metafisica. Milano, 1968.

Phil 7055.310   Pike, James Albert. The other side. Garden City, 1968.

Phil 6315.2.435   Plé, Albert. Freud et la religion. Paris, 1968?

Phil 8140.10   Plebe, Armando. L'estetica italiana dopo Croce. Padova, 1968.

Phil 7150.85   Poeldinger, Walter. Die Abschätzung der Suizidalität. Bern, 1968.

Phil 8416.37.5   Poggioli, Renato. The theory of the avant-garde. Cambridge, 1968.

Phil 6060.65   Pokorny, Richard Raphael. Psychologie der Handschrift. Basel, 1968.

Phil 346.20.4   Polanyi, Michael. Personal knowledge towards a post-critical philosophy. Chicago, 1968[1958]

Chronological Listing

Phil 6140.5   The politics of mental health; organizing community mental health in metropolitan areas. N.Y., 1968.

Phil 1730.32   Ponte Orvieto, Marina da. L'unità di sapere nell'illuminismo. Padova, 1968.

Phil 2805.455   Pontet, Maurice. Pascal et Teilhard, témoins de Jésus-Christ. Paris, 1968.

Phil 4115.110   Portale, Vincenzo. L'ontologismo di Vincenzo Gioberti; antologia sistematica. Cosenza, 1968.

Phil 5225.4.1   Postman, Leo Joseph. Psychology in the making; histories of selected research problems. N.Y., 1968.

Phil 4200.2.01   Premec, Vladimir. Franciskus Patricijus. Beograd, 1968.

Phil 6980.611   Prick, Joseph Jules Guillaume. Human moods. Assen, 1968.

Phil 5066.103   Prior, Arthur Norman. Papers on time and tense. Oxford, 1968.

Phil 8400.60   Priroda i funktsii esteticheskogo. Moskva, 1968.

Phil 210.15   Il problema della domanda. Padova, 1968.

Phil 5039.14   Probleme de logică. Bucuresti, 1968. 3v.

Phil 310.696.5   Problèmes fondamentaux du matérialisme historique. Moscou, 1968.

Phil 8430.50   Problemi na khudozhestvenoto tvorchestvo. Sofiia, 1968.

Phil 6158.30   The problems and prospects of LSD. Springfield, 1968.

Phil 310.101   Problemy dialekticheskoi logiki. Alma-Ata, 1968.

Phil 310.689   Problemy filosofii. Alma-Ata, 1968.

Phil 310.688   Problemy filosofii i sotsiologii. Leningrad, 1968.

Phil 5055.32   Problemy logiki i teorii poznaniia. Moskva, 1968.

Phil 346.33   Problemy poznaniia sotsial'nykh iavlenii. Moskva, 1968.

Phil 70.100.10   Problemy teorii poznaniia i logiki. Moskva, 1968.

Phil 2150.22.97   Proto, Mario. Introduzione a Marcuse. 2. ed. Manduria, 1968.

Phil 5627.268.10   Pruyser, Paul W. A dynamic psychology of religion. N.Y., 1968.

Phil 5520.618   Psikhologiia grammatiki. Moskva, 1968.

Phil 5238.246   Psühholoogia ja kaasaeg. Tallinn, 1968.

Phil 6309.8   Psychoanalyse; zum 60. Geburtstag von Alexander Mitscherlich. Frankfurt am Main, 1968.

Phil 5870.65   Psychologen over het kind. Groningen, 1968.

Phil 5886.5   Psychological functioning in the normal aging and senile aged. Basel, 1968.

Phil 5255.78   Psychologische Testtheorie. Bern, 1968.

Phil 665.110   Queis, Karl. Wege der Seele. Wien, 1968.

Phil 1750.830   Qu'est-ce que le structuralisme? Paris, 1968.

Phil 6327.40   Racker, Heinrich. Transference and counter transference. N.Y., 1968.

Phil 8597.60.2   Radbruch, Gustav. Religionsphilosophie der Kultur. 2. Aufl. Darmstadt, 1968.

Phil 3120.8.160   Rancurello, Antos C. A study of Franz Brentano; his psychological standpoint and his significance in the history of psychology. N.Y., 1968.

Phil 4720.9   Rapp, Friedrich. Gesetz und Determination in der Sowjetphilosophie. Dordrecht, 1968.

Phil 1740.24   Raschini, Maria A. Riflessioni su filosofia e cultura. Milano, 1968.

Phil 7072.22   Raudive, Konstantins. Unhorbares wird Hörbar. Ramagen, 1968.

Phil 5238.220   The reach of mind. N.Y., 1968.

Phil 1817.18   Reck, A.J. The new American philosophers. Baton Rouge, 1968.

Phil 3805.228   Redeker, Martin. Friedrich Schleiermacher. Berlin, 1968.

Phil 6327.42   Ree, Frank van. Botsende Generaties. Assen, 1968.

Phil 165.424   Le réel et l'irréel. Paris, 1968.

Phil 5585.280   Reese, Hayne Waring. The perception of stimulus relations. N.Y., 1968.

Phil 1717.17.7   Reichenbach, Hans. Der Aufsteig der wissenschaftlichen Philosophie. Braunschweig, 1968.

Phil 3640.79.60.5   Reichert, Herbert William. International Nietzsche bibliography. Chapel Hill, 1968.

Phil 3017.9   Reichmann, Eberhard. Die Herrschaft der Zahl. Stuttgart, 1968.

Phil 6327.12.36   Reik, Theodor. The search within; the inner experience of a psychoanalyst. N.Y., 1968.

Phil 5548.135   Reiss, Gretel. Der Einfluss von Erfolgs- und Misserfolgsmotivierung auf das Behalten eigener Leistungen. Inaug. Diss. Münster? 1968?

Phil 8597.3.11   Remarus, Johann Albert Heinrich. Über die Gründe der menschlichen Erkentniss und der natürlichen Religion. Bruxelles, 1968.

Phil 5066.316   Rescher, Nicholas. Topics in philosophical logic. Dordrecht, Holland, 1968.

Phil 6140.6   Research Seminar on the Evaluation of Community Mental Health Programs. Community mental health; an international perspective. San Francisco, 1968.

Phil 2138.175   Restaino, Franco. J.S. Mill e la cultura filosofica britannica. Firenze, 1968.

Phil 192.118   Reuss, Materhus. Vorlesungen über die theoretische und praktische Philosophie. Bruxelles, 1968.

Phil 817.30   Revel, Jean François. Histoire de la philosophie occidentale. Paris, 1968-

Phil 8400.65.5   Revoliutsiia, prekrasnoe, chelovek. Moskva, 1968.

Phil 7010.10   Rhine, Joseph Banks. Parapsychology today. 1. ed. N.Y., 1968-

Phil 2750.11.215   Riccio, Franco. Maritain umano e metafisico. Trapani, 1968.

Phil 5520.145.10   Richards, Ivor Armstrong. Design for escape; world education through modern media. 1. ed. N.Y., 1968.

Phil 5520.145.5   Richards, Ivor Armstrong. So much nearer; essays toward a world English. 1. ed. N.Y., 1968.

Phil 4752.2.185   Richardson, David B. Berdyaev's philosophy of history. The Hague, 1968.

Phil 5585.275   Richerche sperimentali sulla percezione. Trieste, 1968.

Phil 75.86   Richter, Richard. Humdert Jahre philosophische Bibliothek 1868-1968. Hamburg, 1968.

Phil 3790.30.5   Richtscheid, Hans. Helle Nächte; drei Stücke Existenzphilosophie. München, 1968.

Phil 2750.19.115   Ricoeur, Paul. Entretiens Paul Ricoeur, Gabriel Marcel. Paris, 1968.

Phil 5875.125   Rieder, Oskar. Die Entwicklung des kindlichen Fragens. München, 1968.

Phil 585.315   Riedweg, Franz. Konservative Evolution. Müncl en, 1968.

Phil 5350.5.10   Riley, Matilda White. Aging and society. N.Y., 1968. 2v.

Phil 192.67.22   Rintelen, Fritz J. von. Der Aufstieg im Geiste. 2. Aufl. Frankfurt, 1968.

Phil 2905.1.530   Rivière, Claude. En Chine avec Teilhard. Paris, 1968.

Phil 6315.2.390   Roazen, Paul. Freud; political and social thought. 1. ed. N.Y., 1968.

Phil 1817.20   Roberts, James Deotis. From Puritanism to Platonism in seventeenth century England. The Hague, 1968.

Phil 2250.116   Robinson, Daniel Sommer. Royce and Hocking; American idealists. Boston, 1968.

Phil 8642.10   Robinson, John Arthur Thomas. In the end, God. 1. ed. N.Y., 1968.

Phil 2138.155.1   Robson, John Mercel. The improvement of mankind; the social and political thought of John Stuart Mill. Toronto, 1968.

Phil 2138.155   Robson, John Mercel. The improvement of mankind; the social and political thought of John Stuart Mill. Toronto, 1968.

Phil 4080.3.535   Roggerone, Giuseppe A. Prospettive crociane. Lecce, 1968.

Phil 2725.13.85   Roggerone, Giuseppe Agostino. La via nuova di Lequier. Milano, 1968.

Phil 6060.70   Roman, Klara Goldzieher. Encyclopedia of the written word. N.Y., 1968.

Phil 5520.535A   Rommetreit, Ragnar. Words, meanings, and messages. N.Y., 1968.

Phil 2515.6.5   Rons, Ivo. Introduction au socialisme rationnel de Colins. Neuchâtel, 1968.

Phil 8892.82   Roscam Abbing, Pieter Johan. Om de mens. Leiden, 1968.

Phil 5880.5   Roscam Abbing, Pieter Johan. Volwassenheid. Hilversum, 1968.

Phil 6967.25   Rosen, George. Madness in society. London, 1968.

Phil 3120.30.195   Rosenblueth, Pinchas Erich. Martin Buber: sein Denken und Wirken. Hannover, 1968.

Phil 2417.4.5   Rosenfield, Leonora D.C. From beast-machine to man-machine. N.Y., 1968.

Phil 3790.20.10   Rosenstock, Eugen. Ja und Nein. Heidelberg, 1968.

Phil 5257.80   Roskam, Edwarda Elias Charles Iben. Metric analysis of ordinal data in psychology. Proefschrift. Voorschoten, 1968.

Phil 8892.80   Ross, Alf. Directives and norms. London, 1968.

Phil 5520.581   Rossi, Eduard. Das menschliche Begreifen und seine Grenzen. Bonn, 1968.

Phil 1850.147.10   Rossi, Paolo. Francis Baconi from magic to science. London, 1968.

Phil 1740.22   Rossi, Pietro. Lo storicismo contemporaneo. Torino, 1968.

Phil 3837.16   Rousset, Bernard. La perspective finale de l'éthique et le problème de la coherence du Spinozisme. Paris, 1968.

Phil 310.673   Rozhim, Vasilii P. Voprosy filosofii i sotsiologii v reskeniiekh XXIII s'ezda KPSS. Leningrad, 1968.

Phil 4710.50.45   Rozvytok filosofii v Ukrainskii RSR. Kyïv, 1968.

Phil 5535.14   Rubin, Frederick. Current research in hypnopaedia; a symposium of selected literature. London, 1968.

Phil 3790.34   Ruemke, Henricus Cornelius. Levenstijdperken van de naan. Amsterdam, 1968.

VPhil 310.647.10   Rus, Vojan. Sodobna filosofija med dialektiko in metafiziko. Ljubljana, 1968.

Phil 310.686   Rusev, Pancho. Teoriiata na otrazhenieto v domarksovata filosofiia. Sofiia, 1968.

Phil 2255.1.38   Russell, Bertrand Russell. The art of philosophizing. N.Y., 1968.

Phil 8707.16.5   Russell, Bertrand Russell. Religion and science. London, 1968.

Phil 5421.20.55   Russell, Claire. Violence, monkeys, and man. London, 1968.

Phil 6980.661   Rycroft, Charles. Imagination and reality; psycho-analytical essays, 1951-1961. London, 1968.

Phil 5238.224   Sahakian, William S. History of psychology. Itasca, Ill., 1968.

Phil 3500.102   Saher, Hans. Kants Weg vom Krieg zum Frieden. München, 1968-

Phil 4957.65   Salazar, Bondy Augusto. Existe una filosofía de nuestra América? 1. ed. México, 1968[1969]

Phil 2880.2.92   Salmona, Bruno. Il pensiero di Charles Secrétan. Milano, 1968.

Phil 3640.116.2   Salter, William M. Nietzsche the thinker; a study. N.Y., 1968.

Phil 1750.825   Sanborn, Patricia F. Existentialism. N.Y., 1968.

Phil 3801.768   Sandkuehler, Hans-Jörg. Freiheit und Wirklichkeit. Frankfurt, 1968.

Phil 1718.40   Sándor, Pál. A filozófia is közügy! Tanulmányok. Budapest, 1968.

Phil 7082.42   Sanford, John A. Dreams; God's forgotten language. Philadelphia, 1968.

Phil 193.49.12   Santayana, G. The birth of reason and other essays. N.Y., 1968.

Phil 2280.5.79.5   Santayana, George. Selected critical writing. Cambridge, Eng., 1968. 2v.

Phil 5520.575   Santoni, Ronald E. Religious language and problem of religious knowledge. Bloomington, 1968.

Phil 2880.8.70   Sartre, Jean Paul. The communists and peace, with a reply to Claude Lefort. N.Y., 1968.

Phil 3450.19.455   Sass, Hans-Martin. Heidegger-Bibliographie. Meisenheim am Glan, 1968.

Phil 3018.38   Sauer, Ernst Friedrich. Deutsche Philosophen: von Eckhart his Heidegger. Göttingen, 1968.

Phil 5871.35   Savioz, Esther. Die Anfänge der Geschwisterbeziehung. Bern, 1968.

Phil 2477.6.170   Scannone, Juan Carlos. Sein und Inkarnation. Diss. Freiburg, 1968.

Phil 5520.700   Schaefer, Wolfgang von. Was geht uns Noah an? München, 1968.

Phil 5520.325.7   Schaff, Adam. Essays über die Philosophie der Sprache. Frankfurt, 1968.

Phil 8062.9   Schaper, Eva. Prelude to aesthetics. London, 1968.

Phil 6315.2.442   Scharfenberg, Joachim. Sigmund Freud und sein Religionskritik als Herausforderung für den christlichen Glauben. Göttingen, 1968.

Phil 705.70   Schaumann, Johann Christian Gottlieb. Über die transcendentale Ästhetik. Bruxelles, 1968.

Phil 3850.55   Scherrer, Eduard. Wissenschaftslehre. Bern, 1968.

Phil 8708.40   Schiffers, Norbert. Fragen der Physik an die Theologie. 1. Aufl. Düsseldorf, 1968.

Phil 2120.4.95   Schilpp, Paul A. The philosophy of C.I. Lewis. 1. ed. Facsimile. La Salle, 1968.

Phil 8598.135.10   Schlette, Heinz Robert. Philosophie, Theologie, Ideologie. Köln, 1968.

Phil 559.2   Schmida-Wöllersdorfer, Susanna. Perspektiven des Seins. München, 1968. 2v.

Phil 493.12   Schmidt, Karl. Zur Überwindung des wissenschaftlichen Materialismus. Basel, 1968.

Phil 1750.860   Schmidt, Siegfried Josef. Sprache und Denken als sprachphilosophisches Problem von Locke bis Wittgenstein. Den Haag, 1968[1969].

Phil 1750.115.160   Schmitz, Hermann. Subjektivität; Beiträge zur Phänomenologie und Logik. Bonn, 1968.

Phil 6060.84   Schneevoigt, Ihno. Die graphologische Intelligenzdiagnose. Bonn, 1968.

Phil 3801.774.10   Schneiter, Rudolf. Schellings Gesetz der Polarität. Winterthur, 1968.

Phil 5058.98   Schock, Rolf. Logics without existence assumptions. Uppsala, 1968.

Phil 6315.2.430   Schoenan, Walter. Sigmund Freuds Prosa. Stuttgart, 1968.

Phil 978.49.920   Schrey, Helmut. Waldorfpädagogik. Bad Godesberg, 1968.

Phil 7082.4.5   Schubert, Gotthilf Heinrich von. Die Symbolik des Traumes. Heidelberg, 1968.

Phil 3246.315   Schuhmann, Karl. Die Grundlage der Wissenschaftslehre in ihrem Umrisse. Den Haag, 1968[1969]

Phil 7084.12.1   Schultz-Hencke, Harald. Lehrbuch der Traumanalyse. 1. Aufl. Stuttgart, 1968.

Phil 5403.12   Schutz, William Carl. Joy; expanding human awareness. N.Y., 1968.

Phil 3500.17.15   Schwab, J.C. Bemerkungen ueber den Kantischen Begriff...metaphysischen Rechtslehre. Bruxelles, 1968.

Phil 3500.110   Schwab, Johann Christoph. Sendschreiben an einen Recensenten in der Gothaischen gelehrten Zeitung über den gerichtlichen Eyd. v.1-2. Bruxelles, 1968.

Phil 3500.106   Schwartlaender, Johannes. Der Mensch ist Person. Stuttgart, 1968.

Phil 2651.85   Sciacca, Giuseppe Maria. Scetticismo cristiano. Palermo, 1968.

Phil 4225.8.58   Sciacca, Michele Federico. Filosofia e antifilosofia. Milano, 1968.

Phil 4260.195   Sciacca, Michele Federico. Verità e storia in Vico. Roma, 1968.

Phil 8622.88   Scoppio, Domenico. Fede e verità nel Cristianesimo contemporaneo. Bari, 1968.

Phil 5066.24.10   Segerberg, Krister. Results in non-classical propositional logic. Lund, 1968.

Phil 3790.4.95   Seidel, Hermann. Wert und Wirklichkeit in der Philosophie Heinrich Rickerts. Bonn, 1968.

Phil 8673.36   Seidlitz, Carl Siegmund von. Briefe über Gott und Unsterblichkeit. Bruxelles, 1968.

Phil 1619.5   Seigel, Jerrold Edward. Rhetoric and philosophy in Renaissance humanism. Princeton, 1968.

Phil 5421.20.60   Selg, Herbert. Diagnostik der Aggressivität. Habilitationsschrift. Göttingen, 1968.

Phil 2115.205   Seligen, Martin. The liberal politics of John Locke. London, 1968.

Phil 3500.112   Sellars, Wilfrid. Science and metaphysics; variations on Kantian themes. London, 1968.

Phil 8968.22.5   Semaine des Intellectuels Catholiques, 1967. La violenza. Roma, 1968.

Phil 5090.11   Sengupta, Pradip Kumar. Demonstration and logical truth. 1st ed. Calcutta, 1968.

Phil 3552.482   Serres, Michel. Le système de Leibniz et ses modèles mathématiques. Paris, 1968.

Phil 3246.294   Severino, Emanuele. Per un innovamento nella interpretazione della filosofia Fichtiana. Brescia, 1968.

Phil 585.340   Shaffer, Jerome A. Philosophy of mind. Englewood Cliffs, N.J., 1968.

Phil 4710.156   Shein, Louis J. Readings in Russian philosophical thought. The Hague, 1968.

Phil 4769.7.33   Shestov, Lev. Potestas clavium. Athens, Ohio, 1968.

Phil 5058.96.5   Shirwood, William. William of Sherwood's treatise on syncategorematic words. Minneapolis, 1968.

Phil 8980.787.25   Shishkin, Aleksandr F. Dvadtsatyi vek i moral'nye tsennosti chelovechestva. Moskva, 1968.

Phil 310.675   Shliakhtenko, Sergei G. Kategorii kachestva i kolichestva. Leningrad, 1968.

Phil 193.47.2   Sidgwick, Henry. Philosophy; its scope and relations. N.Y., 1968.

Phil 165.412   Sidney Hook and contemporary world; essay on the pragmatic intelligence. N.Y., 1968.

Phil 5875.30.5   Sigel, Irving Edward. Logical thinking in children; research based on Piaget's theory. N.Y., 1968.

Phil 6985.5   Sigrell, B. Group psychotherapy. Stockholm, 1968.

Phil 3850.16.41   Simmel, Georg. The conflict in modern culture and other essays. N.Y., 1968.

Phil 3850.16.45   Simmel, Georg. Das individuelle Gesetz. Frankfurt, 1968.

Phil 3552.476.5   Simonovits, Istvánné. Dialektisches Denken in der Philosophie von Gottfried Wilhelm Leibniz. Budapest, 1968.

Phil 8980.790   Simpozium Posviashchennyi 100-letiiu so Dnia Rozhdeniia V.I. Lenina, Novosibirsk? 1968? Problemy kategorii marksistsko-leninskoi etiki. Novosibirsk, 1968.

Phil 1135.190   Sinnige, Theo G. Matter and infinity in the Presocratic school and Plato. Assen, 1968.

Phil 8140.8   Sinnonini, Augusto. Storia dei movimenti estetici nella cultura italiana. Firenze, 1968.

Phil 4800.22.10   Skarbek, Janusz. Koncepcja nauki w pozytywizmie polskim. Wrocław, 1968.

Phil 5058.102   Skyrms, Brian. Choice and chance; an introduction to inductive logic. Belmont, Calif., 1968.

Phil 5190.24.10   Slaatte, Howard Alexander. The pertinence of the paradox. N.Y., 1968.

Phil 5258.203   Slavskaia, Kseniia A. Mysl' v deistvii. Moskva, 1968.

Phil 8980.795   Slovak, Emil. Desat prikazani. Bratislava, 1968.

Phil 5627.268.5   Smolenaars, A.J. Kerkelijkheid en persoonlijkheidskenmerken in twee Zuiderzeepolders. Amsterdam, 1968.

Phil 818.39   Smuts, Johannes Petrus. Kruispaaie van die filosofie. Kaapstad, 1968.

Phil 8419.64   Sokolov, Aleksandr N. Teoriia stilia. Moskva, 1968.

Phil 5258.204   Sokolov, Aleksandr N. Vnutrenniaia rech' i myshlenie. Moskva, 1968.

Phil 735.270   Solimini, Maria. Genealogia e scienza dei valori. Manduria, 1968.

Phil 1955.6.240   Somjee, Abdulkarim Husseinbhay. The political theory of John Dewey. N.Y., 1968.

Phil 5520.596   Sotnikian, Pogos A. Osnovnye problemy iazyka i myshleniia. Erevan, 1968.

Phil 5374.276   Soznanie i obshchenie. Frunze, 1968.

Phil 3850.32.10.2   Spann, Othmar. Erkenne dich Selbst. 2. Aufl. Graz, 1968.

Phil 3805.226   Spiegel, Yorick. Theologie der bürgerlichen Gesellschaft. München, 1968.

Phil 400.128   Spisani, Franco. Natura e spirito nell'idealismo attuale. Milano, 1968?

Phil 5066.304   Spisani, Franco. Neutralizzazione dello spazio per sintesiproduttiva. 2. ed. Milano, 1968.

Phil 2630.6.85   Spring, Gerald M. Man's invincible surmise; a personal interpretation of Bovarysm. N.Y., 1968.

Phil 8598.144   Standinger, Hugo. Gott: Fehlanzeige? Tries, 1968.

Phil 860.2.2   Staudacher, Willibald. Die Trennung von Himmel und Erde; ein vorgriechischer Schöpfungsmythus bei Hesiod und den Orphikern. 2. Aufl. Darmstadt, 1968.

Phil 978.49.697   Steiner, R. Anthroposophie. 3. Aufl. Dornach, 1968.

Phil 978.49.720   Steiner, R. Anweisungen für eine esoterische Schulung: aus den Inhalten der Esoterischen Schule. Dornach, 1968.

Phil 978.49.525   Steiner, R. Das christliche Mysterium. Dornach, 1968.

Phil 978.49.535   Steiner, R. Die geistige Vereinigung der Menschheit durch den Christus-Impuls. 1. Aufl. Dornach, 1968.

Phil 978.49.705   Steiner, R. Die Geschichte der Menschheit und die Weltanschauungen der Kulturvölker. Dornach, 1968.

Phil 978.49.710   Steiner, R. Der innere Aspekt des sozialen Rätsels. Dornach, 1968.

Phil 978.49.695   Steiner, R. Das Lukas-Evangelium. Ein Zyklus von zehn Vorträgen. 6. Aufl. Dornach, 1968.

Phil 978.49.770   Steiner, R. Die Polarität von Dauer und Entwickelung im Menschenleben. Dornach, 1968.

Phil 978.49.750.8   Steiner, R. Die Rätsel der Philosophie. 8. Aufl. Dornach, 1968.

Phil 978.49.696   Steiner, R. Die Verbindung zwischen Lebenden und Toten; acht Vorträge genalten im verschiedenen Stadten zwischen dem 16. Februar und 3. Dezember, 1916. 1. Aufl. Dornach, 1968.

Phil 978.49.699.2   Steiner, R. Wie Kann die Menschheit den Christus Wiederfinden? 2. Aufl. Dornach, 1968.

Phil 978.49.425   Steiner, R. Der Zusammenhang des Menschen mit der elementarischen Welt. Dornach, 1968.

Phil 6328.21.8   Sterba, Richard. Introduction to the psychoanalytic theory of the libido. 3d ed. N.Y., 1968.

Phil 5402.39   Sternbach, Richard A. Pain; a psychophysiological analysis. N.Y., 1968.

Phil 310.665.5   Stiehler, Gottfried. Dialektik und Praxis. Berlin, 1968.

Phil 5790.35.5   Stoddard, Ellwyn R. Conceptual models of human behavior in disaster. El Paso, 1968.

Phil 5421.20.145   Stokes, Allen W. Aggressive man and aggressive beast. Logan, 1968?

Phil 5590.496   Stoller, Robert J. Sex and gender; on the development of masculinity and feminity. London, 1968.

Phil 5870.80.2   Stone, Lawrence Joseph. Childhood and adolescence. 2nd ed. N.Y., 1968.

Phil 5421.20.40   Storr, Anthony. Human aggression. 1. American ed. N.Y., 1968.

Phil 165.420   Strawson, Peter Frederick. Studies in the philosophy of thought and action. London, 1968.

Phil 165.444   Studenty - Oktiabriu. Moskva, 1968.

Phil 5039.12   Studies in logical theory. Oxford, 1968.

Phil 8870.32   Studies in moral philosophy. Oxford, 1968.

Phil 5590.500   The study of personality. N.Y., 1968.

Phil 5548.146   Stückmann, Günther. Der Berufserfolg als Motivationsphänomen. Berlin, 1968.

Phil 349.61   Sukhotin, Anatoli K. Gnoselogicheskii analiz em kosti znaniia. Tomsk, 1968.

Phil 5058.70.10   Suppes, Patrick. Introduction to logic. Princeton, N.J., 1968.

Phil 310.118   Sviderskii, Vladimir Io. O nekotorykh formakh protivorechivosti v ob'ektivnom mire. Leningrad, 1968.

Phil 4809.814.30   Svitak, Ivan. Lidský smysl kultury. Vyd. 1. Praha, 1968.

VPhil 7069.68   Swanson, Mildred Burris. God bless Ü, daughter. Independance, 1968.

Phil 672.252   Swinburne, Richard. Space and time. London, 1968.

Phil 5500.55   Symposium on Cognition, 3rd, Carnegie Institute of Technology, 1967. Formal representation of human judgment. N.Y., 1968.

VPhil 2280.5.150   Szmyd, Jan. Filozofia moralna Santayany. Wyd. 1. Warszawa, 1968.

Phil 5258.205   Szondi, Lipot. Freiheit und Zwang im Schicksal des Einzelnen. Bern, 1968.

Phil 8430.76   Tagliaferri, Aldo. L'estetica dell'oggettivo. Milano, 1968.

Phil 8420.26   Tartalja, Ivo. Djure Daničiča lekcije iz estetike. Beograd, 1968.

Phil 2725.60   Tedeschi, Paul. Saint-Aubin et son oeuvre. Paris, 1968.

Phil 2905.1.28   Teilhard de Chardin, Pierre. Letters to two friends, 1926-1952. N.Y., 1968.

Phil 2905.1.63   Teilhard de Chardin, Pierre. Science and Christ. London, 1968.

Phil 2905.1.27   Teilhard de Chardin, Pierre. Writings in time of war. London, 1968.

Phil 4320.10A   Le temps et la mort dans la philosophie espagnole contemporaine. Toulouse, 1968.

Phil 7030.2   Tenhaeff, Wilhelm H.C. Parapsychologie. Antwerpen, 1968.

Phil 5520.576   Teoriia rechevoi deiatel'nosti. Moskva, 1968.

Phil 5520.570   Terwilliger, Robert F. Meaning and mind. N.Y., 1968.

Phil 5520.545   Thass-Thienemann, Théodore. Symbolic behavior. N.Y., 1968.

Phil 194.56   Thayer, Horace Standish. Meaning and action. Indianapolis, 1968.

Phil 5259.60   Thines, Georges. La problématique de la psychologie. La Haye, 1968.

Phil 5590.492   Thomae, Hans. Das Idividuum und seine Welt. Göttingen, 1968.

Phil 3890.8.40   Thomasius, Christian. Ausübung der Sittenlehre. Hildesheim, 1968.

Phil 3890.8.45.1   Thomasius, Christian. Ausübung der Vernunftlehre. Hildesheim, 1968.

Phil 3890.8.30.1   Thomasius, Christian. Einleitung zur Sittenlehre. Hildesheim, 1968.

Phil 5059.24.2   Thomasius, Christian. Einleitung zur Vernunftlehre. Hildesheim, 1968.

Phil 8870.18   Thomson, Judith J. Ethics. N.Y., 1968.

Phil 5229.2   Thomson, Robert. The Pelican history of psychology. Harmondsworth, 1968.

Phil 3501.18   Tilling, Christian Gottfried. Gedanken zur Prüfung von Kants...der Sitten. Leipzig, 1789. Bruxelles, 1968.

Phil 2905.1.520   Tilloy, Alain. Teilhard de Chardin, père de l'Église ou pseudo-prophète? Saint Cénére, 1968.

Phil 665.100   Timeless documents of the soul. Evanston, 1968.

Phil 5545.264   Tocquet, Robert. La mémoire, comment l'acquérer, comment la conserver. Paris, 1968.

Phil 400.116   Todd, William. Analytical solipsism. The Hague, 1968.

1968 - cont.

Phil 5548.75.5 — Toman, Walter. Motivation, Persönlichkeit, Umwelt. Göttingen, 1968.

Phil 5627.266.21 — Tournier, Paul. A place for you; psychology and religion. 1st U.S. ed. N.Y., 1968.

Phil 5590.455.1 — Tournier, Paul. Secrets. Richmond, 1968.

Phil 8969.3.5 — Traherne, Thomas. Christian ethicks. Ithaca, 1968.

Phil 6969.14 — The transmission of schizophrenia: proceedings of the second research conference of the Foundations' Fund for Research in Psychiatry. Oxford, 1968.

Phil 5270.8 — Traxel, Werner. Über Gegenstand und Methode der Psychologie. Bern, 1968.

Phil 310.681 — Trendafilov, Nikola. Za deistvieto na zakona za edinstvoto i borbata na protivopolozhnostite pri sotsializma. Sofiia, 1968.

Phil 2905.1.535 — Trinité, Phillipe de la. Teilhard de Chardin. Paris, 1968.

Phil 2475.1.495 — Trotignon, Pierre. L'idée de vie chez Bergson et la critique de la metaphysique. Paris, 1968.

VPhil 585.261 — Trstenjak, Anton. Hoja za človekom. Celje, 1968.

VPhil 8735.59 — Trubnikov, Nikolai N. O kategoriiakh "tsel'", "sredstvo", "rezul'tat". Moskva, 1968.

Phil 3508.4 — Über das Studium der Kantischen Philosophie und ihren Werth. Bruxelles, 1968.

Phil 3120.55.95 — Über Ernst Bloch. Frankfurt, 1968.

Phil 3925.16.205 — Über Ludwig Wittgenstein. Frankfurt, 1968.

Phil 195.13.5 — Ulken, Hilmi Zuja. Varlik ve olus. Ankara, 1968.

Phil 5406.2 — United States. National Institute of Child Health and Human Development. Perspectives on human deprivation: biological, psychological, and sociological. Washington, 1968.

Phil 860.6 — Ushida, Noriko. Étude comparative de la psychologie d'Aristote, d'Avicenne et de St.Thomas d'Aquin. Tokyo, 1968.

Phil 3903.3.43 — Vaihinger, Hans. The philosophy of "As if"; a system of the theoretical, practical and religious fictions of mankind. 2. ed. London, 1968.

Phil 302.4 — Valsardieu, Paul. La révolution totale, en tout. Paris, 1968- 2v.

Phil 3503.25 — Vas, Harmen de. Kant als theoloog. Baarn, 1968.

Phil 1630.35 — Vasoli, Cesare. La dialettica e la retorica dell'Umanesimo. Milano, 1968.

Phil 1622.5 — Vasoli, Cesare. Studi sulla cultura del Rinascimento. Manduria, 1968.

Phil 3805.230 — Vattimo, Gianni. Schleiermacher filosofo dell'interpretazione. Milano, 1968.

Phil 1695.35 — Verstehen und Vertranen. Otto Friedrich Bollnow zum 65. Geburtstag. Stuttgart, 1968.

Phil 5401.54 — Vestdijk, Simon. Het wezen van de angst. Amsterdam, 1968.

Phil 5520.577 — Vetrov, Anatolii A. Semiotika i ee osnovnye problemy. Moskva, 1968.

Phil 6971.5 — Vetter, Harold T. Language behavior in schizophrenia. Springfield, Ill., 1968.

Phil 4260.34.2A — Vico, G.B. The new science of Giambattista Vico. Ithaca, 1968.

Phil 525.260 — Vinkenoog, Simon. Weergaloos. Hilversum, 1968.

Phil 2475.1.485 — Violette, René. La spiritualité de Bergson. Toulouse, 1968.

Phil 4960.625.5 — Vita, Luís Washington. Antologia do pensamento social e político no Brasil, seleção e notas. São Paulo, 1968.

Phil 4080.3.550 — Vitiello, Vincenzo. Storiografia e storia nel pensiero di Benedetto Croce. Napoli, 1968.

Phil 8896.3.10 — Vives, Juan Luis. Vives' introduction to wisdom. N.Y., 1968.

Phil 1750.166.230 — Vogel, Cornelia Johanna de. Het humanisme en zijn historische achtergrond. Assen, 1968.

Phil 8422.17.5 — Volek, Jaroslav. Základy obecné teorie umění. Praha, 1968.

Phil 3640.755 — Volkmann-Schluck, Karl Heinz. Leben und Denken. Frankfurt, 1968.

Phil 310.724 — Voprosy filosofii. Novosibirsk, 1968.

Phil 310.163.5 — Vranicki, Predrag. L'uomo e la storia. Roma, 1968.

Phil 8430.45.5 — Vučković, Vojislav. Studije, eseji, kritike. Beograd, 1968. 2v.

Phil 2255.1.145 — Vuillemin, Jules. Leçons sur la première philosophie de Russell. Paris, 1968.

Phil 5520.500 — Wagner, Geoffrey A. On the wisdom of words. Princeton, 1968.

Phil 303.20.1 — Wagner, Johann Jacob. Von der Natur der Dinge. Mit einer physiognomischen Kupfertafel. Leipzig, 1803. Bruxelles, 1968.

Phil 3925.18.30 — Waismann, Friedrich. How I see philosophy. N.Y., 1968.

Phil 197.95 — Wal, Goossen Albertus van der. Wereldbeschouwelijk denken als filosofisch probleem. Den Haag, 1968.

Phil 8602.80 — Waldmann, Günter. Christliches Glauben und christliche Glaubenslosigkeit. Tübingen, 1968.

Phil 9495.168.5 — Walker, Brooks R. The new immorality. 1st ed. Garden City, 1968.

VPhil 8423.27 — Wallis, Mieczysław. Przeżycie i wartość. Wyd. 1. Kraków, 1968.

Phil 672.240.2 — Wallis, Robert. Time, fourth dimension of the mind. 1st ed. N.Y., 1968.

Phil 5585.265 — Warr, Peter Bryan. The perception of people and events. London, 1968.

Phil 5232.10.2 — Watson, Robert Irving. The great psychologists from Aristotle to Freud. 2. ed. Philadelphia, 1968.

Phil 4655.4.30 — Wedberg, Anders. Philosophical papers. Stockholm, 1968-

Phil 3120.30.190 — Wehr, Gerhard. Martin Buber in Selbstzeugnissen und Bilddokumenten. Reinbek, 1968.

Phil 8712.35 — Weil, Simone. On science, necessity, and the love of God. London, 1968.

Phil 585.120.10 — Wein, Hermann. Kentaurische Philosophie; Vorträge und Abhandlungen. München, 1968.

Phil 5520.600 — Welterfahrung in der Sprache. Freiburg, 1968-

Phil 4752.2.160 — Wernham, James C.S. Two Russian thinkers: essays in Berdyaev and Shestov. Toronto, 1968.

Phil 5262.65 — Westcott, Malcolm Robert. Toward a contemporary psychology of intuition. N.Y., 1968.

Phil 8586.36.70 — Weth, Rudolf. Gott in Jesus; der Ansatz der Christologie Friedrich Gogartens. München, 1968.

Phil 3819.5 — Wetlesen, Jon. A Spinoza bibliography, particularly on the period 1940-1967. Oslo, 1968.

Phil 3450.11.450 — Wewel, Meinolf. Die Konstitution des transzendenten Etevas im Vollzug des Sehens. Düsseldorf, 1968.

Phil 5520.124.3 — Wheelwright, Phillip Ellis. The burning fountain. Bloomington, 1968.

1968 - cont.

Phil 5262.62 — Whitla, Dean. Handbook of measurement and assessment in behavioral sciences. Reading, 1968.

Phil 8602.35.10 — Wieman, Henry Nelson. Religious inquiry; some explorations. Boston, 1968.

Phil 5520.530 — Wiener, Morton. Language within language; immediacy, a channel in verbal communication. N.Y., 1968.

Phil 2050.278 — Wilbanks, Jan. Hume's theory of imagination. The Hague, 1968.

Phil 3801.878 — Wild, Christoph. Reflexion und Erfahrung. Freiburg, 1968.

Phil 5535.16 — Wilde, Henricus Andreas Maria. Coalitie formatie in triades. Rotterdam, 1968.

Phil 2905.1.130.5 — Wildiers, N.M. An introduction to Teilhard de Chardin. 1st American ed. N.Y., 1968.

Phil 3504.55 — Williams, T.C. The concept of the categorical imperative. Oxford, 1968.

Phil 5249.2.81.5 — Wilshire, Bruce. William James and phenomenology. Bloomington, 1968.

Phil 8897.96 — Winch, Peter. Moral integrity: inaugural lecture in the Chair of Philosophy delivered at King's College, London, 9 May 1968. Oxford, 1968.

Phil 8423.16.5 — Winckelmann, Johann Joachim. Kleine Schriften, Vorreden, Entwürfe. Berlin, 1968.

Phil 585.250 — Wirklichkeit der Mitte. Beiträge zu einer Strukturanthropologie. Freiburg, 1968.

Phil 353.21.5 — Wisdom, John. Other minds. Berkeley, 1968.

Phil 3925.16.3 — Wittgenstein, Ludwig. Philosophical investigations. 3rd ed. N.Y., 1968[1958]

Phil 3925.16.3.1 — Wittgenstein, Ludwig. Philosophical investigations. 3rd ed. Oxford, 1968.

Phil 3925.16.3.2 — Wittgenstein, Ludwig. Philosophical investigations. 3rd ed. Oxford, 1968.

Phil 3425.730 — Wolff, Kurt Heinrich. Hingebung und Begriff. Neuwied, 1968.

Phil 9425.10 — Wollgast, Siegfried. Zur Friedensidee in der Reformationszeit. Berlin, 1968.

Phil 5232.12 — Wolman, Benjamin B. Historical roots of contemporary psychology. N.Y., 1968.

VPhil 3925.16.155 — Wolniewicz, Bogusław. Rzeczy i fakty. Warszawa, 1968.

Phil 7055.386 — Woods, Margaret. Mosaic; a psychic autobiography. London, 1968.

Phil 6132.41.5 — Wooldridge, Dean E. Mechanical man. N.Y., 1968.

Phil 165.415 — World perspectives in philosophy, religion and culture. Patna, 1968.

Phil 3310.19.80 — Wucherer-Huldenfeld, Karl. Die Gegensatzphilosophie Romano Guardinis in ihren Grundlagen und Folgerungen. Wien, 1968.

Phil 8897.94 — Wyss, Dieter. Strukturen der Moral. Göttingen, 1968.

Phil 525.266 — Xirau, Ramón. Palabra y silencio. 1. ed. México, 1968.

Phil 4710.50.50 — Z istorii filosofii i sotsiolohii na Ukraini. Kyïv, 1968.

Phil 8900.9 — Zdotusskii, Igor P. Faust i fiziki. Moskva, 1968.

Phil 4957.805 — Zea, Leopoldo. Antología de la filosofía americana contemporánea. México, 1968.

Phil 5235.2 — Zharikbaev, Kubigul B. Razvitie psikhologicheskoi mysli v Kazakhstane (so vtoroi poloviny XIXveka i do nashikh dnei . Alma-Ata, 1968.

Phil 9075.80 — Ziegler, Josef Georg. Vom Gesetz zum Gewissen. Freiburg, 1968.

Phil 665.102 — Zolla, Elémire. Le potenze dell'anima. Milano, 1968.

Phil 70.118 — Zonal'naia Konferentsiia Psikhologov Pribaltki, 5th, Tartu, Kääriku, 1968. Materialy V Zonal'noi Konferentsii Psikhologov Pribaltiki. Tartu, 1968.

Phil 3425.670 — Zuefle, Manfred. Prosa der Welt: die Sprache Hegels. Einsiedeln, 1968.

Phil 3940.4 — Zwanziger, Johann Christian. Die Religion des Philosoph und sein Glaubenskenntniss. Bruxelles, 1968.

Phil 3845.4 — Zweig, Arnold. Baruch Spinoza. Darmstadt, 1968.

Phil 5421.25.40 — Zweig, Paul. The heresy of self-love. N.Y., 1968.

1969

Phil 5590.510 — Aamark, Curt. Individ, persenlighet och medmänsklig miljö. Stolkholm, 1969.

Phil 1750.270.15 — Abbagnano, Nicola. Critical existentialism. 1. ed. Garden City, 1969.

Phil 974.3.170 — Abendroth, Walter. Rudolf Steiner und die heutige Welt. München, 1969.

Phil 6310.2.16 — Abraham, Karl. Psychoanalytische Studien zur Charakterbildung und andere Schriften. Frankfurt, 1969. 2v.

Phil 75.88 — Adorno, Francesco. Il pensiero greco. Orientamenti bibliografici a cura di Francesco Adorno. Bari, 1969.

Phil 3085.7.35 — Adorno, Theodor W. Stichworte. Kritische Modelle. Frankfurt, 1969.

Phil 396.8 — De ag ligt nog voor ons essays van humanisten. 's-Gravenhage, 1969.

Phil 7069.69.10 — Agee, Doris. Edgar Cayce on E.S.P. 1st ed. N.Y., 1969.

Phil 3000.8 — Albrecht, Herbert. Deutsche Philosophie heute. Bremen, 1969.

Phil 3450.11.515 — Altamore, Giovanni. Della fènomenologia all'ontologia. Padova, 1969.

Phil 5240.65 — Alvarez Villar, Alfonso. Psicología de los pueblos primitivos. Madrid, 1969.

Phil 5066.324 — Ambacher, Nicolò. Logica simbolica e diritto. Milano, 1969.

Phil 2150.22.125 — Ambacher, Michel. Marcuse et la critique de la civilisation américaine. Paris, 1969.

Phil 5627.269.15 — Amon, Jesus. Prejuicio antiprotestante y religiosidad utilitaria. Madrid, 1969.

Phil 8654.118 — L'analis del linguaggio teologico: il nome di Dio. Padova, 1969.

Phil 505.6 — Andreev, Edvard P. Prostranstvo mikromira. Moskva, 1969.

Phil 4870.16 — Anikeev, Nikolai Petrovich. Modern ideological struggle for the ancient philosophical heritage of India. Calcutta, 1969.

Phil 5535.40 — Annett, John. Feedback and human behavior. Baltimore, 1969.

Phil 8655.16 — Anonimnye ateisticheskie traktaty. Moskva, 1969.

Phil 8980.159.5 — Arkhangel'skii, Leonid M. Lektsii po marksistskoi etiki. v.1-. Sverdlovsk, 1969.

Phil 720.80 — Armour, Leslie. The concept of truth. Assen, 1969.

Phil 2490.184.5 — Arnaud, Pierre. La pensée d'Auguste Comte. Paris, 1969.

Phil 2490.184 — Arnaud, Pierre. Sociologie de Comte. Paris, 1969.

Phil 8401.40.10 — Arnheim, Rudolf. Visual thinking. Berkeley, 1969.

Phil 8980.162 — Artač, Marija. Gradiva za pouk temeljev socialistične morale. Ljubljana, 1969.

Phil 4751.4.25 — Asmus, Valentin F. Izbrannye filosofskie trudy. v.1- Moskva, 1969- 2v.

Phil 1865.190.7 — Atkinson, Charles. Jeremy Bentham. N.Y., 1969.

Chronological Listing

Phil 2477.8.90   Avanzini, Guy. La contribution de Binet à l'élaboration d'une pédagogie scientifique. Paris, 1969.

Phil 8401.41   Avramov, Dimitur. Estetika na modernoto izkustvo. Sofiia, 1969.

Phil 2445.6.30   Axelos, Kostas. Le jeu du monde. Paris, 1969.

Phil 6998.4.2   Axline, Virginia Mae. Play therapy. N.Y., 1969.

Phil 1845.10.5   Ayer, Alfred Jules. Metaphysics and common sense. London, 1969.

Phil 8876.166   Baader, Franz von. Über die Begründung der Ethik durch die Physik und andere Schriften. Stuttgart, 1969.

Phil 2477.15.8   Bachelard, Gaston. The poetics of reverie. N.Y., 1969.

Phil 5599.85.5   Backes-Thomas, Madeleine. Le test des trois personnages. Neuchâtel, 1969.

Phil 8402.66   Baekkelund, Kjell. Kunst eller kaos? Oslo, 1969.

Phil 310.718   Bagirov, Z.N. V.I. Lenin i dialekticheskoe ponimanie otritsaniia. Baku, 1969.

Phil 8656.40   Balbontín, José A. A la busca del Dios perdido. Madrid, 1969.

Phil 2115.235   Baldini, Artemio Enzo. Il pensiero giovanile di John Locke. Milano, 1969.

Phil 3483.92   Banfi, Antonio. Esegesi e letture kantiane. Urbino, 1969. 2v.

Phil 9070.128   Banowsky, William Slater. It's a playboy world. Old Tappan, 1969.

Phil 3450.11.475   Baratta, Giorgio. L'idealismo fenomenologico di Edmund Husserl. Urbino, 1969.

Phil 5190.75   Barker, John A. A formal analysis of conditionals. Carbondale, 1969.

Phil 5425.114.1   Barlow, F. Mental prodigies. N.Y., 1969.

Phil 3120.3.30   Barnick, Johannes. Vierfaltigkeit in Logik und Welt oder die vier Bücher vom Sinn des Ganzen. Berlin, 1969.

Phil 5871.80   Baroni, Christophe. Les parents, les inconnus. Genève, 1969.

Phil 5421.10.35   Barraud, Jean. L'homme et son angoisse. Paris, 1969.

Phil 8620.64   Barreau, Jean Claude. Où est le mal? Paris, 1969.

Phil 4351.6.85   Barreiro Gomez, José. Sistematización de lo personal y lo sobrenatural. Lugo, 1969.

Phil 2880.8.250   Bauer, George Howard. Sartre and the artist. Chicago, 1969.

Phil 3460.92   Baum, Guenther. Vernunft und Erkenntnis. Bonn, 1969.

Phil 5625.128   Baumstimler, Yves. Automatisation du comportement et commutation. Paris, 1969.

Phil 1701.54   Bausola, Adriano. Indagini di storia della filosofia. Milano, 1969.

Phil 3801.194.5   Bausola, Adriano. Lo svolgimento del pensiero di Schelling. Milano, 1969.

Phil 8876.164   Beardsmore, R.W. Moral reasoning. London, 1969.

Phil 3001.22   Beck, Lewis White. Early German philosophy: Kant and his predecessors. Cambridge, 1969.

Phil 3483.85.5   Beck, Lewis White. Kant studies today. La Salle, 1969.

Phil 5241.174   Becker, Ernest. Angel in armor; a post Freudian perspective on the nature of man. N.Y., 1969.

Phil 3425.738   Becker, Werner. Hegels Begriff der Dialektik und das Prinzip des Idealismus. Stuttgart, 1969.

Phil 332.38   Begiashvili, Archie F. Problema nachala poznaniia v B. Rassela i E. Gusserlia. Tbilisi, 1969.

Phil 5440.38   Behavioral genetics; method and research. N.Y., 1969.

Phil 1540.96   Beierwaltes, Werner. Platonismus in der Philosophie des Mittelalters. Darmstadt, 1969.

Phil 978.59.125   Bercou, Lydia. Krishnamurti, sa vie, sa parole. n.p., 1969.

Phil 5241.180   Berdelle, Philipp. Kleine Theorie des praktischen Denkens. Mainz, 1969.

Phil 5241.182   Berg, Jan Hendrik van den. De zuilen van het Panthéon en andere studies. Nijkerk, 1969.

Phil 2750.19.125   Berg, Randi. Alternativ til det absurde. Oslo, 1969.

Phil 585.385   Berger, Herman. De progressieve en de conservatieve mens in hermeneutisch perspectief. Nijmegen, 1969.

Phil 5421.20.75   Berkowitz, Leonard. Roots of aggression. 1. ed. N.Y., 1969.

Phil 978.6.72   Besant, Annie. Thought-forms. Wheaton, Ill., 1969.

Phil 2648.96   Besthern, Rudolf. Textkritische Studien zum Werk Holbachs. Berlin, 1969.

Phil 176.240   Betancur, Cayetano. Filosofos y filosofias. Bogota, 1969.

Phil 5871.40   Bettelheim, Bruno. The children of the dream. N.Y., 1969.

Phil 4006.5.80   Bibliografia degli scritti di Eugenio Garin. Bari, 1969.

Phil 8092.22   Bignami, Ariel. Notas para la polémica sobre realismo. Buenos Aires, 1969.

Phil 6140.15   Bindman, Arthur J. Perspectives in community mental health. Chicago, 1969.

Phil 5241.54.5   Binet, Alfred. The experimental psychology of Alfred Binet; selected papers. N.Y., 1969.

Phil 5478.14   Birney, Robert Charles. Fear of failure. N.Y., 1969.

Phil 7159.8   Bjornstad, James. Twentieth century prophecy: Jeane Dixon, Edgar Cayce. Minneapolis, 1969.

Phil 5811.24   Blancheteau, Marc. L'orientation spatiale chez l'animal, ses indices et ses repères. Paris, 1969.

Phil 3120.55.25   Bloch, Ernst. Die Kunst, Schiller zu sprechen und andere literarische Aufsätze. Frankfurt, 1969. 14v.

Phil 5548.142   Bloeschl, Lilian. Belohnung und Bestrafung im Lernexperiment. Weinheim, 1969.

Phil 2477.6.180   Blondel, Maurice. Correspondance de Maurice Blondel et Joannès Wehrlé; extraits. Paris, 1969. 2v.

Phil 5545.266   Blum, Herwig. Die antike Mnemotechnik. Thesis. Hildesheim, 1969.

Phil 3425.700   Bodanmer, Theodor. Hegel Deutung der Sprache. Hamburg, 1969.

Phil 3246.320   Boeckelmann, Frank. Die Schriften zu Johann Gottlieb Fichtes Atheismus-Streit. München, 1969.

Phil 577.2   Boehm, Gottfried. Studien zur Perspektivität. Thesis. Heidelberg, 1969.

Phil 5252.164   Boersenverein des deutschen Buchhandels, Frankfurt am Main. Alexander Mitscherlich: Ansprachen anlässlich der Verleihung des Friedenspreises. Frankfurt, 1969.

Phil 176.232   Bogliolo, Luigi. Nuovo corso di filosofia a norma del Concilio Vaticano II. Roma, 1969- 2v.

Phil 3001.20   Bogomolov, A.S. Nemetskaia burzhuaznaia filosofiia posle 1865 goda. Moskva, 1969.

Phil 1750.96.5   Boller, Paul F. American thought in transition: the impact of evolutionary naturalism, 1865-1900. Chicago, 1969.

Phil 3120.2.20   Bolzano, Bernard. Bernard Bolzano - Gesamtausgabe. Stuttgart, 1969.

Phil 3120.2.45   Bolzano, Bernard. Was ist Philosophie? Amsterdam, 1969.

Phil 4073.124   Bonansea, Bernardino M. Tommaso Campanella. Washington, 1969.

Phil 3821.30   Bonfi, Antonio. Spinoza e il suo tempo. Firenze, 1969.

Phil 1602.2   Bonicatti, Maurizio. Studi sull'Umanesimo. Secoli XIV-XVI. Firenze, 1969.

Phil 8430.94   Bono, Pierluigi. La morale dell'artista. Milano, 1969.

Phil 8612.82   Bordoni, Marcello. Dimensioni antropologiche della morte. Roma, 1969.

Phil 332.40   Born, Friedrich Gottlab. Versuch über die ursprünglichen Grundlagen des menschlichen Denkens und die davon Abhängigen Schranken unserer Erkenntniss. Bruxelles, 1969.

Phil 8581.113.5   Bošnjak, Branko. Marksist i kršćanin. Zagreb, 1969.

Phil 3425.688   Bourgeois, Bernard. La pensée politique de Hegel. Paris, 1969.

Phil 1195.21   Bowersock, Glen Warren. Greek sophists in the Roman empire. Oxford, 1969.

Phil 5241.172   Bowlby, John. Attachment and loss. London, 1969.

Phil 4065.50.15   Boyanov, Slavi. Filosofiiata na Dzhordano Bruno. Sofiia, 1969.

Phil 5865.5.35   Boyle, D.G. A student's guide to Piaget. 1st ed. Oxford, 1969.

Phil 1955.6.245   Boyston, JoAnn. John Dewey; a checklist of translations, 1900-1967. Carbondale, 1969.

Phil 9245.136   Bradburn, Norman Marshall. The structure of psychological well-being. Chicago, 1969.

Phil 8876.27.15   Bradley, Francis Herbert. Ethical studies. 2nd ed. London, 1969.

Phil 4260.180   Brancato, Francesco. Vico nel risorgimento. Palermo, 1969.

Phil 5858.5   Branden, Nathaniel. The psychology of self-esteem. Los Angeles, 1969.

Phil 450.12   Braun-Urban, Heiner. Wandlung der Welt durch Wandlung des Bewusstseins. München, 1969.

Phil 4803.454.105   Brawn, Jérzy Bronislaw. Apercu de la philosophie de Wroński. Rome, 1969?

Phil 5238.230   Breger, Louis. Clinical-cognitive psychology. Englewood Cliffs, N.J., 1969.

Phil 801.21.6.1   Bréhier, É. Histoire de la philosophie. Paris, 1969.

Phil 2750.20.130   Brena, Gian Luigi. La struttura della percezione. Milano, 1969.

Phil 6978.10   Bricout, Jacques. L'homme et la douleur. Paris, 1969.

Phil 176.230   Britton, Karl. Philosophy and the meaning of life. London, 1969.

Phil 9400.45   Brøndsted, Holger Valdemar. Tanker til overvejelse for os aeldre. København, 1969.

Phil 4912.5   Brown, Robert. Contemporary philosophy in Australia. London, 1969.

Phil 8402.39.5   Brunius, Teddy. Theory and taste. Uppsala, 1969.

Phil 4065.65.5   Bruno, Giordano. Das Aschermitt Wochsmahl. Frankfurt, 1969.

Phil 8070.2.10   Bruyne, Edgar de. The esthetics of the Middle Ages. N.Y., 1969.

Phil 1750.848   Buchdahl, G. Metaphysics and the philosophy of science. Oxford, 1969.

Phil 5241.88.3.5   Bühler, Charlotte M. Psychology for contemporary living. 1st American ed. N.Y., 1969.

Phil 5627.269.5   Bukin, Viktor R. Psikhologiia veruiushchikh i ateisticheskoe vospitanie. Moskva, 1969.

Phil 3640.790   Bulhof-Rutgers, Ilse Nina. Apollos Wiederkehr; eine Untersuchung der Rolle des Kreises in Nietzsches Denken. 's-Gravenhage, 1969.

Phil 7069.70.15   Burke, Clara Baker. The ghosts about us. Philadelphia, 1969.

Phil 6976.10   Buss, Arnold H. Theories of schizophrenia. N.Y., 1969.

Phil 332.42   Bychko, Ihor Valentynovych. Poznanie i svoboda. Moskva, 1969.

Phil 6480.265   Caligor, Leopold. Dreams and symbols. N.Y., 1969.

Phil 4073.58   Campanella, Tommaso. De dictis Christi. Roma, 1969.

Phil 4073.70   Campanella, Tommaso. Escatologia. Roma, 1969.

Phil 4260.190   Candela, Silvestro. L'unità e la religiosità del pensiero di Giambattista Vico. Napoli, 1969.

Phil 2905.1.650   Canteni, Agostino. Il problema Teilhard de Chardin. Milano, 1969.

Phil 5876.15   Caplan, Gerald. Adolescence: psychosocial perspectives. N.Y., 1969.

Phil 1107.7.3   Carbonara, Cleto. La filosofia greca. Platone. 2. ed. Napoli, 1969.

Phil 848.2.3   Carbonare, Cleto. La filosofia dell'espirenza e la fondazione dell'Umanesimo. 3. ed. Napoli, 1969.

Phil 5100.10   Carcaterra, Gaetano. Il problema della fallacia naturalistica. Milano, 1969.

Phil 4075.79.16   Cardano, Girolamo. Des Girolamo Cardano von Mailand eigene Lebensbeschreibung. München, 1969.

Phil 2905.1.600   Cargas, Harry J. The continuous flame. St. Louis, 1969?

Phil 5853.14   Carkhuff, Robert R. Helping and human relations. N.Y., 1969. 2v.

Phil 5917.168   Carnicer, Ramón. Entre la ciencia y la magia. 1. ed. Barcelona, 1969.

Phil 4080.3.81   Carr, Herbert Wildon. The philosophy of Benedetto Croce. N.Y., 1969.

Phil 680.10   Caruso, Paolo. Conversazioni con Claude Lévi-Straws, Michel Foucault, Jacques Lacan. Milano, 1969.

Phil 6327.21.95   Cattier, Michel. La vie et l'oeuvre du docteur Wilhelm Reich. Lausanne, 1969.

Phil 2880.8.295   Cavaciuti, Santino. L'ontologia di Jean Paul Sartre. Milano, 1969.

Phil 4843.2   Cavarnos, Constantine Peter. Modern Greek thought. Belmont, Mass., 1969.

Phil 1930.20   Cavell, Stanley. Must we mean what we say? N.Y., 1969.

Phil 7069.69.25   Cayce, Edgar. The Edgar Cayce reader. N.Y., 1969.

Phil 5520.738   Centre Regional de Documentation, Pedagogique de Poitiers. Textes et communications sur le thème: philosophie et langage, 24 avril, 1969. Photoreproduction. Paris, 1969?

Phil 3801.272   Cesa, Claudio. La filosofia politica di Schelling. Bari, 1969.

Phil 5520.68.10   Chase, Stuart. Danger: man talking! N.Y., 1969.

Phil 310.555.3   Chesnokov, Dimitrii I. Historical materialism. Moscow, 1969.

Phil 5212.15   Chin, Robert. Psychological research in Communist China, 1949-1966. Cambridge, Mass., 1969.

Phil 210.70.1   Chladenius, Johann Martin. Einleitung zur richtigen Auslegung vernünftiger Reden und Schriften. Düsseldorf, 1969.

Phil 5520.449.5   Chomsky, Noam. Linguistica cartesiana. Madrid, 1969.

Phil 8725.14   Christelijk bestaan in een seculaire cultuur. Roermond, 1969.

Phil 2515.10.10   Cioran, Emile M. Le Mauvais démiurge. Paris, 1969.

Phil 2255.1.150   Clark, Robert J. Bertrand Russell's philosophy of language. The Hague, 1969.

Chronological Listing

1969 - cont.

Phil 6155.10   Clark, Walter Houston. Chemical ecstasy. N.Y., 1969.

Phil 5870.90   Clauser, Günter. Die moderne Elternschule. Freiburg, 1969.

Phil 1133.40.2   Cleve, Felix M. The giants of pre-sophistic Greek philosophy. 2nd ed. The Hague, 1969. 2v.

Phil 5500.70   Cohen, Rudolf. Systematische Tendenzen bei Persönlichkeitsbeurteilungen. Bern, 1969.

Phil 5042.80   Coke, Zachary. The art of logic, 1654. Menston, Eng., 1969.

Phil 4080.3.540   Colapietra, Raffaele. Benedetto Croce e la politica italiana. Bari, 1969.

Phil 5238.226   Cole, Michael. Handbook of contemporary Soviet psychology. N.Y., 1969.

Phil 3425.716   Colletti, Lucio. Il marxismo e Hegel. Bari, 1969.

Phil 5520.675   Colli, Giorgio. Filosofia dell'espressione. Milano, 1969.

Phil 2905.1.590   Combes, André. Teilhard de Chardin et la sainte èvolution. Paris, 1969.

Phil 5080.8   Combès, Michel. Le concept de concept formel. Toulouse, 1969.

Phil 5585.305   Combs, Arthur Wright. Florida studies in the helping professions. Gainesville, 1969.

Phil 8952.23   Comitato Cattolico Docenti Universitari. Il problema morale, oggi. Bologna, 1969.

Phil 6140.25   Community life for the mentally ill; an alternative to institutional care. Chicago, 1969.

Phil 5625.126   Conditioned reinforcement. Homewood, Ill., 1969.

Phil 5625.122   Conference on Punishment. Punishment and aversive behavior. N.Y., 1969.

Phil 310.728   Congrès des Sociétés de Philosophie de Langue Française, 14th, 1969. La dialectique. 1. éd. Paris, 1969.

Phil 4070.7.90   Convegno di Studi Banfiani, Reggio Emilia. Antonio Banfi e il pensiero contemporaneo. Firenze, 1969.

Phil 4060.5.90   Cordaro, Philip. Andrea Angiulli e l'eredità dell'800. Castanissetta, 1969.

Phil 210.72   Coreth, Emerich. Grundfragen der Hermeneutik. Freiburg, 1969.

Phil 680.20   Corvez, Maurice. Les structuralistes: les linguistes, Michel Foucault, Claude Lévi-Strauss, Jacques Lacan, Louis Althusser, les critiques littéraires. Paris, 1969.

Phil 5520.670   Coseriu, Eugenio. Die Geschichte der Sprachphilosophie von der Antike bis zur Gegenwart. Stuttgart, 1969.

Phil 8877.102   Coste, René. Une morale pour un monde en mutation. Gembloux, 1969.

Phil 8657.34   Cottier, Georges. Horizons de l'athéisme. Paris, 1969.

Phil 8905.5   Coulson, Charles Alfred. Faith and technology; being the inaugural lecture of the Luton Industrial College. London, 1969.

Phil 5812.14   Crile, George J. A naturalistic view of man. N.Y., 1969.

Phil 5066.310   Crossley, John N. Constructive order types. London, 1969.

Phil 1702.13   Cruickshank, John. Aspects of the modern European mind. Harlow, 1969.

Phil 3822.12   Curley, E.M. Spinoza's metaphysics. Cambridge, 1969.

Phil 310.796.2   Cvekl, Jiří. Filosofie a soucásnost. 2. vyd. Praha, 1969.

Phil 310.712   Dahm, Helmut. Meuterei auf den Knien. Olten, 1969.

Phil 8583.46   Damiani, Raoul. Cristianesimo-marxismo. Milano, 1969.

Phil 3450.19.465   Dantlo, René. A la rencontre de Martin Heidegger. Toulouse, 1969.

Phil 5520.690   Das Jagannath, Prasad. Verbal conditioning and behavior. 1. ed. Oxford, 1969.

Phil 5039.28   Davis, J.W. Philosophical logic. Dordrecht, 1969.

Phil 5400.198   Davitz, Joel Robert. The language of emotion. N.Y., 1969.

Phil 5520.588   De Bono, Edward. The mechanism of mind. N.Y., 1969.

Phil 4752.2.195   Déchet, Ferruccio. L'ottavo giorno della creazione. Saggio su N. Berdijaev. Milano, 1969.

Phil 8980.320A   De George, Richard T. Soviet ethics and morality. Ann Arbor, 1969.

Phil 1828.6   Delaney, Cornelius F. Mind and nature; a study of the naturalistic philosophies of Cohen. Notre Dame, Ind., 1969.

Phil 2150.22.130   Delbo, Charlotte. La théorie et la pratique, dialogue imaginaire mais non tout à fait apocryphe entre Herbert Marcuse et Henri Lefebvre. Paris, 1969.

Phil 2905.1.115.5   Delfgaauw, B.M.I. Evolution; the theory of Teilhard de Chardin. London, 1969.

Phil 5398.5   Delgado, José M.R. Physical control of the mind. N.Y., 1969.

Phil 3425.748   Dell'Aquila, Michele. Critica e letteratura in tre hegeliani di Napoli. Bari, 1969.

Phil 5243.72   Dembicki, Leo. Psychologie: Modell und Wirklichkeit. Bodman/Bodensee, 1969.

Phil 4803.320.30   Dembowski, Bronisław. Spór o metafizyke. Warszawa, 1969.

Phil 6307.452   Denmark. Statens Andssvageforsorg. Ti ars andssvageforsorg, 1, oktober, 1969. København, 1969.

Phil 178.84   Derisi, Octavio Nicolas. Los fundamentos metafisicos del orden moral. 3. ed. Madrid, 1969.

Phil 8956.20.80   Derungs, Ursicin. Der Moraltheologe Joseph Geishüttner (1763-1805), I. Kant und J.G. Fichte. Regensburg, 1969.

Phil 2520.64   Descartes, René. Descartes. Paris, 1969.

Phil 2477.11.94   Deschoux, Marcel. Léon Brunschvicg ou l'idéalisme à hauteur d'homme. Paris, 1969.

Phil 9320.10   Desjardins, Arnaud. Les chemins de la sagesse. Paris, 1969- 2v.

Phil 8878.11.3   Dewey, John. Outlines of a critical theory of ethics. N.Y., 1969.

Phil 310.770   Dialekticheskii materializm i voprosy estestvosnaniia. Perm', 1969.

Phil 2750.22.120   Diaz, Carlos. Personalismo oberero. Madrid, 1969.

Phil 5043.38   DiBernardo, Giuliano. Logica, norme, azione. Trento, 1969.

Phil 1108.8   Diels, Hermann. Kleine Schriften zur Geschichte der antiken Philosophie. Hildesheim, 1969.

Phil 9255.30   Dikkers, S.J. Ironie als vorm van communicatie. Den Haag, 1969.

Phil 6906.15   Doerner, Klaus. Bürger und Irre. Frankfurt, 1969.

Phil 8448.11   Dorfles, Gillo. Kitsch: an anthology of bad taste. London, 1969.

Phil 2150.22.100   Doria, Francisco Antônio. Marcuse, vida e obra. Rio de Janeiro, 1969.

Phil 5243.41.2   Dreikurs, Rudolf. Grundbegriffe der Individualpsychologie. Stuttgart, 1969.

Phil 334.12   Dretske, Fred I. Seeing and knowing. London, 1969.

Phil 1828.4   Dubois, Pierre. Le problème de la connaissance d'autrui dans la philosophie anglaise contemporaine. Paris, 1969.

Phil 4073.128   Ducros, Franc. Tommaso Campanella, poète. Paris, 1969.

Phil 6400.38   Durieu, Colette. La rééducation des aphasiques. Bruxelles, 1969.

1969 - cont.

Phil 3425.726   Duso, Giuseppe. Hegel interprete di Platone. Padova, 1969.

Phil 8622.78   Duss-von Werdt, Josef. Theologie aus Glaubenserfahrung. Zürich, 1969.

Phil 2255.1.155   Eames, Elizabeth Ramsden. Bertrand Russell's theory of knowledge. London, 1969.

Phil 1750.166.285   Echandia, Dario. Humanismo y tecnica. Bogota, 1969.

Phil 5620.35   Edgley, Roy. Reason in theory and practice. London, 1969.

Phil 8725.10   Edwards, David Lawrence. Religion and change. London, 1969.

Phil 440.8   Edwards, Rem Blanchard. Freedom, responsibiblity and obligation. The Hague, 1969.

Phil 703.3   Ehbinghaus, Julius. Traditionsfeindschaft und Traditionsgehundenheit. Frankfurt, 1969.

Phil 165.448   Einführung in die Psychologie. Frankfurt, 1969.

Phil 5069.4   Eley, Lothar. Metakritik der formalen Logik. Den Haag, 1969.

Phil 285.6.1   Eliade, Mircea. Le mythe de l'eternel retour. Paris, 1969.

Phil 8954.10   Ellul, Jacques. Violence. N.Y., 1969.

Phil 5335.4   Elms, Alan C. Role playing, reward, and attitude change. N.Y., 1969.

Phil 6834.4   Emde Boas, Coenrad van. Essays in erotiek. Amsterdam, 1969.

Phil 5520.632   Engel, S. Morris. Language and illumination. The Hague, 1969.

Phil 978.49.915   Ericsson-Skopnik, Brigitte. Nachweis der Zitate zu Rudolf Steiner Die Rätsel der Philosophie im ihrer Geschichte als Umriss Dargestellt. Dornach, 1969.

Phil 5520.636   Ertel, Suitbert. Psychophonetik; Untersuchungen über Lautsymbolik und Motivation. Göttingen, 1969.

Phil 8629.4   Eschatologie et cosmologie. Bruxelles, 1969.

Phil 5160.6   Espersen, Jon. Logik og argumenter. København, 1969.

Phil 6155.18   Essai sur l'expérience hallucinogène. Paris, 1969.

Phil 8430.83   Estetika i proizvodstvo. Moskva, 1969.

Phil 8870.26   The ethics of change; a symposium. Toronto, 1969.

Phil 2115.220   Euchner, Walter. Naturrecht und Politik bei John Locke. Frankfurt am Main, 1969.

Phil 5593.69   Exner, John E. The Rorschach system. N.Y., 1969.

Phil 5592.196   Eysenck, Hans Jurgen. Personality structure and measurement. London, 1969.

Phil 5520.712   Faccani, Remo. I sistemi di segni e lo strutturalismo sovietico. Milano, 1969.

Phil 180.88.5   Faggiotto, Pietro. Il problema della metafisica nel pensiero moderno. Padova, 1969-

Phil 575.274   Fair, Charles M. The dying self. 1st ed. Middletown, Conn., 1969.

Phil 974.8   Faivre, Antoine. Eckartshausen et la théosophie chrétienne. Thèse. Paris, 1969.

Phil 1845.16.5   Fann, K.T. Symposium on J.L. Austin. London, 1969.

Phil 3925.16.210   Fann, K.T. Wittgenstein's conception of philosophy. Oxford, 1969.

Phil 180.92   Fasel, Georg K. Metaphysik. Duisburg, 1969.

Phil 960.212   Fausset, H.I. Anson. The flame and the light. N.Y., 1969[1958]

Phil 8622.80   Fede e mondo moderno. Roma, 1969.

Phil 2005.9.34   Feibleman, James. The way of a man. N.Y., 1969.

Phil 5590.542   Fel'dshtein, David I. Psikhologicheskie problemy formirovaniia nravstvennykh kachestv lichnosti v podrostkovom vozraste. Dushanbe, 1969.

Phil 1740.12   Ferrater Mora, José. La filosofia actual. Madrid, 1969.

Phil 5066.286   Feys, Robert. Dictionary of symbols of mathematical logic. Amsterdam, 1969.

Phil 400.134   Fichera, Giuseppe. La tematico religiosa nell'idealismo attuale. Catania, 1969.

Phil 3246.44.10.5   Fichte, Johann Gottlieb. Erste Wissenschaftslehre ven 1804. Stuttgart, 1969.

Phil 3246.72.3   Fichte, Johann Gottlieb. Das System der Sittenlehre nach Prinzipien der Wissenschaftslehre, 1798. 2. Aufl. Hamburg, 1969.

Phil 5590.475.5   Filosofsko-sotsiologicheskie problemy seorii lichnosti. Photoreproduction. Moskva, 1969. 2v.

Phil 5590.272   Fingarette, Herbert. Self-deception. London, 1969.

Phil 8612.78   Fink, Eugen. Metaphysik und Tod. Stuttgart, 1969.

Phil 8092.13.5   Fischer, Ernst. Art against ideology. London, 1969.

Phil 310.701   Flam, Léopold. Wording en ontbinding van de filosofie. Amsterdam, 1969.

Phil 310.784   Fleischer, Helmut. Marxismus und Geschichte. Frankfurt, 1969.

Phil 2045.144   Foester, Winfried. Thomas Hobbes und der Puritanismus. Berlin, 1969.

Phil 5870.50   Fordham, Michael Scott Montague. Children as individuals. London, 1969.

Phil 9070.136   Frank, Hannelore. Auf der Suche nach dem eigenen Ich. Stuttgart, 1969.

Phil 5045.19.2   Fraunce, Abraham. The lawyer's logic, 1588. Menston, Eng., 1969.

Phil 5045.19.5   Fraunce, Abraham. The shepherd's logic. Menston, 1969.

Phil 2130.80   Freeman, Kenneth D. The role of reason in religion: a study of Henry Mansel. The Hague, 1969.

Phil 7016.2   Frei, Gebhard. Probleme der Parapsychologie. München, 1969.

Phil 6315.17.30   Freud, Anna. Difficulties in the path of psychoanalysis. N.Y., 1969.

Phil 6315.17.16   Freud, Anna. Indications for child analysis, and other papers, 1945-56. London, 1969.

Phil 6315.2.40   Freud, Sigmund. Studienausgabe. v.1,4,6,8,10. Frankfurt, 1969. 6v.

Phil 3801.406.20   Frigo, Gianfranco. Matematismo e spinozismo nel primo Schelling. Padova, 1969.

Phil 575.286   Frings, Manfred S. Person und Dasein. Zur Frage der Ontologie des Wertseins. Den Haag, 1969.

Phil 5068.75   Frisch, Joseph C. Extension and comprehension in logic. N.Y., 1969.

Phil 5627.107.30   Frossard, Amdre. Díos existe, yo me la encontre. Madrid, 1969.

Phil 3805.260   Fuchs, Emil. Von Schleiermacher zu Marx. Berlin, 1969.

Phil 8955.13.5   Fuchs, Josef. Moral und Moraltheologie nach dem Konzil. Freiburg, 1969.

Phil 8612.76   Fuchs, Werner. Todesbilder in der modernen Gesellschaft. Frankfurt, 1969.

Phil 310.705   Furman, Aleksei E. Materialisticheskaia dialektika. Moskva, 1969.

Phil 5865.5.25   Furth, Hans G. Piaget and knowledge. Englewood Cliffs, 1969.

1969 - cont.

Phil 2477.15.115   Gagey, Jacques. Gaston Bachelard; ou, La conversion à l'imaginaire. Paris, 1969.

Phil 9346.15   Garabedian, John H. Eastern religions in the electric age. N.Y., 1969.

Phil 8696.27   Garadzha, Vikton I. Neotomizm. Razum. Nauka. Moskva, 1969.

Phil 2750.11.220   Garofalo, Gaetano. Jacques Maritain. Saggio critico. Bari, 1969.

Phil 2805.470   Garrone, Gabriel Marie. Ce que croyait Pascal. Tours, 1969.

Phil 3450.19.505   Garulli, Enrico. Problemi dell'Ur-Heidegger. Urbino, 1969.

Phil 2045.146   Gauthier, David Peter. The logic of Leviathan; the moral and political theory of Thomas Hobbes. Oxford, 1969.

Phil 6956.18   Gebhard, Erwin. Psychiatrie in unserer Zeit. Göttingen, 1969.

Phil 8881.82   Gehlen, Arnold. Moral und Hypemoral. Frankfurt, 1969.

Phil 310.745   Georgiev, Filipp I. Problema protivorechiia. Moskva, 1969.

Phil 3310.20   Geyer, H.F. Philosophisches Tagebuch. Freiburg, 1969. 3v.

Phil 8661.40   Giannini, Giorgio. L'ateismo nella filosofia italiana contemporanea. Roma, 1969.

Phil 5585.295   Gibson, Eleanor Jack. Principles of perceptual learning and development. N.Y., 1969.

Phil 3925.16.225   Giegel, Hans Joachim. Die Logik der seelischen Ereignisse. Thesis. Frankfurt, 1969.

Phil 4307.4   Gil Cremades, Juan José. El reformismo español; Krausismo. Barcelona, 1969.

Phil 8696.20.5   Gillispie, C.C. Genesis and geology. Cambridge, 1969.

Phil 5520.605   Gilson, Etienne. Linguistique et philosophie. Paris, 1969.

Phil 8661.35.5   Girardi, Giulio. Credenti e non credenti per un mondo nuovo. Firenze, 1969.

Phil 8661.35   Girardi, Giulio. Dialogue et révolution. Paris, 1969.

Phil 8661.33   Gironella, José María. Cien españoles y Dios. 3. ed. Barcelona, 1969.

Phil 3925.16.220   Glebe Møller, Jens. Wittgenstein or religionen. København, 1969.

Phil 5838.269   Glickman, Stephen E. The neurological basis of motivation. N.Y., 1969.

Phil 337.37   Gnoseologicheskie problemy formalizatsii. Minsk, 1969.

Phil 5270.12   Gobar, Ash. Philosophic foundations of genetic psychology and Gestalt psychology. The Hague, 1969.

Phil 6116.30   Goër de Herve, Jacques de. Mécanisme et intelligence. Paris, 1969.

Phil 310.734   Goerlich, Johann Wolfgang. Semantik und dialektischer Materialismus; Darstellung und Analyse der modernen marxistisch-leninistischen Wissenschaftstheorie in der DDR. Berlin, 1969.

Phil 6140.2   Golann, Stuart E. Coordinate index reference guide to community mental health. N.Y., 1969.

Phil 181.136.5   Goldmann, Lucien. The human sciences and philosophy. London, 1969.

Phil 3120.30.89   Goldstein, Walter Benjamin. Der Glaube Martin Bubers. Jerusalem, 1969.

Phil 3425.744   Golosov, Viktor F. Ratsional'noe i misticheskoe v gegelevskoi teorii iavliaiushchegosia dukha. Krasnoiarsk, 1969.

Phil 4073.126   Gonfunkel', Aleksandrkh. Tommaso Kampanella. Moskva, 1969.

Phil 5850.221.20   Gorden, Raymond L. Interviewing: strategy, techniques, and tactics. Homewood, Ill., 1969.

Phil 3450.18.90   Gornshtein, T.N. Filosofiia Nikolaia Gartmana. Leningrad, 1969.

Phil 9245.138   Gosling, Justin Cyril Bertrand. Pleasure and desire: the case for hedonism reviewed. Oxford, 1969.

Phil 6316.30   Gottschalk, Louis. The measurement of psychological states through the content analysis of verbal behavior. Berkeley, 1969.

Phil 9035.110   Granell Mañiz, Manuel. La recindad humana. Madrid, 1969.

Phil 5520.586   Grava, Arnolds. A structural inquiry into the symbolic representation of ideas. The Hague, 1969.

Phil 2905.1.595   Gray, Donald P. The one and the many. N.Y., 1969.

Phil 9070.121   Green, Celia Elizabeth. The human evasion. London, 1969.

Phil 5535.38   Green, Edward J. An annotated bibliography of visual discrimination learning. N.Y., 1969.

Phil 310.703   Gritsenko, Ivan I. Istoricheskoe i marksistskoi filosofii. Rostov-na-Donn, 1969.

VPhil 3640.766   Grlić, Danko. Ko je Niče. Beograd, 1969.

Phil 4080.36   Grocholl, Wolfgang. Der Mensch in seinem ursprünglichen Sein nach der Lehre Landulfs von Neapel. München, 1969.

Phil 585.422   Groethuysen, Bernhard. Antropoligia filosofica. Napoli, 1969.

Phil 3488.48   Grohmann, Johann Christian August. Dem Andenken Kants. Berlin 1804. Bruxelles, 1969.

Phil 3270.12.110   Grossmann, Reinhardt S. Reflections on Frege's philosophy. Evanston, 1969.

Phil 3640.795   Gruenter, Karlfried. Der Streit um Nietzsches "Geburt der Tragödie". Hildersheim, 1969.

Phil 3425.696   Grujié, P.M. Hegel und Sowjetphilosophie der Gegenwart. Bern, 1969.

Phil 2905.1.645   Grupo Español de Trabajo Teilhard de Chardin. En torno a Teilhard. Madrid, 1969.

Phil 5590.516   Gschwind, Martin. Die Wertfunktion des Menschen. Mainz, 1969.

Phil 8956.24   Guenthöe, Anselm. Entscheidung gegen das Gesetz. Freiburg, 1969.

Phil 3425.682   Guereñu, Ernesto de. Das Gottesbild des Jungen Hegel. Thesis. Freiburg, 1969.

Phil 5841.4   Guérin, Daniel. Essai sur la révolution sexuelle. Paris, 1969.

Phil 1828.10   Guffey, George Robert. Traherne and the seventeenth-century English platonists, 1900-1966. London, 1969.

Phil 2475.1.500   Gunter, Pete Addison Y. Bergson and the evolution of physics. 1st ed. Knoxville, 1969.

Phil 181.79.5   Gutkind, Eric. The body of God. N.Y., 1969.

Phil 3450.19.510   Guzzoni, Giorgio. Considerazioni intorno alla prima sezione de Sein und Zeit. Urbino, 1969.

Phil 585.345   Haeberlin, Paul. Der Mensch, eine philosophische Anthropologie. Zürich, 1969.

Phil 8882.95   Haering, Herman Johan. Ethiek der voorlopigheid. Nijkerk, 1969.

Phil 5411.10   Haesler, Alfred A. Leben mit dem Hass. Reinbeck, 1969.

1969 - cont.

Phil 3425.706   Hagen, Eduard von. Abstraktion und Konkretion bei Hegel und Kierkegaard. Bonn, 1969.

Phil 3425.698   Hahn, Manfred. Bürgerlicher Optimismus im Niedergang. München, 1969.

Phil 6980.347   Haley, Jay. The power tactics of Jesus Christ and other essays. N.Y., 1969.

Phil 9558.50   Hallie, Phillip Paul. The paradox of cruelty. 1. ed. Middletown, Conn., 1969.

Phil 182.140   Hammacher, Klaus. Kritik und Leben. v.2. München, 1969.

Phil 9245.142   Hancerlioğlu, Orhan. Başlangicidan bugüne mutluluk düsüncesi. Istanbul, 1969.

Phil 735.266   Handy, Rollo. Value theory and the behavioral sciences. Springfield, Ill., 1969.

Phil 6317.54   Harris, Thomas Anthony. I'm OK, you are OK: a practical guide to transactional analysis. N.Y., 1969.

Phil 974.3.147   Hartmann, Georg. Erziehung aus Menschenerkenntnis: von pädagogischen Impuls der Anthroposophie Rudolf Steiners. 2. Aufl. Dornach, 1969.

Phil 585.350   Hartmann, Otto Julius. Der Kampf um den Menschen in Natur, Mythos und Geschichte. Freiburg, 1969.

Phil 807.24   Hartnack, Justus. Filosofisns historie. København, 1969.

Phil 8882.90.5   Hedenius, Ingemar. Den omoraliska anständigheten. Stockholm, 1969.

Phil 3425.34.28   Hegel, Georg Wilhelm Friedrich. Hegel's Science of logic. N.Y., 1969.

Phil 3425.13.5   Hegel, Georg Wilhelm Friedrich. Werke. v.1-2,4-20. Frankfurt, 1969- 21v.

Phil 6750.269   Heggland, Ruth. Ti år med Erik; en mors beretning om sin hjerneskadede sønn. Oslo, 1969.

Phil 3450.19.54   Heidegger, Martin. The essence of reasons. Evanston, 1969.

Phil 3450.19.77.5   Heidegger, Martin. Identity and difference. 1st ed. N.Y., 1969.

Phil 3450.19.38   Heidegger, Martin. Martin Heidegger. Frankfurt, 1969.

Phil 3450.19.58   Heidegger, Martin. Zur Sache des Denkens. Tübingen, 1969.

Phil 8525.5   Heimbeck, Raeburne Seeley. Theology and meaning: a critique of metatheological scepticism. Stanford, 1969.

Phil 3090.91   Helberger-Frobenius, Sebastian. Macht und Gewalt in der Philosophie Franz von Baaders. Bonn, 1969.

Phil 5421.10.40   Hellner, Hans. Uber die Angst. Stuttgart, 1969.

Phil 5865.5.30   Helmore, Geoffrey Anthony. Piaget: a practical consideration. 1st ed. N.Y., 1969.

Phil 8882.100   Hemming, James. Individual morality. London, 1969.

Phil 7150.98   Hendin, Herbert. Black suicide. N.Y., 1969.

Phil 8882.108   Hengstenberg, Hans Eduard. Grundlegung der Ethik. Stuttgart, 1969.

Phil 585.408   Hermach, Yiří. Uskutečnění současného dověka. 1. vyd. Praha, 1969.

Phil 8440.5   Hermeren, Göran. Representation and meaning in the visual arts. Lund, 1969.

Phil 5590.534   Herrmann, T. Lehrbuch der empirischen Persönlichkeitsforschung. Göttingen, 1969.

Phil 3195.6.01   Herrmann, Ulrich. Bibliographie Wilhelm Dilthey. Berlin, 1969.

Phil 6315.2.460   Herwig, Hedda Juliane. Therapie der Menscheit. München, 1969.

Phil 5590.572.4   Hiebsch, Hans. Sozialpsychologische Grundlagen der Persönlichrechtsformung. 4. Aufl. Berlin, 1969.

Phil 8697.26   High, Dallas M. New essays on religious language. N.Y., 1969.

Phil 5066.314   Hintikka, Kaarlo Jaakko Johani. Models for modalities. Dordrecht, Holland, 1969.

Phil 4668.123.30   Hintikka, Kaarlo Jaakko Juhani. Tieto on valtaa ja muita aatehistoriallisia esseitä. Porvoo, 1969.

Phil 210.60   Hirsch, Wolfgang. Uber die Grundlagen einer universalen Methode der Philosophie. Bad Homburg, 1969.

Phil 6319.1.260   Hochheimer, Wolfgang. The psychotherapy of C.G. Jung. N.Y., 1969.

Phil 4007.10   Hoellhuber, Ivo. Geschichte der italienischen Philosophie von den Anfängen des 19. Jahrhunderts biz zur Gegenwart. München, 1969.

Phil 402.14   Hoelzle, Erwin. Idee und Ideologie. Bern, 1969.

Phil 338.48   Hoeres, Walter. Kritik der transzendentalphilosophischen Erkenntnistheorie. Stuttgart, 1969.

Phil 8815.5   Hoermann, Karl. Lexikon der christlichen Moral. Innsbruck, 1969.

Phil 288.24   Hoerz, Herbert. Naturphilosophie von der Spekulation zur Wissenschaft. Berlin, 1969.

Phil 8408.50   Hogg, James. Psychology and the visual arts: selected readings. Harmondsworth, 1969.

Phil 7069.69   Holzer, Hans W. Window to the past. Garden City, 1969.

Phil 8589.5.45   Hoover, Dwight W. Henry James. Grand Rapids, 1969.

Phil 3425.692   Horn, András. Kunst und Freiheit. Den Haag, 1969.

Phil 5876.25.3   Horrocks, John Edwin. The psychology of adolescence; behavior and development. 3rd ed. Boston, 1969.

Phil 182.138   Hors'kyï, Vilen S. Sotsial'ne seredovishche ta istoriko-filosofs'kyi protses. Kyïv, 1969.

Phil 5853.2   Hruschka, Erna. Versuch einer theoretischen Grundlegung des Beratungsprozesses. Habilitationsschrift. Meisenheim am Glan, 1969.

Phil 8882.105   Hudson, William Donald. The is-ought question. London, 1969.

Phil 70.6   Human action: conceptual and empirical issues. N.Y., 1969.

Phil 2050.59.4   Hume, David. A treatise of human nature. Harmondsworth, 1969.

Phil 5047.11.25   Husserl, Edmund. Formal and transcendental logic. The Hague, 1969.

Phil 3425.390.5   Hyppolite, Jean. Studies on Marx and Hegel. N.Y., 1969.

Phil 8430.72   Iakovlev, Eugenii G. Esteticheskoe soznanie iskusstvo i religiia. Moskva, 1969.

Phil 4960.270   Influenza italiana nella filosofia rioplatense. Firenze, 1969.

Phil 4803.462.45   Ingarden, Roman. Erlebnis, Kunstwerk und Wert. Tübingen, 1969.

Phil 70.83.16   International Congress of Applied Psychology, 16th, Amsterdam, 1968. Proceedings of the XVIth International Congress of Applied Psychology. Amsterdam, 1969.

Phil 5585.311   International Congress of Psychology, 18th, Moscow, 1966. Vospriiatie prostranstva i vremeni. Leningrad, 1969.

Phil 8400.36.4   International Congress on Aesthetics, 5th, Amsterdam, 1964. Actes du cinquième congrès international d'esthétique, Amsterdam, 1964. La Haye, 1969.

Phil 5545.254.3   International Interdisciplinary Conference on Learning, Remembering and Forgetting. Readiness to remember; proceedings of the third conference on learning, remembering, and forgetting. N.Y., 1969. 2v.

1969 - cont.

Phil 210.40 — Interpretation, theory and practice. Baltimore, 1969.

Phil 808.4 — Iovchuk, Mikhail T. Kratkii ocherk istorii filosofii. 2e Izd. Moskva, 1969.

Phil 8400.59 — Iskusstvo revoliutsiei prizvannoe. Moskva, 1969.

Phil 8905.15 — Iskusstvo uravstvennoe i bezuravstvennoe. Moskva, 1969.

Phil 5520.708 — Ismailov, B. Iazyk i poznanie mira. Tashkent, 1969.

Phil 1735.14 — Istoriko filosofskii sbornik. Moskva, 1969.

Phil 8430.74 — Iuldashev, Lekal G. Esteticheskoe chuvstvo i proizvedenie iskusstva. Moskva, 1969.

Phil 8673.34 — Ivanov, Ivan G. Rol' estestvornaniia v razvitii ateisticheskogo miroponimaniia. Moskva, 1969.

Phil 4710.7.15 — Iz istorii russkoi filosofii XIX-go-nachala XX-go veka. Moskva, 1969.

Phil 3120.55.100 — Jager, Alfred. Reich ohne Gott; zur Eschatologie Ernst Blochs. Zürich, 1969.

Phil 7120.2 — Jagot, Paul Clément. Traité méthodique de magnétisme personnel. Paris, 1969.

Phil 830.5 — James, Edwin Oliver. Creation and cosmology. Leiden, 1969.

Phil 2070.34 — James, William. The moral philosophy of William James. N.Y., 1969.

Phil 2475.1.510 — Janicaud, Dominique. Une généalogie du spiritualisme français. La Haye, 1969.

Phil 2675.4.10 — Jankélévitch, Vladimir. Vladimir Jankélévitch, ou De l'Effectivité. Paris, 1969.

Phil 3491.16 — Jansohn, Heinz. Kants Lehre von der Subjektivität. Bonn, 1969.

Phil 2905.1.630 — Jarque i Jutglar, Joan E. Foi en l'homme; l'apologétique de Teilhard de Chardin. Paris, 1969.

Phil 184.19.11 — Jaspers, K. Philosophy. v.1-. Translation. Chicago, 1969-71. 3v.

Phil 3475.3.220 — Jaspers, Karl. Provokationen; Gespräche und Interviews. München, 1969.

Phil 1809.4 — Jesuit Philosophical Association of the Eastern States. Phases of American culture. Freeport, 1969.

Phil 4720.2 — Jeu, Bernard. La philosophie soviétique et l'Occident. Paris, 1969.

Phil 720.74 — Joachim, Harold Henry. The nature of truth. Ann Arbor, 1969.

Phil 5819.10 — Joffe, J.M. Prenatal determinants of behaviour. 1. ed. Oxford, 1969.

Phil 6319.18 — Johnson, Adelaide McFadyne. Experience, affect and behavior: psychoanalytic explorations of Adelaide McFadyne Johnson. Chicago, 1969.

Phil 8884.25.5 — Johnson, Oliver Adolph. The moral life. London, 1969.

Phil 8090.5 — Johnson, Robert Vincent. Aestheticism. London, 1969.

Phil 5627.269.10 — Johoda, Gustav. The psychology of superstition. London, 1969.

Phil 809.5.2 — Jones, W.T. A history of Western philosophy. 2d ed. N.Y., 1969. 4v.

Phil 6128.17.5 — Jonsson, Inge. Swedenborgs konespondenslära. Stockholm, 1969.

Phil 8589.30 — Jordan, Placidus. Antwort auf Wort. München, 1969.

Phil 8664.12 — Journet, Charles. Connaissance et inconnaissance de Dieu. Paris, 1969.

Phil 5700.6 — Kadinsky, David. Der Mythos der Maschine. Bern, 1969.

Phil 8665.18.1 — Kahl, Joachim. Das Elend des Christentums. Reinbek bei Hamburg, 1969.

Phil 575.253.5 — Kalinin, Ananii I. Rol' truda v razvitii lichnosti v usloviiakh stroitelstva kommunizma. Cheboksary, 1969.

Phil 8885.54 — Kalinowski, Jerzy. Querelle de la science normative, une contribution à la théorie de la science. Paris, 1969.

Phil 3425.566 — Kaminsky, Jack. Hegel on art. N.Y., 1969.

Phil 5520.582 — Kaminsky, Jack. Language and ontology. Carbondale, 1969.

Phil 1750.845 — Kamlah, Wilhelm. Utopie, Eschatologie, Geschichtsteleologie. Mannheim, 1969.

Phil 3850.27.250 — Kantzenbach, Friedrich Wilhelm. Albert Schweitzer, Wirklichkeit und Legende. Göttingen, 1969.

Phil 3549.8.140 — Kasdorff, Hans. Ludwig Klages Werk und Wirkung. Bonn, 1969.

Phil 525.262 — Katsaros, Thomas. The Western mystical tradition. New Haven, 1969-

Phil 5286.10.4 — Katz, David. Gestaltpsychologie. 4. Aufl. Basel, 1969.

Phil 8735.61 — Kazakevich, Tat'iana A. Tselesoobraznost' i tsel' v obshchestvennom razvitii. Leningrad, 1969.

Phil 260.17 — Kedrov, Bonifatii M. Triaspekta atomistiki. Moskva, 1969. 3v.

Phil 5250.86 — Keiter, Friedrich. Verhaltensforschung im Rahmen der Wissenschaften vom Menschen. Göttingen, 1969.

Phil 310.554.2 — Kelle, Vladislav Zh. Kurs istoricheskogo materializma. 2. Izd. Moskva, 1969.

Phil 5279.25.5 — Kelly, Everett Lowell. The prediction of performance in clinical psychology. N.Y., 1969.

Phil 3270.4.86 — Kipper, Eberhard. Johann Paul Anselm Feuerbach. Köln, 1969.

Phil 310.692 — Kirschenmann, Peter. Kybernetik, Information, Widerspiegelung. München, 1969.

Phil 8980.486 — Kiselev, Askol'd A. V.I. Lenin i voprosy etiki. L'vov, 1969.

Phil 5790.40 — Klebelsberg, Dieter von. Risikoverhalten als Persönlichkeitsmerkmal. Bern, 1969.

Phil 2150.18.105.5 — Klemke, E.D. The epistemology of G.E. Moore. Evanston, 1969.

Phil 2150.18.105 — Klemke, E.D. Studies in the philosophy of G.E. Moore. Chicago, 1969.

Phil 5590.538 — Klimov, Evgenii A. Individual'nyi stil' deiatel'nosti v zavisimosti ot tipologicheskikh svoistv nervnoi sistemy. Kazan', 1969.

Phil 3160.9.95 — Kloppe, Wolfgang. Erinnerungen an Carl Gustav Carus. Berlin, 1969.

Phil 3640.780 — Klossowski, Pierre. Nietzsche et le cercle vicieux. Paris, 1969.

Phil 5090.12.2 — Klotz, Hans. Der philosophische Beweis. 2. Aufl. Berlin, 1969.

Phil 7010.7 — Knight, David C. The ESP reader. N.Y., 1969.

Phil 8700.14.5 — Kocher, Paul Harold. Science and religion in Elizabethan England. N.Y., 1969.

Phil 5274.4 — Kochergin, A.N. Problemy modelirovaniia psikhicheskoi deiatel'nosti. v.2. Photoreproduction. Moskva, 1969. 2v.

Phil 5520.706 — Kochergin, Al'bert N. Modelirovanie myshleniia. Moskva, 1969.

Phil 5250.15.18 — Köhler, Wolfgang. The task of Gestalt psychology. Princeton, 1969.

Phil 185.104 — Koerner, Stephan. What is philosophy? London, 1969.

Phil 5465.137.5 — Koestler, Arthur. The act of creation. N.Y., 1969.

1969 - cont.

Phil 3425.321.5 — Kojève, Alexandre. Introduction to the reading of Hegel. N.Y., 1969.

Phil 850.50 — Komarova, Vera Ia. K tekstologicheskomu analizn antichnoi filosofi. Leningrad, 1969.

Phil 5520.628 — Komlev, Nikolai G. Komponenty soderzhatel'noi struktury slova. Moskva, 1969.

Phil 5250.79.4 — Kotarbiński, Tadeusz. Traktat o dobrej robocie. Wyd. 4. Wrocław, 1969.

Phil 95.5 — Kratkii anglo-russkii filosofskii slovar'. Moskva, 1969.

Phil 291.16 — Kremianskii, Viktor I. Strukturnze urovni zhivoi materii. Moskva, 1969.

Phil 978.59.50 — Krishnamurti, J. Freedom from the known. 1st ed. N.Y., 1969.

Phil 5272.22 — Kristof, Walter. Untersuchungen zur Theorie psychologischen Messens. Meisenheim, 1969.

Phil 8665.27 — Kromer, Klaus. Gott und Welt in der klassischen Metaphysik. Stuttgart, 1969.

Phil 3549.11.5 — Kroner, Richard. Freiheit und Gnade. Tübingen, 1969.

Phil 3552.486 — Krueger, Lorenz. Rationalismus und Entwurf einer universalen Logik bei Leibniz. Frankfurt, 1969.

Phil 3528.60.1 — Krug, Wilhelm Traugott. Entwurf eines neuen Organon's der Philosophie. Meissen, 1801. Bruxelles, 1969.

Phil 185.10.2 — Krug, Wilhelm Traugott. Handbuch der Philosophie und der philosophischen Literatur. v.1-2. Düsseldorf, 1969.

Phil 6320.30 — Kruse, Friedrich. Die Anfänge des menschlichen Seelenlebens. Stuttgart, 1969.

Phil 5590.544 — Kucher, Volodymyr. Zorzumiite samykh sebe. Kanada, 1969.

Phil 4803.502.20 — Kuczyński, Janusz. Zyć i filozofować. Wyd. 1. Warszawa, 1969.

Phil 5790.2.15 — Kuebler-Ron, Elisabeth. On death and dying. N.Y., 1969.

Phil 8411.41 — Kuezyńska, Alicja. Przemiany wyobraźni. Wyd. 1. Warszawa, 1969.

Phil 185.106 — Kuspit, Donald Burton. The philosophical life of the senses. N.Y., 1969.

VPhil 310.704 — Kusý, Miroslav. Marxistická filozofia. 2. Vyd. Bratislava, 1969.

Phil 2880.8.255 — Kuznetsov, Vitalii N. Zhan-Pol Sartr i ekzistentsializm. Moskva, 1969.

Phil 1750.115.175 — Kwant, Remigius Cornelis. Phenomonology of expression. Pittsburgh, 1969.

Phil 3493.40 — Lacorte, Carmelo. Kant. Ancora un episodio dell' allanza di religione e filosofia. Urbino, 1969.

Phil 3493.44.3 — Lacroix, Jean. Kant et le Kantisme. 3. éd. Paris, 1969.

Phil 5270.24 — Lagache, Daniel. L'unité de la psychologie. 2. éd. Paris, 1969.

Phil 5241.75.80 — La Garanderie, Antoine de. Le dynamisme des structures inconscientes dans la psychologie d'Albert Burloud. Louvain, 1969.

Phil 6949.369 — Laiblin, Wilhelm. Märchenforschung und Tiefenpsychologie. Darmstadt, 1969.

Phil 6961.19.2 — Laing, Ronald David. Self and others. 2. ed. London, 1969.

Phil 3425.712 — Lakebrink, Bernhard. Studien zur Metaphysik Hegels. Freiburg, 1969.

Phil 3493.46 — Lamacchia, Ada. La filosofia della religione in Kant. Mandeiria, 1969-

Phil 5039.24 — Lambert, Karel. The logical way of doing things. New Haven, 1969.

Phil 5761.24.1 — Lamont, Corliss. Freedom of choice affirmed. Boston, 1969.

Phil 6121.55 — Laszlo, Ervin. System, structure, and experience. N.Y., 1969.

Phil 7069.69.40 — Laubscher, Barend Jacob Frederick. In quest of the unseen. 1st ed. N.Y., 1969.

Phil 3493.42 — Lauener, Henri. Hume und Kant. Bern, 1969.

Phil 8886.91 — Lauth, Reinhard. Ethik in ihrer Grundlage aus Prinzipien entfaltet. Stuttgart, 1969.

Phil 7074.5 — Laval. L'heure des révélations; le livre des temps. Montpellier, 1969.

Phil 978.120 — Leevwen, A.J.H. van. Ganesha. Amsterdam, 1969.

Phil 5051.42 — Lefebvre, Henri. Logique formelle, logique dialectique. 2e éd. Paris, 1969.

Phil 5068.86 — The legacy of logical positivism. Baltimore, 1969.

Phil 2805.465 — Le Guern, Michel. L'image dans l'oeuvre de Pascal. Paris, 1969.

Phil 3493.54 — Lehmann, Gerhard. Beiträge zur Geschichte und Interpretation der Philosophie Kants. Berlin, 1969.

Phil 3552.18.10 — Leibniz, Gottfried Wilhelm. Oeuvres, publiées pour la première fois d'après les manuscrits. v.2-7. N.Y., 1969. 7v.

Phil 3552.32.2 — Leibniz, Gottfried Wilhelm. Philosophical papers and letters. 2nd ed. Dordrecht, 1969.

Phil 635.2 — Leisegang, Dieter. Die drei Potenzen der Relation. Inaug. Diss. Frankfurt, 1969.

Phil 186.158 — Lemos, Ramon M. Experience, mind, and value. Leiden, 1969.

Phil 3425.300.5 — Lenin, V.I. Hefte zu Hegels Dialektik. München, 1969.

Phil 310.710 — Leninskata teoriia na otrazhenieto i sovremennostta. Sofiia, 1969.

Phil 310.716 — Leninskii etap v razvitii marksistskoi filosofii; sbornik nauchnykh rabot kafedry filosofii. Dnepropetrovsk, 1969.

Phil 5520.707 — Leon'tev, Aleksei A. Iazyk, rech', rechevaia deiatel'nost'. Moskva, 1969.

Phil 5520.595 — Leont'ev, Aleksei A. Psikholingvisticheskie edinitsy v porozhdenie rechevogo vyskazyvaniia. Moskva, 1969.

VPhil 9330.10 — Lepenies, Wolf. Melancholie und Gesellschaft. Thesis. Frankfurt, 1969.

Phil 5535.48 — Der Lernprozess. Anthropologie, Psychologie, Biologie des Lernens. Freiburg, 1969.

Phil 585.320 — Lersch, Philipp. Der Mensch als Schnittpunkt. München, 1969.

Phil 1750.166.240 — Letopis' zhizni i deiatel'nosti akademika I.P. Pavlova. Leningrad, 1969.

Phil 2725.42.5 — Levi, Albert William. Humanism and politics. Bloomington, 1969.

Phil 5590.530.3 — Levinas, Emmanuel. Totality and infinity. Pittsburgh, Pennsylvania, 1969.

Phil 5585.340 — Levitov, Nikolai D. Psikologiia kharaktera. 3. izd. Moskva, 1969.

Phil 8886.86 — Lévy, Jean Claude. Le temps psychologique. Paris, 1969.

Phil 8591.44.8 — Lewis, Clarence I. Values and imperatives. Stanford, Calif., 1969.

Phil 5520.571 — Lewis, Clive Staples. The screwtape letters. N.Y., 1969.

— Lewis, David Kellogg. Convention; a philosophical study. Cambridge, 1969.

1969 - cont.

Phil 6121.60 — Lewis, Hywel David. The elusive mind; based on the first series of the Gifford lectures. London, 1969.

Phil 5649.46 — Lézine, Iréne. Les étopes de l'intelligence sensori-motrice. Paris, 1969.

Phil 4160.41.35 — Librizzi, Carmelo. Letteratura, arte, filosofia. Padova, 1969.

Phil 5871.5.5 — Lindeman, Bard. The twins who found each other. N.Y., 1969.

Phil 4960.255 — Lipp, Solomon. Three Argentine thinkers. N.Y., 1969.

Phil 8886.90 — Loiser, Burton M. Custom, law, and morality: conflict and continuity in social behavior. 1st ed. Garden City, 1969.

Phil 5780.25 — London, Perry. Behavior control. 1. ed. N.Y., 1969.

Phil 6682.3.85 — Look, Maria van. Franz Anton Mesmer, Reinhold Schneider. Freiburg, 1969.

Phil 978.124 — Lorenzen, Iwer Thor. Evolution durch Inkarnation und Metamorphose. Hamburg, 1969.

Phil 5068.82 — Lorenzen, Paul. Normative logic and ethics. Mannheim, 1969.

Phil 8062.8 — Losev, Aleksei F. Istoriia antichnoi estetiki. Moskva, 1969.

Phil 5535.22 — Losifeseu, Marius. Random processes and learning. Berlin, 1969.

Phil 6321.56 — Lowe, Gordon Robb. Personal relationships in psychological disorders. Harmondsworth, 1969.

Phil 8666.17.11 — Lubac, Henri de. The drama of atheist humanism. Cleveland, 1969.

Phil 6400.32 — Lubin, Carl Kenneth. Language disturbance and intellectual functioning. The Hague, 1969.

Phil 5790.35 — Lucas, Rex H. Men in crisis; a study of a mine disaster. N.Y., 1969.

Phil 5467.10 — Lueck, Helmut E. Soziale Aktivierung. Köln, 1969.

Phil 5599.52 — Luescher, Max. The Lüscher color test. N.Y., 1969.

Phil 3585.20.30 — Luijpen, Wilhelmus Antonius Maria. Fenomenologie van het natuurrecht door W. Luijpen. Utrecht, 1969.

Phil 3585.20.6 — Luijpen, Wilhelmus Antonius Maria. A first introduction to existential phenomenology. Pittsburgh, 1969.

Phil 3585.20.4 — Luijpen, Wilhelmus Antonius Maria. Nieuwe inleiding tot de existentiële fenomenologie. Utrecht, 1969.

Phil 5590.506 — Lundin, Robert William. Personality; a behavioral analysis. N.Y., 1969.

Phil 3585.32 — Luyten, Norbert Alfons. Ordo rerum. Freiburg, 1969.

Phil 5871.114 — Lynn, David Brandon. Parental and sex-role identification. Berkeley, Calif., 1969.

Phil 575.276 — Maaloee, Erik. Egenskab og faellesskab. København, 1969.

Phil 3625.28.31 — Maass, Johann Gebhard Ehrenreich. Kritische Theorie der Offenbarung. Bruxelles, 1969.

Phil 5465.190 — Maass, Johann Gebhard Ehrenreich. Versuch über die Einbildungskraft. Bruxelles, 1969.

Phil 4983.5.95 — McCadden, Joseph James. Father Varela. N.Y., 1969.

Phil 5548.125 — McClelland, David Clarence. Motivating economic achievement. N.Y., 1969.

Phil 8887.134 — McCloskey, H.J. Meta-ethics and normative ethics. The Hague, 1969.

Phil 5890.2 — McDaniel, James Winnard. Physical disability and human behavior. N.Y., 1969.

Phil 6980.464 — McDougall, Joyce. Dialogue with Sammy; a psycho-analytical contribution to the understanding a child psychosis. London, 1969.

Phil 187.180 — Machado Bandeira de Mello, Lydio. Crítica cosmológica da física quântica. Belo Horizonte, 1969.

Phil 343.55 — McInerny, Ralph M. Studies in analogy. The Hague, 1969.

Phil 165.438 — MacIntosh, John James. The business of reason. London, 1969.

Phil 8667.30 — MacIntyre, Alasdair C. The religious significance of atheism. N.Y., 1969.

Phil 5330.42 — Mackworth, Jane F. Vigilance and habituation: a new psychological approach. Harmondsworth, 1969.

Phil 5222.22 — Madsen, K.B. Moderne psykologiske teorier. 2. oplag. København, 1969.

Phil 8962.28 — Maehl, Sibylle. Quadriga virtutum. Köln, 1969.

Phil 4170.18.30 — Magnini, Carlomagno. Introduzione alla critica della scienza. Bologna, 1969.

Phil 2520.405 — Magnus, Bernd. Cartesian essays; a collection of critical studies. The Hague, 1969.

Phil 5871.55 — Mahler, Margaret S. On human symbiosis and the vicissitudes of individuation. London, 1969-

Phil 1750.115.195 — Mailov, Anatolii Il'ich. Opisanie i ob"iasnenie. Tashkent, 1969.

Phil 3625.5.30 — Maimon, Salomon. Über die Progressen der Philosophie. Bruxelles, 1969.

Phil 8110.16 — Mainusch, Herbert. Romantische Ästhetik. Habilitationsschrift. Bad Homburg, 1969.

Phil 8413.44 — Malecki, Herbert. Spielräume. Frankfurt, 1969.

Phil 8962.24 — Manaranche, André. Y a-t-il une éthique sociale chrétienne? Paris, 1969.

Phil 5421.25.55 — Mannin, Ethel Edith. Practitioners of love: some aspects of the human phenomenon. London, 1969.

Phil 4260.165 — Manson, Richard. The theory of knowledge of Giambattista Vico. Hamden, Conn., 1969.

Phil 5052.44.7 — Marc-Wogau, Konrad. Logik, vetenskapsteori, argumentationsanalys. 2. tryckningen. Stockholm, 1969.

Phil 2150.22.35 — Marcuse, Herbert. An essay on liberation. Boston, 1969.

Phil 2150.22.40.2 — Marcuse, Herbert. Ideen zu einer kritischen Theorie der Gesellschaft. 2e Aufl. Frankfurt, 1969.

Phil 4363.7.6 — Marias Aguilera, Julián. Idée de la métaphysique. Toulouse, 1969.

Phil 7150.95 — Maris, Ronald W. Social forces in urban suicide. Homewood, 1969.

Phil 2750.11.41.1 — Maritain, Jacques. On the grace and humanity of Jesus. N.Y., 1969.

Phil 5401.60 — Marks, Issac M. Fears and phobias. N.Y., 1969.

Phil 5520.720 — Marmy, Emile. La philosophie du signe. Fribourg, 1969.

Phil 5251.41.95 — Marrow, Alfred Jay. The practical theorist; the life and work of Kurt Lewin. N.Y., 1969.

Phil 8725.12 — Martin, David. The religious and the secular. London, 1969.

Phil 3494.45.4 — Martin, Gottfried. Immanuel Kant. 4. Aufl. Berlin, 1969.

Phil 5625.116 — Martin, Irene. The genesis of the classical conditioned response. 1. ed. Oxford, 1969.

Phil 5070.30 — Martin, Richard Milton. Belief, existence, and meaning. N.Y., 1969.

Phil 8725.18 — Marty, Martin E. The modern schism. 1. ed. N.Y., 1969.

Phil 2150.22.140 — Masset, Pierre. La pensée de Herbert Marcuse. Toulouse, 1969.

Phil 3640.830 — Massuh, Victor. Nietzsche y el fin de la religión. Buenos Aires, 1969.

1969 - cont.

Phil 2750.19.120 — Matera, Rocco. Problematico e meta-problematico in Gabriel Marcel. Bari, 1969.

Phil 3832.22 — Matheron, Alexandre. Individu et communauté chez Spinoza. Paris, 1969.

Phil 2905.1.585 — Mathieu, Pierre Louis. La pensée politique et économique de Teilhard de Chardin. Paris, 1969.

Phil 5238.88.2 — May, Rollo. Existential psychology. 2d ed. N.Y., 1969.

Phil 5421.25.60 — May, Rollo. Love and will. 1. ed. N.Y., 1969.

Phil 187.184 — Maziarski, Stanisław. Prolegomena do filozofii przyrody inspiracji arystotelesowsko-tomistycznej. Lublin, 1969.

Phil 3450.19.485 — Mazzantini, Carlo. Il tempo e quattro saggi su Heidegger. Parma, 1969.

Phil 5875.130 — Mecham, Merlin J. Development of audiolinguistic skills in children. St. Louis, 1969.

Phil 3625.1.58A — Mendelssohn, Moses. Jerusalem, and other Jewish writings. N.Y., 1969.

Phil 1170.11.3 — Merlan, Philip. From Platonism to Neoplatonism. 3rd ed. The Hague, 1969.

Phil 2750.20.60 — Merleau-Ponty, Maurice. La prose du monde. Paris, 1969.

Phil 2805.421.1 — Mesnard, Jean. Pascal. University, 1969.

Phil 5270.16 — Metodologicheskie i teoreticheskie problemy psikhologii. Moskva, 1969.

Phil 1750.115.87 — Micallef, John. Philosophy of existence. N.Y., 1969.

Phil 1517.10 — Michalski, Konstanty. La philosophie au XIVe siècle; six études. Frankfurt, 1969.

Phil 7082.2 — Michaux, Henri. Façons d'endormi, façons d'éveillé. Paris, 1969.

Phil 2805.460 — Miel, Jan. Pascal and theology. Baltimore, 1969.

Phil 2190.20 — Miethke, Jürgen. Ockhams Weg zur Sozialphilosophie. Berlin, 1969.

Phil 2138.79.8.6 — Mill, John S. Autobiography. N.Y., 1969.

Phil 2138.45.15 — Mill, John S. Nature, the utility of religion and theism. Westmead, Eng., 1969.

Phil 2138.50.21 — Mill, John S. Utilitarianism. Belmont, Calif., 1969.

Phil 5251.1.30 — Mills, Eugene S. George Trumbull Ladd: pioneer American psychologist. Cleveland, 1969.

Phil 6322.65 — Milner, Marion Blackett. The hands of the living god. London, 1969.

Phil 1930.8.120 — Mink, Louis O. Mind, History, and dialectic: the philosophy of R.G. Collingwood. Bloomington, 1969.

Phil 705.68 — The minor and later transcendentalists; a symposium. Hartford, 1969.

Phil 5052.48.2 — Miro, Quesada Cantuarias. Iniciación lógica. 2. ed. Lima, 1969.

Phil 396.14 — Miro Quesada, Francisco. Humanismo y revolución. Lima, 1969.

Phil 553.2 — Misrahi, Robert. Lumière, commencement, liberté. Thèse. Paris, 1969.

Phil 5421.20.80 — Mitscherlich, Alexander. Bis hierher und nicht weiter. München, 1969.

Phil 5421.20.85 — Mitscherlich, Alexander. Die Idee des Friedens und die menschliche Aggressivität. Frankfurt, 1969.

Phil 5274.5 — Modelirovanie psikhicheskoi deiatel'nosti. Moskva, 1969.

Phil 6322.51 — Modell, Arnold H. Object love and reality: an introduction to a psychoanalytic theory of object relations. London, 1969.

Phil 583.18 — Mokrejš, Antonín. Fenomenologie a problém intersubjektivity. 1. Vyd. Praha, 1969.

Phil 8622.70 — Molevez, Léopold. Pour une théologie de la foi. Paris, 1969.

Phil 8887.135 — Momov, Vasil M. Nravstvenata norma i neinata realizatsiia. Sofiia, 1969.

Phil 2750.33.30 — Monnerot, Jules. Les lois du tragique. Paris, 1969.

Phil 5190.80 — Morales Encina, Carlos. Técnica de la persuasión. Santiago de Chile, 1969.

Phil 8962.26 — Morals, law, and authority. Dayton, Ohio, 1969.

Phil 8962.26.1 — Morals, law and authority. Dublin, 1969.

Phil 5330.38 — Moray, Neville. Listening and attention. Baltimore, 1969.

Phil 3494.68 — Moreau, Joseph. Le Dieu des philosophes. Paris, 1969.

Phil 2070.141.5 — Morris, Lloyd R. William James; the message of a modern mind. N.Y., 1969.

Phil 1730.28 — Mortier, Roland. Clartés et ombres du siècle des lumières. Études sur le 18e siècle littéraire. Genève, 1969.

Phil 5068.102 — Moscato, Alberto. Intenzionalità e dialettica. Firenze, 1969.

Phil 672.266 — Mostepanenko, Aleksandr M. Problema universal'nosti osnovnykh svoistv prostranstva i vremeni. Leningrad, 1969.

Phil 5066.312 — Mostowski, Andrzej. Constructable sets with applications. Warszawa, 1969.

Phil 1712.28 — Motroshilova, Nelli V. Poznanie i obshchestvo. Moskva, 1969.

Phil 3552.462.5 — Mueller, Kurt. Leben und Werk von Gottfried Wilhelm Leibniz. Frankfurt, 1969.

Phil 1750.750.2 — Mueller-Schwefe, Hans Rudolf. Existenzphilosophie. 2. Aufl. Göttingen, 1969.

Phil 5222.9.5 — Muller, Philippe. Psychology in the modern world. N.Y., 1969.

Phil 930.72 — Munro, Donald J. The concept of man in early China. Stanford, 1969.

Phil 5252.160 — Murphy, Gardner. Western psychology. N.Y., 1969.

Phil 5590.512 — Myers, Gerald E. Self; an introduction to philosophical psychology. N.Y., 1969.

Phil 1614.10 — Napoli, Giovanni di. Dal rinascimento all'illuminismo. Roma, 1969.

Phil 310.212 — Narskii, I.S. Problema protivoreckiia v dialekticheskoi logike. Moskva, 1969.

Phil 5068.94 — Narskii, Igor S. Dialekticheskoe protivorechie i logika poznaniia. Moskva, 1969.

Phil 5270.14 — Naturalistic viewpoints in psychological research. N.Y., 1969.

Phil 5867.25 — Neale, Robert Edward. In praise of play; toward a psychology of religion. N.Y., 1969.

Phil 8888.17 — Nedeljković, Dušan. Etika. 2. izd. Beograd, 1969.

Phil 3665.3.31 — Neeb, Johann. Vernunft gegen Vernunft. Frankfurt, 1797. Bruxelles, 1969.

Phil 3425.328.1 — Negri, Enrico de. Interpretazione di Hegel. Firenze, 1969.

Phil 310.805 — Negt, Oskar. Abram Deborin/Nikolai Bucharin: Kontroversen über dialektischen und mechanistischen Materialismus. Frankfurt, 1969.

Phil 813.6 — Negulescu, P.P. Scrieri inedite. Bucuresti, 1969.

Phil 310.749 — Nekotorye voprosy istoricheskogo materializma i nauchnogo kommunizma. Fergana, 1969.

Phil 7069.69.5 — Nelson, Geoffrey K. Spiritualism and society. London, 1969.

Chronological Listing

Phil 8980.604 — Nesteroo, Vladimir G. Trud i moral' v sovetskom doshchestve. Moskva, 1969.

Phil 8888.14.1 — Neumann, Erich. Depth psychology and a new ethic. London, 1969.

Phil 1750.115.180 — New essays in phenomenology. Chicago, 1969.

Phil 2150.22.120 — Nicolas, André. Herbert Marcuse ou la Quête d'un univers trans-prométhéen. Paris, 1969.

Phil 3640.78.5 — Nietzsche, Friedrich. Selected letters of Friedrich Nietzsche. Chicago, 1969.

Phil 3640.27.1 — Nietzsche, Friedrich. Umwertung aller Werte. München, 1969. 2v.

Phil 585.280 — Nobel Conference, 4th, Gustavus Adolphus College. The uniqueness of man. Amsterdam, 1969.

Phil 3925.16.255 — Novielli, Valeria. Wittgenstein e la filosofia. Bari, 1969.

Phil 5253.21 — Novik, Il'ia B. Filosofskie voprosy modelirovaniia psikhiki. Moskva, 1969.

Phil 8980.616.5 — Nravstvennoe razvitie lichnosti. Moskva, 1969.

Phil 5068.56.25 — Nuchelmans, G. O verzicht van de analytische wijsbegeeste. Utrecht, 1969.

Phil 4961.918 — Nuño, Alicia de. Ideas sociales del positivismo en Venezuela. Caracas, 1969.

Phil 8839.5 — Ocherk istorii etiki. Moskva, 1969.

VPhil 310.694 — Ochocki, Aleksander. Materializm historyezny. Warszawa, 1969.

Phil 6124.7 — O'Connor, John. Modern materialism; readings on mind-body identity. N.Y., 1969.

Phil 3030.6 — Oelmueller, W. Die unbefriedigte Aufklärung. Frankfurt, 1969.

Phil 5876.18 — Offer, Daniel. The psychological world of the teen-ager. N.Y., 1969.

Phil 189.34 — Oizerman, Teodor I. Problemy istoriko-filosofskoi nauki. Moskva, 1969.

Phil 3425.678 — Oldrini, Guido. Il primo hegelismo Italiano. Firenze, 1969.

Phil 1400.10 — Olhler, Klaus. Antike Philosophie und byzan tinisches Mittelalter. München, 1969.

Phil 5599.85 — Ombredane, André. L'exploration de la mentalité des noirs, le Congo T.A.T. Paris, 1969.

Phil 5535.36 — On the biology of learning. N.Y., 1969.

Phil 7150.105 — On the nature of suicide. 1st ed. San Francisco, 1969.

Phil 6324.8 — Orgü, Halis. Kampleksler ve insanlar. Istanbul, 1969.

Phil 5585.325 — Orme, John Edward. Time, experience and behavior. London, 1969.

Phil 4365.2.41 — Ortega y Gasset, José. Some lessons in metaphysics. 1st ed. N.Y., 1969.

Phil 8889.8.2 — Ossowska, Maria. Socjologia moralności 2. wyd. Warszawa, 1969.

Phil 4225.8.79 — Ottonello, Pier Paolo. Bibliografia di M.F. Sciacca. Milano, 1969.

Phil 5590.550 — Ozgü, Halis. Şahsiyet. 2. b. Istanbul, 1969.

Phil 815.34 — Pacini, Dante. Crise filosófica do século atual. Rio de Janeiro, 1969.

Phil 210.5 — Palmer, Richard E. Hermeneutics; interpretation theory in Schlelermacher, Dilthey, Heidegger, and Gadamer. Evanston, 1969.

Phil 6321.51.10 — Palmier, Jean Michel. Lacan, le symbolique et l'imaginaire. Paris, 1969.

Phil 2150.22.110 — Palmier, Jean Michel. Présentation d'Herbert Marcuse. Paris, 1969.

VPhil 3425.676 — Panasiuk, R. Lewica Heglowska. wyd. 1. Warszawa, 1969.

Phil 815.33 — Papalexandrou, K. Synoptike historia tes philosophias. 3. ed. Athens, 1969.

Phil 3497.28 — Papi, Fulvio. Cosmologia e civilta. Urbino, 1969.

Phil 2880.8.260 — Papone, Annagrazia. Esistenza e corporeità in Sartre. Firenze, 1969.

Phil 5520.598 — Parain, Brice. Petite métaphysique de la parole. Paris, 1969.

Phil 1750.830.10 — Parain-Vial, Jeanne. Analyses structurales et idéologies structuralistes. Toulouse, 1969.

Phil 3425.666.2 — Parinetto, Luciano. La nozione di alienazione in Hegel, Feuerbach e Marx. 2. ed. Milano, 1969.

Phil 440.10 — Pavidovich, Vsevolod E. Grani svobody. Moskva, 1969.

Phil 4768.5 — Payne, T.R. S.L. Rubinstein and the philosophical foundations of Soviet psychology. Dordrecht, 1969.

Phil 5055.29.5 — Perelman, Chaim. The new rhetoric: a treatise on agrumentation. Notre Dame, Ind., 1969.

Phil 6998.2 — Perls, Frederick S. Ego, hunger, and aggression; the beginning of Gestalt therapy. N.Y., 1969.

Phil 6998.2.11 — Perls, Frederick S. Gestalt therapy. N.Y., 1969.

Phil 6998.2.5 — Perls, Frederick S. In and out the garbage pail. Lafayette, Calif., 1969.

Phil 2150.22.105 — Perroux, François. François Perroux interroge Herbert Marcuse qui repond. Paris, 1969.

Phil 6965.28 — Pesso, Albert. Movement in psychotherapy; psychomotor techniques and training. N.Y., 1969.

Phil 575.294 — Petander, Karl. Västerlandet infor personlighetstanken. Uppsala, 1969.

Phil 2520.435 — Petit, Léon. Descartes et la princesse Elisabeth. Paris, 1969.

Phil 6325.27 — Petrilowitsch, Nikolaus. Charakterstudien. Basel, 1969.

Phil 6890.63 — Petrov, Erik F. Egoizm. Moskva, 1969.

Phil 310.699 — Petrović, Gajo. Mognénost čovjeka. Zagreb, 1969.

Phil 2725.13.80 — Petterlini, Arnaldo. Jules Lequier e il problema della liberta. Milano, 1969.

Phil 3552.478.1 — Peursen, Cornelis Anthonie van. Leibniz. London, 1969.

Phil 3925.16.98.1 — Peursen, Cornelis Anthonie van. Ludwig Wittgenstein: an introduction to his philosophy. London, 1969.

Phil 165.452 — Phaenomenologie, Rechtsphilosophie, Jurisprudenz. Frankfurt, 1969.

Phil 3497.25 — Philonenko, Alexis. L'oeuvre de Kant. Paris, 1969-

Phil 100.15 — La philosophie. Paris, 1969.

Phil 5865.5.22 — Piaget, Jean. The child's conception of time. London, 1969.

Phil 5585.195.5 — Piaget, Jean. The mechanisms of perception. London, 1969.

Phil 5865.5.5 — Piaget, Jean. The psychology of the child. N.Y., 1969.

Phil 705.74 — Piclin, Michel. La notion de transcendance; son sens, son évolution. Paris, 1969.

Phil 8612.68.5 — Pieper, Joel M. Death and immortality. N.Y., 1969.

Phil 5590.526 — Pieter, Józef. Wstęp do nauki o osobowości. Katowice, 1969.

Phil 4897.10.5 — Piovesana, Gino K. Contemporary Japanese philosophical thought. N.Y., 1969.

Phil 8670.24 — Pita Carpenter, Tomás. El ateismo de las masas. Madrid, 1969.

Phil 6325.32 — Plé, Albert. Freud et la morale. Paris, 1969.

Phil 8430.63 — Plebe, Armando. Che cosa è l'estetica sovietica. Roma, 1969.

Phil 75.90 — Plott, John C. Sarva-darsana-sangraha; a bibliographical guide to the global history of philosophy. Leiden, 1969.

Phil 585.335 — Podol'nyi, Roman Grigor'evich. Sviaz' vremen. Moskva, 1969.

Phil 346.20.15 — Polanyi, Michael. Knowing and being. London, 1969.

Phil 2825.35 — Politzer, Georges. Écrits...textes réunis par Jacques Debouzy. Paris, 1969. 2v.

Phil 346.27.8 — Popper, Karl Raimund. Conjectures and refutations: the grouth of scientific knowledge. 3. ed. London, 1969.

Phil 380.4 — Porter, Gene L. The nature of form in process. N.Y., 1969.

Phil 5255.80 — Porteus, Stanley David. A psychologist of sorts. Palo Alto, 1969.

Phil 5475.12 — Portmann, Adolf. Manipulation des Menschen als Schicksal und Bedrohung. Zürich, 1969.

Phil 3246.325 — Preul, Reiner. Reflexion und Gefühl. Berlin, 1969.

Phil 5238.234 — Pribram, Karl H. Brain and behaviour. Harmondsworth, Middlesex, Eng., 1969. 4v.

Phil 5070.28 — Price, Henry Habberley. Belief: the Gifford lectures delivered at the University of Aberdeen in 1960. London, 1969.

Phil 2050.256.5 — Price, John Valdimir. David Hume. N.Y., 1969.

Phil 585.330 — Problema cheloveka v sovremennoi filosofii. Moskva, 1969.

Phil 5520.644 — Problema znaka i znacheniia. Moskva, 1969.

Phil 8980.712.60 — Problemy formirovaniia kommunisticheskogo soznaniia. Ivanovo, 1969.

Phil 310.753 — Problemy istoricheskogo materializma. Moskva, 1969.

Phil 8654.115 — Problemy lichnosti v religii i ateizme. Moskva, 1969.

Phil 310.686.5 — Problemy otrazheniia. Moskva, 1969.

Phil 5545.256 — Problemy psikhologii pamiati. Khar'kov, 1969.

Phil 1750.850 — Protasenko, Zoia M. Lenin kak istorik filosofii. Leningrad, 1969.

Phil 5068.80 — Przelecki, Marian. The logic of empirical theories. London, 1969.

Phil 5520.698 — Psikhologicheskie i psikholingvisticheskie problemy vladeniia i ovladeniia iazykom. Moskva, 1969.

Phil 6155.20 — Psychedelic drugs. N.Y., 1969.

Phil 346.36 — Puntel, L. Analogie und Geschichtlichkeit. Freiburg, 1969.

Phil 8890.64 — Punzo, Vincent C. Reflective naturalism. N.Y., 1969.

Phil 5066.11.50 — Quine, Willard van Orman. Ontological relativity, and other essays. N.Y., 1969.

Phil 2725.35.115 — Quito, Emérita. La notion de la liberté participée dans la philosophie de Louis Lavelle. Fribourg, 1969.

Phil 5485.4 — Raaheim, Kjell. Opplevelse, erfaring og intelligens. Bergen, 1969.

Phil 5627.269 — Rabut, Olivier A. L'expérience religieuse fondamentale. Paris, 1969.

Phil 3425.694 — Rademaker, Hans. Hegels "objektive Logik" eine Einführung. Bonn, 1969.

Phil 8615.28 — Radest, Howard B. Toward common ground; the study of the ethical societies in the United States. N.Y., 1969.

Phil 4872.242.22 — Radhakrishnan, Sarvépalli. Radhakrishnan reader; an anthology. 1st ed. Bombay, 1969.

Phil 8870.31 — Raphael, David Daiches. British moralists, 1650-1800. Oxford, 1969. 2v.

Phil 6980.712.105 — Rattner, Josef. Psychologie der zwischenmenschlichen Beziehungen. Ölten, 1969.

Phil 8418.42 — Razummyi, Vladimir A. Esteticheskoe vospitanie. Moskva, 1969.

Phil 8092.18 — Realizm i khudozhestvennye iskaniia XX veka. Moskva, 1969.

Phil 1133.44 — Regnéll, Hans. Före Sokrates. Stockholm, 1969.

Phil 6327.21.85 — Reich, Ilse Ollendorff. Wilhelm Reich. N.Y., 1969.

Phil 2240.8 — Reid, Thomas. Essays on the active powers of the human mind. Cambridge, Mass., 1969.

Phil 2240.60.31 — Reid, Thomas. Essays on the intellectual powers of man. Cambridge, 1969.

Phil 3425.720 — Reidinger, Otto. Gottes Tod und Hegels Auferstehung. Berlin, 1969.

Phil 5625.117 — Reinforcement and behavior. N.Y., 1969.

Phil 1145.102 — Reinicke, Hans. Das Verhängnis der Übel im Weltbild griechischer Denker. Berlin, 1969.

Phil 348.26 — Reinisch, Leonhard. Grenzen der Erkenntnis. Freiburg, 1969.

Phil 5068.96 — Reintel'dt, Boris K. Zakon edinstva i bor'by protivopolzhnostei. Ioshkar-Ola, 1969.

Phil 165.432 — Rescher, Nicholas. Essays in philosophical analysis. Pittsburg, 1969.

Phil 735.268 — Rescher, Nicholas. Introduction to value theory. Englewood Cliffs, N.J., 1969.

Phil 5856.10 — Reuchlin, Maurice. La psychologie différentielle. Paris, 1969.

Phil 2255.11 — Rhees, Rush. Without answers. London, 1969.

VPhil 9513.40 — Rice, Charles E. The vanishing right to live. 1st ed. Garden City, N.Y., 1969.

Phil 5465.182 — Richardson, Alan. Mental imagery. London, 1969.

Phil 5465.182.1 — Richardson, Alan. Mental imagery. N.Y., 1969.

Phil 210.55 — Ricoeur, Paul. Le conflit des interprétations; essais d'herméneutique. Paris, 1969.

Phil 3808.240 — Riconda, Giuseppe. Schopenhauer interprete dell'occidente. Milano, 1969.

Phil 585.418 — Riedel, Maximilian. Der Mensch und das Ganze. München, 1969.

Phil 6965.3.95 — Riese, Walter. The legacy of Philippe Pinel. N.Y., 1969.

Phil 3499.26.5 — Rink, Friedrich T. Mancherley zur Geschichte der metacritischen Invasion. Bruxelles, 1969.

Phil 1200.70 — Rist, John Michael. Stoic philosophy. London, 1969.

Phil 3425.702 — Ritta, Joachim. Metaphysik und Politik. Frankfurt, 1969.

Phil 1828.8 — Riverso, Emanuele. La filosofia analitica in Inghilterra. Roma, 1969.

Phil 2255.1.180 — Rizzacasa, Aurelio. Il pacifismo nella dottrina politico-pedagogica di Bertrand Russell. Bologna, 1969.

Phil 8672.28 — Rizzacasa, Aurelio. Il problema di Dio nella filosofia occidentale. Viterbo, 1969?

Phil 6329.22 — Roazen, Paul. Brother animal; the story of Freud and Tausk. 1st ed. N.Y., 1969.

Phil 5066.300 — Robbin, Joel W. Mathematical logic; a first course. N.Y., 1969.

Phil 6327.21.90 — Robinson, Paul Arnold. The Freudian left: Wilhelm Reich, Geza Roheim, Albert Marcuse. 1st ed. N.Y., 1969.

Phil 1122.20 — Robinson, Richard. Essays in Greek philosophy. Oxford, 1969.

Phil 5066.288 — Robison, Gerson B. An introduction to mathematical logic. Englewood Cliffs, 1969.

1969 - cont.

Phil 3195.6.200 Rodi, Frithjof. Morphologie und Hermeneutik. Stuttgart, 1969.

Phil 3705.3.95 Rodnyi, Naum I. Vil'gel'm Ostval'd. Moskva, 1969.

Phil 3837.40 Roehrich, Welfried. Staat der Freiheit. Darmstadt, 1969.

Phil 5535.34 Rogers, Carl Ransom. Freedom to learn. Columbus, Ohio, 1969.

Phil 5870.70 Rogers, Dorothy. Issues in child psychology. Belmont, 1969.

Phil 676.2 Rohrbach, Marc Adrien. L'éveil spirituel, accomplissement personnel par la pensée créatrice. Paris, 1969.

Phil 4960.265 Roig, Arturo Andres. Los krausistas argentinos. Puebla, Mexico, 1969.

Phil 735.278 Die Rolle der Werte im Leben. Festschrift für Johannes Hessen zu seinen 80. Geburtstag. Köln, 1969.

Phil 3425.680 Rollwage, Jürgen. Das Modalproblem und die historische Handlung. München, 1969.

Phil 3450.19.495 Romano, Bruno. Tecnica e giustizia nel pensiero di Martin Heidegger. Milano, 1969.

Phil 4979.65.30 Romero, Sylvio. Obra filosófica. Rio de Janeiro, 1969.

Phil 8707.36 Roqueplo, Philippe. La foi d'un mal-eroyant ou mentalité scientifique et vie de foi. Paris, 1969.

Phil 535.45 Rosen, Stanley. Nihilism: a philosophical essay. New Haven, 1969.

Phil 5270.18 Rosenthal, Robert. Artifact in behavioral research. N.Y., 1969.

Phil 5700.2 Rosolato, Guy. Essais sur le symbolique. Paris, 1969.

Phil 3808.246 Rosset, Clément. L'esthetique de Schopenhauer. Paris, 1969.

Phil 4260.175 Rossi, Paolo. Le sterminate antichità. Studi vichiani. Pisa, 1969.

Phil 4110.5.80 Rota Ghibandi, Silvia. Giuseppe Ferrari. L'evoluzione del suo pensiero (1838-1860). Firenze, 1969.

Phil 2070.164 Roth, John K. Freedom and the moral life. Philadelphia, 1969.

Phil 3790.32 Rothert, Helmut. Welt, All, Einheit. München, 1969.

Phil 8892.84 Roubiczek, Paul. Ethical values in the age of science. Cambridge, Eng., 1969.

Phil 2055.7.85 Rouner, Leroy S. Within human experience; the philosophy of William Ernest Hocking. Cambridge, 1969.

Phil 5421.30.5 Rourke, Byron P. Explorations in the psychology of stress and anxiety. Don Mills, Ontario, 1969.

Phil 2880.8.265 Rovatti, Pier Aldo. Che cosa ha veramente detto Sartre. Roma, 1969.

Phil 2250.15 Royce, Josiah. The basic writings of Josiah Royce. Chicago, 1969. 2v.

Phil 8418.40 Rubert de Ventós, Xavier. Teoría de la sensibilidad. 1. ed. Barcelona, 1969.

Phil 1817.22 Rucker, Darnell. The Chicago pragmatists. Minneapolis, 1969.

Phil 9450.61 Rus, Vojan. Kultura, politika in morala. Maribor, 1969.

Phil 2255.1.64 Russell, Bertrand Russell. Dear Bertrand Russell: a selection of his correspondence with the general public, 1950-1968. London, 1969.

Phil 2255.1.74A Russell, Bertrand Russell. Power; a new social analysis. N.Y., 1969.

Phil 3850.18.220 Rutishauser, Bruno. Max Schelers Phänomenologie des Fühlens. Bern, 1969.

Phil 3499.42 Ruvo, Vincenzo de. Il pensiero filosofico di Kant, ovvero problemi di critica Kantiana. Paris, 1969.

Phil 8419.65 Šabouk, Sáva. Jazyk umění. Praha, 1969.

Phil 5421.25.20 Sadler, William Alan. Existence and love. N.Y., 1969.

Phil 6980.666 Sahakian, William S. Psychotherapy and counselling; studies in technique. Chicago, 1969.

Phil 8598.138.1 Saher, Purvezji Jamshedji. Easten wisdom and Western thought. London, 1969.

Phil 5853.6 Saint-Arnaud, Yves. La consultation pastorale d'orientation Rogérienne. Paris, 1969.

Phil 2225.5.175 Salanitro, Niccolò. Peirce e i problemi dell'interpretazione. Roma, 1969.

Phil 5590.508 Salber, Wilhelm. Charakterentwicklung. Wuppertal, 1969.

Phil 3500.114 Salem, Joseph. Immanuel Kants Lehre und ihre Auswirkungen. Gelsenkirchen-Buer, 1969.

Phil 5411.12 Salgado, Enrique. Radiografía del odio. Madrid, 1969.

Phil 4060.1.100 Saloni, Alfredo. Il positivismo e Roberto Ardigò. Roma, 1969.

Phil 5258.208 Salvat, Henri. L'intelligence; mythes et réalités. Paris, 1969.

Phil 5585.345 Sandstroem, Carl Ivar. Iakttagelse och upplevelse. Stockholm, 1969.

Phil 2280.5.91 Santayana, George. Physical order and moral liberty. Nashville, 1969.

Phil 1750.166.290 Santinello, Giovanni. Studi sull'Umanesimo europeo. Padova, 1969.

Phil 2050.282 Santucci, Antonio. Sistema e ricerca in David Hume. Bari, 1969.

Phil 4369.7.3 Sanz del Rio, Julián. Sanz del Río, 1814-1869. Madrid, 1969.

Phil 5520.624 Savigny, Eike von. Die Philosophie der normalen Sprache. Frankfurt, 1969.

Phil 8886.86.5 Saydah, J. Roger. The ethical theory of Clarence Irving Lewis. Athens, Ohio, 1969.

Phil 3500.116 Schaeffer, Wilhelm Friedrich. Inconsequenzen, und auffallende Widersprüche in der Kantischen Philosophie, Dessau, 1792. Bruxelles, 1969.

Phil 9495.169 Schaetzing, Eberhard. Schön wieder ein Aufklärungsbuch? Hamburg, 1969.

Phil 5520.325.1 Schaff, Adam. Einführung in die Semantik. Frankfurt, 1969.

Phil 5520.325.10 Schaff, Adam. Language et connaissance. Paris, 1969.

Phil 3850.62 Schaumann, Johann Christian Gottlieb. Versuch eines neuen Systems des natürlichen Rechts. Bruxelles, 1969.

Phil 845.4 Schiavone, Michel. Problemi ed aspetti dell'Umanesimo. Milano, 1969.

Phil 5520.584 Schiller, Jerome Paul. I.A. Richard's theory of literature. New Haven, 1969.

Phil 5421.20.115 Schindler, Sepp. Aggressionshandlungen Jugendlicher. Wien, 1969.

Phil 3805.18 Schleiermacher, Friedrich. Kleine Schriften und Predigten. Berlin, 1969-70. 3v.

Phil 7160.5 Schmeidler, Gertrude R. Extra-sensory perception. N.Y., 1969.

Phil 5520.580.5 Schmidt, Siegfried J. Bedeutung und Begriff. N.Y., 1969.

Phil 1050.19 Schmiedl, A. Studien über jüdische, Insonders jüdisch-arabische Religionsphilosophie. Wien, 1969.

Phil 3450.19.445 Schmitt, Richard. Martin Heidegger on being human. N.Y., 1969.

1969 - cont.

Phil 3500.88 Schmucker, Josef. Das Problem der Kontingenz der Welt. Freiburg, 1969.

Phil 2138.170 Schneewind, Jerome B. Mill, a collection of critical essays. Notre Dame, 1969.

Phil 5270.20 Schneewind, Klaus Alfred. Methodisches Denken in der Psychologie. Bern, 1969.

Phil 5413.16.5 Schoeck, Helmut. Envy; a theory of social behaviour. London, 1969.

Phil 6109.4 Schoenpflug, Wolfgang. Methoden der Aktivierungsforschung. Bern, 1969.

Phil 5238.236 Schools of psychology. N.Y., 1969.

Phil 3425.728 Schrader-Klebert, Karin. Das Problem des Anfangs in Hegels Philosophie. Wien, 1969.

Phil 349.65 Schrag, Calvin Orville. Experience and being. Evanston, Ill., 1969.

Phil 5642.22 Schroder, Ludwig. Sinne und Sinnesverknüpfungen. Heidelberg, 1969.

Phil 1750.858 Schröder, Erich Christian. Abschied von der Metaphysik? Beiträge zu einer Philosophie der Endlichkeit. Trier, 1969.

Phil 210.74 Schueling, Hermann. Die Geschichte der axiomatischen Methode im 16. und Beginnenden 17. Jahrhundert. Hildesheim, 1969.

Phil 5228.18 Schultz, Duane P. A history of modern psychology. N.Y., 1969.

Phil 6849.2 Schumann, Hans Joachim von. Liebesunfähigkeit bie Frauen und ihre Behandlung. München, 1969.

Phil 3850.27.65.5 Schweitzer, A. Reverence for life. N.Y., 1969.

Phil 4225.8.67.2 Sciacca, Michele Federico. La chiesane la civiltà moderna. 2. ed. Milano, 1969.

Phil 4225.8.48 Sciacca, Michele Federico. Gliarieti contro la verticale. Milano, 1969.

Phil 3850.27.16 Seaver, George. Albert Schweitzer; the man and his mind. 6th ed. London, 1969.

Phil 8598.6.10 Sedgwick, Adam. A discourse on the studies of the university. N.Y., 1969.

Phil 6309.6 Seelische Störungen. Frankfurt am Main, 1969.

Phil 493.6.15 Seely, Charles Sherlock. The essentials of modern materialism. N.Y., 1969.

Phil 5358.2 Seifert, Karl Heinz. Grundformen und theoretische Perspektiven psychologischer Kompensation. Meisenheim, 1969.

Phil 3850.70 Selle, Christian Gottlieb. Grundsätze der reinen Philosophie. Bruxelles, 1969.

Phil 720.78 Semaine des Intellectuels Catholiques, 1969. Chercher la vérité, 5-12 mars 1969. Paris, 1969.

Phil 1718.44 Semerari, Giuseppe. Esperienze del pensiero moderno. Urbino, 1969.

Phil 8980.782 Sevrikov, Konstantin I. Prostye istiny. Moskva, 1969.

Phil 5875.155 Sexuality and aggression in maturation: new facets. London, 1969.

VPhil 7072.21 Shakhnovich, Mikhail I. Primety v svete nauki. 2. izd. Leningrad, 1969.

Phil 960.274 Sharma, Dhirendra. The differentiation theory of meaning in Indian logic. The Hague, 1969.

Phil 2880.8.245 Sheridan, James Francis. Sartre; the radical conversion. Athens, Ohio, 1969.

Phil 5722.83 Sheroziia, Apollon E. K probleme soznaniia i bessoznatel'nogo psikhicheskogo. v.1-. Tbilisi, 1969.

Phil 193.260 Shibles, Warren. Philosophical pictures. Dubuque, 1969.

Phil 3925.16.280 Shibles, Warren. Wittgenstein; language and philosophy. Dubuque, Iowa, 1969.

Phil 5075.7 Shirokanov, Imitri I. Vzaimosviaz' kategorii dialektiki. Minsk, 1969.

Phil 6128.83 Shontz, Frank C. Perceptual and cognitive aspects of body experience. N.Y., 1969.

Phil 6140.10 Shore, Milton F. Mental health and the community; problems, programs and strategies. N.Y., 1969.

Phil 380.6 Shumilin, A.T. Problemy struktuny i soderzhaniia protsessa poznaniia. Moskva, 1969.

Phil 5520.594 Siddiqi, J.A. Experimentelle Untersuchungen über den Zusammenhang von Sprachgestalt und Bedeutung. Meisenheim, 1969.

Phil 5275.15 Simon, Herbert Alexander. The sciences of the artificial. Cambridge, 1969.

Phil 5520.590 Simon, Josef. Sprache und Raum. Berlin, 1969.

Phil 5768.22 Simon, Yves. Freedom of choice. N.Y., 1969.

Phil 3640.825 Simpozium na temu Niče i Marksizam, Belgrade, 1968. Niče i marksizam. Beograd, 1969.

Phil 8419.50.10 Šindelář, Dušan. Tržiště estetiky. Vyd. 1. Praha, 1969.

Phil 728.5 Singevin, Charles. Essai sur l'un. Thèse. Paris, 1969.

Phil 1750.115.145 Sinha, Debabrata. Studies in phenomenology. The Hague, 1969.

Phil 3450.18.195 Sirchia, Francesco. Nicolai Hartmann dal neokantismo all ontologia. Milano, 1969.

Phil 5625.120 Skinner, B.F. Contingencies of reinforcement. N.Y., 1969.

Phil 4803.794.30 Skolimowski, Henryk. Polski Marksizm. Londyn, 1969.

Phil 2266.41.10 Smith, Adam. The theory of moral sentiments. New Rochelle, 1969.

Phil 5374.280 Smith, Kendon Rasey. Behavior and conscious experience. Athens, 1969.

Phil 5599.80 Snider, James G. Semantic differential technique; a sourcebook. Chicago, 1969.

Phil 3808.244 Sørensen, Villy. Schopenhauer. København, 1969.

Phil 720.96 Soggettività e intersoggettività. Padova, 1969.

Phil 3425.718 Soll, Ivan. An introduction to Hegel's metaphysics. Chicago, 1969.

Phil 585.270 Sonnemann, Ulrich. Negative Anthropologie. Reinbeck bei Hamburg, 1969.

Phil 193.256 Sontag, Frederick. The existentialist prolegomena. Chicago, 1969.

Phil 8893.103.2 Sorokin, Pitirim Aleksandrovich. Altruistic love. N.Y., 1969.

Phil 8430.42.1 Souriau, Étienne. La correspondance des arts, éléments d'esthétique comparée. Paris, 1969.

Phil 9513.44 Sozialethik im Umbruch der Gesellschaft. Göttingen, 1969.

Phil 3850.66 Spann, Othmar. Kämpfende Wissenschaft. 2. Aufl. Graz, 1969.

Phil 5075.3.3 Spann, Othmar. Kategorienlehre. 3. Aufl. Graz, 1969.

Phil 400.76.2 Spann, Othmar. Der Schöpfungsgang des Geistes. 2. Aufl. Graz, 1969.

Phil 3925.16.195 Specht, Ernst Konrad. The foundations of Wittgenstein's late philosophy. Manchester, 1969.

Phil 9495.169.10 Speicher, Günter. Die grossen Tabus. Düsseldorf, 1969.

Phil 7150.100 Speijer, Nico. Het zelfmoordvraagstuk. Arnhem, 1969.

1969 - cont.

Phil 5643.172 — Spiekers, Rudolf. Über die optische Unterscheidbarkeit einfacher Zeichen. Thesis. Meisenheim am Glan, 1969.

Phil 4120.4.130 — Spirito, Ugo. Giovanni Gentile. Firenze, 1969.

Phil 310.751 — Spirkin, Aleksandr G. Teoriia, preobrasui ushchaia mir. Moskva, 1969.

Phil 3850.46.1 — Spranger, Eduard. Gesammelte Schriften. v.1-3,8. Tübingen, 1969- 4v.

Phil 8708.42 — Spülbeck, Otto. Zur Begegnung von Naturwissenschaft und Theologie. Einsiedeln, 1969.

Phil 3805.255 — Stalder, Robert. Grundlinien der Theologie Schleiermachers. Wiesbaden, 1969.

Phil 9070.122 — Starcke, Walter. The ultimate revolution. 1st ed. N.Y., 1969.

Phil 7069.69.20 — Stearn, Jess. Adventures into the psychic. N.Y., 1969.

Phil 1740.16.4 — Stegmüller, Wolfgang. Hauptströmungen der Gegenwartsphilosophie. 4. Aufl. Stuttgart, 1969.

Phil 3850.72.2 — Stegmueller, Wolfgang. Metaphysik, Skepsis, Wissenschaft. 2. Aufl. Berlin, 1969.

Phil 582.2 — Stegmueller, Wolfgang. Der Phänomenalismus und seine Schwierigkeiten. Darmstadt, 1969.

Phil 2150.22.115 — Steigerwald, Robert Reinhold. Herbert Marcuses dritter Weg. Köln, 1969.

Phil 8663.3.100 — Stein, Gordon. Robert G. Ingersoll; a checklist. 1. ed. Kent, Ohio? 1969.

Phil 978.49.692.4 — Steiner, R. Aus der Akasha-Chronik. 4. Aufl. Dornach, 1969.

Phil 978.49.735 — Steiner, R. Entwürfe, Fragmente und Paralipomenn zu den vier Mysteriendramen: Die Pforte der Einwiehung. Dornach, 1969.

Phil 978.49.778 — Steiner, R. Die gesunde Entwickelung des Leiblich-Physischen als Grundlage der freien Entfaltung des Seelison-Geistigen. 3. Aufl. Dornach, 1969.

Phil 978.49.759 — Steiner, R. Grenzen der Naturerkenntnis. 4. Aufl. Dornach, 1969.

Phil 978.49.785.3 — Steiner, R. Die Grundsteinlegung der Allgemeinen Anthroposophischen Gesellschaft. 3. Aufl. Dornach, 1969.

Phil 978.49.760 — Steiner, R. Heilfaktoren für den sozialen Organismus. 1. Aufl. Dornach, 1969.

Phil 978.49.77 — Steiner, R. Das Initiaten-Bewusstsein: die Wahren und die falschen Wege der geistigen Forschung. Dornach, 1969.

Phil 978.49.685 — Steiner, R. Menschenfragen und Weltenantworten. 1. Aufl. Dornach, 1969.

Phil 978.49.730 — Steiner, R. Die Naturwissenschaft und die welgeschichtliche Entwicklung der Menschheit seit dem Altertum. Dornach, 1969.

Phil 978.49.173 — Steiner, R. Die okkulte Bewegung im Neunzehnten Jahrhundert und ihre Beiziehung zur Weltkultur. 3. Aufl. Dornach, 1969.

Phil 978.49.745 — Steiner, R. Die Schöpfung der Welt und des Menschen. Dornach, 1969.

Phil 978.49.145.3 — Steiner, R. Sprachgestaltung und dramatische Kunst. 3. Aufl. Dornach, 1969.

Phil 978.49.595 — Steiner, R. Der Tod als Lebenswandlung. 1. Aufl. Dornach, 1969.

Phil 978.49.727 — Steiner, R. Wahrspruchworte: anthroposophischer Selenkalender. 2. Aufl. Dornach, 1969.

Phil 978.49.688 — Steiner, R. Das Wesen des Musikaleschen und das Tonerlebnis im Menschen. 1. Aufl. Dornach, 1969.

Phil 8598.143 — Stenson, Sten H. Sense and nonsense in religion. Nashville, 1969.

Phil 3850.64 — Stern-Mitcherlich, Axel Ludwig. The science of freedom; an essay in applied philosophy. London, 1969.

Phil 299.32 — Sterneder, Hans. Das kosmische Weltbild. Freiburg, 1969.

Phil 5066.242.1 — Stiazhkin, Nikolai Ivanovich. History of mathematical logic from Leibniz to Peano. Cambridge, Mass., 1969.

Phil 5875.160 — Stimulation in early infancy. London, 1969.

Phil 193.130.15 — Stocks, J.L. Morality and purpose. N.Y., 1969.

Phil 6315.2.475 — Stoev, Stoiu G. Froidizmat i preodoliavaneto ma v Bulgariia. Sofiia, 1969.

Phil 8419.66 — Stolovich, Leonid N. Kategoriia prekrasnogo i obshchestvennyi ideal. Moskva, 1969.

Phil 5421.35.15 — Stotland, Ezra. The psychology of hope. 1. ed. San Francisco, 1969.

Phil 1190.30 — Stough, Charlotte L. Greek skepticism; a study in epistemology. Berkeley, 1969.

Phil 2905.1.640 — Straniero, Giorgio. L'ontologia fenomenologica di Teilhard de Chardin. Milano, 1969.

Phil 583.4 — Strasser, Stephan. The idea of dialogal phenomenology. Pittsburgh, 1969.

Phil 3850.68 — Struve, Wolfgang. Der andere Zug. Salzburg, 1969.

Phil 705.72 — Struve, Wolfgang. Philosophie und Transzendenz. Freiburg, 1969.

Phil 5465.186 — Strzalecki, Andrzej. Wybrane zagadnienia psychologii twórczości. Wyd. 1. Warszawa, 1969.

Phil 5870.45 — Studies in cognitive development. N.Y., 1969.

Phil 5520.407.5 — Studies in multilingualism. Leiden, 1969.

Phil 349.58 — Study Group on the Unity of Knowledge. The anatomy of knowledge. Amherst, 1969.

Phil 3838.34 — Stybe, Svend Erik. Spinoza. København, 1969.

Phil 5170.14.5 — Subbotin, Aleksandr L. Traditsionnaia i sovremennaia formal'naia logika. Moskva, 1969.

Phil 6128.13.12 — Swazey, Judith Pound. Reflexes and motor integration; Sherrington's concept of integrative action. Cambridge, 1969.

Phil 3500.108 — Swing, Thomas K. Kant's transcendental logic. New Haven, 1969.

Phil 6328.40.5 — Szondi, Lipot. Kain, Gestalten des Bösen. Bern, 1969.

Phil 4260.160 — Tagliacozzo, Giorgio. Giambattista Vico. Baltimore, 1969.

Phil 3501.22 — Takeda, Sueo. Kant und das Problem der Analogie. Den Haag, 1969.

Phil 5069.6 — Tammelo, Ilmar. Outlines of modern legal logic. Wiesbaden, 1969.

Phil 5374.278 — Tart, Charles T. Altered states of consciousness. N.Y., 1969.

Phil 2905.1.18 — Teilhard de Chardin, Pierre. Human energy. London, 1969.

Phil 2905.1.29.5 — Teilhard de Chardin, Pierre. Letters to Léontine Zanta. London, 1969.

Phil 5190.94 — Thilo, Ingmar. Vom Fragen. Inaug. Diss. München, 1969.

Phil 5590.492.5 — Thomae, Hans. Vita humana. Frankfurt, 1969.

Phil 6980.732 — Thomas, Alexander. Temperament and behavior disorders in children. N.Y., 1969.

Phil 4073.130 — Thomas Campanella, 1568-1639. Milleciquecentoses santotto-milescicentotrentanove. Napoli, 1969.

Phil 5259.7.22 — Thorndike, E.L. Human nature and the social order. Cambridge, 1969.

Phil 3890.16 — Tiedemann, Dieterich. Idealistische Briefe Marburg. Bruxelles, 1969.

Phil 310.760 — Tierno Galvan, Enrique. Razon mecanica y razon dialectica. Madrid, 1969.

Phil 5520.704 — Tikhomirov, Oleg K. Struktura myslitel'noi deiatel'nosti cheloveka. Moskva, 1969.

Phil 8599.50 — Tillich, Paul. What is religion? 1. ed. N.Y., 1969.

Phil 9513.41 — Titarenko, Aleksandr I. Nravstvennyi progress. Moskva, 1969.

Phil 5421.20.70 — Toch, Hans. Violent men; an inquiry into the psychology of violence. Chicago, 1969.

Phil 5190.24.15 — Toensma, E. The paradoxes. Assen, 1969.

Phil 5259.55.2 — Toman, Walter. Family constellation. 2d ed. N.Y., 1969.

Phil 194.58 — Topitsch, Ernst. Mythos, Philosophie, Politik. Freiburg, 1969.

Phil 4060.10.80 — Travaglia, Sandro. La nozione di possibilità nel pensiero di Nicola Abbagnano. Padova, 1969.

Phil 3425.710 — Treher, Wolfgang. Hegels Geisteskrankheit. Emmendin, 1969.

Phil 5865.7 — Trends and issues in developmental psychology. N.Y., 1969.

Phil 9495.169.5 — Trillhaas, Wolfgang. Sexualethik. Göttingen, 1969.

Phil 8400.63 — Trud i esteticheskoe vospitanie. Riga, 1969.

Phil 5722.30.6 — Tucci, Giuseppe. The theory and practice of the Mandala. London, 1969.

Phil 3195.6.205 — Tuttle, Howard Nelson. Wilhelm Dilthey's philosophy of historical understanding. Leiden, 1969.

Phil 5853.10.3 — Tyler, Leona Elizabeth. The work of the counselor. 3d ed. N.Y., 1969.

Phil 310.690 — Ukraintsev, Boris S. Otobrazhenie v nezhivoi prirode. Moskva, 1969.

Phil 2150.22.145 — Ulle, Dieter. E'rivoluzionaria la dottrina di Marcuse? Torino, 1969.

Phil 6330.2 — Ullmann, Leonard P. A psychological approach to abnormal behavior. Englewood, Cliffs, 1969.

Phil 70.105.5 — University of Western Ontario. Philosophy Colloquium. Fact and existence; proceedings of the University of Western Ontario philosophy colloquium, 1966. Toronto, 1969. 2v.

Phil 70.105 — University of Western Ontario. Philosophy Colloquium. Fact and existence; proceedings of the University of Western Ontario philosophy colloquium, 1966. Oxford, 1969.

Phil 6980.760.10 — Urban challenges to psychiatry. 1. ed. Boston, 1969.

Phil 5585.335 — Uslar, Detlev von. Die Wirklichkeit des Psychischen. Pfullingen, 1969.

Phil 3503.35.4 — Valentiner, Theodor. Kant und seine Lehre. Eine Einführung in die kritische Philosophie. 4. Aufl. Stuttgart, 1969.

Phil 6315.2.440 — Vansina, M.J. Het super-ego. Antwerpen, 1969.

Phil 585.397 — Váross, Marian. Estetično, umenie a človek. Bratislava, 1969.

Phil 5061.10 — Veatch, Henry B. Two logics. Evanston, 1969.

Phil 3503.30 — Veca, Salvatore. Fondazione e modalita in Kant. Milano, 1969.

Phil 3808.252 — Vecchiotti, Icilio. La dottrina di Schopenhauer. Roma, 1969.

Phil 5627.266.6 — Vergote, Antoine. The religious man. Dublin, 1969.

Phil 5548.130 — Vernon, Magdalen Dorothea. Human motivation. London, 1969.

Phil 5871.45 — Vernon, Philip Ewart. Intelligence and cultural environment. London, 1969.

Phil 6400.36 — Vetter, Harold J. Language behavior and psychopathology. Chicago, 1969.

Phil 4260.44 — Vico, Giovanni Battista. De antiquissima Italorum sapientia. Roma, 1969.

Phil 4357.2.85 — Villalopos, José. El pensamiento filsofico de Giner. Sevilla, 1969.

Phil 8971.6 — La violenza die cristiani. Assisi, 1969.

Phil 4960.625.15 — Vita, Luís Washington. A filosofía contemporânea em São Paulo nos seus textos. São Paulo, 1969.

Phil 4960.625.10 — Vita, Luís Washington. Panorama da filosofia no Brasil. Pôrto Alegre, 1969.

Phil 1821.15 — Vitoux, Pierre. Hisotire des idées en Grande-Bretagne. Paris, 1969.

Phil 3801.872.25 — Volkmann-Schluck, Karl Heinz. Mythos und Logos. Berlin, 1969.

Phil 821.7 — Vollrath, Ernst. Die These der Metaphysik. Wuppertal, 1969.

Phil 106.1.20 — Voltaire, Francois Marie Arouet de. Philosophical dictionary. N.Y., 1969. 2v.

Phil 310.706 — Voprosy istoricheskogo materializma i kritika nekototorykh kontseptsii burzhnaznoi sotsiologii. Moskva, 1969.

Phil 352.13 — Voprosy teorii poznaniia. Moskva, 1969.

Phil 196.44 — Vries, Joseph de. Philosophie im Grundriss. Würzburg, 1969.

Phil 1750.189.5 — Wahl, Jean André. Philosophies of existence: an introduction to the basic thought of Kierkegaard. London, 1969.

Phil 197.94 — Walendy, Udo. Die Weltanschauung des Wissens. 1. Aufl. Vlotho, 1969. 2v.

Phil 1527.5 — Weber, Hans Emil. Der Einfluss der protestantischen Schulphilosophie auf die orthodox-lutherische Dogmatik. Darmstadt, 1969.

Phil 6319.1.265 — Wehr, Gerhard. C.G. Jung in Selbstzeugnissen und Bilddokumenten. Reinbek, 1969.

Phil 3460.94.5 — Weischedel, Wilhelm. Jacobi und Schelling. Darmstadt, 1969.

Phil 2340.10.235 — Weisenbeck, Jude D. Alfred North Whitehead's philosophy of values. Thesis. Waukesha, Wisconsin, 1969.

Phil 3425.704 — Weiss, Frederich Gustav. Hegel's critique of Aristotle's philosophy of mind. The Hague, 1969.

Phil 5590.470 — Weldes, Göran. Psykologi och mentalhygien. Lund, 1969.

Phil 5286.7 — Wellek, Albert. Ganzheitspsychologie und Strukturtheorie. 2. Aufl. Berlin, 1969. 4v.

Phil 384.15 — Welte, Bernhard. Determination und Freiheit. 1. Aufl. Frankfurt, 1969.

Phil 9450.64 — Wendland, Heinz Dietrich. Politik und Ethik. Darmstadt, 1969.

Phil 530.20.93.3 — Wentzlaff-Eggebert, F.W. Deutsche Mystik zwischen Mittelalter und Neuzeit. 3. Aufl. Berlin, 1969.

Phil 8725.16 — Werhahn, Hans. Das Vorschreiten der Säkularisierung. Bonn, 1969.

Phil 6332.45 — Whitmont, Edward C. The symbolic quest. N.Y., 1969.

Phil 5520.615 — Wierzbicka, Anna. Dociekania semantyczne. Wrocław, 1969.

Phil 6332.55 — Wiesenhuetter, Eckhart. Grundbegriffe der Tiefenpsychologie. Darmstadt, 1969.

Phil 6060.90 — Wieser, Roda. Grundriss der Graphologie. München, 1969.

Phil 2070.158 — Wild, John. The radical empiricism of William James. 1st ed. Garden City, N.Y., 1969.

1969 - cont.

Phil 2070.159 — William James: unfinished business. Washington, 1969.

Phil 5062.30.1 — Wilson, John Cook. Statement and inference. Oxford, 1969. 2v.

Phil 3925.16.200 — Winch, Peter. Studies in the philosophy of Wittgenstein. N.Y., 1969.

Phil 8423.16.15 — Winckelmann, Johann Joachim. Gedanken über die Nachahmung der griechischen Werke in der Malerei und Bildhauerkunst. Stuttgart, 1969.

Phil 8423.16.10 — Winckelmann, Johann Joachim. Werke in einem Band. Berlin, 1969.

Phil 1560.18 — Wippel, John F. Medieval philosophy: from St. Augustine to Nicolas of Cusa. N.Y., 1969.

Phil 3925.16.35A — Wittgenstein, Ludwig. On certainty. Oxford, 1969.

Phil 3925.16.12 — Wittgenstein, Ludwig. Preliminary studies for the "Philosophical investigations" generally known as the Blue and Brown books. 2nd ed. Oxford, 1969.

Phil 2045.148 — Wolf, Friedrich Otto. Die neue Wissenschaft des Thomas Hobbes. Stuttgart, 1969.

Phil 2340.20.30 — Wolff, Charlotte. On the way to myself: communications to a friend. London, 1969.

Phil 5871.75 — Wolff, Sula. Children under stress. London, 1969.

Phil 5425.110 — Wolfle, Dael Lee. The discovery of talent. Cambridge, 1969.

Phil 3842.11.2 — Wolfson, Abraham. Spinoza; a life of reason. 2nd ed. N.Y., 1969.

Phil 1885.93.2 — Wollheim, Richard. F.H. Bradley. 2d ed. Harmondsworth, 1969.

Phil 5627.134.57 — Wolrige Gordon, Anne. Peter Howard: life and letters. London, 1969.

Phil 3120.30.180 — Wood, Robert E. Martin Buber's ontology. Evanston, 1969.

Phil 5066.11.80 — Words and objections. N.Y., 1969.

Phil 3925.16.230 — Wuchteil, Kurt. Strukur und Sprachspiel bei Wittgenstein. Frankfurt, 1969.

Phil 5190.92 — Wybramec-Skardowska, Urszula. Z badań nad seoria zdań odrzuconych. Opole, 1969.

Phil 2115.210 — Yolton, John W. John Locke: problems and perspectives. London, 1969.

Phil 2725.2.125 — Zadei, Guido. Il pensiero socio-politico di Lamennais. Napoli, 1969.

Phil 310.655.5 — Zaječaranovič, Gligorije. Dijalektika ljudskog sveta. Novi Sad, 1969.

Phil 5835.10 — Zajonc, Robert Boleslaw. Animal social psychology. N.Y., 1969.

Phil 4957.810 — Zea, Leopoldo. La filosofía americana como filosofia sin más. 1. ed. México, 1969.

Phil 8426.11 — Zelenov, L.A. Protsess esteticheskogo otrazheniia. Moskva, 1969.

Phil 5650.54 — Zenatti, Arlette. Le développement génétique de la perception musicale. Paris, 1969.

Phil 5265.7 — Zhdanov, D.A. Vozniknovenie abstraktnogo myshleniia. Khar'kov, 1969.

Phil 8900.10 — Ziemba, Zdzisław. Logika deontyczna jako formalizacja rozumowań normatywnych. Wyd. 1. Warszawa, 1969.

Phil 5325.48 — Zimbardo, Philip G. The cognitive control of motivation: the consequences of choice and dissonance. Glenville, Ill., 1969.

Phil 5643.178 — Zinchenko, Vladimir P. Formirovanie zritel'nogo obraza. Moskva, 1969.

Phil 735.274 — Životić, Miladin. Čovek i vrednost. Beograd, 1969.

Phil 5640.136.15 — Zuber, John Peter. Sensory deprivation: fifteen years of research. N.Y., 1969.

Phil 4720.5 — Zuev, Ivan E. Ob"ektivnoe i sub"ektivnoe v poznanii i prakticheskoi deiatel'nosti. Moskva, 1969.

Phil 5873.4 — Zulliger, Hans. Die Angst unserer Kinder. Frankfurt, 1969.

Phil 5870.55 — Zulliger, Hans. Das Kind in der Entwicklung. Bern, 1969.

Phil 5599.98.5 — Zulliger, Hans. The Zulliger individual and group test. N.Y., 1969.

Phil 3507.12 — Zwingelberg, Hans Willi. Kants Ethik und das Problem der Einheit von Freiheit und Gesetz. Thesis. Bonn, 1969.

1970

Phil 9560.62 — Abicht, Johann Heinrich. Neues System einer philosophischen Tugendlehre. Leipzig, 1970.

Phil 3482.20 — Acton, Harry Burrows. Kant's moral philosophy. London, 1970.

Phil 860.4 — Adkins, Arthur William Hope. From the many to the one: a study of personality and views of human nature in the context of ancient Greek society, values and beliefs. London, 1970.

Phil 8875.27.5 — Adler, Mortimer Jerome. The time of our lives. 1st ed. N.Y., 1970.

Phil 75.88.5 — Adorno, Francesco. Il pensiero greco-romano e il cristianesimo. 1. ed. Bari, 1970.

Phil 3085.7.40 — Adorno, Theodor W. Aufsätze zur Gesellschaftstheorie und Methodologie. 1. Aufl. Frankfurt, 1970.

Phil 8448.5 — Ästhetik und Gewalt. Gütersloh, 1970.

Phil 3450.11.505 — Aguirre, Antonio. Genetische Phänomenologie und Reduktion. Den Haag, 1970.

Phil 5066.224.5 — Akademiia Nauk SSSR. Institut Filosofii. Problems of the logic of scientific knowledge. Dordrecht, 1970.

Phil 3850.27.260 — Al'bers Shveitser - velikii gumanist XX veka. Moskva, 1970.

Phil 3850.27.93.1 — The Albert Schweitzer Jubilee Book. Westport, Conn., 1970.

Phil 5040.30 — Alejandro, Jose Maria de. La lógica y el hombre. Madrid, 1970.

Phil 2070.155.1 — Allen, Gay Wilson. William James. Minneapolis, 1970.

Phil 2150.18.110 — Ambrose, Alice. G.E. Moore; essays in retrospect. London, 1970.

Phil 5627.270.5 — Anderson, George Christian. Your religion: neurotic or healthy? 1st ed. Garden City, 1970.

Phil 735.284 — Anisimov, Sergei F. Tseunoi real'nye i mnimye. Moskva, 1970.

Phil 585.375 — Antonovich, Ivan I. Sovremennaia "Anlosofskaia antropoligiia". Minsk, 1970.

Phil 5592.148 — Anzieu, D. Les méthodes projectives. 3e éd. Paris, 1970.

Phil 5274.6 — Apter, Michael John. The computer simulation of behavior. London, 1970.

Phil 535.30 — Arendt, Dieter. Nihilismus. Köln, 1970.

Phil 325.22 — Armstrong, Robert L. Metaphysics and British empiricism. Lincoln, 1970.

Phil 2880.8.275 — Aron, Raymond. Marxism and the existentialists. N.Y., 1970.

Phil 175.63 — Arvasi, S. Ahmet. Insan ve insanötesi. Istanbul, 1970.

Phil 8092.20 — Arvon, Henri. L'esthétique marxiste. Paris, 1970.

1970 - cont.

Phil 3000.6 — Arvon, Henri. La philosophie allemande. Paris, 1970.

Phil 5545.260 — Association de Psychologie Scientifique de Langue Française. La Mémoire. 1. éd. Paris, 1970.

Phil 5465.202 — Astruc, Louis. Créativité et sciences humaines. Paris, 1970.

Phil 5548.108.5 — Atkinson, John W. The dynamics of action. N.Y., 1970.

Phil 8825.10 — Attisam, Adelchi. Saggi di etica e di filosofia del diritto. Napoli, 1970.

Phil 325.18 — Aune, Bruce. Rationalism, empiricism, and pragmatism: an introduction. N.Y., 1970.

Phil 175.52.2 — Austin, John L. Philosophical papers. 2d ed. Oxford, 1970.

Phil 5870.107 — Ausubel, David Paul. Theory and problems of child development. 2nd ed. N.Y., 1970.

Phil 2905.1.635 — Babosov, Evgenii M. Teiiardizm. Minsk, 1970.

Phil 2477.15.32 — Bachelard, Gaston. Le droit de rêver. 2. éd. Paris, 1970.

Phil 2477.15.35 — Bachelard, Gaston. Études. Paris, 1970.

Phil 3808.248 — Bahr, Hans Dieter. Das gefesselte Engagement; zur Ideologie der Kontemplativen Asthetik Schopenhauer. Bonn, 1970.

Phil 5585.310 — Baird, John C. Psychophysical analysis of visual space. 1. ed. Oxford, 1970.

Phil 282.28.2 — Balaban, Grigorii Iu. Real'nyi mir v svete uni persal'noi seorii podoishnogo ravnovesiia. 2. izd. Hamilton, 1970.

Phil 70.114 — Banff Conference on Theoretical Psychology, 1st, 1965. Toward unification in psychology. Toronto, 1970.

Phil 4803.465.86 — Bańka, Józef. Narodziny filozofii nauki o pracy w Polsce. Wyd. 1. Warszawa, 1970.

Phil 5590.514.5 — Bannister, Donald. Perspectives in personal construct theory. London, 1970.

Phil 6642.5 — Barbizet, Jacques. Pathologie de la mémoire. 1. éd. Paris, 1970.

Phil 8656.44 — Barbotin, Edmond. Humanité de Dieu. Paris, 1970.

Phil 585.390 — Barbotin, Edmond. Humanité de l'homme. Paris, 1970.

Phil 6985.45 — Barrucand, Dominique. La catharsis dans le théâtre. Paris, 1970.

Phil 6111.70.5 — Barsley, Michael. Left-handed man in a right-handed world. London, 1970.

Phil 960.40.5 — Barua, B.M. A history of pre-Buddhistic Indian philosophy. Delhi, 1970.

Phil 310.764 — Barulin, Vladimir S. Otnoshenie material'nogo i ideal'nogo v obshchestve kak problema istoricheskogo materializma. Barnaul, 1970.

Phil 6111.88 — Baumer, Franz. Vom Zauberkult zur Psychoanalyse. München, 1970.

Phil 9075.88 — Baumhauer, Otto. Das Vor-Urteil des Gewissens. Limburg, 1970.

Phil 310.732 — Becker, Werner. Idealistische und materialistische Dialektik; das Verhältnis von Herrschaft und Knechtschaft bei Hegel und Marx. Stuttgart, 1970.

Phil 5238.232 — Behavioral and Social Sciences Survey Committe. Psychology. Englewood Cliffs, N.J., 1970.

Phil 5335.2 — Bem, Daryl J. Beliefs, attitudes and human affairs. Belmont, Calif., 1970.

Phil 5414.45 — Benda, Clemens Ernst. Gewissen und Schuld. Stuttgart, 1970.

Phil 7010.5.1 — Bender, Hans. Parapsychologie; ihre Ergebnisse und Probleme. Bremen, 1970.

Phil 1865.28 — Bentham, Jeremy. Of laws in general. London, 1970.

Phil 1865.51.15 — Bentham, Jeremy. An introduction to the principles of morals and legislation. London, 1970.

Phil 2475.1.8 — Bergson, Henri. Oeuvres. 3. éd. Paris, 1970.

Phil 1730.27.1 — Berlin, Isaiah. The age of enlightenment. Freeport, 1970.

Phil 8656.27.5 — Bertocci, Peter Anthony. The person God is. N.Y., 1970.

Phil 9075.86 — Bertola, Ermenegildo. Il problema della coscienza nella téologia Monastica del XII secolo. Padova, 1970.

Phil 5041.58.8 — Beth, Evert Willem. Aspects of modern logic. Dordrecht, 1970.

Phil 1740.20 — Beyer, Wilhelm Raimund. Vier Kritiken. Heidegger, Sartre, Adorno, Lukácz. Köln, 1970.

Phil 525.268 — Bieri, Edgard L. Un concetto dell'aldilà. Roma, 1970.

Phil 6315.2.480 — Birk, Kasimir. Sigmund Freud und die Religion. Münsterschwarzach, 1970.

Phil 3910.132 — Bissinger, Anton. Die Stuktur der Gotteserkenntnis. Bonn, 1970.

Phil 6946.38 — Blatt, Burton. Exodus from pandemonium; human abuse and a reformation of public policy. Boston, 1970.

Phil 8581.120 — Bloch, Ernst. Man on his own. N.Y., 1970.

Phil 3120.55.50 — Bloch, Ernst. A philosophy of the future. N.Y., 1970.

Phil 3425.756 — Bloch, Ernst. Über Methode und System bei Hegel. Frankfurt am Main, 1970.

Phil 5520.728 — Blumenthal, Arthur L. Language and psychology. N.Y., 1970.

Phil 5850.138.5 — Bodalev, Aleksei A. Formirovanie poniatiia o drugom cheloveke kak lichnosti. Leningrad, 1970.

Phil 843.5.5 — Boeckenhoff, J. Die Begegnungsphilosophie. Freiburg, 1970.

Phil 8951.32 — Boeckman, Peter Wilhelm. Liv, felleskap, tjeneste. Oslo, 1970.

Phil 3425.732 — Boey, C. L'aliénation dans la phénoménologie de l'esprit de G.W.F. Hegel. Paris, 1970.

Phil 4710.172.3 — Bogatov, Vitalii V. Istoriia filosofii narodov SSSR. Izd. 3. Moskva, 1970.

Phil 8430.70 — Bolam, David Whielden. Art and belief. N.Y., 1970.

Phil 332.44 — Bollnow, Otto Friedrich. Philosophie der Erkenntnis; das Vorverständnis und die Erfahrung des Neuen. Stuttgart, 1970.

Phil 5525.72 — Borev, Iurii B. Komicheskoe. Moskva, 1970.

Phil 5270.26 — Borger, Robert. Explanation in the behavioral sciences. Cambridge, Eng., 1970.

Phil 6109.2 — Borst, Clive Vernon. The mind-brain identity theory. N.Y., 1970.

Phil 3821.32 — Boschavini, Emilia Giancotti. Lexicon Spinozanum. La Haye, 1970.

Phil 3640.805 — Boudot, Pierre. Nietzsche et l'au-delà de la liberté; Nietzsche et les écrivains français de 1930 à 1960. Paris, 1970.

Phil 3425.758 — Bourgeois, Bernard. Hegel à Francfort; ou Judaisme, christianisme, hégelianisme. Paris, 1970.

Phil 5145.6 — Boursin, Jean Louis. Autopsie du hasard. Paris, 1970.

Phil 9415.14 — Bowker, John. Problems of suffering in religions of the world. Cambridge, 1970.

Phil 2270.90.5 — Bowne, Borden Parker. The philosophy of Herbert Spencer; being an examination of the first principles of his system. New York, 1881. Photoreproduction. Ann Arbor, Michigan, 1970.

1970 - cont.

Phil 5599.95 — Bowyer, Laura Ruth. The Lowenfeld world technique. 1. ed. Oxford, N.Y., 1970.

Phil 5875.65.5 — Brandis, Walter. Social class language and communication. London, 1970.

Phil 2905.1.610 — Bravo, Francisco. Teilhard de Chardin, su concepción de la historia. 1. ed. Barcelona, 1970.

Phil 3425.722 — Brazill, William J. The young Hegelians. New Haven, 1970.

Phil 332.14.2 — Brentano, Franz. Versuch über die Erkenntnis. 2. Aufl. Hamburg, 1970.

Phil 6317.22.85 — Brés, Yvon. Freud et la psychanalyse américaine Karen Horney. Paris, 1970.

Phil 530.155 — Bridges, Leonard Hal. American mysticism, from William James to Zen. 1. ed. N.Y., 1970.

Phil 5520.744 — Brisset, Jean Pierre. La grammaire logique. Paris, 1970.

Phil 5520.642 — Brkić, Jovan. Norm and order; an investigation into logic, semantics, and the theory of law and morals. N.Y., 1970.

Phil 6112.40.12 — Bro, Harmon Hartzell. Dreams in the life of prayer: the approach of Edgar Cayce. 1st ed. N.Y., 1970.

Phil 2520.400 — Broadie, Frederick. An approach to Descartes' meditations. London, 1970.

Phil 3425.754 — Brockard, Hans. Subjekt; Versuch zur Ontologie bei Hegel. München, 1970.

Phil 8581.43.3 — Brod, M. Paganism, Christianity, Judaism; a confession of faith. University, 1970.

Phil 3483.94 — Broecker, Walter. Kant über Metaphysik und Erfahrung. Frankfurt, 1970.

Phil 5871.85 — Bronfenbrenner, Urie. Two worlds of childhood: U.S. and U.S.S.R. N.Y., 1970.

Phil 7052.20 — Brown, Slater. The heyday of spiritualism. N.Y., 1970.

Phil 5520.722 — Brushlinskii, Andrei V. Psikhologiia myshleniia i kibernetika. Moskva, 1970.

Phil 3120.30.44.3 — Buber, Martin. I and thou. N.Y., 1970.

Phil 5241.20.2 — Buchanan, Joseph. The philosophy of human nature. Weston, Mass., 1970.

Phil 176.236 — Bueno Martinez, Gustavo. El papel de la filosofía en el conjunto del saber. Madrid, 1970.

Phil 6350.2 — Buerli, Alois. Indikation zur analytischen Psychotherapie mit Hilfe des "Experimentellen Triebdiagnostik". Bern, 1970.

Phil 615.1 — Buozyńska, Hanna. Wartość i fakt. Wyd. 1. Warszawa, 1970.

Phil 8980.248 — Burdiva, Alla I. Formuvannia komunistychnoi idei nosti osoby. Kyïv, 1970.

Phil 5465.188 — Burnshaw, Stanley. The seamless web; language thinking. N.Y., 1970.

Phil 3160.10.95 — Butrick, Richard. Carnap on meaning and analyticity. The Hague, 1970.

Phil 1870.182 — Bykhovskii, Bernard E. Dzhordzh Berkli. Moskva, 1970.

Phil 1740.26 — Calabró, Gaetano. La società fuori tutela. Napoli, 1970.

Phil 2475.1.505 — Callagher, Idella J. Morality in evolution: the moral philosophy of Henri Bergson. The Hague, 1970.

Phil 1828.2.5 — Cameron, Kenneth Walter. Concord harvest:publications of the Concord school of philosophy and literature. Hartford, 1970.

Phil 4073.72 — Campanella, Tommaso. Le creature sovrannaturali. Roma, 1970.

Phil 8444.2 — Cantoni, Remo. Il significato del tragico. Milano, 1970.

Phil 9495.170.10 — Caraco, Albert. L'ordre et le sexe. Lausanne, 1970.

Phil 4357.12.2 — Carcía Hoz, Victor. El nacimiento de la intimidad, y otros estudios. 2. ed. Madrid, 1970.

Phil 5870.85.3 — Carmichael, Leonard. Carmichael's manual of child psychology. 3rd ed. N.Y., 1970. 2v.

Phil 5405.6.2 — Casaubon, M. A treatise conserning enthusiasme (1655). 2. ed. Gainsville, 1970.

Phil 4080.12.65 — Castelli, Enrico. I paradossi del senso comune. Padova, 1970.

Phil 680.40 — Centro di studi filosofici di gallarate. Strutturalismo filosofico. Padova, 1970.

Phil 1600.20 — Centro di studi umanistici di Montepulciano. Il pensiero italiano del Rinascimento e il tempo Nostro. Firenze, 1970.

Phil 1133.55 — Chanyshev, Arsenii N. Egeiskaia predfilosofiia. Moskva, 1970.

Phil 5545.258 — Chauchard, Paul. Connaissance et maîtrise de la mémoire. Verviers, 1970.

Phil 4753.4 — Chernovolenko, Vilen F. Mirovozzronie i nauchnoe poznanie. Kiev, 1970.

Phil 8980.275.10 — Chevkashyn, D.S. Kommunistychnyi ideal i diisnist'. Kharkiv, 1970.

Phil 8092.32 — Chiari, Joseph. The aesthetics of modernism. London, 1970.

Phil 680.45 — Chvotík, Květoslav. Strukturalismus a avantgarda. 1. vyd. Praha, 1970.

Phil 3552.488 — Cichowicz, Stanislaw. Filosof i istnienie. Wyd. 1. Warszawa, 1970.

Phil 2515.10.16 — Cioran, Émile M. The fall into time. Chicago, 1970.

Phil 585.406.2 — Claessens, Dieter. Instinkt, Psyche, Geltung. 2. Aufl. Köln, 1970.

Phil 1750.856 — Clavel, Maurice. Qui est aliéné? Critique et métaphysique sociale de l'Occident. Paris, 1970.

Phil 5520.630A — Cognition and the development of language. N.Y., 1970.

Phil 5242.56.5 — Cohen, John. Homs psychologicus. London, 1970.

Phil 5125.40 — Cohen, Laurence Jonathan. The implications of induction. London, 1970.

Phil 5244.34 — Coles, Robert. Erik H. Erikson; the growth of his work. 1st ed. Boston, 1970.

Phil 2490.59 — Comte, Auguste. Écrits de jeunesse, 1816-1828. Suivis du Mémoire sur la cosmogonie de Laplace, 1835. Paris, 1970.

Phil 585.420 — Congressus Thomisticus Internationalis. v.1- Romae, 1970.

Phil 1800.2.10 — Contemporary American philosophy: second series. London, 1970.

Phil 70.116 — Contemporary philosophic thought. Albany, 1970. 4v.

Phil 310.756 — Conz, Gianni. Introduzione a una dialettica dei complementari. Padova, 1970.

Phil 4080.3.545 — Cotroneo, Girolamo. Croce e l'illuminismo. Napoli, 1970.

Phil 6952.32 — Cotti, Edelweiss. Contro la psichiatria. 1.ed. Firenze, 1970.

Phil 5520.634 — Cowan, Joseph Lloyd. Studies in thought and language. Tucson, 1970.

Phil 2255.1.185 — Crawshay-Williams, Rupert. Russell remembered. London, 1970.

Phil 2630.13.80 — Crispini, Franco. Lo strutturalismo dialettico di Lucien Goldmann. Napoli, 1970.

Phil 3925.16.250 — Cristaldi, Mariano. Wittgenstein; l'ontologia inibita. Bologna, 1970.

Phil 4140.80 — Cristallini, Alessandro. Il pensiero filosofico di Donato Jaja. Padova, 1970.

1970 - cont.

Phil 8403.46 — Crousaz, Jean Pierre de. Traité du beau, où l'on montre en quoi consiste ce que l'on nomme ainsi, Amsterdam, 1715. Genève, 1970.

Phil 7074.16 — Cummins, Geraldine Dorothy. Swan on a black sea: a study in automatic writing, the Cummins-Willet scripts. London, 1970.

Phil 8952.25 — Cunningham, Robert L. Situationism and the new morality. N.Y., 1970.

Phil 8952.22.5 — Curran, Charles E. Contemporary problems in moral theology. Notre Dame, 1970.

Phil 5042.45 — Czech, Albert. Grundkurs der Logik. Bonn, 1970.

Phil 6834.8 — Dacguino, Giacomo. Diario di un omosessuale. Milano, 1970.

Phil 5243.74 — D'Amato, Michael Richard. Experimental psychology. N.Y., 1970.

Phil 5590.564 — Dantov, Tasbolat M. Lichnost' kak sotsiologicheskaia problema. Alma-Ata, 1970.

Phil 3805.265 — Daur, Martin. Die eine Kirche und das zweifache Recht. Thesis. München, 1970.

Phil 5875.62.5 — De Bono, Edward. The dog exercising machine. London, 1970.

Phil 3450.19.515 — De Cecchi Duso, Gianna. L'interpretazione heideggeriana dei presocratici. Padova, 1970.

Phil 3485.34 — Declève, Henri. Heidegger et Kant. La Haye, 1970.

Phil 5520.626 — Deese, James Earle. Psycholinguistics. Boston, 1970.

Phil 848.10 — DeGrood, David H. Philosophies of essence; an examination of the category of essence. Groningen, 1970.

Phil 6440.5 — Delay, Jean. Les maladies de la mémoire. 5e ed. Paris, 1970.

Phil 3450.19.296 — Demske, James M. Being, man and death: a key to Heidegger. Lexington, 1970.

Phil 2428.15 — Denis, Jacques. Sceptiques ou libertins de la première moitié du XVIIe siècle. Genève, 1970.

Phil 2520.425 — Denissoff, Élie. Descartes, premier théoricien de la physique mathematique. Louvain, 1970.

Phil 5400.204 — Dermon, Emiir. Sinirlenmeden yaşayeniz. Izmir, 1970.

Phil 2520.78.45 — Descartes, René. Philosophical letters. Oxford, 1970.

Phil 2835.89 — Desmaze, Charles. P. Ramus, professeur au Collège de France. Sa vie. Genève, 1970.

Phil 4829.160.80 — Despot, Branko. Filozofija Djue Arnolda. Zagreb, 1970.

Phil 5520.702 — De Vito, Joseph A. The psychology of speech and language. N.Y., 1970.

Phil 5853.12 — Dexter, Lewis Anthony. Elite and specialized interviewing. Evanston, 1970.

Phil 310.744 — Dialektika i sovremennol estestvoznanie. Moskva, 1970.

Phil 178.82 — Diéguez, Manuel de. Science et nescience. Paris, 1970.

Phil 5535.60 — Dienes, Zoltan Paul. The effects of structural relations on transfer. London, 1970.

Phil 8622.84 — Dobraczyński, Jan. W co wierze. Wyd. 1. Warszawa, 1970.

Phil 5585.330 — Dodwell, P.C. Visual pattern recognition. N.Y., 1970.

Phil 4260.210 — Donzelli, Maria. Natura e humanitas nel Giovane Vico. Napoli, 1970.

Phil 8092.28 — Dorfles, Gillo. Comunicazione e struttura nell'analisi di alcumi linguaggi artistici. Milano, 1970.

Phil 5418.6 — Dreitzel, Hans Peter. Die Einsamkeit als soziologisches Problem. Zurich, 1970.

Phil 860.8 — Dreyer, Oskar. Untersuchungen zum Begriff des Gottgeziemenden in der Antike. Hildesheim, 1970.

Phil 8980.3 — Drobnitskii, Oleg G. Slovar po etike. Izd. 2. Moskva, 1970.

Phil 334.16 — Duchenko, Mykola V. Problema ob'iekta v marksysto'ko-lenins'kvi Seorii piznanoria. Kyiv, 1970.

Phil 5590.528 — Duesberg, Hans. Person und Gemeinschaft. Bonn, 1970.

Phil 5886.20 — Duke University. Center for the Study of Aging and Human Development. Normal aging: reports from the Duke longitudinal study, 1955-1969. Durham, N.C., 1970.

Phil 8658.27 — Duluman, Evgraf K. Ideiia boga. Moskva, 1970.

Phil 8658.26 — Duquesne, Jacques. Dieu pour l'homme d'aujourd'hui. Paris, 1970.

Phil 3450.19.480 — Durchblicke: Martin Heidegger zum 80. Geburtstag. Frankfurt, 1970.

Phil 6155.2 — Durr, R.A. Poetic vision and the psychedelic experience. 1st ed. Syracuse, 1970.

Phil 384.10 — Dworkin, Gerald. Determinism, free will, and moral responsibility. Englewood Cliffs, 1970.

Phil 4803.879.95 — Dybiec, Julian. Michał wiszniewski. Wrocław, 1970.

Phil 3549.2.105 — Dyserinck, Hugo. Graf Hermann Keyserling und Frankereich. Bonn, 1970.

Phil 8980.346.5 — Dzhafarli, Teimuraz M. Besedy o kommunisticheskoi morali. Moskva, 1970.

Phil 8828.10 — Dzhafarli, Teimuraz M. Iz istorii domarksistskoi eticheskoi mysli. Tbilisi, 1970.

Phil 630.64 — Eberle, Rolf A. Nominalistic systems. Dordrecht, 1970.

Phil 7069.70 — Ebon, Martin. Test your E.S.P. N.Y., 1970.

Phil 6114.15.5 — Eccles, J.C. Facing reality; philosophical adventures by a brain scientist. London, 1970.

Phil 5270.28 — Eckensberger, Lutz H. Methodenprobleme der kulturvergleichenden Psychologie. Saarbrücken, 1970.

Phil 3200.17 — Edelmann, Johann Christian. Sämtliche Schriften in Einzelausgaben. Stuttgart, 1970. 5v.

Phil 1740.18 — Edmaier, Alois. Die Philosophie der Gegenwart. Aschaffenburg, 1970.

Phil 1828.12 — Ehrle, Franz. Gesammelte Aufsätze zur englischen Scholastik. Roma, 1970.

Phil 5421.20.105 — Eibl-Eibesfeld, Irenäus. Liebe und Hass. München, 1970.

Phil 8820.5 — Eifler, Günter. Ritterliches Tugendsystem. Darmstadt, 1970.

Phil 285.6.2 — Eliade, Mircea. Cosmos and history. N.Y., 1970.

Phil 5865.5.40 — Elkind, David. Children and adolescents. N.Y., 1970.

Phil 6906.10 — Ellenberger, Henri F. The discovery of the unconscious. N.Y., 1970.

Phil 3450.11.470 — Elveton, R.O. The phenomenology of Husserl. Chicago, 1970.

Phil 960.280 — The encyclopedia of Indian philosophies. 1st ed. Delhi, 1970.

Phil 310.768.2 — Enerstvedt, Regi Th. Dialektikk og samfunnsvitenskap. 2. oppl. Oslo, 1970.

Phil 610.2 — Engelhardt, Paulus. Zur Theorie der Praxis. Mainz, 1970.

Phil 3925.16.295 — Engelmann, Paul. Ludwig Wittgenstein: Briefe und Begegnungen. Wien, 1970.

Phil 585.3.6 — Erickson, Stephen A. Language and being: an analytic phenomenology. New Haven, 1970.

Phil 8448.25 — Eriksson, I.O. Estetisk upplevelse. Stockholm, 1970.

Phil 574.8 — Escobar, Edmundo. Francisco Larroyo y su personalismo crítico. 1. ed. México, 1970.

Phil 165.442 — Essays in honor of Carl G. Hempel. Dordrecht, 1970.

1970 - cont.

Phil 165.458   Essays in metaphysics, by members of the philosophy department, the Pennsylvania State University. University Park, 1970.

Phil 5044.12   Essler, Wilhelm Karl. Induktive Logik. Habilitationsschrift. Freiburg, 1970.

Phil 5535.46   Estes, William Kaye. Learning theory and mental development. N.Y., 1970.

Phil 8092.31   Estetischeski idei V.I. Lenina i sovremennost'. Kalinin, 1970.

Phil 575.280   Evans, Cedric Oliver. The subject of consciousness. London, 1970.

Phil 5871.116   Evans, Judith L. Children in Africa: a review of psychological research. N.Y., 1970.

Phil 5240.70   Evans, Richard Isadore. Gordon Allport. 1. ed. N.Y., 1970[1971]

Phil 3486.9.6A   Ewing, Alfred Cyril. A short commentary on Kant's Critique of pure reason. Chicago, 1970.

Phil 5590.45.20   Eysenck, Hans Jürgen. Readings in extraversion-introversion. London, 1970-

Phil 5590.45.13   Eysenck, Hans Jurgen. The structure of human personality. 3. ed. London, 1970.

Phil 1705.6.1   Fabre, Joseph. La pensée moderne [de Luther à Leibniz]. Genève, 1970.

Phil 1020.4.36   Fakhry, Majid. A history of Islamic philosophy. N.Y., 1970.

Phil 2225.5.170   Fann, K.T. Peirce's theory of abduction. The Hague, 1970.

Phil 8406.30   Farner, Konrad. Der Aufstand der Abstrakt-Konkreten. Neuwied, 1970.

Phil 2880.8.305   Fé, Franco. Sartre e il comunismo. Firenze, 1970.

Phil 480.10   Feibleman, James. The new materialism. The Hague, 1970.

Phil 384.20   Fellowship of Religious Humanists. Freedom of choice. Yellow Springs, Ohio, 1970.

Phil 585.402   Ferrater Mora, Jose. Els mots i els homes. 1. ed. Barcelona, 1970.

Phil 5238.240   Festschrift for B.F. Skinner. N.Y., 1970.

Phil 3425.736   Fetscher, Iring. Hegels Lehre von Menschen. Stuttgart, 1970.

Phil 960.284   Filliozat, Jean. Les philosophies de l'Inde. Paris, 1970.

Phil 310.755   Filozofia marksisĺowska. Wyd. 1. Warszawa, 1970.

Phil 252.5   Findlay, John Niemayer. Ascent to the absolute: metaphysical papers and lectures. London, 1970.

Phil 735.280   Findlay, Niemeyer. Axiological ethics. London, 1970.

Phil 8880.68   Fink, Hans. Moralbegrundelse og logik. København, 1970.

Phil 5365.4   Fisch, Rudolf. Konfliktmtivation und Examen. Meisenheim am Glan, 1970.

Phil 5421.10.45   Fischer, William Frank. Theories of anxiety. N.Y., 1970.

Phil 6115.32.5   Fisher, Seymour. Body experience in fantasy and behavior. N.Y., 1970.

Phil 325.20   Formigari, Lia. Linguistica ed empirismo nel Seicento inglese. Bari, 1970.

Phil 5414.50   Fornari, Franco. Psicanalisi della situazione atomica. Milano, 1970.

Phil 6315.2.470   Fougeyrollas, Pierre. La révolution freudienne. Paris, 1970.

Phil 680.55   Francovich, Guillermo. Ensayos sobre el estructuralismo. La Paz, Bolivia, 1970.

Phil 2520.410   Frankfurt, Harry G. Demons, dreamers, and madmen. Indianapolis, 1970.

Phil 5870.75   Freud, Anna. Research at the Hampstead Child-Therapy Clinic and other papers, 1956-1965. London, 1970.

Phil 6315.2.26.6   Freud, Sigmund. The letters of Sigmund Freud and Arnold Zweig. London, 1970.

Phil 6315.2.26.5   Freud, Sigmund. The letters of Sigmund Freud and Arnold Zweig. N.Y., 1970.

Phil 8880.66   Fried, Charles. An anatomy of values; problems of personal and social choice. Cambridge, 1970.

Phil 5867.35   Fried, Edrita. Active/passive: the crucial psychological dimension. N.Y., 1970.

Phil 1133.52   Furley, David J. Studies in presocratic philosophy. London, 1970-

Phil 310.762   Furman, Aleksei E. Istoricheskii materializon. Moskva, 1970.

Phil 2520.430   Gabaude, Jean Marc. Liberté et raison. v. 1- Toulouse, 1970-

Phil 3235.134   Gagen, Michael von. Ludwig Feuerbach. München, 1970.

Phil 5246.82   Gagey, Jacques. Analyse spectacle de la psychologie. Paris, 1970.

Phil 6840.2   Gagey, Roland. La volupté dans la souffrance. Paris, 1970?

Phil 4710.168   Galaktionov, Anatolii A. Russkaia filosofiia XI-XIX vekov. Leningrad, 1970.

Phil 310.643.1   Garaudy, Roger. Marxism in the twentieth century. London, 1970.

Phil 5400.93.1   Gardiner, Harry Norman. Feeling and emotion. Westport, 1970.

Phil 3808.250   Garewicz, Jan. Schopenhauer. Wyd. 1. Warszawa, 1970.

Phil 1730.34   Garin, Eugenio. Dal rinascimento all'illuminismo. Studi e ricerche. Pisa, 1970.

Phil 5853.4   Gauguelin, François. Savoir communiquer. Paris, 1970.

Phil 1706.1.25   Gaultier, Jules de. Bovarysm. N.Y., 1970.

Phil 806.39.5   Gay, Peter. The bridge of criticism. 1st ed. N.Y., 1970.

Phil 365.68   Gebser, Hans. Der unsichtbare Ursprung. Evolution als Nachvollzug. Olten, 1970.

Phil 9495.170.5   Geets, Claude. Psychanalyse et morale sexuelle. Paris, 1970.

Phil 3450.19.10.5   Gelven, Michael. A commentary on Heidegger's Being and time. N.Y., 1970.

Phil 5520.638   George, Frank Honywill. Models of thinking. London, 1970.

VPhil 5590.558   Gerstmann, Stanisĺaw. Osobowość. Wyd. 1. Warszawa, 1970.

Phil 4870.18   Gessler, Clara. Westlicher Wissensdrang-Indische Weisheit. Zürich, 1970.

Phil 287.12   Ghirardi, Olsen A. Cosmología y ciencia ficcion. Córdoba, Argentina, 1970.

Phil 165.454   Giacon, Carlo. Saggi e ricerche su Alessandro di Afrodisia, Avicenna, Miceli, Brentano, Jaspers, Ingarden, Carr. Padova, 1970.

Phil 8586.62   Gibson, Alexander Boyce. Theism and empiricism. London, 1970.

Phil 8696.26   Gilkey, Langdon Brown. Religion and the scientific future; reflections on myth, science, and theology. 1. ed. N.Y., 1970.

Phil 5246.80   Gilmer, Beverly von Haller. Psychology. N.Y., 1970.

Phil 337.4.6   Glanvill, Joseph. The vanity of dogmatizing. Facsimile reprints of the London editions of 1661, 1665 and 1676. Brighton, 1970.

Phil 5850.219   Glidewell, John C. Choice points. Cambridge, Mass., 1970.

1970 - cont.

Phil 3310.8.30   Glockner, Hermann. Bilderbuch meiner Jugend; Erinnerungen. Bonn, 1970. 2v.

Phil 5756.16   Glover, Jonathan. Responsibility. London, 1970.

Phil 672.268   Goelz, Walter. Dasein und Raum. Habilitationsschrift. Tübingen, 1970.

Phil 5520.680   Goessmann, Wilhelm. Glaubwürdigkeit im Sprachgebrauch. 1. Aufl. München, 1970.

Phil 3850.27.255   Götting, Gerald. Albert Schweitzer- Pionier der Menschlichkeit. Berlin, 1970.

Phil 6946.1.16   Goffman, Erving. Asylums: essays on the social situation of mental patients and other inmates. Chicago, 1970.

Phil 5535.58   Goguelin, Pierre. La formation continue des adultes. 1. ed. Paris, 1970.

Phil 5246.84   Goldman, Alvin I. A theory of human action. Englewood Cliffs, N.J., 1970.

Phil 337.38   Golovanov, Viacheslaw N. Zakony v sisteme naukhnogo znaniia. Moskva, 1970.

Phil 8407.35.5   Goranov, Krusto. Istoricheskiias zhivos na izkustvoto. Sofiia, 1970.

Phil 5246.88   Gosselin, Albert. L'homme en ce monde et le sens de la vie. Paris, 1970.

Phil 3640.800   Goth, Joachim. Nietzsche und die Rhetorik. Tübingen, 1970.

Phil 5871.112.2   Graber, Gustav Hans. Ursprung, Einheit und Zwiespalt der Seele. München, 1970.

Phil 450.6   Gradman, Hans. Menschsein ohne Illusionen. München, 1970.

Phil 3488.50   Granel, Gérard. L'équivoque ontologique de la pensée Kantienne. Paris, 1970.

Phil 2150.18.115   Granese, Alberto. G.E. Moore e la filosofia analitica inglese. Firenze, 1970.

Phil 8956.22   Greet, Kenneth. The art of moral judgement. London, 1970.

Phil 8407.44.5   Grenier, Jean. L'art et ses problèmes. Lausanne, 1970.

Phil 5465.184   Groch, Judith. The right to create. 1. ed. Boston, 1970.

Phil 8407.1.5   Gromov, Evgenii S. Khudozhestvennoe tvorchestvo. Moskva, 1970.

Phil 258.15   Gross, Barry R. Analytic philosophy; an historical introduction. N.Y., 1970.

Phil 3935.1.80   Gruender, Karl Fried. Zur Philosophie des Grafen Paul Vorck von Wartenburg. Göttingen, 1970.

Phil 2520.420   Guéroult, Marital. Etudes sur Descartes, Spinoza, Hildesheim, 1970.

Phil 1955.6.250   Guide to the works of John Dewey. Carbondale, 1970.

Phil 2630.11.40   Guitton, Jean. Histoire et destinée. Paris, 1970.

Phil 3425.774   Gulyga, Arsenii V. Gegel'. Moskva, 1970.

Phil 5850.226   Gŭrdev, Dinó. Strukturen analiz na obshtestvenoto Sŭznanie. Sofiia, 1970.

Phil 1135.235   Hager, Fritz-Peter. Der Geist und das Eine. Inaug. Diss. Bern, 1970.

Phil 5590.215.2.2   Hall, Calvin S. Theories of personality. 2. ed. N.Y., 1970.

Phil 6155.12   Hallucinogenic drug research; impact on science and society. Beloit, Wis., 1970.

Phil 5100.8   Hamblin, Charles Leonard. Fallacies. London, 1970.

Phil 9450.66   Hamelin, Jacques. Entretiens sur la justice contemporaire. Paris, 1970.

Phil 807.26   Hançerlióglu, Orhan. Düşünce tarihi. Istanbul, 1970.

Phil 9450.68   Haring, Philip S. Political morality; a general theory of politics. Cambridge, Mass., 1970.

Phil 807.24.7   Hartnack, Justus. Filosofiske problemer og filosofiske argumentation. 2. Opl. København, 1970.

Phil 2055.9.40   Hartshorne, Charles. Creative synthesis and philosophic method. London, 1970.

Phil 5535.62   Haseloff, Otto Walter. Psychologie des Lernens: Methoden, Ergebnisse, Anwendungen. Berlin, 1970.

Phil 5592.198   Hauss, Kurt. Emotionalität und Wahrnehmung. Göttingen, 1970.

Phil 8408.52   Havryliuk, Pedro I. Problema estetychnoko i teoriia upravlinnia. Kyïv, 1970.

Phil 3425.66   Hegel, Georg Wilhelm Friedrich. Der Geist des Christentums und sein Schicksal. Gütersloh, 1970.

Phil 3425.46.12   Hegel, Georg Wilhelm Friedrich. Hegel's philosophy of nature. London, 1970.

Phil 3425.46.10   Hegel, Georg Wilhelm Friedrich. Hegel's philosophy of nature. Oxford, 1970.

Phil 3425.64   Hegel, Georg Wilhelm Friedrich. Das junge Hegel in Stuttgart. Marbach, 1970?

Phil 3450.19.15.1   Heidegger, Martin. Existence and being. Chicago, 1970.

Phil 3425.20.10   Heidegger, Martin. Hegel's concept of experience. 1st ed. N.Y., 1970.

Phil 3425.73.20.10   Heidegger, Martin. Hegel's concept of experience. 1st ed. N.Y., 1970.

Phil 3450.19.76   Heidegger, Martin. Phänomenologie und Theologie. Frankfurt, 1970.

Phil 3450.19.500   Heidegger and the path of thinking. Pittsburgh, 1970.

Phil 3425.724   Heintel, Peter. Hegel. Göttingen, 1970.

Phil 4843.4   Henderson, George Patrick. The revival of Greek thought, 1620-1830. Albany, 1970.

Phil 210.68   Hermeneutik und Dialektik. Aufsätze. Hans-Georg Gadamer zum 70. Geburtstag. Tübingen, 1970. 2v.

Phil 5520.646   Herriot, Peter. An introduction to the psychology of language. London, 1970.

Phil 3270.18.1   Herrmann, Friedrich Wilhelm von. Bibliographie Eugen Fink. Den Haag, 1970.

Phil 6315.2.82.15   Hesnard, Angelo. De Freud à Lacan. Paris, 1970.

Phil 182.144   Hilm, Selhattin. 100 soruda felsefe el kilabi. Istanbul, 1970.

Phil 7118.10   Hilgard, Josephine Rohrs. Personality and hypnosis. Chicago, 1970.

Phil 3480.32.65.2   Hinske, Norbert. Kant-Seitenkondordanz. Darmstadt, 1970.

Phil 3489.47   Hinske, Norbert. Kants Begriff des Transzendentalen. Pt.1. Stuttgart, 1970.

Phil 5520.648   Hintikka, Kaarlo Jaakko Juhani. Information and inference. Dordrecht, 1970.

Phil 4803.454.1   Hoene-Wroński, Józef Maria. Hoëné Wronski. Paris, 1970.

Phil 5520.665   Hoepp, Gerhard. Evolution der Sprache und Vernunft. Berlin, 1970.

Phil 5520.492.2   Hoermann, Hans. Psychologie der Sprache. Berlin, 1970.

Phil 338.47   Hoffman, Robert. Language, minds, and knowledge. N.Y., 1970.

Phil 2648.64   Holbach, Paul Henri T. Bicentenaire du Système de la nature. Paris, 1970.

Phil 2648.34.5   Holbach, Paul Henri T. Le bons sens du Curé Jean Meslier. Hildesheim, 1970.

Phil 2730.118   Holda, Bernard. La pensée de Maine de Biran. Paris, 1970.

1970 - cont.

Phil 5421.20.130 Hollitscher, Walter. Aggression im Menschenbild. Wien, 1970.

Phil 5841.6 Holter, Harriet. Sex roles and social structure. Oslo, 1970.

Phil 7055.310.25 Holzer, Hans W. The psychic world of Bishop Pike. N.Y., 1970.

Phil 3489.50 Holzhey, Helmut. Kants Erfahrungsbegriff. Basel, 1970.

Phil 5627.270 Homans, Peter. Theology after Freud; an interpretive inquiry. Indianapolis, 1970.

Phil 4987.89.90 Homenaje a Xavier Zubiri. Madrid, 1970. 2v.

Phil 3425.770 Hondt, Jacques d'. Hegel et la pensée moderne. 1. éd. Paris, 1970.

Phil 3450.28.20 Horkheimer, Max. Die Sehnsucht nach dem ganz Anderen. Hamburg, 1970.

Phil 1750.166.270 Horosz, William. The promise and peril of human purpose. Saint Louis, 1970.

Phil 5465.182.5 Horowitz, Mardi Jon. Image formation and cognition. N.Y., 1970.

Phil 8697.28 Howe, Günter. Die Christenheit im Atomzeitalter. Stuttgart, 1970.

Phil 182.142 Hrušovský, Igor. Probleme der Philosophie. Bratislava, 1970.

Phil 2215.85 Hudson, William Donald. Reason and right: a critical examination of Richard Price's philosophy. London, 1970.

Phil 5871.90 Hunt, David. Parents and children in history. N.Y., 1970.

Phil 8277.2 Huonder, Quirin. Das Unsterblichkeitsproblem in der abendländischenPhilosophie. Stuttgart, 1970.

Phil 3450.11.62 Husserl, Edmund. The crisis of European sciences and transcendental phenomenology. Evanston, 1970.

Phil 5047.11.4 Husserl, Edmund. Logical investigations. 2nd ed. N.Y., 1970. 2v.

Phil 8980.459 Iakuba, Elena A. Pravoi nravstvennost'kak reguliatory obshchestvennykh otnoshenii pri sotsializme. Khav'kov, 1970.

Phil 1750.852 Ideologiia sovremennogo reformizma. Moskva, 1970.

Phil 8663.6 Illanes, José L. Hablar de Dios. Madrid, 1970.

Phil 9470.16 Ingarden, Roman. Über die Verantwortung. Stuttgart, 1970.

Phil 70.3.90 International Congress of Psychology, 19th, London, 1969. Deviatnadtsatyi mezhdnnarodnyi psikhologicheskii Kongress, 27 iialia - 2 avgusta 1969 g., London, Angliia. Moskva, 1970.

Phil 310.772 Iovchuk, Mikhail T. Leninism, filosofskie traditsii i sovremennost'. Moskva, 1970.

Phil 310.776 Iribadzhakov, Nikolai. Leninizum, filosofiia, ideologicheska borba. Sofiia, 1970.

Phil 5066.326 Issledovanie logicheskikh sistem. Moskva, 1970.

Phil 4822.1 Istoriia na filosofskata misul v Bulgariia. Sofiia, 1970-

Phil 310.750 Iurova, Inna L. Ob otnoshenii marksistski-leninskoi filosofii k estestrosnamiu. Moskva, 1970.

Phil 8171.300 Ivan'o Ivan V. Spetsyfika mystetstva. Kyïv, 1970.

Phil 735.286 Ivin, Aleksandr A. Osnovaniia logiki otsenok. Moskva, 1970.

Phil 6319.1.236 Jaffé, Aniela. The myth of meaning in the work of C.G. Jung. London, 1970.

Phil 4802.1 Jakiej filozofii Polacy potrzebują. Wyd. 1. Warszawa, 1970.

Phil 3246.350 Janke, Wolfgang. Ficht; Sein und Reflexion. Berlin, 1970.

Phil 3450.11.416 Janssen, Paul. Geschichte und Lebenswelt. Den Haag, 1970.

Phil 2905.1.1 Jarque i Jutglar, Joan E. Bibliographie générale des oeuvres et articles sur Pierre Teilhard de Chardin parus jusqu'a fin décembre 1969. Fribourg, 1970.

Phil 3475.3.57 Jaspers, Karl. Chiffren der Transzendenz. München, 1970.

Phil 4803.108.95 Jezierski, Romuald. Poglądy etyczne Edwarda Abramowskiego. Wyd. 1. Poznań, 1970.

Phil 575.284 Johnstone, Henry Webb. The problem of the self. University Park, 1970.

Phil 7082.12.5 Jones, Richard Matthew. The new psychology of dreaming. N.Y., 1970.

Phil 8725.20 Jouguelet, Pierre. Laïcité, liberté et vérité. Tournai, 1970.

Phil 2477.6.185 Jouhaud, Michel. Le problème de l'être et l'expérience morale chez Maurice Blondel. Paris, 1970.

Phil 49.6 Jowett papers, 1968-1969. Oxford, 1970.

Phil 3491.18 Juchem, Hans Georg. Die Entwicklung des Begriffs des Schönen bei Kant, unter besonderer Berücksichtigung des Begriffs verworrenen Erkenntnis. Bonn, 1970.

Phil 5520.654 Juliard, Pierre. Philosophies of language in eighteenth-century France. The Hague, 1970.

Phil 5249.13.28 Jung, Carl G. C.G. Jung: psychological reflections. Princeton, 1970.

Phil 484.4 Juul, Jensen. Uffe sjoel og legeme. København, 1970.

Phil 6112.40.15 Kahn, David E. My life with Edgar Cayce. 1. ed. Garden City, 1970.

Phil 585.396 Kakabadze, Zurab M. Chelovek kak filosofskaia problema. Tbilisi, 1970.

Phil 5325.50 Kallich, Martin. The association of ideas and critical theory in eighteenth-century England. The Hague, 1970.

Phil 3425.766 Kaltenbrunner, Gerd Klaus. Hegel und die Folgen. 1. Aufl. Freiburg, 1970.

Phil 3235.132 Kamenka, Eugene. The philosophy of Ludwig Feuerbach. London, 1970.

Phil 5284.2 Kaminski, Gerhard. Verhaltenstheorie und Verhaltensmodifikation. Stuttgart, 1970.

Phil 341.44 Kanak, Fedvi M. Sub'ieks, ob'iekt i fizychne piznannia. Kyïv, 1970.

Phil 6998.6 Kanfer, Frederick H. Learning foundations of behavior therapy. N.Y., 1970.

Phil 8885.49.5 Kangrga, Milan. Razmisljanja o etici. Zagreb, 1970.

Phil 3480.92.5 Kant, Immanuel. Briefe. Göttingen, 1970.

Phil 3480.50.18.4 Kant, Immanuel. Erste Einleitung in die Kritik der Urteilskraft. 2. Aufl. Hamburg, 1970.

Phil 3480.132 Kant, Immanuel. Kant's political writings. Cambridge, 1970.

Phil 3480.81.4.1 Kant, Immanuel. Metaphysical foundations of natural science. Indianapolis, 1970.

Phil 5190.85.2 Karlins, Marvin. Persuasion; how opinions and attitudes are changed. 2nd ed. N.Y., 1970.

Phil 575.296 Karquel, André. La tragédie cosmique de la conscience. Paris, 1970.

Phil 310.748 Kategorii dialektiki i metodologiia sovremennoi nauki. Voronezh, 1970.

Phil 5465.212 Kaufmann, Arnold. L'inventique. Paris, 1970.

Phil 3425.752 Kaufmann, Walter Arnold. Hegel's political philosophy. 1st ed. N.Y., 1970.

Phil 5421.20.135 Keil, Siegfried. Aggression und Mitmenschlichkeit. Stuttgart, 1970.

1970 - cont.

Phil 5548.144 Keiler, Peter. Wollen und Wert. Berlin, 1970.

Phil 9070.138 Kemelman, Haim. How to live in the present tense. South Brunswick, 1970.

Phil 1750.518 Kern, Edith G. Existential thought and fictional technique; Kierkegaard, Sartre, Beckett. New Haven, 1970.

Phil 310.726 Khotiakova, Valentina Alekseevna. Chelovek i istoriia. Moskva, 1970.

Phil 5535.42 Kintsch, Walter. Learning, memory, and conceptual processes. N.Y., 1970.

Phil 310.692.5 Kirschenmann, Peter Paul. Information and reflection on some problems of cybernetics and how contemporary dialectical materialism copes with them. Dordrecht, 1970.

Phil 310.779 Kissel', Mikhail A. Uchenie o dialektike v burzhnarnoi filosofii XX veka. Leningrad, 1970.

Phil 5220.7 Klein, David Ballin. A history of scientific psychology. N.Y., 1970.

Phil 8430.81 Klein, Robert. La forme et l'intelligible. Paris, 1970.

Phil 2255.1.165 Klemke, E.D. Essays on Bertrand Russell. Urbana, Illinois, 1970.

Phil 8092.19 Klivar, Miroslav. Estetika nových uměni. Vyd. 1. Praha, 1970.

Phil 5421.20.120 Kneutgen, Johannes. Der Mensch, ein kriegerisches Tier. Stuttgart, 1970.

Phil 583.8.5 Kockelmans, Joseph John. Phenomenology and the natural sciences: essays and translations. Evanston, 1970.

Phil 5075.8 Koerner, Stephan. Categorial frameworks. Oxford, 1970.

Phil 8430.89 Kofman, Sarah. L'enfance de l'art. Paris, 1970.

Phil 8411.38.5 Kogan, Lev Naumovich. Iskusstvo i my. Moskva, 1970.

Phil 5520.658 Konczewski, C. La psychologie dynamique et la pensée vécue. Paris, 1970.

Phil 9245.140 Korneva, Mariia N. Kommunizm i problema schast'ia. Moskva, 1970.

Phil 8411.42 Kornienko, Vasilii S. O zakonakh krasoty. Khar'kov, 1970.

Phil 4803.497.6 Kotarbiński, Tadeusz. Studia z zakresu filozofii, etyki i nauk społecznych. Wrocław, 1970.

Phil 3120.55.105 Kraenzle, Karl. Utopie und Ideologie. Bern, 1970.

Phil 95.4.2 Kratki slovar' po filosofii. Izd.2. Moskva, 1970.

Phil 1930.18.85 Krauth, Lothar. Die Philosophie Carnaps. Wien, 1970.

Phil 6120.8.10 Kretschmer, E. Physique and character. 2d ed. N.Y., 1970.

Phil 2045.165 Kriele, Martin. Die Herausforderung des Verfassungsstaates; Hobbes und englische Juristen. Neuwied, 1970.

Phil 978.59.60 Krishnamurti, J. The only revolution. London, 1970.

Phil 978.59.70 Krishnamurti, J. Talks and dialogues, Saanen 1968. Wassenaar, 1970.

Phil 978.59.72 Krishnamurti, J. Talks and discussions at Brockwood Park, 1969. Wassenaar, 1970.

Phil 978.59.74 Krishnamurti, J. Talks with American students, 1968. Wassenaar, 1970.

Phil 8665.30 Kruger, Klaus. Der Gottesbegriff der spekulativen Theologie. Berlin, 1970.

Phil 8980.501 Krutova, Ol'ga Natanouna. Chelovek i moral'. Moskva, 1970.

Phil 4110.11.35 Kuczyńska, Alicja. Filozofia i seoria piękna Marsilia Ficina. Wyd. 1. Warszawa, 1970.

Phil 3549.28.30 Kudszus, Hans. Zaworte, Neimworte, Aphorismen. 1. Aufl. Frankfurt, 1970.

Phil 3549.26 Kulenkampff, Arend. Antinomie und Dialektik. Stuttgart, 1970.

Phil 8885.56 Kupperman, Joel J. Ethical knowledge. London, 1970.

Phil 396.12.2 Kurella, Alfred. Das Eigene und das Fremde. Neue Beiträge zum sozialist. Humanismus. 2. Aufl. Berlin, 1970.

Phil 1135.230 Kurz, Dietrich. Akpibeia. Göppingen, 1970.

Phil 9560.64 Kuş, Nuri. Güneş batidan doğmustur. Kütahya, 1970.

Phil 4065.186 Kuznetsov, Boris G. Dzhordano Bruno i genesis klassicheskoi nauki. Moskva, 1970.

Phil 2410.1 Kuznetsov, Vitalii N. Frantsuzskaia burzhuaznaia filosofiia dvadtsatogo veka. Moskva, 1970.

Phil 3808.90.1 Laban, Ferdinand. Die Schopenhauer-Literatur. N.Y., 1970.

Phil 3831.18 Lacroix, Jean. Spinoza et le problème du salut. Paris, 1970.

Phil 2730.116 Lacroze, René. Maine de Biran. 1. éd. Paris, 1970.

Phil 2880.8.216 Lafarge, René. Jean-Paul Sartre: his philosophy. Notre Dame, 1970.

Phil 6321.53.10 Laing, Roland David. Knots. London, 1970.

Phil 6976.17 Laing, Ronald David. Sanity, madness and family: families of schizophrenics. 2. ed. London, 1970.

Phil 342.26 Landesman, Charles. The foundations of knowledge. Englewood Cliffs, 1970.

Phil 720.88 Lane, Gilles. Être et langage; essai sur la recherche de l'objectivite. Paris, 1970.

Phil 680.25 Lane, Michael. Introduction to structuralism. N.Y., 1970.

Phil 680.26 Lane, Michael. Structuralism: a reader. London, 1970.

Phil 186.160 Lange, John. The cognitivity paradox. Princeton, 1970.

Phil 971.8 Lantier, Jacques. La théosophie. Paris, 1970.

Phil 6321.60 Laplanche, Jean. Vie et mort en psychanalyse. Paris, 1970.

Phil 3270.12.115 Largeault, Jean. Logique et philosophie chez Frege. Paris, 1970.

Phil 2805.495 Larraillet, Paul. Pascal et le problème de la destinée. Paris, 1970.

Phil 5051.44.4 Larroyo, Francisco. Lecciones de lógica y etica. 4. ed. México, 1970.

Phil 4959.5 Lascaris Comneno, Constantino. Historia de las ideas en Centroamerica. 1. ed. San José de Costa Rica, 1970.

Phil 3246.335 Lassahn, Rudolf. Studien zur Wirkungsgeschichte Fichtes als Pädagoge Habilitationsschrift. Heidelberg, 1970.

Phil 2340.10.240 Laszlo, Ervin. La métaphysique de Whitehead: recherche des prolongements anthropologiques. La Hague, 1970.

Phil 5790.45 Latané, Bibb. The unresponsive bystander: why doesn't he help? N.Y., 1970.

Phil 6321.58 Laughlin, Henry Prather. The ego and its defenses. N.Y., 1970.

Phil 5585.291 Laurondeau, Monique. The development of the concept of space in the child. N.Y., 1970.

Phil 3493.52 Lebrun, Gérard. Kant et la mort de la métaphysique. Paris, 1970.

Phil 2905.1.655 Lecourt, Jacques. Cari Gustav Jung et Pierre Teilhard de Chardin. Goële, 1970.

Phil 3925.16.285 Leeds, England. University. Department of Philosophy. A Witttgenstein workbook. Berkeley, 1970.

Phil 408.6 Lefebvre, Henri. Le manifeste différentialiste. Paris, 1970.

Phil 1133.50 Legrand, Gérard. La pensée des présocratiques. Paris, 1970.

764

Chronological Listing

1970 - cont.

Phil 5520.640 Lehrer, Adrienne. Theory of meaning. Englewood Cliffs, N.J., 1970.
Phil 971.10 Leiste, Heinrich. Ein Beitrag zur anthroposophischen Hochschulfrage. Dornach, 1970.
Phil 1750.854 Leminizm i sovremennze problemy istoriko-filosofskoi nauki. Moskva, 1970.
Phil 310.794 Lenin i niakoi problemi na marksistkata filosofiia. Sofiia, 1970.
Phil 310.702 Leninizm i filosofskie problemy sovremennosti. Moskva, 1970.
Phil 310.792 Leninskaia kontseptsiia razvitiia. Gor'kii, 1970.
Phil 8980.898 Leninskoe teoreticheskoe nasledie i nekotorye voprosy marksistkoi etiki. Moskva, 1970.
Phil 3425.778 Léonard, Andre. La foi chez Hegel. Paris, 1970.
Phil 3831.17 Levin, Dan. Spinoza, the young thinker who destroyed the past. N.Y., 1970.
Phil 3450.11.465 Levin, David Michael. Reason and evidence in Husserl's phenomenology. Evanston, 1970.
Phil 342.28 Levin, Grigorii Aronovich. V.I. Lenin i sovremennye problemy teorii poznaniia. Minsk, 1970. 9v.
Phil 5590.540 Levy, Leon Harris. Conception of personality; theories and research. N.Y., 1970.
Phil 2120.18 Lewis, Clarence Irving. Collected papers. Stanford, 1970.
Phil 2725.38.5 Leyvraz, Jean Pierre. Phénoménologie de l'expérience. La Haye, 1970.
Phil 6302.5 Life history research in psychopathology. Minneapolis, 1970.
Phil 5865.12 Life-span developmental psychology. N.Y., 1970.
Phil 6121.62.1 Lilly, John Cunningham. Programming and metaprogramming in the human biocomputer. Berkeley, 1970.
Phil 978.49.910 Lindenberg, Christoph. Individualismus und offenbare Religion. Stuttgart, 1970.
Phil 5416.2 Loeb, Robert H. The sins of bias. N.Y., 1970.
Phil 6961.22 Loechen, Yngvar. Idealer og realiteter i et psykiatrisk sykehus. Oslo, 1970.
Phil 3493.50 Loegstrup, Knud Ejler Christian. Kants Kritik af erkendelsen og refleksionen. København, 1970.
VPhil 3450.11.490 Logar, Cene. Fenomenologija analiza in kritika filosofije Edmunda Husserla. Ljubljana, 1970.
Phil 4160.66.12.2 Lombardi, Franco. Scritti; saggi. v.11- 2. ed. Firenze, 1970-
Phil 8886.73.10 López Aranguren, José Luis. Teoria y sociedad. Barcelona, 1970.
Phil 4312.8 Lopez Quintas, Alfonso. Filosofía española contemporánea; temas y autores. Madrid, 1970.
Phil 258.10 Lorenz, Kuno. Elemente der Sprachkritik; eine Alternative zum Dogmatismus und Skeptizismus in der analytischen Philosophie. 1. Aufl. Frankfurt am Main, 1970.
Phil 5051.46.4 Lorenzen, Paul. Formale Logik. 4. Aufl. Berlin, 1970.
Phil 5700.4 Lorenzer, Alfred. Kritik des psychoanalytischen Symbolbegriffs. 1. Aufl. Frankfurt, 1970.
Phil 811.26 Louisgrand, Jean. De Lucrèce à Camus, littérature et philosophie comme réflexion sur l'homme. Paris, 1970.
Phil 5402.44 Lowen, Alexander. Pleasure: a creative approach to life. N.Y., 1970.
Phil 384.25 Lucas, John Randolph. The freedom of the will. Oxford, 1970.
Phil 5051.28.10 Lukasiewicz, Jan. Selected works. Amsterdam, 1970.
Phil 5545.236 Luriiâ, Aleksandr R. Une prodigieuse mémoire. Neuchâtel, 1970.
Phil 6400.34 Luriia, Aleksandr Romanovich. Traumatic aphasia. The Hague, 1970.
Phil 310.725 Lutai, Vadlen Stepanovich. O metode postroeniia sistemy dialekticheskogo materializma. Kiev, 1970.
Phil 3450.19.525 MacDowell, João Augusto A. Amazonas. A gênese da ontologia fundamental de Martin Heidegger. São Paulo, 1970.
Phil 3494.74 McFarland, John D. Kant's concept of teleology. Edinburgh, 1970.
Phil 2150.22.135 MacIntyre, Alasdair C. Herbert Marcuse: and exposition and a polemic. N.Y., 1970.
Phil 8622.76 McKinnon, Alastair. Falsification and belief. The Hague, 1970.
Phil 680.15 Macksey, Richard. The language of criticism and the science of man. Baltimore, 1970.
Phil 5330.42.5 Mackworth, Jane F. Vigilance and attention; a signal detection approach. Harmondsworth, 1970.
Phil 5222.22.5 Madsen, K.B. Psykologiens udvikling. København, 1970.
Phil 3450.19.540 Magnus, Bernd. Heidegger's metahistory of philosophy: amor fati, being and truth. The Hague, 1970.
Phil 5590.520 Mahrer, Alvin. New approaches to personality classification. N.Y., 1970.
Phil 5052.46 Mała encyklopedia logiki. Wrocław, 1970.
Phil 2733.5.11 Malebranche, Nicolas. Oeuvres complètes. Paris, 1970.
Phil 3425.746 Man'kovski, Boris S. Uchenie Gegelia o gosudarstve i sovremennost. Moskva, 1970.
Phil 6985.10 Mann, John Harvey. Encounter; a weekend with intimate strangers. N.Y., 1970.
Phil 450.4 Mansuy, Michel. Études sur l'imagination de la vie. Paris, 1970.
Phil 310.790 Marc, Alexandre. De la méthodologie à la dialectique. Paris, 1970.
Phil 2150.22.42 Marcuse, Herbert. Five lectures. Boston, 1970.
Phil 2750.23.30 Maréchal, Joseph. A Maréchal reader. N.Y., 1970.
Phil 585.400 Marías Aguilera, Julián. Antropología metafisica. Madrid, 1970.
Phil 2750.11.38 Maritain, Jacques. De l'Église du Christ; la personne de l'Église et son personnel. Paris, 1970.
Phil 5465.210 Markov, Mark E. Iskusstvo nak protsess. Moskva, 1970.
Phil 5190.72 Martin, Robert L. The paradox of the liar. New Haven, 1970.
Phil 3450.19.470 Martin Heidegger im Gespräch. München, 1970.
Phil 5404.4 Martinon, Jean Pierre. Les métamorphoses du désir et l'oeuvre. Paris, 1970.
Phil 3425.372 Marx, Karl. Critique of Hegel's 'Philosophy of right.' Cambridge, Eng., 1970.
Phil 187.186 Marx, Werner. Vernunft und Welt. The Hague, 1970.
Phil 1750.116 Marxist-Non-Marxist Humanist Dialogue, 2d, Herceg-Novi, 1969. Tolerance and revolution. Beograd, 1970.
Phil 6854.6.5 Masaryk, Tomáš Gottigue. Suicide and the meanings of civilization. Chicago, 1970.
Phil 5548.98 Maslow, Abraham Harold. Motivation and personality. 2. ed. N.Y., 1970.
Phil 5066.318 Massey, Gerald J. Understanding symbolic logic. N.Y., 1970.
Phil 5875.145 Mauco, Georges. L'inconscient et la psychologie de l'enfant. 1. éd. Paris, 1970.

1970 - cont.

Phil 8667.50 Mavrodes, George I. Belief in God; a study in the epistemalogy of religion. N.Y., 1970.
Phil 3494.76 May, Joseph Austin. Kant's concept of geography and its relation to recent geographical thought. Toronto, 1970.
Phil 9440.1 Med ideali in resniŏnostjo. Ljubljana, 1970.
Phil 5421.20.100 Megargee, Edwin I. The dynamics of aggression. N.Y., 1970.
Phil 8962.30 Mehl, Roger. Éthique catholique et éthique protestante. Neuchâtel, 1970.
Phil 418.5 Meiland, Jack W. The nature of intention. London, 1970.
Phil 408.4 Meiland, Jack W. Talking about particulars. London, 1970.
Phil 3910.134.1 Meissner, Heinrich Adam. Philosophischer Lexicon aus Christian Wolffs sämtlichen deutschen Schriften. Düsseldorf, 1970.
Phil 5330.40 Meldman, Monte Jay. Diseases of attention and perception. 1st ed. Oxford, 1970.
Phil 8328.2.2 Mello, Mario Vieira de Mello. Desenvolvimento e cultura. 2. ed. Rio de Janeiro, 1970.
Phil 6980.466 Meltzoff, Julian. Research in psychotherapy. 1. ed. N.Y., 1970.
Phil 2750.20.50.5 Merleau-Ponty, Maurice. Themes from the lectures at the Collège de France, 1952-1960. Evanston, 1970.
Phil 4080.3.201 Merlotti, Eric. L'intention spéculative de Benedetto Croce. (Filosofia dello spirito). Neuchâtel, 1970.
Phil 8592.122 Meslier, Jean. Oeuvres complètes. Paris, 1970- 2v.
Phil 8980.572.10 Mikhalevich, Aleksandr Vl. Front dushi. Kiev, 1970.
Phil 8962.32 Milhaven, John Giles. Toward a new Catholic morality. Garden City, 1970.
Phil 2138.40.16 Mill, John S. Die Freiheit (On Liberty) Übers. 3. Aufl. Darmstadt, 1970.
Phil 5867.30 Miller, David LeRoy. Gods and games; toward a theology of play. N.Y., 1970.
Phil 3805.270 Miller, Marlin E. Der Ubergang. 1. Aufl. Gütersloh, 1970.
Phil 3832.24 Millet, Louis. La pensée de Spinoza. Paris, 1970.
Phil 680.30 Millet, Louis. Le structuralisme. Paris, 1970.
Phil 5465.206 Mironov, Alekseĭ V. Minuty poeticheskikh vdokhnovenii. Iavoslavl', 1970.
Phil 8586.64.80 Mitchell, Phillip Marshall. Vilhelm Grønbech. En indføring. København, 1970.
Phil 8667.54 Mizor, Nikolai. Metadologicheski problemi na ateizma. Sofiia, 1970.
Phil 3494.70.2 Mörchen, Hermann. Die Einbildungskraft bei Kant. 2. Aufl. Tübingen, 1970.
Phil 583.12 Mohanty, Jitendra Nath. Phenomenology and ontology. Den Haag, 1970.
Phil 5403.16 Monedero Gil, Carmelo. La alegría. Madrid, 1970.
Phil 6322.70 Monroe, Russell R. Episodic behavioral disorders. Cambridge, 1970.
Phil 5865.5.45 Montada, Leo. Die Lernpsychologie Jean Piagets. Stuttgart, 1970.
Phil 8592.45.6 Montague, W.P. Belief unbound. Freeport, N.Y., 1970.
Phil 9070.148 Montapert, Alfred Armand. The supreme philosophy of man; the laws of life. Englewood Cliffs, N.J., 1970.
Phil 2730.114 Moore, Francis Charles Timothy. The psychology of Maine de Biran. Oxford, 1970.
Phil 3640.840A Morel, Georges. Nietzsche; Introduction à une première lecture. Paris, 1970-71. 3v.
Phil 585.414 Morichon, René. Entretiens sur la destinée humaine. Limoges, 1970.
Phil 8612.45.2 Morin, Edgar. L'homme et la mort. Paris, 1970.
Phil 8592.124 Morra, Gianfranco. Dio senza Dio. Bologna, 1970.
Phil 8092.24 Mozhniagun, Sergei E. O modernizme. Moskva, 1970.
Phil 3425.750 Mueller, Friedrich. Entfremdung. Berlin, 1970.
Phil 8620.62.5 Murdoch, Iris. The sovereignty of good. London, 1970.
Phil 3494.72 Murphy, Jeffrie G. Kant: the philosophy of right. London, 1970.
Phil 8888.18 Nagel, Thomas. The possibility of altruism. Oxford, 1970.
Phil 4013.10 Namer, Émile. La philosophie italienne. Paris, 1970.
Phil 5865.8 Nash, John. Developmental psychology. Englewood Cliffs, N.J., 1970.
Phil 575.282 Natanson, Maurice Alexander. The journeying self; a study in philosophy and social role. Reading, Mass., 1970.
Phil 5585.351 NATO Advanced Study Institute, University of Thessaloniki, 1968. Contemporary problems in perception. London, 1970.
Phil 70.112 The nature of philosophical inquiry. Notre Dame, 1970.
Phil 3425.693 Nedeljković, Dušan. Hegelova estetika, Marksovi osnovi estetike i današnje estetičke perspektive. Beograd, 1970.
Phil 98.3.2 Neff, Vladimir. Filosofiký sborník pro sannonsy neboli autigorgias. 2. vyd. Praha, 1970.
Phil 2520.415 Negri, Antonio. Descartes politico o della ragionevole ideologia. Milano, 1970.
Phil 3425.776 Negt, Oskar. Aktualität und Folgen der Philosophie Hegels. Frankfurt am Main, 1970.
Phil 5066.322 Neklassichesknia logika. Moskva, 1970.
Phil 8888.6.1 Nelson, Leonard. Critique of practical reason. Scarsdale, 1970?
Phil 3665.5.2 Nelson, Leonard. Gesammelte Schriften. v.1-8. Hamburg, 1970. 7v.
Phil 3665.5.32 Nelson, Leonard. Progress and regress in philosophy, from Hume and Kant to Hegel and Fries. Oxford, 1970.
Phil 3425.14.5 Nicolin, Günther. Hegel in Berichten seines Zeitgenossen companion von to Briefe von und an Hegel. Hamburg, 1970.
Phil 344.6 Nikitin, Evgenii P. Ob''iasnenie - funktsiia nauki. Moskva, 1970.
Phil 5465.198 Nobel Conference, 6th, Gustavus Adolphus College, 1970. Creativity. Amsterdam, 1970.
Phil 2905.1.665 Nogare, Pedro Dalle. Pessoa e amor segundo Teilhard de Chardin. São Paulo, 1970.
Phil 6323.26 Nolte, Helmut. Psychoanalyse und Soziologie. Bern, 1970.
Phil 8905.32 Nome, John. Kritisk forskerholdning i etikk og religionsfilosofi. Oslo, 1970.
Phil 9035.111 Norakidze, Vladimir G. Temperament lichnosti i fiksiorovannaia ustanovka. Tbilisi, 1970.
Phil 4372.1.135 Noreña, Carlos G. Juan Luis Vives. The Hague, 1970.
Phil 7053.344 Norman, Diana. Tom Corbett's stately ghosts of England. N.Y., 1970.
Phil 585.410 Nornengast, Urda. Der androgyne Mensch. Bellnhausen, 1970.
Phil 188.30 Nott, Kathleen. Philosophy and human nature. London, 1970.
Phil 4265.1.95 Nowicki, Andrzej. Centralne kategorie filosofii Vaniniego. Wyd. 1. Warszawa, 1970.
Phil 4882.1 Ocherki istorii filosofskoi i obshchestvenno-politicheskoi mysli v Turkmenistane. Ashkhabad, 1970.
Phil 1930.5.80 O'higgins, James. Anthony Collins; the man and his works. The Hague, 1970.

Chronological Listing

Phil 4710.170   Okulov, Aleksandr F. Sovetskaia filosofskaia nauka i ee problemy. Moskva, 1970.

Phil 8964.7   Olejnik, Stanisław. Moralność życia Społecznego. Warszawa, 1970.

Phil 4710.50.55   Oleksiuk, Myroslav M. Borot'ba filosofs'kykh techii na zakhidnoukraïns'kykh zemliak u 20-30kh rokakh XX st. L'viv, 1970.

Phil 3460.96   Olivetti, Marco M. L'esito teologico della filosofia del linguaggio di Jacobi. Padova, 1970.

Phil 1870.175   Olscamp, Paul J. The moral philosophy of George Berkeley. The Hague, 1970.

Phil 2750.20.140   O'Neill, John. Perception, expression, and history. Evanston, 1970.

Phil 396.18   Oppermann, Hans. Humanismus. Darmstadt, 1970.

Phil 295.6   Orban, A.P. Les dénominations du monde chez les premiers auteurs chrétiens. Nijmegen, 1970.

Phil 1714.5.8   Orsi, Domenico d'. Il tramonto della filosofia moderna. 3. ed. Padova, 1970.

Phil 974.5.10   Osborne, Arthur. Ramana Maharshi and the path of sell-knowledge. London, 1970.

Phil 310.5.12   Oshakov, Zhivko. Istoricheskiiat materializum i sotsiologiiatu. 2. izd. Sofiia, 1970.

Phil 8889.8.10   Ossowska, Maria. Normy moralne. Warszawa, 1970.

Phil 8889.8.5   Ossowska, Maria. Social determinants of moral ideas. Philadelphia, 1970.

Phil 7069.70.10   Ostrander, Sheila. Psychic discoveries behind the Iron Curtain. Englewood Cliffs, 1970.

Phil 8415.10.3   Ottaviano, Carmelo. La legge della come legge universale della natura. 3. ed. Padova, 1970.

Phil 2905.1.670   Ouince, René d'. Un prophète en procès. Paris, 1970. 2v.

Phil 2880.8.300   Pagano, Giacoma Maria. Sartre e la dialettica. Napoli, 1970.

Phil 8446.2   Pagliaro, Antonino. Ironia e verità. Milano, 1970.

Phil 3425.762   Palma, Norman. Moment et processus. Paris, 1970-

Phil 972.20   Panet, Edmond. La mort de Canopus. Paris, 1970.

Phil 5055.34   Papanoutsos, Euangelos. Logiké. Athéna, 1970.

Phil 5255.82   Papanoutsos, Euangelos. Psychologia. Athénai, 1970.

Phil 8416.44   Pasi, Isak. Esteticheski studii. Sofiia, 1970.

Phil 585.365   Passmore, John Arthur. The perfectibility of man. London, 1970.

Phil 4065.184   Paterson, Antoinette Mann. The infinite worlds of Giordano Bruno. Springfield, 1970.

Phil 8595.62   Patterson, Robert Leet. A philosophy of religion. Durham, 1970.

Phil 5055.38   Patzig, Günther. Sprache und Logik. Göttingen, 1970.

Phil 5055.36   Paulus Venetus. Logica. Hildesheim, 1970.

Phil 8430.90   Pavlovskii, Boris V. U istokov sovetskoi khudozhestvennoi kritiki. Leningrad, 1970.

Phil 310.740   Pawelzig, Gerd. Dialektik der Entwicklung objektiver Systeme. 1. Aufl. Berlin, 1970.

Phil 3925.16.260   Pear, David Francis. Ludwig Wittgenstein. N.Y., 1970.

Phil 1715.18   Pejović, Danilo. Sistem i egzistencija. Zagreb, 1970.

Phil 8640.16   Penelhum, Terence. Survival and disembodied existence. London, 1970.

Phil 5055.29.15   Perelman, Chaim. Le champ de l'argumentation. Bruxelles, 1970.

Phil 5590.524   Pervin, Lawrence A. Personality: theory, assessment, and research. N.Y., 1970.

Phil 6315.2.140.8   Pesch, Edgar. Pour connaître la pensée de Freud. Evreux, 1970.

Phil 5520.718   Peterfalvi, Jean Michel. Introduction à la psycholinguistique. 1. éd. Paris, 1970.

Phil 5520.732   Peterfalvi, Jean Michel. Recherches experimentales sur le symbolisme phonétique. Paris, 1970.

Phil 585.392   Peterson, Forrest H. A philosophy of man and society. N.Y., 1970.

Phil 815.36   Petruzzellis, Nicola. Maestri di ieri. Napoli, 1970.

Phil 4200.6.32.2   Petruzzellis, Nicola. Problemi e aporie del pensiero contemporaneo. 2. ed. Napoli, 1970.

Phil 165.450   Phenomenology and social reality. The Hague, 1970.

Phil 2905.1.660   Philippe de la Trinité, Father. Pour et contre Teilhard de Chardin, penseur religieux. Saint-Cénéré, 1970.

Phil 5039.22   Philosophical problems in logic. Dordrecht, 1970.

Phil 100.10.7   Philosophisches Wörterbuch. 7. Aufl. Berlin, 1970. 2v.

Phil 5400.206   Physiological correlates of emotion. N.Y., 1970.

Phil 5865.5.20   Piaget, Jean. Genetic epistomology. N.Y., 1970.

Phil 5875.175   Piaget, Jean. Psychologie et épistémologie. Paris, 1970.

Phil 9560.66   Pieper, Josef. Auskunft über die Tugenden. Zürich, 1970.

Phil 8965.13.20   Pieper, Josef. Missbrauch der Sprache, Missbrauch der Macht. Zürich, 1970.

Phil 8670.22   Pike, Nelson craft. God and timelessness. N.Y., 1970.

Phil 310.714   Piroschkow, Vera. Freiheit und Notwendigkeit in der Geschichte; zur Kritik des historischen Materialismus. München, 1970.

Phil 3450.11.480   Pivčević, Edo. Husserl and phenomenology. London, 1970.

Phil 8980.697   Platonov, Rostislav P. Vospitanie kommunisticheskoi soznatel'nosti. Minsk, 1970.

Phil 5525.70   Plessner, Helmuth. Laughing and crying; a study of limits of human behavior. Evanston, 1970.

Phil 3745.2.31   Ploucquet, Gottfried. Sammlung der Schriften welche den logischen calcul Herrn Prof. Ploucquets Betreffen, mit neuen Zusäben, Frankfurt und Leipzig, 1766. Stuttgart, 1970.

Phil 3450.19.460   Poeggeler, Otto. Heidegger; Perspektiven zur Deutung seines Werks. Köln, 1970.

Phil 5055.40   Poern, Ingmar. The logic of power. Oxford, 1970.

Phil 1200.44.2   Pohlenz, Max. Die Stoa. 2. und 4. Aufl. Göttingen, 1970. 2v.

Phil 9513.46   Polishchuk, Nina P. Problema moral'noho idealn. Kyív, 1970.

Phil 4200.1.34.1   Pomponazzi, Pietro. De naturalium effectuum causis, sive, De incantationibus. Hildesheim, 1970.

Phil 680.35   Popovič, Anton. Štrukturalizmus v slovenskej vede. Martin, 1970.

Phil 4015.6   Poppi, Antonino. Introduzione all'aristotelismo padovano. Padova, 1970.

Phil 4200.1.90   Poppi, Antonio. Saggi sul pensiero inedito di Pietri Pomponazzi. Padova, 1970.

Phil 5545.252   Postman, Leo Joseph. Verbal learning and memory; selected readings. N.Y., 1970.

Phil 845.6   Pozzo, Gianni M. Umanesimo moderno o tramonto dell'Umanesimo? Padova, 1970.

Phil 8430.86   Pracht, Erwin. Sozialistischer Realismus-Positionen, Probleme, Perspektiven. 1. Aufl. Berlin, 1970.

Phil 2477.20.80   Pradines, Marie Thérèse. Georges Bastide, philosophe de la valeur. Toulouse, 1970.

Phil 310.742   Problema urovnei i sistem v nauchnom poznanii. Minsk, 1970.

Phil 8980.712.65   Problemy dukhovnoi kul'tury i formirovaniia lichnosti. Sverdlovsk, 1970.

Phil 5066.328   Problemy matematicheskoi logiki. Moskva, 1970.

Phil 1750.115.190   Prohić, Kasim. Odvažnost izricanja; fenomenologije životnih formi. Zagreb, 1970.

Phil 6110.30   Psychological aspects of stress. Springfield, Ill., 1970.

Phil 1750.842   Pucci, Raffaele. La filosofia e l'unità della cultura. Napoli, 1970.

Phil 4210.250   Quacguarelli, Antonio. La lezione liturgica di Antonio Rosmini. Milano, 1970.

Phil 5056.1.25   Quine, Willard Van Orman. Philosophy of logic. Englewood Cliffs, N.J., 1970.

Phil 266.2   Quine, Willard Van Orman. The web of belief. N.Y., 1970.

Phil 1750.862   Radev, R. Kritika va neotomizma. Sofiia, 1970.

Phil 5870.100   Ratcliffe, Tom A. The child and reality. London, 1970.

Phil 5421.20.110   Rattner, Josef. Aggression und menschliche Natur. Olten, 1970.

Phil 720.101   Rauche, Gerhard Albin. Contemporary philosophical alternatives and the crisis of truth; a critical study of positivism, existentialism and Marxism. The Hague, 1970.

Phil 5593.70   Rausch de Traubenberg, Nina. La pratique du Rorschach. 1. éd. Paris, 1970.

Phil 5590.560   Ravzvitie lichnosti v usloviiakh stroitel'stva kommunizma. Cheboksarg, 1970.

Phil 6327.42.5   Ree, Frank van. Colliding generations. Varanasi, 1970.

Phil 3450.19.530   Regina, Umberto. Heidegger. Milano, 1970.

Phil 6327.21.13   Reich, Wilhelm. Character analysis. 3. ed. N.Y., 1970.

Phil 6327.21.40   Reich, Wilhelm. Die sexuelle Revolution. Frankfurt am Main, 1970.

Phil 1750.395.2   Reidemeister, Kurt. Die Unsachlichkeit der Existenzphilosophie. 2. Aufl. Berlin, 1970.

Phil 2225.5.165   Reilly, Francis E. Charles Peirce's theory of scientific method. N.Y., 1970.

Phil 5272.10   Restle, Frank. Introduction to mathematical psychology. Reading, Mass., 1970.

Phil 2905.1.620   Rétif, André. Teilhard et l'évangélisation des temps nouveaux. Paris, 1970.

Phil 6854.10   Retterstøl, Nils. Selvmord. Oslo, 1970.

Phil 2905.1.625   Revol, Enrique Luis. Símbolo y evolución humana. Cordoba, 1970.

Phil 3925.16.235   Rhees, Rush. Discussions of Wittgenstein. London, 1970.

Phil 8448.15   Richter, G. Erbauliches, Belehrendes, wie auch Vergnügliches kitsch Lexion. Gütersloh, 1970.

Phil 2880.8.282   Richter, Liselotte. Jean-Paul Sartre. N.Y., 1970.

Phil 6315.2.444   Ricoeur, Paul. Freud and philosophy. New Haven, 1970.

Phil 3925.16.240   Rielkopf, Charles F. Strict finitism. The Hague, 1970.

Phil 960.282   Riepe, Dale Maurice. The philosophy of India and its impact on American thought. Springfield, 1970.

Phil 8597.66   Riet, Georges van. Philosophie et religion. Louvain, 1970.

Phil 3017.10   Rintelen, Fritz-Joachim von. Contemporary German philosophy and its background. Bonn, 1970.

Phil 2045.81.4   Robertson, George Croan. Hobbes. St. Clair Shores, Michigan, 1970.

Phil 396.16   Rodi, Frithjof. Provokation, Affirmation. Das Dilemma des kritischen Humanismus. Stuttgart, 1970.

Phil 2520.276   Rodis-Lewis, Geneviève. La morale de Descartes. 3e ed. Paris, 1970.

Phil 1200.72   Rodis-Lewis, Geneviève. La morale stoïcienne. Paris, 1970.

Phil 6980.650   Rogow, Arnold A. The psychiatrists. N.Y., 1970.

Phil 310.736   Rohrmoser, Günter. Das Elend der kritischen Theorie. Theodor W. Adorno, Herbert Marcuse, Jürgen Habermas. Freiburg, 1970.

Phil 8597.64   Rohrmoser, Günter. Emanzipation und Freiheit. München, 1970.

Phil 3425.764   Rohrmoser, Günter. Theologie et aliénation dans la pensée du jeune Hegel. Paris, 1970.

Phil 5627.268.18   Rokeach, Milton. Beliefs, attitudes and values; a theory of organization and change. San Francisco, 1970.

Phil 1135.210   Roloff, Dietrich. Gottähnlichkeit, Vergöttlichung und Erhöhung zu seligem Leben. Berlin, 1970.

Phil 3450.19.545   Rosales, Alberto. Transzendenz und Differenz. Den Haag, 1970.

Phil 1030.5A   Rosenthal, Franz. Knowledge triumphant; the concept of knowledge in medieval Islam. Leiden, 1970.

Phil 683.2   Rosenthal, Klaus. Die Überwindung des Subjekt-Objekt-Denkens als philosophisches und theologisches Problem. Göttingen, 1970.

Phil 4210.255   Rosmini e il Rosminianesimo nel veneto. Padova, 1970.

Phil 348.25   Ross, Jacob Joshua. The appeal to the given. London, 1970.

Phil 9120.185   Ross, Ralph Gilbert. Obligation; a social theory. Ann Arbor, 1970.

Phil 3425.740   Rossi, Mario. Da Hegel a Marx. Milano, 1970- 2v.

Phil 1630.23.5   Rossi, Paolo. Philosophy, technology, and the arts in the early modern era. N.Y., 1970.

Phil 8892.88   Rotter, Hans. Strukturen sittlichen Handelns. Mainz, 1970.

Phil 2250.25   Royce, Josiah. Letters. Chicago, 1970.

Phil 5649.44   Roze, Nina A. Psikhomotorika vzroslogo cheloveka. Leningrad, 1970.

Phil 930.76   Rubin, Vitalii A. Ideologiia i kul'tura Drevnego Kitaia. Moskva, 1970.

Phil 1930.8.125   Rubinoff, Lionel. Collingwood and the reform of metaphysics; a study in the philosophy of mind. Toronto, 1970.

Phil 5871.105.2   Ruehle, Otto. Zur Psychologie des proletarischen Kindes. 2. Aufl. Frankfurt, 1970.

Phil 5520.685   Rundle, Clement William Kennedy. A critique of linguistic philosophy. Oxford, 1970.

Phil 5548.150   Russell, Wallace Addison. Milestones in motivation; contributions to the psychology of drive and purpose. N.Y., 1970.

Phil 8980.759   Rutkovs'kyi, Borys O. Katehoriia dovir'ia v marksysts'kii etytsi. Kyiv, 1970.

Phil 720.98   Ruvo, Vincenzo de. Il problema della verità da Spinoza a Hume. Padova, 1970.

Phil 8892.57.2   Ruvo, Vincenzo de. I valori morali. 2. ed. Padora, 1970.

Phil 8597.62   Ruyer, Raymond. Dieu des religious, dieu de la science. Paris, 1970.

Phil 2138.165   Ryan, Alan. John Stuart Mill. N.Y., 1970.

Chronological Listing

Phil 5548.140   Ryan, Thomas Arthur. Intentional behavior; an approach to human motivation. N.Y., 1970.

Phil 7028.2   Rýzl, Milan. Parapsychology. N.Y., 1970.

Phil 910.2   Saddhatissa, Hammalaiva. Buddhist ethics: essence of Buddhism. London, 1970.

Phil 7085.10.1   Sadger, Isidor. Über Nachtwandeln und Mondsucht. Nendeln, 1970.

Phil 349.90   Sadovskii, Grigorii I. Leninskaia kontseptsiia poniatiia i evoliutsiia poniatiia "vid". Minsk, 1970.

Phil 5535.50   Sahakian, William S. Psychology of learning. Chicago, 1970.

Phil 4872.109.80   Sailley, Robert. Crî Aurobindo, philosophe du yoga intégral. Paris, 1970.

Phil 396.20   Salzburger Humanismusgespräch. Die erschreckende Zivilisation. Wien, 1970.

Phil 3585.30.10   Sampaio Ferraz, Torcio. Die Zweidimensionalität des Rechts als Voraussetzung für den Methodendualismus von Emil Lask. Meisenheim am Glan, 1970.

Phil 3801.768.10   Sandkuehler, Hans-Jörg. Friedrich Wilhelm Joseph Schelling. Stuttgart, 1970.

Phil 3475.3.250   Saner, Hans. Karl Jaspers in Selbstzeugnissen und Bilddokumenten. Reinbek, 1970.

Phil 5590.518   Sanford, Nevitt. Issues in personality theory. 1. ed. San Francisco, 1970.

Phil 3450.11.495   Saraiva, Maria Manuela. L'imagination selon Husserl. La Haye, 1970.

Phil 5590.576   Satura, Vladimir. Struktur und Genese der Person. Innsbrück, 1970.

Phil 720.92   Schär, Hans. Was ist Wahrheit? Eine theologisch-psychologische Untersuchung. Zürich, 1970.

Phil 5627.270.10   Scheibe, Karl Edward. Beliefs and values. N.Y., 1970.

Phil 5415.7.9   Scheler, Max. The nature of sympathy. Hamden, 1970.

Phil 2428.20   Schiwy, Günther. Der französische Strukturalismus. Reinbek, 1970.

Phil 5414.40   Schlederer, Franz. Schuld, Reue und Krankheit. München, 1970.

Phil 9495.170.15   Schlegelberger, Bruno. Vor- und ausserehelicher Geschlechtsverkehr. Remscheid, 1970.

Phil 585.416   Schleissheimer, Bernhard. Der Mensch als Wissender und Glaubender. Inaug. Diss. Wien, 1970.

Phil 8598.135.15   Schlette, Heinz Robert. Aporie und Glaube. München, 1970.

Phil 2725.2.130   Schmid, Beat. L'espérance et l'itinéraire de la certitude chez Lamennais. Berne, 1970.

Phil 5643.180   Schmidt, Udo. Figurale Nachwirkungen auf Kinästhetischen Gebeit bei Lageveränderung von Objekt und tastender Hand. Frankfurt, 1970.

Phil 3850.32.80   Schneller, Martin. Zurischen Romantik und Faschismus. 1. Aufl. Stuttgart, 1970.

Phil 308.4   Scholes, Robert E. The philosopher critic. Tulsa, Okla., 1970.

Phil 9075.94   Scholl, Robert. Das Gewissen des Kindes. 2. Aufl. Stuttgart, 1970.

Phil 3808.61.5   Schopenhauer, Arthur. Essays and aphorisms. Harmondsworth, Eng., 1970.

Phil 8698.15   Schueppe, Otto. Gott sprach-es-ward. Bern, 1970.

Phil 440.12   Schuette, Hermann Günther. Freiheit ist anders. München, 1970.

Phil 1750.115.205   Schutz, Alfred. On phenomenology and social relations. Chicago, 1970.

Phil 2280.21.10   Schutz, Alfred. Reflections on the problem of relevance. New Haven, 1970.

Phil 4225.8.62   Sciacca, Michele Federico. L'oscuramento dell'intelligenza. Milano, 1970.

Phil 8689.105   Science et théologie: méthode et langage. Paris, 1970.

Phil 6128.84   Scott, Donald Fletcher. The psychology of work. London, 1970.

Phil 559.4   Seidel, George Joseph. Being nothing and God; a philosophy of appearance. Assen, 1970.

Phil 2805.480   Sellier, Philippe. Pascal et Saint Augustin. Paris, 1970.

Phil 8843.20   Sena, Cemil. Insanlar ve ahlâklar. İstanbul, 1970.

Phil 8673.38   Sencer, Muammer. Allah neden var. Istanbul, 1970.

Phil 9590.32.5   Sendy, Jean. L'ére du verseau. Paris, 1970.

Phil 8419.68   Séran de la Tour. L'art de sentir et de juger en matière de goût. v.1-2. Genève, 1970.

Phil 5058.110   Serebriannikov, Oleg F. Evristicheskie printsipy i logicheskie ischisleniia. Moskva, 1970.

Phil 5520.716   Seuphor, Michel. Le don de la parole. Saint-Aguilin-de-Pacy, 1970.

Phil 5841.8   Sexualité humaine. Paris, 1970.

Phil 1865.200   el Shakankiri, Mohamed Abd el-Hadi. La philosophie juridique de Jeremy Bentham. Paris, 1970.

Phil 6968.39   Shands, Harley C. Semiotic approaches to psychiatry. The Hague, 1970.

Phil 310.782   Shchekina, Liubov' I. Poniatiia "dvizhenie" i razvitie i ikhvol' v izuchsnii fizicheskikh protsessov. Moskva, 1970.

Phil 5485.6   Sheinin, Iulian M. Integral'nyi intelleks. Moskva, 1970.

Phil 6980.685   Shepard, Martin. Games analysts play. N.Y., 1970.

Phil 6985.15   Shepard, Martin. Marathon 16. N.Y., 1970.

Phil 6854.4   Shneidman, Edwin S. The psychology of suicide. N.Y., 1970.

Phil 5465.204   Shouksmith, George. Intelligence, creativity and cognitive style. London, 1970.

Phil 3425.768   Siep, Ludwig. Hegels Fichtekritik und die Wissenschaftslehre von 1804. Freiburg, 1970.

Phil 818.41.3   Sikora, Adam. Spotkania z filozofia. 3. Wyd. Warszawa, 1970.

Phil 8430.77   Sikors'kyi, Qurii P. Estetychna tsinnist' tekhniky. Kyïv, 1970.

Phil 193.185.5   Silva-Tarouca, Amadeo. Aufsätze zur Sozialphilosophie. Wien, 1970.

Phil 6328.64   Silverman, Samuel. Psychologic cues in forecasting physical illness. N.Y., 1970.

Phil 310.778   Simpozium po Teme Ob"ektivnye Zakony Istorii i Nauchnoe Rukovodstov Obshchestvom, Moscow, 1967. Ob"ektirnye zako istorii i nauchnoe rukovodstov obshchestvom. Moskva, 1970.

Phil 2805.490   Sina, Mario. L'anti-Pascal di Voltaire. Milano, 1970.

Phil 2280.5.161   Singer, Beth J. The rational society; a critical study of Santayana's social thought. Cleveland, 1970.

Phil 5058.104   Skolem, Thoralf. Selected works in logic. Oslo, 1970.

Phil 645.60   Slote, Michael A. Reason and scepticism. London, 1970.

Phil 5535.44   Sluckin, Wladyslaw. Early learning in man and animal. London, 1970.

Phil 5590.426.2   Smelser, Neil Joseph. Personality and social systems. 2. ed. N.Y., 1970.

Phil 5520.710   Smerud, Warren B. Can there be a private language? The Hague, 1970.

Phil 2266.35   Smith, Adam. A dissertation on the origin of languages. Tübingen, 1970.

Phil 4120.4.140   Smith, William Aloysius. Giovanni Gentile on the existence of God. Louvain, 1970.

Phil 2805.202.1   Soltau, R.H. Pascal: the man and the message. Westport, 1970.

Phil 5039.32   Sootnoshenie istorii i logiki nauki. Dnepropetrovsk, 1970.

Phil 8893.104.3   Sorokin, Pitirim Aleksandrovich. Explorations in altruistic love and behavior. N.Y., 1970.

Phil 5590.562   Sotsializm i lichnost'. Volgograd, 1970.

Phil 349.92   Sovremennye problemy seorii poznaniia dialekticheskogo materializma. Moskva, 1970. 2v.

Phil 8598.92.2   Spann, Othmhar. Religionsphilosophie auf geschichtlicher Grundlage. 2. Aufl. Graz, 1970.

Phil 193.163.3   Spann, Othmar. Philosophenspiegel; die Hauptlehren der Philosophie begrifflich und geschichtlich dargestellt. 3. Aufl. Graz, 1970.

Phil 5520.726   Spasov, Dobrin I. Filosofiia na lingvistikata sreshchu lingvisticheskata filosofiia. Sofiia, 1970.

Phil 2905.1.456   Speaight, Robert. Teilhard de Chardin: re-mythologization. Chicago, 1970.

Phil 5058.106.1   Spencer, Thomas. The art of logic. 1628. Facsimile. Menston, Eng., 1970.

Phil 8423.16.80   Spengler, Walter Eckehart. Der Begriff des Schönen bei Winckelmann. Göppingen, 1970.

Phil 6310.1.110   Sperker, Manès. Alfred Adler oder das Elénd der Psychologie. 1. Aufl. Wien, 1970.

Phil 585.325   Spicker, Stuart F. The philosophy of the body. Chicago, 1970.

Phil 5070.32   Sprigge, Timothy Lauro Squire. Facts, words, and beliefs. N.Y., 1970.

Phil 8708.42.5   Spülbeck, Otto. Grenzfragen zwischen Naturwissenschaft und Glaube. München, 1970.

Phil 1870.180   Stack, George J. Berkeley's analysis of preception. The Hague, 1970.

Phil 1718.25.1   Stegmüller, W. Main currents in contemporary German, British, and American philosophy. Bloomington, 1970.

Phil 349.94   Stegmueller, Wolfgang. Aufsätze zur Wissenschaftstheorie. Darmstadt, 1970.

Phil 5421.15.12   Stein, Edith. On the problem of empathy. 2d ed. The Hague, 1970.

Phil 2225.2.85   Steinberg, Ira Sherman. Ralph Barton Perry on education for democracy. Columbus, 1970.

Phil 450.10   Steiner, Hans Friedrich. Marxiaten-Lennisten über den Sinn des Lebens. Essen, 1970.

Phil 978.49.767   Steiner, R. Anthroposophie. 2. Aufl. Dornach, 1970.

Phil 978.49.729   Steiner, R. Die Beantwortung von Welt- und Lebensfragen durch Anthroposophie. Dornach, 1970.

Phil 978.49.740   Steiner, R. Das Geheimnis der Trinität. Dornach, 1970.

Phil 978.49.782   Steiner, R. Die neue Geistigkeit und das Christus-Erlebnis des zwanzigsten Jahrhunderts. 2. Aufl. Dornach, 1970.

Phil 5520.730   Stichl, Ulrich. Einführung in die allgemeine Semantik. Bern, 1970.

Phil 400.132   Stiehler, Gottfried. Der Idealismus von Kant bis Hegel. Berlin, 1970.

Phil 4825.16   Stojković, Andrija B. Počeci filosofije Srba od Save do Dositeja na osnovama narodne mudrosti. Beograd, 1970.

Phil 5520.746   Strawson, Peter Frederick. Meaning and truth: an inaugural lecture delivered before the University of Oxford on 5 November 1969. Oxford, 1970.

Phil 8586.36.66   Strohm, Theodor. Theologie im Schatten politischer Romantik. Mainz, 1970.

Phil 5058.108   Strombach, Werner. Die Gesetze unseres Denkens. München, 1970.

Phil 1630.45   Struever, Nancy S. The language of history in the Renaissance. Princeton, N.J., 1970.

Phil 5238.242   Struktur und Dynamik des menschlichen Verhaltens; zum Stand der modernen Psychologie. Stuttgart, 1970.

Phil 8870.40   Struktura morali. Sverdlovsk, 1970.

Phil 1750.830.5   Strukturalizam. Zagreb, 1970.

Phil 165.464   Studi in memoria di Carlo Ascheri. Urbino, 1970.

Phil 165.460   Studi in onore di Antonio Corsano. Manduria, 1970.

Phil 349.85   Studies in the theory of knowledge. Oxford, 1970.

Phil 365.66   Stuttgarter Gemeinschaft "Arzt und Seelsorger." Evolution; Fortschrittsglaube und Heilserwartung. Ein Tagungsbericht. Stuttgart, 1970.

Phil 2880.8.270   Suhl, Benjamin. Jean-Paul Sartre: the philosopher as a literary critic. N.Y., 1970.

Phil 5871.95   Sutton-Smith, Brian. The sibling. N.Y., 1970.

Phil 310.754   Svidenskii, Vladimir I. Novye filosofskie aspekty elementno-strukturnykh otnoshenii. Leningrad, 1970.

Phil 585.370   Sviták, Ivan. Man and his world; a Marxian view. N.Y., 1970.

Phil 5125.38   Swain, Marshall. Induction, acceptance and rational belief. Dordrecht, 1970.

Phil 6328.62   Szasz, Thomas Stephen. Ideology and insanity. Garden City, 1970.

Phil 6980.717.30   Szazs, Thomas Stephen. The manufacture of madness. 1st ed. N.Y., 1970.

Phil 3018.40   Szyszkowka, Maria. Neokantyzm - filozofia społeczna wraz a filozofia prawa natury o zmilnej treści. Wyd. 1. Warszawa, 1970.

Phil 8709.25   Tancher, Volodymyr K. Nauka oprovergaet religioznye dogmaty. Kiçv, 1970.

Phil 8050.95   Tatarkiewicz, Wladyslaw. History of aesthetics. The Hague, 1970.

Phil 6903.10   Tavistock Institute of Human Relations, London. Annotated list of publications, 1946-1970. London, 1970?

Phil 194.60   Taylor, Daniel Malcolm. Explanation and meaning. Cambridge, Eng., 1970.

Phil 3050.8   Taylor, Ronald Jack. The romantic tradition in Germany. London, 1970.

Phil 2905.1.69.1   Teilhard de Chardin, Pierre. Let me explain. London, 1970.

Phil 2905.1.605   Teilhard reassessed: a symposium of critical studies in the thought of Père Teilhard de Chardin attempting an evaluation of his place in contemporary Christian thinking. London, 1970.

Phil 7082.190.5   Teillard, Ania. Ce que disent les rêves. Paris, 1970.

Phil 310.747   Teoreticheskol nasledie V.I. Lenina i meditsina. Moskva, 1970.

Phil 6854.8   Tetaz, Numa. Du darfst Leben. Zürich, 1970.

Phil 3640.810   Thatcher, David S. Nietzsche in England, 1890-1914. Toronto, 1970.

Phil 8599.52   Theill-Wunder, Hella. Die archaische Verborgenheit. München, 1970.

Chronological Listing

Phil 8969.16   Theiner, Johann. Die Entwicklung der Moraltheologie zur eigenständigen Disziplin. Regensburg, 1970.

Phil 2477.15.120   Therrien, Vincent. La révolution de Gaston Bachelard en critique littéraire. Paris, 1970.

Phil 3425.772   Theunissen, Michael. Hegels Lehre vom absoluten Geist als theologisch-politischer Traktat. Berlin, 1970.

Phil 8599.34.5   Thomas, George Finger. Philosophy and religious belief. N.Y., 1970.

Phil 5780.15.20   Thomas, Klaus. Die künstlich gesteuerte Seele. Stuttgart, 1970.

Phil 5465.218   Thomas de Saint-Laurent, Raymond de. L'imagination, son importance, sa nature. Avignon, 1970.

Phil 8420.28   Tilghman, Benjamin R. The expression of emotion in the visual arts: a philosophical inquiry. The Hague, 1970.

Phil 2750.20.145   Tilliette, Xavier. Merleau-Ponty. Paris, 1970.

Phil 3801.837.15   Tilliette, Xavier. Schelling: une philosophie en devenir. Paris, 1970. 2v.

Phil 494.6   Timpanaro, Sebastiano. Sul materialismo. Pisa, 1970.

Phil 5790.50   Tournier, Paul. The meaning of gifts. Richmond, Va., 1970.

Phil 8969.15   Tournier, Paul. The seasons of life. Richmond, Va., 1970[1963]

Phil 194.62   Trias, Eugenio. Metodologia del pensamiento mágico. Bercelona, 1970.

Phil 5402.42   Trigg, Roger. Pain and emotion. Oxford, 1970.

Phil 8969.18.3   Trillhaas, Wolfgang. Ethik. 3. Aufl. Berlin, 1970.

Phil 396.10   Trinkaus, Charles Edward. In our image and likeness; humanity and divinity in Italian humanist thought. London, 1970. 2v.

Phil 2428.12   Trotignon, Pierre. Les philosophes français d'aujourd'hui. 2. éd. Paris, 1970.

Phil 8980.850   Tselikova, Ol'ga P. Kommunisticheskii ideal i nravstvennoe razvitie lichnosti. Moskva, 1970.

Phil 5829.16   Tukh, Nina A. Predystoniia obshehestva. Leningrad, 1970.

Phil 8894.36   Turner, Dean. The autonomous man. St. Louis, 1970.

Phil 8674.16   Tvethoworn, Illtyd. Absolute value: a study in Christian theism. London, 1970.

Phil 6946.42   U.S. President's Task Force on the Mentally Handicapped. Action against mental disability; the report. Washington, 1970.

Phil 5871.106   Ulrich, Ferdinand. Der Mensch als Anfang. Benziger, 1970.

Phil 8905.10   Utz, Arthur Fridolin. Ethik und Politik. Stuttgart, 1970.

Phil 4720.7   V.I. Lenin i istoriia filosofii narodov SSSR. Moskva, 1970.

Phil 1885.97   Vander Veer, Garrett L. Bradley's metaphysics and the self. New Haven, 1970.

Phil 5066.259.5   Van Heijenoort, Jean. Frege and Gödel; two fundamental texts in mathematical logic. Cambridge, 1970.

Phil 5068.98   Vax, Louis. L'empirisme logique. Paris, 1970.

Phil 8846.4   Vázquez, Francisco. Tres éticas del siglo XX. Madrid, 1970.

Phil 8982.2   Vega, Rafael de la. Marxismus und Ethik. 1. Aufl. Frankfurt am Main, 1970.

Phil 2399.1   Vek Prosveshcheniia. Moskva, 1970.

Phil 1730.30   Venturi, Franco. Utopia e riforma nell'iluminismo. Torino, 1970.

Phil 75.72.5   Verbinc, Franc. Filozofski tokovi na Slovenskem. Ljubljana, 1970.

Phil 8612.84   Vernon, Glenn M. Sociology of death; an analysis of death-related behavior. N.Y., 1970.

Phil 5465.200   Vernon, Philip Ewart. Creativity: selected readings. Harmondsworth, 1970.

Phil 6060.92   Vetter, August. Die Zeichensprache von Schrift und Traum. Freiburg, 1970.

Phil 850.48   Vogel, Cornelia Johanna de. Studies in Greek philosophy. Assen, 1970.

Phil 5548.148   Vontobel, Jacques. Leistungsbedürfnis und soziale Umwelt. Bern, 1970.

Phil 8980.872.10   Voprosy marksistko-leninskoi etiki i kommunisticheskogo vospitaniia. Sverdlovsk, 1970.

Phil 8400.66   Voprosy teorii esteticheskogo vospitaniia. Moskva, 1970.

Phil 315.19   Vries, Joseph de. Materie und Geist. München, 1970.

Phil 3841.8   Vries, Theun de. Baruch de Spinoza in Selbstzeugnissen und Bilddokumenten. Reinbek, 1970.

Phil 2520.395   Vrooman, Jack Rochford. René Descartes; a biography. N.Y., 1970.

Phil 1135.14   Wa Saïd, Dibinga. Theosophies of Plato, Aristotle and Plotinus. N.Y., 1970.

Phil 3120.30.205   Wachinger, Lorenz. Der Glaubensbegriff Martin Bubers. 1. Aufl. München, 1970.

Phil 165.446   Wahrheit, Wert und Sein; Festgabe für Dietrich von Hildebrand zum 80. Geburtstag. Regensburg, 1970.

Phil 8870.34   Wallace, Gerald. The definition of morality. London, 1970.

Phil 5590.536.4   Wallon, Henri. Les origines du caractère chez l'enfant. 4. éd. Paris, 1970.

Phil 2340.22.30   Wank, Martin. The real world. N.Y., 1970.

Phil 1750.552.25   Warnock, Mary. Existentialism. London, 1970.

Phil 2255.1.160   Watling, John. Bertrand Russell. Edinburgh, 1970.

Phil 9070.144   Watts, Alan Wilson. Does it matter? N.Y., 1970.

Phil 6032.8   Weber, F. Aptitudes et caractère par la physiognomonie. Genève, 1970.

Phil 822.22   Weier, Winfried. Sinn und Teilhabe. Salzburg, 1970.

Phil 6332.50   Weigert, C. Edith. The courage to love. New Haven, 1970.

Phil 2940.3.20   Weil, Éric. Essais et conférences. Paris, 1970. 2v.

Phil 3504.50.2   Weil, Éric. Problemes kantiens. 2. éd. Paris, 1970.

Phil 5520.25.1   Weiler, Gershon. Mauthner's Critique of language. Cambridge, Eng., 1970.

Phil 5360.36   Weinberg, Julius Rudolph. Ideas and concepts. Milwaukee, 1970.

Phil 3504.60   Weisskopf, Traugott. Immanuel Kant und die Pädagogik. Zürich, 1970.

Phil 7055.156   Weldon, Warren. A happy medium: the life of Caroline Randolph Chapman. Englewood Cliffs, 1970.

Phil 5871.100   Westley, William A. The silent majority; families of emotionally healthy college students. San Francisco, 1970.

Phil 5520.695   Wettler, Manfred. Syntaktische Faktoren im verbalen Lernen. Bern, 1970.

Phil 197.98   Wheatley, Jon. Prolegomena to philosophy. Belmont, Calif., 1970.

Phil 2422.8   White, Reginald James. The anti-philosophers; a study of philosophers in eighteenth century France. London, 1970.

Phil 1135.205   Whittaker, John. God, time, being; studies in the transcendental tradition in Greek philosophy. Thesis. Bergen, 1970.

Phil 585.360   Williams, Gershom Antonio. The measure of a man. 1st ed. Toronto, 1970.

Phil 2045.150   Willms, Bernard. Die Antwort des Leviathan; Thomas Hobbes' politische Theorie. Neuwied, 1970.

Phil 8612.88   Wiplinger, Fridolin. Der personal verstandene Tod. Freiburg, 1970.

Phil 632.15   Das Wirklichkeitsverständnis der Gegenwart. Salzburg, 1970.

Phil 3425.742   Wofford Symposium on Hegel and the Philosophy of Religion, Wofford College, 1968. Hegel and the philosophy of religion; the Wofford Symposium. The Hague, 1970.

Phil 5590.522   Wolberg, Lewis Robert. The dynamics of personality. N.Y., 1970.

Phil 6976.25   Wolfson, Louis. Le schizo et les langues. Paris, 1970.

Phil 6980.780.20   Wolpe, Joseph. The practice of behavior therapy. 1. ed. N.Y., 1970.

Phil 730.36   Wolterstorff, Nicholas Paul. On universals. Chicago, 1970.

Phil 3504.58   Wood, Allen W. Kant's moral religion. Ithaca, 1970.

Phil 7069.70.5   Worrall, Ambrose A. Explore your psychic world. N.Y., 1970.

Phil 8897.94.2   Wyss, Dieter. Strukturen der Moral. 2. Aufl. Göttingen, 1970.

Phil 3235.136   Xhaufflaire, Marcel. Feuerbach et la théologie de la sécularisation. Paris, 1970.

Phil 6334.10A   Yankelovich, Daniel. Ego and instinct; the psychoanalytic view of human nature. N.Y., 1970.

Phil 2115.225   Yolton, John W. Locke and the compass of human understanding; a selective commentary on the Essay. Cambridge, Eng., 1970.

Phil 5234.2   Young, Robert Maxwell. Mind, brain and adaptation in the nineteenth century. Oxford, 1970.

Phil 583.16   Zaner, Richard M. The way of phenomenology. N.Y., 1970.

Phil 5590.556   Zawadski, Bohdan. Wstęp do seorii osobowosci. Wyd. 1. Warszawa, 1970.

Phil 8575.16   Die Zeit Jesu. Freiburg, 1970.

Phil 310.759   Zel'kina, Ol'ga S. Sistemno-strukturnyi analiz osnovnykh kategorii dialektilu. Saratov, 1970.

Phil 6315.62   Zetzel, Elizabeth R. The capacity for emotional growth. London, 1970.

Phil 5066.172   Zinov'ev, Aleksandr A. Kompleksnaia logika. Moskva, 1970.

Phil 8980.896.5   Ziuziukin, Ivan I. Uznaiu cheloveka. Mosva, 1970.

Phil 5590.477   Zurabashvili, Avlippi. Aktual'nye problemy persondogii i klinicheskoi psikhiatrii. Tbilisi, 1970.

1971

Phil 2115.149.3   Aaron, Richard Ithamar. John Locke. 3rd ed. Oxford, 1971.

Phil 3085.7.1   Adorno, Theodor W. Gesammelte Schriften. 1. Aufl. Frankfurt, 1971.

Phil 3085.7.45   Adorno, Theodor W. Kritik: kleine Schriften zur Gesellschaft. 1. Aufl. Frankfurt, 1971.

Phil 8430.92   Afasizhev, Marat Nurbievich. Freĭdizm i burzhuaznoe iskusstvo. Moskva, 1971.

Phil 8980.131.15   Akmambetov, Galikhan G. Problemy nravstvennogo razvitiia lichnosti. Alma-Ata, 1971.

Phil 2445.5.35   Alquié, Ferdinand. Signification de la philosophie. Paris, 1971.

Phil 5190.90   Andersen, Kenneth E. Persuasion: theory and practice. Boston, 1971.

Phil 5270.36   Anderson, Barry F. The psychology experiment. 2d ed. Belmont, Calif., 1971.

Phil 310.774   Andrade, Almir de. Ensaio critico sôbre os fundamentos da filosofia dialética. Rio de Janeiro, 1971.

Phil 1105.14   Anton, John Peter. Essays in ancient Greek philosophy. Albany, 1971.

Phil 5130.4   Antonov, Georgii V. Ot formal'noi logiki k dialektike. Moskva, 1971.

Phil 5590.563   Anufriev, Evgenii A. Sotsial'naia vol' i aktivnost' lichnosti. Moskva, 1971.

Phil 8401.31.5   Astakhov, I.B. Estetika. Moskva, 1971.

Phil 6998.8   Aubin, Henri. Art et magie chez l'enfant. Toulouse, 1971.

Phil 2255.1.170   Ayer, Alfred Jules. Russell and Moore: the analytical heritage. Cambridge, 1971.

Phil 8691.34   Babosov, Evgenii M. Nauchno-teknicheskaia revoliutsiia i modernizatsiia katolitsizma. Minsk, 1971.

Phil 2477.15.22   Bachelard, Gaston. On poetic imagination and reverie; selections from the works of Gaston Bachelard. Indianapolis, 1971.

Phil 575.290   Ban'ka, Józef. Współczesne problemy filosofii aechniki. Poznań, 1971.

Phil 2750.22.130   Barlow, Michel. Le socialisme d'Emmanuel Mounier. Toulouse, 1971.

Phil 585.140.2   Becker, Ernest. The birth and death of meaning. 2. ed. N.Y., 1971.

Phil 6849.4   Bell, Alan P. The personality of a child molester. Chicago, 1971.

Phil 7012.4   Bender, Hans. Unser sechster Sinn. Stuttgart, 1971.

Phil 8594.16.80   Benz, Ernst. Rudolf Otto's Bedeutung für die Religionswissenschaft und die Theologie. Leiden, 1971.

Phil 585.386   Berger, Herman. Progressive and conservative man. Pittsburgh, Pa., 1971.

Phil 8402.70   Berlyne, Daniel Ellis. Aesthetics and psychology. N.Y., 1971.

Phil 5876.35   Bernard, Harold Wright. Adolescent development. Scranton, 1971.

Phil 1750.866   Bernstein, Richard Jacob. Praxis and action. Philadelphia, 1971.

Phil 5871.108   Biller, Henry B. Father, child, and sex role. Lexington, 1971.

Phil 3120.55.60   Bloch, Ernst. Pädagogica. 1.Aufl. Frankfurt, 1971.

Phil 2610.100.5   Bloch, Olivier René. La philosophie de Gassendi. La Haye, 1971.

Phil 3640.845   Boudot, Pierre. L'ontologie de Nietzsche. Paris, 1971.

Phil 5520.714   Bourne, Lyle Eugene. The psychology of thinking. Englewood Cliffs, N.J., 1971.

Phil 1750.115.200   Brand, Gerd. Die Lebenswelt. Berlin, 1971.

Phil 5520.740   Bressanone Conference on Psycholinguistics, University of Padova, 1969. Advances in psycholinguistics. Amsterdam, 1971.

Phil 5352.20   Broadbent, Donald Eric. Decision and stress. London, 1971.

Phil 7074.10   Brown, Rosemary. Unfinished symphonies; voices from the beyond. N.Y., 1971.

Phil 6360.2   Browning, Robert Mitchell. Behavior modification in child treatment. Chicago, 1971.

Chronological Listing

Phil 5625.123   Brush, Franklin Robert. Aversive conditioning and learning. N.Y., 1971.

Phil 3120.61.30   Bueschel, Johann Gabriel Bernhard. Über die Charlatanerie der Gelehrten seit Menken. Leipzig, 1971.

Phil 310.800   Bŭnkov, Angel I. Dialekticheskaia logika. Sofiia, 1971.

Phil 7009.145.1   Byrd, Elizabeth. A strange and seeing time. London, 1971.

Phil 5640.148   Cain, William S. Stimulus and sensation; readings in sensory psychology. Boston, 1971.

Phil 2266.90   Campbell, Thomas Douglas. Adam Smith's science of morals. London, 1971.

Phil 5110.5   Capaldi, Nicholas. The art of deception. N.Y., 1971.

Phil 5585.355   Cappon, Daniel. Technology and perception. Springfield, 1971.

Phil 8877.100   Casey, John. Morality and moral reasoning; five essays in ethics. London, 1971.

Phil 5374.235.10   Castaneda, Carlos. A separate reality; further conversations with Don Juan. N.Y., 1971.

Phil 5485.8   Cattell, Raymond Bernard. Abilities: their structure, growth, and action. Boston, 1971.

Phil 3450.19.535   Cauturier, Fernand. Monde et être chez Heidegger. Montréal, 1971.

Phil 6112.40.20   Cayce, Edgar Evans. The outer limits of Edgar Cayce's power. 1. ed. N.Y., 1971.

Phil 960.272.5   Chethimattam, John B. Patterns of Indian thought. Maryknoll, N.Y., 1971.

Phil 333.28   Chomsky, Noam. Problems of knowledge and freedom: the Russell lectures. 1st ed. N.Y., 1971.

Phil 5841.12   Christenson, Cornelia Vos. Kinsey, a biography. Bloomington, 1971.

Phil 5635.48   Christman, Raymond John. Sensory experience. Scranton, 1971.

Phil 8582.80   Čimić, Esad. Drama ateizacije. Religija, ateizam i odgoj. Sarajevo, 1971.

Phil 5520.734   Cognitive development and epistemology. N.Y., 1971.

Phil 8120.10.5   Coleman, Francis X.J. The aesthetic thought of the French Enlightenment. Pittsburgh, 1971.

Phil 5130.6   Czayka, Lothar. Grundzüge der Aussagenlogik. München, 1971.

Phil 4769.1.140   Dahm, Helmut. Vladimir Solov'ev und Max Scheler. München, 1971.

Phil 1170.26   Descombes, Vincent. Le platonisme. Paris, 1971.

Phil 5520.758   DeVito, Joseph A. Psycholinguistics. Indianapolis, 1971.

Phil 310.656.2   Dialekticheskii i istoricheskii materializm. Izd. 4. Moskva, 1971.

Phil 9070.150   Dilman, Ilhman. Sense and delusion. London, 1971.

Phil 5695.2   Dixon, Norman F. Subliminal perception. London, 1971.

Phil 6113.34   Dubrovskii, David I. Psikhicheskie iavleniia i mozg. Moskva, 1971.

Phil 8404.26   Dzhibladze, Georgii N. Iskusstvo i deistoitel'nost'. Tbilisi, 1971.

Phil 6360.8   Eckensberger, Diethind. Sozialisationsbedingungen der öffentlichen Erziehung. 1. Aufl. Frankfurt am Main, 1971.

Phil 3120.30.210   Edwards, Paul. Buber and Buberism. Lawrence, 1971.

Phil 3925.16.305   Egidi, Rosaria. Studi di logica e filosofia della scienza. Roma, 1971.

Phil 5244.36   Egidius, Henry. Förstå människor. Lund, 1971.

Phil 2070.161   Eisendrath, Craig Ralph. The unifying moment; the psychological philosophy of William James and Alfred North Whitehead. Cambridge, 1971.

Phil 6329.22.5   Eissler, Kurt Robert. Talent and genius. N.Y., 1971.

Phil 5627.134.105   Ekman, Nils Gösta. Experiment med Gud. Stockholm, 1971.

Phil 3235.138   Elez, Iovo. Problema bytiia i myshleniia v filosofii Liudirga Feienbakha. Moskva, 1971.

Phil 5258.7.80   Elschenbroich, Adalbert. Romantische Sehnsucht und Kosmogonie. Tübingen, 1971.

Phil 335.11   Essler, Wilhelm Karl. Wissenschaftstheorie. v.2. Freiburg, 1971.

Phil 8092.30   Esteticheskoe nasledie V.I. Lenina i problemy iskusstva. Moskva, 1971.

Phil 8905.28   Eticheskoe i esteticheskoe. Leningrad, 1971.

Phil 5282.5   Existential humanistic psychology. Belmont, Calif., 1971.

Phil 6321.51.15   Fages, Jean Baptiste. Comprendre Jacques Lacan. Toulouse, 1971.

Phil 5421.20.125   Feshbach, Seymour. Television and aggression. 1. ed. San Francisco, 1971.

Phil 8406.28   Fiedler, Konrad. Schriften zur Kunst. München, 1971. 2v.

Phil 70.100.15   Filosofiia i sovnemennost'. Moskva, 1971.

Phil 3925.16.290   Finch, Henry Leroy. Wittgenstein - the early philosophy. N.Y., 1971.

Phil 310.808   Fiorani, Eleonora. Friedrich Engels e il materialismo dialettico. Milano, 1971.

Phil 5871.118   Föräldrar i 70-talet. Stockholm, 1971.

Phil 4756.1.47.1   Frank, Semen L. Nepostizhimoe. München, 1971.

Phil 6834.20   Freedman, Mark. Homosexuality and psychological functioning. Belmont, Calif., 1971.

Phil 6315.64   Freeman, Erika. Insights: conversations with Theodor Reik. Englewood Cliffs, 1971.

Phil 5335.8   Freyhold, Michaela von. Autoritarismus und politische Apathie. Frankfurt, 1971.

Phil 8905.30   Friedmann, Georges. La puissance et la sagesse. Paris, 1971.

Phil 3460.98   Friedrich, Heinrich Jacobi. Philosoph und Literat der Goethezeit. Frankfurt, 1971.

Phil 5585.315.5   From, Franz. Perception of other people. N.Y., 1971.

Phil 6315.19.16   Fromm, Erich. Psychoanalysis and religion. New Haven, 1971.

Phil 7009.210   Gandee, Lee R. Strange experience; the autobiography of a hexenmeister. Englewood Cliffs, 1971.

Phil 510.1.50   Gasman, Daniel. The scientific origins of National Socialism: Social Darwinism in Ernst Haeckel and the German Monist League. London, 1971.

Phil 5876.30   Gattegno, Caleb. The adolescent and his will. N.Y., 1971.

Phil 5246.86   Gelinas, Robert P. The teenager and psychology. 1. ed. N.Y., 1971.

Phil 2750.20.150   Geraets, Théodore F. Vers une nouvelle philosophie transcendantale. La Haye, 1971.

Phil 575.288   Gergen, Kenneth J. The concept of self. N.Y., 1971.

Phil 4260.200   Giambattista Vico nel terzo centenario della nascita. Napoli, 1971.

Phil 8448.11.7   Giesz, Ludwig. Phanomenologie des Kitsches. 2. Aufl. München, 1971.

Phil 5590.574   Gilligan, Sonja Carl. The heterosexuals are coming; the fusion strategy. N.Y., 1971.

Phil 2725.2.95.2   Gioberti, V. Lettera intorno alle dottrine filosofiche e religiose del sig. di Lamennais. Milano, 1971.

Phil 6760.5   Gjedde, Georg. Bogen om Jesper. København, 1971.

Phil 2905.1.675   Goerres, Ida F.C. Teilhard de Chardin als Christ und als Mensch. Wiesbaden, 1971.

Phil 3488.26.1   Goldmann, L. Immanuel Kant. London, 1971.

Phil 5875.170   Grotloh-Amberg, Heidi. Beeinflussung des Verhaltens durch den Schuleintritt. Bern, 1971.

Phil 8956.26.2   Gruendel, Johannes. Wandelbares und Unwandelbares in der Moraltheologie. 2. Aufl. Düsseldorf, 1971.

Phil 6316.14.10   Guntrip, Henry James Samuel. Psychoanalytic theory, therapy, and the self. N.Y., 1971.

Phil 5046.50   Guttenplan, Samuel D. Logic: a comprehensive introduction. N.Y., 1971.

Phil 338.44.1   Habermas, Jürgen. Knowledge and interests. Boston, 1971.

Phil 3030.8   Habermas, Jürgen. Philosophisch-politische Profile. 7. Aufl. Frankfurt, 1971.

Phil 8957.13.20   Haering, Bernhard. Morality is for persons. N.Y., 1971.

Phil 210.76   Hare, Richard Mervyn. Essays on philosophical method. London, 1971.

Phil 5190.88   Hare, Richard Mervyn. Practical inferences. London, 1971.

Phil 974.2.70   Harris, Iverson L. Mme. Blatavsky defended. San Diego, 1971.

Phil 8882.115   Harrison, Jonathan. Our knowledge of right and wrong. London, 1971.

Phil 5203.11.24   Harvard University. The Harvard list of books in psychology. Compiled and annotated by the psychologists in Harvard University. 4th ed. Cambridge, 1971.

Phil 5878.5   Hauser, Stuart T. Black and white identity formation: studies in the psychosocial development of lower socioeconomic class adolescent boys. N.Y., 1971.

Phil 3450.19.64   Heidegger, Martin. Poetry, language, thought. 1. ed. N.Y., 1971.

Phil 6980.350.25   Henry, William Earl. The fifth profession. 1st ed. San Francisco, 1971.

Phil 210.78   Hermeneutik als Weg heutiger Wissenschaft. Salzburg, 1971.

Phil 3450.11.500   Herrmann, Friedrich-Wilhelm von. Husserl und die Meditationen des Descartes. Frankfurt, 1971.

Phil 3195.6.210   Herrmann, Ulrich. Die Pädagogik Wilhelm Diltheys. Göttingen, 1971.

Phil 5867.40   Herron, R.E. Child's play. N.Y., 1971.

Phil 8587.82   Hildebrand, Alice M. (Jourdain) von. Introduction to a philosophy of religion. Chicago, 1971.

Phil 5069.8   Hilpinen, Risto. Deontic logic: introductory and systematic readings. Dordrecht, 1971.

Phil 3120.30.200   Hodes, Aubrey. Martin Buber; an intimate portrait. N.Y., 1971.

Phil 8855.4   Höffe, Otfried. Praktische Philosophie. München, 1971.

Phil 165.462   Hommage à Jean Hyppolite. 1. ed. Paris, 1971.

Phil 5017.6.5   Howell, W.S. Eighteenth-century British logic and rhetoric. Princeton, 1971.

Phil 6985.30   Howells, John Gwilym. Theory and practice of family psychiatry. N.Y., 1971.

Phil 9530.66   Huber, Richard M. The American idea of success. 1st ed. N.Y., 1971.

Phil 2053.65   Hutcheson, F. Illustrations on the moral sense. Cambridge, 1971.

Phil 5218.5.5   Iaroshevskii, Mikhail G. Psikhologiia v XX stoletii. Moskva, 1971.

Phii 4957.60   The Ibero-American enlightenment. Urbana, 1971.

Phii 274.6   Identity and individuation. N.Y., 1971.

Phil 4803.462.10   Ingarden, Roman. U podsław sevrii poznania. Wyd. 1. Warszawa, 1971.

Phil 8448.20   Introspection: the artist looks at himself. Tulsa, 1971.

Phil 5400.208   Izard, Carroll E. The face of emotion. N.Y., 1971.

Phil 6854.12   Jacobs, Jerry. Adolescent suicide. N.Y., 1971.

Phil 7020.2   Jacobson, Nils-Olof. Liv efter döden? Salna, 1971.

Phil 4803.497.90   Jawonski, Manek. Tadeusz Kotarbiński. Wyd. 1. Warszawa, 1971.

Phil 5051.28.15   Jermen, Frane. Med logiko in filozofijo. Ljubljana, 1971.

Phil 5274.20   Johnson, Homer H. An introduction to experimental design in psychology. N.Y., 1971.

Phil 3491.20   Jones, Hardy E. Kant's principle of personality. Madison, 1971.

Phil 5590.568.1   Jourard, Sidney Marshall. The transparent self. N.Y., 1971.

Phil 5270.32   Jung, John. The experimenter's dilemma. N.Y., 1971.

Phil 8400.41.2   Kagan, Moisei S. Lektsii po marksistsko-leninskoi estetike. Izd. 2. Leningrad, 1971.

Phil 8092.26   Kalelin, Eugene Francis. Art and existence: a phemomenological aesthetics. Lewisburg, Pa. 1971.

Phil 4720.6   Kamenskii, Zakhar A. Filosofskie idei russkogo prosveshcheniia. Moskva, 1971.

Phil 310.786   Kategoriia dialektilei kak stupeni poznaniia. Moskva, 1971.

Phil 1750.455.12   Kaufmann, W.A. From Shakespeare to existentialism. Freeport, N.Y., 1971.

Phil 551.1   Kichanova, Inga M. Desiat' ispovedi. Moskva, 1971.

Phil 5780.27   Kiesler, Charles A. The psychology of commitment. N.Y., 1971.

Phil 8960.20   Kleber, Karl-Heinz. De parvitate materiae in sexto. Regensburg, 1971.

Phil 5590.554   Knowles, Henry P. Personality and leadership behavior. Reading, Mass., 1971.

Phil 270.150   Komarov, Viktor N. Zagadka budushchego. Moskva, 1971.

Phil 8171.100.5   Konan, Uladzimir M. Demokraticheskaia estetika Belorussii (1905-1917 gg). Minsk, 1971.

Phil 5004.1   Kondakov, Nikolai I. Logicheskii slovar'. Moskva, 1971.

Phil 8090.10   Koopmann, Helmut. Beiträge zur Theorie der Künste im 19. Jahrhundert. Frankfurt, 1971-

Phil 5068.29   Korneeva, Anna I. Leninskaia kritika malchizma i bor'ba protiv sovremennogo idealizma. Moskva, 1971.

Phil 552.3   Lanza del Vasto, Joseph Jean. Les quatre fléaux. Paris, 1971.

Phil 342.30   Ławniczak, Włodzimierz. O uzasadniającej roli analogii na przykładzie wnioskowań z zakresu historii sztuki. Poznań, 1971.

Phil 6321.5.8.2   Lawrence, David Herbert. Fantasia of the unconscious and Psychoanalysis and the unconscious. London, 1971.

Phil 6980.413   Lazarus, Arnold A. Behavior therapy and beyond. N.Y., 1971.

Phil 5620.36   Lee, Wayne. Decision, theory and human behavior. N.Y., 1971.

Phil 680.50   Lefebvre, Henri. Au-delà du structuralisme. Paris, 1971.

Phil 585.404   Légaut, Marcel. L'homme à la recherche de son humanité. Paris, 1971.

Phil 8980.516   Leninskoe eticheskoe nasledstvo i sovremennost. Tambov, 1971.

1971 - cont.

Phil 5421.20.140 Lepenies, Wolf. Kritik der Anthropologie. München, 1971.
Phil 2775.6.80   Levert, Paule. Jean Nabert; ou, L'exigence absolue. Paris, 1971.
Phil 6980.518.2 Levi, Vladimir L'. Okhota za mysl'iu. Izd. 2. Moskva, 1971.
Phil 4803.522.30 Libelt, Karol. Pisma o oświacie i wychowaniu. Wrocław, 1971.
Phil 1135.245   Lotz, Johannes Baptist. Die Stufen der Liebe; Eros, Phila, Agape. 1. Aufl. Frankfurt, 1971.
Phil 4809.447.90 Loužil, Jaromír. Ignác Jan Hanuš. Vyd. 1. Praha, 1971.
Phil 5896.5   Lynn, Richard. Personality and national character. 1. ed. Oxford, 1971.
Phil 2138.180   McCloskey, Henry John. John Stuart Mill: a critical study. London, 1971.
Phil 7158.715   MacDermot, Violet. The cult of the seer in the ancient Middle East. Berkeley, 1971.
Phil 8887.138   McGann, Thomas F. Ethics: theory and practice. Chicago, 1971.
Phil 402.22   MacIntyre, Alasdair Chalmers. Against the self-images of the age: essays on ideology and philosophy. London, 1971.
Phil 1133.54   McLean, George F. Ancient Western philosophy: the Hellenic emergence. N.Y., 1971.
Phil 2880.8.287 McMahon, Joseph H. Humans being; the world of Jean-Paul Sartre. Chicago, 1971.
Phil 5627.144.1 Macmurray, John. The structure of religious experience. Hamden, Conn., 1971.
Phil 2725.25.95 Magnani, Giovanni S.I. Itinerario al valore in R. Le Senne. Roma, 1971.
Phil 5252.168   Malcolm, Norman. Problems of mind. N.Y., 1971.
Phil 5052.38.5   Mally, Ernst. Logische Schriften. Dordrecht, 1971.
Phil 5809.102   Man and beast: comparative social behavior. Washington, 1971.
Phil 1735.16   Mandelbaum, Maurice H. History, man, and reason; a study in nineteenth-century thought. Baltimore, 1971.
Phil 672.270   Maneev, Aleksei K. Preemstvennost' v razoitii kategorii prostranstva, vremeni i dvizheniia. Minsk, 1971.
Phil 6315.2.465 Mannoni, O. Freud. 1st American ed. N.Y., 1971.
Phil 3925.16.300 Marconi, Diego. Il mito del linguaggio scientifico. Studi su Wittgenstein. Milano, 1971.
Phil 8887.136   Margolis, Joseph Zalman. Values and conduct. Oxford, 1971.
Phil 310.659.7   Marković, Mihajlo. Dijalektička teorija značenja. 2. izd. Beograd, 1971.
Phil 310.608.7   Marksistsko-leninskaia filosofiia. Moskva, 1971. 2v.
Phil 3850.27.230.5
          Marshall, George N. Schweitzer; a biography. 1st ed. Garden City, 1971.
Phil 6309.2   Massachusetts Commission on Lunacy. Insanity and idiocy in Massachusetts; report of the Commission on lunacy, 1855. Cambridge, 1971.
Phil 583.14   Mathur, Dinesh Chandra. Naturalistic philosophies of experience. St. Louis, 1971.
Phil 9070.142   Mayeroff, Milton. On caring. 1st American ed. N.Y., 1971.
Phil 5627.271.5 Mensching, Gustav. Topos und Typos; Motive und Strukturen religiösen Lebens. Bonn, 1971.
Phil 5875.65.10 Menyuk, Paula. The acquisition and development of language. Englewood Cliffs, 1971.
Phil 8980.572.30 Miladinović, Milan M. Moralno-politicki lik komunista Vojvodine u NOR-u i revoluciji. Beograd, 1971.
Phil 5270.30   Miller, Arthur G. The social psychology of psychological research. N.Y., 1971.
Phil 8980.572.15 Milovidov, Arsenii S. Kommunisticheskaia moral' i voinskii dolg. Moskva, 1971.
Phil 310.798   Mitin, Mark B. V.I. Lenin i aktual'nye problemy filosofii. Moskva, 1971.
Phil 418.16   Mohanty, Jitendra Nath. The concept of intentionality. St. Louis, 1971.
Phil 7077.2   Montgomery, Ruth Shick. A world beyond. N.Y., 1971.
Phil 8612.90   Moos, Peter von. Consolatio; Studien zur mittellateinischen Trostliteratur über den Tod und zum Problem der christlichen Trauer. München, 1971-
Phil 3832.26   Moreau, Joseph. Spinoza et le spinozisme. 1. éd. Paris, 1971.
Phil 5252.170   Morris, Desmond. Intimate behaviour. London, 1971.
Phil 5520.750   Mounin, Georges. Introductions à la sémiologie. Paris, 1971.
Phil 3549.8.145 Mueller, Roland. Das verzwistete Ich-Ludwig Klages und sein philosophisches Hauptwerk Der Geist als Widersacher der Seele. Bern, 1971.
Phil 5274.23   Mulaik, Stanley A. The foundations of factor analysis. N.Y., 1971.
Phil 6834.10   Murphy, John. Homosexual liberation; a personal view. N.Y., 1971.
Phil 4803.592.20 Mysłakowski, Zygmunt. Pisma wybrane. Wyd. 1. Warszawa, 1971.
Phil 6155.22   Mystification and drug misuse; hazards in using psychoactive drugs. 1st ed. San Francisco, 1971.
Phil 344.7   Nauchnoe otknjtie i ego vospriiatie. Moskva, 1971.
Phil 8905.34   Nauka i nravstvennost'. Moskva, 1971.
Phil 4825.11   Nedeljković, Dušan. Od Heraklita do njegoša i Svetozara. Beograd, 1971.
Phil 3640.76.17 Nietzsche, Friedrich. Nietzsche; a self-portrait from his letters. Cambridge, 1971.
Phil 1713.5   Nikolajević, Sietamir B. Misao kas odraz vremens. Beograd, 1971.
Phil 8125.37.2   Nivelle, A. Kunst- und Dichtungstheorien zwischen Aufklärung und Klassik. 2. Aufl. Berlin, 1971.
Phil 9215.2   Norman, Richard. Reasons for actions: a critique of utilitarian rationality. Oxford, 1971.
Phil 3850.27.265 Nosik, Boris M. Shveitser. Moskva, 1971.
Phil 8593.25   Novak, Michael. Ascent of the mountain. 1. ed. N.Y., 1971.
Phil 70.94.10   Oberlin Colloquium in Philosophy. Society, revolution and reform; proceedings. Cleveland, 1971.
Phil 3640.595.5 Oduev, S.F. Tropami Zaratustry. Moskva, 1971.
Phil 310.6.7   Osnovy marksistsko-leninskoi filosofii. Moskva, 1971.
Phil 8082.4   Ossola, Carlo. Autunno del Rinascimento. Firenze, 1971.
Phil 4783.1   Ostrianyn, Danylo Kh. Rozvytok materialistychnoi filosofii na Ukrainii. Kyiv, 1971.
Phil 5280.5   Owens, Thomas J. Phenomenology and intersubjectivity. The Hague, 1971.
Phil 5520.756   Panfilov, Vladimir Z. Vzaimootnoshenie iazyka i myshleniia. Moskva, 1971.
Phil 4845.227.30 Papanoutsos, Euangelos. Ho logos kai ho anthrōpos. Athena, 1971.

1971 - cont.

Phil 8622.86   Parker, Francis H. Reason and faith revisited. Milwaukee, 1971.
Phil 6834.15   Parker, William. Homosexuality: a selective bibliography of over 3000 items. Metuchen, N.J., 1971.
VPhil 5225.11   Pasłuszha, Yózet. Historia psychologii. Lublin, 1971.
Phil 5643.174   Pastore, Nicholas. Selective history of theories of visual perception: 1650-1950. N.Y., 1971.
Phil 8980.676   Pavlova, Liia Jakovlevna. Nravstvennye tsennosti nachego sovremennika. Moskva, 1971.
Phil 346.38   Pears, David Francis. What is knowledge? N.Y., 1971.
Phil 2270.190   Peel, John David Yeadon. Herbert Spencer; the evolution of a sociologist. London, 1971.
Phil 5520.748   Pelc, Jerzy. Semiotyka polska, 1894-1969. Warszawa, 1971.
Phil 5520.748.2 Pelc, Jerzy. Studies in functional logical semiotics of natural language. The Hague, 1971.
Phil 8595.60   Penelhum, Terence. Religion and rationality. 1. ed. N.Y., 1971.
Phil 2855.11.80 Philibert, Michel André Jean. Paul Ricoeur. Paris, 1971.
Phil 190.106.5   Piaget, Jean. Insights and illusions of philosophy. Translation. 1st American ed. N.Y., 1971.
Phil 5465.151   Piaget, Jean. Mental imagery in the child; a study of the development of imaginal representation. London, 1971.
Phil 4195.7F   Pico della Mirandola, Giovanni. Joannes Pieus Mirandulanus Opera omnia. Torino, 1971.
Phil 5640.146   Pitcher, George Willard. A theory of perception. Princeton, N.J., 1971.
Phil 3552.490   Pogrebyskii, Iosif B. Gotfrid Vil'gel'm Leibnits, 1646-1716. Moskva, 1971.
Phil 5893.4   Porter, Judith Deborah Revitch. Black child, white child; the development of racial attitudes. Cambridge, 1971.
Phil 3497.30   Prauss, Gerold. Erscheinung bei Kant. Habilitationsschrift. Berlin, 1971.
Phil 6125.32   Pribram, Karl H. Languages of the brain. Englewood Cliffs, 1971.
Phil 1200.74   Problems in stoicism. London, 1971.
Phil 5465.220   Problemy nauchnogo tvorchestva v sovremennoi psikhologii. Moskva, 1971.
Phil 5284.4   The psychology of private events; perspectives on covert response systems. N.Y., 1971.
Phil 5055.42   Putnam, Hilary. Philosophy of logic. N.Y., 1971.
Phil 6325.28.1   Putnam, James Jackson. James Jackson Putnam and psychoanalysis. Cambridge, 1971.
Phil 6327.4.36   Rank, Otto. The double: a psychoanalytic study. Chapel Hill, 1971.
Phil 402.20   Ratković, Radoslav. Ideologija i politika. Beograd, 1971.
Phil 8656.46.2   Ratschow, Carl Heinz. Atheismus im Christentum? 2. Aufl. Gütersloh, 1971.
Phil 8622.82.2   Ratzinger, Joseph. Glaube und Zukunft. 2. Aufl. München, 1971.
Phil 7072.22.5   Raudive, Konstantins. Breakthrough. N.Y., 1971.
Phil 3425.780   Rebstock, Hans Otto. Hegels Auffassung des Mythos in seinen Frühschriften. Freiburg, 1971.
Phil 5520.754.2 Regnell, Hans. Filosofiska och språkvetenskapliga grundfrågor inom betydelseläran. 2. uppl. Stockholm, 1971.
Phil 6327.21.46 Reich, Wilhelm. The invasion of compulsory sex-morality. N.Y., 1971.
Phil 6327.21.41 Reich, Wilhelm. The sexual revolution. N.Y., 1971.
Phil 5066.316.5 Rescher, Nicholas. Temporal logic. Wien, 1971.
Phil 6967.6   Revault D'Allounes, G. Thèse pour le doctorat en médecine. Paris, 1971.
Phil 3640.850   Rey, Jean Michel. L'enjeu des signes; lecture de Nietzsche. Paris, 1971.
Phil 8892.68   Richards, David A.J. A theory of reasons for action. Oxford, 1971.
Phil 5841.10   Richardson, Herbert Warren. Nun, witch, playmate; the Americanization of sex. 1st ed. N.Y., 1971.
Phil 6360.5   Rie, Herbert E. Perspectives in child psychopathology. Chicago, 1971.
Phil 3850.32.85 Rieber, Arnulf. Vom Positivismus zum Universalismus. Berlin, 1971.
Phil 310.788   Rodin, Davor. Dijalektika gradjanskog drustva. Beograd, 1971.
Phil 4829.749.30 Rodin, Davor. Metafizika i ćudoredje. Zagreb, 1971.
Phil 1717.26   Rossi, Paolo. Aspetti della rivoluzione scientifica. Napoli, 1971.
Phil 2250.70   Royce, Josiah. The philosophy of Josiah Royce. N.Y., 1971.
Phil 2255.12   Ryle. London, 1971.
Phil 5535.54   Saltz, Eli. The cognitive bases of human learning. Homewood, 1971.
Phil 3565.132   Santayana, George. Lotze's system of philosophy. Bloomington, 1971.
Phil 1718.46   Šarčević, Abdulah. Iskon i smisao. Sarajevo, 1971.
Phil 8419.67   Schmidt, Siegfried Josef. Ästhetische Prozesse. Köln, 1971.
Phil 600.64   Schnaedelbach, Herbert. Erfahrung, Begründing und Reflexion. 1. Aufl. Frankfurt, 1971.
Phil 3475.3.245 Schrag, Oswald O. Existence, existenz, and transcendence. Pittsburgh, 1971.
Phil 5520.742   Semanticheskaia struktura slova. Moskva, 1971.
Phil 5520.760   Shands, Harley Cecil. The war with words, structure and transcendence. The Hague, 1971.
Phil 3450.19.520 Sherover, Charles M. Heidegger, Kant and time. Bloomington, 1971.
Phil 310.752   Simpozium po Dialekticheskoi Logike, Alma-Ata, 1968. Aktual'nye problemy dialekticheskoi logiki. Alma-Ata, 1971.
Phil 5258.120.20A Skinner, Burrhus F. Beyond freedom and dignity. 1st ed. N.Y., 1971.
Phil 8419.70   Slattery, Mary Francis. Hazard, form, and value. Detroit, 1971.
Phil 5520.736   Slobin, Dan Isaac. Psycholinguistics. Glenview, Ill., 1971.
Phil 575.292   Slobodianuz, Sergei S. Lichnost' llaaz asennost! Moskva, 1971.
Phil 7055.341   Smith, Susy. Confessions of a psychic. N.Y., 1971.
Phil 8419.43.2   Solger, K.W.F. Erwin. München, 1971.
Phil 8893.104.6 Sorokin, Pitirim Aleksandrovich. Forms and techniques of altruistic and spiritual growth. Boston, 1954. N.Y., 1971.
Phil 5058.82   Spann, Othmar. Ganzheitliche Logik. 2. Aufl. Graz, 1971.
Phil 310.751.6   Spirkin, Aleksandr G. The basic principles of dialectical and historical materialism. Moscow, 1971.
Phil 1135.240   Stachowiak, Herbert. Rationalismus im Ursprung. Wien, 1971.
Phil 2280.23.30 Stern, Alfred. The search for meaning: philosophical vistas. Memphis, 1971.

1971 - cont.

Phil 5374.284   Stevens, John O. Awareness: exploring, experimenting, experiencing. Lafayette, Calif., 1971.

Phil 860.10   Stokes, Michael C. One and many in Presocratic philosophy. Washington, 1971.

Phil 6980.710.80   Strupp, Hans Herman. Psychotherapy and the modification of abnormal behavior. N.Y., 1971.

Phil 5520.724   Studia z dziejów semiotyki. Wrocław, 1971.

Phil 2150.22.150   Szewczyk, Jan. Eros i rewolucja. Wyd. 1. Warszawa, 1971.

Phil 193.262   Szymański, Jesy. Technika i mowa jako narsedsia pornania ludskiego. Pornań, 1971.

Phil 5465.208   Talejko, Eugeniusz. Zagadnienie psychologii twórezoju technïvzncj. Poznań, 1971.

Phil 4803.822.30   Tatarkiewicz, Władysław. Droga do filozofii i inne rozprowy filozoficzne. Wyd. 1. v.1- Warszawa, 1971-

Phil 2905.1.7   Teilhard de Chardin, Pierre. L'oeuvre scientifique. Olten, 1971.

Phil 4235.1.40   Telesius, B. Varii de naturalibus rebus libelli. Hildesheim, 1971.

Phil 6985.35   Therapy with families of sexually acting-out girls. N.Y., 1971.

Phil 1750.864   Tormey, Alan. The concept of expression. Princeton, N.J., 1971.

Phil 8709.26   Torrance, Thomas Forsyth. God and rationality. London, 1971.

Phil 5335.10   Triandis, Harry C. Attitude and attitude change. N.Y., 1971.

Phil 4803.241.90   Trzebuchowski, Pavel. Filozofia pracy Stanisława Brzozowskiego. Wyd. 1. Warszawa, 1971.

Phil 5374.282   Tugarinov, Vasilii P. Filosifiia soznaniia. Moskva, 1971.

Phil 3501.24   Tuschling, Burkhard. Metaphysische und transzendentale Dynamik in Kants opus postumum. Berlin, 1971.

Phil 5272.26.2   Tyler, Leona Elizabeth. Tests and measurements. 2d ed. Englewood Cliffs, 1971.

Phil 4825.18   Urbančič, Juan. Poglavitne ideje slovenskih filozofov med sholastiko in neosholako. Ljubljana, 1971.

Phil 310.777   V.I. Lenin i metodologicheskie voprosy sovremennoi nauki. Kiev, 1971.

Phil 8971.8   Van der Poel, Cornelius J. The search for human values. N.Y., 1971.

Phil 1730.31   Venturi, Franco. Utopia and reform in the enlightenment. Cambridge, Eng., 1971.

Phil 9150.34   Volkova, Emma V. Determinatsaia evoliutsionnogo professor. Minsk, 1971.

Phil 9250.34   Volkova, Emma V. Determinatsiia evoliutsionnogo protsessa. Minsk, 1971.

Phil 254.2   Vuillemin, Jules. La logique et le monde sensible. Paris, 1971.

Phil 3450.11.510   Waldenfels, Bernhard. Das Zwischenreich des Dialogs. Den Haag, 1971.

Phil 8897.90.5   Warnock, Geoffrey James. The object of morality. London, 1971.

Phil 6319.1.266   Wehr, Gerhard. Portrait of Jung; an illustrated biography. N.Y., 1971.

Phil 8897.73.5   Wellman, Carl. Challenge and response. Carbordale, 1971.

Phil 1135.225   West, M.L. Early Greek philosophy and the Orient. Oxford, 1971.

Phil 2750.19.130   Widmer, Charles. Gabriel Marcel et le théisme existentiel. Paris, 1971.

Phil 5520.616   Wierzbicka, Anna. Kocha, lubi, szanuje. Wyd. 1. Warszawa, 1971.

Phil 5272.7   Wike, Edward L. Data analysis. Chicago, 1971.

Phil 165.456   Wolff, Robert Paul. Philosophy. Englewood Cliffs, 1971.

Phil 5520.752   Wormnaes, Odd. Semantikk i teori og praksis. Oslo, 1971.

Phil 270.148   Wright Georg Henrik van. Explanation and understanding. Ithaca, N.Y., 1971.

Phil 2045.155   Wudel, Witold. Filozofia strachu i nadziei. Wyd. 1. Warszawa, 1971.

Phil 5068.100   Zaichenko, Georgii A. K voprosu o kritike sovremennogo angliiskogo pozitivizma. Khar'kov, 1971.

Phil 5066.212   Zinov'ev, Aleksandr A. Logika nauki. Moskva, 1971.

Phil 35.40.2   Zygon. Authors and titles, v. 1-5 (1966-1970). Chicago, 1971.

1972

Phil 6854.16   Alvarez, Alfred. The savage god: a study of suicide. London, 1972.

Phil 5240.58.2   Andreas, Burton G. Experimental psychology. 2. ed. N.Y., 1972.

Phil 2255.1.190   Bertrand Russell; a collection of critical essays. 1st ed. Garden City, 1972.

Phil 6980.141   Bry, Adelaide. Inside psychotherapy. N.Y., 1972.

Phil 6854.14   Choran, Jacques. Suicide. N.Y., 1972.

Phil 2520.13.15.5   Descartes, René. Treatise of man. Cambridge, 1972.

Phil 5374.286   Drury, Michael. The inward sea. 1st ed. Garden City, 1972.

Phil 2030.6.10   Goodman, Nelson. Problems and projects. Indianapolis, 1972.

Phil 2070.76.11   James, William. A William James reader. Boston, 1972.

Phil 6158.50   Lilly, John Cunningham. The center of the cyclone. N.Y., 1972.

Phil 165.466   Logic and art. Indianapolis, 1972.

Phil 5412.20   Madow, Leo. Anger. N.Y., 1972.

Phil 6360.10   Manual of child psychopathology. N.Y., 1972.

Phil 5500.16.5   Newell, Allen. Human problem solving. Englewood Cliffs, 1972.

Phil 1828.14   Petersen, Richard J. Scottish common sense in America, 1768-1850. Thesis. Ann Arbor, 1972.

Phil 6360.12   Quay, Herbert Callister. Psychopathological disorders of childhood. N.Y., 1972.

Phil 6327.21.100   Rycroft, Charles. Wilhelm Reich. N.Y., 1972.

Phil 5545.269   Salaman, Esther Polianowsky. A collection of moments; a study of involuntary memories. N.Y., 1972.

Phil 29.35.2   Triades; revue trimestrielle de culture humaine. Sommaires des numéros parus, 1953-1972. Paris, 1972.

Phil 3903.5.31   Verhoeven, Cornelius Wilhelmus Maria. The philosophy of wonder. N.Y., 1972.

Phil 6976.35   Wechsler, James Arthur. In a darkness. 1. ed. N.Y., 1972.

Phil 8897.98   Wertheimer, Roger. The significance of sense. Ithaca, 1972.